כתובים   KETHUVIM

The Writings

PRESENTED TO
_____

BY
_____

DATE
_____

THIS BIBLE BELONGS TO

_____

SIGNIFICANT FAMILY EVENTS

_____   _____

_____   _____

_____   _____

_____   _____

_____   _____

_____   _____

_____   _____

_____   _____

_____   _____

_____   _____

_____   _____

_____   _____

_____   _____

_____   _____

_____   _____

תנ״ך

JPS
HEBREW-
ENGLISH
TANAKH

TORAH THE FIVE BOOKS OF MOSES תורה

NEVI'IM THE PROPHETS נביאים

KETHUVIM THE WRITINGS כתובים

JPS
HEBREW-
ENGLISH
TANAKH

THE TRADITIONAL HEBREW TEXT AND

THE NEW JPS TRANSLATION – *Second Edition*

THE JEWISH PUBLICATION SOCIETY

Philadelphia   1999 · 5759

The Jewish Publication Society
1930 Chestnut Street
Philadelphia, PA 19103–4599

Hebrew text, based on Biblia Hebraica Stuttgartensia, © 1999 by The Jewish Publication Society
Translation © 1985, 1999 by The Jewish Publication Society
First Edition published 1985. Second Edition 1999

Designed by Adrianne Onderdonk Dudden and R. David E. Sulomm Stein
Composed in Hadassah (Hebrew) and Minion (English) by VARDA Graphics, Skokie, Illinois
Lead typesetter: R. Shimon Deutsch. Computer programmer: Daniel Weisman
Manufactured in the United States of America

00 01 02 03 04 05 06 07 08   10 9 8 7 6 5 4 3 2

Library of Congress Cataloging-in-Publication Data

Bible. O.T. Hebrew. 1999
[Tanakh] = JPS Hebrew-English Tanakh : the traditional Hebrew text
and the new JPS translation. —2nd ed.
p. cm.
"Hebrew text based on Biblia Hebraica Stuttgartensia"—T.p. verso.
ISBN 0-8276-0656-7
I. Jewish Publication Society.   II. Bible. O.T. English. Jewish
Publication Society. 1999.   III. Title.   IV. Title: JPS Hebrew-
English Tanakh.
BS895.J4 1999
221.4′4—dc21   99-11017
                                                                     CIP

NOTE: The second (1999) edition of the translation incorporates many revisions and additions
reflecting archaeological and scholarly research since 1985, as submitted by our readers. Corrections
have been made in typography, punctuation, and in the rendering of references to God. As in the first
edition (and in Hebrew), masculine terms for God such as "He" should be understood as gender
neutral unless the imagery of their context requires otherwise.

This publication was made possible through generous grants from

THE LEONARD AND MADLYN ABRAMSON FOUNDATION

and

THE ARETE FOUNDATION

CONTENTS

תורה TORAH THE FIVE BOOKS OF MOSES

נביאים NEVI'IM THE PROPHETS

כתובים KETHUVIM THE WRITINGS

PREFACE TO THE 1999 HEBREW-ENGLISH EDITION

A court of law relies on witnesses to establish the facts of a case. But for those who seek the "facts" of the original biblical texts, no firsthand witnesses exist. We have only the testimony of various manuscripts, produced hundreds of years after the Bible's books were completed. And even if we had an autograph copy of, say, the Book of Ezra, it would not answer all our questions, for it was created at a time (2400 years ago) when writing was imprecise—even before the invention of punctuation.

Through the intervening centuries, scribes have figured out how to record the oral traditions more precisely. At the same time, during each transmission of the books from person to person, uncertainty has grown. For schools have sometimes disagreed on pronunciation. Handwriting has not always been legible. And every scribe has occasionally made mistakes in copying.

Witnesses testifying in court often disagree. Little surprise, then, that the Bible's textual "witnesses"—farther removed from the original "event"—differ from each other in a wide range of small ways: spelling, punctuation, layout of poetry, and so on. Sometimes entire verses appear in only a few manuscripts.

So which version is true? This was the first question we faced in preparing our Hebrew text.

THE UNBROKEN CHAIN OF UNCERTAINTY

Accuracy has been ensured via side documentation—part of what is called *masorah*.[1] This gives rise to a "masoretic text"—a Bible that accords with the *masorah*. Yet the number of details has been too vast for *masorah* to address all room for disagreement. And the masoretic notes have been neglected through the ages; written in shorthand, they are often vague, and their own textual witnesses sometimes disagree.

---

1   *Masorah* refers to everything transmitted with the biblical text except its consonants. It includes: vowel signs, accent signs, arrangements of poetry, marginal notes and endnotes, as well as separate treatises on the copying and use of manuscripts. *Masorah* exists independently of *halakhah* (rabbinic law). The early medieval masters of the biblical text who developed this documentation are known in English as "masoretes." Many masoretic annotations seem designed to reduce loss or distortion in transmission of the text.

Much *masorah* seems to have been created only after problems arose; in such cases, it could only reinforce the torn textual fabric, not mend the hole. Unable or unwilling to choose between variants, scribes sometimes preserved two versions of a word side by side—transmitting both.

Furthermore, by nature the Bible is not predictable. Because of its spiritual subject matter, its choice of words must be improbable at times. So is a given puzzling phrase due to scribal error—or religious mystery? When to expect the text to follow rules of grammar—and when to allow for artistic expression?

Despite these pitfalls, Bible scholars have always refined the text as they found it. Each expert begins with a different set of available manuscripts, from scribes of varying (and uncertain) reliability. They each use different methods for resolving textual problems. So the experts come to different conclusions as to what is the "best" Bible text.

Ironically, the result is a Bible whose text continually *evolves*—the changes being justified to preserve the accuracy of tradition. Thus, an early printed Bible edited in Italy by R. Jacob ben Ḥayyim Ibn-Adoniyah (1525 C.E.) reconstructed the work of the Tiberian textual tradition from six hundred years earlier. His effort was impressive enough that soon afterward, owners of old manuscripts all across Europe altered their parchments to match his newly authoritative book.

As mistakes were corrected, new ones appeared. R. Meir Letteris of Austria edited a Hebrew Bible first published in 1852 C.E., based on lists of "corrections" by experts who perceived mistakes in earlier editions. It became the standard Hebrew text among many Jews to this day. Yet like all prior printed Bibles, it contained hundreds of its own typographical errors.

Meanwhile, in the modern era, certain early medieval manuscripts—safeguarded in isolated Middle Eastern communities—were brought to the attention of Bible scholars. These have proven to be the oldest known witnesses of the now-standard Tiberian tradition. Only recently has the wider, evolutionary, corrective process taken these unusually reliable texts into account. These manuscripts still contain inconsistencies and differ slightly from each other. But on the whole, they confirm the "received" (evolutionary European) traditions of the Bible text, especially for the Torah.

Amazingly, manuscript differences are truly minor. More than 99.9 percent of the time, the masoretic Bible's witnesses give identical accounts. Rarely does the variation impact the meaning of a given verse. Yet even this small uncertainty can vex a publisher who—for each detail of the text—must pick one possibility over another.

If a definitive text of the Hebrew Bible does not exist, the best a publisher can do is produce *a defensible text that is sufficiently accurate for the edition's intended purpose.* Therefore I shall now explain our text's history and our approach to editing it—and let the reader judge its soundness.

THE HISTORY OF OUR HEBREW TEXT

Since ancient times, Jews have traced the chain of transmission of Scripture: "Moses received Torah at Sinai and handed it on to Joshua, Joshua to the elders, and the elders to the prophets. And the prophets handed it on to the Great Assembly…" (Mishnah *Avot* 1:1). For the present volume, the textual transmission history is as follows.

Aaron ben Moses Ben-Asher (Tiberias, c. 930 C.E.)

An industrious family of masoretes once lived in the Galilean town of Tiberias (an ancient center of Jewish scholarship). The last in their line of scholars was Aaron ben Moses Ben-Asher, who flourished circa 930 C.E. He authored a classic masoretic treatise. He is the first known scribe to complete a manuscript of the entire Bible (whose books had been preserved somewhat independently). An important part of his work included the proofreading of others' manuscripts, which is how he enters into our picture.[2]

Samuel ben Jacob (Egypt, 1010 C.E.)

Two generations later, a scribe in Fostat (Egypt's thriving center of trade and learning) spent years composing a Bible codex.[3] Noting its completion in 4770 A.M. (1010 C.E.), he recorded that he copied from several manuscripts into this one volume: "Samuel ben Jacob wrote out the consonants, vowels, punctuation, accents, and annotations of this codex of Scripture from the texts checked and corrected by the late master Aaron ben Moses Ben-Asher; it has been checked and corrected per tradition."[4]

---

2   Two centuries after Aaron Ben-Asher's death, mastery of the *masorah* vanished (except in the isolated community of Yemen), probably degraded by continual invasions and war in the Land of Israel. Scribes blended different textual traditions and copied the *masorah* without understanding it, multiplying inconsistencies and errors. Ironically, while Ben-Asher's authority was then invoked to the exclusion of other masoretes, manuscripts that consistently reflected his teaching became rare.

3   For about eight hundred years before the invention of printing, Jewish books were written on parchment in two formats, scroll or codex. A *codex* was made of bound folios; it was easier to use for study, and it could hold far more information. In manuscripts, the entire Bible has appeared only as a codex, never as a scroll. Classical Hebrew terms for a codex are *maḥzor, mitzḥaf,* and *keter.*

4   A local teacher and jurisconsult (a public servant of high standing among rabbinic Jews in Egypt) had ordered this codex for his own study. Samuel ben Jacob produced it singlehandedly— a rare feat; usually, a masoretic Bible's three facets (consonants, vowels/accents, and masoretic notes) were each written by a specialist.

Samuel's Bible contains sixty thousand marginal notes on the text, including more than a thousand divergences between consonantal text (*kethib*) and reading tradition (*qere*).[5]

In proofreading and correcting his work, Samuel ben Jacob missed (or let stand) hundreds of errors—which is actually an impressive result, given the millions of characters in a Hebrew Bible. As the contemporary scholar E.J. Revell comments, "This is a long way from perfection, but it is close to ideal when compared to the situation in most [later] medieval manuscripts."

Recent Editions of the Leningrad Codex

Today, Samuel ben Jacob's work is the oldest known complete Hebrew Bible, and the oldest complete representative of the Ben-Asher tradition.[6] For centuries, however, it was kept out of circulation, unknown to historians or Bible editors. Then in 1840 C.E., a manuscript collector announced possession of this Bible—which has since become known as the Leningrad Codex.[7]

Repeatedly since then, international teams of Christian and Jewish scholars (both religious and academic) have edited this codex for modern use. The first group, led by Rudolph Kittel and Paul Kahle, made it the base text for a critical edition, *Biblia Hebraica Kittel* (BHK, 1937). After World War II, another team revised BHK, producing *Biblia Hebraica Stuttgartensia* (BHS, 1967–1977), for which Karl Elliger, Wilhelm Rudolph, and Gérard Weil served as lead editors. Then, at the University of Michigan, H. Van Dyke Parunak and Robert Eckert devised computer-readable codes for the biblical text's characters and main features; Parunak oversaw the transcription of BHS into three megabytes of data (1982). Soon thereafter, Richard E. Whitaker of the Claremont Graduate Schools coordinated revisions. Finally, J. Alan Groves of Westminster Theological Seminary (Philadelphia) with Emanuel Tov of The Hebrew University (Jerusalem) directed a proofreading team (1987), a project that JPS helped to fund.

---

5   The number of words accorded this treatment varies greatly among manuscripts and editions. What the *kethib/qere* system means is not certain; it appears to contain a mix of intended corrections, variant readings, and guidance for pronouncing words with odd spelling. Ultimately, even though the *qere* was preserved only in the margin (if written down at all), the masoretes gave it greater weight, for they transmitted the *kethib* with consonants only. (Therefore, unless stated otherwise, our translation is based on the *qere*.)

6   Only for a few dozen characters is this codex not clearly legible—given some parchment stains, flaked ink, and ambiguous pen strokes.

7   When this manuscript gained renown as the only known direct evidence of Aaron Ben-Asher's work, the city in which it was housed was called Leningrad (now St. Petersburg). There, in the Russian National Library, this codex is officially catalogued as "Firkovich B19A."

The result is called the Michigan-Claremont-Westminster (MCW) electronic BHS. It has provided JPS with a text nearly identical to the Leningrad Codex manuscript. Each round of revision has corrected previous typographic errors and misreadings while introducing a smaller number of other typos and mistakes. Its machine-readable text format has nearly precluded new typos in our own production process. Meanwhile, BHS notes have provided vital supporting documentation.

To aid modern readers, its various editors have brought the codex's outward features in line with the more familiar evolution of Bibles, by:

- adding chapter and verse numbers (invented after the codex was written);

- changing the order of books (putting Chronicles at the end, rather than before Psalms);

- redividing Psalms to show 150 chapters rather than the codex's 149;

- adding end-of-verse punctuation where Samuel ben Jacob had omitted it;

- inserting typographic markers to show the codex's paragraphing;

- placing each *qere* entry in the text (rather than in the margin), following its *kethib*, and transferring pointing to the *qere* consonants— which occasionally meant inferring pointing (a *dagesh* or *maqqef*) not in the codex;

- omitting the diacritical sign *rafé* (ubiquitous in the codex) in all but six places, which most modern Bibles have dropped as superfluous and hard to print;

- turning many marginal notes on superfluous letters (*yatér*) into *qere* entries;

- tripling the number of masoretic notes by filling in cross-references; and

- flagging the apparent scribal errors.

EDITING THE JPS HEBREW BIBLE TEXT

This section details our editing approach, which is summarized by the table on page xv.

Intended Audience. This is a study Bible, for readers who want to explore the meaning of the masoretic Hebrew text. Hence, our designers focused on reducing the work of reading. Our edition features clear type, an engaging and efficient layout that enables readers to move quickly from one language to another, and a format that contemporary English speakers will find familiar.

This edition is not meant for ritual use, and it thus omits some synagogue-related features. It meets only the traditional rabbinic standards (*halakhah*) for formatting a study Bible, which are less stringent than those for ritual texts. And this is not an academic Bible. We did not pack the page with details of interest to scholars alone.

Type Design. Our type design emphasized clarity, reducing the ambiguity common in older editions. We crafted and placed vowels and accents with an eye to making reading—and correct pronunciation—easy.[8]

Language Alignment. Chapter divisions, while not an organic part of the text, provided a regular way to correlate the text with its translation, for we regularly aligned the two columns at the start of each chapter. Matching within one verse at the bottom of each page also helped keep the two columns in near alignment.

Prose Paragraphing. In the absence of standard paragraphing,[9] we adopted a dual layout approach. While showing where paragraph breaks appear in the Leningrad Codex,[10] we paragraphed the Hebrew per contemporary English paragraphing practice.[11] That is, we arranged the prose into logical units according to its plain meaning, as judged by our translators. Advantages of this approach are: (*1*) English readers can more easily grasp the Hebrew prose when it is arranged in familiar units of thought; and (*2*) paragraph correspondence of the two languages greatly aids the reader's movement between text and translation.

Poetry Layout. Traditionally, scribes could lay out a biblical poem any way they saw fit, so long as they placed a gap (blank space) somewhere within each line. The gaps stood for pauses that amplified the rhythm, meaning, and beauty of the recited poem. Now instead of gaps we have used line breaks, in the manner of poetry in more recent centuries. By inserting a line break between poetic phrases—where the

---

8   Similarly, we replaced BHS's vestigial use of the archaic *rafé* symbol with better-known means of showing unusual vocalization.

9   According to an ancient rabbinic teaching, paragraph breaks give us "a chance to reflect while pausing between topics and issues" (*Sifra* I:1.9). But masoretic notes do not address paragraph breaks, nor does rabbinic law recognize one authoritative paragraphing pattern. In fact, no two Bible manuscripts or printed editions agree with regard to paragraphing.

10   Traditionally, the Hebrew Bible has two types of breaks: within a line (*setumot*, "closed"), and starting a new line (*petuhot*, "open")—the latter suggesting a greater shift in content. Like many Bible printers, we have used the letters *samekh* (for *setumot*) and *peh* (for *petuhot*) as markers to show paragraph breaks in the source manuscript.

11   For the sake of column alignment, on a couple of pages we kept the Hebrew text closed up.

EDITING SUMMARY FOR THE HEBREW TEXT

Intended Audience and Use	Readers who want to explore meaning of the masoretic Hebrew text while staying in touch with the translation; for use in study rather than in worship.
Source of Text	*Biblia Hebraica Stuttgartensia* (BHS)* in the form of a 1987 computerized transcription; chosen for optimal accuracy and good documentation.
Type Design	Chose a font known for its clarity (Hadassah) and sized it for readability; custom-designed appearance of vowels and accents to reduce ambiguity.
Language Alignment	Lined up text columns at chapter openings and matched them within one verse at the bottom of each page, aiding the reader's movement between text and translation.
Prose Paragraphing	Matched the English translation; divided text into logical units of prose according to its plain meaning, for ease of reading.
Poetry Layout	Matched the English translation; inserted line break between poetic phrases where the reader would normally pause, so that rhythm is apparent.
Verse Numbering	Placed Arabic numerals within the Hebrew text, for quick correlation with the translation.
Division of Books	Accommodated each of the conventional ways, arranging text both as twenty-four and as thirty-nine books.
Order of Books	Rearranged books as in most Hebrew printed editions, making navigation easy for readers familiar with the "standard" order.
Spelling Variants (Orthography)	Of minor spelling discrepancies between codex text and its marginal notes, resolved twenty-nine in Torah in favor of the notes; in Prophets and Writings, printed spelling as in text, regardless of marginal notes.
Hymns	Set classical, "interwoven" layout for Song of the Sea and Song of Deborah, placing gaps to coincide with syntactic pauses; set line breaks between phrases in the Song of Moses.
Lists	Set special, traditional layout for the conquered kings and Haman's sons.
Weekly Torah Portions	Divided Torah into *parashiyot* (sections according to Babylonian Jewish reading tradition), for study in accord with the weekly cycle.
Reading Tradition vs. Writing Tradition	Set *kethib* (consonantal text as written) in smaller, unpointed type; pointed the *qere* (consantal text as read) placed it in the text after its *kethib*.
Letter Size and Nequdot (Extraordinary Points)	Set unusually large or small letters and placed special points per modern editions in Torah, and per BHS in Prophets and Writings.
Transcription Errors	Corrected hundreds of errors: BHS misreadings of its source manuscript, typos in BHS printing, and mistakes in BHS transcription onto computer.
Scribal Errors	Supplied missing pointing as implied by the text; deleted superfluous pointing; changed the codex text to match "received" texts in thirty-nine words where our manuscript's reading seemed both impossible and glaring.
Hebrew Footnotes	Noted selected anomalies (in spelling, pointing, grammar, or meaning) and verse counts using traditional terms—spelled out and reworded for clarity; showed variant readings from other Bible manuscripts where preferred by our translators; marked ways that our edition differs from its source text.

---

* BHS is a scientific, printed edition of the Leningrad Codex—the oldest complete masoretic manuscript of the Bible (see above, pages xi–xiii).

reader would normally pause—we bring out the poetic rhythm, reduce reading effort, and speed the reader's recourse to the translation.[12]

Verse Numbering. Numerals of the same type font in both columns ease one's navigation through the Bible. The same goes for numbers printed within the text—showing clearly which verse is which. (Many editions have instead used Hebrew letters for verse numbers and placed them in the margin.)

Division of Books. English translations usually list thirty-nine books of the Bible. Meanwhile, Hebrew Bibles classically have presented twenty-four books—counting the following groups as one book each: the two parts of Samuel; the two parts of Kings; the Twelve ("Minor") Prophets; Ezra and Nehemiah; and the two parts of Chronicles.

Some aspects of our book design presume the thirty-nine-book division: the tables, book openings, and chapter numbers. But we ended only the conventional twenty-four books with a closing prayer ("Hereby completed—praise to God, creator of the cosmos!") and with the sum total of verses.[13]

Order of Books. The Leningrad Codex reflects a sequence found in Middle Eastern and Spanish manuscripts. But the Writings are arranged differently in most modern Bibles, following the German manuscript tradition. We chose the modern sequence—more likely to be familiar to our readers—for quicker navigation.

Spelling Variants (Orthography). Many words are not spelled the same way throughout the Bible.[14] In masoretic tradition, a marginal note fixes a correct spelling for nearly all those words in each place they occur (although each manuscript's set of notes is incomplete). However, in the Ben-Asher study Bibles, when their text's spelling was contradicted by a marginal note (written in a later pass through the manuscript), masoretic scribes usually let the "mistake" stand—perhaps because variant spelling affected neither meaning nor pronunciation. We too let stand about ninety spellings known to differ from both "received" and Yemenite Torah texts. At the same time, to represent our codex's Torah accurately, we took into account its marginal notes; sometimes (as BHS's editor of masoretic notes pointed out) the weight of internal evidence favors a marginal note over the text.[15] As a result we altered the spelling

---

12 Poetic line breaks in the two columns do not always match, due to the differing syntax of the two languages.

13 Also, we divided the Book of Psalms into five collections, according to an ancient tradition lacking in the Leningrad Codex.

14 When the letters *alef, heh, waw,* and *yod* represent certain vowel sounds rather than consonants, the same word can be spelled either with or without them.

15 Discrepancies in spelling between a manuscript's text and its marginal notes may be due not only to errors in the text; they may reflect errors in the notes or the traditions of different schools.

of twenty-nine words. Coincidentally, twenty-eight of them now match the "received" and Yemenite texts.

In Prophets and Writings—historically, regulated less precisely than Torah—we printed the codex text regardless of marginal notes. For those two sections, our codex's spelling is already closer to masoretic tradition than that of the "received" editions (as exemplified by Letteris and Koren).

Hymns. Song of the Sea (Exodus 15) and Song of Deborah (Judges 5) are national anthems. We reproduced ancient graphic designs that adorn their lyrics, following the traditionally recommended practice of setting written gaps at syntactic pauses. Another hymn, the Song of Moses (Deuteronomy 32), we treated differently in accord with its lesser distinctiveness in later tradition. In all three cases we enabled the reader to correlate text with translation.

Lists. Our codex displayed many sections in a traditional list format, which we employed only in the cases required by *masorah* and *halakhah*: the conquered kings (Joshua 12) and Haman's sons (Esther 9).

Weekly Torah Portions. We divided the Torah into *parashiyot*—the weekly portions within an annual public reading cycle according to Babylonian Jewish tradition—because contemporary Torah study often refers to them. We did not show the older division into smaller sections (*sedarim*) per Levantine Jewish tradition, no longer in common use.

Reading Tradition Versus Writing Tradition. Previous editions set the *qere* consonants in the margin, which has proven awkward in use; pronouncing the *qere* has required simultaneously looking for consonants in the margin while looking for vowels in the text. In contrast, our side-by-side, in-the-text format preserves the distinctness of the two forms while making it easy to read the *qere*.

This edition contains 1,322 *kethib/qere* instances located as per MCW (see above, page xii note 5 and page xiii), with two cases added for clarity: the form of *na'ara(h)* in Genesis (for which we adopted the masoretic practice in Deuteronomy), and Numbers 10:36.

Letter Size. Masoretic tradition was not consistent about writing certain letters larger or smaller than normal. The meaning of letter size is only occasionally clear. Later manuscripts (and modern printed editions) tend to have more odd-sized letters than earlier ones. In Torah we set odd-sized letters according to modern practice, noting our sources. In Prophets and Writings, we went according to our codex text.

Nequdot (Extraordinary Points). Traditionally, a point that marks uncertainty is placed atop and/or below certain letters. The number and placement of these obscure markers varies among the sources. In Torah, we placed these points at ten locations according to the modern editions.

In Prophets and Writings, we placed them at five locations according to the Leningrad Codex.

Transcription Errors. Research in the past decade with high-resolution photographs of our codex has continued to clear up earlier misreadings and typos. To match revisions in recent editions of BHS (1990, 1997), we corrected MCW (1987) in several hundred places. Then, checking selectively in a large facsimile edition (1998) of the codex, we found eight more instances where BHS editors had misread the manuscript. Further, we found seventeen MCW typos. (All told, this codex is closer to the "received" traditions than previously thought.)

Scribal Errors. Bible scholar and editor R. Mordechai Breuer has noted, "The Leningrad Codex ... is one of the best of the ancient manuscripts as far as its vocalization and accentuation are concerned." Yet a lack of pointing where the rules of Hebrew call for it *must* be a scribal oversight. Conversely, excessive pointing must also be a mistake. Rather than needlessly puzzle our readers, we fixed both types of errors; we added about 150 pointing characters (and subtracted a few) as implied, and in accord with the manuscripts and editions noted by BHS.

Other anomalies may reflect a variant reading tradition, an idiosyncrasy of the scribe's graphical system, a dialect—or an outright error. In any event, we judged the codex's reading to be impossible by modern standards—and significant enough to trip up most readers—in thirty-nine words, which we changed to match the "received" masoretic texts.[16]

Hebrew Footnotes. Like the medieval scribes, we culled most of our nearly six hundred notes from the larger body of masoretic lore (roughly two hundred thousand notes!); we do not pretend to have been exhaustive. We composed such notes either in the classic Aramaic shorthand or in Hebrew terms similar to the Letteris Bible's notes—but spelled out and reworded for clarity. Many of these notes point out a textual anomaly (in spelling, vocalization, accentuation, punctuation, grammar, or meaning), lest the reader be puzzled or think it a mistake. Other notes relate to counting: the total number of verses in each book, halfway point of each book, variant counting traditions, or aspects of the text that affect the count.[17]

16 In those thirty-nine words, we only moved or changed pointing, except for deleting one superfluous *waw* and changing one prefixed *kaf* to a *bet*. Probable scribal errors that we let stand typically involve a missing *dagesh* (a dot to show either that the letter is doubled or pronounced with a stop). Apparent errors in this codex are well documented—in BHS, the Dotan/Adi edition, and R. Breuer's lists. We therefore trust that those for whom such errors matter have the wherewithal to determine a reading that will satisfy them.

17 Where masoretic traditions give more than one verse total or halfway point, we checked the calculations ourselves and noted discrepancies.

We also included notes of our own. Most of these give variant readings preferred by our translators from other Bible manuscripts. A few notes mark where our edition differs from its sources, either BHS or the Leningrad Codex itself (styled as "our manuscript").

In closing, we at the Jewish Publication Society hope that this edition opens up the richness of the Hebrew Bible to our readers. "How much better to acquire wisdom than gold; / To acquire understanding is preferable to silver" (Proverbs 16.16).

Rabbi David E. Sulomm Stein
Managing Editor
February 1, 1999
ט״ו בשבט תשנ״ט

PREFACE TO THE 1985 ENGLISH EDITION

This translation of *Tanakh,* the Holy Scriptures, produced by the Jewish Publication Society, was made directly from the traditional Hebrew text into the idiom of modern English. It represents the collaboration of academic scholars with rabbis from the three largest branches of organized Jewish religious life in America. Begun in 1955, the ongoing translation was published in three main stages: *The Torah* in 1962, *The Prophets (Nevi'im)* in 1978, and *The Writings (Kethuvim)* in 1982. These three volumes, with revisions, are now brought together in a complete English *Tanakh (Torah-Nevi'im-Kethuvim),* the latest link in the chain of Jewish Bible translations.

ON THE HISTORY OF BIBLE TRANSLATION

Bible translation began about 2200 years ago, in the third century B.C.E., as the large Jewish population of Alexandria, Egypt, came under the influence of Hellenism. When the Greek language replaced Hebrew and Aramaic as their vernacular, and the Torah in its Hebrew original was no longer commonly understood, a translation into Greek was made for the Jewish community of Alexandria. This translation came to be known as the Septuagint, Latin for "seventy," because of the legend that the committee of translators numbered seventy-two, six elders from each of the twelve tribes of Israel.

In the last few centuries B.C.E., the Jews who lived to the north and east of Judea also found the Hebrew Bible difficult to understand, for their spoken language had become largely Aramaic. Translations into Aramaic, first of the Torah and then of the rest of the Bible, became known as the Targums.

The Septuagint and the Targums are not only the oldest translations of the Bible but also the most influential. Down to our own day, virtually every Christian translation has followed the methods of the Jewish translators who created the Septuagint, and generally followed their renderings of the Hebrew as well. The Christian translators also were influenced by the interpretation of the Hebrew text set forth in the Targums (much of it in oral form at the time) and by the writings of the Jewish philosopher-interpreter Philo of Alexandria (died about 45 C.E.).

The forerunners and leaders of the Renaissance and the Reformation (fourteenth–fifteenth centuries), and especially Martin Luther and William Tyndale (sixteenth century), made use of Latin translations of the classic Jewish commentators Rashi, Ibn Ezra, and Kimhi (eleventh–thirteenth centuries), whose works were imbued with the direct knowledge of the Targums. Luther was greatly indebted to Nicholas of Lyre (1270–1349), who had adopted Rashi's exegesis for his Latin Bible commentary. Rashi's influence on all authorized and most unofficial English translations of the Hebrew Bible becomes evident when Tyndale's dependence on Luther is considered. Tyndale is central to many subsequent English translations: the King James Version of 1611, the (British) Revised Version of 1881–1885, the American Standard Version of 1901, and especially the Revised Standard Version of 1952.

Alongside the close, literal method of Bible translation, the earliest Jewish translators were also influenced by the widely held view that, along with the Written Law (torah she-bikhtav), God had given Moses on Mount Sinai an Oral Law (torah she-be'al peh) as well; so that to comprehend God's Torah fully and correctly, it was essential to make use of both. Thus, when a translation of the Hebrew Bible into the Judeo-Arabic vernacular was deemed necessary for Jewry in Moslem countries toward the end of the first millennium, the noted philologian, philosopher, and community leader Saadia Gaon (882–942) produced a version that incorporated traditional Jewish interpretation but was not based on word-for-word translation; at the same time, it was a model of clarity and stylistic elegance. The present version is in the spirit of Saadia.

With the growth of Christianity in the first century, the Church adopted the Septuagint as its Bible, and the Septuagint was translated into the languages of the various Christian communities. As Greek began to give way to Latin in the Roman Empire, it was only a matter of time before a Latin translation of Scripture became the recognized Bible of the Church. The Church father Jerome (c. 340–420) produced the official Latin version. Drawing on Jewish tradition and consulting Jewish teachers, he achieved what came to be known as the Vulgate, the Bible in the language of the common people. The Vulgate, the Bible of European Christianity until the Reformation, is clearly the most significant Bible translation after the Septuagint.

With the rise of Protestantism in Europe, scholars within this movement set themselves the task of making the Bible available in the various vernaculars of the time. By 1526 the first parts of two notable translations began to appear: Martin Luther's in German and William Tyndale's in English. The latter, by way of several subsequent revisions, became the King James Version of 1611. The more modern English versions—such as *The Holy Scriptures* by the American rabbi Isaac Leeser (1855), the (British) Revised Version (1881–1885), the American Standard Version (1901), the Jewish Publication Society's *The Holy Scriptures* (1917), and the (American) Revised Standard Version (1952)—made extensive use of the King James.

ON THE MAKING OF THE NEW TRANSLATION

After World War II, when the Jewish Publication Society began to consider a new edition of the Bible, the idea of a modest revision of the 1917 translation met with resistance, and the concept of a completely new translation gradually took hold. The proposed translation would reproduce the Hebrew idiomatically and reflect contemporary scholarship, thus laying emphasis upon intelligibility and correctness. It would make critical use of the early rabbinic and medieval Jewish commentators, grammarians, and philologians and would rely on the traditional Hebrew text, avoiding emendations. The need for this new translation was the focus of the Jewish Publication Society's annual meeting in 1953. Later that year the Society announced its intention to proceed with the project, and in 1955 the committee of translators began their task.

Harry M. Orlinsky, Professor of Bible at Hebrew Union College–Jewish Institute of Religion (New York), was asked to serve as editor-in-chief for the new translation, along with H. L. Ginsberg, Professor of Bible at the Jewish Theological Seminary, and Ephraim A. Speiser, Professor of Semitic and Oriental Languages at the University of Pennsylvania, as fellow editors. Associated with them were three rabbis: Max Arzt, Bernard J. Bamberger, and Harry Freedman, representing the Conservative, Reform, and Orthodox branches of organized Jewish religious life. Solomon Grayzel, editor of the Jewish Publication Society, served as secretary of the committee.

The committee profited much from the work of previous translators; the present rendering, however, is essentially a new translation. A few of its characteristics may be noted. The committee undertook to follow faithfully the traditional Hebrew text, but there were certain points at which footnotes appeared necessary: (*1*) where the committee had to admit that it did not understand a word or passage; (*2*) where an alternative rendering was possible; (*3*) where an old rendering, no longer retained, was so well known that it would very likely be missed, in which case the traditional translation was given in the name of "Others" (usually referring to the Society's version of 1917); (4) where the understanding of a passage could be facilitated by reference to another passage elsewhere in the Bible; and (5) where important textual variants are to be found in some of the ancient manuscripts or versions of the Bible.

The translators avoided obsolete words and phrases and, whenever possible, rendered Hebrew idioms by means of their normal English equivalents. For the second person singular, the modern "you" was used instead of the archaic "thou," even when referring to the Deity ("You"). A further obvious difference between this translation and most of the older ones is in the rendering of the Hebrew particle *waw*, which is usually translated "and." Biblical Hebrew demanded the frequent use of the *waw*, but in that style it had the force not only of "and" but also of "however," "but," "yet," "when," and any number of other such words and particles, or none at all that can be translated into English. Always to render it as "and" is to misrepresent the Hebrew rather than be faithful to it. Consequently, the committee translated the particle as the sense required, or left it untranslated.

The chapter and verse divisions found in the printed Bible are indispensable as a system of precise reference, but they do not always coincide with the organic divisions of the text. The chapter divisions, whose origin is neither ancient nor Jewish but medieval Christian, sometimes join or separate the wrong paragraphs, sentences, or even parts of sentences. The verse divisions, though considerably older and of Jewish origin, sometimes join together parts of different sentences or separate from each other parts of the same sentence. The translation of Saadia Gaon often does not correspond to our chapter divisions, which did not exist in his day. More noteworthy is the readiness with which he joined separate verses of the Hebrew text (whose authority he did not question) into single sentences when the sense required it. Thus, in joining Genesis 7.24 and 8.1 into a single sentence, or combining the last part of 1 Kings 6.38 with 7.1, the present translation is following the example of Saadia. The attentive reader will discover other instances in which the translators have followed what they considered to be the logical units of meaning even when they did not coincide with the conventional chapters and verses. The latter, however, are marked and numbered throughout.

The preface to the first edition of *The Torah* was dated September 25, 1962, Erev Rosh Ha-Shanah 5723. A second edition, incorporating some changes by the translators, came out five years later. The committee also produced translations of *The Five Megilloth and Jonah* (1969), *Isaiah*

(1973), and *Jeremiah* (1974). The latter two books and Jonah were incorporated, with some corrections and revisions, into the complete translation of *The Prophets (Nevi'im)*. For this volume, which was published in 1978, Professor Ginsberg served as editor, in association with Professor Orlinsky. Whereas Professor Orlinsky had initially prepared a draft translation of the entire Torah, individual members of the committee undertook to prepare a draft of an entire prophetic book or part of a book; but, as in translating the Torah, everyone had an opportunity to criticize the draft and to offer detailed suggestions at periodic committee sessions, which were presided over by Rabbi Bamberger. Differences of opinion were settled by majority vote.

In preparing the translation of *The Prophets,* the translators faced a recurring problem that deserves special mention. The prophetic books contain many passages whose meaning is uncertain. Thus, in order to provide an intelligible rendering, modern scholars have resorted to emending the Hebrew text. Some of these emendations derive from the ancient translators, especially of the Septuagint and the Targums, who had before them a Hebrew text that sometimes differed from today's traditional text. Where these ancient versions provide no help, some scholars have made conjectural emendations of their own. Many modern English versions contain translations of emended texts, sometimes without citing any departure from the traditional Hebrew text.

Like the translation of *The Torah,* the present translation of the prophetic books adheres strictly to the traditional Hebrew text; but where the text remains obscure and an alteration provides marked clarification, a footnote is offered with a rendering of the suggested emendation. If the emendation is based on one or two ancient versions, they are mentioned by name; if more than two versions agree, they are summed up as "ancient versions." Conjectural emendations are introduced by "Emendation yields." Sometimes, however, it was deemed sufficient to offer only a change of vowels, and such modifications are indicated by "Change of vocalization yields." In all cases, the emendation is given in a footnote, which may be readily disregarded by those who reject it on either scholarly or religious grounds. The only exceptions involve such changes in grammatical form as those, say, from second person to third or from singular to plural. In such rare instances, the change is incorporated in the text, and the traditional Hebrew is translated in a footnote.

The committee of translators for *The Writings (Kethuvim),* the third part of the Hebrew Bible, was set up by the Jewish Publication Society in 1966. It consisted of Moshe Greenberg, now Professor of Bible at the

Hebrew University, Jonas C. Greenfield, then Professor of Semitic Languages at the Hebrew University, and Nahum M. Sarna, then Professor of Biblical Studies at Brandeis University, in association with Rabbis Saul Leeman, Martin S. Rozenberg, and David Shapiro of the Conservative, Reform, and Orthodox movements. Chaim Potok, then editor of the Society, served as secretary of the committee.

The present English rendering of *Kethuvim*, like *Torah* and *Nevi'im*, is based on the traditional Hebrew text—its consonants, vowels, and syntactical divisions—although the traditional accentuation occasionally has been replaced by an alternative construction. Following the approach of the original committee, the entire gamut of biblical interpretation, ancient and modern, Jewish and non-Jewish, has been consulted, and, whenever possible, the results of modern study of the languages and cultures of the ancient Near East have been brought to bear on the biblical text. In choosing between alternatives, however, just as antiquity was not in itself a disqualification, so modernity was not in itself a recommendation. Divergences of the present translation from recent renderings reflect the committee's judgment that certain innovations, though interesting, are too speculative for adoption in the present state of knowledge. The as-yet-imperfect understanding of the language of the Bible, or what appears to be some disorder in the Hebrew text, makes sure translation of many passages impossible. This uncertainty in *Kethuvim* is indicated in a note, and, where the Hebrew text permits, alternative renderings have been offered. However, emendations of the text of *Kethuvim*—except for the five *Megilloth*—were not proposed, and notes were kept to a minimum.

Some passages in *Kethuvim* are identical or very similar to passages in *Torah* and *Nevi'im*. The rendering of these passages in *Kethuvim* generally follows the wording in the earlier books; on occasion, however, owing to various considerations, divergences in style and translation will be found. For example, in the presentation of the poetry of the Psalms, it was deemed fitting, because of their liturgical use, to indicate the thought units through appropriate indentation. The text of *Kethuvim* frequently presented the translators with extraordinary difficulties, for it is hardly possible to convey in English the fullness of the Hebrew, with its ambiguities, its overtones, and the richness that it carries from centuries of use. Still, it was their goal to transmit something of the directness, the simplicity, and the uniquely Israelite expressions of piety that are so essential to the sublimity of the Hebrew Bible.

The committee's translation of *The Psalms* appeared in 1973; of *The Book of Job*, in 1980. The two were incorporated, with revisions, into the complete translations of *The Writings (Kethuvim)*, which appeared in 1982.

For this one-volume English edition of *Tanakh*, the translation of *The Torah*, first published twenty years earlier, underwent more revision than the more recent publications of *The Prophets* and *The Writings*. A number of the changes had already been projected in *Notes on the New Translation of the Torah*, edited by Harry M. Orlinsky and published by the Society in 1969. Subsequent research on the text has led to further revisions in the translation of *Torah* and some revisions in *Nevi'im* as well.

Ephraim Speiser, of the original committee, died in June 1965. Max Arzt, also an active member of the original committee, died in 1975, when the work of translating the prophetic books was almost complete. Since the appearance of *The Prophets* and *The Writings*, Bernard J. Bamberger, Solomon Grayzel, and Harry Freedman have also passed on.* Their memory, and their scholarship, will be for a blessing.

The Jewish Publication Society joins the members of the committees of translators in the hope that the results of their labors will find favor with God and man.

The Jewish Publication Society
September 15, 1985
ערב ראש השנה תשמ"ו

---

* Deceased and lamented since 1985: H. L. Ginsberg, Harry Orlinsky, and Jonas Greenfield.

TORAH THE FIVE BOOKS OF MOSES

GENESIS	בראשית
EXODUS	שמות
LEVITICUS	ויקרא
NUMBERS	במדבר
DEUTERONOMY	דברים

GENESIS

When God began to create[a] heaven and earth—[2]the earth being unformed and void, with darkness over the surface of the deep and a wind from[b] God sweeping over the water—[3]God said, "Let there be light"; and there was light. [4]God saw that the light was good, and God separated the light from the darkness. [5]God called the light Day, and the darkness He called Night. And there was evening and there was morning, a first day.[c]

[6]God said, "Let there be an expanse in the midst of the water, that it may separate water from water." [7]God made the expanse, and it separated the water which was below the expanse from the water which was above the expanse. And it was so. [8]God called the expanse Sky. And there was evening and there was morning, a second day.

[9]God said, "Let the water below the sky be gathered into one area, that the dry land may appear." And it was so. [10]God called the dry land Earth, and the gathering of waters He called Seas. And God saw that this was good. [11]And God said, "Let the earth sprout vegetation: seed-bearing plants, fruit trees of every kind on earth that bear fruit with the seed in it." And it was so. [12]The earth brought forth vegetation: seed-bearing plants of every kind, and trees of every kind bearing fruit with the seed in it. And God saw that this was good. [13]And there was evening and there was morning, a third day.

[14]God said, "Let there be lights in the expanse

א בְּרֵאשִׁית* בָּרָ֣א אֱלֹהִ֑ים אֵ֥ת הַשָּׁמַ֖יִם וְאֵ֥ת הָאָֽרֶץ: [2]וְהָאָ֗רֶץ הָיְתָ֥ה תֹ֙הוּ֙ וָבֹ֔הוּ וְחֹ֖שֶׁךְ עַל־פְּנֵ֣י תְה֑וֹם וְר֣וּחַ אֱלֹהִ֔ים מְרַחֶ֖פֶת עַל־פְּנֵ֥י הַמָּֽיִם: [3]וַיֹּ֥אמֶר אֱלֹהִ֖ים יְהִ֣י א֑וֹר וַֽיְהִי־אֽוֹר: [4]וַיַּ֧רְא אֱלֹהִ֛ים אֶת־הָא֖וֹר כִּי־ט֑וֹב וַיַּבְדֵּ֣ל אֱלֹהִ֔ים בֵּ֥ין הָא֖וֹר וּבֵ֥ין הַחֹֽשֶׁךְ: [5]וַיִּקְרָ֨א אֱלֹהִ֤ים ׀ לָאוֹר֙ י֔וֹם וְלַחֹ֖שֶׁךְ קָ֣רָא לָ֑יְלָה וַֽיְהִי־עֶ֥רֶב וַֽיְהִי־בֹ֖קֶר י֥וֹם אֶחָֽד: פ

[6]וַיֹּ֣אמֶר אֱלֹהִ֔ים יְהִ֥י רָקִ֖יעַ בְּת֣וֹךְ הַמָּ֑יִם וִיהִ֣י מַבְדִּ֔יל בֵּ֥ין מַ֖יִם לָמָֽיִם: [7]וַיַּ֣עַשׂ אֱלֹהִים֮ אֶת־הָרָקִיעַ֒ וַיַּבְדֵּ֗ל בֵּ֤ין הַמַּ֙יִם֙ אֲשֶׁר֙ מִתַּ֣חַת לָרָקִ֔יעַ וּבֵ֣ין הַמַּ֔יִם אֲשֶׁ֖ר מֵעַ֣ל לָרָקִ֑יעַ וַֽיְהִי־כֵֽן: [8]וַיִּקְרָ֧א אֱלֹהִ֛ים לָֽרָקִ֖יעַ שָׁמָ֑יִם וַֽיְהִי־עֶ֥רֶב וַֽיְהִי־בֹ֖קֶר י֥וֹם שֵׁנִֽי: פ

[9]וַיֹּ֣אמֶר אֱלֹהִ֗ים יִקָּו֨וּ הַמַּ֜יִם מִתַּ֤חַת הַשָּׁמַ֙יִם֙ אֶל־מָק֣וֹם אֶחָ֔ד וְתֵרָאֶ֖ה הַיַּבָּשָׁ֑ה וַֽיְהִי־כֵֽן: [10]וַיִּקְרָ֨א אֱלֹהִ֤ים ׀ לַיַּבָּשָׁה֙ אֶ֔רֶץ וּלְמִקְוֵ֥ה הַמַּ֖יִם קָרָ֣א יַמִּ֑ים וַיַּ֥רְא אֱלֹהִ֖ים כִּי־טֽוֹב: [11]וַיֹּ֣אמֶר אֱלֹהִ֗ים תַּֽדְשֵׁ֤א הָאָ֙רֶץ֙ דֶּ֔שֶׁא עֵ֚שֶׂב מַזְרִ֣יעַ זֶ֔רַע עֵ֣ץ פְּרִ֞י עֹ֤שֶׂה פְּרִי֙ לְמִינ֔וֹ אֲשֶׁ֥ר זַרְעוֹ־ב֖וֹ עַל־הָאָ֑רֶץ וַֽיְהִי־כֵֽן: [12]וַתּוֹצֵ֨א הָאָ֜רֶץ דֶּ֠שֶׁא עֵ֣שֶׂב מַזְרִ֤יעַ זֶ֙רַע֙ לְמִינֵ֔הוּ וְעֵ֧ץ עֹֽשֶׂה־פְּרִ֛י אֲשֶׁ֥ר זַרְעוֹ־ב֖וֹ לְמִינֵ֑הוּ וַיַּ֥רְא אֱלֹהִ֖ים כִּי־טֽוֹב: [13]וַֽיְהִי־עֶ֥רֶב וַֽיְהִי־בֹ֖קֶר י֥וֹם שְׁלִישִֽׁי: פ

[14]וַיֹּ֣אמֶר אֱלֹהִ֗ים יְהִ֤י מְאֹרֹת֙ בִּרְקִ֣יעַ

ב׳ רבתי לפי נוסחים המקובלים   v. 1.

---

a   Others "In the beginning God created."
b   Others "the spirit of."
c   Others "one day."

1

of the sky to separate day from night; they shall serve as signs for the set times—the days and the years; ¹⁵and they shall serve as lights in the expanse of the sky to shine upon the earth." And it was so. ¹⁶God made the two great lights, the greater light to dominate the day and the lesser light to dominate the night, and the stars. ¹⁷And God set them in the expanse of the sky to shine upon the earth, ¹⁸to dominate the day and the night, and to separate light from darkness. And God saw that this was good. ¹⁹And there was evening and there was morning, a fourth day.

²⁰God said, "Let the waters bring forth swarms of living creatures, and birds that fly above the earth across the expanse of the sky." ²¹God created the great sea monsters, and all the living creatures of every kind that creep, which the waters brought forth in swarms, and all the winged birds of every kind. And God saw that this was good. ²²God blessed them, saying, "Be fertile and increase, fill the waters in the seas, and let the birds increase on the earth." ²³And there was evening and there was morning, a fifth day.

²⁴God said, "Let the earth bring forth every kind of living creature: cattle, creeping things, and wild beasts of every kind." And it was so. ²⁵God made wild beasts of every kind and cattle of every kind, and all kinds of creeping things of the earth. And God saw that this was good. ²⁶And God said, "Let us make man in our image, after our likeness. They shall rule the fish of the sea, the birds of the sky, the cattle, the whole earth, and all the creeping things that creep on earth." ²⁷And God created man in His image, in the image of God He created him; male and female He created them. ²⁸God blessed them and God said to them, "Be fertile and increase, fill the earth and master it; and rule the fish of the sea, the birds of the sky, and all the living things that creep on earth."

הַשָּׁמַיִם לְהַבְדִּיל בֵּין הַיּוֹם וּבֵין הַלָּיְלָה וְהָיוּ לְאֹתֹת וּלְמוֹעֲדִים וּלְיָמִים וְשָׁנִים: ¹⁵ וְהָיוּ לִמְאוֹרֹת בִּרְקִיעַ הַשָּׁמַיִם לְהָאִיר עַל־הָאָרֶץ וַיְהִי־כֵן: ¹⁶ וַיַּעַשׂ אֱלֹהִים אֶת־שְׁנֵי הַמְּאֹרֹת הַגְּדֹלִים אֶת־הַמָּאוֹר הַגָּדֹל לְמֶמְשֶׁלֶת הַיּוֹם וְאֶת־הַמָּאוֹר הַקָּטֹן לְמֶמְשֶׁלֶת הַלַּיְלָה וְאֵת הַכּוֹכָבִים: ¹⁷ וַיִּתֵּן אֹתָם אֱלֹהִים בִּרְקִיעַ הַשָּׁמָיִם לְהָאִיר עַל־הָאָרֶץ: ¹⁸ וְלִמְשֹׁל בַּיּוֹם וּבַלַּיְלָה וּלְהַבְדִּיל בֵּין הָאוֹר וּבֵין הַחֹשֶׁךְ וַיַּרְא אֱלֹהִים כִּי־טוֹב: ¹⁹ וַיְהִי־עֶרֶב וַיְהִי־בֹקֶר יוֹם רְבִיעִי: פ

²⁰ וַיֹּאמֶר אֱלֹהִים יִשְׁרְצוּ הַמַּיִם שֶׁרֶץ נֶפֶשׁ חַיָּה וְעוֹף יְעוֹפֵף עַל־הָאָרֶץ עַל־פְּנֵי רְקִיעַ הַשָּׁמָיִם: ²¹ וַיִּבְרָא אֱלֹהִים אֶת־הַתַּנִּינִם* הַגְּדֹלִים וְאֵת כָּל־נֶפֶשׁ הַחַיָּה | הָרֹמֶשֶׂת אֲשֶׁר שָׁרְצוּ הַמַּיִם לְמִינֵהֶם וְאֵת כָּל־עוֹף כָּנָף לְמִינֵהוּ וַיַּרְא אֱלֹהִים כִּי־טוֹב: ²² וַיְבָרֶךְ אֹתָם אֱלֹהִים לֵאמֹר פְּרוּ וּרְבוּ וּמִלְאוּ אֶת־הַמַּיִם בַּיַּמִּים וְהָעוֹף יִרֶב בָּאָרֶץ: ²³ וַיְהִי־עֶרֶב וַיְהִי־בֹקֶר יוֹם חֲמִישִׁי: פ

²⁴ וַיֹּאמֶר אֱלֹהִים תּוֹצֵא הָאָרֶץ נֶפֶשׁ חַיָּה לְמִינָהּ בְּהֵמָה וָרֶמֶשׂ וְחַיְתוֹ־אֶרֶץ לְמִינָהּ וַיְהִי־כֵן: ²⁵ וַיַּעַשׂ אֱלֹהִים אֶת־חַיַּת הָאָרֶץ לְמִינָהּ וְאֶת־הַבְּהֵמָה לְמִינָהּ וְאֵת כָּל־רֶמֶשׂ הָאֲדָמָה לְמִינֵהוּ וַיַּרְא אֱלֹהִים כִּי־טוֹב: ²⁶ וַיֹּאמֶר אֱלֹהִים נַעֲשֶׂה אָדָם בְּצַלְמֵנוּ כִּדְמוּתֵנוּ וְיִרְדּוּ בִדְגַת הַיָּם וּבְעוֹף הַשָּׁמַיִם וּבַבְּהֵמָה וּבְכָל־הָאָרֶץ וּבְכָל־הָרֶמֶשׂ הָרֹמֵשׂ עַל־הָאָרֶץ: ²⁷ וַיִּבְרָא אֱלֹהִים | אֶת־הָאָדָם בְּצַלְמוֹ בְּצֶלֶם אֱלֹהִים בָּרָא אֹתוֹ זָכָר וּנְקֵבָה בָּרָא אֹתָם: ²⁸ וַיְבָרֶךְ אֹתָם אֱלֹהִים וַיֹּאמֶר לָהֶם אֱלֹהִים פְּרוּ וּרְבוּ וּמִלְאוּ אֶת־הָאָרֶץ וְכִבְשֻׁהָ וּרְדוּ בִּדְגַת הַיָּם וּבְעוֹף הַשָּׁמַיִם וּבְכָל־חַיָּה הָרֹמֶשֶׂת עַל־הָאָרֶץ:

²⁹God said, "See, I give you every seed-bearing plant that is upon all the earth, and every tree that has seed-bearing fruit; they shall be yours for food. ³⁰And to all the animals on land, to all the birds of the sky, and to everything that creeps on earth, in which there is the breath of life, [I give] all the green plants for food." And it was so. ³¹And God saw all that He had made, and found it very good. And there was evening and there was morning, the sixth day.

2 The heaven and the earth were finished, and all their array. ²On the seventh day God finished the work that He had been doing, and He ceased[a] on the seventh day from all the work that He had done. ³And God blessed the seventh day and declared it holy, because on it God ceased from all the work of creation that He had done. ⁴Such is the story of heaven and earth when they were created.

When the LORD God made earth and heaven—⁵when no shrub of the field was yet on earth and no grasses of the field had yet sprouted, because the LORD God had not sent rain upon the earth and there was no man to till the soil, ⁶but a flow would well up from the ground and water the whole surface of the earth—⁷the LORD God formed man[b] from the dust of the earth.[c] He blew into his nostrils the breath of life, and man became a living being.

⁸The LORD God planted a garden in Eden, in the east, and placed there the man whom He had formed. ⁹And from the ground the LORD God caused to grow every tree that was pleasing to the sight and good for food, with the tree of life in the middle of the garden, and the tree of knowledge of good and bad.

כט וַיֹּאמֶר אֱלֹהִים הִנֵּה נָתַתִּי לָכֶם אֶת־כָּל־עֵשֶׂב ׀ זֹרֵעַ זֶרַע אֲשֶׁר עַל־פְּנֵי כָל־הָאָרֶץ וְאֶת־כָּל־הָעֵץ אֲשֶׁר־בּוֹ פְרִי־עֵץ זֹרֵעַ זָרַע לָכֶם יִהְיֶה לְאָכְלָה: ל וּלְכָל־חַיַּת הָאָרֶץ וּלְכָל־עוֹף הַשָּׁמַיִם וּלְכֹל ׀ רוֹמֵשׂ עַל־הָאָרֶץ אֲשֶׁר־בּוֹ נֶפֶשׁ חַיָּה אֶת־כָּל־יֶרֶק עֵשֶׂב לְאָכְלָה וַיְהִי־כֵן: לא וַיַּרְא אֱלֹהִים אֶת־כָּל־אֲשֶׁר עָשָׂה וְהִנֵּה־טוֹב מְאֹד וַיְהִי־עֶרֶב וַיְהִי־בֹקֶר יוֹם הַשִּׁשִּׁי: פ

ב וַיְכֻלּוּ הַשָּׁמַיִם וְהָאָרֶץ וְכָל־צְבָאָם: ב וַיְכַל אֱלֹהִים בַּיּוֹם הַשְּׁבִיעִי מְלַאכְתּוֹ אֲשֶׁר עָשָׂה וַיִּשְׁבֹּת בַּיּוֹם הַשְּׁבִיעִי מִכָּל־מְלַאכְתּוֹ אֲשֶׁר עָשָׂה: ג וַיְבָרֶךְ אֱלֹהִים אֶת־יוֹם הַשְּׁבִיעִי וַיְקַדֵּשׁ אֹתוֹ כִּי בוֹ שָׁבַת מִכָּל־מְלַאכְתּוֹ אֲשֶׁר־בָּרָא אֱלֹהִים לַעֲשׂוֹת: פ ד אֵלֶּה תוֹלְדוֹת הַשָּׁמַיִם וְהָאָרֶץ בְּהִבָּרְאָם*

בְּיוֹם עֲשׂוֹת יְהוָה אֱלֹהִים אֶרֶץ וְשָׁמָיִם: ה וְכֹל ׀ שִׂיחַ הַשָּׂדֶה טֶרֶם יִהְיֶה בָאָרֶץ וְכָל־עֵשֶׂב הַשָּׂדֶה טֶרֶם יִצְמָח כִּי לֹא הִמְטִיר יְהוָה אֱלֹהִים עַל־הָאָרֶץ וְאָדָם אַיִן לַעֲבֹד אֶת־הָאֲדָמָה: ו וְאֵד יַעֲלֶה מִן־הָאָרֶץ וְהִשְׁקָה אֶת־כָּל־פְּנֵי־הָאֲדָמָה: ז וַיִּיצֶר יְהוָה אֱלֹהִים אֶת־הָאָדָם עָפָר מִן־הָאֲדָמָה וַיִּפַּח בְּאַפָּיו נִשְׁמַת חַיִּים וַיְהִי הָאָדָם לְנֶפֶשׁ חַיָּה: ח וַיִּטַּע יְהוָה אֱלֹהִים גַּן־בְּעֵדֶן מִקֶּדֶם וַיָּשֶׂם שָׁם אֶת־הָאָדָם אֲשֶׁר יָצָר: ט וַיַּצְמַח יְהוָה אֱלֹהִים מִן־הָאֲדָמָה כָּל־עֵץ נֶחְמָד לְמַרְאֶה וְטוֹב לְמַאֲכָל וְעֵץ הַחַיִּים בְּתוֹךְ הַגָּן וְעֵץ הַדַּעַת טוֹב וָרָע:

ה' זְעֵירָא לְפִי נֻסְחִים הַמְקֻבָּלִים v. 4.

a Or "rested."
b Heb. 'adam.
c Heb. 'adamah.

[10]A river issues from Eden to water the garden, and it then divides and becomes four branches. [11]The name of the first is Pishon, the one that winds through the whole land of Havilah, where the gold is. ([12]The gold of that land is good; bdellium is there, and lapis lazuli.[d]) [13]The name of the second river is Gihon, the one that winds through the whole land of Cush. [14]The name of the third river is Tigris, the one that flows east of Asshur. And the fourth river is the Euphrates.

[15]The LORD God took the man and placed him in the garden of Eden, to till it and tend it. [16]And the LORD God commanded the man, saying, "Of every tree of the garden you are free to eat; [17]but as for the tree of knowledge of good and bad, you must not eat of it; for as soon as you eat of it, you shall die."

[18]The LORD God said, "It is not good for man to be alone; I will make a fitting helper for him." [19]And the LORD God formed out of the earth all the wild beasts and all the birds of the sky, and brought them to the man to see what he would call them; and whatever the man called each living creature, that would be its name. [20]And the man gave names to all the cattle and to the birds of the sky and to all the wild beasts; but for Adam no fitting helper was found. [21]So the LORD God cast a deep sleep upon the man; and, while he slept, He took one of his ribs and closed up the flesh at that spot. [22]And the LORD God fashioned the rib that He had taken from the man into a woman; and He brought her to the man. [23]Then the man said,

"This one at last
Is bone of my bones
And flesh of my flesh.
This one shall be called Woman,[e]
For from man[f] was she taken."

---

d   Others "onyx"; meaning of Heb. shoham uncertain.
e   Heb. 'ishshah.
f   Heb. 'ish.

10 וְנָהָר֙ יֹצֵ֣א מֵעֵ֔דֶן לְהַשְׁק֖וֹת אֶת־הַגָּ֑ן וּמִשָּׁם֙ יִפָּרֵ֔ד וְהָיָ֖ה לְאַרְבָּעָ֥ה רָאשִֽׁים׃ 11 שֵׁ֥ם הָֽאֶחָ֖ד פִּישׁ֑וֹן ה֣וּא הַסֹּבֵ֗ב אֵ֚ת כָּל־אֶ֣רֶץ הַֽחֲוִילָ֔ה אֲשֶׁר־שָׁ֖ם הַזָּהָֽב׃ 12 וּֽזֲהַ֛ב הָאָ֥רֶץ הַהִ֖וא ט֑וֹב שָׁ֥ם הַבְּדֹ֖לַח וְאֶ֥בֶן הַשֹּֽׁהַם׃ 13 וְשֵֽׁם־הַנָּהָ֥ר הַשֵּׁנִ֖י גִּיח֑וֹן ה֣וּא הַסּוֹבֵ֔ב אֵ֖ת כָּל־אֶ֥רֶץ כּֽוּשׁ׃ 14 וְשֵׁ֨ם הַנָּהָ֤ר הַשְּׁלִישִׁי֙ חִדֶּ֔קֶל ה֥וּא הַֽהֹלֵ֖ךְ קִדְמַ֣ת אַשּׁ֑וּר וְהַנָּהָ֥ר הָרְבִיעִ֖י ה֥וּא פְרָֽת׃ 15 וַיִּקַּ֛ח יְהֹוָ֥ה אֱלֹהִ֖ים אֶת־הָֽאָדָ֑ם וַיַּנִּחֵ֣הוּ בְגַן־עֵ֔דֶן לְעָבְדָ֖הּ וּלְשָׁמְרָֽהּ׃ 16 וַיְצַו֙ יְהֹוָ֣ה אֱלֹהִ֔ים עַל־הָֽאָדָ֖ם לֵאמֹ֑ר מִכֹּ֥ל עֵֽץ־הַגָּ֖ן אָכֹ֥ל תֹּאכֵֽל׃ 17 וּמֵעֵ֗ץ הַדַּ֙עַת֙ ט֣וֹב וָרָ֔ע לֹ֥א תֹאכַ֖ל מִמֶּ֑נּוּ כִּ֗י בְּי֛וֹם אֲכׇלְךָ֥ מִמֶּ֖נּוּ מ֥וֹת תָּמֽוּת׃ 18 וַיֹּ֙אמֶר֙ יְהֹוָ֣ה אֱלֹהִ֔ים לֹא־ט֛וֹב הֱי֥וֹת הָֽאָדָ֖ם לְבַדּ֑וֹ אֶֽעֱשֶׂה־לּ֥וֹ עֵ֖זֶר כְּנֶגְדּֽוֹ׃ 19 וַיִּצֶר֩ יְהֹוָ֨ה אֱלֹהִ֜ים מִן־הָֽאֲדָמָ֗ה כָּל־חַיַּ֤ת הַשָּׂדֶה֙ וְאֵת֙ כָּל־ע֣וֹף הַשָּׁמַ֔יִם וַיָּבֵא֙ אֶל־הָ֣אָדָ֔ם לִרְא֖וֹת מַה־יִּקְרָא־ל֑וֹ וְכֹל֩ אֲשֶׁ֨ר יִקְרָא־ל֧וֹ הָֽאָדָ֛ם נֶ֥פֶשׁ חַיָּ֖ה ה֥וּא שְׁמֽוֹ׃ 20 וַיִּקְרָ֨א הָֽאָדָ֜ם שֵׁמ֗וֹת לְכׇל־הַבְּהֵמָה֙ וּלְע֣וֹף הַשָּׁמַ֔יִם וּלְכֹ֖ל חַיַּ֣ת הַשָּׂדֶ֑ה וּלְאָדָ֕ם לֹֽא־מָצָ֥א עֵ֖זֶר כְּנֶגְדּֽוֹ׃ 21 וַיַּפֵּל֩ יְהֹוָ֨ה אֱלֹהִ֧ים ׀ תַּרְדֵּמָ֛ה עַל־הָאָדָ֖ם וַיִּישָׁ֑ן וַיִּקַּ֗ח אַחַת֙ מִצַּלְעֹתָ֔יו וַיִּסְגֹּ֥ר בָּשָׂ֖ר תַּחְתֶּֽנָּה׃ 22 וַיִּ֩בֶן֩ יְהֹוָ֨ה אֱלֹהִ֧ים ׀ אֶֽת־הַצֵּלָ֛ע אֲשֶׁר־לָקַ֥ח מִן־הָֽאָדָ֖ם לְאִשָּׁ֑ה וַיְבִאֶ֖הָ אֶל־הָֽאָדָֽם׃ 23 וַיֹּ֘אמֶר֮ הָֽאָדָם֒ זֹ֣את הַפַּ֗עַם עֶ֚צֶם מֵֽעֲצָמַ֔י וּבָשָׂ֖ר מִבְּשָׂרִ֑י לְזֹאת֙ יִקָּרֵ֣א אִשָּׁ֔ה כִּ֥י מֵאִ֖ישׁ לֻֽקְחָה־זֹּֽאת׃

24Hence a man leaves his father and mother and clings to his wife, so that they become one flesh.

25The two of them were naked,g the man and his wife, yet they felt no shame. 1Now the serpent was the shrewdest of all the wild beasts that the LORD God had made. He said to the woman, "Did God really say: You shall not eat of any tree of the garden?" 2The woman replied to the serpent, "We may eat of the fruit of the other trees of the garden. 3It is only about fruit of the tree in the middle of the garden that God said: 'You shall not eat of it or touch it, lest you die.'" 4And the serpent said to the woman, "You are not going to die, 5but God knows that as soon as you eat of it your eyes will be opened and you will be like a-divine be-ings who know-a good and bad." 6When the woman saw that the tree was good for eating and a delight to the eyes, and that the tree was desirable as a source of wisdom, she took of its fruit and ate. She also gave some to her husband, and he ate. 7Then the eyes of both of them were opened and they perceived that they were na-ked; and they sewed together fig leaves and made themselves loincloths.

8They heard the sound of the LORD God mov-ing about in the garden at the breezy time of day; and the man and his wife hid from the LORD God among the trees of the garden. 9The LORD God called out to the man and said to him, "Where are you?" 10He replied, "I heard the sound of You in the garden, and I was afraid because I was naked, so I hid." 11Then He asked, "Who told you that you were naked? Did you eat of the tree from which I had forbidden you to eat?" 12The man said, "The woman You put at my side—she gave me of the tree, and I ate." 13And the LORD God said to the woman, "What

---

g Heb. 'arummim, *play on* 'arum *"shrewd" in* 3.1.

a-a Others "God, who knows."

24 עַל־כֵּן יַעֲזָב־אִישׁ אֶת־אָבִיו וְאֶת־אִמּוֹ וְדָבַק בְּאִשְׁתּוֹ וְהָיוּ לְבָשָׂר אֶחָד:

25 וַיִּהְיוּ שְׁנֵיהֶם עֲרוּמִּים הָאָדָם וְאִשְׁתּוֹ וְלֹא יִתְבֹּשָׁשׁוּ: 1 וְהַנָּחָשׁ הָיָה עָרוּם מִכֹּל חַיַּת הַשָּׂדֶה אֲשֶׁר עָשָׂה יְהוָה אֱלֹהִים וַיֹּאמֶר אֶל־הָאִשָּׁה אַף כִּי־אָמַר אֱלֹהִים לֹא תֹאכְלוּ מִכֹּל עֵץ הַגָּן: 2 וַתֹּאמֶר הָאִשָּׁה אֶל־הַנָּחָשׁ מִפְּרִי עֵץ־הַגָּן נֹאכֵל: 3 וּמִפְּרִי הָעֵץ אֲשֶׁר בְּתוֹךְ־הַגָּן אָמַר אֱלֹהִים לֹא תֹאכְלוּ מִמֶּנּוּ וְלֹא תִגְּעוּ בּוֹ פֶּן־תְּמֻתוּן: 4 וַיֹּאמֶר הַנָּחָשׁ אֶל־הָאִשָּׁה לֹא־מוֹת תְּמֻתוּן: 5 כִּי יֹדֵעַ אֱלֹהִים כִּי בְּיוֹם אֲכָלְכֶם מִמֶּנּוּ וְנִפְקְחוּ עֵינֵיכֶם וִהְיִיתֶם כֵּאלֹהִים יֹדְעֵי טוֹב וָרָע: 6 וַתֵּרֶא הָאִשָּׁה כִּי טוֹב הָעֵץ לְמַאֲכָל וְכִי תַאֲוָה־הוּא לָעֵינַיִם וְנֶחְמָד הָעֵץ לְהַשְׂכִּיל וַתִּקַּח מִפִּרְיוֹ וַתֹּאכַל וַתִּתֵּן גַּם־לְאִישָׁהּ עִמָּהּ וַיֹּאכַל: 7 וַתִּפָּקַחְנָה עֵינֵי שְׁנֵיהֶם וַיֵּדְעוּ כִּי עֵירֻמִּם הֵם וַיִּתְפְּרוּ עֲלֵה תְאֵנָה וַיַּעֲשׂוּ לָהֶם חֲגֹרֹת:

8 וַיִּשְׁמְעוּ אֶת־קוֹל יְהוָה אֱלֹהִים מִתְהַלֵּךְ בַּגָּן לְרוּחַ הַיּוֹם וַיִּתְחַבֵּא הָאָדָם וְאִשְׁתּוֹ מִפְּנֵי יְהוָה אֱלֹהִים בְּתוֹךְ עֵץ הַגָּן: 9 וַיִּקְרָא יְהוָה אֱלֹהִים אֶל־הָאָדָם וַיֹּאמֶר לוֹ אַיֶּכָּה: 10 וַיֹּאמֶר אֶת־קֹלְךָ שָׁמַעְתִּי בַּגָּן וָאִירָא כִּי־עֵירֹם אָנֹכִי וָאֵחָבֵא: 11 וַיֹּאמֶר מִי הִגִּיד לְךָ כִּי עֵירֹם אָתָּה הֲמִן־הָעֵץ אֲשֶׁר צִוִּיתִיךָ לְבִלְתִּי אֲכָל־מִמֶּנּוּ אָכָלְתָּ: 12 וַיֹּאמֶר הָאָדָם הָאִשָּׁה אֲשֶׁר נָתַתָּה עִמָּדִי הִוא נָתְנָה־לִּי מִן־הָעֵץ וָאֹכֵל: 13 וַיֹּאמֶר יְהוָה אֱלֹהִים לָאִשָּׁה מַה־זֹּאת עָשִׂית וַתֹּאמֶר הָאִשָּׁה הַנָּחָשׁ הִשִּׁיאַנִי וָאֹכֵל: 14 וַיֹּאמֶר יְהוָה אֱלֹהִים | אֶל־הַנָּחָשׁ כִּי עָשִׂיתָ זֹּאת

is this you have done!" The woman replied,
"The serpent duped me, and I ate." ¹⁴Then the
LORD God said to the serpent,

> "Because you did this,
> More cursed shall you be
> Than all cattle
> And all the wild beasts:
> On your belly shall you crawl
> And dirt shall you eat
> All the days of your life.

¹⁵I will put enmity
> Between you and the woman,
> And between your offspring and hers;
> They shall strike at your head,
> And you shall strike at their heel."

¹⁶And to the woman He said,

> "I will make most severe
> Your pangs in childbearing;
> In pain shall you bear children.
> Yet your urge shall be for your husband,
> And he shall rule over you."

¹⁷To Adam He said, "Because you did as your
wife said and ate of the tree about which I
commanded you, 'You shall not eat of it,'

> Cursed be the ground because of you;
> By toil shall you eat of it
> All the days of your life:
> ¹⁸Thorns and thistles shall it sprout for you.
> But your food shall be the grasses of the field;
> ¹⁹By the sweat of your brow
> Shall you get bread to eat,
> Until you return to the ground—
> For from it you were taken.
> For dust you are,
> And to dust you shall return."

²⁰The man named his wife Eve,ᵇ because she
was the mother of all the living.ᶜ ²¹And the
LORD God made garments of skins for Adam
and his wife, and clothed them.

אָר֤וּר אַתָּה֙
מִכָּל־הַבְּהֵמָ֔ה
וּמִכֹּ֖ל חַיַּ֣ת הַשָּׂדֶ֑ה
עַל־גְּחֹנְךָ֣ תֵלֵ֔ךְ
וְעָפָ֥ר תֹּאכַ֖ל
כָּל־יְמֵ֥י חַיֶּֽיךָ׃
15 וְאֵיבָ֣ה ׀ אָשִׁ֗ית
בֵּֽינְךָ֙ וּבֵ֣ין הָֽאִשָּׁ֔ה
וּבֵ֥ין זַרְעֲךָ֖ וּבֵ֣ין זַרְעָ֑הּ
ה֚וּא יְשׁוּפְךָ֣ רֹ֔אשׁ
וְאַתָּ֖ה תְּשׁוּפֶ֥נּוּ עָקֵֽב׃ ס
16 אֶֽל־הָאִשָּׁ֣ה אָמַ֗ר
הַרְבָּ֤ה אַרְבֶּה֙
עִצְּבוֹנֵ֣ךְ וְהֵֽרֹנֵ֔ךְ
בְּעֶ֖צֶב תֵּֽלְדִ֣י בָנִ֑ים
וְאֶל־אִישֵׁךְ֙ תְּשׁ֣וּקָתֵ֔ךְ
וְה֖וּא יִמְשָׁל־בָּֽךְ׃ ס
17 וּלְאָדָ֣ם אָמַ֗ר כִּֽי־שָׁמַעְתָּ֮ לְק֣וֹל אִשְׁתֶּךָ֒
וַתֹּ֙אכַל֙ מִן־הָעֵ֔ץ אֲשֶׁ֣ר צִוִּיתִ֔יךָ לֵאמֹ֖ר לֹ֣א
תֹאכַ֣ל מִמֶּ֑נּוּ
אֲרוּרָ֤ה הָֽאֲדָמָה֙ בַּֽעֲבוּרֶ֔ךָ
בְּעִצָּבוֹן֙ תֹּֽאכֲלֶ֔נָּה
כֹּ֖ל יְמֵ֥י חַיֶּֽיךָ׃
18 וְק֥וֹץ וְדַרְדַּ֖ר תַּצְמִ֣יחַֽ לָ֑ךְ
וְאָֽכַלְתָּ֖ אֶת־עֵ֥שֶׂב הַשָּׂדֶֽה׃
19 בְּזֵעַ֤ת אַפֶּ֙יךָ֙
תֹּ֣אכַל לֶ֔חֶם
עַ֤ד שֽׁוּבְךָ֙ אֶל־הָ֣אֲדָמָ֔ה
כִּ֥י מִמֶּ֖נָּה לֻקָּ֑חְתָּ
כִּֽי־עָפָ֣ר אַ֔תָּה
וְאֶל־עָפָ֖ר תָּשֽׁוּב׃
20 וַיִּקְרָ֧א הָֽאָדָ֛ם שֵׁ֥ם אִשְׁתּ֖וֹ חַוָּ֑ה כִּ֛י
הִ֥וא הָֽיְתָ֖ה אֵ֥ם כָּל־חָֽי׃ 21 וַיַּ֩עַשׂ֩ יְהֹוָ֨ה
אֱלֹהִ֜ים לְאָדָ֧ם וּלְאִשְׁתּ֛וֹ כָּתְנ֥וֹת ע֖וֹר
וַיַּלְבִּשֵֽׁם׃ פ

---

b   Heb. ḥawwah.
c   Heb. ḥay.

22And the Lord God said, "Now that the man has become like one of us, knowing good and bad, what if he should stretch out his hand and take also from the tree of life and eat, and live forever!" 23So the Lord God banished him from the garden of Eden, to till the soil from which he was taken. 24He drove the man out, and stationed east of the garden of Eden the cherubim and the fiery ever-turning sword, to guard the way to the tree of life.

4 Now the man knew[a] his wife Eve, and she conceived and bore Cain, saying, "I have gained[b] a male child with the help of the Lord." 2She then bore his brother Abel. Abel became a keeper of sheep, and Cain became a tiller of the soil. 3In the course of time, Cain brought an offering to the Lord from the fruit of the soil; 4and Abel, for his part, brought the choicest of the firstlings of his flock. The Lord paid heed to Abel and his offering, 5but to Cain and his offering He paid no heed. Cain was much distressed and his face fell. 6And the Lord said to Cain,

"Why are you distressed,
And why is your face fallen?
7cSurely, if you do right,
There is uplift.
But if you do not do right
Sin couches at the door;
Its urge is toward you,
Yet you can be its master."

8Cain said to his brother Abel[d] ... and when they were in the field, Cain set upon his brother Abel and killed him. 9The Lord said to Cain, "Where is your brother Abel?" And he said, "I do not know. Am I my brother's keeper?" 10Then He said, "What have you done? Hark,

22 וַיֹּאמֶר ׀ יְהוָה אֱלֹהִים הֵן הָאָדָם הָיָה כְּאַחַד מִמֶּנּוּ לָדַעַת טוֹב וָרָע וְעַתָּה ׀ פֶּן־יִשְׁלַח יָדוֹ וְלָקַח גַּם מֵעֵץ הַחַיִּים וְאָכַל וָחַי לְעֹלָם: 23 וַיְשַׁלְּחֵהוּ יְהוָה אֱלֹהִים מִגַּן־עֵדֶן לַעֲבֹד אֶת־הָאֲדָמָה אֲשֶׁר לֻקַּח מִשָּׁם: 24 וַיְגָרֶשׁ אֶת־הָאָדָם וַיַּשְׁכֵּן מִקֶּדֶם לְגַן־עֵדֶן אֶת־הַכְּרֻבִים וְאֵת לַהַט הַחֶרֶב הַמִּתְהַפֶּכֶת לִשְׁמֹר אֶת־דֶּרֶךְ עֵץ הַחַיִּים: ס

ד וְהָאָדָם יָדַע אֶת־חַוָּה אִשְׁתּוֹ וַתַּהַר וַתֵּלֶד אֶת־קַיִן וַתֹּאמֶר קָנִיתִי אִישׁ אֶת־יְהוָה: 2 וַתֹּסֶף לָלֶדֶת אֶת־אָחִיו אֶת־הָבֶל וַיְהִי־הֶבֶל רֹעֵה צֹאן וְקַיִן הָיָה עֹבֵד אֲדָמָה: 3 וַיְהִי מִקֵּץ יָמִים וַיָּבֵא קַיִן מִפְּרִי הָאֲדָמָה מִנְחָה לַיהוָה: 4 וְהֶבֶל הֵבִיא גַם־הוּא מִבְּכֹרוֹת צֹאנוֹ וּמֵחֶלְבֵהֶן* וַיִּשַׁע יְהוָה אֶל־הֶבֶל וְאֶל־מִנְחָתוֹ: 5 וְאֶל־קַיִן וְאֶל־מִנְחָתוֹ לֹא שָׁעָה וַיִּחַר לְקַיִן מְאֹד וַיִּפְּלוּ פָּנָיו: 6 וַיֹּאמֶר יְהוָה אֶל־קָיִן

לָמָּה חָרָה לָךְ
וְלָמָּה נָפְלוּ פָנֶיךָ:
7 הֲלוֹא אִם־תֵּיטִיב
שְׂאֵת
וְאִם לֹא תֵיטִיב
לַפֶּתַח חַטָּאת רֹבֵץ
וְאֵלֶיךָ תְּשׁוּקָתוֹ
וְאַתָּה תִּמְשָׁל־בּוֹ:
8 וַיֹּאמֶר קַיִן אֶל־הֶבֶל אָחִיו וַיְהִי בִּהְיוֹתָם בַּשָּׂדֶה וַיָּקָם קַיִן אֶל־הֶבֶל אָחִיו וַיַּהַרְגֵהוּ: 9 וַיֹּאמֶר יְהוָה אֶל־קַיִן אֵי הֶבֶל אָחִיךָ וַיֹּאמֶר לֹא יָדַעְתִּי הֲשֹׁמֵר אָחִי אָנֹכִי: 10 וַיֹּאמֶר מֶה עָשִׂיתָ קוֹל דְּמֵי אָחִיךָ

v. 4. ב' רפה

---

a   Heb. yada', often in a sexual sense.
b   Heb. qanithi, connected with "Cain."
c   Meaning of verse uncertain.
d   Ancient versions, including the Targum, read "Come, let us go out into the field."

your brother's blood cries out to Me from the ground! ¹¹Therefore, you shall be more cursed than the ground,ᵉ which opened its mouth to receive your brother's blood from your hand. ¹²If you till the soil, it shall no longer yield its strength to you. You shall become a ceaseless wanderer on earth."

¹³Cain said to the LORD, "My punishment is too great to bear! ¹⁴Since You have banished me this day from the soil, and I must avoid Your presence and become a restless wanderer on earth—anyone who meets me may kill me!" ¹⁵The LORD said to him, "I promise, if anyone kills Cain, sevenfold vengeance shall be taken on him." And the LORD put a mark on Cain, lest anyone who met him should kill him. ¹⁶Cain left the presence of the LORD and settled in the land of Nod, east of Eden.

¹⁷Cain knew his wife, and she conceived and bore Enoch. And he then founded a city, and named the city after his son Enoch. ¹⁸To Enoch was born Irad, and Irad begot Mehujael, and Mehujaelᶠ begot Methusael, and Methusael begot Lamech. ¹⁹Lamech took to himself two wives: the name of the one was Adah, and the name of the other was Zillah. ²⁰Adah bore Jabal; he was the ancestor of those who dwell in tents and amidst herds. ²¹And the name of his brother was Jubal; he was the ancestor of all who play the lyre and the pipe. ²²As for Zillah, she bore Tubal-cain, who forged all implements of copper and iron. And the sister of Tubal-cain was Naamah.

²³And Lamech said to his wives,

"Adah and Zillah, hear my voice;
O wives of Lamech, give ear to my speech.
I have slain a man for wounding me,
And a lad for bruising me.
²⁴If Cain is avenged sevenfold,
Then Lamech seventy-sevenfold."

צֹעֲקִים אֵלַי מִן־הָאֲדָמָה: ¹¹ וְעַתָּה אָרוּר אָתָּה מִן־הָאֲדָמָה אֲשֶׁר פָּצְתָה אֶת־פִּיהָ לָקַחַת אֶת־דְּמֵי אָחִיךָ מִיָּדֶךָ: ¹² כִּי תַעֲבֹד אֶת־הָאֲדָמָה לֹא־תֹסֵף תֵּת־כֹּחָהּ לָךְ נָע וָנָד תִּהְיֶה בָאָרֶץ:

¹³ וַיֹּאמֶר קַיִן אֶל־יְהֹוָה גָּדוֹל עֲוֹנִי מִנְּשֹׂא: ¹⁴ הֵן גֵּרַשְׁתָּ אֹתִי הַיּוֹם מֵעַל פְּנֵי הָאֲדָמָה וּמִפָּנֶיךָ אֶסָּתֵר וְהָיִיתִי נָע וָנָד בָּאָרֶץ וְהָיָה כָל־מֹצְאִי יַהַרְגֵנִי: ¹⁵ וַיֹּאמֶר לוֹ יְהֹוָה לָכֵן כָּל־הֹרֵג קַיִן שִׁבְעָתַיִם יֻקָּם וַיָּשֶׂם יְהֹוָה לְקַיִן אוֹת לְבִלְתִּי הַכּוֹת־אֹתוֹ כָּל־מֹצְאוֹ: ¹⁶ וַיֵּצֵא קַיִן מִלִּפְנֵי יְהֹוָה וַיֵּשֶׁב בְּאֶרֶץ־נוֹד קִדְמַת־עֵדֶן:

¹⁷ וַיֵּדַע קַיִן אֶת־אִשְׁתּוֹ וַתַּהַר וַתֵּלֶד אֶת־חֲנוֹךְ וַיְהִי בֹּנֶה עִיר וַיִּקְרָא שֵׁם הָעִיר כְּשֵׁם בְּנוֹ חֲנוֹךְ: ¹⁸ וַיִּוָּלֵד לַחֲנוֹךְ אֶת־עִירָד וְעִירָד יָלַד אֶת־מְחוּיָאֵל וּמְחִיָּיאֵל יָלַד אֶת־מְתוּשָׁאֵל וּמְתוּשָׁאֵל יָלַד אֶת־לָמֶךְ: ¹⁹ וַיִּקַּח־לוֹ לֶמֶךְ שְׁתֵּי נָשִׁים שֵׁם הָאַחַת עָדָה וְשֵׁם הַשֵּׁנִית צִלָּה: ²⁰ וַתֵּלֶד עָדָה אֶת־יָבָל הוּא הָיָה אֲבִי יֹשֵׁב אֹהֶל וּמִקְנֶה: ²¹ וְשֵׁם אָחִיו יוּבָל הוּא הָיָה אֲבִי כָּל־תֹּפֵשׂ כִּנּוֹר וְעוּגָב: ²² וְצִלָּה גַם־הִוא יָלְדָה אֶת־תּוּבַל קַיִן לֹטֵשׁ כָּל־חֹרֵשׁ נְחֹשֶׁת וּבַרְזֶל וַאֲחוֹת תּוּבַל־קַיִן נַעֲמָה: ²³ וַיֹּאמֶר לֶמֶךְ לְנָשָׁיו

עָדָה וְצִלָּה שְׁמַעַן קוֹלִי
נְשֵׁי לֶמֶךְ הַאְזֵנָּה אִמְרָתִי
כִּי אִישׁ הָרַגְתִּי לְפִצְעִי
וְיֶלֶד לְחַבֻּרָתִי:
²⁴ כִּי שִׁבְעָתַיִם יֻקַּם־קָיִן
וְלֶמֶךְ שִׁבְעִים וְשִׁבְעָה:

ᵉ See 3.17.
ᶠ Heb. Mehijael.

8

25Adam knew his wife again, and she bore a son and named him Seth, meaning, "God has g-provided me with-g another offspring in place of Abel," for Cain had killed him. 26And to Seth, in turn, a son was born, and he named him Enosh. It was then that men began to invoke the LORD by name.

5 This is the record of Adam's line.—When God created man, He made him in the likeness of God; 2male and female He created them. And when they were created, He blessed them and called them Man.—3When Adam had lived 130 years, he begot a son in his likeness after his image, and he named him Seth. 4After the birth of Seth, Adam lived 800 years and begot sons and daughters. 5All the days that Adam lived came to 930 years; then he died.

6When Seth had lived 105 years, he begot Enosh. 7After the birth of Enosh, Seth lived 807 years and begot sons and daughters. 8All the days of Seth came to 912 years; then he died.

9When Enosh had lived 90 years, he begot Kenan. 10After the birth of Kenan, Enosh lived 815 years and begot sons and daughters. 11All the days of Enosh came to 905 years; then he died.

12When Kenan had lived 70 years, he begot Mahalalel. 13After the birth of Mahalalel, Kenan lived 840 years and begot sons and daughters. 14All the days of Kenan came to 910 years; then he died.

15When Mahalalel had lived 65 years, he begot Jared. 16After the birth of Jared, Mahalalel

g-g   Or "established for me"; Heb. shath, connected with "Seth."

25 וַיֵּ֨דַע אָדָ֥ם עוֹד֙ אֶת־אִשְׁתּ֔וֹ וַתֵּ֣לֶד בֵּ֔ן וַתִּקְרָ֥א אֶת־שְׁמ֖וֹ שֵׁ֑ת כִּ֣י שָֽׁת־לִ֤י אֱלֹהִים֙ זֶ֣רַע אַחֵ֔ר תַּ֥חַת הֶ֖בֶל כִּ֥י הֲרָג֖וֹ קָֽיִן׃ 26 וּלְשֵׁ֤ת גַּם־הוּא֙ יֻלַּד־בֵּ֔ן וַיִּקְרָ֥א אֶת־שְׁמ֖וֹ אֱנ֑וֹשׁ אָ֣ז הוּחַ֔ל לִקְרֹ֖א בְּשֵׁ֥ם יְהֹוָֽה׃ פ

ה זֶ֣ה סֵ֔פֶר תּוֹלְדֹ֖ת אָדָ֑ם בְּי֗וֹם בְּרֹ֤א אֱלֹהִים֙ אָדָ֔ם בִּדְמ֥וּת אֱלֹהִ֖ים עָשָׂ֥ה אֹתֽוֹ׃ 2 זָכָ֥ר וּנְקֵבָ֖ה בְּרָאָ֑ם וַיְבָ֣רֶךְ אֹתָ֗ם וַיִּקְרָ֤א אֶת־שְׁמָם֙ אָדָ֔ם בְּי֖וֹם הִבָּֽרְאָֽם׃ ס 3 וַֽיְחִ֣י אָדָ֗ם שְׁלֹשִׁ֤ים וּמְאַת֙ שָׁנָ֔ה וַיּ֥וֹלֶד בִּדְמוּת֖וֹ כְּצַלְמ֑וֹ וַיִּקְרָ֥א אֶת־שְׁמ֖וֹ שֵֽׁת׃ 4 וַיִּֽהְי֣וּ יְמֵי־אָדָ֗ם אַֽחֲרֵי֙ הוֹלִיד֣וֹ אֶת־שֵׁ֔ת שְׁמֹנֶ֥ה מֵאֹ֖ת שָׁנָ֑ה וַיּ֥וֹלֶד בָּנִ֥ים וּבָנֽוֹת׃ 5 וַיִּֽהְי֞וּ כׇּל־יְמֵ֤י אָדָם֙ אֲשֶׁר־חַ֔י תְּשַׁ֤ע מֵאוֹת֙ שָׁנָ֔ה וּשְׁלֹשִׁ֖ים שָׁנָ֑ה וַיָּמֹֽת׃ ס 6 וַֽיְחִי־שֵׁ֕ת חָמֵ֥שׁ שָׁנִ֖ים וּמְאַ֣ת שָׁנָ֑ה וַיּ֖וֹלֶד אֶת־אֱנֽוֹשׁ׃ 7 וַֽיְחִי־שֵׁ֗ת אַֽחֲרֵי֙ הוֹלִיד֣וֹ אֶת־אֱנ֔וֹשׁ שֶׁ֤בַע שָׁנִים֙ וּשְׁמֹנֶ֣ה מֵא֣וֹת שָׁנָ֔ה וַיּ֥וֹלֶד בָּנִ֥ים וּבָנֽוֹת׃ 8 וַיִּֽהְיוּ֙ כׇּל־יְמֵי־שֵׁ֔ת שְׁתֵּ֤ים עֶשְׂרֵה֙ שָׁנָ֔ה וּתְשַׁ֥ע מֵא֖וֹת שָׁנָ֑ה וַיָּמֹֽת׃ ס 9 וַֽיְחִ֥י אֱנ֖וֹשׁ תִּשְׁעִ֣ים שָׁנָ֑ה וַיּ֖וֹלֶד אֶת־קֵינָֽן׃ 10 וַֽיְחִ֣י אֱנ֗וֹשׁ אַֽחֲרֵי֙ הוֹלִיד֣וֹ אֶת־קֵינָ֔ן חֲמֵ֤שׁ עֶשְׂרֵה֙ שָׁנָ֔ה וּשְׁמֹנֶ֥ה מֵא֖וֹת שָׁנָ֑ה וַיּ֥וֹלֶד בָּנִ֥ים וּבָנֽוֹת׃ 11 וַיִּֽהְיוּ֙ כׇּל־יְמֵ֣י אֱנ֔וֹשׁ חָמֵ֣שׁ שָׁנִ֔ים וּתְשַׁ֥ע מֵא֖וֹת שָׁנָ֑ה וַיָּמֹֽת׃ ס 12 וַֽיְחִ֥י קֵינָ֖ן שִׁבְעִ֣ים שָׁנָ֑ה וַיּ֖וֹלֶד אֶת־מַֽהֲלַלְאֵֽל׃ 13 וַֽיְחִ֣י קֵינָ֗ן אַֽחֲרֵי֙ הוֹלִיד֣וֹ אֶת־מַֽהֲלַלְאֵ֔ל אַרְבָּעִ֣ים שָׁנָ֔ה וּשְׁמֹנֶ֥ה מֵא֖וֹת שָׁנָ֑ה וַיּ֥וֹלֶד בָּנִ֥ים וּבָנֽוֹת׃ 14 וַיִּֽהְיוּ֙ כׇּל־יְמֵ֣י קֵינָ֔ן עֶ֣שֶׂר שָׁנִ֔ים וּתְשַׁ֥ע מֵא֖וֹת שָׁנָ֑ה וַיָּמֹֽת׃ ס 15 וַֽיְחִ֣י מַֽהֲלַלְאֵ֔ל חָמֵ֥שׁ שָׁנִ֖ים וְשִׁשִּׁ֣ים שָׁנָ֑ה וַיּ֖וֹלֶד אֶת־יָֽרֶד׃ 16 וַֽיְחִ֣י מַֽהֲלַלְאֵ֗ל אַֽחֲרֵי֙ הוֹלִיד֣וֹ אֶת־יֶ֔רֶד שְׁלֹשִׁ֥ים שָׁנָ֖ה וּשְׁמֹנֶ֣ה מֵא֣וֹת שָׁנָ֑ה וַיּ֥וֹלֶד

lived 830 years and begot sons and daughters. [17]All the days of Mahalalel came to 895 years; then he died.

[18]When Jared had lived 162 years, he begot Enoch. [19]After the birth of Enoch, Jared lived 800 years and begot sons and daughters. [20]All the days of Jared came to 962 years; then he died.

[21]When Enoch had lived 65 years, he begot Methuselah. [22]After the birth of Methuselah, Enoch walked with God 300 years; and he begot sons and daughters. [23]All the days of Enoch came to 365 years. [24]Enoch walked with God; then he was no more, for God took him.

[25]When Methuselah had lived 187 years, he begot Lamech. [26]After the birth of Lamech, Methuselah lived 782 years and begot sons and daughters. [27]All the days of Methuselah came to 969 years; then he died.

[28]When Lamech had lived 182 years, he begot a son. [29]And he named him Noah, saying, "This one will provide us relief[a] from our work and from the toil of our hands, out of the very soil which the LORD placed under a curse." [30]After the birth of Noah, Lamech lived 595 years and begot sons and daughters. [31]All the days of Lamech came to 777 years; then he died.

[32]When Noah had lived 500 years, Noah begot Shem, Ham, and Japheth.

6 When men began to increase on earth and daughters were born to them, [2]the divine beings[a] saw how beautiful the daughters of men were and took wives from among those that

בָּנִים וּבָנוֹת: 17 וַיִּהְיוּ כָּל־יְמֵי מַהֲלַלְאֵל חָמֵשׁ וְתִשְׁעִים שָׁנָה וּשְׁמֹנֶה מֵאוֹת שָׁנָה וַיָּמֹת: ס 18 וַיְחִי־יֶרֶד שְׁתַּיִם וְשִׁשִּׁים שָׁנָה וּמְאַת שָׁנָה וַיּוֹלֶד אֶת־חֲנוֹךְ: 19 וַיְחִי־יֶרֶד אַחֲרֵי הוֹלִידוֹ אֶת־חֲנוֹךְ שְׁמֹנֶה מֵאוֹת שָׁנָה וַיּוֹלֶד בָּנִים וּבָנוֹת: 20 וַיִּהְיוּ כָּל־יְמֵי־יֶרֶד שְׁתַּיִם וְשִׁשִּׁים שָׁנָה וּתְשַׁע מֵאוֹת שָׁנָה וַיָּמֹת: פ 21 וַיְחִי חֲנוֹךְ חָמֵשׁ וְשִׁשִּׁים שָׁנָה וַיּוֹלֶד אֶת־מְתוּשָׁלַח: 22 וַיִּתְהַלֵּךְ חֲנוֹךְ אֶת־הָאֱלֹהִים אַחֲרֵי הוֹלִידוֹ אֶת־מְתוּשֶׁלַח שְׁלֹשׁ מֵאוֹת שָׁנָה וַיּוֹלֶד בָּנִים וּבָנוֹת: 23 וַיְהִי כָּל־יְמֵי חֲנוֹךְ חָמֵשׁ וְשִׁשִּׁים שָׁנָה וּשְׁלֹשׁ מֵאוֹת שָׁנָה: 24 וַיִּתְהַלֵּךְ חֲנוֹךְ אֶת־הָאֱלֹהִים וְאֵינֶנּוּ כִּי־לָקַח אֹתוֹ אֱלֹהִים: פ 25 וַיְחִי מְתוּשֶׁלַח שֶׁבַע וּשְׁמֹנִים שָׁנָה וּמְאַת שָׁנָה וַיּוֹלֶד אֶת־לָמֶךְ: 26 וַיְחִי מְתוּשֶׁלַח אַחֲרֵי הוֹלִידוֹ אֶת־לֶמֶךְ שְׁתַּיִם וּשְׁמוֹנִים שָׁנָה וּשְׁבַע מֵאוֹת שָׁנָה וַיּוֹלֶד בָּנִים וּבָנוֹת: 27 וַיִּהְיוּ כָּל־יְמֵי מְתוּשֶׁלַח תֵּשַׁע וְשִׁשִּׁים שָׁנָה וּתְשַׁע מֵאוֹת שָׁנָה וַיָּמֹת: פ 28 וַיְחִי־לֶמֶךְ שְׁתַּיִם וּשְׁמֹנִים שָׁנָה וּמְאַת שָׁנָה וַיּוֹלֶד בֵּן: 29 וַיִּקְרָא אֶת־שְׁמוֹ נֹחַ לֵאמֹר זֶה* יְנַחֲמֵנוּ מִמַּעֲשֵׂנוּ וּמֵעִצְּבוֹן יָדֵינוּ מִן־הָאֲדָמָה אֲשֶׁר אֵרְרָהּ יְהֹוָה: 30 וַיְחִי־לֶמֶךְ אַחֲרֵי הוֹלִידוֹ אֶת־נֹחַ חָמֵשׁ וְתִשְׁעִים שָׁנָה וַחֲמֵשׁ מֵאֹת שָׁנָה וַיּוֹלֶד בָּנִים וּבָנוֹת: 31 וַיְהִי כָּל־יְמֵי־לֶמֶךְ שֶׁבַע וְשִׁבְעִים שָׁנָה וּשְׁבַע מֵאוֹת שָׁנָה וַיָּמֹת: ס 32 וַיְהִי־נֹחַ בֶּן־חֲמֵשׁ מֵאוֹת שָׁנָה וַיּוֹלֶד נֹחַ אֶת־שֵׁם אֶת־חָם וְאֶת־יָפֶת:

ו וַיְהִי כִּי־הֵחֵל הָאָדָם לָרֹב עַל־פְּנֵי הָאֲדָמָה וּבָנוֹת יֻלְּדוּ לָהֶם: 2 וַיִּרְאוּ בְנֵי־הָאֱלֹהִים אֶת־בְּנוֹת הָאָדָם כִּי טֹבֹת הֵנָּה

שני טעמים v. 29.

---

a   Connecting Noah with Heb. niḥam "to comfort"; cf. 9.20 ff.
a   Others "the sons of God."

pleased them.—[3]The Lord said, "My breath shall not abide[b] in man forever, since he too is flesh; let the days allowed him be one hundred and twenty years."—[4]It was then, and later too, that the Nephilim appeared on earth—when the divine beings cohabited with the daughters of men, who bore them offspring. They were the heroes of old, the men of renown.

[5]The Lord saw how great was man's wickedness on earth, and how every plan devised by his mind was nothing but evil all the time. [6]And the Lord regretted that He had made man on earth, and His heart was saddened. [7]The Lord said, "I will blot out from the earth the men whom I created—men together with beasts, creeping things, and birds of the sky; for I regret that I made them." [8]But Noah found favor with the Lord.

NOAH

[9]This is the line of Noah.—Noah was a righteous man; he was blameless in his age; Noah walked with God.—[10]Noah begot three sons: Shem, Ham, and Japheth.

[11]The earth became corrupt before God; the earth was filled with lawlessness. [12]When God saw how corrupt the earth was, for all flesh had corrupted its ways on earth, [13]God said to Noah, "I have decided to put an end to all flesh, for the earth is filled with lawlessness because of them: I am about to destroy them with the earth. [14]Make yourself an ark of gopher wood; make it an ark with compartments, and cover it inside and out with pitch. [15]This is how you shall make it: the length of the ark shall be three hundred cubits, its width fifty cubits, and its height thirty cubits. [16]Make an opening for daylight in the ark, and -[c]terminate it within a cubit of the top.-[c] Put the entrance to the ark in its side; make it with bottom, second, and third decks.

---

b   Meaning of Heb. uncertain.
c-c   Meaning of Heb. uncertain.

11

וַיִּקְחוּ לָהֶם נָשִׁים מִכֹּל אֲשֶׁר בָּחָרוּ: 3 וַיֹּאמֶר יְהֹוָה לֹא־יָדוֹן רוּחִי בָאָדָם לְעֹלָם בְּשַׁגַּם הוּא בָשָׂר וְהָיוּ יָמָיו מֵאָה וְעֶשְׂרִים שָׁנָה: 4 הַנְּפִלִים הָיוּ בָאָרֶץ בַּיָּמִים הָהֵם וְגַם אַחֲרֵי־כֵן אֲשֶׁר יָבֹאוּ בְּנֵי הָאֱלֹהִים אֶל־בְּנוֹת הָאָדָם וְיָלְדוּ לָהֶם הֵמָּה הַגִּבֹּרִים אֲשֶׁר מֵעוֹלָם אַנְשֵׁי הַשֵּׁם: פ 5 וַיַּרְא יְהֹוָה כִּי רַבָּה רָעַת הָאָדָם בָּאָרֶץ וְכָל־יֵצֶר מַחְשְׁבֹת לִבּוֹ רַק רַע כָּל־הַיּוֹם: 6 וַיִּנָּחֶם יְהֹוָה כִּי־עָשָׂה אֶת־הָאָדָם בָּאָרֶץ וַיִּתְעַצֵּב אֶל־לִבּוֹ: 7 וַיֹּאמֶר יְהֹוָה אֶמְחֶה אֶת־הָאָדָם אֲשֶׁר־בָּרָאתִי מֵעַל פְּנֵי הָאֲדָמָה מֵאָדָם עַד־בְּהֵמָה עַד־רֶמֶשׂ וְעַד־עוֹף הַשָּׁמָיִם כִּי נִחַמְתִּי כִּי עֲשִׂיתִם: 8 וְנֹחַ מָצָא חֵן בְּעֵינֵי יְהֹוָה: פ

נח

9 אֵלֶּה תּוֹלְדֹת נֹחַ נֹחַ אִישׁ צַדִּיק תָּמִים הָיָה בְּדֹרֹתָיו אֶת־הָאֱלֹהִים הִתְהַלֶּךְ־נֹחַ: 10 וַיּוֹלֶד נֹחַ שְׁלֹשָׁה בָנִים אֶת־שֵׁם אֶת־חָם וְאֶת־יָפֶת: 11 וַתִּשָּׁחֵת הָאָרֶץ לִפְנֵי הָאֱלֹהִים וַתִּמָּלֵא הָאָרֶץ חָמָס: 12 וַיַּרְא אֱלֹהִים אֶת־הָאָרֶץ וְהִנֵּה נִשְׁחָתָה כִּי־הִשְׁחִית כָּל־בָּשָׂר אֶת־דַּרְכּוֹ עַל־הָאָרֶץ: ס 13 וַיֹּאמֶר אֱלֹהִים לְנֹחַ קֵץ כָּל־בָּשָׂר בָּא לְפָנַי כִּי־מָלְאָה הָאָרֶץ חָמָס מִפְּנֵיהֶם וְהִנְנִי מַשְׁחִיתָם אֶת־הָאָרֶץ: 14 עֲשֵׂה לְךָ תֵּבַת עֲצֵי־גֹפֶר קִנִּים תַּעֲשֶׂה אֶת־הַתֵּבָה וְכָפַרְתָּ אֹתָהּ מִבַּיִת וּמִחוּץ בַּכֹּפֶר: 15 וְזֶה אֲשֶׁר תַּעֲשֶׂה אֹתָהּ שְׁלֹשׁ מֵאוֹת אַמָּה אֹרֶךְ הַתֵּבָה חֲמִשִּׁים אַמָּה רָחְבָּהּ וּשְׁלֹשִׁים אַמָּה קוֹמָתָהּ: 16 צֹהַר | תַּעֲשֶׂה לַתֵּבָה וְאֶל־אַמָּה תְּכַלֶּנָּה מִלְמַעְלָה וּפֶתַח הַתֵּבָה בְּצִדָּהּ תָּשִׂים תַּחְתִּיִּם שְׁנִיִּם וּשְׁלִשִׁים תַּעֲשֶׂהָ:

17"For My part, I am about to bring the Flood—waters upon the earth—to destroy all flesh under the sky in which there is breath of life; everything on earth shall perish. 18But I will establish My covenant with you, and you shall enter the ark, with your sons, your wife, and your sons' wives. 19And of all that lives, of all flesh, you shall take two of each into the ark to keep alive with you; they shall be male and female. 20From birds of every kind, cattle of every kind, every kind of creeping thing on earth, two of each shall come to you to stay alive. 21For your part, take of everything that is eaten and store it away, to serve as food for you and for them." 22Noah did so; just as God commanded him, so he did.

7 Then the LORD said to Noah, "Go into the ark, with all your household, for you alone have I found righteous before Me in this generation. 2Of every clean animal you shall take seven pairs, males and their mates, and of every animal that is not clean, two, a male and its mate; 3of the birds of the sky also, seven pairs, male and female, to keep seed alive upon all the earth. 4For in seven days' time I will make it rain upon the earth, forty days and forty nights, and I will blot out from the earth all existence that I created." 5And Noah did just as the LORD commanded him.

6Noah was six hundred years old when the Flood came, waters upon the earth. 7Noah, with his sons, his wife, and his sons' wives, went into the ark because of the waters of the Flood. 8Of the clean animals, of the animals that are not clean, of the birds, and of everything that creeps on the ground, 9two of each, male and female, came to Noah into the ark, as God had commanded Noah. 10And on the seventh day the waters of the Flood came upon the earth.

17 וַאֲנִ֗י הִנְנִ֨י מֵבִ֧יא אֶת־הַמַּבּ֛וּל מַ֖יִם עַל־הָאָ֑רֶץ לְשַׁחֵ֣ת כָּל־בָּשָׂ֗ר אֲשֶׁר־בּוֹ֙ ר֣וּחַ חַיִּ֔ים מִתַּ֖חַת הַשָּׁמָ֑יִם כֹּ֥ל אֲשֶׁר־בָּאָ֖רֶץ יִגְוָֽע: 18 וַהֲקִמֹתִ֥י אֶת־בְּרִיתִ֖י אִתָּ֑ךְ וּבָאתָ֙ אֶל־הַתֵּבָ֔ה אַתָּ֕ה וּבָנֶ֛יךָ וְאִשְׁתְּךָ֥ וּנְשֵֽׁי־בָנֶ֖יךָ אִתָּֽךְ: 19 וּמִכָּל־הָ֠חַ֠י מִֽכָּל־בָּשָׂ֞ר שְׁנַ֤יִם מִכֹּל֙ תָּבִ֣יא אֶל־הַתֵּבָ֔ה לְהַחֲיֹ֖ת אִתָּ֑ךְ זָכָ֥ר וּנְקֵבָ֖ה יִֽהְיֽוּ: 20 מֵהָע֣וֹף לְמִינֵ֗הוּ וּמִן־הַבְּהֵמָה֙ לְמִינָ֔הּ מִכֹּ֛ל רֶ֥מֶשׂ הָֽאֲדָמָ֖ה לְמִינֵ֑הוּ שְׁנַ֧יִם מִכֹּ֛ל יָבֹ֥אוּ אֵלֶ֖יךָ לְהַֽחֲיֽוֹת: 21 וְאַתָּ֣ה קַח־לְךָ֗ מִכָּל־מַֽאֲכָל֙ אֲשֶׁ֣ר יֵֽאָכֵ֔ל וְאָֽסַפְתָּ֖ אֵלֶ֑יךָ וְהָיָ֥ה לְךָ֛ וְלָהֶ֖ם לְאָכְלָֽה: 22 וַיַּ֖עַשׂ נֹ֑חַ כְּ֠כֹ֠ל אֲשֶׁ֨ר צִוָּ֥ה אֹת֛וֹ אֱלֹהִ֖ים כֵּ֥ן עָשָֽׂה: ס

ז וַיֹּ֤אמֶר יְהֹוָה֙ לְנֹ֔חַ בֹּֽא־אַתָּ֥ה וְכָל־בֵּֽיתְךָ֖ אֶל־הַתֵּבָ֑ה כִּֽי־אֹֽתְךָ֥ רָאִ֛יתִי צַדִּ֥יק לְפָנַ֖י בַּדּ֥וֹר הַזֶּֽה: 2 מִכֹּ֣ל ׀ הַבְּהֵמָ֣ה הַטְּהוֹרָ֗ה תִּֽקַּח־לְךָ֛ שִׁבְעָ֥ה שִׁבְעָ֖ה אִ֣ישׁ וְאִשְׁתּ֑וֹ וּמִן־הַבְּהֵמָ֡ה אֲ֠שֶׁ֠ר לֹ֣א טְהֹרָ֥ה הִ֛וא שְׁנַ֖יִם אִ֥ישׁ וְאִשְׁתּֽוֹ: 3 גַּ֣ם מֵע֧וֹף הַשָּׁמַ֛יִם שִׁבְעָ֥ה שִׁבְעָ֖ה זָכָ֣ר וּנְקֵבָ֑ה לְחַיּ֥וֹת זֶ֖רַע עַל־פְּנֵ֥י כָל־הָאָֽרֶץ: 4 כִּי֩ לְיָמִ֨ים ע֜וֹד שִׁבְעָ֗ה אָֽנֹכִי֙ מַמְטִ֣יר עַל־הָאָ֔רֶץ אַרְבָּעִ֣ים י֔וֹם וְאַרְבָּעִ֖ים לָ֑יְלָה וּמָחִ֗יתִי אֶֽת־כָּל־הַיְקוּם֙ אֲשֶׁ֣ר עָשִׂ֔יתִי מֵעַ֖ל פְּנֵ֥י הָֽאֲדָמָֽה: 5 וַיַּ֖עַשׂ נֹ֑חַ כְּכֹ֥ל אֲשֶׁר־צִוָּ֖הוּ יְהֹוָֽה: 6 וְנֹ֕חַ בֶּן־שֵׁ֥שׁ מֵא֖וֹת שָׁנָ֑ה וְהַמַּבּ֣וּל הָיָ֔ה מַ֖יִם עַל־הָאָֽרֶץ: 7 וַיָּ֣בֹא נֹ֗חַ וּ֠בָנָ֠יו וְאִשְׁתּ֧וֹ וּנְשֵֽׁי־בָנָ֛יו אִתּ֖וֹ אֶל־הַתֵּבָ֑ה מִפְּנֵ֖י מֵ֥י הַמַּבּֽוּל: 8 מִן־הַבְּהֵמָה֙ הַטְּהוֹרָ֔ה וּמִ֨ן־הַבְּהֵמָ֔ה אֲשֶׁ֥ר אֵינֶ֖נָּה טְהֹרָ֑ה וּמִ֨ן־הָע֔וֹף וְכֹ֥ל אֲשֶׁר־רֹמֵ֖שׂ עַל־הָֽאֲדָמָֽה: 9 שְׁנַ֨יִם שְׁנַ֜יִם בָּ֤אוּ אֶל־נֹ֨חַ֙ אֶל־הַתֵּבָ֔ה זָכָ֖ר וּנְקֵבָ֑ה כַּֽאֲשֶׁ֛ר צִוָּ֥ה אֱלֹהִ֖ים אֶת־נֹֽחַ: 10 וַֽיְהִ֖י

12

11In the six hundredth year of Noah's life, in the second month, on the seventeenth day of the month, on that day

All the fountains of the great deep burst apart,
And the floodgates of the sky broke open.

(12The rain fell on the earth forty days and forty nights.) 13That same day Noah and Noah's sons, Shem, Ham, and Japheth, went into the ark, with Noah's wife and the three wives of his sons—14they and all beasts of every kind, all cattle of every kind, all creatures of every kind that creep on the earth, and all birds of every kind, every bird, every winged thing. 15They came to Noah into the ark, two each of all flesh in which there was breath of life. 16Thus they that entered comprised male and female of all flesh, as God had commanded him. And the Lord shut him in.

17The Flood continued forty days on the earth, and the waters increased and raised the ark so that it rose above the earth. 18The waters swelled and increased greatly upon the earth, and the ark drifted upon the waters. 19When the waters had swelled much more upon the earth, all the highest mountains everywhere under the sky were covered. 20Fifteen cubits higher did the waters swell, as the mountains were covered. 21And all flesh that stirred on earth perished—birds, cattle, beasts, and all the things that swarmed upon the earth, and all mankind. 22All in whose nostrils was the merest breath of life, all that was on dry land, died. 23All existence on earth was blotted out—man, cattle, creeping things, and birds of the sky; they were blotted out from the earth. Only Noah was left, and those with him in the ark.

לְשִׁבְעַ֣ת הַיָּמִ֔ים וּמֵ֣י הַמַּבּ֔וּל הָי֖וּ עַל־
הָאָֽרֶץ:

11 בִּשְׁנַ֨ת שֵׁשׁ־מֵא֤וֹת שָׁנָה֙ לְחַיֵּי־נֹ֔חַ בַּחֹ֨דֶשׁ
הַשֵּׁנִ֜י בְּשִׁבְעָֽה־עָשָׂ֥ר י֖וֹם לַחֹ֑דֶשׁ בַּיּ֣וֹם
הַזֶּ֗ה
נִבְקְעוּ֙ כָּל־מַעְיְנֹת֙ תְּה֣וֹם רַבָּ֔ה
וַאֲרֻבֹּ֥ת הַשָּׁמַ֖יִם נִפְתָּֽחוּ:

12 וַֽיְהִ֥י הַגֶּ֖שֶׁם עַל־הָאָ֑רֶץ אַרְבָּעִ֣ים י֔וֹם
וְאַרְבָּעִ֖ים לָֽיְלָה: 13 בְּעֶ֨צֶם הַיּ֤וֹם הַזֶּה֙ בָּ֣א
נֹ֔חַ וְשֵׁם־וְחָ֥ם וָיֶ֖פֶת בְּנֵי־נֹ֑חַ וְאֵ֣שֶׁת נֹ֗חַ
וּשְׁלֹ֧שֶׁת נְשֵֽׁי־בָנָ֛יו אִתָּ֖ם אֶל־הַתֵּבָֽה:

14 הֵ֜מָּה וְכָל־הַֽחַיָּ֣ה לְמִינָ֗הּ וְכָל־הַבְּהֵמָה֙
לְמִינָ֔הּ וְכָל־הָרֶ֛מֶשׂ הָרֹמֵ֥שׂ עַל־הָאָ֖רֶץ
לְמִינֵ֑הוּ וְכָל־הָע֣וֹף לְמִינֵ֔הוּ כֹּ֖ל צִפּ֥וֹר
כָּל־כָּנָֽף: 15 וַיָּבֹ֥אוּ אֶל־נֹ֖חַ אֶל־הַתֵּבָ֑ה
שְׁנַ֤יִם שְׁנַ֨יִם֙ מִכָּל־הַבָּשָׂ֔ר אֲשֶׁר־בּ֖וֹ ר֥וּחַ
חַיִּֽים: 16 וְהַבָּאִ֗ים זָכָ֨ר וּנְקֵבָ֤ה מִכָּל־בָּשָׂר֙
בָּ֔אוּ כַּאֲשֶׁ֛ר צִוָּ֥ה אֹת֖וֹ אֱלֹהִ֑ים וַיִּסְגֹּ֥ר יְהוָ֖ה
בַּעֲדֽוֹ:

17 וַֽיְהִ֧י הַמַּבּ֛וּל אַרְבָּעִ֥ים י֖וֹם עַל־הָאָ֑רֶץ
וַיִּרְבּ֣וּ הַמַּ֗יִם וַיִּשְׂאוּ֙ אֶת־הַתֵּבָ֔ה וַתָּ֖רָם
מֵעַ֥ל הָאָֽרֶץ: 18 וַיִּגְבְּר֥וּ הַמַּ֛יִם וַיִּרְבּ֥וּ מְאֹ֖ד
עַל־הָאָ֑רֶץ וַתֵּ֥לֶךְ הַתֵּבָ֖ה עַל־פְּנֵ֥י הַמָּֽיִם:
19 וְהַמַּ֗יִם גָּבְר֛וּ מְאֹ֥ד מְאֹ֖ד עַל־הָאָ֑רֶץ
וַיְכֻסּ֕וּ כָּל־הֶֽהָרִים֙ הַגְּבֹהִ֔ים אֲשֶׁר־תַּ֖חַת
כָּל־הַשָּׁמָֽיִם: 20 חֲמֵ֨שׁ עֶשְׂרֵ֤ה אַמָּה֙
מִלְמַ֔עְלָה גָּבְר֖וּ הַמָּ֑יִם וַיְכֻסּ֖וּ הֶהָרִֽים:
21 וַיִּגְוַ֞ע כָּל־בָּשָׂ֣ר ׀ הָרֹמֵ֣שׂ עַל־הָאָ֗רֶץ
בָּע֤וֹף וּבַבְּהֵמָה֙ וּבַ֣חַיָּ֔ה וּבְכָל־הַשֶּׁ֖רֶץ
הַשֹּׁרֵ֣ץ עַל־הָאָ֑רֶץ וְכֹ֖ל הָאָדָֽם: 22 כֹּ֡ל אֲשֶׁר֩
נִשְׁמַת־ר֨וּחַ חַיִּ֜ים בְּאַפָּ֗יו מִכֹּ֛ל אֲשֶׁ֥ר
בֶּחָֽרָבָ֖ה מֵֽתוּ: 23 וַיִּ֜מַח אֶֽת־כָּל־הַיְק֣וּם ׀
אֲשֶׁ֣ר ׀ עַל־פְּנֵ֣י הָֽאֲדָמָ֗ה מֵאָדָ֤ם עַד־בְּהֵמָה֙
עַד־רֶ֨מֶשׂ֙ וְעַד־ע֣וֹף הַשָּׁמַ֔יִם וַיִּמָּח֖וּ מִן־
הָאָ֑רֶץ וַיִּשָּׁ֧אֶר אַךְ־נֹ֛חַ וַֽאֲשֶׁ֥ר אִתּ֖וֹ בַּתֵּבָֽה:

13

24And when the waters had swelled on the

8 earth one hundred and fifty days, 1God remembered Noah and all the beasts and all the cattle that were with him in the ark, and God caused a wind to blow across the earth, and the waters subsided. 2The fountains of the deep and the floodgates of the sky were stopped up, and the rain from the sky was held back; 3the waters then receded steadily from the earth. At the end of one hundred and fifty days the waters diminished, 4so that in the seventh month, on the seventeenth day of the month, the ark came to rest on the mountains of Ararat. 5The waters went on diminishing until the tenth month; in the tenth month, on the first of the month, the tops of the mountains became visible.

6At the end of forty days, Noah opened the window of the ark that he had made 7and sent out the raven; it went to and fro until the waters had dried up from the earth. 8Then he sent out the dove to see whether the waters had decreased from the surface of the ground. 9But the dove could not find a resting place for its foot, and returned to him to the ark, for there was water over all the earth. So putting out his hand, he took it into the ark with him. 10He waited another seven days, and again sent out the dove from the ark. 11The dove came back to him toward evening, and there in its bill was a plucked-off olive leaf! Then Noah knew that the waters had decreased on the earth. 12He waited still another seven days and sent the dove forth; and it did not return to him any more.

13In the six hundred and first year, in the first month, on the first of the month, the waters began to dry from the earth; and when Noah removed the covering of the ark, he saw that the surface of the ground was drying. 14And in the second month, on the twenty-seventh day of the month, the earth was dry.

15God spoke to Noah, saying, 16"Come out

24 וַיִּגְבְּר֥וּ הַמַּ֖יִם עַל־הָאָ֑רֶץ חֲמִשִּׁ֥ים וּמְאַ֖ת
יֽוֹם: 1 וַיִּזְכֹּ֤ר אֱלֹהִים֙ אֶת־נֹ֔חַ וְאֵ֤ת
כָּל־הַֽחַיָּה֙ וְאֶת־כָּל־הַבְּהֵמָ֔ה אֲשֶׁ֥ר
אִתּ֖וֹ בַּתֵּבָ֑ה וַיַּעֲבֵ֨ר אֱלֹהִ֥ים ר֙וּחַ֙ עַל־הָאָ֔רֶץ
וַיָּשֹׁ֖כּוּ הַמָּֽיִם: 2 וַיִּסָּֽכְרוּ֙ מַעְיְנֹ֣ת תְּה֔וֹם
וַאֲרֻבֹּ֖ת הַשָּׁמָ֑יִם וַיִּכָּלֵ֥א הַגֶּ֖שֶׁם מִן־
הַשָּׁמָֽיִם: 3 וַיָּשֻׁ֧בוּ הַמַּ֛יִם מֵעַ֥ל הָאָ֖רֶץ
הָל֣וֹךְ וָשׁ֑וֹב וַיַּחְסְר֣וּ הַמַּ֔יִם מִקְצֵ֕ה חֲמִשִּׁ֥ים
וּמְאַ֖ת יֽוֹם: 4 וַתָּ֤נַח הַתֵּבָה֙ בַּחֹ֣דֶשׁ
הַשְּׁבִיעִ֔י בְּשִׁבְעָֽה־עָשָׂ֥ר י֖וֹם לַחֹ֑דֶשׁ עַ֖ל
הָרֵ֥י אֲרָרָֽט: 5 וְהַמַּ֗יִם הָיוּ֙ הָל֣וֹךְ וְחָס֔וֹר
עַ֖ד הַחֹ֣דֶשׁ הָֽעֲשִׂירִ֑י בָּֽעֲשִׂירִי֙ בְּאֶחָ֣ד
לַחֹ֔דֶשׁ נִרְא֖וּ רָאשֵׁ֥י הֶהָרִֽים:

6 וַֽיְהִ֕י מִקֵּ֖ץ אַרְבָּעִ֣ים י֑וֹם וַיִּפְתַּ֣ח נֹ֔חַ
אֶת־חַלּ֥וֹן הַתֵּבָ֖ה אֲשֶׁ֥ר עָשָֽׂה: 7 וַיְשַׁלַּ֖ח
אֶת־הָֽעֹרֵ֑ב וַיֵּצֵ֤א יָצוֹא֙ וָשׁ֔וֹב עַד־יְבֹ֥שֶׁת
הַמַּ֖יִם מֵעַ֥ל הָאָֽרֶץ: 8 וַיְשַׁלַּ֥ח אֶת־הַיּוֹנָ֖ה
מֵֽאִתּ֑וֹ לִרְאוֹת֙ הֲקַ֣לּוּ הַמַּ֔יִם מֵעַ֖ל פְּנֵ֥י
הָֽאֲדָמָֽה: 9 וְלֹֽא־מָצְאָה֩ הַיּוֹנָ֨ה מָנ֜וֹחַ לְכַף־
רַגְלָ֗הּ וַתָּ֣שָׁב אֵלָיו֘ אֶל־הַתֵּבָה֒ כִּי־מַ֖יִם
עַל־פְּנֵ֣י כָל־הָאָ֑רֶץ וַיִּשְׁלַ֤ח יָדוֹ֙ וַיִּקָּחֶ֔הָ
וַיָּבֵ֥א אֹתָ֛הּ אֵלָ֖יו אֶל־הַתֵּבָֽה: 10 וַיָּ֣חֶל ע֔וֹד
שִׁבְעַ֥ת יָמִ֖ים אֲחֵרִ֑ים וַיֹּ֛סֶף שַׁלַּ֥ח אֶת־
הַיּוֹנָ֖ה מִן־הַתֵּבָֽה: 11 וַתָּבֹ֨א אֵלָ֤יו הַיּוֹנָה֙
לְעֵ֣ת עֶ֔רֶב וְהִנֵּ֥ה עֲלֵה־זַ֖יִת טָרָ֣ף בְּפִ֑יהָ
וַיֵּ֣דַע נֹ֔חַ כִּי־קַ֥לּוּ הַמַּ֖יִם מֵעַ֥ל הָאָֽרֶץ:
12 וַיִּיָּ֣חֶל ע֔וֹד שִׁבְעַ֥ת יָמִ֖ים אֲחֵרִ֑ים וַיְשַׁלַּח֙
אֶת־הַיּוֹנָ֔ה וְלֹֽא־יָסְפָ֥ה שֽׁוּב־אֵלָ֖יו עֽוֹד:
13 וַ֠יְהִ֠י בְּאַחַ֨ת וְשֵׁשׁ־מֵא֜וֹת שָׁנָ֗ה בָּֽרִאשׁוֹן֙
בְּאֶחָ֣ד לַחֹ֔דֶשׁ חָֽרְב֥וּ הַמַּ֖יִם מֵעַ֣ל הָאָ֑רֶץ
וַיָּ֣סַר נֹ֗חַ אֶת־מִכְסֵ֤ה הַתֵּבָה֙ וַיַּ֔רְא וְהִנֵּ֥ה
חָֽרְב֖וּ פְּנֵ֥י הָֽאֲדָמָֽה: 14 וּבַחֹ֙דֶשׁ֙ הַשֵּׁנִ֔י
בְּשִׁבְעָ֧ה וְעֶשְׂרִ֛ים י֖וֹם לַחֹ֑דֶשׁ יָֽבְשָׁ֖ה
הָאָֽרֶץ: ס

15 וַיְדַבֵּ֥ר אֱלֹהִ֖ים אֶל־נֹ֥חַ לֵאמֹֽר: 16 צֵ֖א
מִן־הַתֵּבָ֑ה אַתָּ֕ה וְאִשְׁתְּךָ֛ וּבָנֶ֥יךָ וּנְשֵֽׁי־בָנֶ֖יךָ

of the ark, together with your wife, your sons, and your sons' wives. 17Bring out with you every living thing of all flesh that is with you: birds, animals, and everything that creeps on earth; and let them swarm on the earth and be fertile and increase on earth." 18So Noah came out, together with his sons, his wife, and his sons' wives. 19Every animal, every creeping thing, and every bird, everything that stirs on earth came out of the ark by families.

20Then Noah built an altar to the LORD and, taking of every clean animal and of every clean bird, he offered burnt offerings on the altar. 21The LORD smelled the pleasing odor, and the LORD said to Himself: "Never again will I doom the earth because of man, since the devisings of man's mind are evil from his youth; nor will I ever again destroy every living being, as I have done.

22So long as the earth endures,
Seedtime and harvest,
Cold and heat,
Summer and winter,
Day and night
Shall not cease."

9 God blessed Noah and his sons, and said to them, "Be fertile and increase, and fill the earth. 2The fear and the dread of you shall be upon all the beasts of the earth and upon all the birds of the sky—everything with which the earth is astir—and upon all the fish of the sea; they are given into your hand. 3Every creature that lives shall be yours to eat; as with the green grasses, I give you all these. 4You must not, however, eat flesh with its life-blood in it. 5But for your own life-blood I will require a reckoning: I will require it of every beast; of man, too, will I require a reckoning for human life, of every man for that of his fellow man!

אִתָּךְ: 17 כָּל־הַחַיָּה אֲשֶׁר־אִתְּךָ מִכָּל־בָּשָׂר בָּעוֹף וּבַבְּהֵמָה וּבְכָל־הָרֶמֶשׂ הָרֹמֵשׂ עַל־הָאָרֶץ הוצא [הַיְצֵא] אִתָּךְ וְשָׁרְצוּ בָאָרֶץ וּפָרוּ וְרָבוּ עַל־הָאָרֶץ: 18 וַיֵּצֵא־נֹחַ וּבָנָיו וְאִשְׁתּוֹ וּנְשֵׁי־בָנָיו אִתּוֹ: 19 כָּל־הַחַיָּה כָּל־הָרֶמֶשׂ וְכָל־הָעוֹף כֹּל רוֹמֵשׂ עַל־הָאָרֶץ לְמִשְׁפְּחֹתֵיהֶם יָצְאוּ מִן־הַתֵּבָה:

20 וַיִּבֶן נֹחַ מִזְבֵּחַ לַיהוָה וַיִּקַּח מִכֹּל | הַבְּהֵמָה הַטְּהוֹרָה וּמִכֹּל הָעוֹף הַטָּהוֹר וַיַּעַל עֹלֹת בַּמִּזְבֵּחַ: 21 וַיָּרַח יְהוָה אֶת־רֵיחַ הַנִּיחֹחַ וַיֹּאמֶר יְהוָה אֶל־לִבּוֹ לֹא־אֹסִף לְקַלֵּל עוֹד אֶת־הָאֲדָמָה בַּעֲבוּר הָאָדָם כִּי יֵצֶר לֵב הָאָדָם רַע מִנְּעֻרָיו וְלֹא־אֹסִף עוֹד לְהַכּוֹת אֶת־כָּל־חַי כַּאֲשֶׁר עָשִׂיתִי:

22 עֹד כָּל־יְמֵי הָאָרֶץ
זֶרַע וְקָצִיר
וְקֹר וָחֹם
וְקַיִץ וָחֹרֶף
וְיוֹם וָלַיְלָה
לֹא יִשְׁבֹּתוּ:

ט וַיְבָרֶךְ אֱלֹהִים אֶת־נֹחַ וְאֶת־בָּנָיו וַיֹּאמֶר לָהֶם פְּרוּ וּרְבוּ וּמִלְאוּ אֶת־הָאָרֶץ: 2 וּמוֹרַאֲכֶם וְחִתְּכֶם יִהְיֶה עַל כָּל־חַיַּת הָאָרֶץ וְעַל כָּל־עוֹף הַשָּׁמָיִם בְּכֹל אֲשֶׁר תִּרְמֹשׂ הָאֲדָמָה וּבְכָל־דְּגֵי הַיָּם בְּיֶדְכֶם נִתָּנוּ: 3 כָּל־רֶמֶשׂ אֲשֶׁר הוּא־חַי לָכֶם יִהְיֶה לְאָכְלָה כְּיֶרֶק עֵשֶׂב נָתַתִּי לָכֶם אֶת־כֹּל: 4 אַךְ־בָּשָׂר בְּנַפְשׁוֹ דָמוֹ לֹא תֹאכֵלוּ: 5 וְאַךְ אֶת־דִּמְכֶם לְנַפְשֹׁתֵיכֶם אֶדְרֹשׁ מִיַּד כָּל־חַיָּה אֶדְרְשֶׁנּוּ וּמִיַּד הָאָדָם מִיַּד אִישׁ אָחִיו אֶדְרֹשׁ אֶת־נֶפֶשׁ הָאָדָם:

6Whoever sheds the blood of man,
By man shall his blood be shed;
For in His image
Did God make man.

7Be fertile, then, and increase; abound on the earth and increase on it."

8And God said to Noah and to his sons with him, 9"I now establish My covenant with you and your offspring to come, 10and with every living thing that is with you—birds, cattle, and every wild beast as well—all that have come out of the ark, every living thing on earth. 11I will maintain My covenant with you: never again shall all flesh be cut off by the waters of a flood, and never again shall there be a flood to destroy the earth."

12God further said, "This is the sign that I set for the covenant between Me and you, and every living creature with you, for all ages to come. 13I have set My bow in the clouds, and it shall serve as a sign of the covenant between Me and the earth. 14When I bring clouds over the earth, and the bow appears in the clouds, 15I will remember My covenant between Me and you and every living creature among all flesh, so that the waters shall never again become a flood to destroy all flesh. 16When the bow is in the clouds, I will see it and remember the everlasting covenant between God and all living creatures, all flesh that is on earth. 17That," God said to Noah, "shall be the sign of the covenant that I have established between Me and all flesh that is on earth."

18The sons of Noah who came out of the ark were Shem, Ham, and Japheth—Ham being the father of Canaan. 19These three were the sons of Noah, and from these the whole world branched out.

20Noah, the tiller of the soil, was the first to plant a vineyard. 21He drank of the wine and

6 שֹׁפֵךְ֙ דַּ֣ם הָֽאָדָ֔ם
בָּֽאָדָ֖ם דָּמ֣וֹ יִשָּׁפֵ֑ךְ
כִּ֚י בְּצֶ֣לֶם אֱלֹהִ֔ים
עָשָׂ֖ה אֶת־הָֽאָדָֽם:
7 וְאַתֶּ֖ם פְּר֣וּ וּרְב֑וּ שִׁרְצ֥וּ בָאָ֖רֶץ וּרְבוּ־
בָֽהּ: ס
8 וַיֹּ֤אמֶר אֱלֹהִים֙ אֶל־נֹ֔חַ וְאֶל־בָּנָ֥יו אִתּ֖וֹ
לֵאמֹֽר: 9 וַֽאֲנִ֗י הִנְנִ֥י מֵקִ֛ים אֶת־בְּרִיתִ֖י
אִתְּכֶ֑ם וְאֶֽת־זַרְעֲכֶ֖ם אַֽחֲרֵיכֶֽם: 10 וְאֵ֣ת
כָּל־נֶ֣פֶשׁ הַֽחַיָּה֙ אֲשֶׁ֣ר אִתְּכֶ֔ם בָּע֧וֹף
בַּבְּהֵמָ֛ה וּֽבְכָל־חַיַּ֥ת הָאָ֖רֶץ אִתְּכֶ֑ם מִכֹּל֙
יֹֽצְאֵ֣י הַתֵּבָ֔ה לְכֹ֖ל חַיַּ֥ת הָאָֽרֶץ: 11 וַֽהֲקִֽמֹתִ֤י
אֶת־בְּרִיתִי֙ אִתְּכֶ֔ם וְלֹֽא־יִכָּרֵ֧ת כָּל־בָּשָׂ֛ר
ע֖וֹד מִמֵּ֣י הַמַּבּ֑וּל וְלֹֽא־יִֽהְיֶ֥ה ע֛וֹד מַבּ֖וּל
לְשַׁחֵ֥ת הָאָֽרֶץ:
12 וַיֹּ֣אמֶר אֱלֹהִ֗ים זֹ֤את אֽוֹת־הַבְּרִית֙ אֲשֶׁר־
אֲנִ֣י נֹתֵ֗ן בֵּינִי֙ וּבֵ֣ינֵיכֶ֔ם וּבֵ֛ין כָּל־נֶ֥פֶשׁ חַיָּ֖ה
אֲשֶׁ֣ר אִתְּכֶ֑ם לְדֹרֹ֖ת עוֹלָֽם: 13 אֶֽת־קַשְׁתִּ֕י
נָתַ֖תִּי בֶּֽעָנָ֑ן וְהָֽיְתָה֙ לְא֣וֹת בְּרִ֔ית בֵּינִ֖י וּבֵ֥ין
הָאָֽרֶץ: 14 וְהָיָ֕ה בְּעַֽנְנִ֥י עָנָ֖ן עַל־הָאָ֑רֶץ
וְנִרְאֲתָ֥ה הַקֶּ֖שֶׁת בֶּֽעָנָֽן: 15 וְזָֽכַרְתִּ֣י אֶת־
בְּרִיתִ֗י אֲשֶׁ֤ר בֵּינִי֙ וּבֵ֣ינֵיכֶ֔ם וּבֵ֛ין כָּל־נֶ֥פֶשׁ
חַיָּ֖ה בְּכָל־בָּשָׂ֑ר וְלֹֽא־יִֽהְיֶ֨ה ע֤וֹד הַמַּ֨יִם֙
לְמַבּ֔וּל לְשַׁחֵ֖ת כָּל־בָּשָֽׂר: 16 וְהָֽיְתָ֤ה
הַקֶּ֨שֶׁת֙ בֶּֽעָנָ֔ן וּרְאִיתִ֗יהָ לִזְכֹּר֙ בְּרִ֣ית עוֹלָ֔ם
בֵּ֣ין אֱלֹהִ֔ים וּבֵין֙ כָּל־נֶ֣פֶשׁ חַיָּ֔ה בְּכָל־בָּשָׂ֖ר
אֲשֶׁ֣ר עַל־הָאָֽרֶץ: 17 וַיֹּ֥אמֶר אֱלֹהִ֖ים אֶל־נֹ֑חַ
זֹ֤את אֽוֹת־הַבְּרִית֙ אֲשֶׁ֣ר הֲקִמֹ֔תִי בֵּינִ֕י וּבֵ֥ין
כָּל־בָּשָׂ֖ר אֲשֶׁ֥ר עַל־הָאָֽרֶץ: פ

18 וַיִּֽהְי֣וּ בְנֵי־נֹ֗חַ הַיֹּֽצְאִים֙ מִן־הַתֵּבָ֔ה שֵׁ֖ם
וְחָ֣ם וָיָ֑פֶת וְחָ֕ם ה֖וּא אֲבִ֥י כְנָֽעַן: 19 שְׁלֹשָׁ֥ה
אֵ֖לֶּה בְּנֵי־נֹ֑חַ וּמֵאֵ֖לֶּה נָֽפְצָ֥ה כָל־הָאָֽרֶץ:
20 וַיָּ֥חֶל נֹ֖חַ אִ֣ישׁ הָֽאֲדָמָ֑ה וַיִּטַּ֖ע כָּֽרֶם:
21 וַיֵּ֥שְׁתְּ מִן־הַיַּ֖יִן וַיִּשְׁכָּ֑ר וַיִּתְגַּ֖ל בְּת֥וֹךְ

became drunk, and he uncovered himself within his tent. 22Ham, the father of Canaan, saw his father's nakedness and told his two brothers outside. 23But Shem and Japheth took a cloth, placed it against both their backs and, walking backward, they covered their father's nakedness; their faces were turned the other way, so that they did not see their father's nakedness. 24When Noah woke up from his wine and learned what his youngest son had done to him, 25he said,

"Cursed be Canaan;
The lowest of slaves
Shall he be to his brothers."

26And he said,

"Blessed be the LORD,
The God of Shem;
Let Canaan be a slave to them.

27May God enlarge[a] Japheth,
And let him dwell in the tents of Shem;
And let Canaan be a slave to them."

28Noah lived after the Flood 350 years. 29And all the days of Noah came to 950 years; then he died.

10 These are the lines of Shem, Ham, and Japheth, the sons of Noah: sons were born to them after the Flood.

2The descendants of Japheth: Gomer, Magog, Madai, Javan, Tubal, Meshech, and Tiras. 3The descendants of Gomer: Ashkenaz, Riphath, and Togarmah. 4The descendants of Javan: Elishah and Tarshish, the Kittim and the Dodanim.[a] 5From these the maritime nations branched out. [These are the descendants of Japheth][b] by their lands—each with its language—their clans and their nations.

6The descendants of Ham: Cush, Mizraim, Put, and Canaan. 7The descendants of Cush:

אֵלֶּה אָהֳלוֹ: 22 וַיַּרְא חָם אֲבִי כְנַעַן אֵת עֶרְוַת אָבִיו וַיַּגֵּד לִשְׁנֵי־אֶחָיו בַּחוּץ: 23 וַיִּקַּח שֵׁם וָיֶפֶת אֶת־הַשִּׂמְלָה וַיָּשִׂימוּ עַל־שְׁכֶם שְׁנֵיהֶם וַיֵּלְכוּ אֲחֹרַנִּית וַיְכַסּוּ אֵת עֶרְוַת אֲבִיהֶם וּפְנֵיהֶם אֲחֹרַנִּית וְעֶרְוַת אֲבִיהֶם לֹא רָאוּ: 24 וַיִּיקֶץ נֹחַ מִיֵּינוֹ וַיֵּדַע אֵת אֲשֶׁר־עָשָׂה־לוֹ בְּנוֹ הַקָּטָן: 25 וַיֹּאמֶר

אָרוּר כְּנָעַן
עֶבֶד עֲבָדִים
יִהְיֶה לְאֶחָיו:

26 וַיֹּאמֶר
בָּרוּךְ יְהֹוָה
אֱלֹהֵי שֵׁם
וִיהִי כְנַעַן עֶבֶד לָמוֹ:

27 יַפְתְּ אֱלֹהִים לְיֶפֶת
וְיִשְׁכֹּן בְּאָהֳלֵי־שֵׁם
וִיהִי כְנַעַן עֶבֶד לָמוֹ:

28 וַיְחִי־נֹחַ אַחַר הַמַּבּוּל שְׁלֹשׁ מֵאוֹת שָׁנָה וַחֲמִשִּׁים שָׁנָה: 29 וַיִּהְיוּ כָּל־יְמֵי־נֹחַ תְּשַׁע מֵאוֹת שָׁנָה וַחֲמִשִּׁים שָׁנָה וַיָּמֹת: פ

י 1 וְאֵלֶּה תּוֹלְדֹת בְּנֵי־נֹחַ שֵׁם חָם וָיָפֶת וַיִּוָּלְדוּ לָהֶם בָּנִים אַחַר הַמַּבּוּל: 2 בְּנֵי יֶפֶת גֹּמֶר וּמָגוֹג וּמָדַי וְיָוָן וְתֻבָל וּמֶשֶׁךְ וְתִירָס: 3 וּבְנֵי גֹּמֶר אַשְׁכְּנַז וְרִיפַת וְתֹגַרְמָה: 4 וּבְנֵי יָוָן אֱלִישָׁה וְתַרְשִׁישׁ כִּתִּים וְדֹדָנִים: 5 מֵאֵלֶּה נִפְרְדוּ אִיֵּי הַגּוֹיִם בְּאַרְצֹתָם אִישׁ לִלְשֹׁנוֹ לְמִשְׁפְּחֹתָם בְּגוֹיֵהֶם:

6 וּבְנֵי חָם כּוּשׁ וּמִצְרַיִם וּפוּט וּכְנָעַן: 7 וּבְנֵי כוּשׁ סְבָא וַחֲוִילָה וְסַבְתָּה וְרַעְמָה וְסַבְתְּכָא וּבְנֵי רַעְמָה שְׁבָא וּדְדָן:

---

a   Heb. yapht, play on Heb. yepheth "Japheth."

a   Septuagint and 1 Chron. 1.7 "Rodanim."

b   Cf. vv. 20 and 31.

Seba, Havilah, Sabtah, Raamah, and Sabteca.
The descendants of Raamah: Sheba and Dedan.

[8]Cush also begot Nimrod, who was the first
man of might on earth. [9]He was a mighty hunter
by the grace of the Lord; hence the saying, "Like
Nimrod a mighty hunter by the grace of the
Lord." [10]The mainstays of his kingdom were
Babylon, Erech, Accad, and Calneh[c] in the land
of Shinar. [11]From that land Asshur went forth
and built Nineveh, Rehoboth-ir, Calah, [12]and
Resen between Nineveh and Calah, that is the
great city.

[13]And Mizraim begot the Ludim, the
Anamim, the Lehabim, the Naphtuhim, [14]the
Pathrusim, the Casluhim, and the Caphtorim,[d]
whence the Philistines came forth.

[15]Canaan begot Sidon, his first-born, and
Heth; [16]and the Jebusites, the Amorites, the
Girgashites, [17]the Hivites, the Arkites, the
Sinites, [18]the Arvadites, the Zemarites, and the
Hamathites. Afterward the clans of the Canaanites spread out. ([19]The [original] Canaanite territory extended from Sidon as far as Gerar, near
Gaza, and as far as Sodom, Gomorrah, Admah,
and Zeboiim, near Lasha.) [20]These are the descendants of Ham, according to their clans and
languages, by their lands and nations.

[21]Sons were also born to Shem, ancestor of
all the descendants of Eber and older brother
of Japheth. [22]The descendants of Shem: Elam,
Asshur, Arpachshad, Lud, and Aram. [23]The descendants of Aram: Uz, Hul, Gether, and Mash.
[24]Arpachshad begot Shelah, and Shelah begot
Eber. [25]Two sons were born to Eber: the name
of the first was Peleg, for in his days the earth
was divided;[e] and the name of his brother was
Joktan. [26]Joktan begot Almodad, Sheleph,
Hazarmaveth, Jerah, [27]Hadoram, Uzal, Diklah,
[28]Obal, Abimael, Sheba, [29]Ophir, Havilah, and

---

c Heb. *we-khalneh, better vocalized we-khullanah* "all of them
   being."
d I.e., the Cretans; moved up for the sake of clarity; cf. Amos 9.7.
e Heb. *niphlegah,* play on "Peleg."

8 וְכ֣וּשׁ יָלַ֖ד אֶת־נִמְרֹ֑ד ה֣וּא הֵחֵ֔ל לִֽהְי֥וֹת
גִּבֹּ֖ר בָּאָֽרֶץ: 9 הֽוּא־הָיָ֥ה גִבֹּֽר־צַ֖יִד לִפְנֵ֣י
יְהֹוָ֑ה עַל־כֵּן֙ יֵֽאָמַ֔ר כְּנִמְרֹ֛ד גִּבּ֥וֹר צַ֖יִד לִפְנֵ֥י
יְהֹוָֽה: 10 וַתְּהִ֨י רֵאשִׁ֤ית מַמְלַכְתּוֹ֙ בָּבֶ֔ל
וְאֶ֖רֶךְ וְאַכַּ֣ד וְכַלְנֵ֑ה בְּאֶ֖רֶץ שִׁנְעָֽר: 11 מִן־
הָאָ֥רֶץ הַהִ֖וא יָצָ֣א אַשּׁ֑וּר וַיִּ֙בֶן֙ אֶת־נִ֣ינְוֵ֔ה
וְאֶת־רְחֹבֹ֥ת עִ֖יר וְאֶת־כָּֽלַח: 12 וְאֶת־רֶ֕סֶן
בֵּ֥ין נִֽינְוֵ֖ה וּבֵ֣ין כָּ֑לַח הִ֖וא הָעִ֥יר הַגְּדֹלָֽה:
13 וּמִצְרַ֡יִם יָלַ֞ד אֶת־לוּדִ֧ים וְאֶת־עֲנָמִ֛ים
וְאֶת־לְהָבִ֖ים וְאֶת־נַפְתֻּחִֽים: 14 וְאֶת־
פַּתְרֻסִ֞ים וְאֶת־כַּסְלֻחִ֗ים אֲשֶׁ֨ר יָֽצְא֤וּ מִשָּׁ֙ם
פְּלִשְׁתִּ֔ים וְאֶת־כַּפְתֹּרִֽים: ס
15 וּכְנַ֗עַן יָלַ֛ד אֶת־צִידֹ֥ן בְּכֹר֖וֹ וְאֶת־
חֵֽת: 16 וְאֶת־הַיְבוּסִי֙ וְאֶת־הָ֣אֱמֹרִ֔י וְאֵ֖ת
הַגִּרְגָּשִֽׁי: 17 וְאֶת־הַֽחִוִּ֥י וְאֶת־הַֽעַרְקִ֖י וְאֶת־
הַסִּינִֽי: 18 וְאֶת־הָֽאַרְוָדִ֥י וְאֶת־הַצְּמָרִ֖י
וְאֶת־הַֽחֲמָתִ֑י וְאַחַ֣ר נָפֹ֔צוּ מִשְׁפְּח֖וֹת
הַֽכְּנַעֲנִֽי: 19 וַֽיְהִ֞י גְּב֤וּל הַֽכְּנַעֲנִי֙ מִצִּידֹ֔ן
בֹּֽאֲכָ֥ה גְרָ֖רָה עַד־עַזָּ֑ה בֹּֽאֲכָ֞ה סְדֹ֧מָה
וַֽעֲמֹרָ֛ה וְאַדְמָ֥ה וּצְבֹיִ֖ם עַד־לָֽשַׁע: 20 אֵ֣לֶּה
בְנֵי־חָ֔ם לְמִשְׁפְּחֹתָ֖ם לִלְשֹֽׁנֹתָ֑ם בְּאַרְצֹתָ֖ם
בְּגֽוֹיֵהֶֽם: ס
21 וּלְשֵׁ֥ם יֻלַּ֖ד גַּם־ה֑וּא אֲבִי֙ כָּל־בְּנֵי־עֵ֔בֶר
אֲחִ֖י יֶ֥פֶת הַגָּדֽוֹל: 22 בְּנֵ֣י שֵׁ֔ם עֵילָ֣ם וְאַשּׁ֑וּר
וְאַרְפַּכְשַׁ֖ד וְל֥וּד וַֽאֲרָֽם: 23 וּבְנֵ֖י אֲרָ֑ם ע֣וּץ
וְח֖וּל וְגֶ֥תֶר וָמַֽשׁ: 24 וְאַרְפַּכְשַׁ֖ד יָלַ֣ד אֶת־
שָׁ֑לַח וְשֶׁ֖לַח יָלַ֥ד אֶת־עֵֽבֶר: 25 וּלְעֵ֥בֶר יֻלַּ֖ד
שְׁנֵ֣י בָנִ֑ים שֵׁ֣ם הָֽאֶחָ֞ד פֶּ֗לֶג כִּ֤י בְיָמָיו֙ נִפְלְגָ֣ה
הָאָ֔רֶץ וְשֵׁ֥ם אָחִ֖יו יָקְטָֽן: 26 וְיָקְטָ֣ן יָלַ֔ד
אֶת־אַלְמוֹדָ֖ד וְאֶת־שָׁ֑לֶף וְאֶת־חֲצַרְמָ֖וֶת
וְאֶת־יָֽרַח: 27 וְאֶת־הֲדוֹרָ֥ם וְאֶת־אוּזָ֖ל
וְאֶת־דִּקְלָֽה: 28 וְאֶת־עוֹבָ֥ל וְאֶת־אֲבִֽימָאֵ֖ל
וְאֶת־שְׁבָֽא: 29 וְאֶת־אוֹפִ֥ר וְאֶת־חֲוִילָ֖ה

Jobab; all these were the descendants of Joktan. ³⁰Their settlements extended from Mesha as far as Sephar, the hill country to the east. ³¹These are the descendants of Shem according to their clans and languages, by their lands, according to their nations.

³²These are the groupings of Noah's descendants, according to their origins, by their nations; and from these the nations branched out over the earth after the Flood.

11 Everyone on earth had the same language and the same words. ²And as they migrated from the east, they came upon a valley in the land of Shinar and settled there. ³They said to one another, "Come, let us make bricks and burn them hard."—Brick served them as stone, and bitumen served them as mortar.— ⁴And they said, "Come, let us build us a city, and a tower with its top in the sky, to make a name for ourselves; else we shall be scattered all over the world." ⁵The Lord came down to look at the city and tower that man had built, ⁶and the Lord said, "If, as one people with one language for all, this is how they have begun to act, then nothing that they may propose to do will be out of their reach. ⁷Let us, then, go down and confound their speech there, so that they shall not understand one another's speech." ⁸Thus the Lord scattered them from there over the face of the whole earth; and they stopped building the city. ⁹That is why it was called Babel,ᵃ because there the Lord confoundedᵇ the speech of the whole earth; and from there the Lord scattered them over the face of the whole earth.

¹⁰This is the line of Shem. Shem was 100 years old when he begot Arpachshad, two years

וְאֶת־יוֹבָ֑ב כָּל־אֵ֖לֶּה בְּנֵ֥י יָקְטָֽן׃ 30 וַֽיְהִ֥י מֽוֹשָׁבָ֖ם מִמֵּשָׁ֑א בֹּאֲכָ֥ה סְפָ֖רָה הַ֥ר הַקֶּֽדֶם׃ 31 אֵ֣לֶּה בְנֵי־שֵׁ֔ם לְמִשְׁפְּחֹתָ֖ם לִלְשֹֽׁנֹתָ֑ם בְּאַרְצֹתָ֖ם לְגֽוֹיֵהֶֽם׃ 32 אֵ֣לֶּה מִשְׁפְּחֹ֧ת בְּנֵי־נֹ֛חַ לְתֽוֹלְדֹתָ֖ם בְּגֽוֹיֵהֶ֑ם וּמֵאֵ֜לֶּה נִפְרְד֧וּ הַגּוֹיִ֛ם בָּאָ֖רֶץ אַחַ֥ר הַמַּבּֽוּל׃ פ

יא וַֽיְהִ֥י כָל־הָאָ֖רֶץ שָׂפָ֣ה אֶחָ֑ת וּדְבָרִ֖ים אֲחָדִֽים׃ 2 וַֽיְהִ֖י בְּנָסְעָ֣ם מִקֶּ֑דֶם וַֽיִּמְצְא֥וּ בִקְעָ֛ה בְּאֶ֥רֶץ שִׁנְעָ֖ר וַיֵּ֥שְׁבוּ שָֽׁם׃ 3 וַיֹּֽאמְר֞וּ אִ֣ישׁ אֶל־רֵעֵ֗הוּ הָ֚בָה נִלְבְּנָ֣ה לְבֵנִ֔ים וְנִשְׂרְפָ֖ה לִשְׂרֵפָ֑ה וַתְּהִ֨י לָהֶ֤ם הַלְּבֵנָה֙ לְאָ֔בֶן וְהַ֣חֵמָ֔ר הָיָ֥ה לָהֶ֖ם לַחֹֽמֶר׃ 4 וַיֹּֽאמְר֞וּ הָ֣בָה ׀ נִבְנֶה־לָּ֣נוּ עִ֗יר וּמִגְדָּל֙ וְרֹאשׁ֣וֹ בַשָּׁמַ֔יִם וְנַֽעֲשֶׂה־לָּ֖נוּ שֵׁ֑ם פֶּן־נָפ֖וּץ עַל־פְּנֵ֥י כָל־הָאָֽרֶץ׃ 5 וַיֵּ֣רֶד יְהֹוָ֔ה לִרְאֹ֥ת אֶת־הָעִ֖יר וְאֶת־הַמִּגְדָּ֑ל אֲשֶׁ֥ר בָּנ֖וּ בְּנֵ֥י הָֽאָדָֽם׃ 6 וַיֹּ֣אמֶר יְהֹוָ֗ה הֵ֣ן עַ֤ם אֶחָד֙ וְשָׂפָ֤ה אַחַת֙ לְכֻלָּ֔ם וְזֶ֖ה הַֽחִלָּ֣ם לַֽעֲשׂ֑וֹת וְעַתָּה֙ לֹֽא־יִבָּצֵ֣ר מֵהֶ֔ם כֹּ֛ל אֲשֶׁ֥ר יָֽזְמ֖וּ לַֽעֲשֽׂוֹת׃ 7 הָ֚בָה נֵֽרְדָ֔ה וְנָֽבְלָ֥ה שָׁ֖ם שְׂפָתָ֑ם אֲשֶׁר֙ לֹ֣א יִשְׁמְע֔וּ אִ֖ישׁ שְׂפַ֥ת רֵעֵֽהוּ׃ 8 וַיָּ֨פֶץ יְהֹוָ֥ה אֹתָ֛ם מִשָּׁ֖ם עַל־פְּנֵ֣י כָל־הָאָ֑רֶץ וַֽיַּחְדְּל֖וּ לִבְנֹ֥ת הָעִֽיר׃ 9 עַל־כֵּ֞ן קָרָ֤א שְׁמָהּ֙ בָּבֶ֔ל כִּי־שָׁ֛ם בָּלַ֥ל יְהֹוָ֖ה שְׂפַ֣ת כָּל־הָאָ֑רֶץ וּמִשָּׁם֙ הֱפִיצָ֣ם יְהֹוָ֔ה עַל־פְּנֵ֖י כָּל־הָאָֽרֶץ׃ פ

10 אֵ֚לֶּה תּֽוֹלְדֹ֣ת שֵׁ֔ם שֵׁ֚ם בֶּן־מְאַ֣ת שָׁנָ֔ה וַיּ֖וֹלֶד אֶת־אַרְפַּכְשָׁ֑ד שְׁנָתַ֖יִם אַחַ֥ר הַמַּבּֽוּל׃ 11 וַֽיְחִי־שֵׁ֗ם אַֽחֲרֵי֙ הֽוֹלִיד֣וֹ אֶת־אַרְפַּכְשָׁ֔ד חֲמֵ֥שׁ מֵא֖וֹת שָׁנָ֑ה וַיּ֥וֹלֶד בָּנִ֖ים

ᵃ   I.e., "Babylon."
ᵇ   Heb. *balal* "confound," play on "Babel."

after the Flood. [11]After the birth of[c] Arpach-shad, Shem lived 500 years and begot sons and daughters.

[12]When Arpachshad had lived 35 years, he begot Shelah. [13]After the birth of Shelah, Arpachshad lived 403 years and begot sons and daughters.

[14]When Shelah had lived 30 years, he begot Eber. [15]After the birth of Eber, Shelah lived 403 years and begot sons and daughters.

[16]When Eber had lived 34 years, he begot Peleg. [17]After the birth of Peleg, Eber lived 430 years and begot sons and daughters.

[18]When Peleg had lived 30 years, he begot Reu. [19]After the birth of Reu, Peleg lived 209 years and begot sons and daughters.

[20]When Reu had lived 32 years, he begot Serug. [21]After the birth of Serug, Reu lived 207 years and begot sons and daughters.

[22]When Serug had lived 30 years, he begot Nahor. [23]After the birth of Nahor, Serug lived 200 years and begot sons and daughters.

[24]When Nahor had lived 29 years, he begot Terah. [25]After the birth of Terah, Nahor lived 119 years and begot sons and daughters.

[26]When Terah had lived 70 years, he begot Abram, Nahor, and Haran. [27]Now this is the line of Terah: Terah begot Abram, Nahor, and Haran; and Haran begot Lot. [28]Haran died in the lifetime of his father Terah, in his native land, Ur of the Chaldeans. [29]Abram and Nahor took to themselves wives, the name of Abram's wife being Sarai and that of Nahor's wife Milcah, the daughter of Haran, the father of Milcah and Iscah. [30]Now Sarai was barren, she had no child.

[31]Terah took his son Abram, his grandson Lot the son of Haran, and his daughter-in-law Sarai, the wife of his son Abram, and they set out to-gether from Ur of the Chaldeans for the land

c   Lit. "After he begot," and so throughout.

‫וּבָנוֹת: ס 12 וְאַרְפַּכְשַׁד חַי חָמֵשׁ‬
‫וּשְׁלֹשִׁים שָׁנָה וַיּוֹלֶד אֶת־שָׁלַח: 13 וַיְחִי‬
‫אַרְפַּכְשַׁד אַחֲרֵי הוֹלִידוֹ אֶת־שֶׁלַח שָׁלֹשׁ‬
‫שָׁנִים וְאַרְבַּע מֵאוֹת שָׁנָה וַיּוֹלֶד בָּנִים‬
‫וּבָנוֹת: ס 14 וְשֶׁלַח חַי שְׁלֹשִׁים שָׁנָה‬
‫וַיּוֹלֶד אֶת־עֵבֶר: 15 וַיְחִי־שֶׁלַח אַחֲרֵי‬
‫הוֹלִידוֹ אֶת־עֵבֶר שָׁלֹשׁ שָׁנִים וְאַרְבַּע‬
‫מֵאוֹת שָׁנָה וַיּוֹלֶד בָּנִים וּבָנוֹת: ס‬
‫16 וַיְחִי־עֵבֶר אַרְבַּע וּשְׁלֹשִׁים שָׁנָה וַיּוֹלֶד‬
‫אֶת־פָּלֶג: 17 וַיְחִי־עֵבֶר אַחֲרֵי הוֹלִידוֹ אֶת־‬
‫פֶּלֶג שְׁלֹשִׁים שָׁנָה וְאַרְבַּע מֵאוֹת שָׁנָה‬
‫וַיּוֹלֶד בָּנִים וּבָנוֹת: ס 18 וַיְחִי־פֶלֶג‬
‫שְׁלֹשִׁים שָׁנָה וַיּוֹלֶד אֶת־רְעוּ: 19 וַיְחִי־פֶלֶג‬
‫אַחֲרֵי הוֹלִידוֹ אֶת־רְעוּ תֵּשַׁע שָׁנִים‬
‫וּמָאתַיִם שָׁנָה וַיּוֹלֶד בָּנִים וּבָנוֹת: ס‬
‫20 וַיְחִי רְעוּ שְׁתַּיִם וּשְׁלֹשִׁים שָׁנָה וַיּוֹלֶד‬
‫אֶת־שְׂרוּג: 21 וַיְחִי רְעוּ אַחֲרֵי הוֹלִידוֹ‬
‫אֶת־שְׂרוּג שֶׁבַע שָׁנִים וּמָאתַיִם שָׁנָה‬
‫וַיּוֹלֶד בָּנִים וּבָנוֹת: ס 22 וַיְחִי שְׂרוּג‬
‫שְׁלֹשִׁים שָׁנָה וַיּוֹלֶד אֶת־נָחוֹר: 23 וַיְחִי‬
‫שְׂרוּג אַחֲרֵי הוֹלִידוֹ אֶת־נָחוֹר מָאתַיִם‬
‫שָׁנָה וַיּוֹלֶד בָּנִים וּבָנוֹת: ס 24 וַיְחִי נָחוֹר‬
‫תֵּשַׁע וְעֶשְׂרִים שָׁנָה וַיּוֹלֶד אֶת־תָּרַח:‬
‫25 וַיְחִי נָחוֹר אַחֲרֵי הוֹלִידוֹ אֶת־תֶּרַח‬
‫תְּשַׁע־עֶשְׂרֵה שָׁנָה וּמְאַת שָׁנָה וַיּוֹלֶד‬
‫בָּנִים וּבָנוֹת: ס 26 וַיְחִי־תֶרַח שִׁבְעִים‬
‫שָׁנָה וַיּוֹלֶד אֶת־אַבְרָם אֶת־נָחוֹר וְאֶת־‬
‫הָרָן: 27 וְאֵלֶּה תּוֹלְדֹת תֶּרַח תֶּרַח הוֹלִיד‬
‫אֶת־אַבְרָם אֶת־נָחוֹר וְאֶת־הָרָן וְהָרָן‬
‫הוֹלִיד אֶת־לוֹט: 28 וַיָּמָת הָרָן עַל־פְּנֵי‬
‫תֶּרַח אָבִיו בְּאֶרֶץ מוֹלַדְתּוֹ בְּאוּר כַּשְׂדִּים:‬
‫29 וַיִּקַּח אַבְרָם וְנָחוֹר לָהֶם נָשִׁים שֵׁם‬
‫אֵשֶׁת־אַבְרָם שָׂרָי וְשֵׁם אֵשֶׁת־נָחוֹר מִלְכָּה‬
‫בַּת־הָרָן אֲבִי־מִלְכָּה וַאֲבִי יִסְכָּה: 30 וַתְּהִי‬
‫שָׂרַי עֲקָרָה אֵין לָהּ וָלָד:‬
‫31 וַיִּקַּח תֶּרַח אֶת־אַבְרָם בְּנוֹ וְאֶת־לוֹט‬

of Canaan; but when they had come as far as Haran, they settled there. [32]The days of Terah came to 205 years; and Terah died in Haran.

12 LEKH LEKHA

The LORD said to Abram, "Go forth from your native land and from your father's house to the land that I will show you.

[2]I will make of you a great nation,
And I will bless you;
I will make your name great,
And you shall be a blessing.[a]
[3]I will bless those who bless you
And curse him that curses you;
And all the families of the earth
Shall bless themselves by you."

[4]Abram went forth as the LORD had commanded him, and Lot went with him. Abram was seventy-five years old when he left Haran. [5]Abram took his wife Sarai and his brother's son Lot, and all the wealth that they had amassed, and the persons that they had acquired in Haran; and they set out for the land of Canaan. When they arrived in the land of Canaan, [6]Abram passed through the land as far as the site of Shechem, at the terebinth of Moreh. The Canaanites were then in the land.

[7]The LORD appeared to Abram and said, "I will assign this land to your offspring." And he built an altar there to the LORD who had appeared to him. [8]From there he moved on to the hill country east of Bethel and pitched his tent, with Bethel on the west and Ai on the east; and he built there an altar to the LORD and invoked the LORD by name. [9]Then Abram journeyed by stages toward the Negeb.

---

a   I.e., a standard by which blessing is invoked; cf. v. 3 end.

בֶּן־הָרָ֔ן בֶּן־בְּנ֑וֹ וְאֵת֙ שָׂרַ֣י כַּלָּת֔וֹ אֵ֖שֶׁת אַבְרָ֣ם בְּנ֑וֹ וַיֵּצְא֨וּ אִתָּ֜ם מֵא֣וּר כַּשְׂדִּ֗ים לָלֶ֙כֶת֙ אַ֣רְצָה כְּנַ֔עַן וַיָּבֹ֥אוּ עַד־חָרָ֖ן וַיֵּ֥שְׁבוּ שָֽׁם: [32] וַיִּהְי֣וּ יְמֵי־תֶ֗רַח חָמֵ֥שׁ שָׁנִ֛ים וּמָאתַ֖יִם שָׁנָ֑ה וַיָּ֥מָת תֶּ֖רַח בְּחָרָֽן: ס

יב לך לך

וַיֹּ֤אמֶר יְהֹוָה֙ אֶל־אַבְרָ֔ם לֶךְ־לְךָ֛ מֵאַרְצְךָ֥ וּמִמּֽוֹלַדְתְּךָ֖ וּמִבֵּ֣ית אָבִ֑יךָ אֶל־הָאָ֖רֶץ אֲשֶׁ֥ר אַרְאֶֽךָּ: [2] וְאֶֽעֶשְׂךָ֙ לְג֣וֹי גָּד֔וֹל וַאֲבָ֣רֶכְךָ֔ וַאֲגַדְּלָ֖ה שְׁמֶ֑ךָ וֶהְיֵ֖ה בְּרָכָֽה: [3] וַאֲבָֽרֲכָה֙ מְבָ֣רְכֶ֔יךָ וּמְקַלֶּלְךָ֖ אָאֹ֑ר וְנִבְרְכ֣וּ בְךָ֔ כֹּ֖ל מִשְׁפְּחֹ֥ת הָאֲדָמָֽה: [4] וַיֵּ֣לֶךְ אַבְרָ֗ם כַּאֲשֶׁ֨ר דִּבֶּ֤ר אֵלָיו֙ יְהֹוָ֔ה וַיֵּ֥לֶךְ אִתּ֖וֹ ל֑וֹט וְאַבְרָ֗ם בֶּן־חָמֵ֤שׁ שָׁנִים֙ וְשִׁבְעִ֣ים שָׁנָ֔ה בְּצֵאת֖וֹ מֵחָרָֽן: [5] וַיִּקַּ֣ח אַבְרָם֩ אֶת־שָׂרַ֨י אִשְׁתּ֜וֹ וְאֶת־ל֣וֹט בֶּן־אָחִ֗יו וְאֶת־כָּל־רְכוּשָׁם֙ אֲשֶׁ֣ר רָכָ֔שׁוּ וְאֶת־הַנֶּ֖פֶשׁ אֲשֶׁר־עָשׂ֣וּ בְחָרָ֑ן וַיֵּצְא֗וּ לָלֶ֙כֶת֙ אַ֣רְצָה כְּנַ֔עַן וַיָּבֹ֖אוּ אַ֥רְצָה כְּנָֽעַן: [6] וַיַּעֲבֹ֤ר אַבְרָם֙ בָּאָ֔רֶץ עַ֚ד מְק֣וֹם שְׁכֶ֔ם עַ֖ד אֵל֣וֹן מוֹרֶ֑ה וְהַֽכְּנַעֲנִ֖י אָ֥ז בָּאָֽרֶץ: [7] וַיֵּרָ֤א יְהֹוָה֙ אֶל־אַבְרָ֔ם וַיֹּ֕אמֶר לְזַ֨רְעֲךָ֔ אֶתֵּ֖ן אֶת־הָאָ֣רֶץ הַזֹּ֑את וַיִּ֤בֶן שָׁם֙ מִזְבֵּ֔חַ לַיהֹוָ֖ה הַנִּרְאֶ֥ה אֵלָֽיו: [8] וַיַּעְתֵּ֨ק מִשָּׁ֜ם הָהָ֗רָה מִקֶּ֛דֶם לְבֵֽית־אֵ֖ל וַיֵּ֣ט אָֽהֳלֹ֑ה בֵּֽית־אֵ֤ל מִיָּם֙ וְהָעַ֣י מִקֶּ֔דֶם וַיִּֽבֶן־שָׁ֤ם מִזְבֵּ֨חַ֙ לַֽיהֹוָ֔ה וַיִּקְרָ֖א בְּשֵׁ֥ם יְהֹוָֽה: [9] וַיִּסַּ֣ע אַבְרָ֔ם הָל֥וֹךְ וְנָס֖וֹעַ הַנֶּֽגְבָּה: פ

10There was a famine in the land, and Abram went down to Egypt to sojourn there, for the famine was severe in the land. 11As he was about to enter Egypt, he said to his wife Sarai, "I know[b] what a beautiful woman you are. 12If the Egyptians see you, and think, 'She is his wife,' they will kill me and let you live. 13Please say that you are my sister, that it may go well with me because of you, and that I may remain alive thanks to you."

14When Abram entered Egypt, the Egyptians saw how very beautiful the woman was. 15Pharaoh's courtiers saw her and praised her to Pharaoh, and the woman was taken into Pharaoh's palace. 16And because of her, it went well with Abram; he acquired sheep, oxen, asses, male and female slaves, she-asses, and camels.

17But the Lord afflicted Pharaoh and his household with mighty plagues on account of Sarai, the wife of Abram. 18Pharaoh sent for Abram and said, "What is this you have done to me! Why did you not tell me that she was your wife? 19Why did you say, 'She is my sister,' so that I took her as my wife? Now, here is your wife; take her and begone!" 20And Pharaoh put men in charge of him, and they sent him off with his wife and all that he possessed.

13 From Egypt, Abram went up into the Negeb, with his wife and all that he possessed, together with Lot. 2Now Abram was very rich in cattle, silver, and gold. 3And he proceeded by stages from the Negeb as far as Bethel, to the place where his tent had been formerly, between Bethel and Ai, 4the site of the altar that he had built there at first; and there Abram invoked the Lord by name.

5Lot, who went with Abram, also had flocks and herds and tents, 6so that the land could not

10 וַיְהִ֥י רָעָ֖ב בָּאָ֑רֶץ וַיֵּ֨רֶד אַבְרָ֤ם מִצְרַ֨יְמָה֙ לָג֣וּר שָׁ֔ם כִּֽי־כָבֵ֥ד הָרָעָ֖ב בָּאָֽרֶץ׃ 11 וַיְהִ֕י כַּאֲשֶׁ֥ר הִקְרִ֖יב לָב֣וֹא מִצְרָ֑יְמָה וַיֹּ֨אמֶר֙ אֶל־שָׂרַ֣י אִשְׁתּ֔וֹ הִנֵּה־נָ֣א יָדַ֔עְתִּי כִּ֛י אִשָּׁ֥ה יְפַת־מַרְאֶ֖ה אָֽתְּ׃ 12 וְהָיָ֗ה כִּֽי־יִרְא֤וּ אֹתָךְ֙ הַמִּצְרִ֔ים וְאָמְר֖וּ אִשְׁתּ֣וֹ זֹ֑את וְהָרְג֥וּ אֹתִ֖י וְאֹתָ֥ךְ יְחַיּֽוּ׃ 13 אִמְרִי־נָ֖א אֲחֹ֣תִי אָ֑תְּ לְמַ֨עַן֙ יִֽיטַב־לִ֣י בַעֲבוּרֵ֔ךְ וְחָיְתָ֥ה נַפְשִׁ֖י בִּגְלָלֵֽךְ׃ 14 וַיְהִ֕י כְּב֥וֹא אַבְרָ֖ם מִצְרָ֑יְמָה וַיִּרְא֤וּ הַמִּצְרִים֙ אֶת־הָ֣אִשָּׁ֔ה כִּֽי־יָפָ֥ה הִ֖וא מְאֹֽד׃ 15 וַיִּרְא֤וּ אֹתָהּ֙ שָׂרֵ֣י פַרְעֹ֔ה וַיְהַֽלְל֥וּ אֹתָ֖הּ אֶל־פַּרְעֹ֑ה וַתֻּקַּ֥ח הָאִשָּׁ֖ה בֵּ֥ית פַּרְעֹֽה׃ 16 וּלְאַבְרָ֥ם הֵיטִ֖יב בַּעֲבוּרָ֑הּ וַֽיְהִי־ל֤וֹ צֹאן־וּבָקָר֙ וַחֲמֹרִ֔ים וַעֲבָדִים֙ וּשְׁפָחֹ֔ת וַאֲתֹנֹ֖ת וּגְמַלִּֽים׃ 17 וַיְנַגַּ֨ע יְהֹוָ֧ה ׀ אֶת־פַּרְעֹ֛ה נְגָעִ֥ים גְּדֹלִ֖ים וְאֶת־בֵּית֑וֹ עַל־דְּבַ֥ר שָׂרַ֖י אֵ֥שֶׁת אַבְרָֽם׃ 18 וַיִּקְרָ֤א פַרְעֹה֙ לְאַבְרָ֔ם וַיֹּ֕אמֶר מַה־זֹּ֖את עָשִׂ֣יתָ לִּ֑י לָ֚מָּה לֹא־הִגַּ֣דְתָּ לִּ֔י כִּ֥י אִשְׁתְּךָ֖ הִֽוא׃ 19 לָמָ֤ה אָמַ֨רְתָּ֙ אֲחֹ֣תִי הִ֔וא וָאֶקַּ֥ח אֹתָ֛הּ לִ֖י לְאִשָּׁ֑ה וְעַתָּ֕ה הִנֵּ֥ה אִשְׁתְּךָ֖ קַ֥ח וָלֵֽךְ׃ 20 וַיְצַ֥ו עָלָ֛יו פַּרְעֹ֖ה אֲנָשִׁ֑ים וַֽיְשַׁלְּח֤וּ אֹתוֹ֙ וְאֶת־אִשְׁתּ֔וֹ וְאֶת־כׇּל־אֲשֶׁר־לֽוֹ׃

יג וַיַּ֩עַל֩ אַבְרָ֨ם מִמִּצְרַ֜יִם ה֠וּא וְאִשְׁתּ֧וֹ וְכׇל־אֲשֶׁר־ל֛וֹ וְל֥וֹט עִמּ֖וֹ הַנֶּֽגְבָּה׃ 2 וְאַבְרָ֖ם כָּבֵ֣ד מְאֹ֑ד בַּמִּקְנֶ֕ה בַּכֶּ֖סֶף וּבַזָּהָֽב׃ 3 וַיֵּ֨לֶךְ֙ לְמַסָּעָ֔יו מִנֶּ֖גֶב וְעַד־בֵּֽית־אֵ֑ל עַד־הַמָּק֗וֹם אֲשֶׁר־הָ֨יָה שָׁ֤ם אׇֽהֳלֹה֙ בַּתְּחִלָּ֔ה בֵּ֥ין בֵּֽית־אֵ֖ל וּבֵ֥ין הָעָֽי׃ 4 אֶל־מְקוֹם֙ הַמִּזְבֵּ֔חַ אֲשֶׁר־עָ֥שָׂה שָׁ֖ם בָּרִֽאשֹׁנָ֑ה וַיִּקְרָ֥א שָׁ֛ם אַבְרָ֖ם בְּשֵׁ֥ם יְהֹוָֽה׃ 5 וְגַ֨ם־לְל֔וֹט הַהֹלֵ֖ךְ אֶת־אַבְרָ֑ם הָיָ֥ה צֹאן־וּבָקָ֖ר וְאֹהָלִֽים׃ 6 וְלֹא־נָשָׂ֥א אֹתָ֛ם הָאָ֖רֶץ

b Or "You"; cf. the second person feminine form -ti in Judg. 5.7; Jer. 2.20; Mic. 4.13, etc.

support them staying together; for their possessions were so great that they could not remain together. 7And there was quarreling between the herdsmen of Abram's cattle and those of Lot's cattle.—The Canaanites and Perizzites were then dwelling in the land.—8Abram said to Lot, "Let there be no strife between you and me, between my herdsmen and yours, for we are kinsmen. 9Is not the whole land before you? Let us separate:ᵃ if you go north, I will go south; and if you go south, I will go north." 10Lot looked about him and saw how well watered was the whole plain of the Jordan, all of it—this was before the LORD had destroyed Sodom and Gomorrah—all the way to Zoar, like the garden of the LORD, like the land of Egypt. 11So Lot chose for himself the whole plain of the Jordan, and Lot journeyed eastward. Thus they parted from each other; 12Abram remained in the land of Canaan, while Lot settled in the cities of the Plain, pitching his tents near Sodom. 13Now the inhabitants of Sodom were very wicked sinners against the LORD.

14And the LORD said to Abram, after Lot had parted from him, "Raise your eyes and look out from where you are, to the north and south, to the east and west, 15for I give all the land that you see to you and your offspring forever. 16I will make your offspring as the dust of the earth, so that if one can count the dust of the earth, then your offspring too can be counted. 17Up, walk about the land, through its length and its breadth, for I give it to you." 18And Abram moved his tent, and came to dwell at the terebinths of Mamre, which are in Hebron; and he built an altar there to the LORD.

14 Now, when King Amraphel of Shinar, King Arioch of Ellasar, King Chedorlaomer of Elam, and King Tidal of Goiim 2made war on

לְשֶׁבֶת יַחְדָּו כִּי־הָיָה רְכוּשָׁם רָב וְלֹא יָכְלוּ לָשֶׁבֶת יַחְדָּו: 7וַיְהִי־רִיב בֵּין רֹעֵי מִקְנֵה־אַבְרָם וּבֵין רֹעֵי מִקְנֵה־לוֹט וְהַכְּנַעֲנִי וְהַפְּרִזִּי אָז יֹשֵׁב בָּאָרֶץ: 8וַיֹּאמֶר אַבְרָם אֶל־לוֹט אַל־נָא תְהִי מְרִיבָה בֵּינִי וּבֵינֶיךָ וּבֵין רֹעַי וּבֵין רֹעֶיךָ כִּי־אֲנָשִׁים אַחִים אֲנָחְנוּ: 9הֲלֹא כָל־הָאָרֶץ לְפָנֶיךָ הִפָּרֶד נָא מֵעָלָי אִם־הַשְּׂמֹאל וְאֵימִנָה וְאִם־הַיָּמִין וְאַשְׂמְאִילָה: 10וַיִּשָּׂא־לוֹט אֶת־עֵינָיו וַיַּרְא אֶת־כָּל־כִּכַּר הַיַּרְדֵּן כִּי כֻלָּהּ מַשְׁקֶה לִפְנֵי | שַׁחֵת יְהֹוָה אֶת־סְדֹם וְאֶת־עֲמֹרָה כְּגַן־יְהֹוָה כְּאֶרֶץ מִצְרַיִם בֹּאֲכָה צֹעַר: 11וַיִּבְחַר־לוֹ לוֹט אֵת כָּל־כִּכַּר הַיַּרְדֵּן וַיִּסַּע לוֹט מִקֶּדֶם וַיִּפָּרְדוּ אִישׁ מֵעַל אָחִיו: 12אַבְרָם יָשַׁב בְּאֶרֶץ־כְּנָעַן וְלוֹט יָשַׁב בְּעָרֵי הַכִּכָּר וַיֶּאֱהַל עַד־סְדֹם: 13וְאַנְשֵׁי סְדֹם רָעִים וְחַטָּאִים לַיהֹוָה מְאֹד:

14וַיהֹוָה אָמַר אֶל־אַבְרָם אַחֲרֵי הִפָּרֶד־לוֹט מֵעִמּוֹ שָׂא נָא עֵינֶיךָ וּרְאֵה מִן־הַמָּקוֹם אֲשֶׁר־אַתָּה שָׁם צָפֹנָה וָנֶגְבָּה וָקֵדְמָה וָיָמָּה: 15כִּי אֶת־כָּל־הָאָרֶץ אֲשֶׁר אַתָּה רֹאֶה לְךָ אֶתְּנֶנָּה וּלְזַרְעֲךָ עַד־עוֹלָם: 16וְשַׂמְתִּי אֶת־זַרְעֲךָ כַּעֲפַר הָאָרֶץ אֲשֶׁר | אִם־יוּכַל אִישׁ לִמְנוֹת אֶת־עֲפַר הָאָרֶץ גַּם־זַרְעֲךָ יִמָּנֶה: 17קוּם הִתְהַלֵּךְ בָּאָרֶץ לְאָרְכָּהּ וּלְרָחְבָּהּ כִּי לְךָ אֶתְּנֶנָּה: 18וַיֶּאֱהַל אַבְרָם וַיָּבֹא וַיֵּשֶׁב בְּאֵלֹנֵי מַמְרֵא אֲשֶׁר בְּחֶבְרוֹן וַיִּבֶן־שָׁם מִזְבֵּחַ לַיהֹוָה: פ

יד וַיְהִי בִּימֵי אַמְרָפֶל מֶלֶךְ־שִׁנְעָר אַרְיוֹךְ מֶלֶךְ אֶלָּסָר כְּדָרְלָעֹמֶר מֶלֶךְ עֵילָם וְתִדְעָל מֶלֶךְ גּוֹיִם: 2עָשׂוּ מִלְחָמָה אֶת־

---

a Lit. *"Please separate from me."*

23

King Bera of Sodom, King Birsha of Gomorrah, King Shinab of Admah, King Shemeber of Zeboiim, and the king of Bela, which is Zoar, ³all the latter joined forces at the Valley of Siddim, now the Dead Sea.ª ⁴Twelve years they served Chedorlaomer, and in the thirteenth year they rebelled. ⁵In the fourteenth year Chedorlaomer and the kings who were with him came and defeated the Rephaim at Ashteroth-karnaim, the Zuzim at Ham, the Emim at Shaveh-kiriathaim, ⁶and the Horites in their hill country of Seir as far as El-paran, which is by the wilderness. ⁷On their way back they came to En-mishpat, which is Kadesh, and subdued all the territory of the Amalekites, and also the Amorites who dwelt in Hazazon-tamar. ⁸Then the king of Sodom, the king of Gomorrah, the king of Admah, the king of Zeboiim, and the king of Bela, which is Zoar, went forth and engaged them in battle in the Valley of Siddim: ⁹King Chedorlaomer of Elam, King Tidal of Goiim, King Amraphel of Shinar, and King Arioch of Ellasar—four kings against those five.

¹⁰Now the Valley of Siddim was dotted with bitumen pits; and the kings of Sodom and Gomorrah, in their flight, threw themselves into them, while the rest escaped to the hill country. ¹¹[The invaders] seized all the wealth of Sodom and Gomorrah and all their provisions, and went their way. ¹²They also took Lot, the son of Abram's brother, and his possessions, and departed; for he had settled in Sodom.

¹³A fugitive brought the news to Abram the Hebrew, who was dwelling at the terebinths of Mamre the Amorite, kinsman of Eshkol and Aner, these being Abram's allies. ¹⁴When Abram heard that his kinsman had been taken captive, he mustered his retainers,ᵇ born into his household, numbering three hundred and eighteen, and went in pursuit as far as Dan. ¹⁵At

בֶּ֫רַע מֶ֣לֶךְ סְדֹם֒ וְאֶת־בִּרְשַׁע֙ מֶ֣לֶךְ עֲמֹרָ֔ה שִׁנְאָ֣ב ׀ מֶ֣לֶךְ אַדְמָ֗ה וְשֶׁמְאֵ֙בֶר֙ מֶ֣לֶךְ צביים צְבוֹיִ֔ם וּמֶ֥לֶךְ בֶּ֖לַע הִיא־צֹֽעַר׃ 3 כָּל־אֵ֙לֶּה֙ חָֽבְר֔וּ אֶל־עֵ֖מֶק הַשִּׂדִּ֑ים ה֖וּא יָ֥ם הַמֶּֽלַח׃ 4 שְׁתֵּ֤ים עֶשְׂרֵה֙ שָׁנָ֔ה עָֽבְד֖וּ אֶת־כְּדׇרְלָעֹ֑מֶר וּשְׁלֹשׁ־עֶשְׂרֵ֥ה שָׁנָ֖ה מָרָֽדוּ׃ 5 וּבְאַרְבַּע֩ עֶשְׂרֵ֙ה שָׁנָ֜ה בָּ֣א כְדׇרְלָעֹ֗מֶר וְהַמְּלָכִים֙ אֲשֶׁ֣ר אִתּ֔וֹ וַיַּכּ֤וּ אֶת־רְפָאִים֙ בְּעַשְׁתְּרֹ֣ת קַרְנַ֔יִם וְאֶת־הַזּוּזִ֖ים בְּהָ֑ם וְאֵת֙ הָֽאֵימִ֔ים בְּשָׁוֵ֖ה קִרְיָתָֽיִם׃ 6 וְאֶת־הַחֹרִ֖י בְּהַרְרָ֣ם שֵׂעִ֑יר עַ֚ד אֵ֣יל פָּארָ֔ן אֲשֶׁ֖ר עַל־הַמִּדְבָּֽר׃ 7 וַ֠יָּשֻׁ֠בוּ וַיָּבֹ֜אוּ אֶל־עֵ֤ין מִשְׁפָּט֙ הִ֣וא קָדֵ֔שׁ וַיַּכּ֕וּ אֶֽת־כָּל־שְׂדֵ֖ה הָעֲמָֽלֵקִ֑י וְגַם֙ אֶת־הָ֣אֱמֹרִ֔י הַיֹּשֵׁ֖ב בְּחַֽצְצֹ֥ן תָּמָֽר׃ 8 וַיֵּצֵ֣א מֶֽלֶךְ־סְדֹ֡ם וּמֶ֣לֶךְ עֲמֹרָה֩ וּמֶ֙לֶךְ אַדְמָ֜ה וּמֶ֣לֶךְ צביים צְבוֹיִ֗ם וּמֶ֛לֶךְ בֶּ֥לַע הִֽוא־צֹ֖עַר וַיַּֽעַרְכ֤וּ אִתָּם֙ מִלְחָמָ֔ה בְּעֵ֖מֶק הַשִּׂדִּֽים׃ 9 אֵ֣ת כְּדׇרְלָעֹ֜מֶר מֶ֣לֶךְ עֵילָ֗ם וְתִדְעָל֙ מֶ֣לֶךְ גּוֹיִ֔ם וְאַמְרָפֶל֙ מֶ֣לֶךְ שִׁנְעָ֔ר וְאַרְי֖וֹךְ מֶ֣לֶךְ אֶלָּסָ֑ר אַרְבָּעָ֧ה מְלָכִ֛ים אֶת־הַחֲמִשָּֽׁה׃ 10 וְעֵ֣מֶק הַשִּׂדִּ֗ים בֶּֽאֱרֹ֤ת בֶּאֱרֹת֙ חֵמָ֔ר וַיָּנֻ֛סוּ מֶֽלֶךְ־סְדֹ֥ם וַעֲמֹרָ֖ה וַיִּפְּלוּ־שָׁ֑מָּה וְהַנִּשְׁאָרִ֖ים הֶ֥רָה נָּֽסוּ׃ 11 וַ֠יִּקְח֠וּ אֶת־כָּל־רְכֻ֙שׁ סְדֹ֧ם וַעֲמֹרָ֛ה וְאֶת־כָּל־אָכְלָ֖ם וַיֵּלֵֽכוּ׃ 12 וַיִּקְח֨וּ אֶת־ל֧וֹט וְאֶת־רְכֻשׁ֛וֹ בֶּן־אֲחִ֥י אַבְרָ֖ם וַיֵּלֵ֑כוּ וְה֥וּא יֹשֵׁ֖ב בִּסְדֹֽם׃ 13 וַיָּבֹא֙ הַפָּלִ֔יט וַיַּגֵּ֖ד לְאַבְרָ֣ם הָעִבְרִ֑י וְהוּא֩ שֹׁכֵ֙ן בְּאֵֽלֹנֵ֜י מַמְרֵ֣א הָאֱמֹרִ֗י אֲחִ֤י אֶשְׁכֹּל֙ וַאֲחִ֣י עָנֵ֔ר וְהֵ֖ם בַּעֲלֵ֥י בְרִית־אַבְרָֽם׃ 14 וַיִּשְׁמַ֣ע אַבְרָ֔ם כִּ֥י נִשְׁבָּ֖ה אָחִ֑יו וַיָּ֨רֶק אֶת־חֲנִיכָ֜יו יְלִידֵ֣י בֵית֗וֹ שְׁמֹנָ֤ה עָשָׂר֙ וּשְׁלֹ֣שׁ מֵא֔וֹת וַיִּרְדֹּ֖ף עַד־דָּֽן׃ 15 וַיֵּחָלֵ֨ק עֲלֵיהֶ֧ם ׀ לַ֛יְלָה ה֥וּא וַעֲבָדָ֖יו וַיַּכֵּ֑ם וַֽיִּרְדְּפֵ֔ם עַד־חוֹבָ֕ה אֲשֶׁ֥ר מִשְּׂמֹ֖אל לְדַמָּֽשֶׂק׃

ª Heb. "Salt Sea."
ᵇ Meaning of Heb. ḥanikh uncertain.

night, he and his servants deployed against them and defeated them; and he pursued them as far as Hobah, which is north of Damascus. ¹⁶He brought back all the possessions; he also brought back his kinsman Lot and his possessions, and the women and the rest of the people.

¹⁷When he returned from defeating Chedorlaomer and the kings with him, the king of Sodom came out to meet him in the Valley of Shaveh, which is the Valley of the King. ¹⁸And King Melchizedek of Salem brought out bread and wine; he was a priest of God Most High.ᶜ ¹⁹He blessed him, saying,

"Blessed be Abram of God Most High,
Creator of heaven and earth.
²⁰And blessed be God Most High,
Who has delivered your foes into your hand."

And [Abram] gave him a tenth of everything.

²¹Then the king of Sodom said to Abram, "Give me the persons, and take the possessions for yourself." ²²But Abram said to the king of Sodom, "I swearᵈ to the Lᴏʀᴅ, God Most High, Creator of heaven and earth: ²³I will not take so much as a thread or a sandal strap of what is yours; you shall not say, 'It is I who made Abram rich.' ²⁴For me, nothing but what my servants have used up; as for the share of the men who went with me—Aner, Eshkol, and Mamre—let them take their share."

15 Some time later, the word of the Lᴏʀᴅ came to Abram in a vision. He said,

"Fear not, Abram,
I am a shield to you;
Your reward shall be very great."

²But Abram said, "O Lord Gᴏᴅ, what can You give me, seeing that I shall die childless, ᵃ-and the one in charge of my household is Dammesek

---

16 וַיָּ֜שֶׁב אֵ֣ת כָּל־הָרְכֻ֗שׁ וְגַ֨ם אֶת־ל֤וֹט אָחִיו֙ וּרְכֻשׁ֣וֹ הֵשִׁ֔יב וְגַ֛ם אֶת־הַנָּשִׁ֖ים וְאֶת־הָעָֽם׃

17 וַיֵּצֵ֣א מֶֽלֶךְ־סְדֹם֮ לִקְרָאתוֹ֒ אַחֲרֵ֣י שׁוּב֗וֹ מֵֽהַכּוֹת֙ אֶת־כְּדָרלָעֹ֔מֶר וְאֶת־הַמְּלָכִ֖ים אֲשֶׁ֣ר אִתּ֑וֹ אֶל־עֵ֣מֶק שָׁוֵ֔ה ה֖וּא עֵ֥מֶק הַמֶּֽלֶךְ׃ 18 וּמַלְכִּי־צֶ֙דֶק֙ מֶ֣לֶךְ שָׁלֵ֔ם הוֹצִ֖יא לֶ֣חֶם וָיָ֑יִן וְה֥וּא כֹהֵ֖ן לְאֵ֥ל עֶלְיֽוֹן׃ 19 וַֽיְבָרְכֵ֖הוּ וַיֹּאמַ֑ר בָּר֤וּךְ אַבְרָם֙ לְאֵ֣ל עֶלְי֔וֹן קֹנֵ֖ה שָׁמַ֥יִם וָאָֽרֶץ׃ 20 וּבָרוּךְ֙ אֵ֣ל עֶלְי֔וֹן אֲשֶׁר־מִגֵּ֥ן צָרֶ֖יךָ בְּיָדֶ֑ךָ וַיִּתֶּן־ל֥וֹ מַעֲשֵׂ֖ר מִכֹּֽל׃ 21 וַיֹּ֥אמֶר מֶֽלֶךְ־סְדֹ֖ם אֶל־אַבְרָ֑ם תֶּן־לִ֣י הַנֶּ֔פֶשׁ וְהָרְכֻ֖שׁ קַֽח־לָֽךְ׃ 22 וַיֹּ֥אמֶר אַבְרָ֖ם אֶל־מֶ֣לֶךְ סְדֹ֑ם הֲרִימֹ֨תִי יָדִ֤י אֶל־יְהוָה֙ אֵ֣ל עֶלְי֔וֹן קֹנֵ֖ה שָׁמַ֥יִם וָאָֽרֶץ׃ 23 אִם־מִחוּט֙ וְעַ֣ד שְׂרֽוֹךְ־נַ֔עַל וְאִם־אֶקַּ֖ח מִכָּל־אֲשֶׁר־לָ֑ךְ וְלֹ֣א תֹאמַ֔ר אֲנִ֖י הֶעֱשַׁ֥רְתִּי אֶת־אַבְרָֽם׃ 24 בִּלְעָדַ֗י רַ֚ק אֲשֶׁ֣ר אָֽכְל֣וּ הַנְּעָרִ֔ים וְחֵ֙לֶק֙ הָֽאֲנָשִׁ֔ים אֲשֶׁ֥ר הָלְכ֖וּ אִתִּ֑י עָנֵר֙ אֶשְׁכֹּ֣ל וּמַמְרֵ֔א הֵ֖ם יִקְח֥וּ חֶלְקָֽם׃ ס

טו אַחַ֣ר ׀ הַדְּבָרִ֣ים הָאֵ֗לֶּה הָיָ֤ה דְבַר־יְהוָה֙ אֶל־אַבְרָ֔ם בַּֽמַּחֲזֶ֖ה לֵאמֹ֑ר אַל־תִּירָ֣א אַבְרָ֗ם אָנֹכִי֙ מָגֵ֣ן לָ֔ךְ שְׂכָרְךָ֖ הַרְבֵּ֥ה מְאֹֽד׃ 2 וַיֹּ֣אמֶר אַבְרָ֗ם אֲדֹנָ֤י יֱהוִה֙ מַה־תִּתֶּן־לִ֔י וְאָנֹכִ֖י הוֹלֵ֣ךְ עֲרִירִ֑י וּבֶן־מֶ֣שֶׁק בֵּיתִ֔י ה֖וּא

ᶜ Heb. El ʿElyon.
ᵈ Lit. "lift up my hand."

ᵃ⁻ᵃ Meaning of Heb. uncertain.

Eliezer!"-ᵃ ³Abram said further, "Since You have granted me no offspring, my steward will be my heir." ⁴The word of the LORD came to him in reply, "That one shall not be your heir; none but your very own issue shall be your heir." ⁵He took him outside and said, "Look toward heaven and count the stars, if you are able to count them." And He added, "So shall your offspring be." ⁶And because he put his trust in the LORD, He reckoned it to his merit.

⁷Then He said to him, "I am the LORD who brought you out from Ur of the Chaldeans to assign this land to you as a possession." ⁸And he said, "O Lord GOD, how shall I know that I am to possess it?" ⁹He answered, "Bring Me a three-year-old heifer, a three-year-old she-goat, a three-year-old ram, a turtledove, and a young bird." ¹⁰He brought Him all these and cut them in two, placing each half opposite the other; but he did not cut up the bird. ¹¹Birds of prey came down upon the carcasses, and Abram drove them away. ¹²As the sun was about to set, a deep sleep fell upon Abram, and a great dark dread descended upon him. ¹³And He said to Abram, "Know well that your offspring shall be strangers in a land not theirs, and they shall be enslaved and oppressed four hundred years; ¹⁴but I will execute judgment on the nation they shall serve, and in the end they shall go free with great wealth. ¹⁵As for you,

You shall go to your fathers in peace;
You shall be buried at a ripe old age.

¹⁶And they shall return here in the fourth generation, for the iniquity of the Amorites is not yet complete."

¹⁷When the sun set and it was very dark, there appeared a smoking oven, and a flaming torch which passed between those pieces. ¹⁸On that day the LORD made a covenant with Abram, saying, "To your offspring I assign this land, from the river of Egypt to the great river, the river Euphrates: ¹⁹the Kenites, the Kenizzites, the

דַּמֶּ֣שֶׂק אֱלִיעֶ֑זֶר: ³וַיֹּ֣אמֶר אַבְרָ֗ם הֵ֣ן לִ֔י לֹ֥א נָתַ֖תָּה זָ֑רַע וְהִנֵּ֥ה בֶן־בֵּיתִ֖י יוֹרֵ֥שׁ אֹתִֽי: ⁴וְהִנֵּ֨ה דְבַר־יְהֹוָ֤ה אֵלָיו֙ לֵאמֹ֔ר לֹ֥א יִירָֽשְׁךָ֖ זֶ֑ה כִּי־אִם֙ אֲשֶׁ֣ר יֵצֵ֣א מִמֵּעֶ֔יךָ ה֖וּא יִֽירָשֶֽׁךָ: ⁵וַיּוֹצֵ֨א אֹתוֹ֙ הַח֔וּצָה וַיֹּ֗אמֶר הַבֶּט־נָ֣א הַשָּׁמַ֗יְמָה וּסְפֹר֙ הַכּ֣וֹכָבִ֔ים אִם־תּוּכַ֖ל לִסְפֹּ֣ר אֹתָ֑ם וַיֹּ֣אמֶר ל֔וֹ כֹּ֥ה יִֽהְיֶ֖ה זַרְעֶֽךָ: ⁶וְהֶֽאֱמִ֖ן בַּֽיהֹוָ֑ה וַיַּחְשְׁבֶ֥הָ לּ֖וֹ צְדָקָֽה: ⁷וַיֹּ֖אמֶר אֵלָ֑יו אֲנִ֣י יְהֹוָ֗ה אֲשֶׁ֤ר הֽוֹצֵאתִ֨יךָ֙ מֵא֣וּר כַּשְׂדִּ֔ים לָ֧תֶת לְךָ֛ אֶת־הָאָ֥רֶץ הַזֹּ֖את לְרִשְׁתָּֽהּ: ⁸וַיֹּאמַ֑ר אֲדֹנָ֣י יֱהֹוִ֔ה בַּמָּ֥ה אֵדַ֖ע כִּ֥י אִֽירָשֶֽׁנָּה: ⁹וַיֹּ֣אמֶר אֵלָ֗יו קְחָ֥ה לִי֙ עֶגְלָ֣ה מְשֻׁלֶּ֗שֶׁת וְעֵ֤ז מְשֻׁלֶּ֨שֶׁת֙ וְאַ֣יִל מְשֻׁלָּ֔שׁ וְתֹ֖ר וְגוֹזָֽל: ¹⁰וַיִּֽקַּֽח־ל֣וֹ אֶת־כָּל־אֵ֗לֶּה וַיְבַתֵּ֤ר אֹתָם֙ בַּתָּ֔וֶךְ וַיִּתֵּ֥ן אִישׁ־בִּתְר֖וֹ לִקְרַ֣את רֵעֵ֑הוּ וְאֶת־הַצִּפֹּ֖ר לֹ֥א בָתָֽר: ¹¹וַיֵּ֥רֶד הָעַ֖יִט עַל־הַפְּגָרִ֑ים וַיַּשֵּׁ֥ב אֹתָ֖ם אַבְרָֽם: ¹²וַיְהִ֤י הַשֶּׁ֨מֶשׁ֙ לָב֔וֹא וְתַרְדֵּמָ֖ה נָפְלָ֣ה עַל־אַבְרָ֑ם וְהִנֵּ֥ה אֵימָ֛ה חֲשֵׁכָ֥ה גְדֹלָ֖ה נֹפֶ֥לֶת עָלָֽיו: ¹³וַיֹּ֣אמֶר לְאַבְרָ֗ם יָדֹ֣עַ תֵּדַ֞ע כִּי־גֵ֣ר | יִֽהְיֶ֣ה זַרְעֲךָ֗ בְּאֶ֨רֶץ֙ לֹ֣א לָהֶ֔ם וַעֲבָד֖וּם וְעִנּ֣וּ אֹתָ֑ם אַרְבַּ֥ע מֵא֖וֹת שָׁנָֽה: ¹⁴וְגַ֧ם אֶת־הַגּ֛וֹי אֲשֶׁ֥ר יַֽעֲבֹ֖דוּ דָּ֣ן אָנֹ֑כִי וְאַֽחֲרֵי־כֵ֥ן יֵֽצְא֖וּ בִּרְכֻ֥שׁ גָּדֽוֹל: ¹⁵וְאַתָּ֛ה תָּב֥וֹא אֶל־אֲבֹתֶ֖יךָ בְּשָׁל֑וֹם תִּקָּבֵ֖ר בְּשֵׂיבָ֥ה טוֹבָֽה: ¹⁶וְד֥וֹר רְבִיעִ֖י יָשׁ֣וּבוּ הֵ֑נָּה כִּ֧י לֹֽא־שָׁלֵ֛ם עֲוֺ֥ן הָאֱמֹרִ֖י עַד־הֵֽנָּה: ¹⁷וַיְהִ֣י הַשֶּׁ֗מֶשׁ בָּ֨אָה֙ וַעֲלָטָ֣ה הָיָ֔ה וְהִנֵּ֨ה תַנּ֤וּר עָשָׁן֙ וְלַפִּ֣יד אֵ֔שׁ אֲשֶׁ֣ר עָבַ֔ר בֵּ֖ין הַגְּזָרִ֥ים הָאֵֽלֶּה: ¹⁸בַּיּ֣וֹם הַה֗וּא כָּרַ֧ת יְהֹוָ֛ה אֶת־אַבְרָ֖ם בְּרִ֣ית לֵאמֹ֑ר לְזַרְעֲךָ֗ נָתַ֨תִּי֙ אֶת־הָאָ֣רֶץ הַזֹּ֔את מִנְּהַ֣ר מִצְרַ֔יִם עַד־הַנָּהָ֥ר הַגָּדֹ֖ל נְהַר־פְּרָֽת: ¹⁹אֶת־הַקֵּינִ֥י וְאֶת־הַקְּנִזִּ֖י וְאֵ֥ת הַקַּדְמֹנִֽי: ²⁰וְאֶת־הַחִתִּ֥י

Kadmonites, 20the Hittites, the Perizzites, the Rephaim, 21the Amorites, the Canaanites, the Girgashites, and the Jebusites."

16 Sarai, Abram's wife, had borne him no children. She had an Egyptian maidservant whose name was Hagar. 2And Sarai said to Abram, "Look, the Lord has kept me from bearing. Consort with my maid; perhaps I shall have a son*a* through her." And Abram heeded Sarai's request. 3So Sarai, Abram's wife, took her maid, Hagar the Egyptian—after Abram had dwelt in the land of Canaan ten years—and gave her to her husband Abram as concubine. 4He cohabited with Hagar and she conceived; and when she saw that she had conceived, her mistress was lowered in her esteem. 5And Sarai said to Abram, "The wrong done me is your fault! I myself put my maid in your bosom; now that she sees that she is pregnant, I am lowered in her esteem. The Lord decide between you and me!" 6Abram said to Sarai, "Your maid is in your hands. Deal with her as you think right." Then Sarai treated her harshly, and she ran away from her.

7An angel of the Lord found her by a spring of water in the wilderness, the spring on the road to Shur, 8and said, "Hagar, slave of Sarai, where have you come from, and where are you going?" And she said, "I am running away from my mistress Sarai."

9And the angel of the Lord said to her, "Go back to your mistress, and submit to her harsh treatment." 10And the angel of the Lord said to her,

"I will greatly increase your offspring,
And they shall be too many to count."

11The angel of the Lord said to her further,
"Behold, you are with child

a   Lit. "be built up," play on ben "son" and banah "build up."

וְאֶת־הַפְּרִזִּי וְאֶת־הָרְפָאִים: 21 וְאֶת־הָאֱמֹרִי וְאֶת־הַכְּנַעֲנִי וְאֶת־הַגִּרְגָּשִׁי וְאֶת־הַיְבוּסִי: ס

טז וְשָׂרַי אֵשֶׁת אַבְרָם לֹא יָלְדָה לוֹ וְלָהּ שִׁפְחָה מִצְרִית וּשְׁמָהּ הָגָר: 2 וַתֹּאמֶר שָׂרַי אֶל־אַבְרָם הִנֵּה־נָא עֲצָרַנִי יְהוָה מִלֶּדֶת בֹּא־נָא אֶל־שִׁפְחָתִי אוּלַי אִבָּנֶה מִמֶּנָּה וַיִּשְׁמַע אַבְרָם לְקוֹל שָׂרָי: 3 וַתִּקַּח שָׂרַי אֵשֶׁת־אַבְרָם אֶת־הָגָר הַמִּצְרִית שִׁפְחָתָהּ מִקֵּץ עֶשֶׂר שָׁנִים לְשֶׁבֶת אַבְרָם בְּאֶרֶץ כְּנָעַן וַתִּתֵּן אֹתָהּ לְאַבְרָם אִישָׁהּ לוֹ לְאִשָּׁה: 4 וַיָּבֹא אֶל־הָגָר וַתַּהַר וַתֵּרֶא כִּי הָרָתָה וַתֵּקַל גְּבִרְתָּהּ בְּעֵינֶיהָ: 5 וַתֹּאמֶר שָׂרַי אֶל־אַבְרָם חֲמָסִי עָלֶיךָ אָנֹכִי נָתַתִּי שִׁפְחָתִי בְּחֵיקֶךָ וַתֵּרֶא כִּי הָרָתָה וָאֵקַל בְּעֵינֶיהָ יִשְׁפֹּט יְהוָה בֵּינִי וּבֵינֶיךָ*: 6 וַיֹּאמֶר אַבְרָם אֶל־שָׂרַי הִנֵּה שִׁפְחָתֵךְ בְּיָדֵךְ עֲשִׂי־לָהּ הַטּוֹב בְּעֵינָיִךְ וַתְּעַנֶּהָ שָׂרַי וַתִּבְרַח מִפָּנֶיהָ: 7 וַיִּמְצָאָהּ מַלְאַךְ יְהוָה עַל־עֵין הַמַּיִם בַּמִּדְבָּר עַל־הָעַיִן בְּדֶרֶךְ שׁוּר: 8 וַיֹּאמַר הָגָר שִׁפְחַת שָׂרַי אֵי־מִזֶּה בָאת וְאָנָה תֵלֵכִי וַתֹּאמֶר מִפְּנֵי שָׂרַי גְּבִרְתִּי אָנֹכִי בֹּרַחַת: 9 וַיֹּאמֶר לָהּ מַלְאַךְ יְהוָה שׁוּבִי אֶל־גְּבִרְתֵּךְ וְהִתְעַנִּי תַּחַת יָדֶיהָ: 10 וַיֹּאמֶר לָהּ מַלְאַךְ יְהוָה הַרְבָּה אַרְבֶּה אֶת־זַרְעֵךְ וְלֹא יִסָּפֵר מֵרֹב: 11 וַיֹּאמֶר לָהּ מַלְאַךְ יְהוָה הִנָּךְ הָרָה

v. 5. נקוד על י' בתראה

And shall bear a son;
You shall call him Ishmael,[b]
For the Lord has paid heed to your suffering.
[12]He shall be a wild ass of a man;
His hand against everyone,
And everyone's hand against him;
He shall dwell alongside of all his kinsmen."
[13]And she called the Lord who spoke to her,
"You Are El-roi,"[c] by which she meant, [d-]"Have
I not gone on seeing after He saw me!"-[d]
[14]Therefore the well was called Beer-lahai-roi;[e]
it is between Kadesh and Bered.—[15]Hagar bore
a son to Abram, and Abram gave the son that
Hagar bore him the name Ishmael. [16]Abram was
eighty-six years old when Hagar bore Ishmael
to Abram.

17 When Abram was ninety-nine years old,
the Lord appeared to Abram and said to him,
"I am El Shaddai.[a] Walk in My ways and be
blameless. [2]I will establish My covenant between Me and you, and I will make you exceedingly numerous."

[3]Abram threw himself on his face; and God
spoke to him further, [4]"As for Me, this is My
covenant with you: You shall be the father of
a multitude of nations. [5]And you shall no longer
be called Abram, but your name shall be
Abraham,[b] for I make you the father of a multitude of nations. [6]I will make you exceedingly
fertile, and make nations of you; and kings shall
come forth from you. [7]I will maintain My covenant between Me and you, and your offspring
to come, as an everlasting covenant throughout
the ages, to be God to you and to your offspring
to come. [8]I assign the land you sojourn in to

וְיָלַדְתְּ בֵּן
וְקָרָאת שְׁמוֹ יִשְׁמָעֵאל
כִּי־שָׁמַע יְהֹוָה אֶל־עָנְיֵךְ:
12 וְהוּא יִהְיֶה פֶּרֶא אָדָם
יָדוֹ בַכֹּל
וְיַד כֹּל בּוֹ
וְעַל־פְּנֵי כָל־אֶחָיו יִשְׁכֹּן:
13 וַתִּקְרָא שֵׁם־יְהֹוָה הַדֹּבֵר אֵלֶיהָ אַתָּה
אֵל רֳאִי כִּי אָמְרָה הֲגַם הֲלֹם רָאִיתִי אַחֲרֵי
רֹאִי: 14 עַל־כֵּן קָרָא לַבְּאֵר בְּאֵר לַחַי רֹאִי
הִנֵּה בֵין־קָדֵשׁ וּבֵין בָּרֶד: 15 וַתֵּלֶד הָגָר
לְאַבְרָם בֵּן וַיִּקְרָא אַבְרָם שֶׁם־בְּנוֹ אֲשֶׁר־
יָלְדָה הָגָר יִשְׁמָעֵאל: 16 וְאַבְרָם בֶּן־
שְׁמֹנִים שָׁנָה וְשֵׁשׁ שָׁנִים בְּלֶדֶת־הָגָר
אֶת־יִשְׁמָעֵאל לְאַבְרָם: ס

יז וַיְהִי אַבְרָם בֶּן־תִּשְׁעִים שָׁנָה וְתֵשַׁע
שָׁנִים וַיֵּרָא יְהֹוָה אֶל־אַבְרָם וַיֹּאמֶר אֵלָיו
אֲנִי־אֵל שַׁדַּי הִתְהַלֵּךְ לְפָנַי וֶהְיֵה תָמִים:
2 וְאֶתְּנָה בְרִיתִי בֵּינִי וּבֵינֶךָ וְאַרְבֶּה אוֹתְךָ
בִּמְאֹד מְאֹד:
3 וַיִּפֹּל אַבְרָם עַל־פָּנָיו וַיְדַבֵּר אִתּוֹ אֱלֹהִים
לֵאמֹר: 4 אֲנִי הִנֵּה בְרִיתִי אִתָּךְ וְהָיִיתָ
לְאַב הֲמוֹן גּוֹיִם: 5 וְלֹא־יִקָּרֵא עוֹד אֶת־
שִׁמְךָ אַבְרָם וְהָיָה שִׁמְךָ אַבְרָהָם כִּי
אַב־הֲמוֹן גּוֹיִם נְתַתִּיךָ: 6 וְהִפְרֵתִי אֹתְךָ
בִּמְאֹד מְאֹד וּנְתַתִּיךָ לְגוֹיִם וּמְלָכִים מִמְּךָ
יֵצֵאוּ: 7 וַהֲקִמֹתִי אֶת־בְּרִיתִי בֵּינִי וּבֵינֶךָ
וּבֵין זַרְעֲךָ אַחֲרֶיךָ לְדֹרֹתָם לִבְרִית עוֹלָם
לִהְיוֹת לְךָ לֵאלֹהִים וּלְזַרְעֲךָ אַחֲרֶיךָ:
8 וְנָתַתִּי לְךָ וּלְזַרְעֲךָ אַחֲרֶיךָ אֵת | אֶרֶץ
מְגֻרֶיךָ אֵת כָּל־אֶרֶץ כְּנַעַן לַאֲחֻזַּת עוֹלָם
וְהָיִיתִי לָהֶם לֵאלֹהִים:

---

b   I.e., "God heeds."
c   Apparently "God of Seeing."
d-d   Meaning of Heb. uncertain.
e   Apparently "the Well of the Living One Who sees me."

a   Traditionally rendered "God Almighty."
b   Understood as "father of a multitude."

you and your offspring to come, all the land of Canaan, as an everlasting holding. I will be their God."

⁹God further said to Abraham, "As for you, you and your offspring to come throughout the ages shall keep My covenant. ¹⁰Such shall be the covenant between Me and you and your offspring to follow which you shall keep: every male among you shall be circumcised. ¹¹You shall circumcise the flesh of your foreskin, and that shall be the sign of the covenant between Me and you. ¹²And throughout the generations, every male among you shall be circumcised at the age of eight days. As for the homeborn slave and the one bought from an outsider who is not of your offspring, ¹³they must be circumcised, homeborn, and purchased alike. Thus shall My covenant be marked in your flesh as an everlasting pact. ¹⁴And if any male who is uncircumcised fails to circumcise the flesh of his foreskin, that person shall be cut off from his kin; he has broken My covenant."

¹⁵And God said to Abraham, "As for your wife Sarai, you shall not call her Sarai, but her name shall be Sarah.ᶜ ¹⁶I will bless her; indeed, I will give you a son by her. I will bless her so that she shall give rise to nations; rulers of peoples shall issue from her." ¹⁷Abraham threw himself on his face and laughed, as he said to himself, "Can a child be born to a man a hundred years old, or can Sarah bear a child at ninety?" ¹⁸And Abraham said to God, "O that Ishmael might live by Your favor!" ¹⁹God said, "Nevertheless, Sarah your wife shall bear you a son, and you shall name him Isaac;ᵈ and I will maintain My covenant with him as an everlasting covenant for his offspring to come. ²⁰As for Ishmael, I have heeded you.ᵉ I hereby bless him. I will make him fertile and exceedingly numerous. He shall be the father of twelve chieftains, and I will make

9 וַיֹּ֤אמֶר אֱלֹהִים֙ אֶל־אַבְרָהָ֔ם וְאַתָּ֖ה אֶת־בְּרִיתִ֣י תִשְׁמֹ֑ר אַתָּ֛ה וְזַרְעֲךָ֥ אַחֲרֶ֖יךָ לְדֹרֹתָֽם׃ 10 זֹ֣את בְּרִיתִ֞י אֲשֶׁ֣ר תִּשְׁמְר֗וּ בֵּינִי֙ וּבֵ֣ינֵיכֶ֔ם וּבֵ֥ין זַרְעֲךָ֖ אַחֲרֶ֑יךָ הִמּ֥וֹל לָכֶ֖ם כָּל־זָכָֽר׃ 11 וּנְמַלְתֶּ֕ם אֵ֖ת בְּשַׂ֣ר עָרְלַתְכֶ֑ם וְהָיָה֙ לְא֣וֹת בְּרִ֔ית בֵּינִ֖י וּבֵינֵיכֶֽם׃ 12 וּבֶן־שְׁמֹנַ֣ת יָמִ֗ים יִמּ֥וֹל לָכֶ֛ם כָּל־זָכָ֖ר לְדֹרֹתֵיכֶ֑ם יְלִ֣יד בָּ֔יִת וּמִקְנַת־כֶּ֙סֶף֙ מִכֹּ֣ל בֶּן־נֵכָ֔ר אֲשֶׁ֛ר לֹ֥א מִזַּרְעֲךָ֖ הֽוּא׃ 13 הִמּ֧וֹל ׀ יִמּ֛וֹל יְלִ֥יד בֵּֽיתְךָ֖ וּמִקְנַ֣ת כַּסְפֶּ֑ךָ וְהָיְתָ֧ה בְרִיתִ֛י בִּבְשַׂרְכֶ֖ם לִבְרִ֥ית עוֹלָֽם׃ 14 וְעָרֵ֣ל ׀ זָכָ֗ר אֲשֶׁ֤ר לֹֽא־יִמּוֹל֙ אֶת־בְּשַׂ֣ר עָרְלָת֔וֹ וְנִכְרְתָ֛ה הַנֶּ֥פֶשׁ הַהִ֖וא מֵעַמֶּ֑יהָ אֶת־בְּרִיתִ֖י הֵפַֽר׃ ס

15 וַיֹּ֤אמֶר אֱלֹהִים֙ אֶל־אַבְרָהָ֔ם שָׂרַ֣י אִשְׁתְּךָ֔ לֹא־תִקְרָ֥א אֶת־שְׁמָ֖הּ שָׂרָ֑י כִּ֥י שָׂרָ֖ה שְׁמָֽהּ׃ 16 וּבֵרַכְתִּ֣י אֹתָ֔הּ וְגַ֨ם נָתַ֧תִּי מִמֶּ֛נָּה לְךָ֖ בֵּ֑ן וּבֵֽרַכְתִּ֗יהָ וְהָֽיְתָה֙ לְגוֹיִ֔ם מַלְכֵ֥י עַמִּ֖ים מִמֶּ֥נָּה יִהְיֽוּ׃ 17 וַיִּפֹּ֧ל אַבְרָהָ֛ם עַל־פָּנָ֖יו וַיִּצְחָ֑ק וַיֹּ֣אמֶר בְּלִבּ֗וֹ הַלְּבֶ֤ן מֵאָֽה־שָׁנָה֙ יִוָּלֵ֔ד וְאִם־שָׂרָ֔ה הֲבַת־תִּשְׁעִ֥ים שָׁנָ֖ה תֵּלֵֽד׃ 18 וַיֹּ֥אמֶר אַבְרָהָ֖ם אֶל־הָֽאֱלֹהִ֑ים ל֥וּ יִשְׁמָעֵ֖אל יִחְיֶ֥ה לְפָנֶֽיךָ׃ 19 וַיֹּ֣אמֶר אֱלֹהִ֗ים אֲבָל֙ שָׂרָ֣ה אִשְׁתְּךָ֗ יֹלֶ֤דֶת לְךָ֙ בֵּ֔ן וְקָרָ֥אתָ אֶת־שְׁמ֖וֹ יִצְחָ֑ק וַהֲקִמֹתִ֨י אֶת־בְּרִיתִ֥י אִתּ֛וֹ לִבְרִ֥ית עוֹלָ֖ם לְזַרְע֥וֹ אַחֲרָֽיו׃ 20 וּֽלְיִשְׁמָעֵאל֮ שְׁמַעְתִּיךָ֒ הִנֵּ֣ה ׀ בֵּרַ֣כְתִּי אֹת֗וֹ וְהִפְרֵיתִ֥י אֹת֛וֹ וְהִרְבֵּיתִ֥י אֹת֖וֹ בִּמְאֹ֣ד מְאֹ֑ד שְׁנֵים־עָשָׂ֤ר נְשִׂיאִם֙ יוֹלִ֔יד וּנְתַתִּ֖יו

---

c   I.e., "princess."
d   Heb. *Yiṣḥaq,* from *ṣaḥaq,* "laugh."
e   Heb. *shemaʿtikha,* play on "Ishmael."

of him a great nation. [21]But My covenant I will maintain with Isaac, whom Sarah shall bear to you at this season next year." [22]And when He was done speaking with him, God was gone from Abraham.

[23]Then Abraham took his son Ishmael, and all his homeborn slaves and all those he had bought, every male in Abraham's household, and he circumcised the flesh of their foreskins on that very day, as God had spoken to him. [24]Abraham was ninety-nine years old when he circumcised the flesh of his foreskin, [25]and his son Ishmael was thirteen years old when he was circumcised in the flesh of his foreskin. [26]Thus Abraham and his son Ishmael were circumcised on that very day; [27]and all his household, his homeborn slaves and those that had been bought from outsiders, were circumcised with him.

18 VA-YERA'

The LORD appeared to him by the terebinths of Mamre; he was sitting at the entrance of the tent as the day grew hot. [2]Looking up, he saw three men standing near him. As soon as he saw them, he ran from the entrance of the tent to greet them and, bowing to the ground, [3]he said, "My lords,[a] if it please you, do not go on past your servant. [4]Let a little water be brought; bathe your feet and recline under the tree. [5]And let me fetch a morsel of bread that you may refresh yourselves; then go on—seeing that you have come your servant's way." They replied, "Do as you have said."

[6]Abraham hastened into the tent to Sarah, and said, "Quick, three *seah*s of choice flour! Knead and make cakes!" [7]Then Abraham ran to the herd, took a calf, tender and choice, and gave it to a servant-boy, who hastened to prepare it. [8]He took curds and milk and the calf that had been prepared and set these before

לְגוֹי גָּדוֹל: 21 וְאֶת־בְּרִיתִי אָקִים אֶת־
יִצְחָק אֲשֶׁר תֵּלֵד לְךָ שָׂרָה לַמּוֹעֵד הַזֶּה
בַּשָּׁנָה הָאַחֶרֶת: 22 וַיְכַל לְדַבֵּר אִתּוֹ וַיַּעַל
אֱלֹהִים מֵעַל אַבְרָהָם:
23 וַיִּקַּח אַבְרָהָם אֶת־יִשְׁמָעֵאל בְּנוֹ וְאֵת
כָּל־יְלִידֵי בֵיתוֹ וְאֵת כָּל־מִקְנַת כַּסְפּוֹ
כָּל־זָכָר בְּאַנְשֵׁי בֵּית אַבְרָהָם וַיָּמָל אֶת־
בְּשַׂר עָרְלָתָם בְּעֶצֶם הַיּוֹם הַזֶּה כַּאֲשֶׁר
דִּבֶּר אִתּוֹ אֱלֹהִים: 24 וְאַבְרָהָם בֶּן־תִּשְׁעִים
וָתֵשַׁע שָׁנָה בְּהִמֹּלוֹ בְּשַׂר עָרְלָתוֹ:
25 וְיִשְׁמָעֵאל בְּנוֹ בֶּן־שְׁלֹשׁ עֶשְׂרֵה שָׁנָה
בְּהִמֹּלוֹ אֵת בְּשַׂר עָרְלָתוֹ: 26 בְּעֶצֶם הַיּוֹם
הַזֶּה נִמּוֹל אַבְרָהָם וְיִשְׁמָעֵאל בְּנוֹ: 27 וְכָל־
אַנְשֵׁי בֵיתוֹ יְלִיד בָּיִת וּמִקְנַת־כֶּסֶף מֵאֵת
בֶּן־נֵכָר נִמֹּלוּ אִתּוֹ: פ

יח וַיֵּרָא אֵלָיו יְהוָה בְּאֵלֹנֵי מַמְרֵא
וְהוּא יֹשֵׁב פֶּתַח־הָאֹהֶל כְּחֹם הַיּוֹם:
2 וַיִּשָּׂא עֵינָיו וַיַּרְא וְהִנֵּה שְׁלֹשָׁה אֲנָשִׁים
נִצָּבִים עָלָיו וַיַּרְא וַיָּרָץ לִקְרָאתָם מִפֶּתַח
הָאֹהֶל וַיִּשְׁתַּחוּ אָרְצָה: 3 וַיֹּאמַר אֲדֹנָי
אִם־נָא מָצָאתִי חֵן בְּעֵינֶיךָ אַל־נָא תַעֲבֹר
מֵעַל עַבְדֶּךָ: 4 יֻקַּח־נָא מְעַט־מַיִם וְרַחֲצוּ
רַגְלֵיכֶם וְהִשָּׁעֲנוּ תַּחַת הָעֵץ: 5 וְאֶקְחָה
פַת־לֶחֶם וְסַעֲדוּ לִבְּכֶם אַחַר תַּעֲבֹרוּ
כִּי־עַל־כֵּן עֲבַרְתֶּם עַל־עַבְדְּכֶם וַיֹּאמְרוּ כֵּן
תַּעֲשֶׂה כַּאֲשֶׁר דִּבַּרְתָּ:
6 וַיְמַהֵר אַבְרָהָם הָאֹהֱלָה אֶל־שָׂרָה
וַיֹּאמֶר מַהֲרִי שְׁלֹשׁ סְאִים קֶמַח סֹלֶת
לוּשִׁי וַעֲשִׂי עֻגוֹת: 7 וְאֶל־הַבָּקָר רָץ
אַבְרָהָם וַיִּקַּח בֶּן־בָּקָר רַךְ וָטוֹב וַיִּתֵּן
אֶל־הַנַּעַר וַיְמַהֵר לַעֲשׂוֹת אֹתוֹ: 8 וַיִּקַּח
חֶמְאָה וְחָלָב וּבֶן־הַבָּקָר אֲשֶׁר עָשָׂה וַיִּתֵּן

---

a   Or "My Lord."

them; and he waited on them under the tree as they ate.

⁹They said to him, "Where is your wife Sarah?" And he replied, "There, in the tent." ¹⁰Then one said, "I will return to you next year,ᵇ and your wife Sarah shall have a son!" Sarah was listening at the entrance of the tent, which was behind him. ¹¹Now Abraham and Sarah were old, advanced in years; Sarah had stopped having the periods of women. ¹²And Sarah laughed to herself, saying, "Now that I am withered, am I to have enjoyment—with my husband so old?" ¹³Then the LORD said to Abraham, "Why did Sarah laugh, saying, 'Shall I in truth bear a child, old as I am?' ¹⁴Is anything too wondrous for the LORD? I will return to you at the same season next year, and Sarah shall have a son." ¹⁵Sarah lied, saying, "I did not laugh," for she was frightened. But He replied, "You did laugh."

¹⁶The men set out from there and looked down toward Sodom, Abraham walking with them to see them off. ¹⁷Now the LORD had said, "Shall I hide from Abraham what I am about to do, ¹⁸since Abraham is to become a great and populous nation and all the nations of the earth are to bless themselves by him? ¹⁹For I have singled him out, that he may instruct his children and his posterity to keep the way of the LORD by doing what is just and right, in order that the LORD may bring about for Abraham what He has promised him." ²⁰Then the LORD said, "The outrage of Sodom and Gomorrah is so great, and their sin so grave! ²¹I will go down to see whether they have acted altogether according to the outcry that has reached Me; if not, I will take note."

²²The men went on from there to Sodom, while Abraham remained standing before the LORD. ²³Abraham came forward and said, "Will You sweep away the innocent along with the

---

ᵇ Cf. Gen. 17.21; 2 Kings 4.16–17.

לִפְנֵיהֶ֥ם וְהֽוּא־עֹמֵ֛ד עֲלֵיהֶ֖ם תַּ֣חַת הָעֵ֑ץ וַיֹּאכֵֽלוּ׃

9 וַיֹּאמְר֣וּ אֵלָ֔יו* אַיֵּ֖ה שָׂרָ֣ה אִשְׁתֶּ֑ךָ וַיֹּ֖אמֶר הִנֵּ֥ה בָאֹֽהֶל׃ 10 וַיֹּ֗אמֶר שׁ֣וֹב אָשׁ֤וּב אֵלֶ֨יךָ֙ כָּעֵ֣ת חַיָּ֔ה וְהִנֵּה־בֵ֖ן לְשָׂרָ֣ה אִשְׁתֶּ֑ךָ וְשָׂרָ֥ה שֹׁמַ֛עַת פֶּ֥תַח הָאֹ֖הֶל וְה֥וּא אַחֲרָֽיו׃ 11 וְאַבְרָהָ֤ם וְשָׂרָה֙ זְקֵנִ֔ים בָּאִ֖ים בַּיָּמִ֑ים חָדַל֙ לִהְי֣וֹת לְשָׂרָ֔ה אֹ֖רַח כַּנָּשִֽׁים׃ 12 וַתִּצְחַ֥ק שָׂרָ֖ה בְּקִרְבָּ֣הּ לֵאמֹ֑ר אַחֲרֵ֤י בְלֹתִי֙ הָֽיְתָה־לִּ֣י עֶדְנָ֔ה וַֽאדֹנִ֖י זָקֵֽן׃ 13 וַיֹּ֥אמֶר יְהֹוָ֖ה אֶל־אַבְרָהָ֑ם לָ֣מָּה זֶּה֩ צָחֲקָ֨ה שָׂרָ֜ה לֵאמֹ֗ר הַאַ֥ף אֻמְנָ֛ם אֵלֵ֖ד וַאֲנִ֥י זָקַֽנְתִּי׃ 14 הֲיִפָּלֵ֥א מֵֽיהֹוָ֖ה דָּבָ֑ר לַמּוֹעֵ֞ד אָשׁ֥וּב אֵלֶ֛יךָ כָּעֵ֥ת חַיָּ֖ה וּלְשָׂרָ֥ה בֵֽן׃ 15 וַתְּכַחֵ֨שׁ שָׂרָ֧ה ׀ לֵאמֹ֛ר לֹ֥א צָחַ֖קְתִּי כִּ֣י ׀ יָרֵ֑אָה וַיֹּ֥אמֶר ׀ לֹ֖א כִּ֥י צָחָֽקְתְּ׃

16 וַיָּקֻ֤מוּ מִשָּׁם֙ הָֽאֲנָשִׁ֔ים וַיַּשְׁקִ֖פוּ עַל־פְּנֵ֣י סְדֹ֑ם וְאַ֨בְרָהָ֔ם הֹלֵ֥ךְ עִמָּ֖ם לְשַׁלְּחָֽם׃ 17 וַֽיהֹוָ֖ה אָמָ֑ר הַֽמְכַסֶּ֤ה אֲנִי֙ מֵֽאַבְרָהָ֔ם אֲשֶׁ֖ר אֲנִ֥י עֹשֶֽׂה׃ 18 וְאַ֨בְרָהָ֔ם הָי֧וֹ יִֽהְיֶ֛ה לְג֥וֹי גָּד֖וֹל וְעָצ֑וּם וְנִ֨בְרְכוּ־ב֔וֹ כֹּ֖ל גּוֹיֵ֥י הָאָֽרֶץ׃ 19 כִּ֣י יְדַעְתִּ֗יו לְמַעַן֩ אֲשֶׁ֨ר יְצַוֶּ֜ה אֶת־בָּנָ֤יו וְאֶת־בֵּיתוֹ֙ אַחֲרָ֔יו וְשָֽׁמְרוּ֙ דֶּ֣רֶךְ יְהֹוָ֔ה לַעֲשׂ֥וֹת צְדָקָ֖ה וּמִשְׁפָּ֑ט לְמַ֗עַן הָבִ֤יא יְהֹוָה֙ עַל־אַבְרָהָ֔ם אֵ֥ת אֲשֶׁר־דִּבֶּ֖ר עָלָֽיו׃ 20 וַיֹּ֣אמֶר יְהֹוָ֔ה זַעֲקַ֛ת סְדֹ֥ם וַעֲמֹרָ֖ה כִּי־רָ֑בָּה וְחַ֨טָּאתָ֔ם כִּ֥י כָבְדָ֖ה מְאֹֽד׃ 21 אֵֽרְדָה־נָּ֣א וְאֶרְאֶ֔ה הַכְּצַעֲקָתָ֛הּ הַבָּ֥אָה אֵלַ֖י עָשׂ֣וּ ׀ כָּלָ֑ה וְאִם־לֹ֖א אֵדָֽעָה׃ 22 וַיִּפְנ֤וּ מִשָּׁם֙ הָֽאֲנָשִׁ֔ים וַיֵּלְכ֖וּ סְדֹ֑מָה וְאַ֨בְרָהָ֔ם עוֹדֶ֥נּוּ עֹמֵ֖ד לִפְנֵ֥י יְהֹוָֽה׃ 23 וַיִּגַּ֥שׁ אַבְרָהָ֖ם וַיֹּאמַ֑ר הַאַ֣ף תִּסְפֶּ֔ה צַדִּ֖יק עִם־רָשָֽׁע׃ 24 אוּלַ֥י יֵ֛שׁ חֲמִשִּׁ֥ים צַדִּיקִ֖ם בְּת֣וֹךְ

---

v. 9. נָקוּד עַל א' י' ו', וּלְפִי נֻסְחָאוֹת הַמְּקֻבָּלִים אֵין נָקוּד עַל לֹ'

---

guilty? 24What if there should be fifty innocent within the city; will You then wipe out the place and not forgive it for the sake of the innocent fifty who are in it? 25Far be it from You to do such a thing, to bring death upon the innocent as well as the guilty, so that innocent and guilty fare alike. Far be it from You! Shall not the Judge of all the earth deal justly?" 26And the Lord answered, "If I find within the city of Sodom fifty innocent ones, I will forgive the whole place for their sake." 27Abraham spoke up, saying, "Here I venture to speak to my Lord, I who am but dust and ashes: 28What if the fifty innocent should lack five? Will You destroy the whole city for want of the five?" And He answered, "I will not destroy if I find forty-five there." 29But he spoke to Him again, and said, "What if forty should be found there?" And He answered, "I will not do it, for the sake of the forty." 30And he said, "Let not my Lord be angry if I go on: What if thirty should be found there?" And He answered, "I will not do it if I find thirty there." 31And he said, "I venture again to speak to my Lord: What if twenty should be found there?" And He answered, "I will not destroy, for the sake of the twenty." 32And he said, "Let not my Lord be angry if I speak but this last time: What if ten should be found there?" And He answered, "I will not destroy, for the sake of the ten."

33When the Lord had finished speaking to Abraham, He departed; and Abraham returned to his place.

19

The two angels arrived in Sodom in the evening, as Lot was sitting in the gate of Sodom. When Lot saw them, he rose to greet them and, bowing low with his face to the ground, 2he said, "Please, my lords, turn aside to your servant's house to spend the night, and bathe your feet; then you may be on your way early." But they

הָעִיר הַאַף תִּסְפֶּה וְלֹא־תִשָּׂא לַמָּקוֹם לְמַעַן חֲמִשִּׁים הַצַּדִּיקִם אֲשֶׁר בְּקִרְבָּהּ: 25 חָלִלָה לְּךָ מֵעֲשֹׂת ׀ כַּדָּבָר הַזֶּה לְהָמִית צַדִּיק עִם־רָשָׁע וְהָיָה כַצַּדִּיק כָּרָשָׁע חָלִלָה לָּךְ הֲשֹׁפֵט כָּל־הָאָרֶץ לֹא יַעֲשֶׂה מִשְׁפָּט: 26 וַיֹּאמֶר יְהֹוָה אִם־אֶמְצָא בִסְדֹם חֲמִשִּׁים צַדִּיקִם בְּתוֹךְ הָעִיר וְנָשָׂאתִי לְכָל־הַמָּקוֹם בַּעֲבוּרָם: 27 וַיַּעַן אַבְרָהָם וַיֹּאמַר הִנֵּה־נָא הוֹאַלְתִּי לְדַבֵּר אֶל־אֲדֹנָי וְאָנֹכִי עָפָר וָאֵפֶר: 28 אוּלַי יַחְסְרוּן חֲמִשִּׁים הַצַּדִּיקִם חֲמִשָּׁה הֲתַשְׁחִית בַּחֲמִשָּׁה אֶת־כָּל־הָעִיר וַיֹּאמֶר לֹא אַשְׁחִית אִם־אֶמְצָא שָׁם אַרְבָּעִים וַחֲמִשָּׁה: 29 וַיֹּסֶף עוֹד לְדַבֵּר אֵלָיו וַיֹּאמַר אוּלַי יִמָּצְאוּן שָׁם אַרְבָּעִים וַיֹּאמֶר לֹא אֶעֱשֶׂה בַּעֲבוּר הָאַרְבָּעִים: 30 וַיֹּאמֶר אַל־נָא יִחַר לַאדֹנָי וַאֲדַבֵּרָה אוּלַי יִמָּצְאוּן שָׁם שְׁלֹשִׁים וַיֹּאמֶר לֹא אֶעֱשֶׂה אִם־אֶמְצָא שָׁם שְׁלֹשִׁים: 31 וַיֹּאמֶר הִנֵּה־נָא הוֹאַלְתִּי לְדַבֵּר אֶל־אֲדֹנָי אוּלַי יִמָּצְאוּן שָׁם עֶשְׂרִים וַיֹּאמֶר לֹא אַשְׁחִית בַּעֲבוּר הָעֶשְׂרִים: 32 וַיֹּאמֶר אַל־נָא יִחַר לַאדֹנָי וַאֲדַבְּרָה אַךְ־הַפַּעַם אוּלַי יִמָּצְאוּן שָׁם עֲשָׂרָה וַיֹּאמֶר לֹא אַשְׁחִית בַּעֲבוּר הָעֲשָׂרָה: 33 וַיֵּלֶךְ יְהֹוָה כַּאֲשֶׁר כִּלָּה לְדַבֵּר אֶל־אַבְרָהָם וְאַבְרָהָם שָׁב לִמְקֹמוֹ:

יט וַיָּבֹאוּ שְׁנֵי הַמַּלְאָכִים סְדֹמָה בָּעֶרֶב וְלוֹט יֹשֵׁב בְּשַׁעַר־סְדֹם וַיַּרְא־לוֹט וַיָּקָם לִקְרָאתָם וַיִּשְׁתַּחוּ אַפַּיִם אָרְצָה: 2 וַיֹּאמֶר הִנֶּה נָּא־אֲדֹנַי סוּרוּ נָא אֶל־בֵּית עַבְדְּכֶם וְלִינוּ וְרַחֲצוּ רַגְלֵיכֶם וְהִשְׁכַּמְתֶּם וַהֲלַכְתֶּם לְדַרְכְּכֶם וַיֹּאמְרוּ לֹּא כִּי בָרְחוֹב

said, "No, we will spend the night in the square." [3] But he urged them strongly, so they turned his way and entered his house. He prepared a feast for them and baked unleavened bread, and they ate.

[4] They had not yet lain down, when the townspeople, the men of Sodom, young and old—all the people to the last man—gathered about the house. [5] And they shouted to Lot and said to him, "Where are the men who came to you tonight? Bring them out to us, that we may be intimate with them." [6] So Lot went out to them to the entrance, shut the door behind him, [7] and said, "I beg you, my friends, do not commit such a wrong. [8] Look, I have two daughters who have not known a man. Let me bring them out to you, and you may do to them as you please; but do not do anything to these men, since they have come under the shelter of my roof." [9] But they said, "Stand back! The fellow," they said, "came here as an alien, and already he acts the ruler! Now we will deal worse with you than with them." And they pressed hard against the person of Lot, and moved forward to break the door. [10] But the men stretched out their hands and pulled Lot into the house with them, and shut the door. [11] And the people who were at the entrance of the house, young and old, they struck with blinding light, so that they were helpless to find the entrance.

[12] Then the men said to Lot, "Whom else have you here? Sons-in-law, your sons and daughters, or anyone else that you have in the city—bring them out of the place. [13] For we are about to destroy this place; because the outcry against them before the LORD has become so great that the LORD has sent us to destroy it." [14] So Lot went out and spoke to his sons-in-law, who had married his daughters, and said, "Up, get out of this place, for the LORD is about to destroy the city." But he seemed to his sons-in-law as one who jests.

נָלִין: 3 וַיִּפְצַר־בָּם מְאֹד וַיָּסֻרוּ אֵלָיו וַיָּבֹאוּ אֶל־בֵּיתוֹ וַיַּעַשׂ לָהֶם מִשְׁתֶּה וּמַצּוֹת אָפָה וַיֹּאכֵלוּ: 4 טֶרֶם יִשְׁכָּבוּ וְאַנְשֵׁי הָעִיר אַנְשֵׁי סְדֹם נָסַבּוּ עַל־הַבַּיִת מִנַּעַר וְעַד־זָקֵן כָּל־הָעָם מִקָּצֶה: 5 וַיִּקְרְאוּ אֶל־לוֹט וַיֹּאמְרוּ לוֹ אַיֵּה הָאֲנָשִׁים אֲשֶׁר־בָּאוּ אֵלֶיךָ הַלָּיְלָה הוֹצִיאֵם אֵלֵינוּ וְנֵדְעָה אֹתָם: 6 וַיֵּצֵא אֲלֵהֶם לוֹט הַפֶּתְחָה וְהַדֶּלֶת סָגַר אַחֲרָיו: 7 וַיֹּאמַר אַל־נָא אַחַי תָּרֵעוּ: 8 הִנֵּה־נָא לִי שְׁתֵּי בָנוֹת אֲשֶׁר לֹא־יָדְעוּ אִישׁ אוֹצִיאָה־נָּא אֶתְהֶן אֲלֵיכֶם וַעֲשׂוּ לָהֶן כַּטּוֹב בְּעֵינֵיכֶם רַק לָאֲנָשִׁים הָאֵל אַל־תַּעֲשׂוּ דָבָר כִּי־עַל־כֵּן בָּאוּ בְּצֵל קֹרָתִי: 9 וַיֹּאמְרוּ ׀ גֶּשׁ־הָלְאָה וַיֹּאמְרוּ הָאֶחָד בָּא־לָגוּר וַיִּשְׁפֹּט שָׁפוֹט עַתָּה נָרַע לְךָ מֵהֶם וַיִּפְצְרוּ בָאִישׁ בְּלוֹט מְאֹד וַיִּגְּשׁוּ לִשְׁבֹּר הַדָּלֶת: 10 וַיִּשְׁלְחוּ הָאֲנָשִׁים אֶת־יָדָם וַיָּבִיאוּ אֶת־לוֹט אֲלֵיהֶם הַבָּיְתָה וְאֶת־הַדֶּלֶת סָגָרוּ: 11 וְאֶת־הָאֲנָשִׁים אֲשֶׁר־פֶּתַח הַבַּיִת הִכּוּ בַּסַּנְוֵרִים מִקָּטֹן וְעַד־גָּדוֹל וַיִּלְאוּ לִמְצֹא הַפָּתַח: 12 וַיֹּאמְרוּ הָאֲנָשִׁים אֶל־לוֹט עֹד מִי־לְךָ פֹה חָתָן וּבָנֶיךָ וּבְנֹתֶיךָ וְכֹל אֲשֶׁר־לְךָ בָּעִיר הוֹצֵא מִן־הַמָּקוֹם: 13 כִּי־מַשְׁחִתִים אֲנַחְנוּ אֶת־הַמָּקוֹם הַזֶּה כִּי־גָדְלָה צַעֲקָתָם אֶת־פְּנֵי יְהוָה וַיְשַׁלְּחֵנוּ יְהוָה לְשַׁחֲתָהּ: 14 וַיֵּצֵא לוֹט וַיְדַבֵּר ׀ אֶל־חֲתָנָיו ׀ לֹקְחֵי בְנֹתָיו וַיֹּאמֶר קוּמוּ צְּאוּ מִן־הַמָּקוֹם הַזֶּה כִּי־מַשְׁחִית יְהוָה אֶת־הָעִיר וַיְהִי כִמְצַחֵק בְּעֵינֵי חֲתָנָיו:

33

15As dawn broke, the angels urged Lot on, saying, "Up, take your wife and your two remaining daughters, lest you be swept away because of the iniquity of the city." 16Still he delayed. So the men seized his hand, and the hands of his wife and his two daughters—in the LORD's mercy on him—and brought him out and left him outside the city. 17When they had brought them outside, one said, "Flee for your life! Do not look behind you, nor stop anywhere in the Plain; flee to the hills, lest you be swept away." 18But Lot said to them, "Oh no, my lord! 19You have been so gracious to your servant, and have already shown me so much kindness in order to save my life; but I cannot flee to the hills, lest the disaster overtake me and I die. 20Look, that town there is near enough to flee to; it is such a little place! Let me flee there—it is such a little place—and let my life be saved." 21He replied, "Very well, I will grant you this favor too, and I will not annihilate the town of which you have spoken. 22Hurry, flee there, for I cannot do anything until you arrive there." Hence the town came to be called Zoar.a

23As the sun rose upon the earth and Lot entered Zoar, 24the LORD rained upon Sodom and Gomorrah sulfurous fire from the LORD out of heaven. 25He annihilated those cities and the entire Plain, and all the inhabitants of the cities and the vegetation of the ground. 26Lot'sb wife looked back,c and she thereupon turned into a pillar of salt.

27Next morning, Abraham hurried to the place where he had stood before the LORD, 28and, looking down toward Sodom and Gomorrah and all the land of the Plain, he saw the smoke of the land rising like the smoke of a kiln.

29Thus it was that, when God destroyed the cities of the Plain and annihilated the cities

---

a Connected with miṣ'ar "a little place," v. 20.
b Lit. "His."
c Lit. "behind him."

---

15 וּכְמוֹ֩ הַשַּׁ֨חַר עָלָ֜ה וַיָּאִ֥יצוּ הַמַּלְאָכִ֛ים בְּל֥וֹט לֵאמֹ֖ר ק֑וּם קַ֣ח אֶֽת־אִשְׁתְּךָ֗ וְאֶת־שְׁתֵּ֤י בְנֹתֶ֙יךָ֙ הַנִּמְצָאֹ֔ת פֶּן־תִּסָּפֶ֖ה בַּעֲוֺ֥ן הָעִֽיר: 16 וַֽיִּתְמַהְמָ֓הּ ׀ וַיַּחֲזִ֨קוּ הָאֲנָשִׁ֜ים בְּיָד֣וֹ וּבְיַד־אִשְׁתּ֗וֹ וּבְיַד֙ שְׁתֵּ֣י בְנֹתָ֔יו בְּחֶמְלַ֥ת יְהוָ֖ה עָלָ֑יו וַיֹּצִאֻ֥הוּ וַיַּנִּחֻ֖הוּ מִח֥וּץ לָעִֽיר: 17 וַיְהִי֩ כְהוֹצִיאָ֨ם אֹתָ֜ם הַח֗וּצָה וַיֹּ֙אמֶר֙ הִמָּלֵ֣ט עַל־נַפְשֶׁ֔ךָ אַל־תַּבִּ֣יט אַחֲרֶ֔יךָ וְאַֽל־תַּעֲמֹ֖ד בְּכָל־הַכִּכָּ֑ר הָהָ֥רָה הִמָּלֵ֖ט פֶּן־תִּסָּפֶֽה: 18 וַיֹּ֥אמֶר ל֖וֹט אֲלֵהֶ֑ם אַל־נָ֖א אֲדֹנָֽי: 19 הִנֵּה־נָ֠א מָצָ֨א עַבְדְּךָ֣ חֵן֮ בְּעֵינֶיךָ֒ וַתַּגְדֵּ֣ל חַסְדְּךָ֗ אֲשֶׁ֤ר עָשִׂ֙יתָ֙ עִמָּדִ֔י לְהַחֲי֖וֹת אֶת־נַפְשִׁ֑י וְאָנֹכִ֗י לֹ֤א אוּכַל֙ לְהִמָּלֵ֣ט הָהָ֔רָה פֶּן־תִּדְבָּקַ֥נִי הָרָעָ֖ה וָמַֽתִּי: 20 הִנֵּה־נָ֠א הָעִ֨יר הַזֹּ֧את קְרֹבָ֛ה לָנ֥וּס שָׁ֖מָּה וְהִ֣יא מִצְעָ֑ר אִמָּלְטָ֨ה נָּ֜א שָׁ֗מָּה הֲלֹ֥א מִצְעָ֛ר הִ֖וא וּתְחִ֥י נַפְשִֽׁי: 21 וַיֹּ֣אמֶר אֵלָ֔יו הִנֵּה֙ נָשָׂ֣אתִי פָנֶ֔יךָ גַּ֖ם לַדָּבָ֣ר הַזֶּ֑ה לְבִלְתִּ֛י הָפְכִּ֥י אֶת־הָעִ֖יר אֲשֶׁ֥ר דִּבַּֽרְתָּ: 22 מַהֵר֙ הִמָּלֵ֣ט שָׁ֔מָּה כִּ֣י לֹ֤א אוּכַל֙ לַעֲשׂ֣וֹת דָּבָ֔ר עַד־בֹּאֲךָ֖ שָׁ֑מָּה עַל־כֵּ֛ן קָרָ֥א שֵׁם־הָעִ֖יר צֽוֹעַר: 23 הַשֶּׁ֖מֶשׁ יָצָ֣א* עַל־הָאָ֑רֶץ וְל֖וֹט בָּ֥א צֹֽעֲרָה: 24 וַֽיהוָ֗ה הִמְטִ֧יר עַל־סְדֹ֛ם וְעַל־עֲמֹרָ֖ה גָּפְרִ֣ית וָאֵ֑שׁ מֵאֵ֥ת יְהוָ֖ה מִן־הַשָּׁמָֽיִם: 25 וַֽיַּהֲפֹךְ֙ אֶת־הֶעָרִ֣ים הָאֵ֔ל וְאֵ֖ת כָּל־הַכִּכָּ֑ר וְאֵת֙ כָּל־יֹשְׁבֵ֣י הֶעָרִ֔ים וְצֶ֖מַח הָאֲדָמָֽה: 26 וַתַּבֵּ֥ט אִשְׁתּ֖וֹ מֵאַחֲרָ֑יו וַתְּהִ֖י נְצִ֥יב מֶֽלַח: 27 וַיַּשְׁכֵּ֥ם אַבְרָהָ֖ם בַּבֹּ֑קֶר אֶל־הַ֨מָּק֔וֹם אֲשֶׁר־עָ֥מַד שָׁ֖ם אֶת־פְּנֵ֥י יְהוָֽה: 28 וַיַּשְׁקֵ֗ף עַל־פְּנֵ֤י סְדֹם֙ וַעֲמֹרָ֔ה וְעַֽל־כָּל־פְּנֵ֖י אֶ֣רֶץ הַכִּכָּ֑ר וַיַּ֗רְא וְהִנֵּ֤ה עָלָה֙ קִיטֹ֣ר הָאָ֔רֶץ כְּקִיטֹ֖ר הַכִּבְשָֽׁן: 29 וַיְהִ֗י בְּשַׁחֵ֤ת אֱלֹהִים֙ אֶת־עָרֵ֣י הַכִּכָּ֔ר

where Lot dwelt, God was mindful of Abraham and removed Lot from the midst of the upheaval.

30Lot went up from Zoar and settled in the hill country with his two daughters, for he was afraid to dwell in Zoar; and he and his two daughters lived in a cave. 31And the older one said to the younger, "Our father is old, and there is not a man on earth to consort with us in the way of all the world. 32Come, let us make our father drink wine, and let us lie with him, that we may maintain life through our father." 33That night they made their father drink wine, and the older one went in and lay with her father; he did not know when she lay down or when she rose. 34The next day the older one said to the younger, "See, I lay with Father last night; let us make him drink wine tonight also, and you go and lie with him, that we may maintain life through our father." 35That night also they made their father drink wine, and the younger one went and lay with him; he did not know when she lay down or when she rose.

36Thus the two daughters of Lot came to be with child by their father. 37The older one bore a son and named him Moab;d he is the father of the Moabites of today. 38And the younger also bore a son, and she called him Ben-ammi;e he is the father of the Ammonites of today.

20

Abraham journeyed from there to the region of the Negeb and settled between Kadesh and Shur. While he was sojourning in Gerar, 2Abraham said of Sarah his wife, "She is my sister." So King Abimelech of Gerar had Sarah brought to him. 3But God came to Abimelech in a dream by night and said to him, "You are to die because of the woman that you have taken, for she is a married woman." 4Now

וַיִּזְכֹּר אֱלֹהִים אֶת־אַבְרָהָם וַיְשַׁלַּח אֶת־לוֹט מִתּוֹךְ הַהֲפֵכָה בַּהֲפֹךְ אֶת־הֶעָרִים אֲשֶׁר־יָשַׁב בָּהֵן לוֹט: 30 וַיַּעַל לוֹט מִצּוֹעַר וַיֵּשֶׁב בָּהָר וּשְׁתֵּי בְנֹתָיו עִמּוֹ כִּי יָרֵא לָשֶׁבֶת בְּצוֹעַר וַיֵּשֶׁב בַּמְּעָרָה הוּא וּשְׁתֵּי בְנֹתָיו: 31 וַתֹּאמֶר הַבְּכִירָה אֶל־הַצְּעִירָה אָבִינוּ זָקֵן וְאִישׁ אֵין בָּאָרֶץ לָבוֹא עָלֵינוּ כְּדֶרֶךְ כָּל־הָאָרֶץ: 32 לְכָה נַשְׁקֶה אֶת־אָבִינוּ יַיִן וְנִשְׁכְּבָה עִמּוֹ וּנְחַיֶּה מֵאָבִינוּ זָרַע: 33 וַתַּשְׁקֶיןָ אֶת־אֲבִיהֶן יַיִן בַּלַּיְלָה הוּא וַתָּבֹא הַבְּכִירָה וַתִּשְׁכַּב אֶת־אָבִיהָ וְלֹא־יָדַע בְּשִׁכְבָהּ וּבְקוּמָהּ*: 34 וַיְהִי מִמָּחֳרָת וַתֹּאמֶר הַבְּכִירָה אֶל־הַצְּעִירָה הֵן־שָׁכַבְתִּי אֶמֶשׁ אֶת־אָבִי נַשְׁקֶנּוּ יַיִן גַּם־הַלַּיְלָה וּבֹאִי שִׁכְבִי עִמּוֹ וּנְחַיֶּה מֵאָבִינוּ זָרַע: 35 וַתַּשְׁקֶיןָ גַּם בַּלַּיְלָה הַהוּא אֶת־אֲבִיהֶן יָיִן וַתָּקָם הַצְּעִירָה וַתִּשְׁכַּב עִמּוֹ וְלֹא־יָדַע בְּשִׁכְבָהּ וּבְקֻמָהּ: 36 וַתַּהֲרֶיןָ שְׁתֵּי בְנוֹת־לוֹט מֵאֲבִיהֶן: 37 וַתֵּלֶד הַבְּכִירָה בֵּן וַתִּקְרָא שְׁמוֹ מוֹאָב הוּא אֲבִי־מוֹאָב עַד־הַיּוֹם: 38 וְהַצְּעִירָה גַם־הִוא יָלְדָה בֵּן וַתִּקְרָא שְׁמוֹ בֶּן־עַמִּי הוּא אֲבִי בְנֵי־עַמּוֹן עַד־הַיּוֹם: ס

כ וַיִּסַּע מִשָּׁם אַבְרָהָם אַרְצָה הַנֶּגֶב וַיֵּשֶׁב בֵּין־קָדֵשׁ וּבֵין שׁוּר וַיָּגָר בִּגְרָר: 2 וַיֹּאמֶר אַבְרָהָם אֶל־שָׂרָה אִשְׁתּוֹ אֲחֹתִי הִוא וַיִּשְׁלַח אֲבִימֶלֶךְ מֶלֶךְ גְּרָר וַיִּקַּח אֶת־שָׂרָה: 3 וַיָּבֹא אֱלֹהִים אֶל־אֲבִימֶלֶךְ בַּחֲלוֹם הַלָּיְלָה וַיֹּאמֶר לוֹ הִנְּךָ מֵת עַל־הָאִשָּׁה אֲשֶׁר־לָקַחְתָּ וְהִוא בְּעֻלַת בָּעַל: 4 וַאֲבִימֶלֶךְ לֹא קָרַב אֵלֶיהָ וַיֹּאמַר אֲדֹנָי

נקוד על ו' v. 33.

---

d　As though me-'ab "from (my) father."
e　As though "son of my (paternal) kindred."

Abimelech had not approached her. He said, "O Lord, will You slay people even though innocent? [5]He himself said to me, 'She is my sister!' And she also said, 'He is my brother.' When I did this, my heart was blameless and my hands were clean." [6]And God said to him in the dream, "I knew that you did this with a blameless heart, and so I kept you from sinning against Me. That was why I did not let you touch her. [7]Therefore, restore the man's wife—since he is a prophet, he will intercede for you—to save your life. If you fail to restore her, know that you shall die, you and all that are yours."

[8]Early next morning, Abimelech called his servants and told them all that had happened; and the men were greatly frightened. [9]Then Abimelech summoned Abraham and said to him, "What have you done to us? What wrong have I done that you should bring so great a guilt upon me and my kingdom? You have done to me things that ought not to be done. [10]What, then," Abimelech demanded of Abraham, "was your purpose in doing this thing?" [11]"I thought," said Abraham, "surely there is no fear of God in this place, and they will kill me because of my wife. [12]And besides, she is in truth my sister, my father's daughter though not my mother's; and she became my wife. [13]So when God made me wander from my father's house, I said to her, 'Let this be the kindness that you shall do me: whatever place we come to, say there of me: He is my brother.'"

[14]Abimelech took sheep and oxen, and male and female slaves, and gave them to Abraham; and he restored his wife Sarah to him. [15]And Abimelech said, "Here, my land is before you; settle wherever you please." [16]And to Sarah he said, "I herewith give your brother a thousand pieces of silver; this will serve you as vindication[a] before all who are with you, and

---

a Lit. "a covering of the eyes"; meaning of latter half of verse uncertain.

הֲגוֹי גַּם־צַדִּיק תַּהֲרֹג: 5 הֲלֹא הוּא אָמַר־ לִי אֲחֹתִי הִוא וְהִיא־גַם־הִוא אָמְרָה אָחִי הוּא בְּתָם־לְבָבִי וּבְנִקְיֹן כַּפַּי עָשִׂיתִי זֹאת: 6 וַיֹּאמֶר אֵלָיו הָאֱלֹהִים בַּחֲלֹם גַּם אָנֹכִי יָדַעְתִּי כִּי בְתָם־לְבָבְךָ עָשִׂיתָ זֹּאת וָאֶחְשֹׂךְ גַּם־אָנֹכִי אוֹתְךָ מֵחֲטוֹ*־לִי עַל־כֵּן לֹא־נְתַתִּיךָ לִנְגֹּעַ אֵלֶיהָ: 7 וְעַתָּה הָשֵׁב אֵשֶׁת־הָאִישׁ כִּי־נָבִיא הוּא וְיִתְפַּלֵּל בַּעַדְךָ וֶחְיֵה וְאִם־אֵינְךָ מֵשִׁיב דַּע כִּי־מוֹת תָּמוּת אַתָּה וְכָל־אֲשֶׁר־לָךְ: 8 וַיַּשְׁכֵּם אֲבִימֶלֶךְ בַּבֹּקֶר וַיִּקְרָא לְכָל־ עֲבָדָיו וַיְדַבֵּר אֶת־כָּל־הַדְּבָרִים הָאֵלֶּה בְּאָזְנֵיהֶם וַיִּירְאוּ הָאֲנָשִׁים מְאֹד: 9 וַיִּקְרָא אֲבִימֶלֶךְ לְאַבְרָהָם וַיֹּאמֶר לוֹ מֶה־עָשִׂיתָ לָּנוּ וּמֶה־חָטָאתִי לָךְ כִּי־הֵבֵאתָ עָלַי וְעַל־ מַמְלַכְתִּי חֲטָאָה גְדֹלָה מַעֲשִׂים אֲשֶׁר לֹא־יֵעָשׂוּ עָשִׂיתָ עִמָּדִי: 10 וַיֹּאמֶר אֲבִימֶלֶךְ אֶל־אַבְרָהָם מָה רָאִיתָ כִּי עָשִׂיתָ אֶת־הַדָּבָר הַזֶּה: 11 וַיֹּאמֶר אַבְרָהָם כִּי אָמַרְתִּי רַק אֵין־יִרְאַת אֱלֹהִים בַּמָּקוֹם הַזֶּה וַהֲרָגוּנִי עַל־דְּבַר אִשְׁתִּי: 12 וְגַם־ אָמְנָה אֲחֹתִי בַת־אָבִי הִוא אַךְ לֹא בַת־אִמִּי וַתְּהִי־לִי לְאִשָּׁה: 13 וַיְהִי כַּאֲשֶׁר הִתְעוּ אֹתִי אֱלֹהִים מִבֵּית אָבִי וָאֹמַר לָהּ זֶה חַסְדֵּךְ אֲשֶׁר תַּעֲשִׂי עִמָּדִי אֶל כָּל־ הַמָּקוֹם אֲשֶׁר נָבוֹא שָׁמָּה אִמְרִי־לִי אָחִי הוּא: 14 וַיִּקַּח אֲבִימֶלֶךְ צֹאן וּבָקָר וַעֲבָדִים וּשְׁפָחֹת וַיִּתֵּן לְאַבְרָהָם וַיָּשֶׁב לוֹ אֵת שָׂרָה אִשְׁתּוֹ: 15 וַיֹּאמֶר אֲבִימֶלֶךְ הִנֵּה אַרְצִי לְפָנֶיךָ בַּטּוֹב בְּעֵינֶיךָ שֵׁב: 16 וּלְשָׂרָה אָמַר הִנֵּה נָתַתִּי אֶלֶף כֶּסֶף לְאָחִיךְ הִנֵּה הוּא־ לָךְ כְּסוּת עֵינַיִם לְכֹל אֲשֶׁר אִתָּךְ וְאֵת כֹּל וְנֹכָחַת: 17 וַיִּתְפַּלֵּל אַבְרָהָם אֶל־הָאֱלֹהִים וַיִּרְפָּא אֱלֹהִים אֶת־אֲבִימֶלֶךְ וְאֶת־אִשְׁתּוֹ

v. 6. חסר א'

36

you are cleared before everyone." [17]Abraham then prayed to God, and God healed Abimelech and his wife and his slave girls, so that they bore children; [18]for the LORD had closed fast every womb of the household of Abimelech because of Sarah, the wife of Abraham.

21 The LORD took note of Sarah as He had promised, and the LORD did for Sarah as He had spoken. [2]Sarah conceived and bore a son to Abraham in his old age, at the set time of which God had spoken. [3]Abraham gave his newborn son, whom Sarah had borne him, the name of Isaac. [4]And when his son Isaac was eight days old, Abraham circumcised him, as God had commanded him. [5]Now Abraham was a hundred years old when his son Isaac was born to him. [6]Sarah said, "God has brought me laughter; everyone who hears will laugh with[a] me." [7]And she added,

"Who would have said to Abraham
That Sarah would suckle children!
Yet I have borne a son in his old age."

[8]The child grew up and was weaned, and Abraham held a great feast on the day that Isaac was weaned.

[9]Sarah saw the son whom Hagar the Egyptian had borne to Abraham playing. [10]She said to Abraham, "Cast out that slave-woman and her son, for the son of that slave shall not share in the inheritance with my son Isaac." [11]The matter distressed Abraham greatly, for it concerned a son of his. [12]But God said to Abraham, "Do not be distressed over the boy or your slave; whatever Sarah tells you, do as she says, for it is through Isaac that offspring shall be continued[b] for you. [13]As for the son of the slave-woman, I will make a nation of him, too, for he is your seed."

---

a Lit. "for."
b Lit. "called."

37

וְאַמְהֹתָיו וַיֵּלֵדוּ: 18 כִּי־עָצֹר עָצַר יְהוָה בְּעַד כָּל־רֶחֶם לְבֵית אֲבִימֶלֶךְ עַל־דְּבַר שָׂרָה אֵשֶׁת אַבְרָהָם: ס

כא וַיהוָה פָּקַד אֶת־שָׂרָה כַּאֲשֶׁר אָמָר וַיַּעַשׂ יְהוָה לְשָׂרָה כַּאֲשֶׁר דִּבֵּר: 2 וַתַּהַר וַתֵּלֶד שָׂרָה לְאַבְרָהָם בֵּן לִזְקֻנָיו לַמּוֹעֵד אֲשֶׁר־דִּבֶּר אֹתוֹ אֱלֹהִים: 3 וַיִּקְרָא אַבְרָהָם אֶת־שֶׁם־בְּנוֹ הַנּוֹלַד־לוֹ אֲשֶׁר־יָלְדָה־לּוֹ שָׂרָה יִצְחָק: 4 וַיָּמָל אַבְרָהָם אֶת־יִצְחָק בְּנוֹ בֶּן־שְׁמֹנַת יָמִים כַּאֲשֶׁר צִוָּה אֹתוֹ אֱלֹהִים: 5 וְאַבְרָהָם בֶּן־מְאַת שָׁנָה בְּהִוָּלֶד לוֹ אֵת יִצְחָק בְּנוֹ: 6 וַתֹּאמֶר שָׂרָה צְחֹק עָשָׂה לִי אֱלֹהִים כָּל־הַשֹּׁמֵעַ יִצְחַק־לִי: 7 וַתֹּאמֶר

מִי מִלֵּל לְאַבְרָהָם
הֵינִיקָה בָנִים שָׂרָה
כִּי־יָלַדְתִּי בֵן לִזְקֻנָיו:

8 וַיִּגְדַּל הַיֶּלֶד וַיִּגָּמַל וַיַּעַשׂ אַבְרָהָם מִשְׁתֶּה גָדוֹל בְּיוֹם הִגָּמֵל אֶת־יִצְחָק: 9 וַתֵּרֶא שָׂרָה אֶת־בֶּן־הָגָר הַמִּצְרִית אֲשֶׁר־יָלְדָה לְאַבְרָהָם מְצַחֵק: 10 וַתֹּאמֶר לְאַבְרָהָם גָּרֵשׁ הָאָמָה הַזֹּאת וְאֶת־בְּנָהּ כִּי לֹא יִירַשׁ בֶּן־הָאָמָה הַזֹּאת עִם־בְּנִי עִם־יִצְחָק: 11 וַיֵּרַע הַדָּבָר מְאֹד בְּעֵינֵי אַבְרָהָם עַל אוֹדֹת בְּנוֹ: 12 וַיֹּאמֶר אֱלֹהִים אֶל־אַבְרָהָם אַל־יֵרַע בְּעֵינֶיךָ עַל־הַנַּעַר וְעַל־אֲמָתֶךָ כֹּל אֲשֶׁר תֹּאמַר אֵלֶיךָ שָׂרָה שְׁמַע בְּקֹלָהּ כִּי בְיִצְחָק יִקָּרֵא לְךָ זָרַע: 13 וְגַם אֶת־בֶּן־הָאָמָה לְגוֹי אֲשִׂימֶנּוּ כִּי זַרְעֲךָ הוּא:

14Early next morning Abraham took some bread and a skin of water, and gave them to Hagar. He placed them over her shoulder, together with the child, and sent her away. And she wandered about in the wilderness of Beer-sheba. 15When the water was gone from the skin, she left the child under one of the bushes, 16and went and sat down at a distance, a bowshot away; for she thought, "Let me not look on as the child dies." And sitting thus afar, she burst into tears.

17God heard the cry of the boy, and an angel of God called to Hagar from heaven and said to her, "What troubles you, Hagar? Fear not, for God has heeded the cry of the boy where he is. 18Come, lift up the boy and hold him by the hand, for I will make a great nation of him." 19Then God opened her eyes and she saw a well of water. She went and filled the skin with water, and let the boy drink. 20God was with the boy and he grew up; he dwelt in the wilderness and became a bowman. 21He lived in the wilderness of Paran; and his mother got a wife for him from the land of Egypt.

22At that time Abimelech and Phicol, chief of his troops, said to Abraham, "God is with you in everything that you do. 23Therefore swear to me here by God that you will not deal falsely with me or with my kith and kin, but will deal with me and with the land in which you have sojourned as loyally as I have dealt with you." 24And Abraham said, "I swear it."

25Then Abraham reproached Abimelech for the well of water which the servants of Abimelech had seized. 26But Abimelech said, "I do not know who did this; you did not tell me, nor have I heard of it until today." 27Abraham took sheep and oxen and gave them to Abimelech, and the two of them made a pact. 28Abraham then set seven ewes of the flock by themselves,

14 וַיַּשְׁכֵּ֨ם אַבְרָהָ֣ם ׀ בַּבֹּ֗קֶר וַיִּֽקַּֽח־לֶ֜חֶם וְחֵ֣מַת מַ֡יִם וַיִּתֵּ֣ן אֶל־הָ֠גָר שָׂ֧ם עַל־שִׁכְמָ֛הּ וְאֶת־הַיֶּ֖לֶד וַֽיְשַׁלְּחֶ֑הָ וַתֵּ֣לֶךְ וַתֵּ֔תַע בְּמִדְבַּ֖ר בְּאֵ֥ר שָֽׁבַע׃ 15 וַיִּכְל֥וּ הַמַּ֖יִם מִן־הַחֵ֑מֶת וַתַּשְׁלֵ֣ךְ אֶת־הַיֶּ֔לֶד תַּ֖חַת אַחַ֥ד הַשִּׂיחִֽם׃ 16 וַתֵּ֩לֶךְ֩ וַתֵּ֨שֶׁב לָ֜הּ מִנֶּ֗גֶד הַרְחֵק֙ כִּמְטַחֲוֵ֣י קֶ֔שֶׁת כִּ֣י אָֽמְרָ֔ה אַל־אֶרְאֶ֖ה בְּמ֣וֹת הַיָּ֑לֶד וַתֵּ֣שֶׁב מִנֶּ֔גֶד וַתִּשָּׂ֥א אֶת־קֹלָ֖הּ וַתֵּֽבְךְּ׃ 17 וַיִּשְׁמַ֣ע אֱלֹהִים֮ אֶת־ק֣וֹל הַנַּעַר֒ וַיִּקְרָא֩ מַלְאַ֨ךְ אֱלֹהִ֤ים ׀ אֶל־הָגָר֙ מִן־הַשָּׁמַ֔יִם וַיֹּ֥אמֶר לָ֖הּ מַה־לָּ֣ךְ הָגָ֑ר אַל־תִּ֣ירְאִ֔י כִּֽי־שָׁמַ֧ע אֱלֹהִ֛ים אֶל־ק֥וֹל הַנַּ֖עַר בַּֽאֲשֶׁ֥ר הוּא־שָֽׁם׃ 18 ק֚וּמִי שְׂאִ֣י אֶת־הַנַּ֔עַר וְהַחֲזִ֥יקִי אֶת־יָדֵ֖ךְ בּ֑וֹ כִּֽי־לְג֥וֹי גָּד֖וֹל אֲשִׂימֶֽנּוּ׃ 19 וַיִּפְקַ֤ח אֱלֹהִים֙ אֶת־עֵינֶ֔יהָ וַתֵּ֖רֶא בְּאֵ֣ר מָ֑יִם וַתֵּ֜לֶךְ וַתְּמַלֵּ֤א אֶת־הַחֵ֙מֶת֙ מַ֔יִם וַתַּ֖שְׁקְ אֶת־הַנָּֽעַר׃ 20 וַיְהִ֧י אֱלֹהִ֛ים אֶת־הַנַּ֖עַר וַיִּגְדָּ֑ל וַיֵּ֙שֶׁב֙ בַּמִּדְבָּ֔ר וַיְהִ֖י רֹבֶ֥ה קַשָּֽׁת׃ 21 וַיֵּ֖שֶׁב בְּמִדְבַּ֣ר פָּארָ֑ן וַתִּֽקַּֽח־ל֥וֹ אִמּ֛וֹ אִשָּׁ֖ה מֵאֶ֥רֶץ מִצְרָֽיִם׃ פ

22 וַֽיְהִי֙ בָּעֵ֣ת הַהִ֔וא וַיֹּ֣אמֶר אֲבִימֶ֗לֶךְ וּפִיכֹל֙ שַׂר־צְבָא֔וֹ אֶל־אַבְרָהָ֖ם לֵאמֹ֑ר אֱלֹהִ֣ים עִמְּךָ֔ בְּכֹ֥ל אֲשֶׁר־אַתָּ֖ה עֹשֶֽׂה׃ 23 וְעַתָּ֗ה הִשָּׁ֨בְעָה לִּ֤י בֵֽאלֹהִים֙ הֵ֔נָּה אִם־תִּשְׁקֹ֣ר לִ֔י וּלְנִינִ֖י וּלְנֶכְדִּ֑י כַּחֶ֜סֶד אֲשֶׁר־עָשִׂ֤יתִי עִמְּךָ֙ תַּעֲשֶׂ֣ה עִמָּדִ֔י וְעִם־הָאָ֖רֶץ אֲשֶׁר־גַּ֥רְתָּה בָּֽהּ׃ 24 וַיֹּ֙אמֶר֙ אַבְרָהָ֔ם אָנֹכִ֖י אִשָּׁבֵֽעַ׃ 25 וְהוֹכִ֥חַ אַבְרָהָ֖ם אֶת־אֲבִימֶ֑לֶךְ עַל־אֹדוֹת֙ בְּאֵ֣ר הַמַּ֔יִם אֲשֶׁ֥ר גָּזְל֖וּ עַבְדֵ֥י אֲבִימֶֽלֶךְ׃ 26 וַיֹּ֣אמֶר אֲבִימֶ֔לֶךְ לֹ֣א יָדַ֔עְתִּי מִ֥י עָשָׂ֖ה אֶת־הַדָּבָ֣ר הַזֶּ֑ה וְגַם־אַתָּ֞ה לֹֽא־הִגַּ֣דְתָּ לִּ֗י וְגַ֧ם אָנֹכִ֛י לֹ֥א שָׁמַ֖עְתִּי בִּלְתִּ֥י הַיּֽוֹם׃ 27 וַיִּקַּ֤ח אַבְרָהָם֙ צֹ֣אן וּבָקָ֔ר וַיִּתֵּ֖ן לַאֲבִימֶ֑לֶךְ וַיִּכְרְת֥וּ שְׁנֵיהֶ֖ם בְּרִֽית׃ 28 וַיַּצֵּ֣ב אַבְרָהָ֗ם אֶת־שֶׁ֛בַע כִּבְשֹׂ֥ת הַצֹּ֖אן לְבַדְּהֶֽן׃

29and Abimelech said to Abraham, "What mean these seven ewes which you have set apart?" 30He replied, "You are to accept these seven ewes from me as proof that I dug this well." 31Hence that place was called Beer-sheba,c for there the two of them swore an oath. 32When they had concluded the pact at Beer-sheba, Abimelech and Phicol, chief of his troops, departed and returned to the land of the Philistines. 33[Abraham] planted a tamarisk at Beer-sheba, and invoked there the name of the LORD, the Everlasting God. 34And Abraham resided in the land of the Philistines a long time.

22 Some time afterward, God put Abraham to the test. He said to him, "Abraham," and he answered, "Here I am." 2And He said, "Take your son, your favored one, Isaac, whom you love, and go to the land of Moriah, and offer him there as a burnt offering on one of the heights that I will point out to you." 3So early next morning, Abraham saddled his ass and took with him two of his servants and his son Isaac. He split the wood for the burnt offering, and he set out for the place of which God had told him. 4On the third day Abraham looked up and saw the place from afar. 5Then Abraham said to his servants, "You stay here with the ass. The boy and I will go up there; we will worship and we will return to you."

6Abraham took the wood for the burnt offering and put it on his son Isaac. He himself took the firestonea and the knife; and the two walked off together. 7Then Isaac said to his father Abraham, "Father!" And he answered, "Yes, my son." And he said, "Here are the firestone and the wood; but where is the sheep for the burnt offering?" 8And Abraham said,

29 וַיֹּאמֶר אֲבִימֶלֶךְ אֶל־אַבְרָהָם מָה הֵנָּה שֶׁבַע כְּבָשֹׂת הָאֵלֶּה אֲשֶׁר הִצַּבְתָּ לְבַדָּנָה: 30 וַיֹּאמֶר כִּי אֶת־שֶׁבַע כְּבָשֹׂת תִּקַּח מִיָּדִי בַּעֲבוּר תִּהְיֶה־לִּי לְעֵדָה כִּי חָפַרְתִּי אֶת־הַבְּאֵר הַזֹּאת: 31 עַל־כֵּן קָרָא לַמָּקוֹם הַהוּא בְּאֵר שָׁבַע כִּי שָׁם נִשְׁבְּעוּ שְׁנֵיהֶם: 32 וַיִּכְרְתוּ בְרִית בִּבְאֵר שָׁבַע וַיָּקָם אֲבִימֶלֶךְ וּפִיכֹל שַׂר־צְבָאוֹ וַיָּשֻׁבוּ אֶל־אֶרֶץ פְּלִשְׁתִּים: 33 וַיִּטַּע אֵשֶׁל בִּבְאֵר שָׁבַע וַיִּקְרָא־שָׁם בְּשֵׁם יְהוָה אֵל עוֹלָם: 34 וַיָּגָר אַבְרָהָם בְּאֶרֶץ פְּלִשְׁתִּים יָמִים רַבִּים: פ

כב וַיְהִי אַחַר הַדְּבָרִים הָאֵלֶּה וְהָאֱלֹהִים נִסָּה אֶת־אַבְרָהָם וַיֹּאמֶר אֵלָיו אַבְרָהָם וַיֹּאמֶר הִנֵּנִי: 2 וַיֹּאמֶר קַח־נָא אֶת־בִּנְךָ אֶת־יְחִידְךָ אֲשֶׁר־אָהַבְתָּ אֶת־יִצְחָק וְלֶךְ־לְךָ אֶל־אֶרֶץ הַמֹּרִיָּה וְהַעֲלֵהוּ שָׁם לְעֹלָה עַל אַחַד הֶהָרִים אֲשֶׁר אֹמַר אֵלֶיךָ: 3 וַיַּשְׁכֵּם אַבְרָהָם בַּבֹּקֶר וַיַּחֲבֹשׁ אֶת־חֲמֹרוֹ וַיִּקַּח אֶת־שְׁנֵי נְעָרָיו אִתּוֹ וְאֵת יִצְחָק בְּנוֹ וַיְבַקַּע עֲצֵי עֹלָה וַיָּקָם וַיֵּלֶךְ אֶל־הַמָּקוֹם אֲשֶׁר־אָמַר־לוֹ הָאֱלֹהִים: 4 בַּיּוֹם הַשְּׁלִישִׁי וַיִּשָּׂא אַבְרָהָם אֶת־עֵינָיו וַיַּרְא אֶת־הַמָּקוֹם מֵרָחֹק: 5 וַיֹּאמֶר אַבְרָהָם אֶל־נְעָרָיו שְׁבוּ־לָכֶם פֹּה עִם־הַחֲמוֹר וַאֲנִי וְהַנַּעַר נֵלְכָה עַד־כֹּה וְנִשְׁתַּחֲוֶה וְנָשׁוּבָה אֲלֵיכֶם: 6 וַיִּקַּח אַבְרָהָם אֶת־עֲצֵי הָעֹלָה וַיָּשֶׂם עַל־יִצְחָק בְּנוֹ וַיִּקַּח בְּיָדוֹ אֶת־הָאֵשׁ וְאֶת־הַמַּאֲכֶלֶת וַיֵּלְכוּ שְׁנֵיהֶם יַחְדָּו: 7 וַיֹּאמֶר יִצְחָק אֶל־אַבְרָהָם אָבִיו וַיֹּאמֶר אָבִי וַיֹּאמֶר הִנֶּנִּי בְנִי וַיֹּאמֶר הִנֵּה הָאֵשׁ וְהָעֵצִים וְאַיֵּה הַשֶּׂה לְעֹלָה: 8 וַיֹּאמֶר

c   I.e., "well of seven" or "well of oath."

a   Lit. "fire."

39

"God will see to the sheep for His burnt offering, my son." And the two of them walked on together.

[9]They arrived at the place of which God had told him. Abraham built an altar there; he laid out the wood; he bound his son Isaac; he laid him on the altar, on top of the wood. [10]And Abraham picked up the knife to slay his son. [11]Then an angel of the Lord called to him from heaven: "Abraham! Abraham!" And he answered, "Here I am." [12]And he said, "Do not raise your hand against the boy, or do anything to him. For now I know that you fear God, since you have not withheld your son, your favored one, from Me." [13]When Abraham looked up, his eye fell upon a[b] ram, caught in the thicket by its horns. So Abraham went and took the ram and offered it up as a burnt offering in place of his son. [14]And Abraham named that site Adonai-yireh,[c] whence the present saying, "On the mount of the Lord there is vision."[d]

[15]The angel of the Lord called to Abraham a second time from heaven, [16]and said, "By Myself I swear, the Lord declares: Because you have done this and have not withheld your son, your favored one, [17]I will bestow My blessing upon you and make your descendants as numerous as the stars of heaven and the sands on the seashore; and your descendants shall seize the gates of their foes. [18]All the nations of the earth shall bless themselves by your descendants, because you have obeyed My command." [19]Abraham then returned to his servants, and they departed together for Beer-sheba; and Abraham stayed in Beer-sheba.

[20]Some time later, Abraham was told, "Milcah too has borne children to your brother Nahor: [21]Uz the first-born, and Buz his brother,

אַבְרָהָם אֱלֹהִים יִרְאֶה־לּוֹ הַשֶּׂה לְעֹלָה בְּנִי וַיֵּלְכוּ שְׁנֵיהֶם יַחְדָּו: 9 וַיָּבֹאוּ אֶל־הַמָּקוֹם אֲשֶׁר אָמַר־לוֹ הָאֱלֹהִים וַיִּבֶן שָׁם אַבְרָהָם אֶת־הַמִּזְבֵּחַ וַיַּעֲרֹךְ אֶת־הָעֵצִים וַיַּעֲקֹד אֶת־יִצְחָק בְּנוֹ וַיָּשֶׂם אֹתוֹ עַל־הַמִּזְבֵּחַ מִמַּעַל לָעֵצִים: 10 וַיִּשְׁלַח אַבְרָהָם אֶת־יָדוֹ וַיִּקַּח אֶת־הַמַּאֲכֶלֶת לִשְׁחֹט אֶת־בְּנוֹ: 11 וַיִּקְרָא אֵלָיו מַלְאַךְ יְהוָה מִן־הַשָּׁמַיִם וַיֹּאמֶר אַבְרָהָם אַבְרָהָם וַיֹּאמֶר הִנֵּנִי: 12 וַיֹּאמֶר אַל־תִּשְׁלַח יָדְךָ אֶל־הַנַּעַר וְאַל־תַּעַשׂ לוֹ מְאוּמָה כִּי עַתָּה יָדַעְתִּי כִּי־יְרֵא אֱלֹהִים אַתָּה וְלֹא חָשַׂכְתָּ אֶת־בִּנְךָ אֶת־יְחִידְךָ מִמֶּנִּי: 13 וַיִּשָּׂא אַבְרָהָם אֶת־עֵינָיו וַיַּרְא וְהִנֵּה־אַיִל אַחַר נֶאֱחַז בַּסְּבַךְ בְּקַרְנָיו וַיֵּלֶךְ אַבְרָהָם וַיִּקַּח אֶת־הָאַיִל וַיַּעֲלֵהוּ לְעֹלָה תַּחַת בְּנוֹ: 14 וַיִּקְרָא אַבְרָהָם שֵׁם־הַמָּקוֹם הַהוּא יְהוָה יִרְאֶה אֲשֶׁר יֵאָמֵר הַיּוֹם בְּהַר יְהוָה יֵרָאֶה: 15 וַיִּקְרָא מַלְאַךְ יְהוָה אֶל־אַבְרָהָם שֵׁנִית מִן־הַשָּׁמָיִם: 16 וַיֹּאמֶר בִּי נִשְׁבַּעְתִּי נְאֻם־יְהוָה כִּי יַעַן אֲשֶׁר עָשִׂיתָ אֶת־הַדָּבָר הַזֶּה וְלֹא חָשַׂכְתָּ אֶת־בִּנְךָ אֶת־יְחִידֶךָ: 17 כִּי־בָרֵךְ אֲבָרֶכְךָ וְהַרְבָּה אַרְבֶּה אֶת־זַרְעֲךָ כְּכוֹכְבֵי הַשָּׁמַיִם וְכַחוֹל אֲשֶׁר עַל־שְׂפַת הַיָּם וְיִרַשׁ זַרְעֲךָ אֵת שַׁעַר אֹיְבָיו: 18 וְהִתְבָּרֲכוּ בְזַרְעֲךָ כֹּל גּוֹיֵי הָאָרֶץ עֵקֶב אֲשֶׁר שָׁמַעְתָּ בְּקֹלִי: 19 וַיָּשָׁב אַבְרָהָם אֶל־נְעָרָיו וַיָּקֻמוּ וַיֵּלְכוּ יַחְדָּו אֶל־בְּאֵר שָׁבַע וַיֵּשֶׁב אַבְרָהָם בִּבְאֵר שָׁבַע: פ

20 וַיְהִי אַחֲרֵי הַדְּבָרִים הָאֵלֶּה וַיֻּגַּד לְאַבְרָהָם לֵאמֹר הִנֵּה יָלְדָה מִלְכָּה גַם־הִוא בָּנִים לְנָחוֹר אָחִיךָ: 21 אֶת־עוּץ בְּכֹרוֹ

---

b Reading 'eḥad with many Heb. mss. and ancient versions; text 'aḥar "after."
c I.e., "the Lord will see"; cf. v. 8.
d Heb. Behar Adonai yera'eh.

and Kemuel the father of Aram; 22and Che-sed, Hazo, Pildash, Jidlaph, and Bethuel"— 23Bethuel being the father of Rebekah. These eight Milcah bore to Nahor, Abraham's brother. 24And his concubine, whose name was Reumah, also bore children: Tebah, Gaham, Tahash, and Maacah.

23 ḤAYYEI SARAH

Sarah's lifetime—the span of Sarah's life—came to one hundred and twenty-seven years. 2Sarah died in Kiriath-arba—now Hebron—in the land of Canaan; and Abraham proceeded to mourn for Sarah and to bewail her. 3Then Abraham rose from beside his dead, and spoke to the Hittites, saying, 4"I am a resident alien among you; sell me a burial site among you, that I may remove my dead for burial." 5And the Hittites replied to Abraham, saying to him, 6"Hear us, my lord: you are the elect of God among us. Bury your dead in the choicest of our burial places; none of us will withhold his burial place from you for burying your dead." 7Thereupon Abraham bowed low to the people of the land, the Hittites, 8and he said to them, "If it is your wish that I remove my dead for burial, you must agree to intercede for me with Ephron son of Zohar. 9Let him sell me the cave of Machpelah that he owns, which is at the edge of his land. Let him sell it to me, at the full price, for a burial site in your midst."

10Ephron was present among the Hittites; so Ephron the Hittite answered Abraham in the hearing of the Hittites, all who entered the gate of his town,ᵃ saying, 11"No, my lord, hear me: I give you the field and I give you the cave that is in it; I give it to you in the presence of my people. Bury your dead." 12Then Abraham bowed low before the people of the land, 13and

וְאֶת־בּ֛וּז אָחִ֖יו וְאֶת־קְמוּאֵ֣ל אֲבִ֣י אֲרָֽם׃ 22 וְאֶת־כֶּ֣שֶׂד וְאֶת־חֲז֗וֹ וְאֶת־פִּלְדָּ֛שׁ וְאֶת־יִדְלָ֖ף וְאֵ֣ת בְּתוּאֵֽל׃ 23 וּבְתוּאֵ֖ל יָלַ֣ד אֶת־רִבְקָ֑ה שְׁמֹנָ֥ה אֵ֙לֶּה֙ יָֽלְדָ֣ה מִלְכָּ֔ה לְנָח֖וֹר אֲחִ֥י אַבְרָהָֽם׃ 24 וּפִֽילַגְשׁ֖וֹ וּשְׁמָ֣הּ רְאוּמָ֑ה וַתֵּ֤לֶד גַּם־הִוא֙ אֶת־טֶ֣בַח וְאֶת־גַּ֔חַם וְאֶת־תַּ֖חַשׁ וְאֶֽת־מַעֲכָֽה׃ ס

חיי שרה

כג וַיִּֽהְיוּ֙ חַיֵּ֣י שָׂרָ֔ה מֵאָ֥ה שָׁנָ֛ה וְעֶשְׂרִ֥ים שָׁנָ֖ה וְשֶׁ֣בַע שָׁנִ֑ים שְׁנֵ֖י חַיֵּ֥י שָׂרָֽה׃ 2 וַתָּ֣מׇת שָׂרָ֗ה בְּקִרְיַ֥ת אַרְבַּ֛ע הִ֥וא חֶבְר֖וֹן בְּאֶ֣רֶץ כְּנָ֑עַן וַיָּבֹא֙ אַבְרָהָ֔ם לִסְפֹּ֥ד לְשָׂרָ֖ה וְלִבְכֹּתָֽהּ*׃ 3 וַיָּ֙קׇם֙ אַבְרָהָ֔ם מֵעַ֖ל פְּנֵ֣י מֵת֑וֹ וַיְדַבֵּ֥ר אֶל־בְּנֵי־חֵ֖ת לֵאמֹֽר׃ 4 גֵּר־וְתוֹשָׁ֥ב אָנֹכִ֖י עִמָּכֶ֑ם תְּנ֨וּ לִ֤י אֲחֻזַּת־קֶ֙בֶר֙ עִמָּכֶ֔ם וְאֶקְבְּרָ֥ה מֵתִ֖י מִלְּפָנָֽי׃ 5 וַיַּעֲנ֧וּ בְנֵי־חֵ֛ת אֶת־אַבְרָהָ֖ם לֵאמֹ֥ר לֽוֹ׃ 6 שְׁמָעֵ֣נוּ ׀ אֲדֹנִ֗י נְשִׂ֨יא אֱלֹהִ֤ים אַתָּה֙ בְּתוֹכֵ֔נוּ בְּמִבְחַ֣ר קְבָרֵ֔ינוּ קְבֹ֖ר אֶת־מֵתֶ֑ךָ אִ֣ישׁ מִמֶּ֔נּוּ אֶת־קִבְר֞וֹ לֹֽא־יִכְלֶ֧ה מִמְּךָ֛ מִקְּבֹ֖ר מֵתֶֽךָ׃ 7 וַיָּ֧קׇם אַבְרָהָ֛ם וַיִּשְׁתַּ֥חוּ לְעַם־הָאָ֖רֶץ לִבְנֵי־חֵֽת׃ 8 וַיְדַבֵּ֥ר אִתָּ֖ם לֵאמֹ֑ר אִם־יֵ֣שׁ אֶֽת־נַפְשְׁכֶ֗ם לִקְבֹּ֤ר אֶת־מֵתִי֙ מִלְּפָנַ֔י שְׁמָע֕וּנִי וּפִגְעוּ־לִ֖י בְּעֶפְר֥וֹן בֶּן־צֹֽחַר׃ 9 וְיִתֶּן־לִ֗י אֶת־מְעָרַ֤ת הַמַּכְפֵּלָה֙ אֲשֶׁר־ל֔וֹ אֲשֶׁ֖ר בִּקְצֵ֣ה שָׂדֵ֑הוּ בְּכֶ֨סֶף מָלֵ֜א יִתְּנֶ֥נָּה לִ֛י בְּתוֹכְכֶ֖ם לַאֲחֻזַּת־קָֽבֶר׃ 10 וְעֶפְר֤וֹן יֹשֵׁב֙ בְּת֣וֹךְ בְּנֵי־חֵ֔ת וַיַּ֩עַן֩ עֶפְר֨וֹן הַחִתִּ֤י אֶת־אַבְרָהָם֙ בְּאׇזְנֵ֣י בְנֵי־חֵ֔ת לְכֹ֛ל בָּאֵ֥י שַֽׁעַר־עִיר֖וֹ לֵאמֹֽר׃ 11 לֹֽא־אֲדֹנִ֣י שְׁמָעֵ֔נִי הַשָּׂדֶה֙ נָתַ֣תִּי לָ֔ךְ וְהַמְּעָרָ֥ה אֲשֶׁר־בּ֖וֹ לְךָ֣ נְתַתִּ֑יהָ לְעֵינֵ֧י בְנֵֽי־עַמִּ֛י נְתַתִּ֥יהָ לָּ֖ךְ קְבֹ֥ר מֵתֶֽךָ׃ 12 וַיִּשְׁתַּ֙חוּ֙ אַבְרָהָ֔ם לִפְנֵ֖י עַ֥ם הָאָֽרֶץ׃ 13 וַיְדַבֵּ֨ר אֶל־עֶפְר֜וֹן בְּאׇזְנֵ֣י עַם־

spoke to Ephron in the hearing of the people of the land, saying, "If only you would hear me out! Let me pay the price of the land; accept it from me, that I may bury my dead there." 14And Ephron replied to Abraham, saying to him, 15"My lord, do hear me! A piece of land worth four hundred shekels of silver—what is that between you and me? Go and bury your dead." 16Abraham accepted Ephron's terms. Abraham paid out to Ephron the money that he had named in the hearing of the Hittites—four hundred shekels of silver at the going merchants' rate.

17So Ephron's land in Machpelah, near Mamre—the field with its cave and all the trees anywhere within the confines of that field—passed 18to Abraham as his possession, in the presence of the Hittites, of all who entered the gate of his town.*a* 19And then Abraham buried his wife Sarah in the cave of the field of Machpelah, facing Mamre—now Hebron—in the land of Canaan. 20Thus the field with its cave passed from the Hittites to Abraham, as a burial site.

24 Abraham was now old, advanced in years, and the Lord had blessed Abraham in all things. 2And Abraham said to the senior servant of his household, who had charge of all that he owned, "Put your hand under my thigh 3and I will make you swear by the Lord, the God of heaven and the God of the earth, that you will not take a wife for my son from the daughters of the Canaanites among whom I dwell, 4but will go to the land of my birth and get a wife for my son Isaac." 5And the servant said to him, "What if the woman does not consent to follow me to this land, shall I then take your son back to the land from which you came?" 6Abraham answered him, "On no account must you take

---

a I.e., all his fellow townsmen.

הָאָ֗רֶץ לֵאמֹר֮ אַ֣ךְ אִם־אַתָּ֣ה ל֣וּ שְׁמָעֵ֒נִי֒ נָתַ֜תִּי כֶּ֤סֶף הַשָּׂדֶה֙ קַ֣ח מִמֶּ֔נִּי וְאֶקְבְּרָ֥ה אֶת־מֵתִ֖י שָֽׁמָּה׃ 14 וַיַּ֧עַן עֶפְר֛וֹן אֶת־אַבְרָהָ֖ם לֵאמֹ֥ר לֽוֹ׃ 15 אֲדֹנִ֣י שְׁמָעֵ֔נִי אֶ֩רֶץ אַרְבַּ֨ע מֵאֹ֧ת שֶֽׁקֶל־כֶּ֛סֶף בֵּינִ֥י וּבֵֽינְךָ֖ מַה־הִ֑וא וְאֶת־מֵתְךָ֖ קְבֹֽר׃ 16 וַיִּשְׁמַ֣ע אַבְרָהָם֮ אֶל־עֶפְרוֹן֒ וַיִּשְׁקֹ֤ל אַבְרָהָם֙ לְעֶפְרֹ֔ן אֶת־הַכֶּ֕סֶף אֲשֶׁ֥ר דִּבֶּ֖ר בְּאָזְנֵ֣י בְנֵי־חֵ֑ת אַרְבַּ֤ע מֵאוֹת֙ שֶׁ֣קֶל כֶּ֔סֶף עֹבֵ֖ר לַסֹּחֵֽר׃

17 וַיָּ֣קׇם ׀ שְׂדֵ֣ה עֶפְר֗וֹן אֲשֶׁר֙ בַּמַּכְפֵּלָ֔ה אֲשֶׁ֖ר לִפְנֵ֣י מַמְרֵ֑א הַשָּׂדֶה֙ וְהַמְּעָרָ֣ה אֲשֶׁר־בּ֔וֹ וְכׇל־הָעֵץ֙ אֲשֶׁ֣ר בַּשָּׂדֶ֔ה אֲשֶׁ֥ר בְּכׇל־גְּבֻל֖וֹ סָבִֽיב׃ 18 לְאַבְרָהָ֥ם לְמִקְנָ֖ה לְעֵינֵ֣י בְנֵי־חֵ֑ת בְּכֹ֖ל בָּאֵ֥י שַֽׁעַר־עִירֽוֹ׃ 19 וְאַחֲרֵי־כֵן֩ קָבַ֨ר אַבְרָהָ֜ם אֶת־שָׂרָ֣ה אִשְׁתּ֗וֹ אֶל־מְעָרַ֞ת שְׂדֵ֧ה הַמַּכְפֵּלָ֛ה עַל־פְּנֵ֥י מַמְרֵ֖א הִ֣וא חֶבְר֑וֹן בְּאֶ֖רֶץ כְּנָֽעַן׃ 20 וַיָּ֨קׇם הַשָּׂדֶ֜ה וְהַמְּעָרָ֧ה אֲשֶׁר־בּ֛וֹ לְאַבְרָהָ֖ם לַאֲחֻזַּת־קָ֑בֶר מֵאֵ֖ת בְּנֵי־חֵֽת׃ ס

כד וְאַבְרָהָ֣ם זָקֵ֔ן בָּ֖א בַּיָּמִ֑ים וַֽיהֹוָ֛ה בֵּרַ֥ךְ אֶת־אַבְרָהָ֖ם בַּכֹּֽל׃ 2 וַיֹּ֣אמֶר אַבְרָהָ֗ם אֶל־עַבְדּוֹ֙ זְקַ֣ן בֵּית֔וֹ הַמֹּשֵׁ֖ל בְּכׇל־אֲשֶׁר־ל֑וֹ שִֽׂים־נָ֥א יָדְךָ֖ תַּ֥חַת יְרֵכִֽי׃ 3 וְאַשְׁבִּ֣יעֲךָ֔ בַּֽיהֹוָה֙ אֱלֹהֵ֣י הַשָּׁמַ֔יִם וֵֽאלֹהֵ֖י הָאָ֑רֶץ אֲשֶׁ֨ר לֹֽא־תִקַּ֤ח אִשָּׁה֙ לִבְנִ֔י מִבְּנוֹת֙ הַֽכְּנַעֲנִ֔י אֲשֶׁ֥ר אָנֹכִ֖י יוֹשֵׁ֥ב בְּקִרְבּֽוֹ׃ 4 כִּ֧י אֶל־אַרְצִ֛י וְאֶל־מוֹלַדְתִּ֖י תֵּלֵ֑ךְ וְלָקַחְתָּ֥ אִשָּׁ֖ה לִבְנִ֥י לְיִצְחָֽק׃ 5 וַיֹּ֤אמֶר אֵלָיו֙ הָעֶ֔בֶד אוּלַי֙ לֹא־תֹאבֶ֣ה הָֽאִשָּׁ֔ה לָלֶ֥כֶת אַחֲרַ֖י אֶל־הָאָ֣רֶץ הַזֹּ֑את הֶֽהָשֵׁ֤ב אָשִׁיב֙ אֶת־בִּנְךָ֔ אֶל־הָאָ֖רֶץ אֲשֶׁר־יָצָ֥אתָ מִשָּֽׁם׃ 6 וַיֹּ֥אמֶר אֵלָ֖יו אַבְרָהָ֑ם הִשָּׁ֣מֶר לְךָ֔ פֶּן־תָּשִׁ֥יב אֶת־בְּנִ֖י שָֽׁמָּה׃

42

my son back there! [7]The LORD, the God of
heaven, who took me from my father's house
and from my native land, who promised me on
oath, saying, 'I will assign this land to your
offspring'—He will send His angel before you,
and you will get a wife for my son from there.
[8]And if the woman does not consent to follow
you, you shall then be clear of this oath to me;
but do not take my son back there." [9]So the servant put his hand under the thigh of his master
Abraham and swore to him as bidden.[a]

[10]Then the servant took ten of his master's
camels and set out, taking with him all the
bounty of his master; and he made his way to
Aram-naharaim, to the city of Nahor. [11]He
made the camels kneel down by the well outside
the city, at evening time, the time when women
come out to draw water. [12]And he said, "O
LORD, God of my master Abraham, grant me
good fortune this day, and deal graciously with
my master Abraham: [13]Here I stand by the
spring as the daughters of the townsmen come
out to draw water; [14]let the maiden to whom I
say, 'Please, lower your jar that I may drink,'
and who replies, 'Drink, and I will also water
your camels'—let her be the one whom You
have decreed for Your servant Isaac. Thereby
shall I know that You have dealt graciously with
my master."

[15]He had scarcely finished speaking, when
Rebekah, who was born to Bethuel, the son of
Milcah the wife of Abraham's brother Nahor,
came out with her jar on her shoulder. [16]The
maiden was very beautiful, a virgin whom no
man had known. She went down to the spring,
filled her jar, and came up. [17]The servant ran
toward her and said, "Please, let me sip a little
water from your jar." [18]"Drink, my lord," she
said, and she quickly lowered her jar upon her
hand and let him drink. [19]When she had let him
drink his fill, she said, "I will also draw for your

7 יְהֹוָה ׀ אֱלֹהֵי הַשָּׁמַיִם אֲשֶׁר לְקָחַנִי מִבֵּית
אָבִי וּמֵאֶרֶץ מוֹלַדְתִּי וַאֲשֶׁר דִּבֶּר־לִי וַאֲשֶׁר
נִשְׁבַּע־לִי לֵאמֹר לְזַרְעֲךָ אֶתֵּן אֶת־הָאָרֶץ
הַזֹּאת הוּא יִשְׁלַח מַלְאָכוֹ לְפָנֶיךָ וְלָקַחְתָּ
אִשָּׁה לִבְנִי מִשָּׁם: 8 וְאִם־לֹא תֹאבֶה
הָאִשָּׁה לָלֶכֶת אַחֲרֶיךָ וְנִקִּיתָ מִשְּׁבֻעָתִי
זֹאת רַק אֶת־בְּנִי לֹא תָשֵׁב שָׁמָּה: 9 וַיָּשֶׂם
הָעֶבֶד אֶת־יָדוֹ תַּחַת יֶרֶךְ אַבְרָהָם אֲדֹנָיו
וַיִּשָּׁבַע לוֹ עַל־הַדָּבָר הַזֶּה:
10 וַיִּקַּח הָעֶבֶד עֲשָׂרָה גְמַלִּים מִגְּמַלֵּי
אֲדֹנָיו וַיֵּלֶךְ וְכָל־טוּב אֲדֹנָיו בְּיָדוֹ וַיָּקָם
וַיֵּלֶךְ אֶל־אֲרַם נַהֲרַיִם אֶל־עִיר נָחוֹר:
11 וַיַּבְרֵךְ הַגְּמַלִּים מִחוּץ לָעִיר אֶל־בְּאֵר
הַמָּיִם לְעֵת עֶרֶב לְעֵת צֵאת הַשֹּׁאֲבֹת:
12 וַיֹּאמַר ׀ יְהֹוָה אֱלֹהֵי אֲדֹנִי אַבְרָהָם
הַקְרֵה־נָא לְפָנַי הַיּוֹם וַעֲשֵׂה־חֶסֶד עִם
אֲדֹנִי אַבְרָהָם: 13 הִנֵּה אָנֹכִי נִצָּב עַל־עֵין
הַמָּיִם וּבְנוֹת אַנְשֵׁי הָעִיר יֹצְאֹת לִשְׁאֹב
מָיִם: 14 וְהָיָה הַנַּעֲרָה אֲשֶׁר אֹמַר
אֵלֶיהָ הַטִּי־נָא כַדֵּךְ וְאֶשְׁתֶּה וְאָמְרָה שְׁתֵה
וְגַם־גְּמַלֶּיךָ אַשְׁקֶה אֹתָהּ הֹכַחְתָּ לְעַבְדְּךָ
לְיִצְחָק וּבָהּ אֵדַע כִּי־עָשִׂיתָ חֶסֶד עִם־
אֲדֹנִי:
15 וַיְהִי־הוּא טֶרֶם כִּלָּה לְדַבֵּר וְהִנֵּה רִבְקָה
יֹצֵאת אֲשֶׁר יֻלְּדָה לִבְתוּאֵל בֶּן־מִלְכָּה
אֵשֶׁת נָחוֹר אֲחִי אַבְרָהָם וְכַדָּהּ עַל־
שִׁכְמָהּ: 16 וְהַנַּעֲרָה טֹבַת מַרְאֶה
מְאֹד בְּתוּלָה וְאִישׁ לֹא יְדָעָהּ וַתֵּרֶד
הָעַיְנָה וַתְּמַלֵּא כַדָּהּ וַתָּעַל: 17 וַיָּרָץ הָעֶבֶד
לִקְרָאתָהּ וַיֹּאמֶר הַגְמִיאִינִי נָא מְעַט־מַיִם
מִכַּדֵּךְ: 18 וַתֹּאמֶר שְׁתֵה אֲדֹנִי וַתְּמַהֵר
וַתֹּרֶד כַּדָּהּ עַל־יָדָהּ וַתַּשְׁקֵהוּ: 19 וַתְּכַל
לְהַשְׁקֹתוֹ וַתֹּאמֶר גַּם לִגְמַלֶּיךָ אֶשְׁאָב עַד

---

a Lit. "about this matter."

camels, until they finish drinking." ²⁰Quickly emptying her jar into the trough, she ran back to the well to draw, and she drew for all his camels.

²¹The man, meanwhile, stood gazing at her, silently wondering whether the LORD had made his errand successful or not. ²²When the camels had finished drinking, the man took a gold nose-ring weighing a half-shekel,ᵇ and two gold bands for her arms, ten shekels in weight. ²³"Pray tell me," he said, "whose daughter are you? Is there room in your father's house for us to spend the night?" ²⁴She replied, "I am the daughter of Bethuel the son of Milcah, whom she bore to Nahor." ²⁵And she went on, "There is plenty of strawᶜ and feed at home, and also room to spend the night." ²⁶The man bowed low in homage to the LORD ²⁷and said, "Blessed be the LORD, the God of my master Abraham, who has not withheld His steadfast faithfulness from my master. For I have been guided on my errand by the LORD, to the house of my master's kinsmen."

²⁸The maiden ran and told all this to her mother's household. ²⁹Now Rebekah had a brother whose name was Laban. Laban ran out to the man at the spring—³⁰when he saw the nose-ring and the bands on his sister's arms, and when he heard his sister Rebekah say, "Thus the man spoke to me." He went up to the man, who was still standing beside the camels at the spring. ³¹"Come in, O blessed of the LORD," he said, "why do you remain outside, when I have made ready the house and a place for the camels?" ³²So the man entered the house, and the camels were unloaded. The camels were given straw and feed, and water was brought to bathe his feet and the feet of the men with him. ³³But when food was set before him, he said, "I will not eat

אִם־כִּלּוּ לִשְׁתֹּת׃ 20 וַתְּמַהֵר וַתְּעַר כַּדָּהּ אֶל־הַשֹּׁקֶת וַתָּרָץ עוֹד אֶל־הַבְּאֵר לִשְׁאֹב וַתִּשְׁאַב לְכָל־גְּמַלָּיו׃ 21 וְהָאִישׁ מִשְׁתָּאֵה לָהּ מַחֲרִישׁ לָדַעַת הַהִצְלִיחַ יְהֹוָה דַּרְכּוֹ אִם־לֹא׃ 22 וַיְהִי כַּאֲשֶׁר כִּלּוּ הַגְּמַלִּים לִשְׁתּוֹת וַיִּקַּח הָאִישׁ נֶזֶם זָהָב בֶּקַע מִשְׁקָלוֹ וּשְׁנֵי צְמִידִים עַל־יָדֶיהָ עֲשָׂרָה זָהָב מִשְׁקָלָם׃ 23 וַיֹּאמֶר בַּת־מִי אַתְּ הַגִּידִי נָא לִי הֲיֵשׁ בֵּית־אָבִיךְ מָקוֹם לָנוּ לָלִין׃ 24 וַתֹּאמֶר אֵלָיו בַּת־בְּתוּאֵל אָנֹכִי בֶּן־מִלְכָּה אֲשֶׁר יָלְדָה לְנָחוֹר׃ 25 וַתֹּאמֶר אֵלָיו גַּם־תֶּבֶן גַּם־מִסְפּוֹא רַב עִמָּנוּ גַּם־מָקוֹם לָלוּן׃ 26 וַיִּקֹּד הָאִישׁ וַיִּשְׁתַּחוּ לַיהֹוָה׃ 27 וַיֹּאמֶר בָּרוּךְ יְהֹוָה אֱלֹהֵי אֲדֹנִי אַבְרָהָם אֲשֶׁר לֹא־עָזַב חַסְדּוֹ וַאֲמִתּוֹ מֵעִם אֲדֹנִי אָנֹכִי בַּדֶּרֶךְ נָחַנִי יְהֹוָה בֵּית אֲחֵי אֲדֹנִי׃ 28 וַתָּרָץ הַנַּעֲרָה וַתַּגֵּד לְבֵית אִמָּהּ כַּדְּבָרִים הָאֵלֶּה׃ 29 וּלְרִבְקָה אָח וּשְׁמוֹ לָבָן וַיָּרָץ לָבָן אֶל־הָאִישׁ הַחוּצָה אֶל־הָעָיִן׃ 30 וַיְהִי ׀ כִּרְאֹת אֶת־הַנֶּזֶם וְאֶת־הַצְּמִדִים עַל־יְדֵי אֲחֹתוֹ וּכְשָׁמְעוֹ אֶת־דִּבְרֵי רִבְקָה אֲחֹתוֹ לֵאמֹר כֹּה־דִבֶּר אֵלַי הָאִישׁ וַיָּבֹא אֶל־הָאִישׁ וְהִנֵּה עֹמֵד עַל־הַגְּמַלִּים עַל־הָעָיִן׃ 31 וַיֹּאמֶר בּוֹא בְּרוּךְ יְהֹוָה לָמָּה תַעֲמֹד בַּחוּץ וְאָנֹכִי פִּנִּיתִי הַבַּיִת וּמָקוֹם לַגְּמַלִּים׃ 32 וַיָּבֹא הָאִישׁ הַבַּיְתָה וַיְפַתַּח הַגְּמַלִּים וַיִּתֵּן תֶּבֶן וּמִסְפּוֹא לַגְּמַלִּים וּמַיִם לִרְחֹץ רַגְלָיו וְרַגְלֵי הָאֲנָשִׁים אֲשֶׁר אִתּוֹ׃ 33 וַיּוּשַׂם וַיִּישַׂם לְפָנָיו לֶאֱכֹל וַיֹּאמֶר לֹא אֹכַל עַד אִם־דִּבַּרְתִּי דְּבָרָי וַיֹּאמֶר דַּבֵּר׃

ᵇ   *Heb.* beqaʻ.
ᶜ   *Heb.* teben, *shredded straw, which in the East is mixed with feed;* cf. v. 32.

until I have told my tale." He said, "Speak, then."

34"I am Abraham's servant," he began. 35"The LORD has greatly blessed my master, and he has become rich: He has given him sheep and cattle, silver and gold, male and female slaves, camels and asses. 36And Sarah, my master's wife, bore my master a son in her old age, and he has assigned to him everything he owns. 37Now my master made me swear, saying, 'You shall not get a wife for my son from the daughters of the Canaanites in whose land I dwell; 38but you shall go to my father's house, to my kindred, and get a wife for my son.' 39And I said to my master, 'What if the woman does not follow me?' 40He replied to me, 'The LORD, whose ways I have followed, will send His angel with you and make your errand successful; and you will get a wife for my son from my kindred, from my father's house. 41Thus only shall you be freed from my adjuration: if, when you come to my kindred, they refuse you—only then shall you be freed from my adjuration.'

42"I came today to the spring, and I said: O LORD, God of my master Abraham, if You would indeed grant success to the errand on which I am engaged! 43As I stand by the spring of water, let the young woman who comes out to draw and to whom I say, 'Please, let me drink a little water from your jar,' 44and who answers, 'You may drink, and I will also draw for your camels'—let her be the wife whom the LORD has decreed for my master's son.' 45I had scarcely finished praying in my heart, when Rebekah came out with her jar on her shoulder, and went down to the spring and drew. And I said to her, 'Please give me a drink.' 46She quickly lowered her jar and said, 'Drink, and I will also water your camels.' So I drank, and she also watered the camels. 47I inquired of her, 'Whose daughter are you?' And she said, 'The daughter of

34 וַיֹּאמַ֑ר עֶ֥בֶד אַבְרָהָ֖ם אָנֹֽכִי׃ 35 וַֽיהֹוָ֞ה בֵּרַ֧ךְ אֶת־אֲדֹנִ֛י מְאֹ֖ד וַיִּגְדָּ֑ל וַיִּתֶּן־ל֗וֹ צֹ֤אן וּבָקָר֙ וְכֶ֣סֶף וְזָהָ֔ב וַעֲבָדִם֙ וּשְׁפָחֹ֔ת וּגְמַלִּ֖ים וַחֲמֹרִֽים׃ 36 וַתֵּ֡לֶד שָׂרָה֩ אֵ֨שֶׁת אֲדֹנִ֤י בֵן֙ לַֽאדֹנִ֔י אַחֲרֵ֖י זִקְנָתָ֑הּ וַיִּתֶּן־ל֖וֹ אֶת־כׇּל־אֲשֶׁר־לֽוֹ׃ 37 וַיַּשְׁבִּעֵ֥נִי אֲדֹנִ֖י לֵאמֹ֑ר לֹֽא־תִקַּ֤ח אִשָּׁה֙ לִבְנִ֔י מִבְּנוֹת֙ הַֽכְּנַעֲנִ֔י אֲשֶׁ֥ר אָנֹכִ֖י יֹשֵׁ֥ב בְּאַרְצֽוֹ׃ 38 אִם־לֹ֧א אֶל־בֵּית־אָבִ֛י תֵּלֵ֖ךְ וְאֶל־מִשְׁפַּחְתִּ֑י וְלָקַחְתָּ֥ אִשָּׁ֖ה לִבְנִֽי׃ 39 וָאֹמַ֖ר אֶל־אֲדֹנִ֑י אֻלַ֛י לֹא־תֵלֵ֥ךְ הָאִשָּׁ֖ה אַחֲרָֽי׃ 40 וַיֹּ֖אמֶר אֵלָ֑י יְהֹוָ֞ה אֲשֶׁר־הִתְהַלַּ֣כְתִּי לְפָנָ֗יו יִשְׁלַ֨ח מַלְאָכ֤וֹ אִתָּךְ֙ וְהִצְלִ֣יחַ דַּרְכֶּ֔ךָ וְלָקַחְתָּ֤ אִשָּׁה֙ לִבְנִ֔י מִמִּשְׁפַּחְתִּ֖י וּמִבֵּ֥ית אָבִֽי׃ 41 אָ֤ז תִּנָּקֶה֙ מֵאָ֣לָתִ֔י כִּ֥י תָב֖וֹא אֶל־מִשְׁפַּחְתִּ֑י וְאִם־לֹ֤א יִתְּנוּ֙ לָ֔ךְ וְהָיִ֥יתָ נָקִ֖י מֵאָלָתִֽי׃ 42 וָאָבֹ֥א הַיּ֖וֹם אֶל־הָעָ֑יִן וָאֹמַ֗ר יְהֹוָה֙ אֱלֹהֵי֙ אֲדֹנִ֣י אַבְרָהָ֔ם אִם־יֶשְׁךָ־נָּא֙ מַצְלִ֣יחַ דַּרְכִּ֔י אֲשֶׁ֥ר אָנֹכִ֖י הֹלֵ֥ךְ עָלֶֽיהָ׃ 43 הִנֵּ֛ה אָנֹכִ֥י נִצָּ֖ב עַל־עֵ֣ין הַמָּ֑יִם וְהָיָ֤ה הָֽעַלְמָה֙ הַיֹּצֵ֣את לִשְׁאֹ֔ב וְאָמַרְתִּ֣י אֵלֶ֔יהָ הַשְׁקִֽינִי־נָ֥א מְעַט־מַ֖יִם מִכַּדֵּֽךְ׃ 44 וְאָמְרָ֤ה אֵלַי֙ גַּם־אַתָּ֣ה שְׁתֵ֔ה וְגַ֥ם לִגְמַלֶּ֖יךָ אֶשְׁאָ֑ב הִ֣וא הָֽאִשָּׁ֔ה אֲשֶׁר־הֹכִ֥יחַ יְהֹוָ֖ה לְבֶן־אֲדֹנִֽי׃ 45 אֲנִ֩י טֶ֨רֶם אֲכַלֶּ֜ה לְדַבֵּ֣ר אֶל־לִבִּ֗י וְהִנֵּ֨ה רִבְקָ֤ה יֹצֵאת֙ וְכַדָּ֣הּ עַל־שִׁכְמָ֔הּ וַתֵּ֥רֶד הָעַ֖יְנָה וַתִּשְׁאָ֑ב וָאֹמַ֥ר אֵלֶ֖יהָ הַשְׁקִ֥ינִי נָֽא׃ 46 וַתְּמַהֵ֗ר וַתּ֤וֹרֶד כַּדָּהּ֙ מֵֽעָלֶ֔יהָ וַתֹּ֣אמֶר שְׁתֵ֔ה וְגַם־גְּמַלֶּ֖יךָ אַשְׁקֶ֑ה וָאֵ֕שְׁתְּ וְגַ֥ם הַגְּמַלִּ֖ים הִשְׁקָֽתָה׃ 47 וָאֶשְׁאַ֣ל אֹתָ֗הּ וָאֹמַר֙ בַּת־מִ֣י אַ֔תְּ וַתֹּ֗אמֶר בַּת־בְּתוּאֵל֙ בֶּן־נָח֔וֹר אֲשֶׁ֥ר יָֽלְדָה־לּ֖וֹ

Bethuel, son of Nahor, whom Milcah bore to him.' And I put the ring on her nose and the bands on her arms. [48]Then I bowed low in homage to the LORD and blessed the LORD, the God of my master Abraham, who led me on the right way to get the daughter of my master's brother for his son. [49]And now, if you mean to treat my master with true kindness, tell me; and if not, tell me also, that I may turn right or left."

[50]Then Laban and Bethuel answered, "The matter was decreed by the LORD; we cannot speak to you bad or good. [51]Here is Rebekah before you; take her and go, and let her be a wife to your master's son, as the LORD has spoken." [52]When Abraham's servant heard their words, he bowed low to the ground before the LORD. [53]The servant brought out objects of silver and gold, and garments, and gave them to Rebekah; and he gave presents to her brother and her mother. [54]Then he and the men with him ate and drank, and they spent the night. When they arose next morning, he said, "Give me leave to go to my master." [55]But her brother and her mother said, "Let the maiden remain with us [d]-some ten days;-[d] then you may go." [56]He said to them, "Do not delay me, now that the LORD has made my errand successful. Give me leave that I may go to my master." [57]And they said, "Let us call the girl and ask for her reply." [58]They called Rebekah and said to her, "Will you go with this man?" And she said, "I will." [59]So they sent off their sister Rebekah and her nurse along with Abraham's servant and his men. [60]And they blessed Rebekah and said to her,

"O sister!
May you grow
Into thousands of myriads;
May your offspring seize
The gates of their foes."

[61]Then Rebekah and her maids arose, mounted

מִלְכָּה וָאָשִׂם הַנֶּ֫זֶם עַל־אַפָּהּ וְהַצְּמִידִים עַל־יָדֶיהָ: [48]וָאֶקֹּד וָאֶֽשְׁתַּחֲוֶה לַֽיהֹוָה וָאֲבָרֵךְ אֶת־יְהֹוָה אֱלֹהֵי אֲדֹנִי אַבְרָהָם אֲשֶׁר הִנְחַ֫נִי בְּדֶרֶךְ אֱמֶת לָקַחַת אֶת־בַּת־אֲחִי אֲדֹנִי לִבְנֽוֹ: [49]וְעַתָּה אִם־יֶשְׁכֶם עֹשִׂים חֶסֶד וֶאֱמֶת אֶת־אֲדֹנִי הַגִּידוּ לִי וְאִם־לֹא הַגִּידוּ לִי וְאֶפְנֶה עַל־יָמִין אוֹ עַל־שְׂמֹֽאל:

[50]וַיַּעַן לָבָן וּבְתוּאֵל וַיֹּֽאמְרוּ מֵֽיְהֹוָה יָצָא הַדָּבָר לֹא נוּכַל דַּבֵּר אֵלֶיךָ רַע אוֹ־טֽוֹב: [51]הִנֵּֽה־רִבְקָה לְפָנֶיךָ קַח וָלֵךְ וּתְהִי אִשָּׁה לְבֶן־אֲדֹנֶיךָ כַּֽאֲשֶׁר דִּבֶּר יְהֹוָֽה: [52]וַיְהִי כַּֽאֲשֶׁר שָׁמַע עֶבֶד אַבְרָהָם אֶת־דִּבְרֵיהֶם וַיִּשְׁתַּחוּ אַ֫רְצָה לַֽיהֹוָֽה: [53]וַיּוֹצֵא הָעֶבֶד כְּלֵי־כֶסֶף וּכְלֵי זָהָב וּבְגָדִים וַיִּתֵּן לְרִבְקָה וּמִגְדָּנֹת נָתַן לְאָחִיהָ וּלְאִמָּֽהּ: [54]וַיֹּֽאכְלוּ וַיִּשְׁתּוּ ה֫וּא וְהָֽאֲנָשִׁים אֲשֶׁר־עִמּוֹ וַיָּלִינוּ וַיָּקוּמוּ בַבֹּקֶר וַיֹּאמֶר שַׁלְּחֻנִי לַֽאדֹנִֽי: [55]וַיֹּאמֶר אָחִיהָ וְאִמָּהּ תֵּשֵׁב הַנַּֽעֲרָ֫ אִתָּנוּ יָמִים אוֹ עָשׂוֹר אַחַר תֵּלֵֽךְ: [56]וַיֹּאמֶר אֲלֵהֶם אַל־תְּאַֽחֲרוּ אֹתִי וַֽיהֹוָה הִצְלִיחַ דַּרְכִּי שַׁלְּחוּנִי וְאֵֽלְכָה לַֽאדֹנִֽי: [57]וַיֹּֽאמְרוּ נִקְרָא לַֽנַּֽעֲרָ וְנִשְׁאֲלָה אֶת־פִּֽיהָ: [58]וַיִּקְרְאוּ לְרִבְקָה וַיֹּֽאמְרוּ אֵלֶיהָ הֲתֵֽלְכִי עִם־הָאִישׁ הַזֶּה וַתֹּאמֶר אֵלֵֽךְ: [59]וַֽיְשַׁלְּחוּ אֶת־רִבְקָה אֲחֹתָם וְאֶת־מֵֽנִקְתָּהּ וְאֶת־עֶבֶד אַבְרָהָם וְאֶת־אֲנָשָֽׁיו: [60]וַיְבָֽרְכוּ אֶת־רִבְקָה וַיֹּאמְרוּ לָהּ

אֲחֹתֵנוּ

אַתְּ הֲיִי

לְאַלְפֵי רְבָבָה

וְיִירַשׁ זַרְעֵךְ

אֵת שַׁעַר שֹֽׂנְאָֽיו:

[61]וַתָּקָם רִבְקָה וְנַֽעֲרֹתֶיהָ וַתִּרְכַּבְנָה עַל־הַגְּמַלִּים וַתֵּלַכְנָה אַֽחֲרֵי הָאִישׁ וַיִּקַּח הָעֶבֶד אֶת־רִבְקָה וַיֵּלַֽךְ:

the camels, and followed the man. So the servant took Rebekah and went his way.

⁶²Isaac had just come back from the vicinity of Beer-lahai-roi, for he was settled in the region of the Negeb. ⁶³And Isaac went out walkingᵉ in the field toward evening and, looking up, he saw camels approaching. ⁶⁴Raising her eyes, Rebekah saw Isaac. She alighted from the camel ⁶⁵and said to the servant, "Who is that man walking in the field toward us?" And the servant said, "That is my master." So she took her veil and covered herself. ⁶⁶The servant told Isaac all the things that he had done. ⁶⁷Isaac then brought her into the tent of his mother Sarah, and he took Rebekah as his wife. Isaac loved her, and thus found comfort after his mother's death.

25 Abraham took another wife, whose name was Keturah. ²She bore him Zimran, Jokshan, Medan, Midian, Ishbak, and Shuah. ³Jokshan begot Sheba and Dedan. The descendants of Dedan were the Asshurim, the Letushim, and the Leummim. ⁴The descendants of Midian were Ephah, Epher, Enoch,ᵃ Abida, and Eldaah. All these were descendants of Keturah. ⁵Abraham willed all that he owned to Isaac; ⁶but to Abraham's sons by concubines Abraham gave gifts while he was still living, and he sent them away from his son Isaac eastward, to the land of the East.

⁷This was the total span of Abraham's life: one hundred and seventy-five years. ⁸And Abraham breathed his last, dying at a good ripe age, old and contented; and he was gathered to his kin. ⁹His sons Isaac and Ishmael buried him in the cave of Machpelah, in the field of Ephron son of Zohar the Hittite, facing Mamre, ¹⁰the field

---

e   Others "to meditate"; meaning of Heb. uncertain.

a   Or "Hanoch."

---

62 וְיִצְחָק֙ בָּ֣א מִבּ֔וֹא בְּאֵ֥ר לַחַ֖י רֹאִ֑י וְה֥וּא יוֹשֵׁ֖ב בְּאֶ֥רֶץ הַנֶּֽגֶב׃ 63 וַיֵּצֵ֥א יִצְחָ֛ק לָשׂ֥וּחַ בַּשָּׂדֶ֖ה לִפְנ֣וֹת עָ֑רֶב וַיִּשָּׂ֤א עֵינָיו֙ וַיַּ֔רְא וְהִנֵּ֥ה גְמַלִּ֖ים בָּאִֽים׃ 64 וַתִּשָּׂ֤א רִבְקָה֙ אֶת־עֵינֶ֔יהָ וַתֵּ֖רֶא אֶת־יִצְחָ֑ק וַתִּפֹּ֖ל מֵעַ֥ל הַגָּמָֽל׃ 65 וַתֹּ֣אמֶר אֶל־הָעֶ֗בֶד מִֽי־הָאִ֤ישׁ הַלָּזֶה֙ הַהֹלֵ֤ךְ בַּשָּׂדֶה֙ לִקְרָאתֵ֔נוּ וַיֹּ֥אמֶר הָעֶ֖בֶד ה֣וּא אֲדֹנִ֑י וַתִּקַּ֥ח הַצָּעִ֖יף וַתִּתְכָּֽס׃ 66 וַיְסַפֵּ֥ר הָעֶ֖בֶד לְיִצְחָ֑ק אֵ֥ת כָּל־הַדְּבָרִ֖ים אֲשֶׁ֥ר עָשָֽׂה׃ 67 וַיְבִאֶ֣הָ יִצְחָ֗ק הָאֹ֙הֱלָה֙ שָׂרָ֣ה אִמּ֔וֹ וַיִּקַּ֧ח אֶת־רִבְקָ֛ה וַתְּהִי־ל֥וֹ לְאִשָּׁ֖ה וַיֶּאֱהָבֶ֑הָ וַיִּנָּחֵ֥ם יִצְחָ֖ק אַחֲרֵ֥י אִמּֽוֹ׃ פ

כה וַיֹּ֧סֶף אַבְרָהָ֛ם וַיִּקַּ֥ח אִשָּׁ֖ה וּשְׁמָ֥הּ קְטוּרָֽה׃ 2 וַתֵּ֣לֶד ל֗וֹ אֶת־זִמְרָן֙ וְאֶת־יָקְשָׁ֔ן וְאֶת־מְדָ֖ן וְאֶת־מִדְיָ֑ן וְאֶת־יִשְׁבָּ֖ק וְאֶת־שֽׁוּחַ׃ 3 וְיָקְשָׁ֣ן יָלַ֔ד אֶת־שְׁבָ֖א וְאֶת־דְּדָ֑ן וּבְנֵ֣י דְדָ֗ן הָי֛וּ אַשּׁוּרִ֥ם וּלְטוּשִׁ֖ים וּלְאֻמִּֽים׃ 4 וּבְנֵ֣י מִדְיָ֗ן עֵיפָ֤ה וָעֵ֙פֶר֙ וַחֲנֹ֔ךְ וַאֲבִידָ֖ע וְאֶלְדָּעָ֑ה כָּל־אֵ֖לֶּה בְּנֵ֥י קְטוּרָֽה׃ 5 וַיִּתֵּ֧ן אַבְרָהָ֛ם אֶת־כָּל־אֲשֶׁר־ל֖וֹ לְיִצְחָֽק׃ 6 וְלִבְנֵ֤י הַפִּֽילַגְשִׁים֙ אֲשֶׁ֣ר לְאַבְרָהָ֔ם נָתַ֧ן אַבְרָהָ֛ם מַתָּנֹ֖ת וַֽיְשַׁלְּחֵ֡ם מֵעַ֣ל יִצְחָ֣ק בְּנ֗וֹ בְּעוֹדֶ֣נּוּ חַ֔י קֵ֖דְמָה אֶל־אֶ֥רֶץ קֶֽדֶם׃ 7 וְאֵ֗לֶּה יְמֵ֛י שְׁנֵֽי־חַיֵּ֥י אַבְרָהָ֖ם אֲשֶׁר־חָ֑י מְאַ֥ת שָׁנָ֛ה וְשִׁבְעִ֥ים שָׁנָ֖ה וְחָמֵ֥שׁ שָׁנִֽים׃ 8 וַיִּגְוַ֨ע וַיָּ֧מָת אַבְרָהָ֛ם בְּשֵׂיבָ֥ה טוֹבָ֖ה זָקֵ֣ן וְשָׂבֵ֑עַ וַיֵּאָ֖סֶף אֶל־עַמָּֽיו׃ 9 וַיִּקְבְּר֨וּ אֹת֜וֹ יִצְחָ֤ק וְיִשְׁמָעֵאל֙ בָּנָ֔יו אֶל־מְעָרַ֖ת הַמַּכְפֵּלָ֑ה אֶל־שְׂדֵ֞ה עֶפְרֹ֤ן בֶּן־צֹ֙חַר֙ הַֽחִתִּ֔י אֲשֶׁ֖ר עַל־פְּנֵ֥י מַמְרֵֽא׃ 10 הַשָּׂדֶ֛ה אֲשֶׁר־קָנָ֥ה

that Abraham had bought from the Hittites; there Abraham was buried, and Sarah his wife. [11]After the death of Abraham, God blessed his son Isaac. And Isaac settled near Beer-lahai-roi.

[12]This is the line of Ishmael, Abraham's son, whom Hagar the Egyptian, Sarah's slave, bore to Abraham. [13]These are the names of the sons of Ishmael, by their names, in the order of their birth: Nebaioth, the first-born of Ishmael, Kedar, Adbeel, Mibsam, [14]Mishma, Dumah, Massa, [15]Hadad, Tema, Jetur, Naphish, and Kedmah. [16]These are the sons of Ishmael and these are their names by their villages and by their encampments: twelve chieftains of as many tribes.—[17]These were the years of the life of Ishmael: one hundred and thirty-seven years; then he breathed his last and died, and was gathered to his kin.—[18]They dwelt from Havilah, by Shur, which is close to Egypt, all the way to Asshur; they camped alongside all their kinsmen.

TOLEDOT

[19]This is the story of Isaac, son of Abraham. Abraham begot Isaac. [20]Isaac was forty years old when he took to wife Rebekah, daughter of Bethuel the Aramean of Paddan-aram, sister of Laban the Aramean. [21]Isaac pleaded with the LORD on behalf of his wife, because she was barren; and the LORD responded to his plea, and his wife Rebekah conceived. [22]But the children struggled in her womb, and she said, "If so, why do I exist?"[b] She went to inquire of the LORD, [23]and the LORD answered her,

"Two nations are in your womb,
Two separate peoples shall issue from your
    body;
One people shall be mightier than the other,
And the older shall serve the younger."

[24]When her time to give birth was at hand, there

אַבְרָהָם מֵאֵת בְּנֵי־חֵת שָׁמָּה קֻבַּר
אַבְרָהָם וְשָׂרָה אִשְׁתּוֹ: 11 וַיְהִי אַחֲרֵי מוֹת
אַבְרָהָם וַיְבָרֶךְ אֱלֹהִים אֶת־יִצְחָק בְּנוֹ
וַיֵּשֶׁב יִצְחָק עִם־בְּאֵר לַחַי רֹאִי: ס
12 וְאֵלֶּה תֹּלְדֹת יִשְׁמָעֵאל בֶּן־אַבְרָהָם
אֲשֶׁר יָלְדָה הָגָר הַמִּצְרִית שִׁפְחַת שָׂרָה
לְאַבְרָהָם: 13 וְאֵלֶּה שְׁמוֹת בְּנֵי יִשְׁמָעֵאל
בִּשְׁמֹתָם לְתוֹלְדֹתָם בְּכֹר יִשְׁמָעֵאל נְבָיֹת
וְקֵדָר וְאַדְבְּאֵל וּמִבְשָׂם: 14 וּמִשְׁמָע וְדוּמָה
וּמַשָּׂא: 15 חֲדַד וְתֵימָא יְטוּר נָפִישׁ
וָקֵדְמָה: 16 אֵלֶּה הֵם בְּנֵי יִשְׁמָעֵאל וְאֵלֶּה
שְׁמֹתָם בְּחַצְרֵיהֶם וּבְטִירֹתָם שְׁנֵים־עָשָׂר
נְשִׂיאִם לְאֻמֹּתָם: 17 וְאֵלֶּה שְׁנֵי חַיֵּי
יִשְׁמָעֵאל מְאַת שָׁנָה וּשְׁלֹשִׁים שָׁנָה וְשֶׁבַע
שָׁנִים וַיִּגְוַע וַיָּמָת וַיֵּאָסֶף אֶל־עַמָּיו:
18 וַיִּשְׁכְּנוּ מֵחֲוִילָה עַד־שׁוּר אֲשֶׁר עַל־פְּנֵי
מִצְרַיִם בֹּאֲכָה אַשּׁוּרָה עַל־פְּנֵי כָל־אֶחָיו
נָפָל: פ

תולדות

19 וְאֵלֶּה תּוֹלְדֹת יִצְחָק בֶּן־אַבְרָהָם
אַבְרָהָם הוֹלִיד אֶת־יִצְחָק: 20 וַיְהִי יִצְחָק
בֶּן־אַרְבָּעִים שָׁנָה בְּקַחְתּוֹ אֶת־רִבְקָה בַּת־
בְּתוּאֵל הָאֲרַמִּי מִפַּדַּן אֲרָם אֲחוֹת לָבָן
הָאֲרַמִּי לוֹ לְאִשָּׁה: 21 וַיֶּעְתַּר יִצְחָק לַיהוָה
לְנֹכַח אִשְׁתּוֹ כִּי עֲקָרָה הִוא וַיֵּעָתֶר לוֹ
יְהוָה וַתַּהַר רִבְקָה אִשְׁתּוֹ: 22 וַיִּתְרֹצֲצוּ
הַבָּנִים בְּקִרְבָּהּ וַתֹּאמֶר אִם־כֵּן לָמָּה זֶּה
אָנֹכִי וַתֵּלֶךְ לִדְרֹשׁ אֶת־יְהוָה: 23 וַיֹּאמֶר
יְהוָה לָהּ

שְׁנֵי גיים גוֹיִם בְּבִטְנֵךְ
וּשְׁנֵי לְאֻמִּים מִמֵּעַיִךְ יִפָּרֵדוּ
וּלְאֹם מִלְאֹם יֶאֱמָץ
וְרַב יַעֲבֹד צָעִיר:
24 וַיִּמְלְאוּ יָמֶיהָ לָלֶדֶת וְהִנֵּה תוֹמִם*

*חסר א׳ ו׳   v. 24.

_b_ _Meaning of Heb. uncertain._

were twins in her womb. ²⁵The first one emerged red, like a hairy mantle all over; so they named him Esau.*c* ²⁶Then his brother emerged, holding on to the heel of Esau; so they named him Jacob.*d* Isaac was sixty years old when they were born.

²⁷When the boys grew up, Esau became a skillful hunter, a man of the outdoors; but Jacob was a mild man who stayed in camp. ²⁸Isaac favored Esau because *e*-he had a taste for game;-*e* but Rebekah favored Jacob. ²⁹Once when Jacob was cooking a stew, Esau came in from the open, famished. ³⁰And Esau said to Jacob, "Give me some of that red stuff to gulp down, for I am famished"—which is why he was named Edom.*f* ³¹Jacob said, "First sell me your birthright." ³²And Esau said, "I am at the point of death, so of what use is my birthright to me?" ³³But Jacob said, "Swear to me first." So he swore to him, and sold his birthright to Jacob. ³⁴Jacob then gave Esau bread and lentil stew; he ate and drank, and he rose and went away. Thus did Esau spurn the birthright.

26 There was a famine in the land—aside from the previous famine that had occurred in the days of Abraham—and Isaac went to Abimelech, king of the Philistines, in Gerar. ²The LORD had appeared to him and said, "Do not go down to Egypt; stay in the land which I point out to you. ³Reside in this land, and I will be with you and bless you; I will assign all these lands to you and to your heirs, fulfilling the oath that I swore to your father Abraham. ⁴I will make your heirs as numerous as the stars of heaven, and assign to your heirs all these lands, so that all the nations of the earth shall bless themselves by your heirs—⁵inasmuch as Abra-

25 וַיֵּצֵ֤א הָרִאשׁוֹן֙ אַדְמוֹנִ֔י כֻּלּ֖וֹ כְּאַדֶּ֣רֶת שֵׂעָ֑ר וַיִּקְרְא֥וּ שְׁמ֖וֹ עֵשָֽׂו׃ 26 וְאַֽחֲרֵי־כֵ֞ן יָצָ֣א אָחִ֗יו וְיָד֤וֹ אֹחֶ֙זֶת֙ בַּעֲקֵ֣ב עֵשָׂ֔ו וַיִּקְרָ֥א שְׁמ֖וֹ יַעֲקֹ֑ב וְיִצְחָ֛ק בֶּן־שִׁשִּׁ֥ים שָׁנָ֖ה בְּלֶ֥דֶת אֹתָֽם׃ 27 וַֽיִּגְדְּלוּ֙ הַנְּעָרִ֔ים וַיְהִ֣י עֵשָׂ֗ו אִ֛ישׁ יֹדֵ֥עַ צַ֖יִד אִ֣ישׁ שָׂדֶ֑ה וְיַעֲקֹב֙ אִ֣ישׁ תָּ֔ם יֹשֵׁ֖ב אֹהָלִֽים׃ 28 וַיֶּאֱהַ֥ב יִצְחָ֛ק אֶת־עֵשָׂ֖ו כִּי־צַ֣יִד בְּפִ֑יו וְרִבְקָ֖ה אֹהֶ֥בֶת אֶֽת־יַעֲקֹֽב׃ 29 וַיָּ֥זֶד יַעֲקֹ֖ב נָזִ֑יד וַיָּבֹ֥א עֵשָׂ֛ו מִן־הַשָּׂדֶ֖ה וְה֥וּא עָיֵֽף׃ 30 וַיֹּ֨אמֶר עֵשָׂ֜ו אֶֽל־יַעֲקֹ֗ב הַלְעִיטֵ֤נִי נָא֙ מִן־הָֽאָדֹ֤ם הָאָדֹם֙ הַזֶּ֔ה כִּ֥י עָיֵ֖ף אָנֹ֑כִי עַל־כֵּ֥ן קָרָֽא־שְׁמ֖וֹ אֱדֽוֹם׃ 31 וַיֹּ֖אמֶר יַעֲקֹ֑ב מִכְרָ֥ה כַיּ֛וֹם אֶת־בְּכֹרָֽתְךָ֖ לִֽי׃ 32 וַיֹּ֣אמֶר עֵשָׂ֗ו הִנֵּ֛ה אָנֹכִ֥י הוֹלֵ֖ךְ לָמ֑וּת וְלָמָּה־זֶּ֥ה לִ֖י בְּכֹרָֽה׃ 33 וַיֹּ֣אמֶר יַעֲקֹ֗ב הִשָּׁ֤בְעָה לִּי֙ כַּיּ֔וֹם וַיִּשָּׁבַ֖ע ל֑וֹ וַיִּמְכֹּ֥ר אֶת־בְּכֹרָת֖וֹ לְיַעֲקֹֽב׃ 34 וְיַעֲקֹ֞ב נָתַ֣ן לְעֵשָׂ֗ו לֶ֚חֶם וּנְזִ֣יד עֲדָשִׁ֔ים וַיֹּ֣אכַל וַיֵּ֔שְׁתְּ וַיָּ֖קָם וַיֵּלַ֑ךְ וַיִּ֥בֶז עֵשָׂ֖ו אֶת־הַבְּכֹרָֽה׃ ס

כו וַיְהִ֤י רָעָב֙ בָּאָ֔רֶץ מִלְּבַד֙ הָרָעָ֣ב הָרִאשׁ֔וֹן אֲשֶׁ֥ר הָיָ֖ה בִּימֵ֣י אַבְרָהָ֑ם וַיֵּ֧לֶךְ יִצְחָ֛ק אֶל־אֲבִימֶ֥לֶךְ מֶֽלֶךְ־פְּלִשְׁתִּ֖ים גְּרָֽרָה׃ 2 וַיֵּרָ֤א אֵלָיו֙ יְהֹוָ֔ה וַיֹּ֖אמֶר אַל־תֵּרֵ֣ד מִצְרָ֑יְמָה שְׁכֹ֣ן בָּאָ֔רֶץ אֲשֶׁ֖ר אֹמַ֥ר אֵלֶֽיךָ׃ 3 גּ֚וּר בָּאָ֣רֶץ הַזֹּ֔את וְאֶֽהְיֶ֥ה עִמְּךָ֖ וַאֲבָרְכֶ֑ךָּ כִּֽי־לְךָ֣ וּֽלְזַרְעֲךָ֗ אֶתֵּן֙ אֶת־כׇּל־הָֽאֲרָצֹ֣ת הָאֵ֔ל וַהֲקִֽמֹתִי֙ אֶת־הַשְּׁבֻעָ֔ה אֲשֶׁ֥ר נִשְׁבַּ֖עְתִּי לְאַבְרָהָ֥ם אָבִֽיךָ׃ 4 וְהִרְבֵּיתִ֤י אֶֽת־זַרְעֲךָ֙ כְּכוֹכְבֵ֣י הַשָּׁמַ֔יִם וְנָתַתִּ֣י לְזַרְעֲךָ֔ אֵ֥ת כׇּל־הָאֲרָצֹ֖ת הָאֵ֑ל וְהִתְבָּרְכ֣וּ בְזַרְעֲךָ֔ כֹּ֖ל גּוֹיֵ֥י הָאָֽרֶץ׃ 5 עֵ֕קֶב אֲשֶׁר־שָׁמַ֥ע

---

c Synonym of "Seir," play on Heb. *se'ar* "hair."
d Play on Heb. *'aqeb* "heel."
e-e Lit. "game was in his mouth."
f Play on Heb. *'adom* "red."

ham obeyed Me and kept My charge: My commandments, My laws, and My teachings."

6So Isaac stayed in Gerar. 7When the men of the place asked him about his wife, he said, "She is my sister," for he was afraid to say "my wife," thinking, "The men of the place might kill me on account of Rebekah, for she is beautiful." 8When some time had passed, Abimelech king of the Philistines, looking out of the window, saw Isaac fondling his wife Rebekah. 9Abimelech sent for Isaac and said, "So she is your wife! Why then did you say: 'She is my sister?'" Isaac said to him, "Because I thought I might lose my life on account of her." 10Abimelech said, "What have you done to us! One of the people might have lain with your wife, and you would have brought guilt upon us." 11Abimelech then charged all the people, saying, "Anyone who molests this man or his wife shall be put to death."

12Isaac sowed in that land and reaped a hundredfold the same year. The LORD blessed him, 13and the man grew richer and richer until he was very wealthy: 14he acquired flocks and herds, and a large household, so that the Philistines envied him. 15And the Philistines stopped up all the wells which his father's servants had dug in the days of his father Abraham, filling them with earth. 16And Abimelech said to Isaac, "Go away from us, for you have become far too big for us."

17So Isaac departed from there and encamped in the wadi of Gerar, where he settled. 18Isaac dug anew the wells which had been dug in the days of his father Abraham and which the Philistines had stopped up after Abraham's death; and he gave them the same names that his father had given them. 19But when Isaac's servants, digging in the wadi, found there a well of spring water, 20the herdsmen of Gerar quarreled with Isaac's herdsmen, saying, "The water is ours."

אַבְרָהָ֖ם בְּקֹלִ֑י וַיִּשְׁמֹר֙ מִשְׁמַרְתִּ֔י מִצְוֺתַ֖י חֻקּוֹתַ֥י וְתוֹרֹתָֽי׃

6וַיֵּ֥שֶׁב יִצְחָ֖ק בִּגְרָֽר׃ 7וַֽיִּשְׁאֲל֞וּ אַנְשֵׁ֤י הַמָּקוֹם֙ לְאִשְׁתּ֔וֹ וַיֹּ֖אמֶר אֲחֹ֣תִי הִ֑וא כִּ֤י יָרֵא֙ לֵאמֹ֣ר אִשְׁתִּ֔י פֶּן־יַֽהַרְגֻ֜נִי אַנְשֵׁ֤י הַמָּקוֹם֙ עַל־רִבְקָ֔ה כִּֽי־טוֹבַ֥ת מַרְאֶ֖ה הִֽיא׃ 8וַיְהִ֗י כִּ֣י אָֽרְכוּ־ל֥וֹ שָׁם֙ הַיָּמִ֔ים וַיַּשְׁקֵ֗ף אֲבִימֶ֙לֶךְ֙ מֶ֣לֶךְ פְּלִשְׁתִּ֔ים בְּעַ֖ד הַֽחַלּ֑וֹן וַיַּ֗רְא וְהִנֵּ֤ה יִצְחָק֙ מְצַחֵ֔ק אֵ֖ת רִבְקָ֥ה אִשְׁתּֽוֹ׃ 9וַיִּקְרָ֨א אֲבִימֶ֜לֶךְ לְיִצְחָ֗ק וַיֹּ֙אמֶר֙ אַ֣ךְ הִנֵּ֤ה אִשְׁתְּךָ֙ הִ֔וא וְאֵ֥יךְ אָמַ֖רְתָּ אֲחֹ֣תִי הִ֑וא וַיֹּ֤אמֶר אֵלָיו֙ יִצְחָ֔ק כִּ֣י אָמַ֔רְתִּי פֶּן־אָמ֖וּת עָלֶֽיהָ׃ 10וַיֹּ֣אמֶר אֲבִימֶ֔לֶךְ מַה־זֹּ֖את עָשִׂ֣יתָ לָּ֑נוּ כִּ֠מְעַ֠ט שָׁכַ֞ב אַחַ֤ד הָעָם֙ אֶת־אִשְׁתֶּ֔ךָ וְהֵבֵאתָ֥ עָלֵ֖ינוּ אָשָֽׁם׃ 11וַיְצַ֣ו אֲבִימֶ֔לֶךְ אֶת־כׇּל־הָעָ֖ם לֵאמֹ֑ר הַנֹּגֵ֜עַ בָּאִ֥ישׁ הַזֶּ֛ה וּבְאִשְׁתּ֖וֹ מ֥וֹת יוּמָֽת׃

12וַיִּזְרַ֤ע יִצְחָק֙ בָּאָ֣רֶץ הַהִ֔וא וַיִּמְצָ֛א בַּשָּׁנָ֥ה הַהִ֖וא מֵאָ֣ה שְׁעָרִ֑ים וַֽיְבָרְכֵ֖הוּ יְהֹוָֽה׃ 13וַיִּגְדַּ֖ל הָאִ֑ישׁ וַיֵּ֤לֶךְ הָלוֹךְ֙ וְגָדֵ֔ל עַ֥ד כִּֽי־גָדַ֖ל מְאֹֽד׃ 14וַֽיְהִי־ל֤וֹ מִקְנֵה־צֹאן֙ וּמִקְנֵ֣ה בָקָ֔ר וַעֲבֻדָּ֖ה רַבָּ֑ה וַיְקַנְא֥וּ אֹת֖וֹ פְּלִשְׁתִּֽים׃ 15וְכׇל־הַבְּאֵרֹ֗ת אֲשֶׁ֤ר חָֽפְרוּ֙ עַבְדֵ֣י אָבִ֔יו בִּימֵ֖י אַבְרָהָ֣ם אָבִ֑יו סִתְּמ֣וּם פְּלִשְׁתִּ֔ים וַיְמַלְא֖וּם עָפָֽר׃ 16וַיֹּ֥אמֶר אֲבִימֶ֖לֶךְ אֶל־יִצְחָ֑ק לֵ֚ךְ מֵֽעִמָּ֔נוּ כִּֽי־עָצַ֥מְתָּ מִמֶּ֖נּוּ מְאֹֽד׃

17וַיֵּ֥לֶךְ מִשָּׁ֖ם יִצְחָ֑ק וַיִּ֥חַן בְּנַֽחַל־גְּרָ֖ר וַיֵּ֥שֶׁב שָֽׁם׃ 18וַיָּ֨שׇׁב יִצְחָ֜ק וַיַּחְפֹּ֣ר ׀ אֶת־בְּאֵרֹ֣ת הַמַּ֗יִם אֲשֶׁ֤ר חָֽפְרוּ֙ בִּימֵי֙ אַבְרָהָ֣ם אָבִ֔יו וַיְסַתְּמ֣וּם פְּלִשְׁתִּ֔ים אַחֲרֵ֖י מ֣וֹת אַבְרָהָ֑ם וַיִּקְרָ֤א לָהֶן֙ שֵׁמ֔וֹת כַּשֵּׁמֹ֕ת אֲשֶׁר־קָרָ֥א לָהֶ֖ן אָבִֽיו׃ 19וַיַּחְפְּר֥וּ עַבְדֵֽי־יִצְחָ֖ק בַּנָּ֑חַל וַיִּ֨מְצְאוּ־שָׁ֔ם בְּאֵ֖ר מַ֥יִם חַיִּֽים׃ 20וַיָּרִ֜יבוּ רֹעֵ֣י גְרָ֗ר עִם־רֹעֵ֥י יִצְחָ֛ק לֵאמֹ֖ר לָ֣נוּ הַמָּ֑יִם

He named that well Esek,ᵃ because they contended with him. ²¹And when they dug another well, they disputed over that one also; so he named it Sitnah.ᵇ ²²He moved from there and dug yet another well, and they did not quarrel over it; so he called it Rehoboth, saying, "Now at last the LORD has granted us ample spaceᶜ to increase in the land."

²³From there he went up to Beer-sheba. ²⁴That night the LORD appeared to him and said, "I am the God of your father Abraham. Fear not, for I am with you, and I will bless you and increase your offspring for the sake of My servant Abraham." ²⁵So he built an altar there and invoked the LORD by name. Isaac pitched his tent there and his servants started digging a well. ²⁶And Abimelech came to him from Gerar, with Ahuzzath his councilor and Phicol chief of his troops. ²⁷Isaac said to them, "Why have you come to me, seeing that you have been hostile to me and have driven me away from you?" ²⁸And they said, "We now see plainly that the LORD has been with you, and we thought: Let there be a sworn treaty between our two parties, between you and us. Let us make a pact with you ²⁹that you will not do us harm, just as we have not molested you but have always dealt kindly with you and sent you away in peace. From now on, be you blessed of the LORD!" ³⁰Then he made for them a feast, and they ate and drank.

³¹Early in the morning, they exchanged oaths. Isaac then bade them farewell, and they departed from him in peace. ³²That same day Isaac's servants came and told him about the well they had dug, and said to him, "We have found water!" ³³He named it Shibah;ᵈ therefore the name of the city is Beer-sheba to this day.

וַיִּקְרָ֤א שֵֽׁם־הַבְּאֵר֙ עֵ֔שֶׂק כִּ֥י הִֽתְעַשְּׂק֖וּ עִמּ֑וֹ ²¹ וַֽיַּחְפְּרוּ֙ בְּאֵ֣ר אַחֶ֔רֶת וַיָּרִ֖יבוּ גַּם־עָלֶ֑יהָ וַיִּקְרָ֥א שְׁמָ֖הּ שִׂטְנָֽה: ²² וַיַּעְתֵּ֣ק מִשָּׁ֗ם וַיַּחְפֹּר֙ בְּאֵ֣ר אַחֶ֔רֶת וְלֹ֥א רָב֖וּ עָלֶ֑יהָ וַיִּקְרָ֤א שְׁמָהּ֙ רְחֹב֔וֹת וַיֹּ֗אמֶר כִּֽי־עַתָּ֞ה הִרְחִ֧יב יְהוָ֛ה לָ֖נוּ וּפָרִ֥ינוּ בָאָֽרֶץ: ²³ וַיַּ֥עַל מִשָּׁ֖ם בְּאֵ֥ר שָֽׁבַע: ²⁴ וַיֵּרָ֨א אֵלָ֤יו יְהוָה֙ בַּלַּ֣יְלָה הַה֔וּא וַיֹּ֕אמֶר אָֽנֹכִ֕י אֱלֹהֵ֖י אַבְרָהָ֣ם אָבִ֑יךָ אַל־תִּירָא֙ כִּֽי־אִתְּךָ֣ אָנֹ֔כִי וּבֵֽרַכְתִּ֙יךָ֙ וְהִרְבֵּיתִ֣י אֶֽת־זַרְעֲךָ֔ בַּֽעֲב֖וּר אַבְרָהָ֥ם עַבְדִּֽי: ²⁵ וַיִּ֧בֶן שָׁ֣ם מִזְבֵּ֗חַ וַיִּקְרָא֙ בְּשֵׁ֣ם יְהוָ֔ה וַיֶּט־שָׁ֖ם אָֽהֳל֑וֹ וַיִּכְרוּ־שָׁ֥ם עַבְדֵֽי־יִצְחָ֖ק בְּאֵֽר: ²⁶ וַֽאֲבִימֶ֕לֶךְ הָלַ֥ךְ אֵלָ֖יו מִגְּרָ֑ר וַֽאֲחֻזַּת֙ מֵֽרֵעֵ֔הוּ וּפִיכֹ֖ל שַׂר־צְבָאֽוֹ: ²⁷ וַיֹּ֤אמֶר אֲלֵהֶם֙ יִצְחָ֔ק מַדּ֖וּעַ בָּאתֶ֣ם אֵלָ֑י וְאַתֶּם֙ שְׂנֵאתֶ֣ם אֹתִ֔י וַתְּשַׁלְּח֖וּנִי מֵֽאִתְּכֶֽם: ²⁸ וַיֹּֽאמְר֗וּ רָא֣וֹ רָאִ֘ינוּ֮ כִּֽי־הָיָ֣ה יְהוָ֣ה ׀ עִמָּךְ֒ וַנֹּ֗אמֶר תְּהִ֨י נָ֥א אָלָ֛ה בֵּֽינוֹתֵ֖ינוּ בֵּינֵ֣ינוּ וּבֵינֶ֑ךָ וְנִכְרְתָ֥ה בְרִ֖ית עִמָּֽךְ: ²⁹ אִם־תַּֽעֲשֵׂ֨ה עִמָּ֜נוּ רָעָ֗ה כַּֽאֲשֶׁר֙ לֹ֣א נְגַֽעֲנ֔וּךָ וְכַֽאֲשֶׁ֨ר עָשִׂ֤ינוּ עִמְּךָ֙ רַק־ט֔וֹב וַנְּשַׁלֵּֽחֲךָ֖ בְּשָׁל֑וֹם אַתָּ֥ה עַתָּ֖ה בְּר֥וּךְ יְהוָֽה: ³⁰ וַיַּ֤עַשׂ לָהֶם֙ מִשְׁתֶּ֔ה וַיֹּֽאכְל֖וּ וַיִּשְׁתּֽוּ: ³¹ וַיַּשְׁכִּ֣ימוּ בַבֹּ֔קֶר וַיִּשָּֽׁבְע֖וּ אִ֣ישׁ לְאָחִ֑יו וַיְשַׁלְּחֵ֤ם יִצְחָק֙ וַיֵּֽלְכ֣וּ מֵֽאִתּ֔וֹ בְּשָׁלֽוֹם: ³² וַיְהִ֣י ׀ בַּיּ֣וֹם הַה֗וּא וַיָּבֹ֨אוּ֙ עַבְדֵ֣י יִצְחָ֔ק וַיַּגִּ֣דוּ ל֔וֹ עַל־אֹד֥וֹת הַבְּאֵ֖ר אֲשֶׁ֣ר חָפָ֑רוּ וַיֹּ֥אמְרוּ ל֖וֹ מָצָ֥אנוּ מָֽיִם: ³³ וַיִּקְרָ֥א אֹתָ֖הּ שִׁבְעָ֑ה עַל־כֵּ֤ן שֵׁם־הָעִיר֙ בְּאֵ֣ר שֶׁ֔בַע עַ֖ד הַיּ֥וֹם הַזֶּֽה: ס

ᵃ I.e., "contention."
ᵇ I.e., "harassment."
ᶜ Heb. hirḥib, connected with "Rehoboth."
ᵈ As though "oath."

³⁴When Esau was forty years old, he took to wife Judith daughter of Beeri the Hittite, and Basemath daughter of Elon the Hittite; ³⁵and they were a source of bitterness to Isaac and Rebekah.

27 When Isaac was old and his eyes were too dim to see, he called his older son Esau and said to him, "My son." He answered, "Here I am." ²And he said, "I am old now, and I do not know how soon I may die. ³Take your gear, your quiver and bow, and go out into the open and hunt me some game. ⁴Then prepare a dish for me such as I like, and bring it to me to eat, so that I may give you my innermost blessing before I die."

⁵Rebekah had been listening as Isaac spoke to his son Esau. When Esau had gone out into the open to hunt game to bring home, ⁶Rebekah said to her son Jacob, "I overheard your father speaking to your brother Esau, saying, ⁷'Bring me some game and prepare a dish for me to eat, that I may bless you, with the LORD's approval, before I die.' ⁸Now, my son, listen carefully as I instruct you. ⁹Go to the flock and fetch me two choice kids, and I will make of them a dish for your father, such as he likes. ¹⁰Then take it to your father to eat, in order that he may bless you before he dies." ¹¹Jacob answered his mother Rebekah, "But my brother Esau is a hairy man and I am smooth-skinned. ¹²If my father touches me, I shall appear to him as a trickster and bring upon myself a curse, not a blessing." ¹³But his mother said to him, "Your curse, my son, be upon me! Just do as I say and go fetch them for me."

¹⁴He got them and brought them to his mother, and his mother prepared a dish such as his father liked. ¹⁵Rebekah then took the best

‎34 וַיְהִ֤י עֵשָׂו֙ בֶּן־אַרְבָּעִ֣ים שָׁנָ֔ה וַיִּקַּ֤ח אִשָּׁה֙ אֶת־יְהוּדִ֔ית בַּת־בְּאֵרִ֖י הַֽחִתִּ֑י וְאֶת־בָּ֣שְׂמַ֔ת בַּת־אֵילֹ֖ן הַֽחִתִּֽי׃ 35 וַתִּהְיֶ֖יןָ מֹ֣רַת ר֑וּחַ לְיִצְחָ֖ק וּלְרִבְקָֽה׃ ס

כז וַיְהִי֙ כִּֽי־זָקֵ֣ן יִצְחָ֔ק וַתִּכְהֶ֥יןָ עֵינָ֖יו מֵֽרְאֹ֑ת וַיִּקְרָ֞א אֶת־עֵשָׂ֣ו ׀ בְּנ֣וֹ הַגָּדֹ֗ל וַיֹּ֤אמֶר אֵלָיו֙ בְּנִ֔י וַיֹּ֥אמֶר אֵלָ֖יו הִנֵּֽנִי׃ 2 וַיֹּ֕אמֶר הִנֵּה־נָ֖א זָקַ֑נְתִּי לֹ֥א יָדַ֖עְתִּי י֥וֹם מוֹתִֽי׃ 3 וְעַתָּה֙ שָׂא־נָ֣א כֵלֶ֔יךָ תֶּלְיְךָ֖ וְקַשְׁתֶּ֑ךָ וְצֵא֙ הַשָּׂדֶ֔ה וְצ֥וּדָה לִּ֖י צידה צָֽיִד׃ 4 וַעֲשֵׂה־לִ֨י מַטְעַמִּ֜ים כַּאֲשֶׁ֥ר אָהַ֛בְתִּי וְהָבִ֥יאָה לִּ֖י וְאֹכֵ֑לָה בַּעֲב֛וּר תְּבָרֶכְךָ֥ נַפְשִׁ֖י בְּטֶ֥רֶם אָמֽוּת׃

5 וְרִבְקָ֣ה שֹׁמַ֔עַת בְּדַבֵּ֣ר יִצְחָ֔ק אֶל־עֵשָׂ֖ו בְּנ֑וֹ וַיֵּ֤לֶךְ עֵשָׂו֙ הַשָּׂדֶ֔ה לָצ֥וּד צַ֖יִד לְהָבִֽיא׃ 6 וְרִבְקָה֙ אָֽמְרָ֔ה אֶל־יַעֲקֹ֥ב בְּנָ֖הּ לֵאמֹ֑ר הִנֵּ֤ה שָׁמַ֙עְתִּי֙ אֶת־אָבִ֔יךָ מְדַבֵּ֥ר אֶל־עֵשָׂ֛ו אָחִ֖יךָ לֵאמֹֽר׃ 7 הָבִ֨יאָה לִּ֥י צַ֛יִד וַעֲשֵׂה־לִ֥י מַטְעַמִּ֖ים וְאֹכֵ֑לָה וַאֲבָרֶכְכָ֛ה לִפְנֵ֥י יְהוָ֖ה לִפְנֵ֥י מוֹתִֽי׃ 8 וְעַתָּ֥ה בְנִ֖י שְׁמַ֣ע בְּקֹלִ֑י לַאֲשֶׁ֥ר אֲנִ֖י מְצַוָּ֥ה אֹתָֽךְ׃ 9 לֶךְ־נָא֙ אֶל־הַצֹּ֔אן וְקַֽח־לִ֣י מִשָּׁ֗ם שְׁנֵ֛י גְּדָיֵ֥י עִזִּ֖ים טֹבִ֑ים וְאֶֽעֱשֶׂ֨ה אֹתָ֧ם מַטְעַמִּ֛ים לְאָבִ֖יךָ כַּאֲשֶׁ֥ר אָהֵֽב׃ 10 וְהֵבֵאתָ֥ לְאָבִ֖יךָ וְאָכָ֑ל בַּעֲבֻ֛ר אֲשֶׁ֥ר יְבָרֶכְךָ֖ לִפְנֵ֥י מוֹתֽוֹ׃ 11 וַיֹּ֣אמֶר יַעֲקֹ֔ב אֶל־רִבְקָ֖ה אִמּ֑וֹ הֵ֣ן עֵשָׂ֤ו אָחִי֙ אִ֣ישׁ שָׂעִ֔ר וְאָנֹכִ֖י אִ֥ישׁ חָלָֽק׃ 12 אוּלַ֤י יְמֻשֵּׁ֙נִי֙ אָבִ֔י וְהָיִ֥יתִי בְעֵינָ֖יו כִּמְתַעְתֵּ֑עַ וְהֵבֵאתִ֥י עָלַ֛י קְלָלָ֖ה וְלֹ֥א בְרָכָֽה׃ 13 וַתֹּ֤אמֶר לוֹ֙ אִמּ֔וֹ עָלַ֥י קִלְלָתְךָ֖ בְּנִ֑י אַ֛ךְ שְׁמַ֥ע בְּקֹלִ֖י וְלֵ֥ךְ קַֽח־לִֽי׃ 14 וַיֵּ֙לֶךְ֙ וַיִּקַּ֔ח וַיָּבֵ֖א לְאִמּ֑וֹ וַתַּ֤עַשׂ אִמּוֹ֙ מַטְעַמִּ֔ים כַּאֲשֶׁ֖ר אָהֵ֥ב אָבִֽיו׃ 15 וַתִּקַּ֣ח רִבְקָ֡ה אֶת־בִּגְדֵי֩ עֵשָׂ֨ו בְּנָ֤הּ הַגָּדֹל֙ הַחֲמֻדֹ֔ת

clothes of her older son Esau, which were there in the house, and had her younger son Jacob put them on; ¹⁶and she covered his hands and the hairless part of his neck with the skins of the kids. ¹⁷Then she put in the hands of her son Jacob the dish and the bread that she had prepared.

¹⁸He went to his father and said, "Father." And he said, "Yes, which of my sons are you?" ¹⁹Jacob said to his father, "I am Esau, your first-born; I have done as you told me. Pray sit up and eat of my game, that you may give me your innermost blessing." ²⁰Isaac said to his son, "How did you succeed so quickly, my son?" And he said, "Because the LORD your God granted me good fortune." ²¹Isaac said to Jacob, "Come closer that I may feel you, my son—whether you are really my son Esau or not." ²²So Jacob drew close to his father Isaac, who felt him and wondered. "The voice is the voice of Jacob, yet the hands are the hands of Esau." ²³He did not recognize him, because his hands were hairy like those of his brother Esau; and so he blessed him.

²⁴He asked, "Are you really my son Esau?" And when he said, "I am," ²⁵he said, "Serve me and let me eat of my son's game that I may give you my innermost blessing." So he served him and he ate, and he brought him wine and he drank. ²⁶Then his father Isaac said to him, "Come close and kiss me, my son"; ²⁷and he went up and kissed him. And he smelled his clothes and he blessed him, saying, "Ah, the smell of my son is like the smell of the fields that the LORD has blessed.

²⁸"May God give you
Of the dew of heaven and the fat of the earth,
Abundance of new grain and wine.
²⁹Let peoples serve you,
And nations bow to you;
Be master over your brothers,
And let your mother's sons bow to you.

Cursed be they who curse you,
Blessed they who bless you."

³⁰No sooner had Jacob left the presence of his father Isaac—after Isaac had finished blessing Jacob—than his brother Esau came back from his hunt. ³¹He too prepared a dish and brought it to his father. And he said to his father, "Let my father sit up and eat of his son's game, so that you may give me your innermost blessing." ³²His father Isaac said to him, "Who are you?" And he said, "I am your son, Esau, your first-born!" ³³Isaac was seized with very violent trembling. "Who was it then," he demanded, "that hunted game and brought it to me? Moreover, I ate of it before you came, and I blessed him; now he must remain blessed!" ³⁴When Esau heard his father's words, he burst into wild and bitter sobbing, and said to his father, "Bless me too, Father!" ³⁵But he answered, "Your brother came with guile and took away your blessing." ³⁶[Esau] said, "Was he, then, named Jacob that he might supplant meᵃ these two times? First he took away my birthright and now he has taken away my blessing!" And he added, "Have you not reserved a blessing for me?" ³⁷Isaac answered, saying to Esau, "But I have made him master over you: I have given him all his brothers for servants, and sustained him with grain and wine. What, then, can I still do for you, my son?" ³⁸And Esau said to his father, "Have you but one blessing, Father? Bless me too, Father!" And Esau wept aloud. ³⁹And his father Isaac answered, saying to him,

"See, your abode shall ᵇ-enjoy the fat of the earth
And-ᵇ the dew of heaven above.
⁴⁰Yet by your sword you shall live,
And you shall serve your brother;
But when you grow restive,
You shall break his yoke from your neck."

אֹרְרֶ֣יךָ אָר֔וּר
וּֽמְבָרֲכֶ֖יךָ בָּרֽוּךְ׃
³⁰ וַיְהִ֗י כַּאֲשֶׁ֨ר כִּלָּ֣ה יִצְחָק֮ לְבָרֵ֣ךְ אֶֽת־יַעֲקֹב֒ וַיְהִ֗י אַ֣ךְ יָצֹ֤א יָצָא֙ יַעֲקֹ֔ב מֵאֵ֥ת פְּנֵ֖י יִצְחָ֣ק אָבִ֑יו וְעֵשָׂ֣ו אָחִ֔יו בָּ֖א מִצֵּידֽוֹ׃ ³¹ וַיַּ֤עַשׂ גַּם־הוּא֙ מַטְעַמִּ֔ים וַיָּבֵ֖א לְאָבִ֑יו וַיֹּ֣אמֶר לְאָבִ֗יו יָקֻ֤ם אָבִי֙ וְיֹאכַל֙ מִצֵּ֣יד בְּנ֔וֹ בַּעֲב֖וּר תְּבָרֲכַ֥נִּי נַפְשֶֽׁךָ׃ ³² וַיֹּ֥אמֶר ל֛וֹ יִצְחָ֥ק אָבִ֖יו מִי־אָ֑תָּה וַיֹּ֕אמֶר אֲנִ֛י בִּנְךָ֥ בְכֹֽרְךָ֖ עֵשָֽׂו׃ ³³ וַיֶּחֱרַ֨ד יִצְחָ֣ק חֲרָדָה֮ גְּדֹלָ֣ה עַד־מְאֹד֒ וַיֹּ֡אמֶר מִֽי־אֵפ֡וֹא ה֣וּא הַצָּֽד־צַ֩יִד֩ וַיָּ֨בֵא לִ֜י וָאֹכַ֥ל מִכֹּ֛ל בְּטֶ֥רֶם תָּב֖וֹא וָאֲבָרֲכֵ֑הוּ גַּם־בָּר֖וּךְ יִהְיֶֽה׃ ³⁴ כִּשְׁמֹ֤עַ עֵשָׂו֙ אֶת־דִּבְרֵ֣י אָבִ֔יו וַיִּצְעַ֣ק צְעָקָ֔ה גְּדֹלָ֥ה וּמָרָ֖ה עַד־מְאֹ֑ד וַיֹּ֣אמֶר לְאָבִ֔יו בָּרֲכֵ֥נִי גַם־אָ֖נִי אָבִֽי׃ ³⁵ וַיֹּ֕אמֶר בָּ֥א אָחִ֖יךָ בְּמִרְמָ֑ה וַיִּקַּ֖ח בִּרְכָתֶֽךָ׃ ³⁶ וַיֹּ֡אמֶר הֲכִי֩ קָרָ֨א שְׁמ֜וֹ יַעֲקֹ֗ב וַֽיַּעְקְבֵ֙נִי֙ זֶ֣ה פַעֲמַ֔יִם אֶת־בְּכֹרָתִ֣י לָקָ֔ח וְהִנֵּ֥ה עַתָּ֖ה לָקַ֣ח בִּרְכָתִ֑י וַיֹּאמַ֕ר הֲלֹא־אָצַ֥לְתָּ לִּ֖י בְּרָכָֽה׃ ³⁷ וַיַּ֨עַן יִצְחָ֜ק וַיֹּ֣אמֶר לְעֵשָׂ֗ו הֵ֣ן גְּבִ֞יר שַׂמְתִּ֥יו לָךְ֙ וְאֶת־כׇּל־אֶחָ֗יו נָתַ֤תִּי לוֹ֙ לַעֲבָדִ֔ים וְדָגָ֥ן וְתִירֹ֖שׁ סְמַכְתִּ֑יו וּלְכָ֣ה אֵפ֔וֹא מָ֥ה אֶֽעֱשֶׂ֖ה בְּנִֽי׃ ³⁸ וַיֹּ֨אמֶר עֵשָׂ֜ו אֶל־אָבִ֗יו הַֽבְרָכָ֨ה אַחַ֤ת הִֽוא־לְךָ֙ אָבִ֔י בָּרֲכֵ֥נִי גַם־אָ֖נִי אָבִ֑י וַיִּשָּׂ֥א עֵשָׂ֛ו קֹל֖וֹ וַיֵּֽבְךְּ׃ ³⁹ וַיַּ֛עַן יִצְחָ֥ק אָבִ֖יו וַיֹּ֣אמֶר אֵלָ֑יו הִנֵּ֞ה מִשְׁמַנֵּ֤י הָאָ֙רֶץ֙ יִהְיֶ֣ה מֽוֹשָׁבֶ֔ךָ וּמִטַּ֥ל הַשָּׁמַ֖יִם מֵעָֽל׃ ⁴⁰ *וְעַל־חַרְבְּךָ֣ תִֽחְיֶ֔ה וְאֶת־אָחִ֖יךָ תַּעֲבֹ֑ד וְהָיָה֙ כַּאֲשֶׁ֣ר תָּרִ֔יד וּפָרַקְתָּ֥ עֻלּ֖וֹ מֵעַ֥ל צַוָּארֶֽךָ׃

ᵃ Heb. 'aqab, connected with "Jacob."
ᵇ-ᵇ Others "be away from the fat of the earth and from."

41Now Esau harbored a grudge against Jacob because of the blessing which his father had given him, and Esau said to himself, "Let but the mourning period of my father come, and I will kill my brother Jacob." 42When the words of her older son Esau were reported to Rebekah, she sent for her younger son Jacob and said to him, "Your brother Esau is consoling himself by planning to kill you. 43Now, my son, listen to me. Flee at once to Haran, to my brother La-ban. 44Stay with him a while, until your broth-er's fury subsides—45until your brother's anger against you subsides—and he forgets what you have done to him. Then I will fetch you from there. Let me not lose you both in one day!"

46Rebekah said to Isaac, "I am disgusted with my life because of the Hittite women. If Jacob marries a Hittite woman like these, from among the native women, what good will life be to me?"

28 1So Isaac sent for Jacob and blessed him. He instructed him, saying, "You shall not take a wife from among the Canaanite women. 2Up, go to Paddan-aram, to the house of Bethuel, your mother's father, and take a wife there from among the daughters of Laban, your mother's brother, 3May El Shaddaia bless you, make you fertile and numerous, so that you be-come an assembly of peoples. 4May He grant the blessing of Abraham to you and your offspring, that you may possess the land where you are sojourning, which God assigned to Abraham."

5Then Isaac sent Jacob off, and he went to Paddan-aram, to Laban the son of Bethuel the Aramean, the brother of Rebekah, mother of Jacob and Esau.

6When Esau saw that Isaac had blessed Jacob and sent him off to Paddan-aram to take a wife from there, charging him, as he blessed him,

a See note at 17.1.

41 וַיִּשְׂטֹם עֵשָׂו אֶת־יַעֲקֹב עַל־הַבְּרָכָה אֲשֶׁר בֵּרֲכוֹ אָבִיו וַיֹּאמֶר עֵשָׂו בְּלִבּוֹ יִקְרְבוּ יְמֵי אֵבֶל אָבִי וְאַהַרְגָה אֶת־יַעֲקֹב אָחִי: 42 וַיֻּגַּד לְרִבְקָה אֶת־דִּבְרֵי עֵשָׂו בְּנָהּ הַגָּדֹל וַתִּשְׁלַח וַתִּקְרָא לְיַעֲקֹב בְּנָהּ הַקָּטֹן וַתֹּאמֶר אֵלָיו הִנֵּה עֵשָׂו אָחִיךָ מִתְנַחֵם לְךָ לְהָרְגֶךָ: 43 וְעַתָּה בְנִי שְׁמַע בְּקֹלִי וְקוּם בְּרַח־לְךָ אֶל־לָבָן אָחִי חָרָנָה: 44 וְיָשַׁבְתָּ עִמּוֹ יָמִים אֲחָדִים עַד אֲשֶׁר־תָּשׁוּב חֲמַת אָחִיךָ: 45 עַד־שׁוּב אַף־אָחִיךָ מִמְּךָ וְשָׁכַח אֵת אֲשֶׁר־עָשִׂיתָ לּוֹ וְשָׁלַחְתִּי וּלְקַחְתִּיךָ מִשָּׁם לָמָה אֶשְׁכַּל גַּם־שְׁנֵיכֶם יוֹם אֶחָד:

46 וַתֹּאמֶר רִבְקָה אֶל־יִצְחָק קַצְתִּי בְחַיַּי מִפְּנֵי בְּנוֹת חֵת אִם־לֹקֵחַ יַעֲקֹב אִשָּׁה מִבְּנוֹת־חֵת כָּאֵלֶּה מִבְּנוֹת הָאָרֶץ לָמָה לִּי חַיִּים: כח 1 וַיִּקְרָא יִצְחָק אֶל־יַעֲקֹב וַיְבָרֶךְ אֹתוֹ וַיְצַוֵּהוּ וַיֹּאמֶר לוֹ לֹא־תִקַּח אִשָּׁה מִבְּנוֹת כְּנָעַן: 2 קוּם לֵךְ פַּדֶּנָה אֲרָם בֵּיתָה בְתוּאֵל אֲבִי אִמֶּךָ וְקַח־לְךָ מִשָּׁם אִשָּׁה מִבְּנוֹת לָבָן אֲחִי אִמֶּךָ: 3 וְאֵל שַׁדַּי יְבָרֵךְ אֹתְךָ וְיַפְרְךָ וְיַרְבֶּךָ וְהָיִיתָ לִקְהַל עַמִּים: 4 וְיִתֶּן־לְךָ אֶת־בִּרְכַּת אַבְרָהָם לְךָ וּלְזַרְעֲךָ אִתָּךְ לְרִשְׁתְּךָ אֶת־אֶרֶץ מְגֻרֶיךָ אֲשֶׁר־נָתַן אֱלֹהִים לְאַבְרָהָם:

5 וַיִּשְׁלַח יִצְחָק אֶת־יַעֲקֹב וַיֵּלֶךְ פַּדֶּנָה אֲרָם אֶל־לָבָן בֶּן־בְּתוּאֵל הָאֲרַמִּי אֲחִי רִבְקָה אֵם יַעֲקֹב וְעֵשָׂו:

6 וַיַּרְא עֵשָׂו כִּי־בֵרַךְ יִצְחָק אֶת־יַעֲקֹב וְשִׁלַּח אֹתוֹ פַּדֶּנָה אֲרָם לָקַחַת־לוֹ מִשָּׁם אִשָּׁה בְּבָרֲכוֹ אֹתוֹ וַיְצַו עָלָיו לֵאמֹר לֹא־תִקַּח אִשָּׁה מִבְּנוֹת כְּנָעַן: 7 וַיִּשְׁמַע

v. 46. קְרֵי זְעִירָא לְפִי נֻסְחִים הַמְקֻבָּלִים

55

"You shall not take a wife from among the Canaanite women," [7]and that Jacob had obeyed
his father and mother and gone to Paddan-
aram, [8]Esau realized that the Canaanite women
displeased his father Isaac. [9]So Esau went to Ishmael and took to wife, in addition to the wives
he had, Mahalath the daughter of Ishmael son
of Abraham, sister of Nebaioth.

VA-YETSE'

[10]Jacob left Beer-sheba, and set out for Haran.
[11]He came upon a certain place and stopped
there for the night, for the sun had set. Taking
one of the stones of that place, he put it under
his head and lay down in that place. [12]He had
a dream; a stairway[b] was set on the ground and
its top reached to the sky, and angels of God
were going up and down on it. [13]And the LORD
was standing beside him and He said, "I am the
LORD, the God of your father Abraham and the
God of Isaac: the ground on which you are lying
I will assign to you and to your offspring. [14]Your
descendants shall be as the dust of the earth; you
shall spread out to the west and to the east, to
the north and to the south. All the families of
the earth shall bless themselves by you and your
descendants. [15]Remember, I am with you: I will
protect you wherever you go and will bring you
back to this land. I will not leave you until I have
done what I have promised you."

[16]Jacob awoke from his sleep and said,
"Surely the LORD is present in this place, and
I did not know it!" [17]Shaken, he said, "How awesome is this place! This is none other than the
abode of God, and that is the gateway to
heaven." [18]Early in the morning, Jacob took the
stone that he had put under his head and set
it up as a pillar and poured oil on the top of it.
[19]He named that site Bethel;[c] but previously the
name of the city had been Luz.

יַעֲקֹב אֶל־אָבִיו וְאֶל־אִמּוֹ וַיֵּלֶךְ פַּדֶּנָה
אֲרָם: [8]וַיַּרְא עֵשָׂו כִּי רָעוֹת בְּנוֹת כְּנָעַן
בְּעֵינֵי יִצְחָק אָבִיו: [9]וַיֵּלֶךְ עֵשָׂו אֶל־
יִשְׁמָעֵאל וַיִּקַּח אֶת־מָחֲלַת ׀ בַּת־יִשְׁמָעֵאל
בֶּן־אַבְרָהָם אֲחוֹת נְבָיוֹת עַל־נָשָׁיו לוֹ
לְאִשָּׁה: ס

וַיֵּצֵא

[10]וַיֵּצֵא יַעֲקֹב מִבְּאֵר שָׁבַע וַיֵּלֶךְ חָרָנָה:
[11]וַיִּפְגַּע בַּמָּקוֹם וַיָּלֶן שָׁם כִּי־בָא הַשֶּׁמֶשׁ
וַיִּקַּח מֵאַבְנֵי הַמָּקוֹם וַיָּשֶׂם מְרַאֲשֹׁתָיו
וַיִּשְׁכַּב בַּמָּקוֹם הַהוּא: [12]וַיַּחֲלֹם וְהִנֵּה
סֻלָּם מֻצָּב אַרְצָה וְרֹאשׁוֹ מַגִּיעַ הַשָּׁמָיְמָה
וְהִנֵּה מַלְאֲכֵי אֱלֹהִים עֹלִים וְיֹרְדִים בּוֹ:
[13]וְהִנֵּה יְהֹוָה נִצָּב עָלָיו וַיֹּאמַר אֲנִי יְהֹוָה
אֱלֹהֵי אַבְרָהָם אָבִיךָ וֵאלֹהֵי יִצְחָק הָאָרֶץ
אֲשֶׁר אַתָּה שֹׁכֵב עָלֶיהָ לְךָ אֶתְּנֶנָּה
וּלְזַרְעֶךָ: [14]וְהָיָה זַרְעֲךָ כַּעֲפַר הָאָרֶץ
וּפָרַצְתָּ יָמָּה וָקֵדְמָה וְצָפֹנָה וָנֶגְבָּה וְנִבְרְכוּ
בְךָ כָּל־מִשְׁפְּחֹת הָאֲדָמָה וּבְזַרְעֶךָ:
[15]וְהִנֵּה אָנֹכִי עִמָּךְ וּשְׁמַרְתִּיךָ בְּכֹל אֲשֶׁר־
תֵּלֵךְ וַהֲשִׁבֹתִיךָ אֶל־הָאֲדָמָה הַזֹּאת כִּי
לֹא אֶעֱזָבְךָ עַד אֲשֶׁר אִם־עָשִׂיתִי אֵת
אֲשֶׁר־דִּבַּרְתִּי לָךְ: [16]וַיִּיקַץ יַעֲקֹב מִשְּׁנָתוֹ וַיֹּאמֶר אָכֵן יֵשׁ
יְהֹוָה בַּמָּקוֹם הַזֶּה וְאָנֹכִי לֹא יָדָעְתִּי:
[17]וַיִּירָא וַיֹּאמַר מַה־נּוֹרָא הַמָּקוֹם הַזֶּה
אֵין זֶה כִּי אִם־בֵּית אֱלֹהִים וְזֶה שַׁעַר
הַשָּׁמָיִם: [18]וַיַּשְׁכֵּם יַעֲקֹב בַּבֹּקֶר וַיִּקַּח
אֶת־הָאֶבֶן אֲשֶׁר־שָׂם מְרַאֲשֹׁתָיו וַיָּשֶׂם
אֹתָהּ מַצֵּבָה וַיִּצֹק שֶׁמֶן עַל־רֹאשָׁהּ:
[19]וַיִּקְרָא אֶת־שֵׁם־הַמָּקוֹם הַהוּא בֵּית־אֵל
וְאוּלָם לוּז שֵׁם־הָעִיר לָרִאשֹׁנָה:

---

b   Or "ramp"; others "ladder."
c   I.e., "house of God."

20Jacob then made a vow, saying, "If God remains with me, if He protects me on this journey that I am making, and gives me bread to eat and clothing to wear, 21and if I return safe to my father's house—the Lord shall be my God. 22And this stone, which I have set up as a pillar, shall be God's abode; and of all that You give me, I will set aside a tithe for You."

29

Jacob a-resumed his journey-a and came to the land of the Easterners. 2There before his eyes was a well in the open. Three flocks of sheep were lying there beside it, for the flocks were watered from that well. The stone on the mouth of the well was large. 3When all the flocks were gathered there, the stone would be rolled from the mouth of the well and the sheep watered; then the stone would be put back in its place on the mouth of the well.

4Jacob said to them, "My friends, where are you from?" And they said, "We are from Haran." 5He said to them, "Do you know Laban the son of Nahor?" And they said, "Yes, we do." 6He continued, "Is he well?" They answered, "Yes, he is; and there is his daughter Rachel, coming with the flock." 7He said, "It is still broad daylight, too early to round up the animals; water the flock and take them to pasture." 8But they said, "We cannot, until all the flocks are rounded up; then the stone is rolled off the mouth of the well and we water the sheep."

9While he was still speaking with them, Rachel came with her father's flock; for she was a shepherdess. 10And when Jacob saw Rachel, the daughter of his uncleb Laban, and the flock of his uncle Laban, Jacob went up and rolled the stone off the mouth of the well, and watered the flock of his uncle Laban. 11Then Jacob kissed Rachel, and broke into tears. 12Jacob told Rachel

a-a Lit. "lifted up his feet."
b Lit. "his mother's brother."

20 וַיִּדַּר יַעֲקֹב נֶדֶר לֵאמֹר אִם־יִהְיֶה אֱלֹהִים עִמָּדִי וּשְׁמָרַנִי בַּדֶּרֶךְ הַזֶּה אֲשֶׁר אָנֹכִי הוֹלֵךְ וְנָתַן־לִי לֶחֶם לֶאֱכֹל וּבֶגֶד לִלְבֹּשׁ: 21 וְשַׁבְתִּי בְשָׁלוֹם אֶל־בֵּית אָבִי וְהָיָה יְהֹוָה לִי לֵאלֹהִים: 22 וְהָאֶבֶן הַזֹּאת אֲשֶׁר־שַׂמְתִּי מַצֵּבָה יִהְיֶה בֵּית אֱלֹהִים וְכֹל אֲשֶׁר תִּתֶּן־לִי עַשֵּׂר אֲעַשְּׂרֶנּוּ לָךְ:

כט

וַיִּשָּׂא יַעֲקֹב רַגְלָיו וַיֵּלֶךְ אַרְצָה בְנֵי־קֶדֶם: 2 וַיַּרְא וְהִנֵּה בְאֵר בַּשָּׂדֶה וְהִנֵּה־שָׁם שְׁלֹשָׁה עֶדְרֵי־צֹאן רֹבְצִים עָלֶיהָ כִּי מִן־הַבְּאֵר הַהִוא יַשְׁקוּ הָעֲדָרִים וְהָאֶבֶן גְּדֹלָה עַל־פִּי הַבְּאֵר: 3 וְנֶאֶסְפוּ־שָׁמָּה כָל־הָעֲדָרִים וְגָלֲלוּ אֶת־הָאֶבֶן מֵעַל פִּי הַבְּאֵר וְהִשְׁקוּ אֶת־הַצֹּאן וְהֵשִׁיבוּ אֶת־הָאֶבֶן עַל־פִּי הַבְּאֵר לִמְקֹמָהּ: 4 וַיֹּאמֶר לָהֶם יַעֲקֹב אַחַי מֵאַיִן אַתֶּם וַיֹּאמְרוּ מֵחָרָן אֲנָחְנוּ: 5 וַיֹּאמֶר לָהֶם הַיְדַעְתֶּם אֶת־לָבָן בֶּן־נָחוֹר וַיֹּאמְרוּ יָדָעְנוּ: 6 וַיֹּאמֶר לָהֶם הֲשָׁלוֹם לוֹ וַיֹּאמְרוּ שָׁלוֹם וְהִנֵּה רָחֵל בִּתּוֹ בָּאָה עִם־הַצֹּאן: 7 וַיֹּאמֶר הֵן עוֹד הַיּוֹם גָּדוֹל לֹא־עֵת הֵאָסֵף הַמִּקְנֶה הַשְׁקוּ הַצֹּאן וּלְכוּ רְעוּ: 8 וַיֹּאמְרוּ לֹא נוּכַל עַד אֲשֶׁר יֵאָסְפוּ כָּל־הָעֲדָרִים וְגָלֲלוּ אֶת־הָאֶבֶן מֵעַל פִּי הַבְּאֵר וְהִשְׁקִינוּ הַצֹּאן: 9 עוֹדֶנּוּ מְדַבֵּר עִמָּם וְרָחֵל | בָּאָה עִם־הַצֹּאן אֲשֶׁר לְאָבִיהָ כִּי רֹעָה הִוא: 10 וַיְהִי כַּאֲשֶׁר רָאָה יַעֲקֹב אֶת־רָחֵל בַּת־לָבָן אֲחִי אִמּוֹ וְאֶת־צֹאן לָבָן אֲחִי אִמּוֹ וַיִּגַּשׁ יַעֲקֹב וַיָּגֶל אֶת־הָאֶבֶן מֵעַל פִּי הַבְּאֵר וַיַּשְׁקְ אֶת־צֹאן לָבָן אֲחִי אִמּוֹ: 11 וַיִּשַּׁק יַעֲקֹב לְרָחֵל וַיִּשָּׂא אֶת־קֹלוֹ וַיֵּבְךְּ: 12 וַיַּגֵּד יַעֲקֹב

that he was her father's kinsman, that he was Rebekah's son; and she ran and told her father. ¹³On hearing the news of his sister's son Jacob, Laban ran to greet him; he embraced him and kissed him, and took him into his house. He told Laban all that had happened, ¹⁴and Laban said to him, "You are truly my bone and flesh."

When he had stayed with him a month's time, ¹⁵Laban said to Jacob, "Just because you are a kinsman, should you serve me for nothing? Tell me, what shall your wages be?" ¹⁶Now Laban had two daughters; the name of the older one was Leah, and the name of the younger was Rachel. ¹⁷Leah had weak eyes; Rachel was shapely and beautiful. ¹⁸Jacob loved Rachel; so he answered, "I will serve you seven years for your younger daughter Rachel." ¹⁹Laban said, "Better that I give her to you than that I should give her to an outsider. Stay with me." ²⁰So Jacob served seven years for Rachel and they seemed to him but a few days because of his love for her.

²¹Then Jacob said to Laban, "Give me my wife, for my time is fulfilled, that I may cohabit with her." ²²And Laban gathered all the people of the place and made a feast. ²³When evening came, he took his daughter Leah and brought her to him; and he cohabited with her.— ²⁴Laban had given his maidservant Zilpah to his daughter Leah as her maid.—²⁵When morning came, there was Leah! So he said to Laban, "What is this you have done to me? I was in your service for Rachel! Why did you deceive me?" ²⁶Laban said, "It is not the practice in our place to marry off the younger before the older. ²⁷Wait until the bridal week of this one is over and we will give you that one too, provided you serve me another seven years." ²⁸Jacob did so; he waited out the bridal week of the one, and then he gave him his daughter Rachel as wife.— ²⁹Laban had given his maidservant Bilhah to his

לְרָחֵל כִּי אֲחִי אָבִיהָ הוּא וְכִי בֶן־רִבְקָה הוּא וַתָּרָץ וַתַּגֵּד לְאָבִיהָ: 13 וַיְהִי כִשְׁמֹעַ לָבָן אֶת־שֵׁמַע ׀ יַעֲקֹב בֶּן־אֲחֹתוֹ וַיָּרָץ לִקְרָאתוֹ וַיְחַבֶּק־לוֹ וַיְנַשֶּׁק־לוֹ וַיְבִיאֵהוּ אֶל־בֵּיתוֹ וַיְסַפֵּר לְלָבָן אֵת כָּל־הַדְּבָרִים הָאֵלֶּה: 14 וַיֹּאמֶר לוֹ לָבָן אַךְ עַצְמִי וּבְשָׂרִי אָתָּה

וַיֵּשֶׁב עִמּוֹ חֹדֶשׁ יָמִים: 15 וַיֹּאמֶר לָבָן לְיַעֲקֹב הֲכִי־אָחִי אַתָּה וַעֲבַדְתַּנִי חִנָּם הַגִּידָה לִּי מַה־מַּשְׂכֻּרְתֶּךָ: 16 וּלְלָבָן שְׁתֵּי בָנוֹת שֵׁם הַגְּדֹלָה לֵאָה וְשֵׁם הַקְּטַנָּה רָחֵל: 17 וְעֵינֵי לֵאָה רַכּוֹת וְרָחֵל הָיְתָה יְפַת־תֹּאַר וִיפַת מַרְאֶה: 18 וַיֶּאֱהַב יַעֲקֹב אֶת־רָחֵל וַיֹּאמֶר אֶעֱבָדְךָ שֶׁבַע שָׁנִים בְּרָחֵל בִּתְּךָ הַקְּטַנָּה: 19 וַיֹּאמֶר לָבָן טוֹב תִּתִּי אֹתָהּ לָךְ מִתִּתִּי אֹתָהּ לְאִישׁ אַחֵר שְׁבָה עִמָּדִי: 20 וַיַּעֲבֹד יַעֲקֹב בְּרָחֵל שֶׁבַע שָׁנִים וַיִּהְיוּ בְעֵינָיו כְּיָמִים אֲחָדִים בְּאַהֲבָתוֹ אֹתָהּ:

21 וַיֹּאמֶר יַעֲקֹב אֶל־לָבָן הָבָה אֶת־אִשְׁתִּי כִּי מָלְאוּ יָמָי וְאָבוֹאָה אֵלֶיהָ: 22 וַיֶּאֱסֹף לָבָן אֶת־כָּל־אַנְשֵׁי הַמָּקוֹם וַיַּעַשׂ מִשְׁתֶּה: 23 וַיְהִי בָעֶרֶב וַיִּקַּח אֶת־לֵאָה בִתּוֹ וַיָּבֵא אֹתָהּ אֵלָיו וַיָּבֹא אֵלֶיהָ: 24 וַיִּתֵּן לָבָן לָהּ אֶת־זִלְפָּה שִׁפְחָתוֹ לְלֵאָה בִתּוֹ שִׁפְחָה: 25 וַיְהִי בַבֹּקֶר וְהִנֵּה־הִוא לֵאָה וַיֹּאמֶר אֶל־לָבָן מַה־זֹּאת עָשִׂיתָ לִּי הֲלֹא בְרָחֵל עָבַדְתִּי עִמָּךְ וְלָמָּה רִמִּיתָנִי: 26 וַיֹּאמֶר לָבָן לֹא־יֵעָשֶׂה כֵן בִּמְקוֹמֵנוּ לָתֵת הַצְּעִירָה לִפְנֵי הַבְּכִירָה: 27 מַלֵּא שְׁבֻעַ זֹאת וְנִתְּנָה לְךָ גַּם־אֶת־זֹאת בַּעֲבֹדָה אֲשֶׁר תַּעֲבֹד עִמָּדִי עוֹד שֶׁבַע־שָׁנִים אֲחֵרוֹת: 28 וַיַּעַשׂ יַעֲקֹב כֵּן וַיְמַלֵּא שְׁבֻעַ זֹאת וַיִּתֶּן־לוֹ אֶת־רָחֵל בִּתּוֹ לוֹ לְאִשָּׁה: 29 וַיִּתֵּן לָבָן

daughter Rachel as her maid.—³⁰And Jacob cohabited with Rachel also; indeed, he loved Rachel more than Leah. And he served him another seven years.

³¹The LORD saw that Leah was unloved and he opened her womb; but Rachel was barren. ³²Leah conceived and bore a son, and named him Reuben;c for she declared, "It means: 'The LORD has seend my affliction'; it also means: 'Now my husband will love me.'"e ³³She conceived again and bore a son, and declared, "This is because the LORD heardf that I was unloved and has given me this one also"; so she named him Simeon. ³⁴Again she conceived and bore a son and declared, "This time my husband will become attachedg to me, for I have borne him three sons." Therefore he was named Levi. ³⁵She conceived again and bore a son, and declared, "This time I will praiseh the LORD." Therefore she named him Judah. Then she stopped bearing.

30 When Rachel saw that she had borne Jacob no children, she became envious of her sister; and Rachel said to Jacob, "Give me children, or I shall die." ²Jacob was incensed at Rachel, and said, "Can I take the place of God, who has denied you fruit of the womb?" ³She said, "Here is my maid Bilhah. Consort with her, that she may bear on my knees and that through her I too may have children." ⁴So she gave him her maid Bilhah as concubine, and Jacob cohabited with her. ⁵Bilhah conceived and bore Jacob a son. ⁶And Rachel said, "God has vindicated me;a indeed, He has heeded my plea and given me a son." Therefore she named him Dan.

---

c   Understood as "See a son."
d   Heb. ra'ah, connected with the first part of "Reuben."
e   Heb. ye'ehabani, connected with the last part of "Reuben."
f   Heb. shama', connected with "Simeon."
g   Heb. yillaweh, connected with "Levi."
h   Heb. 'odeh, connected with "Judah."

a   Heb. dananni, connected with "Dan."

59

לְרָחֵל בִּתּוֹ אֶת־בִּלְהָה שִׁפְחָתוֹ לָהּ לְשִׁפְחָה: 30 וַיָּבֹא גַּם אֶל־רָחֵל וַיֶּאֱהַב גַּם־אֶת־רָחֵל מִלֵּאָה וַיַּעֲבֹד עִמּוֹ עוֹד שֶׁבַע־שָׁנִים אֲחֵרוֹת:

31 וַיַּרְא יְהוָה כִּי־שְׂנוּאָה לֵאָה וַיִּפְתַּח אֶת־רַחְמָהּ וְרָחֵל עֲקָרָה: 32 וַתַּהַר לֵאָה וַתֵּלֶד בֵּן וַתִּקְרָא שְׁמוֹ רְאוּבֵן כִּי אָמְרָה כִּי־רָאָה יְהוָה בְּעָנְיִי כִּי עַתָּה יֶאֱהָבַנִי אִישִׁי: 33 וַתַּהַר עוֹד וַתֵּלֶד בֵּן וַתֹּאמֶר כִּי־שָׁמַע יְהוָה כִּי־שְׂנוּאָה אָנֹכִי וַיִּתֶּן־לִי גַּם־אֶת־זֶה וַתִּקְרָא שְׁמוֹ שִׁמְעוֹן: 34 וַתַּהַר עוֹד וַתֵּלֶד בֵּן וַתֹּאמֶר עַתָּה הַפַּעַם יִלָּוֶה אִישִׁי אֵלַי כִּי־יָלַדְתִּי לוֹ שְׁלֹשָׁה בָנִים עַל־כֵּן קָרָא־שְׁמוֹ לֵוִי: 35 וַתַּהַר עוֹד וַתֵּלֶד בֵּן וַתֹּאמֶר הַפַּעַם אוֹדֶה אֶת־יְהוָה עַל־כֵּן קָרְאָה שְׁמוֹ יְהוּדָה וַתַּעֲמֹד מִלֶּדֶת:

ל וַתֵּרֶא רָחֵל כִּי לֹא יָלְדָה לְיַעֲקֹב וַתְּקַנֵּא רָחֵל בַּאֲחֹתָהּ וַתֹּאמֶר אֶל־יַעֲקֹב הָבָה־לִּי בָנִים וְאִם־אַיִן מֵתָה אָנֹכִי: 2 וַיִּחַר־אַף יַעֲקֹב בְּרָחֵל וַיֹּאמֶר הֲתַחַת אֱלֹהִים אָנֹכִי אֲשֶׁר־מָנַע מִמֵּךְ פְּרִי־בָטֶן: 3 וַתֹּאמֶר הִנֵּה אֲמָתִי בִלְהָה בֹּא אֵלֶיהָ וְתֵלֵד עַל־בִּרְכַּי וְאִבָּנֶה גַם־אָנֹכִי מִמֶּנָּה: 4 וַתִּתֶּן־לוֹ אֶת־בִּלְהָה שִׁפְחָתָהּ לְאִשָּׁה וַיָּבֹא אֵלֶיהָ יַעֲקֹב: 5 וַתַּהַר בִּלְהָה וַתֵּלֶד לְיַעֲקֹב בֵּן: 6 וַתֹּאמֶר רָחֵל דָּנַנִּי אֱלֹהִים וְגַם שָׁמַע בְּקֹלִי וַיִּתֶּן־לִי בֵּן עַל־כֵּן קָרְאָה שְׁמוֹ דָּן: 7 וַתַּהַר עוֹד וַתֵּלֶד בִּלְהָה שִׁפְחַת

7Rachel's maid Bilhah conceived again and bore Jacob a second son. 8And Rachel said, b-"A fateful contest I waged-b with my sister; yes, and I have prevailed." So she named him Naphtali.

9When Leah saw that she had stopped bearing, she took her maid Zilpah and gave her to Jacob as concubine. 10And when Leah's maid Zilpah bore Jacob a son, 11Leah said, "What luck!"c So she named him Gad. 12When Leah's maid Zilpah bore Jacob a second son, 13Leah declared, "What fortune!"d meaning, "Women will deem me fortunate." So she named him Asher.

14Once, at the time of the wheat harvest, Reuben came upon some mandrakes in the field and brought them to his mother Leah. Rachel said to Leah, "Please give me some of your son's mandrakes." 15But she said to her, "Was it not enough for you to take away my husband, that you would also take my son's mandrakes?" Rachel replied, "I promise, he shall lie with you tonight, in return for your son's mandrakes." 16When Jacob came home from the field in the evening, Leah went out to meet him and said, "You are to sleep with me, for I have hired you with my son's mandrakes." And he lay with her that night. 17God heeded Leah, and she conceived and bore him a fifth son. 18And Leah said, "God has given me my rewarde for having given my maid to my husband." So she named him Issachar. 19When Leah conceived again and bore Jacob a sixth son, 20Leah said, "God has given me a choice gift;f this time my husband will exalt me,g for I have borne him six sons." So she named him Zebulun. 21Last, she bore him a daughter, and named her Dinah.

22Now God remembered Rachel; God heeded

8 וַתֹּאמֶר רָחֵל נַפְתּוּלֵי אֱלֹהִים ׀ נִפְתַּלְתִּי עִם־אֲחֹתִי גַּם־יָכֹלְתִּי וַתִּקְרָא שְׁמוֹ נַפְתָּלִי׃
9 וַתֵּרֶא לֵאָה כִּי עָמְדָה מִלֶּדֶת וַתִּקַּח אֶת־זִלְפָּה שִׁפְחָתָהּ וַתִּתֵּן אֹתָהּ לְיַעֲקֹב לְאִשָּׁה׃ 10 וַתֵּלֶד זִלְפָּה שִׁפְחַת לֵאָה לְיַעֲקֹב בֵּן׃ 11 וַתֹּאמֶר לֵאָה בגד בָּא גָד וַתִּקְרָא אֶת־שְׁמוֹ גָּד׃ 12 וַתֵּלֶד זִלְפָּה שִׁפְחַת לֵאָה בֵּן שֵׁנִי לְיַעֲקֹב׃ 13 וַתֹּאמֶר לֵאָה בְּאָשְׁרִי כִּי אִשְּׁרוּנִי בָּנוֹת וַתִּקְרָא אֶת־שְׁמוֹ אָשֵׁר׃
14 וַיֵּלֶךְ רְאוּבֵן בִּימֵי קְצִיר־חִטִּים וַיִּמְצָא דוּדָאִים בַּשָּׂדֶה וַיָּבֵא אֹתָם אֶל־לֵאָה אִמּוֹ וַתֹּאמֶר רָחֵל אֶל־לֵאָה תְּנִי־נָא לִי מִדּוּדָאֵי בְּנֵךְ׃ 15 וַתֹּאמֶר לָהּ הַמְעַט קַחְתֵּךְ אֶת־אִישִׁי וְלָקַחַת גַּם אֶת־דּוּדָאֵי בְּנִי וַתֹּאמֶר רָחֵל לָכֵן יִשְׁכַּב עִמָּךְ הַלַּיְלָה תַּחַת דּוּדָאֵי בְּנֵךְ׃ 16 וַיָּבֹא יַעֲקֹב מִן־הַשָּׂדֶה בָּעֶרֶב וַתֵּצֵא לֵאָה לִקְרָאתוֹ וַתֹּאמֶר אֵלַי תָּבוֹא כִּי שָׂכֹר שְׂכַרְתִּיךָ בְּדוּדָאֵי בְּנִי וַיִּשְׁכַּב עִמָּהּ בַּלַּיְלָה הוּא׃ 17 וַיִּשְׁמַע אֱלֹהִים אֶל־לֵאָה וַתַּהַר וַתֵּלֶד לְיַעֲקֹב בֵּן חֲמִישִׁי׃ 18 וַתֹּאמֶר לֵאָה נָתַן אֱלֹהִים שְׂכָרִי אֲשֶׁר־נָתַתִּי שִׁפְחָתִי לְאִישִׁי וַתִּקְרָא שְׁמוֹ יִשָּׂשכָר׃ 19 וַתַּהַר עוֹד לֵאָה וַתֵּלֶד בֵּן־שִׁשִּׁי לְיַעֲקֹב׃ 20 וַתֹּאמֶר לֵאָה זְבָדַנִי אֱלֹהִים ׀ אֹתִי זֶבֶד טוֹב הַפַּעַם יִזְבְּלֵנִי אִישִׁי כִּי־יָלַדְתִּי לוֹ שִׁשָּׁה בָנִים וַתִּקְרָא אֶת־שְׁמוֹ זְבֻלוּן׃ 21 וְאַחַר יָלְדָה בַּת וַתִּקְרָא אֶת־שְׁמָהּ דִּינָה׃
22 וַיִּזְכֹּר אֱלֹהִים אֶת־רָחֵל וַיִּשְׁמַע אֵלֶיהָ

---

b-b   *Heb.* naphtule … naphtalti, *connected with* "Naphtali." Lit. "A contest of God …"

c   *Kethib* begad; *the qere reads* ba gad "luck has come"; *connected with* "Gad."

d   *Heb.* be'oshri, *connected with* "Asher."

e   *Heb.* sekhari, *connected with* "Issachar."

f   *Heb.* zebadani … zebed.

g   *Heb.* yizbeleni; *others* "will dwell with me."

her and opened her womb. ²³She conceived and bore a son, and said, "God has taken away^h my disgrace." ²⁴So she named him Joseph, which is to say, "May the Lord add^i another son for me."

²⁵After Rachel had borne Joseph, Jacob said to Laban, "Give me leave to go back to my own homeland. ²⁶Give me my wives and my children, for whom I have served you, that I may go; for well you know what services I have rendered you." ²⁷But Laban said to him, "If you will indulge me,^j I have learned by divination that the Lord has blessed me on your account." ²⁸And he continued, "Name the wages due from me, and I will pay you." ²⁹But he said, "You know well how I have served you and how your livestock has fared with me. ³⁰For the little you had before I came has grown to much, since the Lord has blessed you wherever I turned. And now, when shall I make provision for my own household?" ³¹He said, "What shall I pay you?" And Jacob said, "Pay me nothing! If you will do this thing for me, I will again pasture and keep your flocks: ³²let me pass through your whole flock today, removing from there every speckled and spotted animal—every dark-colored sheep and every spotted and speckled goat. Such shall be my wages. ³³In the future when you go over my wages, let my honesty toward you testify for me: if there are among my goats any that are not speckled or spotted or any sheep that are not dark-colored, they got there by theft." ³⁴And Laban said, "Very well, let it be as you say."

³⁵But that same day he removed the streaked and spotted he-goats and all the speckled and spotted she-goats—every one that had white on it—and all the dark-colored sheep, and left them in the charge of his sons. ³⁶And he put a

אֱלֹהִים וַיִּפְתַּח אֶת־רַחְמָהּ: 23 וַתַּהַר וַתֵּלֶד בֵּן וַתֹּאמֶר אָסַף אֱלֹהִים אֶת־חֶרְפָּתִי: 24 וַתִּקְרָא אֶת־שְׁמוֹ יוֹסֵף לֵאמֹר יֹסֵף יְהֹוָה לִי בֵּן אַחֵר:

25 וַיְהִי כַּאֲשֶׁר יָלְדָה רָחֵל אֶת־יוֹסֵף וַיֹּאמֶר יַעֲקֹב אֶל־לָבָן שַׁלְּחֵנִי וְאֵלְכָה אֶל־מְקוֹמִי וּלְאַרְצִי: 26 תְּנָה אֶת־נָשַׁי וְאֶת־יְלָדַי אֲשֶׁר עָבַדְתִּי אֹתְךָ בָּהֵן וְאֵלֵכָה כִּי אַתָּה יָדַעְתָּ אֶת־עֲבֹדָתִי אֲשֶׁר עֲבַדְתִּיךָ: 27 וַיֹּאמֶר אֵלָיו לָבָן אִם־נָא מָצָאתִי חֵן בְּעֵינֶיךָ נִחַשְׁתִּי וַיְבָרֲכֵנִי יְהֹוָה בִּגְלָלֶךָ: 28 וַיֹּאמַר נׇקְבָה שְׂכָרְךָ עָלַי וְאֶתֵּנָה: 29 וַיֹּאמֶר אֵלָיו אַתָּה יָדַעְתָּ אֵת אֲשֶׁר עֲבַדְתִּיךָ וְאֵת אֲשֶׁר־הָיָה מִקְנְךָ אִתִּי: 30 כִּי מְעַט אֲשֶׁר־הָיָה לְךָ לְפָנַי וַיִּפְרֹץ לָרֹב וַיְבָרֶךְ יְהֹוָה אֹתְךָ לְרַגְלִי וְעַתָּה מָתַי אֶעֱשֶׂה גַם־אָנֹכִי לְבֵיתִי: 31 וַיֹּאמֶר מָה אֶתֶּן־לָךְ וַיֹּאמֶר יַעֲקֹב לֹא־תִתֶּן־לִי מְאוּמָה אִם־תַּעֲשֶׂה־לִּי הַדָּבָר הַזֶּה אָשׁוּבָה אֶרְעֶה צֹאנְךָ אֶשְׁמֹר: 32 אֶעֱבֹר בְּכׇל־צֹאנְךָ הַיּוֹם הָסֵר מִשָּׁם כׇּל־שֶׂה נָקֹד וְטָלוּא וְכׇל־שֶׂה־חוּם בַּכְּשָׂבִים וְטָלוּא וְנָקֹד בָּעִזִּים וְהָיָה שְׂכָרִי: 33 וְעָנְתָה־בִּי צִדְקָתִי בְּיוֹם מָחָר כִּי־תָבוֹא עַל־שְׂכָרִי לְפָנֶיךָ כֹּל אֲשֶׁר־אֵינֶנּוּ נָקֹד וְטָלוּא בָּעִזִּים וְחוּם בַּכְּשָׂבִים גָּנוּב הוּא אִתִּי: 34 וַיֹּאמֶר לָבָן הֵן לוּ יְהִי כִדְבָרֶךָ: 35 וַיָּסַר בַּיּוֹם הַהוּא אֶת־הַתְּיָשִׁים הָעֲקֻדִּים וְהַטְּלֻאִים וְאֵת כׇּל־הָעִזִּים הַנְּקֻדּוֹת וְהַטְּלֻאֹת כֹּל אֲשֶׁר־לָבָן בּוֹ וְכׇל־חוּם בַּכְּשָׂבִים וַיִּתֵּן בְּיַד־בָּנָיו: 36 וַיָּשֶׂם דֶּרֶךְ שְׁלֹשֶׁת יָמִים בֵּינוֹ וּבֵין יַעֲקֹב וְיַעֲקֹב רֹעֶה אֶת־צֹאן לָבָן הַנּוֹתָרֹת:

---

h   Heb. 'asaph.
i   Heb. yoseph.
j   Lit. "If I have found favor in your eyes."

distance of three days' journey between himself and Jacob, while Jacob was pasturing the rest of Laban's flock.

³⁷Jacob then got fresh shoots of poplar, and of almond and plane, and peeled white stripes in them, laying bare the white of the shoots. ³⁸The rods that he had peeled he set up in front of the goats*ᵏ* in the troughs, the water receptacles, that the goats came to drink from. Their mating occurred when they came to drink, ³⁹and since the goats mated by the rods, the goats brought forth streaked, speckled, and spotted young. ⁴⁰But Jacob dealt separately with the sheep; he made these animals face the streaked or wholly dark-colored animals in Laban's flock. And so he produced special flocks for himself, which he did not put with Laban's flocks. ⁴¹Moreover, when the sturdier*ˡ* animals were mating, Jacob would place the rods in the troughs, in full view of the animals, so that they mated by the rods; ⁴²but with the feebler*ᵐ* animals he would not place them there. Thus the feeble ones*ᵐ* went to Laban and the sturdy to Jacob. ⁴³So the man grew exceedingly prosperous, and came to own large flocks, maidservants and menservants, camels and asses.

31 Now he heard the things that Laban's sons were saying: "Jacob has taken all that was our father's, and from that which was our father's he has built up all this wealth." ²Jacob also saw that Laban's manner toward him was not as it had been in the past. ³Then the Lᴏʀᴅ said to Jacob, "Return to the land of your fathers where you were born, and I will be with you." ⁴Jacob had Rachel and Leah called to the field, where his flock was, ⁵and said to them, "I see that your father's manner toward me is not as

---

k Lit. "flocks."
l Or "early-breeding."
m Or "late-breeding."

³⁷וַיִּקַּח־לוֹ יַעֲקֹב מַקַּל לִבְנֶה לַח וְלוּז וְעַרְמוֹן וַיְפַצֵּל בָּהֵן פְּצָלוֹת לְבָנוֹת מַחְשֹׂף הַלָּבָן אֲשֶׁר עַל־הַמַּקְלוֹת: ³⁸וַיַּצֵּג אֶת־הַמַּקְלוֹת אֲשֶׁר פִּצֵּל בָּרְהָטִים בְּשִׁקֲתוֹת הַמָּיִם אֲשֶׁר תָּבֹאןָ הַצֹּאן לִשְׁתּוֹת לְנֹכַח הַצֹּאן וַיֵּחַמְנָה בְּבֹאָן לִשְׁתּוֹת: ³⁹וַיֶּחֱמוּ הַצֹּאן אֶל־הַמַּקְלוֹת וַתֵּלַדְןָ הַצֹּאן עֲקֻדִּים נְקֻדִּים וּטְלֻאִים: ⁴⁰וְהַכְּשָׂבִים הִפְרִיד יַעֲקֹב וַיִּתֵּן פְּנֵי הַצֹּאן אֶל־עָקֹד וְכָל־חוּם בְּצֹאן לָבָן וַיָּשֶׁת־לוֹ עֲדָרִים לְבַדּוֹ וְלֹא שָׁתָם עַל־צֹאן לָבָן: ⁴¹וְהָיָה בְּכָל־יַחֵם הַצֹּאן הַמְקֻשָּׁרוֹת וְשָׂם יַעֲקֹב אֶת־הַמַּקְלוֹת לְעֵינֵי הַצֹּאן בָּרְהָטִים לְיַחְמֵנָּה בַּמַּקְלוֹת: ⁴²וּבְהַעֲטִיף* הַצֹּאן לֹא יָשִׂים וְהָיָה הָעֲטֻפִים לְלָבָן וְהַקְּשֻׁרִים לְיַעֲקֹב: ⁴³וַיִּפְרֹץ הָאִישׁ מְאֹד מְאֹד וַיְהִי־לוֹ צֹאן רַבּוֹת וּשְׁפָחוֹת וַעֲבָדִים וּגְמַלִּים וַחֲמֹרִים:

לא וַיִּשְׁמַע אֶת־דִּבְרֵי בְנֵי־לָבָן לֵאמֹר לָקַח יַעֲקֹב אֵת כָּל־אֲשֶׁר לְאָבִינוּ וּמֵאֲשֶׁר לְאָבִינוּ עָשָׂה אֵת כָּל־הַכָּבֹד הַזֶּה: ²וַיַּרְא יַעֲקֹב אֶת־פְּנֵי לָבָן וְהִנֵּה אֵינֶנּוּ עִמּוֹ כִּתְמוֹל שִׁלְשׁוֹם: ³וַיֹּאמֶר יְהֹוָה אֶל־יַעֲקֹב שׁוּב אֶל־אֶרֶץ אֲבוֹתֶיךָ וּלְמוֹלַדְתֶּךָ וְאֶהְיֶה עִמָּךְ: ⁴וַיִּשְׁלַח יַעֲקֹב וַיִּקְרָא לְרָחֵל וּלְלֵאָה הַשָּׂדֶה אֶל־צֹאנוֹ: ⁵וַיֹּאמֶר לָהֶן רֹאֶה אָנֹכִי אֶת־פְּנֵי אֲבִיכֶן כִּי־אֵינֶנּוּ אֵלַי כִּתְמֹל שִׁלְשֹׁם וֵאלֹהֵי אָבִי

v. 42. ף' רבתי לפי מהדורת לעטעריס

it has been in the past. But the God of my father has been with me. 6As you know, I have served your father with all my might; 7but your father has cheated me, changing my wages time and again.ᵃ God, however, would not let him do me harm. 8If he said thus, 'The speckled shall be your wages,' then all the flocks would drop speckled young; and if he said thus, 'The streaked shall be your wages,' then all the flocks would drop streaked young. 9God has taken away your father's livestock and given it to me.

10"Once, at the mating time of the flocks, ᵇ-I had a dream in which I saw-ᵇ that the he-goats mating with the flock were streaked, speckled, and mottled. 11And in the dream an angel of God said to me, 'Jacob!' 'Here,' I answered. 12And he said, 'Note well that all the he-goats which are mating with the flock are streaked, speckled, and mottled; for I have noted all that Laban has been doing to you. 13I am the God of Beth-el, where you anointed a pillar and where you made a vow to Me. Now, arise and leave this land and return to your native land.'"

14Then Rachel and Leah answered him, saying, "Have we still a share in the inheritance of our father's house? 15Surely, he regards us as outsiders, now that he has sold us and has used up our purchase price. 16Truly, all the wealth that God has taken away from our father belongs to us and to our children. Now then, do just as God has told you."

17Thereupon Jacob put his children and wives on camels; 18and he drove off all his livestock and all the wealth that he had amassed, the livestock in his possession that he had acquired in Paddan-aram, to go to his father Isaac in the land of Canaan.

19Meanwhile Laban had gone to shear his sheep, and Rachel stole her father's household

---

ᵃ   Lit. "ten times."
ᵇ-ᵇ   Lit. "I raised my eyes and saw in a dream, behold."

הָיָה עִמָּדִי: 6 וְאַתֵּנָה יְדַעְתֶּן כִּי בְּכָל־כֹּחִי עָבַדְתִּי אֶת־אֲבִיכֶן: 7 וַאֲבִיכֶן הֵתֶל בִּי וְהֶחֱלִף אֶת־מַשְׂכֻּרְתִּי עֲשֶׂרֶת מֹנִים וְלֹא־נְתָנוֹ אֱלֹהִים לְהָרַע עִמָּדִי: 8 אִם־כֹּה יֹאמַר נְקֻדִּים יִהְיֶה שְׂכָרֶךָ וְיָלְדוּ כָל־הַצֹּאן נְקֻדִּים וְאִם־כֹּה יֹאמַר עֲקֻדִּים יִהְיֶה שְׂכָרֶךָ וְיָלְדוּ כָל־הַצֹּאן עֲקֻדִּים: 9 וַיַּצֵּל אֱלֹהִים אֶת־מִקְנֵה אֲבִיכֶם וַיִּתֶּן־לִי:

10 וַיְהִי בְּעֵת יַחֵם הַצֹּאן וָאֶשָּׂא עֵינַי וָאֵרֶא בַּחֲלוֹם וְהִנֵּה הָעַתֻּדִים הָעֹלִים עַל־הַצֹּאן עֲקֻדִּים נְקֻדִּים וּבְרֻדִּים: 11 וַיֹּאמֶר אֵלַי מַלְאַךְ הָאֱלֹהִים בַּחֲלוֹם יַעֲקֹב וָאֹמַר הִנֵּנִי: 12 וַיֹּאמֶר שָׂא־נָא עֵינֶיךָ וּרְאֵה כָּל־הָעַתֻּדִים הָעֹלִים עַל־הַצֹּאן עֲקֻדִּים נְקֻדִּים וּבְרֻדִּים כִּי רָאִיתִי אֵת כָּל־אֲשֶׁר לָבָן עֹשֶׂה לָּךְ: 13 אָנֹכִי הָאֵל בֵּית־אֵל אֲשֶׁר מָשַׁחְתָּ שָּׁם מַצֵּבָה אֲשֶׁר נָדַרְתָּ לִּי שָׁם נֶדֶר עַתָּה קוּם צֵא מִן־הָאָרֶץ הַזֹּאת וְשׁוּב אֶל־אֶרֶץ מוֹלַדְתֶּךָ:

14 וַתַּעַן רָחֵל וְלֵאָה וַתֹּאמַרְנָה לוֹ הַעוֹד לָנוּ חֵלֶק וְנַחֲלָה בְּבֵית אָבִינוּ: 15 הֲלוֹא נָכְרִיּוֹת נֶחְשַׁבְנוּ לוֹ כִּי מְכָרָנוּ וַיֹּאכַל גַּם־אָכוֹל אֶת־כַּסְפֵּנוּ: 16 כִּי כָל־הָעֹשֶׁר אֲשֶׁר הִצִּיל אֱלֹהִים מֵאָבִינוּ לָנוּ הוּא וּלְבָנֵינוּ וְעַתָּה כֹּל אֲשֶׁר אָמַר אֱלֹהִים אֵלֶיךָ עֲשֵׂה:

17 וַיָּקָם יַעֲקֹב וַיִּשָּׂא אֶת־בָּנָיו וְאֶת־נָשָׁיו עַל־הַגְּמַלִּים: 18 וַיִּנְהַג אֶת־כָּל־מִקְנֵהוּ וְאֶת־כָּל־רְכֻשׁוֹ אֲשֶׁר רָכָשׁ מִקְנֵה קִנְיָנוֹ אֲשֶׁר רָכַשׁ בְּפַדַּן אֲרָם לָבוֹא אֶל־יִצְחָק אָבִיו אַרְצָה כְּנָעַן:

19 וְלָבָן הָלַךְ לִגְזֹז אֶת־צֹאנוֹ וַתִּגְנֹב רָחֵל אֶת־הַתְּרָפִים אֲשֶׁר לְאָבִיהָ: 20 וַיִּגְנֹב

idols. 20Jacob c-kept Laban the Aramean in the dark,-c not telling him that he was fleeing, 21and fled with all that he had. Soon he was across the Euphrates and heading toward the hill country of Gilead.

22On the third day, Laban was told that Jacob had fled. 23So he took his kinsmen with him and pursued him a distance of seven days, catching up with him in the hill country of Gilead. 24But God appeared to Laban the Aramean in a dream by night and said to him, "Beware of attempting anything with Jacob, good or bad."

25Laban overtook Jacob. Jacob had pitched his tent on the Height, and Laban with his kins-men encamped in the hill country of Gilead. 26And Laban said to Jacob, "What did you mean by keeping me in the dark and carrying off my daughters like captives of the sword? 27Why did you flee in secrecy and mislead me and not tell me? I would have sent you off with festive music, with timbrel and lyre. 28You did not even let me kiss my sons and daughters good-by! It was a foolish thing for you to do. 29I have it in my power to do you harm; but the God of your fa-ther said to me last night, 'Beware of attempting anything with Jacob, good or bad.' 30Very well, you had to leave because you were longing for your father's house; but why did you steal my gods?"

31Jacob answered Laban, saying, "I was afraid because I thought you would take your daugh-ters from me by force. 32But anyone with whom you find your gods shall not remain alive! In the presence of our kinsmen, point out what I have of yours and take it." Jacob, of course, did not know that Rachel had stolen them.

33So Laban went into Jacob's tent and Leah's tent and the tents of the two maidservants; but he did not find them. Leaving Leah's tent, he entered Rachel's tent. 34Rachel, meanwhile, had

יַעֲקֹב אֶת־לֵב לָבָן הָאֲרַמִּי עַל־בְּלִי הִגִּיד לוֹ כִּי בֹרֵחַ הוּא: 21 וַיִּבְרַח הוּא וְכָל־אֲשֶׁר־לוֹ וַיָּקָם וַיַּעֲבֹר אֶת־הַנָּהָר וַיָּשֶׂם אֶת־פָּנָיו הַר הַגִּלְעָד:

22 וַיֻּגַּד לְלָבָן בַּיּוֹם הַשְּׁלִישִׁי כִּי בָרַח יַעֲקֹב: 23 וַיִּקַּח אֶת־אֶחָיו עִמּוֹ וַיִּרְדֹּף אַחֲרָיו דֶּרֶךְ שִׁבְעַת יָמִים וַיַּדְבֵּק אֹתוֹ בְּהַר הַגִּלְעָד: 24 וַיָּבֹא אֱלֹהִים אֶל־לָבָן הָאֲרַמִּי בַּחֲלֹם הַלָּיְלָה וַיֹּאמֶר לוֹ הִשָּׁמֶר לְךָ פֶּן־תְּדַבֵּר עִם־יַעֲקֹב מִטּוֹב עַד־רָע:

25 וַיַּשֵּׂג לָבָן אֶת־יַעֲקֹב וְיַעֲקֹב תָּקַע אֶת־אָהֳלוֹ בָּהָר וְלָבָן תָּקַע אֶת־אֶחָיו בְּהַר הַגִּלְעָד: 26 וַיֹּאמֶר לָבָן לְיַעֲקֹב מֶה עָשִׂיתָ וַתִּגְנֹב אֶת־לְבָבִי וַתְּנַהֵג אֶת־בְּנֹתַי כִּשְׁבֻיוֹת חָרֶב: 27 לָמָּה נַחְבֵּאתָ לִבְרֹחַ וַתִּגְנֹב אֹתִי וְלֹא־הִגַּדְתָּ לִּי וָאֲשַׁלֵּחֲךָ בְּשִׂמְחָה וּבְשִׁרִים בְּתֹף וּבְכִנּוֹר: 28 וְלֹא נְטַשְׁתַּנִי לְנַשֵּׁק לְבָנַי וְלִבְנֹתָי עַתָּה הִסְכַּלְתָּ עֲשׂוֹ: 29 יֶשׁ־לְאֵל יָדִי לַעֲשׂוֹת עִמָּכֶם רָע וֵאלֹהֵי אֲבִיכֶם אֶמֶשׁ ׀ אָמַר אֵלַי לֵאמֹר הִשָּׁמֶר לְךָ מִדַּבֵּר עִם־יַעֲקֹב מִטּוֹב עַד־רָע: 30 וְעַתָּה הָלֹךְ הָלַכְתָּ כִּי־נִכְסֹף נִכְסַפְתָּה לְבֵית אָבִיךָ לָמָּה גָנַבְתָּ אֶת־אֱלֹהָי:

31 וַיַּעַן יַעֲקֹב וַיֹּאמֶר לְלָבָן כִּי יָרֵאתִי כִּי אָמַרְתִּי פֶּן־תִּגְזֹל אֶת־בְּנוֹתֶיךָ מֵעִמִּי: 32 עִם אֲשֶׁר תִּמְצָא אֶת־אֱלֹהֶיךָ לֹא יִחְיֶה נֶגֶד אַחֵינוּ הַכֶּר־לְךָ מָה עִמָּדִי וְקַח־לָךְ וְלֹא־יָדַע יַעֲקֹב כִּי רָחֵל גְּנָבָתַם: 33 וַיָּבֹא לָבָן בְּאֹהֶל יַעֲקֹב ׀ וּבְאֹהֶל לֵאָה וּבְאֹהֶל שְׁתֵּי הָאֲמָהֹת וְלֹא מָצָא וַיֵּצֵא מֵאֹהֶל לֵאָה וַיָּבֹא בְּאֹהֶל רָחֵל: 34 וְרָחֵל לָקְחָה אֶת־הַתְּרָפִים וַתְּשִׂמֵם בְּכַר הַגָּמָל

---

c-c　Lit. "stole the mind of Laban the Aramean"; similarly in v. 26.

taken the idols and placed them in the camel cushion and sat on them; and Laban rummaged through the tent without finding them. ³⁵For she said to her father, "Let not my lord take it amiss that I cannot rise before you, for the period of women is upon me." Thus he searched, but could not find the household idols.

³⁶Now Jacob became incensed and took up his grievance with Laban. Jacob spoke up and said to Laban, "What is my crime, what is my guilt that you should pursue me? ³⁷You rummaged through all my things; what have you found of all your household objects? Set it here, before my kinsmen and yours, and let them decide between us two.

³⁸"These twenty years I have spent in your service, your ewes and she-goats never miscarried, nor did I feast on rams from your flock. ³⁹That which was torn by beasts I never brought to you; I myself made good the loss; you exacted it of me, whether snatched by day or snatched by night. ⁴⁰Often,ᵈ scorching heat ravaged me by day and frost by night; and sleep fled from my eyes. ⁴¹Of the twenty years that I spent in your household, I served you fourteen years for your two daughters, and six years for your flocks; and you changed my wages time and again.ᵉ ⁴²Had not the God of my father, the God of Abraham and the Fearᶠ of Isaac, been with me, you would have sent me away empty-handed. But God took notice of my plight and the toil of my hands, and He gave judgment last night."

⁴³Then Laban spoke up and said to Jacob, "The daughters are my daughters, the children are my children, and the flocks are my flocks; all that you see is mine. Yet what can I do now about my daughters or the children they have borne? ⁴⁴Come, then, let us make a pact, you

---

d Lit. "I was."
e Lit. "ten times."
f Meaning of Heb. paḥad uncertain.

65

וַתֵּשֶׁב עֲלֵיהֶם וַיְמַשֵּׁשׁ לָבָן אֶת־כָּל־הָאֹהֶל וְלֹא מָצָא: 35 וַתֹּאמֶר אֶל־אָבִיהָ אַל־יִחַר בְּעֵינֵי אֲדֹנִי כִּי לוֹא* אוּכַל לָקוּם מִפָּנֶיךָ כִּי־דֶרֶךְ נָשִׁים לִי וַיְחַפֵּשׂ וְלֹא מָצָא אֶת־הַתְּרָפִים:

36 וַיִּחַר לְיַעֲקֹב וַיָּרֶב בְּלָבָן וַיַּעַן יַעֲקֹב וַיֹּאמֶר לְלָבָן מַה־פִּשְׁעִי מַה חַטָּאתִי כִּי דָלַקְתָּ אַחֲרָי: 37 כִּי־מִשַּׁשְׁתָּ אֶת־כָּל־כֵּלַי מַה־מָּצָאתָ מִכֹּל כְּלֵי־בֵיתֶךָ שִׂים כֹּה נֶגֶד אַחַי וְאַחֶיךָ וְיוֹכִיחוּ בֵּין שְׁנֵינוּ:

38 זֶה עֶשְׂרִים שָׁנָה אָנֹכִי עִמָּךְ רְחֵלֶיךָ וְעִזֶּיךָ לֹא שִׁכֵּלוּ וְאֵילֵי צֹאנְךָ לֹא אָכָלְתִּי: 39 טְרֵפָה לֹא־הֵבֵאתִי אֵלֶיךָ אָנֹכִי אֲחַטֶּנָּה מִיָּדִי תְּבַקְשֶׁנָּה גְּנֻבְתִי יוֹם וּגְנֻבְתִי לָיְלָה: 40 הָיִיתִי בַיּוֹם אֲכָלַנִי חֹרֶב וְקֶרַח בַּלָּיְלָה וַתִּדַּד שְׁנָתִי מֵעֵינָי: 41 זֶה־לִּי עֶשְׂרִים שָׁנָה בְּבֵיתֶךָ עֲבַדְתִּיךָ אַרְבַּע־עֶשְׂרֵה שָׁנָה בִּשְׁתֵּי בְנֹתֶיךָ וְשֵׁשׁ שָׁנִים בְּצֹאנֶךָ וַתַּחֲלֵף אֶת־מַשְׂכֻּרְתִּי עֲשֶׂרֶת מֹנִים: 42 לוּלֵי אֱלֹהֵי אָבִי אֱלֹהֵי אַבְרָהָם וּפַחַד יִצְחָק הָיָה לִי כִּי עַתָּה רֵיקָם שִׁלַּחְתָּנִי אֶת־עָנְיִי וְאֶת־יְגִיעַ כַּפַּי רָאָה אֱלֹהִים וַיּוֹכַח אָמֶשׁ:

43 וַיַּעַן לָבָן וַיֹּאמֶר אֶל־יַעֲקֹב הַבָּנוֹת בְּנֹתַי וְהַבָּנִים בָּנַי וְהַצֹּאן צֹאנִי וְכֹל אֲשֶׁר־אַתָּה רֹאֶה לִי־הוּא וְלִבְנֹתַי מָה־אֶעֱשֶׂה לָאֵלֶּה הַיּוֹם אוֹ לִבְנֵיהֶן אֲשֶׁר יָלָדוּ: 44 וְעַתָּה לְכָה נִכְרְתָה בְרִית אֲנִי וָאָתָּה וְהָיָה לְעֵד

מלא ו׳　v. 35.

and I, that there may be a witness between you and me." ⁴⁵Thereupon Jacob took a stone and set it up as a pillar. ⁴⁶And Jacob said to his kinsmen, "Gather stones." So they took stones and made a mound; and they partook of a meal there by the mound. ⁴⁷Laban named it Yegar-sahadutha,ᵍ but Jacob named it Gal-ed.ʰ ⁴⁸And Laban declared, "This mound is a witness between you and me this day." That is why it was named Gal-ed; ⁴⁹and [it was called] Mizpah, because he said, "May the Lord watchⁱ between you and me, when we are out of sight of each other. ⁵⁰If you ill-treat my daughters or take other wives besides my daughters—though no one else be about, remember, God Himself will be witness between you and me."

⁵¹And Laban said to Jacob, "Here is this mound and here the pillar which I have set up between you and me: ⁵²this mound shall be witness and this pillar shall be witness that I am not to cross to you past this mound, and that you are not to cross to me past this mound and this pillar, with hostile intent. ⁵³May the God of Abraham and the god of Nahor"—their ancestral deities—"judge between us." And Jacob swore by the Fearʲ of his father Isaac. ⁵⁴Jacob then offered up a sacrifice on the Height, and invited his kinsmen to partake of the meal. After the meal, they spent the night on the Height.

32 Early in the morning, Laban kissed his sons and daughters and bade them good-by; then Laban left on his journey homeward. ²Jacob went on his way, and angels of God encountered him. ³When he saw them, Jacob said, "This is God's camp." So he named that place Mahanaim.ᵃ

בֵּינִי וּבֵינֶךָ: ⁴⁵ וַיִּקַּח יַעֲקֹב אָבֶן וַיְרִימֶהָ מַצֵּבָה: ⁴⁶ וַיֹּאמֶר יַעֲקֹב לְאֶחָיו לִקְטוּ אֲבָנִים וַיִּקְחוּ אֲבָנִים וַיַּעֲשׂוּ־גָל וַיֹּאכְלוּ שָׁם עַל־הַגָּל: ⁴⁷ וַיִּקְרָא־לוֹ לָבָן יְגַר שָׂהֲדוּתָא וְיַעֲקֹב קָרָא לוֹ גַּלְעֵד: ⁴⁸ וַיֹּאמֶר לָבָן הַגַּל הַזֶּה עֵד בֵּינִי וּבֵינְךָ הַיּוֹם עַל־כֵּן קָרָא־שְׁמוֹ גַּלְעֵד: ⁴⁹ וְהַמִּצְפָּה אֲשֶׁר אָמַר יִצֶף יְהוָה בֵּינִי וּבֵינֶךָ כִּי נִסָּתֵר אִישׁ מֵרֵעֵהוּ: ⁵⁰ אִם־תְּעַנֶּה אֶת־בְּנֹתַי וְאִם־תִּקַּח נָשִׁים עַל־בְּנֹתַי אֵין אִישׁ עִמָּנוּ רְאֵה אֱלֹהִים עֵד בֵּינִי וּבֵינֶךָ: ⁵¹ וַיֹּאמֶר לָבָן לְיַעֲקֹב הִנֵּה ׀ הַגַּל הַזֶּה וְהִנֵּה הַמַּצֵּבָה אֲשֶׁר יָרִיתִי בֵּינִי וּבֵינֶךָ: ⁵² עֵד הַגַּל הַזֶּה וְעֵדָה הַמַּצֵּבָה אִם־אָנִי לֹא־אֶעֱבֹר אֵלֶיךָ אֶת־הַגַּל הַזֶּה וְאִם־אַתָּה לֹא־תַעֲבֹר אֵלַי אֶת־הַגַּל הַזֶּה וְאֶת־הַמַּצֵּבָה הַזֹּאת לְרָעָה: ⁵³ אֱלֹהֵי אַבְרָהָם וֵאלֹהֵי נָחוֹר יִשְׁפְּטוּ בֵינֵינוּ אֱלֹהֵי אֲבִיהֶם וַיִּשָּׁבַע יַעֲקֹב בְּפַחַד אָבִיו יִצְחָק: ⁵⁴ וַיִּזְבַּח יַעֲקֹב זֶבַח בָּהָר וַיִּקְרָא לְאֶחָיו לֶאֱכָל־לָחֶם וַיֹּאכְלוּ לֶחֶם וַיָּלִינוּ בָּהָר:

לב וַיַּשְׁכֵּם לָבָן בַּבֹּקֶר וַיְנַשֵּׁק לְבָנָיו וְלִבְנוֹתָיו וַיְבָרֶךְ אֶתְהֶם וַיֵּלֶךְ וַיָּשָׁב לָבָן לִמְקֹמוֹ: ² וְיַעֲקֹב הָלַךְ לְדַרְכּוֹ וַיִּפְגְּעוּ־בוֹ מַלְאֲכֵי אֱלֹהִים: ³ וַיֹּאמֶר יַעֲקֹב כַּאֲשֶׁר רָאָם מַחֲנֵה אֱלֹהִים זֶה וַיִּקְרָא שֵׁם־הַמָּקוֹם הַהוּא מַחֲנָיִם: פ

---

g   Aramaic for "the mound (or, stone-heap) of witness."
h   Heb. for "the mound (or, stone-heap) of witness," reflecting the
    name Gilead, v. 23.
i   Heb. yiseph, associated with Mizpah.
j   Meaning of Heb. paḥad uncertain.

a   Connected with Heb. maḥaneh, "camp."

וישלח

VA-YISHLAH

4Jacob sent messengers ahead to his brother Esau in the land of Seir, the country of Edom, 5and instructed them as follows, *b-*"Thus shall you say, 'To my lord Esau, thus says your servant Jacob:*-b* I stayed with Laban and remained until now; 6I have acquired cattle, asses, sheep, and male and female slaves; and I send this message to my lord in the hope of gaining your favor.'" 7The messengers returned to Jacob, saying, "We came to your brother Esau; he himself is coming to meet you, and there are four hundred men with him." 8Jacob was greatly frightened; in his anxiety, he divided the people with him, and the flocks and herds and camels, into two camps, 9thinking, "If Esau comes to the one camp and attacks it, the other camp may yet escape."

10Then Jacob said, "O God of my father Abraham and God of my father Isaac, O LORD, who said to me, 'Return to your native land and I will deal bountifully with you'! 11I am unworthy of all the kindness that You have so steadfastly shown Your servant: with my staff alone I crossed this Jordan, and now I have become two camps. 12Deliver me, I pray, from the hand of my brother, from the hand of Esau; else, I fear, he may come and strike me down, mothers and children alike. 13Yet You have said, 'I will deal bountifully with you and make your offspring as the sands of the sea, which are too numerous to count.'"

14After spending the night there, he selected from what was at hand these presents for his brother Esau: 15200 she-goats and 20 he-goats; 200 ewes and 20 rams; 1630 milch camels with their colts; 40 cows and 10 bulls; 20 she-asses and 10 he-asses. 17These he put in the charge of his servants, drove by drove, and he told his servants, "Go on ahead, and keep a distance between droves." 18He instructed the one in front

4 וַיִּשְׁלַ֨ח יַעֲקֹ֤ב מַלְאָכִים֙ לְפָנָ֔יו אֶל־עֵשָׂ֖ו אָחִ֑יו אַ֥רְצָה שֵׂעִ֖יר שְׂדֵ֥ה אֱדֽוֹם: 5 וַיְצַ֤ו אֹתָם֙ לֵאמֹ֔ר כֹּ֣ה תֹאמְר֔וּן לַֽאדֹנִ֖י לְעֵשָׂ֑ו כֹּ֤ה אָמַר֙ עַבְדְּךָ֣ יַעֲקֹ֔ב עִם־לָבָ֣ן גַּ֔רְתִּי וָאֵחַ֖ר עַד־עָֽתָּה: 6 וַֽיְהִי־לִי֙ שׁ֣וֹר וַחֲמ֔וֹר צֹ֖אן וְעֶ֣בֶד וְשִׁפְחָ֑ה וָֽאֶשְׁלְחָה֙ לְהַגִּ֣יד לַֽאדֹנִ֔י לִמְצֹא־חֵ֖ן בְּעֵינֶֽיךָ: 7 וַיָּשֻׁ֨בוּ֙ הַמַּלְאָכִ֔ים אֶֽל־יַעֲקֹ֖ב לֵאמֹ֑ר בָּ֤אנוּ אֶל־אָחִ֨יךָ֙ אֶל־עֵשָׂ֔ו וְגַם֙ הֹלֵ֣ךְ לִקְרָֽאתְךָ֔ וְאַרְבַּע־מֵא֥וֹת אִ֖ישׁ עִמּֽוֹ: 8 וַיִּירָ֧א יַעֲקֹ֛ב מְאֹ֖ד וַיֵּ֣צֶר ל֑וֹ וַיַּ֜חַץ אֶת־הָעָ֣ם אֲשֶׁר־אִתּ֗וֹ וְאֶת־הַצֹּ֛אן וְאֶת־הַבָּקָ֥ר וְהַגְּמַלִּ֖ים לִשְׁנֵ֥י מַחֲנֽוֹת: 9 וַיֹּ֕אמֶר אִם־יָב֥וֹא עֵשָׂ֛ו אֶל־הַמַּחֲנֶ֥ה הָאַחַ֖ת וְהִכָּ֑הוּ וְהָיָ֛ה הַמַּחֲנֶ֥ה הַנִּשְׁאָ֖ר לִפְלֵיטָֽה: 10 וַיֹּאמֶר֮ יַעֲקֹב֒ אֱלֹהֵי֙ אָבִ֣י אַבְרָהָ֔ם וֵאלֹהֵ֖י אָבִ֣י יִצְחָ֑ק יְהֹוָ֞ה הָאֹמֵ֣ר אֵלַ֗י שׁ֤וּב לְאַרְצְךָ֙ וּלְמֽוֹלַדְתְּךָ֖ וְאֵיטִ֥יבָה עִמָּֽךְ: 11 קָטֹ֜נְתִּי מִכֹּ֤ל הַחֲסָדִים֙ וּמִכָּל־הָ֣אֱמֶ֔ת אֲשֶׁ֥ר עָשִׂ֖יתָ אֶת־עַבְדֶּ֑ךָ כִּ֣י בְמַקְלִ֗י עָבַ֨רְתִּי֙ אֶת־הַיַּרְדֵּ֣ן הַזֶּ֔ה וְעַתָּ֥ה הָיִ֖יתִי לִשְׁנֵ֥י מַחֲנֽוֹת: 12 הַצִּילֵ֥נִי נָ֛א מִיַּ֥ד אָחִ֖י מִיַּ֣ד עֵשָׂ֑ו כִּֽי־יָרֵ֤א אָנֹכִי֙ אֹת֔וֹ פֶּן־יָב֣וֹא וְהִכַּ֔נִי אֵ֖ם עַל־בָּנִֽים: 13 וְאַתָּ֣ה אָמַ֔רְתָּ הֵיטֵ֥ב אֵיטִ֖יב עִמָּ֑ךְ וְשַׂמְתִּ֣י אֶֽת־זַרְעֲךָ֙ כְּח֣וֹל הַיָּ֔ם אֲשֶׁ֥ר לֹא־יִסָּפֵ֖ר מֵרֹֽב: 14 וַיָּ֥לֶן שָׁ֖ם בַּלַּ֣יְלָה הַה֑וּא וַיִּקַּ֞ח מִן־הַבָּ֧א בְיָד֛וֹ מִנְחָ֖ה לְעֵשָׂ֥ו אָחִֽיו: 15 עִזִּ֣ים מָאתַ֔יִם וּתְיָשִׁ֖ים עֶשְׂרִ֑ים רְחֵלִ֥ים מָאתַ֖יִם וְאֵילִ֥ים עֶשְׂרִֽים: 16 גְּמַלִּ֧ים מֵינִיק֛וֹת וּבְנֵיהֶ֖ם שְׁלֹשִׁ֑ים פָּר֤וֹת אַרְבָּעִים֙ וּפָרִ֣ים עֲשָׂרָ֔ה אֲתֹנֹ֣ת עֶשְׂרִ֔ים וַעְיָרִ֖ם עֲשָׂרָֽה: 17 וַיִּתֵּן֙ בְּיַד־עֲבָדָ֔יו עֵ֥דֶר עֵ֖דֶר לְבַדּ֑וֹ וַיֹּ֤אמֶר אֶל־עֲבָדָיו֙ עִבְר֣וּ לְפָנַ֔י וְרֶ֣וַח תָּשִׂ֔ימוּ בֵּ֥ין עֵ֖דֶר וּבֵ֥ין עֵֽדֶר: 18 וַיְצַ֥ו אֶת־הָרִאשׁ֖וֹן לֵאמֹ֑ר כִּ֣י

---

b-b Or "Thus you shall say to my lord Esau, 'Thus says your servant Jacob:…'"

as follows, "When my brother Esau meets you and asks you, 'Whose man are you? Where are you going? And whose [animals] are these ahead of you?' ¹⁹you shall answer, 'Your servant Jacob's; they are a gift sent to my lord Esau; and [Jacob] himself is right behind us.'" ²⁰He gave similar instructions to the second one, and the third, and all the others who followed the droves, namely, "Thus and so shall you say to Esau when you reach him. ²¹And you shall add, 'And your servant Jacob himself is right behind us.'" For he reasoned, "If I propitiate him with presents in advance, and then face him, perhaps he will show me favor." ²²And so the gift went on ahead, while he remained in camp that night.

²³That same night he arose, and taking his two wives, his two maidservants, and his eleven children, he crossed the ford of the Jabbok. ²⁴After taking them across the stream, he sent across all his possessions. ²⁵Jacob was left alone. And a man wrestled with him until the break of dawn. ²⁶When he saw that he had not prevailed against him, he wrenched Jacob's hip at its socket, so that the socket of his hip was strained as he wrestled with him. ²⁷Then he said, "Let me go, for dawn is breaking." But he answered, "I will not let you go, unless you bless me." ²⁸Said the other, "What is your name?" He replied, "Jacob." ²⁹Said he, "Your name shall no longer be Jacob, but Israel, for you have strivenᶜ with ᵈbeings divine and human,-ᵈ and have prevailed." ³⁰Jacob asked, "Pray tell me your name." But he said, "You must not ask my name!" And he took leave of him there. ³¹So Jacob named the place Peniel,ᵉ meaning, "I have seen a divine being face to face, yet my life has been preserved." ³²The sun rose upon him as he passed Penuel, limping on his hip. ³³That is

c   Heb. saritha, connected with first part of "Israel."
d-d   Or "God (Elohim, connected with second part of 'Israel') and men."
e   Understood as "face of God."

יִפְגָּשְׁךָ֙ עֵשָׂ֣ו אָחִ֔י וּשְׁאֵֽלְךָ֣ לֵאמֹ֔ר לְמִי־
אַ֙תָּה֙ וְאָ֣נָה תֵלֵ֔ךְ וּלְמִ֖י אֵ֥לֶּה לְפָנֶֽיךָ׃ 19 וְאָֽמַרְתָּ֙ לְעַבְדְּךָ֣ לְיַעֲקֹ֔ב מִנְחָ֥ה הִוא֙ שְׁלוּחָ֖ה לַֽאדֹנִ֣י לְעֵשָׂ֑ו וְהִנֵּ֥ה גַם־ה֖וּא אַחֲרֵֽינוּ׃ 20 וַיְצַ֞ו גַּ֣ם אֶת־הַשֵּׁנִ֗י גַּ֚ם אֶת־הַשְּׁלִישִׁ֔י גַּ֚ם אֶֽת־כָּל־הַהֹ֣לְכִ֔ים אַחֲרֵ֥י הָעֲדָרִ֖ים לֵאמֹ֑ר כַּדָּבָ֤ר הַזֶּה֙ תְּדַבְּר֣וּן אֶל־עֵשָׂ֔ו בְּמֹצַאֲכֶ֖ם אֹתֽוֹ׃ 21 וַאֲמַרְתֶּ֕ם גַּ֗ם הִנֵּ֛ה עַבְדְּךָ֥ יַעֲקֹ֖ב אַחֲרֵ֑ינוּ כִּֽי־אָמַ֞ר אֲכַפְּרָ֣ה פָנָ֗יו בַּמִּנְחָה֙ הַהֹלֶ֣כֶת לְפָנָ֔י וְאַחֲרֵי־כֵן֙ אֶרְאֶ֣ה פָנָ֔יו אוּלַ֖י יִשָּׂ֥א פָנָֽי׃ 22 וַתַּעֲבֹ֥ר הַמִּנְחָ֖ה עַל־פָּנָ֑יו וְה֛וּא לָ֥ן בַּלַּֽיְלָה־הַה֖וּא בַּֽמַּחֲנֶֽה׃ 23 וַיָּ֣קָם ׀ בַּלַּ֣יְלָה ה֗וּא וַיִּקַּ֞ח אֶת־שְׁתֵּ֤י נָשָׁיו֙ וְאֶת־שְׁתֵּ֣י שִׁפְחֹתָ֔יו וְאֶת־אַחַ֥ד עָשָׂ֖ר יְלָדָ֑יו וַֽיַּעֲבֹ֔ר אֵ֖ת מַעֲבַ֥ר יַבֹּֽק׃ 24 וַיִּקָּחֵ֔ם וַיַּֽעֲבִרֵ֖ם אֶת־הַנָּ֑חַל וַֽיַּעֲבֵ֖ר אֶת־אֲשֶׁר־לֽוֹ׃ 25 וַיִּוָּתֵ֥ר יַעֲקֹ֖ב לְבַדּ֑וֹ וַיֵּֽאָבֵ֥ק אִישׁ֙ עִמּ֔וֹ עַ֖ד עֲל֥וֹת הַשָּֽׁחַר׃ 26 וַיַּ֗רְא כִּ֣י לֹ֤א יָכֹל֙ ל֔וֹ וַיִּגַּ֖ע בְּכַף־יְרֵכ֑וֹ וַתֵּ֨קַע֙ כַּף־יֶ֣רֶךְ יַעֲקֹ֔ב בְּהֵֽאָבְק֖וֹ עִמּֽוֹ׃ 27 וַיֹּ֣אמֶר שַׁלְּחֵ֔נִי כִּ֥י עָלָ֖ה הַשָּׁ֑חַר וַיֹּ֙אמֶר֙ לֹ֣א אֲשַֽׁלֵּֽחֲךָ֔ כִּ֖י אִם־בֵּרַכְתָּֽנִי׃ 28 וַיֹּ֥אמֶר אֵלָ֖יו מַה־שְּׁמֶ֑ךָ וַיֹּ֖אמֶר יַעֲקֹֽב׃ 29 וַיֹּ֗אמֶר לֹ֤א יַעֲקֹב֙ יֵאָמֵ֥ר עוֹד֙ שִׁמְךָ֔ כִּ֖י אִם־יִשְׂרָאֵ֑ל כִּֽי־שָׂרִ֧יתָ עִם־אֱלֹהִ֛ים וְעִם־אֲנָשִׁ֖ים וַתּוּכָֽל׃ 30 וַיִּשְׁאַ֣ל יַעֲקֹ֗ב וַיֹּ֙אמֶר֙ הַגִּֽידָה־נָּ֣א שְׁמֶ֔ךָ וַיֹּ֕אמֶר לָ֥מָּה זֶּ֖ה תִּשְׁאַ֣ל לִשְׁמִ֑י וַיְבָ֥רֶךְ אֹת֖וֹ שָֽׁם׃ 31 וַיִּקְרָ֧א יַעֲקֹ֛ב שֵׁ֥ם הַמָּק֖וֹם פְּנִיאֵ֑ל כִּֽי־רָאִ֤יתִי אֱלֹהִים֙ פָּנִ֣ים אֶל־פָּנִ֔ים וַתִּנָּצֵ֖ל נַפְשִֽׁי׃ 32 וַיִּֽזְרַֽח־ל֣וֹ הַשֶּׁ֔מֶשׁ כַּאֲשֶׁ֥ר עָבַ֖ר אֶת־פְּנוּאֵ֑ל וְה֥וּא צֹלֵ֖עַ עַל־יְרֵכֽוֹ׃ 33 עַל־כֵּ֡ן לֹֽא־יֹאכְל֨וּ בְנֵֽי־יִשְׂרָאֵ֜ל אֶת־גִּ֣יד הַנָּשֶׁ֗ה אֲשֶׁר֙ עַל־כַּ֣ף הַיָּרֵ֔ךְ

עַד הַיּ֣וֹם הַזֶּ֑ה כִּ֤י נָגַע֙ בְּכַף־יֶ֣רֶךְ יַעֲקֹ֔ב
בְּגִ֖יד הַנָּשֶֽׁה׃

33 Looking up, Jacob saw Esau coming, accompanied by four hundred men. He divided the children among Leah, Rachel, and the two maids, [2] putting the maids and their children first, Leah and her children next, and Rachel and Joseph last. [3] He himself went on ahead and bowed low to the ground seven times until he was near his brother. [4] Esau ran to greet him. He embraced him and, falling on his neck, he kissed him; and they wept. [5] Looking about, he saw the women and the children. "Who," he asked, "are these with you?" He answered, "The children with whom God has favored your servant." [6] Then the maids, with their children, came forward and bowed low; [7] next Leah, with her children, came forward and bowed low; and last, Joseph and Rachel came forward and bowed low; [8] And he asked, "What do you mean by all this company which I have met?" He answered, "To gain my lord's favor." [9] Esau said, "I have enough, my brother; let what you have remain yours." [10] But Jacob said, "No, I pray you; if you would do me this favor, accept from me this gift; for to see your face is like seeing the face of God, and you have received me favorably. [11] Please accept my present which has been brought to you, for God has favored me and I have plenty." And when he urged him, he accepted.

[12] And [Esau] said, "Let us start on our journey, and I will proceed at your pace." [13] But he said to him, "My lord knows that the children are frail and that the flocks and herds, which are nursing, are a care to me; if they are driven hard a single day, all the flocks will die. [14] Let

לג וַיִּשָּׂ֨א יַעֲקֹ֜ב עֵינָ֗יו וַיַּרְא֙ וְהִנֵּ֣ה עֵשָׂ֣ו
בָּ֔א וְעִמּ֕וֹ אַרְבַּ֥ע מֵא֖וֹת אִ֑ישׁ וַיַּ֣חַץ אֶת־
הַיְלָדִ֗ים עַל־לֵאָה֙ וְעַל־רָחֵ֔ל וְעַ֖ל שְׁתֵּ֥י
הַשְּׁפָחֽוֹת׃ [2] וַיָּ֣שֶׂם אֶת־הַשְּׁפָח֧וֹת וְאֶת־
יַלְדֵיהֶ֛ן רִֽאשֹׁנָ֖ה וְאֶת־לֵאָ֣ה וִֽילָדֶ֣יהָ
אַחֲרֹנִ֑ים וְאֶת־רָחֵ֥ל וְאֶת־יוֹסֵ֖ף אַחֲרֹנִֽים׃
[3] וְה֖וּא עָבַ֣ר לִפְנֵיהֶ֑ם וַיִּשְׁתַּ֤חוּ אַ֙רְצָה֙ שֶׁ֣בַע
פְּעָמִ֔ים עַד־גִּשְׁתּ֖וֹ עַד־אָחִֽיו׃ [4] וַיָּ֨רׇץ עֵשָׂ֤ו
לִקְרָאתוֹ֙ וַֽיְחַבְּקֵ֔הוּ וַיִּפֹּ֥ל עַל־צַוָּארָ֖ו וַֽיִּשָּׁקֵ֑הוּ* וַיִּבְכּֽוּ׃ [5] וַיִּשָּׂ֣א אֶת־עֵינָ֗יו
וַיַּ֤רְא אֶת־הַנָּשִׁים֙ וְאֶת־הַיְלָדִ֔ים וַיֹּ֖אמֶר
מִי־אֵ֣לֶּה לָּ֑ךְ וַיֹּאמַ֕ר הַיְלָדִ֕ים אֲשֶׁר־חָנַ֥ן
אֱלֹהִ֖ים אֶת־עַבְדֶּֽךָ׃ [6] וַתִּגַּ֧שְׁןָ הַשְּׁפָח֛וֹת
הֵ֥נָּה וְיַלְדֵיהֶ֖ן וַתִּֽשְׁתַּחֲוֶֽיןָ׃ [7] וַתִּגַּ֧שׁ גַּם־
לֵאָ֛ה וִֽילָדֶ֖יהָ וַיִּֽשְׁתַּחֲו֑וּ וְאַחַ֗ר נִגַּ֥שׁ יוֹסֵ֛ף
וְרָחֵ֖ל וַיִּֽשְׁתַּחֲוֽוּ׃ [8] וַיֹּ֕אמֶר מִ֥י לְךָ֛ כׇּל־
הַמַּחֲנֶ֥ה הַזֶּ֖ה אֲשֶׁ֣ר פָּגָ֑שְׁתִּי וַיֹּ֕אמֶר לִמְצֹא־
חֵ֖ן בְּעֵינֵ֥י אֲדֹנִֽי׃ [9] וַיֹּ֥אמֶר עֵשָׂ֖ו יֶשׁ־לִ֣י רָ֑ב
אָחִ֕י יְהִ֥י לְךָ֖ אֲשֶׁר־לָֽךְ׃ [10] וַיֹּ֣אמֶר יַעֲקֹ֗ב
אַל־נָא֙ אִם־נָ֨א מָצָ֤אתִי חֵן֙ בְּעֵינֶ֔יךָ וְלָקַחְתָּ֥
מִנְחָתִ֖י מִיָּדִ֑י כִּ֣י עַל־כֵּ֞ן רָאִ֣יתִי פָנֶ֗יךָ כִּרְאֹ֛ת
פְּנֵ֥י אֱלֹהִ֖ים וַתִּרְצֵֽנִי׃ [11] קַח־נָ֤א אֶת־
בִּרְכָתִי֙ אֲשֶׁ֣ר הֻבָ֣את לָ֔ךְ כִּֽי־חַנַּ֥נִי אֱלֹהִ֖ים
וְכִ֣י יֶשׁ־לִי־כֹ֑ל וַיִּפְצַר־בּ֖וֹ וַיִּקָּֽח׃
[12] וַיֹּ֖אמֶר נִסְעָ֣ה וְנֵלֵ֑כָה וְאֵלְכָ֖ה לְנֶגְדֶּֽךָ׃
[13] וַיֹּ֣אמֶר אֵלָ֗יו אֲדֹנִ֤י יֹדֵ֙עַ֙ כִּֽי־הַיְלָדִ֣ים
רַכִּ֔ים וְהַצֹּ֥אן וְהַבָּקָ֖ר עָל֣וֹת עָלָ֑י וּדְפָק֣וּם
י֣וֹם אֶחָ֔ד וָמֵ֖תוּ כׇּל־הַצֹּֽאן׃ [14] יַעֲבׇר־נָ֥א
אֲדֹנִ֖י לִפְנֵ֣י עַבְדּ֑וֹ וַאֲנִ֞י אֶֽתְנָהֲלָ֣ה לְאִטִּ֗י

my lord go on ahead of his servant, while I travel slowly, at the pace of the cattle before me and at the pace of the children, until I come to my lord in Seir."

15Then Esau said, "Let me assign to you some of the men who are with me." But he said, "Oh no, my lord is too kind to me!" 16So Esau started back that day on his way to Seir. 17But Jacob journeyed on to Succoth, and built a house for himself and made stalls for his cattle; that is why the place was called Succoth.a

18Jacob arrived safe in the city of Shechem which is in the land of Canaan—having come thus from Paddan-aram—and he encamped before the city. 19The parcel of land where he pitched his tent he purchased from the children of Hamor, Shechem's father, for a hundred kesitahs.b 20He set up an altar there, and called it El-elohe-yisrael.c

34 Now Dinah, the daughter whom Leah had borne to Jacob, went out to visit the daughters of the land. 2Shechem son of Hamor the Hivite, chief of the country, saw her, and took her and lay with her by force. 3Being strongly drawn to Dinah daughter of Jacob, and in love with the maiden, he spoke to the maiden tenderly. 4So Shechem said to his father Hamor, "Get me this girl as a wife."

5Jacob heard that he had defiled his daughter Dinah; but since his sons were in the field with his cattle, Jacob kept silent until they came home. 6Then Shechem's father Hamor came out to Jacob to speak to him. 7Meanwhile Jacob's sons, having heard the news, came in from the field. The men were distressed and very angry, because he had committed an outrage in

לְרֶגֶל הַמְּלָאכָה אֲשֶׁר־לְפָנַי וּלְרֶגֶל הַיְלָדִים עַד אֲשֶׁר־אָבֹא אֶל־אֲדֹנִי שֵׂעִירָה: 15 וַיֹּאמֶר עֵשָׂו אַצִּיגָה־נָּא עִמְּךָ מִן־הָעָם אֲשֶׁר אִתִּי וַיֹּאמֶר לָמָּה זֶּה אֶמְצָא־חֵן בְּעֵינֵי אֲדֹנִי: 16 וַיָּשָׁב בַּיּוֹם הַהוּא עֵשָׂו לְדַרְכּוֹ שֵׂעִירָה: 17 וְיַעֲקֹב נָסַע סֻכֹּתָה וַיִּבֶן לוֹ בָּיִת וּלְמִקְנֵהוּ עָשָׂה סֻכֹּת עַל־כֵּן קָרָא שֵׁם־הַמָּקוֹם סֻכּוֹת: ס

18 וַיָּבֹא יַעֲקֹב שָׁלֵם עִיר שְׁכֶם אֲשֶׁר בְּאֶרֶץ כְּנַעַן בְּבֹאוֹ מִפַּדַּן אֲרָם וַיִּחַן אֶת־פְּנֵי הָעִיר: 19 וַיִּקֶן אֶת־חֶלְקַת הַשָּׂדֶה אֲשֶׁר נָטָה־שָׁם אָהֳלוֹ מִיַּד בְּנֵי־חֲמוֹר אֲבִי שְׁכֶם בְּמֵאָה קְשִׂיטָה: 20 וַיַּצֶּב־שָׁם מִזְבֵּחַ וַיִּקְרָא־לוֹ אֵל אֱלֹהֵי יִשְׂרָאֵל: ס

לד וַתֵּצֵא דִינָה בַּת־לֵאָה אֲשֶׁר יָלְדָה לְיַעֲקֹב לִרְאוֹת בִּבְנוֹת הָאָרֶץ: 2 וַיַּרְא אֹתָהּ שְׁכֶם בֶּן־חֲמוֹר הַחִוִּי נְשִׂיא הָאָרֶץ וַיִּקַּח אֹתָהּ וַיִּשְׁכַּב אֹתָהּ וַיְעַנֶּהָ: 3 וַתִּדְבַּק נַפְשׁוֹ בְּדִינָה בַּת־יַעֲקֹב וַיֶּאֱהַב אֶת־הַנַּעֲרָ וַיְדַבֵּר עַל־לֵב הַנַּעֲרָ: 4 וַיֹּאמֶר שְׁכֶם אֶל־חֲמוֹר אָבִיו לֵאמֹר קַח־לִי אֶת־הַיַּלְדָּה הַזֹּאת לְאִשָּׁה: 5 וְיַעֲקֹב שָׁמַע כִּי טִמֵּא אֶת־דִּינָה בִתּוֹ וּבָנָיו הָיוּ אֶת־מִקְנֵהוּ בַּשָּׂדֶה וְהֶחֱרִשׁ יַעֲקֹב עַד־בֹּאָם: 6 וַיֵּצֵא חֲמוֹר אֲבִי־שְׁכֶם אֶל־יַעֲקֹב לְדַבֵּר אִתּוֹ: 7 וּבְנֵי יַעֲקֹב בָּאוּ מִן־הַשָּׂדֶה כְּשָׁמְעָם וַיִּתְעַצְּבוּ הָאֲנָשִׁים וַיִּחַר לָהֶם מְאֹד כִּי־נְבָלָה עָשָׂה בְיִשְׂרָאֵל לִשְׁכַּב אֶת־בַּת־יַעֲקֹב וְכֵן לֹא יֵעָשֶׂה:

---

a   Meaning "stalls," "huts," "booths."
b   Heb. qesiṭah, a unit of unknown value.
c   "El, God of Israel."

70

Israel by lying with Jacob's daughter—a thing not to be done.

8And Hamor spoke with them, saying, "My son Shechem longs for your daughter. Please give her to him in marriage. 9Intermarry with us: give your daughters to us, and take our daughters for yourselves: 10You will dwell among us, and the land will be open before you; settle, move about, and acquire holdings in it." 11Then Shechem said to her father and brothers, "Do me this favor, and I will pay whatever you tell me. 12Ask of me a bride-price ever so high, as well as gifts, and I will pay what you tell me; only give me the maiden for a wife."

13Jacob's sons answered Shechem and his father Hamor—speaking with guile because he had defiled their sister Dinah—14and said to them, "We cannot do this thing, to give our sister to a man who is uncircumcised, for that is a disgrace among us. 15Only on this condition will we agree with you; that you will become like us in that every male among you is circumcised. 16Then we will give our daughters to you and take your daughters to ourselves; and we will dwell among you and become as one kindred. 17But if you will not listen to us and become circumcised, we will take our daughter and go."

18Their words pleased Hamor and Hamor's son Shechem. 19And the youth lost no time in doing the thing, for he wanted Jacob's daughter. Now he was the most respected in his father's house. 20So Hamor and his son Shechem went to the a-public place-a of their town and spoke to their fellow townsmen, saying, 21"These people are our friends; let them settle in the land and move about in it, for the land is large enough for them; we will take their daughters to ourselves as wives and give our daughters to them. 22But only on this condition will the men agree with us to dwell among us and be as one kindred: that all our males become circumcised

a-a Lit. "gate."

71

וַיְדַבֵּר חֲמוֹר אִתָּם לֵאמֹר שְׁכֶם בְּנִי 8
חָשְׁקָה נַפְשׁוֹ בְּבִתְּכֶם תְּנוּ נָא אֹתָהּ
לוֹ לְאִשָּׁה: 9וְהִתְחַתְּנוּ אֹתָנוּ בְּנֹתֵיכֶם
תִּתְּנוּ־לָנוּ וְאֶת־בְּנֹתֵינוּ תִּקְחוּ לָכֶם:
10וְאִתָּנוּ תֵּשֵׁבוּ וְהָאָרֶץ תִּהְיֶה לִפְנֵיכֶם
שְׁבוּ וּסְחָרוּהָ וְהֵאָחֲזוּ בָּהּ: 11וַיֹּאמֶר
שְׁכֶם אֶל־אָבִיהָ וְאֶל־אַחֶיהָ אֶמְצָא־חֵן
בְּעֵינֵיכֶם וַאֲשֶׁר תֹּאמְרוּ אֵלַי אֶתֵּן:
12הַרְבּוּ עָלַי מְאֹד מֹהַר וּמַתָּן וְאֶתְּנָה
כַּאֲשֶׁר תֹּאמְרוּ אֵלָי וּתְנוּ־לִי אֶת־הַנַּעֲרָ
הַנַּעֲרָה לְאִשָּׁה:
13וַיַּעֲנוּ בְנֵי־יַעֲקֹב אֶת־שְׁכֶם וְאֶת־חֲמוֹר
אָבִיו בְּמִרְמָה וַיְדַבֵּרוּ אֲשֶׁר טִמֵּא אֵת דִּינָה
אֲחֹתָם: 14וַיֹּאמְרוּ אֲלֵיהֶם לֹא נוּכַל
לַעֲשׂוֹת הַדָּבָר הַזֶּה לָתֵת אֶת־אֲחֹתֵנוּ
לְאִישׁ אֲשֶׁר־לוֹ עָרְלָה כִּי־חֶרְפָּה הִוא לָנוּ:
15אַךְ־בְּזֹאת נֵאוֹת לָכֶם אִם תִּהְיוּ כָמֹנוּ
לְהִמֹּל לָכֶם כָּל־זָכָר: 16וְנָתַנּוּ אֶת־בְּנֹתֵינוּ
לָכֶם וְאֶת־בְּנֹתֵיכֶם נִקַּח־לָנוּ וְיָשַׁבְנוּ
אִתְּכֶם וְהָיִינוּ לְעַם אֶחָד: 17וְאִם־לֹא
תִשְׁמְעוּ אֵלֵינוּ לְהִמּוֹל וְלָקַחְנוּ אֶת־בִּתֵּנוּ
וְהָלָכְנוּ:
18וַיִּיטְבוּ דִבְרֵיהֶם בְּעֵינֵי חֲמוֹר וּבְעֵינֵי
שְׁכֶם בֶּן־חֲמוֹר: 19וְלֹא־אֵחַר הַנַּעַר
לַעֲשׂוֹת הַדָּבָר כִּי חָפֵץ בְּבַת־יַעֲקֹב וְהוּא
נִכְבָּד מִכֹּל בֵּית אָבִיו: 20וַיָּבֹא חֲמוֹר
וּשְׁכֶם בְּנוֹ אֶל־שַׁעַר עִירָם וַיְדַבְּרוּ אֶל־
אַנְשֵׁי עִירָם לֵאמֹר: 21הָאֲנָשִׁים הָאֵלֶּה
שְׁלֵמִים הֵם אִתָּנוּ וְיֵשְׁבוּ בָאָרֶץ וְיִסְחֲרוּ
אֹתָהּ וְהָאָרֶץ הִנֵּה רַחֲבַת־יָדַיִם לִפְנֵיהֶם
אֶת־בְּנֹתָם נִקַּח־לָנוּ לְנָשִׁים וְאֶת־בְּנֹתֵינוּ
נִתֵּן לָהֶם: 22אַךְ־בְּזֹאת יֵאֹתוּ לָנוּ
הָאֲנָשִׁים לָשֶׁבֶת אִתָּנוּ לִהְיוֹת לְעַם אֶחָד
בְּהִמּוֹל לָנוּ כָּל־זָכָר כַּאֲשֶׁר הֵם נִמֹּלִים:

as they are circumcised. 23Their cattle and substance and all their beasts will be ours, if we only agree to their terms, so that they will settle among us." 24All b-who went out of the gate of his town-b heeded Hamor and his son Shechem, and all males, b-all those who went out of the gate of his town,-b were circumcised.

25On the third day, when they were in pain, Simeon and Levi, two of Jacob's sons, brothers of Dinah, took each his sword, came upon the city unmolested, and slew all the males. 26They put Hamor and his son Shechem to the sword, took Dinah out of Shechem's house, and went away. 27The other sons of Jacob came upon the slain and plundered the town, because their sister had been defiled. 28They seized their flocks and herds and asses, all that was inside the town and outside; 29all their wealth, all their children, and their wives, all that was in the houses, they took as captives and booty.

30Jacob said to Simeon and Levi, "You have brought trouble on me, making me odious among the inhabitants of the land, the Canaanites and the Perizzites; my men are few in number, so that if they unite against me and attack me, I and my house will be destroyed." 31But they answered, "Should our sister be treated like a whore?"

35 God said to Jacob, "Arise, go up to Bethel and remain there; and build an altar there to the God who appeared to you when you were fleeing from your brother Esau." 2So Jacob said to his household and to all who were with him, "Rid yourselves of the alien gods in your midst, purify yourselves, and change your clothes. 3Come, let us go up to Bethel, and I will build an altar there to the God who answered me when I was in distress and who has been with

23 מִקְנֵהֶם וְקִנְיָנָם וְכָל־בְּהֶמְתָּם הֲלוֹא לָנוּ הֵם אַךְ נֵאוֹתָה לָהֶם וְיֵשְׁבוּ אִתָּנוּ: 24 וַיִּשְׁמְעוּ אֶל־חֲמוֹר וְאֶל־שְׁכֶם בְּנוֹ כָּל־יֹצְאֵי שַׁעַר עִירוֹ וַיִּמֹּלוּ כָּל־זָכָר כָּל־יֹצְאֵי שַׁעַר עִירוֹ: 25 וַיְהִי בַיּוֹם הַשְּׁלִישִׁי בִּהְיוֹתָם כֹּאֲבִים וַיִּקְחוּ שְׁנֵי־בְנֵי־יַעֲקֹב שִׁמְעוֹן וְלֵוִי אֲחֵי דִינָה אִישׁ חַרְבּוֹ וַיָּבֹאוּ עַל־הָעִיר בֶּטַח וַיַּהַרְגוּ כָּל־זָכָר: 26 וְאֶת־חֲמוֹר וְאֶת־שְׁכֶם בְּנוֹ הָרְגוּ לְפִי־חָרֶב וַיִּקְחוּ אֶת־דִּינָה מִבֵּית שְׁכֶם וַיֵּצֵאוּ: 27 בְּנֵי יַעֲקֹב בָּאוּ עַל־הַחֲלָלִים וַיָּבֹזּוּ הָעִיר אֲשֶׁר טִמְּאוּ אֲחוֹתָם: 28 אֶת־צֹאנָם וְאֶת־בְּקָרָם וְאֶת־חֲמֹרֵיהֶם וְאֵת אֲשֶׁר־בָּעִיר וְאֶת־אֲשֶׁר בַּשָּׂדֶה לָקָחוּ: 29 וְאֶת־כָּל־חֵילָם וְאֶת־כָּל־טַפָּם וְאֶת־נְשֵׁיהֶם שָׁבוּ וַיָּבֹזּוּ וְאֵת כָּל־אֲשֶׁר בַּבָּיִת: 30 וַיֹּאמֶר יַעֲקֹב אֶל־שִׁמְעוֹן וְאֶל־לֵוִי עֲכַרְתֶּם אֹתִי לְהַבְאִישֵׁנִי בְּיֹשֵׁב הָאָרֶץ בַּכְּנַעֲנִי וּבַפְּרִזִּי וַאֲנִי מְתֵי מִסְפָּר וְנֶאֶסְפוּ עָלַי וְהִכּוּנִי וְנִשְׁמַדְתִּי אֲנִי וּבֵיתִי: 31 וַיֹּאמְרוּ הַכְזוֹנָה* יַעֲשֶׂה אֶת־אֲחוֹתֵנוּ: פ

לה וַיֹּאמֶר אֱלֹהִים אֶל־יַעֲקֹב קוּם עֲלֵה בֵית־אֵל וְשֶׁב־שָׁם וַעֲשֵׂה־שָׁם מִזְבֵּחַ לָאֵל הַנִּרְאֶה אֵלֶיךָ בְּבָרְחֲךָ מִפְּנֵי עֵשָׂו אָחִיךָ: 2 וַיֹּאמֶר יַעֲקֹב אֶל־בֵּיתוֹ וְאֶל כָּל־אֲשֶׁר עִמּוֹ הָסִרוּ אֶת־אֱלֹהֵי הַנֵּכָר אֲשֶׁר בְּתֹכְכֶם וְהִטַּהֲרוּ וְהַחֲלִיפוּ שִׂמְלֹתֵיכֶם: 3 וְנָקוּמָה וְנַעֲלֶה בֵּית־אֵל וְאֶעֱשֶׂה־שָּׁם מִזְבֵּחַ לָאֵל הָעֹנֶה אֹתִי בְּיוֹם צָרָתִי וַיְהִי עִמָּדִי בַּדֶּרֶךְ אֲשֶׁר הָלָכְתִּי: 4 וַיִּתְּנוּ אֶל־

---

b-b I.e., all his fellow townsmen.   ז׳ רבתי לפי מהדורת לעטעריס   v. 31.

me wherever I have gone." ⁴They gave to Jacob all the alien gods that they had, and the rings that were in their ears, and Jacob buried them under the terebinth that was near Shechem. ⁵As they set out, a terror from God fell on the cities round about, so that they did not pursue the sons of Jacob.

⁶Thus Jacob came to Luz—that is, Bethel—in the land of Canaan, he and all the people who were with him. ⁷There he built an altar and named the site El-bethel,ᵃ for it was there that God had revealed Himself to him when he was fleeing from his brother.

⁸Deborah, Rebekah's nurse, died, and was buried under the oak below Bethel; so it was named Allon-bacuth.ᵇ

⁹God appeared again to Jacob on his arrival from Paddan-aram, and He blessed him. ¹⁰God said to him,

"You whose name is Jacob,
You shall be called Jacob no more,
But Israel shall be your name."
Thus He named him Israel.

¹¹And God said to him,

"I am El Shaddai.ᶜ
Be fertile and increase;
A nation, yea an assembly of nations,
Shall descend from you.
Kings shall issue from your loins.
¹²The land that I assigned to Abraham and
    Isaac
I assign to you;
And to your offspring to come
Will I assign the land."

¹³God parted from him at the spot where He had spoken to him; ¹⁴and Jacob set up a pillar at the site where He had spoken to him, a pillar of stone, and he offered a libation on it and poured oil upon it. ¹⁵Jacob gave the site,

יַעֲקֹב אֵת כָּל־אֱלֹהֵי הַנֵּכָר אֲשֶׁר בְּיָדָם
וְאֶת־הַנְּזָמִים אֲשֶׁר בְּאָזְנֵיהֶם וַיִּטְמֹן אֹתָם
יַעֲקֹב תַּחַת הָאֵלָה אֲשֶׁר עִם־שְׁכֶם: ⁵ וַיִּסָּעוּ וַיְהִי ׀ חִתַּת אֱלֹהִים עַל־הֶעָרִים
אֲשֶׁר סְבִיבֹתֵיהֶם וְלֹא רָדְפוּ אַחֲרֵי בְּנֵי
יַעֲקֹב:

⁶ וַיָּבֹא יַעֲקֹב לוּזָה אֲשֶׁר בְּאֶרֶץ כְּנַעַן הִוא
בֵּית־אֵל הוּא וְכָל־הָעָם אֲשֶׁר־עִמּוֹ: ⁷ וַיִּבֶן
שָׁם מִזְבֵּחַ וַיִּקְרָא לַמָּקוֹם אֵל בֵּית־אֵל כִּי
שָׁם נִגְלוּ אֵלָיו הָאֱלֹהִים בְּבָרְחוֹ מִפְּנֵי
אָחִיו:

⁸ וַתָּמָת דְּבֹרָה מֵינֶקֶת רִבְקָה וַתִּקָּבֵר
מִתַּחַת לְבֵית־אֵל תַּחַת הָאַלּוֹן וַיִּקְרָא
שְׁמוֹ אַלּוֹן בָּכוּת: פ

⁹ וַיֵּרָא אֱלֹהִים אֶל־יַעֲקֹב עוֹד בְּבֹאוֹ מִפַּדַּן
אֲרָם וַיְבָרֶךְ אֹתוֹ: ¹⁰ וַיֹּאמֶר־לוֹ אֱלֹהִים
שִׁמְךָ יַעֲקֹב

לֹא־יִקָּרֵא שִׁמְךָ עוֹד יַעֲקֹב
כִּי אִם־יִשְׂרָאֵל יִהְיֶה שְׁמֶךָ
וַיִּקְרָא אֶת־שְׁמוֹ יִשְׂרָאֵל:

¹¹ וַיֹּאמֶר לוֹ אֱלֹהִים
אֲנִי אֵל שַׁדַּי
פְּרֵה וּרְבֵה
גּוֹי וּקְהַל גּוֹיִם
יִהְיֶה מִמֶּךָּ
וּמְלָכִים מֵחֲלָצֶיךָ יֵצֵאוּ:
¹² וְאֶת־הָאָרֶץ אֲשֶׁר נָתַתִּי לְאַבְרָהָם
וּלְיִצְחָק
לְךָ אֶתְּנֶנָּה
וּלְזַרְעֲךָ אַחֲרֶיךָ
אֶתֵּן אֶת־הָאָרֶץ:
¹³ וַיַּעַל מֵעָלָיו אֱלֹהִים בַּמָּקוֹם אֲשֶׁר־דִּבֶּר
אִתּוֹ: ¹⁴ וַיַּצֵּב יַעֲקֹב מַצֵּבָה בַּמָּקוֹם אֲשֶׁר־
דִּבֶּר אִתּוֹ מַצֶּבֶת אָבֶן וַיַּסֵּךְ עָלֶיהָ נֶסֶךְ
וַיִּצֹק עָלֶיהָ שָׁמֶן: ¹⁵ וַיִּקְרָא יַעֲקֹב אֶת־שֵׁם

---

a   "The God of Bethel."
b   Understood as "the oak of the weeping."
c   Cf. 17.1.

where God had spoken to him, the name of Bethel.

16They set out from Bethel; but when they were still some distance short of Ephrath, Rachel was in childbirth, and she had hard labor. 17When her labor was at its hardest, the midwife said to her, "Have no fear, for it is another boy for you." 18But as she breathed her last—for she was dying—she named him Ben-oni;d but his father called him Benjamin.e 19Thus Rachel died. She was buried on the road to Ephrath—now Bethlehem. 20Over her grave Jacob set up a pillar; it is the pillar at Rachel's grave to this day. 21Israel journeyed on, and pitched his tent beyond Migdal-eder.

22While Israel stayed in that land, Reuben went and lay with Bilhah, his father's concubine; and Israel found out.

Now the sons of Jacob were twelve in number. 23The sons of Leah: Reuben—Jacob's first-born—Simeon, Levi, Judah, Issachar, and Zebulun. 24The sons of Rachel: Joseph and Benjamin. 25The sons of Bilhah, Rachel's maid: Dan and Naphtali. 26And the sons of Zilpah, Leah's maid: Gad and Asher. These are the sons of Jacob who were born to him in Paddan-aram.

27And Jacob came to his father Isaac at Mamre, at Kiriath-arba—now Hebron—where Abraham and Isaac had sojourned. 28Isaac was a hundred and eighty years old 29when he breathed his last and died. Hef was gathered to his kin in ripe old age; and he was buried by his sons Esau and Jacob.

36 This is the line of Esau—that is, Edom.

2Esau took his wives from among the Canaanite women—Adah daughter of Elon the Hittite, and Oholibamah daughter of Anah

הַמָּקוֹם אֲשֶׁר דִּבֶּר אִתּוֹ שָׁם אֱלֹהִים בֵּית־אֵל׃

16 וַיִּסְעוּ מִבֵּית אֵל וַיְהִי־עוֹד כִּבְרַת־הָאָרֶץ לָבוֹא אֶפְרָתָה וַתֵּלֶד רָחֵל וַתְּקַשׁ בְּלִדְתָּהּ׃ 17 וַיְהִי בְהַקְשֹׁתָהּ בְּלִדְתָּהּ וַתֹּאמֶר לָהּ הַמְיַלֶּדֶת אַל־תִּירְאִי כִּי־גַם־זֶה לָךְ בֵּן׃ 18 וַיְהִי בְּצֵאת נַפְשָׁהּ כִּי מֵתָה וַתִּקְרָא שְׁמוֹ בֶּן־אוֹנִי וְאָבִיו קָרָא־לוֹ בִנְיָמִין׃ 19 וַתָּמָת רָחֵל וַתִּקָּבֵר בְּדֶרֶךְ אֶפְרָתָה הִוא בֵּית לָחֶם׃ 20 וַיַּצֵּב יַעֲקֹב מַצֵּבָה עַל־קְבֻרָתָהּ הִוא מַצֶּבֶת קְבֻרַת־רָחֵל עַד־הַיּוֹם׃ 21 וַיִּסַּע יִשְׂרָאֵל וַיֵּט אָהֳלֹה מֵהָלְאָה לְמִגְדַּל־עֵדֶר׃

22 וַיְהִי בִּשְׁכֹּן יִשְׂרָאֵל בָּאָרֶץ הַהִוא וַיֵּלֶךְ רְאוּבֵן וַיִּשְׁכַּב אֶת־בִּלְהָה פִּילֶגֶשׁ אָבִיו וַיִּשְׁמַע יִשְׂרָאֵל׃ פ*

וַיִּהְיוּ בְנֵי־יַעֲקֹב שְׁנֵים עָשָׂר׃ 23 בְּנֵי לֵאָה בְּכוֹר יַעֲקֹב רְאוּבֵן וְשִׁמְעוֹן וְלֵוִי וִיהוּדָה וְיִשָּׂשכָר וּזְבֻלוּן׃ 24 בְּנֵי רָחֵל יוֹסֵף וּבִנְיָמִן׃ 25 וּבְנֵי בִלְהָה שִׁפְחַת רָחֵל דָּן וְנַפְתָּלִי׃ 26 וּבְנֵי זִלְפָּה שִׁפְחַת לֵאָה גָּד וְאָשֵׁר אֵלֶּה בְּנֵי יַעֲקֹב אֲשֶׁר יֻלַּד־לוֹ בְּפַדַּן אֲרָם׃

27 וַיָּבֹא יַעֲקֹב אֶל־יִצְחָק אָבִיו מַמְרֵא קִרְיַת הָאַרְבַּע הִוא חֶבְרוֹן אֲשֶׁר־גָּר־שָׁם אַבְרָהָם וְיִצְחָק׃ 28 וַיִּהְיוּ יְמֵי יִצְחָק מְאַת שָׁנָה וּשְׁמֹנִים שָׁנָה׃ 29 וַיִּגְוַע יִצְחָק וַיָּמָת וַיֵּאָסֶף אֶל־עַמָּיו זָקֵן וּשְׂבַע יָמִים וַיִּקְבְּרוּ אֹתוֹ עֵשָׂו וְיַעֲקֹב בָּנָיו׃ פ

לו

וְאֵלֶּה תֹּלְדוֹת עֵשָׂו הוּא אֱדוֹם׃ 2 עֵשָׂו לָקַח אֶת־נָשָׁיו מִבְּנוֹת כְּנָעַן אֶת־עָדָה בַּת־אֵילוֹן הַחִתִּי וְאֶת־אָהֳלִיבָמָה בַּת־עֲנָה בַּת־צִבְעוֹן הַחִוִּי׃ 3 וְאֶת־בָּשְׂמַת

---

d   Understood as "son of my suffering (or, strength)."
e   I.e., "son of the right hand," or "son of the south."
f   Lit. "Isaac."

v. 22.   למדינחאי סוף פסוק, ולמערבאי פיסקא באמצע פסוק

daughter of Zibeon the Hivite[a]—³and also Basemath daughter of Ishmael and sister of Nebaioth. ⁴Adah bore to Esau Eliphaz; Basemath bore Reuel; ⁵and Oholibamah bore Jeush, Jalam, and Korah. Those were the sons of Esau, who were born to him in the land of Canaan.

⁶Esau took his wives, his sons and daughters, and all the members of his household, his cattle and all his livestock, and all the property that he had acquired in the land of Canaan, and went to another land because of his brother Jacob. ⁷For their possessions were too many for them to dwell together, and the land where they sojourned could not support them because of their livestock. ⁸So Esau settled in the hill country of Seir—Esau being Edom.

⁹This, then, is the line of Esau, the ancestor of the Edomites, in the hill country of Seir.

¹⁰These are the names of Esau's sons: Eliphaz, the son of Esau's wife Adah; Reuel, the son of Esau's wife Basemath. ¹¹The sons of Eliphaz were Teman, Omar, Zepho, Gatam, and Kenaz. ¹²Timna was a concubine of Esau's son Eliphaz; she bore Amalek to Eliphaz. Those were the descendants of Esau's wife Adah. ¹³And these were the sons of Reuel: Nahath, Zerah, Shammah, and Mizzah. Those were the descendants of Esau's wife Basemath. ¹⁴And these were the sons of Esau's wife Oholibamah, daughter of Anah daughter of Zibeon: she bore to Esau Jeush, Jalam, and Korah.

¹⁵These are the clans of the children of Esau. The descendants of Esau's first-born Eliphaz: the clans Teman, Omar, Zepho, Kenaz, ¹⁶Korah, Gatam, and Amalek; these are the clans of Eliphaz in the land of Edom. Those are the descendants of Adah. ¹⁷And these are the descendants of Esau's son Reuel: the clans Nahath, Zerah, Shammah, and Mizzah; these are the clans of Reuel in the land of Edom. Those

---

a Cf. v. 20, "Horite."

בַּת־יִשְׁמָעֵאל אֲחוֹת נְבָיֽוֹת׃ 4 וַתֵּלֶד עָדָה לְעֵשָׂו אֶת־אֱלִיפָז וּבָשְׂמַת יָֽלְדָה אֶת־רְעוּאֵֽל׃ 5 וְאָהֳלִֽיבָמָה יָֽלְדָה אֶת־יְעוּשׁ וְאֶת־יַעְלָם וְאֶת־קֹרַח אֵלֶּה בְּנֵי עֵשָׂו אֲשֶׁר יֻלְּדוּ־לוֹ בְּאֶרֶץ כְּנָֽעַן׃

6 וַיִּקַּח עֵשָׂו אֶת־נָשָׁיו וְאֶת־בָּנָיו וְאֶת־בְּנֹתָיו וְאֶת־כָּל־נַפְשׁוֹת בֵּיתוֹ וְאֶת־מִקְנֵהוּ וְאֶת־כָּל־בְּהֶמְתּוֹ וְאֵת כָּל־קִנְיָנוֹ אֲשֶׁר רָכַשׁ בְּאֶרֶץ כְּנָעַן וַיֵּלֶךְ אֶל־אֶרֶץ מִפְּנֵי יַעֲקֹב אָחִֽיו׃ 7 כִּֽי־הָיָה רְכוּשָׁם רָב מִשֶּׁבֶת יַחְדָּו וְלֹא יָֽכְלָה אֶרֶץ מְגֽוּרֵיהֶם לָשֵׂאת אֹתָם מִפְּנֵי מִקְנֵיהֶֽם׃ 8 וַיֵּשֶׁב עֵשָׂו בְּהַר שֵׂעִיר עֵשָׂו הוּא אֱדֽוֹם׃

9 וְאֵלֶּה תֹּֽלְדוֹת עֵשָׂו אֲבִי אֱדוֹם בְּהַר שֵׂעִֽיר׃

10 אֵלֶּה שְׁמוֹת בְּנֵֽי־עֵשָׂו אֱלִיפַז בֶּן־עָדָה אֵשֶׁת עֵשָׂו רְעוּאֵל בֶּן־בָּשְׂמַת אֵשֶׁת עֵשָֽׂו׃ 11 וַיִּֽהְיוּ בְּנֵי אֱלִיפָז תֵּימָן אוֹמָר צְפוֹ וְגַעְתָּם וּקְנַֽז׃ 12 וְתִמְנַע ׀ הָֽיְתָה פִילֶגֶשׁ לֶֽאֱלִיפַז בֶּן־עֵשָׂו וַתֵּלֶד לֶאֱלִיפַז אֶת־עֲמָלֵק אֵלֶּה בְּנֵי עָדָה אֵשֶׁת עֵשָֽׂו׃ 13 וְאֵלֶּה בְּנֵי רְעוּאֵל נַחַת וָזֶרַח שַׁמָּה וּמִזָּה אֵלֶּה הָיוּ בְּנֵי בָשְׂמַת אֵשֶׁת עֵשָֽׂו׃ 14 וְאֵלֶּה הָיוּ בְּנֵי אָהֳלִֽיבָמָה בַת־עֲנָה בַּת־צִבְעוֹן אֵשֶׁת עֵשָׂו וַתֵּלֶד לְעֵשָׂו אֶת־יעיש וְאֶת־יַעְלָם וְאֶת־קֹֽרַח׃

15 אֵלֶּה אַלּוּפֵי בְנֵֽי־עֵשָׂו בְּנֵי אֱלִיפַז בְּכוֹר עֵשָׂו אַלּוּף תֵּימָן אַלּוּף אוֹמָר אַלּוּף צְפוֹ אַלּוּף קְנַֽז׃ 16 אַלּֽוּף־קֹרַח אַלּוּף גַּעְתָּם אַלּוּף עֲמָלֵק אֵלֶּה אַלּוּפֵי אֱלִיפַז בְּאֶרֶץ אֱדוֹם אֵלֶּה בְּנֵי עָדָֽה׃ 17 וְאֵלֶּה בְּנֵי רְעוּאֵל בֶּן־עֵשָׂו אַלּוּף נַחַת אַלּוּף זֶרַח אַלּוּף שַׁמָּה אַלּוּף מִזָּה אֵלֶּה אַלּוּפֵי רְעוּאֵל בְּאֶרֶץ אֱדוֹם אֵלֶּה בְּנֵי בָשְׂמַת אֵשֶׁת עֵשָֽׂו׃

are the descendants of Esau's wife Basemath. [18]And these are the descendants of Esau's wife Oholibamah: the clans Jeush, Jalam, and Korah; these are the clans of Esau's wife Oholibamah, the daughter of Anah. [19]Those were the sons of Esau—that is, Edom—and those are their clans.

[20]These were the sons of Seir the Horite, who were settled in the land: Lotan, Shobal, Zibeon, Anah, [21]Dishon, Ezer, and Dishan. Those are the clans of the Horites, the descendants of Seir, in the land of Edom.

[22]The sons of Lotan were Hori and Hemam; and Lotan's sister was Timna. [23]The sons of Shobal were these: Alvan, Manahath, Ebal, Shepho, and Onam. [24]The sons of Zibeon were these: Aiah[b] and Anah—that was the Anah who discovered the hot springs[c] in the wilderness while pasturing the asses of his father Zibeon. [25]The children of Anah were these: Dishon and Anah's daughter Oholibamah. [26]The sons of Dishon[d] were these: Hemdan, Eshban, Ithran, and Cheran. [27]The sons of Ezer were these: Bilhan, Zaavan, and Akan. [28]And the sons of Dishan were these: Uz and Aran.

[29]These are the clans of the Horites: the clans Lotan, Shobal, Zibeon, Anah, [30]Dishon, Ezer, and Dishan. Those are the clans of the Horites, clan by clan, in the land of Seir.

[31]These are the kings who reigned in the land of Edom before any king reigned over the Israelites. [32]Bela son of Beor reigned in Edom, and the name of his city was Dinhabah. [33]When Bela died, Jobab son of Zerah, from Bozrah, succeeded him as king. [34]When Jobab died, Husham of the land of the Temanites succeeded him as king. [35]When Husham died, Hadad son of Bedad, who defeated the Midianites in the country of Moab, succeeded him as king; the name of his city was Avith. [36]When Hadad died,

18 וְאֵ֣לֶּה בְּנֵ֞י אָהֳלִֽיבָמָ֛ה אֵ֥שֶׁת עֵשָׂ֖ו אַלּ֥וּף יְע֛וּשׁ אַלּ֥וּף יַעְלָ֖ם אַלּ֣וּף קֹ֑רַח אֵ֣לֶּה אַלּוּפֵ֞י אָהֳלִֽיבָמָ֛ה בַּת־עֲנָ֖ה אֵ֥שֶׁת עֵשָֽׂו׃ 19 אֵ֧לֶּה בְנֵי־עֵשָׂ֛ו וְאֵ֥לֶּה אַלּוּפֵיהֶ֖ם ה֥וּא אֱדֽוֹם׃ ס 20 אֵ֤לֶּה בְנֵֽי־שֵׂעִיר֙ הַחֹרִ֔י יֹשְׁבֵ֖י הָאָ֑רֶץ לוֹטָ֥ן וְשׁוֹבָ֖ל וְצִבְע֥וֹן וַעֲנָֽה׃ 21 וְדִשׁ֥וֹן וְאֵ֖צֶר וְדִישָׁ֑ן אֵ֣לֶּה אַלּוּפֵ֧י הַחֹרִ֛י בְּנֵ֥י שֵׂעִ֖יר בְּאֶ֥רֶץ אֱדֽוֹם׃ 22 וַיִּהְי֥וּ בְנֵֽי־לוֹטָ֖ן חֹרִ֣י וְהֵימָ֑ם וַאֲח֥וֹת לוֹטָ֖ן תִּמְנָֽע׃ 23 וְאֵ֙לֶּה֙ בְּנֵ֣י שׁוֹבָ֔ל עַלְוָ֥ן וּמָנַ֖חַת וְעֵיבָ֑ל שְׁפ֖וֹ וְאוֹנָֽם׃ 24 וְאֵ֥לֶּה בְנֵֽי־צִבְע֖וֹן וְאַיָּ֣ה וַעֲנָ֑ה ה֣וּא עֲנָ֗ה אֲשֶׁ֨ר מָצָ֤א אֶת־הַיֵּמִם֙ בַּמִּדְבָּ֔ר בִּרְעֹת֥וֹ אֶת־הַחֲמֹרִ֖ים לְצִבְע֥וֹן אָבִֽיו׃ 25 וְאֵ֥לֶּה בְנֵֽי־עֲנָ֖ה דִּשֹׁ֑ן וְאָהֳלִֽיבָמָ֖ה בַּת־עֲנָֽה׃ 26 וְאֵ֖לֶּה בְּנֵ֣י דִישָׁ֑ן חֶמְדָּ֥ן וְאֶשְׁבָּ֖ן וְיִתְרָ֥ן וּכְרָֽן׃ 27 אֵ֖לֶּה בְּנֵי־אֵ֑צֶר בִּלְהָ֥ן וְזַעֲוָ֖ן וַעֲקָֽן׃ 28 אֵ֥לֶּה בְנֵֽי־דִישָׁ֖ן ע֥וּץ וַאֲרָֽן׃ 29 אֵ֖לֶּה אַלּוּפֵ֣י הַחֹרִ֑י אַלּ֤וּף לוֹטָן֙ אַלּ֣וּף שׁוֹבָ֔ל אַלּ֥וּף צִבְע֖וֹן אַלּ֥וּף עֲנָֽה׃ 30 אַלּ֥וּף דִּשֹׁ֛ן אַלּ֥וּף אֵ֖צֶר אַלּ֣וּף דִּישָׁ֑ן אֵ֣לֶּה אַלּוּפֵ֧י הַחֹרִ֛י לְאַלֻּפֵיהֶ֖ם בְּאֶ֥רֶץ שֵׂעִֽיר׃ פ 31 וְאֵ֙לֶּה֙ הַמְּלָכִ֔ים אֲשֶׁ֥ר מָלְכ֖וּ בְּאֶ֣רֶץ אֱד֑וֹם לִפְנֵ֥י מְלָךְ־מֶ֖לֶךְ לִבְנֵ֥י יִשְׂרָאֵֽל׃ 32 וַיִּמְלֹ֣ךְ בֶּאֱד֔וֹם בֶּ֖לַע בֶּן־בְּע֑וֹר וְשֵׁ֥ם עִיר֖וֹ דִּנְהָֽבָה׃ 33 וַיָּ֖מָת בָּ֑לַע וַיִּמְלֹ֣ךְ תַּחְתָּ֗יו יוֹבָ֛ב בֶּן־זֶ֖רַח מִבָּצְרָֽה׃ 34 וַיָּ֖מָת יוֹבָ֑ב וַיִּמְלֹ֣ךְ תַּחְתָּ֔יו חֻשָׁ֖ם מֵאֶ֥רֶץ הַתֵּימָנִֽי׃ 35 וַיָּ֖מָת חֻשָׁ֑ם וַיִּמְלֹ֨ךְ תַּחְתָּ֜יו הֲדַ֣ד בֶּן־בְּדַ֗ד הַמַּכֶּ֤ה אֶת־מִדְיָן֙ בִּשְׂדֵ֣ה מוֹאָ֔ב וְשֵׁ֥ם עִיר֖וֹ עֲוִֽית׃ 36 וַיָּ֖מָת הֲדָ֑ד וַיִּמְלֹ֣ךְ תַּחְתָּ֔יו שַׂמְלָ֖ה

b   Heb. "and Aiah."
c   Meaning of Heb. yemim uncertain.
d   Heb. Dishan; but cf. vv. 21, 25, 28, and 30, and 1 Chron. 1.41.

Samlah of Masrekah succeeded him as king. [37]When Samlah died, Saul[e] of Rehoboth-on-the-river succeeded him as king. [38]When Saul died, Baal-hanan son of Achbor succeeded him as king. [39]And when Baal-hanan son of Achbor died, Hadar succeeded him as king; the name of his city was Pau, and his wife's name was Mehetabel daughter of Matred daughter of Me-zahab.

[40]These are the names of the clans of Esau, each with its families and locality, name by name: the clans Timna, Alvah, Jetheth, [41]Oholibamah, Elah, Pinon, [42]Kenaz, Teman, Mibzar, [43]Magdiel, and Iram. Those are the clans of Edom—that is, of Esau, father of the Edomites—by their settlements in the land which they hold.

37 VA-YESHEV

Now Jacob was settled in the land where his father had sojourned, the land of Canaan. [2]This, then, is the line of Jacob:

At seventeen years of age, Joseph tended the flocks with his brothers, as a helper to the sons of his father's wives Bilhah and Zilpah. And Joseph brought bad reports of them to their father. [3]Now Israel loved Joseph best of all his sons, for he was the child of his old age; and he had made him an ornamented tunic.[a] [4]And when his brothers saw that their father loved him more than any of his brothers, they hated him so that they could not speak a friendly word to him.

[5]Once Joseph had a dream which he told to his brothers; and they hated him even more. [6]He said to them, "Hear this dream which I have dreamed: [7]There we were binding sheaves in the field, when suddenly my sheaf stood up and remained upright; then your sheaves gathered around and bowed low to my sheaf." [8]His

מִמַּשְׂרֵקָה: 37 וַיָּמָת שַׂמְלָה וַיִּמְלֹךְ תַּחְתָּיו שָׁאוּל מֵרְחֹבוֹת הַנָּהָר: 38 וַיָּמָת שָׁאוּל וַיִּמְלֹךְ תַּחְתָּיו בַּעַל חָנָן בֶּן־עַכְבּוֹר: 39 וַיָּמָת בַּעַל חָנָן בֶּן־עַכְבּוֹר וַיִּמְלֹךְ תַּחְתָּיו הֲדַר וְשֵׁם עִירוֹ פָּעוּ וְשֵׁם אִשְׁתּוֹ מְהֵיטַבְאֵל בַּת־מַטְרֵד בַּת מֵי זָהָב: 40 וְאֵלֶּה שְׁמוֹת אַלּוּפֵי עֵשָׂו לְמִשְׁפְּחֹתָם לִמְקֹמֹתָם בִּשְׁמֹתָם אַלּוּף תִּמְנָע אַלּוּף עַלְוָה אַלּוּף יְתֵת: 41 אַלּוּף אָהֳלִיבָמָה אַלּוּף אֵלָה אַלּוּף פִּינֹן: 42 אַלּוּף קְנַז אַלּוּף תֵּימָן אַלּוּף מִבְצָר: 43 אַלּוּף מַגְדִּיאֵל אַלּוּף עִירָם אֵלֶּה | אַלּוּפֵי אֱדוֹם לְמֹשְׁבֹתָם בְּאֶרֶץ אֲחֻזָּתָם הוּא עֵשָׂו אֲבִי אֱדוֹם: פ

לז וישב

וַיֵּשֶׁב יַעֲקֹב בְּאֶרֶץ מְגוּרֵי אָבִיו בְּאֶרֶץ כְּנָעַן: 2 אֵלֶּה | תֹּלְדוֹת יַעֲקֹב יוֹסֵף בֶּן־שְׁבַע־עֶשְׂרֵה שָׁנָה הָיָה רֹעֶה אֶת־אֶחָיו בַּצֹּאן וְהוּא נַעַר אֶת־בְּנֵי בִלְהָה וְאֶת־בְּנֵי זִלְפָּה נְשֵׁי אָבִיו וַיָּבֵא יוֹסֵף אֶת־דִּבָּתָם רָעָה אֶל־אֲבִיהֶם: 3 וְיִשְׂרָאֵל אָהַב אֶת־יוֹסֵף מִכָּל־בָּנָיו כִּי־בֶן־זְקֻנִים הוּא לוֹ וְעָשָׂה לוֹ כְּתֹנֶת פַּסִּים: 4 וַיִּרְאוּ אֶחָיו כִּי־אֹתוֹ אָהַב אֲבִיהֶם מִכָּל־אֶחָיו וַיִּשְׂנְאוּ אֹתוֹ וְלֹא יָכְלוּ דַּבְּרוֹ לְשָׁלֹם: 5 וַיַּחֲלֹם יוֹסֵף חֲלוֹם וַיַּגֵּד לְאֶחָיו וַיּוֹסִפוּ עוֹד שְׂנֹא אֹתוֹ: 6 וַיֹּאמֶר אֲלֵיהֶם שִׁמְעוּ־נָא הַחֲלוֹם הַזֶּה אֲשֶׁר חָלָמְתִּי: 7 וְהִנֵּה אֲנַחְנוּ מְאַלְּמִים אֲלֻמִּים בְּתוֹךְ הַשָּׂדֶה וְהִנֵּה קָמָה אֲלֻמָּתִי וְגַם־נִצָּבָה וְהִנֵּה תְסֻבֶּינָה אֲלֻמֹּתֵיכֶם וַתִּשְׁתַּחֲוֶיןָ לַאֲלֻמָּתִי: 8 וַיֹּאמְרוּ לוֹ אֶחָיו הֲמָלֹךְ תִּמְלֹךְ עָלֵינוּ

---

e   Or "Shaul."

a   Or "a coat of many colors"; meaning of Heb. uncertain.

brothers answered, "Do you mean to reign over us? Do you mean to rule over us?" And they hated him even more for his talk about his dreams.

⁹He dreamed another dream and told it to his brothers, saying, "Look, I have had another dream: And this time, the sun, the moon, and eleven stars were bowing down to me." ¹⁰And when he told it to his father and brothers, his father berated him. "What," he said to him, "is this dream you have dreamed? Are we to come, I and your mother and your brothers, and bow low to you to the ground?" ¹¹So his brothers were wrought up at him, and his father kept the matter in mind.

¹²One time, when his brothers had gone to pasture their father's flock at Shechem, ¹³Israel said to Joseph, "Your brothers are pasturing at Shechem. Come, I will send you to them." He answered, "I am ready." ¹⁴And he said to him, "Go and see how your brothers are and how the flocks are faring, and bring me back word." So he sent him from the valley of Hebron.

When he reached Shechem, ¹⁵a man came upon him wandering in the fields. The man asked him, "What are you looking for?" ¹⁶He answered, "I am looking for my brothers. Could you tell me where they are pasturing?" ¹⁷The man said, "They have gone from here, for I heard them say: Let us go to Dothan." So Joseph followed his brothers and found them at Dothan.

¹⁸They saw him from afar, and before he came close to them they conspired to kill him. ¹⁹They said to one another, "Here comes that dreamer! ²⁰Come now, let us kill him and throw him into one of the pits; and we can say, 'A savage beast devoured him.' We shall see what comes of his dreams!" ²¹But when Reuben heard it, he tried to save him from them. He said, "Let us not take his life." ²²And Reuben went on, "Shed no

אִם־מָשׁוֹל תִּמְשֹׁל בָּנוּ וַיּוֹסִפוּ עוֹד שְׂנֹא אֹתוֹ עַל־חֲלֹמֹתָיו וְעַל־דְּבָרָיו: ⁹ וַיַּחֲלֹם עוֹד חֲלוֹם אַחֵר וַיְסַפֵּר אֹתוֹ לְאֶחָיו וַיֹּאמֶר הִנֵּה חָלַמְתִּי חֲלוֹם עוֹד וְהִנֵּה הַשֶּׁמֶשׁ וְהַיָּרֵחַ וְאַחַד עָשָׂר כּוֹכָבִים מִשְׁתַּחֲוִים לִי: ¹⁰ וַיְסַפֵּר אֶל־אָבִיו וְאֶל־אֶחָיו וַיִּגְעַר־בּוֹ אָבִיו וַיֹּאמֶר לוֹ מָה הַחֲלוֹם הַזֶּה אֲשֶׁר חָלָמְתָּ הֲבוֹא נָבוֹא אֲנִי וְאִמְּךָ וְאַחֶיךָ לְהִשְׁתַּחֲוֹת לְךָ אָרְצָה: ¹¹ וַיְקַנְאוּ־בוֹ אֶחָיו וְאָבִיו שָׁמַר אֶת־הַדָּבָר: ¹² וַיֵּלְכוּ אֶחָיו לִרְעוֹת אֶת־*צֹאן אֲבִיהֶם בִּשְׁכֶם: ¹³ וַיֹּאמֶר יִשְׂרָאֵל אֶל־יוֹסֵף הֲלוֹא אַחֶיךָ רֹעִים בִּשְׁכֶם לְכָה וְאֶשְׁלָחֲךָ אֲלֵיהֶם וַיֹּאמֶר לוֹ הִנֵּנִי: ¹⁴ וַיֹּאמֶר לוֹ לֶךְ־נָא רְאֵה אֶת־שְׁלוֹם אַחֶיךָ וְאֶת־שְׁלוֹם הַצֹּאן וַהֲשִׁבֵנִי דָּבָר וַיִּשְׁלָחֵהוּ מֵעֵמֶק חֶבְרוֹן וַיָּבֹא שְׁכֶמָה: ¹⁵ וַיִּמְצָאֵהוּ אִישׁ וְהִנֵּה תֹעֶה בַּשָּׂדֶה וַיִּשְׁאָלֵהוּ הָאִישׁ לֵאמֹר מַה־תְּבַקֵּשׁ: ¹⁶ וַיֹּאמֶר אֶת־אַחַי אָנֹכִי מְבַקֵּשׁ הַגִּידָה־נָּא לִי אֵיפֹה הֵם רֹעִים: ¹⁷ וַיֹּאמֶר הָאִישׁ נָסְעוּ מִזֶּה כִּי שָׁמַעְתִּי אֹמְרִים נֵלְכָה דֹּתָיְנָה וַיֵּלֶךְ יוֹסֵף אַחַר אֶחָיו וַיִּמְצָאֵם בְּדֹתָן: ¹⁸ וַיִּרְאוּ אֹתוֹ מֵרָחֹק וּבְטֶרֶם יִקְרַב אֲלֵיהֶם וַיִּתְנַכְּלוּ אֹתוֹ לַהֲמִיתוֹ: ¹⁹ וַיֹּאמְרוּ אִישׁ אֶל־אָחִיו הִנֵּה בַּעַל הַחֲלֹמוֹת הַלָּזֶה בָּא: ²⁰ וְעַתָּה לְכוּ וְנַהַרְגֵהוּ וְנַשְׁלִכֵהוּ בְּאַחַד הַבֹּרוֹת וְאָמַרְנוּ חַיָּה רָעָה אֲכָלָתְהוּ וְנִרְאֶה מַה־יִּהְיוּ חֲלֹמֹתָיו: ²¹ וַיִּשְׁמַע רְאוּבֵן וַיַּצִּלֵהוּ מִיָּדָם וַיֹּאמֶר לֹא נַכֶּנּוּ נָפֶשׁ: ²² וַיֹּאמֶר אֲלֵהֶם רְאוּבֵן אַל־תִּשְׁפְּכוּ־דָם הַשְׁלִיכוּ אֹתוֹ אֶל־הַבּוֹר הַזֶּה אֲשֶׁר בַּמִּדְבָּר וְיָד אַל־תִּשְׁלְחוּ־בוֹ לְמַעַן

v. 12. נקוד על א' ת'

78

blood! Cast him into that pit out in the wilderness, but do not touch him yourselves"—intending to save him from them and restore him to his father. ²³When Joseph came up to his brothers, they stripped Joseph of his tunic, the ornamented tunic that he was wearing, ²⁴and took him and cast him into the pit. The pit was empty; there was no water in it.

²⁵Then they sat down to a meal. Looking up, they saw a caravan of Ishmaelites coming from Gilead, their camels bearing gum, balm, and ladanum to be taken to Egypt. ²⁶Then Judah said to his brothers, "What do we gain by killing our brother and covering up his blood? ²⁷Come, let us sell him to the Ishmaelites, but let us not do away with him ourselves. After all, he is our brother, our own flesh." His brothers agreed. ²⁸When Midianite traders passed by, they pulled Joseph up out of the pit. They sold Joseph for twenty pieces of silver to the Ishmaelites, who brought Joseph to Egypt.

²⁹When Reuben returned to the pit and saw that Joseph was not in the pit, he rent his clothes. ³⁰Returning to his brothers, he said, "The boy is gone! Now, what am I to do?" ³¹Then they took Joseph's tunic, slaughtered a kid, and dipped the tunic in the blood. ³²They had the ornamented tunic taken to their father, and they said, "We found this. Please examine it; is it your son's tunic or not?" ³³He recognized it, and said, "My son's tunic! A savage beast devoured him! Joseph was torn by a beast!" ³⁴Jacob rent his clothes, put sackcloth on his loins, and observed mourning for his son many days. ³⁵All his sons and daughters sought to comfort him; but he refused to be comforted, saying, "No, I will go down mourning to my son in Sheol." Thus his father bewailed him.

³⁶The Midianites,ᵇ meanwhile, sold him in Egypt to Potiphar, a courtier of Pharaoh and his chief steward.

הִצִּיל אֹתוֹ מִיָּדָם לַהֲשִׁיבוֹ אֶל־אָבִיו: ²³ וַיְהִי כַּאֲשֶׁר־בָּא יוֹסֵף אֶל־אֶחָיו וַיַּפְשִׁיטוּ אֶת־יוֹסֵף אֶת־כֻּתָּנְתּוֹ אֶת־כְּתֹנֶת הַפַּסִּים אֲשֶׁר עָלָיו: ²⁴ וַיִּקָּחֻהוּ וַיַּשְׁלִכוּ אֹתוֹ הַבֹּרָה וְהַבּוֹר רֵק אֵין בּוֹ מָיִם:

²⁵ וַיֵּשְׁבוּ לֶאֱכָל־לֶחֶם וַיִּשְׂאוּ עֵינֵיהֶם וַיִּרְאוּ וְהִנֵּה אֹרְחַת יִשְׁמְעֵאלִים בָּאָה מִגִּלְעָד וּגְמַלֵּיהֶם נֹשְׂאִים נְכֹאת וּצְרִי וָלֹט הוֹלְכִים לְהוֹרִיד מִצְרָיְמָה: ²⁶ וַיֹּאמֶר יְהוּדָה אֶל־אֶחָיו מַה־בֶּצַע כִּי נַהֲרֹג אֶת־אָחִינוּ וְכִסִּינוּ אֶת־דָּמוֹ: ²⁷ לְכוּ וְנִמְכְּרֶנּוּ לַיִּשְׁמְעֵאלִים וְיָדֵנוּ אַל־תְּהִי־בוֹ כִּי־אָחִינוּ בְשָׂרֵנוּ הוּא וַיִּשְׁמְעוּ אֶחָיו: ²⁸ וַיַּעַבְרוּ אֲנָשִׁים מִדְיָנִים סֹחֲרִים וַיִּמְשְׁכוּ וַיַּעֲלוּ אֶת־יוֹסֵף מִן־הַבּוֹר וַיִּמְכְּרוּ אֶת־יוֹסֵף לַיִּשְׁמְעֵאלִים בְּעֶשְׂרִים כָּסֶף וַיָּבִיאוּ אֶת־יוֹסֵף מִצְרָיְמָה:

²⁹ וַיָּשָׁב רְאוּבֵן אֶל־הַבּוֹר וְהִנֵּה אֵין־יוֹסֵף בַּבּוֹר וַיִּקְרַע אֶת־בְּגָדָיו: ³⁰ וַיָּשָׁב אֶל־אֶחָיו וַיֹּאמַר הַיֶּלֶד אֵינֶנּוּ וַאֲנִי אָנָה אֲנִי־בָא: ³¹ וַיִּקְחוּ אֶת־כְּתֹנֶת יוֹסֵף וַיִּשְׁחֲטוּ שְׂעִיר עִזִּים וַיִּטְבְּלוּ אֶת־הַכֻּתֹּנֶת בַּדָּם: ³² וַיְשַׁלְּחוּ אֶת־כְּתֹנֶת הַפַּסִּים וַיָּבִיאוּ אֶל־אֲבִיהֶם וַיֹּאמְרוּ זֹאת מָצָאנוּ הַכֶּר־נָא הַכְּתֹנֶת בִּנְךָ הִוא אִם־לֹא: ³³ וַיַּכִּירָהּ וַיֹּאמֶר כְּתֹנֶת בְּנִי חַיָּה רָעָה אֲכָלָתְהוּ טָרֹף טֹרַף יוֹסֵף: ³⁴ וַיִּקְרַע יַעֲקֹב שִׂמְלֹתָיו וַיָּשֶׂם שַׂק בְּמָתְנָיו וַיִּתְאַבֵּל עַל־בְּנוֹ יָמִים רַבִּים: ³⁵ וַיָּקֻמוּ כָל־בָּנָיו וְכָל־בְּנֹתָיו לְנַחֲמוֹ וַיְמָאֵן לְהִתְנַחֵם וַיֹּאמֶר כִּי־אֵרֵד אֶל־בְּנִי אָבֵל שְׁאֹלָה וַיֵּבְךְּ אֹתוֹ אָבִיו: ³⁶ וְהַמְּדָנִים מָכְרוּ אֹתוֹ אֶל־מִצְרָיִם לְפוֹטִיפַר סְרִיס פַּרְעֹה שַׂר הַטַּבָּחִים: פ

ᵇ Heb. "Medanites."

38

About that time Judah left his brothers and camped near a certain Adullamite whose name was Hirah. [2]There Judah saw the daughter of a certain Canaanite whose name was Shua, and he married her and cohabited with her. [3]She conceived and bore a son, and he named him Er. [4]She conceived again and bore a son, and named him Onan. [5]Once again she bore a son, and named him Shelah; he was at Chezib when she bore him.

[6]Judah got a wife for Er his first-born; her name was Tamar. [7]But Er, Judah's first-born, was displeasing to the LORD, and the LORD took his life. [8]Then Judah said to Onan, "Join with your brother's wife and do your duty by her as a brother-in-law,[a] and provide offspring for your brother." [9]But Onan, knowing that the seed would not count as his, let it go to waste[b] whenever he joined with his brother's wife, so as not to provide offspring for his brother. [10]What he did was displeasing to the LORD, and He took his life also. [11]Then Judah said to his daughter-in-law Tamar, "Stay as a widow in your father's house until my son Shelah grows up"—for he thought, "He too might die like his brothers." So Tamar went to live in her father's house.

[12]A long time afterward, Shua's daughter, the wife of Judah, died. When [c]his period of mourning was over,[c] Judah went up to Timnah to his sheepshearers, together with his friend Hirah the Adullamite. [13]And Tamar was told, "Your father-in-law is coming up to Timnah for the sheepshearing." [14]So she took off her widow's garb, covered her face with a veil, and, wrapping herself up, sat down at the entrance to Enaim,[d] which is on the road to Timnah; for

לח וַיְהִי בָּעֵת הַהִוא וַיֵּרֶד יְהוּדָה מֵאֵת אֶחָיו וַיֵּט עַד־אִישׁ עֲדֻלָּמִי וּשְׁמוֹ חִירָה: 2 וַיַּרְא־שָׁם יְהוּדָה בַּת־אִישׁ כְּנַעֲנִי וּשְׁמוֹ שׁוּעַ וַיִּקָּחֶהָ וַיָּבֹא אֵלֶיהָ: 3 וַתַּהַר וַתֵּלֶד בֵּן וַיִּקְרָא אֶת־שְׁמוֹ עֵר: 4 וַתַּהַר עוֹד וַתֵּלֶד בֵּן וַתִּקְרָא אֶת־שְׁמוֹ אוֹנָן: 5 וַתֹּסֶף עוֹד וַתֵּלֶד בֵּן וַתִּקְרָא אֶת־שְׁמוֹ שֵׁלָה וְהָיָה בִכְזִיב בְּלִדְתָּהּ אֹתוֹ: 6 וַיִּקַּח יְהוּדָה אִשָּׁה לְעֵר בְּכוֹרוֹ וּשְׁמָהּ תָּמָר: 7 וַיְהִי עֵר בְּכוֹר יְהוּדָה רַע בְּעֵינֵי יְהֹוָה וַיְמִתֵהוּ יְהֹוָה: 8 וַיֹּאמֶר יְהוּדָה לְאוֹנָן בֹּא אֶל־אֵשֶׁת אָחִיךָ וְיַבֵּם אֹתָהּ וְהָקֵם זֶרַע לְאָחִיךָ: 9 וַיֵּדַע אוֹנָן כִּי לֹא לוֹ יִהְיֶה הַזָּרַע וְהָיָה אִם־בָּא אֶל־אֵשֶׁת אָחִיו וְשִׁחֵת אַרְצָה לְבִלְתִּי נְתָן־זֶרַע לְאָחִיו: 10 וַיֵּרַע בְּעֵינֵי יְהֹוָה אֲשֶׁר עָשָׂה וַיָּמֶת גַּם־אֹתוֹ: 11 וַיֹּאמֶר יְהוּדָה לְתָמָר כַּלָּתוֹ שְׁבִי אַלְמָנָה בֵית־אָבִיךְ עַד־יִגְדַּל שֵׁלָה בְנִי כִּי אָמַר פֶּן־יָמוּת גַּם־הוּא כְּאֶחָיו וַתֵּלֶךְ תָּמָר וַתֵּשֶׁב בֵּית אָבִיהָ: 12 וַיִּרְבּוּ הַיָּמִים וַתָּמָת בַּת־שׁוּעַ אֵשֶׁת־יְהוּדָה וַיִּנָּחֶם יְהוּדָה וַיַּעַל עַל־גֹּזְזֵי צֹאנוֹ הוּא וְחִירָה רֵעֵהוּ הָעֲדֻלָּמִי תִּמְנָתָה: 13 וַיֻּגַּד לְתָמָר לֵאמֹר הִנֵּה חָמִיךְ עֹלֶה תִמְנָתָה לָגֹז צֹאנוֹ: 14 וַתָּסַר בִּגְדֵי אַלְמְנוּתָהּ מֵעָלֶיהָ וַתְּכַס בַּצָּעִיף וַתִּתְעַלָּף וַתֵּשֶׁב בְּפֶתַח עֵינַיִם אֲשֶׁר עַל־דֶּרֶךְ תִּמְנָתָה כִּי רָאֲתָה כִּי־גָדַל שֵׁלָה וְהִוא

---

a   Cf. Deut. 25.5.
b   Lit. "spoil on the ground."
c-c Lit. "he was comforted."
d   Cf. Enam, Josh. 15.34. Others "in an open place" or "at the
     crossroad."

she saw that Shelah was grown up, yet she had not been given to him as wife. 15When Judah saw her, he took her for a harlot; for she had covered her face. 16So he turned aside to her by the road and said, "Here, let me sleep with you"—for he did not know that she was his daughter-in-law. "What," she asked, "will you pay for sleeping with me?" 17He replied, "I will send a kid from my flock." But she said, "You must leave a pledge until you have sent it." 18And he said, "What pledge shall I give you?" She replied, "Your seal and cord, and the staff which you carry." So he gave them to her and slept with her, and she conceived by him. 19Then she went on her way. She took off her veil and again put on her widow's garb.

20Judah sent the kid by his friend the Adullamite, to redeem the pledge from the woman; but he could not find her. 21He inquired of the people of that town, "Where is the cult prostitute, the one at Enaim, by the road?" But they said, "There has been no prostitute here." 22So he returned to Judah and said, "I could not find her; moreover, the townspeople said: There has been no prostitute here." 23Judah said, "Let her keep them, lest we become a laughingstock. I did send her this kid, but you did not find her."

24About three months later, Judah was told, "Your daughter-in-law Tamar has played the harlot; in fact, she is with child by harlotry." "Bring her out," said Judah, "and let her be burned." 25As she was being brought out, she sent this message to her father-in-law, "I am with child by the man to whom these belong." And she added, "Examine these: whose seal and cord and staff are these?" 26Judah recognized them, and said, "She is more in the right than I, inasmuch as I did not give her to my son Shelah." And he was not intimate with her again.

לֹא־נִתְּנָ֥ה ל֖וֹ לְאִשָּֽׁה׃ 15 וַיִּרְאֶ֣הָ יְהוּדָ֔ה וַֽיַּחְשְׁבֶ֖הָ לְזוֹנָ֑ה כִּ֥י כִסְּתָ֖ה פָּנֶֽיהָ׃ 16 וַיֵּ֣ט אֵלֶ֣יהָ אֶל־הַדֶּ֗רֶךְ וַיֹּ֙אמֶר֙ הָֽבָה־נָּא֙ אָב֣וֹא אֵלַ֔יִךְ כִּ֚י לֹ֣א יָדַ֔ע כִּ֥י כַלָּת֖וֹ הִ֑וא וַתֹּ֕אמֶר מַה־תִּתֶּן־לִ֔י כִּ֥י תָב֖וֹא אֵלָֽי׃ 17 וַיֹּ֕אמֶר אָנֹכִ֛י אֲשַׁלַּ֥ח גְּדִֽי־עִזִּ֖ים מִן־הַצֹּ֑אן וַתֹּ֕אמֶר אִם־תִּתֵּ֥ן עֵרָב֖וֹן עַ֥ד שָׁלְחֶֽךָ׃ 18 וַיֹּ֡אמֶר מָ֣ה הָעֵֽרָבוֹן֮ אֲשֶׁ֣ר אֶתֶּן־לָךְ֒ וַתֹּ֗אמֶר חֹתָֽמְךָ֙ וּפְתִילֶ֔ךָ וּמַטְּךָ֖ אֲשֶׁ֣ר בְּיָדֶ֑ךָ וַיִּתֶּן־לָ֛הּ וַיָּבֹ֥א אֵלֶ֖יהָ וַתַּ֥הַר לֽוֹ׃ 19 וַתָּ֣קָם וַתֵּ֔לֶךְ וַתָּ֥סַר צְעִיפָ֖הּ מֵֽעָלֶ֑יהָ וַתִּלְבַּ֖שׁ בִּגְדֵ֥י אַלְמְנוּתָֽהּ׃ 20 וַיִּשְׁלַ֨ח יְהוּדָ֜ה אֶת־גְּדִ֣י הָֽעִזִּ֗ים בְּיַד֙ רֵעֵ֣הוּ הָֽעֲדֻלָּמִ֔י לָקַ֥חַת הָעֵֽרָב֖וֹן מִיַּ֣ד הָֽאִשָּׁ֑ה וְלֹ֖א מְצָאָֽהּ׃ 21 וַיִּשְׁאַ֞ל אֶת־אַנְשֵׁ֤י מְקֹמָהּ֙ לֵאמֹ֔ר אַיֵּ֧ה הַקְּדֵשָׁ֛ה הִ֥וא בָעֵינַ֖יִם עַל־הַדָּ֑רֶךְ וַיֹּ֣אמְר֔וּ לֹא־הָיְתָ֥ה בָזֶ֖ה קְדֵשָֽׁה׃ 22 וַיָּ֙שָׁב֙ אֶל־יְהוּדָ֔ה וַיֹּ֖אמֶר לֹ֣א מְצָאתִ֑יהָ וְגַ֙ם אַנְשֵׁ֤י הַמָּקוֹם֙ אָֽמְר֔וּ לֹא־הָיְתָ֥ה בָזֶ֖ה קְדֵשָֽׁה׃ 23 וַיֹּ֤אמֶר יְהוּדָה֙ תִּֽקַּֽח־לָ֔הּ פֶּ֖ן נִהְיֶ֣ה לָב֑וּז הִנֵּ֤ה שָׁלַ֙חְתִּי֙ הַגְּדִ֣י הַזֶּ֔ה וְאַתָּ֖ה לֹ֥א מְצָאתָֽהּ׃ 24 וַיְהִ֣י ׀ כְּמִשְׁלֹ֣שׁ חֳדָשִׁ֗ים וַיֻּגַּ֨ד לִֽיהוּדָ֤ה לֵֽאמֹר֙ זָֽנְתָה֙ תָּמָ֣ר כַּלָּתֶ֔ךָ וְגַ֛ם הִנֵּ֥ה הָרָ֖ה לִזְנוּנִ֑ים וַיֹּ֣אמֶר יְהוּדָ֔ה הֽוֹצִיא֖וּהָ וְתִשָּׂרֵֽף׃ 25 הִ֣וא מוּצֵ֗את וְהִ֨יא שָֽׁלְחָ֤ה אֶל־חָמִ֙יהָ֙ לֵאמֹ֔ר לְאִישׁ֙ אֲשֶׁר־אֵ֣לֶּה לּ֔וֹ אָנֹכִ֖י הָרָ֑ה וַתֹּ֙אמֶר֙ הַכֶּר־נָ֔א לְמִ֞י הַחֹתֶ֧מֶת וְהַפְּתִילִ֛ים וְהַמַּטֶּ֖ה הָאֵֽלֶּה׃ 26 וַיַּכֵּ֣ר יְהוּדָ֗ה וַיֹּ֙אמֶר֙ צָֽדְקָ֣ה מִמֶּ֔נִּי כִּֽי־עַל־כֵּ֥ן לֹא־נְתַתִּ֖יהָ לְשֵׁלָ֣ה בְנִ֑י וְלֹֽא־יָסַ֥ף ע֖וֹד לְדַעְתָּֽהּ׃

27When the time came for her to give birth, there were twins in her womb! 28While she was in labor, one of them put out his hand, and the midwife tied a crimson thread on that hand, to signify: This one came out first. 29But just then he drew back his hand, and out came his brother; and she said, "What a breach[e] you have made for yourself!" So he was named Perez. 30Afterward his brother came out, on whose hand was the crimson thread; he was named Zerah.[f]

39

When Joseph was taken down to Egypt, a certain Egyptian, Potiphar, a courtier of Pharaoh and his chief steward, bought him from the Ishmaelites who had brought him there. 2The LORD was with Joseph, and he was a successful man; and he stayed in the house of his Egyptian master. 3And when his master saw that the LORD was with him and that the LORD lent success to everything he undertook, 4he took a liking to Joseph. He made him his personal attendant and put him in charge of his household, placing in his hands all that he owned. 5And from the time that the Egyptian put him in charge of his household and of all that he owned, the LORD blessed his house for Joseph's sake, so that the blessing of the LORD was upon everything that he owned, in the house and outside. 6He left all that he had in Joseph's hands and, with him there, he paid attention to nothing save the food that he ate. Now Joseph was well built and handsome.

7After a time, his master's wife cast her eyes upon Joseph and said, "Lie with me." 8But he refused. He said to his master's wife, "Look, with me here, my master gives no thought to anything in this house, and all that he owns he has placed in my hands. 9He wields no more authority in this house than I, and he has withheld

וַיְהִי בְּעֵת לִדְתָּהּ וְהִנֵּה תְאוֹמִים 27
בְּבִטְנָהּ: 28 וַיְהִי בְלִדְתָּהּ וַיִּתֶּן־יָד וַתִּקַּח
הַמְיַלֶּדֶת וַתִּקְשֹׁר עַל־יָדוֹ שָׁנִי לֵאמֹר זֶה
יָצָא רִאשֹׁנָה: 29 וַיְהִי ׀ כְּמֵשִׁיב יָדוֹ וְהִנֵּה
יָצָא אָחִיו וַתֹּאמֶר מַה־פָּרַצְתָּ עָלֶיךָ
פָּרֶץ וַיִּקְרָא שְׁמוֹ פָּרֶץ: 30 וְאַחַר יָצָא
אָחִיו אֲשֶׁר עַל־יָדוֹ הַשָּׁנִי וַיִּקְרָא שְׁמוֹ
זָרַח: ס

לט

וְיוֹסֵף הוּרַד מִצְרָיְמָה וַיִּקְנֵהוּ
פּוֹטִיפַר סְרִיס פַּרְעֹה שַׂר הַטַּבָּחִים אִישׁ
מִצְרִי מִיַּד הַיִּשְׁמְעֵאלִים אֲשֶׁר הוֹרִדֻהוּ
שָׁמָּה: 2 וַיְהִי יְהוָה אֶת־יוֹסֵף וַיְהִי אִישׁ
מַצְלִיחַ וַיְהִי בְּבֵית אֲדֹנָיו הַמִּצְרִי: 3 וַיַּרְא
אֲדֹנָיו כִּי יְהוָה אִתּוֹ וְכֹל אֲשֶׁר־הוּא עֹשֶׂה
יְהוָה מַצְלִיחַ בְּיָדוֹ: 4 וַיִּמְצָא יוֹסֵף חֵן
בְּעֵינָיו וַיְשָׁרֶת אֹתוֹ וַיַּפְקִדֵהוּ עַל־בֵּיתוֹ
וְכָל־יֶשׁ־לוֹ נָתַן בְּיָדוֹ: 5 וַיְהִי מֵאָז הִפְקִיד
אֹתוֹ בְּבֵיתוֹ וְעַל כָּל־אֲשֶׁר יֶשׁ־לוֹ וַיְבָרֶךְ
יְהוָה אֶת־בֵּית הַמִּצְרִי בִּגְלַל יוֹסֵף וַיְהִי
בִּרְכַּת יְהוָה בְּכָל־אֲשֶׁר יֶשׁ־לוֹ בַּבַּיִת
וּבַשָּׂדֶה: 6 וַיַּעֲזֹב כָּל־אֲשֶׁר־לוֹ בְּיַד־יוֹסֵף
וְלֹא־יָדַע אִתּוֹ מְאוּמָה כִּי אִם־הַלֶּחֶם
אֲשֶׁר־הוּא אוֹכֵל וַיְהִי יוֹסֵף יְפֵה־תֹאַר
וִיפֵה מַרְאֶה:
7 וַיְהִי אַחַר הַדְּבָרִים הָאֵלֶּה וַתִּשָּׂא אֵשֶׁת־
אֲדֹנָיו אֶת־עֵינֶיהָ אֶל־יוֹסֵף וַתֹּאמֶר שִׁכְבָה
עִמִּי: 8 וַיְמָאֵן ׀ וַיֹּאמֶר אֶל־אֵשֶׁת אֲדֹנָיו
הֵן אֲדֹנִי לֹא־יָדַע אִתִּי מַה־בַּבָּיִת וְכֹל
אֲשֶׁר־יֶשׁ־לוֹ נָתַן בְּיָדִי: 9 אֵינֶנּוּ גָדוֹל בַּבַּיִת
הַזֶּה מִמֶּנִּי וְלֹא־חָשַׂךְ מִמֶּנִּי מְאוּמָה כִּי
אִם־אוֹתָךְ בַּאֲשֶׁר אַתְּ־אִשְׁתּוֹ וְאֵיךְ אֶעֱשֶׂה

---

e Heb. pereṣ
f I.e., "brightness," perhaps alluding to the crimson thread.

nothing from me except yourself, since you are his wife. How then could I do this most wicked thing, and sin before God?" ¹⁰And much as she coaxed Joseph day after day, he did not yield to her request to lie beside her, to be with her.

¹¹One such day, he came into the house to do his work. None of the household being there inside, ¹²she caught hold of him by his garment and said, "Lie with me!" But he left his garment in her hand and got away and fled outside. ¹³When she saw that he had left it in her hand and had fled outside, ¹⁴she called out to her servants and said to them, "Look, he had to bring us a Hebrew to dally with us! This one came to lie with me; but I screamed loud. ¹⁵And when he heard me screaming at the top of my voice, he left his garment with me and got away and fled outside." ¹⁶She kept his garment beside her, until his master came home. ¹⁷Then she told him the same story, saying, "The Hebrew slave whom you brought into our house came to me to dally with me; ¹⁸but when I screamed at the top of my voice, he left his garment with me and fled outside."

¹⁹When his master heard the story that his wife told him, namely, "Thus and so your slave did to me," he was furious. ²⁰So Joseph's master had him put in prison, where the king's prisoners were confined. But even while he was there in prison, ²¹the Lord was with Joseph: He extended kindness to him and disposed the chief jailer favorably toward him. ²²The chief jailer put in Joseph's charge all the prisoners who were in that prison, and he was the one to carry out everything that was done there. ²³The chief jailer did not supervise anything that was in Joseph'sᵃ charge, because the Lord was with him, and whatever he did the Lord made successful.

ᵃ Lit. "his."

הָרָעָה הַגְּדֹלָה הַזֹּאת וְחָטָאתִי לֵאלֹהִים: ¹⁰ וַיְהִי כְּדַבְּרָהּ אֶל־יוֹסֵף יוֹם | יוֹם וְלֹא־שָׁמַע אֵלֶיהָ לִשְׁכַּב אֶצְלָהּ לִהְיוֹת עִמָּהּ: ¹¹ וַיְהִי כְּהַיּוֹם הַזֶּה וַיָּבֹא הַבַּיְתָה לַעֲשׂוֹת מְלַאכְתּוֹ וְאֵין אִישׁ מֵאַנְשֵׁי הַבַּיִת שָׁם בַּבָּיִת: ¹² וַתִּתְפְּשֵׂהוּ בְּבִגְדוֹ לֵאמֹר שִׁכְבָה עִמִּי וַיַּעֲזֹב בִּגְדוֹ בְּיָדָהּ וַיָּנָס וַיֵּצֵא הַחוּצָה: ¹³ וַיְהִי כִּרְאוֹתָהּ כִּי־עָזַב בִּגְדוֹ בְּיָדָהּ וַיָּנָס הַחוּצָה: ¹⁴ וַתִּקְרָא לְאַנְשֵׁי בֵיתָהּ וַתֹּאמֶר לָהֶם לֵאמֹר רְאוּ הֵבִיא לָנוּ אִישׁ עִבְרִי לְצַחֶק בָּנוּ בָּא אֵלַי לִשְׁכַּב עִמִּי וָאֶקְרָא בְּקוֹל גָּדוֹל: ¹⁵ וַיְהִי כְשָׁמְעוֹ כִּי־הֲרִימֹתִי קוֹלִי וָאֶקְרָא וַיַּעֲזֹב בִּגְדוֹ אֶצְלִי וַיָּנָס וַיֵּצֵא הַחוּצָה: ¹⁶ וַתַּנַּח בִּגְדוֹ אֶצְלָהּ עַד־בּוֹא אֲדֹנָיו אֶל־בֵּיתוֹ: ¹⁷ וַתְּדַבֵּר אֵלָיו כַּדְּבָרִים הָאֵלֶּה לֵאמֹר בָּא־אֵלַי הָעֶבֶד הָעִבְרִי אֲשֶׁר־הֵבֵאתָ לָּנוּ לְצַחֶק בִּי: ¹⁸ וַיְהִי כַּהֲרִימִי קוֹלִי וָאֶקְרָא וַיַּעֲזֹב בִּגְדוֹ אֶצְלִי וַיָּנָס הַחוּצָה:

¹⁹ וַיְהִי כִשְׁמֹעַ אֲדֹנָיו אֶת־דִּבְרֵי אִשְׁתּוֹ אֲשֶׁר דִּבְּרָה אֵלָיו לֵאמֹר כַּדְּבָרִים הָאֵלֶּה עָשָׂה לִי עַבְדֶּךָ וַיִּחַר אַפּוֹ: ²⁰ וַיִּקַּח אֲדֹנֵי יוֹסֵף אֹתוֹ וַיִּתְּנֵהוּ אֶל־בֵּית הַסֹּהַר מְקוֹם אֲשֶׁר־אֲסוּרֵי הַמֶּלֶךְ אֲסוּרִים וַיְהִי־שָׁם בְּבֵית הַסֹּהַר: ²¹ וַיְהִי יְהֹוָה אֶת־יוֹסֵף וַיֵּט אֵלָיו חָסֶד וַיִּתֵּן חִנּוֹ בְּעֵינֵי שַׂר בֵּית־הַסֹּהַר: ²² וַיִּתֵּן שַׂר בֵּית־הַסֹּהַר בְּיַד־יוֹסֵף אֵת כָּל־הָאֲסִירִם אֲשֶׁר בְּבֵית הַסֹּהַר וְאֵת כָּל־אֲשֶׁר עֹשִׂים שָׁם הוּא הָיָה עֹשֶׂה: ²³ אֵין | שַׂר בֵּית־הַסֹּהַר רֹאֶה אֶת־כָּל־מְאוּמָה בְּיָדוֹ בַּאֲשֶׁר יְהֹוָה אִתּוֹ וַאֲשֶׁר־הוּא עֹשֶׂה יְהֹוָה מַצְלִיחַ: ס

40 Some time later, the cupbearer and the baker of the king of Egypt gave offense to their lord the king of Egypt. ²Pharaoh was angry with his two courtiers, the chief cupbearer and the chief baker, ³and put them in custody, in the house of the chief steward, in the same prison house where Joseph was confined. ⁴The chief steward assigned Joseph to them, and he attended them.

When they had been in custody for some time, ⁵both of them—the cupbearer and the baker of the king of Egypt, who were confined in the prison—dreamed in the same night, each his own dream and each dream with its own meaning. ⁶When Joseph came to them in the morning, he saw that they were distraught. ⁷He asked Pharaoh's courtiers, who were with him in custody in his master's house, saying, "Why do you appear downcast today?" ⁸And they said to him, "We had dreams, and there is no one to interpret them." So Joseph said to them, "Surely God can interpret! Tell me [your dreams]."

⁹Then the chief cupbearer told his dream to Joseph. He said to him, "In my dream, there was a vine in front of me. ¹⁰On the vine were three branches. It had barely budded, when out came its blossoms and its clusters ripened into grapes. ¹¹Pharaoh's cup was in my hand, and I took the grapes, pressed them into Pharaoh's cup, and placed the cup in Pharaoh's hand." ¹²Joseph said to him, "This is its interpretation: The three branches are three days. ¹³In three days Pharaoh will pardon you[a] and restore you to your post; you will place Pharaoh's cup in his hand, as was your custom formerly when you were his cupbearer. ¹⁴But think of me when all is well with you again, and do me the kindness of mentioning me to Pharaoh, so as to free me from this

---

a Lit. "lift up your head."

מ וַיְהִי אַחַר הַדְּבָרִים הָאֵלֶּה חָטְאוּ מַשְׁקֵה מֶלֶךְ־מִצְרַיִם וְהָאֹפֶה לַאֲדֹנֵיהֶם לְמֶלֶךְ מִצְרָיִם: 2 וַיִּקְצֹף פַּרְעֹה עַל שְׁנֵי סָרִיסָיו עַל שַׂר הַמַּשְׁקִים וְעַל שַׂר הָאוֹפִים: 3 וַיִּתֵּן אֹתָם בְּמִשְׁמַר בֵּית שַׂר הַטַּבָּחִים אֶל־בֵּית הַסֹּהַר מְקוֹם אֲשֶׁר יוֹסֵף אָסוּר שָׁם: 4 וַיִּפְקֹד שַׂר הַטַּבָּחִים אֶת־יוֹסֵף אִתָּם וַיְשָׁרֶת אֹתָם וַיִּהְיוּ יָמִים בְּמִשְׁמָר: 5 וַיַּחַלְמוּ חֲלוֹם שְׁנֵיהֶם אִישׁ חֲלֹמוֹ בְּלַיְלָה אֶחָד אִישׁ כְּפִתְרוֹן חֲלֹמוֹ הַמַּשְׁקֶה וְהָאֹפֶה אֲשֶׁר לְמֶלֶךְ מִצְרַיִם אֲשֶׁר אֲסוּרִים בְּבֵית הַסֹּהַר: 6 וַיָּבֹא אֲלֵיהֶם יוֹסֵף בַּבֹּקֶר וַיַּרְא אֹתָם וְהִנָּם זֹעֲפִים: 7 וַיִּשְׁאַל אֶת־סְרִיסֵי פַרְעֹה אֲשֶׁר אִתּוֹ בְמִשְׁמַר בֵּית אֲדֹנָיו לֵאמֹר מַדּוּעַ פְּנֵיכֶם רָעִים הַיּוֹם: 8 וַיֹּאמְרוּ אֵלָיו חֲלוֹם חָלַמְנוּ וּפֹתֵר אֵין אֹתוֹ וַיֹּאמֶר אֲלֵהֶם יוֹסֵף הֲלוֹא לֵאלֹהִים פִּתְרֹנִים סַפְּרוּ־נָא לִי: 9 וַיְסַפֵּר שַׂר־הַמַּשְׁקִים אֶת־חֲלֹמוֹ לְיוֹסֵף וַיֹּאמֶר לוֹ בַּחֲלוֹמִי וְהִנֵּה־גֶפֶן לְפָנָי: 10 וּבַגֶּפֶן שְׁלֹשָׁה שָׂרִיגִם וְהִיא כְפֹרַחַת עָלְתָה נִצָּהּ הִבְשִׁילוּ אַשְׁכְּלֹתֶיהָ עֲנָבִים: 11 וְכוֹס פַּרְעֹה בְּיָדִי וָאֶקַּח אֶת־הָעֲנָבִים וָאֶשְׂחַט אֹתָם אֶל־כּוֹס פַּרְעֹה וָאֶתֵּן אֶת־הַכּוֹס עַל־כַּף פַּרְעֹה: 12 וַיֹּאמֶר לוֹ יוֹסֵף זֶה פִּתְרֹנוֹ שְׁלֹשֶׁת הַשָּׂרִגִים שְׁלֹשֶׁת יָמִים הֵם: 13 בְּעוֹד | שְׁלֹשֶׁת יָמִים יִשָּׂא פַרְעֹה אֶת־רֹאשֶׁךָ וַהֲשִׁיבְךָ עַל־כַּנֶּךָ וְנָתַתָּ כוֹס־פַּרְעֹה בְּיָדוֹ כַּמִּשְׁפָּט הָרִאשׁוֹן אֲשֶׁר הָיִיתָ מַשְׁקֵהוּ: 14 כִּי אִם־זְכַרְתַּנִי אִתְּךָ כַּאֲשֶׁר יִיטַב לָךְ וְעָשִׂיתָ־נָּא עִמָּדִי חָסֶד וְהִזְכַּרְתַּנִי אֶל־פַּרְעֹה וְהוֹצֵאתַנִי מִן־הַבַּיִת הַזֶּה:

place. ¹⁵For in truth, I was kidnapped from the land of the Hebrews; nor have I done anything here that they should have put me in the dungeon."

¹⁶When the chief baker saw how favorably he had interpreted, he said to Joseph, "In my dream, similarly, there were three openwork baskets[b] on my head. ¹⁷In the uppermost basket were all kinds of food for Pharaoh that a baker prepares; and the birds were eating it out of the basket above my head." ¹⁸Joseph answered, "This is its interpretation: The three baskets are three days. ¹⁹In three days Pharaoh will lift off your head and impale you upon a pole; and the birds will pick off your flesh."

²⁰On the third day—his birthday—Pharaoh made a banquet for all his officials, and he singled out[c] his chief cupbearer and his chief baker from among his officials. ²¹He restored the chief cupbearer to his cupbearing, and he placed the cup in Pharaoh's hand; ²²but the chief baker he impaled—just as Joseph had interpreted to them.

²³Yet the chief cupbearer did not think of Joseph; he forgot him.

41 MIKKETS
After two years' time, Pharaoh dreamed that he was standing by the Nile, ²when out of the Nile there came up seven cows, handsome and sturdy, and they grazed in the reed grass. ³But presently, seven other cows came up from the Nile close behind them, ugly and gaunt, and stood beside the cows on the bank of the Nile; ⁴and the ugly gaunt cows ate up the seven handsome sturdy cows. And Pharaoh awoke. ⁵He fell asleep and dreamed a second time: Seven ears of grain, solid and healthy, grew on a single stalk. ⁶But close behind them sprouted seven ears, thin and scorched by the east wind.

---

b   *Others "baskets with white bread" or "white baskets"; meaning of Heb. ḥori uncertain.*
c   *Lit. "lifted the head of."*

15 כִּי־גֻנֹּב גֻּנַּ֔בְתִּי מֵאֶ֖רֶץ הָעִבְרִ֑ים וְגַם־פֹּה֙ לֹא־עָשִׂ֣יתִי מְא֔וּמָה כִּֽי־שָׂמ֥וּ אֹתִ֖י בַּבּֽוֹר׃ 16 וַיַּ֥רְא שַׂר־הָאֹפִ֖ים כִּ֣י ט֣וֹב פָּתָ֑ר וַיֹּ֙אמֶר֙ אֶל־יוֹסֵ֔ף אַף־אֲנִי֙ בַּחֲלוֹמִ֔י וְהִנֵּ֗ה שְׁלֹשָׁ֛ה סַלֵּ֥י חֹרִ֖י עַל־רֹאשִֽׁי׃ 17 וּבַסַּ֣ל הָֽעֶלְי֗וֹן מִכֹּ֛ל מַאֲכַ֥ל פַּרְעֹ֖ה מַעֲשֵׂ֣ה אֹפֶ֑ה וְהָע֗וֹף אֹכֵ֥ל אֹתָ֛ם מִן־הַסַּ֖ל מֵעַ֥ל רֹאשִֽׁי׃ 18 וַיַּ֤עַן יוֹסֵף֙ וַיֹּ֔אמֶר זֶ֖ה פִּתְרֹנ֑וֹ שְׁלֹ֙שֶׁת֙ הַסַּלִּ֔ים שְׁלֹ֥שֶׁת יָמִ֖ים הֵֽם׃ 19 בְּע֣וֹד ׀ שְׁלֹ֣שֶׁת יָמִ֗ים יִשָּׂ֨א פַרְעֹ֤ה אֶת־רֹֽאשְׁךָ֙ מֵֽעָלֶ֔יךָ וְתָלָ֥ה אוֹתְךָ֖ עַל־עֵ֑ץ וְאָכַ֥ל הָע֛וֹף אֶת־בְּשָׂרְךָ֖ מֵעָלֶֽיךָ׃ 20 וַיְהִ֣י ׀ בַּיּ֣וֹם הַשְּׁלִישִׁ֗י י֚וֹם הֻלֶּ֣דֶת אֶת־פַּרְעֹ֔ה וַיַּ֥עַשׂ מִשְׁתֶּ֖ה לְכׇל־עֲבָדָ֑יו וַיִּשָּׂ֞א אֶת־רֹ֣אשׁ ׀ שַׂ֣ר הַמַּשְׁקִ֗ים וְאֶת־רֹ֛אשׁ שַׂ֥ר הָאֹפִ֖ים בְּת֥וֹךְ עֲבָדָֽיו׃ 21 וַיָּ֛שֶׁב אֶת־שַׂ֥ר הַמַּשְׁקִ֖ים עַל־מַשְׁקֵ֑הוּ וַיִּתֵּ֥ן הַכּ֖וֹס עַל־כַּ֥ף פַּרְעֹֽה׃ 22 וְאֵ֛ת שַׂ֥ר הָאֹפִ֖ים תָּלָ֑ה כַּאֲשֶׁ֥ר פָּתַ֛ר לָהֶ֖ם יוֹסֵֽף׃ 23 וְלֹֽא־זָכַ֧ר שַֽׂר־הַמַּשְׁקִ֛ים אֶת־יוֹסֵ֖ף וַיִּשְׁכָּחֵֽהוּ׃ פ

מא **מקץ** 41 וַיְהִ֕י מִקֵּ֖ץ שְׁנָתַ֣יִם יָמִ֑ים וּפַרְעֹ֣ה חֹלֵ֔ם וְהִנֵּ֖ה עֹמֵ֥ד עַל־הַיְאֹֽר׃ 2 וְהִנֵּ֣ה מִן־הַיְאֹ֗ר עֹלֹת֙ שֶׁ֣בַע פָּר֔וֹת יְפ֥וֹת מַרְאֶ֖ה וּבְרִיאֹ֣ת בָּשָׂ֑ר וַתִּרְעֶ֖ינָה בָּאָֽחוּ׃ 3 וְהִנֵּ֞ה שֶׁ֧בַע פָּר֣וֹת אֲחֵר֗וֹת עֹל֤וֹת אַחֲרֵיהֶן֙ מִן־הַיְאֹ֔ר רָע֥וֹת מַרְאֶ֖ה וְדַקּ֣וֹת בָּשָׂ֑ר וַֽתַּעֲמֹ֛דְנָה אֵ֥צֶל הַפָּר֖וֹת עַל־שְׂפַ֥ת הַיְאֹֽר׃ 4 וַתֹּאכַ֣לְנָה הַפָּר֗וֹת רָע֤וֹת הַמַּרְאֶה֙ וְדַקֹּ֣ת הַבָּשָׂ֔ר אֵ֣ת שֶׁ֧בַע הַפָּר֛וֹת יְפֹ֥ת הַמַּרְאֶ֖ה וְהַבְּרִיאֹ֑ת וַיִּיקַ֖ץ פַּרְעֹֽה׃ 5 וַיִּישָׁ֕ן וַֽיַּחֲלֹ֖ם שֵׁנִ֑ית וְהִנֵּ֣ה ׀ שֶׁ֣בַע שִׁבֳּלִ֗ים עֹל֛וֹת בְּקָנֶ֥ה אֶחָ֖ד בְּרִיא֥וֹת וְטֹבֽוֹת׃ 6 וְהִנֵּה֙

7And the thin ears swallowed up the seven solid and full ears. Then Pharaoh awoke: it was a dream!

8Next morning, his spirit was agitated, and he sent for all the magicians of Egypt, and all its wise men; and Pharaoh told them his dreams, but none could interpret them for Pharaoh.

9The chief cupbearer then spoke up and said to Pharaoh, "I must make mention today of my offenses. 10Once Pharaoh was angry with his servants, and placed me in custody in the house of the chief steward, together with the chief baker. 11We had dreams the same night, he and I, each of us a dream with a meaning of its own. 12A Hebrew youth was there with us, a servant of the chief steward; and when we told him our dreams, he interpreted them for us, telling each of the meaning of his dream. 13And as he interpreted for us, so it came to pass: I was restored to my post, and the other was impaled."

14Thereupon Pharaoh sent for Joseph, and he was rushed from the dungeon. He had his hair cut and changed his clothes, and he appeared before Pharaoh. 15And Pharaoh said to Joseph, "I have had a dream, but no one can interpret it. Now I have heard it said of you that for you to hear a dream is to tell its meaning." 16Joseph answered Pharaoh, saying, "Not I! God will see to Pharaoh's welfare."

17Then Pharaoh said to Joseph, "In my dream, I was standing on the bank of the Nile, 18when out of the Nile came up seven sturdy and well-formed cows and grazed in the reed grass. 19Presently there followed them seven other cows, scrawny, ill-formed, and emaciated—never had I seen their likes for ugliness in all the land of Egypt! 20And the seven lean and ugly cows ate up the first seven cows, the sturdy ones; 21but when they had consumed them, one could not tell that they had consumed them, for they looked just as bad as before. And

שֶׁבַע שִׁבֳּלִים דַּקּוֹת וּשְׁדוּפֹת קָדִים צֹמְחוֹת אַחֲרֵיהֶן׃ 7 וַתִּבְלַעְןָ הַשִּׁבֳּלִים הַדַּקּוֹת אֵת שֶׁבַע הַשִּׁבֳּלִים הַבְּרִיאוֹת וְהַמְּלֵאוֹת וַיִּיקַץ פַּרְעֹה וְהִנֵּה חֲלוֹם׃ 8 וַיְהִי בַבֹּקֶר וַתִּפָּעֶם רוּחוֹ וַיִּשְׁלַח וַיִּקְרָא אֶת־כָּל־חַרְטֻמֵּי מִצְרַיִם וְאֶת־כָּל־חֲכָמֶיהָ וַיְסַפֵּר פַּרְעֹה לָהֶם אֶת־חֲלֹמוֹ וְאֵין־פּוֹתֵר אוֹתָם לְפַרְעֹה׃ 9 וַיְדַבֵּר שַׂר הַמַּשְׁקִים אֶת־פַּרְעֹה לֵאמֹר אֶת־חֲטָאַי אֲנִי מַזְכִּיר הַיּוֹם׃ 10 פַּרְעֹה קָצַף עַל־עֲבָדָיו וַיִּתֵּן אֹתִי בְּמִשְׁמַר בֵּית שַׂר הַטַּבָּחִים אֹתִי וְאֵת שַׂר הָאֹפִים׃ 11 וַנַּחַלְמָה חֲלוֹם בְּלַיְלָה אֶחָד אֲנִי וָהוּא אִישׁ כְּפִתְרוֹן חֲלֹמוֹ חָלָמְנוּ׃ 12 וְשָׁם אִתָּנוּ נַעַר עִבְרִי עֶבֶד לְשַׂר הַטַּבָּחִים וַנְּסַפֶּר־לוֹ וַיִּפְתָּר־לָנוּ אֶת־חֲלֹמֹתֵינוּ אִישׁ כַּחֲלֹמוֹ פָּתָר׃ 13 וַיְהִי כַּאֲשֶׁר פָּתַר־לָנוּ כֵּן הָיָה אֹתִי הֵשִׁיב עַל־כַּנִּי וְאֹתוֹ תָלָה׃ 14 וַיִּשְׁלַח פַּרְעֹה וַיִּקְרָא אֶת־יוֹסֵף וַיְרִיצֻהוּ מִן־הַבּוֹר וַיְגַלַּח וַיְחַלֵּף שִׂמְלֹתָיו וַיָּבֹא אֶל־פַּרְעֹה׃ 15 וַיֹּאמֶר פַּרְעֹה אֶל־יוֹסֵף חֲלוֹם חָלַמְתִּי וּפֹתֵר אֵין אֹתוֹ וַאֲנִי שָׁמַעְתִּי עָלֶיךָ לֵאמֹר תִּשְׁמַע חֲלוֹם לִפְתֹּר אֹתוֹ׃ 16 וַיַּעַן יוֹסֵף אֶת־פַּרְעֹה לֵאמֹר בִּלְעָדָי אֱלֹהִים יַעֲנֶה אֶת־שְׁלוֹם פַּרְעֹה׃ 17 וַיְדַבֵּר פַּרְעֹה אֶל־יוֹסֵף בַּחֲלֹמִי הִנְנִי עֹמֵד עַל־שְׂפַת הַיְאֹר׃ 18 וְהִנֵּה מִן־הַיְאֹר עֹלֹת שֶׁבַע פָּרוֹת בְּרִיאוֹת בָּשָׂר וִיפֹת תֹּאַר וַתִּרְעֶינָה בָּאָחוּ׃ 19 וְהִנֵּה שֶׁבַע־פָּרוֹת אֲחֵרוֹת עֹלוֹת אַחֲרֵיהֶן דַּלּוֹת וְרָעוֹת תֹּאַר מְאֹד וְרַקּוֹת בָּשָׂר לֹא־רָאִיתִי כָהֵנָּה בְּכָל־אֶרֶץ מִצְרַיִם לָרֹעַ׃ 20 וַתֹּאכַלְנָה הַפָּרוֹת הָרַקּוֹת וְהָרָעוֹת אֵת שֶׁבַע הַפָּרוֹת הָרִאשֹׁנוֹת הַבְּרִיאֹת׃ 21 וַתָּבֹאנָה אֶל־קִרְבֶּנָה וְלֹא נוֹדַע כִּי־בָאוּ אֶל־קִרְבֶּנָה וּמַרְאֵיהֶן רַע כַּאֲשֶׁר בַּתְּחִלָּה וָאִיקָץ׃

I awoke. 22In my other dream, I saw seven ears of grain, full and healthy, growing on a single stalk; 23but right behind them sprouted seven ears, shriveled, thin, and scorched by the east wind. 24And the thin ears swallowed the seven healthy ears. I have told my magicians, but none has an explanation for me."

25And Joseph said to Pharaoh, "Pharaoh's dreams are one and the same: God has told Pharaoh what He is about to do. 26The seven healthy cows are seven years, and the seven healthy ears are seven years; it is the same dream. 27The seven lean and ugly cows that followed are seven years, as are also the seven empty ears scorched by the east wind; they are seven years of famine. 28It is just as I have told Pharaoh: God has revealed to Pharaoh what He is about to do. 29Immediately ahead are seven years of great abundance in all the land of Egypt. 30After them will come seven years of famine, and all the abundance in the land of Egypt will be forgotten. As the land is ravaged by famine, 31no trace of the abundance will be left in the land because of the famine thereafter, for it will be very severe. 32As for Pharaoh having had the same dream twice, it means that the matter has been determined by God, and that God will soon carry it out.

33"Accordingly, let Pharaoh find a man of discernment and wisdom, and set him over the land of Egypt. 34And let Pharaoh take steps to appoint overseers over the land, and organize[a] the land of Egypt in the seven years of plenty. 35Let all the food of these good years that are coming be gathered, and let the grain be collected under Pharaoh's authority as food to be stored in the cities. 36Let that food be a reserve for the land for the seven years of famine which will come upon the land of Egypt, so that the land may not perish in the famine."

37The plan pleased Pharaoh and all his court-

22 וָאֵרֶא בַּחֲלֹמִי וְהִנֵּה ׀ שֶׁבַע שִׁבֳּלִים עֹלֹת בְּקָנֶה אֶחָד מְלֵאֹת וְטֹבֽוֹת: 23 וְהִנֵּה שֶׁבַע שִׁבֳּלִים צְנֻמוֹת דַּקּוֹת שְׁדֻפוֹת קָדִים צֹמְחוֹת אַחֲרֵיהֶֽם: 24 וַתִּבְלַעְןָ הָשִׁבֳּלִים הַדַּקֹּת אֵת שֶׁבַע הַשִּׁבֳּלִים הַטֹּבוֹת וָאֹמַר אֶל־הַחַרְטֻמִּים וְאֵין מַגִּיד לִֽי:

25 וַיֹּאמֶר יוֹסֵף אֶל־פַּרְעֹה חֲלוֹם פַּרְעֹה אֶחָד הוּא אֵת אֲשֶׁר הָאֱלֹהִים עֹשֶׂה הִגִּיד לְפַרְעֹֽה: 26 שֶׁבַע פָּרֹת הַטֹּבֹת שֶׁבַע שָׁנִים הֵנָּה וְשֶׁבַע הַשִּׁבֳּלִים הַטֹּבֹת שֶׁבַע שָׁנִים הֵנָּה חֲלוֹם אֶחָד הֽוּא: 27 וְשֶׁבַע הַפָּרוֹת הָרַקּוֹת וְהָרָעֹת הָעֹלֹת אַחֲרֵיהֶן שֶׁבַע שָׁנִים הֵנָּה וְשֶׁבַע הַשִּׁבֳּלִים הָרֵקוֹת שְׁדֻפוֹת הַקָּדִים יִהְיוּ שֶׁבַע שְׁנֵי רָעָֽב: 28 הוּא הַדָּבָר אֲשֶׁר דִּבַּרְתִּי אֶל־פַּרְעֹה אֲשֶׁר הָאֱלֹהִים עֹשֶׂה הֶרְאָה אֶת־פַּרְעֹֽה: 29 הִנֵּה שֶׁבַע שָׁנִים בָּאוֹת שָׂבָע גָּדוֹל בְּכָל־אֶרֶץ מִצְרָֽיִם: 30 וְקָמוּ שֶׁבַע שְׁנֵי רָעָב אַחֲרֵיהֶן וְנִשְׁכַּח כָּל־הַשָּׂבָע בְּאֶרֶץ מִצְרָיִם וְכִלָּה הָרָעָב אֶת־הָאָֽרֶץ: 31 וְלֹא־יִוָּדַע הַשָּׂבָע בָּאָרֶץ מִפְּנֵי הָרָעָב הַהוּא אַחֲרֵי־כֵן כִּֽי־כָבֵד הוּא מְאֹֽד: 32 וְעַל הִשָּׁנוֹת הַחֲלוֹם אֶל־פַּרְעֹה פַּעֲמָיִם כִּי־נָכוֹן הַדָּבָר מֵעִם הָאֱלֹהִים וּמְמַהֵר הָאֱלֹהִים לַעֲשֹׂתֽוֹ: 33 וְעַתָּה יֵרֶא פַרְעֹה אִישׁ נָבוֹן וְחָכָם וִישִׁיתֵהוּ עַל־אֶרֶץ מִצְרָֽיִם: 34 יַעֲשֶׂה פַרְעֹה וְיַפְקֵד פְּקִדִים עַל־הָאָרֶץ וְחִמֵּשׁ אֶת־אֶרֶץ מִצְרַיִם בְּשֶׁבַע שְׁנֵי הַשָּׂבָֽע: 35 וְיִקְבְּצוּ אֶת־כָּל־אֹכֶל הַשָּׁנִים הַטֹּבֹת הַבָּאֹת הָאֵלֶּה וְיִצְבְּרוּ־בָר תַּחַת יַד־פַּרְעֹה אֹכֶל בֶּעָרִים וְשָׁמָֽרוּ: 36 וְהָיָה הָאֹכֶל לְפִקָּדוֹן לָאָרֶץ לְשֶׁבַע שְׁנֵי הָרָעָב אֲשֶׁר תִּהְיֶיןָ בְּאֶרֶץ מִצְרָיִם וְלֹא־תִכָּרֵת הָאָרֶץ בָּרָעָֽב:

37 וַיִּיטַב הַדָּבָר בְּעֵינֵי פַרְעֹה וּבְעֵינֵי כָּל־עֲבָדָֽיו: 38 וַיֹּאמֶר פַּרְעֹה אֶל־עֲבָדָיו

---

a   Others "take a fifth part of"; meaning of Heb. uncertain.

iers. ³⁸And Pharaoh said to his courtiers, "Could we find another like him, a man in whom is the spirit of God?" ³⁹So Pharaoh said to Joseph, "Since God has made all this known to you, there is none so discerning and wise as you. ⁴⁰You shall be in charge of my court, and by your command shall all my people be directed;^b only with respect to the throne shall I be superior to you." ⁴¹Pharaoh further said to Joseph, "See, I put you in charge of all the land of Egypt." ⁴²And removing his signet ring from his hand, Pharaoh put it on Joseph's hand; and he had him dressed in robes of fine linen, and put a gold chain about his neck. ⁴³He had him ride in the chariot of his second-in-command, and they cried before him, "Abrek!"^c Thus he placed him over all the land of Egypt.

⁴⁴Pharaoh said to Joseph, "I am Pharaoh; yet without you, no one shall lift up hand or foot in all the land of Egypt." ⁴⁵Pharaoh then gave Joseph the name Zaphenath-paneah;^d and he gave him for a wife Asenath daughter of Poti-phera, priest of On. Thus Joseph emerged in charge of the land of Egypt.—⁴⁶Joseph was thirty years old when he entered the service of Pharaoh king of Egypt.—Leaving Pharaoh's presence, Joseph traveled through all the land of Egypt.

⁴⁷During the seven years of plenty, the land produced in abundance. ⁴⁸And he gathered all the grain of ^{e-}the seven years that the land of Egypt was enjoying,^{-e} and stored the grain in the cities; he put in each city the grain of the fields around it. ⁴⁹So Joseph collected produce in very large quantity, like the sands of the sea, until he ceased to measure it, for it could not be measured.

---

b   *Others "order themselves" or "pay homage"; meaning of Heb. yishshaq uncertain.*

c   *Others "Bow the knee," as though from Heb. barakh "to kneel"; perhaps from an Egyptian word of unknown meaning.*

d   *Egyptian for "God speaks; he lives," or "creator of life."*

e-e   *Lit. "the seven years that were in the land of Egypt."*

הֲנִמְצָ֣א כָזֶ֔ה אִ֕ישׁ אֲשֶׁ֛ר ר֥וּחַ אֱלֹהִ֖ים בּֽוֹ׃

³⁹ וַיֹּ֤אמֶר פַּרְעֹה֙ אֶל־יוֹסֵ֔ף אַחֲרֵ֨י הוֹדִ֧יעַ אֱלֹהִ֛ים אוֹתְךָ֖ אֶת־כָּל־זֹ֑את אֵין־נָב֥וֹן וְחָכָ֖ם כָּמֽוֹךָ׃ ⁴⁰ אַתָּה֙ תִּהְיֶ֣ה עַל־בֵּיתִ֔י וְעַל־פִּ֖יךָ יִשַּׁ֣ק כָּל־עַמִּ֑י רַ֥ק הַכִּסֵּ֖א אֶגְדַּ֥ל מִמֶּֽךָּ׃ ⁴¹ וַיֹּ֥אמֶר פַּרְעֹ֖ה אֶל־יוֹסֵ֑ף רְאֵה֙ נָתַ֣תִּי אֹֽתְךָ֔ עַ֖ל כָּל־אֶ֥רֶץ מִצְרָֽיִם׃ ⁴² וַיָּ֨סַר פַּרְעֹ֤ה אֶת־טַבַּעְתּוֹ֙ מֵעַ֣ל יָד֔וֹ וַיִּתֵּ֥ן אֹתָ֖הּ עַל־יַ֣ד יוֹסֵ֑ף וַיַּלְבֵּ֤שׁ אֹתוֹ֙ בִּגְדֵי־שֵׁ֔שׁ וַיָּ֛שֶׂם רְבִ֥ד הַזָּהָ֖ב עַל־צַוָּארֽוֹ׃ ⁴³ וַיַּרְכֵּ֣ב אֹת֗וֹ בְּמִרְכֶּ֤בֶת הַמִּשְׁנֶה֙ אֲשֶׁר־ל֔וֹ וַיִּקְרְא֥וּ לְפָנָ֖יו אַבְרֵ֑ךְ וְנָת֣וֹן אֹת֔וֹ עַ֖ל כָּל־אֶ֥רֶץ מִצְרָֽיִם׃ ⁴⁴ וַיֹּ֧אמֶר פַּרְעֹ֛ה אֶל־יוֹסֵ֖ף אֲנִ֣י פַרְעֹ֑ה וּבִלְעָדֶ֗יךָ לֹֽא־יָרִ֨ים אִ֧ישׁ אֶת־יָד֛וֹ וְאֶת־רַגְל֖וֹ בְּכָל־אֶ֥רֶץ מִצְרָֽיִם׃ ⁴⁵ וַיִּקְרָ֨א פַרְעֹ֣ה שֵׁם־יוֹסֵף֮ צָֽפְנַ֣ת פַּעְנֵחַ֒ וַיִּתֶּן־ל֣וֹ אֶת־אָֽסְנַ֗ת בַּת־פּ֥וֹטִי פֶ֛רַע כֹּהֵ֥ן אֹ֖ן לְאִשָּׁ֑ה וַיֵּצֵ֥א יוֹסֵ֖ף עַל־אֶ֥רֶץ מִצְרָֽיִם׃ ⁴⁶ וְיוֹסֵף֙ בֶּן־שְׁלֹשִׁ֣ים שָׁנָ֔ה בְּעָמְד֕וֹ לִפְנֵ֖י פַּרְעֹ֣ה מֶֽלֶךְ־מִצְרָ֑יִם וַיֵּצֵ֤א יוֹסֵף֙ מִלִּפְנֵ֣י פַרְעֹ֔ה וַֽיַּעֲבֹ֖ר בְּכָל־אֶ֥רֶץ מִצְרָֽיִם׃ ⁴⁷ וַתַּ֣עַשׂ הָאָ֔רֶץ בְּשֶׁ֖בַע שְׁנֵ֣י הַשָּׂבָ֑ע לִקְמָצִֽים׃ ⁴⁸ וַיִּקְבֹּ֞ץ אֶת־כָּל־אֹ֣כֶל ׀ שֶׁ֣בַע שָׁנִ֗ים אֲשֶׁ֤ר הָיוּ֙ בְּאֶ֣רֶץ מִצְרַ֔יִם וַיִּתֶּן־אֹ֖כֶל בֶּעָרִ֑ים אֹ֧כֶל שְׂדֵה־הָעִ֛יר אֲשֶׁ֥ר סְבִיבֹתֶ֖יהָ נָתַ֥ן בְּתוֹכָֽהּ׃ ⁴⁹ וַיִּצְבֹּ֨ר יוֹסֵ֥ף בָּ֛ר כְּח֥וֹל הַיָּ֖ם הַרְבֵּ֣ה מְאֹ֑ד עַ֛ד כִּֽי־חָדַ֥ל לִסְפֹּ֖ר כִּי־אֵ֥ין מִסְפָּֽר׃

50Before the years of famine came, Joseph became the father of two sons, whom Asenath daughter of Poti-phera, priest of On, bore to him. 51Joseph named the first-born Manasseh, meaning, "God has made me forget*f* completely my hardship and my parental home." 52And the second he named Ephraim, meaning, "God has made me fertile*g* in the land of my affliction."

53The seven years of abundance that the land of Egypt enjoyed came to an end, 54and the seven years of famine set in, just as Joseph had foretold. There was famine in all lands, but throughout the land of Egypt there was bread. 55And when all the land of Egypt felt the hunger, the people cried out to Pharaoh for bread; and Pharaoh said to all the Egyptians, "Go to Joseph; whatever he tells you, you shall do."— 56Accordingly, when the famine became severe in the land of Egypt, Joseph laid open all that was within, and rationed out grain to the Egyptians. The famine, however, spread over the whole world. 57So all the world came to Joseph in Egypt to procure rations, for the famine had become severe throughout the world.

42 When Jacob saw that there were food rations to be had in Egypt, he*a* said to his sons, "Why do you keep looking at one another? 2Now I hear," he went on, "that there are rations to be had in Egypt. Go down and procure rations for us there, that we may live and not die." 3So ten of Joseph's brothers went down to get grain rations in Egypt; 4for Jacob did not send Joseph's brother Benjamin with his brothers, since he feared that he might meet with disaster. 5Thus the sons of Israel were among those who came to procure rations, for the famine extended to the land of Canaan.

---

f Heb. nashshani, connected with "Manasseh" (Menashsheh).
g Heb. hiphrani, connected with "Ephraim."

a Lit. "Jacob."

50 וּלְיוֹסֵף יֻלַּד שְׁנֵי בָנִים בְּטֶרֶם תָּבוֹא שְׁנַת הָרָעָב אֲשֶׁר יָלְדָה־לּוֹ אָסְנַת בַּת־פּוֹטִי פֶרַע כֹּהֵן אוֹן: 51 וַיִּקְרָא יוֹסֵף אֶת־שֵׁם הַבְּכוֹר מְנַשֶּׁה כִּי־נַשַּׁנִי אֱלֹהִים אֶת־כָּל־עֲמָלִי וְאֵת כָּל־בֵּית אָבִי: 52 וְאֵת שֵׁם הַשֵּׁנִי קָרָא אֶפְרָיִם כִּי־הִפְרַנִי אֱלֹהִים בְּאֶרֶץ עָנְיִי: 53 וַתִּכְלֶינָה שֶׁבַע שְׁנֵי הַשָּׂבָע אֲשֶׁר הָיָה בְּאֶרֶץ מִצְרָיִם: 54 וַתְּחִלֶּינָה שֶׁבַע שְׁנֵי הָרָעָב לָבוֹא כַּאֲשֶׁר אָמַר יוֹסֵף וַיְהִי רָעָב בְּכָל־הָאֲרָצוֹת וּבְכָל־אֶרֶץ מִצְרַיִם הָיָה לָחֶם: 55 וַתִּרְעַב כָּל־אֶרֶץ מִצְרַיִם וַיִּצְעַק הָעָם אֶל־פַּרְעֹה לַלָּחֶם וַיֹּאמֶר פַּרְעֹה לְכָל־מִצְרַיִם לְכוּ אֶל־יוֹסֵף אֲשֶׁר־יֹאמַר לָכֶם תַּעֲשׂוּ: 56 וְהָרָעָב הָיָה עַל כָּל־פְּנֵי הָאָרֶץ וַיִּפְתַּח יוֹסֵף אֶת־כָּל־אֲשֶׁר בָּהֶם וַיִּשְׁבֹּר לְמִצְרַיִם וַיֶּחֱזַק הָרָעָב בְּאֶרֶץ מִצְרָיִם: 57 וְכָל־הָאָרֶץ בָּאוּ מִצְרַיְמָה לִשְׁבֹּר אֶל־יוֹסֵף כִּי־חָזַק הָרָעָב בְּכָל־הָאָרֶץ:

מב וַיַּרְא יַעֲקֹב כִּי יֶשׁ־שֶׁבֶר בְּמִצְרָיִם וַיֹּאמֶר יַעֲקֹב לְבָנָיו לָמָּה תִּתְרָאוּ: 2 וַיֹּאמֶר הִנֵּה שָׁמַעְתִּי כִּי יֶשׁ־שֶׁבֶר בְּמִצְרָיִם רְדוּ־שָׁמָּה וְשִׁבְרוּ־לָנוּ מִשָּׁם וְנִחְיֶה וְלֹא נָמוּת: 3 וַיֵּרְדוּ אֲחֵי־יוֹסֵף עֲשָׂרָה לִשְׁבֹּר בָּר מִמִּצְרָיִם: 4 וְאֶת־בִּנְיָמִין אֲחִי יוֹסֵף לֹא־שָׁלַח יַעֲקֹב אֶת־אֶחָיו כִּי אָמַר פֶּן־יִקְרָאֶנּוּ אָסוֹן: 5 וַיָּבֹאוּ בְּנֵי יִשְׂרָאֵל לִשְׁבֹּר בְּתוֹךְ הַבָּאִים כִּי־הָיָה הָרָעָב בְּאֶרֶץ כְּנָעַן:

⁶Now Joseph was the vizier of the land; it was he who dispensed rations to all the people of the land. And Joseph's brothers came and bowed low to him, with their faces to the ground. ⁷When Joseph saw his brothers, he recognized them; but he acted like a stranger toward them and spoke harshly to them. He asked them, "Where do you come from?" And they said, "From the land of Canaan, to procure food." ⁸For though Joseph recognized his brothers, they did not recognize him. ⁹Recalling the dreams that he had dreamed about them, Joseph said to them, "You are spies, you have come to see the land in its nakedness." ¹⁰But they said to him, "No, my lord! Truly, your servants have come to procure food. ¹¹We are all of us sons of the same man; we are honest men; your servants have never been spies!" ¹²And he said to them, "No, you have come to see the land in its nakedness!" ¹³And they replied, "We your servants were twelve brothers, sons of a certain man in the land of Canaan; the youngest, however, is now with our father, and one is no more." ¹⁴But Joseph said to them, "It is just as I have told you: You are spies! ¹⁵By this you shall be put to the test: unless your youngest brother comes here, by Pharaoh, you shall not depart from this place! ¹⁶Let one of you go and bring your brother, while the rest of you remain confined, that your words may be put to the test whether there is truth in you. Else, by Pharaoh, you are nothing but spies!" ¹⁷And he confined them in the guardhouse for three days.

¹⁸On the third day Joseph said to them, "Do this and you shall live, for I am a God-fearing man. ¹⁹If you are honest men, let one of you brothers be held in your place of detention, while the rest of you go and take home rations for your starving households; ²⁰but you must bring me your youngest brother, that your words may be verified and that you may not

6 וְיוֹסֵ֗ף ה֚וּא הַשַּׁלִּ֣יט עַל־הָאָ֔רֶץ ה֥וּא הַמַּשְׁבִּ֖יר לְכָל־עַ֣ם הָאָ֑רֶץ וַיָּבֹ֙אוּ֙ אֲחֵ֣י יוֹסֵ֔ף וַיִּשְׁתַּחֲווּ־ל֥וֹ אַפַּ֖יִם אָֽרְצָה: 7 וַיַּ֥רְא יוֹסֵ֖ף אֶת־אֶחָ֑יו וַיַּכִּרֵ֗ם וַיִּתְנַכֵּ֤ר אֲלֵיהֶם֙ וַיְדַבֵּ֨ר אִתָּ֜ם קָשׁ֗וֹת וַיֹּ֤אמֶר אֲלֵהֶם֙ מֵאַ֣יִן בָּאתֶ֔ם וַיֹּ֣אמְר֔וּ מֵאֶ֥רֶץ כְּנַ֖עַן לִשְׁבָּר־אֹֽכֶל: 8 וַיַּכֵּ֥ר יוֹסֵ֖ף אֶת־אֶחָ֑יו וְהֵ֖ם לֹ֥א הִכִּרֻֽהוּ: 9 וַיִּזְכֹּ֣ר יוֹסֵ֔ף אֵ֚ת הַחֲלֹמ֔וֹת אֲשֶׁ֥ר חָלַ֖ם לָהֶ֑ם וַיֹּ֤אמֶר אֲלֵהֶם֙ מְרַגְּלִ֣ים אַתֶּ֔ם לִרְא֛וֹת אֶת־עֶרְוַ֥ת הָאָ֖רֶץ בָּאתֶֽם: 10 וַיֹּאמְר֥וּ אֵלָ֖יו לֹ֣א אֲדֹנִ֑י וַעֲבָדֶ֥יךָ בָּ֖אוּ לִשְׁבָּר־אֹֽכֶל: 11 כֻּלָּ֕נוּ בְּנֵ֥י אִישׁ־אֶחָ֖ד נָ֑חְנוּ כֵּנִ֣ים אֲנַ֔חְנוּ לֹא־הָי֥וּ עֲבָדֶ֖יךָ מְרַגְּלִֽים: 12 וַיֹּ֖אמֶר אֲלֵהֶ֑ם לֹ֕א כִּֽי־עֶרְוַ֥ת הָאָ֖רֶץ בָּאתֶ֥ם לִרְאֽוֹת: 13 וַיֹּאמְר֗וּ שְׁנֵ֣ים עָשָׂר֩ עֲבָדֶ֨יךָ אַחִ֥ים | אֲנַ֛חְנוּ בְּנֵ֥י אִישׁ־אֶחָ֖ד בְּאֶ֣רֶץ כְּנָ֑עַן וְהִנֵּ֨ה הַקָּטֹ֤ן אֶת־אָבִ֙ינוּ֙ הַיּ֔וֹם וְהָאֶחָ֖ד אֵינֶֽנּוּ: 14 וַיֹּ֥אמֶר אֲלֵהֶ֖ם יוֹסֵ֑ף ה֗וּא אֲשֶׁ֨ר דִּבַּ֧רְתִּי אֲלֵכֶ֛ם לֵאמֹ֖ר מְרַגְּלִ֥ים אַתֶּֽם: 15 בְּזֹ֖את תִּבָּחֵ֑נוּ חֵ֤י פַרְעֹה֙ אִם־תֵּצְא֣וּ מִזֶּ֔ה כִּ֧י אִם־בְּב֛וֹא אֲחִיכֶ֥ם הַקָּטֹ֖ן הֵֽנָּה: 16 שִׁלְח֨וּ מִכֶּ֣ם אֶחָד֮ וְיִקַּ֣ח אֶת־אֲחִיכֶם֒ וְאַתֶּם֙ הֵאָ֣סְר֔וּ וְיִבָּֽחֲנוּ֙ דִּבְרֵיכֶ֔ם הַֽאֱמֶ֖ת אִתְּכֶ֑ם וְאִם־לֹ֕א חֵ֣י פַרְעֹ֔ה כִּ֥י מְרַגְּלִ֖ים אַתֶּֽם: 17 וַיֶּאֱסֹ֥ף אֹתָ֛ם אֶל־מִשְׁמָ֖ר שְׁלֹ֥שֶׁת יָמִֽים: 18 וַיֹּ֨אמֶר אֲלֵהֶ֤ם יוֹסֵף֙ בַּיּ֣וֹם הַשְּׁלִישִׁ֔י זֹ֥את עֲשׂ֖וּ וִֽחְי֑וּ אֶת־הָאֱלֹהִ֖ים אֲנִ֥י יָרֵֽא: 19 אִם־כֵּנִ֣ים אַתֶּ֔ם אֲחִיכֶ֣ם אֶחָ֔ד יֵֽאָסֵ֖ר בְּבֵ֣ית מִשְׁמַרְכֶ֑ם וְאַתֶּם֙ לְכ֣וּ הָבִ֔יאוּ שֶׁ֖בֶר רַעֲב֥וֹן בָּתֵּיכֶֽם: 20 וְאֶת־אֲחִיכֶ֤ם הַקָּטֹן֙ תָּבִ֣יאוּ אֵלַ֔י וְיֵאָמְנ֥וּ דִבְרֵיכֶ֖ם וְלֹ֣א תָמ֑וּתוּ וַיַּֽעֲשׂוּ

die." And they did accordingly. ²¹They said to one another, "Alas, we are being punished on account of our brother, because we looked on at his anguish, yet paid no heed as he pleaded with us. That is why this distress has come upon us." ²²Then Reuben spoke up and said to them, "Did I not tell you, 'Do no wrong to the boy'? But you paid no heed. Now comes the reckoning for his blood." ²³They did not know that Joseph understood, for there was an interpreter between him and them. ²⁴He turned away from them and wept. But he came back to them and spoke to them; and he took Simeon from among them and had him bound before their eyes. ²⁵Then Joseph gave orders to fill their bags with grain, return each one's money to his sack, and give them provisions for the journey; and this was done for them. ²⁶So they loaded their asses with the rations and departed from there.

²⁷As one of them was opening his sack to give feed to his ass at the night encampment, he saw his money right there at the mouth of his bag. ²⁸And he said to his brothers, "My money has been returned! It is here in my bag!" Their hearts sank; and, trembling, they turned to one another, saying, "What is this that God has done to us?"

²⁹When they came to their father Jacob in the land of Canaan, they told him all that had befallen them, saying, ³⁰"The man who is lord of the land spoke harshly to us and accused us of spying on the land. ³¹We said to him, 'We are honest men; we have never been spies! ³²There were twelve of us brothers, sons by the same father; but one is no more, and the youngest is now with our father in the land of Canaan.' ³³But the man who is lord of the land said to us, 'By this I shall know that you are honest men: leave one of your brothers with me, and take something for your starving households and be off. ³⁴And bring your youngest brother to me,

21 וַיֹּאמְרוּ אִישׁ אֶל־אָחִיו אֲבָל ...

כֵּן׃ 21 וַיֹּאמְרוּ אִישׁ אֶל־אָחִיו אֲבָל אֲשֵׁמִים ׀ אֲנַחְנוּ עַל־אָחִינוּ אֲשֶׁר רָאִינוּ צָרַת נַפְשׁוֹ בְּהִתְחַנְנוֹ אֵלֵינוּ וְלֹא שָׁמָעְנוּ עַל־כֵּן בָּאָה אֵלֵינוּ הַצָּרָה הַזֹּאת׃ 22 וַיַּעַן רְאוּבֵן אֹתָם לֵאמֹר הֲלוֹא אָמַרְתִּי אֲלֵיכֶם ׀ לֵאמֹר אַל־תֶּחֶטְאוּ בַיֶּלֶד וְלֹא שְׁמַעְתֶּם וְגַם־דָּמוֹ הִנֵּה נִדְרָשׁ׃ 23 וְהֵם לֹא יָדְעוּ כִּי שֹׁמֵעַ יוֹסֵף כִּי הַמֵּלִיץ בֵּינֹתָם׃ 24 וַיִּסֹּב מֵעֲלֵיהֶם וַיֵּבְךְּ וַיָּשָׁב אֲלֵהֶם וַיְדַבֵּר אֲלֵהֶם וַיִּקַּח מֵאִתָּם אֶת־שִׁמְעוֹן וַיֶּאֱסֹר אֹתוֹ לְעֵינֵיהֶם׃ 25 וַיְצַו יוֹסֵף וַיְמַלְאוּ אֶת־כְּלֵיהֶם בָּר וּלְהָשִׁיב כַּסְפֵּיהֶם אִישׁ אֶל־שַׂקּוֹ וְלָתֵת לָהֶם צֵדָה לַדָּרֶךְ וַיַּעַשׂ לָהֶם כֵּן׃ 26 וַיִּשְׂאוּ אֶת־שִׁבְרָם עַל־חֲמֹרֵיהֶם וַיֵּלְכוּ מִשָּׁם׃ 27 וַיִּפְתַּח הָאֶחָד אֶת־שַׂקּוֹ לָתֵת מִסְפּוֹא לַחֲמֹרוֹ בַּמָּלוֹן וַיַּרְא אֶת־כַּסְפּוֹ וְהִנֵּה־הוּא בְּפִי אַמְתַּחְתּוֹ׃ 28 וַיֹּאמֶר אֶל־אֶחָיו הוּשַׁב כַּסְפִּי וְגַם הִנֵּה בְאַמְתַּחְתִּי וַיֵּצֵא לִבָּם וַיֶּחֶרְדוּ אִישׁ אֶל־אָחִיו לֵאמֹר מַה־זֹּאת עָשָׂה אֱלֹהִים לָנוּ׃ 29 וַיָּבֹאוּ אֶל־יַעֲקֹב אֲבִיהֶם אַרְצָה כְּנָעַן וַיַּגִּידוּ לוֹ אֵת כָּל־הַקֹּרֹת אֹתָם לֵאמֹר׃ 30 דִּבֶּר הָאִישׁ אֲדֹנֵי הָאָרֶץ אִתָּנוּ קָשׁוֹת וַיִּתֵּן אֹתָנוּ כִּמְרַגְּלִים אֶת־הָאָרֶץ׃ 31 וַנֹּאמֶר אֵלָיו כֵּנִים אֲנָחְנוּ לֹא הָיִינוּ מְרַגְּלִים׃ 32 שְׁנֵים־עָשָׂר אֲנַחְנוּ אַחִים בְּנֵי אָבִינוּ הָאֶחָד אֵינֶנּוּ וְהַקָּטֹן הַיּוֹם אֶת־אָבִינוּ בְּאֶרֶץ כְּנָעַן׃ 33 וַיֹּאמֶר אֵלֵינוּ הָאִישׁ אֲדֹנֵי הָאָרֶץ בְּזֹאת אֵדַע כִּי כֵנִים אַתֶּם אֲחִיכֶם הָאֶחָד הַנִּיחוּ אִתִּי וְאֶת־רַעֲבוֹן בָּתֵּיכֶם קְחוּ וָלֵכוּ׃ 34 וְהָבִיאוּ אֶת־אֲחִיכֶם הַקָּטֹן אֵלַי וְאֵדְעָה כִּי לֹא מְרַגְּלִים אַתֶּם

91

that I may know that you are not spies but hon-est men. I will then restore your brother to you, and you shall be free to move about in the land.'"

35As they were emptying their sacks, there, in each one's sack, was his money-bag! When they and their father saw their money-bags, they were dismayed. 36Their father Jacob said to them, "It is always me that you bereave: Joseph is no more and Simeon is no more, and now you would take away Benjamin. These things always happen to me!" 37Then Reuben said to his father, "You may kill my two sons if I do not bring him back to you. Put him in my care, and I will return him to you." 38But he said, "My son must not go down with you, for his brother is dead and he alone is left. If he meets with dis-aster on the journey you are taking, you will send my white head down to Sheol in grief."

43 But the famine in the land was severe. 2And when they had eaten up the rations which they had brought from Egypt, their father said to them, "Go again and procure some food for us." 3But Judah said to him, "The man warned us, a-'Do not let me see your faces-a unless your brother is with you.' 4If you will let our brother go with us, we will go down and procure food for you; 5but if you will not let him go, we will not go down, for the man said to us, a-'Do not let me see your faces-a unless your brother is with you.'" 6And Israel said, "Why did you serve me so ill as to tell the man that you had another brother?" 7They replied, "But the man kept ask-ing about us and our family, saying, 'Is your fa-ther still living? Have you another brother?' And we answered him accordingly. How were we to know that he would say, 'Bring your brother here'?"

8Then Judah said to his father Israel, "Send

כִּי כֵנִים אַתֶּם אֶת־אֲחִיכֶם אֶתֵּן לָכֶם וְאֶת־הָאָרֶץ תִּסְחָרוּ: 35 וַיְהִי הֵם מְרִיקִים שַׂקֵּיהֶם וְהִנֵּה־אִישׁ צְרוֹר־כַּסְפּוֹ בְּשַׂקּוֹ וַיִּרְאוּ אֶת־צְרֹרוֹת כַּסְפֵּיהֶם הֵמָּה וַאֲבִיהֶם וַיִּירָאוּ: 36 וַיֹּאמֶר אֲלֵהֶם יַעֲקֹב אֲבִיהֶם אֹתִי שִׁכַּלְתֶּם יוֹסֵף אֵינֶנּוּ וְשִׁמְעוֹן אֵינֶנּוּ וְאֶת־בִּנְיָמִן תִּקָּחוּ עָלַי הָיוּ כֻלָּנָה: 37 וַיֹּאמֶר רְאוּבֵן אֶל־אָבִיו לֵאמֹר אֶת־שְׁנֵי בָנַי תָּמִית אִם־לֹא אֲבִיאֶנּוּ אֵלֶיךָ תְּנָה אֹתוֹ עַל־יָדִי וַאֲנִי אֲשִׁיבֶנּוּ אֵלֶיךָ: 38 וַיֹּאמֶר לֹא־יֵרֵד בְּנִי עִמָּכֶם כִּי־אָחִיו מֵת וְהוּא לְבַדּוֹ נִשְׁאָר וּקְרָאָהוּ אָסוֹן בַּדֶּרֶךְ אֲשֶׁר תֵּלְכוּ־בָהּ וְהוֹרַדְתֶּם אֶת־שֵׂיבָתִי בְּיָגוֹן שְׁאוֹלָה:

מג וְהָרָעָב כָּבֵד בָּאָרֶץ: 2 וַיְהִי כַּאֲשֶׁר כִּלּוּ לֶאֱכֹל אֶת־הַשֶּׁבֶר אֲשֶׁר הֵבִיאוּ מִמִּצְרָיִם וַיֹּאמֶר אֲלֵיהֶם אֲבִיהֶם שֻׁבוּ שִׁבְרוּ־לָנוּ מְעַט־אֹכֶל: 3 וַיֹּאמֶר אֵלָיו יְהוּדָה לֵאמֹר הָעֵד הֵעִד בָּנוּ הָאִישׁ לֵאמֹר לֹא־תִרְאוּ פָנַי בִּלְתִּי אֲחִיכֶם אִתְּכֶם: 4 אִם־יֶשְׁךָ מְשַׁלֵּחַ אֶת־אָחִינוּ אִתָּנוּ נֵרְדָה וְנִשְׁבְּרָה לְךָ אֹכֶל: 5 וְאִם־אֵינְךָ מְשַׁלֵּחַ לֹא נֵרֵד כִּי־הָאִישׁ אָמַר אֵלֵינוּ לֹא־תִרְאוּ פָנַי בִּלְתִּי אֲחִיכֶם אִתְּכֶם: 6 וַיֹּאמֶר יִשְׂרָאֵל לָמָה הֲרֵעֹתֶם לִי לְהַגִּיד לָאִישׁ הַעוֹד לָכֶם אָח: 7 וַיֹּאמְרוּ שָׁאוֹל שָׁאַל־הָאִישׁ לָנוּ וּלְמוֹלַדְתֵּנוּ לֵאמֹר הַעוֹד אֲבִיכֶם חַי הֲיֵשׁ לָכֶם אָח וַנַּגֶּד־לוֹ עַל־פִּי הַדְּבָרִים הָאֵלֶּה הֲיָדוֹעַ נֵדַע כִּי יֹאמַר הוֹרִידוּ אֶת־אֲחִיכֶם: 8 וַיֹּאמֶר יְהוּדָה אֶל־יִשְׂרָאֵל אָבִיו שִׁלְחָה

---

a-a   Lit. "Do not see my face."

the boy in my care, and let us be on our way, that we may live and not die—you and we and our children. 9I myself will be surety for him; you may hold me responsible: if I do not bring him back to you and set him before you, I shall stand guilty before you forever. 10For we could have been there and back twice if we had not dawdled."

11Then their father Israel said to them, "If it must be so, do this: take some of the choice products of the land in your baggage, and carry them down as a gift for the man—some balm and some honey, gum, ladanum, pistachio nuts, and almonds. 12And take with you double the money, carrying back with you the money that was replaced in the mouths of your bags; perhaps it was a mistake. 13Take your brother too; and go back at once to the man. 14And may El Shaddai dispose the man to mercy toward you, that he may release to you your other brother, as well as Benjamin. As for me, if I am to be bereaved, I shall be bereaved."

15So the men took that gift, and they took with them double the money, as well as Benjamin. They made their way down to Egypt, where they presented themselves to Joseph. 16When Joseph saw Benjamin with them, he said to his house steward, "Take the men into the house; slaughter and prepare an animal, for the men will dine with me at noon." 17The man did as Joseph said, and he brought the men into Joseph's house. 18But the men were frightened at being brought into Joseph's house. "It must be," they thought, "because of the money replaced in our bags the first time that we have been brought inside, as a pretext to attack us and seize us as slaves, with our pack animals." 19So they went up to Joseph's house steward and spoke to him at the entrance of the house. 20"If you please, my lord," they said, "we came down once before to procure food. 21But when we arrived at the night en-

הַנַּעַר אִתִּי וְנָק֫וּמָה וְנֵלֵ֫כָה וְנִֽחְיֶה֙ וְלֹ֣א נָמ֔וּת גַּם־אֲנַ֖חְנוּ גַם־אַתָּ֑ה גַּם־טַפֵּֽנוּ׃ 9 אָֽנֹכִי֙ אֶֽעֶרְבֶ֔נּוּ מִיָּדִ֖י תְּבַקְשֶׁ֑נּוּ אִם־לֹ֨א הֲבִיאֹתִ֤יו אֵלֶ֙יךָ֙ וְהִצַּגְתִּ֣יו לְפָנֶ֔יךָ וְחָטָ֥אתִי לְךָ֖ כָּל־הַיָּמִֽים׃ 10 כִּ֖י לוּלֵ֣א הִתְמַהְמָ֑הְנוּ כִּֽי־עַתָּ֥ה שַׁ֖בְנוּ זֶ֥ה פַעֲמָֽיִם׃

11 וַיֹּ֨אמֶר אֲלֵהֶ֜ם יִשְׂרָאֵ֣ל אֲבִיהֶ֗ם אִם־כֵּ֣ן ׀ אֵפוֹא֮ זֹ֣את עֲשׂוּ֒ קְח֞וּ מִזִּמְרַ֤ת הָאָ֙רֶץ֙ בִּכְלֵיכֶ֔ם וְהוֹרִ֥ידוּ לָאִ֖ישׁ מִנְחָ֑ה מְעַ֤ט צֳרִי֙ וּמְעַ֣ט דְּבַ֔שׁ נְכֹ֣את וָלֹ֔ט בָּטְנִ֖ים וּשְׁקֵדִֽים׃ 12 וְכֶ֥סֶף מִשְׁנֶ֖ה קְח֣וּ בְיֶדְכֶ֑ם וְאֶת־הַכֶּ֜סֶף הַמּוּשָׁ֨ב בְּפִ֤י אַמְתְּחֹֽתֵיכֶם֙ תָּשִׁ֣יבוּ בְיֶדְכֶ֔ם אוּלַ֥י מִשְׁגֶּ֖ה הֽוּא׃ 13 וְאֶת־אֲחִיכֶ֖ם קָ֑חוּ וְק֖וּמוּ שׁ֥וּבוּ אֶל־הָאִֽישׁ׃ 14 וְאֵ֣ל שַׁדַּ֗י יִתֵּ֨ן לָכֶ֤ם רַחֲמִים֙ לִפְנֵ֣י הָאִ֔ישׁ וְשִׁלַּ֥ח לָכֶ֛ם אֶת־אֲחִיכֶ֥ם אַחֵ֖ר וְאֶת־בִּנְיָמִ֑ין וַאֲנִ֕י כַּאֲשֶׁ֥ר שָׁכֹ֖לְתִּי שָׁכָֽלְתִּי׃

15 וַיִּקְח֤וּ הָֽאֲנָשִׁים֙ אֶת־הַמִּנְחָ֣ה הַזֹּ֔את וּמִשְׁנֶה־כֶּ֛סֶף לָקְח֥וּ בְיָדָ֖ם וְאֶת־בִּנְיָמִ֑ן וַיָּקֻ֙מוּ֙ וַיֵּרְד֣וּ מִצְרַ֔יִם וַיַּֽעַמְד֖וּ לִפְנֵ֥י יוֹסֵֽף׃ 16 וַיַּ֨רְא יוֹסֵ֣ף אִתָּם֮ אֶת־בִּנְיָמִין֒ וַיֹּ֗אמֶר לַֽאֲשֶׁר֙ עַל־בֵּית֔וֹ הָבֵ֥א אֶת־הָאֲנָשִׁ֖ים הַבָּ֑יְתָה וּטְבֹ֤חַ טֶ֙בַח֙ וְהָכֵ֔ן כִּ֥י אִתִּ֛י יֹאכְל֥וּ הָאֲנָשִׁ֖ים בַּֽצָּהֳרָֽיִם׃ 17 וַיַּ֣עַשׂ הָאִ֔ישׁ כַּֽאֲשֶׁ֖ר אָמַ֣ר יוֹסֵ֑ף וַיָּבֵ֥א הָאִ֛ישׁ אֶת־הָאֲנָשִׁ֖ים בֵּ֥יתָה יוֹסֵֽף׃ 18 וַיִּֽירְא֣וּ הָֽאֲנָשִׁ֗ים כִּ֣י הֽוּבְאוּ֮ בֵּ֣ית יוֹסֵף֒ וַיֹּאמְר֗וּ עַל־דְּבַ֤ר הַכֶּ֙סֶף֙ הַשָּׁ֣ב בְּאַמְתְּחֹתֵ֜ינוּ בַּתְּחִלָּ֗ה אֲנַ֣חְנוּ מֽוּבָאִ֔ים לְהִתְגֹּלֵ֤ל עָלֵ֙ינוּ֙ וּלְהִתְנַפֵּ֣ל עָלֵ֔ינוּ וְלָקַ֧חַת אֹתָ֛נוּ לַעֲבָדִ֖ים וְאֶת־חֲמֹרֵֽינוּ׃ 19 וַֽיִּגְּשׁוּ֙ אֶל־הָאִ֔ישׁ אֲשֶׁ֖ר עַל־בֵּ֣ית יוֹסֵ֑ף וַיְדַבְּר֥וּ אֵלָ֖יו פֶּ֥תַח הַבָּֽיִת׃ 20 וַיֹּאמְר֖וּ בִּ֣י אֲדֹנִ֑י יָרֹ֥ד יָרַ֛דְנוּ בַּתְּחִלָּ֖ה לִשְׁבָּר־אֹֽכֶל׃ 21 וַֽיְהִ֞י כִּֽי־בָ֣אנוּ אֶל־הַמָּל֗וֹן וַֽנִּפְתְּחָה֙ אֶת־

campment and opened our bags, there was each one's money in the mouth of his bag, our money in full.*b* So we have brought it back with us. 22And we have brought down with us other money to procure food. We do not know who put the money in our bags." 23He replied, "All is well with you; do not be afraid. Your God, the God of your father, must have put treasure in your bags for you. I got your payment." And he brought out Simeon to them.

24Then the man brought the men into Joseph's house; he gave them water to bathe their feet, and he provided feed for their asses. 25They laid out their gifts to await Joseph's arrival at noon, for they had heard that they were to dine there.

26When Joseph came home, they presented to him the gifts that they had brought with them into the house, bowing low before him to the ground. 27He greeted them, and he said, "How is your aged father of whom you spoke? Is he still in good health?" 28They replied, "It is well with your servant our father; he is still in good health." And they bowed and made obeisance.

29Looking about, he saw his brother Benjamin, his mother's son, and asked, "Is this your youngest brother of whom you spoke to me?" And he went on, "May God be gracious to you, my boy." 30With that, Joseph hurried out, for he was overcome with feeling toward his brother and was on the verge of tears; he went into a room and wept there. 31Then he washed his face, reappeared, and—now in control of himself—gave the order, "Serve the meal." 32They served him by himself, and them by themselves, and the Egyptians who ate with him by themselves; for the Egyptians could not dine with the Hebrews, since that would be abhorrent to the Egyptians. 33As they were seated by his direction, from the oldest in the order of his

אַמְתְּחֹתֵינוּ וְהִנֵּה כֶסֶף־אִישׁ בְּפִי אַמְתַּחְתּוֹ כַּסְפֵּנוּ בְּמִשְׁקָלוֹ וַנָּשֶׁב אֹתוֹ בְּיָדֵנוּ: 22 וְכֶסֶף אַחֵר הוֹרַדְנוּ בְיָדֵנוּ לִשְׁבָּר־אֹכֶל לֹא יָדַעְנוּ מִי־שָׂם כַּסְפֵּנוּ בְּאַמְתְּחֹתֵינוּ: 23 וַיֹּאמֶר שָׁלוֹם לָכֶם אַל־תִּירָאוּ אֱלֹהֵיכֶם וֵאלֹהֵי אֲבִיכֶם נָתַן לָכֶם מַטְמוֹן בְּאַמְתְּחֹתֵיכֶם כַּסְפְּכֶם בָּא אֵלָי וַיּוֹצֵא אֲלֵהֶם אֶת־שִׁמְעוֹן:

24 וַיָּבֵא הָאִישׁ אֶת־הָאֲנָשִׁים בֵּיתָה יוֹסֵף וַיִּתֶּן־מַיִם וַיִּרְחֲצוּ רַגְלֵיהֶם וַיִּתֵּן מִסְפּוֹא לַחֲמֹרֵיהֶם: 25 וַיָּכִינוּ אֶת־הַמִּנְחָה עַד־בּוֹא יוֹסֵף בַּצָּהֳרָיִם כִּי שָׁמְעוּ כִּי־שָׁם יֹאכְלוּ לָחֶם:

26 וַיָּבֹא יוֹסֵף הַבַּיְתָה וַיָּבִיאוּ* לוֹ אֶת־הַמִּנְחָה אֲשֶׁר־בְּיָדָם הַבָּיְתָה וַיִּשְׁתַּחֲווּ־לוֹ אָרְצָה: 27 וַיִּשְׁאַל לָהֶם לְשָׁלוֹם וַיֹּאמֶר הֲשָׁלוֹם אֲבִיכֶם הַזָּקֵן אֲשֶׁר אֲמַרְתֶּם הַעוֹדֶנּוּ חָי: 28 וַיֹּאמְרוּ שָׁלוֹם לְעַבְדְּךָ לְאָבִינוּ עוֹדֶנּוּ חָי וַיִּקְּדוּ וישתחו וַיִּשְׁתַּחֲווּ: 29 וַיִּשָּׂא עֵינָיו וַיַּרְא אֶת־בִּנְיָמִין אָחִיו בֶּן־אִמּוֹ וַיֹּאמֶר הֲזֶה אֲחִיכֶם הַקָּטֹן אֲשֶׁר אֲמַרְתֶּם אֵלָי וַיֹּאמַר אֱלֹהִים יָחְנְךָ בְּנִי: 30 וַיְמַהֵר יוֹסֵף כִּי־נִכְמְרוּ רַחֲמָיו אֶל־אָחִיו וַיְבַקֵּשׁ לִבְכּוֹת וַיָּבֹא הַחַדְרָה וַיֵּבְךְּ שָׁמָּה: 31 וַיִּרְחַץ פָּנָיו וַיֵּצֵא וַיִּתְאַפַּק וַיֹּאמֶר שִׂימוּ לָחֶם: 32 וַיָּשִׂימוּ לוֹ לְבַדּוֹ וְלָהֶם לְבַדָּם וְלַמִּצְרִים הָאֹכְלִים אִתּוֹ לְבַדָּם כִּי לֹא יוּכְלוּן הַמִּצְרִים לֶאֱכֹל אֶת־הָעִבְרִים לֶחֶם כִּי־תוֹעֵבָה הִוא לְמִצְרָיִם: 33 וַיֵּשְׁבוּ לְפָנָיו הַבְּכֹר כִּבְכֹרָתוֹ וְהַצָּעִיר כִּצְעִרָתוֹ

---

b Lit. "by its weight."   א׳ דגושה   v. 26.

seniority to the youngest in the order of his youth, the men looked at one another in astonishment. ³⁴Portions were served them from his table; but Benjamin's portion was several[c] times that of anyone else. And they drank their fill with him.

44 Then he instructed his house steward as follows, "Fill the men's bags with food, as much as they can carry, and put each one's money in the mouth of his bag. ²Put my silver goblet in the mouth of the bag of the youngest one, together with his money for the rations." And he did as Joseph told him.

³With the first light of morning, the men were sent off with their pack animals. ⁴They had just left the city and had not gone far, when Joseph said to his steward, "Up, go after the men! And when you overtake them, say to them, 'Why did you repay good with evil? ⁵It is the very one from which my master drinks and which he uses for divination. It was a wicked thing for you to do!'"

⁶He overtook them and spoke those words to them. ⁷And they said to him, "Why does my lord say such things? Far be it from your servants to do anything of the kind! ⁸Here we brought back to you from the land of Canaan the money that we found in the mouths of our bags. How then could we have stolen any silver or gold from your master's house! ⁹Whichever of your servants it is found with shall die; the rest of us, moreover, shall become slaves to my lord." ¹⁰He replied, "Although what you are proposing is right, only the one with whom it is found shall be my slave; but the rest of you shall go free."

¹¹So each one hastened to lower his bag to the ground, and each one opened his bag. ¹²He searched, beginning with the oldest and ending with the youngest; and the goblet turned up in

---

c Lit. "five."

וַיִּתְמְה֣וּ הָאֲנָשִׁ֔ים אִ֖ישׁ אֶל־רֵעֵ֑הוּ: ³⁴וַיִּשָּׂ֨א מַשְׂאֹ֜ת מֵאֵ֣ת פָּנָיו֮ אֲלֵהֶם֒ וַתֵּ֜רֶב מַשְׂאַ֤ת בִּנְיָמִן֙ מִמַּשְׂאֹ֣ת כֻּלָּ֔ם חָמֵ֖שׁ יָד֑וֹת וַיִּשְׁתּ֥וּ וַיִּשְׁכְּר֖וּ עִמּֽוֹ:

מד וַיְצַ֞ו אֶת־אֲשֶׁ֣ר עַל־בֵּיתוֹ֮ לֵאמֹר֒ מַלֵּ֞א אֶת־אַמְתְּחֹ֤ת הָֽאֲנָשִׁים֙ אֹ֔כֶל כַּאֲשֶׁ֥ר יוּכְל֖וּן שְׂאֵ֑ת וְשִׂ֥ים כֶּֽסֶף־אִ֖ישׁ בְּפִ֥י אַמְתַּחְתּֽוֹ: ²וְאֶת־גְּבִיעִ֞י גְּבִ֣יעַ הַכֶּ֗סֶף תָּשִׂים֙ בְּפִי֙ אַמְתַּ֣חַת הַקָּטֹ֔ן וְאֵ֖ת כֶּ֣סֶף שִׁבְר֑וֹ וַיַּ֕עַשׂ כִּדְבַ֥ר יוֹסֵ֖ף אֲשֶׁ֥ר דִּבֵּֽר: ³הַבֹּ֖קֶר א֑וֹר וְהָאֲנָשִׁ֣ים שֻׁלְּח֔וּ הֵ֖מָּה וַחֲמֹרֵיהֶֽם: ⁴הֵ֠ם יָֽצְא֣וּ אֶת־הָעִיר֮ לֹ֣א הִרְחִ֒יקוּ֒ וְיוֹסֵ֞ף אָמַ֣ר לַֽאֲשֶׁ֣ר עַל־בֵּית֗וֹ ק֚וּם רְדֹ֣ף אַחֲרֵ֣י הָֽאֲנָשִׁ֔ים וְהִשַּׂגְתָּם֙ וְאָמַרְתָּ֣ אֲלֵהֶ֔ם לָ֛מָּה שִׁלַּמְתֶּ֥ם רָעָ֖ה תַּ֥חַת טוֹבָֽה: ⁵הֲל֣וֹא זֶ֗ה אֲשֶׁ֨ר יִשְׁתֶּ֤ה אֲדֹנִי֙ בּ֔וֹ וְה֕וּא נַחֵ֥שׁ יְנַחֵ֖שׁ בּ֑וֹ הֲרֵעֹתֶ֖ם אֲשֶׁ֥ר עֲשִׂיתֶֽם: ⁶וַֽיַּשִּׂגֵ֑ם וַיְדַבֵּ֣ר אֲלֵהֶ֔ם אֶת־הַדְּבָרִ֖ים הָאֵֽלֶּה: ⁷וַיֹּאמְר֣וּ אֵלָ֔יו לָ֛מָּה יְדַבֵּ֥ר אֲדֹנִ֖י כַּדְּבָרִ֣ים הָאֵ֑לֶּה חָלִ֙ילָה֙ לַעֲבָדֶ֔יךָ מֵעֲשׂ֖וֹת כַּדָּבָ֥ר הַזֶּֽה: ⁸הֵ֣ן כֶּ֗סֶף אֲשֶׁ֤ר מָצָ֙אנוּ֙ בְּפִ֣י אַמְתְּחֹתֵ֔ינוּ הֱשִׁיבֹ֥נוּ אֵלֶ֖יךָ מֵאֶ֣רֶץ כְּנָ֑עַן וְאֵ֗יךְ נִגְנֹב֙ מִבֵּ֣ית אֲדֹנֶ֔יךָ כֶּ֖סֶף א֥וֹ זָהָֽב: ⁹אֲשֶׁ֨ר יִמָּצֵ֥א אִתּ֛וֹ מֵעֲבָדֶ֖יךָ וָמֵ֑ת וְגַם־אֲנַ֕חְנוּ נִֽהְיֶ֥ה לַֽאדֹנִ֖י לַעֲבָדִֽים: ¹⁰וַיֹּ֕אמֶר גַּם־עַתָּ֥ה כְדִבְרֵיכֶ֖ם כֶּן־ה֑וּא אֲשֶׁ֨ר יִמָּצֵ֤א אִתּוֹ֙ יִהְיֶה־לִּ֣י עָ֔בֶד וְאַתֶּ֖ם תִּהְי֥וּ נְקִיִּֽם: ¹¹וַֽיְמַהֲר֗וּ וַיּוֹרִ֛דוּ אִ֥ישׁ אֶת־אַמְתַּחְתּ֖וֹ אָ֑רְצָה וַֽיִּפְתְּח֖וּ אִ֥ישׁ אַמְתַּחְתּֽוֹ: ¹²וַיְחַפֵּ֕שׂ בַּגָּד֣וֹל הֵחֵ֔ל וּבַקָּטֹ֖ן כִּלָּ֑ה וַיִּמָּצֵא֙ הַגָּבִ֔יעַ

Benjamin's bag. 13At this they rent their clothes. Each reloaded his pack animal, and they returned to the city.

14When Judah and his brothers reentered the house of Joseph, who was still there, they threw themselves on the ground before him. 15Joseph said to them, "What is this deed that you have done? Do you not know that a man like me practices divination?" 16Judah replied, "What can we say to my lord? How can we plead, how can we prove our innocence? God has uncovered the crime of your servants. Here we are, then, slaves of my lord, the rest of us as much as he in whose possession the goblet was found." 17But he replied, "Far be it from me to act thus! Only he in whose possession the goblet was found shall be my slave; the rest of you go back in peace to your father."

VA-YIGGASH

18Then Judah went up to him and said, "Please, my lord, let your servant appeal to my lord, and do not be impatient with your servant, you who are the equal of Pharaoh. 19My lord asked his servants, 'Have you a father or another brother?' 20We told my lord, 'We have an old father, and there is a child of his old age, the youngest; his full brother is dead, so that he alone is left of his mother, and his father dotes on him.' 21Then you said to your servants, 'Bring him down to me, that I may set eyes on him.' 22We said to my lord, 'The boy cannot leave his father; if he were to leave him, his father would die.' 23But you said to your servants, 'Unless your youngest brother comes down with you, do not let me see your faces.' 24When we came back to your servant my father, we reported my lord's words to him.

25"Later our father said, 'Go back and procure some food for us.' 26We answered, 'We cannot go down; only if our youngest brother is with

בְּאַמְתַּחַת בִּנְיָמִן: 13 וַיִּקְרְעוּ שִׂמְלֹתָם וַיַּעֲמֹס אִישׁ עַל־חֲמֹרוֹ וַיָּשֻׁבוּ הָעִירָה: 14 וַיָּבֹא יְהוּדָה וְאֶחָיו בֵּיתָה יוֹסֵף וְהוּא עוֹדֶנּוּ שָׁם וַיִּפְּלוּ לְפָנָיו אָרְצָה: 15 וַיֹּאמֶר לָהֶם יוֹסֵף מָה־הַמַּעֲשֶׂה הַזֶּה אֲשֶׁר עֲשִׂיתֶם הֲלוֹא יְדַעְתֶּם כִּי־נַחֵשׁ יְנַחֵשׁ אִישׁ אֲשֶׁר כָּמֹנִי: 16 וַיֹּאמֶר יְהוּדָה מַה־נֹּאמַר לַאדֹנִי מַה־נְּדַבֵּר וּמַה־נִּצְטַדָּק הָאֱלֹהִים מָצָא אֶת־עֲוֺן עֲבָדֶיךָ הִנֶּנּוּ עֲבָדִים לַאדֹנִי גַּם־אֲנַחְנוּ גַּם אֲשֶׁר־נִמְצָא הַגָּבִיעַ בְּיָדוֹ: 17 וַיֹּאמֶר חָלִילָה לִּי מֵעֲשׂוֹת זֹאת הָאִישׁ אֲשֶׁר נִמְצָא הַגָּבִיעַ בְּיָדוֹ הוּא יִהְיֶה־לִּי עָבֶד וְאַתֶּם עֲלוּ לְשָׁלוֹם אֶל־אֲבִיכֶם: פ

וַיִּגַּשׁ

18 וַיִּגַּשׁ אֵלָיו יְהוּדָה וַיֹּאמֶר בִּי אֲדֹנִי יְדַבֶּר־נָא עַבְדְּךָ דָבָר בְּאָזְנֵי אֲדֹנִי וְאַל־יִחַר אַפְּךָ בְּעַבְדֶּךָ כִּי כָמוֹךָ כְּפַרְעֹה: 19 אֲדֹנִי שָׁאַל אֶת־עֲבָדָיו לֵאמֹר הֲיֵשׁ־לָכֶם אָב אוֹ־אָח: 20 וַנֹּאמֶר אֶל־אֲדֹנִי יֶשׁ־לָנוּ אָב זָקֵן וְיֶלֶד זְקֻנִים קָטָן וְאָחִיו מֵת וַיִּוָּתֵר הוּא לְבַדּוֹ לְאִמּוֹ וְאָבִיו אֲהֵבוֹ: 21 וַתֹּאמֶר אֶל־עֲבָדֶיךָ הוֹרִדֻהוּ אֵלָי וְאָשִׂימָה עֵינִי עָלָיו: 22 וַנֹּאמֶר אֶל־אֲדֹנִי לֹא־יוּכַל הַנַּעַר לַעֲזֹב אֶת־אָבִיו וְעָזַב אֶת־אָבִיו וָמֵת: 23 וַתֹּאמֶר אֶל־עֲבָדֶיךָ אִם־לֹא יֵרֵד אֲחִיכֶם הַקָּטֹן אִתְּכֶם לֹא תֹסִפוּן לִרְאוֹת פָּנָי: 24 וַיְהִי כִּי עָלִינוּ אֶל־עַבְדְּךָ אָבִי וַנַּגֶּד־לוֹ אֵת דִּבְרֵי אֲדֹנִי: 25 וַיֹּאמֶר אָבִינוּ שֻׁבוּ שִׁבְרוּ־לָנוּ מְעַט־אֹכֶל: 26 וַנֹּאמֶר לֹא נוּכַל לָרֶדֶת אִם־יֵשׁ

us can we go down, for we may not ^a-show our faces to the man-^a unless our youngest brother is with us.' ²⁷Your servant my father said to us, 'As you know, my wife bore me two sons. ²⁸But one is gone from me, and I said: Alas, he was torn by a beast! And I have not seen him since. ²⁹If you take this one from me, too, and he meets with disaster, you will send my white head down to Sheol in sorrow.'

³⁰"Now, if I come to your servant my father and the boy is not with us—since his own life is so bound up with his—³¹when he sees that the boy is not with us, he will die, and your servants will send the white head of your servant our father down to Sheol in grief. ³²Now your servant has pledged himself for the boy to my father, saying, 'If I do not bring him back to you, I shall stand guilty before my father forever.' ³³Therefore, please let your servant remain as a slave to my lord instead of the boy, and let the boy go back with his brothers. ³⁴For how can I go back to my father unless the boy is with me? Let me not be witness to the woe that would overtake my father!"

45 Joseph could no longer control himself before all his attendants, and he cried out, "Have everyone withdraw from me!" So there was no one else about when Joseph made himself known to his brothers. ²His sobs were so loud that the Egyptians could hear, and so the news reached Pharaoh's palace.

³Joseph said to his brothers, "I am Joseph. Is my father still well?" But his brothers could not answer him, so dumfounded were they on account of him.

⁴Then Joseph said to his brothers, "Come forward to me." And when they came forward, he said, "I am your brother Joseph, he whom you

אָחִינוּ הַקָּטֹן אִתָּנוּ וְיָרַדְנוּ כִּי־לֹא נוּכַל לִרְאוֹת פְּנֵי הָאִישׁ וְאָחִינוּ הַקָּטֹן אֵינֶנּוּ אִתָּנוּ: 27 וַיֹּאמֶר עַבְדְּךָ אָבִי אֵלֵינוּ אַתֶּם יְדַעְתֶּם כִּי שְׁנַיִם יָלְדָה־לִּי אִשְׁתִּי: 28 וַיֵּצֵא הָאֶחָד מֵאִתִּי וָאֹמַר אַךְ טָרֹף טֹרָף וְלֹא רְאִיתִיו עַד־הֵנָּה: 29 וּלְקַחְתֶּם גַּם־אֶת־זֶה מֵעִם פָּנַי וְקָרָהוּ* אָסוֹן וְהוֹרַדְתֶּם אֶת־שֵׂיבָתִי בְּרָעָה שְׁאֹלָה:

30 וְעַתָּה כְּבֹאִי אֶל־עַבְדְּךָ אָבִי וְהַנַּעַר אֵינֶנּוּ אִתָּנוּ וְנַפְשׁוֹ קְשׁוּרָה בְנַפְשׁוֹ: 31 וְהָיָה כִּרְאוֹתוֹ כִּי־אֵין הַנַּעַר וָמֵת וְהוֹרִידוּ עֲבָדֶיךָ אֶת־שֵׂיבַת עַבְדְּךָ אָבִינוּ בְּיָגוֹן שְׁאֹלָה: 32 כִּי עַבְדְּךָ עָרַב אֶת־הַנַּעַר מֵעִם אָבִי לֵאמֹר אִם־לֹא אֲבִיאֶנּוּ אֵלֶיךָ וְחָטָאתִי לְאָבִי כָּל־הַיָּמִים: 33 וְעַתָּה יֵשֶׁב־נָא עַבְדְּךָ תַּחַת הַנַּעַר עֶבֶד לַאדֹנִי וְהַנַּעַר יַעַל עִם־אֶחָיו: 34 כִּי־אֵיךְ אֶעֱלֶה אֶל־אָבִי וְהַנַּעַר אֵינֶנּוּ אִתִּי פֶּן אֶרְאֶה בָרָע אֲשֶׁר יִמְצָא אֶת־אָבִי:

מה וְלֹא־יָכֹל יוֹסֵף לְהִתְאַפֵּק לְכֹל הַנִּצָּבִים עָלָיו וַיִּקְרָא הוֹצִיאוּ כָל־אִישׁ מֵעָלָי וְלֹא־עָמַד אִישׁ אִתּוֹ בְּהִתְוַדַּע יוֹסֵף אֶל־אֶחָיו: 2 וַיִּתֵּן אֶת־קֹלוֹ בִּבְכִי וַיִּשְׁמְעוּ מִצְרַיִם וַיִּשְׁמַע בֵּית פַּרְעֹה: 3 וַיֹּאמֶר יוֹסֵף אֶל־אֶחָיו אֲנִי יוֹסֵף הַעוֹד אָבִי חָי וְלֹא־יָכְלוּ אֶחָיו לַעֲנוֹת אֹתוֹ כִּי נִבְהֲלוּ מִפָּנָיו: 4 וַיֹּאמֶר יוֹסֵף אֶל־אֶחָיו גְּשׁוּ־נָא אֵלַי וַיִּגָּשׁוּ וַיֹּאמֶר אֲנִי יוֹסֵף אֲחִיכֶם אֲשֶׁר־מְכַרְתֶּם

חסר א' ‏ v. 29.

a-a Lit. "see the man's face."

97

sold into Egypt. 5Now, do not be distressed or reproach yourselves because you sold me hither; it was to save life that God sent me ahead of you. 6It is now two years that there has been famine in the land, and there are still five years to come in which there shall be no yield from tilling. 7God has sent me ahead of you to ensure your survival on earth, and to save your lives in an extraordinary deliverance. 8So, it was not you who sent me here, but God; and He has made me a father to Pharaoh, lord of all his household, and ruler over the whole land of Egypt.

9"Now, hurry back to my father and say to him: Thus says your son Joseph, 'God has made me lord of all Egypt; come down to me without delay. 10You will dwell in the region of Goshen, where you will be near me—you and your children and your grandchildren, your flocks and herds, and all that is yours. 11There I will provide for you—for there are yet five years of famine to come—that you and your household and all that is yours may not suffer want.' 12You can see for yourselves, and my brother Benjamin for himself, that it is indeed I who am speaking to you. 13And you must tell my father everything about my high station in Egypt and all that you have seen; and bring my father here with all speed."

14With that he embraced*a* his brother Benjamin around the neck and wept, and Benjamin wept on his neck. 15He kissed all his brothers and wept upon them; only then were his brothers able to talk to him.

16The news reached Pharaoh's palace: "Joseph's brothers have come." Pharaoh and his courtiers were pleased. 17And Pharaoh said to Joseph, "Say to your brothers, 'Do as follows: load up your beasts and go at once to the land of Canaan. 18Take your father and your house-

a Lit. "fell on."

אֹתִ֖י מִצְרָֽיְמָה׃ 5 וְעַתָּ֣ה ׀ אַל־תֵּעָ֣צְב֗וּ וְאַל־יִ֨חַר֙ בְּעֵ֣ינֵיכֶ֔ם כִּֽי־מְכַרְתֶּ֥ם אֹתִ֖י הֵ֑נָּה כִּ֣י לְמִֽחְיָ֔ה שְׁלָחַ֥נִי אֱלֹהִ֖ים לִפְנֵיכֶֽם׃ 6 כִּי־זֶ֛ה שְׁנָתַ֥יִם הָרָעָ֖ב בְּקֶ֣רֶב הָאָ֑רֶץ וְעוֹד֙ חָמֵ֣שׁ שָׁנִ֔ים אֲשֶׁ֥ר אֵֽין־חָרִ֖ישׁ וְקָצִֽיר׃ 7 וַיִּשְׁלָחֵ֣נִי אֱלֹהִים֮ לִפְנֵיכֶם֒ לָשׂ֥וּם לָכֶ֛ם שְׁאֵרִ֖ית בָּאָ֑רֶץ וּלְהַחֲי֣וֹת לָכֶ֔ם לִפְלֵיטָ֖ה גְּדֹלָֽה׃ 8 וְעַתָּ֗ה לֹֽא־אַתֶּ֞ם שְׁלַחְתֶּ֤ם אֹתִי֙ הֵ֔נָּה כִּ֖י הָאֱלֹהִ֑ים וַיְשִׂימֵ֨נִי לְאָ֜ב לְפַרְעֹ֗ה וּלְאָדוֹן֙ לְכָל־בֵּית֔וֹ וּמֹשֵׁ֖ל בְּכָל־אֶ֥רֶץ מִצְרָֽיִם׃ 9 מַהֲרוּ֮ וַעֲל֣וּ אֶל־אָבִי֒ וַאֲמַרְתֶּ֣ם אֵלָ֗יו כֹּ֤ה אָמַר֙ בִּנְךָ֣ יוֹסֵ֔ף שָׂמַ֧נִי אֱלֹהִ֛ים לְאָד֖וֹן לְכָל־מִצְרָ֑יִם רְדָ֥ה אֵלַ֖י אַֽל־תַּעֲמֹֽד׃ 10 וְיָשַׁבְתָּ֣ בְאֶֽרֶץ־גֹּ֗שֶׁן וְהָיִ֤יתָ קָרוֹב֙ אֵלַ֔י אַתָּ֕ה וּבָנֶ֖יךָ וּבְנֵ֣י בָנֶ֑יךָ וְצֹאנְךָ֥ וּבְקָרְךָ֖ וְכָל־אֲשֶׁר־לָֽךְ׃ 11 וְכִלְכַּלְתִּ֤י אֹֽתְךָ֙ שָׁ֔ם כִּי־ע֛וֹד חָמֵ֥שׁ שָׁנִ֖ים רָעָ֑ב פֶּן־תִּוָּרֵ֛שׁ אַתָּ֥ה וּבֵֽיתְךָ֖ וְכָל־אֲשֶׁר־לָֽךְ׃ 12 וְהִנֵּ֤ה עֵֽינֵיכֶם֙ רֹא֔וֹת וְעֵינֵ֖י אָחִ֣י בִנְיָמִ֑ין כִּי־פִ֖י הַֽמְדַבֵּ֥ר אֲלֵיכֶֽם׃ 13 וְהִגַּדְתֶּ֣ם לְאָבִ֗י אֶת־כָּל־כְּבוֹדִי֙ בְּמִצְרַ֔יִם וְאֵ֖ת כָּל־אֲשֶׁ֣ר רְאִיתֶ֑ם וּמִֽהַרְתֶּ֛ם וְהוֹרַדְתֶּ֥ם אֶת־אָבִ֖י הֵֽנָּה׃ 14 וַיִּפֹּ֛ל עַל־צַוְּארֵ֥י בִנְיָמִֽן־אָחִ֖יו וַיֵּ֑בְךְּ וּבִ֨נְיָמִ֔ן בָּכָ֖ה עַל־צַוָּארָֽיו׃ 15 וַיְנַשֵּׁ֥ק לְכָל־אֶחָ֖יו וַיֵּ֣בְךְּ עֲלֵהֶ֑ם וְאַ֣חֲרֵי כֵ֔ן דִּבְּר֥וּ אֶחָ֖יו אִתּֽוֹ׃ 16 וְהַקֹּ֣ל נִשְׁמַ֗ע בֵּ֤ית פַּרְעֹה֙ לֵאמֹ֔ר בָּ֖אוּ אֲחֵ֣י יוֹסֵ֑ף וַיִּיטַב֙ בְּעֵינֵ֣י פַרְעֹ֔ה וּבְעֵינֵ֖י עֲבָדָֽיו׃ 17 וַיֹּ֤אמֶר פַּרְעֹה֙ אֶל־יוֹסֵ֔ף אֱמֹ֥ר אֶל־אַחֶ֖יךָ זֹ֣את עֲשׂ֑וּ טַֽעֲנוּ֙ אֶת־בְּעִ֣ירְכֶ֔ם וּלְכוּ־בֹ֖אוּ אַ֥רְצָה כְּנָֽעַן׃ 18 וּקְח֥וּ אֶת־

holds and come to me; I will give you the best of the land of Egypt and you shall live off the fat of the land.' [19]And you are bidden [to add], 'Do as follows: take from the land of Egypt wagons for your children and your wives, and bring your father here. [20]And never mind your belongings, for the best of all the land of Egypt shall be yours.'"

[21]The sons of Israel did so; Joseph gave them wagons as Pharaoh had commanded, and he supplied them with provisions for the journey. [22]To each of them, moreover, he gave a change of clothing; but to Benjamin he gave three hundred pieces of silver and several[b] changes of clothing. [23]And to his father he sent the following: ten he-asses laden with the best things of Egypt, and ten she-asses laden with grain, bread, and provisions for his father on the journey. [24]As he sent his brothers off on their way, he told them, "Do not be quarrelsome on the way."

[25]They went up from Egypt and came to their father Jacob in the land of Canaan. [26]And they told him, "Joseph is still alive; yes, he is ruler over the whole land of Egypt." His heart went numb, for he did not believe them. [27]But when they recounted all that Joseph had said to them, and when he saw the wagons that Joseph had sent to transport him, the spirit of their father Jacob revived. [28]"Enough!" said Israel. "My son Joseph is still alive! I must go and see him before I die."

46

So Israel set out with all that was his, and he came to Beer-sheba, where he offered sacrifices to the God of his father Isaac. [2]God called to Israel in a vision by night: "Jacob! Jacob!" He answered, "Here." [3]And He said, "I am God, the God of your father. Fear not to go down to Egypt, for I will make you there into

---

אֲבִיכֶם וְאֶת־בָּתֵּיכֶם וּבֹאוּ אֵלָי וְאֶתְּנָה לָכֶם אֶת־טוּב אֶרֶץ מִצְרַיִם וְאִכְלוּ אֶת־חֵלֶב הָאָרֶץ: 19 וְאַתָּה צֻוֵּיתָה זֹאת עֲשׂוּ קְחוּ־לָכֶם מֵאֶרֶץ מִצְרַיִם עֲגָלוֹת לְטַפְּכֶם וְלִנְשֵׁיכֶם וּנְשָׂאתֶם אֶת־אֲבִיכֶם וּבָאתֶם: 20 וְעֵינְכֶם אַל־תָּחֹס עַל־כְּלֵיכֶם כִּי־טוּב כָּל־אֶרֶץ מִצְרַיִם לָכֶם הוּא: 21 וַיַּעֲשׂוּ־כֵן בְּנֵי יִשְׂרָאֵל וַיִּתֵּן לָהֶם יוֹסֵף עֲגָלוֹת עַל־פִּי פַרְעֹה וַיִּתֵּן לָהֶם צֵדָה לַדָּרֶךְ: 22 לְכֻלָּם נָתַן לָאִישׁ חֲלִפוֹת שְׂמָלֹת וּלְבִנְיָמִן נָתַן שְׁלֹשׁ מֵאוֹת כֶּסֶף וְחָמֵשׁ חֲלִפֹת שְׂמָלֹת: 23 וּלְאָבִיו שָׁלַח כְּזֹאת עֲשָׂרָה חֲמֹרִים נֹשְׂאִים מִטּוּב מִצְרָיִם וְעֶשֶׂר אֲתֹנֹת נֹשְׂאֹת בָּר וָלֶחֶם וּמָזוֹן לְאָבִיו לַדָּרֶךְ: 24 וַיְשַׁלַּח אֶת־אֶחָיו וַיֵּלֵכוּ וַיֹּאמֶר אֲלֵהֶם אַל־תִּרְגְּזוּ בַּדָּרֶךְ: 25 וַיַּעֲלוּ מִמִּצְרָיִם וַיָּבֹאוּ אֶרֶץ* כְּנַעַן אֶל־יַעֲקֹב אֲבִיהֶם: 26 וַיַּגִּדוּ לוֹ לֵאמֹר עוֹד יוֹסֵף חַי וְכִי־הוּא מֹשֵׁל בְּכָל־אֶרֶץ מִצְרָיִם וַיָּפָג לִבּוֹ כִּי לֹא־הֶאֱמִין לָהֶם: 27 וַיְדַבְּרוּ אֵלָיו אֵת כָּל־דִּבְרֵי יוֹסֵף אֲשֶׁר דִּבֶּר אֲלֵהֶם וַיַּרְא אֶת־הָעֲגָלוֹת אֲשֶׁר־שָׁלַח יוֹסֵף לָשֵׂאת אֹתוֹ וַתְּחִי רוּחַ יַעֲקֹב אֲבִיהֶם: 28 וַיֹּאמֶר יִשְׂרָאֵל רַב עוֹד־יוֹסֵף בְּנִי חָי אֵלְכָה וְאֶרְאֶנּוּ בְּטֶרֶם אָמוּת:

מו וַיִּסַּע יִשְׂרָאֵל וְכָל־אֲשֶׁר־לוֹ וַיָּבֹא בְּאֵרָה שָּׁבַע וַיִּזְבַּח זְבָחִים לֵאלֹהֵי אָבִיו יִצְחָק: 2 וַיֹּאמֶר אֱלֹהִים | לְיִשְׂרָאֵל בְּמַרְאֹת הַלַּיְלָה וַיֹּאמֶר יַעֲקֹב | יַעֲקֹב וַיֹּאמֶר הִנֵּנִי: 3 וַיֹּאמֶר אָנֹכִי הָאֵל אֱלֹהֵי אָבִיךָ אַל־תִּירָא מֵרְדָה מִצְרַיְמָה כִּי־לְגוֹי

---

b Lit. "five"; cf. 43.34.

a great nation. [4]I Myself will go down with you to Egypt, and I Myself will also bring you back; and Joseph's hand shall close your eyes."

[5]So Jacob set out from Beer-sheba. The sons of Israel put their father Jacob and their children and their wives in the wagons that Pharaoh had sent to transport him; [6]and they took along their livestock and the wealth that they had amassed in the land of Canaan. Thus Jacob and all his offspring with him came to Egypt: [7]he brought with him to Egypt his sons and grandsons, his daughters and granddaughters—all his offspring.

[8]These are the names of the Israelites, Jacob and his descendants, who came to Egypt.

Jacob's first-born Reuben; [9]Reuben's sons: Enoch,[a] Pallu, Hezron, and Carmi. [10]Simeon's sons: Jemuel, Jamin, Ohad, Jachin, Zohar, and Saul[b] the son of a Canaanite woman. [11]Levi's sons: Gershon, Kohath, and Merari. [12]Judah's sons: Er, Onan, Shelah, Perez, and Zerah—but Er and Onan had died in the land of Canaan; and Perez's sons were Hezron and Hamul. [13]Issachar's sons: Tola, Puvah, Iob, and Shimron. [14]Zebulun's sons: Sered, Elon, and Jahleel. [15]Those were the sons whom Leah bore to Jacob in Paddan-aram, in addition to his daughter Dinah. Persons in all, male and female: 33.[c]

[16]Gad's sons: Ziphion, Haggi, Shuni, Ezbon, Eri, Arodi, and Areli. [17]Asher's sons: Imnah, Ishvah, Ishvi, and Beriah, and their sister Serah. Beriah's sons: Heber and Malchiel. [18]These were the descendants of Zilpah, whom Laban had given to his daughter Leah. These she bore to Jacob—16 persons.

[19]The sons of Jacob's wife Rachel were Joseph and Benjamin. [20]To Joseph were born in the land of Egypt Manasseh and Ephraim, whom Asenath daughter of Poti-phera priest of On bore to him. [21]Benjamin's sons: Bela, Becher,

גָּדוֹל אֲשִׂימְךָ שָׁם: 4 אָנֹכִי אֵרֵד עִמְּךָ מִצְרַיְמָה וְאָנֹכִי אַעַלְךָ גַם־עָלֹה וְיוֹסֵף יָשִׁית יָדוֹ עַל־עֵינֶיךָ: 5 וַיָּקָם יַעֲקֹב מִבְּאֵר שָׁבַע וַיִּשְׂאוּ בְנֵי־יִשְׂרָאֵל אֶת־יַעֲקֹב אֲבִיהֶם וְאֶת־טַפָּם וְאֶת־נְשֵׁיהֶם בָּעֲגָלוֹת אֲשֶׁר־שָׁלַח פַּרְעֹה לָשֵׂאת אֹתוֹ: 6 וַיִּקְחוּ אֶת־מִקְנֵיהֶם וְאֶת־רְכוּשָׁם אֲשֶׁר רָכְשׁוּ בְּאֶרֶץ כְּנַעַן וַיָּבֹאוּ מִצְרַיְמָה יַעֲקֹב וְכָל־זַרְעוֹ אִתּוֹ: 7 בָּנָיו וּבְנֵי בָנָיו אִתּוֹ בְּנֹתָיו וּבְנוֹת בָּנָיו וְכָל־זַרְעוֹ הֵבִיא אִתּוֹ מִצְרָיְמָה: ס 8 וְאֵלֶּה שְׁמוֹת בְּנֵי־יִשְׂרָאֵל הַבָּאִים מִצְרַיְמָה יַעֲקֹב וּבָנָיו בְּכֹר יַעֲקֹב רְאוּבֵן: 9 וּבְנֵי רְאוּבֵן חֲנוֹךְ וּפַלּוּא וְחֶצְרוֹן וְכַרְמִי: 10 וּבְנֵי שִׁמְעוֹן יְמוּאֵל וְיָמִין וְאֹהַד וְיָכִין וְצֹחַר וְשָׁאוּל בֶּן־הַכְּנַעֲנִית: 11 וּבְנֵי לֵוִי גֵּרְשׁוֹן קְהָת וּמְרָרִי: 12 וּבְנֵי יְהוּדָה עֵר וְאוֹנָן וְשֵׁלָה וָפֶרֶץ וָזָרַח וַיָּמָת עֵר וְאוֹנָן בְּאֶרֶץ כְּנַעַן וַיִּהְיוּ בְנֵי־פֶרֶץ חֶצְרוֹן וְחָמוּל: 13 וּבְנֵי יִשָּׂשכָר תּוֹלָע וּפֻוָּה וְיוֹב וְשִׁמְרוֹן: 14 וּבְנֵי זְבֻלוּן סֶרֶד וְאֵלוֹן וְיַחְלְאֵל: 15 אֵלֶּה | בְּנֵי לֵאָה אֲשֶׁר יָלְדָה לְיַעֲקֹב בְּפַדַּן אֲרָם וְאֵת דִּינָה בִתּוֹ כָּל־נֶפֶשׁ בָּנָיו וּבְנוֹתָיו שְׁלֹשִׁים וְשָׁלֹשׁ: 16 וּבְנֵי גָד צִפְיוֹן וְחַגִּי שׁוּנִי וְאֶצְבֹּן עֵרִי וַאֲרוֹדִי וְאַרְאֵלִי: 17 וּבְנֵי אָשֵׁר יִמְנָה וְיִשְׁוָה וְיִשְׁוִי וּבְרִיעָה וְשֶׂרַח אֲחֹתָם וּבְנֵי בְרִיעָה חֶבֶר וּמַלְכִּיאֵל: 18 אֵלֶּה בְּנֵי זִלְפָּה אֲשֶׁר־נָתַן לָבָן לְלֵאָה בִתּוֹ וַתֵּלֶד אֶת־אֵלֶּה לְיַעֲקֹב שֵׁשׁ עֶשְׂרֵה נָפֶשׁ: 19 בְּנֵי רָחֵל אֵשֶׁת יַעֲקֹב יוֹסֵף וּבִנְיָמִן: 20 וַיִּוָּלֵד לְיוֹסֵף בְּאֶרֶץ מִצְרַיִם אֲשֶׁר יָלְדָה־לּוֹ אָסְנַת בַּת־פּוֹטִי פֶרַע כֹּהֵן אֹן אֶת־מְנַשֶּׁה וְאֶת־אֶפְרָיִם: 21 וּבְנֵי בִנְיָמִן בֶּלַע

---

a   Or "Hanoch."
b   Or "Shaul."
c   Including Jacob.

Ashbel, Gera, Naaman, Ehi, Rosh, Muppim, Huppim, and Ard. 22These were the descendants of Rachel who were born to Jacob—14 persons in all.

23Dan's son:*d* Hushim. 24Naphtali's sons: Jahzeel, Guni, Jezer, and Shillem. 25These were the descendants of Bilhah, whom Laban had given to his daughter Rachel. These she bore to Jacob—7 persons in all.

26All the persons belonging to Jacob who came to Egypt*e*—his own issue, aside from the wives of Jacob's sons—all these persons numbered 66. 27And Joseph's sons who were born to him in Egypt were two in number. Thus the total of Jacob's household who came to Egypt was seventy persons.*f*

28He had sent Judah ahead of him to Joseph, to point the way before him to Goshen. So when they came to the region of Goshen, 29Joseph ordered*g* his chariot and went to Goshen to meet his father Israel; he presented himself to him and, embracing him around the neck, he wept on his neck a good while. 30Then Israel said to Joseph, "Now I can die, having seen for myself that you are still alive."

31Then Joseph said to his brothers and to his father's household, "I will go up and tell the news to Pharaoh, and say to him, 'My brothers and my father's household, who were in the land of Canaan, have come to me. 32The men are shepherds; they have always been breeders of livestock, and they have brought with them their flocks and herds and all that is theirs.' 33So when Pharaoh summons you and asks, 'What is your occupation?' 34you shall answer, 'Your servants have been breeders of livestock from the start until now, both we and our fathers'— so that you may stay in the region of Goshen. For all shepherds are abhorrent to Egyptians."

וָבֶ֫כֶר וְאַשְׁבֵּ֖ל גֵּרָ֣א וְנַעֲמָ֑ן אֵחִ֖י וָרֹ֑אשׁ מֻפִּ֥ים וְחֻפִּ֖ים וָאָֽרְדְּ׃ 22 אֵ֚לֶּה בְּנֵ֣י רָחֵ֔ל אֲשֶׁ֥ר יֻלַּ֖ד לְיַעֲקֹ֑ב כָּל־נֶ֖פֶשׁ אַרְבָּעָ֥ה עָשָֽׂר׃ 23 וּבְנֵי־דָ֖ן חֻשִׁ֑ים׃ 24 וּבְנֵ֣י נַפְתָּלִ֔י יַחְצְאֵ֥ל וְגוּנִ֖י וְיֵ֥צֶר וְשִׁלֵּֽם׃ 25 אֵ֚לֶּה בְּנֵ֣י בִלְהָ֔ה אֲשֶׁר־נָתַ֥ן לָבָ֖ן לְרָחֵ֣ל בִּתּ֑וֹ וַתֵּ֧לֶד אֶת־אֵ֛לֶּה לְיַעֲקֹ֖ב כָּל־נֶ֥פֶשׁ שִׁבְעָֽה׃

26 כָּל־הַ֠נֶּ֠פֶשׁ הַבָּאָ֨ה לְיַעֲקֹ֤ב מִצְרַ֙יְמָה֙ יֹצְאֵ֣י יְרֵכ֔וֹ מִלְּבַ֖ד נְשֵׁ֣י בְנֵֽי־יַעֲקֹ֑ב כָּל־נֶ֖פֶשׁ שִׁשִּׁ֥ים וָשֵֽׁשׁ׃ 27 וּבְנֵ֥י יוֹסֵ֛ף אֲשֶׁר־יֻלַּד־ל֥וֹ בְמִצְרַ֖יִם נֶ֣פֶשׁ שְׁנָ֑יִם כָּל־הַנֶּ֧פֶשׁ לְבֵ֛ית־יַעֲקֹ֖ב הַבָּ֣אָה מִצְרַ֖יְמָה שִׁבְעִֽים׃ פ

28 וְאֶת־יְהוּדָ֞ה שָׁלַ֤ח לְפָנָיו֙ אֶל־יוֹסֵ֔ף לְהוֹרֹ֥ת לְפָנָ֖יו גֹּ֑שְׁנָה וַיָּבֹ֖אוּ אַ֥רְצָה גֹּֽשֶׁן׃ 29 וַיֶּאְסֹ֤ר יוֹסֵף֙ מֶרְכַּבְתּ֔וֹ וַיַּ֛עַל לִקְרַֽאת־יִשְׂרָאֵ֥ל אָבִ֖יו גֹּ֑שְׁנָה וַיֵּרָ֣א אֵלָ֗יו וַיִּפֹּל֙ עַל־צַוָּארָ֔יו וַיֵּ֥בְךְּ עַל־צַוָּארָ֖יו עֽוֹד׃ 30 וַיֹּ֧אמֶר יִשְׂרָאֵ֛ל אֶל־יוֹסֵ֖ף אָמ֣וּתָה הַפָּ֑עַם אַחֲרֵ֥י רְאוֹתִ֖י אֶת־פָּנֶ֑יךָ כִּ֥י עֽוֹדְךָ֖ חָֽי׃ 31 וַיֹּ֨אמֶר יוֹסֵ֜ף אֶל־אֶחָ֗יו וְאֶל־בֵּ֣ית אָבִיו֒ אֶעֱלֶ֣ה וְאַגִּ֣ידָה לְפַרְעֹ֑ה וְאֹמְרָ֣ה אֵלָ֔יו אַחַ֥י וּבֵית־אָבִ֛י אֲשֶׁ֥ר בְּאֶֽרֶץ־כְּנַ֖עַן בָּ֥אוּ אֵלָֽי׃ 32 וְהָאֲנָשִׁים֙ רֹ֣עֵי צֹ֔אן כִּֽי־אַנְשֵׁ֥י מִקְנֶ֖ה הָי֑וּ וְצֹאנָ֧ם וּבְקָרָ֛ם וְכָל־אֲשֶׁ֥ר לָהֶ֖ם הֵבִֽיאוּ׃ 33 וְהָיָ֕ה כִּֽי־יִקְרָ֥א לָכֶ֖ם פַּרְעֹ֑ה וְאָמַ֖ר מַה־מַּעֲשֵׂיכֶֽם׃ 34 וַאֲמַרְתֶּ֗ם אַנְשֵׁ֨י מִקְנֶ֜ה הָי֤וּ עֲבָדֶ֙יךָ֙ מִנְּעוּרֵ֣ינוּ וְעַד־עַ֔תָּה גַּם־אֲנַ֖חְנוּ גַּם־אֲבֹתֵ֑ינוּ בַּעֲב֗וּר תֵּֽשְׁבוּ֙ בְּאֶ֣רֶץ גֹּ֔שֶׁן כִּֽי־תוֹעֲבַ֥ת מִצְרַ֖יִם כָּל־רֹ֥עֵה צֹֽאן׃

---

d Heb. "sons."
e Not including Joseph and Joseph's two sons.
f Including Jacob and Joseph.
g Lit. "hitched."

47 Then Joseph came and reported to Pharaoh, saying, "My father and my brothers, with their flocks and herds and all that is theirs, have come from the land of Canaan and are now in the region of Goshen." [2]And selecting a few[a] of his brothers, he presented them to Pharaoh. [3]Pharaoh said to his brothers, "What is your occupation?" They answered Pharaoh, "We your servants are shepherds, as were also our fathers. [4]We have come," they told Pharaoh, "to sojourn in this land, for there is no pasture for your servants' flocks, the famine being severe in the land of Canaan. Pray, then, let your servants stay in the region of Goshen." [5]Then Pharaoh said to Joseph, "As regards your father and your brothers who have come to you, [6]the land of Egypt is open before you: settle your father and your brothers in the best part of the land; let them stay in the region of Goshen. And if you know any capable men among them, put them in charge of my livestock."

[7]Joseph then brought his father Jacob and presented him to Pharaoh; and Jacob greeted Pharaoh. [8]Pharaoh asked Jacob, "How many are the years of your life?" [9]And Jacob answered Pharaoh, "The years of my sojourn [on earth] are one hundred and thirty. Few and hard have been the years of my life, nor do they come up to the life spans of my fathers during their sojourns." [10]Then Jacob bade Pharaoh farewell, and left Pharaoh's presence.

[11]So Joseph settled his father and his brothers, giving them holdings in the choicest part of the land of Egypt, in the region of Rameses, as Pharaoh had commanded. [12]Joseph sustained his father, and his brothers, and all his father's household with bread, down to the little ones.

[13]Now there was no bread in all the world, for the famine was very severe; both the land

מז וַיָּבֹא יוֹסֵף וַיַּגֵּד לְפַרְעֹה וַיֹּאמֶר אָבִי וְאַחַי וְצֹאנָם וּבְקָרָם וְכָל־אֲשֶׁר לָהֶם בָּאוּ מֵאֶרֶץ כְּנָעַן וְהִנָּם בְּאֶרֶץ גֹּשֶׁן: [2]וּמִקְצֵה אֶחָיו לָקַח חֲמִשָּׁה אֲנָשִׁים וַיַּצִּגֵם לִפְנֵי פַרְעֹה: [3]וַיֹּאמֶר פַּרְעֹה אֶל־אֶחָיו מַה־מַּעֲשֵׂיכֶם וַיֹּאמְרוּ אֶל־פַּרְעֹה רֹעֵה צֹאן עֲבָדֶיךָ גַּם־אֲנַחְנוּ גַּם־אֲבוֹתֵינוּ: [4]וַיֹּאמְרוּ אֶל־פַּרְעֹה לָגוּר בָּאָרֶץ בָּאנוּ כִּי־אֵין מִרְעֶה לַצֹּאן אֲשֶׁר לַעֲבָדֶיךָ כִּי־כָבֵד הָרָעָב בְּאֶרֶץ כְּנָעַן וְעַתָּה יֵשְׁבוּ־נָא עֲבָדֶיךָ בְּאֶרֶץ גֹּשֶׁן: [5]וַיֹּאמֶר פַּרְעֹה אֶל־יוֹסֵף לֵאמֹר אָבִיךָ וְאַחֶיךָ בָּאוּ אֵלֶיךָ: [6]אֶרֶץ מִצְרַיִם לְפָנֶיךָ הִוא בְּמֵיטַב הָאָרֶץ הוֹשֵׁב אֶת־אָבִיךָ וְאֶת־אַחֶיךָ יֵשְׁבוּ בְּאֶרֶץ גֹּשֶׁן וְאִם־יָדַעְתָּ וְיֶשׁ־בָּם אַנְשֵׁי־חַיִל וְשַׂמְתָּם שָׂרֵי מִקְנֶה עַל־אֲשֶׁר־לִי: [7]וַיָּבֵא יוֹסֵף אֶת־יַעֲקֹב אָבִיו וַיַּעֲמִדֵהוּ לִפְנֵי פַרְעֹה וַיְבָרֶךְ יַעֲקֹב אֶת־פַּרְעֹה: [8]וַיֹּאמֶר פַּרְעֹה אֶל־יַעֲקֹב כַּמָּה יְמֵי שְׁנֵי חַיֶּיךָ: [9]וַיֹּאמֶר יַעֲקֹב אֶל־פַּרְעֹה יְמֵי שְׁנֵי מְגוּרַי שְׁלֹשִׁים וּמְאַת שָׁנָה מְעַט וְרָעִים הָיוּ יְמֵי שְׁנֵי חַיַּי וְלֹא הִשִּׂיגוּ אֶת־יְמֵי שְׁנֵי חַיֵּי אֲבֹתַי בִּימֵי מְגוּרֵיהֶם: [10]וַיְבָרֶךְ יַעֲקֹב אֶת־פַּרְעֹה וַיֵּצֵא מִלִּפְנֵי פַרְעֹה: [11]וַיּוֹשֵׁב יוֹסֵף אֶת־אָבִיו וְאֶת־אֶחָיו וַיִּתֵּן לָהֶם אֲחֻזָּה בְּאֶרֶץ מִצְרַיִם בְּמֵיטַב הָאָרֶץ בְּאֶרֶץ רַעְמְסֵס כַּאֲשֶׁר צִוָּה פַרְעֹה: [12]וַיְכַלְכֵּל יוֹסֵף אֶת־אָבִיו וְאֶת־אֶחָיו וְאֵת כָּל־בֵּית אָבִיו לֶחֶם לְפִי הַטָּף: [13]וְלֶחֶם אֵין בְּכָל־הָאָרֶץ כִּי־כָבֵד הָרָעָב מְאֹד וַתֵּלַהּ אֶרֶץ מִצְרַיִם וְאֶרֶץ כְּנָעַן מִפְּנֵי

---

a Lit. "five."

of Egypt and the land of Canaan languished because of the famine. [14]Joseph gathered in all the money that was to be found in the land of Egypt and in the land of Canaan, as payment for the rations that were being procured, and Joseph brought the money into Pharaoh's palace. [15]And when the money gave out in the land of Egypt and in the land of Canaan, all the Egyptians came to Joseph and said, "Give us bread, lest we die before your very eyes; for the money is gone!" [16]And Joseph said, "Bring your livestock, and I will sell to you against your livestock, if the money is gone." [17]So they brought their livestock to Joseph, and Joseph gave them bread in exchange for the horses, for the stocks of sheep and cattle, and the asses; thus he provided them with bread that year in exchange for all their livestock. [18]And when that year was ended, they came to him the next year and said to him, "We cannot hide from my lord that, with all the money and animal stocks consigned to my lord, nothing is left at my lord's disposal save our persons and our farmland. [19]Let us not perish before your eyes, both we and our land. Take us and our land in exchange for bread, and we with our land will be serfs to Pharaoh; provide the seed, that we may live and not die, and that the land may not become a waste."

[20]So Joseph gained possession of all the farm land of Egypt for Pharaoh, every Egyptian having sold his field because the famine was too much for them; thus the land passed over to Pharaoh. [21]And he removed the population town by town,[b] from one end of Egypt's border to the other. [22]Only the land of the priests he did not take over, for the priests had an allotment from Pharaoh, and they lived off the allotment which Pharaoh had made to them; therefore they did not sell their land.

[23]Then Joseph said to the people, "Whereas I have this day acquired you and your land for

הָרָעָב: 14 וַיְלַקֵּט יוֹסֵף אֶת־כָּל־הַכֶּסֶף הַנִּמְצָא בְאֶרֶץ־מִצְרַיִם וּבְאֶרֶץ כְּנַעַן בַּשֶּׁבֶר אֲשֶׁר־הֵם שֹׁבְרִים וַיָּבֵא יוֹסֵף אֶת־הַכֶּסֶף בֵּיתָה פַרְעֹה: 15 וַיִּתֹּם הַכֶּסֶף מֵאֶרֶץ מִצְרַיִם וּמֵאֶרֶץ כְּנַעַן וַיָּבֹאוּ כָל־מִצְרַיִם אֶל־יוֹסֵף לֵאמֹר הָבָה־לָּנוּ לֶחֶם וְלָמָּה נָמוּת נֶגְדֶּךָ כִּי אָפֵס כָּסֶף: 16 וַיֹּאמֶר יוֹסֵף הָבוּ מִקְנֵיכֶם וְאֶתְּנָה לָכֶם בְּמִקְנֵיכֶם אִם־אָפֵס כָּסֶף: 17 וַיָּבִיאוּ אֶת־מִקְנֵיהֶם אֶל־יוֹסֵף וַיִּתֵּן לָהֶם יוֹסֵף לֶחֶם בַּסּוּסִים וּבְמִקְנֵה הַצֹּאן וּבְמִקְנֵה הַבָּקָר וּבַחֲמֹרִים וַיְנַהֲלֵם בַּלֶּחֶם בְּכָל־מִקְנֵהֶם בַּשָּׁנָה הַהִוא: 18 וַתִּתֹּם הַשָּׁנָה הַהִוא וַיָּבֹאוּ אֵלָיו בַּשָּׁנָה הַשֵּׁנִית וַיֹּאמְרוּ לוֹ לֹא־נְכַחֵד מֵאֲדֹנִי כִּי אִם־תַּם הַכֶּסֶף וּמִקְנֵה הַבְּהֵמָה אֶל־אֲדֹנִי לֹא נִשְׁאַר לִפְנֵי אֲדֹנִי בִּלְתִּי אִם־גְּוִיָּתֵנוּ וְאַדְמָתֵנוּ: 19 לָמָּה נָמוּת לְעֵינֶיךָ גַּם־אֲנַחְנוּ גַּם אַדְמָתֵנוּ קְנֵה־אֹתָנוּ וְאֶת־אַדְמָתֵנוּ בַּלָּחֶם וְנִהְיֶה אֲנַחְנוּ וְאַדְמָתֵנוּ עֲבָדִים לְפַרְעֹה וְתֶן־זֶרַע וְנִחְיֶה וְלֹא נָמוּת וְהָאֲדָמָה לֹא תֵשָׁם: 20 וַיִּקֶן יוֹסֵף אֶת־כָּל־אַדְמַת מִצְרַיִם לְפַרְעֹה כִּי־מָכְרוּ מִצְרַיִם אִישׁ שָׂדֵהוּ כִּי־חָזַק עֲלֵהֶם הָרָעָב וַתְּהִי הָאָרֶץ לְפַרְעֹה: 21 וְאֶת־הָעָם הֶעֱבִיר אֹתוֹ לֶעָרִים מִקְצֵה גְבוּל־מִצְרַיִם וְעַד־קָצֵהוּ: 22 רַק אַדְמַת הַכֹּהֲנִים לֹא קָנָה כִּי חֹק לַכֹּהֲנִים מֵאֵת פַּרְעֹה וְאָכְלוּ אֶת־חֻקָּם אֲשֶׁר נָתַן לָהֶם פַּרְעֹה עַל־כֵּן לֹא מָכְרוּ אֶת־אַדְמָתָם: 23 וַיֹּאמֶר יוֹסֵף אֶל־הָעָם הֵן קָנִיתִי אֶתְכֶם הַיּוֹם וְאֶת־אַדְמַתְכֶם לְפַרְעֹה הֵא־לָכֶם

---

b   *Meaning of Heb. uncertain.*

Pharaoh, here is seed for you to sow the land.
²⁴And when harvest comes, you shall give
one-fifth to Pharaoh, and four-fifths shall be
yours as seed for the fields and as food for you
and those in your households, and as nourishment for your children." ²⁵And they said, "You
have saved our lives! We are grateful to my lord,
and we shall be serfs to Pharaoh." ²⁶And Joseph
made it into a land law in Egypt, which is still
valid, that a fifth should be Pharaoh's; only the
land of the priests did not become Pharaoh's.

²⁷Thus Israel settled in the country of Egypt,
in the region of Goshen; they acquired holdings
in it, and were fertile and increased greatly.

VA-YEḤI

²⁸Jacob lived seventeen years in the land of
Egypt, so that the span of Jacob's life came to
one hundred and forty-seven years. ²⁹And when
the time approached for Israel to die, he summoned his son Joseph and said to him, "Do me
this favor, place your hand under my thigh as
a pledge of your steadfast loyalty: please do not
bury me in Egypt. ³⁰When I lie down with my
fathers, take me up from Egypt and bury me in
their burial-place." He replied, "I will do as you
have spoken." ³¹And he said, "Swear to me."
And he swore to him. Then Israel bowed at the
head of the bed.

48
Some time afterward, Joseph was told,
"Your father is ill." So he took with him his two
sons, Manasseh and Ephraim. ²When Jacob was
told, "Your son Joseph has come to see you,"
Israel summoned his strength and sat up in bed.

³And Jacob said to Joseph, "El Shaddai appeared to me at Luz in the land of Canaan, and
He blessed me, ⁴and said to me, 'I will make you
fertile and numerous, making of you a community of peoples; and I will assign this land

זֶ֥רַע וּזְרַעְתֶּ֖ם אֶת־הָאֲדָמָֽה: 24 וְהָיָה֙
בַּתְּבוּאֹ֔ת וּנְתַתֶּ֥ם חֲמִישִׁ֖ית לְפַרְעֹ֑ה
וְאַרְבַּ֣ע הַיָּדֹ֡ת יִהְיֶ֣ה לָכֶם֩ לְזֶ֨רַע הַשָּׂדֶ֤ה
וּֽלְאָכְלְכֶם֙ וְלַאֲשֶׁ֣ר בְּבָתֵּיכֶ֔ם וְלֶאֱכֹ֖ל
לְטַפְּכֶֽם: 25 וַיֹּאמְר֖וּ הֶחֱיִתָ֑נוּ נִמְצָא־חֵן֙
בְּעֵינֵ֣י אֲדֹנִ֔י וְהָיִ֥ינוּ עֲבָדִ֖ים לְפַרְעֹֽה:
26 וַיָּ֣שֶׂם אֹתָ֣הּ יוֹסֵ֡ף לְחֹק֩ עַד־הַיּ֨וֹם הַזֶּ֜ה
עַל־אַדְמַ֤ת מִצְרַ֙יִם֙ לְפַרְעֹ֖ה לַחֹ֑מֶשׁ רַ֗ק
אַדְמַ֤ת הַכֹּֽהֲנִים֙ לְבַדָּ֔ם לֹ֥א הָיְתָ֖ה
לְפַרְעֹֽה:
27 וַיֵּ֧שֶׁב יִשְׂרָאֵ֛ל בְּאֶ֥רֶץ מִצְרַ֖יִם בְּאֶ֣רֶץ גֹּ֑שֶׁן
וַיֵּאָחֲז֣וּ בָ֔הּ וַיִּפְר֥וּ וַיִּרְבּ֖וּ מְאֹֽד:

ויחי

28 וַיְחִ֤י יַֽעֲקֹב֙ בְּאֶ֣רֶץ מִצְרַ֔יִם שְׁבַ֥ע עֶשְׂרֵ֖ה
שָׁנָ֑ה וַיְהִ֤י יְמֵֽי־יַֽעֲקֹב֙ שְׁנֵ֣י חַיָּ֔יו שֶׁ֤בַע שָׁנִים֙
וְאַרְבָּעִ֣ים וּמְאַ֣ת שָׁנָֽה: 29 וַיִּקְרְב֣וּ יְמֵֽי־
יִשְׂרָאֵל֮ לָמוּת֒ וַיִּקְרָ֣א ׀ לִבְנ֣וֹ לְיוֹסֵ֗ף וַיֹּ֤אמֶר
ל֙וֹ אִם־נָ֨א מָצָ֤אתִי חֵן֙ בְּעֵינֶ֔יךָ שִֽׂים־נָ֥א
יָדְךָ֖ תַּ֣חַת יְרֵכִ֑י וְעָשִׂ֤יתָ עִמָּדִי֙ חֶ֣סֶד וֶאֱמֶ֔ת
אַל־נָ֥א תִקְבְּרֵ֖נִי בְּמִצְרָֽיִם: 30 וְשָֽׁכַבְתִּי֙ עִם־
אֲבֹתַ֔י וּנְשָׂאתַ֙נִי֙ מִמִּצְרַ֔יִם וּקְבַרְתַּ֖נִי
בִּקְבֻֽרָתָ֑ם וַיֹּאמַ֕ר אָֽנֹכִ֖י אֶֽעֱשֶׂ֥ה כִדְבָרֶֽךָ:
31 וַיֹּ֗אמֶר הִשָּֽׁבְעָה֙ לִ֔י וַיִּשָּׁבַ֖ע ל֑וֹ וַיִּשְׁתַּ֥חוּ
יִשְׂרָאֵ֖ל עַל־רֹ֥אשׁ הַמִּטָּֽה: פ

מח
וַיְהִ֗י אַֽחֲרֵי֙ הַדְּבָרִ֣ים הָאֵ֔לֶּה
וַיֹּ֣אמֶר לְיוֹסֵ֔ף הִנֵּ֥ה אָבִ֖יךָ חֹלֶ֑ה וַיִּקַּ֞ח
אֶת־שְׁנֵ֤י בָנָיו֙ עִמּ֔וֹ אֶת־מְנַשֶּׁ֖ה וְאֶת־
אֶפְרָֽיִם: 2 וַיַּגֵּ֣ד לְיַֽעֲקֹ֗ב וַיֹּ֕אמֶר הִנֵּ֛ה בִּנְךָ֥
יוֹסֵ֖ף בָּ֣א אֵלֶ֑יךָ וַיִּתְחַזֵּק֙ יִשְׂרָאֵ֔ל וַיֵּ֖שֶׁב
עַל־הַמִּטָּֽה:
3 וַיֹּ֤אמֶר יַֽעֲקֹב֙ אֶל־יוֹסֵ֔ף אֵ֥ל שַׁדַּ֛י נִרְאָֽה־
אֵלַ֥י בְּל֖וּז בְּאֶ֣רֶץ כְּנָ֑עַן וַיְבָ֖רֶךְ אֹתִֽי:
4 וַיֹּ֣אמֶר אֵלַ֗י הִנְנִ֤י מַפְרְךָ֙ וְהִרְבִּיתִ֔ךָ

to your offspring to come for an everlasting possession.' 5Now, your two sons, who were born to you in the land of Egypt before I came to you in Egypt, shall be mine; Ephraim and Manasseh shall be mine no less than Reuben and Simeon. 6But progeny born to you after them shall be yours; they shall be recorded instead*a* of their brothers in their inheritance. 7I [do this because], when I was returning from Paddan, Rachel died, to my sorrow, while I was journeying in the land of Canaan, when still some distance short of Ephrath; and I buried her there on the road to Ephrath"—now Bethlehem.

8Noticing Joseph's sons, Israel asked, "Who are these?" 9And Joseph said to his father, "They are my sons, whom God has given me here." "Bring them up to me," he said, "that I may bless them." 10Now Israel's eyes were dim with age; he could not see. So [Joseph] brought them close to him, and he kissed them and embraced them. 11And Israel said to Joseph, "I never expected to see you again, and here God has let me see your children as well."

12Joseph then removed them from his knees, and bowed low with his face to the ground. 13Joseph took the two of them, Ephraim with his right hand—to Israel's left—and Manasseh with his left hand—to Israel's right—and brought them close to him. 14But Israel stretched out his right hand and laid it on Ephraim's head, though he was the younger, and his left hand on Manasseh's head—thus crossing his hands—although Manasseh was the first-born. 15And he blessed Joseph, saying,

"The God in whose ways my fathers Abraham
  and Isaac walked,
The God who has been my shepherd from my
  birth to this day—
16The Angel who has redeemed me from all
  harm—
Bless the lads.

---

a Lit. "under the name."

105

וּנְתַתִּ֜יךָ לִקְהַ֣ל עַמִּ֗ים וְנָ֨תַתִּ֜י אֶת־הָאָ֧רֶץ הַזֹּ֛את לְזַרְעֲךָ֥ אַחֲרֶ֖יךָ אֲחֻזַּ֥ת עוֹלָֽם׃ 5וְעַתָּ֡ה שְׁנֵֽי־בָנֶיךָ֩ הַנּוֹלָדִ֨ים לְךָ֜ בְּאֶ֣רֶץ מִצְרַ֗יִם עַד־בֹּאִ֥י אֵלֶ֛יךָ מִצְרַ֖יְמָה לִי־הֵ֑ם אֶפְרַ֙יִם֙ וּמְנַשֶּׁ֔ה כִּרְאוּבֵ֥ן וְשִׁמְע֖וֹן יִֽהְיוּ־לִֽי׃ 6וּמוֹלַדְתְּךָ֛ אֲשֶׁר־הוֹלַ֥דְתָּ אַחֲרֵיהֶ֖ם לְךָ֣ יִֽהְי֑וּ עַ֣ל שֵׁ֧ם אֲחֵיהֶ֛ם יִקָּרְא֖וּ בְּנַחֲלָתָֽם׃ 7וַאֲנִ֣י ׀ בְּבֹאִ֣י מִפַּדָּ֗ן מֵ֩תָה֩ עָלַ֨י רָחֵ֜ל בְּאֶ֤רֶץ כְּנַ֙עַן֙ בַּדֶּ֔רֶךְ בְּע֥וֹד כִּבְרַת־אֶ֖רֶץ לָבֹ֣א אֶפְרָ֑תָה וָאֶקְבְּרֶ֤הָ שָּׁם֙ בְּדֶ֣רֶךְ אֶפְרָ֔ת הִ֖וא בֵּ֥ית לָֽחֶם׃ 8וַיַּ֥רְא יִשְׂרָאֵ֖ל אֶת־בְּנֵ֣י יוֹסֵ֑ף וַיֹּ֖אמֶר מִי־אֵֽלֶּה׃ 9וַיֹּ֤אמֶר יוֹסֵף֙ אֶל־אָבִ֔יו בָּנַ֣י הֵ֔ם אֲשֶׁר־נָֽתַן־לִ֥י אֱלֹהִ֖ים בָּזֶ֑ה וַיֹּאמַ֕ר קָֽחֶם־נָ֥א אֵלַ֖י וַאֲבָרֲכֵֽם׃ 10וְעֵינֵ֤י יִשְׂרָאֵל֙ כָּֽבְד֣וּ מִזֹּ֔קֶן לֹ֥א יוּכַ֖ל לִרְא֑וֹת וַיַּגֵּ֤שׁ אֹתָם֙ אֵלָ֔יו וַיִּשַּׁ֥ק לָהֶ֖ם וַיְחַבֵּ֥ק לָהֶֽם׃ 11וַיֹּ֤אמֶר יִשְׂרָאֵל֙ אֶל־יוֹסֵ֔ף רְאֹ֥ה פָנֶ֖יךָ לֹ֣א פִלָּ֑לְתִּי וְהִנֵּ֨ה הֶרְאָ֥ה אֹתִ֛י אֱלֹהִ֖ים גַּ֥ם אֶת־זַרְעֶֽךָ׃ 12וַיּוֹצֵ֥א יוֹסֵ֛ף אֹתָ֖ם מֵעִ֣ם בִּרְכָּ֑יו וַיִּשְׁתַּ֥חוּ לְאַפָּ֖יו אָֽרְצָה׃ 13וַיִּקַּ֣ח יוֹסֵף֮ אֶת־שְׁנֵיהֶם֒ אֶת־אֶפְרַ֤יִם בִּֽימִינוֹ֙ מִשְּׂמֹ֣אל יִשְׂרָאֵ֔ל וְאֶת־מְנַשֶּׁ֥ה בִשְׂמֹאל֖וֹ מִימִ֣ין יִשְׂרָאֵ֑ל וַיַּגֵּ֖שׁ אֵלָֽיו׃ 14וַיִּשְׁלַח֩ יִשְׂרָאֵ֨ל אֶת־יְמִינ֜וֹ וַיָּ֣שֶׁת עַל־רֹ֣אשׁ אֶפְרַ֗יִם וְה֣וּא הַצָּעִ֔יר וְאֶת־שְׂמֹאל֖וֹ עַל־רֹ֣אשׁ מְנַשֶּׁ֑ה שִׂכֵּל֙ אֶת־יָדָ֔יו כִּ֥י מְנַשֶּׁ֖ה הַבְּכֽוֹר׃ 15וַיְבָ֥רֶךְ אֶת־יוֹסֵ֖ף וַיֹּאמַ֑ר הָֽאֱלֹהִ֡ים אֲשֶׁר֩ הִתְהַלְּכ֨וּ אֲבֹתַ֤י לְפָנָיו֙ אַבְרָהָ֣ם וְיִצְחָ֔ק הָֽאֱלֹהִים֙ הָרֹעֶ֣ה אֹתִ֔י מֵעוֹדִ֖י עַד־הַיּ֥וֹם הַזֶּֽה׃ 16הַמַּלְאָךְ֩ הַגֹּאֵ֨ל אֹתִ֜י מִכָּל־רָ֗ע יְבָרֵךְ֮ אֶת־הַנְּעָרִים֒

In them may my name be recalled,
And the names of my fathers Abraham and
   Isaac,
And may they be teeming multitudes upon
   the earth."

[17] When Joseph saw that his father was placing his right hand on Ephraim's head, he thought it wrong; so he took hold of his father's hand to move it from Ephraim's head to Manasseh's. [18] "Not so, Father," Joseph said to his father, "for the other is the first-born; place your right hand on his head." [19] But his father objected, saying, "I know, my son, I know. He too shall become a people, and he too shall be great. Yet his younger brother shall be greater than he, and his offspring shall be plentiful enough for nations." [20] So he blessed them that day, saying, "By you shall Israel invoke blessings, saying: God make you like Ephraim and Manasseh." Thus he put Ephraim before Manasseh.

[21] Then Israel said to Joseph, "I am about to die; but God will be with you and bring you back to the land of your fathers. [22] And now, I assign to you one portion[b] more than to your brothers, which I wrested from the Amorites with my sword and bow."

49

And Jacob called his sons and said, "Come together that I may tell you what is to befall you in days to come.

[2] Assemble and hearken, O sons of Jacob;
Hearken to Israel your father:

[3] Reuben, you are my first-born,
My might and first fruit of my vigor,
Exceeding in rank
And exceeding in honor.
[4] Unstable as water, you shall excel no longer;
For when you mounted your father's bed,
You brought disgrace—my couch he
   mounted!

ויִּקְרָא בָהֶם שְׁמִי
וְשֵׁם אֲבֹתַי אַבְרָהָם וְיִצְחָק
וְיִדְגּוּ לָרֹב בְּקֶרֶב הָאָרֶץ:
17 וַיַּרְא יוֹסֵף כִּי־יָשִׁית אָבִיו יַד־יְמִינוֹ
עַל־רֹאשׁ אֶפְרַיִם וַיֵּרַע בְּעֵינָיו וַיִּתְמֹךְ
יַד־אָבִיו לְהָסִיר אֹתָהּ מֵעַל רֹאשׁ־אֶפְרַיִם
עַל־רֹאשׁ מְנַשֶּׁה: 18 וַיֹּאמֶר יוֹסֵף אֶל־אָבִיו
לֹא־כֵן אָבִי כִּי־זֶה הַבְּכֹר שִׂים יְמִינְךָ
עַל־רֹאשׁוֹ: 19 וַיְמָאֵן אָבִיו וַיֹּאמֶר יָדַעְתִּי
בְנִי יָדַעְתִּי גַּם־הוּא יִהְיֶה־לְּעָם וְגַם־הוּא
יִגְדָּל וְאוּלָם אָחִיו הַקָּטֹן יִגְדַּל מִמֶּנּוּ וְזַרְעוֹ
יִהְיֶה מְלֹא־הַגּוֹיִם: 20 וַיְבָרֲכֵם בַּיּוֹם הַהוּא
לֵאמוֹר בְּךָ יְבָרֵךְ יִשְׂרָאֵל לֵאמֹר יְשִׂמְךָ
אֱלֹהִים כְּאֶפְרַיִם וְכִמְנַשֶּׁה וַיָּשֶׂם אֶת־
אֶפְרַיִם לִפְנֵי מְנַשֶּׁה:
21 וַיֹּאמֶר יִשְׂרָאֵל אֶל־יוֹסֵף הִנֵּה אָנֹכִי מֵת
וְהָיָה אֱלֹהִים עִמָּכֶם וְהֵשִׁיב אֶתְכֶם אֶל־
אֶרֶץ אֲבֹתֵיכֶם: 22 וַאֲנִי נָתַתִּי לְךָ שְׁכֶם
אַחַד עַל־אַחֶיךָ אֲשֶׁר לָקַחְתִּי מִיַּד הָאֱמֹרִי
בְּחַרְבִּי וּבְקַשְׁתִּי: פ

מט וַיִּקְרָא יַעֲקֹב אֶל־בָּנָיו וַיֹּאמֶר
הֵאָסְפוּ וְאַגִּידָה לָכֶם אֵת אֲשֶׁר־יִקְרָא
אֶתְכֶם בְּאַחֲרִית הַיָּמִים:
2 הִקָּבְצוּ וְשִׁמְעוּ בְּנֵי יַעֲקֹב
וְשִׁמְעוּ אֶל־יִשְׂרָאֵל אֲבִיכֶם:

3 רְאוּבֵן בְּכֹרִי אַתָּה
כֹּחִי וְרֵאשִׁית אוֹנִי
יֶתֶר שְׂאֵת
וְיֶתֶר עָז:
4 פַּחַז כַּמַּיִם אַל־תּוֹתַר
כִּי עָלִיתָ מִשְׁכְּבֵי אָבִיךָ
אָז חִלַּלְתָּ יְצוּעִי עָלָה: פ

---

b   *Meaning of Heb.* shekhem *uncertain; others "mountain slope."*

⁵Simeon and Levi are a pair;
Their weapons are tools of lawlessness.
⁶Let not my person be included in their
   council,
Let not my being be counted in their assem-
   bly.
For when angry they slay men,
And when pleased they maim oxen.
⁷Cursed be their anger so fierce,
And their wrath so relentless.
I will divide them in Jacob,
Scatter them in Israel.

⁸You, O Judah, your brothers shall praise;
Your hand shall be on the nape of your foes;
Your father's sons shall bow low to you.
⁹Judah is a lion's whelp;
On prey, my son, have you grown.
He crouches, lies down like a lion,
Like *a*-the king of beasts-*a*—who dare rouse
   him?
¹⁰The scepter shall not depart from Judah,
Nor the ruler's staff from between his feet;
So that tribute shall come to him^b
And the homage of peoples be his.

¹¹He tethers his ass to a vine,
His ass's foal to a choice vine;
He washes his garment in wine,
His robe in blood of grapes.
^{12c}-His eyes are darker than wine;
His teeth are whiter than milk.-^c

¹³Zebulun shall dwell by the seashore;
He shall be a haven for ships,
And his flank shall rest on Sidon.

¹⁴Issachar is a strong-boned ass,
Crouching among the sheepfolds.

5 שִׁמְע֥וֹן וְלֵוִ֖י אַחִ֑ים
כְּלֵ֥י חָמָ֖ס מְכֵרֹתֵיהֶֽם:
6 בְּסֹדָם֙ אַל־תָּבֹ֣א נַפְשִׁ֔י
בִּקְהָלָ֖ם אַל־תֵּחַ֣ד כְּבֹדִ֑י
כִּ֤י בְאַפָּם֙ הָ֣רְגוּ אִ֔ישׁ
וּבִרְצֹנָ֖ם עִקְּרוּ־שֽׁוֹר:
7 אָר֤וּר אַפָּם֙ כִּ֣י עָ֔ז
וְעֶבְרָתָ֖ם כִּ֣י קָשָׁ֑תָה
אֲחַלְּקֵ֣ם בְּיַעֲקֹ֔ב
וַאֲפִיצֵ֖ם בְּיִשְׂרָאֵֽל: ס

8 יְהוּדָ֗ה אַתָּה֙ יוֹד֣וּךָ אַחֶ֔יךָ
יָדְךָ֖ בְּעֹ֣רֶף אֹיְבֶ֑יךָ
יִשְׁתַּחֲו֥וּ לְךָ֖ בְּנֵ֥י אָבִֽיךָ:
9 גּ֤וּר אַרְיֵה֙ יְהוּדָ֔ה
מִטֶּ֖רֶף בְּנִ֣י עָלִ֑יתָ
כָּרַ֨ע רָבַ֧ץ כְּאַרְיֵ֛ה
וּכְלָבִ֖יא מִ֥י יְקִימֶֽנּוּ:
10 לֹֽא־יָס֥וּר שֵׁ֙בֶט֙ מִֽיהוּדָ֔ה
וּמְחֹקֵ֖ק מִבֵּ֣ין רַגְלָ֑יו
עַ֚ד כִּֽי־יָבֹ֣א שילה שִׁילֹ֔ה
וְל֖וֹ יִקְּהַ֥ת עַמִּֽים:

11 אֹסְרִ֤י לַגֶּ֙פֶן֙ עירה עִיר֔וֹ
וְלַשֹּׂרֵקָ֖ה בְּנִ֣י אֲתֹנ֑וֹ
כִּבֵּ֤ס בַּיַּ֙יִן֙ לְבֻשׁ֔וֹ
וּבְדַם־עֲנָבִ֖ים סוּתֹֽה:
12 חַכְלִילִ֥י עֵינַ֖יִם מִיָּ֑יִן
וּלְבֶן־שִׁנַּ֖יִם מֵחָלָֽב: פ

13 זְבוּלֻ֕ן לְח֥וֹף יַמִּ֖ים יִשְׁכֹּ֑ן
וְהוּא֙ לְח֣וֹף אֳנִיֹּ֔ת
וְיַרְכָת֖וֹ עַל־צִידֹֽן: ס

14 יִשָּׂשכָ֖ר חֲמֹ֣ר גָּ֑רֶם
רֹבֵ֖ץ בֵּ֥ין הַֽמִּשְׁפְּתָֽיִם:

---

a-a   Heb. *labi, another word for "lion."*
b   *Shiloh, understood as shai loh "tribute to him," following*
    Midrash; cf. Isa. 18.7. Meaning of Heb. uncertain; lit. "Until he
    comes to Shiloh."
c-c   Or "His eyes are dark from wine,
    And his teeth are white from milk."

¹⁵When he saw how good was security,
And how pleasant was the country,
He bent his shoulder to the burden,
And became a toiling serf.

¹⁶Dan shall govern his people,
As one of the tribes of Israel.
¹⁷Dan shall be a serpent by the road,
A viper by the path,
That bites the horse's heels
So that his rider is thrown backward.

¹⁸I wait for Your deliverance, O LORD!

¹⁹Gad shall be raided by raiders,
But he shall raid at their heels.

²⁰Asher's bread shall be rich,
And he shall yield royal dainties.

²¹Naphtali is a hind let loose,
Which yields lovely fawns.

²²ᵈ⁻Joseph is a wild ass,
A wild ass by a spring
—Wild colts on a hillside.⁻ᵈ

²³Archers bitterly assailed him;
They shot at him and harried him.
²⁴Yet his bow stayed taut,
And his armsᵉ were made firm
By the hands of the Mighty One of Jacob—
There, the Shepherd, the Rock of Israel—
²⁵The God of your father who helps you,
And Shaddai who blesses you
With blessings of heaven above,
Blessings of the deep that couches below,
Blessings of the breast and womb.

---

d-d   Others "Joseph is a fruitful bough,
      A fruitful bough by a spring,
      Its branches run over a wall."
e   Heb. "the arms of his hands."

15 וַיַּרְא מְנֻחָה כִּי טוֹב
וְאֶת־הָאָרֶץ כִּי נָעֵמָה
וַיֵּט שִׁכְמוֹ לִסְבֹּל
וַיְהִי לְמַס־עֹבֵד׃ ס

16 דָּן יָדִין עַמּוֹ
כְּאַחַד שִׁבְטֵי יִשְׂרָאֵל׃
17 יְהִי־דָן נָחָשׁ עֲלֵי־דֶרֶךְ
שְׁפִיפֹן עֲלֵי־אֹרַח
הַנֹּשֵׁךְ עִקְּבֵי־סוּס
וַיִּפֹּל רֹכְבוֹ אָחוֹר׃

18 לִישׁוּעָתְךָ קִוִּיתִי יְהוָה׃

19 גָּד גְּדוּד יְגוּדֶנּוּ
וְהוּא יָגֻד עָקֵב׃ ס

20 מֵאָשֵׁר שְׁמֵנָה לַחְמוֹ
וְהוּא יִתֵּן מַעֲדַנֵּי־מֶלֶךְ׃ ס

21 נַפְתָּלִי אַיָּלָה שְׁלֻחָה
הַנֹּתֵן אִמְרֵי־שָׁפֶר׃ ס

22 בֵּן פֹּרָת יוֹסֵף
בֵּן פֹּרָת עֲלֵי־עָיִן
בָּנוֹת צָעֲדָה עֲלֵי־שׁוּר׃

23 וַיְמָרֲרֻהוּ וָרֹבּוּ
וַיִּשְׂטְמֻהוּ בַּעֲלֵי חִצִּים׃
24 וַתֵּשֶׁב בְּאֵיתָן קַשְׁתּוֹ
וַיָּפֹזּוּ זְרֹעֵי יָדָיו
מִידֵי אֲבִיר יַעֲקֹב
מִשָּׁם רֹעֶה אֶבֶן יִשְׂרָאֵל׃
25 מֵאֵל אָבִיךָ וְיַעְזְרֶךָ
וְאֵת שַׁדַּי וִיבָרְכֶךָּ
בִּרְכֹת שָׁמַיִם מֵעָל
בִּרְכֹת תְּהוֹם רֹבֶצֶת תָּחַת
בִּרְכֹת שָׁדַיִם וָרָחַם׃

26 f-The blessings of your father
Surpass the blessings of my ancestors,
To the utmost bounds of the eternal hills.-f
May they rest on the head of Joseph,
On the brow of the elect of his brothers.

27Benjamin is a ravenous wolf;
In the morning he consumes the foe,g
And in the evening he divides the spoil."

28All these were the tribes of Israel, twelve in number, and this is what their father said to them as he bade them farewell, addressing to each a parting word appropriate to him.

29Then he instructed them, saying to them, "I am about to be gathered to my kin. Bury me with my fathers in the cave which is in the field of Ephron the Hittite, 30the cave which is in the field of Machpelah, facing Mamre, in the land of Canaan, the field that Abraham bought from Ephron the Hittite for a burial site—31there Abraham and his wife Sarah were buried; there Isaac and his wife Rebekah were buried; and there I buried Leah—32the field and the cave in it, bought from the Hittites." 33When Jacob finished his instructions to his sons, he drew his feet into the bed and, breathing his last, he was gathered to his people.

50 Joseph flung himself upon his father's face and wept over him and kissed him. 2Then Joseph ordered the physicians in his service to embalm his father, and the physicians embalmed Israel. 3It required forty days, for such is the full period of embalming. The Egyptians bewailed him seventy days; 4and when the wailing period was over, Joseph spoke to Pharaoh's court, saying, "Do me this favor, and lay this

26 בִּרְכֹ֣ת אָבִ֗יךָ
גָּֽבְרוּ֙ עַל־בִּרְכֹ֣ת הוֹרַ֔י
עַֽד־תַּאֲוַ֖ת גִּבְעֹ֣ת עוֹלָ֑ם
תִּֽהְיֶ֙יןָ֙ לְרֹ֣אשׁ יוֹסֵ֔ף
וּלְקָדְקֹ֖ד נְזִ֥יר אֶחָֽיו׃ פ

27 בִּנְיָמִין֙ זְאֵ֣ב יִטְרָ֔ף
בַּבֹּ֖קֶר יֹ֣אכַל עַ֑ד
וְלָעֶ֖רֶב יְחַלֵּ֥ק שָׁלָֽל׃

28 כָּל־אֵ֛לֶּה שִׁבְטֵ֥י יִשְׂרָאֵ֖ל שְׁנֵ֣ים עָשָׂ֑ר וְ֠זֹאת אֲשֶׁר־דִּבֶּ֨ר לָהֶ֤ם אֲבִיהֶם֙ וַיְבָ֣רֶךְ אוֹתָ֔ם אִ֗ישׁ אֲשֶׁ֧ר כְּבִרְכָת֛וֹ בֵּרַ֖ךְ אֹתָֽם׃ 29 וַיְצַ֣ו אוֹתָ֗ם וַיֹּ֤אמֶר אֲלֵהֶם֙ אֲנִי֙ נֶאֱסָ֣ף אֶל־עַמִּ֔י קִבְר֥וּ אֹתִ֖י אֶל־אֲבֹתָ֑י אֶל־הַ֨מְּעָרָ֔ה אֲשֶׁ֥ר בִּשְׂדֵ֖ה עֶפְר֥וֹן הַֽחִתִּֽי׃ 30 בַּ֠מְּעָרָ֞ה אֲשֶׁ֨ר בִּשְׂדֵ֤ה הַמַּכְפֵּלָה֙ אֲשֶׁ֣ר עַל־פְּנֵי־מַמְרֵ֔א בְּאֶ֖רֶץ כְּנָ֑עַן אֲשֶׁר֩ קָנָ֨ה אַבְרָהָ֜ם אֶת־הַשָּׂדֶ֗ה מֵאֵ֛ת עֶפְרֹ֥ן הַֽחִתִּ֖י לַאֲחֻזַּת־קָֽבֶר׃ 31 שָׁ֣מָּה קָֽבְר֞וּ אֶת־אַבְרָהָ֗ם וְאֵת֙ שָׂרָ֣ה אִשְׁתּ֔וֹ שָׁ֚מָּה קָֽבְר֣וּ אֶת־יִצְחָ֔ק וְאֵ֖ת רִבְקָ֣ה אִשְׁתּ֑וֹ וְשָׁ֥מָּה קָבַ֖רְתִּי אֶת־לֵאָֽה׃ 32 מִקְנֵ֧ה הַשָּׂדֶ֛ה וְהַמְּעָרָ֥ה אֲשֶׁר־בּ֖וֹ מֵאֵ֥ת בְּנֵי־חֵֽת׃ 33 וַיְכַ֤ל יַעֲקֹב֙ לְצַוֺּ֣ת אֶת־בָּנָ֔יו וַיֶּאֱסֹ֥ף רַגְלָ֖יו אֶל־הַמִּטָּ֑ה וַיִּגְוַ֖ע וַיֵּאָ֥סֶף אֶל־עַמָּֽיו׃

נ וַיִּפֹּ֥ל יוֹסֵ֖ף עַל־פְּנֵ֣י אָבִ֑יו וַיֵּ֥בְךְּ עָלָ֖יו וַיִּשַּׁק־לֽוֹ׃ 2 וַיְצַ֨ו יוֹסֵ֤ף אֶת־עֲבָדָיו֙ אֶת־הָרֹ֣פְאִ֔ים לַחֲנֹ֖ט אֶת־אָבִ֑יו וַיַּחַנְט֥וּ הָרֹפְאִ֖ים אֶת־יִשְׂרָאֵֽל׃ 3 וַיִּמְלְאוּ־לוֹ֙ אַרְבָּעִ֣ים י֔וֹם כִּ֛י כֵּ֥ן יִמְלְא֖וּ יְמֵ֣י הַחֲנֻטִ֑ים וַיִּבְכּ֥וּ אֹת֛וֹ מִצְרַ֖יִם שִׁבְעִ֥ים יֽוֹם׃ 4 וַיַּֽעַבְרוּ֙ יְמֵ֣י בְכִית֔וֹ וַיְדַבֵּ֣ר יוֹסֵ֔ף אֶל־בֵּ֥ית פַּרְעֹ֖ה לֵאמֹ֑ר אִם־נָ֨א מָצָ֤אתִי חֵן֙ בְּעֵ֣ינֵיכֶ֔ם דַּבְּרוּ־

---

f-f Meaning of Heb. uncertain.
g Meaning of Heb. uncertain; others "booty."

appeal before Pharaoh: 5'My father made me swear, saying, "I am about to die. Be sure to bury me in the grave which I made ready for myself in the land of Canaan." Now, therefore, let me go up and bury my father; then I shall return.'"
6And Pharaoh said, "Go up and bury your father, as he made you promise on oath."

7So Joseph went up to bury his father; and with him went up all the officials of Pharaoh, the senior members of his court, and all of Egypt's dignitaries, 8together with all of Joseph's household, his brothers, and his father's household; only their children, their flocks, and their herds were left in the region of Goshen. 9Chariots, too, and horsemen went up with him; it was a very large troop.

10When they came to Goren^a ha-Atad, which is beyond the Jordan, they held there a very great and solemn lamentation; and he observed a mourning period of seven days for his father. 11And when the Canaanite inhabitants of the land saw the mourning at Goren ha-Atad, they said, "This is a solemn mourning on the part of the Egyptians." That is why it was named Abel-mizraim,^b which is beyond the Jordan. 12Thus his sons did for him as he had instructed them. 13His sons carried him to the land of Canaan, and buried him in the cave of the field of Machpelah, the field near Mamre, which Abraham had bought for a burial site from Ephron the Hittite. 14After burying his father, Joseph returned to Egypt, he and his brothers and all who had gone up with him to bury his father.

15When Joseph's brothers saw that their father was dead, they said, "What if Joseph still bears a grudge against us and pays us back for all the wrong that we did him!" 16So they sent this message to Joseph, "Before his death your

נָא בְּאׇזְנֵי פַרְעֹה לֵאמֹר: 5 אָבִי הִשְׁבִּיעַנִי לֵאמֹר הִנֵּה אָנֹכִי מֵת בְּקִבְרִי אֲשֶׁר כָּרִיתִי לִי בְּאֶרֶץ כְּנַעַן שָׁמָּה תִּקְבְּרֵנִי וְעַתָּה אֶעֱלֶה־נָּא וְאֶקְבְּרָה אֶת־אָבִי וְאָשׁוּבָה: 6 וַיֹּאמֶר פַּרְעֹה עֲלֵה וּקְבֹר אֶת־אָבִיךָ כַּאֲשֶׁר הִשְׁבִּיעֶךָ: 7 וַיַּעַל יוֹסֵף לִקְבֹּר אֶת־אָבִיו וַיַּעֲלוּ אִתּוֹ כׇּל־עַבְדֵי פַרְעֹה זִקְנֵי בֵיתוֹ וְכֹל זִקְנֵי אֶרֶץ־מִצְרָיִם: 8 וְכֹל בֵּית יוֹסֵף וְאֶחָיו וּבֵית אָבִיו רַק טַפָּם וְצֹאנָם וּבְקָרָם עָזְבוּ בְּאֶרֶץ גֹּשֶׁן: 9 וַיַּעַל עִמּוֹ גַּם־רֶכֶב גַּם־פָּרָשִׁים וַיְהִי הַמַּחֲנֶה כָּבֵד מְאֹד: 10 וַיָּבֹאוּ עַד־גֹּרֶן הָאָטָד אֲשֶׁר בְּעֵבֶר הַיַּרְדֵּן וַיִּסְפְּדוּ־שָׁם מִסְפֵּד גָּדוֹל וְכָבֵד מְאֹד וַיַּעַשׂ לְאָבִיו אֵבֶל שִׁבְעַת יָמִים: 11 וַיַּרְא יוֹשֵׁב הָאָרֶץ הַכְּנַעֲנִי אֶת־הָאֵבֶל בְּגֹרֶן הָאָטָד וַיֹּאמְרוּ אֵבֶל־כָּבֵד זֶה לְמִצְרָיִם עַל־כֵּן קָרָא שְׁמָהּ אָבֵל מִצְרַיִם אֲשֶׁר בְּעֵבֶר הַיַּרְדֵּן: 12 וַיַּעֲשׂוּ בָנָיו לוֹ כֵּן כַּאֲשֶׁר צִוָּם: 13 וַיִּשְׂאוּ אֹתוֹ בָנָיו אַרְצָה כְּנַעַן וַיִּקְבְּרוּ אֹתוֹ בִּמְעָרַת שְׂדֵה הַמַּכְפֵּלָה אֲשֶׁר קָנָה אַבְרָהָם אֶת־הַשָּׂדֶה לַאֲחֻזַּת־קֶבֶר מֵאֵת עֶפְרֹן הַחִתִּי עַל־פְּנֵי מַמְרֵא: 14 וַיָּשׇׁב יוֹסֵף מִצְרַיְמָה הוּא וְאֶחָיו וְכׇל־הָעֹלִים אִתּוֹ לִקְבֹּר אֶת־אָבִיו אַחֲרֵי קׇבְרוֹ אֶת־אָבִיו:

15 וַיִּרְאוּ אֲחֵי־יוֹסֵף כִּי־מֵת אֲבִיהֶם וַיֹּאמְרוּ לוּ יִשְׂטְמֵנוּ יוֹסֵף וְהָשֵׁב יָשִׁיב לָנוּ אֵת כׇּל־הָרָעָה אֲשֶׁר גָּמַלְנוּ אֹתוֹ: 16 וַיְצַוּוּ אֶל־יוֹסֵף לֵאמֹר אָבִיךָ צִוָּה לִפְנֵי מוֹתוֹ לֵאמֹר: 17 כֹּה־תֹאמְרוּ לְיוֹסֵף אָנָּא שָׂא

---

a Or "the threshing floor of."
b Interpreted as "the mourning of the Egyptians."

father left this instruction: [17]So shall you say to Joseph, 'Forgive, I urge you, the offense and guilt of your brothers who treated you so harshly.' Therefore, please forgive the offense of the servants of the God of your father." And Joseph was in tears as they spoke to him.

[18]His brothers went to him themselves, flung themselves before him, and said, "We are prepared to be your slaves." [19]But Joseph said to them, "Have no fear! Am I a substitute for God? [20]Besides, although you intended me harm, God intended it for good, so as to bring about the present result—the survival of many people. [21]And so, fear not. I will sustain you and your children." Thus he reassured them, speaking kindly to them.

[22]So Joseph and his father's household remained in Egypt. Joseph lived one hundred and ten years. [23]Joseph lived to see children of the third generation of Ephraim; the children of Machir son of Manasseh were likewise born upon Joseph's knees. [24]At length, Joseph said to his brothers, "I am about to die. God will surely take notice of you and bring you up from this land to the land that He promised on oath to Abraham, to Isaac, and to Jacob." [25]So Joseph made the sons of Israel swear, saying, "When God has taken notice of you, you shall carry up my bones from here."

[26]Joseph died at the age of one hundred and ten years; and he was embalmed and placed in a coffin in Egypt.

נָא פֶּשַׁע אַחֶיךָ וְחַטָּאתָם כִּי־רָעָה גְמָלוּךָ וְעַתָּה שָׂא נָא לְפֶשַׁע עַבְדֵי אֱלֹהֵי אָבִיךָ וַיֵּבְךְּ יוֹסֵף בְּדַבְּרָם אֵלָיו: [18]וַיֵּלְכוּ גַּם־אֶחָיו וַיִּפְּלוּ לְפָנָיו וַיֹּאמְרוּ הִנֶּנּוּ לְךָ לַעֲבָדִים: [19]וַיֹּאמֶר אֲלֵהֶם יוֹסֵף אַל־תִּירָאוּ כִּי הֲתַחַת אֱלֹהִים אָנִי: [20]וְאַתֶּם חֲשַׁבְתֶּם עָלַי רָעָה אֱלֹהִים חֲשָׁבָהּ לְטֹבָה לְמַעַן עֲשֹׂה כַּיּוֹם הַזֶּה לְהַחֲיֹת עַם־רָב: [21]וְעַתָּה אַל־תִּירָאוּ אָנֹכִי אֲכַלְכֵּל אֶתְכֶם וְאֶת־טַפְּכֶם וַיְנַחֵם אוֹתָם וַיְדַבֵּר עַל־לִבָּם:

[22]וַיֵּשֶׁב יוֹסֵף בְּמִצְרַיִם הוּא וּבֵית אָבִיו וַיְחִי יוֹסֵף מֵאָה וָעֶשֶׂר שָׁנִים: [23]וַיַּרְא יוֹסֵף לְאֶפְרַיִם בְּנֵי שִׁלֵּשִׁים* גַּם בְּנֵי מָכִיר בֶּן־מְנַשֶּׁה יֻלְּדוּ עַל־בִּרְכֵּי יוֹסֵף: [24]וַיֹּאמֶר יוֹסֵף אֶל־אֶחָיו אָנֹכִי מֵת וֵאלֹהִים פָּקֹד יִפְקֹד אֶתְכֶם וְהֶעֱלָה אֶתְכֶם מִן־הָאָרֶץ הַזֹּאת אֶל־הָאָרֶץ אֲשֶׁר נִשְׁבַּע לְאַבְרָהָם לְיִצְחָק וּלְיַעֲקֹב: [25]וַיַּשְׁבַּע יוֹסֵף אֶת־בְּנֵי יִשְׂרָאֵל לֵאמֹר פָּקֹד יִפְקֹד אֱלֹהִים אֶתְכֶם וְהַעֲלִתֶם אֶת־עַצְמֹתַי מִזֶּה: [26]וַיָּמָת יוֹסֵף בֶּן־מֵאָה וָעֶשֶׂר שָׁנִים וַיַּחַנְטוּ אֹתוֹ וַיִּישֶׂם בָּאָרוֹן בְּמִצְרָיִם:*

תם ונשלם תהילה לאל בורא עולם

v. 23. ס׳ רבתי לפי מהדורת לעטעריס
v. 26. למדינחאי סכום הפסוקים של ספר 1,534 וחציו
27.40

EXODUS

1 **SHEMOT**
These are the names of the sons of Israel who came to Egypt with Jacob, each coming with his household: [2]Reuben, Simeon, Levi, and Judah; [3]Issachar, Zebulun, and Benjamin; [4]Dan and Naphtali, Gad and Asher. [5]The total number of persons that were of Jacob's issue came to seventy, Joseph being already in Egypt. [6]Joseph died, and all his brothers, and all that generation. [7]But the Israelites were fertile and prolific; they multiplied and increased very greatly, so that the land was filled with them.

[8]A new king arose over Egypt who did not know Joseph. [9]And he said to his people, "Look, the Israelite people are much too numerous for us. [10]Let us deal shrewdly with them, so that they may not increase; otherwise in the event of war they may join our enemies in fighting against us and [a]-rise from the ground."-[a] [11]So they set taskmasters over them to oppress them with forced labor; and they built garrison cities[b] for Pharaoh: Pithom and Raamses. [12]But the more they were oppressed, the more they increased and spread out, so that the [Egyptians] came to dread the Israelites.

[13]The Egyptians ruthlessly imposed upon the Israelites [14c]-the various labors that they made them perform. Ruthlessly-[c] they made life bitter for them with harsh labor at mortar and bricks and with all sorts of tasks in the field.

[15]The king of Egypt spoke to the Hebrew midwives, one of whom was named Shiphrah and

שמות

א וְאֵ֗לֶּה שְׁמוֹת֙ בְּנֵ֣י יִשְׂרָאֵ֔ל הַבָּאִ֖ים מִצְרָ֑יְמָה אֵ֣ת יַעֲקֹ֔ב אִ֥ישׁ וּבֵית֖וֹ בָּֽאוּ: ² רְאוּבֵ֣ן שִׁמְע֔וֹן לֵוִ֖י וִֽיהוּדָֽה: ³ יִשָּׂשכָ֥ר זְבוּלֻ֖ן וּבִנְיָמִֽן: ⁴ דָּ֥ן וְנַפְתָּלִ֖י גָּ֥ד וְאָשֵֽׁר: ⁵ וַֽיְהִ֗י כָּל־נֶ֛פֶשׁ יֹצְאֵ֥י יֶֽרֶךְ־יַעֲקֹ֖ב שִׁבְעִ֣ים נָ֑פֶשׁ וְיוֹסֵ֖ף הָיָ֥ה בְמִצְרָֽיִם: ⁶ וַיָּ֤מָת יוֹסֵף֙ וְכָל־אֶחָ֔יו וְכֹ֖ל הַדּ֥וֹר הַהֽוּא: ⁷ וּבְנֵ֣י יִשְׂרָאֵ֗ל פָּר֧וּ וַֽיִּשְׁרְצ֛וּ וַיִּרְבּ֥וּ וַיַּֽעַצְמ֖וּ בִּמְאֹ֣ד מְאֹ֑ד וַתִּמָּלֵ֥א הָאָ֖רֶץ אֹתָֽם: פ

⁸ וַיָּ֥קָם מֶֽלֶךְ־חָדָ֖שׁ עַל־מִצְרָ֑יִם אֲשֶׁ֥ר לֹֽא־יָדַ֖ע אֶת־יוֹסֵֽף: ⁹ וַיֹּ֖אמֶר אֶל־עַמּ֑וֹ הִנֵּ֗ה עַ֚ם בְּנֵ֣י יִשְׂרָאֵ֔ל רַ֥ב וְעָצ֖וּם מִמֶּֽנּוּ: ¹⁰ הָ֚בָה נִֽתְחַכְּמָ֖ה ל֑וֹ פֶּן־יִרְבֶּ֗ה וְהָיָ֞ה כִּֽי־תִקְרֶ֤אנָה מִלְחָמָה֙ וְנוֹסַ֤ף גַּם־הוּא֙ עַל־שֹׂ֣נְאֵ֔ינוּ וְנִלְחַם־בָּ֖נוּ וְעָלָ֥ה מִן־הָאָֽרֶץ: ¹¹ וַיָּשִׂ֤ימוּ עָלָיו֙ שָׂרֵ֣י מִסִּ֔ים לְמַ֥עַן עַנֹּת֖וֹ בְּסִבְלֹתָ֑ם וַיִּ֜בֶן עָרֵ֤י מִסְכְּנוֹת֙ לְפַרְעֹ֔ה אֶת־פִּתֹ֖ם וְאֶת־רַֽעַמְסֵֽס: ¹² וְכַֽאֲשֶׁר֙ יְעַנּ֣וּ אֹת֔וֹ כֵּ֥ן יִרְבֶּ֖ה וְכֵ֣ן יִפְרֹ֑ץ וַיָּקֻ֕צוּ מִפְּנֵ֖י בְּנֵ֥י יִשְׂרָאֵֽל:

¹³ וַיַּעֲבִ֧דוּ מִצְרַ֛יִם אֶת־בְּנֵ֥י יִשְׂרָאֵ֖ל בְּפָֽרֶךְ: ¹⁴ וַיְמָרֲר֨וּ אֶת־חַיֵּיהֶ֜ם בַּעֲבֹדָ֣ה קָשָׁ֗ה בְּחֹ֨מֶר֙ וּבִלְבֵנִ֔ים וּבְכָל־עֲבֹדָ֖ה בַּשָּׂדֶ֑ה אֵ֚ת כָּל־עֲבֹ֣דָתָ֔ם אֲשֶׁר־עָבְד֥וּ בָהֶ֖ם בְּפָֽרֶךְ: ¹⁵ וַיֹּ֨אמֶר֙ מֶ֣לֶךְ מִצְרַ֔יִם לַֽמְיַלְּדֹ֖ת הָֽעִבְרִיֹּ֑ת אֲשֶׁ֨ר שֵׁ֤ם הָֽאַחַת֙ שִׁפְרָ֔ה וְשֵׁ֥ם הַשֵּׁנִ֖ית

---

a-a Meaning perhaps from their wretched condition, cf. Hos. 2.2; or "gain ascendancy over the country." Others "get them up out of the land."

b Others "store cities."

c-c Brought up from the end of the verse for clarity.

the other Puah, 16saying, "When you deliver the Hebrew women, look at the birthstool:*d* if it is a boy, kill him; if it is a girl, let her live." 17The midwives, fearing God, did not do as the king of Egypt had told them; they let the boys live. 18So the king of Egypt summoned the midwives and said to them, "Why have you done this thing, letting the boys live?" 19The midwives said to Pharaoh, "Because the Hebrew women are not like the Egyptian women: they are vigorous. Before the midwife can come to them, they have given birth." 20And God dealt well with the midwives; and the people multiplied and increased greatly. 21And because the midwives feared God, He established households*e* for them. 22Then Pharaoh charged all his people, saying, "Every boy that is born you shall throw into the Nile, but let every girl live."

2 A certain man of the house of Levi went and married a Levite woman. 2The woman conceived and bore a son; and when she saw how beautiful he was, she hid him for three months. 3When she could hide him no longer, she got a wicker basket for him and caulked it with bitumen and pitch. She put the child into it and placed it among the reeds by the bank of the Nile. 4And his sister stationed herself at a distance, to learn what would befall him.

5The daughter of Pharaoh came down to bathe in the Nile, while her maidens walked along the Nile. She spied the basket among the reeds and sent her slave girl to fetch it. 6When she opened it, she saw that it was a child, a boy crying. She took pity on it and said, "This must be a Hebrew child." 7Then his sister said to Pharaoh's daughter, "Shall I go and get you a Hebrew nurse to suckle the child for you?" 8And

---

פּוּעָה: 16 וַיֹּאמֶר בְּיַלֶּדְכֶן אֶת־הָעִבְרִיּוֹת וּרְאִיתֶן עַל־הָאָבְנָיִם אִם־בֵּן הוּא וַהֲמִתֶּן אֹתוֹ וְאִם־בַּת הִיא וָחָיָה: 17 וַתִּירֶאןָ הַמְיַלְּדֹת אֶת־הָאֱלֹהִים וְלֹא עָשׂוּ כַּאֲשֶׁר דִּבֶּר אֲלֵיהֶן מֶלֶךְ מִצְרָיִם וַתְּחַיֶּיןָ אֶת־הַיְלָדִים: 18 וַיִּקְרָא מֶלֶךְ־מִצְרַיִם לַמְיַלְּדֹת וַיֹּאמֶר לָהֶן מַדּוּעַ עֲשִׂיתֶן הַדָּבָר הַזֶּה וַתְּחַיֶּיןָ אֶת־הַיְלָדִים: 19 וַתֹּאמַרְןָ הַמְיַלְּדֹת אֶל־פַּרְעֹה כִּי לֹא כַנָּשִׁים הַמִּצְרִיֹּת הָעִבְרִיֹּת כִּי־חָיוֹת הֵנָּה בְּטֶרֶם תָּבוֹא אֲלֵהֶן הַמְיַלֶּדֶת וְיָלָדוּ: 20 וַיֵּיטֶב אֱלֹהִים לַמְיַלְּדֹת וַיִּרֶב הָעָם וַיַּעַצְמוּ מְאֹד: 21 וַיְהִי כִּי־יָרְאוּ הַמְיַלְּדֹת אֶת־הָאֱלֹהִים וַיַּעַשׂ לָהֶם בָּתִּים: 22 וַיְצַו פַּרְעֹה לְכָל־עַמּוֹ לֵאמֹר כָּל־הַבֵּן הַיִּלּוֹד הַיְאֹרָה תַּשְׁלִיכֻהוּ וְכָל־הַבַּת תְּחַיּוּן: ס

ב וַיֵּלֶךְ אִישׁ מִבֵּית לֵוִי וַיִּקַּח אֶת־בַּת־לֵוִי: 2 וַתַּהַר הָאִשָּׁה וַתֵּלֶד בֵּן וַתֵּרֶא אֹתוֹ כִּי־טוֹב הוּא וַתִּצְפְּנֵהוּ שְׁלֹשָׁה יְרָחִים: 3 וְלֹא־יָכְלָה עוֹד הַצְּפִינוֹ וַתִּקַּח־לוֹ תֵּבַת גֹּמֶא וַתַּחְמְרָה בַחֵמָר וּבַזָּפֶת וַתָּשֶׂם בָּהּ אֶת־הַיֶּלֶד וַתָּשֶׂם בַּסּוּף עַל־שְׂפַת הַיְאֹר: 4 וַתֵּתַצַּב אֲחֹתוֹ מֵרָחֹק לְדֵעָה מַה־יֵּעָשֶׂה לוֹ:

5 וַתֵּרֶד בַּת־פַּרְעֹה לִרְחֹץ עַל־הַיְאֹר וְנַעֲרֹתֶיהָ הֹלְכֹת עַל־יַד הַיְאֹר וַתֵּרֶא אֶת־הַתֵּבָה בְּתוֹךְ הַסּוּף וַתִּשְׁלַח אֶת־אֲמָתָהּ וַתִּקָּחֶהָ: 6 וַתִּפְתַּח וַתִּרְאֵהוּ אֶת־הַיֶּלֶד וְהִנֵּה־נַעַר בֹּכֶה וַתַּחְמֹל עָלָיו וַתֹּאמֶר מִיַּלְדֵי הָעִבְרִים זֶה: 7 וַתֹּאמֶר אֲחֹתוֹ אֶל־בַּת־פַּרְעֹה הַאֵלֵךְ וְקָרָאתִי לָךְ אִשָּׁה מֵינֶקֶת מִן הָעִבְרִיֹּת וְתֵינִק לָךְ אֶת־הַיָּלֶד: 8 וַתֹּאמֶר־לָהּ בַּת־פַּרְעֹה לְכִי

---

d   More exactly, the brick or stone supports used by Egyptian women during childbirth.
e   Meaning of Heb. batim uncertain.

114

Pharaoh's daughter answered, "Yes." So the girl went and called the child's mother. 9And Pharaoh's daughter said to her, "Take this child and nurse it for me, and I will pay your wages." So the woman took the child and nursed it. 10When the child grew up, she brought him to Pharaoh's daughter, who made him her son. She named him Moses,[a] explaining, "I drew him out of the water."

11Some time after that, when Moses had grown up, he went out to his kinsfolk and witnessed their labors. He saw an Egyptian beating a Hebrew, one of his kinsmen. 12He turned this way and that and, seeing no one about, he struck down the Egyptian and hid him in the sand. 13When he went out the next day, he found two Hebrews fighting; so he said to the offender, "Why do you strike your fellow?" 14He retorted, "Who made you chief and ruler over us? Do you mean to kill me as you killed the Egyptian?" Moses was frightened, and thought: Then the matter is known! 15When Pharaoh learned of the matter, he sought to kill Moses; but Moses fled from Pharaoh. He arrived[b] in the land of Midian, and sat down beside a well.

16Now the priest of Midian had seven daughters. They came to draw water, and filled the troughs to water their father's flock; 17but shepherds came and drove them off. Moses rose to their defense, and he watered their flock. 18When they returned to their father Reuel, he said, "How is it that you have come back so soon today?" 19They answered, "An Egyptian rescued us from the shepherds; he even drew water for us and watered the flock." 20He said to his daughters, "Where is he then? Why did you leave the man? Ask him in to break bread." 21Moses consented to stay with the man, and

וַתֵּלֶךְ הָעַלְמָה וַתִּקְרָא אֶת־אֵם הַיָּלֶד: 9 וַתֹּאמֶר לָהּ בַּת־פַּרְעֹה הֵילִיכִי אֶת־הַיֶּלֶד הַזֶּה וְהֵינִקִהוּ לִי וַאֲנִי אֶתֵּן אֶת־שְׂכָרֵךְ וַתִּקַּח הָאִשָּׁה הַיֶּלֶד וַתְּנִיקֵהוּ: 10 וַיִּגְדַּל הַיֶּלֶד וַתְּבִאֵהוּ לְבַת־פַּרְעֹה וַיְהִי־לָהּ לְבֵן וַתִּקְרָא שְׁמוֹ מֹשֶׁה וַתֹּאמֶר כִּי מִן־הַמַּיִם מְשִׁיתִהוּ:

11 וַיְהִי | בַּיָּמִים הָהֵם וַיִּגְדַּל מֹשֶׁה וַיֵּצֵא אֶל־אֶחָיו וַיַּרְא בְּסִבְלֹתָם וַיַּרְא אִישׁ מִצְרִי מַכֶּה אִישׁ־עִבְרִי מֵאֶחָיו: 12 וַיִּפֶן כֹּה וָכֹה וַיַּרְא כִּי אֵין אִישׁ וַיַּךְ אֶת־הַמִּצְרִי וַיִּטְמְנֵהוּ בַּחוֹל: 13 וַיֵּצֵא בַּיּוֹם הַשֵּׁנִי וְהִנֵּה שְׁנֵי־אֲנָשִׁים עִבְרִים נִצִּים וַיֹּאמֶר לָרָשָׁע לָמָּה תַכֶּה רֵעֶךָ: 14 וַיֹּאמֶר מִי שָׂמְךָ לְאִישׁ שַׂר וְשֹׁפֵט עָלֵינוּ הַלְהָרְגֵנִי אַתָּה אֹמֵר כַּאֲשֶׁר הָרַגְתָּ אֶת־הַמִּצְרִי וַיִּירָא מֹשֶׁה וַיֹּאמֶר אָכֵן נוֹדַע הַדָּבָר: 15 וַיִּשְׁמַע פַּרְעֹה אֶת־הַדָּבָר הַזֶּה וַיְבַקֵּשׁ לַהֲרֹג אֶת־מֹשֶׁה וַיִּבְרַח מֹשֶׁה מִפְּנֵי פַרְעֹה וַיֵּשֶׁב בְּאֶרֶץ־מִדְיָן וַיֵּשֶׁב עַל־הַבְּאֵר:

16 וּלְכֹהֵן מִדְיָן שֶׁבַע בָּנוֹת וַתָּבֹאנָה וַתִּדְלֶנָה וַתְּמַלֶּאנָה אֶת־הָרְהָטִים לְהַשְׁקוֹת צֹאן אֲבִיהֶן: 17 וַיָּבֹאוּ הָרֹעִים וַיְגָרְשׁוּם וַיָּקָם מֹשֶׁה וַיּוֹשִׁעָן וַיַּשְׁקְ אֶת־צֹאנָם: 18 וַתָּבֹאנָה אֶל־רְעוּאֵל אֲבִיהֶן וַיֹּאמֶר מַדּוּעַ מִהַרְתֶּן בֹּא הַיּוֹם: 19 וַתֹּאמַרְןָ אִישׁ מִצְרִי הִצִּילָנוּ מִיַּד הָרֹעִים וְגַם־דָּלֹה דָלָה לָנוּ וַיַּשְׁקְ אֶת־הַצֹּאן: 20 וַיֹּאמֶר אֶל־בְּנֹתָיו וְאַיּוֹ לָמָּה זֶּה עֲזַבְתֶּן אֶת־הָאִישׁ קִרְאֶן לוֹ וְיֹאכַל לָחֶם: 21 וַיּוֹאֶל מֹשֶׁה לָשֶׁבֶת אֶת־הָאִישׁ וַיִּתֵּן

---

a   Heb. Mosheh *from Egyptian for "born of"; here associated with*
    mashah *"draw out."*
b   Lit. *"sat" or "settled."*

he gave Moses his daughter Zipporah as wife. [22]She bore a son whom he named Gershom,[c] for he said, "I have been a stranger in a foreign land."

[23]A long time after that, the king of Egypt died. The Israelites were groaning under the bondage and cried out; and their cry for help from the bondage rose up to God. [24]God heard their moaning, and God remembered His covenant with Abraham and Isaac and Jacob. [25]God looked upon the Israelites, and God took notice of them.

3 Now Moses, tending the flock of his father-in-law Jethro, the priest of Midian, drove the flock into the wilderness, and came to Horeb, the mountain of God. [2]An angel of the LORD appeared to him in a blazing fire out of a bush. He gazed, and there was a bush all aflame, yet the bush was not consumed. [3]Moses said, "I must turn aside to look at this marvelous sight; why doesn't the bush burn up?" [4]When the LORD saw that he had turned aside to look, God called to him out of the bush: "Moses! Moses!" He answered, "Here I am." [5]And He said, "Do not come closer. Remove your sandals from your feet, for the place on which you stand is holy ground. [6]I am," He said, "the God of your father, the God of Abraham, the God of Isaac, and the God of Jacob." And Moses hid his face, for he was afraid to look at God.

[7]And the LORD continued, "I have marked well the plight of My people in Egypt and have heeded their outcry because of their taskmasters; yes, I am mindful of their sufferings. [8]I have come down to rescue them from the Egyptians and to bring them out of that land to a good and spacious land, a land flowing with milk and honey, the region of the Canaanites, the Hit-

אֶת־צִפֹּרָה בִתּוֹ לְמֹשֶׁה: 22 וַתֵּלֶד בֵּן וַיִּקְרָא אֶת־שְׁמוֹ גֵּרְשֹׁם כִּי אָמַר גֵּר הָיִיתִי בְּאֶרֶץ נָכְרִיָּה: פ

23 וַיְהִי בַיָּמִים הָרַבִּים הָהֵם וַיָּמָת מֶלֶךְ מִצְרַיִם וַיֵּאָנְחוּ בְנֵי־יִשְׂרָאֵל מִן־הָעֲבֹדָה וַיִּזְעָקוּ וַתַּעַל שַׁוְעָתָם אֶל־הָאֱלֹהִים מִן־ הָעֲבֹדָה: 24 וַיִּשְׁמַע אֱלֹהִים אֶת־נַאֲקָתָם וַיִּזְכֹּר אֱלֹהִים אֶת־בְּרִיתוֹ אֶת־אַבְרָהָם אֶת־יִצְחָק וְאֶת־יַעֲקֹב: 25 וַיַּרְא אֱלֹהִים אֶת־בְּנֵי יִשְׂרָאֵל וַיֵּדַע אֱלֹהִים: ס

ג וּמֹשֶׁה הָיָה רֹעֶה אֶת־צֹאן יִתְרוֹ חֹתְנוֹ כֹּהֵן מִדְיָן וַיִּנְהַג אֶת־הַצֹּאן אַחַר הַמִּדְבָּר וַיָּבֹא אֶל־הַר הָאֱלֹהִים חֹרֵבָה: 2 וַיֵּרָא מַלְאַךְ יְהֹוָה אֵלָיו בְּלַבַּת־אֵשׁ מִתּוֹךְ הַסְּנֶה וַיַּרְא וְהִנֵּה הַסְּנֶה בֹּעֵר בָּאֵשׁ וְהַסְּנֶה אֵינֶנּוּ אֻכָּל: 3 וַיֹּאמֶר מֹשֶׁה אָסֻרָה־נָּא וְאֶרְאֶה אֶת־הַמַּרְאֶה הַגָּדֹל הַזֶּה מַדּוּעַ לֹא־יִבְעַר הַסְּנֶה: 4 וַיַּרְא יְהֹוָה כִּי סָר לִרְאוֹת וַיִּקְרָא אֵלָיו אֱלֹהִים מִתּוֹךְ הַסְּנֶה וַיֹּאמֶר מֹשֶׁה מֹשֶׁה וַיֹּאמֶר הִנֵּנִי: 5 וַיֹּאמֶר אַל־תִּקְרַב הֲלֹם שַׁל־נְעָלֶיךָ מֵעַל רַגְלֶיךָ כִּי הַמָּקוֹם אֲשֶׁר אַתָּה עוֹמֵד עָלָיו אַדְמַת־קֹדֶשׁ הוּא: 6 וַיֹּאמֶר אָנֹכִי אֱלֹהֵי אָבִיךָ אֱלֹהֵי אַבְרָהָם אֱלֹהֵי יִצְחָק וֵאלֹהֵי יַעֲקֹב וַיַּסְתֵּר מֹשֶׁה פָּנָיו כִּי יָרֵא מֵהַבִּיט אֶל־הָאֱלֹהִים: 7 וַיֹּאמֶר יְהֹוָה רָאֹה רָאִיתִי אֶת־עֳנִי עַמִּי אֲשֶׁר בְּמִצְרָיִם וְאֶת־צַעֲקָתָם שָׁמַעְתִּי מִפְּנֵי נֹגְשָׂיו כִּי יָדַעְתִּי אֶת־מַכְאֹבָיו: 8 וָאֵרֵד לְהַצִּילוֹ ׀ מִיַּד מִצְרַיִם וּלְהַעֲלֹתוֹ מִן־הָאָרֶץ הַהִוא אֶל־אֶרֶץ טוֹבָה וּרְחָבָה אֶל־אֶרֶץ זָבַת חָלָב וּדְבָשׁ אֶל־מְקוֹם הַכְּנַעֲנִי וְהַחִתִּי וְהָאֱמֹרִי וְהַפְּרִזִּי וְהַחִוִּי וְהַיְבוּסִי: 9 וְעַתָּה הִנֵּה צַעֲקַת בְּנֵי־יִשְׂרָאֵל

c   *Associated with* ger sham, *"a stranger there."*

116

tites, the Amorites, the Perizzites, the Hivites, and the Jebusites. [9]Now the cry of the Israelites has reached Me; moreover, I have seen how the Egyptians oppress them. [10]Come, therefore, I will send you to Pharaoh, and you shall free My people, the Israelites, from Egypt."

[11]But Moses said to God, "Who am I that I should go to Pharaoh and free the Israelites from Egypt?" [12]And He said, "I will be with you; that shall be your sign that it was I who sent you. And when you have freed the people from Egypt, you shall worship God at this mountain."

[13]Moses said to God, "When I come to the Israelites and say to them, 'The God of your fathers has sent me to you,' and they ask me, 'What is His name?' what shall I say to them?" [14]And God said to Moses, "Ehyeh-Asher-Ehyeh."[a] He continued, "Thus shall you say to the Israelites, 'Ehyeh[b] sent me to you.'" [15]And God said further to Moses, "Thus shall you speak to the Israelites: The LORD,[c] the God of your fathers, the God of Abraham, the God of Isaac, and the God of Jacob, has sent me to you:

This shall be My name forever,
This My appellation for all eternity.

[16]"Go and assemble the elders of Israel and say to them: the LORD, the God of your fathers, the God of Abraham, Isaac, and Jacob, has appeared to me and said, 'I have taken note of you and of what is being done to you in Egypt, [17]and I have declared: I will take you out of the misery of Egypt to the land of the Canaanites, the Hittites, the Amorites, the Perizzites, the Hivites, and the Jebusites, to a land flowing with milk and honey.' [18]They will listen to you; then you shall go with the elders of Israel to the king of Egypt and you shall say to him, 'The LORD, the God of the Hebrews, manifested Himself to us.

בָּאָה אֵלָי וְגַם־רָאִיתִי אֶת־הַלַּחַץ אֲשֶׁר מִצְרַיִם לֹחֲצִים אֹתָם: 10 וְעַתָּה לְכָה וְאֶשְׁלָחֲךָ אֶל־פַּרְעֹה וְהוֹצֵא אֶת־עַמִּי בְנֵי־יִשְׂרָאֵל מִמִּצְרָיִם: 11 וַיֹּאמֶר מֹשֶׁה אֶל־הָאֱלֹהִים מִי אָנֹכִי כִּי אֵלֵךְ אֶל־פַּרְעֹה וְכִי אוֹצִיא אֶת־בְּנֵי יִשְׂרָאֵל מִמִּצְרָיִם: 12 וַיֹּאמֶר כִּי־אֶהְיֶה עִמָּךְ וְזֶה־לְּךָ הָאוֹת כִּי אָנֹכִי שְׁלַחְתִּיךָ בְּהוֹצִיאֲךָ אֶת־הָעָם מִמִּצְרַיִם תַּעַבְדוּן אֶת־הָאֱלֹהִים עַל הָהָר הַזֶּה: 13 וַיֹּאמֶר מֹשֶׁה אֶל־הָאֱלֹהִים הִנֵּה אָנֹכִי בָא אֶל־בְּנֵי יִשְׂרָאֵל וְאָמַרְתִּי לָהֶם אֱלֹהֵי אֲבוֹתֵיכֶם שְׁלָחַנִי אֲלֵיכֶם וְאָמְרוּ־לִי מַה־שְּׁמוֹ מָה אֹמַר אֲלֵהֶם: 14 וַיֹּאמֶר אֱלֹהִים אֶל־מֹשֶׁה אֶהְיֶה אֲשֶׁר אֶהְיֶה וַיֹּאמֶר כֹּה תֹאמַר לִבְנֵי יִשְׂרָאֵל אֶהְיֶה שְׁלָחַנִי אֲלֵיכֶם: 15 וַיֹּאמֶר עוֹד אֱלֹהִים אֶל־מֹשֶׁה כֹּה־תֹאמַר אֶל־בְּנֵי יִשְׂרָאֵל יְהוָֹה אֱלֹהֵי אֲבֹתֵיכֶם אֱלֹהֵי אַבְרָהָם אֱלֹהֵי יִצְחָק וֵאלֹהֵי יַעֲקֹב שְׁלָחַנִי אֲלֵיכֶם זֶה־שְּׁמִי לְעֹלָם וְזֶה זִכְרִי לְדֹר דֹּר: 16 לֵךְ וְאָסַפְתָּ אֶת־זִקְנֵי יִשְׂרָאֵל וְאָמַרְתָּ אֲלֵהֶם יְהוָֹה אֱלֹהֵי אֲבֹתֵיכֶם נִרְאָה אֵלַי אֱלֹהֵי אַבְרָהָם יִצְחָק וְיַעֲקֹב לֵאמֹר פָּקֹד פָּקַדְתִּי אֶתְכֶם וְאֶת־הֶעָשׂוּי לָכֶם בְּמִצְרָיִם: 17 וָאֹמַר אַעֲלֶה אֶתְכֶם מֵעֳנִי מִצְרַיִם אֶל־אֶרֶץ הַכְּנַעֲנִי וְהַחִתִּי וְהָאֱמֹרִי וְהַפְּרִזִּי וְהַחִוִּי וְהַיְבוּסִי אֶל־אֶרֶץ זָבַת חָלָב וּדְבָשׁ: 18 וְשָׁמְעוּ לְקֹלֶךָ וּבָאתָ אַתָּה וְזִקְנֵי יִשְׂרָאֵל אֶל־מֶלֶךְ מִצְרַיִם וַאֲמַרְתֶּם אֵלָיו יְהוָֹה אֱלֹהֵי הָעִבְרִיִּים נִקְרָה עָלֵינוּ וְעַתָּה נֵלֲכָה־נָּא דֶּרֶךְ שְׁלֹשֶׁת יָמִים

---

a   *Meaning of Heb. uncertain; variously translated: "I Am That I Am"; "I Am Who I Am"; "I Will Be What I Will Be"; etc.*

b   *Others "I Am" or "I Will Be."*

c   *The name YHWH (traditionally read Adonai "the LORD") is here associated with the root hayah "to be."*

Now therefore, let us go a distance of three days into the wilderness to sacrifice to the LORD our God.' [19]Yet I know that the king of Egypt will let you go only because of a greater might. [20]So I will stretch out My hand and smite Egypt with various wonders which I will work upon them; after that he shall let you go. [21]And I will dispose the Egyptians favorably toward this people, so that when you go, you will not go away empty-handed. [22]Each woman shall borrow from her neighbor and the lodger in her house objects of silver and gold, and clothing, and you shall put these on your sons and daughters, thus stripping the Egyptians."

4 But Moses spoke up and said, "What if they do not believe me and do not listen to me, but say: The LORD did not appear to you?" [2]The LORD said to him, "What is that in your hand?" And he replied, "A rod." [3]He said, "Cast it on the ground." He cast it on the ground and it became a snake; and Moses recoiled from it. [4]Then the LORD said to Moses, "Put out your hand and grasp it by the tail"—he put out his hand and seized it, and it became a rod in his hand—[5]"that they may believe that the LORD, the God of their fathers, the God of Abraham, the God of Isaac, and the God of Jacob, did appear to you."

[6]The LORD said to him further, "Put your hand into your bosom." He put his hand into his bosom; and when he took it out, his hand was encrusted with snowy scales![a] [7]And He said, "Put your hand back into your bosom."—He put his hand back into his bosom; and when he took it out of his bosom, there it was again like the rest of his body.—[8]"And if they do not believe you or pay heed to the first sign, they will believe the second. [9]And if they are not con-

---

a Cf. Lev. 13.2–3.

בַּמִּדְבָּ֑ר וְנִזְבְּחָ֖ה לַיהֹוָ֥ה אֱלֹהֵֽינוּ: 19 וַאֲנִ֣י יָדַ֔עְתִּי כִּ֣י לֹֽא־יִתֵּ֥ן אֶתְכֶ֛ם מֶ֥לֶךְ מִצְרַ֖יִם לַהֲלֹ֑ךְ וְלֹ֖א בְּיָ֥ד חֲזָקָֽה: 20 וְשָׁלַחְתִּ֤י אֶת־יָדִי֙ וְהִכֵּיתִ֣י אֶת־מִצְרַ֔יִם בְּכֹל֙ נִפְלְאֹתַ֔י אֲשֶׁ֥ר אֶֽעֱשֶׂ֖ה בְּקִרְבּ֑וֹ וְאַחֲרֵי־כֵ֖ן יְשַׁלַּ֥ח אֶתְכֶֽם: 21 וְנָתַתִּ֛י אֶת־חֵ֥ן הָֽעָם־הַזֶּ֖ה בְּעֵינֵ֣י מִצְרָ֑יִם וְהָיָה֙ כִּ֣י תֵֽלֵכ֔וּן לֹ֥א תֵלְכ֖וּ רֵיקָֽם: 22 וְשָׁאֲלָ֨ה אִשָּׁ֤ה מִשְּׁכֶנְתָּהּ֙ וּמִגָּרַ֣ת בֵּיתָ֔הּ כְּלֵי־כֶ֛סֶף וּכְלֵ֥י זָהָ֖ב וּשְׂמָלֹ֑ת וְשַׂמְתֶּ֗ם עַל־בְּנֵיכֶם֙ וְעַל־בְּנֹ֣תֵיכֶ֔ם וְנִצַּלְתֶּ֖ם אֶת־מִצְרָֽיִם:

ד וַיַּ֤עַן מֹשֶׁה֙ וַיֹּ֔אמֶר וְהֵן֙ לֹֽא־יַֽאֲמִ֣ינוּ לִ֔י וְלֹ֥א יִשְׁמְע֖וּ בְּקֹלִ֑י כִּ֣י יֹֽאמְר֔וּ לֹֽא־נִרְאָ֥ה אֵלֶ֖יךָ יְהֹוָֽה: 2 וַיֹּ֧אמֶר אֵלָ֛יו יְהֹוָ֖ה מַזֶּ֣ה בְיָדֶ֑ךָ וַיֹּ֖אמֶר מַטֶּֽה: 3 וַיֹּ֗אמֶר הַשְׁלִיכֵ֣הוּ אַ֔רְצָה וַיַּשְׁלִכֵ֥הוּ אַ֖רְצָה וַיְהִ֣י לְנָחָ֑שׁ וַיָּ֥נׇס מֹשֶׁ֖ה מִפָּנָֽיו: 4 וַיֹּ֤אמֶר יְהֹוָה֙ אֶל־מֹשֶׁ֔ה שְׁלַח֙ יָֽדְךָ֔ וֶֽאֱחֹ֖ז בִּזְנָב֑וֹ וַיִּשְׁלַ֤ח יָדוֹ֙ וַיַּ֣חֲזֶק בּ֔וֹ וַיְהִ֥י לְמַטֶּ֖ה בְּכַפּֽוֹ: 5 לְמַ֣עַן יַֽאֲמִ֔ינוּ כִּֽי־נִרְאָ֥ה אֵלֶ֛יךָ יְהֹוָ֖ה אֱלֹהֵ֣י אֲבֹתָ֑ם אֱלֹהֵ֧י אַבְרָהָ֛ם אֱלֹהֵ֥י יִצְחָ֖ק וֵאלֹהֵ֥י יַעֲקֹֽב:

6 וַיֹּ֩אמֶר֩ יְהֹוָ֨ה ל֜וֹ ע֗וֹד הָֽבֵא־נָ֤א יָֽדְךָ֙ בְּחֵיקֶ֔ךָ וַיָּבֵ֥א יָד֖וֹ בְּחֵיק֑וֹ וַיּ֣וֹצִאָ֔הּ וְהִנֵּ֥ה יָד֖וֹ מְצֹרַ֥עַת כַּשָּֽׁלֶג: 7 וַיֹּ֗אמֶר הָשֵׁ֤ב יָֽדְךָ֙ אֶל־חֵיקֶ֔ךָ וַיָּ֥שֶׁב יָד֖וֹ אֶל־חֵיק֑וֹ וַיּֽוֹצִאָהּ֙ מֵֽחֵיק֔וֹ וְהִנֵּה־שָׁ֖בָה כִּבְשָׂרֽוֹ: 8 וְהָיָה֙ אִם־לֹ֣א יַֽאֲמִ֣ינוּ לָ֔ךְ וְלֹ֣א יִשְׁמְע֔וּ לְקֹ֖ל הָאֹ֣ת הָֽרִאשׁ֑וֹן וְהֶֽאֱמִ֔ינוּ לְקֹ֖ל הָאֹ֥ת הָאַֽחֲרֽוֹן: 9 וְהָיָ֡ה אִם־לֹ֣א יַֽאֲמִ֡ינוּ גַּם֩ לִשְׁנֵ֨י הָֽאֹת֜וֹת הָאֵ֗לֶּה וְלֹ֤א יִשְׁמְעוּן֙ לְקֹלֶ֔ךָ וְלָֽקַחְתָּ֙ מִמֵּימֵ֣י

vinced by both these signs and still do not heed you, take some water from the Nile and pour it on the dry ground, and it—the water that you take from the Nile—will turn to blood on the dry ground."

[10]But Moses said to the LORD, "Please, O Lord, I have never been a man of words, either in times past or now that You have spoken to Your servant; I am slow of speech and slow of tongue." [11]And the LORD said to him, "Who gives man speech? Who makes him dumb or deaf, seeing or blind? Is it not I, the LORD? [12]Now go, and I will be with you as you speak and will instruct you what to say." [13]But he said, "Please, O Lord, make someone else Your agent."[b] [14]The LORD became angry with Moses, and He said, "There is your brother Aaron the Levite. He, I know, speaks readily. Even now he is setting out to meet you, and he will be happy to see you. [15]You shall speak to him and put the words in his mouth—I will be with you and with him as you speak, and tell both of you what to do—[16]and he shall speak for you to the people. Thus he shall serve as your spokesman, with you playing the role of God[c] to him, [17]and take with you this rod, with which you shall perform the signs."

[18]Moses went back to his father-in-law Jether[d] and said to him, "Let me go back to my kinsmen in Egypt and see how they are faring."[e] And Jethro said to Moses, "Go in peace."

[19]The LORD said to Moses in Midian, "Go back to Egypt, for all the men who sought to kill you are dead." [20]So Moses took his wife and sons, mounted them on an ass, and went back to the land of Egypt; and Moses took the rod of God with him.

[21]And the LORD said to Moses, "When you return to Egypt, see that you perform before

הַיְאֹר וְשָׁפַכְתָּ הַיַּבָּשָׁה וְהָיוּ הַמַּיִם אֲשֶׁר תִּקַּח מִן־הַיְאֹר וְהָיוּ לְדָם בַּיַּבָּשֶׁת: 10 וַיֹּאמֶר מֹשֶׁה אֶל־יְהֹוָה בִּי אֲדֹנָי לֹא אִישׁ דְּבָרִים אָנֹכִי גַּם מִתְּמוֹל גַּם מִשִּׁלְשֹׁם גַּם מֵאָז דַּבֶּרְךָ אֶל־עַבְדֶּךָ כִּי כְבַד־פֶּה וּכְבַד לָשׁוֹן אָנֹכִי: 11 וַיֹּאמֶר יְהֹוָה אֵלָיו מִי שָׂם פֶּה לָאָדָם אוֹ מִי־יָשׂוּם אִלֵּם אוֹ חֵרֵשׁ אוֹ פִקֵּחַ אוֹ עִוֵּר הֲלֹא אָנֹכִי יְהֹוָה: 12 וְעַתָּה לֵךְ וְאָנֹכִי אֶהְיֶה עִם־פִּיךָ וְהוֹרֵיתִיךָ אֲשֶׁר תְּדַבֵּר: 13 וַיֹּאמֶר בִּי אֲדֹנָי שְׁלַח־נָא בְּיַד־תִּשְׁלָח: 14 וַיִּחַר־אַף יְהֹוָה בְּמֹשֶׁה וַיֹּאמֶר הֲלֹא אַהֲרֹן אָחִיךָ הַלֵּוִי יָדַעְתִּי כִּי־דַבֵּר יְדַבֵּר הוּא וְגַם הִנֵּה־הוּא יֹצֵא לִקְרָאתֶךָ וְרָאֲךָ וְשָׂמַח בְּלִבּוֹ: 15 וְדִבַּרְתָּ אֵלָיו וְשַׂמְתָּ אֶת־הַדְּבָרִים בְּפִיו וְאָנֹכִי אֶהְיֶה עִם־פִּיךָ וְעִם־פִּיהוּ וְהוֹרֵיתִי אֶתְכֶם אֵת אֲשֶׁר תַּעֲשׂוּן: 16 וְדִבֶּר־הוּא לְךָ אֶל־הָעָם וְהָיָה הוּא יִהְיֶה־לְּךָ לְפֶה וְאַתָּה תִּהְיֶה־לּוֹ לֵאלֹהִים: 17 וְאֶת־הַמַּטֶּה הַזֶּה תִּקַּח בְּיָדֶךָ אֲשֶׁר תַּעֲשֶׂה־בּוֹ אֶת־הָאֹתֹת: פ 18 וַיֵּלֶךְ מֹשֶׁה וַיָּשָׁב אֶל־יֶתֶר חֹתְנוֹ וַיֹּאמֶר לוֹ אֵלְכָה נָּא וְאָשׁוּבָה אֶל־אַחַי אֲשֶׁר־בְּמִצְרַיִם וְאֶרְאֶה הַעוֹדָם חַיִּים וַיֹּאמֶר יִתְרוֹ לְמֹשֶׁה לֵךְ לְשָׁלוֹם: 19 וַיֹּאמֶר יְהֹוָה אֶל־מֹשֶׁה בְּמִדְיָן לֵךְ שֻׁב מִצְרָיִם כִּי־מֵתוּ כָּל־הָאֲנָשִׁים הַמְבַקְשִׁים אֶת־נַפְשֶׁךָ: 20 וַיִּקַּח מֹשֶׁה אֶת־אִשְׁתּוֹ וְאֶת־בָּנָיו וַיַּרְכִּבֵם עַל־הַחֲמֹר וַיָּשָׁב אַרְצָה מִצְרָיִם וַיִּקַּח מֹשֶׁה אֶת־מַטֵּה הָאֱלֹהִים בְּיָדוֹ: 21 וַיֹּאמֶר יְהֹוָה אֶל־מֹשֶׁה בְּלֶכְתְּךָ לָשׁוּב מִצְרַיְמָה רְאֵה כָּל־הַמֹּפְתִים אֲשֶׁר־שַׂמְתִּי

---

b   Lit. "send through whomever You will send."
c   Cf. 7.1.
d   I.e., Jethro.
e   Lit. "whether they are still alive."

Pharaoh all the marvels that I have put within your power. I, however, will stiffen his heart so that he will not let the people go. [22]Then you shall say to Pharaoh, 'Thus says the LORD: Israel is My first-born son. [23]I have said to you, "Let My son go, that he may worship Me," yet you refuse to let him go. Now I will slay your first-born son.'"

[24]At a night encampment on the way, the LORD encountered him and sought to kill him. [25]f So Zipporah took a flint and cut off her son's foreskin, and touched his legs with it, saying, "You are truly a bridegroom of blood to me!" [26]And when He let him alone, she added, "A bridegroom of blood because of the circumcision."

[27]The LORD said to Aaron, "Go to meet Moses in the wilderness." He went and met him at the mountain of God, and he kissed him. [28]Moses told Aaron about all the things that the LORD had committed to him and all the signs about which He had instructed him. [29]Then Moses and Aaron went and assembled all the elders of the Israelites. [30]Aaron repeated all the words that the LORD had spoken to Moses, and he performed the signs in the sight of the people, [31]and the people were convinced. When they heard that the LORD had taken note of the Israelites and that He had seen their plight, they bowed low in homage.

5 Afterward Moses and Aaron went and said to Pharaoh, "Thus says the LORD, the God of Israel: Let My people go that they may celebrate a festival for Me in the wilderness." [2]But Pharaoh said, "Who is the LORD that I should heed Him and let Israel go? I do not know the LORD,

בְּיָדֶ֔ךָ וַעֲשִׂיתָ֥ם לִפְנֵ֖י פַרְעֹ֑ה וַאֲנִי֙ אֲחַזֵּ֣ק אֶת־לִבּ֔וֹ וְלֹ֥א יְשַׁלַּ֖ח אֶת־הָעָֽם׃ 22 וְאָמַרְתָּ֖ אֶל־פַּרְעֹ֑ה כֹּ֚ה אָמַ֣ר יְהֹוָ֔ה בְּנִ֥י בְכֹרִ֖י יִשְׂרָאֵֽל׃ 23 וָאֹמַ֣ר אֵלֶ֗יךָ שַׁלַּ֤ח אֶת־בְּנִי֙ וְיַ֣עַבְדֵ֔נִי וַתְּמָאֵ֖ן לְשַׁלְּח֑וֹ הִנֵּה֙ אָנֹכִ֣י הֹרֵ֔ג אֶת־בִּנְךָ֖ בְּכֹרֶֽךָ׃

24 וַיְהִ֥י בַדֶּ֖רֶךְ בַּמָּל֑וֹן וַיִּפְגְּשֵׁ֣הוּ יְהֹוָ֔ה וַיְבַקֵּ֖שׁ הֲמִיתֽוֹ׃ 25 וַתִּקַּ֣ח צִפֹּרָ֣ה צֹ֗ר וַתִּכְרֹת֙ אֶת־עׇרְלַ֣ת בְּנָ֔הּ וַתַּגַּ֖ע לְרַגְלָ֑יו וַתֹּ֕אמֶר כִּ֧י חֲתַן־דָּמִ֛ים אַתָּ֖ה לִֽי׃ 26 וַיִּ֖רֶף מִמֶּ֑נּוּ אָ֚ז אָֽמְרָ֔ה חֲתַ֥ן דָּמִ֖ים לַמּוּלֹֽת׃ פ

27 וַיֹּ֤אמֶר יְהֹוָה֙ אֶֽל־אַהֲרֹ֔ן לֵ֛ךְ לִקְרַ֥את מֹשֶׁ֖ה הַמִּדְבָּ֑רָה וַיֵּ֗לֶךְ וַֽיִּפְגְּשֵׁ֛הוּ בְּהַ֥ר הָאֱלֹהִ֖ים וַיִּשַּׁק־לֽוֹ׃ 28 וַיַּגֵּ֤ד מֹשֶׁה֙ לְאַ֣הֲרֹ֔ן אֵ֛ת כׇּל־דִּבְרֵ֥י יְהֹוָ֖ה אֲשֶׁ֣ר שְׁלָח֑וֹ וְאֵ֥ת כׇּל־הָאֹתֹ֖ת אֲשֶׁ֥ר צִוָּֽהוּ׃ 29 וַיֵּ֥לֶךְ מֹשֶׁ֖ה וְאַהֲרֹ֑ן וַיַּ֣אַסְפ֔וּ אֶת־כׇּל־זִקְנֵ֖י בְּנֵ֥י יִשְׂרָאֵֽל׃ 30 וַיְדַבֵּ֣ר אַהֲרֹ֔ן אֵ֚ת כׇּל־הַדְּבָרִ֔ים אֲשֶׁר־דִּבֶּ֥ר יְהֹוָ֖ה אֶל־מֹשֶׁ֑ה וַיַּ֥עַשׂ הָאֹתֹ֖ת לְעֵינֵ֥י הָעָֽם׃ 31 וַֽיַּאֲמֵ֖ן הָעָ֑ם וַֽיִּשְׁמְע֡וּ כִּֽי־פָקַ֨ד יְהֹוָ֜ה אֶת־בְּנֵ֣י יִשְׂרָאֵ֗ל וְכִ֤י רָאָה֙ אֶת־עׇנְיָ֔ם וַֽיִּקְּד֖וּ וַיִּֽשְׁתַּחֲוֽוּ׃

ה וְאַחַ֗ר בָּ֚אוּ מֹשֶׁ֣ה וְאַהֲרֹ֔ן וַיֹּאמְר֖וּ אֶל־פַּרְעֹ֑ה כֹּֽה־אָמַ֤ר יְהֹוָה֙ אֱלֹהֵ֣י יִשְׂרָאֵ֔ל שַׁלַּח֙ אֶת־עַמִּ֔י וְיָחֹ֥גּוּ לִ֖י בַּמִּדְבָּֽר׃ 2 וַיֹּ֣אמֶר פַּרְעֹ֔ה מִ֤י יְהֹוָה֙ אֲשֶׁ֣ר אֶשְׁמַ֣ע בְּקֹל֔וֹ לְשַׁלַּ֖ח אֶת־יִשְׂרָאֵ֑ל לֹ֤א יָדַ֙עְתִּי֙ אֶת־יְהֹוָ֔ה וְגַ֥ם

---

f *Meaning of vv. 25–26 uncertain.*

nor will I let Israel go." ³They answered, "The God of the Hebrews has manifested Himself to us. Let us go, we pray, a distance of three days into the wilderness to sacrifice to the LORD our God, lest He strike us with pestilence or sword." ⁴But the king of Egypt said to them, "Moses and Aaron, why do you distract the people from their tasks! Get to your labors!" ⁵And Pharaoh continued, *a*-"The people of the land are already so numerous,-*a* and you would have them cease from their labors!"*b*

⁶That same day Pharaoh charged the task-masters and foremen of the people, saying, ⁷"You shall no longer provide the people with straw for making bricks as heretofore; let them go and gather straw for themselves. ⁸But impose upon them the same quota of bricks as they have been making heretofore; do not reduce it, for they are shirkers; that is why they cry, 'Let us go and sacrifice to our God!' ⁹Let heavier work be laid upon the men; let them keep at it and not pay attention to deceitful promises."

¹⁰So the taskmasters and foremen of the people went out and said to the people, "Thus says Pharaoh: I will not give you any straw. ¹¹You must go and get the straw yourselves wherever you can find it; but there shall be no decrease whatever in your work." ¹²Then the people scattered throughout the land of Egypt to gather stubble for straw. ¹³And the taskmasters pressed them, saying, "You must complete the same work assignment each day as when you had straw." ¹⁴And the foremen of the Israelites, whom Pharaoh's taskmasters had set over them, were beaten. "Why," they were asked, "did you not complete the prescribed amount of bricks, either yesterday or today, as you did before?"

¹⁵Then the foremen of the Israelites came to Pharaoh and cried: "Why do you deal thus with

אֶת־יִשְׂרָאֵל לֹא אֲשַׁלֵּחַ: 3 וַיֹּאמְרוּ אֱלֹהֵי הָעִבְרִים נִקְרָא עָלֵינוּ נֵלֲכָה נָּא דֶּרֶךְ שְׁלֹשֶׁת יָמִים בַּמִּדְבָּר וְנִזְבְּחָה לַיהוָה אֱלֹהֵינוּ פֶּן־יִפְגָּעֵנוּ בַּדֶּבֶר אוֹ בֶחָרֶב: 4 וַיֹּאמֶר אֲלֵהֶם מֶלֶךְ מִצְרַיִם לָמָּה מֹשֶׁה וְאַהֲרֹן תַּפְרִיעוּ אֶת־הָעָם מִמַּעֲשָׂיו לְכוּ לְסִבְלֹתֵיכֶם: 5 וַיֹּאמֶר פַּרְעֹה הֵן־רַבִּים עַתָּה עַם הָאָרֶץ וְהִשְׁבַּתֶּם אֹתָם מִסִּבְלֹתָם: 6 וַיְצַו פַּרְעֹה בַּיּוֹם הַהוּא אֶת־הַנֹּגְשִׂים בָּעָם וְאֶת־שֹׁטְרָיו לֵאמֹר: 7 לֹא תֹאסִפוּן* לָתֵת תֶּבֶן לָעָם לִלְבֹּן הַלְּבֵנִים כִּתְמוֹל שִׁלְשֹׁם הֵם יֵלְכוּ וְקֹשְׁשׁוּ לָהֶם תֶּבֶן: 8 וְאֶת־מַתְכֹּנֶת הַלְּבֵנִים אֲשֶׁר הֵם עֹשִׂים תְּמוֹל שִׁלְשֹׁם תָּשִׂימוּ עֲלֵיהֶם לֹא תִגְרְעוּ מִמֶּנּוּ כִּי־נִרְפִּים הֵם עַל־כֵּן הֵם צֹעֲקִים לֵאמֹר נֵלְכָה נִזְבְּחָה לֵאלֹהֵינוּ: 9 תִּכְבַּד הָעֲבֹדָה עַל־הָאֲנָשִׁים וְיַעֲשׂוּ־בָהּ וְאַל־יִשְׁעוּ בְּדִבְרֵי־שָׁקֶר: 10 וַיֵּצְאוּ נֹגְשֵׂי הָעָם וְשֹׁטְרָיו וַיֹּאמְרוּ אֶל־הָעָם לֵאמֹר כֹּה אָמַר פַּרְעֹה אֵינֶנִּי נֹתֵן לָכֶם תֶּבֶן: 11 אַתֶּם לְכוּ קְחוּ לָכֶם תֶּבֶן מֵאֲשֶׁר תִּמְצָאוּ כִּי אֵין נִגְרָע מֵעֲבֹדַתְכֶם דָּבָר: 12 וַיָּפֶץ הָעָם בְּכָל־אֶרֶץ מִצְרָיִם לְקֹשֵׁשׁ קַשׁ לַתֶּבֶן: 13 וְהַנֹּגְשִׂים אָצִים לֵאמֹר כַּלּוּ מַעֲשֵׂיכֶם דְּבַר־יוֹם בְּיוֹמוֹ כַּאֲשֶׁר בִּהְיוֹת הַתֶּבֶן: 14 וַיֻּכּוּ שֹׁטְרֵי בְּנֵי יִשְׂרָאֵל אֲשֶׁר־שָׂמוּ עֲלֵהֶם נֹגְשֵׂי פַרְעֹה לֵאמֹר מַדּוּעַ לֹא כִלִּיתֶם חָקְכֶם לִלְבֹּן כִּתְמוֹל שִׁלְשֹׁם גַּם־תְּמוֹל גַּם־הַיּוֹם: 15 וַיָּבֹאוּ שֹׁטְרֵי בְּנֵי יִשְׂרָאֵל וַיִּצְעֲקוּ אֶל־פַּרְעֹה לֵאמֹר לָמָּה תַעֲשֶׂה כֹה לַעֲבָדֶיךָ:

v. 7. יתיר א'

---

a-a   Samaritan "Even now they are more numerous than the people of the land," i.e., than the native population (cf. Gen. 23.7).
b   See 1.5–11.

your servants? 16No straw is issued to your servants, yet they demand of us: Make bricks! Thus your servants are being beaten, when the fault is with your own people." 17He replied, "You are shirkers, shirkers! That is why you say, 'Let us go and sacrifice to the Lord.' 18Be off now to your work! No straw shall be issued to you, but you must produce your quota of bricks!"

19Now the foremen of the Israelites found themselves in trouble because of the order, "You must not reduce your daily quantity of bricks." 20As they left Pharaoh's presence, they came upon Moses and Aaron standing in their path, 21and they said to them, "May the Lord look upon you and punish you for making us loathsome to Pharaoh and his courtiers—putting a sword in their hands to slay us." 22Then Moses returned to the Lord and said, "O Lord, why did You bring harm upon this people? Why did You send me? 23Ever since I came to Pharaoh to speak in Your name, he has dealt worse with this people; and still You have not delivered Your people."

6 Then the Lord said to Moses, "You shall soon see what I will do to Pharaoh: he shall let them go because of a greater might; indeed, because of a greater might he shall drive them from his land."

VA'ERA'

2God spoke to Moses and said to him, "I am the Lord. 3I appeared to Abraham, Isaac, and Jacob as El Shaddai, but I did not make Myself known to them by My name יהוה.ᵃ 4I also established My covenant with them, to give them the land of Canaan, the land in which they lived as sojourners. 5I have now heard the moaning of the Israelites because the Egyptians are hold-

---

a   This divine name is traditionally not pronounced; instead, Adonai, "(the) Lord," is regularly substituted for it.

---

16 תֶּ֣בֶן אֵ֥ין נִתָּ֖ן לַעֲבָדֶ֑יךָ וּלְבֵנִ֤ים אֹמְרִ֣ים לָ֙נוּ֙ עֲשׂ֔וּ וְהִנֵּ֧ה עֲבָדֶ֛יךָ מֻכִּ֖ים וְחָטָ֥את עַמֶּֽךָ׃ 17 וַיֹּ֛אמֶר נִרְפִּ֥ים אַתֶּ֖ם נִרְפִּ֑ים עַל־כֵּן֙ אַתֶּ֣ם אֹֽמְרִ֔ים נֵלְכָ֖ה נִזְבְּחָ֥ה לַֽיהוָֽה׃ 18 וְעַתָּה֙ לְכ֣וּ עִבְד֔וּ וְתֶ֖בֶן לֹא־יִנָּתֵ֣ן לָכֶ֑ם וְתֹ֥כֶן לְבֵנִ֖ים תִּתֵּֽנּוּ׃ 19 וַיִּרְא֞וּ שֹֽׁטְרֵ֣י בְנֵֽי־יִשְׂרָאֵ֗ל אֹתָ֖ם בְּרָ֣ע לֵאמֹ֑ר לֹא־תִגְרְע֥וּ מִלִּבְנֵיכֶ֖ם דְּבַר־יֹ֥ום בְּיֹומֹֽו׃ 20 וַֽיִּפְגְּעוּ֙ אֶת־מֹשֶׁ֣ה וְאֶֽת־אַהֲרֹ֔ן נִצָּבִ֖ים לִקְרָאתָ֑ם בְּצֵאתָ֖ם מֵאֵ֥ת פַּרְעֹֽה׃ 21 וַיֹּאמְר֣וּ אֲלֵהֶ֔ם יֵ֧רֶא יְהוָ֛ה עֲלֵיכֶ֖ם וְיִשְׁפֹּ֑ט אֲשֶׁ֧ר הִבְאַשְׁתֶּ֣ם אֶת־רֵיחֵ֗נוּ בְּעֵינֵ֤י פַרְעֹה֙ וּבְעֵינֵ֣י עֲבָדָ֔יו לָֽתֶת־חֶ֥רֶב בְּיָדָ֖ם לְהָרְגֵֽנוּ׃ 22 וַיָּ֧שָׁב מֹשֶׁ֛ה אֶל־יְהוָ֖ה וַיֹּאמַ֑ר אֲדֹנָ֗י לָמָ֤ה הֲרֵעֹ֙תָה֙ לָעָ֣ם הַזֶּ֔ה לָ֥מָּה זֶּ֖ה שְׁלַחְתָּֽנִי׃ 23 וּמֵאָ֞ז בָּ֤אתִי אֶל־פַּרְעֹה֙ לְדַבֵּ֣ר בִּשְׁמֶ֔ךָ הֵרַ֖ע לָעָ֣ם הַזֶּ֑ה וְהַצֵּ֥ל לֹא־הִצַּ֖לְתָּ אֶת־עַמֶּֽךָ׃

ו 1 וַיֹּ֥אמֶר יְהוָ֖ה אֶל־מֹשֶׁ֑ה עַתָּ֣ה תִרְאֶ֔ה אֲשֶׁ֥ר אֶֽעֱשֶׂ֖ה לְפַרְעֹ֑ה כִּ֣י בְיָ֤ד חֲזָקָה֙ יְשַׁלְּחֵ֔ם וּבְיָ֣ד חֲזָקָ֔ה יְגָרְשֵׁ֖ם מֵאַרְצֹֽו׃ ס

ואֵרָא

2 וַיְדַבֵּ֥ר אֱלֹהִ֖ים אֶל־מֹשֶׁ֑ה וַיֹּ֥אמֶר אֵלָ֖יו אֲנִ֥י יְהוָֽה׃ 3 וָאֵרָ֗א אֶל־אַבְרָהָ֛ם אֶל־יִצְחָ֥ק וְאֶֽל־יַעֲקֹ֖ב בְּאֵ֣ל שַׁדָּ֑י וּשְׁמִ֣י יְהוָ֔ה לֹ֥א נֹודַ֖עְתִּי לָהֶֽם׃ 4 וְגַ֨ם הֲקִמֹ֤תִי אֶת־בְּרִיתִי֙ אִתָּ֔ם לָתֵ֥ת לָהֶ֖ם אֶת־אֶ֣רֶץ כְּנָ֑עַן אֵ֛ת אֶ֥רֶץ מְגֻרֵיהֶ֖ם אֲשֶׁר־גָּ֥רוּ בָֽהּ׃ 5 וְגַ֣ם ׀ אֲנִ֣י שָׁמַ֗עְתִּי אֶֽת־נַאֲקַת֙ בְּנֵ֣י יִשְׂרָאֵ֔ל אֲשֶׁ֥ר

ing them in bondage, and I have remembered My covenant. [6]Say, therefore, to the Israelite people: I am the LORD. I will free you from the labors of the Egyptians and deliver you from their bondage. I will redeem you with an outstretched arm and through extraordinary chastisements. [7]And I will take you to be My people, and I will be your God. And you shall know that I, the LORD, am your God who freed you from the labors of the Egyptians. [8]I will bring you into the land which I swore[b] to give to Abraham, Isaac, and Jacob, and I will give it to you for a possession, I the LORD." [9]But when Moses told this to the Israelites, they would not listen to Moses, their spirits crushed by cruel bondage.

[10]The LORD spoke to Moses, saying, [11]"Go and tell Pharaoh king of Egypt to let the Israelites depart from his land." [12]But Moses appealed to the LORD, saying, "The Israelites would not listen to me; how then should Pharaoh heed me, a man of impeded speech!" [13]So the LORD spoke to both Moses and Aaron in regard to the Israelites and Pharaoh king of Egypt, instructing them to deliver the Israelites from the land of Egypt.

[14]The following are the heads of their respective clans.

The sons of Reuben, Israel's first-born: Enoch[c] and Pallu, Hezron and Carmi; those are the families of Reuben. [15]The sons of Simeon: Jemuel, Jamin, Ohad, Jachin, Zohar, and Saul[d] the son of a Canaanite woman; those are the families of Simeon. [16]These are the names of Levi's sons by their lineage: Gershon, Kohath, and Merari; and the span of Levi's life was 137 years. [17]The sons of Gershon: Libni and Shimei, by their families. [18]The sons of Kohath: Amram, Izhar, Hebron, and Uzziel; and the span of

מִצְרַיִם מַעֲבִדִים אֹתָם וָאֶזְכֹּר אֶת־בְּרִיתִֽי׃
[6] לָכֵן אֱמֹר לִבְנֵֽי־יִשְׂרָאֵל אֲנִי יְהֹוָה וְהוֹצֵאתִי אֶתְכֶם מִתַּחַת סִבְלֹת מִצְרַיִם וְהִצַּלְתִּי אֶתְכֶם מֵעֲבֹדָתָם וְגָאַלְתִּי אֶתְכֶם בִּזְרוֹעַ נְטוּיָה וּבִשְׁפָטִים גְּדֹלִֽים׃ [7] וְלָקַחְתִּי אֶתְכֶם לִי לְעָם וְהָיִיתִי לָכֶם לֵֽאלֹהִים וִֽידַעְתֶּם כִּי אֲנִי יְהֹוָה אֱלֹֽהֵיכֶם הַמּוֹצִיא אֶתְכֶם מִתַּחַת סִבְלוֹת מִצְרָֽיִם׃ [8] וְהֵבֵאתִי אֶתְכֶם אֶל־הָאָרֶץ אֲשֶׁר נָשָׂאתִי אֶת־יָדִי לָתֵת אֹתָהּ לְאַבְרָהָם לְיִצְחָק וּֽלְיַעֲקֹב וְנָתַתִּי אֹתָהּ לָכֶם מוֹרָשָׁה אֲנִי יְהֹוָֽה׃ [9] וַיְדַבֵּר מֹשֶׁה כֵּן אֶל־בְּנֵי יִשְׂרָאֵל וְלֹא שָׁמְעוּ אֶל־מֹשֶׁה מִקֹּצֶר רוּחַ וּמֵעֲבֹדָה קָשָֽׁה׃ פ

[10] וַיְדַבֵּר יְהֹוָה אֶל־מֹשֶׁה לֵּאמֹֽר׃ [11] בֹּא דַבֵּר אֶל־פַּרְעֹה מֶלֶךְ מִצְרָיִם וִֽישַׁלַּח אֶת־בְּנֵֽי־יִשְׂרָאֵל מֵאַרְצֽוֹ׃ [12] וַיְדַבֵּר מֹשֶׁה לִפְנֵי יְהֹוָה לֵאמֹר הֵן בְּנֵֽי־יִשְׂרָאֵל לֹֽא־שָׁמְעוּ אֵלַי וְאֵיךְ יִשְׁמָעֵנִי פַרְעֹה וַאֲנִי עֲרַל שְׂפָתָֽיִם׃ פ [13] וַיְדַבֵּר יְהֹוָה אֶל־מֹשֶׁה וְאֶֽל־אַהֲרֹן וַיְצַוֵּם אֶל־בְּנֵי יִשְׂרָאֵל וְאֶל־פַּרְעֹה מֶלֶךְ מִצְרָיִם לְהוֹצִיא אֶת־בְּנֵֽי־יִשְׂרָאֵל מֵאֶרֶץ מִצְרָֽיִם׃ ס

[14] אֵלֶּה רָאשֵׁי בֵית־אֲבֹתָם בְּנֵי רְאוּבֵן בְּכֹר יִשְׂרָאֵל חֲנוֹךְ וּפַלּוּא חֶצְרוֹן וְכַרְמִי אֵלֶּה מִשְׁפְּחֹת רְאוּבֵֽן׃ [15] וּבְנֵי שִׁמְעוֹן יְמוּאֵל וְיָמִין וְאֹהַד וְיָכִין וְצֹחַר וְשָׁאוּל בֶּן־הַֽכְּנַעֲנִית אֵלֶּה מִשְׁפְּחֹת שִׁמְעֽוֹן׃ [16] וְאֵלֶּה שְׁמוֹת בְּנֵֽי־לֵוִי לְתֹלְדֹתָם גֵּרְשׁוֹן וּקְהָת וּמְרָרִי וּשְׁנֵי חַיֵּי לֵוִי שֶׁבַע וּשְׁלֹשִׁים וּמְאַת שָׁנָֽה׃ [17] בְּנֵי גֵרְשׁוֹן לִבְנִי וְשִׁמְעִי לְמִשְׁפְּחֹתָֽם׃ [18] וּבְנֵי קְהָת עַמְרָם וְיִצְהָר וְחֶבְרוֹן וְעֻזִּיאֵל וּשְׁנֵי חַיֵּי קְהָת

---

b   Lit. "raised My hand."
c   Or "Hanoch"; cf. on Gen. 46.9.
d   Or "Shaul"; cf. on Gen. 46.10.

Kohath's life was 133 years. ¹⁹The sons of Merari: Mahli and Mushi. These are the families of the Levites by their lineage.

²⁰Amram took to wife his father's sister Jochebed, and she bore him Aaron and Moses; and the span of Amram's life was 137 years. ²¹The sons of Izhar: Korah, Nepheg, and Zichri. ²²The sons of Uzziel: Mishael, Elzaphan, and Sithri. ²³Aaron took to wife Elisheba, daughter of Amminadab and sister of Nahshon, and she bore him Nadab and Abihu, Eleazar and Ithamar. ²⁴The sons of Korah: Assir, Elkanah, and Abiasaph. Those are the families of the Korahites. ²⁵And Aaron's son Eleazar took to wife one of Putiel's daughters, and she bore him Phinehas. Those are the heads of the fathers' houses of the Levites by their families.

²⁶It is the same Aaron and Moses to whom the LORD said, "Bring forth the Israelites from the land of Egypt, troop by troop." ²⁷It was they who spoke to Pharaoh king of Egypt to free the Israelites from the Egyptians; these are the same Moses and Aaron. ²⁸For when the LORD spoke to Moses in the land of Egypt ²⁹and the LORD said to Moses, "I am the LORD; speak to Pharaoh king of Egypt all that I will tell you," ³⁰Moses appealed to the LORD, saying, "See, I am of impeded speech; how then should Pharaoh heed me!"

7 The LORD replied to Moses, "See, I place you in the role of God to Pharaoh, with your brother Aaron as your prophet.ᵃ ²You shall repeat all that I command you, and your brother Aaron shall speak to Pharaoh to let the Israelites depart from his land. ³But I will harden Pharaoh's heart, that I may multiply My signs and marvels in the land of Egypt. ⁴When Pharaoh

---

שָׁלֹשׁ וּשְׁלֹשִׁים וּמְאַת שָׁנָה: ¹⁹ וּבְנֵי מְרָרִי מַחְלִי וּמוּשִׁי אֵלֶּה מִשְׁפְּחֹת הַלֵּוִי לְתֹלְדֹתָם:

²⁰ וַיִּקַּח עַמְרָם אֶת־יוֹכֶבֶד דֹּדָתוֹ לוֹ לְאִשָּׁה וַתֵּלֶד לוֹ אֶת־אַהֲרֹן וְאֶת־מֹשֶׁה וּשְׁנֵי חַיֵּי עַמְרָם שֶׁבַע וּשְׁלֹשִׁים וּמְאַת שָׁנָה: ²¹ וּבְנֵי יִצְהָר קֹרַח וָנֶפֶג וְזִכְרִי: ²² וּבְנֵי עֻזִּיאֵל מִישָׁאֵל וְאֶלְצָפָן וְסִתְרִי: ²³ וַיִּקַּח אַהֲרֹן אֶת־אֱלִישֶׁבַע בַּת־עַמִּינָדָב אֲחוֹת נַחְשׁוֹן לוֹ לְאִשָּׁה וַתֵּלֶד לוֹ אֶת־נָדָב וְאֶת־אֲבִיהוּא אֶת־אֶלְעָזָר וְאֶת־אִיתָמָר: ²⁴ וּבְנֵי קֹרַח אַסִּיר וְאֶלְקָנָה וַאֲבִיאָסָף אֵלֶּה מִשְׁפְּחֹת הַקָּרְחִי: ²⁵ וְאֶלְעָזָר בֶּן־אַהֲרֹן לָקַח־לוֹ מִבְּנוֹת פּוּטִיאֵל לוֹ לְאִשָּׁה וַתֵּלֶד לוֹ אֶת־פִּינְחָס אֵלֶּה רָאשֵׁי אֲבוֹת הַלְוִיִּם לְמִשְׁפְּחֹתָם:

²⁶ הוּא אַהֲרֹן וּמֹשֶׁה אֲשֶׁר אָמַר יְהוָה לָהֶם הוֹצִיאוּ אֶת־בְּנֵי יִשְׂרָאֵל מֵאֶרֶץ מִצְרַיִם עַל־צִבְאֹתָם: ²⁷ הֵם הַמְדַבְּרִים אֶל־פַּרְעֹה מֶלֶךְ־מִצְרַיִם לְהוֹצִיא אֶת־בְּנֵי־יִשְׂרָאֵל מִמִּצְרָיִם הוּא מֹשֶׁה וְאַהֲרֹן: ²⁸ וַיְהִי בְּיוֹם דִּבֶּר יְהוָה אֶל־מֹשֶׁה בְּאֶרֶץ מִצְרָיִם: פ ²⁹ וַיְדַבֵּר יְהוָה אֶל־מֹשֶׁה לֵּאמֹר אֲנִי יְהוָה דַּבֵּר אֶל־פַּרְעֹה מֶלֶךְ מִצְרַיִם אֵת כָּל־אֲשֶׁר אֲנִי דֹּבֵר אֵלֶיךָ: ³⁰ וַיֹּאמֶר מֹשֶׁה לִפְנֵי יְהוָה הֵן אֲנִי עֲרַל שְׂפָתַיִם וְאֵיךְ יִשְׁמַע אֵלַי פַּרְעֹה: פ

ז וַיֹּאמֶר יְהוָה אֶל־מֹשֶׁה רְאֵה נְתַתִּיךָ אֱלֹהִים לְפַרְעֹה וְאַהֲרֹן אָחִיךָ יִהְיֶה נְבִיאֶךָ: ² אַתָּה תְדַבֵּר אֵת כָּל־אֲשֶׁר אֲצַוֶּךָּ וְאַהֲרֹן אָחִיךָ יְדַבֵּר אֶל־פַּרְעֹה וְשִׁלַּח אֶת־בְּנֵי־יִשְׂרָאֵל מֵאַרְצוֹ: ³ וַאֲנִי אַקְשֶׁה אֶת־לֵב פַּרְעֹה וְהִרְבֵּיתִי אֶת־אֹתֹתַי וְאֶת־ מוֹפְתַי בְּאֶרֶץ מִצְרָיִם: ⁴ וְלֹא־יִשְׁמַע

ᵃ Cf. 4.16.

does not heed you, I will lay My hand upon Egypt and deliver My ranks, My people the Israelites, from the land of Egypt with extraordinary chastisements. [5]And the Egyptians shall know that I am the LORD, when I stretch out My hand over Egypt and bring out the Israelites from their midst." [6]This Moses and Aaron did; as the LORD commanded them, so they did. [7]Moses was eighty years old and Aaron eighty-three, when they made their demand on Pharaoh.

[8]The LORD said to Moses and Aaron, [9]"When Pharaoh speaks to you and says, 'Produce your marvel,' you shall say to Aaron, 'Take your rod and cast it down before Pharaoh.' It shall turn into a serpent." [10]So Moses and Aaron came before Pharaoh and did just as the LORD had commanded: Aaron cast down his rod in the presence of Pharaoh and his courtiers, and it turned into a serpent. [11]Then Pharaoh, for his part, summoned the wise men and the sorcerers; and the Egyptian magicians, in turn, did the same with their spells; [12]each cast down his rod, and they turned into serpents. But Aaron's rod swallowed their rods. [13]Yet Pharaoh's heart stiffened and he did not heed them, as the LORD had said.

[14]And the LORD said to Moses, "Pharaoh is stubborn; he refuses to let the people go. [15]Go to Pharaoh in the morning, as he is coming out to the water, and station yourself before him at the edge of the Nile, taking with you the rod that turned into a snake. [16]And say to him, 'The LORD, the God of the Hebrews, sent me to you to say, "Let My people go that they may worship Me in the wilderness." But you have paid no heed until now. [17]Thus says the LORD, "By this you shall know that I am the LORD." See, I shall strike the water in the Nile with the rod that is in my hand, and it will be turned into blood; [18]and the fish in the Nile will die. The Nile will

אֲלֵכֶם֙ פַּרְעֹ֔ה וְנָתַתִּ֥י אֶת־יָדִ֖י בְּמִצְרָ֑יִם וְהוֹצֵאתִ֨י אֶת־צִבְאֹתַ֜י אֶת־עַמִּ֤י בְנֵֽי־יִשְׂרָאֵל֙ מֵאֶ֣רֶץ מִצְרַ֔יִם בִּשְׁפָטִ֖ים גְּדֹלִֽים׃ [5] וְיָדְע֤וּ מִצְרַ֙יִם֙ כִּֽי־אֲנִ֣י יְהֹוָ֔ה בִּנְטֹתִ֥י אֶת־יָדִ֖י עַל־מִצְרָ֑יִם וְהוֹצֵאתִ֥י אֶת־בְּנֵֽי־יִשְׂרָאֵ֖ל מִתּוֹכָֽם׃ [6] וַיַּ֥עַשׂ מֹשֶׁ֖ה וְאַהֲרֹ֑ן כַּאֲשֶׁ֨ר צִוָּ֧ה יְהֹוָ֛ה אֹתָ֖ם כֵּ֥ן עָשֽׂוּ׃ [7] וּמֹשֶׁה֙ בֶּן־שְׁמֹנִ֣ים שָׁנָ֔ה וְאַֽהֲרֹ֔ן בֶּן־שָׁלֹ֥שׁ וּשְׁמֹנִ֖ים שָׁנָ֑ה בְּדַבְּרָ֖ם אֶל־פַּרְעֹֽה׃ פ

[8] וַיֹּ֤אמֶר יְהֹוָה֙ אֶל־מֹשֶׁ֣ה וְאֶֽל־אַהֲרֹ֔ן לֵאמֹֽר׃ [9] כִּי֩ יְדַבֵּ֨ר אֲלֵכֶ֤ם פַּרְעֹה֙ לֵאמֹ֔ר תְּנ֥וּ לָכֶ֖ם מוֹפֵ֑ת וְאָמַרְתָּ֣ אֶֽל־אַהֲרֹ֗ן קַ֧ח אֶֽת־מַטְּךָ֛ וְהַשְׁלֵ֥ךְ לִפְנֵֽי־פַרְעֹ֖ה יְהִ֥י לְתַנִּֽין׃ [10] וַיָּבֹ֨א מֹשֶׁ֤ה וְאַֽהֲרֹן֙ אֶל־פַּרְעֹ֔ה וַיַּ֣עֲשׂוּ כֵ֔ן כַּאֲשֶׁ֖ר צִוָּ֣ה יְהֹוָ֑ה וַיַּשְׁלֵ֣ךְ אַהֲרֹ֗ן אֶת־מַטֵּ֛הוּ לִפְנֵ֥י פַרְעֹ֖ה וְלִפְנֵ֣י עֲבָדָ֑יו וַיְהִ֖י לְתַנִּֽין׃ [11] וַיִּקְרָא֙ גַּם־פַּרְעֹ֔ה לַחֲכָמִ֖ים וְלַֽמְכַשְּׁפִ֑ים וַיַּֽעֲשׂ֨וּ גַם־הֵ֜ם חַרְטֻמֵּ֥י מִצְרַ֛יִם בְּלַהֲטֵיהֶ֖ם כֵּֽן׃ [12] וַיַּשְׁלִ֙יכוּ֙ אִ֣ישׁ מַטֵּ֔הוּ וַיִּהְי֖וּ לְתַנִּינִ֑ם וַיִּבְלַ֥ע מַטֵּֽה־אַהֲרֹ֖ן אֶת־מַטֹּתָֽם׃ [13] וַיֶּחֱזַק֙ לֵ֣ב פַּרְעֹ֔ה וְלֹ֥א שָׁמַ֖ע אֲלֵהֶ֑ם כַּאֲשֶׁ֖ר דִּבֶּ֥ר יְהֹוָֽה׃ פ

[14] וַיֹּ֤אמֶר יְהֹוָה֙ אֶל־מֹשֶׁ֔ה כָּבֵ֖ד לֵ֣ב פַּרְעֹ֑ה מֵאֵ֖ן לְשַׁלַּ֥ח הָעָֽם׃ [15] לֵ֣ךְ אֶל־פַּרְעֹ֞ה בַּבֹּ֗קֶר הִנֵּה֙ יֹצֵ֣א הַמַּ֔יְמָה וְנִצַּבְתָּ֥ לִקְרָאת֖וֹ עַל־שְׂפַ֣ת הַיְאֹ֑ר וְהַמַּטֶּ֛ה אֲשֶׁר־נֶהְפַּ֥ךְ לְנָחָ֖שׁ תִּקַּ֥ח בְּיָדֶֽךָ׃ [16] וְאָמַרְתָּ֣ אֵלָ֗יו יְהֹוָ֞ה אֱלֹהֵ֤י הָֽעִבְרִים֙ שְׁלָחַ֣נִי אֵלֶ֣יךָ לֵאמֹ֔ר שַׁלַּח֙ אֶת־עַמִּ֔י וְיַֽעַבְדֻ֖נִי בַּמִּדְבָּ֑ר וְהִנֵּ֥ה לֹא־שָׁמַ֖עְתָּ עַד־כֹּֽה׃ [17] כֹּ֚ה אָמַ֣ר יְהֹוָ֔ה בְּזֹ֣את תֵּדַ֔ע כִּ֖י אֲנִ֣י יְהֹוָ֑ה הִנֵּ֨ה אָנֹכִ֜י מַכֶּ֣ה ׀ בַּמַּטֶּ֣ה אֲשֶׁר־בְּיָדִ֗י עַל־הַמַּ֛יִם אֲשֶׁ֥ר בַּיְאֹ֖ר וְנֶהֶפְכ֥וּ לְדָֽם׃ [18] וְהַדָּגָ֧ה אֲשֶׁר־בַּיְאֹ֛ר תָּמ֖וּת וּבָאַ֣שׁ הַיְאֹ֑ר וְנִלְא֣וּ מִצְרַ֔יִם לִשְׁתּ֥וֹת מַ֖יִם מִן־הַיְאֹֽר׃ ס

stink so that the Egyptians will find it impossible to drink the water of the Nile.'"

[19] And the LORD said to Moses, "Say to Aaron: Take your rod and hold out your arm over the waters of Egypt—its rivers, its canals, its ponds, all its bodies of water—that they may turn to blood; there shall be blood throughout the land of Egypt, even in vessels of wood and stone." [20] Moses and Aaron did just as the LORD commanded: he lifted up the rod and struck the water in the Nile in the sight of Pharaoh and his courtiers, and all the water in the Nile was turned into blood [21] and the fish in the Nile died. The Nile stank so that the Egyptians could not drink water from the Nile; and there was blood throughout the land of Egypt. [22] But when the Egyptian magicians did the same with their spells, Pharaoh's heart stiffened and he did not heed them—as the LORD had spoken. [23] Pharaoh turned and went into his palace, paying no regard even to this. [24] And all the Egyptians had to dig round about the Nile for drinking water, because they could not drink the water of the Nile.

[25] When seven days had passed after the LORD struck the Nile, [26] the LORD said to Moses, "Go to Pharaoh and say to him, 'Thus says the LORD: Let My people go that they may worship Me. [27] If you refuse to let them go, then I will plague your whole country with frogs. [28] The Nile shall swarm with frogs, and they shall come up and enter your palace, your bedchamber and your bed, the houses of your courtiers and your people, and your ovens and your kneading bowls. [29] The frogs shall come up on you and on your people and on all your courtiers.'"

8 And the LORD said to Moses, "Say to Aaron: Hold out your arm with the rod over the rivers,

19 וַיֹּאמֶר יְהוָה אֶל־מֹשֶׁה אֱמֹר אֶל־אַהֲרֹן קַח מַטְּךָ וּנְטֵה־יָדְךָ עַל־מֵימֵי מִצְרַיִם עַל־נַהֲרֹתָם ׀ עַל־יְאֹרֵיהֶם וְעַל־אַגְמֵיהֶם וְעַל כָּל־מִקְוֵה מֵימֵיהֶם וְיִהְיוּ־דָם וְהָיָה דָם בְּכָל־אֶרֶץ מִצְרַיִם וּבָעֵצִים וּבָאֲבָנִים: 20 וַיַּעֲשׂוּ־כֵן מֹשֶׁה וְאַהֲרֹן כַּאֲשֶׁר ׀ צִוָּה יְהוָה וַיָּרֶם בַּמַּטֶּה וַיַּךְ אֶת־הַמַּיִם אֲשֶׁר בַּיְאֹר לְעֵינֵי פַרְעֹה וּלְעֵינֵי עֲבָדָיו וַיֵּהָפְכוּ כָּל־הַמַּיִם אֲשֶׁר־בַּיְאֹר לְדָם: 21 וְהַדָּגָה אֲשֶׁר־בַּיְאֹר מֵתָה וַיִּבְאַשׁ הַיְאֹר וְלֹא־יָכְלוּ מִצְרַיִם לִשְׁתּוֹת מַיִם מִן־הַיְאֹר וַיְהִי הַדָּם בְּכָל־אֶרֶץ מִצְרָיִם: 22 וַיַּעֲשׂוּ־כֵן חַרְטֻמֵּי מִצְרַיִם בְּלָטֵיהֶם וַיֶּחֱזַק לֵב־פַּרְעֹה וְלֹא־שָׁמַע אֲלֵהֶם כַּאֲשֶׁר דִּבֶּר יְהוָה: 23 וַיִּפֶן פַּרְעֹה וַיָּבֹא אֶל־בֵּיתוֹ וְלֹא־שָׁת לִבּוֹ גַּם־לָזֹאת: 24 וַיַּחְפְּרוּ כָל־מִצְרַיִם סְבִיבֹת הַיְאֹר מַיִם לִשְׁתּוֹת כִּי לֹא יָכְלוּ לִשְׁתֹּת מִמֵּימֵי הַיְאֹר:

25 וַיִּמָּלֵא שִׁבְעַת יָמִים אַחֲרֵי הַכּוֹת־יְהוָה אֶת־הַיְאֹר: פ 26 וַיֹּאמֶר יְהוָה אֶל־מֹשֶׁה בֹּא אֶל־פַּרְעֹה וְאָמַרְתָּ אֵלָיו כֹּה אָמַר יְהוָה שַׁלַּח אֶת־עַמִּי וְיַעַבְדֻנִי: 27 וְאִם־מָאֵן אַתָּה לְשַׁלֵּחַ הִנֵּה אָנֹכִי נֹגֵף אֶת־כָּל־גְּבוּלְךָ בַּצְפַרְדְּעִים: 28 וְשָׁרַץ הַיְאֹר צְפַרְדְּעִים וְעָלוּ וּבָאוּ בְּבֵיתֶךָ וּבַחֲדַר מִשְׁכָּבְךָ וְעַל־מִטָּתֶךָ וּבְבֵית עֲבָדֶיךָ וּבְעַמֶּךָ וּבְתַנּוּרֶיךָ וּבְמִשְׁאֲרוֹתֶיךָ: 29 וּבְכָה* וּבְעַמְּךָ וּבְכָל־עֲבָדֶיךָ יַעֲלוּ הַצְפַרְדְּעִים:

ח וַיֹּאמֶר יְהוָה אֶל־מֹשֶׁה אֱמֹר אֶל־אַהֲרֹן נְטֵה אֶת־יָדְךָ בְּמַטֶּךָ עַל־הַנְּהָרֹת

the canals, and the ponds, and bring up the frogs on the land of Egypt." [2]Aaron held out his arm over the waters of Egypt, and the frogs came up and covered the land of Egypt. [3]But the magicians did the same with their spells, and brought frogs upon the land of Egypt.

[4]Then Pharaoh summoned Moses and Aaron and said, "Plead with the Lord to remove the frogs from me and my people, and I will let the people go to sacrifice to the Lord." [5]And Moses said to Pharaoh, "You may have this triumph over me: for what time shall I plead in behalf of you and your courtiers and your people, that the frogs be cut off from you and your houses, to remain only in the Nile?" [6]"For tomorrow," he replied. And [Moses] said, "As you say—that you may know that there is none like the Lord our God; [7]the frogs shall retreat from you and your courtiers and your people; they shall remain only in the Nile." [8]Then Moses and Aaron left Pharaoh's presence, and Moses cried out to the Lord in the matter of the frogs which He had inflicted upon Pharaoh. [9]And the Lord did as Moses asked; the frogs died out in the houses, the courtyards, and the fields. [10]And they piled them up in heaps, till the land stank. [11]But when Pharaoh saw that there was relief, he became stubborn and would not heed them, as the Lord had spoken.

[12]Then the Lord said to Moses, "Say to Aaron: Hold out your rod and strike the dust of the earth, and it shall turn to lice throughout the land of Egypt." [13]And they did so. Aaron held out his arm with the rod and struck the dust of the earth, and vermin came upon man and beast; all the dust of the earth turned to lice throughout the land of Egypt. [14]The magicians did the like with their spells to produce lice, but they could not. The vermin remained upon man and beast; [15]and the magicians said to Pharaoh, "This is the finger of God!" But Pharaoh's heart

עַל־הַיְאֹרִים וְעַל־הָאֲגַמִּים וְהַעַל אֶת־ הַצְפַרְדְּעִים עַל־אֶרֶץ מִצְרָיִם: [2] וַיֵּט אַהֲרֹן אֶת־יָדוֹ עַל מֵימֵי מִצְרָיִם וַתַּעַל הַצְפַרְדֵּעַ וַתְּכַס אֶת־אֶרֶץ מִצְרָיִם: [3] וַיַּעֲשׂוּ־כֵן הַחַרְטֻמִּים בְּלָטֵיהֶם וַיַּעֲלוּ אֶת־הַצְפַרְדְּעִים עַל־אֶרֶץ מִצְרָיִם:

[4] וַיִּקְרָא פַרְעֹה לְמֹשֶׁה וּלְאַהֲרֹן וַיֹּאמֶר הַעְתִּירוּ אֶל־יְהוָה וְיָסֵר הַצְפַרְדְּעִים מִמֶּנִּי וּמֵעַמִּי וַאֲשַׁלְּחָה אֶת־הָעָם וְיִזְבְּחוּ לַיהוָה: [5] וַיֹּאמֶר מֹשֶׁה לְפַרְעֹה הִתְפָּאֵר עָלַי לְמָתַי ׀ אַעְתִּיר לְךָ וְלַעֲבָדֶיךָ וּלְעַמְּךָ לְהַכְרִית הַצְפַרְדְּעִים מִמְּךָ וּמִבָּתֶּיךָ רַק בַּיְאֹר תִּשָּׁאַרְנָה: [6] וַיֹּאמֶר לְמָחָר וַיֹּאמֶר כִּדְבָרְךָ לְמַעַן תֵּדַע כִּי־אֵין כַּיהוָה אֱלֹהֵינוּ: [7] וְסָרוּ הַצְפַרְדְּעִים מִמְּךָ וּמִבָּתֶּיךָ וּמֵעֲבָדֶיךָ וּמֵעַמֶּךָ רַק בַּיְאֹר תִּשָּׁאַרְנָה: [8] וַיֵּצֵא מֹשֶׁה וְאַהֲרֹן מֵעִם פַּרְעֹה וַיִּצְעַק מֹשֶׁה אֶל־יְהוָה עַל־דְּבַר הַצְפַרְדְּעִים אֲשֶׁר־שָׂם לְפַרְעֹה: [9] וַיַּעַשׂ יְהוָה כִּדְבַר מֹשֶׁה וַיָּמֻתוּ הַצְפַרְדְּעִים מִן־הַבָּתִּים מִן־ הַחֲצֵרֹת וּמִן־הַשָּׂדֹת: [10] וַיִּצְבְּרוּ אֹתָם חֳמָרִם חֳמָרִם וַתִּבְאַשׁ הָאָרֶץ: [11] וַיַּרְא פַּרְעֹה כִּי הָיְתָה הָרְוָחָה וְהַכְבֵּד אֶת־לִבּוֹ וְלֹא שָׁמַע אֲלֵהֶם כַּאֲשֶׁר דִּבֶּר יְהוָה: ס

[12] וַיֹּאמֶר יְהוָה אֶל־מֹשֶׁה אֱמֹר אֶל־אַהֲרֹן נְטֵה אֶת־מַטְּךָ וְהַךְ אֶת־עֲפַר הָאָרֶץ וְהָיָה לְכִנִּם בְּכָל־אֶרֶץ מִצְרָיִם: [13] וַיַּעֲשׂוּ־כֵן וַיֵּט אַהֲרֹן אֶת־יָדוֹ בְמַטֵּהוּ וַיַּךְ אֶת־עֲפַר הָאָרֶץ וַתְּהִי הַכִּנָּם בָּאָדָם וּבַבְּהֵמָה כָּל־ עֲפַר הָאָרֶץ הָיָה כִנִּים בְּכָל־אֶרֶץ מִצְרָיִם: [14] וַיַּעֲשׂוּ־כֵן הַחַרְטֻמִּים בְּלָטֵיהֶם לְהוֹצִיא אֶת־הַכִּנִּים וְלֹא יָכֹלוּ וַתְּהִי הַכִּנָּם בָּאָדָם וּבַבְּהֵמָה: [15] וַיֹּאמְרוּ הַחַרְטֻמִּם אֶל־פַּרְעֹה אֶצְבַּע אֱלֹהִים הִוא וַיֶּחֱזַק

stiffened and he would not heed them, as the LORD had spoken.

16And the LORD said to Moses, "Early in the morning present yourself to Pharaoh, as he is coming out to the water, and say to him, 'Thus says the LORD: Let My people go that they may worship Me. 17For if you do not let My people go, I will let loose *a-swarms of insects-a* against you and your courtiers and your people and your houses; the houses of the Egyptians, and the very ground they stand on, shall be filled with swarms of insects. 18But on that day I will set apart the region of Goshen, where My people dwell, so that no swarms of insects shall be there, that you may know that I the LORD am in the midst of the land. 19And I will make a distinction*b* between My people and your people. Tomorrow this sign shall come to pass.'" 20And the LORD did so. Heavy swarms of insects invaded Pharaoh's palace and the houses of his courtiers; throughout the country of Egypt the land was ruined because of the swarms of insects.

21Then Pharaoh summoned Moses and Aaron and said, "Go and sacrifice to your God within the land." 22But Moses replied, "It would not be right to do this, for what we sacrifice to the LORD our God is untouchable to the Egyptians. If we sacrifice that which is untouchable to the Egyptians before their very eyes, will they not stone us! 23So we must go a distance of three days into the wilderness and sacrifice to the LORD our God as He may command us." 24Pharaoh said, "I will let you go to sacrifice to the LORD your God in the wilderness; but do not go very far. Plead, then, for me." 25And Moses said, "When I leave your presence, I will plead with the LORD that the swarms of insects depart tomorrow from Pharaoh and his courtiers and his people; but let not Pharaoh again

---

לֵב־פַּרְעֹה וְלֹא־שָׁמַע אֲלֵהֶם כַּאֲשֶׁר דִּבֶּר יְהוָֹה: ס

16 וַיֹּאמֶר יְהוָֹה אֶל־מֹשֶׁה הַשְׁכֵּם בַּבֹּקֶר וְהִתְיַצֵּב לִפְנֵי פַרְעֹה הִנֵּה יוֹצֵא הַמָּיְמָה וְאָמַרְתָּ אֵלָיו כֹּה אָמַר יְהוָֹה שַׁלַּח עַמִּי וְיַעַבְדֻנִי: 17 כִּי אִם־אֵינְךָ מְשַׁלֵּחַ אֶת־עַמִּי הִנְנִי מַשְׁלִיחַ בְּךָ וּבַעֲבָדֶיךָ וּבְעַמְּךָ וּבְבָתֶּיךָ אֶת־הֶעָרֹב וּמָלְאוּ בָּתֵּי מִצְרַיִם אֶת־הֶעָרֹב וְגַם הָאֲדָמָה אֲשֶׁר־הֵם עָלֶיהָ: 18 וְהִפְלֵיתִי בַיּוֹם הַהוּא אֶת־אֶרֶץ גֹּשֶׁן אֲשֶׁר עַמִּי עֹמֵד עָלֶיהָ לְבִלְתִּי הֱיוֹת־שָׁם עָרֹב לְמַעַן תֵּדַע כִּי אֲנִי יְהוָֹה בְּקֶרֶב הָאָרֶץ: 19 וְשַׂמְתִּי פְדֻת בֵּין עַמִּי וּבֵין עַמֶּךָ לְמָחָר יִהְיֶה הָאֹת הַזֶּה: 20 וַיַּעַשׂ יְהוָֹה כֵּן וַיָּבֹא עָרֹב כָּבֵד בֵּיתָה פַרְעֹה וּבֵית* עֲבָדָיו וּבְכָל־אֶרֶץ מִצְרַיִם תִּשָּׁחֵת הָאָרֶץ מִפְּנֵי הֶעָרֹב:

21 וַיִּקְרָא פַרְעֹה אֶל־מֹשֶׁה וּלְאַהֲרֹן וַיֹּאמֶר לְכוּ זִבְחוּ לֵאלֹהֵיכֶם בָּאָרֶץ: 22 וַיֹּאמֶר מֹשֶׁה לֹא נָכוֹן לַעֲשׂוֹת כֵּן כִּי תּוֹעֲבַת מִצְרַיִם נִזְבַּח לַיהוָֹה אֱלֹהֵינוּ הֵן נִזְבַּח אֶת־תּוֹעֲבַת מִצְרַיִם לְעֵינֵיהֶם וְלֹא יִסְקְלֻנוּ: 23 דֶּרֶךְ שְׁלֹשֶׁת יָמִים נֵלֵךְ בַּמִּדְבָּר וְזָבַחְנוּ לַיהוָֹה אֱלֹהֵינוּ כַּאֲשֶׁר יֹאמַר אֵלֵינוּ: 24 וַיֹּאמֶר פַּרְעֹה אָנֹכִי אֲשַׁלַּח אֶתְכֶם וּזְבַחְתֶּם לַיהוָֹה אֱלֹהֵיכֶם בַּמִּדְבָּר רַק הַרְחֵק לֹא־תַרְחִיקוּ לָלֶכֶת הַעְתִּירוּ בַּעֲדִי: 25 וַיֹּאמֶר מֹשֶׁה הִנֵּה אָנֹכִי יוֹצֵא מֵעִמָּךְ וְהַעְתַּרְתִּי אֶל־יְהוָֹה וְסָר הֶעָרֹב מִפַּרְעֹה מֵעֲבָדָיו וּמֵעַמּוֹ מָחָר רַק אַל־יֹסֵף פַּרְעֹה הָתֵל לְבִלְתִּי שַׁלַּח אֶת־הָעָם לִזְבֹּחַ לַיהוָֹה:

---

a-a   *Others "wild beasts."*
b   *Meaning of* peduth *uncertain.*

act deceitfully, not letting the people go to sacrifice to the LORD."

26So Moses left Pharaoh's presence and pleaded with the LORD. 27And the LORD did as Moses asked: He removed the swarms of insects from Pharaoh, from his courtiers, and from his people; not one remained. 28But Pharaoh became stubborn this time also, and would not let the people go.

9 The LORD said to Moses, "Go to Pharaoh and say to him, 'Thus says the LORD, the God of the Hebrews: Let My people go to worship Me. 2For if you refuse to let them go, and continue to hold them, 3then the hand of the LORD will strike your livestock in the fields—the horses, the asses, the camels, the cattle, and the sheep—with a very severe pestilence. 4But the LORD will make a distinction between the livestock of Israel and the livestock of the Egyptians, so that nothing shall die of all that belongs to the Israelites. 5The LORD has fixed the time: tomorrow the LORD will do this thing in the land.'" 6And the LORD did so the next day: all the livestock of the Egyptians died, but of the livestock of the Israelites not a beast died. 7When Pharaoh inquired, he found that not a head of the livestock of Israel had died; yet Pharaoh remained stubborn, and he would not let the people go.

8Then the LORD said to Moses and Aaron, "Each of you take handfuls of soot from the kiln, and let Moses throw it toward the sky in the sight of Pharaoh. 9It shall become a fine dust all over the land of Egypt, and cause an inflammation breaking out in boils on man and beast throughout the land of Egypt." 10So they took soot of the kiln and appeared before Pharaoh; Moses threw it toward the sky, and it caused an inflammation breaking out in boils on man and beast. [11]The magicians were unable to confront Moses because of the inflammation, for the inflammation afflicted the magicians as well as all the other Egyptians. [12]But the LORD stiffened the heart of Pharaoh, and he would not heed them, just as the LORD had told Moses.

[13]The LORD said to Moses, "Early in the morning present yourself to Pharaoh and say to him, 'Thus says the LORD, the God of the Hebrews: Let My people go to worship Me. [14]For this time I will send all My plagues upon your person, and your courtiers, and your people, in order that you may know that there is none like Me in all the world. [15]I could have stretched forth My hand and stricken you and your people with pestilence, and you would have been effaced from the earth. [16]Nevertheless I have spared you for this purpose: in order to show you My power, and in order that My fame may resound throughout the world. [17]Yet you continue to thwart[a] My people, and do not let them go! [18]This time tomorrow I will rain down a very heavy hail, such as has not been in Egypt from the day it was founded until now. [19]Therefore, order your livestock and everything you have in the open brought under shelter; every man and beast that is found outside, not having been brought indoors, shall perish when the hail comes down upon them!'" [20]Those among Pharaoh's courtiers who feared the LORD's word brought their slaves and livestock indoors to safety; [21]but those who paid no regard to the word of the LORD left their slaves and livestock in the open.

[22]The LORD said to Moses, "Hold out your arm toward the sky that hail may fall on all the land of Egypt, upon man and beast and all the grasses of the field in the land of Egypt." [23]So Moses held out his rod toward the sky, and the LORD sent thunder and hail, and fire streamed

---

a   Others "exalt yourself over."

אַבְעַבֻּעֹת פֹּרֵחַ בָּאָדָם וּבַבְּהֵמָה: 11 וְלֹא־
יָכְלוּ הַחַרְטֻמִּים לַעֲמֹד לִפְנֵי מֹשֶׁה מִפְּנֵי
הַשְּׁחִין כִּי־הָיָה הַשְּׁחִין בַּחַרְטֻמִּם וּבְכָל־
מִצְרָיִם: 12 וַיְחַזֵּק יְהֹוָה אֶת־לֵב פַּרְעֹה
וְלֹא שָׁמַע אֲלֵהֶם כַּאֲשֶׁר דִּבֶּר יְהֹוָה
אֶל־מֹשֶׁה: ס

13 וַיֹּאמֶר יְהֹוָה אֶל־מֹשֶׁה הַשְׁכֵּם בַּבֹּקֶר
וְהִתְיַצֵּב לִפְנֵי פַרְעֹה וְאָמַרְתָּ אֵלָיו כֹּה־
אָמַר יְהֹוָה אֱלֹהֵי הָעִבְרִים שַׁלַּח אֶת־עַמִּי
וְיַעַבְדֻנִי: 14 כִּי ׀ בַּפַּעַם הַזֹּאת אֲנִי שֹׁלֵחַ
אֶת־כָּל־מַגֵּפֹתַי אֶל־לִבְּךָ וּבַעֲבָדֶיךָ וּבְעַמֶּךָ
בַּעֲבוּר תֵּדַע כִּי אֵין כָּמֹנִי בְּכָל־הָאָרֶץ:
15 כִּי עַתָּה שָׁלַחְתִּי אֶת־יָדִי וָאַךְ אוֹתְךָ
וְאֶת־עַמְּךָ בַּדָּבֶר וַתִּכָּחֵד מִן־הָאָרֶץ:
16 וְאוּלָם בַּעֲבוּר זֹאת הֶעֱמַדְתִּיךָ בַּעֲבוּר
הַרְאֹתְךָ אֶת־כֹּחִי וּלְמַעַן סַפֵּר שְׁמִי בְּכָל־
הָאָרֶץ: 17 עוֹדְךָ מִסְתּוֹלֵל בְּעַמִּי לְבִלְתִּי
שַׁלְּחָם: 18 הִנְנִי מַמְטִיר כָּעֵת מָחָר בָּרָד
כָּבֵד מְאֹד אֲשֶׁר לֹא־הָיָה כָמֹהוּ בְּמִצְרַיִם
לְמִן־הַיּוֹם הִוָּסְדָה וְעַד־עָתָּה: 19 וְעַתָּה
שְׁלַח הָעֵז אֶת־מִקְנְךָ וְאֵת כָּל־אֲשֶׁר לְךָ
בַּשָּׂדֶה כָּל־הָאָדָם וְהַבְּהֵמָה אֲשֶׁר־יִמָּצֵא
בַשָּׂדֶה וְלֹא יֵאָסֵף הַבַּיְתָה וְיָרַד עֲלֵהֶם
הַבָּרָד וָמֵתוּ: 20 הַיָּרֵא אֶת־דְּבַר יְהֹוָה
מֵעַבְדֵי פַּרְעֹה הֵנִיס אֶת־עֲבָדָיו וְאֶת־
מִקְנֵהוּ אֶל־הַבָּתִּים: 21 וַאֲשֶׁר לֹא־שָׂם לִבּוֹ
אֶל־דְּבַר יְהֹוָה וַיַּעֲזֹב אֶת־עֲבָדָיו וְאֶת־
מִקְנֵהוּ בַּשָּׂדֶה: פ

22 וַיֹּאמֶר יְהֹוָה אֶל־מֹשֶׁה נְטֵה אֶת־יָדְךָ
עַל־הַשָּׁמַיִם וִיהִי בָרָד בְּכָל־אֶרֶץ מִצְרָיִם
עַל־הָאָדָם וְעַל־הַבְּהֵמָה וְעַל כָּל־עֵשֶׂב
הַשָּׂדֶה בְּאֶרֶץ מִצְרָיִם: 23 וַיֵּט מֹשֶׁה אֶת־
מַטֵּהוּ עַל־הַשָּׁמַיִם וַיהֹוָה נָתַן קֹלֹת וּבָרָד
וַתִּהֲלַךְ אֵשׁ אַרְצָה וַיַּמְטֵר יְהֹוָה בָּרָד

down to the ground, as the Lord rained down hail upon the land of Egypt. [24]The hail was very heavy—fire flashing in the midst of the hail—such as had not fallen on the land of Egypt since it had become a nation. [25]Throughout the land of Egypt the hail struck down all that were in the open, both man and beast; the hail also struck down all the grasses of the field and shattered all the trees of the field. [26]Only in the region of Goshen, where the Israelites were, there was no hail.

[27]Thereupon Pharaoh sent for Moses and Aaron and said to them, "I stand guilty this time. The Lord is in the right, and I and my people are in the wrong. [28]Plead with the Lord that there may be an end of God's thunder and of hail. I will let you go; you need stay no longer." [29]Moses said to him, "As I go out of the city, I shall spread out my hands to the Lord; the thunder will cease and the hail will fall no more, so that you may know that the earth is the Lord's. [30]But I know that you and your courtiers do not yet fear the Lord God."—[31]Now the flax and barley were ruined, for the barley was in the ear and the flax was in bud; [32]but the wheat and the emmer*b* were not hurt, for they ripen late.—[33]Leaving Pharaoh, Moses went outside the city and spread out his hands to the Lord: the thunder and the hail ceased, and no rain came pouring down upon the earth. [34]But when Pharaoh saw that the rain and the hail and the thunder had ceased, he became stubborn and reverted to his guilty ways, as did his courtiers. [35]So Pharaoh's heart stiffened and he would not let the Israelites go, just as the Lord had foretold through Moses.

10 BO'
Then the Lord said to Moses, "Go to Pharaoh. For I have hardened his heart and the

b A kind of wheat.

עַל־אֶרֶץ מִצְרָיִם: 24 וַיְהִי בָרָד וְאֵשׁ מִתְלַקַּחַת בְּתוֹךְ הַבָּרָד כָּבֵד מְאֹד אֲשֶׁר לֹא־הָיָה כָמֹהוּ בְּכָל־אֶרֶץ מִצְרַיִם מֵאָז הָיְתָה לְגוֹי: 25 וַיַּךְ הַבָּרָד בְּכָל־אֶרֶץ מִצְרַיִם אֵת כָּל־אֲשֶׁר בַּשָּׂדֶה מֵאָדָם וְעַד־בְּהֵמָה וְאֵת כָּל־עֵשֶׂב הַשָּׂדֶה הִכָּה הַבָּרָד וְאֶת־כָּל־עֵץ הַשָּׂדֶה שִׁבֵּר: 26 רַק בְּאֶרֶץ גֹּשֶׁן אֲשֶׁר־שָׁם בְּנֵי יִשְׂרָאֵל לֹא הָיָה בָּרָד: 27 וַיִּשְׁלַח פַּרְעֹה וַיִּקְרָא לְמֹשֶׁה וּלְאַהֲרֹן וַיֹּאמֶר אֲלֵהֶם חָטָאתִי הַפָּעַם יְהוָה הַצַּדִּיק וַאֲנִי וְעַמִּי הָרְשָׁעִים: 28 הַעְתִּירוּ אֶל־יְהוָה וְרַב מִהְיֹת קֹלֹת אֱלֹהִים וּבָרָד וַאֲשַׁלְּחָה אֶתְכֶם וְלֹא תֹסִפוּן לַעֲמֹד: 29 וַיֹּאמֶר אֵלָיו מֹשֶׁה כְּצֵאתִי אֶת־הָעִיר אֶפְרֹשׂ אֶת־כַּפַּי אֶל־יְהוָה הַקֹּלוֹת יֶחְדָּלוּן וְהַבָּרָד לֹא יִהְיֶה־עוֹד לְמַעַן תֵּדַע כִּי לַיהוָה הָאָרֶץ: 30 וְאַתָּה וַעֲבָדֶיךָ יָדַעְתִּי כִּי טֶרֶם תִּירְאוּן מִפְּנֵי יְהוָה אֱלֹהִים: 31 וְהַפִּשְׁתָּה וְהַשְּׂעֹרָה נֻכָּתָה כִּי הַשְּׂעֹרָה אָבִיב וְהַפִּשְׁתָּה גִּבְעֹל: 32 וְהַחִטָּה וְהַכֻּסֶּמֶת לֹא נֻכּוּ כִּי אֲפִילֹת הֵנָּה: 33 וַיֵּצֵא מֹשֶׁה מֵעִם פַּרְעֹה אֶת־הָעִיר וַיִּפְרֹשׂ כַּפָּיו אֶל־יְהוָה וַיַּחְדְּלוּ הַקֹּלוֹת וְהַבָּרָד וּמָטָר לֹא־נִתַּךְ אָרְצָה: 34 וַיַּרְא פַּרְעֹה כִּי־חָדַל הַמָּטָר וְהַבָּרָד וְהַקֹּלֹת וַיֹּסֶף לַחֲטֹא וַיַּכְבֵּד לִבּוֹ הוּא וַעֲבָדָיו: 35 וַיֶּחֱזַק לֵב פַּרְעֹה וְלֹא שִׁלַּח אֶת־בְּנֵי יִשְׂרָאֵל כַּאֲשֶׁר דִּבֶּר יְהוָה בְּיַד־מֹשֶׁה: פ

בא

ר
וַיֹּאמֶר יְהוָה אֶל־מֹשֶׁה בֹּא אֶל־פַּרְעֹה כִּי־אֲנִי הִכְבַּדְתִּי אֶת־לִבּוֹ וְאֶת־לֵב עֲבָדָיו

hearts of his courtiers, in order that I may display these My signs among them, [2]and that you may recount in the hearing of your sons and of your sons' sons how I made a mockery of the Egyptians and how I displayed My signs among them—in order that you may know that I am the LORD." [3]So Moses and Aaron went to Pharaoh and said to him, "Thus says the LORD, the God of the Hebrews, 'How long will you refuse to humble yourself before Me? Let My people go that they may worship Me. [4]For if you refuse to let My people go, tomorrow I will bring locusts on your territory. [5]They shall cover the surface of the land, so that no one will be able to see the land. They shall devour the surviving remnant that was left to you after the hail; and they shall eat away all your trees that grow in the field. [6]Moreover, they shall fill your palaces and the houses of all your courtiers and of all the Egyptians—something that neither your fathers nor fathers' fathers have seen from the day they appeared on earth to this day.'" With that he turned and left Pharaoh's presence.

[7]Pharaoh's courtiers said to him, "How long shall this one be a snare to us? Let the men go to worship the LORD their God! Are you not yet aware that Egypt is lost?" [8]So Moses and Aaron were brought back to Pharaoh and he said to them, "Go, worship the LORD your God! Who are the ones to go?" [9]Moses replied, "We will all go, young and old: we will go with our sons and daughters, our flocks and herds; for we must observe the LORD's festival." [10]But he said to them, "The LORD be with you the same as I mean to let your children go with you! Clearly, you are bent on mischief. [11]No! You menfolk go and worship the LORD, since that is what you want." And they were expelled from Pharaoh's presence.

[12]Then the LORD said to Moses, "Hold out your arm over the land of Egypt for the locusts,

לְמַעַן שִׁתִי אֹתֹתַי אֵלֶּה בְּקִרְבּוֹ: 2וּלְמַעַן תְּסַפֵּר בְּאָזְנֵי בִנְךָ וּבֶן־בִּנְךָ אֵת אֲשֶׁר הִתְעַלַּלְתִּי בְּמִצְרַיִם וְאֶת־אֹתֹתַי אֲשֶׁר־שַׂמְתִּי בָם וִידַעְתֶּם כִּי־אֲנִי יְהֹוָה: 3וַיָּבֹא מֹשֶׁה וְאַהֲרֹן אֶל־פַּרְעֹה וַיֹּאמְרוּ אֵלָיו כֹּה־אָמַר יְהֹוָה אֱלֹהֵי הָעִבְרִים עַד־מָתַי מֵאַנְתָּ לֵעָנֹת מִפָּנָי שַׁלַּח עַמִּי וְיַעַבְדֻנִי: 4כִּי אִם־מָאֵן אַתָּה לְשַׁלֵּחַ אֶת־עַמִּי הִנְנִי מֵבִיא מָחָר אַרְבֶּה בִּגְבֻלֶךָ: 5וְכִסָּה אֶת־עֵין הָאָרֶץ וְלֹא יוּכַל לִרְאֹת אֶת־הָאָרֶץ וְאָכַל | אֶת־יֶתֶר הַפְּלֵטָה הַנִּשְׁאֶרֶת לָכֶם מִן־הַבָּרָד וְאָכַל אֶת־כָּל־הָעֵץ הַצֹּמֵחַ לָכֶם מִן־הַשָּׂדֶה: 6וּמָלְאוּ בָתֶּיךָ וּבָתֵּי כָל־עֲבָדֶיךָ וּבָתֵּי כָל־מִצְרַיִם אֲשֶׁר לֹא־רָאוּ אֲבֹתֶיךָ וַאֲבוֹת אֲבֹתֶיךָ מִיּוֹם הֱיוֹתָם עַל־הָאֲדָמָה עַד הַיּוֹם הַזֶּה וַיִּפֶן וַיֵּצֵא מֵעִם פַּרְעֹה:

7וַיֹּאמְרוּ עַבְדֵי פַרְעֹה אֵלָיו עַד־מָתַי יִהְיֶה זֶה לָנוּ לְמוֹקֵשׁ שַׁלַּח אֶת־הָאֲנָשִׁים וְיַעַבְדוּ אֶת־יְהֹוָה אֱלֹהֵיהֶם הֲטֶרֶם תֵּדַע כִּי אָבְדָה מִצְרָיִם: 8וַיּוּשַׁב אֶת־מֹשֶׁה וְאֶת־אַהֲרֹן אֶל־פַּרְעֹה וַיֹּאמֶר אֲלֵהֶם לְכוּ עִבְדוּ אֶת־יְהֹוָה אֱלֹהֵיכֶם מִי וָמִי הַהֹלְכִים: 9וַיֹּאמֶר מֹשֶׁה בִּנְעָרֵינוּ וּבִזְקֵנֵינוּ נֵלֵךְ בְּבָנֵינוּ וּבִבְנוֹתֵנוּ בְּצֹאנֵנוּ וּבִבְקָרֵנוּ נֵלֵךְ כִּי חַג־יְהֹוָה לָנוּ: 10וַיֹּאמֶר אֲלֵהֶם יְהִי כֵן יְהֹוָה עִמָּכֶם כַּאֲשֶׁר אֲשַׁלַּח אֶתְכֶם וְאֶת־טַפְּכֶם רְאוּ כִּי רָעָה נֶגֶד פְּנֵיכֶם: 11לֹא כֵן לְכוּ־נָא הַגְּבָרִים וְעִבְדוּ אֶת־יְהֹוָה כִּי אֹתָהּ אַתֶּם מְבַקְשִׁים וַיְגָרֶשׁ אֹתָם מֵאֵת פְּנֵי פַרְעֹה: פ

12וַיֹּאמֶר יְהֹוָה אֶל־מֹשֶׁה נְטֵה יָדְךָ עַל־אֶרֶץ מִצְרַיִם בָּאַרְבֶּה וְיַעַל עַל־אֶרֶץ

that they may come upon the land of Egypt and eat up all the grasses in the land, whatever the hail has left." [13]So Moses held out his rod over the land of Egypt, and the LORD drove an east wind over the land all that day and all night; and when morning came, the east wind had brought the locusts. [14]Locusts invaded all the land of Egypt and settled within all the territory of Egypt in a thick mass; never before had there been so many, nor will there ever be so many again. [15]They hid all the land from view, and the land was darkened; and they ate up all the grasses of the field and all the fruit of the trees which the hail had left, so that nothing green was left, of tree or grass of the field, in all the land of Egypt.

[16]Pharaoh hurriedly summoned Moses and Aaron and said, "I stand guilty before the LORD your God and before you. [17]Forgive my offense just this once, and plead with the LORD your God that He but remove this death from me." [18]So he left Pharaoh's presence and pleaded with the LORD. [19]The LORD caused a shift to a very strong west wind, which lifted the locusts and hurled them into the Sea of Reeds;[a] not a single locust remained in all the territory of Egypt. [20]But the LORD stiffened Pharaoh's heart, and he would not let the Israelites go.

[21]Then the LORD said to Moses, "Hold out your arm toward the sky that there may be darkness upon the land of Egypt, a darkness that can be touched." [22]Moses held out his arm toward the sky and thick darkness descended upon all the land of Egypt for three days. [23]People could not see one another, and for three days no one could get up from where he was; but all the Israelites enjoyed light in their dwellings.

[24]Pharaoh then summoned Moses and said, "Go, worship the LORD! Only your flocks and your herds shall be left behind; even your chil-

מִצְרַיִם וְיֹאכַל֙ אֶת־כָּל־עֵ֣שֶׂב הָאָ֔רֶץ אֵ֛ת כָּל־אֲשֶׁ֥ר הִשְׁאִ֖יר הַבָּרָֽד: 13 וַיֵּ֨ט מֹשֶׁ֜ה אֶת־מַטֵּ֘הוּ֮ עַל־אֶ֣רֶץ מִצְרַיִם֒ וַֽיהֹוָ֗ה נִהַ֣ג ר֤וּחַ קָדִים֙ בָּאָ֔רֶץ כָּל־הַיּ֥וֹם הַה֖וּא וְכָל־הַלָּ֑יְלָה הַבֹּ֣קֶר הָיָ֔ה וְר֙וּחַ֙ הַקָּדִ֔ים נָשָׂ֖א אֶת־הָֽאַרְבֶּֽה: 14 וַיַּ֣עַל הָֽאַרְבֶּ֗ה עַ֚ל כָּל־אֶ֣רֶץ מִצְרַ֔יִם וַיָּ֕נַח בְּכֹ֖ל גְּב֣וּל מִצְרָ֑יִם כָּבֵ֣ד מְאֹ֔ד לְ֠פָנָ֠יו לֹא־הָ֨יָה כֵ֤ן אַרְבֶּה֙ כָּמֹ֔הוּ וְאַחֲרָ֖יו לֹ֥א יִֽהְיֶה־כֵּֽן: 15 וַיְכַ֞ס אֶת־עֵ֣ין כָּל־הָאָרֶץ֮ וַתֶּחְשַׁ֣ךְ הָאָרֶץ֒ וַיֹּ֜אכַל אֶת־כָּל־עֵ֣שֶׂב הָאָ֗רֶץ וְאֵת֙ כָּל־פְּרִ֣י הָעֵ֔ץ אֲשֶׁ֥ר הוֹתִ֖יר הַבָּרָ֑ד וְלֹא־נוֹתַ֨ר כָּל־יֶ֧רֶק בָּעֵ֛ץ וּבְעֵ֥שֶׂב הַשָּׂדֶ֖ה בְּכָל־אֶ֥רֶץ מִצְרָֽיִם: 16 וַיְמַהֵ֣ר פַּרְעֹ֔ה לִקְרֹ֖א לְמֹשֶׁ֣ה וּֽלְאַֽהֲרֹ֑ן וַיֹּ֗אמֶר חָטָ֛אתִי לַֽיהֹוָ֥ה אֱלֹֽהֵיכֶ֖ם וְלָכֶֽם: 17 וְעַתָּ֗ה שָׂ֣א נָ֤א חַטָּאתִי֙ אַ֣ךְ הַפַּ֔עַם וְהַעְתִּ֖ירוּ לַֽיהֹוָ֣ה אֱלֹֽהֵיכֶ֑ם וְיָסֵר֙ מֵֽעָלַ֔י רַ֖ק אֶת־הַמָּ֥וֶת הַזֶּֽה: 18 וַיֵּצֵ֖א מֵעִ֣ם פַּרְעֹ֑ה וַיֶּעְתַּ֖ר אֶל־יְהֹוָֽה: 19 וַיַּֽהֲפֹ֙ךְ יְהֹוָ֤ה רֽוּחַ־יָם֙ חָזָ֣ק מְאֹ֔ד וַיִּשָּׂא֙ אֶת־הָ֣אַרְבֶּ֔ה וַיִּתְקָעֵ֖הוּ יָ֣מָּה סּ֑וּף לֹ֤א נִשְׁאַר֙ אַרְבֶּ֣ה אֶחָ֔ד בְּכֹ֖ל גְּב֥וּל מִצְרָֽיִם: 20 וַיְחַזֵּ֥ק יְהֹוָ֖ה אֶת־לֵ֣ב פַּרְעֹ֑ה וְלֹ֥א שִׁלַּ֖ח אֶת־בְּנֵ֥י יִשְׂרָאֵֽל: פ 21 וַיֹּ֨אמֶר יְהֹוָ֜ה אֶל־מֹשֶׁ֗ה נְטֵ֤ה יָֽדְךָ֙ עַל־הַשָּׁמַ֔יִם וִ֥יהִי חֹ֖שֶׁךְ עַל־אֶ֣רֶץ מִצְרָ֑יִם וְיָמֵ֖שׁ חֹֽשֶׁךְ: 22 וַיֵּ֥ט מֹשֶׁ֛ה אֶת־יָד֖וֹ עַל־הַשָּׁמָ֑יִם וַיְהִ֧י חֹֽשֶׁךְ־אֲפֵלָ֛ה בְּכָל־אֶ֥רֶץ מִצְרַ֖יִם שְׁלֹ֥שֶׁת יָמִֽים: 23 לֹֽא־רָא֞וּ אִ֣ישׁ אֶת־אָחִ֗יו וְלֹא־קָ֛מוּ אִ֥ישׁ מִתַּחְתָּ֖יו שְׁלֹ֣שֶׁת יָמִ֑ים וּֽלְכָל־בְּנֵ֧י יִשְׂרָאֵ֛ל הָ֥יָה א֖וֹר בְּמֽוֹשְׁבֹתָֽם: 24 וַיִּקְרָ֨א פַרְעֹ֜ה אֶל־מֹשֶׁ֗ה וַיֹּ֨אמֶר֙ לְכוּ֙ עִבְד֣וּ אֶת־יְהֹוָ֔ה רַ֛ק צֹֽאנְכֶ֥ם וּבְקַרְכֶ֖ם יֻצָּ֑ג

---

[a] Traditionally, but incorrectly, "Red Sea."

dren may go with you." 25But Moses said, "You yourself must provide us with sacrifices and burnt offerings to offer up to the Lord our God; 26our own livestock, too, shall go along with us—not a hoof shall remain behind: for we must select from it for the worship of the Lord our God; and we shall not know with what we are to worship the Lord until we arrive there." 27But the Lord stiffened Pharaoh's heart and he would not agree to let them go. 28Pharaoh said to him, "Be gone from me! Take care not to see me again, for the moment you look upon my face you shall die." 29And Moses replied, "You have spoken rightly. I shall not see your face again!"

11 And the Lord said to Moses, "I will bring but one more plague upon Pharaoh and upon Egypt; after that he shall let you go from here; indeed, when he lets you go, he will drive you out of here one and all. 2Tell the people to borrow, each man from his neighbor and each woman from hers, objects of silver and gold." 3The Lord disposed the Egyptians favorably toward the people. Moreover, Moses himself was much esteemed in the land of Egypt, among Pharaoh's courtiers and among the people.

4Moses said, "Thus says the Lord: Toward midnight I will go forth among the Egyptians, 5and every first-born in the land of Egypt shall die, from the first-born of Pharaoh who sits on his throne to the first-born of the slave girl who is behind the millstones; and all the first-born of the cattle. 6And there shall be a loud cry in all the land of Egypt, such as has never been or will ever be again; 7but not a dog shall snarl[a] at any of the Israelites, at man or beast—in order that you may know that the Lord makes a distinction between Egypt and Israel. 8Then all

25 וַיֹּאמֶר מֹשֶׁה גַּם־אַתָּה תִּתֵּן בְּיָדֵנוּ זְבָחִים וְעֹלֹת וְעָשִׂינוּ לַיהֹוָה אֱלֹהֵינוּ: 26 וְגַם־מִקְנֵנוּ יֵלֵךְ עִמָּנוּ לֹא תִשָּׁאֵר פַּרְסָה כִּי מִמֶּנּוּ נִקַּח לַעֲבֹד אֶת־יְהֹוָה אֱלֹהֵינוּ וַאֲנַחְנוּ לֹא־נֵדַע מַה־נַּעֲבֹד אֶת־יְהֹוָה עַד־בֹּאֵנוּ שָׁמָּה: 27 וַיְחַזֵּק יְהֹוָה אֶת־לֵב פַּרְעֹה וְלֹא אָבָה לְשַׁלְּחָם: 28 וַיֹּאמֶר־לוֹ פַרְעֹה לֵךְ מֵעָלָי הִשָּׁמֶר לְךָ אַל־תֹּסֶף רְאוֹת פָּנַי כִּי בְּיוֹם רְאֹתְךָ פָנַי תָּמוּת: 29 וַיֹּאמֶר מֹשֶׁה כֵּן דִּבַּרְתָּ לֹא־אֹסִף עוֹד רְאוֹת פָּנֶיךָ: פ

יא וַיֹּאמֶר יְהֹוָה אֶל־מֹשֶׁה עוֹד נֶגַע אֶחָד אָבִיא עַל־פַּרְעֹה וְעַל־מִצְרַיִם אַחֲרֵי־כֵן יְשַׁלַּח אֶתְכֶם מִזֶּה כְּשַׁלְּחוֹ כָּלָה גָּרֵשׁ יְגָרֵשׁ אֶתְכֶם מִזֶּה: 2 דַּבֶּר־נָא בְּאָזְנֵי הָעָם וְיִשְׁאֲלוּ אִישׁ ׀ מֵאֵת רֵעֵהוּ וְאִשָּׁה מֵאֵת רְעוּתָהּ כְּלֵי־כֶסֶף וּכְלֵי זָהָב: 3 וַיִּתֵּן יְהֹוָה אֶת־חֵן הָעָם בְּעֵינֵי מִצְרָיִם גַּם ׀ הָאִישׁ מֹשֶׁה גָּדוֹל מְאֹד בְּאֶרֶץ מִצְרַיִם בְּעֵינֵי עַבְדֵי־פַרְעֹה וּבְעֵינֵי הָעָם: ס 4 וַיֹּאמֶר מֹשֶׁה כֹּה אָמַר יְהֹוָה כַּחֲצֹת הַלַּיְלָה אֲנִי יוֹצֵא בְּתוֹךְ מִצְרָיִם: 5 וּמֵת כָּל־בְּכוֹר בְּאֶרֶץ מִצְרַיִם מִבְּכוֹר פַּרְעֹה הַיֹּשֵׁב עַל־כִּסְאוֹ עַד בְּכוֹר הַשִּׁפְחָה אֲשֶׁר אַחַר הָרֵחָיִם וְכֹל בְּכוֹר בְּהֵמָה: 6 וְהָיְתָה צְעָקָה גְדֹלָה בְּכָל־אֶרֶץ מִצְרָיִם אֲשֶׁר כָּמֹהוּ לֹא נִהְיָתָה וְכָמֹהוּ לֹא תֹסִף: 7 וּלְכֹל ׀ בְּנֵי יִשְׂרָאֵל לֹא יֶחֱרַץ־כֶּלֶב לְשֹׁנוֹ לְמֵאִישׁ וְעַד־בְּהֵמָה לְמַעַן תֵּדְעוּן אֲשֶׁר יַפְלֶה יְהֹוָה בֵּין מִצְרַיִם וּבֵין יִשְׂרָאֵל: 8 וְיָרְדוּ כָל־עֲבָדֶיךָ אֵלֶּה אֵלַי וְהִשְׁתַּחֲווּ־לִי

---

a Others "move (or whet) his tongue."

these courtiers of yours shall come down to me and bow low to me, saying, 'Depart, you and all the people who follow you!' After that I will depart." And he left Pharaoh's presence in hot anger.

9Now the LORD had said to Moses, "Pharaoh will not heed you, in order that My marvels may be multiplied in the land of Egypt." 10Moses and Aaron had performed all these marvels before Pharaoh, but the LORD had stiffened the heart of Pharaoh so that he would not let the Israelites go from his land.

12

The LORD said to Moses and Aaron in the land of Egypt: 2This month shall mark for you the beginning of the months; it shall be the first of the months of the year for you. 3Speak to the whole community of Israel and say that on the tenth of this month each of them shall take a lamb*a* to a family, a lamb to a household. 4But if the household is too small for a lamb, let him share one with a neighbor who dwells nearby, in proportion to the number of persons: you shall contribute for the lamb according to what each household will eat. 5Your lamb shall be without blemish, a yearling male; you may take it from the sheep or from the goats. 6You shall keep watch over it until the fourteenth day of this month; and all the assembled congregation of the Israelites shall slaughter it at twilight. 7They shall take some of the blood and put it on the two doorposts and the lintel of the houses in which they are to eat it. 8They shall eat the flesh that same night; they shall eat it roasted over the fire, with unleavened bread and with bitter herbs. 9Do not eat any of it raw, or cooked in any way with water, but roasted— head, legs, and entrails—over the fire. 10You shall not leave any of it over until morning;

לֵאמֹר צֵא אַתָּה וְכָל־הָעָם אֲשֶׁר־בְּרַגְלֶיךָ וְאַחֲרֵי־כֵן אֵצֵא וַיֵּצֵא מֵעִם־פַּרְעֹה בׇּחֳרִי־ אָף׃ ס

9וַיֹּאמֶר יְהֹוָה אֶל־מֹשֶׁה לֹא־יִשְׁמַע אֲלֵיכֶם פַּרְעֹה לְמַעַן רְבוֹת מוֹפְתַי בְּאֶרֶץ מִצְרָיִם׃ 10וּמֹשֶׁה וְאַהֲרֹן עָשׂוּ אֶת־כׇּל־ הַמֹּפְתִים הָאֵלֶּה לִפְנֵי פַרְעֹה וַיְחַזֵּק יְהֹוָה אֶת־לֵב פַּרְעֹה וְלֹא־שִׁלַּח אֶת־בְּנֵי־יִשְׂרָאֵל מֵאַרְצוֹ׃ פ

יב וַיֹּאמֶר יְהֹוָה אֶל־מֹשֶׁה וְאֶל־אַהֲרֹן בְּאֶרֶץ מִצְרַיִם לֵאמֹר׃ 2הַחֹדֶשׁ הַזֶּה לָכֶם רֹאשׁ חֳדָשִׁים רִאשׁוֹן הוּא לָכֶם לְחׇדְשֵׁי הַשָּׁנָה׃ 3דַּבְּרוּ אֶל־כׇּל־עֲדַת יִשְׂרָאֵל לֵאמֹר בֶּעָשֹׂר לַחֹדֶשׁ הַזֶּה וְיִקְחוּ לָהֶם אִישׁ שֶׂה לְבֵית־אָבֹת שֶׂה לַבָּיִת׃ 4וְאִם־ יִמְעַט הַבַּיִת מִהְיֹת מִשֶּׂה וְלָקַח הוּא וּשְׁכֵנוֹ הַקָּרֹב אֶל־בֵּיתוֹ בְּמִכְסַת נְפָשֹׁת אִישׁ לְפִי אׇכְלוֹ תָּכֹסּוּ עַל־הַשֶּׂה׃ 5שֶׂה תָמִים זָכָר בֶּן־שָׁנָה יִהְיֶה לָכֶם מִן־ הַכְּבָשִׂים וּמִן־הָעִזִּים תִּקָּחוּ׃ 6וְהָיָה לָכֶם לְמִשְׁמֶרֶת עַד אַרְבָּעָה עָשָׂר יוֹם לַחֹדֶשׁ הַזֶּה וְשָׁחֲטוּ אֹתוֹ כֹּל קְהַל עֲדַת־יִשְׂרָאֵל בֵּין הָעַרְבָּיִם׃ 7וְלָקְחוּ מִן־הַדָּם וְנָתְנוּ עַל־שְׁתֵּי הַמְּזוּזֹת וְעַל־הַמַּשְׁקוֹף עַל הַבָּתִּים אֲשֶׁר־יֹאכְלוּ אֹתוֹ בָּהֶם׃ 8וְאָכְלוּ אֶת־הַבָּשָׂר בַּלַּיְלָה הַזֶּה צְלִי־אֵשׁ וּמַצּוֹת עַל־מְרֹרִים יֹאכְלֻהוּ׃ 9אַל־תֹּאכְלוּ מִמֶּנּוּ נָא וּבָשֵׁל מְבֻשָּׁל בַּמָּיִם כִּי אִם־צְלִי־אֵשׁ רֹאשׁוֹ עַל־כְּרָעָיו וְעַל־קִרְבּוֹ׃ 10וְלֹא־ תוֹתִירוּ מִמֶּנּוּ עַד־בֹּקֶר וְהַנֹּתָר מִמֶּנּוּ עַד־ בֹּקֶר בָּאֵשׁ תִּשְׂרֹפוּ׃

---

a　Or "kid." Heb. *seh* means either "sheep" or "goat"; cf. v. 5.

if any of it is left until morning, you shall burn it.

¹¹This is how you shall eat it: your loins girded, your sandals on your feet, and your staff in your hand; and you shall eat it hurriedly: it is a passover offering[b] to the LORD. ¹²For that night I will go through the land of Egypt and strike down every first-born in the land of Egypt, both man and beast; and I will mete out punishments to all the gods of Egypt, I the LORD. ¹³And the blood on the houses where you are staying shall be a sign for you: when I see the blood I will pass over you, so that no plague will destroy you when I strike the land of Egypt.

¹⁴This day shall be to you one of remembrance: you shall celebrate it as a festival to the LORD throughout the ages; you shall celebrate it as an institution for all time. ¹⁵Seven days you shall eat unleavened bread; on the very first day you shall remove leaven from your houses, for whoever eats leavened bread from the first day to the seventh day, that person shall be cut off from Israel.

¹⁶You shall celebrate a sacred occasion on the first day, and a sacred occasion on the seventh day; no work at all shall be done on them; only what every person is to eat, that alone may be prepared for you. ¹⁷You shall observe the [Feast of] Unleavened Bread, for on this very day I brought your ranks out of the land of Egypt; you shall observe this day throughout the ages as an institution for all time. ¹⁸In the first month, from the fourteenth day of the month at evening, you shall eat unleavened bread until the twenty-first day of the month at evening. ¹⁹No leaven shall be found in your houses for seven days. For whoever eats what is leavened, that person shall be cut off from the community of Israel, whether he is a stranger or a citizen of the country. ²⁰You shall eat nothing leavened;

---

b Or "protective offering"; Heb. pesaḥ.

---

11 וְכָכָה֮ תֹּאכְל֣וּ אֹתוֹ֒ מָתְנֵיכֶ֣ם חֲגֻרִ֔ים נַֽעֲלֵיכֶם֙ בְּרַגְלֵיכֶ֔ם וּמַקֶּלְכֶ֖ם בְּיֶדְכֶ֑ם וַאֲכַלְתֶּ֤ם אֹתוֹ֙ בְּחִפָּז֔וֹן פֶּ֥סַח ה֖וּא לַיהוָֽה׃ 12 וְעָבַרְתִּ֣י בְאֶֽרֶץ־מִצְרַ֘יִם֮ בַּלַּ֣יְלָה הַזֶּה֒ וְהִכֵּיתִ֤י כָל־בְּכוֹר֙ בְּאֶ֣רֶץ מִצְרַ֔יִם מֵאָדָ֖ם וְעַד־בְּהֵמָ֑ה וּבְכָל־אֱלֹהֵ֥י מִצְרַ֛יִם אֶֽעֱשֶׂ֥ה שְׁפָטִ֖ים אֲנִ֥י יְהוָֽה׃ 13 וְהָיָה֩ הַדָּ֨ם לָכֶ֜ם לְאֹ֗ת עַ֤ל הַבָּתִּים֙ אֲשֶׁ֣ר אַתֶּ֣ם שָׁ֔ם וְרָאִ֙יתִי֙ אֶת־הַדָּ֔ם וּפָסַחְתִּ֖י עֲלֵכֶ֑ם וְלֹֽא־יִֽהְיֶ֨ה בָכֶ֥ם נֶ֙גֶף֙ לְמַשְׁחִ֔ית בְּהַכֹּתִ֖י בְּאֶ֥רֶץ מִצְרָֽיִם׃ 14 וְהָיָה֩ הַיּ֨וֹם הַזֶּ֜ה לָכֶ֣ם לְזִכָּר֗וֹן וְחַגֹּתֶ֤ם אֹתוֹ֙ חַ֣ג לַֽיהוָ֔ה לְדֹרֹ֣תֵיכֶ֔ם חֻקַּ֥ת עוֹלָ֖ם תְּחָגֻּֽהוּ׃ 15 שִׁבְעַ֤ת יָמִים֙ מַצּ֣וֹת תֹּאכֵ֔לוּ אַ֚ךְ בַּיּ֣וֹם הָֽרִאשׁ֔וֹן תַּשְׁבִּ֥יתוּ שְּׂאֹ֖ר מִבָּֽתֵּיכֶ֑ם כִּ֣י ׀ כָּל־אֹכֵ֣ל חָמֵ֗ץ וְנִכְרְתָ֞ה הַנֶּ֤פֶשׁ הַהִוא֙ מִיִּשְׂרָאֵ֔ל מִיּ֥וֹם הָרִאשֹׁ֖ן עַד־י֥וֹם הַשְּׁבִעִֽי׃ 16 וּבַיּ֤וֹם הָרִאשׁוֹן֙ מִקְרָא־קֹ֔דֶשׁ וּבַיּוֹם֙ הַשְּׁבִיעִ֔י מִקְרָא־קֹ֖דֶשׁ יִהְיֶ֣ה לָכֶ֑ם כָּל־מְלָאכָה֙ לֹא־יֵעָשֶׂ֣ה בָהֶ֔ם אַ֣ךְ אֲשֶׁ֞ר יֵאָכֵ֣ל לְכָל־נֶ֗פֶשׁ ה֧וּא לְבַדּ֛וֹ יֵעָשֶׂ֖ה לָכֶֽם׃ 17 וּשְׁמַרְתֶּם֮ אֶת־הַמַּצּוֹת֒ כִּ֗י בְּעֶ֙צֶם֙ הַיּ֣וֹם הַזֶּ֔ה הוֹצֵ֥אתִי אֶת־צִבְאוֹתֵיכֶ֖ם מֵאֶ֣רֶץ מִצְרָ֑יִם וּשְׁמַרְתֶּ֞ם אֶת־הַיּ֥וֹם הַזֶּ֛ה לְדֹרֹתֵיכֶ֖ם חֻקַּ֥ת עוֹלָֽם׃ 18 בָּֽרִאשֹׁ֡ן בְּאַרְבָּעָה֩ עָשָׂ֨ר י֤וֹם לַחֹ֙דֶשׁ֙ בָּעֶ֔רֶב תֹּאכְל֖וּ מַצֹּ֑ת עַ֠ד י֣וֹם הָֽאֶחָ֧ד וְעֶשְׂרִ֛ים לַחֹ֖דֶשׁ בָּעָֽרֶב׃ 19 שִׁבְעַ֣ת יָמִ֔ים שְׂאֹ֕ר לֹ֥א יִמָּצֵ֖א בְּבָתֵּיכֶ֑ם כִּ֣י ׀ כָּל־אֹכֵ֣ל מַחְמֶ֗צֶת וְנִכְרְתָ֞ה הַנֶּ֤פֶשׁ הַהִוא֙ מֵעֲדַ֣ת יִשְׂרָאֵ֔ל בַּגֵּ֖ר וּבְאֶזְרַ֥ח הָאָֽרֶץ׃ 20 כָּל־מַחְמֶ֖צֶת לֹ֣א תֹאכֵ֑לוּ בְּכֹל֙ מוֹשְׁבֹ֣תֵיכֶ֔ם תֹּאכְל֖וּ מַצּֽוֹת׃ פ

---

in all your settlements you shall eat unleavened bread.

[21]Moses then summoned all the elders of Israel and said to them, "Go, pick out lambs for your families, and slaughter the passover offering. [22]Take a bunch of hyssop, dip it in the blood that is in the basin, and apply some of the blood that is in the basin to the lintel and to the two doorposts. None of you shall go outside the door of his house until morning. [23]For when the LORD goes through to smite the Egyptians, He will see the blood on the lintel and the two doorposts, and the LORD will pass over[c] the door and not let the Destroyer enter and smite your home.

[24]"You shall observe this as an institution for all time, for you and for your descendants. [25]And when you enter the land that the LORD will give you, as He has promised, you shall observe this rite. [26]And when your children ask you, 'What do you mean by this rite?' [27]you shall say, 'It is the passover sacrifice to the LORD, because He passed over the houses of the Israelites in Egypt when He smote the Egyptians, but saved our houses.'"

The people then bowed low in homage. [28]And the Israelites went and did so; just as the LORD had commanded Moses and Aaron, so they did.

[29]In the middle of the night the LORD struck down all the first-born in the land of Egypt, from the first-born of Pharaoh who sat on the throne to the first-born of the captive who was in the dungeon, and all the first-born of the cattle. [30]And Pharaoh arose in the night, with all his courtiers and all the Egyptians—because there was a loud cry in Egypt; for there was no house where there was not someone dead. [31]He summoned Moses and Aaron in the night and said, "Up, depart from among my people, you

21 וַיִּקְרָ֥א מֹשֶׁ֛ה לְכָל־זִקְנֵ֥י יִשְׂרָאֵ֖ל וַיֹּ֣אמֶר אֲלֵהֶ֑ם מִֽשְׁכ֗וּ וּקְח֨וּ לָכֶ֥ם צֹ֛אן לְמִשְׁפְּחֹֽתֵיכֶ֖ם וְשַׁחֲט֥וּ הַפָּֽסַח׃ 22 וּלְקַחְתֶּ֞ם אֲגֻדַּ֣ת אֵז֗וֹב וּטְבַלְתֶּם֮ בַּדָּ֣ם אֲשֶׁר־בַּסַּף֒ וְהִגַּעְתֶּ֤ם אֶל־הַמַּשְׁקוֹף֙ וְאֶל־שְׁתֵּ֣י הַמְּזוּזֹ֔ת מִן־הַדָּ֖ם אֲשֶׁ֣ר בַּסָּ֑ף וְאַתֶּ֗ם לֹ֥א תֵצְא֛וּ אִ֥ישׁ מִפֶּֽתַח־בֵּית֖וֹ עַד־בֹּֽקֶר׃ 23 וְעָבַ֣ר יְהוָה֮ לִנְגֹּ֣ף אֶת־מִצְרַיִם֒ וְרָאָ֤ה אֶת־הַדָּם֙ עַל־הַמַּשְׁק֔וֹף וְעַ֖ל שְׁתֵּ֣י הַמְּזוּזֹ֑ת וּפָסַ֤ח יְהוָה֙ עַל־הַפֶּ֔תַח וְלֹ֤א יִתֵּן֙ הַמַּשְׁחִ֔ית לָבֹ֥א אֶל־בָּתֵּיכֶ֖ם לִנְגֹּֽף׃

24 וּשְׁמַרְתֶּ֖ם אֶת־הַדָּבָ֣ר הַזֶּ֑ה לְחָק־לְךָ֥ וּלְבָנֶ֖יךָ עַד־עוֹלָֽם׃ 25 וְהָיָ֞ה כִּֽי־תָבֹ֣אוּ אֶל־הָאָ֗רֶץ אֲשֶׁ֨ר יִתֵּ֧ן יְהוָ֛ה לָכֶ֖ם כַּאֲשֶׁ֣ר דִּבֵּ֑ר וּשְׁמַרְתֶּ֖ם אֶת־הָעֲבֹדָ֥ה הַזֹּֽאת׃ 26 וְהָיָ֕ה כִּֽי־יֹאמְר֥וּ אֲלֵיכֶ֖ם בְּנֵיכֶ֑ם מָ֛ה הָעֲבֹדָ֥ה הַזֹּ֖את לָכֶֽם׃ 27 וַאֲמַרְתֶּ֡ם זֶֽבַח־פֶּ֨סַח ה֜וּא לַֽיהוָ֗ה אֲשֶׁ֣ר פָּ֠סַח עַל־בָּתֵּ֤י בְנֵֽי־יִשְׂרָאֵל֙ בְּמִצְרַ֔יִם בְּנָגְפּ֥וֹ אֶת־מִצְרַ֖יִם וְאֶת־בָּתֵּ֣ינוּ הִצִּ֑יל וַיִּקֹּ֥ד הָעָ֖ם וַיִּֽשְׁתַּחֲוֽוּ׃ 28 וַיֵּלְכ֥וּ וַיַּעֲשׂ֖וּ בְּנֵ֣י יִשְׂרָאֵ֑ל כַּאֲשֶׁ֨ר צִוָּ֧ה יְהוָ֛ה אֶת־מֹשֶׁ֥ה וְאַהֲרֹ֖ן כֵּ֥ן עָשֽׂוּ׃ ס

29 וַיְהִ֣י ׀ בַּחֲצִ֣י הַלַּ֗יְלָה וַֽיהוָה֮ הִכָּ֣ה כָל־בְּכוֹר֮ בְּאֶ֣רֶץ מִצְרַיִם֒ מִבְּכֹ֤ר פַּרְעֹה֙ הַיֹּשֵׁ֣ב עַל־כִּסְא֔וֹ עַ֚ד בְּכ֣וֹר הַשְּׁבִ֔י אֲשֶׁ֖ר בְּבֵ֣ית הַבּ֑וֹר וְכֹ֖ל בְּכ֥וֹר בְּהֵמָֽה׃ 30 וַיָּ֨קָם פַּרְעֹ֜ה לַ֗יְלָה ה֤וּא וְכָל־עֲבָדָיו֙ וְכָל־מִצְרַ֔יִם וַתְּהִ֛י צְעָקָ֥ה גְדֹלָ֖ה בְּמִצְרָ֑יִם כִּֽי־אֵ֣ין בַּ֔יִת אֲשֶׁ֥ר אֵֽין־שָׁ֖ם מֵֽת׃ 31 וַיִּקְרָא֩ לְמֹשֶׁ֨ה וּֽלְאַהֲרֹ֜ן לַ֗יְלָה וַיֹּ֙אמֶר֙ ק֤וּמוּ צְּאוּ֙ מִתּ֣וֹךְ עַמִּ֔י גַּם־

---

c Or "protect"; cf. v. 11, note b.

137

and the Israelites with you! Go, worship the
LORD as you said! [32]Take also your flocks and
your herds, as you said, and begone! And may
you bring a blessing upon me also!"

[33]The Egyptians urged the people on, impatient to have them leave the country, for they
said, "We shall all be dead." [34]So the people took
their dough before it was leavened, their kneading bowls wrapped in their cloaks upon their
shoulders. [35]The Israelites had done Moses' bidding and borrowed from the Egyptians objects
of silver and gold, and clothing. [36]And the LORD
had disposed the Egyptians favorably toward
the people, and they let them have their request;
thus they stripped the Egyptians.

[37]The Israelites journeyed from Raamses to
Succoth, about six hundred thousand men on
foot, aside from children. [38]Moreover, a mixed
multitude went up with them, and very much
livestock, both flocks and herds. [39]And they
baked unleavened cakes of the dough that they
had taken out of Egypt, for it was not leavened,
since they had been driven out of Egypt and
could not delay; nor had they prepared any provisions for themselves.

[40]The length of time that the Israelites lived
in Egypt was four hundred and thirty years; [41]at
the end of the four hundred and thirtieth year,
to the very day, all the ranks of the LORD departed from the land of Egypt. [42]That was for
the LORD a night of vigil to bring them out of
the land of Egypt; that same night is the LORD's,
one of vigil for all the children of Israel throughout the ages.

[43]The LORD said to Moses and Aaron: This
is the law of the passover offering: No foreigner
shall eat of it. [44]But any slave a man has bought
may eat of it once he has been circumcised. [45]No
bound or hired laborer shall eat of it. [46]It shall
be eaten in one house: you shall not take any

אַתֶּם גַּם־בְּנֵי יִשְׂרָאֵל וּלְכוּ עִבְדוּ אֶת־
יְהֹוָה כְּדַבֶּרְכֶם: 32 גַּם־צֹאנְכֶם גַּם־בְּקַרְכֶם
קְחוּ כַּאֲשֶׁר דִּבַּרְתֶּם וָלֵכוּ וּבֵרַכְתֶּם גַּם־
אֹתִי:
33 וַתֶּחֱזַק מִצְרַיִם עַל־הָעָם לְמַהֵר
לְשַׁלְּחָם מִן־הָאָרֶץ כִּי אָמְרוּ כֻּלָּנוּ מֵתִים:
34 וַיִּשָּׂא הָעָם אֶת־בְּצֵקוֹ טֶרֶם יֶחְמָץ
מִשְׁאֲרֹתָם צְרֻרֹת בְּשִׂמְלֹתָם עַל־שִׁכְמָם:
35 וּבְנֵי־יִשְׂרָאֵל עָשׂוּ כִּדְבַר מֹשֶׁה וַיִּשְׁאֲלוּ
מִמִּצְרַיִם כְּלֵי־כֶסֶף וּכְלֵי זָהָב וּשְׂמָלֹת:
36 וַיהֹוָה נָתַן אֶת־חֵן הָעָם בְּעֵינֵי מִצְרַיִם
וַיַּשְׁאִלוּם וַיְנַצְּלוּ אֶת־מִצְרָיִם: פ
37 וַיִּסְעוּ בְנֵי־יִשְׂרָאֵל מֵרַעְמְסֵס סֻכֹּתָה
כְּשֵׁשׁ־מֵאוֹת אֶלֶף רַגְלִי הַגְּבָרִים לְבַד
מִטָּף: 38 וְגַם־עֵרֶב רַב עָלָה אִתָּם וְצֹאן
וּבָקָר מִקְנֶה כָּבֵד מְאֹד: 39 וַיֹּאפוּ אֶת־
הַבָּצֵק אֲשֶׁר הוֹצִיאוּ מִמִּצְרַיִם עֻגֹת מַצּוֹת
כִּי לֹא חָמֵץ כִּי־גֹרְשׁוּ מִמִּצְרַיִם וְלֹא יָכְלוּ
לְהִתְמַהְמֵהַּ וְגַם־צֵדָה לֹא־עָשׂוּ לָהֶם:
40 וּמוֹשַׁב בְּנֵי יִשְׂרָאֵל אֲשֶׁר יָשְׁבוּ בְּמִצְרָיִם
שְׁלֹשִׁים שָׁנָה וְאַרְבַּע מֵאוֹת שָׁנָה: 41 וַיְהִי
מִקֵּץ שְׁלֹשִׁים שָׁנָה וְאַרְבַּע מֵאוֹת שָׁנָה
וַיְהִי בְּעֶצֶם הַיּוֹם הַזֶּה יָצְאוּ כָּל־צִבְאוֹת
יְהֹוָה מֵאֶרֶץ מִצְרָיִם: 42 לֵיל שִׁמֻּרִים הוּא
לַיהֹוָה לְהוֹצִיאָם מֵאֶרֶץ מִצְרָיִם הוּא־
הַלַּיְלָה הַזֶּה לַיהֹוָה שִׁמֻּרִים לְכָל־בְּנֵי
יִשְׂרָאֵל לְדֹרֹתָם: פ

43 וַיֹּאמֶר יְהֹוָה אֶל־מֹשֶׁה וְאַהֲרֹן זֹאת
חֻקַּת הַפָּסַח כָּל־בֶּן־נֵכָר לֹא־יֹאכַל בּוֹ:
44 וְכָל־עֶבֶד אִישׁ מִקְנַת־כָּסֶף וּמַלְתָּה אֹתוֹ
אָז יֹאכַל בּוֹ: 45 תּוֹשָׁב וְשָׂכִיר לֹא־יֹאכַל־
בּוֹ: 46 בְּבַיִת אֶחָד יֵאָכֵל לֹא־תוֹצִיא
מִן־הַבַּיִת מִן־הַבָּשָׂר חוּצָה וְעֶצֶם לֹא

of the flesh outside the house; nor shall you break a bone of it. ⁴⁷The whole community of Israel shall offer it. ⁴⁸If a stranger who dwells with you would offer the passover to the LORD, all his males must be circumcised; then he shall be admitted to offer it; he shall then be as a citizen of the country. But no uncircumcised person may eat of it. ⁴⁹There shall be one law for the citizen and for the stranger who dwells among you.

⁵⁰And all the Israelites did so; as the LORD had commanded Moses and Aaron, so they did.

⁵¹That very day the LORD freed the Israelites from the land of Egypt, troop by troop.

13

The LORD spoke further to Moses, saying, ²"Consecrate to Me every first-born; man and beast, the first issue of every womb among the Israelites is Mine."

³And Moses said to the people,

"Remember this day, on which you went free from Egypt, the house of bondage, how the LORD freed you from it with a mighty hand: no leavened bread shall be eaten. ⁴You go free on this day, in the month^a of Abib. ⁵So, when the LORD has brought you into the land of the Canaanites, the Hittites, the Amorites, the Hivites, and the Jebusites, which He swore to your fathers to give you, a land flowing with milk and honey, you shall observe in this month the following practice:

⁶"Seven days you shall eat unleavened bread, and on the seventh day there shall be a festival of the LORD. ⁷Throughout the seven days unleavened bread shall be eaten; no leavened bread shall be found with you, and no leaven shall be found in all your territory. ⁸And you shall explain to your son on that day, 'It is because of

---

a   Or "on the new moon."

תִּשְׁבְּרוּ־בֽוֹ: 47 כָּל־עֲדַ֥ת יִשְׂרָאֵ֖ל יַעֲשׂ֥וּ אֹתֽוֹ: 48 וְכִֽי־יָג֨וּר אִתְּךָ֜ גֵּ֗ר וְעָ֣שָׂה פֶ֨סַח לַֽיהוָ֗ה הִמּ֧וֹל ל֣וֹ כָל־זָכָ֗ר וְאָז֙ יִקְרַ֣ב לַעֲשֹׂת֔וֹ וְהָיָ֖ה כְּאֶזְרַ֣ח הָאָ֑רֶץ וְכָל־עָרֵ֖ל לֹֽא־יֹ֥אכַל בּֽוֹ: 49 תּוֹרָ֣ה אַחַ֔ת יִהְיֶ֖ה לָֽאֶזְרָ֑ח וְלַגֵּ֖ר הַגָּ֥ר בְּתוֹכְכֶֽם:

50 וַיַּעֲשׂ֖וּ כָּל־בְּנֵ֣י יִשְׂרָאֵ֑ל כַּאֲשֶׁ֨ר צִוָּ֤ה יְהוָה֙ אֶת־מֹשֶׁ֣ה וְאֶֽת־אַהֲרֹ֔ן כֵּ֥ן עָשֽׂוּ: ס

51 וַיְהִ֕י בְּעֶ֖צֶם הַיּ֣וֹם הַזֶּ֑ה הוֹצִ֨יא יְהוָ֜ה אֶת־בְּנֵ֧י יִשְׂרָאֵ֛ל מֵאֶ֥רֶץ מִצְרַ֖יִם עַל־צִבְאֹתָֽם: פ

יג וַיְדַבֵּ֥ר יְהוָ֖ה אֶל־מֹשֶׁ֥ה לֵּאמֹֽר: 2 קַדֶּשׁ־לִ֨י כָל־בְּכ֜וֹר פֶּ֤טֶר כָּל־רֶ֨חֶם֙ בִּבְנֵ֣י יִשְׂרָאֵ֔ל בָּאָדָ֖ם וּבַבְּהֵמָ֑ה לִ֥י הֽוּא:

3 וַיֹּ֨אמֶר מֹשֶׁ֜ה אֶל־הָעָ֗ם זָכ֞וֹר אֶת־הַיּ֤וֹם הַזֶּה֙ אֲשֶׁ֨ר יְצָאתֶ֤ם מִמִּצְרַ֨יִם֙ מִבֵּ֣ית עֲבָדִ֔ים כִּ֚י בְּחֹ֣זֶק יָ֔ד הוֹצִ֧יא יְהוָ֛ה אֶתְכֶ֖ם מִזֶּ֑ה וְלֹ֥א יֵאָכֵ֖ל חָמֵֽץ: 4 הַיּ֖וֹם אַתֶּ֣ם יֹצְאִ֑ים בְּחֹ֖דֶשׁ הָאָבִֽיב: 5 וְהָיָ֣ה כִֽי־יְבִֽיאֲךָ֣ יְהוָ֡ה אֶל־אֶ֣רֶץ הַֽכְּנַעֲנִ֣י וְהַחִתִּ֣י וְהָאֱמֹרִ֣י וְהַחִוִּ֣י וְהַיְבוּסִ֗י אֲשֶׁ֨ר נִשְׁבַּ֤ע לַאֲבֹתֶ֨יךָ֙ לָ֣תֶת לָ֔ךְ אֶ֛רֶץ זָבַ֥ת חָלָ֖ב וּדְבָ֑שׁ וְעָבַדְתָּ֛ אֶת־הָעֲבֹדָ֥ה הַזֹּ֖את בַּחֹ֥דֶשׁ הַזֶּֽה:

6 שִׁבְעַ֥ת יָמִ֖ים תֹּאכַ֣ל מַצֹּ֑ת וּבַיּוֹם֙ הַשְּׁבִיעִ֔י חַ֖ג לַיהוָֽה: 7 מַצּוֹת֙ יֵֽאָכֵ֔ל אֵ֖ת שִׁבְעַ֣ת הַיָּמִ֑ים וְלֹֽא־יֵרָאֶ֨ה לְךָ֜ חָמֵ֗ץ וְלֹֽא־יֵרָאֶ֥ה לְךָ֛ שְׂאֹ֖ר בְּכָל־גְּבֻלֶֽךָ: 8 וְהִגַּדְתָּ֣ לְבִנְךָ֔ בַּיּ֥וֹם הַה֖וּא לֵאמֹ֑ר בַּעֲב֣וּר זֶ֗ה עָשָׂ֤ה יְהוָה֙ לִ֔י בְּצֵאתִ֖י מִמִּצְרָֽיִם:

what the LORD did for me when I went free from Egypt.'

9"And this shall serve you as a sign on your hand and as a reminder on your forehead[b]—in order that the Teaching of the LORD may be in your mouth—that with a mighty hand the LORD freed you from Egypt. 10You shall keep this institution at its set time from year to year.

11"And when the LORD has brought you into the land of the Canaanites, as He swore to you and to your fathers, and has given it to you, 12you shall set apart for the LORD every first issue of the womb: every male firstling that your cattle drop shall be the LORD's. 13But every firstling ass you shall redeem with a sheep; if you do not redeem it, you must break its neck. And you must redeem every first-born male among your children. 14And when, in time to come, your son asks you, saying, 'What does this mean?' you shall say to him, 'It was with a mighty hand that the LORD brought us out from Egypt, the house of bondage. 15When Pharaoh stubbornly refused to let us go, the LORD slew every first-born in the land of Egypt, the first-born of both man and beast. Therefore I sacrifice to the LORD every first male issue of the womb, but redeem every first-born among my sons.'

16"And so it shall be as a sign upon your hand and as a symbol[c] on your forehead that with a mighty hand the LORD freed us from Egypt."

BE-SHALLAḤ

17Now when Pharaoh let the people go, God did not lead them by way of the land of the Philistines, although it was nearer; for God said, "The people may have a change of heart when they see war, and return to Egypt." 18So God led the people roundabout, by way of the wilderness at the Sea of Reeds.

---

b Lit. "between your eyes."
c Others "frontlet."

9 וְהָיָה֩ לְךָ֨ לְא֜וֹת עַל־יָדְךָ֗ וּלְזִכָּרוֹן֙ בֵּ֣ין עֵינֶ֔יךָ לְמַ֗עַן תִּהְיֶ֛ה תּוֹרַ֥ת יְהֹוָ֖ה בְּפִ֑יךָ כִּ֚י בְּיָ֣ד חֲזָקָ֔ה הוֹצִֽאֲךָ֥ יְהֹוָ֖ה מִמִּצְרָֽיִם: 10 וְשָׁמַרְתָּ֛ אֶת־הַֽחֻקָּ֥ה הַזֹּ֖את לְמוֹעֲדָ֑הּ מִיָּמִ֖ים יָמִֽימָה: ס

11 וְהָיָ֞ה כִּֽי־יְבִֽאֲךָ֤ יְהֹוָה֙ אֶל־אֶ֣רֶץ הַֽכְּנַעֲנִ֔י כַּֽאֲשֶׁ֛ר נִשְׁבַּ֥ע לְךָ֖ וְלַֽאֲבֹתֶ֑יךָ וּנְתָנָ֖הּ לָֽךְ: 12 וְהַֽעֲבַרְתָּ֥ כָל־פֶּֽטֶר־רֶ֖חֶם לַֽיהֹוָ֑ה וְכָל־פֶּ֣טֶר ׀ שֶׁ֣גֶר בְּהֵמָ֗ה אֲשֶׁ֨ר יִֽהְיֶ֥ה לְךָ֛ הַזְּכָרִ֖ים לַֽיהֹוָֽה: 13 וְכָל־פֶּ֤טֶר חֲמֹר֙ תִּפְדֶּ֣ה בְשֶׂ֔ה וְאִם־לֹ֥א תִפְדֶּ֖ה וַֽעֲרַפְתּ֑וֹ וְכֹ֨ל בְּכ֥וֹר אָדָ֛ם בְּבָנֶ֖יךָ תִּפְדֶּֽה: 14 וְהָיָ֞ה כִּֽי־יִשְׁאָֽלְךָ֥ בִנְךָ֛ מָחָ֖ר לֵאמֹ֣ר מַה־זֹּ֑את וְאָֽמַרְתָּ֣ אֵלָ֔יו בְּחֹ֣זֶק יָ֗ד הֽוֹצִיאָ֧נוּ יְהֹוָ֛ה מִמִּצְרַ֖יִם מִבֵּ֥ית עֲבָדִֽים: 15 וַיְהִ֗י כִּֽי־הִקְשָׁ֣ה פַרְעֹה֮ לְשַׁלְּחֵנוּ֒ וַיַּֽהֲרֹ֨ג יְהֹוָ֤ה כָּל־בְּכוֹר֙ בְּאֶ֣רֶץ מִצְרַ֔יִם מִבְּכֹ֥ר אָדָ֖ם וְעַד־בְּכ֣וֹר בְּהֵמָ֑ה עַל־כֵּן֩ אֲנִ֨י זֹבֵ֜חַ לַֽיהֹוָ֗ה כָּל־פֶּ֤טֶר רֶ֨חֶם֙ הַזְּכָרִ֔ים וְכָל־בְּכ֥וֹר בָּנַ֖י אֶפְדֶּֽה: 16 וְהָיָ֤ה לְא֨וֹת֙ עַל־יָ֣דְכָ֗ה* וּלְטֽוֹטָפֹ֖ת בֵּ֣ין עֵינֶ֑יךָ כִּ֚י בְּחֹ֣זֶק יָ֔ד הֽוֹצִיאָ֥נוּ יְהֹוָ֖ה מִמִּצְרָֽיִם: ס

בשלח

17 וַיְהִ֗י בְּשַׁלַּ֣ח פַּרְעֹה֮ אֶת־הָעָם֒ וְלֹֽא־נָחָ֣ם אֱלֹהִ֗ים דֶּ֚רֶךְ אֶ֣רֶץ פְּלִשְׁתִּ֔ים כִּ֥י קָר֖וֹב ה֑וּא כִּ֣י ׀ אָמַ֣ר אֱלֹהִ֗ים פֶּֽן־יִנָּחֵ֥ם הָעָ֛ם בִּרְאֹתָ֥ם מִלְחָמָ֖ה וְשָׁ֥בוּ מִצְרָֽיְמָה: 18 וַיַּסֵּ֨ב אֱלֹהִ֧ים ׀ אֶת־הָעָ֛ם דֶּ֥רֶךְ הַמִּדְבָּ֖ר יַם־ס֑וּף

v. 16. יתיר ה'

140

Now the Israelites went up armed[d] out of the land of Egypt. [19]And Moses took with him the bones of Joseph, who had exacted an oath from the children of Israel, saying, "God will be sure to take notice of you: then you shall carry up my bones from here with you."

[20]They set out from Succoth, and encamped at Etham, at the edge of the wilderness. [21]The LORD went before them in a pillar of cloud by day, to guide them along the way, and in a pillar of fire by night, to give them light, that they might travel day and night. [22]The pillar of cloud by day and the pillar of fire by night did not depart from before the people.

14 The LORD said to Moses: [2]Tell the Israelites to turn back and encamp before Pi-hahiroth, between Migdol and the sea, before Baal-zephon; you shall encamp facing it, by the sea. [3]Pharaoh will say of the Israelites, "They are astray in the land; the wilderness has closed in on them." [4]Then I will stiffen Pharaoh's heart and he will pursue them, that I may gain glory through Pharaoh and all his host; and the Egyptians shall know that I am the LORD.

And they did so.

[5]When the king of Egypt was told that the people had fled, Pharaoh and his courtiers had a change of heart about the people and said, "What is this we have done, releasing Israel from our service?" [6]He ordered[a] his chariot and took his men with him; [7]he took six hundred of his picked chariots, and the rest of the chariots of Egypt, with officers[b] in all of them. [8]The LORD stiffened the heart of Pharaoh king of Egypt, and he gave chase to the Israelites. As the Israelites were departing defiantly,[c] [9]the Egyptians gave

וַחֲמֻשִׁים עָלוּ בְנֵי־יִשְׂרָאֵל מֵאֶרֶץ מִצְרָיִם: ¹⁹ וַיִּקַּח מֹשֶׁה אֶת־עַצְמוֹת יוֹסֵף עִמּוֹ כִּי הַשְׁבֵּעַ הִשְׁבִּיעַ אֶת־בְּנֵי יִשְׂרָאֵל לֵאמֹר פָּקֹד יִפְקֹד אֱלֹהִים אֶתְכֶם וְהַעֲלִיתֶם אֶת־עַצְמֹתַי מִזֶּה אִתְּכֶם: ²⁰ וַיִּסְעוּ מִסֻּכֹּת וַיַּחֲנוּ בְאֵתָם בִּקְצֵה הַמִּדְבָּר: ²¹ וַיהֹוָה הֹלֵךְ לִפְנֵיהֶם יוֹמָם בְּעַמּוּד עָנָן לַנְחֹתָם הַדֶּרֶךְ וְלַיְלָה בְּעַמּוּד אֵשׁ לְהָאִיר לָהֶם לָלֶכֶת יוֹמָם וָלָיְלָה: ²² לֹא־יָמִישׁ עַמּוּד הֶעָנָן יוֹמָם וְעַמּוּד הָאֵשׁ לָיְלָה לִפְנֵי הָעָם: פ

יד

וַיְדַבֵּר יְהֹוָה אֶל־מֹשֶׁה לֵּאמֹר: ² דַּבֵּר אֶל־בְּנֵי יִשְׂרָאֵל וְיָשֻׁבוּ וְיַחֲנוּ לִפְנֵי פִּי הַחִירֹת בֵּין מִגְדֹּל וּבֵין הַיָּם לִפְנֵי בַּעַל צְפֹן נִכְחוֹ תַחֲנוּ עַל־הַיָּם: ³ וְאָמַר פַּרְעֹה לִבְנֵי יִשְׂרָאֵל נְבֻכִים הֵם בָּאָרֶץ סָגַר עֲלֵיהֶם הַמִּדְבָּר: ⁴ וְחִזַּקְתִּי אֶת־לֵב־פַּרְעֹה וְרָדַף אַחֲרֵיהֶם וְאִכָּבְדָה בְּפַרְעֹה וּבְכָל־חֵילוֹ וְיָדְעוּ מִצְרַיִם כִּי־אֲנִי יְהֹוָה וַיַּעֲשׂוּ־כֵן: ⁵ וַיֻּגַּד לְמֶלֶךְ מִצְרַיִם כִּי בָרַח הָעָם וַיֵּהָפֵךְ לְבַב פַּרְעֹה וַעֲבָדָיו אֶל־הָעָם וַיֹּאמְרוּ מַה־זֹּאת עָשִׂינוּ כִּי־שִׁלַּחְנוּ אֶת־יִשְׂרָאֵל מֵעָבְדֵנוּ: ⁶ וַיֶּאְסֹר אֶת־רִכְבּוֹ וְאֶת־עַמּוֹ לָקַח עִמּוֹ: ⁷ וַיִּקַּח שֵׁשׁ־מֵאוֹת רֶכֶב בָּחוּר וְכֹל רֶכֶב מִצְרָיִם וְשָׁלִשִׁם עַל־כֻּלּוֹ: ⁸ וַיְחַזֵּק יְהֹוָה אֶת־לֵב פַּרְעֹה מֶלֶךְ מִצְרַיִם וַיִּרְדֹּף אַחֲרֵי בְּנֵי יִשְׂרָאֵל וּבְנֵי יִשְׂרָאֵל יֹצְאִים בְּיָד רָמָה: ⁹ וַיִּרְדְּפוּ מִצְרַיִם

---

d   *Meaning of Heb. ḥamushim uncertain.*

a   *See on Gen. 46.29.*

b   *Heb. shalish; originally "third man on royal chariot"; hence "adjutant," "officer."*

c   *Lit. "with upraised hand."*

chase to them, and all the chariot horses of Pharaoh, his horsemen, and his warriors overtook them encamped by the sea, near Pi-hahiroth, before Baal-zephon.

10As Pharaoh drew near, the Israelites caught sight of the Egyptians advancing upon them. Greatly frightened, the Israelites cried out to the LORD. 11And they said to Moses, "Was it for want of graves in Egypt that you brought us to die in the wilderness? What have you done to us, taking us out of Egypt? 12Is this not the very thing we told you in Egypt, saying, 'Let us be, and we will serve the Egyptians, for it is better for us to serve the Egyptians than to die in the wilderness'?" 13But Moses said to the people, "Have no fear! Stand by, and witness the deliverance which the LORD will work for you today; for the Egyptians whom you see today you will never see again. 14The LORD will battle for you; you hold your peace!"

15Then the LORD said to Moses, "Why do you cry out to Me? Tell the Israelites to go forward. 16And you lift up your rod and hold out your arm over the sea and split it, so that the Israelites may march into the sea on dry ground. 17And I will stiffen the hearts of the Egyptians so that they go in after them; and I will gain glory through Pharaoh and all his warriors, his chariots and his horsemen. 18Let the Egyptians know that I am LORD, when I gain glory through Pharaoh, his chariots, and his horsemen."

19The angel of God, who had been going ahead of the Israelite army, now moved and followed behind them; and the pillar of cloud shifted from in front of them and took up a place behind them, 20and it came between the army of the Egyptians and the army of Israel. Thus there was the cloud with the darkness, and it cast a spell[d] upon the night, so that the one could not come near the other all through the night.

---

d   From root 'rr, "cast a spell" or "curse." Others "and it lit up."

אַחֲרֵיהֶם וַיַּשִּׂיגוּ אוֹתָם חֹנִים עַל־הַיָּם כָּל־סוּס רֶכֶב פַּרְעֹה וּפָרָשָׁיו וְחֵילוֹ עַל־פִּי הַחִירֹת לִפְנֵי בַּעַל צְפֹן: 10 וּפַרְעֹה הִקְרִיב וַיִּשְׂאוּ בְנֵי־יִשְׂרָאֵל אֶת־עֵינֵיהֶם וְהִנֵּה מִצְרַיִם ׀ נֹסֵעַ אַחֲרֵיהֶם וַיִּירְאוּ מְאֹד וַיִּצְעֲקוּ בְנֵי־יִשְׂרָאֵל אֶל־יְהֹוָה: 11 וַיֹּאמְרוּ אֶל־מֹשֶׁה הֲמִבְּלִי אֵין־קְבָרִים בְּמִצְרַיִם לְקַחְתָּנוּ לָמוּת בַּמִּדְבָּר מַה־זֹּאת עָשִׂיתָ לָּנוּ לְהוֹצִיאָנוּ מִמִּצְרָיִם: 12 הֲלֹא־זֶה הַדָּבָר אֲשֶׁר דִּבַּרְנוּ אֵלֶיךָ בְמִצְרַיִם לֵאמֹר חֲדַל מִמֶּנּוּ וְנַעַבְדָה אֶת־מִצְרָיִם כִּי טוֹב לָנוּ עֲבֹד אֶת־מִצְרַיִם מִמֻּתֵנוּ בַּמִּדְבָּר: 13 וַיֹּאמֶר מֹשֶׁה אֶל־הָעָם אַל־תִּירָאוּ הִתְיַצְּבוּ וּרְאוּ אֶת־יְשׁוּעַת יְהֹוָה אֲשֶׁר־יַעֲשֶׂה לָכֶם הַיּוֹם כִּי אֲשֶׁר רְאִיתֶם אֶת־מִצְרַיִם הַיּוֹם לֹא תֹסִפוּ לִרְאֹתָם עוֹד עַד־עוֹלָם: 14 יְהֹוָה יִלָּחֵם לָכֶם וְאַתֶּם תַּחֲרִשׁוּן: פ 15 וַיֹּאמֶר יְהֹוָה אֶל־מֹשֶׁה מַה־תִּצְעַק אֵלָי דַּבֵּר אֶל־בְּנֵי־יִשְׂרָאֵל וְיִסָּעוּ: 16 וְאַתָּה הָרֵם אֶת־מַטְּךָ וּנְטֵה אֶת־יָדְךָ עַל־הַיָּם וּבְקָעֵהוּ וְיָבֹאוּ בְנֵי־יִשְׂרָאֵל בְּתוֹךְ הַיָּם בַּיַּבָּשָׁה: 17 וַאֲנִי הִנְנִי מְחַזֵּק אֶת־לֵב מִצְרַיִם וְיָבֹאוּ אַחֲרֵיהֶם וְאִכָּבְדָה בְּפַרְעֹה וּבְכָל־חֵילוֹ בְּרִכְבּוֹ וּבְפָרָשָׁיו: 18 וְיָדְעוּ מִצְרַיִם כִּי־אֲנִי יְהֹוָה בְּהִכָּבְדִי בְּפַרְעֹה בְּרִכְבּוֹ וּבְפָרָשָׁיו: 19 וַיִּסַּע מַלְאַךְ הָאֱלֹהִים הַהֹלֵךְ לִפְנֵי מַחֲנֵה יִשְׂרָאֵל וַיֵּלֶךְ מֵאַחֲרֵיהֶם וַיִּסַּע עַמּוּד הֶעָנָן מִפְּנֵיהֶם וַיַּעֲמֹד מֵאַחֲרֵיהֶם: 20 וַיָּבֹא בֵּין ׀ מַחֲנֵה מִצְרַיִם וּבֵין מַחֲנֵה יִשְׂרָאֵל וַיְהִי הֶעָנָן וְהַחֹשֶׁךְ וַיָּאֶר אֶת־הַלָּיְלָה וְלֹא־קָרַב זֶה אֶל־זֶה כָּל־הַלָּיְלָה:

²¹Then Moses held out his arm over the sea and the LORD drove back the sea with a strong east wind all that night, and turned the sea into dry ground. The waters were split, ²²and the Israelites went into the sea on dry ground, the waters forming a wall for them on their right and on their left. ²³The Egyptians came in pursuit after them into the sea, all of Pharaoh's horses, chariots, and horsemen. ²⁴At the morning watch, the LORD looked down upon the Egyptian army from a pillar of fire and cloud, and threw the Egyptian army into panic. ²⁵He locked[e] the wheels of their chariots so that they moved forward with difficulty. And the Egyptians said, "Let us flee from the Israelites, for the LORD is fighting for them against Egypt."

²⁶Then the LORD said to Moses, "Hold out your arm over the sea, that the waters may come back upon the Egyptians and upon their chariots and upon their horsemen." ²⁷Moses held out his arm over the sea, and at daybreak the sea returned to its normal state, and the Egyptians fled at its approach. But the LORD hurled the Egyptians into the sea. ²⁸The waters turned back and covered the chariots and the horsemen—Pharaoh's entire army that followed them into the sea; not one of them remained. ²⁹But the Israelites had marched through the sea on dry ground, the waters forming a wall for them on their right and on their left.

³⁰Thus the LORD delivered Israel that day from the Egyptians. Israel saw the Egyptians dead on the shore of the sea. ³¹And when Israel saw the wondrous power which the LORD had wielded against the Egyptians, the people feared the LORD; they had faith in the LORD and His servant Moses.

---

e   *From root* 'sr, *with several ancient versions. Others* "took off."

וַיֵּ֨ט מֹשֶׁ֣ה אֶת־יָדוֹ֮ עַל־הַיָּם֒ וַיּ֣וֹלֶךְ יְהֹוָ֣ה ׀ 21 אֶת־הַיָּ֠ם בְּר֨וּחַ קָדִ֤ים עַזָּה֙ כׇּל־הַלַּ֔יְלָה וַיָּ֥שֶׂם אֶת־הַיָּ֖ם לֶחָרָבָ֑ה וַיִּבָּקְע֖וּ הַמָּֽיִם׃ וַיָּבֹ֧אוּ בְנֵֽי־יִשְׂרָאֵ֛ל בְּת֥וֹךְ הַיָּ֖ם בַּיַּבָּשָׁ֑ה 22 וְהַמַּ֤יִם לָהֶם֙ חֹמָ֔ה מִֽימִינָ֖ם וּמִשְּׂמֹאלָֽם׃ וַיִּרְדְּפ֤וּ מִצְרַ֙יִם֙ וַיָּבֹ֣אוּ אַחֲרֵיהֶ֔ם כֹּ֚ל ס֣וּס 23 פַּרְעֹ֔ה רִכְבּ֖וֹ וּפָרָשָׁ֑יו אֶל־תּ֖וֹךְ הַיָּֽם׃ וַֽיְהִי֙ 24 בְּאַשְׁמֹ֣רֶת הַבֹּ֔קֶר וַיַּשְׁקֵ֤ף יְהֹוָה֙ אֶל־מַחֲנֵ֣ה מִצְרַ֔יִם בְּעַמּ֥וּד אֵ֖שׁ וְעָנָ֑ן וַיָּ֕הׇם אֵ֖ת מַחֲנֵ֥ה מִצְרָֽיִם׃ וַיָּ֗סַר אֵ֚ת אֹפַ֣ן מַרְכְּבֹתָ֔יו 25 וַֽיְנַהֲגֵ֖הוּ בִּכְבֵדֻ֑ת וַיֹּ֣אמֶר* מִצְרַ֗יִם אָנ֙וּסָה֙ מִפְּנֵ֣י יִשְׂרָאֵ֔ל כִּ֣י יְהֹוָ֔ה נִלְחָ֥ם לָהֶ֖ם בְּמִצְרָֽיִם׃ פ

וַיֹּ֤אמֶר יְהֹוָה֙ אֶל־מֹשֶׁ֔ה נְטֵ֥ה אֶת־יָדְךָ֖ 26 עַל־הַיָּ֑ם וְיָשֻׁ֤בוּ הַמַּ֙יִם֙ עַל־מִצְרַ֔יִם עַל־ רִכְבּ֖וֹ וְעַל־פָּרָשָֽׁיו׃ וַיֵּט֩ מֹשֶׁ֨ה אֶת־יָד֜וֹ 27 עַל־הַיָּ֗ם וַיָּ֨שׇׁב הַיָּ֜ם לִפְנ֥וֹת בֹּ֙קֶר֙ לְאֵ֣יתָנ֔וֹ וּמִצְרַ֖יִם נָסִ֣ים לִקְרָאת֑וֹ וַיְנַעֵ֧ר יְהֹוָ֛ה אֶת־ מִצְרַ֖יִם בְּת֥וֹךְ הַיָּֽם׃ וַיָּשֻׁ֣בוּ הַמַּ֗יִם וַיְכַסּ֤וּ 28 אֶת־הָרֶ֙כֶב֙ וְאֶת־הַפָּ֣רָשִׁ֔ים לְכֹל֙ חֵ֣יל פַּרְעֹ֔ה הַבָּאִ֥ים אַחֲרֵיהֶ֖ם בַּיָּ֑ם לֹֽא־נִשְׁאַ֥ר בָּהֶ֖ם עַד־אֶחָֽד׃ וּבְנֵ֧י יִשְׂרָאֵ֛ל הָלְכ֥וּ 29 בַיַּבָּשָׁ֖ה בְּת֣וֹךְ הַיָּ֑ם וְהַמַּ֤יִם לָהֶם֙ חֹמָ֔ה מִֽימִינָ֖ם וּמִשְּׂמֹאלָֽם׃

וַיּ֨וֹשַׁע יְהֹוָ֜ה בַּיּ֥וֹם הַה֛וּא אֶת־יִשְׂרָאֵ֖ל 30 מִיַּ֣ד מִצְרָ֑יִם וַיַּ֤רְא יִשְׂרָאֵל֙ אֶת־מִצְרַ֔יִם מֵ֖ת עַל־שְׂפַ֥ת הַיָּֽם׃ וַיַּ֨רְא יִשְׂרָאֵ֜ל אֶת־הַיָּ֣ד 31 הַגְּדֹלָ֗ה אֲשֶׁ֨ר עָשָׂ֤ה יְהֹוָה֙ בְּמִצְרַ֔יִם וַיִּֽירְא֥וּ הָעָ֖ם אֶת־יְהֹוָ֑ה וַיַּֽאֲמִ֙ינוּ֙ בַּֽיהֹוָ֔ה וּבְמֹשֶׁ֖ה עַבְדּֽוֹ׃ פ

v. 25.   סבירין ומטעין לשון רבים

טו

אָז יָשִׁיר־מֹשֶׁה וּבְנֵי יִשְׂרָאֵל אֶת־הַשִּׁירָה הַזֹּאת לַיהוָה וַיֹּאמְרוּ

לֵאמֹר*   אָשִׁירָה לַיהוָה כִּי־גָאֹה גָּאָה   סוּס

וְרֹכְבוֹ רָמָה בַיָּם: 2 עָזִּי וְזִמְרָת יָהּ וַיְהִי־לִי

לִישׁוּעָה   זֶה אֵלִי וְאַנְוֵהוּ   אֱלֹהֵי

אָבִי וַאֲרֹמְמֶנְהוּ: 3 יְהוָה אִישׁ מִלְחָמָה יְהוָה

שְׁמוֹ:   4 מַרְכְּבֹת פַּרְעֹה וְחֵילוֹ יָרָה בַיָּם   וּמִבְחַר

שָׁלִשָׁיו טֻבְּעוּ בְיַם־סוּף: 5 תְּהֹמֹת יְכַסְיֻמוּ יָרְדוּ בִמְצוֹלֹת כְּמוֹ־

אָבֶן: 6 יְמִינְךָ יְהוָה נֶאְדָּרִי בַּכֹּחַ   יְמִינְךָ

יְהוָה תִּרְעַץ אוֹיֵב: 7 וּבְרֹב גְּאוֹנְךָ תַּהֲרֹס

קָמֶיךָ   תְּשַׁלַּח חֲרֹנְךָ יֹאכְלֵמוֹ כַּקַּשׁ:   8 וּבְרוּחַ

אַפֶּיךָ נֶעֶרְמוּ מַיִם   נִצְּבוּ כְמוֹ־נֵד

נֹזְלִים   קָפְאוּ תְהֹמֹת בְּלֶב־יָם: 9 אָמַר

אוֹיֵב אֶרְדֹּף אַשִּׂיג   אֲחַלֵּק שָׁלָל תִּמְלָאֵמוֹ

נַפְשִׁי   אָרִיק חַרְבִּי תּוֹרִישֵׁמוֹ יָדִי: 10 נָשַׁפְתָּ

בְרוּחֲךָ כִּסָּמוֹ יָם   צָלֲלוּ כַּעוֹפֶרֶת בְּמַיִם

אַדִּירִים: 11 מִי־כָמֹכָה* בָּאֵלִם יְהוָה   מִי

כָּמֹכָה* נֶאְדָּר בַּקֹּדֶשׁ   נוֹרָא תְהִלֹּת עֹשֵׂה

פֶלֶא: 12 נָטִיתָ יְמִינְךָ תִּבְלָעֵמוֹ אָרֶץ: 13 נָחִיתָ

בְחַסְדְּךָ עַם־זוּ גָּאָלְתָּ   נֵהַלְתָּ בְעָזְּךָ אֶל־נְוֵה

קָדְשֶׁךָ:   14 שָׁמְעוּ עַמִּים יִרְגָּזוּן   חִיל

אָחַז יֹשְׁבֵי פְּלָשֶׁת: 15 אָז נִבְהֲלוּ אַלּוּפֵי

אֱדוֹם   אֵילֵי מוֹאָב יֹאחֲזֵמוֹ רָעַד   נָמֹגוּ

כֹּל יֹשְׁבֵי כְנָעַן: 16 תִּפֹּל עֲלֵיהֶם אֵימָתָה

וָפַחַד   בִּגְדֹל זְרוֹעֲךָ יִדְּמוּ כָּאָבֶן   עַד־

יַעֲבֹר עַמְּךָ יְהוָה   עַד־יַעֲבֹר עַם־זוּ

קָנִיתָ:   17 תְּבִאֵמוֹ וְתִטָּעֵמוֹ בְּהַר נַחֲלָתְךָ   מָכוֹן

לְשִׁבְתְּךָ פָּעַלְתָּ יְהוָה   מִקְּדָשׁ אֲדֹנָי כּוֹנֲנוּ

יָדֶיךָ:   18 יְהוָה | יִמְלֹךְ לְעֹלָם וָעֶד:

---

v. 1.   צורת השירה לפי כתב היד שלנו, והיא כהלכה

v. 11.   יתיר ה' פעמיים

15 Then Moses and the Israelites sang this song to the LORD. They said:
I will sing to the LORD, for He has triumphed gloriously;
Horse and driver He has hurled into the sea.
²The LORD*ᵃ* is my strength and might;*ᵇ*
He is become my deliverance.
This is my God and I will enshrine*ᶜ* Him;
The God of my father, and I will exalt Him.
³The LORD, the Warrior—
LORD is His name!
⁴Pharaoh's chariots and his army
He has cast into the sea;
And the pick of his officers
Are drowned in the Sea of Reeds.
⁵The deeps covered them;
They went down into the depths like a stone.
⁶Your right hand, O LORD, glorious in power,
Your right hand, O LORD, shatters the foe!
⁷In Your great triumph You break Your opponents;
You send forth Your fury, it consumes them like straw.
⁸At the blast of Your nostrils the waters piled up,
The floods stood straight like a wall;
The deeps froze in the heart of the sea.
⁹The foe said,
"I will pursue, I will overtake,
I will divide the spoil;
My desire shall have its fill of them.
I will bare my sword—
My hand shall subdue them."
¹⁰You made Your wind blow, the sea covered them;
They sank like lead in the majestic waters.
¹¹Who is like You, O LORD, among the celestials;*ᵈ*
Who is like You, majestic in holiness,
Awesome in splendor, working wonders!
¹²You put out Your right hand,
The earth swallowed them.
¹³In Your love You lead the people You redeemed;
In Your strength You guide them to Your holy abode.
¹⁴The peoples hear, they tremble;
Agony grips the dwellers in Philistia.
¹⁵Now are the clans of Edom dismayed;
The tribes of Moab—trembling grips them;
All the dwellers in Canaan are aghast.
¹⁶Terror and dread descend upon them;
Through the might of Your arm they are still as stone—
Till Your people cross over, O LORD,
Till Your people cross whom You have ransomed.
¹⁷You will bring them and plant them in Your own mountain,
The place You made to dwell in, O LORD,
The sanctuary, O LORD, which Your hands established.
¹⁸The LORD will reign for ever and ever!

a Heb. Yah.   *b* Others "song."   *c* Others "glorify."   *d* Others "mighty."

¹⁹For the horses of Pharaoh, with his chariots and horsemen, went into the sea; and the LORD turned back on them the waters of the sea; but the Israelites marched on dry ground in the midst of the sea.

²⁰Then Miriam the prophetess, Aaron's sister, took a timbrel in her hand, and all the women went out after her in dance with timbrels. ²¹And Miriam chanted for them:

Sing to the LORD, for He has triumphed gloriously;
Horse and driver He has hurled into the sea.

²²Then Moses caused Israel to set out from the Sea of Reeds. They went on into the wilderness of Shur; they traveled three days in the wilderness and found no water. ²³They came to Marah, but they could not drink the water of Marah because it was bitter; that is why it was named Marah.^e ²⁴And the people grumbled against Moses, saying, "What shall we drink?" ²⁵So he cried out to the LORD, and the LORD showed him a piece of wood; he threw it into the water and the water became sweet.

There He made for them a fixed rule, and there He put them to the test. ²⁶He said, "If you will heed the LORD your God diligently, doing what is upright in His sight, giving ear to His commandments and keeping all His laws, then I will not bring upon you any of the diseases that I brought upon the Egyptians, for I the LORD am your healer."

²⁷And they came to Elim, where there were twelve springs of water and seventy palm trees; and they encamped there beside the water.

---

^e I.e., "bitter."

וַיֵּשֶׁב יְהוָה עֲלֵהֶם אֶת־מֵי הַיָּם וּבְנֵי
יִשְׂרָאֵל הָלְכוּ בַיַּבָּשָׁה בְּתוֹךְ הַיָּם: פ

כִּי בָא סוּס פַּרְעֹה בְּרִכְבּוֹ וּבְפָרָשָׁיו בַּיָּם 19

וַתִּקַּח מִרְיָם הַנְּבִיאָה אֲחוֹת אַהֲרֹן 20
אֶת־הַתֹּף בְּיָדָהּ וַתֵּצֶאןָ כָל־הַנָּשִׁים
אַחֲרֶיהָ בְּתֻפִּים וּבִמְחֹלֹת: 21 וַתַּעַן לָהֶם
מִרְיָם

שִׁירוּ לַיהוָה כִּי־גָאֹה גָּאָה
סוּס וְרֹכְבוֹ רָמָה בַיָּם: ס

וַיַּסַּע מֹשֶׁה אֶת־יִשְׂרָאֵל מִיַּם־סוּף וַיֵּצְאוּ 22
אֶל־מִדְבַּר־שׁוּר וַיֵּלְכוּ שְׁלֹשֶׁת־יָמִים
בַּמִּדְבָּר וְלֹא־מָצְאוּ מָיִם: 23 וַיָּבֹאוּ מָרָתָה
וְלֹא יָכְלוּ לִשְׁתֹּת מַיִם מִמָּרָה כִּי מָרִים
הֵם עַל־כֵּן קָרָא־שְׁמָהּ מָרָה: 24 וַיִּלֹּנוּ הָעָם
עַל־מֹשֶׁה לֵּאמֹר מַה־נִּשְׁתֶּה: 25 וַיִּצְעַק
אֶל־יְהוָה וַיּוֹרֵהוּ יְהוָה עֵץ וַיַּשְׁלֵךְ אֶל־
הַמַּיִם וַיִּמְתְּקוּ הַמָּיִם
שָׁם שָׂם לוֹ חֹק וּמִשְׁפָּט וְשָׁם נִסָּהוּ:
26 וַיֹּאמֶר אִם־שָׁמוֹעַ תִּשְׁמַע לְקוֹל | יְהוָה
אֱלֹהֶיךָ וְהַיָּשָׁר בְּעֵינָיו תַּעֲשֶׂה וְהַאֲזַנְתָּ
לְמִצְוֹתָיו וְשָׁמַרְתָּ כָּל־חֻקָּיו כָּל־הַמַּחֲלָה
אֲשֶׁר־שַׂמְתִּי בְמִצְרַיִם לֹא־אָשִׂים עָלֶיךָ
כִּי אֲנִי יְהוָה רֹפְאֶךָ: ס
27 וַיָּבֹאוּ אֵילִמָה וְשָׁם שְׁתֵּים עֶשְׂרֵה עֵינֹת
מַיִם וְשִׁבְעִים תְּמָרִים וַיַּחֲנוּ־שָׁם עַל־
הַמָּיִם:

146

16 Setting out from Elim, the whole Israelite community came to the wilderness of Sin, which is between Elim and Sinai, on the fifteenth day of the second month after their departure from the land of Egypt. [2]In the wilderness, the whole Israelite community grumbled against Moses and Aaron. [3]The Israelites said to them, "If only we had died by the hand of the LORD in the land of Egypt, when we sat by the fleshpots, when we ate our fill of bread! For you have brought us out into this wilderness to starve this whole congregation to death."

[4]And the LORD said to Moses, "I will rain down bread for you from the sky, and the people shall go out and gather each day that day's portion—that I may thus test them, to see whether they will follow My instructions or not. [5]But on the sixth day, when they apportion what they have brought in, it shall prove to be double the amount they gather each day." [6]So Moses and Aaron said to all the Israelites, "By evening you shall know it was the LORD who brought you out from the land of Egypt; [7]and in the morning you shall behold the Presence[a] of the LORD, because He has heard your grumblings against the LORD. For who are we that you should grumble against us? [8]Since it is the LORD," Moses continued, "who will give you flesh to eat in the evening and bread in the morning to the full, because the LORD has heard the grumblings you utter against Him, what is our part? Your grumbling is not against us, but against the LORD!"

[9]Then Moses said to Aaron, "Say to the whole Israelite community: Advance toward the LORD, for He has heard your grumbling." [10]And as Aaron spoke to the whole Israelite community, they turned toward the wilderness, and

---

a Others "glory."

טז וַיִּסְעוּ מֵאֵילִם וַיָּבֹאוּ כָּל־עֲדַת בְּנֵי־יִשְׂרָאֵל אֶל־מִדְבַּר־סִין אֲשֶׁר בֵּין־אֵילִם וּבֵין סִינָי בַּחֲמִשָּׁה עָשָׂר יוֹם לַחֹדֶשׁ הַשֵּׁנִי לְצֵאתָם מֵאֶרֶץ מִצְרָיִם: 2 וַיִּלּוֹנוּ כָּל־עֲדַת בְּנֵי־יִשְׂרָאֵל עַל־מֹשֶׁה וְעַל־אַהֲרֹן בַּמִּדְבָּר: 3 וַיֹּאמְרוּ אֲלֵהֶם בְּנֵי יִשְׂרָאֵל מִי־יִתֵּן מוּתֵנוּ בְיַד־יְהוָה בְּאֶרֶץ מִצְרַיִם בְּשִׁבְתֵּנוּ עַל־סִיר הַבָּשָׂר בְּאָכְלֵנוּ לֶחֶם לָשֹׂבַע כִּי־הוֹצֵאתֶם אֹתָנוּ אֶל־הַמִּדְבָּר הַזֶּה לְהָמִית אֶת־כָּל־הַקָּהָל הַזֶּה בָּרָעָב: ס

4 וַיֹּאמֶר יְהוָה אֶל־מֹשֶׁה הִנְנִי מַמְטִיר לָכֶם לֶחֶם מִן־הַשָּׁמָיִם וְיָצָא הָעָם וְלָקְטוּ דְּבַר־יוֹם בְּיוֹמוֹ לְמַעַן אֲנַסֶּנּוּ הֲיֵלֵךְ בְּתוֹרָתִי אִם־לֹא: 5 וְהָיָה בַּיּוֹם הַשִּׁשִּׁי וְהֵכִינוּ אֵת אֲשֶׁר־יָבִיאוּ וְהָיָה מִשְׁנֶה עַל אֲשֶׁר־יִלְקְטוּ יוֹם ׀ יוֹם: ס 6 וַיֹּאמֶר מֹשֶׁה וְאַהֲרֹן אֶל־כָּל־בְּנֵי יִשְׂרָאֵל עֶרֶב וִידַעְתֶּם כִּי יְהוָה הוֹצִיא אֶתְכֶם מֵאֶרֶץ מִצְרָיִם: 7 וּבֹקֶר וּרְאִיתֶם אֶת־כְּבוֹד יְהוָה בְּשָׁמְעוֹ אֶת־תְּלֻנֹּתֵיכֶם עַל־יְהוָה וְנַחְנוּ מָה כִּי תַלּוֹנוּ עָלֵינוּ: 8 וַיֹּאמֶר מֹשֶׁה בְּתֵת יְהוָה לָכֶם בָּעֶרֶב בָּשָׂר לֶאֱכֹל וְלֶחֶם בַּבֹּקֶר לִשְׂבֹּעַ בִּשְׁמֹעַ יְהוָה אֶת־תְּלֻנֹּתֵיכֶם אֲשֶׁר־אַתֶּם מַלִּינִם עָלָיו וְנַחְנוּ מָה לֹא־עָלֵינוּ תְלֻנֹּתֵיכֶם כִּי עַל־יְהוָה:

9 וַיֹּאמֶר מֹשֶׁה אֶל־אַהֲרֹן אֱמֹר אֶל־כָּל־עֲדַת בְּנֵי יִשְׂרָאֵל קִרְבוּ לִפְנֵי יְהוָה כִּי שָׁמַע אֵת תְּלֻנֹּתֵיכֶם: 10 וַיְהִי כְּדַבֵּר אַהֲרֹן אֶל־כָּל־עֲדַת בְּנֵי־יִשְׂרָאֵל וַיִּפְנוּ אֶל־הַמִּדְבָּר וְהִנֵּה כְּבוֹד יְהוָה נִרְאָה בֶּעָנָן: פ

there, in a cloud, appeared the Presence of the LORD.

[11]The LORD spoke to Moses: [12]"I have heard the grumbling of the Israelites. Speak to them and say: By evening you shall eat flesh, and in the morning you shall have your fill of bread; and you shall know that I the LORD am your God."

[13]In the evening quail appeared and covered the camp; in the morning there was a fall of dew about the camp. [14]When the fall of dew lifted, there, over the surface of the wilderness, lay a fine and flaky substance, as fine as frost on the ground. [15]When the Israelites saw it, they said to one another, "What is it?"[b]—for they did not know what it was. And Moses said to them, "That is the bread which the LORD has given you to eat. [16]This is what the LORD has commanded: Gather as much of it as each of you requires to eat, an *omer* to a person for as many of you as there are; each of you shall fetch for those in his tent."

[17]The Israelites did so, some gathering much, some little. [18]But when they measured it by the *omer*, he who had gathered much had no excess, and he who had gathered little had no deficiency: they had gathered as much as they needed to eat. [19]And Moses said to them, "Let no one leave any of it over until morning." [20]But they paid no attention to Moses; some of them left of it until morning, and it became infested with maggots and stank. And Moses was angry with them.

[21]So they gathered it every morning, each as much as he needed to eat; for when the sun grew hot, it would melt. [22]On the sixth day they gathered double the amount of food, two *omer*s for each; and when all the chieftains of the community came and told Moses, [23]he said to them, "This is what the LORD meant: Tomorrow is a

11 וַיְדַבֵּ֥ר יְהוָ֖ה אֶל־מֹשֶׁ֥ה לֵּאמֹֽר׃ 12 שָׁמַ֗עְתִּי אֶת־תְּלוּנֹּת֮ בְּנֵ֣י יִשְׂרָאֵל֒ דַּבֵּ֨ר אֲלֵהֶ֜ם לֵאמֹ֗ר בֵּ֤ין הָֽעַרְבַּ֙יִם֙ תֹּאכְל֣וּ בָשָׂ֔ר וּבַבֹּ֖קֶר תִּשְׂבְּעוּ־לָ֑חֶם וִֽידַעְתֶּ֕ם כִּ֛י אֲנִ֥י יְהוָ֖ה אֱלֹהֵיכֶֽם׃ 13 וַיְהִ֣י בָעֶ֔רֶב וַתַּ֣עַל הַשְּׂלָ֔ו וַתְּכַ֖ס אֶת־הַֽמַּחֲנֶ֑ה וּבַבֹּ֗קֶר הָֽיְתָה֙ שִׁכְבַ֣ת הַטַּ֔ל סָבִ֖יב לַֽמַּחֲנֶֽה׃ 14 וַתַּ֖עַל שִׁכְבַ֣ת הַטָּ֑ל וְהִנֵּ֞ה עַל־פְּנֵ֤י הַמִּדְבָּר֙ דַּ֣ק מְחֻסְפָּ֔ס דַּ֥ק כַּכְּפֹ֖ר עַל־הָאָֽרֶץ׃ 15 וַיִּרְא֣וּ בְנֵֽי־יִשְׂרָאֵ֗ל וַיֹּ֨אמְר֜וּ אִ֤ישׁ אֶל־אָחִיו֙ מָ֣ן ה֔וּא כִּ֛י לֹ֥א יָֽדְע֖וּ מַה־ה֑וּא וַיֹּ֤אמֶר מֹשֶׁה֙ אֲלֵהֶ֔ם ה֣וּא הַלֶּ֔חֶם אֲשֶׁ֨ר נָתַ֧ן יְהוָ֛ה לָכֶ֖ם לְאָכְלָֽה׃ 16 זֶ֤ה הַדָּבָר֙ אֲשֶׁ֣ר צִוָּ֣ה יְהוָ֔ה לִקְט֣וּ מִמֶּ֔נּוּ אִ֖ישׁ לְפִ֣י אָכְל֑וֹ עֹ֣מֶר לַגֻּלְגֹּ֗לֶת מִסְפַּר֙ נַפְשֹׁ֣תֵיכֶ֔ם אִ֛ישׁ לַֽאֲשֶׁ֥ר בְּאָהֳל֖וֹ תִּקָּֽחוּ׃ 17 וַיַּֽעֲשׂוּ־כֵ֖ן בְּנֵ֣י יִשְׂרָאֵ֑ל וַֽיִּלְקְט֔וּ הַמַּרְבֶּ֖ה וְהַמַּמְעִֽיט׃ 18 וַיָּמֹ֣דּוּ בָעֹ֔מֶר וְלֹ֤א הֶעְדִּיף֙ הַמַּרְבֶּ֔ה וְהַמַּמְעִ֖יט לֹ֣א הֶחְסִ֑יר אִ֖ישׁ לְפִֽי־אָכְל֖וֹ לָקָֽטוּ׃ 19 וַיֹּ֥אמֶר מֹשֶׁ֖ה אֲלֵהֶ֑ם אִ֕ישׁ אַל־יוֹתֵ֥ר מִמֶּ֖נּוּ עַד־בֹּֽקֶר׃ 20 וְלֹא־שָֽׁמְע֣וּ אֶל־מֹשֶׁ֗ה וַיּוֹתִ֨רוּ אֲנָשִׁ֤ים מִמֶּ֙נּוּ֙ עַד־בֹּ֔קֶר וַיָּ֥רֻם תּֽוֹלָעִ֖ים וַיִּבְאַ֑שׁ וַיִּקְצֹ֥ף עֲלֵהֶ֖ם מֹשֶֽׁה׃ 21 וַיִּלְקְט֤וּ אֹתוֹ֙ בַּבֹּ֣קֶר בַּבֹּ֔קֶר אִ֖ישׁ כְּפִ֣י אָכְל֑וֹ וְחַ֥ם הַשֶּׁ֖מֶשׁ וְנָמָֽס׃ 22 וַיְהִ֣י ׀ בַּיּ֣וֹם הַשִּׁשִּׁ֗י לָֽקְט֥וּ לֶ֙חֶם֙ מִשְׁנֶ֔ה שְׁנֵ֥י הָעֹ֖מֶר לָֽאֶחָ֑ד וַיָּבֹ֙אוּ֙ כָּל־נְשִׂיאֵ֣י הָֽעֵדָ֔ה וַיַּגִּ֖ידוּ לְמֹשֶֽׁה׃ 23 וַיֹּ֣אמֶר אֲלֵהֶ֗ם ה֚וּא אֲשֶׁ֣ר דִּבֶּ֣ר יְהוָ֔ה שַׁבָּת֧וֹן שַׁבַּת־קֹ֛דֶשׁ לַֽיהוָ֖ה מָחָ֑ר אֵ֣ת

---

b Heb. *man hu; others* "It is manna."

day of rest, a holy sabbath of the LORD. Bake what you would bake and boil what you would boil; and all that is left put aside to be kept until morning." ²⁴So they put it aside until morning, as Moses had ordered; and it did not turn foul, and there were no maggots in it. ²⁵Then Moses said, "Eat it today, for today is a sabbath of the LORD; you will not find it today on the plain. ²⁶Six days you shall gather it; on the seventh day, the sabbath, there will be none."

²⁷Yet some of the people went out on the seventh day to gather, but they found nothing. ²⁸And the LORD said to Moses, "How long will you men refuse to obey My commandments and My teachings? ²⁹Mark that the LORD has given you the sabbath; therefore He gives you two days' food on the sixth day. Let everyone remain where he is: let no one leave his place on the seventh day." ³⁰So the people remained inactive on the seventh day.

³¹The house of Israel named it manna;^c it was like coriander seed, white, and it tasted like wafers^d in honey. ³²Moses said, "This is what the LORD has commanded: Let one *omer* of it be kept throughout the ages, in order that they may see the bread that I fed you in the wilderness when I brought you out from the land of Egypt." ³³And Moses said to Aaron, "Take a jar, put one *omer* of manna in it, and place it before the LORD, to be kept throughout the ages." ³⁴As the LORD had commanded Moses, Aaron placed it before the Pact,^e to be kept. ³⁵And the Israelites ate manna forty years, until they came to a settled land; they ate the manna until they came to the border of the land of Canaan. ³⁶The *omer* is a tenth of an *ephah*.

---

c Heb. man.
d Meaning of Heb. ṣappiḥith uncertain.
e Others "Testimony."

אֲשֶׁר־תֹּאפוּ אֵפֹוּ וְאֵת אֲשֶׁר־תְּבַשְּׁלוּ בַּשֵּׁלוּ וְאֵת כָּל־הָעֹדֵף הַנִּיחוּ לָכֶם לְמִשְׁמֶרֶת עַד־הַבֹּקֶר: 24 וַיַּנִּיחוּ אֹתוֹ עַד־ הַבֹּקֶר כַּאֲשֶׁר צִוָּה מֹשֶׁה וְלֹא הִבְאִישׁ וְרִמָּה לֹא־הָיְתָה בּוֹ: 25 וַיֹּאמֶר מֹשֶׁה אִכְלֻהוּ הַיּוֹם כִּי־שַׁבָּת הַיּוֹם לַיהוָה הַיּוֹם לֹא תִמְצָאֻהוּ בַּשָּׂדֶה: 26 שֵׁשֶׁת יָמִים תִּלְקְטֻהוּ וּבַיּוֹם הַשְּׁבִיעִי שַׁבָּת לֹא יִהְיֶה־ בּוֹ:

27 וַיְהִי בַּיּוֹם הַשְּׁבִיעִי יָצְאוּ מִן־הָעָם לִלְקֹט וְלֹא מָצָאוּ: ס 28 וַיֹּאמֶר יְהוָה אֶל־מֹשֶׁה עַד־אָנָה מֵאַנְתֶּם לִשְׁמֹר מִצְוֹתַי וְתוֹרֹתָי: 29 רְאוּ כִּי־יְהוָה נָתַן לָכֶם הַשַּׁבָּת עַל־כֵּן הוּא נֹתֵן לָכֶם בַּיּוֹם הַשִּׁשִּׁי לֶחֶם יוֹמָיִם שְׁבוּ | אִישׁ תַּחְתָּיו אַל־יֵצֵא אִישׁ מִמְּקֹמוֹ בַּיּוֹם הַשְּׁבִיעִי: 30 וַיִּשְׁבְּתוּ הָעָם בַּיּוֹם הַשְּׁבִעִי:

31 וַיִּקְרְאוּ בֵית־יִשְׂרָאֵל אֶת־שְׁמוֹ מָן וְהוּא כְּזֶרַע גַּד לָבָן וְטַעְמוֹ כְּצַפִּיחִת בִּדְבָשׁ: 32 וַיֹּאמֶר מֹשֶׁה זֶה הַדָּבָר אֲשֶׁר צִוָּה יְהוָה מְלֹא הָעֹמֶר מִמֶּנּוּ לְמִשְׁמֶרֶת לְדֹרֹתֵיכֶם לְמַעַן | יִרְאוּ אֶת־הַלֶּחֶם אֲשֶׁר הֶאֱכַלְתִּי אֶתְכֶם בַּמִּדְבָּר בְּהוֹצִיאִי אֶתְכֶם מֵאֶרֶץ מִצְרָיִם: 33 וַיֹּאמֶר מֹשֶׁה אֶל־אַהֲרֹן קַח צִנְצֶנֶת אַחַת וְתֶן־שָׁמָּה מְלֹא־הָעֹמֶר מָן וְהַנַּח אֹתוֹ לִפְנֵי יְהוָה לְמִשְׁמֶרֶת לְדֹרֹתֵיכֶם: 34 כַּאֲשֶׁר צִוָּה יְהוָה אֶל־מֹשֶׁה וַיַּנִּיחֵהוּ אַהֲרֹן לִפְנֵי הָעֵדֻת לְמִשְׁמָרֶת: 35 וּבְנֵי יִשְׂרָאֵל אָכְלוּ אֶת־הַמָּן אַרְבָּעִים שָׁנָה עַד־בֹּאָם אֶל־אֶרֶץ נוֹשָׁבֶת אֶת־הַמָּן אָכְלוּ עַד־בֹּאָם אֶל־קְצֵה אֶרֶץ כְּנָעַן: 36 וְהָעֹמֶר עֲשִׂרִית הָאֵיפָה הוּא: פ

17 From the wilderness of Sin the whole Israelite community continued by stages as the LORD would command. They encamped at Rephidim, and there was no water for the people to drink. ²The people quarreled with Moses. "Give us water to drink," they said; and Moses replied to them, "Why do you quarrel with me? Why do you try the LORD?" ³But the people thirsted there for water; and the people grumbled against Moses and said, "Why did you bring us up from Egypt, to kill us and our children and livestock with thirst?" ⁴Moses cried out to the LORD, saying, "What shall I do with this people? Before long they will be stoning me!" ⁵Then the LORD said to Moses, "Pass before the people; take with you some of the elders of Israel, and take along the rod with which you struck the Nile, and set out. ⁶I will be standing there before you on the rock at Horeb. Strike the rock and water will issue from it, and the people will drink." And Moses did so in the sight of the elders of Israel. ⁷The place was named Massah*a* and Meribah,*b* because the Israelites quarreled and because they tried the LORD, saying, "Is the LORD present among us or not?"

⁸Amalek came and fought with Israel at Rephidim. ⁹Moses said to Joshua, "Pick some men for us, and go out and do battle with Amalek. Tomorrow I will station myself on the top of the hill, with the rod of God in my hand." ¹⁰Joshua did as Moses told him and fought with Amalek, while Moses, Aaron, and Hur went up to the top of the hill. ¹¹Then, whenever Moses held up his hand, Israel prevailed; but whenever he let down his hand, Amalek prevailed. ¹²But Moses' hands grew heavy; so they took a stone and put it under him and he sat on it, while

רז ¹וַיִּסְעוּ כָּל־עֲדַת בְּנֵי־יִשְׂרָאֵל מִמִּדְבַּר־סִין לְמַסְעֵיהֶם עַל־פִּי יְהֹוָה וַיַּחֲנוּ בִּרְפִידִים וְאֵין מַיִם לִשְׁתֹּת הָעָם: ²וַיָּרֶב הָעָם עִם־מֹשֶׁה וַיֹּאמְרוּ תְּנוּ־לָנוּ מַיִם וְנִשְׁתֶּה וַיֹּאמֶר לָהֶם מֹשֶׁה מַה־תְּרִיבוּן עִמָּדִי מַה־תְּנַסּוּן אֶת־יְהֹוָה: ³וַיִּצְמָא שָׁם הָעָם לַמַּיִם וַיָּלֶן הָעָם עַל־מֹשֶׁה וַיֹּאמֶר לָמָּה זֶּה הֶעֱלִיתָנוּ מִמִּצְרַיִם לְהָמִית אֹתִי וְאֶת־בָּנַי וְאֶת־מִקְנַי בַּצָּמָא: ⁴וַיִּצְעַק מֹשֶׁה אֶל־יְהֹוָה לֵאמֹר מָה אֶעֱשֶׂה לָעָם הַזֶּה עוֹד מְעַט וּסְקָלֻנִי: ⁵וַיֹּאמֶר יְהֹוָה אֶל־מֹשֶׁה עֲבֹר לִפְנֵי הָעָם וְקַח אִתְּךָ מִזִּקְנֵי יִשְׂרָאֵל וּמַטְּךָ אֲשֶׁר הִכִּיתָ בּוֹ אֶת־הַיְאֹר קַח בְּיָדְךָ וְהָלָכְתָּ: ⁶הִנְנִי עֹמֵד לְפָנֶיךָ שָּׁם ׀ עַל־הַצּוּר בְּחֹרֵב וְהִכִּיתָ בַצּוּר וְיָצְאוּ מִמֶּנּוּ מַיִם וְשָׁתָה הָעָם וַיַּעַשׂ כֵּן מֹשֶׁה לְעֵינֵי זִקְנֵי יִשְׂרָאֵל: ⁷וַיִּקְרָא שֵׁם הַמָּקוֹם מַסָּה וּמְרִיבָה עַל־רִיב ׀ בְּנֵי יִשְׂרָאֵל וְעַל נַסֹּתָם אֶת־יְהֹוָה לֵאמֹר הֲיֵשׁ יְהֹוָה בְּקִרְבֵּנוּ אִם־אָיִן: פ

⁸וַיָּבֹא עֲמָלֵק וַיִּלָּחֶם עִם־יִשְׂרָאֵל בִּרְפִידִם: ⁹וַיֹּאמֶר מֹשֶׁה אֶל־יְהוֹשֻׁעַ בְּחַר־לָנוּ אֲנָשִׁים וְצֵא הִלָּחֵם בַּעֲמָלֵק מָחָר אָנֹכִי נִצָּב עַל־רֹאשׁ הַגִּבְעָה וּמַטֵּה הָאֱלֹהִים בְּיָדִי: ¹⁰וַיַּעַשׂ יְהוֹשֻׁעַ כַּאֲשֶׁר אָמַר־לוֹ מֹשֶׁה לְהִלָּחֵם בַּעֲמָלֵק וּמֹשֶׁה אַהֲרֹן וְחוּר עָלוּ רֹאשׁ הַגִּבְעָה: ¹¹וְהָיָה כַּאֲשֶׁר יָרִים מֹשֶׁה יָדוֹ וְגָבַר יִשְׂרָאֵל וְכַאֲשֶׁר יָנִיחַ יָדוֹ וְגָבַר עֲמָלֵק: ¹²וִידֵי מֹשֶׁה כְּבֵדִים וַיִּקְחוּ־אֶבֶן וַיָּשִׂימוּ תַחְתָּיו וַיֵּשֶׁב עָלֶיהָ וְאַהֲרֹן וְחוּר תָּמְכוּ בְיָדָיו מִזֶּה אֶחָד

---

a   I.e., "Trial."
b   I.e., "Quarrel."

Aaron and Hur, one on each side, supported his hands; thus his hands remained steady until the sun set. [13]And Joshua overwhelmed the people of Amalek[c] with the sword.

[14]Then the LORD said to Moses, "Inscribe this in a document as a reminder, and read it aloud to Joshua: I will utterly blot out the memory of Amalek from under heaven!" [15]And Moses built an altar and named it Adonai-nissi.[d] [16]He said, "It means, 'Hand upon the throne[e] of the LORD!' The LORD will be at war with Amalek throughout the ages."

18 YITRO
Jethro priest of Midian, Moses' father-in-law, heard all that God had done for Moses and for Israel His people, how the LORD had brought Israel out from Egypt. [2]So Jethro, Moses' father-in-law, took Zipporah, Moses' wife, after she had been sent home, [3]and her two sons—of whom one was named Gershom, that is to say, "I have been a stranger[a] in a foreign land"; [4]and the other was named Eliezer,[b] meaning, "The God of my father was my help, and He delivered me from the sword of Pharaoh." [5]Jethro, Moses' father-in-law, brought Moses' sons and wife to him in the wilderness, where he was encamped at the mountain of God. [6]He sent word to Moses, "I, your father-in-law Jethro, am coming to you, with your wife and her two sons." [7]Moses went out to meet his father-in-law; he bowed low and kissed him; each asked after the other's welfare, and they went into the tent.

[8]Moses then recounted to his father-in-law everything that the LORD had done to Pharaoh and to the Egyptians for Israel's sake, all the

וּמִזֶּ֣ה אֶחָ֔ד וַיְהִ֥י יָדָ֛יו אֱמוּנָ֖ה עַד־בֹּ֣א הַשָּׁ֑מֶשׁ: 13 וַיַּחֲלֹ֧שׁ יְהוֹשֻׁ֛עַ אֶת־עֲמָלֵ֥ק וְאֶת־עַמּ֖וֹ לְפִי־חָֽרֶב: פ

14 וַיֹּ֨אמֶר יְהֹוָ֜ה אֶל־מֹשֶׁ֗ה כְּתֹ֨ב זֹ֤את זִכָּרוֹן֙ בַּסֵּ֔פֶר וְשִׂ֖ים בְּאָזְנֵ֣י יְהוֹשֻׁ֑עַ כִּֽי־מָחֹ֤ה אֶמְחֶה֙ אֶת־זֵ֣כֶר עֲמָלֵ֔ק מִתַּ֖חַת הַשָּׁמָֽיִם: 15 וַיִּ֥בֶן מֹשֶׁ֖ה מִזְבֵּ֑חַ וַיִּקְרָ֥א שְׁמ֖וֹ יְהֹוָ֥ה | נִסִּֽי: 16 וַיֹּ֗אמֶר כִּֽי־יָד֙ עַל־כֵּ֣ס יָ֔הּ מִלְחָמָ֥ה לַֽיהֹוָ֖ה בַּֽעֲמָלֵ֑ק מִדֹּ֖ר דֹּֽר: פ

יח   יתרו
וַיִּשְׁמַ֞ע יִתְר֨וֹ כֹהֵ֤ן מִדְיָן֙ חֹתֵ֣ן מֹשֶׁ֔ה אֵת֩ כָּל־אֲשֶׁ֨ר עָשָׂ֤ה אֱלֹהִים֙ לְמֹשֶׁ֔ה וּלְיִשְׂרָאֵ֖ל עַמּ֑וֹ כִּֽי־הוֹצִ֧יא יְהֹוָ֛ה אֶת־יִשְׂרָאֵ֖ל מִמִּצְרָֽיִם: 2 וַיִּקַּ֗ח יִתְרוֹ֙ חֹתֵ֣ן מֹשֶׁ֔ה אֶת־צִפֹּרָ֖ה אֵ֣שֶׁת מֹשֶׁ֑ה אַחַ֖ר שִׁלּוּחֶֽיהָ: 3 וְאֵ֖ת שְׁנֵ֣י בָנֶ֑יהָ אֲשֶׁ֨ר שֵׁ֤ם הָֽאֶחָד֙ גֵּֽרְשֹׁ֔ם כִּ֣י אָמַ֔ר גֵּ֣ר הָיִ֔יתִי בְּאֶ֖רֶץ נָכְרִיָּֽה: 4 וְשֵׁ֥ם הָֽאֶחָ֖ד אֱלִיעֶ֑זֶר כִּֽי־אֱלֹהֵ֤י אָבִי֙ בְּעֶזְרִ֔י וַיַּצִּלֵ֖נִי מֵחֶ֥רֶב פַּרְעֹֽה: 5 וַיָּבֹ֞א יִתְר֨וֹ חֹתֵ֥ן מֹשֶׁ֛ה וּבָנָ֥יו וְאִשְׁתּ֖וֹ אֶל־מֹשֶׁ֑ה אֶל־הַמִּדְבָּ֕ר אֲשֶׁר־ה֥וּא חֹנֶ֛ה שָׁ֖ם הַ֥ר הָֽאֱלֹהִֽים: 6 וַיֹּ֙אמֶר֙ אֶל־מֹשֶׁ֔ה אֲנִ֛י חֹתֶנְךָ֥ יִתְר֖וֹ בָּ֣א אֵלֶ֑יךָ וְאִ֨שְׁתְּךָ֔ וּשְׁנֵ֥י בָנֶ֖יהָ עִמָּֽהּ: 7 וַיֵּצֵ֨א מֹשֶׁ֜ה לִקְרַ֣את חֹֽתְנ֗וֹ וַיִּשְׁתַּ֙חוּ֙ וַיִּשַּׁק־ל֔וֹ וַיִּשְׁאֲל֥וּ אִישׁ־לְרֵעֵ֖הוּ לְשָׁל֑וֹם וַיָּבֹ֖אוּ הָאֹֽהֱלָה: 8 וַיְסַפֵּ֤ר מֹשֶׁה֙ לְחֹ֣תְנ֔וֹ אֵת֩ כָּל־אֲשֶׁ֨ר עָשָׂ֤ה יְהֹוָה֙ לְפַרְעֹ֣ה וּלְמִצְרַ֔יִם עַ֖ל אוֹדֹ֣ת יִשְׂרָאֵ֑ל אֵ֤ת כָּל־הַתְּלָאָה֙ אֲשֶׁ֣ר מְצָאָ֣תַם בַּדֶּ֔רֶךְ

---

c   Lit. "Amalek and his people."
d   I.e., "The LORD is my banner."
e   Meaning of Heb. kes uncertain.

a   Heb. ger.
b   Lit. "(My) God is help."

hardships that had befallen them on the way, and how the LORD had delivered them. 9And Jethro rejoiced over all the kindness that the LORD had shown Israel when He delivered them from the Egyptians. 10"Blessed be the LORD," Jethro said, "who delivered you from the Egyptians and from Pharaoh, and who delivered the people from under the hand of the Egyptians. 11Now I know that the LORD is greater than all gods, c-yes, by the result of their very schemes against [the people]."-c 12And Jethro, Moses' father-in-law, brought a burnt offering and sacrifices for God; and Aaron came with all the elders of Israel to partake of the meal before God with Moses' father-in-law.

13Next day, Moses sat as magistrate among the people, while the people stood about Moses from morning until evening. 14But when Moses' father-in-law saw how much he had to do for the people, he said, "What is this thing that you are doing to the people? Why do you actd alone, while all the people stand about you from morning until evening?" 15Moses replied to his father-in-law, "It is because the people come to me to inquire of God. 16When they have a dispute, it comes before me, and I decide between one person and another, and I make known the laws and teachings of God."

17But Moses' father-in-law said to him, "The thing you are doing is not right; 18you will surely wear yourself out, and these people as well. For the task is too heavy for you; you cannot do it alone. 19Now listen to me. I will give you counsel, and God be with you! You represent the people before God: you bring the disputes before God, 20and enjoin upon them the laws and the teachings, and make known to them the way they are to go and the practices they are to follow. 21You shall also seek out from among all

---

c-c Meaning of Heb. uncertain.
d Lit. "sit" as magistrate; cf. v. 13.

וַיַּצִּלֵם יְהֹוָה׃ 9וַיִּחַדְּ יִתְרוֹ עַל כָּל־הַטּוֹבָה אֲשֶׁר־עָשָׂה יְהֹוָה לְיִשְׂרָאֵל אֲשֶׁר הִצִּילוֹ מִיַּד מִצְרָיִם׃ 10וַיֹּאמֶר יִתְרוֹ בָּרוּךְ יְהֹוָה אֲשֶׁר הִצִּיל אֶתְכֶם מִיַּד מִצְרַיִם וּמִיַּד פַּרְעֹה אֲשֶׁר הִצִּיל אֶת־הָעָם מִתַּחַת יַד־מִצְרָיִם׃ 11עַתָּה יָדַעְתִּי כִּי־גָדוֹל יְהֹוָה מִכָּל־הָאֱלֹהִים כִּי בַדָּבָר אֲשֶׁר זָדוּ עֲלֵיהֶם׃ 12וַיִּקַּח יִתְרוֹ חֹתֵן מֹשֶׁה עֹלָה וּזְבָחִים לֵאלֹהִים וַיָּבֹא אַהֲרֹן וְכֹל ׀ זִקְנֵי יִשְׂרָאֵל לֶאֱכָל־לֶחֶם עִם־חֹתֵן מֹשֶׁה לִפְנֵי הָאֱלֹהִים׃

13וַיְהִי מִמׇּחֳרָת וַיֵּשֶׁב מֹשֶׁה לִשְׁפֹּט אֶת־הָעָם וַיַּעֲמֹד הָעָם עַל־מֹשֶׁה מִן־הַבֹּקֶר עַד־הָעָרֶב׃ 14וַיַּרְא חֹתֵן מֹשֶׁה אֵת כָּל־אֲשֶׁר־הוּא עֹשֶׂה לָעָם וַיֹּאמֶר מָה־הַדָּבָר הַזֶּה אֲשֶׁר אַתָּה עֹשֶׂה לָעָם מַדּוּעַ אַתָּה יוֹשֵׁב לְבַדֶּךָ וְכָל־הָעָם נִצָּב עָלֶיךָ מִן־בֹּקֶר עַד־עָרֶב׃ 15וַיֹּאמֶר מֹשֶׁה לְחֹתְנוֹ כִּי־יָבֹא אֵלַי הָעָם לִדְרֹשׁ אֱלֹהִים׃ 16כִּי־יִהְיֶה לָהֶם דָּבָר בָּא אֵלַי וְשָׁפַטְתִּי בֵּין אִישׁ וּבֵין רֵעֵהוּ וְהוֹדַעְתִּי אֶת־חֻקֵּי הָאֱלֹהִים וְאֶת־תּוֹרֹתָיו׃ 17וַיֹּאמֶר חֹתֵן מֹשֶׁה אֵלָיו לֹא־טוֹב הַדָּבָר אֲשֶׁר אַתָּה עֹשֶׂה׃ 18נָבֹל תִּבֹּל גַּם־אַתָּה גַּם־הָעָם הַזֶּה אֲשֶׁר עִמָּךְ כִּי־כָבֵד מִמְּךָ הַדָּבָר לֹא־תוּכַל עֲשֹׂהוּ לְבַדֶּךָ׃ 19עַתָּה שְׁמַע בְּקֹלִי אִיעָצְךָ וִיהִי אֱלֹהִים עִמָּךְ הֱיֵה אַתָּה לָעָם מוּל הָאֱלֹהִים וְהֵבֵאתָ אַתָּה אֶת־הַדְּבָרִים אֶל־הָאֱלֹהִים׃ 20וְהִזְהַרְתָּה אֶתְהֶם אֶת־הַחֻקִּים וְאֶת־הַתּוֹרֹת וְהוֹדַעְתָּ לָהֶם אֶת־הַדֶּרֶךְ יֵלְכוּ בָהּ וְאֶת־הַמַּעֲשֶׂה אֲשֶׁר יַעֲשׂוּן׃ 21וְאַתָּה תֶחֱזֶה מִכָּל־הָעָם אַנְשֵׁי־חַיִל יִרְאֵי

the people capable men who fear God, trustworthy men who spurn ill-gotten gain. Set these over them as chiefs of thousands, hundreds, fifties, and tens, and 22let them judge the people at all times. Have them bring every major dispute to you, but let them decide every minor dispute themselves. Make it easier for yourself by letting them share the burden with you. 23If you do this—and God so commands you—you will be able to bear up; and all these people too will go home unwearied."

24Moses heeded his father-in-law and did just as he had said. 25Moses chose capable men out of all Israel, and appointed them heads over the people—chiefs of thousands, hundreds, fifties, and tens; 26and they judged the people at all times: the difficult matters they would bring to Moses, and all the minor matters they would decide themselves. 27Then Moses bade his father-in-law farewell, and he went his way to his own land.

19 On the third new moon after the Israelites had gone forth from the land of Egypt, on that very day, they entered the wilderness of Sinai. 2Having journeyed from Rephidim, they entered the wilderness of Sinai and encamped in the wilderness. Israel encamped there in front of the mountain, 3and Moses went up to God. The LORD called to him from the mountain, saying, "Thus shall you say to the house of Jacob and declare to the children of Israel: 4'You have seen what I did to the Egyptians, how I bore you on eagles' wings and brought you to Me. 5Now then, if you will obey Me faithfully and keep My covenant, you shall be My treasured possession among all the peoples. Indeed, all the earth is Mine, 6but you shall be to Me a kingdom of priests and a holy nation.' These are the words that you shall speak to the children of Israel."

אֱלֹהִים אַנְשֵׁי אֱמֶת שֹׂנְאֵי בָצַע וְשַׂמְתָּ עֲלֵהֶם שָׂרֵי אֲלָפִים שָׂרֵי מֵאוֹת שָׂרֵי חֲמִשִּׁים וְשָׂרֵי עֲשָׂרֹת: 22 וְשָׁפְטוּ אֶת־הָעָם בְּכָל־עֵת וְהָיָה כָּל־הַדָּבָר הַגָּדֹל יָבִיאוּ אֵלֶיךָ וְכָל־הַדָּבָר הַקָּטֹן יִשְׁפְּטוּ־הֵם וְהָקֵל מֵעָלֶיךָ וְנָשְׂאוּ אִתָּךְ: 23 אִם אֶת־הַדָּבָר הַזֶּה תַּעֲשֶׂה וְצִוְּךָ אֱלֹהִים וְיָכָלְתָּ עֲמֹד וְגַם כָּל־הָעָם הַזֶּה עַל־מְקֹמוֹ יָבֹא בְשָׁלוֹם: 24 וַיִּשְׁמַע מֹשֶׁה לְקוֹל חֹתְנוֹ וַיַּעַשׂ כֹּל אֲשֶׁר אָמָר: 25 וַיִּבְחַר מֹשֶׁה אַנְשֵׁי־חַיִל מִכָּל־יִשְׂרָאֵל וַיִּתֵּן אֹתָם רָאשִׁים עַל־הָעָם שָׂרֵי אֲלָפִים שָׂרֵי מֵאוֹת שָׂרֵי חֲמִשִּׁים וְשָׂרֵי עֲשָׂרֹת: 26 וְשָׁפְטוּ אֶת־הָעָם בְּכָל־עֵת אֶת־הַדָּבָר הַקָּשֶׁה יְבִיאוּן אֶל־מֹשֶׁה וְכָל־הַדָּבָר הַקָּטֹן יִשְׁפּוּטוּ הֵם: 27 וַיְשַׁלַּח מֹשֶׁה אֶת־חֹתְנוֹ וַיֵּלֶךְ לוֹ אֶל־אַרְצוֹ: פ

יט בַּחֹדֶשׁ הַשְּׁלִישִׁי לְצֵאת בְּנֵי־יִשְׂרָאֵל מֵאֶרֶץ מִצְרָיִם בַּיּוֹם הַזֶּה בָּאוּ מִדְבַּר סִינָי: 2 וַיִּסְעוּ מֵרְפִידִים וַיָּבֹאוּ מִדְבַּר סִינַי וַיַּחֲנוּ בַּמִּדְבָּר וַיִּחַן־שָׁם יִשְׂרָאֵל נֶגֶד הָהָר: 3 וּמֹשֶׁה עָלָה אֶל־הָאֱלֹהִים וַיִּקְרָא אֵלָיו יְהוָֹה מִן־הָהָר לֵאמֹר כֹּה תֹאמַר לְבֵית יַעֲקֹב וְתַגֵּיד לִבְנֵי יִשְׂרָאֵל: 4 אַתֶּם רְאִיתֶם אֲשֶׁר עָשִׂיתִי לְמִצְרָיִם וָאֶשָּׂא אֶתְכֶם עַל־כַּנְפֵי נְשָׁרִים וָאָבִא אֶתְכֶם אֵלָי: 5 וְעַתָּה אִם־שָׁמוֹעַ תִּשְׁמְעוּ בְּקֹלִי וּשְׁמַרְתֶּם אֶת־בְּרִיתִי וִהְיִיתֶם לִי סְגֻלָּה מִכָּל־הָעַמִּים כִּי־לִי כָּל־הָאָרֶץ: 6 וְאַתֶּם תִּהְיוּ־לִי מַמְלֶכֶת כֹּהֲנִים וְגוֹי קָדוֹשׁ אֵלֶּה הַדְּבָרִים אֲשֶׁר תְּדַבֵּר אֶל־בְּנֵי יִשְׂרָאֵל:

7Moses came and summoned the elders of the people and put before them all that the LORD had commanded him. 8All the people answered as one, saying, "All that the LORD has spoken we will do!" And Moses brought back the people's words to the LORD. 9And the LORD said to Moses, "I will come to you in a thick cloud, in order that the people may hear when I speak with you and so trust you ever after." Then Moses reported the people's words to the LORD, 10and the LORD said to Moses, "Go to the people and warn them to stay pure[a] today and tomorrow. Let them wash their clothes. 11Let them be ready for the third day; for on the third day the LORD will come down, in the sight of all the people, on Mount Sinai. 12You shall set bounds for the people round about, saying, 'Beware of going up the mountain or touching the border of it. Whoever touches the mountain shall be put to death: 13no hand shall touch him, but he shall be either stoned or shot; beast or man, he shall not live.' When the ram's horn [b]-sounds a long blast,-[b] they may go up on the mountain."

14Moses came down from the mountain to the people and warned the people to stay pure, and they washed their clothes. 15And he said to the people, "Be ready for the third day: do not go near a woman."

16On the third day, as morning dawned, there was thunder, and lightning, and a dense cloud upon the mountain, and a very loud blast of the horn; and all the people who were in the camp trembled. 17Moses led the people out of the camp toward God, and they took their places at the foot of the mountain.

18Now Mount Sinai was all in smoke, for the LORD had come down upon it in fire; the smoke rose like the smoke of a kiln, and the whole

7וַיָּבֹא מֹשֶׁה וַיִּקְרָא לְזִקְנֵי הָעָם וַיָּשֶׂם לִפְנֵיהֶם אֵת כָּל־הַדְּבָרִים הָאֵלֶּה אֲשֶׁר צִוָּהוּ יְהוָה: 8וַיַּעֲנוּ כָל־הָעָם יַחְדָּו וַיֹּאמְרוּ כֹּל אֲשֶׁר־דִּבֶּר יְהוָה נַעֲשֶׂה וַיָּשֶׁב מֹשֶׁה אֶת־דִּבְרֵי הָעָם אֶל־יְהוָה: 9וַיֹּאמֶר יְהוָה אֶל־מֹשֶׁה הִנֵּה אָנֹכִי בָּא אֵלֶיךָ בְּעַב הֶעָנָן בַּעֲבוּר יִשְׁמַע הָעָם בְּדַבְּרִי עִמָּךְ וְגַם־בְּךָ יַאֲמִינוּ לְעוֹלָם וַיַּגֵּד מֹשֶׁה אֶת־דִּבְרֵי הָעָם אֶל־יְהוָה: 10וַיֹּאמֶר יְהוָה אֶל־מֹשֶׁה לֵךְ אֶל־הָעָם וְקִדַּשְׁתָּם הַיּוֹם וּמָחָר וְכִבְּסוּ שִׂמְלֹתָם: 11וְהָיוּ נְכֹנִים לַיּוֹם הַשְּׁלִישִׁי כִּי | בַּיּוֹם הַשְּׁלִישִׁי יֵרֵד יְהוָה לְעֵינֵי כָל־הָעָם עַל־הַר סִינָי: 12וְהִגְבַּלְתָּ אֶת־הָעָם סָבִיב לֵאמֹר הִשָּׁמְרוּ לָכֶם עֲלוֹת בָּהָר וּנְגֹעַ בְּקָצֵהוּ כָּל־הַנֹּגֵעַ בָּהָר מוֹת יוּמָת: 13לֹא־תִגַּע בּוֹ יָד כִּי־סָקוֹל יִסָּקֵל אוֹ־יָרֹה יִיָּרֶה אִם־בְּהֵמָה אִם־אִישׁ לֹא יִחְיֶה בִּמְשֹׁךְ הַיֹּבֵל הֵמָּה יַעֲלוּ בָהָר:

14וַיֵּרֶד מֹשֶׁה מִן־הָהָר אֶל־הָעָם וַיְקַדֵּשׁ אֶת־הָעָם וַיְכַבְּסוּ שִׂמְלֹתָם: 15וַיֹּאמֶר אֶל־הָעָם הֱיוּ נְכֹנִים לִשְׁלֹשֶׁת יָמִים אַל־תִּגְּשׁוּ אֶל־אִשָּׁה:

16וַיְהִי בַיּוֹם הַשְּׁלִישִׁי בִּהְיֹת הַבֹּקֶר וַיְהִי קֹלֹת וּבְרָקִים וְעָנָן כָּבֵד עַל־הָהָר וְקֹל שֹׁפָר חָזָק מְאֹד וַיֶּחֱרַד כָּל־הָעָם אֲשֶׁר בַּמַּחֲנֶה: 17וַיּוֹצֵא מֹשֶׁה אֶת־הָעָם לִקְרַאת הָאֱלֹהִים מִן־הַמַּחֲנֶה וַיִּתְיַצְּבוּ בְּתַחְתִּית הָהָר: 18וְהַר סִינַי עָשַׁן כֻּלּוֹ מִפְּנֵי אֲשֶׁר יָרַד עָלָיו יְהוָה בָּאֵשׁ וַיַּעַל עֲשָׁנוֹ כְּעֶשֶׁן הַכִּבְשָׁן וַיֶּחֱרַד כָּל־הָהָר מְאֹד: 19וַיְהִי קוֹל הַשּׁוֹפָר

---

a Cf. v. 15.
b-b Meaning of Heb. uncertain.

mountain^c trembled violently. ¹⁹The blare of the horn grew louder and louder. As Moses spoke, God answered him in thunder. ²⁰The LORD came down upon Mount Sinai, on the top of the mountain, and the LORD called Moses to the top of the mountain and Moses went up. ²¹The LORD said to Moses, "Go down, warn the people not to break through to the LORD to gaze, lest many of them perish. ²²The priests also, who come near the LORD, must stay pure, lest the LORD break out against them." ²³But Moses said to the LORD, "The people cannot come up to Mount Sinai, for You warned us saying, 'Set bounds about the mountain and sanctify it.'" ²⁴So the LORD said to him, "Go down, and come back together with Aaron; but let not the priests or the people break through to come up to the LORD, lest He break out against them." ²⁵And Moses went down to the people and spoke to them.

20 God spoke all these words,^a saying:

²I the LORD am your God who brought you out of the land of Egypt, the house of bondage: ³You shall have no other gods besides Me.

⁴You shall not make for yourself a sculptured image, or any likeness of what is in the heavens above, or on the earth below, or in the waters under the earth. ⁵You shall not bow down to them or serve them. For I the LORD your God am an impassioned God, visiting the guilt of the parents upon the children, upon the third and upon the fourth generations of those who reject Me, ⁶but showing kindness to the thousandth generation of those who love Me and keep My commandments.

⁷You shall not ^bswear falsely by-^b the name

---

c *Some Hebrew manuscripts and the Greek read "all the people";*
   cf. v. 16.

a *Tradition varies as to the division of the Commandments in*
   vv. 2–14, and as to the numbering of the verses from 13 on.

b-b *Others "take in vain."*

הוֹלֵךְ וְחָזֵק מְאֹד מֹשֶׁה יְדַבֵּר וְהָאֱלֹהִים יַעֲנֶנּוּ בְקוֹל: 20 וַיֵּרֶד יְהוָה עַל־הַר סִינַי אֶל־רֹאשׁ הָהָר וַיִּקְרָא יְהוָה לְמֹשֶׁה אֶל־רֹאשׁ הָהָר וַיַּעַל מֹשֶׁה: 21 וַיֹּאמֶר יְהוָה אֶל־מֹשֶׁה רֵד הָעֵד בָּעָם פֶּן־יֶהֶרְסוּ אֶל־יְהוָה לִרְאוֹת וְנָפַל מִמֶּנּוּ רָב: 22 וְגַם הַכֹּהֲנִים הַנִּגָּשִׁים אֶל־יְהוָה יִתְקַדָּשׁוּ פֶּן־יִפְרֹץ בָּהֶם יְהוָה: 23 וַיֹּאמֶר מֹשֶׁה אֶל־יְהוָה לֹא־יוּכַל הָעָם לַעֲלֹת אֶל־הַר סִינָי כִּי־אַתָּה הַעֵדֹתָה בָּנוּ לֵאמֹר הַגְבֵּל אֶת־הָהָר וְקִדַּשְׁתּוֹ: 24 וַיֹּאמֶר אֵלָיו יְהוָה לֶךְ־רֵד וְעָלִיתָ אַתָּה וְאַהֲרֹן עִמָּךְ וְהַכֹּהֲנִים וְהָעָם אַל־יֶהֶרְסוּ לַעֲלֹת אֶל־יְהוָה פֶּן־יִפְרָץ־בָּם: 25 וַיֵּרֶד מֹשֶׁה אֶל־הָעָם וַיֹּאמֶר אֲלֵהֶם: ס

כ וַיְדַבֵּר אֱלֹהִים אֵת כָּל־הַדְּבָרִים הָאֵלֶּה לֵאמֹר: ס

2 *אָנֹכִי יְהוָה אֱלֹהֶיךָ אֲשֶׁר הוֹצֵאתִיךָ מֵאֶרֶץ מִצְרַיִם מִבֵּית עֲבָדִים: 3 *לֹא־יִהְיֶה לְךָ אֱלֹהִים אֲחֵרִים עַל־פָּנָי:

4 לֹא תַעֲשֶׂה־לְךָ פֶסֶל וְכָל־תְּמוּנָה אֲשֶׁר בַּשָּׁמַיִם מִמַּעַל וַאֲשֶׁר בָּאָרֶץ מִתָּחַת וַאֲשֶׁר בַּמַּיִם מִתַּחַת לָאָרֶץ: 5 לֹא־תִשְׁתַּחְוֶה לָהֶם וְלֹא תָעָבְדֵם כִּי אָנֹכִי יְהוָה אֱלֹהֶיךָ אֵל קַנָּא פֹּקֵד עֲוֹן אָבֹת עַל־בָּנִים עַל־שִׁלֵּשִׁים וְעַל־רִבֵּעִים לְשֹׂנְאָי: 6 וְעֹשֶׂה חֶסֶד לַאֲלָפִים לְאֹהֲבַי וּלְשֹׁמְרֵי מִצְוֹתָי: ס

7 לֹא תִשָּׂא אֶת־שֵׁם־יְהוָה אֱלֹהֶיךָ לַשָּׁוְא

---

vv. 2–16. נדפס טעם התחתון בלבד והוא למערבאי,
והפסוקים נספר לפי מהדורת לעטעריס
v. 3. למערבאי לא נספר בסכום הפסוקים

of the Lord your God; for the Lord will not clear one who swears falsely by His name.

8Remember the sabbath day and keep it holy. 9Six days you shall labor and do all your work, 10but the seventh day is a sabbath of the Lord your God: you shall not do any work—you, your son or daughter, your male or female slave, or your cattle, or the stranger who is within your settlements. 11For in six days the Lord made heaven and earth and sea, and all that is in them, and He rested on the seventh day; therefore the Lord blessed the sabbath day and hallowed it.

12Honor your father and your mother, that you may long endure on the land that the Lord your God is assigning to you.

13You shall not murder.

You shall not commit adultery.

You shall not steal.

You shall not bear false witness against your neighbor.

14You shall not covet your neighbor's house: you shall not covet your neighbor's wife, or his male or female slave, or his ox or his ass, or anything that is your neighbor's.

15All the people witnessed the thunder and lightning, the blare of the horn and the mountain smoking; and when the people saw it, they fell back and stood at a distance. 16"You speak to us," they said to Moses, "and we will obey; but let not God speak to us, lest we die." 17Moses answered the people, "Be not afraid; for God has come only in order to test you, and in order that the fear of Him may be ever with you, so that you do not go astray." 18So the people remained at a distance, while Moses approached the thick cloud where God was.

19The Lord said to Moses:

Thus shall you say to the Israelites: You yourselves saw that I spoke to you from the very

כִּ֣י לֹ֤א יְנַקֶּה֙ יְהֹוָ֔ה אֵ֛ת אֲשֶׁר־יִשָּׂ֥א אֶת־שְׁמ֖וֹ לַשָּֽׁוְא׃ פ

8זָכ֛וֹר֩ אֶת־י֥֨וֹם הַשַּׁבָּ֖ת לְקַדְּשֽׁ֑וֹ׃ 9שֵׁ֤֣שֶׁת יָמִ֣ים֙ תַּֽעֲבֹ֔ד֮ וְעָשִׂ֣֖יתָ כׇּל־מְלַאכְתֶּ֑ךָ׃ 10וְי֙֡וֹם הַשְּׁבִיעִ֜֔י שַׁבָּ֖֣ת ׀ לַיהֹוָ֣ה אֱלֹהֶ֑֗יךָ לֹֽא־תַעֲשֶׂ֣ה כׇל־מְלָאכָ֡֡ה אַתָּ֣ה ׀ וּבִנְךָֽ֣־וּ֠בִתֶּ֗ךָ עַבְדְּךָ֤֨ וַאֲמָֽתְ֜ךָ֙ וּבְהֶמְתֶּ֔ךָ וְגֵרְךָ֖ אֲשֶׁ֥ר בִּשְׁעָרֶֽיךָ׃ 11כִּ֣י שֵֽׁשֶׁת־יָמִים֩ עָשָׂ֨ה יְהֹוָ֜ה אֶת־הַשָּׁמַ֣יִם וְאֶת־הָאָ֗רֶץ אֶת־הַיָּם֙ וְאֶת־כׇּל־אֲשֶׁר־בָּ֔ם וַיָּ֖נַח בַּיּ֣וֹם הַשְּׁבִיעִ֑י עַל־כֵּ֗ן בֵּרַ֧ךְ יְהֹוָ֛ה אֶת־י֥וֹם הַשַּׁבָּ֖ת וַֽיְקַדְּשֵֽׁהוּ׃ ס

12כַּבֵּ֥ד אֶת־אָבִ֖יךָ וְאֶת־אִמֶּ֑ךָ לְמַ֙עַן֙ יַאֲרִכ֣וּן יָמֶ֔יךָ עַ֚ל הָאֲדָמָ֔ה אֲשֶׁר־יְהֹוָ֥ה אֱלֹהֶ֖יךָ נֹתֵ֥ן לָֽךְ׃ ס

13*לֹ֥֖א תִּֿרְצָֽ֖ח׃ ס

לֹ֣֖א תִּֿנְאָֽ֑ף׃ ס

לֹ֣֖א תִּֿגְנֹֽ֔ב׃ ס

לֹֽא־תַעֲנֶ֥ה בְרֵעֲךָ֖ עֵ֥ד שָֽׁקֶר׃ ס

14לֹ֥א תַחְמֹ֖ד בֵּ֣ית רֵעֶ֑ךָ לֹֽא־תַחְמֹ֞ד אֵ֣שֶׁת רֵעֶ֗ךָ וְעַבְדּ֤וֹ וַאֲמָתוֹ֙ וְשׁוֹר֣וֹ וַחֲמֹר֔וֹ וְכֹ֖ל אֲשֶׁ֥ר לְרֵעֶֽךָ׃ פ

15וְכׇל־הָעָם֩ רֹאִ֨ים אֶת־הַקּוֹלֹ֜ת וְאֶת־הַלַּפִּידִ֗ם וְאֵת֙ ק֣וֹל הַשֹּׁפָ֔ר וְאֶת־הָהָ֖ר עָשֵׁ֑ן וַיַּ֣רְא הָעָ֔ם וַיָּנֻ֖עוּ וַיַּֽעַמְד֥וּ מֵֽרָחֹֽק׃ 16וַיֹּֽאמְרוּ֙ אֶל־מֹשֶׁ֔ה דַּבֵּר־אַתָּ֥ה עִמָּ֖נוּ וְנִשְׁמָ֑עָה וְאַל־יְדַבֵּ֥ר עִמָּ֛נוּ אֱלֹהִ֖ים פֶּן־נָמֽוּת׃ 17וַיֹּ֨אמֶר מֹשֶׁ֣ה אֶל־הָעָם֮ אַל־תִּירָ֒אוּ֒ כִּ֗י לְבַֽעֲבוּר֙ נַסּ֣וֹת אֶתְכֶ֔ם בָּ֖א הָאֱלֹהִ֑ים וּבַעֲב֗וּר תִּהְיֶ֧ה יִרְאָת֛וֹ עַל־פְּנֵיכֶ֖ם לְבִלְתִּ֥י תֶחֱטָֽאוּ׃ 18וַיַּעֲמֹ֥ד הָעָ֖ם מֵֽרָחֹ֑ק וּמֹשֶׁה֙ נִגַּ֣שׁ אֶל־הָ֣עֲרָפֶ֔ל אֲשֶׁר־שָׁ֖ם הָאֱלֹהִֽים׃ פ

19וַיֹּ֥אמֶר יְהֹוָ֖ה אֶל־מֹשֶׁ֑ה כֹּ֤ה תֹאמַר֙ אֶל־בְּנֵ֣י יִשְׂרָאֵ֔ל אַתֶּ֣ם רְאִיתֶ֔ם

heavens: ²⁰With Me, therefore, you shall not make any gods of silver, nor shall you make for yourselves any gods of gold. ²¹Make for Me an altar of earth and sacrifice on it your burnt offerings and your sacrifices of well-being,^c your sheep and your oxen; in every place where I cause My name to be mentioned I will come to you and bless you. ²²And if you make for Me an altar of stones, do not build it of hewn stones; for by wielding your tool upon them you have profaned them. ²³Do not ascend My altar by steps, that your nakedness may not be exposed upon it.

21 MISHPATIM
These are the rules that you shall set before them:

²When you acquire a Hebrew slave, he shall serve six years; in the seventh year he shall go free, without payment. ³If he came single, he shall leave single; if he had a wife, his wife shall leave with him. ⁴If his master gave him a wife, and she has borne him children, the wife and her children shall belong to the master, and he shall leave alone. ⁵But if the slave declares, "I love my master, and my wife and children: I do not wish to go free," ⁶his master shall take him before God.^a He shall be brought to the door or the doorpost, and his master shall pierce his ear with an awl; and he shall then remain his slave for life.

⁷When a man sells his daughter as a slave, she shall not be freed as male slaves are. ⁸If she proves to be displeasing to her master, who designated her for himself, he must let her be redeemed; he shall not have the right to sell her to outsiders, since he broke faith with her. ⁹And if he designated her for his son, he shall deal with

___
c   Others "peace-offering." Meaning of shelamim uncertain.

a   Others "to the judges."

---

20 כִּי מִן־הַשָּׁמַ֫יִם דִּבַּ֫רְתִּי עִמָּכֶ֑ם לֹ֣א תַעֲשׂ֣וּן אִתִּ֔י אֱלֹ֤הֵי כֶ֫סֶף֙ וֵֽאלֹהֵ֣י זָהָ֔ב לֹ֥א תַעֲשׂ֖וּ לָכֶֽם׃ 21 מִזְבַּ֣ח אֲדָמָה֮ תַּעֲשֶׂה־לִּי֒ וְזָבַחְתָּ֣ עָלָ֗יו אֶת־עֹלֹתֶ֨יךָ֙ וְאֶת־שְׁלָמֶ֔יךָ אֶת־צֹֽאנְךָ֖ וְאֶת־בְּקָרֶ֑ךָ בְּכׇל־הַמָּקוֹם֙ אֲשֶׁ֣ר אַזְכִּ֣יר אֶת־שְׁמִ֔י אָב֥וֹא אֵלֶ֖יךָ וּבֵרַכְתִּֽיךָ׃ 22 וְאִם־מִזְבַּ֤ח אֲבָנִים֙ תַּֽעֲשֶׂה־לִּ֔י לֹֽא־תִבְנֶ֥ה אֶתְהֶ֖ן גָּזִ֑ית כִּ֧י חַרְבְּךָ֛ הֵנַ֥פְתָּ עָלֶ֖יהָ וַתְּחַלְלֶֽהָ׃ 23 וְלֹֽא־תַעֲלֶ֥ה בְמַעֲלֹ֖ת עַֽל־מִזְבְּחִ֑י אֲשֶׁ֛ר לֹֽא־תִגָּלֶ֥ה עֶרְוָתְךָ֖ עָלָֽיו׃ פ

כא משפטים
וְאֵ֙לֶּה֙ הַמִּשְׁפָּטִ֔ים אֲשֶׁ֥ר תָּשִׂ֖ים לִפְנֵיהֶֽם׃ 2 כִּ֤י תִקְנֶה֙ עֶ֣בֶד עִבְרִ֔י שֵׁ֥שׁ שָׁנִ֖ים יַעֲבֹ֑ד וּבַ֨שְּׁבִעִ֔ת יֵצֵ֥א לַֽחׇפְשִׁ֖י חִנָּֽם׃ 3 אִם־בְּגַפּ֥וֹ יָבֹ֖א בְּגַפּ֣וֹ יֵצֵ֑א אִם־בַּ֤עַל אִשָּׁה֙ ה֔וּא וְיָצְאָ֥ה אִשְׁתּ֖וֹ עִמּֽוֹ׃ 4 אִם־אֲדֹנָיו֙ יִתֶּן־ל֣וֹ אִשָּׁ֔ה וְיָלְדָה־ל֥וֹ בָנִ֖ים א֣וֹ בָנ֑וֹת הָאִשָּׁ֣ה וִילָדֶ֗יהָ תִּהְיֶה֙ לַֽאדֹנֶ֔יהָ וְה֖וּא יֵצֵ֥א בְגַפּֽוֹ׃ 5 וְאִם־אָמֹ֤ר יֹאמַר֙ הָעֶ֔בֶד אָהַ֙בְתִּי֙ אֶת־אֲדֹנִ֔י אֶת־אִשְׁתִּ֖י וְאֶת־בָּנָ֑י לֹ֥א אֵצֵ֖א חׇפְשִֽׁי׃ 6 וְהִגִּישׁ֤וֹ אֲדֹנָיו֙ אֶל־הָ֣אֱלֹהִ֔ים וְהִגִּישׁוֹ֙ אֶל־הַדֶּ֔לֶת א֖וֹ אֶל־הַמְּזוּזָ֑ה וְרָצַ֨ע אֲדֹנָ֤יו אֶת־אׇזְנוֹ֙ בַּמַּרְצֵ֔עַ וַעֲבָד֖וֹ לְעֹלָֽם׃ ס 7 וְכִֽי־יִמְכֹּ֥ר אִ֛ישׁ אֶת־בִּתּ֖וֹ לְאָמָ֑ה לֹ֥א תֵצֵ֖א כְּצֵ֥את הָעֲבָדִֽים׃ 8 אִם־רָעָ֞ה בְּעֵינֵ֧י אֲדֹנֶ֛יהָ אֲשֶׁר־ל֥וֹ יְעָדָ֖הּ וְהֶפְדָּ֑הּ לְעַ֥ם נׇכְרִ֛י לֹא־יִמְשֹׁ֥ל לְמׇכְרָ֖הּ בְּבִגְדוֹ־בָֽהּ׃ 9 וְאִם־לִבְנ֖וֹ יִֽיעָדֶ֑נָּה כְּמִשְׁפַּ֥ט הַבָּנ֖וֹת

her as is the practice with free maidens. [10]If he marries another, he must not withhold from this one her food, her clothing, or her conjugal rights.[b] [11]If he fails her in these three ways, she shall go free, without payment.

[12]He who fatally strikes a man shall be put to death. [13]If he did not do it by design, but it came about by an act of God, I will assign you a place to which he can flee.

[14]When a man schemes against another and kills him treacherously, you shall take him from My very altar to be put to death.

[15]He who strikes his father or his mother shall be put to death.

[16]He who kidnaps a man—whether he has sold him or is still holding him—shall be put to death.

[17]He who insults[c] his father or his mother shall be put to death.

[18]When men quarrel and one strikes the other with stone or fist, and he does not die but has to take to his bed—[19]if he then gets up and walks outdoors upon his staff, the assailant shall go unpunished, except that he must pay for his idleness and his cure.

[20]When a man strikes his slave, male or female, with a rod, and he dies there and then,[d] he must be avenged. [21]But if he survives a day or two, he is not to be avenged, since he is the other's property.

[22]When men fight, and one of them pushes a pregnant woman and a miscarriage results, but no other damage ensues, the one responsible[e] shall be fined according as the woman's husband may exact from him, the payment to be based on reckoning.[f] [23]But if other damage ensues, the penalty shall be life for life, [24]eye for eye, tooth for tooth, hand for hand, foot for foot,

יַעֲשֶׂה־לָּהּ: 10 אִם־אַחֶרֶת יִקַּח־לֹו שְׁאֵרָהּ כְּסוּתָהּ וְעֹנָתָהּ לֹא יִגְרָע: 11 וְאִם־שְׁלָשׁ־אֵלֶּה לֹא יַעֲשֶׂה לָהּ וְיָצְאָה חִנָּם אֵין כָּסֶף: ס

12 מַכֵּה אִישׁ וָמֵת מֹות יוּמָת: 13 וַאֲשֶׁר לֹא צָדָה וְהָאֱלֹהִים אִנָּה לְיָדֹו וְשַׂמְתִּי לְךָ מָקֹום אֲשֶׁר יָנוּס שָׁמָּה: ס

14 וְכִי־יָזִד אִישׁ עַל־רֵעֵהוּ לְהָרְגֹו בְעָרְמָה מֵעִם מִזְבְּחִי תִּקָּחֶנּוּ לָמוּת: ס

15 וּמַכֵּה אָבִיו וְאִמֹּו מֹות יוּמָת:

16 וְגֹנֵב אִישׁ וּמְכָרֹו וְנִמְצָא בְיָדֹו מֹות יוּמָת: ס

17 וּמְקַלֵּל אָבִיו וְאִמֹּו מֹות יוּמָת: ס

18 וְכִי־יְרִיבֻן אֲנָשִׁים וְהִכָּה־אִישׁ אֶת־רֵעֵהוּ בְּאֶבֶן אֹו בְאֶגְרֹף וְלֹא יָמוּת וְנָפַל לְמִשְׁכָּב: 19 אִם־יָקוּם וְהִתְהַלֵּךְ בַּחוּץ עַל־מִשְׁעַנְתֹּו וְנִקָּה הַמַּכֶּה רַק שִׁבְתֹּו יִתֵּן וְרַפֹּא יְרַפֵּא: ס

20 וְכִי־יַכֶּה אִישׁ אֶת־עַבְדֹּו אֹו אֶת־אֲמָתֹו בַּשֵּׁבֶט וּמֵת תַּחַת יָדֹו נָקֹם יִנָּקֵם: 21 אַךְ אִם־יֹום אֹו יֹומַיִם יַעֲמֹד לֹא יֻקַּם כִּי כַסְפֹּו הוּא: ס

22 וְכִי־יִנָּצוּ אֲנָשִׁים וְנָגְפוּ אִשָּׁה הָרָה וְיָצְאוּ יְלָדֶיהָ וְלֹא יִהְיֶה אָסֹון עָנֹושׁ יֵעָנֵשׁ כַּאֲשֶׁר יָשִׁית עָלָיו בַּעַל הָאִשָּׁה וְנָתַן בִּפְלִלִים: 23 וְאִם־אָסֹון יִהְיֶה וְנָתַתָּה נֶפֶשׁ תַּחַת נָפֶשׁ: 24 עַיִן תַּחַת עַיִן שֵׁן תַּחַת שֵׁן יָד תַּחַת יָד רֶגֶל תַּחַת רָגֶל: 25 כְּוִיָּה תַּחַת

---

b   Or "ointments."
c   Or "reviles."
d   Lit. "under his hand."
e   Heb. "he."
f   Others "as the judges determine."

²⁵burn for burn, wound for wound, bruise for bruise.

²⁶When a man strikes the eye of his slave, male or female, and destroys it, he shall let him go free on account of his eye. ²⁷If he knocks out the tooth of his slave, male or female, he shall let him go free on account of his tooth.

²⁸When an ox gores a man or a woman to death, the ox shall be stoned and its flesh shall not be eaten, but the owner of the ox is not to be punished. ²⁹If, however, that ox has been in the habit of goring, and its owner, though warned, has failed to guard it, and it kills a man or a woman—the ox shall be stoned and its owner, too, shall be put to death. ³⁰If ransom is laid upon him, he must pay whatever is laid upon him to redeem his life. ³¹So, too, if it gores a minor, male or female, [the owner] shall be dealt with according to the same rule. ³²But if the ox gores a slave, male or female, he shall pay thirty shekels of silver to the master, and the ox shall be stoned.

³³When a man opens a pit, or digs a pit and does not cover it, and an ox or an ass falls into it, ³⁴the one responsible for the pit must make restitution; he shall pay the price to the owner, but shall keep the dead animal.

³⁵When a man's ox injures his neighbor's ox and it dies, they shall sell the live ox and divide its price; they shall also divide the dead animal. ³⁶If, however, it is known that the ox was in the habit of goring, and its owner has failed to guard it, he must restore ox for ox, but shall keep the dead animal.

³⁷gWhen a man steals an ox or a sheep, and slaughters it or sells it, he shall pay five oxen for the ox, and four sheep for the sheep.—

22

¹If the thief is seized while tunneling,ᵃ and he is beaten to death, there is no bloodguilt

כְּוִיָּה פֶּצַע תַּחַת פָּצַע חַבּוּרָה תַּחַת חַבּוּרָה: ס

²⁶ וְכִי־יַכֶּה אִישׁ אֶת־עֵין עַבְדּוֹ אוֹ־אֶת־עֵין אֲמָתוֹ וְשִׁחֲתָהּ לַחָפְשִׁי יְשַׁלְּחֶנּוּ תַּחַת עֵינוֹ: ס ²⁷ וְאִם־שֵׁן עַבְדּוֹ אוֹ־שֵׁן אֲמָתוֹ יַפִּיל לַחָפְשִׁי יְשַׁלְּחֶנּוּ תַּחַת שִׁנּוֹ: פ ²⁸ וְכִי־יִגַּח שׁוֹר אֶת־אִישׁ אוֹ אֶת־אִשָּׁה וָמֵת סָקוֹל יִסָּקֵל הַשּׁוֹר וְלֹא יֵאָכֵל אֶת־בְּשָׂרוֹ וּבַעַל הַשּׁוֹר נָקִי: ²⁹ וְאִם שׁוֹר נַגָּח הוּא מִתְּמֹל שִׁלְשֹׁם וְהוּעַד בִּבְעָלָיו וְלֹא יִשְׁמְרֶנּוּ וְהֵמִית אִישׁ אוֹ אִשָּׁה הַשּׁוֹר יִסָּקֵל וְגַם־בְּעָלָיו יוּמָת: ³⁰ אִם־כֹּפֶר יוּשַׁת עָלָיו וְנָתַן פִּדְיֹן נַפְשׁוֹ כְּכֹל אֲשֶׁר־יוּשַׁת עָלָיו: ³¹ אוֹ־בֵן יִגָּח אוֹ־בַת יִגָּח כַּמִּשְׁפָּט הַזֶּה יֵעָשֶׂה לּוֹ: ³² אִם־עֶבֶד יִגַּח הַשּׁוֹר אוֹ אָמָה כֶּסֶף ׀ שְׁלֹשִׁים שְׁקָלִים יִתֵּן לַאדֹנָיו וְהַשּׁוֹר יִסָּקֵל: ס

³³ וְכִי־יִפְתַּח אִישׁ בּוֹר אוֹ כִּי־יִכְרֶה אִישׁ בֹּר וְלֹא יְכַסֶּנּוּ וְנָפַל־שָׁמָּה שּׁוֹר אוֹ חֲמוֹר: ³⁴ בַּעַל הַבּוֹר יְשַׁלֵּם כֶּסֶף יָשִׁיב לִבְעָלָיו וְהַמֵּת יִהְיֶה־לּוֹ: ס

³⁵ וְכִי־יִגֹּף שׁוֹר־אִישׁ אֶת־שׁוֹר רֵעֵהוּ וָמֵת וּמָכְרוּ אֶת־הַשּׁוֹר הַחַי וְחָצוּ אֶת־כַּסְפּוֹ וְגַם אֶת־הַמֵּת יֶחֱצוּן: ³⁶ אוֹ נוֹדַע כִּי שׁוֹר נַגָּח הוּא מִתְּמוֹל שִׁלְשֹׁם וְלֹא יִשְׁמְרֶנּוּ בְּעָלָיו שַׁלֵּם יְשַׁלֵּם שׁוֹר תַּחַת הַשּׁוֹר וְהַמֵּת יִהְיֶה־לּוֹ: ס

³⁷ כִּי יִגְנֹב־אִישׁ שׁוֹר אוֹ־שֶׂה וּטְבָחוֹ אוֹ מְכָרוֹ חֲמִשָּׁה בָקָר יְשַׁלֵּם תַּחַת הַשּׁוֹר וְאַרְבַּע־צֹאן תַּחַת הַשֶּׂה: כב ¹ אִם־בַּמַּחְתֶּרֶת יִמָּצֵא הַגַּנָּב וְהֻכָּה וָמֵת אֵין לוֹ דָּמִים: ² אִם־זָרְחָה הַשֶּׁמֶשׁ

---

g   *This constitutes chap. 22.1 in some editions.*

a   *I.e, under a wall for housebreaking.*

in his case. ²If the sun has risen on him, there is bloodguilt in that case.—He[b] must make restitution; if he lacks the means, he shall be sold for his theft. ³But if what he stole—whether ox or ass or sheep—is found alive in his possession, he shall pay double.

⁴When a man lets his livestock loose to graze in another's land, and so allows a field or a vineyard to be grazed bare, he must make restitution for the impairment[c] of that field or vineyard.

⁵When a fire is started and spreads to thorns, so that stacked, standing, or growing[d] grain is consumed, he who started the fire must make restitution.

⁶When a man gives money or goods to another for safekeeping, and they are stolen from the man's house—if the thief is caught, he shall pay double; ⁷if the thief is not caught, the owner of the house shall depose before God[e] that he has not laid hands on the other's property. ⁸In all charges of misappropriation—pertaining to an ox, an ass, a sheep, a garment, or any other loss, whereof one party alleges, "This is it"—the case of both parties shall come before God: he whom God declares guilty shall pay double to the other.

⁹When a man gives to another an ass, an ox, a sheep or any other animal to guard, and it dies or is injured or is carried off, with no witness about, ¹⁰an oath before the LORD shall decide between the two of them that the one has not laid hands on the property of the other; the owner must acquiesce, and no restitution shall be made. ¹¹But if [the animal] was stolen from him, he shall make restitution to its owner. ¹²If it was torn by beasts, he shall bring it as evidence; he need not replace what has been torn by beasts.

¹³When a man borrows [an animal] from an-

עָלָיו דָּמִים לוֹ שַׁלֵּם יְשַׁלֵּם אִם־אֵין לוֹ וְנִמְכַּר בִּגְנֵבָתוֹ׃ 3 אִם־הִמָּצֵא תִמָּצֵא בְיָדוֹ הַגְּנֵבָה מִשּׁוֹר עַד־חֲמוֹר עַד־שֶׂה חַיִּים שְׁנַיִם יְשַׁלֵּם׃ ס

4 כִּי יַבְעֶר־אִישׁ שָׂדֶה אוֹ־כֶרֶם וְשִׁלַּח אֶת־בְּעִירוֹ וּבִעֵר בִּשְׂדֵה אַחֵר מֵיטַב שָׂדֵהוּ וּמֵיטַב כַּרְמוֹ יְשַׁלֵּם׃ ס

5 כִּי־תֵצֵא אֵשׁ וּמָצְאָה קֹצִים וְנֶאֱכַל גָּדִישׁ אוֹ הַקָּמָה אוֹ הַשָּׂדֶה שַׁלֵּם יְשַׁלֵּם הַמַּבְעִר אֶת־הַבְּעֵרָה׃ ס

6 כִּי־יִתֵּן אִישׁ אֶל־רֵעֵהוּ כֶּסֶף אוֹ־כֵלִים לִשְׁמֹר וְגֻנַּב מִבֵּית הָאִישׁ אִם־יִמָּצֵא הַגַּנָּב יְשַׁלֵּם שְׁנָיִם׃ 7 אִם־לֹא יִמָּצֵא הַגַּנָּב וְנִקְרַב בַּעַל־הַבַּיִת אֶל־הָאֱלֹהִים אִם־לֹא שָׁלַח יָדוֹ בִּמְלֶאכֶת רֵעֵהוּ׃ 8 עַל־כָּל־דְּבַר־פֶּשַׁע עַל־שׁוֹר עַל־חֲמוֹר עַל־שֶׂה עַל־שַׂלְמָה עַל־כָּל־אֲבֵדָה אֲשֶׁר יֹאמַר כִּי־הוּא זֶה עַד הָאֱלֹהִים יָבֹא דְּבַר־שְׁנֵיהֶם אֲשֶׁר יַרְשִׁיעֻן אֱלֹהִים יְשַׁלֵּם שְׁנַיִם לְרֵעֵהוּ׃ ס

9 כִּי־יִתֵּן אִישׁ אֶל־רֵעֵהוּ חֲמוֹר אוֹ־שׁוֹר אוֹ־שֶׂה וְכָל־בְּהֵמָה לִשְׁמֹר וּמֵת אוֹ־נִשְׁבַּר אוֹ־נִשְׁבָּה אֵין רֹאֶה׃ 10 שְׁבֻעַת יְהֹוָה תִּהְיֶה בֵּין שְׁנֵיהֶם אִם־לֹא שָׁלַח יָדוֹ בִּמְלֶאכֶת רֵעֵהוּ וְלָקַח בְּעָלָיו וְלֹא יְשַׁלֵּם׃ 11 וְאִם־גָּנֹב יִגָּנֵב מֵעִמּוֹ יְשַׁלֵּם לִבְעָלָיו׃ 12 אִם־טָרֹף יִטָּרֵף יְבִאֵהוּ עֵד הַטְּרֵפָה לֹא יְשַׁלֵּם׃ פ

13 וְכִי־יִשְׁאַל אִישׁ מֵעִם רֵעֵהוּ וְנִשְׁבַּר

---

b   I.e, the thief of 21.37.
c   Lit. "excellence."
d   Lit. "field."
e   See note on 21.6.

other and it dies or is injured, its owner not being with it, he must make restitution. [14]If its owner was with it, no restitution need be made; but if it was hired, he is entitled to the hire.

[15]If a man seduces a virgin for whom the bride-price has not been paid,*f* and lies with her, he must make her his wife by payment of a bride-price. [16]If her father refuses to give her to him, he must still weigh out silver in accordance with the bride-price for virgins.

[17]You shall not tolerate*g* a sorceress.

[18]Whoever lies with a beast shall be put to death.

[19]Whoever sacrifices to a god other than the LORD alone shall be proscribed.*h*

[20]You shall not wrong a stranger or oppress him, for you were strangers in the land of Egypt.

[21]You shall not ill-treat any widow or orphan. [22]If you do mistreat them, I will heed their outcry as soon as they cry out to Me, [23]and My anger shall blaze forth and I will put you to the sword, and your own wives shall become widows and your children orphans.

[24]If you lend money to My people, to the poor among you, do not act toward them as a creditor; exact no interest from them. [25]If you take your neighbor's garment in pledge, you must return it to him before the sun sets; [26]it is his only clothing, the sole covering for his skin. In what else shall he sleep? Therefore, if he cries out to Me, I will pay heed, for I am compassionate.

[27]You shall not revile God, nor put a curse upon a chieftain among your people.

[28]You shall not *i-*put off the skimming of the first yield of your vats.*-i* You shall give Me the first-born among your sons. [29]You shall do the same with your cattle and your flocks: seven

אוֹ־מֵ֛ת בְּעָלָ֥יו אֵין־עִמּ֖וֹ שַׁלֵּ֥ם יְשַׁלֵּֽם׃ 14 אִם־בְּעָלָ֥יו עִמּ֖וֹ לֹ֣א יְשַׁלֵּ֑ם אִם־שָׂכִ֣יר ה֔וּא בָּ֖א בִּשְׂכָרֽוֹ׃ ס 15 וְכִֽי־יְפַתֶּ֣ה אִ֗ישׁ בְּתוּלָ֛ה אֲשֶׁ֥ר לֹא־אֹרָ֖שָׂה וְשָׁכַ֣ב עִמָּ֑הּ מָהֹ֛ר יִמְהָרֶ֥נָּה לּ֖וֹ לְאִשָּֽׁה׃ 16 אִם־מָאֵ֧ן יְמָאֵ֛ן אָבִ֖יהָ לְתִתָּ֣הּ ל֑וֹ כֶּ֣סֶף יִשְׁקֹ֔ל כְּמֹ֖הַר הַבְּתוּלֹֽת׃ ס 17 מְכַשֵּׁפָ֖ה לֹ֥א תְחַיֶּֽה׃ ס 18 כָּל־שֹׁכֵ֥ב עִם־בְּהֵמָ֖ה מ֥וֹת יוּמָֽת׃ ס 19 זֹבֵ֥חַ לָֽאֱלֹהִ֖ים יָֽחֳרָ֑ם בִּלְתִּ֥י לַֽיהוָ֖ה לְבַדּֽוֹ׃ 20 וְגֵ֥ר לֹא־תוֹנֶ֖ה וְלֹ֣א תִלְחָצֶ֑נּוּ כִּֽי־גֵרִ֥ים הֱיִיתֶ֖ם בְּאֶ֥רֶץ מִצְרָֽיִם׃ 21 כָּל־אַלְמָנָ֥ה וְיָת֖וֹם לֹ֥א תְעַנּֽוּן׃ 22 אִם־עַנֵּ֥ה תְעַנֶּ֖ה אֹת֑וֹ כִּ֣י אִם־צָעֹ֤ק יִצְעַק֙ אֵלַ֔י שָׁמֹ֥עַ אֶשְׁמַ֖ע צַֽעֲקָתֽוֹ׃ 23 וְחָרָ֣ה אַפִּ֔י וְהָרַגְתִּ֥י אֶתְכֶ֖ם בֶּחָ֑רֶב וְהָי֤וּ נְשֵׁיכֶם֙ אַלְמָנ֔וֹת וּבְנֵיכֶ֖ם יְתֹמִֽים׃ פ 24 אִם־כֶּ֣סֶף ׀ תַּלְוֶ֣ה אֶת־עַמִּ֗י אֶת־הֶֽעָנִי֙ עִמָּ֔ךְ לֹא־תִהְיֶ֥ה ל֖וֹ כְּנֹשֶׁ֑ה לֹֽא־תְשִׂימ֥וּן עָלָ֖יו נֶֽשֶׁךְ׃ 25 אִם־חָבֹ֥ל תַּחְבֹּ֖ל שַׂלְמַ֣ת רֵעֶ֑ךָ עַד־בֹּ֥א הַשֶּׁ֖מֶשׁ תְּשִׁיבֶ֥נּוּ לֽוֹ׃ 26 כִּ֣י הִ֤וא כְסוּתֹה֙ לְבַדָּ֔הּ הִ֥וא שִׂמְלָת֖וֹ לְעֹר֑וֹ בַּמֶּ֣ה יִשְׁכָּ֔ב וְהָיָה֙ כִּֽי־יִצְעַ֣ק אֵלַ֔י וְשָֽׁמַעְתִּ֖י כִּֽי־חַנּ֥וּן אָֽנִי׃ ס 27 *אֱלֹהִ֖ים לֹ֣א תְקַלֵּ֑ל וְנָשִׂ֥יא בְעַמְּךָ֖ לֹ֥א תָאֹֽר׃ 28 מְלֵאָֽתְךָ֥ וְדִמְעֲךָ֖ לֹ֣א תְאַחֵ֑ר בְּכ֥וֹר בָּנֶ֖יךָ תִּתֶּן־לִּֽי׃ 29 כֵּֽן־תַּעֲשֶׂ֥ה לְשֹֽׁרְךָ֖ לְצֹאנֶ֑ךָ

---

f So that she is unmarried; cf. Deut. 20.7; 22.23 ff.
g Lit. "let live."
h See Lev. 27.29.
i-i Meaning of Heb. uncertain.

למערבאי חצי הספר בפסוקים   v. 27.

days it[j] shall remain with its mother; on the eighth day you shall give it to Me.

30You shall be holy people to Me: you must not eat flesh torn by beasts in the field; you shall cast it to the dogs.

23 You must not carry false rumors; you shall not join hands with the guilty to act as a malicious witness: 2You shall neither side with the mighty[a] to do wrong—you shall not give perverse testimony in a dispute so as to pervert it in favor of the mighty[a] —3nor shall you show deference to a poor man in his dispute.

4When you encounter your enemy's ox or ass wandering, you must take it back to him.

5When you see the ass of your enemy lying under its burden and would refrain from raising[b] it, you must nevertheless raise it with him.

6You shall not subvert the rights of your needy in their disputes. 7Keep far from a false charge; do not bring death on those who are innocent and in the right, for I will not acquit the wrongdoer. 8Do not take bribes, for bribes blind the clear-sighted and upset the pleas of those who are in the right.

9You shall not oppress a stranger, for you know the feelings of the stranger, having yourselves been strangers in the land of Egypt.

10Six years you shall sow your land and gather in its yield; 11but in the seventh you shall let it rest and lie fallow. Let the needy among your people eat of it, and what they leave let the wild beasts eat. You shall do the same with your vineyards and your olive groves.

12Six days you shall do your work, but on the seventh day you shall cease from labor, in order

---

j   I.e., the male first-born.

a   Others "multitude."

b   For this use of the verb 'zb, cf. Neh. 3.8, 34. For the whole verse see Deut. 22.4.

שִׁבְעַת יָמִים יִהְיֶה עִם־אִמּוֹ בַּיּוֹם הַשְּׁמִינִי תִּתְּנוֹ־לִי:

30 וְאַנְשֵׁי־קֹדֶשׁ תִּהְיוּן לִי וּבָשָׂר בַּשָּׂדֶה טְרֵפָה לֹא תֹאכֵלוּ לַכֶּלֶב תַּשְׁלִכוּן אֹתוֹ: ס

כג לֹא תִשָּׂא שֵׁמַע שָׁוְא אַל־תָּשֶׁת יָדְךָ עִם־רָשָׁע לִהְיֹת עֵד חָמָס: ס 2 לֹא־תִהְיֶה אַחֲרֵי־רַבִּים לְרָעֹת וְלֹא־תַעֲנֶה עַל־רִב לִנְטֹת אַחֲרֵי רַבִּים לְהַטֹּת: 3 וְדָל לֹא תֶהְדַּר בְּרִיבוֹ: ס

4 כִּי תִפְגַּע שׁוֹר אֹיִבְךָ אוֹ חֲמֹרוֹ תֹּעֶה הָשֵׁב תְּשִׁיבֶנּוּ לוֹ: ס

5 כִּי־תִרְאֶה חֲמוֹר שֹׂנַאֲךָ רֹבֵץ תַּחַת מַשָּׂאוֹ וְחָדַלְתָּ מֵעֲזֹב לוֹ עָזֹב תַּעֲזֹב עִמּוֹ: ס

6 לֹא תַטֶּה מִשְׁפַּט אֶבְיֹנְךָ בְּרִיבוֹ: 7 מִדְּבַר־שֶׁקֶר תִּרְחָק וְנָקִי וְצַדִּיק אַל־תַּהֲרֹג כִּי לֹא־אַצְדִּיק רָשָׁע: 8 וְשֹׁחַד לֹא תִקָּח כִּי הַשֹּׁחַד יְעַוֵּר פִּקְחִים וִיסַלֵּף דִּבְרֵי צַדִּיקִים: 9 וְגֵר לֹא תִלְחָץ וְאַתֶּם יְדַעְתֶּם אֶת־נֶפֶשׁ הַגֵּר כִּי־גֵרִים הֱיִיתֶם בְּאֶרֶץ מִצְרָיִם:

10 וְשֵׁשׁ שָׁנִים תִּזְרַע אֶת־אַרְצֶךָ וְאָסַפְתָּ אֶת־תְּבוּאָתָהּ: 11 וְהַשְּׁבִיעִת תִּשְׁמְטֶנָּה וּנְטַשְׁתָּהּ וְאָכְלוּ אֶבְיֹנֵי עַמֶּךָ וְיִתְרָם תֹּאכַל חַיַּת הַשָּׂדֶה כֵּן־תַּעֲשֶׂה לְכַרְמְךָ לְזֵיתֶךָ: 12 שֵׁשֶׁת יָמִים תַּעֲשֶׂה מַעֲשֶׂיךָ וּבַיּוֹם

that your ox and your ass may rest, and that your bondman and the stranger may be refreshed.

13Be on guard concerning all that I have told you. Make no mention of the names of other gods; they shall not be heard on your lips.

14Three times a year you shall hold a festival for Me: 15You shall observe the Feast of Unleavened Bread—eating unleavened bread for seven days as I have commanded you—at the set time in the monthᶜ of Abib, for in it you went forth from Egypt; and none shall appear before Me empty-handed; 16and the Feast of the Harvest, of the first fruits of your work, of what you sow in the field; and the Feast of Ingathering at the end of the year, when you gather in the results of your work from the field. 17Three times a year all your males shall appear before the Sovereign, the LORD.

18You shall not offer the blood of My sacrifice with anything leavened; and the fat of My festal offering shall not be left lying until morning.

19The choice first fruits of your soil you shall bring to the house of the LORD your God.

You shall not boil a kid in its mother's milk.

20I am sending an angel before you to guard you on the way and to bring you to the place that I have made ready. 21Pay heed to him and obey him. Do not defy him, for he will not pardon your offenses, since My Name is in him; 22but if you obey him and do all that I say, I will be an enemy to your enemies and a foe to your foes.

23When My angel goes before you and brings you to the Amorites, the Hittites, the Perizzites, the Canaanites, the Hivites, and the Jebusites, and I annihilate them, 24you shall not bow down to their gods in worship or follow their practices, but shall tear them down and smash their pillars to bits. 25You shall serve the LORD your God, and He will bless your bread and your wa-

ᶜ See note at 13.4.

הַשְּׁבִיעִי תִּשְׁבֹּת לְמַעַן יָנוּחַ שׁוֹרְךָ וַחֲמֹרֶךָ וְיִנָּפֵשׁ בֶּן־אֲמָתְךָ וְהַגֵּר:

13 וּבְכֹל אֲשֶׁר־אָמַרְתִּי אֲלֵיכֶם תִּשָּׁמֵרוּ וְשֵׁם אֱלֹהִים אֲחֵרִים לֹא תַזְכִּירוּ לֹא יִשָּׁמַע עַל־פִּיךָ:

14 שָׁלֹשׁ רְגָלִים תָּחֹג לִי בַּשָּׁנָה: 15 אֶת־חַג הַמַּצּוֹת תִּשְׁמֹר שִׁבְעַת יָמִים תֹּאכַל מַצּוֹת כַּאֲשֶׁר צִוִּיתִךָ לְמוֹעֵד חֹדֶשׁ הָאָבִיב כִּי־בוֹ יָצָאתָ מִמִּצְרָיִם וְלֹא־יֵרָאוּ פָנַי רֵיקָם: 16 וְחַג הַקָּצִיר בִּכּוּרֵי מַעֲשֶׂיךָ אֲשֶׁר תִּזְרַע בַּשָּׂדֶה וְחַג הָאָסִף בְּצֵאת הַשָּׁנָה בְּאָסְפְּךָ אֶת־מַעֲשֶׂיךָ מִן־הַשָּׂדֶה: 17 שָׁלֹשׁ פְּעָמִים בַּשָּׁנָה יֵרָאֶה כָּל־זְכוּרְךָ אֶל־פְּנֵי הָאָדֹן | יְהוָה:

18 לֹא־תִזְבַּח עַל־חָמֵץ דַּם־זִבְחִי וְלֹא־יָלִין חֵלֶב־חַגִּי עַד־בֹּקֶר:

19 רֵאשִׁית בִּכּוּרֵי אַדְמָתְךָ תָּבִיא בֵּית יְהוָה אֱלֹהֶיךָ לֹא־תְבַשֵּׁל גְּדִי בַּחֲלֵב אִמּוֹ: ס

20 הִנֵּה אָנֹכִי שֹׁלֵחַ מַלְאָךְ לְפָנֶיךָ לִשְׁמָרְךָ בַּדָּרֶךְ וְלַהֲבִיאֲךָ אֶל־הַמָּקוֹם אֲשֶׁר הֲכִנֹתִי: 21 הִשָּׁמֶר מִפָּנָיו וּשְׁמַע בְּקֹלוֹ אַל־תַּמֵּר בּוֹ כִּי לֹא יִשָּׂא לְפִשְׁעֲכֶם כִּי שְׁמִי בְּקִרְבּוֹ: 22 כִּי אִם־שָׁמוֹעַ תִּשְׁמַע בְּקֹלוֹ וְעָשִׂיתָ כֹּל אֲשֶׁר אֲדַבֵּר וְאָיַבְתִּי אֶת־אֹיְבֶיךָ וְצַרְתִּי אֶת־צֹרְרֶיךָ:

23 כִּי־יֵלֵךְ מַלְאָכִי לְפָנֶיךָ וֶהֱבִיאֲךָ אֶל־הָאֱמֹרִי וְהַחִתִּי וְהַפְּרִזִּי וְהַכְּנַעֲנִי הַחִוִּי וְהַיְבוּסִי וְהִכְחַדְתִּיו: 24 לֹא־תִשְׁתַּחֲוֶה לֵאלֹהֵיהֶם וְלֹא תָעָבְדֵם וְלֹא תַעֲשֶׂה כְּמַעֲשֵׂיהֶם כִּי הָרֵס תְּהָרְסֵם וְשַׁבֵּר תְּשַׁבֵּר מַצֵּבֹתֵיהֶם: 25 וַעֲבַדְתֶּם אֵת יְהוָה אֱלֹהֵיכֶם וּבֵרַךְ אֶת־לַחְמְךָ וְאֶת־מֵימֶיךָ

ter. And I will remove sickness from your midst. [26]No woman in your land shall miscarry or be barren. I will let you enjoy the full count of your days.

[27]I will send forth My terror before you, and I will throw into panic all the people among whom you come, and I will make all your enemies turn tail[d] before you. [28]I will send a plague[e] ahead of you, and it shall drive out before you the Hivites, the Canaanites, and the Hittites. [29]I will not drive them out before you in a single year, lest the land become desolate and the wild beasts multiply to your hurt. [30]I will drive them out before you little by little, until you have increased and possess the land. [31]I will set your borders from the Sea of Reeds to the Sea of Philistia, and from the wilderness to the Euphrates; for I will deliver the inhabitants of the land into your hands, and you will drive them out before you. [32]You shall make no covenant with them and their gods. [33]They shall not remain in your land, lest they cause you to sin against Me; for you will serve their gods—and it will prove a snare to you.

24

Then He said to Moses, "Come up to the LORD, with Aaron, Nadab and Abihu, and seventy elders of Israel, and bow low from afar. [2]Moses alone shall come near the LORD; but the others shall not come near, nor shall the people come up with him."

[3]Moses went and repeated to the people all the commands of the LORD and all the rules; and all the people answered with one voice, saying, "All the things that the LORD has commanded we will do!" [4]Moses then wrote down all the commands of the LORD.

Early in the morning, he set up an altar at the foot of the mountain, with twelve pillars for the

וַהֲסִרֹתִ֥י מַחֲלָ֖ה מִקִּרְבֶּֽךָ׃ 26 לֹ֥א תִהְיֶ֛ה מְשַׁכֵּלָ֥ה וַעֲקָרָ֖ה בְּאַרְצֶ֑ךָ אֶת־מִסְפַּ֥ר יָמֶ֖יךָ אֲמַלֵּֽא׃ 27 אֶת־אֵֽימָתִי֙ אֲשַׁלַּ֣ח לְפָנֶ֔יךָ וְהַמֹּתִי֙ אֶת־ כׇּל־הָעָ֔ם אֲשֶׁ֥ר תָּבֹ֖א בָּהֶ֑ם וְנָתַתִּ֧י אֶת־ כׇּל־אֹיְבֶ֛יךָ אֵלֶ֖יךָ עֹֽרֶף׃ 28 וְשָׁלַחְתִּ֥י אֶת־ הַצִּרְעָ֖ה לְפָנֶ֑יךָ וְגֵרְשָׁ֗ה אֶת־הַחִוִּ֛י אֶת־ הַֽכְּנַעֲנִ֥י וְאֶת־הַֽחִתִּ֖י מִלְּפָנֶֽיךָ׃ 29 לֹ֧א אֲגָרְשֶׁ֛נּוּ מִפָּנֶ֖יךָ בְּשָׁנָ֣ה אֶחָ֑ת פֶּן־תִּהְיֶ֤ה הָאָ֙רֶץ֙ שְׁמָמָ֔ה וְרַבָּ֥ה עָלֶ֖יךָ חַיַּ֥ת הַשָּׂדֶֽה׃ 30 מְעַ֥ט מְעַ֛ט אֲגָרְשֶׁ֖נּוּ מִפָּנֶ֑יךָ עַ֚ד אֲשֶׁ֣ר תִּפְרֶ֔ה וְנָחַלְתָּ֖ אֶת־הָאָֽרֶץ׃ 31 וְשַׁתִּ֣י אֶת־ גְּבֻלְךָ֗ מִיַּם־סוּף֙ וְעַד־יָ֣ם פְּלִשְׁתִּ֔ים וּמִמִּדְבָּ֖ר עַד־הַנָּהָ֑ר כִּ֣י ׀ אֶתֵּ֣ן בְּיֶדְכֶ֗ם אֵ֚ת יֹשְׁבֵ֣י הָאָ֔רֶץ וְגֵרַשְׁתָּ֖מוֹ מִפָּנֶֽיךָ׃ 32 לֹֽא־תִכְרֹ֥ת לָהֶ֛ם וְלֵאלֹֽהֵיהֶ֖ם בְּרִֽית׃ 33 לֹ֤א יֵשְׁבוּ֙ בְּאַרְצְךָ֔ פֶּן־יַחֲטִ֥יאוּ אֹתְךָ֖ לִ֑י כִּ֤י תַעֲבֹד֙ אֶת־אֱלֹ֣הֵיהֶ֔ם כִּי־יִהְיֶ֥ה לְךָ֖ לְמוֹקֵֽשׁ׃ פ

כד וְאֶל־מֹשֶׁ֨ה אָמַ֜ר עֲלֵ֣ה אֶל־יְהֹוָ֗ה אַתָּה֙ וְאַהֲרֹן֙ נָדָ֣ב וַאֲבִיה֔וּא וְשִׁבְעִ֖ים מִזִּקְנֵ֣י יִשְׂרָאֵ֑ל וְהִשְׁתַּחֲוִיתֶ֖ם מֵֽרָחֹֽק׃ 2 וְנִגַּ֨שׁ מֹשֶׁ֤ה לְבַדּוֹ֙ אֶל־יְהֹוָ֔ה וְהֵ֖ם לֹ֣א יִגָּ֑שׁוּ וְהָעָ֕ם לֹ֥א יַעֲל֖וּ עִמּֽוֹ׃ 3 וַיָּבֹ֣א מֹשֶׁ֗ה וַיְסַפֵּ֤ר לָעָם֙ אֵ֚ת כׇּל־דִּבְרֵ֣י יְהֹוָ֔ה וְאֵ֖ת כׇּל־הַמִּשְׁפָּטִ֑ים וַיַּ֨עַן כׇּל־הָעָ֜ם ק֤וֹל אֶחָד֙ וַיֹּ֣אמְר֔וּ כׇּל־הַדְּבָרִ֛ים אֲשֶׁר־דִּבֶּ֥ר יְהֹוָ֖ה נַעֲשֶֽׂה׃ 4 וַיִּכְתֹּ֣ב מֹשֶׁ֔ה אֵ֖ת כׇּל־דִּבְרֵ֥י יְהֹוָ֑ה וַיַּשְׁכֵּ֣ם בַּבֹּ֔קֶר וַיִּ֥בֶן מִזְבֵּ֖חַ תַּ֣חַת הָהָ֑ר וּשְׁתֵּ֤ים עֶשְׂרֵה֙ מַצֵּבָ֔ה לִשְׁנֵ֥ים עָשָׂ֖ר שִׁבְטֵ֥י

---

d   Lit. "back."
e   Others "hornet"; meaning of Heb. uncertain.

twelve tribes of Israel. [5]He designated some young men among the Israelites, and they offered burnt offerings and sacrificed bulls as offerings of well-being to the LORD. [6]Moses took one part of the blood and put it in basins, and the other part of the blood he dashed against the altar. [7]Then he took the record of the covenant and read it aloud to the people. And they said, "All that the LORD has spoken [a]-we will faithfully do!"-[a] [8]Moses took the blood and dashed it on the people and said, "This is the blood of the covenant that the LORD now makes with you concerning all these commands."

[9]Then Moses and Aaron, Nadab and Abihu, and seventy elders of Israel ascended; [10]and they saw the God of Israel: under His feet there was the likeness of a pavement of sapphire, like the very sky for purity. [11]Yet He did not raise His hand against the leaders[b] of the Israelites; they beheld God, and they ate and drank.

[12]The LORD said to Moses, "Come up to Me on the mountain and wait there, and I will give you the stone tablets with the teachings and commandments which I have inscribed to instruct them." [13]So Moses and his attendant Joshua arose, and Moses ascended the mountain of God. [14]To the elders he had said, "Wait here for us until we return to you. You have Aaron and Hur with you; let anyone who has a legal matter approach them."

[15]When Moses had ascended the mountain, the cloud covered the mountain. [16]The Presence of the LORD abode on Mount Sinai, and the cloud hid it for six days. On the seventh day He called to Moses from the midst of the cloud. [17]Now the Presence of the LORD appeared in the sight of the Israelites as a consuming fire on the top of the mountain. [18]Moses went inside the cloud and ascended the mountain; and Moses remained on the mountain forty days and forty nights.

יִשְׂרָאֵל: 5 וַיִּשְׁלַח אֶת־נַעֲרֵי בְּנֵי יִשְׂרָאֵל וַיַּעֲלוּ עֹלֹת וַיִּזְבְּחוּ זְבָחִים שְׁלָמִים לַיהוָה פָּרִים: 6 וַיִּקַּח מֹשֶׁה חֲצִי הַדָּם וַיָּשֶׂם בָּאַגָּנֹת וַחֲצִי הַדָּם זָרַק עַל־הַמִּזְבֵּחַ: 7 וַיִּקַּח סֵפֶר הַבְּרִית וַיִּקְרָא בְּאָזְנֵי הָעָם וַיֹּאמְרוּ כֹּל אֲשֶׁר־דִּבֶּר יְהוָה נַעֲשֶׂה וְנִשְׁמָע: 8 וַיִּקַּח מֹשֶׁה אֶת־הַדָּם וַיִּזְרֹק עַל־הָעָם וַיֹּאמֶר הִנֵּה דַם־הַבְּרִית אֲשֶׁר כָּרַת יְהוָה עִמָּכֶם עַל כָּל־הַדְּבָרִים הָאֵלֶּה:

9 וַיַּעַל מֹשֶׁה וְאַהֲרֹן נָדָב וַאֲבִיהוּא וְשִׁבְעִים מִזִּקְנֵי יִשְׂרָאֵל: 10 וַיִּרְאוּ אֵת אֱלֹהֵי יִשְׂרָאֵל וְתַחַת רַגְלָיו כְּמַעֲשֵׂה לִבְנַת הַסַּפִּיר וּכְעֶצֶם הַשָּׁמַיִם לָטֹהַר: 11 וְאֶל־אֲצִילֵי בְּנֵי יִשְׂרָאֵל לֹא שָׁלַח יָדוֹ וַיֶּחֱזוּ אֶת־הָאֱלֹהִים וַיֹּאכְלוּ וַיִּשְׁתּוּ: ס

12 וַיֹּאמֶר יְהוָה אֶל־מֹשֶׁה עֲלֵה אֵלַי הָהָרָה וֶהְיֵה־שָׁם וְאֶתְּנָה לְךָ אֶת־לֻחֹת הָאֶבֶן וְהַתּוֹרָה וְהַמִּצְוָה אֲשֶׁר כָּתַבְתִּי לְהוֹרֹתָם: 13 וַיָּקָם מֹשֶׁה וִיהוֹשֻׁעַ מְשָׁרְתוֹ וַיַּעַל מֹשֶׁה אֶל־הַר הָאֱלֹהִים: 14 וְאֶל־הַזְּקֵנִים אָמַר שְׁבוּ־לָנוּ בָזֶה עַד אֲשֶׁר־נָשׁוּב אֲלֵיכֶם וְהִנֵּה אַהֲרֹן וְחוּר עִמָּכֶם מִי־בַעַל דְּבָרִים יִגַּשׁ אֲלֵהֶם:

15 וַיַּעַל מֹשֶׁה אֶל־הָהָר וַיְכַס הֶעָנָן אֶת־הָהָר: 16 וַיִּשְׁכֹּן כְּבוֹד־יְהוָה עַל־הַר סִינַי וַיְכַסֵּהוּ הֶעָנָן שֵׁשֶׁת יָמִים וַיִּקְרָא אֶל־מֹשֶׁה בַּיּוֹם הַשְּׁבִיעִי מִתּוֹךְ הֶעָנָן: 17 וּמַרְאֵה כְּבוֹד יְהוָה כְּאֵשׁ אֹכֶלֶת בְּרֹאשׁ הָהָר לְעֵינֵי בְּנֵי יִשְׂרָאֵל: 18 וַיָּבֹא מֹשֶׁה בְּתוֹךְ הֶעָנָן וַיַּעַל אֶל־הָהָר וַיְהִי מֹשֶׁה בָּהָר אַרְבָּעִים יוֹם וְאַרְבָּעִים לָיְלָה: פ

---

a-a Lit. "we will do and obey."
b Meaning of Heb. 'aṣilim uncertain.

25 TERUMAH

The LORD spoke to Moses, saying: [2]Tell the Israelite people to bring Me gifts; you shall accept gifts for Me from every person whose heart so moves him. [3]And these are the gifts that you shall accept from them: gold, silver, and copper; [4]blue, purple, and crimson yarns, fine linen, goats' hair; [5]tanned ram skins,[a] dolphin[b] skins, and acacia wood; [6]oil for lighting, spices for the anointing oil and for the aromatic incense; [7]lapis lazuli[c] and other stones for setting, for the ephod and for the breastpiece. [8]And let them make Me a sanctuary that I may dwell among them. [9]Exactly as I show you—the pattern of the Tabernacle and the pattern of all its furnishings—so shall you make it.

[10]They shall make an ark of acacia wood, two and a half cubits long, a cubit and a half wide, and a cubit and a half high. [11]Overlay it with pure gold—overlay it inside and out—and make upon it a gold molding round about. [12]Cast four gold rings for it, to be attached to its four feet, two rings on one of its side walls and two on the other. [13]Make poles of acacia wood and overlay them with gold; [14]then insert the poles into the rings on the side walls of the ark, for carrying the ark. [15]The poles shall remain in the rings of the ark: they shall not be removed from it. [16]And deposit in the Ark [the tablets of] the Pact which I will give you.

[17]You shall make a cover of pure gold, two and a half cubits long and a cubit and a half wide. [18]Make two cherubim of gold—make them of hammered work—at the two ends of the cover. [19]Make one cherub at one end and the other cherub at the other end; of one piece with the cover shall you make the cherubim at its two ends. [20]The cherubim shall have their wings spread out above, shielding the cover with their

---

a   *Others "rams' skins dyed red."*
b   *Or "dugong"; meaning of Hebrew* taḥash *uncertain.*
c   *Cf. Gen. 2.12 and note.*

כה תרומה

וַיְדַבֵּ֥ר יְהֹוָ֖ה אֶל־מֹשֶׁ֥ה לֵּאמֹֽר׃ ²דַּבֵּר֙ אֶל־בְּנֵ֣י יִשְׂרָאֵ֔ל וְיִקְחוּ־לִ֖י תְּרוּמָ֑ה מֵאֵ֤ת כׇּל־אִישׁ֙ אֲשֶׁ֣ר יִדְּבֶ֣נּוּ לִבּ֔וֹ תִּקְח֖וּ אֶת־תְּרוּמָתִֽי׃ ³וְזֹאת֙ הַתְּרוּמָ֔ה אֲשֶׁ֥ר תִּקְח֖וּ מֵאִתָּ֑ם זָהָ֥ב וָכֶ֖סֶף וּנְחֹֽשֶׁת׃ ⁴וּתְכֵ֧לֶת וְאַרְגָּמָ֛ן וְתוֹלַ֥עַת שָׁנִ֖י וְשֵׁ֥שׁ וְעִזִּֽים׃ ⁵וְעֹרֹ֨ת אֵילִ֧ם מְאׇדָּמִ֛ים וְעֹרֹ֥ת תְּחָשִׁ֖ים וַעֲצֵ֥י שִׁטִּֽים׃ ⁶שֶׁ֖מֶן לַמָּאֹ֑ר בְּשָׂמִים֙ לְשֶׁ֣מֶן הַמִּשְׁחָ֔ה וְלִקְטֹ֖רֶת הַסַּמִּֽים׃ ⁷אַבְנֵי־שֹׁ֕הַם וְאַבְנֵ֖י מִלֻּאִ֑ים לָאֵפֹ֖ד וְלַחֹֽשֶׁן׃ ⁸וְעָ֥שׂוּ לִ֖י מִקְדָּ֑שׁ וְשָׁכַנְתִּ֖י בְּתוֹכָֽם׃ ⁹כְּכֹ֗ל אֲשֶׁ֤ר אֲנִי֙ מַרְאֶ֣ה אוֹתְךָ֔ אֵ֚ת תַּבְנִ֣ית הַמִּשְׁכָּ֔ן וְאֵ֖ת תַּבְנִ֣ית כׇּל־כֵּלָ֑יו וְכֵ֖ן תַּעֲשֽׂוּ׃ ס

¹⁰וְעָשׂ֥וּ אֲר֖וֹן עֲצֵ֣י שִׁטִּ֑ים אַמָּתַ֨יִם וָחֵ֜צִי אׇרְכּ֗וֹ וְאַמָּ֤ה וָחֵ֙צִי֙ רׇחְבּ֔וֹ וְאַמָּ֥ה וָחֵ֖צִי קֹמָתֽוֹ׃ ¹¹וְצִפִּיתָ֤ אֹתוֹ֙ זָהָ֣ב טָה֔וֹר מִבַּ֥יִת וּמִח֖וּץ תְּצַפֶּ֑נּוּ וְעָשִׂ֧יתָ עָלָ֛יו זֵ֥ר זָהָ֖ב סָבִֽיב׃ ¹²וְיָצַ֣קְתָּ לּ֗וֹ אַרְבַּע֙ טַבְּעֹ֣ת זָהָ֔ב וְנָ֣תַתָּ֔ה עַ֖ל אַרְבַּ֣ע פַּעֲמֹתָ֑יו וּשְׁתֵּ֣י טַבָּעֹ֗ת עַל־צַלְעוֹ֙ הָֽאֶחָ֔ת וּשְׁתֵּי֙ טַבָּעֹ֔ת עַל־צַלְע֖וֹ הַשֵּׁנִֽית׃ ¹³וְעָשִׂ֥יתָ בַדֵּ֖י עֲצֵ֣י שִׁטִּ֑ים וְצִפִּיתָ֥ אֹתָ֖ם זָהָֽב׃ ¹⁴וְהֵֽבֵאתָ֤ אֶת־הַבַּדִּים֙ בַּטַּבָּעֹ֔ת עַ֖ל צַלְעֹ֣ת הָאָרֹ֑ן לָשֵׂ֥את אֶת־הָאָרֹ֖ן בָּהֶֽם׃ ¹⁵בְּטַבְּעֹת֙ הָֽאָרֹ֔ן יִהְי֖וּ הַבַּדִּ֑ים לֹ֥א יָסֻ֖רוּ מִמֶּֽנּוּ׃ ¹⁶וְנָתַתָּ֖ אֶל־הָאָרֹ֑ן אֵ֚ת הָעֵדֻ֔ת אֲשֶׁ֖ר אֶתֵּ֥ן אֵלֶֽיךָ׃

¹⁷וְעָשִׂ֥יתָ כַפֹּ֖רֶת זָהָ֣ב טָה֑וֹר אַמָּתַ֤יִם וָחֵ֙צִי֙ אׇרְכָּ֔הּ וְאַמָּ֥ה וָחֵ֖צִי רׇחְבָּֽהּ׃ ¹⁸וְעָשִׂ֛יתָ שְׁנַ֥יִם כְּרֻבִ֖ים זָהָ֑ב מִקְשָׁה֙ תַּעֲשֶׂ֣ה אֹתָ֔ם מִשְּׁנֵ֖י קְצ֥וֹת הַכַּפֹּֽרֶת׃ ¹⁹וַ֠עֲשֵׂ֠ה כְּר֨וּב אֶחָ֤ד מִקָּצָה֙ מִזֶּ֔ה וּכְרוּב־אֶחָ֥ד מִקָּצָ֖ה מִזֶּ֑ה מִן־הַכַּפֹּ֛רֶת תַּעֲשׂ֥וּ אֶת־הַכְּרֻבִ֖ים עַל־שְׁנֵ֥י קְצוֹתָֽיו׃ ²⁰וְהָי֣וּ הַכְּרֻבִים֩ פֹּרְשֵׂ֨י כְנָפַ֜יִם

wings. They shall confront each other, the faces of the cherubim being turned toward the cover. [21]Place the cover on top of the Ark, after depositing inside the Ark the Pact that I will give you. [22]There I will meet with you, and I will impart to you—from above the cover, from between the two cherubim that are on top of the Ark of the Pact—all that I will command you concerning the Israelite people.

[23]You shall make a table of acacia wood, two cubits long, one cubit wide, and a cubit and a half high. [24]Overlay it with pure gold, and make a gold molding around it. [25]Make a rim of a hand's breadth around it, and make a gold molding for its rim round about. [26]Make four gold rings for it, and attach the rings to the four corners at its four legs. [27]The rings shall be next to the rim, as holders for poles to carry the table. [28]Make the poles of acacia wood, and overlay them with gold; by these the table shall be carried. [29]Make its bowls, ladles, jars and jugs with which to offer libations; make them of pure gold. [30]And on the table you shall set the bread of display, to be before Me always.

[31]You shall make a lampstand of pure gold; the lampstand shall be made of hammered work; its base and its shaft, its cups, calyxes, and petals shall be of one piece. [32]Six branches shall issue from its sides; three branches from one side of the lampstand and three branches from the other side of the lampstand. [33]On one branch there shall be three cups shaped like almond-blossoms, each with calyx and petals, and on the next branch there shall be three cups shaped like almond-blossoms, each with calyx and petals; so for all six branches issuing from the lampstand. [34]And on the lampstand itself there shall be four cups shaped like almond-blossoms, each with calyx and petals: [35]a calyx, of one piece with it, under a pair of branches; and a calyx, of one piece with it, under the sec-

לְמַעְלָה סֹכְכִים בְּכַנְפֵיהֶם עַל־הַכַּפֹּרֶת וּפְנֵיהֶם אִישׁ אֶל־אָחִיו אֶל־הַכַּפֹּרֶת יִהְיוּ פְּנֵי הַכְּרֻבִים: 21 וְנָתַתָּ אֶת־הַכַּפֹּרֶת עַל־הָאָרֹן מִלְמָעְלָה וְאֶל־הָאָרֹן תִּתֵּן אֶת־הָעֵדֻת אֲשֶׁר אֶתֵּן אֵלֶיךָ: 22 וְנוֹעַדְתִּי לְךָ שָׁם וְדִבַּרְתִּי אִתְּךָ מֵעַל הַכַּפֹּרֶת מִבֵּין שְׁנֵי הַכְּרֻבִים אֲשֶׁר עַל־אֲרֹן הָעֵדֻת אֵת כָּל־אֲשֶׁר אֲצַוֶּה אוֹתְךָ אֶל־בְּנֵי יִשְׂרָאֵל: פ

23 וְעָשִׂיתָ שֻׁלְחָן עֲצֵי שִׁטִּים אַמָּתַיִם אָרְכּוֹ וְאַמָּה רָחְבּוֹ וְאַמָּה וָחֵצִי קֹמָתוֹ: 24 וְצִפִּיתָ אֹתוֹ זָהָב טָהוֹר וְעָשִׂיתָ לּוֹ זֵר זָהָב סָבִיב: 25 וְעָשִׂיתָ לּוֹ מִסְגֶּרֶת טֹפַח סָבִיב וְעָשִׂיתָ זֵר־זָהָב לְמִסְגַּרְתּוֹ סָבִיב: 26 וְעָשִׂיתָ לּוֹ אַרְבַּע טַבְּעֹת זָהָב וְנָתַתָּ אֶת־הַטַּבָּעֹת עַל אַרְבַּע הַפֵּאֹת אֲשֶׁר לְאַרְבַּע רַגְלָיו: 27 לְעֻמַּת הַמִּסְגֶּרֶת תִּהְיֶיןָ הַטַּבָּעֹת לְבָתִּים לְבַדִּים לָשֵׂאת אֶת־הַשֻּׁלְחָן: 28 וְעָשִׂיתָ אֶת־הַבַּדִּים עֲצֵי שִׁטִּים וְצִפִּיתָ אֹתָם זָהָב וְנִשָּׂא־בָם אֶת־הַשֻּׁלְחָן: 29 וְעָשִׂיתָ קְּעָרֹתָיו וְכַפֹּתָיו וּקְשׂוֹתָיו וּמְנַקִּיֹּתָיו אֲשֶׁר יֻסַּךְ בָּהֵן זָהָב טָהוֹר תַּעֲשֶׂה אֹתָם: 30 וְנָתַתָּ עַל־הַשֻּׁלְחָן לֶחֶם פָּנִים לְפָנַי תָּמִיד: פ

31 וְעָשִׂיתָ מְנֹרַת זָהָב טָהוֹר מִקְשָׁה תֵּעָשֶׂה הַמְּנוֹרָה יְרֵכָהּ וְקָנָהּ גְּבִיעֶיהָ כַּפְתֹּרֶיהָ וּפְרָחֶיהָ מִמֶּנָּה יִהְיוּ: 32 וְשִׁשָּׁה קָנִים יֹצְאִים מִצִּדֶּיהָ שְׁלֹשָׁה | קְנֵי מְנֹרָה מִצִּדָּהּ הָאֶחָד וּשְׁלֹשָׁה קְנֵי מְנֹרָה מִצִּדָּהּ הַשֵּׁנִי: 33 שְׁלֹשָׁה גְבִעִים מְשֻׁקָּדִים בַּקָּנֶה הָאֶחָד כַּפְתֹּר וָפֶרַח וּשְׁלֹשָׁה גְבִעִים מְשֻׁקָּדִים בַּקָּנֶה הָאֶחָד כַּפְתֹּר וָפָרַח כֵּן לְשֵׁשֶׁת הַקָּנִים הַיֹּצְאִים מִן־הַמְּנֹרָה: 34 וּבַמְּנֹרָה אַרְבָּעָה גְבִעִים מְשֻׁקָּדִים כַּפְתֹּרֶיהָ וּפְרָחֶיהָ: 35 וְכַפְתֹּר תַּחַת שְׁנֵי הַקָּנִים מִמֶּנָּה וְכַפְתֹּר תַּחַת שְׁנֵי הַקָּנִים

ond pair of branches, and a calyx, of one piece with it, under the last pair of branches; so for all six branches issuing from the lampstand. ³⁶Their calyxes and their stems shall be of one piece with it, the whole of it a single hammered piece of pure gold. ³⁷Make its seven lamps—the lamps shall be so mounted as to give the light on its front side—³⁸and its tongs and fire pans of pure gold. ³⁹It shall be made, with all these furnishings, out of a talent of pure gold. ⁴⁰Note well, and follow the patterns for them that are being shown you on the mountain.

26

As for the Tabernacle,ᵃ make it of ten strips of cloth; make these of fine twisted linen, of blue, purple, and crimson yarns, with a design of cherubim worked into them. ²The length of each cloth shall be twenty-eight cubits, and the width of each cloth shall be four cubits, all the cloths to have the same measurements. ³Five of the cloths shall be joined to one another, and the other five cloths shall be joined to one another. ⁴Make loops of blue wool on the edge of the outermost cloth of the one set; and do likewise on the edge of the outermost cloth of the other set: ⁵make fifty loops on the one cloth, and fifty loops on the edge of the end cloth of the other set, the loops to be opposite one another. ⁶And make fifty gold clasps, and couple the cloths to one another with the clasps, so that the Tabernacle becomes one whole.

⁷You shall then make cloths of goats' hair for a tent over the Tabernacle; make the cloths eleven in number. ⁸The length of each cloth shall be thirty cubits, and the width of each cloth shall be four cubits, the eleven cloths to have the same measurements. ⁹Join five of the cloths by themselves, and the other six cloths by themselves; and fold over the sixth cloth at the front

מִמֶּנָּה וְכַפְתֹּר תַּחַת־שְׁנֵי הַקָּנִים מִמֶּנָּה לְשֵׁשֶׁת הַקָּנִים הַיֹּצְאִים מִן־הַמְּנֹרָה: ³⁶ כַּפְתֹּרֵיהֶם וּקְנֹתָם מִמֶּנָּה יִהְיוּ כֻּלָּהּ מִקְשָׁה אַחַת זָהָב טָהוֹר: ³⁷ וְעָשִׂיתָ אֶת־ נֵרֹתֶיהָ שִׁבְעָה וְהֶעֱלָה אֶת־נֵרֹתֶיהָ וְהֵאִיר עַל־עֵבֶר פָּנֶיהָ: ³⁸ וּמַלְקָחֶיהָ וּמַחְתֹּתֶיהָ זָהָב טָהוֹר: ³⁹ כִּכָּר זָהָב טָהוֹר יַעֲשֶׂה אֹתָהּ אֵת כָּל־הַכֵּלִים הָאֵלֶּה: ⁴⁰ וּרְאֵה וַעֲשֵׂה בְּתַבְנִיתָם אֲשֶׁר־אַתָּה מָרְאֶה בָּהָר: ס

כו וְאֶת־הַמִּשְׁכָּן תַּעֲשֶׂה עֶשֶׂר יְרִיעֹת שֵׁשׁ מָשְׁזָר וּתְכֵלֶת וְאַרְגָּמָן וְתֹלַעַת שָׁנִי כְּרֻבִים מַעֲשֵׂה חֹשֵׁב תַּעֲשֶׂה אֹתָם: ² אֹרֶךְ ׀ הַיְרִיעָה הָאַחַת שְׁמֹנֶה וְעֶשְׂרִים בָּאַמָּה וְרֹחַב אַרְבַּע בָּאַמָּה הַיְרִיעָה הָאֶחָת מִדָּה אַחַת לְכָל־הַיְרִיעֹת: ³ חֲמֵשׁ הַיְרִיעֹת תִּהְיֶיןָ חֹבְרֹת אִשָּׁה אֶל־אֲחֹתָהּ וְחָמֵשׁ יְרִיעֹת חֹבְרֹת אִשָּׁה אֶל־אֲחֹתָהּ: ⁴ וְעָשִׂיתָ לֻלְאֹת תְּכֵלֶת עַל שְׂפַת הַיְרִיעָה הָאֶחָת מִקָּצָה בַּחֹבָרֶת וְכֵן תַּעֲשֶׂה בִּשְׂפַת הַיְרִיעָה הַקִּיצוֹנָה בַּמַּחְבֶּרֶת הַשֵּׁנִית: ⁵ חֲמִשִּׁים לֻלָאֹת תַּעֲשֶׂה בַּיְרִיעָה הָאֶחָת וַחֲמִשִּׁים לֻלָאֹת תַּעֲשֶׂה בִּקְצֵה הַיְרִיעָה אֲשֶׁר בַּמַּחְבֶּרֶת הַשֵּׁנִית מַקְבִּילֹת הַלֻּלָאֹת אִשָּׁה אֶל־אֲחֹתָהּ: ⁶ וְעָשִׂיתָ חֲמִשִּׁים קַרְסֵי זָהָב וְחִבַּרְתָּ אֶת־הַיְרִיעֹת אִשָּׁה אֶל־ אֲחֹתָהּ בַּקְּרָסִים וְהָיָה הַמִּשְׁכָּן אֶחָד: פ ⁷ וְעָשִׂיתָ יְרִיעֹת עִזִּים לְאֹהֶל עַל־הַמִּשְׁכָּן עַשְׁתֵּי־עֶשְׂרֵה יְרִיעֹת תַּעֲשֶׂה אֹתָם: ⁸ אֹרֶךְ ׀ הַיְרִיעָה הָאַחַת שְׁלֹשִׁים בָּאַמָּה וְרֹחַב אַרְבַּע בָּאַמָּה הַיְרִיעָה הָאֶחָת מִדָּה אַחַת לְעַשְׁתֵּי עֶשְׂרֵה יְרִיעֹת: ⁹ וְחִבַּרְתָּ אֶת־חֲמֵשׁ הַיְרִיעֹת לְבָד וְאֶת־שֵׁשׁ

ᵃ Here the lowest of the covers of the Tabernacle.

of the tent. [10]Make fifty loops on the edge of the outermost cloth of the one set, and fifty loops on the edge of the cloth of the other set. [11]Make fifty copper clasps, and fit the clasps into the loops, and couple the tent together so that it becomes one whole. [12]As for the overlapping excess of the cloths of the tent, the extra half-cloth shall overlap the back of the Tabernacle, [13]while the extra cubit at either end of each length of tent cloth shall hang down to the bottom of the two sides of the Tabernacle and cover it. [14]And make for the tent a covering of tanned ram skins, and a covering of dolphin skins above.

[15]You shall make the planks for the Tabernacle of acacia wood, upright. [16]The length of each plank shall be ten cubits and the width of each plank a cubit and a half. [17]Each plank shall have two tenons, parallel[b] to each other; do the same with all the planks of the Tabernacle. [18]Of the planks of the Tabernacle, make twenty planks on the south[c] side: [19]making forty silver sockets under the twenty planks, two sockets under the one plank for its two tenons and two sockets under each following plank for its two tenons; [20]and for the other side wall of the Tabernacle, on the north side, twenty planks, [21]with their forty silver sockets, two sockets under the one plank and two sockets under each following plank. [22]And for the rear of the Tabernacle, to the west, make six planks; [23]and make two planks for the corners of the Tabernacle at the rear. [24]*d*-They shall match at the bottom, and terminate alike at the top inside one ring;-*d* thus shall it be with both of them: they shall form the two corners. [25]Thus there shall be eight planks with their sockets of silver: sixteen sockets, two sockets under the first plank, and two sockets under each of the other planks.

---

b   *Meaning of Heb.* meshullaboth *uncertain.*
c   *Heb. uses two terms for "south."*
d-d *Meaning of Heb. uncertain.*

הַיְרִיעֹת לְבָד וְכָפַלְתָּ אֶת־הַיְרִיעָה הַשִּׁשִּׁית אֶל־מוּל פְּנֵי הָאֹהֶל: 10 וְעָשִׂיתָ חֲמִשִּׁים לֻלָאֹת עַל שְׂפַת הַיְרִיעָה הָאֶחָת הַקִּיצֹנָה בַּחֹבָרֶת וַחֲמִשִּׁים לֻלָאֹת עַל שְׂפַת הַיְרִיעָה הַחֹבֶרֶת הַשֵּׁנִית: 11 וְעָשִׂיתָ קַרְסֵי נְחֹשֶׁת חֲמִשִּׁים וְהֵבֵאתָ אֶת־ הַקְּרָסִים בַּלֻּלָאֹת וְחִבַּרְתָּ אֶת־הָאֹהֶל וְהָיָה אֶחָד: 12 וְסֶרַח הָעֹדֵף בִּירִיעֹת הָאֹהֶל חֲצִי הַיְרִיעָה הָעֹדֶפֶת תִּסְרַח עַל אֲחֹרֵי הַמִּשְׁכָּן: 13 וְהָאַמָּה מִזֶּה וְהָאַמָּה מִזֶּה בָּעֹדֵף בְּאֹרֶךְ יְרִיעֹת הָאֹהֶל יִהְיֶה סָרוּחַ עַל־צִדֵּי הַמִּשְׁכָּן מִזֶּה וּמִזֶּה לְכַסֹּתוֹ: 14 וְעָשִׂיתָ מִכְסֶה לָאֹהֶל עֹרֹת אֵילִם מְאָדָּמִים וּמִכְסֵה עֹרֹת תְּחָשִׁים מִלְמָעְלָה: פ

15 וְעָשִׂיתָ אֶת־הַקְּרָשִׁים לַמִּשְׁכָּן עֲצֵי שִׁטִּים עֹמְדִים: 16 עֶשֶׂר אַמּוֹת אֹרֶךְ הַקָּרֶשׁ וְאַמָּה וַחֲצִי הָאַמָּה רֹחַב הַקֶּרֶשׁ הָאֶחָד: 17 שְׁתֵּי יָדוֹת לַקֶּרֶשׁ הָאֶחָד מְשֻׁלָּבֹת אִשָּׁה אֶל־אֲחֹתָהּ כֵּן תַּעֲשֶׂה לְכֹל קַרְשֵׁי הַמִּשְׁכָּן: 18 וְעָשִׂיתָ אֶת־הַקְּרָשִׁים לַמִּשְׁכָּן עֶשְׂרִים קֶרֶשׁ לִפְאַת נֶגְבָּה תֵימָנָה: 19 וְאַרְבָּעִים אַדְנֵי־כֶסֶף תַּעֲשֶׂה תַּחַת עֶשְׂרִים הַקָּרֶשׁ שְׁנֵי אֲדָנִים תַּחַת־הַקֶּרֶשׁ הָאֶחָד לִשְׁתֵּי יְדֹתָיו וּשְׁנֵי אֲדָנִים תַּחַת־ הַקֶּרֶשׁ הָאֶחָד לִשְׁתֵּי יְדֹתָיו: 20 וּלְצֶלַע הַמִּשְׁכָּן הַשֵּׁנִית לִפְאַת צָפוֹן עֶשְׂרִים קָרֶשׁ: 21 וְאַרְבָּעִים אַדְנֵיהֶם כָּסֶף שְׁנֵי אֲדָנִים תַּחַת הַקֶּרֶשׁ הָאֶחָד וּשְׁנֵי אֲדָנִים תַּחַת הַקֶּרֶשׁ הָאֶחָד: 22 וּלְיַרְכְּתֵי הַמִּשְׁכָּן יָמָּה תַּעֲשֶׂה שִׁשָּׁה קְרָשִׁים: 23 וּשְׁנֵי קְרָשִׁים תַּעֲשֶׂה לִמְקֻצְעֹת הַמִּשְׁכָּן בַּיַּרְכָתָיִם: 24 וְיִהְיוּ תֹאֲמִים מִלְּמַטָּה וְיַחְדָּו יִהְיוּ תַמִּים עַל־רֹאשׁוֹ אֶל־הַטַּבַּעַת הָאֶחָת כֵּן יִהְיֶה לִשְׁנֵיהֶם לִשְׁנֵי הַמִּקְצֹעֹת יִהְיוּ: 25 וְהָיוּ שְׁמֹנָה קְרָשִׁים וְאַדְנֵיהֶם

26You shall make bars of acacia wood: five for the planks of the one side wall of the Tabernacle, 27five bars for the planks of the other side wall of the Tabernacle, and five bars for the planks of the wall of the Tabernacle at the rear to the west. 28The center bar halfway up the planks shall run from end to end. 29Overlay the planks with gold, and make their rings of gold, as holders for the bars; and overlay the bars with gold. 30Then set up the Tabernacle according to the manner of it that you were shown on the mountain.

31You shall make a curtain of blue, purple, and crimson yarns, and fine twisted linen; it shall have a design of cherubim worked into it. 32Hang it upon four posts of acacia wood overlaid with gold and having hooks of gold, [set] in four sockets of silver. 33Hang the curtain under the clasps, and carry the Ark of the Pact there, behind the curtain, so that the curtain shall serve you as a partition between the Holy and the Holy of Holies. 34Place the cover upon the Ark of the Pact in the Holy of Holies. 35Place the table outside the curtain, and the lampstand by the south wall of the Tabernacle opposite the table, which is to be placed by the north wall.

36You shall make a screen for the entrance of the Tent, of blue, purple, and crimson yarns, and fine twisted linen, done in embroidery. 37Make five posts of acacia wood for the screen and overlay them with gold—their hooks being of gold—and cast for them five sockets of copper.

כֶּסֶף שִׁשָּׁה עָשָׂר אֲדָנִים שְׁנֵי אֲדָנִים תַּחַת הַקֶּרֶשׁ הָאֶחָד וּשְׁנֵי אֲדָנִים תַּחַת הַקֶּרֶשׁ הָאֶחָד:

26 וְעָשִׂיתָ בְרִיחִם עֲצֵי שִׁטִּים חֲמִשָּׁה לְקַרְשֵׁי צֶלַע־הַמִּשְׁכָּן הָאֶחָד: 27 וַחֲמִשָּׁה בְרִיחִם לְקַרְשֵׁי צֶלַע־הַמִּשְׁכָּן הַשֵּׁנִית וַחֲמִשָּׁה בְרִיחִם לְקַרְשֵׁי צֶלַע הַמִּשְׁכָּן לַיַּרְכָתַיִם יָמָּה: 28 וְהַבְּרִיחַ הַתִּיכֹן בְּתוֹךְ הַקְּרָשִׁים מַבְרִחַ מִן־הַקָּצֶה אֶל־הַקָּצֶה: 29 וְאֶת־הַקְּרָשִׁים תְּצַפֶּה זָהָב וְאֶת־טַבְּעֹתֵיהֶם תַּעֲשֶׂה זָהָב בָּתִּים לַבְּרִיחִם וְצִפִּיתָ אֶת־הַבְּרִיחִם זָהָב: 30 וַהֲקֵמֹתָ אֶת־הַמִּשְׁכָּן כְּמִשְׁפָּטוֹ אֲשֶׁר הָרְאֵיתָ בָּהָר: ס

31 וְעָשִׂיתָ פָרֹכֶת תְּכֵלֶת וְאַרְגָּמָן וְתוֹלַעַת שָׁנִי וְשֵׁשׁ מָשְׁזָר מַעֲשֵׂה חֹשֵׁב יַעֲשֶׂה אֹתָהּ כְּרֻבִים: 32 וְנָתַתָּה אֹתָהּ עַל־אַרְבָּעָה עַמּוּדֵי שִׁטִּים מְצֻפִּים זָהָב וָוֵיהֶם זָהָב עַל־אַרְבָּעָה אַדְנֵי־כָסֶף: 33 וְנָתַתָּה אֶת־הַפָּרֹכֶת תַּחַת הַקְּרָסִים וְהֵבֵאתָ שָׁמָּה מִבֵּית לַפָּרֹכֶת אֵת אֲרוֹן הָעֵדוּת וְהִבְדִּילָה הַפָּרֹכֶת לָכֶם בֵּין הַקֹּדֶשׁ וּבֵין קֹדֶשׁ הַקֳּדָשִׁים: 34 וְנָתַתָּ אֶת־הַכַּפֹּרֶת עַל אֲרוֹן הָעֵדֻת בְּקֹדֶשׁ הַקֳּדָשִׁים: 35 וְשַׂמְתָּ אֶת־הַשֻּׁלְחָן מִחוּץ לַפָּרֹכֶת וְאֶת־הַמְּנֹרָה נֹכַח הַשֻּׁלְחָן עַל צֶלַע הַמִּשְׁכָּן תֵּימָנָה וְהַשֻּׁלְחָן תִּתֵּן עַל־צֶלַע צָפוֹן:

36 וְעָשִׂיתָ מָסָךְ לְפֶתַח הָאֹהֶל תְּכֵלֶת וְאַרְגָּמָן וְתוֹלַעַת שָׁנִי וְשֵׁשׁ מָשְׁזָר מַעֲשֵׂה רֹקֵם: 37 וְעָשִׂיתָ לַמָּסָךְ חֲמִשָּׁה עַמּוּדֵי שִׁטִּים וְצִפִּיתָ אֹתָם זָהָב וָוֵיהֶם זָהָב וְיָצַקְתָּ לָהֶם חֲמִשָּׁה אַדְנֵי נְחֹשֶׁת: ס

27 You shall make the altar of acacia wood, five cubits long and five cubits wide—the altar is to be square—and three cubits high. ²Make its horns on the four corners, the horns to be of one piece with it; and overlay it with copper. ³Make the pails for removing its ashes, as well as its scrapers, basins, flesh hooks, and fire pans—make all its utensils of copper. ⁴Make for it a grating of meshwork in copper; and on the mesh make four copper rings at its four corners. ⁵Set the mesh below, under the ledge of the altar, so that it extends to the middle of the altar. ⁶And make poles for the altar, poles of acacia wood, and overlay them with copper. ⁷The poles shall be inserted into the rings, so that the poles remain on the two sides of the altar when it is carried. ⁸Make it hollow, of boards. As you were shown on the mountain, so shall they be made.

⁹You shall make the enclosure of the Tabernacle:

On the south side,ᵃ a hundred cubits of hangings of fine twisted linen for the length of the enclosure on that side—¹⁰with its twenty posts and their twenty sockets of copper, the hooks and bands of the posts to be of silver.

¹¹Again a hundred cubits of hangings for its length along the north side—with its twenty posts and their twenty sockets of copper, the hooks and bands of the posts to be of silver.

¹²For the width of the enclosure, on the west side, fifty cubits of hangings, with their ten posts and their ten sockets.

¹³For the width of the enclosure on the front, or east side, fifty cubits: ¹⁴fifteen cubits of hangings on the one flank, with their three posts and their three sockets; ¹⁵fifteen cubits of hangings on the other flank, with their three posts and their three sockets; ¹⁶and for the gate of the en-

---

ᵃ   *Cf. note at 26.18.*

כז וְעָשִׂיתָ אֶת־הַמִּזְבֵּחַ עֲצֵי שִׁטִּים חָמֵשׁ אַמּוֹת אֹרֶךְ וְחָמֵשׁ אַמּוֹת רֹחַב רָבוּעַ יִהְיֶה הַמִּזְבֵּחַ וְשָׁלֹשׁ אַמּוֹת קֹמָתוֹ: ² וְעָשִׂיתָ קַרְנֹתָיו עַל אַרְבַּע פִּנֹּתָיו מִמֶּנּוּ תִּהְיֶיןָ קַרְנֹתָיו וְצִפִּיתָ אֹתוֹ נְחֹשֶׁת: ³ וְעָשִׂיתָ סִּירֹתָיו לְדַשְּׁנוֹ וְיָעָיו וּמִזְרְקֹתָיו וּמִזְלְגֹתָיו וּמַחְתֹּתָיו לְכָל־כֵּלָיו תַּעֲשֶׂה נְחֹשֶׁת: ⁴ וְעָשִׂיתָ לּוֹ מִכְבָּר מַעֲשֵׂה רֶשֶׁת נְחֹשֶׁת וְעָשִׂיתָ עַל־הָרֶשֶׁת אַרְבַּע טַבְּעֹת נְחֹשֶׁת עַל אַרְבַּע קְצוֹתָיו: ⁵ וְנָתַתָּה אֹתָהּ תַּחַת כַּרְכֹּב הַמִּזְבֵּחַ מִלְמָטָּה וְהָיְתָה הָרֶשֶׁת עַד חֲצִי הַמִּזְבֵּחַ: ⁶ וְעָשִׂיתָ בַדִּים לַמִּזְבֵּחַ בַּדֵּי עֲצֵי שִׁטִּים וְצִפִּיתָ אֹתָם נְחֹשֶׁת: ⁷ וְהוּבָא אֶת־בַּדָּיו בַּטַּבָּעֹת וְהָיוּ הַבַּדִּים עַל־שְׁתֵּי צַלְעֹת הַמִּזְבֵּחַ בִּשְׂאֵת אֹתוֹ: ⁸ נְבוּב לֻחֹת תַּעֲשֶׂה אֹתוֹ כַּאֲשֶׁר הֶרְאָה אֹתְךָ בָּהָר כֵּן יַעֲשׂוּ: ס

⁹ וְעָשִׂיתָ אֵת חֲצַר הַמִּשְׁכָּן לִפְאַת נֶגֶב־תֵּימָנָה קְלָעִים לֶחָצֵר שֵׁשׁ מָשְׁזָר מֵאָה בָאַמָּה אֹרֶךְ לַפֵּאָה הָאֶחָת: ¹⁰ וְעַמֻּדָיו עֶשְׂרִים וְאַדְנֵיהֶם עֶשְׂרִים נְחֹשֶׁת וָוֵי הָעַמֻּדִים וַחֲשֻׁקֵיהֶם כָּסֶף: ¹¹ וְכֵן לִפְאַת צָפוֹן בָּאֹרֶךְ קְלָעִים מֵאָה אֹרֶךְ וְעַמּוּדָו עֶשְׂרִים וְאַדְנֵיהֶם עֶשְׂרִים נְחֹשֶׁת וָוֵי הָעַמֻּדִים וַחֲשֻׁקֵיהֶם כָּסֶף: ¹² וְרֹחַב הֶחָצֵר לִפְאַת־יָם קְלָעִים חֲמִשִּׁים אַמָּה עַמֻּדֵיהֶם עֲשָׂרָה וְאַדְנֵיהֶם עֲשָׂרָה: ¹³ וְרֹחַב הֶחָצֵר לִפְאַת קֵדְמָה מִזְרָחָה חֲמִשִּׁים אַמָּה: ¹⁴ וַחֲמֵשׁ עֶשְׂרֵה אַמָּה קְלָעִים לַכָּתֵף עַמֻּדֵיהֶם שְׁלֹשָׁה וְאַדְנֵיהֶם שְׁלֹשָׁה: ¹⁵ וְלַכָּתֵף הַשֵּׁנִית חֲמֵשׁ עֶשְׂרֵה קְלָעִים עַמֻּדֵיהֶם שְׁלֹשָׁה וְאַדְנֵיהֶם

closure, a screen of twenty cubits, of blue, purple, and crimson yarns, and fine twisted linen, done in embroidery, with their four posts and their four sockets.

¹⁷All the posts round the enclosure shall be banded with silver and their hooks shall be of silver; their sockets shall be of copper.

¹⁸The length of the enclosure shall be a hundred cubits, and the width fifty throughout; and the height five cubits—[with hangings] of fine twisted linen. The sockets shall be of copper: ¹⁹all the utensils of the Tabernacle,[b] for all its service, as well as all its pegs and all the pegs of the court, shall be of copper.

TETSAVVEH

²⁰You shall further instruct the Israelites to bring you clear oil of beaten olives for lighting, for kindling lamps regularly. ²¹Aaron and his sons shall set them up in the Tent of Meeting, outside the curtain which is over [the Ark of] the Pact, [to burn] from evening to morning before the Lord. It shall be a due from the Israelites for all time, throughout the ages.

28 You shall bring forward your brother Aaron, with his sons, from among the Israelites, to serve Me as priests: Aaron, Nadab and Abihu, Eleazar and Ithamar, the sons of Aaron. ²Make sacral vestments for your brother Aaron, for dignity and adornment. ³Next you shall instruct all who are ᵃ-skillful, whom I have endowed with the gift of skill,-ᵃ to make Aaron's vestments, for consecrating him to serve Me as priest. ⁴These are the vestments they are to make: a breastpiece, an ephod, a robe, a fringed[b] tunic, a headdress, and a sash. They shall make those

שְׁלֹשָׁה׃ 16 וּלְשַׁ֣עַר הֶֽחָצֵ֗ר מָסָךְ֮ | עֶשְׂרִ֣ים אַמָּה֒ תְּכֵ֨לֶת וְאַרְגָּמָ֜ן וְתוֹלַ֧עַת שָׁנִ֛י וְשֵׁ֥שׁ מָשְׁזָ֖ר מַעֲשֵׂ֣ה רֹקֵ֑ם עַמֻּֽדֵיהֶ֣ם אַרְבָּעָ֔ה וְאַדְנֵיהֶ֖ם אַרְבָּעָֽה׃ 17 כׇּל־עַמּוּדֵ֨י הֶֽחָצֵ֤ר סָבִיב֙ מְחֻשָּׁקִ֣ים כֶּ֔סֶף וָוֵיהֶ֖ם כָּ֑סֶף וְאַדְנֵיהֶ֖ם נְחֹֽשֶׁת׃ 18 אֹ֣רֶךְ הֶֽחָצֵר֩ מֵאָ֨ה בָֽאַמָּ֜ה וְרֹ֣חַב | חֲמִשִּׁ֣ים בַּחֲמִשִּׁ֗ים וְקֹמָ֛ה חָמֵ֥שׁ אַמּ֖וֹת שֵׁ֣שׁ מׇשְׁזָ֑ר וְאַדְנֵיהֶ֖ם נְחֹֽשֶׁת׃ 19 לְכֹל֙ כְּלֵ֣י הַמִּשְׁכָּ֔ן בְּכֹ֖ל עֲבֹדָת֑וֹ וְכׇל־יְתֵֽדֹתָ֛יו וְכׇל־ יִתְדֹ֥ת הֶחָצֵ֖ר נְחֹֽשֶׁת׃ ס

תצוה

20 וְאַתָּ֞ה תְּצַוֶּ֣ה | אֶת־בְּנֵ֣י יִשְׂרָאֵ֗ל וְיִקְח֨וּ אֵלֶ֜יךָ שֶׁ֣מֶן זַ֥יִת זָ֛ךְ כָּתִ֖ית לַמָּא֑וֹר לְהַעֲלֹ֥ת נֵ֖ר תָּמִֽיד׃ 21 בְּאֹ֣הֶל מוֹעֵד֩ מִח֨וּץ לַפָּרֹ֜כֶת אֲשֶׁ֣ר עַל־הָעֵדֻ֗ת יַעֲרֹךְ֩ אֹת֨וֹ אַהֲרֹ֤ן וּבָנָיו֙ מֵעֶ֣רֶב עַד־בֹּ֔קֶר לִפְנֵ֖י יְהֹוָ֑ה חֻקַּ֤ת עוֹלָם֙ לְדֹ֣רֹתָ֔ם מֵאֵ֖ת בְּנֵ֥י יִשְׂרָאֵֽל׃ ס

כח וְאַתָּ֡ה הַקְרֵ֣ב אֵלֶ֩יךָ֩ אֶת־אַהֲרֹ֨ן אָחִ֜יךָ וְאֶת־בָּנָ֣יו אִתּ֗וֹ מִתּ֛וֹךְ בְּנֵ֥י יִשְׂרָאֵ֖ל לְכַהֲנוֹ־לִ֑י אַהֲרֹ֕ן נָדָ֧ב וַאֲבִיה֛וּא אֶלְעָזָ֥ר וְאִֽיתָמָ֖ר בְּנֵ֥י אַהֲרֹֽן׃ 2 וְעָשִׂ֥יתָ בִגְדֵי־קֹ֖דֶשׁ לְאַהֲרֹ֣ן אָחִ֑יךָ לְכָב֖וֹד וּלְתִפְאָֽרֶת׃ 3 וְאַתָּ֗ה תְּדַבֵּר֙ אֶל־כׇּל־חַכְמֵי־לֵ֔ב אֲשֶׁ֥ר מִלֵּאתִ֖יו ר֣וּחַ חׇכְמָ֑ה וְעָשׂ֞וּ אֶת־בִּגְדֵ֧י אַהֲרֹ֛ן לְקַדְּשׁ֖וֹ לְכַהֲנוֹ־לִֽי׃ 4 וְאֵ֨לֶּה הַבְּגָדִ֜ים אֲשֶׁ֣ר יַעֲשׂ֗וּ חֹ֤שֶׁן וְאֵפוֹד֙ וּמְעִ֔יל וּכְתֹ֥נֶת תַּשְׁבֵּ֖ץ מִצְנֶ֣פֶת וְאַבְנֵ֑ט וְעָשׂ֨וּ בִגְדֵי־קֹ֜דֶשׁ לְאַהֲרֹ֥ן אָחִ֛יךָ

---

b   *I.e., of the Tabernacle enclosure; the furnishings inside were of gold.*

a-a   *Lit. "wise of heart, whom I have filled with a spirit of wisdom."*
b   *Others "checkered."*

sacral vestments for your brother Aaron and his sons, for priestly service to Me; [5]they, therefore, shall receive the gold, the blue, purple, and crimson yarns, and the fine linen.

[6]They shall make the ephod of gold, of blue, purple, and crimson yarns, and of fine twisted linen, worked into designs. [7]It shall have two shoulder-pieces attached; they shall be attached at its two ends. [8]And the decorated band that is upon it shall be made like it, of one piece with it: of gold, of blue, purple, and crimson yarns, and of fine twisted linen. [9]Then take two lazuli stones and engrave on them the names of the sons of Israel: [10]six of their names on the one stone, and the names of the remaining six on the other stone, in the order of their birth. [11]On the two stones you shall make seal engravings—the work of a lapidary—of the names of the sons of Israel. Having bordered them with frames of gold, [12]attach the two stones to the shoulder-pieces of the ephod, as stones for remembrance of the Israelite people, whose names Aaron shall carry upon his two shoulder-pieces for remembrance before the LORD.

[13]Then make frames of gold [14]and two chains of pure gold; braid these like corded work, and fasten the corded chains to the frames.

[15]You shall make a breastpiece of decision,[c] worked into a design; make it in the style of the ephod: make it of gold, of blue, purple, and crimson yarns, and of fine twisted linen. [16]It shall be square and doubled, a span in length and a span in width. [17]Set in it mounted stones, in four rows of stones. The first row shall be a row of [d]carnelian, chrysolite, and emerald; [18]the second row: a turquoise, a sapphire, and an amethyst; [19]the third row: a jacinth, an agate, and a crystal; [20]and the fourth row: a beryl, a lapis lazuli, and a jasper. They shall be framed with

וּלְבָנָיו לְכַהֲנוֹ־לִי: 5 וְהֵם יִקְחוּ אֶת־הַזָּהָב וְאֶת־הַתְּכֵלֶת וְאֶת־הָאַרְגָּמָן וְאֶת־תּוֹלַעַת הַשָּׁנִי וְאֶת־הַשֵּׁשׁ: פ

6 וְעָשׂוּ אֶת־הָאֵפֹד זָהָב תְּכֵלֶת וְאַרְגָּמָן תּוֹלַעַת שָׁנִי וְשֵׁשׁ מָשְׁזָר מַעֲשֵׂה חֹשֵׁב: 7 שְׁתֵּי כְתֵפֹת חֹבְרֹת יִהְיֶה־לּוֹ אֶל־שְׁנֵי קְצוֹתָיו וְחֻבָּר: 8 וְחֵשֶׁב אֲפֻדָּתוֹ אֲשֶׁר עָלָיו כְּמַעֲשֵׂהוּ מִמֶּנּוּ יִהְיֶה זָהָב תְּכֵלֶת וְאַרְגָּמָן וְתוֹלַעַת שָׁנִי וְשֵׁשׁ מָשְׁזָר: 9 וְלָקַחְתָּ אֶת־שְׁתֵּי אַבְנֵי־שֹׁהַם וּפִתַּחְתָּ עֲלֵיהֶם שְׁמוֹת בְּנֵי יִשְׂרָאֵל: 10 שִׁשָּׁה מִשְּׁמֹתָם עַל הָאֶבֶן הָאֶחָת וְאֶת־שְׁמוֹת הַשִּׁשָּׁה הַנּוֹתָרִים עַל־הָאֶבֶן הַשֵּׁנִית כְּתוֹלְדֹתָם: 11 מַעֲשֵׂה חָרַשׁ אֶבֶן פִּתּוּחֵי חֹתָם תְּפַתַּח אֶת־שְׁתֵּי הָאֲבָנִים עַל־שְׁמֹת בְּנֵי יִשְׂרָאֵל מֻסַבֹּת מִשְׁבְּצוֹת זָהָב תַּעֲשֶׂה אֹתָם: 12 וְשַׂמְתָּ אֶת־שְׁתֵּי הָאֲבָנִים עַל כִּתְפֹת הָאֵפֹד אַבְנֵי זִכָּרֹן לִבְנֵי יִשְׂרָאֵל וְנָשָׂא אַהֲרֹן אֶת־שְׁמוֹתָם לִפְנֵי יְהוָה עַל־שְׁתֵּי כְתֵפָיו לְזִכָּרֹן: ס

13 וְעָשִׂיתָ מִשְׁבְּצֹת זָהָב: 14 וּשְׁתֵּי שַׁרְשְׁרֹת זָהָב טָהוֹר מִגְבָּלֹת תַּעֲשֶׂה אֹתָם מַעֲשֵׂה עֲבֹת וְנָתַתָּה אֶת־שַׁרְשְׁרֹת הָעֲבֹתֹת עַל־הַמִּשְׁבְּצֹת: ס

15 וְעָשִׂיתָ חֹשֶׁן מִשְׁפָּט מַעֲשֵׂה חֹשֵׁב כְּמַעֲשֵׂה אֵפֹד תַּעֲשֶׂנּוּ זָהָב תְּכֵלֶת וְאַרְגָּמָן וְתוֹלַעַת שָׁנִי וְשֵׁשׁ מָשְׁזָר תַּעֲשֶׂה אֹתוֹ: 16 רָבוּעַ יִהְיֶה כָּפוּל זֶרֶת אָרְכּוֹ וְזֶרֶת רָחְבּוֹ: 17 וּמִלֵּאתָ בוֹ מִלֻּאַת אֶבֶן אַרְבָּעָה טוּרִים אָבֶן טוּר אֹדֶם פִּטְדָה וּבָרֶקֶת הַטּוּר הָאֶחָד: 18 וְהַטּוּר הַשֵּׁנִי נֹפֶךְ סַפִּיר וְיָהֲלֹם: 19 וְהַטּוּר הַשְּׁלִישִׁי לֶשֶׁם שְׁבוֹ וְאַחְלָמָה: 20 וְהַטּוּר הָרְבִיעִי תַּרְשִׁישׁ וְשֹׁהַם וְיָשְׁפֵה מְשֻׁבָּצִים זָהָב יִהְיוּ בְּמִלּוּאֹתָם:

---

c   See v. 30 below; others "judgment."
d   The identity of several of these twelve stones is uncertain.

gold in their mountings. ²¹The stones shall correspond [in number] to the names of the sons
of Israel: twelve, corresponding to their names.
They shall be engraved like seals, each with its
name, for the twelve tribes.

²²On the breastpiece make braided chains of
corded work in pure gold. ²³Make two rings of
gold on the breastpiece, and fasten the two rings
at the two ends of the breastpiece, ²⁴attaching
the two golden cords to the two rings at the ends
of the breastpiece. ²⁵Then fasten the two ends
of the cords to the two frames, which you shall
attach to the shoulder-pieces of the ephod, at
the front. ²⁶Make two rings of gold and attach
them to the two ends of the breastpiece, at its
inner edge, which faces the ephod. ²⁷And make
two other rings of gold and fasten them on the
front of the ephod, low on the two shoulder-
pieces, close to its seam above the decorated
band. ²⁸The breastpiece shall be held in place
by a cord of blue from its rings to the rings of
the ephod, so that the breastpiece rests on the
decorated band and does not come loose from
the ephod. ²⁹Aaron shall carry the names of the
sons of Israel on the breastpiece of decision over
his heart, when he enters the sanctuary, for remembrance before the LORD at all times. ³⁰In-
side the breastpiece of decision you shall place
the Urim and Thummim,^e so that they are over
Aaron's heart when he comes before the LORD.
Thus Aaron shall carry the instrument of decision for the Israelites over his heart before the
LORD at all times.

³¹You shall make the robe of the ephod of
pure blue.^f ³²The opening for the head shall be
in the middle of it; the opening shall have a bind-
ing of woven work round about—it shall be like
the opening of a coat of mail—so that it does
not tear. ³³On its hem make pomegranates of

---

e   *Meaning of these two words uncertain. They designate a kind*
    of oracle; cf. Num. 27.21.
f   *Others "all of blue."*

---

21 וְהָאֲבָנִים תִּהְיֶ֫יןָ עַל־שְׁמֹ֣ת בְּנֵי־יִשְׂרָאֵ֗ל
שְׁתֵּ֥ים עֶשְׂרֵ֖ה עַל־שְׁמֹתָ֑ם פִּתּוּחֵ֣י חוֹתָ֗ם
אִ֤ישׁ עַל־שְׁמוֹ֙ תִּֽהְיֶ֔יןָ לִשְׁנֵ֖י עָשָׂ֥ר שָֽׁבֶט׃
22 וְעָשִׂ֧יתָ עַל־הַחֹ֛שֶׁן שַׁרְשֹׁ֥ת גַּבְלֻ֖ת
מַעֲשֵׂ֣ה עֲבֹ֑ת זָהָ֖ב טָהֽוֹר׃ 23 וְעָשִׂ֣יתָ עַל־
הַחֹ֗שֶׁן שְׁתֵּי֙ טַבְּע֣וֹת זָהָ֔ב וְנָתַתָּ֗ אֶת־שְׁתֵּי֙
הַטַּבָּע֔וֹת עַל־שְׁנֵ֖י קְצ֥וֹת הַחֹֽשֶׁן׃ 24 וְנָֽתַתָּ֗ה
אֶת־שְׁתֵּי֙ עֲבֹתֹ֣ת הַזָּהָ֔ב עַל־שְׁתֵּ֖י הַטַּבָּעֹ֑ת
אֶל־קְצ֖וֹת הַחֹֽשֶׁן׃ 25 וְאֵ֨ת שְׁתֵּ֤י קְצוֹת֙ שְׁתֵּ֣י
הָעֲבֹתֹ֔ת תִּתֵּ֖ן עַל־שְׁתֵּ֣י הַֽמִּשְׁבְּצ֑וֹת
וְנָתַתָּ֛ה עַל־כִּתְפ֥וֹת הָאֵפֹ֖ד אֶל־מ֥וּל פָּנָֽיו׃
26 וְעָשִׂ֗יתָ שְׁתֵּי֙ טַבְּע֣וֹת זָהָ֔ב וְשַׂמְתָּ֣ אֹתָ֔ם
עַל־שְׁנֵ֖י קְצ֣וֹת הַחֹ֑שֶׁן עַל־שְׂפָת֕וֹ אֲשֶׁ֛ר
אֶל־עֵ֥בֶר הָאֵפֹ֖ד בָּֽיְתָה׃ 27 וְעָשִׂ֘יתָ֮ שְׁתֵּ֣י
טַבְּע֣וֹת זָהָב֒ וְנָתַתָּ֣ה אֹתָ֗ם עַל־שְׁתֵּ֣י
כִתְפ֣וֹת הָאֵפ֞וֹד מִלְּמַ֗טָּה מִמּ֣וּל פָּנָ֔יו
לְעֻמַּ֖ת מֶחְבַּרְתּ֑וֹ מִמַּ֕עַל לְחֵ֖שֶׁב הָאֵפֽוֹד׃
28 וְיִרְכְּס֣וּ אֶת־הַ֠חֹשֶׁן מִֽטַּבְּעֹתָ֞יו
אֶל־טַבְּעֹ֤ת הָאֵפֹד֙ בִּפְתִ֣יל תְּכֵ֔לֶת לִֽהְי֖וֹת
עַל־חֵ֣שֶׁב הָאֵפ֑וֹד וְלֹֽא־יִזַּ֣ח הַחֹ֔שֶׁן מֵעַ֖ל
הָאֵפֽוֹד׃ 29 וְנָשָׂ֣א אַ֠הֲרֹן אֶת־שְׁמ֨וֹת בְּנֵֽי־
יִשְׂרָאֵ֜ל בְּחֹ֧שֶׁן הַמִּשְׁפָּ֛ט עַל־לִבּ֖וֹ בְּבֹא֣וֹ
אֶל־הַקֹּ֑דֶשׁ לְזִכָּרֹ֥ן לִפְנֵֽי־יְהוָ֖ה תָּמִֽיד׃
30 וְנָתַתָּ֞ אֶל־חֹ֣שֶׁן הַמִּשְׁפָּ֗ט אֶת־הָאוּרִים֙
וְאֶת־הַתֻּמִּ֔ים וְהָיוּ֙ עַל־לֵ֣ב אַהֲרֹ֔ן בְּבֹא֖וֹ
לִפְנֵ֣י יְהוָ֑ה וְנָשָׂ֣א אַ֠הֲרֹן אֶת־מִשְׁפַּ֨ט בְּנֵֽי־
יִשְׂרָאֵ֧ל עַל־לִבּ֛וֹ לִפְנֵ֥י יְהוָ֖ה תָּמִֽיד׃ ס
31 וְעָשִׂ֛יתָ אֶת־מְעִ֥יל הָאֵפ֖וֹד כְּלִ֥יל תְּכֵֽלֶת׃
32 וְהָיָ֥ה פִֽי־רֹאשׁ֖וֹ בְּתוֹכ֑וֹ שָׂפָ֡ה יִֽהְיֶה֩ לְפִ֨יו
סָבִ֜יב מַעֲשֵׂ֣ה אֹרֵ֗ג כְּפִ֤י תַחְרָא֙ יִֽהְיֶה־לּ֔וֹ
לֹ֖א יִקָּרֵֽעַ׃ 33 וְעָשִׂ֣יתָ עַל־שׁוּלָ֗יו רִמֹּנֵ֤י

blue, purple, and crimson yarns, all around the hem, with bells of gold between them all around: ³⁴a golden bell and a pomegranate, a golden bell and a pomegranate, all around the hem of the robe. ³⁵Aaron shall wear it while officiating, so that the sound of it is heard when he comes into the sanctuary before the LORD and when he goes out—that he may not die.

³⁶You shall make a frontlet of pure gold and engrave on it the seal inscription: "Holy to the LORD." ³⁷Suspend it on a cord of blue, so that it may remain on the headdress; it shall remain on the front of the headdress. ³⁸It shall be on Aaron's forehead, that Aaron may take away any sin arising from the holy things that the Israelites consecrate, from any of their sacred donations; it shall be on his forehead at all times, to win acceptance for them before the LORD.

³⁹You shall make the fringed tunic of fine linen.

You shall make the headdress of fine linen.

You shall make the sash of embroidered work.

⁴⁰And for Aaron's sons also you shall make tunics, and make sashes for them, and make turbans for them, for dignity and adornment. ⁴¹Put these on your brother Aaron and on his sons as well; anoint them, and ordain themᵍ and consecrate them to serve Me as priests.

⁴²You shall also make for them linen breeches to cover their nakedness; they shall extend from the hips to the thighs. ⁴³They shall be worn by Aaron and his sons when they enter the Tent of Meeting or when they approach the altar to officiate in the sanctuary, so that they do not incur punishment and die. It shall be a law for all time for him and for his offspring to come.

29
This is what you shall do to them in consecrating them to serve Me as priests: Take a

ᵍ Lit. "and fill their hands."

175

young bull of the herd and two rams without blemish; [2]also unleavened bread, unleavened cakes with oil mixed in, and unleavened wafers spread with oil—make these of choice wheat flour. [3]Place these in one basket and present them in the basket, along with the bull and the two rams. [4]Lead Aaron and his sons up to the entrance of the Tent of Meeting, and wash them with water. [5]Then take the vestments, and clothe Aaron with the tunic, the robe of the ephod, the ephod, and the breastpiece, and gird him with the decorated band of the ephod. [6]Put the headdress on his head, and place the holy diadem upon the headdress. [7]Take the anointing oil and pour it on his head and anoint him. [8]Then bring his sons forward; clothe them with tunics [9]and wind turbans upon them. And gird both Aaron and his sons with sashes. And so they shall have priesthood as their right for all time.

You shall then ordain Aaron and his sons. [10]Lead the bull up to the front of the Tent of Meeting, and let Aaron and his sons lay their hands upon the head of the bull. [11]Slaughter the bull before the Lord, at the entrance of the Tent of Meeting, [12]and take some of the bull's blood and put it on the horns of the altar with your finger; then pour out the rest of the blood at the base of the altar. [13]Take all the fat that covers the entrails, the protuberance on the liver, and the two kidneys with the fat on them, and turn them into smoke upon the altar. [14]The rest of the flesh of the bull, its hide, and its dung shall be put to the fire outside the camp; it is a sin offering.

[15]Next take the one ram, and let Aaron and his sons lay their hands upon the ram's head. [16]Slaughter the ram, and take its blood and dash it against all sides of the altar. [17]Cut up the ram into sections, wash its entrails and legs, and put them with its quarters and its head. [18]Turn all

בֶּן־בָּקָר וְאֵילִם שְׁנַיִם תְּמִימִם: 2 וְלֶחֶם מַצּוֹת וְחַלֹּת מַצֹּת בְּלוּלֹת בַּשֶּׁמֶן וּרְקִיקֵי מַצּוֹת מְשֻׁחִים בַּשָּׁמֶן סֹלֶת חִטִּים תַּעֲשֶׂה אֹתָם: 3 וְנָתַתָּ אוֹתָם עַל־סַל אֶחָד וְהִקְרַבְתָּ אֹתָם בַּסָּל וְאֶת־הַפָּר וְאֵת שְׁנֵי הָאֵילִם: 4 וְאֶת־אַהֲרֹן וְאֶת־בָּנָיו תַּקְרִיב אֶל־פֶּתַח אֹהֶל מוֹעֵד וְרָחַצְתָּ אֹתָם בַּמָּיִם: 5 וְלָקַחְתָּ אֶת־הַבְּגָדִים וְהִלְבַּשְׁתָּ אֶת־אַהֲרֹן אֶת־הַכֻּתֹּנֶת וְאֵת מְעִיל הָאֵפֹד וְאֶת־הָאֵפֹד וְאֶת־הַחֹשֶׁן וְאָפַדְתָּ לוֹ בְּחֵשֶׁב הָאֵפֹד: 6 וְשַׂמְתָּ הַמִּצְנֶפֶת עַל־רֹאשׁוֹ וְנָתַתָּ אֶת־נֵזֶר הַקֹּדֶשׁ עַל־הַמִּצְנָפֶת: 7 וְלָקַחְתָּ אֶת־שֶׁמֶן הַמִּשְׁחָה וְיָצַקְתָּ עַל־רֹאשׁוֹ וּמָשַׁחְתָּ אֹתוֹ: 8 וְאֶת־בָּנָיו תַּקְרִיב וְהִלְבַּשְׁתָּם כֻּתֳּנֹת: 9 וְחָגַרְתָּ אֹתָם אַבְנֵט אַהֲרֹן וּבָנָיו וְחָבַשְׁתָּ לָהֶם מִגְבָּעֹת וְהָיְתָה לָהֶם כְּהֻנָּה לְחֻקַּת עוֹלָם וּמִלֵּאתָ יַד־אַהֲרֹן וְיַד־בָּנָיו: 10 וְהִקְרַבְתָּ אֶת־הַפָּר לִפְנֵי אֹהֶל מוֹעֵד וְסָמַךְ אַהֲרֹן וּבָנָיו אֶת־יְדֵיהֶם עַל־רֹאשׁ הַפָּר: 11 וְשָׁחַטְתָּ אֶת־הַפָּר לִפְנֵי יְהֹוָה פֶּתַח אֹהֶל מוֹעֵד: 12 וְלָקַחְתָּ מִדַּם הַפָּר וְנָתַתָּה עַל־קַרְנֹת הַמִּזְבֵּחַ בְּאֶצְבָּעֶךָ וְאֶת־כָּל־הַדָּם תִּשְׁפֹּךְ אֶל־יְסוֹד הַמִּזְבֵּחַ: 13 וְלָקַחְתָּ אֶת־כָּל־הַחֵלֶב הַמְכַסֶּה אֶת־הַקֶּרֶב וְאֵת הַיֹּתֶרֶת עַל־הַכָּבֵד וְאֵת שְׁתֵּי הַכְּלָיֹת וְאֶת־הַחֵלֶב אֲשֶׁר עֲלֵיהֶן וְהִקְטַרְתָּ הַמִּזְבֵּחָה: 14 וְאֶת־בְּשַׂר הַפָּר וְאֶת־עֹרוֹ וְאֶת־פִּרְשׁוֹ תִּשְׂרֹף בָּאֵשׁ מִחוּץ לַמַּחֲנֶה חַטָּאת הוּא: 15 וְאֶת־הָאַיִל הָאֶחָד תִּקָּח וְסָמְכוּ אַהֲרֹן וּבָנָיו אֶת־יְדֵיהֶם עַל־רֹאשׁ הָאָיִל: 16 וְשָׁחַטְתָּ אֶת־הָאָיִל וְלָקַחְתָּ אֶת־דָּמוֹ וְזָרַקְתָּ עַל־הַמִּזְבֵּחַ סָבִיב: 17 וְאֶת־הָאַיִל תְּנַתֵּחַ לִנְתָחָיו וְרָחַצְתָּ קִרְבּוֹ וּכְרָעָיו וְנָתַתָּ עַל־נְתָחָיו וְעַל־רֹאשׁוֹ: 18 וְהִקְטַרְתָּ

of the ram into smoke upon the altar. It is a burnt offering to the Lord, a pleasing odor, an offering by fire to the Lord.

19Then take the other ram, and let Aaron and his sons lay their hands upon the ram's head. 20Slaughter the ram, and take some of its blood and put it on the ridge[a] of Aaron's right ear and on the ridges of his sons' right ears, and on the thumbs of their right hands, and on the big toes of their right feet; and dash the rest of the blood against every side of the altar round about. 21Take some of the blood that is on the altar and some of the anointing oil and sprinkle upon Aaron and his vestments, and also upon his sons and his sons' vestments. Thus shall he and his vestments be holy, as well as his sons and his sons' vestments.

22You shall take from the ram the fat parts—the broad tail, the fat that covers the entrails, the protuberance on the liver, the two kidneys with the fat on them—and the right thigh; for this is a ram of ordination. 23Add one flat loaf of bread, one cake of oil bread, and one wafer, from the basket of unleavened bread that is before the Lord. 24Place all these on the palms of Aaron and his sons, and offer them as an elevation offering before the Lord. 25Take them from their hands and turn them into smoke upon the altar with the burnt offering, as a pleasing odor before the Lord; it is an offering by fire to the Lord.

26Then take the breast of Aaron's ram of ordination and offer it as an elevation offering before the Lord; it shall be your portion. 27You shall consecrate the breast that was offered as an elevation offering and the thigh that was offered as a gift offering from the ram of ordination—from that which was Aaron's and from that which was his sons'—28and those parts shall be a due for all time from the Israelites

a Or "lobe."

177

to Aaron and his descendants. For they are a gift; and so shall they be a gift from the Israelites, their gift to the LORD out of their sacrifices of well-being.

29The sacral vestments of Aaron shall pass on to his sons after him, for them to be anointed and ordained in. 30He among his sons who becomes priest in his stead, who enters the Tent of Meeting to officiate within the sanctuary, shall wear them seven days.

31You shall take the ram of ordination and boil its flesh in the sacred precinct; 32and Aaron and his sons shall eat the flesh of the ram, and the bread that is in the basket, at the entrance of the Tent of Meeting. 33These things shall be eaten only by those for whom expiation was made with them when they were ordained and consecrated; they may not be eaten by a layman, for they are holy. 34And if any of the flesh of ordination, or any of the bread, is left until morning, you shall put what is left to the fire; it shall not be eaten, for it is holy.

35Thus you shall do to Aaron and his sons, just as I have commanded you. You shall ordain them through seven days, 36and each day you shall prepare a bull as a sin offering for expiation; you shall purge the altar by performing purification upon it, and you shall anoint it to consecrate it. 37Seven days you shall perform purification for the altar to consecrate it, and the altar shall become most holy; whatever touches the altar shall become consecrated.

38Now this is what you shall offer upon the altar: two yearling lambs each day, regularly. 39You shall offer the one lamb in the morning, and you shall offer the other lamb at twilight. 40There shall be a tenth of a measure of choice flour with a quarter of a *hin* of beaten oil mixed in, and a libation of a quarter *hin* of wine for one lamb; 41and you shall offer the other lamb at twilight, repeating with it the meal offering

יִשְׂרָאֵל֙ מִזְבְחֵ֣י שַׁלְמֵיהֶ֔ם תְּרוּמָתָ֖ם לַֽיהוָֽה׃
29 וּבִגְדֵ֤י הַקֹּ֙דֶשׁ֙ אֲשֶׁ֣ר לְאַהֲרֹ֔ן יִהְי֥וּ לְבָנָ֖יו אַחֲרָ֑יו לְמָשְׁחָ֣ה בָהֶ֔ם וּלְמַלֵּֽא־בָ֖ם אֶת־יָדָֽם׃ 30 שִׁבְעַ֣ת יָמִ֗ים יִלְבָּשָׁ֧ם הַכֹּהֵ֛ן תַּחְתָּ֖יו מִבָּנָ֑יו אֲשֶׁ֥ר יָבֹ֛א אֶל־אֹ֥הֶל מוֹעֵ֖ד לְשָׁרֵ֥ת בַּקֹּֽדֶשׁ׃
31 וְאֵ֛ת אֵ֥יל הַמִּלֻּאִ֖ים תִּקָּ֑ח וּבִשַּׁלְתָּ֥ אֶת־בְּשָׂר֖וֹ בְּמָקֹ֥ם קָדֹֽשׁ׃ 32 וְאָכַ֨ל אַהֲרֹ֤ן וּבָנָיו֙ אֶת־בְּשַׂ֣ר הָאַ֔יִל וְאֶת־הַלֶּ֖חֶם אֲשֶׁ֣ר בַּסָּ֑ל פֶּ֖תַח אֹ֥הֶל מוֹעֵֽד׃ 33 וְאָכְל֤וּ אֹתָם֙ אֲשֶׁ֣ר כֻּפַּ֣ר בָּהֶ֔ם לְמַלֵּ֥א אֶת־יָדָ֖ם לְקַדֵּ֣שׁ אֹתָ֑ם וְזָ֥ר לֹא־יֹאכַ֖ל כִּי־קֹ֥דֶשׁ הֵֽם׃ 34 וְאִם־יִוָּתֵ֞ר מִבְּשַׂ֧ר הַמִּלֻּאִ֛ים וּמִן־הַלֶּ֖חֶם עַד־הַבֹּ֑קֶר וְשָׂרַפְתָּ֤ אֶת־הַנּוֹתָר֙ בָּאֵ֔שׁ לֹ֥א יֵאָכֵ֖ל כִּי־קֹ֥דֶשׁ הֽוּא׃
35 וְעָשִׂ֜יתָ לְאַהֲרֹ֤ן וּלְבָנָיו֙ כָּ֔כָה כְּכֹ֥ל אֲשֶׁר־צִוִּ֖יתִי אֹתָ֑כָה שִׁבְעַ֥ת יָמִ֖ים תְּמַלֵּ֥א יָדָֽם׃ 36 וּפַ֨ר חַטָּ֜את תַּעֲשֶׂ֤ה לַיּוֹם֙ עַל־הַכִּפֻּרִ֔ים וְחִטֵּאתָ֙ עַל־הַמִּזְבֵּ֔חַ בְּכַפֶּרְךָ֖ עָלָ֑יו וּמָשַׁחְתָּ֥ אֹת֖וֹ לְקַדְּשֽׁוֹ׃ 37 שִׁבְעַ֣ת יָמִ֗ים תְּכַפֵּר֙ עַל־הַמִּזְבֵּ֔חַ וְקִדַּשְׁתָּ֖ אֹת֑וֹ וְהָיָ֤ה הַמִּזְבֵּ֙חַ֙ קֹ֣דֶשׁ קָֽדָשִׁ֔ים כָּל־הַנֹּגֵ֥עַ בַּמִּזְבֵּ֖חַ יִקְדָּֽשׁ׃ ס
38 וְזֶ֕ה אֲשֶׁ֥ר תַּעֲשֶׂ֖ה עַל־הַמִּזְבֵּ֑חַ כְּבָשִׂ֧ים בְּנֵֽי־שָׁנָ֛ה שְׁנַ֖יִם לַיּ֥וֹם תָּמִֽיד׃ 39 אֶת־הַכֶּ֥בֶשׂ הָאֶחָ֖ד תַּעֲשֶׂ֣ה בַבֹּ֑קֶר וְאֵת֙ הַכֶּ֣בֶשׂ הַשֵּׁנִ֔י תַּעֲשֶׂ֖ה בֵּ֥ין הָעַרְבָּֽיִם׃ 40 וְעִשָּׂרֹ֨ן סֹ֜לֶת בָּל֨וּל בְּשֶׁ֤מֶן כָּתִית֙ רֶ֣בַע הַהִ֔ין וְנֵ֕סֶךְ רְבִעִ֥ית הַהִ֖ין יָ֑יִן לַכֶּ֖בֶשׂ הָאֶחָֽד׃ 41 וְאֵת֙ הַכֶּ֣בֶשׂ הַשֵּׁנִ֔י תַּעֲשֶׂ֖ה בֵּ֣ין הָעַרְבָּ֑יִם כְּמִנְחַ֨ת הַבֹּ֤קֶר וּכְנִסְכָּהּ֙ תַּעֲשֶׂה־לָּ֔הּ לְרֵ֥יחַ נִיחֹ֖חַ

of the morning with its libation—an offering by fire for a pleasing odor to the LORD, [42]a regular burnt offering throughout the generations, at the entrance of the Tent of Meeting before the LORD.

For there I will meet with you, and there I will speak with you, [43]and there I will meet with the Israelites, and it shall be sanctified by My Presence. [44]I will sanctify the Tent of Meeting and the altar, and I will consecrate Aaron and his sons to serve Me as priests. [45]I will abide among the Israelites, and I will be their God. [46]And they shall know that I the LORD am their God, who brought them out from the land of Egypt that I might abide among them, I the LORD their God.

30 You shall make an altar for burning incense; make it of acacia wood. [2]It shall be a cubit long and a cubit wide—it shall be square—and two cubits high, its horns of one piece with it. [3]Overlay it with pure gold: its top, its sides round about, and its horns; and make a gold molding for it round about. [4]And make two gold rings for it under its molding; make them on its two side walls, on opposite[a] sides. They shall serve as holders for poles with which to carry it. [5]Make the poles of acacia wood, and overlay them with gold.

[6]Place it in front of the curtain that is over the Ark of the Pact—in front of the cover that is over the Pact—where I will meet with you. [7]On it Aaron shall burn aromatic incense: he shall burn it every morning when he tends the lamps, [8]and Aaron shall burn it at twilight when he lights the lamps—a regular incense offering before the LORD throughout the ages. [9]You shall not offer alien incense on it, or a burnt offering or a meal offering; neither shall you pour a

אִשֶּׁה לַיהֹוָה: 42 עֹלַת תָּמִיד לְדֹרֹתֵיכֶם פֶּתַח אֹהֶל־מוֹעֵד לִפְנֵי יְהֹוָה אֲשֶׁר אִוָּעֵד לָכֶם שָׁמָּה לְדַבֵּר אֵלֶיךָ שָׁם: 43 וְנֹעַדְתִּי שָׁמָּה לִבְנֵי יִשְׂרָאֵל וְנִקְדַּשׁ בִּכְבֹדִי: 44 וְקִדַּשְׁתִּי אֶת־אֹהֶל מוֹעֵד וְאֶת־הַמִּזְבֵּחַ וְאֶת־אַהֲרֹן וְאֶת־בָּנָיו אֲקַדֵּשׁ לְכַהֵן לִי: 45 וְשָׁכַנְתִּי בְּתוֹךְ בְּנֵי יִשְׂרָאֵל וְהָיִיתִי לָהֶם לֵאלֹהִים: 46 וְיָדְעוּ כִּי אֲנִי יְהֹוָה אֱלֹהֵיהֶם אֲשֶׁר הוֹצֵאתִי אֹתָם מֵאֶרֶץ מִצְרַיִם לְשָׁכְנִי בְתוֹכָם אֲנִי יְהֹוָה אֱלֹהֵיהֶם: פ

ל וְעָשִׂיתָ מִזְבֵּחַ מִקְטַר קְטֹרֶת עֲצֵי שִׁטִּים תַּעֲשֶׂה אֹתוֹ: 2 אַמָּה אָרְכּוֹ וְאַמָּה רָחְבּוֹ רָבוּעַ יִהְיֶה וְאַמָּתַיִם קֹמָתוֹ מִמֶּנּוּ קַרְנֹתָיו: 3 וְצִפִּיתָ אֹתוֹ זָהָב טָהוֹר אֶת־גַּגּוֹ וְאֶת־קִירֹתָיו סָבִיב וְאֶת־קַרְנֹתָיו וְעָשִׂיתָ לּוֹ זֵר זָהָב סָבִיב: 4 וּשְׁתֵּי טַבְּעֹת זָהָב תַּעֲשֶׂה־לּוֹ | מִתַּחַת לְזֵרוֹ עַל שְׁתֵּי צַלְעֹתָיו תַּעֲשֶׂה עַל־שְׁנֵי צִדָּיו וְהָיָה לְבָתִּים לְבַדִּים לָשֵׂאת אֹתוֹ בָּהֵמָּה: 5 וְעָשִׂיתָ אֶת־הַבַּדִּים עֲצֵי שִׁטִּים וְצִפִּיתָ אֹתָם זָהָב: 6 וְנָתַתָּה אֹתוֹ לִפְנֵי הַפָּרֹכֶת אֲשֶׁר עַל־אֲרֹן הָעֵדֻת לִפְנֵי הַכַּפֹּרֶת אֲשֶׁר עַל־הָעֵדֻת אֲשֶׁר אִוָּעֵד לְךָ שָׁמָּה: 7 וְהִקְטִיר עָלָיו אַהֲרֹן קְטֹרֶת סַמִּים בַּבֹּקֶר בַּבֹּקֶר בְּהֵיטִיבוֹ אֶת־הַנֵּרֹת יַקְטִירֶנָּה: 8 וּבְהַעֲלֹת אַהֲרֹן אֶת־הַנֵּרֹת בֵּין הָעַרְבַּיִם יַקְטִירֶנָּה קְטֹרֶת תָּמִיד לִפְנֵי יְהֹוָה לְדֹרֹתֵיכֶם: 9 לֹא־תַעֲלוּ עָלָיו קְטֹרֶת זָרָה וְעֹלָה וּמִנְחָה וְנֵסֶךְ לֹא

---

a   Lit. "its two."

179

libation on it. ¹⁰Once a year Aaron shall perform purification upon its horns with blood of the sin offering of purification; purification shall be performed upon it once a year throughout the ages. It is most holy to the LORD.

תִּסְכּוּ עָלָיו: 10 וְכִפֶּר אַהֲרֹן עַל־קַרְנֹתָיו אַחַת בַּשָּׁנָה מִדַּם חַטַּאת הַכִּפֻּרִים אַחַת בַּשָּׁנָה יְכַפֵּר עָלָיו לְדֹרֹתֵיכֶם קֹדֶשׁ־קָדָשִׁים הוּא לַיהוָה: פ

KI TISSA'

כי תשא

¹¹The LORD spoke to Moses, saying: ¹²When you take a census of the Israelite people according to their enrollment, each shall pay the LORD a ransom for himself on being enrolled, that no plague may come upon them through their being enrolled. ¹³This is what everyone who is entered in the records shall pay: a half-shekel by the sanctuary weight—twenty *gerah*s to the shekel—a half-shekel as an offering to the LORD. ¹⁴Everyone who is entered in the records, from the age of twenty years up, shall give the LORD's offering: ¹⁵the rich shall not pay more and the poor shall not pay less than half a shekel when giving the LORD's offering as expiation for your persons. ¹⁶You shall take the expiation money from the Israelites and assign it to the service of the Tent of Meeting; it shall serve the Israelites as a reminder before the LORD, as expiation for your persons.

11 וַיְדַבֵּר יְהוָה אֶל־מֹשֶׁה לֵּאמֹר: 12 כִּי תִשָּׂא אֶת־רֹאשׁ בְּנֵי־יִשְׂרָאֵל לִפְקֻדֵיהֶם וְנָתְנוּ אִישׁ כֹּפֶר נַפְשׁוֹ לַיהוָה בִּפְקֹד אֹתָם וְלֹא־יִהְיֶה בָהֶם נֶגֶף בִּפְקֹד אֹתָם: 13 זֶה | יִתְּנוּ כָּל־הָעֹבֵר עַל־הַפְּקֻדִים מַחֲצִית הַשֶּׁקֶל בְּשֶׁקֶל הַקֹּדֶשׁ עֶשְׂרִים גֵּרָה הַשֶּׁקֶל מַחֲצִית הַשֶּׁקֶל תְּרוּמָה לַיהוָה: 14 כֹּל הָעֹבֵר עַל־הַפְּקֻדִים מִבֶּן עֶשְׂרִים שָׁנָה וָמָעְלָה יִתֵּן תְּרוּמַת יְהוָה: 15 הֶעָשִׁיר לֹא־יַרְבֶּה וְהַדַּל לֹא יַמְעִיט מִמַּחֲצִית הַשָּׁקֶל לָתֵת אֶת־תְּרוּמַת יְהוָה לְכַפֵּר עַל־נַפְשֹׁתֵיכֶם: 16 וְלָקַחְתָּ אֶת־כֶּסֶף הַכִּפֻּרִים מֵאֵת בְּנֵי יִשְׂרָאֵל וְנָתַתָּ אֹתוֹ עַל־עֲבֹדַת אֹהֶל מוֹעֵד וְהָיָה לִבְנֵי יִשְׂרָאֵל לְזִכָּרוֹן לִפְנֵי יְהוָה לְכַפֵּר עַל־נַפְשֹׁתֵיכֶם: פ

¹⁷The LORD spoke to Moses, saying: ¹⁸Make a laver of copper and a stand of copper for it, for washing; and place it between the Tent of Meeting and the altar. Put water in it, ¹⁹and let Aaron and his sons wash their hands and feet [in water drawn] from it. ²⁰When they enter the Tent of Meeting they shall wash with water, that they may not die; or when they approach the altar to serve, to turn into smoke an offering by fire to the LORD, ²¹they shall wash their hands and feet, that they may not die. It shall be a law for all time for them—for him and his offspring—throughout the ages.

17 וַיְדַבֵּר יְהוָה אֶל־מֹשֶׁה לֵּאמֹר: 18 וְעָשִׂיתָ כִּיּוֹר נְחֹשֶׁת וְכַנּוֹ נְחֹשֶׁת לְרָחְצָה וְנָתַתָּ אֹתוֹ בֵּין־אֹהֶל מוֹעֵד וּבֵין הַמִּזְבֵּחַ וְנָתַתָּ שָׁמָּה מָיִם: 19 וְרָחֲצוּ אַהֲרֹן וּבָנָיו מִמֶּנּוּ אֶת־יְדֵיהֶם וְאֶת־רַגְלֵיהֶם: 20 בְּבֹאָם אֶל־אֹהֶל מוֹעֵד יִרְחֲצוּ־מַיִם וְלֹא יָמֻתוּ אוֹ בְגִשְׁתָּם אֶל־הַמִּזְבֵּחַ לְשָׁרֵת לְהַקְטִיר אִשֶּׁה לַיהוָה: 21 וְרָחֲצוּ יְדֵיהֶם וְרַגְלֵיהֶם וְלֹא יָמֻתוּ וְהָיְתָה לָהֶם חָק־עוֹלָם לוֹ וּלְזַרְעוֹ לְדֹרֹתָם: פ

22The Lord spoke to Moses, saying: 23Next take choice spices: five hundred weight of solidified[b] myrrh, half as much—two hundred and fifty—of fragrant cinnamon, two hundred and fifty of aromatic cane, 24five hundred—by the sanctuary weight—of cassia, and a *hin* of olive oil. 25Make of this a sacred anointing oil, a compound of ingredients expertly blended, to serve as sacred anointing oil. 26With it anoint the Tent of Meeting, the Ark of the Pact, 27the table and all its utensils, the lampstand and all its fittings, the altar of incense, 28the altar of burnt offering and all its utensils, and the laver and its stand. 29Thus you shall consecrate them so that they may be most holy; whatever touches them shall be consecrated. 30You shall also anoint Aaron and his sons, consecrating them to serve Me as priests.

31And speak to the Israelite people, as follows: This shall be an anointing oil sacred to Me throughout the ages. 32It must not be rubbed on any person's body, and you must not make anything like it in the same proportions; it is sacred, to be held sacred by you. 33Whoever compounds its like, or puts any of it on a layman, shall be cut off from his kin.

34And the Lord said to Moses: Take the herbs stacte, onycha, and galbanum—these herbs together with pure frankincense; let there be an equal part of each. 35Make them into incense, a compound expertly blended, refined, pure, sacred. 36Beat some of it into powder, and put some before the Pact in the Tent of Meeting, where I will meet with you; it shall be most holy to you. 37But when you make this incense, you must not make any in the same proportions for yourselves; it shall be held by you sacred to the Lord. Whoever makes any like it, to smell of it, shall be cut off from his kin.

b   Others "*flowing*."

22 וַיְדַבֵּ֥ר יְהֹוָ֖ה אֶל־מֹשֶׁ֥ה לֵּאמֹֽר׃ 23 וְאַתָּ֣ה קַח־לְךָ֮ בְּשָׂמִ֣ים רֹאשׁ֒ מׇר־דְּרוֹר֙ חֲמֵ֣שׁ מֵא֔וֹת וְקִנְּמׇן־בֶּ֥שֶׂם מַחֲצִית֖וֹ חֲמִשִּׁ֣ים וּמָאתָ֑יִם וּקְנֵה־בֹ֖שֶׂם חֲמִשִּׁ֥ים וּמָאתָֽיִם׃ 24 וְקִדָּ֕ה חֲמֵ֥שׁ מֵא֖וֹת בְּשֶׁ֣קֶל הַקֹּ֑דֶשׁ וְשֶׁ֥מֶן זַ֖יִת הִֽין׃ 25 וְעָשִׂ֣יתָ אֹת֗וֹ שֶׁ֚מֶן מִשְׁחַת־קֹ֔דֶשׁ רֹ֥קַח מִרְקַ֖חַת מַעֲשֵׂ֣ה רֹקֵ֑חַ שֶׁ֥מֶן מִשְׁחַת־קֹ֖דֶשׁ יִהְיֶֽה׃ 26 וּמָשַׁחְתָּ֥ ב֖וֹ אֶת־אֹ֣הֶל מוֹעֵ֑ד וְאֵ֖ת אֲר֥וֹן הָעֵדֻֽת׃ 27 וְאֶת־הַשֻּׁלְחָן֙ וְאֶת־כׇּל־כֵּלָ֔יו וְאֶת־הַמְּנֹרָ֖ה וְאֶת־כֵּלֶ֑יהָ וְאֵ֖ת מִזְבַּ֥ח הַקְּטֹֽרֶת׃ 28 וְאֶת־מִזְבַּ֥ח הָעֹלָ֖ה וְאֶת־כׇּל־כֵּלָ֑יו וְאֶת־הַכִּיֹּ֖ר וְאֶת־כַּנּֽוֹ׃ 29 וְקִדַּשְׁתָּ֣ אֹתָ֔ם וְהָי֖וּ קֹ֣דֶשׁ קׇדָשִׁ֑ים כׇּל־הַנֹּגֵ֥עַ בָּהֶ֖ם יִקְדָּֽשׁ׃ 30 וְאֶת־אַהֲרֹ֥ן וְאֶת־בָּנָ֖יו תִּמְשָׁ֑ח וְקִדַּשְׁתָּ֥ אֹתָ֖ם לְכַהֵ֥ן לִֽי׃ 31 וְאֶל־בְּנֵ֥י יִשְׂרָאֵ֖ל תְּדַבֵּ֣ר לֵאמֹ֑ר שֶׁ֠מֶן מִשְׁחַת־קֹ֨דֶשׁ יִהְיֶ֥ה זֶ֛ה לִ֖י לְדֹרֹתֵיכֶֽם׃ 32 עַל־בְּשַׂ֤ר אָדָם֙ לֹ֣א יִיסָ֔ךְ וּבְמַ֨תְכֻּנְתּ֔וֹ לֹ֥א תַעֲשׂ֖וּ כָּמֹ֑הוּ קֹ֣דֶשׁ ה֔וּא קֹ֖דֶשׁ יִהְיֶ֥ה לָכֶֽם׃ 33 אִ֚ישׁ אֲשֶׁ֣ר יִרְקַ֣ח כָּמֹ֔הוּ וַאֲשֶׁ֥ר יִתֵּ֛ן מִמֶּ֖נּוּ עַל־זָ֑ר וְנִכְרַ֖ת מֵעַמָּֽיו׃ ס 34 וַיֹּ֩אמֶר֩ יְהֹוָ֨ה אֶל־מֹשֶׁ֜ה קַח־לְךָ֣ סַמִּ֗ים נָטָ֤ף ׀ וּשְׁחֵ֙לֶת֙ וְחֶלְבְּנָ֔ה סַמִּ֖ים וּלְבֹנָ֣ה זַכָּ֑ה בַּ֥ד בְּבַ֖ד יִהְיֶֽה׃ 35 וְעָשִׂ֤יתָ אֹתָהּ֙ קְטֹ֔רֶת רֹ֖קַח מַעֲשֵׂ֣ה רוֹקֵ֑חַ מְמֻלָּ֖ח טָה֥וֹר קֹֽדֶשׁ׃ 36 וְשָֽׁחַקְתָּ֣ מִמֶּ֘נָּה֮ הָדֵק֒ וְנָתַתָּ֨ה מִמֶּ֜נָּה לִפְנֵ֤י הָעֵדֻת֙ בְּאֹ֣הֶל מוֹעֵ֔ד אֲשֶׁ֛ר אִוָּעֵ֥ד לְךָ֖ שָׁ֑מָּה קֹ֥דֶשׁ קׇדָשִׁ֖ים תִּהְיֶ֥ה לָכֶֽם׃ 37 וְהַקְּטֹ֙רֶת֙ אֲשֶׁ֣ר תַּעֲשֶׂ֔ה בְּמַ֨תְכֻּנְתָּ֔הּ לֹ֥א תַעֲשׂ֖וּ לָכֶ֑ם קֹ֛דֶשׁ תִּהְיֶ֥ה לְךָ֖ לַיהֹוָֽה׃ 38 אִ֛ישׁ אֲשֶׁר־יַעֲשֶׂ֥ה כָמ֖וֹהָ לְהָרִ֣יחַ בָּ֑הּ וְנִכְרַ֖ת מֵעַמָּֽיו׃ ס

31 The LORD spoke to Moses: ²See, I have singled out by name Bezalel son of Uri son of Hur, of the tribe of Judah. ³I have endowed him with a divine spirit of skill, ability, and knowledge in every kind of craft; ⁴to make designs for work in gold, silver, and copper, ⁵to cut stones for setting and to carve wood—to work in every kind of craft. ⁶Moreover, I have assigned to him Oholiab son of Ahisamach, of the tribe of Dan; and I have also granted skill to all who are skillful, that they may make everything that I have commanded you: ⁷the Tent of Meeting, the Ark for the Pact and the cover upon it, and all the furnishings of the Tent; ⁸the table and its utensils, the pure lampstand*a* and all its fittings, and the altar of incense; ⁹the altar of burnt offering and all its utensils, and the laver and its stand; ¹⁰the service*b* vestments, the sacral vestments of Aaron the priest and the vestments of his sons, for their service as priests; ¹¹as well as the anointing oil and the aromatic incense for the sanctuary. Just as I have commanded you, they shall do.

¹²And the LORD said to Moses: ¹³Speak to the Israelite people and say: Nevertheless, you must keep My sabbaths, for this is a sign between Me and you throughout the ages, that you may know that I the LORD have consecrated you. ¹⁴You shall keep the sabbath, for it is holy for you. He who profanes it shall be put to death: whoever does work on it, that person shall be cut off from among his kin. ¹⁵Six days may work be done, but on the seventh day there shall be a sabbath of complete rest, holy to the LORD; whoever does work on the sabbath day shall be put to death. ¹⁶The Israelite people shall keep the sabbath, observing the sabbath throughout the ages as a covenant for all time: ¹⁷it shall be a sign for all time between Me and the people

---

a Or "lampstand of pure gold."
b Others "plaited."

לֹא וַיְדַבֵּ֥ר יְהוָ֖ה אֶל־מֹשֶׁ֥ה לֵּאמֹֽר׃ ²רְאֵ֖ה קָרָ֣אתִי בְשֵׁ֑ם בְּצַלְאֵ֛ל בֶּן־אוּרִ֥י בֶן־ח֖וּר לְמַטֵּ֥ה יְהוּדָֽה׃ ³וָאֲמַלֵּ֥א אֹת֖וֹ ר֣וּחַ אֱלֹהִ֑ים בְּחָכְמָ֥ה וּבִתְבוּנָ֛ה וּבְדַ֖עַת וּבְכָל־מְלָאכָֽה׃ ⁴לַחְשֹׁ֖ב מַחֲשָׁבֹ֑ת לַעֲשֹׂ֛ות בַּזָּהָ֥ב וּבַכֶּ֖סֶף וּבַנְּחֹֽשֶׁת׃ ⁵וּבַחֲרֹ֥שֶׁת אֶ֙בֶן֙ לְמַלֹּ֔את וּבַחֲרֹ֖שֶׁת עֵ֑ץ לַעֲשֹׂ֥ות בְּכָל־מְלָאכָֽה׃ ⁶וַאֲנִ֞י הִנֵּ֧ה נָתַ֣תִּי אִתּ֗וֹ אֵ֣ת אָהֳלִיאָ֞ב בֶּן־אֲחִֽיסָמָךְ֙ לְמַטֵּה־דָ֔ן וּבְלֵ֥ב כָּל־חֲכַם־לֵ֖ב נָתַ֣תִּי חָכְמָ֑ה וְעָשׂ֕וּ אֵ֖ת כָּל־אֲשֶׁ֥ר צִוִּיתִֽךָ׃ ⁷אֵ֣ת ׀ אֹ֣הֶל מוֹעֵ֗ד וְאֶת־הָֽאָרֹן֙ לָֽעֵדֻ֔ת וְאֶת־הַכַּפֹּ֖רֶת אֲשֶׁ֣ר עָלָ֑יו וְאֵ֖ת כָּל־כְּלֵ֥י הָאֹֽהֶל׃ ⁸וְאֶת־הַשֻּׁלְחָ֣ן וְאֶת־כֵּלָ֗יו וְאֶת־הַמְּנֹרָ֛ה הַטְּהֹרָ֖ה וְאֶת־כָּל־כֵּלֶ֑יהָ וְאֵ֖ת מִזְבַּ֥ח הַקְּטֹֽרֶת׃ ⁹וְאֶת־מִזְבַּ֥ח הָעֹלָ֖ה וְאֶת־כָּל־כֵּלָ֑יו וְאֶת־הַכִּיּ֖וֹר וְאֶת־כַּנּֽוֹ׃ ¹⁰וְאֵ֖ת בִּגְדֵ֣י הַשְּׂרָ֑ד וְאֶת־בִּגְדֵ֤י הַקֹּ֙דֶשׁ֙ לְאַֽהֲרֹ֣ן הַכֹּהֵ֔ן וְאֶת־בִּגְדֵ֥י בָנָ֖יו לְכַהֵֽן׃ ¹¹וְאֵ֨ת שֶׁ֧מֶן הַמִּשְׁחָ֛ה וְאֶת־קְטֹ֥רֶת הַסַּמִּ֖ים לַקֹּ֑דֶשׁ כְּכֹ֥ל אֲשֶׁר־צִוִּיתִ֖ךָ יַעֲשֽׂוּ׃ פ

¹²וַיֹּ֥אמֶר יְהוָ֖ה אֶל־מֹשֶׁ֥ה לֵּאמֹֽר׃ ¹³וְאַתָּ֞ה דַּבֵּ֨ר אֶל־בְּנֵ֤י יִשְׂרָאֵל֙ לֵאמֹ֔ר אַ֥ךְ אֶת־שַׁבְּתֹתַ֖י תִּשְׁמֹ֑רוּ כִּ֡י א֠וֹת הִ֣וא בֵּינִ֤י וּבֵֽינֵיכֶם֙ לְדֹרֹ֣תֵיכֶ֔ם לָדַ֕עַת כִּ֛י אֲנִ֥י יְהוָ֖ה מְקַדִּשְׁכֶֽם׃ ¹⁴וּשְׁמַרְתֶּם֙ אֶת־הַשַּׁבָּ֔ת כִּ֣י קֹ֥דֶשׁ הִ֖וא לָכֶ֑ם מְחַֽלְלֶ֙יהָ֙ מ֣וֹת יוּמָ֔ת כִּ֗י כָּל־הָעֹשֶׂ֥ה בָהּ֙ מְלָאכָ֔ה וְנִכְרְתָ֛ה הַנֶּ֥פֶשׁ הַהִ֖וא מִקֶּ֥רֶב עַמֶּֽיהָ׃ ¹⁵שֵׁ֣שֶׁת יָמִים֮ יֵעָשֶׂ֣ה מְלָאכָה֒ וּבַיּ֣וֹם הַשְּׁבִיעִ֗י שַׁבַּ֧ת שַׁבָּת֛וֹן קֹ֖דֶשׁ לַיהוָ֑ה כָּל־הָעֹשֶׂ֧ה מְלָאכָ֛ה בְּי֥וֹם הַשַּׁבָּ֖ת מ֥וֹת יוּמָֽת׃ ¹⁶וְשָׁמְר֥וּ בְנֵֽי־יִשְׂרָאֵ֖ל אֶת־הַשַּׁבָּ֑ת לַעֲשׂ֧וֹת אֶת־הַשַּׁבָּ֛ת לְדֹרֹתָ֖ם בְּרִ֥ית עוֹלָֽם׃ ¹⁷בֵּינִ֗י וּבֵין֙ בְּנֵ֣י יִשְׂרָאֵ֔ל א֥וֹת

of Israel. For in six days the LORD made heaven and earth, and on the seventh day He ceased from work and was refreshed.

18When He finished speaking with him on Mount Sinai, He gave Moses the two tablets of the Pact, stone tablets inscribed with the finger of God.

32 When the people saw that Moses was so long in coming down from the mountain, the people gathered against Aaron and said to him, "Come, make us a god who shall go before us, for that man Moses, who brought us from the land of Egypt—we do not know what has happened to him." 2Aaron said to them, "Take off the gold rings that are on the ears of your wives, your sons, and your daughters, and bring them to me." 3And all the people took off the gold rings that were in their ears and brought them to Aaron. 4This he took from them and a-cast in a mold,-a and made it into a molten calf. And they exclaimed, b-"This is your god,-b O Israel, who brought you out of the land of Egypt!" 5When Aaron saw this, he built an altar before it; and Aaron announced: "Tomorrow shall be a festival of the LORD!" 6Early next day, the people offered up burnt offerings and brought sacrifices of well-being; they sat down to eat and drink, and then rose to dance.

7The LORD spoke to Moses, "Hurry down, for your people, whom you brought out of the land of Egypt, have acted basely. 8They have been quick to turn aside from the way that I enjoined upon them. They have made themselves a molten calf and bowed low to it and sacrificed to it, saying: 'This is your god, O Israel, who brought you out of the land of Egypt!'"

הוּא לְעֹלָם כִּי־שֵׁשֶׁת יָמִים עָשָׂה יְהוָה אֶת־הַשָּׁמַיִם וְאֶת־הָאָרֶץ וּבַיּוֹם הַשְּׁבִיעִי שָׁבַת וַיִּנָּפַשׁ: ס

18 וַיִּתֵּן אֶל־מֹשֶׁה כְּכַלֹּתוֹ לְדַבֵּר אִתּוֹ בְּהַר סִינַי שְׁנֵי לֻחֹת הָעֵדֻת לֻחֹת אֶבֶן כְּתֻבִים בְּאֶצְבַּע אֱלֹהִים:

לב וַיַּרְא הָעָם כִּי־בֹשֵׁשׁ מֹשֶׁה לָרֶדֶת מִן־הָהָר וַיִּקָּהֵל הָעָם עַל־אַהֲרֹן וַיֹּאמְרוּ אֵלָיו קוּם | עֲשֵׂה־לָנוּ אֱלֹהִים אֲשֶׁר יֵלְכוּ לְפָנֵינוּ כִּי־זֶה | מֹשֶׁה הָאִישׁ אֲשֶׁר הֶעֱלָנוּ מֵאֶרֶץ מִצְרַיִם לֹא יָדַעְנוּ מֶה־הָיָה לוֹ: 2 וַיֹּאמֶר אֲלֵהֶם אַהֲרֹן פָּרְקוּ נִזְמֵי הַזָּהָב אֲשֶׁר בְּאָזְנֵי נְשֵׁיכֶם בְּנֵיכֶם וּבְנֹתֵיכֶם וְהָבִיאוּ אֵלָי: 3 וַיִּתְפָּרְקוּ כָּל־הָעָם אֶת־נִזְמֵי הַזָּהָב אֲשֶׁר בְּאָזְנֵיהֶם וַיָּבִיאוּ אֶל־אַהֲרֹן: 4 וַיִּקַּח מִיָּדָם וַיָּצַר אֹתוֹ בַּחֶרֶט וַיַּעֲשֵׂהוּ עֵגֶל מַסֵּכָה וַיֹּאמְרוּ אֵלֶּה אֱלֹהֶיךָ יִשְׂרָאֵל אֲשֶׁר הֶעֱלוּךָ מֵאֶרֶץ מִצְרָיִם: 5 וַיַּרְא אַהֲרֹן וַיִּבֶן מִזְבֵּחַ לְפָנָיו וַיִּקְרָא אַהֲרֹן וַיֹּאמַר חַג לַיהוָה מָחָר: 6 וַיַּשְׁכִּימוּ מִמָּחֳרָת וַיַּעֲלוּ עֹלֹת וַיַּגִּשׁוּ שְׁלָמִים וַיֵּשֶׁב הָעָם לֶאֱכֹל וְשָׁתוֹ וַיָּקֻמוּ לְצַחֵק: פ 7 וַיְדַבֵּר יְהוָה אֶל־מֹשֶׁה לֶךְ־רֵד כִּי שִׁחֵת עַמְּךָ אֲשֶׁר הֶעֱלֵיתָ מֵאֶרֶץ מִצְרָיִם: 8 סָרוּ מַהֵר מִן־הַדֶּרֶךְ אֲשֶׁר צִוִּיתִם עָשׂוּ לָהֶם עֵגֶל מַסֵּכָה וַיִּשְׁתַּחֲווּ־לוֹ וַיִּזְבְּחוּ־לוֹ וַיֹּאמְרוּ אֵלֶּה אֱלֹהֶיךָ יִשְׂרָאֵל אֲשֶׁר הֶעֱלוּךָ מֵאֶרֶץ מִצְרָיִם:

---

a-a Cf. Zech. 11.13 (beth hayyoṣer, "foundry"); others "fashioned it with a graving tool."
b-b Others "These are your gods."

⁹The Lord further said to Moses, "I see that this is a stiffnecked people. ¹⁰Now, let Me be, that My anger may blaze forth against them and that I may destroy them, and make of you a great nation." ¹¹But Moses implored the Lord his God, saying, "Let not Your anger, O Lord, blaze forth against Your people, whom You delivered from the land of Egypt with great power and with a mighty hand. ¹²Let not the Egyptians say, 'It was with evil intent that He delivered them, only to kill them off in the mountains and annihilate them from the face of the earth.' Turn from Your blazing anger, and renounce the plan to punish Your people. ¹³Remember Your servants, Abraham, Isaac, and Israel, how You swore to them by Your Self and said to them: I will make your offspring as numerous as the stars of heaven, and I will give to your offspring this whole land of which I spoke, to possess forever." ¹⁴And the Lord renounced the punishment He had planned to bring upon His people.

¹⁵Thereupon Moses turned and went down from the mountain bearing the two tablets of the Pact, tablets inscribed on both their surfaces: they were inscribed on the one side and on the other. ¹⁶The tablets were God's work, and the writing was God's writing, incised upon the tablets. ¹⁷When Joshua heard the sound of the people in its boisterousness, he said to Moses, "There is a cry of war in the camp." ¹⁸But he answered,

"It is not the sound of the tune of triumph,
Or the sound of the tune of defeat;
It is the sound of song that I hear!"

¹⁹As soon as Moses came near the camp and saw the calf and the dancing, he became enraged; and he hurled the tablets from his hands and shattered them at the foot of the mountain. ²⁰He took the calf that they had made and burned it; he ground it to powder and strewed

9 וַיֹּאמֶר יְהֹוָה אֶל־מֹשֶׁה רָאִיתִי אֶת־הָעָם הַזֶּה וְהִנֵּה עַם־קְשֵׁה־עֹרֶף הוּא: 10 וְעַתָּה הַנִּיחָה לִּי וְיִחַר־אַפִּי בָהֶם וַאֲכַלֵּם וְאֶעֱשֶׂה אוֹתְךָ לְגוֹי גָּדוֹל: 11 וַיְחַל מֹשֶׁה אֶת־פְּנֵי יְהֹוָה אֱלֹהָיו וַיֹּאמֶר לָמָה יְהֹוָה יֶחֱרֶה אַפְּךָ בְּעַמֶּךָ אֲשֶׁר הוֹצֵאתָ מֵאֶרֶץ מִצְרַיִם בְּכֹחַ גָּדוֹל וּבְיָד חֲזָקָה: 12 לָמָה יֹאמְרוּ מִצְרַיִם לֵאמֹר בְּרָעָה הוֹצִיאָם לַהֲרֹג אֹתָם בֶּהָרִים וּלְכַלֹּתָם מֵעַל פְּנֵי הָאֲדָמָה שׁוּב מֵחֲרוֹן אַפֶּךָ וְהִנָּחֵם עַל־הָרָעָה לְעַמֶּךָ: 13 זְכֹר לְאַבְרָהָם לְיִצְחָק וּלְיִשְׂרָאֵל עֲבָדֶיךָ אֲשֶׁר נִשְׁבַּעְתָּ לָהֶם בָּךְ וַתְּדַבֵּר אֲלֵהֶם אַרְבֶּה אֶת־זַרְעֲכֶם כְּכוֹכְבֵי הַשָּׁמָיִם וְכָל־הָאָרֶץ הַזֹּאת אֲשֶׁר אָמַרְתִּי אֶתֵּן לְזַרְעֲכֶם וְנָחֲלוּ לְעֹלָם: 14 וַיִּנָּחֶם יְהֹוָה עַל־הָרָעָה אֲשֶׁר דִּבֶּר לַעֲשׂוֹת לְעַמּוֹ: פ

15 וַיִּפֶן וַיֵּרֶד מֹשֶׁה מִן־הָהָר וּשְׁנֵי לֻחֹת הָעֵדֻת בְּיָדוֹ לֻחֹת כְּתֻבִים מִשְּׁנֵי עֶבְרֵיהֶם מִזֶּה וּמִזֶּה הֵם כְּתֻבִים: 16 וְהַלֻּחֹת מַעֲשֵׂה אֱלֹהִים הֵמָּה וְהַמִּכְתָּב מִכְתַּב אֱלֹהִים הוּא חָרוּת עַל־הַלֻּחֹת: 17 וַיִּשְׁמַע יְהוֹשֻׁעַ אֶת־קוֹל הָעָם בְּרֵעֹה וַיֹּאמֶר אֶל־מֹשֶׁה קוֹל מִלְחָמָה בַּמַּחֲנֶה: 18 וַיֹּאמֶר אֵין קוֹל עֲנוֹת גְּבוּרָה וְאֵין קוֹל עֲנוֹת חֲלוּשָׁה קוֹל עַנּוֹת אָנֹכִי שֹׁמֵעַ: 19 וַיְהִי כַּאֲשֶׁר קָרַב אֶל־הַמַּחֲנֶה וַיַּרְא אֶת־הָעֵגֶל וּמְחֹלֹת וַיִּחַר־אַף מֹשֶׁה וַיַּשְׁלֵךְ מִיָּדָו אֶת־הַלֻּחֹת וַיְשַׁבֵּר אֹתָם תַּחַת הָהָר: 20 וַיִּקַּח אֶת־הָעֵגֶל אֲשֶׁר עָשׂוּ וַיִּשְׂרֹף בָּאֵשׁ וַיִּטְחַן עַד אֲשֶׁר־דָּק וַיִּזֶר עַל־פְּנֵי הַמַּיִם וַיַּשְׁקְ אֶת־בְּנֵי יִשְׂרָאֵל:

it upon the water and so made the Israelites drink it.

21Moses said to Aaron, "What did this people do to you that you have brought such great sin upon them?" 22Aaron said, "Let not my lord be enraged. You know that this people is bent on evil. 23They said to me, 'Make us a god to lead us; for that man Moses, who brought us from the land of Egypt—we do not know what has happened to him.' 24So I said to them, 'Whoever has gold, take it off!' They gave it to me and I hurled it into the fire and out came this calf!"

25Moses saw that the people were out of control—since Aaron had let them get out of control—so that they were a menace[c] to any who might oppose them. 26Moses stood up in the gate of the camp and said, "Whoever is for the Lord, come here!" And all the Levites rallied to him. 27He said to them, "Thus says the Lord, the God of Israel: Each of you put sword on thigh, go back and forth from gate to gate throughout the camp, and slay brother, neighbor, and kin." 28The Levites did as Moses had bidden; and some three thousand of the people fell that day. 29And Moses said, "Dedicate yourselves[d] to the Lord this day—for each of you has been against son and brother—that He may bestow a blessing upon you today."

30The next day Moses said to the people, "You have been guilty of a great sin. Yet I will now go up to the Lord; perhaps I may win forgiveness for your sin." 31Moses went back to the Lord and said, "Alas, this people is guilty of a great sin in making for themselves a god of gold. 32Now, if You will forgive their sin [well and good]; but if not, erase me from the record which You have written!" 33But the Lord said to Moses, "He who has sinned against Me, him only will I erase from My record. 34Go now, lead the people where I told you. See, My angel shall

---

c   Others "an object of derision."
d   Lit. "fill your hands."

185

21 וַיֹּ֤אמֶר מֹשֶׁה֙ אֶֽל־אַהֲרֹ֔ן מֶֽה־עָשָׂ֥ה לְךָ֖ הָעָ֣ם הַזֶּ֑ה כִּֽי־הֵבֵ֥אתָ עָלָ֖יו חֲטָאָ֥ה גְדֹלָֽה׃ 22 וַיֹּ֣אמֶר אַהֲרֹ֔ן אַל־יִ֥חַר אַ֖ף אֲדֹנִ֑י אַתָּה֙ יָדַ֣עְתָּ אֶת־הָעָ֔ם כִּ֥י בְרָ֖ע הֽוּא׃ 23 וַיֹּ֣אמְרוּ לִ֔י עֲשֵׂה־לָ֣נוּ אֱלֹהִ֔ים אֲשֶׁ֥ר יֵלְכ֖וּ לְפָנֵ֑ינוּ כִּי־זֶ֣ה ׀ מֹשֶׁ֣ה הָאִ֗ישׁ אֲשֶׁ֤ר הֶֽעֱלָ֙נוּ֙ מֵאֶ֣רֶץ מִצְרַ֔יִם לֹ֥א יָדַ֖עְנוּ מֶה־הָ֥יָה לֽוֹ׃ 24 וָאֹמַ֤ר לָהֶם֙ לְמִ֣י זָהָ֔ב הִתְפָּרָ֖קוּ וַיִּתְּנוּ־לִ֑י וָאַשְׁלִכֵ֣הוּ בָאֵ֔שׁ וַיֵּצֵ֖א הָעֵ֥גֶל הַזֶּֽה׃ 25 וַיַּ֤רְא מֹשֶׁה֙ אֶת־הָעָ֔ם כִּ֥י פָרֻ֖עַ ה֑וּא כִּֽי־פְרָעֹ֣ה אַהֲרֹ֔ן לְשִׁמְצָ֖ה בְּקָמֵיהֶֽם׃ 26 וַיַּעֲמֹ֤ד מֹשֶׁה֙ בְּשַׁ֣עַר הַֽמַּחֲנֶ֔ה וַיֹּ֕אמֶר מִ֥י לַֽיהוָ֖ה אֵלָ֑י וַיֵּאָסְפ֥וּ אֵלָ֖יו כָּל־בְּנֵ֥י לֵוִֽי׃ 27 וַיֹּ֣אמֶר לָהֶ֗ם כֹּֽה־אָמַ֤ר יְהוָה֙ אֱלֹהֵ֣י יִשְׂרָאֵ֔ל שִׂ֥ימוּ אִישׁ־חַרְבּ֖וֹ עַל־יְרֵכ֑וֹ עִבְר֨וּ וָשׁ֜וּבוּ מִשַּׁ֤עַר לָשַׁ֙עַר֙ בַּֽמַּחֲנֶ֔ה וְהִרְג֧וּ אִֽישׁ־אֶת־אָחִ֛יו וְאִ֥ישׁ אֶת־רֵעֵ֖הוּ וְאִ֥ישׁ אֶת־קְרֹבֽוֹ׃ 28 וַיַּֽעֲשׂ֥וּ בְנֵֽי־לֵוִ֖י כִּדְבַ֣ר מֹשֶׁ֑ה וַיִּפֹּ֤ל מִן־הָעָם֙ בַּיּ֣וֹם הַה֔וּא כִּשְׁלֹ֥שֶׁת אַלְפֵ֖י אִֽישׁ׃ 29 וַיֹּ֣אמֶר מֹשֶׁ֗ה מִלְא֨וּ יֶדְכֶ֤ם הַיּוֹם֙ לַֽיהוָ֔ה כִּ֣י אִ֣ישׁ בִּבְנ֖וֹ וּבְאָחִ֑יו וְלָתֵ֧ת עֲלֵיכֶ֛ם הַיּ֖וֹם בְּרָכָֽה׃ 30 וַיְהִי֙ מִֽמָּחֳרָ֔ת וַיֹּ֤אמֶר מֹשֶׁה֙ אֶל־הָעָ֔ם אַתֶּ֥ם חֲטָאתֶ֖ם חֲטָאָ֣ה גְדֹלָ֑ה וְעַתָּה֙ אֶֽעֱלֶ֣ה אֶל־יְהוָ֔ה אוּלַ֥י אֲכַפְּרָ֖ה בְּעַ֥ד חַטַּאתְכֶֽם׃ 31 וַיָּ֧שָׁב מֹשֶׁ֛ה אֶל־יְהוָ֖ה וַיֹּאמַ֑ר אָ֣נָּא חָטָ֞א הָעָ֤ם הַזֶּה֙ חֲטָאָ֣ה גְדֹלָ֔ה וַיַּֽעֲשׂ֥וּ לָהֶ֖ם אֱלֹהֵ֥י זָהָֽב׃ 32 וְעַתָּ֖ה אִם־תִּשָּׂ֣א חַטָּאתָ֑ם וְאִם־אַ֕יִן מְחֵ֣נִי נָ֔א מִֽסִּפְרְךָ֖ אֲשֶׁ֥ר כָּתָֽבְתָּ׃ 33 וַיֹּ֥אמֶר יְהוָ֖ה אֶל־מֹשֶׁ֑ה מִ֚י אֲשֶׁ֣ר חָֽטָא־לִ֔י אֶמְחֶ֖נּוּ מִסִּפְרִֽי׃ 34 וְעַתָּ֞ה לֵ֣ךְ ׀ נְחֵ֣ה אֶת־הָעָ֗ם אֶ֤ל אֲשֶׁר־דִּבַּ֙רְתִּי֙ לָ֔ךְ הִנֵּ֥ה*

go before you. But when I make an accounting, I will bring them to account for their sins."

35Then the LORD sent a plague upon the people, e-for what they did with the calf that Aaron made.-e

33 Then the LORD said to Moses, "Set out from here, you and the people that you have brought up from the land of Egypt, to the land of which I swore to Abraham, Isaac, and Jacob, saying, 'To your offspring will I give it'—2I will send an angel before you, and I will drive out the Canaanites, the Amorites, the Hittites, the Perizzites, the Hivites, and the Jebusites—3a land flowing with milk and honey. But I will not go in your midst, since you are a stiffnecked people, lest I destroy you on the way."

4When the people heard this harsh word, they went into mourning, and none put on his finery.

5The LORD said to Moses, "Say to the Israelite people, 'You are a stiffnecked people. If I were to go in your midst for one moment, I would destroy you. Now, then, leave off your finery, and I will consider what to do to you.'" 6So the Israelites remained stripped of the finery from Mount Horeb on.

7Now Moses would take the Tent and pitch it outside the camp, at some distance from the camp. It was called the Tent of Meeting, and whoever sought the LORD would go out to the Tent of Meeting that was outside the camp. 8Whenever Moses went out to the Tent, all the people would rise and stand, each at the entrance of his tent, and gaze after Moses until he had entered the Tent. 9And when Moses entered the Tent, the pillar of cloud would descend and stand at the entrance of the Tent, while He spoke with Moses. 10When all the people saw the pillar of cloud poised at the entrance of the Tent, all

מַלְאָכִי יֵלֵךְ לְפָנֶיךָ וּבְיוֹם פָּקְדִי וּפָקַדְתִּי עֲלֵהֶם חַטָּאתָם׃ 35 וַיִּגֹּף יְהוָה אֶת־הָעָם עַל אֲשֶׁר עָשׂוּ אֶת־הָעֵגֶל אֲשֶׁר עָשָׂה אַהֲרֹן׃ ס

לג וַיְדַבֵּר יְהוָה אֶל־מֹשֶׁה לֵךְ עֲלֵה מִזֶּה אַתָּה וְהָעָם אֲשֶׁר הֶעֱלִיתָ מֵאֶרֶץ מִצְרָיִם אֶל־הָאָרֶץ אֲשֶׁר נִשְׁבַּעְתִּי לְאַבְרָהָם לְיִצְחָק וּלְיַעֲקֹב לֵאמֹר לְזַרְעֲךָ אֶתְּנֶנָּה׃ 2 וְשָׁלַחְתִּי לְפָנֶיךָ מַלְאָךְ וְגֵרַשְׁתִּי אֶת־הַכְּנַעֲנִי הָאֱמֹרִי וְהַחִתִּי וְהַפְּרִזִּי הַחִוִּי וְהַיְבוּסִי׃ 3 אֶל־אֶרֶץ זָבַת חָלָב וּדְבָשׁ כִּי לֹא אֶעֱלֶה בְּקִרְבְּךָ כִּי עַם־קְשֵׁה־עֹרֶף אַתָּה פֶּן־אֲכֶלְךָ בַּדָּרֶךְ׃ 4 וַיִּשְׁמַע הָעָם אֶת־הַדָּבָר הָרָע הַזֶּה וַיִּתְאַבָּלוּ וְלֹא־שָׁתוּ אִישׁ עֶדְיוֹ עָלָיו׃ 5 וַיֹּאמֶר יְהוָה אֶל־מֹשֶׁה אֱמֹר אֶל־בְּנֵי־יִשְׂרָאֵל אַתֶּם עַם־קְשֵׁה־עֹרֶף רֶגַע אֶחָד אֶעֱלֶה בְקִרְבְּךָ וְכִלִּיתִיךָ וְעַתָּה הוֹרֵד עֶדְיְךָ מֵעָלֶיךָ וְאֵדְעָה מָה אֶעֱשֶׂה־לָּךְ׃ 6 וַיִּתְנַצְּלוּ בְנֵי־יִשְׂרָאֵל אֶת־עֶדְיָם מֵהַר חוֹרֵב׃

7 וּמֹשֶׁה יִקַּח אֶת־הָאֹהֶל וְנָטָה־לוֹ ׀ מִחוּץ לַמַּחֲנֶה הַרְחֵק מִן־הַמַּחֲנֶה וְקָרָא לוֹ אֹהֶל מוֹעֵד וְהָיָה כָּל־מְבַקֵּשׁ יְהוָה יֵצֵא אֶל־אֹהֶל מוֹעֵד אֲשֶׁר מִחוּץ לַמַּחֲנֶה׃ 8 וְהָיָה כְּצֵאת מֹשֶׁה אֶל־הָאֹהֶל יָקוּמוּ כָּל־הָעָם וְנִצְּבוּ אִישׁ פֶּתַח אָהֳלוֹ וְהִבִּיטוּ אַחֲרֵי מֹשֶׁה עַד־בֹּאוֹ הָאֹהֱלָה׃ 9 וְהָיָה כְּבֹא מֹשֶׁה הָאֹהֱלָה יֵרֵד עַמּוּד הֶעָנָן וְעָמַד פֶּתַח הָאֹהֶל וְדִבֶּר עִם־מֹשֶׁה׃ 10 וְרָאָה כָל־הָעָם אֶת־עַמּוּד הֶעָנָן עֹמֵד פֶּתַח

---

e-e   Meaning of Heb. uncertain.

the people would rise and bow low, each at the entrance of his tent. [11]The LORD would speak to Moses face to face, as one man speaks to another. And he would then return to the camp; but his attendant, Joshua son of Nun, a youth, would not stir out of the Tent.

[12]Moses said to the LORD, "See, You say to me, 'Lead this people forward,' but You have not made known to me whom You will send with me. Further, You have said, 'I have singled you out by name, and you have, indeed, gained My favor.' [13]Now, if I have truly gained Your favor, pray let me know Your ways, that I may know You and continue in Your favor. Consider, too, that this nation is Your people." [14]And He said, *a*-"I will go in the lead and will-*a* lighten your burden." [15]And he said to Him, "Unless You go in the lead, do not make us leave this place. [16]For how shall it be known that Your people have gained Your favor unless You go with us, so that we may be distinguished, Your people and I, from every people on the face of the earth?"

[17]And the LORD said to Moses, "I will also do this thing that you have asked; for you have truly gained My favor and I have singled you out by name." [18]He said, "Oh, let me behold Your Presence!" [19]And He answered, "I will make all My goodness pass before you, and I will proclaim before you the name LORD, *b*-and the grace that I grant and the compassion that I show.-*b* [20]But," He said, "you cannot see My face, for man may not see Me and live." [21]And the LORD said, "See, there is a place near Me. Station yourself on the rock [22]and, as My Presence passes by, I will put you in a cleft of the rock and shield you with My hand until I have passed by. [23]Then I will take My hand away and you will see My back; but My face must not be seen."

הָאֹ֔הֶל וְקָ֤ם כָּל־הָעָם֙ וְהִֽשְׁתַּחֲוֹ֔וּ אִ֕ישׁ פֶּ֖תַח אָהֳל֑וֹ: 11 וְדִבֶּ֨ר יְהֹוָ֤ה אֶל־מֹשֶׁה֙ פָּנִ֣ים אֶל־פָּנִ֔ים כַּֽאֲשֶׁ֛ר יְדַבֵּ֥ר אִ֖ישׁ אֶל־רֵעֵ֑הוּ וְשָׁב֙ אֶל־הַֽמַּחֲנֶ֔ה וּמְשָׁ֨רְת֜וֹ יְהוֹשֻׁ֤עַ בִּן־נוּן֙ נַ֔עַר לֹ֥א יָמִ֖ישׁ מִתּ֥וֹךְ הָאֹֽהֶל: ס

12 וַיֹּ֨אמֶר מֹשֶׁ֜ה אֶל־יְהֹוָ֗ה רְאֵ֞ה אַתָּ֣ה אֹמֵ֣ר אֵלַ֗י הַ֚עַל אֶת־הָעָ֣ם הַזֶּ֔ה וְאַתָּה֙ לֹ֣א הֽוֹדַעְתַּ֔נִי אֵ֥ת אֲשֶׁר־תִּשְׁלַ֖ח עִמִּ֑י וְאַתָּ֣ה אָמַ֗רְתָּ יְדַעְתִּ֣יךָֽ בְשֵׁ֔ם וְגַם־מָצָ֥אתָ חֵ֖ן בְּעֵינָֽי: 13 וְעַתָּ֡ה אִם־נָא֩ מָצָ֨אתִי חֵ֜ן בְּעֵינֶ֗יךָ הֽוֹדִעֵ֤נִי נָא֙ אֶת־דְּרָכֶ֔ךָ וְאֵדָ֣עֲךָ֔ לְמַ֥עַן אֶמְצָא־חֵ֖ן בְּעֵינֶ֑יךָ וּרְאֵ֕ה כִּ֥י עַמְּךָ֖ הַגּ֥וֹי הַזֶּֽה: 14 וַיֹּאמַ֑ר פָּנַ֥י יֵלֵ֖כוּ וַהֲנִחֹ֥תִי לָֽךְ: 15 וַיֹּ֖אמֶר אֵלָ֑יו אִם־אֵ֤ין פָּנֶ֙יךָ֙ הֹֽלְכִ֔ים אַֽל־תַּֽעֲלֵ֖נוּ מִזֶּֽה: 16 וּבַמֶּ֣ה ׀ יִוָּדַ֣ע אֵפ֗וֹא כִּֽי־מָצָ֨אתִי חֵ֤ן בְּעֵינֶ֙יךָ֙ אֲנִ֣י וְעַמֶּ֔ךָ הֲל֖וֹא בְּלֶכְתְּךָ֣ עִמָּ֑נוּ וְנִפְלִ֗ינוּ אֲנִ֤י וְעַמְּךָ֙ מִכָּל־הָעָ֔ם אֲשֶׁ֖ר עַל־פְּנֵ֥י הָאֲדָמָֽה: פ

17 וַיֹּ֤אמֶר יְהֹוָה֙ אֶל־מֹשֶׁ֔ה גַּ֣ם אֶת־הַדָּבָ֥ר הַזֶּ֛ה אֲשֶׁ֥ר דִּבַּ֖רְתָּ אֶֽעֱשֶׂ֑ה כִּֽי־מָצָ֤אתָ חֵן֙ בְּעֵינַ֔י וָאֵדָֽעֲךָ֖ בְּשֵֽׁם: 18 וַיֹּאמַ֑ר הַרְאֵ֥נִי נָ֖א אֶת־כְּבֹדֶֽךָ: 19 וַיֹּ֗אמֶר אֲנִ֨י אַֽעֲבִ֤יר כָּל־טוּבִי֙ עַל־פָּנֶ֔יךָ וְקָרָ֧אתִי בְשֵׁ֛ם יְהֹוָ֖ה לְפָנֶ֑יךָ וְחַנֹּתִי֙ אֶת־אֲשֶׁ֣ר אָחֹ֔ן וְרִֽחַמְתִּ֖י אֶת־אֲשֶׁ֥ר אֲרַחֵֽם: 20 וַיֹּ֕אמֶר לֹ֥א תוּכַ֖ל לִרְאֹ֣ת אֶת־פָּנָ֑י כִּ֛י לֹֽא־יִרְאַ֥נִי הָאָדָ֖ם וָחָֽי: 21 וַיֹּ֣אמֶר יְהֹוָ֔ה הִנֵּ֥ה מָק֖וֹם אִתִּ֑י וְנִצַּבְתָּ֖ עַל־הַצּֽוּר: 22 וְהָיָה֙ בַּֽעֲבֹ֣ר כְּבֹדִ֔י וְשַׂמְתִּ֖יךָ בְּנִקְרַ֣ת הַצּ֑וּר וְשַׂכֹּתִ֥י כַפִּ֛י עָלֶ֖יךָ עַד־עָבְרִֽי: 23 וַהֲסִֽרֹתִי֙ אֶת־כַּפִּ֔י וְרָאִ֖יתָ אֶת־אֲחֹרָ֑י וּפָנַ֖י לֹ֥א יֵרָאֽוּ: ס

---

a-a Lit. "My face will go and I will."
b-b Lit. "and I will grant the grace that I will grant and show the compassion that I will show."

34 The LORD said to Moses: "Carve two tablets of stone like the first, and I will inscribe upon the tablets the words that were on the first tablets, which you shattered. ²Be ready by morning, and in the morning come up to Mount Sinai and present yourself there to Me, on the top of the mountain. ³No one else shall come up with you, and no one else shall be seen anywhere on the mountain; neither shall the flocks and the herds graze at the foot of this mountain."

⁴So Moses carved two tablets of stone, like the first, and early in the morning he went up on Mount Sinai, as the LORD had commanded him, taking the two stone tablets with him. ⁵The LORD came down in a cloud; He stood with him there, and proclaimed the name LORD. ⁶The LORD passed before him ᵃ-and proclaimed: "The LORD! the LORD!-ᵃ a God compassionate and gracious, slow to anger, abounding in kindness and faithfulness, ⁷extending kindness to the thousandth generation, forgiving iniquity, transgression, and sin; yet He does not remit all punishment, but visits the iniquity of parents upon children and children's children, upon the third and fourth generations."

⁸Moses hastened to bow low to the ground in homage, ⁹and said, "If I have gained Your favor, O Lord, pray, let the Lord go in our midst, even though this is a stiffnecked people. Pardon our iniquity and our sin, and take us for Your own!"

¹⁰He said: I hereby make a covenant. Before all your people I will work such wonders as have not been wrought on all the earth or in any nation; and all the people ᵇ-who are with you-ᵇ shall see how awesome are the LORD's deeds which I will perform for you. ¹¹Mark well what

לד וַיֹּ֤אמֶר יְהוָה֙ אֶל־מֹשֶׁ֔ה פְּסָל־לְךָ֛ שְׁנֵֽי־לֻחֹ֥ת אֲבָנִ֖ים כָּרִֽאשֹׁנִ֑ים וְכָתַבְתִּי֙ עַל־הַלֻּחֹ֔ת אֶת־הַדְּבָרִ֔ים אֲשֶׁ֥ר הָי֛וּ עַל־הַלֻּחֹ֥ת הָרִֽאשֹׁנִ֖ים אֲשֶׁ֥ר שִׁבַּֽרְתָּ׃ ²וֶהְיֵ֥ה נָכ֖וֹן לַבֹּ֑קֶר וְעָלִ֤יתָ בַבֹּ֙קֶר֙ אֶל־הַ֣ר סִינַ֔י וְנִצַּבְתָּ֥ לִ֛י שָׁ֖ם עַל־רֹ֥אשׁ הָהָֽר׃ ³וְאִישׁ֩ לֹֽא־יַעֲלֶ֨ה עִמָּ֜ךְ וְגַם־אִ֗ישׁ אַל־יֵרָא֙ בְּכָל־הָהָ֔ר גַּם־הַצֹּ֥אן וְהַבָּקָ֖ר אַל־יִרְע֑וּ אֶל־מ֖וּל הָהָ֥ר הַהֽוּא׃

⁴וַיִּפְסֹ֡ל שְׁנֵֽי־לֻחֹ֨ת אֲבָנִ֜ים כָּרִֽאשֹׁנִ֗ים וַיַּשְׁכֵּ֨ם מֹשֶׁ֤ה בַבֹּ֙קֶר֙ וַיַּ֙עַל֙ אֶל־הַ֣ר סִינַ֔י כַּאֲשֶׁ֛ר צִוָּ֥ה יְהוָ֖ה אֹת֑וֹ וַיִּקַּ֣ח בְּיָד֔וֹ שְׁנֵ֖י לֻחֹ֥ת אֲבָנִֽים׃ ⁵וַיֵּ֤רֶד יְהוָה֙ בֶּֽעָנָ֔ן וַיִּתְיַצֵּ֥ב עִמּ֖וֹ שָׁ֑ם וַיִּקְרָ֥א בְשֵׁ֖ם יְהוָֽה׃ ⁶וַיַּעֲבֹ֨ר יְהוָ֥ה ׀ עַל־פָּנָיו֮ וַיִּקְרָא֒ יְהוָ֣ה ׀ יְהוָ֔ה אֵ֥ל רַח֖וּם וְחַנּ֑וּן אֶ֥רֶךְ אַפַּ֖יִם וְרַב־חֶ֥סֶד וֶאֱמֶֽת׃ ⁷נֹצֵ֥ר* חֶ֙סֶד֙ לָאֲלָפִ֔ים נֹשֵׂ֥א עָוֺ֛ן וָפֶ֖שַׁע וְחַטָּאָ֑ה וְנַקֵּה֙ לֹ֣א יְנַקֶּ֔ה פֹּקֵ֣ד ׀ עֲוֺ֣ן אָב֗וֹת עַל־בָּנִים֙ וְעַל־בְּנֵ֣י בָנִ֔ים עַל־שִׁלֵּשִׁ֖ים וְעַל־רִבֵּעִֽים׃

⁸וַיְמַהֵ֖ר מֹשֶׁ֑ה וַיִּקֹּ֥ד אַ֖רְצָה וַיִּשְׁתָּֽחוּ׃ ⁹וַיֹּ֡אמֶר אִם־נָא֩ מָצָ֨אתִי חֵ֤ן בְּעֵינֶ֙יךָ֙ אֲדֹנָ֔י יֵֽלֶךְ־נָ֥א אֲדֹנָ֖י בְּקִרְבֵּ֑נוּ כִּ֤י עַם־קְשֵׁה־עֹ֙רֶף֙ ה֔וּא וְסָלַחְתָּ֛ לַעֲוֺנֵ֥נוּ וּלְחַטָּאתֵ֖נוּ וּנְחַלְתָּֽנוּ׃

¹⁰וַיֹּ֗אמֶר הִנֵּ֣ה אָנֹכִי֮ כֹּרֵ֣ת בְּרִית֒ נֶ֤גֶד כָּֽל־עַמְּךָ֙ אֶעֱשֶׂ֣ה נִפְלָאֹ֔ת אֲשֶׁ֛ר לֹֽא־נִבְרְא֥וּ בְכָל־הָאָ֖רֶץ וּבְכָל־הַגּוֹיִ֑ם וְרָאָ֣ה כָל־הָ֠עָם אֲשֶׁר־אַתָּ֨ה בְקִרְבּ֜וֹ אֶת־מַעֲשֵׂ֤ה יְהוָה֙ כִּֽי־נוֹרָ֣א ה֔וּא אֲשֶׁ֥ר אֲנִ֖י עֹשֶׂ֥ה עִמָּֽךְ׃ ¹¹שְׁמָ֨ר־לְךָ֔ אֵ֛ת אֲשֶׁ֥ר אָנֹכִ֖י מְצַוְּךָ֣ הַיּ֑וֹם הִנְנִ֧י גֹרֵ֣שׁ

---

a-a   Or "and the Lord proclaimed: The LORD! a God compassionate," etc.; cf. Num. 14.17–18.

b-b   Lit. "in whose midst you are."

נ' רבתי לפי נוסחים המקובלים v. 7.

I command you this day. I will drive out before you the Amorites, the Canaanites, the Hittites, the Perizzites, the Hivites, and the Jebusites. 12Beware of making a covenant with the inhabitants of the land against which you are advancing, lest they be a snare in your midst. 13No, you must tear down their altars, smash their pillars, and cut down their sacred posts; 14for you must not worship any other god, because the LORD, whose name is Impassioned, is an impassioned God. 15You must not make a covenant with the inhabitants of the land, for they will lust after their gods and sacrifice to their gods and invite you, and you will eat of their sacrifices. 16And when you take wives from among their daughters for your sons, their daughters will lust after their gods and will cause your sons to lust after their gods.

17You shall not make molten gods for yourselves.

18You shall observe the Feast of Unleavened Bread—eating unleavened bread for seven days, as I have commanded you—at the set time of the month c of Abib, for in the month of Abib you went forth from Egypt.

19Every first issue of the womb is Mine, from all your livestock that drop a male d as firstling, whether cattle or sheep. 20But the firstling of an ass you shall redeem with a sheep; if you do not redeem it, you must break its neck. And you must redeem every first-born among your sons.

None shall appear before Me empty-handed.

21Six days you shall work, but on the seventh day you shall cease from labor; you shall cease from labor even at plowing time and harvest time.

22You shall observe the Feast of Weeks, of the first fruits of the wheat harvest; and the Feast of Ingathering at the turn of the year. 23Three times a year all your males shall appear before

מִפָּנֶ֑יךָ אֶת־הָאֱמֹרִי֙ וְהַכְּנַעֲנִ֔י וְהַחִתִּ֔י
וְהַפְּרִזִּ֖י וְהַחִוִּ֥י וְהַיְבוּסִֽי: 12 הִשָּׁ֣מֶר לְךָ֗
פֶּן־תִּכְרֹ֤ת בְּרִית֙ לְיוֹשֵׁ֣ב הָאָ֔רֶץ אֲשֶׁ֥ר אַתָּ֖ה
בָּ֣א עָלֶ֑יהָ פֶּן־יִהְיֶ֥ה לְמוֹקֵ֖שׁ בְּקִרְבֶּֽךָ: 13 כִּ֤י
אֶת־מִזְבְּחֹתָם֙ תִּתֹּצ֔וּן וְאֶת־מַצֵּבֹתָ֖ם
תְּשַׁבֵּר֑וּן וְאֶת־אֲשֵׁרָ֖יו תִּכְרֹתֽוּן: 14 כִּ֛י לֹ֥א
תִֽשְׁתַּחֲוֶ֖ה לְאֵ֣ל אַחֵ֑ר* כִּ֤י יְהֹוָה֙ קַנָּ֣א שְׁמ֔וֹ
אֵ֥ל קַנָּ֖א הֽוּא: 15 פֶּן־תִּכְרֹ֥ת בְּרִ֖ית לְיוֹשֵׁ֣ב
הָאָ֑רֶץ וְזָנ֣וּ | אַחֲרֵ֣י אֱלֹֽהֵיהֶ֗ם וְזָבְחוּ֙
לֵאלֹ֣הֵיהֶ֔ם וְקָרָ֣א לְךָ֔ וְאָכַלְתָּ֖ מִזִּבְחֽוֹ: 16
וְלָקַחְתָּ֣ מִבְּנֹתָ֔יו לְבָנֶ֑יךָ וְזָנ֣וּ בְנֹתָ֗יו אַחֲרֵי֙
אֱלֹ֣הֵיהֶ֔ן וְהִזְנוּ֙ אֶת־בָּנֶ֔יךָ אַחֲרֵ֖י אֱלֹהֵיהֶֽן:
17 אֱלֹהֵ֥י מַסֵּכָ֖ה לֹ֥א תַעֲשֶׂה־לָּֽךְ:
18 אֶת־חַ֣ג הַמַּצּוֹת֮ תִּשְׁמֹר֒ שִׁבְעַ֣ת יָמִ֗ים
תֹּאכַ֤ל מַצּוֹת֙ אֲשֶׁ֣ר צִוִּיתִ֔ךָ לְמוֹעֵ֖ד חֹ֣דֶשׁ
הָֽאָבִ֑יב כִּ֚י בְּחֹ֣דֶשׁ הָֽאָבִ֔יב יָצָ֖אתָ
מִמִּצְרָֽיִם: 19 כָּל־פֶּ֥טֶר רֶ֖חֶם לִ֑י וְכָל־מִקְנְךָ֙ תִּזָּכָ֔ר פֶּ֖טֶר
שׁ֥וֹר וָשֶֽׂה: 20 וּפֶ֤טֶר חֲמוֹר֙ תִּפְדֶּ֣ה בְשֶׂ֔ה
וְאִם־לֹ֥א תִפְדֶּ֖ה וַעֲרַפְתּ֑וֹ כֹּ֣ל בְּכ֤וֹר בָּנֶ֙יךָ֙
תִּפְדֶּ֔ה
וְלֹֽא־יֵרָא֥וּ פָנַ֖י רֵיקָֽם:
21 שֵׁ֤שֶׁת יָמִים֙ תַּעֲבֹ֔ד וּבַיּ֥וֹם הַשְּׁבִיעִ֖י
תִּשְׁבֹּ֑ת בֶּחָרִ֥ישׁ וּבַקָּצִ֖יר תִּשְׁבֹּֽת:
22 וְחַ֤ג שָׁבֻעֹת֙ תַּעֲשֶׂ֣ה לְךָ֔ בִּכּוּרֵ֖י קְצִ֣יר
חִטִּ֑ים וְחַג֙ הָֽאָסִ֔יף תְּקוּפַ֖ת הַשָּׁנָֽה:
23 שָׁלֹ֥שׁ פְּעָמִ֖ים בַּשָּׁנָ֑ה יֵֽרָאֶה֙ כָּל־זְכ֣וּרְךָ֔
אֶת־פְּנֵ֛י הָֽאָדֹ֥ן | יְהֹוָ֖ה אֱלֹהֵ֥י יִשְׂרָאֵֽל:

---

c   See note at 13.4.
d   Heb. tizzakhar, form uncertain.

ר׳ רבתי לפי נוסחים המקובלים   v. 14.

the Sovereign LORD, the God of Israel. 24I will drive out nations from your path and enlarge your territory; no one will covet your land when you go up to appear before the LORD your God three times a year.

25You shall not offer the blood of My sacrifice with anything leavened; and the sacrifice of the Feast of Passover shall not be left lying until morning.

26The choice first fruits of your soil you shall bring to the house of the LORD your God.

You shall not boil a kid in its mother's milk.

27And the LORD said to Moses: Write down these commandments, for in accordance with these commandments I make a covenant with you and with Israel.

28And he was there with the LORD forty days and forty nights; he ate no bread and drank no water; and he wrote down on the tablets the terms of the covenant, the Ten Commandments.

29So Moses came down from Mount Sinai. And as Moses came down from the mountain bearing the two tablets of the Pact, Moses was not aware that the skin of his face was radiant, since he had spoken with Him. 30Aaron and all the Israelites saw that the skin of Moses' face was radiant; and they shrank from coming near him. 31But Moses called to them, and Aaron and all the chieftains in the assembly returned to him, and Moses spoke to them. 32Afterward all the Israelites came near, and he instructed them concerning all that the LORD had imparted to him on Mount Sinai. 33And when Moses had finished speaking with them, he put a veil over his face.

34Whenever Moses went in before the LORD to speak with Him, he would leave the veil off until he came out; and when he came out and told the Israelites what he had been com-

24 כִּי־אוֹרִישׁ גּוֹיִם מִפָּנֶיךָ וְהִרְחַבְתִּי אֶת־גְּבוּלֶךָ וְלֹא־יַחְמֹד אִישׁ אֶת־אַרְצְךָ בַּעֲלֹתְךָ לֵרָאוֹת אֶת־פְּנֵי יְהוָה אֱלֹהֶיךָ שָׁלֹשׁ פְּעָמִים בַּשָּׁנָה:

25 לֹא־תִשְׁחַט עַל־חָמֵץ דַּם־זִבְחִי וְלֹא־יָלִין לַבֹּקֶר זֶבַח חַג הַפָּסַח:

26 רֵאשִׁית בִּכּוּרֵי אַדְמָתְךָ תָּבִיא בֵּית יְהוָה אֱלֹהֶיךָ

לֹא־תְבַשֵּׁל גְּדִי בַּחֲלֵב אִמּוֹ: פ

27 וַיֹּאמֶר יְהוָה אֶל־מֹשֶׁה כְּתָב־לְךָ אֶת־הַדְּבָרִים הָאֵלֶּה כִּי עַל־פִּי | הַדְּבָרִים הָאֵלֶּה כָּרַתִּי אִתְּךָ בְּרִית וְאֶת־יִשְׂרָאֵל:

28 וַיְהִי־שָׁם עִם־יְהוָה אַרְבָּעִים יוֹם וְאַרְבָּעִים לַיְלָה לֶחֶם לֹא אָכַל וּמַיִם לֹא שָׁתָה וַיִּכְתֹּב עַל־הַלֻּחֹת אֵת דִּבְרֵי הַבְּרִית עֲשֶׂרֶת הַדְּבָרִים:

29 וַיְהִי בְּרֶדֶת מֹשֶׁה מֵהַר סִינַי וּשְׁנֵי לֻחֹת הָעֵדֻת בְּיַד־מֹשֶׁה בְּרִדְתּוֹ מִן־הָהָר וּמֹשֶׁה לֹא־יָדַע כִּי קָרַן עוֹר פָּנָיו בְּדַבְּרוֹ אִתּוֹ:

30 וַיַּרְא אַהֲרֹן וְכָל־בְּנֵי יִשְׂרָאֵל אֶת־מֹשֶׁה וְהִנֵּה קָרַן עוֹר פָּנָיו וַיִּירְאוּ מִגֶּשֶׁת אֵלָיו:

31 וַיִּקְרָא אֲלֵהֶם מֹשֶׁה וַיָּשֻׁבוּ אֵלָיו אַהֲרֹן וְכָל־הַנְּשִׂאִים בָּעֵדָה וַיְדַבֵּר מֹשֶׁה אֲלֵהֶם:

32 וְאַחֲרֵי־כֵן נִגְּשׁוּ כָּל־בְּנֵי יִשְׂרָאֵל וַיְצַוֵּם אֵת כָּל־אֲשֶׁר דִּבֶּר יְהוָה אִתּוֹ בְּהַר סִינָי:

33 וַיְכַל מֹשֶׁה מִדַּבֵּר אִתָּם וַיִּתֵּן עַל־פָּנָיו מַסְוֶה:

34 וּבְבֹא מֹשֶׁה לִפְנֵי יְהוָה לְדַבֵּר אִתּוֹ יָסִיר אֶת־הַמַּסְוֶה עַד־צֵאתוֹ וְיָצָא וְדִבֶּר אֶל־בְּנֵי יִשְׂרָאֵל אֵת אֲשֶׁר יְצֻוֶּה: 35 וְרָאוּ בְנֵי־

manded, [35]the Israelites would see how radiant the skin of Moses' face was. Moses would then put the veil back over his face until he went in to speak with Him.

35 VA-YAKHEL

Moses then convoked the whole Israelite community and said to them:

These are the things that the LORD has commanded you to do: [2]On six days work may be done, but on the seventh day you shall have a sabbath of complete rest, holy to the LORD; whoever does any work on it shall be put to death. [3]You shall kindle no fire throughout your settlements on the sabbath day.

[4]Moses said further to the whole community of Israelites:

This is what the LORD has commanded: [5]Take from among you gifts to the LORD; everyone whose heart so moves him shall bring them— gifts for the LORD: gold, silver, and copper; [6a]blue, purple, and crimson yarns, fine linen, and goats' hair; [7]tanned ram skins, dolphin skins, and acacia wood; [8]oil for lighting, spices for the anointing oil and for the aromatic incense; [9]lapis lazuli and other stones for setting, for the ephod and the breastpiece.

[10]And let all among you who are skilled come and make all that the LORD has commanded: [11]the Tabernacle, its tent and its covering, its clasps and its planks, its bars, its posts, and its sockets; [12]the ark and its poles, the cover, and the curtain for the screen; [13]the table, and its poles and all its utensils; and the bread of display; [14]the lampstand for lighting, its furnishings and its lamps, and the oil for lighting; [15]the altar of incense and its poles; the anointing oil and the aromatic incense; and the entrance screen for the entrance of the Tabernacle; [16]the

יִשְׂרָאֵל֙ אֶת־פְּנֵ֣י מֹשֶׁ֔ה כִּ֣י קָרַ֔ן ע֖וֹר פְּנֵ֣י מֹשֶׁ֑ה וְהֵשִׁ֨יב מֹשֶׁ֤ה אֶת־הַמַּסְוֶה֙ עַל־פָּנָ֔יו עַד־בֹּא֖וֹ לְדַבֵּ֥ר אִתּֽוֹ׃ ס

לה ויקהל

וַיַּקְהֵ֣ל מֹשֶׁ֗ה אֶֽת־כָּל־עֲדַ֛ת בְּנֵ֥י יִשְׂרָאֵ֖ל וַיֹּ֣אמֶר אֲלֵהֶ֑ם
אֵ֚לֶּה הַדְּבָרִ֔ים אֲשֶׁר־צִוָּ֥ה יְהוָ֖ה לַעֲשֹׂ֥ת אֹתָֽם׃ [2]שֵׁ֣שֶׁת יָמִים֮ תֵּעָשֶׂ֣ה מְלָאכָה֒ וּבַיּ֣וֹם הַשְּׁבִיעִ֗י יִהְיֶ֨ה לָכֶ֥ם קֹ֛דֶשׁ שַׁבַּ֥ת שַׁבָּת֖וֹן לַיהוָ֑ה כָּל־הָעֹשֶׂ֥ה ב֛וֹ מְלָאכָ֖ה יוּמָֽת׃ [3]לֹא־תְבַעֲר֣וּ אֵ֔שׁ בְּכֹ֖ל מֹשְׁבֹֽתֵיכֶ֑ם בְּי֖וֹם הַשַּׁבָּֽת׃ פ

[4]וַיֹּ֣אמֶר מֹשֶׁ֔ה אֶל־כָּל־עֲדַ֥ת בְּנֵֽי־יִשְׂרָאֵ֖ל לֵאמֹ֑ר
זֶ֣ה הַדָּבָ֔ר אֲשֶׁר־צִוָּ֥ה יְהוָ֖ה לֵאמֹֽר׃ [5]קְח֨וּ מֵֽאִתְּכֶ֤ם תְּרוּמָה֙ לַֽיהוָ֔ה כֹּ֚ל נְדִ֣יב לִבּ֔וֹ יְבִיאֶ֕הָ אֵ֖ת תְּרוּמַ֣ת יְהוָ֑ה זָהָ֥ב וָכֶ֖סֶף וּנְחֹֽשֶׁת׃ [6]וּתְכֵ֧לֶת וְאַרְגָּמָ֛ן וְתוֹלַ֥עַת שָׁנִ֖י וְשֵׁ֥שׁ וְעִזִּֽים׃ [7]וְעֹרֹ֨ת אֵילִ֧ם מְאָדָּמִ֛ים וְעֹרֹ֥ת תְּחָשִׁ֖ים וַעֲצֵ֥י שִׁטִּֽים׃ [8]וְשֶׁ֖מֶן לַמָּא֑וֹר וּבְשָׂמִים֙ לְשֶׁ֣מֶן הַמִּשְׁחָ֔ה וְלִקְטֹ֖רֶת הַסַּמִּֽים׃ [9]וְאַבְנֵי־שֹׁ֕הַם וְאַבְנֵ֖י מִלֻּאִ֑ים לָאֵפ֖וֹד וְלַחֹֽשֶׁן׃

[10]וְכָל־חֲכַם־לֵ֖ב בָּכֶ֑ם יָבֹ֣אוּ וְיַעֲשֹׂ֔וּ אֵ֖ת כָּל־אֲשֶׁ֥ר צִוָּ֖ה יְהוָֽה׃ [11]אֶת־הַמִּשְׁכָּ֕ן אֶֽת־אָהֳל֖וֹ וְאֶת־מִכְסֵ֑הוּ אֶת־קְרָסָיו֙ וְאֶת־קְרָשָׁ֔יו אֶת־בְּרִיחָ֕ו בְּרִיחָ֖יו אֶת־עַמֻּדָ֥יו וְאֶת־אֲדָנָֽיו׃ [12]אֶת־הָֽאָרֹ֥ן וְאֶת־בַּדָּ֖יו אֶת־הַכַּפֹּ֑רֶת וְאֵ֖ת פָּרֹ֥כֶת הַמָּסָֽךְ׃ [13]אֶת־הַשֻּׁלְחָ֥ן וְאֶת־בַּדָּ֖יו וְאֶת־כָּל־כֵּלָ֑יו וְאֵ֖ת לֶ֥חֶם הַפָּנִֽים׃ [14]וְאֶת־מְנֹרַ֧ת הַמָּא֛וֹר וְאֶת־כֵּלֶ֖יהָ וְאֶת־נֵרֹתֶ֑יהָ וְאֵ֖ת שֶׁ֥מֶן הַמָּאֽוֹר׃ [15]וְאֶת־מִזְבַּ֤ח הַקְּטֹ֙רֶת֙ וְאֶת־בַּדָּ֔יו וְאֵת֙

---

a   See 25.4 ff. and the notes there.

altar of burnt offering, its copper grating, its poles, and all its furnishings; the laver and its stand; [17]the hangings of the enclosure, its posts and its sockets, and the screen for the gate of the court; [18]the pegs for the Tabernacle, the pegs for the enclosure, and their cords; [19]the service vestments for officiating in the sanctuary, the sacral vestments of Aaron the priest and the vestments of his sons for priestly service.

[20]So the whole community of the Israelites left Moses' presence. [21]And everyone who excelled in ability and everyone whose spirit moved him came, bringing to the LORD his offering for the work of the Tent of Meeting and for all its service and for the sacral vestments. [22]Men and women, all whose hearts moved them, all who would make an elevation offering of gold to the LORD, came bringing brooches, earrings, rings, and pendants[b]—gold objects of all kinds. [23]And everyone who had in his possession blue, purple, and crimson yarns, fine linen, goats' hair, tanned ram skins, and dolphin skins, brought them; [24]everyone who would make gifts of silver or copper brought them as gifts for the LORD; and everyone who had in his possession acacia wood for any work of the service brought that. [25]And all the skilled women spun with their own hands, and brought what they had spun, in blue, purple, and crimson yarns, and in fine linen. [26]And all the women who excelled in that skill spun the goats' hair. [27]And the chieftains brought lapis lazuli and other stones for setting, for the ephod and for the breastpiece; [28]and spices and oil for lighting, for the anointing oil, and for the aromatic incense. [29]Thus the Israelites, all the men and women whose hearts moved them to bring anything for the work that the LORD, through Moses, had commanded to be done, brought it as a freewill offering to the LORD.

---

b *Meaning of Heb.* kumaz *uncertain.*

שֶׁמֶן הַמִּשְׁחָה וְאֵת קְטֹרֶת הַסַּמִּים וְאֶת־
מָסַךְ הַפֶּתַח לְפֶתַח הַמִּשְׁכָּן: 16 אֵת ׀
מִזְבַּח הָעֹלָה וְאֶת־מִכְבַּר הַנְּחֹשֶׁת אֲשֶׁר־
לוֹ אֶת־בַּדָּיו וְאֶת־כָּל־כֵּלָיו אֶת־הַכִּיֹּר
וְאֶת־כַּנּוֹ: 17 אֵת קַלְעֵי הֶחָצֵר אֶת־עַמֻּדָיו
וְאֶת־אֲדָנֶיהָ וְאֵת מָסַךְ שַׁעַר הֶחָצֵר:
18 אֶת־יִתְדֹת הַמִּשְׁכָּן וְאֶת־יִתְדֹת הֶחָצֵר
וְאֶת־מֵיתְרֵיהֶם: 19 אֶת־בִּגְדֵי הַשְּׂרָד
לְשָׁרֵת בַּקֹּדֶשׁ אֶת־בִּגְדֵי הַקֹּדֶשׁ לְאַהֲרֹן
הַכֹּהֵן וְאֶת־בִּגְדֵי בָנָיו לְכַהֵן:
20 וַיֵּצְאוּ כָּל־עֲדַת בְּנֵי־יִשְׂרָאֵל מִלִּפְנֵי
מֹשֶׁה: 21 וַיָּבֹאוּ כָּל־אִישׁ אֲשֶׁר־נְשָׂאוֹ לִבּוֹ
וְכֹל אֲשֶׁר נָדְבָה רוּחוֹ אֹתוֹ הֵבִיאוּ אֶת־
תְּרוּמַת יְהֹוָה לִמְלֶאכֶת אֹהֶל מוֹעֵד
וּלְכָל־עֲבֹדָתוֹ וּלְבִגְדֵי הַקֹּדֶשׁ: 22 וַיָּבֹאוּ
הָאֲנָשִׁים עַל־הַנָּשִׁים כֹּל ׀ נְדִיב לֵב הֵבִיאוּ
חָח וָנֶזֶם וְטַבַּעַת וְכוּמָז כָּל־כְּלִי זָהָב
וְכָל־אִישׁ אֲשֶׁר הֵנִיף תְּנוּפַת זָהָב לַיהֹוָה:
23 וְכָל־אִישׁ אֲשֶׁר־נִמְצָא אִתּוֹ תְּכֵלֶת
וְאַרְגָּמָן וְתוֹלַעַת שָׁנִי וְשֵׁשׁ וְעִזִּים וְעֹרֹת
אֵילִם מְאָדָּמִים וְעֹרֹת תְּחָשִׁים הֵבִיאוּ:
24 כָּל־מֵרִים תְּרוּמַת כֶּסֶף וּנְחֹשֶׁת הֵבִיאוּ
אֵת תְּרוּמַת יְהֹוָה וְכֹל אֲשֶׁר נִמְצָא אִתּוֹ
עֲצֵי שִׁטִּים לְכָל־מְלֶאכֶת הָעֲבֹדָה הֵבִיאוּ:
25 וְכָל־אִשָּׁה חַכְמַת־לֵב בְּיָדֶיהָ טָווּ
וַיָּבִיאוּ מַטְוֶה אֶת־הַתְּכֵלֶת וְאֶת־הָאַרְגָּמָן
אֶת־תּוֹלַעַת הַשָּׁנִי וְאֶת־הַשֵּׁשׁ: 26 וְכָל־
הַנָּשִׁים אֲשֶׁר נָשָׂא לִבָּן אֹתָנָה בְּחָכְמָה
טָווּ אֶת־הָעִזִּים: 27 וְהַנְּשִׂאִם הֵבִיאוּ אֵת
אַבְנֵי הַשֹּׁהַם וְאֵת אַבְנֵי הַמִּלֻּאִים לָאֵפוֹד
וְלַחֹשֶׁן: 28 וְאֶת־הַבֹּשֶׂם וְאֶת־הַשָּׁמֶן
לְמָאוֹר וּלְשֶׁמֶן הַמִּשְׁחָה וְלִקְטֹרֶת
הַסַּמִּים: 29 כָּל־אִישׁ וְאִשָּׁה אֲשֶׁר נָדַב
לִבָּם אֹתָם לְהָבִיא לְכָל־הַמְּלָאכָה אֲשֶׁר
צִוָּה יְהֹוָה לַעֲשׂוֹת בְּיַד־מֹשֶׁה הֵבִיאוּ
בְנֵי־יִשְׂרָאֵל נְדָבָה לַיהֹוָה: פ

30And Moses said to the Israelites: See, the LORD has singled out by name Bezalel, son of Uri son of Hur, of the tribe of Judah. 31He has endowed him with a divine spirit of skill, ability, and knowledge in every kind of craft 32and c-has inspired him-c to make designs for work in gold, silver, and copper, 33to cut stones for setting and to carve wood—to work in every kind of designer's craft—34and to give directions. He and Oholiab son of Ahisamach of the tribe of Dan 35have been endowed with the skill to do any work—of the carver, the designer, the embroiderer in blue, purple, crimson yarns, and in fine linen, and of the weaver—as workers in all crafts

36 and as makers of designs. 1Let, then, Bezalel and Oholiab and all the skilled persons whom the LORD has endowed with skill and ability to perform expertly all the tasks connected with the service of the sanctuary carry out all that the LORD has commanded.

2Moses then called Bezalel and Oholiab, and every skilled person whom the LORD had endowed with skill, everyone who excelled in ability, to undertake the task and carry it out. 3They took over from Moses all the gifts that the Israelites had brought, to carry out the tasks connected with the service of the sanctuary. But when these continued to bring freewill offerings to him morning after morning, 4all the artisans who were engaged in the tasks of the sanctuary came, each from the task upon which he was engaged, 5and said to Moses, "The people are bringing more than is needed for the tasks entailed in the work that the LORD has commanded to be done." 6Moses thereupon had this proclamation made throughout the camp: "Let no man or woman make further effort toward gifts for the sanctuary!" So the people stopped bringing: 7their efforts had been more than enough for all the tasks to be done.

30 וַיֹּ֤אמֶר מֹשֶׁה֙ אֶל־בְּנֵ֣י יִשְׂרָאֵ֔ל רְא֛וּ קָרָ֥א יְהוָ֖ה בְּשֵׁ֑ם בְּצַלְאֵ֛ל בֶּן־אוּרִ֥י בֶן־ח֖וּר לְמַטֵּ֥ה יְהוּדָֽה: 31 וַיְמַלֵּ֥א אֹת֖וֹ ר֣וּחַ אֱלֹהִ֑ים בְּחָכְמָ֛ה בִּתְבוּנָ֥ה וּבְדַ֖עַת וּבְכָל־מְלָאכָֽה: 32 וְלַחְשֹׁ֖ב מַֽחֲשָׁבֹ֑ת לַעֲשֹׂ֛ת בַּזָּהָ֥ב וּבַכֶּ֖סֶף וּבַנְּחֹֽשֶׁת: 33 וּבַחֲרֹ֥שֶׁת אֶ֛בֶן לְמַלֹּ֖את וּבַחֲרֹ֣שֶׁת עֵ֑ץ לַעֲשֹׂ֖ות בְּכָל־מְלֶ֥אכֶת מַחֲשָֽׁבֶת: 34 וּלְהוֹרֹ֖ת נָתַ֣ן בְּלִבּ֑וֹ ה֕וּא וְאָֽהֳלִיאָ֖ב בֶּן־אֲחִיסָמָ֥ךְ לְמַטֵּה־דָֽן: 35 מִלֵּ֨א אֹתָ֜ם חָכְמַת־לֵ֗ב לַעֲשׂוֹת֮ כָּל־מְלֶ֣אכֶת חָרָ֣שׁ ׀ וְחֹשֵׁ֣ב וְרֹקֵ֗ם בַּתְּכֵ֨לֶת וּבָֽאַרְגָּמָ֜ן בְּתוֹלַ֧עַת הַשָּׁנִ֛י וּבַשֵּׁ֖שׁ וְאֹרֵ֑ג עֹשֵׂי֙ כָּל־מְלָאכָ֔ה וְחֹשְׁבֵ֖י מַחֲשָׁבֹֽת:

לו 1 וְעָשָׂה֩ בְצַלְאֵ֨ל וְאָֽהֳלִיאָ֜ב וְכֹ֣ל ׀ אִ֣ישׁ חֲכַם־לֵ֗ב אֲשֶׁר֩ נָתַ֨ן יְהֹוָ֜ה חָכְמָ֤ה וּתְבוּנָה֙ בָּהֵ֔מָּה לָדַ֣עַת לַעֲשֹׂ֔ת אֶֽת־כָּל־מְלֶ֖אכֶת עֲבֹדַ֣ת הַקֹּ֑דֶשׁ לְכֹ֥ל אֲשֶׁר־צִוָּ֖ה יְהוָֽה:

2 וַיִּקְרָ֣א מֹשֶׁ֗ה אֶל־בְּצַלְאֵל֮ וְאֶל־אָֽהֳלִיאָב֒ וְאֶל֙ כָּל־אִ֣ישׁ חֲכַם־לֵ֔ב אֲשֶׁ֨ר נָתַ֧ן יְהוָ֛ה חָכְמָ֖ה בְּלִבּ֑וֹ כֹּ֚ל אֲשֶׁ֣ר נְשָׂא֣וֹ לִבּ֔וֹ לְקָרְבָ֥ה אֶל־הַמְּלָאכָ֖ה לַעֲשֹׂ֥ת אֹתָֽהּ: 3 וַיִּקְח֣וּ מִלִּפְנֵ֣י מֹשֶׁ֗ה אֵ֤ת כָּל־הַתְּרוּמָה֙ אֲשֶׁ֨ר הֵבִ֜יאוּ בְּנֵ֣י יִשְׂרָאֵ֗ל לִמְלֶ֛אכֶת עֲבֹדַ֥ת הַקֹּ֖דֶשׁ לַעֲשֹׂ֣ת אֹתָ֑הּ וְ֠הֵם הֵבִ֨יאוּ אֵלָ֥יו ע֛וֹד נְדָבָ֖ה בַּבֹּ֥קֶר בַּבֹּֽקֶר: 4 וַיָּבֹ֨אוּ֙ כָּל־הַ֣חֲכָמִ֔ים הָעֹשִׂ֕ים אֵ֖ת כָּל־מְלֶ֣אכֶת הַקֹּ֑דֶשׁ אִֽישׁ־אִ֥ישׁ מִמְּלַאכְתּ֖וֹ אֲשֶׁר־הֵ֥מָּה עֹשִֽׂים: 5 וַיֹּאמְרוּ֙ אֶל־מֹשֶׁ֣ה לֵּאמֹ֔ר מַרְבִּ֥ים הָעָ֖ם לְהָבִ֑יא מִדֵּ֤י הָֽעֲבֹדָה֙ לַמְּלָאכָ֔ה אֲשֶׁר־צִוָּ֥ה יְהוָ֖ה לַעֲשֹׂ֥ת אֹתָֽהּ: 6 וַיְצַ֣ו מֹשֶׁ֗ה וַיַּעֲבִ֨ירוּ֙ ק֣וֹל בַּֽמַּחֲנֶה֮ לֵאמֹר֒ אִ֣ישׁ וְאִשָּׁ֗ה אַל־יַֽעֲשׂוּ־ע֛וֹד מְלָאכָ֖ה לִתְרוּמַ֣ת הַקֹּ֑דֶשׁ וַיִּכָּלֵ֥א הָעָ֖ם מֵהָבִֽיא: 7 וְהַמְּלָאכָ֗ה הָיְתָ֥ה דַיָּ֛ם לְכָל־הַמְּלָאכָ֖ה לַעֲשׂ֣וֹת אֹתָ֑הּ וְהוֹתֵֽר: ס

---

c-c Moved up from v. 34 for clarity.

8Then all the skilled among those engaged in the work made the Tabernacle of ten strips of cloth, which they made of fine twisted linen, blue, purple, and crimson yarns; into these they worked a design of cherubim. 9The length of each cloth was twenty-eight cubits, and the width of each cloth was four cubits, all cloths having the same measurements. 10They joined five of the cloths to one another, and they joined the other five cloths to one another. 11They made loops of blue wool on the edge of the outermost cloth of the one set, and did the same on the edge of the outermost cloth of the other set: 12they made fifty loops on the one cloth, and they made fifty loops on the edge of the end cloth of the other set, the loops being opposite one another. 13And they made fifty gold clasps and coupled the units*a* to one another with the clasps, so that the Tabernacle became one whole.

14They made cloths of goats' hair for a tent over the Tabernacle; they made the cloths eleven in number. 15The length of each cloth was thirty cubits, and the width of each cloth was four cubits, the eleven cloths having the same measurements. 16They joined five of the cloths by themselves, and the other six cloths by themselves. 17They made fifty loops on the edge of the outermost cloth of the one set, and they made fifty loops on the edge of the end cloth of the other set. 18They made fifty copper clasps to couple the Tent together so that it might become one whole. 19And they made a covering of tanned ram skins for the tent, and a covering of dolphin skins above.

20They made the planks for the Tabernacle of acacia wood, upright. 21The length of each plank was ten cubits, the width of each plank a cubit and a half. 22Each plank had two tenons, parallel*b* to each other; they did the same with

---

a Lit. *"strip of cloth,"* here used collectively.
b See note at 26.17.

---

8 וַיַּעֲשׂוּ כָל־חֲכַם־לֵ֞ב בְּעֹשֵׂ֤י הַמְּלָאכָה֙ אֶת־הַמִּשְׁכָּ֔ן עֶ֥שֶׂר יְרִיעֹ֑ת שֵׁ֣שׁ מָשְׁזָ֗ר וּתְכֵ֤לֶת וְאַרְגָּמָן֙ וְתוֹלַ֣עַת שָׁנִ֔י כְּרֻבִ֛ים מַעֲשֵׂ֥ה חֹשֵׁ֖ב עָשָׂ֥ה אֹתָֽם: 9 אֹ֣רֶךְ הַיְרִיעָ֣ה הָֽאַחַ֗ת שְׁמֹנֶ֤ה וְעֶשְׂרִים֙ בָּֽאַמָּ֔ה וְרֹ֨חַב֙ אַרְבַּ֣ע בָּֽאַמָּ֔ה הַיְרִיעָ֖ה הָֽאֶחָ֑ת מִדָּ֥ה אַחַ֖ת לְכָל־הַיְרִיעֹֽת: 10 וַיְחַבֵּר֙ אֶת־חֲמֵ֣שׁ הַיְרִיעֹ֔ת אַחַ֖ת אֶל־אֶחָ֑ת וְחָמֵ֤שׁ יְרִיעֹת֙ חִבַּ֔ר אַחַ֖ת אֶל־אֶחָֽת: 11 וַיַּ֜עַשׂ לֻלְאֹ֣ת תְּכֵ֗לֶת עַ֣ל שְׂפַ֤ת הַיְרִיעָה֙ הָֽאֶחָ֔ת מִקָּצָ֖ה בַּמַּחְבָּ֑רֶת כֵּ֤ן עָשָׂה֙ בִּשְׂפַ֣ת הַיְרִיעָ֔ה הַקִּ֣יצוֹנָ֔ה בַּמַּחְבֶּ֖רֶת הַשֵּׁנִֽית: 12 חֲמִשִּׁ֣ים לֻלָאֹ֗ת עָשָׂה֙ בַּיְרִיעָ֣ה הָֽאֶחָ֔ת וַחֲמִשִּׁ֣ים לֻלָאֹ֗ת עָשָׂה֙ בִּקְצֵ֣ה הַיְרִיעָ֔ה אֲשֶׁ֖ר בַּמַּחְבֶּ֣רֶת הַשֵּׁנִ֑ית מַקְבִּילֹת֙ הַלֻּ֣לָאֹ֔ת אַחַ֖ת אֶל־אֶחָֽת: 13 וַיַּ֕עַשׂ חֲמִשִּׁ֖ים קַרְסֵ֣י זָהָ֑ב וַיְחַבֵּ֨ר אֶת־הַיְרִיעֹ֜ת אַחַ֤ת אֶל־אַחַת֙ בַּקְּרָסִ֔ים וַֽיְהִ֥י הַמִּשְׁכָּ֖ן אֶחָֽד: ס 14 וַיַּ֨עַשׂ֙ יְרִיעֹ֣ת עִזִּ֔ים לְאֹ֖הֶל עַל־הַמִּשְׁכָּ֑ן עַשְׁתֵּֽי־עֶשְׂרֵ֥ה יְרִיעֹ֖ת עָשָׂ֥ה אֹתָֽם: 15 אֹ֜רֶךְ הַיְרִיעָ֣ה הָֽאַחַ֗ת שְׁלֹשִׁים֙ בָּֽאַמָּ֔ה וְאַרְבַּ֣ע אַמּ֗וֹת רֹ֚חַב הַיְרִיעָ֣ה הָֽאֶחָ֔ת מִדָּ֣ה אַחַ֔ת לְעַשְׁתֵּ֥י עֶשְׂרֵ֖ה יְרִיעֹֽת: 16 וַיְחַבֵּ֛ר אֶת־חֲמֵ֥שׁ הַיְרִיעֹ֖ת לְבָ֑ד וְאֶת־שֵׁ֥שׁ הַיְרִיעֹ֖ת לְבָֽד: 17 וַיַּ֜עַשׂ לֻלָאֹ֣ת חֲמִשִּׁ֗ים עַ֚ל שְׂפַ֣ת הַיְרִיעָ֔ה הַקִּ֣יצֹנָ֔ה בַּמַּחְבָּ֑רֶת וַחֲמִשִּׁ֣ים לֻלָאֹ֗ת עָשָׂה֙ עַל־שְׂפַ֣ת הַיְרִיעָ֔ה הַחֹבֶ֖רֶת הַשֵּׁנִֽית: 18 וַיַּ֛עַשׂ קַרְסֵ֥י נְחֹ֖שֶׁת חֲמִשִּׁ֑ים לְחַבֵּ֥ר אֶת־הָאֹ֖הֶל לִֽהְיֹ֥ת אֶחָֽד: 19 וַיַּ֤עַשׂ מִכְסֶה֙ לָאֹ֔הֶל עֹרֹ֥ת אֵלִ֖ם מְאׇדָּמִ֑ים וּמִכְסֵ֛ה עֹרֹ֥ת תְּחָשִׁ֖ים מִלְמָֽעְלָה: ס 20 וַיַּ֥עַשׂ אֶת־הַקְּרָשִׁ֖ים לַמִּשְׁכָּ֑ן עֲצֵ֥י שִׁטִּ֖ים עֹמְדִֽים: 21 עֶ֥שֶׂר אַמֹּ֖ת אֹ֣רֶךְ הַקָּ֑רֶשׁ וְאַמָּה֙ וַחֲצִ֣י הָֽאַמָּ֔ה רֹ֖חַב הַקֶּ֥רֶשׁ הָֽאֶחָֽד: 22 שְׁתֵּ֣י יָדֹ֗ת לַקֶּ֙רֶשׁ֙ הָֽאֶחָ֔ד מְשֻׁלָּבֹ֔ת אַחַ֖ת אֶל־

all the planks of the Tabernacle. 23Of the planks of the Tabernacle, they made twenty planks for the south side,c 24making forty silver sockets under the twenty planks, two sockets under one plank for its two tenons and two sockets under each following plank for its two tenons; 25and for the other side wall of the Tabernacle, the north side, twenty planks, 26with their forty silver sockets, two sockets under one plank and two sockets under each following plank. 27And for the rear of the Tabernacle, to the west, they made six planks; 28and they made two planks for the corners of the Tabernacle at the rear. 29d-They matched at the bottom, but terminated as one at the top into one ring;-d they did so with both of them at the two corners. 30Thus there were eight planks with their sockets of silver: sixteen sockets, two under each plank.

31They made bars of acacia wood, five for the planks of the one side wall of the Tabernacle, 32five bars for the planks of the other side wall of the Tabernacle, and five bars for the planks of the wall of the Tabernacle at the rear, to the west; 33they made the center bar to run, halfway up the planks, from end to end. 34They overlaid the planks with gold, and made their rings of gold, as holders for the bars; and they overlaid the bars with gold.

35They made the curtain of blue, purple, and crimson yarns, and fine twisted linen, working into it a design of cherubim. 36They made for it four posts of acacia wood and overlaid them with gold, with their hooks of gold; and they cast for them four silver sockets.

37They made the screen for the entrance of the Tent, of blue, purple, and crimson yarns, and fine twisted linen, done in embroidery;

c See note at 26.18.
d-d See note at 26.24.

אַחַ֣ת כֵּ֣ן עָשָׂ֔ה לְכֹ֖ל קַרְשֵׁ֥י הַמִּשְׁכָּֽן׃ 23 וַיַּ֥עַשׂ אֶת־הַקְּרָשִׁ֖ים לַמִּשְׁכָּ֑ן עֶשְׂרִ֣ים קְרָשִׁ֔ים לִפְאַ֖ת נֶ֥גֶב תֵּימָֽנָה׃ 24 וְאַרְבָּעִ֣ים אַדְנֵי־כֶ֗סֶף עָשָׂ֔ה תַּ֖חַת עֶשְׂרִ֣ים הַקְּרָשִׁ֑ים שְׁנֵ֣י אֲדָנִ֗ים תַּֽחַת־הַקֶּ֤רֶשׁ הָֽאֶחָד֙ לִשְׁתֵּ֣י יְדֹתָ֔יו וּשְׁנֵ֣י אֲדָנִ֗ים תַּֽחַת־הַקֶּ֥רֶשׁ הָֽאֶחָ֖ד לִשְׁתֵּ֥י יְדֹתָֽיו׃ 25 וּלְצֶ֜לַע הַמִּשְׁכָּ֤ן הַשֵּׁנִית֙ לִפְאַ֣ת צָפ֔וֹן עָשָׂ֖ה עֶשְׂרִ֥ים קְרָשִֽׁים׃ 26 וְאַרְבָּעִ֥ים אַדְנֵיהֶ֖ם כָּ֑סֶף שְׁנֵ֣י אֲדָנִ֗ים תַּ֚חַת הַקֶּ֣רֶשׁ הָֽאֶחָ֔ד וּשְׁנֵ֣י אֲדָנִ֗ים תַּ֖חַת הַקֶּ֥רֶשׁ הָֽאֶחָֽד׃ 27 וּֽלְיַרְכְּתֵ֥י הַמִּשְׁכָּ֖ן יָ֑מָּה עָשָׂ֖ה שִׁשָּׁ֥ה קְרָשִֽׁים׃ 28 וּשְׁנֵ֣י קְרָשִׁ֗ים עָשָׂ֛ה לִמְקֻצְעֹ֥ת הַמִּשְׁכָּ֖ן בַּיַּרְכָתָֽיִם׃ 29 וְהָי֣וּ תוֹאֲמִם֮ מִלְּמַ֒טָּה֒ וְיַחְדָּ֗ו יִהְי֤וּ תַמִּים֙ אֶל־רֹאשׁ֔וֹ אֶל־הַטַּבַּ֖עַת הָאֶחָ֑ת כֵּ֚ן עָשָׂ֣ה לִשְׁנֵיהֶ֔ם לִשְׁנֵ֖י הַמִּקְצֹעֹֽת׃ 30 וְהָיוּ֙ שְׁמֹנָ֣ה קְרָשִׁ֗ים וְאַדְנֵיהֶ֥ם כֶּ֖סֶף שִׁשָּׁ֣ה עָשָׂ֣ר אֲדָנִ֑ים שְׁנֵ֤י אֲדָנִים֙ שְׁנֵ֣י אֲדָנִ֔ים תַּ֖חַת הַקֶּ֥רֶשׁ הָֽאֶחָֽד׃ 31 וַיַּ֥עַשׂ בְּרִיחֵ֖י עֲצֵ֣י שִׁטִּ֑ים חֲמִשָּׁ֕ה לְקַרְשֵׁ֥י צֶֽלַע־הַמִּשְׁכָּ֖ן הָאֶחָֽת׃ 32 וַחֲמִשָּׁ֣ה בְרִיחִ֗ם לְקַרְשֵׁ֤י צֶֽלַע־הַמִּשְׁכָּן֙ הַשֵּׁנִ֔ית וַחֲמִשָּׁ֤ה בְרִיחִם֙ לְקַרְשֵׁ֣י הַמִּשְׁכָּ֔ן לַיַּרְכָתַ֖יִם יָֽמָּה׃ 33 וַיַּ֖עַשׂ אֶת־הַבְּרִ֣יחַ הַתִּיכֹ֑ן לִבְרֹ֙חַ֙ בְּת֣וֹךְ הַקְּרָשִׁ֔ים מִן־הַקָּצֶ֖ה אֶל־הַקָּצֶֽה׃ 34 וְֽאֶת־הַקְּרָשִׁ֞ים צִפָּ֣ה זָהָ֗ב וְאֶת־טַבְּעֹתָם֙ עָשָׂ֣ה זָהָ֔ב בָּתִּ֖ים לַבְּרִיחִ֑ם וַיְצַ֥ף אֶת־הַבְּרִיחִ֖ם זָהָֽב׃ 35 וַיַּ֙עַשׂ֙ אֶת־הַפָּרֹ֔כֶת תְּכֵ֥לֶת וְאַרְגָּמָ֖ן וְתוֹלַ֣עַת שָׁנִ֑י וְשֵׁ֣שׁ מָשְׁזָ֔ר מַעֲשֵׂ֥ה חֹשֵׁ֛ב עָשָׂ֥ה אֹתָ֖הּ כְּרֻבִֽים׃ 36 וַיַּ֣עַשׂ לָ֗הּ אַרְבָּעָה֙ עַמּוּדֵ֣י שִׁטִּ֔ים וַיְצַפֵּ֣ם זָהָ֔ב וָוֵיהֶ֖ם זָהָ֑ב וַיִּצֹ֣ק לָהֶ֔ם אַרְבָּעָ֖ה אַדְנֵי־כָֽסֶף׃ 37 וַיַּ֤עַשׂ מָסָךְ֙ לְפֶ֣תַח הָאֹ֔הֶל תְּכֵ֥לֶת

195

38and five posts for it with their hooks. They overlaid their tops and their bands with gold; but the five sockets were of copper.

37 Bezalel made the ark of acacia wood, two and a half cubits long, a cubit and a half wide, and a cubit and a half high. 2He overlaid it with pure gold, inside and out; and he made a gold molding for it round about. 3He cast four gold rings for it, for its four feet: two rings on one of its side walls and two rings on the other. 4He made poles of acacia wood, overlaid them with gold, 5and inserted the poles into the rings on the side walls of the ark for carrying the ark.

6He made a cover of pure gold, two and a half cubits long and a cubit and a half wide. 7He made two cherubim of gold; he made them of hammered work, at the two ends of the cover: 8one cherub at one end and the other cherub at the other end; he made the cherubim of one piece with the cover, at its two ends. 9The cherubim had their wings spread out above, shielding the cover with their wings. They faced each other; the faces of the cherubim were turned toward the cover.

10He made the table of acacia wood, two cubits long, one cubit wide, and a cubit and a half high; 11he overlaid it with pure gold and made a gold molding around it. 12He made a rim of a hand's breadth around it and made a gold molding for its rim round about. 13He cast four gold rings for it and attached the rings to the four corners at its four legs. 14The rings were next to the rim, as holders for the poles to carry the table. 15He made the poles of acacia wood for carrying the table, and overlaid them with gold. 16The utensils that were to be upon the table—its bowls, ladles, jugs, and jars with which to offer libations—he made of pure gold.

וְאַרְגָּמָ֤ן וְתוֹלַ֙עַת֙ שָׁנִ֔י וְשֵׁ֥שׁ מָשְׁזָ֖ר מַעֲשֵׂ֣ה רֹקֵ֑ם: 38 וְאֶת־עַמּוּדָ֤יו חֲמִשָּׁה֙ וְאֶת־וָ֣וֵיהֶ֔ם וְצִפָּ֧ה רָאשֵׁיהֶ֛ם וַחֲשֻׁקֵיהֶ֖ם זָהָ֑ב וְאַדְנֵיהֶ֥ם חֲמִשָּׁ֖ה נְחֹֽשֶׁת: פ

לז וַיַּ֧עַשׂ בְּצַלְאֵ֛ל אֶת־הָאָרֹ֖ן עֲצֵ֣י שִׁטִּ֑ים אַמָּתַ֨יִם וָחֵ֜צִי אָרְכּ֗וֹ וְאַמָּ֤ה וָחֵ֙צִי֙ רָחְבּ֔וֹ וְאַמָּ֥ה וָחֵ֖צִי קֹמָתֽוֹ: 2 וַיְצַפֵּ֜הוּ זָהָ֥ב טָה֛וֹר מִבַּ֥יִת וּמִח֖וּץ וַיַּ֧עַשׂ ל֛וֹ זֵ֥ר זָהָ֖ב סָבִֽיב: 3 וַיִּצֹ֣ק ל֗וֹ אַרְבַּע֙ טַבְּעֹ֣ת זָהָ֔ב עַ֖ל אַרְבַּ֣ע פַּעֲמֹתָ֑יו וּשְׁתֵּ֣י טַבָּעֹ֗ת עַל־צַלְעוֹ֙ הָֽאֶחָ֔ת וּשְׁתֵּי֙ טַבָּע֔וֹת עַל־צַלְע֖וֹ הַשֵּׁנִֽית: 4 וַיַּ֥עַשׂ בַּדֵּ֖י עֲצֵ֣י שִׁטִּ֑ים וַיְצַ֥ף אֹתָ֖ם זָהָֽב: 5 וַיָּבֵ֤א אֶת־הַבַּדִּים֙ בַּטַּבָּעֹ֔ת עַ֖ל צַלְעֹ֣ת הָאָרֹ֑ן לָשֵׂ֖את אֶת־הָאָרֹֽן:

6 וַיַּ֥עַשׂ כַּפֹּ֖רֶת זָהָ֣ב טָה֑וֹר אַמָּתַ֤יִם וָחֵ֙צִי֙ אָרְכָּ֔הּ וְאַמָּ֥ה וָחֵ֖צִי רָחְבָּֽהּ: 7 וַיַּ֛עַשׂ שְׁנֵ֥י כְרֻבִ֖ים זָהָ֑ב מִקְשָׁה֙ עָשָׂ֣ה אֹתָ֔ם מִשְּׁנֵ֖י קְצ֥וֹת הַכַּפֹּֽרֶת: 8 כְּרֽוּב־אֶחָ֤ד מִקָּצָה֙ מִזֶּ֔ה וּכְרֽוּב־אֶחָ֥ד מִקָּצָ֖ה מִזֶּ֑ה מִן־הַכַּפֹּ֛רֶת עָשָׂ֥ה אֶת־הַכְּרֻבִ֖ים מִשְּׁנֵ֥י קצוותו קְצוֹתָֽיו: 9 וַיִּהְי֣וּ הַכְּרֻבִים֩ פֹּרְשֵׂ֨י כְנָפַ֜יִם לְמַ֗עְלָה סֹֽכְכִ֤ים בְּכַנְפֵיהֶם֙ עַל־הַכַּפֹּ֔רֶת וּפְנֵיהֶ֖ם אִ֣ישׁ אֶל־אָחִ֑יו אֶל־הַכַּפֹּ֔רֶת הָי֖וּ פְּנֵ֥י הַכְּרֻבִֽים: פ

10 וַיַּ֥עַשׂ אֶת־הַשֻּׁלְחָ֖ן עֲצֵ֣י שִׁטִּ֑ים אַמָּתַ֤יִם אָרְכּוֹ֙ וְאַמָּ֣ה רָחְבּ֔וֹ וְאַמָּ֥ה וָחֵ֖צִי קֹמָתֽוֹ: 11 וַיְצַ֥ף אֹת֖וֹ זָהָ֣ב טָה֑וֹר וַיַּ֥עַשׂ ל֛וֹ זֵ֥ר זָהָ֖ב סָבִֽיב: 12 וַיַּ֨עַשׂ ל֤וֹ מִסְגֶּ֙רֶת֙ טֹ֣פַח סָבִ֔יב וַיַּ֧עַשׂ זֵר־זָהָ֛ב לְמִסְגַּרְתּ֖וֹ סָבִֽיב: 13 וַיִּצֹ֣ק ל֗וֹ אַרְבַּע֙ טַבְּעֹ֣ת זָהָ֔ב וַיִּתֵּן֙ אֶת־הַטַּבָּעֹ֔ת עַ֚ל אַרְבַּ֣ע הַפֵּאֹ֔ת אֲשֶׁ֖ר לְאַרְבַּ֥ע רַגְלָֽיו: 14 לְעֻמַּת֙ הַמִּסְגֶּ֔רֶת הָי֖וּ הַטַּבָּעֹ֑ת בָּתִּים֙ לַבַּדִּ֔ים לָשֵׂ֖את אֶת־הַשֻּׁלְחָֽן: 15 וַיַּ֤עַשׂ אֶת־הַבַּדִּים֙ עֲצֵ֣י שִׁטִּ֔ים וַיְצַ֥ף אֹתָ֖ם זָהָ֑ב לָשֵׂ֖את אֶת־הַשֻּׁלְחָֽן: 16 וַיַּ֜עַשׂ אֶֽת־הַכֵּלִ֣ים ׀ אֲשֶׁ֣ר

17He made the lampstand of pure gold. He made the lampstand—its base and its shaft—of hammered work; its cups, calyxes, and petals were of one piece with it. 18Six branches issued from its sides: three branches from one side of the lampstand, and three branches from the other side of the lampstand. 19There were three cups shaped like almond-blossoms, each with calyx and petals, on one branch; and there were three cups shaped like almond-blossoms, each with calyx and petals, on the next branch; so for all six branches issuing from the lampstand. 20On the lampstand itself there were four cups shaped like almond-blossoms, each with calyx and petals: 21a calyx, of one piece with it, under a pair of branches; and a calyx, of one piece with it, under the second pair of branches; and a calyx, of one piece with it, under the last pair of branches; so for all six branches issuing from it. 22Their calyxes and their stems were of one piece with it, the whole of it a single hammered piece of pure gold. 23He made its seven lamps, its tongs, and its fire pans of pure gold. 24He made it and all its furnishings out of a talent of pure gold.

25He made the incense altar of acacia wood, a cubit long and a cubit wide—square—and two cubits high; its horns were of one piece with it. 26He overlaid it with pure gold: its top, its sides round about, and its horns; and he made a gold molding for it round about. 27He made two gold rings for it under its molding, on its two walls—on opposite sides—as holders for the poles with which to carry it. 28He made the poles of acacia wood, and overlaid them with gold. 29He prepared the sacred anointing oil and the pure aromatic incense, expertly blended.

עַל־הַשֻּׁלְחָן אֶת־קְעָרֹתָיו וְאֶת־כַּפֹּתָיו וְאֵת מְנַקִּיֹּתָיו וְאֶת־הַקְּשָׂוֹת אֲשֶׁר יֻסַּךְ בָּהֵן זָהָב טָהוֹר: פ

17 וַיַּעַשׂ אֶת־הַמְּנֹרָה זָהָב טָהוֹר מִקְשָׁה עָשָׂה אֶת־הַמְּנֹרָה יְרֵכָהּ וְקָנָהּ גְּבִיעֶיהָ כַּפְתֹּרֶיהָ וּפְרָחֶיהָ מִמֶּנָּה הָיוּ: 18 וְשִׁשָּׁה קָנִים יֹצְאִים מִצִּדֶּיהָ שְׁלֹשָׁה ׀ קְנֵי מְנֹרָה מִצִּדָּהּ הָאֶחָד וּשְׁלֹשָׁה קְנֵי מְנֹרָה מִצִּדָּהּ הַשֵּׁנִי: 19 שְׁלֹשָׁה גְבִעִים מְשֻׁקָּדִים בַּקָּנֶה הָאֶחָד כַּפְתֹּר וָפֶרַח וּשְׁלֹשָׁה גְבִעִים מְשֻׁקָּדִים בְּקָנֶה אֶחָד כַּפְתֹּר וָפָרַח כֵּן לְשֵׁשֶׁת הַקָּנִים הַיֹּצְאִים מִן־הַמְּנֹרָה: 20 וּבַמְּנֹרָה אַרְבָּעָה גְבִעִים מְשֻׁקָּדִים כַּפְתֹּרֶיהָ וּפְרָחֶיהָ: 21 וְכַפְתֹּר תַּחַת שְׁנֵי הַקָּנִים מִמֶּנָּה וְכַפְתֹּר תַּחַת שְׁנֵי הַקָּנִים מִמֶּנָּה וְכַפְתֹּר תַּחַת־שְׁנֵי הַקָּנִים מִמֶּנָּה לְשֵׁשֶׁת הַקָּנִים הַיֹּצְאִים מִמֶּנָּה: 22 כַּפְתֹּרֵיהֶם וּקְנֹתָם מִמֶּנָּה הָיוּ כֻּלָּהּ מִקְשָׁה אַחַת זָהָב טָהוֹר: 23 וַיַּעַשׂ אֶת־נֵרֹתֶיהָ שִׁבְעָה וּמַלְקָחֶיהָ וּמַחְתֹּתֶיהָ זָהָב טָהוֹר: 24 כִּכָּר זָהָב טָהוֹר עָשָׂה אֹתָהּ וְאֵת כָּל־כֵּלֶיהָ: פ

25 וַיַּעַשׂ אֶת־מִזְבַּח הַקְּטֹרֶת עֲצֵי שִׁטִּים אַמָּה אָרְכּוֹ וְאַמָּה רָחְבּוֹ רָבוּעַ וְאַמָּתַיִם קֹמָתוֹ מִמֶּנּוּ הָיוּ קַרְנֹתָיו: 26 וַיְצַף אֹתוֹ זָהָב טָהוֹר אֶת־גַּגּוֹ וְאֶת־קִירֹתָיו סָבִיב וְאֶת־קַרְנֹתָיו וַיַּעַשׂ לוֹ זֵר זָהָב סָבִיב: 27 וּשְׁתֵּי טַבְּעֹת זָהָב עָשָׂה־לוֹ ׀ מִתַּחַת לְזֵרוֹ עַל שְׁתֵּי צַלְעֹתָיו עַל שְׁנֵי צִדָּיו לְבָתִּים לְבַדִּים לָשֵׂאת אֹתוֹ בָּהֶם: 28 וַיַּעַשׂ אֶת־הַבַּדִּים עֲצֵי שִׁטִּים וַיְצַף אֹתָם זָהָב: 29 וַיַּעַשׂ אֶת־שֶׁמֶן הַמִּשְׁחָה קֹדֶשׁ וְאֶת־קְטֹרֶת הַסַּמִּים טָהוֹר מַעֲשֵׂה רֹקֵחַ: פ

38 He made the altar for burnt offering of acacia wood, five cubits long and five cubits wide—square—and three cubits high. [2]He made horns for it on its four corners, the horns being of one piece with it; and he overlaid it with copper. [3]He made all the utensils of the altar—the pails, the scrapers, the basins, the flesh hooks, and the fire pans; he made all these utensils of copper. [4]He made for the altar a grating of meshwork in copper, extending below, under its ledge, to its middle. [5]He cast four rings, at the four corners of the copper grating, as holders for the poles. [6]He made the poles of acacia wood and overlaid them with copper; [7]and he inserted the poles into the rings on the side walls of the altar, to carry it by them. He made it hollow, of boards.

[8]He made the laver of copper and its stand of copper, from the mirrors of the women who performed tasks[a] at the entrance of the Tent of Meeting.

[9]He made the enclosure:

On the south[b] side, a hundred cubits of hangings of fine twisted linen for the enclosure—[10]with their twenty posts and their twenty sockets of copper, the hooks and bands of the posts being silver.

[11]On the north side, a hundred cubits—with their twenty posts and their twenty sockets of copper, the hooks and bands of the posts being silver.

[12]On the west side, fifty cubits of hangings—with their ten posts and their ten sockets, the hooks and bands of the posts being silver.

[13]And on the front side, to the east, fifty cubits: [14]fifteen cubits of hangings on the one flank, with their three posts and their three sockets, [15]and fifteen cubits of hangings on the other

---

a   Meaning of Heb. uncertain.
b   Cf. note at 26.18.

לח

וַיַּעַשׂ אֶת־מִזְבַּח הָעֹלָה עֲצֵי שִׁטִּים חָמֵשׁ אַמּוֹת אָרְכּוֹ וְחָמֵשׁ־אַמּוֹת רָחְבּוֹ רָבוּעַ וְשָׁלֹשׁ אַמּוֹת קֹמָתוֹ: 2 וַיַּעַשׂ קַרְנֹתָיו עַל אַרְבַּע פִּנֹּתָיו מִמֶּנּוּ הָיוּ קַרְנֹתָיו וַיְצַף אֹתוֹ נְחֹשֶׁת: 3 וַיַּעַשׂ אֶת־כָּל־כְּלֵי הַמִּזְבֵּחַ אֶת־הַסִּירֹת וְאֶת־הַיָּעִים וְאֶת־הַמִּזְרָקֹת אֶת־הַמִּזְלָגֹת וְאֶת־הַמַּחְתֹּת כָּל־כֵּלָיו עָשָׂה נְחֹשֶׁת: 4 וַיַּעַשׂ לַמִּזְבֵּחַ מִכְבָּר מַעֲשֵׂה רֶשֶׁת נְחֹשֶׁת תַּחַת כַּרְכֻּבּוֹ מִלְמַטָּה עַד־חֶצְיוֹ: 5 וַיִּצֹק אַרְבַּע טַבָּעֹת בְּאַרְבַּע הַקְּצָוֺת לְמִכְבַּר הַנְּחֹשֶׁת בָּתִּים לַבַּדִּים: 6 וַיַּעַשׂ אֶת־הַבַּדִּים עֲצֵי שִׁטִּים וַיְצַף אֹתָם נְחֹשֶׁת: 7 וַיָּבֵא אֶת־הַבַּדִּים בַּטַּבָּעֹת עַל צַלְעֹת הַמִּזְבֵּחַ לָשֵׂאת אֹתוֹ בָּהֶם נְבוּב לֻחֹת עָשָׂה אֹתוֹ: ס

8 וַיַּעַשׂ אֵת הַכִּיּוֹר נְחֹשֶׁת וְאֵת כַּנּוֹ נְחֹשֶׁת בְּמַרְאֹת הַצֹּבְאֹת אֲשֶׁר צָבְאוּ פֶּתַח אֹהֶל מוֹעֵד: ס

9 וַיַּעַשׂ אֶת־הֶחָצֵר לִפְאַת | נֶגֶב תֵּימָנָה קַלְעֵי הֶחָצֵר שֵׁשׁ מָשְׁזָר מֵאָה בָּאַמָּה: 10 עַמּוּדֵיהֶם עֶשְׂרִים וְאַדְנֵיהֶם עֶשְׂרִים נְחֹשֶׁת וָוֵי הָעַמֻּדִים וַחֲשֻׁקֵיהֶם כָּסֶף:

11 וְלִפְאַת צָפוֹן מֵאָה בָאַמָּה עַמּוּדֵיהֶם עֶשְׂרִים וְאַדְנֵיהֶם עֶשְׂרִים נְחֹשֶׁת וָוֵי הָעַמּוּדִים וַחֲשֻׁקֵיהֶם כָּסֶף:

12 וְלִפְאַת־יָם קְלָעִים חֲמִשִּׁים בָּאַמָּה עַמּוּדֵיהֶם עֲשָׂרָה וְאַדְנֵיהֶם עֲשָׂרָה וָוֵי הָעַמֻּדִים וַחֲשׁוּקֵיהֶם כָּסֶף:

13 וְלִפְאַת קֵדְמָה מִזְרָחָה חֲמִשִּׁים אַמָּה: 14 קְלָעִים חֲמֵשׁ־עֶשְׂרֵה אַמָּה אֶל־הַכָּתֵף עַמֻּדֵיהֶם שְׁלֹשָׁה וְאַדְנֵיהֶם שְׁלֹשָׁה:

flank—on each side of the gate of the enclo-sure[c]—with their three posts and their three sockets.

16All the hangings around the enclosure were of fine twisted linen. 17The sockets for the posts were of copper, the hooks and bands of the posts were of silver, the overlay of their tops was of silver; all the posts of the enclosure were banded with silver.—18The screen of the gate of the en-closure, done in embroidery, was of blue, pur-ple, and crimson yarns, and fine twisted linen. It was twenty cubits long. [d]-Its height—or width—was five cubits, like that of-[d] the hang-ings of the enclosure. 19The posts were four; their four sockets were of copper, their hooks of silver; and the overlay of their tops was of silver, as were also their bands.—20All the pegs of the Tabernacle and of the enclosure round about were of copper.

PEKUDEI

21These are the records of the Tabernacle, the Tabernacle of the Pact, which were drawn up at Moses' bidding—the work of the Levites un-der the direction of Ithamar son of Aaron the priest. 22Now Bezalel, son of Uri son of Hur, of the tribe of Judah, had made all that the LORD had commanded Moses; 23at his side was Oholiab son of Ahisamach, of the tribe of Dan, carver and designer, and embroiderer in blue, purple, and crimson yarns and in fine linen.

24All the gold that was used for the work, in all the work of the sanctuary—the elevation offering of gold—came to 29 talents[e] and 730 shekels by the sanctuary weight. 25The silver of those of the community who were recorded came to 100 talents and 1,775 shekels by the sanc-tuary weight: 26a half-shekel[f] a head, half a shekel by the sanctuary weight, for each one

15 וְלַכָּתֵף הַשֵּׁנִית מִזֶּה וּמִזֶּה לְשַׁעַר הֶחָצֵר קְלָעִים חֲמֵשׁ עֶשְׂרֵה אַמָּה עַמֻּדֵיהֶם שְׁלֹשָׁה וְאַדְנֵיהֶם שְׁלֹשָׁה: 16 כָּל־קַלְעֵי הֶחָצֵר סָבִיב שֵׁשׁ מָשְׁזָר: 17 וְהָאֲדָנִים לָעַמֻּדִים נְחֹשֶׁת וָוֵי הָעַמּוּדִים וַחֲשׁוּקֵיהֶם כֶּסֶף וְצִפּוּי רָאשֵׁיהֶם כֶּסֶף וְהֵם מְחֻשָּׁקִים כֶּסֶף כֹּל עַמֻּדֵי הֶחָצֵר: 18 וּמָסַךְ שַׁעַר הֶחָצֵר מַעֲשֵׂה רֹקֵם תְּכֵלֶת וְאַרְגָּמָן וְתוֹלַעַת שָׁנִי וְשֵׁשׁ מָשְׁזָר וְעֶשְׂרִים אַמָּה אֹרֶךְ וְקוֹמָה בְרֹחַב חָמֵשׁ אַמּוֹת לְעֻמַּת קַלְעֵי הֶחָצֵר: 19 וְעַמֻּדֵיהֶם אַרְבָּעָה וְאַדְנֵיהֶם אַרְבָּעָה נְחֹשֶׁת וָוֵיהֶם כֶּסֶף וְצִפּוּי רָאשֵׁיהֶם וַחֲשֻׁקֵיהֶם כָּסֶף: 20 וְכָל־הַיְתֵדֹת לַמִּשְׁכָּן וְלֶחָצֵר סָבִיב נְחֹשֶׁת: ס

פקודי

21 אֵלֶּה פְקוּדֵי הַמִּשְׁכָּן מִשְׁכַּן הָעֵדֻת אֲשֶׁר פֻּקַּד עַל־פִּי מֹשֶׁה עֲבֹדַת הַלְוִיִּם בְּיַד אִיתָמָר בֶּן־אַהֲרֹן הַכֹּהֵן: 22 וּבְצַלְאֵל בֶּן־אוּרִי בֶן־חוּר לְמַטֵּה יְהוּדָה עָשָׂה אֵת כָּל־אֲשֶׁר־צִוָּה יְהוָה אֶת־מֹשֶׁה: 23 וְאִתּוֹ אָהֳלִיאָב בֶּן־אֲחִיסָמָךְ לְמַטֵּה־דָן חָרָשׁ וְחֹשֵׁב וְרֹקֵם בַּתְּכֵלֶת וּבָאַרְגָּמָן וּבְתוֹלַעַת הַשָּׁנִי וּבַשֵּׁשׁ: ס 24 כָּל־הַזָּהָב הֶעָשׂוּי לַמְּלָאכָה בְּכֹל מְלֶאכֶת הַקֹּדֶשׁ וַיְהִי זְהַב הַתְּנוּפָה תֵּשַׁע וְעֶשְׂרִים כִּכָּר וּשְׁבַע מֵאוֹת וּשְׁלֹשִׁים שֶׁקֶל בְּשֶׁקֶל הַקֹּדֶשׁ: 25 וְכֶסֶף פְּקוּדֵי הָעֵדָה מְאַת כִּכָּר וְאֶלֶף וּשְׁבַע מֵאוֹת וַחֲמִשָּׁה וְשִׁבְעִים שֶׁקֶל בְּשֶׁקֶל הַקֹּדֶשׁ: 26 בֶּקַע לַגֻּלְגֹּלֶת מַחֲצִית הַשֶּׁקֶל בְּשֶׁקֶל הַקֹּדֶשׁ לְכֹל הָעֹבֵר עַל־הַפְּקֻדִים מִבֶּן עֶשְׂרִים

---

c   Which accounts for the remaining 20 cubits; cf. v. 18.
d-d   Meaning of Heb. uncertain.
e   A talent here equals 3,000 shekels.
f   Heb. beqa'.

who was entered in the records, from the age of twenty years up, 603,550 men. ²⁷The 100 talents of silver were for casting the sockets of the sanctuary and the sockets for the curtain, 100 sockets to the 100 talents, a talent a socket. ²⁸And of the 1,775 shekels he made hooks for the posts, overlay for their tops, and bands around them.

²⁹The copper from the elevation offering came to 70 talents and 2,400 shekels. ³⁰Of it he made the sockets for the entrance of the Tent of Meeting; the copper altar and its copper grating and all the utensils of the altar; ³¹the sockets of the enclosure round about and the sockets of the gate of the enclosure; and all the pegs of the Tabernacle and all the pegs of the enclosure round about.

39

Of the blue, purple, and crimson yarns they also[a] made the service vestments for officiating in the sanctuary; they made Aaron's sacral vestments—as the LORD had commanded Moses.

²The ephod was made[b] of gold, blue, purple, and crimson yarns, and fine twisted linen. ³They hammered out sheets of gold and cut threads to be worked into designs among the blue, the purple, and the crimson yarns, and the fine linen. ⁴They made for it attaching shoulder-pieces; they were attached at its two ends. ⁵The decorated band that was upon it was made like it, of one piece with it; of gold, blue, purple, and crimson yarns, and fine twisted linen—as the LORD had commanded Moses.

⁶They bordered the lazuli stones with frames of gold, engraved with seal engravings of the names of the sons of Israel. ⁷They were set on the shoulder-pieces of the ephod, as stones of

שָׁנָה֙ וָמַ֔עְלָה לְשֵׁשׁ־מֵא֥וֹת אֶ֖לֶף וּשְׁלֹ֣שֶׁת אֲלָפִ֑ים וַחֲמֵ֥שׁ מֵא֖וֹת וַחֲמִשִּֽׁים׃ 27 וַיְהִ֗י מְאַת֙ כִּכַּ֣ר הַכֶּ֔סֶף לָצֶ֕קֶת אֵ֖ת אַדְנֵ֣י הַקֹּ֑דֶשׁ וְאֵ֖ת אַדְנֵ֣י הַפָּרֹ֑כֶת מְאַ֣ת אֲדָנִ֔ים לִמְאַ֥ת הַכִּכָּ֖ר כִּכָּ֥ר לָאָֽדֶן׃ 28 וְאֶת־הָאֶ֜לֶף וּשְׁבַ֣ע הַמֵּא֗וֹת וַחֲמִשָּׁ֤ה וְשִׁבְעִים֙ עָשָׂ֣ה וָוִ֣ים לָעַמּוּדִ֑ים וְצִפָּ֥ה רָאשֵׁיהֶ֖ם וְחִשַּׁ֥ק אֹתָֽם׃ 29 וּנְחֹ֥שֶׁת הַתְּנוּפָ֖ה שִׁבְעִ֣ים כִּכָּ֑ר וְאַלְפַּ֛יִם וְאַרְבַּע־מֵא֖וֹת שָֽׁקֶל׃ 30 וַיַּ֣עַשׂ בָּ֗הּ אֶת־אַדְנֵי֙ פֶּ֚תַח אֹ֣הֶל מוֹעֵ֔ד וְאֵת֙ מִזְבַּ֣ח הַנְּחֹ֔שֶׁת וְאֶת־מִכְבַּ֥ר הַנְּחֹ֖שֶׁת אֲשֶׁר־ל֑וֹ וְאֵ֖ת כָּל־כְּלֵ֥י הַמִּזְבֵּֽחַ׃ 31 וְאֶת־אַדְנֵ֤י הֶֽחָצֵר֙ סָבִ֔יב וְאֶת־אַדְנֵ֖י שַׁ֣עַר הֶחָצֵ֑ר וְאֵ֨ת כָּל־יִתְדֹ֤ת הַמִּשְׁכָּן֙ וְאֶת־כָּל־יִתְדֹ֥ת הֶחָצֵ֖ר סָבִֽיב׃

לט

וּמִן־הַתְּכֵ֤לֶת וְהָֽאַרְגָּמָן֙ וְתוֹלַ֣עַת הַשָּׁנִ֔י עָשׂ֥וּ בִגְדֵי־שְׂרָ֖ד לְשָׁרֵ֣ת בַּקֹּ֑דֶשׁ וַיַּֽעֲשׂ֞וּ אֶת־בִּגְדֵ֤י הַקֹּ֙דֶשׁ֙ אֲשֶׁ֣ר לְאַהֲרֹ֔ן כַּאֲשֶׁ֛ר צִוָּ֥ה יְהוָ֖ה אֶת־מֹשֶֽׁה׃ פ 2 וַיַּ֖עַשׂ אֶת־הָאֵפֹ֑ד זָהָ֗ב תְּכֵ֧לֶת וְאַרְגָּמָ֛ן וְתוֹלַ֥עַת שָׁנִ֖י וְשֵׁ֥שׁ מָשְׁזָֽר׃ 3 וַֽיְרַקְּע֞וּ אֶת־פַּחֵ֣י הַזָּהָב֮ וְקִצֵּ֣ץ פְּתִילִם֒ לַעֲשׂ֗וֹת בְּת֤וֹךְ הַתְּכֵ֙לֶת֙ וּבְת֣וֹךְ הָֽאַרְגָּמָ֔ן וּבְת֛וֹךְ תּוֹלַ֥עַת הַשָּׁנִ֖י וּבְת֣וֹךְ הַשֵּׁ֑שׁ מַעֲשֵׂ֖ה חֹשֵֽׁב׃ 4 כְּתֵפֹ֥ת עָֽשׂוּ־ל֖וֹ חֹבְרֹ֑ת עַל־שְׁנֵ֥י קצוותו קְצוֹתָ֖יו חֻבָּֽר׃ 5 וְחֵ֨שֶׁב אֲפֻדָּת֜וֹ אֲשֶׁ֣ר עָלָ֗יו מִמֶּ֣נּוּ הוּא֙ כְּמַעֲשֵׂ֔הוּ זָהָ֗ב תְּכֵ֧לֶת וְאַרְגָּמָ֛ן וְתוֹלַ֥עַת שָׁנִ֖י וְשֵׁ֣שׁ מָשְׁזָ֑ר כַּאֲשֶׁ֛ר צִוָּ֥ה יְהוָ֖ה אֶת־מֹשֶֽׁה׃ 6 וַֽיַּעֲשׂוּ֙ אֶת־אַבְנֵ֣י הַשֹּׁ֔הַם מֻסַבֹּ֖ת מִשְׁבְּצֹ֣ת זָהָ֑ב מְפֻתָּחֹת֙ פִּתּוּחֵ֣י חוֹתָ֔ם עַל־שְׁמ֖וֹת בְּנֵ֣י יִשְׂרָאֵֽל׃ 7 וַיָּ֣שֶׂם אֹתָ֗ם עַ֚ל כִּתְפֹ֣ת

---

a   *See 36.8.*
b   *Here and elsewhere in this chapter the singular active verb (lit.* "he made") *is used impersonally.*

remembrance for the Israelites—as the Lord had commanded Moses.

8The breastpiece was made in the style of the ephod: of gold, blue, purple, and crimson yarns, and fine twisted linen. 9It was square; they made the breastpiece doubled—a span in length and a span in width, doubled. 10They set in it four rows of stones. The first row was a row of *car-nelian, chrysolite, and emerald; 11the second row: a turquoise, a sapphire, and an amethyst; 12the third row: a jacinth, an agate, and a crystal; 13and the fourth row: a beryl, a lapis lazuli, and a jasper. They were encircled in their mountings with frames of gold. 14The stones corresponded [in number] to the names of the sons of Israel: twelve, corresponding to their names; engraved like seals, each with its name, for the twelve tribes.

15On the breastpiece they made braided chains of corded work in pure gold. 16They made two frames of gold and two rings of gold, and fastened the two rings at the two ends of the breastpiece, 17attaching the two golden cords to the two rings at the ends of the breastpiece. 18They then fastened the two ends of the cords to the two frames, attaching them to the shoulder-pieces of the ephod, at the front. 19They made two rings of gold and attached them to the two ends of the breastpiece, at its inner edge, which faced the ephod. 20They made two other rings of gold and fastened them on the front of the ephod, low on the two shoulder-pieces, close to its seam above the dec-orated band. 21The breastpiece was held in place by a cord of blue from its rings to the rings of the ephod, so that the breastpiece rested on the decorated band and did not come loose from the ephod—as the Lord had commanded Moses.

22The robe for the ephod was made of woven

הָאֵפֹד אַבְנֵי זִכָּרֹן לִבְנֵי יִשְׂרָאֵל כַּאֲשֶׁר צִוָּה יְהוָה אֶת־מֹשֶׁה: פ 8וַיַּעַשׂ אֶת־הַחֹשֶׁן מַעֲשֵׂה חֹשֵׁב כְּמַעֲשֵׂה אֵפֹד זָהָב תְּכֵלֶת וְאַרְגָּמָן וְתוֹלַעַת שָׁנִי וְשֵׁשׁ מָשְׁזָר: 9רָבוּעַ הָיָה כָּפוּל עָשׂוּ אֶת־הַחֹשֶׁן זֶרֶת אָרְכּוֹ וְזֶרֶת רָחְבּוֹ כָּפוּל: 10וַיְמַלְאוּ־בוֹ אַרְבָּעָה טוּרֵי אָבֶן טוּר אֹדֶם פִּטְדָה וּבָרֶקֶת הַטּוּר הָאֶחָד: 11וְהַטּוּר הַשֵּׁנִי נֹפֶךְ סַפִּיר וְיָהֲלֹם: 12וְהַטּוּר הַשְּׁלִישִׁי לֶשֶׁם שְׁבוֹ וְאַחְלָמָה: 13וְהַטּוּר הָרְבִיעִי תַּרְשִׁישׁ שֹׁהַם וְיָשְׁפֵה מוּסַבֹּת מִשְׁבְּצוֹת זָהָב בְּמִלֻּאֹתָם: 14וְהָאֲבָנִים עַל־שְׁמֹת בְּנֵי־יִשְׂרָאֵל הֵנָּה שְׁתֵּים עֶשְׂרֵה עַל־שְׁמֹתָם פִּתּוּחֵי חֹתָם אִישׁ עַל־שְׁמוֹ לִשְׁנֵים עָשָׂר שָׁבֶט: 15וַיַּעֲשׂוּ עַל־הַחֹשֶׁן שַׁרְשְׁרֹת גַּבְלֻת מַעֲשֵׂה עֲבֹת זָהָב טָהוֹר: 16וַיַּעֲשׂוּ שְׁתֵּי מִשְׁבְּצֹת זָהָב וּשְׁתֵּי טַבְּעֹת זָהָב וַיִּתְּנוּ אֶת־שְׁתֵּי הַטַּבָּעֹת עַל־שְׁנֵי קְצוֹת הַחֹשֶׁן: 17וַיִּתְּנוּ שְׁתֵּי הָעֲבֹתֹת הַזָּהָב עַל־שְׁתֵּי הַטַּבָּעֹת עַל־קְצוֹת הַחֹשֶׁן: 18וְאֵת שְׁתֵּי קְצוֹת שְׁתֵּי הָעֲבֹתֹת נָתְנוּ עַל־שְׁתֵּי הַמִּשְׁבְּצֹת וַיִּתְּנֻם עַל־כִּתְפֹת הָאֵפֹד אֶל־מוּל פָּנָיו: 19וַיַּעֲשׂוּ שְׁתֵּי טַבְּעֹת זָהָב וַיָּשִׂימוּ עַל־שְׁנֵי קְצוֹת הַחֹשֶׁן עַל־שְׂפָתוֹ אֲשֶׁר אֶל־עֵבֶר הָאֵפֹד בָּיְתָה: 20וַיַּעֲשׂוּ שְׁתֵּי טַבְּעֹת זָהָב וַיִּתְּנֻם עַל־שְׁתֵּי כִתְפֹת הָאֵפֹד מִלְמַטָּה מִמּוּל פָּנָיו לְעֻמַּת מֶחְבַּרְתּוֹ מִמַּעַל לְחֵשֶׁב הָאֵפֹד: 21וַיִּרְכְּסוּ אֶת־הַחֹשֶׁן מִטַּבְּעֹתָיו אֶל־טַבְּעֹת הָאֵפֹד בִּפְתִיל תְּכֵלֶת לִהְיֹת עַל־חֵשֶׁב הָאֵפֹד וְלֹא־יִזַּח הַחֹשֶׁן מֵעַל הָאֵפֹד כַּאֲשֶׁר צִוָּה יְהוָה אֶת־מֹשֶׁה: 22וַיַּעַשׂ אֶת־מְעִיל הָאֵפֹד מַעֲשֵׂה אֹרֵג

c See note at 28.17.

work, of pure blue.*d* 23The opening of the robe, in the middle of it, was like the opening of a coat of mail, with a binding around the opening, so that it would not tear. 24On the hem of the robe they made pomegranates of blue, purple, and crimson yarns, twisted. 25They also made bells of pure gold, and attached the bells between the pomegranates, all around the hem of the robe, between the pomegranates: 26a bell and a pomegranate, a bell and a pomegranate, all around the hem of the robe for officiating in—as the Lord had commanded Moses.

27They made the tunics of fine linen, of woven work, for Aaron and his sons; 28and the headdress of fine linen, and the decorated turbans of fine linen, and the linen breeches of fine twisted linen; 29and sashes of fine twisted linen, blue, purple, and crimson yarns, done in embroidery—as the Lord had commanded Moses.

30They made the frontlet for the holy diadem of pure gold, and incised upon it the seal inscription: "Holy to the Lord." 31They attached to it a cord of blue to fix it upon the headdress above—as the Lord had commanded Moses.

32Thus was completed all the work of the Tabernacle of the Tent of Meeting. The Israelites did so; just as the Lord had commanded Moses, so they did.

33Then they brought the Tabernacle to Moses, with the Tent and all its furnishings: its clasps, its planks, its bars, its posts, and its sockets; 34the covering of tanned ram skins, the covering of dolphin skins, and the curtain for the screen; 35the Ark of the Pact and its poles, and the cover; 36the table and all its utensils, and the bread of display; 37the pure lampstand,*e* its lamps—lamps in due order—and all its fittings, and the oil for lighting; 38the altar of gold, the

---

d   See note at 28.31.
e   See note at 31.8.

23 וּפִֽי־הַמְּעִיל בְּתוֹכוֹ כְּפִי תַחְרָא שָׂפָה לְפִיו סָבִיב לֹא יִקָּרֵֽעַ: 24 וַֽיַּעֲשׂוּ עַל־שׁוּלֵי הַמְּעִיל רִמּוֹנֵי תְּכֵלֶת וְאַרְגָּמָן וְתוֹלַעַת שָׁנִי מָשְׁזָֽר: 25 וַיַּעֲשׂוּ פַעֲמֹנֵי זָהָב טָהוֹר וַיִּתְּנוּ אֶת־הַפַּֽעֲמֹנִים בְּתוֹךְ הָרִמֹּנִים עַל־שׁוּלֵי הַמְּעִיל סָבִיב בְּתוֹךְ הָרִמֹּנִֽים: 26 פַּעֲמֹן וְרִמֹּן פַּֽעֲמֹן וְרִמֹּן עַל־שׁוּלֵי הַמְּעִיל סָבִיב לְשָׁרֵת כַּאֲשֶׁר צִוָּה יְהוָֹה אֶת־מֹשֶֽׁה: ס 27 וַֽיַּעֲשׂוּ אֶת־הַכָּתְנֹת שֵׁשׁ מַעֲשֵׂה אֹרֵג לְאַהֲרֹן וּלְבָנָֽיו: 28 וְאֵת הַמִּצְנֶפֶת שֵׁשׁ וְאֶת־פַּאֲרֵי הַמִּגְבָּעֹת שֵׁשׁ וְאֶת־מִכְנְסֵי הַבָּד שֵׁשׁ מָשְׁזָֽר: 29 וְאֶת־הָאַבְנֵט שֵׁשׁ מָשְׁזָר וּתְכֵלֶת וְאַרְגָּמָן וְתוֹלַעַת שָׁנִי מַעֲשֵׂה רֹקֵם כַּאֲשֶׁר צִוָּה יְהוָֹה אֶת־מֹשֶֽׁה: ס 30 וַֽיַּעֲשׂוּ אֶת־צִיץ נֵֽזֶר־הַקֹּדֶשׁ זָהָב טָהוֹר וַיִּכְתְּבוּ עָלָיו מִכְתַּב פִּתּוּחֵי חוֹתָם קֹדֶשׁ לַֽיהוָֹה: 31 וַיִּתְּנוּ עָלָיו פְּתִיל תְּכֵלֶת לָתֵת עַל־הַמִּצְנֶפֶת מִלְמָעְלָה כַּאֲשֶׁר צִוָּה יְהוָֹה אֶת־מֹשֶֽׁה: ס

32 וַתֵּכֶל כָּל־עֲבֹדַת מִשְׁכַּן אֹהֶל מוֹעֵד וַיַּֽעֲשׂוּ בְּנֵי יִשְׂרָאֵל כְּכֹל אֲשֶׁר צִוָּה יְהוָֹה אֶת־מֹשֶׁה כֵּן עָשֽׂוּ: פ 33 וַיָּבִיאוּ אֶת־הַמִּשְׁכָּן אֶל־מֹשֶׁה אֶת־הָאֹהֶל וְאֶת־כָּל־כֵּלָיו קְרָסָיו קְרָשָׁיו בְּרִיחָו בְּרִיחָיו וְעַמֻּדָיו וַאֲדָנָֽיו: 34 וְאֶת־מִכְסֵה עוֹרֹת הָֽאֵילִם הַֽמְאָדָּמִים וְאֶת־מִכְסֵה עֹרֹת הַתְּחָשִׁים וְאֵת פָּרֹכֶת הַמָּסָֽךְ: 35 אֶת־אֲרֹן הָעֵדֻת וְאֶת־בַּדָּיו וְאֵת הַכַּפֹּֽרֶת: 36 אֶת־הַשֻּׁלְחָן אֶת־כָּל־כֵּלָיו וְאֵת לֶחֶם הַפָּנִֽים: 37 אֶת־הַמְּנֹרָה הַטְּהֹרָה אֶת־נֵרֹתֶיהָ נֵרֹת הַמַּֽעֲרָכָה וְאֶת־כָּל־כֵּלֶיהָ וְאֵת שֶׁמֶן הַמָּאֽוֹר: 38 וְאֶת

oil for anointing, the aromatic incense, and the screen for the entrance of the Tent; 39the copper altar with its copper grating, its poles and all its utensils, and the laver and its stand; 40the hangings of the enclosure, its posts and its sockets, the screen for the gate of the enclosure, its cords and its pegs—all the furnishings for the service of the Tabernacle, the Tent of Meeting; 41the service vestments for officiating in the sanctuary, the sacral vestments of Aaron the priest, and the vestments of his sons for priestly service. 42Just as the LORD had commanded Moses, so the Israelites had done all the work. 43And when Moses saw that they had performed all the tasks—as the LORD had commanded, so they had done—Moses blessed them.

40 And the LORD spoke to Moses, saying: 2On the first day of the first month you shall set up the Tabernacle of the Tent of Meeting. 3Place there the Ark of the Pact, and screen off the ark with the curtain. 4Bring in the table and lay out its due setting; bring in the lampstand and light its lamps; 5and place the gold altar of incense before the Ark of the Pact. Then put up the screen for the entrance of the Tabernacle.

6You shall place the altar of burnt offering before the entrance of the Tabernacle of the Tent of Meeting. 7Place the laver between the Tent of Meeting and the altar, and put water in it. 8Set up the enclosure round about, and put in place the screen for the gate of the enclosure.

9You shall take the anointing oil and anoint the Tabernacle and all that is in it to consecrate it and all its furnishings, so that it shall be holy. 10Then anoint the altar of burnt offering and all its utensils to consecrate the altar, so that the altar shall be most holy. 11And anoint the laver and its stand to consecrate it.

מִזְבַּ֤ח הַזָּהָב֙ וְאֵת֙ שֶׁ֣מֶן הַמִּשְׁחָ֔ה וְאֵ֖ת קְטֹ֣רֶת הַסַּמִּ֑ים וְאֵ֕ת מָסַ֖ךְ פֶּ֥תַח הָאֹֽהֶל: 39 אֵ֣ת | מִזְבַּ֣ח הַנְּחֹ֗שֶׁת וְאֶת־מִכְבַּ֤ר הַנְּחֹ֙שֶׁת֙ אֲשֶׁר־ל֔וֹ אֶת־בַּדָּ֖יו וְאֶת־כָּל־כֵּלָ֑יו אֶת־הַכִּיֹּ֖ר וְאֶת־כַּנּֽוֹ: 40 אֵת֩ קַלְעֵ֨י הֶחָצֵ֜ר אֶת־עַמֻּדֶ֣יהָ וְאֶת־אֲדָנֶ֗יהָ וְאֶת־הַמָּסָךְ֙ לְשַׁ֣עַר הֶֽחָצֵ֔ר אֶת־מֵיתָרָ֖יו וִיתֵדֹתֶ֑יהָ וְאֵ֗ת כָּל־כְּלֵ֛י עֲבֹדַ֥ת הַמִּשְׁכָּ֖ן לְאֹ֥הֶל מוֹעֵֽד: 41 אֶת־בִּגְדֵ֥י הַשְּׂרָ֖ד לְשָׁרֵ֣ת בַּקֹּ֑דֶשׁ אֶת־בִּגְדֵ֤י הַקֹּ֙דֶשׁ֙ לְאַהֲרֹ֣ן הַכֹּהֵ֔ן וְאֶת־בִּגְדֵ֥י בָנָ֖יו לְכַהֵֽן: 42 כְּכֹ֛ל אֲשֶׁר־צִוָּ֥ה יְהֹוָ֖ה אֶת־מֹשֶׁ֑ה כֵּ֤ן עָשׂוּ֙ בְּנֵ֣י יִשְׂרָאֵ֔ל אֵ֖ת כָּל־הָעֲבֹדָֽה: 43 וַיַּ֨רְא מֹשֶׁ֜ה אֶת־כָּל־הַמְּלָאכָ֗ה וְהִנֵּה֙ עָשׂ֣וּ אֹתָ֔הּ כַּאֲשֶׁ֛ר צִוָּ֥ה יְהֹוָ֖ה כֵּ֣ן עָשׂ֑וּ וַיְבָ֥רֶךְ אֹתָ֖ם מֹשֶֽׁה: פ

מ וַיְדַבֵּ֥ר יְהֹוָ֖ה אֶל־מֹשֶׁ֥ה לֵּאמֹֽר: 2 בְּיוֹם־הַחֹ֥דֶשׁ הָרִאשׁ֖וֹן בְּאֶחָ֣ד לַחֹ֑דֶשׁ תָּקִ֕ים אֶת־מִשְׁכַּ֖ן אֹ֥הֶל מוֹעֵֽד: 3 וְשַׂמְתָּ֣ שָׁ֔ם אֵ֖ת אֲר֣וֹן הָעֵד֑וּת וְסַכֹּתָ֥ עַל־הָאָרֹ֖ן אֶת־הַפָּרֹֽכֶת: 4 וְהֵבֵאתָ֙ אֶת־הַשֻּׁלְחָ֔ן וְעָרַכְתָּ֖ אֶת־עֶרְכּ֑וֹ וְהֵבֵאתָ֙ אֶת־הַמְּנֹרָ֔ה וְהַעֲלֵיתָ֖ אֶת־נֵרֹתֶֽיהָ: 5 וְנָתַתָּ֞ה אֶת־מִזְבַּ֤ח הַזָּהָב֙ לִקְטֹ֔רֶת לִפְנֵ֖י אֲר֣וֹן הָעֵדֻ֑ת וְשַׂמְתָּ֛ אֶת־מָסַ֥ךְ הַפֶּ֖תַח לַמִּשְׁכָּֽן: 6 וְנָ֣תַתָּ֔ה אֵ֖ת מִזְבַּ֣ח הָעֹלָ֑ה לִפְנֵ֕י פֶּ֖תַח מִשְׁכַּ֥ן אֹֽהֶל־מוֹעֵֽד: 7 וְנָֽתַתָּ֙ אֶת־הַכִּיֹּ֔ר בֵּֽין־אֹ֥הֶל מוֹעֵ֖ד וּבֵ֣ין הַמִּזְבֵּ֑חַ וְנָתַתָּ֥ שָׁ֖ם מָֽיִם: 8 וְשַׂמְתָּ֥ אֶת־הֶחָצֵ֖ר סָבִ֑יב וְנָ֣תַתָּ֔ אֶת־מָסַ֖ךְ שַׁ֥עַר הֶחָצֵֽר: 9 וְלָקַחְתָּ֙ אֶת־שֶׁ֣מֶן הַמִּשְׁחָ֔ה וּמָשַׁחְתָּ֥ אֶת־הַמִּשְׁכָּ֖ן וְאֶת־כָּל־אֲשֶׁר־בּ֑וֹ וְקִדַּשְׁתָּ֥ אֹת֛וֹ וְאֶת־כָּל־כֵּלָ֖יו וְהָ֥יָה קֹֽדֶשׁ: 10 וּמָשַׁחְתָּ֛ אֶת־מִזְבַּ֥ח הָעֹלָ֖ה וְאֶת־כָּל־כֵּלָ֑יו וְקִדַּשְׁתָּ֙ אֶת־הַמִּזְבֵּ֔חַ וְהָיָ֥ה הַמִּזְבֵּ֖חַ

12You shall bring Aaron and his sons forward to the entrance of the Tent of Meeting and wash them with the water. 13Put the sacral vestments on Aaron, and anoint him and consecrate him, that he may serve Me as priest. 14Then bring his sons forward, put tunics on them, 15and anoint them as you have anointed their father, that they may serve Me as priests. This their anointing shall serve them for everlasting priesthood throughout the ages.

16This Moses did; just as the LORD had commanded him, so he did.

17In the first month of the second year, on the first of the month, the Tabernacle was set up. 18Moses set up the Tabernacle, placing its sockets, setting up its planks, inserting its bars, and erecting its posts. 19He spread the tent over the Tabernacle, placing the covering of the tent on top of it—just as the LORD had commanded Moses.

20He took the Pact and placed it in the ark; he fixed the poles to the ark, placed the cover on top of the ark, 21and brought the ark inside the Tabernacle. Then he put up the curtain for screening, and screened off the Ark of the Pact—just as the LORD had commanded Moses.

22He placed the table in the Tent of Meeting, outside the curtain, on the north side of the Tabernacle. 23Upon it he laid out the setting of bread before the LORD—as the LORD had commanded Moses. 24He placed the lampstand in the Tent of Meeting opposite the table, on the south side of the Tabernacle. 25And he lit the lamps before the LORD—as the LORD had commanded Moses. 26He placed the altar of gold in the Tent of Meeting, before the curtain. 27On it he burned aromatic incense—as the LORD had commanded Moses.

קֹדֶשׁ קָדָשִׁים: 11 וּמָשַׁחְתָּ אֶת־הַכִּיֹּר וְאֶת־
כַּנּוֹ וְקִדַּשְׁתָּ אֹתוֹ: 12 וְהִקְרַבְתָּ אֶת־אַהֲרֹן וְאֶת־בָּנָיו אֶל־פֶּתַח
אֹהֶל מוֹעֵד וְרָחַצְתָּ אֹתָם בַּמָּיִם: 13 וְהִלְבַּשְׁתָּ אֶת־אַהֲרֹן אֵת בִּגְדֵי הַקֹּדֶשׁ
וּמָשַׁחְתָּ אֹתוֹ וְקִדַּשְׁתָּ אֹתוֹ וְכִהֵן לִי: 14 וְאֶת־בָּנָיו תַּקְרִיב וְהִלְבַּשְׁתָּ אֹתָם
כֻּתֳּנֹת: 15 וּמָשַׁחְתָּ אֹתָם כַּאֲשֶׁר מָשַׁחְתָּ אֶת־אֲבִיהֶם וְכִהֲנוּ לִי וְהָיְתָה לִהְיֹת לָהֶם
מָשְׁחָתָם לִכְהֻנַּת עוֹלָם לְדֹרֹתָם: 16 וַיַּעַשׂ מֹשֶׁה כְּכֹל אֲשֶׁר צִוָּה יְהֹוָה אֹתוֹ
כֵּן עָשָׂה: ס

17 וַיְהִי בַּחֹדֶשׁ הָרִאשׁוֹן בַּשָּׁנָה הַשֵּׁנִית בְּאֶחָד לַחֹדֶשׁ הוּקַם הַמִּשְׁכָּן: 18 וַיָּקֶם
מֹשֶׁה אֶת־הַמִּשְׁכָּן וַיִּתֵּן אֶת־אֲדָנָיו וַיָּשֶׂם אֶת־קְרָשָׁיו וַיִּתֵּן אֶת־בְּרִיחָיו וַיָּקֶם אֶת־
עַמּוּדָיו: 19 וַיִּפְרֹשׂ אֶת־הָאֹהֶל עַל־הַמִּשְׁכָּן וַיָּשֶׂם אֶת־מִכְסֵה הָאֹהֶל עָלָיו
מִלְמָעְלָה כַּאֲשֶׁר צִוָּה יְהֹוָה אֶת־מֹשֶׁה: ס
20 וַיִּקַּח וַיִּתֵּן אֶת־הָעֵדֻת אֶל־הָאָרֹן וַיָּשֶׂם אֶת־הַבַּדִּים עַל־הָאָרֹן וַיִּתֵּן אֶת־הַכַּפֹּרֶת
עַל־הָאָרֹן מִלְמָעְלָה: 21 וַיָּבֵא אֶת־הָאָרֹן אֶל־הַמִּשְׁכָּן וַיָּשֶׂם אֵת פָּרֹכֶת הַמָּסָךְ וַיָּסֶךְ
עַל אֲרוֹן הָעֵדוּת כַּאֲשֶׁר צִוָּה יְהֹוָה אֶת־מֹשֶׁה: ס
22 וַיִּתֵּן אֶת־הַשֻּׁלְחָן בְּאֹהֶל מוֹעֵד עַל יֶרֶךְ הַמִּשְׁכָּן צָפֹנָה מִחוּץ לַפָּרֹכֶת: 23 וַיַּעֲרֹךְ
עָלָיו עֵרֶךְ לֶחֶם לִפְנֵי יְהֹוָה כַּאֲשֶׁר צִוָּה יְהֹוָה אֶת־מֹשֶׁה: ס 24 וַיָּשֶׂם אֶת־הַמְּנֹרָה בְּאֹהֶל מוֹעֵד נֹכַח הַשֻּׁלְחָן עַל
יֶרֶךְ הַמִּשְׁכָּן נֶגְבָּה: 25 וַיַּעַל הַנֵּרֹת לִפְנֵי יְהֹוָה כַּאֲשֶׁר צִוָּה יְהֹוָה אֶת־מֹשֶׁה: ס
26 וַיָּשֶׂם אֶת־מִזְבַּח הַזָּהָב בְּאֹהֶל מוֹעֵד

204

28Then he put up the screen for the entrance of the Tabernacle. 29At the entrance of the Tabernacle of the Tent of Meeting he placed the altar of burnt offering. On it he offered up the burnt offering and the meal offering—as the Lord had commanded Moses. 30He placed the laver between the Tent of Meeting and the altar, and put water in it for washing. 31From it Moses and Aaron and his sons would wash their hands and feet; 32they washed when they entered the Tent of Meeting and when they approached the altar—as the Lord had commanded Moses. 33And he set up the enclosure around the Tabernacle and the altar, and put up the screen for the gate of the enclosure.

When Moses had finished the work, 34the cloud covered the Tent of Meeting, and the Presence of the Lord filled the Tabernacle. 35Moses could not enter the Tent of Meeting, because the cloud had settled upon it and the Presence of the Lord filled the Tabernacle. 36When the cloud lifted from the Tabernacle, the Israelites would set out, on their various journeys; 37but if the cloud did not lift, they would not set out until such time as it did lift. 38For over the Tabernacle a cloud of the Lord rested by day, and fire would appear in it[a] by night, in the view of all the house of Israel throughout their journeys.

לִפְנֵי הַפָּרֹכֶת: 27 וַיַּקְטֵר עָלָיו קְטֹרֶת סַמִּים כַּאֲשֶׁר צִוָּה יְהֹוָה אֶת־מֹשֶׁה: פ 28 וַיָּשֶׂם אֶת־מָסַךְ הַפֶּתַח לַמִּשְׁכָּן: 29 וְאֵת מִזְבַּח הָעֹלָה שָׂם פֶּתַח מִשְׁכַּן אֹהֶל־מוֹעֵד וַיַּעַל עָלָיו אֶת־הָעֹלָה וְאֶת־הַמִּנְחָה כַּאֲשֶׁר צִוָּה יְהֹוָה אֶת־מֹשֶׁה: ס 30 וַיָּשֶׂם אֶת־הַכִּיֹּר בֵּין־אֹהֶל מוֹעֵד וּבֵין הַמִּזְבֵּחַ וַיִּתֵּן שָׁמָּה מַיִם לְרָחְצָה: 31 וְרָחֲצוּ מִמֶּנּוּ מֹשֶׁה וְאַהֲרֹן וּבָנָיו אֶת־יְדֵיהֶם וְאֶת־רַגְלֵיהֶם: 32 בְּבֹאָם אֶל־אֹהֶל מוֹעֵד וּבְקָרְבָתָם אֶל־הַמִּזְבֵּחַ יִרְחָצוּ כַּאֲשֶׁר צִוָּה יְהֹוָה אֶת־מֹשֶׁה: ס 33 וַיָּקֶם אֶת־הֶחָצֵר סָבִיב לַמִּשְׁכָּן וְלַמִּזְבֵּחַ וַיִּתֵּן אֶת־מָסַךְ שַׁעַר הֶחָצֵר

וַיְכַל מֹשֶׁה אֶת־הַמְּלָאכָה: פ 34 וַיְכַס הֶעָנָן אֶת־אֹהֶל מוֹעֵד וּכְבוֹד יְהֹוָה מָלֵא אֶת־הַמִּשְׁכָּן: 35 וְלֹא־יָכֹל מֹשֶׁה לָבוֹא אֶל־אֹהֶל מוֹעֵד כִּי־שָׁכַן עָלָיו הֶעָנָן וּכְבוֹד יְהֹוָה מָלֵא אֶת־הַמִּשְׁכָּן: 36 וּבְהֵעָלוֹת הֶעָנָן מֵעַל הַמִּשְׁכָּן יִסְעוּ בְּנֵי יִשְׂרָאֵל בְּכֹל מַסְעֵיהֶם: 37 וְאִם־לֹא יֵעָלֶה הֶעָנָן וְלֹא יִסְעוּ עַד־יוֹם הֵעָלֹתוֹ: 38 כִּי עֲנַן יְהֹוָה עַל־הַמִּשְׁכָּן יוֹמָם וְאֵשׁ תִּהְיֶה לַיְלָה בּוֹ לְעֵינֵי כָל־בֵּית־יִשְׂרָאֵל בְּכָל־מַסְעֵיהֶם: *

תם ונשלם תהילה לאל בורא עולם

---

a I.e., in the cloud.

למערבאי סכום הפסוקים של ספר 1,209 וחציו   v. 38. 22.27

LEVITICUS

VA-YIKRA'

1 The LORD called to Moses and spoke to him from the Tent of Meeting, saying: ²Speak to the Israelite people, and say to them:

When any of you presents an offering of cattle to the LORD, a-he shall choose his-a offering from the herd or from the flock.

³If his offering is a burnt offering from the herd, he shall make his offering a male without blemish. He shall bring it to the entrance of the Tent of Meeting, for acceptance in his behalf before the LORD. ⁴He shall lay his hand upon the head of the burnt offering, that it may be acceptable in his behalf, in expiation for him. ⁵The bull shall be slaughtered before the LORD; and Aaron's sons, the priests, shall offer the blood, dashing the blood against all sides of the altar which is at the entrance of the Tent of Meeting. ⁶The burnt offering shall be flayed and cut up into sections. ⁷The sons of Aaron the priest shall put fire on the altar and lay out wood upon the fire; ⁸and Aaron's sons, the priests, shall lay out the sections, with the head and the suet, on the wood that is on the fire upon the altar. ⁹Its entrails and legs shall be washed with water, and the priest shall turn the whole into smoke on the altar as a burnt offering, an offering by fire of pleasing odor to the LORD.

¹⁰If his offering for a burnt offering is from the flock, of sheep or of goats, he shall make his offering a male without blemish. ¹¹It shall be slaughtered before the LORD on the north side of the altar, and Aaron's sons, the priests, shall dash its blood against all sides of the altar.

a-a Lit. "you shall offer your."

וַיִּקְרָא

אַ וַיִּקְרָא* אֶל־מֹשֶׁה וַיְדַבֵּר יְהֹוָה אֵלָיו מֵאֹהֶל מוֹעֵד לֵאמֹר: 2 דַּבֵּר אֶל־בְּנֵי יִשְׂרָאֵל וְאָמַרְתָּ אֲלֵהֶם אָדָם כִּי־יַקְרִיב מִכֶּם קָרְבָּן לַיהֹוָה מִן־הַבְּהֵמָה מִן־הַבָּקָר וּמִן־הַצֹּאן תַּקְרִיבוּ אֶת־קָרְבַּנְכֶם: 3 אִם־עֹלָה קָרְבָּנוֹ מִן־הַבָּקָר זָכָר תָּמִים יַקְרִיבֶנּוּ אֶל־פֶּתַח אֹהֶל מוֹעֵד יַקְרִיב אֹתוֹ לִרְצֹנוֹ לִפְנֵי יְהֹוָה: 4 וְסָמַךְ יָדוֹ עַל רֹאשׁ הָעֹלָה וְנִרְצָה לוֹ לְכַפֵּר עָלָיו: 5 וְשָׁחַט אֶת־בֶּן הַבָּקָר לִפְנֵי יְהֹוָה וְהִקְרִיבוּ בְּנֵי אַהֲרֹן הַכֹּהֲנִים אֶת־הַדָּם וְזָרְקוּ אֶת־הַדָּם עַל־הַמִּזְבֵּחַ סָבִיב אֲשֶׁר־פֶּתַח אֹהֶל מוֹעֵד: 6 וְהִפְשִׁיט אֶת־הָעֹלָה וְנִתַּח אֹתָהּ לִנְתָחֶיהָ: 7 וְנָתְנוּ בְּנֵי אַהֲרֹן הַכֹּהֵן אֵשׁ עַל־הַמִּזְבֵּחַ וְעָרְכוּ עֵצִים עַל־הָאֵשׁ: 8 וְעָרְכוּ בְּנֵי אַהֲרֹן הַכֹּהֲנִים אֵת הַנְּתָחִים אֶת־הָרֹאשׁ וְאֶת־הַפָּדֶר עַל־הָעֵצִים אֲשֶׁר עַל־הָאֵשׁ אֲשֶׁר עַל־הַמִּזְבֵּחַ: 9 וְקִרְבּוֹ וּכְרָעָיו יִרְחַץ בַּמָּיִם וְהִקְטִיר הַכֹּהֵן אֶת־הַכֹּל הַמִּזְבֵּחָה עֹלָה אִשֵּׁה רֵיחַ־נִיחוֹחַ לַיהֹוָה: ס

10 וְאִם־מִן־הַצֹּאן קָרְבָּנוֹ מִן־הַכְּשָׂבִים אוֹ מִן־הָעִזִּים לְעֹלָה זָכָר תָּמִים יַקְרִיבֶנּוּ: 11 וְשָׁחַט אֹתוֹ עַל יֶרֶךְ הַמִּזְבֵּחַ צָפֹנָה לִפְנֵי יְהֹוָה וְזָרְקוּ בְּנֵי אַהֲרֹן הַכֹּהֲנִים אֶת־דָּמוֹ עַל־הַמִּזְבֵּחַ סָבִיב: 12 וְנִתַּח אֹתוֹ לִנְתָחָיו

אַ זְעִירָא לְפִי נֻסְחִים הַמְקֻבָּלִים v. 1. א׳

¹²When it has been cut up into sections, the priest shall lay them out, with the head and the suet, on the wood that is on the fire upon the altar. ¹³The entrails and the legs shall be washed with water; the priest shall offer up and turn the whole into smoke on the altar. It is a burnt offering, an offering by fire, of pleasing odor to the LORD.

¹⁴If his offering to the LORD is a burnt offering of birds, he shall choose his offering from turtledoves or pigeons. ¹⁵The priest shall bring it to the altar, pinch off its head, and turn it into smoke on the altar; and its blood shall be drained out against the side of the altar. ¹⁶He shall remove its crop with its contents,[b] and cast it into the place of the ashes, at the east side of the altar. ¹⁷The priest shall tear it open by its wings, without severing it, and turn it into smoke on the altar, upon the wood that is on the fire. It is a burnt offering, an offering by fire, of pleasing odor to the LORD.

2 When a person presents an offering of meal to the LORD, his offering shall be of choice flour; he shall pour oil upon it, lay frankincense on it, ²and present it to Aaron's sons, the priests. The priest shall scoop out of it a handful of its choice flour and oil, as well as all of its frankincense; and this token portion he shall turn into smoke on the altar, as an offering by fire, of pleasing odor to the LORD. ³And the remainder of the meal offering shall be for Aaron and his sons, a most holy portion from the LORD's offerings by fire.

⁴When you present an offering of meal baked in the oven, [it shall be of] choice flour: unleavened cakes with oil mixed in, or unleavened wafers spread with oil.

⁵If your offering is a meal offering on a griddle, it shall be of choice flour with oil mixed in,

---

וְאֶת־הָרֹאשׁ וְאֶת־הַפֶּדֶר וְעָרַךְ הַכֹּהֵן אֹתָם
עַל־הָעֵצִים אֲשֶׁר עַל־הָאֵשׁ אֲשֶׁר עַל־
הַמִּזְבֵּחַ: ¹³ וְהַקֶּרֶב וְהַכְּרָעַיִם יִרְחַץ בַּמָּיִם
וְהִקְרִיב הַכֹּהֵן אֶת־הַכֹּל וְהִקְטִיר
הַמִּזְבֵּחָה עֹלָה הוּא אִשֵּׁה רֵיחַ נִיחֹחַ
לַיהוָה: פ
¹⁴ וְאִם מִן־הָעוֹף עֹלָה קָרְבָּנוֹ לַיהוָה
וְהִקְרִיב מִן־הַתֹּרִים אוֹ מִן־בְּנֵי הַיּוֹנָה
אֶת־קָרְבָּנוֹ: ¹⁵ וְהִקְרִיבוֹ הַכֹּהֵן אֶל־הַמִּזְבֵּחַ
וּמָלַק אֶת־רֹאשׁוֹ וְהִקְטִיר הַמִּזְבֵּחָה
וְנִמְצָה דָמוֹ עַל קִיר הַמִּזְבֵּחַ: ¹⁶ וְהֵסִיר
אֶת־מֻרְאָתוֹ בְּנֹצָתָהּ וְהִשְׁלִיךְ אֹתָהּ אֵצֶל
הַמִּזְבֵּחַ קֵדְמָה אֶל־מְקוֹם הַדָּשֶׁן: ¹⁷ וְשִׁסַּע
אֹתוֹ בִכְנָפָיו לֹא יַבְדִּיל וְהִקְטִיר אֹתוֹ
הַכֹּהֵן הַמִּזְבֵּחָה עַל־הָעֵצִים אֲשֶׁר עַל־
הָאֵשׁ עֹלָה הוּא אִשֵּׁה רֵיחַ נִיחֹחַ
לַיהוָה: ס

ב וְנֶפֶשׁ כִּי־תַקְרִיב קָרְבַּן מִנְחָה לַיהוָה
סֹלֶת יִהְיֶה קָרְבָּנוֹ וְיָצַק עָלֶיהָ שֶׁמֶן וְנָתַן
עָלֶיהָ לְבֹנָה: ² וֶהֱבִיאָהּ אֶל־בְּנֵי אַהֲרֹן
הַכֹּהֲנִים וְקָמַץ מִשָּׁם מְלֹא קֻמְצוֹ מִסָּלְתָּהּ
וּמִשַּׁמְנָהּ עַל כָּל־לְבֹנָתָהּ וְהִקְטִיר הַכֹּהֵן
אֶת־אַזְכָּרָתָהּ הַמִּזְבֵּחָה אִשֵּׁה רֵיחַ נִיחֹחַ
לַיהוָה: ³ וְהַנּוֹתֶרֶת מִן־הַמִּנְחָה לְאַהֲרֹן
וּלְבָנָיו קֹדֶשׁ קָדָשִׁים מֵאִשֵּׁי יְהוָה: ס
⁴ וְכִי תַקְרִב קָרְבַּן מִנְחָה מַאֲפֵה תַנּוּר
סֹלֶת חַלּוֹת מַצֹּת בְּלוּלֹת בַּשֶּׁמֶן וּרְקִיקֵי
מַצּוֹת מְשֻׁחִים בַּשָּׁמֶן: ס
⁵ וְאִם־מִנְחָה עַל־הַמַּחֲבַת קָרְבָּנֶךָ סֹלֶת

---

b Others "feathers."

unleavened. 6Break it into bits and pour oil on it; it is a meal offering.

7If your offering is a meal offering in a pan, it shall be made of choice flour in oil.

8When you present to the LORD a meal offering that is made in any of these ways, it shall be brought to the priest who shall take it up to the altar. 9The priest shall remove the token portion from the meal offering and turn it into smoke on the altar as an offering by fire, of pleasing odor to the LORD. 10And the remainder of the meal offering shall be for Aaron and his sons, a most holy portion from the LORD's offerings by fire.

11No meal offering that you offer to the LORD shall be made with leaven, for no leaven or honey may be turned into smoke as an offering by fire to the LORD. 12You may bring them to the LORD as an offering of choice products;a but they shall not be offered up on the altar for a pleasing odor. 13You shall season your every offering of meal with salt; you shall not omit from your meal offering the salt of your covenant with God; with all your offerings you must offer salt.

14If you bring a meal offering of first fruits to the LORD, you shall bring new ears parched with fire, grits of the fresh grain, as your meal offering of first fruits. 15You shall add oil to it and lay frankincense on it; it is a meal offering. 16And the priest shall turn a token portion of it into smoke: some of the grits and oil, with all of the frankincense, as an offering by fire to the LORD.

3

If his offering is a sacrifice of well-beinga—

If he offers of the herd, whether a male or a female, he shall bring before the LORD one without blemish. 2He shall lay his hand upon the

בְּלוּלָה בַשֶּׁמֶן מַצָּה תִהְיֶה: 6 פָּתוֹת אֹתָהּ פִּתִּים וְיָצַקְתָּ עָלֶיהָ שָׁמֶן מִנְחָה הִוא: ס 7 וְאִם־מִנְחַת מַרְחֶשֶׁת קָרְבָּנֶךָ סֹלֶת בַּשֶּׁמֶן תֵּעָשֶׂה: 8 וְהֵבֵאתָ אֶת־הַמִּנְחָה אֲשֶׁר יֵעָשֶׂה מֵאֵלֶּה לַיהוָה וְהִקְרִיבָהּ אֶל־הַכֹּהֵן וְהִגִּישָׁהּ אֶל־הַמִּזְבֵּחַ: 9 וְהֵרִים הַכֹּהֵן מִן־הַמִּנְחָה אֶת־אַזְכָּרָתָהּ וְהִקְטִיר הַמִּזְבֵּחָה אִשֵּׁה רֵיחַ נִיחֹחַ לַיהוָה: 10 וְהַנּוֹתֶרֶת מִן־הַמִּנְחָה לְאַהֲרֹן וּלְבָנָיו קֹדֶשׁ קָדָשִׁים מֵאִשֵּׁי יְהוָה: 11 כָּל־הַמִּנְחָה אֲשֶׁר תַּקְרִיבוּ לַיהוָה לֹא תֵעָשֶׂה חָמֵץ כִּי כָל־שְׂאֹר וְכָל־דְּבַשׁ לֹא־תַקְטִירוּ מִמֶּנּוּ אִשֶּׁה לַיהוָה: 12 קָרְבַּן רֵאשִׁית תַּקְרִיבוּ אֹתָם לַיהוָה וְאֶל־הַמִּזְבֵּחַ לֹא־יַעֲלוּ לְרֵיחַ נִיחֹחַ: 13 וְכָל־קָרְבַּן מִנְחָתְךָ בַּמֶּלַח תִּמְלָח וְלֹא תַשְׁבִּית מֶלַח בְּרִית אֱלֹהֶיךָ מֵעַל מִנְחָתֶךָ עַל כָּל־קָרְבָּנְךָ תַּקְרִיב מֶלַח: ס 14 וְאִם־תַּקְרִיב מִנְחַת בִּכּוּרִים לַיהוָה אָבִיב קָלוּי בָּאֵשׁ גֶּרֶשׂ כַּרְמֶל תַּקְרִיב אֵת מִנְחַת בִּכּוּרֶיךָ: 15 וְנָתַתָּ עָלֶיהָ שֶׁמֶן וְשַׂמְתָּ עָלֶיהָ לְבֹנָה מִנְחָה הִוא: 16 וְהִקְטִיר הַכֹּהֵן אֶת־אַזְכָּרָתָהּ מִגִּרְשָׂהּ וּמִשַּׁמְנָהּ עַל כָּל־לְבֹנָתָהּ אִשֶּׁה לַיהוָה: פ

ג וְאִם־זֶבַח שְׁלָמִים קָרְבָּנוֹ אִם מִן־הַבָּקָר הוּא מַקְרִיב אִם־זָכָר אִם־נְקֵבָה תָּמִים יַקְרִיבֶנּוּ לִפְנֵי יְהוָה: 2 וְסָמַךְ

---

a *Exact meaning of Heb. uncertain.*

a *Others "peace offering." Exact meaning of shelamim uncertain.*

head of his offering and slaughter it at the entrance of the Tent of Meeting; and Aaron's sons,
the priests, shall dash the blood against all sides
of the altar. ³He shall then present from the
sacrifice of well-being, as an offering by fire to
the LORD, the fat that covers the entrails and all
the fat that is about the entrails; ⁴the two kidneys
and the fat that is on them, that is at the loins;
and the protuberance on the liver, which he
shall remove with the kidneys. ⁵Aaron's sons
shall turn these into smoke on the altar, with
the burnt offering which is upon the wood that
is on the fire, as an offering by fire, of pleasing
odor to the LORD.

⁶And if his offering for a sacrifice of well-being
to the LORD is from the flock, whether a male
or a female, he shall offer one without blemish.
⁷If he presents a sheep as his offering, he shall
bring it before the LORD ⁸and lay his hand upon
the head of his offering. It shall be slaughtered
before the Tent of Meeting, and Aaron's sons
shall dash its blood against all sides of the altar.
⁹He shall then present, as an offering by fire to
the LORD, the fat from the sacrifice of well-
being: the whole broad tail, which shall be removed close to the backbone; the fat that covers
the entrails and all the fat that is about the entrails; ¹⁰the two kidneys and the fat that is on
them, that is at the loins; and the protuberance
on the liver, which he shall remove with the kidneys. ¹¹The priest shall turn these into smoke
on the altar as food, an offering by fire to the
LORD.

¹²And if his offering is a goat, he shall bring
it before the LORD ¹³and lay his hand upon its
head. It shall be slaughtered before the Tent of
Meeting, and Aaron's sons shall dash its blood
against all sides of the altar. ¹⁴He shall then present as his offering from it, as an offering by fire
to the LORD, the fat that covers the entrails and
all the fat that is about the entrails; ¹⁵the two

יָדוֹ עַל־רֹאשׁ קָרְבָּנוֹ וּשְׁחָטוֹ פֶּתַח אֹהֶל
מוֹעֵד וְזָרְקוּ בְּנֵי אַהֲרֹן הַכֹּהֲנִים אֶת־
הַדָּם עַל־הַמִּזְבֵּחַ סָבִיב: ³ וְהִקְרִיב מִזֶּבַח
הַשְּׁלָמִים אִשֶּׁה לַיהוָה אֶת־הַחֵלֶב
הַמְכַסֶּה אֶת־הַקֶּרֶב וְאֵת כָּל־הַחֵלֶב אֲשֶׁר
עַל־הַקֶּרֶב: ⁴ וְאֵת שְׁתֵּי הַכְּלָיֹת וְאֶת־
הַחֵלֶב אֲשֶׁר עֲלֵהֶן אֲשֶׁר עַל־הַכְּסָלִים
וְאֶת־הַיֹּתֶרֶת עַל־הַכָּבֵד עַל־הַכְּלָיוֹת
יְסִירֶנָּה: ⁵ וְהִקְטִירוּ אֹתוֹ בְנֵי־אַהֲרֹן
הַמִּזְבֵּחָה עַל־הָעֹלָה אֲשֶׁר עַל־הָעֵצִים
אֲשֶׁר עַל־הָאֵשׁ אִשֵּׁה רֵיחַ נִיחֹחַ
לַיהוָה: פ

⁶ וְאִם־מִן־הַצֹּאן קָרְבָּנוֹ לְזֶבַח שְׁלָמִים
לַיהוָה זָכָר אוֹ נְקֵבָה תָּמִים יַקְרִיבֶנּוּ:
⁷ אִם־כֶּשֶׂב הוּא־מַקְרִיב אֶת־קָרְבָּנוֹ
וְהִקְרִיב אֹתוֹ לִפְנֵי יְהוָה: ⁸ וְסָמַךְ אֶת־יָדוֹ
עַל־רֹאשׁ קָרְבָּנוֹ וְשָׁחַט אֹתוֹ לִפְנֵי אֹהֶל
מוֹעֵד וְזָרְקוּ בְּנֵי אַהֲרֹן אֶת־דָּמוֹ עַל־
הַמִּזְבֵּחַ סָבִיב: ⁹ וְהִקְרִיב מִזֶּבַח הַשְּׁלָמִים
אִשֶּׁה לַיהוָה חֶלְבּוֹ הָאַלְיָה תְמִימָה
לְעֻמַּת הֶעָצֶה יְסִירֶנָּה וְאֶת־הַחֵלֶב
הַמְכַסֶּה אֶת־הַקֶּרֶב וְאֵת כָּל־הַחֵלֶב אֲשֶׁר
עַל־הַקֶּרֶב: ¹⁰ וְאֵת שְׁתֵּי הַכְּלָיֹת וְאֶת־
הַחֵלֶב אֲשֶׁר עֲלֵהֶן אֲשֶׁר עַל־הַכְּסָלִים
וְאֶת־הַיֹּתֶרֶת עַל־הַכָּבֵד עַל־הַכְּלָיֹת
יְסִירֶנָּה: ¹¹ וְהִקְטִירוֹ הַכֹּהֵן הַמִּזְבֵּחָה לֶחֶם
אִשֶּׁה לַיהוָה: פ

¹² וְאִם עֵז קָרְבָּנוֹ וְהִקְרִיבוֹ לִפְנֵי יְהוָה:
¹³ וְסָמַךְ אֶת־יָדוֹ עַל־רֹאשׁוֹ וְשָׁחַט אֹתוֹ
לִפְנֵי אֹהֶל מוֹעֵד וְזָרְקוּ בְּנֵי אַהֲרֹן אֶת־
דָּמוֹ עַל־הַמִּזְבֵּחַ סָבִיב: ¹⁴ וְהִקְרִיב מִמֶּנּוּ
קָרְבָּנוֹ אִשֶּׁה לַיהוָה אֶת־הַחֵלֶב הַמְכַסֶּה
אֶת־הַקֶּרֶב וְאֵת כָּל־הַחֵלֶב אֲשֶׁר עַל־
הַקֶּרֶב: ¹⁵ וְאֵת שְׁתֵּי הַכְּלָיֹת וְאֶת־הַחֵלֶב

kidneys and the fat that is on them, that is at the loins; and the protuberance on the liver, which he shall remove with the kidneys. [16]The priest shall turn these into smoke on the altar as food, an offering by fire, of pleasing odor.

All fat is the LORD's. [17]It is a law for all time throughout the ages, in all your settlements: you must not eat any fat or any blood.

4 The LORD spoke to Moses, saying: [2]Speak to the Israelite people thus:

When a person unwittingly incurs guilt in regard to any of the LORD's commandments about things not to be done, and does one of them—

[3]If it is the anointed priest who has incurred guilt, so that blame falls upon the people, he shall offer for the sin of which he is guilty a bull of the herd without blemish as a sin offering[a] to the LORD. [4]He shall bring the bull to the entrance of the Tent of Meeting, before the Lord, and lay his hand upon the head of the bull. The bull shall be slaughtered before the LORD, [5]and the anointed priest shall take some of the bull's blood and bring it into the Tent of Meeting. [6]The priest shall dip his finger in the blood, and sprinkle of the blood seven times before the LORD, in front of the curtain of the Shrine. [7]The priest shall put some of the blood on the horns of the altar of aromatic incense, which is in the Tent of Meeting, before the LORD; and all the rest of the bull's blood he shall pour out at the base of the altar of burnt offering, which is at the entrance of the Tent of Meeting. [8]He shall remove all the fat from the bull of sin offering: the fat that covers the entrails and all the fat that is about the entrails; [9]the two kidneys and the fat that is on them, that is at the loins; and the protuberance on the liver, which he shall remove with the kidneys—[10]just as it is removed

אֲשֶׁ֣ר עֲלֵהֶ֗ן אֲשֶׁר֙ עַל־הַכְּסָלִ֔ים וְאֶת־הַיֹּתֶ֙רֶת֙ עַל־הַכָּבֵ֔ד עַל־הַכְּלָיֹ֖ת יְסִירֶֽנָּה: [16]וְהִקְטִירָ֥ם הַכֹּהֵ֖ן הַמִּזְבֵּ֑חָה לֶ֤חֶם אִשֶּׁה֙ לְרֵ֣יחַ נִיחֹ֔חַ

כָּל־חֵ֖לֶב לַיהוָֽה: [17]חֻקַּ֤ת עוֹלָם֙ לְדֹרֹ֣תֵיכֶ֔ם בְּכֹ֖ל מֽוֹשְׁבֹֽתֵיכֶ֑ם כָּל־חֵ֥לֶב וְכָל־דָּ֖ם לֹ֥א תֹאכֵֽלוּ: פ

ד וַיְדַבֵּ֥ר יְהוָ֖ה אֶל־מֹשֶׁ֥ה לֵּאמֹֽר: [2]דַּבֵּ֞ר אֶל־בְּנֵ֣י יִשְׂרָאֵל֮ לֵאמֹר֒ נֶ֗פֶשׁ כִּֽי־תֶחֱטָ֤א בִשְׁגָגָה֙ מִכֹּל֙ מִצְוֺ֣ת יְהוָ֔ה אֲשֶׁ֖ר לֹ֣א תֵעָשֶׂ֑ינָה וְעָשָׂ֕ה מֵֽאַחַ֖ת מֵהֵֽנָּה:

[3]אִ֣ם הַכֹּהֵ֧ן הַמָּשִׁ֛יחַ יֶחֱטָ֖א לְאַשְׁמַ֣ת הָעָ֑ם וְהִקְרִ֡יב עַ֣ל חַטָּאתוֹ֩ אֲשֶׁ֨ר חָטָ֜א פַּ֣ר בֶּן־בָּקָ֥ר תָּמִ֛ים לַיהוָ֖ה לְחַטָּֽאת: [4]וְהֵבִ֣יא אֶת־הַפָּ֗ר אֶל־פֶּ֛תַח אֹ֥הֶל מוֹעֵ֖ד לִפְנֵ֣י יְהוָ֑ה וְסָמַ֤ךְ אֶת־יָדוֹ֙ עַל־רֹ֣אשׁ הַפָּ֔ר וְשָׁחַ֥ט אֶת־הַפָּ֖ר לִפְנֵ֥י יְהוָֽה: [5]וְלָקַ֛ח הַכֹּהֵ֥ן הַמָּשִׁ֖יחַ מִדַּ֣ם הַפָּ֑ר וְהֵבִ֥יא אֹתֹ֖ו אֶל־אֹ֥הֶל מוֹעֵֽד: [6]וְטָבַ֧ל הַכֹּהֵ֛ן אֶת־אֶצְבָּע֖וֹ בַּדָּ֑ם וְהִזָּ֨ה מִן־הַדָּ֜ם שֶׁ֤בַע פְּעָמִים֙ לִפְנֵ֣י יְהוָ֔ה אֶת־פְּנֵ֖י פָּרֹ֥כֶת הַקֹּֽדֶשׁ: [7]וְנָתַן֩ הַכֹּהֵ֨ן מִן־הַדָּ֜ם עַל־קַרְנֹ֞ת מִזְבַּ֣ח קְטֹ֣רֶת הַסַּמִּים֮ לִפְנֵ֣י יְהוָה֒ אֲשֶׁ֖ר בְּאֹ֣הֶל מוֹעֵ֑ד וְאֵ֣ת ׀ כָּל־דַּ֣ם הַפָּ֗ר יִשְׁפֹּךְ֙ אֶל־יְסוֹד֙ מִזְבַּ֣ח הָֽעֹלָ֔ה אֲשֶׁר־פֶּ֖תַח אֹ֥הֶל מוֹעֵֽד: [8]וְאֶת־כָּל־חֵ֛לֶב פַּ֥ר הַֽחַטָּ֖את יָרִ֣ים מִמֶּ֑נּוּ אֶת־הַחֵ֙לֶב֙ הַֽמְכַסֶּ֣ה עַל־הַקֶּ֔רֶב וְאֵת֙ כָּל־הַחֵ֔לֶב אֲשֶׁ֖ר עַל־הַקֶּֽרֶב: [9]וְאֵת֙ שְׁתֵּ֣י הַכְּלָיֹ֔ת וְאֶת־הַחֵ֙לֶב֙ אֲשֶׁ֣ר עֲלֵיהֶ֔ן אֲשֶׁ֖ר עַל־הַכְּסָלִ֑ים וְאֶת־הַיֹּתֶ֙רֶת֙ עַל־הַכָּבֵ֔ד עַל־הַכְּלָיֹ֖ות יְסִירֶֽנָּה: [10]כַּֽאֲשֶׁ֣ר יוּרַ֔ם מִשֹּׁ֖ור זֶ֥בַח הַשְּׁלָמִ֑ים

---

[a] So traditionally; more precisely "offering of purgation."

from the ox of the sacrifice of well-being. The priest shall turn them into smoke on the altar of burnt offering. ¹¹But the hide of the bull, and all its flesh, as well as its head and legs, its entrails and its dung—¹²all the rest of the bull—he shall carry to a clean place outside the camp, to the ash heap, and burn it up in a wood fire; it shall be burned on the ash heap.

¹³If it is the whole community of Israel that has erred and the matter escapes the notice of the congregation, so that they do any of the things which by the LORD's commandments ought not to be done, and they realize their guilt—¹⁴when the sin through which they incurred guilt becomes known, the congregation shall offer a bull of the herd as a sin offering, and bring it before the Tent of Meeting. ¹⁵The elders of the community shall lay their hands upon the head of the bull before the LORD, and the bull shall be slaughtered before the LORD. ¹⁶The anointed priest shall bring some of the blood of the bull into the Tent of Meeting, ¹⁷and the priest shall dip his finger in the blood and sprinkle of it seven times before the LORD, in front of the curtain. ¹⁸Some of the blood he shall put on the horns of the altar which is before the LORD in the Tent of Meeting, and all the rest of the blood he shall pour out at the base of the altar of burnt offering, which is at the entrance of the Tent of Meeting. ¹⁹He shall remove all its fat from it and turn it into smoke on the altar. ²⁰He shall do with this bull just as is done with the [priest's] bull of sin offering; he shall do the same with it. Thus the priest shall make expiation for them, and they shall be forgiven. ²¹He shall carry the bull outside the camp and burn it as he burned the first bull; it is the sin offering of the congregation.

²²In case it is a chieftain who incurs guilt by doing unwittingly any of the things which by the commandment of the LORD his God ought

וְהִקְטִירָם֙ הַכֹּהֵ֔ן עַ֖ל מִזְבַּ֥ח הָעֹלָֽה׃ 11 וְאֶת־ע֤וֹר הַפָּר֙ וְאֶת־כָּל־בְּשָׂר֔וֹ עַל־רֹאשׁ֖וֹ וְעַל־כְּרָעָ֑יו וְקִרְבּ֖וֹ וּפִרְשֽׁוֹ׃ 12 וְהוֹצִ֣יא אֶת־כָּל־הַ֠פָּ֠ר אֶל־מִח֨וּץ לַֽמַּחֲנֶ֜ה אֶל־מָק֤וֹם טָהוֹר֙ אֶל־שֶׁ֣פֶךְ הַדֶּ֔שֶׁן וְשָׂרַ֥ף אֹת֛וֹ עַל־עֵצִ֖ים בָּאֵ֑שׁ עַל־שֶׁ֥פֶךְ הַדֶּ֖שֶׁן יִשָּׂרֵֽף׃ פ 13 וְאִ֨ם כָּל־עֲדַ֤ת יִשְׂרָאֵל֙ יִשְׁגּ֔וּ וְנֶעְלַ֣ם דָּבָ֔ר מֵעֵינֵ֖י הַקָּהָ֑ל וְ֠עָשׂ֠וּ אַחַ֨ת מִכָּל־מִצְוֺ֧ת יְהוָ֛ה אֲשֶׁ֥ר לֹא־תֵעָשֶׂ֖ינָה וְאָשֵֽׁמוּ׃ 14 וְנֽוֹדְעָה֙ הַֽחַטָּ֔את אֲשֶׁ֥ר חָטְא֖וּ עָלֶ֑יהָ וְהִקְרִ֨יבוּ הַקָּהָ֜ל פַּ֤ר בֶּן־בָּקָר֙ לְחַטָּ֔את וְהֵבִ֣יאוּ אֹת֔וֹ לִפְנֵ֖י אֹ֥הֶל מוֹעֵֽד׃ 15 וְֽסָמְכ֡וּ זִקְנֵ֣י הָעֵדָ֩ה אֶת־יְדֵיהֶ֨ם עַל־רֹ֤אשׁ הַפָּר֙ לִפְנֵ֣י יְהוָ֔ה וְשָׁחַ֥ט אֶת־הַפָּ֖ר לִפְנֵ֥י יְהוָֽה׃ 16 וְהֵבִ֛יא הַכֹּהֵ֥ן הַמָּשִׁ֖יחַ מִדַּ֣ם הַפָּ֑ר אֶל־אֹ֖הֶל מוֹעֵֽד׃ 17 וְטָבַ֧ל הַכֹּהֵ֛ן אֶצְבָּע֖וֹ מִן־הַדָּ֑ם וְהִזָּ֞ה שֶׁ֤בַע פְּעָמִים֙ לִפְנֵ֣י יְהוָ֔ה אֵ֖ת פְּנֵ֥י הַפָּרֹֽכֶת׃ 18 וּמִן־הַדָּ֞ם יִתֵּ֣ן ׀ עַל־קַרְנֹ֣ת הַמִּזְבֵּ֗חַ אֲשֶׁר֙ לִפְנֵ֣י יְהוָ֔ה אֲשֶׁ֖ר בְּאֹ֣הֶל מוֹעֵ֑ד וְאֵ֣ת כָּל־הַדָּ֗ם יִשְׁפֹּךְ֙ אֶל־יְסוֹד֙ מִזְבַּ֣ח הָֽעֹלָ֔ה אֲשֶׁר־פֶּ֖תַח אֹ֥הֶל מוֹעֵֽד׃ 19 וְאֵ֥ת כָּל־חֶלְבּ֖וֹ יָרִ֣ים מִמֶּ֑נּוּ וְהִקְטִ֖יר הַמִּזְבֵּֽחָה׃ 20 וְעָשָׂ֣ה לַפָּ֔ר כַּאֲשֶׁ֤ר עָשָׂה֙ לְפַ֣ר הַֽחַטָּ֔את כֵּ֖ן יַעֲשֶׂה־לּ֑וֹ וְכִפֶּ֧ר עֲלֵהֶ֛ם הַכֹּהֵ֖ן וְנִסְלַ֥ח לָהֶֽם׃ 21 וְהוֹצִ֣יא אֶת־הַפָּ֗ר אֶל־מִחוּץ֙ לַֽמַּחֲנֶ֔ה וְשָׂרַ֣ף אֹת֔וֹ כַּאֲשֶׁ֣ר שָׂרַ֔ף אֵ֖ת הַפָּ֣ר הָרִאשׁ֑וֹן חַטַּ֥את הַקָּהָ֖ל הֽוּא׃ פ 22 אֲשֶׁ֥ר נָשִׂ֖יא יֶֽחֱטָ֑א וְעָשָׂ֡ה אַחַ֣ת מִכָּל־מִצְוֺ֩ת יְהוָ֨ה אֱלֹהָ֜יו אֲשֶׁ֧ר לֹא־תֵעָשֶׂ֛ינָה

not to be done, and he realizes his guilt—23or the sin of which he is guilty is brought to his knowledge—he shall bring as his offering a male goat without blemish. 24He shall lay his hand upon the goat's head, and it shall be slaughtered at the spot where the burnt offering is slaughtered[b] before the LORD; it is a sin offering. 25The priest shall take with his finger some of the blood of the sin offering and put it on the horns of the altar of burnt offering; and the rest of its blood he shall pour out at the base of the altar of burnt offering. 26All its fat he shall turn into smoke on the altar, like the fat of the sacrifice of well-being. Thus the priest shall make expiation on his behalf for his sin, and he shall be forgiven.

27If any person from among the populace[c] unwittingly incurs guilt by doing any of the things which by the LORD's commandments ought not to be done, and he realizes his guilt—28or the sin of which he is guilty is brought to his knowledge—he shall bring a female goat without blemish as his offering for the sin of which he is guilty. 29He shall lay his hand upon the head of the sin offering, and the sin offering shall be slaughtered at the place of the burnt offering. 30The priest shall take with his finger some of its blood and put it on the horns of the altar of burnt offering; and all the rest of its blood he shall pour out at the base of the altar. 31He shall remove all its fat, just as the fat is removed from the sacrifice of well-being; and the priest shall turn it into smoke on the altar, for a pleasing odor to the LORD. Thus the priest shall make expiation for him, and he shall be forgiven.

32If the offering he brings as a sin offering is a sheep, he shall bring a female without blemish. 33He shall lay his hand upon the head of the sin offering, and it shall be slaughtered as a sin offering at the spot where the burnt offering is

בִּשְׁגָגָה וְאָשֵׁם: 23 אוֹ־הוֹדַע אֵלָיו חַטָּאתוֹ אֲשֶׁר חָטָא בָּהּ וְהֵבִיא אֶת־קָרְבָּנוֹ שְׂעִיר עִזִּים זָכָר תָּמִים: 24 וְסָמַךְ יָדוֹ עַל־רֹאשׁ הַשָּׂעִיר וְשָׁחַט אֹתוֹ בִּמְקוֹם אֲשֶׁר־יִשְׁחַט אֶת־הָעֹלָה לִפְנֵי יְהוָה חַטָּאת הוּא: 25 וְלָקַח הַכֹּהֵן מִדַּם הַחַטָּאת בְּאֶצְבָּעוֹ וְנָתַן עַל־קַרְנֹת מִזְבַּח הָעֹלָה וְאֶת־דָּמוֹ יִשְׁפֹּךְ אֶל־יְסוֹד מִזְבַּח הָעֹלָה: 26 וְאֶת־כָּל־ חֶלְבּוֹ יַקְטִיר הַמִּזְבֵּחָה כְּחֵלֶב זֶבַח הַשְּׁלָמִים וְכִפֶּר עָלָיו הַכֹּהֵן מֵחַטָּאתוֹ וְנִסְלַח לוֹ: פ

27 וְאִם־נֶפֶשׁ אַחַת תֶּחֱטָא בִשְׁגָגָה מֵעַם הָאָרֶץ בַּעֲשֹׂתָהּ אַחַת מִמִּצְוֺת יְהוָה אֲשֶׁר לֹא־תֵעָשֶׂינָה וְאָשֵׁם: 28 אוֹ הוֹדַע אֵלָיו חַטָּאתוֹ אֲשֶׁר חָטָא וְהֵבִיא קָרְבָּנוֹ שְׂעִירַת עִזִּים תְּמִימָה נְקֵבָה עַל־חַטָּאתוֹ אֲשֶׁר חָטָא: 29 וְסָמַךְ אֶת־יָדוֹ עַל רֹאשׁ הַחַטָּאת וְשָׁחַט אֶת־הַחַטָּאת בִּמְקוֹם הָעֹלָה: 30 וְלָקַח הַכֹּהֵן מִדָּמָהּ בְּאֶצְבָּעוֹ וְנָתַן עַל־ קַרְנֹת מִזְבַּח הָעֹלָה וְאֶת־כָּל־דָּמָהּ יִשְׁפֹּךְ אֶל־יְסוֹד הַמִּזְבֵּחַ: 31 וְאֶת־כָּל־חֶלְבָּהּ יָסִיר כַּאֲשֶׁר הוּסַר חֵלֶב מֵעַל זֶבַח הַשְּׁלָמִים וְהִקְטִיר הַכֹּהֵן הַמִּזְבֵּחָה לְרֵיחַ נִיחֹחַ לַיהוָה וְכִפֶּר עָלָיו הַכֹּהֵן וְנִסְלַח לוֹ: פ 32 וְאִם־כֶּבֶשׂ יָבִיא קָרְבָּנוֹ לְחַטָּאת נְקֵבָה תְמִימָה יְבִיאֶנָּה: 33 וְסָמַךְ אֶת־יָדוֹ עַל רֹאשׁ הַחַטָּאת וְשָׁחַט אֹתָהּ לְחַטָּאת בִּמְקוֹם אֲשֶׁר יִשְׁחַט אֶת־הָעֹלָה: 34 וְלָקַח

---

b Cf. 1.11.
c Lit. "people of the country."

slaughtered. ³⁴The priest shall take with his finger some of the blood of the sin offering and put it on the horns of the altar of burnt offering, and all the rest of its blood he shall pour out at the base of the altar. ³⁵And all its fat he shall remove just as the fat of the sheep of the sacrifice of well-being is removed; and this the priest shall turn into smoke on the altar, over the LORD's offering by fire. Thus the priest shall make expiation on his behalf for the sin of which he is guilty, and he shall be forgiven.

5

If a person incurs guilt—

When he has heard a public imprecation[a] and—although able to testify as one who has either seen or learned of the matter—he does not give information, so that he is subject to punishment;

²Or when a person touches any unclean thing—be it the carcass of an unclean beast or the carcass of unclean cattle or the carcass of an unclean creeping thing—and the fact has escaped him, and then, being unclean, he realizes his guilt;

³Or when he touches human uncleanness—any such uncleanness whereby one becomes unclean—and, though he has known it, the fact has escaped him, but later he realizes his guilt;

⁴Or when a person utters[b] an oath to bad or good purpose—whatever a man may utter in an oath—and, though he has known it, the fact has escaped him, but later he realizes his guilt in any of these matters—

⁵when he realizes his guilt in any of these matters, he shall confess that wherein he has sinned. ⁶And he shall bring as his penalty to the LORD, for the sin of which he is guilty, a female from the flock, sheep or goat, as a sin offering; and

הַכֹּהֵן מִדַּם הַחַטָּאת בְּאֶצְבָּעוֹ וְנָתַן עַל־קַרְנֹת מִזְבַּח הָעֹלָה וְאֶת־כָּל־דָּמָהּ יִשְׁפֹּךְ אֶל־יְסוֹד הַמִּזְבֵּחַ: ³⁵ וְאֶת־כָּל־חֶלְבָּהּ יָסִיר כַּאֲשֶׁר יוּסַר חֵלֶב־הַכֶּשֶׂב מִזֶּבַח הַשְּׁלָמִים וְהִקְטִיר הַכֹּהֵן אֹתָם הַמִּזְבֵּחָה עַל אִשֵּׁי יְהוָה וְכִפֶּר עָלָיו הַכֹּהֵן עַל־חַטָּאתוֹ אֲשֶׁר־חָטָא וְנִסְלַח לוֹ: פ

ה וְנֶפֶשׁ כִּי־תֶחֱטָא וְשָׁמְעָה קוֹל אָלָה וְהוּא עֵד אוֹ רָאָה אוֹ יָדָע אִם־לוֹא יַגִּיד וְנָשָׂא עֲוֹנוֹ: ² אוֹ נֶפֶשׁ אֲשֶׁר תִּגַּע בְּכָל־דָּבָר טָמֵא אוֹ בְנִבְלַת חַיָּה טְמֵאָה אוֹ בְּנִבְלַת בְּהֵמָה טְמֵאָה אֹו בְּנִבְלַת שֶׁרֶץ טָמֵא וְנֶעְלַם מִמֶּנּוּ וְהוּא טָמֵא וְאָשֵׁם: ³ אוֹ כִי יִגַּע בְּטֻמְאַת אָדָם לְכֹל טֻמְאָתוֹ אֲשֶׁר יִטְמָא בָּהּ וְנֶעְלַם מִמֶּנּוּ וְהוּא יָדַע וְאָשֵׁם: ⁴ אוֹ נֶפֶשׁ כִּי תִשָּׁבַע לְבַטֵּא בִשְׂפָתַיִם לְהָרַע אוֹ לְהֵיטִיב לְכֹל אֲשֶׁר יְבַטֵּא הָאָדָם בִּשְׁבֻעָה וְנֶעְלַם מִמֶּנּוּ וְהוּא־יָדַע וְאָשֵׁם לְאַחַת מֵאֵלֶּה: ⁵ וְהָיָה כִי־יֶאְשַׁם לְאַחַת מֵאֵלֶּה וְהִתְוַדָּה אֲשֶׁר חָטָא עָלֶיהָ: ⁶ וְהֵבִיא אֶת־אֲשָׁמוֹ לַיהוָה עַל חַטָּאתוֹ אֲשֶׁר חָטָא נְקֵבָה מִן־הַצֹּאן כִּשְׂבָּה אוֹ־שְׂעִירַת עִזִּים לְחַטָּאת וְכִפֶּר עָלָיו הַכֹּהֵן מֵחַטָּאתוֹ:

---

a Namely, against one who withholds testimony.
b Lit. "utters with his lips."

the priest shall make expiation on his behalf for his sin.

[7]But if his means do not suffice for a sheep, he shall bring to the LORD, as his penalty for that of which he is guilty, two turtledoves or two pigeons, one for a sin offering and the other for a burnt offering. [8]He shall bring them to the priest, who shall offer first the one for the sin offering, pinching its head at the nape without severing it. [9]He shall sprinkle some of the blood of the sin offering on the side of the altar, and what remains of the blood shall be drained out at the base of the altar; it is a sin offering. [10]And the second he shall prepare as a burnt offering, according to regulation. Thus the priest shall make expiation on his behalf for the sin of which he is guilty, and he shall be forgiven.

[11]And if his means do not suffice for two turtledoves or two pigeons, he shall bring as his offering for that of which he is guilty a tenth of an *ephah* of choice flour for a sin offering; he shall not add oil to it or lay frankincense on it, for it is a sin offering. [12]He shall bring it to the priest, and the priest shall scoop out of it a handful as a token portion of it and turn it into smoke on the altar, with the LORD's offerings by fire; it is a sin offering. [13]Thus the priest shall make expiation on his behalf for whichever of these sins he is guilty, and he shall be forgiven. It shall belong to the priest, like the meal offering.

[14]And the LORD spoke to Moses, saying:

[15]When a person commits a trespass, being unwittingly remiss about any of the LORD's sacred things, he shall bring as his penalty to the LORD a ram without blemish from the flock, convertible into payment in silver by the sanctuary weight, as a guilt offering. [16]He shall make restitution for that wherein he was remiss about the sacred things, and he shall add a fifth part

וְאִם־לֹא תַגִּיעַ יָדוֹ דֵּי שֶׂה וְהֵבִיא אֶת־ 7
אֲשָׁמוֹ אֲשֶׁר חָטָא שְׁתֵּי תֹרִים אוֹ־שְׁנֵי
בְנֵי־יוֹנָה לַיהוָה אֶחָד לְחַטָּאת וְאֶחָד
לְעֹלָה: 8 וְהֵבִיא אֹתָם אֶל־הַכֹּהֵן וְהִקְרִיב
אֶת־אֲשֶׁר לַחַטָּאת רִאשׁוֹנָה וּמָלַק אֶת־
רֹאשׁוֹ מִמּוּל עָרְפּוֹ וְלֹא יַבְדִּיל: 9 וְהִזָּה
מִדַּם הַחַטָּאת עַל־קִיר הַמִּזְבֵּחַ וְהַנִּשְׁאָר
בַּדָּם יִמָּצֵה אֶל־יְסוֹד הַמִּזְבֵּחַ חַטָּאת הוּא
10 וְאֶת־הַשֵּׁנִי יַעֲשֶׂה עֹלָה כַּמִּשְׁפָּט וְכִפֶּר
עָלָיו הַכֹּהֵן מֵחַטָּאתוֹ אֲשֶׁר־חָטָא וְנִסְלַח
לוֹ: ס

11 וְאִם־לֹא תַשִּׂיג יָדוֹ לִשְׁתֵּי תֹרִים אוֹ
לִשְׁנֵי בְנֵי־יוֹנָה וְהֵבִיא אֶת־קָרְבָּנוֹ אֲשֶׁר
חָטָא עֲשִׂירִת הָאֵפָה סֹלֶת לְחַטָּאת לֹא־
יָשִׂים עָלֶיהָ שֶׁמֶן וְלֹא־יִתֵּן עָלֶיהָ לְבֹנָה
כִּי חַטָּאת הִיא: 12 וֶהֱבִיאָהּ אֶל־הַכֹּהֵן
וְקָמַץ הַכֹּהֵן | מִמֶּנָּה מְלוֹא קֻמְצוֹ אֶת־
אַזְכָּרָתָהּ וְהִקְטִיר הַמִּזְבֵּחָה עַל אִשֵּׁי יְהוָה
חַטָּאת הִוא: 13 וְכִפֶּר עָלָיו הַכֹּהֵן עַל־
חַטָּאתוֹ אֲשֶׁר־חָטָא מֵאַחַת מֵאֵלֶּה וְנִסְלַח
לוֹ וְהָיְתָה לַכֹּהֵן כַּמִּנְחָה: ס

14 וַיְדַבֵּר יְהוָה אֶל־מֹשֶׁה לֵּאמֹר:
15 נֶפֶשׁ כִּי־תִמְעֹל מַעַל וְחָטְאָה בִּשְׁגָגָה
מִקָּדְשֵׁי יְהוָה וְהֵבִיא אֶת־אֲשָׁמוֹ לַיהוָה
אַיִל תָּמִים מִן־הַצֹּאן בְּעֶרְכְּךָ כֶּסֶף־
שְׁקָלִים בְּשֶׁקֶל־הַקֹּדֶשׁ לְאָשָׁם: 16 וְאֵת
אֲשֶׁר חָטָא מִן־הַקֹּדֶשׁ יְשַׁלֵּם וְאֶת־
חֲמִישִׁתוֹ יוֹסֵף עָלָיו וְנָתַן אֹתוֹ לַכֹּהֵן
וְהַכֹּהֵן יְכַפֵּר עָלָיו בְּאֵיל הָאָשָׁם וְנִסְלַח
לוֹ: פ

to it and give it to the priest. The priest shall make expiation on his behalf with the ram of the guilt offering, and he shall be forgiven.

[17]And when a person, without knowing it, sins in regard to any of the LORD's commandments about things not to be done, and then realizes his guilt, he shall be subject to punishment. [18]He shall bring to the priest a ram without blemish from the flock, or the equivalent,[c] as a guilt offering. The priest shall make expiation on his behalf for the error that he committed unwittingly, and he shall be forgiven. [19]It is a guilt offering; he has incurred guilt before the LORD.

[20]The LORD spoke to Moses, saying: [21]When a person sins and commits a trespass against the LORD by dealing deceitfully with his fellow in the matter of a deposit or a pledge,[d] or through robbery, or by defrauding his fellow, [22]or by finding something lost and lying about it; if he swears falsely regarding any one of the various things that one may do and sin thereby— [23]when one has thus sinned and, realizing his guilt, would restore that which he got through robbery or fraud, or the deposit that was entrusted to him, or the lost thing that he found, [24]or anything else about which he swore falsely, he shall repay the principal amount and add a fifth part to it. He shall pay it to its owner when he realizes his guilt. [25]Then he shall bring to the priest, as his penalty to the LORD, a ram without blemish from the flock, or the equivalent,[e] as a guilt offering. [26]The priest shall make expiation on his behalf before the LORD, and he shall be forgiven for whatever he may have done to draw blame thereby.

c *I.e., in currency; cf. v. 15.*
d *Meaning of Heb. uncertain.*
e *I.e., in currency; cf. v. 15.*

17 וְאִם־נֶ֙פֶשׁ֙ כִּ֣י תֶחֱטָ֔א וְעָֽשְׂתָ֗ה אַחַ֤ת
מִכָּל־מִצְוֺ֣ת יְהֹוָ֔ה אֲשֶׁ֖ר לֹ֣א תֵעָשֶׂ֑ינָה
וְלֹֽא־יָדַ֥ע וְאָשֵׁ֖ם וְנָשָׂ֥א עֲוֺנֽוֹ׃ 18 וְ֠הֵבִ֠יא אַ֣יִל
תָּמִ֧ים מִן־הַצֹּ֛אן בְּעֶרְכְּךָ֥ לְאָשָׁ֖ם אֶל־הַכֹּהֵ֑ן
וְכִפֶּר֩ עָלָ֨יו הַכֹּהֵ֜ן עַ֣ל שִׁגְגָת֧וֹ אֲשֶׁר־שָׁגָ֛ג
וְה֥וּא לֹֽא־יָדַ֖ע וְנִסְלַ֥ח לֽוֹ׃ 19 אָשָׁ֖ם ה֑וּא
אָשֹׁ֥ם אָשַׁ֖ם לַֽיהֹוָֽה׃ פ

20 וַיְדַבֵּ֥ר יְהֹוָ֖ה אֶל־מֹשֶׁ֥ה לֵּאמֹֽר׃ 21 נֶ֚פֶשׁ
כִּ֣י תֶחֱטָ֔א וּמָעֲלָ֥ה מַ֖עַל בַּֽיהֹוָ֑ה וְכִחֵ֨שׁ
בַּעֲמִית֜וֹ בְּפִקָּד֗וֹן אֽוֹ־בִתְשֽׂוּמֶת יָד֙ א֣וֹ בְגָזֵ֔ל
א֖וֹ עָשַׁ֥ק אֶת־עֲמִיתֽוֹ׃ 22 אֽוֹ־מָצָ֨א אֲבֵדָ֜ה
וְכִ֣חֶשׁ בָּ֗הּ וְנִשְׁבַּ֖ע עַל־שָׁ֑קֶר עַל־אַחַ֗ת
מִכֹּ֛ל אֲשֶׁר־יַעֲשֶׂ֥ה הָאָדָ֖ם לַחֲטֹ֥א בָהֵֽנָּה׃
23 וְהָיָה֮ כִּֽי־יֶחֱטָ֣א וְאָשֵׁם֒ וְהֵשִׁ֨יב אֶת־
הַגְּזֵלָ֜ה אֲשֶׁ֣ר גָּזָ֗ל א֤וֹ אֶת־הָעֹ֙שֶׁק֙ אֲשֶׁ֣ר
עָשָׁ֔ק א֚וֹ אֶת־הַפִּקָּד֔וֹן אֲשֶׁ֥ר הׇפְקַ֖ד אִתּ֑וֹ
א֥וֹ אֶת־הָאֲבֵדָ֖ה אֲשֶׁ֥ר מָצָֽא׃ 24 א֠וֹ מִכֹּ֞ל
אֲשֶׁר־יִשָּׁבַ֣ע עָלָיו֮ לַשֶּׁקֶר֒ וְשִׁלַּ֤ם אֹתוֹ֙
בְּרֹאשׁ֔וֹ וַחֲמִשִׁתָ֖יו יֹסֵ֣ף עָלָ֑יו לַאֲשֶׁ֨ר ה֥וּא
ל֛וֹ יִתְּנֶ֖נּוּ בְּי֥וֹם אַשְׁמָתֽוֹ׃ 25 וְאֶת־אֲשָׁמ֥וֹ
יָבִ֖יא לַֽיהֹוָ֑ה אַ֣יִל תָּמִ֧ים מִן־הַצֹּ֛אן בְּעֶרְכְּךָ֥
לְאָשָׁ֖ם אֶל־הַכֹּהֵֽן׃ 26 וְכִפֶּ֨ר עָלָ֧יו הַכֹּהֵ֛ן
לִפְנֵ֥י יְהֹוָ֖ה וְנִסְלַ֣ח ל֑וֹ עַל־אַחַ֛ת מִכֹּ֥ל
אֲשֶׁר־יַעֲשֶׂ֖ה לְאַשְׁמָ֥ה בָֽהּ׃ פ

6 TSAV

The LORD spoke to Moses, saying: ²Command Aaron and his sons thus:

This is the ritual of the burnt offering: The burnt offering itself shall remain where it is burned upon the altar all night until morning, while the fire on the altar is kept going on it. ³The priest shall dress in linen raiment, with linen breeches next to his body; and he shall take up the ashes to which the fire has reduced the burnt offering on the altar and place them beside the altar. ⁴He shall then take off his vestments and put on other vestments, and carry the ashes outside the camp to a clean place. ⁵The fire on the altar shall be kept burning, not to go out: every morning the priest shall feed wood to it, lay out the burnt offering on it, and turn into smoke the fat parts of the offerings of well-being. ⁶A perpetual fire shall be kept burning on the altar, not to go out.

⁷And this is the ritual of the meal offering: Aaron's sons shall present it before the LORD, in front of the altar. ⁸A handful of the choice flour and oil of the meal offering shall be taken from it, with all the frankincense that is on the meal offering, and this token portion shall be turned into smoke on the altar as a pleasing odor to the LORD. ⁹What is left of it shall be eaten by Aaron and his sons; it shall be eaten as unleavened cakes, in the sacred precinct; they shall eat it in the enclosure of the Tent of Meeting. ¹⁰It shall not be baked with leaven; I have given it as their portion from My offerings by fire; it is most holy, like the sin offering and the guilt offering. ¹¹Only the males among Aaron's descendants may eat of it, as their due for all time throughout the ages from the LORD's offerings by fire. Anything that touches these shall become holy.

¹²The LORD spoke to Moses, saying: ¹³This is the offering that Aaron and his sons shall offer

צו

‏וַיְדַבֵּ֥ר יְהֹוָ֖ה אֶל־מֹשֶׁ֥ה לֵּאמֹֽר: ‏2 ‏צַ֤ו
‏אֶֽת־אַהֲרֹן֙ וְאֶת־בָּנָ֣יו לֵאמֹ֔ר
‏זֹ֥את תּוֹרַ֖ת הָֽעֹלָ֑ה הִ֣וא הָֽעֹלָ֡ה עַ֣ל
‏מֽוֹקְדָה֩* עַל־הַמִּזְבֵּ֨חַ כׇּל־הַלַּ֜יְלָה עַד־
‏הַבֹּ֗קֶר וְאֵ֥שׁ הַמִּזְבֵּ֖חַ תּ֥וּקַד בּֽוֹ: ‏3 ‏וְלָבַ֨שׁ
‏הַכֹּהֵ֜ן מִדּ֣וֹ בַ֗ד וּמִכְנְסֵי־בַד֮ יִלְבַּ֣שׁ עַל־
‏בְּשָׂרוֹ֒ וְהֵרִ֣ים אֶת־הַדֶּ֗שֶׁן אֲשֶׁ֨ר תֹּאכַ֥ל
‏הָאֵ֛שׁ אֶת־הָֽעֹלָ֖ה עַל־הַמִּזְבֵּ֑חַ וְשָׂמ֕וֹ אֵ֖צֶל
‏הַמִּזְבֵּֽחַ: ‏4 ‏וּפָשַׁט֙ אֶת־בְּגָדָ֔יו וְלָבַ֖שׁ בְּגָדִ֣ים
‏אֲחֵרִ֑ים וְהוֹצִ֤יא אֶת־הַדֶּ֙שֶׁן֙ אֶל־מִח֣וּץ
‏לַֽמַּחֲנֶ֔ה אֶל־מָק֖וֹם טָהֽוֹר: ‏5 ‏וְהָאֵ֨שׁ עַל־
‏הַמִּזְבֵּ֤חַ תּֽוּקַד־בּוֹ֙ לֹ֣א תִכְבֶּ֔ה וּבִעֵ֨ר עָלֶ֧יהָ
‏הַכֹּהֵ֛ן עֵצִ֖ים בַּבֹּ֣קֶר בַּבֹּ֑קֶר וְעָרַ֤ךְ עָלֶ֙יהָ֙
‏הָֽעֹלָ֔ה וְהִקְטִ֥יר עָלֶ֖יהָ חֶלְבֵ֥י הַשְּׁלָמִֽים:
‏6 ‏אֵ֗שׁ תָּמִ֛יד תּוּקַ֥ד עַל־הַמִּזְבֵּ֖חַ לֹ֥א
‏תִכְבֶּֽה: ס

‏7 ‏וְזֹ֥את תּוֹרַ֖ת הַמִּנְחָ֑ה הַקְרֵ֨ב אֹתָ֤הּ בְּנֵֽי־
‏אַהֲרֹן֙ לִפְנֵ֣י יְהֹוָ֔ה אֶל־פְּנֵ֖י הַמִּזְבֵּֽחַ:
‏8 ‏וְהֵרִ֨ים מִמֶּ֜נּוּ* בְּקֻמְצ֗וֹ מִסֹּ֤לֶת הַמִּנְחָה֙
‏וּמִשַּׁמְנָ֔הּ וְאֵת֙ כׇּל־הַלְּבֹנָ֔ה אֲשֶׁ֖ר עַל־
‏הַמִּנְחָ֑ה וְהִקְטִ֣יר הַמִּזְבֵּ֗חַ רֵ֧יחַ נִיחֹ֛חַ
‏אַזְכָּרָתָ֖הּ לַֽיהֹוָֽה: ‏9 ‏וְהַנּוֹתֶ֣רֶת מִמֶּ֔נָּה
‏יֹאכְל֖וּ אַהֲרֹ֣ן וּבָנָ֑יו מַצּ֤וֹת תֵּֽאָכֵל֙ בְּמָק֣וֹם
‏קָדֹ֔שׁ בַּחֲצַ֥ר אֹֽהֶל־מוֹעֵ֖ד יֹאכְלֽוּהָ: ‏10 ‏לֹ֤א
‏תֵֽאָפֶה֙ חָמֵ֔ץ חֶלְקָ֛ם נָתַ֥תִּי אֹתָ֖הּ מֵֽאִשָּׁ֑י
‏קֹ֤דֶשׁ קׇֽדָשִׁים֙ הִ֔וא כַּחַטָּ֖את וְכָֽאָשָֽׁם:
‏11 ‏כׇּל־זָכָ֞ר בִּבְנֵ֤י אַהֲרֹן֙ יֹֽאכְלֶ֔נָּה חׇק־עוֹלָ֤ם
‏לְדֹרֹֽתֵיכֶם֙ מֵֽאִשֵּׁ֣י יְהֹוָ֔ה כֹּ֛ל אֲשֶׁר־יִגַּ֥ע בָּהֶ֖ם
‏יִקְדָּֽשׁ: פ

‏12 ‏וַיְדַבֵּ֥ר יְהֹוָ֖ה אֶל־מֹשֶׁ֥ה לֵּאמֹֽר: ‏13 ‏זֶ֡ה
‏קׇרְבַּן֩ אַהֲרֹ֨ן וּבָנָ֜יו אֲשֶׁר־יַקְרִ֣יבוּ לַיהֹוָ֗ה

‏*v. 2. מ' זעירא לפי נוסחים המקובלים
‏*v. 8. סבירין ומטעין "ממנה"

217

to the LORD on the occasion of his[a] anointment: a tenth of an *ephah* of choice flour as a regular meal offering, half of it in the morning and half of it in the evening, [14]shall be prepared with oil on a griddle. You shall bring it well soaked, and offer it as a meal offering of baked slices,[b] of pleasing odor to the LORD. [15]And so shall the priest, anointed from among his sons to succeed him, prepare it; it is the LORD's—a law for all time—to be turned entirely into smoke. [16]So, too, every meal offering of a priest shall be a whole offering: it shall not be eaten.

[17]The LORD spoke to Moses, saying: [18]Speak to Aaron and his sons thus: This is the ritual of the sin offering: the sin offering shall be slaughtered before the LORD, at the spot[c] where the burnt offering is slaughtered: it is most holy. [19]The priest who offers it as a sin offering shall eat of it; it shall be eaten in the sacred precinct, in the enclosure of the Tent of Meeting. [20]Anything that touches its flesh shall become holy; and if any of its blood is spattered upon a garment, you shall wash the bespattered part in the sacred precinct. [21]An earthen vessel in which it was boiled shall be broken; if it was boiled in a copper vessel, [the vessel] shall be scoured and rinsed with water. [22]Only the males in the priestly line may eat of it: it is most holy. [23]But no sin offering may be eaten from which any blood is brought into the Tent of Meeting for expiation in the sanctuary; any such shall be consumed in fire.

7 This is the ritual of the guilt offering: it is most holy. [2]The guilt offering shall be slaughtered at the spot where the burnt offering is slaughtered, and the blood shall be dashed on all sides of the altar. [3]All its fat shall be offered:

בְּיוֹם הִמָּשַׁח אֹתוֹ עֲשִׂירִת הָאֵפָה סֹלֶת מִנְחָה תָּמִיד מַחֲצִיתָהּ בַּבֹּקֶר וּמַחֲצִיתָהּ בָּעָרֶב: 14 עַל־מַחֲבַת בַּשֶּׁמֶן תֵּעָשֶׂה מֻרְבֶּכֶת תְּבִיאֶנָּה תֻּפִינֵי מִנְחַת פִּתִּים תַּקְרִיב רֵיחַ־נִיחֹחַ לַיהוָה: 15 וְהַכֹּהֵן הַמָּשִׁיחַ תַּחְתָּיו מִבָּנָיו יַעֲשֶׂה אֹתָהּ חָק־עוֹלָם לַיהוָה כָּלִיל תָּקְטָר: 16 וְכָל־מִנְחַת כֹּהֵן כָּלִיל תִּהְיֶה לֹא תֵאָכֵל: פ

17 וַיְדַבֵּר יְהוָה אֶל־מֹשֶׁה לֵּאמֹר: 18 דַּבֵּר אֶל־אַהֲרֹן וְאֶל־בָּנָיו לֵאמֹר זֹאת תּוֹרַת הַחַטָּאת בִּמְקוֹם אֲשֶׁר תִּשָּׁחֵט הָעֹלָה תִּשָּׁחֵט הַחַטָּאת לִפְנֵי יְהוָה קֹדֶשׁ קָדָשִׁים הִוא: 19 הַכֹּהֵן הַמְחַטֵּא אֹתָהּ יֹאכְלֶנָּה בְּמָקוֹם קָדֹשׁ תֵּאָכֵל בַּחֲצַר אֹהֶל מוֹעֵד: 20 כֹּל אֲשֶׁר־יִגַּע בִּבְשָׂרָהּ יִקְדָּשׁ וַאֲשֶׁר יִזֶּה מִדָּמָהּ עַל־הַבֶּגֶד אֲשֶׁר יִזֶּה עָלֶיהָ תְּכַבֵּס בְּמָקוֹם קָדֹשׁ: 21 וּכְלִי־חֶרֶשׂ אֲשֶׁר תְּבֻשַּׁל־בּוֹ יִשָּׁבֵר וְאִם־בִּכְלִי נְחֹשֶׁת בֻּשָּׁלָה וּמֹרַק וְשֻׁטַּף בַּמָּיִם: 22 כָּל־זָכָר בַּכֹּהֲנִים יֹאכַל אֹתָהּ קֹדֶשׁ קָדָשִׁים הִוא: 23 וְכָל־חַטָּאת אֲשֶׁר יוּבָא מִדָּמָהּ אֶל־אֹהֶל מוֹעֵד לְכַפֵּר בַּקֹּדֶשׁ לֹא תֵאָכֵל בָּאֵשׁ תִּשָּׂרֵף: פ

ז וְזֹאת תּוֹרַת הָאָשָׁם קֹדֶשׁ קָדָשִׁים הוּא: 2 בִּמְקוֹם אֲשֶׁר יִשְׁחֲטוּ אֶת־הָעֹלָה יִשְׁחֲטוּ אֶת־הָאָשָׁם וְאֶת־דָּמוֹ יִזְרֹק עַל־הַמִּזְבֵּחַ סָבִיב: 3 וְאֵת כָּל־חֶלְבּוֹ יַקְרִיב מִמֶּנּוּ אֶת

the broad tail; the fat that covers the entrails; [4]the two kidneys and the fat that is on them at the loins; and the protuberance on the liver, which shall be removed with the kidneys. [5]The priest shall turn them into smoke on the altar as an offering by fire to the LORD; it is a guilt offering. [6]Only the males in the priestly line may eat of it; it shall be eaten in the sacred precinct: it is most holy.

[7]The guilt offering is like the sin offering. The same rule applies to both: it shall belong to the priest who makes expiation thereby. [8]So, too, the priest who offers a man's burnt offering shall keep the skin of the burnt offering that he offered. [9]Further, any meal offering that is baked in an oven, and any that is prepared in a pan or on a griddle, shall belong to the priest who offers it. [10]But every other meal offering, with oil mixed in or dry, shall go to the sons of Aaron all alike.

[11]This is the ritual of the sacrifice of well-being that one may offer to the LORD:

[12]If he offers it for thanksgiving, he shall offer together with the sacrifice of thanksgiving unleavened cakes with oil mixed in, unleavened wafers spread with oil, and cakes of choice flour with oil mixed in, well soaked. [13]This offering, with cakes of leavened bread added, he shall offer along with his thanksgiving sacrifice of well-being. [14]Out of this he shall offer one of each kind[a] as a gift to the LORD; it shall go to the priest who dashes the blood of the offering of well-being. [15]And the flesh of his thanksgiving sacrifice of well-being shall be eaten on the day that it is offered; none of it shall be set aside until morning.

[16]If, however, the sacrifice he offers is a votive or a freewill offering, it shall be eaten on the day that he offers his sacrifice, and what is left of it

---

a   Lit. "offering."

הָאַלְיָ֕ה וְאֶת־הַחֵ֖לֶב הַֽמְכַסֶּ֣ה אֶת־הַקֶּֽרֶב׃ 4 וְאֵת֙ שְׁתֵּ֣י הַכְּלָיֹ֔ת וְאֶת־הַחֵ֙לֶב֙ אֲשֶׁ֣ר עֲלֵיהֶ֔ן אֲשֶׁ֖ר עַל־הַכְּסָלִ֑ים וְאֶת־הַיֹּתֶ֙רֶת֙ עַל־הַכָּבֵ֔ד עַל־הַכְּלָיֹ֖ת יְסִירֶֽנָּה׃ 5 וְהִקְטִ֙יר אֹתָ֤ם הַכֹּהֵן֙ הַמִּזְבֵּ֔חָה אִשֶּׁ֖ה לַֽיהֹוָ֑ה אָשָׁ֖ם הֽוּא׃ 6 כָּל־זָכָ֥ר בַּכֹּהֲנִ֖ים יֹֽאכְלֶ֑נּוּ בְּמָק֤וֹם קָדוֹשׁ֙ יֵֽאָכֵ֔ל קֹ֥דֶשׁ קָֽדָשִׁ֖ים הֽוּא׃ 7 כַּֽחַטָּאת֙ כָּֽאָשָׁ֔ם תּוֹרָ֥ה אַחַ֖ת לָהֶ֑ם הַכֹּהֵ֛ן אֲשֶׁ֥ר יְכַפֶּר־בּ֖וֹ ל֥וֹ יִהְיֶֽה׃ 8 וְהַ֙כֹּהֵ֔ן הַמַּקְרִ֖יב אֶת־עֹ֣לַת אִ֑ישׁ ע֤וֹר הָֽעֹלָה֙ אֲשֶׁ֣ר הִקְרִ֔יב לַכֹּהֵ֖ן ל֥וֹ יִהְיֶֽה׃ 9 וְכָל־מִנְחָ֗ה אֲשֶׁ֤ר תֵּֽאָפֶה֙ בַּתַּנּ֔וּר וְכָל־נַֽעֲשָׂ֥ה בַמַּרְחֶ֖שֶׁת וְעַל־מַֽחֲבַ֑ת לַכֹּהֵ֛ן הַמַּקְרִ֥יב אֹתָ֖הּ ל֥וֹ תִֽהְיֶֽה׃ 10 וְכָל־מִנְחָ֥ה בְלוּלָֽה־בַשֶּׁ֖מֶן וַֽחֲרֵבָ֑ה לְכָל־בְּנֵ֧י אַהֲרֹ֛ן תִּֽהְיֶ֖ה אִ֥ישׁ כְּאָחִֽיו׃ פ

11 וְזֹ֥את תּוֹרַ֖ת זֶ֣בַח הַשְּׁלָמִ֑ים אֲשֶׁ֥ר יַקְרִ֖יב לַֽיהֹוָֽה׃ 12 אִ֣ם עַל־תּוֹדָה֮ יַקְרִיבֶ֒נּוּ֒ וְהִקְרִ֣יב ׀ עַל־זֶ֣בַח הַתּוֹדָ֗ה חַלּ֤וֹת מַצּוֹת֙ בְּלוּלֹ֣ת בַּשֶּׁ֔מֶן וּרְקִיקֵ֥י מַצּ֖וֹת מְשֻׁחִ֣ים בַּשָּׁ֑מֶן וְסֹ֣לֶת מֻרְבֶּ֔כֶת חַלֹּ֖ת בְּלוּלֹ֥ת בַּשָּֽׁמֶן׃ 13 עַל־חַלֹּת֙ לֶ֣חֶם חָמֵ֔ץ יַקְרִ֖יב קׇרְבָּנ֑וֹ עַל־זֶ֖בַח תּוֹדַ֥ת שְׁלָמָֽיו׃ 14 וְהִקְרִ֨יב מִמֶּ֤נּוּ אֶחָד֙ מִכׇּל־קׇרְבָּ֔ן תְּרוּמָ֖ה לַֽיהֹוָ֑ה לַכֹּהֵ֗ן הַזֹּרֵ֛ק אֶת־דַּ֥ם הַשְּׁלָמִ֖ים ל֥וֹ יִהְיֶֽה׃ 15 וּבְשַׂ֗ר זֶ֚בַח תּוֹדַ֣ת שְׁלָמָ֔יו בְּי֥וֹם קׇרְבָּנ֖וֹ יֵאָכֵ֑ל לֹֽא־יַנִּ֥יחַ מִמֶּ֖נּוּ עַד־בֹּֽקֶר׃

16 וְאִם־נֶ֣דֶר ׀ א֣וֹ נְדָבָ֗ה זֶ֚בַח קׇרְבָּנ֔וֹ בְּי֛וֹם הַקְרִיב֥וֹ אֶת־זִבְח֖וֹ יֵֽאָכֵ֑ל וּמִֽמׇּחֳרָ֕ת

shall be eaten on the morrow. [17]What is then left of the flesh of the sacrifice shall be consumed in fire on the third day. [18]If any of the flesh of his sacrifice of well-being is eaten on the third day, it shall not be acceptable; it shall not count for him who offered it. It is an offensive thing, and the person who eats of it shall bear his guilt.

[19]Flesh that touches anything unclean shall not be eaten; it shall be consumed in fire. As for other flesh, only he who is clean may eat such flesh. [20]But the person who, in a state of uncleanness, eats flesh from the LORD's sacrifices of well-being, that person shall be cut off from his kin. [21]When a person touches anything unclean, be it human uncleanness or an unclean animal or any unclean creature,[b] and eats flesh from the LORD's sacrifices of well-being, that person shall be cut off from his kin.

[22]And the LORD spoke to Moses, saying: [23]Speak to the Israelite people thus: You shall eat no fat[c] of ox or sheep or goat. [24]Fat from animals that died or were torn by beasts may be put to any use, but you must not eat it. [25]If anyone eats the fat of animals from which offerings by fire may be made to the LORD, the person who eats it shall be cut off from his kin. [26]And you must not consume any blood, either of bird or of animal, in any of your settlements. [27]Anyone who eats blood shall be cut off from his kin.

[28]And the LORD spoke to Moses, saying: [29]Speak to the Israelite people thus: The offering to the LORD from a sacrifice of well-being must be presented by him who offers his sacrifice of well-being to the LORD: [30]his own hands shall present the LORD's offerings by fire. He shall present the fat with the breast, the breast to be elevated as an elevation offering before the

וְהַנּוֹתָר מִמֶּנּוּ יֵאָכֵל: 17 וְהַנּוֹתָר מִבְּשַׂר הַזֶּבַח בַּיּוֹם הַשְּׁלִישִׁי בָּאֵשׁ יִשָּׂרֵף: 18 וְאִם הֵאָכֹל יֵאָכֵל מִבְּשַׂר־זֶבַח שְׁלָמָיו בַּיּוֹם הַשְּׁלִישִׁי לֹא יֵרָצֶה הַמַּקְרִיב אֹתוֹ לֹא יֵחָשֵׁב לוֹ פִּגּוּל יִהְיֶה וְהַנֶּפֶשׁ הָאֹכֶלֶת מִמֶּנּוּ עֲוֺנָהּ תִּשָּׂא:

19 וְהַבָּשָׂר אֲשֶׁר־יִגַּע בְּכָל־טָמֵא לֹא יֵאָכֵל בָּאֵשׁ יִשָּׂרֵף וְהַבָּשָׂר כָּל־טָהוֹר יֹאכַל בָּשָׂר: 20 וְהַנֶּפֶשׁ אֲשֶׁר־תֹּאכַל בָּשָׂר מִזֶּבַח הַשְּׁלָמִים אֲשֶׁר לַיהוָה וְטֻמְאָתוֹ עָלָיו וְנִכְרְתָה הַנֶּפֶשׁ הַהִוא מֵעַמֶּיהָ: 21 וְנֶפֶשׁ כִּי־תִגַּע בְּכָל־טָמֵא בְּטֻמְאַת אָדָם אוֹ בִּבְהֵמָה טְמֵאָה אוֹ בְּכָל־שֶׁקֶץ טָמֵא וְאָכַל מִבְּשַׂר־זֶבַח הַשְּׁלָמִים אֲשֶׁר לַיהוָה וְנִכְרְתָה הַנֶּפֶשׁ הַהִוא מֵעַמֶּיהָ: פ

22 וַיְדַבֵּר יְהוָה אֶל־מֹשֶׁה לֵּאמֹר: 23 דַּבֵּר אֶל־בְּנֵי יִשְׂרָאֵל לֵאמֹר כָּל־חֵלֶב שׁוֹר וְכֶשֶׂב וָעֵז לֹא תֹאכֵלוּ: 24 וְחֵלֶב נְבֵלָה וְחֵלֶב טְרֵפָה יֵעָשֶׂה לְכָל־מְלָאכָה וְאָכֹל לֹא תֹאכְלֻהוּ: 25 כִּי כָּל־אֹכֵל חֵלֶב מִן הַבְּהֵמָה אֲשֶׁר יַקְרִיב מִמֶּנָּה אִשֶּׁה לַיהוָה וְנִכְרְתָה הַנֶּפֶשׁ הָאֹכֶלֶת מֵעַמֶּיהָ: 26 וְכָל־ דָּם לֹא תֹאכְלוּ בְּכֹל מוֹשְׁבֹתֵיכֶם לָעוֹף וְלַבְּהֵמָה: 27 כָּל־נֶפֶשׁ אֲשֶׁר־תֹּאכַל כָּל־ דָּם וְנִכְרְתָה הַנֶּפֶשׁ הַהִוא מֵעַמֶּיהָ: פ

28 וַיְדַבֵּר יְהוָה אֶל־מֹשֶׁה לֵּאמֹר: 29 דַּבֵּר אֶל־בְּנֵי יִשְׂרָאֵל לֵאמֹר הַמַּקְרִיב אֶת־זֶבַח שְׁלָמָיו לַיהוָה יָבִיא אֶת־קָרְבָּנוֹ לַיהוָה מִזֶּבַח שְׁלָמָיו: 30 יָדָיו תְּבִיאֶינָה אֵת אִשֵּׁי יְהוָה אֶת־הַחֵלֶב עַל־הֶחָזֶה יְבִיאֶנּוּ אֵת הֶחָזֶה לְהָנִיף אֹתוֹ תְּנוּפָה לִפְנֵי יְהוָה:

---

b   Heb. sheqeṣ, lit. "abomination"; several mss. and ancient versions read shereṣ "swarming things."
c   I.e., hard, coarse fat (suet); cf. 3.3–5.

LORD; [31]the priest shall turn the fat into smoke on the altar, and the breast shall go to Aaron and his sons. [32]And the right thigh from your sacrifices of well-being you shall present to the priest as a gift; [33]he from among Aaron's sons who offers the blood and the fat of the offering of well-being shall get the right thigh as his portion. [34]For I have taken the breast of elevation offering and the thigh of gift offering from the Israelites, from their sacrifices of well-being, and given them to Aaron the priest and to his sons as their due from the Israelites for all time.

[35]Those shall be the perquisites[d] of Aaron and the perquisites of his sons from the LORD's offerings by fire, once they have been inducted[e] to serve the LORD as priests; [36]these the LORD commanded to be given them, once they had been anointed, as a due from the Israelites for all time throughout the ages.

[37]Such are the rituals of the burnt offering, the meal offering, the sin offering, the guilt offering, the offering of ordination, and the sacrifice of well-being, [38]with which the LORD charged Moses on Mount Sinai, when He commanded that the Israelites present their offerings to the LORD, in the wilderness of Sinai.

8

The LORD spoke to Moses, saying: [2]Take Aaron along with his sons, and the vestments, the anointing oil, the bull of sin offering, the two rams, and the basket of unleavened bread; [3]and assemble the whole community at the entrance of the Tent of Meeting. [4]Moses did as the LORD commanded him. And when the community was assembled at the entrance of the Tent of Meeting, [5]Moses said to the community, "This is what the LORD has commanded to be done."

---

d Lit. "anointment," i.e., accruing from anointment.
e Lit. "brought forward."

31 וְהִקְטִיר הַכֹּהֵן אֶת־הַחֵ֫לֶב הַמִּזְבֵּ֫חָה וְהָיָה֙ הֶחָזֶ֔ה לְאַהֲרֹ֖ן וּלְבָנָֽיו׃ 32 וְאֵת֙ שׁ֣וֹק הַיָּמִ֔ין תִּתְּנ֥וּ תְרוּמָ֖ה לַכֹּהֵ֑ן מִזִּבְחֵ֖י שַׁלְמֵיכֶֽם׃ 33 הַמַּקְרִ֞יב אֶת־דַּ֣ם הַשְּׁלָמִ֗ים וְאֶת־הַחֵ֛לֶב מִבְּנֵ֥י אַהֲרֹ֖ן ל֣וֹ תִֽהְיֶ֑ה שׁ֥וֹק הַיָּמִ֖ין לְמָנָֽה׃ 34 כִּי֩ אֶת־חֲזֵ֨ה הַתְּנוּפָ֜ה וְאֵ֣ת ׀ שׁ֣וֹק הַתְּרוּמָ֗ה לָקַ֙חְתִּי֙ מֵאֵ֣ת בְּנֵֽי־יִשְׂרָאֵ֔ל מִזִּבְחֵ֖י שַׁלְמֵיהֶ֑ם וָאֶתֵּ֣ן אֹתָ֡ם לְאַהֲרֹ֨ן הַכֹּהֵ֤ן וּלְבָנָיו֙ לְחׇק־עוֹלָ֔ם מֵאֵ֖ת בְּנֵ֥י יִשְׂרָאֵֽל׃

35 זֹ֣את מִשְׁחַ֤ת אַהֲרֹן֙ וּמִשְׁחַ֣ת בָּנָ֔יו מֵאִשֵּׁ֖י יְהֹוָ֑ה בְּיוֹם֙ הִקְרִ֣יב אֹתָ֔ם לְכַהֵ֖ן לַֽיהֹוָֽה׃ 36 אֲשֶׁר֩ צִוָּ֨ה יְהֹוָ֜ה לָתֵ֣ת לָהֶ֗ם בְּיוֹם֙ מׇשְׁח֣וֹ אֹתָ֔ם מֵאֵ֖ת בְּנֵ֣י יִשְׂרָאֵ֑ל חֻקַּ֥ת עוֹלָ֖ם לְדֹרֹתָֽם׃

37 זֹ֣את הַתּוֹרָ֗ה לָֽעֹלָה֙ לַמִּנְחָ֔ה וְלַֽחַטָּ֖את וְלָֽאָשָׁ֑ם וְלַ֨מִּלּוּאִ֔ים וּלְזֶ֖בַח הַשְּׁלָמִֽים׃ 38 אֲשֶׁ֨ר צִוָּ֧ה יְהֹוָ֛ה אֶת־מֹשֶׁ֖ה בְּהַ֣ר סִינָ֑י בְּי֨וֹם צַוֺּת֜וֹ אֶת־בְּנֵ֤י יִשְׂרָאֵל֙ לְהַקְרִ֣יב אֶת־קׇרְבְּנֵיהֶ֖ם לַֽיהֹוָ֑ה בְּמִדְבַּ֥ר סִינָֽי׃ פ

ח וַיְדַבֵּ֥ר יְהֹוָ֖ה אֶל־מֹשֶׁ֥ה לֵּאמֹֽר׃ 2 קַ֤ח אֶֽת־אַהֲרֹן֙ וְאֶת־בָּנָ֣יו אִתּ֔וֹ וְאֵת֙ הַבְּגָדִ֔ים וְאֵ֖ת שֶׁ֣מֶן הַמִּשְׁחָ֑ה וְאֵ֣ת ׀ פַּ֣ר הַֽחַטָּ֗את וְאֵת֙ שְׁנֵ֣י הָֽאֵילִ֔ים וְאֵ֖ת סַ֥ל הַמַּצּֽוֹת׃ 3 וְאֵ֥ת כׇּל־הָעֵדָ֖ה הַקְהֵ֑ל אֶל־פֶּ֖תַח אֹ֥הֶל מוֹעֵֽד׃ 4 וַיַּ֣עַשׂ מֹשֶׁ֔ה כַּֽאֲשֶׁ֛ר צִוָּ֥ה יְהֹוָ֖ה אֹת֑וֹ וַתִּקָּהֵל֙ הָֽעֵדָ֔ה אֶל־פֶּ֖תַח אֹ֥הֶל מוֹעֵֽד׃ 5 וַיֹּ֥אמֶר מֹשֶׁ֖ה אֶל־הָֽעֵדָ֑ה זֶ֣ה הַדָּבָ֔ר אֲשֶׁר־צִוָּ֥ה יְהֹוָ֖ה לַֽעֲשֽׂוֹת׃

⁶Then Moses brought Aaron and his sons forward and washed them with water. ⁷He put the tunic on him, girded him with the sash, clothed him with the robe, and put the ephod on him, girding him with the decorated band with which he tied it to him. ⁸He put the breastpiece on him, and put into the breastpiece the Urim and Thummim.ᵃ ⁹And he set the headdress on his head; and on the headdress, in front, he put the gold frontlet, the holy diadem—as the LORD had commanded Moses.

¹⁰Moses took the anointing oil and anointed the Tabernacle and all that was in it, thus consecrating them. ¹¹He sprinkled some of it on the altar seven times, anointing the altar, all its utensils, and the laver with its stand, to consecrate them. ¹²He poured some of the anointing oil upon Aaron's head and anointed him, to consecrate him. ¹³Moses then brought Aaron's sons forward, clothed them in tunics, girded them with sashes, and wound turbans upon them, as the LORD had commanded Moses.

¹⁴He led forward the bull of sin offering. Aaron and his sons laid their hands upon the head of the bull of sin offering, ¹⁵and it was slaughtered. Moses took the blood and with his finger put some on each of the horns of the altar, cleansing the altar; then he poured out the blood at the base of the altar. Thus he consecrated it in order to make expiation upon it.

¹⁶Moses then took all the fat that was about the entrails, and the protuberance of the liver, and the two kidneys and their fat, and turned them into smoke on the altar. ¹⁷The rest of the bull, its hide, its flesh, and its dung, he put to the fire outside the camp—as the LORD had commanded Moses.

¹⁸Then he brought forward the ram of burnt offering. Aaron and his sons laid their hands upon the ram's head, ¹⁹and it was slaughtered.

ᵃ See note on Exod. 28.30.

6 וַיַּקְרֵב מֹשֶׁה אֶת־אַהֲרֹן וְאֶת־בָּנָיו וַיִּרְחַץ אֹתָם בַּמָּיִם: 7 וַיִּתֵּן עָלָיו אֶת־הַכֻּתֹּנֶת וַיַּחְגֹּר אֹתוֹ בָּאַבְנֵט וַיַּלְבֵּשׁ אֹתוֹ אֶת־הַמְּעִיל וַיִּתֵּן עָלָיו אֶת־הָאֵפֹד וַיַּחְגֹּר אֹתוֹ בְּחֵשֶׁב הָאֵפֹד וַיֶּאְפֹּד לוֹ בּוֹ: 8 וַיָּשֶׂם עָלָיו אֶת־הַחֹשֶׁן וַיִּתֵּן אֶל־הַחֹשֶׁן אֶת־הָאוּרִים וְאֶת־הַתֻּמִּים: 9 וַיָּשֶׂם אֶת־הַמִּצְנֶפֶת עַל־רֹאשׁוֹ וַיָּשֶׂם עַל־הַמִּצְנֶפֶת אֶל־מוּל פָּנָיו אֵת צִיץ הַזָּהָב נֵזֶר הַקֹּדֶשׁ כַּאֲשֶׁר צִוָּה יְהוָה אֶת־מֹשֶׁה:

10 וַיִּקַּח מֹשֶׁה אֶת־שֶׁמֶן הַמִּשְׁחָה וַיִּמְשַׁח אֶת־הַמִּשְׁכָּן וְאֶת־כָּל־אֲשֶׁר־בּוֹ וַיְקַדֵּשׁ אֹתָם: 11 וַיַּז מִמֶּנּוּ עַל־הַמִּזְבֵּחַ שֶׁבַע פְּעָמִים וַיִּמְשַׁח אֶת־הַמִּזְבֵּחַ וְאֶת־כָּל־כֵּלָיו וְאֶת־הַכִּיֹּר וְאֶת־כַּנּוֹ לְקַדְּשָׁם: 12 וַיִּצֹק מִשֶּׁמֶן הַמִּשְׁחָה עַל רֹאשׁ אַהֲרֹן וַיִּמְשַׁח אֹתוֹ לְקַדְּשׁוֹ: 13 וַיַּקְרֵב מֹשֶׁה אֶת־בְּנֵי אַהֲרֹן וַיַּלְבִּשֵׁם כֻּתֳּנֹת וַיַּחְגֹּר אֹתָם אַבְנֵט וַיַּחֲבֹשׁ לָהֶם מִגְבָּעוֹת כַּאֲשֶׁר צִוָּה יְהוָה אֶת־מֹשֶׁה:

14 וַיַּגֵּשׁ אֵת פַּר הַחַטָּאת וַיִּסְמֹךְ אַהֲרֹן וּבָנָיו אֶת־יְדֵיהֶם עַל־רֹאשׁ פַּר הַחַטָּאת: 15 וַיִּשְׁחָט וַיִּקַּח מֹשֶׁה אֶת־הַדָּם וַיִּתֵּן עַל־קַרְנוֹת הַמִּזְבֵּחַ סָבִיב בְּאֶצְבָּעוֹ וַיְחַטֵּא אֶת־הַמִּזְבֵּחַ וְאֶת־הַדָּם יָצַק אֶל־יְסוֹד הַמִּזְבֵּחַ וַיְקַדְּשֵׁהוּ לְכַפֵּר עָלָיו: 16 וַיִּקַּח אֶת־כָּל־הַחֵלֶב אֲשֶׁר עַל־הַקֶּרֶב וְאֵת יֹתֶרֶת הַכָּבֵד וְאֶת־שְׁתֵּי הַכְּלָיֹת וְאֶת־חֶלְבְּהֶן וַיַּקְטֵר מֹשֶׁה הַמִּזְבֵּחָה: 17 וְאֶת־הַפָּר וְאֶת־עֹרוֹ וְאֶת־בְּשָׂרוֹ וְאֶת־פִּרְשׁוֹ שָׂרַף בָּאֵשׁ מִחוּץ לַמַּחֲנֶה כַּאֲשֶׁר צִוָּה יְהוָה אֶת־מֹשֶׁה: 18 וַיַּקְרֵב אֵת אֵיל הָעֹלָה וַיִּסְמְכוּ אַהֲרֹן וּבָנָיו אֶת־יְדֵיהֶם עַל־רֹאשׁ הָאָיִל: 19 וַיִּשְׁחָט וַיִּזְרֹק מֹשֶׁה אֶת־הַדָּם עַל־

Moses dashed the blood against all sides of the altar. [20]The ram was cut up into sections and Moses turned the head, the sections, and the suet into smoke on the altar; [21]Moses washed the entrails and the legs with water and turned all of the ram into smoke. That was a burnt offering for a pleasing odor, an offering by fire to the Lord—as the Lord had commanded Moses.

[22]He brought forward the second ram, the ram of ordination. Aaron and his sons laid their hands upon the ram's head, [23]and it was slaughtered. Moses took some of its blood and put it on the ridge[b] of Aaron's right ear, and on the thumb of his right hand, and on the big toe of his right foot. [24]Moses then brought forward the sons of Aaron, and put some of the blood on the ridges of their right ears, and on the thumbs of their right hands, and on the big toes of their right feet; and the rest of the blood Moses dashed against every side of the altar. [25]He took the fat—the broad tail, all the fat about the entrails, the protuberance of the liver, and the two kidneys and their fat—and the right thigh. [26]From the basket of unleavened bread that was before the Lord, he took one cake of unleavened bread, one cake of oil bread, and one wafer, and placed them on the fat parts and on the right thigh. [27]He placed all these on the palms of Aaron and on the palms of his sons, and elevated them as an elevation offering before the Lord. [28]Then Moses took them from their hands and turned them into smoke on the altar with the burnt offering. This was an ordination offering for a pleasing odor; it was an offering by fire to the Lord. [29]Moses took the breast and elevated it as an elevation offering before the Lord; it was Moses' portion of the ram of ordination—as the Lord had commanded Moses.

[30]And Moses took some of the anointing oil and some of the blood that was on the altar and

---

b   Or "lobe."

הַמִּזְבֵּ֖חַ סָבִֽיב׃ 20 וְאֶ֨ת־הָאַ֔יִל נִתַּ֖ח לִנְתָחָ֑יו וַיַּקְטֵ֤ר מֹשֶׁה֙ אֶת־הָרֹ֔אשׁ וְאֶת־ הַנְּתָחִ֖ים וְאֶת־הַפָּֽדֶר׃ 21 וְאֶת־הַקֶּ֣רֶב וְאֶת־הַכְּרָעַ֖יִם רָחַ֣ץ בַּמָּ֑יִם וַיַּקְטֵר֩ מֹשֶׁ֨ה אֶת־כׇּל־הָאַ֜יִל הַמִּזְבֵּ֗חָה עֹלָ֨ה ה֤וּא לְרֵֽיחַ־ נִיחֹ֙חַ֙ אִשֶּׁ֥ה הוּא֙ לַֽיהֹוָ֔ה כַּאֲשֶׁ֛ר צִוָּ֥ה יְהֹוָ֖ה אֶת־מֹשֶֽׁה׃ 22 וַיַּקְרֵב֙ אֶת־הָאַ֣יִל הַשֵּׁנִ֔י אֵ֖יל הַמִּלֻּאִ֑ים וַֽיִּסְמְכ֞וּ אַהֲרֹ֧ן וּבָנָ֛יו אֶת־יְדֵיהֶ֖ם עַל־רֹ֥אשׁ הָאָֽיִל׃ 23 וַיִּשְׁחָ֓ט ׀ וַיִּקַּ֤ח מֹשֶׁה֙ מִדָּמ֔וֹ וַיִּתֵּ֛ן עַל־תְּנ֥וּךְ אֹֽזֶן־אַהֲרֹ֖ן הַיְמָנִ֑ית וְעַל־בֹּ֤הֶן יָדוֹ֙ הַיְמָנִ֔ית וְעַל־בֹּ֥הֶן רַגְל֖וֹ הַיְמָנִֽית׃ 24 וַיַּקְרֵ֞ב אֶת־בְּנֵ֣י אַהֲרֹ֗ן וַיִּתֵּ֨ן מֹשֶׁ֤ה מִן־הַדָּם֙ עַל־ תְּנ֤וּךְ אׇזְנָם֙ הַיְמָנִ֔ית וְעַל־בֹּ֤הֶן יָדָם֙ הַיְמָנִ֔ית וְעַל־בֹּ֖הֶן רַגְלָ֣ם הַיְמָנִ֑ית וַיִּזְרֹ֨ק מֹשֶׁ֧ה אֶת־הַדָּ֛ם עַל־הַֽמִּזְבֵּ֖חַ סָבִֽיב׃ 25 וַיִּקַּ֞ח אֶת־הַחֵ֣לֶב וְאֶת־הָֽאַלְיָ֗ה וְאֶֽת־ כׇּל־הַחֵ֘לֶב֮ אֲשֶׁ֣ר עַל־הַקֶּ֒רֶב֒ וְאֵת֙ יֹתֶ֣רֶת הַכָּבֵ֔ד וְאֶת־שְׁתֵּ֥י הַכְּלָיֹ֖ת וְאֶת־חֶלְבְּהֶ֑ן וְאֵ֖ת שׁ֥וֹק הַיָּמִֽין׃ 26 וּמִסַּ֨ל הַמַּצּ֜וֹת אֲשֶׁ֣ר ׀ לִפְנֵ֣י יְהֹוָ֗ה לָקַ֞ח חַלַּ֤ת מַצָּה֙ אַחַ֔ת וְֽחַלַּ֨ת לֶ֧חֶם שֶׁ֛מֶן אַחַ֖ת וְרָקִ֣יק אֶחָ֑ד וַיָּ֙שֶׂם֙ עַל־ הַ֣חֲלָבִ֔ים וְעַ֖ל שׁ֥וֹק הַיָּמִֽין׃ 27 וַיִּתֵּ֣ן אֶת־ הַכֹּ֔ל עַ֚ל כַּפֵּ֣י אַהֲרֹ֔ן וְעַ֖ל כַּפֵּ֣י בָנָ֑יו וַיָּ֧נֶף אֹתָ֛ם תְּנוּפָ֖ה לִפְנֵ֥י יְהֹוָֽה׃ 28 וַיִּקַּ֨ח מֹשֶׁ֤ה אֹתָם֙ מֵעַ֣ל כַּפֵּיהֶ֔ם וַיַּקְטֵ֥ר הַמִּזְבֵּ֖חָה עַל־הָעֹלָ֑ה מִלֻּאִ֥ים הֵם֙ לְרֵ֣יחַ נִיחֹ֔חַ אִשֶּׁ֥ה ה֖וּא לַֽיהֹוָֽה׃ 29 וַיִּקַּ֤ח מֹשֶׁה֙ אֶת־ הֶ֣חָזֶ֔ה וַיְנִיפֵ֥הוּ תְנוּפָ֖ה לִפְנֵ֣י יְהֹוָ֑ה מֵאֵ֣יל הַמִּלֻּאִ֗ים לְמֹשֶׁ֤ה הָיָה֙ לְמָנָ֔ה כַּאֲשֶׁ֛ר צִוָּ֥ה יְהֹוָ֖ה אֶת־מֹשֶֽׁה׃ 30 וַיִּקַּ֨ח מֹשֶׁ֜ה מִשֶּׁ֣מֶן הַמִּשְׁחָ֗ה וּמִן־הַדָּם֙ אֲשֶׁ֣ר עַל־הַמִּזְבֵּ֔חַ וַיַּ֥ז עַֽל־אַהֲרֹ֖ן עַל־בְּגָדָ֡יו

sprinkled it upon Aaron and upon his vestments, and also upon his sons and upon their
vestments. Thus he consecrated Aaron and his
vestments, and also his sons and their vestments.

31Moses said to Aaron and his sons: Boil the
flesh at the entrance of the Tent of Meeting and
eat it there with the bread that is in the basket
of ordination—as I commanded:c Aaron and
his sons shall eat it; 32and what is left over of
the flesh and the bread you shall consume in
fire. 33You shall not go outside the entrance of
the Tent of Meeting for seven days, until the
day that your period of ordination is completed.
For your ordination will require seven days.
34Everything done today, the LORD has commanded to be done [seven days], to make expiation for you. 35You shall remain at the
entrance of the Tent of Meeting day and night
for seven days, keeping the LORD's charge—that
you may not die—for so I have been commanded.

36And Aaron and his sons did all the things
that the LORD had commanded through Moses.

9 SHEMINI

On the eighth day Moses called Aaron and
his sons, and the elders of Israel. 2He said to
Aaron: "Take a calf of the herd for a sin offering
and a ram for a burnt offering, without blemish,
and bring them before the LORD. 3And speak
to the Israelites, saying: Take a he-goat for a sin
offering; a calf and a lamb, yearlings without
blemish, for a burnt offering; 4and an ox and
a ram for an offering of well-being to sacrifice
before the LORD; and a meal offering with oil
mixed in. For today the LORD will appear to
you."

5They brought to the front of the Tent of
Meeting the things that Moses had com-

וְעַל־בָּנָיו וְעַל־בִּגְדֵי בָנָיו אִתּוֹ וַיְקַדֵּשׁ
אֶת־אַהֲרֹן אֶת־בְּגָדָיו וְאֶת־בָּנָיו וְאֶת־בִּגְדֵי
בָנָיו אִתּוֹ:
31 וַיֹּאמֶר מֹשֶׁה אֶל־אַהֲרֹן וְאֶל־בָּנָיו בַּשְּׁלוּ
אֶת־הַבָּשָׂר פֶּתַח אֹהֶל מוֹעֵד וְשָׁם תֹּאכְלוּ
אֹתוֹ וְאֶת־הַלֶּחֶם אֲשֶׁר בְּסַל הַמִּלֻּאִים
כַּאֲשֶׁר צִוֵּיתִי לֵאמֹר אַהֲרֹן וּבָנָיו יֹאכְלֻהוּ:
32 וְהַנּוֹתָר בַּבָּשָׂר וּבַלָּחֶם בָּאֵשׁ תִּשְׂרֹפוּ:
33 וּמִפֶּתַח אֹהֶל מוֹעֵד לֹא תֵצְאוּ שִׁבְעַת
יָמִים עַד יוֹם מְלֹאת יְמֵי מִלֻּאֵיכֶם כִּי
שִׁבְעַת יָמִים יְמַלֵּא אֶת־יֶדְכֶם: 34 כַּאֲשֶׁר
עָשָׂה בַּיּוֹם הַזֶּה צִוָּה יְהוָה לַעֲשֹׂת לְכַפֵּר
עֲלֵיכֶם: 35 וּפֶתַח אֹהֶל מוֹעֵד תֵּשְׁבוּ יוֹמָם
וָלַיְלָה שִׁבְעַת יָמִים וּשְׁמַרְתֶּם אֶת־
מִשְׁמֶרֶת יְהוָה וְלֹא תָמוּתוּ כִּי־כֵן צֻוֵּיתִי:
36 וַיַּעַשׂ אַהֲרֹן וּבָנָיו אֵת כָּל־הַדְּבָרִים
אֲשֶׁר־צִוָּה יְהוָה בְּיַד־מֹשֶׁה: ס

שמיני ט
וַיְהִי בַּיּוֹם הַשְּׁמִינִי קָרָא מֹשֶׁה
לְאַהֲרֹן וּלְבָנָיו וּלְזִקְנֵי יִשְׂרָאֵל: 2 וַיֹּאמֶר
אֶל־אַהֲרֹן קַח־לְךָ עֵגֶל בֶּן־בָּקָר לְחַטָּאת
וְאַיִל לְעֹלָה תְּמִימִם וְהַקְרֵב לִפְנֵי יְהוָה:
3 וְאֶל־בְּנֵי יִשְׂרָאֵל תְּדַבֵּר לֵאמֹר קְחוּ
שְׂעִיר־עִזִּים לְחַטָּאת וְעֵגֶל וָכֶבֶשׂ בְּנֵי־
שָׁנָה תְּמִימִם לְעֹלָה: 4 וְשׁוֹר וָאַיִל
לִשְׁלָמִים לִזְבֹּחַ לִפְנֵי יְהוָה וּמִנְחָה בְּלוּלָה
בַשָּׁמֶן כִּי הַיּוֹם יְהוָה נִרְאָה אֲלֵיכֶם:
5 וַיִּקְחוּ אֵת אֲשֶׁר צִוָּה מֹשֶׁה אֶל־פְּנֵי אֹהֶל
מוֹעֵד וַיִּקְרְבוּ כָּל־הָעֵדָה וַיַּעַמְדוּ לִפְנֵי

---

c Or, vocalizing ṣuwwethi, "I have been commanded"; cf. below,
   vv. 35 and 10.13.

manded, and the whole community came forward and stood before the LORD. ⁶Moses said: "This is what the LORD has commanded that you do, that the Presence of the LORD may appear to you." ⁷Then Moses said to Aaron: "Come forward to the altar and sacrifice your sin offering and your burnt offering, making expiation for yourself and for the people; and sacrifice the people's offering and make expiation for them, as the LORD has commanded."

⁸Aaron came forward to the altar and slaughtered his calf of sin offering. ⁹Aaron's sons brought the blood to him; he dipped his finger in the blood and put it on the horns of the altar; and he poured out the rest of the blood at the base of the altar. ¹⁰The fat, the kidneys, and the protuberance of the liver from the sin offering he turned into smoke on the altar—as the LORD had commanded Moses; ¹¹and the flesh and the skin were consumed in fire outside the camp. ¹²Then he slaughtered the burnt offering. Aaron's sons passed the blood to him, and he dashed it against all sides of the altar. ¹³They passed the burnt offering to him in sections, as well as the head, and he turned it into smoke on the altar. ¹⁴He washed the entrails and the legs, and turned them into smoke on the altar with the burnt offering.

¹⁵Next he brought forward the people's offering. He took the goat for the people's sin offering, and slaughtered it, and presented it as a sin offering like the previous one. ¹⁶He brought forward the burnt offering and sacrificed it according to regulation. ¹⁷He then brought forward the meal offering and, taking a handful of it, he turned it into smoke on the altar—in addition to the burnt offering of the morning.ᵃ ¹⁸He slaughtered the ox and the ram, the people's sacrifice of well-being. Aaron's sons passed the blood to him—which he dashed

---

יְהוָֹה: 6 וַיֹּאמֶר מֹשֶׁה זֶה הַדָּבָר אֲשֶׁר־צִוָּה יְהוָֹה תַּעֲשֹׂוּ וְיֵרָא אֲלֵיכֶם כְּבוֹד יְהוָֹה: 7 וַיֹּאמֶר מֹשֶׁה אֶל־אַהֲרֹן קְרַב אֶל־הַמִּזְבֵּחַ וַעֲשֵׂה אֶת־חַטָּאתְךָ וְאֶת־עֹלָתֶךָ וְכַפֵּר בַּעַדְךָ וּבְעַד הָעָם וַעֲשֵׂה אֶת־קָרְבַּן הָעָם וְכַפֵּר בַּעֲדָם כַּאֲשֶׁר צִוָּה יְהוָֹה: 8 וַיִּקְרַב אַהֲרֹן אֶל־הַמִּזְבֵּחַ וַיִּשְׁחַט אֶת־עֵגֶל הַחַטָּאת אֲשֶׁר־לוֹ: 9 וַיַּקְרִבוּ בְּנֵי אַהֲרֹן אֶת־הַדָּם אֵלָיו וַיִּטְבֹּל אֶצְבָּעוֹ בַּדָּם וַיִּתֵּן עַל־קַרְנוֹת הַמִּזְבֵּחַ וְאֶת־הַדָּם יָצַק אֶל־יְסוֹד הַמִּזְבֵּחַ: 10 וְאֶת־הַחֵלֶב וְאֶת־הַכְּלָיֹת וְאֶת־הַיֹּתֶרֶת מִן־הַכָּבֵד מִן־הַחַטָּאת הִקְטִיר הַמִּזְבֵּחָה כַּאֲשֶׁר צִוָּה יְהוָֹה אֶת־מֹשֶׁה: 11 וְאֶת־הַבָּשָׂר וְאֶת־הָעוֹר שָׂרַף בָּאֵשׁ מִחוּץ לַמַּחֲנֶה: 12 וַיִּשְׁחַט אֶת־הָעֹלָה וַיַּמְצִאוּ בְּנֵי אַהֲרֹן אֵלָיו אֶת־הַדָּם וַיִּזְרְקֵהוּ עַל־הַמִּזְבֵּחַ סָבִיב: 13 וְאֶת־הָעֹלָה הִמְצִיאוּ אֵלָיו לִנְתָחֶיהָ וְאֶת־הָרֹאשׁ וַיַּקְטֵר עַל־הַמִּזְבֵּחַ: 14 וַיִּרְחַץ אֶת־הַקֶּרֶב וְאֶת־הַכְּרָעָיִם וַיַּקְטֵר עַל־הָעֹלָה הַמִּזְבֵּחָה: 15 וַיַּקְרֵב אֵת קָרְבַּן הָעָם וַיִּקַּח אֶת־שְׂעִיר הַחַטָּאת אֲשֶׁר לָעָם וַיִּשְׁחָטֵהוּ וַיְחַטְּאֵהוּ כָּרִאשׁוֹן: 16 וַיַּקְרֵב אֶת־הָעֹלָה וַיַּעֲשֶׂהָ כַּמִּשְׁפָּט: 17 וַיַּקְרֵב אֶת־הַמִּנְחָה וַיְמַלֵּא כַפּוֹ מִמֶּנָּה וַיַּקְטֵר עַל־הַמִּזְבֵּחַ מִלְּבַד עֹלַת הַבֹּקֶר: 18 וַיִּשְׁחַט אֶת־הַשּׁוֹר וְאֶת־הָאַיִל זֶבַח הַשְּׁלָמִים אֲשֶׁר לָעָם וַיַּמְצִאוּ בְּנֵי אַהֲרֹן אֶת־הַדָּם אֵלָיו וַיִּזְרְקֵהוּ עַל־

ᵃ   See Exod. 29.38–46.

225

against every side of the altar—¹⁹and the fat parts of the ox and the ram: the broad tail, the covering [fat], the kidneys, and the protuberances of the livers. ²⁰They laid these fat parts over the breasts; and Aaron*b* turned the fat parts into smoke on the altar, ²¹and elevated the breasts and the right thighs as an elevation offering before the LORD—as Moses had commanded.

²²Aaron lifted his hands toward the people and blessed them; and he stepped down after offering the sin offering, the burnt offering, and the offering of well-being. ²³Moses and Aaron then went inside the Tent of Meeting. When they came out, they blessed the people; and the Presence of the LORD appeared to all the people. ²⁴Fire came forth from before the LORD and consumed the burnt offering and the fat parts on the altar. And all the people saw, and shouted, and fell on their faces.

10 Now Aaron's sons Nadab and Abihu each took his fire pan, put fire in it, and laid incense on it; and they offered before the LORD alien fire, which He had not enjoined upon them. ²And fire came forth from the LORD and consumed them; thus they died *a*-at the instance of-*a* the LORD. ³Then Moses said to Aaron, "This is what the LORD meant when He said:

Through those near to Me I show Myself holy,
And gain glory before all the people."
And Aaron was silent.

⁴Moses called Mishael and Elzaphan, sons of Uzziel the uncle of Aaron, and said to them, "Come forward and carry your kinsmen away from the front of the sanctuary to a place outside the camp." ⁵They came forward and carried them out of the camp by their tunics, as Moses

הַמִּזְבֵּחַ סָבִיב׃ 19 וְאֶת־הַחֲלָבִים מִן־הַשּׁוֹר וּמִן־הָאַיִל הָאַלְיָה וְהַמְכַסֶּה וְהַכְּלָיֹת וְיֹתֶרֶת הַכָּבֵד׃ 20 וַיָּשִׂימוּ אֶת־הַחֲלָבִים עַל־הֶחָזוֹת וַיַּקְטֵר הַחֲלָבִים הַמִּזְבֵּחָה׃ 21 וְאֵת הֶחָזוֹת וְאֵת שׁוֹק הַיָּמִין הֵנִיף אַהֲרֹן תְּנוּפָה לִפְנֵי יְהוָה כַּאֲשֶׁר צִוָּה מֹשֶׁה׃

22 וַיִּשָּׂא אַהֲרֹן אֶת־יָדָו אֶל־הָעָם וַיְבָרְכֵם וַיֵּרֶד מֵעֲשֹׂת הַחַטָּאת וְהָעֹלָה וְהַשְּׁלָמִים׃ 23 וַיָּבֹא מֹשֶׁה וְאַהֲרֹן אֶל־אֹהֶל מוֹעֵד וַיֵּצְאוּ וַיְבָרְכוּ אֶת־הָעָם וַיֵּרָא כְבוֹד־יְהוָה אֶל־כָּל־הָעָם׃ 24 וַתֵּצֵא אֵשׁ מִלִּפְנֵי יְהוָה וַתֹּאכַל עַל־הַמִּזְבֵּחַ אֶת־הָעֹלָה וְאֶת־הַחֲלָבִים וַיַּרְא כָּל־הָעָם וַיָּרֹנּוּ וַיִּפְּלוּ עַל־פְּנֵיהֶם׃

י וַיִּקְחוּ בְנֵי־אַהֲרֹן נָדָב וַאֲבִיהוּא אִישׁ מַחְתָּתוֹ וַיִּתְּנוּ בָהֵן אֵשׁ וַיָּשִׂימוּ עָלֶיהָ קְטֹרֶת וַיַּקְרִבוּ לִפְנֵי יְהוָה אֵשׁ זָרָה אֲשֶׁר לֹא צִוָּה אֹתָם׃ 2 וַתֵּצֵא אֵשׁ מִלִּפְנֵי יְהוָה וַתֹּאכַל אוֹתָם וַיָּמֻתוּ לִפְנֵי יְהוָה׃ 3 וַיֹּאמֶר מֹשֶׁה אֶל־אַהֲרֹן הוּא אֲשֶׁר־דִּבֶּר יְהוָה ׀ לֵאמֹר

בִּקְרֹבַי אֶקָּדֵשׁ

וְעַל־פְּנֵי כָל־הָעָם אֶכָּבֵד

וַיִּדֹּם אַהֲרֹן׃

4 וַיִּקְרָא מֹשֶׁה אֶל־מִישָׁאֵל וְאֶל אֶלְצָפָן בְּנֵי עֻזִּיאֵל דֹּד אַהֲרֹן וַיֹּאמֶר אֲלֵהֶם קִרְבוּ* שְׂאוּ אֶת־אֲחֵיכֶם מֵאֵת פְּנֵי־הַקֹּדֶשׁ אֶל־מִחוּץ לַמַּחֲנֶה׃ 5 וַיִּקְרְבוּ וַיִּשָּׂאֻם בְּכֻתֳּנֹתָם אֶל־מִחוּץ לַמַּחֲנֶה כַּאֲשֶׁר דִּבֶּר מֹשֶׁה׃

---

b   *This word moved up from v. 21 for clarity.*

a-a   Others "before."

שני טעמים   v. 4.

had ordered. 6And Moses said to Aaron and to his sons Eleazar and Ithamar, "Do not *b*-bare your heads-*b* and do not rend your clothes, lest you die and anger strike the whole community. But your kinsmen, all the house of Israel, shall bewail the burning that the LORD has wrought. 7And so do not go outside the entrance of the Tent of Meeting, lest you die, for the LORD's anointing oil is upon you." And they did as Moses had bidden.

8And the LORD spoke to Aaron, saying: 9Drink no wine or other intoxicant, you or your sons, when you enter the Tent of Meeting, that you may not die. This is a law for all time throughout the ages, 10for you must distinguish between the sacred and the profane, and between the unclean and the clean; 11and you must teach the Israelites all the laws which the LORD has imparted to them through Moses.

12Moses spoke to Aaron and to his remaining sons, Eleazar and Ithamar: Take the meal offering that is left over from the LORD's offerings by fire and eat it unleavened beside the altar, for it is most holy. 13You shall eat it in the sacred precinct, inasmuch as it is your due, and that of your children, from the LORD's offerings by fire; for so I have been commanded. 14But the breast of elevation offering and the thigh of gift offering you, and your sons and daughters with you, may eat in any clean place, for they have been assigned as a due to you and your children from the Israelites' sacrifices of well-being. 15Together with the fat of fire offering, they must present the thigh of gift offering and the breast of elevation offering, which are to be elevated as an elevation offering before the LORD, and which are to be your due and that of your children with you for all time—as the LORD has commanded.

---

b-b Or "dishevel your hair."

6 וַיֹּאמֶר מֹשֶׁה אֶל־אַהֲרֹן וּלְאֶלְעָזָר וּלְאִיתָמָר ׀ בָּנָיו רָאשֵׁיכֶם אַל־תִּפְרָעוּ וּבִגְדֵיכֶם לֹא־תִפְרֹמוּ וְלֹא תָמֻתוּ וְעַל כָּל־הָעֵדָה יִקְצֹף וַאֲחֵיכֶם כָּל־בֵּית יִשְׂרָאֵל יִבְכּוּ אֶת־הַשְּׂרֵפָה אֲשֶׁר שָׂרַף יְהוָה: 7 וּמִפֶּתַח אֹהֶל מוֹעֵד לֹא תֵצְאוּ פֶּן־תָּמֻתוּ כִּי־שֶׁמֶן מִשְׁחַת יְהוָה עֲלֵיכֶם וַיַּעֲשׂוּ כִּדְבַר מֹשֶׁה: פ

8 וַיְדַבֵּר יְהוָה אֶל־אַהֲרֹן לֵאמֹר: 9 יַיִן וְשֵׁכָר אַל־תֵּשְׁתְּ ׀ אַתָּה ׀ וּבָנֶיךָ אִתָּךְ בְּבֹאֲכֶם אֶל־אֹהֶל מוֹעֵד וְלֹא תָמֻתוּ חֻקַּת עוֹלָם לְדֹרֹתֵיכֶם: 10 וּלֲהַבְדִּיל בֵּין הַקֹּדֶשׁ וּבֵין הַחֹל וּבֵין הַטָּמֵא וּבֵין הַטָּהוֹר: 11 וּלְהוֹרֹת אֶת־בְּנֵי יִשְׂרָאֵל אֵת כָּל־הַחֻקִּים אֲשֶׁר דִּבֶּר יְהוָה אֲלֵיהֶם בְּיַד־מֹשֶׁה: פ

12 וַיְדַבֵּר מֹשֶׁה אֶל־אַהֲרֹן וְאֶל אֶלְעָזָר וְאֶל־אִיתָמָר ׀ בָּנָיו הַנּוֹתָרִים קְחוּ אֶת־הַמִּנְחָה הַנּוֹתֶרֶת מֵאִשֵּׁי יְהוָה וְאִכְלוּהָ מַצּוֹת אֵצֶל הַמִּזְבֵּחַ כִּי קֹדֶשׁ קָדָשִׁים הִוא: 13 וַאֲכַלְתֶּם אֹתָהּ בְּמָקוֹם קָדֹשׁ כִּי חָקְךָ וְחָק־בָּנֶיךָ הִוא מֵאִשֵּׁי יְהוָה כִּי־כֵן צֻוֵּיתִי: 14 וְאֵת חֲזֵה הַתְּנוּפָה וְאֵת ׀ שׁוֹק הַתְּרוּמָה תֹּאכְלוּ בְּמָקוֹם טָהוֹר אַתָּה וּבָנֶיךָ וּבְנֹתֶיךָ אִתָּךְ כִּי־חָקְךָ וְחָק־בָּנֶיךָ נִתְּנוּ מִזִּבְחֵי שַׁלְמֵי בְּנֵי יִשְׂרָאֵל: 15 שׁוֹק הַתְּרוּמָה וַחֲזֵה הַתְּנוּפָה עַל אִשֵּׁי הַחֲלָבִים יָבִיאוּ לְהָנִיף תְּנוּפָה לִפְנֵי יְהוָה וְהָיָה לְךָ וּלְבָנֶיךָ אִתְּךָ לְחָק־עוֹלָם כַּאֲשֶׁר צִוָּה יְהוָה:

16Then Moses inquired about the goat of sin offering, and it had already been burned! He was angry with Eleazar and Ithamar, Aaron's remaining sons, and said, 17"Why did you not eat the sin offering in the sacred area? For it is most holy, and He has given it to you to remove the guilt of the community and to make expiation for them before the Lord. 18Since its blood was not brought inside the sanctuary,c you should certainly have eaten it in the sanctuary, as I commanded." 19And Aaron spoke to Moses, "See, this day they brought their sin offering and their burnt offering before the Lord, and such things have befallen me! Had I eaten sin offering today, would the Lord have approved?" 20And when Moses heard this, he approved.

11 The Lord spoke to Moses and Aaron, saying to them: 2Speak to the Israelite people thus:

These are the creatures that you may eat from among all the land animals: 3any animal that has true hoofs, with clefts through the hoofs, and that chewsa the cud—such you may eat. 4The following, however, of those that either chew the cud or have true hoofs, you shall not eat: the camel—although it chews the cud, it has no true hoofs: it is unclean for you; 5the daman—although it chews the cud, it has no true hoofs: it is unclean for you; 6the hare—although it chews the cud, it has no true hoofs: it is unclean for you; 7and the swine—although it has true hoofs, with the hoofs cleft through, it does not chew the cud: it is unclean for you. 8You shall not eat of their flesh or touch their carcasses; they are unclean for you.

9These you may eat of all that live in water: anything in water, whether in the seas or in the

---

c As is done in the case of the most solemn offerings; see 4.3–21; 16.11–17.

a Lit. "brings up."

---

16 וְאֵ֣ת ׀ שְׂעִ֣יר הַֽחַטָּ֗את דָּרֹ֥שׁ* דָּרַ֛שׁ מֹשֶׁ֖ה וְהִנֵּ֣ה שֹׂרָ֑ף וַ֠יִּקְצֹף עַל־אֶלְעָזָ֤ר וְעַל־אִֽיתָמָר֙ בְּנֵ֣י אַהֲרֹ֔ן הַנּוֹתָרִ֖ם לֵאמֹֽר: 17 מַדּ֗וּעַ לֹֽא־אֲכַלְתֶּ֤ם אֶת־הַֽחַטָּאת֙ בִּמְק֣וֹם הַקֹּ֔דֶשׁ כִּ֛י קֹ֥דֶשׁ קָֽדָשִׁ֖ים הִ֑וא וְאֹתָ֣הּ ׀ נָתַ֣ן לָכֶ֗ם לָשֵׂאת֙ אֶת־עֲוֺ֣ן הָֽעֵדָ֔ה לְכַפֵּ֥ר עֲלֵיהֶ֖ם לִפְנֵ֥י יְהֹוָֽה: 18 הֵ֣ן לֹא־הוּבָ֤א אֶת־דָּמָהּ֙ אֶל־הַקֹּ֣דֶשׁ פְּנִ֔ימָה אָכ֨וֹל תֹּֽאכְל֥וּ אֹתָ֛הּ בַּקֹּ֖דֶשׁ כַּֽאֲשֶׁ֥ר צִוֵּֽיתִי: 19 וַיְדַבֵּ֨ר אַֽהֲרֹ֜ן אֶל־מֹשֶׁ֗ה הֵ֣ן הַ֠יּוֹם הִקְרִ֨יבוּ אֶת־חַטָּאתָ֤ם וְאֶת־עֹֽלָתָם֙ לִפְנֵ֣י יְהֹוָ֔ה וַתִּקְרֶ֥אנָה אֹתִ֖י כָּאֵ֑לֶּה וְאָכַ֤לְתִּי חַטָּאת֙ הַיּ֔וֹם הַיִּיטַ֖ב בְּעֵינֵ֥י יְהֹוָֽה: 20 וַיִּשְׁמַ֣ע מֹשֶׁ֔ה וַיִּיטַ֖ב בְּעֵינָֽיו: פ

יא וַיְדַבֵּ֧ר יְהֹוָ֛ה אֶל־מֹשֶׁ֥ה וְאֶֽל־אַהֲרֹ֖ן לֵאמֹ֥ר אֲלֵהֶֽם: 2 דַּבְּר֛וּ אֶל־בְּנֵ֥י יִשְׂרָאֵ֖ל לֵאמֹ֑ר זֹ֤את הַֽחַיָּה֙ אֲשֶׁ֣ר תֹּֽאכְל֔וּ מִכָּל־הַבְּהֵמָ֖ה אֲשֶׁ֥ר עַל־הָאָֽרֶץ: 3 כֹּ֣ל ׀ מַפְרֶ֣סֶת פַּרְסָ֗ה וְשֹׁסַ֤עַת שֶׁ֨סַע֙ פְּרָסֹ֔ת מַֽעֲלַ֥ת גֵּרָ֖ה בַּבְּהֵמָ֑ה אֹתָ֖הּ תֹּאכֵֽלוּ: 4 אַ֤ךְ אֶת־זֶה֙ לֹ֣א תֹֽאכְל֔וּ מִֽמַּֽעֲלֵי֙ הַגֵּרָ֔ה וּמִמַּפְרִיסֵ֖י הַפַּרְסָ֑ה אֶֽת־הַ֠גָּמָל כִּֽי־מַֽעֲלֵ֨ה גֵרָ֜ה ה֗וּא וּפַרְסָה֙ אֵינֶ֣נּוּ מַפְרִ֔יס טָמֵ֥א ה֖וּא לָכֶֽם: 5 וְאֶת־הַשָּׁפָ֗ן כִּֽי־מַֽעֲלֵ֤ה גֵרָה֙ ה֔וּא וּפַרְסָ֖ה לֹ֣א יַפְרִ֑יס טָמֵ֥א ה֖וּא לָכֶֽם: 6 וְאֶת־הָֽאַרְנֶ֗בֶת כִּֽי־מַֽעֲלַ֤ת גֵּרָה֙ ה֔וּא וּפַרְסָ֖ה לֹ֣א הִפְרִ֑יסָה טְמֵאָ֥ה ה֖וּא לָכֶֽם: 7 וְאֶת־הַ֠חֲזִיר כִּֽי־מַפְרִ֨יס פַּרְסָ֤ה הוּא֙ וְשֹׁסַ֣ע שֶׁ֔סַע פַּרְסָ֔ה וְה֖וּא גֵּרָ֣ה לֹֽא־יִגָּ֑ר טָמֵ֥א ה֖וּא לָכֶֽם: 8 מִבְּשָׂרָם֙ לֹ֣א תֹאכֵ֔לוּ וּבְנִבְלָתָ֖ם לֹ֣א תִגָּ֑עוּ טְמֵאִ֥ים הֵ֖ם לָכֶֽם: 9 אֶת־זֶה֙ תֹּֽאכְל֔וּ מִכֹּ֖ל אֲשֶׁ֣ר בַּמָּ֑יִם כֹּ֣ל

v. 16. דרך המדרש נסמן חצי התורה בתיבות

228

streams, that has fins and scales—these you may eat. [10]But anything in the seas or in the streams that has no fins and scales, among all the swarming things of the water and among all the other living creatures that are in the water—they are an abomination for you [11]and an abomination for you they shall remain: you shall not eat of their flesh and you shall abominate their carcasses. [12]Everything in water that has no fins and scales shall be an abomination for you.

[13]The following[b] you shall abominate among the birds—they shall not be eaten, they are an abomination: the eagle, the vulture, and the black vulture; [14]the kite, falcons of every variety; [15]all varieties of raven; [16]the ostrich, the nighthawk, the sea gull; hawks of every variety; [17]the little owl, the cormorant, and the great owl; [18]the white owl, the pelican, and the bustard; [19]the stork; herons of every variety; the hoopoe, and the bat.

[20]All winged swarming things that walk on fours shall be an abomination for you. [21]But these you may eat among all the winged swarming things that walk on fours: all that have, above their feet, jointed legs to leap with on the ground—[22]of these you may eat the following:[b] locusts of every variety; all varieties of bald locust; crickets of every variety; and all varieties of grasshopper. [23]But all other winged swarming things that have four legs shall be an abomination for you.

[24]And the following shall make you unclean—whoever touches their carcasses shall be unclean until evening, [25]and whoever carries the carcasses of any of them shall wash his clothes and be unclean until evening—[26]every animal that has true hoofs but without clefts through the hoofs, or that does not chew the cud. They are unclean for you; whoever touches them shall be unclean. [27]Also all animals that

אֲשֶׁר־לוֹ סְנַפִּיר וְקַשְׂקֶשֶׂת בַּמַּיִם בַּיַּמִּים
וּבַנְּחָלִים אֹתָם תֹּאכֵלוּ: 10 וְכֹל אֲשֶׁר
אֵין־לוֹ סְנַפִּיר וְקַשְׂקֶשֶׂת בַּיַּמִּים וּבַנְּחָלִים
מִכֹּל שֶׁרֶץ הַמַּיִם וּמִכֹּל נֶפֶשׁ הַחַיָּה
אֲשֶׁר בַּמָּיִם שֶׁקֶץ הֵם לָכֶם: 11 וְשֶׁקֶץ יִהְיוּ
לָכֶם מִבְּשָׂרָם לֹא תֹאכֵלוּ וְאֶת־נִבְלָתָם
תְּשַׁקֵּצוּ: 12 כֹּל אֲשֶׁר אֵין־לוֹ סְנַפִּיר
וְקַשְׂקֶשֶׂת בַּמָּיִם שֶׁקֶץ הוּא לָכֶם:
13 וְאֶת־אֵלֶּה תְּשַׁקְּצוּ מִן־הָעוֹף לֹא יֵאָכְלוּ
שֶׁקֶץ הֵם אֶת־הַנֶּשֶׁר וְאֶת־הַפֶּרֶס וְאֵת
הָעָזְנִיָּה: 14 וְאֶת־הַדָּאָה וְאֶת־הָאַיָּה
לְמִינָהּ: 15 אֵת כָּל־עֹרֵב לְמִינוֹ: 16 וְאֵת
בַּת הַיַּעֲנָה וְאֶת־הַתַּחְמָס וְאֶת־הַשָּׁחַף
וְאֶת־הַנֵּץ לְמִינֵהוּ: 17 וְאֶת־הַכּוֹס וְאֶת־
הַשָּׁלָךְ וְאֶת־הַיַּנְשׁוּף: 18 וְאֶת־הַתִּנְשֶׁמֶת
וְאֶת־הַקָּאָת וְאֶת־הָרָחָם: 19 וְאֵת
הַחֲסִידָה הָאֲנָפָה לְמִינָהּ וְאֶת־הַדּוּכִיפַת
וְאֶת־הָעֲטַלֵּף:
20 כֹּל שֶׁרֶץ הָעוֹף הַהֹלֵךְ עַל־אַרְבַּע שֶׁקֶץ
הוּא לָכֶם: ס 21 אַךְ אֶת־זֶה תֹּאכֵלוּ
מִכֹּל שֶׁרֶץ הָעוֹף הַהֹלֵךְ עַל־אַרְבַּע אֲשֶׁר־
לא לוֹ כְרָעַיִם מִמַּעַל לְרַגְלָיו לְנַתֵּר בָּהֵן
עַל־הָאָרֶץ: 22 אֶת־אֵלֶּה מֵהֶם תֹּאכֵלוּ
אֶת־הָאַרְבֶּה לְמִינוֹ וְאֶת־הַסָּלְעָם לְמִינֵהוּ
וְאֶת־הַחַרְגֹּל לְמִינֵהוּ וְאֶת־הֶחָגָב
לְמִינֵהוּ: 23 וְכֹל שֶׁרֶץ הָעוֹף אֲשֶׁר־לוֹ
אַרְבַּע רַגְלָיִם שֶׁקֶץ הוּא לָכֶם:
24 וּלְאֵלֶּה תִּטַּמָּאוּ כָּל־הַנֹּגֵעַ בְּנִבְלָתָם
יִטְמָא עַד־הָעָרֶב: 25 וְכָל־הַנֹּשֵׂא מִנִּבְלָתָם
יְכַבֵּס בְּגָדָיו וְטָמֵא עַד־הָעָרֶב: 26 לְכָל־
הַבְּהֵמָה אֲשֶׁר הִוא מַפְרֶסֶת פַּרְסָה וְשֶׁסַע |
אֵינֶנָּה שֹׁסַעַת וְגֵרָה אֵינֶנָּה מַעֲלָה טְמֵאִים
הֵם לָכֶם כָּל־הַנֹּגֵעַ בָּהֶם יִטְמָא: 27 וְכֹל |
הוֹלֵךְ עַל־כַּפָּיו בְּכָל־הַחַיָּה הַהֹלֶכֶת עַל־

---

b   *A number of these cannot be identified with certainty.*

walk on paws, among those that walk on fours, are unclean for you; whoever touches their carcasses shall be unclean until evening. ²⁸And anyone who carries their carcasses shall wash his clothes and remain unclean until evening. They are unclean for you.

²⁹The following[b] shall be unclean for you from among the things that swarm on the earth: the mole, the mouse, and great lizards of every variety; ³⁰the gecko, the land crocodile, the lizard, the sand lizard, and the chameleon. ³¹Those are for you the unclean among all the swarming things; whoever touches them when they are dead shall be unclean until evening. ³²And anything on which one of them falls when dead shall be unclean: be it any article of wood, or a cloth, or a skin, or a sack—any such article that can be put to use shall be dipped in water, and it shall remain unclean until evening; then it shall be clean. ³³And if any of those falls into an earthen vessel, everything inside it shall be unclean and [the vessel] itself you shall break. ³⁴As to any food that may be eaten, it shall become unclean if it came in contact with water;[c] as to any liquid that may be drunk, it shall become unclean if it was inside any vessel.[d] ³⁵Everything on which the carcass of any of them falls shall be unclean: an oven or stove shall be smashed. They are unclean and unclean they shall remain for you. ³⁶However, a spring or cistern in which water is collected shall be clean, but whoever touches such a carcass in it shall be unclean. ³⁷If such a carcass falls upon seed grain that is to be sown, it is clean; ³⁸but if water is put on the seed and any part of a carcass falls upon it, it shall be unclean for you.

³⁹If an animal that you may eat has died, anyone who touches its carcass shall be unclean until evening; ⁴⁰anyone who eats of its carcass shall wash his clothes and remain unclean until

אַרְבַּ֖ע טְמֵאִ֥ים הֵ֛ם לָכֶ֖ם כָּל־הַנֹּגֵ֥עַ בְּנִבְלָתָ֖ם יִטְמָ֥א עַד־הָעָֽרֶב׃ 28 וְהַנֹּשֵׂא֙ אֶת־נִבְלָתָ֔ם יְכַבֵּ֥ס בְּגָדָ֖יו וְטָמֵ֣א עַד־הָעָ֑רֶב טְמֵאִ֥ים הֵ֖מָּה לָכֶֽם׃ ס 29 וְזֶ֤ה לָכֶם֙ הַטָּמֵ֔א בַּשֶּׁ֖רֶץ הַשֹּׁרֵ֣ץ עַל־הָאָ֑רֶץ הַחֹ֥לֶד וְהָעַכְבָּ֖ר וְהַצָּ֥ב לְמִינֵֽהוּ׃ 30 וְהָאֲנָקָ֥ה וְהַכֹּ֖חַ וְהַלְּטָאָ֑ה וְהַחֹ֖מֶט וְהַתִּנְשָֽׁמֶת׃ 31 אֵ֛לֶּה הַטְּמֵאִ֥ים לָכֶ֖ם בְּכָל־הַשָּׁ֑רֶץ כָּל־הַנֹּגֵ֧עַ בָּהֶ֛ם בְּמֹתָ֖ם יִטְמָ֥א עַד־הָעָֽרֶב׃ 32 וְכֹ֣ל אֲשֶׁר־יִפֹּל־עָלָיו֩ מֵהֶ֨ם ׀ בְּמֹתָ֜ם יִטְמָ֗א מִכָּל־כְּלִי־עֵץ֙ א֣וֹ בֶ֤גֶד אוֹ־ע֙וֹר֙ א֣וֹ שָׂ֔ק כָּל־כְּלִ֕י אֲשֶׁר־יֵעָשֶׂ֥ה מְלָאכָ֖ה בָּהֶ֑ם בַּמַּ֥יִם יוּבָ֛א וְטָמֵ֥א עַד־הָעֶ֖רֶב וְטָהֵֽר׃ 33 וְכָל־כְּלִי־חֶ֔רֶשׂ אֲשֶׁר־יִפֹּ֥ל מֵהֶ֖ם אֶל־תּוֹכ֑וֹ כֹּ֣ל אֲשֶׁ֧ר בְּתוֹכ֛וֹ יִטְמָ֖א וְאֹת֥וֹ תִשְׁבֹּֽרוּ׃ 34 מִכָּל־הָאֹ֜כֶל אֲשֶׁ֣ר יֵאָכֵ֗ל אֲשֶׁ֨ר יָב֥וֹא עָלָ֛יו מַ֖יִם יִטְמָ֑א וְכָל־מַשְׁקֶה֙ אֲשֶׁ֣ר יִשָּׁתֶ֔ה בְּכָל־כְּלִ֖י יִטְמָֽא׃ 35 וְ֠כֹל אֲשֶׁר־יִפֹּ֨ל מִנִּבְלָתָ֥ם ׀ עָלָיו֮ יִטְמָא֒ תַּנּ֧וּר וְכִירַ֛יִם יֻתָּ֖ץ טְמֵאִ֣ים הֵ֑ם וּטְמֵאִ֖ים יִהְי֥וּ לָכֶֽם׃ 36 אַ֣ךְ מַעְיָ֥ן וּב֛וֹר מִקְוֵה־מַ֖יִם יִהְיֶ֣ה טָה֑וֹר וְנֹגֵ֥עַ בְּנִבְלָתָ֖ם יִטְמָֽא׃ 37 וְכִ֤י יִפֹּל֙ מִנִּבְלָתָ֔ם עַל־כָּל־זֶ֥רַע זֵר֖וּעַ אֲשֶׁ֣ר יִזָּרֵ֑עַ טָה֖וֹר הֽוּא׃ 38 וְכִ֤י יֻתַּן־מַ֙יִם֙ עַל־זֶ֔רַע וְנָפַ֥ל מִנִּבְלָתָ֖ם עָלָ֑יו טָמֵ֥א ה֖וּא לָכֶֽם׃ ס 39 וְכִ֤י יָמוּת֙ מִן־הַבְּהֵמָ֔ה אֲשֶׁר־הִ֥יא לָכֶ֖ם לְאָכְלָ֑ה הַנֹּגֵ֥עַ בְּנִבְלָתָ֖הּ יִטְמָ֥א עַד־הָעָֽרֶב׃ 40 וְהָֽאֹכֵל֙ מִנִּבְלָתָ֔הּ יְכַבֵּ֥ס בְּגָדָ֖יו וְטָמֵ֣א עַד־הָעָ֑רֶב וְהַנֹּשֵׂא֙ אֶת־נִבְלָתָ֔הּ יְכַבֵּ֥ס בְּגָדָ֖יו וְטָמֵ֥א עַד־הָעָֽרֶב׃

---

c   *I.e., if the food then came in contact with the carcass of any animal named in vv. 29–30.*

d   *I.e., a vessel that had become contaminated by such contact.*

evening; and anyone who carries its carcass shall wash his clothes and remain unclean until evening.

41All the things that swarm upon the earth are an abomination; they shall not be eaten. 42You shall not eat, among all things that swarm upon the earth, anything that crawls on its belly, or anything that walks on fours, or anything that has many legs; for they are an abomination. 43You shall not draw abomination upon yourselves through anything that swarms; you shall not make yourselves unclean therewith and thus become unclean. 44For I the Lord am your God: you shall sanctify yourselves and be holy, for I am holy. You shall not make yourselves unclean through any swarming thing that moves upon the earth. 45For I the Lord am He who brought you up from the land of Egypt to be your God: you shall be holy, for I am holy.

46These are the instructions concerning animals, birds, all living creatures that move in water, and all creatures that swarm on earth, 47for distinguishing between the unclean and the clean, between the living things that may be eaten and the living things that may not be eaten.

12 TAZRIA‘

The Lord spoke to Moses, saying: 2Speak to the Israelite people thus: When a woman at childbirth*a* bears a male, she shall be unclean seven days; she shall be unclean as at the time of her menstrual infirmity.—3On the eighth day the flesh of his foreskin shall be circumcised.—4She shall remain in a state of blood purification*b* for thirty-three days: she shall not touch any consecrated thing, nor enter the sanctuary until her period of purification is completed. 5If she bears a female, she shall be

---

41 וְכָל־הַשֶּׁרֶץ הַשֹּׁרֵץ עַל־הָאָרֶץ שֶׁקֶץ הוּא לֹא יֵאָכֵל: 42 כֹּל הוֹלֵךְ עַל־גָּחוֹן* וְכֹל ׀ הוֹלֵךְ עַל־אַרְבַּע עַד כָּל־מַרְבֵּה רַגְלַיִם לְכָל־הַשֶּׁרֶץ הַשֹּׁרֵץ עַל־הָאָרֶץ לֹא תֹאכְלוּם כִּי־שֶׁקֶץ הֵם: 43 אַל־תְּשַׁקְּצוּ אֶת־נַפְשֹׁתֵיכֶם בְּכָל־הַשֶּׁרֶץ הַשֹּׁרֵץ וְלֹא תִטַּמְּאוּ בָּהֶם וְנִטְמֵתֶם* בָּם: 44 כִּי אֲנִי יְהֹוָה אֱלֹהֵיכֶם וְהִתְקַדִּשְׁתֶּם וִהְיִיתֶם קְדֹשִׁים כִּי קָדוֹשׁ אָנִי וְלֹא תְטַמְּאוּ אֶת־נַפְשֹׁתֵיכֶם בְּכָל־הַשֶּׁרֶץ הָרֹמֵשׂ עַל־הָאָרֶץ: 45 כִּי ׀ אֲנִי יְהֹוָה הַמַּעֲלֶה אֶתְכֶם מֵאֶרֶץ מִצְרַיִם לִהְיֹת לָכֶם לֵאלֹהִים וִהְיִיתֶם קְדֹשִׁים כִּי קָדוֹשׁ אָנִי: 46 זֹאת תּוֹרַת הַבְּהֵמָה וְהָעוֹף וְכֹל נֶפֶשׁ הַחַיָּה הָרֹמֶשֶׂת בַּמָּיִם וּלְכָל־נֶפֶשׁ הַשֹּׁרֶצֶת עַל־הָאָרֶץ: 47 לְהַבְדִּיל בֵּין הַטָּמֵא וּבֵין הַטָּהֹר וּבֵין הַחַיָּה הַנֶּאֱכֶלֶת וּבֵין הַחַיָּה אֲשֶׁר לֹא תֵאָכֵל: פ

יב וַיְדַבֵּר יְהֹוָה אֶל־מֹשֶׁה לֵּאמֹר: 2 דַּבֵּר אֶל־בְּנֵי יִשְׂרָאֵל לֵאמֹר אִשָּׁה כִּי תַזְרִיעַ וְיָלְדָה זָכָר וְטָמְאָה שִׁבְעַת יָמִים כִּימֵי נִדַּת דְּוֹתָהּ תִּטְמָא: 3 וּבַיּוֹם הַשְּׁמִינִי יִמּוֹל בְּשַׂר עָרְלָתוֹ: 4 וּשְׁלֹשִׁים יוֹם וּשְׁלֹשֶׁת יָמִים תֵּשֵׁב בִּדְמֵי טָהֳרָה בְּכָל־קֹדֶשׁ לֹא־תִגָּע וְאֶל־הַמִּקְדָּשׁ לֹא תָבֹא עַד־מְלֹאת יְמֵי טָהֳרָהּ: 5 וְאִם־נְקֵבָה תֵלֵד

v. 42. ר' רבתי, ובמסורה היא חצי התורה באותיות

v. 43. חסר א'

---

a   Heb. tazria‘, lit. “brings forth seed.”
b   Meaning of Heb. uncertain.

unclean two weeks as during her menstruation, and she shall remain in a state of blood purification[b] for sixty-six days.

[6]On the completion of her period of purification, for either son or daughter, she shall bring to the priest, at the entrance of the Tent of Meeting, a lamb in its first year for a burnt offering, and a pigeon or a turtledove for a sin offering.[c] [7]He shall offer it before the LORD and make expiation on her behalf; she shall then be clean from her flow of blood. Such are the rituals concerning her who bears a child, male or female. [8]If, however, her means do not suffice for a sheep, she shall take two turtledoves or two pigeons, one for a burnt offering and the other for a sin offering. The priest shall make expiation on her behalf, and she shall be clean.

13 The LORD spoke to Moses and Aaron, saying:

[2]When a person has on the skin of his body a swelling, a rash, or a discoloration, and it develops into a scaly affection on the skin of his body, it shall be reported[a] to Aaron the priest or to one of his sons, the priests. [3]The priest shall examine the affection on the skin of his body: if hair in the affected patch has turned white and the affection appears to be deeper than the skin of his body, it is a leprous affection;[b] when the priest sees it, he shall pronounce him unclean. [4]But if it is a white discoloration on the skin of his body which does not appear to be deeper than the skin and the hair in it has not turned white, the priest shall isolate the affected person for seven days. [5]On the seventh day the priest shall examine him, and if the affection has remained unchanged in color and the disease has

וְטָמְאָה שְׁבֻעַיִם כְּנִדָּתָהּ וְשִׁשִּׁים יוֹם וְשֵׁשֶׁת יָמִים תֵּשֵׁב עַל־דְּמֵי טׇהֳרָה: 6 וּבִמְלֹאת ׀ יְמֵי טׇהֳרָהּ לְבֵן אוֹ לְבַת תָּבִיא כֶּבֶשׂ בֶּן־שְׁנָתוֹ לְעֹלָה וּבֶן־יוֹנָה אוֹ־תֹר לְחַטָּאת אֶל־פֶּתַח אֹהֶל־מוֹעֵד אֶל־הַכֹּהֵן: 7 וְהִקְרִיבוֹ לִפְנֵי יְהֹוָה וְכִפֶּר עָלֶיהָ וְטׇהֲרָה מִמְּקֹר דָּמֶיהָ זֹאת תּוֹרַת הַיֹּלֶדֶת לַזָּכָר אוֹ לַנְּקֵבָה: 8 וְאִם־לֹא תִמְצָא יָדָהּ דֵּי שֶׂה וְלָקְחָה שְׁתֵּי־תֹרִים אוֹ שְׁנֵי בְּנֵי יוֹנָה אֶחָד לְעֹלָה וְאֶחָד לְחַטָּאת וְכִפֶּר עָלֶיהָ הַכֹּהֵן וְטׇהֵרָה: פ

יג וַיְדַבֵּר יְהֹוָה אֶל־מֹשֶׁה וְאֶל־אַהֲרֹן לֵאמֹר: 2 אָדָם כִּי־יִהְיֶה בְעוֹר־בְּשָׂרוֹ שְׂאֵת אוֹ־סַפַּחַת אוֹ בַהֶרֶת וְהָיָה בְעוֹר־בְּשָׂרוֹ לְנֶגַע צָרָעַת וְהוּבָא אֶל־אַהֲרֹן הַכֹּהֵן אוֹ אֶל־אַחַד מִבָּנָיו הַכֹּהֲנִים: 3 וְרָאָה הַכֹּהֵן אֶת־הַנֶּגַע בְּעוֹר־הַבָּשָׂר וְשֵׂעָר בַּנֶּגַע הָפַךְ ׀ לָבָן וּמַרְאֵה הַנֶּגַע עָמֹק מֵעוֹר בְּשָׂרוֹ נֶגַע צָרַעַת הוּא וְרָאָהוּ הַכֹּהֵן וְטִמֵּא אֹתוֹ: 4 וְאִם־בַּהֶרֶת לְבָנָה הִוא בְּעוֹר בְּשָׂרוֹ וְעָמֹק אֵין־מַרְאֶהָ מִן־הָעוֹר וּשְׂעָרָה לֹא־הָפַךְ לָבָן וְהִסְגִּיר הַכֹּהֵן אֶת־הַנֶּגַע שִׁבְעַת יָמִים: 5 וְרָאָהוּ הַכֹּהֵן בַּיּוֹם הַשְּׁבִיעִי וְהִנֵּה הַנֶּגַע עָמַד בְּעֵינָיו לֹא־פָשָׂה הַנֶּגַע בָּעוֹר וְהִסְגִּירוֹ הַכֹּהֵן שִׁבְעַת יָמִים שֵׁנִית:

---

c *See note at 4.3.*

a *Or "he shall be brought."*

b *Heb.* ṣara'ath *is used for a variety of diseases. Where a human being is declared unclean by reason of* ṣara'ath, *the traditional translation "leprosy" has been retained without regard to modern medical terminology.*

not spread on the skin, the priest shall isolate him for another seven days. 6On the seventh day the priest shall examine him again: if the affection has faded and has not spread on the skin, the priest shall pronounce him clean. It is a rash; he shall wash his clothes, and he shall be clean. 7But if the rash should spread on the skin after he has presented himself to the priest and been pronounced clean, he shall present himself again to the priest. 8And if the priest sees that the rash has spread on the skin, the priest shall pronounce him unclean; it is leprosy.

9When a person has a scaly affection, it shall be reported[c] to the priest. 10If the priest finds on the skin a white swelling which has turned some hair white, with [d]-a patch of undiscolored flesh-[d] in the swelling, 11it is chronic leprosy on the skin of his body, and the priest shall pronounce him unclean; he need not isolate him, for he is unclean. 12If the eruption spreads out over the skin so that it covers all the skin of the affected person from head to foot, wherever the priest can see—13if the priest sees that the eruption has covered the whole body—he shall pronounce the affected person clean; he is clean, for he has turned all white. 14But as soon as undiscolored flesh appears in it, he shall be unclean; 15when the priest sees the undiscolored flesh, he shall pronounce him unclean. The undiscolored flesh is unclean; it is leprosy. 16But if the undiscolored flesh again turns white, he shall come to the priest, 17and the priest shall examine him: if the affection has turned white, the priest shall pronounce the affected person clean; he is clean.

18When an inflammation appears on the skin of one's body and it heals, 19and a white swelling or a white discoloration streaked with red develops where the inflammation was, he shall present himself to the priest. 20If the priest finds

6 וְרָאָ֨ה הַכֹּהֵ֜ן אֹת֗וֹ בַּיּ֤וֹם הַשְּׁבִיעִי֙ שֵׁנִ֔ית וְהִנֵּה֙ כֵּהָ֣ה הַנֶּ֔גַע וְלֹא־פָשָׂ֥ה הַנֶּ֖גַע בָּע֑וֹר וְטִֽהֲר֤וֹ הַכֹּהֵן֙ מִסְפַּ֣חַת הִ֔יא וְכִבֶּ֥ס בְּגָדָ֖יו וְטָהֵֽר: 7 וְאִם־פָּשֹׂ֨ה תִפְשֶׂ֤ה הַמִּסְפַּ֙חַת֙ בָּע֔וֹר אַחֲרֵ֧י הֵרָאֹת֛וֹ אֶל־הַכֹּהֵ֖ן לְטָהֳרָת֑וֹ וְנִרְאָ֥ה שֵׁנִ֖ית אֶל־הַכֹּהֵֽן: 8 וְרָאָה֙ הַכֹּהֵ֔ן וְהִנֵּ֛ה פָּשְׂתָ֥ה הַמִּסְפַּ֖חַת בָּע֑וֹר וְטִמְּא֥וֹ הַכֹּהֵ֖ן צָרַ֥עַת הִֽוא: פ

9 נֶ֣גַע צָרַ֔עַת כִּ֥י תִהְיֶ֖ה בְּאָדָ֑ם וְהוּבָ֖א אֶל־הַכֹּהֵֽן: 10 וְרָאָ֣ה הַכֹּהֵ֗ן וְהִנֵּ֤ה שְׂאֵת־לְבָנָה֙ בָּע֔וֹר וְהִ֕יא הָפְכָ֖ה שֵׂעָ֣ר לָבָ֑ן וּמִֽחְיַ֛ת בָּשָׂ֥ר חַ֖י בַּשְׂאֵֽת: 11 צָרַ֨עַת נוֹשֶׁ֤נֶת הִוא֙ בְּע֣וֹר בְּשָׂר֔וֹ וְטִמְּא֖וֹ הַכֹּהֵ֑ן לֹ֣א יַסְגִּרֶ֔נּוּ כִּ֥י טָמֵ֖א הֽוּא: 12 וְאִם־פָּר֨וֹחַ תִּפְרַ֤ח הַצָּרַ֙עַת֙ בָּע֔וֹר וְכִסְּתָ֣ה הַצָּרַ֗עַת אֵ֚ת כָּל־ע֣וֹר הַנֶּ֔גַע מֵרֹאשׁ֖וֹ וְעַד־רַגְלָ֑יו לְכָל־מַרְאֵ֖ה עֵינֵ֥י הַכֹּהֵֽן: 13 וְרָאָ֣ה הַכֹּהֵ֗ן וְהִנֵּ֨ה כִסְּתָ֤ה הַצָּרַ֙עַת֙ אֶת־כָּל־בְּשָׂר֔וֹ וְטִהַ֖ר אֶת־הַנָּ֑גַע כֻּלּ֛וֹ הָפַ֥ךְ לָבָ֖ן טָה֥וֹר הֽוּא: 14 וּבְי֨וֹם הֵרָא֥וֹת בּ֛וֹ בָּשָׂ֥ר חַ֖י יִטְמָֽא: 15 וְרָאָ֣ה הַכֹּהֵ֗ן אֶת־הַבָּשָׂ֤ר הַחַי֙ וְטִמְּא֔וֹ הַבָּשָׂ֥ר הַחַ֛י טָמֵ֥א ה֖וּא צָרַ֥עַת הֽוּא: 16 א֣וֹ כִ֤י יָשׁוּב֙ הַבָּשָׂ֣ר הַחַ֔י וְנֶהְפַּ֖ךְ לְלָבָ֑ן וּבָ֖א אֶל־הַכֹּהֵֽן: 17 וְרָאָ֙הוּ֙ הַכֹּהֵ֔ן וְהִנֵּ֛ה נֶהְפַּ֥ךְ הַנֶּ֖גַע לְלָבָ֑ן וְטִהַ֧ר הַכֹּהֵ֛ן אֶת־הַנֶּ֖גַע טָה֥וֹר הֽוּא: פ

18 וּבָשָׂ֕ר כִּֽי־יִהְיֶ֥ה בֽוֹ־בְעֹר֖וֹ שְׁחִ֑ין וְנִרְפָּֽא: 19 וְהָיָ֞ה בִּמְק֤וֹם הַשְּׁחִין֙ שְׂאֵ֣ת לְבָנָ֔ה א֥וֹ בַהֶ֖רֶת לְבָנָ֣ה אֲדַמְדָּ֑מֶת וְנִרְאָ֖ה אֶל־הַכֹּהֵֽן: 20 וְרָאָ֣ה הַכֹּהֵ֗ן וְהִנֵּ֤ה מַרְאֶ֙הָ֙ שָׁפָ֣ל מִן־

---

c   See note a at 13.2.

d-d   Others "quick raw flesh."

that it appears lower than the rest of the skin and that the hair in it has turned white, the priest shall pronounce him unclean; it is a leprous affection that has broken out in the inflammation. [21]But if the priest finds that there is no white hair in it and it is not lower than the rest of the skin, and it is faded, the priest shall isolate him for seven days. [22]If it should spread in the skin, the priest shall pronounce him unclean; it is an affection. [23]But if the discoloration remains stationary, not having spread, it is the scar of the inflammation; the priest shall pronounce him clean.

[24]When the skin of one's body sustains a burn by fire, and the patch from the burn is a discoloration, either white streaked with red, or white, [25]the priest shall examine it. If some hair has turned white in the discoloration, which itself appears to go deeper than the skin, it is leprosy that has broken out in the burn. The priest shall pronounce him unclean; it is a leprous affection. [26]But if the priest finds that there is no white hair in the discoloration, and that it is not lower than the rest of the skin, and it is faded, the priest shall isolate him for seven days. [27]On the seventh day the priest shall examine him: if it has spread in the skin, the priest shall pronounce him unclean; it is a leprous affection. [28]But if the discoloration has remained stationary, not having spread on the skin, and it is faded, it is the swelling from the burn. The priest shall pronounce him clean, for it is the scar of the burn.

[29]If a man or a woman has an affection on the head or in the beard, [30]the priest shall examine the affection. If it appears to go deeper than the skin and there is thin yellow hair in it, the priest shall pronounce him unclean; it is a scall, a scaly eruption in the hair or beard. [31]But if the priest finds that the scall affection does not appear to go deeper than the skin, yet there

הָעוֹר וּשְׂעָרָהּ הָפַךְ לָבָן וְטִמְּאוֹ הַכֹּהֵן נֶגַע־צָרַעַת הִוא בַּשְּׁחִין פָּרָחָה׃ 21 וְאִם ׀ יִרְאֶנָּה הַכֹּהֵן וְהִנֵּה אֵין־בָּהּ שֵׂעָר לָבָן וּשְׁפָלָה אֵינֶנָּה מִן־הָעוֹר וְהִיא כֵהָה וְהִסְגִּירוֹ הַכֹּהֵן שִׁבְעַת יָמִים׃ 22 וְאִם־פָּשֹׂה תִפְשֶׂה בָּעוֹר וְטִמֵּא הַכֹּהֵן אֹתוֹ נֶגַע הִוא׃ 23 וְאִם־תַּחְתֶּיהָ תַּעֲמֹד הַבַּהֶרֶת לֹא פָשָׂתָה צָרֶבֶת הַשְּׁחִין הִוא וְטִהֲרוֹ הַכֹּהֵן׃ ס

24 אוֹ בָשָׂר כִּי־יִהְיֶה בְעֹרוֹ מִכְוַת־אֵשׁ וְהָיְתָה מִחְיַת הַמִּכְוָה בַּהֶרֶת לְבָנָה אֲדַמְדֶּמֶת אוֹ לְבָנָה׃ 25 וְרָאָה אֹתָהּ הַכֹּהֵן וְהִנֵּה נֶהְפַּךְ שֵׂעָר לָבָן בַּבַּהֶרֶת וּמַרְאֶהָ עָמֹק מִן־הָעוֹר צָרַעַת הִוא בַּמִּכְוָה פָּרָחָה וְטִמֵּא אֹתוֹ הַכֹּהֵן נֶגַע צָרַעַת הִוא׃ 26 וְאִם ׀ יִרְאֶנָּה הַכֹּהֵן וְהִנֵּה אֵין־בַּבֶּהֶרֶת שֵׂעָר לָבָן וּשְׁפָלָה אֵינֶנָּה מִן־הָעוֹר וְהִוא כֵהָה וְהִסְגִּירוֹ הַכֹּהֵן שִׁבְעַת יָמִים׃ 27 וְרָאָהוּ הַכֹּהֵן בַּיּוֹם הַשְּׁבִיעִי אִם־פָּשֹׂה תִפְשֶׂה בָּעוֹר וְטִמֵּא הַכֹּהֵן אֹתוֹ נֶגַע צָרַעַת הִוא׃ 28 וְאִם־תַּחְתֶּיהָ תַעֲמֹד הַבַּהֶרֶת לֹא־פָשְׂתָה בָעוֹר וְהִוא כֵהָה שְׂאֵת הַמִּכְוָה הִוא וְטִהֲרוֹ הַכֹּהֵן כִּי־צָרֶבֶת הַמִּכְוָה הִוא׃ פ

29 וְאִישׁ אוֹ אִשָּׁה כִּי־יִהְיֶה בוֹ נָגַע בְּרֹאשׁ אוֹ בְזָקָן׃ 30 וְרָאָה הַכֹּהֵן אֶת־הַנֶּגַע וְהִנֵּה מַרְאֵהוּ עָמֹק מִן־הָעוֹר וּבוֹ שֵׂעָר צָהֹב דָּק וְטִמֵּא אֹתוֹ הַכֹּהֵן נֶתֶק הוּא צָרַעַת הָרֹאשׁ אוֹ הַזָּקָן הוּא׃ 31 וְכִי־יִרְאֶה הַכֹּהֵן אֶת־נֶגַע הַנֶּתֶק וְהִנֵּה אֵין־מַרְאֵהוּ עָמֹק מִן־הָעוֹר וְשֵׂעָר שָׁחֹר אֵין בּוֹ וְהִסְגִּיר הַכֹּהֵן

is no black hair in it, the priest shall isolate the person with the scall affection for seven days. ³²On the seventh day the priest shall examine the affection. If the scall has not spread and no yellow hair has appeared in it, and the scall does not appear to go deeper than the skin, ³³the person with the scall shall shave himself, but without shaving the scall; the priest shall isolate him for another seven days. ³⁴On the seventh day the priest shall examine the scall. If the scall has not spread on the skin, and does not appear to go deeper than the skin, the priest shall pronounce him clean; he shall wash his clothes, and he shall be clean. ³⁵If, however, the scall should spread on the skin after he has been pronounced clean, ³⁶the priest shall examine him. If the scall has spread on the skin, the priest need not look for yellow hair: he is unclean. ³⁷But if the scall has remained unchanged in color, and black hair has grown in it, the scall is healed; he is clean. The priest shall pronounce him clean.

³⁸If a man or a woman has the skin of the body streaked with white discolorations, ³⁹and the priest sees that the discolorations on the skin of the body are of a dull white, it is a tetter broken out on the skin; he is clean.

⁴⁰If a man loses the hair of his head and becomes bald, he is clean. ⁴¹If he loses the hair on the front part of his head and becomes bald at the forehead, he is clean. ⁴²But if a white affection streaked with red appears on the bald part in the front or at the back of the head, it is a scaly eruption that is spreading over the bald part in the front or at the back of the head. ⁴³The priest shall examine him: if the swollen affection on the bald part in the front or at the back of his head is white streaked with red, like the leprosy of body skin in appearance, ⁴⁴the man is leprous; he is unclean. The priest shall pronounce him unclean; he has the affection on his head.

אֶת־נֶגַע הַנֶּתֶק שִׁבְעַת יָמִים: 32 וְרָאָה הַכֹּהֵן אֶת־הַנֶּגַע בַּיּוֹם הַשְּׁבִיעִי וְהִנֵּה לֹא־פָשָׂה הַנֶּתֶק וְלֹא־הָיָה בוֹ שֵׂעָר צָהֹב וּמַרְאֵה הַנֶּתֶק אֵין עָמֹק מִן־הָעוֹר: 33 וְהִתְגַּלָּח* וְאֶת־הַנֶּתֶק לֹא יְגַלֵּחַ וְהִסְגִּיר הַכֹּהֵן אֶת־הַנֶּתֶק שִׁבְעַת יָמִים שֵׁנִית: 34 וְרָאָה הַכֹּהֵן אֶת־הַנֶּתֶק בַּיּוֹם הַשְּׁבִיעִי וְהִנֵּה לֹא־פָשָׂה הַנֶּתֶק בָּעוֹר וּמַרְאֵהוּ אֵינֶנּוּ עָמֹק מִן־הָעוֹר וְטִהַר אֹתוֹ הַכֹּהֵן וְכִבֶּס בְּגָדָיו וְטָהֵר: 35 וְאִם־פָּשֹׂה יִפְשֶׂה הַנֶּתֶק בָּעוֹר אַחֲרֵי טָהֳרָתוֹ: 36 וְרָאָהוּ הַכֹּהֵן וְהִנֵּה פָּשָׂה הַנֶּתֶק בָּעוֹר לֹא־יְבַקֵּר הַכֹּהֵן לַשֵּׂעָר הַצָּהֹב טָמֵא הוּא: 37 וְאִם־בְּעֵינָיו עָמַד הַנֶּתֶק וְשֵׂעָר שָׁחֹר צָמַח־בּוֹ נִרְפָּא הַנֶּתֶק טָהוֹר הוּא וְטִהֲרוֹ הַכֹּהֵן: ס 38 וְאִישׁ אוֹ־אִשָּׁה כִּי־יִהְיֶה בְעוֹר־בְּשָׂרָם בֶּהָרֹת בֶּהָרֹת לְבָנֹת: 39 וְרָאָה הַכֹּהֵן וְהִנֵּה בְעוֹר־בְּשָׂרָם בֶּהָרֹת כֵּהוֹת לְבָנֹת בֹּהַק הוּא פָּרַח בָּעוֹר טָהוֹר הוּא: ס 40 וְאִישׁ כִּי יִמָּרֵט רֹאשׁוֹ קֵרֵחַ הוּא טָהוֹר הוּא: 41 וְאִם מִפְּאַת פָּנָיו יִמָּרֵט רֹאשׁוֹ גִּבֵּחַ הוּא טָהוֹר הוּא: 42 וְכִי־יִהְיֶה בַקָּרַחַת אוֹ בַגַּבַּחַת נֶגַע לָבָן אֲדַמְדָּם צָרַעַת פֹּרַחַת הִוא בְּקָרַחְתּוֹ אוֹ בְגַבַּחְתּוֹ: 43 וְרָאָה אֹתוֹ הַכֹּהֵן וְהִנֵּה שְׂאֵת־הַנֶּגַע לְבָנָה אֲדַמְדֶּמֶת בְּקָרַחְתּוֹ אוֹ בְגַבַּחְתּוֹ כְּמַרְאֵה צָרַעַת עוֹר בָּשָׂר: 44 אִישׁ־צָרוּעַ הוּא טָמֵא הוּא טַמֵּא יְטַמְּאֶנּוּ הַכֹּהֵן בְּרֹאשׁוֹ נִגְעוֹ:

v. 33. ג׳ רבתי לפי נוסחים המקובלים

⁴⁵As for the person with a leprous affection, his clothes shall be rent, his head shall be left bare,ᵉ and he shall cover over his upper lip; and he shall call out, "Unclean! Unclean!" ⁴⁶He shall be unclean as long as the disease is on him. Being unclean, he shall dwell apart; his dwelling shall be outside the camp.

⁴⁷When an eruptive affection occurs in a cloth of wool or linen fabric, ⁴⁸in the warp or in the woof of the linen or the wool, or in a skin or in anything made of skin; ⁴⁹if the affection in the cloth or the skin, in the warp or the woof, or in any article of skin, is streaky greenᶠ or red, it is an eruptive affection. It shall be shown to the priest; ⁵⁰and the priest, after examining the affection, shall isolate the affected article for seven days. ⁵¹On the seventh day he shall examine the affection: if the affection has spread in the cloth—whether in the warp or the woof, or in the skin, for whatever purpose the skin may be used—the affection is a malignant eruption; it is unclean. ⁵²The cloth—whether warp or woof in wool or linen, or any article of skin—in which the affection is found, shall be burned, for it is a malignant eruption; it shall be consumed in fire. ⁵³But if the priest sees that the affection in the cloth—whether in warp or in woof, or in any article of skin—has not spread, ⁵⁴the priest shall order the affected article washed, and he shall isolate it for another seven days. ⁵⁵And if, after the affected article has been washed, the priest sees that the affection has not changed color and that it has not spread, it is unclean. It shall be consumed in fire; it is a fret,ᵍ whether on its inner side or on its outer side. ⁵⁶But if the priest sees that the affected part, after it has been washed, is faded, he shall tear it out from the cloth or skin, whether in the warp or in the woof; ⁵⁷and if it occurs again in the

---

⁴⁵ וְהַצָּר֜וּעַ אֲשֶׁר־בּ֣וֹ הַנֶּ֗גַע בְּגָדָ֞יו יִהְי֤וּ פְרֻמִים֙ וְרֹאשׁוֹ֙ יִהְיֶ֣ה פָר֔וּעַ וְעַל־שָׂפָ֖ם יַעְטֶ֑ה וְטָמֵ֥א ׀ טָמֵ֖א יִקְרָֽא׃ ⁴⁶ כָּל־יְמֵ֞י אֲשֶׁ֨ר הַנֶּ֥גַע בּ֛וֹ יִטְמָ֖א טָמֵ֣א ה֑וּא בָּדָ֣ד יֵשֵׁ֔ב מִח֥וּץ לַֽמַּחֲנֶ֖ה מוֹשָׁבֽוֹ׃ ס

⁴⁷ וְהַבֶּ֕גֶד כִּֽי־יִהְיֶ֥ה ב֖וֹ נֶ֣גַע צָרָ֑עַת בְּבֶ֣גֶד צֶ֔מֶר א֖וֹ בְּבֶ֥גֶד פִּשְׁתִּֽים׃ ⁴⁸ א֤וֹ בִֽשְׁתִי֙ א֣וֹ בְעֵ֔רֶב לַפִּשְׁתִּ֖ים וְלַצָּ֑מֶר א֤וֹ בְעוֹר֙ א֣וֹ בְּכָל־מְלֶ֥אכֶת עֽוֹר׃ ⁴⁹ וְהָיָ֨ה הַנֶּ֜גַע יְרַקְרַ֣ק ׀ א֣וֹ אֲדַמְדָּ֗ם בַּבֶּ֩גֶד֩ א֨וֹ בָע֜וֹר אֽוֹ־בַשְּׁתִ֤י אֽוֹ־בָעֵ֙רֶב֙ א֣וֹ בְכָל־כְּלִי־ע֔וֹר נֶ֥גַע צָרַ֖עַת ה֑וּא וְהָרְאָ֖ה אֶת־הַכֹּהֵֽן׃ ⁵⁰ וְרָאָ֥ה הַכֹּהֵ֖ן אֶת־הַנָּ֑גַע וְהִסְגִּ֥יר אֶת־הַנֶּ֖גַע שִׁבְעַ֥ת יָמִֽים׃ ⁵¹ וְרָאָ֣ה אֶת־הַנֶּ֡גַע בַּיּוֹם֩ הַשְּׁבִיעִ֨י כִּֽי־פָשָׂ֤ה הַנֶּ֙גַע֙ בַּבֶּ֗גֶד אֽוֹ־בַשְּׁתִ֤י אֽוֹ־בָעֵ֙רֶב֙ א֣וֹ בָע֔וֹר לְכֹ֛ל אֲשֶׁר־יֵעָשֶׂ֥ה הָע֖וֹר לִמְלָאכָ֑ה צָרַ֨עַת מַמְאֶ֧רֶת הַנֶּ֛גַע טָמֵ֖א הֽוּא׃ ⁵² וְשָׂרַ֨ף אֶת־הַבֶּ֜גֶד א֥וֹ אֶֽת־הַשְּׁתִ֣י ׀ א֣וֹ אֶת־הָעֵ֗רֶב בַּצֶּ֙מֶר֙ א֣וֹ בַפִּשְׁתִּ֔ים א֣וֹ אֶת־כָּל־כְּלִ֣י הָע֔וֹר אֲשֶׁר־יִהְיֶ֥ה ב֖וֹ הַנָּ֑גַע כִּֽי־צָרַ֤עַת מַמְאֶ֙רֶת֙ ה֔וּא בָּאֵ֖שׁ תִּשָּׂרֵֽף׃ ⁵³ וְאִם֮ יִרְאֶ֣ה הַכֹּהֵן֒ וְהִנֵּה֙ לֹא־פָשָׂ֣ה הַנֶּ֔גַע בַּבֶּ֕גֶד א֥וֹ בַשְּׁתִ֖י א֣וֹ בָעֵ֑רֶב א֖וֹ בְּכָל־כְּלִי־עֽוֹר׃ ⁵⁴ וְצִוָּה֙ הַכֹּהֵ֔ן וְכִ֨בְּס֔וּ אֵ֥ת אֲשֶׁר־בּ֖וֹ הַנָּ֑גַע וְהִסְגִּיר֥וֹ שִׁבְעַת־יָמִ֖ים שֵׁנִֽית׃ ⁵⁵ וְרָאָ֣ה הַכֹּהֵ֗ן אַחֲרֵ֣י ׀ הֻכַּבֵּ֣ס אֶת־הַנֶּ֗גַע וְ֠הִנֵּה לֹֽא־הָפַ֨ךְ הַנֶּ֤גַע אֶת־עֵינוֹ֙ וְהַנֶּ֣גַע לֹֽא־פָשָׂ֔ה טָמֵ֣א ה֔וּא בָּאֵ֖שׁ תִּשְׂרְפֶ֑נּוּ פְּחֶ֣תֶת הִ֔וא בְּקָרַחְתּ֖וֹ א֥וֹ בְגַבַּחְתּֽוֹ׃ ⁵⁶ וְאִם֮ רָאָ֣ה הַכֹּהֵן֒ וְהִנֵּה֙ כֵּהָ֣ה הַנֶּ֔גַע אַחֲרֵ֖י הֻכַּבֵּ֣ס אֹת֑וֹ וְקָרַ֣ע אֹת֗וֹ מִן־הַבֶּ֙גֶד֙ א֣וֹ מִן־הָע֔וֹר א֥וֹ מִן־הַשְּׁתִ֖י א֥וֹ מִן־הָעֵֽרֶב׃ ⁵⁷ וְאִם־תֵּרָאֶ֨ה ע֜וֹד בַּבֶּ֤גֶד אֽוֹ־בַשְּׁתִ֣י אֽוֹ־בָעֵ֗רֶב א֤וֹ

---

e   *See note at 10.6.*
f   *Or "yellow."*
g   *Meaning of Heb.* peḥetheth *uncertain.*

236

cloth—whether in warp or in woof—or in any article of skin, it is a wild growth; the affected article shall be consumed in fire. [58]If, however, the affection disappears from the cloth—warp or woof—or from any article of skin that has been washed, it shall be washed again, and it shall be clean.

[59]Such is the procedure for eruptive affections of cloth, woolen or linen, in warp or in woof, or of any article of skin, for pronouncing it clean or unclean.

14 METSORA῾
The LORD spoke to Moses, saying: [2]This shall be the ritual for a leper at the time that he is to be cleansed.

When it has been reported[a] to the priest, [3]the priest shall go outside the camp. If the priest sees that the leper has been healed of his scaly affection, [4]the priest shall order two live clean birds, cedar wood, crimson stuff, and hyssop to be brought for him who is to be cleansed. [5]The priest shall order one of the birds slaughtered over fresh water in an earthen vessel; [6]and he shall take the live bird, along with the cedar wood, the crimson stuff, and the hyssop, and dip them together with the live bird in the blood of the bird that was slaughtered over the fresh water. [7]He shall then sprinkle it seven times on him who is to be cleansed of the eruption and cleanse him; and he shall set the live bird free in the open country. [8]The one to be cleansed shall wash his clothes, shave off all his hair, and bathe in water; then he shall be clean. After that he may enter the camp, but he must remain outside his tent seven days. [9]On the seventh day he shall shave off all his hair—of head, beard, and eyebrows. When he has shaved off all his hair, he shall wash his clothes and bathe his body in water; then he shall be clean. [10]On the eighth

a   Cf. note a at 13.2.

בְּכָל־כְּלִי־ע֖וֹר פֹּרַ֣חַת הִ֑וא בָּאֵ֖שׁ תִּשְׂרְפֶ֑נּוּ אֵ֥ת אֲשֶׁר־בּ֖וֹ הַנָּֽגַע׃ 58 וְהַבֶּ֣גֶד אֽוֹ־הַשְּׁתִ֞י אֽוֹ־הָעֵ֗רֶב אֽוֹ־כָל־כְּלִ֤י הָעוֹר֙ אֲשֶׁ֣ר תְּכַבֵּ֔ס וְסָ֥ר מֵהֶ֖ם הַנָּ֑גַע וְכֻבַּ֥ס שֵׁנִ֖ית וְטָהֵֽר׃ 59 זֹ֠את תּוֹרַ֨ת נֶֽגַע־צָרַ֜עַת בֶּ֥גֶד הַצֶּ֣מֶר ׀ א֣וֹ הַפִּשְׁתִּ֗ים א֤וֹ הַשְּׁתִי֙ א֣וֹ הָעֵ֔רֶב א֖וֹ כָּל־כְּלִי־ע֑וֹר לְטַהֲר֖וֹ א֥וֹ לְטַמְּאֽוֹ׃ פ

יד מצרע
וַיְדַבֵּ֥ר יְהֹוָ֖ה אֶל־מֹשֶׁ֥ה לֵּאמֹֽר׃ 2 זֹ֤את תִּֽהְיֶה֙ תּוֹרַ֣ת הַמְּצֹרָ֔ע בְּי֖וֹם טׇהֳרָת֑וֹ וְהוּבָ֖א אֶל־הַכֹּהֵֽן׃ 3 וְיָצָא֙ הַכֹּהֵ֔ן אֶל־מִח֖וּץ לַֽמַּחֲנֶ֑ה וְרָאָה֙ הַכֹּהֵ֔ן וְהִנֵּ֛ה נִרְפָּ֥א נֶֽגַע־הַצָּרַ֖עַת מִן־הַצָּרֽוּעַ׃ 4 וְצִוָּה֙ הַכֹּהֵ֔ן וְלָקַ֣ח לַמִּטַּהֵ֗ר שְׁתֵּֽי־צִפֳּרִ֛ים חַיּ֖וֹת טְהֹר֑וֹת וְעֵ֣ץ אֶ֔רֶז וּשְׁנִ֥י תוֹלַ֖עַת וְאֵזֹֽב׃ 5 וְצִוָּה֙ הַכֹּהֵ֔ן וְשָׁחַ֖ט אֶת־הַצִּפּ֣וֹר הָֽאֶחָ֑ת אֶל־כְּלִי־חֶ֖רֶשׂ עַל־מַ֥יִם חַיִּֽים׃ 6 אֶת־הַצִּפֹּ֤ר הַֽחַיָּה֙ יִקַּ֣ח אֹתָ֔הּ וְאֶת־עֵ֥ץ הָאֶ֛רֶז וְאֶת־שְׁנִ֥י הַתּוֹלַ֖עַת וְאֶת־הָֽאֵזֹ֑ב וְטָבַ֣ל אוֹתָ֗ם וְאֵ֣ת ׀ הַצִּפֹּ֣ר הַֽחַיָּ֔ה בְּדַם֙ הַצִּפֹּ֣ר הַשְּׁחֻטָ֔ה עַ֖ל הַמַּ֥יִם הַֽחַיִּֽים׃ 7 וְהִזָּ֗ה עַ֧ל הַמִּטַּהֵ֛ר מִן־הַצָּרַ֖עַת שֶׁ֣בַע פְּעָמִ֑ים וְטִ֣הֲר֔וֹ וְשִׁלַּ֛ח אֶת־הַצִּפֹּ֥ר הַֽחַיָּ֖ה עַל־פְּנֵ֥י הַשָּׂדֶֽה׃ 8 וְכִבֶּס֩ הַמִּטַּהֵ֨ר אֶת־בְּגָדָ֜יו וְגִלַּ֣ח אֶת־כׇּל־שְׂעָר֗וֹ וְרָחַ֤ץ בַּמַּ֙יִם֙ וְטָהֵ֔ר וְאַחַ֖ר יָב֣וֹא אֶל־הַֽמַּחֲנֶ֑ה וְיָשַׁ֛ב מִח֥וּץ לְאׇהֳל֖וֹ שִׁבְעַ֥ת יָמִֽים׃ 9 וְהָיָה֩ בַיּ֨וֹם הַשְּׁבִיעִ֜י יְגַלַּ֣ח אֶת־כׇּל־שְׂעָר֗וֹ אֶת־רֹאשׁ֤וֹ וְאֶת־זְקָנוֹ֙ וְאֵת֙ גַּבֹּ֣ת עֵינָ֔יו וְאֶת־כׇּל־שְׂעָר֖וֹ יְגַלֵּ֑חַ וְכִבֶּ֣ס אֶת־בְּגָדָ֗יו וְרָחַ֧ץ אֶת־בְּשָׂר֛וֹ בַּמַּ֖יִם וְטָהֵֽר׃ 10 וּבַיּ֣וֹם הַשְּׁמִינִ֗י

day he shall take two male lambs without blemish, one ewe lamb in its first year without blemish, three-tenths of a measure of choice flour with oil mixed in for a meal offering, and one *log* of oil. [11]These shall be presented before the LORD, with the man to be cleansed, at the entrance of the Tent of Meeting, by the priest who performs the cleansing.

[12]The priest shall take one of the male lambs and offer it with the *log* of oil as a guilt offering, and he shall elevate them as an elevation offering before the LORD. [13]The lamb shall be slaughtered at the spot in the sacred area where the sin offering and the burnt offering are slaughtered.[b] For the guilt offering, like the sin offering, goes to the priest; it is most holy. [14]The priest shall take some of the blood of the guilt offering, and the priest shall put it on the ridge of the right ear of him who is being cleansed, and on the thumb of his right hand, and on the big toe of his right foot. [15]The priest shall then take some of the *log* of oil and pour it into the palm of his own left hand. [16]And the priest shall dip his right finger in the oil that is in the palm of his left hand and sprinkle some of the oil with his finger seven times before the LORD. [17]Some of the oil left in his palm shall be put by the priest on the ridge of the right ear of the one being cleansed, on the thumb of his right hand, and on the big toe of his right foot—over the blood of the guilt offering. [18]The rest of the oil in his palm the priest shall put on the head of the one being cleansed. Thus the priest shall make expiation for him before the LORD. [19]The priest shall then offer the sin offering and make expiation for the one being cleansed of his uncleanness. Last, the burnt offering shall be slaughtered, [20]and the priest shall offer the burnt offering and the meal offering on the altar, and the priest shall make expiation for him. Then he shall be clean.

b *See 1.11; 4.24.*

יִקַּח שְׁנֵי־כְבָשִׂים תְּמִימִם וְכַבְשָׂה אַחַת בַּת־שְׁנָתָהּ תְּמִימָה וּשְׁלֹשָׁה עֶשְׂרֹנִים סֹלֶת מִנְחָה בְּלוּלָה בַשֶּׁמֶן וְלֹג אֶחָד שָׁמֶן: [11] וְהֶעֱמִיד הַכֹּהֵן הַמְטַהֵר אֵת הָאִישׁ הַמִּטַּהֵר וְאֹתָם לִפְנֵי יְהֹוָה פֶּתַח אֹהֶל מוֹעֵד:

[12] וְלָקַח הַכֹּהֵן אֶת־הַכֶּבֶשׂ הָאֶחָד וְהִקְרִיב אֹתוֹ לְאָשָׁם וְאֶת־לֹג הַשָּׁמֶן וְהֵנִיף אֹתָם תְּנוּפָה לִפְנֵי יְהֹוָה: [13] וְשָׁחַט אֶת־הַכֶּבֶשׂ בִּמְקוֹם אֲשֶׁר יִשְׁחַט אֶת־הַחַטָּאת וְאֶת־הָעֹלָה בִּמְקוֹם הַקֹּדֶשׁ כִּי כַּחַטָּאת הָאָשָׁם הוּא לַכֹּהֵן קֹדֶשׁ קָדָשִׁים הוּא: [14] וְלָקַח הַכֹּהֵן מִדַּם הָאָשָׁם וְנָתַן הַכֹּהֵן עַל־תְּנוּךְ אֹזֶן הַמִּטַּהֵר הַיְמָנִית וְעַל־בֹּהֶן יָדוֹ הַיְמָנִית וְעַל־בֹּהֶן רַגְלוֹ הַיְמָנִית: [15] וְלָקַח הַכֹּהֵן מִלֹּג הַשָּׁמֶן וְיָצַק עַל־כַּף הַכֹּהֵן הַשְּׂמָאלִית: [16] וְטָבַל הַכֹּהֵן אֶת־אֶצְבָּעוֹ הַיְמָנִית מִן־הַשֶּׁמֶן אֲשֶׁר עַל־כַּפּוֹ הַשְּׂמָאלִית וְהִזָּה מִן־הַשֶּׁמֶן בְּאֶצְבָּעוֹ שֶׁבַע פְּעָמִים לִפְנֵי יְהֹוָה: [17] וּמִיֶּתֶר הַשֶּׁמֶן אֲשֶׁר עַל־כַּפּוֹ יִתֵּן הַכֹּהֵן עַל־תְּנוּךְ אֹזֶן הַמִּטַּהֵר הַיְמָנִית וְעַל־בֹּהֶן יָדוֹ הַיְמָנִית וְעַל־בֹּהֶן רַגְלוֹ הַיְמָנִית עַל דַּם הָאָשָׁם: [18] וְהַנּוֹתָר בַּשֶּׁמֶן אֲשֶׁר עַל־כַּף הַכֹּהֵן יִתֵּן עַל־רֹאשׁ הַמִּטַּהֵר וְכִפֶּר עָלָיו הַכֹּהֵן לִפְנֵי יְהֹוָה: [19] וְעָשָׂה הַכֹּהֵן אֶת־הַחַטָּאת וְכִפֶּר עַל־הַמִּטַּהֵר מִטֻּמְאָתוֹ וְאַחַר יִשְׁחַט אֶת־הָעֹלָה: [20] וְהֶעֱלָה הַכֹּהֵן אֶת־הָעֹלָה וְאֶת־הַמִּנְחָה הַמִּזְבֵּחָה וְכִפֶּר עָלָיו הַכֹּהֵן וְטָהֵר: ס

21If, however, he is poor and his means are insufficient, he shall take one male lamb for a guilt offering, to be elevated in expiation for him, one-tenth of a measure of choice flour with oil mixed in for a meal offering, and a *log* of oil; 22and two turtledoves or two pigeons, depending on his means, the one to be the sin offering and the other the burnt offering. 23On the eighth day of his cleansing he shall bring them to the priest at the entrance of the Tent of Meeting, before the Lord. 24The priest shall take the lamb of guilt offering and the *log* of oil, and elevate them as an elevation offering before the Lord. 25When the lamb of guilt offering has been slaughtered, the priest shall take some of the blood of the guilt offering and put it on the ridge of the right ear of the one being cleansed, on the thumb of his right hand, and on the big toe of his right foot. 26The priest shall then pour some of the oil into the palm of his own left hand, 27and with the finger of his right hand the priest shall sprinkle some of the oil that is in the palm of his left hand seven times before the Lord. 28Some of the oil in his palm shall be put by the priest on the ridge of the right ear of the one being cleansed, on the thumb of his right hand, and on the big toe of his right foot, over the same places as the blood of the guilt offering; 29and what is left of the oil in his palm the priest shall put on the head of the one being cleansed, to make expiation for him before the Lord. 30He shall then offer one of the turtledoves or pigeons, depending on his means—31whichever he can afford—the one as a sin offering and the other as a burnt offering, together with the meal offering. Thus the priest shall make expiation before the Lord for the one being cleansed. 32Such is the ritual for him who has a scaly affection and whose means for his cleansing are limited.

21 וְאִם־דַּל הוּא וְאֵין יָדוֹ מַשֶּׂגֶת וְלָקַח כֶּבֶשׂ אֶחָד אָשָׁם לִתְנוּפָה לְכַפֵּר עָלָיו וְעִשָּׂרוֹן סֹלֶת אֶחָד בָּלוּל בַּשֶּׁמֶן לְמִנְחָה וְלֹג שָׁמֶן: 22 וּשְׁתֵּי תֹרִים אוֹ שְׁנֵי בְּנֵי יוֹנָה אֲשֶׁר תַּשִּׂיג יָדוֹ וְהָיָה אֶחָד חַטָּאת וְהָאֶחָד עֹלָה: 23 וְהֵבִיא אֹתָם בַּיּוֹם הַשְּׁמִינִי לְטָהֳרָתוֹ אֶל־הַכֹּהֵן אֶל־פֶּתַח אֹהֶל־מוֹעֵד לִפְנֵי יְהוָה: 24 וְלָקַח הַכֹּהֵן אֶת־כֶּבֶשׂ הָאָשָׁם וְאֶת־לֹג הַשָּׁמֶן וְהֵנִיף אֹתָם הַכֹּהֵן תְּנוּפָה לִפְנֵי יְהוָה: 25 וְשָׁחַט אֶת־כֶּבֶשׂ הָאָשָׁם וְלָקַח הַכֹּהֵן מִדַּם הָאָשָׁם וְנָתַן עַל־תְּנוּךְ אֹזֶן־הַמִּטַּהֵר הַיְמָנִית וְעַל־בֹּהֶן יָדוֹ הַיְמָנִית וְעַל־בֹּהֶן רַגְלוֹ הַיְמָנִית: 26 וּמִן־הַשֶּׁמֶן יִצֹק הַכֹּהֵן עַל־כַּף הַכֹּהֵן הַשְּׂמָאלִית: 27 וְהִזָּה הַכֹּהֵן בְּאֶצְבָּעוֹ הַיְמָנִית מִן־הַשֶּׁמֶן אֲשֶׁר עַל־כַּפּוֹ הַשְּׂמָאלִית שֶׁבַע פְּעָמִים לִפְנֵי יְהוָה: 28 וְנָתַן הַכֹּהֵן מִן־הַשֶּׁמֶן אֲשֶׁר עַל־כַּפּוֹ עַל־תְּנוּךְ אֹזֶן הַמִּטַּהֵר הַיְמָנִית וְעַל־בֹּהֶן יָדוֹ הַיְמָנִית וְעַל־בֹּהֶן רַגְלוֹ הַיְמָנִית עַל־מְקוֹם דַּם הָאָשָׁם: 29 וְהַנּוֹתָר מִן־הַשֶּׁמֶן אֲשֶׁר עַל־כַּף הַכֹּהֵן יִתֵּן עַל־רֹאשׁ הַמִּטַּהֵר לְכַפֵּר עָלָיו לִפְנֵי יְהוָה: 30 וְעָשָׂה אֶת־הָאֶחָד מִן־הַתֹּרִים אוֹ מִן־בְּנֵי הַיּוֹנָה מֵאֲשֶׁר תַּשִּׂיג יָדוֹ: 31 אֵת אֲשֶׁר־תַּשִּׂיג יָדוֹ אֶת־הָאֶחָד חַטָּאת וְאֶת־הָאֶחָד עֹלָה עַל־הַמִּנְחָה וְכִפֶּר הַכֹּהֵן עַל הַמִּטַּהֵר לִפְנֵי יְהוָה: 32 זֹאת תּוֹרַת אֲשֶׁר־בּוֹ נֶגַע צָרָעַת אֲשֶׁר לֹא־תַשִּׂיג יָדוֹ בְּטָהֳרָתוֹ: פ

33The LORD spoke to Moses and Aaron, saying:

34When you enter the land of Canaan that I give you as a possession, and I inflict an eruptive plague upon a house in the land you possess, 35the owner of the house shall come and tell the priest, saying, "Something like a plague has appeared upon my house." 36The priest shall order the house cleared before the priest enters to examine the plague, so that nothing in the house may become unclean; after that the priest shall enter to examine the house. 37If, when he examines the plague, the plague in the walls of the house is found to consist of greenish[c] or reddish streaks[d] that appear to go deep into the wall, 38the priest shall come out of the house to the entrance of the house, and close up the house for seven days. 39On the seventh day the priest shall return. If he sees that the plague has spread on the walls of the house, 40the priest shall order the stones with the plague in them to be pulled out and cast outside the city into an unclean place. 41The house shall be scraped inside all around, and the coating[e] that is scraped off shall be dumped outside the city in an unclean place. 42They shall take other stones and replace those stones with them, and take other coating and plaster the house.

43If the plague again breaks out in the house, after the stones have been pulled out and after the house has been scraped and replastered, 44the priest shall come to examine: if the plague has spread in the house, it is a malignant eruption in the house; it is unclean. 45The house shall be torn down—its stones and timber and all the coating on the house—and taken to an unclean place outside the city.

46Whoever enters the house while it is closed up shall be unclean until evening. 47Whoever

---

c Or "yellowish."
d Meaning of Heb. sheqa'aruroth uncertain.
e Lit. "dust," "mud."

33 וַיְדַבֵּ֣ר יְהֹוָ֔ה אֶל־מֹשֶׁ֥ה וְאֶֽל־אַהֲרֹ֖ן לֵאמֹֽר׃

34 כִּ֤י תָבֹ֙אוּ֙ אֶל־אֶ֣רֶץ כְּנַ֔עַן אֲשֶׁ֥ר אֲנִ֖י נֹתֵ֣ן לָכֶ֣ם לַאֲחֻזָּ֑ה וְנָתַתִּי֙ נֶ֣גַע צָרַ֔עַת בְּבֵ֖ית אֶ֥רֶץ אֲחֻזַּתְכֶֽם׃ 35 וּבָא֙ אֲשֶׁר־ל֣וֹ הַבַּ֔יִת וְהִגִּ֥יד לַכֹּהֵ֖ן לֵאמֹ֑ר כְּנֶ֕גַע נִרְאָ֥ה לִ֖י בַּבָּֽיִת׃ 36 וְצִוָּ֨ה הַכֹּהֵ֜ן וּפִנּ֣וּ אֶת־הַבַּ֗יִת בְּטֶ֜רֶם יָבֹ֤א הַכֹּהֵן֙ לִרְא֣וֹת אֶת־הַנֶּ֔גַע וְלֹ֥א יִטְמָ֖א כׇּל־אֲשֶׁ֣ר בַּבָּ֑יִת וְאַ֥חַר כֵּ֛ן יָבֹ֥א הַכֹּהֵ֖ן לִרְא֥וֹת אֶת־הַבָּֽיִת׃ 37 וְרָאָ֣ה אֶת־הַנֶּ֗גַע וְהִנֵּ֤ה הַנֶּ֙גַע֙ בְּקִירֹ֣ת הַבַּ֔יִת שְׁקַֽעֲרוּרֹת֙ יְרַקְרַקֹּ֔ת א֖וֹ אֲדַמְדַּמֹּ֑ת וּמַרְאֵיהֶ֥ן שָׁפָ֖ל מִן־הַקִּֽיר׃ 38 וְיָצָ֧א הַכֹּהֵ֛ן מִן־הַבַּ֖יִת אֶל־פֶּ֣תַח הַבָּ֑יִת וְהִסְגִּ֥יר אֶת־הַבַּ֖יִת שִׁבְעַ֥ת יָמִֽים׃ 39 וְשָׁ֥ב הַכֹּהֵ֖ן בַּיּ֣וֹם הַשְּׁבִיעִ֑י וְרָאָ֕ה וְהִנֵּ֛ה פָּשָׂ֥ה הַנֶּ֖גַע בְּקִירֹ֥ת הַבָּֽיִת׃ 40 וְצִוָּה֙ הַכֹּהֵ֔ן וְחִלְּצוּ֙ אֶת־הָ֣אֲבָנִ֔ים אֲשֶׁ֥ר בָּהֵ֖ן הַנָּ֑גַע וְהִשְׁלִ֤יכוּ אֶתְהֶן֙ אֶל־מִח֣וּץ לָעִ֔יר אֶל־מָק֖וֹם טָמֵֽא׃ 41 וְאֶת־הַבַּ֛יִת יַקְצִ֥עַ מִבַּ֖יִת סָבִ֑יב וְשָׁפְכ֗וּ אֶת־הֶֽעָפָר֙ אֲשֶׁ֣ר הִקְצ֔וּ אֶל־מִח֣וּץ לָעִ֔יר אֶל־מָק֖וֹם טָמֵֽא׃ 42 וְלָקְחוּ֙ אֲבָנִ֣ים אֲחֵר֔וֹת וְהֵבִ֖יאוּ אֶל־תַּ֣חַת הָאֲבָנִ֑ים וְעָפָ֥ר אַחֵ֛ר יִקַּ֖ח וְטָ֥ח אֶת־הַבָּֽיִת׃ 43 וְאִם־יָשׁ֤וּב הַנֶּ֙גַע֙ וּפָרַ֣ח בַּבַּ֔יִת אַחַ֖ר חִלֵּ֣ץ אֶת־הָאֲבָנִ֑ים וְאַחֲרֵ֛י הִקְצ֥וֹת אֶת־הַבַּ֖יִת וְאַחֲרֵ֥י הִטּֽוֹחַ׃ 44 וּבָא֙ הַכֹּהֵ֔ן וְרָאָ֕ה וְהִנֵּ֛ה פָּשָׂ֥ה הַנֶּ֖גַע בַּבָּ֑יִת צָרַ֨עַת מַמְאֶ֥רֶת הִ֛וא בַּבַּ֖יִת טָמֵ֥א הֽוּא׃ 45 וְנָתַ֣ץ אֶת־הַבַּ֗יִת אֶת־אֲבָנָיו֙ וְאֶת־עֵצָ֔יו וְאֵ֖ת כׇּל־עֲפַ֣ר הַבָּ֑יִת וְהוֹצִיא֙ אֶל־מִח֣וּץ לָעִ֔יר אֶל־מָק֖וֹם טָמֵֽא׃ 46 וְהַבָּא֙ אֶל־הַבַּ֔יִת כׇּל־יְמֵ֖י הִסְגִּ֣יר אֹת֑וֹ

240

sleeps in the house must wash his clothes, and whoever eats in the house must wash his clothes.

⁴⁸If, however, the priest comes and sees that the plague has not spread in the house after the house was replastered, the priest shall pronounce the house clean, for the plague has healed. ⁴⁹To purge the house, he shall take two birds, cedar wood, crimson stuff, and hyssop. ⁵⁰He shall slaughter the one bird over fresh water in an earthen vessel. ⁵¹He shall take the cedar wood, the hyssop, the crimson stuff, and the live bird, and dip them in the blood of the slaughtered bird and the fresh water, and sprinkle on the house seven times. ⁵²Having purged the house with the blood of the bird, the fresh water, the live bird, the cedar wood, the hyssop, and the crimson stuff, ⁵³he shall set the live bird free outside the city in the open country. Thus he shall make expiation for the house, and it shall be clean.

⁵⁴Such is the ritual for every eruptive affection—for scalls, ⁵⁵for an eruption on a cloth or a house, ⁵⁶for swellings, for rashes, or for discolorations—⁵⁷to determine when they are unclean and when they are clean.

Such is the ritual concerning eruptions.

15 The LORD spoke to Moses and Aaron, saying: ²Speak to the Israelite people and say to them:

When any man has a discharge issuing from his member,ᵃ he is unclean. ³The uncleanness from his discharge shall mean the following— whether his member runs with the discharge or is stopped up so that there is no discharge, his uncleanness means this: ⁴Any bedding on which the one with the discharge lies shall be unclean, and every object on which he sits shall be un-

אֶת־בְּגָדָיו וְהָאֹכֵל בַּבַּיִת יְכַבֵּס יִטְמָא עַד־הָעָרֶב: 47 וְהַשֹּׁכֵב בַּבַּיִת יְכַבֵּס אֶת־בְּגָדָיו: 48 וְאִם־בֹּא יָבֹא הַכֹּהֵן וְרָאָה וְהִנֵּה לֹא־פָשָׂה הַנֶּגַע בַּבַּיִת אַחֲרֵי הִטֹּחַ אֶת־הַבָּיִת וְטִהַר הַכֹּהֵן אֶת־הַבַּיִת כִּי נִרְפָּא הַנָּגַע: 49 וְלָקַח לְחַטֵּא אֶת־הַבַּיִת שְׁתֵּי צִפֳּרִים וְעֵץ אֶרֶז וּשְׁנִי תוֹלַעַת וְאֵזֹב: 50 וְשָׁחַט אֶת־הַצִּפֹּר הָאֶחָת אֶל־כְּלִי־חֶרֶשׂ עַל־מַיִם חַיִּים: 51 וְלָקַח אֶת־עֵץ־הָאֶרֶז וְאֶת־הָאֵזֹב וְאֵת שְׁנִי הַתּוֹלַעַת וְאֵת הַצִּפֹּר הַחַיָּה וְטָבַל אֹתָם בְּדַם הַצִּפֹּר הַשְּׁחוּטָה וּבַמַּיִם הַחַיִּים וְהִזָּה אֶל־הַבַּיִת שֶׁבַע פְּעָמִים: 52 וְחִטֵּא אֶת־הַבַּיִת בְּדַם הַצִּפּוֹר וּבַמַּיִם הַחַיִּים וּבַצִּפֹּר הַחַיָּה וּבְעֵץ הָאֶרֶז וּבָאֵזֹב וּבִשְׁנִי הַתּוֹלָעַת: 53 וְשִׁלַּח אֶת־הַצִּפֹּר הַחַיָּה אֶל־מִחוּץ לָעִיר אֶל־פְּנֵי הַשָּׂדֶה וְכִפֶּר עַל־הַבַּיִת וְטָהֵר:

54 זֹאת הַתּוֹרָה לְכָל־נֶגַע הַצָּרַעַת וְלַנָּתֶק: 55 וּלְצָרַעַת הַבֶּגֶד וְלַבָּיִת: 56 וְלַשְׂאֵת וְלַסַּפַּחַת וְלַבֶּהָרֶת: 57 לְהוֹרֹת בְּיוֹם הַטָּמֵא וּבְיוֹם הַטָּהֹר זֹאת תּוֹרַת הַצָּרָעַת: ס

טו וַיְדַבֵּר יְהֹוָה אֶל־מֹשֶׁה וְאֶל־אַהֲרֹן לֵאמֹר: 2 דַּבְּרוּ אֶל־בְּנֵי יִשְׂרָאֵל וַאֲמַרְתֶּם אֲלֵהֶם אִישׁ אִישׁ כִּי יִהְיֶה זָב מִבְּשָׂרוֹ זוֹבוֹ טָמֵא הוּא: 3 וְזֹאת תִּהְיֶה טֻמְאָתוֹ בְּזוֹבוֹ רָר בְּשָׂרוֹ אֶת־זוֹבוֹ אוֹ־הֶחְתִּים בְּשָׂרוֹ מִזּוֹבוֹ טֻמְאָתוֹ הִוא: 4 כָּל־הַמִּשְׁכָּב אֲשֶׁר יִשְׁכַּב עָלָיו הַזָּב יִטְמָא וְכָל־הַכְּלִי אֲשֶׁר־יֵשֵׁב

ᵃ Lit. "flesh."

clean. 5Anyone who touches his bedding shall wash his clothes, bathe in water, and remain unclean until evening. 6Whoever sits on an object on which the one with the discharge has sat shall wash his clothes, bathe in water, and remain unclean until evening. 7Whoever touches the body of the one with the discharge shall wash his clothes, bathe in water, and remain unclean until evening. 8If one with a discharge spits on one who is clean, the latter shall wash his clothes, bathe in water, and remain unclean until evening. 9Any means for riding that one with a discharge has mounted shall be unclean; 10whoever touches anything that was under him shall be unclean until evening; and whoever carries such things shall wash his clothes, bathe in water, and remain unclean until evening. 11If one with a discharge, without having rinsed his hands in water, touches another person, that person shall wash his clothes, bathe in water, and remain unclean until evening. 12An earthen vessel that one with a discharge touches shall be broken; and any wooden implement shall be rinsed with water.

13When one with a discharge becomes clean of his discharge, he shall count off seven days for his cleansing, wash his clothes, and bathe his body in fresh water; then he shall be clean. 14On the eighth day he shall take two turtledoves or two pigeons and come before the Lord at the entrance of the Tent of Meeting and give them to the priest. 15The priest shall offer them, the one as a sin offering and the other as a burnt offering. Thus the priest shall make expiation on his behalf, for his discharge, before the Lord.

16When a man has an emission of semen, he shall bathe his whole body in water and remain unclean until evening. 17All cloth or leather on which semen falls shall be washed in water and remain unclean until evening. 18And if a man has carnal relations with a woman, they

עָלָ֖יו יִטְמָֽא: 5 וְאִ֕ישׁ אֲשֶׁ֥ר יִגַּ֖ע בְּמִשְׁכָּב֑וֹ יְכַבֵּ֣ס בְּגָדָ֗יו וְרָחַ֥ץ בַּמַּ֖יִם וְטָמֵ֥א עַד־הָעָֽרֶב: 6 וְהַיֹּשֵׁב֙ עַל־הַכְּלִ֔י אֲשֶׁר־יֵשֵׁ֥ב עָלָ֖יו הַזָּ֑ב יְכַבֵּ֣ס בְּגָדָ֗יו וְרָחַ֥ץ בַּמַּ֖יִם וְטָמֵ֥א עַד־הָעָֽרֶב: 7 *וְהַנֹּגֵ֖עַ בִּבְשַׂ֣ר הַזָּ֑ב יְכַבֵּ֣ס בְּגָדָ֗יו וְרָחַ֥ץ בַּמַּ֖יִם וְטָמֵ֥א עַד־הָעָֽרֶב: 8 וְכִֽי־יָרֹ֥ק הַזָּ֖ב בַּטָּה֑וֹר וְכִבֶּ֣ס בְּגָדָ֗יו וְרָחַ֥ץ בַּמַּ֖יִם וְטָמֵ֥א עַד־הָעָֽרֶב: 9 וְכָל־הַמֶּרְכָּ֗ב אֲשֶׁ֨ר יִרְכַּ֥ב עָלָ֛יו הַזָּ֖ב יִטְמָֽא: 10 וְכָל־הַנֹּגֵ֗עַ בְּכֹל֙ אֲשֶׁ֣ר יִהְיֶ֣ה תַחְתָּ֔יו יִטְמָ֖א עַד־הָעָ֑רֶב וְהַנּוֹשֵׂ֣א אוֹתָ֗ם יְכַבֵּ֧ס בְּגָדָ֛יו וְרָחַ֥ץ בַּמַּ֖יִם וְטָמֵ֥א עַד־הָעָֽרֶב: 11 וְכֹ֨ל אֲשֶׁ֤ר יִגַּע־בּוֹ֙ הַזָּ֔ב וְיָדָ֖יו לֹא־שָׁטַ֣ף בַּמָּ֑יִם וְכִבֶּ֧ס בְּגָדָ֛יו וְרָחַ֥ץ בַּמַּ֖יִם וְטָמֵ֥א עַד־הָעָֽרֶב: 12 וּכְלִי־חֶ֛רֶשׂ אֲשֶׁר־יִגַּע־בּ֥וֹ הַזָּ֖ב יִשָּׁבֵ֑ר וְכָל־כְּלִי־עֵ֔ץ יִשָּׁטֵ֖ף בַּמָּֽיִם:

13 וְכִֽי־יִטְהַ֤ר הַזָּב֙ מִזּוֹב֔וֹ וְסָ֥פַר ל֛וֹ שִׁבְעַ֥ת יָמִ֛ים לְטָהֳרָת֖וֹ וְכִבֶּ֣ס בְּגָדָ֑יו וְרָחַ֧ץ בְּשָׂר֛וֹ בְּמַ֥יִם חַיִּ֖ים וְטָהֵֽר: 14 וּבַיּ֣וֹם הַשְּׁמִינִ֗י יִקַּֽח־לוֹ֙ שְׁתֵּ֣י תֹרִ֔ים א֥וֹ שְׁנֵ֖י בְּנֵ֣י יוֹנָ֑ה וּבָ֣א ׀ לִפְנֵ֣י יְהֹוָ֗ה אֶל־פֶּ֙תַח֙ אֹ֣הֶל מוֹעֵ֔ד וּנְתָנָ֖ם אֶל־הַכֹּהֵֽן: 15 וְעָשָׂ֤ה אֹתָם֙ הַכֹּהֵ֔ן אֶחָ֣ד חַטָּ֔את וְהָאֶחָ֖ד עֹלָ֑ה וְכִפֶּ֨ר עָלָ֧יו הַכֹּהֵ֛ן לִפְנֵ֥י יְהֹוָ֖ה מִזּוֹבֽוֹ: ס

16 וְאִ֕ישׁ כִּֽי־תֵצֵ֥א מִמֶּ֖נּוּ שִׁכְבַת־זָ֑רַע וְרָחַ֥ץ בַּמַּ֛יִם אֶת־כָּל־בְּשָׂר֖וֹ וְטָמֵ֥א עַד־הָעָֽרֶב: 17 וְכָל־בֶּ֣גֶד וְכָל־ע֔וֹר אֲשֶׁר־יִהְיֶ֥ה עָלָ֖יו שִׁכְבַת־זָ֑רַע וְכֻבַּ֥ס בַּמַּ֖יִם וְטָמֵ֥א עַד־הָעָֽרֶב: פ 18 וְאִשָּׁ֕ה אֲשֶׁ֨ר יִשְׁכַּ֥ב אִ֛ישׁ אֹתָ֖הּ שִׁכְבַת־זָ֑רַע וְרָחֲצ֣וּ בַמַּ֔יִם וְטָמְא֖וּ עַד־הָעָֽרֶב:

shall bathe in water and remain unclean until evening.

¹⁹When a woman has a discharge, her discharge being blood from her body, she shall remain in her impurity seven days; whoever touches her shall be unclean until evening. ²⁰Anything that she lies on during her impurity shall be unclean; and anything that she sits on shall be unclean. ²¹Anyone who touches her bedding shall wash his clothes, bathe in water, and remain unclean until evening; ²²and anyone who touches any object on which she has sat shall wash his clothes, bathe in water, and remain unclean until evening. ²³Be it the bedding or be it the object on which she has sat, on touching it he shall be unclean until evening. ²⁴And if a man lies with her, her impurity is communicated to him; he shall be unclean seven days, and any bedding on which he lies shall become unclean.

²⁵When a woman has had a discharge of blood for many days, not at the time of her impurity, or when she has a discharge beyond her period of impurity, she shall be unclean, as though at the time of her impurity, as long as her discharge lasts. ²⁶Any bedding on which she lies while her discharge lasts shall be for her like bedding during her impurity; and any object on which she sits shall become unclean, as it does during her impurity: ²⁷whoever touches them shall be unclean; he shall wash his clothes, bathe in water, and remain unclean until evening.

²⁸When she becomes clean of her discharge, she shall count off seven days, and after that she shall be clean. ²⁹On the eighth day she shall take two turtledoves or two pigeons, and bring them to the priest at the entrance of the Tent of Meeting. ³⁰The priest shall offer the one as a sin offering and the other as a burnt offering; and the priest shall make expiation on her behalf, for her unclean discharge, before the LORD.

19 וְאִשָּׁה֙ כִּֽי־תִהְיֶ֣ה זָבָ֔ה דָּ֛ם יִהְיֶ֥ה זֹבָ֖הּ בִּבְשָׂרָ֑הּ שִׁבְעַ֤ת יָמִים֙ תִּהְיֶ֣ה בְנִדָּתָ֔הּ וְכָל־הַנֹּגֵ֥עַ בָּ֖הּ יִטְמָ֥א עַד־הָעָֽרֶב׃ 20 וְכֹל֩ אֲשֶׁ֨ר תִּשְׁכַּ֥ב עָלָ֛יו בְּנִדָּתָ֖הּ יִטְמָ֑א וְכֹ֛ל אֲשֶׁר־תֵּשֵׁ֥ב עָלָ֖יו יִטְמָֽא׃ 21 וְכָל־הַנֹּגֵ֖עַ בְּמִשְׁכָּבָ֑הּ יְכַבֵּ֧ס בְּגָדָ֛יו וְרָחַ֥ץ בַּמַּ֖יִם וְטָמֵ֥א עַד־הָעָֽרֶב׃ 22 וְכָ֨ל־הַנֹּגֵ֔עַ בְּכָל־כְּלִ֖י אֲשֶׁר־תֵּשֵׁ֣ב עָלָ֑יו יְכַבֵּ֧ס בְּגָדָ֛יו וְרָחַ֥ץ בַּמַּ֖יִם וְטָמֵ֥א עַד־הָעָֽרֶב׃ 23 וְאִ֨ם עַל־הַמִּשְׁכָּ֜ב ה֗וּא א֤וֹ עַֽל־הַכְּלִי֙ אֲשֶׁר־הִ֣וא יֹשֶֽׁבֶת־עָלָ֔יו בְּנָגְעוֹ־ב֖וֹ יִטְמָ֥א עַד־הָעָֽרֶב׃ 24 וְאִ֡ם שָׁכֹב֩ יִשְׁכַּ֨ב אִ֜ישׁ אֹתָ֗הּ וּתְהִ֤י נִדָּתָהּ֙ עָלָ֔יו וְטָמֵ֖א שִׁבְעַ֣ת יָמִ֑ים וְכָל־הַמִּשְׁכָּ֛ב אֲשֶׁר־יִשְׁכַּ֥ב עָלָ֖יו יִטְמָֽא׃ פ

25 וְאִשָּׁ֡ה כִּֽי־יָזוּב֩ ז֨וֹב דָּמָ֜הּ יָמִ֣ים רַבִּ֗ים בְּלֹא֙ עֶת־נִדָּתָ֔הּ א֥וֹ כִֽי־תָז֖וּב עַל־נִדָּתָ֑הּ כָּל־יְמֵ֞י ז֣וֹב טֻמְאָתָ֗הּ כִּימֵ֧י נִדָּתָ֛הּ תִּהְיֶ֖ה טְמֵאָ֥ה הִֽוא׃ 26 כָּל־הַמִּשְׁכָּ֞ב אֲשֶׁר־תִּשְׁכַּ֤ב עָלָיו֙ כָּל־יְמֵ֣י זוֹבָ֔הּ כְּמִשְׁכַּ֥ב נִדָּתָ֖הּ יִֽהְיֶה־לָּ֑הּ וְכָֽל־הַכְּלִי֙ אֲשֶׁ֣ר תֵּשֵׁ֣ב עָלָ֔יו טָמֵ֣א יִהְיֶ֔ה כְּטֻמְאַ֖ת נִדָּתָֽהּ׃ 27 וְכָל־הַנּוֹגֵ֥עַ בָּ֖ם יִטְמָ֑א וְכִבֶּ֧ס בְּגָדָ֛יו וְרָחַ֥ץ בַּמַּ֖יִם וְטָמֵ֥א עַד־הָעָֽרֶב׃

28 וְאִֽם־טָהֲרָ֖ה מִזּוֹבָ֑הּ וְסָ֥פְרָה לָּ֛הּ שִׁבְעַ֥ת יָמִ֖ים וְאַחַ֥ר תִּטְהָֽר׃ 29 וּבַיּ֣וֹם הַשְּׁמִינִ֗י תִּֽקַּח־לָהּ֙ שְׁתֵּ֣י תֹרִ֔ים א֥וֹ שְׁנֵ֖י בְּנֵ֣י יוֹנָ֑ה וְהֵבִיאָ֤ה אוֹתָם֙ אֶל־הַכֹּהֵ֔ן אֶל־פֶּ֖תַח אֹ֥הֶל מוֹעֵֽד׃ 30 וְעָשָׂ֣ה הַכֹּהֵ֗ן אֶת־הָֽאֶחָד֙ חַטָּ֔את וְאֶת־הָֽאֶחָ֖ד עֹלָ֑ה וְכִפֶּ֨ר עָלֶ֤יהָ הַכֹּהֵן֙ לִפְנֵ֣י יְהֹוָ֔ה מִזּ֖וֹב טֻמְאָתָֽהּ׃

31You shall put the Israelites on guard against their uncleanness, lest they die through their uncleanness by defiling My Tabernacle which is among them.

32Such is the ritual concerning him who has a discharge: concerning him who has an emission of semen and becomes unclean thereby, 33and concerning her who is in menstrual infirmity, and concerning anyone, male or female, who has a discharge, and concerning a man who lies with an unclean woman.

16 'AHAREI MOT

The Lord spoke to Moses after the death of the two sons of Aaron who died when they drew too close to the presence of the Lord. 2The Lord said to Moses:

Tell your brother Aaron that he is not to come at willa into the Shrine behind the curtain, in front of the cover that is upon the ark, lest he die; for I appear in the cloud over the cover. 3Thus only shall Aaron enter the Shrine: with a bull of the herd for a sin offering and a ram for a burnt offering.—4He shall be dressed in a sacral linen tunic, with linen breeches next to his flesh, and be girt with a linen sash, and he shall wear a linen turban. They are sacral vestments; he shall bathe his body in water and then put them on.—5And from the Israelite community he shall take two he-goats for a sin offering and a ram for a burnt offering.

6Aaron is to offer his own bull of sin offering, to make expiation for himself and for his household. 7Aaronb shall take the two he-goats and let them stand before the Lord at the entrance of the Tent of Meeting; 8and he shall place lots upon the two goats, one marked for the Lord and the other marked for Azazel. 9Aaron shall bring forward the goat designated by lot for the Lord, which he is to offer as a sin offering;

31 וְהִזַּרְתֶּ֥ם אֶת־בְּנֵֽי־יִשְׂרָאֵ֖ל מִטֻּמְאָתָ֑ם וְלֹ֤א יָמֻ֨תוּ֙ בְּטֻמְאָתָ֔ם בְּטַמְּאָ֥ם אֶת־מִשְׁכָּנִ֖י אֲשֶׁ֥ר בְּתוֹכָֽם׃ 32 זֹ֥את תּוֹרַ֖ת הַזָּ֑ב וַאֲשֶׁ֨ר תֵּצֵ֤א מִמֶּ֨נּוּ֙ שִׁכְבַת־זֶ֔רַע לְטָמְאָה־בָֽהּ׃ 33 וְהַדָּוָה֙ בְּנִדָּתָ֔הּ וְהַזָּב֙ אֶת־זוֹב֔וֹ לַזָּכָ֖ר וְלַנְּקֵבָ֑ה וּלְאִ֕ישׁ אֲשֶׁ֥ר יִשְׁכַּ֖ב עִם־טְמֵאָֽה׃ פ

טז אחרי מות

וַיְדַבֵּ֤ר יְהוָה֙ אֶל־מֹשֶׁ֔ה אַחֲרֵ֣י מ֔וֹת שְׁנֵ֖י בְּנֵ֣י אַהֲרֹ֑ן בְּקָרְבָתָ֥ם לִפְנֵֽי־יְהוָ֖ה וַיָּמֻֽתוּ׃ 2 וַיֹּ֨אמֶר יְהוָ֜ה אֶל־מֹשֶׁ֗ה דַּבֵּר֮ אֶל־אַהֲרֹ֣ן אָחִיךָ֒ וְאַל־יָבֹ֤א בְכָל־עֵת֙ אֶל־הַקֹּ֜דֶשׁ מִבֵּ֣ית לַפָּרֹ֗כֶת אֶל־פְּנֵ֨י הַכַּפֹּ֜רֶת אֲשֶׁ֤ר עַל־הָאָרֹן֙ וְלֹ֣א יָמ֔וּת כִּ֚י בֶּֽעָנָ֔ן אֵרָאֶ֖ה עַל־הַכַּפֹּֽרֶת׃ 3 בְּזֹ֛את יָבֹ֥א אַהֲרֹ֖ן אֶל־הַקֹּ֑דֶשׁ בְּפַ֧ר בֶּן־בָּקָ֛ר לְחַטָּ֖את וְאַ֥יִל לְעֹלָֽה׃ 4 כְּתֹֽנֶת־בַּ֨ד קֹ֜דֶשׁ יִלְבָּ֗שׁ וּמִֽכְנְסֵי־בַד֮ יִהְי֣וּ עַל־בְּשָׂרוֹ֒ וּבְאַבְנֵ֥ט בַּד֙ יַחְגֹּ֔ר וּבְמִצְנֶ֥פֶת בַּ֖ד יִצְנֹ֑ף בִּגְדֵי־קֹ֣דֶשׁ הֵ֔ם וְרָחַ֥ץ בַּמַּ֛יִם אֶת־בְּשָׂר֖וֹ וּלְבֵשָֽׁם׃ 5 וּמֵאֵ֗ת עֲדַת֙ בְּנֵ֣י יִשְׂרָאֵ֔ל יִקַּ֛ח שְׁנֵֽי־שְׂעִירֵ֥י עִזִּ֖ים לְחַטָּ֑את וְאַ֥יִל אֶחָ֖ד לְעֹלָֽה׃ 6 וְהִקְרִ֧יב אַהֲרֹ֛ן אֶת־פַּ֥ר הַחַטָּ֖את אֲשֶׁר־ל֑וֹ וְכִפֶּ֥ר בַּעֲד֖וֹ וּבְעַ֥ד בֵּיתֽוֹ׃ 7 וְלָקַ֖ח אֶת־שְׁנֵ֣י הַשְּׂעִירִ֑ם וְהֶעֱמִ֤יד אֹתָם֙ לִפְנֵ֣י יְהוָ֔ה פֶּ֖תַח אֹ֥הֶל מוֹעֵֽד׃ 8 וְנָתַ֧ן אַהֲרֹ֛ן עַל־שְׁנֵ֥י הַשְּׂעִירִ֖ם גֹּרָל֑וֹת גּוֹרָ֤ל אֶחָד֙ לַֽיהוָ֔ה וְגוֹרָ֥ל אֶחָ֖ד לַעֲזָאזֵֽל׃ 9 וְהִקְרִ֤יב אַהֲרֹן֙ אֶת־הַשָּׂעִ֔יר אֲשֶׁ֨ר עָלָ֥ה עָלָ֛יו הַגּוֹרָ֖ל לַיהוָ֑ה

---

a   Lit. "at any time."
b   Moved up from v. 8 for clarity.

244

10while the goat designated by lot for Azazel shall be left standing alive before the LORD, to make expiation with it and to send it off to the wilderness for Azazel.

11Aaron shall then offer his bull of sin offering, to make expiation for himself and his household. He shall slaughter his bull of sin offering, 12and he shall take a panful of glowing coals scooped from the altar before the LORD, and two handfuls of finely ground aromatic incense, and bring this behind the curtain. 13He shall put the incense on the fire before the LORD, so that the cloud from the incense screens the cover that is over [the Ark of] the Pact, lest he die. 14He shall take some of the blood of the bull and sprinkle it with his finger over the cover on the east side; and in front of the cover he shall sprinkle some of the blood with his finger seven times. 15He shall then slaughter the people's goat of sin offering, bring its blood behind the curtain, and do with its blood as he has done with the blood of the bull: he shall sprinkle it over the cover and in front of the cover.

16Thus he shall purge the Shrine of the uncleanness and transgression of the Israelites, whatever their sins; and he shall do the same for the Tent of Meeting, which abides with them in the midst of their uncleanness. 17When he goes in to make expiation in the Shrine, nobody else shall be in the Tent of Meeting until he comes out.

When he has made expiation for himself and his household, and for the whole congregation of Israel, 18he shall go out to the altar that is before the LORD and purge it: he shall take some of the blood of the bull and of the goat and apply it to each of the horns of the altar; 19and the rest of the blood he shall sprinkle on it with his finger seven times. Thus he shall cleanse it of the uncleanness of the Israelites and consecrate it.

וְעָשָׂהוּ חַטָּאת: 10 וְהַשָּׂעִיר אֲשֶׁר עָלָה עָלָיו הַגּוֹרָל לַעֲזָאזֵל יָעֳמַד־חַי לִפְנֵי יְהֹוָה לְכַפֵּר עָלָיו לְשַׁלַּח אֹתוֹ לַעֲזָאזֵל הַמִּדְבָּרָה:

11 וְהִקְרִיב אַהֲרֹן אֶת־פַּר הַחַטָּאת אֲשֶׁר־לוֹ וְכִפֶּר בַּעֲדוֹ וּבְעַד בֵּיתוֹ וְשָׁחַט אֶת־פַּר הַחַטָּאת אֲשֶׁר־לוֹ: 12 וְלָקַח מְלֹא־הַמַּחְתָּה גַּחֲלֵי־אֵשׁ מֵעַל הַמִּזְבֵּחַ מִלִּפְנֵי יְהֹוָה וּמְלֹא חָפְנָיו קְטֹרֶת סַמִּים דַּקָּה וְהֵבִיא מִבֵּית לַפָּרֹכֶת: 13 וְנָתַן אֶת־הַקְּטֹרֶת עַל־הָאֵשׁ לִפְנֵי יְהֹוָה וְכִסָּה | עֲנַן הַקְּטֹרֶת אֶת־הַכַּפֹּרֶת אֲשֶׁר עַל־הָעֵדוּת וְלֹא יָמוּת: 14 וְלָקַח מִדַּם הַפָּר וְהִזָּה בְאֶצְבָּעוֹ עַל־פְּנֵי הַכַּפֹּרֶת קֵדְמָה וְלִפְנֵי הַכַּפֹּרֶת יַזֶּה שֶׁבַע־פְּעָמִים מִן־הַדָּם בְּאֶצְבָּעוֹ: 15 וְשָׁחַט אֶת־שְׂעִיר הַחַטָּאת אֲשֶׁר לָעָם וְהֵבִיא אֶת־דָּמוֹ אֶל־מִבֵּית לַפָּרֹכֶת וְעָשָׂה אֶת־דָּמוֹ כַּאֲשֶׁר עָשָׂה לְדַם הַפָּר וְהִזָּה אֹתוֹ עַל־הַכַּפֹּרֶת וְלִפְנֵי הַכַּפֹּרֶת:

16 וְכִפֶּר עַל־הַקֹּדֶשׁ מִטֻּמְאֹת בְּנֵי יִשְׂרָאֵל וּמִפִּשְׁעֵיהֶם לְכָל־חַטֹּאתָם וְכֵן יַעֲשֶׂה לְאֹהֶל מוֹעֵד הַשֹּׁכֵן אִתָּם בְּתוֹךְ טֻמְאֹתָם: 17 וְכָל־אָדָם לֹא־יִהְיֶה | בְּאֹהֶל מוֹעֵד בְּבֹאוֹ לְכַפֵּר בַּקֹּדֶשׁ עַד־צֵאתוֹ וְכִפֶּר בַּעֲדוֹ וּבְעַד בֵּיתוֹ וּבְעַד כָּל־קְהַל יִשְׂרָאֵל: 18 וְיָצָא אֶל־הַמִּזְבֵּחַ אֲשֶׁר לִפְנֵי־יְהֹוָה וְכִפֶּר עָלָיו וְלָקַח מִדַּם הַפָּר וּמִדַּם הַשָּׂעִיר וְנָתַן עַל־קַרְנוֹת הַמִּזְבֵּחַ סָבִיב: 19 וְהִזָּה עָלָיו מִן־הַדָּם בְּאֶצְבָּעוֹ שֶׁבַע פְּעָמִים וְטִהֲרוֹ וְקִדְּשׁוֹ מִטֻּמְאֹת בְּנֵי יִשְׂרָאֵל:

20When he has finished purging the Shrine, the Tent of Meeting, and the altar, the live goat shall be brought forward. 21Aaron shall lay both his hands upon the head of the live goat and confess over it all the iniquities and transgressions of the Israelites, whatever their sins, putting them on the head of the goat; and it shall be sent off to the wilderness through a designated* man. 22Thus the goat shall carry on it all their iniquities to an inaccessible region; and the goat shall be set free in the wilderness.

23And Aaron shall go into the Tent of Meeting, take off the linen vestments that he put on when he entered the Shrine, and leave them there. 24He shall bathe his body in water in the holy precinct and put on his vestments; then he shall come out and offer his burnt offering and the burnt offering of the people, making expiation for himself and for the people. 25The fat of the sin offering he shall turn into smoke on the altar.

26He who set the Azazel-goat free shall wash his clothes and bathe his body in water; after that he may reenter the camp.

27The bull of sin offering and the goat of sin offering whose blood was brought in to purge the Shrine shall be taken outside the camp; and their hides, flesh, and dung shall be consumed in fire. 28He who burned them shall wash his clothes and bathe his body in water; after that he may re-enter the camp.

29And this shall be to you a law for all time: In the seventh month, on the tenth day of the month, you shall practice self-denial; and you shall do no manner of work, neither the citizen nor the alien who resides among you. 30For on this day atonement shall be made for you to cleanse you of all your sins; you shall be clean before the LORD. 31It shall be a sabbath of complete rest for you, and you shall practice self-denial; it is a law for all time. 32The priest who

c   *Meaning of Heb. 'itti uncertain.*

20 וְכִלָּה֙ מִכַּפֵּ֣ר אֶת־הַקֹּ֔דֶשׁ וְאֶת־אֹ֥הֶל מוֹעֵ֖ד וְאֶת־הַמִּזְבֵּ֑חַ וְהִקְרִ֖יב אֶת־הַשָּׂעִ֥יר הֶחָֽי׃ 21 וְסָמַ֨ךְ אַהֲרֹ֜ן אֶת־שְׁתֵּ֣י ידו יָדָ֗יו עַ֣ל רֹ֣אשׁ הַשָּׂעִיר֮ הַחַי֒ וְהִתְוַדָּ֣ה עָלָ֗יו אֶת־כָּל־עֲוֺנֹת֙ בְּנֵ֣י יִשְׂרָאֵ֔ל וְאֶת־כָּל־פִּשְׁעֵיהֶ֖ם לְכָל־חַטֹּאתָ֑ם וְנָתַ֤ן אֹתָם֙ עַל־רֹ֣אשׁ הַשָּׂעִ֔יר וְשִׁלַּ֛ח בְּיַד־אִ֥ישׁ עִתִּ֖י הַמִּדְבָּֽרָה׃ 22 וְנָשָׂ֨א הַשָּׂעִ֥יר עָלָ֛יו אֶת־כָּל־עֲוֺנֹתָ֖ם אֶל־אֶ֣רֶץ גְּזֵרָ֑ה וְשִׁלַּ֥ח אֶת־הַשָּׂעִ֖יר בַּמִּדְבָּֽר׃

23 וּבָ֤א אַהֲרֹן֙ אֶל־אֹ֣הֶל מוֹעֵ֔ד וּפָשַׁט֙ אֶת־בִּגְדֵ֣י הַבָּ֔ד אֲשֶׁ֥ר לָבַ֖שׁ בְּבֹא֣וֹ אֶל־הַקֹּ֑דֶשׁ וְהִנִּיחָ֖ם שָֽׁם׃ 24 וְרָחַ֨ץ אֶת־בְּשָׂר֤וֹ בַמַּ֙יִם֙ בְּמָק֣וֹם קָד֔וֹשׁ וְלָבַ֖שׁ אֶת־בְּגָדָ֑יו וְיָצָ֗א וְעָשָׂ֤ה אֶת־עֹֽלָתוֹ֙ וְאֶת־עֹלַ֣ת הָעָ֔ם וְכִפֶּ֥ר בַּעֲד֖וֹ וּבְעַ֥ד הָעָֽם׃ 25 וְאֵ֛ת חֵ֥לֶב הַחַטָּ֖את יַקְטִ֥יר הַמִּזְבֵּֽחָה׃

26 וְהַֽמְשַׁלֵּ֤חַ אֶת־הַשָּׂעִיר֙ לַֽעֲזָאזֵ֔ל יְכַבֵּ֣ס בְּגָדָ֔יו וְרָחַ֥ץ אֶת־בְּשָׂר֖וֹ בַּמָּ֑יִם וְאַחֲרֵי־כֵ֖ן יָב֥וֹא אֶל־הַֽמַּחֲנֶֽה׃

27 וְאֵת֩ פַּ֨ר הַֽחַטָּ֜את וְאֵ֣ת ׀ שְׂעִ֣יר הַֽחַטָּ֗את אֲשֶׁ֨ר הוּבָ֤א אֶת־דָּמָם֙ לְכַפֵּ֣ר בַּקֹּ֔דֶשׁ יוֹצִ֖יא אֶל־מִח֣וּץ לַֽמַּחֲנֶ֑ה וְשָׂרְפ֣וּ בָאֵ֔שׁ אֶת־עֹרֹתָ֥ם וְאֶת־בְּשָׂרָ֖ם וְאֶת־פִּרְשָֽׁם׃ 28 וְהַשֹּׂרֵ֣ף אֹתָ֗ם יְכַבֵּ֣ס בְּגָדָ֔יו וְרָחַ֥ץ אֶת־בְּשָׂר֖וֹ בַּמָּ֑יִם וְאַחֲרֵי־כֵ֖ן יָב֥וֹא אֶל־הַֽמַּחֲנֶֽה׃

29 וְהָיְתָ֥ה לָכֶ֖ם לְחֻקַּ֣ת עוֹלָ֑ם בַּחֹ֣דֶשׁ הַשְּׁבִיעִ֣י בֶּֽעָשׂ֣וֹר לַחֹ֗דֶשׁ תְּעַנּ֣וּ אֶת־נַפְשֹֽׁתֵיכֶ֗ם וְכָל־מְלָאכָה֙ לֹ֣א תַעֲשׂ֔וּ הָֽאֶזְרָ֔ח וְהַגֵּ֖ר הַגָּ֣ר בְּתוֹכְכֶֽם׃ 30 כִּֽי־בַיּ֥וֹם הַזֶּ֛ה יְכַפֵּ֥ר עֲלֵיכֶ֖ם לְטַהֵ֣ר אֶתְכֶ֑ם מִכֹּל֙ חַטֹּ֣אתֵיכֶ֔ם לִפְנֵ֥י יְהֹוָ֖ה תִּטְהָֽרוּ׃ 31 שַׁבַּ֧ת שַׁבָּת֛וֹן הִיא֙ לָכֶ֔ם וְעִנִּיתֶ֖ם אֶת־נַפְשֹֽׁתֵיכֶ֑ם

246

has been anointed and ordained to serve as priest in place of his father shall make expiation. He shall put on the linen vestments, the sacral vestments. ³³He shall purge the innermost Shrine; he shall purge the Tent of Meeting and the altar; and he shall make expiation for the priests and for all the people of the congregation.

³⁴This shall be to you a law for all time: to make atonement for the Israelites for all their sins once a year.

And Moses did as the LORD had commanded him.

17

The LORD spoke to Moses, saying:

²Speak to Aaron and his sons and to all the Israelite people and say to them:

This is what the LORD has commanded: ³if anyone of the house of Israel slaughters an ox or sheep or goat in the camp, or does so outside the camp, ⁴and does not bring it to the entrance of the Tent of Meeting to present it as an offering to the LORD, before the LORD's Tabernacle, bloodguilt shall be imputed to that man: he has shed blood; that man shall be cut off from among his people. ⁵This is in order that the Israelites may bring the sacrifices which they have been making in the open—that they may bring them before the LORD, to the priest, at the entrance of the Tent of Meeting, and offer them as sacrifices of well-being to the LORD; ⁶that the priest may dash the blood against the altar of the LORD at the entrance of the Tent of Meeting, and turn the fat into smoke as a pleasing odor to the LORD; ⁷and that they may offer their sacrifices no more to the goat-demons after whom they stray. This shall be to them a law for all time, throughout the ages.

⁸Say to them further: If anyone of the house of Israel or of the strangers who reside among

חֻקַּת עוֹלָם: 32 וְכִפֶּר הַכֹּהֵן אֲשֶׁר־יִמְשַׁח אֹתוֹ וַאֲשֶׁר יְמַלֵּא אֶת־יָדוֹ לְכַהֵן תַּחַת אָבִיו וְלָבַשׁ אֶת־בִּגְדֵי הַבָּד בִּגְדֵי הַקֹּדֶשׁ: 33 וְכִפֶּר אֶת־מִקְדַּשׁ הַקֹּדֶשׁ וְאֶת־אֹהֶל מוֹעֵד וְאֶת־הַמִּזְבֵּחַ יְכַפֵּר וְעַל הַכֹּהֲנִים וְעַל־כָּל־עַם הַקָּהָל יְכַפֵּר: 34 וְהָיְתָה־זֹּאת לָכֶם לְחֻקַּת עוֹלָם לְכַפֵּר עַל־בְּנֵי יִשְׂרָאֵל מִכָּל־חַטֹּאתָם אַחַת בַּשָּׁנָה וַיַּעַשׂ כַּאֲשֶׁר צִוָּה יְהוָה אֶת־מֹשֶׁה: פ

יז וַיְדַבֵּר יְהוָה אֶל־מֹשֶׁה לֵּאמֹר: 2 דַּבֵּר אֶל־אַהֲרֹן וְאֶל־בָּנָיו וְאֶל כָּל־בְּנֵי יִשְׂרָאֵל וְאָמַרְתָּ אֲלֵיהֶם זֶה הַדָּבָר אֲשֶׁר־צִוָּה יְהוָה לֵאמֹר: 3 אִישׁ אִישׁ מִבֵּית יִשְׂרָאֵל אֲשֶׁר יִשְׁחַט שׁוֹר אוֹ־כֶשֶׂב אוֹ־עֵז בַּמַּחֲנֶה אוֹ אֲשֶׁר יִשְׁחַט מִחוּץ לַמַּחֲנֶה: 4 וְאֶל־פֶּתַח אֹהֶל מוֹעֵד לֹא הֱבִיאוֹ לְהַקְרִיב קָרְבָּן לַיהוָה לִפְנֵי מִשְׁכַּן יְהוָה דָּם יֵחָשֵׁב לָאִישׁ הַהוּא דָּם שָׁפָךְ וְנִכְרַת הָאִישׁ הַהוּא מִקֶּרֶב עַמּוֹ: 5 לְמַעַן אֲשֶׁר יָבִיאוּ בְּנֵי יִשְׂרָאֵל אֶת־ זִבְחֵיהֶם אֲשֶׁר הֵם זֹבְחִים עַל־פְּנֵי הַשָּׂדֶה וֶהֱבִיאֻם לַיהוָה אֶל־פֶּתַח אֹהֶל מוֹעֵד אֶל־הַכֹּהֵן וְזָבְחוּ זִבְחֵי שְׁלָמִים לַיהוָה אוֹתָם: 6 וְזָרַק הַכֹּהֵן אֶת־הַדָּם עַל־מִזְבַּח יְהוָה פֶּתַח אֹהֶל מוֹעֵד וְהִקְטִיר הַחֵלֶב לְרֵיחַ נִיחֹחַ לַיהוָה: 7 וְלֹא־יִזְבְּחוּ עוֹד אֶת־זִבְחֵיהֶם לַשְּׂעִירִם אֲשֶׁר הֵם זֹנִים אַחֲרֵיהֶם חֻקַּת עוֹלָם תִּהְיֶה־זֹּאת לָהֶם לְדֹרֹתָם: 8 וַאֲלֵהֶם תֹּאמַר אִישׁ אִישׁ מִבֵּית יִשְׂרָאֵל וּמִן־הַגֵּר אֲשֶׁר־יָגוּר בְּתוֹכְכֶם אֲשֶׁר־יַעֲלֶה

them offers a burnt offering or a sacrifice, ⁹and does not bring it to the entrance of the Tent of Meeting to offer it to the Lord, that person shall be cut off from his people.

¹⁰And if anyone of the house of Israel or of the strangers who reside among them partakes of any blood, I will set My face against the person who partakes of the blood, and I will cut him off from among his kin. ¹¹For the life of the flesh is in the blood, and I have assigned it to you for making expiation for your lives upon the altar; it is the blood, as life, that effects expiation. ¹²Therefore I say to the Israelite people: No person among you shall partake of blood, nor shall the stranger who resides among you partake of blood.

¹³And if any Israelite or any stranger who resides among them hunts down an animal or a bird that may be eaten, he shall pour out its blood and cover it with earth. ¹⁴For the life of all flesh—its blood is its life. Therefore I say to the Israelite people: You shall not partake of the blood of any flesh, for the life of all flesh is its blood. Anyone who partakes of it shall be cut off.

¹⁵Any person, whether citizen or stranger, who eats what has died or has been torn by beasts shall wash his clothes, bathe in water, and remain unclean until evening; then he shall be clean. ¹⁶But if he does not wash [his clothes] and bathe his body, he shall bear his guilt.

18

The Lord spoke to Moses, saying: ²Speak to the Israelite people and say to them:

I the Lord am your God. ³You shall not copy the practices of the land of Egypt where you dwelt, or of the land of Canaan to which I am taking you; nor shall you follow their laws. ⁴My rules alone shall you observe, and faithfully follow My laws: I the Lord am your God.

עֹלֶה אוֹ־זֶבַח: ⁹וְאֶל־פֶּתַח אֹהֶל מוֹעֵד לֹא יְבִיאֶנּוּ לַעֲשׂוֹת אֹתוֹ לַיהוָה וְנִכְרַת הָאִישׁ הַהוּא מֵעַמָּיו: ¹⁰וְאִישׁ אִישׁ מִבֵּית יִשְׂרָאֵל וּמִן־הַגֵּר הַגָּר בְּתוֹכָם אֲשֶׁר יֹאכַל כָּל־דָּם וְנָתַתִּי פָנַי בַּנֶּפֶשׁ הָאֹכֶלֶת אֶת־הַדָּם וְהִכְרַתִּי אֹתָהּ מִקֶּרֶב עַמָּהּ: ¹¹כִּי נֶפֶשׁ הַבָּשָׂר בַּדָּם הִוא וַאֲנִי נְתַתִּיו לָכֶם עַל־הַמִּזְבֵּחַ לְכַפֵּר עַל־נַפְשֹׁתֵיכֶם כִּי־הַדָּם הוּא בַּנֶּפֶשׁ יְכַפֵּר: ¹²עַל־כֵּן אָמַרְתִּי לִבְנֵי יִשְׂרָאֵל כָּל־נֶפֶשׁ מִכֶּם לֹא־תֹאכַל דָּם וְהַגֵּר הַגָּר בְּתוֹכְכֶם לֹא־יֹאכַל דָּם: ס ¹³וְאִישׁ אִישׁ מִבְּנֵי יִשְׂרָאֵל וּמִן־הַגֵּר הַגָּר בְּתוֹכָם אֲשֶׁר יָצוּד צֵיד חַיָּה אוֹ־עוֹף אֲשֶׁר יֵאָכֵל וְשָׁפַךְ אֶת־דָּמוֹ וְכִסָּהוּ בֶּעָפָר: ¹⁴כִּי־נֶפֶשׁ כָּל־בָּשָׂר דָּמוֹ בְנַפְשׁוֹ הוּא וָאֹמַר לִבְנֵי יִשְׂרָאֵל דַּם כָּל־בָּשָׂר לֹא תֹאכֵלוּ כִּי נֶפֶשׁ כָּל־בָּשָׂר דָּמוֹ הִוא כָּל־אֹכְלָיו יִכָּרֵת: ¹⁵וְכָל־נֶפֶשׁ אֲשֶׁר תֹּאכַל נְבֵלָה וּטְרֵפָה בָּאֶזְרָח וּבַגֵּר וְכִבֶּס בְּגָדָיו וְרָחַץ בַּמַּיִם וְטָמֵא עַד־הָעֶרֶב וְטָהֵר: ¹⁶וְאִם לֹא יְכַבֵּס וּבְשָׂרוֹ לֹא יִרְחָץ וְנָשָׂא עֲוֹנוֹ: פ

יח

וַיְדַבֵּר יְהוָה אֶל־מֹשֶׁה לֵּאמֹר: ²דַּבֵּר אֶל־בְּנֵי יִשְׂרָאֵל וְאָמַרְתָּ אֲלֵהֶם אֲנִי יְהוָה אֱלֹהֵיכֶם: ³כְּמַעֲשֵׂה אֶרֶץ־מִצְרַיִם אֲשֶׁר יְשַׁבְתֶּם־בָּהּ לֹא תַעֲשׂוּ וּכְמַעֲשֵׂה אֶרֶץ־כְּנַעַן אֲשֶׁר אֲנִי מֵבִיא אֶתְכֶם שָׁמָּה לֹא תַעֲשׂוּ וּבְחֻקֹּתֵיהֶם לֹא תֵלֵכוּ: ⁴אֶת־מִשְׁפָּטַי תַּעֲשׂוּ וְאֶת־

5You shall keep My laws and My rules, by the pursuit of which man shall live: I am the LORD.

6None of you shall come near anyone of his own flesh to uncover nakedness: I am the LORD.

7a-Your father's nakedness, that is, the nakedness of your mother, you shall not uncover; she is your mother—you shall not uncover her nakedness.

8Do not uncover the nakedness of your father's wife;-a it is the nakedness of your father.

9The nakedness of your sister—your father's daughter or your mother's, whether born into the household or outside—do not uncover their nakedness.

10The nakedness of your son's daughter, or of your daughter's daughter—do not uncover their nakedness; for their nakedness is yours.b

11The nakedness of your father's wife's daughter, who has born into your father's household—she is your sister; do not uncover her nakedness.

12Do not uncover the nakedness of your father's sister; she is your father's flesh.

13Do not uncover the nakedness of your mother's sister; for she is your mother's flesh.

14Do not uncover the nakedness of your father's brother: do not approach his wife; she is your aunt.

15Do not uncover the nakedness of your daughter-in-law: she is your son's wife; you shall not uncover her nakedness.

16a-Do not uncover the nakedness of your brother's wife; it is the nakedness of your brother.-a

17Do not uncover the nakedness of a woman and her daughter; nor shall you marry her son's daughter or her daughter's daughter and uncover her nakedness: they are kindred; it is depravity.

חֻקֹּתַי תִּשְׁמְרוּ לָלֶכֶת בָּהֶם אֲנִי יְהֹוָה אֱלֹהֵיכֶם:

5 וּשְׁמַרְתֶּם אֶת־חֻקֹּתַי וְאֶת־מִשְׁפָּטַי אֲשֶׁר יַעֲשֶׂה אֹתָם הָאָדָם וָחַי בָּהֶם אֲנִי יְהֹוָה: ס

6 אִישׁ אִישׁ אֶל־כָּל־שְׁאֵר בְּשָׂרוֹ לֹא תִקְרְבוּ לְגַלּוֹת עֶרְוָה אֲנִי יְהֹוָה: ס

7 עֶרְוַת אָבִיךָ וְעֶרְוַת אִמְּךָ לֹא תְגַלֵּה אִמְּךָ הִוא לֹא תְגַלֶּה עֶרְוָתָהּ: ס

8 עֶרְוַת אֵשֶׁת־אָבִיךָ לֹא תְגַלֵּה עֶרְוַת אָבִיךָ הִוא: ס

9 עֶרְוַת אֲחוֹתְךָ בַת־אָבִיךָ אוֹ בַת־אִמֶּךָ מוֹלֶדֶת בַּיִת אוֹ מוֹלֶדֶת חוּץ לֹא תְגַלֶּה עֶרְוָתָן: ס

10 עֶרְוַת בַּת־בִּנְךָ אוֹ בַת־בִּתְּךָ לֹא תְגַלֶּה עֶרְוָתָן כִּי עֶרְוָתְךָ הֵנָּה: ס

11 עֶרְוַת בַּת־אֵשֶׁת אָבִיךָ מוֹלֶדֶת אָבִיךָ אֲחוֹתְךָ הִוא לֹא תְגַלֶּה עֶרְוָתָהּ: ס

12 עֶרְוַת אֲחוֹת־אָבִיךָ לֹא תְגַלֵּה שְׁאֵר אָבִיךָ הִוא: ס

13 עֶרְוַת אֲחוֹת־אִמְּךָ לֹא תְגַלֵּה כִּי־שְׁאֵר אִמְּךָ הִוא: ס

14 עֶרְוַת אֲחִי־אָבִיךָ לֹא תְגַלֵּה אֶל־אִשְׁתּוֹ לֹא תִקְרָב דֹּדָתְךָ הִוא: ס

15 עֶרְוַת כַּלָּתְךָ לֹא תְגַלֵּה אֵשֶׁת בִּנְךָ הִוא לֹא תְגַלֶּה עֶרְוָתָהּ: ס

16 עֶרְוַת אֵשֶׁת־אָחִיךָ לֹא תְגַלֵּה עֶרְוַת אָחִיךָ הִוא: ס

17 עֶרְוַת אִשָּׁה וּבִתָּהּ לֹא תְגַלֵּה אֶת־בַּת־בְּנָהּ וְאֶת־בַּת־בִּתָּהּ לֹא תִקַּח לְגַלּוֹת עֶרְוָתָהּ שַׁאֲרָה הֵנָּה זִמָּה הִוא:

---

a-a A man and his wife are one flesh (Gen. 2.24), even if he should die or divorce her.

b Meaning uncertain.

¹⁸Do not marry a woman as a rival to her sister and uncover her nakedness in the other's lifetime.

¹⁹Do not come near a woman during her period of uncleanness to uncover her nakedness.

²⁰Do not have carnal relations with your neighbor's wife and defile yourself with her.

²¹Do not allow any of your offspring to be offered up to Molech, and do not profane the name of your God: I am the Lord.

²²Do not lie with a male as one lies with a woman; it is an abhorrence.

²³Do not have carnal relations with any beast and defile yourself thereby; and let no woman lend herself to a beast to mate with it; it is perversion.

²⁴Do not defile yourselves in any of those ways, for it is by such that the nations that I am casting out before you defiled themselves. ²⁵Thus the land became defiled; and I called it to account for its iniquity, and the land spewed out its inhabitants. ²⁶But you must keep My laws and My rules, and you must not do any of those abhorrent things, neither the citizen nor the stranger who resides among you; ²⁷for all those abhorrent things were done by the people who were in the land before you, and the land became defiled. ²⁸So let not the land spew you out for defiling it, as it spewed out the nation that came before you. ²⁹All who do any of those abhorrent things—such persons shall be cut off from their people. ³⁰You shall keep My charge not to engage in any of the abhorrent practices that were carried on before you, and you shall not defile yourselves through them: I the Lord am your God.

18 וְאִשָּׁה אֶל־אֲחֹתָהּ לֹא תִקָּח לִצְרֹר לְגַלּוֹת עֶרְוָתָהּ עָלֶיהָ בְּחַיֶּיהָ:

19 וְאֶל־אִשָּׁה בְּנִדַּת טֻמְאָתָהּ לֹא תִקְרַב לְגַלּוֹת עֶרְוָתָהּ:

20 וְאֶל־אֵשֶׁת עֲמִיתְךָ לֹא־תִתֵּן שְׁכָבְתְּךָ לְזָרַע לְטָמְאָה־בָהּ:

21 וּמִזַּרְעֲךָ לֹא־תִתֵּן לְהַעֲבִיר לַמֹּלֶךְ וְלֹא תְחַלֵּל אֶת־שֵׁם אֱלֹהֶיךָ אֲנִי יְהוָה:

22 וְאֶת־זָכָר לֹא תִשְׁכַּב מִשְׁכְּבֵי אִשָּׁה תּוֹעֵבָה הִוא:

23 וּבְכָל־בְּהֵמָה לֹא־תִתֵּן שְׁכָבְתְּךָ לְטָמְאָה־בָהּ וְאִשָּׁה לֹא־תַעֲמֹד לִפְנֵי בְהֵמָה לְרִבְעָהּ תֶּבֶל הוּא:

24 אַל־תִּטַּמְּאוּ בְּכָל־אֵלֶּה כִּי בְכָל־אֵלֶּה נִטְמְאוּ הַגּוֹיִם אֲשֶׁר־אֲנִי מְשַׁלֵּחַ מִפְּנֵיכֶם:

25 וַתִּטְמָא הָאָרֶץ וָאֶפְקֹד עֲוֺנָהּ עָלֶיהָ וַתָּקִא הָאָרֶץ אֶת־יֹשְׁבֶיהָ: 26 וּשְׁמַרְתֶּם אַתֶּם אֶת־חֻקֹּתַי וְאֶת־מִשְׁפָּטַי וְלֹא תַעֲשׂוּ מִכֹּל הַתּוֹעֵבֹת הָאֵלֶּה הָאֶזְרָח וְהַגֵּר הַגָּר בְּתוֹכְכֶם: 27 כִּי אֶת־כָּל־הַתּוֹעֵבֹת הָאֵל עָשׂוּ אַנְשֵׁי־הָאָרֶץ אֲשֶׁר לִפְנֵיכֶם וַתִּטְמָא הָאָרֶץ: 28 וְלֹא־תָקִיא הָאָרֶץ אֶתְכֶם בְּטַמַּאֲכֶם אֹתָהּ כַּאֲשֶׁר קָאָה אֶת־הַגּוֹי אֲשֶׁר לִפְנֵיכֶם: 29 כִּי כָּל־אֲשֶׁר יַעֲשֶׂה מִכֹּל הַתּוֹעֵבוֹת הָאֵלֶּה וְנִכְרְתוּ הַנְּפָשׁוֹת הָעֹשֹׂת מִקֶּרֶב עַמָּם: 30 וּשְׁמַרְתֶּם אֶת־מִשְׁמַרְתִּי לְבִלְתִּי עֲשׂוֹת מֵחֻקּוֹת הַתּוֹעֵבֹת אֲשֶׁר נַעֲשׂוּ לִפְנֵיכֶם וְלֹא תִטַּמְּאוּ בָּהֶם אֲנִי יְהוָה אֱלֹהֵיכֶם: פ

19 KEDOSHIM

The LORD spoke to Moses, saying: [2]Speak to the whole Israelite community and say to them:

You shall be holy, for I, the LORD your God, am holy.

[3]You shall each revere his mother and his father, and keep My sabbaths: I the LORD am your God.

[4]Do not turn to idols or make molten gods for yourselves: I the LORD am your God.

[5]When you sacrifice an offering of well-being to the LORD, sacrifice it so that it may be accepted on your behalf. [6]It shall be eaten on the day you sacrifice it, or on the day following; but what is left by the third day must be consumed in fire. [7]If it should be eaten on the third day, it is an offensive thing, it will not be acceptable. [8]And he who eats of it shall bear his guilt, for he has profaned what is sacred to the LORD; that person shall be cut off from his kin.

[9]When you reap the harvest of your land, you shall not reap all the way to the edges of your field, or gather the gleanings of your harvest. [10]You shall not pick your vineyard bare, or gather the fallen fruit of your vineyard; you shall leave them for the poor and the stranger: I the LORD am your God.

[11]You shall not steal; you shall not deal deceitfully or falsely with one another. [12]You shall not swear falsely by My name, profaning the name of your God: I am the LORD.

[13]You shall not defraud your fellow. You shall not commit robbery. The wages of a laborer shall not remain with you until morning.

[14]You shall not insult the deaf, or place a stumbling block before the blind. You shall fear your God: I am the LORD.

[15]You shall not render an unfair decision: do not favor the poor or show deference to the rich;

קדשים **יט**

וַיְדַבֵּ֥ר יְהֹוָ֖ה אֶל־מֹשֶׁ֥ה לֵּאמֹֽר: [2]דַּבֵּ֞ר אֶל־כׇּל־עֲדַ֧ת בְּנֵֽי־יִשְׂרָאֵ֛ל וְאָמַרְתָּ֥ אֲלֵהֶ֖ם קְדֹשִׁ֣ים תִּהְי֑וּ כִּ֣י קָד֔וֹשׁ אֲנִ֖י יְהֹוָ֥ה אֱלֹהֵיכֶֽם: [3]אִ֣ישׁ אִמּ֤וֹ וְאָבִיו֙ תִּירָ֔אוּ וְאֶת־שַׁבְּתֹתַ֖י תִּשְׁמֹ֑רוּ אֲנִ֖י יְהֹוָ֥ה אֱלֹהֵיכֶֽם: [4]אַל־תִּפְנוּ֙ אֶל־הָ֣אֱלִילִ֔ים וֵֽאלֹהֵי֙ מַסֵּכָ֔ה לֹ֥א תַעֲשׂ֖וּ לָכֶ֑ם אֲנִ֖י יְהֹוָ֥ה אֱלֹהֵיכֶֽם: [5]וְכִ֧י תִזְבְּח֛וּ זֶ֥בַח שְׁלָמִ֖ים לַיהֹוָ֑ה לִֽרְצֹנְכֶ֖ם תִּזְבָּחֻֽהוּ: [6]בְּי֧וֹם זִבְחֲכֶ֛ם יֵאָכֵ֖ל וּמִֽמׇּחֳרָ֑ת וְהַנּוֹתָר֙ עַד־י֣וֹם הַשְּׁלִישִׁ֔י בָּאֵ֖שׁ יִשָּׂרֵֽף: [7]וְאִ֛ם הֵֽאָכֹ֥ל יֵאָכֵ֖ל בַּיּ֣וֹם הַשְּׁלִישִׁ֑י פִּגּ֥וּל ה֖וּא לֹ֥א יֵֽרָצֶֽה: [8]וְאֹֽכְלָיו֙ עֲוֺנ֣וֹ יִשָּׂ֔א כִּֽי־אֶת־קֹ֥דֶשׁ יְהֹוָ֖ה חִלֵּ֑ל וְנִכְרְתָ֛ה הַנֶּ֥פֶשׁ הַהִ֖וא מֵעַמֶּֽיהָ: [9]וּֽבְקֻצְרְכֶם֙ אֶת־קְצִ֣יר אַרְצְכֶ֔ם לֹ֧א תְכַלֶּ֛ה פְּאַ֥ת שָׂדְךָ֖ לִקְצֹ֑ר וְלֶ֥קֶט קְצִֽירְךָ֖ לֹ֥א תְלַקֵּֽט: [10]וְכַרְמְךָ֙ לֹ֣א תְעוֹלֵ֔ל וּפֶ֥רֶט כַּרְמְךָ֖ לֹ֣א תְלַקֵּ֑ט לֶֽעָנִ֤י וְלַגֵּר֙ תַּעֲזֹ֣ב אֹתָ֔ם אֲנִ֖י יְהֹוָ֥ה אֱלֹהֵיכֶֽם: [11]לֹ֖א תִּגְנֹ֑בוּ וְלֹא־תְכַחֲשׁ֥וּ וְלֹֽא־תְשַׁקְּר֖וּ אִ֥ישׁ בַּעֲמִיתֽוֹ: [12]וְלֹֽא־תִשָּׁבְע֥וּ בִשְׁמִ֖י לַשָּׁ֑קֶר וְחִלַּלְתָּ֛ אֶת־שֵׁ֥ם אֱלֹהֶ֖יךָ אֲנִ֥י יְהֹוָֽה: [13]לֹֽא־תַעֲשֹׁ֣ק אֶת־רֵֽעֲךָ֮ וְלֹ֣א תִגְזֹל֒ לֹֽא־תָלִ֞ין פְּעֻלַּ֧ת שָׂכִ֛יר אִתְּךָ֖ עַד־בֹּֽקֶר: [14]לֹא־תְקַלֵּ֣ל חֵרֵ֔שׁ וְלִפְנֵ֣י עִוֵּ֔ר לֹ֥א תִתֵּ֖ן מִכְשֹׁ֑ל וְיָרֵ֥אתָ מֵּֽאֱלֹהֶ֖יךָ אֲנִ֥י יְהֹוָֽה: [15]לֹא־תַעֲשׂ֥וּ עָ֙וֶל֙ בַּמִּשְׁפָּ֔ט לֹא־תִשָּׂ֣א פְנֵי־דָ֔ל וְלֹ֥א תֶהְדַּ֖ר פְּנֵ֣י גָד֑וֹל בְּצֶ֖דֶק תִּשְׁפֹּ֥ט

judge your kinsman fairly. [16]Do not *a*-deal basely with-*a* your countrymen. Do not *b*-profit by-*b* the blood of your fellow: I am the Lord.

[17]You shall not hate your kinsfolk in your heart. Reprove your kinsman but*c* incur no guilt because of him. [18]You shall not take vengeance or bear a grudge against your countrymen. Love your fellow as yourself: I am the Lord.

[19]You shall observe My laws.

You shall not let your cattle mate with a different kind; you shall not sow your field with two kinds of seed; you shall not put on cloth from a mixture of two kinds of material.

[20]If a man has carnal relations with a woman who is a slave and has been designated for another man, but has not been redeemed or given her freedom, there shall be an indemnity; they shall not, however, be put to death, since she has not been freed. [21]But he must bring to the entrance of the Tent of Meeting, as his guilt offering to the Lord, a ram of guilt offering. [22]With the ram of guilt offering the priest shall make expiation for him before the Lord for the sin that he committed; and the sin that he committed will be forgiven him.

[23]When you enter the land and plant any tree for food, you shall regard its fruit as forbidden.*d* Three years it shall be forbidden*d* for you, not to be eaten. [24]In the fourth year all its fruit shall be set aside for jubilation before the Lord; [25]and only in the fifth year may you use its fruit—that its yield to you may be increased: I the Lord am your God.

[26]You shall not eat anything with its blood. You shall not practice divination or soothsaying. [27]You shall not round off the side-growth on your head, or destroy the side-growth of your beard. [28]You shall not make gashes in your

---

a-a Others "go about as a talebearer among"; meaning of Heb. uncertain.
b-b Lit. "stand upon"; precise meaning of Heb. phrase uncertain.
c   Exact force of we- uncertain.
d   Heb. root 'rl, commonly "to be uncircumcised."

עֲמִיתֶֽךָ: 16 לֹא־תֵלֵ֤ךְ רָכִיל֙ בְּעַמֶּ֔יךָ לֹ֥א תַעֲמֹ֖ד עַל־דַּ֣ם רֵעֶ֑ךָ אֲנִ֖י יְהוָֽה:

17 לֹֽא־תִשְׂנָ֥א אֶת־אָחִ֖יךָ בִּלְבָבֶ֑ךָ הוֹכֵ֤חַ תּוֹכִ֙יחַ֙ אֶת־עֲמִיתֶ֔ךָ וְלֹא־תִשָּׂ֥א עָלָ֖יו חֵֽטְא: 18 לֹֽא־תִקֹּ֤ם וְלֹֽא־תִטֹּר֙ אֶת־בְּנֵ֣י עַמֶּ֔ךָ וְאָֽהַבְתָּ֥ לְרֵעֲךָ֖ כָּמ֑וֹךָ אֲנִ֖י יְהוָֽה:

19 אֶֽת־חֻקֹּתַי֮ תִּשְׁמֹ֒רוּ֒ בְּהֶמְתְּךָ֞ לֹא־תַרְבִּ֣יעַ כִּלְאַ֗יִם שָֽׂדְךָ֙ לֹא־תִזְרַ֣ע כִּלְאָ֑יִם וּבֶ֤גֶד כִּלְאַ֙יִם֙ שַֽׁעַטְנֵ֔ז לֹ֥א יַעֲלֶ֖ה עָלֶֽיךָ: פ

20 וְ֠אִ֠ישׁ כִּֽי־יִשְׁכַּ֨ב אֶת־אִשָּׁ֜ה שִׁכְבַת־זֶ֗רַע וְהִ֤וא שִׁפְחָה֙ נֶחֱרֶ֣פֶת לְאִ֔ישׁ וְהָפְדֵּה֙ לֹ֣א נִפְדָּ֔תָה א֖וֹ חֻפְשָׁ֣ה לֹ֣א נִתַּן־לָ֑הּ בִּקֹּ֧רֶת תִּֽהְיֶ֛ה לֹ֥א יוּמְת֖וּ כִּי־לֹ֥א חֻפָּֽשָׁה: 21 וְהֵבִ֤יא אֶת־אֲשָׁמוֹ֙ לַֽיהֹוָ֔ה אֶל־פֶּ֖תַח אֹ֣הֶל מוֹעֵ֑ד אֵ֖יל אָשָֽׁם: 22 וְכִפֶּר֩ עָלָ֨יו הַכֹּהֵ֜ן בְּאֵ֣יל הָֽאָשָׁם֮ לִפְנֵ֣י יְהוָה֒ עַל־חַטָּאת֖וֹ אֲשֶׁ֣ר חָטָ֑א וְנִסְלַ֣ח ל֔וֹ מֵֽחַטָּאת֖וֹ אֲשֶׁ֥ר חָטָֽא: פ

23 וְכִֽי־תָבֹ֣אוּ אֶל־הָאָ֗רֶץ וּנְטַעְתֶּם֙ כָּל־עֵ֣ץ מַֽאֲכָ֔ל וַֽעֲרַלְתֶּ֥ם עָרְלָת֖וֹ אֶת־פִּרְי֑וֹ שָׁלֹ֣שׁ שָׁנִ֗ים יִהְיֶ֥ה לָכֶ֛ם עֲרֵלִ֖ים לֹ֥א יֵֽאָכֵֽל: 24 וּבַשָּׁנָה֙ הָֽרְבִיעִ֔ת יִהְיֶ֖ה כָּל־פִּרְי֑וֹ קֹ֥דֶשׁ הִלּוּלִ֖ים לַֽיהוָֽה: 25 וּבַשָּׁנָ֣ה הַֽחֲמִישִׁ֗ת תֹּֽאכְלוּ֙ אֶת־פִּרְי֔וֹ לְהוֹסִ֥יף לָכֶ֖ם תְּבֽוּאָת֑וֹ אֲנִ֖י יְהוָ֥ה אֱלֹֽהֵיכֶֽם:

26 לֹ֥א תֹֽאכְל֖וּ עַל־הַדָּ֑ם לֹ֥א תְנַֽחֲשׁ֖וּ וְלֹ֥א תְעוֹנֵֽנוּ: 27 לֹ֣א תַקִּ֔פוּ פְּאַ֖ת רֹֽאשְׁכֶ֑ם וְלֹ֣א תַשְׁחִ֔ית אֵ֖ת פְּאַ֥ת זְקָנֶֽךָ: 28 וְשֶׂ֣רֶט לָנֶ֗פֶשׁ לֹ֤א תִתְּנוּ֙ בִּבְשַׂרְכֶ֔ם וּכְתֹ֣בֶת קַֽעֲקַ֔ע לֹ֥א תִתְּנ֖וּ בָּכֶ֑ם אֲנִ֖י יְהוָֽה:

flesh for the dead, or incise any marks on your-selves: I am the LORD.

²⁹Do not degrade your daughter and make her a harlot, lest the land fall into harlotry and the land be filled with depravity. ³⁰You shall keep My sabbaths and venerate My sanctuary: I am the LORD.

³¹Do not turn to ghosts and do not inquire of familiar spirits, to be defiled by them: I the LORD am your God.

³²You shall rise before the aged and show def-erence to the old; you shall fear your God: I am the LORD.

³³When a stranger resides with you in your land, you shall not wrong him. ³⁴The stranger who resides with you shall be to you as one of your citizens; you shall love him as yourself, for you were strangers in the land of Egypt: I the LORD am your God.

³⁵You shall not falsify measures of length, weight, or capacity. ³⁶You shall have an honest balance, honest weights, an honest *ephah*, and an honest *hin*.

I the LORD am your God who freed you from the land of Egypt. ³⁷You shall faithfully observe all My laws and all My rules: I am the LORD.

20 And the LORD spoke to Moses: ²Say fur-ther to the Israelite people:

Anyone among the Israelites, or among the strangers residing in Israel, who gives any of his offspring to Molech, shall be put to death; the people of the land shall pelt him with stones. ³And I will set My face against that man and will cut him off from among his people, because he gave of his offspring to Molech and so defiled My sanctuary and profaned My holy name. ⁴And if the people of the land should shut their eyes to that man when he gives of his offspring to Molech, and should not put him to death,

---

29 אַל־תְּחַלֵּ֤ל אֶֽת־בִּתְּךָ֙ לְהַזְנוֹתָ֔הּ וְלֹא־ תִזְנֶ֣ה הָאָ֔רֶץ וּמָלְאָ֥ה הָאָ֖רֶץ זִמָּֽה: 30 אֶת־ שַׁבְּתֹתַ֣י תִּשְׁמֹ֔רוּ וּמִקְדָּשִׁ֖י תִּירָ֑אוּ אֲנִ֖י יְהוָֽה:

31 אַל־תִּפְנ֤וּ אֶל־הָֽאֹבֹת֙ וְאֶל־הַיִּדְּעֹנִ֔ים אַל־תְּבַקְשׁ֖וּ לְטׇמְאָ֣ה בָהֶ֑ם אֲנִ֖י יְהוָ֥ה אֱלֹהֵיכֶֽם:

32 מִפְּנֵ֤י שֵׂיבָה֙ תָּק֔וּם וְהָדַרְתָּ֖ פְּנֵ֣י זָקֵ֑ן וְיָרֵ֥אתָ מֵּאֱלֹהֶ֖יךָ אֲנִ֥י יְהוָֽה: פ

33 וְכִֽי־יָג֧וּר אִתְּךָ֛ גֵּ֖ר בְּאַרְצְכֶ֑ם לֹ֥א תוֹנ֖וּ אֹתֽוֹ: 34 כְּאֶזְרָ֣ח מִכֶּם֩ יִהְיֶ֨ה לָכֶ֜ם הַגֵּ֣ר ׀ הַגָּ֣ר אִתְּכֶ֗ם וְאָהַבְתָּ֥ לוֹ֙ כָּמ֔וֹךָ כִּֽי־גֵרִ֥ים הֱיִיתֶ֖ם בְּאֶ֣רֶץ מִצְרָ֑יִם אֲנִ֖י יְהוָ֥ה אֱלֹהֵיכֶֽם:

35 לֹא־תַעֲשׂ֥וּ עָ֖וֶל בַּמִּשְׁפָּ֑ט בַּמִּדָּ֕ה בַּמִּשְׁקָ֖ל וּבַמְּשׂוּרָֽה: 36 מֹ֧אזְנֵי צֶ֣דֶק אַבְנֵי־צֶ֗דֶק אֵ֤יפַת צֶ֙דֶק֙ וְהִ֣ין צֶ֔דֶק יִהְיֶ֖ה לָכֶ֑ם אֲנִי֙ יְהוָ֣ה אֱלֹ֣הֵיכֶ֔ם אֲשֶׁר־הוֹצֵ֥אתִי אֶתְכֶ֖ם מֵאֶ֣רֶץ מִצְרָֽיִם: 37 וּשְׁמַרְתֶּ֤ם אֶת־כׇּל־ חֻקֹּתַי֙ וְאֶת־כׇּל־מִשְׁפָּטַ֔י וַעֲשִׂיתֶ֖ם אֹתָ֑ם אֲנִ֖י יְהוָֽה: פ

כ וַיְדַבֵּ֥ר יְהוָ֖ה אֶל־מֹשֶׁ֥ה לֵּאמֹֽר: 2 וְאֶל־ בְּנֵ֣י יִשְׂרָאֵ֘ל֮ תֹּאמַר֒ אִ֣ישׁ אִישׁ֩ מִבְּנֵ֨י יִשְׂרָאֵ֜ל וּמִן־הַגֵּ֣ר ׀ הַגָּ֣ר בְּיִשְׂרָאֵ֗ל אֲשֶׁ֨ר יִתֵּ֧ן מִזַּרְע֛וֹ לַמֹּ֖לֶךְ מ֣וֹת יוּמָ֑ת עַ֥ם הָאָ֖רֶץ יִרְגְּמֻ֥הוּ בָאָֽבֶן: 3 וַאֲנִ֞י אֶתֵּ֤ן אֶת־פָּנַי֙ בָּאִ֣ישׁ הַה֔וּא וְהִכְרַתִּ֥י אֹת֖וֹ מִקֶּ֣רֶב עַמּ֑וֹ כִּ֤י מִזַּרְעוֹ֙ נָתַ֣ן לַמֹּ֔לֶךְ לְמַ֗עַן טַמֵּא֙ אֶת־מִקְדָּשִׁ֔י וּלְחַלֵּ֖ל אֶת־שֵׁ֥ם קׇדְשִֽׁי: 4 וְאִ֡ם הַעְלֵ֣ם יַעְלִ֩ימוּ֩ עַ֨ם הָאָ֜רֶץ אֶת־ עֵֽינֵיהֶם֙ מִן־הָאִ֣ישׁ הַה֔וּא בְּתִתּ֥וֹ מִזַּרְע֖וֹ לַמֹּ֑לֶךְ לְבִלְתִּ֖י הָמִ֣ית אֹת֑וֹ: 5 וְשַׂמְתִּ֨י אֲנִ֤י

⁵I Myself will set My face against that man and his kin, and will cut off from among their people both him and all who follow him in going astray after Molech. ⁶And if any person turns to ghosts and familiar spirits and goes astray after them, I will set My face against that person and cut him off from among his people.

⁷You shall sanctify yourselves and be holy, for I the Lord am your God. ⁸You shall faithfully observe My laws: I the Lord make you holy.

⁹If anyone insults his father or his mother, he shall be put to death; he has insulted his father and his mother—his bloodguilt is upon him.

¹⁰If a man commits adultery with a married woman, committing adultery with another man's wife, the adulterer and the adulteress shall be put to death. ¹¹If a man lies with his father's wife, it is the nakedness of his father that he has uncovered; the two shall be put to death—their bloodguilt is upon them. ¹²If a man lies with his daughter-in-law, both of them shall be put to death; they have committed incest—their bloodguilt is upon them. ¹³If a man lies with a male as one lies with a woman, the two of them have done an abhorrent thing; they shall be put to death—their bloodguilt is upon them. ¹⁴If a man marries a woman and her mother, it is depravity; both he and they shall be put to the fire, that there be no depravity among you. ¹⁵If a man has carnal relations with a beast, he shall be put to death; and you shall kill the beast. ¹⁶If a woman approaches any beast to mate with it, you shall kill the woman and the beast; they shall be put to death—their bloodguilt is upon them.

¹⁷If a man marries his sister, the daughter of either his father or his mother, so that he sees her nakedness and she sees his nakedness, it is a disgrace; they shall be excommunicated*ᵃ* in the sight of their kinsfolk. He has uncovered the na-

---

ᵃ Lit. "cut off."

אֶת־פָּנַ֤י בָּאִישׁ֙ הַה֔וּא וּבְמִשְׁפַּחְתּ֑וֹ
וְהִכְרַתִּ֣י אֹת֗וֹ וְאֵ֤ת ׀ כָּל־הַזֹּנִים֙ אַחֲרָ֔יו
לִזְנ֖וֹת אַחֲרֵ֣י הַמֹּ֑לֶךְ מִקֶּ֥רֶב עַמָּֽם׃ 6 וְהַנֶּ֗פֶשׁ
אֲשֶׁ֨ר תִּפְנֶ֜ה אֶל־הָאֹבֹת֙ וְאֶל־הַיִּדְּעֹנִ֔ים
לִזְנ֖וֹת אַחֲרֵיהֶ֑ם וְנָתַתִּ֤י אֶת־פָּנַי֙ בַּנֶּ֣פֶשׁ
הַה֔וּא וְהִכְרַתִּ֥י אֹת֖וֹ מִקֶּ֥רֶב עַמּֽוֹ׃
7 וְהִ֨תְקַדִּשְׁתֶּ֔ם וִהְיִיתֶ֖ם קְדֹשִׁ֑ים כִּ֛י אֲנִ֥י
יְהוָ֖ה אֱלֹהֵיכֶֽם׃ 8 וּשְׁמַרְתֶּם֙ אֶת־חֻקֹּתַ֔י
וַעֲשִׂיתֶ֖ם אֹתָ֑ם אֲנִ֥י יְהוָ֖ה מְקַדִּשְׁכֶֽם׃
9 כִּֽי־אִ֣ישׁ אִ֗ישׁ אֲשֶׁ֨ר יְקַלֵּ֧ל אֶת־אָבִ֛יו
וְאֶת־אִמּ֖וֹ מ֣וֹת יוּמָ֑ת אָבִ֧יו וְאִמּ֛וֹ קִלֵּ֖ל
דָּמָ֥יו בּֽוֹ׃
10 וְאִ֗ישׁ אֲשֶׁ֤ר יִנְאַף֙ אֶת־אֵ֣שֶׁת אִ֔ישׁ אֲשֶׁ֥ר
יִנְאַ֖ף אֶת־אֵ֣שֶׁת רֵעֵ֑הוּ מֽוֹת־יוּמַ֥ת הַנֹּאֵ֖ף
וְהַנֹּאָֽפֶת׃ 11 וְאִ֗ישׁ אֲשֶׁ֤ר יִשְׁכַּב֙ אֶת־אֵ֣שֶׁת
אָבִ֔יו עֶרְוַ֥ת אָבִ֖יו גִּלָּ֑ה מֽוֹת־יוּמְת֥וּ שְׁנֵיהֶ֖ם
דְּמֵיהֶ֥ם בָּֽם׃ 12 וְאִ֗ישׁ אֲשֶׁ֤ר יִשְׁכַּב֙ אֶת־
כַּלָּת֔וֹ מ֥וֹת יוּמְת֖וּ שְׁנֵיהֶ֑ם תֶּ֧בֶל עָשׂ֛וּ
דְּמֵיהֶ֥ם בָּֽם׃ 13 וְאִ֗ישׁ אֲשֶׁ֨ר יִשְׁכַּ֤ב אֶת־זָכָר֙
מִשְׁכְּבֵ֣י אִשָּׁ֔ה תּוֹעֵבָ֥ה עָשׂ֖וּ שְׁנֵיהֶ֑ם מ֣וֹת
יוּמָ֖תוּ דְּמֵיהֶ֥ם בָּֽם׃ 14 וְאִ֗ישׁ אֲשֶׁ֨ר יִקַּ֤ח
אֶת־אִשָּׁה֙ וְאֶת־אִמָּ֔הּ זִמָּ֖ה הִ֑וא בָּאֵ֞שׁ
יִשְׂרְפ֤וּ אֹתוֹ֙ וְאֶתְהֶ֔ן וְלֹא־תִהְיֶ֥ה זִמָּ֖ה
בְּתוֹכְכֶֽם׃ 15 וְאִ֗ישׁ אֲשֶׁ֨ר יִתֵּ֧ן שְׁכָבְתּ֛וֹ
בִּבְהֵמָ֖ה מ֣וֹת יוּמָ֑ת וְאֶת־הַבְּהֵמָ֖ה
תַּהֲרֹֽגוּ׃ 16 וְאִשָּׁ֗ה אֲשֶׁ֨ר תִּקְרַ֤ב אֶל־כָּל־
בְּהֵמָה֙ לְרִבְעָ֣ה אֹתָ֔הּ וְהָרַגְתָּ֥ אֶת־הָאִשָּׁ֖ה
וְאֶת־הַבְּהֵמָ֑ה מ֥וֹת יוּמָ֖תוּ דְּמֵיהֶ֥ם בָּֽם׃
17 וְאִ֗ישׁ אֲשֶׁר־יִקַּ֨ח אֶת־אֲחֹת֜וֹ בַּת־אָבִ֣יו
א֣וֹ בַת־אִמּ֗וֹ וְרָאָ֤ה אֶת־עֶרְוָתָהּ֙ וְהִֽיא־
תִרְאֶ֣ה אֶת־עֶרְוָת֔וֹ חֶ֣סֶד ה֑וּא וְנִ֨כְרְת֔וּ
לְעֵינֵ֖י בְּנֵ֣י עַמָּ֑ם עֶרְוַ֧ת אֲחֹת֛וֹ גִּלָּ֖ה עֲוֺנ֥וֹ

254

kedness of his sister, he shall bear his guilt. ¹⁸If a man lies with a woman in her infirmity and uncovers her nakedness, he has laid bare her flow and she has exposed her blood flow; both of them shall be cut off from among their people. ¹⁹You shall not uncover the nakedness of your mother's sister or of your father's sister, for that is laying bare one's own flesh; they shall bear their guilt. ²⁰If a man lies with his uncle's wife, it is his uncle's nakedness that he has uncovered. They shall bear their guilt: they shall die childless. ²¹If a man marries the wife of his brother, it is indecency. It is the nakedness of his brother that he has uncovered; they shall remain childless.

²²You shall faithfully observe all My laws and all My regulations, lest the land to which I bring you to settle in spew you out. ²³You shall not follow the practices of the nation that I am driving out before you. For it is because they did all these things that I abhorred them ²⁴and said to you: You shall possess their land, for I will give it to you to possess, a land flowing with milk and honey. I the Lord am your God who has set you apart from other peoples. ²⁵So you shall set apart the clean beast from the unclean, the unclean bird from the clean. You shall not draw abomination upon yourselves through beast or bird or anything with which the ground is alive, which I have set apart for you to treat as unclean. ²⁶You shall be holy to Me, for I the Lord am holy, and I have set you apart from other peoples to be Mine.

²⁷A man or a woman who has a ghost or a familiar spirit shall be put to death; they shall be pelted with stones—their bloodguilt shall be upon them.

יִשָּֽׂא׃ 18 וְ֠אִ֠ישׁ אֲשֶׁר־יִשְׁכַּ֨ב אֶת־אִשָּׁ֜ה דָּוָ֗ה וְגִלָּ֤ה אֶת־עֶרְוָתָהּ֙ אֶת־מְקֹרָ֣הּ הֶֽעֱרָ֔ה וְהִ֕וא גִּלְּתָ֖ה אֶת־מְק֣וֹר דָּמֶ֑יהָ וְנִכְרְת֥וּ שְׁנֵיהֶ֖ם מִקֶּ֥רֶב עַמָּֽם׃ 19 וְעֶרְוַ֨ת אֲח֧וֹת אִמְּךָ֛ וַאֲח֥וֹת אָבִ֖יךָ לֹ֣א תְגַלֵּ֑ה כִּ֧י אֶת־שְׁאֵר֛וֹ הֶעֱרָ֖ה עֲוֺנָ֥ם יִשָּֽׂאוּ׃ 20 וְאִ֗ישׁ אֲשֶׁ֤ר יִשְׁכַּב֙ אֶת־דֹּ֣דָת֔וֹ עֶרְוַ֥ת דֹּד֖וֹ גִּלָּ֑ה חֶטְאָ֥ם יִשָּׂ֖אוּ עֲרִירִ֥ים יָמֻֽתוּ׃ 21 וְאִ֗ישׁ אֲשֶׁ֥ר יִקַּ֛ח אֶת־אֵ֥שֶׁת אָחִ֖יו נִדָּ֣ה הִ֑וא עֶרְוַ֥ת אָחִ֛יו גִּלָּ֖ה עֲרִירִ֥ים יִהְיֽוּ׃

22 וּשְׁמַרְתֶּ֤ם אֶת־כׇּל־חֻקֹּתַי֙ וְאֶת־כׇּל־מִשְׁפָּטַ֔י וַעֲשִׂיתֶ֖ם אֹתָ֑ם וְלֹא־תָקִ֤יא אֶתְכֶם֙ הָאָ֔רֶץ אֲשֶׁ֨ר אֲנִ֜י מֵבִ֥יא אֶתְכֶ֛ם שָׁ֖מָּה לָשֶׁ֥בֶת בָּֽהּ׃ 23 וְלֹ֤א תֵֽלְכוּ֙ בְּחֻקֹּ֣ת הַגּ֔וֹי אֲשֶׁר־אֲנִ֥י מְשַׁלֵּ֖חַ מִפְּנֵיכֶ֑ם כִּ֤י אֶת־כׇּל־אֵ֙לֶּה֙ עָשׂ֔וּ וָאָקֻ֖ץ בָּֽם׃ 24 וָאֹמַ֣ר לָכֶ֗ם אַתֶּם֮ תִּֽירְשׁ֣וּ אֶת־אַדְמָתָם֒ וַאֲנִ֞י אֶתְּנֶ֤נָּה לָכֶם֙ לָרֶ֣שֶׁת אֹתָ֔הּ אֶ֛רֶץ זָבַ֥ת חָלָ֖ב וּדְבָ֑שׁ אֲנִי֙ יְהֹוָ֣ה אֱלֹֽהֵיכֶ֔ם אֲשֶׁר־הִבְדַּ֥לְתִּי אֶתְכֶ֖ם מִן־הָֽעַמִּֽים׃ 25 וְהִבְדַּלְתֶּ֞ם בֵּֽין־הַבְּהֵמָ֤ה הַטְּהֹרָה֙ לַטְּמֵאָ֔ה וּבֵֽין־הָע֥וֹף הַטָּמֵ֖א לַטָּהֹ֑ר וְלֹֽא־תְשַׁקְּצ֨וּ אֶת־נַפְשֹֽׁתֵיכֶ֜ם בַּבְּהֵמָ֣ה וּבָע֗וֹף וּבְכֹל֙ אֲשֶׁ֣ר תִּרְמֹ֣שׂ הָֽאֲדָמָ֔ה אֲשֶׁר־הִבְדַּ֥לְתִּי לָכֶ֖ם לְטַמֵּֽא׃ 26 וִהְיִ֤יתֶם לִי֙ קְדֹשִׁ֔ים כִּ֥י קָד֖וֹשׁ אֲנִ֣י יְהֹוָ֑ה וָאַבְדִּ֥ל אֶתְכֶ֛ם מִן־הָֽעַמִּ֖ים לִהְי֥וֹת לִֽי׃ 27 וְאִ֣ישׁ אֽוֹ־אִשָּׁ֗ה כִּֽי־יִהְיֶ֨ה בָהֶ֥ם א֛וֹב א֥וֹ יִדְּעֹנִ֖י מ֣וֹת יוּמָ֑תוּ בָּאֶ֛בֶן יִרְגְּמ֥וּ אֹתָ֖ם דְּמֵיהֶ֥ם בָּֽם׃ פ

21 'EMOR

The LORD said to Moses: Speak to the priests, the sons of Aaron, and say to them:

None shall defile himself for any [dead] person among his kin, 2except for the relatives that are closest to him: his mother, his father, his son, his daughter, and his brother; 3also for a virgin sister, close to him because she has not married, for her he may defile himself. 4But he shall not defile himself a-as a kinsman by marriage,-a and so profane himself.

5They shall not shave smooth any part of their heads, or cut the side-growth of their beards, or make gashes in their flesh. 6They shall be holy to their God and not profane the name of their God; for they offer the LORD's offerings by fire, the food of their God, and so must be holy.

7They shall not marry a woman defiled by harlotry, nor shall they marry one divorced from her husband. For they are holy to their God 8and you must treat them as holy, since they offer the food of your God; they shall be holy to you, for I the LORD who sanctify you am holy.

9When the daughter of a priest defiles herself through harlotry, it is her father whom she defiles; she shall be put to the fire.

10The priest who is exalted above his fellows, on whose head the anointing oil has been poured and who has been ordained to wear the vestments, shall not bare his head*b* or rend his vestments. 11He shall not go in where there is any dead body; he shall not defile himself even for his father or mother. 12He shall not go outside the sanctuary and profane the sanctuary of his God, for upon him is the distinction of the anointing oil of his God, Mine the LORD's. 13He may marry only a woman who is a virgin. 14A widow, or a divorced woman, or one who is degraded by harlotry—such he may not marry.

כא וַיֹּאמֶר יְהוָה אֶל־מֹשֶׁה אֱמֹר אֶל־הַכֹּהֲנִים בְּנֵי אַהֲרֹן וְאָמַרְתָּ אֲלֵהֶם לְנֶפֶשׁ לֹא־יִטַּמָּא בְּעַמָּיו: 2 כִּי אִם־לִשְׁאֵרוֹ הַקָּרֹב אֵלָיו לְאִמּוֹ וּלְאָבִיו וְלִבְנוֹ וּלְבִתּוֹ וּלְאָחִיו: 3 וְלַאֲחֹתוֹ הַבְּתוּלָה הַקְּרוֹבָה אֵלָיו אֲשֶׁר לֹא־הָיְתָה לְאִישׁ לָהּ יִטַּמָּא: 4 לֹא יִטַּמָּא בַּעַל בְּעַמָּיו לְהֵחַלּוֹ: 5 לֹא־יִקְרְחָה קָרְחָה בְּרֹאשָׁם וּפְאַת זְקָנָם לֹא יְגַלֵּחוּ וּבִבְשָׂרָם לֹא יִשְׂרְטוּ שָׂרָטֶת: 6 קְדֹשִׁים יִהְיוּ לֵאלֹהֵיהֶם וְלֹא יְחַלְּלוּ שֵׁם אֱלֹהֵיהֶם כִּי אֶת־אִשֵּׁי יְהוָה לֶחֶם אֱלֹהֵיהֶם הֵם מַקְרִיבִם וְהָיוּ קֹדֶשׁ: 7 אִשָּׁה זֹנָה וַחֲלָלָה לֹא יִקָּחוּ וְאִשָּׁה גְּרוּשָׁה מֵאִישָׁהּ לֹא יִקָּחוּ כִּי־קָדֹשׁ הוּא לֵאלֹהָיו: 8 וְקִדַּשְׁתּוֹ כִּי־אֶת־לֶחֶם אֱלֹהֶיךָ הוּא מַקְרִיב קָדֹשׁ יִהְיֶה־לָּךְ כִּי קָדוֹשׁ אֲנִי יְהוָה מְקַדִּשְׁכֶם: 9 וּבַת אִישׁ כֹּהֵן כִּי תֵחֵל לִזְנוֹת אֶת־אָבִיהָ הִיא מְחַלֶּלֶת בָּאֵשׁ תִּשָּׂרֵף: ס 10 וְהַכֹּהֵן הַגָּדוֹל מֵאֶחָיו אֲשֶׁר־יוּצַק עַל־רֹאשׁוֹ ׀ שֶׁמֶן הַמִּשְׁחָה וּמִלֵּא אֶת־יָדוֹ לִלְבֹּשׁ אֶת־הַבְּגָדִים אֶת־רֹאשׁוֹ לֹא יִפְרָע וּבְגָדָיו לֹא יִפְרֹם: 11 וְעַל כָּל־נַפְשֹׁת מֵת לֹא יָבֹא לְאָבִיו וּלְאִמּוֹ לֹא יִטַּמָּא: 12 וּמִן־הַמִּקְדָּשׁ לֹא יֵצֵא וְלֹא יְחַלֵּל אֵת מִקְדַּשׁ אֱלֹהָיו כִּי נֵזֶר שֶׁמֶן מִשְׁחַת אֱלֹהָיו עָלָיו אֲנִי יְהוָה: 13 וְהוּא אִשָּׁה בִבְתוּלֶיהָ יִקָּח: 14 אַלְמָנָה וּגְרוּשָׁה וַחֲלָלָה זֹנָה אֶת־אֵלֶּה לֹא יִקָּח כִּי אִם־בְּתוּלָה מֵעַמָּיו יִקָּח

---

a-a   Lit. "as a husband among his kin"; meaning uncertain.
b   See note at 10.6.

Only a virgin of his own kin may he take to wife—[15]that he may not profane his offspring among his kin, for I the LORD have sanctified him.

[16]The LORD spoke further to Moses: [17]Speak to Aaron and say: No man of your offspring throughout the ages who has a defect shall be qualified to offer the food of his God. [18]No one at all who has a defect shall be qualified: no man who is blind, or lame, or c-has a limb too short or too long;-c [19]no man who has a broken leg or a broken arm; [20]or who is a hunchback, or a dwarf, or who has a growth in his eye, or who has a boil-scar, or scurvy, or crushed testes. [21]No man among the offspring of Aaron the priest who has a defect shall be qualified to offer the LORD's offering by fire; having a defect, he shall not be qualified to offer the food of his God. [22]He may eat of the food of his God, of the most holy as well as of the holy; [23]but he shall not enter behind the curtain or come near the altar, for he has a defect. He shall not profane these places sacred to Me, for I the LORD have sanctified them.

[24]Thus Moses spoke to Aaron and his sons and to all the Israelites.

22 The LORD spoke to Moses, saying: [2]Instruct Aaron and his sons to be scrupulous about the sacred donations that the Israelite people consecrate to Me, lest they profane My holy name, Mine the LORD's. [3]Say to them:

Throughout the ages, if any man among your offspring, while in a state of uncleanness, partakes of any sacred donation that the Israelite people may consecrate to the LORD, that person shall be cut off from before Me: I am the LORD. [4]No man of Aaron's offspring who has an eruption or a discharge[a] shall eat of the sacred do-

---

c-c   Or "mutilated or has a limb too long."

a   See chapters 13 and 15.

אִשָּׁה: 15 וְלֹא־יְחַלֵּל זַרְעוֹ בְּעַמָּיו כִּי אֲנִי יְהוָה מְקַדְּשׁוֹ: פ 16 וַיְדַבֵּר יְהוָה אֶל־מֹשֶׁה לֵּאמֹר: 17 דַּבֵּר אֶל־אַהֲרֹן לֵאמֹר אִישׁ מִזַּרְעֲךָ לְדֹרֹתָם אֲשֶׁר יִהְיֶה בוֹ מוּם לֹא יִקְרַב לְהַקְרִיב לֶחֶם אֱלֹהָיו: 18 כִּי כָל־אִישׁ אֲשֶׁר־בּוֹ מוּם לֹא יִקְרָב אִישׁ עִוֵּר אוֹ פִסֵּחַ אוֹ חָרֻם אוֹ שָׂרוּעַ: 19 אוֹ אִישׁ אֲשֶׁר־יִהְיֶה בוֹ שֶׁבֶר רֶגֶל אוֹ שֶׁבֶר יָד: 20 אוֹ־גִבֵּן אוֹ־דַק אוֹ תְּבַלֻּל בְּעֵינוֹ אוֹ גָרָב אוֹ יַלֶּפֶת אוֹ מְרוֹחַ אָשֶׁךְ: 21 כָּל־אִישׁ אֲשֶׁר־בּוֹ מוּם מִזֶּרַע אַהֲרֹן הַכֹּהֵן לֹא יִגַּשׁ לְהַקְרִיב אֶת־אִשֵּׁי יְהוָה מוּם בּוֹ אֵת לֶחֶם אֱלֹהָיו לֹא יִגַּשׁ לְהַקְרִיב: 22 לֶחֶם אֱלֹהָיו מִקָּדְשֵׁי הַקֳּדָשִׁים וּמִן־הַקֳּדָשִׁים יֹאכֵל: 23 אַךְ אֶל־ הַפָּרֹכֶת לֹא יָבֹא וְאֶל־הַמִּזְבֵּחַ לֹא יִגַּשׁ כִּי־מוּם בּוֹ וְלֹא יְחַלֵּל אֶת־מִקְדָּשַׁי כִּי אֲנִי יְהוָה מְקַדְּשָׁם: 24 וַיְדַבֵּר מֹשֶׁה אֶל־אַהֲרֹן וְאֶל־בָּנָיו וְאֶל־ כָּל־בְּנֵי יִשְׂרָאֵל: פ

כב וַיְדַבֵּר יְהוָה אֶל־מֹשֶׁה לֵּאמֹר: 2 דַּבֵּר אֶל־אַהֲרֹן וְאֶל־בָּנָיו וְיִנָּזְרוּ מִקָּדְשֵׁי בְנֵי־יִשְׂרָאֵל וְלֹא יְחַלְּלוּ אֶת־שֵׁם קָדְשִׁי אֲשֶׁר הֵם מַקְדִּשִׁים לִי אֲנִי יְהוָה: 3 אֱמֹר אֲלֵהֶם לְדֹרֹתֵיכֶם כָּל־אִישׁ ׀ אֲשֶׁר־יִקְרַב מִכָּל־ זַרְעֲכֶם אֶל־הַקֳּדָשִׁים אֲשֶׁר יַקְדִּישׁוּ בְנֵי־ יִשְׂרָאֵל לַיהוָה וְטֻמְאָתוֹ עָלָיו וְנִכְרְתָה הַנֶּפֶשׁ הַהִוא מִלְּפָנַי אֲנִי יְהוָה: 4 אִישׁ אִישׁ מִזֶּרַע אַהֲרֹן וְהוּא צָרוּעַ אוֹ זָב

nations until he is clean. If one touches anything made unclean by a corpse, or if a man has an emission of semen, [5]or if a man touches any swarming thing by which he is made unclean or any human being by whom he is made unclean—whatever his uncleanness—[6]the person who touches such shall be unclean until evening and shall not eat of the sacred donations unless he has washed his body in water. [7]As soon as the sun sets, he shall be clean; and afterward he may eat of the sacred donations, for they are his food. [8]He shall not eat anything that died or was torn by beasts, thereby becoming unclean: I am the LORD. [9]They shall keep My charge, lest they incur guilt thereby and die for it, having committed profanation: I the LORD consecrate them.

[10]No lay person shall eat of the sacred donations. No bound or hired laborer of a priest shall eat of the sacred donations; [11]but a person who is a priest's property by purchase may eat of them; and those that are born into his household may eat of his food. [12]If a priest's daughter marries a layman, she may not eat of the sacred gifts; [13]but if the priest's daughter is widowed or divorced and without offspring, and is back in her father's house as in her youth, she may eat of her father's food. No lay person may eat of it: [14]but if a man eats of a sacred donation unwittingly, he shall pay the priest for the sacred donation, adding one-fifth of its value. [15]But [the priests] must not allow the Israelites to profane the sacred donations that they set aside for the LORD, [16]or to incur guilt requiring a penalty payment, by eating such sacred donations: for it is I the LORD who make them sacred.

[17]The LORD spoke to Moses, saying: [18]Speak to Aaron and his sons, and to all the Israelite people, and say to them:

When any man of the house of Israel or of the strangers in Israel presents a burnt offering

בַּקֳּדָשִׁים֙ לֹ֣א יֹאכַ֔ל עַ֖ד אֲשֶׁ֣ר יִטְהָ֑ר וְהַנֹּגֵ֙עַ֙ בְּכָל־טְמֵא־נֶ֔פֶשׁ א֣וֹ אִ֔ישׁ אֲשֶׁר־תֵּצֵ֥א מִמֶּ֖נּוּ שִׁכְבַת־זָ֑רַע: 5 אֽוֹ־אִ֗ישׁ אֲשֶׁ֤ר יִגַּע֙ בְּכָל־שֶׁ֔רֶץ אֲשֶׁ֥ר יִטְמָא־ל֑וֹ א֤וֹ בְאָדָם֙ אֲשֶׁ֣ר יִטְמָא־ל֔וֹ לְכֹ֖ל טֻמְאָתֽוֹ: 6 נֶ֚פֶשׁ אֲשֶׁ֣ר תִּגַּע־בּ֔וֹ וְטָמְאָ֖ה עַד־הָעָ֑רֶב וְלֹ֤א יֹאכַל֙ מִן־הַקֳּדָשִׁ֔ים כִּ֛י אִם־רָחַ֥ץ בְּשָׂר֖וֹ בַּמָּֽיִם: 7 וּבָ֣א הַשֶּׁ֔מֶשׁ וְטָהֵ֑ר וְאַחַר֙ יֹאכַ֣ל מִן־הַקֳּדָשִׁ֔ים כִּ֥י לַחְמ֖וֹ הֽוּא: 8 נְבֵלָ֧ה וּטְרֵפָ֛ה לֹ֥א יֹאכַ֖ל לְטָמְאָה־בָ֑הּ אֲנִ֖י יְהוָֽה: 9 וְשָׁמְר֣וּ אֶת־מִשְׁמַרְתִּ֗י וְלֹֽא־יִשְׂא֤וּ עָלָיו֙ חֵ֔טְא וּמֵ֥תוּ ב֖וֹ כִּ֣י יְחַלְּלֻ֑הוּ אֲנִ֥י יְהוָ֖ה מְקַדְּשָֽׁם: 10 וְכָל־זָ֖ר לֹא־יֹ֣אכַל קֹ֑דֶשׁ תּוֹשַׁ֧ב כֹּהֵ֛ן וְשָׂכִ֖יר לֹא־יֹ֥אכַל קֹֽדֶשׁ: 11 וְכֹהֵ֗ן כִּֽי־יִקְנֶ֥ה נֶ֙פֶשׁ֙ קִנְיַ֣ן כַּסְפּ֔וֹ ה֖וּא יֹ֣אכַל בּ֑וֹ וִילִ֣יד בֵּית֔וֹ הֵ֖ם יֹאכְל֥וּ בְלַחְמֽוֹ: 12 וּבַת־כֹּהֵ֔ן כִּ֥י תִהְיֶ֖ה לְאִ֣ישׁ זָ֑ר הִ֕וא בִּתְרוּמַ֥ת הַקֳּדָשִׁ֖ים לֹ֥א תֹאכֵֽל: 13 וּבַת־כֹּהֵן֩ כִּ֨י תִהְיֶ֜ה אַלְמָנָ֣ה וּגְרוּשָׁ֗ה וְזֶ֘רַע֘ אֵ֣ין לָהּ֒ וְשָׁבָ֞ה אֶל־בֵּ֤ית אָבִ֙יהָ֙ כִּנְעוּרֶ֔יהָ מִלֶּ֥חֶם אָבִ֖יהָ תֹּאכֵ֑ל וְכָל־זָ֖ר לֹא־יֹ֥אכַל בּֽוֹ: ס 14 וְאִ֕ישׁ כִּֽי־יֹאכַ֥ל קֹ֖דֶשׁ בִּשְׁגָגָ֑ה וְיָסַ֤ף חֲמִֽשִׁיתוֹ֙ עָלָ֔יו וְנָתַ֥ן לַכֹּהֵ֖ן אֶת־הַקֹּֽדֶשׁ: 15 וְלֹ֣א יְחַלְּל֔וּ אֶת־קָדְשֵׁ֖י בְּנֵ֣י יִשְׂרָאֵ֑ל אֵ֥ת אֲשֶׁר־יָרִ֖ימוּ לַֽיהוָֽה: 16 וְהִשִּׂ֤יאוּ אוֹתָם֙ עֲוֺ֣ן אַשְׁמָ֔ה בְּאָכְלָ֖ם אֶת־קָדְשֵׁיהֶ֑ם כִּ֛י אֲנִ֥י יְהוָ֖ה מְקַדְּשָֽׁם: פ 17 וַיְדַבֵּ֥ר יְהוָ֖ה אֶל־מֹשֶׁ֥ה לֵּאמֹֽר: 18 דַּבֵּ֨ר אֶֽל־אַהֲרֹ֜ן וְאֶל־בָּנָ֗יו וְאֶל֙ כָּל־בְּנֵ֣י יִשְׂרָאֵ֔ל וְאָמַרְתָּ֖ אֲלֵהֶ֑ם אִ֣ישׁ אִישׁ֩ מִבֵּ֨ית יִשְׂרָאֵ֜ל וּמִן־הַגֵּ֣ר בְּיִשְׂרָאֵ֗ל אֲשֶׁ֨ר יַקְרִ֧יב קָרְבָּנ֛וֹ לְכָל־נִדְרֵיהֶם֙

as his offering for any of the votive or any of the freewill offerings that they offer to the LORD, [19]it must, to be acceptable in your favor, be a male without blemish, from cattle or sheep or goats. [20]You shall not offer any that has a defect, for it will not be accepted in your favor.

[21]And when a man offers, from the herd or the flock, a sacrifice of well-being to the LORD for an explicit[b] vow or as a freewill offering, it must, to be acceptable, be without blemish; there must be no defect in it. [22]Anything blind, or injured, or maimed, or with a wen, boil-scar, or scurvy—such you shall not offer to the LORD; you shall not put any of them on the altar as offerings by fire to the LORD. [23]You may, however, present as a freewill offering an ox or a sheep with a limb extended or contracted; but it will not be accepted for a vow. [24]You shall not offer to the LORD anything [with its testes] bruised or crushed or torn or cut. You shall have no such practices[c] in your own land, [25]nor shall you accept such [animals] from a foreigner for offering as food for your God, for they are mutilated, they have a defect; they shall not be accepted in your favor.

[26]The LORD spoke to Moses, saying: [27]When an ox or a sheep or a goat is born, it shall stay seven days with its mother, and from the eighth day on it shall be acceptable as an offering by fire to the LORD. [28]However, no animal from the herd or from the flock shall be slaughtered on the same day with its young.

[29]When you sacrifice a thanksgiving offering to the LORD, sacrifice it so that it may be acceptable in your favor. [30]It shall be eaten on the same day; you shall not leave any of it until morning: I am the LORD.

[31]You shall faithfully observe My commandments: I am the LORD. [32]You shall not profane My holy name, that I may be sanctified in the

וּלְכָל־נִדְבוֹתָ֔ם אֲשֶׁר־יַקְרִ֥יבוּ לַיהוָ֖ה לְעֹלָֽה׃ 19 לִֽרְצֹנְכֶ֑ם תָּמִ֣ים זָכָ֔ר בַּבָּקָ֕ר בַּכְּשָׂבִ֖ים וּבָֽעִזִּֽים׃ 20 כֹּ֛ל אֲשֶׁר־בּ֥וֹ מ֖וּם לֹ֣א תַקְרִ֑יבוּ כִּי־לֹ֥א לְרָצ֖וֹן יִֽהְיֶ֥ה לָכֶֽם׃ 21 וְאִ֗ישׁ כִּֽי־יַקְרִ֤יב זֶֽבַח־שְׁלָמִים֙ לַֽיהוָ֔ה לְפַלֵּא־נֶ֙דֶר֙ א֣וֹ לִנְדָבָ֔ה בַּבָּקָ֖ר א֣וֹ בַצֹּ֑אן תָּמִ֤ים יִֽהְיֶה֙ לְרָצ֔וֹן כָּל־מ֖וּם לֹ֥א יִֽהְיֶה־בּֽוֹ׃ 22 עַוֶּרֶת֩ א֨וֹ שָׁב֜וּר אֽוֹ־חָר֣וּץ אֽוֹ־יַבֶּ֗לֶת א֤וֹ גָרָב֙ א֣וֹ יַלֶּ֔פֶת לֹֽא־תַקְרִ֥יבוּ אֵ֖לֶּה לַֽיהוָ֑ה וְאִשֶּׁ֗ה לֹֽא־תִתְּנ֥וּ מֵהֶ֛ם עַל־הַמִּזְבֵּ֖חַ לַֽיהוָֽה׃ 23 וְשׁ֣וֹר וָשֶׂ֗ה שָׂר֤וּעַ וְקָלוּט֙ נְדָבָ֣ה תַּעֲשֶׂ֣ה אֹת֔וֹ וּלְנֵ֖דֶר לֹ֥א יֵֽרָצֶֽה׃ 24 וּמָע֤וּךְ וְכָתוּת֙ וְנָת֣וּק וְכָר֔וּת לֹ֥א תַקְרִ֖יבוּ לַֽיהוָ֑ה וּבְאַרְצְכֶ֖ם לֹ֥א תַעֲשֽׂוּ׃ 25 וּמִיַּ֣ד בֶּן־נֵכָ֗ר לֹ֥א תַקְרִ֛יבוּ אֶת־לֶ֥חֶם אֱלֹֽהֵיכֶ֖ם מִכָּל־אֵ֑לֶּה כִּ֣י מָשְׁחָתָ֤ם בָּהֶם֙ מ֣וּם בָּ֔ם לֹ֥א יֵרָצ֖וּ לָכֶֽם׃ פ

26 וַיְדַבֵּ֥ר יְהוָ֖ה אֶל־מֹשֶׁ֥ה לֵּאמֹֽר׃ 27 שׁ֣וֹר אוֹ־כֶ֤שֶׂב אוֹ־עֵז֙ כִּ֣י יִוָּלֵ֔ד וְהָיָ֛ה שִׁבְעַ֥ת יָמִ֖ים תַּ֣חַת אִמּ֑וֹ וּמִיּ֤וֹם הַשְּׁמִינִי֙ וָהָ֔לְאָה יֵֽרָצֶ֔ה לְקָרְבַּ֥ן אִשֶּׁ֖ה לַֽיהוָֽה׃ 28 וְשׁ֖וֹר אוֹ־שֶׂ֑ה אֹת֣וֹ וְאֶת־בְּנ֔וֹ לֹ֥א תִשְׁחֲט֖וּ בְּי֥וֹם אֶחָֽד׃ 29 וְכִֽי־תִזְבְּח֥וּ זֶֽבַח־תּוֹדָ֖ה לַֽיהוָ֑ה לִֽרְצֹנְכֶ֖ם תִּזְבָּֽחוּ׃ 30 בַּיּ֤וֹם הַהוּא֙ יֵֽאָכֵ֔ל לֹֽא־תוֹתִ֥ירוּ מִמֶּ֖נּוּ עַד־בֹּ֑קֶר אֲנִ֖י יְהוָֽה׃ 31 וּשְׁמַרְתֶּם֙ מִצְוֺתַ֔י וַעֲשִׂיתֶ֖ם אֹתָ֑ם אֲנִ֖י יְהוָֽה׃ 32 וְלֹ֤א תְחַלְּלוּ֙ אֶת־שֵׁ֣ם קָדְשִׁ֔י וְנִ֨קְדַּשְׁתִּ֔י בְּת֖וֹךְ בְּנֵ֣י יִשְׂרָאֵ֑ל אֲנִ֥י יְהוָֽה

---

b Or "unspecified" or "extraordinary"; meaning of Heb. lephalle uncertain.
c I.e., mutilations.

midst of the Israelite people—I the Lord who sanctify you, 33I who brought you out of the land of Egypt to be your God, I the Lord.

23

The Lord spoke to Moses, saying: 2Speak to the Israelite people and say to them:

These are My fixed times, the fixed times of the Lord, which you shall proclaim as sacred occasions.

3On six days work may be done, but on the seventh day there shall be a sabbath of complete rest, a sacred occasion. You shall do no work; it shall be a sabbath of the Lord throughout your settlements.

4These are the set times of the Lord, the sacred occasions, which you shall celebrate each at its appointed time: 5In the first month, on the fourteenth day of the month, at twilight, there shall be a passover offering to the Lord, 6and on the fifteenth day of that month the Lord's Feast of Unleavened Bread. You shall eat unleavened bread for seven days. 7On the first day you shall celebrate a sacred occasion: you shall not work at your occupations. 8Seven days you shall make offerings by fire to the Lord. The seventh day shall be a sacred occasion: you shall not work at your occupations.

9The Lord spoke to Moses, saying: 10Speak to the Israelite people and say to them:

When you enter the land that I am giving to you and you reap its harvest, you shall bring the first sheaf of your harvest to the priest. 11He shall elevate the sheaf before the Lord for acceptance in your behalf; the priest shall elevate it on the day after the sabbath. 12On the day that you elevate the sheaf, you shall offer as a burnt offering to the Lord a lamb of the first year without blemish. 13The meal offering with it shall be two-tenths of a measure of choice flour with oil

מִקְדִּשְׁכֶם: 33 הַמּוֹצִיא אֶתְכֶם מֵאֶרֶץ מִצְרַיִם לִהְיוֹת לָכֶם לֵאלֹהִים אֲנִי יְהוָה: פ

כג וַיְדַבֵּר יְהוָה אֶל־מֹשֶׁה לֵּאמֹר: 2 דַּבֵּר אֶל־בְּנֵי יִשְׂרָאֵל וְאָמַרְתָּ אֲלֵהֶם מוֹעֲדֵי יְהוָה אֲשֶׁר־תִּקְרְאוּ אֹתָם מִקְרָאֵי קֹדֶשׁ אֵלֶּה הֵם מוֹעֲדָי: 3 שֵׁשֶׁת יָמִים תֵּעָשֶׂה מְלָאכָה וּבַיּוֹם הַשְּׁבִיעִי שַׁבַּת שַׁבָּתוֹן מִקְרָא־קֹדֶשׁ כָּל־מְלָאכָה לֹא תַעֲשׂוּ שַׁבָּת הִוא לַיהוָה בְּכֹל מוֹשְׁבֹתֵיכֶם: פ 4 אֵלֶּה מוֹעֲדֵי יְהוָה מִקְרָאֵי קֹדֶשׁ אֲשֶׁר־תִּקְרְאוּ אֹתָם בְּמוֹעֲדָם: 5 בַּחֹדֶשׁ הָרִאשׁוֹן בְּאַרְבָּעָה עָשָׂר לַחֹדֶשׁ בֵּין הָעַרְבָּיִם פֶּסַח לַיהוָה: 6 וּבַחֲמִשָּׁה עָשָׂר יוֹם לַחֹדֶשׁ הַזֶּה חַג הַמַּצּוֹת לַיהוָה שִׁבְעַת יָמִים מַצּוֹת תֹּאכֵלוּ: 7 בַּיּוֹם הָרִאשׁוֹן מִקְרָא־קֹדֶשׁ יִהְיֶה לָכֶם כָּל־מְלֶאכֶת עֲבֹדָה לֹא תַעֲשׂוּ: 8 וְהִקְרַבְתֶּם אִשֶּׁה לַיהוָה שִׁבְעַת יָמִים בַּיּוֹם הַשְּׁבִיעִי מִקְרָא־קֹדֶשׁ כָּל־מְלֶאכֶת עֲבֹדָה לֹא תַעֲשׂוּ: פ

9 וַיְדַבֵּר יְהוָה אֶל־מֹשֶׁה לֵּאמֹר: 10 דַּבֵּר אֶל־בְּנֵי יִשְׂרָאֵל וְאָמַרְתָּ אֲלֵהֶם כִּי־תָבֹאוּ אֶל־הָאָרֶץ אֲשֶׁר אֲנִי נֹתֵן לָכֶם וּקְצַרְתֶּם אֶת־קְצִירָהּ וַהֲבֵאתֶם אֶת־עֹמֶר רֵאשִׁית קְצִירְכֶם אֶל־הַכֹּהֵן: 11 וְהֵנִיף אֶת־הָעֹמֶר לִפְנֵי יְהוָה לִרְצֹנְכֶם מִמָּחֳרַת הַשַּׁבָּת יְנִיפֶנּוּ הַכֹּהֵן: 12 וַעֲשִׂיתֶם בְּיוֹם הֲנִיפְכֶם אֶת־הָעֹמֶר כֶּבֶשׂ תָּמִים בֶּן־שְׁנָתוֹ לְעֹלָה לַיהוָה: 13 וּמִנְחָתוֹ שְׁנֵי עֶשְׂרֹנִים סֹלֶת בְּלוּלָה בַשֶּׁמֶן אִשֶּׁה לַיהוָה רֵיחַ

mixed in, an offering by fire of pleasing odor to the LORD; and the libation with it shall be of wine, a quarter of a *hin.* [14]Until that very day, until you have brought the offering of your God, you shall eat no bread or parched grain or fresh ears;[a] it is a law for all time throughout the ages in all your settlements.

[15]And from the day on which you bring the sheaf of elevation offering—the day after the sabbath—you shall count off seven weeks. They must be complete: [16]you must count until the day after the seventh week—fifty days; then you shall bring an offering of new grain to the LORD. [17]You shall bring from your settlements two loaves of bread as an elevation offering; each shall be made of two-tenths of a measure of choice flour, baked after leavening, as first fruits to the LORD. [18]With the bread you shall present, as burnt offerings to the LORD, seven yearling lambs without blemish, one bull of the herd, and two rams, with their meal offerings and libations, an offering by fire of pleasing odor to the LORD. [19]You shall also offer one he-goat as a sin offering and two yearling lambs as a sacrifice of well-being. [20]The priest shall elevate these—the two lambs[b]—together with the bread of first fruits as an elevation offering before the LORD; they shall be holy to the LORD, for the priest. [21]On that same day you shall hold a celebration; it shall be a sacred occasion for you; you shall not work at your occupations. This is a law for all time in all your settlements, throughout the ages.

[22]And when you reap the harvest of your land, you shall not reap all the way to the edges of your field, or gather the gleanings of your harvest; you shall leave them for the poor and the stranger: I the LORD am your God.

[23]The LORD spoke to Moses, saying: [24]Speak to the Israelite people thus: In the seventh

נִיחֹ֔חַ וְנִסְכֹּ֖ה יַ֥יִן רְבִיעִ֥ת הַהִֽין: 14 וְלֶ֩חֶם֩ וְקָלִ֨י וְכַרְמֶ֜ל לֹ֣א תֹֽאכְל֗וּ עַד־ עֶ֙צֶם֙ הַיּ֣וֹם הַזֶּ֔ה עַ֚ד הֲבִ֣יאֲכֶ֔ם אֶת־קָרְבַּ֖ן אֱלֹֽהֵיכֶ֑ם חֻקַּ֤ת עוֹלָם֙ לְדֹרֹ֣תֵיכֶ֔ם בְּכֹ֖ל מֹשְׁבֹֽתֵיכֶֽם: ס

15 וּסְפַרְתֶּ֤ם לָכֶם֙ מִמָּֽחֳרַ֣ת הַשַּׁבָּ֔ת מִיּוֹם֙ הֲבִ֣יאֲכֶ֔ם אֶת־עֹ֖מֶר הַתְּנוּפָ֑ה שֶׁ֥בַע שַׁבָּת֖וֹת תְּמִימֹ֥ת תִּהְיֶֽינָה: 16 עַ֣ד מִמָּֽחֳרַ֤ת הַשַּׁבָּת֙ הַשְּׁבִיעִ֔ת תִּסְפְּר֖וּ חֲמִשִּׁ֣ים י֑וֹם וְהִקְרַבְתֶּ֛ם מִנְחָ֥ה חֲדָשָׁ֖ה לַֽיהוָֽה: 17 מִמּֽוֹשְׁבֹ֨תֵיכֶ֜ם תָּבִ֣יאּוּ‎ * ׀ לֶ֣חֶם תְּנוּפָ֗ה שְׁתַּ֙יִם֙ שְׁנֵ֣י עֶשְׂרֹנִ֔ים סֹ֣לֶת תִּהְיֶ֔ינָה חָמֵ֖ץ תֵּֽאָפֶ֑ינָה בִּכּוּרִ֖ים לַֽיהוָֽה: 18 וְהִקְרַבְתֶּ֣ם עַל־הַלֶּ֗חֶם שִׁבְעַ֤ת כְּבָשִׂים֙ תְּמִימִם֙ בְּנֵ֣י שָׁנָ֔ה וּפַ֧ר בֶּן־בָּקָ֛ר אֶחָ֖ד וְאֵילִ֣ם שְׁנָ֑יִם יִֽהְי֤וּ עֹלָה֙ לַֽיהוָ֔ה וּמִנְחָתָם֙ וְנִסְכֵּיהֶ֔ם אִשֵּׁ֥ה רֵֽיחַ־נִיחֹ֖חַ לַֽיהוָֽה: 19 וַֽעֲשִׂיתֶ֛ם שְׂעִיר־ עִזִּ֥ים אֶחָ֖ד לְחַטָּ֑את וּשְׁנֵ֧י כְבָשִׂ֛ים בְּנֵ֥י שָׁנָ֖ה לְזֶ֥בַח שְׁלָמִֽים: 20 וְהֵנִ֣יף הַכֹּהֵ֣ן ׀ אֹתָ֡ם עַל֩ לֶ֨חֶם הַבִּכּוּרִ֤ים תְּנוּפָה֙ לִפְנֵ֣י יְהוָ֔ה עַל־שְׁנֵ֖י כְּבָשִׂ֑ים קֹ֛דֶשׁ יִֽהְי֥וּ לַֽיהוָ֖ה לַכֹּהֵֽן: 21 וּקְרָאתֶ֞ם בְּעֶ֣צֶם ׀ הַיּ֣וֹם הַזֶּ֗ה מִֽקְרָא־קֹ֙דֶשׁ֙ יִהְיֶ֣ה לָכֶ֔ם כָּל־מְלֶ֥אכֶת עֲבֹדָ֖ה לֹ֣א תַעֲשׂ֑וּ חֻקַּ֥ת עוֹלָ֛ם בְּכָל־ מֹשְׁבֹֽתֵיכֶ֖ם לְדֹרֹֽתֵיכֶֽם:

22 וּֽבְקֻצְרְכֶ֞ם אֶת־קְצִ֣יר אַרְצְכֶ֗ם לֹֽא־ תְכַלֶּ֞ה פְּאַ֤ת שָֽׂדְךָ֙ בְּקֻצְרֶ֔ךָ וְלֶ֥קֶט קְצִֽירְךָ֖ לֹ֣א תְלַקֵּ֑ט לֶֽעָנִ֤י וְלַגֵּר֙ תַּעֲזֹ֣ב אֹתָ֔ם אֲנִ֖י יְהוָ֥ה אֱלֹֽהֵיכֶֽם: ס

23 וַיְדַבֵּ֥ר יְהוָ֖ה אֶל־מֹשֶׁ֥ה לֵּאמֹֽר: 24 דַּבֵּ֞ר אֶל־בְּנֵ֤י יִשְׂרָאֵל֙ לֵאמֹ֔ר בַּחֹ֣דֶשׁ הַשְּׁבִיעִ֗י בְּאֶחָ֤ד לַחֹ֙דֶשׁ֙ יִהְיֶ֤ה לָכֶם֙ שַׁבָּת֔וֹן זִכְר֖וֹן

---

month, on the first day of the month, you shall observe complete rest, a sacred occasion commemorated with loud blasts. 25You shall not work at your occupations; and you shall bring an offering by fire to the LORD.

26The LORD spoke to Moses, saying: 27Mark, the tenth day of this seventh month is the Day of Atonement. It shall be a sacred occasion for you: you shall practice self-denial, and you shall bring an offering by fire to the LORD; 28you shall do no work throughout that day. For it is a Day of Atonement, on which expiation is made on your behalf before the LORD your God. 29Indeed, any person who does not practice self-denial throughout that day shall be cut off from his kin; 30and whoever does any work throughout that day, I will cause that person to perish from among his people. 31Do no work whatever; it is a law for all time, throughout the ages in all your settlements. 32It shall be a sabbath of complete rest for you, and you shall practice self-denial; on the ninth day of the month at evening, from evening to evening, you shall observe this your sabbath.

33The LORD spoke to Moses, saying: 34Say to the Israelite people:

On the fifteenth day of this seventh month there shall be the Feast of Booths[c] to the LORD, [to last] seven days. 35The first day shall be a sacred occasion: you shall not work at your occupations; 36seven days you shall bring offerings by fire to the LORD. On the eighth day you shall observe a sacred occasion and bring an offering by fire to the LORD; it is a solemn gathering:[d] you shall not work at your occupations.

37Those are the set times of the LORD that you shall celebrate as sacred occasions, bringing offerings by fire to the LORD—burnt offerings,

---

c   Others "Tabernacles."
d   Precise meaning of Heb. 'aṣereth uncertain.

---

25 כָּל־מְלֶאכֶת   תְּרוּעָה מִקְרָא־קֹדֶשׁ:
עֲבֹדָה לֹא תַעֲשׂוּ וְהִקְרַבְתֶּם אִשֶּׁה
לַיהוָה: ס
26 וַיְדַבֵּר יְהוָה אֶל־מֹשֶׁה לֵּאמֹר: 27 אַ֣ךְ
בֶּעָשׂוֹר לַחֹדֶשׁ הַשְּׁבִיעִי הַזֶּה יוֹם הַכִּפֻּרִים
הוּא מִקְרָא־קֹדֶשׁ יִהְיֶה לָכֶם וְעִנִּיתֶם
אֶת־נַפְשֹׁתֵיכֶם וְהִקְרַבְתֶּם אִשֶּׁה לַיהוָה:
28 וְכָל־מְלָאכָה לֹא תַעֲשׂוּ בְּעֶצֶם הַיּוֹם
הַזֶּה כִּי יוֹם כִּפֻּרִים הוּא לְכַפֵּר עֲלֵיכֶם
לִפְנֵי יְהוָה אֱלֹהֵיכֶם: 29 כִּי כָל־הַנֶּפֶשׁ
אֲשֶׁר לֹא־תְעֻנֶּה בְּעֶצֶם הַיּוֹם הַזֶּה
וְנִכְרְתָה מֵעַמֶּיהָ: 30 וְכָל־הַנֶּפֶשׁ אֲשֶׁר
תַּעֲשֶׂה כָּל־מְלָאכָה בְּעֶצֶם הַיּוֹם הַזֶּה
וְהַאֲבַדְתִּי אֶת־הַנֶּפֶשׁ הַהִוא מִקֶּרֶב עַמָּהּ:
31 כָּל־מְלָאכָה לֹא תַעֲשׂוּ חֻקַּת עוֹלָם
לְדֹרֹתֵיכֶם בְּכֹל מֹשְׁבֹתֵיכֶם: 32 שַׁבַּת
שַׁבָּתוֹן הוּא לָכֶם וְעִנִּיתֶם אֶת־נַפְשֹׁתֵיכֶם
בְּתִשְׁעָה לַחֹדֶשׁ בָּעֶרֶב מֵעֶרֶב עַד־עֶרֶב
תִּשְׁבְּתוּ שַׁבַּתְּכֶם: פ

33 וַיְדַבֵּר יְהוָה אֶל־מֹשֶׁה לֵּאמֹר: 34 דַּבֵּר
אֶל־בְּנֵי יִשְׂרָאֵל לֵאמֹר
בַּחֲמִשָּׁה עָשָׂר יוֹם לַחֹדֶשׁ הַשְּׁבִיעִי הַזֶּה
חַג הַסֻּכּוֹת שִׁבְעַת יָמִים לַיהוָה: 35 בַּיּוֹם
הָרִאשׁוֹן מִקְרָא־קֹדֶשׁ כָּל־מְלֶאכֶת עֲבֹדָה
לֹא תַעֲשׂוּ: 36 שִׁבְעַת יָמִים תַּקְרִיבוּ אִשֶּׁה
לַיהוָה בַּיּוֹם הַשְּׁמִינִי מִקְרָא־קֹדֶשׁ יִהְיֶה
לָכֶם וְהִקְרַבְתֶּם אִשֶּׁה לַיהוָה עֲצֶרֶת הִוא
כָּל־מְלֶאכֶת עֲבֹדָה לֹא תַעֲשׂוּ:

37 אֵלֶּה מוֹעֲדֵי יְהוָה אֲשֶׁר־תִּקְרְאוּ אֹתָם
מִקְרָאֵי קֹדֶשׁ לְהַקְרִיב אִשֶּׁה לַיהוָה עֹלָה
וּמִנְחָה זֶבַח וּנְסָכִים דְּבַר־יוֹם בְּיוֹמוֹ:

meal offerings, sacrifices, and libations, on each day what is proper to it—³⁸apart from the sabbaths of the Lord, and apart from your gifts and from all your votive offerings and from all your freewill offerings that you give to the Lord.

³⁹Mark, on the fifteenth day of the seventh month, when you have gathered in the yield of your land, you shall observe the festival of the Lord [to last] seven days: a complete rest on the first day, and a complete rest on the eighth day. ⁴⁰On the first day you shall take the product of *hadar*[e] trees, branches of palm trees, boughs of leafy[f] trees, and willows of the brook, and you shall rejoice before the Lord your God seven days. ⁴¹You shall observe it as a festival of the Lord for seven days in the year; you shall observe it in the seventh month as a law for all time, throughout the ages. ⁴²You shall live in booths seven days; all citizens in Israel shall live in booths, ⁴³in order that future generations may know that I made the Israelite people live in booths when I brought them out of the land of Egypt, I the Lord your God.

⁴⁴So Moses declared to the Israelites the set times of the Lord.

24

The Lord spoke to Moses, saying:

²Command the Israelite people to bring you clear oil of beaten olives for lighting, for kindling lamps regularly. ³Aaron shall set them up in the Tent of Meeting outside the curtain of the Pact [to burn] from evening to morning before the Lord regularly; it is a law for all time throughout the ages. ⁴He shall set up the lamps on the pure[a] lampstand before the Lord [to burn] regularly.

---

e   *Others "goodly"; exact meaning of Heb.* hadar *uncertain. Traditionally the product is understood as "citron."*

f   *Meaning of Heb.* aboth *uncertain.*

a   *See note at Exod. 31.8.*

Hebrew column:

³⁸ מִלְּבַ֖ד שַׁבְּתֹ֣ת יְהֹוָ֑ה וּמִלְּבַ֣ד מַתְּנֽוֹתֵיכֶ֗ם וּמִלְּבַד֙ כָּל־נִדְרֵיכֶ֔ם וּמִלְּבַד֙ כָּל־ נִדְבֽוֹתֵיכֶ֔ם אֲשֶׁ֥ר תִּתְּנ֖וּ לַיהֹוָֽה׃

³⁹ אַ֡ךְ בַּחֲמִשָּׁה֩ עָשָׂ֨ר י֜וֹם לַחֹ֣דֶשׁ הַשְּׁבִיעִ֗י בְּאָסְפְּכֶם֙ אֶת־תְּבוּאַ֣ת הָאָ֔רֶץ תָּחֹ֥גּוּ אֶת־ חַג־יְהֹוָ֖ה שִׁבְעַ֣ת יָמִ֑ים בַּיּ֤וֹם הָֽרִאשׁוֹן֙ שַׁבָּת֔וֹן וּבַיּ֥וֹם הַשְּׁמִינִ֖י שַׁבָּתֽוֹן׃ ⁴⁰ וּלְקַחְתֶּ֨ם לָכֶ֜ם בַּיּ֣וֹם הָרִאשׁ֗וֹן פְּרִ֨י עֵ֤ץ הָדָר֙ כַּפֹּ֣ת תְּמָרִ֔ים וַעֲנַ֥ף עֵץ־עָבֹ֖ת וְעַרְבֵי־ נָ֑חַל וּשְׂמַחְתֶּ֗ם לִפְנֵ֛י יְהֹוָ֥ה אֱלֹהֵיכֶ֖ם שִׁבְעַ֥ת יָמִֽים׃ ⁴¹ וְחַגֹּתֶ֤ם אֹתוֹ֙ חַ֣ג לַֽיהֹוָ֔ה שִׁבְעַ֥ת יָמִ֖ים בַּשָּׁנָ֑ה חֻקַּ֤ת עוֹלָם֙ לְדֹרֹ֣תֵיכֶ֔ם בַּחֹ֥דֶשׁ הַשְּׁבִיעִ֖י תָּחֹ֥גּוּ אֹתֽוֹ׃ ⁴² בַּסֻּכֹּ֥ת תֵּשְׁב֖וּ שִׁבְעַ֣ת יָמִ֑ים כָּל־הָֽאֶזְרָח֙ בְּיִשְׂרָאֵ֔ל יֵשְׁב֖וּ בַּסֻּכֹּֽת׃ ⁴³ לְמַ֘עַן֮ יֵדְע֣וּ דֹרֹֽתֵיכֶם֒ כִּ֣י בַסֻּכּ֗וֹת הוֹשַׁ֙בְתִּי֙ אֶת־בְּנֵ֣י יִשְׂרָאֵ֔ל בְּהוֹצִיאִ֥י אוֹתָ֖ם מֵאֶ֣רֶץ מִצְרָ֑יִם אֲנִ֖י יְהֹוָ֥ה אֱלֹהֵיכֶֽם׃ ⁴⁴ וַיְדַבֵּ֣ר מֹשֶׁ֔ה אֶֽת־מֹעֲדֵ֖י יְהֹוָ֑ה אֶל־בְּנֵ֖י יִשְׂרָאֵֽל׃ פ

כד וַיְדַבֵּ֥ר יְהֹוָ֖ה אֶל־מֹשֶׁ֥ה לֵּאמֹֽר׃ ² צַ֞ו אֶת־בְּנֵ֣י יִשְׂרָאֵ֗ל וְיִקְח֨וּ אֵלֶ֜יךָ שֶׁ֣מֶן זַ֥יִת זָ֛ךְ כָּתִ֖ית לַמָּא֑וֹר לְהַעֲלֹ֥ת נֵ֖ר תָּמִֽיד׃ ³ מִח֩וּץ לְפָרֹ֨כֶת הָעֵדֻ֜ת בְּאֹ֣הֶל מוֹעֵ֗ד יַעֲרֹ֩ךְ אֹת֨וֹ אַהֲרֹ֜ן מֵעֶ֧רֶב עַד־בֹּ֛קֶר לִפְנֵ֥י יְהֹוָ֖ה תָּמִ֑יד חֻקַּ֥ת עוֹלָ֖ם לְדֹרֹֽתֵיכֶֽם׃ ⁴ עַ֚ל הַמְּנֹרָ֣ה הַטְּהֹרָ֔ה יַעֲרֹ֖ךְ אֶת־הַנֵּר֑וֹת לִפְנֵ֥י יְהֹוָ֖ה תָּמִֽיד׃ פ

⁵You shall take choice flour and bake of it twelve loaves, two-tenths of a measure for each loaf. ⁶Place them on the pureᵃ table before the Lord in two rows, six to a row. ⁷With each row you shall place pure frankincense, which is to be a token offeringᵇ for the bread, as an offering by fire to the Lord. ⁸He shall arrange them before the Lord regularly every sabbath day—it is a commitment for all time on the part of the Israelites. ⁹They shall belong to Aaron and his sons, who shall eat them in the sacred precinct; for they are his as most holy things from the Lord's offerings by fire, a due for all time.

¹⁰There came out among the Israelites one whose mother was Israelite and whose father was Egyptian. And a fight broke out in the camp between that half-Israeliteᶜ and a certain Israelite. ¹¹The son of the Israelite woman pronounced the Name in blasphemy, and he was brought to Moses—now his mother's name was Shelomith daughter of Dibri of the tribe of Dan—¹²and he was placed in custody, until the decision of the Lord should be made clear to them.

¹³And the Lord spoke to Moses, saying: ¹⁴Take the blasphemer outside the camp; and let all who were within hearing lay their hands upon his head, and let the whole community stone him.

¹⁵And to the Israelite people speak thus: Anyone who blasphemes his God shall bear his guilt; ¹⁶if he also pronounces the name Lord, he shall be put to death. The whole community shall stone him; stranger or citizen, if he has thus pronounced the Name, he shall be put to death.

¹⁷If anyone kills any human being, he shall be put to death. ¹⁸One who kills a beast shall make restitution for it: life for life. ¹⁹If anyone maims his fellow, as he has done so shall it be

---

ה וְלָקַחְתָּ סֹּלֶת וְאָפִיתָ אֹתָהּ שְׁתֵּים עֶשְׂרֵה חַלּוֹת שְׁנֵי עֶשְׂרֹנִים יִהְיֶה הַחַלָּה הָאֶחָת: ו וְשַׂמְתָּ אוֹתָם שְׁתַּיִם מַעֲרָכוֹת שֵׁשׁ הַמַּעֲרָכֶת עַל הַשֻּׁלְחָן הַטָּהֹר לִפְנֵי יְהֹוָה: ז וְנָתַתָּ עַל־הַמַּעֲרֶכֶת לְבֹנָה זַכָּה וְהָיְתָה לַלֶּחֶם לְאַזְכָּרָה אִשֶּׁה לַיהֹוָה: ח בְּיוֹם הַשַּׁבָּת בְּיוֹם הַשַּׁבָּת יַעַרְכֶנּוּ לִפְנֵי יְהֹוָה תָּמִיד מֵאֵת בְּנֵי־יִשְׂרָאֵל בְּרִית עוֹלָם: ט וְהָיְתָה לְאַהֲרֹן וּלְבָנָיו וַאֲכָלֻהוּ בְּמָקוֹם קָדֹשׁ כִּי קֹדֶשׁ קָדָשִׁים הוּא* לוֹ מֵאִשֵּׁי יְהֹוָה חָק־עוֹלָם: ס

י וַיֵּצֵא בֶּן־אִשָּׁה יִשְׂרְאֵלִית וְהוּא בֶּן־אִישׁ מִצְרִי בְּתוֹךְ בְּנֵי יִשְׂרָאֵל וַיִּנָּצוּ בַּמַּחֲנֶה בֶּן הַיִּשְׂרְאֵלִית וְאִישׁ הַיִּשְׂרְאֵלִי: יא וַיִּקֹּב בֶּן־הָאִשָּׁה הַיִּשְׂרְאֵלִית אֶת־הַשֵּׁם וַיְקַלֵּל וַיָּבִיאוּ אֹתוֹ אֶל־מֹשֶׁה וְשֵׁם אִמּוֹ שְׁלֹמִית בַּת־דִּבְרִי לְמַטֵּה־דָן: יב וַיַּנִּיחֻהוּ בַּמִּשְׁמָר לִפְרֹשׁ לָהֶם עַל־פִּי יְהֹוָה: פ

יג וַיְדַבֵּר יְהֹוָה אֶל־מֹשֶׁה לֵּאמֹר: יד הוֹצֵא אֶת־הַמְקַלֵּל אֶל־מִחוּץ לַמַּחֲנֶה וְסָמְכוּ כָל־הַשֹּׁמְעִים אֶת־יְדֵיהֶם עַל־רֹאשׁוֹ וְרָגְמוּ אֹתוֹ כָּל־הָעֵדָה:

טו וְאֶל־בְּנֵי יִשְׂרָאֵל תְּדַבֵּר לֵאמֹר אִישׁ אִישׁ כִּי־יְקַלֵּל אֱלֹהָיו וְנָשָׂא חֶטְאוֹ: טז וְנֹקֵב שֵׁם־יְהֹוָה מוֹת יוּמָת רָגוֹם יִרְגְּמוּ־בוֹ כָּל־הָעֵדָה כַּגֵּר כָּאֶזְרָח בְּנָקְבוֹ־שֵׁם יוּמָת:

יז וְאִישׁ כִּי יַכֶּה כָּל־נֶפֶשׁ אָדָם מוֹת יוּמָת: יח וּמַכֵּה נֶפֶשׁ־בְּהֵמָה יְשַׁלְּמֶנָּה נֶפֶשׁ תַּחַת נָפֶשׁ: יט וְאִישׁ כִּי־יִתֵּן מוּם בַּעֲמִיתוֹ כַּאֲשֶׁר עָשָׂה כֵּן יֵעָשֶׂה לּוֹ: כ שֶׁבֶר תַּחַת

---

b   See Lev. 2.2.
c   Lit. "the son of an Israelite woman."

v. 9.   סבירין ומטעין "היא"

done to him: [20]fracture for fracture, eye for eye, tooth for tooth. The injury he inflicted on another shall be inflicted on him. [21]One who kills a beast shall make restitution for it; but one who kills a human being shall be put to death. [22]You shall have one standard for stranger and citizen alike: for I the LORD am your God.

[23]Moses spoke thus to the Israelites. And they took the blasphemer outside the camp and pelted him with stones. The Israelites did as the LORD had commanded Moses.

25 BE-HAR
The LORD spoke to Moses on Mount Sinai: [2]Speak to the Israelite people and say to them:

When you enter the land that I assign to you, the land shall observe a sabbath of the LORD. [3]Six years you may sow your field and six years you may prune your vineyard and gather in the yield. [4]But in the seventh year the land shall have a sabbath of complete rest, a sabbath of the LORD: you shall not sow your field or prune your vineyard. [5]You shall not reap the aftergrowth of your harvest or gather the grapes of your untrimmed vines; it shall be a year of complete rest for the land. [6]But you may eat whatever the land during its sabbath will produce—you, your male and female slaves, the hired and bound laborers who live with you, [7]and your cattle and the beasts in your land may eat all its yield.

[8]You shall count off seven weeks of years—seven times seven years—so that the period of seven weeks of years gives you a total of forty-nine years. [9]Then you shall sound the horn loud; in the seventh month, on the tenth day of the month—the Day of Atonement—you shall have the horn sounded throughout your land [10]and you shall hallow the fiftieth year. You shall proclaim release[a] throughout the land for

a   Others "liberty."

שֶׁבֶר עַ֫יִן תַּ֤חַת עַ֙יִן֙ שֵׁ֣ן תַּ֣חַת שֵׁ֔ן כַּאֲשֶׁ֨ר 21 וּמַכֵּ֥ה יִתֵּ֥ן מוּם֙ בָּֽאָדָ֔ם כֵּ֖ן יִנָּ֥תֶן בּֽוֹ׃ בְהֵמָ֖ה יְשַׁלְּמֶ֑נָּה וּמַכֵּ֥ה אָדָ֖ם יוּמָֽת׃ 22 מִשְׁפַּ֤ט אֶחָד֙ יִהְיֶ֣ה לָכֶ֔ם כַּגֵּ֥ר כָּאֶזְרָ֖ח יִהְיֶ֑ה כִּ֛י אֲנִ֥י יְהוָ֖ה אֱלֹהֵיכֶֽם׃ 23 וַיְדַבֵּ֣ר מֹשֶׁה֮ אֶל־בְּנֵ֣י יִשְׂרָאֵל֒ וַיּוֹצִ֣יאוּ אֶת־הַֽמְקַלֵּ֗ל אֶל־מִחוּץ֙ לַֽמַּחֲנֶ֔ה וַיִּרְגְּמ֥וּ אֹת֖וֹ אָ֑בֶן וּבְנֵֽי־יִשְׂרָאֵ֣ל עָשׂ֔וּ כַּאֲשֶׁ֛ר צִוָּ֥ה יְהוָ֖ה אֶת־מֹשֶֽׁה׃ פ

בהר
כה וַיְדַבֵּ֤ר יְהוָה֙ אֶל־מֹשֶׁ֔ה בְּהַ֥ר סִינַ֖י לֵאמֹֽר׃ 2 דַּבֵּ֞ר אֶל־בְּנֵ֤י יִשְׂרָאֵל֙ וְאָמַרְתָּ֣ אֲלֵהֶ֔ם כִּ֤י תָבֹ֙אוּ֙ אֶל־הָאָ֔רֶץ אֲשֶׁ֥ר אֲנִ֖י נֹתֵ֣ן לָכֶ֑ם וְשָׁבְתָ֣ה הָאָ֔רֶץ שַׁבָּ֖ת לַֽיהוָֽה׃ 3 שֵׁ֤שׁ שָׁנִים֙ תִּזְרַ֣ע שָׂדֶ֔ךָ וְשֵׁ֥שׁ שָׁנִ֖ים תִּזְמֹ֣ר כַּרְמֶ֑ךָ וְאָסַפְתָּ֖ אֶת־תְּבוּאָתָֽהּ׃ 4 וּבַשָּׁנָ֣ה הַשְּׁבִיעִ֗ת שַׁבַּ֤ת שַׁבָּתוֹן֙ יִהְיֶ֣ה לָאָ֔רֶץ שַׁבָּ֖ת לַֽיהוָ֑ה שָֽׂדְךָ֙ לֹ֣א תִזְרָ֔ע וְכַרְמְךָ֖ לֹ֥א תִזְמֹֽר׃ 5 אֵ֣ת סְפִ֤יחַ קְצִֽירְךָ֙ לֹ֣א תִקְצ֔וֹר וְאֶת־עִנְּבֵ֥י נְזִירֶ֖ךָ לֹ֣א תִבְצֹ֑ר שְׁנַ֥ת שַׁבָּת֖וֹן יִהְיֶ֥ה לָאָֽרֶץ׃ 6 וְֽהָיְתָ֞ה שַׁבַּ֤ת הָאָ֙רֶץ֙ לָכֶ֣ם לְאָכְלָ֔ה לְךָ֖ וּלְעַבְדְּךָ֣ וְלַאֲמָתֶ֑ךָ וְלִשְׂכִֽירְךָ֙ וּלְתוֹשָׁ֣בְךָ֔ הַגָּרִ֖ים עִמָּֽךְ׃ 7 וְלִ֨בְהֶמְתְּךָ֔ וְלַֽחַיָּ֖ה אֲשֶׁ֣ר בְּאַרְצֶ֑ךָ תִּהְיֶ֥ה כָל־תְּבוּאָתָ֖הּ לֶאֱכֹֽל׃ ס 8 וְסָפַרְתָּ֣ לְךָ֗ שֶׁ֤בַע שַׁבְּתֹ֣ת שָׁנִ֔ים שֶׁ֥בַע שָׁנִ֖ים שֶׁ֣בַע פְּעָמִ֑ים וְהָי֣וּ לְךָ֗ יְמֵי֙ שֶׁ֣בַע שַׁבְּתֹ֣ת הַשָּׁנִ֔ים תֵּ֥שַׁע וְאַרְבָּעִ֖ים שָׁנָֽה׃ 9 וְהַֽעֲבַרְתָּ֞ שׁוֹפַ֤ר תְּרוּעָה֙ בַּחֹ֣דֶשׁ הַשְּׁבִעִ֔י בֶּעָשׂ֖וֹר לַחֹ֑דֶשׁ בְּיוֹם֙ הַכִּפֻּרִ֔ים תַּעֲבִ֥ירוּ שׁוֹפָ֖ר בְּכָל־אַרְצְכֶֽם׃ 10 וְקִדַּשְׁתֶּ֗ם אֵ֣ת שְׁנַ֤ת הַחֲמִשִּׁים֙ שָׁנָ֔ה וּקְרָאתֶ֥ם דְּר֛וֹר

all its inhabitants. It shall be a jubilee[b] for you: each of you shall return to his holding and each of you shall return to his family. [11]That fiftieth year shall be a jubilee for you: you shall not sow, neither shall you reap the aftergrowth or harvest the untrimmed vines, [12]for it is a jubilee. It shall be holy to you: you may only eat the growth direct from the field.

[13]In this year of jubilee, each of you shall return to his holding. [14]When you sell property to your neighbor,[c] or buy any from your neighbor, you shall not wrong one another. [15]In buying from your neighbor, you shall deduct only for the number of years since the jubilee; and in selling to you, he shall charge you only for the remaining crop years: [16]the more such years, the higher the price you pay; the fewer such years, the lower the price; for what he is selling you is a number of harvests. [17]Do not wrong one another, but fear your God; for I the LORD am your God.

[18]You shall observe My laws and faithfully keep My rules, that you may live upon the land in security; [19]the land shall yield its fruit and you shall eat your fill, and you shall live upon it in security. [20]And should you ask, "What are we to eat in the seventh year, if we may neither sow nor gather in our crops?" [21]I will ordain My blessing for you in the sixth year, so that it shall yield a crop sufficient for three years. [22]When you sow in the eighth year, you will still be eating old grain of that crop; you will be eating the old until the ninth year, until its crops come in.

[23]But the land must not be sold beyond reclaim, for the land is Mine; you are but strangers resident with Me. [24]Throughout the land that you hold, you must provide for the redemption of the land.

[25]If your kinsman is in straits and has to sell part of his holding, his nearest redeemer[d] shall

בָּאָ֗רֶץ לְכָל־יֹשְׁבֶ֑יהָ יוֹבֵ֥ל הִוא֙ תִּהְיֶ֣ה לָכֶ֔ם וְשַׁבְתֶּ֗ם אִ֚ישׁ אֶל־אֲחֻזָּת֔וֹ וְאִ֖ישׁ אֶל־מִשְׁפַּחְתּ֥וֹ תָּשֻֽׁבוּ׃ [11] יוֹבֵ֣ל הִ֗וא שְׁנַ֛ת הַחֲמִשִּׁ֥ים שָׁנָ֖ה תִּהְיֶ֣ה לָכֶ֑ם לֹ֣א תִזְרָ֗עוּ וְלֹ֤א תִקְצְרוּ֙ אֶת־סְפִיחֶ֔יהָ וְלֹ֥א תִבְצְר֖וּ אֶת־נְזִרֶֽיהָ׃ [12] כִּ֚י יוֹבֵ֣ל הִ֔וא קֹ֖דֶשׁ תִּהְיֶ֣ה לָכֶ֑ם מִ֨ן־הַשָּׂדֶ֔ה תֹּאכְל֖וּ אֶת־תְּבוּאָתָֽהּ׃ [13] בִּשְׁנַ֥ת הַיּוֹבֵ֖ל הַזֹּ֑את תָּשֻׁ֕בוּ אִ֖ישׁ אֶל־אֲחֻזָּתֽוֹ׃ [14] וְכִֽי־תִמְכְּר֤וּ מִמְכָּר֙ לַעֲמִיתֶ֔ךָ א֥וֹ קָנֹ֖ה מִיַּ֣ד עֲמִיתֶ֑ךָ אַל־תּוֹנ֖וּ אִ֥ישׁ אֶת־אָחִֽיו׃ [15] בְּמִסְפַּ֤ר שָׁנִים֙ אַחַ֣ר הַיּוֹבֵ֔ל תִּקְנֶ֖ה מֵאֵ֣ת עֲמִיתֶ֑ךָ בְּמִסְפַּ֥ר שְׁנֵֽי־תְבוּאֹ֖ת יִמְכָּר־לָֽךְ׃ [16] לְפִ֣י ׀ רֹ֣ב הַשָּׁנִ֗ים תַּרְבֶּה֙ מִקְנָת֔וֹ וּלְפִי֙ מְעֹ֣ט הַשָּׁנִ֔ים תַּמְעִ֖יט מִקְנָת֑וֹ כִּ֚י מִסְפַּ֣ר תְּבוּאֹ֔ת ה֖וּא מֹכֵ֥ר לָֽךְ׃ [17] וְלֹ֤א תוֹנוּ֙ אִ֣ישׁ אֶת־עֲמִית֔וֹ וְיָרֵ֖אתָ מֵֽאֱלֹהֶ֑יךָ כִּ֛י אֲנִ֥י יְהֹוָ֖ה אֱלֹהֵיכֶֽם׃ [18] וַעֲשִׂיתֶם֙ אֶת־חֻקֹּתַ֔י וְאֶת־מִשְׁפָּטַ֥י תִּשְׁמְר֖וּ וַעֲשִׂיתֶ֣ם אֹתָ֑ם וִֽישַׁבְתֶּ֥ם עַל־הָאָ֖רֶץ לָבֶֽטַח׃ [19] וְנָתְנָ֤ה הָאָ֙רֶץ֙ פִּרְיָ֔הּ וַאֲכַלְתֶּ֖ם לָשֹׂ֑בַע וִֽישַׁבְתֶּ֥ם לָבֶ֖טַח עָלֶֽיהָ׃ [20] וְכִ֣י תֹאמְר֔וּ מַה־נֹּאכַ֖ל בַּשָּׁנָ֣ה הַשְּׁבִיעִ֑ת הֵ֚ן לֹ֣א נִזְרָ֔ע וְלֹ֥א נֶאֱסֹ֖ף אֶת־תְּבוּאָתֵֽנוּ׃ [21] וְצִוִּ֤יתִי אֶת־בִּרְכָתִי֙ לָכֶ֔ם בַּשָּׁנָ֖ה הַשִּׁשִּׁ֑ית וְעָשָׂת֙ אֶת־הַתְּבוּאָ֔ה לִשְׁלֹ֖שׁ הַשָּׁנִֽים׃ [22] וּזְרַעְתֶּ֗ם אֵ֚ת הַשָּׁנָ֣ה הַשְּׁמִינִ֔ת וַאֲכַלְתֶּ֖ם מִן־הַתְּבוּאָ֣ה יָשָׁ֑ן עַ֣ד ׀ הַשָּׁנָ֣ה הַתְּשִׁיעִ֗ת עַד־בּוֹא֙ תְּבֽוּאָתָ֔הּ תֹּאכְל֖וּ יָשָֽׁן׃ [23] וְהָאָ֗רֶץ לֹ֤א תִמָּכֵר֙ לִצְמִתֻ֔ת כִּי־לִ֖י הָאָ֑רֶץ כִּֽי־גֵרִ֧ים וְתוֹשָׁבִ֛ים אַתֶּ֖ם עִמָּדִֽי׃ [24] וּבְכֹ֖ל אֶ֣רֶץ אֲחֻזַּתְכֶ֑ם גְּאֻלָּ֖ה תִּתְּנ֥וּ לָאָֽרֶץ׃ ס [25] כִּֽי־יָמ֣וּךְ אָחִ֔יךָ וּמָכַ֖ר מֵאֲחֻזָּת֑וֹ וּבָ֤א גֹֽאֲלוֹ֙ הַקָּרֹ֣ב אֵלָ֔יו וְגָאַ֕ל אֵ֖ת מִמְכַּ֥ר אָחִֽיו׃

---

b Heb. *yobel*, "ram" or "ram's horn."
c I.e., fellow Israelite; see v. 46.
d I.e., the closest relative able to redeem the land.

come and redeem what his kinsman has sold. [26]If a man has no one to redeem for him, but prospers and acquires enough to redeem with, [27]he shall compute the years since its sale, refund the difference to the man to whom he sold it, and return to his holding. [28]If he lacks sufficient means to recover it, what he sold shall remain with the purchaser until the jubilee; in the jubilee year it shall be released, and he shall return to his holding.

[29]If a man sells a dwelling house in a walled city, it may be redeemed until a year has elapsed since its sale; the redemption period shall be a year. [30]If it is not redeemed before a full year has elapsed, the house in the walled city shall pass to the purchaser beyond reclaim throughout the ages; it shall not be released in the jubilee. [31]But houses in villages that have no encircling walls shall be classed as open country: they may be redeemed, and they shall be released through the jubilee. [32]As for the cities of the Levites, the houses in the cities they hold—the Levites shall forever have the right of redemption. [33]e Such property as may be redeemed from the Levites—houses sold in a city they hold—shall be released through the jubilee; for the houses in the cities of the Levites are their holding among the Israelites. [34]But the unenclosed land about their cities cannot be sold, for that is their holding for all time.

[35]If your kinsman, being in straits, comes under your authority, and you hold him as though a resident alien, let him live by your side: [36]do not exact from him advance or accrued interest,f but fear your God. Let him live by your side as your kinsman. [37]Do not lend him your money at advance interest, or give him your food at accrued interest. [38]I the LORD am your God, who brought you out of the land of Egypt, to give you the land of Canaan, to be your God.

וְאִ֗ישׁ כִּ֣י לֹ֤א יִהְיֶה־לּוֹ֙ גֹּאֵ֔ל וְהִשִּׂ֖יגָה יָד֑וֹ 26 וּמָצָ֖א כְּדֵ֥י גְאֻלָּתֽוֹ׃ 27 וְחִשַּׁב֙ אֶת־שְׁנֵ֣י מִמְכָּר֔וֹ וְהֵשִׁיב֙ אֶת־הָ֣עֹדֵ֔ף לָאִ֖ישׁ אֲשֶׁ֣ר מָֽכַר־ל֑וֹ וְשָׁ֖ב לַאֲחֻזָּתֽוֹ׃ 28 וְאִ֨ם לֹֽא־מָצְאָ֜ה יָד֗וֹ דֵּי֮ הָשִׁ֣יב לוֹ֒ וְהָיָ֣ה מִמְכָּר֗וֹ בְּיַד֙ הַקֹּנֶ֣ה אֹת֔וֹ עַ֖ד שְׁנַ֣ת הַיּוֹבֵ֑ל וְיָצָא֙ בַּיֹּבֵ֔ל וְשָׁ֖ב לַאֲחֻזָּתֽוֹ׃

29 וְאִ֗ישׁ כִּֽי־יִמְכֹּ֤ר בֵּית־מוֹשַׁב֙ עִ֣יר חוֹמָ֔ה וְהָיְתָה֙ גְּאֻלָּת֔וֹ עַד־תֹּ֖ם שְׁנַ֣ת מִמְכָּר֑וֹ יָמִ֖ים תִּהְיֶ֥ה גְאֻלָּתֽוֹ׃ 30 וְאִ֣ם לֹֽא־יִגָּאֵ֡ל עַד־ מְלֹאת֩ לוֹ֙ שָׁנָ֣ה תְמִימָ֗ה וְ֠קָם הַבַּ֨יִת אֲשֶׁר־בָּעִ֜יר אֲשֶׁר־לֹ֣א לוֹ֮ חֹמָה֒ לַצְּמִיתֻ֛ת לַקֹּנֶ֥ה אֹת֖וֹ לְדֹרֹתָ֑יו לֹ֥א יֵצֵ֖א בַּיֹּבֵֽל׃ 31 וּבָתֵּ֣י הַחֲצֵרִ֗ים אֲשֶׁ֨ר אֵֽין־לָהֶ֤ם חֹמָה֙ סָבִ֔יב עַל־שְׂדֵ֥ה הָאָ֖רֶץ יֵחָשֵׁ֑ב גְּאֻלָּה֙ תִּֽהְיֶה־לּ֔וֹ וּבַיֹּבֵ֖ל יֵצֵֽא׃ 32 וְעָרֵי֙ הַלְוִיִּ֔ם בָּתֵּ֖י עָרֵ֣י אֲחֻזָּתָ֑ם גְּאֻלַּ֥ת עוֹלָ֖ם תִּהְיֶ֥ה לַלְוִיִּֽם׃ 33 וַאֲשֶׁ֨ר יִגְאַ֜ל מִן־הַלְוִיִּ֗ם וְיָצָ֨א מִמְכַּר־ בַּ֧יִת וְעִ֣יר אֲחֻזָּת֛וֹ בַּיֹּבֵ֑ל כִּ֣י בָתֵּ֞י עָרֵ֣י הַלְוִיִּ֗ם הִ֚וא אֲחֻזָּתָ֔ם בְּת֖וֹךְ בְּנֵ֥י יִשְׂרָאֵֽל׃ 34 וּֽשְׂדֵ֛ה מִגְרַ֥שׁ עָרֵיהֶ֖ם לֹ֣א יִמָּכֵ֑ר כִּֽי־ אֲחֻזַּ֥ת עוֹלָ֛ם ה֖וּא לָהֶֽם׃ ס

35 וְכִֽי־יָמ֣וּךְ אָחִ֔יךָ וּמָ֥טָה יָד֖וֹ עִמָּ֑ךְ וְהֶֽחֱזַ֣קְתָּ בּ֔וֹ גֵּ֧ר וְתוֹשָׁ֛ב וָחַ֖י עִמָּֽךְ׃ 36 אַל־ תִּקַּ֤ח מֵֽאִתּוֹ֙ נֶ֣שֶׁךְ וְתַרְבִּ֔ית וְיָרֵ֖אתָ מֵֽאֱלֹהֶ֑יךָ וְחֵ֥י אָחִ֖יךָ עִמָּֽךְ׃ 37 אֶ֨ת־כַּסְפְּךָ֔ לֹֽא־תִתֵּ֥ן ל֖וֹ בְּנֶ֑שֶׁךְ וּבְמַרְבִּ֖ית לֹא־תִתֵּ֥ן אָכְלֶֽךָ׃ 38 אֲנִ֗י יְהֹוָה֙ אֱלֹ֣הֵיכֶ֔ם אֲשֶׁר־ הוֹצֵ֤אתִי אֶתְכֶם֙ מֵאֶ֣רֶץ מִצְרָ֔יִם לָתֵ֤ת לָכֶם֙ אֶת־אֶ֣רֶץ כְּנַ֔עַן לִהְי֥וֹת לָכֶ֖ם לֵאלֹהִֽים׃ ס

---

e *Meaning of first half of verse uncertain.*
f *I.e., interest deducted in advance, or interest added at the time of repayment.*

³⁹If your kinsman under you continues in straits and must give himself over to you, do not subject him to the treatment of a slave. ⁴⁰He shall remain with you as a hired or bound laborer; he shall serve with you only until the jubilee year. ⁴¹Then he and his children with him shall be free of your authority; he shall go back to his family and return to his ancestral holding.—⁴²For they are My servants, whom I freed from the land of Egypt; they may not give themselves over into servitude.—⁴³You shall not rule over him ruthlessly; you shall fear your God. ⁴⁴Such male and female slaves as you may have—it is from the nations round about you that you may acquire male and female slaves. ⁴⁵You may also buy them from among the children of aliens resident among you, or from their families that are among you, whom they begot in your land. These shall become your property: ⁴⁶you may keep them as a possession for your children after you, for them to inherit as property for all time. Such you may treat as slaves. But as for your Israelite kinsmen, no one shall rule ruthlessly over the other.

⁴⁷If a resident alien among you has prospered, and your kinsman being in straits, comes under his authority and gives himself over to the resident alien among you, or to an offshoot of an alien's family, ⁴⁸he shall have the right of redemption even after he has given himself over. One of his kinsmen shall redeem him, ⁴⁹or his uncle or his uncle's son shall redeem him, or anyone of his family who is of his own flesh shall redeem him; or, if he prospers, he may redeem himself. ⁵⁰He shall compute with his purchaser the total from the year he gave himself over to him until the jubilee year; the price of his sale shall be applied to the number of years, as though it were for a term as a hired laborer under the other's authority. ⁵¹If many years remain, he shall pay back for his redemption in

כֹּה וְכִי־יָמ֣וּךְ אָחִ֣יךָ עִמָּ֔ךְ וְנִמְכַּר־לָ֖ךְ לֹא־ תַעֲבֹ֥ד בּ֖וֹ עֲבֹ֥דַת עָֽבֶד׃ 40 כְּשָׂכִ֥יר כְּתוֹשָׁ֛ב יִהְיֶ֥ה עִמָּ֖ךְ עַד־שְׁנַ֥ת הַיֹּבֵ֖ל יַעֲבֹ֥ד עִמָּֽךְ׃ 41 וְיָצָא֙ מֵֽעִמָּ֔ךְ ה֖וּא וּבָנָ֣יו עִמּ֑וֹ וְשָׁב֙ אֶל־מִשְׁפַּחְתּ֔וֹ וְאֶל־אֲחֻזַּ֥ת אֲבֹתָ֖יו יָשֽׁוּב׃ 42 כִּֽי־עֲבָדַ֣י הֵ֔ם אֲשֶׁר־הוֹצֵ֥אתִי אֹתָ֖ם מֵאֶ֣רֶץ מִצְרָ֑יִם לֹ֥א יִמָּכְר֖וּ מִמְכֶּ֥רֶת עָֽבֶד׃ 43 לֹא־תִרְדֶּ֥ה ב֖וֹ בְּפָ֑רֶךְ וְיָרֵ֖אתָ מֵאֱלֹהֶֽיךָ׃ 44 וְעַבְדְּךָ֥ וַאֲמָֽתְךָ֖ אֲשֶׁ֣ר יִהְיוּ־לָ֑ךְ מֵאֵ֣ת הַגּוֹיִ֗ם אֲשֶׁר֙ סְבִיבֹ֣תֵיכֶ֔ם מֵהֶ֥ם תִּקְנ֖וּ עֶ֥בֶד וְאָמָֽה׃ 45 וְ֠גַם מִבְּנֵ֨י הַתּוֹשָׁבִ֜ים הַגָּרִ֤ים עִמָּכֶם֙ מֵהֶ֣ם תִּקְנ֔וּ וּמִמִּשְׁפַּחְתָּם֙ אֲשֶׁ֣ר עִמָּכֶ֔ם אֲשֶׁ֥ר הוֹלִ֖ידוּ בְּאַרְצְכֶ֑ם וְהָי֥וּ לָכֶ֖ם לַֽאֲחֻזָּֽה׃ 46 וְהִתְנַחֲלְתֶּ֨ם אֹתָ֜ם לִבְנֵיכֶ֤ם אַחֲרֵיכֶם֙ לָרֶ֣שֶׁת אֲחֻזָּ֔ה לְעֹלָ֖ם בָּהֶ֣ם תַּעֲבֹ֑דוּ וּבְאַ֨חֵיכֶ֤ם בְּנֵֽי־יִשְׂרָאֵל֙ אִ֣ישׁ בְּאָחִ֔יו לֹא־תִרְדֶּ֥ה ב֖וֹ בְּפָֽרֶךְ׃ ס 47 וְכִ֣י תַשִּׂיג֩ יַ֨ד גֵּ֤ר וְתוֹשָׁב֙ עִמָּ֔ךְ וּמָ֥ךְ אָחִ֖יךָ עִמּ֑וֹ וְנִמְכַּ֗ר לְגֵ֤ר תּוֹשָׁב֙ עִמָּ֔ךְ א֥וֹ לְעֵ֖קֶר מִשְׁפַּ֥חַת גֵּֽר׃ 48 אַחֲרֵ֣י נִמְכַּ֔ר גְּאֻלָּ֖ה תִּהְיֶה־לּ֑וֹ אֶחָ֥ד מֵאֶחָ֖יו יִגְאָלֶֽנּוּ׃ 49 אֽוֹ־דֹד֞וֹ א֤וֹ בֶן־דֹּדוֹ֙ יִגְאָלֶ֔נּוּ אֽוֹ־מִשְּׁאֵ֧ר בְּשָׂר֛וֹ מִמִּשְׁפַּחְתּ֖וֹ יִגְאָלֶ֑נּוּ אֽוֹ־הִשִּׂ֥יגָה יָד֖וֹ וְנִגְאָֽל׃ 50 וְחִשַּׁב֙ עִם־קֹנֵ֔הוּ מִשְּׁנַת֙ הִמָּ֣כְרוֹ ל֔וֹ עַ֖ד שְׁנַ֣ת הַיֹּבֵ֑ל וְהָיָ֞ה כֶּ֤סֶף מִמְכָּרוֹ֙ בְּמִסְפַּ֣ר שָׁנִ֔ים כִּימֵ֥י שָׂכִ֖יר יִהְיֶ֥ה עִמּֽוֹ׃ 51 אִם־ע֥וֹד רַבּ֖וֹת בַּשָּׁנִ֑ים לְפִיהֶ֕ן יָשִׁ֥יב גְּאֻלָּת֖וֹ מִכֶּ֥סֶף

proportion to his purchase price; 52and if few years remain until the jubilee year, he shall so compute: he shall make payment for his redemption according to the years involved. 53He shall be under his authority as a laborer hired by the year; he shall not rule ruthlessly over him in your sight. 54If he has not been redeemed in any of those ways, he and his children with him shall go free in the jubilee year. 55For it is to Me that the Israelites are servants: they are My servants, whom I freed from the land of Egypt, I the LORD your God.

26

You shall not make idols for yourselves, or set up for yourselves carved images or pillars, or place figured[a] stones in your land to worship upon, for I the LORD am your God. 2You shall keep My sabbaths and venerate My sanctuary, Mine, the LORD's.

BE-ḤUKKOTAI

3If you follow My laws and faithfully observe My commandments, 4I will grant your rains in their season, so that the earth shall yield its produce and the trees of the field their fruit. 5Your threshing shall overtake the vintage, and your vintage shall overtake the sowing; you shall eat your fill of bread and dwell securely in your land.

6I will grant peace in the land, and you shall lie down untroubled by anyone; I will give the land respite from vicious beasts, and no sword shall cross your land. 7You shall give chase to your enemies, and they shall fall before you by the sword. 8Five of you shall give chase to a hundred, and a hundred of you shall give chase to ten thousand; your enemies shall fall before you by the sword.

9I will look with favor upon you, and make

---

a Meaning of Heb. maskith *uncertain.*

מִקְנָתוֹ: 52 וְאִם־מְעַט נִשְׁאַר בַּשָּׁנִים עַד־שְׁנַת הַיֹּבֵל וְחִשַּׁב־לוֹ כְּפִי שָׁנָיו יָשִׁיב אֶת־גְּאֻלָּתוֹ: 53 כִּשְׂכִיר שָׁנָה בְּשָׁנָה יִהְיֶה עִמּוֹ לֹא־יִרְדֶּנּוּ בְּפֶרֶךְ לְעֵינֶיךָ: 54 וְאִם־לֹא יִגָּאֵל בְּאֵלֶּה וְיָצָא בִּשְׁנַת הַיֹּבֵל הוּא וּבָנָיו עִמּוֹ: 55 כִּי־לִי בְנֵי־יִשְׂרָאֵל עֲבָדִים עֲבָדַי הֵם אֲשֶׁר־הוֹצֵאתִי אוֹתָם מֵאֶרֶץ מִצְרָיִם אֲנִי יְהוָה אֱלֹהֵיכֶם:

כו לֹא־תַעֲשׂוּ לָכֶם אֱלִילִם וּפֶסֶל וּמַצֵּבָה לֹא־תָקִימוּ לָכֶם וְאֶבֶן מַשְׂכִּית לֹא תִתְּנוּ בְּאַרְצְכֶם לְהִשְׁתַּחֲוֺת עָלֶיהָ כִּי אֲנִי יְהוָה אֱלֹהֵיכֶם: 2 אֶת־שַׁבְּתֹתַי תִּשְׁמֹרוּ וּמִקְדָּשִׁי תִּירָאוּ אֲנִי יְהוָה: ס

בחקתי

3 אִם־בְּחֻקֹּתַי תֵּלֵכוּ וְאֶת־מִצְוֺתַי תִּשְׁמְרוּ וַעֲשִׂיתֶם אֹתָם: 4 וְנָתַתִּי גִשְׁמֵיכֶם בְּעִתָּם וְנָתְנָה הָאָרֶץ יְבוּלָהּ וְעֵץ הַשָּׂדֶה יִתֵּן פִּרְיוֹ: 5 וְהִשִּׂיג לָכֶם דַּיִשׁ אֶת־בָּצִיר וּבָצִיר יַשִּׂיג אֶת־זָרַע וַאֲכַלְתֶּם לַחְמְכֶם לָשֹׂבַע וִישַׁבְתֶּם לָבֶטַח בְּאַרְצְכֶם: 6 וְנָתַתִּי שָׁלוֹם בָּאָרֶץ וּשְׁכַבְתֶּם וְאֵין מַחֲרִיד וְהִשְׁבַּתִּי חַיָּה רָעָה מִן־הָאָרֶץ וְחֶרֶב לֹא־תַעֲבֹר בְּאַרְצְכֶם: 7 וּרְדַפְתֶּם אֶת־אֹיְבֵיכֶם וְנָפְלוּ לִפְנֵיכֶם לֶחָרֶב: 8 וְרָדְפוּ מִכֶּם חֲמִשָּׁה מֵאָה וּמֵאָה מִכֶּם רְבָבָה יִרְדֹּפוּ וְנָפְלוּ אֹיְבֵיכֶם לִפְנֵיכֶם לֶחָרֶב: 9 וּפָנִיתִי אֲלֵיכֶם וְהִפְרֵיתִי אֶתְכֶם

you fertile and multiply you; and I will maintain My covenant with you. ¹⁰You shall eat old grain long stored, and you shall have to clear out the old to make room for the new.

¹¹I will establish My abode in your midst, and I will not spurn you. ¹²I will be ever present in your midst: I will be your God, and you shall be My people. ¹³I the LORD am your God who brought you out from the land of the Egyptians to be their slaves no more, who broke the bars of your yoke and made you walk erect.

¹⁴But if you do not obey Me and do not observe all these commandments, ¹⁵if you reject My laws and spurn My rules, so that you do not observe all My commandments and you break My covenant, ¹⁶I in turn will do this to you: I will wreak misery upon you—*b*consumption and fever, which cause the eyes to pine and the body to languish; you shall sow your seed to no purpose, for your enemies shall eat it. ¹⁷I will set My face against you: you shall be routed by your enemies, and your foes shall dominate you. You shall flee though none pursues.

¹⁸And if, for all that, you do not obey Me, I will go on to discipline you sevenfold for your sins, ¹⁹and I will break your proud glory. I will make your skies like iron and your earth like copper, ²⁰so that your strength shall be spent to no purpose. Your land shall not yield its produce, nor shall the trees of the land yield their fruit.

²¹And if you remain hostile toward Me and refuse to obey Me, I will go on smiting you sevenfold for your sins. ²²I will loose wild beasts against you, and they shall bereave you of your children and wipe out your cattle. They shall decimate you, and your roads shall be deserted.

²³And if these things fail to discipline you for Me, and you remain hostile to Me, ²⁴I too will

וְהִרְבֵּיתִי אֶתְכֶם וַהֲקִימֹתִי אֶת־בְּרִיתִי
אִתְּכֶם: 10 וַאֲכַלְתֶּם יָשָׁן נוֹשָׁן וְיָשָׁן מִפְּנֵי
חָדָשׁ תּוֹצִיאוּ:
11 וְנָתַתִּי מִשְׁכָּנִי בְּתוֹכְכֶם וְלֹא־תִגְעַל
נַפְשִׁי אֶתְכֶם: 12 וְהִתְהַלַּכְתִּי בְּתוֹכְכֶם
וְהָיִיתִי לָכֶם לֵאלֹהִים וְאַתֶּם תִּהְיוּ־לִי
לְעָם: 13 אֲנִי יְהֹוָה אֱלֹהֵיכֶם אֲשֶׁר
הוֹצֵאתִי אֶתְכֶם מֵאֶרֶץ מִצְרַיִם מִהְיֹת
לָהֶם עֲבָדִים וָאֶשְׁבֹּר מֹטֹת עֻלְּכֶם וָאוֹלֵךְ
אֶתְכֶם קוֹמְמִיּוּת: פ

14 וְאִם־לֹא תִשְׁמְעוּ לִי וְלֹא תַעֲשׂוּ אֵת
כָּל־הַמִּצְוֺת הָאֵלֶּה: 15 וְאִם־בְּחֻקֹּתַי
תִּמְאָסוּ וְאִם אֶת־מִשְׁפָּטַי תִּגְעַל נַפְשְׁכֶם
לְבִלְתִּי עֲשׂוֹת אֶת־כָּל־מִצְוֺתַי לְהַפְרְכֶם
אֶת־בְּרִיתִי: 16 אַף־אֲנִי אֶעֱשֶׂה־זֹּאת לָכֶם
וְהִפְקַדְתִּי עֲלֵיכֶם בֶּהָלָה אֶת־הַשַּׁחֶפֶת
וְאֶת־הַקַּדַּחַת מְכַלּוֹת עֵינַיִם וּמְדִיבֹת נָפֶשׁ
וּזְרַעְתֶּם לָרִיק זַרְעֲכֶם וַאֲכָלֻהוּ אֹיְבֵיכֶם:
17 וְנָתַתִּי פָנַי בָּכֶם וְנִגַּפְתֶּם לִפְנֵי אֹיְבֵיכֶם
וְרָדוּ בָכֶם שֹׂנְאֵיכֶם וְנַסְתֶּם וְאֵין־רֹדֵף
אֶתְכֶם: ס
18 וְאִם־עַד־אֵלֶּה לֹא תִשְׁמְעוּ לִי וְיָסַפְתִּי
לְיַסְּרָה אֶתְכֶם שֶׁבַע עַל־חַטֹּאתֵיכֶם:
19 וְשָׁבַרְתִּי אֶת־גְּאוֹן עֻזְּכֶם וְנָתַתִּי אֶת־
שְׁמֵיכֶם כַּבַּרְזֶל וְאֶת־אַרְצְכֶם כַּנְּחֻשָׁה:
20 וְתַם לָרִיק כֹּחֲכֶם וְלֹא־תִתֵּן אַרְצְכֶם
אֶת־יְבוּלָהּ וְעֵץ הָאָרֶץ לֹא יִתֵּן פִּרְיוֹ:
21 וְאִם־תֵּלְכוּ עִמִּי קֶרִי וְלֹא תֹאבוּ
לִשְׁמֹעַ לִי וְיָסַפְתִּי עֲלֵיכֶם מַכָּה שֶׁבַע
כְּחַטֹּאתֵיכֶם: 22 וְהִשְׁלַחְתִּי בָכֶם אֶת־חַיַּת
הַשָּׂדֶה וְשִׁכְּלָה אֶתְכֶם וְהִכְרִיתָה אֶת־
בְּהֶמְתְּכֶם וְהִמְעִיטָה אֶתְכֶם וְנָשַׁמּוּ
דַּרְכֵיכֶם:
23 וְאִם־בְּאֵלֶּה לֹא תִוָּסְרוּ לִי וַהֲלַכְתֶּם עִמִּי

---

b Precise nature of these ills is uncertain.

remain hostile to you: I in turn will smite you sevenfold for your sins. 25I will bring a sword against you to wreak vengeance for the covenant; and if you withdraw into your cities, I will send pestilence among you, and you shall be delivered into enemy hands. 26When I break your staff of bread, ten women shall bake your bread in a single oven; they shall dole out your bread by weight, and though you eat, you shall not be satisfied.

27But if, despite this, you disobey Me and remain hostile to Me, 28I will act against you in wrathful hostility; I, for My part, will discipline you sevenfold for your sins. 29You shall eat the flesh of your sons and the flesh of your daughters. 30I will destroy your cult places and cut down your incense stands, and I will heap your carcasses upon your lifeless fetishes.

I will spurn you. 31I will lay your cities in ruin and make your sanctuaries desolate, and I will not savor your pleasing odors. 32I will make the land desolate, so that your enemies who settle in it shall be appalled by it. 33And you I will scatter among the nations, and I will unsheath the sword against you. Your land shall become a desolation and your cities a ruin.

34Then shall the land make up for its sabbath years throughout the time that it is desolate and you are in the land of your enemies; then shall the land rest and make up for its sabbath years. 35Throughout the time that it is desolate, it shall observe the rest that it did not observe in your sabbath years while you were dwelling upon it. 36As for those of you who survive, I will cast a faintness into their hearts in the land of their enemies. The sound of a driven leaf shall put them to flight. Fleeing as though from the sword, they shall fall though none pursues. 37With no one pursuing, they shall stumble over one another as before the sword. You shall not be able to stand your ground before your en-

קֶּֽרִי: 24 וְהָלַכְתִּ֤י אַף־אֲנִי֙ עִמָּכֶ֣ם בְּקֶ֔רִי וְהִכֵּיתִ֥י אֶתְכֶ֖ם גַּם־אָ֑נִי שֶׁ֖בַע עַל־חַטֹּאתֵיכֶֽם: 25 וְהֵבֵאתִ֨י עֲלֵיכֶ֜ם חֶ֗רֶב נֹקֶ֙מֶת֙ נְקַם־בְּרִ֔ית וְנֶֽאֱסַפְתֶּ֖ם אֶל־עָֽרֵיכֶ֑ם וְשִׁלַּ֤חְתִּי דֶ֙בֶר֙ בְּת֣וֹכְכֶ֔ם וְנִתַּתֶּ֖ם בְּיַד־אוֹיֵֽב: 26 בְּשִׁבְרִ֣י לָכֶם֮ מַטֵּה־לֶ֒חֶם֒ וְ֠אָפ֠וּ עֶ֣שֶׂר נָשִׁ֤ים לַחְמְכֶם֙ בְּתַנּ֣וּר אֶחָ֔ד וְהֵשִׁ֥יבוּ לַחְמְכֶ֖ם בַּמִּשְׁקָ֑ל וַאֲכַלְתֶּ֖ם וְלֹ֥א תִשְׂבָּֽעוּ: ס

27 וְאִם־בְּזֹ֕את לֹ֥א תִשְׁמְע֖וּ לִ֑י וַהֲלַכְתֶּ֥ם עִמִּ֖י בְּקֶֽרִי: 28 וְהָלַכְתִּ֥י עִמָּכֶ֖ם בַּֽחֲמַת־קֶ֑רִי וְיִסַּרְתִּ֤י אֶתְכֶם֙ אַף־אָ֔נִי שֶׁ֖בַע עַל־חַטֹּאתֵיכֶֽם: 29 וַאֲכַלְתֶּ֖ם בְּשַׂ֣ר בְּנֵיכֶ֑ם וּבְשַׂ֥ר בְּנֹֽתֵיכֶ֖ם תֹּאכֵֽלוּ: 30 וְהִשְׁמַדְתִּ֞י אֶת־בָּמֹֽתֵיכֶ֗ם וְהִכְרַתִּי֙ אֶת־חַמָּ֣נֵיכֶ֔ם וְנָֽתַתִּי֙ אֶת־פִּגְרֵיכֶ֔ם עַל־פִּגְרֵ֖י גִּלּֽוּלֵיכֶ֑ם וְגָעֲלָ֥ה נַפְשִׁ֖י אֶתְכֶֽם: 31 וְנָֽתַתִּ֤י אֶת־עָֽרֵיכֶם֙ חָרְבָּ֔ה וַהֲשִׁמּוֹתִ֖י אֶת־מִקְדְּשֵׁיכֶ֑ם וְלֹ֣א אָרִ֔יחַ בְּרֵ֖יחַ נִיחֹֽחֲכֶֽם: 32 וַהֲשִׁמֹּתִ֥י אֲנִ֖י אֶת־הָאָ֑רֶץ וְשָֽׁמְמ֤וּ עָלֶ֙יהָ֙ אֹֽיְבֵיכֶ֔ם הַיֹּֽשְׁבִ֖ים בָּֽהּ: 33 וְאֶתְכֶם֙ אֱזָרֶ֣ה בַגּוֹיִ֔ם וַהֲרִֽיקֹתִ֥י אַחֲרֵיכֶ֖ם חָ֑רֶב וְהָיְתָ֤ה אַרְצְכֶם֙ שְׁמָמָ֔ה וְעָרֵיכֶ֖ם יִהְי֥וּ חָרְבָּֽה: 34 אָ֣ז תִּרְצֶ֤ה הָאָ֙רֶץ֙ אֶת־שַׁבְּתֹתֶ֔יהָ כֹּ֖ל יְמֵ֣י הֳשַּׁמָּ֑ה וְאַתֶּ֖ם בְּאֶ֣רֶץ אֹיְבֵיכֶ֑ם אָ֚ז תִּשְׁבַּ֣ת הָאָ֔רֶץ וְהִרְצָ֖ת אֶת־שַׁבְּתֹתֶֽיהָ: 35 כָּל־יְמֵ֥י הָשַּׁמָּ֖ה תִּשְׁבֹּ֑ת אֵ֣ת אֲשֶׁ֧ר לֹֽא־שָֽׁבְתָ֛ה בְּשַׁבְּתֹֽתֵיכֶ֖ם בְּשִׁבְתְּכֶ֥ם עָלֶֽיהָ: 36 וְהַנִּשְׁאָרִ֣ים בָּכֶ֔ם וְהֵבֵ֤אתִי מֹ֙רֶךְ֙ בִּלְבָבָ֔ם בְּאַרְצֹ֖ת אֹֽיְבֵיהֶ֑ם וְרָדַ֣ף אֹתָ֗ם ק֚וֹל עָלֶ֣ה נִדָּ֔ף וְנָ֛סוּ מְנֻֽסַת־חֶ֖רֶב וְנָפְל֥וּ וְאֵ֥ין רֹדֵֽף: 37 וְכָשְׁל֧וּ אִישׁ־בְּאָחִ֛יו כְּמִפְּנֵי־חֶ֖רֶב וְרֹדֵ֣ף אָ֑יִן וְלֹֽא־תִהְיֶ֤ה לָכֶם֙ תְּקוּמָ֔ה לִפְנֵ֖י

emies, [38]but shall perish among the nations; and the land of your enemies shall consume you.

[39]Those of you who survive shall be heartsick over their iniquity in the land of your enemies; more, they shall be heartsick over the iniquities of their fathers; [40]and they shall confess their iniquity and the iniquity of their fathers, in that they trespassed against Me, yea, were hostile to Me. [41]When I, in turn, have been hostile to them and have removed them into the land of their enemies, then at last shall their obdurate[c] heart humble itself, and they shall atone for their iniquity. [42]Then will I remember My covenant with Jacob; I will remember also My covenant with Isaac, and also My covenant with Abraham; and I will remember the land.

[43]For the land shall be forsaken of them, making up for its sabbath years by being desolate of them, while they atone for their iniquity; for the abundant reason that they rejected My rules and spurned My laws. [44]Yet, even then, when they are in the land of their enemies, I will not reject them or spurn them so as to destroy them, annulling My covenant with them: for I the LORD am their God. [45]I will remember in their favor the covenant with the ancients, whom I freed from the land of Egypt in the sight of the nations to be their God: I, the LORD.

[46]These are the laws, rules, and instructions that the LORD established, through Moses on Mount Sinai, between Himself and the Israelite people.

27

The LORD spoke to Moses, saying: [2]Speak to the Israelite people and say to them: When anyone explicitly[a] vows to the LORD the equivalent for a human being, [3]the following scale shall apply: If it is a male from twenty to

---

38 וַאֲבַדְתֶּ֖ם בַּגּוֹיִ֑ם וְאָכְלָ֣ה אֶתְכֶ֔ם אֶ֖רֶץ אֹיְבֵיכֶֽם׃

39 וְהַנִּשְׁאָרִ֣ים בָּכֶ֗ם יִמַּ֙קּוּ֙ בַּֽעֲוֺנָ֔ם בְּאַרְצֹ֖ת אֹיְבֵיכֶ֑ם וְאַ֛ף בַּעֲוֺנֹ֥ת אֲבֹתָ֖ם אִתָּ֥ם יִמָּֽקּוּ׃

40 וְהִתְוַדּ֤וּ אֶת־עֲוֺנָם֙ וְאֶת־עֲוֺ֣ן אֲבֹתָ֔ם בְּמַעֲלָ֖ם אֲשֶׁ֣ר מָֽעֲלוּ־בִ֑י וְאַ֕ף אֲשֶׁר־הָֽלְכ֥וּ עִמִּ֖י בְּקֶֽרִי׃

41 אַף־אֲנִ֗י אֵלֵ֤ךְ עִמָּם֙ בְּקֶ֔רִי וְהֵבֵאתִ֣י אֹתָ֔ם בְּאֶ֖רֶץ אֹיְבֵיהֶ֑ם אוֹ־אָ֣ז יִכָּנַ֗ע לְבָבָם֙ הֶֽעָרֵ֔ל וְאָ֖ז יִרְצ֥וּ אֶת־עֲוֺנָֽם׃

42 וְזָכַרְתִּ֖י אֶת־בְּרִיתִ֣י יַעֲק֑וֹב וְאַף֩ אֶת־בְּרִיתִ֨י יִצְחָ֜ק וְאַ֨ף אֶת־בְּרִיתִ֧י אַבְרָהָ֛ם אֶזְכֹּ֖ר וְהָאָ֥רֶץ אֶזְכֹּֽר׃

43 וְהָאָ֩רֶץ֩ תֵּעָזֵ֨ב מֵהֶ֜ם וְתִ֣רֶץ אֶת־שַׁבְּתֹתֶ֗יהָ בׇּהְשַׁמָּה֙ מֵהֶ֔ם וְהֵ֖ם יִרְצ֣וּ אֶת־עֲוֺנָ֑ם יַ֣עַן וּבְיַ֔עַן בְּמִשְׁפָּטַ֣י מָאָ֔סוּ וְאֶת־חֻקֹּתַ֖י גָּעֲלָ֥ה נַפְשָֽׁם׃

44 וְאַף־גַּם־זֹ֠את בִּֽהְיוֹתָ֞ם בְּאֶ֣רֶץ אֹֽיְבֵיהֶ֗ם לֹֽא־מְאַסְתִּ֤ים וְלֹֽא־גְעַלְתִּים֙ לְכַלֹּתָ֔ם לְהָפֵ֥ר בְּרִיתִ֖י אִתָּ֑ם כִּ֛י אֲנִ֥י יְהֹוָ֖ה אֱלֹֽהֵיהֶֽם׃

45 וְזָכַרְתִּ֥י לָהֶ֖ם בְּרִ֣ית רִֽאשֹׁנִ֑ים אֲשֶׁ֣ר הוֹצֵֽאתִי־אֹתָם֩ מֵאֶ֨רֶץ מִצְרַ֜יִם לְעֵינֵ֣י הַגּוֹיִ֗ם לִהְי֥וֹת לָהֶ֛ם לֵאלֹהִ֖ים אֲנִ֥י יְהֹוָֽה׃

46 אֵ֠לֶּה הַֽחֻקִּ֣ים וְהַמִּשְׁפָּטִים֮ וְהַתּוֹרֹת֒ אֲשֶׁר֙ נָתַ֣ן יְהֹוָ֔ה בֵּינ֕וֹ וּבֵ֖ין בְּנֵ֣י יִשְׂרָאֵ֑ל בְּהַ֥ר סִינַ֖י בְּיַד־מֹשֶֽׁה׃ פ

כז

וַיְדַבֵּ֥ר יְהֹוָ֖ה אֶל־מֹשֶׁ֥ה לֵּאמֹֽר׃ 2 דַּבֵּ֞ר אֶל־בְּנֵ֤י יִשְׂרָאֵל֙ וְאָמַרְתָּ֣ אֲלֵהֶ֔ם אִ֕ישׁ כִּ֥י יַפְלִ֖א נֶ֑דֶר בְּעֶרְכְּךָ֥ נְפָשֹׁ֖ת לַֽיהֹוָֽה׃ 3 וְהָיָ֤ה עֶרְכְּךָ֙ הַזָּכָ֔ר מִבֶּן֙ עֶשְׂרִ֣ים שָׁנָ֔ה

---

c   Others "uncircumcised"; lit. "blocked."

a   Cf. note at Lev. 22.21.

sixty years of age, the equivalent is fifty shekels of silver by the sanctuary weight; ⁴if it is a female, the equivalent is thirty shekels. ⁵If the age is from five years to twenty years, the equivalent is twenty shekels for a male and ten shekels for a female. ⁶If the age is from one month to five years, the equivalent for a male is five shekels of silver, and the equivalent for a female is three shekels of siiver. ⁷If the age is sixty years or over, the equivalent is fifteen shekels in the case of a male and ten shekels for a female. ⁸But if one cannot afford the equivalent, he shall be presented before the priest, and the priest shall assess him; the priest shall assess him according to what the vower can afford.

⁹If [the vow concerns] any animal that may be brought as an offering to the Lord, any such that may be given to the Lord shall be holy. ¹⁰One may not exchange or substitute another for it, either good for bad, or bad for good; if one does substitute one animal for another, the thing vowed and its substitute shall both be holy. ¹¹If [the vow concerns] any unclean animal that may not be brought as an offering to the Lord, the animal shall be presented before the priest, ¹²and the priest shall assess it. Whether *ᵇ*high or low,*-ᵇ* whatever assessment is set by the priest shall stand; ¹³and if he wishes to redeem it, he must add one-fifth to its assessment.

¹⁴If anyone consecrates his house to the Lord, the priest shall assess it. Whether *ᵇ*high or low,*-ᵇ* as the priest assesses it, so it shall stand; ¹⁵and if he who has consecrated his house wishes to redeem it, he must add one-fifth to the sum at which it was assessed, and it shall be his.

¹⁶If anyone consecrates to the Lord any land that he holds, its assessment shall be in accordance with its seed requirement: fifty shekels of silver to a *homer* of barley seed. ¹⁷If he conse-

וְעַד בֶּן־שִׁשִּׁים שָׁנָה וְהָיָה עֶרְכְּךָ חֲמִשִּׁים שֶׁקֶל כֶּסֶף בְּשֶׁקֶל הַקֹּדֶשׁ: 4 וְאִם־נְקֵבָה הִוא וְהָיָה עֶרְכְּךָ שְׁלֹשִׁים שָׁקֶל: 5 וְאִם מִבֶּן־חָמֵשׁ שָׁנִים וְעַד בֶּן־עֶשְׂרִים שָׁנָה וְהָיָה עֶרְכְּךָ הַזָּכָר עֶשְׂרִים שְׁקָלִים וְלַנְּקֵבָה עֲשֶׂרֶת שְׁקָלִים: 6 וְאִם מִבֶּן־חֹדֶשׁ וְעַד בֶּן־חָמֵשׁ שָׁנִים וְהָיָה עֶרְכְּךָ הַזָּכָר חֲמִשָּׁה שְׁקָלִים כָּסֶף וְלַנְּקֵבָה עֶרְכְּךָ שְׁלֹשֶׁת שְׁקָלִים כָּסֶף: 7 וְאִם מִבֶּן־שִׁשִּׁים שָׁנָה וָמַעְלָה אִם־זָכָר וְהָיָה עֶרְכְּךָ חֲמִשָּׁה עָשָׂר שָׁקֶל וְלַנְּקֵבָה עֲשָׂרָה שְׁקָלִים: 8 וְאִם־מָךְ הוּא מֵעֶרְכֶּךָ וְהֶעֱמִידוֹ לִפְנֵי הַכֹּהֵן וְהֶעֱרִיךְ אֹתוֹ הַכֹּהֵן עַל־פִּי אֲשֶׁר תַּשִּׂיג יַד הַנֹּדֵר יַעֲרִיכֶנּוּ הַכֹּהֵן: ס 9 וְאִם־בְּהֵמָה אֲשֶׁר יַקְרִיבוּ מִמֶּנָּה קָרְבָּן לַיהוָה כֹּל אֲשֶׁר יִתֵּן מִמֶּנּוּ* לַיהוָה יִהְיֶה־קֹּדֶשׁ: 10 לֹא יַחֲלִיפֶנּוּ וְלֹא־יָמִיר אֹתוֹ טוֹב בְּרָע אוֹ־רַע בְּטוֹב וְאִם־הָמֵר יָמִיר בְּהֵמָה בִּבְהֵמָה וְהָיָה־הוּא וּתְמוּרָתוֹ יִהְיֶה־קֹּדֶשׁ: 11 וְאִם כָּל־בְּהֵמָה טְמֵאָה אֲשֶׁר לֹא־יַקְרִיבוּ מִמֶּנָּה קָרְבָּן לַיהוָה וְהֶעֱמִיד אֶת־הַבְּהֵמָה לִפְנֵי הַכֹּהֵן: 12 וְהֶעֱרִיךְ הַכֹּהֵן אֹתָהּ בֵּין טוֹב וּבֵין רָע כְּעֶרְכְּךָ הַכֹּהֵן כֵּן יִהְיֶה: 13 וְאִם־גָּאֹל יִגְאָלֶנָּה וְיָסַף חֲמִישִׁתוֹ עַל־עֶרְכֶּךָ: 14 וְאִישׁ כִּי־יַקְדִּשׁ אֶת־בֵּיתוֹ קֹדֶשׁ לַיהוָה וְהֶעֱרִיכוֹ הַכֹּהֵן בֵּין טוֹב וּבֵין רָע כַּאֲשֶׁר יַעֲרִיךְ אֹתוֹ הַכֹּהֵן כֵּן יָקוּם: 15 וְאִם־הַמַּקְדִּישׁ יִגְאַל אֶת־בֵּיתוֹ וְיָסַף חֲמִישִׁית כֶּסֶף־עֶרְכְּךָ עָלָיו וְהָיָה לוֹ: 16 וְאִם | מִשְּׂדֵה אֲחֻזָּתוֹ יַקְדִּישׁ אִישׁ לַיהוָה וְהָיָה עֶרְכְּךָ לְפִי זַרְעוֹ זֶרַע חֹמֶר שְׂעֹרִים בַּחֲמִשִּׁים שֶׁקֶל כָּסֶף: 17 אִם־

---

b-b Lit. "good or bad."

סְבִירִין וּמַטְעִין "מִמֶּנָּה" v. 9.

crates his land as of the jubilee year, its assessment stands. 18But if he consecrates his land after the jubilee, the priest shall compute the price according to the years that are left until the jubilee year, and its assessment shall be so reduced; 19and if he who consecrated the land wishes to redeem it, he must add one-fifth to the sum at which it was assessed, and it shall pass to him. 20But if he does not redeem the land, and the land is sold to another, it shall no longer be redeemable: 21when it is released in the jubilee, the land shall be holy to the LORD, as land proscribed; it becomes the priest's holding.

22If he consecrates to the LORD land that he purchased, which is not land of his holding, 23the priest shall compute for him the proportionate assessment up to the jubilee year, and he shall pay the assessment as of that day, a sacred donation to the LORD. 24In the jubilee year the land shall revert to him from whom it was bought, whose holding the land is. 25All assessments shall be by the sanctuary weight, the shekel being twenty *gerah*s.

26A firstling of animals, however, which—as a firstling—is the LORD's, cannot be consecrated by anybody; whether ox or sheep, it is the LORD's. 27But if it is of unclean animals, it may be ransomed as its assessment, with one-fifth added; if it is not redeemed, it shall be sold at its assessment.

28But of all that anyone owns, be it man or beast or land of his holding, nothing that he has proscribed for the LORD may be sold or redeemed; every proscribed thing is totally consecrated to the LORD. 29No human being who has been proscribed can be ransomed: he shall be put to death.

30All tithes from the land, whether seed from the ground or fruit from the tree, are the LORD's; they are holy to the LORD. 31If anyone wishes

מִשְׁנַת הַיּבֵל יַקְדִּישׁ שָׂדֵהוּ כְּעֶרְכְּךָ יָקוּם: 18 וְאִם־אַחַר הַיּבֵל יַקְדִּישׁ שָׂדֵהוּ וְחִשַּׁב־לוֹ הַכֹּהֵן אֶת־הַכֶּסֶף עַל־פִּי הַשָּׁנִים הַנּוֹתָרֹת עַד שְׁנַת הַיּבֵל וְנִגְרַע מֵעֶרְכֶּךָ: 19 וְאִם־גָּאֹל יִגְאַל אֶת־הַשָּׂדֶה הַמַּקְדִּישׁ אֹתוֹ וְיָסַף חֲמִשִׁית כֶּסֶף־עֶרְכְּךָ עָלָיו וְקָם לוֹ: 20 וְאִם־לֹא יִגְאַל אֶת־הַשָּׂדֶה וְאִם־מָכַר אֶת־הַשָּׂדֶה לְאִישׁ אַחֵר לֹא יִגָּאֵל עוֹד: 21 וְהָיָה הַשָּׂדֶה בְּצֵאתוֹ בַיֹּבֵל קֹדֶשׁ לַיהוָה כִּשְׂדֵה הַחֵרֶם לַכֹּהֵן תִּהְיֶה אֲחֻזָּתוֹ:

22 וְאִם אֶת־שְׂדֵה מִקְנָתוֹ אֲשֶׁר לֹא מִשְׂדֵה אֲחֻזָּתוֹ יַקְדִּישׁ לַיהוָה: 23 וְחִשַּׁב־לוֹ הַכֹּהֵן אֵת מִכְסַת הָעֶרְכְּךָ עַד שְׁנַת הַיֹּבֵל וְנָתַן אֶת־הָעֶרְכְּךָ בַּיּוֹם הַהוּא קֹדֶשׁ לַיהוָה: 24 בִּשְׁנַת הַיּוֹבֵל יָשׁוּב הַשָּׂדֶה לַאֲשֶׁר קָנָהוּ מֵאִתּוֹ לַאֲשֶׁר־לוֹ אֲחֻזַּת הָאָרֶץ: 25 וְכָל־עֶרְכְּךָ יִהְיֶה בְּשֶׁקֶל הַקֹּדֶשׁ עֶשְׂרִים גֵּרָה יִהְיֶה הַשָּׁקֶל: ס

26 אַךְ־בְּכוֹר אֲשֶׁר־יְבֻכַּר לַיהוָה בִּבְהֵמָה לֹא־יַקְדִּישׁ אִישׁ אֹתוֹ אִם־שׁוֹר אִם־שֶׂה לַיהוָה הוּא: 27 וְאִם בַּבְּהֵמָה הַטְּמֵאָה וּפָדָה בְעֶרְכֶּךָ וְיָסַף חֲמִשִׁתוֹ עָלָיו וְאִם־לֹא יִגָּאֵל וְנִמְכַּר בְּעֶרְכֶּךָ:

28 אַךְ־כָּל־חֵרֶם אֲשֶׁר יַחֲרִם אִישׁ לַיהוָה מִכָּל־אֲשֶׁר־לוֹ מֵאָדָם וּבְהֵמָה וּמִשְּׂדֵה אֲחֻזָּתוֹ לֹא יִמָּכֵר וְלֹא יִגָּאֵל כָּל־חֵרֶם קֹדֶשׁ־קָדָשִׁים הוּא לַיהוָה: 29 כָּל־חֵרֶם אֲשֶׁר יָחֳרַם מִן־הָאָדָם לֹא יִפָּדֶה מוֹת יוּמָת:

30 וְכָל־מַעְשַׂר הָאָרֶץ מִזֶּרַע הָאָרֶץ מִפְּרִי הָעֵץ לַיהוָה הוּא קֹדֶשׁ לַיהוָה: 31 וְאִם־

to redeem any of his tithes, he must add one-fifth to them. ³²All tithes of the herd or flock—of all that passes under the shepherd's staff, every tenth one—shall be holy to the LORD. ³³He must not look out for good as against bad, or make substitution for it. If he does make substitution for it, then it and its substitute shall both be holy: it cannot be redeemed.

³⁴These are the commandments that the LORD gave Moses for the Israelite people on Mount Sinai.

גָּאֹל יִגְאַל אִישׁ מִמַּעַשְׂרוֹ חֲמִשִׁיתוֹ יֹסֵף עָלָיו: 32 וְכָל־מַעְשַׂר בָּקָר וָצֹאן כֹּל אֲשֶׁר־יַעֲבֹר תַּחַת הַשָּׁבֶט הָעֲשִׂירִי יִהְיֶה־קֹּדֶשׁ לַיהוָה: 33 לֹא יְבַקֵּר בֵּין־טוֹב לָרַע וְלֹא יְמִירֶנּוּ וְאִם־הָמֵר יְמִירֶנּוּ וְהָיָה־הוּא וּתְמוּרָתוֹ יִהְיֶה־קֹּדֶשׁ לֹא יִגָּאֵל:

34 אֵלֶּה הַמִּצְוֹת אֲשֶׁר צִוָּה יְהוָה אֶת־מֹשֶׁה אֶל־בְּנֵי יִשְׂרָאֵל בְּהַר סִינָי: *

תם ונשלם תהילה לאל בורא עולם

NUMBERS

במדבר

1 BE-MIDBAR
On the first day of the second month, in the second year following the exodus from the land of Egypt, the Lord spoke to Moses in the wilderness of Sinai, in the Tent of Meeting, saying:

²Take a census of the whole Israelite community by the clans of *ª*-its ancestral houses,-*ª* listing the names, every male, head by head. ³You and Aaron shall record them by their groups, from the age of twenty years up, all those in Israel who are able to bear arms. ⁴Associated with you shall be a man from each tribe, each one the head of his ancestral house.

⁵These are the names of the men who shall assist you:

From Reuben, Elizur son of Shedeur.

⁶From Simeon, Shelumiel son of Zuri-shaddai.

⁷From Judah, Nahshon son of Amminadab.

⁸From Issachar, Nethanel son of Zuar.

⁹From Zebulun, Eliab son of Helon.

¹⁰From the sons of Joseph:

from Ephraim, Elishama son of Ammihud;

from Manasseh, Gamaliel son of Pedahzur.

¹¹From Benjamin, Abidan son of Gideoni.

¹²From Dan, Ahiezer son of Ammishaddai.

¹³From Asher, Pagiel son of Ochran.

¹⁴From Gad, Eliasaph son of Deuel.

¹⁵From Naphtali, Ahira son of Enan.

¹⁶Those are the elected of the assembly, the chieftains of their ancestral tribes: they are the heads of the contingents of Israel.

---

a-a I.e., of its tribes.

א בְּמִדְבַּר וַיְדַבֵּ֣ר יְהוָ֧ה אֶל־מֹשֶׁ֛ה בְּמִדְבַּ֥ר סִינַ֖י בְּאֹ֣הֶל מוֹעֵ֑ד בְּאֶחָד֩ לַחֹ֨דֶשׁ הַשֵּׁנִ֜י בַּשָּׁנָ֣ה הַשֵּׁנִ֗ית לְצֵאתָ֛ם מֵאֶ֥רֶץ מִצְרַ֖יִם לֵאמֹֽר ׃ 2 שְׂא֗וּ אֶת־רֹאשׁ֙ כָּל־עֲדַ֣ת בְּנֵֽי־יִשְׂרָאֵ֔ל לְמִשְׁפְּחֹתָ֖ם לְבֵ֣ית אֲבֹתָ֑ם בְּמִסְפַּ֣ר שֵׁמ֔וֹת כָּל־זָכָ֖ר לְגֻלְגְּלֹתָֽם ׃ 3 מִבֶּ֨ן עֶשְׂרִ֤ים שָׁנָה֙ וָמַ֔עְלָה כָּל־יֹצֵ֥א צָבָ֖א בְּיִשְׂרָאֵ֑ל תִּפְקְד֥וּ אֹתָ֛ם לְצִבְאֹתָ֖ם אַתָּ֥ה וְאַהֲרֹֽן ׃ 4 וְאִתְּכֶ֣ם יִהְי֔וּ אִ֥ישׁ אִ֖ישׁ לַמַּטֶּ֑ה אִ֛ישׁ רֹ֥אשׁ לְבֵית־אֲבֹתָ֖יו הֽוּא ׃ 5 וְאֵ֙לֶּה֙ שְׁמ֣וֹת הָֽאֲנָשִׁ֔ים אֲשֶׁ֥ר יַֽעַמְד֖וּ אִתְּכֶ֑ם

לִרְאוּבֵ֕ן אֱלִיצ֖וּר בֶּן־שְׁדֵיאֽוּר ׃

6 לְשִׁמְע֕וֹן שְׁלֻֽמִיאֵ֖ל בֶּן־צוּרִֽישַׁדָּֽי ׃

7 לִֽיהוּדָ֕ה נַחְשׁ֖וֹן בֶּן־עַמִּֽינָדָֽב ׃

8 לְיִ֨שָּׂשכָ֔ר נְתַנְאֵ֖ל בֶּן־צוּעָֽר ׃

9 לִזְבוּלֻ֕ן אֱלִיאָ֖ב בֶּן־חֵלֹֽן ׃

10 לִבְנֵ֣י יוֹסֵ֔ף לְאֶפְרַ֕יִם אֱלִישָׁמָ֖ע בֶּן־עַמִּיה֑וּד לִמְנַשֶּׁ֕ה גַּמְלִיאֵ֖ל בֶּן־פְּדָהצֽוּר ׃

11 לְבִ֨נְיָמִ֔ן אֲבִידָ֖ן בֶּן־גִּדְעֹנִֽי ׃

12 לְדָ֕ן אֲחִיעֶ֖זֶר בֶּן־עַמִּֽישַׁדָּֽי ׃

13 לְאָשֵׁ֕ר פַּגְעִיאֵ֖ל בֶּן־עָכְרָֽן ׃

14 לְגָ֕ד אֶלְיָסָ֖ף בֶּן־דְּעוּאֵֽל ׃

15 לְנַ֨פְתָּלִ֔י אֲחִירַ֖ע בֶּן־עֵינָֽן ׃

16 אֵ֚לֶּה קְרוּאֵ֣י הָֽעֵדָ֔ה נְשִׂיאֵ֖י מַטּ֣וֹת אֲבוֹתָ֑ם רָאשֵׁ֛י אַלְפֵ֥י יִשְׂרָאֵ֖ל הֵֽם ׃

¹⁷So Moses and Aaron took those men, who were designated by name, ¹⁸and on the first day of the second month they convoked the whole community, who were registered by the clans of their ancestral houses—the names of those aged twenty years and over being listed head by head. ¹⁹As the LORD had commanded Moses, so he recorded them in the wilderness of Sinai.

²⁰They totaled as follows:

The descendants of Reuben, Israel's first-born, the registration of the clans of their ancestral house, as listed by name, head by head, all males aged twenty years and over, all who were able to bear arms—²¹those enrolled from the tribe of Reuben: 46,500.

²²Of the descendants of Simeon, the registration of the clans of their ancestral house, their enrollment as listed by name, head by head, all males aged twenty years and over, all who were able to bear arms—²³those enrolled from the tribe of Simeon: 59,300.

²⁴Of the descendants of Gad, the registration of the clans of their ancestral house, as listed by name, aged twenty years and over, all who were able to bear arms—²⁵those enrolled from the tribe of Gad: 45,650.

²⁶Of the descendants of Judah, the registration of the clans of their ancestral house, as listed by name, aged twenty years and over, all who were able to bear arms—²⁷those enrolled from the tribe of Judah: 74,600.

²⁸Of the descendants of Issachar, the registration of the clans of their ancestral house, as listed by name, aged twenty years and over, all who were able to bear arms—²⁹those enrolled from the tribe of Issachar: 54,400.

³⁰Of the descendants of Zebulun, the registration of the clans of their ancestral house, as listed by name, aged twenty years and over, all who were able to bear arms—³¹those enrolled from the tribe of Zebulun: 57,400.

17 וַיִּקַּ֤ח מֹשֶׁה֙ וְאַֽהֲרֹ֔ן אֵ֖ת הָאֲנָשִׁ֣ים הָאֵ֑לֶּה אֲשֶׁ֥ר נִקְּב֖וּ בְּשֵׁמֽוֹת׃ 18 וְאֵ֣ת כָּל־הָעֵדָ֗ה הִקְהִ֜ילוּ בְּאֶחָד֙ לַחֹ֣דֶשׁ הַשֵּׁנִ֔י וַיִּתְיַֽלְד֥וּ עַל־מִשְׁפְּחֹתָ֖ם לְבֵ֣ית אֲבֹתָ֑ם בְּמִסְפַּ֣ר שֵׁמ֗וֹת מִבֶּ֨ן עֶשְׂרִ֥ים שָׁנָ֛ה וָמַ֖עְלָה לְגֻלְגְּלֹתָֽם׃ 19 כַּֽאֲשֶׁ֛ר צִוָּ֥ה יְהוָ֖ה אֶת־מֹשֶׁ֑ה וַֽיִּפְקְדֵ֖ם בְּמִדְבַּ֥ר סִינָֽי׃ פ

20 וַיִּֽהְי֤וּ בְנֵֽי־רְאוּבֵן֙ בְּכֹ֣ר יִשְׂרָאֵ֔ל תּֽוֹלְדֹתָ֥ם לְמִשְׁפְּחֹתָ֖ם לְבֵ֣ית אֲבֹתָ֑ם בְּמִסְפַּ֣ר שֵׁמוֹת֙ לְגֻלְגְּלֹתָ֔ם כָּל־זָכָ֗ר מִבֶּ֨ן עֶשְׂרִ֤ים שָׁנָה֙ וָמַ֔עְלָה כֹּ֖ל יֹצֵ֥א צָבָֽא׃ 21 פְּקֻֽדֵיהֶ֖ם לְמַטֵּ֣ה רְאוּבֵ֑ן שִׁשָּׁ֧ה וְאַרְבָּעִ֛ים אֶ֖לֶף וַֽחֲמֵ֥שׁ מֵאֽוֹת׃ פ 22 לִבְנֵ֣י שִׁמְעוֹן֮ תּֽוֹלְדֹתָ֣ם לְמִשְׁפְּחֹתָם֮ לְבֵ֣ית אֲבֹתָם֒ פְּקֻדָ֗יו בְּמִסְפַּ֤ר שֵׁמוֹת֙ לְגֻלְגְּלֹתָ֔ם כָּל־זָכָ֗ר מִבֶּ֨ן עֶשְׂרִ֤ים שָׁנָה֙ וָמַ֔עְלָה כֹּ֖ל יֹצֵ֥א צָבָֽא׃ 23 פְּקֻֽדֵיהֶ֖ם לְמַטֵּ֣ה שִׁמְע֑וֹן תִּשְׁעָ֧ה וַֽחֲמִשִּׁ֛ים אֶ֖לֶף וּשְׁלֹ֥שׁ מֵאֽוֹת׃ פ 24 לִבְנֵ֣י גָד֮ תּֽוֹלְדֹתָ֣ם לְמִשְׁפְּחֹתָם֮ לְבֵ֣ית אֲבֹתָם֒ בְּמִסְפַּ֣ר שֵׁמ֗וֹת מִבֶּ֨ן עֶשְׂרִ֤ים שָׁנָה֙ וָמַ֔עְלָה כֹּ֖ל יֹצֵ֥א צָבָֽא׃ 25 פְּקֻֽדֵיהֶ֖ם לְמַטֵּ֣ה גָ֑ד חֲמִשָּׁ֣ה וְאַרְבָּעִ֥ים אֶ֛לֶף וְשֵׁ֥שׁ מֵא֖וֹת וַֽחֲמִשִּֽׁים׃ פ 26 לִבְנֵ֣י יְהוּדָ֗ה תּֽוֹלְדֹתָ֛ם לְמִשְׁפְּחֹתָ֖ם לְבֵ֣ית אֲבֹתָ֑ם בְּמִסְפַּ֣ר שֵׁמֹ֗ת מִבֶּ֨ן עֶשְׂרִ֤ים שָׁנָה֙ וָמַ֔עְלָה כֹּ֖ל יֹצֵ֥א צָבָֽא׃ 27 פְּקֻֽדֵיהֶ֖ם לְמַטֵּ֣ה יְהוּדָ֑ה אַרְבָּעָ֧ה וְשִׁבְעִ֛ים אֶ֖לֶף וְשֵׁ֥שׁ מֵאֽוֹת׃ פ 28 לִבְנֵ֣י יִשָּׂשכָר֮ תּֽוֹלְדֹתָ֣ם לְמִשְׁפְּחֹתָם֮ לְבֵ֣ית אֲבֹתָם֒ בְּמִסְפַּ֣ר שֵׁמֹ֗ת מִבֶּ֨ן עֶשְׂרִ֤ים שָׁנָה֙ וָמַ֔עְלָה כֹּ֖ל יֹצֵ֥א צָבָֽא׃ 29 פְּקֻֽדֵיהֶ֖ם לְמַטֵּ֣ה יִשָּׂשכָ֑ר אַרְבָּעָ֧ה וַֽחֲמִשִּׁ֛ים אֶ֖לֶף וְאַרְבַּ֥ע מֵאֽוֹת׃ פ 30 לִבְנֵ֣י זְבוּלֻן֮ תּֽוֹלְדֹתָ֣ם לְמִשְׁפְּחֹתָם֮ לְבֵ֣ית אֲבֹתָם֒ בְּמִסְפַּ֣ר שֵׁמֹ֗ת מִבֶּ֨ן עֶשְׂרִ֤ים שָׁנָה֙ וָמַ֔עְלָה כֹּ֖ל יֹצֵ֥א צָבָֽא׃ 31 פְּקֻֽדֵיהֶ֖ם לְמַטֵּ֣ה זְבוּלֻ֑ן שִׁבְעָ֧ה וַֽחֲמִשִּׁ֛ים אֶ֖לֶף וְאַרְבַּ֥ע מֵאֽוֹת׃ פ 32 לִבְנֵ֣י יוֹסֵף֮ לִבְנֵ֣י אֶפְרַיִם֒

32Of the descendants of Joseph:

Of the descendants of Ephraim, the registration of the clans of their ancestral house, as listed by name, aged twenty years and over, all who were able to bear arms—33those enrolled from the tribe of Ephraim: 40,500.

34Of the descendants of Manasseh, the registration of the clans of their ancestral house, as listed by name, aged twenty years and over, all who were able to bear arms—35those enrolled from the tribe of Manasseh: 32,200.

36Of the descendants of Benjamin, the registration of the clans of their ancestral house, as listed by name, aged twenty years and over, all who were able to bear arms—37those enrolled from the tribe of Benjamin: 35,400.

38Of the descendants of Dan, the registration of the clans of their ancestral house, as listed by name, aged twenty years and over, all who were able to bear arms—39those enrolled from the tribe of Dan: 62,700.

40Of the descendants of Asher, the registration of the clans of their ancestral house, as listed by name, aged twenty years and over, all who were able to bear arms—41those enrolled from the tribe of Asher: 41,500.

42[Of] the descendants of Naphtali, the registration of the clans of their ancestral house as listed by name, aged twenty years and over, all who were able to bear arms—43those enrolled from the tribe of Naphtali: 53,400.

44Those are the enrollments recorded by Moses and Aaron and by the chieftains of Israel, who were twelve in number, one man to each ancestral house. 45All the Israelites, aged twenty years and over, enrolled by ancestral houses, all those in Israel who were able to bear arms—46all who were enrolled came to 603,550.

47The Levites, however, were not recorded among them by their ancestral tribe. 48For the LORD had spoken to Moses, saying: 49Do not

תּוֹלְדֹתָם לְמִשְׁפְּחֹתָם לְבֵית אֲבֹתָם בְּמִסְפַּר שֵׁמֹת מִבֶּן עֶשְׂרִים שָׁנָה וָמַעְלָה כֹּל יֹצֵא צָבָא: 33 פְּקֻדֵיהֶם לְמַטֵּה אֶפְרָיִם אַרְבָּעִים אֶלֶף וַחֲמֵשׁ מֵאוֹת: פ 34 לִבְנֵי מְנַשֶּׁה תּוֹלְדֹתָם לְמִשְׁפְּחֹתָם לְבֵית אֲבֹתָם בְּמִסְפַּר שֵׁמוֹת מִבֶּן עֶשְׂרִים שָׁנָה וָמַעְלָה כֹּל יֹצֵא צָבָא: 35 פְּקֻדֵיהֶם לְמַטֵּה מְנַשֶּׁה שְׁנַיִם וּשְׁלֹשִׁים אֶלֶף וּמָאתָיִם: פ 36 לִבְנֵי בִנְיָמִן תּוֹלְדֹתָם לְמִשְׁפְּחֹתָם לְבֵית אֲבֹתָם בְּמִסְפַּר שֵׁמֹת מִבֶּן עֶשְׂרִים שָׁנָה וָמַעְלָה כֹּל יֹצֵא צָבָא: 37 פְּקֻדֵיהֶם לְמַטֵּה בִנְיָמִן חֲמִשָּׁה וּשְׁלֹשִׁים אֶלֶף וְאַרְבַּע מֵאוֹת: פ 38 לִבְנֵי דָן תּוֹלְדֹתָם לְמִשְׁפְּחֹתָם לְבֵית אֲבֹתָם בְּמִסְפַּר שֵׁמֹת מִבֶּן עֶשְׂרִים שָׁנָה וָמַעְלָה כֹּל יֹצֵא צָבָא: 39 פְּקֻדֵיהֶם לְמַטֵּה דָן שְׁנַיִם וְשִׁשִּׁים אֶלֶף וּשְׁבַע מֵאוֹת: פ 40 לִבְנֵי אָשֵׁר תּוֹלְדֹתָם לְמִשְׁפְּחֹתָם לְבֵית אֲבֹתָם בְּמִסְפַּר שֵׁמֹת מִבֶּן עֶשְׂרִים שָׁנָה וָמַעְלָה כֹּל יֹצֵא צָבָא: 41 פְּקֻדֵיהֶם לְמַטֵּה אָשֵׁר אֶחָד וְאַרְבָּעִים אֶלֶף וַחֲמֵשׁ מֵאוֹת: פ 42 בְּנֵי נַפְתָּלִי תּוֹלְדֹתָם לְמִשְׁפְּחֹתָם לְבֵית אֲבֹתָם בְּמִסְפַּר שֵׁמֹת מִבֶּן עֶשְׂרִים שָׁנָה וָמַעְלָה כֹּל יֹצֵא צָבָא: 43 פְּקֻדֵיהֶם לְמַטֵּה נַפְתָּלִי שְׁלֹשָׁה וַחֲמִשִּׁים אֶלֶף וְאַרְבַּע מֵאוֹת: פ

44 אֵלֶּה הַפְּקֻדִים אֲשֶׁר פָּקַד מֹשֶׁה וְאַהֲרֹן וּנְשִׂיאֵי יִשְׂרָאֵל שְׁנֵים עָשָׂר אִישׁ אִישׁ־אֶחָד לְבֵית־אֲבֹתָיו הָיוּ: 45 וַיִּהְיוּ כָּל־פְּקוּדֵי בְנֵי־יִשְׂרָאֵל לְבֵית אֲבֹתָם מִבֶּן עֶשְׂרִים שָׁנָה וָמַעְלָה כָּל־יֹצֵא צָבָא בְּיִשְׂרָאֵל: 46 וַיִּהְיוּ כָּל־הַפְּקֻדִים שֵׁשׁ־מֵאוֹת אֶלֶף וּשְׁלֹשֶׁת אֲלָפִים וַחֲמֵשׁ מֵאוֹת וַחֲמִשִּׁים:

47 וְהַלְוִיִּם לְמַטֵּה אֲבֹתָם לֹא הָתְפָּקְדוּ בְּתוֹכָם: פ 48 וַיְדַבֵּר יְהוָה אֶל־מֹשֶׁה

on any account enroll the tribe of Levi or take a census of them with the Israelites. [50]You shall put the Levites in charge of the Tabernacle of the Pact, all its furnishings, and everything that pertains to it: they shall carry the Tabernacle and all its furnishings, and they shall tend it; and they shall camp around the Tabernacle. [51]When the Tabernacle is to set out, the Levites shall take it down, and when the Tabernacle is to be pitched, the Levites shall set it up; any outsider who encroaches shall be put to death. [52]The Israelites shall encamp troop by troop, each man with his division and each under his standard. [53]The Levites, however, shall camp around the Tabernacle of the Pact, that wrath may not strike the Israelite community; the Levites shall stand guard around the Tabernacle of the Pact.

[54]The Israelites did accordingly; just as the LORD had commanded Moses, so they did.

2 The LORD spoke to Moses and Aaron, saying: [2]The Israelites shall camp each with his standard, under the banners of their ancestral house; they shall camp around the Tent of Meeting at a distance.

[3]Camped on the front, or east side: the standard of the division of Judah, troop by troop.
Chieftain of the Judites: Nahshon son of Amminadab. [4]His troop, as enrolled: 74,600.
[5]Camping next to it:
The tribe of Issachar.
Chieftain of the Issacharites: Nethanel son of Zuar. [6]His troop, as enrolled: 54,400.
[7]The tribe of Zebulun.
Chieftain of the Zebulunites: Eliab son of Helon. [8]His troop, as enrolled: 57,400.
[9]The total enrolled in the division of Judah: 186,400, for all troops. These shall march first.

לֵאמֹֽר: 49 אַ֣ךְ אֶת־מַטֵּ֤ה לֵוִי֙ לֹ֣א תִפְקֹ֔ד וְאֶת־רֹאשָׁ֖ם לֹ֣א תִשָּׂ֑א בְּת֖וֹךְ בְּנֵ֥י יִשְׂרָאֵֽל: 50 וְאַתָּ֡ה הַפְקֵ֣ד אֶת־הַלְוִיִּם֩ עַל־מִשְׁכַּ֨ן הָעֵדֻ֜ת וְעַ֣ל כָּל־כֵּלָיו֮ וְעַ֣ל כָּל־אֲשֶׁר־לוֹ֒ הֵ֜מָּה יִשְׂא֣וּ אֶת־הַמִּשְׁכָּ֗ן וְאֶת־כָּל־כֵּלָ֔יו וְהֵ֖ם יְשָׁרְתֻ֑הוּ וְסָבִ֥יב לַמִּשְׁכָּ֖ן יַחֲנֽוּ: 51 וּבִנְסֹ֣עַ הַמִּשְׁכָּ֗ן יוֹרִ֤ידוּ אֹתוֹ֙ הַלְוִיִּ֔ם וּבַחֲנֹת֙ הַמִּשְׁכָּ֔ן יָקִ֥ימוּ אֹת֖וֹ הַלְוִיִּ֑ם וְהַזָּ֥ר הַקָּרֵ֖ב יוּמָֽת: 52 וְחָנ֖וּ בְּנֵ֣י יִשְׂרָאֵ֑ל אִ֧ישׁ עַֽל־מַחֲנֵ֛הוּ וְאִ֥ישׁ עַל־דִּגְל֖וֹ לְצִבְאֹתָֽם: 53 וְהַלְוִיִּ֞ם יַחֲנ֤וּ סָבִיב֙ לְמִשְׁכַּ֣ן הָעֵדֻ֔ת וְלֹֽא־יִהְיֶ֣ה קֶ֔צֶף עַל־עֲדַ֖ת בְּנֵ֣י יִשְׂרָאֵ֑ל וְשָׁמְרוּ֙ הַלְוִיִּ֔ם אֶת־מִשְׁמֶ֖רֶת מִשְׁכַּ֥ן הָעֵדֽוּת: 54 וַֽיַּעֲשׂ֖וּ בְּנֵ֣י יִשְׂרָאֵ֑ל כְּ֠כֹל אֲשֶׁ֨ר צִוָּ֤ה יְהוָֹה֙ אֶת־מֹשֶׁ֔ה כֵּ֖ן עָשֽׂוּ: פ

ב וַיְדַבֵּ֣ר יְהוָֹ֔ה אֶל־מֹשֶׁ֥ה וְאֶֽל־אַהֲרֹ֖ן לֵאמֹֽר: 2 אִ֣ישׁ עַל־דִּגְל֤וֹ בְאֹתֹת֙ לְבֵ֣ית אֲבֹתָ֔ם יַחֲנ֖וּ בְּנֵ֣י יִשְׂרָאֵ֑ל מִנֶּ֕גֶד סָבִ֥יב לְאֹֽהֶל־מוֹעֵ֖ד יַחֲנֽוּ:

3 וְהַֽחֹנִים֙ קֵ֣דְמָה מִזְרָ֔חָה דֶּ֛גֶל מַחֲנֵ֥ה יְהוּדָ֖ה לְצִבְאֹתָ֑ם וְנָשִׂיא֙ לִבְנֵ֣י יְהוּדָ֔ה נַחְשׁ֖וֹן בֶּן־עַמִּֽינָדָֽב: 4 וּצְבָא֖וֹ וּפְקֻדֵיהֶ֑ם אַרְבָּעָ֧ה וְשִׁבְעִ֛ים אֶ֖לֶף וְשֵׁ֥שׁ מֵאֽוֹת: 5 וְהַחֹנִ֥ים עָלָ֖יו מַטֵּ֣ה יִשָּׂשׂכָ֑ר וְנָשִׂיא֙ לִבְנֵ֣י יִשָּׂשׂכָ֔ר נְתַנְאֵ֖ל בֶּן־צוּעָֽר: 6 וּצְבָא֖וֹ וּפְקֻדָ֑יו אַרְבָּעָ֧ה וַחֲמִשִּׁ֛ים אֶ֖לֶף וְאַרְבַּ֥ע מֵאֽוֹת: ס 7 מַטֵּ֖ה זְבוּלֻ֑ן וְנָשִׂיא֙ לִבְנֵ֣י זְבוּלֻ֔ן אֱלִיאָ֖ב בֶּן־חֵלֹֽן: 8 וּצְבָא֖וֹ וּפְקֻדָ֑יו שִׁבְעָ֧ה וַחֲמִשִּׁ֛ים אֶ֖לֶף וְאַרְבַּ֥ע מֵאֽוֹת: 9 כָּֽל־הַפְּקֻדִ֞ים לְמַחֲנֵ֣ה יְהוּדָ֗ה מְאַ֨ת אֶ֜לֶף

10On the south: the standard of the division of Reuben, troop by troop.

Chieftain of the Reubenites: Elizur son of Shedeur. 11His troop, as enrolled: 46,500. 12Camping next to it:

The tribe of Simeon.

Chieftain of the Simeonites: Shelumiel son of Zurishaddai.

13His troop, as enrolled: 59,300.

14And the tribe of Gad.

Chieftain of the Gadites: Eliasaph son of Reuel. 15His troop, as enrolled: 45,650.

16The total enrolled in the division of Reuben: 151,450, for all troops. These shall march second.

17Then, midway between the divisions, the Tent of Meeting, the division of the Levites, shall move. As they camp, so they shall march, each in position, by their standards.

18On the west: the standard of the division of Ephraim, troop by troop.

Chieftain of the Ephraimites: Elishama son of Ammihud. 19His troop, as enrolled: 40,500.

20Next to it:

The tribe of Manasseh.

Chieftain of the Manassites: Gamaliel son of Pedahzur. 21His troop, as enrolled: 32,200.

22And the tribe of Benjamin.

Chieftain of the Benjaminites: Abidan son of Gideoni. 23His troop, as enrolled: 35,400.

24The total enrolled in the division of Ephraim: 108,100 for all troops. These shall march third.

25On the north: the standard of the division of Dan, troop by troop.

וּשְׁמֹנִים אֶלֶף וְשֵׁשֶׁת־אֲלָפִים וְאַרְבַּע־
מֵאוֹת לְצִבְאֹתָם רִאשֹׁנָה יִסָּעוּ: ס

10 דֶּגֶל מַחֲנֵה רְאוּבֵן תֵּימָנָה לְצִבְאֹתָם
וְנָשִׂיא לִבְנֵי רְאוּבֵן אֱלִיצוּר בֶּן־שְׁדֵיאוּר:
11 וּצְבָאוֹ וּפְקֻדָיו שִׁשָּׁה וְאַרְבָּעִים אֶלֶף
וַחֲמֵשׁ מֵאוֹת:
12 וְהַחֹנִם עָלָיו מַטֵּה שִׁמְעוֹן וְנָשִׂיא לִבְנֵי
שִׁמְעוֹן שְׁלֻמִיאֵל בֶּן־צוּרִי־שַׁדָּי: 13 וּצְבָאוֹ
וּפְקֻדֵיהֶם תִּשְׁעָה וַחֲמִשִּׁים אֶלֶף וּשְׁלֹשׁ
מֵאוֹת: 14 וּמַטֵּה גָּד וְנָשִׂיא לִבְנֵי גָד אֶלְיָסָף
בֶּן־רְעוּאֵל: 15 וּצְבָאוֹ וּפְקֻדֵיהֶם חֲמִשָּׁה
וְאַרְבָּעִים אֶלֶף וְשֵׁשׁ מֵאוֹת וַחֲמִשִּׁים:
16 כָּל־הַפְּקֻדִים לְמַחֲנֵה רְאוּבֵן מְאַת אֶלֶף
וְאֶחָד וַחֲמִשִּׁים אֶלֶף וְאַרְבַּע־מֵאוֹת
וַחֲמִשִּׁים לְצִבְאֹתָם וּשְׁנִיִם יִסָּעוּ: ס

17 וְנָסַע אֹהֶל־מוֹעֵד מַחֲנֵה הַלְוִיִּם בְּתוֹךְ
הַמַּחֲנֹת כַּאֲשֶׁר יַחֲנוּ כֵּן יִסָּעוּ אִישׁ עַל־יָדוֹ
לְדִגְלֵיהֶם: ס

18 דֶּגֶל מַחֲנֵה אֶפְרַיִם לְצִבְאֹתָם יָמָּה
וְנָשִׂיא לִבְנֵי אֶפְרַיִם אֱלִישָׁמָע בֶּן־
עַמִּיהוּד: 19 וּצְבָאוֹ וּפְקֻדֵיהֶם אַרְבָּעִים
אֶלֶף וַחֲמֵשׁ מֵאוֹת:
20 וְעָלָיו מַטֵּה מְנַשֶּׁה וְנָשִׂיא לִבְנֵי מְנַשֶּׁה
גַּמְלִיאֵל בֶּן־פְּדָהצוּר: 21 וּצְבָאוֹ וּפְקֻדֵיהֶם
שְׁנַיִם וּשְׁלֹשִׁים אֶלֶף וּמָאתָיִם: 22 וּמַטֵּה
בִּנְיָמִן וְנָשִׂיא לִבְנֵי בִנְיָמִן אֲבִידָן בֶּן־
גִּדְעֹנִי: 23 וּצְבָאוֹ וּפְקֻדֵיהֶם חֲמִשָּׁה
וּשְׁלֹשִׁים אֶלֶף וְאַרְבַּע מֵאוֹת:
24 כָּל־הַפְּקֻדִים לְמַחֲנֵה אֶפְרַיִם מְאַת
אֶלֶף וּשְׁמֹנַת־אֲלָפִים וּמֵאָה לְצִבְאֹתָם
וּשְׁלִשִׁים יִסָּעוּ: ס

Chieftain of the Danites: Ahiezer son of Ammishaddai. ²⁶His troop, as enrolled: 62,700.

²⁷Camping next to it:

The tribe of Asher.

Chieftain of the Asherites: Pagiel son of Ochran. ²⁸His troop, as enrolled: 41,500.

²⁹And the tribe of Naphtali.

Chieftain of the Naphtalites: Ahira son of Enan. ³⁰His troop, as enrolled: 53,400.

³¹The total enrolled in the division of Dan: 157,600. These shall march last, by their standards.

³²Those are the enrollments of the Israelites by ancestral houses. The total enrolled in the divisions, for all troops: 603,550. ³³The Levites, however, were not recorded among the Israelites, as the LORD had commanded Moses.

³⁴The Israelites did accordingly; just as the LORD had commanded Moses, so they camped by their standards, and so they marched, each with his clan according to his ancestral house.

3 This is the line of Aaron and Moses at the time that the LORD spoke with Moses on Mount Sinai. ²These were the names of Aaron's sons: Nadab, the first-born, and Abihu, Eleazar and Ithamar; ³those were the names of Aaron's sons, the anointed priests who were ordained for priesthood. ⁴But Nadab and Abihu died ᵃ-by the will of-ᵃ the LORD, when they offered alien fire before the LORD in the wilderness of Sinai; and they left no sons. So it was Eleazar and Ithamar who served as priests in the lifetime of their father Aaron.

⁵The LORD spoke to Moses, saying: ⁶Advance the tribe of Levi and place them in attendance

²⁵ דֶּגֶל מַחֲנֵה דָן צָפֹנָה לְצִבְאֹתָם וְנָשִׂיא לִבְנֵי דָן אֲחִיעֶזֶר בֶּן־עַמִּישַׁדָּי׃ 26 וּצְבָאוֹ וּפְקֻדֵיהֶם שְׁנַיִם וְשִׁשִּׁים אֶלֶף וּשְׁבַע מֵאוֹת׃

²⁷ וְהַחֹנִים עָלָיו מַטֵּה אָשֵׁר וְנָשִׂיא לִבְנֵי אָשֵׁר פַּגְעִיאֵל בֶּן־עָכְרָן׃ 28 וּצְבָאוֹ וּפְקֻדֵיהֶם אֶחָד וְאַרְבָּעִים אֶלֶף וַחֲמֵשׁ מֵאוֹת׃ 29 וּמַטֵּה נַפְתָּלִי וְנָשִׂיא לִבְנֵי נַפְתָּלִי אֲחִירַע בֶּן־עֵינָן׃ 30 וּצְבָאוֹ וּפְקֻדֵיהֶם שְׁלֹשָׁה וַחֲמִשִּׁים אֶלֶף וְאַרְבַּע מֵאוֹת׃

³¹ כָּל־הַפְּקֻדִים לְמַחֲנֵה דָן מְאַת אֶלֶף וְשִׁבְעָה וַחֲמִשִּׁים אֶלֶף וְשֵׁשׁ מֵאוֹת לָאַחֲרֹנָה יִסְעוּ לְדִגְלֵיהֶם׃ פ 32 אֵלֶּה פְּקוּדֵי בְנֵי־יִשְׂרָאֵל לְבֵית אֲבֹתָם כָּל־פְּקוּדֵי הַמַּחֲנֹת לְצִבְאֹתָם שֵׁשׁ־מֵאוֹת אֶלֶף וּשְׁלֹשֶׁת אֲלָפִים וַחֲמֵשׁ מֵאוֹת וַחֲמִשִּׁים׃ 33 וְהַלְוִיִּם לֹא הָתְפָּקְדוּ בְּתוֹךְ בְּנֵי יִשְׂרָאֵל כַּאֲשֶׁר צִוָּה יְהוָה אֶת־מֹשֶׁה׃ 34 וַיַּעֲשׂוּ בְּנֵי יִשְׂרָאֵל כְּכֹל אֲשֶׁר־צִוָּה יְהוָה אֶת־מֹשֶׁה כֵּן־חָנוּ לְדִגְלֵיהֶם וְכֵן נָסָעוּ אִישׁ לְמִשְׁפְּחֹתָיו עַל־בֵּית אֲבֹתָיו׃

ג וְאֵלֶּה תּוֹלְדֹת אַהֲרֹן וּמֹשֶׁה בְּיוֹם דִּבֶּר יְהוָה אֶת־מֹשֶׁה בְּהַר סִינָי׃ 2 וְאֵלֶּה שְׁמוֹת בְּנֵי־אַהֲרֹן הַבְּכֹר ׀ נָדָב וַאֲבִיהוּא אֶלְעָזָר וְאִיתָמָר׃ 3 אֵלֶּה שְׁמוֹת בְּנֵי אַהֲרֹן הַכֹּהֲנִים הַמְּשֻׁחִים אֲשֶׁר־מִלֵּא יָדָם לְכַהֵן׃ 4 וַיָּמָת נָדָב וַאֲבִיהוּא לִפְנֵי יְהוָה בְּהַקְרִבָם אֵשׁ זָרָה לִפְנֵי יְהוָה בְּמִדְבַּר סִינַי וּבָנִים לֹא־הָיוּ לָהֶם וַיְכַהֵן אֶלְעָזָר וְאִיתָמָר עַל־פְּנֵי אַהֲרֹן אֲבִיהֶם׃ פ 5 וַיְדַבֵּר יְהוָה אֶל־מֹשֶׁה לֵּאמֹר׃ 6 הַקְרֵב אֶת־מַטֵּה לֵוִי וְהַעֲמַדְתָּ אֹתוֹ לִפְנֵי אַהֲרֹן

ᵃ⁻ᵃ Others "before."

upon Aaron the priest to serve him. 7They shall perform duties for him and for the whole community before the Tent of Meeting, doing the work of the Tabernacle. 8They shall take charge of all the furnishings of the Tent of Meeting—a duty on behalf of the Israelites—doing the work of the Tabernacle. 9You shall assign the Levites to Aaron and to his sons: they are formally assigned to him from among the Israelites. 10You shall make Aaron and his sons responsible for observing their priestly duties; and any outsider who encroaches shall be put to death.

11The LORD spoke to Moses, saying: 12I hereby take the Levites from among the Israelites in place of all the first-born, the first issue of the womb among the Israelites: the Levites shall be Mine. 13For every first-born is Mine: at the time that I smote every first-born in the land of Egypt, I consecrated every first-born in Israel, man and beast, to Myself, to be Mine, the LORD's.

14The LORD spoke to Moses in the wilderness of Sinai, saying: 15Record the Levites by ancestral house and by clan; record every male among them from the age of one month up. 16So Moses recorded them at the command of the LORD, as he was bidden. 17These were the sons of Levi by name: Gershon, Kohath, and Merari. 18These were the names of the sons of Gershon by clan: Libni and Shimei. 19The sons of Kohath by clan: Amram and Izhar, Hebron and Uzziel. 20The sons of Merari by clan: Mahli and Mushi.

These were the clans of the Levites within their ancestral houses:

21To Gershon belonged the clan of the Libnites and the clan of the Shimeites; those were the clans of the Gershonites. 22The recorded entries of all their males from the age of one month up, as recorded, came to 7,500. 23The clans of the Gershonites were to camp behind the Tabernacle, to the west. 24The chieftain of the ancestral house of the Gershonites was

הַכֹּהֵן וְשֵׁרְתוּ אֹתוֹ: 7 וְשָׁמְרוּ אֶת־מִשְׁמַרְתּוֹ וְאֶת־מִשְׁמֶרֶת כָּל־הָעֵדָה לִפְנֵי אֹהֶל מוֹעֵד לַעֲבֹד אֶת־עֲבֹדַת הַמִּשְׁכָּן: 8 וְשָׁמְרוּ אֶת־כָּל־כְּלֵי אֹהֶל מוֹעֵד וְאֶת־מִשְׁמֶרֶת בְּנֵי יִשְׂרָאֵל לַעֲבֹד אֶת־עֲבֹדַת הַמִּשְׁכָּן: 9 וְנָתַתָּה אֶת־הַלְוִיִּם לְאַהֲרֹן וּלְבָנָיו נְתוּנִם נְתוּנִם הֵמָּה לוֹ מֵאֵת בְּנֵי יִשְׂרָאֵל: 10 וְאֶת־אַהֲרֹן וְאֶת־בָּנָיו תִּפְקֹד וְשָׁמְרוּ אֶת־כְּהֻנָּתָם וְהַזָּר הַקָּרֵב יוּמָת: פ

11 וַיְדַבֵּר יְהוָה אֶל־מֹשֶׁה לֵּאמֹר: 12 וַאֲנִי הִנֵּה לָקַחְתִּי אֶת־הַלְוִיִּם מִתּוֹךְ בְּנֵי יִשְׂרָאֵל תַּחַת כָּל־בְּכוֹר פֶּטֶר רֶחֶם מִבְּנֵי יִשְׂרָאֵל וְהָיוּ לִי הַלְוִיִּם: 13 כִּי לִי כָּל־בְּכוֹר בְּיוֹם הַכֹּתִי כָל־בְּכוֹר בְּאֶרֶץ מִצְרַיִם הִקְדַּשְׁתִּי לִי כָל־בְּכוֹר בְּיִשְׂרָאֵל מֵאָדָם עַד־בְּהֵמָה לִי יִהְיוּ אֲנִי יְהוָה: ס

14 וַיְדַבֵּר יְהוָה אֶל־מֹשֶׁה בְּמִדְבַּר סִינַי לֵאמֹר: 15 פְּקֹד אֶת־בְּנֵי לֵוִי לְבֵית אֲבֹתָם לְמִשְׁפְּחֹתָם כָּל־זָכָר מִבֶּן־חֹדֶשׁ וָמַעְלָה תִּפְקְדֵם: 16 וַיִּפְקֹד אֹתָם מֹשֶׁה עַל־פִּי יְהוָה כַּאֲשֶׁר צֻוָּה: 17 וַיִּהְיוּ־אֵלֶּה בְנֵי־לֵוִי בִּשְׁמֹתָם גֵּרְשׁוֹן וּקְהָת וּמְרָרִי: 18 וְאֵלֶּה שְׁמוֹת בְּנֵי־גֵרְשׁוֹן לְמִשְׁפְּחֹתָם לִבְנִי וְשִׁמְעִי: 19 וּבְנֵי קְהָת לְמִשְׁפְּחֹתָם עַמְרָם וְיִצְהָר חֶבְרוֹן וְעֻזִּיאֵל: 20 וּבְנֵי מְרָרִי לְמִשְׁפְּחֹתָם מַחְלִי וּמוּשִׁי אֵלֶּה הֵם מִשְׁפְּחֹת הַלֵּוִי לְבֵית אֲבֹתָם: 21 לְגֵרְשׁוֹן מִשְׁפַּחַת הַלִּבְנִי וּמִשְׁפַּחַת הַשִּׁמְעִי אֵלֶּה הֵם מִשְׁפְּחֹת הַגֵּרְשֻׁנִּי: 22 פְּקֻדֵיהֶם בְּמִסְפַּר כָּל־זָכָר מִבֶּן־חֹדֶשׁ וָמָעְלָה פְּקֻדֵיהֶם שִׁבְעַת אֲלָפִים וַחֲמֵשׁ מֵאוֹת: 23 מִשְׁפְּחֹת הַגֵּרְשֻׁנִּי אַחֲרֵי הַמִּשְׁכָּן יַחֲנוּ יָמָּה: 24 וּנְשִׂיא בֵית־אָב לַגֵּרְשֻׁנִּי אֶלְיָסָף בֶּן־לָאֵל: 25 וּמִשְׁמֶרֶת בְּנֵי־

Eliasaph son of Lael. 25The duties of the Gershonites in the Tent of Meeting comprised: the Tabernacle,[b] the tent, its covering, and the screen for the entrance of the Tent of Meeting; 26the hangings of the enclosure, the screen for the entrance of the enclosure which surrounds the Tabernacle, the cords thereof, and the altar—all the service connected with these.

27To Kohath belonged the clan of the Amramites, the clan of the Izharites, the clan of the Hebronites, and the clan of the Uzzielites; those were the clans of the Kohathites. 28All the listed males from the age of one month up came to 8,600, attending to the duties of the sanctuary. 29The clans of the Kohathites were to camp along the south side of the Tabernacle. 30The chieftain of the ancestral house of the Kohathite clans was Elizaphan son of Uzziel. 31Their duties comprised: the ark, the table, the lampstand, the altars, and the sacred utensils that were used with them, and the screen[c]—all the service connected with these. 32The head chieftain of the Levites was Eleazar son of Aaron the priest, in charge of those attending to the duties of the sanctuary.

33To Merari belonged the clan of the Mahlites and the clan of the Mushites; those were the clans of Merari. 34The recorded entries of all their males from the age of one month up came to 6,200. 35The chieftain of the ancestral house of the clans of Merari was Zuriel son of Abihail. They were to camp along the north side of the Tabernacle. 36The assigned duties of the Merarites comprised: the planks of the Tabernacle, its bars, posts, and sockets, and all its furnishings—all the service connected with these; 37also the posts around the enclosure and their sockets, pegs, and cords.

38Those who were to camp before the Tabernacle, in front—before the Tent of Meeting,

גֵּרְשׁוֹן בְּאֹהֶל מוֹעֵד הַמִּשְׁכָּן וְהָאֹהֶל מִכְסֵהוּ וּמָסַ֗ךְ פֶּ֖תַח אֹ֥הֶל מוֹעֵֽד׃ 26 וְקַלְעֵ֣י הֶֽחָצֵ֗ר וְאֶת־מָסַךְ֙ פֶּ֣תַח הֶֽחָצֵ֔ר אֲשֶׁ֧ר עַל־הַמִּשְׁכָּ֛ן וְעַל־הַמִּזְבֵּ֖חַ סָבִ֑יב וְאֵת֙ מֵֽיתָרָ֔יו לְכֹ֖ל עֲבֹֽדָתֽוֹ׃

27 וְלִקְהָ֗ת מִשְׁפַּ֤חַת הָֽעַמְרָמִי֙ וּמִשְׁפַּ֣חַת הַיִּצְהָרִ֔י וּמִשְׁפַּ֖חַת הַֽחֶבְרֹנִ֑י וּמִשְׁפַּ֖חַת הָֽעָזִּֽיאֵלִ֑י אֵ֥לֶּה הֵ֖ם מִשְׁפְּחֹ֥ת הַקְּהָתִֽי׃ 28 בְּמִסְפַּר֙ כָּל־זָכָ֔ר מִבֶּן־חֹ֖דֶשׁ וָמָ֑עְלָה שְׁמֹנַ֤ת אֲלָפִים֙ וְשֵׁ֣שׁ מֵא֔וֹת שֹׁמְרֵ֖י מִשְׁמֶ֥רֶת הַקֹּֽדֶשׁ׃ 29 מִשְׁפְּחֹ֥ת בְּנֵֽי־קְהָ֖ת יַֽחֲנ֑וּ עַ֛ל יֶ֥רֶךְ הַמִּשְׁכָּ֖ן תֵּימָֽנָה׃ 30 וּנְשִׂ֥יא בֵֽית־אָ֖ב לְמִשְׁפְּחֹ֣ת הַקְּהָתִ֑י אֱלִֽיצָפָ֖ן בֶּן־עֻזִּיאֵֽל׃ 31 וּמִשְׁמַרְתָּ֗ם הָֽאָרֹ֤ן וְהַשֻּׁלְחָן֙ וְהַמְּנֹרָ֣ה וְהַֽמִּזְבְּחֹ֔ת וּכְלֵ֣י הַקֹּ֔דֶשׁ אֲשֶׁ֥ר יְשָֽׁרְת֖וּ בָּהֶ֑ם וְהַמָּסָ֖ךְ וְכֹ֥ל עֲבֹֽדָתֽוֹ׃ 32 וּנְשִׂיא֙ נְשִׂיאֵ֣י הַלֵּוִ֔י אֶלְעָזָ֖ר בֶּן־אַֽהֲרֹ֣ן הַכֹּהֵ֑ן פְּקֻדַּ֕ת שֹׁמְרֵ֖י מִשְׁמֶ֥רֶת הַקֹּֽדֶשׁ׃

33 לִמְרָרִ֕י מִשְׁפַּ֙חַת֙ הַמַּחְלִ֔י וּמִשְׁפַּ֖חַת הַמּוּשִׁ֑י אֵ֥לֶּה הֵ֖ם מִשְׁפְּחֹ֥ת מְרָרִֽי׃ 34 וּפְקֻדֵיהֶ֣ם בְּמִסְפַּ֗ר כָּל־זָכָ֔ר מִבֶּן־חֹ֖דֶשׁ וָמָ֑עְלָה שֵׁ֥שֶׁת אֲלָפִ֖ים וּמָאתָֽיִם׃ 35 וּנְשִׂ֤יא בֵֽית־אָב֙ לְמִשְׁפְּחֹ֣ת מְרָרִ֔י צֽוּרִיאֵ֖ל בֶּן־אֲבִיחָ֑יִל עַ֣ל יֶ֧רֶךְ הַמִּשְׁכָּ֛ן יַֽחֲנ֖וּ צָפֹֽנָה׃ 36 וּפְקֻדַּ֣ת מִשְׁמֶרֶת֮ בְּנֵ֣י מְרָרִי֒ קַרְשֵׁי֙ הַמִּשְׁכָּ֔ן וּבְרִיחָ֖יו וְעַמֻּדָ֣יו וַֽאֲדָנָ֑יו וְכָ֨ל־כֵּלָ֔יו וְכֹ֖ל עֲבֹֽדָתֽוֹ׃ 37 וְעַמֻּדֵ֧י הֶֽחָצֵ֛ר סָבִ֖יב וְאַדְנֵיהֶ֑ם וִיתֵֽדֹתָ֖ם וּמֵֽיתְרֵיהֶֽם׃

38 וְהַֽחֹנִ֣ים לִפְנֵ֣י הַמִּשְׁכָּ֡ן קֵ֣דְמָה לִפְנֵי֩ אֹֽהֶל־מוֹעֵ֨ד ׀ מִזְרָ֜חָה מֹשֶׁ֣ה ׀ וְאַֽהֲרֹ֣ן וּבָנָ֗יו

---

b   See note on Exod. 26.1.
c   I.e., the screening curtain; cf. 4–5.

on the east—were Moses and Aaron and his sons, attending to the duties of the sanctuary, as a duty on behalf of the Israelites; and any outsider who encroached was to be put to death. [39]All the Levites who were recorded, whom at the LORD's command Moses and Aaron recorded by their clans, all the males from the age of one month up, came to 22,000.

[40]The LORD said to Moses: Record every first-born male of the Israelite people from the age of one month up, and make a list of their names; [41]and take the Levites for Me, the LORD, in place of every first-born among the Israelite people, and the cattle of the Levites in place of every first-born among the cattle of the Israelites. [42]So Moses recorded all the first-born among the Israelites, as the LORD had commanded him. [43]All the first-born males as listed by name, recorded from the age of one month up, came to 22,273.

[44]The LORD spoke to Moses, saying: [45]Take the Levites in place of all the first-born among the Israelite people, and the cattle of the Levites in place of their cattle; and the Levites shall be Mine, the LORD's. [46]And as the redemption price of the 273 Israelite first-born over and above the number of the Levites, [47]take five shekels per head—take this by the sanctuary weight, twenty *gerahs* to the shekel—[48]and give the money to Aaron and his sons as the redemption price for those who are in excess. [49]So Moses took the redemption money from those over and above the ones redeemed by the Levites; [50]he took the money from the first-born of the Israelites, 1,365 sanctuary shekels. [51]And Moses gave the redemption money to Aaron and his sons at the LORD's bidding, as the LORD had commanded Moses.

שְׁמְרִים מִשְׁמֶרֶת הַמִּקְדָּשׁ לְמִשְׁמֶרֶת בְּנֵי יִשְׂרָאֵל וְהַזָּר הַקָּרֵב יוּמָת: 39 כָּל־פְּקוּדֵי הַלְוִיִּם אֲשֶׁר פָּקַד מֹשֶׁה וְאַהֲרֹן* עַל־פִּי יְהוָה לְמִשְׁפְּחֹתָם כָּל־זָכָר מִבֶּן־חֹדֶשׁ וָמַעְלָה שְׁנַיִם וְעֶשְׂרִים אָלֶף: ס 40 וַיֹּאמֶר יְהוָה אֶל־מֹשֶׁה פְּקֹד כָּל־בְּכֹר זָכָר לִבְנֵי יִשְׂרָאֵל מִבֶּן־חֹדֶשׁ וָמַעְלָה וְשָׂא אֵת מִסְפַּר שְׁמֹתָם: 41 וְלָקַחְתָּ אֶת־הַלְוִיִּם לִי אֲנִי יְהוָה תַּחַת כָּל־בְּכֹר בִּבְנֵי יִשְׂרָאֵל וְאֵת בֶּהֱמַת הַלְוִיִּם תַּחַת כָּל־בְּכוֹר בְּבֶהֱמַת בְּנֵי יִשְׂרָאֵל: 42 וַיִּפְקֹד מֹשֶׁה כַּאֲשֶׁר צִוָּה יְהוָה אֹתוֹ אֶת־כָּל־בְּכֹר בִּבְנֵי יִשְׂרָאֵל: 43 וַיְהִי כָל־בְּכוֹר זָכָר בְּמִסְפַּר שֵׁמֹת מִבֶּן־חֹדֶשׁ וָמַעְלָה לִפְקֻדֵיהֶם שְׁנַיִם וְעֶשְׂרִים אָלֶף שְׁלֹשָׁה וְשִׁבְעִים וּמָאתָיִם: פ 44 וַיְדַבֵּר יְהוָה אֶל־מֹשֶׁה לֵּאמֹר: 45 קַח אֶת־הַלְוִיִּם תַּחַת כָּל־בְּכוֹר בִּבְנֵי יִשְׂרָאֵל וְאֶת־בֶּהֱמַת הַלְוִיִּם תַּחַת בְּהֶמְתָּם וְהָיוּ־לִי הַלְוִיִּם אֲנִי יְהוָה: 46 וְאֵת פְּדוּיֵי הַשְּׁלֹשָׁה וְהַשִּׁבְעִים וְהַמָּאתָיִם הָעֹדְפִים עַל־הַלְוִיִּם מִבְּכוֹר בְּנֵי יִשְׂרָאֵל: 47 וְלָקַחְתָּ חֲמֵשֶׁת חֲמֵשֶׁת שְׁקָלִים לַגֻּלְגֹּלֶת בְּשֶׁקֶל הַקֹּדֶשׁ תִּקָּח עֶשְׂרִים גֵּרָה הַשָּׁקֶל: 48 וְנָתַתָּה הַכֶּסֶף לְאַהֲרֹן וּלְבָנָיו פְּדוּיֵי הָעֹדְפִים בָּהֶם: 49 וַיִּקַּח מֹשֶׁה אֵת כֶּסֶף הַפִּדְיוֹם מֵאֵת הָעֹדְפִים עַל פְּדוּיֵי הַלְוִיִּם: 50 מֵאֵת בְּכוֹר בְּנֵי יִשְׂרָאֵל לָקַח אֶת־הַכָּסֶף חֲמִשָּׁה וְשִׁשִּׁים וּשְׁלֹשׁ מֵאוֹת וָאֶלֶף בְּשֶׁקֶל הַקֹּדֶשׁ: 51 וַיִּתֵּן מֹשֶׁה אֶת־כֶּסֶף הַפְּדֻיִם* לְאַהֲרֹן וּלְבָנָיו עַל־פִּי יְהוָה כַּאֲשֶׁר צִוָּה יְהוָה אֶת־מֹשֶׁה: פ

4 The LORD spoke to Moses and Aaron, saying:

²Take a [separate] census of the Kohathites among the Levites, by the clans of their ancestral house, ³from the age of thirty years up to the age of fifty, all who are subject to service, to perform tasks for the Tent of Meeting. ⁴This is the responsibility of the Kohathites in the Tent of Meeting: the most sacred objects.

⁵At the breaking of camp, Aaron and his sons shall go in and take down the screening curtain and cover the Ark of the Pact with it. ⁶They shall lay a covering of dolphin*a* skin over it and spread a cloth of pure blue on top; and they shall put its poles in place.

⁷Over the table of display they shall spread a blue cloth; they shall place upon it the bowls, the ladles, the jars, and the libation jugs; and the regular bread shall rest upon it. ⁸They shall spread over these a crimson cloth which they shall cover with a covering of dolphin skin; and they shall put the poles in place.

⁹Then they shall take a blue cloth and cover the lampstand for lighting, with its lamps, its tongs, and its fire pans, as well as all the oil vessels that are used in its service. ¹⁰They shall put it and all its furnishings into a covering of dolphin skin, which they shall then place on a carrying frame.

¹¹Next they shall spread a blue cloth over the altar of gold and cover it with a covering of dolphin skin; and they shall put its poles in place. ¹²They shall take all the service vessels with which the service in the sanctuary is performed, put them into a blue cloth and cover them with a covering of dolphin skin, which they shall then place on a carrying frame. ¹³They shall remove the ashes from the [copper] altar and spread a

---

a See note at Exod. 25.5.

ד וַיְדַבֵּ֣ר יְהֹוָ֔ה אֶל־מֹשֶׁ֥ה וְאֶֽל־אַהֲרֹ֖ן לֵאמֹֽר:

2 נָשֹׂ֗א אֶת־רֹאשׁ֙ בְּנֵ֣י קְהָ֔ת מִתּ֖וֹךְ בְּנֵ֣י לֵוִ֑י לְמִשְׁפְּחֹתָ֖ם לְבֵ֥ית אֲבֹתָֽם: 3 מִבֶּ֨ן שְׁלֹשִׁ֤ים שָׁנָה֙ וָמַ֔עְלָה וְעַ֖ד בֶּן־חֲמִשִּׁ֣ים שָׁנָ֑ה כָּל־בָּא֙ לַצָּבָ֔א לַעֲשׂ֥וֹת מְלָאכָ֖ה בְּאֹ֥הֶל מוֹעֵֽד: 4 זֹ֛את עֲבֹדַ֥ת בְּנֵֽי־קְהָ֖ת בְּאֹ֣הֶל מוֹעֵ֑ד קֹ֖דֶשׁ הַקֳּדָשִֽׁים:

5 וּבָ֨א אַהֲרֹ֤ן וּבָנָיו֙ בִּנְסֹ֣עַ הַֽמַּחֲנֶ֔ה וְהוֹרִ֕דוּ אֵ֖ת פָּרֹ֣כֶת הַמָּסָ֑ךְ וְכִ֨סּוּ־בָ֔הּ אֵ֖ת אֲרֹ֥ן הָעֵדֻֽת: 6 וְנָתְנ֣וּ עָלָ֗יו כְּסוּי֙ ע֣וֹר תַּ֔חַשׁ וּפָרְשׂ֧וּ בֶֽגֶד־כְּלִ֛יל תְּכֵ֖לֶת מִלְמָ֑עְלָה וְשָׂמ֖וּ בַּדָּֽיו:

7 וְעַ֣ל ׀ שֻׁלְחַ֣ן הַפָּנִ֗ים יִפְרְשׂוּ֙ בֶּ֣גֶד תְּכֵ֔לֶת וְנָתְנ֣וּ עָ֠לָ֠יו אֶת־הַקְּעָרֹ֤ת וְאֶת־הַכַּפֹּת֙ וְאֶת־הַמְּנַקִּיֹּ֔ת וְאֵ֖ת קְשׂ֣וֹת הַנָּ֑סֶךְ וְלֶ֥חֶם הַתָּמִ֖יד עָלָ֥יו יִהְיֶֽה: 8 וּפָרְשׂ֣וּ עֲלֵיהֶ֗ם בֶּ֚גֶד תּוֹלַ֣עַת שָׁנִ֔י וְכִסּ֣וּ אֹת֔וֹ בְּמִכְסֵ֖ה ע֣וֹר תָּ֑חַשׁ וְשָׂמ֖וּ אֶת־בַּדָּֽיו:

9 וְלָקְח֣וּ ׀ בֶּ֣גֶד תְּכֵ֗לֶת וְכִסּ֞וּ אֶת־מְנֹרַ֤ת הַמָּאוֹר֙ וְאֶת־נֵ֣רֹתֶ֔יהָ וְאֶת־מַלְקָחֶ֖יהָ וְאֶת־מַחְתֹּתֶ֑יהָ וְאֵת֙ כָּל־כְּלֵ֣י שַׁמְנָ֔הּ אֲשֶׁ֥ר יְשָֽׁרְתוּ־לָ֖הּ בָּהֶֽם: 10 וְנָתְנ֣וּ אֹתָ֗הּ וְאֶת־כָּל־כֵּלֶ֔יהָ אֶל־מִכְסֵ֖ה ע֣וֹר תָּ֑חַשׁ וְנָתְנ֖וּ עַל־הַמּֽוֹט:

11 וְעַ֣ל ׀ מִזְבַּ֣ח הַזָּהָ֗ב יִפְרְשׂוּ֙ בֶּ֣גֶד תְּכֵ֔לֶת וְכִסּ֣וּ אֹת֔וֹ בְּמִכְסֵ֖ה ע֣וֹר תָּ֑חַשׁ וְשָׂמ֖וּ אֶת־בַּדָּֽיו: 12 וְלָקְחוּ֩ אֶת־כָּל־כְּלֵ֨י הַשָּׁרֵ֜ת אֲשֶׁ֧ר יְשָֽׁרְתוּ־בָ֣ם בַּקֹּ֗דֶשׁ וְנָֽתְנוּ֙ אֶל־בֶּ֣גֶד תְּכֵ֔לֶת וְכִסּ֣וּ אוֹתָ֔ם בְּמִכְסֵ֖ה ע֣וֹר תָּ֑חַשׁ וְנָתְנ֖וּ עַל־הַמּֽוֹט: 13 וְדִשְּׁנ֖וּ אֶת־הַמִּזְבֵּ֑חַ

286

purple cloth over it. ¹⁴Upon it they shall place all the vessels that are used in its service: the fire pans, the flesh hooks, the scrapers, and the basins—all the vessels of the altar—and over it they shall spread a covering of dolphin skin; and they shall put its poles in place.

¹⁵When Aaron and his sons have finished covering the sacred objects and all the furnishings of the sacred objects at the breaking of camp, only then shall the Kohathites come and lift them, so that they do not come in contact with the sacred objects and die. These things in the Tent of Meeting shall be the porterage of the Kohathites.

¹⁶Responsibility shall rest with Eleazar son of Aaron the priest for the lighting oil, the aromatic incense, the regular meal offering, and the anointing oil—responsibility for the whole Tabernacle and for everything consecrated that is in it or in its vessels.

¹⁷The LORD spoke to Moses and Aaron, saying: ¹⁸Do not let the group of Kohathite clans be cut off from the Levites. ¹⁹Do this with them, that they may live and not die when they approach the most sacred objects: let Aaron and his sons go in and assign each of them to his duties and to his porterage. ²⁰But let not [the Kohathites] go inside and ᵇ-witness the dismantling of the sanctuary,-ᵇ lest they die.

NASO'

²¹The LORD spoke to Moses: ²²Take a census of the Gershonites also, by their ancestral house and by their clans. ²³Record them from the age of thirty years up to the age of fifty, all who are subject to service in the performance of tasks for the Tent of Meeting. ²⁴These are the duties of the Gershonite clans as to labor and porterage: ²⁵they shall carry the cloths of the Taber-

וּפָרְשׂוּ עָלָיו בֶּגֶד אַרְגָּמָן ׃ 14 וְנָתְנוּ עָלָיו
אֶת־כָּל־כֵּלָיו אֲשֶׁר יְשָׁרְתוּ עָלָיו בָּהֶם
אֶת־הַמַּחְתֹּת אֶת־הַמִּזְלָגֹת וְאֶת־הַיָּעִים
וְאֶת־הַמִּזְרָקֹת כֹּל כְּלֵי הַמִּזְבֵּחַ וּפָרְשׂוּ
עָלָיו כְּסוּי עוֹר תַּחַשׁ וְשָׂמוּ בַדָּיו ׃

15 וְכִלָּה אַהֲרֹן־וּבָנָיו לְכַסֹּת אֶת־הַקֹּדֶשׁ
וְאֶת־כָּל־כְּלֵי הַקֹּדֶשׁ בִּנְסֹעַ הַמַּחֲנֶה
וְאַחֲרֵי־כֵן יָבֹאוּ בְנֵי־קְהָת לָשֵׂאת וְלֹא־
יִגְּעוּ אֶל־הַקֹּדֶשׁ וָמֵתוּ אֵלֶּה מַשָּׂא בְנֵי־
קְהָת בְּאֹהֶל מוֹעֵד ׃

16 וּפְקֻדַּת אֶלְעָזָר ׀ בֶּן־אַהֲרֹן הַכֹּהֵן שֶׁמֶן
הַמָּאוֹר וּקְטֹרֶת הַסַּמִּים וּמִנְחַת הַתָּמִיד
וְשֶׁמֶן הַמִּשְׁחָה פְּקֻדַּת כָּל־הַמִּשְׁכָּן וְכָל־
אֲשֶׁר־בּוֹ בְּקֹדֶשׁ וּבְכֵלָיו ׃ ס

17 וַיְדַבֵּר יְהֹוָה אֶל־מֹשֶׁה וְאֶל־אַהֲרֹן
לֵאמֹר ׃ 18 אַל־תַּכְרִיתוּ אֶת־שֵׁבֶט מִשְׁפְּחֹת
הַקְּהָתִי מִתּוֹךְ הַלְוִיִּם ׃ 19 וְזֹאת ׀ עֲשׂוּ
לָהֶם וְחָיוּ וְלֹא יָמֻתוּ בְּגִשְׁתָּם אֶת־קֹדֶשׁ
הַקֳּדָשִׁים אַהֲרֹן וּבָנָיו יָבֹאוּ וְשָׂמוּ אוֹתָם
אִישׁ אִישׁ עַל־עֲבֹדָתוֹ וְאֶל־מַשָּׂאוֹ ׃
20 וְלֹא־יָבֹאוּ לִרְאוֹת כְּבַלַּע אֶת־הַקֹּדֶשׁ
וָמֵתוּ ׃ פ

נשא

21 וַיְדַבֵּר יְהֹוָה אֶל־מֹשֶׁה לֵּאמֹר ׃ 22 נָשֹׂא
אֶת־רֹאשׁ בְּנֵי גֵרְשׁוֹן גַּם־הֵם לְבֵית אֲבֹתָם
לְמִשְׁפְּחֹתָם ׃ 23 מִבֶּן שְׁלֹשִׁים שָׁנָה וָמַעְלָה
עַד בֶּן־חֲמִשִּׁים שָׁנָה תִּפְקֹד אוֹתָם כָּל־
הַבָּא לִצְבֹא צָבָא לַעֲבֹד עֲבֹדָה בְּאֹהֶל
מוֹעֵד ׃ 24 זֹאת עֲבֹדַת מִשְׁפְּחֹת הַגֵּרְשֻׁנִּי
לַעֲבֹד וּלְמַשָּׂא ׃ 25 וְנָשְׂאוּ אֶת־יְרִיעֹת

ᵇ-ᵇ Others "look at the sacred objects even for a moment."

nacle, the Tent of Meeting with its covering, the covering of dolphin skin that is on top of it, and the screen for the entrance of the Tent of Meeting; 26the hangings of the enclosure, the screen at the entrance of the gate of the enclosure that surrounds the Tabernacle, the cords thereof, and the altar, and all their service equipment and all their accessories; and they shall perform the service. 27All the duties of the Gershonites, all their porterage and all their service, shall be performed on orders from Aaron and his sons; you shall make them responsible for attending to all their porterage. 28Those are the duties of the Gershonite clans for the Tent of Meeting; they shall attend to them under the direction of Ithamar son of Aaron the priest.

29As for the Merarites, you shall record them by the clans of their ancestral house; 30you shall record them from the age of thirty years up to the age of fifty, all who are subject to service in the performance of the duties for the Tent of Meeting. 31These are their porterage tasks in connection with their various duties for the Tent of Meeting: the planks, the bars, the posts, and the sockets of the Tabernacle; 32the posts around the enclosure and their sockets, pegs, and cords—all these furnishings and their service: you shall list by name the objects that are their porterage tasks. 33Those are the duties of the Merarite clans, pertaining to their various duties in the Tent of Meeting under the direction of Ithamar son of Aaron the priest.

34So Moses, Aaron, and the chieftains of the community recorded the Kohathites by the clans of their ancestral house, 35from the age of thirty years up to the age of fifty, all who were subject to service for work relating to the Tent of Meeting. 36Those recorded by their clans came to 2,750. 37That was the enrollment of the Kohathite clans, all those who performed duties relating to the Tent of Meeting, whom Moses

הַמִּשְׁכָּן וְאֶת־אֹהֶל מוֹעֵד מִכְסֵהוּ וּמִכְסֵה הַתַּחַשׁ אֲשֶׁר־עָלָיו מִלְמָעְלָה וְאֶת־מָסַךְ פֶּתַח אֹהֶל מוֹעֵד: 26 וְאֵת קַלְעֵי הֶחָצֵר וְאֶת־מָסַךְ ׀ פֶּתַח ׀ שַׁעַר הֶחָצֵר אֲשֶׁר עַל־הַמִּשְׁכָּן וְעַל־הַמִּזְבֵּחַ סָבִיב וְאֵת מֵיתְרֵיהֶם וְאֶת־כָּל־כְּלֵי עֲבֹדָתָם וְאֵת כָּל־אֲשֶׁר יֵעָשֶׂה לָהֶם וְעָבָדוּ: 27 עַל־פִּי אַהֲרֹן וּבָנָיו תִּהְיֶה כָּל־עֲבֹדַת בְּנֵי הַגֵּרְשֻׁנִּי לְכָל־מַשָּׂאָם וּלְכֹל עֲבֹדָתָם וּפְקַדְתֶּם עֲלֵהֶם בְּמִשְׁמֶרֶת אֵת כָּל־מַשָּׂאָם: 28 זֹאת עֲבֹדַת מִשְׁפְּחֹת בְּנֵי הַגֵּרְשֻׁנִּי בְּאֹהֶל מוֹעֵד וּמִשְׁמַרְתָּם בְּיַד אִיתָמָר בֶּן־אַהֲרֹן הַכֹּהֵן: פ

29 בְּנֵי מְרָרִי לְמִשְׁפְּחֹתָם לְבֵית־אֲבֹתָם תִּפְקֹד אֹתָם: 30 מִבֶּן שְׁלֹשִׁים שָׁנָה וָמַעְלָה וְעַד בֶּן־חֲמִשִּׁים שָׁנָה תִּפְקְדֵם כָּל־הַבָּא לַצָּבָא לַעֲבֹד אֶת־עֲבֹדַת אֹהֶל מוֹעֵד: 31 וְזֹאת מִשְׁמֶרֶת מַשָּׂאָם לְכָל־עֲבֹדָתָם בְּאֹהֶל מוֹעֵד קַרְשֵׁי הַמִּשְׁכָּן וּבְרִיחָיו וְעַמּוּדָיו וַאֲדָנָיו: 32 וְעַמּוּדֵי הֶחָצֵר סָבִיב וְאַדְנֵיהֶם וִיתֵדֹתָם וּמֵיתְרֵיהֶם לְכָל־כְּלֵיהֶם וּלְכֹל עֲבֹדָתָם וּבְשֵׁמֹת תִּפְקְדוּ אֶת־כְּלֵי מִשְׁמֶרֶת מַשָּׂאָם: 33 זֹאת עֲבֹדַת מִשְׁפְּחֹת בְּנֵי מְרָרִי לְכָל־עֲבֹדָתָם בְּאֹהֶל מוֹעֵד בְּיַד אִיתָמָר בֶּן־אַהֲרֹן הַכֹּהֵן: 34 וַיִּפְקֹד מֹשֶׁה וְאַהֲרֹן וּנְשִׂיאֵי הָעֵדָה אֶת־בְּנֵי הַקְּהָתִי לְמִשְׁפְּחֹתָם וּלְבֵית אֲבֹתָם: 35 מִבֶּן שְׁלֹשִׁים שָׁנָה וָמַעְלָה וְעַד בֶּן־חֲמִשִּׁים שָׁנָה כָּל־הַבָּא לַצָּבָא לַעֲבֹדָה בְּאֹהֶל מוֹעֵד: 36 וַיִּהְיוּ פְקֻדֵיהֶם לְמִשְׁפְּחֹתָם אַלְפַּיִם שְׁבַע מֵאוֹת וַחֲמִשִּׁים: 37 אֵלֶּה פְקוּדֵי מִשְׁפְּחֹת הַקְּהָתִי כָּל־הָעֹבֵד בְּאֹהֶל מוֹעֵד אֲשֶׁר פָּקַד מֹשֶׁה וְאַהֲרֹן עַל־פִּי יְהוָה בְּיַד־מֹשֶׁה: ס

and Aaron recorded at the command of the LORD through Moses.

38The Gershonites who were recorded by the clans of their ancestral house, 39from the age of thirty years up to the age of fifty, all who were subject to service for work relating to the Tent of Meeting—40those recorded by the clans of their ancestral house came to 2,630. 41That was the enrollment of the Gershonite clans, all those performing duties relating to the Tent of Meeting whom Moses and Aaron recorded at the command of the LORD.

42The enrollment of the Merarite clans by the clans of their ancestral house, 43from the age of thirty years up to the age of fifty, all who were subject to service for work relating to the Tent of Meeting—44those recorded by their clans came to 3,200. 45That was the enrollment of the Merarite clans which Moses and Aaron recorded at the command of the LORD through Moses.

46All the Levites whom Moses, Aaron, and the chieftains of Israel recorded by the clans of their ancestral houses, 47from the age of thirty years up to the age of fifty, all who were subject to duties of service and porterage relating to the Tent of Meeting—48those recorded came to 8,580. 49Each one was given responsibility for his service and porterage at the command of the LORD through Moses, and each was recorded as the LORD had commanded Moses.

5 The LORD spoke to Moses, saying: 2Instruct the Israelites to remove from camp anyone with an *a*-eruption or a discharge-*a* and anyone defiled by a corpse. 3Remove male and female alike; put them outside the camp so that they do not defile the camp of those in whose midst I dwell.

---

a-a See Lev. 13, 15.

38 וּפְקוּדֵי בְּנֵי גֵרְשׁוֹן לְמִשְׁפְּחוֹתָם וּלְבֵית אֲבֹתָם: 39 מִבֶּן שְׁלֹשִׁים שָׁנָה וָמַעְלָה וְעַד בֶּן־חֲמִשִּׁים שָׁנָה כָּל־הַבָּא לַצָּבָא לַעֲבֹדָה בְּאֹהֶל מוֹעֵד: 40 וַיִּהְיוּ פְּקֻדֵיהֶם לְמִשְׁפְּחֹתָם לְבֵית אֲבֹתָם אַלְפַּיִם וְשֵׁשׁ מֵאוֹת וּשְׁלֹשִׁים: 41 אֵלֶּה פְקוּדֵי מִשְׁפְּחֹת בְּנֵי גֵרְשׁוֹן כָּל־הָעֹבֵד בְּאֹהֶל מוֹעֵד אֲשֶׁר פָּקַד מֹשֶׁה וְאַהֲרֹן עַל־פִּי יְהוָה:

42 וּפְקוּדֵי מִשְׁפְּחֹת בְּנֵי מְרָרִי לְמִשְׁפְּחֹתָם לְבֵית אֲבֹתָם: 43 מִבֶּן שְׁלֹשִׁים שָׁנָה וָמַעְלָה וְעַד בֶּן־חֲמִשִּׁים שָׁנָה כָּל־הַבָּא לַצָּבָא לַעֲבֹדָה בְּאֹהֶל מוֹעֵד: 44 וַיִּהְיוּ פְקֻדֵיהֶם לְמִשְׁפְּחֹתָם שְׁלֹשֶׁת אֲלָפִים וּמָאתָיִם: 45 אֵלֶּה פְקוּדֵי מִשְׁפְּחֹת בְּנֵי מְרָרִי אֲשֶׁר פָּקַד מֹשֶׁה וְאַהֲרֹן עַל־פִּי יְהוָה בְּיַד־מֹשֶׁה:

46 כָּל־הַפְּקֻדִים אֲשֶׁר פָּקַד מֹשֶׁה וְאַהֲרֹן וּנְשִׂיאֵי יִשְׂרָאֵל אֶת־הַלְוִיִּם לְמִשְׁפְּחֹתָם וּלְבֵית אֲבֹתָם: 47 מִבֶּן שְׁלֹשִׁים שָׁנָה וָמַעְלָה וְעַד בֶּן־חֲמִשִּׁים שָׁנָה כָּל־הַבָּא לַעֲבֹד עֲבֹדַת עֲבֹדָה וַעֲבֹדַת מַשָּׂא בְּאֹהֶל מוֹעֵד: 48 וַיִּהְיוּ פְּקֻדֵיהֶם שְׁמֹנַת אֲלָפִים וַחֲמֵשׁ מֵאוֹת וּשְׁמֹנִים: 49 עַל־פִּי יְהוָה פָּקַד אוֹתָם בְּיַד־מֹשֶׁה אִישׁ אִישׁ עַל־עֲבֹדָתוֹ וְעַל־מַשָּׂאוֹ וּפְקֻדָיו אֲשֶׁר־צִוָּה יְהוָה אֶת־מֹשֶׁה: פ

ה וַיְדַבֵּר יְהוָה אֶל־מֹשֶׁה לֵּאמֹר: 2 צַו אֶת־בְּנֵי יִשְׂרָאֵל וִישַׁלְּחוּ מִן־הַמַּחֲנֶה כָּל־צָרוּעַ וְכָל־זָב וְכֹל טָמֵא לָנָפֶשׁ: 3 מִזָּכָר עַד־נְקֵבָה תְּשַׁלֵּחוּ אֶל־מִחוּץ לַמַּחֲנֶה תְּשַׁלְּחוּם וְלֹא יְטַמְּאוּ אֶת־מַחֲנֵיהֶם אֲשֶׁר אֲנִי שֹׁכֵן בְּתוֹכָם:

⁴The Israelites did so, putting them outside the camp; as the LORD had spoken to Moses, so the Israelites did.

⁵The LORD spoke to Moses, saying: ⁶Speak to the Israelites: When a man or woman commits any wrong toward a fellow man, thus breaking faith with the LORD, and that person realizes his guilt, ⁷he shall confess the wrong that he has done. He shall make restitution in the principal amount and add one-fifth to it, giving it to him whom he has wronged. ⁸If the man has no kinsman[b] to whom restitution can be made, the amount repaid shall go to the LORD for the priest—in addition to the ram of expiation with which expiation is made on his behalf.[c] ⁹So, too, any gift among the sacred donations that the Israelites offer shall be the priest's. ¹⁰And each shall retain his sacred donations: each priest shall keep what is given to him.

¹¹The LORD spoke to Moses, saying: ¹²Speak to the Israelite people and say to them:

If any man's wife has gone astray and broken faith with him ¹³in that a man has had carnal relations with her unbeknown to her husband, and she keeps secret the fact that she has defiled herself without being forced, and there is no witness against her—¹⁴but a fit of jealousy comes over him and he is wrought up about the wife who has defiled herself; or if a fit of jealousy comes over one and he is wrought up about his wife although she has not defiled herself—¹⁵the man shall bring his wife to the priest. And he shall bring as an offering for her one-tenth of an *ephah* of barley flour. No oil shall be poured upon it and no frankincense shall be laid on it, for it is a meal offering of jealousy, a meal offering of remembrance which recalls wrongdoing.

4 וַיַּעֲשׂוּ־כֵן בְּנֵי יִשְׂרָאֵל וַיְשַׁלְּחוּ אוֹתָם אֶל־מִחוּץ לַמַּחֲנֶה כַּאֲשֶׁר דִּבֶּר יְהֹוָה אֶל־מֹשֶׁה כֵּן עָשׂוּ בְּנֵי יִשְׂרָאֵל: פ

5 וַיְדַבֵּר יְהֹוָה אֶל־מֹשֶׁה לֵּאמֹר: 6 דַּבֵּר אֶל־בְּנֵי יִשְׂרָאֵל אִישׁ אוֹ־אִשָּׁה כִּי יַעֲשׂוּ מִכָּל־חַטֹּאת הָאָדָם לִמְעֹל מַעַל בַּיהֹוָה וְאָשְׁמָה הַנֶּפֶשׁ הַהִוא: 7 וְהִתְוַדּוּ אֶת־חַטָּאתָם אֲשֶׁר עָשׂוּ וְהֵשִׁיב אֶת־אֲשָׁמוֹ בְּרֹאשׁוֹ וַחֲמִישִׁתוֹ יֹסֵף עָלָיו וְנָתַן לַאֲשֶׁר אָשַׁם לוֹ: 8 וְאִם־אֵין לָאִישׁ גֹּאֵל לְהָשִׁיב הָאָשָׁם אֵלָיו הָאָשָׁם הַמּוּשָׁב לַיהֹוָה לַכֹּהֵן מִלְּבַד אֵיל הַכִּפֻּרִים אֲשֶׁר יְכַפֶּר־בּוֹ עָלָיו: 9 וְכָל־תְּרוּמָה לְכָל־קָדְשֵׁי בְנֵי־יִשְׂרָאֵל אֲשֶׁר־יַקְרִיבוּ לַכֹּהֵן לוֹ יִהְיֶה: 10 וְאִישׁ אֶת־קֳדָשָׁיו לוֹ יִהְיוּ אִישׁ אֲשֶׁר־יִתֵּן לַכֹּהֵן לוֹ יִהְיֶה: פ

11 וַיְדַבֵּר יְהֹוָה אֶל־מֹשֶׁה לֵּאמֹר: 12 דַּבֵּר אֶל־בְּנֵי יִשְׂרָאֵל וְאָמַרְתָּ אֲלֵהֶם אִישׁ אִישׁ כִּי־תִשְׂטֶה אִשְׁתּוֹ וּמָעֲלָה בוֹ מָעַל: 13 וְשָׁכַב אִישׁ אֹתָהּ שִׁכְבַת־זֶרַע וְנֶעְלַם מֵעֵינֵי אִישָׁהּ וְנִסְתְּרָה וְהִיא נִטְמָאָה וְעֵד אֵין בָּהּ וְהִוא לֹא נִתְפָּשָׂה: 14 וְעָבַר עָלָיו רוּחַ־קִנְאָה וְקִנֵּא אֶת־אִשְׁתּוֹ וְהִוא נִטְמָאָה אוֹ־עָבַר עָלָיו רוּחַ־קִנְאָה וְקִנֵּא אֶת־אִשְׁתּוֹ וְהִיא לֹא נִטְמָאָה: 15 וְהֵבִיא הָאִישׁ אֶת־אִשְׁתּוֹ אֶל־הַכֹּהֵן וְהֵבִיא אֶת־קָרְבָּנָהּ עָלֶיהָ עֲשִׂירִת הָאֵיפָה קֶמַח שְׂעֹרִים לֹא־יִצֹק עָלָיו שֶׁמֶן וְלֹא־יִתֵּן עָלָיו לְבֹנָה כִּי־מִנְחַת קְנָאֹת הוּא* מִנְחַת זִכָּרוֹן מַזְכֶּרֶת עָוֹן:

---

b Lit. "redeemer."
c Cf. Lev. 5.15 f.

סבירין ומטעין "הִיא"   v. 15.

16The priest shall bring her forward and have her stand before the LORD. 17The priest shall take sacral water in an earthen vessel and, taking some of the earth that is on the floor of the Tabernacle, the priest shall put it into the water. 18After he has made the woman stand before the LORD, the priest shall bare the woman's head[d] and place upon her hands the meal offering of remembrance, which is a meal offering of jealousy. And in the priest's hands shall be the water of bitterness [e-that induces the spell.-e] 19The priest shall adjure the woman, saying to her, "If no man has lain with you, if you have not gone astray in defilement while married to your husband, be immune to harm from this water of bitterness that induces the spell. 20But if you have gone astray while married to your husband and have defiled yourself, if a man other than your husband has had carnal relations with you"—21here the priest shall administer the curse of adjuration to the woman, as the priest goes on to say to the woman—"may the LORD make you a curse and an imprecation among your people, as the LORD causes your thigh to sag and your belly to distend; 22may this water that induces the spell enter your body, causing the belly to distend and the thigh to sag." And the woman shall say, "Amen, amen!"

23The priest shall put these curses down in writing and rub it off into the water of bitterness. 24He is to make the woman drink the water of bitterness that induces the spell, so that the spell-inducing water may enter into her to bring on bitterness. 25Then the priest shall take from the woman's hand the meal offering of jealousy, elevate the meal offering before the LORD, and present it on the altar. 26The priest shall scoop out of the meal offering a token part of it and turn it into smoke on the altar. Last, he shall make the woman drink the water.

16 וְהִקְרִיב אֹתָהּ הַכֹּהֵן וְהֶעֱמִדָהּ לִפְנֵי יְהוָה: 17 וְלָקַח הַכֹּהֵן מַיִם קְדֹשִׁים בִּכְלִי־חָרֶשׂ וּמִן־הֶעָפָר אֲשֶׁר יִהְיֶה בְּקַרְקַע הַמִּשְׁכָּן יִקַּח הַכֹּהֵן וְנָתַן אֶל־הַמָּיִם: 18 וְהֶעֱמִיד הַכֹּהֵן אֶת־הָאִשָּׁה לִפְנֵי יְהוָה וּפָרַע אֶת־רֹאשׁ הָאִשָּׁה וְנָתַן עַל־כַּפֶּיהָ אֵת מִנְחַת הַזִּכָּרוֹן מִנְחַת קְנָאֹת הִוא וּבְיַד הַכֹּהֵן יִהְיוּ מֵי הַמָּרִים הַמְאָרֲרִים: 19 וְהִשְׁבִּיעַ אֹתָהּ הַכֹּהֵן וְאָמַר אֶל־הָאִשָּׁה אִם־לֹא שָׁכַב אִישׁ אֹתָךְ וְאִם־לֹא שָׂטִית טֻמְאָה תַּחַת אִישֵׁךְ הִנָּקִי מִמֵּי הַמָּרִים הַמְאָרֲרִים הָאֵלֶּה: 20 וְאַתְּ כִּי שָׂטִית תַּחַת אִישֵׁךְ וְכִי נִטְמֵאת וַיִּתֵּן אִישׁ בָּךְ אֶת־שְׁכָבְתּוֹ מִבַּלְעֲדֵי אִישֵׁךְ: 21 וְהִשְׁבִּיעַ הַכֹּהֵן אֶת־הָאִשָּׁה בִּשְׁבֻעַת הָאָלָה וְאָמַר הַכֹּהֵן לָאִשָּׁה יִתֵּן יְהוָה אוֹתָךְ לְאָלָה וְלִשְׁבֻעָה בְּתוֹךְ עַמֵּךְ בְּתֵת יְהוָה אֶת־יְרֵכֵךְ נֹפֶלֶת וְאֶת־בִּטְנֵךְ צָבָה: 22 וּבָאוּ הַמַּיִם הַמְאָרֲרִים הָאֵלֶּה בְּמֵעַיִךְ לַצְבּוֹת בֶּטֶן וְלַנְפִּל יָרֵךְ וְאָמְרָה הָאִשָּׁה אָמֵן | אָמֵן: 23 וְכָתַב אֶת־הָאָלֹת הָאֵלֶּה הַכֹּהֵן בַּסֵּפֶר וּמָחָה אֶל־מֵי הַמָּרִים: 24 וְהִשְׁקָה אֶת־הָאִשָּׁה אֶת־מֵי הַמָּרִים הַמְאָרֲרִים וּבָאוּ בָהּ הַמַּיִם הַמְאָרֲרִים לְמָרִים: 25 וְלָקַח הַכֹּהֵן מִיַּד הָאִשָּׁה אֵת מִנְחַת הַקְּנָאֹת וְהֵנִיף אֶת־הַמִּנְחָה לִפְנֵי יְהוָה וְהִקְרִיב אֹתָהּ אֶל־הַמִּזְבֵּחַ: 26 וְקָמַץ הַכֹּהֵן מִן־הַמִּנְחָה אֶת־אַזְכָּרָתָהּ וְהִקְטִיר הַמִּזְבֵּחָה וְאַחַר יַשְׁקֶה אֶת־הָאִשָּׁה אֶת־הַמָּיִם:

---

d   See note at Lev. 10.6.
e-e   Meaning of Heb. uncertain.

27Once he has made her drink the water—if she has defiled herself by breaking faith with her husband, the spell-inducing water shall enter into her to bring on bitterness, so that her belly shall distend and her thigh shall sag; and the woman shall become a curse among her people. 28But if the woman has not defiled herself and is pure, she shall be unharmed and able to retain seed.

29This is the ritual in cases of jealousy, when a woman goes astray while married to her husband and defiles herself, 30or when a fit of jealousy comes over a man and he is wrought up over his wife: the woman shall be made to stand before the Lord and the priest shall carry out all this ritual with her. 31The man shall be clear of guilt; but that woman shall suffer for her guilt.

6 The Lord spoke to Moses, saying: 2Speak to the Israelites and say to them: If anyone, man or woman, explicitly^a utters a nazirite's vow, to set himself apart for the Lord, 3he shall abstain from wine and any other intoxicant; he shall not drink vinegar of wine or of any other intoxicant, neither shall he drink anything in which grapes have been steeped, nor eat grapes fresh or dried. 4Throughout his term as nazirite, he may not eat anything that is obtained from the grapevine, even seeds or skin.^{b}

5Throughout the term of his vow as nazirite, no razor shall touch his head; it shall remain consecrated until the completion of his term as nazirite of the Lord, the hair of his head being left to grow untrimmed. 6Throughout the term that he has set apart for the Lord, he shall not go in where there is a dead person. 7Even if his father or mother, or his brother or sister should die, he must not defile himself for them, since

27 וְהִשְׁקָהּ אֶת־הַמַּיִם וְהָיְתָה אִם־נִטְמְאָה וַתִּמְעֹל מַעַל בְּאִישָׁהּ וּבָאוּ בָהּ הַמַּיִם הַמְאָרְרִים לְמָרִים וְצָבְתָה בִטְנָהּ וְנָפְלָה יְרֵכָהּ וְהָיְתָה הָאִשָּׁה לְאָלָה בְּקֶרֶב עַמָּהּ: 28 וְאִם־לֹא נִטְמְאָה הָאִשָּׁה וּטְהֹרָה הִוא וְנִקְּתָה וְנִזְרְעָה זָרַע: 29 זֹאת תּוֹרַת הַקְּנָאֹת אֲשֶׁר תִּשְׂטֶה אִשָּׁה תַּחַת אִישָׁהּ וְנִטְמָאָה: 30 אוֹ אִישׁ אֲשֶׁר תַּעֲבֹר עָלָיו רוּחַ קִנְאָה וְקִנֵּא אֶת־אִשְׁתּוֹ וְהֶעֱמִיד אֶת־הָאִשָּׁה לִפְנֵי יְהֹוָה וְעָשָׂה לָהּ הַכֹּהֵן אֵת כָּל־הַתּוֹרָה הַזֹּאת: 31 וְנִקָּה הָאִישׁ מֵעָו‍ֹן וְהָאִשָּׁה הַהִוא תִּשָּׂא אֶת־עֲוֺנָהּ: פ

2 וַיְדַבֵּר יְהֹוָה אֶל־מֹשֶׁה לֵּאמֹר: דַּבֵּר אֶל־בְּנֵי יִשְׂרָאֵל וְאָמַרְתָּ אֲלֵהֶם אִישׁ אוֹ־אִשָּׁה כִּי יַפְלִא לִנְדֹּר נֶדֶר נָזִיר לְהַזִּיר לַיהֹוָה: 3 מִיַּיִן וְשֵׁכָר יַזִּיר חֹמֶץ יַיִן וְחֹמֶץ שֵׁכָר לֹא יִשְׁתֶּה וְכָל־מִשְׁרַת עֲנָבִים לֹא יִשְׁתֶּה וַעֲנָבִים לַחִים וִיבֵשִׁים לֹא יֹאכֵל: 4 כֹּל יְמֵי נִזְרוֹ מִכֹּל אֲשֶׁר יֵעָשֶׂה מִגֶּפֶן הַיַּיִן מֵחַרְצַנִּים וְעַד־זָג לֹא יֹאכֵל: 5 כָּל־יְמֵי נֶדֶר נִזְרוֹ תַּעַר לֹא־יַעֲבֹר עַל־רֹאשׁוֹ עַד־מְלֹאת הַיָּמִם אֲשֶׁר־יַזִּיר לַיהֹוָה קָדֹשׁ יִהְיֶה גַּדֵּל פֶּרַע שְׂעַר רֹאשׁוֹ: 6 כָּל־יְמֵי הַזִּירוֹ לַיהֹוָה עַל־נֶפֶשׁ מֵת לֹא יָבֹא: 7 לְאָבִיו וּלְאִמּוֹ לְאָחִיו וּלְאַחֹתוֹ לֹא יִטַּמָּא לָהֶם בְּמֹתָם כִּי נֵזֶר אֱלֹהָיו עַל־

_____
a　See note at Lev. 22.21.
b　Meaning of Heb. ḥarṣannim and zag uncertain.

c-hair set apart for his God-c is upon his head: 8throughout his term as nazirite he is consecrated to the LORD.

9If a person dies suddenly near him,d defiling his consecrated hair, he shall shave his head on the day he becomes clean; he shall shave it on the seventh day. 10On the eighth day he shall bring two turtledoves or two pigeons to the priest, at the entrance of the Tent of Meeting. 11The priest shall offer one as a sin offering and the other as a burnt offering, and make expiation on his behalf for the guilt that he incurred through the corpse. That same day he shall reconsecrate his head 12and rededicate to the LORD his term as nazirite; and he shall bring a lamb in its first year as a penalty offering. The previous period shall be void, since his consecrated hair was defiled.

13This is the ritual for the nazirite: On the day that his term as nazirite is completed, hee shall be brought to the entrance of the Tent of Meeting. 14As his offering to the LORD he shall present: one male lamb in its first year, without blemish, for a burnt offering; one ewe lamb in its first year, without blemish, for a sin offering; one ram without blemish for an offering of well-being; 15a basket of unleavened cakes of choice flour with oil mixed in, and unleavened wafers spread with oil; and the proper meal offerings and libations.

16The priest shall present them before the LORD and offer the sin offering and the burnt offering. 17He shall offer the ram as a sacrifice of well-being to the LORD, together with the basket of unleavened cakes; the priest shall also offer the meal offerings and the libations. 18The nazirite shall then shave his consecrated hair, at the entrance of the Tent of Meeting, and take the locks of his consecrated hair and put them

רֹאשֽׁוֹ׃ 8 כֹּ֖ל יְמֵ֣י נִזְר֑וֹ קָדֹ֥שׁ ה֖וּא לַיהוָֽה׃ 9 וְכִֽי־יָמ֨וּת מֵ֤ת עָלָיו֙ בְּפֶ֣תַע פִּתְאֹ֔ם וְטִמֵּ֖א רֹ֣אשׁ נִזְר֑וֹ וְגִלַּ֤ח רֹאשׁוֹ֙ בְּי֣וֹם טׇהֳרָת֔וֹ בַּיּ֥וֹם הַשְּׁבִיעִ֖י יְגַלְּחֶֽנּוּ׃ 10 וּבַיּ֣וֹם הַשְּׁמִינִ֗י יָבִא֙ שְׁתֵּ֣י תֹרִ֔ים א֥וֹ שְׁנֵ֖י בְּנֵ֣י יוֹנָ֑ה אֶל־הַ֨כֹּהֵ֔ן אֶל־פֶּ֖תַח אֹ֥הֶל מוֹעֵֽד׃ 11 וְעָשָׂ֣ה הַכֹּהֵ֗ן אֶחָ֤ד לְחַטָּאת֙ וְאֶחָ֣ד לְעֹלָ֔ה וְכִפֶּ֣ר עָלָ֔יו מֵאֲשֶׁ֥ר חָטָ֖א עַל־הַנָּ֑פֶשׁ וְקִדַּ֥שׁ אֶת־רֹאשׁ֖וֹ בַּיּ֥וֹם הַהֽוּא׃ 12 וְהִזִּ֤יר לַֽיהוָה֙ אֶת־יְמֵ֣י נִזְר֔וֹ וְהֵבִ֛יא כֶּ֥בֶשׂ בֶּן־שְׁנָת֖וֹ לְאָשָׁ֑ם וְהַיָּמִ֤ים הָרִֽאשֹׁנִים֙ יִפְּל֔וּ כִּ֥י טָמֵ֖א נִזְרֽוֹ׃ 13 וְזֹ֥את תּוֹרַ֖ת הַנָּזִ֑יר בְּי֗וֹם מְלֹאת֙ יְמֵ֣י נִזְר֔וֹ יָבִ֣יא אֹת֔וֹ אֶל־פֶּ֖תַח אֹ֥הֶל מוֹעֵֽד׃ 14 וְהִקְרִ֣יב אֶת־קׇרְבָּנ֣וֹ לַיהוָ֡ה כֶּ֩בֶשׂ֩ בֶּן־שְׁנָת֨וֹ תָמִ֤ים אֶחָד֙ לְעֹלָ֔ה וְכַבְשָׂ֨ה אַחַ֧ת בַּת־שְׁנָתָ֛הּ תְּמִימָ֖ה לְחַטָּ֑את וְאַֽיִל־אֶחָ֥ד תָּמִ֖ים לִשְׁלָמִֽים׃ 15 וְסַ֣ל מַצּ֗וֹת סֹ֤לֶת חַלֹּת֙ בְּלוּלֹ֣ת בַּשֶּׁ֔מֶן וּרְקִיקֵ֥י מַצּ֖וֹת מְשֻׁחִ֣ים בַּשָּׁ֑מֶן וּמִנְחָתָ֖ם וְנִסְכֵּיהֶֽם׃ 16 וְהִקְרִ֥יב הַכֹּהֵ֖ן לִפְנֵ֣י יְהוָ֑ה וְעָשָׂ֥ה אֶת־חַטָּאת֖וֹ וְאֶת־עֹלָתֽוֹ׃ 17 וְאֶת־הָאַ֜יִל יַעֲשֶׂ֤ה זֶ֣בַח שְׁלָמִים֙ לַֽיהוָ֔ה עַ֖ל סַ֣ל הַמַּצּ֑וֹת וְעָשָׂה֙ הַכֹּהֵ֔ן אֶת־מִנְחָת֖וֹ וְאֶת־נִסְכּֽוֹ׃ 18 וְגִלַּ֣ח הַנָּזִ֗יר פֶּ֛תַח אֹ֥הֶל מוֹעֵ֖ד אֶת־רֹ֣אשׁ נִזְר֑וֹ וְלָקַ֗ח אֶת־שְׂעַר֙ רֹ֣אשׁ נִזְר֔וֹ וְנָתַן֙ עַל־הָאֵ֔שׁ אֲשֶׁר־תַּ֖חַת זֶ֥בַח הַשְּׁלָמִֽים׃

---

c-c　Others "his consecration unto God."
d　Cf. Num. 19.14–16.
e　Or "it," i.e., the consecrated hair; cf. v. 19.

on the fire that is under the sacrifice of well-being.

¹⁹The priest shall take the shoulder of the ram when it has been boiled, one unleavened cake from the basket, and one unleavened wafer, and place them on the hands of the nazirite after he has shaved his consecrated hair. ²⁰The priest shall elevate them as an elevation offering before the LORD; and this shall be a sacred donation for the priest, in addition to the breast of the elevation offering and the thigh of gift offering. After that the nazirite may drink wine.

²¹Such is the obligation of a nazirite; except that he who vows an offering to the LORD of what he can afford, beyond his nazirite requirements, must do exactly according to the vow that he has made beyond his obligation as a nazirite.

²²The LORD spoke to Moses: ²³Speak to Aaron and his sons: Thus shall you bless the people of Israel. Say to them:

²⁴The LORD bless you and protect you!

²⁵The LORD f-deal kindly and graciously with you!-f

²⁶The LORD g-bestow His favor-g upon you and grant you peace!ʰ

²⁷Thus they shall link My name with the people of Israel, and I will bless them.

7 On the day that Moses finished setting up the Tabernacle, he anointed and consecrated it and all its furnishings, as well as the altar and its utensils. When he had anointed and consecrated them, ²the chieftains of Israel, the heads of ancestral houses, namely, the chieftains of the tribes, those who were in charge of enrollment,

19 וְלָקַח הַכֹּהֵן אֶת־הַזְּרֹעַ בְּשֵׁלָה מִן־הָאַיִל וְחַלַּת מַצָּה אַחַת מִן־הַסַּל וּרְקִיק מַצָּה אֶחָד וְנָתַן עַל־כַּפֵּי הַנָּזִיר אַחַר הִתְגַּלְּחוֹ אֶת־נִזְרוֹ: 20 וְהֵנִיף אוֹתָם הַכֹּהֵן ׀ תְּנוּפָה לִפְנֵי יְהוָה קֹדֶשׁ הוּא לַכֹּהֵן עַל חֲזֵה הַתְּנוּפָה וְעַל שׁוֹק הַתְּרוּמָה וְאַחַר יִשְׁתֶּה הַנָּזִיר יָיִן: 21 זֹאת תּוֹרַת הַנָּזִיר אֲשֶׁר יִדֹּר קָרְבָּנוֹ לַיהוָה עַל־נִזְרוֹ מִלְּבַד אֲשֶׁר־תַּשִּׂיג יָדוֹ כְּפִי נִדְרוֹ אֲשֶׁר יִדֹּר כֵּן יַעֲשֶׂה עַל תּוֹרַת נִזְרוֹ: פ

22 וַיְדַבֵּר יְהוָה אֶל־מֹשֶׁה לֵּאמֹר: 23 דַּבֵּר אֶל־אַהֲרֹן וְאֶל־בָּנָיו לֵאמֹר כֹּה תְבָרֲכוּ אֶת־בְּנֵי יִשְׂרָאֵל אָמוֹר לָהֶם: ס

24 יְבָרֶכְךָ יְהוָה וְיִשְׁמְרֶךָ: ס

25 יָאֵר יְהוָה ׀ פָּנָיו אֵלֶיךָ וִיחֻנֶּךָּ: ס

26 יִשָּׂא יְהוָה ׀ פָּנָיו אֵלֶיךָ וְיָשֵׂם לְךָ שָׁלוֹם: ס

27 וְשָׂמוּ אֶת־שְׁמִי עַל־בְּנֵי יִשְׂרָאֵל וַאֲנִי אֲבָרֲכֵם: פ

ז 1 וַיְהִי בְּיוֹם כַּלּוֹת מֹשֶׁה לְהָקִים אֶת־הַמִּשְׁכָּן וַיִּמְשַׁח אֹתוֹ וַיְקַדֵּשׁ אֹתוֹ וְאֶת־כָּל־כֵּלָיו וְאֶת־הַמִּזְבֵּחַ וְאֶת־כָּל־כֵּלָיו וַיִּמְשָׁחֵם וַיְקַדֵּשׁ אֹתָם: 2 וַיַּקְרִיבוּ נְשִׂיאֵי יִשְׂרָאֵל רָאשֵׁי בֵּית אֲבֹתָם הֵם נְשִׂיאֵי הַמַּטֹּת הֵם הָעֹמְדִים עַל־הַפְּקֻדִים:

---

f-f   Others "make His face to shine upon thee and be gracious to thee."

g-g   Others "lift up His countenance."

h   Or "friendship."

drew near[a] 3and brought their offering before the LORD: six draught carts and twelve oxen, a cart for every two chieftains and an ox for each one.

When they had brought them before the Tabernacle, 4the LORD said to Moses: 5Accept these from them for use in the service of the Tent of Meeting, and give them to the Levites according to their respective services.

6Moses took the carts and the oxen and gave them to the Levites. 7Two carts and four oxen he gave to the Gershonites, as required for their service, 8and four carts and eight oxen he gave to the Merarites, as required for their service—under the direction of Ithamar son of Aaron the priest. 9But to the Kohathites he did not give any; since theirs was the service of the [most] sacred objects, their porterage was by shoulder.

10The chieftains also brought the dedication offering for the altar upon its being anointed. As the chieftains were presenting their offerings before the altar, 11the LORD said to Moses: Let them present their offerings for the dedication of the altar, one chieftain each day.

12The one who presented his offering on the first day was Nahshon son of Amminadab of the tribe of Judah. 13His offering: one silver bowl weighing 130 shekels and one silver basin of 70 shekels by the sanctuary weight, both filled with choice flour with oil mixed in, for a meal offering; 14one gold ladle of 10 shekels, filled with incense; 15one bull of the herd, one ram, and one lamb in its first year, for a burnt offering; 16one goat for a sin offering; 17and for his sacrifice of well-being: two oxen, five rams, five he-goats, and five yearling lambs. That was the offering of Nahshon son of Amminadab.

18On the second day, Nethanel son of Zuar, chieftain of Issachar, made his offering. 19He presented as his offering: one silver bowl weigh-

3 וַיָּבִ֨יאוּ אֶת־קָרְבָּנָ֜ם לִפְנֵ֣י יְהוָ֗ה שֵׁשׁ־עֶגְלֹ֥ת צָב֙ וּשְׁנֵ֣י עָשָׂ֣ר בָּקָ֔ר עֲגָלָ֛ה עַל־שְׁנֵ֥י הַנְּשִׂאִ֖ים וְשׁ֣וֹר לְאֶחָ֑ד וַיַּקְרִ֥יבוּ אוֹתָ֖ם לִפְנֵ֥י הַמִּשְׁכָּֽן: 4 וַיֹּ֥אמֶר יְהוָ֖ה אֶל־מֹשֶׁ֥ה לֵּאמֹֽר: 5 קַ֚ח מֵֽאִתָּ֔ם וְהָי֕וּ לַעֲבֹ֕ד אֶת־עֲבֹדַ֖ת אֹ֣הֶל מוֹעֵ֑ד וְנָתַתָּ֤ה אוֹתָם֙ אֶל־הַלְוִיִּ֔ם אִ֖ישׁ כְּפִ֥י עֲבֹדָתֽוֹ: 6 וַיִּקַּ֣ח מֹשֶׁ֔ה אֶת־הָעֲגָלֹ֖ת וְאֶת־הַבָּקָ֑ר וַיִּתֵּ֥ן אוֹתָ֖ם אֶל־הַלְוִיִּֽם: 7 אֵ֣ת ׀ שְׁתֵּ֣י הָעֲגָלֹ֗ת וְאֵת֙ אַרְבַּ֣עַת הַבָּקָ֔ר נָתַ֖ן לִבְנֵ֣י גֵרְשׁ֑וֹן כְּפִ֖י עֲבֹדָתָֽם: 8 וְאֵ֣ת ׀ אַרְבַּ֣ע הָעֲגָלֹ֗ת וְאֵת֙ שְׁמֹנַ֣ת הַבָּקָ֔ר נָתַ֖ן לִבְנֵ֣י מְרָרִ֑י כְּפִי֙ עֲבֹ֣דָתָ֔ם בְּיַד֙ אִֽיתָמָ֔ר בֶּֽן־אַהֲרֹ֖ן הַכֹּהֵֽן: 9 וְלִבְנֵ֥י קְהָ֖ת לֹ֣א נָתָ֑ן כִּֽי־עֲבֹדַ֤ת הַקֹּ֙דֶשׁ֙ עֲלֵהֶ֔ם בַּכָּתֵ֖ף יִשָּֽׂאוּ: 10 וַיַּקְרִ֣יבוּ הַנְּשִׂאִ֗ים אֵ֚ת חֲנֻכַּ֣ת הַמִּזְבֵּ֔חַ בְּי֖וֹם הִמָּשַׁ֣ח אֹת֑וֹ וַיַּקְרִ֧יבוּ הַנְּשִׂיאִ֛ם אֶת־קָרְבָּנָ֖ם לִפְנֵ֥י הַמִּזְבֵּֽחַ: 11 וַיֹּ֥אמֶר יְהוָ֖ה אֶל־מֹשֶׁ֑ה נָשִׂ֞יא אֶחָ֣ד לַיּ֗וֹם נָשִׂ֤יא אֶחָד֙ לַיּ֔וֹם יַקְרִ֙יבוּ֙ אֶת־קָרְבָּנָ֔ם לַחֲנֻכַּ֖ת הַמִּזְבֵּֽחַ: ס

12 וַיְהִ֗י הַמַּקְרִ֛יב בַּיּ֥וֹם הָרִאשׁ֖וֹן אֶת־קָרְבָּנ֑וֹ נַחְשׁ֥וֹן בֶּן־עַמִּינָדָ֖ב לְמַטֵּ֥ה יְהוּדָֽה: 13 וְקָרְבָּנ֞וֹ קַֽעֲרַת־כֶּ֣סֶף אַחַ֗ת שְׁלֹשִׁ֣ים וּמֵאָה֮ מִשְׁקָלָהּ֒ מִזְרָ֤ק אֶחָד֙ כֶּ֔סֶף שִׁבְעִ֥ים שֶׁ֖קֶל בְּשֶׁ֣קֶל הַקֹּ֑דֶשׁ שְׁנֵיהֶ֣ם ׀ מְלֵאִ֗ים סֹ֛לֶת בְּלוּלָ֥ה בַשֶּׁ֖מֶן לְמִנְחָֽה: 14 כַּ֚ף אַחַ֣ת עֲשָׂרָ֣ה זָהָ֔ב מְלֵאָ֖ה קְטֹֽרֶת: 15 פַּ֣ר אֶחָ֞ד בֶּן־בָּקָ֗ר אַ֧יִל אֶחָ֛ד כֶּֽבֶשׂ־אֶחָ֥ד בֶּן־שְׁנָת֖וֹ לְעֹלָֽה: 16 שְׂעִיר־עִזִּ֥ים אֶחָ֖ד לְחַטָּֽאת: 17 וּלְזֶ֣בַח הַשְּׁלָמִים֮ בָּקָ֣ר שְׁנַיִם֒ אֵילִ֤ם חֲמִשָּׁה֙ עַתּוּדִ֣ים חֲמִשָּׁ֔ה כְּבָשִׂ֥ים בְּנֵֽי־שָׁנָ֖ה חֲמִשָּׁ֑ה זֶ֛ה קָרְבַּ֥ן נַחְשׁ֖וֹן בֶּן־עַמִּינָדָֽב: פ

18 בַּיּוֹם֙ הַשֵּׁנִ֔י הִקְרִ֖יב נְתַנְאֵ֣ל בֶּן־צוּעָ֑ר נְשִׂ֖יא יִשָּׂשכָֽר: 19 הִקְרִ֥ב אֶת־קָרְבָּנ֖וֹ

---

a Cf. Exod. 14.10.

ing 130 shekels and one silver basin of 70 shekels by the sanctuary weight, both filled with choice flour with oil mixed in, for a meal offering; 20one gold ladle of 10 shekels, filled with incense; 21one bull of the herd, one ram, and one lamb in its first year, for a burnt offering; 22one goat for a sin offering; 23and for his sacrifice of well-being: two oxen, five rams, five he-goats, and five yearling lambs. That was the offering of Nethanel son of Zuar.

24On the third day, it was the chieftain of the Zebulunites, Eliab son of Helon. 25His offering: one silver bowl weighing 130 shekels and one silver basin of 70 shekels by the sanctuary weight, both filled with choice flour with oil mixed in, for a meal offering; 26one gold ladle of 10 shekels, filled with incense; 27one bull of the herd, one ram, and one lamb in its first year, for a burnt offering; 28one goat for a sin offering; 29and for his sacrifice of well-being: two oxen, five rams, five he-goats, and five yearling lambs. That was the offering of Eliab son of Helon.

30On the fourth day, it was the chieftain of the Reubenites, Elizur son of Shedeur. 31His offering: one silver bowl weighing 130 shekels and one silver basin of 70 shekels by the sanctuary weight, both filled with choice flour with oil mixed in, for a meal offering; 32one gold ladle of 10 shekels, filled with incense; 33one bull of the herd, one ram, and one lamb in its first year, for a burnt offering; 34one goat for a sin offering; 35and for his sacrifice of well-being: two oxen, five rams, five he-goats, and five yearling lambs. That was the offering of Elizur son of Shedeur.

36On the fifth day, it was the chieftain of the Simeonites, Shelumiel son of Zurishaddai. 37His offering: one silver bowl weighing 130 shekels and one silver basin of 70 shekels by the sanctuary weight, both filled with choice flour

קַעֲרַת־כֶּסֶף אַחַת שְׁלֹשִׁים וּמֵאָה מִשְׁקָלָהּ מִזְרָק אֶחָד כֶּסֶף שִׁבְעִים שֶׁקֶל בְּשֶׁקֶל הַקֹּדֶשׁ שְׁנֵיהֶם ׀ מְלֵאִים סֹלֶת בְּלוּלָה בַשֶּׁמֶן לְמִנְחָה: 20 כַּף אַחַת עֲשָׂרָה זָהָב מְלֵאָה קְטֹרֶת: 21 פַּר אֶחָד בֶּן־בָּקָר אַיִל אֶחָד כֶּבֶשׂ־אֶחָד בֶּן־שְׁנָתוֹ לְעֹלָה: 22 שְׂעִיר־עִזִּים אֶחָד לְחַטָּאת: 23 וּלְזֶבַח הַשְּׁלָמִים בָּקָר שְׁנַיִם אֵילִם חֲמִשָּׁה עַתֻּדִים חֲמִשָּׁה כְּבָשִׂים בְּנֵי־שָׁנָה חֲמִשָּׁה זֶה קָרְבַּן נְתַנְאֵל בֶּן־צוּעָר: פ
24 בַּיּוֹם הַשְּׁלִישִׁי נָשִׂיא לִבְנֵי זְבוּלֻן אֱלִיאָב בֶּן־חֵלֹן: 25 קָרְבָּנוֹ קַעֲרַת־כֶּסֶף אַחַת שְׁלֹשִׁים וּמֵאָה מִשְׁקָלָהּ מִזְרָק אֶחָד כֶּסֶף שִׁבְעִים שֶׁקֶל בְּשֶׁקֶל הַקֹּדֶשׁ שְׁנֵיהֶם ׀ מְלֵאִים סֹלֶת בְּלוּלָה בַשֶּׁמֶן לְמִנְחָה: 26 כַּף אַחַת עֲשָׂרָה זָהָב מְלֵאָה קְטֹרֶת: 27 פַּר אֶחָד בֶּן־בָּקָר אַיִל אֶחָד כֶּבֶשׂ־אֶחָד בֶּן־שְׁנָתוֹ לְעֹלָה: 28 שְׂעִיר־עִזִּים אֶחָד לְחַטָּאת: 29 וּלְזֶבַח הַשְּׁלָמִים בָּקָר שְׁנַיִם אֵילִם חֲמִשָּׁה עַתֻּדִים חֲמִשָּׁה כְּבָשִׂים בְּנֵי־שָׁנָה חֲמִשָּׁה זֶה קָרְבַּן אֱלִיאָב בֶּן־חֵלֹן: פ
30 בַּיּוֹם הָרְבִיעִי נָשִׂיא לִבְנֵי רְאוּבֵן אֱלִיצוּר בֶּן־שְׁדֵיאוּר: 31 קָרְבָּנוֹ קַעֲרַת־כֶּסֶף אַחַת שְׁלֹשִׁים וּמֵאָה מִשְׁקָלָהּ מִזְרָק אֶחָד כֶּסֶף שִׁבְעִים שֶׁקֶל בְּשֶׁקֶל הַקֹּדֶשׁ שְׁנֵיהֶם ׀ מְלֵאִים סֹלֶת בְּלוּלָה בַשֶּׁמֶן לְמִנְחָה: 32 כַּף אַחַת עֲשָׂרָה זָהָב מְלֵאָה קְטֹרֶת: 33 פַּר אֶחָד בֶּן־בָּקָר אַיִל אֶחָד כֶּבֶשׂ־אֶחָד בֶּן־שְׁנָתוֹ לְעֹלָה: 34 שְׂעִיר־עִזִּים אֶחָד לְחַטָּאת: 35 וּלְזֶבַח הַשְּׁלָמִים בָּקָר שְׁנַיִם אֵילִם חֲמִשָּׁה עַתֻּדִים חֲמִשָּׁה כְּבָשִׂים בְּנֵי־שָׁנָה חֲמִשָּׁה זֶה קָרְבַּן אֱלִיצוּר בֶּן־שְׁדֵיאוּר: פ
36 בַּיּוֹם הַחֲמִישִׁי נָשִׂיא לִבְנֵי שִׁמְעוֹן שְׁלֻמִיאֵל בֶּן־צוּרִישַׁדָּי: 37 קָרְבָּנוֹ קַעֲרַת־

with oil mixed in, for a meal offering; ³⁸one gold ladle of 10 shekels, filled with incense; ³⁹one bull of the herd, one ram, and one lamb in its first year, for a burnt offering; ⁴⁰one goat for a sin offering; ⁴¹and for his sacrifice of well-being: two oxen, five rams, five he-goats, and five yearling lambs. That was the offering of Shelumiel son of Zurishaddai.

⁴²On the sixth day, it was the chieftain of the Gadites, Eliasaph son of Deuel. ⁴³His offering: one silver bowl weighing 130 shekels and one silver basin of 70 shekels by the sanctuary weight, both filled with choice flour with oil mixed in, for a meal offering; ⁴⁴one gold ladle of 10 shekels, filled with incense; ⁴⁵one bull of the herd, one ram, and one lamb in its first year, for a burnt offering; ⁴⁶one goat for a sin offering; ⁴⁷and for his sacrifice of well-being: two oxen, five rams, five he-goats, and five yearling lambs. That was the offering of Eliasaph son of Deuel.

⁴⁸On the seventh day, it was the chieftain of the Ephraimites, Elishama son of Ammihud. ⁴⁹His offering: one silver bowl weighing 130 shekels and one silver basin of 70 shekels by the sanctuary weight, both filled with choice flour with oil mixed in, for a meal offering; ⁵⁰one gold ladle of 10 shekels, filled with incense; ⁵¹one bull of the herd, one ram, and one lamb in its first year, for a burnt offering; ⁵²one goat for a sin offering; ⁵³and for his sacrifice of well-being: two oxen, five rams, five he-goats, and five yearling lambs. That was the offering of Elishama son of Ammihud.

⁵⁴On the eighth day, it was the chieftain of the Manassites, Gamaliel son of Pedahzur. ⁵⁵His

כֶּסֶף אַחַת שְׁלֹשִׁים וּמֵאָה מִשְׁקָלָהּ מִזְרָק אֶחָד כֶּסֶף שִׁבְעִים שֶׁקֶל בְּשֶׁקֶל הַקֹּדֶשׁ שְׁנֵיהֶם ׀ מְלֵאִים סֹלֶת בְּלוּלָה בַשֶּׁמֶן לְמִנְחָה: 38 כַּף אַחַת עֲשָׂרָה זָהָב מְלֵאָה קְטֹרֶת: 39 פַּר אֶחָד בֶּן־בָּקָר אַיִל אֶחָד כֶּבֶשׂ־אֶחָד בֶּן־שְׁנָתוֹ לְעֹלָה: 40 שְׂעִיר־עִזִּים אֶחָד לְחַטָּאת: 41 וּלְזֶבַח הַשְּׁלָמִים בָּקָר שְׁנַיִם אֵילִם חֲמִשָּׁה עַתֻּדִים חֲמִשָּׁה כְּבָשִׂים בְּנֵי־שָׁנָה חֲמִשָּׁה זֶה קָרְבַּן שְׁלֻמִיאֵל בֶּן־צוּרִישַׁדָּי: פ

42 בַּיּוֹם הַשִּׁשִּׁי נָשִׂיא לִבְנֵי גָד אֶלְיָסָף בֶּן־דְּעוּאֵל: 43 קָרְבָּנוֹ קַעֲרַת־כֶּסֶף אַחַת שְׁלֹשִׁים וּמֵאָה מִשְׁקָלָהּ מִזְרָק אֶחָד כֶּסֶף שִׁבְעִים שֶׁקֶל בְּשֶׁקֶל הַקֹּדֶשׁ שְׁנֵיהֶם ׀ מְלֵאִים סֹלֶת בְּלוּלָה בַשֶּׁמֶן לְמִנְחָה: 44 כַּף אַחַת עֲשָׂרָה זָהָב מְלֵאָה קְטֹרֶת: 45 פַּר אֶחָד בֶּן־בָּקָר אַיִל אֶחָד כֶּבֶשׂ־אֶחָד בֶּן־שְׁנָתוֹ לְעֹלָה: 46 שְׂעִיר־עִזִּים אֶחָד לְחַטָּאת: 47 וּלְזֶבַח הַשְּׁלָמִים בָּקָר שְׁנַיִם אֵילִם חֲמִשָּׁה עַתֻּדִים חֲמִשָּׁה כְּבָשִׂים בְּנֵי־שָׁנָה חֲמִשָּׁה זֶה קָרְבַּן אֶלְיָסָף בֶּן־דְּעוּאֵל: פ

48 בַּיּוֹם הַשְּׁבִיעִי נָשִׂיא לִבְנֵי אֶפְרָיִם אֱלִישָׁמָע בֶּן־עַמִּיהוּד: 49 קָרְבָּנוֹ קַעֲרַת־כֶּסֶף אַחַת שְׁלֹשִׁים וּמֵאָה מִשְׁקָלָהּ מִזְרָק אֶחָד כֶּסֶף שִׁבְעִים שֶׁקֶל בְּשֶׁקֶל הַקֹּדֶשׁ שְׁנֵיהֶם ׀ מְלֵאִים סֹלֶת בְּלוּלָה בַשֶּׁמֶן לְמִנְחָה: 50 כַּף אַחַת עֲשָׂרָה זָהָב מְלֵאָה קְטֹרֶת: 51 פַּר אֶחָד בֶּן־בָּקָר אַיִל אֶחָד כֶּבֶשׂ־אֶחָד בֶּן־שְׁנָתוֹ לְעֹלָה: 52 שְׂעִיר־עִזִּים אֶחָד לְחַטָּאת: 53 וּלְזֶבַח הַשְּׁלָמִים בָּקָר שְׁנַיִם אֵילִם חֲמִשָּׁה עַתֻּדִים חֲמִשָּׁה כְּבָשִׂים בְּנֵי־שָׁנָה חֲמִשָּׁה זֶה קָרְבַּן אֱלִישָׁמָע בֶּן־עַמִּיהוּד: פ

54 בַּיּוֹם הַשְּׁמִינִי נָשִׂיא לִבְנֵי מְנַשֶּׁה גַּמְלִיאֵל בֶּן־פְּדָהצוּר: 55 קָרְבָּנוֹ קַעֲרַת־

offering: one silver bowl weighing 130 shekels and one silver basin of 70 shekels by the sanctuary weight, both filled with choice flour with oil mixed in, for a meal offering; [56] one gold ladle of 10 shekels, filled with incense; [57] one bull of the herd, one ram, and one lamb in its first year, for a burnt offering; [58] one goat for a sin offering; [59] and for his sacrifice of well-being: two oxen, five rams, five he-goats, and five yearling lambs. That was the offering of Gamaliel son of Pedahzur.

[60] On the ninth day, it was the chieftain of the Benjaminites, Abidan son of Gideoni. [61] His offering: one silver bowl weighing 130 shekels and one silver basin of 70 shekels by the sanctuary weight, both filled with choice flour with oil mixed in, for a meal offering; [62] one gold ladle of 10 shekels, filled with incense; [63] one bull of the herd, one ram, and one lamb in its first year, for a burnt offering; [64] one goat for a sin offering; [65] and for his sacrifice of well-being: two oxen, five rams, five he-goats, and five yearling lambs. That was the offering of Abidan son of Gideoni.

[66] On the tenth day, it was the chieftain of the Danites, Ahiezer son of Ammishaddai. [67] His offering: one silver bowl weighing 130 shekels and one silver basin of 70 shekels by the sanctuary weight, both filled with choice flour with oil mixed in, for a meal offering; [68] one gold ladle of 10 shekels, filled with incense; [69] one bull of the herd, one ram, and one lamb in its first year, for a burnt offering; [70] one goat for a sin offering; [71] and for his sacrifice of well-being: two oxen, five rams, five he-goats, and five yearling lambs. That was the offering of Ahiezer son of Ammishaddai.

[72] On the eleventh day, it was the chieftain of the Asherites, Pagiel son of Ochran. [73] His offering: one silver bowl weighing 130 shekels

כֶּסֶף אַחַת שְׁלֹשִׁים וּמֵאָה מִשְׁקָלָהּ מִזְרָק אֶחָד כֶּסֶף שִׁבְעִים שֶׁקֶל בְּשֶׁקֶל הַקֹּדֶשׁ שְׁנֵיהֶם ׀ מְלֵאִים סֹלֶת בְּלוּלָה בַשֶּׁמֶן לְמִנְחָה: 56 כַּף אַחַת עֲשָׂרָה זָהָב מְלֵאָה קְטֹרֶת: 57 פַּר אֶחָד בֶּן־בָּקָר אַיִל אֶחָד כֶּבֶשׂ־אֶחָד בֶּן־שְׁנָתוֹ לְעֹלָה: 58 שְׂעִיר־עִזִּים אֶחָד לְחַטָּאת: 59 וּלְזֶבַח הַשְּׁלָמִים בָּקָר שְׁנַיִם אֵילִם חֲמִשָּׁה עַתֻּדִים חֲמִשָּׁה כְּבָשִׂים בְּנֵי־שָׁנָה חֲמִשָּׁה זֶה קָרְבַּן גַּמְלִיאֵל בֶּן־פְּדָהצוּר: פ

60 בַּיּוֹם הַתְּשִׁיעִי נָשִׂיא לִבְנֵי בִנְיָמִן אֲבִידָן בֶּן־גִּדְעֹנִי: 61 קָרְבָּנוֹ קַעֲרַת־כֶּסֶף אַחַת שְׁלֹשִׁים וּמֵאָה מִשְׁקָלָהּ מִזְרָק אֶחָד כֶּסֶף שִׁבְעִים שֶׁקֶל בְּשֶׁקֶל הַקֹּדֶשׁ שְׁנֵיהֶם ׀ מְלֵאִים סֹלֶת בְּלוּלָה בַשֶּׁמֶן לְמִנְחָה: 62 כַּף אַחַת עֲשָׂרָה זָהָב מְלֵאָה קְטֹרֶת: 63 פַּר אֶחָד בֶּן־בָּקָר אַיִל אֶחָד כֶּבֶשׂ־אֶחָד בֶּן־שְׁנָתוֹ לְעֹלָה: 64 שְׂעִיר־עִזִּים אֶחָד לְחַטָּאת: 65 וּלְזֶבַח הַשְּׁלָמִים בָּקָר שְׁנַיִם אֵילִם חֲמִשָּׁה עַתֻּדִים חֲמִשָּׁה כְּבָשִׂים בְּנֵי־שָׁנָה חֲמִשָּׁה זֶה קָרְבַּן אֲבִידָן בֶּן־גִּדְעֹנִי: פ

66 בַּיּוֹם הָעֲשִׂירִי נָשִׂיא לִבְנֵי דָן אֲחִיעֶזֶר בֶּן־עַמִּישַׁדָּי: 67 קָרְבָּנוֹ קַעֲרַת־כֶּסֶף אַחַת שְׁלֹשִׁים וּמֵאָה מִשְׁקָלָהּ מִזְרָק אֶחָד כֶּסֶף שִׁבְעִים שֶׁקֶל בְּשֶׁקֶל הַקֹּדֶשׁ שְׁנֵיהֶם ׀ מְלֵאִים סֹלֶת בְּלוּלָה בַשֶּׁמֶן לְמִנְחָה: 68 כַּף אַחַת עֲשָׂרָה זָהָב מְלֵאָה קְטֹרֶת: 69 פַּר אֶחָד בֶּן־בָּקָר אַיִל אֶחָד כֶּבֶשׂ־אֶחָד בֶּן־שְׁנָתוֹ לְעֹלָה: 70 שְׂעִיר־עִזִּים אֶחָד לְחַטָּאת: 71 וּלְזֶבַח הַשְּׁלָמִים בָּקָר שְׁנַיִם אֵילִם חֲמִשָּׁה עַתֻּדִים חֲמִשָּׁה כְּבָשִׂים בְּנֵי־שָׁנָה חֲמִשָּׁה זֶה קָרְבַּן אֲחִיעֶזֶר בֶּן־עַמִּישַׁדָּי: פ

72 בְּיוֹם עַשְׁתֵּי עָשָׂר יוֹם נָשִׂיא לִבְנֵי אָשֵׁר פַּגְעִיאֵל בֶּן־עָכְרָן: 73 קָרְבָּנוֹ קַעֲרַת־כֶּסֶף

and one silver basin of 70 shekels by the sanctuary weight, both filled with choice flour with oil mixed in, for a meal offering; ⁷⁴one gold ladle of 10 shekels, filled with incense; ⁷⁵one bull of the herd, one ram, and one lamb in its first year, for a burnt offering; ⁷⁶one goat for a sin offering; ⁷⁷and for his sacrifice of well-being: two oxen, five rams, five he-goats, and five yearling lambs. That was the offering of Pagiel son of Ochran.

⁷⁸On the twelfth day, it was the chieftain of the Naphtalites, Ahira son of Enan. ⁷⁹His offering: one silver bowl weighing 130 shekels and one silver basin of 70 shekels by the sanctuary weight, both filled with choice flour with oil mixed in, for a meal offering; ⁸⁰one gold ladle of 10 shekels, filled with incense; ⁸¹one bull of the herd, one ram, and one lamb in its first year, for a burnt offering; ⁸²one goat for a sin offering; ⁸³and for his sacrifice of well-being: two oxen, five rams, five he-goats, and five yearling lambs. That was the offering of Ahira son of Enan.

⁸⁴This was the dedication offering for the altar from the chieftains of Israel upon its being anointed: silver bowls, 12; silver basins, 12; gold ladles, 12. ⁸⁵Silver per bowl, 130; per basin, 70. Total silver of vessels, 2,400 sanctuary shekels. ⁸⁶The 12 gold ladles filled with incense—10 sanctuary shekels per ladle—total gold of the ladles, 120.

⁸⁷Total of herd animals for burnt offerings, 12 bulls; of rams, 12; of yearling lambs, 12—with their proper meal offerings; of goats for sin offerings, 12. ⁸⁸Total of herd animals for sacrifices of well-being, 24 bulls; of rams, 60; of

אַחַת שְׁלֹשִׁים וּמֵאָה֙ מִשְׁקָלָ֔הּ מִזְרָ֥ק אֶחָ֛ד
כֶּ֥סֶף שִׁבְעִ֛ים שֶׁ֖קֶל בְּשֶׁ֣קֶל הַקֹּ֑דֶשׁ שְׁנֵיהֶ֣ם ׀
מְלֵאִ֗ים סֹ֛לֶת בְּלוּלָ֥ה בַשֶּׁ֖מֶן לְמִנְחָֽה:
‏⁷⁴ כַּ֥ף אַחַ֛ת עֲשָׂרָ֥ה זָהָ֖ב מְלֵאָ֥ה קְטֹֽרֶת:
‏⁷⁵ פַּ֣ר אֶחָ֞ד בֶּן־בָּקָ֗ר אַ֧יִל אֶחָ֛ד כֶּֽבֶשׂ־אֶחָ֥ד
בֶּן־שְׁנָת֖וֹ לְעֹלָֽה: ‏⁷⁶ שְׂעִיר־עִזִּ֥ים אֶחָ֖ד
לְחַטָּֽאת: ‏⁷⁷ וּלְזֶ֣בַח הַשְּׁלָמִים֮ בָּקָ֣ר שְׁנַ֒יִם֒
אֵילִ֤ם חֲמִשָּׁה֙ עַתֻּדִ֣ים חֲמִשָּׁ֔ה כְּבָשִׂ֥ים
בְּנֵֽי־שָׁנָ֖ה חֲמִשָּׁ֑ה זֶ֛ה קָרְבַּ֥ן פַּגְעִיאֵ֖ל בֶּן־
עָכְרָֽן: פ

‏⁷⁸ בְּיוֹם֙ שְׁנֵ֣ים עָשָׂ֣ר י֔וֹם נָשִׂ֖יא לִבְנֵ֣י נַפְתָּלִ֑י
אֲחִירַ֖ע בֶּן־עֵינָֽן: ‏⁷⁹ קָרְבָּנ֞וֹ קַֽעֲרַת־כֶּ֣סֶף
אַחַ֗ת שְׁלֹשִׁ֣ים וּמֵאָה֮ מִשְׁקָלָהּ֒ מִזְרָ֣ק אֶחָד֮
כֶּ֣סֶף שִׁבְעִ֣ים שֶׁקֶל֒ בְּשֶׁ֣קֶל הַקֹּ֑דֶשׁ שְׁנֵיהֶ֣ם ׀
מְלֵאִ֗ים סֹ֛לֶת בְּלוּלָ֥ה בַשֶּׁ֖מֶן לְמִנְחָֽה:
‏⁸⁰ כַּ֥ף אַחַ֛ת עֲשָׂרָ֥ה זָהָ֖ב מְלֵאָ֥ה קְטֹֽרֶת:
‏⁸¹ פַּ֣ר אֶחָ֞ד בֶּן־בָּקָ֗ר אַ֧יִל אֶחָ֛ד כֶּֽבֶשׂ־אֶחָ֥ד
בֶּן־שְׁנָת֖וֹ לְעֹלָֽה: ‏⁸² שְׂעִיר־עִזִּ֥ים אֶחָ֖ד
לְחַטָּֽאת: ‏⁸³ וּלְזֶ֣בַח הַשְּׁלָמִים֮ בָּקָ֣ר שְׁנַ֒יִם֒
אֵילִ֤ם חֲמִשָּׁה֙ עַתֻּדִ֣ים חֲמִשָּׁ֔ה כְּבָשִׂ֥ים
בְּנֵֽי־שָׁנָ֖ה חֲמִשָּׁ֑ה זֶ֛ה קָרְבַּ֥ן אֲחִירַ֖ע בֶּן־
עֵינָֽן: פ

‏⁸⁴ זֹ֣את ׀ חֲנֻכַּ֣ת הַמִּזְבֵּ֗חַ בְּיוֹם֙ הִמָּשַׁ֣ח אֹת֔וֹ
מֵאֵ֖ת נְשִׂיאֵ֣י יִשְׂרָאֵ֑ל קַעֲרֹ֨ת כֶּ֜סֶף שְׁתֵּ֣ים
עֶשְׂרֵ֗ה מִֽזְרְקֵי־כֶ֨סֶף֙ שְׁנֵ֣ים עָשָׂ֔ר כַּפּ֥וֹת זָהָ֖ב
שְׁתֵּ֥ים עֶשְׂרֵֽה: ‏⁸⁵ שְׁלֹשִׁ֣ים וּמֵאָ֗ה הַקְּעָרָ֤ה
הָֽאַחַת֙ כֶּ֔סֶף וְשִׁבְעִ֖ים הַמִּזְרָ֣ק הָאֶחָ֑ד כֹּ֚ל
כֶּ֣סֶף הַכֵּלִ֔ים אַלְפַּ֥יִם וְאַרְבַּע־מֵא֖וֹת בְּשֶׁ֥קֶל
הַקֹּֽדֶשׁ: ‏⁸⁶ כַּפּ֨וֹת זָהָ֤ב שְׁתֵּים־עֶשְׂרֵה֙
מְלֵאֹ֣ת קְטֹ֔רֶת עֲשָׂרָ֧ה עֲשָׂרָ֛ה הַכַּ֖ף בְּשֶׁ֣קֶל
הַקֹּ֑דֶשׁ כָּל־זְהַ֣ב הַכַּפּ֔וֹת עֶשְׂרִ֖ים וּמֵאָֽה:
‏⁸⁷ כָּל־הַבָּקָ֨ר לָעֹלָ֜ה שְׁנֵ֧ים עָשָׂ֣ר פָּרִ֗ים
אֵילִ֤ם שְׁנֵים־עָשָׂר֙ כְּבָשִׂ֤ים בְּנֵֽי־שָׁנָה֙ שְׁנֵ֣ים
עָשָׂ֔ר וּמִנְחָתָ֑ם וּשְׂעִירֵ֥י עִזִּ֛ים שְׁנֵ֥ים עָשָׂ֖ר
לְחַטָּֽאת: ‏⁸⁸ וְכֹ֞ל בְּקַ֣ר ׀ זֶ֣בַח הַשְּׁלָמִ֗ים
עֶשְׂרִ֣ים וְאַרְבָּעָה֙ פָּרִים֙ אֵילִ֣ם שִׁשִּׁ֔ים

he-goats, 60; of yearling lambs, 60. That was the dedication offering for the altar after its anointing.

⁸⁹When Moses went into the Tent of Meeting to speak with Him, he would hear the Voice addressing him from above the cover that was on top of the Ark of the Pact between the two cherubim; thus He spoke to him.

8 BE-HA'ALOTEKHA

The LORD spoke to Moses, saying: ²Speak to Aaron and say to him, "When you mount[a] the lamps, let the seven lamps give light at the front of the lampstand." ³Aaron did so; he mounted the lamps at the front of the lampstand, as the LORD had commanded Moses.—⁴Now this is how the lampstand was made: it was hammered work of gold, hammered from base to petal. According to the pattern that the LORD had shown Moses, so was the lampstand made.

⁵The LORD spoke to Moses, saying: ⁶Take the Levites from among the Israelites and cleanse them. ⁷This is what you shall do to them to cleanse them: sprinkle on them water of purification, and let them go over their whole body with a razor, and wash their clothes; thus they shall be cleansed. ⁸Let them take a bull of the herd, and with it a meal offering of choice flour with oil mixed in, and you take a second bull of the herd for a sin offering. ⁹You shall bring the Levites forward before the Tent of Meeting. Assemble the whole Israelite community, ¹⁰and bring the Levites forward before the LORD. Let the Israelites lay their hands upon the Levites, ¹¹and let Aaron designate[b] the Levites before the LORD as an elevation offering from

---

a   Cf. Exod. 25.37.
b   Lit. "elevate."

עַתֻּדִים שִׁשִּׁים כְּבָשִׂים בְּנֵי־שָׁנָה שִׁשִּׁים זֹאת חֲנֻכַּת הַמִּזְבֵּחַ אַחֲרֵי הִמָּשַׁח אֹתוֹ:

89 וּבְבֹא מֹשֶׁה אֶל־אֹהֶל מוֹעֵד לְדַבֵּר אִתּוֹ וַיִּשְׁמַע אֶת־הַקּוֹל מִדַּבֵּר אֵלָיו מֵעַל הַכַּפֹּרֶת אֲשֶׁר עַל־אֲרֹן הָעֵדֻת מִבֵּין שְׁנֵי הַכְּרֻבִים וַיְדַבֵּר אֵלָיו: פ

בהעלתך

ח וַיְדַבֵּר יְהֹוָה אֶל־מֹשֶׁה לֵּאמֹר: 2 דַּבֵּר אֶל־אַהֲרֹן וְאָמַרְתָּ אֵלָיו בְּהַעֲלֹתְךָ אֶת־הַנֵּרֹת אֶל־מוּל פְּנֵי הַמְּנוֹרָה יָאִירוּ שִׁבְעַת הַנֵּרוֹת: 3 וַיַּעַשׂ כֵּן אַהֲרֹן אֶל־מוּל פְּנֵי הַמְּנוֹרָה הֶעֱלָה נֵרֹתֶיהָ כַּאֲשֶׁר צִוָּה יְהֹוָה אֶת־מֹשֶׁה: 4 וְזֶה מַעֲשֵׂה הַמְּנֹרָה מִקְשָׁה זָהָב עַד־יְרֵכָהּ עַד־פִּרְחָהּ מִקְשָׁה הִוא כַּמַּרְאֶה אֲשֶׁר הֶרְאָה יְהֹוָה אֶת־מֹשֶׁה כֵּן עָשָׂה אֶת־הַמְּנֹרָה: פ

5 וַיְדַבֵּר יְהֹוָה אֶל־מֹשֶׁה לֵּאמֹר: 6 קַח אֶת־הַלְוִיִּם מִתּוֹךְ בְּנֵי יִשְׂרָאֵל וְטִהַרְתָּ אֹתָם: 7 וְכֹה־תַעֲשֶׂה לָהֶם לְטַהֲרָם הַזֵּה עֲלֵיהֶם מֵי חַטָּאת וְהֶעֱבִירוּ תַעַר עַל־כָּל־בְּשָׂרָם וְכִבְּסוּ בִגְדֵיהֶם וְהִטֶּהָרוּ: 8 וְלָקְחוּ פַּר בֶּן־בָּקָר וּמִנְחָתוֹ סֹלֶת בְּלוּלָה בַשָּׁמֶן וּפַר־שֵׁנִי בֶן־בָּקָר תִּקַּח לְחַטָּאת: 9 וְהִקְרַבְתָּ אֶת־הַלְוִיִּם לִפְנֵי אֹהֶל מוֹעֵד וְהִקְהַלְתָּ אֶת־כָּל־עֲדַת בְּנֵי יִשְׂרָאֵל: 10 וְהִקְרַבְתָּ אֶת־הַלְוִיִּם לִפְנֵי יְהֹוָה וְסָמְכוּ בְנֵי־יִשְׂרָאֵל אֶת־יְדֵיהֶם עַל־הַלְוִיִּם: 11 וְהֵנִיף אַהֲרֹן אֶת־הַלְוִיִּם תְּנוּפָה לִפְנֵי יְהֹוָה מֵאֵת בְּנֵי יִשְׂרָאֵל וְהָיוּ לַעֲבֹד אֶת־

the Israelites, that they may perform the service of the Lord. 12The Levites shall now lay their hands upon the heads of the bulls; one shall be offered to the Lord as a sin offering and the other as a burnt offering, to make expiation for the Levites.

13You shall place the Levites in attendance upon Aaron and his sons, and designate them as an elevation offering to the Lord. 14Thus you shall set the Levites apart from the Israelites, and the Levites shall be Mine. 15Thereafter the Levites shall be qualified for the service of the Tent of Meeting, once you have cleansed them and designated them as an elevation offering. 16For they are formally assigned to Me from among the Israelites: I have taken them for Myself in place of all the first issue of the womb, of all the first-born of the Israelites. 17For every first-born among the Israelites, man as well as beast, is Mine; I consecrated them to Myself at the time that I smote every first-born in the land of Egypt. 18Now I take the Levites instead of every first-born of the Israelites; 19and from among the Israelites I formally assign the Levites to Aaron and his sons, to perform the service for the Israelites in the Tent of Meeting and to make expiation for the Israelites, so that no plague may afflict the Israelites c-for coming-c too near the sanctuary.

20Moses, Aaron, and the whole Israelite community did with the Levites accordingly; just as the Lord had commanded Moses in regard to the Levites, so the Israelites did with them. 21The Levites purified themselves and washed their clothes; and Aaron designated them as an elevation offering before the Lord, and Aaron made expiation for them to cleanse them. 22Thereafter the Levites were qualified to perform their service in the Tent of Meeting, under Aaron and his sons. As the Lord had com-

עֲבֹדַת יְהוָה: 12 וְהַלְוִיִּם יִסְמְכוּ אֶת־יְדֵיהֶם עַל רֹאשׁ הַפָּרִים וַעֲשֵׂה אֶת־הָאֶחָד חַטָּאת וְאֶת־הָאֶחָד עֹלָה לַיהוָה לְכַפֵּר עַל־הַלְוִיִּם: 13 וְהַעֲמַדְתָּ אֶת־הַלְוִיִּם לִפְנֵי אַהֲרֹן וְלִפְנֵי בָנָיו וְהֵנַפְתָּ אֹתָם תְּנוּפָה לַיהוָה: 14 וְהִבְדַּלְתָּ אֶת־הַלְוִיִּם מִתּוֹךְ בְּנֵי יִשְׂרָאֵל וְהָיוּ לִי הַלְוִיִּם: 15 וְאַחֲרֵי־כֵן יָבֹאוּ הַלְוִיִּם לַעֲבֹד אֶת־אֹהֶל מוֹעֵד וְטִהַרְתָּ אֹתָם וְהֵנַפְתָּ אֹתָם תְּנוּפָה: 16 כִּי נְתֻנִים נְתֻנִים הֵמָּה לִי מִתּוֹךְ בְּנֵי יִשְׂרָאֵל תַּחַת פִּטְרַת כָּל־רֶחֶם בְּכוֹר כֹּל מִבְּנֵי יִשְׂרָאֵל לָקַחְתִּי אֹתָם לִי: 17 כִּי לִי כָל־בְּכוֹר בִּבְנֵי יִשְׂרָאֵל בָּאָדָם וּבַבְּהֵמָה בְּיוֹם הַכֹּתִי כָל־בְּכוֹר בְּאֶרֶץ מִצְרַיִם הִקְדַּשְׁתִּי אֹתָם לִי: 18 וָאֶקַּח אֶת־הַלְוִיִּם תַּחַת כָּל־בְּכוֹר בִּבְנֵי יִשְׂרָאֵל: 19 וָאֶתְּנָה אֶת־הַלְוִיִּם נְתֻנִים | לְאַהֲרֹן וּלְבָנָיו מִתּוֹךְ בְּנֵי יִשְׂרָאֵל לַעֲבֹד אֶת־עֲבֹדַת בְּנֵי־יִשְׂרָאֵל בְּאֹהֶל מוֹעֵד וּלְכַפֵּר עַל־בְּנֵי יִשְׂרָאֵל וְלֹא יִהְיֶה בִּבְנֵי יִשְׂרָאֵל נֶגֶף בְּגֶשֶׁת בְּנֵי־יִשְׂרָאֵל אֶל־הַקֹּדֶשׁ: 20 וַיַּעַשׂ מֹשֶׁה וְאַהֲרֹן וְכָל־עֲדַת בְּנֵי־יִשְׂרָאֵל לַלְוִיִּם כְּכֹל אֲשֶׁר־צִוָּה יְהוָה אֶת־מֹשֶׁה לַלְוִיִּם כֵּן־עָשׂוּ לָהֶם בְּנֵי יִשְׂרָאֵל: 21 וַיִּתְחַטְּאוּ הַלְוִיִּם וַיְכַבְּסוּ בִּגְדֵיהֶם וַיָּנֶף אַהֲרֹן אֹתָם תְּנוּפָה לִפְנֵי יְהוָה וַיְכַפֵּר עֲלֵיהֶם אַהֲרֹן לְטַהֲרָם: 22 וְאַחֲרֵי־כֵן בָּאוּ הַלְוִיִּם לַעֲבֹד אֶת־עֲבֹדָתָם בְּאֹהֶל מוֹעֵד לִפְנֵי אַהֲרֹן וְלִפְנֵי

---

c-c Lit. "when the Israelites come."

301

manded Moses in regard to the Levites, so they did to them.

בָּנָיו כַּאֲשֶׁר צִוָּה יְהוָה אֶת־מֹשֶׁה עַל־הַלְוִיִּם כֵּן עָשׂוּ לָהֶם: ס

23The Lord spoke to Moses, saying: 24This is the rule for the Levites. From twenty-five years of age up they shall participate in the work force in the service of the Tent of Meeting; 25but at the age of fifty they shall retire from the work force and shall serve no more. 26They may assist their brother Levites at the Tent of Meeting by standing guard, but they shall perform no labor. Thus you shall deal with the Levites in regard to their duties.

23 וַיְדַבֵּר יְהוָה אֶל־מֹשֶׁה לֵּאמֹר: 24 זֹאת אֲשֶׁר לַלְוִיִּם מִבֶּן חָמֵשׁ וְעֶשְׂרִים שָׁנָה וָמַעְלָה יָבוֹא לִצְבֹא צָבָא בַּעֲבֹדַת אֹהֶל מוֹעֵד: 25 וּמִבֶּן חֲמִשִּׁים שָׁנָה יָשׁוּב מִצְּבָא הָעֲבֹדָה וְלֹא יַעֲבֹד עוֹד: 26 וְשֵׁרֵת אֶת־אֶחָיו בְּאֹהֶל מוֹעֵד לִשְׁמֹר מִשְׁמֶרֶת וַעֲבֹדָה לֹא יַעֲבֹד כָּכָה תַּעֲשֶׂה לַלְוִיִּם בְּמִשְׁמְרֹתָם: פ

9 The Lord spoke to Moses in the wilderness of Sinai, on the first new moon of the second year following the exodus from the land of Egypt, saying: 2Let the Israelite people offer the passover sacrifice at its set time: 3you shall offer it on the fourteenth day of this month, at twilight, at its set time; you shall offer it in accordance with all its rules and rites.

ט וַיְדַבֵּר יְהוָה אֶל־מֹשֶׁה בְמִדְבַּר־סִינַי בַּשָּׁנָה הַשֵּׁנִית לְצֵאתָם מֵאֶרֶץ מִצְרַיִם בַּחֹדֶשׁ הָרִאשׁוֹן לֵאמֹר: 2 וְיַעֲשׂוּ בְנֵי־יִשְׂרָאֵל אֶת־הַפָּסַח בְּמוֹעֲדוֹ: 3 בְּאַרְבָּעָה עָשָׂר־יוֹם בַּחֹדֶשׁ הַזֶּה בֵּין הָעַרְבַּיִם תַּעֲשׂוּ אֹתוֹ בְּמוֹעֲדוֹ כְּכָל־חֻקֹּתָיו וּכְכָל־מִשְׁפָּטָיו תַּעֲשׂוּ אֹתוֹ:

4Moses instructed the Israelites to offer the passover sacrifice; 5and they offered the passover sacrifice in the first month, on the fourteenth day of the month, at twilight, in the wilderness of Sinai. Just as the Lord had commanded Moses, so the Israelites did.

4 וַיְדַבֵּר מֹשֶׁה אֶל־בְּנֵי יִשְׂרָאֵל לַעֲשֹׂת הַפָּסַח: 5 וַיַּעֲשׂוּ אֶת־הַפֶּסַח בָּרִאשׁוֹן בְּאַרְבָּעָה עָשָׂר יוֹם לַחֹדֶשׁ בֵּין הָעַרְבַּיִם בְּמִדְבַּר סִינָי כְּכֹל אֲשֶׁר צִוָּה יְהוָה אֶת־מֹשֶׁה כֵּן עָשׂוּ בְּנֵי יִשְׂרָאֵל:

6But there were some men who were unclean by reason of a corpse and could not offer the passover sacrifice on that day. Appearing that same day before Moses and Aaron, 7those men said to them,a "Unclean though we are by reason of a corpse, why must we be debarred from presenting the Lord's offering at its set time with the rest of the Israelites?" 8Moses said to them, "Stand by, and let me hear what instructions the Lord gives about you."

6 וַיְהִי אֲנָשִׁים אֲשֶׁר הָיוּ טְמֵאִים לְנֶפֶשׁ אָדָם וְלֹא־יָכְלוּ לַעֲשֹׂת־הַפֶּסַח בַּיּוֹם הַהוּא וַיִּקְרְבוּ לִפְנֵי מֹשֶׁה וְלִפְנֵי אַהֲרֹן בַּיּוֹם הַהוּא: 7 וַיֹּאמְרוּ הָאֲנָשִׁים הָהֵמָּה אֵלָיו אֲנַחְנוּ טְמֵאִים לְנֶפֶשׁ אָדָם לָמָּה נִגָּרַע לְבִלְתִּי הַקְרִב אֶת־קָרְבַּן יְהוָה בְּמֹעֲדוֹ בְּתוֹךְ בְּנֵי יִשְׂרָאֵל: 8 וַיֹּאמֶר אֲלֵהֶם מֹשֶׁה עִמְדוּ וְאֶשְׁמְעָה מַה־יְצַוֶּה יְהוָה לָכֶם: פ

9And the Lord spoke to Moses, saying:

9 וַיְדַבֵּר יְהוָה אֶל־מֹשֶׁה לֵּאמֹר: 10 דַּבֵּר

a Lit. "him."

10Speak to the Israelite people, saying: When any of you or of your posterity who are defiled by a corpse or are on a long journey would offer a passover sacrifice to the Lord, 11they shall offer it in the second month, on the fourteenth day of the month, at twilight. They shall eat it with unleavened bread and bitter herbs, 12and they shall not leave any of it over until morning. They shall not break a bone of it. They shall offer it in strict accord with the law of the passover sacrifice. 13But if a man who is clean and not on a journey refrains from offering the passover sacrifice, that person shall be cut off from his kin, for he did not present the Lord's offering at its set time; that man shall bear his guilt.

14And when a stranger who resides with you would offer a passover sacrifice to the Lord, he must offer it in accordance with the rules and rites of the passover sacrifice. There shall be one law for you, whether stranger or citizen of the country.

15On the day that the Tabernacle was set up, the cloud covered the Tabernacle, the Tent of the Pact; and in the evening it rested over the Tabernacle in the likeness of fire until morning. 16It was always so: the cloud covered it, appearing as fire by night. 17And whenever the cloud lifted from the Tent, the Israelites would set out accordingly; and at the spot where the cloud settled, there the Israelites would make camp. 18At a command of the Lord the Israelites broke camp, and at a command of the Lord they made camp: they remained encamped as long as the cloud stayed over the Tabernacle. 19When the cloud lingered over the Tabernacle many days, the Israelites observed the Lord's mandate and did not journey on. 20At such times as the cloud rested over the Tabernacle for but a few days, they remained encamped at a command of the Lord, and broke camp at a command of the

אֶל־בְּנֵי יִשְׂרָאֵל לֵאמֹר אִישׁ אִישׁ כִּי־ יִהְיֶה־טָמֵא ׀ לָנֶפֶשׁ אוֹ בְדֶרֶךְ רְחֹקָה* לָכֶם אוֹ לְדֹרֹתֵיכֶם וְעָשָׂה פֶסַח לַיהוָה: 11 בַּחֹדֶשׁ הַשֵּׁנִי בְּאַרְבָּעָה עָשָׂר יוֹם בֵּין הָעַרְבַּיִם יַעֲשׂוּ אֹתוֹ עַל־מַצּוֹת וּמְרֹרִים יֹאכְלֻהוּ: 12 לֹא־יַשְׁאִירוּ מִמֶּנּוּ עַד־בֹּקֶר וְעֶצֶם לֹא יִשְׁבְּרוּ־בוֹ כְּכָל־חֻקַּת הַפֶּסַח יַעֲשׂוּ אֹתוֹ: 13 וְהָאִישׁ אֲשֶׁר־הוּא טָהוֹר וּבְדֶרֶךְ לֹא־הָיָה וְחָדַל לַעֲשׂוֹת הַפֶּסַח וְנִכְרְתָה הַנֶּפֶשׁ הַהִוא מֵעַמֶּיהָ כִּי ׀ קָרְבַּן יְהוָה לֹא הִקְרִיב בְּמֹעֲדוֹ חֶטְאוֹ יִשָּׂא הָאִישׁ הַהוּא:

14 וְכִי־יָגוּר אִתְּכֶם גֵּר וְעָשָׂה פֶסַח לַיהוָה כְּחֻקַּת הַפֶּסַח וּכְמִשְׁפָּטוֹ כֵּן יַעֲשֶׂה חֻקָּה אַחַת יִהְיֶה לָכֶם וְלַגֵּר וּלְאֶזְרַח הָאָרֶץ: פ

15 וּבְיוֹם הָקִים אֶת־הַמִּשְׁכָּן כִּסָּה הֶעָנָן אֶת־הַמִּשְׁכָּן לְאֹהֶל הָעֵדֻת וּבָעֶרֶב יִהְיֶה עַל־הַמִּשְׁכָּן כְּמַרְאֵה־אֵשׁ עַד־בֹּקֶר: 16 כֵּן יִהְיֶה תָמִיד הֶעָנָן יְכַסֶּנּוּ וּמַרְאֵה־אֵשׁ לָיְלָה: 17 וּלְפִי הֵעָלוֹת הֶעָנָן מֵעַל הָאֹהֶל וְאַחֲרֵי־כֵן יִסְעוּ בְּנֵי יִשְׂרָאֵל וּבִמְקוֹם אֲשֶׁר יִשְׁכָּן־שָׁם הֶעָנָן שָׁם יַחֲנוּ בְּנֵי יִשְׂרָאֵל: 18 עַל־פִּי יְהוָה יִסְעוּ בְּנֵי יִשְׂרָאֵל וְעַל־פִּי יְהוָה יַחֲנוּ כָּל־יְמֵי אֲשֶׁר יִשְׁכֹּן הֶעָנָן עַל־הַמִּשְׁכָּן יַחֲנוּ: 19 וּבְהַאֲרִיךְ הֶעָנָן עַל־ הַמִּשְׁכָּן יָמִים רַבִּים וְשָׁמְרוּ בְנֵי־יִשְׂרָאֵל אֶת־מִשְׁמֶרֶת יְהוָה וְלֹא יִסָּעוּ: 20 וְיֵשׁ אֲשֶׁר יִהְיֶה הֶעָנָן יָמִים מִסְפָּר עַל־הַמִּשְׁכָּן עַל־פִּי יְהוָה יַחֲנוּ וְעַל־פִּי יְהוָה יִסָּעוּ:

LORD. 21And at such times as the cloud stayed from evening until morning, they broke camp as soon as the cloud lifted in the morning. Day or night, whenever the cloud lifted, they would break camp. 22Whether it was two days or a month or a year—however long the cloud lingered over the Tabernacle—the Israelites remained encamped and did not set out; only when it lifted did they break camp. 23On a sign from the LORD they made camp and on a sign from the LORD they broke camp; they observed the LORD's mandate at the LORD's bidding through Moses.

10 The LORD spoke to Moses, saying: 2Have two silver trumpets made; make them of hammered work. They shall serve you to summon the community and to set the divisions in motion. 3When both are blown in long blasts,*a* the whole community shall assemble before you at the entrance of the Tent of Meeting; 4and if only one is blown, the chieftains, heads of Israel's contingents, shall assemble before you. 5But when you sound short blasts,*a* the divisions encamped on the east shall move forward; 6and when you sound short blasts a second time, those encamped on the south shall move forward. Thus short blasts shall be blown for setting them in motion, 7while to convoke the congregation you shall blow long blasts, not short ones. 8The trumpets shall be blown by Aaron's sons, the priests; they shall be for you an institution for all time throughout the ages.

9*a*-When you are at war-*a* in your land against an aggressor who attacks you, you shall sound short blasts on the trumpets, that you may be remembered before the LORD your God and be delivered from your enemies. 10And on your joyous occasions—your fixed festivals and new

---

21 וְיֵ֣שׁ אֲשֶׁ֣ר יִהְיֶ֣ה הֶֽעָנָ֡ן מֵעֶ֣רֶב עַד־בֹּ֒קֶר֒ וְנַעֲלָ֤ה הֶֽעָנָן֙ בַּבֹּ֔קֶר וְנָסָ֑עוּ א֥וֹ יוֹמָ֛ם וָלַ֖יְלָה וְנַעֲלָ֥ה הֶעָנָ֖ן וְנָסָֽעוּ: 22 אֽוֹ־יֹמַ֙יִם֙ אֽוֹ־חֹ֜דֶשׁ אֽוֹ־יָמִ֗ים בְּהַאֲרִ֙יךְ֙ הֶֽעָנָ֤ן עַל־הַמִּשְׁכָּן֙ לִשְׁכֹּ֣ן עָלָ֔יו יַחֲנ֥וּ בְנֵֽי־יִשְׂרָאֵ֖ל וְלֹ֣א יִסָּ֑עוּ וּבְהֵעָלֹת֖וֹ יִסָּֽעוּ: 23 עַל־פִּ֤י יְהֹוָה֙ יַחֲנ֔וּ וְעַל־פִּ֥י יְהֹוָ֖ה יִסָּ֑עוּ אֶת־מִשְׁמֶ֤רֶת יְהֹוָה֙ שָׁמָ֔רוּ עַל־פִּ֥י יְהֹוָ֖ה בְּיַד־מֹשֶֽׁה: פ

י וַיְדַבֵּ֥ר יְהֹוָ֖ה אֶל־מֹשֶׁ֥ה לֵּאמֹֽר: 2 עֲשֵׂ֣ה לְךָ֗ שְׁתֵּי֙ חֲצֽוֹצְרֹ֣ת כֶּ֔סֶף מִקְשָׁ֖ה תַּעֲשֶׂ֣ה אֹתָ֑ם וְהָי֤וּ לְךָ֙ לְמִקְרָ֣א הָֽעֵדָ֔ה וּלְמַסַּ֖ע אֶת־הַֽמַּחֲנֽוֹת: 3 וְתָקְע֖וּ בָּהֵ֑ן וְנֽוֹעֲד֤וּ אֵלֶ֙יךָ֙ כׇּל־הָ֣עֵדָ֔ה אֶל־פֶּ֖תַח אֹ֥הֶל מוֹעֵֽד: 4 וְאִם־ בְּאַחַ֖ת יִתְקָ֑עוּ וְנֽוֹעֲד֤וּ אֵלֶ֙יךָ֙ הַנְּשִׂיאִ֔ים רָאשֵׁ֖י אַלְפֵ֥י יִשְׂרָאֵֽל: 5 וּתְקַעְתֶּ֖ם תְּרוּעָ֑ה וְנָֽסְעוּ֙ הַֽמַּחֲנ֔וֹת הַֽחֹנִ֖ים קֵֽדְמָה: 6 וּתְקַעְתֶּ֤ם תְּרוּעָה֙ שֵׁנִ֔ית וְנָֽסְעוּ֙ הַֽמַּחֲנ֔וֹת הַֽחֹנִ֖ים תֵּימָ֑נָה תְּרוּעָ֥ה יִתְקְע֖וּ לְמַסְעֵיהֶֽם: 7 וּבְהַקְהִ֖יל אֶת־הַקָּהָ֑ל תִּתְקְע֖וּ וְלֹ֥א תָרִֽיעוּ: 8 וּבְנֵ֤י אַהֲרֹן֙ הַכֹּ֣הֲנִ֔ים יִתְקְע֖וּ בַּֽחֲצֹֽצְר֑וֹת וְהָי֥וּ לָכֶ֛ם לְחֻקַּ֥ת עוֹלָ֖ם לְדֹרֹתֵיכֶֽם: 9 וְכִֽי־תָבֹ֨אוּ מִלְחָמָ֜ה בְּאַרְצְכֶ֗ם עַל־הַצַּר֙ הַצֹּרֵ֣ר אֶתְכֶ֔ם וַהֲרֵעֹתֶ֖ם בַּֽחֲצֹֽצְרֹ֑ת וְנִזְכַּרְתֶּ֗ם לִפְנֵי֙ יְהֹוָ֣ה אֱלֹֽהֵיכֶ֔ם וְנֽוֹשַׁעְתֶּ֖ם מֵאֹֽיְבֵיכֶֽם: 10 וּבְי֨וֹם שִׂמְחַתְכֶ֜ם וּֽבְמוֹעֲדֵיכֶ֗ם וּבְרָאשֵׁ֣י חׇדְשֵׁיכֶ֔ם וּתְקַעְתֶּ֣ם

---

a Meaning of Heb. uncertain.

moon days—you shall sound the trumpets over your burnt offerings and your sacrifices of well-being. They shall be a reminder of you before your God: I, the LORD, am your God.

¹¹In the second year, on the twentieth day of the second month, the cloud lifted from the Tabernacle of the Pact ¹²and the Israelites set out on their journeys from the wilderness of Sinai. The cloud came to rest in the wilderness of Paran.

¹³When the march was to begin, at the LORD's command through Moses, ¹⁴the first standard to set out, troop by troop, was the division of Judah. In command of its troops was Nahshon son of Amminadab; ¹⁵in command of the tribal troop of Issachar, Nethanel son of Zuar; ¹⁶and in command of the tribal troop of Zebulun, Eliab son of Helon.

¹⁷Then the Tabernacle would be taken apart; and the Gershonites and the Merarites, who carried the Tabernacle, would set out.

¹⁸The next standard to set out, troop by troop, was the division of Reuben. In command of its troop was Elizur son of Shedeur; ¹⁹in command of the tribal troop of Simeon, Shelumiel son of Zurishaddai; ²⁰and in command of the tribal troop of Gad, Eliasaph son of Deuel.

²¹Then the Kohathites, who carried the sacred objects, would set out; and by the time they arrived, the Tabernacle would be set up again.

²²The next standard to set out, troop by troop, was the division of Ephraim. In command of its troop was Elishama son of Ammihud; ²³in command of the tribal troop of Manasseh, Gamaliel son of Pedahzur; ²⁴and in command of the tribal troop of Benjamin, Abidan son of Gideoni.

²⁵Then, as the rear guard of all the divisions, the standard of the division of Dan would set out, troop by troop. In command of its troop

בַּחֲצֹצְרֹת עַל עֹלֹתֵיכֶ֔ם וְעַ֖ל זִבְחֵ֣י שַׁלְמֵיכֶ֑ם וְהָי֨וּ לָכֶ֤ם לְזִכָּרוֹן֙ לִפְנֵ֣י אֱלֹֽהֵיכֶ֔ם אֲנִ֖י יְהֹוָ֥ה אֱלֹהֵיכֶֽם: פ

¹¹וַיְהִ֞י בַּשָּׁנָ֧ה הַשֵּׁנִ֛ית בַּחֹ֥דֶשׁ הַשֵּׁנִ֖י בְּעֶשְׂרִ֣ים בַּחֹ֑דֶשׁ נַעֲלָה֙ הֶֽעָנָ֔ן מֵעַ֖ל מִשְׁכַּ֥ן הָעֵדֻֽת: ¹²וַיִּסְע֧וּ בְנֵֽי־יִשְׂרָאֵ֛ל לְמַסְעֵיהֶ֖ם מִמִּדְבַּ֣ר סִינָ֑י וַיִּשְׁכֹּ֥ן הֶעָנָ֖ן בְּמִדְבַּ֥ר פָּארָֽן: ¹³וַיִּסְע֖וּ בָּרִֽאשֹׁנָ֑ה עַל־פִּ֥י יְהֹוָ֖ה בְּיַד־ מֹשֶֽׁה: ¹⁴וַיִּסַּ֞ע דֶּ֣גֶל מַחֲנֵ֧ה בְנֵֽי־יְהוּדָ֛ה בָּרִֽאשֹׁנָ֖ה לְצִבְאֹתָ֑ם וְעַ֨ל־צְבָא֔וֹ נַחְשׁ֖וֹן בֶּן־עַמִּֽינָדָֽב: ¹⁵וְעַ֨ל־צְבָ֔א מַטֵּ֖ה בְּנֵ֣י יִשָּׂשכָ֑ר נְתַנְאֵ֖ל בֶּן־צוּעָֽר: ¹⁶וְעַ֨ל־צְבָ֔א מַטֵּ֖ה בְּנֵ֣י זְבוּלֻ֑ן אֱלִיאָ֖ב בֶּן־חֵלֹֽן: ¹⁷וְהוּרַ֖ד הַמִּשְׁכָּ֑ן וְנָסְע֤וּ בְנֵֽי־גֵרְשׁוֹן֙ וּבְנֵ֣י מְרָרִ֔י נֹשְׂאֵ֖י הַמִּשְׁכָּֽן: ס ¹⁸וְנָסַ֗ע דֶּ֛גֶל מַחֲנֵ֥ה רְאוּבֵ֖ן לְצִבְאֹתָ֑ם וְעַ֨ל־צְבָא֔וֹ אֱלִיצ֖וּר בֶּן־שְׁדֵיאֽוּר: ¹⁹וְעַ֨ל־צְבָ֔א מַטֵּ֖ה בְּנֵ֣י שִׁמְע֑וֹן שְׁלֻֽמִיאֵ֖ל בֶּן־צוּרִֽי־שַׁדָּֽי: ²⁰וְעַ֨ל־צְבָ֔א מַטֵּ֖ה בְּנֵי־גָ֑ד אֶלְיָסָ֖ף בֶּן־דְּעוּאֵֽל: ²¹וְנָסְעוּ֙ הַקְּהָתִ֔ים נֹשְׂאֵ֖י הַמִּקְדָּ֑שׁ וְהֵקִ֥ימוּ אֶת־הַמִּשְׁכָּ֖ן עַד־בֹּאָֽם: ס ²²וְנָסַ֗ע דֶּ֛גֶל מַחֲנֵ֥ה בְנֵֽי־אֶפְרַ֖יִם לְצִבְאֹתָ֑ם וְעַ֨ל־צְבָא֔וֹ אֱלִֽישָׁמָ֖ע בֶּן־עַמִּיהֽוּד: ²³וְעַ֨ל־צְבָ֔א מַטֵּ֖ה בְּנֵ֣י מְנַשֶּׁ֑ה גַּמְלִיאֵ֖ל בֶּן־פְּדָהצֽוּר: ²⁴וְעַ֨ל־צְבָ֔א מַטֵּ֖ה בְּנֵ֣י בִנְיָמִ֑ן אֲבִידָ֖ן בֶּן־גִּדְעוֹנִֽי: ס ²⁵וְנָסַ֗ע דֶּ֚גֶל מַחֲנֵ֣ה בְנֵי־דָ֔ן מְאַסֵּ֖ף לְכָל־ הַמַּחֲנֹ֑ת לְצִבְאֹתָ֑ם וְעַ֨ל־צְבָא֔וֹ אֲחִיעֶ֖זֶר

was Ahiezer son of Ammishaddai; [26]in command of the tribal troop of Asher, Pagiel son of Ochran; [27]and in command of the tribal troop of Naphtali, Ahira son of Enan.

[28]Such was the order of march of the Israelites, as they marched troop by troop.

[29]Moses said to Hobab son of Reuel the Midianite, Moses' father-in-law, "We are setting out for the place of which the LORD has said, 'I will give it to you.' Come with us and we will be generous with you; for the LORD has promised to be generous to Israel."

[30]"I will not go," he replied to him, "but will return to my native land." [31]He said, "Please do not leave us, inasmuch as you know where we should camp in the wilderness and can be our guide.[b] [32]So if you come with us, we will extend to you the same bounty that the LORD grants us."

[33]They marched from the mountain of the LORD a distance of three days. The Ark of the Covenant of the LORD traveled in front of them on that three days' journey to seek out a resting place for them; [34]and the LORD's cloud kept above them by day, as they moved on from camp.

[35]When the Ark was to set out, Moses would say:

Advance, O LORD!
May Your enemies be scattered,
And may Your foes flee before You!
[36]And when it halted, he would say:
[c]Return, O LORD,
You who are Israel's myriads of thousands![c]

בֶּן־עַמִּֽישַׁדָּֽי: [26] וְעַל־צְבָ֗א מַטֵּ֖ה בְּנֵ֣י אָשֵׁ֑ר
פַּגְעִיאֵ֖ל בֶּן־עָכְרָֽן: [27] וְעַל־צְבָ֕א מַטֵּ֖ה בְּנֵ֣י
נַפְתָּלִ֑י אֲחִירַ֖ע בֶּן־עֵינָֽן: [28] אֵ֛לֶּה מַסְעֵ֥י
בְנֵֽי־יִשְׂרָאֵ֖ל לְצִבְאֹתָ֑ם
וַיִּסָּֽעוּ: ס

[29] וַיֹּ֣אמֶר מֹשֶׁ֗ה לְ֠חֹבָב בֶּן־רְעוּאֵ֣ל הַמִּדְיָנִי֮
חֹתֵ֣ן מֹשֶׁה֒ נֹסְעִ֣ים ׀ אֲנַ֗חְנוּ אֶל־הַמָּקוֹם֙
אֲשֶׁ֣ר אָמַ֣ר יְהוָ֔ה אֹת֖וֹ אֶתֵּ֣ן לָכֶ֑ם לְכָ֤ה
אִתָּ֨נוּ֙ וְהֵטַ֣בְנוּ לָ֔ךְ כִּֽי־יְהוָ֥ה דִּבֶּר־ט֖וֹב
עַל־יִשְׂרָאֵֽל:

[30] וַיֹּ֥אמֶר אֵלָ֖יו לֹ֣א אֵלֵ֑ךְ כִּ֧י אִם־אֶל־אַרְצִ֛י
וְאֶל־מֽוֹלַדְתִּ֖י אֵלֵֽךְ: [31] וַיֹּ֨אמֶר֙ אַל־נָ֖א
תַּעֲזֹ֣ב אֹתָ֑נוּ כִּ֣י ׀ עַל־כֵּ֣ן יָדַ֗עְתָּ חֲנֹתֵ֙נוּ֙
בַּמִּדְבָּ֔ר וְהָיִ֥יתָ לָּ֖נוּ לְעֵינָֽיִם: [32] וְהָיָ֖ה כִּֽי־
תֵלֵ֣ךְ עִמָּ֑נוּ וְהָיָ֣ה ׀ הַטּ֣וֹב הַה֗וּא אֲשֶׁ֨ר
יֵיטִ֤יב יְהוָה֙ עִמָּ֔נוּ וְהֵטַ֖בְנוּ לָֽךְ:

[33] וַיִּסְעוּ֙ מֵהַ֣ר יְהוָ֔ה דֶּ֖רֶךְ שְׁלֹ֣שֶׁת יָמִ֑ים
וַאֲר֨וֹן בְּרִית־יְהוָ֜ה נֹסֵ֣עַ לִפְנֵיהֶ֗ם דֶּ֚רֶךְ
שְׁלֹ֣שֶׁת יָמִ֔ים לָת֥וּר לָהֶ֖ם מְנוּחָֽה: [34] וַעֲנַ֧ן
יְהוָ֛ה עֲלֵיהֶ֖ם יוֹמָ֑ם בְּנָסְעָ֖ם מִן־
הַֽמַּחֲנֶֽה: ׆* ס

[35] וַיְהִ֛י בִּנְסֹ֥עַ הָאָרֹ֖ן וַיֹּ֣אמֶר מֹשֶׁ֑ה
קוּמָ֣ה ׀ יְהוָ֗ה
וְיָפֻ֙צוּ֙ אֹֽיְבֶ֔יךָ
וְיָנֻ֛סוּ מְשַׂנְאֶ֖יךָ מִפָּנֶֽיךָ: [36] וּבְנֻחֹ֖ה יֹאמַ֑ר
שׁוּבָ֣ה יְהוָ֔ה
רִֽבְב֖וֹת אַלְפֵ֥י יִשְׂרָאֵֽל: ׆* פ

v. 35. סימנית מנוזרת וגם נקרא נ' הפוכה
v. 36. סימנית מנוזרת וגם נקרא נ' הפוכה

---

b   Lit. "eyes."
c-c   Others "Return, O LORD, unto the
      ten thousands of the families of Israel!"

11

The people took to complaining bitterly before the Lord. The Lord heard and was incensed: a fire of the Lord broke out against them, ravaging the outskirts of the camp. ²The people cried out to Moses. Moses prayed to the Lord, and the fire died down. ³That place was named Taberah,*a* because a fire of the Lord had broken out against them.

⁴The riffraff in their midst felt a gluttonous craving; and then the Israelites wept and said, "If only we had meat to eat! ⁵We remember the fish that we used to eat free in Egypt, the cucumbers, the melons, the leeks, the onions, and the garlic. ⁶Now our gullets are shriveled. There is nothing at all! Nothing but this manna to look to!"

⁷Now the manna was like coriander seed, and in color it was like bdellium. ⁸The people would go about and gather it, grind it between millstones or pound it in a mortar, boil it in a pot, and make it into cakes. It tasted like rich cream.*b* ⁹When the dew fell on the camp at night, the manna would fall upon it.

¹⁰Moses heard the people weeping, every clan apart, each person at the entrance of his tent. The Lord was very angry, and Moses was distressed. ¹¹And Moses said to the Lord, "Why have You dealt ill with Your servant, and why have I not enjoyed Your favor, that You have laid the burden of all this people upon me? ¹²Did I conceive all this people, did I bear them, that You should say to me, 'Carry them in your bosom as a nurse carries an infant,' to the land that You have promised on oath to their fathers? ¹³Where am I to get meat to give to all this people, when they whine before me and say, 'Give us meat to eat!' ¹⁴I cannot carry all this people

יא וַיְהִ֤י הָעָם֙ כְּמִתְאֹ֣נְנִ֔ים רַ֖ע בְּאׇזְנֵ֣י יְהֹוָ֑ה וַיִּשְׁמַ֤ע יְהֹוָה֙ וַיִּ֣חַר אַפּ֔וֹ וַתִּבְעַר־בָּם֙ אֵ֣שׁ יְהֹוָ֔ה וַתֹּ֖אכַל בִּקְצֵ֥ה הַֽמַּחֲנֶֽה: ² וַיִּצְעַ֥ק הָעָ֖ם אֶל־מֹשֶׁ֑ה וַיִּתְפַּלֵּ֤ל מֹשֶׁה֙ אֶל־יְהֹוָ֔ה וַתִּשְׁקַ֖ע הָאֵֽשׁ: ³ וַיִּקְרָ֛א שֵֽׁם־הַמָּק֥וֹם הַה֖וּא תַּבְעֵרָ֑ה כִּֽי־בָעֲרָ֥ה בָ֖ם אֵ֥שׁ יְהֹוָֽה: ⁴ וְהָֽאסַפְסֻף֙* אֲשֶׁ֣ר בְּקִרְבּ֔וֹ הִתְאַוּ֖וּ תַּֽאֲוָ֑ה וַיָּשֻׁ֣בוּ וַיִּבְכּ֗וּ גַּ֚ם בְּנֵ֣י יִשְׂרָאֵ֔ל וַיֹּ֣אמְר֔וּ מִ֥י יַֽאֲכִלֵ֖נוּ בָּשָֽׂר: ⁵ זָכַ֙רְנוּ֙ אֶת־הַדָּגָ֔ה אֲשֶׁר־נֹאכַ֥ל בְּמִצְרַ֖יִם חִנָּ֑ם אֵ֣ת הַקִּשֻּׁאִ֗ים וְאֵת֙ הָֽאֲבַטִּחִ֔ים וְאֶת־הֶֽחָצִ֥יר וְאֶת־הַבְּצָלִ֖ים וְאֶת־הַשּׁוּמִֽים: ⁶ וְעַתָּ֛ה נַפְשֵׁ֥נוּ יְבֵשָׁ֖ה אֵ֣ין כֹּ֑ל בִּלְתִּ֖י אֶל־הַמָּ֥ן עֵינֵֽינוּ: ⁷ וְהַמָּ֕ן כִּזְרַע־גַּ֖ד ה֑וּא וְעֵינ֖וֹ כְּעֵ֥ין הַבְּדֹֽלַח: ⁸ שָׁ֩טוּ֩ הָעָ֨ם וְלָֽקְט֜וּ וְטָֽחֲנ֣וּ בָֽרֵחַ֗יִם א֤וֹ דָכוּ֙ בַּמְּדֹכָ֔ה וּבִשְּׁלוּ֙ בַּפָּר֔וּר וְעָשׂ֥וּ אֹת֖וֹ עֻג֑וֹת וְהָיָ֣ה טַעְמ֔וֹ כְּטַ֖עַם לְשַׁ֥ד הַשָּֽׁמֶן: ⁹ וּבְרֶ֧דֶת הַטַּ֛ל עַל־הַֽמַּחֲנֶ֖ה לָ֑יְלָה יֵרֵ֥ד הַמָּ֖ן עָלָֽיו:

¹⁰ וַיִּשְׁמַ֨ע מֹשֶׁ֜ה אֶת־הָעָ֗ם בֹּכֶה֙ לְמִשְׁפְּחֹתָ֔יו אִ֖ישׁ לְפֶ֣תַח אׇהֳל֑וֹ וַיִּֽחַר־אַ֤ף יְהֹוָה֙ מְאֹ֔ד וּבְעֵינֵ֥י מֹשֶׁ֖ה רָֽע: ¹¹ וַיֹּ֨אמֶר מֹשֶׁ֜ה אֶל־יְהֹוָ֗ה לָמָ֤ה הֲרֵעֹ֙תָ֙ לְעַבְדֶּ֔ךָ וְלָ֛מָּה לֹֽא־מָצָ֥תִי* חֵ֖ן בְּעֵינֶ֑יךָ לָשׂ֗וּם אֶת־מַשָּׂ֛א כׇּל־הָעָ֥ם הַזֶּ֖ה עָלָֽי: ¹² הֶאָֽנֹכִ֣י הָרִ֗יתִי אֵ֚ת כׇּל־הָעָ֣ם הַזֶּ֔ה אִם־אָֽנֹכִ֖י יְלִדְתִּ֑יהוּ כִּֽי־תֹאמַ֣ר אֵלַ֗י שָׂאֵ֤הוּ בְחֵיקֶ֙ךָ֙ כַּֽאֲשֶׁ֨ר יִשָּׂ֤א הָֽאֹמֵן֙ אֶת־הַיֹּנֵ֔ק עַ֚ל הָֽאֲדָמָ֔ה אֲשֶׁ֥ר נִשְׁבַּ֖עְתָּ לַֽאֲבֹתָֽיו: ¹³ מֵאַ֤יִן לִי֙ בָּשָׂ֔ר לָתֵ֖ת לְכׇל־הָעָ֣ם הַזֶּ֑ה כִּֽי־יִבְכּ֤וּ עָלַי֙ לֵאמֹ֔ר תְּנָה־לָּ֥נוּ בָשָׂ֖ר וְנֹאכֵֽלָה: ¹⁴ לֹֽא־אוּכַ֤ל אָֽנֹכִי֙ לְבַדִּ֔י לָשֵׂ֕את אֶת־כׇּל־הָעָ֥ם הַזֶּ֖ה כִּ֥י

א' נחה v. 4.
חסר א' v. 11.

---

a From root b'r, "to burn."
b Lit. "cream of oil (or, fat)."

by myself, for it is too much for me. ¹⁵If You would deal thus with me, kill me rather, I beg You, and let me see no more of my wretchedness!"

¹⁶Then the LORD said to Moses, "Gather for Me seventy of Israel's elders of whom you have experience as elders and officers of the people, and bring them to the Tent of Meeting and let them take their place there with you. ¹⁷I will come down and speak with you there, and I will draw upon the spirit that is on you and put it upon them; they shall share the burden of the people with you, and you shall not bear it alone. ¹⁸And say to the people: ^c-Purify yourselves-^c for tomorrow and you shall eat meat, for you have kept whining before the LORD and saying, 'If only we had meat to eat! Indeed, we were better off in Egypt!' The LORD will give you meat and you shall eat. ¹⁹You shall eat not one day, not two, not even five days or ten or twenty, ²⁰but a whole month, until it comes out of your nostrils and becomes loathsome to you. For you have rejected the LORD who is among you, by whining before Him and saying, 'Oh, why did we ever leave Egypt!'"

²¹But Moses said, "The people ^d-who are with me-^d number six hundred thousand men; yet You say, 'I will give them enough meat to eat for a whole month.' ²²Could enough flocks and herds be slaughtered to suffice them? Or could all the fish of the sea be gathered for them to suffice them?" ²³And the LORD answered Moses, ^e-"Is there a limit to the LORD's power?-^e You shall soon see whether what I have said happens to you or not!"

²⁴Moses went out and reported the words of the LORD to the people. He gathered seventy of the people's elders and stationed them around the Tent. ²⁵Then the LORD came down in a cloud

כָּבֵ֖ד מִמֶּֽנִּי׃ ¹⁵ וְאִם־כָּ֣כָה ׀ אַתְּ־עֹ֣שֶׂה לִּ֗י הָרְגֵ֤נִי נָא֙ הָרֹ֔ג אִם־מָצָ֥אתִי חֵ֖ן בְּעֵינֶ֑יךָ וְאַל־אֶרְאֶ֖ה בְּרָעָתִֽי׃ פ ¹⁶ וַיֹּ֨אמֶר יְהֹוָ֜ה אֶל־מֹשֶׁ֗ה אֶסְפָה־לִּ֞י שִׁבְעִ֣ים אִישׁ֮ מִזִּקְנֵ֣י יִשְׂרָאֵל֒ אֲשֶׁ֣ר יָדַ֔עְתָּ כִּי־הֵ֛ם זִקְנֵ֥י הָעָ֖ם וְשֹׁטְרָ֑יו וְלָקַחְתָּ֤ אֹתָם֙ אֶל־אֹ֣הֶל מוֹעֵ֔ד וְהִֽתְיַצְּב֥וּ שָׁ֖ם עִמָּֽךְ׃ ¹⁷ וְיָרַדְתִּ֗י וְדִבַּרְתִּ֣י עִמְּךָ֮ שָׁם֒ וְאָצַלְתִּ֗י מִן־הָר֛וּחַ אֲשֶׁ֥ר עָלֶ֖יךָ וְשַׂמְתִּ֣י עֲלֵיהֶ֑ם וְנָשְׂא֤וּ אִתְּךָ֙ בְּמַשָּׂ֣א הָעָ֔ם וְלֹא־תִשָּׂ֥א אַתָּ֖ה לְבַדֶּֽךָ׃ ¹⁸ וְאֶל־הָעָ֨ם תֹּאמַ֜ר הִתְקַדְּשׁ֣וּ לְמָחָר֮ וַאֲכַלְתֶּ֣ם בָּשָׂר֒ כִּ֡י בְּכִיתֶם֩ בְּאׇזְנֵ֨י יְהֹוָ֜ה לֵאמֹ֗ר מִ֤י יַאֲכִלֵ֙נוּ֙ בָּשָׂ֔ר כִּי־ט֥וֹב לָ֖נוּ בְּמִצְרָ֑יִם וְנָתַ֨ן יְהֹוָ֥ה לָכֶ֛ם בָּשָׂ֖ר וַאֲכַלְתֶּֽם׃ ¹⁹ לֹ֣א י֥וֹם אֶחָ֛ד תֹּֽאכְל֖וּן וְלֹ֣א יוֹמָ֑יִם וְלֹ֣א ׀ חֲמִשָּׁ֣ה יָמִ֗ים וְלֹא֙ עֲשָׂרָ֣ה יָמִ֔ים וְלֹ֖א עֶשְׂרִ֥ים יֽוֹם׃ ²⁰ עַ֣ד ׀ חֹ֣דֶשׁ יָמִ֗ים עַ֤ד אֲשֶׁר־יֵצֵא֙ מֵֽאַפְּכֶ֔ם וְהָיָ֥ה לָכֶ֖ם לְזָרָ֑א יַ֗עַן כִּֽי־מְאַסְתֶּ֤ם אֶת־יְהֹוָה֙ אֲשֶׁ֣ר בְּקִרְבְּכֶ֔ם וַתִּבְכּ֤וּ לְפָנָיו֙ לֵאמֹ֔ר לָ֥מָּה זֶּ֖ה יָצָ֥אנוּ מִמִּצְרָֽיִם׃ ²¹ וַיֹּ֘אמֶר֮ מֹשֶׁה֒ שֵׁשׁ־מֵא֥וֹת אֶ֙לֶף֙ רַגְלִ֔י הָעָ֕ם אֲשֶׁ֥ר אָנֹכִ֖י בְּקִרְבּ֑וֹ וְאַתָּ֣ה אָמַ֗רְתָּ בָּשָׂר֙ אֶתֵּ֣ן לָהֶ֔ם וְאָכְל֖וּ חֹ֥דֶשׁ יָמִֽים׃ ²² הֲצֹ֧אן וּבָקָ֛ר יִשָּׁחֵ֥ט לָהֶ֖ם וּמָצָ֣א לָהֶ֑ם אִ֣ם אֶֽת־כׇּל־דְּגֵ֥י הַיָּ֛ם יֵאָסֵ֥ף לָהֶ֖ם וּמָצָ֥א לָהֶֽם׃ פ ²³ וַיֹּ֤אמֶר יְהֹוָה֙ אֶל־מֹשֶׁ֔ה הֲיַ֥ד יְהֹוָ֖ה תִּקְצָ֑ר עַתָּ֥ה תִרְאֶ֛ה הֲיִקְרְךָ֥ דְבָרִ֖י אִם־לֹֽא׃ ²⁴ וַיֵּצֵ֣א מֹשֶׁ֗ה וַיְדַבֵּר֙ אֶל־הָעָ֔ם אֵ֖ת דִּבְרֵ֣י יְהֹוָ֑ה וַיֶּאֱסֹ֞ף שִׁבְעִ֥ים אִישׁ֙ מִזִּקְנֵ֣י הָעָ֔ם וַֽיַּעֲמֵ֥ד אֹתָ֖ם סְבִיבֹ֥ת הָאֹֽהֶל׃ ²⁵ וַיֵּ֤רֶד יְהֹוָ֣ה ׀ בֶּעָנָן֮ וַיְדַבֵּ֣ר אֵלָיו֒ וַיָּ֙אצֶל֙* מִן־

---

c-c I.e., as for a sacrificial meal.
d-d Lit. "in whose midst I am."
e-e Lit. "Is the LORD's hand too short?"

and spoke to him; He drew upon the spirit that was on him and put it upon the seventy elders. And when the spirit rested upon them, they f-spoke in ecstasy,-f but did not continue.

26Two men, one named Eldad and the other Medad, had remained in camp; yet the spirit rested upon them—they were among those recorded, but they had not gone out to the Tent—and they f-spoke in ecstasy-f in the camp. 27A youth ran out and told Moses, saying, "Eldad and Medad are acting the prophet in the camp!" 28And Joshua son of Nun, Moses' attendant from his youth, spoke up and said, "My lord Moses, restrain them!" 29But Moses said to him, "Are you wrought up on my account? Would that all the LORD's people were prophets, that the LORD put His spirit upon them!" 30Moses then reentered the camp together with the elders of Israel.

31A wind from the LORD started up, swept quail from the sea and strewed them over the camp, about a day's journey on this side and about a day's journey on that side, all around the camp, and some two cubits deep on the ground. 32The people set to gathering quail all that day and night and all the next day—even he who gathered least had ten *homers*—and they spread them out all around the camp. 33The meat was still between their teeth, nor yet chewed,g when the anger of the LORD blazed forth against the people and the LORD struck the people with a very severe plague. 34That place was named Kibroth-hattaavah,h because the people who had the craving were buried there.

35Then the people set out from Kibroth-hattaavah for Hazeroth.

הָרוּחַ אֲשֶׁר עָלָיו וַיִּתֵּן עַל־שִׁבְעִים אִישׁ הַזְּקֵנִים וַיְהִי כְּנוֹחַ עֲלֵיהֶם הָרוּחַ וַיִּתְנַבְּאוּ וְלֹא יָסָפוּ:

26 וַיִּשָּׁאֲרוּ שְׁנֵי־אֲנָשִׁים ׀ בַּמַּחֲנֶה שֵׁם הָאֶחָד ׀ אֶלְדָּד וְשֵׁם הַשֵּׁנִי מֵידָד וַתָּנַח עֲלֵהֶם הָרוּחַ וְהֵמָּה בַּכְּתֻבִים וְלֹא יָצְאוּ הָאֹהֱלָה וַיִּתְנַבְּאוּ בַּמַּחֲנֶה: 27 וַיָּרָץ הַנַּעַר וַיַּגֵּד לְמֹשֶׁה וַיֹּאמַר אֶלְדָּד וּמֵידָד מִתְנַבְּאִים בַּמַּחֲנֶה: 28 וַיַּעַן יְהוֹשֻׁעַ בִּן־נוּן מְשָׁרֵת מֹשֶׁה מִבְּחֻרָיו וַיֹּאמַר אֲדֹנִי מֹשֶׁה כְּלָאֵם: 29 וַיֹּאמֶר לוֹ מֹשֶׁה הַמְקַנֵּא אַתָּה לִי וּמִי יִתֵּן כָּל־עַם יְהוָה נְבִיאִים כִּי־יִתֵּן יְהוָה אֶת־רוּחוֹ עֲלֵיהֶם: 30 וַיֵּאָסֵף מֹשֶׁה אֶל־הַמַּחֲנֶה הוּא וְזִקְנֵי יִשְׂרָאֵל:

31 וְרוּחַ נָסַע ׀ מֵאֵת יְהוָה וַיָּגָז שַׂלְוִים מִן־הַיָּם וַיִּטֹּשׁ עַל־הַמַּחֲנֶה כְּדֶרֶךְ יוֹם כֹּה וּכְדֶרֶךְ יוֹם כֹּה סְבִיבוֹת הַמַּחֲנֶה וּכְאַמָּתַיִם עַל־פְּנֵי הָאָרֶץ: 32 וַיָּקָם הָעָם כָּל־הַיּוֹם הַהוּא וְכָל־הַלַּיְלָה וְכֹל ׀ יוֹם הַמָּחֳרָת וַיַּאַסְפוּ אֶת־הַשְּׂלָו הַמַּמְעִיט אָסַף עֲשָׂרָה חֳמָרִים וַיִּשְׁטְחוּ לָהֶם שָׁטוֹחַ סְבִיבוֹת הַמַּחֲנֶה: 33 הַבָּשָׂר עוֹדֶנּוּ בֵּין שִׁנֵּיהֶם טֶרֶם יִכָּרֵת וְאַף יְהוָה חָרָה בָעָם וַיַּךְ יְהוָה בָּעָם מַכָּה רַבָּה מְאֹד: 34 וַיִּקְרָא אֶת־שֵׁם־הַמָּקוֹם הַהוּא קִבְרוֹת הַתַּאֲוָה כִּי־שָׁם קָבְרוּ אֶת־הָעָם הַמִּתְאַוִּים:

35 מִקִּבְרוֹת הַתַּאֲוָה נָסְעוּ הָעָם חֲצֵרוֹת וַיִּהְיוּ בַּחֲצֵרוֹת: פ

---

f-f Others "prophesied."
g Meaning of Heb. *yikkareth* uncertain.
h I.e., "the graves of craving."

12

When they were in Hazeroth, [1]Miriam and Aaron spoke against Moses because of the Cushite woman he had married: "He married a Cushite woman!"

[2]They said, "Has the LORD spoken only through Moses? Has He not spoken through us as well?" The LORD heard it. [3]Now Moses was a very humble man, more so than any other man on earth. [4]Suddenly the LORD called to Moses, Aaron, and Miriam, "Come out, you three, to the Tent of Meeting." So the three of them went out. [5]The LORD came down in a pillar of cloud, stopped at the entrance of the Tent, and called out, "Aaron and Miriam!" The two of them came forward; [6]and He said, "Hear these My words: a-When a prophet of the LORD arises among you, I-a make Myself known to him in a vision, I speak with him in a dream. [7]Not so with My servant Moses; he is trusted throughout My household. [8]With him I speak mouth to mouth, plainly and not in riddles, and he beholds the likeness of the LORD. How then did you not shrink from speaking against My servant Moses!" [9]Still incensed with them, the LORD departed.

[10]As the cloud withdrew from the Tent, there was Miriam stricken with snow-white scales![b] When Aaron turned toward Miriam, he saw that she was stricken with scales. [11]And Aaron said to Moses, "O my lord, account not to us the sin which we committed in our folly. [12]Let her not be as one dead, who emerges from his mother's womb with half his flesh eaten away." [13]So Moses cried out to the LORD, saying, "O God, pray heal her!"

[14]But the LORD said to Moses, "If her father spat in her face, would she not bear her shame for seven days? Let her be shut out of camp for

---

יב וַתְּדַבֵּר מִרְיָם וְאַהֲרֹן בְּמֹשֶׁה עַל־
אֹדֹת הָאִשָּׁה הַכֻּשִׁית אֲשֶׁר לָקָח כִּי־
אִשָּׁה כֻשִׁית לָקָח: 2 וַיֹּאמְרוּ הֲרַק אַךְ־בְּמֹשֶׁה דִּבֶּר יְהוָה הֲלֹא
גַם־בָּנוּ דִבֵּר וַיִּשְׁמַע יְהוָה: 3 וְהָאִישׁ מֹשֶׁה
עָנָיו מְאֹד מִכֹּל הָאָדָם אֲשֶׁר עַל־
פְּנֵי הָאֲדָמָה: ס 4 וַיֹּאמֶר יְהוָה פִּתְאֹם
אֶל־מֹשֶׁה וְאֶל־אַהֲרֹן וְאֶל־מִרְיָם צְאוּ
שְׁלָשְׁתְּכֶם אֶל־אֹהֶל מוֹעֵד וַיֵּצְאוּ
שְׁלָשְׁתָּם: 5 וַיֵּרֶד יְהוָה בְּעַמּוּד עָנָן וַיַּעֲמֹד
פֶּתַח הָאֹהֶל וַיִּקְרָא אַהֲרֹן וּמִרְיָם וַיֵּצְאוּ
שְׁנֵיהֶם: 6 וַיֹּאמֶר שִׁמְעוּ־נָא דְבָרָי אִם־
יִהְיֶה נְבִיאֲכֶם יְהוָה בַּמַּרְאָה אֵלָיו אֶתְוַדָּע
בַּחֲלוֹם אֲדַבֶּר־בּוֹ: 7 לֹא־כֵן עַבְדִּי מֹשֶׁה
בְּכָל־בֵּיתִי נֶאֱמָן הוּא: 8 פֶּה אֶל־פֶּה
אֲדַבֶּר־בּוֹ וּמַרְאֶה וְלֹא בְחִידֹת וּתְמֻנַת
יְהוָה יַבִּיט וּמַדּוּעַ לֹא יְרֵאתֶם לְדַבֵּר
בְּעַבְדִּי בְמֹשֶׁה: 9 וַיִּחַר־אַף יְהוָה בָּם
וַיֵּלַךְ:
10 וְהֶעָנָן סָר מֵעַל הָאֹהֶל וְהִנֵּה מִרְיָם
מְצֹרַעַת כַּשָּׁלֶג וַיִּפֶן אַהֲרֹן אֶל־מִרְיָם וְהִנֵּה
מְצֹרָעַת: 11 וַיֹּאמֶר אַהֲרֹן אֶל־מֹשֶׁה בִּי
אֲדֹנִי אַל־נָא תָשֵׁת עָלֵינוּ חַטָּאת אֲשֶׁר
נוֹאַלְנוּ וַאֲשֶׁר חָטָאנוּ: 12 אַל־נָא תְהִי כַּמֵּת
אֲשֶׁר בְּצֵאתוֹ מֵרֶחֶם אִמּוֹ וַיֵּאָכֵל חֲצִי
בְשָׂרוֹ: 13 וַיִּצְעַק מֹשֶׁה אֶל־יְהוָה לֵאמֹר
אֵל נָא רְפָא נָא לָהּ: פ
14 וַיֹּאמֶר יְהוָה אֶל־מֹשֶׁה וְאָבִיהָ יָרֹק יָרַק
בְּפָנֶיהָ הֲלֹא תִכָּלֵם שִׁבְעַת יָמִים תִּסָּגֵר
שִׁבְעַת יָמִים מִחוּץ לַמַּחֲנֶה וְאַחַר תֵּאָסֵף:

---

a-a   *Meaning of Heb. uncertain. Others "If there be a prophet among you, I the* LORD."
b   *Cf. Lev. 13.2–3.*

seven days, and then let her be readmitted." [15]So Miriam was shut out of camp seven days; and the people did not march on until Miriam was readmitted. [16]After that the people set out from Hazeroth and encamped in the wilderness of Paran.

13 SHELAḤ-LEKHA
The Lord spoke to Moses, saying, [2]"Send men to scout the land of Canaan, which I am giving to the Israelite people; send one man from each of their ancestral tribes, each one a chieftain among them." [3]So Moses, by the Lord's command, sent them out from the wilderness of Paran, all the men being leaders of the Israelites. [4]And these were their names:

From the tribe of Reuben, Shammua son of Zaccur.

[5]From the tribe of Simeon, Shaphat son of Hori.

[6]From the tribe of Judah, Caleb son of Jephunneh.

[7]From the tribe of Issachar, Igal son of Joseph.

[8]From the tribe of Ephraim, Hosea[a] son of Nun.

[9]From the tribe of Benjamin, Palti son of Rafu.

[10]From the tribe of Zebulun, Gaddiel son of Sodi.

[11]From the tribe of Joseph, namely, the tribe of Manasseh, Gaddi son of Susi.

[12]From the tribe of Dan, Ammiel son of Gemalli.

[13]From the tribe of Asher, Sethur son of Michael.

[14]From the tribe of Naphtali, Nahbi son of Vophsi.

[15]From the tribe of Gad, Geuel son of Machi.

[16]Those were the names of the men whom Moses sent to scout the land; but Moses changed the name of Hosea[a] son of Nun to Joshua.

a   Or "Hoshea."

וַתִּסָּגֵ֞ר מִרְיָ֛ם מִח֥וּץ לַֽמַּחֲנֶ֖ה שִׁבְעַ֣ת 15 יָמִ֑ים וְהָעָם֙ לֹ֣א נָסַ֔ע עַד־הֵאָסֵ֖ף מִרְיָֽם׃ וְאַחַ֛ר נָסְע֥וּ הָעָ֖ם מֵֽחֲצֵר֑וֹת וַֽיַּחֲנ֖וּ 16 בְּמִדְבַּ֥ר פָּארָֽן׃ פ

יג שלח לך
וַיְדַבֵּ֥ר יְהֹוָ֖ה אֶל־מֹשֶׁ֥ה לֵּאמֹֽר׃ שְׁלַח־לְךָ֣ אֲנָשִׁ֗ים וְיָתֻ֙רוּ֙ אֶת־אֶ֣רֶץ כְּנַ֔עַן 2 אֲשֶׁר־אֲנִ֥י נֹתֵ֖ן לִבְנֵ֣י יִשְׂרָאֵ֑ל אִ֣ישׁ אֶחָד֩ אִ֨ישׁ אֶחָ֜ד לְמַטֵּ֤ה אֲבֹתָיו֙ תִּשְׁלָ֔חוּ כֹּ֖ל נָשִׂ֥יא בָהֶֽם׃ וַיִּשְׁלַ֨ח אֹתָ֥ם מֹשֶׁ֛ה מִמִּדְבַּ֥ר 3 פָּארָ֖ן עַל־פִּ֣י יְהֹוָ֑ה כֻּלָּ֣ם אֲנָשִׁ֔ים רָאשֵׁ֥י בְנֵֽי־יִשְׂרָאֵ֖ל הֵֽמָּה׃ וְאֵ֖לֶּה שְׁמוֹתָ֑ם 4 לְמַטֵּ֣ה רְאוּבֵ֔ן שַׁמּ֖וּעַ בֶּן־זַכּֽוּר׃ לְמַטֵּ֣ה שִׁמְע֔וֹן שָׁפָ֖ט בֶּן־חוֹרִֽי׃ 5 לְמַטֵּ֣ה יְהוּדָ֔ה כָּלֵ֖ב בֶּן־יְפֻנֶּֽה׃ 6 לְמַטֵּ֣ה יִשָּׂשכָ֔ר יִגְאָ֖ל בֶּן־יוֹסֵֽף׃ 7 לְמַטֵּ֥ה אֶפְרָ֖יִם הוֹשֵׁ֥עַ בִּן־נֽוּן׃ 8 לְמַטֵּ֣ה בִנְיָמִ֔ן פַּלְטִ֖י בֶּן־רָפֽוּא׃ 9 לְמַטֵּ֣ה זְבוּלֻ֔ן גַּדִּיאֵ֖ל בֶּן־סוֹדִֽי׃ 10 לְמַטֵּ֣ה יוֹסֵ֔ף לְמַטֵּ֣ה מְנַשֶּׁ֔ה גַּדִּ֖י בֶּן־ 11 סוּסִֽי׃ לְמַטֵּ֣ה דָ֔ן עַמִּיאֵ֖ל בֶּן־גְּמַלִּֽי׃ 12 לְמַטֵּ֣ה אָשֵׁ֔ר סְת֖וּר בֶּן־מִיכָאֵֽל׃ 13 לְמַטֵּ֣ה נַפְתָּלִ֔י נַחְבִּ֖י בֶּן־וׇפְסִֽי׃ 14 לְמַטֵּ֣ה גָ֔ד גְּאוּאֵ֖ל בֶּן־מָכִֽי׃ 15 אֵ֚לֶּה שְׁמ֣וֹת הָֽאֲנָשִׁ֔ים אֲשֶׁר־שָׁלַ֥ח מֹשֶׁ֖ה 16 לָת֣וּר אֶת־הָאָ֑רֶץ וַיִּקְרָ֥א מֹשֶׁ֛ה לְהוֹשֵׁ֥עַ בִּן־נ֖וּן יְהוֹשֻֽׁעַ׃

17When Moses sent them to scout the land of Canaan, he said to them, "Go up there into the Negeb and on into the hill country, 18and see what kind of country it is. Are the people who dwell in it strong or weak, few or many? 19Is the country in which they dwell good or bad? Are the towns they live in open or fortified? 20Is the soil rich or poor? Is it wooded or not? And take pains to bring back some of the fruit of the land."—Now it happened to be the season of the first ripe grapes.

21They went up and scouted the land, from the wilderness of Zin to Rehob, at Lebo-hamath.b 22They went up into the Negeb and came to Hebron, where lived Ahiman, Sheshai, and Talmai, the Anakites.—Now Hebron was founded seven years before Zoan of Egypt.—23They reached the wadi Eshcol, and there they cut down a branch with a single cluster of grapes—it had to be borne on a carrying frame by two of them—and some pomegranates and figs. 24That place was named the wadi Eshcolc because of the cluster that the Israelites cut down there.

25At the end of forty days they returned from scouting the land. 26They went straight to Moses and Aaron and the whole Israelite community at Kadesh in the wilderness of Paran, and they made their report to them and to the whole community, as they showed them the fruit of the land. 27This is what they told him: "We came to the land you sent us to; it does indeed flow with milk and honey, and this is its fruit. 28However, the people who inhabit the country are powerful, and the cities are fortified and very large; moreover, we saw the Anakites there. 29Amalekites dwell in the Negeb region; Hittites, Jebusites, and Amorites inhabit the hill country; and Canaanites dwell by the Sea and along the Jordan."

17 וַיִּשְׁלַ֤ח אֹתָם֙ מֹשֶׁ֔ה לָת֖וּר אֶת־אֶ֣רֶץ כְּנָ֑עַן וַיֹּ֣אמֶר אֲלֵהֶ֗ם עֲל֥וּ זֶה֙ בַּנֶּ֔גֶב וַעֲלִיתֶ֖ם אֶת־הָהָֽר׃ 18 וּרְאִיתֶ֥ם אֶת־הָאָ֖רֶץ מַה־הִ֑וא וְאֶת־הָעָם֙ הַיֹּשֵׁ֣ב עָלֶ֔יהָ הֶחָזָ֥ק הוּא֙ הֲרָפֶ֔ה הַמְעַ֥ט ה֖וּא אִם־רָֽב׃ 19 וּמָ֣ה הָאָ֗רֶץ אֲשֶׁר־הוּא֙ יֹשֵׁ֣ב בָּ֔הּ הֲטוֹבָ֥ה הִ֖וא אִם־רָעָ֑ה וּמָ֣ה הֶֽעָרִ֗ים אֲשֶׁר־הוּא֙ יוֹשֵׁ֣ב בָּהֵ֔נָּה הַבְּמַֽחֲנִ֖ים אִ֥ם בְּמִבְצָרִֽים׃ 20 וּמָ֣ה הָ֠אָ֠רֶץ הַשְּׁמֵנָ֨ה הִ֜וא אִם־רָזָ֗ה הֲיֵֽשׁ־בָּ֥הּ עֵץ֙ אִם־אַ֔יִן וְהִ֨תְחַזַּקְתֶּ֔ם וּלְקַחְתֶּ֖ם מִפְּרִ֣י הָאָ֑רֶץ וְהַ֨יָּמִ֔ים יְמֵ֖י בִּכּוּרֵ֥י עֲנָבִֽים׃

21 וַֽיַּעֲל֖וּ וַיָּתֻ֣רוּ אֶת־הָאָ֑רֶץ מִמִּדְבַּר־צִ֥ן עַד־רְחֹ֖ב לְבֹ֥א חֲמָֽת׃ 22 וַיַּעֲל֣וּ בַנֶּגֶב֮ וַיָּבֹ֣א* עַד־חֶבְרוֹן֒ וְשָׁ֤ם אֲחִימַן֙ שֵׁשַׁ֣י וְתַלְמַ֔י יְלִידֵ֖י הָעֲנָ֑ק וְחֶבְר֗וֹן שֶׁ֤בַע שָׁנִים֙ נִבְנְתָ֔ה לִפְנֵ֖י צֹ֥עַן מִצְרָֽיִם׃ 23 וַיָּבֹ֜אוּ עַד־נַ֣חַל אֶשְׁכֹּ֗ל וַיִּכְרְת֨וּ מִשָּׁ֤ם זְמוֹרָה֙ וְאֶשְׁכּ֤וֹל עֲנָבִים֙ אֶחָ֔ד וַיִּשָּׂאֻ֥הוּ בַמּ֖וֹט בִּשְׁנָ֑יִם וּמִן־הָרִמֹּנִ֖ים וּמִן־הַתְּאֵנִֽים׃ 24 לַמָּק֣וֹם הַה֔וּא קָרָ֖א נַ֣חַל אֶשְׁכּ֑וֹל עַ֚ל אֹד֣וֹת הָֽאֶשְׁכּ֔וֹל אֲשֶׁר־כָּרְת֥וּ מִשָּׁ֖ם בְּנֵ֥י יִשְׂרָאֵֽל׃

25 וַיָּשֻׁ֖בוּ מִתּ֣וּר הָאָ֑רֶץ מִקֵּ֖ץ אַרְבָּעִ֥ים יֽוֹם׃ 26 וַיֵּלְכ֡וּ וַיָּבֹאוּ֩ אֶל־מֹשֶׁ֨ה וְאֶֽל־אַהֲרֹ֜ן וְאֶל־כָּל־עֲדַ֧ת בְּנֵֽי־יִשְׂרָאֵ֛ל אֶל־מִדְבַּ֥ר פָּארָ֖ן קָדֵ֑שָׁה וַיָּשִׁ֨יבוּ אֹתָ֤ם דָּבָר֙ וְאֶת־כָּל־הָ֣עֵדָ֔ה וַיַּרְא֖וּם אֶת־פְּרִ֥י הָאָֽרֶץ׃ 27 וַיְסַפְּרוּ־לוֹ֙ וַיֹּ֣אמְר֔וּ בָּ֕אנוּ אֶל־הָאָ֖רֶץ אֲשֶׁ֣ר שְׁלַחְתָּ֑נוּ וְ֠גַ֠ם זָבַ֨ת חָלָ֥ב וּדְבַ֛שׁ הִ֖וא וְזֶה־פִּרְיָֽהּ׃ 28 אֶ֚פֶס כִּֽי־עַ֣ז הָעָ֔ם הַיֹּשֵׁ֖ב בָּאָ֑רֶץ וְהֶֽעָרִ֗ים בְּצֻר֤וֹת גְּדֹלֹת֙ מְאֹ֔ד וְגַם־יְלִדֵ֥י הָעֲנָ֖ק רָאִ֥ינוּ שָֽׁם׃ 29 עֲמָלֵ֥ק יוֹשֵׁ֖ב בְּאֶ֣רֶץ הַנֶּ֑גֶב וְ֠הַֽחִתִּ֠י וְהַיְבוּסִ֤י וְהָֽאֱמֹרִי֙ יוֹשֵׁ֣ב בָּהָ֔ר וְהַֽכְּנַעֲנִי֙ יוֹשֵׁ֣ב עַל־הַיָּ֔ם וְעַ֖ל יַ֥ד הַיַּרְדֵּֽן׃

v. 22. סבירין ומטעין לשון רבים

---

b   Others "the entrance to Hamath."
c   I.e., "cluster."

30Caleb hushed the people before Moses and said, "Let us by all means go up, and we shall gain possession of it, for we shall surely overcome it."

31But the men who had gone up with him said, "We cannot attack that people, for it is stronger than we." 32Thus they spread calumnies among the Israelites about the land they had scouted, saying, "The country that we traversed and scouted is one that devours its settlers. All the people that we saw in it are men of great size; 33we saw the Nephilim[d] there—the Anakites are part of the Nephilim—and we looked like grasshoppers to ourselves, and so we must have looked to them."

14 The whole community broke into loud cries, and the people wept that night. 2All the Israelites railed against Moses and Aaron. "If only we had died in the land of Egypt," the whole community shouted at them, "or if only we might die in this wilderness! 3Why is the LORD taking us to that land to fall by the sword? Our wives and children will be carried off! It would be better for us to go back to Egypt!" 4And they said to one another, "Let us [a-]head back for[-a] Egypt."

5Then Moses and Aaron fell on their faces before all the assembled congregation of the Israelites. 6And Joshua son of Nun and Caleb son of Jephunneh, of those who had scouted the land, rent their clothes 7and exhorted the whole Israelite community: "The land that we traversed and scouted is an exceedingly good land. 8If the LORD is pleased with us, He will bring us into that land, a land that flows with milk and honey, and give it to us; 9only you must not rebel against the LORD. Have no fear then of the

---

d See Gen. 6.4.

a-a Lit. "set the head and return to"; cf. Neh. 9.17. Others "Let us make a captain and return to."

30 וַיַּ֧הַס כָּלֵ֛ב אֶת־הָעָ֖ם אֶל־מֹשֶׁ֑ה וַיֹּ֗אמֶר עָלֹ֤ה נַעֲלֶה֙ וְיָרַ֣שְׁנוּ אֹתָ֔הּ כִּֽי־יָכ֥וֹל נוּכַ֖ל לָֽהּ׃

31 וְהָ֣אֲנָשִׁ֗ים אֲשֶׁר־עָל֤וּ עִמּוֹ֙ אָֽמְר֔וּ לֹ֥א נוּכַ֖ל לַעֲל֣וֹת אֶל־הָעָ֑ם כִּֽי־חָזָ֥ק ה֖וּא מִמֶּֽנּוּ׃ 32 וַיּוֹצִ֜יאוּ דִּבַּ֤ת הָאָ֙רֶץ֙ אֲשֶׁ֣ר תָּר֣וּ אֹתָ֔הּ אֶל־בְּנֵ֥י יִשְׂרָאֵ֖ל לֵאמֹ֑ר הָאָ֡רֶץ אֲשֶׁר֩ עָבַ֨רְנוּ בָ֜הּ לָת֣וּר אֹתָ֗הּ אֶ֣רֶץ אֹכֶ֤לֶת יוֹשְׁבֶ֙יהָ֙ הִ֔וא וְכָל־הָעָ֛ם אֲשֶׁר־רָאִ֥ינוּ בְתוֹכָ֖הּ אַנְשֵׁ֥י מִדּֽוֹת׃ 33 וְשָׁ֣ם רָאִ֗ינוּ אֶת־הַנְּפִילִ֛ים בְּנֵ֥י עֲנָ֖ק מִן־הַנְּפִלִ֑ים וַנְּהִ֤י בְעֵינֵ֙ינוּ֙ כַּֽחֲגָבִ֔ים וְכֵ֥ן הָיִ֖ינוּ בְּעֵינֵיהֶֽם׃

יד וַתִּשָּׂא֙ כָּל־הָ֣עֵדָ֔ה וַֽיִּתְּנ֖וּ אֶת־קוֹלָ֑ם וַיִּבְכּ֥וּ הָעָ֖ם בַּלַּ֥יְלָה הַהֽוּא׃ 2 וַיִּלֹּ֙נוּ֙ עַל־מֹשֶׁ֣ה וְעַֽל־אַהֲרֹ֔ן כֹּ֖ל בְּנֵ֣י יִשְׂרָאֵ֑ל וַיֹּאמְר֨וּ אֲלֵהֶ֜ם כָּל־הָעֵדָ֗ה לוּ־מַ֙תְנוּ֙ בְּאֶ֣רֶץ מִצְרַ֔יִם א֛וֹ בַּמִּדְבָּ֥ר הַזֶּ֖ה לוּ־מָֽתְנוּ׃ 3 וְלָמָ֣ה יְ֠הוָה מֵבִ֨יא אֹתָ֜נוּ אֶל־הָאָ֤רֶץ הַזֹּאת֙ לִנְפֹּ֣ל בַּחֶ֔רֶב נָשֵׁ֥ינוּ וְטַפֵּ֖נוּ יִהְי֣וּ לָבַ֑ז הֲל֧וֹא ט֛וֹב לָ֖נוּ שׁ֥וּב מִצְרָֽיְמָה׃ 4 וַיֹּאמְר֖וּ אִ֣ישׁ אֶל־אָחִ֑יו נִתְּנָ֥ה רֹ֖אשׁ וְנָשׁ֥וּבָה מִצְרָֽיְמָה׃ 5 וַיִּפֹּ֥ל מֹשֶׁ֛ה וְאַהֲרֹ֖ן עַל־פְּנֵיהֶ֑ם לִפְנֵ֕י כָּל־קְהַ֥ל עֲדַ֖ת בְּנֵ֥י יִשְׂרָאֵֽל׃ 6 וִיהוֹשֻׁ֣עַ בִּן־נ֗וּן וְכָלֵב֙ בֶּן־יְפֻנֶּ֔ה מִן־הַתָּרִ֖ים אֶת־הָאָ֑רֶץ קָרְע֖וּ בִּגְדֵיהֶֽם׃ 7 וַיֹּ֣אמְר֔וּ אֶל־כָּל־עֲדַ֥ת בְּנֵֽי־יִשְׂרָאֵ֖ל לֵאמֹ֑ר הָאָ֗רֶץ אֲשֶׁ֨ר עָבַ֤רְנוּ בָהּ֙ לָת֣וּר אֹתָ֔הּ טוֹבָ֥ה הָאָ֖רֶץ מְאֹ֥ד מְאֹֽד׃ 8 אִם־חָפֵ֥ץ בָּ֙נוּ֙ יְהוָ֔ה וְהֵבִ֤יא אֹתָ֙נוּ֙ אֶל־הָאָ֣רֶץ הַזֹּ֔את וּנְתָנָ֖הּ לָ֑נוּ אֶ֕רֶץ אֲשֶׁר־הִ֛וא זָבַ֥ת חָלָ֖ב וּדְבָֽשׁ׃ 9 אַ֣ךְ בַּֽיהוָה֮ אַל־תִּמְרֹ֒דוּ֒ וְאַתֶּ֗ם אַל־תִּֽירְאוּ֙ אֶת־עַ֣ם הָאָ֔רֶץ

people of the country, for they are our prey:*b*
their protection has departed from them, but
the LORD is with us. Have no fear of them!" 10As
the whole community threatened to pelt them
with stones, the Presence of the LORD appeared
in the Tent of Meeting to all the Israelites.

11And the LORD said to Moses, "How long will
this people spurn Me, and how long will they
have no faith in Me despite all the signs that I
have performed in their midst? 12I will strike
them with pestilence and disown them, and I
will make of you a nation far more numerous
than they!" 13But Moses said to the LORD,
"When the Egyptians, from whose midst You
brought up this people in Your might, hear the
news, 14they will tell it to the inhabitants of that
land. Now they have heard that You, O LORD,
are in the midst of this people; that You, O LORD,
appear in plain sight when Your cloud rests over
them and when You go before them in a pillar
of cloud by day and in a pillar of fire by night.
15If then You slay this people to a man, the nations who have heard Your fame will say, 16'It
must be because the LORD was powerless to
bring that people into the land He had promised
them on oath that He slaughtered them in the
wilderness.' 17Therefore, I pray, let my Lord's
forbearance be great, as You have declared,
saying,*c* 18'The LORD! slow to anger and
abounding in kindness; forgiving iniquity and
transgression; yet not remitting all punishment,
but visiting the iniquity of fathers upon children, upon the third and fourth generations.'
19Pardon, I pray, the iniquity of this people according to Your great kindness, as You have forgiven this people ever since Egypt."

20And the LORD said, "I pardon, as you have
asked. 21Nevertheless, as I live and as the LORD's
Presence fills the whole world, 22none of the
men who have seen My Presence and the signs

כִּי לַחְמֵנוּ הֵם סָר צִלָּם מֵעֲלֵיהֶם וַיהֹוָה
אִתָּנוּ אַל־תִּירָאֻם׃ 10 וַיֹּאמְרוּ כָּל־הָעֵדָה
לִרְגּוֹם אֹתָם בָּאֲבָנִים וּכְבוֹד יְהֹוָה נִרְאָה
בְּאֹהֶל מוֹעֵד אֶל־כָּל־בְּנֵי יִשְׂרָאֵל׃ פ
11 וַיֹּאמֶר יְהֹוָה אֶל־מֹשֶׁה עַד־אָנָה יְנַאֲצֻנִי
הָעָם הַזֶּה וְעַד־אָנָה לֹא־יַאֲמִינוּ בִי בְּכֹל
הָאֹתוֹת אֲשֶׁר עָשִׂיתִי בְּקִרְבּוֹ׃ 12 אַכֶּנּוּ
בַדֶּבֶר וְאוֹרִשֶׁנּוּ וְאֶעֱשֶׂה אֹתְךָ לְגוֹי־גָּדוֹל
וְעָצוּם מִמֶּנּוּ׃ 13 וַיֹּאמֶר מֹשֶׁה אֶל־יְהֹוָה
וְשָׁמְעוּ מִצְרַיִם כִּי־הֶעֱלִיתָ בְכֹחֲךָ אֶת־
הָעָם הַזֶּה מִקִּרְבּוֹ׃ 14 וְאָמְרוּ אֶל־יוֹשֵׁב
הָאָרֶץ הַזֹּאת שָׁמְעוּ כִּי־אַתָּה יְהֹוָה בְּקֶרֶב
הָעָם הַזֶּה אֲשֶׁר־עַיִן בְּעַיִן נִרְאָה | אַתָּה
יְהֹוָה וַעֲנָנְךָ עֹמֵד עֲלֵהֶם וּבְעַמֻּד עָנָן אַתָּה
הֹלֵךְ לִפְנֵיהֶם יוֹמָם וּבְעַמּוּד אֵשׁ לָיְלָה׃
15 וְהֵמַתָּה אֶת־הָעָם הַזֶּה כְּאִישׁ אֶחָד
וְאָמְרוּ הַגּוֹיִם אֲשֶׁר־שָׁמְעוּ אֶת־שִׁמְעֲךָ
לֵאמֹר׃ 16 מִבִּלְתִּי יְכֹלֶת יְהֹוָה לְהָבִיא
אֶת־הָעָם הַזֶּה אֶל־הָאָרֶץ אֲשֶׁר־נִשְׁבַּע
לָהֶם וַיִּשְׁחָטֵם בַּמִּדְבָּר׃ 17 וְעַתָּה יִגְדַּל־
נָא* כֹּחַ אֲדֹנָי כַּאֲשֶׁר דִּבַּרְתָּ לֵאמֹר׃
18 יְהֹוָה אֶרֶךְ אַפַּיִם וְרַב־חֶסֶד נֹשֵׂא עָוֹן
וָפֶשַׁע וְנַקֵּה לֹא יְנַקֶּה פֹּקֵד עֲוֹן אָבוֹת
עַל־בָּנִים עַל־שִׁלֵּשִׁים וְעַל־רִבֵּעִים׃
19 סְלַח־נָא לַעֲוֹן הָעָם הַזֶּה כְּגֹדֶל חַסְדֶּךָ
וְכַאֲשֶׁר נָשָׂאתָה לָעָם הַזֶּה מִמִּצְרַיִם
וְעַד־הֵנָּה׃
20 וַיֹּאמֶר יְהֹוָה סָלַחְתִּי כִּדְבָרֶךָ׃ 21 וְאוּלָם
חַי־אָנִי וְיִמָּלֵא כְבוֹד־יְהֹוָה אֶת־כָּל־
הָאָרֶץ׃ 22 כִּי כָל־הָאֲנָשִׁים הָרֹאִים אֶת־
כְּבֹדִי וְאֶת־אֹתֹתַי אֲשֶׁר־עָשִׂיתִי בְמִצְרַיִם

---

b   Lit. "food (or, bread)."
c   Cf. Exod. 34.6–7.

that I have performed in Egypt and in the wilderness, and who have tried Me these many[d] times and have disobeyed Me, [23]shall see the land that I promised on oath to their fathers; none of those who spurn Me shall see it. [24]But My servant Caleb, because he was imbued with a different spirit and remained loyal to Me—him will I bring into the land that he entered, and his offspring shall hold it as a possession. [25]Now the Amalekites and the Canaanites occupy the valleys. Start out, then, tomorrow and march into the wilderness by way of the Sea of Reeds."[e]

[26]The LORD spoke further to Moses and Aaron, [27]"How much longer shall that wicked community keep muttering against Me? Very well, I have heeded the incessant muttering of the Israelites against Me. [28]Say to them: 'As I live,' says the LORD, 'I will do to you just as you have urged Me. [29]In this very wilderness shall your carcasses drop. Of all of you who were recorded in your various lists from the age of twenty years up, you who have muttered against Me, [30]not one shall enter the land in which I swore[f] to settle you—save Caleb son of Jephunneh and Joshua son of Nun. [31]Your children who, you said, would be carried off—these will I allow to enter; they shall know the land that you have rejected. [32]But your carcasses shall drop in this wilderness, [33]while your children roam the wilderness for forty years, suffering for your faithlessness, until the last of your carcasses is down in the wilderness. [34]You shall bear your punishment for forty years, corresponding to the number of days—forty days—that you scouted the land: a year for each day. Thus you shall know what it means to thwart Me. [35]I the LORD have spoken: Thus will I do to all that wicked band that has banded together against

וּבַמִּדְבָּר וַיְנַסּוּ אֹתִי זֶה עֶשֶׂר פְּעָמִים וְלֹא שָׁמְעוּ בְּקוֹלִי: 23 אִם־יִרְאוּ אֶת־הָאָרֶץ אֲשֶׁר נִשְׁבַּעְתִּי לַאֲבֹתָם וְכָל־מְנַאֲצַי לֹא יִרְאוּהָ: 24 וְעַבְדִּי כָלֵב עֵקֶב הָיְתָה רוּחַ אַחֶרֶת עִמּוֹ וַיְמַלֵּא אַחֲרָי וַהֲבִיאֹתִיו אֶל־הָאָרֶץ אֲשֶׁר־בָּא שָׁמָּה וְזַרְעוֹ יוֹרִשֶׁנָּה: 25 וְהָעֲמָלֵקִי וְהַכְּנַעֲנִי יוֹשֵׁב בָּעֵמֶק מָחָר פְּנוּ וּסְעוּ לָכֶם הַמִּדְבָּר דֶּרֶךְ יַם־סוּף: פ 26 וַיְדַבֵּר יְהֹוָה אֶל־מֹשֶׁה וְאֶל־אַהֲרֹן לֵאמֹר: 27 עַד־מָתַי לָעֵדָה הָרָעָה הַזֹּאת אֲשֶׁר הֵמָּה מַלִּינִים עָלָי אֶת־תְּלֻנּוֹת בְּנֵי יִשְׂרָאֵל אֲשֶׁר הֵמָּה מַלִּינִים עָלַי שָׁמָעְתִּי: 28 אֱמֹר אֲלֵהֶם חַי־אָנִי נְאֻם־יְהֹוָה אִם־לֹא כַּאֲשֶׁר דִּבַּרְתֶּם בְּאָזְנָי כֵּן אֶעֱשֶׂה לָכֶם: 29 בַּמִּדְבָּר הַזֶּה יִפְּלוּ פִגְרֵיכֶם וְכָל־פְּקֻדֵיכֶם לְכָל־מִסְפַּרְכֶם מִבֶּן עֶשְׂרִים שָׁנָה וָמָעְלָה אֲשֶׁר הֲלִינֹתֶם עָלָי: 30 אִם־אַתֶּם תָּבֹאוּ אֶל־הָאָרֶץ אֲשֶׁר נָשָׂאתִי אֶת־יָדִי לְשַׁכֵּן אֶתְכֶם בָּהּ כִּי אִם־כָּלֵב בֶּן־יְפֻנֶּה וִיהוֹשֻׁעַ בִּן־נוּן: 31 וְטַפְּכֶם אֲשֶׁר אֲמַרְתֶּם לָבַז יִהְיֶה וְהֵבֵיאתִי אֹתָם וְיָדְעוּ אֶת־הָאָרֶץ אֲשֶׁר מְאַסְתֶּם בָּהּ: 32 וּפִגְרֵיכֶם אַתֶּם יִפְּלוּ בַּמִּדְבָּר הַזֶּה: 33 וּבְנֵיכֶם יִהְיוּ רֹעִים בַּמִּדְבָּר אַרְבָּעִים שָׁנָה וְנָשְׂאוּ אֶת־זְנוּתֵיכֶם עַד־תֹּם פִּגְרֵיכֶם בַּמִּדְבָּר: 34 בְּמִסְפַּר הַיָּמִים אֲשֶׁר־תַּרְתֶּם אֶת־הָאָרֶץ אַרְבָּעִים יוֹם יוֹם לַשָּׁנָה יוֹם לַשָּׁנָה תִּשְׂאוּ אֶת־עֲוֺנֹתֵיכֶם אַרְבָּעִים שָׁנָה וִידַעְתֶּם אֶת־תְּנוּאָתִי: 35 אֲנִי יְהֹוָה דִּבַּרְתִּי אִם־לֹא ׀ זֹאת אֶעֱשֶׂה לְכָל־הָעֵדָה

---

d   Lit. "ten"; cf. note at Gen. 31.41.
e   See note at Exod. 10.19.
f   Lit. "raised My hand."

Me: in this very wilderness they shall die to the last man.'"

36As for the men whom Moses sent to scout the land, those who came back and caused the whole community to mutter against him by spreading calumnies about the land—37those who spread such calumnies about the land died of plague, by the will of the LORD. 38Of those men who had gone to scout the land, only Joshua son of Nun and Caleb son of Jephunneh survived.

39When Moses repeated these words to all the Israelites, the people were overcome by grief. 40Early next morning they set out toward the crest of the hill country, saying, "We are prepared to go up to the place that the LORD has spoken of, for we were wrong." 41But Moses said, "Why do you transgress the LORD's command? This will not succeed. 42Do not go up, lest you be routed by your enemies, for the LORD is not in your midst. 43For the Amalekites and the Canaanites will be there to face you, and you will fall by the sword, inasmuch as you have turned from following the LORD and the LORD will not be with you."

44Yet defiantly[g] they marched toward the crest of the hill country, though neither the LORD's Ark of the Covenant nor Moses stirred from the camp. 45And the Amalekites and the Canaanites who dwelt in that hill country came down and dealt them a shattering blow at Hormah.

15

The LORD spoke to Moses, saying: 2Speak to the Israelite people and say to them:

When you enter the land that I am giving you to settle in, 3and would present an offering by fire to the LORD from the herd or from the flock, be it burnt offering or sacrifice, in fulfillment

---

הָרָעָ֣ה הַזֹּ֗את הַנּוֹעָדִ֛ים עָלַ֖י בַּמִּדְבָּ֣ר הַזֶּ֑ה יִתַּ֖מּוּ וְשָׁ֥ם יָמֻֽתוּ׃ 36 וְהָ֣אֲנָשִׁ֔ים אֲשֶׁר־שָׁלַ֥ח מֹשֶׁ֖ה לָת֣וּר אֶת־הָאָ֑רֶץ וַיָּשֻׁ֙בוּ֙ וילינו [וַיַּלִּ֤ינוּ] עָלָיו֙ אֶת־כׇּל־הָ֣עֵדָ֔ה לְהוֹצִ֥יא דִבָּ֖ה עַל־הָאָֽרֶץ׃ 37 וַיָּמֻ֙תוּ֙ הָֽאֲנָשִׁ֔ים מוֹצִאֵ֥י דִבַּת־הָאָ֖רֶץ רָעָ֑ה בַּמַּגֵּפָ֖ה לִפְנֵ֥י יְהֹוָֽה׃ 38 וִיהוֹשֻׁ֣עַ בִּן־נ֔וּן וְכָלֵ֖ב בֶּן־יְפֻנֶּ֑ה חָיוּ֙ מִן־הָאֲנָשִׁ֣ים הָהֵ֔ם הַהֹֽלְכִ֖ים לָת֥וּר אֶת־הָאָֽרֶץ׃ 39 וַיְדַבֵּ֤ר מֹשֶׁה֙ אֶת־הַדְּבָרִ֣ים הָאֵ֔לֶּה אֶל־כׇּל־בְּנֵ֖י יִשְׂרָאֵ֑ל וַיִּֽתְאַבְּל֥וּ הָעָ֖ם מְאֹֽד׃ 40 וַיַּשְׁכִּ֣מוּ בַבֹּ֔קֶר וַיַּֽעֲל֥וּ אֶל־רֹאשׁ־הָהָ֖ר לֵאמֹ֑ר הִנֶּ֗נּוּ וְעָלִ֛ינוּ אֶל־הַמָּק֛וֹם אֲשֶׁר־אָמַ֥ר יְהֹוָ֖ה כִּ֥י חָטָֽאנוּ׃ 41 וַיֹּ֣אמֶר מֹשֶׁ֔ה לָ֥מָּה זֶּ֛ה אַתֶּ֥ם עֹבְרִ֖ים אֶת־פִּ֣י יְהֹוָ֑ה וְהִ֖וא לֹ֥א תִצְלָֽח׃ 42 אַֽל־תַּֽעֲל֔וּ כִּ֛י אֵ֥ין יְהֹוָ֖ה בְּקִרְבְּכֶ֑ם וְלֹא֙ תִּנָּ֣גְפ֔וּ לִפְנֵ֖י אֹיְבֵיכֶֽם׃ 43 כִּי֩ הָעֲמָלֵקִ֨י וְהַכְּנַעֲנִ֥י שָׁם֙ לִפְנֵיכֶ֔ם וּנְפַלְתֶּ֖ם בֶּחָ֑רֶב כִּֽי־עַל־כֵּ֤ן שַׁבְתֶּם֙ מֵאַחֲרֵ֣י יְהֹוָ֔ה וְלֹא־יִהְיֶ֥ה יְהֹוָ֖ה עִמָּכֶֽם׃ 44 וַיַּעְפִּ֕לוּ לַעֲל֖וֹת אֶל־רֹ֣אשׁ הָהָ֑ר וַאֲר֤וֹן בְּרִית־יְהֹוָה֙ וּמֹשֶׁ֔ה לֹא־מָ֖שׁוּ מִקֶּ֥רֶב הַֽמַּחֲנֶֽה׃ 45 וַיֵּ֤רֶד הָעֲמָלֵקִי֙ וְהַֽכְּנַעֲנִ֔י הַיֹּשֵׁ֖ב בָּהָ֣ר הַה֑וּא וַיַּכּ֥וּם וַֽיַּכְּת֖וּם עַד־הַֽחׇרְמָֽה׃ פ

טו

וַיְדַבֵּ֥ר יְהֹוָ֖ה אֶל־מֹשֶׁ֥ה לֵּאמֹֽר׃ 2 דַּבֵּר֙ אֶל־בְּנֵ֣י יִשְׂרָאֵ֔ל וְאָמַרְתָּ֖ אֲלֵהֶ֑ם כִּ֣י תָבֹ֗אוּ אֶל־אֶ֙רֶץ֙ מוֹשְׁבֹ֣תֵיכֶ֔ם אֲשֶׁ֥ר אֲנִ֖י נֹתֵ֥ן לָכֶֽם׃ 3 וַעֲשִׂיתֶ֨ם אִשֶּׁ֤ה לַֽיהֹוָה֙ עֹלָ֣ה אוֹ־זֶ֔בַח לְפַלֵּא־נֶ֙דֶר֙ א֣וֹ בִנְדָבָ֔ה א֖וֹ

---

g *Meaning of Heb. uncertain.*

of a vow explicitly uttered,ᵃ or as a freewill offering, or at your fixed occasions, producing an odor pleasing to the LORD:

⁴The person who presents the offering to the LORD shall bring as a meal offering: a tenth of a measure of choice flour with a quarter of a *hin* of oil mixed in. ⁵You shall also offer, with the burnt offering or the sacrifice, a quarter of a *hin* of wine as a libation for each sheep.

⁶In the case of a ram, you shall present as a meal offering: two-tenths of a measure of choice flour with a third of a *hin* of oil mixed in; ⁷and a third of a *hin* of wine as a libation—as an offering of pleasing odor to the LORD.

⁸And if it is an animal from the herd that you offer to the LORD as a burnt offering or as a sacrifice, in fulfillment of a vow explicitly uttered or as an offering of well-being, ⁹there shall be offered a meal offering along with the animal: three-tenths of a measure of choice flour with half a *hin* of oil mixed in; ¹⁰and as libation you shall offer half a *hin* of wine—these being offerings by fire of pleasing odor to the LORD.

¹¹Thus shall be done with each ox, with each ram, and with any sheep or goat, ¹²as many as you offer; you shall do thus with each one, as many as there are. ¹³Every citizen, when presenting an offering by fire of pleasing odor to the LORD, shall do so with them.

¹⁴And when, throughout the ages, a stranger who has taken up residence with you, or one who lives among you, would present an offering by fire of pleasing odor to the LORD—as you do, so ᵇ-shall it be done by ¹⁵the rest of the congregation.-ᵇ There shall be one law for you and for the resident stranger; it shall be a law for all time throughout the ages. You and the stranger shall be alike before the LORD; ¹⁶the same ritual and the same rule shall apply to you and to the stranger who resides among you.

בְּמֹעֲדֵיכֶ֑ם לַעֲשׂ֞וֹת רֵ֤יחַ נִיחֹ֙חַ֙ לַֽיהֹוָ֔ה מִן־הַבָּקָ֖ר א֥וֹ מִן־הַצֹּֽאן׃

⁴ וְהִקְרִ֛יב הַמַּקְרִ֥יב קׇרְבָּנ֖וֹ לַֽיהֹוָ֑ה מִנְחָה֙ סֹ֣לֶת עִשָּׂר֔וֹן בָּל֕וּל בִּרְבִעִ֥ית הַהִ֖ין שָֽׁמֶן׃ ⁵ וְיַ֤יִן לַנֶּ֙סֶךְ֙ רְבִיעִ֣ית הַהִ֔ין תַּעֲשֶׂ֥ה עַל־הָעֹלָ֖ה א֣וֹ לַזָּ֑בַח לַכֶּ֖בֶשׂ הָאֶחָֽד׃

⁶ א֤וֹ לָאַ֙יִל֙ תַּעֲשֶׂ֣ה מִנְחָ֔ה סֹ֖לֶת שְׁנֵ֣י עֶשְׂרֹנִ֑ים בְּלוּלָ֥ה בַשֶּׁ֖מֶן שְׁלִשִׁ֥ית הַהִֽין׃ ⁷ וְיַ֥יִן לַנֶּ֖סֶךְ שְׁלִשִׁ֣ית הַהִ֑ין תַּקְרִ֥יב רֵֽיחַ־נִיחֹ֖חַ לַֽיהֹוָֽה׃

⁸ וְכִֽי־תַעֲשֶׂ֥ה בֶן־בָּקָ֖ר עֹלָ֣ה אוֹ־זָ֑בַח לְפַלֵּא־נֶ֥דֶר אֽוֹ־שְׁלָמִ֖ים לַֽיהֹוָֽה׃ ⁹ וְהִקְרִ֤יב עַל־בֶּן־הַבָּקָר֙ מִנְחָ֔ה סֹ֖לֶת שְׁלֹשָׁ֣ה עֶשְׂרֹנִ֑ים בָּל֥וּל בַּשֶּׁ֖מֶן חֲצִ֥י הַהִֽין׃ ¹⁰ וְיַ֛יִן תַּקְרִ֥יב לַנֶּ֖סֶךְ חֲצִ֣י הַהִ֑ין אִשֵּׁ֥ה רֵֽיחַ־נִיחֹ֖חַ לַֽיהֹוָֽה׃

¹¹ כָּ֣כָה יֵעָשֶׂ֗ה לַשּׁוֹר֙ הָֽאֶחָ֔ד א֖וֹ לָאַ֣יִל הָאֶחָ֑ד אֽוֹ־לַשֶּׂ֥ה בַכְּבָשִׂ֖ים א֥וֹ בָעִזִּֽים׃ ¹² כַּמִּסְפָּ֖ר אֲשֶׁ֣ר תַּעֲשׂ֑וּ כָּ֣כָה תַּעֲשׂ֥וּ לָאֶחָ֖ד כְּמִסְפָּרָֽם׃ ¹³ כׇּל־הָאֶזְרָ֥ח יַעֲשֶׂה־כָּ֖כָה אֶת־אֵ֑לֶּה לְהַקְרִ֛יב אִשֵּׁ֥ה רֵֽיחַ־נִיחֹ֖חַ לַֽיהֹוָֽה׃

¹⁴ וְכִֽי־יָגוּר֩ אִתְּכֶ֨ם גֵּ֜ר א֤וֹ אֲשֶֽׁר־בְּתֽוֹכְכֶם֙ לְדֹרֹ֣תֵיכֶ֔ם וְעָשָׂ֛ה אִשֵּׁ֥ה רֵֽיחַ־נִיחֹ֖חַ לַֽיהֹוָ֑ה כַּאֲשֶׁ֥ר תַּעֲשׂ֖וּ כֵּ֥ן יַעֲשֶֽׂה׃ ¹⁵ הַקָּהָ֕ל חֻקָּ֥ה אַחַ֛ת לָכֶ֖ם וְלַגֵּ֣ר הַגָּ֑ר חֻקַּ֤ת עוֹלָם֙ לְדֹרֹ֣תֵיכֶ֔ם כָּכֶ֛ם כַּגֵּ֥ר יִהְיֶ֖ה לִפְנֵ֥י יְהֹוָֽה׃ ¹⁶ תּוֹרָ֥ה אַחַ֛ת וּמִשְׁפָּ֥ט אֶחָ֖ד יִהְיֶ֣ה לָכֶ֑ם וְלַגֵּ֖ר הַגָּ֥ר אִתְּכֶֽם׃ פ

ᵃ   *See note at Lev. 22.21.*
ᵇ-ᵇ   *Meaning of Heb. uncertain.*

17The Lord spoke to Moses, saying: 18Speak to the Israelite people and say to them:

When you enter the land to which I am taking you 19and you eat of the bread of the land, you shall set some aside as a gift to the Lord: 20as the first yield of your baking,c you shall set aside a loaf as a gift; you shall set it aside as a gift like the gift from the threshing floor. 21You shall make a gift to the Lord from the first yield of your baking, throughout the ages.

22If you unwittingly fail to observe any one of the commandments that the Lord has declared to Moses—23anything that the Lord has enjoined upon you through Moses—from the day that the Lord gave the commandment and on through the ages:

24If this was done unwittingly, through the inadvertence of the community, the whole community shall present one bull of the herd as a burnt offering of pleasing odor to the Lord, with its proper meal offering and libation, and one he-goat as a sin offering. 25The priest shall make expiation for the whole Israelite community and they shall be forgiven; for it was an error, and for their error they have brought their offering, an offering by fire to the Lord and their sin offering before the Lord. 26The whole Israelite community and the stranger residing among them shall be forgiven, for it happened to the entire people through error.

27In case it is an individual who has sinned unwittingly, he shall offer a she-goat in its first year as a sin offering. 28The priest shall make expiation before the Lord on behalf of the person who erred, for he sinned unwittingly, making such expiation for him that he may be forgiven. 29For the citizen among the Israelites and for the stranger who resides among them—you shall have one ritual for anyone who acts in error.

---

c Meaning of Heb. 'arisah uncertain.

17 וַיְדַבֵּר יְהוָה אֶל־מֹשֶׁה לֵּאמֹר: 18 דַּבֵּר אֶל־בְּנֵי יִשְׂרָאֵל וְאָמַרְתָּ אֲלֵהֶם בְּבֹאֲכֶם אֶל־הָאָרֶץ אֲשֶׁר אֲנִי מֵבִיא אֶתְכֶם שָׁמָּה: 19 וְהָיָה בַּאֲכָלְכֶם מִלֶּחֶם הָאָרֶץ תָּרִימוּ תְרוּמָה לַיהוָה: 20 רֵאשִׁית עֲרִסֹתֵכֶם חַלָּה תָּרִימוּ תְרוּמָה כִּתְרוּמַת גֹּרֶן כֵּן תָּרִימוּ אֹתָהּ: 21 מֵרֵאשִׁית עֲרִסֹתֵיכֶם תִּתְּנוּ לַיהוָה תְּרוּמָה לְדֹרֹתֵיכֶם: ס

22 וְכִי תִשְׁגּוּ וְלֹא תַעֲשׂוּ אֵת כָּל־הַמִּצְוֹת הָאֵלֶּה אֲשֶׁר־דִּבֶּר יְהוָה אֶל־מֹשֶׁה: 23 אֵת כָּל־אֲשֶׁר צִוָּה יְהוָה אֲלֵיכֶם בְּיַד־מֹשֶׁה מִן־הַיּוֹם אֲשֶׁר צִוָּה יְהוָה וָהָלְאָה לְדֹרֹתֵיכֶם: 24 וְהָיָה אִם מֵעֵינֵי הָעֵדָה נֶעֶשְׂתָה לִשְׁגָגָה וְעָשׂוּ כָל־הָעֵדָה פַּר בֶּן־בָּקָר אֶחָד לְעֹלָה לְרֵיחַ נִיחֹחַ לַיהוָה וּמִנְחָתוֹ וְנִסְכּוֹ כַּמִּשְׁפָּט וּשְׂעִיר־עִזִּים אֶחָד לְחַטָּת*: 25 וְכִפֶּר הַכֹּהֵן עַל־כָּל־עֲדַת בְּנֵי יִשְׂרָאֵל וְנִסְלַח לָהֶם כִּי־שְׁגָגָה הִוא וְהֵם הֵבִיאוּ אֶת־קָרְבָּנָם אִשֶּׁה לַיהוָה וְחַטָּאתָם לִפְנֵי יְהוָה עַל־שִׁגְגָתָם: 26 וְנִסְלַח לְכָל־עֲדַת בְּנֵי יִשְׂרָאֵל וְלַגֵּר הַגָּר בְּתוֹכָם כִּי לְכָל־הָעָם בִּשְׁגָגָה: ס

27 וְאִם־נֶפֶשׁ אַחַת תֶּחֱטָא בִשְׁגָגָה וְהִקְרִיבָה עֵז בַּת־שְׁנָתָהּ לְחַטָּאת: 28 וְכִפֶּר הַכֹּהֵן עַל־הַנֶּפֶשׁ הַשֹּׁגֶגֶת בְּחֶטְאָה בִשְׁגָגָה לִפְנֵי יְהוָה לְכַפֵּר עָלָיו וְנִסְלַח לוֹ: 29 הָאֶזְרָח בִּבְנֵי יִשְׂרָאֵל וְלַגֵּר הַגָּר בְּתוֹכָם תּוֹרָה אַחַת יִהְיֶה לָכֶם לָעֹשֶׂה בִּשְׁגָגָה:

³⁰But the person, be he citizen or stranger, who acts defiantly^d reviles the Lord; that person shall be cut off from among his people. ³¹Because he has spurned the word of the Lord and violated His commandment, that person shall be cut off—he bears his guilt.

³²Once, when the Israelites were in the wilderness, they came upon a man gathering wood on the sabbath day. ³³Those who found him as he was gathering wood brought him before Moses, Aaron, and the whole community. ³⁴He was placed in custody, for it had not been specified what should be done to him. ³⁵Then the Lord said to Moses, "The man shall be put to death: the whole community shall pelt him with stones outside the camp." ³⁶So the whole community took him outside the camp and stoned him to death—as the Lord had commanded Moses.

³⁷The Lord said to Moses as follows: ³⁸Speak to the Israelite people and instruct them to make for themselves fringes on the corners of their garments throughout the ages; let them attach a cord of blue to the fringe at each corner. ³⁹That shall be your fringe; look at it and recall all the commandments of the Lord and observe them, so that you do not follow your heart and eyes in your lustful urge. ⁴⁰Thus you shall be reminded to observe all My commandments and to be holy to your God. ⁴¹I the Lord am your God, who brought you out of the land of Egypt to be your God: I, the Lord your God.

16 KORAḤ
Now Korah, son of Izhar son of Kohath son of Levi, ^a-betook himself,-^a along with

---

³⁰ וְהַנֶּ֜פֶשׁ אֲשֶׁר־תַּעֲשֶׂ֣ה ׀ בְּיָ֣ד רָמָ֗ה מִן־הָֽאֶזְרָח֙ וּמִן־הַגֵּ֔ר אֶת־יְהֹוָ֖ה ה֣וּא מְגַדֵּ֑ף וְנִכְרְתָ֛ה הַנֶּ֥פֶשׁ הַהִ֖וא מִקֶּ֥רֶב עַמָּֽהּ׃ ³¹ כִּ֤י דְבַר־יְהֹוָה֙ בָּזָ֔ה וְאֶת־מִצְוָת֖וֹ הֵפַ֑ר הִכָּרֵ֧ת ׀ תִּכָּרֵ֛ת הַנֶּ֥פֶשׁ הַהִ֖וא עֲוֺנָ֥ה בָֽהּ׃ פ

³² וַיִּהְי֥וּ בְנֵֽי־יִשְׂרָאֵ֖ל בַּמִּדְבָּ֑ר וַֽיִּמְצְא֗וּ אִ֛ישׁ מְקֹשֵׁ֥שׁ עֵצִ֖ים בְּי֥וֹם הַשַּׁבָּֽת׃ ³³ וַיַּקְרִ֣יבוּ אֹת֔וֹ הַמֹּצְאִ֥ים אֹת֖וֹ מְקֹשֵׁ֣שׁ עֵצִ֑ים אֶל־מֹשֶׁה֙ וְאֶֽל־אַהֲרֹ֔ן וְאֶ֖ל כׇּל־הָעֵדָֽה׃ ³⁴ וַיַּנִּ֥יחוּ אֹת֖וֹ בַּמִּשְׁמָ֑ר כִּ֛י לֹ֥א פֹרַ֖שׁ מַה־יֵּעָשֶׂ֥ה לֽוֹ׃ ס ³⁵ וַיֹּ֤אמֶר יְהֹוָה֙ אֶל־מֹשֶׁ֔ה מ֥וֹת יוּמַ֖ת הָאִ֑ישׁ רָג֨וֹם אֹת֤וֹ בָֽאֲבָנִים֙ כׇּל־הָ֣עֵדָ֔ה מִח֖וּץ לַֽמַּחֲנֶֽה׃ ³⁶ וַיֹּצִ֨יאוּ אֹת֜וֹ כׇּל־הָעֵדָ֗ה אֶל־מִחוּץ֙ לַֽמַּחֲנֶ֔ה וַיִּרְגְּמ֥וּ אֹת֛וֹ בָּאֲבָנִ֖ים וַיָּמֹ֑ת כַּאֲשֶׁ֛ר צִוָּ֥ה יְהֹוָ֖ה אֶת־מֹשֶֽׁה׃ פ

³⁷ וַיֹּ֥אמֶר יְהֹוָ֖ה אֶל־מֹשֶׁ֥ה לֵּאמֹֽר׃ ³⁸ דַּבֵּ֞ר אֶל־בְּנֵ֤י יִשְׂרָאֵל֙ וְאָמַרְתָּ֣ אֲלֵהֶ֔ם וְעָשׂ֨וּ לָהֶ֥ם צִיצִ֛ת עַל־כַּנְפֵ֥י בִגְדֵיהֶ֖ם לְדֹרֹתָ֑ם וְנָ֥תְנ֛וּ עַל־צִיצִ֥ת הַכָּנָ֖ף פְּתִ֥יל תְּכֵֽלֶת׃ ³⁹ וְהָיָ֣ה לָכֶם֮ לְצִיצִת֒ וּרְאִיתֶ֣ם אֹת֗וֹ וּזְכַרְתֶּם֙ אֶת־כׇּל־מִצְוֺ֣ת יְהֹוָ֔ה וַעֲשִׂיתֶ֖ם אֹתָ֑ם וְלֹֽא־תָת֜וּרוּ אַחֲרֵ֤י לְבַבְכֶם֙ וְאַחֲרֵ֣י עֵֽינֵיכֶ֔ם אֲשֶׁר־אַתֶּ֥ם זֹנִ֖ים אַחֲרֵיהֶֽם׃ ⁴⁰ לְמַ֣עַן תִּזְכְּר֔וּ וַעֲשִׂיתֶ֖ם אֶת־כׇּל־מִצְוֺתָ֑י וִהְיִיתֶ֥ם קְדֹשִׁ֖ים לֵֽאלֹהֵיכֶֽם׃ ⁴¹ אֲנִ֞י יְהֹוָ֣ה אֱלֹֽהֵיכֶ֗ם אֲשֶׁ֨ר הוֹצֵ֤אתִי אֶתְכֶם֙ מֵאֶ֣רֶץ מִצְרַ֔יִם לִהְי֥וֹת לָכֶ֖ם לֵאלֹהִ֑ים אֲנִ֖י יְהֹוָ֥ה אֱלֹהֵיכֶֽם׃ פ

טז קרח
¹ וַיִּקַּ֣ח קֹ֔רַח בֶּן־יִצְהָ֥ר בֶּן־קְהָ֖ת בֶּן־לֵוִ֑י וְדָתָ֨ן וַאֲבִירָ֜ם בְּנֵ֧י אֱלִיאָ֛ב וְא֥וֹן

---

^d Lit. "with upraised hand."

^{a-a} Lit. "took"; meaning of Heb. uncertain.

Dathan and Abiram sons of Eliab, *b-*and On son of Peleth—descendants of Reuben-*b*—²to rise up against Moses, together with two hundred and fifty Israelites, chieftains of the community, chosen in the assembly, men of repute. ³They combined against Moses and Aaron and said to them, "You have gone too far! For all the community are holy, all of them, and the LORD is in their midst. Why then do you raise yourselves above the LORD's congregation?"

⁴When Moses heard this, he fell on his face.*c* ⁵Then he spoke to Korah and all his company, saying, "Come morning, the LORD will make known who is His and who is holy, and will grant him access to Himself; He will grant access to the one He has chosen. ⁶Do this: You, Korah and all your*d* band, take fire pans, ⁷and tomorrow put fire in them and lay incense on them before the LORD. Then the man whom the LORD chooses, he shall be the holy one. You have gone too far, sons of Levi!"

⁸Moses said further to Korah, "Hear me, sons of Levi. ⁹Is it not enough for you that the God of Israel has set you apart from the community of Israel and given you access to Him, to perform the duties of the LORD's Tabernacle and to minister to the community and serve them? ¹⁰Now that He has advanced you and all your fellow Levites with you, do you seek the priesthood too? ¹¹Truly, it is against the LORD that you and all your company have banded together. For who is Aaron that you should rail against him?"

¹²Moses sent for Dathan and Abiram, sons of Eliab; but they said, "We will not come! ¹³Is it not enough that you brought us from a land flowing with milk and honey to have us die in the wilderness, that you would also lord it over us? ¹⁴*e-*Even if you had-*e* brought us to a land

בֶּן־פֶּ֫לֶת֙ בְּנֵ֣י רְאוּבֵֽן׃ ²וַיָּקֻ֙מוּ֙ לִפְנֵ֣י מֹשֶׁ֔ה וַאֲנָשִׁ֥ים מִבְּנֵֽי־יִשְׂרָאֵ֖ל חֲמִשִּׁ֣ים וּמָאתָ֑יִם נְשִׂיאֵ֥י עֵדָ֛ה קְרִאֵ֥י מוֹעֵ֖ד אַנְשֵׁי־שֵֽׁם׃ ³וַיִּקָּהֲל֞וּ עַל־מֹשֶׁ֣ה וְעַֽל־אַהֲרֹ֗ן וַיֹּאמְר֣וּ אֲלֵהֶם֮ רַב־לָכֶם֒ כִּ֤י כָל־הָֽעֵדָה֙ כֻּלָּ֣ם קְדֹשִׁ֔ים וּבְתוֹכָ֖ם יְהֹוָ֑ה וּמַדּ֥וּעַ תִּֽתְנַשְּׂא֖וּ עַל־קְהַ֥ל יְהֹוָֽה׃ ⁴וַיִּשְׁמַ֣ע מֹשֶׁ֔ה וַיִּפֹּ֖ל עַל־פָּנָֽיו׃ ⁵וַיְדַבֵּ֨ר אֶל־קֹ֜רַח וְאֶֽל־כׇּל־עֲדָתוֹ֮ לֵאמֹר֒ בֹּ֠קֶר וְיֹדַ֨ע יְהֹוָ֧ה אֶת־אֲשֶׁר־ל֛וֹ וְאֶת־הַקָּד֖וֹשׁ וְהִקְרִ֣יב אֵלָ֑יו וְאֵ֛ת אֲשֶׁ֥ר יִבְחַר־בּ֖וֹ יַקְרִ֥יב אֵלָֽיו׃ ⁶זֹ֖את עֲשׂ֑וּ קְחוּ־לָכֶ֣ם מַחְתּ֔וֹת קֹ֖רַח וְכׇל־עֲדָתֽוֹ׃ ⁷וּתְנ֣וּ בָהֵ֣ן ׀ אֵ֡שׁ וְשִׂ֩ימוּ֩ עֲלֵיהֶ֨ן קְטֹ֜רֶת לִפְנֵ֤י יְהֹוָה֙ מָחָ֔ר וְהָיָ֗ה הָאִ֛ישׁ אֲשֶׁר־יִבְחַ֥ר יְהֹוָ֖ה ה֣וּא הַקָּד֑וֹשׁ רַב־לָכֶ֖ם בְּנֵ֥י לֵוִֽי׃ ⁸וַיֹּ֥אמֶר מֹשֶׁ֖ה אֶל־קֹ֑רַח שִׁמְעוּ־נָ֖א בְּנֵ֥י לֵוִֽי׃ ⁹הַמְעַ֣ט מִכֶּ֗ם כִּֽי־הִבְדִּיל֩ אֱלֹהֵ֨י יִשְׂרָאֵ֤ל אֶתְכֶם֙ מֵעֲדַ֣ת יִשְׂרָאֵ֔ל לְהַקְרִ֥יב אֶתְכֶ֖ם אֵלָ֑יו לַעֲבֹ֗ד אֶת־עֲבֹדַת֙ מִשְׁכַּ֣ן יְהֹוָ֔ה וְלַעֲמֹ֛ד לִפְנֵ֥י הָעֵדָ֖ה לְשָׁרְתָֽם׃ ¹⁰וַיַּקְרֵב֙ אֹֽתְךָ֔ וְאֶת־כׇּל־אַחֶ֥יךָ בְנֵֽי־לֵוִ֖י אִתָּ֑ךְ וּבִקַּשְׁתֶּ֖ם גַּם־כְּהֻנָּֽה׃ ¹¹לָכֵ֗ן אַתָּה֙ וְכׇל־עֲדָ֣תְךָ֔ הַנֹּעָדִ֖ים עַל־יְהֹוָ֑ה וְאַהֲרֹ֣ן מַה־ה֔וּא כִּ֥י תַלִּ֖ינוּ עָלָֽיו׃ ¹²וַיִּשְׁלַ֣ח מֹשֶׁ֔ה לִקְרֹ֛א לְדָתָ֥ן וְלַאֲבִירָ֖ם בְּנֵ֣י אֱלִיאָ֑ב וַיֹּאמְר֖וּ לֹ֥א נַעֲלֶֽה׃ ¹³הַמְעַ֗ט כִּ֤י הֶעֱלִיתָ֙נוּ֙ מֵאֶ֨רֶץ זָבַ֤ת חָלָב֙ וּדְבַ֔שׁ לַהֲמִיתֵ֖נוּ בַּמִּדְבָּ֑ר כִּֽי־תִשְׂתָּרֵ֥ר עָלֵ֖ינוּ גַּם־הִשְׂתָּרֵֽר׃ ¹⁴אַ֡ף לֹ֣א אֶל־אֶ֩רֶץ֩ זָבַ֨ת חָלָ֤ב

---

b-b   *According to Num. 26.5, 8–9, Eliab was son of Pallu, son of Reuben.*

c   *Perhaps in the sense of "his face fell."*

d   *Lit. "his."*

e-e   *Lit. "You have not even."*

flowing with milk and honey, and given us possession of fields and vineyards, should you gouge out those men's eyes?*f* We will not come!" 15Moses was much aggrieved and he said to the LORD, "Pay no regard to their oblation. I have not taken the ass of any one of them, nor have I wronged any one of them."

16And Moses said to Korah, "Tomorrow, you and all your company appear before the LORD, you and they and Aaron. 17Each of you take his fire pan and lay incense on it, and each of you bring his fire pan before the LORD, two hundred and fifty fire pans; you and Aaron also [bring] your fire pans." 18Each of them took his fire pan, put fire in it, laid incense on it, and took his place at the entrance of the Tent of Meeting, as did Moses and Aaron. 19Korah gathered the whole community against them at the entrance of the Tent of Meeting.

Then the Presence of the LORD appeared to the whole community, 20and the LORD spoke to Moses and Aaron, saying, 21"Stand back from this community that I may annihilate them in an instant!" 22But they fell on their faces and said, "O God, Source*g* of the breath of all flesh! When one man sins, will You be wrathful with the whole community?"

23The LORD spoke to Moses, saying, 24"Speak to the community and say: Withdraw from about the abodes of Korah, Dathan, and Abiram."

25Moses rose and went to Dathan and Abiram, the elders of Israel following him. 26He addressed the community, saying, "Move away from the tents of these wicked men and touch nothing that belongs to them, lest you be wiped out for all their sins." 27So they withdrew from about the abodes of Korah, Dathan, and Abiram.

וּדְבַ֔שׁ הֲבִיאֹתָ֔נוּ וַתִּתֶּן־לָ֕נוּ נַחֲלַ֖ת שָׂדֶ֣ה וָכָ֑רֶם הַעֵינֵ֞י הָאֲנָשִׁ֤ים הָהֵם֙ תְּנַקֵּ֔ר לֹ֖א נַעֲלֶֽה׃ 15 וַיִּ֤חַר לְמֹשֶׁה֙ מְאֹ֔ד וַיֹּ֙אמֶר֙ אֶל־יְהֹוָ֔ה אַל־תֵּ֖פֶן אֶל־מִנְחָתָ֑ם לֹ֠א חֲמ֨וֹר אֶחָ֤ד מֵהֶם֙ נָשָׂ֔אתִי וְלֹ֥א הֲרֵעֹ֖תִי אֶת־אַחַ֥ד מֵהֶֽם׃ 16 וַיֹּ֤אמֶר מֹשֶׁה֙ אֶל־קֹ֔רַח אַתָּה֙ וְכׇל־עֲדָ֣תְךָ֔ הֱי֖וּ לִפְנֵ֣י יְהֹוָ֑ה אַתָּ֥ה וָהֵ֛ם וְאַהֲרֹ֖ן מָחָֽר׃ 17 וּקְח֣וּ ׀ אִ֣ישׁ מַחְתָּת֗וֹ וּנְתַתֶּ֣ם עֲלֵיהֶם֮ קְטֹ֒רֶת֒ וְהִקְרַבְתֶּ֞ם לִפְנֵ֤י יְהֹוָה֙ אִ֣ישׁ מַחְתָּת֔וֹ חֲמִשִּׁ֥ים וּמָאתַ֖יִם מַחְתֹּ֑ת וְאַתָּ֥ה וְאַהֲרֹ֖ן אִ֥ישׁ מַחְתָּתֽוֹ׃ 18 וַיִּקְח֞וּ אִ֣ישׁ מַחְתָּת֗וֹ וַיִּתְּנ֤וּ עֲלֵיהֶם֙ אֵ֔שׁ וַיָּשִׂ֥ימוּ עֲלֵיהֶ֖ם קְטֹ֑רֶת וַיַּֽעַמְד֗וּ פֶּ֛תַח אֹ֥הֶל מוֹעֵ֖ד וּמֹשֶׁ֥ה וְאַהֲרֹֽן׃ 19 וַיַּקְהֵ֨ל עֲלֵיהֶ֥ם קֹ֙רַח֙ אֶת־כׇּל־הָ֣עֵדָ֔ה אֶל־פֶּ֖תַח אֹ֣הֶל מוֹעֵ֑ד וַיֵּרָ֥א כְבוֹד־יְהֹוָ֖ה אֶל־כׇּל־הָעֵדָֽה׃ פ 20 וַיְדַבֵּ֣ר יְהֹוָ֔ה אֶל־מֹשֶׁ֥ה וְאֶֽל־אַהֲרֹ֖ן לֵאמֹֽר׃ 21 הִבָּ֣דְל֔וּ מִתּ֖וֹךְ הָעֵדָ֣ה הַזֹּ֑את וַאֲכַלֶּ֥ה אֹתָ֖ם כְּרָֽגַע׃ 22 וַיִּפְּל֤וּ עַל־פְּנֵיהֶם֙ וַיֹּ֣אמְר֔וּ אֵ֕ל אֱלֹהֵ֥י הָרוּחֹ֖ת לְכׇל־בָּשָׂ֑ר הָאִ֤ישׁ אֶחָד֙ יֶחֱטָ֔א וְעַ֥ל כׇּל־הָעֵדָ֖ה תִּקְצֹֽף׃ פ 23 וַיְדַבֵּ֥ר יְהֹוָ֖ה אֶל־מֹשֶׁ֥ה לֵּאמֹֽר׃ 24 דַּבֵּ֥ר אֶל־הָעֵדָ֖ה לֵאמֹ֑ר הֵֽעָלוּ֙ מִסָּבִ֔יב לְמִשְׁכַּן־קֹ֖רַח דָּתָ֥ן וַאֲבִירָֽם׃ 25 וַיָּ֣קׇם מֹשֶׁ֔ה וַיֵּ֖לֶךְ אֶל־דָּתָ֣ן וַאֲבִירָ֑ם וַיֵּלְכ֥וּ אַחֲרָ֖יו זִקְנֵ֥י יִשְׂרָאֵֽל׃ 26 וַיְדַבֵּ֨ר אֶל־הָעֵדָ֜ה לֵאמֹ֗ר ס֣וּרוּ נָ֡א מֵעַל֩ אׇהֳלֵ֨י הָאֲנָשִׁ֤ים הָֽרְשָׁעִים֙ הָאֵ֔לֶּה וְאַֽל־תִּגְּע֖וּ בְּכׇל־אֲשֶׁ֣ר לָהֶ֑ם פֶּן־תִּסָּפ֖וּ בְּכׇל־חַטֹּאתָֽם׃ 27 וַיֵּעָל֗וּ מֵעַ֧ל מִשְׁכַּן־קֹ֛רַח דָּתָ֥ן וַאֲבִירָ֖ם מִסָּבִ֑יב

---

f "Those men's" is a euphemism for "our"; cf. 1 Sam 29.4. Gouging out the eyes was punishment for runaway slaves and rebellious vassals; cf. 2 Kings 25.4–7; Jer. 39.4–7, 52.7–11.
g Lit. "God."

Now Dathan and Abiram had come out and they stood at the entrance of their tents, with their wives, their children, and their little ones. [28]And Moses said, "By this you shall know that it was the LORD who sent me to do all these things; that they are not of my own devising: [29]if these men die as all men do, if their lot be the common fate of all mankind, it was not the LORD who sent me. [30]But if the LORD brings about something unheard-of, so that the ground opens its mouth and swallows them up with all that belongs to them, and they go down alive into Sheol, you shall know that these men have spurned the LORD." [31]Scarcely had he finished speaking all these words when the ground under them burst asunder, [32]and the earth opened its mouth and swallowed them up with their households, all Korah's people and all their possessions. [33]They went down alive into Sheol, with all that belonged to them; the earth closed over them and they vanished from the midst of the congregation. [34]All Israel around them fled at their shrieks, for they said, "The earth might swallow us!"

[35]And a fire went forth from the LORD and consumed the two hundred and fifty men offering the incense.

17

The LORD spoke to Moses, saying: [2]Order Eleazar son of Aaron the priest to remove the fire pans—for they have become sacred—from among the charred remains; and scatter the coals abroad. [3][a][Remove] the fire pans of those who have sinned at the cost of their lives, and let them be made into hammered sheets as plating for the altar—for once they have been used for offering to the LORD, they have become sacred—and let them serve as a warning to the people of Israel. [4]Eleazar the priest took the cop-

וְדָתָ֤ן וַאֲבִירָם֙ יָצְא֣וּ נִצָּבִ֔ים פֶּ֖תַח אָֽהֳלֵיהֶ֑ם וּנְשֵׁיהֶ֥ם וּבְנֵיהֶ֖ם וְטַפָּֽם: 28 וַיֹּ֘אמֶר֮ מֹשֶׁה֒ בְּזֹאת֙ תֵּֽדְע֔וּן כִּֽי־יְהֹוָ֣ה שְׁלָחַ֔נִי לַעֲשׂ֕וֹת אֵ֖ת כָּל־הַמַּעֲשִׂ֣ים הָאֵ֑לֶּה כִּי־לֹ֖א מִלִּבִּֽי: 29 אִם־כְּמ֤וֹת כָּל־הָֽאָדָם֙ יְמֻת֣וּן אֵ֔לֶּה וּפְקֻדַּת֙ כָּל־הָ֣אָדָ֔ם יִפָּקֵ֖ד עֲלֵיהֶ֑ם לֹ֥א יְהֹוָ֖ה שְׁלָחָֽנִי: 30 וְאִם־בְּרִיאָ֞ה יִבְרָ֣א יְהֹוָ֗ה וּפָֽצְתָ֨ה הָֽאֲדָמָ֤ה אֶת־פִּ֨יהָ֙ וּבָלְעָ֤ה אֹתָם֙ וְאֶת־כָּל־אֲשֶׁ֣ר לָהֶ֔ם וְיָֽרְד֥וּ חַיִּ֖ים שְׁאֹ֑לָה וִֽידַעְתֶּ֕ם כִּ֧י נִֽאֲצ֛וּ הָֽאֲנָשִׁ֥ים הָאֵ֖לֶּה אֶת־יְהֹוָֽה: 31 וַֽיְהִי֙ כְּכַלֹּת֔וֹ לְדַבֵּ֕ר אֵ֥ת כָּל־הַדְּבָרִ֖ים הָאֵ֑לֶּה וַתִּבָּקַ֥ע הָֽאֲדָמָ֖ה אֲשֶׁ֥ר תַּחְתֵּיהֶֽם: 32 וַתִּפְתַּ֤ח הָאָ֨רֶץ֙ אֶת־פִּ֔יהָ וַתִּבְלַ֥ע אֹתָ֖ם וְאֶת־בָּֽתֵּיהֶ֑ם וְאֵ֤ת כָּל־הָֽאָדָם֙ אֲשֶׁ֣ר לְקֹ֔רַח וְאֵ֖ת כָּל־הָֽרְכֽוּשׁ: 33 וַיֵּ֨רְד֜וּ הֵ֣ם וְכָל־אֲשֶׁ֥ר לָהֶ֛ם חַיִּ֖ים שְׁאֹ֑לָה וַתְּכַ֤ס עֲלֵיהֶם֙ הָאָ֔רֶץ וַיֹּֽאבְד֖וּ מִתּ֥וֹךְ הַקָּהָֽל: 34 וְכָל־יִשְׂרָאֵ֗ל אֲשֶׁ֛ר סְבִיבֹֽתֵיהֶ֖ם נָ֣סוּ לְקֹלָ֑ם כִּ֣י אָֽמְר֔וּ פֶּן־תִּבְלָעֵ֖נוּ הָאָֽרֶץ: 35 וְאֵ֥שׁ יָֽצְאָ֖ה מֵאֵ֣ת יְהֹוָ֑ה וַתֹּ֗אכַל אֵ֣ת הַחֲמִשִּׁ֤ים וּמָאתַ֨יִם֙ אִ֔ישׁ מַקְרִיבֵ֖י הַקְּטֹֽרֶת: פ

רז

וַיְדַבֵּ֥ר יְהֹוָ֖ה אֶל־מֹשֶׁ֥ה לֵּאמֹֽר: 2 אֱמֹ֨ר אֶל־אֶלְעָזָ֜ר בֶּן־אַֽהֲרֹ֣ן הַכֹּהֵ֗ן וְיָרֵ֤ם אֶת־הַמַּחְתֹּת֙ מִבֵּ֣ין הַשְּׂרֵפָ֔ה וְאֶת־הָאֵ֖שׁ זְרֵה־הָ֑לְאָה כִּ֖י קָדֵֽשׁוּ: 3 אֵ֡ת מַחְתּוֹת֩ הַֽחַטָּאִ֨ים הָאֵ֜לֶּה בְּנַפְשֹׁתָ֗ם וְעָשׂ֨וּ אֹתָ֜ם רִקֻּעֵ֤י פַחִים֙ צִפּ֣וּי לַמִּזְבֵּ֔חַ כִּֽי־הִקְרִיבֻ֥ם לִפְנֵֽי־יְהֹוָ֖ה וַיִּקְדָּ֑שׁוּ וְיִֽהְי֥וּ לְא֖וֹת לִבְנֵ֥י יִשְׂרָאֵֽל: 4 וַיִּקַּ֞ח אֶלְעָזָ֤ר הַכֹּהֵן֙ אֵ֖ת מַחְתּ֣וֹת

---

a   *Meaning of parts of verse uncertain.*

per fire pans which had been used for offering by those who died in the fire; and they were hammered into plating for the altar, [5]as the LORD had ordered him through Moses. It was to be a reminder to the Israelites, so that no outsider—one not of Aaron's offspring—should presume to offer incense before the LORD and suffer the fate of Korah and his band.

[6]Next day the whole Israelite community railed against Moses and Aaron, saying, "You two have brought death upon the LORD's people!" [7]But as the community gathered against them, Moses and Aaron turned toward the Tent of Meeting; the cloud had covered it and the Presence of the LORD appeared.

[8]When Moses and Aaron reached the Tent of Meeting, [9]the LORD spoke to Moses, saying, [10]"Remove yourselves from this community, that I may annihilate them in an instant." They fell on their faces. [11]Then Moses said to Aaron, "Take the fire pan, and put on it fire from the altar. Add incense and take it quickly to the community and make expiation for them. For wrath has gone forth from the LORD: the plague has begun!" [12]Aaron took it, as Moses had ordered, and ran to the midst of the congregation, where the plague had begun among the people. He put on the incense and made expiation for the people; [13]he stood between the dead and the living until the plague was checked. [14]Those who died of the plague came to fourteen thousand and seven hundred, aside from those who died on account of Korah. [15]Aaron then returned to Moses at the entrance of the Tent of Meeting, since the plague was checked.

[16]The LORD spoke to Moses, saying: [17]Speak to the Israelite people and take from them—from the chieftains of their ancestral houses[b] —one staff for each chieftain of an ancestral house: twelve staffs in all. Inscribe each man's

---

b   I.e., of their tribes.

הַנְּחֹשֶׁת אֲשֶׁר הִקְרִיבוּ הַשְּׂרֻפִים וַיְרַקְּעוּם צִפּוּי לַמִּזְבֵּחַ: 5 זִכָּרוֹן לִבְנֵי יִשְׂרָאֵל לְמַעַן אֲשֶׁר לֹא־יִקְרַב אִישׁ זָר אֲשֶׁר לֹא מִזֶּרַע אַהֲרֹן הוּא לְהַקְטִיר קְטֹרֶת לִפְנֵי יְהוָה וְלֹא־יִהְיֶה כְקֹרַח וְכַעֲדָתוֹ כַּאֲשֶׁר דִּבֶּר יְהוָה בְּיַד־מֹשֶׁה לוֹ:

6 וַיִּלֹּנוּ כָּל־עֲדַת בְּנֵי־יִשְׂרָאֵל מִמָּחֳרָת עַל־מֹשֶׁה וְעַל־אַהֲרֹן לֵאמֹר אַתֶּם הֲמִתֶּם אֶת־עַם יְהוָה: 7 וַיְהִי בְּהִקָּהֵל הָעֵדָה עַל־מֹשֶׁה וְעַל־אַהֲרֹן וַיִּפְנוּ אֶל־אֹהֶל מוֹעֵד וְהִנֵּה כִסָּהוּ הֶעָנָן וַיֵּרָא כְּבוֹד יְהוָה: 8 וַיָּבֹא מֹשֶׁה וְאַהֲרֹן אֶל־פְּנֵי אֹהֶל מוֹעֵד: פ 9 וַיְדַבֵּר יְהוָה אֶל־מֹשֶׁה לֵּאמֹר: 10 הֵרֹמּוּ מִתּוֹךְ הָעֵדָה הַזֹּאת וַאֲכַלֶּה אֹתָם כְּרָגַע וַיִּפְּלוּ עַל־פְּנֵיהֶם: 11 וַיֹּאמֶר מֹשֶׁה אֶל־אַהֲרֹן קַח אֶת־הַמַּחְתָּה וְתֶן־עָלֶיהָ אֵשׁ מֵעַל הַמִּזְבֵּחַ וְשִׂים קְטֹרֶת וְהוֹלֵךְ מְהֵרָה אֶל־הָעֵדָה וְכַפֵּר עֲלֵיהֶם כִּי־יָצָא הַקֶּצֶף מִלִּפְנֵי יְהוָה הֵחֵל הַנָּגֶף: 12 וַיִּקַּח אַהֲרֹן כַּאֲשֶׁר דִּבֶּר מֹשֶׁה וַיָּרָץ אֶל־תּוֹךְ הַקָּהָל וְהִנֵּה הֵחֵל הַנֶּגֶף בָּעָם וַיִּתֵּן אֶת־הַקְּטֹרֶת וַיְכַפֵּר עַל־הָעָם: 13 וַיַּעֲמֹד בֵּין־הַמֵּתִים וּבֵין הַחַיִּים וַתֵּעָצַר הַמַּגֵּפָה: 14 וַיִּהְיוּ הַמֵּתִים בַּמַּגֵּפָה אַרְבָּעָה עָשָׂר אֶלֶף וּשְׁבַע מֵאוֹת מִלְּבַד הַמֵּתִים עַל־דְּבַר־קֹרַח: 15 וַיָּשָׁב אַהֲרֹן אֶל־מֹשֶׁה אֶל־פֶּתַח אֹהֶל מוֹעֵד וְהַמַּגֵּפָה נֶעֱצָרָה: פ

16 וַיְדַבֵּר יְהוָה אֶל־מֹשֶׁה לֵּאמֹר: 17 דַּבֵּר ׀ אֶל־בְּנֵי יִשְׂרָאֵל וְקַח מֵאִתָּם מַטֶּה מַטֶּה לְבֵית אָב מֵאֵת כָּל־נְשִׂיאֵהֶם לְבֵית אֲבֹתָם שְׁנֵים עָשָׂר מַטּוֹת אִישׁ אֶת־שְׁמוֹ

name on his staff, 18there being one staff for each head of an ancestral house; also inscribe Aaron's name on the staff of Levi. 19Deposit them in the Tent of Meeting before the Pact, where I meet with you. 20The staff of the man whom I choose shall sprout, and I will rid^c Myself of the incessant mutterings of the Israelites against you.

21Moses spoke thus to the Israelites. Their chieftains gave him a staff for each chieftain of an ancestral house, twelve staffs in all; among these staffs was that of Aaron. 22Moses deposited the staffs before the LORD, in the Tent of the Pact. 23The next day Moses entered the Tent of the Pact, and there the staff of Aaron of the house of Levi had sprouted: it had brought forth sprouts, produced blossoms, and borne almonds. 24Moses then brought out all the staffs from before the LORD to all the Israelites; each identified and recovered his staff.

25The LORD said to Moses, "Put Aaron's staff back before the Pact, to be kept as a lesson to rebels, so that their mutterings against Me may cease, lest they die." 26This Moses did; just as the LORD had commanded him, so he did.

27But the Israelites said to Moses, "Lo, we perish! We are lost, all of us lost! 28Everyone who so much as ventures near the LORD's Tabernacle must die. Alas, we are doomed to perish!"

18

The LORD said to Aaron: You and your sons and the ancestral house under your charge shall bear any guilt connected with the sanctuary; you and your sons alone shall bear any guilt connected with your priesthood. 2You shall also associate with yourself your kinsmen the tribe of Levi, your ancestral tribe, to be attached to you and to minister to you, while you and your

18 וְאֶת־שֵׁם אַהֲרֹן תִּכְתֹּב עַל־מַטֵּהוּ׃ תִּכְתֹּב עַל־מַטֵּה לֵוִי כִּי מַטֶּה אֶחָד לְרֹאשׁ בֵּית אֲבוֹתָם׃ 19 וְהִנַּחְתָּם בְּאֹהֶל מוֹעֵד לִפְנֵי הָעֵדוּת אֲשֶׁר אִוָּעֵד לָכֶם שָׁמָּה׃ 20 *וְהָיָה הָאִישׁ אֲשֶׁר אֶבְחַר־בּוֹ מַטֵּהוּ יִפְרָח וַהֲשִׁכֹּתִי מֵעָלַי אֶת־תְּלֻנּוֹת בְּנֵי יִשְׂרָאֵל אֲשֶׁר הֵם מַלִּינִם עֲלֵיכֶם׃

21 וַיְדַבֵּר מֹשֶׁה אֶל־בְּנֵי יִשְׂרָאֵל וַיִּתְּנוּ אֵלָיו ׀ כָּל־נְשִׂיאֵיהֶם מַטֶּה לְנָשִׂיא אֶחָד מַטֶּה לְנָשִׂיא אֶחָד לְבֵית אֲבֹתָם שְׁנֵים עָשָׂר מַטּוֹת וּמַטֵּה אַהֲרֹן בְּתוֹךְ מַטּוֹתָם׃ 22 וַיַּנַּח מֹשֶׁה אֶת־הַמַּטֹּת לִפְנֵי יְהֹוָה בְּאֹהֶל הָעֵדֻת׃ 23 וַיְהִי מִמׇּחֳרָת וַיָּבֹא מֹשֶׁה אֶל־אֹהֶל הָעֵדוּת וְהִנֵּה פָּרַח מַטֵּה־אַהֲרֹן לְבֵית לֵוִי וַיֹּצֵא פֶרַח וַיָּצֵץ צִיץ וַיִּגְמֹל שְׁקֵדִים׃ 24 וַיֹּצֵא מֹשֶׁה אֶת־כָּל־הַמַּטֹּת מִלִּפְנֵי יְהֹוָה אֶל־כָּל־בְּנֵי יִשְׂרָאֵל וַיִּרְאוּ וַיִּקְחוּ אִישׁ מַטֵּהוּ׃ ס

25 וַיֹּאמֶר יְהֹוָה אֶל־מֹשֶׁה הָשֵׁב אֶת־מַטֵּה אַהֲרֹן לִפְנֵי הָעֵדוּת לְמִשְׁמֶרֶת לְאוֹת לִבְנֵי־מֶרִי וּתְכַל תְּלוּנֹּתָם מֵעָלַי וְלֹא יָמֻתוּ׃ 26 וַיַּעַשׂ מֹשֶׁה כַּאֲשֶׁר צִוָּה יְהֹוָה אֹתוֹ כֵּן עָשָׂה׃ ס

27 וַיֹּאמְרוּ בְּנֵי יִשְׂרָאֵל אֶל־מֹשֶׁה לֵאמֹר הֵן גָּוַעְנוּ אָבַדְנוּ כֻּלָּנוּ אָבָדְנוּ׃ 28 כֹּל הַקָּרֵב ׀ הַקָּרֵב אֶל־מִשְׁכַּן יְהֹוָה יָמוּת הַאִם תַּמְנוּ לִגְוֺעַ׃ ס

יח וַיֹּאמֶר יְהֹוָה אֶל־אַהֲרֹן אַתָּה וּבָנֶיךָ וּבֵית־אָבִיךָ אִתָּךְ תִּשְׂאוּ אֶת־עֲוֺן הַמִּקְדָּשׁ וְאַתָּה וּבָנֶיךָ אִתָּךְ תִּשְׂאוּ אֶת־עֲוֺן כְּהֻנַּתְכֶם׃ 2 וְגַם אֶת־אַחֶיךָ מַטֵּה לֵוִי שֵׁבֶט אָבִיךָ הַקְרֵב אִתָּךְ וְיִלָּווּ עָלֶיךָ וִישָׁרְתוּךָ וְאַתָּה וּבָנֶיךָ אִתָּךְ לִפְנֵי אֹהֶל

חצי הספר בפסוקים   v. 20.

---

c   Meaning of Heb. wahashikkothi uncertain.

324

sons under your charge are before the Tent of the Pact.[a] [3]They shall discharge their duties to you and to the Tent as a whole, but they must not have any contact with the furnishings of the Shrine or with the altar, lest both they and you die. [4]They shall be attached to you and discharge the duties of the Tent of Meeting, all the service of the Tent; but no outsider shall intrude upon you [5]as you discharge the duties connected with the Shrine and the altar, that wrath may not again strike the Israelites.

[6]I hereby take your fellow Levites from among the Israelites; they are assigned to you in dedication to the LORD, to do the work of the Tent of Meeting; [7]while you and your sons shall be careful to perform your priestly duties in everything pertaining to the altar and to what is behind the curtain. I make your priesthood a service of dedication; any outsider who encroaches shall be put to death.

[8]The LORD spoke further to Aaron: I hereby give you charge of My gifts, all the sacred donations of the Israelites; I grant them to you and to your sons as a perquisite,[b] a due for all time. [9]This shall be yours from the most holy sacrifices, [c]the offerings by fire:[c] every such offering that they render to Me as most holy sacrifices, namely, every meal offering, sin offering, and guilt offering of theirs, shall belong to you and your sons. [10]You shall partake of them as most sacred donations: only males may eat them; you shall treat them as consecrated.[d]

[11]This, too, shall be yours: the gift offerings[e] of their contributions, all the elevation offerings of the Israelites, I give to you, to your sons, and to the daughters that are with you, as a due for all time; everyone of your household who is clean may eat it.

הָעֵדָת: 3 וְשָׁמְרוּ מִשְׁמַרְתְּךָ וּמִשְׁמֶרֶת כָּל־הָאֹהֶל אַךְ אֶל־כְּלֵי הַקֹּדֶשׁ וְאֶל־הַמִּזְבֵּחַ לֹא יִקְרָבוּ וְלֹא־יָמֻתוּ גַם־הֵם גַּם־אַתֶּם: 4 וְנִלְווּ עָלֶיךָ וְשָׁמְרוּ אֶת־מִשְׁמֶרֶת אֹהֶל מוֹעֵד לְכֹל עֲבֹדַת הָאֹהֶל וְזָר לֹא־יִקְרַב אֲלֵיכֶם: 5 וּשְׁמַרְתֶּם אֵת מִשְׁמֶרֶת הַקֹּדֶשׁ וְאֵת מִשְׁמֶרֶת הַמִּזְבֵּחַ וְלֹא־יִהְיֶה עוֹד קֶצֶף עַל־בְּנֵי יִשְׂרָאֵל: 6 וַאֲנִי הִנֵּה לָקַחְתִּי אֶת־אֲחֵיכֶם הַלְוִיִּם מִתּוֹךְ בְּנֵי יִשְׂרָאֵל לָכֶם מַתָּנָה נְתֻנִים לַיהֹוָה לַעֲבֹד אֶת־עֲבֹדַת אֹהֶל מוֹעֵד: 7 וְאַתָּה וּבָנֶיךָ אִתְּךָ תִּשְׁמְרוּ אֶת־כְּהֻנַּתְכֶם לְכָל־דְּבַר הַמִּזְבֵּחַ וּלְמִבֵּית לַפָּרֹכֶת וַעֲבַדְתֶּם עֲבֹדַת מַתָּנָה אֶתֵּן אֶת־כְּהֻנַּתְכֶם וְהַזָּר הַקָּרֵב יוּמָת: ס 8 וַיְדַבֵּר יְהֹוָה אֶל־אַהֲרֹן וַאֲנִי הִנֵּה נָתַתִּי לְךָ אֶת־מִשְׁמֶרֶת תְּרוּמֹתָי לְכָל־קָדְשֵׁי בְנֵי־יִשְׂרָאֵל לְךָ נְתַתִּים לְמָשְׁחָה וּלְבָנֶיךָ לְחָק־עוֹלָם: 9 זֶה־יִהְיֶה לְךָ מִקֹּדֶשׁ הַקֳּדָשִׁים מִן־הָאֵשׁ כָּל־קָרְבָּנָם לְכָל־מִנְחָתָם וּלְכָל־חַטָּאתָם וּלְכָל־אֲשָׁמָם אֲשֶׁר יָשִׁיבוּ לִי קֹדֶשׁ קָדָשִׁים לְךָ הוּא וּלְבָנֶיךָ: 10 בְּקֹדֶשׁ הַקֳּדָשִׁים תֹּאכְלֶנּוּ כָּל־זָכָר יֹאכַל אֹתוֹ קֹדֶשׁ יִהְיֶה־לָּךְ: 11 וְזֶה־לְּךָ תְּרוּמַת מַתָּנָם לְכָל־תְּנוּפֹת בְּנֵי יִשְׂרָאֵל לְךָ נְתַתִּים וּלְבָנֶיךָ וְלִבְנֹתֶיךָ אִתְּךָ לְחָק־עוֹלָם כָּל־טָהוֹר בְּבֵיתְךָ יֹאכַל אֹתוֹ:

---

a   *Meaning of latter part of verse uncertain.*
b   *See note at Lev. 7.35.*
c-c   *Meaning of Heb. uncertain; lit. "from the fire."*
d   *Or "they are consecrated for your use."*
e   *Cf. Lev. 7.29 ff.*

12All the best of the new oil, wine, and grain—the choice parts that they present to the LORD—I give to you. 13The first fruits of everything in their land, that they bring to the LORD, shall be yours; everyone of your household who is clean may eat them. 14Everything that has been proscribed in Israel*f* shall be yours. 15The first issue of the womb of every being, man or beast, that is offered to the LORD, shall be yours; but you shall have the first-born of man redeemed, and you shall also have the firstling of unclean animals redeemed. 16Take as their redemption price,*g* from the age of one month up, the money equivalent of five shekels by the sanctuary weight, which is twenty *gerah*s. 17But the firstlings of cattle, sheep, or goats may not be redeemed; they are consecrated. You shall dash their blood against the altar, and turn their fat into smoke as an offering by fire for a pleasing odor to the LORD. 18But their meat shall be yours: it shall be yours like the breast of elevation offering and like the right thigh.

19All the sacred gifts that the Israelites set aside for the LORD I give to you, to your sons, and to the daughters that are with you, as a due for all time. It shall be an everlasting covenant of salt*h* before the LORD for you and for your offspring as well. 20And the LORD said to Aaron: You shall, however, have no territorial share among them or own any portion in their midst; I am your portion and your share among the Israelites.

21And to the Levites I hereby give all the tithes in Israel as their share in return for the services that they perform, the services of the Tent of Meeting. 22Henceforth, Israelites shall not trespass on the Tent of Meeting, and thus incur guilt and die: 23only Levites shall perform the services of the Tent of Meeting; others*i* would incur

12 כֹּל חֵלֶב יִצְהָר וְכָל־חֵלֶב תִּירוֹשׁ וְדָגָן רֵאשִׁיתָם אֲשֶׁר־יִתְּנוּ לַיהוָה לְךָ נְתַתִּים׃ 13 בִּכּוּרֵי כָּל־אֲשֶׁר בְּאַרְצָם אֲשֶׁר־יָבִיאוּ לַיהוָה לְךָ יִהְיֶה כָּל־טָהוֹר בְּבֵיתְךָ יֹאכֲלֶנּוּ׃ 14 כָּל־חֵרֶם בְּיִשְׂרָאֵל לְךָ יִהְיֶה׃ 15 כָּל־פֶּטֶר רֶחֶם לְכָל־בָּשָׂר אֲשֶׁר־יַקְרִיבוּ לַיהוָה בָּאָדָם וּבַבְּהֵמָה יִהְיֶה־לָּךְ אַךְ ׀ פָּדֹה תִפְדֶּה אֵת בְּכוֹר הָאָדָם וְאֵת בְּכוֹר־הַבְּהֵמָה הַטְּמֵאָה תִּפְדֶּה׃ 16 וּפְדוּיָו מִבֶּן־חֹדֶשׁ תִּפְדֶּה בְּעֶרְכְּךָ כֶּסֶף חֲמֵשֶׁת שְׁקָלִים בְּשֶׁקֶל הַקֹּדֶשׁ עֶשְׂרִים גֵּרָה הוּא׃ 17 אַךְ בְּכוֹר־שׁוֹר אוֹ־בְכוֹר כֶּשֶׂב אוֹ־בְכוֹר עֵז לֹא תִפְדֶּה קֹדֶשׁ הֵם אֶת־דָּמָם תִּזְרֹק עַל־הַמִּזְבֵּחַ וְאֶת־חֶלְבָּם תַּקְטִיר אִשֶּׁה לְרֵיחַ נִיחֹחַ לַיהוָה׃ 18 וּבְשָׂרָם יִהְיֶה־לָּךְ כַּחֲזֵה הַתְּנוּפָה וּכְשׁוֹק הַיָּמִין לְךָ יִהְיֶה׃ 19 כֹּל ׀ תְּרוּמֹת הַקֳּדָשִׁים אֲשֶׁר יָרִימוּ בְנֵי־יִשְׂרָאֵל לַיהוָה נָתַתִּי לְךָ וּלְבָנֶיךָ וְלִבְנֹתֶיךָ אִתְּךָ לְחָק־עוֹלָם בְּרִית מֶלַח עוֹלָם הִוא לִפְנֵי יְהוָה לְךָ וּלְזַרְעֲךָ אִתָּךְ׃ 20 וַיֹּאמֶר יְהוָה אֶל־אַהֲרֹן בְּאַרְצָם לֹא תִנְחָל וְחֵלֶק לֹא־יִהְיֶה לְךָ בְּתוֹכָם אֲנִי חֶלְקְךָ וְנַחֲלָתְךָ בְּתוֹךְ בְּנֵי יִשְׂרָאֵל׃ ס 21 וְלִבְנֵי לֵוִי הִנֵּה נָתַתִּי כָּל־מַעֲשֵׂר בְּיִשְׂרָאֵל לְנַחֲלָה חֵלֶף עֲבֹדָתָם אֲשֶׁר־הֵם עֹבְדִים אֶת־עֲבֹדַת אֹהֶל מוֹעֵד׃ 22 וְלֹא־יִקְרְבוּ עוֹד בְּנֵי יִשְׂרָאֵל אֶל־אֹהֶל מוֹעֵד לָשֵׂאת חֵטְא לָמוּת׃ 23 וְעָבַד הַלֵּוִי הוּא אֶת־עֲבֹדַת אֹהֶל מוֹעֵד וְהֵם יִשְׂאוּ עֲוֹנָם

---

f   See Lev. 27.28.
g   I.e., for human first-born; cf. Num. 3.44 ff. For animals see Exod. 34.19 f.
h   See Lev. 2.13.
i   Lit. "they."

guilt. It is the law for all time throughout the ages. But they shall have no territorial share among the Israelites; [24]for it is the tithes set aside by the Israelites as a gift to the LORD that I give to the Levites as their share. Therefore I have said concerning them: They shall have no territorial share among the Israelites.

[25]The LORD spoke to Moses, saying: [26]Speak to the Levites and say to them: When you receive from the Israelites their tithes, which I have assigned to you as your share, you shall set aside from them one-tenth of the tithe as a gift to the LORD. [27]This shall be accounted to you as your gift. As with the new grain from the threshing floor or the flow from the vat, [28]so shall you on your part set aside a gift for the LORD from all the tithes that you receive from the Israelites; and from them you shall bring the gift for the LORD to Aaron the priest. [29]You shall set aside all gifts due to the LORD from everything that is donated to you, from each thing its best portion, the part thereof that is to be consecrated.

[30]Say to them further: When you have removed the best part from it, you Levites may consider it the same as the yield of threshing floor or vat. [31]You and your households may eat it anywhere, for it is your recompense for your services in the Tent of Meeting. [32]You will incur no guilt through it, once you have removed the best part from it; but you must not profane the sacred donations of the Israelites, lest you die.

19 ḤUKKAT

The LORD spoke to Moses and Aaron, saying: [2]This is the ritual law that the LORD has commanded:

Instruct the Israelite people to bring you a red cow without blemish, in which there is no defect and on which no yoke has been laid. [3]You shall give it to Eleazar the priest. It shall be taken out-

חֻקַּת עוֹלָם לְדֹרֹתֵיכֶם וּבְתוֹךְ בְּנֵי יִשְׂרָאֵל לֹא יִנְחֲלוּ נַחֲלָה: 24 כִּי אֶת־מַעְשַׂר בְּנֵי־ יִשְׂרָאֵל אֲשֶׁר יָרִימוּ לַיהוָה תְּרוּמָה נָתַתִּי לַלְוִיִּם לְנַחֲלָה עַל־כֵּן אָמַרְתִּי לָהֶם בְּתוֹךְ בְּנֵי יִשְׂרָאֵל לֹא יִנְחֲלוּ נַחֲלָה: פ 25 וַיְדַבֵּר יְהוָה אֶל־מֹשֶׁה לֵּאמֹר: 26 וְאֶל־ הַלְוִיִּם תְּדַבֵּר וְאָמַרְתָּ אֲלֵהֶם כִּי־תִקְחוּ מֵאֵת בְּנֵי־יִשְׂרָאֵל אֶת־הַמַּעֲשֵׂר אֲשֶׁר נָתַתִּי לָכֶם מֵאִתָּם בְּנַחֲלַתְכֶם וַהֲרֵמֹתֶם מִמֶּנּוּ תְּרוּמַת יְהוָה מַעֲשֵׂר מִן־הַמַּעֲשֵׂר: 27 וְנֶחְשַׁב לָכֶם תְּרוּמַתְכֶם כַּדָּגָן מִן־הַגֹּרֶן וְכַמְלֵאָה מִן־הַיָּקֶב: 28 כֵּן תָּרִימוּ גַם־ אַתֶּם תְּרוּמַת יְהוָה מִכֹּל מַעְשְׂרֹתֵיכֶם אֲשֶׁר תִּקְחוּ מֵאֵת בְּנֵי יִשְׂרָאֵל וּנְתַתֶּם מִמֶּנּוּ אֶת־תְּרוּמַת יְהוָה לְאַהֲרֹן הַכֹּהֵן: 29 מִכֹּל מַתְּנֹתֵיכֶם תָּרִימוּ אֵת כָּל־תְּרוּמַת יְהוָה מִכָּל־חֶלְבּוֹ אֶת־מִקְדְּשׁוֹ מִמֶּנּוּ: 30 וְאָמַרְתָּ אֲלֵהֶם בַּהֲרִימְכֶם אֶת־חֶלְבּוֹ מִמֶּנּוּ וְנֶחְשַׁב לַלְוִיִּם כִּתְבוּאַת גֹּרֶן וְכִתְבוּאַת יָקֶב: 31 וַאֲכַלְתֶּם אֹתוֹ בְּכָל־ מָקוֹם אַתֶּם וּבֵיתְכֶם כִּי־שָׂכָר הוּא לָכֶם חֵלֶף עֲבֹדַתְכֶם בְּאֹהֶל מוֹעֵד: 32 וְלֹא־ תִשְׂאוּ עָלָיו חֵטְא בַּהֲרִימְכֶם אֶת־חֶלְבּוֹ מִמֶּנּוּ וְאֶת־קָדְשֵׁי בְנֵי־יִשְׂרָאֵל לֹא תְחַלְּלוּ וְלֹא תָמוּתוּ: פ

יט חקת וַיְדַבֵּר יְהוָה אֶל־מֹשֶׁה וְאֶל־אַהֲרֹן לֵאמֹר: 2 זֹאת חֻקַּת הַתּוֹרָה אֲשֶׁר־צִוָּה יְהוָה לֵאמֹר דַּבֵּר ׀ אֶל־בְּנֵי יִשְׂרָאֵל וְיִקְחוּ אֵלֶיךָ פָרָה אֲדֻמָּה תְּמִימָה אֲשֶׁר אֵין־בָּהּ מוּם אֲשֶׁר לֹא־עָלָה עָלֶיהָ עֹל: 3 וּנְתַתֶּם אֹתָהּ אֶל־

side the camp and slaughtered in his presence. [4]Eleazar the priest shall take some of its blood with his finger and sprinkle it seven times toward the front of the Tent of Meeting. [5]The cow shall be burned in his sight—its hide, flesh, and blood shall be burned, its dung included—[6]and the priest shall take cedar wood, hyssop, and crimson stuff, and throw them into the fire consuming the cow. [7]The priest shall wash his garments and bathe his body in water; after that the priest may reenter the camp, but he shall be unclean until evening. [8]He who performed the burning shall also wash his garments in water, bathe his body in water, and be unclean until evening. [9]A man who is clean shall gather up the ashes of the cow and deposit them outside the camp in a clean place, to be kept for water of lustration[a] for the Israelite community. It is for cleansing. [10]He who gathers up the ashes of the cow shall also wash his clothes and be unclean until evening.

This shall be a permanent law for the Israelites and for the strangers who reside among you.

[11]He who touches the corpse of any human being shall be unclean for seven days. [12]He shall cleanse himself with it[b] on the third day and on the seventh day, and then be clean; if he fails to cleanse himself on the third and seventh days, he shall not be clean. [13]Whoever touches a corpse, the body of a person who has died, and does not cleanse himself, defiles the LORD's Tabernacle; that person shall be cut off from Israel. Since the water of lustration was not dashed on him, he remains unclean; his uncleanness is still upon him.

[14]This is the ritual: When a person dies in a tent, whoever enters the tent and whoever is in the tent shall be unclean seven days; [15]and every open vessel, with no lid fastened down, shall be unclean. [16]And in the open, anyone who

אֶלְעָזָ֣ר הַכֹּהֵ֑ן וְהוֹצִ֤יא אֹתָהּ֙ אֶל־מִח֣וּץ לַֽמַּחֲנֶ֔ה וְשָׁחַ֥ט אֹתָ֖הּ לְפָנָֽיו׃ 4 וְלָקַ֞ח אֶלְעָזָ֧ר הַכֹּהֵ֛ן מִדָּמָ֖הּ בְּאֶצְבָּע֑וֹ וְהִזָּ֞ה אֶל־נֹ֨כַח פְּנֵ֧י אֹֽהֶל־מוֹעֵ֛ד מִדָּמָ֖הּ שֶׁ֥בַע פְּעָמִֽים׃ 5 וְשָׂרַ֥ף אֶת־הַפָּרָ֖ה לְעֵינָ֑יו אֶת־עֹרָ֤הּ וְאֶת־בְּשָׂרָהּ֙ וְאֶת־דָּמָ֔הּ עַל־פִּרְשָׁ֖הּ יִשְׂרֹֽף׃ 6 וְלָקַ֣ח הַכֹּהֵ֗ן עֵ֥ץ אֶ֛רֶז וְאֵז֖וֹב וּשְׁנִ֣י תוֹלָ֑עַת וְהִשְׁלִ֕יךְ אֶל־תּ֖וֹךְ שְׂרֵפַ֥ת הַפָּרָֽה׃ 7 וְכִבֶּ֨ס בְּגָדָ֜יו הַכֹּהֵ֗ן וְרָחַ֤ץ בְּשָׂרוֹ֙ בַּמַּ֔יִם וְאַחַ֖ר יָבֹ֣א אֶל־הַֽמַּחֲנֶ֑ה וְטָמֵ֥א הַכֹּהֵ֖ן עַד־הָעָֽרֶב׃ 8 וְהַשֹּׂרֵ֣ף אֹתָ֔הּ יְכַבֵּ֤ס בְּגָדָיו֙ בַּמַּ֔יִם וְרָחַ֥ץ בְּשָׂר֖וֹ בַּמָּ֑יִם וְטָמֵ֖א עַד־הָעָֽרֶב׃ 9 וְאָסַ֣ף ׀ אִ֣ישׁ טָה֗וֹר אֵ֚ת אֵ֣פֶר הַפָּרָ֔ה וְהִנִּ֛יחַ מִח֥וּץ לַֽמַּחֲנֶ֖ה בְּמָק֣וֹם טָה֑וֹר וְ֠הָיְתָ֠ה לַעֲדַ֨ת בְּנֵֽי־יִשְׂרָאֵ֧ל לְמִשְׁמֶ֛רֶת לְמֵ֥י נִדָּ֖ה חַטָּ֥את הִֽוא׃ 10 וְ֠כִבֶּ֠ס הָאֹסֵ֨ף אֶת־אֵ֤פֶר הַפָּרָה֙ אֶת־בְּגָדָ֔יו וְטָמֵ֖א עַד־הָעָ֑רֶב וְֽהָיְתָ֞ה לִבְנֵ֣י יִשְׂרָאֵ֗ל וְלַגֵּ֛ר הַגָּ֥ר בְּתוֹכָ֖ם לְחֻקַּ֥ת עוֹלָֽם׃ 11 הַנֹּגֵ֥עַ בְּמֵ֖ת לְכָל־נֶ֣פֶשׁ אָדָ֑ם וְטָמֵ֖א שִׁבְעַ֥ת יָמִֽים׃ 12 ה֣וּא יִתְחַטָּא־ב֗וֹ בַּיּ֧וֹם הַשְּׁלִישִׁ֛י וּבַיּ֥וֹם הַשְּׁבִיעִ֖י יִטְהָ֑ר וְאִם־לֹ֨א יִתְחַטָּ֜א בַּיּ֧וֹם הַשְּׁלִישִׁ֛י וּבַיּ֥וֹם הַשְּׁבִיעִ֖י לֹ֥א יִטְהָֽר׃ 13 כָּֽל־הַנֹּגֵ֡עַ בְּמֵ֣ת בְּנֶפֶשׁ֩ הָאָדָ֨ם אֲשֶׁר־יָמ֜וּת וְלֹ֣א יִתְחַטָּ֗א אֶת־מִשְׁכַּ֤ן יְהֹוָה֙ טִמֵּ֔א וְנִכְרְתָ֛ה הַנֶּ֥פֶשׁ הַהִ֖וא מִיִּשְׂרָאֵ֑ל כִּ֣י מֵ֨י נִדָּ֜ה לֹא־זֹרַ֤ק עָלָיו֙ טָמֵ֣א יִהְיֶ֔ה ע֖וֹד טֻמְאָת֥וֹ בֽוֹ׃ 14 זֹ֚את הַתּוֹרָ֔ה אָדָ֖ם כִּֽי־יָמ֣וּת בְּאֹ֑הֶל כָּל־הַבָּ֤א אֶל־הָאֹ֙הֶל֙ וְכָל־אֲשֶׁ֣ר בָּאֹ֔הֶל יִטְמָ֖א שִׁבְעַ֥ת יָמִֽים׃ 15 וְכֹל֙ כְּלִ֣י פָת֔וּחַ אֲשֶׁ֛ר אֵין־צָמִ֥יד פָּתִ֖יל עָלָ֑יו טָמֵ֥א הֽוּא׃ 16 וְכֹ֠ל אֲשֶׁר־יִגַּ֨ע עַל־פְּנֵ֤י הַשָּׂדֶה֙ בַּֽחֲלַל־

---

touches a person who was killed[c] or who died naturally, or human bone, or a grave, shall be unclean seven days. [17]Some of the ashes[d] from the fire of cleansing shall be taken for the unclean person, and fresh water shall be added to them in a vessel. [18]A person who is clean shall take hyssop, dip it in the water, and sprinkle on the tent and on all the vessels and people who were there, or on him who touched the bones or the person who was killed or died naturally or the grave. [19]The clean person shall sprinkle it upon the unclean person on the third day and on the seventh day, thus cleansing him by the seventh day. He[e] shall then wash his clothes and bathe in water, and at nightfall he shall be clean. [20]If anyone who has become unclean fails to cleanse himself, that person shall be cut off from the congregation, for he has defiled the LORD's sanctuary. The water of lustration was not dashed on him: he is unclean.

[21]That shall be for them a law for all time. Further, he who sprinkled the water of lustration shall wash his clothes; and whoever touches the water of lustration shall be unclean until evening. [22]Whatever that unclean person touches shall be unclean; and the person who touches him shall be unclean until evening.

20

The Israelites arrived in a body at the wilderness of Zin on the first new moon,[a] and the people stayed at Kadesh. Miriam died there and was buried there.

[2]The community was without water, and they joined against Moses and Aaron. [3]The people quarreled with Moses, saying, "If only we had perished when our brothers perished at the instance of the LORD! [4]Why have you brought the LORD's congregation into this wilderness for us

חֶרֶב אוֹ בְמֵת אוֹ־בְעֶצֶם אָדָם אוֹ בְקָבֶר יִטְמָא שִׁבְעַת יָמִים: 17 וְלָקְחוּ לַטָּמֵא מֵעֲפַר שְׂרֵפַת הַחַטָּאת וְנָתַן עָלָיו מַיִם חַיִּים אֶל־כֶּלִי: 18 וְלָקַח אֵזוֹב וְטָבַל בַּמַּיִם אִישׁ טָהוֹר וְהִזָּה עַל־הָאֹהֶל וְעַל־כָּל־הַכֵּלִים וְעַל־הַנְּפָשׁוֹת אֲשֶׁר הָיוּ־שָׁם וְעַל־הַנֹּגֵעַ בַּעֶצֶם אוֹ בֶחָלָל אוֹ בַמֵּת אוֹ בַקָּבֶר: 19 וְהִזָּה הַטָּהֹר עַל־הַטָּמֵא בַּיּוֹם הַשְּׁלִישִׁי וּבַיּוֹם הַשְּׁבִיעִי וְחִטְּאוֹ בַּיּוֹם הַשְּׁבִיעִי וְכִבֶּס בְּגָדָיו וְרָחַץ בַּמַּיִם וְטָהֵר בָּעָרֶב: 20 וְאִישׁ אֲשֶׁר־יִטְמָא וְלֹא יִתְחַטָּא וְנִכְרְתָה הַנֶּפֶשׁ הַהִוא מִתּוֹךְ הַקָּהָל כִּי אֶת־מִקְדַּשׁ יְהוָה טִמֵּא מֵי נִדָּה לֹא־זֹרַק עָלָיו טָמֵא הוּא: 21 וְהָיְתָה לָהֶם לְחֻקַּת עוֹלָם וּמַזֵּה מֵי־הַנִּדָּה יְכַבֵּס בְּגָדָיו וְהַנֹּגֵעַ בְּמֵי הַנִּדָּה יִטְמָא עַד־הָעָרֶב: 22 וְכֹל אֲשֶׁר־יִגַּע־בּוֹ הַטָּמֵא יִטְמָא וְהַנֶּפֶשׁ הַנֹּגַעַת תִּטְמָא עַד־הָעָרֶב: פ

כ וַיָּבֹאוּ בְנֵי־יִשְׂרָאֵל כָּל־הָעֵדָה מִדְבַּר־צִן בַּחֹדֶשׁ הָרִאשׁוֹן וַיֵּשֶׁב הָעָם בְּקָדֵשׁ וַתָּמָת שָׁם מִרְיָם וַתִּקָּבֵר שָׁם: 2 וְלֹא־הָיָה מַיִם לָעֵדָה וַיִּקָּהֲלוּ עַל־מֹשֶׁה וְעַל־אַהֲרֹן: 3 וַיָּרֶב הָעָם עִם־מֹשֶׁה וַיֹּאמְרוּ לֵאמֹר וְלוּ גָוַעְנוּ בִּגְוַע אַחֵינוּ לִפְנֵי יְהוָה: 4 וְלָמָה הֲבֵאתֶם אֶת־קְהַל יְהוָה אֶל־הַמִּדְבָּר הַזֶּה לָמוּת שָׁם אֲנַחְנוּ

---

c　Lit. "slain by the sword."
d　Lit. "earth" or "dust."
e　I.e., the person being cleansed.

a　Of the fortieth year; cf. Num. 33.36–38.

and our beasts to die there? 5Why did you make us leave Egypt to bring us to this wretched place, a place with no grain or figs or vines or pomegranates? There is not even water to drink!"

6Moses and Aaron came away from the congregation to the entrance of the Tent of Meeting, and fell on their faces. The Presence of the LORD appeared to them, 7and the LORD spoke to Moses, saying, 8"You and your brother Aaron take the rod and assemble the community, and before their very eyes order the rock to yield its water. Thus you shall produce water for them from the rock and provide drink for the congregation and their beasts."

9Moses took the rod from before the LORD, as He had commanded him. 10Moses and Aaron assembled the congregation in front of the rock; and he said to them, "Listen, you rebels, shall we get water for you out of this rock?" 11And Moses raised his hand and struck the rock twice with his rod. Out came copious water, and the community and their beasts drank.

12But the LORD said to Moses and Aaron, "Because you did not trust Me enough to affirm My sanctity in the sight of the Israelite people, therefore you shall not lead this congregation into the land that I have given them." 13Those are the Waters of Meribah[b]—meaning that the Israelites quarrelled with the LORD—through which He affirmed His sanctity.

14From Kadesh, Moses sent messengers to the king of Edom: "Thus says your brother Israel: You know all the hardships that have befallen us; 15that our ancestors went down to Egypt, that we dwelt in Egypt a long time, and that the Egyptians dealt harshly with us and our ancestors. 16We cried to the LORD and He heard our plea, and He sent a messenger[c] who freed us

---

b I.e., "Quarrel"; cf. Exod. 17.7 and note b there.
c Or "angel."

וּבְעִירֵנוּ: 5 וְלָמָה הֶעֱלִיתֻנוּ מִמִּצְרַיִם לְהָבִיא אֹתָנוּ אֶל־הַמָּקוֹם הָרָע הַזֶּה לֹא ׀ מְקוֹם זֶרַע וּתְאֵנָה וְגֶפֶן וְרִמּוֹן וּמַיִם אַיִן לִשְׁתּוֹת:

6 וַיָּבֹא מֹשֶׁה וְאַהֲרֹן מִפְּנֵי הַקָּהָל אֶל־פֶּתַח אֹהֶל מוֹעֵד וַיִּפְּלוּ עַל־פְּנֵיהֶם וַיֵּרָא כְבוֹד־יְהוָה אֲלֵיהֶם: פ 7 וַיְדַבֵּר יְהוָה אֶל־מֹשֶׁה לֵּאמֹר: 8 קַח אֶת־הַמַּטֶּה וְהַקְהֵל אֶת־הָעֵדָה אַתָּה וְאַהֲרֹן אָחִיךָ וְדִבַּרְתֶּם אֶל־הַסֶּלַע לְעֵינֵיהֶם וְנָתַן מֵימָיו וְהוֹצֵאתָ לָהֶם מַיִם מִן־הַסֶּלַע וְהִשְׁקִיתָ אֶת־הָעֵדָה וְאֶת־בְּעִירָם:

9 וַיִּקַּח מֹשֶׁה אֶת־הַמַּטֶּה מִלִּפְנֵי יְהוָה כַּאֲשֶׁר צִוָּהוּ: 10 וַיַּקְהִלוּ מֹשֶׁה וְאַהֲרֹן אֶת־הַקָּהָל אֶל־פְּנֵי הַסָּלַע וַיֹּאמֶר לָהֶם שִׁמְעוּ־נָא הַמֹּרִים הֲמִן־הַסֶּלַע הַזֶּה נוֹצִיא לָכֶם מָיִם: 11 וַיָּרֶם מֹשֶׁה אֶת־יָדוֹ וַיַּךְ אֶת־הַסֶּלַע בְּמַטֵּהוּ פַּעֲמָיִם וַיֵּצְאוּ מַיִם רַבִּים וַתֵּשְׁתְּ הָעֵדָה וּבְעִירָם: ס

12 וַיֹּאמֶר יְהוָה אֶל־מֹשֶׁה וְאֶל־אַהֲרֹן יַעַן לֹא־הֶאֱמַנְתֶּם בִּי לְהַקְדִּישֵׁנִי לְעֵינֵי בְּנֵי יִשְׂרָאֵל לָכֵן לֹא תָבִיאוּ אֶת־הַקָּהָל הַזֶּה אֶל־הָאָרֶץ אֲשֶׁר־נָתַתִּי לָהֶם: 13 הֵמָּה מֵי מְרִיבָה אֲשֶׁר־רָבוּ בְנֵי־יִשְׂרָאֵל אֶת־יְהוָה וַיִּקָּדֵשׁ בָּם: ס

14 וַיִּשְׁלַח מֹשֶׁה מַלְאָכִים מִקָּדֵשׁ אֶל־מֶלֶךְ אֱדוֹם כֹּה אָמַר אָחִיךָ יִשְׂרָאֵל אַתָּה יָדַעְתָּ אֵת כָּל־הַתְּלָאָה אֲשֶׁר מְצָאָתְנוּ: 15 וַיֵּרְדוּ אֲבֹתֵינוּ מִצְרַיְמָה וַנֵּשֶׁב בְּמִצְרַיִם יָמִים רַבִּים וַיָּרֵעוּ לָנוּ מִצְרַיִם וְלַאֲבֹתֵינוּ: 16 וַנִּצְעַק אֶל־יְהוָה וַיִּשְׁמַע קֹלֵנוּ וַיִּשְׁלַח מַלְאָךְ וַיֹּצִאֵנוּ מִמִּצְרָיִם וְהִנֵּה אֲנַחְנוּ

from Egypt. Now we are in Kadesh, the town on the border of your territory. [17]Allow us, then, to cross your country. We will not pass through fields or vineyards, and we will not drink water from wells. We will follow the king's highway, turning off neither to the right nor to the left until we have crossed your territory."

[18]But Edom answered him, "You shall not pass through us, else we will go out against you with the sword." [19]"We will keep to the beaten track," the Israelites said to them, "and if we or our cattle drink your water, we will pay for it. We ask only for passage on foot—it is but a small matter." [20]But they replied, "You shall not pass through!" And Edom went out against them in heavy force, strongly armed. [21]So Edom would not let Israel cross their territory, and Israel turned away from them.

[22]Setting out from Kadesh, the Israelites arrived in a body at Mount Hor. [23]At Mount Hor, on the boundary of the land of Edom, the LORD said to Moses and Aaron, [24]"Let Aaron be gathered to his kin: he is not to enter the land that I have assigned to the Israelite people, because you disobeyed my command about the waters of Meribah. [25]Take Aaron and his son Eleazar and bring them up on Mount Hor. [26]Strip Aaron of his vestments and put them on his son Eleazar. There Aaron shall be gathered *d*-unto the dead."-*d*

[27]Moses did as the LORD had commanded. They ascended Mount Hor in the sight of the whole community. [28]Moses stripped Aaron of his vestments and put them on his son Eleazar, and Aaron died there on the summit of the mountain. When Moses and Eleazar came down from the mountain, [29]the whole community knew that Aaron had breathed his last. All the house of Israel bewailed Aaron thirty days.

d-d Lit. "and die."

בְּקָדֵשׁ עִיר קְצֵה גְבוּלֶךָ: 17 נַעְבְּרָה־נָּא בְאַרְצֶךָ לֹא נַעֲבֹר בְּשָׂדֶה וּבְכֶרֶם וְלֹא נִשְׁתֶּה מֵי בְאֵר דֶּרֶךְ הַמֶּלֶךְ נֵלֵךְ לֹא נִטֶּה יָמִין וּשְׂמֹאול עַד אֲשֶׁר־נַעֲבֹר גְּבוּלֶךָ: 18 וַיֹּאמֶר אֵלָיו אֱדוֹם לֹא תַעֲבֹר בִּי פֶּן־בַּחֶרֶב אֵצֵא לִקְרָאתֶךָ: 19 וַיֹּאמְרוּ אֵלָיו בְּנֵי־יִשְׂרָאֵל בַּמְסִלָּה נַעֲלֶה וְאִם־מֵימֶיךָ נִשְׁתֶּה אֲנִי וּמִקְנַי וְנָתַתִּי מִכְרָם רַק אֵין־דָּבָר בְּרַגְלַי אֶעֱבֹרָה: 20 וַיֹּאמֶר לֹא תַעֲבֹר וַיֵּצֵא אֱדוֹם לִקְרָאתוֹ בְּעַם כָּבֵד וּבְיָד חֲזָקָה: 21 וַיְמָאֵן ׀ אֱדוֹם נְתֹן אֶת־יִשְׂרָאֵל עֲבֹר בִּגְבֻלוֹ וַיֵּט יִשְׂרָאֵל מֵעָלָיו: פ

22 וַיִּסְעוּ מִקָּדֵשׁ וַיָּבֹאוּ בְנֵי־יִשְׂרָאֵל כָּל־הָעֵדָה הֹר הָהָר: 23 וַיֹּאמֶר יְהוָה אֶל־מֹשֶׁה וְאֶל־אַהֲרֹן בְּהֹר הָהָר עַל־גְּבוּל אֶרֶץ־אֱדוֹם לֵאמֹר: 24 יֵאָסֵף אַהֲרֹן אֶל־עַמָּיו כִּי לֹא יָבֹא אֶל־הָאָרֶץ אֲשֶׁר נָתַתִּי לִבְנֵי יִשְׂרָאֵל עַל אֲשֶׁר־מְרִיתֶם אֶת־פִּי לְמֵי מְרִיבָה: 25 קַח אֶת־אַהֲרֹן וְאֶת־אֶלְעָזָר בְּנוֹ וְהַעַל אֹתָם הֹר הָהָר: 26 וְהַפְשֵׁט אֶת־אַהֲרֹן אֶת־בְּגָדָיו וְהִלְבַּשְׁתָּם אֶת־אֶלְעָזָר בְּנוֹ וְאַהֲרֹן יֵאָסֵף וּמֵת שָׁם: 27 וַיַּעַשׂ מֹשֶׁה כַּאֲשֶׁר צִוָּה יְהוָה וַיַּעֲלוּ אֶל־הֹר הָהָר לְעֵינֵי כָּל־הָעֵדָה: 28 וַיַּפְשֵׁט מֹשֶׁה אֶת־אַהֲרֹן אֶת־בְּגָדָיו וַיַּלְבֵּשׁ אֹתָם אֶת־אֶלְעָזָר בְּנוֹ וַיָּמָת אַהֲרֹן שָׁם בְּרֹאשׁ הָהָר וַיֵּרֶד מֹשֶׁה וְאֶלְעָזָר מִן־הָהָר: 29 וַיִּרְאוּ כָּל־הָעֵדָה כִּי גָוַע אַהֲרֹן וַיִּבְכּוּ אֶת־אַהֲרֹן שְׁלֹשִׁים יוֹם כֹּל בֵּית יִשְׂרָאֵל: ס

21

When the Canaanite, king of Arad, who dwelt in the Negeb, learned that Israel was coming by the way of Atharim,[a] he engaged Israel in battle and took some of them captive. [2]Then Israel made a vow to the LORD and said, "If You deliver this people into our hand, we will proscribe[b] their towns." [3]The LORD heeded Israel's plea and delivered up the Canaanites; and they and their cities were proscribed. So that place was named Hormah.[c]

[4]They set out from Mount Hor by way of the Sea of Reeds[d] to skirt the land of Edom. But the people grew restive on the journey, [5]and the people spoke against God and against Moses, "Why did you make us leave Egypt to die in the wilderness? There is no bread and no water, and we have come to loathe this miserable food." [6]The LORD sent seraph[e] serpents against the people. They bit the people and many of the Israelites died. [7]The people came to Moses and said, "We sinned by speaking against the LORD and against you. Intercede with the LORD to take away the serpents from us!" And Moses interceded for the people. [8]Then the LORD said to Moses, "Make a seraph[e] figure and mount it on a standard. And if anyone who is bitten looks at it, he shall recover." [9]Moses made a copper serpent and mounted it on a standard; and when anyone was bitten by a serpent, he would look at the copper serpent and recover.

[10]The Israelites marched on and encamped at Oboth. [11]They set out from Oboth and encamped at Iye-abarim, in the wilderness bordering on Moab to the east. [12]From there they

כא וַיִּשְׁמַ֞ע הַכְּנַעֲנִ֤י מֶֽלֶךְ־עֲרָד֙ יֹשֵׁ֣ב
הַנֶּ֔גֶב כִּ֚י בָּ֣א יִשְׂרָאֵ֔ל דֶּ֖רֶךְ הָאֲתָרִ֑ים וַיִּלָּ֙חֶם֙
בְּיִשְׂרָאֵ֔ל וַיִּ֥שְׁבְּ ׀ מִמֶּ֖נּוּ שֶֽׁבִי׃ 2 וַיִּדַּ֨ר יִשְׂרָאֵ֥ל
נֶ֛דֶר לַֽיהֹוָ֖ה וַיֹּאמַ֑ר אִם־נָתֹ֨ן תִּתֵּ֤ן אֶת־
הָעָ֤ם הַזֶּה֙ בְּיָדִ֔י וְהַֽחֲרַמְתִּ֖י אֶת־עָרֵיהֶֽם׃
3 וַיִּשְׁמַ֨ע יְהֹוָ֜ה בְּק֣וֹל יִשְׂרָאֵ֗ל וַיִּתֵּן֙ אֶת־
הַֽכְּנַעֲנִ֔י וַיַּֽחֲרֵ֥ם אֶתְהֶ֖ם וְאֶת־עָרֵיהֶ֑ם
וַיִּקְרָ֥א שֵׁם־הַמָּק֖וֹם חׇרְמָֽה׃ פ

4 וַיִּסְע֞וּ מֵהֹ֤ר הָהָר֙ דֶּ֣רֶךְ יַם־ס֔וּף לִסְבֹ֖ב
אֶת־אֶ֣רֶץ אֱד֑וֹם וַתִּקְצַ֥ר נֶֽפֶשׁ־הָעָ֖ם בַּדָּֽרֶךְ׃
5 וַיְדַבֵּ֣ר הָעָ֗ם בֵּֽאלֹהִים֮ וּבְמֹשֶׁה֒ לָמָ֤ה
הֶֽעֱלִיתֻ֙נוּ֙ מִמִּצְרַ֔יִם לָמ֖וּת בַּמִּדְבָּ֑ר כִּ֣י אֵ֥ין
לֶ֙חֶם֙ וְאֵ֣ין מַ֔יִם וְנַפְשֵׁ֣נוּ קָ֔צָה בַּלֶּ֖חֶם
הַקְּלֹקֵֽל׃ 6 וַיְשַׁלַּ֨ח יְהֹוָ֜ה בָּעָ֗ם אֵ֚ת
הַנְּחָשִׁ֣ים הַשְּׂרָפִ֔ים וַֽיְנַשְּׁכ֖וּ אֶת־הָעָ֑ם
וַיָּ֥מׇת עַם־רָ֖ב מִיִּשְׂרָאֵֽל׃ 7 וַיָּבֹא֩ הָעָ֨ם
אֶל־מֹשֶׁ֜ה וַיֹּאמְר֣וּ חָטָ֗אנוּ כִּֽי־דִבַּ֤רְנוּ
בַֽיהֹוָה֙ וָבָ֔ךְ הִתְפַּלֵּל֙ אֶל־יְהֹוָ֔ה וְיָסֵ֥ר
מֵֽעָלֵ֖ינוּ אֶת־הַנָּחָ֑שׁ וַיִּתְפַּלֵּ֥ל מֹשֶׁ֖ה בְּעַ֥ד
הָעָֽם׃ 8 וַיֹּ֨אמֶר יְהֹוָ֜ה אֶל־מֹשֶׁ֗ה עֲשֵׂ֤ה לְךָ֙
שָׂרָ֔ף וְשִׂ֥ים אֹת֖וֹ עַל־נֵ֑ס וְהָיָה֙ כׇּל־הַנָּשׁ֔וּךְ
וְרָאָ֥ה אֹת֖וֹ וָחָֽי׃ 9 וַיַּ֤עַשׂ מֹשֶׁה֙ נְחַ֣שׁ נְחֹ֔שֶׁת
וַיְשִׂמֵ֖הוּ עַל־הַנֵּ֑ס וְהָיָ֗ה אִם־נָשַׁ֤ךְ הַנָּחָשׁ֙
אֶת־אִ֔ישׁ וְהִבִּ֛יט אֶל־נְחַ֥שׁ הַנְּחֹ֖שֶׁת וָחָֽי׃

10 וַיִּסְע֖וּ בְּנֵ֣י יִשְׂרָאֵ֑ל וַיַּֽחֲנ֖וּ בְּאֹבֹֽת׃
11 וַיִּסְע֖וּ מֵאֹבֹ֑ת וַֽיַּחֲנ֞וּ בְּעִיֵּ֣י הָֽעֲבָרִ֗ים
בַּמִּדְבָּר֙ אֲשֶׁר֙ עַל־פְּנֵ֣י מוֹאָ֔ב מִמִּזְרַ֖ח
הַשָּֽׁמֶשׁ׃ 12 מִשָּׁ֖ם נָסָ֑עוּ וַֽיַּחֲנ֖וּ בְּנַ֥חַל זָֽרֶד׃

---

a   *Meaning of Heb.* ha-'atharim *uncertain. Targum and other ancient versions render "the way [taken by] the scouts."*

b   *I.e., utterly destroy, reserving no booty except what is deposited in the Sanctuary; see Josh. 6.24.*

c   *Connected with* heḥerim *"to proscribe."*

d   *See Exod. 10.19 note.*

e   *Cf. Isa. 14.29; 30.6. Others "fiery"; exact meaning of Heb.* saraph *uncertain.*

set out and encamped at the wadi Zered. [13]From there they set out and encamped beyond the Arnon, that is, in the wilderness that extends from the territory of the Amorites. For the Arnon is the boundary of Moab, between Moab and the Amorites. [14]Therefore the Book of the Wars of the LORD speaks of *f* "...Waheb in Suphah, and the wadis: the Arnon [15]with its tributary wadis, stretched along the settled country of Ar, hugging the territory of Moab..."

[16]And from there to Beer,*g* which is the well where the LORD said to Moses, "Assemble the people that I may give them water." [17]Then Israel sang this song:

Spring up, O well—sing to it—
[18]The well which the chieftains dug,
Which the nobles of the people started
With maces, with their own staffs.
And from Midbar*h* to Mattanah, [19]and from Mattanah to Nahaliel, and from Nahaliel to Bamoth, [20]and from Bamoth to the valley that is in the country of Moab, at the peak of Pisgah, overlooking the wasteland.*i*

[21]Israel now sent messengers to Sihon king of the Amorites, saying, [22]"Let me pass through your country. We will not turn off into fields or vineyards, and we will not drink water from wells. We will follow the king's highway until we have crossed your territory." [23]But Sihon would not let Israel pass through his territory. Sihon gathered all his people and went out against Israel in the wilderness. He came to Jahaz and engaged Israel in battle. [24]But Israel put them to the sword, and took possession of their land, from the Arnon to the Jabbok, as far as [Az] of the Ammonites, for Az*j* marked the boundary of the Ammonites. [25]Israel took all

---

13 מִשָּׁם֙ נָסָ֔עוּ וַֽיַּחֲנ֖וּ מֵעֵ֣בֶר אַרְנ֑וֹן אֲשֶׁ֣ר בַּמִּדְבָּ֗ר הַיֹּצֵ֖א מִגְּבֻ֣ל הָֽאֱמֹרִ֑י כִּ֤י אַרְנוֹן֙ גְּב֣וּל מוֹאָ֔ב בֵּ֥ין מוֹאָ֖ב וּבֵ֥ין הָאֱמֹרִֽי: 14 עַל־כֵּן֙ יֵֽאָמַ֔ר בְּסֵ֖פֶר מִלְחֲמֹ֣ת יְהוָ֑ה אֶת־וָהֵ֣ב בְּסוּפָ֔ה וְאֶת־הַנְּחָלִ֖ים אַרְנֽוֹן: 15 וְאֶ֙שֶׁד֙ הַנְּחָלִ֔ים אֲשֶׁ֥ר נָטָ֖ה לְשֶׁ֣בֶת עָ֑ר וְנִשְׁעַ֖ן לִגְב֥וּל מוֹאָֽב: 16 וּמִשָּׁ֖ם בְּאֵ֑רָה הִ֣וא הַבְּאֵ֔ר אֲשֶׁ֣ר אָמַ֤ר יְהוָה֙ לְמֹשֶׁ֔ה אֱסֹף֙ אֶת־הָעָ֔ם וְאֶתְּנָ֥ה לָהֶ֖ם מָֽיִם: ס 17 אָ֚ז יָשִׁ֣יר יִשְׂרָאֵ֔ל אֶת־הַשִּׁירָ֖ה הַזֹּ֑את עֲלִ֥י בְאֵ֖ר עֱנוּ־לָֽהּ: 18 בְּאֵ֞ר חֲפָר֣וּהָ שָׂרִ֗ים כָּר֙וּהָ֙ נְדִיבֵ֣י הָעָ֔ם בִּמְחֹקֵ֖ק בְּמִשְׁעֲנֹתָ֑ם וּמִמִּדְבָּ֖ר מַתָּנָֽה: 19 וּמִמַּתָּנָ֖ה נַחֲלִיאֵ֑ל וּמִנַּחֲלִיאֵ֖ל בָּמֽוֹת: 20 וּמִבָּמ֗וֹת הַגַּיְא֙ אֲשֶׁר֙ בִּשְׂדֵ֣ה מוֹאָ֔ב רֹ֖אשׁ הַפִּסְגָּ֑ה וְנִשְׁקָ֖פָה עַל־פְּנֵ֥י הַיְשִׁימֹֽן: פ

21 וַיִּשְׁלַ֤ח יִשְׂרָאֵל֙ מַלְאָכִ֔ים אֶל־סִיחֹ֥ן מֶֽלֶךְ־הָאֱמֹרִ֖י לֵאמֹֽר: 22 אֶעְבְּרָ֣ה בְאַרְצֶ֗ךָ לֹ֤א נִטֶּה֙ בְּשָׂדֶ֣ה וּבְכֶ֔רֶם לֹ֥א נִשְׁתֶּ֖ה מֵ֣י בְאֵ֑ר בְּדֶ֤רֶךְ הַמֶּ֙לֶךְ֙ נֵלֵ֔ךְ עַ֥ד אֲשֶֽׁר־נַעֲבֹ֖ר גְּבֻלֶֽךָ: 23 וְלֹא־נָתַ֨ן סִיחֹ֣ן אֶת־יִשְׂרָאֵל֮ עֲבֹ֣ר בִּגְבֻלוֹ֒ וַיֶּאֱסֹ֨ף סִיחֹ֜ן אֶת־כָּל־עַמּ֗וֹ וַיֵּצֵ֞א לִקְרַ֤את יִשְׂרָאֵל֙ הַמִּדְבָּ֔רָה וַיָּבֹ֖א יָ֑הְצָה וַיִּלָּ֖חֶם בְּיִשְׂרָאֵֽל: 24 וַיַּכֵּ֥הוּ יִשְׂרָאֵ֖ל לְפִי־חָ֑רֶב וַיִּירַ֨שׁ אֶת־אַרְצ֜וֹ מֵֽאַרְנֹ֗ן עַד־יַבֹּק֙ עַד־בְּנֵ֣י עַמּ֔וֹן כִּ֣י עַ֔ז גְּב֖וּל בְּנֵ֥י עַמּֽוֹן: 25 וַיִּקַּח֙ יִשְׂרָאֵ֔ל אֵ֥ת כָּל־הֶעָרִ֖ים הָאֵ֑לֶּה וַיֵּ֤שֶׁב יִשְׂרָאֵל֙ בְּכָל־עָרֵ֣י הָֽאֱמֹרִ֔י בְּחֶשְׁבּ֖וֹן וּבְכָל־בְּנֹתֶֽיהָ:

---

f   *The quotation that follows is a fragment; text and meaning are uncertain.*
g   *Lit. "well."*
h   *Septuagint "the well" (=Beer); cf. v. 16.*
i   *Or "Jeshimon."*
j   *Septuagint "Jazer," cf. v. 32. Others "for the boundary of the Ammonites was strong."*

those towns. And Israel settled in all the towns of the Amorites, in Heshbon and all its dependencies.

26Now Heshbon was the city of Sihon king of the Amorites, who had fought against a former king of Moab and taken all his land from him as far as the Arnon. 27Therefore the bards would recite:

k"Come to Heshbon; firmly built
And well founded is Sihon's city.
28For fire went forth from Heshbon,
Flame from Sihon's city,
Consuming Ar of Moab,
The lords of Bamoth*l* by the Arnon.
29Woe to you, O Moab!
You are undone, O people of Chemosh!
His sons are rendered fugitive
And his daughters captive
By an Amorite king, Sihon."
30*m*Yet we have cast them down utterly,
Heshbon along with Dibon;
We have wrought desolation at Nophah,
Which is hard by Medeba.
31So Israel occupied the land of the Amorites. 32Then Moses sent to spy out Jazer, and they captured its dependencies and dispossessed the Amorites who were there.

33They marched on and went up the road to Bashan, and King Og of Bashan, with all his people, came out to Edrei to engage them in battle. 34But the Lord said to Moses, "Do not fear him, for I give him and all his people and his land into your hand. You shall do to him as you did to Sihon king of the Amorites who dwelt in Heshbon." 35They defeated him and his sons and all his people, until no remnant was left

26 כִּי חֶשְׁבּוֹן עִיר סִיחֹן מֶלֶךְ הָאֱמֹרִי הִוא
וְהוּא נִלְחַם בְּמֶלֶךְ מוֹאָב הָרִאשׁוֹן וַיִּקַּח
אֶת־כָּל־אַרְצוֹ מִיָּדוֹ עַד־אַרְנֹן: 27 עַל־כֵּן
יֹאמְרוּ הַמֹּשְׁלִים
בֹּאוּ חֶשְׁבּוֹן תִּבָּנֶה
וְתִכּוֹנֵן עִיר סִיחוֹן:
28 כִּי־אֵשׁ יָצְאָה מֵחֶשְׁבֹּן
לֶהָבָה מִקִּרְיַת סִיחֹן
אָכְלָה עָר מוֹאָב
בַּעֲלֵי בָּמוֹת אַרְנֹן:
29 אוֹי־לְךָ מוֹאָב
אָבַדְתָּ עַם־כְּמוֹשׁ
נָתַן בָּנָיו פְּלֵיטִם
וּבְנֹתָיו בַּשְּׁבִית
לְמֶלֶךְ אֱמֹרִי סִיחוֹן:
30 וַנִּירָם אָבַד
חֶשְׁבּוֹן עַד־דִּיבוֹן
וַנַּשִּׁים עַד־נֹפַח
אֲשֶׁר* עַד־מֵידְבָא:
31 וַיֵּשֶׁב יִשְׂרָאֵל בְּאֶרֶץ הָאֱמֹרִי: 32 וַיִּשְׁלַח
מֹשֶׁה לְרַגֵּל אֶת־יַעְזֵר וַיִּלְכְּדוּ בְּנֹתֶיהָ וייריש
וַיּוֹרֶשׁ אֶת־הָאֱמֹרִי אֲשֶׁר־שָׁם:

33 וַיִּפְנוּ וַיַּעֲלוּ דֶּרֶךְ הַבָּשָׁן וַיֵּצֵא עוֹג
מֶלֶךְ־הַבָּשָׁן לִקְרָאתָם הוּא וְכָל־עַמּוֹ
לַמִּלְחָמָה אֶדְרֶעִי: 34 וַיֹּאמֶר יְהוָה אֶל־
מֹשֶׁה אַל־תִּירָא אֹתוֹ כִּי בְיָדְךָ נָתַתִּי אֹתוֹ
וְאֶת־כָּל־עַמּוֹ וְאֶת־אַרְצוֹ וְעָשִׂיתָ לּוֹ
כַּאֲשֶׁר עָשִׂיתָ לְסִיחֹן מֶלֶךְ הָאֱמֹרִי אֲשֶׁר
יוֹשֵׁב בְּחֶשְׁבּוֹן: 35 וַיַּכּוּ אֹתוֹ וְאֶת־בָּנָיו

v. 30. נקוד על ר'

---

k   The meaning of several parts of this ancient poem is no longer
    certain.
l   Cf. vv. 19 and 20 and Num. 22.21.
m   Meaning of verse uncertain. Alternatively:
      "Their dominion is at an end
      From Heshbon to Dibon
      And from Nashim to Nophah,
      Which is hard by Medeba."

him; and they took possession of his country.

22 ¹The Israelites then marched on and encamped in the steppes of Moab, across the Jordan from Jericho.

BALAK

²Balak son of Zippor saw all that Israel had done to the Amorites.

³Moab was alarmed because that people was so numerous. Moab dreaded the Israelites, ⁴and Moab said to the elders of Midian, "Now this horde will lick clean all that is about us as an ox licks up the grass of the field."

Balak son of Zippor, who was king of Moab at that time, ⁵sent messengers to Balaam son of Beor in Pethor, which is by the Euphrates,ᵃ in the land of his kinsfolk, to invite him, saying, "There is a people that came out of Egypt; it hides the earth from view, and it is settled next to me. ⁶Come then, put a curse upon this people for me, since they are too numerous for me; perhaps I can thus defeat them and drive them out of the land. For I know that he whom you bless is blessed indeed, and he whom you curse is cursed."

⁷The elders of Moab and the elders of Midian, ᵇversed in divination,ᵇ set out. They came to Balaam and gave him Balak's message. ⁸He said to them, "Spend the night here, and I shall reply to you as the LORD may instruct me." So the Moabite dignitaries stayed with Balaam.

⁹God came to Balaam and said, "What do these people want of you?" ¹⁰Balaam said to God, "Balak son of Zippor, king of Moab, sent me this message: ¹¹Here is a people that came out from Egypt and hides the earth from view. Come now and curse them for me; perhaps I can engage them in battle and drive them off." ¹²But God said to Balaam, "Do not go with

וְאֶת־כָּל־עַמּוֹ עַד־בִּלְתִּי הִשְׁאִיר־לוֹ שָׂרִיד וַיִּירְשׁוּ אֶת־אַרְצוֹ: **כב** ¹וַיִּסְעוּ בְּנֵי יִשְׂרָאֵל וַיַּחֲנוּ בְּעַרְבוֹת מוֹאָב מֵעֵבֶר לְיַרְדֵּן יְרֵחוֹ: ס

בלק

²וַיַּרְא בָּלָק בֶּן־צִפּוֹר אֵת כָּל־אֲשֶׁר־עָשָׂה יִשְׂרָאֵל לָאֱמֹרִי: ³וַיָּגָר מוֹאָב מִפְּנֵי הָעָם מְאֹד כִּי רַב־הוּא וַיָּקָץ מוֹאָב מִפְּנֵי בְּנֵי יִשְׂרָאֵל: ⁴וַיֹּאמֶר מוֹאָב אֶל־זִקְנֵי מִדְיָן עַתָּה יְלַחֲכוּ הַקָּהָל אֶת־כָּל־סְבִיבֹתֵינוּ כִּלְחֹךְ הַשּׁוֹר אֵת יֶרֶק הַשָּׂדֶה וּבָלָק בֶּן־צִפּוֹר מֶלֶךְ לְמוֹאָב בָּעֵת הַהִוא: ⁵וַיִּשְׁלַח מַלְאָכִים אֶל־בִּלְעָם בֶּן־בְּעוֹר פְּתוֹרָה אֲשֶׁר עַל־הַנָּהָר אֶרֶץ בְּנֵי־עַמּוֹ לִקְרֹא־לוֹ לֵאמֹר הִנֵּה עַם יָצָא מִמִּצְרַיִם הִנֵּה כִסָּה אֶת־עֵין הָאָרֶץ וְהוּא יֹשֵׁב מִמֻּלִי: ⁶וְעַתָּה לְכָה־נָּא אָרָה־לִּי אֶת־הָעָם הַזֶּה כִּי־עָצוּם הוּא מִמֶּנִּי אוּלַי אוּכַל נַכֶּה־בּוֹ וַאֲגָרְשֶׁנּוּ מִן־הָאָרֶץ כִּי יָדַעְתִּי אֵת אֲשֶׁר־תְּבָרֵךְ מְבֹרָךְ וַאֲשֶׁר תָּאֹר יוּאָר: ⁷וַיֵּלְכוּ זִקְנֵי מוֹאָב וְזִקְנֵי מִדְיָן וּקְסָמִים בְּיָדָם וַיָּבֹאוּ אֶל־בִּלְעָם וַיְדַבְּרוּ אֵלָיו דִּבְרֵי בָלָק: ⁸וַיֹּאמֶר אֲלֵיהֶם לִינוּ פֹה הַלַּיְלָה וַהֲשִׁבֹתִי אֶתְכֶם דָּבָר כַּאֲשֶׁר יְדַבֵּר יְהוָה אֵלָי וַיֵּשְׁבוּ שָׂרֵי־מוֹאָב עִם־בִּלְעָם: ⁹וַיָּבֹא אֱלֹהִים אֶל־בִּלְעָם וַיֹּאמֶר מִי הָאֲנָשִׁים הָאֵלֶּה עִמָּךְ: ¹⁰וַיֹּאמֶר בִּלְעָם אֶל־הָאֱלֹהִים בָּלָק בֶּן־צִפֹּר מֶלֶךְ מוֹאָב שָׁלַח אֵלָי: ¹¹הִנֵּה הָעָם הַיֹּצֵא מִמִּצְרַיִם וַיְכַס אֶת־עֵין הָאָרֶץ עַתָּה לְכָה קָבָה־לִּי אֹתוֹ אוּלַי אוּכַל לְהִלָּחֶם בּוֹ וְגֵרַשְׁתִּיו: ¹²וַיֹּאמֶר אֱלֹהִים אֶל־בִּלְעָם לֹא תֵלֵךְ

ᵃ Lit. "the River."
ᵇ⁻ᵇ Lit. "with divination in their power (hand)."

them. You must not curse that people, for they are blessed."

13Balaam arose in the morning and said to Balak's dignitaries, "Go back to your own country, for the Lord will not let me go with you." 14The Moabite dignitaries left, and they came to Balak and said, "Balaam refused to come with us."

15Then Balak sent other dignitaries, more numerous and distinguished than the first. 16They came to Balaam and said to him, "Thus says Balak son of Zippor: Please do not refuse to come to me. 17I will reward you richly and I will do anything you ask of me. Only come and damn this people for me." 18Balaam replied to Balak's officials, "Though Balak were to give me his house full of silver and gold, I could not do anything, big or little, contrary to the command of the Lord my God. 19So you, too, stay here overnight, and let me find out what else the Lord may say to me." 20That night God came to Balaam and said to him, "If these men have come to invite you, you may go with them. But whatever I command you, that you shall do."

21When he arose in the morning, Balaam saddled his ass and departed with the Moabite dignitaries. 22But God was incensed at his going; so an angel of the Lord placed himself in his way as an adversary.

He was riding on his she-ass, with his two servants alongside, 23when the ass caught sight of the angel of the Lord standing in the way, with his drawn sword in his hand. The ass swerved from the road and went into the fields; and Balaam beat the ass to turn her back onto the road. 24The angel of the Lord then stationed himself in a lane between the vineyards, with a fence on either side. 25The ass, seeing the angel of the Lord, pressed herself against the wall and squeezed Balaam's foot against the wall; so he beat her again. 26Once more the angel of the Lord moved forward and stationed himself on

עִמָּהֶ֖ם לֹ֥א תָאֹ֣ר אֶת־הָעָ֑ם כִּ֥י בָר֖וּךְ הֽוּא׃
13 וַיָּ֤קׇם בִּלְעָם֙ בַּבֹּ֔קֶר וַיֹּ֨אמֶר֙ אֶל־שָׂרֵ֣י בָלָ֔ק לְכ֖וּ אֶֽל־אַרְצְכֶ֑ם כִּ֚י מֵאֵ֣ן יְהֹוָ֔ה לְתִתִּ֖י לַהֲלֹ֥ךְ עִמָּכֶֽם׃ 14 וַיָּק֙וּמוּ֙ שָׂרֵ֣י מוֹאָ֔ב וַיָּבֹ֖אוּ אֶל־בָּלָ֑ק וַיֹּ֣אמְר֔וּ מֵאֵ֥ן בִּלְעָ֖ם הֲלֹ֥ךְ עִמָּֽנוּ׃
15 וַיֹּ֥סֶף ע֖וֹד בָּלָ֑ק שְׁלֹ֣חַ שָׂרִ֔ים רַבִּ֥ים וְנִכְבָּדִ֖ים מֵאֵֽלֶּה׃ 16 וַיָּבֹ֖אוּ אֶל־בִּלְעָ֑ם וַיֹּ֣אמְרוּ ל֗וֹ כֹּ֤ה אָמַר֙ בָּלָ֣ק בֶּן־צִפּ֔וֹר אַל־נָ֥א תִמָּנַ֖ע מֵהֲלֹ֥ךְ אֵלָֽי׃ 17 כִּֽי־כַבֵּ֤ד אֲכַבֶּדְךָ֙ מְאֹ֔ד וְכֹ֛ל אֲשֶׁר־תֹּאמַ֥ר אֵלַ֖י אֶֽעֱשֶׂ֑ה וּלְכָה־נָּא֙ קׇֽבָה־לִּ֔י אֵ֖ת הָעָ֥ם הַזֶּֽה׃ 18 וַיַּ֣עַן בִּלְעָ֗ם וַיֹּ֙אמֶר֙ אֶל־עַבְדֵ֣י בָלָ֔ק אִם־יִתֶּן־לִ֥י בָלָ֛ק מְלֹ֥א בֵית֖וֹ כֶּ֣סֶף וְזָהָ֑ב לֹ֣א אוּכַ֗ל לַעֲבֹר֙ אֶת־פִּי֙ יְהֹוָ֣ה אֱלֹהָ֔י לַעֲשׂ֥וֹת קְטַנָּ֖ה א֥וֹ גְדוֹלָֽה׃ 19 וְעַתָּ֗ה שְׁב֨וּ נָ֥א בָזֶ֛ה גַּם־אַתֶּ֖ם הַלָּ֑יְלָה וְאֵ֣דְעָ֔ה מַה־יֹּסֵ֥ף יְהֹוָ֖ה דַּבֵּ֥ר עִמִּֽי׃ 20 וַיָּבֹ֨א אֱלֹהִ֥ים ׀ אֶל־בִּלְעָם֮ לַ֒יְלָה֒ וַיֹּ֣אמֶר ל֗וֹ אִם־לִקְרֹ֤א לְךָ֙ בָּ֣אוּ הָֽאֲנָשִׁ֔ים ק֖וּם לֵ֣ךְ אִתָּ֑ם וְאַ֗ךְ אֶת־הַדָּבָ֛ר אֲשֶׁר־אֲדַבֵּ֥ר אֵלֶ֖יךָ אֹת֥וֹ תַעֲשֶֽׂה׃
21 וַיָּ֤קׇם בִּלְעָם֙ בַּבֹּ֔קֶר וַֽיַּחֲבֹ֖שׁ אֶת־אֲתֹנ֑וֹ וַיֵּ֖לֶךְ עִם־שָׂרֵ֥י מוֹאָֽב׃ 22 וַיִּֽחַר־אַ֣ף אֱלֹהִים֮ כִּֽי־הוֹלֵ֣ךְ הוּא֒ וַיִּתְיַצֵּ֞ב מַלְאַ֧ךְ יְהֹוָ֛ה בַּדֶּ֖רֶךְ לְשָׂטָ֣ן ל֑וֹ וְהוּא֙ רֹכֵ֣ב עַל־אֲתֹנ֔וֹ וּשְׁנֵ֥י נְעָרָ֖יו עִמּֽוֹ׃ 23 וַתֵּ֣רֶא הָאָת֡וֹן אֶת־מַלְאַךְ֩ יְהֹוָ֨ה נִצָּ֜ב בַּדֶּ֗רֶךְ וְחַרְבּ֤וֹ שְׁלוּפָה֙ בְּיָד֔וֹ וַתֵּ֤ט הָֽאָתוֹן֙ מִן־הַדֶּ֔רֶךְ וַתֵּ֖לֶךְ בַּשָּׂדֶ֑ה וַיַּ֤ךְ בִּלְעָם֙ אֶת־הָ֣אָת֔וֹן לְהַטֹּתָ֖הּ הַדָּֽרֶךְ׃ 24 וַֽיַּעֲמֹד֙ מַלְאַ֣ךְ יְהֹוָ֔ה בְּמִשְׁע֖וֹל הַכְּרָמִ֑ים גָּדֵ֥ר מִזֶּ֖ה וְגָדֵ֥ר מִזֶּֽה׃ 25 וַתֵּ֨רֶא הָאָת֜וֹן אֶת־מַלְאַ֣ךְ יְהֹוָ֗ה וַתִּלָּחֵץ֙ אֶל־הַקִּ֔יר וַתִּלְחַ֛ץ אֶת־רֶ֥גֶל בִּלְעָ֖ם אֶל־הַקִּ֑יר וַיֹּ֖סֶף לְהַכֹּתָֽהּ׃ 26 וַיּ֥וֹסֶף מַלְאַךְ־יְהֹוָ֖ה עֲב֑וֹר וַֽיַּעֲמֹד֙ בְּמָק֣וֹם צָ֔ר אֲשֶׁ֛ר

a spot so narrow that there was no room to swerve right or left. ²⁷When the ass now saw the angel of the LORD, she lay down under Balaam; and Balaam was furious and beat the ass with his stick.

²⁸Then the LORD opened the ass's mouth, and she said to Balaam, "What have I done to you that you have beaten me these three times?" ²⁹Balaam said to the ass, "You have made a mockery of me! If I had a sword with me, I'd kill you." ³⁰The ass said to Balaam, "Look, I am the ass that you have been riding all along until this day! Have I been in the habit of doing thus to you?" And he answered, "No."

³¹Then the LORD uncovered Balaam's eyes, and he saw the angel of the LORD standing in the way, his drawn sword in his hand; thereupon he bowed ᶜ-right down to the ground.-ᶜ ³²The angel of the LORD said to him, "Why have you beaten your ass these three times? It is I who came out as an adversary, for the errand is obnoxiousᵈ to me. ³³And when the ass saw me, she shied away because of me those three times. If she had not shied away from me, you are the one I should have killed, while sparing her." ³⁴Balaam said to the angel of the LORD, "I erred because I did not know that you were standing in my way. If you still disapprove, I will turn back." ³⁵But the angel of the LORD said to Balaam, "Go with the men. But you must say nothing except what I tell you." So Balaam went on with Balak's dignitaries.

³⁶When Balak heard that Balaam was coming, he went out to meet him at Ir-moab, which is on the Arnon border, at its farthest point. ³⁷Balak said to Balaam, "When I first sent to invite you, why didn't you come to me? Am I really unable to reward you?" ³⁸But Balaam said to Balak, "And now that I have come to you, have I

---

c-c Lit. "and prostrated himself to his nostrils."
d Precise meaning of Heb. uncertain.

²⁷ וַתֵּ֣רֶא אֵין־דֶּ֔רֶךְ לִנְט֖וֹת יָמִ֥ין וּשְׂמֹֽאול׃ הָֽאָת֗וֹן אֶת־מַלְאַ֣ךְ יְהֹוָה֒ וַתִּרְבַּץ֙ תַּ֣חַת בִּלְעָ֔ם וַיִּֽחַר־אַ֣ף בִּלְעָ֔ם וַיַּ֥ךְ אֶת־הָאָת֖וֹן בַּמַּקֵּֽל׃ ²⁸ וַיִּפְתַּ֥ח יְהֹוָ֖ה אֶת־פִּ֣י הָאָת֑וֹן וַתֹּ֤אמֶר לְבִלְעָם֙ מֶה־עָשִׂ֣יתִי לְךָ֔ כִּ֣י הִכִּיתַ֔נִי זֶ֖ה שָׁלֹ֥שׁ רְגָלִֽים׃ ²⁹ וַיֹּ֤אמֶר בִּלְעָם֙ לָֽאָת֔וֹן כִּ֥י הִתְעַלַּ֖לְתְּ בִּ֑י ל֤וּ יֶשׁ־חֶ֙רֶב֙ בְּיָדִ֔י כִּ֥י עַתָּ֖ה הֲרַגְתִּֽיךְ׃ ³⁰ וַתֹּ֨אמֶר הָאָת֜וֹן אֶל־בִּלְעָ֗ם הֲלוֹא֩ אָנֹכִ֨י אֲתֹֽנְךָ֜ אֲשֶׁר־רָכַ֣בְתָּ עָלַ֗י מֵעֽוֹדְךָ֙ עַד־הַיּ֣וֹם הַזֶּ֔ה הַֽהַסְכֵּ֣ן הִסְכַּ֔נְתִּי לַעֲשׂ֥וֹת לְךָ֖ כֹּ֑ה וַיֹּ֖אמֶר לֹֽא׃ ³¹ וַיְגַ֣ל יְהֹוָה֮ אֶת־עֵינֵ֣י בִלְעָם֒ וַיַּ֞רְא אֶת־מַלְאַ֤ךְ יְהֹוָה֙ נִצָּ֣ב בַּדֶּ֔רֶךְ וְחַרְבּ֥וֹ שְׁלֻפָ֖ה בְּיָד֑וֹ וַיִּקֹּ֥ד וַיִּשְׁתַּ֖חוּ לְאַפָּֽיו׃ ³² וַיֹּ֤אמֶר אֵלָיו֙ מַלְאַ֣ךְ יְהֹוָ֔ה עַל־מָ֗ה הִכִּ֙יתָ֙ אֶת־אֲתֹ֣נְךָ֔ זֶ֖ה שָׁל֣וֹשׁ רְגָלִ֑ים הִנֵּ֧ה אָנֹכִ֛י יָצָ֥אתִי לְשָׂטָ֖ן כִּֽי־יָרַ֥ט הַדֶּ֖רֶךְ לְנֶגְדִּֽי׃ ³³ וַתִּרְאַ֙נִי֙ הָֽאָת֔וֹן וַתֵּ֣ט לְפָנַ֔י זֶ֖ה שָׁלֹ֣שׁ רְגָלִ֑ים אוּלַי֙ נָטְתָ֣ה מִפָּנַ֔י כִּ֥י עַתָּ֛ה גַּם־אֹתְכָ֖ה הָרַ֣גְתִּי וְאוֹתָ֥הּ הֶחֱיֵֽיתִי׃ ³⁴ וַיֹּ֨אמֶר בִּלְעָ֜ם אֶל־מַלְאַ֤ךְ יְהֹוָה֙ חָטָ֔אתִי כִּ֚י לֹ֣א יָדַ֔עְתִּי כִּ֥י אַתָּ֛ה נִצָּ֥ב לִקְרָאתִ֖י בַּדָּ֑רֶךְ וְעַתָּ֛ה אִם־רַ֥ע בְּעֵינֶ֖יךָ אָשׁ֥וּבָה לִּֽי׃ ³⁵ וַיֹּ֩אמֶר֩ מַלְאַ֨ךְ יְהֹוָ֜ה אֶל־בִּלְעָ֗ם לֵ֚ךְ עִם־הָ֣אֲנָשִׁ֔ים וְאֶ֗פֶס אֶת־הַדָּבָ֛ר אֲשֶׁר־אֲדַבֵּ֥ר אֵלֶ֖יךָ אֹת֣וֹ תְדַבֵּ֑ר וַיֵּ֥לֶךְ בִּלְעָ֖ם עִם־שָׂרֵ֥י בָלָֽק׃ ³⁶ וַיִּשְׁמַ֥ע בָּלָ֖ק כִּ֣י בָ֣א בִלְעָ֑ם וַיֵּצֵ֨א לִקְרָאת֜וֹ אֶל־עִ֣יר מוֹאָ֗ב אֲשֶׁר֙ עַל־גְּב֣וּל אַרְנֹ֔ן אֲשֶׁ֖ר בִּקְצֵ֥ה הַגְּבֽוּל׃ ³⁷ וַיֹּ֨אמֶר בָּלָ֜ק אֶל־בִּלְעָ֗ם הֲלֹא֩ שָׁלֹ֨חַ שָׁלַ֤חְתִּי אֵלֶ֙יךָ֙ לִקְרֹא־לָ֔ךְ לָ֥מָּה לֹא־הָלַ֖כְתָּ אֵלָ֑י הַֽאֻמְנָ֔ם לֹ֥א אוּכַ֖ל כַּבְּדֶֽךָ׃ ³⁸ וַיֹּ֨אמֶר בִּלְעָ֜ם אֶל־בָּלָ֗ק הִֽנֵּה־בָ֙אתִי֙ אֵלֶ֔יךָ עַתָּ֕ה הֲיָכֹ֥ל אוּכַ֖ל דַּבֵּ֣ר

v. 33. יתיר ה'

the power to speak freely? I can utter only the word that God puts into my mouth."

³⁹Balaam went with Balak and they came to Kiriath-huzoth.

⁴⁰Balak sacrificed oxen and sheep, and had them served to Balaam and the dignitaries with him. ⁴¹In the morning Balak took Balaam up to Bamoth-baal. From there he could see a portion of the people.

23

Balaam said to Balak, "Build me seven altars here and have seven bulls and seven rams ready here for me." ²Balak did as Balaam directed; and Balak and Balaam offered up a bull and a ram on each altar. ³Then Balaam said to Balak, "Stay here beside your offerings while I am gone. Perhaps the LORD will grant me a manifestation, and whatever He reveals to me I will tell you." And he went off alone.[a]

⁴God manifested Himself to Balaam, who said to Him, "I have set up the seven altars and offered up a bull and a ram on each altar." ⁵And the LORD put a word in Balaam's mouth and said, "Return to Balak and speak thus."

⁶So he returned to him and found him standing beside his offerings, and all the Moabite dignitaries with him. ⁷He took up his theme, and said:

From Aram has Balak brought me,
Moab's king from the hills of the East:
Come, curse me Jacob,
Come, tell Israel's doom!
⁸How can I damn whom God[b] has not damned,
How doom when the LORD has not doomed?
⁹As I see them from the mountain tops,
Gaze on them from the heights,
There is a people that dwells apart,
Not reckoned among the nations,

מֵאוּמָה הַדָּבָ֗ר אֲשֶׁ֨ר יָשִׂ֧ים אֱלֹהִ֛ים בְּפִ֖י אֹת֥וֹ אֲדַבֵּֽר׃

³⁹וַיֵּ֥לֶךְ בִּלְעָ֖ם עִם־בָּלָ֑ק וַיָּבֹ֖אוּ קִרְיַ֥ת חֻצֽוֹת׃ ⁴⁰וַיִּזְבַּ֥ח בָּלָ֖ק בָּקָ֣ר וָצֹ֑אן וַיְשַׁלַּ֣ח לְבִלְעָ֔ם וְלַשָּׂרִ֖ים אֲשֶׁ֥ר אִתּֽוֹ׃ ⁴¹וַיְהִ֣י בַבֹּ֔קֶר וַיִּקַּ֤ח בָּלָק֙ אֶת־בִּלְעָ֔ם וַֽיַּעֲלֵ֖הוּ בָּמ֣וֹת בָּ֑עַל וַיַּ֥רְא מִשָּׁ֖ם קְצֵ֥ה הָעָֽם׃

כג וַיֹּ֤אמֶר בִּלְעָם֙ אֶל־בָּלָ֔ק בְּנֵה־לִ֥י בָזֶ֖ה שִׁבְעָ֣ה מִזְבְּחֹ֑ת וְהָכֵ֥ן לִ֛י בָּזֶ֖ה שִׁבְעָ֣ה פָרִ֖ים וְשִׁבְעָ֥ה אֵילִֽים׃ ²וַיַּ֣עַשׂ בָּלָ֔ק כַּאֲשֶׁ֖ר דִּבֶּ֣ר בִּלְעָ֑ם וַיַּ֨עַל בָּלָ֧ק וּבִלְעָ֛ם פָּ֥ר וָאַ֖יִל בַּמִּזְבֵּֽחַ׃ ³וַיֹּ֨אמֶר בִּלְעָ֜ם לְבָלָ֗ק הִתְיַצֵּב֮ עַל־עֹלָתֶךָ֒ וְאֵֽלְכָ֗ה אוּלַ֞י יִקָּרֵ֤ה יְהֹוָה֙ לִקְרָאתִ֔י וּדְבַ֥ר מַה־יַּרְאֵ֖נִי וְהִגַּ֣דְתִּי לָ֑ךְ וַיֵּ֖לֶךְ שֶֽׁפִי׃ ⁴וַיִּקָּ֥ר אֱלֹהִ֖ים אֶל־בִּלְעָ֑ם וַיֹּ֣אמֶר אֵלָ֗יו אֶת־שִׁבְעַ֤ת הַֽמִּזְבְּחֹת֙ עָרַ֔כְתִּי וָאַ֛עַל פָּ֥ר וָאַ֖יִל בַּמִּזְבֵּֽחַ׃ ⁵וַיָּ֧שֶׂם יְהֹוָ֛ה דָּבָ֖ר בְּפִ֣י בִלְעָ֑ם וַיֹּ֛אמֶר שׁ֥וּב אֶל־בָּלָ֖ק וְכֹ֥ה תְדַבֵּֽר׃ ⁶וַיָּ֣שׇׁב אֵלָ֔יו וְהִנֵּ֥ה נִצָּ֖ב עַל־עֹלָת֑וֹ ה֥וּא וְכׇל־שָׂרֵ֥י מוֹאָֽב׃ ⁷וַיִּשָּׂ֥א מְשָׁל֖וֹ וַיֹּאמַ֑ר

מִן־אֲ֠רָ֠ם יַנְחֵ֨נִי בָלָ֤ק
מֶֽלֶךְ־מוֹאָב֙ מֵֽהַרְרֵי־קֶ֔דֶם
לְכָה֙ אָֽרָה־לִּ֣י יַעֲקֹ֔ב
וּלְכָ֖ה זֹעֲמָ֥ה יִשְׂרָאֵֽל׃
⁸מָ֣ה אֶקֹּ֔ב לֹ֥א קַבֹּ֖ה אֵ֑ל
וּמָ֣ה אֶזְעֹ֔ם לֹ֥א זָעַ֖ם יְהֹוָֽה׃
⁹כִּֽי־מֵרֹ֤אשׁ צֻרִים֙ אֶרְאֶ֔נּוּ
וּמִגְּבָע֖וֹת אֲשׁוּרֶ֑נּוּ
הֶן־עָם֙ לְבָדָ֣ד יִשְׁכֹּ֔ן
וּבַגּוֹיִ֖ם לֹ֥א יִתְחַשָּֽׁב׃

---

^a Others "to a bare height"; exact meaning of Heb. shephi uncertain.
^b Heb. El, as often in these poems.

10Who can count the dust[c] of Jacob,
Number[d] the dust-cloud of Israel?
May I die the death of the upright,[e]
May my fate be like theirs!

11Then Balak said to Balaam, "What have you done to me? Here I brought you to damn my enemies, and instead you have blessed them!" 12He replied, "I can only repeat faithfully what the LORD puts in my mouth." 13Then Balak said to him, "Come with me to another place from which you can see them—you will see only a portion of them; you will not see all of them—and damn them for me from there." 14With that, he took him to Sedehzophim,[f] on the summit of Pisgah. He built seven altars and offered a bull and a ram on each altar. 15And [Balaam] said to Balak, "Stay here beside your offerings, while I seek a manifestation yonder."

16The LORD manifested Himself to Balaam and put a word in his mouth, saying, "Return to Balak and speak thus." 17He went to him and found him standing beside his offerings, and the Moabite dignitaries with him. Balak asked him, "What did the LORD say?" 18And he took up his theme, and said:

Up, Balak, attend,
Give ear unto me, son of Zippor!
19God is not man to be capricious,
Or mortal to change His mind.
Would He speak and not act,
Promise and not fulfill?
20My message was to bless:
When He blesses, I cannot reverse it.
21No harm is in sight for Jacob,
No woe in view for Israel.
The LORD their God is with them,

10 מִי מָנָה עֲפַר יַעֲקֹב
וּמִסְפָּר אֶת־רֹבַע יִשְׂרָאֵל
תָּמֹת נַפְשִׁי מוֹת יְשָׁרִים
וּתְהִי אַחֲרִיתִי כָּמֹהוּ:

11 וַיֹּאמֶר בָּלָק אֶל־בִּלְעָם מֶה עָשִׂיתָ לִי לָקֹב אֹיְבַי לְקַחְתִּיךָ וְהִנֵּה בֵּרַכְתָּ בָרֵךְ: 12 וַיַּעַן וַיֹּאמַר הֲלֹא אֵת אֲשֶׁר יָשִׂים יְהוָה בְּפִי אֹתוֹ אֶשְׁמֹר לְדַבֵּר: 13 וַיֹּאמֶר אֵלָיו בָּלָק לך נָא אִתִּי אֶל־מָקוֹם אַחֵר אֲשֶׁר תִּרְאֶנּוּ מִשָּׁם אֶפֶס קָצֵהוּ תִרְאֶה וְכֻלּוֹ לֹא תִרְאֶה וְקָבְנוֹ־לִי מִשָּׁם: 14 וַיִּקָּחֵהוּ שְׂדֵה צֹפִים אֶל־רֹאשׁ הַפִּסְגָּה וַיִּבֶן שִׁבְעָה מִזְבְּחֹת וַיַּעַל פָּר וָאַיִל בַּמִּזְבֵּחַ: 15 וַיֹּאמֶר אֶל־בָּלָק הִתְיַצֵּב כֹּה עַל־עֹלָתֶךָ וְאָנֹכִי אִקָּרֶה כֹּה:
16 וַיִּקָּר יְהוָה אֶל־בִּלְעָם וַיָּשֶׂם דָּבָר בְּפִיו וַיֹּאמֶר שׁוּב אֶל־בָּלָק וְכֹה תְדַבֵּר: 17 וַיָּבֹא אֵלָיו וְהִנּוֹ נִצָּב עַל־עֹלָתוֹ וְשָׂרֵי מוֹאָב אִתּוֹ וַיֹּאמֶר לוֹ בָּלָק מַה־דִּבֶּר יְהוָה: 18 וַיִּשָּׂא מְשָׁלוֹ וַיֹּאמַר

קוּם בָּלָק וּשֲׁמָע
הַאֲזִינָה עָדַי בְּנוֹ צִפֹּר:
19 לֹא אִישׁ אֵל וִיכַזֵּב
וּבֶן־אָדָם וְיִתְנֶחָם
הַהוּא אָמַר וְלֹא יַעֲשֶׂה
וְדִבֶּר וְלֹא יְקִימֶנָּה:
20 הִנֵּה בָרֵךְ לָקָחְתִּי
וּבֵרֵךְ וְלֹא אֲשִׁיבֶנָּה:
21 לֹא־הִבִּיט אָוֶן בְּיַעֲקֹב
וְלֹא־רָאָה עָמָל בְּיִשְׂרָאֵל
יְהוָה אֱלֹהָיו עִמּוֹ
וּתְרוּעַת מֶלֶךְ בּוֹ:

---

c Cf. Gen. 13.16.
d Lit. "and the number of."
e Heb. yesharim, a play on yeshurun (Jeshurun in Deut. 32.15), a name for Israel.
f Or "Lookout Point."

And their King's acclaim in their midst.
²²God who freed them from Egypt
Is for them like the horns^g of the wild ox.
²³Lo, there is no augury in Jacob,
No divining in Israel:^h
Jacob is told at once,
Yea Israel, what God has planned.ⁱ
²⁴Lo, a people that rises like a lion,
Leaps up like the ^j-king of beasts,^{-j}
Rests not till it has feasted on prey
And drunk the blood of the slain.

²⁵Thereupon Balak said to Balaam, "Don't curse them and don't bless them!" ²⁶In reply, Balaam said to Balak, "But I told you: Whatever the LORD says, that I must do." ²⁷Then Balak said to Balaam, "Come now, I will take you to another place. Perhaps God will deem it right that you damn them for me there." ²⁸Balak took Balaam to the peak of Peor, which overlooks the wasteland.^k ²⁹Balaam said to Balak, "Build me here seven altars, and have seven bulls and seven rams ready for me here." ³⁰Balak did as Balaam said: he offered up a bull and a ram on each altar.

24 Now Balaam, seeing that it pleased the LORD to bless Israel, did not, as on previous occasions, go in search of omens, but turned his face toward the wilderness. ²As Balaam looked up and saw Israel encamped tribe by tribe, the spirit of God came upon him. ³Taking up his theme, he said:

22 אֵ֚ל מוֹצִיאָ֣ם מִמִּצְרַ֔יִם
כְּתוֹעֲפֹ֥ת רְאֵ֖ם לֽוֹ׃
23 כִּ֤י לֹא־נַ֨חַשׁ֙ בְּֽיַעֲקֹ֔ב
וְלֹא־קֶ֖סֶם בְּיִשְׂרָאֵ֑ל
כָּעֵ֗ת יֵאָמֵ֤ר לְיַעֲקֹב֙
וּלְיִשְׂרָאֵ֔ל מַה־פָּ֖עַל אֵֽל׃
24 הֶן־עָם֙ כְּלָבִ֣יא יָק֔וּם
וְכַאֲרִ֖י יִתְנַשָּׂ֑א
לֹ֤א יִשְׁכַּב֙ עַד־יֹ֣אכַל טֶ֔רֶף
וְדַם־חֲלָלִ֖ים יִשְׁתֶּֽה׃

25 וַיֹּ֤אמֶר בָּלָק֙ אֶל־בִּלְעָ֔ם גַּם־קֹ֖ב לֹ֣א
תִקֳּבֶ֑נּוּ גַּם־בָּרֵ֖ךְ לֹ֥א תְבָרֲכֶֽנּוּ׃ 26 וַיַּ֣עַן
בִּלְעָ֗ם וַיֹּ֨אמֶר֙ אֶל־בָּלָ֔ק הֲלֹ֗א דִּבַּ֤רְתִּי אֵלֶ֨יךָ֙
לֵאמֹ֔ר כֹּ֛ל אֲשֶׁר־יְדַבֵּ֥ר יְהוָ֖ה אֹת֥וֹ אֶעֱשֶֽׂה׃
27 וַיֹּ֤אמֶר בָּלָק֙ אֶל־בִּלְעָ֔ם לְכָה־נָּא֙ אֶקָּ֣חֲךָ֔
אֶל־מָק֖וֹם אַחֵ֑ר אוּלַ֤י יִישַׁר֙ בְּעֵינֵ֣י
הָאֱלֹהִ֔ים וְקַבֹּ֥תוֹ לִ֖י מִשָּֽׁם׃ 28 וַיִּקַּ֥ח בָּלָ֖ק
אֶת־בִּלְעָ֑ם רֹ֚אשׁ הַפְּע֔וֹר הַנִּשְׁקָ֖ף עַל־פְּנֵ֥י
הַיְשִׁימֹֽן׃ 29 וַיֹּ֤אמֶר בִּלְעָם֙ אֶל־בָּלָ֔ק בְּנֵה־
לִ֥י בָזֶ֖ה שִׁבְעָ֣ה מִזְבְּחֹ֑ת וְהָכֵ֥ן לִי֙ בָּזֶ֔ה
שִׁבְעָ֥ה פָרִ֖ים וְשִׁבְעָ֥ה אֵילִֽים׃ 30 וַיַּ֣עַשׂ
בָּלָ֗ק כַּאֲשֶׁ֛ר אָמַ֥ר בִּלְעָ֖ם וַיַּ֛עַל פָּ֥ר וָאַ֖יִל
בַּמִּזְבֵּֽחַ׃

כד וַיַּ֣רְא בִּלְעָ֗ם כִּ֣י ט֞וֹב בְּעֵינֵ֤י יְהוָה֙
לְבָרֵ֣ךְ אֶת־יִשְׂרָאֵ֔ל וְלֹא־הָלַ֥ךְ כְּפַֽעַם־
בְּפַ֖עַם לִקְרַ֣את נְחָשִׁ֑ים וַיָּ֥שֶׁת אֶל־הַמִּדְבָּ֖ר
פָּנָֽיו׃ 2 וַיִּשָּׂ֨א בִלְעָ֜ם אֶת־עֵינָ֗יו וַיַּרְא֙ אֶת־
יִשְׂרָאֵ֔ל שֹׁכֵ֖ן לִשְׁבָטָ֑יו וַתְּהִ֥י עָלָ֖יו ר֥וּחַ
אֱלֹהִֽים׃ 3 וַיִּשָּׂ֥א מְשָׁל֖וֹ וַיֹּאמַֽר׃

---

g Lit. "eminences," used figuratively.
h Cf. Deut. 18.10–15.
i Or, "Else would it be told to Jacob, / Yea to Israel, what God has planned."
j-j Heb. 'ari, another term for "lion."
k Cf. note on 21.20.

a Some of the poetic portions of this chapter are unclear.

*a*Word of Balaam son of Beor,
Word of the man whose eye is true,*b*
⁴Word of him who hears God's speech,
Who beholds visions from the Almighty,
Prostrate, but with eyes unveiled:
⁵How fair are your tents, O Jacob,
Your dwellings, O Israel!
⁶Like palm-groves that stretch out,
Like gardens beside a river,
Like aloes planted by the LORD,
Like cedars beside the water;
⁷Their boughs drip with moisture,
Their roots*c* have abundant water.
Their king shall rise above Agag,
Their kingdom shall be exalted.
⁸God who freed them from Egypt
Is for them like the horns*d* of the wild ox.
They shall devour enemy nations,
Crush their bones,
And smash their arrows.
⁹They crouch, they lie down like a lion,
Like the king of beasts;*e* who dare rouse them?
Blessed are they who bless you,
Accursed they who curse you!

¹⁰Enraged at Balaam, Balak struck his hands together. "I called you," Balak said to Balaam, "to damn my enemies, and instead you have blessed them these three times! ¹¹Back with you at once to your own place! I was going to reward you richly, but the LORD has denied you the reward." ¹²Balaam replied to Balak, "But I even told the messengers you sent to me, ¹³'Though Balak were to give me his house full of silver and gold, I could not of my own accord do anything good or bad contrary to the LORD's command. What the LORD says, that I must say.' ¹⁴And now, as I go back to my people, let me inform you of what this people will do to your

נְאֻם בִּלְעָם בְּנוֹ בְעֹר
וּנְאֻם הַגֶּבֶר שְׁתֻם הָעָיִן:
⁴ נְאֻם שֹׁמֵעַ אִמְרֵי־אֵל
אֲשֶׁר מַחֲזֵה שַׁדַּי יֶחֱזֶה
נֹפֵל וּגְלוּי עֵינָיִם:
⁵ מַה־טֹּבוּ אֹהָלֶיךָ יַעֲקֹב
מִשְׁכְּנֹתֶיךָ יִשְׂרָאֵל:
⁶ כִּנְחָלִים נִטָּיוּ
כְּגַנֹּת עֲלֵי נָהָר
כַּאֲהָלִים נָטַע יְהוָה
כַּאֲרָזִים עֲלֵי־מָיִם:
⁷ יִזַּל־מַיִם מִדָּלְיָו
וְזַרְעוֹ בְּמַיִם רַבִּים
וְיָרֹם מֵאֲגַג מַלְכּוֹ
וְתִנַּשֵּׂא מַלְכֻתוֹ:
⁸ אֵל מוֹצִיאוֹ מִמִּצְרַיִם
כְּתוֹעֲפֹת רְאֵם לוֹ
יֹאכַל גּוֹיִם צָרָיו
וְעַצְמֹתֵיהֶם יְגָרֵם
וְחִצָּיו יִמְחָץ:
⁹ כָּרַע שָׁכַב כַּאֲרִי
וּכְלָבִיא מִי יְקִימֶנּוּ
מְבָרְכֶיךָ בָרוּךְ
וְאֹרְרֶיךָ אָרוּר:

¹⁰ וַיִּחַר־אַף בָּלָק אֶל־בִּלְעָם וַיִּסְפֹּק אֶת־כַּפָּיו וַיֹּאמֶר בָּלָק אֶל־בִּלְעָם לָקֹב אֹיְבַי קְרָאתִיךָ וְהִנֵּה בֵּרַכְתָּ בָרֵךְ זֶה שָׁלֹשׁ פְּעָמִים: ¹¹ וְעַתָּה בְּרַח־לְךָ אֶל־מְקוֹמֶךָ אָמַרְתִּי כַּבֵּד אֲכַבֶּדְךָ וְהִנֵּה מְנָעֲךָ יְהוָה מִכָּבוֹד: ¹² וַיֹּאמֶר בִּלְעָם אֶל־בָּלָק הֲלֹא גַּם אֶל־מַלְאָכֶיךָ אֲשֶׁר־שָׁלַחְתָּ אֵלַי דִּבַּרְתִּי לֵאמֹר: ¹³ אִם־יִתֶּן־לִי בָלָק מְלֹא בֵיתוֹ כֶּסֶף וְזָהָב לֹא אוּכַל לַעֲבֹר אֶת־פִּי יְהוָה לַעֲשׂוֹת טוֹבָה אוֹ רָעָה מִלִּבִּי אֲשֶׁר־יְדַבֵּר יְהוָה אֹתוֹ אֲדַבֵּר: ¹⁴ וְעַתָּה הִנְנִי הוֹלֵךְ לְעַמִּי לְכָה אִיעָצְךָ אֲשֶׁר יַעֲשֶׂה הָעָם הַזֶּה

---

b Others "whose eye is (or, eyes are) open"; meaning of Heb. uncertain.
c Lit. "and its seed."
d See note at 23.22.
e Heb. labi, another word for "lion"; cf. note at 23.24.

341

people in days to come." 15He took up his
theme, and said:

Word of Balaam son of Beor,
Word of the man whose eye is true,
16Word of him who hears God's speech,
Who obtains knowledge from the Most High,
And beholds visions from the Almighty,
Prostrate, but with eyes unveiled:
17What I see for them is not yet,
What I behold will not be soon:
A star rises from Jacob,
A scepter comes forth from Israel;
It smashes the brow of Moab,
The foundation off all children of Seth.
18Edom becomes a possession,
Yea, Seir a possession of its enemies;
But Israel is triumphant.
19A victor issues from Jacob
To wipe out what is left of Ir.

20He saw Amalek and, taking up his theme, he
said:

A leading nation is Amalek;
But its fate is to perish forever.

21He saw the Kenites and, taking up his theme,
he said:

Though your abode be secure,
And your nest be set among cliffs,
22Yet shall Kaing be consumed,
When Asshur takes you captive.

23He took up his theme and said:

Alas, who can survive except God has willed
it!
24Ships come from the quarter of Kittim;
They subject Asshur, subject Eber.
They, too, shall perish forever.

25Then Balaam set out on his journey back
home; and Balak also went his way.

לְעַמְּךָ בְּאַחֲרִית הַיָּמִים׃ 15 וַיִּשָּׂא מְשָׁלוֹ
וַיֹּאמַר

נְאֻם בִּלְעָם בְּנוֹ בְעֹר
וּנְאֻם הַגֶּבֶר שְׁתֻם הָעָיִן׃
16 נְאֻם שֹׁמֵעַ אִמְרֵי־אֵל
וְיֹדֵעַ דַּעַת עֶלְיוֹן
מַחֲזֵה שַׁדַּי יֶחֱזֶה
נֹפֵל וּגְלוּי עֵינָיִם׃
17 אֶרְאֶנּוּ וְלֹא עַתָּה
אֲשׁוּרֶנּוּ וְלֹא קָרוֹב
דָּרַךְ כּוֹכָב מִיַּעֲקֹב
וְקָם שֵׁבֶט מִיִּשְׂרָאֵל
וּמָחַץ פַּאֲתֵי מוֹאָב
וְקַרְקַר כָּל־בְּנֵי־שֵׁת׃
18 וְהָיָה אֱדוֹם יְרֵשָׁה
וְהָיָה יְרֵשָׁה שֵׂעִיר אֹיְבָיו
וְיִשְׂרָאֵל עֹשֶׂה חָיִל׃
19 וְיֵרְדְּ מִיַּעֲקֹב
וְהֶאֱבִיד שָׂרִיד מֵעִיר׃
20 וַיַּרְא אֶת־עֲמָלֵק וַיִּשָּׂא מְשָׁלוֹ וַיֹּאמַר
רֵאשִׁית גּוֹיִם עֲמָלֵק
וְאַחֲרִיתוֹ עֲדֵי אֹבֵד׃
21 וַיַּרְא אֶת־הַקֵּינִי וַיִּשָּׂא מְשָׁלוֹ וַיֹּאמַר
אֵיתָן מוֹשָׁבֶךָ
וְשִׂים בַּסֶּלַע קִנֶּךָ׃
22 כִּי אִם־יִהְיֶה לְבָעֵר קָיִן
עַד־מָה אַשּׁוּר תִּשְׁבֶּךָּ׃
23 וַיִּשָּׂא מְשָׁלוֹ וַיֹּאמַר
אוֹי מִי יִחְיֶה מִשֻּׂמוֹ אֵל׃
24 וְצִים מִיַּד כִּתִּים
וְעִנּוּ אַשּׁוּר וְעִנּוּ־עֵבֶר
וְגַם־הוּא עֲדֵי אֹבֵד׃
25 וַיָּקָם בִּלְעָם וַיֵּלֶךְ וַיָּשָׁב לִמְקֹמוֹ וְגַם־
בָּלָק הָלַךְ לְדַרְכּוֹ׃ פ

---

f Samaritan "the pate of," cf. Jer. 48.45; others "breaks down."
g I.e., the Kenites.

25 While Israel was staying at Shittim, the people *a-profaned themselves by whoring-a* with the Moabite women, ²who invited the people to the sacrifices for their god. The people partook of them and worshiped that god. ³Thus Israel attached itself to Baal-peor, and the LORD was incensed with Israel. ⁴The LORD said to Moses, "Take all the ringleaders[b] and have them publicly[c] impaled before the LORD, so that the LORD's wrath may turn away from Israel." ⁵So Moses said to Israel's officials, "Each of you slay those of his men who attached themselves to Baal-peor."

⁶Just then one of the Israelites came and brought a Midianite woman over to his companions, in the sight of Moses and of the whole Israelite community who were weeping at the entrance of the Tent of Meeting. ⁷When Phinehas, son of Eleazar son of Aaron the priest, saw this, he left the assembly and, taking a spear in his hand, ⁸he followed the Israelite into the chamber and stabbed both of them, the Israelite and the woman, through the belly. Then the plague against the Israelites was checked. ⁹Those who died of the plague numbered twenty-four thousand.

PINHAS

¹⁰The LORD spoke to Moses, saying, ¹¹"Phinehas, son of Eleazar son of Aaron the priest, has turned back My wrath from the Israelites by displaying among them his passion for Me, so that I did not wipe out the Israelite people in My passion. ¹²Say, therefore, 'I grant him My pact of friendship. ¹³It shall be for him and his descendants after him a pact of priesthood for all time, because he took impassioned action for his God, thus making expiation for the Israelites.'"

---

a-a   *Others "began to commit harlotry."*
b   *Lit. "heads of the people."*
c   *Others "in face of the sun."*

כה וַיֵּ֥שֶׁב יִשְׂרָאֵ֖ל בַּשִּׁטִּ֑ים וַיָּ֣חֶל הָעָ֔ם לִזְנֹ֖ות אֶל־בְּנֹ֥ות מֹואָֽב: 2 וַתִּקְרֶ֣אןָ לָעָ֔ם לְזִבְחֵ֖י אֱלֹהֵיהֶ֑ן וַיֹּ֣אכַל הָעָ֔ם וַיִּֽשְׁתַּחֲוֻ֖ לֵאלֹֽהֵיהֶֽן: 3 וַיִּצָּ֥מֶד יִשְׂרָאֵ֖ל לְבַ֣עַל פְּעֹ֑ור וַיִּֽחַר־אַ֥ף יְהוָ֖ה בְּיִשְׂרָאֵֽל: 4 וַיֹּ֨אמֶר יְהוָ֜ה אֶל־מֹשֶׁ֗ה קַ֚ח אֶת־כָּל־רָאשֵׁ֣י הָעָ֔ם וְהֹוקַ֥ע אֹותָ֛ם לַֽיהוָ֖ה נֶ֣גֶד הַשָּׁ֑מֶשׁ וְיָשֹׁ֛ב חֲרֹ֥ון אַף־יְהוָ֖ה מִיִּשְׂרָאֵֽל: 5 וַיֹּ֣אמֶר מֹשֶׁ֗ה אֶל־שֹׁפְטֵ֖י יִשְׂרָאֵ֑ל הִרְגוּ֙ אִ֣ישׁ אֲנָשָׁ֔יו הַנִּצְמָדִ֖ים לְבַ֥עַל פְּעֹֽור: 6 וְהִנֵּ֡ה אִישׁ֩ מִבְּנֵ֨י יִשְׂרָאֵ֜ל בָּ֗א וַיַּקְרֵ֤ב אֶל־אֶחָיו֙ אֶת־הַמִּדְיָנִ֔ית לְעֵינֵ֣י מֹשֶׁ֔ה וּלְעֵינֵ֖י כָּל־עֲדַ֣ת בְּנֵֽי־יִשְׂרָאֵ֑ל וְהֵ֣מָּה בֹכִ֔ים פֶּ֖תַח אֹ֥הֶל מֹועֵֽד: 7 וַיַּ֗רְא פִּֽינְחָס֙ בֶּן־אֶלְעָזָ֔ר בֶּֽן־אַהֲרֹ֖ן הַכֹּהֵ֑ן וַיָּ֙קָם֙ מִתֹּ֣וךְ הָֽעֵדָ֔ה וַיִּקַּ֥ח רֹ֖מַח בְּיָדֹֽו: 8 וַ֠יָּבֹא אַחַ֨ר אִֽישׁ־יִשְׂרָאֵ֜ל אֶל־הַקֻּבָּ֗ה וַיִּדְקֹר֙ אֶת־שְׁנֵיהֶ֔ם אֵ֚ת אִ֣ישׁ יִשְׂרָאֵ֔ל וְאֶת־הָאִשָּׁ֖ה אֶל־קֳבָתָ֑הּ וַתֵּֽעָצַר֙ הַמַּגֵּפָ֔ה מֵעַ֖ל בְּנֵ֥י יִשְׂרָאֵֽל: 9 וַיִּהְי֕וּ הַמֵּתִ֖ים בַּמַּגֵּפָ֑ה אַרְבָּעָ֥ה וְעֶשְׂרִ֖ים אָֽלֶף: פ

פינחס

10 וַיְדַבֵּ֥ר יְהוָ֖ה אֶל־מֹשֶׁ֥ה לֵּאמֹֽר: 11 פִּֽינְחָ֨ס בֶּן־אֶלְעָזָ֜ר בֶּֽן־אַהֲרֹ֣ן הַכֹּהֵ֗ן הֵשִׁ֤יב אֶת־חֲמָתִי֙ מֵעַ֣ל בְּנֵֽי־יִשְׂרָאֵ֔ל בְּקַנְאֹ֥ו אֶת־קִנְאָתִ֖י בְּתֹוכָ֑ם וְלֹֽא־כִלִּ֥יתִי אֶת־בְּנֵֽי־יִשְׂרָאֵ֖ל בְּקִנְאָתִֽי: 12 לָכֵ֖ן אֱמֹ֑ר הִנְנִ֨י נֹתֵ֥ן לֹ֛ו אֶת־בְּרִיתִ֖י שָׁלֹֽום: 13 וְהָ֤יְתָה לֹּו֙ וּלְזַרְעֹ֣ו אַחֲרָ֔יו בְּרִ֖ית כְּהֻנַּ֣ת עֹולָ֑ם תַּ֗חַת אֲשֶׁ֤ר קִנֵּא֙ לֵֽאלֹהָ֔יו וַיְכַפֵּ֖ר עַל־בְּנֵ֥י יִשְׂרָאֵֽל:

14The name of the Israelite who was killed, the one who was killed with the Midianite woman, was Zimri son of Salu, chieftain of a Simeonite ancestral house. 15The name of the Midianite woman who was killed was Cozbi daughter of Zur; he was the tribal head of an ancestral house in Midian.

16The LORD spoke to Moses, saying, 17"Assail the Midianites and defeat them—18for they assailed you by the trickery they practiced against you—because of the affair of Peor and because of the affair of their kinswoman Cozbi, daughter of the Midianite chieftain, who was killed at the time of the plague on account of Peor."

26

19When the plague was over, 1the LORD said to Moses and to Eleazar son of Aaron the priest, 2"Take a census of the whole Israelite community from the age of twenty years up, by their ancestral houses, all Israelites able to bear arms." 3aSo Moses and Eleazar the priest, on the steppes of Moab, at the Jordan near Jericho, gave instructions about them, namely, 4those from twenty years up, as the LORD had commanded Moses.

The descendants of the Israelites who came out of the land of Egypt were:

5Reuben, Israel's first-born. Descendants of Reuben: [Of] Enoch,b the clan of the Enochites; of Pallu, the clan of the Palluites; 6of Hezron, the clan of the Hezronites; of Carmi, the clan of the Carmites. 7Those are the clans of the Reubenites. The persons enrolled came to 43,730.

8c-Born to-c Pallu: Eliab. 9The sons of Eliab were Nemuel, and Dathan and Abiram. These are the same Dathan and Abiram, chosen in the assembly, who agitated against Moses and

---

a Meaning of parts of vv. 3 and 4 uncertain.
b Or "Hanoch."
c-c Or "descendants of."

---

14 וְשֵׁם֩ אִ֨ישׁ יִשְׂרָאֵ֜ל הַמֻּכֶּ֗ה אֲשֶׁ֤ר הֻכָּה֙ אֶת־הַמִּדְיָנִ֔ית זִמְרִ֖י בֶּן־סָל֑וּא נְשִׂ֥יא בֵית־אָ֖ב לַשִּׁמְעֹנִֽי: 15 וְשֵׁ֨ם הָֽאִשָּׁ֧ה הַמֻּכָּ֛ה הַמִּדְיָנִ֖ית כָּזְבִּ֣י בַת־צ֑וּר רֹ֧אשׁ אֻמּ֛וֹת בֵּֽית־אָ֥ב בְּמִדְיָ֖ן הֽוּא: פ

16 וַיְדַבֵּ֥ר יְהוָ֖ה אֶל־מֹשֶׁ֥ה לֵּאמֹֽר: 17 צָר֖וֹר אֶת־הַמִּדְיָנִ֑ים וְהִכִּיתֶ֖ם אוֹתָֽם: 18 כִּ֣י צֹרְרִ֥ים הֵם֙ לָכֶ֔ם בְּנִכְלֵיהֶ֛ם אֲשֶׁר־נִכְּל֥וּ לָכֶ֖ם עַל־דְּבַר־פְּע֑וֹר וְעַל־דְּבַ֞ר כָּזְבִּ֣י בַת־נְשִׂ֣יא מִדְיָ֗ן אֲחֹתָ֛ם הַמֻּכָּ֥ה בְיוֹם־הַמַּגֵּפָ֖ה עַל־דְּבַר־פְּעֽוֹר:

כו

19 וַיְהִ֖י אַחֲרֵ֣י הַמַּגֵּפָ֑ה* פ

1 וַיֹּ֤אמֶר יְהוָה֙ אֶל־מֹשֶׁ֔ה וְאֶ֧ל אֶלְעָזָ֛ר בֶּן־אַהֲרֹ֥ן הַכֹּהֵ֖ן לֵאמֹֽר: 2 שְׂא֞וּ אֶת־רֹ֣אשׁ ׀ כָּל־עֲדַ֣ת בְּנֵֽי־יִשְׂרָאֵ֗ל מִבֶּ֨ן עֶשְׂרִ֥ים שָׁנָ֛ה וָמַ֖עְלָה לְבֵ֣ית אֲבֹתָ֑ם כָּל־יֹצֵ֥א צָבָ֖א בְּיִשְׂרָאֵֽל: 3 וַיְדַבֵּ֨ר מֹשֶׁ֜ה וְאֶלְעָזָ֧ר הַכֹּהֵ֛ן אֹתָ֖ם בְּעַֽרְבֹ֣ת מוֹאָ֑ב עַל־יַרְדֵּ֥ן יְרֵח֖וֹ לֵאמֹֽר: 4 מִבֶּ֛ן עֶשְׂרִ֥ים שָׁנָ֖ה וָמָ֑עְלָה כַּאֲשֶׁר֩ צִוָּ֨ה יְהוָ֤ה אֶת־מֹשֶׁה֙ וּבְנֵ֣י יִשְׂרָאֵ֔ל הַיֹּצְאִ֖ים מֵאֶ֥רֶץ מִצְרָֽיִם:

5 רְאוּבֵ֖ן בְּכ֣וֹר יִשְׂרָאֵ֑ל בְּנֵ֣י רְאוּבֵ֗ן חֲנוֹךְ֙ מִשְׁפַּ֣חַת הַחֲנֹכִ֔י לְפַלּ֕וּא מִשְׁפַּ֖חַת הַפַּלֻּאִֽי: 6 לְחֶצְרֹ֕ן מִשְׁפַּ֖חַת הַחֶצְרוֹנִ֑י לְכַרְמִ֕י מִשְׁפַּ֖חַת הַכַּרְמִֽי: 7 אֵ֖לֶּה מִשְׁפְּחֹ֣ת הָרֻֽאוּבֵנִ֑י וַיִּהְי֣וּ פְקֻדֵיהֶ֗ם שְׁלֹשָׁ֤ה וְאַרְבָּעִים֙ אֶ֔לֶף וּשְׁבַ֥ע מֵא֖וֹת וּשְׁלֹשִֽׁים: 8 וּבְנֵ֥י פַלּ֖וּא אֱלִיאָֽב: 9 וּבְנֵ֣י אֱלִיאָ֔ב נְמוּאֵ֕ל וְדָתָ֖ן וַאֲבִירָ֑ם הֽוּא־דָתָ֨ן וַאֲבִירָ֜ם קרואי קְרִיאֵ֣י הָעֵדָ֗ה אֲשֶׁ֨ר הִצּ֜וּ עַל־מֹשֶׁ֤ה וְעַֽל־אַהֲרֹן֙ בַּעֲדַת־קֹ֔רַח בְּהַצֹּתָ֖ם עַל־יְהוָֽה:

---

v. 19. פיסקא באמצע פסוק, ונספר כאחד בסכום הפסוקים

תורה במדבר כו פינחס

Aaron as part of Korah's band when they agitated against the Lord. ¹⁰Whereupon the earth opened its mouth and swallowed them up with Korah—when that band died, when the fire consumed the two hundred and fifty men—and they became an example. ¹¹The sons of Korah, however, did not die.

¹²Descendants of Simeon by their clans: Of Nemuel, the clan of the Nemuelites; of Jamin, the clan of the Jaminites; of Jachin, the clan of the Jachinites; ¹³of Zerah, the clan of the Zerahites; of Saul,^d the clan of the Saulites. ¹⁴Those are the clans of the Simeonites; [persons enrolled:] 22,200.

¹⁵Descendants of Gad by their clans: Of Zephon, the clan of the Zephonites; of Haggi, the clan of the Haggites; of Shuni, the clan of the Shunites; ¹⁶of Ozni, the clan of the Oznites; of Eri, the clan of the Erites; ¹⁷of Arod, the clan of the Arodites; of Areli, the clan of the Arelites. ¹⁸Those are the clans of Gad's descendants; persons enrolled: 40,500.

^{19c-}Born to-^c Judah: Er and Onan. Er and Onan died in the land of Canaan.

²⁰Descendants of Judah by their clans: Of Shelah, the clan of the Shelanites; of Perez, the clan of the Perezites; of Zerah, the clan of the Zerahites. ²¹Descendants of Perez: of Hezron, the clan of the Hezronites; of Hamul, the clan of the Hamulites. ²²Those are the clans of Judah; persons enrolled: 76,500.

²³Descendants of Issachar by their clans: [Of] Tola, the clan of the Tolaites; of Puvah, the clan of the Punites; ²⁴of Jashub, the clan of the Jashubites; of Shimron, the clan of the Shimronites. ²⁵Those are the clans of Issachar; persons enrolled: 64,300.

²⁶Descendants of Zebulun by their clans: Of Sered, the clan of the Seredites; of Elon, the clan

---

d Or "Shaul."

¹⁰ וַתִּפְתַּ֨ח הָאָ֜רֶץ אֶת־פִּ֗יהָ וַתִּבְלַ֤ע אֹתָם֙ וְאֶת־קֹ֔רַח בְּמ֖וֹת הָעֵדָ֑ה בַּאֲכֹ֣ל הָאֵ֗שׁ אֵ֣ת חֲמִשִּׁ֤ים וּמָאתַ֙יִם֙ אִ֔ישׁ וַיִּהְי֖וּ לְנֵֽס׃

¹¹ וּבְנֵי־קֹ֖רַח לֹא־מֵֽתוּ׃ ס

¹² בְּנֵ֣י שִׁמְעוֹן֮ לְמִשְׁפְּחֹתָם֒ לִנְמוּאֵ֗ל מִשְׁפַּ֙חַת֙ הַנְּמ֣וּאֵלִ֔י לְיָמִ֕ין מִשְׁפַּ֖חַת הַיָּמִינִ֑י לְיָכִ֕ין מִשְׁפַּ֖חַת הַיָּכִינִֽי׃ ¹³ לְזֶ֕רַח מִשְׁפַּ֖חַת הַזַּרְחִ֑י לְשָׁא֕וּל מִשְׁפַּ֖חַת הַשָּׁאוּלִֽי׃ ¹⁴ אֵ֖לֶּה מִשְׁפְּחֹ֣ת הַשִּׁמְעֹנִ֑י שְׁנַ֧יִם וְעֶשְׂרִ֛ים אֶ֖לֶף וּמָאתָֽיִם׃ ס

¹⁵ בְּנֵ֣י גָד֮ לְמִשְׁפְּחֹתָם֒ לִצְפ֗וֹן מִשְׁפַּ֙חַת֙ הַצְּפוֹנִ֔י לְחַגִּ֕י מִשְׁפַּ֖חַת הַֽחַגִּ֑י לְשׁוּנִ֕י מִשְׁפַּ֖חַת הַשּׁוּנִֽי׃ ¹⁶ לְאָזְנִ֕י מִשְׁפַּ֖חַת הָאָזְנִ֑י לְעֵרִ֕י מִשְׁפַּ֖חַת הָעֵרִֽי׃ ¹⁷ לַאֲר֕וֹד מִשְׁפַּ֖חַת הָאֲרוֹדִ֑י לְאַ֣רְאֵלִ֔י מִשְׁפַּ֖חַת הָאַרְאֵלִֽי׃ ¹⁸ אֵ֛לֶּה מִשְׁפְּחֹ֥ת בְּנֵֽי־גָ֖ד לִפְקֻדֵיהֶ֑ם אַרְבָּעִ֥ים אֶ֖לֶף וַחֲמֵ֥שׁ מֵאֽוֹת׃ ס

¹⁹ בְּנֵ֥י יְהוּדָ֖ה עֵ֣ר וְאוֹנָ֑ן וַיָּ֥מׇת עֵ֛ר וְאוֹנָ֖ן בְּאֶ֥רֶץ כְּנָֽעַן׃

²⁰ וַיִּהְי֣וּ בְנֵי־יְהוּדָה֮ לְמִשְׁפְּחֹתָם֒ לְשֵׁלָ֗ה מִשְׁפַּ֙חַת֙ הַשֵּׁ֣לָנִ֔י לְפֶ֕רֶץ מִשְׁפַּ֖חַת הַפַּרְצִ֑י לְזֶ֕רַח מִשְׁפַּ֖חַת הַזַּרְחִֽי׃ ²¹ וַיִּהְי֣וּ בְנֵי־פֶ֗רֶץ לְחֶצְרֹן֙ מִשְׁפַּ֣חַת הַֽחֶצְרֹנִ֔י לְחָמ֕וּל מִשְׁפַּ֖חַת הֶחָמוּלִֽי׃ ²² אֵ֛לֶּה מִשְׁפְּחֹ֥ת יְהוּדָ֖ה לִפְקֻדֵיהֶ֑ם שִׁשָּׁ֧ה וְשִׁבְעִ֛ים אֶ֖לֶף וַחֲמֵ֥שׁ מֵאֽוֹת׃ ס

²³ בְּנֵ֤י יִשָּׂשכָר֙ לְמִשְׁפְּחֹתָ֔ם תּוֹלָ֕ע מִשְׁפַּ֖חַת הַתּוֹלָעִ֑י לְפֻוָ֕ה מִשְׁפַּ֖חַת הַפּוּנִֽי׃ ²⁴ לְיָשׁ֕וּב מִשְׁפַּ֖חַת הַיָּשֻׁבִ֑י לְשִׁמְרֹ֕ן מִשְׁפַּ֖חַת הַשִּׁמְרֹנִֽי׃ ²⁵ אֵ֛לֶּה מִשְׁפְּחֹ֥ת יִשָּׂשכָ֖ר לִפְקֻדֵיהֶ֑ם אַרְבָּעָ֧ה וְשִׁשִּׁ֛ים אֶ֖לֶף וּשְׁלֹ֥שׁ מֵאֽוֹת׃ ס

²⁶ בְּנֵ֣י זְבוּלֻן֮ לְמִשְׁפְּחֹתָם֒ לְסֶ֗רֶד מִשְׁפַּ֙חַת֙ הַסַּרְדִּ֔י לְאֵל֕וֹן מִשְׁפַּ֖חַת הָאֵלֹנִ֑י לְיַחְלְאֵ֕ל

345

of the Elonites; of Jahleel, the clan of the Jahleelites. 27Those are the clans of the Zebulunites; persons enrolled: 60,500.

28The sons of Joseph were Manasseh and Ephraim—by their clans.

29Descendants of Manasseh: Of Machir, the clan of the Machirites.—Machir begot Gilead.—Of Gilead, the clan of the Gileadites. 30These were the descendants of Gilead: [Of] Iezer, the clan of the Iezerites; of Helek, the clan of the Helekites; 31[of] Asriel, the clan of the Asrielites; [of] Shechem, the clan of the Shechemites; 32[of] Shemida, the clan of the Shemidaites; [of] Hepher, the clan of the Hepherites.—33Now Zelophehad son of Hepher had no sons, only daughters. The names of Zelophehad's daughters were Mahlah, Noah, Hoglah, Milcah, and Tirzah.—34Those are the clans of Manasseh; persons enrolled: 52,700.

35These are the descendants of Ephraim by their clans: Of Shuthelah, the clan of the Shuthelahites; of Becher, the clan of the Becherites; of Tahan, the clan of the Tahanites. 36These are the descendants of Shuthelah: Of Eran, the clan of the Eranites. 37Those are the clans of Ephraim's descendants; persons enrolled: 32,500.

Those are the descendants of Joseph by their clans.

38The descendants of Benjamin by their clans: Of Bela, the clan of the Belaites; of Ashbel, the clan of the Ashbelites; of Ahiram, the clan of the Ahiramites; 39of Shephupham, the clan of the Shuphamites; of Hupham, the clan of the Huphamites. 40The sons of Bela were Ard and Naaman: [Of Ard,] the clan of the Ardites; of Naaman, the clan of the Naamanites. 41Those are the descendants of Benjamin by their clans; persons enrolled: 45,600.

42These are the descendants of Dan by their clans: Of Shuham, the clan of the Shuhamites.

מִשְׁפַּ֖חַת הַיַּחְלְאֵלִ֑י: 27 אֵ֥לֶּה מִשְׁפְּחֹ֖ת הַזְּבֽוּלֹנִי֙ לִפְקֻ֣דֵיהֶ֔ם שִׁשִּׁ֥ים אֶ֖לֶף וַחֲמֵ֥שׁ מֵאֽוֹת: ס

28 בְּנֵ֥י יוֹסֵ֖ף לְמִשְׁפְּחֹתָ֑ם מְנַשֶּׁ֖ה וְאֶפְרָֽיִם: 29 בְּנֵ֣י מְנַשֶּׁ֗ה לְמָכִיר֙ מִשְׁפַּ֣חַת הַמָּכִירִ֔י וּמָכִ֖יר הוֹלִ֣יד אֶת־גִּלְעָ֑ד לְגִלְעָ֕ד מִשְׁפַּ֖חַת הַגִּלְעָדִֽי: 30 אֵ֚לֶּה בְּנֵ֣י גִלְעָ֔ד אִיעֶ֕זֶר מִשְׁפַּ֖חַת הָאִֽיעֶזְרִ֑י לְחֵ֕לֶק מִשְׁפַּ֖חַת הַֽחֶלְקִֽי: 31 וְאַ֨שְׂרִיאֵ֔ל מִשְׁפַּ֖חַת הָֽאַשְׂרִאֵלִ֑י וְשֶׁ֕כֶם מִשְׁפַּ֖חַת הַשִּׁכְמִֽי: 32 וּשְׁמִידָ֕ע מִשְׁפַּ֖חַת הַשְּׁמִֽידָעִ֑י וְחֵ֕פֶר מִשְׁפַּ֖חַת הַֽחֶפְרִֽי: 33 וּצְלָפְחָ֣ד בֶּן־חֵ֗פֶר לֹא־הָ֥יוּ ל֛וֹ בָּנִ֖ים כִּ֣י אִם־בָּנ֑וֹת וְשֵׁם֙ בְּנ֣וֹת צְלָפְחָ֔ד מַחְלָ֣ה וְנֹעָ֔ה חָגְלָ֥ה מִלְכָּ֖ה וְתִרְצָֽה: 34 אֵ֖לֶּה מִשְׁפְּחֹ֣ת מְנַשֶּׁ֑ה וּפְקֻ֣דֵיהֶ֔ם שְׁנַ֧יִם וַחֲמִשִּׁ֛ים אֶ֖לֶף וּשְׁבַ֥ע מֵאֽוֹת: ס

35 אֵ֣לֶּה בְנֵֽי־אֶפְרַ֘יִם֒ לְמִשְׁפְּחֹתָ֗ם לְשׁוּתֶ֙לַח֙ מִשְׁפַּ֣חַת הַשֻּׁתַלְחִ֔י לְבֶ֕כֶר מִשְׁפַּ֖חַת הַבַּכְרִ֑י לְתַ֕חַן מִשְׁפַּ֖חַת הַתַּחֲנִֽי: 36 וְאֵ֖לֶּה בְּנֵ֣י שׁוּתָ֑לַח לְעֵרָ֕ן מִשְׁפַּ֖חַת הָעֵרָנִֽי: 37 אֵ֣לֶּה מִשְׁפְּחֹ֤ת בְּנֵֽי־אֶפְרַ֙יִם֙ לִפְקֻ֣דֵיהֶ֔ם שְׁנַ֧יִם וּשְׁלֹשִׁ֛ים אֶ֖לֶף וַחֲמֵ֣שׁ מֵא֑וֹת אֵ֥לֶּה בְנֵֽי־יוֹסֵ֖ף לְמִשְׁפְּחֹתָֽם: ס

38 בְּנֵ֣י בִנְיָמִן֮ לְמִשְׁפְּחֹתָם֒ לְבֶ֗לַע מִשְׁפַּ֙חַת֙ הַבַּלְעִ֔י לְאַשְׁבֵּ֕ל מִשְׁפַּ֖חַת הָֽאַשְׁבֵּלִ֑י לַאֲחִירָ֕ם מִשְׁפַּ֖חַת הָאֲחִֽירָמִֽי: 39 לִשְׁפוּפָ֕ם מִשְׁפַּ֖חַת הַשּׁוּפָמִ֑י לְחוּפָ֕ם מִשְׁפַּ֖חַת הַחוּפָמִֽי: 40 וַיִּהְי֥וּ בְנֵי־בֶ֖לַע אַ֣רְדְּ וְנַעֲמָ֑ן מִשְׁפַּ֙חַת֙ הָֽאַרְדִּ֔י לְנַֽעֲמָ֕ן מִשְׁפַּ֖חַת הַֽנַּעֲמִֽי: 41 אֵ֥לֶּה בְנֵֽי־בִנְיָמִ֖ן לְמִשְׁפְּחֹתָ֑ם וּפְקֻ֣דֵיהֶ֔ם חֲמִשָּׁ֧ה וְאַרְבָּעִ֛ים אֶ֖לֶף וְשֵׁ֥שׁ מֵאֽוֹת: ס

42 אֵ֤לֶּה בְנֵי־דָן֙ לְמִשְׁפְּחֹתָ֔ם לְשׁוּחָ֕ם מִשְׁפַּ֖חַת הַשּׁוּחָמִ֑י אֵ֥לֶּה מִשְׁפְּחֹ֖ת דָּ֑ן

Those are the clans of Dan,^e by their clans. ^43All the clans of the Shuhamites; persons enrolled: 64,400.

^44Descendants of Asher by their clans: Of Imnah, the clan of the Imnites; of Ishvi, the clan of the Ishvites; of Beriah, the clan of the Beriites. ^45Of the descendants of Beriah: Of Heber, the clan of the Heberites; of Malchiel, the clan of the Malchielites.—^46The name of Asher's daughter was Serah.—^47These are the clans of Asher's descendants; persons enrolled: 53,400.

^48Descendants of Naphtali by their clans: Of Jahzeel, the clan of the Jahzeelites; of Guni, the clan of the Gunites; ^49of Jezer, the clan of the Jezerites; of Shillem, the clan of the Shillemites. ^50Those are the clans of the Naphtalites, clan by clan; persons enrolled: 45,400.

^51This is the enrollment of the Israelites: 601,730.

^52The LORD spoke to Moses, saying, ^53"Among these shall the land be apportioned as shares, according to the listed names: ^54with larger groups increase the share, with smaller groups reduce the share. Each is to be assigned its share according to its enrollment. ^55The land, moreover, is to be apportioned by lot; and the allotment shall be made according to the listings of their ancestral tribes. ^56Each portion shall be assigned by lot, whether for larger or smaller groups."

^57This is the enrollment of the Levites by their clans: Of Gershon, the clan of the Gershonites; of Kohath, the clan of the Kohathites; of Merari, the clan of the Merarites. ^58These are the clans of Levi: The clan of the Libnites, the clan of the Hebronites, the clan of the Mahlites, the clan of the Mushites, the clan of the Korahites.— Kohath begot Amram. ^59The name of Amram's wife was Jochebed daughter of Levi, who was born to Levi in Egypt; she bore to Amram Aaron and Moses and their sister Miriam. ^60To Aaron

43 כָּל־מִשְׁפְּחֹת הַשּׁוּחָמִי לִמִשְׁפְּחֹתָם: לִפְקֻדֵיהֶם אַרְבָּעָה וְשִׁשִּׁים אֶלֶף וְאַרְבַּע מֵאוֹת: ס

44 בְּנֵי אָשֵׁר לְמִשְׁפְּחֹתָם לְיִמְנָה מִשְׁפַּחַת הַיִּמְנָה לְיִשְׁוִי מִשְׁפַּחַת הַיִּשְׁוִי לִבְרִיעָה מִשְׁפַּחַת הַבְּרִיעִי: 45 לִבְנֵי בְרִיעָה לְחֶבֶר מִשְׁפַּחַת הַחֶבְרִי לְמַלְכִּיאֵל מִשְׁפַּחַת הַמַּלְכִּיאֵלִי: 46 וְשֵׁם בַּת־אָשֵׁר שָׂרַח: 47 אֵלֶּה מִשְׁפְּחֹת בְּנֵי־אָשֵׁר לִפְקֻדֵיהֶם שְׁלֹשָׁה וַחֲמִשִּׁים אֶלֶף וְאַרְבַּע מֵאוֹת: ס

48 בְּנֵי נַפְתָּלִי לְמִשְׁפְּחֹתָם לְיַחְצְאֵל מִשְׁפַּחַת הַיַּחְצְאֵלִי לְגוּנִי מִשְׁפַּחַת הַגּוּנִי: 49 לְיֵצֶר מִשְׁפַּחַת הַיִּצְרִי לְשִׁלֵּם מִשְׁפַּחַת הַשִּׁלֵּמִי: 50 אֵלֶּה מִשְׁפְּחֹת נַפְתָּלִי לְמִשְׁפְּחֹתָם וּפְקֻדֵיהֶם חֲמִשָּׁה וְאַרְבָּעִים אֶלֶף וְאַרְבַּע מֵאוֹת:

51 אֵלֶּה פְּקוּדֵי בְּנֵי יִשְׂרָאֵל שֵׁשׁ־מֵאוֹת אֶלֶף וָאֶלֶף שְׁבַע מֵאוֹת וּשְׁלֹשִׁים: פ

52 וַיְדַבֵּר יְהֹוָה אֶל־מֹשֶׁה לֵּאמֹר: 53 לָאֵלֶּה תֵּחָלֵק הָאָרֶץ בְּנַחֲלָה בְּמִסְפַּר שֵׁמוֹת: 54 לָרַב תַּרְבֶּה נַחֲלָתוֹ וְלַמְעַט תַּמְעִיט נַחֲלָתוֹ אִישׁ לְפִי פְקֻדָיו יֻתַּן נַחֲלָתוֹ: 55 אַךְ־בְּגוֹרָל יֵחָלֵק אֶת־הָאָרֶץ לִשְׁמוֹת מַטּוֹת־אֲבֹתָם יִנְחָלוּ: 56 עַל־פִּי הַגּוֹרָל תֵּחָלֵק נַחֲלָתוֹ בֵּין רַב לִמְעָט: ס

57 וְאֵלֶּה פְקוּדֵי הַלֵּוִי לְמִשְׁפְּחֹתָם לְגֵרְשׁוֹן מִשְׁפַּחַת הַגֵּרְשֻׁנִּי לִקְהָת מִשְׁפַּחַת הַקְּהָתִי לִמְרָרִי מִשְׁפַּחַת הַמְּרָרִי: 58 אֵלֶּה מִשְׁפְּחֹת לֵוִי מִשְׁפַּחַת הַלִּבְנִי מִשְׁפַּחַת הַחֶבְרֹנִי מִשְׁפַּחַת הַמַּחְלִי מִשְׁפַּחַת הַמּוּשִׁי מִשְׁפַּחַת הַקָּרְחִי וּקְהָת הוֹלִד אֶת־עַמְרָם: 59 וְשֵׁם אֵשֶׁת עַמְרָם יוֹכֶבֶד בַּת־לֵוִי אֲשֶׁר יָלְדָה אֹתָהּ לְלֵוִי בְּמִצְרָיִם וַתֵּלֶד לְעַמְרָם אֶת־אַהֲרֹן וְאֶת־מֹשֶׁה וְאֵת מִרְיָם אֲחֹתָם: 60 וַיִּוָּלֵד לְאַהֲרֹן אֶת־נָדָב

---

e *Meaning of parts of vv. 42 and 43 uncertain.*

were born Nadab and Abihu, Eleazar and Ithamar. [61]Nadab and Abihu died when they offered alien fire before the LORD.—[62]Their enrollment of 23,000 comprised all males from a month up. They were not part of the regular enrollment of the Israelites, since no share was assigned to them among the Israelites.

[63]These are the persons enrolled by Moses and Eleazar the priest who registered the Israelites on the steppes of Moab, at the Jordan near Jericho. [64]Among these there was not one of those enrolled by Moses and Aaron the priest when they recorded the Israelites in the wilderness of Sinai. [65]For the LORD had said of them, "They shall die in the wilderness." Not one of them survived, except Caleb son of Jephunneh and Joshua son of Nun.

27 The daughters of Zelophehad, of Manassite family—son of Hepher son of Gilead son of Machir son of Manasseh son of Joseph—came forward. The names of the daughters were Mahlah, Noah, Hoglah, Milcah, and Tirzah. [2]They stood before Moses, Eleazar the priest, the chieftains, and the whole assembly, at the entrance of the Tent of Meeting, and they said, [3]"Our father died in the wilderness. He was not one of the faction, Korah's faction, which banded together against the LORD, but died for his own sin; and he has left no sons. [4]Let not our father's name be lost to his clan just because he had no son! Give us a holding among our father's kinsmen!"

[5]Moses brought their case before the LORD.

[6]And the LORD said to Moses, [7]"The plea of Zelophehad's daughters is just: you should give them a hereditary holding among their father's kinsmen; transfer their father's share to them.

וְאֶת־אֲבִיהוּא אֶת־אֶלְעָזָר וְאֶת־אִיתָמָר: 61 וַיָּמָת נָדָב וַאֲבִיהוּא בְּהַקְרִיבָם אֵשׁ־זָרָה לִפְנֵי יְהוָה: 62 וַיִּהְיוּ פְקֻדֵיהֶם שְׁלֹשָׁה וְעֶשְׂרִים אֶלֶף כָּל־זָכָר מִבֶּן־חֹדֶשׁ וָמָעְלָה כִּי | לֹא הָתְפָּקְדוּ בְּתוֹךְ בְּנֵי יִשְׂרָאֵל כִּי לֹא־נִתַּן לָהֶם נַחֲלָה בְּתוֹךְ בְּנֵי יִשְׂרָאֵל:

63 אֵלֶּה פְּקוּדֵי מֹשֶׁה וְאֶלְעָזָר הַכֹּהֵן אֲשֶׁר פָּקְדוּ אֶת־בְּנֵי יִשְׂרָאֵל בְּעַרְבֹת מוֹאָב עַל יַרְדֵּן יְרֵחוֹ: 64 וּבְאֵלֶּה לֹא־הָיָה אִישׁ מִפְּקוּדֵי מֹשֶׁה וְאַהֲרֹן הַכֹּהֵן אֲשֶׁר פָּקְדוּ אֶת־בְּנֵי יִשְׂרָאֵל בְּמִדְבַּר סִינָי: 65 כִּי־אָמַר יְהוָה לָהֶם מוֹת יָמֻתוּ בַּמִּדְבָּר וְלֹא־נוֹתַר מֵהֶם אִישׁ כִּי אִם־כָּלֵב בֶּן־יְפֻנֶּה וִיהוֹשֻׁעַ בִּן־נוּן: ס

כז וַתִּקְרַבְנָה בְּנוֹת צְלָפְחָד בֶּן־חֵפֶר בֶּן־גִּלְעָד בֶּן־מָכִיר בֶּן־מְנַשֶּׁה לְמִשְׁפְּחֹת מְנַשֶּׁה בֶן־יוֹסֵף וְאֵלֶּה שְׁמוֹת בְּנֹתָיו מַחְלָה נֹעָה וְחָגְלָה וּמִלְכָּה וְתִרְצָה: 2 וַתַּעֲמֹדְנָה לִפְנֵי מֹשֶׁה וְלִפְנֵי אֶלְעָזָר הַכֹּהֵן וְלִפְנֵי הַנְּשִׂיאִם וְכָל־הָעֵדָה פֶּתַח אֹהֶל־מוֹעֵד לֵאמֹר: 3 אָבִינוּ מֵת בַּמִּדְבָּר וְהוּא לֹא־הָיָה בְּתוֹךְ הָעֵדָה הַנּוֹעָדִים עַל־יְהוָה בַּעֲדַת־קֹרַח כִּי־בְחֶטְאוֹ מֵת וּבָנִים לֹא־הָיוּ לוֹ: 4 לָמָּה יִגָּרַע שֵׁם־אָבִינוּ מִתּוֹךְ מִשְׁפַּחְתּוֹ כִּי אֵין לוֹ בֵּן תְּנָה־לָּנוּ אֲחֻזָּה בְּתוֹךְ אֲחֵי אָבִינוּ: 5 וַיַּקְרֵב מֹשֶׁה אֶת־מִשְׁפָּטָן* לִפְנֵי יְהוָה: ס

6 וַיֹּאמֶר יְהוָה אֶל־מֹשֶׁה לֵּאמֹר: 7 כֵּן בְּנוֹת צְלָפְחָד דֹּבְרֹת נָתֹן תִּתֵּן לָהֶם אֲחֻזַּת נַחֲלָה בְּתוֹךְ אֲחֵי אֲבִיהֶם וְהַעֲבַרְתָּ אֶת־נַחֲלַת אֲבִיהֶן לָהֶן:

v. 5. ן׳ רבתי

8"Further, speak to the Israelite people as follows: 'If a man dies without leaving a son, you shall transfer his property to his daughter. 9If he has no daughter, you shall assign his property to his brothers. 10If he has no brothers, you shall assign his property to his father's brothers. 11If his father had no brothers, you shall assign his property to his nearest relative in his own clan, and he shall inherit it.' This shall be the law of procedure for the Israelites, in accordance with the LORD's command to Moses."

12The LORD said to Moses, "Ascend these heights of Abarim and view the land that I have given to the Israelite people. 13When you have seen it, you too shall be gathered to your kin, just as your brother Aaron was. 14For, in the wilderness of Zin, when the community was contentious, you disobeyed My command to uphold My sanctity in their sight by means of the water." Those are the Waters of Meribath-kadesh,ᵃ in the wilderness of Zin.

15Moses spoke to the LORD, saying, 16"Let the LORD, Source of the breath of all flesh, appoint someone over the community 17b-who shall go out before them and come in before them, and who shall take them out and bring them in,-b so that the LORD's community may not be like sheep that have no shepherd." 18And the LORD answered Moses, "Single out Joshua son of Nun, an inspired man, and lay your hand upon him. 19Have him stand before Eleazar the priest and before the whole community, and commission him in their sight. 20Invest him with some of your authority, so that the whole Israelite community may obey. 21But he shall present himself to Eleazar the priest, who shall on his behalf seek the decision of the Urim before the LORD. By such instruction they shall go out and by such

---

ᵃ   See note at 20.13.
b-b   I.e., who shall lead them in all matters and whom they shall follow in all matters.

---

8 וְאֶל־בְּנֵי יִשְׂרָאֵל תְּדַבֵּר לֵאמֹר אִישׁ כִּי־יָמוּת וּבֵן אֵין לוֹ וְהַעֲבַרְתֶּם אֶת־נַחֲלָתוֹ לְבִתּוֹ: 9 וְאִם־אֵין לוֹ בַּת וּנְתַתֶּם אֶת־נַחֲלָתוֹ לְאֶחָיו: 10 וְאִם־אֵין לוֹ אַחִים וּנְתַתֶּם אֶת־נַחֲלָתוֹ לַאֲחֵי אָבִיו: 11 וְאִם־אֵין אַחִים לְאָבִיו וּנְתַתֶּם אֶת־נַחֲלָתוֹ לִשְׁאֵרוֹ הַקָּרֹב אֵלָיו מִמִּשְׁפַּחְתּוֹ וְיָרַשׁ אֹתָהּ וְהָיְתָה לִבְנֵי יִשְׂרָאֵל לְחֻקַּת מִשְׁפָּט כַּאֲשֶׁר צִוָּה יְהוָה אֶת־מֹשֶׁה: ס

12 וַיֹּאמֶר יְהוָה אֶל־מֹשֶׁה עֲלֵה אֶל־הַר הָעֲבָרִים הַזֶּה וּרְאֵה אֶת־הָאָרֶץ אֲשֶׁר נָתַתִּי לִבְנֵי יִשְׂרָאֵל: 13 וְרָאִיתָה אֹתָהּ וְנֶאֱסַפְתָּ אֶל־עַמֶּיךָ גַּם־אָתָּה כַּאֲשֶׁר נֶאֱסַף אַהֲרֹן אָחִיךָ: 14 כַּאֲשֶׁר מְרִיתֶם פִּי בְּמִדְבַּר־צִן בִּמְרִיבַת הָעֵדָה לְהַקְדִּישֵׁנִי בַמַּיִם לְעֵינֵיהֶם הֵם מֵי־מְרִיבַת קָדֵשׁ מִדְבַּר־צִן: פ

15 וַיְדַבֵּר מֹשֶׁה אֶל־יְהוָה לֵאמֹר: 16 יִפְקֹד יְהוָה אֱלֹהֵי הָרוּחֹת לְכָל־בָּשָׂר אִישׁ עַל־הָעֵדָה: 17 אֲשֶׁר־יֵצֵא לִפְנֵיהֶם וַאֲשֶׁר יָבֹא לִפְנֵיהֶם וַאֲשֶׁר יוֹצִיאֵם וַאֲשֶׁר יְבִיאֵם וְלֹא תִהְיֶה עֲדַת יְהוָה כַּצֹּאן אֲשֶׁר אֵין־לָהֶם רֹעֶה: 18 וַיֹּאמֶר יְהוָה אֶל־מֹשֶׁה קַח־לְךָ אֶת־יְהוֹשֻׁעַ בִּן־נוּן אִישׁ אֲשֶׁר־רוּחַ בּוֹ וְסָמַכְתָּ אֶת־יָדְךָ עָלָיו: 19 וְהַעֲמַדְתָּ אֹתוֹ לִפְנֵי אֶלְעָזָר הַכֹּהֵן וְלִפְנֵי כָּל־הָעֵדָה וְצִוִּיתָה אֹתוֹ לְעֵינֵיהֶם: 20 וְנָתַתָּה מֵהוֹדְךָ עָלָיו לְמַעַן יִשְׁמְעוּ כָּל־עֲדַת בְּנֵי יִשְׂרָאֵל: 21 וְלִפְנֵי אֶלְעָזָר הַכֹּהֵן יַעֲמֹד וְשָׁאַל לוֹ בְּמִשְׁפַּט הָאוּרִים לִפְנֵי יְהוָה עַל־פִּיו יֵצְאוּ

instruction they shall come in, he and all the Israelites, the whole community."

22Moses did as the LORD commanded him. He took Joshua and had him stand before Eleazar the priest and before the whole community. 23He laid his hands upon him and commissioned him—as the LORD had spoken through Moses.

28

The LORD spoke to Moses, saying: 2Command the Israelite people and say to them: Be punctilious in presenting to Me at stated times a-the offerings of food due Me,-a as offerings by fire of pleasing odor to Me.

3Say to them: These are the offerings by fire that you are to present to the LORD:

As a regular burnt offering every day, two yearling lambs without blemish. 4You shall offer one lamb in the morning, and the other lamb you shall offer at twilight. 5And as a meal offering, there shall be a tenth of an *ephah* of choice flour with a quarter of a *hin* of beaten oil mixed in—6the regular burnt offering instituted at Mount Sinaib—an offering by fire of pleasing odor to the LORD.

7The libation with it shall be a quarter of a *hin* for each lamb, to be poured in the sacred precinct as an offering of fermented drinkc to the LORD. 8The other lamb you shall offer at twilight, preparing the same meal offering and libation as in the morning—an offering by fire of pleasing odor to the LORD.

9On the sabbath day: two yearling lambs without blemish, together with two-tenths of a measured of choice flour with oil mixed in as a meal offering, and with the proper libation—10a burnt offering for every sabbath, in addition to the regular burnt offering and its libation.

וְעַל־פִּיו יָבֹאוּ הֻוּא וְכָל־בְּנֵי־יִשְׂרָאֵל אִתּוֹ וְכָל־הָעֵדָה: 22וַיַּעַשׂ מֹשֶׁה כַּאֲשֶׁר צִוָּה יְהֹוָה אֹתוֹ וַיִּקַּח אֶת־יְהוֹשֻׁעַ וַיַּעֲמִדֵהוּ לִפְנֵי אֶלְעָזָר הַכֹּהֵן וְלִפְנֵי כָּל־הָעֵדָה: 23וַיִּסְמֹךְ אֶת־יָדָיו עָלָיו וַיְצַוֵּהוּ כַּאֲשֶׁר דִּבֶּר יְהֹוָה בְּיַד־מֹשֶׁה: פ

כח

וַיְדַבֵּר יְהֹוָה אֶל־מֹשֶׁה לֵּאמֹר: 2צַו אֶת־בְּנֵי יִשְׂרָאֵל וְאָמַרְתָּ אֲלֵהֶם אֶת־קָרְבָּנִי לַחְמִי לְאִשַּׁי רֵיחַ נִיחֹחִי תִּשְׁמְרוּ לְהַקְרִיב לִי בְּמוֹעֲדוֹ: 3וְאָמַרְתָּ לָהֶם זֶה הָאִשֶּׁה אֲשֶׁר תַּקְרִיבוּ לַיהֹוָה כְּבָשִׂים בְּנֵי־שָׁנָה תְמִימִם שְׁנַיִם לַיּוֹם עֹלָה תָמִיד: 4אֶת־הַכֶּבֶשׂ אֶחָד תַּעֲשֶׂה בַבֹּקֶר וְאֵת הַכֶּבֶשׂ הַשֵּׁנִי תַּעֲשֶׂה בֵּין הָעַרְבָּיִם: 5וַעֲשִׂירִית הָאֵיפָה סֹלֶת לְמִנְחָה בְּלוּלָה בְּשֶׁמֶן כָּתִית רְבִיעִת הַהִין: 6עֹלַת תָּמִיד הָעֲשֻׂיָה בְּהַר סִינַי לְרֵיחַ נִיחֹחַ אִשֶּׁה לַיהֹוָה: 7וְנִסְכּוֹ רְבִיעִת הַהִין לַכֶּבֶשׂ הָאֶחָד בַּקֹּדֶשׁ הַסֵּךְ נֶסֶךְ שֵׁכָר לַיהֹוָה: 8וְאֵת הַכֶּבֶשׂ הַשֵּׁנִי תַּעֲשֶׂה בֵּין הָעַרְבָּיִם כְּמִנְחַת הַבֹּקֶר וּכְנִסְכּוֹ תַּעֲשֶׂה אִשֵּׁה רֵיחַ נִיחֹחַ לַיהֹוָה: פ 9וּבְיוֹם הַשַּׁבָּת שְׁנֵי־כְבָשִׂים בְּנֵי־שָׁנָה תְּמִימִם וּשְׁנֵי עֶשְׂרֹנִים סֹלֶת מִנְחָה בְּלוּלָה בַשֶּׁמֶן וְנִסְכּוֹ: 10עֹלַת שַׁבַּת בְּשַׁבַּתּוֹ עַל־עֹלַת הַתָּמִיד וְנִסְכָּהּ: ס

---

a-a   Lit. "My offering, My food."
b   Exod. 29.38–41.
c   I.e., wine.
d   I.e., of an ephah.

11On your new moons you shall present a burnt offering to the Lord: two bulls of the herd, one ram, and seven yearling lambs, without blemish. 12As meal offering for each bull: three-tenths of a measure of choice flour with oil mixed in. As meal offering for each ram: two-tenths of a measure of choice flour with oil mixed in. 13As meal offering for each lamb: a tenth of a measure of fine flour with oil mixed in. Such shall be the burnt offering of pleasing odor, an offering by fire to the Lord. 14Their libations shall be: half a *hin* of wine for a bull, a third of a *hin* for a ram, and a quarter of a *hin* for a lamb. That shall be the monthly burnt offering for each new moon of the year. 15And there shall be one goat as a sin offering to the Lord, to be offered in addition to the regular burnt offering and its libation.

16In the first month, on the fourteenth day of the month, there shall be a passover sacrifice to the Lord, 17and on the fifteenth day of that month a festival. Unleavened bread shall be eaten for seven days. 18The first day shall be a sacred occasion: you shall not work at your occupations. 19You shall present an offering by fire, a burnt offering, to the Lord: two bulls of the herd, one ram, and seven yearling lambs—*e*-see that they are-*e* without blemish. 20The meal offering with them shall be of choice flour with oil mixed in: prepare three-tenths of a measure for a bull, two-tenths for a ram; 21and for each of the seven lambs prepare one-tenth of a measure. 22And there shall be one goat for a sin offering, to make expiation in your behalf. 23You shall present these in addition to the morning portion of the regular burnt offering. 24You shall offer the like daily for seven days as food, an offering by fire of pleasing odor to the Lord; they shall be offered, with their libations, in addition to the regular burnt offering. 25And

e-e Lit. "they shall be to you."

11 וּבְרָאשֵׁי֙ חָדְשֵׁיכֶ֔ם תַּקְרִ֥יבוּ עֹלָ֖ה לַֽיהוָ֑ה פָּרִ֨ים בְּנֵֽי־בָקָ֤ר שְׁנַ֙יִם֙ וְאַ֣יִל אֶחָ֔ד כְּבָשִׂ֧ים בְּנֵֽי־שָׁנָ֛ה שִׁבְעָ֖ה תְּמִימִֽם׃ 12 וּשְׁלֹשָׁ֣ה עֶשְׂרֹנִ֗ים סֹ֤לֶת מִנְחָה֙ בְּלוּלָ֣ה בַשֶּׁ֔מֶן לַפָּ֖ר הָֽאֶחָ֑ד וּשְׁנֵ֣י עֶשְׂרֹנִ֗ים סֹ֤לֶת מִנְחָה֙ בְּלוּלָ֣ה בַשֶּׁ֔מֶן לָאַ֖יִל הָֽאֶחָֽד׃ 13 וְעִשָּׂרֹ֣ן עִשָּׂר֗וֹן סֹ֤לֶת מִנְחָה֙ בְּלוּלָ֣ה בַשֶּׁ֔מֶן לַכֶּ֖בֶשׂ הָֽאֶחָ֑ד עֹלָה֙ רֵ֣יחַ נִיחֹ֔חַ אִשֶּׁ֖ה לַֽיהוָֽה׃ 14 וְנִסְכֵּיהֶ֗ם חֲצִ֣י הַהִ֣ין יִהְיֶ֣ה לַפָּ֡ר וּשְׁלִישִׁ֣ת הַהִין֩ לָאַ֨יִל וּרְבִיעִ֧ת הַהִ֛ין לַכֶּ֖בֶשׂ יָ֑יִן זֹ֣את עֹלַ֥ת חֹ֙דֶשׁ֙ בְּחָדְשׁ֔וֹ לְחָדְשֵׁ֖י הַשָּׁנָֽה׃ 15 וּשְׂעִ֨יר עִזִּ֥ים אֶחָ֛ד לְחַטָּ֖את לַֽיהוָ֑ה עַל־עֹלַ֧ת הַתָּמִ֛יד יֵֽעָשֶׂ֖ה וְנִסְכּֽוֹ׃ ס

16 וּבַחֹ֣דֶשׁ הָֽרִאשׁ֗וֹן בְּאַרְבָּעָ֥ה עָשָׂ֛ר י֖וֹם לַחֹ֑דֶשׁ פֶּ֖סַח לַֽיהוָֽה׃ 17 וּבַחֲמִשָּׁ֨ה עָשָׂ֥ר י֛וֹם לַחֹ֥דֶשׁ הַזֶּ֖ה חָ֑ג שִׁבְעַ֣ת יָמִ֔ים מַצּ֖וֹת יֵֽאָכֵֽל׃ 18 בַּיּ֥וֹם הָרִאשׁ֖וֹן מִקְרָא־קֹ֑דֶשׁ כָּל־מְלֶ֥אכֶת עֲבֹדָ֖ה לֹ֥א תַֽעֲשֽׂוּ׃ 19 וְהִקְרַבְתֶּ֨ם אִשֶּׁ֤ה עֹלָה֙ לַֽיהוָ֔ה פָּרִ֧ים בְּנֵֽי־בָקָ֛ר שְׁנַ֖יִם וְאַ֣יִל אֶחָ֑ד וְשִׁבְעָ֤ה כְבָשִׂים֙ בְּנֵ֣י שָׁנָ֔ה תְּמִימִ֖ם יִהְי֥וּ לָכֶֽם׃ 20 וּמִ֨נְחָתָ֔ם סֹ֖לֶת בְּלוּלָ֣ה בַשָּׁ֑מֶן שְׁלֹשָׁ֨ה עֶשְׂרֹנִ֜ים לַפָּ֗ר וּשְׁנֵ֤י עֶשְׂרֹנִים֙ לָאַ֣יִל תַּֽעֲשֽׂוּ׃ 21 עִשָּׂר֤וֹן עִשָּׂרוֹן֙ תַּֽעֲשֶׂ֔ה לַכֶּ֖בֶשׂ הָֽאֶחָ֑ד לְשִׁבְעַ֖ת הַכְּבָשִֽׂים׃ 22 וּשְׂעִ֥יר חַטָּ֖את אֶחָ֑ד לְכַפֵּ֖ר עֲלֵיכֶֽם׃ 23 מִלְּבַ֗ד עֹלַ֤ת הַבֹּ֙קֶר֙ אֲשֶׁ֣ר לְעֹלַ֣ת הַתָּמִ֔יד תַּֽעֲשׂ֖וּ אֶת־אֵֽלֶּה׃ 24 כָּאֵ֜לֶּה תַּֽעֲשׂ֤וּ לַיּוֹם֙ שִׁבְעַ֣ת יָמִ֔ים לֶ֛חֶם אִשֵּׁ֥ה רֵֽיחַ־נִיחֹ֖חַ לַֽיהוָ֑ה עַל־עוֹלַ֧ת הַתָּמִ֛יד יֵֽעָשֶׂ֖ה וְנִסְכּֽוֹ׃

the seventh day shall be a sacred occasion for you: you shall not work at your occupations.

²⁶On the day of the first fruits, your Feast of Weeks, when you bring an offering of new grain to the LORD, you shall observe a sacred occasion: you shall not work at your occupations. ²⁷You shall present a burnt offering of pleasing odor to the LORD: two bulls of the herd, one ram, seven yearling lambs. ²⁸The meal offering with them shall be of choice flour with oil mixed in, three-tenths of a measure for a bull, two-tenths for a ram, ²⁹and one-tenth for each of the seven lambs. ³⁰And there shall be one goat for expiation in your behalf. ³¹You shall present them—e-see that they are-e without blemish—with their libations, in addition to the regular burnt offering and its meal offering.

29 In the seventh month, on the first day of the month, you shall observe a sacred occasion: you shall not work at your occupations. You shall observe it as ᵃ-a day when the horn is sounded.-ᵃ ²You shall present a burnt offering of pleasing odor to the LORD: one bull of the herd, one ram, and seven yearling lambs, without blemish. ³The meal offering with them—choice flour with oil mixed in—shall be: three-tenths of a measure for a bull, two-tenths for a ram, ⁴and one-tenth for each of the seven lambs. ⁵And there shall be one goat for a sin offering, to make expiation in your behalf—⁶in addition to the burnt offering of the new moon with its meal offering and the regular burnt offering with its meal offering, each with its libation as prescribed, offerings by fire of pleasing odor to the LORD.

⁷On the tenth day of the same seventh month you shall observe a sacred occasion when you shall practice self-denial. You shall do no work.

---

a-a Or "a day of festivity."

²⁵ וּבַיּוֹם֙ הַשְּׁבִיעִ֔י מִקְרָא־קֹ֖דֶשׁ יִהְיֶ֣ה לָכֶ֑ם כָּל־מְלֶ֥אכֶת עֲבֹדָ֖ה לֹ֥א תַעֲשֽׂוּ׃ ס ²⁶ וּבְי֣וֹם הַבִּכּוּרִ֗ים בְּהַקְרִֽיבְכֶ֞ם מִנְחָ֤ה חֲדָשָׁה֙ לַֽיהֹוָ֔ה בְּשָׁבֻעֹֽתֵיכֶ֑ם מִֽקְרָא־קֹ֙דֶשׁ֙ יִהְיֶ֣ה לָכֶ֔ם כָּל־מְלֶ֥אכֶת עֲבֹדָ֖ה לֹ֥א תַעֲשֽׂוּ׃ ²⁷ וְהִקְרַבְתֶּ֨ם עוֹלָ֜ה לְרֵ֤יחַ נִיחֹ֙חַ֙ לַֽיהֹוָ֔ה פָּרִ֧ים בְּנֵֽי־בָקָ֛ר שְׁנַ֖יִם אַ֣יִל אֶחָ֑ד שִׁבְעָ֥ה כְבָשִׂ֖ים בְּנֵ֥י שָׁנָֽה׃ ²⁸ וּמִנְחָתָ֔ם סֹ֖לֶת בְּלוּלָ֣ה בַשָּׁ֑מֶן שְׁלֹשָׁ֤ה עֶשְׂרֹנִים֙ לַפָּ֣ר הָֽאֶחָ֔ד שְׁנֵ֣י עֶשְׂרֹנִ֔ים לָאַ֖יִל הָֽאֶחָֽד׃ ²⁹ עִשָּׂרוֹן֙ עִשָּׂר֔וֹן לַכֶּ֖בֶשׂ הָֽאֶחָ֑ד לְשִׁבְעַ֖ת הַכְּבָשִֽׂים׃ ³⁰ שְׂעִ֥יר עִזִּ֖ים אֶחָ֑ד לְכַפֵּ֖ר עֲלֵיכֶֽם׃ ³¹ מִלְּבַ֞ד עֹלַ֤ת הַתָּמִיד֙ וּמִנְחָת֔וֹ תַּעֲשׂ֑וּ תְּמִימִ֥ם יִהְיוּ־לָכֶ֖ם וְנִסְכֵּיהֶֽם׃ פ

כט וּבַחֹ֙דֶשׁ֙ הַשְּׁבִיעִ֔י בְּאֶחָ֖ד לַחֹ֑דֶשׁ מִֽקְרָא־קֹ֙דֶשׁ֙ יִהְיֶ֣ה לָכֶ֔ם כָּל־מְלֶ֥אכֶת עֲבֹדָ֖ה לֹ֣א תַעֲשׂ֑וּ י֥וֹם תְּרוּעָ֖ה יִהְיֶ֥ה לָכֶֽם׃ ² וַעֲשִׂיתֶ֨ם עֹלָ֜ה לְרֵ֤יחַ נִיחֹ֙חַ֙ לַֽיהֹוָ֔ה פַּ֧ר בֶּן־בָּקָ֛ר אֶחָ֖ד אַ֣יִל אֶחָ֑ד כְּבָשִׂ֧ים בְּנֵֽי־שָׁנָ֛ה שִׁבְעָ֖ה תְּמִימִֽם׃ ³ וּמִנְחָתָ֔ם סֹ֖לֶת בְּלוּלָ֣ה בַשָּׁ֑מֶן שְׁלֹשָׁ֤ה עֶשְׂרֹנִים֙ לַפָּ֔ר שְׁנֵ֥י עֶשְׂרֹנִ֖ים לָאָֽיִל׃ ⁴ וְעִשָּׂר֣וֹן אֶחָ֔ד לַכֶּ֖בֶשׂ הָֽאֶחָ֑ד לְשִׁבְעַ֖ת הַכְּבָשִֽׂים׃ ⁵ וּשְׂעִיר־עִזִּ֥ים אֶחָ֖ד חַטָּ֑את לְכַפֵּ֖ר עֲלֵיכֶֽם׃ ⁶ מִלְּבַד֩ עֹלַ֨ת הַחֹ֜דֶשׁ וּמִנְחָתָ֗הּ וְעֹלַ֤ת הַתָּמִיד֙ וּמִנְחָתָ֔הּ וְנִסְכֵּיהֶ֖ם כְּמִשְׁפָּטָ֑ם לְרֵ֣יחַ נִיחֹ֔חַ אִשֶּׁ֖ה לַֽיהֹוָֽה׃ ס ⁷ וּבֶעָשׂוֹר֩ לַחֹ֨דֶשׁ הַשְּׁבִיעִ֜י הַזֶּ֗ה מִֽקְרָא־קֹ֙דֶשׁ֙ יִהְיֶ֣ה לָכֶ֔ם וְעִנִּיתֶ֖ם אֶת־נַפְשֹׁתֵיכֶ֑ם כָּל־מְלָאכָ֖ה לֹ֥א תַעֲשֽׂוּ׃ ⁸ וְהִקְרַבְתֶּ֨ם עֹלָ֤ה

352

8You shall present to the LORD a burnt offering of pleasing odor: one bull of the herd, one ram, seven yearling lambs; see that they are[b] without blemish. 9The meal offering with them—of choice flour with oil mixed in—shall be: three-tenths of a measure for a bull, two-tenths for the one ram, 10one-tenth for each of the seven lambs. 11And there shall be one goat for a sin offering, in addition to the sin offering of expiation and the regular burnt offering with its meal offering, each with its libation.

12On the fifteenth day of the seventh month, you shall observe a sacred occasion: you shall not work at your occupations.—Seven days you shall observe a festival of the LORD.—13You shall present a burnt offering, an offering by fire of pleasing odor to the LORD: Thirteen bulls of the herd, two rams, fourteen yearling lambs; they shall be without blemish. 14The meal offerings with them—of choice flour with oil mixed in—shall be: three-tenths of a measure for each of the thirteen bulls, two-tenths for each of the two rams, 15and one-tenth for each of the fourteen lambs. 16And there shall be one goat for a sin offering—in addition to the regular burnt offering, its meal offering and libation.

17Second day: Twelve bulls of the herd, two rams, fourteen yearling lambs, without blemish; 18the meal offerings and libations for the bulls, rams, and lambs, in the quantities prescribed; 19and one goat for a sin offering—in addition to the regular burnt offering, its meal offering and libations.

20Third day: Eleven bulls, two rams, fourteen yearling lambs, without blemish; 21the meal offerings and libations for the bulls, rams, and lambs, in the quantities prescribed; 22and one goat for a sin offering—in addition to the regular burnt offering, its meal offering and libation.

לַיהֹוָה רֵיחַ נִיחֹחַ פַּר בֶּן־בָּקָר אֶחָד אַיִל
אֶחָד כְּבָשִׂים בְּנֵי־שָׁנָה שִׁבְעָה תְּמִימִם
יִהְיוּ לָכֶם: 9 וּמִנְחָתָם סֹלֶת בְּלוּלָה בַשֶּׁמֶן
שְׁלֹשָׁה עֶשְׂרֹנִים לַפָּר שְׁנֵי עֶשְׂרֹנִים לָאַיִל
הָאֶחָד: 10 עִשָּׂרוֹן עִשָּׂרוֹן לַכֶּבֶשׂ הָאֶחָד
לְשִׁבְעַת הַכְּבָשִׂים: 11 שְׂעִיר־עִזִּים אֶחָד
חַטָּאת מִלְּבַד חַטַּאת הַכִּפֻּרִים וְעֹלַת
הַתָּמִיד וּמִנְחָתָהּ וְנִסְכֵּיהֶם: פ

12 וּבַחֲמִשָּׁה עָשָׂר יוֹם לַחֹדֶשׁ הַשְּׁבִיעִי
מִקְרָא־קֹדֶשׁ יִהְיֶה לָכֶם כָּל־מְלֶאכֶת
עֲבֹדָה לֹא תַעֲשׂוּ וְחַגֹּתֶם חַג לַיהֹוָה
שִׁבְעַת יָמִים: 13 וְהִקְרַבְתֶּם עֹלָה אִשֵּׁה
רֵיחַ נִיחֹחַ לַיהֹוָה פָּרִים בְּנֵי־בָקָר שְׁלֹשָׁה
עָשָׂר אֵילִם שְׁנָיִם כְּבָשִׂים בְּנֵי־שָׁנָה
אַרְבָּעָה עָשָׂר תְּמִימִם יִהְיוּ: 14 וּמִנְחָתָם
סֹלֶת בְּלוּלָה בַשֶּׁמֶן שְׁלֹשָׁה עֶשְׂרֹנִים לַפָּר
הָאֶחָד לִשְׁלֹשָׁה עָשָׂר פָּרִים שְׁנֵי עֶשְׂרֹנִים
לָאַיִל הָאֶחָד לִשְׁנֵי הָאֵילִם: 15 וְעִשָּׂרוֹן*
עִשָּׂרוֹן לַכֶּבֶשׂ הָאֶחָד לְאַרְבָּעָה עָשָׂר
כְּבָשִׂים: 16 וּשְׂעִיר־עִזִּים אֶחָד חַטָּאת
מִלְּבַד עֹלַת הַתָּמִיד מִנְחָתָהּ וְנִסְכָּהּ: ס

17 וּבַיּוֹם הַשֵּׁנִי פָּרִים בְּנֵי־בָקָר שְׁנֵים עָשָׂר
אֵילִם שְׁנָיִם כְּבָשִׂים בְּנֵי־שָׁנָה אַרְבָּעָה
עָשָׂר תְּמִימִם: 18 וּמִנְחָתָם וְנִסְכֵּיהֶם
לַפָּרִים לָאֵילִם וְלַכְּבָשִׂים בְּמִסְפָּרָם
כַּמִּשְׁפָּט: 19 וּשְׂעִיר־עִזִּים אֶחָד חַטָּאת
מִלְּבַד עֹלַת הַתָּמִיד וּמִנְחָתָהּ
וְנִסְכֵּיהֶם: ס

20 וּבַיּוֹם הַשְּׁלִישִׁי פָּרִים עַשְׁתֵּי־עָשָׂר
אֵילִם שְׁנָיִם כְּבָשִׂים בְּנֵי־שָׁנָה אַרְבָּעָה
עָשָׂר תְּמִימִם: 21 וּמִנְחָתָם וְנִסְכֵּיהֶם
לַפָּרִים לָאֵילִם וְלַכְּבָשִׂים בְּמִסְפָּרָם
כַּמִּשְׁפָּט: 22 וּשְׂעִיר חַטָּאת אֶחָד מִלְּבַד
עֹלַת הַתָּמִיד וּמִנְחָתָהּ וְנִסְכָּהּ: ס

v. 15. נקוד על ו' בתראה

b   See note at 28.19.

23Fourth day: Ten bulls, two rams, fourteen yearling lambs, without blemish; 24the meal offerings and libations for the bulls, rams, and lambs, in the quantities prescribed; 25and one goat for a sin offering—in addition to the regular burnt offering, its meal offering and libation.

26Fifth day: Nine bulls, two rams, fourteen yearling lambs, without blemish; 27the meal offerings and libations for the bulls, rams, and lambs, in the quantities prescribed; 28and one goat for a sin offering—in addition to the regular burnt offering, its meal offering and libation.

29Sixth day: Eight bulls, two rams, fourteen yearling lambs, without blemish; 30the meal offerings and libations for the bulls, rams, and lambs, in the quantities prescribed; 31and one goat for a sin offering—in addition to the regular burnt offering, its meal offering and libations.

32Seventh day: Seven bulls, two rams, fourteen yearling lambs, without blemish; 33the meal offerings and libations for the bulls, rams, and lambs, in the quantities prescribed; 34and one goat for a sin offering—in addition to the regular burnt offering, its meal offering and libation.

35On the eighth day you shall hold a solemn gathering;c you shall not work at your occupations. 36You shall present a burnt offering, an offering by fire of pleasing odor to the LORD; one bull, one ram, seven yearling lambs, without blemish; 37the meal offerings and libations for the bull, the ram, and the lambs, in the quantities prescribed; 38and one goat for a sin offering—in addition to the regular burnt offering, its meal offering and libation.

39All these you shall offer to the LORD at the stated times, in addition to your votive and free-

---

c See note at Lev. 23.36.

23 וּבַיּוֹם הָרְבִיעִי פָּרִים עֲשָׂרָה אֵילִם שְׁנָיִם כְּבָשִׂים בְּנֵי־שָׁנָה אַרְבָּעָה עָשָׂר תְּמִימִם: 24 מִנְחָתָם וְנִסְכֵּיהֶם לַפָּרִים לָאֵילִם וְלַכְּבָשִׂים בְּמִסְפָּרָם כַּמִּשְׁפָּט: 25 וּשְׂעִיר־עִזִּים אֶחָד חַטָּאת מִלְּבַד עֹלַת הַתָּמִיד מִנְחָתָהּ וְנִסְכָּהּ: ס

26 וּבַיּוֹם הַחֲמִישִׁי פָּרִים תִּשְׁעָה אֵילִם שְׁנָיִם כְּבָשִׂים בְּנֵי־שָׁנָה אַרְבָּעָה עָשָׂר תְּמִימִם: 27 וּמִנְחָתָם וְנִסְכֵּיהֶם לַפָּרִים לָאֵילִם וְלַכְּבָשִׂים בְּמִסְפָּרָם כַּמִּשְׁפָּט: 28 וּשְׂעִיר חַטָּאת אֶחָד מִלְּבַד עֹלַת הַתָּמִיד וּמִנְחָתָהּ וְנִסְכָּהּ: ס

29 וּבַיּוֹם הַשִּׁשִּׁי פָּרִים שְׁמֹנָה אֵילִם שְׁנָיִם כְּבָשִׂים בְּנֵי־שָׁנָה אַרְבָּעָה עָשָׂר תְּמִימִם: 30 וּמִנְחָתָם וְנִסְכֵּיהֶם לַפָּרִים לָאֵילִם וְלַכְּבָשִׂים בְּמִסְפָּרָם כַּמִּשְׁפָּט: 31 וּשְׂעִיר חַטָּאת אֶחָד מִלְּבַד עֹלַת הַתָּמִיד מִנְחָתָהּ וּנְסָכֶיהָ: פ

32 וּבַיּוֹם הַשְּׁבִיעִי פָּרִים שִׁבְעָה אֵילִם שְׁנָיִם כְּבָשִׂים בְּנֵי־שָׁנָה אַרְבָּעָה עָשָׂר תְּמִימִם: 33 וּמִנְחָתָם וְנִסְכֵּהֶם* לַפָּרִים לָאֵילִם וְלַכְּבָשִׂים בְּמִסְפָּרָם כְּמִשְׁפָּטָם: 34 וּשְׂעִיר חַטָּאת אֶחָד מִלְּבַד עֹלַת הַתָּמִיד מִנְחָתָהּ וְנִסְכָּהּ: פ

35 בַּיּוֹם הַשְּׁמִינִי עֲצֶרֶת תִּהְיֶה לָכֶם כָּל־מְלֶאכֶת עֲבֹדָה לֹא תַעֲשׂוּ: 36 וְהִקְרַבְתֶּם עֹלָה אִשֵּׁה רֵיחַ נִיחֹחַ לַיהוָה פַּר אֶחָד אַיִל אֶחָד כְּבָשִׂים בְּנֵי־שָׁנָה שִׁבְעָה תְּמִימִם: 37 מִנְחָתָם וְנִסְכֵּיהֶם לַפָּר לָאַיִל וְלַכְּבָשִׂים בְּמִסְפָּרָם כַּמִּשְׁפָּט: 38 וּשְׂעִיר חַטָּאת אֶחָד מִלְּבַד עֹלַת הַתָּמִיד וּמִנְחָתָהּ וְנִסְכָּהּ:

39 אֵלֶּה תַּעֲשׂוּ לַיהוָה בְּמוֹעֲדֵיכֶם לְבַד מִנִּדְרֵיכֶם וְנִדְבֹתֵיכֶם לְעֹלֹתֵיכֶם

v. 33. חסר י'

will offerings, be they burnt offerings, meal offerings, libations, or offerings of well-being. [1]So Moses spoke to the Israelites just as the Lord had commanded Moses.

MATTOT

[2]Moses spoke to the heads of the Israelite tribes, saying: This is what the Lord has commanded:

[3]If a man makes a vow to the Lord or takes an oath imposing an obligation[a] on himself, he shall not break his pledge; he must carry out all that has [b-]crossed his lips.[-b]

[4]If a woman makes a vow to the Lord or assumes an obligation while still in her father's household by reason of her youth, [5]and her father learns of her vow or her self-imposed obligation and offers no objection, all her vows shall stand and every self-imposed obligation shall stand. [6]But if her father restrains her on the day he finds out, none of her vows or self-imposed obligations shall stand; and the Lord will forgive her, since her father restrained her.

[7]If she should marry while her vow or the commitment[c] to which she bound herself is still in force, [8]and her husband learns of it and offers no objection on the day he finds out, her vows shall stand and her self-imposed obligations shall stand. [9]But if her husband restrains her on the day that he learns of it, he thereby annuls her vow which was in force or the commitment[c] to which she bound herself; and the Lord will forgive her.—[10]The vow of a widow or of a divorced woman, however, whatever she has imposed on herself, shall be binding upon her.—[11]So, too, if, while in her husband's household, she makes a vow or imposes an obligation on herself by oath, [12]and her husband learns of it,

---

a   Or "a prohibition."
b-b   Lit. "come out of his mouth."
c   Lit. "utterance of her lips."

וְלִמְנְחֹתֵיכֶ֖ם וּלְנִסְכֵּיכֶ֑ם וּלְשַׁלְמֵיכֶֽם׃
1 וַיֹּ֤אמֶר מֹשֶׁה֙ אֶל־בְּנֵ֣י יִשְׂרָאֵ֔ל כְּכֹ֛ל
אֲשֶׁר־צִוָּ֥ה יְהוָ֖ה אֶת־מֹשֶֽׁה׃ פ

מטות

2 וַיְדַבֵּ֤ר מֹשֶׁה֙ אֶל־רָאשֵׁ֣י הַמַּטּ֔וֹת לִבְנֵ֥י
יִשְׂרָאֵ֖ל לֵאמֹ֑ר זֶ֣ה הַדָּבָ֔ר אֲשֶׁ֖ר צִוָּ֥ה יְהוָֽה׃
3 אִישׁ֩ כִּֽי־יִדֹּ֨ר נֶ֜דֶר לַֽיהוָ֗ה אֽוֹ־הִשָּׁ֤בַע
שְׁבֻעָה֙ לֶאְסֹ֤ר אִסָּר֙ עַל־נַפְשׁ֔וֹ לֹ֥א יַחֵ֖ל
דְּבָר֑וֹ כְּכָל־הַיֹּצֵ֥א מִפִּ֖יו יַעֲשֶֽׂה׃
4 וְאִשָּׁ֕ה כִּֽי־תִדֹּ֥ר נֶ֖דֶר לַֽיהוָ֑ה וְאָסְרָ֥ה אִסָּ֖ר
בְּבֵ֥ית אָבִ֖יהָ בִּנְעֻרֶֽיהָ׃ 5 וְשָׁמַ֨ע אָבִ֜יהָ
אֶת־נִדְרָ֗הּ וֶאֱסָרָהּ֙ אֲשֶׁ֣ר אָֽסְרָ֣ה עַל־נַפְשָׁ֔הּ
וְהֶחֱרִ֥ישׁ לָ֖הּ אָבִ֑יהָ וְקָ֙מוּ֙ כָּל־נְדָרֶ֔יהָ וְכָל־
אִסָּ֛ר אֲשֶׁר־אָסְרָ֥ה עַל־נַפְשָׁ֖הּ יָקֽוּם׃
6 וְאִם־הֵנִ֨יא אָבִ֣יהָ אֹתָהּ֮ בְּי֣וֹם שָׁמְעוֹ֒
כָּל־נְדָרֶ֗יהָ וֶֽאֱסָרֶ֙יהָ֙ אֲשֶׁר־אָֽסְרָ֣ה עַל־
נַפְשָׁ֔הּ לֹ֣א יָק֑וּם וַֽיהוָה֙ יִֽסְלַח־לָ֔הּ כִּֽי־הֵנִ֥יא
אָבִ֖יהָ אֹתָֽהּ׃
7 וְאִם־הָי֤וֹ תִֽהְיֶה֙ לְאִ֔ישׁ וּנְדָרֶ֖יהָ עָלֶ֑יהָ א֚וֹ
מִבְטָ֣א שְׂפָתֶ֔יהָ אֲשֶׁ֥ר אָסְרָ֖ה עַל־נַפְשָֽׁהּ׃
8 וְשָׁמַ֤ע אִישָׁהּ֙ בְּי֣וֹם שָׁמְע֔וֹ וְהֶחֱרִ֖ישׁ לָ֑הּ
וְקָ֣מוּ נְדָרֶ֗יהָ וֶֽאֱסָרֶ֛הָ אֲשֶׁר־אָסְרָ֥ה עַל־
נַפְשָׁ֖הּ יָקֻֽמוּ׃ 9 וְ֠אִם בְּי֨וֹם שְׁמֹ֣עַ אִישָׁהּ֮
יָנִ֣יא אוֹתָהּ֒ וְהֵפֵ֗ר אֶת־נִדְרָהּ֙ אֲשֶׁ֣ר עָלֶ֔יהָ
וְאֵת֙ מִבְטָ֣א שְׂפָתֶ֔יהָ אֲשֶׁ֥ר אָסְרָ֖ה עַל־
נַפְשָׁ֑הּ וַֽיהוָ֖ה יִֽסְלַֽח־לָֽהּ׃ 10 וְנֵ֥דֶר אַלְמָנָ֖ה
וּגְרוּשָׁ֑ה כֹּ֛ל אֲשֶׁר־אָסְרָ֥ה עַל־נַפְשָׁ֖הּ יָק֥וּם
עָלֶֽיהָ׃ 11 וְאִם־בֵּ֥ית אִישָׁ֖הּ נָדָ֑רָה אֽוֹ־
אָֽסְרָ֥ה אִסָּ֛ר עַל־נַפְשָׁ֖הּ בִּשְׁבֻעָֽה׃ 12 וְשָׁמַ֤ע
אִישָׁהּ֙ וְהֶחֱרִ֣שׁ לָ֔הּ לֹ֥א הֵנִ֖יא אֹתָ֑הּ וְקָ֙מוּ֙

yet offers no objection—thus failing to restrain her—all her vows shall stand and all her self-imposed obligations shall stand. [13]But if her husband does annul them on the day he finds out, then nothing that has crossed her lips shall stand, whether vows or self-imposed obligations. Her husband has annulled them, and the LORD will forgive her. [14]Every vow and every sworn obligation of self-denial may be upheld by her husband or annulled by her husband. [15]If her husband offers no objection from that day to the next, he has upheld all the vows or obligations she has assumed: he has upheld them by offering no objection on the day he found out. [16]But if he annuls them after [the day] he finds out, he shall bear her guilt.

[17]Those are the laws that the LORD enjoined upon Moses between a man and his wife, and as between a father and his daughter while in her father's household by reason of her youth.

31

The LORD spoke to Moses, saying, [2]"Avenge the Israelite people on the Midianites; then you shall be gathered to your kin."

[3]Moses spoke to the people, saying, "Let men be picked out from among you for a campaign, and let them fall upon Midian to wreak the LORD's vengeance on Midian. [4]You shall dispatch on the campaign a thousand from every one of the tribes of Israel."

[5]So a thousand from each tribe were furnished from the divisions of Israel, twelve thousand picked for the campaign. [6]Moses dispatched them on the campaign, a thousand from each tribe, with Phinehas son of Eleazar serving as a priest on the campaign, equipped with the sacred utensils[a] and the trumpets for sounding the blasts. [7]They took the field against Midian, as the LORD had commanded Moses,

כָּל־נְדָרֶ֙יהָ֙ וְכָל־אִסָּ֔ר אֲשֶׁר־אָסְרָ֖ה עַל־נַפְשָׁ֖הּ יָקֽוּם׃ 13 וְאִם־הָפֵ֙ר יָפֵ֤ר אֹתָם֙ ׀ אִישָׁ֔הּ בְּי֖וֹם שָׁמְע֑וֹ כָּל־מוֹצָ֙א שְׂפָתֶ֜יהָ לִנְדָרֶ֙יהָ וּלְאִסַּ֤ר נַפְשָׁהּ֙ לֹ֣א יָק֔וּם אִישָׁ֥הּ הֲפֵרָ֖ם וַיהֹוָ֥ה יִֽסְלַֽח־לָֽהּ׃ 14 כָּל־נֵ֥דֶר וְכָל־שְׁבֻעַ֛ת אִסָּ֖ר לְעַנֹּ֣ת נָ֑פֶשׁ אִישָׁ֥הּ יְקִימֶ֖נּוּ וְאִישָׁ֥הּ יְפֵרֶֽנּוּ׃ 15 וְאִם־הַחֲרֵשׁ֩ יַחֲרִ֙ישׁ לָ֜הּ אִישָׁ֗הּ מִיּ֣וֹם אֶל־י֔וֹם וְהֵקִים֙ אֶת־כָּל־נְדָרֶ֔יהָ א֥וֹ אֶת־כָּל־אֱסָרֶ֖יהָ אֲשֶׁ֣ר עָלֶ֑יהָ הֵקִ֣ים אֹתָ֔ם כִּי־הֶחֱרִ֥שׁ לָ֖הּ בְּי֥וֹם שָׁמְעֽוֹ׃ 16 וְאִם־הָפֵ֥ר יָפֵ֛ר אֹתָ֖ם אַחֲרֵ֣י שָׁמְע֑וֹ וְנָשָׂ֖א אֶת־עֲוֺנָֽהּ׃

17 אֵ֣לֶּה הַֽחֻקִּ֗ים אֲשֶׁ֙ר צִוָּ֤ה יְהֹוָה֙ אֶת־מֹשֶׁ֔ה בֵּ֥ין אִ֖ישׁ לְאִשְׁתּ֑וֹ בֵּֽין־אָ֣ב לְבִתּ֔וֹ בִּנְעֻרֶ֖יהָ בֵּ֥ית אָבִֽיהָ׃ פ

לא

וַיְדַבֵּ֥ר יְהֹוָ֖ה אֶל־מֹשֶׁ֥ה לֵּאמֹֽר׃ 2 נְקֹ֗ם נִקְמַת֙ בְּנֵ֣י יִשְׂרָאֵ֔ל מֵאֵ֖ת הַמִּדְיָנִ֑ים אַחַ֖ר תֵּאָסֵ֥ף אֶל־עַמֶּֽיךָ׃ 3 וַיְדַבֵּ֤ר מֹשֶׁה֙ אֶל־הָעָ֣ם לֵאמֹ֔ר הֵחָלְצ֧וּ מֵאִתְּכֶ֛ם אֲנָשִׁ֖ים לַצָּבָ֑א וְיִהְיוּ֙ עַל־מִדְיָ֔ן לָתֵ֥ת נִקְמַת־יְהֹוָ֖ה בְּמִדְיָֽן׃ 4 אֶ֚לֶף לַמַּטֶּ֔ה אֶ֖לֶף לַמַּטֶּ֑ה לְכֹל֙ מַטּ֣וֹת יִשְׂרָאֵ֔ל תִּשְׁלְח֖וּ לַצָּבָֽא׃ 5 וַיִּמָּֽסְרוּ֙ מֵאַלְפֵ֣י יִשְׂרָאֵ֔ל אֶ֖לֶף לַמַּטֶּ֑ה שְׁנֵים־עָשָׂ֥ר אֶ֖לֶף חֲלוּצֵ֥י צָבָֽא׃ 6 וַיִּשְׁלַ֙ח אֹתָ֣ם מֹשֶׁ֥ה אֶ֛לֶף לַמַּטֶּ֖ה לַצָּבָ֑א אֹתָ֡ם וְאֶת־פִּֽינְחָס֩ בֶּן־אֶלְעָזָ֙ר הַכֹּהֵ֜ן לַצָּבָ֗א וּכְלֵ֙י הַקֹּ֤דֶשׁ וַחֲצֹצְר֥וֹת הַתְּרוּעָ֖ה בְּיָדֽוֹ׃ 7 וַֽיִּצְבְּאוּ֙ עַל־מִדְיָ֔ן כַּאֲשֶׁ֛ר צִוָּ֥ה יְהֹוָ֖ה אֶת־מֹשֶׁ֑ה וַיַּֽהַרְג֖וּ כָּל־זָכָֽר׃ 8 וְאֶת־מַלְכֵ֣י מִדְיָ֗ן

---

a   *Perhaps the Urim; cf. 27.21.*

and slew every male. 8Along with their other victims, they slew the kings of Midian: Evi, Rekem, Zur, Hur, and Reba, the five kings of Midian. They also put Balaam son of Beor to the sword.

9The Israelites took the women and children of the Midianites captive, and seized as booty all their beasts, all their herds, and all their wealth. 10And they destroyed by fire all the towns in which they were settled, and their encampments. 11They gathered all the spoil and all the booty, man and beast, 12and they brought the captives, the booty, and the spoil to Moses, Eleazar the priest, and the whole Israelite community, at the camp in the steppes of Moab, at the Jordan near Jericho.

13Moses, Eleazar the priest, and all the chieftains of the community came out to meet them outside the camp. 14Moses became angry with the commanders of the army, the officers of thousands and the officers of hundreds, who had come back from the military campaign. 15Moses said to them, "You have spared every female! 16Yet they are the very ones who, at the bidding of Balaam, induced[b] the Israelites to trespass against the LORD in the matter of Peor, so that the LORD's community was struck by the plague. 17Now, therefore, slay every male among the children, and slay also every woman who has known a man carnally; 18but spare every young woman who has not had carnal relations with a man.

19"You shall then stay outside the camp seven days; every one among you or among your captives who has slain a person or touched a corpse shall cleanse himself on the third and seventh days. 20You shall also cleanse every cloth, every article of skin, everything made of goats' hair, and every object of wood."

21Eleazar the priest said to the troops who had taken part in the fighting, "This is the ritual law

הָרְגוּ עַל־חַלְלֵיהֶם אֶת־אֱוִי וְאֶת־רֶ֫קֶם וְאֶת־צוּר וְאֶת־חוּר וְאֶת־רֶ֫בַע חֲמֵשֶׁת מַלְכֵי מִדְיָן וְאֵת בִּלְעָם בֶּן־בְּעוֹר הָרְגוּ בֶּחָֽרֶב: 9 וַיִּשְׁבּוּ בְנֵי־יִשְׂרָאֵל אֶת־נְשֵׁי מִדְיָן וְאֶת־טַפָּם וְאֵת כָּל־בְּהֶמְתָּם וְאֶת־כָּל־מִקְנֵהֶם וְאֶת־כָּל־חֵילָם בָּזָֽזוּ: 10 וְאֵת כָּל־עָרֵיהֶם בְּמוֹשְׁבֹתָם וְאֵת כָּל־טִירֹתָם שָׂרְפוּ בָּאֵֽשׁ: 11 וַיִּקְחוּ אֶת־כָּל־הַשָּׁלָל וְאֵת כָּל־הַמַּלְקוֹחַ בָּאָדָם וּבַבְּהֵמָֽה: 12 וַיָּבִאוּ אֶל־מֹשֶׁה וְאֶל־אֶלְעָזָר הַכֹּהֵן וְאֶל־עֲדַת בְּנֵי־יִשְׂרָאֵל אֶת־הַשְּׁבִי וְאֶת־הַמַּלְקוֹחַ וְאֶת־הַשָּׁלָל אֶל־הַמַּחֲנֶה אֶל־עַרְבֹת מוֹאָב אֲשֶׁר עַל־יַרְדֵּן יְרֵחֽוֹ: ס 13 וַיֵּצְאוּ מֹשֶׁה וְאֶלְעָזָר הַכֹּהֵן וְכָל־נְשִׂיאֵי הָעֵדָה לִקְרָאתָם אֶל־מִחוּץ לַמַּחֲנֶֽה: 14 וַיִּקְצֹף מֹשֶׁה עַל פְּקוּדֵי הֶחָיִל שָׂרֵי הָאֲלָפִים וְשָׂרֵי הַמֵּאוֹת הַבָּאִים מִצְּבָא הַמִּלְחָמָֽה: 15 וַיֹּאמֶר אֲלֵיהֶם מֹשֶׁה הַחִיִּיתֶם כָּל־נְקֵבָֽה: 16 הֵן הֵנָּה הָיוּ לִבְנֵי יִשְׂרָאֵל בִּדְבַר בִּלְעָם לִמְסָר־מַעַל בַּיהוָה עַל־דְּבַר־פְּעוֹר וַתְּהִי הַמַּגֵּפָה בַּעֲדַת יְהוָֽה: 17 וְעַתָּה הִרְגוּ כָל־זָכָר בַּטָּף וְכָל־אִשָּׁה יֹדַעַת אִישׁ לְמִשְׁכַּב זָכָר הֲרֹֽגוּ: 18 וְכֹל הַטַּף בַּנָּשִׁים אֲשֶׁר לֹא־יָדְעוּ מִשְׁכַּב זָכָר הַחֲיוּ לָכֶֽם: 19 וְאַתֶּם חֲנוּ מִחוּץ לַמַּחֲנֶה שִׁבְעַת יָמִים כֹּל הֹרֵג נֶפֶשׁ וְכֹל | נֹגֵעַ בֶּחָלָל תִּֽתְחַטְּאוּ בַּיּוֹם הַשְּׁלִישִׁי וּבַיּוֹם הַשְּׁבִיעִי אַתֶּם וּשְׁבִיכֶֽם: 20 וְכָל־בֶּגֶד וְכָל־כְּלִי־עוֹר וְכָל־מַעֲשֵׂה עִזִּים וְכָל־כְּלִי־עֵץ תִּתְחַטָּֽאוּ: ס 21 וַיֹּאמֶר אֶלְעָזָר הַכֹּהֵן אֶל־אַנְשֵׁי הַצָּבָא הַבָּאִים לַמִּלְחָמָה זֹאת חֻקַּת הַתּוֹרָה

---

b Meaning of Heb. hayu…limsor uncertain.

that the LORD has enjoined upon Moses: 22Gold and silver, copper, iron, tin, and lead—23any article that can withstand fire—these you shall pass through fire and they shall be clean, except that they must be cleansed with water of lustration; and anything that cannot withstand fire you must pass through water. 24On the seventh day you shall wash your clothes and be clean, and after that you may enter the camp."

25The LORD said to Moses: 26"You and Eleazar the priest and the family heads of the community take an inventory of the booty that was captured, man and beast, 27and divide the booty equally between the combatants who engaged in the campaign and the rest of the community. 28You shall exact a levy for the LORD: in the case of the warriors who engaged in the campaign, one item in five hundred, of persons, oxen, asses, and sheep, 29shall be taken from their half-share and given to Eleazar the priest as a contribution to the LORD; 30and from the half-share of the other Israelites you shall withhold one in every fifty human beings as well as cattle, asses, and sheep—all the animals—and give them to the Levites, who attend to the duties of the LORD's Tabernacle."

31Moses and Eleazar the priest did as the LORD commanded Moses. 32The amount of booty, other than the spoil that the troops had plundered, came to 675,000 sheep, 3372,000 head of cattle, 3461,000 asses, 35and a total of 32,000 human beings, namely, the women who had not had carnal relations.

36Thus, the half-share of those who had engaged in the campaign [was as follows]: The number of sheep was 337,500, 37and the LORD's levy from the sheep was 675; 38the cattle came

אֲשֶׁר־צִוָּ֥ה יְהֹוָ֖ה אֶת־מֹשֶֽׁה: 22 אַ֣ךְ אֶת־ הַזָּהָ֣ב וְאֶת־הַכָּ֗סֶף אֶֽת־הַנְּחֹ֙שֶׁת֙ אֶת־ הַבַּרְזֶ֔ל אֶֽת־הַבְּדִ֖יל וְאֶת־הָעֹפָֽרֶת: 23 כָּל־ דָּבָ֞ר אֲשֶׁר־יָבֹ֣א בָאֵ֗שׁ תַּעֲבִ֤ירוּ בָאֵשׁ֙ וְטָהֵ֔ר אַ֕ךְ בְּמֵ֥י נִדָּ֖ה יִתְחַטָּ֑א וְכֹ֛ל אֲשֶׁ֥ר לֹֽא־יָבֹ֛א בָּאֵ֖שׁ תַּעֲבִ֥ירוּ בַמָּֽיִם: 24 וְכִבַּסְתֶּ֧ם בִּגְדֵיכֶ֛ם בַּיּ֥וֹם הַשְּׁבִיעִ֖י וּטְהַרְתֶּ֑ם וְאַחַ֖ר תָּבֹ֥אוּ אֶל־הַֽמַּחֲנֶֽה: פ

25 וַיֹּ֥אמֶר יְהֹוָ֖ה אֶל־מֹשֶׁ֥ה לֵּאמֹֽר: 26 שָׂ֗א אֵ֣ת רֹ֤אשׁ מַלְק֙וֹחַ֙ הַשְּׁבִ֔י בָּאָדָ֖ם וּבַבְּהֵמָ֑ה אַתָּה֙ וְאֶלְעָזָ֣ר הַכֹּהֵ֔ן וְרָאשֵׁ֖י אֲב֥וֹת הָעֵדָֽה: 27 וְחָצִ֙יתָ֙ אֶת־הַמַּלְק֔וֹחַ בֵּ֚ין תֹּפְשֵׂ֣י הַמִּלְחָמָ֔ה הַיֹּצְאִ֖ים לַצָּבָ֑א וּבֵ֖ין כָּל־ הָעֵדָֽה: 28 וַהֲרֵמֹתָ֨ מֶ֜כֶס לַֽיהֹוָ֗ה מֵאֵ֞ת אַנְשֵׁ֤י הַמִּלְחָמָה֙ הַיֹּצְאִ֣ים לַצָּבָ֔א אֶחָ֣ד נֶ֔פֶשׁ מֵחֲמֵ֖שׁ הַמֵּא֑וֹת מִן־הָֽאָדָם֙ וּמִן־ הַבָּקָ֔ר וּמִן־הַחֲמֹרִ֖ים וּמִן־הַצֹּֽאן: 29 מִמַּֽחֲצִיתָ֖ם תִּקָּ֑חוּ וְנָתַתָּ֛ה לְאֶלְעָזָ֥ר הַכֹּהֵ֖ן תְּרוּמַ֥ת יְהֹוָֽה: 30 וּמִמַּחֲצִ֨ת בְּנֵֽי־ יִשְׂרָאֵ֜ל תִּקַּ֣ח ׀ אֶחָ֣ד ׀ אָחֻ֣ז מִן־הַחֲמִשִּׁ֗ים מִן־הָֽאָדָם֙ מִן־הַבָּקָ֤ר מִן־הַחֲמֹרִים֙ וּמִן־ הַצֹּ֔אן מִכָּל־הַבְּהֵמָ֑ה וְנָתַתָּ֤ה אֹתָם֙ לַלְוִיִּ֔ם שֹׁמְרֵ֕י מִשְׁמֶ֖רֶת מִשְׁכַּ֥ן יְהֹוָֽה: 31 וַיַּ֣עַשׂ מֹשֶׁ֔ה וְאֶלְעָזָ֖ר הַכֹּהֵ֑ן כַּאֲשֶׁ֛ר צִוָּ֥ה יְהֹוָ֖ה אֶת־מֹשֶֽׁה: 32 וַיְהִי֙ הַמַּלְק֔וֹחַ יֶ֖תֶר הַבָּ֑ז אֲשֶׁ֥ר בָּזְז֖וּ עַ֣ם הַצָּבָ֑א צֹ֗אן שֵׁשׁ־מֵא֥וֹת אֶ֛לֶף וְשִׁבְעִ֥ים אֶ֖לֶף וַחֲמֵ֥שֶׁת־אֲלָפִֽים: 33 וּבָקָ֕ר שְׁנַ֥יִם וְשִׁבְעִ֖ים אָֽלֶף: 34 וַחֲמֹרִ֕ים אֶחָ֥ד וְשִׁשִּׁ֖ים אָֽלֶף: 35 וְנֶ֣פֶשׁ אָדָ֔ם מִן־ הַנָּשִׁ֕ים אֲשֶׁ֥ר לֹֽא־יָדְע֖וּ מִשְׁכַּ֣ב זָכָ֑ר כָּל־ נֶ֕פֶשׁ שְׁנַ֥יִם וּשְׁלֹשִׁ֖ים אָֽלֶף: 36 וַתְּהִי֙ הַֽמֶּחֱצָ֔ה חֵ֕לֶק הַיֹּצְאִ֖ים בַּצָּבָ֑א מִסְפַּ֣ר הַצֹּ֗אן שְׁלֹשׁ־מֵא֥וֹת אֶ֙לֶף֙ וּשְׁלֹשִׁ֣ים אֶ֔לֶף וְשִׁבְעַ֥ת אֲלָפִ֖ים וַחֲמֵ֥שׁ מֵאֽוֹת: 37 וַיְהִ֛י הַמֶּ֥כֶס לַֽיהֹוָ֖ה מִן־הַצֹּ֑אן שֵׁ֥שׁ מֵא֖וֹת חָמֵ֥שׁ וְשִׁבְעִֽים: 38 וְהַ֨בָּקָ֔ר שִׁשָּׁ֥ה

to 36,000, from which the LORD's levy was 72; [39]the asses came to 30,500, from which the LORD's levy was 61. [40]And the number of human beings was 16,000, from which the LORD's levy was 32. [41]Moses gave the contributions levied for the LORD to Eleazar the priest, as the LORD had commanded Moses.

[42]As for the half-share of the other Israelites, which Moses withdrew from the men who had taken the field, [43]that half-share of the community consisted of 337,500 sheep, [44]36,000 head of cattle, [45]30,500 asses, [46]and 16,000 human beings. [47]From this half-share of the Israelites, Moses withheld one in every fifty humans and animals; and he gave them to the Levites, who attended to the duties of the LORD's Tabernacle, as the LORD had commanded Moses.

[48]The commanders of the troop divisions, the officers of thousands and the officers of hundreds, approached Moses. [49]They said to Moses, "Your servants have made a check of the warriors in our charge, and not one of us is missing. [50]So we have brought as an offering to the LORD such articles of gold as each of us came upon: armlets, bracelets, signet rings, earrings, and pendants,c that expiation may be made for our persons before the LORD." [51]Moses and Eleazar the priest accepted the gold from them, all kinds of wrought articles. [52]All the gold that was offered by the officers of thousands and the officers of hundreds as a contribution to the LORD came to 16,750 shekels.—[53]But in the ranks, everyone kept his booty for himself.—[54]So Moses and Eleazar the priest accepted the gold from the officers of thousands and the officers of hundreds and brought it to the Tent of Meeting, as a reminder in behalf of the Israelites before the LORD.

c See note at Exod. 35.22.

וּשְׁלֹשִׁים אֶלֶף וּמִכְסָם לַיהֹוָה שְׁנַיִם וְשִׁבְעִים: 39 וַחֲמֹרִים שְׁלֹשִׁים אֶלֶף וַחֲמֵשׁ מֵאוֹת וּמִכְסָם לַיהֹוָה אֶחָד וְשִׁשִּׁים: 40 וְנֶפֶשׁ אָדָם שִׁשָּׁה עָשָׂר אָלֶף וּמִכְסָם לַיהֹוָה שְׁנַיִם וּשְׁלֹשִׁים נָפֶשׁ: 41 וַיִּתֵּן מֹשֶׁה אֶת־מֶכֶס תְּרוּמַת יְהֹוָה לְאֶלְעָזָר הַכֹּהֵן כַּאֲשֶׁר צִוָּה יְהֹוָה אֶת־מֹשֶׁה:

42 וּמִמַּחֲצִית בְּנֵי יִשְׂרָאֵל אֲשֶׁר חָצָה מֹשֶׁה מִן־הָאֲנָשִׁים הַצֹּבְאִים: 43 וַתְּהִי מֶחֱצַת הָעֵדָה מִן־הַצֹּאן שְׁלֹשׁ־מֵאוֹת אֶלֶף וּשְׁלֹשִׁים אֶלֶף שִׁבְעַת אֲלָפִים וַחֲמֵשׁ מֵאוֹת: 44 וּבָקָר שִׁשָּׁה וּשְׁלֹשִׁים אָלֶף: 45 וַחֲמֹרִים שְׁלֹשִׁים אֶלֶף וַחֲמֵשׁ מֵאוֹת: 46 וְנֶפֶשׁ אָדָם שִׁשָּׁה עָשָׂר אָלֶף: 47 וַיִּקַּח מֹשֶׁה מִמַּחֲצִת בְּנֵי־יִשְׂרָאֵל אֶת־הָאָחֻז אֶחָד מִן־הַחֲמִשִּׁים מִן־הָאָדָם וּמִן־הַבְּהֵמָה וַיִּתֵּן אֹתָם לַלְוִיִּם שֹׁמְרֵי מִשְׁמֶרֶת מִשְׁכַּן יְהֹוָה כַּאֲשֶׁר צִוָּה יְהֹוָה אֶת־מֹשֶׁה:

48 וַיִּקְרְבוּ אֶל־מֹשֶׁה הַפְּקֻדִים אֲשֶׁר לְאַלְפֵי הַצָּבָא שָׂרֵי הָאֲלָפִים וְשָׂרֵי הַמֵּאוֹת: 49 וַיֹּאמְרוּ אֶל־מֹשֶׁה עֲבָדֶיךָ נָשְׂאוּ אֶת־רֹאשׁ אַנְשֵׁי הַמִּלְחָמָה אֲשֶׁר בְּיָדֵנוּ וְלֹא־נִפְקַד מִמֶּנּוּ אִישׁ: 50 וַנַּקְרֵב אֶת־קָרְבַּן יְהֹוָה אִישׁ אֲשֶׁר מָצָא כְלִי־זָהָב אֶצְעָדָה וְצָמִיד טַבַּעַת עָגִיל וְכוּמָז לְכַפֵּר עַל־נַפְשֹׁתֵינוּ לִפְנֵי יְהֹוָה: 51 וַיִּקַּח מֹשֶׁה וְאֶלְעָזָר הַכֹּהֵן אֶת־הַזָּהָב מֵאִתָּם כֹּל כְּלִי מַעֲשֶׂה: 52 וַיְהִי ׀ כָּל־זְהַב הַתְּרוּמָה אֲשֶׁר הֵרִימוּ לַיהֹוָה שִׁשָּׁה עָשָׂר אֶלֶף שְׁבַע־מֵאוֹת וַחֲמִשִּׁים שָׁקֶל מֵאֵת שָׂרֵי הָאֲלָפִים וּמֵאֵת שָׂרֵי הַמֵּאוֹת: 53 אַנְשֵׁי הַצָּבָא בָּזְזוּ אִישׁ לוֹ: 54 וַיִּקַּח מֹשֶׁה וְאֶלְעָזָר הַכֹּהֵן אֶת־הַזָּהָב מֵאֵת שָׂרֵי הָאֲלָפִים וְהַמֵּאוֹת וַיָּבִאוּ אֹתוֹ אֶל־אֹהֶל מוֹעֵד זִכָּרוֹן לִבְנֵי־יִשְׂרָאֵל לִפְנֵי יְהֹוָה: פ

32

The Reubenites and the Gadites owned cattle in very great numbers. Noting that the lands of Jazer and Gilead were a region suitable for cattle, [2] the Gadites and the Reubenites came to Moses, Eleazar the priest, and the chieftains of the community, and said, [3] "Ataroth, Dibon, Jazer, Nimrah, Heshbon, Elealeh, Sebam, Nebo, and Beon— [4] the land that the Lord has conquered for the community of Israel is cattle country, and your servants have cattle. [5] It would be a favor to us," they continued, "if this land were given to your servants as a holding; do not move us across the Jordan."

[6] Moses replied to the Gadites and the Reubenites, "Are your brothers to go to war while you stay here? [7] Why will you turn the minds of the Israelites from crossing into the land that the Lord has given them? [8] That is what your fathers did when I sent them from Kadesh-barnea to survey the land. [9] After going up to the wadi Eshcol and surveying the land, they turned the minds of the Israelites from invading the land that the Lord had given them. [10] Thereupon the Lord was incensed and He swore, [11] 'None of the men from twenty years up who came out of Egypt shall see the land that I promised on oath to Abraham, Isaac, and Jacob, for they did not remain loyal to Me— [12] none except Caleb son of Jephunneh the Kenizzite and Joshua son of Nun, for they remained loyal to the Lord.' [13] The Lord was incensed at Israel, and for forty years He made them wander in the wilderness, until the whole generation that had provoked the Lord's displeasure was gone. [14] And now you, a breed of sinful men, have replaced your fathers, to add still further to the Lord's wrath against Israel. [15] If you turn away from Him and He abandons them once more in the wilderness, you will bring calamity upon all this people."

לב

וּמִקְנֶה ׀ רַב הָיָה לִבְנֵי רְאוּבֵן וְלִבְנֵי־גָד עָצוּם מְאֹד וַיִּרְאוּ אֶת־אֶרֶץ יַעְזֵר וְאֶת־אֶרֶץ גִּלְעָד וְהִנֵּה הַמָּקוֹם מְקוֹם מִקְנֶה: 2 וַיָּבֹאוּ בְנֵי־גָד וּבְנֵי רְאוּבֵן וַיֹּאמְרוּ אֶל־מֹשֶׁה וְאֶל־אֶלְעָזָר הַכֹּהֵן וְאֶל־נְשִׂיאֵי הָעֵדָה לֵאמֹר: 3 עֲטָרוֹת וְדִיבֹן וְיַעְזֵר וְנִמְרָה וְחֶשְׁבּוֹן וְאֶלְעָלֵה וּשְׂבָם וּנְבוֹ וּבְעֹן: 4 הָאָרֶץ אֲשֶׁר הִכָּה יְהוָה לִפְנֵי עֲדַת יִשְׂרָאֵל אֶרֶץ מִקְנֶה הִוא וְלַעֲבָדֶיךָ מִקְנֶה: ס 5 וַיֹּאמְרוּ אִם־מָצָאנוּ חֵן בְּעֵינֶיךָ יֻתַּן אֶת־הָאָרֶץ הַזֹּאת לַעֲבָדֶיךָ לַאֲחֻזָּה אַל־תַּעֲבִרֵנוּ אֶת־הַיַּרְדֵּן: 6 וַיֹּאמֶר מֹשֶׁה לִבְנֵי־גָד וְלִבְנֵי רְאוּבֵן הַאַחֵיכֶם יָבֹאוּ לַמִּלְחָמָה וְאַתֶּם תֵּשְׁבוּ פֹה: 7 וְלָמָּה תְנִואוּן אֶת־לֵב בְּנֵי יִשְׂרָאֵל מֵעֲבֹר אֶל־הָאָרֶץ אֲשֶׁר־נָתַן לָהֶם יְהוָה: 8 כֹּה עָשׂוּ אֲבֹתֵיכֶם בְּשָׁלְחִי אֹתָם מִקָּדֵשׁ בַּרְנֵעַ לִרְאוֹת אֶת־הָאָרֶץ: 9 וַיַּעֲלוּ עַד־נַחַל אֶשְׁכּוֹל וַיִּרְאוּ אֶת־הָאָרֶץ וַיָּנִיאוּ אֶת־לֵב בְּנֵי יִשְׂרָאֵל לְבִלְתִּי־בֹא אֶל־הָאָרֶץ אֲשֶׁר־נָתַן לָהֶם יְהוָה: 10 וַיִּחַר־אַף יְהוָה בַּיּוֹם הַהוּא וַיִּשָּׁבַע לֵאמֹר: 11 אִם־יִרְאוּ הָאֲנָשִׁים הָעֹלִים מִמִּצְרַיִם מִבֶּן עֶשְׂרִים שָׁנָה וָמַעְלָה אֵת הָאֲדָמָה אֲשֶׁר נִשְׁבַּעְתִּי לְאַבְרָהָם לְיִצְחָק וּלְיַעֲקֹב כִּי לֹא־מִלְאוּ אַחֲרָי: 12 בִּלְתִּי כָּלֵב בֶּן־יְפֻנֶּה הַקְּנִזִּי וִיהוֹשֻׁעַ בִּן־נוּן כִּי מִלְאוּ אַחֲרֵי יְהוָה: 13 וַיִּחַר־אַף יְהוָה בְּיִשְׂרָאֵל וַיְנִעֵם בַּמִּדְבָּר אַרְבָּעִים שָׁנָה עַד־תֹּם כָּל־הַדּוֹר הָעֹשֶׂה הָרַע בְּעֵינֵי יְהוָה: 14 וְהִנֵּה קַמְתֶּם תַּחַת אֲבֹתֵיכֶם תַּרְבּוּת אֲנָשִׁים חַטָּאִים לִסְפּוֹת עוֹד עַל חֲרוֹן אַף־יְהוָה אֶל־יִשְׂרָאֵל: 15 כִּי תְשׁוּבֻן מֵאַחֲרָיו וְיָסַף עוֹד לְהַנִּיחוֹ בַּמִּדְבָּר וְשִׁחַתֶּם לְכָל־הָעָם הַזֶּה: ס

16Then they stepped up to him and said, "We will build here sheepfolds for our flocks and towns for our children. 17And we will hasten[a] as shock-troops in the van of the Israelites until we have established them in their home, while our children stay in the fortified towns because of the inhabitants of the land. 18We will not return to our homes until every one of the Israelites is in possession of his portion. 19But we will not have a share with them in the territory beyond the Jordan, for we have received our share on the east side of the Jordan."

20Moses said to them, "If you do this, if you go to battle as shock-troops, at the instance of the Lord, 21and every shock-fighter among you crosses the Jordan, at the instance of the Lord, until He has dispossessed His enemies before Him, 22and the land has been subdued, at the instance of the Lord, and then you return—you shall be clear before the Lord and before Israel; and this land shall be your holding under the Lord. 23But if you do not do so, you will have sinned against the Lord; and know that your sin will overtake you. 24Build towns for your children and sheepfolds for your flocks, but do what you have promised."

25The Gadites and the Reubenites answered Moses, "Your servants will do as my lord commands. 26Our children, our wives, our flocks, and all our other livestock will stay behind[b] in the towns of Gilead; 27while your servants, all those recruited for war, cross over, at the instance of the Lord, to engage in battle—as my lord orders."

28Then Moses gave instructions concerning them to Eleazar the priest, Joshua son of Nun, and the family heads of the Israelite tribes. 29Moses said to them, "If every shock-fighter among the Gadites and the Reubenites crosses

16 וַיִּגְּשׁוּ אֵלָיו וַיֹּאמְרוּ גִּדְרֹת צֹאן נִבְנֶה לְמִקְנֵנוּ פֹּה וְעָרִים לְטַפֵּנוּ: 17 וַאֲנַחְנוּ נֵחָלֵץ חֻשִׁים לִפְנֵי בְּנֵי יִשְׂרָאֵל עַד אֲשֶׁר אִם־הֲבִיאֹנֻם אֶל־מְקוֹמָם וְיָשַׁב טַפֵּנוּ בְּעָרֵי הַמִּבְצָר מִפְּנֵי יֹשְׁבֵי הָאָרֶץ: 18 לֹא נָשׁוּב אֶל־בָּתֵּינוּ עַד הִתְנַחֵל בְּנֵי יִשְׂרָאֵל אִישׁ נַחֲלָתוֹ: 19 כִּי לֹא נִנְחַל אִתָּם מֵעֵבֶר לַיַּרְדֵּן וָהָלְאָה כִּי בָאָה נַחֲלָתֵנוּ אֵלֵינוּ מֵעֵבֶר הַיַּרְדֵּן מִזְרָחָה: פ
20 וַיֹּאמֶר אֲלֵיהֶם מֹשֶׁה אִם־תַּעֲשׂוּן אֶת־הַדָּבָר הַזֶּה אִם־תֵּחָלְצוּ לִפְנֵי יְהוָה לַמִּלְחָמָה: 21 וְעָבַר לָכֶם כָּל־חָלוּץ אֶת־הַיַּרְדֵּן לִפְנֵי יְהוָה עַד הוֹרִישׁוֹ אֶת־אֹיְבָיו מִפָּנָיו: 22 וְנִכְבְּשָׁה הָאָרֶץ לִפְנֵי יְהוָה וְאַחַר תָּשֻׁבוּ וִהְיִיתֶם נְקִיִּם מֵיְהוָה וּמִיִּשְׂרָאֵל וְהָיְתָה הָאָרֶץ הַזֹּאת לָכֶם לַאֲחֻזָּה לִפְנֵי יְהוָה: 23 וְאִם־לֹא תַעֲשׂוּן כֵּן הִנֵּה* חֲטָאתֶם לַיהוָה וּדְעוּ חַטַּאתְכֶם אֲשֶׁר תִּמְצָא אֶתְכֶם: 24 בְּנוּ־לָכֶם עָרִים לְטַפְּכֶם וּגְדֵרֹת לְצֹנַאֲכֶם וְהַיֹּצֵא מִפִּיכֶם תַּעֲשׂוּ:
25 וַיֹּאמֶר* בְּנֵי־גָד וּבְנֵי רְאוּבֵן אֶל־מֹשֶׁה לֵאמֹר עֲבָדֶיךָ יַעֲשׂוּ כַּאֲשֶׁר אֲדֹנִי מְצַוֶּה: 26 טַפֵּנוּ נָשֵׁינוּ מִקְנֵנוּ וְכָל־בְּהֶמְתֵּנוּ יִהְיוּ־שָׁם בְּעָרֵי הַגִּלְעָד: 27 וַעֲבָדֶיךָ יַעַבְרוּ כָּל־חֲלוּץ צָבָא לִפְנֵי יְהוָה לַמִּלְחָמָה כַּאֲשֶׁר אֲדֹנִי דֹּבֵר:
28 וַיְצַו לָהֶם מֹשֶׁה אֵת אֶלְעָזָר הַכֹּהֵן וְאֵת יְהוֹשֻׁעַ בִּן־נוּן וְאֶת־רָאשֵׁי אֲבוֹת הַמַּטּוֹת לִבְנֵי יִשְׂרָאֵל: 29 וַיֹּאמֶר מֹשֶׁה אֲלֵהֶם אִם־יַעַבְרוּ בְנֵי־גָד וּבְנֵי־רְאוּבֵן אִתְּכֶם אֶת־הַיַּרְדֵּן כָּל־חָלוּץ לַמִּלְחָמָה לִפְנֵי יְהוָה וְנִכְבְּשָׁה הָאָרֶץ לִפְנֵיכֶם וּנְתַתֶּם לָהֶם אֶת־אֶרֶץ הַגִּלְעָד לַאֲחֻזָּה: 30 וְאִם־

---

a Meaning of Heb. hushim uncertain.
b Lit. "there."

the Jordan with you to do battle, at the instance of the LORD, and the land is subdued before you, you shall give them the land of Gilead as a holding. [30]But if they do not cross over with you as shock-troops, they shall receive holdings among you in the land of Canaan."

[31]The Gadites and the Reubenites said in reply, "Whatever the LORD has spoken concerning your servants, that we will do. [32]We ourselves will cross over as shock-troops, at the instance of the LORD, into the land of Canaan; and we shall keep our hereditary holding across the Jordan."[c]

[33]So Moses assigned to them—to the Gadites, the Reubenites, and the half-tribe of Manasseh son of Joseph—the kingdom of Sihon king of the Amorites and the kingdom of King Og of Bashan, the land with its various cities and the territories of their surrounding towns. [34]The Gadites rebuilt Dibon, Ataroth, Aroer, [35]Atroth-shophan, Jazer, Jogbehah, [36]Beth-nimrah, and Beth-haran as fortified towns or as enclosures for flocks. [37]The Reubenites rebuilt Heshbon, Elealeh, Kiriathaim, [38]Nebo, Baal-meon—some names being changed—and Sibmah; they gave [their own] names to towns that they rebuilt.[d] [39]The descendants of Machir son of Manasseh went to Gilead and captured it, dispossessing the Amorites who were there; [40]so Moses gave Gilead to Machir son of Manasseh, and he settled there. [41]Jair son of Manasseh went and captured [e]their villages,[-e] which he renamed Havvoth-jair.[f] [42]And Nobah went and captured Kenath and its dependencies, renaming it Nobah after himself.

33 MASE'EI
These were the marches of the Israelites who started out from the land of Egypt, troop

לֹא יַעַבְרוּ חֲלוּצִים אִתְּכֶם וְנֹאחֲזוּ בְתֹכְכֶם בְּאֶרֶץ כְּנָעַן: [31]וַיַּעֲנוּ בְנֵי־גָד וּבְנֵי רְאוּבֵן לֵאמֹר אֵת אֲשֶׁר דִּבֶּר יְהוָה אֶל־עֲבָדֶיךָ כֵּן נַעֲשֶׂה: [32]נַחְנוּ נַעֲבֹר חֲלוּצִים לִפְנֵי יְהוָה אֶרֶץ* כְּנָעַן וְאִתָּנוּ אֲחֻזַּת נַחֲלָתֵנוּ מֵעֵבֶר לַיַּרְדֵּן: [33]וַיִּתֵּן לָהֶם ׀ מֹשֶׁה לִבְנֵי־גָד וְלִבְנֵי רְאוּבֵן וְלַחֲצִי ׀ שֵׁבֶט ׀ מְנַשֶּׁה בֶן־יוֹסֵף אֶת־מַמְלֶכֶת סִיחֹן מֶלֶךְ הָאֱמֹרִי וְאֶת־מַמְלֶכֶת עוֹג מֶלֶךְ הַבָּשָׁן הָאָרֶץ לְעָרֶיהָ בִּגְבֻלֹת עָרֵי הָאָרֶץ סָבִיב: [34]וַיִּבְנוּ בְנֵי־גָד אֶת־דִּיבֹן וְאֶת־עֲטָרֹת וְאֵת עֲרֹעֵר: [35]וְאֶת־עַטְרֹת שׁוֹפָן וְאֶת־יַעְזֵר וְיָגְבֳּהָה: [36]וְאֶת־בֵּית נִמְרָה וְאֶת־בֵּית הָרָן עָרֵי מִבְצָר וְגִדְרֹת צֹאן: [37]וּבְנֵי רְאוּבֵן בָּנוּ אֶת־חֶשְׁבּוֹן וְאֶת־אֶלְעָלֵא וְאֵת קִרְיָתָיִם: [38]וְאֶת־נְבוֹ וְאֶת־בַּעַל מְעוֹן מוּסַבֹּת שֵׁם וְאֶת־שִׂבְמָה וַיִּקְרְאוּ בְשֵׁמֹת אֶת־שְׁמוֹת הֶעָרִים אֲשֶׁר בָּנוּ: [39]וַיֵּלְכוּ בְּנֵי מָכִיר בֶּן־מְנַשֶּׁה גִּלְעָדָה וַיִּלְכְּדֻהָ וַיּוֹרֶשׁ אֶת־הָאֱמֹרִי אֲשֶׁר־בָּהּ: [40]וַיִּתֵּן מֹשֶׁה אֶת־הַגִּלְעָד לְמָכִיר בֶּן־מְנַשֶּׁה וַיֵּשֶׁב בָּהּ: [41]וְיָאִיר בֶּן־מְנַשֶּׁה הָלַךְ וַיִּלְכֹּד אֶת־חַוֺּתֵיהֶם וַיִּקְרָא אֶתְהֶן חַוֺּת יָאִיר: [42]וְנֹבַח הָלַךְ וַיִּלְכֹּד אֶת־קְנָת וְאֶת־בְּנֹתֶיהָ וַיִּקְרָא לָה נֹבַח בִּשְׁמוֹ: פ

לג מסעי
אֵלֶּה מַסְעֵי בְנֵי־יִשְׂרָאֵל אֲשֶׁר יָצְאוּ מֵאֶרֶץ מִצְרַיִם לְצִבְאֹתָם בְּיַד־מֹשֶׁה

v. 32. סבירין ומטעין "ארצה"

---

c   I.e., in Transjordan.
d   Cf. vv. 41, 42.
e-e   Or "the villages of Ham"; cf. Gen. 14.5.
f   I.e., "the villages of Jair."

by troop, in the charge of Moses and Aaron. [2]Moses recorded the starting points of their various marches as directed by the LORD. Their marches, by starting points, were as follows:

[3]They set out from Rameses in the first month, on the fifteenth day of the first month. It was on the morrow of the passover offering that the Israelites started out defiantly,[a] in plain view of all the Egyptians. [4]The Egyptians meanwhile were burying those among them whom the LORD had struck down, every first-born—whereby the LORD executed judgment on their gods.

[5]The Israelites set out from Rameses and encamped at Succoth. [6]They set out from Succoth and encamped at Etham, which is on the edge of the wilderness. [7]They set out from Etham and turned about toward Pi-hahiroth, which faces Baal-zephon, and they encamped before Migdol. [8]They set out from Pene[b]-hahiroth and passed through the sea into the wilderness; and they made a three-days' journey in the wilderness of Etham and encamped at Marah. [9]They set out from Marah and came to Elim. There were twelve springs in Elim and seventy palm trees, so they encamped there. [10]They set out from Elim and encamped by the Sea of Reeds.[c] [11]They set out from the Sea of Reeds and encamped in the wilderness of Sin. [12]They set out from the wilderness of Sin and encamped at Dophkah. [13]They set out from Dophkah and encamped at Alush. [14]They set out from Alush and encamped at Rephidim; it was there that the people had no water to drink. [15]They set out from Rephidim and encamped in the wilderness of Sinai. [16]They set out from the wilderness of Sinai and encamped at Kibroth-hattaavah. [17]They set out from Kibroth-hattaavah and encamped at Hazeroth. [18]They set out from

וְאַהֲרֹן: ²וַיִּכְתֹּב מֹשֶׁה אֶת־מוֹצָאֵיהֶם לְמַסְעֵיהֶם עַל־פִּי יְהוָה וְאֵלֶּה מַסְעֵיהֶם לְמוֹצָאֵיהֶם: ³וַיִּסְעוּ מֵרַעְמְסֵס בַּחֹדֶשׁ הָרִאשׁוֹן בַּחֲמִשָּׁה עָשָׂר יוֹם לַחֹדֶשׁ הָרִאשׁוֹן מִמָּחֳרַת הַפֶּסַח יָצְאוּ בְנֵי־יִשְׂרָאֵל בְּיָד רָמָה לְעֵינֵי כָּל־מִצְרָיִם: ⁴וּמִצְרַיִם מְקַבְּרִים אֵת אֲשֶׁר הִכָּה יְהוָה בָּהֶם כָּל־בְּכוֹר וּבֵאלֹהֵיהֶם עָשָׂה יְהוָה שְׁפָטִים: ⁵וַיִּסְעוּ בְנֵי־יִשְׂרָאֵל מֵרַעְמְסֵס וַיַּחֲנוּ בְּסֻכֹּת: ⁶וַיִּסְעוּ מִסֻּכֹּת וַיַּחֲנוּ בְאֵתָם אֲשֶׁר בִּקְצֵה הַמִּדְבָּר: ⁷וַיִּסְעוּ מֵאֵתָם וַיָּשָׁב עַל־פִּי הַחִירֹת אֲשֶׁר עַל־פְּנֵי בַּעַל צְפוֹן וַיַּחֲנוּ לִפְנֵי מִגְדֹּל: ⁸וַיִּסְעוּ מִפְּנֵי* הַחִירֹת וַיַּעַבְרוּ בְתוֹךְ־הַיָּם הַמִּדְבָּרָה וַיֵּלְכוּ דֶּרֶךְ שְׁלֹשֶׁת יָמִים בְּמִדְבַּר אֵתָם וַיַּחֲנוּ בְּמָרָה: ⁹וַיִּסְעוּ מִמָּרָה וַיָּבֹאוּ אֵילִמָה וּבְאֵילִם שְׁתֵּים עֶשְׂרֵה עֵינֹת מַיִם וְשִׁבְעִים תְּמָרִים וַיַּחֲנוּ־שָׁם: ¹⁰וַיִּסְעוּ מֵאֵילִם וַיַּחֲנוּ עַל־יַם־סוּף: ¹¹וַיִּסְעוּ מִיַּם־סוּף וַיַּחֲנוּ בְּמִדְבַּר־סִין: ¹²וַיִּסְעוּ מִמִּדְבַּר־סִין וַיַּחֲנוּ בְּדָפְקָה: ¹³וַיִּסְעוּ מִדָּפְקָה וַיַּחֲנוּ בְּאָלוּשׁ: ¹⁴וַיִּסְעוּ מֵאָלוּשׁ וַיַּחֲנוּ בִּרְפִידִם וְלֹא־הָיָה שָׁם מַיִם לָעָם לִשְׁתּוֹת: ¹⁵וַיִּסְעוּ מֵרְפִידִם וַיַּחֲנוּ בְּמִדְבַּר סִינָי: ¹⁶וַיִּסְעוּ מִמִּדְבַּר סִינָי וַיַּחֲנוּ בְּקִבְרֹת הַתַּאֲוָה: ¹⁷וַיִּסְעוּ מִקִּבְרֹת הַתַּאֲוָה וַיַּחֲנוּ בַּחֲצֵרֹת: ¹⁸וַיִּסְעוּ מֵחֲצֵרֹת

v. 8. סְבִירִין וּמַטְעִין "מִפִּי"

---

a   *See note at Exod. 14.8.*
b   *Many Hebrew manuscripts and ancient versions read "Pi."*
c   *See note at Exod. 10.19.*

Hazeroth and encamped at Rithmah. ¹⁹They set out from Rithmah and encamped at Rimmon-perez. ²⁰They set out from Rimmon-perez and encamped at Libnah. ²¹They set out from Libnah and encamped at Rissah. ²²They set out from Rissah and encamped at Kehelath. ²³They set out from Kehelath and encamped at Mount Shepher. ²⁴They set out from Mount Shepher and encamped at Haradah. ²⁵They set out from Haradah and encamped at Makheloth. ²⁶They set out from Makheloth and encamped at Tahath. ²⁷They set out from Tahath and encamped at Terah. ²⁸They set out from Terah and encamped at Mithkah. ²⁹They set out from Mithkah and encamped at Hashmonah. ³⁰They set out from Hashmonah and encamped at Moseroth. ³¹They set out from Moseroth and encamped at Bene-jaakan. ³²They set out from Bene-jaakan and encamped at Hor-haggidgad. ³³They set out from Hor-haggidgad and encamped at Jotbath. ³⁴They set out from Jotbath and encamped at Abronah. ³⁵They set out from Abronah and encamped at Ezion-geber. ³⁶They set out from Ezion-geber and encamped in the wilderness of Zin, that is, Kadesh. ³⁷They set out from Kadesh and encamped at Mount Hor, on the edge of the land of Edom.

³⁸Aaron the priest ascended Mount Hor at the command of the LORD and died there, in the fortieth year after the Israelites had left the land of Egypt, on the first day of the fifth month. ³⁹Aaron was a hundred and twenty-three years old when he died on Mount Hor. ⁴⁰And the Canaanite, king of Arad, who dwelt in the Negeb, in the land of Canaan, learned of the coming of the Israelites.ᵈ

⁴¹They set out from Mount Hor and encamped at Zalmonah. ⁴²They set out from Zalmonah and encamped at Punon. ⁴³They set

---

וַיַּחֲנוּ בְּרִתְמָה: ¹⁹ וַיִּסְעוּ מֵרִתְמָה וַיַּחֲנוּ בְּרִמֹּן פָּרֶץ: ²⁰ וַיִּסְעוּ מֵרִמֹּן פֶּרֶץ וַיַּחֲנוּ בְּלִבְנָה: ²¹ וַיִּסְעוּ מִלִּבְנָה וַיַּחֲנוּ בְּרִסָּה: ²² וַיִּסְעוּ מֵרִסָּה וַיַּחֲנוּ בִּקְהֵלָתָה: ²³ וַיִּסְעוּ מִקְּהֵלָתָה וַיַּחֲנוּ בְּהַר־שָׁפֶר: ²⁴ וַיִּסְעוּ מֵהַר־שָׁפֶר וַיַּחֲנוּ בַּחֲרָדָה: ²⁵ וַיִּסְעוּ מֵחֲרָדָה וַיַּחֲנוּ בְּמַקְהֵלֹת: ²⁶ וַיִּסְעוּ מִמַּקְהֵלֹת וַיַּחֲנוּ בְּתָחַת: ²⁷ וַיִּסְעוּ מִתָּחַת וַיַּחֲנוּ בְּתָרַח: ²⁸ וַיִּסְעוּ מִתָּרַח וַיַּחֲנוּ בְּמִתְקָה: ²⁹ וַיִּסְעוּ מִמִּתְקָה וַיַּחֲנוּ בְּחַשְׁמֹנָה: ³⁰ וַיִּסְעוּ מֵחַשְׁמֹנָה וַיַּחֲנוּ בְּמֹסֵרוֹת: ³¹ וַיִּסְעוּ מִמֹּסֵרוֹת וַיַּחֲנוּ בִּבְנֵי יַעֲקָן: ³² וַיִּסְעוּ מִבְּנֵי יַעֲקָן וַיַּחֲנוּ בְּחֹר הַגִּדְגָּד: ³³ וַיִּסְעוּ מֵחֹר הַגִּדְגָּד וַיַּחֲנוּ בְּיָטְבָתָה: ³⁴ וַיִּסְעוּ מִיָּטְבָתָה וַיַּחֲנוּ בְּעַבְרֹנָה: ³⁵ וַיִּסְעוּ מֵעַבְרֹנָה וַיַּחֲנוּ בְּעֶצְיוֹן גָּבֶר: ³⁶ וַיִּסְעוּ מֵעֶצְיוֹן גָּבֶר וַיַּחֲנוּ בְמִדְבַּר־צִן הִוא קָדֵשׁ: ³⁷ וַיִּסְעוּ מִקָּדֵשׁ וַיַּחֲנוּ בְּהֹר הָהָר בִּקְצֵה אֶרֶץ אֱדוֹם: ³⁸ וַיַּעַל אַהֲרֹן הַכֹּהֵן אֶל־הֹר הָהָר עַל־פִּי יְהוָה וַיָּמָת שָׁם בִּשְׁנַת הָאַרְבָּעִים לְצֵאת בְּנֵי־יִשְׂרָאֵל מֵאֶרֶץ מִצְרַיִם בַּחֹדֶשׁ הַחֲמִישִׁי בְּאֶחָד לַחֹדֶשׁ: ³⁹ וְאַהֲרֹן בֶּן־שָׁלֹשׁ וְעֶשְׂרִים וּמְאַת שָׁנָה בְּמֹתוֹ בְּהֹר הָהָר: ס ⁴⁰ וַיִּשְׁמַע הַכְּנַעֲנִי מֶלֶךְ עֲרָד וְהוּא־יֹשֵׁב בַּנֶּגֶב בְּאֶרֶץ כְּנָעַן בְּבֹא בְּנֵי יִשְׂרָאֵל: ⁴¹ וַיִּסְעוּ מֵהֹר הָהָר וַיַּחֲנוּ בְּצַלְמֹנָה: ⁴² וַיִּסְעוּ מִצַּלְמֹנָה וַיַּחֲנוּ בְּפוּנֹן: ⁴³ וַיִּסְעוּ

ᵈ See 21.1–3.

out from Punon and encamped at Oboth. ⁴⁴They set out from Oboth and encamped at Iye-abarim, in the territory of Moab. ⁴⁵They set out from Iyim and encamped at Dibon-gad. ⁴⁶They set out from Dibon-gad and encamped at Almon-diblathaim. ⁴⁷They set out from Almon-diblathaim and encamped in the hills of Abarim, before Nebo. ⁴⁸They set out from the hills of Abarim and encamped in the steppes of Moab, at the Jordan near Jericho; ⁴⁹they encamped by the Jordan from Beth-jeshimoth as far as Abel-shittim, in the steppes of Moab.

⁵⁰In the steppes of Moab, at the Jordan near Jericho, the Lord spoke to Moses, saying: ⁵¹Speak to the Israelite people and say to them: When you cross the Jordan into the land of Canaan, ⁵²you shall dispossess all the inhabitants of the land; you shall destroy all their figured*ᵉ* objects; you shall destroy all their molten images, and you shall demolish all their cult places. ⁵³And you shall take possession of the land and settle in it, for I have assigned the land to you to possess. ⁵⁴You shall apportion the land among yourselves by lot, clan by clan: with larger groups increase the share, with smaller groups reduce the share. Wherever the lot falls for anyone, that shall be his. You shall have your portions according to your ancestral tribes. ⁵⁵But if you do not dispossess the inhabitants of the land, those whom you allow to remain shall be stings in your eyes and thorns in your sides, and they shall harass you in the land in which you live; ⁵⁶so that I will do to you what I planned to do to them.

34

The Lord spoke to Moses, saying: ²Instruct the Israelite people and say to them: When you enter the land of Canaan, this is the

---

ᵉ   *See note at Lev. 26.1.*

מִפּוּנֹ֖ן וַיַּחֲנ֥וּ בְּאֹבֹֽת׃ ⁴⁴ וַיִּסְע֖וּ מֵאֹבֹ֑ת וַֽיַּחֲנ֛וּ בְּעִיֵּ֥י הָעֲבָרִ֖ים בִּגְב֥וּל מוֹאָֽב׃ ⁴⁵ וַיִּסְע֖וּ מֵעִיִּ֑ים וַֽיַּחֲנ֖וּ בְּדִיבֹ֥ן גָּֽד׃ ⁴⁶ וַיִּסְעוּ֙ מִדִּיבֹ֣ן גָּ֔ד וַֽיַּחֲנ֖וּ בְּעַלְמֹ֥ן דִּבְלָתָֽיְמָה׃ ⁴⁷ וַיִּסְע֖וּ מֵעַלְמֹ֣ן דִּבְלָתָ֑יְמָה וַֽיַּחֲנ֛וּ בְּהָרֵ֥י הָעֲבָרִ֖ים לִפְנֵ֥י נְבֽוֹ׃ ⁴⁸ וַיִּסְע֖וּ מֵהָרֵ֣י הָעֲבָרִ֑ים וַֽיַּחֲנוּ֙ בְּעַרְבֹ֣ת מוֹאָ֔ב עַ֖ל יַרְדֵּ֥ן יְרֵחֽוֹ׃ ⁴⁹ וַיַּחֲנ֤וּ עַל־הַיַּרְדֵּן֙ מִבֵּ֣ית הַיְשִׁמֹ֔ת עַ֖ד אָבֵ֣ל הַשִּׁטִּ֑ים בְּעַרְבֹ֖ת מוֹאָֽב׃ ס

⁵⁰ וַיְדַבֵּ֧ר יְהֹוָ֛ה אֶל־מֹשֶׁ֖ה בְּעַרְבֹ֣ת מוֹאָ֑ב עַל־יַרְדֵּ֥ן יְרֵח֖וֹ לֵאמֹֽר׃ ⁵¹ דַּבֵּר֙ אֶל־בְּנֵ֣י יִשְׂרָאֵ֔ל וְאָמַרְתָּ֖ אֲלֵהֶ֑ם כִּ֥י אַתֶּ֛ם עֹבְרִ֥ים אֶת־הַיַּרְדֵּ֖ן אֶל־אֶ֥רֶץ כְּנָֽעַן׃ ⁵² וְה֣וֹרַשְׁתֶּ֗ם אֶת־כׇּל־יֹשְׁבֵ֤י הָאָ֙רֶץ֙ מִפְּנֵיכֶ֔ם וְאִבַּדְתֶּ֗ם אֵ֚ת כׇּל־מַשְׂכִּיֹּתָ֔ם וְאֵ֨ת כׇּל־צַלְמֵ֤י מַסֵּֽכֹתָם֙ תְּאַבֵּ֔דוּ וְאֵ֥ת כׇּל־בָּמֹתָ֖ם תַּשְׁמִֽידוּ׃ ⁵³ וְה֥וֹרַשְׁתֶּ֛ם אֶת־הָאָ֖רֶץ וִישַׁבְתֶּם־בָּ֑הּ כִּ֥י לָכֶ֛ם נָתַ֥תִּי אֶת־הָאָ֖רֶץ לָרֶ֥שֶׁת אֹתָֽהּ׃ ⁵⁴ וְהִתְנַחַלְתֶּם֩ אֶת־הָאָ֨רֶץ בְּגוֹרָ֜ל לְמִשְׁפְּחֹֽתֵיכֶ֗ם לָרַ֞ב תַּרְבּ֤וּ אֶת־נַחֲלָתוֹ֙ וְלַמְעַט֙ תַּמְעִ֣יט אֶת־נַחֲלָת֔וֹ אֶל֩ אֲשֶׁר־יֵ֨צֵא ל֥וֹ שָׁ֛מָּה הַגּוֹרָ֖ל ל֣וֹ יִהְיֶ֑ה לְמַטּ֥וֹת אֲבֹתֵיכֶ֖ם תִּתְנֶחָֽלוּ׃ ⁵⁵ וְאִם־לֹ֨א תוֹרִ֜ישׁוּ אֶת־יֹשְׁבֵ֣י הָאָרֶץ֮ מִפְּנֵיכֶם֒ וְהָיָ֗ה אֲשֶׁ֤ר תּוֹתִ֙ירוּ֙ מֵהֶ֔ם לְשִׂכִּים֙ בְּעֵ֣ינֵיכֶ֔ם וְלִצְנִינִ֖ם בְּצִדֵּיכֶ֑ם וְצָרְר֣וּ אֶתְכֶ֔ם עַל־הָאָ֕רֶץ אֲשֶׁ֥ר אַתֶּ֖ם יֹשְׁבִ֥ים בָּֽהּ׃ ⁵⁶ וְהָיָ֗ה כַּאֲשֶׁ֥ר דִּמִּ֛יתִי לַעֲשׂ֥וֹת לָהֶ֖ם אֶֽעֱשֶׂ֥ה לָכֶֽם׃ פ

לד

⁵⁰ וַיְדַבֵּ֥ר יְהֹוָ֖ה אֶל־מֹשֶׁ֥ה לֵּאמֹֽר׃ ² צַ֞ו אֶת־בְּנֵ֤י יִשְׂרָאֵל֙ וְאָמַרְתָּ֣ אֲלֵהֶ֔ם כִּֽי־אַתֶּ֥ם בָּאִ֖ים אֶל־הָאָ֣רֶץ כְּנָ֑עַן זֹ֣את הָאָ֗רֶץ

land that shall fall to you as your portion, the land of Canaan with its various boundaries:

[3]Your southern sector shall extend from the wilderness of Zin alongside Edom. Your southern boundary shall start on the east from the tip of the Dead Sea. [4]Your boundary shall then turn to pass south of the ascent of Akrabbim and continue to Zin, and its limits shall be south of Kadesh-barnea, reaching Hazar-addar and continuing to Azmon. [5]From Azmon the boundary shall turn toward the Wadi of Egypt and terminate at the Sea.[a]

[6]For the western boundary you shall have the coast of the Great Sea;[a] that shall serve as your western boundary.

[7]This shall be your northern boundary: Draw a line from the Great Sea to Mount Hor; [8]from Mount Hor draw a line to Lebo-hamath,[b] and let the boundary reach Zedad. [9]The boundary shall then run to Ziphron and terminate at Hazar-enan. That shall be your northern boundary.

[10]For your eastern boundary you shall draw a line from Hazar-enan to Shepham. [11]From Shepham the boundary shall descend to Riblah on the east side of Ain; from there the boundary shall continue downward and abut on the eastern slopes of the Sea of Chinnereth.[c] [12]The boundary shall then descend along the Jordan and terminate at the Dead Sea.

That shall be your land as defined by its boundaries on all sides.

[13]Moses instructed the Israelites, saying: This is the land you are to receive by lot as your hereditary portion, which the Lord has commanded to be given to the nine and a half tribes. [14]For the Reubenite tribe by its ancestral houses, the Gadite tribe by its ancestral houses, and the

אֲשֶׁר תִּפֹּל לָכֶם בְּנַחֲלָה אֶרֶץ כְּנַעַן לִגְבֻלֹתֶיהָ:

3 וְהָיָה לָכֶם פְּאַת־נֶגֶב מִמִּדְבַּר־צִן עַל־יְדֵי אֱדוֹם וְהָיָה לָכֶם גְּבוּל נֶגֶב מִקְצֵה יָם־הַמֶּלַח קֵדְמָה: 4 וְנָסַב לָכֶם הַגְּבוּל מִנֶּגֶב לְמַעֲלֵה עַקְרַבִּים וְעָבַר צִנָה והיה וְהָיוּ תּוֹצְאֹתָיו מִנֶּגֶב לְקָדֵשׁ בַּרְנֵעַ וְיָצָא חֲצַר־אַדָּר וְעָבַר עַצְמֹנָה: 5 וְנָסַב הַגְּבוּל מֵעַצְמוֹן נַחְלָה מִצְרָיִם וְהָיוּ תוֹצְאֹתָיו הַיָּמָּה:

6 וּגְבוּל יָם וְהָיָה לָכֶם הַיָּם הַגָּדוֹל וּגְבוּל זֶה־יִהְיֶה לָכֶם גְּבוּל יָם:

7 וְזֶה־יִהְיֶה לָכֶם גְּבוּל צָפוֹן מִן־הַיָּם הַגָּדֹל תְּתָאוּ לָכֶם הֹר הָהָר: 8 מֵהֹר הָהָר תְּתָאוּ לְבֹא חֲמָת וְהָיוּ תּוֹצְאֹת הַגְּבֻל צְדָדָה: 9 וְיָצָא הַגְּבֻל זִפְרֹנָה וְהָיוּ תוֹצְאֹתָיו חֲצַר עֵינָן זֶה־יִהְיֶה לָכֶם גְּבוּל צָפוֹן:

10 וְהִתְאַוִּיתֶם לָכֶם לִגְבוּל קֵדְמָה מֵחֲצַר עֵינָן שְׁפָמָה: 11 וְיָרַד הַגְּבֻל מִשְּׁפָם הָרִבְלָה מִקֶּדֶם לָעָיִן וְיָרַד הַגְּבֻל וּמָחָה עַל־כֶּתֶף יָם־כִּנֶּרֶת קֵדְמָה: 12 וְיָרַד הַגְּבוּל הַיַּרְדֵּנָה וְהָיוּ תוֹצְאֹתָיו יָם הַמֶּלַח זֹאת תִּהְיֶה לָכֶם הָאָרֶץ לִגְבֻלֹתֶיהָ סָבִיב:

13 וַיְצַו מֹשֶׁה אֶת־בְּנֵי יִשְׂרָאֵל לֵאמֹר זֹאת הָאָרֶץ אֲשֶׁר תִּתְנַחֲלוּ אֹתָהּ בְּגוֹרָל אֲשֶׁר צִוָּה יְהֹוָה לָתֵת לְתִשְׁעַת הַמַּטּוֹת וַחֲצִי הַמַּטֶּה: 14 כִּי לָקְחוּ מַטֵּה בְנֵי הָראוּבֵנִי לְבֵית אֲבֹתָם וּמַטֵּה בְנֵי־הַגָּדִי לְבֵית אֲבֹתָם וַחֲצִי מַטֵּה מְנַשֶּׁה לָקְחוּ נַחֲלָתָם:

---

a   I.e., the Mediterranean Sea.
b   See note at 13.21.
c   I.e., the Sea (or Lake) of Galilee.

half-tribe of Manasseh have already received their portions: 15those two and a half tribes have received their portions across the Jordan, opposite Jericho, on the east, the orient side.

16The LORD spoke to Moses, saying: 17These are the names of the men through whom the land shall be apportioned for you: Eleazar the priest and Joshua son of Nun. 18And you shall also take a chieftain from each tribe through whom the land shall be apportioned. 19These are the names of the men: from the tribe of Judah: Caleb son of Jephunneh. 20From the Simeonite tribe: Samuel*d* son of Ammihud. 21From the tribe of Benjamin: Elidad son of Chislon. 22From the Danite tribe: a chieftain, Bukki son of Jogli. 23For the descendants of Joseph: from the Manassite tribe: a chieftain, Hanniel son of Ephod; 24and from the Ephraimite tribe: a chieftain, Kemuel son of Shiphtan. 25From the Zebulunite tribe: a chieftain, Elizaphan son of Parnach. 26From the Issacharite tribe: a chieftain, Paltiel son of Azzan. 27From the Asherite tribe: a chieftain, Ahihud son of Shelomi. 28From the Naphtalite tribe: a chieftain, Pedahel son of Ammihud.

29It was these whom the LORD designated to allot portions to the Israelites in the land of Canaan.

35

The LORD spoke to Moses in the steppes of Moab at the Jordan near Jericho, saying: 2Instruct the Israelite people to assign, out of the holdings apportioned to them, towns for the Levites to dwell in; you shall also assign to the Levites pasture land around their towns. 3The towns shall be theirs to dwell in, and the pasture shall be for the cattle they own and all their other beasts. 4The town pasture that you are to assign to the Levites shall extend a thousand cubits

15 שְׁנֵי הַמַּטּוֹת וַחֲצִי הַמַּטֶּה לָקְחוּ נַחֲלָתָם
מֵעֵבֶר לְיַרְדֵּן יְרֵחוֹ קֵדְמָה מִזְרָחָה: פ
16 וַיְדַבֵּר יְהֹוָה אֶל־מֹשֶׁה לֵּאמֹר: 17 אֵלֶּה
שְׁמוֹת הָאֲנָשִׁים אֲשֶׁר־יִנְחֲלוּ לָכֶם אֶת־
הָאָרֶץ אֶלְעָזָר הַכֹּהֵן וִיהוֹשֻׁעַ בִּן־נוּן:
18 וְנָשִׂיא אֶחָד נָשִׂיא אֶחָד מִמַּטֶּה תִּקְחוּ
לִנְחֹל אֶת־הָאָרֶץ: 19 וְאֵלֶּה שְׁמוֹת
הָאֲנָשִׁים לְמַטֵּה יְהוּדָה כָּלֵב בֶּן־יְפֻנֶּה:
20 וּלְמַטֵּה בְּנֵי שִׁמְעוֹן שְׁמוּאֵל בֶּן־
עַמִּיהוּד: 21 לְמַטֵּה בִנְיָמִן אֱלִידָד בֶּן־
כִּסְלוֹן: 22 וּלְמַטֵּה בְנֵי־דָן נָשִׂיא בֻּקִּי בֶּן־
יָגְלִי: 23 לִבְנֵי יוֹסֵף לְמַטֵּה בְנֵי־מְנַשֶּׁה
נָשִׂיא חַנִּיאֵל בֶּן־אֵפֹד: 24 וּלְמַטֵּה בְנֵי־
אֶפְרַיִם נָשִׂיא קְמוּאֵל בֶּן־שִׁפְטָן:
25 וּלְמַטֵּה בְנֵי־זְבוּלֻן נָשִׂיא אֱלִיצָפָן בֶּן־
פַּרְנָךְ: 26 וּלְמַטֵּה בְנֵי־יִשָּׂשכָר נָשִׂיא
פַּלְטִיאֵל בֶּן־עַזָּן: 27 וּלְמַטֵּה בְנֵי־אָשֵׁר
נָשִׂיא אֲחִיהוּד בֶּן־שְׁלֹמִי: 28 וּלְמַטֵּה בְנֵי־
נַפְתָּלִי נָשִׂיא פְּדַהְאֵל בֶּן־עַמִּיהוּד:
29 אֵלֶּה אֲשֶׁר צִוָּה יְהֹוָה לְנַחֵל אֶת־בְּנֵי־
יִשְׂרָאֵל בְּאֶרֶץ כְּנָעַן: פ

לה וַיְדַבֵּר יְהֹוָה אֶל־מֹשֶׁה בְּעַרְבֹת
מוֹאָב עַל־יַרְדֵּן יְרֵחוֹ לֵאמֹר: 2 צַו אֶת־בְּנֵי
יִשְׂרָאֵל וְנָתְנוּ לַלְוִיִּם מִנַּחֲלַת אֲחֻזָּתָם
עָרִים לָשָׁבֶת וּמִגְרָשׁ לֶעָרִים סְבִיבֹתֵיהֶם
תִּתְּנוּ לַלְוִיִּם: 3 וְהָיוּ הֶעָרִים לָהֶם לָשָׁבֶת
וּמִגְרְשֵׁיהֶם יִהְיוּ לִבְהֶמְתָּם וְלִרְכֻשָׁם
וּלְכֹל חַיָּתָם: 4 וּמִגְרְשֵׁי הֶעָרִים אֲשֶׁר
תִּתְּנוּ לַלְוִיִּם מִקִּיר הָעִיר וָחוּצָה אֶלֶף

---

d   Or "Shemuel."

outside the town wall all around. ⁵You shall measure off two thousand cubits outside the town on the east side, two thousand on the south side, two thousand on the west side, and two thousand on the north side, with the town in the center. That shall be the pasture for their towns.

⁶The towns that you assign to the Levites shall comprise the six cities of refuge that you are to designate for a manslayer to flee to, to which you shall add forty-two towns. ⁷Thus the total of the towns that you assign to the Levites shall be forty-eight towns, with their pasture. ⁸In assigning towns from the holdings of the Israelites, take more from the larger groups and less from the smaller, so that each assigns towns to the Levites in proportion to the share it receives.

⁹The Lord spoke further to Moses: ¹⁰Speak to the Israelite people and say to them: When you cross the Jordan into the land of Canaan, ¹¹you shall provide yourselves with places to serve you as cities of refuge to which a manslayer who has killed a person unintentionally may flee. ¹²The cities shall serve you as a refuge from the avenger,ᵃ so that the manslayer may not die unless he has stood trial before the assembly. ¹³The towns that you thus assign shall be six cities of refuge in all. ¹⁴Three cities shall be designated beyond the Jordan, and the other three shall be designated in the land of Canaan: they shall serve as cities of refuge. ¹⁵These six cities shall serve the Israelites and the resident aliens among them for refuge, so that anyone who kills a person unintentionally may flee there.

¹⁶Anyone, however, who strikes another with an iron object so that death results is a murderer; the murderer must be put to death. ¹⁷If he struck him with a stone toolᵇ that could cause death,

אַמָּה סָבִיב: 5 וּמַדֹּתֶם מִחוּץ לָעִיר אֶת־
פְּאַת־קֵדְמָה אַלְפַּיִם בָּאַמָּה וְאֶת־פְּאַת־
נֶגֶב אַלְפַּיִם בָּאַמָּה וְאֶת־פְּאַת־יָם |
אַלְפַּיִם בָּאַמָּה וְאֵת פְּאַת צָפוֹן אַלְפַּיִם
בָּאַמָּה וְהָעִיר בַּתָּוֶךְ זֶה יִהְיֶה לָהֶם מִגְרְשֵׁי
הֶעָרִים:
6 וְאֵת הֶעָרִים אֲשֶׁר תִּתְּנוּ לַלְוִיִּם אֵת
שֵׁשׁ־עָרֵי הַמִּקְלָט אֲשֶׁר תִּתְּנוּ לָנֻס שָׁמָּה
הָרֹצֵחַ וַעֲלֵיהֶם תִּתְּנוּ אַרְבָּעִים וּשְׁתַּיִם
עִיר: 7 כָּל־הֶעָרִים אֲשֶׁר תִּתְּנוּ לַלְוִיִּם
אַרְבָּעִים וּשְׁמֹנֶה עִיר אֶתְהֶן וְאֶת־
מִגְרְשֵׁיהֶן: 8 וְהֶעָרִים אֲשֶׁר תִּתְּנוּ מֵאֲחֻזַּת
בְּנֵי־יִשְׂרָאֵל מֵאֵת הָרַב תַּרְבּוּ וּמֵאֵת
הַמְעַט תַּמְעִיטוּ אִישׁ כְּפִי נַחֲלָתוֹ אֲשֶׁר
יִנְחָלוּ יִתֵּן מֵעָרָיו לַלְוִיִּם: פ

9 וַיְדַבֵּר יְהוָה אֶל־מֹשֶׁה לֵּאמֹר: 10 דַּבֵּר
אֶל־בְּנֵי יִשְׂרָאֵל וְאָמַרְתָּ אֲלֵהֶם כִּי
אַתֶּם עֹבְרִים אֶת־הַיַּרְדֵּן אַרְצָה כְּנָעַן:
11 וְהִקְרִיתֶם לָכֶם עָרִים עָרֵי מִקְלָט
תִּהְיֶינָה לָכֶם וְנָס שָׁמָּה רֹצֵחַ מַכֵּה־נֶפֶשׁ
בִּשְׁגָגָה: 12 וְהָיוּ לָכֶם הֶעָרִים לְמִקְלָט
מִגֹּאֵל וְלֹא יָמוּת הָרֹצֵחַ עַד־עָמְדוֹ לִפְנֵי
הָעֵדָה לַמִּשְׁפָּט:
13 וְהֶעָרִים אֲשֶׁר תִּתֵּנוּ שֵׁשׁ־עָרֵי מִקְלָט
תִּהְיֶינָה לָכֶם: 14 אֵת | שְׁלֹשׁ הֶעָרִים תִּתְּנוּ
מֵעֵבֶר לַיַּרְדֵּן וְאֵת שְׁלֹשׁ הֶעָרִים תִּתְּנוּ
בְּאֶרֶץ כְּנָעַן עָרֵי מִקְלָט תִּהְיֶינָה: 15 לִבְנֵי
יִשְׂרָאֵל וְלַגֵּר וְלַתּוֹשָׁב בְּתוֹכָם תִּהְיֶינָה
שֵׁשׁ־הֶעָרִים הָאֵלֶּה לְמִקְלָט לָנוּס שָׁמָּה
כָּל־מַכֵּה־נֶפֶשׁ בִּשְׁגָגָה:
16 וְאִם־בִּכְלִי בַרְזֶל | הִכָּהוּ וַיָּמֹת רֹצֵחַ
הוּא מוֹת יוּמַת הָרֹצֵחַ: 17 וְאִם בְּאֶבֶן יָד
אֲשֶׁר־יָמוּת בָּהּ הִכָּהוּ וַיָּמֹת רֹצֵחַ הוּא

ᵃ Lit. "redeemer," i.e., next of kin; cf. note at Lev. 25.25.
ᵇ Lit. "of the hand."

and death resulted, he is a murderer; the murderer must be put to death. [18]Similarly, if the object with which he struck him was a wooden tool[b] that could cause death, and death resulted, he is a murderer; the murderer must be put to death. [19]The blood-avenger himself shall put the murderer to death; it is he who shall put him to death upon encounter. [20]So, too, if he pushed him in hate or hurled something at him on purpose and death resulted, [21]or if he struck him with his hand in enmity and death resulted, the assailant shall be put to death; he is a murderer. The blood-avenger shall put the murderer to death upon encounter.

[22]But if he pushed him without malice aforethought or hurled any object at him unintentionally, [23]or inadvertently[c] dropped upon him any deadly object of stone, and death resulted—though he was not an enemy of his and did not seek his harm—[24]in such cases the assembly shall decide between the slayer and the blood-avenger. [25]The assembly shall protect the manslayer from the blood-avenger, and the assembly shall restore him to the city of refuge to which he fled, and there he shall remain until the death of the high priest who was anointed with the sacred oil. [26]But if the manslayer ever goes outside the limits of the city of refuge to which he has fled, [27]and the blood-avenger comes upon him outside the limits of his city of refuge, and the blood-avenger kills the manslayer, there is no bloodguilt on his account. [28]For he must remain inside his city of refuge until the death of the high priest; after the death of the high priest, the manslayer may return to his land holding.

[29]Such shall be your law of procedure throughout the ages in all your settlements.

[30]If anyone kills a person, the manslayer may be executed only on the evidence of witnesses;

מ֣וֹת יוּמַ֣ת הָרֹצֵ֑חַ׃ 18 א֡וֹ בִּכְלִי֩ עֵֽץ־יָ֨ד אֲשֶׁר־יָמ֥וּת בּ֛וֹ הִכָּ֖הוּ וַיָּמֹ֑ת רֹצֵ֣חַ ה֔וּא מ֥וֹת יוּמַ֖ת הָרֹצֵֽחַ׃ 19 גֹּאֵ֣ל הַדָּ֔ם ה֥וּא יָמִ֖ית אֶת־הָרֹצֵ֑חַ בְּפִגְעוֹ־ב֖וֹ ה֥וּא יְמִיתֶֽנּוּ׃ 20 וְאִם־בְּשִׂנְאָ֖ה יֶהְדֳּפֶ֑נּוּ אֽוֹ־הִשְׁלִ֥יךְ עָלָ֛יו בִּצְדִיָּ֖ה וַיָּמֹֽת׃ 21 א֣וֹ בְאֵיבָ֞ה הִכָּ֤הוּ בְיָדוֹ֙ וַיָּמֹ֔ת מֽוֹת־יוּמַ֥ת הַמַּכֶּ֖ה רֹצֵ֣חַ ה֑וּא גֹּאֵ֣ל הַדָּ֗ם יָמִ֛ית אֶת־הָרֹצֵ֖חַ בְּפִגְעוֹ־בֽוֹ׃ 22 וְאִם־בְּפֶ֥תַע בְּלֹא־אֵיבָ֖ה הֲדָפ֑וֹ אֽוֹ־הִשְׁלִ֥יךְ עָלָ֛יו כָּל־כְּלִ֖י בְּלֹ֥א צְדִיָּֽה׃ 23 א֣וֹ בְכָל־אֶ֜בֶן אֲשֶׁר־יָמ֥וּת בָּהּ֙ בְּלֹ֣א רְא֔וֹת וַיַּפֵּ֥ל עָלָ֖יו וַיָּמֹ֑ת וְהוּא֙ לֹֽא־אוֹיֵ֣ב ל֔וֹ וְלֹ֥א מְבַקֵּ֖שׁ רָעָתֽוֹ׃ 24 וְשָֽׁפְטוּ֙ הָֽעֵדָ֔ה בֵּ֚ין הַמַּכֶּ֔ה וּבֵ֖ין גֹּאֵ֣ל הַדָּ֑ם עַ֥ל הַמִּשְׁפָּטִ֖ים הָאֵֽלֶּה׃ 25 וְהִצִּ֨ילוּ הָעֵדָ֜ה אֶת־הָרֹצֵ֗חַ מִיַּד֮ גֹּאֵ֣ל הַדָּם֒ וְהֵשִׁ֤יבוּ אֹתוֹ֙ הָֽעֵדָ֔ה אֶל־עִ֥יר מִקְלָט֖וֹ אֲשֶׁר־נָ֣ס שָׁ֑מָּה וְיָ֣שַׁב בָּ֗הּ עַד־מוֹת֙ הַכֹּהֵ֣ן הַגָּדֹ֔ל אֲשֶׁר־מָשַׁ֥ח אֹת֖וֹ בְּשֶׁ֥מֶן הַקֹּֽדֶשׁ׃ 26 וְאִם־יָצֹ֥א יֵצֵ֖א הָרֹצֵ֑חַ אֶת־גְּבוּל֙ עִ֣יר מִקְלָט֔וֹ אֲשֶׁ֥ר יָנ֖וּס שָֽׁמָּה׃ 27 וּמָצָ֤א אֹתוֹ֙ גֹּאֵ֣ל הַדָּ֔ם מִח֕וּץ לִגְב֖וּל עִ֣יר מִקְלָט֑וֹ וְרָצַ֞ח גֹּאֵ֤ל הַדָּם֙ אֶת־הָ֣רֹצֵ֔חַ אֵ֥ין ל֖וֹ דָּֽם׃ 28 כִּ֣י בְעִ֤יר מִקְלָטוֹ֙ יֵשֵׁ֔ב עַד־מ֖וֹת הַכֹּהֵ֣ן הַגָּדֹ֑ל וְאַֽחֲרֵ֥י מוֹת֙ הַכֹּהֵ֣ן הַגָּדֹ֔ל יָשׁוּב֙ הָֽרֹצֵ֔חַ אֶל־אֶ֖רֶץ אֲחֻזָּתֽוֹ׃ 29 וְהָי֨וּ אֵ֧לֶּה לָכֶ֛ם לְחֻקַּ֥ת מִשְׁפָּ֖ט לְדֹרֹֽתֵיכֶ֑ם בְּכֹ֖ל מֽוֹשְׁבֹֽתֵיכֶֽם׃ 30 כָּל־מַ֨כֵּה־נֶ֔פֶשׁ לְפִ֣י עֵדִ֔ים יִרְצַ֖ח אֶת־הָֽרֹצֵ֑חַ וְעֵ֣ד אֶחָ֔ד לֹא־יַֽעֲנֶ֥ה בְנֶ֖פֶשׁ לָמֽוּת׃

---

c   *Lit. "without seeing."*

the testimony of a single witness against a person shall not suffice for a sentence of death. [31]You may not accept a ransom for the life of a murderer who is guilty of a capital crime; he must be put to death. [32]Nor may you accept ransom in lieu of flight to a city of refuge, enabling one to return to live on his land before the death of the priest. [33]You shall not pollute the land in which you live; for blood pollutes the land, and the land can have no expiation for blood that is shed on it, except by the blood of him who shed it. [34]You shall not defile the land in which you live, in which I Myself abide, for I the Lord abide among the Israelite people.

36

The family heads in the clan of the descendants of Gilead son of Machir son of Manasseh, one of the Josephite clans, came forward and appealed to Moses and the chieftains, family heads[a] of the Israelites. [2]They said, "The Lord commanded my lord to assign the land to the Israelites as shares by lot, and my lord was further commanded by the Lord to assign the share of our kinsman Zelophehad to his daughters. [3]Now, if they marry persons from another Israelite tribe, their share will be cut off from our ancestral portion and be added to the portion of the tribe into which they marry; thus our allotted portion will be diminished. [4]And even when the Israelites observe the jubilee, their share will be added to that of the tribe into which they marry, and their share will be cut off from the ancestral portion of our tribe."

[5]So Moses, at the Lord's bidding, instructed the Israelites, saying: "The plea of the Josephite tribe is just. [6]This is what the Lord has commanded concerning the daughters of Zelophehad: They may marry anyone they wish, provided they marry into a clan of their father's

a   I.e., tribal heads.

31 וְלֹא־תִקְח֤וּ כֹ֙פֶר֙ לְנֶ֣פֶשׁ רֹצֵ֔חַ אֲשֶׁר־ה֥וּא רָשָׁ֖ע לָמ֑וּת כִּי־מ֖וֹת יוּמָֽת: 32 וְלֹא־תִקְח֣וּ כֹ֗פֶר לָנ֨וּס אֶל־עִ֣יר מִקְלָט֔וֹ לָשׁוּב֙ לָשֶׁ֣בֶת בָּאָ֔רֶץ עַד־מ֖וֹת הַכֹּהֵֽן: 33 וְלֹא־תַחֲנִ֣יפוּ אֶת־הָאָ֗רֶץ אֲשֶׁ֤ר אַתֶּם֙ בָּ֔הּ כִּ֣י הַדָּ֗ם ה֚וּא יַחֲנִ֣יף אֶת־הָאָ֔רֶץ וְלָאָ֣רֶץ לֹֽא־יְכֻפַּ֗ר לַדָּם֙ אֲשֶׁ֣ר שֻׁפַּךְ־בָּ֔הּ כִּי־אִ֖ם בְּדַ֥ם שֹׁפְכֽוֹ: 34 וְלֹ֧א תְטַמֵּ֣א אֶת־הָאָ֗רֶץ אֲשֶׁ֤ר אַתֶּם֙ יֹשְׁבִ֣ים בָּ֔הּ אֲשֶׁ֥ר אֲנִ֖י שֹׁכֵ֣ן בְּתוֹכָ֑הּ כִּ֚י אֲנִ֣י יְהֹוָ֔ה שֹׁכֵ֕ן בְּת֖וֹךְ בְּנֵ֥י יִשְׂרָאֵֽל: פ

לו 1 וַיִּקְרְב֞וּ רָאשֵׁ֣י הָֽאָב֗וֹת לְמִשְׁפַּ֜חַת בְּנֵֽי־גִלְעָ֣ד בֶּן־מָכִ֣יר בֶּן־מְנַשֶּׁ֗ה מִֽמִּשְׁפְּחֹ֖ת בְּנֵ֣י יוֹסֵ֑ף וַֽיְדַבְּר֞וּ לִפְנֵ֤י מֹשֶׁה֙ וְלִפְנֵ֣י הַנְּשִׂאִ֔ים רָאשֵׁ֥י אָב֖וֹת לִבְנֵ֥י יִשְׂרָאֵֽל: 2 וַיֹּאמְר֗וּ אֶת־אֲדֹנִי֙ צִוָּ֣ה יְהֹוָ֔ה לָתֵ֨ת אֶת־הָאָ֧רֶץ בְּנַחֲלָ֛ה בְּגוֹרָ֖ל לִבְנֵ֣י יִשְׂרָאֵ֑ל וַֽאדֹנִי֙ צֻוָּ֣ה בַֽיהֹוָ֔ה לָתֵ֗ת אֶֽת־נַחֲלַ֛ת צְלָפְחָ֥ד אָחִ֖ינוּ לִבְנֹתָֽיו: 3 וְ֠הָי֠וּ לְאֶחָ֞ד מִבְּנֵ֨י שִׁבְטֵ֤י בְנֵֽי־יִשְׂרָאֵל֙ לְנָשִׁ֔ים וְנִגְרְעָ֤ה נַחֲלָתָן֙ מִנַּחֲלַ֣ת אֲבֹתֵ֔ינוּ וְנוֹסַ֕ף עַ֖ל נַחֲלַ֣ת הַמַּטֶּ֑ה אֲשֶׁ֥ר תִּהְיֶ֖ינָה לָהֶ֑ם וּמִגֹּרַ֥ל נַחֲלָתֵ֖נוּ יִגָּרֵֽעַ: 4 וְאִם־יִהְיֶ֣ה הַיֹּבֵל֮ לִבְנֵ֣י יִשְׂרָאֵל֒ וְנֽוֹסְפָה֙ נַחֲלָתָ֔ן עַ֚ל נַחֲלַ֣ת הַמַּטֶּ֔ה אֲשֶׁ֥ר תִּהְיֶ֖ינָה לָהֶ֑ם וּמִֽנַּחֲלַת֙ מַטֵּ֣ה אֲבֹתֵ֔ינוּ יִגָּרַ֖ע נַחֲלָתָֽן: 5 וַיְצַ֤ו מֹשֶׁה֙ אֶת־בְּנֵ֣י יִשְׂרָאֵ֔ל עַל־פִּ֥י יְהֹוָ֖ה לֵאמֹ֑ר כֵּ֛ן מַטֵּ֥ה בְנֵֽי־יוֹסֵ֖ף דֹּבְרִֽים: 6 זֶ֣ה הַדָּבָ֞ר אֲשֶׁר־צִוָּ֣ה יְהֹוָ֗ה לִבְנ֤וֹת צְלָפְחָד֙ לֵאמֹ֔ר לַטּ֧וֹב בְּעֵינֵיהֶ֛ם תִּהְיֶ֖ינָה לְנָשִׁ֑ים אַ֗ךְ לְמִשְׁפַּ֛חַת מַטֵּ֥ה אֲבִיהֶ֖ם תִּהְיֶ֥ינָה לְנָשִֽׁים: 7 וְלֹֽא־תִסֹּ֤ב נַחֲלָה֙ לִבְנֵ֣י יִשְׂרָאֵ֔ל

tribe. 7No inheritance of the Israelites may pass over from one tribe to another, but the Israelites must remain bound each to the ancestral portion of his tribe. 8Every daughter among the Israelite tribes who inherits a share must marry someone from a clan of her father's tribe, in order that every Israelite may keep his ancestral share. 9Thus no inheritance shall pass over from one tribe to another, but the Israelite tribes shall remain bound each to its portion."

10The daughters of Zelophehad did as the LORD had commanded Moses: 11Mahlah, Tirzah, Hoglah, Milcah, and Noah, Zelophehad's daughters, were married to sons of their uncles, 12marrying into clans of descendants of Manasseh son of Joseph; and so their share remained in the tribe of their father's clan.

13These are the commandments and regulations that the LORD enjoined upon the Israelites, through Moses, on the steppes of Moab, at the Jordan near Jericho.

מִמַּטֶּה אֶל־מַטֶּה כִּי אִישׁ בְּנַחֲלַת מַטֵּה אֲבֹתָיו יִדְבְּקוּ בְּנֵי יִשְׂרָאֵל: 8 וְכָל־בַּת יֹרֶשֶׁת נַחֲלָה מִמַּטּוֹת בְּנֵי יִשְׂרָאֵל לְאֶחָד מִמִּשְׁפַּחַת מַטֵּה אָבִיהָ תִּהְיֶה לְאִשָּׁה לְמַעַן יִירְשׁוּ בְּנֵי יִשְׂרָאֵל אִישׁ נַחֲלַת אֲבֹתָיו: 9 וְלֹא־תִסֹּב נַחֲלָה מִמַּטֶּה לְמַטֶּה אַחֵר כִּי־אִישׁ בְּנַחֲלָתוֹ יִדְבְּקוּ מַטּוֹת בְּנֵי יִשְׂרָאֵל:

10 כַּאֲשֶׁר צִוָּה יְהוָה אֶת־מֹשֶׁה כֵּן עָשׂוּ בְּנוֹת צְלָפְחָד: 11 וַתִּהְיֶינָה מַחְלָה תִרְצָה וְחָגְלָה וּמִלְכָּה וְנֹעָה בְּנוֹת צְלָפְחָד לִבְנֵי דֹדֵיהֶן לְנָשִׁים: 12 מִמִּשְׁפְּחֹת בְּנֵי־מְנַשֶּׁה בֶן־יוֹסֵף הָיוּ לְנָשִׁים וַתְּהִי נַחֲלָתָן עַל־מַטֵּה מִשְׁפַּחַת אֲבִיהֶן:

13 אֵלֶּה הַמִּצְוֹת וְהַמִּשְׁפָּטִים אֲשֶׁר צִוָּה יְהוָה בְּיַד־מֹשֶׁה אֶל־בְּנֵי יִשְׂרָאֵל בְּעַרְבֹת מוֹאָב עַל יַרְדֵּן יְרֵחוֹ: *

תם ונשלם תהילה לאל בורא עולם

DEUTERONOMY

1 DEVARIM

These are the words that Moses addressed to all Israel on the other side of the Jordan.—[a]Through the wilderness, in the Arabah near Suph, between Paran and Tophel, Laban, Hazeroth, and Di-zahab, [2]it is eleven days from Horeb to Kadesh-barnea by the Mount Seir route.—[3]It was in the fortieth year, on the first day of the eleventh month, that Moses addressed the Israelites in accordance with the instructions that the LORD had given him for them, [4]after he had defeated Sihon king of the Amorites, who dwelt in Heshbon, and King Og of Bashan, who dwelt at Ashtaroth [and[b]] Edrei. [5]On the other side of the Jordan, in the land of Moab, Moses undertook to expound this Teaching. He said:

[6]The LORD our God spoke to us at Horeb, saying: You have stayed long enough at this mountain. [7]Start out and make your way to the hill country of the Amorites and to all their neighbors in the Arabah, the hill country, the Shephelah,[c] the Negeb, the seacoast, the land of the Canaanites,[d] and the Lebanon, as far as the Great River, the river Euphrates. [8]See, I place the land at your disposal. Go, take possession of the land that the LORD swore to your fathers, Abraham, Isaac, and Jacob, to assign to them and to their heirs after them.

[9]Thereupon I said to you, "I cannot bear the burden of you by myself. [10]The LORD your God has multiplied you until you are today as nu-

---

a The rest of this verse and v. 2 are unclear; cf. v. 19 and Num. 33.16–36.
b Cf. Josh. 12.4; 13.12, 31.
c Others "Lowland."
d I.e., Phoenicia.

דברים

א אֵלֶּה הַדְּבָרִים אֲשֶׁר דִּבֶּר מֹשֶׁה אֶל־כָּל־יִשְׂרָאֵל בְּעֵבֶר הַיַּרְדֵּן בַּמִּדְבָּר בָּעֲרָבָה מוֹל סוּף בֵּין־פָּארָן וּבֵין־תֹּפֶל וְלָבָן וַחֲצֵרֹת וְדִי זָהָב: 2 אַחַד עָשָׂר יוֹם מֵחֹרֵב דֶּרֶךְ הַר־שֵׂעִיר עַד קָדֵשׁ בַּרְנֵעַ: 3 וַיְהִי בְּאַרְבָּעִים שָׁנָה בְּעַשְׁתֵּי־עָשָׂר חֹדֶשׁ בְּאֶחָד לַחֹדֶשׁ דִּבֶּר מֹשֶׁה אֶל־בְּנֵי יִשְׂרָאֵל כְּכֹל אֲשֶׁר צִוָּה יְהוָה אֹתוֹ אֲלֵהֶם: 4 אַחֲרֵי הַכֹּתוֹ אֵת סִיחֹן מֶלֶךְ הָאֱמֹרִי אֲשֶׁר יוֹשֵׁב בְּחֶשְׁבּוֹן וְאֵת עוֹג מֶלֶךְ הַבָּשָׁן אֲשֶׁר־יוֹשֵׁב בְּעַשְׁתָּרֹת בְּאֶדְרֶעִי: 5 בְּעֵבֶר הַיַּרְדֵּן בְּאֶרֶץ מוֹאָב הוֹאִיל מֹשֶׁה בֵּאֵר אֶת־הַתּוֹרָה הַזֹּאת לֵאמֹר:

6 יְהוָה אֱלֹהֵינוּ דִּבֶּר אֵלֵינוּ בְּחֹרֵב לֵאמֹר רַב־לָכֶם שֶׁבֶת בָּהָר הַזֶּה: 7 פְּנוּ | וּסְעוּ לָכֶם וּבֹאוּ הַר הָאֱמֹרִי וְאֶל־כָּל־שְׁכֵנָיו בָּעֲרָבָה בָהָר וּבַשְּׁפֵלָה וּבַנֶּגֶב וּבְחוֹף הַיָּם אֶרֶץ הַכְּנַעֲנִי וְהַלְּבָנוֹן עַד־הַנָּהָר הַגָּדֹל נְהַר־פְּרָת: 8 רְאֵה נָתַתִּי לִפְנֵיכֶם אֶת־הָאָרֶץ בֹּאוּ וּרְשׁוּ אֶת־הָאָרֶץ אֲשֶׁר נִשְׁבַּע יְהוָה לַאֲבֹתֵיכֶם לְאַבְרָהָם לְיִצְחָק וּלְיַעֲקֹב לָתֵת לָהֶם וּלְזַרְעָם אַחֲרֵיהֶם: 9 וָאֹמַר אֲלֵכֶם בָּעֵת הַהִוא לֵאמֹר לֹא־אוּכַל לְבַדִּי שְׂאֵת אֶתְכֶם: 10 יְהוָה אֱלֹהֵיכֶם הִרְבָּה אֶתְכֶם וְהִנְּכֶם הַיּוֹם

merous as the stars in the sky.—11May the LORD, the God of your fathers, increase your numbers a thousandfold, and bless you as He promised you.—12How can I bear unaided the trouble of you, and the burden, and the bickering! 13Pick from each of your tribes men who are wise, discerning, and experienced, and I will appoint them as your heads." 14You answered me and said, "What you propose to do is good." 15So I took your tribal leaders, wise and experienced men, and appointed them heads over you: chiefs of thousands, chiefs of hundreds, chiefs of fifties, and chiefs of tens, and officials for your tribes. 16I charged your magistrates at that time as follows, "Hear out your fellow men, and decide justly between any man and a fellow Israelite or a stranger. 17You shall not be partial in judgment: hear out low and high alike. Fear no man, for judgment is God's. And any matter that is too difficult for you, you shall bring to me and I will hear it." 18Thus I instructed you, at that time, about the various things that you should do.

19We set out from Horeb and traveled the great and terrible wilderness that you saw, along the road to the hill country of the Amorites, as the LORD our God had commanded us. When we reached Kadesh-barnea, 20I said to you, "You have come to the hill country of the Amorites which the LORD our God is giving to us. 21See, the LORD your God has placed the land at your disposal. Go up, take possession, as the LORD, the God of your fathers, promised you. Fear not and be not dismayed."

22Then all of you came to me and said, "Let us send men ahead to reconnoiter the land for us and bring back word on the route we shall follow and the cities we shall come to." 23I approved of the plan, and so I selected twelve of your men, one from each tribe. 24They made for the hill country, came to the wadi Eshcol,

כְּכוֹכְבֵי הַשָּׁמַיִם לָרֹב: 11 יְהֹוָה אֱלֹהֵי אֲבֽוֹתֵכֶם יֹסֵף עֲלֵיכֶם כָּכֶם אֶלֶף פְּעָמִים וִיבָרֵךְ אֶתְכֶם כַּאֲשֶׁר דִּבֶּר לָכֶם: 12 אֵיכָה אֶשָּׂא לְבַדִּי טָרְחֲכֶם וּמַשַּׂאֲכֶם וְרִיבְכֶם: 13 הָבוּ לָכֶם אֲנָשִׁים חֲכָמִים וּנְבֹנִים וִידֻעִים לְשִׁבְטֵיכֶם וַאֲשִׂימֵם בְּרָאשֵׁיכֶם: 14 וַתַּעֲנוּ אֹתִי וַתֹּאמְרוּ טֽוֹב־הַדָּבָר אֲשֶׁר־ דִּבַּרְתָּ לַעֲשֽׂוֹת: 15 וָאֶקַּח אֶת־רָאשֵׁי שִׁבְטֵיכֶם אֲנָשִׁים חֲכָמִים וִידֻעִים וָאֶתֵּן אֹתָם רָאשִׁים עֲלֵיכֶם שָׂרֵי אֲלָפִים וְשָׂרֵי מֵאוֹת וְשָׂרֵי חֲמִשִּׁים וְשָׂרֵי עֲשָׂרֹת וְשֹׁטְרִים לְשִׁבְטֵיכֶם: 16 וָאֲצַוֶּה אֶת־ שֹׁפְטֵיכֶם בָּעֵת הַהִוא לֵאמֹר שָׁמֹעַ בֵּין־ אֲחֵיכֶם וּשְׁפַטְתֶּם צֶדֶק בֵּין־אִישׁ וּבֵין־ אָחִיו וּבֵין גֵּרֽוֹ: 17 לֹא־תַכִּירוּ פָנִים בַּמִּשְׁפָּט כַּקָּטֹן כַּגָּדֹל תִּשְׁמָעוּן לֹא תָגוּרוּ מִפְּנֵי־אִישׁ כִּי הַמִּשְׁפָּט לֵאלֹהִים הוּא וְהַדָּבָר אֲשֶׁר יִקְשֶׁה מִכֶּם תַּקְרִבוּן אֵלַי וּשְׁמַעְתִּֽיו: 18 וָאֲצַוֶּה אֶתְכֶם בָּעֵת הַהִוא אֵת כָּל־הַדְּבָרִים אֲשֶׁר תַּעֲשֽׂוּן: 19 וַנִּסַּע מֵחֹרֵב וַנֵּלֶךְ אֵת כָּל־הַמִּדְבָּר הַגָּדוֹל וְהַנּוֹרָא הַהוּא אֲשֶׁר רְאִיתֶם דֶּרֶךְ הַר הָאֱמֹרִי כַּאֲשֶׁר צִוָּה יְהֹוָה אֱלֹהֵינוּ אֹתָנוּ וַנָּבֹא עַד קָדֵשׁ בַּרְנֵעַ: 20 וָאֹמַר אֲלֵכֶם בָּאתֶם עַד־הַר הָאֱמֹרִי אֲשֶׁר־יְהֹוָה אֱלֹהֵינוּ נֹתֵן לָנוּ: 21 רְאֵה נָתַן יְהֹוָה אֱלֹהֶיךָ לְפָנֶיךָ אֶת־הָאָרֶץ עֲלֵה רֵשׁ כַּאֲשֶׁר דִּבֶּר יְהֹוָה אֱלֹהֵי אֲבֹתֶיךָ לָךְ אַל־תִּירָא וְאַל־ תֵּחָֽת: 22 וַתִּקְרְבוּן אֵלַי כֻּלְּכֶם וַתֹּאמְרוּ נִשְׁלְחָה אֲנָשִׁים לְפָנֵינוּ וְיַחְפְּרוּ־לָנוּ אֶת־הָאָרֶץ וְיָשִׁבוּ אֹתָנוּ דָּבָר אֶת־הַדֶּרֶךְ אֲשֶׁר נַעֲלֶה־ בָּהּ וְאֵת הֶעָרִים אֲשֶׁר נָבֹא אֲלֵיהֶן: 23 וַיִּיטַב בְּעֵינַי הַדָּבָר וָאֶקַּח מִכֶּם שְׁנֵים עָשָׂר אֲנָשִׁים אִישׁ אֶחָד לַשָּׁבֶט: 24 וַיִּפְנוּ וַיַּעֲלוּ הָהָרָה וַיָּבֹאוּ עַד־נַחַל אֶשְׁכֹּל

and spied it out. 25They took some of the fruit of the land with them and brought it down to us. And they gave us this report: "It is a good land that the LORD our God is giving to us."

26Yet you refused to go up, and flouted the command of the LORD your God. 27You sulked[e] in your tents and said, "It is because the LORD hates us that He brought us out of the land of Egypt, to hand us over to the Amorites to wipe us out. 28-f What kind of place-f are we going to? Our kinsmen have taken the heart out of us, saying, 'We saw there a people stronger and taller than we, large cities with walls sky-high, and even Anakites.'"

29I said to you, "Have no dread or fear of them. 30None other than the LORD your God, who goes before you, will fight for you, just as He did for you in Egypt before your very eyes, 31and in the wilderness, where you saw how the LORD your God carried you, as a man carries his son, all the way that you traveled until you came to this place. 32Yet for all that, you have no faith in the LORD your God, 33who goes before you on your journeys—to scout the place where you are to encamp—in fire by night and in cloud by day, in order to guide you on the route you are to follow."

34When the LORD heard your loud complaint, He was angry. He vowed: 35Not one of these men, this evil generation, shall see the good land that I swore to give to your fathers—36none except Caleb son of Jephunneh; he shall see it, and to him and his descendants will I give the land on which he set foot, because he remained loyal to the LORD.

37Because of you the LORD was incensed with me too, and He said: You shall not enter it either. 38Joshua son of Nun, who attends you, he shall enter it. Imbue him with strength, for he shall allot it to Israel. 39Moreover, your little ones

---

וַיְרַגְּל֖וּ אֹתָֽהּ׃ 25 וַיִּקְח֤וּ בְיָדָם֙ מִפְּרִ֣י הָאָ֔רֶץ
וַיּוֹרִ֖דוּ אֵלֵ֑ינוּ וַיָּשִׁ֨בוּ אֹתָ֤נוּ דָבָר֙ וַיֹּ֣אמְר֔וּ
טוֹבָ֣ה הָאָ֔רֶץ אֲשֶׁר־יְהֹוָ֥ה אֱלֹהֵ֖ינוּ נֹתֵ֥ן לָֽנוּ׃
26 וְלֹ֥א אֲבִיתֶ֖ם לַעֲלֹ֑ת וַתַּמְר֕וּ אֶת־פִּ֖י
יְהֹוָ֥ה אֱלֹהֵיכֶֽם׃ 27 וַתֵּרָגְנ֤וּ בְאׇהֳלֵיכֶם֙
וַתֹּ֣אמְר֔וּ בְּשִׂנְאַ֤ת יְהֹוָה֙ אֹתָ֔נוּ הוֹצִיאָ֖נוּ
מֵאֶ֣רֶץ מִצְרָ֑יִם לָתֵ֥ת אֹתָ֛נוּ בְּיַ֥ד הָאֱמֹרִ֖י
לְהַשְׁמִידֵֽנוּ׃ 28 אָנָ֣ה ׀ אֲנַ֣חְנוּ עֹלִ֗ים אַחֵ֩ינוּ֩
הֵמַ֨סּוּ אֶת־לְבָבֵ֜נוּ לֵאמֹ֗ר עַ֣ם גָּד֤וֹל וָרָם֙
מִמֶּ֔נּוּ עָרִ֛ים גְּדֹלֹ֥ת וּבְצוּרֹ֖ת בַּשָּׁמָ֑יִם וְגַם־
בְּנֵ֥י עֲנָקִ֖ים רָאִ֥ינוּ שָֽׁם׃
29 וָאֹמַ֖ר אֲלֵכֶ֑ם לֹא־תַֽעַרְצ֥וּן וְֽלֹא־תִֽירְא֖וּן
מֵהֶֽם׃ 30 יְהֹוָ֤ה אֱלֹֽהֵיכֶם֙ הַהֹלֵ֣ךְ לִפְנֵיכֶ֔ם
ה֖וּא יִלָּחֵ֣ם לָכֶ֑ם כְּ֠כֹ֠ל אֲשֶׁ֨ר עָשָׂ֧ה אִתְּכֶ֛ם
בְּמִצְרַ֖יִם לְעֵינֵיכֶֽם׃ 31 וּבַמִּדְבָּר֙ אֲשֶׁ֣ר
רָאִ֔יתָ אֲשֶׁ֤ר נְשָׂאֲךָ֙ יְהֹוָ֣ה אֱלֹהֶ֔יךָ כַּאֲשֶׁ֥ר
יִשָּׂא־אִ֖ישׁ אֶת־בְּנ֑וֹ בְּכׇל־הַדֶּ֙רֶךְ֙ אֲשֶׁ֣ר
הֲלַכְתֶּ֔ם עַד־בֹּאֲכֶ֖ם עַד־הַמָּק֥וֹם הַזֶּֽה׃
32 וּבַדָּבָ֖ר הַזֶּ֑ה אֵֽינְכֶם֙ מַאֲמִינִ֔ם בַּֽיהֹוָ֖ה
אֱלֹהֵיכֶֽם׃ 33 הַהֹלֵ֣ךְ לִפְנֵיכֶ֗ם בַּדֶּ֙רֶךְ֙ לָת֣וּר
לָכֶ֣ם מָק֔וֹם לַחֲנֹֽתְכֶ֑ם בָּאֵ֣שׁ ׀ לַ֗יְלָה
לַרְאֹֽתְכֶ֤ם בַּדֶּ֙רֶךְ֙ אֲשֶׁ֣ר תֵּֽלְכוּ־בָ֔הּ וּבֶעָנָ֖ן
יוֹמָֽם׃
34 וַיִּשְׁמַ֥ע יְהֹוָ֖ה אֶת־ק֣וֹל דִּבְרֵיכֶ֑ם וַיִּקְצֹ֖ף
וַיִּשָּׁבַ֥ע לֵאמֹֽר׃ 35 אִם־יִרְאֶ֥ה אִישׁ֙
בָּאֲנָשִׁ֣ים הָאֵ֔לֶּה הַדּ֥וֹר הָרָ֖ע הַזֶּ֑ה אֵ֚ת
הָאָ֣רֶץ הַטּוֹבָ֔ה אֲשֶׁ֣ר נִשְׁבַּ֔עְתִּי לָתֵ֖ת
לַאֲבֹתֵיכֶֽם׃ 36 זֽוּלָתִ֞י כָּלֵ֤ב בֶּן־יְפֻנֶּה֙ ה֣וּא
יִרְאֶ֔נָּה וְלֽוֹ־אֶתֵּ֧ן אֶת־הָאָ֛רֶץ אֲשֶׁ֥ר דָּֽרַךְ־בָּ֖הּ
וּלְבָנָ֑יו יַ֕עַן אֲשֶׁ֥ר מִלֵּ֖א אַחֲרֵ֥י יְהֹוָֽה׃
37 גַּם־בִּי֙ הִתְאַנַּ֣ף יְהֹוָ֔ה בִּגְלַלְכֶ֖ם לֵאמֹ֑ר
גַּם־אַתָּ֖ה לֹא־תָבֹ֥א שָֽׁם׃ 38 יְהוֹשֻׁ֤עַ בִּן־נוּן֙
הָעֹמֵ֣ד לְפָנֶ֔יךָ ה֖וּא יָ֣בֹא שָׁ֑מָּה אֹת֣וֹ חַזֵּ֔ק
כִּי־ה֖וּא יַנְחִלֶ֥נָּה אֶת־יִשְׂרָאֵֽל׃ 39 וְטַפְּכֶם֩
אֲשֶׁ֨ר אֲמַרְתֶּ֜ם לָבַ֣ז יִהְיֶ֗ה וּבְנֵיכֶ֤ם אֲשֶׁר֙

who you said would be carried off, your children who do not yet know good from bad, they shall enter it; to them will I give it and they shall possess it. 40As for you, turn about and march into the wilderness by the way of the Sea of Reeds.

41You replied to me, saying, "We stand guilty before the LORD. We will go up now and fight, just as the LORD our God commanded us." And you all girded yourselves with war gear and recklessly*g* started for the hill country. 42But the LORD said to me, "Warn them: Do not go up and do not fight, since I am not in your midst; else you will be routed by your enemies." 43I spoke to you, but you would not listen; you flouted the LORD's command and willfully marched into the hill country. 44Then the Amorites who lived in those hills came out against you like so many bees and chased you, and they crushed you at Hormah in Seir. 45Again you wept before the LORD; but the LORD would not heed your cry or give ear to you.

2 46Thus, after you had remained at Kadesh *h*-all that long time,-*h* 1we marched back into the wilderness by the way of the Sea of Reeds, as the LORD had spoken to me, and skirted the hill country of Seir a long time.

2Then the LORD said to me: 3You have been skirting this hill country long enough; now turn north. 4And charge the people as follows: You will be passing through the territory of your kinsmen, the descendants of Esau, who live in Seir. Though they will be afraid of you, be very careful 5not to provoke them. For I will not give you of their land so much as a foot can tread on; I have given the hill country of Seir as a possession to Esau. 6*a*-What food you eat you shall obtain from them for money; even the water

לֹא־יָדְעוּ הַיּוֹם טוֹב וָרָע הֵמָּה יָבֹאוּ שָׁמָּה וְלָהֶם אֶתְּנֶנָּה וְהֵם יִירָשׁוּהָ׃ 40 וְאַתֶּם פְּנוּ לָכֶם וּסְעוּ הַמִּדְבָּרָה דֶּרֶךְ יַם־סוּף׃ 41 וַתַּעֲנוּ | וַתֹּאמְרוּ אֵלַי חָטָאנוּ לַיהוָה אֲנַחְנוּ נַעֲלֶה וְנִלְחַמְנוּ כְּכֹל אֲשֶׁר־צִוָּנוּ יְהוָה אֱלֹהֵינוּ וַתַּחְגְּרוּ אִישׁ אֶת־כְּלֵי מִלְחַמְתּוֹ וַתָּהִינוּ לַעֲלֹת הָהָרָה׃ 42 וַיֹּאמֶר יְהוָה אֵלַי אֱמֹר לָהֶם לֹא תַעֲלוּ וְלֹא־תִלָּחֲמוּ כִּי אֵינֶנִּי בְּקִרְבְּכֶם וְלֹא תִּנָּגְפוּ לִפְנֵי אֹיְבֵיכֶם׃ 43 וָאֲדַבֵּר אֲלֵיכֶם וְלֹא שְׁמַעְתֶּם וַתַּמְרוּ אֶת־פִּי יְהוָה וַתָּזִדוּ וַתַּעֲלוּ הָהָרָה׃ 44 וַיֵּצֵא הָאֱמֹרִי הַיֹּשֵׁב בָּהָר הַהוּא לִקְרַאתְכֶם וַיִּרְדְּפוּ אֶתְכֶם כַּאֲשֶׁר תַּעֲשֶׂינָה הַדְּבֹרִים וַיַּכְּתוּ אֶתְכֶם בְּשֵׂעִיר עַד־חָרְמָה׃ 45 וַתָּשֻׁבוּ וַתִּבְכּוּ לִפְנֵי יְהוָה וְלֹא־שָׁמַע יְהוָה בְּקֹלְכֶם וְלֹא הֶאֱזִין אֲלֵיכֶם׃

ב 46 וַתֵּשְׁבוּ בְקָדֵשׁ יָמִים רַבִּים כַּיָּמִים אֲשֶׁר יְשַׁבְתֶּם׃ 1 וַנֵּפֶן וַנִּסַּע הַמִּדְבָּרָה דֶּרֶךְ יַם־סוּף כַּאֲשֶׁר דִּבֶּר יְהוָה אֵלָי וַנָּסָב אֶת־הַר־שֵׂעִיר יָמִים רַבִּים׃ ס 2 וַיֹּאמֶר יְהוָה אֵלַי לֵאמֹר׃ 3 רַב־לָכֶם סֹב אֶת־הָהָר הַזֶּה פְּנוּ לָכֶם צָפֹנָה׃ 4 וְאֶת־הָעָם צַו לֵאמֹר אַתֶּם עֹבְרִים בִּגְבוּל אֲחֵיכֶם בְּנֵי־עֵשָׂו הַיֹּשְׁבִים בְּשֵׂעִיר וְיִירְאוּ מִכֶּם וְנִשְׁמַרְתֶּם מְאֹד׃ 5 אַל־תִּתְגָּרוּ בָם כִּי לֹא־אֶתֵּן לָכֶם מֵאַרְצָם עַד מִדְרַךְ כַּף־רָגֶל כִּי־יְרֻשָּׁה לְעֵשָׂו נָתַתִּי אֶת־הַר שֵׂעִיר׃ 6 אֹכֶל תִּשְׁבְּרוּ מֵאִתָּם בַּכֶּסֶף וַאֲכַלְתֶּם וְגַם־מַיִם תִּכְרוּ מֵאִתָּם בַּכֶּסֶף

---

g Meaning of Heb. uncertain.
h-h Lit. "many days, like the days that you remained."

a-a Or "You may obtain food from them to eat for money; and you may also procure water from them to drink for money."

you drink you shall procure from them for money.-ᵃ ⁷Indeed, the LORD your God has blessed you in all your undertakings. He has watched over your wanderings through this great wilderness; the LORD your God has been with you these past forty years: you have lacked nothing.

⁸We then moved on, away from our kinsmen, the descendants of Esau, who live in Seir, away from the road of the Arabah, away from Elath and Ezion-geber; and we marched on in the direction of the wilderness of Moab. ⁹And the LORD said to me: Do not harass the Moabites or provoke them to war. For I will not give you any of their land as a possession; I have assigned Ar as a possession to the descendants of Lot.—

¹⁰It was formerly inhabited by the Emim, a people great and numerous, and as tall as the Anakites. ¹¹Like the Anakites, they are counted as Rephaim; but the Moabites call them Emim. ¹²Similarly, Seir was formerly inhabited by the Horites; but the descendants of Esau dispossessed them, wiping them out and settling in their place, just as Israel did in the land they were to possess, which the LORD had given to them.—

¹³Up now! Cross the wadi Zered!

So we crossed the wadi Zered. ¹⁴The time that we spent in travel from Kadesh-barnea until we crossed the wadi Zered was thirty-eight years, until that whole generation of warriors had perished from the camp, as the LORD had sworn concerning them. ¹⁵Indeed, the hand of the LORD struck them, to root them out from the camp to the last man.

¹⁶When all the warriors among the people had died off, ¹⁷the LORD spoke to me, saying: ¹⁸You are now passing through the territory of Moab, through Ar. ¹⁹You will then be close to the Ammonites; do not harass them or start a fight with them. For I will not give any part of

וּשְׁתִיתֶֽם׃ 7 כִּ֤י יְהֹוָ֣ה אֱלֹהֶ֙יךָ֙ בֵּֽרַכְךָ֔ בְּכֹל֙ מַעֲשֵׂ֣ה יָדֶ֔ךָ יָדַ֣ע לֶכְתְּךָ֔ אֶת־הַמִּדְבָּ֥ר הַגָּדֹ֖ל הַזֶּ֑ה זֶ֣ה ׀ אַרְבָּעִ֣ים שָׁנָ֗ה יְהֹוָ֤ה אֱלֹהֶ֙יךָ֙ עִמָּ֔ךְ לֹ֥א חָסַ֖רְתָּ דָּבָֽר׃

8 וַֽנַּעֲבֹ֞ר מֵאֵ֧ת אַחֵ֣ינוּ בְנֵֽי־עֵשָׂ֗ו הַיֹּֽשְׁבִים֙ בְּשֵׂעִ֔יר מִדֶּ֙רֶךְ֙ הָֽעֲרָבָ֔ה מֵֽאֵילַ֖ת וּמֵעֶצְיֹ֣ן גָּ֑בֶר ס וַנֵּ֙פֶן֙ וַֽנַּעֲבֹ֔ר דֶּ֖רֶךְ מִדְבַּ֥ר מוֹאָֽב׃ 9 וַיֹּ֨אמֶר יְהֹוָ֜ה אֵלַ֗י אַל־תָּ֙צַר֙ אֶת־מוֹאָ֔ב וְאַל־תִּתְגָּ֥ר בָּ֖ם מִלְחָמָ֑ה כִּ֠י לֹֽא־אֶתֵּ֨ן לְךָ֤ מֵֽאַרְצוֹ֙ יְרֻשָּׁ֔ה כִּ֣י לִבְנֵי־ל֔וֹט נָתַ֖תִּי אֶת־עָ֥ר יְרֻשָּֽׁה׃

10 הָֽאֵמִ֥ים לְפָנִ֖ים יָ֣שְׁבוּ בָ֑הּ עַ֣ם גָּד֥וֹל וְרַ֖ב וָרָ֥ם כָּעֲנָקִֽים׃ 11 רְפָאִ֛ים יֵחָֽשְׁב֥וּ אַף־הֵ֖ם כָּעֲנָקִ֑ים וְהַמֹּ֣אָבִ֔ים יִקְרְא֥וּ לָהֶ֖ם אֵמִֽים׃ 12 וּבְשֵׂעִ֞יר יָֽשְׁב֣וּ הַחֹרִים֮ לְפָנִים֒ וּבְנֵ֧י עֵשָׂ֣ו יִֽירָשׁ֗וּם וַיַּשְׁמִידוּם֙ מִפְּנֵיהֶ֔ם וַיֵּֽשְׁב֖וּ תַּחְתָּ֑ם כַּאֲשֶׁ֧ר עָשָׂ֣ה יִשְׂרָאֵ֗ל לְאֶ֙רֶץ֙ יְרֻשָּׁת֔וֹ אֲשֶׁר־נָתַ֥ן יְהֹוָ֖ה לָהֶֽם׃

13 עַתָּ֗ה קֻ֚מוּ וְעִבְר֣וּ לָכֶ֔ם אֶת־נַ֖חַל זָ֑רֶד וַֽנַּעֲבֹ֖ר אֶת־נַ֥חַל זָֽרֶד׃ 14 וְהַיָּמִ֞ים אֲשֶׁר־הָלַ֣כְנוּ ׀ מִקָּדֵ֣שׁ בַּרְנֵ֗עַ עַ֤ד אֲשֶׁר־עָבַ֙רְנוּ֙ אֶת־נַ֣חַל זֶ֔רֶד שְׁלֹשִׁ֥ים וּשְׁמֹנֶ֖ה שָׁנָ֑ה עַד־תֹּ֩ם כׇּל־הַדּ֨וֹר אַנְשֵׁ֤י הַמִּלְחָמָה֙ מִקֶּ֣רֶב הַֽמַּחֲנֶ֔ה כַּאֲשֶׁ֛ר נִשְׁבַּ֥ע יְהֹוָ֖ה לָהֶֽם׃ 15 וְגַ֤ם יַד־יְהֹוָה֙ הָ֣יְתָה בָּ֔ם לְהֻמָּ֖ם מִקֶּ֣רֶב הַֽמַּחֲנֶ֑ה עַ֖ד תֻּמָּֽם׃

16 וַיְהִ֨י כַאֲשֶׁר־תַּ֜מּוּ כׇּל־אַנְשֵׁ֧י הַמִּלְחָמָ֛ה לָמ֖וּת מִקֶּ֥רֶב הָעָֽם׃ ס 17 וַיְדַבֵּ֥ר יְהֹוָ֖ה אֵלַ֥י לֵאמֹֽר׃ 18 אַתָּ֨ה עֹבֵ֥ר הַיּ֛וֹם אֶת־גְּב֥וּל מוֹאָ֖ב אֶת־עָֽר׃ 19 וְקָרַבְתָּ֗ מ֚וּל בְּנֵ֣י עַמּ֔וֹן אַל־תְּצֻרֵ֖ם וְאַל־תִּתְגָּ֣ר בָּ֑ם כִּ֣י לֹֽא־אֶתֵּ֠ן

the land of the Ammonites to you as a possession; I have assigned it as a possession to the
descendants of Lot.—

20It, too, is counted as Rephaim country. It
was formerly inhabited by Rephaim, whom
the Ammonites call Zamzummim, 21a people
great and numerous and as tall as the
Anakites. The LORD wiped them out, so that
[the Ammonites] dispossessed them and
settled in their place, 22as He did for the
descendants of Esau who live in Seir, when
He wiped out the Horites before them, so that
they dispossessed them and settled in their
place, as is still the case.b 23So, too, with the
Avvim who dwelt in villages in the vicinity
of Gaza: the Caphtorim, who came from
Crete,c wiped them out and settled in their
place.—

24Up! Set out across the wadi Arnon! See, I give
into your power Sihon the Amorite, king of
Heshbon, and his land. Begin the occupation:
engage him in battle. 25This day I begin to put
the dread and fear of you upon the peoples
everywhere under heaven, so that they shall
tremble and quake because of you whenever
they hear you mentioned.

26Then I sent messengers from the wilderness
of Kedemoth to King Sihon of Heshbon with
an offer of peace, as follows, 27"Let me pass
through your country. I will keep strictly to the
highway, turning off neither to the right nor to
the left. 28What food I eat you will supply for
money, and what water I drink you will furnish
for money; just let me pass throughd—29as the
descendants of Esau who dwell in Seir did for
me, and the Moabites who dwell in Ar—that I
may cross the Jordan into the land that the LORD
our God is giving us."

30But King Sihon of Heshbon refused to let

מֵאֶ֖רֶץ בְּנֵֽי־עַמּ֑וֹן לְךָ֤ יְרֻשָּׁה֙ כִּ֣י לִבְנֵי־ל֔וֹט
נְתַתִּ֖יהָ יְרֻשָּֽׁה׃

20 אֶֽרֶץ־רְפָאִ֥ים תֵּחָשֵׁ֖ב אַף־הִ֑וא רְפָאִ֤ים
יָֽשְׁבוּ־בָהּ֙ לְפָנִ֔ים וְהָֽעַמֹּנִ֔ים יִקְרְא֥וּ לָהֶ֖ם
זַמְזֻמִּֽים׃ 21 עַ֣ם גָּד֥וֹל וְרַ֛ב וָרָ֖ם כָּעֲנָקִ֑ים
וַיַּשְׁמִידֵ֤ם יְהוָה֙ מִפְּנֵיהֶ֔ם וַיִּֽירָשֻׁ֖ם וַיֵּשְׁב֥וּ
תַחְתָּֽם׃ 22 כַּאֲשֶׁ֤ר עָשָׂה֙ לִבְנֵ֣י עֵשָׂ֔ו
הַיֹּֽשְׁבִ֖ים בְּשֵׂעִ֑יר אֲשֶׁ֨ר הִשְׁמִ֜יד אֶת־
הַחֹרִי֙ מִפְּנֵיהֶ֔ם וַיִּֽירָשֻׁם֙ וַיֵּשְׁב֣וּ תַחְתָּ֔ם
עַ֖ד הַיּ֥וֹם הַזֶּֽה׃ 23 וְהָֽעַוִּ֛ים הַיֹּֽשְׁבִ֥ים
בַּֽחֲצֵרִ֖ים עַד־עַזָּ֑ה כַּפְתֹּרִים֙ הַיֹּֽצְאִ֣ים
מִכַּפְתֹּ֔ר הִשְׁמִידֻ֖ם וַיֵּֽשְׁב֥וּ תַחְתָּֽם׃

24 ק֣וּמוּ סְּע֗וּ וְעִבְרוּ֮ אֶת־נַ֣חַל אַרְנֹן֒ רְאֵ֣ה
נָתַ֣תִּי בְ֠יָֽדְךָ אֶת־סִיחֹ֨ן מֶֽלֶךְ־חֶשְׁבּ֧וֹן
הָֽאֱמֹרִ֛י וְאֶת־אַרְצ֖וֹ הָחֵ֣ל רָ֑שׁ וְהִתְגָּ֥ר בּ֖וֹ
מִלְחָמָֽה׃ 25 הַיּ֣וֹם הַזֶּ֗ה אָחֵל֙ תֵּ֣ת פַּחְדְּךָ֣
וְיִרְאָ֣תְךָ֔ עַל־פְּנֵי֙ הָֽעַמִּ֔ים תַּ֖חַת כָּל־
הַשָּׁמָ֑יִם אֲשֶׁ֤ר יִשְׁמְעוּן֙ שִׁמְעֲךָ֔ וְרָגְז֥וּ וְחָל֖וּ
מִפָּנֶֽיךָ׃

26 וָאֶשְׁלַ֤ח מַלְאָכִים֙ מִמִּדְבַּ֣ר קְדֵמ֔וֹת אֶל־
סִיח֖וֹן מֶ֣לֶךְ חֶשְׁבּ֑וֹן דִּבְרֵ֥י שָׁל֖וֹם לֵאמֹֽר׃
27 אֶעְבְּרָ֣ה בְאַרְצֶ֔ךָ בַּדֶּ֥רֶךְ בַּדֶּ֖רֶךְ אֵלֵ֑ךְ לֹ֣א
אָס֖וּר יָמִ֥ין וּשְׂמֹֽאול׃* 28 אֹ֣כֶל בַּכֶּ֤סֶף
תַּשְׁבִּרֵ֙נִי֙ וְאָכַ֔לְתִּי וּמַ֛יִם בַּכֶּ֥סֶף תִּתֶּן־לִ֖י
וְשָׁתִ֑יתִי רַ֖ק אֶעְבְּרָ֥ה בְרַגְלָֽי׃ 29 כַּאֲשֶׁ֨ר
עָֽשׂוּ־לִ֜י בְּנֵ֣י עֵשָׂ֗ו הַיֹּֽשְׁבִים֙ בְּשֵׂעִ֔יר
וְהַמּ֣וֹאָבִ֔ים הַיֹּֽשְׁבִ֖ים בְּעָ֑ר עַ֤ד אֲשֶֽׁר־אֶֽעֱבֹר֙
אֶת־הַיַּרְדֵּ֔ן אֶל־הָאָ֕רֶץ אֲשֶׁר־יְהוָ֥ה אֱלֹהֵ֖ינוּ
נֹתֵ֥ן לָֽנוּ׃

30 וְלֹ֣א אָבָ֗ה סִיחֹן֙ מֶ֣לֶךְ חֶשְׁבּ֔וֹן הַעֲבִרֵ֖נוּ

---

b   Lit. "until this day."
c   Heb. "Caphtor."
d   Lit. "with my feet."

מלא ו׳   v. 27.

378

us pass through, because the LORD had stiffened his will and hardened his heart in order to deliver him into your power—as is now the case. [31]And the LORD said to me: See, I begin by placing Sihon and his land at your disposal. Begin the occupation; take possession of his land.

[32]Sihon with all his men took the field against us at Jahaz, [33]and the LORD our God delivered him to us and we defeated him and his sons and all his men. [34]At that time we captured all his towns, and we doomed[e] every town—men, women, and children—leaving no survivor. [35]We retained as booty only the cattle and the spoil of the cities that we captured. [36]From Aroer on the edge of the Arnon valley, including the town[f] in the valley itself, to Gilead, not a city was too mighty for us; the LORD our God delivered everything to us. [37]But you did not encroach upon the land of the Ammonites, all along the wadi Jabbok and the towns of the hill country, just as the LORD our God had commanded.

3 We made our way up the road toward Bashan, and King Og of Bashan with all his men took the field against us at Edrei. [2]But the LORD said to me: Do not fear him, for I am delivering him and all his men and his country into your power, and you will do to him as you did to Sihon king of the Amorites, who lived in Heshbon.

[3]So the LORD our God also delivered into our power King Og of Bashan, with all his men, and we dealt them such a blow that no survivor was left. [4]At that time we captured all his towns; there was not a town that we did not take from them: sixty towns, the whole district of Argob, the kingdom of Og in Bashan—[5]all those towns

---

e I.e., placed under ḥerem, which meant the annihilation of the population. Cf. note b at Num. 21.2; Josh. 6.24.
f Meaning of Heb. uncertain.

תורה דברים ג דברים

ל בּוֹ כִּי־הִקְשָׁה֩ יְהֹוָ֨ה אֱלֹהֶ֜יךָ אֶת־רוּחוֹ֗ וְאִמֵּץ֙ אֶת־לְבָב֔וֹ לְמַ֛עַן תִּתּ֥וֹ בְיָדְךָ֖ כַּיּ֥וֹם הַזֶּֽה: ס 31 וַיֹּ֤אמֶר יְהֹוָה֙ אֵלַ֔י רְאֵ֗ה הַֽחִלֹּ֙תִי֙ תֵּ֣ת לְפָנֶ֔יךָ אֶת־סִיחֹ֖ן וְאֶת־אַרְצ֑וֹ הָחֵ֣ל רָ֔שׁ לָרֶ֖שֶׁת אֶת־אַרְצֽוֹ: 32 וַיֵּצֵא֩ סִיחֹ֨ן לִקְרָאתֵ֜נוּ ה֧וּא וְכָל־עַמּ֛וֹ לַמִּלְחָמָ֖ה יָֽהְצָה: 33 וַֽיִּתְּנֵ֛הוּ יְהֹוָ֥ה אֱלֹהֵ֖ינוּ לְפָנֵ֑ינוּ וַנַּ֥ךְ אֹת֛וֹ וְאֶת־בָּנָ֖ו וְאֶת־כָּל־עַמּֽוֹ: 34 וַנִּלְכֹּ֤ד אֶת־כָּל־עָרָיו֙ בָּעֵ֣ת הַהִ֔וא וַֽנַּחֲרֵ֗ם אֶת־כָּל־עִיר֙ מְתִ֣ם וְהַנָּשִׁ֣ים וְהַטָּ֔ף לֹ֥א הִשְׁאַ֖רְנוּ שָׂרִֽיד: 35 רַ֥ק הַבְּהֵמָ֖ה בָּזַ֣זְנוּ לָ֑נוּ וּשְׁלַ֥ל הֶעָרִ֖ים אֲשֶׁ֥ר לָכָֽדְנוּ: 36 מֵֽעֲרֹעֵ֡ר אֲשֶׁר֩ עַל־שְׂפַת־נַ֨חַל אַרְנֹ֜ן וְהָעִ֨יר אֲשֶׁ֤ר בַּנַּ֙חַל֙ וְעַד־הַגִּלְעָ֔ד לֹ֤א הָֽיְתָה֙ קִרְיָ֔ה אֲשֶׁ֥ר שָֽׂגְבָ֖ה מִמֶּ֑נּוּ אֶת־הַכֹּ֗ל נָתַ֛ן יְהֹוָ֥ה אֱלֹהֵ֖ינוּ לְפָנֵֽינוּ: 37 רַ֛ק אֶל־אֶ֥רֶץ בְּנֵֽי־עַמּ֖וֹן לֹ֣א קָרָ֑בְתָּ כָּל־יַ֞ד נַ֤חַל יַבֹּק֙ וְעָרֵ֣י הָהָ֔ר וְכֹ֥ל אֲשֶׁר־צִוָּ֖ה יְהֹוָ֥ה אֱלֹהֵֽינוּ:

ג וַנֵּ֣פֶן וַנַּ֔עַל דֶּ֖רֶךְ הַבָּשָׁ֑ן וַיֵּצֵ֣א עוֹג֩ מֶֽלֶךְ־הַבָּשָׁ֨ן לִקְרָאתֵ֜נוּ ה֧וּא וְכָל־עַמּ֛וֹ לַמִּלְחָמָ֖ה אֶדְרֶֽעִי: 2 וַיֹּ֨אמֶר יְהֹוָ֤ה אֵלַי֙ אַל־תִּירָ֣א אֹת֔וֹ כִּ֣י בְיָֽדְךָ֞ נָתַ֧תִּי אֹת֛וֹ וְאֶת־כָּל־עַמּ֖וֹ וְאֶת־אַרְצ֑וֹ וְעָשִׂ֣יתָ לּ֔וֹ כַּֽאֲשֶׁ֣ר עָשִׂ֗יתָ לְסִיחֹן֙ מֶ֣לֶךְ הָֽאֱמֹרִ֔י אֲשֶׁ֥ר יוֹשֵׁ֖ב בְּחֶשְׁבּֽוֹן: 3 וַיִּתֵּן֩ יְהֹוָ֨ה אֱלֹהֵ֜ינוּ בְּיָדֵ֗נוּ גַּ֛ם אֶת־ע֥וֹג מֶֽלֶךְ־הַבָּשָׁ֖ן וְאֶת־כָּל־עַמּ֑וֹ וַנַּכֵּ֕הוּ עַד־בִּלְתִּ֥י הִשְׁאִֽיר־ל֖וֹ שָׂרִֽיד: 4 וַנִּלְכֹּ֤ד אֶת־כָּל־עָרָיו֙ בָּעֵ֣ת הַהִ֔וא לֹ֤א הָֽיְתָה֙ קִרְיָ֔ה אֲשֶׁ֥ר לֹֽא־לָקַ֖חְנוּ מֵֽאִתָּ֑ם שִׁשִּׁ֥ים עִיר֙ כָּל־חֶ֣בֶל אַרְגֹּ֔ב מַמְלֶ֥כֶת ע֖וֹג בַּבָּשָֽׁן: 5 כָּל־

were fortified with high walls, gates,[a] and bars—apart from a great number of unwalled towns. [6]We doomed them as we had done in the case of King Sihon of Heshbon; we doomed every town—men, women, and children—[7]and retained as booty all the cattle and the spoil of the towns.

[8]Thus we seized, at that time, from the two Amorite kings, the country beyond the Jordan, from the wadi Arnon to Mount Hermon—[9]Sidonians called Hermon Sirion, and the Amorites call it Senir—[10]all the towns of the Tableland and the whole of Gilead and Bashan as far as Salcah[b] and Edrei, the towns of Og's kingdom in Bashan. [11]Only King Og of Bashan was left of the remaining Rephaim. His bedstead, an iron bedstead, is now in Rabbah of the Ammonites; it is nine cubits long and four cubits wide, by [c]the standard cubit![-c]

[12d]And this is the land which we apportioned at that time: The part from Aroer along the wadi Arnon, with part of the hill country of Gilead and its towns, I assigned to the Reubenites and the Gadites. [13]The rest of Gilead, and all of Bashan under Og's rule—the whole Argob district, all that part of Bashan which is called Rephaim country—I assigned to the half-tribe of Manasseh. [14]Jair son of Manasseh received the whole Argob district (that is, Bashan) as far as the boundary of the Geshurites and the Maacathites, and named it after himself: Havvoth-jair[e]—as is still the case. [15]To Machir I assigned Gilead. [16]And to the Reubenites and the Gadites I assigned the part from Gilead down to the wadi Arnon, the middle of the wadi being the boundary, and up to the wadi Jabbok, the boundary of the Ammonites.

[17f][We also seized] the Arabah, from the foot

אֵלֶּה עָרִים בְּצֻרֹת חוֹמָה גְבֹהָה דְּלָתַיִם וּבְרִיחַ לְבַד מֵעָרֵי הַפְּרָזִי הַרְבֵּה מְאֹד: [6] וַנַּחֲרֵם אוֹתָם כַּאֲשֶׁר עָשִׂינוּ לְסִיחֹן מֶלֶךְ חֶשְׁבּוֹן הַחֲרֵם כָּל־עִיר מְתִם הַנָּשִׁים וְהַטָּף: [7] וְכָל־הַבְּהֵמָה וּשְׁלַל הֶעָרִים בַּזּוֹנוּ לָנוּ: [8] וַנִּקַּח בָּעֵת הַהִוא אֶת־הָאָרֶץ מִיַּד שְׁנֵי מַלְכֵי הָאֱמֹרִי אֲשֶׁר בְּעֵבֶר הַיַּרְדֵּן מִנַּחַל אַרְנֹן עַד־הַר חֶרְמוֹן: [9] צִידֹנִים יִקְרְאוּ לְחֶרְמוֹן שִׂרְיֹן וְהָאֱמֹרִי יִקְרְאוּ־לוֹ שְׂנִיר: [10] כֹּל | עָרֵי הַמִּישֹׁר וְכָל־הַגִּלְעָד וְכָל־הַבָּשָׁן עַד־סַלְכָה וְאֶדְרֶעִי עָרֵי מַמְלֶכֶת עוֹג בַּבָּשָׁן: [11] כִּי רַק־עוֹג מֶלֶךְ הַבָּשָׁן נִשְׁאַר מִיֶּתֶר הָרְפָאִים הִנֵּה* עַרְשׂוֹ עֶרֶשׂ בַּרְזֶל הֲלֹה* הִוא בְּרַבַּת בְּנֵי עַמּוֹן תֵּשַׁע אַמּוֹת אָרְכָּהּ וְאַרְבַּע אַמּוֹת רָחְבָּהּ בְּאַמַּת־אִישׁ: [12] וְאֶת־הָאָרֶץ הַזֹּאת יָרַשְׁנוּ בָּעֵת הַהִוא מֵעֲרֹעֵר אֲשֶׁר־עַל־נַחַל אַרְנֹן וַחֲצִי הַר־הַגִּלְעָד וְעָרָיו נָתַתִּי לָרֻאוּבֵנִי וְלַגָּדִי: [13] וְיֶתֶר הַגִּלְעָד וְכָל־הַבָּשָׁן מַמְלֶכֶת עוֹג נָתַתִּי לַחֲצִי שֵׁבֶט הַמְנַשֶּׁה כֹּל חֶבֶל הָאַרְגֹּב לְכָל־הַבָּשָׁן הַהוּא יִקָּרֵא אֶרֶץ רְפָאִים: [14] יָאִיר בֶּן־מְנַשֶּׁה לָקַח אֶת־כָּל־חֶבֶל אַרְגֹּב עַד־גְּבוּל הַגְּשׁוּרִי וְהַמַּעֲכָתִי וַיִּקְרָא אֹתָם עַל־שְׁמוֹ אֶת־הַבָּשָׁן חַוֹּת יָאִיר עַד הַיּוֹם הַזֶּה: [15] וּלְמָכִיר נָתַתִּי אֶת־הַגִּלְעָד: [16] וְלָרֻאוּבֵנִי וְלַגָּדִי נָתַתִּי מִן־הַגִּלְעָד וְעַד־נַחַל אַרְנֹן תּוֹךְ הַנַּחַל וּגְבֻל וְעַד יַבֹּק הַנַּחַל גְּבוּל בְּנֵי עַמּוֹן: [17] וְהָעֲרָבָה וְהַיַּרְדֵּן וּגְבֻל מִכִּנֶּרֶת וְעַד יָם

---

a   *I.e., two-leaf doors.*
b   *Others "Salecah" or "Salchah."*
c-c   *Lit. "by a man's forearm."*
d   *Vv. 12–13 proceed from south to north; vv. 14–16 from north to south.*
e   *I.e., "villages of Jair."*
f   *Continuing vv. 8–10; cf. 4.47–49.*

     סבירין ומטעין "והנה"   v. 11.
     ה' במקום א'   v. 11.

of the slopes of Pisgah on the east, to the edge of the Jordan, and from Chinnereth down to the sea of the Arabah, the Dead Sea.

¹⁸At that time I charged you,^g saying, "The LORD your God has given you this country to possess. You must go as shock-troops, warriors all, at the head of your Israelite kinsmen. ¹⁹Only your wives, children, and livestock—I know that you have much livestock—shall be left in the towns I have assigned to you, ²⁰until the LORD has granted your kinsmen a haven such as you have, and they too have taken possession of the land that the LORD your God is assigning them, beyond the Jordan. Then you may return each to the homestead that I have assigned to him."

²¹I also charged Joshua at that time, saying, "You have seen with your own eyes all that the LORD your God has done to these two kings; so shall the LORD do to all the kingdoms into which you shall cross over. ²²Do not fear them, for it is the LORD your God who will battle for you."

VA-'ETHANNAN

²³I pleaded with the LORD at that time, saying, ²⁴"O Lord GOD, You who let Your servant see the first works of Your greatness and Your mighty hand, You whose powerful deeds no god in heaven or on earth can equal! ²⁵Let me, I pray, cross over and see the good land on the other side of the Jordan, that good hill country, and the Lebanon." ²⁶But the LORD was wrathful with me on your account and would not listen to me. The LORD said to me, "Enough! Never speak to Me of this matter again! ²⁷Go up to the summit of Pisgah and gaze about, to the west, the north, the south, and the east. Look at it well, for you shall not go across yonder Jordan. ²⁸Give Joshua his instructions, and imbue him with strength

הָעֲרָבָה֙ יָ֣ם הַמֶּ֔לַח תַּ֖חַת אַשְׁדֹּ֣ת הַפִּסְגָּ֑ה מִזְרָֽחָה׃

¹⁸ וָאֲצַ֣ו אֶתְכֶ֔ם בָּעֵ֥ת הַהִ֖וא לֵאמֹ֑ר יְהֹוָ֣ה אֱלֹהֵיכֶ֗ם נָתַ֨ן לָכֶ֜ם אֶת־הָאָ֤רֶץ הַזֹּאת֙ לְרִשְׁתָּ֔הּ חֲלוּצִ֣ים תַּֽעַבְר֗וּ לִפְנֵ֛י אֲחֵיכֶ֥ם בְּנֵֽי־יִשְׂרָאֵ֖ל כָּל־בְּנֵי־חָֽיִל׃ ¹⁹ רַ֣ק נְשֵׁיכֶ֤ם וְטַפְּכֶם֙ וּמִקְנֵכֶ֔ם יָדַ֕עְתִּי כִּֽי־מִקְנֶ֥ה רַ֖ב לָכֶ֑ם יֵֽשְׁבוּ֙ בְּעָ֣רֵיכֶ֔ם אֲשֶׁ֥ר נָתַ֖תִּי לָכֶֽם׃ ²⁰ עַ֠ד אֲשֶׁר־יָנִ֨יחַ יְהֹוָ֥ה ׀ לַֽאֲחֵיכֶם֮ כָּכֶם֒ וְיָרְשׁ֣וּ גַם־הֵ֔ם אֶת־הָאָ֕רֶץ אֲשֶׁ֨ר יְהֹוָ֧ה אֱלֹהֵיכֶ֛ם נֹתֵ֥ן לָהֶ֖ם בְּעֵ֣בֶר הַיַּרְדֵּ֑ן וְשַׁבְתֶּ֗ם אִ֚ישׁ לִֽירֻשָּׁת֔וֹ אֲשֶׁ֥ר נָתַ֖תִּי לָכֶֽם׃

²¹ וְאֶת־יְהוֹשׁ֣וּעַ צִוֵּ֔יתִי בָּעֵ֥ת הַהִ֖וא לֵאמֹ֑ר עֵינֶ֣יךָ הָרֹאֹ֗ת אֵת֩ כָּל־אֲשֶׁ֨ר עָשָׂ֜ה יְהֹוָ֤ה אֱלֹהֵיכֶם֙ לִשְׁנֵי֙ הַמְּלָכִ֣ים הָאֵ֔לֶּה כֵּֽן־יַעֲשֶׂ֤ה יְהֹוָה֙ לְכָל־הַמַּמְלָכ֔וֹת אֲשֶׁ֥ר אַתָּ֖ה עֹבֵ֥ר שָֽׁמָּה׃ ²² לֹ֖א תִּֽירָא֑וּם כִּ֚י יְהֹוָ֣ה אֱלֹהֵיכֶ֔ם ה֖וּא הַנִּלְחָ֥ם לָכֶֽם׃ ס

ואתחנן

²³ וָאֶתְחַנַּ֖ן אֶל־יְהֹוָ֑ה בָּעֵ֥ת הַהִ֖וא לֵאמֹֽר׃ ²⁴ אֲדֹנָ֣י יֱהֹוִ֗ה אַתָּ֤ה הַֽחִלּ֙וֹתָ֙ לְהַרְא֣וֹת אֶֽת־עַבְדְּךָ֔ אֶ֨ת־גׇּדְלְךָ֔ וְאֶת־יָדְךָ֖ הַחֲזָקָ֑ה אֲשֶׁ֤ר מִי־אֵל֙ בַּשָּׁמַ֣יִם וּבָאָ֔רֶץ אֲשֶׁר־יַעֲשֶׂ֥ה כְמַעֲשֶׂ֖יךָ וְכִגְבוּרֹתֶֽךָ׃ ²⁵ אֶעְבְּרָה־נָּ֗א וְאֶרְאֶה֙ אֶת־הָאָ֣רֶץ הַטּוֹבָ֔ה אֲשֶׁ֖ר בְּעֵ֣בֶר הַיַּרְדֵּ֑ן הָהָ֥ר הַטּ֛וֹב הַזֶּ֖ה וְהַלְּבָנֹֽן׃ ²⁶ וַיִּתְעַבֵּ֨ר יְהֹוָ֥ה בִּי֙ לְמַ֣עַנְכֶ֔ם וְלֹ֥א שָׁמַ֖ע אֵלָ֑י וַיֹּ֨אמֶר יְהֹוָ֤ה אֵלַי֙ רַב־לָ֔ךְ אַל־תּ֗וֹסֶף דַּבֵּ֥ר אֵלַ֛י ע֖וֹד בַּדָּבָ֥ר הַזֶּֽה׃ ²⁷ עֲלֵ֣ה ׀ רֹ֣אשׁ הַפִּסְגָּ֗ה וְשָׂ֥א עֵינֶ֛יךָ יָ֧מָּה וְצָפֹ֛נָה וְתֵימָ֖נָה וּמִזְרָ֑חָה וּרְאֵ֣ה בְעֵינֶ֑יךָ כִּי־לֹ֥א תַעֲבֹ֖ר אֶת־הַיַּרְדֵּ֥ן הַזֶּֽה׃ ²⁸ וְצַ֥ו אֶת־יְהוֹשֻׁ֖עַ

---

g I.e., the two and a half tribes.

and courage, for he shall go across at the head of this people, and he shall allot to them the land that you may only see."

²⁹Meanwhile we stayed on in the valley near Beth-peor.

4 And now, O Israel, give heed to the laws and rules that I am instructing you to observe, so that you may live to enter and occupy the land that the LORD, the God of your fathers, is giving you. ²You shall not add anything to what I command you or take anything away from it, but keep the commandments of the LORD your God that I enjoin upon you. ³You saw with your own eyes what the LORD did in the matter of Baal-peor, that the LORD your God wiped out from among you every person who followed Baal-peor; ⁴while you, who held fast to the LORD your God, are all alive today.

⁵See, I have imparted to you laws and rules, as the LORD my God has commanded me, for you to abide by in the land that you are about to enter and occupy. ⁶Observe them faithfully, for that will be proof of your wisdom and discernment to other peoples, who on hearing of all these laws will say, "Surely, that great nation is a wise and discerning people." ⁷For what great nation is there that has a god so close at hand as is the LORD our God whenever we call upon Him? ⁸Or what great nation has laws and rules as perfect as all this Teaching that I set before you this day?

⁹But take utmost care and watch yourselves scrupulously, so that you do not forget the things that you saw with your own eyes and so that they do not fade from your mind as long as you live. And make them known to your children and to your children's children: ¹⁰The day you stood before the LORD your God at Horeb, when the LORD said to Me, "Gather the people

וְחַזְּקֵהוּ וְאַמְּצֵהוּ כִּי־הוּא יַעֲבֹר לִפְנֵי הָעָם הַזֶּה וְהוּא יַנְחִיל אוֹתָם אֶת־הָאָרֶץ אֲשֶׁר תִּרְאֶה: ²⁹ וַנֵּשֶׁב בַּגָּיְא מוּל בֵּית פְּעוֹר: פ

ד וְעַתָּה יִשְׂרָאֵל שְׁמַע אֶל־הַחֻקִּים וְאֶל־הַמִּשְׁפָּטִים אֲשֶׁר אָנֹכִי מְלַמֵּד אֶתְכֶם לַעֲשׂוֹת לְמַעַן תִּחְיוּ וּבָאתֶם וִירִשְׁתֶּם אֶת־הָאָרֶץ אֲשֶׁר יְהֹוָה אֱלֹהֵי אֲבֹתֵיכֶם נֹתֵן לָכֶם: ² לֹא תֹסִפוּ עַל־הַדָּבָר אֲשֶׁר אָנֹכִי מְצַוֶּה אֶתְכֶם וְלֹא תִגְרְעוּ מִמֶּנּוּ לִשְׁמֹר אֶת־מִצְוֺת יְהֹוָה אֱלֹהֵיכֶם אֲשֶׁר אָנֹכִי מְצַוֶּה אֶתְכֶם: ³ עֵינֵיכֶם הָרֹאֹת אֵת אֲשֶׁר־עָשָׂה יְהֹוָה בְּבַעַל פְּעוֹר כִּי כָל־הָאִישׁ אֲשֶׁר הָלַךְ אַחֲרֵי בַעַל־פְּעוֹר הִשְׁמִידוֹ יְהֹוָה אֱלֹהֶיךָ מִקִּרְבֶּךָ: ⁴ וְאַתֶּם הַדְּבֵקִים בַּיהֹוָה אֱלֹהֵיכֶם חַיִּים כֻּלְּכֶם הַיּוֹם:

⁵ רְאֵה | לִמַּדְתִּי אֶתְכֶם חֻקִּים וּמִשְׁפָּטִים כַּאֲשֶׁר צִוַּנִי יְהֹוָה אֱלֹהָי לַעֲשׂוֹת כֵּן בְּקֶרֶב הָאָרֶץ אֲשֶׁר אַתֶּם בָּאִים שָׁמָּה לְרִשְׁתָּהּ: ⁶ וּשְׁמַרְתֶּם וַעֲשִׂיתֶם כִּי הִוא חָכְמַתְכֶם וּבִינַתְכֶם לְעֵינֵי הָעַמִּים אֲשֶׁר יִשְׁמְעוּן אֵת כָּל־הַחֻקִּים הָאֵלֶּה וְאָמְרוּ רַק עַם־חָכָם וְנָבוֹן הַגּוֹי הַגָּדוֹל הַזֶּה: ⁷ כִּי מִי־גוֹי גָּדוֹל אֲשֶׁר־לוֹ אֱלֹהִים קְרֹבִים אֵלָיו כַּיהֹוָה אֱלֹהֵינוּ בְּכָל־קָרְאֵנוּ אֵלָיו: ⁸ וּמִי גּוֹי גָּדוֹל אֲשֶׁר־לוֹ חֻקִּים וּמִשְׁפָּטִים צַדִּיקִם כְּכֹל הַתּוֹרָה הַזֹּאת אֲשֶׁר אָנֹכִי נֹתֵן לִפְנֵיכֶם הַיּוֹם:

⁹ רַק הִשָּׁמֶר לְךָ וּשְׁמֹר נַפְשְׁךָ מְאֹד פֶּן־תִּשְׁכַּח אֶת־הַדְּבָרִים אֲשֶׁר־רָאוּ עֵינֶיךָ וּפֶן־יָסוּרוּ מִלְּבָבְךָ כֹּל יְמֵי חַיֶּיךָ וְהוֹדַעְתָּם לְבָנֶיךָ וְלִבְנֵי בָנֶיךָ: ¹⁰ יוֹם אֲשֶׁר עָמַדְתָּ לִפְנֵי יְהֹוָה אֱלֹהֶיךָ בְּחֹרֵב בֶּאֱמֹר יְהֹוָה

to Me that I may let them hear My words, in order that they may learn to revere Me as long as they live on earth, and may so teach their children." [11]You came forward and stood at the foot of the mountain. The mountain was ablaze with flames to the very skies, dark with densest clouds. [12]The LORD spoke to you out of the fire; you heard the sound of words but perceived no shape—nothing but a voice. [13]He declared to you the covenant that He commanded you to observe, the Ten Commandments; and He inscribed them on two tablets of stone. [14]At the same time the LORD commanded me to impart to you laws and rules for you to observe in the land that you are about to cross into and occupy.

[15]For your own sake, therefore, be most careful—since you saw no shape when the LORD your God spoke to you at Horeb out of the fire—[16]not to act wickedly and make for yourselves a sculptured image in any likeness whatever: the form of a man or a woman, [17]the form of any beast on earth, the form of any winged bird that flies in the sky, [18]the form of anything that creeps on the ground, the form of any fish that is in the waters below the earth. [19]And when you look up to the sky and behold the sun and the moon and the stars, the whole heavenly host, you must not be lured into bowing down to them or serving them. These the LORD your God allotted to other peoples everywhere under heaven; [20]but you the LORD took and brought out of Egypt, that iron blast furnace, to be His very own people, as is now the case.

[21]Now the LORD was angry with me on your account and swore that I should not cross the Jordan and enter the good land that the LORD your God is assigning you as a heritage. [22]For I must die in this land; I shall not cross the Jordan. But you will cross and take possession of that good land. [23]Take care, then, not to forget the covenant that the LORD your God concluded

אֵלַ֗י הַקְהֶל־לִי֙ אֶת־הָעָ֔ם וְאַשְׁמִעֵ֖ם אֶת־
דְּבָרָ֑י אֲשֶׁ֨ר יִלְמְד֜וּן לְיִרְאָ֣ה אֹתִ֗י כָּל־
הַיָּמִים֙ אֲשֶׁ֨ר הֵ֤ם חַיִּים֙ עַל־הָ֣אֲדָמָ֔ה וְאֶת־
בְּנֵיהֶ֖ם יְלַמֵּדֽוּן׃ 11 וַתִּקְרְב֥וּן וַתַּֽעַמְד֖וּן
תַּ֣חַת הָהָ֑ר וְהָהָ֞ר בֹּעֵ֤ר בָּאֵשׁ֙ עַד־לֵ֣ב
הַשָּׁמַ֔יִם חֹ֖שֶׁךְ עָנָ֥ן וַעֲרָפֶֽל׃ 12 וַיְדַבֵּ֧ר יְהֹוָ֛ה
אֲלֵיכֶ֖ם מִתּ֣וֹךְ הָאֵ֑שׁ ק֤וֹל דְּבָרִים֙ אַתֶּ֣ם
שֹׁמְעִ֔ים וּתְמוּנָ֛ה אֵינְכֶ֥ם רֹאִ֖ים זוּלָתִ֥י
ק֑וֹל׃ 13 וַיַּגֵּ֨ד לָכֶ֜ם אֶת־בְּרִית֗וֹ אֲשֶׁ֨ר צִוָּ֤ה
אֶתְכֶם֙ לַעֲשׂ֔וֹת עֲשֶׂ֖רֶת הַדְּבָרִ֑ים וַֽיִּכְתְּבֵ֔ם
עַל־שְׁנֵ֖י לֻח֥וֹת אֲבָנִֽים׃ 14 וְאֹתִ֞י צִוָּ֤ה
יְהֹוָה֙ בָּעֵ֣ת הַהִ֔וא לְלַמֵּ֣ד אֶתְכֶ֔ם חֻקִּ֖ים
וּמִשְׁפָּטִ֑ים לַעֲשֹׂתְכֶ֣ם אֹתָ֔ם בָּאָ֕רֶץ אֲשֶׁ֥ר
אַתֶּ֛ם עֹבְרִ֥ים שָׁ֖מָּה לְרִשְׁתָּֽהּ׃ 15 וְנִשְׁמַרְתֶּ֥ם
מְאֹ֖ד לְנַפְשֹׁתֵיכֶ֑ם כִּ֣י לֹ֤א
רְאִיתֶם֙ כָּל־תְּמוּנָ֔ה בְּי֗וֹם דִּבֶּ֨ר יְהֹוָ֧ה
אֲלֵיכֶ֛ם בְּחֹרֵ֖ב מִתּ֥וֹךְ הָאֵֽשׁ׃ 16 פֶּן־
תַּשְׁחִת֗וּן וַעֲשִׂיתֶ֥ם לָכֶ֛ם פֶּ֖סֶל תְּמוּנַ֣ת
כָּל־סָ֑מֶל תַּבְנִ֥ית זָכָ֖ר א֥וֹ נְקֵבָֽה׃ 17 תַּבְנִ֕ית
כָּל־בְּהֵמָ֖ה אֲשֶׁ֣ר בָּאָ֑רֶץ תַּבְנִית֙ כָּל־צִפּ֣וֹר
כָּנָ֔ף אֲשֶׁ֥ר תָּע֖וּף בַּשָּׁמָֽיִם׃ 18 תַּבְנִ֕ית כָּל־
רֹמֵ֖שׂ בָּאֲדָמָ֑ה תַּבְנִ֥ית כָּל־דָּגָ֛ה אֲשֶׁר־
בַּמַּ֖יִם מִתַּ֥חַת לָאָֽרֶץ׃ 19 וּפֶן־תִּשָּׂ֨א עֵינֶ֜יךָ
הַשָּׁמַ֗יְמָה וְֽרָאִ֞יתָ אֶת־הַשֶּׁ֣מֶשׁ וְאֶת־הַיָּרֵ֗חַ
וְאֶת־הַכּֽוֹכָבִ֞ים כֹּ֚ל צְבָ֣א הַשָּׁמַ֔יִם וְנִדַּחְתָּ֗
וְהִשְׁתַּחֲוִ֤יתָ לָהֶם֙ וַעֲבַדְתָּ֔ם אֲשֶׁ֤ר חָלַ֣ק
יְהֹוָ֣ה אֱלֹהֶ֔יךָ אֹתָ֔ם לְכֹל֙ הָֽעַמִּ֔ים תַּ֖חַת
כָּל־הַשָּׁמָֽיִם׃ 20 וְאֶתְכֶם֙ לָקַ֣ח יְהֹוָ֔ה וַיּוֹצִ֥א
אֶתְכֶ֛ם מִכּ֥וּר הַבַּרְזֶ֖ל מִמִּצְרָ֑יִם לִהְי֥וֹת ל֛וֹ
לְעַ֥ם נַחֲלָ֖ה כַּיּ֥וֹם הַזֶּֽה׃ 21 וַֽיהֹוָ֥ה
הִתְאַנַּף־בִּ֖י עַל־דִּבְרֵיכֶ֑ם וַיִּשָּׁבַ֗ע
לְבִלְתִּ֤י עָבְרִי֙ אֶת־הַיַּרְדֵּ֔ן וּלְבִלְתִּי־בֹא֙ אֶל־
הָאָ֣רֶץ הַטּוֹבָ֔ה אֲשֶׁר֙ יְהֹוָ֣ה אֱלֹהֶ֔יךָ נֹתֵ֥ן
לְךָ֖ נַחֲלָֽה׃ 22 כִּ֣י אָנֹכִ֥י מֵת֙ בָּאָ֣רֶץ הַזֹּ֔את
אֵינֶ֥נִּי עֹבֵ֖ר אֶת־הַיַּרְדֵּ֑ן וְאַתֶּם֙ עֹֽבְרִ֔ים
וִֽירִשְׁתֶּ֕ם אֶת־הָאָ֥רֶץ הַטּוֹבָ֖ה הַזֹּֽאת׃

with you, and not to make for yourselves a sculptured image in any likeness, against which the LORD your God has enjoined you. 24For the LORD your God is a consuming fire, an impassioned God.

25When you have begotten children and children's children and are long established in the land, should you act wickedly and make for yourselves a sculptured image in any likeness, causing the LORD your God displeasure and vexation, 26I call heaven and earth this day to witness against you that you shall soon perish from the land that you are crossing the Jordan to possess; you shall not long endure in it, but shall be utterly wiped out. 27The LORD will scatter you among the peoples, and only a scant few of you shall be left among the nations to which the LORD will drive you. 28There you will serve man-made gods of wood and stone, that cannot see or hear or eat or smell.

29But if you search there for the LORD your God, you will find Him, if only you seek Him with all your heart and soul—30when you are in distress because all these things have befallen you and, in the end, return to the LORD your God and obey Him. 31For the LORD your God is a compassionate God: He will not fail you nor will He let you perish; He will not forget the covenant which He made on oath with your fathers.

32You have but to inquire about bygone ages that came before you, ever since God created man on earth, from one end of heaven to the other: has anything as grand as this ever happened, or has its like ever been known? 33Has any people heard the voice of a god speaking out of a fire, as you have, and survived? 34Or has any god ventured to go and take for himself one nation from the midst of another by prodigious acts, by signs and portents, by war, by a mighty and an outstretched arm and awesome

23 הִשָּׁמְר֣וּ לָכֶ֗ם פֶּֽן־תִּשְׁכְּחוּ֙ אֶת־בְּרִ֤ית יְהֹוָה֙ אֱלֹֽהֵיכֶ֔ם אֲשֶׁ֥ר כָּרַ֖ת עִמָּכֶ֑ם וַעֲשִׂיתֶ֨ם לָכֶ֥ם פֶּ֙סֶל֙ תְּמ֣וּנַת כֹּ֔ל אֲשֶׁ֥ר צִוְּךָ֖ יְהֹוָ֥ה אֱלֹהֶֽיךָ: 24 כִּ֚י יְהֹוָ֣ה אֱלֹהֶ֔יךָ אֵ֖שׁ אֹכְלָ֣ה ה֑וּא אֵ֖ל קַנָּֽא: פ

25 כִּֽי־תוֹלִ֤יד בָּנִים֙ וּבְנֵ֣י בָנִ֔ים וְנוֹשַׁנְתֶּ֖ם בָּאָ֑רֶץ וְהִשְׁחַתֶּ֗ם וַעֲשִׂ֤יתֶם פֶּ֙סֶל֙ תְּמ֣וּנַת כֹּ֔ל וַעֲשִׂיתֶ֥ם הָרַ֛ע בְּעֵינֵ֥י יְהֹוָֽה־אֱלֹהֶ֖יךָ לְהַכְעִיסֽוֹ: 26 הַעִידֹ֩תִי֩ בָכֶ֨ם הַיּ֜וֹם אֶת־הַשָּׁמַ֣יִם וְאֶת־הָאָ֗רֶץ כִּֽי־אָבֹ֣ד תֹּאבֵדוּן֮ מַהֵר֒ מֵעַ֣ל הָאָ֔רֶץ אֲשֶׁ֨ר אַתֶּ֜ם עֹבְרִ֧ים אֶת־הַיַּרְדֵּ֛ן שָׁ֖מָּה לְרִשְׁתָּ֑הּ לֹֽא־תַאֲרִיכֻ֤ן יָמִים֙ עָלֶ֔יהָ כִּ֥י הִשָּׁמֵ֖ד תִּשָּׁמֵדֽוּן: 27 וְהֵפִ֧יץ יְהֹוָ֛ה אֶתְכֶ֖ם בָּעַמִּ֑ים וְנִשְׁאַרְתֶּם֙ מְתֵ֣י מִסְפָּ֔ר בַּגּוֹיִ֕ם אֲשֶׁ֨ר יְנַהֵ֧ג יְהֹוָ֛ה אֶתְכֶ֖ם שָֽׁמָּה: 28 וַעֲבַדְתֶּם־שָׁ֣ם אֱלֹהִ֔ים מַעֲשֵׂ֖ה יְדֵ֣י אָדָ֑ם עֵ֣ץ וָאֶ֔בֶן אֲשֶׁ֤ר לֹֽא־יִרְאוּן֙ וְלֹ֣א יִשְׁמְע֔וּן וְלֹ֥א יֹֽאכְל֖וּן וְלֹ֥א יְרִיחֻֽן: 29 וּבִקַּשְׁתֶּ֥ם מִשָּׁ֛ם אֶת־יְהֹוָ֥ה אֱלֹהֶ֖יךָ וּמָצָ֑אתָ כִּ֣י תִדְרְשֶׁ֔נּוּ בְּכָל־לְבָבְךָ֖ וּבְכָל־נַפְשֶֽׁךָ: 30 בַּצַּ֣ר לְךָ֔ וּמְצָא֕וּךָ כֹּ֖ל הַדְּבָרִ֣ים הָאֵ֑לֶּה בְּאַחֲרִית֙ הַיָּמִ֔ים וְשַׁבְתָּ֙ עַד־יְהֹוָ֣ה אֱלֹהֶ֔יךָ וְשָׁמַעְתָּ֖ בְּקֹלֽוֹ: 31 כִּ֣י אֵ֤ל רַחוּם֙ יְהֹוָ֣ה אֱלֹהֶ֔יךָ לֹ֥א יַרְפְּךָ֖ וְלֹ֣א יַשְׁחִיתֶ֑ךָ וְלֹ֤א יִשְׁכַּח֙ אֶת־בְּרִ֣ית אֲבֹתֶ֔יךָ אֲשֶׁ֥ר נִשְׁבַּ֖ע לָהֶֽם:

32 כִּ֣י שְׁאַל־נָא֩ לְיָמִ֨ים רִֽאשֹׁנִ֜ים אֲשֶׁר־הָי֣וּ לְפָנֶ֗יךָ לְמִן־הַיּוֹם֙ אֲשֶׁר֩ בָּרָ֨א אֱלֹהִ֤ים ׀ אָדָם֙ עַל־הָאָ֔רֶץ וּלְמִקְצֵ֥ה הַשָּׁמַ֖יִם וְעַד־קְצֵ֣ה הַשָּׁמָ֑יִם הֲנִהְיָ֗ה כַּדָּבָ֤ר הַגָּדוֹל֙ הַזֶּ֔ה א֥וֹ הֲנִשְׁמַ֖ע כָּמֹֽהוּ: 33 הֲשָׁ֣מַֽע עָם֩ קוֹל֨ אֱלֹהִ֜ים מְדַבֵּ֧ר מִתּוֹךְ־הָאֵ֛שׁ כַּאֲשֶׁר־שָׁמַ֥עְתָּ אַתָּ֖ה וַיֶּֽחִי: 34 א֣וֹ ׀ הֲנִסָּ֣ה אֱלֹהִ֗ים לָבוֹא֩ לָקַ֨חַת ל֣וֹ גוֹי֮ מִקֶּ֣רֶב גּוֹי֒ בְּמַסֹּת֩ בְּאֹתֹ֨ת וּבְמֽוֹפְתִ֜ים וּבְמִלְחָמָ֗ה וּבְיָ֤ד חֲזָקָה֙ וּבִזְר֣וֹעַ

power, as the Lord your God did for you in Egypt before your very eyes? [35a]-It has been clearly demonstrated to you-[a] that the Lord alone is God; there is none beside Him. [36]From the heavens He let you hear His voice to discipline you; on earth He let you see His great fire; and from amidst that fire you heard His words. [37]And because He loved your fathers, He chose their heirs after them; He Himself,[b] in His great might, led you out of Egypt, [38]to drive from your path nations greater and more populous than you, to take you into their land and assign it to you as a heritage, as is still the case. [39]Know therefore this day and keep in mind that the Lord alone is God in heaven above and on earth below; there is no other. [40]Observe His laws and commandments, which I enjoin upon you this day, that it may go well with you and your children after you, and that you may long remain in the land that the Lord your God is assigning to you for all time.

[41]Then Moses set aside three cities on the east side of the Jordan [42]to which a manslayer could escape, one who unwittingly slew a fellow man without having been hostile to him in the past; he could flee to one of these cities and live: [43]Bezer, in the wilderness in the Tableland, belonging to the Reubenites; Ramoth, in Gilead, belonging to the Gadites; and Golan, in Bashan, belonging to the Manassites.

[44]This is the Teaching that Moses set before the Israelites: [45]these are the decrees, laws, and rules that Moses addressed to the people of Israel, after they had left Egypt, [46]beyond the Jordan, in the valley at Beth-peor, in the land of King Sihon of the Amorites, who dwelt in Heshbon, whom Moses and the Israelites defeated after they had left Egypt. [47]They had taken possession of his country and that of King

נְטוּיָה וּבְמוֹרָאִים גְּדֹלִים כְּכֹל אֲשֶׁר־עָשָׂה לָכֶם יְהוָה אֱלֹהֵיכֶם בְּמִצְרַיִם לְעֵינֶיךָ: 35 אַתָּה הָרְאֵתָ לָדַעַת כִּי יְהוָה הוּא הָאֱלֹהִים אֵין עוֹד מִלְבַדּוֹ: 36 מִן־הַשָּׁמַיִם הִשְׁמִיעֲךָ אֶת־קֹלוֹ לְיַסְּרֶךָּ וְעַל־הָאָרֶץ הֶרְאֲךָ אֶת־אִשּׁוֹ הַגְּדוֹלָה וּדְבָרָיו שָׁמַעְתָּ מִתּוֹךְ הָאֵשׁ: 37 וְתַחַת כִּי אָהַב אֶת־אֲבֹתֶיךָ וַיִּבְחַר בְּזַרְעוֹ אַחֲרָיו וַיּוֹצִאֲךָ בְּפָנָיו בְּכֹחוֹ הַגָּדֹל מִמִּצְרָיִם: 38 לְהוֹרִישׁ גּוֹיִם גְּדֹלִים וַעֲצֻמִים מִמְּךָ מִפָּנֶיךָ לַהֲבִיאֲךָ לָתֶת־לְךָ אֶת־אַרְצָם נַחֲלָה כַּיּוֹם הַזֶּה: 39 וְיָדַעְתָּ הַיּוֹם וַהֲשֵׁבֹתָ אֶל־לְבָבֶךָ כִּי יְהוָה הוּא הָאֱלֹהִים בַּשָּׁמַיִם מִמַּעַל וְעַל־הָאָרֶץ מִתָּחַת אֵין עוֹד: 40 וְשָׁמַרְתָּ אֶת־חֻקָּיו וְאֶת־מִצְוֹתָיו אֲשֶׁר אָנֹכִי מְצַוְּךָ הַיּוֹם אֲשֶׁר יִיטַב לְךָ וּלְבָנֶיךָ אַחֲרֶיךָ וּלְמַעַן תַּאֲרִיךְ יָמִים עַל־הָאֲדָמָה אֲשֶׁר יְהוָה אֱלֹהֶיךָ נֹתֵן לְךָ כָּל־הַיָּמִים: פ

41 אָז יַבְדִּיל מֹשֶׁה שָׁלֹשׁ עָרִים בְּעֵבֶר הַיַּרְדֵּן מִזְרְחָה שָׁמֶשׁ: 42 לָנֻס שָׁמָּה רוֹצֵחַ אֲשֶׁר יִרְצַח אֶת־רֵעֵהוּ בִּבְלִי־דַעַת וְהוּא לֹא־שֹׂנֵא לוֹ מִתְּמֹל שִׁלְשֹׁם וְנָס אֶל־אַחַת מִן־הֶעָרִים הָאֵל וָחָי: 43 אֶת־בֶּצֶר בַּמִּדְבָּר בְּאֶרֶץ הַמִּישֹׁר לָרֻאוּבֵנִי וְאֶת־רָאמֹת בַּגִּלְעָד לַגָּדִי וְאֶת־גּוֹלָן בַּבָּשָׁן לַמְנַשִּׁי:

44 וְזֹאת הַתּוֹרָה אֲשֶׁר־שָׂם מֹשֶׁה לִפְנֵי בְּנֵי יִשְׂרָאֵל: 45 אֵלֶּה הָעֵדֹת וְהַחֻקִּים וְהַמִּשְׁפָּטִים אֲשֶׁר דִּבֶּר מֹשֶׁה אֶל־בְּנֵי יִשְׂרָאֵל בְּצֵאתָם מִמִּצְרָיִם: 46 בְּעֵבֶר הַיַּרְדֵּן בַּגַּיְא מוּל בֵּית פְּעוֹר בְּאֶרֶץ סִיחֹן מֶלֶךְ הָאֱמֹרִי אֲשֶׁר יוֹשֵׁב בְּחֶשְׁבּוֹן אֲשֶׁר הִכָּה מֹשֶׁה וּבְנֵי יִשְׂרָאֵל בְּצֵאתָם מִמִּצְרָיִם: 47 וַיִּירְשׁוּ אֶת־אַרְצוֹ וְאֶת־

a-a   *Lit.* "You have been shown to know."
b   *Lit.* "With His face (or Presence)"; *cf.* note at Exod. 33.14.

385

Og of Bashan—the two kings of the Amorites—
which were on the east side of the Jordan ⁴⁸from
Aroer on the banks of the wadi Arnon, as far
as Mount Sion,ᶜ that is, Hermon; ⁴⁹also the
whole Arabah on the east side of the Jordan, as
far as the Sea of the Arabah, at the foot of the
slopes of Pisgah.

5 Moses summoned all the Israelites and said
to them: Hear, O Israel, the laws and rules that
I proclaim to you this day! Study them and observe them faithfully!

²The LORD our God made a covenant with
us at Horeb. ³It was not with our fathers that
the LORD made this covenant, but with us, the
living, every one of us who is here today. ⁴Face
to face the LORD spoke to you on the mountain
out of the fire—⁵I stood between the LORD and
you at that time to convey the LORD's words to
you, for you were afraid of the fire and did not
go up the mountain—saying:

⁶ᵃI the LORD am your God who brought you
out of the land of Egypt, the house of bondage:
⁷You shall have no other gods beside Me.

⁸You shall not make for yourself a sculptured
image, any likeness of what is in the heavens
above, or on the earth below, or in the waters
below the earth. ⁹You shall not bow down to
them or serve them. For I the LORD your God
am an impassioned God, visiting the guilt of the
parents upon the children, upon the third and
upon the fourth generations of those who reject
Me, ¹⁰but showing kindness to the thousandth
generation of those who love Me and keep My
commandments.

¹¹You shall not swear falsely by the name of
the LORD your God; for the LORD will not clear
one who swears falsely by His name.

ᶜ Cf. "Sirion," 3.9.

ᵃ Tradition varies as to the divisions of the Commandments in
vv. 6–18 and the numbering of the verses. Cf. Exod. 20, note a.

אֶרֶץ ׀ עוֹג מֶלֶךְ־הַבָּשָׁן שְׁנֵי מַלְכֵי הָאֱמֹרִי
אֲשֶׁר בְּעֵבֶר הַיַּרְדֵּן מִזְרַח שָׁמֶשׁ: ⁴⁸ מֵעֲרֹעֵר אֲשֶׁר עַל־שְׂפַת־נַחַל אַרְנֹן וְעַד־
הַר שִׂיאֹן הוּא חֶרְמוֹן: ⁴⁹ וְכָל־הָעֲרָבָה
עֵבֶר הַיַּרְדֵּן מִזְרָחָה וְעַד יָם הָעֲרָבָה תַּחַת
אַשְׁדֹּת הַפִּסְגָּה: פ

ה וַיִּקְרָא מֹשֶׁה אֶל־כָּל־יִשְׂרָאֵל וַיֹּאמֶר
אֲלֵהֶם שְׁמַע יִשְׂרָאֵל אֶת־הַחֻקִּים וְאֶת־
הַמִּשְׁפָּטִים אֲשֶׁר אָנֹכִי דֹּבֵר בְּאָזְנֵיכֶם הַיּוֹם
וּלְמַדְתֶּם אֹתָם וּשְׁמַרְתֶּם לַעֲשֹׂתָם:
² יְהוָה אֱלֹהֵינוּ כָּרַת עִמָּנוּ בְּרִית בְּחֹרֵב:
³ לֹא אֶת־אֲבֹתֵינוּ כָּרַת יְהוָה אֶת־הַבְּרִית
הַזֹּאת כִּי אִתָּנוּ אֲנַחְנוּ אֵלֶּה פֹה הַיּוֹם
כֻּלָּנוּ חַיִּים: ⁴ פָּנִים ׀ בְּפָנִים דִּבֶּר יְהוָה
עִמָּכֶם בָּהָר מִתּוֹךְ הָאֵשׁ: ⁵ אָנֹכִי עֹמֵד
בֵּין־יְהוָה וּבֵינֵיכֶם בָּעֵת הַהִוא לְהַגִּיד
לָכֶם אֶת־דְּבַר יְהוָה כִּי יְרֵאתֶם מִפְּנֵי
הָאֵשׁ וְלֹא־עֲלִיתֶם בָּהָר לֵאמֹר: ס
⁶*אָנֹכִי יְהוָה אֱלֹהֶיךָ אֲשֶׁר הוֹצֵאתִיךָ
מֵאֶרֶץ מִצְרַיִם מִבֵּית עֲבָדִים: ⁷*לֹא יִהְיֶה
לְךָ אֱלֹהִים אֲחֵרִים עַל־פָּנָי:
⁸ לֹא־תַעֲשֶׂה־לְךָ פֶסֶל ׀ כָּל־תְּמוּנָה אֲשֶׁר
בַּשָּׁמַיִם ׀ מִמַּעַל וַאֲשֶׁר בָּאָרֶץ מִתַּחַת
וַאֲשֶׁר בַּמַּיִם ׀ מִתַּחַת לָאָרֶץ: ⁹ לֹא־
תִשְׁתַּחֲוֶה לָהֶם וְלֹא תָעָבְדֵם כִּי אָנֹכִי
יְהוָה אֱלֹהֶיךָ אֵל קַנָּא פֹּקֵד עֲוֹן אָבוֹת
עַל־בָּנִים וְעַל־שִׁלֵּשִׁים וְעַל־רִבֵּעִים
לְשֹׂנְאָי: ¹⁰ וְעֹשֶׂה חֶסֶד לַאֲלָפִים לְאֹהֲבַי
וּלְשֹׁמְרֵי מִצְוֹתו מִצְוֹתָי: ס
¹¹ לֹא תִשָּׂא אֶת־שֵׁם־יְהוָה אֱלֹהֶיךָ לַשָּׁוְא
כִּי לֹא יְנַקֶּה יְהוָה אֵת אֲשֶׁר־יִשָּׂא אֶת־
שְׁמוֹ לַשָּׁוְא: ס

v. 6–18. נדפס בטעם התחתון בלבד, והוא למערבאי,
והפסוקים נספר לפי מהדורת לעטעריס
v. 7. למערבאי לא נספר בסכום הפסוקים

386

12Observe the sabbath day and keep it holy, as the Lord your God has commanded you. 13Six days you shall labor and do all your work, 14but the seventh day is a sabbath of the Lord your God; you shall not do any work—you, your son or your daughter, your male or female slave, your ox or your ass, or any of your cattle, or the stranger in your settlements, so that your male and female slave may rest as you do. 15Remember that you were a slave in the land of Egypt and the Lord your God freed you from there with a mighty hand and an outstretched arm; therefore the Lord your God has commanded you to observe the sabbath day.

16Honor your father and your mother, as the Lord your God has commanded you, that you may long endure, and that you may fare well, in the land that the Lord your God is assigning to you.

17You shall not murder.

You shall not commit adultery.

You shall not steal.

You shall not bear false witness against your neighbor.

18You shall not covet your neighbor's wife. You shall not crave your neighbor's house, or his field, or his male or female slave, or his ox, or his ass, or anything that is your neighbor's.

19The Lord spoke those words—those and no more—to your whole congregation at the mountain, with a mighty voice out of the fire and the dense clouds. He inscribed them on two tablets of stone, which He gave to me. 20When you heard the voice out of the darkness, while the mountain was ablaze with fire, you came up to me, all your tribal heads and elders, 21and said, "The Lord our God has just shown us His majestic Presence, and we have heard His voice out of the fire; we have seen this day that man may live though God has spoken to him. 22Let us not die, then, for this fearsome fire will con-

12 שָׁמ֣וֹר אֶת־י֥וֹם הַשַּׁבָּ֖ת לְקַדְּשׁ֑וֹ כַּאֲשֶׁ֥ר צִוְּךָ֖ ׀ יְהוָ֣ה אֱלֹהֶֽיךָ׃ 13 שֵׁ֤שֶׁת יָמִים֙ תַּֽעֲבֹ֔ד וְעָשִׂ֖יתָ כָּֽל־מְלַאכְתֶּֽךָ׃ 14 וְי֙וֹם֙ הַשְּׁבִיעִ֔י שַׁבָּ֖ת לַיהוָ֣ה אֱלֹהֶ֑יךָ לֹ֣א תַעֲשֶׂ֣ה כָל־מְלָאכָ֡ה אַתָּ֣ה וּבִנְךָֽ־וּבִתֶּ֣ךָ וְעַבְדְּךָֽ־וַ֠אֲמָתֶ֠ךָ וְשׁוֹרְךָ֙ וַחֲמֹֽרְךָ֜ וְכָל־בְּהֶמְתֶּ֗ךָ וְגֵֽרְךָ֙ אֲשֶׁ֣ר בִּשְׁעָרֶ֔יךָ לְמַ֗עַן יָנ֛וּחַ עַבְדְּךָ֥ וַאֲמָתְךָ֖ כָּמֽוֹךָ׃ 15 וְזָכַרְתָּ֞ כִּ֣י עֶ֣בֶד הָיִ֣יתָ ׀ בְּאֶ֣רֶץ מִצְרַ֗יִם וַיֹּצִ֨אֲךָ֜ יְהוָ֤ה אֱלֹהֶ֙יךָ֙ מִשָּׁ֔ם בְּיָ֥ד חֲזָקָ֖ה וּבִזְרֹ֣עַ נְטוּיָ֑ה עַל־כֵּ֗ן צִוְּךָ֙ יְהוָ֣ה אֱלֹהֶ֔יךָ לַעֲשׂ֖וֹת אֶת־י֥וֹם הַשַּׁבָּֽת׃ ס 16 כַּבֵּ֤ד אֶת־אָבִ֙יךָ֙ וְאֶת־אִמֶּ֔ךָ כַּאֲשֶׁ֥ר צִוְּךָ֖ יְהוָ֣ה אֱלֹהֶ֑יךָ לְמַ֣עַן ׀ יַאֲרִיכֻ֣ן יָמֶ֗יךָ וּלְמַ֙עַן֙ יִ֣יטַב לָ֔ךְ עַ֚ל הָֽאֲדָמָ֔ה אֲשֶׁר־יְהוָ֥ה אֱלֹהֶ֖יךָ נֹתֵ֥ן לָֽךְ׃ ס

17 *לֹ֥א תִּרְצָֽח׃ ס

וְלֹ֖א תִּנְאָֽף׃ ס

וְלֹ֖א תִּגְנֹֽב׃ ס

וְלֹֽא־תַעֲנֶ֥ה בְרֵֽעֲךָ֖ עֵ֥ד שָֽׁוְא׃ ס

18 וְלֹ֥א תַחְמֹ֖ד אֵ֣שֶׁת רֵעֶ֑ךָ* ס וְלֹ֣א תִתְאַוֶּ֜ה בֵּ֣ית רֵעֶ֗ךָ שָׂדֵ֜הוּ וְעַבְדּ֤וֹ וַאֲמָתוֹ֙ שׁוֹר֣וֹ וַחֲמֹר֔וֹ וְכֹ֖ל אֲשֶׁ֥ר לְרֵעֶֽךָ׃ ס

19 אֶֽת־הַדְּבָרִ֣ים הָאֵ֡לֶּה דִּבֶּר֩ יְהוָ֨ה אֶל־כָּל־קְהַלְכֶ֜ם בָּהָ֗ר מִתּ֤וֹךְ הָאֵשׁ֙ הֶֽעָנָ֣ן וְהָֽעֲרָפֶ֔ל ק֥וֹל גָּד֖וֹל וְלֹ֣א יָסָ֑ף וַֽיִּכְתְּבֵ֗ם עַל־שְׁנֵי֙ לֻחֹ֣ת אֲבָנִ֔ים וַֽיִּתְּנֵ֖ם אֵלָֽי׃ 20 וַֽיְהִ֗י כְּשָׁמְעֲכֶ֤ם אֶת־הַקּוֹל֙ מִתּ֣וֹךְ הַחֹ֔שֶׁךְ וְהָהָ֖ר בֹּעֵ֣ר בָּאֵ֑שׁ וַתִּקְרְב֣וּן אֵלַ֔י כָּל־רָאשֵׁ֥י שִׁבְטֵיכֶ֖ם וְזִקְנֵיכֶֽם׃ 21 וַתֹּאמְר֗וּ הֵ֣ן הֶרְאָ֜נוּ יְהוָ֤ה אֱלֹהֵ֙ינוּ֙ אֶת־כְּבֹד֣וֹ וְאֶת־גָּדְל֔וֹ וְאֶת־קֹל֥וֹ שָׁמַ֖עְנוּ מִתּ֣וֹךְ הָאֵ֑שׁ הַיּ֤וֹם הַזֶּה֙ רָאִ֔ינוּ כִּֽי־יְדַבֵּ֧ר אֱלֹהִ֛ים אֶת־הָֽאָדָ֖ם וָחָֽי׃ 22 וְעַתָּה֙ לָ֣מָּה נָמ֔וּת כִּ֣י תֹֽאכְלֵ֔נוּ הָאֵ֥שׁ הַגְּדֹלָ֖ה הַזֹּ֑את אִם־יֹסְפִ֣ים ׀ אֲנַ֗חְנוּ לִשְׁמֹ֛עַ

sume us; if we hear the voice of the Lord our God any longer, we shall die. [23]For what mortal ever heard the voice of the living God speak out of the fire, as we did, and lived? [24]You go closer and hear all that the Lord our God says, and then you tell us everything that the Lord our God tells you, and we will willingly do it."

[25]The Lord heard the plea that you made to me, and the Lord said to me, "I have heard the plea that this people made to you; they did well to speak thus. [26]May they always be of such mind, to revere Me and follow all My commandments, that it may go well with them and with their children forever! [27]Go, say to them, 'Return to your tents.' [28]But you remain here with Me, and I will give you the whole Instruction—the laws and the rules—that you shall impart to them, for them to observe in the land that I am giving them to possess."

[29]Be careful, then, to do as the Lord your God has commanded you. Do not turn aside to the right or to the left: [30]follow only the path that the Lord your God has enjoined upon you, so that you may thrive and that it may go well with you, and that you may long endure in the land you are to possess.

6 And this is the Instruction—the laws and the rules—that the Lord your God has commanded [me] to impart to you, to be observed in the land that you are about to cross into and occupy, [2]so that you, your children, and your children's children may revere the Lord your God and follow, as long as you live, all His laws and commandments that I enjoin upon you, to the end that you may long endure. [3]Obey, O Israel, willingly and faithfully, that it may go well with you and that you may increase greatly [in] *a*-a land flowing with milk and honey,-*a* as the Lord, the God of your fathers, spoke to you.

אֶת־קוֹל יְהוָה אֱלֹהֵינוּ עוֹד וָמָתְנוּ׃ [23] כִּי מִי כָל־בָּשָׂר אֲשֶׁר שָׁמַע קוֹל אֱלֹהִים חַיִּים מְדַבֵּר מִתּוֹךְ־הָאֵשׁ כָּמֹנוּ וַיֶּחִי׃ [24] קְרַב אַתָּה וּשֲׁמָע אֵת כָּל־אֲשֶׁר יֹאמַר יְהוָה אֱלֹהֵינוּ וְאַתְּ ׀ תְּדַבֵּר אֵלֵינוּ אֵת כָּל־אֲשֶׁר יְדַבֵּר יְהוָה אֱלֹהֵינוּ אֵלֶיךָ וְשָׁמַעְנוּ וְעָשִׂינוּ׃

[25] וַיִּשְׁמַע יְהוָה אֶת־קוֹל דִּבְרֵיכֶם בְּדַבֶּרְכֶם אֵלָי וַיֹּאמֶר יְהוָה אֵלַי שָׁמַעְתִּי אֶת־קוֹל דִּבְרֵי הָעָם הַזֶּה אֲשֶׁר דִּבְּרוּ אֵלֶיךָ הֵיטִיבוּ כָּל־אֲשֶׁר דִּבֵּרוּ׃ [26] מִי־יִתֵּן וְהָיָה לְבָבָם זֶה לָהֶם לְיִרְאָה אֹתִי וְלִשְׁמֹר אֶת־כָּל־מִצְוֹתַי כָּל־הַיָּמִים לְמַעַן יִיטַב לָהֶם וְלִבְנֵיהֶם לְעֹלָם׃ [27] לֵךְ אֱמֹר לָהֶם שׁוּבוּ לָכֶם לְאָהֳלֵיכֶם׃ [28] וְאַתָּה פֹּה עֲמֹד עִמָּדִי וַאֲדַבְּרָה אֵלֶיךָ אֵת כָּל־הַמִּצְוָה וְהַחֻקִּים וְהַמִּשְׁפָּטִים אֲשֶׁר תְּלַמְּדֵם וְעָשׂוּ בָאָרֶץ אֲשֶׁר אָנֹכִי נֹתֵן לָהֶם לְרִשְׁתָּהּ׃

[29] וּשְׁמַרְתֶּם לַעֲשׂוֹת כַּאֲשֶׁר צִוָּה יְהוָה אֱלֹהֵיכֶם אֶתְכֶם לֹא תָסֻרוּ יָמִין וּשְׂמֹאל׃ [30] בְּכָל־הַדֶּרֶךְ אֲשֶׁר צִוָּה יְהוָה אֱלֹהֵיכֶם אֶתְכֶם תֵּלֵכוּ לְמַעַן תִּחְיוּן וְטוֹב לָכֶם וְהַאֲרַכְתֶּם יָמִים בָּאָרֶץ אֲשֶׁר תִּירָשׁוּן׃

ו וְזֹאת הַמִּצְוָה הַחֻקִּים וְהַמִּשְׁפָּטִים אֲשֶׁר צִוָּה יְהוָה אֱלֹהֵיכֶם לְלַמֵּד אֶתְכֶם לַעֲשׂוֹת בָּאָרֶץ אֲשֶׁר אַתֶּם עֹבְרִים שָׁמָּה לְרִשְׁתָּהּ׃ [2] לְמַעַן תִּירָא אֶת־יְהוָה אֱלֹהֶיךָ לִשְׁמֹר אֶת־כָּל־חֻקֹּתָיו וּמִצְוֹתָיו אֲשֶׁר אָנֹכִי מְצַוֶּךָ אַתָּה וּבִנְךָ וּבֶן־בִּנְךָ כֹּל יְמֵי חַיֶּיךָ וּלְמַעַן יַאֲרִכֻן יָמֶיךָ׃ [3] וְשָׁמַעְתָּ יִשְׂרָאֵל וְשָׁמַרְתָּ לַעֲשׂוֹת אֲשֶׁר יִיטַב לְךָ וַאֲשֶׁר תִּרְבּוּן מְאֹד כַּאֲשֶׁר דִּבֶּר יְהוָה אֱלֹהֵי אֲבֹתֶיךָ לָךְ אֶרֶץ זָבַת חָלָב וּדְבָשׁ׃ פ

---

a-a According to Ibn Ezra this phrase connects with the end of v. 1.

388

⁴Hear, O Israel! The LORD is our God, the LORD alone.ᵇ ⁵You shall love the LORD your God with all your heart and with all your soul and with all your might. ⁶Take to heart these instructions with which I charge you this day. ⁷Impress them upon your children. Recite them when you stay at home and when you are away, when you lie down and when you get up. ⁸Bind them as a sign on your hand and let them serve as a symbolᶜ on your forehead;ᵈ ⁹inscribe them on the doorposts of your house and on your gates.

¹⁰When the LORD your God brings you into the land that He swore to your fathers, Abraham, Isaac, and Jacob, to assign to you—great and flourishing cities that you did not build, ¹¹houses full of all good things that you did not fill, hewn cisterns that you did not hew, vineyards and olive groves that you did not plant—and you eat your fill, ¹²take heed that you do not forget the LORD who freed you from the land of Egypt, the house of bondage. ¹³Revere only the LORD your God and worship Him alone, and swear only by His name. ¹⁴Do not follow other gods, any gods of the peoples about you—¹⁵for the LORD your God in your midst is an impassioned God—lest the anger of the LORD your God blaze forth against you and He wipe you off the face of the earth.

¹⁶Do not try the LORD your God, as you did at Massah.ᵉ ¹⁷Be sure to keep the commandments, decrees, and laws that the LORD your God has enjoined upon you. ¹⁸Do what is right and good in the sight of the LORD, that it may go well with you and that you may be able to possess the good land that the LORD your God promised on oath to your fathers, ¹⁹and that all your enemies may be driven out before you, as the LORD has spoken.

⁴ שְׁמַ֖ע יִשְׂרָאֵ֑ל יְהֹוָ֥ה אֱלֹהֵ֖ינוּ יְהֹוָ֥ה ׀ אֶחָֽד׃ ⁵ וְאָ֣הַבְתָּ֔ אֵ֖ת יְהֹוָ֣ה אֱלֹהֶ֑יךָ בְּכׇל־לְבָבְךָ֥ וּבְכׇל־נַפְשְׁךָ֖ וּבְכׇל־מְאֹדֶֽךָ׃ ⁶ וְהָי֞וּ הַדְּבָרִ֣ים הָאֵ֗לֶּה אֲשֶׁ֨ר אָנֹכִ֧י מְצַוְּךָ֛ הַיּ֖וֹם עַל־לְבָבֶֽךָ׃ ⁷ וְשִׁנַּנְתָּ֣ם לְבָנֶ֔יךָ וְדִבַּרְתָּ֖ בָּ֑ם בְּשִׁבְתְּךָ֤ בְּבֵיתֶ֙ךָ֙ וּבְלֶכְתְּךָ֣ בַדֶּ֔רֶךְ וּֽבְשׇׁכְבְּךָ֖ וּבְקוּמֶֽךָ׃ ⁸ וּקְשַׁרְתָּ֥ם לְא֖וֹת עַל־יָדֶ֑ךָ וְהָי֥וּ לְטֹטָפֹ֖ת בֵּ֥ין עֵינֶֽיךָ׃ ⁹ וּכְתַבְתָּ֛ם עַל־מְזֻז֥וֹת בֵּיתֶ֖ךָ וּבִשְׁעָרֶֽיךָ׃ ס

¹⁰ וְהָיָ֞ה כִּ֥י יְבִֽיאֲךָ֣ ׀ יְהֹוָ֣ה אֱלֹהֶ֗יךָ אֶל־הָאָ֜רֶץ אֲשֶׁ֨ר נִשְׁבַּ֧ע לַאֲבֹתֶ֛יךָ לְאַבְרָהָ֧ם לְיִצְחָ֛ק וּֽלְיַעֲקֹ֖ב לָ֣תֶת לָ֑ךְ עָרִ֛ים גְּדֹלֹ֥ת וְטֹבֹ֖ת אֲשֶׁ֥ר לֹא־בָנִֽיתָ׃ ¹¹ וּבָ֨תִּ֜ים מְלֵאִ֣ים כׇּל־טוּב֮ אֲשֶׁ֣ר לֹא־מִלֵּ֒אתָ֒ וּבֹרֹ֤ת חֲצוּבִים֙ אֲשֶׁ֣ר לֹא־חָצַ֔בְתָּ כְּרָמִ֥ים וְזֵיתִ֖ים אֲשֶׁ֣ר לֹא־נָטָ֑עְתָּ וְאָכַלְתָּ֖ וְשָׂבָֽעְתָּ׃ ¹² הִשָּׁ֣מֶר לְךָ֔ פֶּן־תִּשְׁכַּ֖ח אֶת־יְהֹוָ֑ה אֲשֶׁ֧ר הוֹצִֽיאֲךָ֛ מֵאֶ֥רֶץ מִצְרַ֖יִם מִבֵּ֥ית עֲבָדִֽים׃ ¹³ אֶת־יְהֹוָ֧ה אֱלֹהֶ֛יךָ תִּירָ֖א וְאֹת֣וֹ תַעֲבֹ֑ד וּבִשְׁמ֖וֹ תִּשָּׁבֵֽעַ׃ ¹⁴ לֹ֣א תֵֽלְכ֔וּן אַחֲרֵ֖י אֱלֹהִ֣ים אֲחֵרִ֑ים מֵאֱלֹהֵי֙ הָֽעַמִּ֔ים אֲשֶׁ֖ר סְבִיבוֹתֵיכֶֽם׃ ¹⁵ כִּ֣י אֵ֥ל קַנָּ֛א יְהֹוָ֥ה אֱלֹהֶ֖יךָ בְּקִרְבֶּ֑ךָ פֶּן־יֶ֠חֱרֶ֠ה אַף־יְהֹוָ֤ה אֱלֹהֶ֙יךָ֙ בָּ֔ךְ וְהִשְׁמִ֣ידְךָ֔ מֵעַ֖ל פְּנֵ֥י הָאֲדָמָֽה׃ ס

¹⁶ לֹ֣א תְנַסּ֔וּ אֶת־יְהֹוָ֖ה אֱלֹהֵיכֶ֑ם כַּאֲשֶׁ֥ר נִסִּיתֶ֖ם בַּמַּסָּֽה׃ ¹⁷ שָׁמ֣וֹר תִּשְׁמְר֔וּן אֶת־מִצְוֺ֖ת יְהֹוָ֣ה אֱלֹהֵיכֶ֑ם וְעֵדֹתָ֖יו וְחֻקָּ֥יו אֲשֶׁ֥ר צִוָּֽךְ׃ ¹⁸ וְעָשִׂ֛יתָ הַיָּשָׁ֥ר וְהַטּ֖וֹב בְּעֵינֵ֣י יְהֹוָ֑ה לְמַ֙עַן֙ יִ֣יטַב לָ֔ךְ וּבָ֗אתָ וְיָֽרַשְׁתָּ֙ אֶת־הָאָ֣רֶץ הַטֹּבָ֔ה אֲשֶׁר־נִשְׁבַּ֥ע יְהֹוָ֖ה לַאֲבֹתֶֽיךָ׃ ¹⁹ לַהֲדֹ֥ף אֶת־כׇּל־אֹיְבֶ֖יךָ מִפָּנֶ֑יךָ כַּאֲשֶׁ֖ר דִּבֶּ֥ר יְהֹוָֽה׃ ס

v. 4. ע׳ ד׳ רבתי

ᵇ Cf. Rashbam and Ibn Ezra; see Zech. 14.9. Others "The LORD our God, the LORD is one."
ᶜ Others "frontlet"; cf. Exod. 13.16.
ᵈ Lit. "between your eyes"; cf. Exod. 13.9.
ᵉ Cf. Exod. 17.1–7.

20When, in time to come, your children ask you, "What mean the decrees, laws, and rules that the Lord our God has enjoined upon you?"f 21you shall say to your children, "We were slaves to Pharaoh in Egypt and the Lord freed us from Egypt with a mighty hand. 22The Lord wrought before our eyes marvelous and destructive signs and portents in Egypt, against Pharaoh and all his household; 23and us He freed from there, that He might take us and give us the land that He had promised on oath to our fathers. 24Then the Lord commanded us to observe all these laws, to revere the Lord our God, for our lasting good and for our survival, as is now the case. 25It will be therefore to our merit before the Lord our God to observe faithfully this whole Instruction, as He has commanded us."

7 When the Lord your God brings you to the land that you are about to enter and possess, and He dislodges many nations before you— the Hittites, Girgashites, Amorites, Canaanites, Perizzites, Hivites, and Jebusites, seven nations much larger than you—2and the Lord your God delivers them to you and you defeat them, you must doom them to destruction: grant them no terms and give them no quarter. 3You shall not intermarry with them: do not give your daughters to their sons or take their daughters for your sons. 4For they will turn your children away from Me to worship other gods, and the Lord's anger will blaze forth against you and He will promptly wipe you out. 5Instead, this is what you shall do to them: you shall tear down their altars, smash their pillars, cut down their sacred posts, and consign their images to the fire.

6For you are a people consecrated to the Lord your God: of all the peoples on earth the Lord your God chose you to be His treasured people.

20 כִּי־יִשְׁאָלְךָ בִנְךָ מָחָר לֵאמֹר מָה הָעֵדֹת וְהַחֻקִּים וְהַמִּשְׁפָּטִים אֲשֶׁר צִוָּה יְהוָה אֱלֹהֵינוּ אֶתְכֶם: 21 וְאָמַרְתָּ לְבִנְךָ עֲבָדִים הָיִינוּ לְפַרְעֹה בְּמִצְרָיִם וַיּוֹצִיאֵנוּ יְהוָה מִמִּצְרַיִם בְּיָד חֲזָקָה: 22 וַיִּתֵּן יְהוָה אוֹתֹת וּמֹפְתִים גְּדֹלִים וְרָעִים בְּמִצְרַיִם בְּפַרְעֹה וּבְכָל־בֵּיתוֹ לְעֵינֵינוּ: 23 וְאוֹתָנוּ הוֹצִיא מִשָּׁם לְמַעַן הָבִיא אֹתָנוּ לָתֶת לָנוּ אֶת־הָאָרֶץ אֲשֶׁר נִשְׁבַּע לַאֲבֹתֵינוּ: 24 וַיְצַוֵּנוּ יְהוָה לַעֲשׂוֹת אֶת־כָּל־הַחֻקִּים הָאֵלֶּה לְיִרְאָה אֶת־יְהוָה אֱלֹהֵינוּ לְטוֹב לָנוּ כָּל־הַיָּמִים לְחַיֹּתֵנוּ כְּהַיּוֹם הַזֶּה: 25 וּצְדָקָה תִּהְיֶה־לָּנוּ כִּי־נִשְׁמֹר לַעֲשׂוֹת אֶת־כָּל־הַמִּצְוָה הַזֹּאת לִפְנֵי יְהוָה אֱלֹהֵינוּ כַּאֲשֶׁר צִוָּנוּ: ס

ז כִּי יְבִיאֲךָ יְהוָה אֱלֹהֶיךָ אֶל־הָאָרֶץ אֲשֶׁר־אַתָּה בָא־שָׁמָּה לְרִשְׁתָּהּ וְנָשַׁל גּוֹיִם־רַבִּים | מִפָּנֶיךָ הַחִתִּי וְהַגִּרְגָּשִׁי וְהָאֱמֹרִי וְהַכְּנַעֲנִי וְהַפְּרִזִּי וְהַחִוִּי וְהַיְבוּסִי שִׁבְעָה גוֹיִם רַבִּים וַעֲצוּמִים מִמֶּךָּ: 2 וּנְתָנָם יְהוָה אֱלֹהֶיךָ לְפָנֶיךָ וְהִכִּיתָם הַחֲרֵם תַּחֲרִים אֹתָם לֹא־תִכְרֹת לָהֶם בְּרִית וְלֹא תְחָנֵּם: 3 וְלֹא תִתְחַתֵּן בָּם בִּתְּךָ לֹא־תִתֵּן לִבְנוֹ וּבִתּוֹ לֹא־תִקַּח לִבְנֶךָ: 4 כִּי־יָסִיר אֶת־בִּנְךָ מֵאַחֲרַי וְעָבְדוּ אֱלֹהִים אֲחֵרִים וְחָרָה אַף־יְהוָה בָּכֶם וְהִשְׁמִידְךָ מַהֵר: 5 כִּי־אִם־כֹּה תַעֲשׂוּ לָהֶם מִזְבְּחֹתֵיהֶם תִּתֹּצוּ וּמַצֵּבֹתָם תְּשַׁבֵּרוּ וַאֲשֵׁירֵהֶם תְּגַדֵּעוּן וּפְסִילֵיהֶם תִּשְׂרְפוּן בָּאֵשׁ: 6 כִּי עַם קָדוֹשׁ אַתָּה לַיהוָה אֱלֹהֶיךָ בְּךָ בָּחַר | יְהוָה אֱלֹהֶיךָ לִהְיוֹת לוֹ לְעַם סְגֻלָּה

___
f Septuagint and rabbinic quotations read "us."

7It is not because you are the most numerous of peoples that the LORD set His heart on you and chose you—indeed, you are the smallest of peoples; 8but it was because the LORD favored you and kept the oath He made to your fathers that the LORD freed you with a mighty hand and rescued you from the house of bondage, from the power of Pharaoh king of Egypt.

9Know, therefore, that only the LORD your God is God, the steadfast God who keeps His covenant faithfully to the thousandth generation of those who love Him and keep His commandments, 10but who instantly requites with destruction those who reject Him—never slow with those who reject Him, but requiting them instantly. 11Therefore, observe faithfully the Instruction—the laws and the rules—with which I charge you today.

'EKEV

12And if you do obey these rules and observe them carefully, the LORD your God will maintain faithfully for you the covenant that He made on oath with your fathers: 13He will favor you and bless you and multiply you; He will bless the issue of your womb and the produce of your soil, your new grain and wine and oil, the calving of your herd and the lambing of your flock, in the land that He swore to your fathers to assign to you. 14You shall be blessed above all other peoples: there shall be no sterile male or female among you or among your livestock. 15The LORD will ward off from you all sickness; He will not bring upon you any of the dreadful diseases of Egypt, about which you know, but will inflict them upon all your enemies.

16You shall destroy all the peoples that the LORD your God delivers to you, showing them no pity. And you shall not worship their gods, for that would be a snare to you. 17Should you say to yourselves, "These nations are more nu-

מִכֹּל הָעַמִּים אֲשֶׁר עַל־פְּנֵי הָאֲדָמָה: ס 7 לֹא מֵרֻבְּכֶם מִכָּל־הָעַמִּים חָשַׁק יְהֹוָה בָּכֶם וַיִּבְחַר בָּכֶם כִּי־אַתֶּם הַמְעַט מִכָּל־הָעַמִּים: 8 כִּי מֵאַהֲבַת יְהֹוָה אֶתְכֶם וּמִשָּׁמְרוֹ אֶת־הַשְּׁבֻעָה אֲשֶׁר נִשְׁבַּע לַאֲבֹתֵיכֶם הוֹצִיא יְהֹוָה אֶתְכֶם בְּיָד חֲזָקָה וַיִּפְדְּךָ מִבֵּית עֲבָדִים מִיַּד פַּרְעֹה מֶלֶךְ־מִצְרָיִם: 9 וְיָדַעְתָּ כִּי־יְהֹוָה אֱלֹהֶיךָ הוּא הָאֱלֹהִים הָאֵל הַנֶּאֱמָן שֹׁמֵר הַבְּרִית וְהַחֶסֶד לְאֹהֲבָיו וּלְשֹׁמְרֵי מִצְוֹתָו לְאֶלֶף דּוֹר: 10 וּמְשַׁלֵּם לְשֹׂנְאָיו אֶל־פָּנָיו לְהַאֲבִידוֹ לֹא יְאַחֵר לְשֹׂנְאוֹ אֶל־פָּנָיו יְשַׁלֶּם־לוֹ: 11 וְשָׁמַרְתָּ אֶת־הַמִּצְוָה וְאֶת־הַחֻקִּים וְאֶת־הַמִּשְׁפָּטִים אֲשֶׁר אָנֹכִי מְצַוְּךָ הַיּוֹם לַעֲשׂוֹתָם: פ

עקב

12 וְהָיָה | עֵקֶב תִּשְׁמְעוּן אֵת הַמִּשְׁפָּטִים הָאֵלֶּה וּשְׁמַרְתֶּם וַעֲשִׂיתֶם אֹתָם וְשָׁמַר יְהֹוָה אֱלֹהֶיךָ לְךָ אֶת־הַבְּרִית וְאֶת־הַחֶסֶד אֲשֶׁר נִשְׁבַּע לַאֲבֹתֶיךָ: 13 וַאֲהֵבְךָ וּבֵרַכְךָ וְהִרְבֶּךָ וּבֵרַךְ פְּרִי־בִטְנְךָ וּפְרִי־אַדְמָתֶךָ דְּגָנְךָ וְתִירֹשְׁךָ וְיִצְהָרֶךָ שְׁגַר־אֲלָפֶיךָ וְעַשְׁתְּרֹת צֹאנֶךָ עַל הָאֲדָמָה אֲשֶׁר־נִשְׁבַּע לַאֲבֹתֶיךָ לָתֶת לָךְ: 14 בָּרוּךְ תִּהְיֶה מִכָּל־הָעַמִּים לֹא־יִהְיֶה בְךָ עָקָר וַעֲקָרָה וּבִבְהֶמְתֶּךָ: 15 וְהֵסִיר יְהֹוָה מִמְּךָ כָּל־חֹלִי וְכָל־מַדְוֵי מִצְרַיִם הָרָעִים אֲשֶׁר יָדַעְתָּ לֹא יְשִׂימָם בָּךְ וּנְתָנָם בְּכָל־שֹׂנְאֶיךָ: 16 וְאָכַלְתָּ אֶת־כָּל־הָעַמִּים אֲשֶׁר יְהֹוָה אֱלֹהֶיךָ נֹתֵן לָךְ לֹא־תָחֹס עֵינְךָ עֲלֵיהֶם וְלֹא תַעֲבֹד אֶת־אֱלֹהֵיהֶם כִּי־מוֹקֵשׁ הוּא לָךְ: ס 17 כִּי תֹאמַר בִּלְבָבְךָ רַבִּים הַגּוֹיִם הָאֵלֶּה מִמֶּנִּי אֵיכָה אוּכַל

merous than we; how can we dispossess them?"
18You need have no fear of them. You have but
to bear in mind what the Lord your God did
to Pharaoh and all the Egyptians: 19the wondrous acts that you saw with your own eyes, the
signs and the portents, the mighty hand, and
the outstretched arm by which the Lord your
God liberated you. Thus will the Lord your God
do to all the peoples you now fear. 20The Lord
your God will also send a plague*a* against them,
until those who are left in hiding perish before
you. 21Do not stand in dread of them, for the
Lord your God is in your midst, a great and
awesome God.

22The Lord your God will dislodge those peoples before you little by little; you will not be
able to put an end to them at once, else the wild
beasts would multiply to your hurt. 23The Lord
your God will deliver them up to you, throwing
them into utter panic until they are wiped out.
24He will deliver their kings into your hand, and
you shall obliterate their name from under the
heavens; no man shall stand up to you, until you
have wiped them out.

25You shall consign the images of their gods
to the fire; you shall not covet the silver and gold
on them and keep it for yourselves, lest you be
ensnared thereby; for that is abhorrent to the
Lord your God. 26You must not bring an abhorrent thing into your house, or you will be
proscribed like it; you must reject it as abominable and abhorrent, for it is proscribed.

8 You shall faithfully observe all the Instruction that I enjoin upon you today, that you may
thrive and increase and be able to possess the
land that the Lord promised on oath to your
fathers.

2Remember the long way that the Lord your

לְהוֹרִישָׁם: 18 לֹא תִירָא מֵהֶם זָכֹר תִּזְכֹּר
אֵת אֲשֶׁר־עָשָׂה יְהוָה אֱלֹהֶיךָ לְפַרְעֹה
וּלְכָל־מִצְרָיִם: 19 הַמַּסֹּת הַגְּדֹלֹת אֲשֶׁר־
רָאוּ עֵינֶיךָ וְהָאֹתֹת וְהַמֹּפְתִים וְהַיָּד
הַחֲזָקָה וְהַזְּרֹעַ הַנְּטוּיָה אֲשֶׁר הוֹצִאֲךָ
יְהוָה אֱלֹהֶיךָ כֵּן־יַעֲשֶׂה יְהוָה אֱלֹהֶיךָ
לְכָל־הָעַמִּים אֲשֶׁר־אַתָּה יָרֵא מִפְּנֵיהֶם:
20 וְגַם אֶת־הַצִּרְעָה יְשַׁלַּח יְהוָה אֱלֹהֶיךָ
בָּם עַד־אֲבֹד הַנִּשְׁאָרִים וְהַנִּסְתָּרִים
מִפָּנֶיךָ: 21 לֹא תַעֲרֹץ מִפְּנֵיהֶם כִּי־יְהוָה
אֱלֹהֶיךָ בְּקִרְבֶּךָ אֵל גָּדוֹל וְנוֹרָא:
22 וְנָשַׁל יְהוָה אֱלֹהֶיךָ אֶת־הַגּוֹיִם הָאֵל
מִפָּנֶיךָ מְעַט מְעָט לֹא תוּכַל כַּלֹּתָם מַהֵר
פֶּן־תִּרְבֶּה עָלֶיךָ חַיַּת הַשָּׂדֶה: 23 וּנְתָנָם
יְהוָה אֱלֹהֶיךָ לְפָנֶיךָ וְהָמָם מְהוּמָה גְדֹלָה
עַד הִשָּׁמְדָם: 24 וְנָתַן מַלְכֵיהֶם בְּיָדֶךָ
וְהַאֲבַדְתָּ אֶת־שְׁמָם מִתַּחַת הַשָּׁמָיִם לֹא־
יִתְיַצֵּב אִישׁ בְּפָנֶיךָ עַד הִשְׁמִדְךָ אֹתָם:
25 פְּסִילֵי אֱלֹהֵיהֶם תִּשְׂרְפוּן בָּאֵשׁ לֹא־
תַחְמֹד כֶּסֶף וְזָהָב עֲלֵיהֶם וְלָקַחְתָּ לָךְ פֶּן
תִּוָּקֵשׁ בּוֹ כִּי תוֹעֲבַת יְהוָה אֱלֹהֶיךָ הוּא:
26 וְלֹא־תָבִיא תוֹעֵבָה אֶל־בֵּיתֶךָ וְהָיִיתָ
חֵרֶם כָּמֹהוּ שַׁקֵּץ | תְּשַׁקְּצֶנּוּ וְתַעֵב |
תְּתַעֲבֶנּוּ כִּי־חֵרֶם הוּא: פ

ח כָּל־הַמִּצְוָה אֲשֶׁר אָנֹכִי מְצַוְּךָ הַיּוֹם
תִּשְׁמְרוּן לַעֲשׂוֹת לְמַעַן תִּחְיוּן וּרְבִיתֶם
וּבָאתֶם וִירִשְׁתֶּם אֶת־הָאָרֶץ אֲשֶׁר־נִשְׁבַּע
יְהוָה לַאֲבֹתֵיכֶם:
2 וְזָכַרְתָּ אֶת־כָּל־הַדֶּרֶךְ אֲשֶׁר הֹלִיכֲךָ יְהוָה

---

*a   Others "hornet"; meaning of Heb. uncertain. Cf. note at Exod.
23.28.*

God has made you travel in the wilderness these past forty years, that He might test you by hardships to learn what was in your hearts: whether you would keep His commandments or not. 3He subjected you to the hardship of hunger and then gave you manna to eat, which neither you nor your fathers had ever known, in order to teach you that man does not live on bread alone, but that man may live on anything that the LORD decrees. 4The clothes upon you did not wear out, nor did your feet swell these forty years. 5Bear in mind that the LORD your God disciplines you just as a man disciplines his son. 6Therefore keep the commandments of the LORD your God: walk in His ways and revere Him.

7For the LORD your God is bringing you into a good land, a land with streams and springs and fountains issuing from plain and hill; 8a land of wheat and barley, of vines, figs, and pomegranates, a land of olive trees and honey; 9a land where you may eat food without stint, where you will lack nothing; a land whose rocks are iron and from whose hills you can mine copper. 10When you have eaten your fill, give thanks to the LORD your God for the good land which He has given you.

11Take care lest you forget the LORD your God and fail to keep His commandments, His rules, and His laws, which I enjoin upon you today. 12When you have eaten your fill, and have built fine houses to live in, 13and your herds and flocks have multiplied, and your silver and gold have increased, and everything you own has prospered, 14beware lest[a] your heart grow haughty and you forget the LORD your God— who freed you from the land of Egypt, the house of bondage; 15who led you through the great and terrible wilderness with its *seraph*[b] serpents and scorpions, a parched land with no water in it,

אֱלֹהֶ֗יךָ זֶ֣ה אַרְבָּעִ֥ים שָׁנָ֖ה בַּמִּדְבָּ֑ר לְמַ֨עַן עַנֹּֽתְךָ֜ לְנַסֹּֽתְךָ֗ לָדַ֜עַת אֶת־אֲשֶׁ֧ר בִּֽלְבָבְךָ֛ הֲתִשְׁמֹ֥ר מִצְוֹתָ֖ו אִם־לֹֽא׃ 3 וַֽיְעַנְּךָ֮ וַיַּרְעִבֶךָ֒ וַיַּֽאֲכִֽלְךָ֤ אֶת־הַמָּן֙ אֲשֶׁ֣ר לֹא־יָדַ֔עְתָּ וְלֹ֥א יָדְע֖וּן אֲבֹתֶ֑יךָ לְמַ֣עַן הוֹדִֽעֲךָ֗ כִּ֠י לֹ֣א עַל־הַלֶּ֤חֶם לְבַדּוֹ֙ יִחְיֶ֣ה הָֽאָדָ֔ם כִּ֛י עַל־כָּל־ מוֹצָ֥א פִֽי־יְהוָ֖ה יִחְיֶ֥ה הָֽאָדָֽם׃ 4 שִׂמְלָ֨תְךָ֜ לֹ֤א בָֽלְתָה֙ מֵֽעָלֶ֔יךָ וְרַגְלְךָ֖ לֹ֣א בָצֵ֑קָה זֶ֖ה אַרְבָּעִ֥ים שָׁנָֽה׃ 5 וְיָֽדַעְתָּ֖ עִם־לְבָבֶ֑ךָ כִּ֗י כַּֽאֲשֶׁ֨ר יְיַסֵּ֥ר אִישׁ֙ אֶת־בְּנ֔וֹ יְהוָ֥ה אֱלֹהֶ֖יךָ מְיַסְּרֶֽךָּ׃ 6 וְשָׁ֣מַרְתָּ֔ אֶת־מִצְוֹ֖ת יְהוָ֣ה אֱלֹהֶ֑יךָ לָלֶ֥כֶת בִּדְרָכָ֖יו וּלְיִרְאָ֥ה אֹתֽוֹ׃ 7 כִּ֚י יְהוָ֣ה אֱלֹהֶ֔יךָ מְבִֽיאֲךָ֖ אֶל־אֶ֣רֶץ טוֹבָ֑ה אֶ֚רֶץ נַ֣חֲלֵי מָ֔יִם עֲיָנֹת֙ וּתְהֹמֹ֔ת יֹצְאִ֥ים בַּבִּקְעָ֖ה וּבָהָֽר׃ 8 אֶ֤רֶץ חִטָּה֙ וּשְׂעֹרָ֔ה וְגֶ֥פֶן וּתְאֵנָ֖ה וְרִמּ֑וֹן אֶֽרֶץ־זֵ֥ית שֶׁ֖מֶן וּדְבָֽשׁ׃ 9 אֶ֗רֶץ אֲשֶׁ֨ר לֹ֤א בְמִסְכֵּנֻת֙ תֹּֽאכַל־בָּ֣הּ לֶ֔חֶם לֹֽא־תֶחְסַ֥ר כֹּ֖ל בָּ֑הּ אֶ֚רֶץ אֲשֶׁ֣ר אֲבָנֶ֣יהָ בַרְזֶ֔ל וּמֵֽהֲרָרֶ֖יהָ תַּחְצֹ֥ב נְחֹֽשֶׁת׃ 10 וְאָֽכַלְתָּ֖ וְשָׂבָ֑עְתָּ וּבֵֽרַכְתָּ֙ אֶת־יְהוָ֣ה אֱלֹהֶ֔יךָ עַל־ הָאָ֥רֶץ הַטֹּבָ֖ה אֲשֶׁ֥ר נָֽתַן־לָֽךְ׃ 11 הִשָּׁ֣מֶר לְךָ֔ פֶּן־תִּשְׁכַּ֖ח אֶת־יְהוָ֣ה אֱלֹהֶ֑יךָ לְבִלְתִּ֨י שְׁמֹ֤ר מִצְוֹתָיו֙ וּמִשְׁפָּטָ֣יו וְחֻקֹּתָ֔יו אֲשֶׁ֛ר אָֽנֹכִ֥י מְצַוְּךָ֖ הַיּֽוֹם׃ 12 פֶּן־תֹּאכַ֖ל וְשָׂבָ֑עְתָּ וּבָתִּ֥ים טוֹבִ֛ים תִּבְנֶ֖ה וְיָשָֽׁבְתָּ׃ 13 וּבְקָֽרְךָ֤ וְצֹֽאנְךָ֙ יִרְבְּיֻ֔ן וְכֶ֥סֶף וְזָהָ֖ב יִרְבֶּה־ לָּ֑ךְ וְכֹ֥ל אֲשֶׁר־לְךָ֖ יִרְבֶּֽה׃ 14 וְרָ֖ם לְבָבֶ֑ךָ וְשָֽׁכַחְתָּ֙ אֶת־יְהוָ֣ה אֱלֹהֶ֔יךָ הַמּֽוֹצִֽיאֲךָ֛ מֵאֶ֥רֶץ מִצְרַ֖יִם מִבֵּ֥ית עֲבָדִֽים׃ 15 הַמּֽוֹלִֽיכֲךָ֗ בַּמִּדְבָּ֣ר ׀ הַגָּדֹ֣ל וְהַנּוֹרָ֗א נָחָ֤שׁ ׀ שָׂרָף֙ וְעַקְרָ֔ב וְצִמָּא֖וֹן אֲשֶׁ֣ר אֵֽין־מָ֑יִם הַמּוֹצִ֤יא

---

a   *Heb. pen moved down from v. 12 for clarity.*
b   *See note at Num. 21.6.*

who brought forth water for you from the flinty rock; 16who fed you in the wilderness with manna, which your fathers had never known, in order to test you by hardships only to benefit you in the end—17and you say to yourselves, "My own power and the might of my own hand have won this wealth for me." 18Remember that it is the LORD your God who gives you the power to get wealth, in fulfillment of the covenant that He made on oath with your fathers, as is still the case.

19If you do forget the LORD your God and follow other gods to serve them or bow down to them, I warn you this day that you shall certainly perish; 20like the nations that the LORD will cause to perish before you, so shall you perish—because you did not heed the LORD your God.

9

Hear, O Israel! You are about to cross the Jordan to go in and dispossess nations greater and more populous than you: great cities with walls sky-high; 2a people great and tall, the Anakites, of whom you have knowledge; for you have heard it said, "Who can stand up to the children of Anak?" 3Know then this day that none other than the LORD your God is crossing at your head, a devouring fire; it is He who will wipe them out. He will subdue them before you, that you may quickly dispossess and destroy them, as the LORD promised you. 4And when the LORD your God has thrust them from your path, say not to yourselves, "The LORD has enabled us to possess this land because of our virtues"; it is rather because of the wickedness of those nations that the LORD is dispossessing them before you. 5It is not because of your virtues and your rectitude that you will be able to possess their country; but it is because of their wickedness that the LORD your God is dispossessing those nations before you, and in order

16 הַמַּאֲכִלְךָ מָן לְךָ מַיִם מִצּוּר הַחַלָּמִישׁ:
בַּמִּדְבָּר אֲשֶׁר לֹא־יָדְעוּן אֲבֹתֶיךָ לְמַעַן
עַנֹּתְךָ וּלְמַעַן נַסֹּתֶךָ לְהֵיטִבְךָ בְּאַחֲרִיתֶךָ:
17 וְאָמַרְתָּ בִּלְבָבֶךָ כֹּחִי וְעֹצֶם יָדִי עָשָׂה
לִי אֶת־הַחַיִל הַזֶּה: 18 וְזָכַרְתָּ אֶת־יְהֹוָה
אֱלֹהֶיךָ כִּי הוּא הַנֹּתֵן לְךָ כֹּחַ לַעֲשׂוֹת חָיִל
לְמַעַן הָקִים אֶת־בְּרִיתוֹ אֲשֶׁר־נִשְׁבַּע
לַאֲבֹתֶיךָ כַּיּוֹם הַזֶּה: פ
19 וְהָיָה אִם־שָׁכֹחַ תִּשְׁכַּח אֶת־יְהֹוָה
אֱלֹהֶיךָ וְהָלַכְתָּ אַחֲרֵי אֱלֹהִים אֲחֵרִים
וַעֲבַדְתָּם וְהִשְׁתַּחֲוִיתָ לָהֶם הַעִדֹתִי בָכֶם
הַיּוֹם כִּי אָבֹד תֹּאבֵדוּן: 20 כַּגּוֹיִם אֲשֶׁר
יְהֹוָה מַאֲבִיד מִפְּנֵיכֶם כֵּן תֹּאבֵדוּן עֵקֶב
לֹא תִשְׁמְעוּן בְּקוֹל יְהֹוָה אֱלֹהֵיכֶם: פ

ט שְׁמַע יִשְׂרָאֵל אַתָּה עֹבֵר הַיּוֹם
אֶת־הַיַּרְדֵּן לָבֹא לָרֶשֶׁת גּוֹיִם גְּדֹלִים
וַעֲצֻמִים מִמֶּךָּ עָרִים גְּדֹלֹת וּבְצֻרֹת
בַּשָּׁמָיִם: 2 עַם־גָּדוֹל וָרָם בְּנֵי עֲנָקִים אֲשֶׁר
אַתָּה יָדַעְתָּ וְאַתָּה שָׁמַעְתָּ מִי יִתְיַצֵּב לִפְנֵי
בְּנֵי עֲנָק: 3 וְיָדַעְתָּ הַיּוֹם כִּי יְהֹוָה אֱלֹהֶיךָ
הוּא־הָעֹבֵר לְפָנֶיךָ אֵשׁ אֹכְלָה הוּא
יַשְׁמִידֵם וְהוּא יַכְנִיעֵם לְפָנֶיךָ וְהוֹרַשְׁתָּם
וְהַאֲבַדְתָּם מַהֵר כַּאֲשֶׁר דִּבֶּר יְהֹוָה לָךְ:
4 אַל־תֹּאמַר בִּלְבָבְךָ בַּהֲדֹף יְהֹוָה אֱלֹהֶיךָ
אֹתָם ׀ מִלְּפָנֶיךָ לֵאמֹר בְּצִדְקָתִי הֱבִיאַנִי
יְהֹוָה לָרֶשֶׁת אֶת־הָאָרֶץ הַזֹּאת וּבְרִשְׁעַת
הַגּוֹיִם הָאֵלֶּה יְהֹוָה מוֹרִישָׁם מִפָּנֶיךָ: 5 לֹא
בְצִדְקָתְךָ וּבְיֹשֶׁר לְבָבְךָ אַתָּה בָא לָרֶשֶׁת
אֶת־אַרְצָם כִּי בְּרִשְׁעַת ׀ הַגּוֹיִם הָאֵלֶּה
יְהֹוָה אֱלֹהֶיךָ מוֹרִישָׁם מִפָּנֶיךָ וּלְמַעַן

to fulfill the oath that the Lord made to your fathers, Abraham, Isaac, and Jacob.

6Know, then, that it is not for any virtue of yours that the Lord your God is giving you this good land to possess; for you are a stiffnecked people. 7Remember, never forget, how you provoked the Lord your God to anger in the wilderness: from the day that you left the land of Egypt until you reached this place, you have continued defiant toward the Lord.

8At Horeb you so provoked the Lord that the Lord was angry enough with you to have destroyed you. 9I had ascended the mountain to receive the tablets of stone, the Tablets of the Covenant that the Lord had made with you, and I stayed on the mountain forty days and forty nights, eating no bread and drinking no water. 10And the Lord gave me the two tablets of stone inscribed by the finger of God, with the exact words that the Lord had addressed to you on the mountain out of the fire on the day of the Assembly.

11At the end of those forty days and forty nights, the Lord gave me the two tablets of stone, the Tablets of the Covenant. 12And the Lord said to me, "Hurry, go down from here at once, for the people whom you brought out of Egypt have acted wickedly; they have been quick to stray from the path that I enjoined upon them; they have made themselves a molten image." 13The Lord further said to me, "I see that this is a stiffnecked people. 14Let Me alone and I will destroy them and blot out their name from under heaven, and I will make you a nation far more numerous than they."

15I started down the mountain, a mountain ablaze with fire, the two Tablets of the Covenant in my two hands. 16I saw how you had sinned against the Lord your God: you had made yourselves a molten calf; you had been quick to stray from the path that the Lord had enjoined upon

הָקֵים אֶת־הַדָּבָ֗ר אֲשֶׁ֨ר נִשְׁבַּ֤ע יְהוָה֙ לַאֲבֹתֶ֔יךָ לְאַבְרָהָ֥ם לְיִצְחָ֖ק וּֽלְיַעֲקֹֽב׃ 6וְיָ֣דַעְתָּ֔ כִּ֠י לֹ֤א בְצִדְקָֽתְךָ֙ יְהוָ֣ה אֱלֹהֶ֗יךָ נֹתֵ֨ן לְךָ֜ אֶת־הָאָ֧רֶץ הַטּוֹבָ֛ה הַזֹּ֖את לְרִשְׁתָּ֑הּ כִּ֥י עַם־קְשֵׁה־עֹ֖רֶף אָֽתָּה׃ 7זְכֹר֙ אַל־תִּשְׁכַּ֔ח אֵ֧ת אֲשֶׁר־הִקְצַ֛פְתָּ אֶת־יְהוָ֥ה אֱלֹהֶ֖יךָ בַּמִּדְבָּ֑ר לְמִן־הַיּ֞וֹם אֲשֶׁר־יָצָ֣אתָ ׀ מֵאֶ֣רֶץ מִצְרַ֗יִם עַד־בֹּֽאֲכֶם֙ עַד־הַמָּק֣וֹם הַזֶּ֔ה מַמְרִ֥ים הֱיִיתֶ֖ם עִם־יְהוָֽה׃ 8וּבְחֹרֵ֥ב הִקְצַפְתֶּ֖ם אֶת־יְהוָ֑ה וַיִּתְאַנַּ֧ף יְהוָ֛ה בָּכֶ֖ם לְהַשְׁמִ֥יד אֶתְכֶֽם׃ 9בַּעֲלֹתִ֣י הָהָ֗רָה לָקַ֜חַת לוּחֹ֤ת הָֽאֲבָנִים֙ לוּחֹ֣ת הַבְּרִ֔ית אֲשֶׁר־כָּרַ֥ת יְהוָ֖ה עִמָּכֶ֑ם וָאֵשֵׁ֣ב בָּהָ֗ר אַרְבָּעִ֥ים יוֹם֙ וְאַרְבָּעִ֣ים לַ֔יְלָה לֶ֚חֶם לֹ֣א אָכַ֔לְתִּי וּמַ֖יִם לֹ֥א שָׁתִֽיתִי׃ 10וַיִּתֵּ֨ן יְהוָ֜ה אֵלַ֗י אֶת־שְׁנֵי֙ לוּחֹ֣ת הָֽאֲבָנִ֔ים כְּתֻבִ֖ים בְּאֶצְבַּ֣ע אֱלֹהִ֑ים וַעֲלֵיהֶ֗ם כְּֽכָל־הַדְּבָרִ֡ים אֲשֶׁ֣ר דִּבֶּר֩ יְהוָ֨ה עִמָּכֶ֥ם בָּהָ֛ר מִתּ֥וֹךְ הָאֵ֖שׁ בְּי֥וֹם הַקָּהָֽל׃ 11וַיְהִ֗י מִקֵּץ֙ אַרְבָּעִ֥ים יוֹם֙ וְאַרְבָּעִ֣ים לַ֔יְלָה נָתַ֨ן יְהוָ֜ה אֵלַ֗י אֶת־שְׁנֵ֛י לֻחֹ֥ת הָאֲבָנִ֖ים לֻח֥וֹת הַבְּרִֽית׃ 12וַיֹּ֨אמֶר יְהוָ֜ה אֵלַ֗י ק֣וּם רֵ֤ד מַהֵר֙ מִזֶּ֔ה כִּ֚י שִׁחֵ֣ת עַמְּךָ֔ אֲשֶׁ֥ר הוֹצֵ֖אתָ מִמִּצְרָ֑יִם סָ֣רוּ מַהֵ֗ר מִן־הַדֶּ֙רֶךְ֙ אֲשֶׁ֣ר צִוִּיתִ֔ם עָשׂ֥וּ לָהֶ֖ם מַסֵּכָֽה׃ 13וַיֹּ֥אמֶר יְהוָ֖ה אֵלַ֣י לֵאמֹ֑ר רָאִ֙יתִי֙ אֶת־הָעָ֣ם הַזֶּ֔ה וְהִנֵּ֥ה עַם־קְשֵׁה־עֹ֖רֶף הֽוּא׃ 14הֶ֤רֶף מִמֶּ֙נִּי֙ וְאַשְׁמִידֵ֔ם וְאֶמְחֶ֣ה אֶת־שְׁמָ֔ם מִתַּ֖חַת הַשָּׁמָ֑יִם וְאֶֽעֱשֶׂה֙ אֽוֹתְךָ֔ לְגוֹי־עָצ֥וּם וָרָ֖ב מִמֶּֽנּוּ׃ 15וָאֵ֗פֶן וָֽאֵרֵד֙ מִן־הָהָ֔ר וְהָהָ֖ר בֹּעֵ֣ר בָּאֵ֑שׁ וּשְׁנֵי֙ לוּחֹ֣ת הַבְּרִ֔ית עַ֖ל שְׁתֵּ֥י יָדָֽי׃ 16וָאֵ֗רֶא וְהִנֵּ֤ה חֲטָאתֶם֙ לַיהוָ֣ה אֱלֹֽהֵיכֶ֔ם עֲשִׂיתֶ֣ם לָכֶ֔ם עֵ֖גֶל מַסֵּכָ֑ה סַרְתֶּ֣ם מַהֵ֔ר מִן־הַדֶּ֔רֶךְ אֲשֶׁר־צִוָּ֥ה יְהוָ֖ה אֶתְכֶֽם׃ 17וָאֶתְפֹּשׂ֙ בִּשְׁנֵ֣י

you. ¹⁷Thereupon I gripped the two tablets and flung them away with both my hands, smashing them before your eyes. ¹⁸I threw myself down before the LORD—eating no bread and drinking no water forty days and forty nights, as before—because of the great wrong you had committed, doing what displeased the LORD and vexing Him. ¹⁹For I was in dread of the LORD's fierce anger against you, which moved Him to wipe you out. And that time, too, the LORD gave heed to me.—²⁰Moreover, the LORD was angry enough with Aaron to have destroyed him; so I also interceded for Aaron at that time.—²¹As for that sinful thing you had made, the calf, I took it and put it to the fire; I broke it to bits and ground it thoroughly until it was fine as dust, and I threw its dust into the brook that comes down from the mountain.

²²Again you provoked the LORD at Taberah, and at Massah, and at Kibroth-hattaavah.

²³And when the LORD sent you on from Kadesh-barnea, saying, "Go up and take possession of the land that I am giving you," you flouted the command of the LORD your God; you did not put your trust in Him and did not obey Him.

²⁴As long as I have known you, you have been defiant toward the LORD.

²⁵When I lay prostrate before the LORD ^a-those forty days and forty nights,-^a because the LORD was determined to destroy you, ²⁶I prayed to the LORD and said, "O Lord GOD, do not annihilate Your very own people, whom You redeemed in Your majesty and whom You freed from Egypt with a mighty hand. ²⁷Give thought to Your servants, Abraham, Isaac, and Jacob, and pay no heed to the stubbornness of this people, its wickedness, and its sinfulness. ²⁸Else the country from which You freed us will say, 'It

הַלֻּחֹת וָאַשְׁלִכֵם מֵעַל שְׁתֵּי יָדָי וָאֲשַׁבְּרֵם לְעֵינֵיכֶם׃ 18 וָאֶתְנַפַּל לִפְנֵי יְהוָה כָּרִאשֹׁנָה אַרְבָּעִים יוֹם וְאַרְבָּעִים לַיְלָה לֶחֶם לֹא אָכַלְתִּי וּמַיִם לֹא שָׁתִיתִי עַל כָּל־חַטַּאתְכֶם אֲשֶׁר חֲטָאתֶם לַעֲשׂוֹת הָרַע בְּעֵינֵי יְהוָה לְהַכְעִיסוֹ׃ 19 כִּי יָגֹרְתִּי מִפְּנֵי הָאַף וְהַחֵמָה אֲשֶׁר קָצַף יְהוָה עֲלֵיכֶם לְהַשְׁמִיד אֶתְכֶם וַיִּשְׁמַע יְהוָה אֵלַי גַּם בַּפַּעַם הַהִוא׃ 20 וּבְאַהֲרֹן הִתְאַנַּף יְהוָה מְאֹד לְהַשְׁמִידוֹ וָאֶתְפַּלֵּל גַּם־בְּעַד אַהֲרֹן בָּעֵת הַהִוא׃ 21 וְאֶת־חַטַּאתְכֶם אֲשֶׁר־עֲשִׂיתֶם אֶת־הָעֵגֶל לָקַחְתִּי וָאֶשְׂרֹף אֹתוֹ ׀ בָּאֵשׁ וָאֶכֹּת אֹתוֹ טָחוֹן הֵיטֵב עַד אֲשֶׁר־דַּק לְעָפָר וָאַשְׁלִךְ אֶת־עֲפָרוֹ אֶל־הַנַּחַל הַיֹּרֵד מִן־הָהָר׃

22 וּבְתַבְעֵרָה וּבְמַסָּה וּבְקִבְרֹת הַתַּאֲוָה מַקְצִפִים הֱיִיתֶם אֶת־יְהוָה׃ 23 וּבִשְׁלֹחַ יְהוָה אֶתְכֶם מִקָּדֵשׁ בַּרְנֵעַ לֵאמֹר עֲלוּ וּרְשׁוּ אֶת־הָאָרֶץ אֲשֶׁר נָתַתִּי לָכֶם וַתַּמְרוּ אֶת־פִּי יְהוָה אֱלֹהֵיכֶם וְלֹא הֶאֱמַנְתֶּם לוֹ וְלֹא שְׁמַעְתֶּם בְּקֹלוֹ׃ 24 מַמְרִים* הֱיִיתֶם עִם־יְהוָה מִיּוֹם דַּעְתִּי אֶתְכֶם׃

25 וָאֶתְנַפַּל לִפְנֵי יְהוָה אֵת אַרְבָּעִים הַיּוֹם וְאֶת־אַרְבָּעִים הַלַּיְלָה אֲשֶׁר הִתְנַפָּלְתִּי כִּי־אָמַר יְהוָה לְהַשְׁמִיד אֶתְכֶם׃ 26 וָאֶתְפַּלֵּל אֶל־יְהוָה וָאֹמַר אֲדֹנָי יְהוִה אַל־תַּשְׁחֵת עַמְּךָ וְנַחֲלָתְךָ אֲשֶׁר פָּדִיתָ בְּגָדְלֶךָ אֲשֶׁר־הוֹצֵאתָ מִמִּצְרַיִם בְּיָד חֲזָקָה׃ 27 זְכֹר לַעֲבָדֶיךָ לְאַבְרָהָם לְיִצְחָק וּלְיַעֲקֹב אַל־תֵּפֶן אֶל־קְשִׁי הָעָם הַזֶּה וְאֶל־רִשְׁעוֹ וְאֶל־חַטָּאתוֹ׃ 28 פֶּן־יֹאמְרוּ הָאָרֶץ אֲשֶׁר הוֹצֵאתָנוּ מִשָּׁם מִבְּלִי

מ׳ זעירא   v. 24.

---

a-a   Lit. "the forty days and forty nights that I lay prostrate."

was because the LORD was powerless to bring them into the land that He had promised them, and because He rejected them, that He brought them out to have them die in the wilderness.' [29]Yet they are Your very own people, whom You freed with Your great might and Your outstretched arm."

10 Thereupon the LORD said to me, "Carve out two tablets of stone like the first, and come up to Me on the mountain; and make an ark of wood. [2]I will inscribe on the tablets the commandments that were on the first tablets that you smashed, and you shall deposit them in the ark."

[3]I made an ark of acacia wood and carved out two tablets of stone like the first; I took the two tablets with me and went up the mountain. [4]The LORD inscribed on the tablets the same text as on the first, the Ten Commandments that He addressed to you on the mountain out of the fire on the day of the Assembly; and the LORD gave them to me. [5]Then I left and went down from the mountain, and I deposited the tablets in the ark that I had made, where they still are, as the LORD had commanded me.

[6]From Beeroth-bene-jaakan[a] the Israelites marched to Moserah. Aaron died there and was buried there; and his son Eleazar became priest in his stead. [7]From there they marched to Gudgod,[b] and from Gudgod to Jotbath, a region of running brooks.

[8]At that time the LORD set apart the tribe of Levi to carry the Ark of the LORD's Covenant, to stand in attendance upon the LORD, and to bless in His name, as is still the case. [9]That is why the Levites have received no hereditary portion along with their kinsmen: the LORD is their portion, as the LORD your God spoke concerning them.

יָכֹ֣לֶת יְהוָה֮ לַהֲבִיאָם֒ אֶל־הָאָ֖רֶץ אֲשֶׁר־
דִּבֶּ֣ר לָהֶ֔ם וּמִשִּׂנְאָת֖וֹ אוֹתָ֑ם הוֹצִיאָ֛ם
לַהֲמִתָ֖ם בַּמִּדְבָּֽר׃ 29 וְהֵ֥ם עַמְּךָ֖ וְנַחֲלָתֶ֑ךָ
אֲשֶׁ֤ר הוֹצֵ֙אתָ֙ בְּכֹחֲךָ֣ הַגָּדֹ֔ל וּבִזְרֹעֲךָ֖
הַנְּטוּיָֽה׃ פ

ר בָּעֵ֨ת הַהִ֜וא אָמַ֧ר יְהוָ֣ה אֵלַ֗י פְּסָל־לְךָ֞
שְׁנֵֽי־לוּחֹ֤ת אֲבָנִים֙ כָּרִ֣אשֹׁנִ֔ים וַעֲלֵ֥ה אֵלַ֖י
הָהָ֑רָה וְעָשִׂ֥יתָ לְּךָ֖ אֲר֥וֹן עֵֽץ׃ 2 וְאֶכְתֹּב֙
עַל־הַלֻּחֹ֔ת אֶת־הַדְּבָרִ֔ים אֲשֶׁ֥ר הָי֛וּ עַל־
הַלֻּחֹ֥ת הָרִאשֹׁנִ֖ים אֲשֶׁ֣ר שִׁבַּ֑רְתָּ וְשַׂמְתָּ֖ם
בָּאָרֽוֹן׃

3 וָאַ֤עַשׂ אֲרוֹן֙ עֲצֵ֣י שִׁטִּ֔ים וָאֶפְסֹ֛ל שְׁנֵֽי־
לֻחֹ֥ת אֲבָנִ֖ים כָּרִֽאשֹׁנִ֑ים וָאַ֣עַל הָהָ֔רָה וּשְׁנֵ֥י
הַלֻּחֹ֖ת בְּיָדִֽי׃ 4 וַיִּכְתֹּ֨ב עַֽל־הַלֻּחֹ֜ת כַּמִּכְתָּ֣ב
הָרִאשׁ֗וֹן אֵ֚ת עֲשֶׂ֣רֶת הַדְּבָרִ֔ים אֲשֶׁ֨ר דִּבֶּר֩
יְהוָ֨ה אֲלֵיכֶ֥ם בָּהָ֛ר מִתּ֥וֹךְ הָאֵ֖שׁ בְּי֣וֹם
הַקָּהָ֑ל וַיִּתְּנֵ֥ם יְהוָ֖ה אֵלָֽי׃ 5 וָאֵ֗פֶן וָאֵרֵד֙
מִן־הָהָ֔ר וָאָשִׂם֙ אֶת־הַלֻּחֹ֔ת בָּאָר֖וֹן אֲשֶׁ֣ר
עָשִׂ֑יתִי וַיִּ֣הְיוּ שָׁ֔ם כַּאֲשֶׁ֖ר צִוַּ֥נִי יְהוָֽה׃

6 וּבְנֵ֣י יִשְׂרָאֵ֗ל נָֽסְע֛וּ מִבְּאֵרֹ֥ת בְּנֵי־יַעֲקָ֖ן
מוֹסֵרָ֑ה שָׁ֣ם מֵ֤ת אַהֲרֹן֙ וַיִּקָּבֵ֣ר שָׁ֔ם וַיְכַהֵ֧ן
אֶלְעָזָ֛ר בְּנ֖וֹ תַּחְתָּֽיו׃ 7 מִשָּׁ֥ם נָסְע֖וּ הַגֻּדְגֹּ֑דָה
וּמִן־הַגֻּדְגֹּ֔דָה יָטְבָ֔תָה אֶ֖רֶץ נַֽחֲלֵי מָֽיִם׃
8 בָּעֵ֣ת הַהִ֗וא הִבְדִּ֤יל יְהוָה֙ אֶת־שֵׁ֣בֶט הַלֵּוִ֔י
לָשֵׂ֖את אֶת־אֲר֣וֹן בְּרִית־יְהוָ֑ה לַעֲמֹד֩ לִפְנֵ֨י
יְהוָ֤ה לְשָֽׁרְתוֹ֙ וּלְבָרֵ֣ךְ בִּשְׁמ֔וֹ עַ֖ד הַיּ֣וֹם
הַזֶּֽה׃ 9 עַל־כֵּ֡ן לֹֽא־הָיָה֩ לְלֵוִ֨י חֵ֤לֶק וְנַחֲלָה֙
עִם־אֶחָ֔יו יְהוָה֙ ה֣וּא נַחֲלָת֔וֹ כַּאֲשֶׁ֥ר דִּבֶּ֛ר
יְהוָ֥ה אֱלֹהֶ֖יךָ לֽוֹ׃

---

a   Lit. "wells of Bene-jaakan"; cf. Num. 33.31–32.
b   "Hor-haggidgad" in Num. 33.32–33.

10I had stayed on the mountain, as I did the first time, forty days and forty nights; and the LORD heeded me once again: the LORD agreed not to destroy you. 11And the LORD said to me, "Up, resume the march at the head of the people, that they may go in and possess the land that I swore to their fathers to give them."

12And now, O Israel, what does the LORD your God demand of you? Only this: to revere the LORD your God, to walk only in His paths, to love Him, and to serve the LORD your God with all your heart and soul, 13keeping the LORD's commandments and laws, which I enjoin upon you today, for your good. 14Mark, the heavens c-to their uttermost reaches-c belong to the LORD your God, the earth and all that is on it! 15Yet it was to your fathers that the LORD was drawn in His love for them, so that He chose you, their lineal descendants, from among all peoples—as is now the case. 16Cut away, therefore, the thickening about your hearts and stiffen your necks no more. 17For the LORD your God is d-God supreme and Lord supreme,-d the great, the mighty, and the awesome God, who shows no favor and takes no bribe, 18but upholds the cause of the fatherless and the widow, and befriends the stranger, providing him with food and clothing.—19You too must befriend the stranger, for you were strangers in the land of Egypt.

20You must revere the LORD your God: only Him shall you worship, to Him shall you hold fast, and by His name shall you swear. 21He is your glory and He is your God, who wrought for you those marvelous, awesome deeds that you saw with your own eyes. 22Your ancestors went down to Egypt seventy persons in all; and now the LORD your God has made you as numerous as the stars of heaven.

10 וְאָנֹכִי עָמַדְתִּי בָהָר כַּיָּמִים הָרִאשֹׁנִים אַרְבָּעִים יוֹם וְאַרְבָּעִים לַיְלָה וַיִּשְׁמַע יְהוָה אֵלַי גַּם בַּפַּעַם הַהִוא לֹא־אָבָה יְהוָה הַשְׁחִיתֶךָ׃ 11 וַיֹּאמֶר יְהוָה אֵלַי קוּם לֵךְ לְמַסַּע לִפְנֵי הָעָם וְיָבֹאוּ וְיִרְשׁוּ אֶת־הָאָרֶץ אֲשֶׁר־נִשְׁבַּעְתִּי לַאֲבֹתָם לָתֵת לָהֶם׃ פ

12 וְעַתָּה יִשְׂרָאֵל מָה יְהוָה אֱלֹהֶיךָ שֹׁאֵל מֵעִמָּךְ כִּי אִם־לְיִרְאָה אֶת־יְהוָה אֱלֹהֶיךָ לָלֶכֶת בְּכָל־דְּרָכָיו וּלְאַהֲבָה אֹתוֹ וְלַעֲבֹד אֶת־יְהוָה אֱלֹהֶיךָ בְּכָל־לְבָבְךָ וּבְכָל־נַפְשֶׁךָ׃ 13 לִשְׁמֹר אֶת־מִצְוֺת יְהוָה וְאֶת־חֻקֹּתָיו אֲשֶׁר אָנֹכִי מְצַוְּךָ הַיּוֹם לְטוֹב לָךְ׃ 14 הֵן לַיהוָה אֱלֹהֶיךָ הַשָּׁמַיִם וּשְׁמֵי הַשָּׁמָיִם הָאָרֶץ וְכָל־אֲשֶׁר־בָּהּ׃ 15 רַק בַּאֲבֹתֶיךָ חָשַׁק יְהוָה לְאַהֲבָה אוֹתָם וַיִּבְחַר בְּזַרְעָם אַחֲרֵיהֶם בָּכֶם מִכָּל־הָעַמִּים כַּיּוֹם הַזֶּה׃ 16 וּמַלְתֶּם אֵת עָרְלַת לְבַבְכֶם וְעָרְפְּכֶם לֹא תַקְשׁוּ עוֹד׃ 17 כִּי יְהוָה אֱלֹהֵיכֶם הוּא אֱלֹהֵי הָאֱלֹהִים וַאֲדֹנֵי הָאֲדֹנִים הָאֵל הַגָּדֹל הַגִּבֹּר וְהַנּוֹרָא אֲשֶׁר לֹא־יִשָּׂא פָנִים וְלֹא יִקַּח שֹׁחַד׃ 18 עֹשֶׂה מִשְׁפַּט יָתוֹם וְאַלְמָנָה וְאֹהֵב גֵּר לָתֶת לוֹ לֶחֶם וְשִׂמְלָה׃ 19 וַאֲהַבְתֶּם אֶת־הַגֵּר כִּי־גֵרִים הֱיִיתֶם בְּאֶרֶץ מִצְרָיִם׃

20 אֶת־יְהוָה אֱלֹהֶיךָ תִּירָא אֹתוֹ תַעֲבֹד וּבוֹ תִדְבָּק וּבִשְׁמוֹ תִּשָּׁבֵעַ׃ 21 הוּא תְהִלָּתְךָ וְהוּא אֱלֹהֶיךָ אֲשֶׁר־עָשָׂה אִתְּךָ אֶת־הַגְּדֹלֹת וְאֶת־הַנּוֹרָאֹת הָאֵלֶּה אֲשֶׁר רָאוּ עֵינֶיךָ׃ 22 בְּשִׁבְעִים נֶפֶשׁ יָרְדוּ אֲבֹתֶיךָ מִצְרָיְמָה וְעַתָּה שָׂמְךָ יְהוָה אֱלֹהֶיךָ כְּכוֹכְבֵי הַשָּׁמַיִם לָרֹב׃

---

c-c   Lit. "and the heaven of heavens."
d-d   Lit. "the God of gods and the Lord of lords."

11 Love, therefore, the Lord your God, and always keep His charge, His laws, His rules, and His commandments.

2^aTake thought this day that it was not your children, who neither experienced nor witnessed the lesson of the Lord your God—

His majesty, His mighty hand, His outstretched arm; 3the signs and the deeds that He performed in Egypt against Pharaoh king of Egypt and all his land; 4what He did to Egypt's army, its horses and chariots; how the Lord rolled back upon them the waters of the Sea of Reeds when they were pursuing you, thus destroying them ^bonce and for all;^{-b} 5what He did for you in the wilderness before you arrived in this place; 6and what He did to Dathan and Abiram, sons of Eliab son of Reuben, when the earth opened her mouth and swallowed them, along with their households, their tents, and every living thing in their train, from amidst all Israel—

7but that it was you who saw with your own eyes all the marvelous deeds that the Lord performed.

8Keep, therefore, all the Instruction that I enjoin upon you today, so that you may have the strength to enter and take possession of the land that you are about to cross into and possess, 9and that you may long endure upon the soil that the Lord swore to your fathers to assign to them and to their heirs, a land flowing with milk and honey.

10For the land that you are about to enter and possess is not like the land of Egypt from which you have come. There the grain you sowed had to be watered by your own labors,^c like a vegetable garden; 11but the land you are about to cross into and possess, a land of hills and valleys,

יא וְאָהַבְתָּ֗ אֵ֚ת יְהוָ֣ה אֱלֹהֶ֔יךָ וְשָׁמַרְתָּ֣
מִשְׁמַרְתּ֗וֹ וְחֻקֹּתָ֧יו וּמִשְׁפָּטָ֛יו וּמִצְוֹתָ֖יו כָּל־
הַיָּמִֽים: 2 וִֽידַעְתֶּם֮ הַיּוֹם֒ כִּ֣י ׀ לֹ֣א אֶת־בְּנֵיכֶ֗ם אֲשֶׁ֤ר
לֹֽא־יָֽדְעוּ֙ וַֽאֲשֶׁ֣ר לֹֽא־רָא֔וּ אֶת־מוּסַ֖ר יְהוָ֣ה
אֱלֹֽהֵיכֶ֑ם אֶת־גָּדְל֔וֹ אֶת־יָדוֹ֙ הַֽחֲזָקָ֔ה וּזְרֹע֖וֹ
הַנְּטוּיָֽה: 3 וְאֶת־אֹֽתֹתָיו֙ וְאֶֽת־מַֽעֲשָׂ֔יו
אֲשֶׁ֥ר עָשָׂ֖ה בְּת֣וֹךְ מִצְרָ֑יִם לְפַרְעֹ֥ה מֶֽלֶךְ־
מִצְרַ֖יִם וּלְכָל־אַרְצֽוֹ: 4 וַֽאֲשֶׁ֣ר עָשָׂה֩
לְחֵ֨יל מִצְרַ֜יִם לְסוּסָ֣יו וּלְרִכְבּ֗וֹ אֲשֶׁ֨ר
הֵצִ֜יף אֶת־מֵ֤י יַם־סוּף֙ עַל־פְּנֵיהֶ֔ם
בְּרָדְפָ֖ם אַֽחֲרֵיכֶ֑ם וַיְאַבְּדֵ֣ם יְהוָ֔ה עַ֖ד
הַיּ֥וֹם הַזֶּֽה: 5 וַֽאֲשֶׁ֥ר עָשָׂ֛ה לָכֶ֖ם בַּמִּדְבָּ֑ר
עַד־בֹּֽאֲכֶ֖ם עַד־הַמָּק֥וֹם הַזֶּֽה: 6 וַֽאֲשֶׁ֨ר
עָשָׂ֜ה לְדָתָ֣ן וְלַֽאֲבִירָ֗ם בְּנֵ֣י אֱלִיאָב֮ בֶּן־
רְאוּבֵן֒ אֲשֶׁ֨ר פָּֽצְתָ֤ה הָאָ֨רֶץ֙ אֶת־פִּ֔יהָ
וַתִּבְלָעֵ֥ם וְאֶת־בָּֽתֵּיהֶ֖ם וְאֶת־אָֽהֳלֵיהֶ֑ם
וְאֵ֤ת כָּל־הַיְקוּם֙ אֲשֶׁ֣ר בְּרַגְלֵיהֶ֔ם בְּקֶ֖רֶב
כָּל־יִשְׂרָאֵֽל: 7 כִּ֤י עֵֽינֵיכֶם֙ הָֽרֹאֹ֔ת אֶת־כָּל־מַֽעֲשֵׂ֥ה יְהוָ֖ה
הַגָּדֹ֑ל אֲשֶׁ֖ר עָשָֽׂה: 8 וּשְׁמַרְתֶּם֙ אֶת־כָּל־הַמִּצְוָ֔ה אֲשֶׁ֛ר אָֽנֹכִ֥י
מְצַוְּךָ֖ הַיּ֑וֹם לְמַ֣עַן תֶּֽחֶזְק֗וּ וּבָאתֶם֙
וִֽירִשְׁתֶּ֣ם אֶת־הָאָ֔רֶץ אֲשֶׁ֥ר אַתֶּ֛ם עֹֽבְרִ֥ים
שָׁ֖מָּה לְרִשְׁתָּֽהּ: 9 וּלְמַ֣עַן תַּֽאֲרִ֣יכוּ יָמִ֗ים
עַל־הָֽאֲדָמָה֙ אֲשֶׁר֩ נִשְׁבַּ֨ע יְהוָ֤ה לַֽאֲבֹֽתֵיכֶם֙
לָתֵ֣ת לָהֶ֔ם וּלְזַרְעָ֑ם אֶ֛רֶץ זָבַ֥ת חָלָ֖ב
וּדְבָֽשׁ: ס 10 כִּ֣י הָאָ֗רֶץ אֲשֶׁ֨ר אַתָּ֤ה בָא־שָׁ֨מָּה֙
לְרִשְׁתָּ֔הּ לֹ֣א כְאֶ֤רֶץ מִצְרַ֨יִם֙ הִ֔וא אֲשֶׁ֥ר
יְצָאתֶ֖ם מִשָּׁ֑ם אֲשֶׁ֤ר תִּזְרַע֙ אֶֽת־זַרְעֲךָ֔
וְהִשְׁקִ֥יתָ בְרַגְלְךָ֖ כְּגַ֥ן הַיָּרָֽק: 11 וְהָאָ֗רֶץ

---

a   *Syntax of Heb. uncertain.*
b-b   *Lit. "to this day."*
c   *Lit. "by your foot."*

soaks up its water from the rains of heaven. 12It is a land which the LORD your God looks after, on which the LORD your God always keeps His eye, from year's beginning to year's end.

13If, then, you obey the commandments that I enjoin upon you this day, loving the LORD your God and serving Him with all your heart and soul, 14I[d] will grant the rain for your land in season, the early rain and the late. You shall gather in your new grain and wine and oil— 15I[d] will also provide grass in the fields for your cattle—and thus you shall eat your fill. 16Take care not to be lured away to serve other gods and bow to them. 17For the LORD's anger will flare up against you, and He will shut up the skies so that there will be no rain and the ground will not yield its produce; and you will soon perish from the good land that the LORD is assigning to you.

18Therefore impress these My words upon your e-very heart:-e bind them as a sign on your hand and let them serve as a f-symbol on your forehead,-f 19and teach them to your children— reciting them when you stay at home and when you are away, when you lie down and when you get up; 20and inscribe them on the doorposts of your house and on your gates—21to the end that you and your children may endure, in the land that the LORD swore to your fathers to assign to them, as long as there is a heaven over the earth.

22If, then, you faithfully keep all this Instruction that I command you, loving the LORD your God, walking in all His ways, and holding fast to Him, 23the LORD will dislodge before you all these nations: you will dispossess nations greater and more numerous than you. 24Every spot on which your foot treads shall be yours; your territory shall extend from the wilderness to the Lebanon and from the River—the

אֲשֶׁ֣ר אַתֶּ֤ם עֹבְרִים֙ שָׁ֔מָּה לְרִשְׁתָּ֑הּ אֶ֥רֶץ הָרִ֖ים וּבְקָעֹ֑ת לִמְטַ֥ר הַשָּׁמַ֖יִם תִּשְׁתֶּה־ מָּֽיִם׃ 12 אֶ֕רֶץ אֲשֶׁר־יְהוָ֥ה אֱלֹהֶ֖יךָ דֹּרֵ֣שׁ אֹתָ֑הּ תָּמִ֗יד עֵינֵ֨י יְהוָ֤ה אֱלֹהֶ֨יךָ֙ בָּ֔הּ מֵֽרֵשִׁית֙* הַשָּׁנָ֔ה וְעַ֖ד אַחֲרִ֥ית שָׁנָֽה׃ ס 13 וְהָיָ֗ה אִם־שָׁמֹ֤עַ תִּשְׁמְעוּ֙ אֶל־מִצְוֺתַ֔י אֲשֶׁ֧ר אָנֹכִ֛י מְצַוֶּ֥ה אֶתְכֶ֖ם הַיּ֑וֹם לְאַהֲבָ֞ה אֶת־יְהוָ֤ה אֱלֹֽהֵיכֶם֙ וּלְעׇבְד֔וֹ בְּכׇל־לְבַבְכֶ֖ם וּבְכׇל־נַפְשְׁכֶֽם׃ 14 וְנָתַתִּ֧י מְטַֽר־אַרְצְכֶ֛ם בְּעִתּ֖וֹ יוֹרֶ֣ה וּמַלְק֑וֹשׁ וְאָסַפְתָּ֣ דְגָנֶ֔ךָ וְתִירֹֽשְׁךָ֖ וְיִצְהָרֶֽךָ׃ 15 וְנָתַתִּ֛י עֵ֥שֶׂב בְּשָׂדְךָ֖ לִבְהֶמְתֶּ֑ךָ וְאָכַלְתָּ֖ וְשָׂבָֽעְתָּ׃ 16 הִשָּׁ֣מְר֣וּ לָכֶ֔ם פֶּ֥ן יִפְתֶּ֖ה לְבַבְכֶ֑ם וְסַרְתֶּ֗ם וַעֲבַדְתֶּם֙ אֱלֹהִ֣ים אֲחֵרִ֔ים וְהִשְׁתַּחֲוִיתֶ֖ם לָהֶֽם׃ 17 וְחָרָ֨ה אַף־יְהוָ֜ה בָּכֶ֗ם וְעָצַ֤ר אֶת־ הַשָּׁמַ֨יִם֙ וְלֹֽא־יִהְיֶ֣ה מָטָ֔ר וְהָ֣אֲדָמָ֔ה לֹ֥א תִתֵּ֖ן אֶת־יְבוּלָ֑הּ וַאֲבַדְתֶּ֣ם מְהֵרָ֗ה מֵעַל֙ הָאָ֣רֶץ הַטֹּבָ֔ה אֲשֶׁ֥ר יְהוָ֖ה נֹתֵ֥ן לָכֶֽם׃ 18 וְשַׂמְתֶּם֙ אֶת־דְּבָרַ֣י אֵ֔לֶּה עַל־לְבַבְכֶ֖ם וְעַֽל־נַפְשְׁכֶ֑ם וּקְשַׁרְתֶּ֨ם אֹתָ֤ם לְאוֹת֙ עַל־ יֶדְכֶ֔ם וְהָי֥וּ לְטוֹטָפֹ֖ת בֵּ֥ין עֵינֵיכֶֽם׃ 19 וְלִמַּדְתֶּ֥ם אֹתָ֛ם אֶת־בְּנֵיכֶ֖ם לְדַבֵּ֣ר בָּ֑ם בְּשִׁבְתְּךָ֤ בְּבֵיתֶ֨ךָ֙ וּבְלֶכְתְּךָ֣ בַדֶּ֔רֶךְ וּֽבְשׇׁכְבְּךָ֖ וּבְקוּמֶֽךָ׃ 20 וּכְתַבְתָּ֛ם עַל־מְזוּז֥וֹת בֵּיתֶ֖ךָ וּבִשְׁעָרֶֽיךָ׃ 21 לְמַ֨עַן יִרְבּ֤וּ יְמֵיכֶם֙ וִימֵ֣י בְנֵיכֶ֔ם עַ֚ל הָֽאֲדָמָ֔ה אֲשֶׁ֨ר נִשְׁבַּ֧ע יְהוָ֛ה לַאֲבֹתֵיכֶ֖ם לָתֵ֣ת לָהֶ֑ם כִּימֵ֥י הַשָּׁמַ֖יִם עַל־הָאָֽרֶץ׃ ס 22 כִּי֩ אִם־שָׁמֹ֨ר תִּשְׁמְר֜וּן אֶת־כׇּל־הַמִּצְוָ֣ה הַזֹּ֗את אֲשֶׁ֧ר אָנֹכִ֛י מְצַוֶּ֥ה אֶתְכֶ֖ם לַעֲשֹׂתָ֑הּ לְאַהֲבָ֞ה אֶת־יְהוָ֧ה אֱלֹהֵיכֶ֛ם לָלֶ֥כֶת בְּכׇל־ דְּרָכָ֖יו וּלְדׇבְקָה־בֽוֹ׃ 23 וְהוֹרִ֧ישׁ יְהוָ֛ה אֶת־ כׇּל־הַגּוֹיִ֥ם הָאֵ֖לֶּה מִלִּפְנֵיכֶ֑ם וִירִשְׁתֶּ֣ם גּוֹיִ֔ם גְּדֹלִ֥ים וַעֲצֻמִ֖ים מִכֶּֽם׃ 24 כׇּל־הַמָּק֗וֹם אֲשֶׁ֨ר תִּדְרֹ֧ךְ כַּֽף־רַגְלְכֶ֛ם בּ֖וֹ לָכֶ֣ם יִהְיֶ֑ה

v. 12. חסר א'

---

d   I.e., the LORD; Samaritan reads "He."
e-e   Lit. "heart and self."
f-f   See notes on 6.8.

Euphrates—to the Western[g] Sea. [25]No man shall stand up to you: the LORD your God will put the dread and the fear of you over the whole land in which you set foot, as He promised you.

RE'EH

[26]See, this day I set before you blessing and curse: [27]blessing, if you obey the commandments of the LORD your God that I enjoin upon you this day; [28]and curse, if you do not obey the commandments of the LORD your God, but turn away from the path that I enjoin upon you this day and follow other gods, [h]whom you have not experienced.[-h] [29]When the LORD your God brings you into the land that you are about to enter and possess, you shall pronounce the blessing at Mount Gerizim and the curse at Mount Ebal.—[30]Both are on the other side of the Jordan, beyond the west road that is in the land of the Canaanites who dwell in the Arabah—near Gilgal, by the terebinths of Moreh.

[31]For you are about to cross the Jordan to enter and possess the land that the LORD your God is assigning to you. When you have occupied it and are settled in it, [32]take care to observe all the laws and rules that I have set before you this day.

12 These are the laws and rules that you must carefully observe in the land that the LORD, God of your fathers, is giving you to possess, as long as you live on earth.

[2]You must destroy all the sites at which the nations you are to dispossess worshiped their gods, whether on lofty mountains and on hills

---

מִן־הַמִּדְבָּר וְהַלְּבָנוֹן מִן־הַנָּהָר נְהַר־פְּרָת וְעַד הַיָּם הָאַחֲרוֹן יִהְיֶה גְּבֻלְכֶם: 25 לֹא־יִתְיַצֵּב אִישׁ בִּפְנֵיכֶם פַּחְדְּכֶם וּמוֹרַאֲכֶם יִתֵּן ׀ יְהֹוָה אֱלֹהֵיכֶם עַל־פְּנֵי כָל־הָאָרֶץ אֲשֶׁר תִּדְרְכוּ־בָהּ כַּאֲשֶׁר דִּבֶּר לָכֶם: ס

ראה

26 רְאֵה אָנֹכִי נֹתֵן לִפְנֵיכֶם הַיּוֹם בְּרָכָה וּקְלָלָה: 27 אֶת־הַבְּרָכָה אֲשֶׁר תִּשְׁמְעוּ אֶל־מִצְוֺת יְהֹוָה אֱלֹהֵיכֶם אֲשֶׁר אָנֹכִי מְצַוֶּה אֶתְכֶם הַיּוֹם: 28 וְהַקְּלָלָה אִם־לֹא תִשְׁמְעוּ אֶל־מִצְוֺת יְהֹוָה אֱלֹהֵיכֶם וְסַרְתֶּם מִן־הַדֶּרֶךְ אֲשֶׁר אָנֹכִי מְצַוֶּה אֶתְכֶם הַיּוֹם לָלֶכֶת אַחֲרֵי אֱלֹהִים אֲחֵרִים אֲשֶׁר לֹא־יְדַעְתֶּם: ס 29 וְהָיָה כִּי יְבִיאֲךָ יְהֹוָה אֱלֹהֶיךָ אֶל־הָאָרֶץ אֲשֶׁר־אַתָּה בָא־שָׁמָּה לְרִשְׁתָּהּ וְנָתַתָּה אֶת־הַבְּרָכָה עַל־הַר גְּרִזִים וְאֶת־הַקְּלָלָה עַל־הַר עֵיבָל: 30 הֲלֹא־הֵמָּה בְּעֵבֶר הַיַּרְדֵּן אַחֲרֵי דֶּרֶךְ מְבוֹא הַשֶּׁמֶשׁ בְּאֶרֶץ הַכְּנַעֲנִי הַיֹּשֵׁב בָּעֲרָבָה מוּל הַגִּלְגָּל אֵצֶל אֵלוֹנֵי מֹרֶה: 31 כִּי אַתֶּם עֹבְרִים אֶת־הַיַּרְדֵּן לָבֹא לָרֶשֶׁת אֶת־הָאָרֶץ אֲשֶׁר־יְהֹוָה אֱלֹהֵיכֶם נֹתֵן לָכֶם וִירִשְׁתֶּם אֹתָהּ וִישַׁבְתֶּם־בָּהּ: 32 וּשְׁמַרְתֶּם לַעֲשׂוֹת אֵת כָּל־הַחֻקִּים וְאֶת־הַמִּשְׁפָּטִים אֲשֶׁר אָנֹכִי נֹתֵן לִפְנֵיכֶם הַיּוֹם:

יב אֵלֶּה הַחֻקִּים וְהַמִּשְׁפָּטִים אֲשֶׁר תִּשְׁמְרוּן לַעֲשׂוֹת בָּאָרֶץ אֲשֶׁר נָתַן יְהֹוָה אֱלֹהֵי אֲבֹתֶיךָ לְךָ לְרִשְׁתָּהּ כָּל־הַיָּמִים אֲשֶׁר־אַתֶּם חַיִּים עַל־הָאֲדָמָה: 2 אַבֵּד תְּאַבְּדוּן אֶת־כָּל־הַמְּקֹמוֹת אֲשֶׁר עָבְדוּ־שָׁם הַגּוֹיִם אֲשֶׁר אַתֶּם יֹרְשִׁים אֹתָם

---

g   I.e., Mediterranean.
h-h   I.e., who have not proved themselves to you; cf. Hos. 13.4.

or under any luxuriant tree. ³Tear down their altars, smash their pillars, put their sacred posts to the fire, and cut down the images of their gods, obliterating their name from that site.

⁴Do not worship the LORD your God in like manner, ⁵but look only to the site that the LORD your God will choose amidst all your tribes as His habitation, to establish His name there. There you are to go, ⁶and there you are to bring your burnt offerings and other sacrifices, your tithes and contributions,ᵃ your votive and free-will offerings, and the firstlings of your herds and flocks. ⁷Together with your households, you shall feast there before the LORD your God, happy in all the undertakings in which the LORD your God has blessed you.

⁸You shall not act at all as we now act here, every man as he pleases, ⁹because you have not yet come to the allotted haven that the LORD your God is giving you. ¹⁰When you cross the Jordan and settle in the land that the LORD your God is allotting to you, and He grants you safety from all your enemies around you and you live in security, ¹¹then you must bring everything that I command you to the site where the LORD your God will choose to establish His name: your burnt offerings and other sacrifices, your tithes and contributions,ᵃ and all the choice votive offerings that you vow to the LORD. ¹²And you shall rejoice before the LORD your God with your sons and daughters and with your male and female slaves, along with the Levite in your settlements, for he has no territorial allotment among you.

¹³Take care not to sacrifice your burnt offerings in any place you like, ¹⁴but only in the place that the LORD will choose in one of your tribal territories. There you shall sacrifice your burnt offerings and there you shall observe all that I enjoin upon you. ¹⁵But whenever you de-

---

אֶת־אֱלֹהֵיהֶם עַל־הֶהָרִים הָרָמִים וְעַל־הַגְּבָעוֹת וְתַחַת כָּל־עֵץ רַעֲנָן: 3 וְנִתַּצְתֶּם אֶת־מִזְבְּחֹתָם וְשִׁבַּרְתֶּם אֶת־מַצֵּבֹתָם וַאֲשֵׁרֵיהֶם תִּשְׂרְפוּן בָּאֵשׁ וּפְסִילֵי אֱלֹהֵיהֶם תְּגַדֵּעוּן וְאִבַּדְתֶּם אֶת־שְׁמָם מִן־הַמָּקוֹם הַהוּא:

4 לֹא־תַעֲשׂוּן כֵּן לַיהוָה אֱלֹהֵיכֶם: 5 כִּי אִם־אֶל־הַמָּקוֹם אֲשֶׁר־יִבְחַר יְהוָה אֱלֹהֵיכֶם מִכָּל־שִׁבְטֵיכֶם לָשׂוּם אֶת־שְׁמוֹ שָׁם לְשִׁכְנוֹ תִדְרְשׁוּ וּבָאתָ שָּׁמָּה: 6 וַהֲבֵאתֶם שָׁמָּה עֹלֹתֵיכֶם וְזִבְחֵיכֶם וְאֵת מַעְשְׂרֹתֵיכֶם וְאֵת תְּרוּמַת יֶדְכֶם וְנִדְרֵיכֶם וְנִדְבֹתֵיכֶם וּבְכֹרֹת בְּקַרְכֶם וְצֹאנְכֶם: 7 וַאֲכַלְתֶּם־שָׁם לִפְנֵי יְהוָה אֱלֹהֵיכֶם וּשְׂמַחְתֶּם בְּכֹל מִשְׁלַח יֶדְכֶם אַתֶּם וּבָתֵּיכֶם אֲשֶׁר בֵּרַכְךָ יְהוָה אֱלֹהֶיךָ: 8 לֹא תַעֲשׂוּן כְּכֹל אֲשֶׁר אֲנַחְנוּ עֹשִׂים פֹּה הַיּוֹם אִישׁ כָּל־הַיָּשָׁר בְּעֵינָיו: 9 כִּי לֹא־בָאתֶם עַד־עָתָּה אֶל־הַמְּנוּחָה וְאֶל־הַנַּחֲלָה אֲשֶׁר־יְהוָה אֱלֹהֶיךָ נֹתֵן לָךְ: 10 וַעֲבַרְתֶּם אֶת־הַיַּרְדֵּן וִישַׁבְתֶּם בָּאָרֶץ אֲשֶׁר־יְהוָה אֱלֹהֵיכֶם מַנְחִיל אֶתְכֶם וְהֵנִיחַ לָכֶם מִכָּל־אֹיְבֵיכֶם מִסָּבִיב וִישַׁבְתֶּם־בֶּטַח: 11 וְהָיָה הַמָּקוֹם אֲשֶׁר־יִבְחַר יְהוָה אֱלֹהֵיכֶם בּוֹ לְשַׁכֵּן שְׁמוֹ שָׁם שָׁמָּה תָבִיאוּ אֵת כָּל־אֲשֶׁר אָנֹכִי מְצַוֶּה אֶתְכֶם עוֹלֹתֵיכֶם וְזִבְחֵיכֶם מַעְשְׂרֹתֵיכֶם וּתְרֻמַת יֶדְכֶם וְכֹל מִבְחַר נִדְרֵיכֶם אֲשֶׁר תִּדְּרוּ לַיהוָה: 12 וּשְׂמַחְתֶּם לִפְנֵי יְהוָה אֱלֹהֵיכֶם אַתֶּם וּבְנֵיכֶם וּבְנֹתֵיכֶם וְעַבְדֵיכֶם וְאַמְהֹתֵיכֶם וְהַלֵּוִי אֲשֶׁר בְּשַׁעֲרֵיכֶם כִּי אֵין לוֹ חֵלֶק וְנַחֲלָה אִתְּכֶם:

13 הִשָּׁמֶר לְךָ פֶּן־תַּעֲלֶה עֹלֹתֶיךָ בְּכָל־מָקוֹם אֲשֶׁר תִּרְאֶה: 14 כִּי אִם־בַּמָּקוֹם

ᵃ   Lit. "the contribution(s) of your hands."

402

sire, you may slaughter and eat meat in any of your settlements, according to the blessing that the LORD your God has granted you. The unclean and the clean alike may partake of it, as of the gazelle and the deer.[b] 16But you must not partake of the blood; you shall pour it out on the ground like water.

17You may not partake in your settlements of the tithes of your new grain or wine or oil, or of the firstlings of your herds and flocks, or of any of the votive offerings that you vow, or of your freewill offerings, or of your contributions.[a] 18These you must consume before the LORD your God in the place that the LORD your God will choose—you and your sons and your daughters, your male and female slaves, and the Levite in your settlements—happy before the LORD your God in all your undertakings. 19Be sure not to neglect the Levite as long as you live in your land.

20When the LORD enlarges your territory, as He has promised you, and you say, "I shall eat some meat," for you have the urge to eat meat, you may eat meat whenever you wish. 21If the place where the LORD has chosen to establish His name is too far from you, you may slaughter any of the cattle or sheep that the LORD gives you, as I have instructed you; and you may eat to your heart's content in your settlements. 22Eat it, however, as the gazelle and the deer are eaten: the unclean may eat it together with the clean. 23But make sure that you do not partake of the blood; for the blood is the life, and you must not consume the life with the flesh. 24You must not partake of it; you must pour it out on the ground like water: 25you must not partake of it, in order that it may go well with you and with your descendants to come, for you will be doing what is right in the sight of the LORD.

26But such sacred and votive donations as you

אֲשֶׁר־יִבְחַ֣ר יְהֹוָ֔ה בְּאַחַ֖ד שְׁבָטֶ֑יךָ שָׁ֣ם
תַּעֲלֶ֣ה עֹלֹתֶ֗יךָ וְשָׁ֣ם תַּעֲשֶׂ֔ה כֹּ֛ל אֲשֶׁ֥ר אָנֹכִ֖י
מְצַוֶּֽךָּ׃ 15 רַק֩ בְּכָל־אַוַּ֨ת נַפְשְׁךָ֜ תִּזְבַּ֣ח ׀
וְאָכַלְתָּ֣ בָשָׂ֗ר כְּבִרְכַּ֨ת יְהֹוָ֧ה אֱלֹהֶ֛יךָ אֲשֶׁ֥ר
נָֽתַן־לְךָ֖ בְּכָל־שְׁעָרֶ֑יךָ הַטָּמֵ֤א וְהַטָּהוֹר֙
יֹאכְלֶ֔נּוּ כַּצְּבִ֖י וְכָאַיָּֽל׃ 16 רַ֥ק הַדָּ֖ם לֹ֣א
תֹאכֵ֑לוּ עַל־הָאָ֥רֶץ תִּשְׁפְּכֶ֖נּוּ כַּמָּֽיִם׃
17 לֹֽא־תוּכַ֞ל לֶאֱכֹ֣ל בִּשְׁעָרֶ֗יךָ מַעְשַׂ֤ר דְּגָֽנְךָ֙
וְתִירֹֽשְׁךָ֣ וְיִצְהָרֶ֔ךָ וּבְכֹרֹ֥ת בְּקָרְךָ֖ וְצֹאנֶ֑ךָ
וְכָל־נְדָרֶ֙יךָ֙ אֲשֶׁ֣ר תִּדֹּ֔ר וְנִדְבֹתֶ֖יךָ וּתְרוּמַ֥ת
יָדֶֽךָ׃ 18 כִּ֡י אִם־לִפְנֵי֩ יְהֹוָ֨ה אֱלֹהֶ֜יךָ תֹּאכְלֶ֗נּוּ
בַּמָּקוֹם֙ אֲשֶׁ֨ר יִבְחַ֜ר יְהֹוָ֣ה אֱלֹהֶ֘יךָ֘ בּוֹ֒ אַתָּ֨ה
וּבִנְךָ֤ וּבִתֶּ֙ךָ֙ וְעַבְדְּךָ֣ וַאֲמָתֶ֔ךָ וְהַלֵּוִ֖י אֲשֶׁ֣ר
בִּשְׁעָרֶ֑יךָ וְשָׂמַחְתָּ֗ לִפְנֵי֙ יְהֹוָ֣ה אֱלֹהֶ֔יךָ בְּכֹ֖ל
מִשְׁלַ֥ח יָדֶֽךָ׃ 19 הִשָּׁ֣מֶר לְךָ֔ פֶּֽן־תַּעֲזֹ֖ב אֶת־
הַלֵּוִ֑י כָּל־יָמֶ֖יךָ עַל־אַדְמָתֶֽךָ׃ ס
20 כִּֽי־יַרְחִיב֩ יְהֹוָ֨ה אֱלֹהֶ֜יךָ אֶֽת־גְּבֻֽלְךָ֗
כַּאֲשֶׁ֣ר דִּבֶּר־לָ֔ךְ וְאָמַרְתָּ֙ אֹכְלָ֣ה בָשָׂ֔ר כִּֽי־
תְאַוֶּ֥ה נַפְשְׁךָ֖ לֶאֱכֹ֣ל בָּשָׂ֑ר בְּכָל־אַוַּ֥ת נַפְשְׁךָ֖
תֹּאכַ֥ל בָּשָֽׂר׃ 21 כִּֽי־יִרְחַ֨ק מִמְּךָ֜ הַמָּק֗וֹם
אֲשֶׁ֨ר יִבְחַ֜ר יְהֹוָ֣ה אֱלֹהֶ֘יךָ֘ לָשׂ֣וּם שְׁמ֣וֹ שָׁם֒
וְזָבַחְתָּ֞ מִבְּקָרְךָ֣ וּמִצֹּֽאנְךָ֗ אֲשֶׁ֨ר נָתַ֤ן יְהֹוָה֙
לְךָ֙ כַּאֲשֶׁ֣ר צִוִּיתִ֔ךָ* וְאָ֣כַלְתָּ֔ בִּשְׁעָרֶ֑יךָ בְּכֹ֖ל
אַוַּ֥ת נַפְשֶֽׁךָ׃ 22 אַ֗ךְ כַּאֲשֶׁ֨ר יֵאָכֵ֤ל אֶֽת־הַצְּבִי֙
וְאֶת־הָ֣אַיָּ֔ל כֵּ֖ן תֹּאכְלֶ֑נּוּ הַטָּמֵא֙ וְהַטָּה֔וֹר
יַחְדָּ֖ו יֹאכְלֶֽנּוּ׃ 23 רַ֣ק חֲזַ֗ק לְבִלְתִּי֙ אֲכֹ֣ל
הַדָּ֔ם כִּ֥י הַדָּ֖ם ה֣וּא הַנָּ֑פֶשׁ וְלֹא־תֹאכַ֥ל
הַנֶּ֖פֶשׁ עִם־הַבָּשָֽׂר׃ 24 לֹ֖א תֹּאכְלֶ֑נּוּ עַל־
הָאָ֥רֶץ תִּשְׁפְּכֶ֖נּוּ כַּמָּֽיִם׃ 25 לֹ֖א תֹּאכְלֶ֑נּוּ
לְמַ֨עַן יִיטַ֤ב לְךָ֙ וּלְבָנֶ֣יךָ אַחֲרֶ֔יךָ כִּֽי־תַעֲשֶׂ֥ה
הַיָּשָׁ֖ר בְּעֵינֵ֥י יְהֹוָֽה׃
26 רַ֣ק קָֽדָשֶׁ֧יךָ אֲשֶׁר־יִהְי֛וּ לְךָ֖ וּנְדָרֶ֑יךָ תִּשָּׂ֣א

---

b   I.e., animals that may be eaten (cf. 14.5; Lev. 11.1 ff.), but not specified (Lev. 1.1 ff.).

may have ᶜ-shall be taken by you-ᶜ to the site that the Lᴏʀᴅ will choose. 27You shall offer your burnt offerings, both the flesh and the blood, on the altar of the Lᴏʀᴅ your God; and of your other sacrifices, the blood shall be poured out on the altar of the Lᴏʀᴅ your God, and you shall eat the flesh.

28Be careful to heed all these commandments that I enjoin upon you; thus it will go well with you and with your descendants after you for-ever, for you will be doing what is good and right in the sight of the Lᴏʀᴅ your God.

29When the Lᴏʀᴅ your God has cut down be-fore you the nations that you are about to enter and dispossess, and you have dispossessed them and settled in their land, 30beware of being lured into their ways after they have been wiped out before you! Do not inquire about their gods, saying, "How did those nations worship their gods? I too will follow those practices." 31You shall not act thus toward the Lᴏʀᴅ your God, for they perform for their gods every abhorrent act that the Lᴏʀᴅ detests; they even offer up their

13 sons and daughters in fire to their gods. 1Be careful to observe only that which I enjoin upon you: neither add to it nor take away from it.

2If there appears among you a prophet or a dream-diviner and he gives you a sign or a por-tent, 3saying, "Let us follow and worship an-other god"—whom you have not experiencedᵃ —even if the sign or portent that he named to you comes true, 4do not heed the words of that prophet or that dream-diviner. For the Lᴏʀᴅ your God is testing you to see whether you really love the Lᴏʀᴅ your God with all your heart and soul. 5Follow none but the Lᴏʀᴅ your God, and revere none but Him; observe His command-

---

וּבָאתָ אֶל־הַמָּקוֹם אֲשֶׁר־יִבְחַר יְהֹוָה:

27 וְעָשִׂיתָ עֹלֹתֶיךָ הַבָּשָׂר וְהַדָּם עַל־מִזְבַּח יְהֹוָה אֱלֹהֶיךָ וְדַם־זְבָחֶיךָ יִשָּׁפֵךְ עַל־מִזְבַּח יְהֹוָה אֱלֹהֶיךָ וְהַבָּשָׂר תֹּאכֵל:

28 שְׁמֹר וְשָׁמַעְתָּ אֵת כָּל־הַדְּבָרִים הָאֵלֶּה אֲשֶׁר אָנֹכִי מְצַוֶּךָּ לְמַעַן יִיטַב לְךָ וּלְבָנֶיךָ אַחֲרֶיךָ עַד־עוֹלָם כִּי תַעֲשֶׂה הַטּוֹב וְהַיָּשָׁר בְּעֵינֵי יְהֹוָה אֱלֹהֶיךָ: ס

29 כִּי־יַכְרִית יְהֹוָה אֱלֹהֶיךָ אֶת־הַגּוֹיִם אֲשֶׁר אַתָּה בָא־שָׁמָּה לָרֶשֶׁת אוֹתָם מִפָּנֶיךָ וְיָרַשְׁתָּ אֹתָם וְיָשַׁבְתָּ בְּאַרְצָם:

30 הִשָּׁמֶר לְךָ פֶּן־תִּנָּקֵשׁ אַחֲרֵיהֶם אַחֲרֵי הִשָּׁמְדָם מִפָּנֶיךָ וּפֶן־תִּדְרֹשׁ לֵאלֹהֵיהֶם לֵאמֹר אֵיכָה יַעַבְדוּ הַגּוֹיִם הָאֵלֶּה אֶת־ אֱלֹהֵיהֶם וְאֶעֱשֶׂה־כֵּן גַּם־אָנִי: 31 לֹא־ תַעֲשֶׂה כֵן לַיהֹוָה אֱלֹהֶיךָ כִּי כָל־תּוֹעֲבַת יְהֹוָה אֲשֶׁר שָׂנֵא עָשׂוּ לֵאלֹהֵיהֶם כִּי גַם אֶת־בְּנֵיהֶם וְאֶת־בְּנֹתֵיהֶם יִשְׂרְפוּ בָאֵשׁ לֵאלֹהֵיהֶם: **לג** 1 אֵת כָּל־הַדָּבָר אֲשֶׁר אָנֹכִי מְצַוֶּה אֶתְכֶם אֹתוֹ תִשְׁמְרוּ לַעֲשׂוֹת לֹא־תֹסֵף עָלָיו וְלֹא תִגְרַע מִמֶּנּוּ: פ

2 כִּי־יָקוּם בְּקִרְבְּךָ נָבִיא אוֹ חֹלֵם חֲלוֹם וְנָתַן אֵלֶיךָ אוֹת אוֹ מוֹפֵת: 3 וּבָא הָאוֹת וְהַמּוֹפֵת אֲשֶׁר־דִּבֶּר אֵלֶיךָ לֵאמֹר נֵלְכָה אַחֲרֵי אֱלֹהִים אֲחֵרִים אֲשֶׁר לֹא־יְדַעְתָּם וְנָעָבְדֵם: 4 לֹא תִשְׁמַע אֶל־דִּבְרֵי הַנָּבִיא הַהוּא אוֹ אֶל־חוֹלֵם הַחֲלוֹם הַהוּא כִּי מְנַסֶּה יְהֹוָה אֱלֹהֵיכֶם אֶתְכֶם לָדַעַת הֲיִשְׁכֶם אֹהֲבִים אֶת־יְהֹוָה אֱלֹהֵיכֶם בְּכָל־ לְבַבְכֶם וּבְכָל־נַפְשְׁכֶם: 5 אַחֲרֵי יְהֹוָה אֱלֹהֵיכֶם תֵּלֵכוּ וְאֹתוֹ תִירָאוּ וְאֶת־מִצְוֹתָיו

ᶜ-ᶜ   Lit. "you shall pick up and come."

ᵃ   See note on 11.28.

ments alone, and heed only His orders; worship none but Him, and hold fast to Him. ⁶As for that prophet or dream-diviner, he shall be put to death; for he urged disloyalty to the LORD your God—who freed you from the land of Egypt and who redeemed you from the house of bondage—to make you stray from the path that the LORD your God commanded you to follow. Thus you will sweep out evil from your midst.

⁷If your brother, *b-your own mother's son,-b* or your son or daughter, or the wife of your bosom, or your *c-closest friend-c* entices you in secret, saying, "Come let us worship other gods"—whom neither you nor your fathers have experienced*a* —⁸from among the gods of the peoples around you, either near to you or distant, anywhere from one end of the earth to the other: ⁹do not assent or give heed to him. Show him no pity or compassion, and do not shield him; ¹⁰but take his life. Let your hand be the first against him to put him to death, and the hand of the rest of the people thereafter. ¹¹Stone him to death, for he sought to make you stray from the LORD your God, who brought you out of the land of Egypt, out of the house of bondage. ¹²Thus all Israel will hear and be afraid, and such evil things will not be done again in your midst.

¹³If you hear it said, of one of the towns that the LORD your God is giving you to dwell in, ¹⁴that some scoundrels from among you have gone and subverted the inhabitants of their town, saying, "Come let us worship other gods"—whom you have not experienced— ¹⁵you shall investigate and inquire and interrogate thoroughly. If it is true, the fact is established—that abhorrent thing was perpetrated in your midst—¹⁶put the inhabitants of

תִּשְׁמֹרוּ וּבְקֹלוֹ תִשְׁמָעוּ וְאֹתוֹ תַעֲבֹדוּ וּבוֹ
תִדְבָּקוּן: ⁶ וְהַנָּבִיא הַהוּא אוֹ חֹלֵם
הַחֲלוֹם הַהוּא יוּמָת כִּי דִבֶּר־סָרָה עַל־
יְהֹוָה אֱלֹהֵיכֶם הַמּוֹצִיא אֶתְכֶם ׀ מֵאֶרֶץ
מִצְרַיִם וְהַפֹּדְךָ מִבֵּית עֲבָדִים לְהַדִּיחֲךָ
מִן־הַדֶּרֶךְ אֲשֶׁר צִוְּךָ יְהֹוָה אֱלֹהֶיךָ לָלֶכֶת
בָּהּ וּבִעַרְתָּ הָרָע מִקִּרְבֶּךָ: ⁷ כִּי יְסִיתְךָ אָחִיךָ בֶן־אִמֶּךָ אוֹ־בִנְךָ אוֹ־
בִתְּךָ אוֹ ׀ אֵשֶׁת חֵיקֶךָ אוֹ רֵעֲךָ אֲשֶׁר
כְּנַפְשְׁךָ בַּסֵּתֶר לֵאמֹר נֵלְכָה וְנַעַבְדָה
אֱלֹהִים אֲחֵרִים אֲשֶׁר לֹא יָדַעְתָּ אַתָּה
וַאֲבֹתֶיךָ: ⁸ מֵאֱלֹהֵי הָעַמִּים אֲשֶׁר
סְבִיבֹתֵיכֶם הַקְּרֹבִים אֵלֶיךָ אוֹ הָרְחֹקִים
מִמֶּךָּ מִקְצֵה הָאָרֶץ וְעַד־קְצֵה הָאָרֶץ:
⁹ לֹא־תֹאבֶה לוֹ וְלֹא תִשְׁמַע אֵלָיו וְלֹא־
תָחוֹס עֵינְךָ עָלָיו וְלֹא־תַחְמֹל וְלֹא־תְכַסֶּה
עָלָיו: ¹⁰ כִּי הָרֹג תַּהַרְגֶנּוּ יָדְךָ תִּהְיֶה־
בּוֹ בָרִאשׁוֹנָה לַהֲמִיתוֹ וְיַד כָּל־הָעָם
בָּאַחֲרֹנָה: ¹¹ וּסְקַלְתּוֹ בָאֲבָנִים וָמֵת כִּי
בִקֵּשׁ לְהַדִּיחֲךָ מֵעַל יְהֹוָה אֱלֹהֶיךָ
הַמּוֹצִיאֲךָ מֵאֶרֶץ מִצְרַיִם מִבֵּית עֲבָדִים:
¹² וְכָל־יִשְׂרָאֵל יִשְׁמְעוּ וְיִרָאוּן וְלֹא־יוֹסִפוּ
לַעֲשׂוֹת כַּדָּבָר הָרָע הַזֶּה בְּקִרְבֶּךָ: ס
¹³ כִּי־תִשְׁמַע בְּאַחַת עָרֶיךָ אֲשֶׁר יְהֹוָה
אֱלֹהֶיךָ נֹתֵן לְךָ לָשֶׁבֶת שָׁם לֵאמֹר:
¹⁴ יָצְאוּ אֲנָשִׁים בְּנֵי־בְלִיַּעַל מִקִּרְבֶּךָ וַיַּדִּיחוּ
אֶת־יֹשְׁבֵי עִירָם לֵאמֹר נֵלְכָה וְנַעַבְדָה
אֱלֹהִים אֲחֵרִים אֲשֶׁר לֹא־יְדַעְתֶּם:
¹⁵ וְדָרַשְׁתָּ וְחָקַרְתָּ וְשָׁאַלְתָּ הֵיטֵב וְהִנֵּה
אֱמֶת נָכוֹן הַדָּבָר נֶעֶשְׂתָה הַתּוֹעֵבָה הַזֹּאת
בְּקִרְבֶּךָ: ¹⁶ הַכֵּה תַכֶּה אֶת־יֹשְׁבֵי הָעִיר

---

b-b Samaritan reads, "the son of your father or the son of your mother."

c-c Lit. "your friend who is as yourself."

that town to the sword and put its cattle to the sword. Doom it and all that is in it to destruction: [17]gather all its spoil into the open square, and burn the town and all its spoil as a holocaust to the LORD your God. And it shall remain an everlasting ruin, never to be rebuilt. [18]Let nothing that has been doomed stick to your hand, in order that the LORD may turn from His blazing anger and show you compassion, and in His compassion increase you as He promised your fathers on oath—[19]for you will be heeding the LORD your God, obeying all His commandments that I enjoin upon you this day, doing what is right in the sight of the LORD your God.

14 You are children of the LORD your God. You shall not gash yourselves or shave the front of your heads because of the dead. [2]For you are a people consecrated to the LORD your God: the LORD your God chose you from among all other peoples on earth to be His treasured people.

[3]You shall not eat anything abhorrent. [4]These are the animals that you may eat: the ox, the sheep, and the goat; [5a] the deer, the gazelle, the roebuck, the wild goat, the ibex, the antelope, the mountain sheep, [6]and any other animal that has true hoofs which are cleft in two and brings up the cud—such you may eat. [7]But the following, which do bring up the cud or have true hoofs which are cleft through, you may not eat: the camel, the hare, and the daman—for although they bring up the cud, they have no true hoofs—they are unclean for you; [8]also the swine—for although it has true hoofs, it does not bring up the cud—is unclean for you. You shall not eat of their flesh or touch their carcasses.

[9]These you may eat of all that live in water: you may eat anything that has fins and scales.

---

a   A number of these creatures cannot be identified with certainty.

הַהִוא לְפִי־חֶ֔רֶב הַחֲרֵ֨ם אֹתָ֧הּ וְאֶת־
כָּל־אֲשֶׁר־בָּ֛הּ וְאֶת־בְּהֶמְתָּ֖הּ לְפִי־חָֽרֶב׃
[17]וְאֶת־כָּל־שְׁלָלָ֗הּ תִּקְבֹּץ֮ אֶל־תּ֣וֹךְ רְחֹבָהּ֒
וְשָׂרַפְתָּ֣ בָאֵ֗שׁ אֶת־הָעִ֤יר וְאֶת־כָּל־שְׁלָלָהּ֙
כָּלִ֔יל לַיהוָ֖ה אֱלֹהֶ֑יךָ וְהָֽיְתָה֙ תֵּ֣ל עוֹלָ֔ם
לֹ֥א תִבָּנֶ֖ה עֽוֹד׃ [18]וְלֹֽא־יִדְבַּ֧ק בְּיָֽדְךָ֛
מְא֖וּמָה מִן־הַחֵ֑רֶם לְמַעַן֩ יָשׁ֨וּב יְהוָ֜ה
מֵחֲר֣וֹן אַפּ֗וֹ וְנָֽתַן־לְךָ֤ רַֽחֲמִים֙ וְרִֽחַמְךָ֣
וְהִרְבֶּ֔ךָ כַּֽאֲשֶׁ֥ר נִשְׁבַּ֖ע לַֽאֲבֹתֶֽיךָ׃ [19]כִּ֣י
תִשְׁמַ֗ע בְּקוֹל֙ יְהוָ֣ה אֱלֹהֶ֔יךָ לִשְׁמֹר֙ אֶת־
כָּל־מִצְוֺתָ֔יו אֲשֶׁ֛ר אָֽנֹכִ֥י מְצַוְּךָ֖ הַיּ֑וֹם
לַֽעֲשׂוֹת֙ הַיָּשָׁ֔ר בְּעֵינֵ֖י יְהוָ֥ה אֱלֹהֶֽיךָ׃ ס

יד בָּנִ֣ים אַתֶּ֔ם לַֽיהוָ֖ה אֱלֹֽהֵיכֶ֑ם
לֹ֣א תִתְגֹּֽדְד֗וּ וְלֹֽא־תָשִׂ֧ימוּ קָרְחָ֛ה בֵּ֥ין
עֵֽינֵיכֶ֖ם לָמֵֽת׃ [2]כִּ֣י עַ֤ם קָדוֹשׁ֙ אַתָּ֔ה לַֽיהוָ֖ה
אֱלֹהֶ֑יךָ וּבְךָ֞ בָּחַ֣ר יְהוָ֗ה לִֽהְי֥וֹת לוֹ֙
לְעַ֣ם סְגֻלָּ֔ה מִכֹּל֙ הָֽעַמִּ֔ים אֲשֶׁ֖ר עַל־פְּנֵ֥י
הָֽאֲדָמָֽה׃ ס
[3]לֹ֥א תֹאכַ֖ל כָּל־תּוֹעֵבָֽה׃ [4]זֹ֥את הַבְּהֵמָ֖ה
אֲשֶׁ֣ר תֹּאכֵ֑לוּ שׁ֕וֹר שֵׂ֥ה כְשָׂבִ֖ים וְשֵׂ֥ה עִזִּֽים׃
[5]אַיָּ֥ל וּצְבִ֖י וְיַחְמ֑וּר וְאַקּ֥וֹ וְדִישֹׁ֖ן וּתְא֥וֹ
וָזָֽמֶר׃ [6]וְכָל־בְּהֵמָ֞ה מַפְרֶ֣סֶת פַּרְסָ֗ה
וְשֹׁסַ֤עַת שֶׁ֨סַע֙ שְׁתֵּ֣י פְרָס֔וֹת מַֽעֲלַ֥ת גֵּרָ֖ה
בַּבְּהֵמָ֑ה אֹתָ֖הּ תֹּאכֵֽלוּ׃ [7]אַ֣ךְ אֶת־זֶ֞ה לֹ֤א
תֹֽאכְלוּ֙ מִֽמַּֽעֲלֵ֣י הַגֵּרָ֔ה וּמִמַּפְרִיסֵ֥י הַפַּרְסָ֖ה
הַשְּׁסוּעָ֑ה אֶֽת־הַ֠גָּמָל וְאֶת־הָֽאַרְנֶ֨בֶת וְאֶת־
הַשָּׁפָ֜ן כִּֽי־מַֽעֲלֵ֧ה גֵרָ֣ה הֵ֗מָּה וּפַרְסָה֙ לֹ֣א
הִפְרִ֔יסוּ טְמֵאִ֥ים הֵ֖ם לָכֶֽם׃ [8]וְאֶת־הַ֠חֲזִיר
כִּֽי־מַפְרִ֨יס פַּרְסָ֥ה הוּא֙ וְלֹ֣א גֵרָ֔ה טָמֵ֥א
ה֖וּא לָכֶ֑ם מִבְּשָׂרָם֙ לֹ֣א תֹאכֵ֔לוּ וּבְנִבְלָתָ֖ם
לֹ֥א תִגָּֽעוּ׃ ס
[9]אֶת־זֶה֙ תֹּֽאכְל֔וּ מִכֹּ֖ל אֲשֶׁ֣ר בַּמָּ֑יִם כֹּ֣ל

10But you may not eat anything that has no fins and scales: it is unclean for you.

11You may eat any clean bird. 12The following you may not eat: athe eagle, the vulture, and the black vulture; 13the kite, the falcon, and the buzzard of any variety; 14every variety of raven; 15the ostrich, the nighthawk, the sea gull, and the hawk of any variety; 16the little owl, the great owl, and the white owl; 17the pelican, the bustard, and the cormorant; 18the stork, any variety of heron, the hoopoe, and the bat.

19All winged swarming things are unclean for you: they may not be eaten. 20You may eat only clean winged creatures.

21You shall not eat anything that has died a natural death; give it to the stranger in your community to eat, or you may sell it to a foreigner. For you are a people consecrated to the Lord your God.

You shall not boil a kid in its mother's milk.

22You shall set aside every year a tenth part of all the yield of your sowing that is brought from the field. 23You shall consume the tithes of your new grain and wine and oil, and the firstlings of your herds and flocks, in the presence of the Lord your God, in the place where He will choose to establish His name, so that you may learn to revere the Lord your God forever. 24Should the distance be too great for you, should you be unable to transport them, because the place where the Lord your God has chosen to establish His name is far from you and because the Lord your God has blessed you,b 25you may convert them into money. Wrap up the money and take it with you to the place that the Lord your God has chosen, 26and spend the money on anything you want—cattle, sheep, wine, or other intoxicant, or anything you may desire. And you shall feast there, in the

b I.e., with abundant crops.

אֲשֶׁר־לֹ֥ו סְנַפִּ֖יר וְקַשְׂקֶ֑שֶׂת תֹּאכֵֽלוּ׃ 10 וְכֹ֡ל אֲשֶׁ֣ר אֵֽין־לֹו֩ סְנַפִּ֨יר וְקַשְׂקֶ֜שֶׂת לֹ֣א תֹאכֵ֗לוּ טָמֵ֥א ה֖וּא לָכֶֽם׃ ס

11 כָּל־צִפֹּ֥ור טְהֹרָ֖ה תֹּאכֵֽלוּ׃ 12 וְזֶ֕ה אֲשֶׁ֥ר לֹֽא־תֹאכְל֖וּ מֵהֶ֑ם הַנֶּ֥שֶׁר וְהַפֶּ֖רֶס וְהָֽעָזְנִיָּֽה׃ 13 וְהָרָאָה֙ וְאֶת־הָ֣אַיָּ֔ה וְהַדַּיָּ֖ה לְמִינָֽהּ׃ 14 וְאֵ֥ת כָּל־עֹרֵ֖ב לְמִינֹֽו׃ 15 וְאֵת֙ בַּ֣ת הַֽיַּעֲנָ֔ה וְאֶת־הַתַּחְמָ֖ס וְאֶת־הַשָּׁ֑חַף וְאֶת־הַנֵּ֖ץ לְמִינֵֽהוּ׃ 16 אֶת־הַכֹּ֥וס וְאֶת־הַיַּנְשׁ֖וּף וְהַתִּנְשָֽׁמֶת׃ 17 וְהַקָּאָ֥ת וְאֶת־הָֽרָחָ֖מָה וְאֶת־הַשָּׁלָֽךְ׃ 18 וְהַ֣חֲסִידָ֔ה וְהָאֲנָפָ֖ה לְמִינָ֑הּ וְהַדּֽוּכִיפַ֖ת וְהָעֲטַלֵּֽף׃ 19 וְכֹל֙ שֶׁ֣רֶץ הָעֹ֔וף טָמֵ֥א ה֖וּא לָכֶ֑ם לֹ֖א יֵאָכֵֽלוּ׃ 20 כָּל־עֹ֥וף טָהֹ֖ור תֹּאכֵֽלוּ׃

21 לֹ֣א תֹאכְל֣וּ כָל־נְבֵלָ֡ה לַגֵּ֣ר אֲשֶׁר־בִּשְׁעָרֶ֜יךָ תִּתְּנֶ֣נָּה וַאֲכָלָ֗הּ אֹ֤ו מָכֹר֙ לְנָכְרִ֔י כִּ֣י עַ֤ם קָדֹושׁ֙ אַתָּ֔ה לַיהוָ֖ה אֱלֹהֶ֑יךָ לֹֽא־תְבַשֵּׁ֥ל גְּדִ֖י בַּחֲלֵ֥ב אִמֹּֽו׃ פ

22 עַשֵּׂ֣ר תְּעַשֵּׂ֔ר אֵ֖ת כָּל־תְּבוּאַ֣ת זַרְעֶ֑ךָ הַיֹּצֵ֥א הַשָּׂדֶ֖ה שָׁנָ֥ה שָׁנָֽה׃ 23 וְאָכַלְתָּ֞ לִפְנֵ֣י ׀ יְהוָ֣ה אֱלֹהֶ֗יךָ בַּמָּקֹ֣ום אֲשֶׁר־יִבְחַר�’ לְשַׁכֵּ֤ן שְׁמֹו֙ שָׁ֔ם מַעְשַׂ֤ר דְּגָֽנְךָ֙ תִּֽירֹשְׁךָ֣ וְיִצְהָרֶ֔ךָ וּבְכֹרֹ֥ת בְּקָרְךָ֖ וְצֹאנֶ֑ךָ לְמַ֣עַן תִּלְמַ֗ד לְיִרְאָ֛ה אֶת־יְהוָ֥ה אֱלֹהֶ֖יךָ כָּל־הַיָּמִֽים׃ 24 וְכִֽי־יִרְבֶּ֨ה מִמְּךָ֜ הַדֶּ֗רֶךְ כִּ֣י לֹ֣א תוּכַל֘ שְׂאֵתֹו֒ כִּֽי־יִרְחַ֤ק מִמְּךָ֙ הַמָּקֹ֔ום אֲשֶׁ֤ר יִבְחַר֙ יְהוָ֣ה אֱלֹהֶ֔יךָ לָשׂ֥וּם שְׁמֹ֖ו שָׁ֑ם כִּ֥י יְבָרֶכְךָ֖ יְהוָ֥ה אֱלֹהֶֽיךָ׃ 25 וְנָתַתָּ֖ה בַּכָּ֑סֶף וְצַרְתָּ֤ הַכֶּ֨סֶף֙ בְּיָ֣דְךָ֔ וְהָֽלַכְתָּ֙ אֶל־הַמָּקֹ֔ום אֲשֶׁ֥ר יִבְחַ֛ר יְהוָ֥ה אֱלֹהֶ֖יךָ בֹּֽו׃ 26 וְנָתַתָּ֣ה הַכֶּ֡סֶף בְּכֹל֩ אֲשֶׁר־תְּאַוֶּ֨ה נַפְשְׁךָ֜ בַּבָּקָ֣ר וּבַצֹּ֗אן וּבַיַּ֨יִן֙ וּבַשֵּׁכָ֔ר וּבְכֹ֛ל אֲשֶׁ֥ר תִּֽשְׁאָלְךָ֖ נַפְשֶׁ֑ךָ וְאָכַ֣לְתָּ

presence of the Lord your God, and rejoice with
your household.

27But do not neglect the Levite in your community, for he has no hereditary portion as you
have. 28c-Every third year-c you shall bring out
the full tithe of your yield of that year, but leave
it within your settlements. 29Then the Levite,
who has no hereditary portion as you have, and
the stranger, the fatherless, and the widow in
your settlements shall come and eat their fill,
so that the Lord your God may bless you in all
the enterprises you undertake.

15 a-Every seventh year-a you shall practice
remission of debts. 2This shall be the nature of
the remission: every creditor shall remit the due
that he claims from his fellow; he shall not dun
his fellow or kinsman, for the remission proclaimed is of the Lord. 3You may dun the foreigner; but you must remit whatever is due you
from your kinsmen.

4There shall be no needy among you—since
the Lord your God will bless you in the land
that the Lord your God is giving you as a hereditary portion—5if only you heed the Lord
your God and take care to keep all this Instruction that I enjoin upon you this day. 6For the
Lord your God will bless you as He has promised you: you will extend loans to many nations,
but require none yourself; you will dominate
many nations, but they will not dominate you.

7If, however, there is a needy person among
you, one of your kinsmen in any of your settlements in the land that the Lord your God
is giving you, do not harden your heart and
shut your hand against your needy kinsman.
8Rather, you must open your hand and lend him
sufficient for whatever he needs. 9Beware lest
you harbor the base thought, "The seventh year,

שָׁם לִפְנֵי יְהֹוָה אֱלֹהֶיךָ וְשָׂמַחְתָּ אַתָּה
וּבֵיתֶךָ: 27וְהַלֵּוִי אֲשֶׁר־בִּשְׁעָרֶיךָ לֹא תַעַזְבֶנּוּ כִּי
אֵין לוֹ חֵלֶק וְנַחֲלָה עִמָּךְ: ס 28מִקְצֵה ׀
שָׁלֹשׁ שָׁנִים תּוֹצִיא אֶת־כָּל־מַעְשַׂר
תְּבוּאָתְךָ בַּשָּׁנָה הַהִוא וְהִנַּחְתָּ בִּשְׁעָרֶיךָ:
29וּבָא הַלֵּוִי כִּי אֵין־לוֹ חֵלֶק וְנַחֲלָה עִמָּךְ
וְהַגֵּר וְהַיָּתוֹם וְהָאַלְמָנָה אֲשֶׁר בִּשְׁעָרֶיךָ
וְאָכְלוּ וְשָׂבֵעוּ לְמַעַן יְבָרֶכְךָ יְהֹוָה אֱלֹהֶיךָ
בְּכָל־מַעֲשֵׂה יָדְךָ אֲשֶׁר תַּעֲשֶׂה: ס

טו מִקֵּץ שֶׁבַע־שָׁנִים תַּעֲשֶׂה שְׁמִטָּה:
2וְזֶה דְּבַר הַשְּׁמִטָּה שָׁמוֹט כָּל־בַּעַל מַשֵּׁה
יָדוֹ אֲשֶׁר יַשֶּׁה בְּרֵעֵהוּ לֹא־יִגֹּשׂ אֶת־רֵעֵהוּ
וְאֶת־אָחִיו כִּי־קָרָא שְׁמִטָּה לַיהֹוָה: 3אֶת־
הַנָּכְרִי תִּגֹּשׂ וַאֲשֶׁר יִהְיֶה לְךָ אֶת־אָחִיךָ
תַּשְׁמֵט יָדֶךָ:
4אֶפֶס כִּי לֹא יִהְיֶה־בְּךָ אֶבְיוֹן כִּי־בָרֵךְ
יְבָרֶכְךָ יְהֹוָה בָּאָרֶץ אֲשֶׁר יְהֹוָה אֱלֹהֶיךָ
נֹתֵן לְךָ נַחֲלָה לְרִשְׁתָּהּ: 5רַק אִם־שָׁמוֹעַ
תִּשְׁמַע בְּקוֹל יְהֹוָה אֱלֹהֶיךָ לִשְׁמֹר לַעֲשׂוֹת
אֶת־כָּל־הַמִּצְוָה הַזֹּאת אֲשֶׁר אָנֹכִי מְצַוְּךָ
הַיּוֹם: 6כִּי־יְהֹוָה אֱלֹהֶיךָ בֵּרַכְךָ כַּאֲשֶׁר
דִּבֶּר־לָךְ וְהַעֲבַטְתָּ גּוֹיִם רַבִּים וְאַתָּה לֹא
תַעֲבֹט וּמָשַׁלְתָּ בְּגוֹיִם רַבִּים וּבְךָ לֹא
יִמְשֹׁלוּ: ס
7כִּי־יִהְיֶה בְךָ אֶבְיוֹן מֵאַחַד אַחֶיךָ בְּאַחַד
שְׁעָרֶיךָ בְּאַרְצְךָ אֲשֶׁר־יְהֹוָה אֱלֹהֶיךָ נֹתֵן
לָךְ לֹא תְאַמֵּץ אֶת־לְבָבְךָ וְלֹא תִקְפֹּץ
אֶת־יָדְךָ מֵאָחִיךָ הָאֶבְיוֹן: 8כִּי־פָתֹחַ
תִּפְתַּח אֶת־יָדְךָ לוֹ וְהַעֲבֵט תַּעֲבִיטֶנּוּ דֵּי
מַחְסֹרוֹ אֲשֶׁר יֶחְסַר לוֹ: 9הִשָּׁמֶר לְךָ
פֶּן־יִהְיֶה דָבָר עִם־לְבָבְךָ בְלִיַּעַל לֵאמֹר

---

c-c Lit. "After a period of three years"; cf. Deut. 26.12.

a-a Cf. 14.28.

the year of remission, is approaching," so that you are mean to your needy kinsman and give him nothing. He will cry out to the Lord against you, and you will incur guilt. ¹⁰Give to him readily and have no regrets when you do so, for in return the Lord your God will bless you in all your efforts and in all your undertakings. ¹¹For there will never cease to be needy ones in your land, which is why I command you: open your hand to the poor and needy kinsman in your land.

¹²If a fellow Hebrew, man or woman, is sold to you, he shall serve you six years, and in the seventh year you shall set him free. ¹³When you set him free, do not let him go empty-handed: ¹⁴Furnish him out of the flock, threshing floor, and vat; with which the Lord your God has blessed you. ¹⁵Bear in mind that you were slaves in the land of Egypt and the Lord your God redeemed you; therefore I enjoin this commandment upon you today.

¹⁶But should he say to you, "I do not want to leave you"—for he loves you and your household and is happy with you—¹⁷you shall take an awl and put it through his ear into the door, and he shall become your slave in perpetuity. Do the same with your female slave. ¹⁸When you do set him free, do not feel aggrieved; for in the six years he has given you double the service of a hired man. Moreover, the Lord your God will bless you in all you do.

¹⁹You shall consecrate to the Lord your God all male firstlings that are born in your herd and in your flock: you must not work your firstling ox or shear your firstling sheep. ²⁰You and your household shall eat it annually before the Lord your God in the place that the Lord will choose. ²¹But if it has a defect, lameness or blindness, any serious defect, you shall not sacrifice it to the Lord your God. ²²Eat it in your settlements,

קָרְבָ֞ה שְׁנַֽת־הַשֶּׁ֣בַע שְׁנַ֣ת הַשְּׁמִטָּה֮ וְרָעָ֣ה עֵֽינְךָ֣ בְּאָחִ֨יךָ֙ הָֽאֶבְי֔וֹן וְלֹ֥א תִתֵּ֖ן ל֑וֹ וְקָרָ֤א עָלֶ֨יךָ֙ אֶל־יְהֹוָ֔ה וְהָיָ֥ה בְךָ֖ חֵֽטְא: ¹⁰ נָת֨וֹן תִּתֵּ֜ן ל֗וֹ וְלֹא־יֵרַ֤ע לְבָֽבְךָ֙ בְּתִתְּךָ֣ ל֔וֹ כִּ֞י בִּגְלַ֣ל ׀ הַדָּבָ֣ר הַזֶּ֗ה יְבָרֶכְךָ֙ יְהֹוָ֣ה אֱלֹהֶ֔יךָ בְּכָֽל־מַֽעֲשֶׂ֔ךָ וּבְכֹ֖ל מִשְׁלַ֥ח יָדֶֽךָ: ¹¹ כִּ֛י לֹֽא־יֶחְדַּ֥ל אֶבְי֖וֹן מִקֶּ֣רֶב הָאָ֑רֶץ עַל־כֵּ֞ן אָֽנֹכִ֤י מְצַוְּךָ֙ לֵאמֹ֔ר פָּ֠תֹ֠חַ תִּפְתַּ֨ח אֶת־יָֽדְךָ֜ לְאָחִ֧יךָ לַֽעֲנִיֶּ֛ךָ וּלְאֶבְיֹֽנְךָ֖ בְּאַרְצֶֽךָ: ס

¹² כִּֽי־יִמָּכֵ֨ר לְךָ֜ אָחִ֣יךָ הָֽעִבְרִ֗י א֚וֹ הָֽעִבְרִיָּ֔ה וַֽעֲבָֽדְךָ֖ שֵׁ֣שׁ שָׁנִ֑ים וּבַשָּׁנָה֙ הַשְּׁבִיעִ֔ת תְּשַׁלְּחֶ֥נּוּ חָפְשִׁ֖י מֵֽעִמָּֽךְ: ¹³ וְכִֽי־תְשַׁלְּחֶ֥נּוּ חָפְשִׁ֖י מֵֽעִמָּ֑ךְ לֹ֥א תְשַׁלְּחֶ֖נּוּ רֵיקָֽם: ¹⁴ הַֽעֲנֵ֤יק תַּֽעֲנִיק֙ ל֔וֹ מִצֹּֽאנְךָ֖ וּמִֽגָּרְנְךָ֣ וּמִיִּקְבֶ֑ךָ אֲשֶׁ֧ר בֵּֽרַכְךָ֛ יְהֹוָ֥ה אֱלֹהֶ֖יךָ תִּתֶּן־ ל֥וֹ: ¹⁵ וְזָֽכַרְתָּ֗ כִּ֣י עֶ֤בֶד הָיִ֨יתָ֙ בְּאֶ֣רֶץ מִצְרַ֔יִם וַֽיִּפְדְּךָ֖ יְהֹוָ֣ה אֱלֹהֶ֑יךָ עַל־כֵּ֞ן אָֽנֹכִ֧י מְצַוְּךָ֛ אֶת־הַדָּבָ֥ר הַזֶּ֖ה הַיּֽוֹם:

¹⁶ וְהָיָה֙ כִּֽי־יֹאמַ֣ר אֵלֶ֔יךָ לֹ֥א אֵצֵ֖א מֵֽעִמָּ֑ךְ כִּ֤י אֲהֵֽבְךָ֙ וְאֶת־בֵּיתֶ֔ךָ כִּי־ט֥וֹב ל֖וֹ עִמָּֽךְ: ¹⁷ וְלָֽקַחְתָּ֣ אֶת־הַמַּרְצֵ֗עַ וְנָֽתַתָּ֤ה בְאָזְנוֹ֙ וּבַדֶּ֔לֶת וְהָיָ֥ה לְךָ֖ עֶ֣בֶד עוֹלָ֑ם וְאַ֥ף לַֽאֲמָֽתְךָ֖ תַּֽעֲשֶׂה־כֵּֽן: ¹⁸ לֹֽא־יִקְשֶׁ֣ה בְעֵינֶ֗ךָ בְּשַׁלֵּֽחֲךָ֙ אֹת֤וֹ חָפְשִׁי֙ מֵֽעִמָּ֔ךְ כִּ֗י מִשְׁנֶה֙ שְׂכַ֣ר שָׂכִ֔יר עֲבָֽדְךָ֖ שֵׁ֣שׁ שָׁנִ֑ים וּבֵֽרַכְךָ֙ יְהֹוָ֣ה אֱלֹהֶ֔יךָ בְּכֹ֖ל אֲשֶׁ֥ר תַּֽעֲשֶֽׂה: פ

¹⁹ כָּל־הַבְּכ֡וֹר אֲשֶׁר֩ יִוָּלֵ֨ד בִּבְקָֽרְךָ֤ וּבְצֹֽאנְךָ֙ הַזָּכָ֔ר תַּקְדִּ֖ישׁ לַֽיהֹוָ֣ה אֱלֹהֶ֑יךָ לֹ֤א תַֽעֲבֹד֙ בִּבְכֹ֣ר שׁוֹרֶ֔ךָ וְלֹ֥א תָגֹ֖ז בְּכ֥וֹר צֹאנֶֽךָ: ²⁰ לִפְנֵי֩ יְהֹוָ֨ה אֱלֹהֶ֤יךָ תֹֽאכְלֶ֨נּוּ֙ שָׁנָ֣ה בְשָׁנָ֔ה בַּמָּק֖וֹם אֲשֶׁר־יִבְחַ֣ר יְהֹוָ֑ה אַתָּ֖ה וּבֵיתֶֽךָ: ²¹ וְכִֽי־ יִהְיֶ֨ה ב֜וֹ מ֗וּם פִּסֵּ֨חַ֙ א֣וֹ עִוֵּ֔ר כֹּ֖ל מ֣וּם רָ֑ע לֹ֣א תִזְבָּחֶ֔נּוּ לַֽיהֹוָ֖ה אֱלֹהֶֽיךָ: ²² בִּשְׁעָרֶ֖יךָ

the unclean among you no less than the clean, just like the gazelle and the deer. ²³Only you must not partake of its blood; you shall pour it out on the ground like water.

16 Observe the month[a] of Abib and offer a passover sacrifice to the LORD your God, for it was in the month[a] of Abib, at night, that the LORD your God freed you from Egypt. ²You shall slaughter the passover sacrifice for the LORD your God, from the flock and the herd, in the place where the LORD will choose to establish His name. ³You shall not eat anything leavened with it; for seven days thereafter[b] you shall eat unleavened bread, bread of distress—for you departed from the land of Egypt hurriedly—so that you may remember the day of your departure from the land of Egypt as long as you live. ⁴For seven days no leaven shall be found with you in all your territory, and none of the flesh of what you slaughter on the evening of the first day shall be left until morning.

⁵You are not permitted to slaughter the passover sacrifice in any of the settlements that the LORD your God is giving you; ⁶but at the place where the LORD your God will choose to establish His name, there alone shall you slaughter the passover sacrifice, in the evening, at sundown, the time of day when you departed from Egypt. ⁷You shall cook and eat it at the place that the LORD your God will choose; and in the morning you may start back on your journey home. ⁸After eating unleavened bread six days, you shall hold a solemn gathering[c] for the LORD your God on the seventh day: you shall do no work.

⁹You shall count off seven weeks; start to count the seven weeks when the sickle is first put to the standing grain. ¹⁰Then you shall ob-

תֹּאכֲלֶנּוּ הַטָּמֵא וְהַטָּהוֹר יַחְדָּו כַּצְּבִי וְכָאַיָּל׃ 23 רַק אֶת־דָּמוֹ לֹא תֹאכֵל עַל־הָאָרֶץ תִּשְׁפְּכֶנּוּ כַּמָּיִם׃ פ

טז שָׁמוֹר אֶת־חֹדֶשׁ הָאָבִיב וְעָשִׂיתָ פֶּסַח לַיהוָה אֱלֹהֶיךָ כִּי בְּחֹדֶשׁ הָאָבִיב הוֹצִיאֲךָ יְהוָה אֱלֹהֶיךָ מִמִּצְרַיִם לָיְלָה׃ 2 וְזָבַחְתָּ פֶּסַח לַיהוָה אֱלֹהֶיךָ צֹאן וּבָקָר בַּמָּקוֹם אֲשֶׁר־יִבְחַר יְהוָה לְשַׁכֵּן שְׁמוֹ שָׁם׃ 3 לֹא־תֹאכַל עָלָיו חָמֵץ שִׁבְעַת יָמִים תֹּאכַל־עָלָיו מַצּוֹת לֶחֶם עֹנִי כִּי בְחִפָּזוֹן יָצָאתָ מֵאֶרֶץ מִצְרַיִם לְמַעַן תִּזְכֹּר אֶת־יוֹם צֵאתְךָ מֵאֶרֶץ מִצְרַיִם כֹּל יְמֵי חַיֶּיךָ׃ 4 וְלֹא־יֵרָאֶה לְךָ שְׂאֹר בְּכָל־גְּבֻלְךָ שִׁבְעַת יָמִים וְלֹא־יָלִין מִן־הַבָּשָׂר אֲשֶׁר תִּזְבַּח בָּעֶרֶב בַּיּוֹם הָרִאשׁוֹן לַבֹּקֶר׃ 5 לֹא תוּכַל לִזְבֹּחַ אֶת־הַפָּסַח בְּאַחַד שְׁעָרֶיךָ אֲשֶׁר־יְהוָה אֱלֹהֶיךָ נֹתֵן לָךְ׃ 6 כִּי אִם־אֶל־הַמָּקוֹם אֲשֶׁר־יִבְחַר יְהוָה אֱלֹהֶיךָ לְשַׁכֵּן שְׁמוֹ שָׁם תִּזְבַּח אֶת־הַפֶּסַח בָּעֶרֶב כְּבוֹא הַשֶּׁמֶשׁ מוֹעֵד צֵאתְךָ מִמִּצְרָיִם׃ 7 וּבִשַּׁלְתָּ וְאָכַלְתָּ בַּמָּקוֹם אֲשֶׁר יִבְחַר יְהוָה אֱלֹהֶיךָ בּוֹ וּפָנִיתָ בַבֹּקֶר וְהָלַכְתָּ לְאֹהָלֶיךָ׃ 8 שֵׁשֶׁת יָמִים תֹּאכַל מַצּוֹת וּבַיּוֹם הַשְּׁבִיעִי עֲצֶרֶת לַיהוָה אֱלֹהֶיךָ לֹא תַעֲשֶׂה מְלָאכָה׃ ס 9 שִׁבְעָה שָׁבֻעֹת תִּסְפָּר־לָךְ מֵהָחֵל חֶרְמֵשׁ בַּקָּמָה תָּחֵל לִסְפֹּר שִׁבְעָה שָׁבֻעוֹת׃ 10 וְעָשִׂיתָ חַג שָׁבֻעוֹת לַיהוָה אֱלֹהֶיךָ מִסַּת

---

a Cf. Exod. 13.4; 23.15; 34.18.
b Lit. "upon it."
c See note at Lev. 23.36.

serve the Feast of Weeks for the Lord your God, offering your freewill contribution according as the Lord your God has blessed you. [11]You shall rejoice before the Lord your God with your son and daughter, your male and female slave, the Levite in your communities, and the stranger, the fatherless, and the widow in your midst, at the place where the Lord your God will choose to establish His name. [12]Bear in mind that you were slaves in Egypt, and take care to obey these laws.

[13]After the ingathering from your threshing floor and your vat, you shall hold the Feast of Booths for seven days. [14]You shall rejoice in your festival, with your son and daughter, your male and female slave, the Levite, the stranger, the fatherless, and the widow in your communities. [15]You shall hold a festival for the Lord your God seven days, in the place that the Lord will choose; for the Lord your God will bless all[d] your crops and all your undertakings, and you shall have nothing but joy.

[16]Three times a year—on the Feast of Unleavened Bread, on the Feast of Weeks, and on the Feast of Booths—all your males shall appear before the Lord your God in the place that He will choose. They shall not appear before the Lord empty-handed, [17]but each with his own gift, according to the blessing that the Lord your God has bestowed upon you.

SHOFETIM

[18]You shall appoint magistrates and officials for your tribes, in all the settlements that the Lord your God is giving you, and they shall govern the people with due justice. [19]You shall not judge unfairly: you shall show no partiality; you shall not take bribes, for bribes blind the eyes of the discerning and upset the plea of the just. [20]Justice, justice shall you pursue, that you may

---

נְדְבַ֣ת יָדְךָ֗ אֲשֶׁ֥ר תִּתֵּ֖ן כַּאֲשֶׁ֥ר יְבָרֶכְךָ֖ יְהֹוָ֥ה
אֱלֹהֶֽיךָ׃ 11 וְשָׂמַחְתָּ֞ לִפְנֵ֣י ׀ יְהֹוָ֣ה אֱלֹהֶ֗יךָ
אַתָּ֨ה וּבִנְךָ֣ וּבִתֶּךָ֮ וְעַבְדְּךָ֣ וַאֲמָתֶךָ֒ וְהַלֵּוִ֜י
אֲשֶׁ֣ר בִּשְׁעָרֶ֗יךָ וְהַגֵּ֤ר וְהַיָּתוֹם֙ וְהָֽאַלְמָנָ֔ה
אֲשֶׁ֖ר בְּקִרְבֶּ֑ךָ בַּמָּק֔וֹם אֲשֶׁ֤ר יִבְחַר֙ יְהֹוָ֣ה
אֱלֹהֶ֔יךָ לְשַׁכֵּ֥ן שְׁמ֖וֹ שָֽׁם׃ 12 וְזָ֣כַרְתָּ֔ כִּי־עֶ֥בֶד
הָיִ֖יתָ בְּמִצְרָ֑יִם וְשָֽׁמַרְתָּ֣ וְעָשִׂ֔יתָ אֶת־
הַֽחֻקִּ֖ים הָאֵֽלֶּה׃ פ

13 חַ֧ג הַסֻּכֹּ֛ת תַּעֲשֶׂ֥ה לְךָ֖ שִׁבְעַ֣ת יָמִ֑ים
בְּאָ֨סְפְּךָ֔ מִֽגָּרְנְךָ֖ וּמִיִּקְבֶֽךָ׃ 14 וְשָׂמַחְתָּ֖ בְּחַגֶּ֑ךָ
אַתָּ֨ה וּבִנְךָ֤ וּבִתֶּ֙ךָ֙ וְעַבְדְּךָ֣ וַאֲמָתֶ֔ךָ וְהַלֵּוִ֗י
וְהַגֵּ֛ר וְהַיָּת֥וֹם וְהָאַלְמָנָ֖ה אֲשֶׁ֥ר בִּשְׁעָרֶֽיךָ׃
15 שִׁבְעַ֣ת יָמִ֗ים תָּחֹג֙ לַֽיהֹוָ֣ה אֱלֹהֶ֔יךָ
בַּמָּק֖וֹם אֲשֶׁר־יִבְחַ֣ר יְהֹוָ֑ה כִּ֣י יְבָרֶכְךָ֞ יְהֹוָ֣ה
אֱלֹהֶ֗יךָ בְּכֹ֤ל תְּבוּאָֽתְךָ֙ וּבְכֹל֙ מַעֲשֵׂ֣ה יָדֶ֔יךָ
וְהָיִ֖יתָ אַ֥ךְ שָׂמֵֽחַ׃

16 שָׁל֣וֹשׁ פְּעָמִ֣ים ׀ בַּשָּׁנָ֡ה יֵרָאֶ֨ה כָל־זְכוּרְךָ֜
אֶת־פְּנֵ֣י ׀ יְהֹוָ֣ה אֱלֹהֶ֗יךָ בַּמָּקוֹם֙ אֲשֶׁ֣ר יִבְחָ֔ר
בְּחַ֧ג הַמַּצּ֛וֹת וּבְחַ֥ג הַשָּׁבֻע֖וֹת וּבְחַ֣ג
הַסֻּכּ֑וֹת וְלֹ֧א יֵרָאֶ֛ה אֶת־פְּנֵ֥י יְהֹוָ֖ה רֵיקָֽם׃
17 אִ֖ישׁ כְּמַתְּנַ֣ת יָד֑וֹ כְּבִרְכַּ֛ת יְהֹוָ֥ה אֱלֹהֶ֖יךָ
אֲשֶׁ֥ר נָֽתַן־לָֽךְ׃ ס

שופטים

18 שֹׁפְטִ֣ים וְשֹֽׁטְרִ֗ים תִּֽתֶּן־לְךָ֙ בְּכָל־שְׁעָרֶ֔יךָ
אֲשֶׁ֨ר יְהֹוָ֧ה אֱלֹהֶ֛יךָ נֹתֵ֥ן לְךָ֖ לִשְׁבָטֶ֑יךָ
וְשָׁפְט֥וּ אֶת־הָעָ֖ם מִשְׁפַּט־צֶֽדֶק׃ 19 לֹא־
תַטֶּ֣ה מִשְׁפָּ֔ט לֹ֥א תַכִּ֖יר פָּנִ֑ים וְלֹא־תִקַּ֣ח
שֹׁ֔חַד כִּ֣י הַשֹּׁ֗חַד יְעַוֵּר֙ עֵינֵ֣י חֲכָמִ֔ים וִֽיסַלֵּ֖ף
דִּבְרֵ֣י צַדִּיקִֽם׃ 20 צֶ֥דֶק צֶ֖דֶק תִּרְדֹּ֑ף לְמַ֙עַן֙

---

d Lit. "you in all."

thrive and occupy the land that the LORD your God is giving you.

21You shall not set up a sacred post—any kind of pole beside the altar of the LORD your God that you may make—22or erect a stone pillar; for such the LORD your God detests.

17

You shall not sacrifice to the LORD your God an ox or a sheep that has any defect of a serious kind, for that is abhorrent to the LORD your God.

2If there is found among you, in one of the settlements that the LORD your God is giving you, a man or woman who has affronted the LORD your God and transgressed His covenant—3turning to the worship of other gods and bowing down to them, to the sun or the moon or any of the heavenly host, something I never commanded—4and you have been informed or have learned of it, then you shall make a thorough inquiry. If it is true, the fact is established, that abhorrent thing was perpetrated in Israel, 5you shall take the man or the woman who did that wicked thing out to the public place, and you shall stone them, man or woman, to death.—6A person shall be put to death only on the testimony of two or more[a] witnesses; he must not be put to death on the testimony of a single witness.—7Let the hands of the witnesses be the first against him to put him to death, and the hands of the rest of the people thereafter. Thus you will sweep out evil from your midst.

8If a case is too baffling for you to decide, be it a controversy over homicide, civil law, or assault—matters of dispute in your courts— you shall promptly repair to the place that the

תִּחְיֶה וְיָרַשְׁתָּ אֶת־הָאָרֶץ אֲשֶׁר־יְהוָה
אֱלֹהֶיךָ נֹתֵן לָךְ: ס
21 לֹא־תִטַּע לְךָ אֲשֵׁרָה כָּל־עֵץ אֵצֶל מִזְבַּח
יְהוָה אֱלֹהֶיךָ אֲשֶׁר תַּעֲשֶׂה־לָּךְ: ס
22 וְלֹא־תָקִים לְךָ מַצֵּבָה אֲשֶׁר שָׂנֵא יְהוָה
אֱלֹהֶיךָ: ס

יז לֹא־תִזְבַּח לַיהוָה אֱלֹהֶיךָ שׁוֹר וָשֶׂה
אֲשֶׁר יִהְיֶה בוֹ מוּם כֹּל דָּבָר רָע כִּי תוֹעֲבַת
יְהוָה אֱלֹהֶיךָ הוּא: ס

2 כִּי־יִמָּצֵא בְקִרְבְּךָ בְּאַחַד שְׁעָרֶיךָ אֲשֶׁר־
יְהוָה אֱלֹהֶיךָ נֹתֵן לָךְ אִישׁ אוֹ־אִשָּׁה
אֲשֶׁר יַעֲשֶׂה אֶת־הָרַע בְּעֵינֵי יְהוָה־אֱלֹהֶיךָ
לַעֲבֹר בְּרִיתוֹ: 3 וַיֵּלֶךְ וַיַּעֲבֹד אֱלֹהִים
אֲחֵרִים וַיִּשְׁתַּחוּ לָהֶם וְלַשֶּׁמֶשׁ אוֹ לַיָּרֵחַ
אוֹ לְכָל־צְבָא הַשָּׁמַיִם אֲשֶׁר לֹא־צִוִּיתִי:
4 וְהֻגַּד־לְךָ וְשָׁמָעְתָּ וְדָרַשְׁתָּ הֵיטֵב וְהִנֵּה
אֱמֶת נָכוֹן הַדָּבָר נֶעֶשְׂתָה הַתּוֹעֵבָה הַזֹּאת
בְּיִשְׂרָאֵל: 5 וְהוֹצֵאתָ אֶת־הָאִישׁ הַהוּא אוֹ
אֶת־הָאִשָּׁה הַהִוא אֲשֶׁר עָשׂוּ אֶת־הַדָּבָר
הָרָע הַזֶּה אֶל־שְׁעָרֶיךָ אֶת־הָאִישׁ אוֹ
אֶת־הָאִשָּׁה וּסְקַלְתָּם בָּאֲבָנִים וָמֵתוּ:
6 עַל־פִּי שְׁנַיִם עֵדִים אוֹ שְׁלֹשָׁה עֵדִים
יוּמַת הַמֵּת לֹא יוּמַת עַל־פִּי עֵד אֶחָד:
7 יַד הָעֵדִים תִּהְיֶה־בּוֹ בָרִאשֹׁנָה לַהֲמִיתוֹ
וְיַד כָּל־הָעָם בָּאַחֲרֹנָה וּבִעַרְתָּ הָרָע
מִקִּרְבֶּךָ: פ

8 כִּי יִפָּלֵא מִמְּךָ דָבָר לַמִּשְׁפָּט בֵּין־דָּם |
לְדָם בֵּין־דִּין לְדִין וּבֵין נֶגַע לָנֶגַע דִּבְרֵי
רִיבֹת בִּשְׁעָרֶיךָ וְקַמְתָּ וְעָלִיתָ אֶל־הַמָּקוֹם
אֲשֶׁר יִבְחַר יְהוָה אֱלֹהֶיךָ בּוֹ: 9 וּבָאתָ

---

a Lit. "three."

LORD your God will have chosen, ⁹and appear before the levitical priests, or the magistrate in charge at the time, and present your problem. When they have announced to you the verdict in the case, ¹⁰you shall carry out the verdict that is announced to you from that place that the LORD chose, observing scrupulously all their instructions to you. ¹¹You shall act in accordance with the instructions given you and the ruling handed down to you; you must not deviate from the verdict that they announce to you either to the right or to the left. ¹²Should a man act presumptuously and disregard the priest charged with serving there the LORD your God, or the magistrate, that man shall die. Thus you will sweep out evil from Israel: ¹³all the people will hear and be afraid and will not act presumptuously again.

¹⁴If, after you have entered the land that the LORD your God has assigned to you, and taken possession of it and settled in it, you decide, "I will set a king over me, as do all the nations about me," ¹⁵you shall be free to set a king over yourself, one chosen by the LORD your God. Be sure to set as king over yourself one of your own people; you must not set a foreigner over you, one who is not your kinsman. ¹⁶Moreover, he shall not keep many horses or send people back to Egypt to add to his horses, since the LORD has warned you, "You must not go back that way again." ¹⁷And he shall not have many wives, lest his heart go astray; nor shall he amass silver and gold to excess.

¹⁸When he is seated on his royal throne, he shall have a copy of this Teaching written for him on a scroll by[b] the levitical priests. ¹⁹Let it remain with him and let him read in it all his life, so that he may learn to revere the LORD his God, to observe faithfully every word of this Teaching as well as these laws. ²⁰Thus he will

---

b Nuance of Heb. milliphne uncertain.

אֶל־הַכֹּהֲנִים הַלְוִיִּם וְאֶל־הַשֹּׁפֵט אֲשֶׁר יִהְיֶה בַּיָּמִים הָהֵם וְדָרַשְׁתָּ וְהִגִּידוּ לְךָ אֵת דְּבַר הַמִּשְׁפָּט: 10 *וְעָשִׂיתָ עַל־פִּי הַדָּבָר אֲשֶׁר יַגִּידוּ לְךָ מִן־הַמָּקוֹם הַהוּא אֲשֶׁר יִבְחַר יְהוָה וְשָׁמַרְתָּ לַעֲשׂוֹת כְּכֹל אֲשֶׁר יוֹרוּךָ: 11 עַל־פִּי הַתּוֹרָה אֲשֶׁר יוֹרוּךָ וְעַל־הַמִּשְׁפָּט אֲשֶׁר־יֹאמְרוּ לְךָ תַּעֲשֶׂה לֹא תָסוּר מִן־הַדָּבָר אֲשֶׁר־יַגִּידוּ לְךָ יָמִין וּשְׂמֹאל: 12 וְהָאִישׁ אֲשֶׁר־יַעֲשֶׂה בְזָדוֹן לְבִלְתִּי שְׁמֹעַ אֶל־הַכֹּהֵן הָעֹמֵד לְשָׁרֶת שָׁם אֶת־יְהוָה אֱלֹהֶיךָ אוֹ אֶל־הַשֹּׁפֵט וּמֵת הָאִישׁ הַהוּא וּבִעַרְתָּ הָרָע מִיִּשְׂרָאֵל: 13 וְכָל־הָעָם יִשְׁמְעוּ וְיִרָאוּ וְלֹא יְזִידוּן עוֹד: ס

14 כִּי־תָבֹא אֶל־הָאָרֶץ אֲשֶׁר יְהוָה אֱלֹהֶיךָ נֹתֵן לָךְ וִירִשְׁתָּהּ וְיָשַׁבְתָּה בָּהּ וְאָמַרְתָּ אָשִׂימָה עָלַי מֶלֶךְ כְּכָל־הַגּוֹיִם אֲשֶׁר סְבִיבֹתָי: 15 שׂוֹם תָּשִׂים עָלֶיךָ מֶלֶךְ אֲשֶׁר יִבְחַר יְהוָה אֱלֹהֶיךָ בּוֹ מִקֶּרֶב אַחֶיךָ תָּשִׂים עָלֶיךָ מֶלֶךְ לֹא תוּכַל לָתֵת עָלֶיךָ אִישׁ נָכְרִי אֲשֶׁר לֹא־אָחִיךָ הוּא: 16 רַק לֹא־יַרְבֶּה־לּוֹ סוּסִים וְלֹא־יָשִׁיב אֶת־הָעָם מִצְרַיְמָה לְמַעַן הַרְבּוֹת סוּס וַיהוָה אָמַר לָכֶם לֹא תֹסִפוּן לָשׁוּב בַּדֶּרֶךְ הַזֶּה עוֹד: 17 וְלֹא יַרְבֶּה־לּוֹ נָשִׁים וְלֹא יָסוּר לְבָבוֹ וְכֶסֶף וְזָהָב לֹא יַרְבֶּה־לּוֹ מְאֹד:

18 וְהָיָה כְשִׁבְתּוֹ עַל כִּסֵּא מַמְלַכְתּוֹ וְכָתַב לוֹ אֶת־מִשְׁנֵה הַתּוֹרָה הַזֹּאת עַל־סֵפֶר מִלִּפְנֵי הַכֹּהֲנִים הַלְוִיִּם: 19 וְהָיְתָה עִמּוֹ וְקָרָא בוֹ כָּל־יְמֵי חַיָּיו לְמַעַן יִלְמַד לְיִרְאָה אֶת־יְהוָה אֱלֹהָיו לִשְׁמֹר אֶת־כָּל־דִּבְרֵי הַתּוֹרָה הַזֹּאת וְאֶת־הַחֻקִּים הָאֵלֶּה לַעֲשֹׂתָם: 20 לְבִלְתִּי רוּם־לְבָבוֹ מֵאֶחָיו

not act haughtily toward his fellows or deviate from the Instruction to the right or to the left, to the end that he and his descendants may reign long in the midst of Israel.

18 The levitical priests, the whole tribe of Levi, shall have no territorial portion with Israel. They shall live only off the LORD's offerings by fire as their*a* portion, [2]and shall have no portion among their brother tribes: the LORD is their portion, as He promised them.

[3]This then shall be the priests' due from the people: Everyone who offers a sacrifice, whether an ox or a sheep, must give the shoulder, the cheeks, and the stomach to the priest. [4]You shall also give him the first fruits of your new grain and wine and oil, and the first shearing of your sheep. [5]For the LORD your God has chosen him and his descendants, out of all your tribes, to be in attendance for service in the name of the LORD for all time.

[6]If a Levite would go, from any of the settlements throughout Israel where he has been residing, to the place that the LORD has chosen, he may do so whenever he pleases. [7]He may serve in the name of the LORD his God like all his fellow Levites who are there in attendance before the LORD. [8]They shall receive equal shares of the dues, *b-without regard to personal gifts or patrimonies.-b*

[9]When you enter the land that the LORD your God is giving you, you shall not learn to imitate the abhorrent practices of those nations. [10]Let no one be found among you who consigns his son or daughter to the fire, or who is an augur, a soothsayer, a diviner, a sorcerer, [11]one who casts spells, or one who consults ghosts or fa-

וּלְבִלְתִּי סוּר מִן־הַמִּצְוָה יָמִין וּשְׂמֹאול*
לְמַעַן יַאֲרִיךְ יָמִים עַל־מַמְלַכְתּוֹ הוּא
וּבָנָיו בְּקֶרֶב יִשְׂרָאֵל: ס

יח לֹא־יִהְיֶה לַכֹּהֲנִים הַלְוִיִּם כָּל־
שֵׁבֶט לֵוִי חֵלֶק וְנַחֲלָה עִם־יִשְׂרָאֵל אִשֵּׁי
יְהוָה וְנַחֲלָתוֹ יֹאכֵלוּן: 2 וְנַחֲלָה לֹא־
יִהְיֶה־לּוֹ בְּקֶרֶב אֶחָיו יְהוָה הוּא נַחֲלָתוֹ
כַּאֲשֶׁר דִּבֶּר־לוֹ: ס

3 וְזֶה יִהְיֶה מִשְׁפַּט הַכֹּהֲנִים מֵאֵת הָעָם
מֵאֵת זֹבְחֵי הַזֶּבַח אִם־שׁוֹר אִם־שֶׂה וְנָתַן
לַכֹּהֵן הַזְּרֹעַ וְהַלְּחָיַיִם וְהַקֵּבָה: 4 רֵאשִׁית
דְּגָנְךָ תִּירֹשְׁךָ וְיִצְהָרֶךָ וְרֵאשִׁית גֵּז צֹאנְךָ
תִּתֶּן־לוֹ: 5 כִּי בוֹ בָּחַר יְהוָה אֱלֹהֶיךָ
מִכָּל־שְׁבָטֶיךָ לַעֲמֹד לְשָׁרֵת בְּשֵׁם־יְהוָה
הוּא וּבָנָיו כָּל־הַיָּמִים: ס

6 וְכִי־יָבֹא הַלֵּוִי מֵאַחַד שְׁעָרֶיךָ מִכָּל־
יִשְׂרָאֵל אֲשֶׁר־הוּא גָּר שָׁם וּבָא בְּכָל־
אַוַּת נַפְשׁוֹ אֶל־הַמָּקוֹם אֲשֶׁר־יִבְחַר
יְהוָה: 7 וְשֵׁרֵת בְּשֵׁם יְהוָה אֱלֹהָיו כְּכָל־
אֶחָיו הַלְוִיִּם הָעֹמְדִים שָׁם לִפְנֵי יְהוָה:
8 חֵלֶק כְּחֵלֶק יֹאכֵלוּ לְבַד מִמְכָּרָיו עַל־
הָאָבוֹת: ס

9 כִּי אַתָּה בָּא אֶל־הָאָרֶץ אֲשֶׁר־יְהוָה
אֱלֹהֶיךָ נֹתֵן לָךְ לֹא־תִלְמַד לַעֲשׂוֹת
כְּתוֹעֲבֹת הַגּוֹיִם הָהֵם: 10 לֹא־יִמָּצֵא בְךָ
מַעֲבִיר בְּנוֹ־וּבִתּוֹ בָּאֵשׁ קֹסֵם קְסָמִים
מְעוֹנֵן וּמְנַחֵשׁ וּמְכַשֵּׁף: 11 וְחֹבֵר חָבֶר
וְשֹׁאֵל אוֹב וְיִדְּעֹנִי וְדֹרֵשׁ אֶל־הַמֵּתִים:

---

a   Lit. "its," i.e., the tribe's.
b-b   Meaning of Heb. uncertain.

miliar spirits, or one who inquires of the dead. [12]For anyone who does such things is abhorrent to the Lord, and it is because of these abhorrent things that the Lord your God is dispossessing them before you. [13]You must be wholehearted with the Lord your God. [14]Those nations that you are about to dispossess do indeed resort to soothsayers and augurs; to you, however, the Lord your God has not assigned the like.

[15]The Lord your God will raise up for you a prophet from among your own people, like myself; him you shall heed. [16]This is just what you asked of the Lord your God at Horeb, on the day of the Assembly, saying, "Let me not hear the voice of the Lord my God any longer or see this wondrous fire any more, lest I die." [17]Whereupon the Lord said to me, "They have done well in speaking thus. [18]I will raise up a prophet for them from among their own people, like yourself: I will put My words in his mouth and he will speak to them all that I command him; [19]and if anybody fails to heed the words he speaks in My name, I Myself will call him to account. [20]But any prophet who presumes to speak in My name an oracle that I did not command him to utter, or who speaks in the name of other gods—that prophet shall die." [21]And should you ask yourselves, "How can we know that the oracle was not spoken by the Lord?"—[22]if the prophet speaks in the name of the Lord and the oracle does not come true, that oracle was not spoken by the Lord; the prophet has uttered it presumptuously: do not stand in dread of him.

19 When the Lord your God has cut down the nations whose land the Lord your God is assigning to you, and you have dispossessed them and settled in their towns and homes, [2]you shall set aside three cities in the land that the

12 כִּי־תוֹעֲבַ֧ת יְהוָ֛ה כָּל־עֹ֥שֵׂה אֵ֖לֶּה וּבִגְלַל֙ הַתּוֹעֵבֹ֣ת הָאֵ֔לֶּה יְהוָ֥ה אֱלֹהֶ֖יךָ מוֹרִ֣ישׁ אוֹתָ֖ם מִפָּנֶֽיךָ׃ 13 תָּמִ֣ים תִּֽהְיֶ֔ה עִ֖ם יְהוָ֥ה אֱלֹהֶֽיךָ׃ ס 14 כִּ֣י ׀ הַגּוֹיִ֣ם הָאֵ֗לֶּה אֲשֶׁ֤ר אַתָּה֙ יוֹרֵ֣שׁ אוֹתָ֔ם אֶל־מְעֹנְנִ֥ים וְאֶל־קֹסְמִ֖ים יִשְׁמָ֑עוּ וְאַתָּ֕ה לֹ֣א כֵ֔ן נָ֥תַן לְךָ֖ יְהוָ֥ה אֱלֹהֶֽיךָ׃

15 נָבִ֨יא מִקִּרְבְּךָ֤ מֵאַחֶ֙יךָ֙ כָּמֹ֔נִי יָקִ֥ים לְךָ֖ יְהוָ֣ה אֱלֹהֶ֑יךָ אֵלָ֖יו תִּשְׁמָעֽוּן׃ 16 כְּכֹ֨ל אֲשֶׁר־שָׁאַ֜לְתָּ מֵעִ֨ם יְהוָ֤ה אֱלֹהֶ֙יךָ֙ בְּחֹרֵ֔ב בְּי֥וֹם הַקָּהָ֖ל לֵאמֹ֑ר לֹ֣א אֹסֵ֗ף לִשְׁמֹ֙עַ֙ אֶת־קוֹל֙ יְהוָ֣ה אֱלֹהָ֔י וְאֶת־הָאֵ֥שׁ הַגְּדֹלָ֤ה הַזֹּאת֙ לֹֽא־אֶרְאֶ֣ה ע֔וֹד וְלֹ֖א אָמֽוּת׃ 17 וַיֹּ֥אמֶר יְהוָ֖ה אֵלָ֑י הֵיטִ֖יבוּ אֲשֶׁ֥ר דִּבֵּֽרוּ׃ 18 נָבִ֨יא אָקִ֥ים לָהֶ֛ם מִקֶּ֥רֶב אֲחֵיהֶ֖ם כָּמ֑וֹךָ וְנָתַתִּ֤י דְבָרַי֙ בְּפִ֔יו וְדִבֶּ֣ר אֲלֵיהֶ֔ם אֵ֖ת כָּל־אֲשֶׁ֥ר אֲצַוֶּֽנּוּ׃ 19 וְהָיָ֗ה הָאִישׁ֙ אֲשֶׁ֤ר לֹֽא־יִשְׁמַע֙ אֶל־דְּבָרַ֔י אֲשֶׁ֥ר יְדַבֵּ֖ר בִּשְׁמִ֑י אָנֹכִ֖י אֶדְרֹ֥שׁ מֵעִמּֽוֹ׃ 20 אַ֣ךְ הַנָּבִ֡יא אֲשֶׁ֣ר יָזִיד֩ לְדַבֵּ֨ר דָּבָ֜ר בִּשְׁמִ֗י אֵ֣ת אֲשֶׁ֤ר לֹֽא־צִוִּיתִיו֙ לְדַבֵּ֔ר וַאֲשֶׁ֣ר יְדַבֵּ֔ר בְּשֵׁ֖ם אֱלֹהִ֣ים אֲחֵרִ֑ים וּמֵ֖ת הַנָּבִ֥יא הַהֽוּא׃ 21 וְכִ֥י תֹאמַ֖ר בִּלְבָבֶ֑ךָ אֵיכָה֙ נֵדַ֣ע אֶת־הַדָּבָ֔ר אֲשֶׁ֥ר לֹֽא־דִבְּר֖וֹ יְהוָֽה׃ 22 אֲשֶׁר֩ יְדַבֵּ֨ר הַנָּבִ֜יא בְּשֵׁ֣ם יְהוָ֗ה וְלֹֽא־יִהְיֶ֤ה הַדָּבָר֙ וְלֹ֣א יָב֔וֹא ה֣וּא הַדָּבָ֔ר אֲשֶׁ֥ר לֹֽא־דִבְּר֖וֹ יְהוָ֑ה בְּזָדוֹן֙ דִּבְּר֣וֹ הַנָּבִ֔יא לֹ֥א תָג֖וּר מִמֶּֽנּוּ׃ ס

יט כִּֽי־יַכְרִ֞ית יְהוָ֤ה אֱלֹהֶ֙יךָ֙ אֶת־הַגּוֹיִ֔ם אֲשֶׁר֙ יְהוָ֣ה אֱלֹהֶ֔יךָ נֹתֵ֥ן לְךָ֖ אֶת־אַרְצָ֑ם וִֽירִשְׁתָּ֔ם וְיָשַׁבְתָּ֥ בְעָרֵיהֶ֖ם וּבְבָתֵּיהֶֽם׃ 2 שָׁל֥וֹשׁ עָרִ֖ים תַּבְדִּ֣יל לָ֑ךְ

LORD your God is giving you to possess. [3]You shall survey the distances, and divide into three parts the territory of the country that the LORD your God has allotted to you, so that any man-slayer may have a place to flee to.—[4]Now this is the case of the manslayer who may flee there and live: one who has killed another unwittingly, without having been his enemy in the past. [5]For instance, a man goes with his neighbor into a grove to cut wood; as his hand swings the ax to cut down a tree, the ax-head flies off the handle and strikes the other so that he dies. That man shall flee to one of these cities and live.—[6]Otherwise, when the distance is great, the blood-avenger, pursuing the manslayer in hot anger, may overtake him and kill him; yet he did not incur the death penalty, since he had never been the other's enemy. [7]That is why I command you: set aside three cities.

[8]And when the LORD your God enlarges your territory, as He swore to your fathers, and gives you all the land that He promised to give your fathers—[9]if you faithfully observe all this In-struction that I enjoin upon you this day, to love the LORD your God and to walk in His ways at all times—then you shall add three more towns to those three. [10]Thus blood of the innocent will not be shed, bringing bloodguilt upon you in the land that the LORD your God is allotting to you.

[11]If, however, a person who is the enemy of another lies in wait for him and sets upon him and strikes him a fatal blow and then flees to one of these towns, [12]the elders of his town shall have him brought back from there and shall hand him over to the blood-avenger to be put to death; [13]you must show him no pity. Thus you will purge Israel of the blood of the innocent,[a] and it will go well with you.

[14]You shall not move your countryman's

---

a   Cf. Num. 35.33–34.

בְּתוֹךְ אַרְצְךָ אֲשֶׁר יְהוָה אֱלֹהֶיךָ נֹתֵן לְךָ לְרִשְׁתָּהּ: 3 תָּכִין לְךָ הַדֶּרֶךְ וְשִׁלַּשְׁתָּ אֶת־גְּבוּל אַרְצְךָ אֲשֶׁר יַנְחִילְךָ יְהוָה אֱלֹהֶיךָ וְהָיָה לָנוּס שָׁמָּה כָּל־רֹצֵחַ: 4 וְזֶה דְּבַר הָרֹצֵחַ אֲשֶׁר־יָנוּס שָׁמָּה וָחָי אֲשֶׁר יַכֶּה אֶת־רֵעֵהוּ בִּבְלִי־דַעַת וְהוּא לֹא־שֹׂנֵא לוֹ מִתְּמֹל שִׁלְשֹׁם: 5 וַאֲשֶׁר יָבֹא אֶת־רֵעֵהוּ בַיַּעַר לַחְטֹב עֵצִים וְנִדְּחָה יָדוֹ בַגַּרְזֶן לִכְרֹת הָעֵץ וְנָשַׁל הַבַּרְזֶל מִן־הָעֵץ וּמָצָא אֶת־רֵעֵהוּ וָמֵת הוּא יָנוּס אֶל־אַחַת הֶעָרִים־הָאֵלֶּה וָחָי: 6 פֶּן־יִרְדֹּף גֹּאֵל הַדָּם אַחֲרֵי הָרֹצֵחַ כִּי־יֵחַם לְבָבוֹ וְהִשִּׂיגוֹ כִּי־יִרְבֶּה הַדֶּרֶךְ וְהִכָּהוּ נָפֶשׁ וְלוֹ אֵין מִשְׁפַּט־מָוֶת כִּי לֹא שֹׂנֵא הוּא לוֹ מִתְּמוֹל שִׁלְשׁוֹם: 7 עַל־כֵּן אָנֹכִי מְצַוְּךָ לֵאמֹר שָׁלֹשׁ עָרִים תַּבְדִּיל לָךְ: ס

8 וְאִם־יַרְחִיב יְהוָה אֱלֹהֶיךָ אֶת־גְּבֻלְךָ כַּאֲשֶׁר נִשְׁבַּע לַאֲבֹתֶיךָ וְנָתַן לְךָ אֶת־כָּל־הָאָרֶץ אֲשֶׁר דִּבֶּר לָתֵת לַאֲבֹתֶיךָ: 9 כִּי־תִשְׁמֹר אֶת־כָּל־הַמִּצְוָה הַזֹּאת לַעֲשֹׂתָהּ אֲשֶׁר אָנֹכִי מְצַוְּךָ הַיּוֹם לְאַהֲבָה אֶת־יְהוָה אֱלֹהֶיךָ וְלָלֶכֶת בִּדְרָכָיו כָּל־הַיָּמִים וְיָסַפְתָּ לְךָ עוֹד שָׁלֹשׁ עָרִים עַל הַשָּׁלֹשׁ הָאֵלֶּה: 10 וְלֹא יִשָּׁפֵךְ דָּם נָקִי בְּקֶרֶב אַרְצְךָ אֲשֶׁר יְהוָה אֱלֹהֶיךָ נֹתֵן לְךָ נַחֲלָה וְהָיָה עָלֶיךָ דָּמִים: ס

11 וְכִי־יִהְיֶה אִישׁ שֹׂנֵא לְרֵעֵהוּ וְאָרַב לוֹ וְקָם עָלָיו וְהִכָּהוּ נֶפֶשׁ וָמֵת וְנָס אֶל־אַחַת הֶעָרִים הָאֵל: 12 וְשָׁלְחוּ זִקְנֵי עִירוֹ וְלָקְחוּ אֹתוֹ מִשָּׁם וְנָתְנוּ אֹתוֹ בְּיַד גֹּאֵל הַדָּם וָמֵת: 13 לֹא־תָחוֹס עֵינְךָ עָלָיו וּבִעַרְתָּ דַם־הַנָּקִי מִיִּשְׂרָאֵל וְטוֹב לָךְ: ס

14 לֹא תַסִּיג גְּבוּל רֵעֲךָ אֲשֶׁר גָּבְלוּ רִאשֹׁנִים

landmarks, set up by previous generations, in the property that will be allotted to you in the land that the Lord your God is giving you to possess.

¹⁵A single witness may not validate against a person any guilt or blame for any offense that may be committed; a case can be valid only on the testimony of two witnesses or more.*b* ¹⁶If a man appears against another to testify maliciously and gives false testimony against him, ¹⁷the two parties to the dispute shall appear before the Lord, before the priests or magistrates in authority at the time, ¹⁸and the magistrates shall make a thorough investigation. If the man who testified is a false witness, if he has testified falsely against his fellow, ¹⁹you shall do to him as he schemed to do to his fellow. Thus you will sweep out evil from your midst; ²⁰others will hear and be afraid, and such evil things will not again be done in your midst. ²¹Nor must you show pity: life for life, eye for eye, tooth for tooth, hand for hand, foot for foot.

20 When you take the field against your enemies, and see horses and chariots—forces larger than yours—have no fear of them, for the Lord your God, who brought you from the land of Egypt, is with you. ²Before you join battle, the priest shall come forward and address the troops. ³He shall say to them, "Hear, O Israel! You are about to join battle with your enemy. Let not your courage falter. Do not be in fear, or in panic, or in dread of them. ⁴For it is the Lord your God who marches with you to do battle for you against your enemy, to bring you victory."

⁵Then the officials shall address the troops, as follows: "Is there anyone who has built a new house but has not dedicated it? Let him go back

בְּנַחֲלָתְךָ֙ אֲשֶׁ֣ר תִּנְחַ֔ל בָּאָ֕רֶץ אֲשֶׁר֙ יְהֹוָ֣ה אֱלֹהֶ֔יךָ נֹתֵ֥ן לְךָ֖ לְרִשְׁתָּֽהּ׃ ס 15 לֹא־יָק֠וּם עֵ֨ד אֶחָ֤ד בְּאִישׁ֙ לְכָל־עָוֺ֣ן וּלְכָל־חַטָּ֔את בְּכָל־חֵ֖טְא אֲשֶׁ֣ר יֶֽחֱטָ֑א עַל־פִּ֣י ׀ שְׁנֵ֣י עֵדִ֗ים א֛וֹ עַל־פִּ֥י שְׁלֹשָֽׁה־עֵדִ֖ים יָק֥וּם דָּבָֽר׃ 16 כִּֽי־יָק֥וּם עֵד־חָמָ֖ס בְּאִ֑ישׁ לַעֲנ֥וֹת בּ֖וֹ סָרָֽה׃ 17 וְעָמְד֧וּ שְׁנֵֽי־הָאֲנָשִׁ֛ים אֲשֶׁר־לָהֶ֥ם הָרִ֖יב לִפְנֵ֣י יְהֹוָ֑ה לִפְנֵ֤י הַכֹּֽהֲנִים֙ וְהַשֹּׁ֣פְטִ֔ים אֲשֶׁ֥ר יִהְי֖וּ בַּיָּמִ֥ים הָהֵֽם׃ 18 וְדָרְשׁ֥וּ הַשֹּׁפְטִ֖ים הֵיטֵ֑ב וְהִנֵּ֤ה עֵֽד־שֶׁ֨קֶר֙ הָעֵ֔ד שֶׁ֖קֶר עָנָ֥ה בְאָחִֽיו׃ 19 וַעֲשִׂ֣יתֶם ל֔וֹ כַּאֲשֶׁ֥ר זָמַ֖ם לַעֲשׂ֣וֹת לְאָחִ֑יו וּבִֽעַרְתָּ֥ הָרָ֖ע מִקִּרְבֶּֽךָ׃ 20 וְהַנִּשְׁאָרִ֖ים יִשְׁמְע֣וּ וְיִרָ֑אוּ וְלֹֽא־יֹסִ֨פוּ לַעֲשׂ֜וֹת ע֗וֹד כַּדָּבָ֥ר הָרָ֛ע הַזֶּ֖ה בְּקִרְבֶּֽךָ׃ 21 וְלֹ֥א תָח֖וֹס עֵינֶ֑ךָ נֶ֣פֶשׁ בְּנֶ֗פֶשׁ עַ֤יִן בְּעַ֨יִן֙ שֵׁ֣ן בְּשֵׁ֔ן יָ֥ד בְּיָ֖ד רֶ֥גֶל בְּרָֽגֶל׃ ס

כ כִּֽי־תֵצֵ֨א לַמִּלְחָמָ֜ה עַל־אֹ֣יְבֶ֗ךָ וְֽרָאִ֜יתָ ס֤וּס וָרֶ֨כֶב֙ עַ֚ם רַ֣ב מִמְּךָ֔ לֹ֥א תִירָ֖א מֵהֶ֑ם כִּֽי־יְהֹוָ֤ה אֱלֹהֶ֨יךָ֙ עִמָּ֔ךְ הַמַּֽעַלְךָ֖ מֵאֶ֥רֶץ מִצְרָֽיִם׃ 2 וְהָיָ֕ה כְּקָֽרׇבְכֶ֖ם אֶל־הַמִּלְחָמָ֑ה וְנִגַּ֥שׁ הַכֹּהֵ֖ן וְדִבֶּ֥ר אֶל־הָעָֽם׃ 3 וְאָמַ֤ר אֲלֵהֶם֙ שְׁמַ֣ע יִשְׂרָאֵ֔ל אַתֶּ֨ם קְרֵבִ֥ים הַיּ֛וֹם לַמִּלְחָמָ֖ה עַל־אֹיְבֵיכֶ֑ם אַל־יֵרַ֣ךְ לְבַבְכֶ֗ם אַל־תִּֽירְא֧וּ וְאַֽל־תַּחְפְּז֛וּ וְאַל־תַּֽעַרְצ֖וּ מִפְּנֵיהֶֽם׃ 4 כִּ֚י יְהֹוָ֣ה אֱלֹֽהֵיכֶ֔ם הַהֹלֵ֖ךְ עִמָּכֶ֑ם לְהִלָּחֵ֥ם לָכֶ֛ם עִם־אֹיְבֵיכֶ֖ם לְהוֹשִׁ֥יעַ אֶתְכֶֽם׃ 5 וְדִבְּר֣וּ הַשֹּֽׁטְרִים֮ אֶל־הָעָ֣ם לֵאמֹר֒ מִֽי־הָאִ֞ישׁ אֲשֶׁ֨ר בָּנָ֤ה בַֽיִת־חָדָשׁ֙ וְלֹ֣א חֲנָכ֔וֹ יֵלֵ֖ךְ וְיָשֹׁ֣ב לְבֵית֑וֹ פֶּן־יָמוּת֙ בַּמִּלְחָמָ֔ה

---

b See note at 17.6.

to his home, lest he die in battle and another dedicate it. 6Is there anyone who has planted a vineyard but has never harvested it? Let him go back to his home, lest he die in battle and another harvest it. 7Is there anyone who has paid the bride-price for a wife,*a* but who has not yet married her? Let him go back to his home, lest he die in battle and another marry her." 8The officials shall go on addressing the troops and say, "Is there anyone afraid and disheartened? Let him go back to his home, lest the courage of his comrades flag like his." 9When the officials have finished addressing the troops, army commanders shall assume command of the troops.

10When you approach a town to attack it, you shall *b-*offer it terms of peace.*-b* 11If it responds peaceably and lets you in, all the people present there shall serve you at forced labor. 12If it does not surrender to you, but would join battle with you, you shall lay siege to it; 13and when the LORD your God delivers it into your hand, you shall put all its males to the sword. 14You may, however, take as your booty the women, the children, the livestock, and everything in the town—all its spoil—and enjoy the use of the spoil of your enemy, which the LORD your God gives you.

15Thus you shall deal with all towns that lie very far from you, towns that do not belong to nations hereabout. 16In the towns of the latter peoples, however, which the LORD your God is giving you as a heritage, you shall not let a soul remain alive. 17No, you must proscribe*c* them— the Hittites and the Amorites, the Canaanites and the Perizzites, the Hivites and the Jebusites—as the LORD your God has commanded you, 18lest they lead you into doing all the abhorrent things that they have done for their gods and you stand guilty before the LORD your God.

וְאִישׁ אַחֵר יַחְנְכֶנּוּ: 6 וּמִי־הָאִישׁ אֲשֶׁר־
נָטַע כֶּרֶם וְלֹא חִלְּלוֹ יֵלֵךְ וְיָשֹׁב לְבֵיתוֹ
פֶּן־יָמוּת בַּמִּלְחָמָה וְאִישׁ אַחֵר יְחַלְּלֶנּוּ:
7 וּמִי־הָאִישׁ אֲשֶׁר־אֵרַשׂ אִשָּׁה וְלֹא לְקָחָהּ
יֵלֵךְ וְיָשֹׁב לְבֵיתוֹ פֶּן־יָמוּת בַּמִּלְחָמָה
וְאִישׁ אַחֵר יִקָּחֶנָּה: 8 וְיָסְפוּ הַשֹּׁטְרִים
לְדַבֵּר אֶל־הָעָם וְאָמְרוּ מִי־הָאִישׁ הַיָּרֵא
וְרַךְ הַלֵּבָב יֵלֵךְ וְיָשֹׁב לְבֵיתוֹ וְלֹא יִמַּס
אֶת־לְבַב אֶחָיו כִּלְבָבוֹ: 9 וְהָיָה כְּכַלֹּת
הַשֹּׁטְרִים לְדַבֵּר אֶל־הָעָם וּפָקְדוּ שָׂרֵי
צְבָאוֹת בְּרֹאשׁ הָעָם: ס

10 כִּי־תִקְרַב אֶל־עִיר לְהִלָּחֵם עָלֶיהָ
וְקָרָאתָ אֵלֶיהָ לְשָׁלוֹם: 11 וְהָיָה אִם־שָׁלוֹם
תַּעַנְךָ וּפָתְחָה לָךְ וְהָיָה כָּל־הָעָם
הַנִּמְצָא־בָהּ יִהְיוּ לְךָ לָמַס וַעֲבָדוּךָ:
12 וְאִם־לֹא תַשְׁלִים עִמָּךְ וְעָשְׂתָה עִמְּךָ
מִלְחָמָה וְצַרְתָּ עָלֶיהָ: 13 וּנְתָנָהּ יְהוָה
אֱלֹהֶיךָ בְּיָדֶךָ וְהִכִּיתָ אֶת־כָּל־זְכוּרָהּ לְפִי־
חָרֶב: 14 רַק הַנָּשִׁים וְהַטַּף וְהַבְּהֵמָה וְכֹל
אֲשֶׁר יִהְיֶה בָעִיר כָּל־שְׁלָלָהּ תָּבֹז לָךְ
וְאָכַלְתָּ אֶת־שְׁלַל אֹיְבֶיךָ אֲשֶׁר נָתַן יְהוָה
אֱלֹהֶיךָ לָךְ:

15 כֵּן תַּעֲשֶׂה לְכָל־הֶעָרִים הָרְחֹקֹת מִמְּךָ
מְאֹד אֲשֶׁר לֹא־מֵעָרֵי הַגּוֹיִם־הָאֵלֶּה הֵנָּה:
16 רַק מֵעָרֵי הָעַמִּים הָאֵלֶּה אֲשֶׁר יְהוָה
אֱלֹהֶיךָ נֹתֵן לְךָ נַחֲלָה לֹא תְחַיֶּה כָּל־
נְשָׁמָה: 17 כִּי־הַחֲרֵם תַּחֲרִימֵם הַחִתִּי
וְהָאֱמֹרִי הַכְּנַעֲנִי וְהַפְּרִזִּי הַחִוִּי וְהַיְבוּסִי
כַּאֲשֶׁר צִוְּךָ יְהוָה אֱלֹהֶיךָ: 18 לְמַעַן אֲשֶׁר
לֹא־יְלַמְּדוּ אֶתְכֶם לַעֲשׂוֹת כְּכֹל תּוֹעֲבֹתָם
אֲשֶׁר עָשׂוּ לֵאלֹהֵיהֶם וַחֲטָאתֶם לַיהוָה
אֱלֹהֵיכֶם: ס

---

a Thereby making her his wife legally, even though the marriage has not yet taken place.
b-b Or "call on it to surrender."
c See Lev. 27.29.

418

19When in your war against a city you have to besiege it a long time in order to capture it, you must not destroy its trees, wielding the ax against them. You may eat of them, but you must not cut them down. Are trees of the field human to withdraw before you into the besieged city? 20Only trees that you know do not yield food may be destroyed; you may cut them down for constructing siegeworks against the city that is waging war on you, until it has been reduced.

21 If, in the land that the LORD your God is assigning you to possess, someone slain is found lying in the open, the identity of the slayer not being known, 2your elders and magistrates shall go out and measure the distances from the corpse to the nearby towns. 3The elders of the town nearest to the corpse shall then take a heifer which has never been worked, which has never pulled in a yoke; 4and the elders of that town shall bring the heifer down to an everflowing wadi, which is not tilled or sown. There, in the wadi, they shall break the heifer's neck. 5The priests, sons of Levi, shall come forward; for the LORD your God has chosen them to minister to Him and to pronounce blessing in the name of the LORD, and every lawsuit and case of assault[a] is subject to their ruling. 6Then all the elders of the town nearest to the corpse shall wash their hands over the heifer whose neck was broken in the wadi. 7And they shall make this declaration: "Our hands did not shed this blood, nor did our eyes see it done. 8Absolve, O LORD, Your people Israel whom You redeemed, and do not let guilt for the blood of the innocent remain among Your people Israel." And they will be absolved of bloodguilt. 9Thus you will remove from your midst guilt for the blood of the innocent, for you will be doing what is right in the sight of the LORD.

19 כִּי־תָצ֨וּר אֶל־עִ֜יר יָמִ֣ים רַבִּים֮ לְהִלָּחֵ֣ם עָלֶ֣יהָ לְתׇפְשָׂהּ֒ לֹֽא־תַשְׁחִ֤ית אֶת־עֵצָהּ֙ לִנְדֹּ֤חַ עָלָיו֙ גַּרְזֶ֔ן כִּ֚י מִמֶּ֣נּוּ תֹאכֵ֔ל וְאֹת֖וֹ לֹ֣א תִכְרֹ֑ת כִּ֤י הָֽאָדָם֙ עֵ֣ץ הַשָּׂדֶ֔ה לָבֹ֥א מִפָּנֶ֖יךָ בַּמָּצֽוֹר׃ 20 רַ֞ק עֵ֣ץ אֲשֶׁר־תֵּדַ֗ע כִּי־לֹא־עֵ֤ץ מַֽאֲכָל֙ ה֔וּא אֹת֥וֹ תַשְׁחִ֖ית וְכָרָ֑תָּ וּבָנִ֣יתָ מָצ֗וֹר עַל־הָעִיר֙ אֲשֶׁר־הִ֨וא עֹשָׂ֧ה עִמְּךָ֛ מִלְחָמָ֖ה עַ֥ד רִדְתָּֽהּ׃ פ

כא כִּֽי־יִמָּצֵ֣א חָלָ֗ל בָּאֲדָמָה֙ אֲשֶׁר֩ יְהֹוָ֨ה אֱלֹהֶ֜יךָ נֹתֵ֤ן לְךָ֙ לְרִשְׁתָּ֔הּ נֹפֵ֖ל בַּשָּׂדֶ֑ה לֹ֥א נוֹדַ֖ע מִ֥י הִכָּֽהוּ׃ 2 וְיָצְא֥וּ זְקֵנֶ֖יךָ וְשֹׁפְטֶ֑יךָ וּמָדְד֖וּ אֶל־הֶ֣עָרִ֑ים אֲשֶׁ֖ר סְבִיבֹ֥ת הֶחָלָֽל׃ 3 וְהָיָ֣ה הָעִ֔יר הַקְּרֹבָ֖ה אֶל־הֶחָלָ֑ל וְלָֽקְח֡וּ זִקְנֵי֩ הָעִ֨יר הַהִ֜וא עֶגְלַ֣ת בָּקָ֗ר אֲשֶׁ֤ר לֹֽא־עֻבַּד֙ בָּ֔הּ אֲשֶׁ֥ר לֹא־מָשְׁכָ֖ה בְּעֹֽל׃ 4 וְהוֹרִ֡דוּ זִקְנֵי֩ הָעִ֨יר הַהִ֤וא אֶת־הָעֶגְלָה֙ אֶל־נַ֣חַל אֵיתָ֔ן אֲשֶׁ֛ר לֹא־יֵעָבֵ֥ד בּ֖וֹ וְלֹ֣א יִזָּרֵ֑עַ וְעָֽרְפוּ־שָׁ֥ם אֶת־הָעֶגְלָ֖ה בַּנָּֽחַל׃ 5 וְנִגְּשׁ֣וּ הַכֹּהֲנִים֮ בְּנֵ֣י לֵוִי֒ כִּ֣י בָ֗ם בָּחַ֞ר יְהֹוָ֤ה אֱלֹהֶ֨יךָ֙ לְשָׁ֣רְת֔וֹ וּלְבָרֵ֖ךְ בְּשֵׁ֣ם יְהֹוָ֑ה וְעַל־פִּיהֶ֥ם יִהְיֶ֖ה כׇּל־רִ֥יב וְכׇל־נָֽגַע׃ 6 וְכֹ֗ל זִקְנֵי֙ הָעִ֣יר הַהִ֔וא הַקְּרֹבִ֖ים אֶל־הֶחָלָ֑ל יִרְחֲצוּ֙ אֶת־יְדֵיהֶ֔ם עַל־הָעֶגְלָ֖ה הָעֲרוּפָ֥ה בַנָּֽחַל׃ 7 וְעָנ֖וּ וְאָמְר֑וּ יָדֵ֗ינוּ לֹ֤א שפכה [שָֽׁפְכוּ֙] אֶת־הַדָּ֣ם הַזֶּ֔ה וְעֵינֵ֖ינוּ לֹ֥א רָאֽוּ׃ 8 כַּפֵּר֩ לְעַמְּךָ֨ יִשְׂרָאֵ֤ל אֲשֶׁר־פָּדִ֨יתָ֙ יְהֹוָ֔ה וְאַל־תִּתֵּן֙ דָּ֣ם נָקִ֔י בְּקֶ֖רֶב עַמְּךָ֣ יִשְׂרָאֵ֑ל וְנִכַּפֵּ֥ר לָהֶ֖ם הַדָּֽם׃ 9 וְאַתָּ֗ה תְּבַעֵ֛ר הַדָּ֥ם הַנָּקִ֖י מִקִּרְבֶּ֑ךָ כִּֽי־תַעֲשֶׂ֥ה הַיָּשָׁ֖ר בְּעֵינֵ֥י יְהֹוָֽה׃ ס

    a Cf. 17.8. Or "skin affection"; cf. 24.8.

KI TETSE'

כי תצא

10When you take the field against your enemies, and the LORD your God delivers them into your power and you take some of them captive, 11and you see among the captives a beautiful woman and you desire her and would take her to wife, 12you shall bring her into your house, and she shall trim her hair, pare her nails, 13and discard her captive's garb. She shall spend a month's time in your house lamenting her father and mother; after that you may come to her and possess her, and she shall be your wife. 14Then, should you no longer want her, you must release her outright. You must not sell her for money: since you had your will of her, you must not enslave her.

15If a man has two wives, one loved and the other unloved, and both the loved and the unloved have borne him sons, but the first-born is the son of the unloved one—16when he wills his property to his sons, he may not treat as first-born the son of the loved one in disregard of the son of the unloved one who is older. 17Instead, he must accept the first-born, the son of the unloved one, and allot to him a double portion[b] of all he possesses; since he is the first fruit of his vigor, the birthright is his due.

18If a man has a wayward and defiant son, who does not heed his father or mother and does not obey them even after they discipline him, 19his father and mother shall take hold of him and bring him out to the elders of his town at the public place of his community. 20They shall say to the elders of his town, "This son of ours is disloyal and defiant; he does not heed us. He is a glutton and a drunkard." 21Thereupon the men of his town shall stone him to death. Thus you will sweep out evil from your midst: all Israel will hear and be afraid.

10 כִּי־תֵצֵא לַמִּלְחָמָה עַל־אֹיְבֶיךָ וּנְתָנוֹ יְהוָה אֱלֹהֶיךָ בְּיָדֶךָ וְשָׁבִיתָ שִׁבְיוֹ: 11 וְרָאִיתָ בַּשִּׁבְיָה אֵשֶׁת יְפַת־תֹּאַר וְחָשַׁקְתָּ בָהּ וְלָקַחְתָּ לְךָ לְאִשָּׁה: 12 וַהֲבֵאתָהּ אֶל־תּוֹךְ בֵּיתֶךָ וְגִלְּחָה אֶת־רֹאשָׁהּ וְעָשְׂתָה אֶת־צִפָּרְנֶיהָ: 13 וְהֵסִירָה אֶת־שִׂמְלַת שִׁבְיָהּ מֵעָלֶיהָ וְיָשְׁבָה בְּבֵיתֶךָ וּבָכְתָה אֶת־אָבִיהָ וְאֶת־אִמָּהּ יֶרַח יָמִים וְאַחַר כֵּן תָּבוֹא אֵלֶיהָ וּבְעַלְתָּהּ וְהָיְתָה לְךָ לְאִשָּׁה: 14 וְהָיָה אִם־לֹא חָפַצְתָּ בָּהּ וְשִׁלַּחְתָּהּ לְנַפְשָׁהּ וּמָכֹר לֹא־תִמְכְּרֶנָּה בַּכָּסֶף לֹא־תִתְעַמֵּר בָּהּ תַּחַת אֲשֶׁר עִנִּיתָהּ: ס

15 כִּי־תִהְיֶיןָ לְאִישׁ שְׁתֵּי נָשִׁים הָאַחַת אֲהוּבָה וְהָאַחַת שְׂנוּאָה וְיָלְדוּ־לוֹ בָנִים הָאֲהוּבָה וְהַשְּׂנוּאָה וְהָיָה הַבֵּן הַבְּכוֹר לַשְּׂנִיאָה: 16 וְהָיָה בְּיוֹם הַנְחִילוֹ אֶת־בָּנָיו אֵת אֲשֶׁר־יִהְיֶה לוֹ לֹא יוּכַל לְבַכֵּר אֶת־בֶּן־הָאֲהוּבָה עַל־פְּנֵי בֶן־הַשְּׂנוּאָה הַבְּכֹר: 17 כִּי אֶת־הַבְּכֹר בֶּן־הַשְּׂנוּאָה יַכִּיר לָתֶת לוֹ פִּי שְׁנַיִם בְּכֹל אֲשֶׁר־יִמָּצֵא לוֹ כִּי־הוּא רֵאשִׁית אֹנוֹ לוֹ מִשְׁפַּט הַבְּכֹרָה: ס

18 כִּי־יִהְיֶה לְאִישׁ בֵּן סוֹרֵר וּמוֹרֶה אֵינֶנּוּ שֹׁמֵעַ בְּקוֹל אָבִיו וּבְקוֹל אִמּוֹ וְיִסְּרוּ אֹתוֹ וְלֹא יִשְׁמַע אֲלֵיהֶם: 19 וְתָפְשׂוּ בוֹ אָבִיו וְאִמּוֹ וְהוֹצִיאוּ אֹתוֹ אֶל־זִקְנֵי עִירוֹ וְאֶל־שַׁעַר מְקֹמוֹ: 20 וְאָמְרוּ אֶל־זִקְנֵי עִירוֹ בְּנֵנוּ זֶה סוֹרֵר וּמֹרֶה אֵינֶנּוּ שֹׁמֵעַ בְּקֹלֵנוּ זוֹלֵל וְסֹבֵא: 21 וּרְגָמֻהוּ כָּל־אַנְשֵׁי עִירוֹ בָאֲבָנִים וָמֵת וּבִעַרְתָּ הָרָע מִקִּרְבֶּךָ וְכָל־יִשְׂרָאֵל יִשְׁמְעוּ וְיִרָאוּ: ס

---

b Lit. two-thirds.

²²If a man is guilty of a capital offense and is put to death, and you impale him on a stake, ²³you must not let his corpse remain on the stake overnight, but must bury him the same day. For an impaled body is an affront to God: you shall not defile the land that the LORD your God is giving you to possess.

22 If you see your fellow's ox or sheep gone astray, do not ignore it; you must take it back to your fellow. ²If your fellow does not live near you or you do not know who he is, you shall bring it home and it shall remain with you until your fellow claims it; then you shall give it back to him. ³You shall do the same with his ass; you shall do the same with his garment; and so too shall you do with anything that your fellow loses and you find: you must not remain indifferent.

⁴If you see your fellow's ass or ox fallen on the road, do not ignore it; you must help him raise it.

⁵A woman must not put on man's apparel, nor shall a man wear woman's clothing; for whoever does these things is abhorrent to the LORD your God.

⁶If, along the road, you chance upon a bird's nest, in any tree or on the ground, with fledglings or eggs and the mother sitting over the fledglings or on the eggs, do not take the mother together with her young. ⁷Let the mother go, and take only the young, in order that you may fare well and have a long life.

⁸When you build a new house, you shall make a parapet for your roof, so that you do not bring bloodguilt on your house if anyone should fall from it.

⁹You shall not sow your vineyard with a second kind of seed, else the crop—from the seed you have sown—and the yield of the vineyard may not be used. ¹⁰You shall not plow with an

²² וְכִי־יִהְיֶ֣ה בְאִ֗ישׁ חֵ֛טְא מִשְׁפַּט־מָ֖וֶת וְהוּמָ֑ת וְתָלִ֥יתָ אֹת֖וֹ עַל־עֵֽץ׃ ²³ לֹא־תָלִ֨ין נִבְלָת֜וֹ עַל־הָעֵ֗ץ כִּֽי־קָב֤וֹר תִּקְבְּרֶ֙נּוּ֙ בַּיּ֣וֹם הַה֔וּא כִּֽי־קִלְלַ֥ת אֱלֹהִ֖ים תָּל֑וּי וְלֹ֤א תְטַמֵּא֙ אֶת־אַדְמָ֣תְךָ֔ אֲשֶׁר֙ יְהֹוָ֣ה אֱלֹהֶ֔יךָ נֹתֵ֥ן לְךָ֖ נַחֲלָֽה׃ ס

כב לֹֽא־תִרְאֶה֩ אֶת־שׁ֨וֹר אָחִ֜יךָ א֤וֹ אֶת־שֵׂיוֹ֙ נִדָּחִ֔ים וְהִתְעַלַּמְתָּ֖ מֵהֶ֑ם הָשֵׁ֥ב תְּשִׁיבֵ֖ם לְאָחִֽיךָ׃ ² וְאִם־לֹ֨א קָר֤וֹב אָחִ֙יךָ֙ אֵלֶ֔יךָ וְלֹ֥א יְדַעְתּ֖וֹ וַאֲסַפְתּוֹ֙ אֶל־תּ֣וֹךְ בֵּיתֶ֔ךָ וְהָיָ֣ה עִמְּךָ֗ עַ֣ד דְּרֹ֤שׁ אָחִ֙יךָ֙ אֹת֔וֹ וַהֲשֵׁבֹת֖וֹ לֽוֹ׃ ³ וְכֵ֧ן תַּעֲשֶׂ֣ה לַחֲמֹר֗וֹ וְכֵ֣ן תַּעֲשֶׂה֮ לְשִׂמְלָתוֹ֒ וְכֵ֣ן תַּעֲשֶׂ֗ה לְכׇל־אֲבֵדַ֥ת אָחִ֛יךָ אֲשֶׁר־תֹּאבַ֥ד מִמֶּ֖נּוּ וּמְצָאתָ֑הּ לֹ֥א תוּכַ֖ל לְהִתְעַלֵּֽם׃ ס ⁴ לֹא־תִרְאֶה֩ אֶת־חֲמ֨וֹר אָחִ֜יךָ א֤וֹ שׁוֹרוֹ֙ נֹפְלִ֣ים בַּדֶּ֔רֶךְ וְהִתְעַלַּמְתָּ֖ מֵהֶ֑ם הָקֵ֥ם תָּקִ֖ים עִמּֽוֹ׃ ס ⁵ לֹא־יִהְיֶ֤ה כְלִי־גֶ֙בֶר֙ עַל־אִשָּׁ֔ה וְלֹא־יִלְבַּ֥שׁ גֶּ֖בֶר שִׂמְלַ֣ת אִשָּׁ֑ה כִּ֧י תוֹעֲבַ֛ת יְהֹוָ֥ה אֱלֹהֶ֖יךָ כׇּל־עֹ֥שֵׂה אֵֽלֶּה׃ פ ⁶ כִּ֣י יִקָּרֵ֣א קַן־צִפּ֣וֹר ׀ לְפָנֶ֡יךָ בַּדֶּ֜רֶךְ בְּכׇל־עֵ֣ץ ׀ א֣וֹ עַל־הָאָ֗רֶץ אֶפְרֹחִים֙ א֣וֹ בֵיצִ֔ים וְהָאֵ֤ם רֹבֶ֙צֶת֙ עַל־הָֽאֶפְרֹחִ֔ים א֖וֹ עַל־הַבֵּיצִ֑ים לֹא־תִקַּ֥ח הָאֵ֖ם עַל־הַבָּנִֽים׃ ⁷ שַׁלֵּ֤חַ תְּשַׁלַּח֙ אֶת־הָאֵ֔ם וְאֶת־הַבָּנִ֖ים תִּֽקַּֽח־לָ֑ךְ לְמַ֙עַן֙ יִ֣יטַב לָ֔ךְ וְהַאֲרַכְתָּ֖ יָמִֽים׃ ס ⁸ כִּ֤י תִבְנֶה֙ בַּ֣יִת חָדָ֔שׁ וְעָשִׂ֥יתָ מַעֲקֶ֖ה לְגַגֶּ֑ךָ וְלֹֽא־תָשִׂ֤ים דָּמִים֙ בְּבֵיתֶ֔ךָ כִּֽי־יִפֹּ֥ל הַנֹּפֵ֖ל מִמֶּֽנּוּ׃ ס ⁹ לֹא־תִזְרַ֥ע כַּרְמְךָ֖ כִּלְאָ֑יִם פֶּן־תִּקְדַּ֗שׁ הַֽמְלֵאָ֤ה הַזֶּ֙רַע֙ אֲשֶׁ֣ר תִּזְרָ֔ע וּתְבוּאַ֖ת הַכָּֽרֶם׃ ס ¹⁰ לֹֽא־תַחֲרֹ֥שׁ בְּשׁוֹר־וּבַחֲמֹ֖ר

ox and an ass together. [11]You shall not wear cloth combining wool and linen.

[12]You shall make tassels on the four corners of the garment with which you cover yourself.

[13]A man marries a woman and cohabits with her. Then he takes an aversion to her [14]and makes up charges against her and defames her, saying, "I married this woman; but when I approached her, I found that she was not a virgin." [15]In such a case, the girl's father and mother shall produce the evidence of the girl's virginity before the elders of the town at the gate. [16]And the girl's father shall say to the elders, "I gave this man my daughter to wife, but he has taken an aversion to her; [17]so he has made up charges, saying, 'I did not find your daughter a virgin.' But here is the evidence of my daughter's virginity!" And they shall spread out the cloth before the elders of the town. [18]The elders of that town shall then take the man and flog him, [19]and they shall fine him a hundred [shekels of] silver and give it to the girl's father; for the man has defamed a virgin in Israel. Moreover, she shall remain his wife; he shall never have the right to divorce her.

[20]But if the charge proves true, the girl was found not to have been a virgin, [21]then the girl shall be brought out to the entrance of her father's house, and the men of her town shall stone her to death; for she did a shameful thing in Israel, committing fornication while under her father's authority. Thus you will sweep away evil from your midst.

[22]If a man is found lying with another man's wife, both of them—the man and the woman with whom he lay—shall die. Thus you will sweep away evil from Israel.

[23]In the case of a virgin who is *a*-engaged to a man-*a*—if a man comes upon her in town and

---

a-a　I.e., for whom a bride-price has been paid; see 20.7.

יַחְדָּו: ס 11 לֹא תִלְבַּשׁ שַׁעַטְנֵז צֶמֶר
וּפִשְׁתִּים יַחְדָּו: ס
12 גְּדִלִים תַּעֲשֶׂה־לָּךְ עַל־אַרְבַּע כַּנְפוֹת
כְּסוּתְךָ אֲשֶׁר תְּכַסֶּה־בָּהּ: ס
13 כִּי־יִקַּח אִישׁ אִשָּׁה וּבָא אֵלֶיהָ וּשְׂנֵאָהּ:
14 וְשָׂם לָהּ עֲלִילֹת דְּבָרִים וְהוֹצִיא עָלֶיהָ
שֵׁם רָע וְאָמַר אֶת־הָאִשָּׁה הַזֹּאת לָקַחְתִּי
וָאֶקְרַב אֵלֶיהָ וְלֹא־מָצָאתִי לָהּ בְּתוּלִים:
15 וְלָקַח אֲבִי הנער הַנַּעֲרָה וְאִמָּהּ וְהוֹצִיאוּ
אֶת־בְּתוּלֵי הנער הַנַּעֲרָה אֶל־זִקְנֵי הָעִיר
הַשָּׁעְרָה: 16 וְאָמַר אֲבִי הנער הַנַּעֲרָה
אֶל־הַזְּקֵנִים אֶת־בִּתִּי נָתַתִּי לָאִישׁ הַזֶּה
לְאִשָּׁה וַיִּשְׂנָאֶהָ: 17 וְהִנֵּה־הוּא שָׂם
עֲלִילֹת דְּבָרִים לֵאמֹר לֹא־מָצָאתִי לְבִתְּךָ
בְּתוּלִים וְאֵלֶּה בְּתוּלֵי בִתִּי וּפָרְשׂוּ
הַשִּׂמְלָה לִפְנֵי זִקְנֵי הָעִיר: 18 וְלָקְחוּ זִקְנֵי
הָעִיר־הַהִוא אֶת־הָאִישׁ וְיִסְּרוּ אֹתוֹ:
19 וְעָנְשׁוּ אֹתוֹ מֵאָה כֶסֶף וְנָתְנוּ לַאֲבִי
הַנַּעֲרָה כִּי הוֹצִיא שֵׁם רָע עַל בְּתוּלַת
יִשְׂרָאֵל וְלוֹ־תִהְיֶה לְאִשָּׁה לֹא־יוּכַל
לְשַׁלְּחָהּ כָּל־יָמָיו: ס
20 וְאִם־אֱמֶת הָיָה הַדָּבָר הַזֶּה לֹא־נִמְצְאוּ
בְתוּלִים לַנַּעֲרָ: 21 וְהוֹצִיאוּ אֶת־
הנער הַנַּעֲרָה אֶל־פֶּתַח בֵּית־אָבִיהָ
וּסְקָלוּהָ אַנְשֵׁי עִירָהּ בָּאֲבָנִים וָמֵתָה
כִּי־עָשְׂתָה נְבָלָה בְּיִשְׂרָאֵל לִזְנוֹת בֵּית
אָבִיהָ וּבִעַרְתָּ הָרָע מִקִּרְבֶּךָ: ס
22 כִּי־יִמָּצֵא אִישׁ שֹׁכֵב | עִם־אִשָּׁה בְעֻלַת־
בַּעַל וּמֵתוּ גַּם־שְׁנֵיהֶם הָאִישׁ הַשֹּׁכֵב
עִם־הָאִשָּׁה וְהָאִשָּׁה וּבִעַרְתָּ הָרָע
מִיִּשְׂרָאֵל: ס

23 כִּי יִהְיֶה נער נַעֲרָה בְתוּלָה מְאֹרָשָׂה
לְאִישׁ וּמְצָאָהּ אִישׁ בָּעִיר וְשָׁכַב עִמָּהּ:

lies with her, 24you shall take the two of them out to the gate of that town and stone them to death: the girl because she did not cry for help in the town, and the man because he violated another man's wife. Thus you will sweep away evil from your midst. 25But if the man comes upon the engaged girl in the open country, and the man lies with her by force, only the man who lay with her shall die, 26but you shall do nothing to the girl. The girl did not incur the death penalty, for this case is like that of a man attacking another and murdering him. 27He came upon her in the open; though the engaged girl cried for help, there was no one to save her.

28If a man comes upon a virgin who is not engaged and he seizes her and lies with her, and they are discovered, 29the man who lay with her shall pay the girl's father fifty [shekels of] silver, and she shall be his wife. Because he has violated her, he can never have the right to divorce her.

23

No man shall marry his father's former wife, so as a-to remove his father's garment.-a

2No one whose testes are crushed or whose member is cut off shall be admitted into the congregation of the Lord.

3No one misbegottenb shall be admitted into the congregation of the Lord; none of his descendants, even in the tenth generation, shall be admitted into the congregation of the Lord.

4No Ammonite or Moabite shall be admitted into the congregation of the Lord; none of their descendants, even in the tenth generation, shall ever be admitted into the congregation of the Lord, 5because they did not meet you with food and water on your journey after you left Egypt, and because they hired Balaam son of

24 וְהוֹצֵאתֶ֣ם אֶת־שְׁנֵיהֶם֮ אֶל־שַׁ֣עַר ׀ הָעִ֣יר הַהִוא֒ וּסְקַלְתֶּ֥ם אֹתָ֛ם בָּאֲבָנִ֖ים וָמֵ֑תוּ אֶת־הַֽנַּעֲרָ֗ עַל־דְּבַר֙ אֲשֶׁ֣ר לֹא־צָעֲקָ֣ה בָעִ֔יר וְאֶ֨ת־הָאִ֔ישׁ עַל־דְּבַ֥ר אֲשֶׁר־עִנָּ֖ה אֶת־אֵ֣שֶׁת רֵעֵ֑הוּ וּבִֽעַרְתָּ֥ הָרָ֖ע מִקִּרְבֶּֽךָ׃ ס 25 וְֽאִם־בַּשָּׂדֶ֞ה יִמְצָ֣א הָאִ֗ישׁ אֶת־הַֽנַּעֲרָ֙ הַמְאֹ֣רָשָׂ֔ה וְהֶֽחֱזִֽיק־בָּ֥הּ הָאִ֖ישׁ וְשָׁכַ֣ב עִמָּ֑הּ וּמֵ֗ת הָאִ֛ישׁ אֲשֶׁר־שָׁכַ֥ב עִמָּ֖הּ לְבַדּֽוֹ׃ 26 ולנער וְלַֽנַּעֲרָ֙ לֹא־תַֽעֲשֶׂ֣ה דָבָ֔ר אֵ֥ין לנער לַֽנַּעֲרָ֖ חֵ֣טְא מָ֑וֶת כִּ֡י כַּֽאֲשֶׁר֩ יָק֨וּם אִ֤ישׁ עַל־רֵעֵ֙הוּ֙ וּרְצָח֣וֹ נֶ֔פֶשׁ כֵּ֖ן הַדָּבָ֥ר הַזֶּֽה׃ 27 כִּ֥י בַשָּׂדֶ֖ה מְצָאָ֑הּ צָעֲקָ֗ה הנער הַֽנַּעֲרָ֙ הַמְאֹ֣רָשָׂ֔ה וְאֵ֥ין מוֹשִׁ֖יעַ לָֽהּ׃ ס

28 כִּֽי־יִמְצָ֣א אִ֗ישׁ נער נַעֲרָ֤ בְתוּלָה֙ אֲשֶׁ֣ר לֹא־אֹרָ֔שָׂה וּתְפָשָׂ֖הּ וְשָׁכַ֣ב עִמָּ֑הּ וְנִמְצָֽאוּ׃ 29 וְ֠נָתַ֠ן הָאִ֨ישׁ הַשֹּׁכֵ֥ב עִמָּ֛הּ לַֽאֲבִ֥י הַֽנַּעֲרָ֖ חֲמִשִּׁ֣ים כָּ֑סֶף וְלֽוֹ־תִֽהְיֶ֣ה לְאִשָּׁ֗ה תַּ֚חַת אֲשֶׁ֣ר עִנָּ֔הּ לֹא־יוּכַ֥ל שַׁלְּחָ֖הּ כָּל־יָמָֽיו׃ ס

כג לֹא־יִקַּ֥ח אִ֖ישׁ אֶת־אֵ֣שֶׁת אָבִ֑יו וְלֹ֥א יְגַלֶּ֖ה כְּנַ֥ף אָבִֽיו׃ ס 2 לֹֽא־יָבֹ֧א פְצֽוּעַ־דַּכָּ֛א וּכְר֥וּת שָׁפְכָ֖ה בִּקְהַ֥ל יְהֹוָֽה׃ ס 3 לֹֽא־יָבֹ֥א מַמְזֵ֖ר בִּקְהַ֣ל יְהֹוָ֑ה גַּ֚ם דּ֣וֹר עֲשִׂירִ֔י לֹא־יָ֥בֹא ל֖וֹ בִּקְהַ֥ל יְהֹוָֽה׃ ס 4 לֹֽא־יָבֹ֧א עַמּוֹנִ֛י וּמֽוֹאָבִ֖י בִּקְהַ֣ל יְהֹוָ֑ה גַּ֚ם דּ֣וֹר עֲשִׂירִ֔י לֹא־יָבֹ֥א לָהֶ֛ם בִּקְהַ֥ל יְהֹוָ֖ה עַד־עוֹלָֽם׃ 5 עַל־דְּבַ֞ר אֲשֶׁ֨ר לֹֽא־קִדְּמ֤וּ אֶתְכֶם֙ בַּלֶּ֣חֶם וּבַמַּ֔יִם בַּדֶּ֖רֶךְ בְּצֵֽאתְכֶ֣ם מִמִּצְרָ֑יִם וַֽאֲשֶׁר֩ שָׂכַ֨ר עָלֶ֜יךָ אֶת־בִּלְעָ֨ם

---

a-a I.e., lay claim to what his father had possessed. Cf. Lev. 18.8, 20.11; Ezek. 16.8; Ruth 3.9.

b Meaning of Heb. mamzer uncertain; in Jewish law, the offspring of adultery or incest between Jews.

Beor, from Pethor of Aram-naharaim, to curse you.—⁶But the LORD your God refused to heed Balaam; instead, the LORD your God turned the curse into a blessing for you, for the LORD your God loves you.—⁷You shall never concern yourself with their welfare or benefit as long as you live.

⁸You shall not abhor an Edomite, for he is your kinsman. You shall not abhor an Egyptian, for you were a stranger in his land. ⁹Children born to them may be admitted into the congregation of the LORD in the third generation.ᶜ

¹⁰When you go out as a troop against your enemies, be on your guard against anything untoward. ¹¹If anyone among you has been rendered unclean by a nocturnal emission, he must leave the camp, and he must not reenter the camp. ¹²Toward evening he shall bathe in water, and at sundown he may reenter the camp. ¹³Further, there shall be an area for you outside the camp, where you may relieve yourself. ¹⁴With your gear you shall have a spike, and when you have squatted you shall dig a hole with it and cover up your excrement. ¹⁵Since the LORD your God moves about in your camp to protect you and to deliver your enemies to you, let your camp be holy; let Him not find anything unseemly among you and turn away from you.

¹⁶You shall not turn over to his master a slave who seeks refuge with you from his master. ¹⁷He shall live with you in any place he may choose among the settlements in your midst, wherever he pleases; you must not ill-treat him.

¹⁸No Israelite woman shall be a cult prostitute, nor shall any Israelite man be a cult prostitute. ¹⁹You shall not bring the fee of a whore or the pay of a dogᵈ into the house of the LORD your God in fulfillment of any vow, for both are abhorrent to the LORD your God.

בֶּן־בְּעוֹר מִפְּתוֹר אֲרַם נַהֲרַיִם לְקַלְלֶךָּ׃
⁶וְלֹא־אָבָה יְהֹוָה אֱלֹהֶיךָ לִשְׁמֹעַ אֶל־
בִּלְעָם וַיַּהֲפֹךְ יְהֹוָה אֱלֹהֶיךָ לְּךָ אֶת־
הַקְּלָלָה לִבְרָכָה כִּי אֲהֵבְךָ יְהֹוָה אֱלֹהֶיךָ׃
⁷לֹא־תִדְרֹשׁ שְׁלֹמָם וְטֹבָתָם כָּל־יָמֶיךָ
לְעוֹלָם׃ ס
⁸לֹא־תְתַעֵב אֲדֹמִי כִּי אָחִיךָ הוּא* ס
לֹא־תְתַעֵב מִצְרִי כִּי־גֵר הָיִיתָ בְאַרְצוֹ׃
⁹בָּנִים אֲשֶׁר־יִוָּלְדוּ לָהֶם דּוֹר שְׁלִישִׁי יָבֹא
לָהֶם בִּקְהַל יְהֹוָה׃ ס

¹⁰כִּי־תֵצֵא מַחֲנֶה עַל־אֹיְבֶיךָ וְנִשְׁמַרְתָּ
מִכֹּל דָּבָר רָע׃ ¹¹כִּי־יִהְיֶה בְךָ אִישׁ אֲשֶׁר
לֹא־יִהְיֶה טָהוֹר מִקְּרֵה־לָיְלָה וְיָצָא אֶל־
מִחוּץ לַמַּחֲנֶה לֹא יָבֹא אֶל־תּוֹךְ הַמַּחֲנֶה׃
¹²וְהָיָה לִפְנוֹת־עֶרֶב יִרְחַץ בַּמָּיִם וּכְבֹא
הַשֶּׁמֶשׁ יָבֹא אֶל־תּוֹךְ הַמַּחֲנֶה׃ ¹³וְיָד
תִּהְיֶה לְךָ מִחוּץ לַמַּחֲנֶה וְיָצָאתָ שָּׁמָּה
חוּץ׃ ¹⁴וְיָתֵד תִּהְיֶה לְךָ עַל־אֲזֵנֶךָ וְהָיָה
בְּשִׁבְתְּךָ חוּץ וְחָפַרְתָּה בָהּ וְשַׁבְתָּ וְכִסִּיתָ
אֶת־צֵאָתֶךָ׃ ¹⁵כִּי יְהֹוָה אֱלֹהֶיךָ מִתְהַלֵּךְ ׀
בְּקֶרֶב מַחֲנֶךָ לְהַצִּילְךָ וְלָתֵת אֹיְבֶיךָ לְפָנֶיךָ
וְהָיָה מַחֲנֶיךָ קָדוֹשׁ וְלֹא־יִרְאֶה בְךָ עֶרְוַת
דָּבָר וְשָׁב מֵאַחֲרֶיךָ׃ ס
¹⁶לֹא־תַסְגִּיר עֶבֶד אֶל־אֲדֹנָיו אֲשֶׁר־יִנָּצֵל
אֵלֶיךָ מֵעִם אֲדֹנָיו׃ ¹⁷עִמְּךָ יֵשֵׁב בְּקִרְבְּךָ
בַּמָּקוֹם אֲשֶׁר־יִבְחַר בְּאַחַד שְׁעָרֶיךָ בַּטּוֹב
לוֹ לֹא תּוֹנֶנּוּ׃ ס
¹⁸לֹא־תִהְיֶה קְדֵשָׁה מִבְּנוֹת יִשְׂרָאֵל וְלֹא־
יִהְיֶה קָדֵשׁ מִבְּנֵי יִשְׂרָאֵל׃ ¹⁹לֹא־תָבִיא
אֶתְנַן זוֹנָה וּמְחִיר כֶּלֶב בֵּית יְהֹוָה אֱלֹהֶיךָ
לְכָל־נֶדֶר כִּי תוֹעֲבַת יְהֹוָה אֱלֹהֶיךָ גַּם־
שְׁנֵיהֶם׃

פיסקא באמצע פסוק   v. 8.

ᶜ I.e., of residence in Israel's territory.
ᵈ I.e., a male prostitute.

20You shall not deduct interest from loans to your countrymen, whether in money or food or anything else that can be deducted as interest; 21but you may deduct interest from loans to foreigners. Do not deduct interest from loans to your countrymen, so that the LORD your God may bless you in all your undertakings in the land that you are about to enter and possess.

22When you make a vow to the LORD your God, do not put off fulfilling it, for the LORD your God will require it of you, and you will have incurred guilt; 23whereas you incur no guilt if you refrain from vowing. 24You must fulfill what has crossed your lips and perform what you have voluntarily vowed to the LORD your God, having made the promise with your own mouth.

25When you enter another man's vineyard, you may eat as many grapes as you want, until you are full, but you must not put any in your vessel. 26When you enter another man's field of standing grain, you may pluck ears with your hand; but you must not put a sickle to your neighbor's grain.

24
A man takes a wife and possesses her. She fails to please him because he finds something obnoxious about her, and he writes her a bill of divorcement, hands it to her, and sends her away from his house; 2she leaves his household and becomes the wife of another man; 3then this latter man rejects her, writes her a bill of divorcement, hands it to her, and sends her away from his house; or the man who married her last dies. 4Then the first husband who divorced her shall not take her to wife again, since she has been defiled*a*—for that would be abhorrent to the LORD. You must not bring sin upon the land that the LORD your God is giving you as a heritage.

---

a I.e., disqualified for him.

20 לֹא־תַשִּׁיךְ לְאָחִיךָ נֶשֶׁךְ כֶּסֶף נֶשֶׁךְ אֹכֶל נֶשֶׁךְ כָּל־דָּבָר אֲשֶׁר יִשָּׁךְ: 21 לַנָּכְרִי תַשִּׁיךְ וּלְאָחִיךָ לֹא תַשִּׁיךְ לְמַעַן יְבָרֶכְךָ יְהוָה אֱלֹהֶיךָ בְּכֹל מִשְׁלַח יָדֶךָ עַל־הָאָרֶץ אֲשֶׁר־אַתָּה בָא־שָׁמָּה לְרִשְׁתָּהּ: ס 22 כִּי־תִדֹּר נֶדֶר לַיהוָה אֱלֹהֶיךָ לֹא תְאַחֵר לְשַׁלְּמוֹ כִּי־דָרֹשׁ יִדְרְשֶׁנּוּ יְהוָה אֱלֹהֶיךָ מֵעִמָּךְ וְהָיָה בְךָ חֵטְא: 23 וְכִי תֶחְדַּל לִנְדֹּר לֹא־יִהְיֶה בְךָ חֵטְא: 24 מוֹצָא שְׂפָתֶיךָ תִּשְׁמֹר וְעָשִׂיתָ כַּאֲשֶׁר נָדַרְתָּ לַיהוָה אֱלֹהֶיךָ נְדָבָה אֲשֶׁר דִּבַּרְתָּ בְּפִיךָ: ס 25 כִּי תָבֹא בְּכֶרֶם רֵעֶךָ וְאָכַלְתָּ עֲנָבִים כְּנַפְשְׁךָ שָׂבְעֶךָ וְאֶל־כֶּלְיְךָ לֹא תִתֵּן: ס 26 כִּי תָבֹא בְּקָמַת רֵעֶךָ וְקָטַפְתָּ מְלִילֹת בְּיָדֶךָ וְחֶרְמֵשׁ לֹא תָנִיף עַל קָמַת רֵעֶךָ: ס

כד כִּי־יִקַּח אִישׁ אִשָּׁה וּבְעָלָהּ וְהָיָה אִם־לֹא תִמְצָא־חֵן בְּעֵינָיו כִּי־מָצָא בָהּ עֶרְוַת דָּבָר וְכָתַב לָהּ סֵפֶר כְּרִיתֻת וְנָתַן בְּיָדָהּ וְשִׁלְּחָהּ מִבֵּיתוֹ: 2 וְיָצְאָה מִבֵּיתוֹ וְהָלְכָה וְהָיְתָה לְאִישׁ־אַחֵר: 3 וּשְׂנֵאָהּ הָאִישׁ הָאַחֲרוֹן וְכָתַב לָהּ סֵפֶר כְּרִיתֻת וְנָתַן בְּיָדָהּ וְשִׁלְּחָהּ מִבֵּיתוֹ אוֹ כִי יָמוּת הָאִישׁ הָאַחֲרוֹן אֲשֶׁר־לְקָחָהּ לוֹ לְאִשָּׁה: 4 לֹא־יוּכַל בַּעְלָהּ הָרִאשׁוֹן אֲשֶׁר־שִׁלְּחָהּ לָשׁוּב לְקַחְתָּהּ לִהְיוֹת לוֹ לְאִשָּׁה אַחֲרֵי אֲשֶׁר הֻטַּמָּאָה כִּי־תוֹעֵבָה הִוא לִפְנֵי יְהוָה וְלֹא תַחֲטִיא אֶת־הָאָרֶץ אֲשֶׁר יְהוָה אֱלֹהֶיךָ נֹתֵן לְךָ נַחֲלָה: ס

⁵When a man has taken a bride, he shall not go out with the army or be assigned to it for any purpose; he shall be exempt one year for the sake of his household, to give happiness to the woman he has married.

⁶A handmill or an upper millstone shall not be taken in pawn, for that would be taking someone's life in pawn.

⁷If a man is found to have kidnapped a fellow Israelite, enslaving him or selling him, that kidnapper shall die; thus you will sweep out evil from your midst.

⁸In cases of a skin affection[b] be most careful to do exactly as the levitical priests instruct you. Take care to do as I have commanded them. ⁹Remember what the LORD your God did to Miriam on the journey after you left Egypt.[c]

¹⁰When you make a loan of any sort to your countryman, you must not enter his house to seize his pledge. ¹¹You must remain outside, while the man to whom you made the loan brings the pledge out to you. ¹²If he is a needy man, you shall not go to sleep in his pledge; ¹³you must return the pledge to him at sundown, that he may sleep in his cloth and bless you; and it will be to your merit before the LORD your God.

¹⁴You shall not abuse a needy and destitute laborer, whether a fellow countryman or a stranger in one of the communities of your land. ¹⁵You must pay him his wages on the same day, before the sun sets, for he is needy and urgently depends on it; else he will cry to the LORD against you and you will incur guilt.

¹⁶Parents shall not be put to death for children, nor children be put to death for parents: a person shall be put to death only for his own crime.

¹⁷You shall not subvert the rights of the stranger or the fatherless; you shall not take a

---

5 כִּי־יִקַּח אִישׁ אִשָּׁה חֲדָשָׁה לֹא יֵצֵא בַּצָּבָא וְלֹא־יַעֲבֹר עָלָיו לְכָל־דָּבָר נָקִי יִהְיֶה לְבֵיתוֹ שָׁנָה אֶחָת וְשִׂמַּח אֶת־אִשְׁתּוֹ אֲשֶׁר־לָקָח: ס

6 לֹא־יַחֲבֹל רֵחַיִם וָרָכֶב כִּי־נֶפֶשׁ הוּא חֹבֵל: ס

7 כִּי־יִמָּצֵא אִישׁ גֹּנֵב נֶפֶשׁ מֵאֶחָיו מִבְּנֵי יִשְׂרָאֵל וְהִתְעַמֶּר־בּוֹ וּמְכָרוֹ וּמֵת הַגַּנָּב הַהוּא וּבִעַרְתָּ הָרָע מִקִּרְבֶּךָ:

8 הִשָּׁמֶר בְּנֶגַע־הַצָּרַעַת לִשְׁמֹר מְאֹד וְלַעֲשׂוֹת כְּכֹל אֲשֶׁר־יוֹרוּ אֶתְכֶם הַכֹּהֲנִים הַלְוִיִּם כַּאֲשֶׁר צִוִּיתִם תִּשְׁמְרוּ לַעֲשׂוֹת: ס

9 זָכוֹר אֵת אֲשֶׁר־עָשָׂה יְהוָה אֱלֹהֶיךָ לְמִרְיָם בַּדֶּרֶךְ בְּצֵאתְכֶם מִמִּצְרָיִם: ס

10 כִּי־תַשֶּׁה בְרֵעֲךָ מַשַּׁאת* מְאוּמָה לֹא־תָבֹא אֶל־בֵּיתוֹ לַעֲבֹט עֲבֹטוֹ: 11 בַּחוּץ תַּעֲמֹד וְהָאִישׁ אֲשֶׁר אַתָּה נֹשֶׁה בוֹ יוֹצִיא אֵלֶיךָ אֶת־הַעֲבוֹט הַחוּצָה: 12 וְאִם־אִישׁ עָנִי הוּא לֹא תִשְׁכַּב בַּעֲבֹטוֹ: 13 הָשֵׁב תָּשִׁיב לוֹ אֶת־הַעֲבוֹט כְּבֹא הַשֶּׁמֶשׁ וְשָׁכַב בְּשַׂלְמָתוֹ וּבֵרֲכֶךָּ וּלְךָ תִּהְיֶה צְדָקָה לִפְנֵי יְהוָה אֱלֹהֶיךָ: ס

14 לֹא־תַעֲשֹׁק שָׂכִיר עָנִי וְאֶבְיוֹן מֵאַחֶיךָ אוֹ מִגֵּרְךָ אֲשֶׁר בְּאַרְצְךָ בִּשְׁעָרֶיךָ: 15 בְּיוֹמוֹ תִתֵּן שְׂכָרוֹ וְלֹא־תָבוֹא עָלָיו הַשֶּׁמֶשׁ כִּי עָנִי הוּא וְאֵלָיו הוּא נֹשֵׂא אֶת־נַפְשׁוֹ וְלֹא־יִקְרָא עָלֶיךָ אֶל־יְהֹוָה וְהָיָה בְךָ חֵטְא: ס

16 לֹא־יוּמְתוּ אָבוֹת עַל־בָּנִים וּבָנִים לֹא־יוּמְתוּ עַל־אָבוֹת אִישׁ בְּחֶטְאוֹ יוּמָתוּ: ס

17 לֹא תַטֶּה מִשְׁפַּט גֵּר יָתוֹם וְלֹא תַחֲבֹל בֶּגֶד אַלְמָנָה: 18 וְזָכַרְתָּ כִּי עֶבֶד הָיִיתָ

א' נחה v. 10.

---

b Cf. Lev. 13.1 ff.
c See Num. 12.10 ff.

widow's garment in pawn. 18Remember that you were a slave in Egypt and that the LORD your God redeemed you from there; therefore do I enjoin you to observe this commandment.

19When you reap the harvest in your field and overlook a sheaf in the field, do not turn back to get it; it shall go to the stranger, the fatherless, and the widow—in order that the LORD your God may bless you in all your undertakings.

20When you beat down the fruit of your olive trees, do not go over them again; that shall go to the stranger, the fatherless, and the widow. 21When you gather the grapes of your vineyard, do not pick it over again; that shall go to the stranger, the fatherless, and the widow. 22Always remember that you were a slave in the land of Egypt; therefore do I enjoin you to observe this commandment.

25

When there is a dispute between men and they go to law, and a decision is rendered declaring the one in the right and the other in the wrong—2if the guilty one is to be flogged, the magistrate shall have him lie down and be given lashes in his presence, by count, as his guilt warrants. 3He may be given up to forty lashes, but not more, lest being flogged further, to excess, your brother be degraded before your eyes.

4You shall not muzzle an ox while it is threshing.

5When brothers dwell together and one of them dies and leaves no son, the wife of the deceased shall not be married to a stranger, outside the family. Her husband's brother shall unite with her: he shall take her as his wife and perform the levir's duty. 6The first son that she bears shall be accounted to the dead brother, that his name may not be blotted out in Israel. 7But if the man does not want to marry his brother's widow, his brother's widow shall ap-

בְּמִצְרַיִם וַיִּפְדְּךָ יְהֹוָה אֱלֹהֶיךָ מִשָּׁם עַל־
כֵּן אָנֹכִי מְצַוְּךָ לַעֲשׂוֹת אֶת־הַדָּבָר
הַזֶּה: ס
19 כִּי תִקְצֹר קְצִירְךָ בְשָׂדֶךָ וְשָׁכַחְתָּ עֹמֶר
בַּשָּׂדֶה לֹא תָשׁוּב לְקַחְתּוֹ לַגֵּר לַיָּתוֹם
וְלָאַלְמָנָה יִהְיֶה לְמַעַן יְבָרֶכְךָ יְהֹוָה
אֱלֹהֶיךָ בְּכֹל מַעֲשֵׂה יָדֶיךָ:
20 כִּי תַחְבֹּט זֵיתְךָ לֹא תְפַאֵר אַחֲרֶיךָ לַגֵּר
לַיָּתוֹם וְלָאַלְמָנָה יִהְיֶה: ס 21 כִּי תִבְצֹר
כַּרְמְךָ לֹא תְעוֹלֵל אַחֲרֶיךָ לַגֵּר לַיָּתוֹם
וְלָאַלְמָנָה יִהְיֶה: 22 וְזָכַרְתָּ כִּי־עֶבֶד הָיִיתָ
בְּאֶרֶץ מִצְרָיִם עַל־כֵּן אָנֹכִי מְצַוְּךָ לַעֲשׂוֹת
אֶת־הַדָּבָר הַזֶּה: ס

כה כִּי־יִהְיֶה רִיב בֵּין אֲנָשִׁים וְנִגְּשׁוּ
אֶל־הַמִּשְׁפָּט וּשְׁפָטוּם וְהִצְדִּיקוּ אֶת־
הַצַּדִּיק וְהִרְשִׁיעוּ אֶת־הָרָשָׁע: 2 וְהָיָה
אִם־בִּן הַכּוֹת הָרָשָׁע וְהִפִּילוֹ הַשֹּׁפֵט
וְהִכָּהוּ לְפָנָיו כְּדֵי רִשְׁעָתוֹ בְּמִסְפָּר:
3 אַרְבָּעִים יַכֶּנּוּ לֹא יֹסִיף פֶּן־יֹסִיף לְהַכֹּתוֹ
עַל־אֵלֶּה מַכָּה רַבָּה וְנִקְלָה אָחִיךָ
לְעֵינֶיךָ: ס
4 לֹא־תַחְסֹם שׁוֹר בְּדִישׁוֹ: ס
5 כִּי־יֵשְׁבוּ אַחִים יַחְדָּו וּמֵת אַחַד מֵהֶם
וּבֵן אֵין־לוֹ לֹא־תִהְיֶה אֵשֶׁת־הַמֵּת
הַחוּצָה לְאִישׁ זָר יְבָמָהּ יָבֹא עָלֶיהָ
וּלְקָחָהּ לוֹ לְאִשָּׁה וְיִבְּמָהּ: 6 וְהָיָה הַבְּכוֹר
אֲשֶׁר תֵּלֵד יָקוּם עַל־שֵׁם אָחִיו הַמֵּת
וְלֹא־יִמָּחֶה שְׁמוֹ מִיִּשְׂרָאֵל: 7 וְאִם־לֹא
יַחְפֹּץ הָאִישׁ לָקַחַת אֶת־יְבִמְתּוֹ וְעָלְתָה
יְבִמְתּוֹ הַשַּׁעְרָה אֶל־הַזְּקֵנִים וְאָמְרָה

pear before the elders in the gate and declare, "My husband's brother refuses to establish a name in Israel for his brother; he will not perform the duty of a levir." [8]The elders of his town shall then summon him and talk to him. If he insists, saying, "I do not want to marry her," [9]his brother's widow shall go up to him in the presence of the elders, pull the sandal off his foot, spit in his face, and make this declaration: Thus shall be done to the man who will not build up his brother's house! [10]And he shall go in Israel by the name of "the family of the unsandaled one."

[11]If two men get into a fight with each other, and the wife of one comes up to save her husband from his antagonist and puts out her hand and seizes him by his genitals, [12]you shall cut off her hand; show no pity.

[13]You shall not have in your pouch alternate weights, larger and smaller. [14]You shall not have in your house alternate measures, a larger and a smaller. [15]You must have completely honest weights and completely honest measures, if you are to endure long on the soil that the LORD your God is giving you. [16]For everyone who does those things, everyone who deals dishonestly, is abhorrent to the LORD your God.

[17]Remember what Amalek did to you on your journey, after you left Egypt—[18]how, undeterred by fear of God, he surprised you on the march, when you were famished and weary, and cut down all the stragglers in your rear. [19]Therefore, when the LORD your God grants you safety from all your enemies around you, in the land that the LORD your God is giving you as a hereditary portion, you shall blot out the memory of Amalek from under heaven. Do not forget!

מֵאֵ֤ן֙* יְבָמִי֙ לְהָקִ֨ים לְאָחִ֥יו שֵׁ֖ם בְּיִשְׂרָאֵ֑ל לֹ֥א אָבָ֖ה יַבְּמִֽי׃ 8 וְקָֽרְאוּ־ל֥וֹ זִקְנֵֽי־עִיר֖וֹ וְדִבְּר֣וּ אֵלָ֑יו וְעָמַ֣ד וְאָמַ֔ר לֹ֥א חָפַ֖צְתִּי לְקַחְתָּֽהּ׃ 9 וְנִגְּשָׁ֨ה יְבִמְתּ֣וֹ אֵלָיו֮ לְעֵינֵ֣י הַזְּקֵנִים֒ וְחָֽלְצָ֤ה נַֽעֲלוֹ֙ מֵעַ֣ל רַגְל֔וֹ וְיָֽרְקָ֖ה בְּפָנָ֑יו וְעָֽנְתָה֙ וְאָ֣מְרָ֔ה כָּ֚כָה יֵֽעָשֶׂ֣ה לָאִ֔ישׁ אֲשֶׁ֥ר לֹֽא־יִבְנֶ֖ה אֶת־בֵּ֥ית אָחִֽיו׃ 10 וְנִקְרָ֥א שְׁמ֖וֹ בְּיִשְׂרָאֵ֑ל בֵּ֖ית חֲל֥וּץ הַנָּֽעַל׃ ס

11 כִּֽי־יִנָּצ֨וּ אֲנָשִׁ֤ים יַחְדָּו֙ אִ֣ישׁ וְאָחִ֔יו וְקָֽרְבָה֙ אֵ֣שֶׁת הָֽאֶחָ֔ד לְהַצִּ֥יל אֶת־אִישָׁ֖הּ מִיַּ֣ד מַכֵּ֑הוּ וְשָֽׁלְחָ֣ה יָדָ֔הּ וְהֶֽחֱזִ֖יקָה בִּמְבֻשָֽׁיו׃ 12 וְקַצֹּתָ֖ה אֶת־כַּפָּ֑הּ לֹ֥א תָח֖וֹס עֵינֶֽךָ׃ ס

13 לֹֽא־יִהְיֶ֥ה לְךָ֛ בְּכִֽיסְךָ֖ אֶ֣בֶן וָאָ֑בֶן גְּדוֹלָ֖ה וּקְטַנָּֽה׃ ס 14 לֹא־יִהְיֶ֥ה לְךָ֛ בְּבֵֽיתְךָ֖ אֵיפָ֣ה וְאֵיפָ֑ה גְּדוֹלָ֖ה וּקְטַנָּֽה׃ 15 אֶ֣בֶן שְׁלֵמָ֤ה וָצֶ֙דֶק֙ יִֽהְיֶה־לָּ֔ךְ אֵיפָ֧ה שְׁלֵמָ֛ה וָצֶ֖דֶק יִֽהְיֶה־לָּ֑ךְ לְמַ֙עַן֙ יַֽאֲרִ֣יכוּ יָמֶ֔יךָ עַ֚ל הָ֣אֲדָמָ֔ה אֲשֶׁר־יְהוָ֥ה אֱלֹהֶ֖יךָ נֹתֵ֥ן לָֽךְ׃ 16 כִּ֧י תֽוֹעֲבַ֛ת יְהוָ֥ה אֱלֹהֶ֖יךָ כָּל־עֹ֣שֵׂה אֵ֑לֶּה כֹּ֖ל עֹ֥שֵׂה עָֽוֶל׃ פ

17 זָכ֕וֹר אֵ֛ת אֲשֶׁר־עָשָׂ֥ה לְךָ֖ עֲמָלֵ֑ק בַּדֶּ֖רֶךְ בְּצֵֽאתְכֶ֥ם מִמִּצְרָֽיִם׃ 18 אֲשֶׁ֨ר קָֽרְךָ֜ בַּדֶּ֗רֶךְ וַיְזַנֵּ֤ב בְּךָ֙ כָּל־הַנֶּֽחֱשָׁלִ֣ים אַֽחֲרֶ֔יךָ וְאַתָּ֖ה עָיֵ֣ף וְיָגֵ֑עַ וְלֹ֥א יָרֵ֖א אֱלֹהִֽים׃ 19 וְהָיָ֡ה בְּהָנִ֣יחַ יְהוָ֣ה אֱלֹהֶ֣יךָ ׀ לְ֠ךָ מִכָּל־אֹ֨יְבֶ֜יךָ מִסָּבִ֗יב בָּאָ֨רֶץ֙ אֲשֶׁ֣ר יְהוָ֣ה־אֱ֠לֹהֶיךָ נֹתֵ֨ן לְךָ֤ נַֽחֲלָה֙ לְרִשְׁתָּ֔הּ תִּמְחֶה֙ אֶת־זֵ֣כֶר עֲמָלֵ֔ק מִתַּ֖חַת הַשָּׁמָ֑יִם לֹ֖א תִּשְׁכָּֽח׃ פ

v. 7. יתיר ו' בכתב היד שלנו

26 KI TAVO'

When you enter the land that the LORD your God is giving you as a heritage, and you possess it and settle in it, [2]you shall take some of every first fruit of the soil, which you harvest from the land that the LORD your God is giving you, put it in a basket and go to the place where the LORD your God will choose to establish His name. [3]You shall go to the priest in charge at that time and say to him, "I acknowledge this day before the LORD your God that I have entered the land that the LORD swore to our fathers to assign us."

[4]The priest shall take the basket from your hand and set it down in front of the altar of the LORD your God.

[5]You shall then recite as follows before the LORD your God: "My father was a fugitive Aramean. He went down to Egypt with meager numbers and sojourned there; but there he became a great and very populous nation. [6]The Egyptians dealt harshly with us and oppressed us; they imposed heavy labor upon us. [7]We cried to the LORD, the God of our fathers, and the LORD heard our plea and saw our plight, our misery, and our oppression. [8]The LORD freed us from Egypt by a mighty hand, by an outstretched arm and awesome power, and by signs and portents. [9]He brought us to this place and gave us this land, a land flowing with milk and honey. [10]Wherefore I now bring the first fruits of the soil which You, O LORD, have given me."

You shall leave it[a] before the LORD your God and bow low before the LORD your God. [11]And you shall enjoy, together with the Levite and the stranger in your midst, all the bounty that the LORD your God has bestowed upon you and your household.

[12]When you have set aside in full the tenth part of your yield—in the third year, the year

---

a   I.e., the basket of v. 4.

כו כי תבוא

כו וְהָיָה֙ כִּי־תָב֣וֹא אֶל־הָאָ֔רֶץ אֲשֶׁר֙
יְהוָ֣ה אֱלֹהֶ֔יךָ נֹתֵ֥ן לְךָ֖ נַחֲלָ֑ה וִֽירִשְׁתָּ֖הּ
וְיָשַׁ֥בְתָּ בָּֽהּ׃ 2 וְלָקַחְתָּ֞ מֵרֵאשִׁ֣ית ׀ כָּל־פְּרִ֣י
הָאֲדָמָ֗ה אֲשֶׁ֨ר תָּבִ֧יא מֵֽאַרְצְךָ֛ אֲשֶׁ֨ר יְהוָ֧ה
אֱלֹהֶ֛יךָ נֹתֵ֥ן לָ֖ךְ וְשַׂמְתָּ֣ בַטֶּ֑נֶא וְהָ֣לַכְתָּ֔
אֶל־הַמָּק֔וֹם אֲשֶׁ֤ר יִבְחַר֙ יְהוָ֣ה אֱלֹהֶ֔יךָ
לְשַׁכֵּ֥ן שְׁמ֖וֹ שָֽׁם׃ 3 וּבָאתָ֙ אֶל־הַכֹּהֵ֔ן אֲשֶׁ֥ר
יִֽהְיֶ֖ה בַּיָּמִ֣ים הָהֵ֑ם וְאָמַרְתָּ֣ אֵלָ֗יו הִגַּ֤דְתִּי
הַיּוֹם֙ לַֽיהוָ֣ה אֱלֹהֶ֔יךָ כִּי־בָ֨אתִי֙ אֶל־הָאָ֔רֶץ
אֲשֶׁ֨ר נִשְׁבַּ֧ע יְהוָ֛ה לַאֲבֹתֵ֖ינוּ לָ֥תֶת לָֽנוּ׃
4 וְלָקַ֧ח הַכֹּהֵ֛ן הַטֶּ֖נֶא מִיָּדֶ֑ךָ וְהִ֨נִּיח֔וֹ לִפְנֵ֕י
מִזְבַּ֖ח יְהוָ֥ה אֱלֹהֶֽיךָ׃
5 וְעָנִ֨יתָ וְאָמַרְתָּ֜ לִפְנֵ֣י ׀ יְהוָ֣ה אֱלֹהֶ֗יךָ אֲרַמִּי֙
אֹבֵ֣ד אָבִ֔י וַיֵּ֣רֶד מִצְרַ֔יְמָה וַיָּ֥גָר שָׁ֖ם בִּמְתֵ֣י
מְעָ֑ט וַֽיְהִי־שָׁ֕ם לְג֥וֹי גָּד֖וֹל עָצ֥וּם וָרָֽב׃ 6 וַיָּרֵ֧עוּ אֹתָ֛נוּ הַמִּצְרִ֖ים וַיְעַנּ֑וּנוּ וַיִּתְּנ֥וּ
עָלֵ֖ינוּ עֲבֹדָ֥ה קָשָֽׁה׃ 7 וַנִּצְעַ֕ק אֶל־יְהוָ֖ה
אֱלֹהֵ֣י אֲבֹתֵ֑ינוּ וַיִּשְׁמַ֤ע יְהוָה֙ אֶת־קֹלֵ֔נוּ
וַיַּ֧רְא אֶת־עָנְיֵ֛נוּ וְאֶת־עֲמָלֵ֖נוּ וְאֶת־לַחֲצֵֽנוּ׃
8 וַיּוֹצִאֵ֤נוּ יְהוָה֙ מִמִּצְרַ֔יִם בְּיָ֤ד חֲזָקָה֙ וּבִזְרֹ֣עַ
נְטוּיָ֔ה וּבְמֹרָ֖א גָּדֹ֑ל וּבְאֹת֖וֹת וּבְמֹפְתִֽים׃
9 וַיְבִאֵ֖נוּ אֶל־הַמָּק֣וֹם הַזֶּ֑ה וַיִּתֶּן־לָ֨נוּ֙ אֶת־
הָאָ֣רֶץ הַזֹּ֔את אֶ֛רֶץ זָבַ֥ת חָלָ֖ב וּדְבָֽשׁ׃
10 וְעַתָּ֗ה הִנֵּ֤ה הֵבֵ֨אתִי֙ אֶת־רֵאשִׁית֙ פְּרִ֣י
הָאֲדָמָ֔ה אֲשֶׁר־נָתַ֥תָּה לִּ֖י יְהוָ֑ה
וְהִנַּחְתּ֗וֹ לִפְנֵי֙ יְהוָ֣ה אֱלֹהֶ֔יךָ וְהִֽשְׁתַּחֲוִ֔יתָ
לִפְנֵ֖י יְהוָ֥ה אֱלֹהֶֽיךָ׃ 11 וְשָׂמַחְתָּ֣ בְכָל־הַטּ֗וֹב
אֲשֶׁ֧ר נָֽתַן־לְךָ֛ יְהוָ֥ה אֱלֹהֶ֖יךָ וּלְבֵיתֶ֑ךָ אַתָּה֙
וְהַלֵּוִ֔י וְהַגֵּ֖ר אֲשֶׁ֥ר בְּקִרְבֶּֽךָ׃ ס
12 כִּ֣י תְכַלֶּ֞ה לַ֠עְשֵׂר אֶת־כָּל־מַעְשַׂ֧ר
תְּבוּאָֽתְךָ֛ בַּשָּׁנָ֥ה הַשְּׁלִישִׁ֖ת שְׁנַ֣ת הַֽמַּעֲשֵׂ֑ר

of the tithe[b]—and have given it to the Levite, the stranger, the fatherless, and the widow, that they may eat their fill in your settlements, [13]you shall declare before the LORD your God: "I have cleared out the consecrated portion from the house; and I have given it to the Levite, the stranger, the fatherless, and the widow, just as You commanded me; I have neither transgressed nor neglected any of Your commandments: [14c] I have not eaten of it while in mourning, I have not cleared out any of it while I was unclean, and I have not deposited any of it with the dead.[d] I have obeyed the LORD my God; I have done just as You commanded me. [15]Look down from Your holy abode, from heaven, and bless Your people Israel and the soil You have given us, a land flowing with milk and honey, as You swore to our fathers."

[16]The LORD your God commands you this day to observe these laws and rules; observe them faithfully with all your heart and soul. [17]You have affirmed[e] this day that the LORD is your God, that you will walk in His ways, that you will observe His laws and commandments and rules, and that you will obey Him. [18]And the LORD has affirmed[e] this day that you are, as He promised you, His treasured people who shall observe all His commandments, [19]and that He will set you, in fame and renown and glory, high above all the nations that He has made; and that you shall be, as He promised, a holy people to the LORD your God.

27
Moses and the elders of Israel charged the people, saying: Observe all the Instruction that I enjoin upon you this day. [2a]As soon as you have crossed the Jordan into the land that

---

וְנָתַתָּ֣ה לַלֵּוִ֡י לַגֵּ֣ר לַיָּתוֹם֩ וְלָֽאַלְמָנָה֙ וְאָכְל֥וּ בִשְׁעָרֶ֖יךָ וְשָׂבֵֽעוּ: 13 וְאָמַרְתָּ֡ לִפְנֵי֩ יְהֹוָ֨ה אֱלֹהֶ֜יךָ בִּעַ֧רְתִּי הַקֹּ֣דֶשׁ מִן־הַבַּ֗יִת וְגַ֨ם נְתַתִּ֤יו לַלֵּוִי֙ וְלַגֵּר֙ לַיָּת֣וֹם וְלָֽאַלְמָנָ֔ה כְּכָל־מִצְוָתְךָ֖ אֲשֶׁ֣ר צִוִּיתָ֑נִי לֹֽא־עָבַ֥רְתִּי מִמִּצְוֺתֶ֖יךָ וְלֹ֥א שָׁכָֽחְתִּי: 14 לֹא־אָכַ֨לְתִּי בְאֹנִ֜י מִמֶּ֗נּוּ וְלֹֽא־בִעַ֤רְתִּי מִמֶּ֙נּוּ֙ בְּטָמֵ֔א וְלֹֽא־נָתַ֥תִּי מִמֶּ֖נּוּ לְמֵ֑ת שָׁמַ֗עְתִּי בְּקוֹל֙ יְהֹוָ֣ה אֱלֹהָ֔י עָשִׂ֕יתִי כְּכֹ֖ל אֲשֶׁ֥ר צִוִּיתָֽנִי: 15 הַשְׁקִ֩יפָה֩ מִמְּע֨וֹן קׇדְשְׁךָ֜ מִן־הַשָּׁמַ֗יִם וּבָרֵ֤ךְ אֶֽת־עַמְּךָ֙ אֶת־יִשְׂרָאֵ֔ל וְאֵת֙ הָֽאֲדָמָ֔ה אֲשֶׁ֥ר נָתַ֖תָּה לָ֑נוּ כַּֽאֲשֶׁ֤ר נִשְׁבַּ֙עְתָּ֙ לַֽאֲבֹתֵ֔ינוּ אֶ֛רֶץ זָבַ֥ת חָלָ֖ב וּדְבָֽשׁ: ס

16 הַיּ֣וֹם הַזֶּ֗ה יְהֹוָ֤ה אֱלֹהֶ֙יךָ֙ מְצַוְּךָ֣ לַֽעֲשׂ֔וֹת אֶת־הַֽחֻקִּ֥ים הָאֵ֖לֶּה וְאֶת־הַמִּשְׁפָּטִ֑ים וְשָׁמַרְתָּ֤ וְעָשִׂ֙יתָ֙ אוֹתָ֔ם בְּכׇל־לְבָבְךָ֖ וּבְכׇל־נַפְשֶֽׁךָ: 17 אֶת־יְהֹוָ֥ה הֶֽאֱמַ֖רְתָּ הַיּ֑וֹם לִֽהְי֨וֹת לְךָ֜ לֵֽאלֹהִ֗ים וְלָלֶ֣כֶת בִּדְרָכָ֗יו וְלִשְׁמֹ֨ר חֻקָּ֧יו וּמִצְוֺתָ֛יו וּמִשְׁפָּטָ֖יו וְלִשְׁמֹ֥עַ בְּקֹלֽוֹ: 18 וַֽיהֹוָ֞ה הֶֽאֱמִֽירְךָ֣ הַיּ֗וֹם לִֽהְי֥וֹת לוֹ֙ לְעַ֣ם סְגֻלָּ֔ה כַּֽאֲשֶׁ֖ר דִּבֶּר־לָ֑ךְ וְלִשְׁמֹ֖ר כׇּל־מִצְוֺתָֽיו: 19 וּֽלְתִתְּךָ֣ עֶלְי֗וֹן עַ֤ל כׇּל־הַגּוֹיִם֙ אֲשֶׁ֣ר עָשָׂ֔ה לִתְהִלָּ֖ה וּלְשֵׁ֣ם וּלְתִפְאָ֑רֶת וְלִֽהְיֹֽתְךָ֧ עַם־קָדֹ֛שׁ לַֽיהֹוָ֥ה אֱלֹהֶ֖יךָ כַּֽאֲשֶׁ֥ר דִּבֵּֽר: ס

כז וַיְצַ֤ו מֹשֶׁה֙ וְזִקְנֵ֣י יִשְׂרָאֵ֔ל אֶת־הָעָ֖ם לֵאמֹ֑ר שָׁמֹר֙ אֶת־כׇּל־הַמִּצְוָ֔ה אֲשֶׁ֧ר אָֽנֹכִ֛י מְצַוֶּ֥ה אֶתְכֶ֖ם הַיּֽוֹם: 2 וְהָיָ֗ה בַּיּוֹם֙ אֲשֶׁ֣ר תַּֽעַבְר֣וּ אֶת־הַיַּרְדֵּ֗ן אֶל־הָאָ֙רֶץ֙ אֲשֶׁר־יְהֹוָ֣ה

---

b   *See Deut. 14.28–29.*
c   *Meaning of first part of verse uncertain.*
d   *No part of the tithe may be left as food for the dead.*
e   *Exact nuance of Heb. uncertain.*

a   *Construction of vv. 2–4 uncertain.*

the LORD your God is giving you, you shall set up large stones. Coat them with plaster [3]and inscribe upon them all the words of this Teaching. When you cross over to enter the land that the LORD your God is giving you, a land flowing with milk and honey, as the LORD, the God of your fathers, promised you—[4]upon crossing the Jordan, you shall set up these stones, about which I charge you this day, on Mount Ebal, and coat them with plaster. [5]There, too, you shall build an altar to the LORD your God, an altar of stones. Do not wield an iron tool over them; [6]you must build the altar of the LORD your God of unhewn[b] stones. You shall offer on it burnt offerings to the LORD your God, [7]and you shall sacrifice there offerings of well-being and eat them, rejoicing before the LORD your God. [8]And on those stones you shall inscribe every word of this Teaching most distinctly.

[9]Moses and the levitical priests spoke to all Israel, saying: Silence! Hear, O Israel! Today you have become the people of the LORD your God: [10]Heed the LORD your God and observe His commandments and His laws, which I enjoin upon you this day.

[11]Thereupon Moses charged the people, saying: [12c]After you have crossed the Jordan, the following shall stand on Mount Gerizim when the blessing for the people is spoken: Simeon, Levi, Judah, Issachar, Joseph, and Benjamin. [13]And for the curse, the following shall stand on Mount Ebal: Reuben, Gad, Asher, Zebulun, Dan, and Naphtali. [14]The Levites shall then proclaim in a loud voice to all the people of Israel:

[15]Cursed be anyone who makes a sculptured or molten image, abhorred by the LORD, a craftsman's handiwork, and sets it up in secret.—And all the people shall respond, Amen.

---

b Lit. "whole."
c Construction of vv. 12–13 uncertain.

אֱלֹהֶ֨יךָ נֹתֵ֤ן לָךְ֙ וַהֲקֵמֹתָ֤ לְךָ֙ אֲבָנִ֣ים גְּדֹל֔וֹת וְשַׂדְתָּ֥ אֹתָ֖ם בַּשִּֽׂיד׃ 3 וְכָתַבְתָּ֣ עֲלֵיהֶ֗ן אֶֽת־כָּל־דִּבְרֵ֛י הַתּוֹרָ֥ה הַזֹּ֖את בְּעָבְרֶ֑ךָ לְמַ֡עַן אֲשֶׁר֩ תָּבֹ֨א אֶל־הָאָ֜רֶץ אֲשֶׁר־יְהוָ֧ה אֱלֹהֶ֣יךָ ׀ נֹתֵ֣ן לְךָ֗ אֶ֚רֶץ זָבַ֤ת חָלָב֙ וּדְבַ֔שׁ כַּאֲשֶׁ֥ר דִּבֶּ֛ר יְהוָ֥ה אֱלֹהֵֽי־אֲבֹתֶ֖יךָ לָֽךְ׃ 4 וְהָיָה֮ בְּעָבְרְכֶ֣ם אֶת־הַיַּרְדֵּן֒ תָּקִ֣ימוּ אֶת־הָאֲבָנִ֣ים הָאֵ֗לֶּה אֲשֶׁ֨ר אָנֹכִ֜י מְצַוֶּ֥ה אֶתְכֶ֛ם הַיּ֖וֹם בְּהַ֣ר עֵיבָ֑ל וְשַׂדְתָּ֥ אוֹתָ֖ם בַּשִּֽׂיד׃ 5 וּבָנִ֤יתָ שָּׁם֙ מִזְבֵּ֔חַ לַיהוָ֖ה אֱלֹהֶ֑יךָ מִזְבַּ֣ח אֲבָנִ֔ים לֹא־תָנִ֥יף עֲלֵיהֶ֖ם בַּרְזֶֽל׃ 6 אֲבָנִ֤ים שְׁלֵמוֹת֙ תִּבְנֶ֔ה אֶת־מִזְבַּ֖ח יְהוָ֣ה אֱלֹהֶ֑יךָ וְהַעֲלִ֤יתָ עָלָיו֙ עוֹלֹ֔ת לַיהוָ֖ה אֱלֹהֶֽיךָ׃ 7 וְזָבַחְתָּ֥ שְׁלָמִ֖ים וְאָכַ֣לְתָּ שָּׁ֑ם וְשָׂ֣מַחְתָּ֔ לִפְנֵ֖י יְהוָ֥ה אֱלֹהֶֽיךָ׃ 8 וְכָתַבְתָּ֣ עַל־הָאֲבָנִ֗ים אֶֽת־כָּל־דִּבְרֵ֛י הַתּוֹרָ֥ה הַזֹּ֖את בַּאֵ֥ר הֵיטֵֽב׃ ס

9 וַיְדַבֵּ֤ר מֹשֶׁה֙ וְהַכֹּהֲנִ֣ים הַלְוִיִּ֔ם אֶ֥ל כָּל־יִשְׂרָאֵ֖ל לֵאמֹ֑ר הַסְכֵּ֤ת ׀ וּשְׁמַ֣ע יִשְׂרָאֵ֔ל הַיּ֤וֹם הַזֶּה֙ נִהְיֵ֣יתָֽ לְעָ֔ם לַיהוָ֖ה אֱלֹהֶֽיךָ׃ 10 וְשָׁמַעְתָּ֖ בְּק֣וֹל יְהוָ֣ה אֱלֹהֶ֑יךָ וְעָשִׂ֤יתָ אֶת־מִצְוֺתָו֙ וְאֶת־חֻקָּ֔יו אֲשֶׁ֛ר אָנֹכִ֥י מְצַוְּךָ֖ הַיּֽוֹם׃ ס

11 וַיְצַ֤ו מֹשֶׁה֙ אֶת־הָעָ֔ם בַּיּ֥וֹם הַה֖וּא לֵאמֹֽר׃ 12 אֵ֠לֶּה יַֽעַמְד֞וּ לְבָרֵ֤ךְ אֶת־הָעָם֙ עַל־הַ֣ר גְּרִזִ֔ים בְּעָבְרְכֶ֖ם אֶת־הַיַּרְדֵּ֑ן שִׁמְעוֹן֙ וְלֵוִ֣י וִֽיהוּדָ֔ה וְיִשָּׂשכָ֖ר וְיוֹסֵ֥ף וּבִנְיָמִֽן׃ 13 וְאֵ֛לֶּה יַֽעַמְד֥וּ עַל־הַקְּלָלָ֖ה בְּהַ֣ר עֵיבָ֑ל רְאוּבֵן֙ גָּ֣ד וְאָשֵׁ֔ר וּזְבוּלֻ֖ן דָּ֥ן וְנַפְתָּלִֽי׃ 14 וְעָנ֣וּ הַלְוִיִּ֗ם וְאָֽמְר֛וּ אֶל־כָּל־אִ֥ישׁ יִשְׂרָאֵ֖ל ק֥וֹל רָֽם׃ ס

15 אָר֣וּר הָאִ֡ישׁ אֲשֶׁ֣ר יַעֲשֶׂה֩ פֶ֨סֶל וּמַסֵּכָ֜ה תּוֹעֲבַ֣ת יְהוָ֗ה מַעֲשֵׂ֛ה יְדֵ֥י חָרָ֖שׁ וְשָׂ֣ם בַּסָּ֑תֶר וְעָנ֧וּ כָל־הָעָ֛ם וְאָמְר֖וּ אָמֵֽן׃ ס

16Cursed be he who insults his father or mother.—And all the people shall say, Amen.

17Cursed be he who moves his fellow countryman's landmark.—And all the people shall say, Amen.

18Cursed be he who misdirects a blind person on his way.—And all the people shall say, Amen.

19Cursed be he who subverts the rights of the stranger, the fatherless, and the widow.—And all the people shall say, Amen.

20Cursed be he who lies with his father's wife, for he has removed his father's garment.d—And all the people shall say, Amen.

21Cursed be he who lies with any beast.—And all the people shall say, Amen.

22Cursed be he who lies with his sister, whether daughter of his father or of his mother.—And all the people shall say, Amen.

23Cursed be he who lies with his mother-in-law.—And all the people shall say, Amen.

24Cursed be he who strikes down his fellow countryman in secret.—And all the people shall say, Amen.

25Cursed be he who accepts a bribe e-in the case of the murder of-e an innocent person.—And all the people shall say, Amen.

26Cursed be he who will not uphold the terms of this Teaching and observe them.—And all the people shall say, Amen.

28 Now, if you obey the Lord your God, to observe faithfully all His commandments which I enjoin upon you this day, the Lord your God will set you high above all the nations of the earth. 2All these blessings shall come upon you and take effect, if you will but heed the word of the Lord your God:

---

d   See note at 23.1.
e-e   I.e., to acquit the murderer; others "to slay."

16 אָר֣וּר מַקְלֶ֥ה אָבִ֖יו וְאִמּ֑וֹ וְאָמַ֥ר כָּל־הָעָ֖ם
אָמֵ֖ן ׃ ס
17 אָר֕וּר מַסִּ֖יג גְּב֣וּל רֵעֵ֑הוּ וְאָמַ֥ר כָּל־הָעָ֖ם
אָמֵ֖ן ׃ ס
18 אָר֕וּר מַשְׁגֶּ֥ה עִוֵּ֖ר בַּדָּ֑רֶךְ וְאָמַ֥ר כָּל־הָעָ֖ם
אָמֵ֖ן ׃ ס
19 אָר֗וּר מַטֶּ֛ה מִשְׁפַּ֥ט גֵּר־יָת֖וֹם וְאַלְמָנָ֑ה
וְאָמַ֥ר כָּל־הָעָ֖ם אָמֵֽן ׃ ס
20 אָר֗וּר שֹׁכֵב֙ עִם־אֵ֣שֶׁת אָבִ֔יו כִּ֥י גִלָּ֖ה כְּנַ֣ף
אָבִ֑יו וְאָמַ֥ר כָּל־הָעָ֖ם אָמֵֽן ׃ ס
21 אָר֗וּר שֹׁכֵ֖ב עִם־כָּל־בְּהֵמָ֑ה וְאָמַ֥ר כָּל־
הָעָ֖ם אָמֵֽן ׃ ס
22 אָר֗וּר שֹׁכֵב֙ עִם־אֲחֹת֔וֹ בַּת־אָבִ֖יו א֣וֹ
בַת־אִמּ֑וֹ וְאָמַ֥ר כָּל־הָעָ֖ם אָמֵֽן ׃ ס
23 אָר֕וּר שֹׁכֵ֖ב עִם־חֹֽתַנְתּ֑וֹ וְאָמַ֥ר כָּל־הָעָ֖ם
אָמֵֽן ׃ ס
24 אָר֕וּר מַכֵּ֥ה רֵעֵ֖הוּ בַּסָּ֑תֶר וְאָמַ֥ר כָּל־
הָעָ֖ם אָמֵֽן ׃ ס
25 אָר֗וּר לֹקֵ֥חַ שֹׁ֙חַד֙ לְהַכּ֣וֹת נֶ֣פֶשׁ דָּ֣ם נָקִ֑י
וְאָמַ֥ר כָּל־הָעָ֖ם אָמֵֽן ׃ ס
26 אָר֗וּר אֲשֶׁ֧ר לֹא־יָקִ֛ים אֶת־דִּבְרֵ֥י
הַתּוֹרָֽה־הַזֹּ֖את לַעֲשׂ֣וֹת אוֹתָ֑ם וְאָמַ֥ר כָּל־
הָעָ֖ם אָמֵֽן ׃ פ

כח וְהָיָ֗ה אִם־שָׁמ֤וֹעַ תִּשְׁמַע֙ בְּקוֹל֙
יְהֹוָ֣ה אֱלֹהֶ֔יךָ לִשְׁמֹ֤ר לַעֲשׂוֹת֙ אֶת־כָּל־
מִצְוֺתָ֔יו אֲשֶׁ֛ר אָנֹכִ֥י מְצַוְּךָ֖ הַיּ֑וֹם וּנְתָ֨נְךָ֜
יְהֹוָ֤ה אֱלֹהֶ֙יךָ֙ עֶלְי֔וֹן עַ֖ל כָּל־גּוֹיֵ֥י הָאָֽרֶץ ׃
2 וּבָ֧אוּ עָלֶ֛יךָ כָּל־הַבְּרָכ֥וֹת הָאֵ֖לֶּה וְהִשִּׂיגֻ֑ךָ
כִּ֥י תִשְׁמַ֖ע בְּק֥וֹל יְהֹוָ֥ה אֱלֹהֶֽיךָ ׃

³Blessed shall you be in the city and blessed shall you be in the country.

⁴Blessed shall be the issue of your womb, the produce of your soil, and the offspring of your cattle, the calving of your herd and the lambing of your flock.

⁵Blessed shall be your basket and your kneading bowl.

⁶Blessed shall you be in your comings and blessed shall you be in your goings.

⁷The LORD will put to rout before you the enemies who attack you; they will march out against you by a single road, but flee from you by many*a* roads. ⁸The LORD will ordain blessings for you upon your barns and upon all your undertakings: He will bless you in the land that the LORD your God is giving you. ⁹The LORD will establish you as His holy people, as He swore to you, if you keep the commandments of the LORD your God and walk in His ways. ¹⁰And all the peoples of the earth shall see that the LORD's name is proclaimed over you,*b* and they shall stand in fear of you. ¹¹The LORD will give you abounding prosperity in the issue of your womb, the offspring of your cattle, and the produce of your soil in the land that the LORD swore to your fathers to assign to you. ¹²The LORD will open for you His bounteous store, the heavens, to provide rain for your land in season and to bless all your undertakings. You will be creditor to many nations, but debtor to none.

¹³The LORD will make you the head, not the tail; you will always be at the top and never at the bottom—if only you obey and faithfully observe the commandments of the LORD your God that I enjoin upon you this day, ¹⁴and do not deviate to the right or to the left from any of the commandments that I enjoin upon you this day and turn to the worship of other gods.

---

a Lit. "seven."
b I.e., the LORD recognizes you as His own; cf. Isa. 4.1.

³ בָּרוּךְ אַתָּה בָּעִיר וּבָרוּךְ אַתָּה בַּשָּׂדֶה:
⁴ בָּרוּךְ פְּרִי־בִטְנְךָ וּפְרִי אַדְמָתְךָ וּפְרִי בְהֶמְתֶּךָ שְׁגַר אֲלָפֶיךָ וְעַשְׁתְּרוֹת צֹאנֶךָ:
⁵ בָּרוּךְ טַנְאֲךָ וּמִשְׁאַרְתֶּךָ:
⁶ בָּרוּךְ אַתָּה בְּבֹאֶךָ וּבָרוּךְ אַתָּה בְּצֵאתֶךָ:
⁷ יִתֵּן יְהוָה אֶת־אֹיְבֶיךָ הַקָּמִים עָלֶיךָ נִגָּפִים לְפָנֶיךָ בְּדֶרֶךְ אֶחָד יֵצְאוּ אֵלֶיךָ וּבְשִׁבְעָה דְרָכִים יָנוּסוּ לְפָנֶיךָ: ⁸ יְצַו יְהוָה אִתְּךָ אֶת־הַבְּרָכָה בַּאֲסָמֶיךָ וּבְכֹל מִשְׁלַח יָדֶךָ וּבֵרַכְךָ בָּאָרֶץ אֲשֶׁר־יְהוָה אֱלֹהֶיךָ נֹתֵן לָךְ: ⁹ יְקִימְךָ יְהוָה לוֹ לְעַם קָדוֹשׁ כַּאֲשֶׁר נִשְׁבַּע־לָךְ כִּי תִשְׁמֹר אֶת־מִצְוֹת יְהוָה אֱלֹהֶיךָ וְהָלַכְתָּ בִּדְרָכָיו: ¹⁰ וְרָאוּ כָּל־עַמֵּי הָאָרֶץ כִּי שֵׁם יְהוָה נִקְרָא עָלֶיךָ וְיָרְאוּ מִמֶּךָּ: ¹¹ וְהוֹתִרְךָ יְהוָה לְטוֹבָה בִּפְרִי בִטְנְךָ וּבִפְרִי בְהֶמְתְּךָ וּבִפְרִי אַדְמָתֶךָ עַל הָאֲדָמָה אֲשֶׁר נִשְׁבַּע יְהוָה לַאֲבֹתֶיךָ לָתֶת לָךְ: ¹² יִפְתַּח יְהוָה ׀ לְךָ אֶת־אוֹצָרוֹ הַטּוֹב אֶת־הַשָּׁמַיִם לָתֵת מְטַר־אַרְצְךָ בְּעִתּוֹ וּלְבָרֵךְ אֵת כָּל־מַעֲשֵׂה יָדֶךָ וְהִלְוִיתָ גּוֹיִם רַבִּים וְאַתָּה לֹא תִלְוֶה:
¹³ וּנְתָנְךָ יְהוָה לְרֹאשׁ וְלֹא לְזָנָב וְהָיִיתָ רַק לְמַעְלָה וְלֹא תִהְיֶה לְמָטָּה כִּי־תִשְׁמַע אֶל־מִצְוֹת ׀ יְהוָה אֱלֹהֶיךָ אֲשֶׁר אָנֹכִי מְצַוְּךָ הַיּוֹם לִשְׁמֹר וְלַעֲשׂוֹת: ¹⁴ וְלֹא תָסוּר מִכָּל־הַדְּבָרִים אֲשֶׁר אָנֹכִי מְצַוֶּה אֶתְכֶם הַיּוֹם יָמִין וּשְׂמֹאול* לָלֶכֶת אַחֲרֵי אֱלֹהִים אֲחֵרִים לְעָבְדָם: ס

15But if you do not obey the LORD your God to observe faithfully all His commandments and laws which I enjoin upon you this day, all these curses shall come upon you and take effect:

16Cursed shall you be in the city and cursed shall you be in the country.

17Cursed shall be your basket and your kneading bowl.

18Cursed shall be the issue of your womb and the produce of your soil, the calving of your herd and the lambing of your flock.

19Cursed shall you be in your comings and cursed shall you be in your goings.

20The LORD will let loose against you calamity, panic, and frustration in all the enterprises you undertake, so that you shall soon be utterly wiped out because of your evildoing in forsaking Me. 21The LORD will make pestilence cling to you, until He has put an end to you in the land that you are entering to possess. 22The LORD will strike you with c consumption, fever, and inflammation, with scorching heat and drought, with blight and mildew; they shall hound you until you perish. 23The skies above your head shall be copper and the earth under you iron. 24The LORD will make the rain of your land dust, and sand shall drop on you from the sky, until you are wiped out.

25The LORD will put you to rout before your enemies; you shall march out against them by a single road, but flee from them by many^a roads; and you shall become a horror to all the kingdoms of the earth. 26Your carcasses shall become food for all the birds of the sky and all the beasts of the earth, with none to frighten them off.

27The LORD will strike you with the Egyptian inflammation,^{d} with hemorrhoids, boil-scars, and itch, from which you shall never recover.

15 וְהָיָה אִם־לֹא תִשְׁמַע בְּקוֹל יְהוָה אֱלֹהֶיךָ לִשְׁמֹר לַעֲשׂוֹת אֶת־כָּל־מִצְוֺתָיו וְחֻקֹּתָיו אֲשֶׁר אָנֹכִי מְצַוְּךָ הַיּוֹם וּבָאוּ עָלֶיךָ כָּל־הַקְּלָלוֹת הָאֵלֶּה וְהִשִּׂיגוּךָ: 16 אָרוּר אַתָּה בָּעִיר וְאָרוּר אַתָּה בַּשָּׂדֶה: 17 אָרוּר טַנְאֲךָ וּמִשְׁאַרְתֶּךָ: 18 אָרוּר פְּרִי־בִטְנְךָ וּפְרִי אַדְמָתֶךָ שְׁגַר אֲלָפֶיךָ וְעַשְׁתְּרוֹת צֹאנֶךָ: 19 אָרוּר אַתָּה בְּבֹאֶךָ וְאָרוּר אַתָּה בְּצֵאתֶךָ: 20 יְשַׁלַּח יְהוָה בְּךָ אֶת־הַמְּאֵרָה אֶת־הַמְּהוּמָה וְאֶת־הַמִּגְעֶרֶת בְּכָל־מִשְׁלַח יָדְךָ אֲשֶׁר תַּעֲשֶׂה עַד הִשָּׁמֶדְךָ וְעַד־אֲבָדְךָ מַהֵר מִפְּנֵי רֹעַ מַעֲלָלֶיךָ אֲשֶׁר עֲזַבְתָּנִי: 21 יַדְבֵּק יְהוָה בְּךָ אֶת־הַדָּבֶר עַד כַּלֹּתוֹ אֹתְךָ מֵעַל הָאֲדָמָה אֲשֶׁר־אַתָּה בָא־שָׁמָּה לְרִשְׁתָּהּ: 22 יַכְּכָה יְהוָה בַּשַּׁחֶפֶת וּבַקַּדַּחַת וּבַדַּלֶּקֶת וּבַחַרְחֻר וּבַחֶרֶב וּבַשִּׁדָּפוֹן וּבַיֵּרָקוֹן וּרְדָפוּךָ עַד אָבְדֶךָ: 23 וְהָיוּ שָׁמֶיךָ אֲשֶׁר עַל־רֹאשְׁךָ נְחֹשֶׁת וְהָאָרֶץ אֲשֶׁר־תַּחְתֶּיךָ בַּרְזֶל: 24 יִתֵּן יְהוָה אֶת־מְטַר אַרְצְךָ אָבָק וְעָפָר מִן־הַשָּׁמַיִם יֵרֵד עָלֶיךָ עַד הִשָּׁמְדָךְ: 25 יִתֶּנְךָ יְהוָה נִגָּף לִפְנֵי אֹיְבֶיךָ בְּדֶרֶךְ אֶחָד תֵּצֵא אֵלָיו וּבְשִׁבְעָה דְרָכִים תָּנוּס לְפָנָיו וְהָיִיתָ לְזַעֲוָה לְכֹל מַמְלְכוֹת הָאָרֶץ: 26 וְהָיְתָה נִבְלָתְךָ לְמַאֲכָל לְכָל־עוֹף הַשָּׁמַיִם וּלְבֶהֱמַת הָאָרֶץ וְאֵין מַחֲרִיד: 27 יַכְּכָה יְהוָה בִּשְׁחִין מִצְרַיִם וּבַעֳפָלִים וּבַגָּרָב וּבֶחָרֶס אֲשֶׁר לֹא־תוּכַל לְהֵרָפֵא:

---

c   Exact nature of these afflictions uncertain.
d   See Exod. 9.9–10.

434

28The LORD will strike you with madness, blindness, and dismay.e 29You shall grope at noon as a blind man gropes in the dark; you shall not prosper in your ventures, but shall be constantly abused and robbed, with none to give help.

30If you pay the bride-price for a wife, another man shall enjoy her. If you build a house, you shall not live in it. If you plant a vineyard, you shall not harvest it.f 31Your ox shall be slaughtered before your eyes, but you shall not eat of it; your ass shall be seized in front of you, and it shall not be returned to you; your flock shall be delivered to your enemies, with none to help you. 32Your sons and daughters shall be delivered to another people, while you look on; and your eyes shall strain for them constantly, but you shall be helpless. 33A people you do not know shall eat up the produce of your soil and all your gains; you shall be abused and downtrodden continually, 34until you are driven mad by what your eyes behold. 35The LORD will afflict you at the knees and thighs with a severe inflammation, from which you shall never recover—from the sole of your foot to the crown of your head.

36The LORD will drive you, and the king you have set over you, to a nation unknown to you or your fathers, where you shall serve other gods, of wood and stone. 37You shall be a consternation, a proverb, and a byword among all the peoples to which the LORD will drive you.

38Though you take much seed out to the field, you shall gather in little, for the locust shall consume it. 39Though you plant vineyards and till them, you shall have no wine to drink or store, for the worm shall devour them. 40Though you have olive trees throughout your territory, you shall have no oil for anointment, for your olives shall drop off. 41Though you beget sons and

---

e Lit. "numbness of heart."
f Cf. 20.6.

435

28 יַכְּכָ֣ה יְהֹוָ֔ה בְּשִׁגָּע֖וֹן וּבְעִוָּר֑וֹן וּבְתִמְה֖וֹן לֵבָֽב: 29 וְהָיִ֜יתָ מְמַשֵּׁ֣שׁ בַּֽצׇּהֳרַ֗יִם כַּאֲשֶׁ֨ר יְמַשֵּׁ֤שׁ הָֽעִוֵּר֙ בָּאֲפֵלָ֔ה וְלֹ֥א תַצְלִ֖יחַ אֶת־דְּרָכֶ֑יךָ וְהָיִ֜יתָ אַ֣ךְ עָשׁ֧וּק וְגָז֛וּל כׇּל־הַיָּמִ֖ים וְאֵ֥ין מוֹשִֽׁיעַ:

30 אִשָּׁ֣ה תְאָרֵ֗שׂ וְאִ֤ישׁ אַחֵר֙ יִשְׁגָּלֶ֔נָּה בַּ֥יִת תִּבְנֶ֖ה וְלֹא־תֵשֵׁ֣ב בּ֑וֹ כֶּ֥רֶם תִּטַּ֖ע וְלֹ֥א תְחַלְּלֶֽנּוּ: 31 שׁוֹרְךָ֞ טָב֣וּחַ לְעֵינֶ֗יךָ וְלֹ֣א תֹאכַל֮ מִמֶּנּוּ֒ חֲמֹֽרְךָ֙ גָּז֣וּל מִלְּפָנֶ֔יךָ וְלֹ֥א יָשׁ֖וּב לָ֑ךְ צֹֽאנְךָ֙ נְתֻנ֣וֹת לְאֹיְבֶ֔יךָ וְאֵ֥ין לְךָ֖ מוֹשִֽׁיעַ: 32 בָּנֶ֨יךָ וּבְנֹתֶ֜יךָ נְתֻנִ֨ים לְעַ֤ם אַחֵר֙ וְעֵינֶ֣יךָ רֹא֔וֹת וְכָל֥וֹת אֲלֵיהֶ֖ם כׇּל־הַיּ֑וֹם וְאֵ֥ין לְאֵ֖ל יָדֶֽךָ: 33 פְּרִ֤י אַדְמָֽתְךָ֙ וְכׇל־יְגִ֣יעֲךָ֔ יֹאכַ֥ל עַ֖ם אֲשֶׁ֣ר לֹא־יָדָ֑עְתָּ וְהָיִ֗יתָ רַ֛ק עָשׁ֥וּק וְרָצ֖וּץ כׇּל־הַיָּמִֽים: 34 וְהָיִ֖יתָ מְשֻׁגָּ֑ע מִמַּרְאֵ֥ה עֵינֶ֖יךָ אֲשֶׁ֥ר תִּרְאֶֽה: 35 יַכְּכָ֨ה יְהֹוָ֜ה בִּשְׁחִ֣ין רָ֗ע עַל־הַבִּרְכַּ֙יִם֙ וְעַל־הַשֹּׁקַ֔יִם אֲשֶׁ֥ר לֹא־תוּכַ֖ל לְהֵרָפֵ֑א מִכַּ֥ף רַגְלְךָ֖ וְעַ֥ד קׇדְקֳדֶֽךָ:

36 יוֹלֵ֨ךְ יְהֹוָ֜ה אֹֽתְךָ֗ וְאֶֽת־מַלְכְּךָ֙ אֲשֶׁ֣ר תָּקִ֣ים עָלֶ֔יךָ אֶל־גּ֕וֹי אֲשֶׁ֥ר לֹא־יָדַ֖עְתָּ אַתָּ֣ה וַאֲבֹתֶ֑יךָ וְעָבַ֥דְתָּ שָּׁ֛ם אֱלֹהִ֥ים אֲחֵרִ֖ים עֵ֥ץ וָאָֽבֶן: 37 וְהָיִ֣יתָ לְשַׁמָּ֔ה לְמָשָׁ֖ל וְלִשְׁנִינָ֑ה בְּכֹל֙ הָֽעַמִּ֔ים אֲשֶׁר־יְנַהֶגְךָ֥ יְהֹוָ֖ה שָֽׁמָּה: 38 זֶ֥רַע רַ֖ב תּוֹצִ֣יא הַשָּׂדֶ֑ה וּמְעַ֣ט תֶּאֱסֹ֔ף כִּ֥י יַחְסְלֶ֖נּוּ הָאַרְבֶּֽה: 39 כְּרָמִ֥ים תִּטַּ֖ע וְעָבָ֑דְתָּ וְיַ֤יִן לֹֽא־תִשְׁתֶּה֙ וְלֹ֣א תֶאֱגֹ֔ר כִּ֥י תֹאכְלֶ֖נּוּ הַתֹּלָֽעַת: 40 זֵיתִ֛ים יִהְי֥וּ לְךָ֖ בְּכׇל־גְּבוּלֶ֑ךָ וְשֶׁ֙מֶן֙ לֹ֣א תָס֔וּךְ כִּ֥י יִשַּׁ֖ל זֵיתֶֽךָ: 41 בָּנִ֥ים וּבָנ֖וֹת תּוֹלִ֑יד וְלֹא־יִהְי֣וּ לָ֔ךְ כִּ֥י

daughters, they shall not remain with you, for they shall go into captivity. 42The cricket shall take over all the trees and produce of your land.

43The stranger in your midst shall rise above you higher and higher, while you sink lower and lower: 44he shall be your creditor, but you shall not be his; he shall be the head and you the tail.

45All these curses shall befall you; they shall pursue you and overtake you, until you are wiped out, because you did not heed the Lord your God and keep the commandments and laws that He enjoined upon you. 46They shall serve as signs and proofs against you and your offspring for all time. 47Because you would not serve the Lord your God in joy and gladness over the abundance of everything, 48you shall have to serve—in hunger and thirst, naked and lacking everything—the enemies whom the Lord will let loose against you. He will put an iron yoke upon your neck until He has wiped you out.

49The Lord will bring a nation against you from afar, from the end of the earth, which will swoop down like the eagle—a nation whose language you do not understand, 50a ruthless nation, that will show the old no regard and the young no mercy. 51It shall devour the offspring of your cattle and the produce of your soil, until you have been wiped out, leaving you nothing of new grain, wine, or oil, of the calving of your herds and the lambing of your flocks, until it has brought you to ruin. 52It shall shut you up in all your towns throughout your land until every mighty, towering wall in which you trust has come down. And when you are shut up in all your towns throughout your land that the Lord your God has assigned to you, 53you shall eat your own issue, the flesh of your sons and daughters that the Lord your God has assigned to you, because of the desperate straits to which your enemy shall reduce you. 54He who is most

יֵלְכוּ בַשֶּׁבִי: 42 כָּל־עֵצְךָ וּפְרִי אַדְמָתֶךָ יְיָרֵשׁ הַצְּלָצַל: 43 הַגֵּר אֲשֶׁר בְּקִרְבְּךָ יַעֲלֶה עָלֶיךָ מַעְלָה מָּעְלָה וְאַתָּה תֵרֵד מַטָּה מָּטָּה: 44 הוּא יַלְוְךָ וְאַתָּה לֹא תַלְוֶנּוּ הוּא יִהְיֶה לְרֹאשׁ וְאַתָּה תִּהְיֶה לְזָנָב: 45 וּבָאוּ עָלֶיךָ כָּל־הַקְּלָלוֹת הָאֵלֶּה וּרְדָפוּךָ וְהִשִּׂיגוּךָ עַד הִשָּׁמְדָךְ כִּי־לֹא שָׁמַעְתָּ בְּקוֹל יְהוָה אֱלֹהֶיךָ לִשְׁמֹר מִצְוֹתָיו וְחֻקֹּתָיו אֲשֶׁר צִוָּךְ: 46 וְהָיוּ בְךָ לְאוֹת וּלְמוֹפֵת וּבְזַרְעֲךָ עַד־עוֹלָם: 47 תַּחַת אֲשֶׁר לֹא־עָבַדְתָּ אֶת־יְהוָה אֱלֹהֶיךָ בְּשִׂמְחָה וּבְטוּב לֵבָב מֵרֹב כֹּל: 48 וְעָבַדְתָּ אֶת־אֹיְבֶיךָ אֲשֶׁר יְשַׁלְּחֶנּוּ יְהוָה בָּךְ בְּרָעָב וּבְצָמָא וּבְעֵירֹם וּבְחֹסֶר כֹּל וְנָתַן עֹל בַּרְזֶל עַל־צַוָּארֶךָ עַד הִשְׁמִידוֹ אֹתָךְ: 49 יִשָּׂא יְהוָה עָלֶיךָ גּוֹי מֵרָחֹק מִקְצֵה הָאָרֶץ כַּאֲשֶׁר יִדְאֶה הַנָּשֶׁר גּוֹי אֲשֶׁר לֹא־תִשְׁמַע לְשֹׁנוֹ: 50 גּוֹי עַז פָּנִים אֲשֶׁר לֹא־יִשָּׂא פָנִים לְזָקֵן וְנַעַר לֹא יָחֹן: 51 וְאָכַל פְּרִי בְהֶמְתְּךָ וּפְרִי־אַדְמָתְךָ עַד הִשָּׁמְדָךְ אֲשֶׁר לֹא־יַשְׁאִיר לְךָ דָּגָן תִּירוֹשׁ וְיִצְהָר שְׁגַר אֲלָפֶיךָ וְעַשְׁתְּרֹת צֹאנֶךָ עַד הַאֲבִידוֹ אֹתָךְ: 52 וְהֵצַר לְךָ בְּכָל־שְׁעָרֶיךָ עַד רֶדֶת חֹמֹתֶיךָ הַגְּבֹהוֹת וְהַבְּצֻרוֹת אֲשֶׁר אַתָּה בֹּטֵחַ בָּהֵן בְּכָל־אַרְצֶךָ וְהֵצַר לְךָ בְּכָל־שְׁעָרֶיךָ בְּכָל־אַרְצְךָ אֲשֶׁר נָתַן יְהוָה אֱלֹהֶיךָ לָךְ: 53 וְאָכַלְתָּ פְרִי־בִטְנְךָ בְּשַׂר בָּנֶיךָ וּבְנֹתֶיךָ אֲשֶׁר נָתַן־לְךָ יְהוָה אֱלֹהֶיךָ בְּמָצוֹר וּבְמָצוֹק אֲשֶׁר־יָצִיק לְךָ אֹיְבֶךָ:

tender and fastidious among you shall be too mean to his brother and the wife of his bosom and the children he has spared [55]to share with any of them the flesh of the children that he eats, because he has nothing else left as a result of the desperate straits to which your enemy shall reduce you in all your towns. [56]And she who is most tender and dainty among you, so tender and dainty that she would never venture to set a foot on the ground, shall begrudge the husband of her bosom, and her son and her daughter, [57]the afterbirth that issues from between her legs and the babies she bears; she shall eat them secretly, because of utter want, in the desperate straits to which your enemy shall reduce you in your towns.

[58]If you fail to observe faithfully all the terms of this Teaching that are written in this book, to reverence this honored and awesome Name, the LORD your God, [59]the LORD will inflict extraordinary plagues upon you and your offspring, strange and lasting plagues, malignant and chronic diseases. [60]He will bring back upon you all the sicknesses of Egypt that you dreaded so, and they shall cling to you. [61]Moreover, the LORD will bring upon you all the other diseases and plagues that are not mentioned in this book of Teaching, until you are wiped out. [62]You shall be left a scant few, after having been as numerous as the stars in the skies, because you did not heed the command of the LORD your God. [63]And as the LORD once delighted in making you prosperous and many, so will the LORD now delight in causing you to perish and in wiping you out; you shall be torn from the land that you are about to enter and possess.

[64]The LORD will scatter you among all the peoples from one end of the earth to the other, and there you shall serve other gods, wood and stone, whom neither you nor your ancestors have experienced.g [65]Yet even among those na-

54 הָאִישׁ הָרַךְ בְּךָ וְהֶעָנֹג מְאֹד תֵּרַע עֵינוֹ בְאָחִיו וּבְאֵשֶׁת חֵיקוֹ וּבְיֶתֶר בָּנָיו אֲשֶׁר יוֹתִיר: 55 מִתֵּת ׀ לְאַחַד מֵהֶם מִבְּשַׂר בָּנָיו אֲשֶׁר יֹאכֵל מִבְּלִי הִשְׁאִיר־לוֹ כֹּל בְּמָצוֹר וּבְמָצוֹק אֲשֶׁר יָצִיק לְךָ אֹיִבְךָ בְּכָל־ שְׁעָרֶיךָ: 56 הָרַכָּה בְךָ וְהָעֲנֻגָּה אֲשֶׁר לֹא־ נִסְּתָה כַף־רַגְלָהּ הַצֵּג עַל־הָאָרֶץ מֵהִתְעַנֵּג וּמֵרֹךְ תֵּרַע עֵינָהּ בְּאִישׁ חֵיקָהּ וּבִבְנָהּ וּבְבִתָּהּ: 57 וּבְשִׁלְיָתָהּ הַיּוֹצֵת* ׀ מִבֵּין רַגְלֶיהָ וּבְבָנֶיהָ אֲשֶׁר תֵּלֵד כִּי־תֹאכְלֵם בְּחֹסֶר־כֹּל בַּסָּתֶר בְּמָצוֹר וּבְמָצוֹק אֲשֶׁר יָצִיק לְךָ אֹיִבְךָ בִּשְׁעָרֶיךָ:

58 אִם־לֹא תִשְׁמֹר לַעֲשׂוֹת אֶת־כָּל־דִּבְרֵי הַתּוֹרָה הַזֹּאת הַכְּתוּבִים בַּסֵּפֶר הַזֶּה לְיִרְאָה אֶת־הַשֵּׁם הַנִּכְבָּד וְהַנּוֹרָא הַזֶּה אֵת יְהֹוָה אֱלֹהֶיךָ: 59 וְהִפְלָא יְהֹוָה אֶת־ מַכֹּתְךָ וְאֵת מַכּוֹת זַרְעֶךָ מַכּוֹת גְּדֹלוֹת וְנֶאֱמָנוֹת וָחֳלָיִם רָעִים וְנֶאֱמָנִים: 60 וְהֵשִׁיב בְּךָ אֵת כָּל־מַדְוֵה מִצְרַיִם אֲשֶׁר יָגֹרְתָּ מִפְּנֵיהֶם וְדָבְקוּ בָּךְ: 61 גַּם כָּל־חֳלִי וְכָל־מַכָּה אֲשֶׁר לֹא כָתוּב בְּסֵפֶר הַתּוֹרָה הַזֹּאת יַעְלֵם יְהֹוָה עָלֶיךָ עַד הִשָּׁמְדָךְ: 62 וְנִשְׁאַרְתֶּם בִּמְתֵי מְעָט תַּחַת אֲשֶׁר הֱיִיתֶם כְּכוֹכְבֵי הַשָּׁמַיִם לָרֹב כִּי־לֹא שָׁמַעְתָּ בְּקוֹל יְהֹוָה אֱלֹהֶיךָ: 63 וְהָיָה כַּאֲשֶׁר־שָׂשׂ יְהֹוָה עֲלֵיכֶם לְהֵיטִיב אֶתְכֶם וּלְהַרְבּוֹת אֶתְכֶם כֵּן יָשִׂישׂ יְהֹוָה עֲלֵיכֶם לְהַאֲבִיד אֶתְכֶם וּלְהַשְׁמִיד אֶתְכֶם וְנִסַּחְתֶּם מֵעַל הָאֲדָמָה אֲשֶׁר־אַתָּה בָא־ שָׁמָּה לְרִשְׁתָּהּ: 64 וֶהֱפִיצְךָ יְהֹוָה בְּכָל־הָעַמִּים מִקְצֵה הָאָרֶץ וְעַד־קְצֵה הָאָרֶץ וְעָבַדְתָּ שָּׁם אֱלֹהִים אֲחֵרִים אֲשֶׁר לֹא־יָדַעְתָּ אַתָּה וַאֲבֹתֶיךָ עֵץ וָאָבֶן: 65 וּבַגּוֹיִם הָהֵם לֹא

g　See note at 11.28.

tions you shall find no peace, nor shall your foot find a place to rest. The LORD will give you there an anguished heart and eyes that pine and a despondent spirit. 66The life you face shall be precarious; you shall be in terror, night and day, with no assurance of survival. 67In the morning you shall say, "If only it were evening!" and in the evening you shall say, "If only it were morning!"—because of what your heart shall dread and your eyes shall see. 68The LORD will send you back to Egypt in galleys, by a route which I told you you should not see again. There you shall offer yourselves for sale to your enemies as male and female slaves, but none will buy.

69These are the terms of the covenant which the LORD commanded Moses to conclude with the Israelites in the land of Moab, in addition to the covenant which He had made with them at Horeb.

29

Moses summoned all Israel and said to them:

You have seen all that the LORD did before your very eyes in the land of Egypt, to Pharaoh and to all his courtiers and to his whole country: 2the wondrous feats that you saw with your own eyes, those prodigious signs and marvels. 3Yet to this day the LORD has not given you a mind to understand or eyes to see or ears to hear.

4I led you through the wilderness forty years; the clothes on your back did not wear out, nor did the sandals on your feet; 5you had no bread to eat and no wine or other intoxicant to drink—that you might know that I the LORD am your God.

6When you reached this place, King Sihon of Heshbon and King Og of Bashan came out to engage us in battle, but we defeated them. 7We

תַּרְגִּיעַ וְלֹא־יִהְיֶה מָנוֹחַ לְכַף־רַגְלֶךָ וְנָתַן
יְהוָה לְךָ שָׁם לֵב רַגָּז וְכִלְיוֹן עֵינַיִם וְדַאֲבוֹן
נָפֶשׁ: 66 וְהָיוּ חַיֶּיךָ תְּלֻאִים לְךָ מִנֶּגֶד
וּפָחַדְתָּ לַיְלָה וְיוֹמָם וְלֹא תַאֲמִין בְּחַיֶּיךָ:
67 בַּבֹּקֶר תֹּאמַר מִי־יִתֵּן עֶרֶב וּבָעֶרֶב
תֹּאמַר מִי־יִתֵּן בֹּקֶר מִפַּחַד לְבָבְךָ אֲשֶׁר
תִּפְחָד וּמִמַּרְאֵה עֵינֶיךָ אֲשֶׁר תִּרְאֶה:
68 וֶהֱשִׁיבְךָ יְהוָה ׀ מִצְרַיִם בָּאֳנִיּוֹת בַּדֶּרֶךְ
אֲשֶׁר אָמַרְתִּי לְךָ לֹא־תֹסִיף עוֹד לִרְאֹתָהּ
וְהִתְמַכַּרְתֶּם שָׁם לְאֹיְבֶיךָ לַעֲבָדִים
וְלִשְׁפָחוֹת וְאֵין קֹנֶה: ס

69 אֵלֶּה דִבְרֵי הַבְּרִית אֲשֶׁר־צִוָּה יְהוָה
אֶת־מֹשֶׁה לִכְרֹת אֶת־בְּנֵי יִשְׂרָאֵל בְּאֶרֶץ
מוֹאָב מִלְּבַד הַבְּרִית אֲשֶׁר־כָּרַת אִתָּם
בְּחֹרֵב: פ

כט וַיִּקְרָא מֹשֶׁה אֶל־כָּל־יִשְׂרָאֵל
וַיֹּאמֶר אֲלֵהֶם
אַתֶּם רְאִיתֶם אֵת כָּל־אֲשֶׁר עָשָׂה יְהוָה
לְעֵינֵיכֶם בְּאֶרֶץ מִצְרַיִם לְפַרְעֹה וּלְכָל־
עֲבָדָיו וּלְכָל־אַרְצוֹ: 2 הַמַּסּוֹת הַגְּדֹלֹת
אֲשֶׁר רָאוּ עֵינֶיךָ הָאֹתֹת וְהַמֹּפְתִים
הַגְּדֹלִים הָהֵם: 3 וְלֹא־נָתַן יְהוָה לָכֶם לֵב
לָדַעַת וְעֵינַיִם לִרְאוֹת וְאָזְנַיִם לִשְׁמֹעַ עַד
הַיּוֹם הַזֶּה:
4 וָאוֹלֵךְ אֶתְכֶם אַרְבָּעִים שָׁנָה בַּמִּדְבָּר
לֹא־בָלוּ שַׂלְמֹתֵיכֶם מֵעֲלֵיכֶם וְנַעַלְךָ לֹא־
בָלְתָה מֵעַל רַגְלֶךָ: 5 לֶחֶם לֹא אֲכַלְתֶּם
וְיַיִן וְשֵׁכָר לֹא שְׁתִיתֶם לְמַעַן תֵּדְעוּ כִּי
אֲנִי יְהוָה אֱלֹהֵיכֶם:
6 וַתָּבֹאוּ אֶל־הַמָּקוֹם הַזֶּה וַיֵּצֵא סִיחֹן
מֶלֶךְ־חֶשְׁבּוֹן וְעוֹג מֶלֶךְ־הַבָּשָׁן לִקְרָאתֵנוּ

took their land and gave it to the Reubenites, the Gadites, and the half-tribe of Manasseh as their heritage. [8]Therefore observe faithfully all the terms of this covenant, that you may succeed in all that you undertake.

NITSAVIM

[9]You stand this day, all of you, before the LORD your God—your tribal heads, your elders and your officials, all the men of Israel, [10]your children, your wives, even the stranger within your camp, from woodchopper to water drawer—[11]to enter into the covenant of the LORD your God, which the LORD your God is concluding with you this day, with its sanctions;[a] [12]to the end that He may establish you this day as His people and be your God, as He promised you and as He swore to your fathers, Abraham, Isaac, and Jacob. [13]I make this covenant, with its sanctions, not with you alone, [14]but both with those who are standing here with us this day before the LORD our God and with those who are not with us here this day.

[15]Well you know that we dwelt in the land of Egypt and that we passed through the midst of various other nations through which you passed; [16]and you have seen the detestable things and the fetishes of wood and stone, silver and gold, that they keep. [17]Perchance there is among you some man or woman, or some clan or tribe, whose heart is even now turning away from the LORD our God to go and worship the gods of those nations—perchance there is among you a stock sprouting poison weed and wormwood. [18]When such a one hears the words of these sanctions, he may fancy himself immune, thinking, "I shall be safe, though I follow my own willful heart"—to the utter ruin of moist and dry alike.[b] [19]The LORD will never for-

---

a I.e., the curses that violations of the covenant will entail.
b I.e., everything.

לַמִּלְחָמָ֑ה וַנַּכֵּ֑ם: 7 וַנִּקַּח֙ אֶת־אַרְצָ֔ם וַנִּתְּנָ֣הּ לְנַחֲלָ֗ה לָרֽאוּבֵנִי֙ וְלַגָּדִ֔י וְלַחֲצִ֖י שֵׁ֣בֶט הַֽמְנַשִּֽׁי׃ 8 וּשְׁמַרְתֶּ֗ם אֶת־דִּבְרֵי֙ הַבְּרִ֣ית הַזֹּ֔את וַעֲשִׂיתֶ֖ם אֹתָ֑ם לְמַ֣עַן תַּשְׂכִּ֔ילוּ אֵ֖ת כָּל־אֲשֶׁ֥ר תַּעֲשֽׂוּן׃ פ

נצבים

9 אַתֶּ֨ם נִצָּבִ֤ים הַיּוֹם֙ כֻּלְּכֶ֔ם לִפְנֵ֖י יְהוָ֣ה אֱלֹהֵיכֶ֑ם רָאשֵׁיכֶ֣ם שִׁבְטֵיכֶ֗ם זִקְנֵיכֶם֙ וְשֹׁ֣טְרֵיכֶ֔ם כֹּ֖ל אִ֥ישׁ יִשְׂרָאֵֽל׃ 10 טַפְּכֶ֣ם נְשֵׁיכֶ֔ם וְגֵ֣רְךָ֔ אֲשֶׁ֖ר בְּקֶ֣רֶב מַחֲנֶ֑יךָ מֵחֹטֵ֣ב עֵצֶ֔יךָ עַ֖ד שֹׁאֵ֥ב מֵימֶֽיךָ׃ 11 לְעָבְרְךָ֗ בִּבְרִ֛ית יְהוָ֥ה אֱלֹהֶ֖יךָ וּבְאָלָת֑וֹ אֲשֶׁר֙ יְהוָ֣ה אֱלֹהֶ֔יךָ כֹּרֵ֥ת עִמְּךָ֖ הַיּֽוֹם׃ 12 לְמַ֣עַן הָקִֽים־אֹתְךָ֩ הַיּ֨וֹם ׀ ל֜וֹ לְעָ֗ם וְה֤וּא יִֽהְיֶה־לְּךָ֙ לֵֽאלֹהִ֔ים כַּאֲשֶׁ֖ר דִּבֶּר־לָ֑ךְ וְכַאֲשֶׁ֥ר נִשְׁבַּ֖ע לַאֲבֹתֶ֔יךָ לְאַבְרָהָ֥ם לְיִצְחָ֖ק וּֽלְיַעֲקֹֽב׃ 13 וְלֹ֥א אִתְּכֶ֖ם לְבַדְּכֶ֑ם אָנֹכִ֗י כֹּרֵת֙ אֶת־הַבְּרִ֣ית הַזֹּ֔את וְאֶת־הָאָלָ֖ה הַזֹּֽאת׃ 14 כִּי֩ אֶת־אֲשֶׁ֨ר יֶשְׁנ֜וֹ פֹּ֗ה עִמָּ֙נוּ֙ עֹמֵ֣ד הַיּ֔וֹם לִפְנֵ֖י יְהוָ֣ה אֱלֹהֵ֑ינוּ וְאֵ֨ת אֲשֶׁ֥ר אֵינֶ֛נּוּ פֹּ֖ה עִמָּ֥נוּ הַיּֽוֹם׃ 15 כִּֽי־אַתֶּ֣ם יְדַעְתֶּ֔ם אֵ֥ת אֲשֶׁר־יָשַׁ֖בְנוּ בְּאֶ֣רֶץ מִצְרָ֑יִם וְאֵ֧ת אֲשֶׁר־עָבַ֛רְנוּ בְּקֶ֥רֶב הַגּוֹיִ֖ם אֲשֶׁ֥ר עֲבַרְתֶּֽם׃ 16 וַתִּרְאוּ֙ אֶת־שִׁקּ֣וּצֵיהֶ֔ם וְאֵ֖ת גִּלֻּלֵיהֶ֑ם עֵ֣ץ וָאֶ֔בֶן כֶּ֥סֶף וְזָהָ֖ב אֲשֶׁ֥ר עִמָּהֶֽם׃ 17 פֶּן־יֵ֣שׁ בָּכֶ֡ם אִ֣ישׁ אֽוֹ־אִשָּׁה֩ א֨וֹ מִשְׁפָּחָ֜ה אֽוֹ־שֵׁ֗בֶט אֲשֶׁר֩ לְבָב֨וֹ פֹנֶ֤ה הַיּוֹם֙ מֵעִם֙ יְהוָ֣ה אֱלֹהֵ֔ינוּ לָלֶ֣כֶת לַעֲבֹ֔ד אֶת־אֱלֹהֵ֖י הַגּוֹיִ֣ם הָהֵ֑ם פֶּן־יֵ֣שׁ בָּכֶ֗ם שֹׁ֛רֶשׁ פֹּרֶ֥ה רֹ֖אשׁ וְלַעֲנָֽה׃ 18 וְהָיָ֡ה בְּשָׁמְעוֹ֩ אֶת־דִּבְרֵ֨י הָֽאָלָ֜ה הַזֹּ֗את וְהִתְבָּרֵ֤ךְ בִּלְבָבוֹ֙ לֵאמֹר֙ שָׁל֣וֹם יִֽהְיֶה־לִּ֔י כִּ֛י בִּשְׁרִר֥וּת לִבִּ֖י אֵלֵ֑ךְ לְמַ֛עַן סְפ֥וֹת הָרָוָ֖ה אֶת־הַצְּמֵאָֽה׃ 19 לֹא־יֹאבֶ֣ה יְהוָה֮ סְלֹ֣חַ לוֹ֒

give him; rather will the Lord's anger and passion rage against that man, till every sanction recorded in this book comes down upon him, and the Lord blots out his name from under heaven.

20The Lord will single them[c] out from all the tribes of Israel for misfortune, in accordance with all the sanctions of the covenant recorded in this book of Teaching. 21And later generations will ask—the children who succeed you, and foreigners who come from distant lands and see the plagues and diseases that the Lord has inflicted upon that land, 22all its soil devastated by sulfur and salt, beyond sowing and producing, no grass growing in it, just like the upheaval of Sodom and Gomorrah, Admah and Zeboiim, which the Lord overthrew in His fierce anger—23all nations will ask, "Why did the Lord do thus to this land? Wherefore that awful wrath?" 24They will be told, "Because they forsook the covenant that the Lord, God of their fathers, made with them when He freed them from the land of Egypt; 25they turned to the service of other gods and worshiped them, gods whom they had not experienced[d] and whom He had not allotted[e] to them. 26So the Lord was incensed at that land and brought upon it all the curses recorded in this book. 27The Lord uprooted them from their soil in anger, fury, and great wrath, and cast them into another land, as is still the case."

28Concealed acts concern the Lord our God; but with overt acts, it is for us and our children ever to apply all the provisions of this Teaching.

30

When all these things befall you—the blessing and the curse that I have set before you—and you take them to heart amidst the

---

c *I.e., clan or tribe, v. 17.*
d *See note at 11.28.*
e *See 4.19–20.*

כִּי אָז יֶעְשַׁן אַף־יְהֹוָה וְקִנְאָתוֹ בָּאִישׁ הַהוּא וְרָבְצָה בּוֹ כׇּל־הָאָלָה הַכְּתוּבָה בַּסֵּפֶר הַזֶּה וּמָחָה יְהֹוָה אֶת־שְׁמוֹ מִתַּחַת הַשָּׁמָיִם:

20וְהִבְדִּילוֹ יְהֹוָה לְרָעָה מִכֹּל שִׁבְטֵי יִשְׂרָאֵל כְּכֹל אָלוֹת הַבְּרִית הַכְּתוּבָה בְּסֵפֶר הַתּוֹרָה הַזֶּה: 21וְאָמַר הַדּוֹר הָאַחֲרוֹן בְּנֵיכֶם אֲשֶׁר יָקוּמוּ מֵאַחֲרֵיכֶם וְהַנׇּכְרִי אֲשֶׁר יָבֹא מֵאֶרֶץ רְחוֹקָה וְרָאוּ אֶת־מַכּוֹת הָאָרֶץ הַהִוא וְאֶת־תַּחֲלֻאֶיהָ אֲשֶׁר־חִלָּה יְהֹוָה בָּהּ: 22גׇּפְרִית וָמֶלַח שְׂרֵפָה כׇל־אַרְצָהּ לֹא תִזָּרַע וְלֹא תַצְמִחַ וְלֹא־יַעֲלֶה בָהּ כׇּל־עֵשֶׂב כְּמַהְפֵּכַת סְדֹם וַעֲמֹרָה אַדְמָה וּצְבֹיִים אֲשֶׁר הָפַךְ יְהֹוָה בְּאַפּוֹ וּבַחֲמָתוֹ: 23וְאָמְרוּ כׇּל־הַגּוֹיִם עַל־מֶה עָשָׂה יְהֹוָה כָּכָה לָאָרֶץ הַזֹּאת מֶה חֳרִי הָאַף הַגָּדוֹל הַזֶּה: 24וְאָמְרוּ עַל אֲשֶׁר עָזְבוּ אֶת־בְּרִית יְהֹוָה אֱלֹהֵי אֲבֹתָם אֲשֶׁר כָּרַת עִמָּם בְּהוֹצִיאוֹ אֹתָם מֵאֶרֶץ מִצְרָיִם: 25וַיֵּלְכוּ וַיַּעַבְדוּ אֱלֹהִים אֲחֵרִים וַיִּשְׁתַּחֲווּ לָהֶם אֱלֹהִים אֲשֶׁר לֹא־יְדָעוּם וְלֹא חָלַק לָהֶם: 26וַיִּחַר־אַף יְהֹוָה בָּאָרֶץ הַהִוא לְהָבִיא עָלֶיהָ אֶת־כׇּל־הַקְּלָלָה הַכְּתוּבָה בַּסֵּפֶר הַזֶּה: 27וַיִּתְּשֵׁם יְהֹוָה מֵעַל אַדְמָתָם בְּאַף וּבְחֵמָה וּבְקֶצֶף גָּדוֹל וַיַּשְׁלִכֵם* אֶל־אֶרֶץ אַחֶרֶת כַּיּוֹם הַזֶּה: 28הַנִּסְתָּרֹת לַיהֹוָה אֱלֹהֵינוּ וְהַנִּגְלֹת לָנוּ וּלְבָנֵינוּ* עַד־עוֹלָם לַעֲשׂוֹת אֶת־כׇּל־דִּבְרֵי הַתּוֹרָה הַזֹּאת: ס

לוְהָיָה כִי־יָבֹאוּ עָלֶיךָ כׇּל־הַדְּבָרִים הָאֵלֶּה הַבְּרָכָה וְהַקְּלָלָה אֲשֶׁר נָתַתִּי לְפָנֶיךָ וַהֲשֵׁבֹתָ אֶל־לְבָבֶךָ בְּכׇל־הַגּוֹיִם

---

v. 27. ל׳ רבתי לפי נוסחים המקובלים

v. 28. נקוד על ל׳ נ׳ י׳ ו׳ ו׳ ל׳ ב׳ נ׳ י׳ נ׳ ו׳, ולפי נוסחים המקובלים גם נקוד על ע׳

various nations to which the LORD your God has banished you, ²and you return to the LORD your God, and you and your children heed His command with all your heart and soul, just as I enjoin upon you this day, ³then the LORD your God will restore your fortunes*a* and take you back in love. He will bring you together again from all the peoples where the LORD your God has scattered you. ⁴Even if your outcasts are at the ends of the world,*b* from there the LORD your God will gather you, from there He will fetch you. ⁵And the LORD your God will bring you to the land that your fathers possessed, and you shall possess it; and He will make you more prosperous and more numerous than your fathers.

⁶Then the LORD your God will open up*c* your heart and the hearts of your offspring to love the LORD your God with all your heart and soul, in order that you may live. ⁷The LORD your God will inflict all those curses upon the enemies and foes who persecuted you. ⁸You, however, will again heed the LORD and obey all His commandments that I enjoin upon you this day. ⁹And the LORD your God will grant you abounding prosperity in all your undertakings, in the issue of your womb, the offspring of your cattle, and the produce of your soil. For the LORD will again delight in your well-being, as He did in that of your fathers, ¹⁰since you will be heeding the LORD your God and keeping His commandments and laws that are recorded in this book of the Teaching—once you return to the LORD your God with all your heart and soul.

¹¹Surely, this Instruction which I enjoin upon you this day is not too baffling for you, nor is it beyond reach. ¹²It is not in the heavens, that you should say, "Who among us can go up to the heavens and get it for us and impart it to us, that we may observe it?" ¹³Neither is it be-

---

אֲשֶׁ֨ר הִדִּיחֲךָ֜ יְהֹוָ֧ה אֱלֹהֶ֛יךָ שָֽׁמָּה׃ 2 וְשַׁבְתָּ֞ עַד־יְהֹוָ֤ה אֱלֹהֶ֙יךָ֙ וְשָׁמַעְתָּ֣ בְקֹל֔וֹ כְּכֹ֛ל אֲשֶׁר־אָנֹכִ֥י מְצַוְּךָ֖ הַיּ֑וֹם אַתָּ֣ה וּבָנֶ֔יךָ בְּכׇל־לְבָבְךָ֖ וּבְכׇל־נַפְשֶֽׁךָ׃ 3 וְשָׁ֨ב יְהֹוָ֧ה אֱלֹהֶ֛יךָ אֶת־שְׁבוּתְךָ֖ וְרִחֲמֶ֑ךָ וְשָׁ֗ב וְקִבֶּצְךָ֙ מִכׇּל־הָ֣עַמִּ֔ים אֲשֶׁ֧ר הֱפִֽיצְךָ֛ יְהֹוָ֥ה אֱלֹהֶ֖יךָ שָֽׁמָּה׃ 4 אִם־יִהְיֶ֥ה נִֽדַּחֲךָ֖ בִּקְצֵ֣ה הַשָּׁמָ֑יִם מִשָּׁ֗ם יְקַבֶּצְךָ֙ יְהֹוָ֣ה אֱלֹהֶ֔יךָ וּמִשָּׁ֖ם יִקָּחֶֽךָ׃ 5 וֶהֱבִֽיאֲךָ֞ יְהֹוָ֣ה אֱלֹהֶ֗יךָ אֶל־הָאָ֛רֶץ אֲשֶׁר־יָרְשׁ֥וּ אֲבֹתֶ֖יךָ וִֽירִשְׁתָּ֑הּ וְהֵיטִֽבְךָ֥ וְהִרְבְּךָ֖ מֵאֲבֹתֶֽיךָ׃ 6 וּמָ֨ל יְהֹוָ֧ה אֱלֹהֶ֛יךָ אֶת־לְבָבְךָ֖ וְאֶת־לְבַ֣ב זַרְעֶ֑ךָ לְאַהֲבָ֞ה אֶת־יְהֹוָ֧ה אֱלֹהֶ֛יךָ בְּכׇל־לְבָבְךָ֥ וּבְכׇל־נַפְשְׁךָ֖ לְמַ֥עַן חַיֶּֽיךָ׃ 7 וְנָתַן֙ יְהֹוָ֣ה אֱלֹהֶ֔יךָ אֵ֥ת כׇּל־הָאָל֖וֹת הָאֵ֑לֶּה עַל־אֹיְבֶ֥יךָ וְעַל־שֹׂנְאֶ֖יךָ אֲשֶׁ֥ר רְדָפֽוּךָ׃ 8 וְאַתָּ֣ה תָשׁ֔וּב וְשָׁמַעְתָּ֖ בְּק֣וֹל יְהֹוָ֑ה וְעָשִׂ֙יתָ֙ אֶת־כׇּל־מִצְוֺתָ֔יו אֲשֶׁ֛ר אָנֹכִ֥י מְצַוְּךָ֖ הַיּֽוֹם׃ 9 וְהוֹתִֽירְךָ֩ יְהֹוָ֨ה אֱלֹהֶ֜יךָ בְּכֹ֣ל ׀ מַעֲשֵׂ֣ה יָדֶ֗ךָ בִּפְרִ֨י בִטְנְךָ֜ וּבִפְרִ֧י בְהֶמְתְּךָ֛ וּבִפְרִ֥י אַדְמָתְךָ֖ לְטֹבָ֑ה כִּ֣י ׀ יָשׁ֣וּב יְהֹוָ֗ה לָשׂ֤וּשׂ עָלֶ֙יךָ֙ לְט֔וֹב כַּאֲשֶׁר־שָׂ֖שׂ עַל־אֲבֹתֶֽיךָ׃ 10 כִּ֣י תִשְׁמַ֗ע בְּקוֹל֙ יְהֹוָ֣ה אֱלֹהֶ֔יךָ לִשְׁמֹ֤ר מִצְוֺתָיו֙ וְחֻקֹּתָ֔יו הַכְּתוּבָ֕ה בְּסֵ֖פֶר הַתּוֹרָ֣ה הַזֶּ֑ה כִּ֤י תָשׁוּב֙ אֶל־יְהֹוָ֣ה אֱלֹהֶ֔יךָ בְּכׇל־לְבָבְךָ֖ וּבְכׇל־נַפְשֶֽׁךָ׃ פ 11 כִּ֚י הַמִּצְוָ֣ה הַזֹּ֔את אֲשֶׁ֛ר אָנֹכִ֥י מְצַוְּךָ֖ הַיּ֑וֹם לֹֽא־נִפְלֵ֥את הִוא֙ מִמְּךָ֔ וְלֹ֥א רְחֹקָ֖ה הִֽוא׃ 12 לֹ֥א בַשָּׁמַ֖יִם הִ֑וא לֵאמֹ֗ר מִ֣י יַעֲלֶה־לָּ֤נוּ הַשָּׁמַ֙יְמָה֙ וְיִקָּחֶ֣הָ לָּ֔נוּ וְיַשְׁמִעֵ֥נוּ אֹתָ֖הּ וְנַעֲשֶֽׂנָּה׃ 13 וְלֹא־מֵעֵ֥בֶר לַיָּ֖ם הִ֑וא

---

a Others "captivity."
b Lit. "sky."
c Others "circumcise."

yond the sea, that you should say, "Who among us can cross to the other side of the sea and get it for us and impart it to us, that we may observe it?" [14]No, the thing is very close to you, in your mouth and in your heart, to observe it.

[15]See, I set before you this day life and prosperity, death and adversity. [16]For[d] I command you this day, to love the LORD your God, to walk in His ways, and to keep His commandments, His laws, and His rules, that you may thrive and increase, and that the LORD your God may bless you in the land that you are about to enter and possess. [17]But if your heart turns away and you give no heed, and are lured into the worship and service of other gods, [18]I declare to you this day that you shall certainly perish; you shall not long endure on the soil that you are crossing the Jordan to enter and possess. [19]I call heaven and earth to witness against you this day: I have put before you life and death, blessing and curse. Choose life—if you and your offspring would live—[20]by loving the LORD your God, heeding His commands, and holding fast to Him. For thereby you shall have life and shall long endure upon the soil that the LORD swore to your ancestors, Abraham, Isaac, and Jacob, to give to them.

31 VA-YELEKH

[a-]Moses went and spoke[-a] these things to all Israel. [2]He said to them:

I am now one hundred and twenty years old, I can no longer [b-]be active.[-b] Moreover, the LORD has said to me, "You shall not go across yonder Jordan." [3]The LORD your God Himself will cross over before you; and He Himself will wipe out those nations from your path and you shall dispossess them.—Joshua is the one who

לֵאמֹר מִי יַעֲבָר־לָנוּ אֶל־עֵבֶר הַיָּם וְיִקָּחֶהָ לָּנוּ וְיַשְׁמִעֵנוּ אֹתָהּ וְנַעֲשֶׂנָּה: 14 כִּי־קָרוֹב אֵלֶיךָ הַדָּבָר מְאֹד בְּפִיךָ וּבִלְבָבְךָ לַעֲשֹׂתוֹ: ס

15 רְאֵה נָתַתִּי לְפָנֶיךָ הַיּוֹם אֶת־הַחַיִּים וְאֶת־הַטּוֹב וְאֶת־הַמָּוֶת וְאֶת־הָרָע: 16 אֲשֶׁר אָנֹכִי מְצַוְּךָ הַיּוֹם לְאַהֲבָה אֶת־יְהוָה אֱלֹהֶיךָ לָלֶכֶת בִּדְרָכָיו וְלִשְׁמֹר מִצְוֺתָיו וְחֻקֹּתָיו וּמִשְׁפָּטָיו וְחָיִיתָ וְרָבִיתָ וּבֵרַכְךָ יְהוָה אֱלֹהֶיךָ בָּאָרֶץ אֲשֶׁר־אַתָּה בָא־שָׁמָּה לְרִשְׁתָּהּ: 17 וְאִם־יִפְנֶה לְבָבְךָ וְלֹא תִשְׁמָע וְנִדַּחְתָּ וְהִשְׁתַּחֲוִיתָ לֵאלֹהִים אֲחֵרִים וַעֲבַדְתָּם: 18 הִגַּדְתִּי לָכֶם הַיּוֹם כִּי אָבֹד תֹּאבֵדוּן לֹא־תַאֲרִיכֻן יָמִים עַל־הָאֲדָמָה אֲשֶׁר אַתָּה עֹבֵר אֶת־הַיַּרְדֵּן לָבֹא שָׁמָּה לְרִשְׁתָּהּ: 19 הַעִדֹתִי בָכֶם הַיּוֹם אֶת־הַשָּׁמַיִם וְאֶת־הָאָרֶץ הַחַיִּים וְהַמָּוֶת נָתַתִּי לְפָנֶיךָ הַבְּרָכָה וְהַקְּלָלָה וּבָחַרְתָּ בַּחַיִּים לְמַעַן תִּחְיֶה אַתָּה וְזַרְעֶךָ: 20 לְאַהֲבָה אֶת־יְהוָה אֱלֹהֶיךָ לִשְׁמֹעַ בְּקֹלוֹ וּלְדָבְקָה־בוֹ כִּי הוּא חַיֶּיךָ וְאֹרֶךְ יָמֶיךָ לָשֶׁבֶת עַל־הָאֲדָמָה אֲשֶׁר נִשְׁבַּע יְהוָה לַאֲבֹתֶיךָ לְאַבְרָהָם לְיִצְחָק וּלְיַעֲקֹב לָתֵת לָהֶם: פ

לא וַיֵּלֶךְ

וַיֵּלֶךְ מֹשֶׁה וַיְדַבֵּר אֶת־הַדְּבָרִים הָאֵלֶּה אֶל־כָּל־יִשְׂרָאֵל: 2 וַיֹּאמֶר אֲלֵהֶם בֶּן־מֵאָה וְעֶשְׂרִים שָׁנָה אָנֹכִי הַיּוֹם לֹא־אוּכַל עוֹד לָצֵאת וְלָבוֹא וַיהוָה אָמַר אֵלַי לֹא תַעֲבֹר אֶת־הַיַּרְדֵּן הַזֶּה: 3 יְהוָה אֱלֹהֶיךָ הוּא עֹבֵר לְפָנֶיךָ הוּא־יַשְׁמִיד אֶת־הַגּוֹיִם הָאֵלֶּה מִלְּפָנֶיךָ וִירִשְׁתָּם

---

d Septuagint reads "If you obey the commandments of the LORD your God, which."

a-a An ancient Heb. ms. and the Septuagint read: "When Moses had finished speaking …"; cf. 29.1.

b-b Lit. "come and go."

shall cross before you, as the LORD has spoken.—[4]The LORD will do to them as He did to Sihon and Og, kings of the Amorites, and to their countries, when He wiped them out. [5]The LORD will deliver them up to you, and you shall deal with them in full accordance with the Instruction that I have enjoined upon you. [6]Be strong and resolute, be not in fear or in dread of them; for the LORD your God Himself marches with you: He will not fail you or forsake you.

[7]Then Moses called Joshua and said to him in the sight of all Israel: "Be strong and resolute, for it is you who shall go with this people into the land that the LORD swore to their fathers to give them, and it is you who shall apportion it to them. [8]And the LORD Himself will go before you. He will be with you; He will not fail you or forsake you. Fear not and be not dismayed!"

[9]Moses wrote down this Teaching and gave it to the priests, sons of Levi, who carried the Ark of the LORD's Covenant, and to all the elders of Israel.

[10]And Moses instructed them as follows: Every seventh year,[c] the year set for remission, at the Feast of Booths, [11]when all Israel comes to appear before the LORD your God in the place that He will choose, you shall read this Teaching aloud in the presence of all Israel. [12]Gather the people—men, women, children, and the strangers in your communities—that they may hear and so learn to revere the LORD your God and to observe faithfully every word of this Teaching. [13]Their children, too, who have not had the experience, shall hear and learn to revere the LORD your God as long as they live in the land that you are about to cross the Jordan to possess.

[14]The LORD said to Moses: The time is drawing near for you to die. Call Joshua and present

c *See note at 15.1.*

443

יְהוֹשֻׁעַ הוּא עֹבֵר לְפָנֶיךָ כַּאֲשֶׁר דִּבֶּר יְהוָה: [4] וְעָשָׂה יְהוָה לָהֶם כַּאֲשֶׁר עָשָׂה לְסִיחוֹן וּלְעוֹג מַלְכֵי הָאֱמֹרִי וּלְאַרְצָם אֲשֶׁר הִשְׁמִיד אֹתָם: [5] וּנְתָנָם יְהוָה לִפְנֵיכֶם וַעֲשִׂיתֶם לָהֶם כְּכָל־הַמִּצְוָה אֲשֶׁר צִוִּיתִי אֶתְכֶם: [6] חִזְקוּ וְאִמְצוּ אַל־תִּירְאוּ וְאַל־תַּעַרְצוּ מִפְּנֵיהֶם כִּי ׀ יְהוָה אֱלֹהֶיךָ הוּא הַהֹלֵךְ עִמָּךְ לֹא יַרְפְּךָ וְלֹא יַעַזְבֶךָּ: פ

[7] וַיִּקְרָא מֹשֶׁה לִיהוֹשֻׁעַ וַיֹּאמֶר אֵלָיו לְעֵינֵי כָל־יִשְׂרָאֵל חֲזַק וֶאֱמָץ כִּי אַתָּה תָּבוֹא אֶת־הָעָם הַזֶּה אֶל־הָאָרֶץ אֲשֶׁר נִשְׁבַּע יְהוָה לַאֲבֹתָם לָתֵת לָהֶם וְאַתָּה תַּנְחִילֶנָּה אוֹתָם: [8] וַיהוָֹה הוּא ׀ הַהֹלֵךְ לְפָנֶיךָ הוּא יִהְיֶה עִמָּךְ לֹא יַרְפְּךָ וְלֹא יַעַזְבֶךָּ לֹא תִירָא וְלֹא תֵחָת: [9] וַיִּכְתֹּב מֹשֶׁה אֶת־הַתּוֹרָה הַזֹּאת וַיִּתְּנָהּ אֶל־הַכֹּהֲנִים בְּנֵי לֵוִי הַנֹּשְׂאִים אֶת־אֲרוֹן בְּרִית יְהוָה וְאֶל־כָּל־זִקְנֵי יִשְׂרָאֵל: [10] וַיְצַו מֹשֶׁה אוֹתָם לֵאמֹר מִקֵּץ ׀ שֶׁבַע שָׁנִים בְּמֹעֵד שְׁנַת הַשְּׁמִטָּה בְּחַג הַסֻּכּוֹת: [11] בְּבוֹא כָל־יִשְׂרָאֵל לֵרָאוֹת אֶת־פְּנֵי יְהוָה אֱלֹהֶיךָ בַּמָּקוֹם אֲשֶׁר יִבְחָר תִּקְרָא אֶת־הַתּוֹרָה הַזֹּאת נֶגֶד כָּל־יִשְׂרָאֵל בְּאָזְנֵיהֶם: [12] הַקְהֵל אֶת־הָעָם הָאֲנָשִׁים וְהַנָּשִׁים וְהַטַּף וְגֵרְךָ אֲשֶׁר בִּשְׁעָרֶיךָ לְמַעַן יִשְׁמְעוּ וּלְמַעַן יִלְמְדוּ וְיָרְאוּ אֶת־יְהוָה אֱלֹהֵיכֶם וְשָׁמְרוּ לַעֲשׂוֹת אֶת־כָּל־דִּבְרֵי הַתּוֹרָה הַזֹּאת: [13] וּבְנֵיהֶם אֲשֶׁר לֹא־יָדְעוּ יִשְׁמְעוּ וְלָמְדוּ לְיִרְאָה אֶת־יְהוָה אֱלֹהֵיכֶם כָּל־הַיָּמִים אֲשֶׁר אַתֶּם חַיִּים עַל־הָאֲדָמָה אֲשֶׁר אַתֶּם עֹבְרִים אֶת־הַיַּרְדֵּן שָׁמָּה לְרִשְׁתָּהּ: פ

[14] וַיֹּאמֶר יְהוָה אֶל־מֹשֶׁה הֵן קָרְבוּ יָמֶיךָ לָמוּת קְרָא אֶת־יְהוֹשֻׁעַ וְהִתְיַצְּבוּ בְּאֹהֶל

yourselves in the Tent of Meeting, that I may instruct him. Moses and Joshua went and presented themselves in the Tent of Meeting. [15]The LORD appeared in the Tent, in a pillar of cloud, the pillar of cloud having come to rest at the entrance of the tent.

[16]The LORD said to Moses: You are soon to lie with your fathers. This people will thereupon go astray after the alien gods in their midst, in the land that they are about to enter; they will forsake Me and break My covenant that I made with them. [17]Then My anger will flare up against them, and I will abandon them and hide My countenance from them. They shall be ready prey; and many evils and troubles shall befall them. And they shall say on that day, "Surely it is because our God is not in our midst that these evils have befallen us." [18]Yet I will keep My countenance hidden on that day, because of all the evil they have done in turning to other gods. [19]Therefore, write down this poem and teach it to the people of Israel; put it in their mouths, in order that this poem may be My witness against the people of Israel. [20]When I bring them into the land flowing with milk and honey that I promised on oath to their fathers, and they eat their fill and grow fat and turn to other gods and serve them, spurning Me and breaking My covenant, [21]and the many evils and troubles befall them—then this poem shall confront them as a witness, since it will never be lost from the mouth of their offspring. For I know what plans they are devising even now, before I bring them into the land that I promised on oath.

[22]That day, Moses wrote down this poem and taught it to the Israelites.

[23]And He charged Joshua son of Nun: "Be strong and resolute: for you shall bring the Israelites into the land that I promised them on oath, and I will be with you."

[24]When Moses had put down in writing the

מוֹעֵד וַאֲצַוֶּנּוּ וַיֵּלֶךְ מֹשֶׁה וִיהוֹשֻׁעַ וַיִּתְיַצְּבוּ
בְּאֹהֶל מוֹעֵד: 15 וַיֵּרָא יְהֹוָה בָּאֹהֶל בְּעַמּוּד
עָנָן וַיַּעֲמֹד עַמּוּד הֶעָנָן עַל־פֶּתַח
הָאֹהֶל: ס
16 וַיֹּאמֶר יְהֹוָה אֶל־מֹשֶׁה הִנְּךָ שֹׁכֵב עִם־
אֲבֹתֶיךָ וְקָם הָעָם הַזֶּה וְזָנָה ׀ אַחֲרֵי ׀
אֱלֹהֵי נֵכַר־הָאָרֶץ אֲשֶׁר הוּא בָא־שָׁמָּה
בְּקִרְבּוֹ וַעֲזָבַנִי וְהֵפֵר אֶת־בְּרִיתִי אֲשֶׁר
כָּרַתִּי אִתּוֹ: 17 וְחָרָה אַפִּי בוֹ בַיּוֹם־הַהוּא
וַעֲזַבְתִּים וְהִסְתַּרְתִּי פָנַי מֵהֶם וְהָיָה
לֶאֱכֹל וּמְצָאֻהוּ רָעוֹת רַבּוֹת וְצָרוֹת וְאָמַר
בַּיּוֹם הַהוּא הֲלֹא עַל כִּי־אֵין אֱלֹהַי בְּקִרְבִּי
מְצָאוּנִי הָרָעוֹת הָאֵלֶּה: 18 וְאָנֹכִי הַסְתֵּר
אַסְתִּיר פָּנַי בַּיּוֹם הַהוּא עַל כָּל־הָרָעָה
אֲשֶׁר עָשָׂה כִּי פָנָה אֶל־אֱלֹהִים אֲחֵרִים:
19 וְעַתָּה כִּתְבוּ לָכֶם אֶת־הַשִּׁירָה הַזֹּאת
וְלַמְּדָהּ אֶת־בְּנֵי־יִשְׂרָאֵל שִׂימָהּ בְּפִיהֶם
לְמַעַן תִּהְיֶה־לִּי הַשִּׁירָה הַזֹּאת לְעֵד בִּבְנֵי
יִשְׂרָאֵל: 20 כִּי־אֲבִיאֶנּוּ אֶל־הָאֲדָמָה ׀
אֲשֶׁר־נִשְׁבַּעְתִּי לַאֲבֹתָיו זָבַת חָלָב וּדְבַשׁ
וְאָכַל וְשָׂבַע וְדָשֵׁן וּפָנָה אֶל־אֱלֹהִים
אֲחֵרִים וַעֲבָדוּם וְנִאֲצוּנִי וְהֵפֵר אֶת־
בְּרִיתִי: 21 וְהָיָה כִּי־תִמְצֶאןָ אֹתוֹ רָעוֹת
רַבּוֹת וְצָרוֹת וְעָנְתָה הַשִּׁירָה הַזֹּאת
לְפָנָיו לְעֵד כִּי לֹא תִשָּׁכַח מִפִּי זַרְעוֹ
כִּי יָדַעְתִּי אֶת־יִצְרוֹ אֲשֶׁר הוּא עֹשֶׂה
הַיּוֹם בְּטֶרֶם אֲבִיאֶנּוּ אֶל־הָאָרֶץ אֲשֶׁר
נִשְׁבָּעְתִּי:
22 וַיִּכְתֹּב מֹשֶׁה אֶת־הַשִּׁירָה הַזֹּאת בַּיּוֹם
הַהוּא וַיְלַמְּדָהּ אֶת־בְּנֵי יִשְׂרָאֵל:
23 וַיְצַו אֶת־יְהוֹשֻׁעַ בִּן־נוּן וַיֹּאמֶר חֲזַק
וֶאֱמָץ כִּי אַתָּה תָּבִיא אֶת־בְּנֵי יִשְׂרָאֵל
אֶל־הָאָרֶץ אֲשֶׁר־נִשְׁבַּעְתִּי לָהֶם וְאָנֹכִי
אֶהְיֶה עִמָּךְ:
24 וַיְהִי ׀ כְּכַלּוֹת מֹשֶׁה לִכְתֹּב אֶת־דִּבְרֵי

words of this Teaching to the very end, 25Moses charged the Levites who carried the Ark of the Covenant of the LORD, saying: 26Take this book of Teaching and place it beside the Ark of the Covenant of the LORD your God, and let it remain there as a witness against you. 27Well I know how defiant and stiffnecked you are: even now, while I am still alive in your midst, you have been defiant toward the LORD; how much more, then, when I am dead! 28Gather to me all the elders of your tribes and your officials, that I may speak all these words to them and that I may call heaven and earth to witness against them. 29For I know that, when I am dead, you will act wickedly and turn away from the path that I enjoined upon you, and that in time to come misfortune will befall you for having done evil in the sight of the LORD and vexed Him by your deeds.

30Then Moses recited the words of this poem to the very end, in the hearing of the whole congregation of Israel:

32 HA'AZINU

Give ear, O heavens, let me speak;
Let the earth hear the words I utter!
2May my discourse come down as the rain,
My speech distill as the dew,
Like showers on young growth,
Like droplets on the grass.*a*
3For the name of the LORD I proclaim;
Give glory to our God!

4The Rock!—His deeds are perfect,
Yea, all His ways are just;
A faithful God, never false,
True and upright is He.
5*b*Children unworthy of Him—
That crooked, perverse generation—
Their baseness has played Him false.

---

a I.e., may my words be received eagerly; cf. Job 29.22–23.
b Meaning of Heb. uncertain.

הַתּוֹרָה־הַזֹּאת עַל־סֵפֶר עַד תֻּמָּם: 25 וַיְצַו
מֹשֶׁה אֶת־הַלְוִיִּם נֹשְׂאֵי אֲרוֹן בְּרִית־יְהוָה
לֵאמֹר: 26 לָקֹחַ אֵת סֵפֶר הַתּוֹרָה הַזֶּה
וְשַׂמְתֶּם אֹתוֹ מִצַּד אֲרוֹן בְּרִית־יְהוָה
אֱלֹהֵיכֶם וְהָיָה־שָׁם בְּךָ לְעֵד: 27 כִּי אָנֹכִי
יָדַעְתִּי אֶת־מֶרְיְךָ וְאֶת־עָרְפְּךָ הַקָּשֶׁה הֵן
בְּעוֹדֶנִּי חַי עִמָּכֶם הַיּוֹם מַמְרִים הֱיִתֶם
עִם־יְהוָה וְאַף כִּי־אַחֲרֵי מוֹתִי: 28 הַקְהִילוּ
אֵלַי אֶת־כָּל־זִקְנֵי שִׁבְטֵיכֶם וְשֹׁטְרֵיכֶם
וַאֲדַבְּרָה בְאָזְנֵיהֶם אֵת הַדְּבָרִים הָאֵלֶּה
וְאָעִידָה בָּם אֶת־הַשָּׁמַיִם וְאֶת־הָאָרֶץ:
29 כִּי יָדַעְתִּי אַחֲרֵי מוֹתִי כִּי־הַשְׁחֵת
תַּשְׁחִתוּן וְסַרְתֶּם מִן־הַדֶּרֶךְ אֲשֶׁר צִוִּיתִי
אֶתְכֶם וְקָרָאת אֶתְכֶם הָרָעָה בְּאַחֲרִית
הַיָּמִים כִּי־תַעֲשׂוּ אֶת־הָרַע בְּעֵינֵי יְהוָה
לְהַכְעִיסוֹ בְּמַעֲשֵׂה יְדֵיכֶם:
30 וַיְדַבֵּר מֹשֶׁה בְּאָזְנֵי כָּל־קְהַל יִשְׂרָאֵל
אֶת־דִּבְרֵי הַשִּׁירָה הַזֹּאת עַד תֻּמָּם: פ

לב האזינו

*הַאֲזִינוּ הַשָּׁמַיִם וַאֲדַבֵּרָה
וְתִשְׁמַע הָאָרֶץ אִמְרֵי־פִי:
2 יַעֲרֹף כַּמָּטָר לִקְחִי
תִּזַּל כַּטַּל אִמְרָתִי
כִּשְׂעִירִם עֲלֵי־דֶשֶׁא
וְכִרְבִיבִים עֲלֵי־עֵשֶׂב:
3 כִּי שֵׁם יְהוָה אֶקְרָא
הָבוּ גֹדֶל לֵאלֹהֵינוּ:
4 הַצּוּר תָּמִים פָּעֳלוֹ
כִּי כָל־דְּרָכָיו מִשְׁפָּט
אֵל אֱמוּנָה וְאֵין עָוֶל
צַדִּיק וְיָשָׁר הוּא:
5 שִׁחֵת לוֹ לֹא בָּנָיו מוּמָם
דּוֹר עִקֵּשׁ וּפְתַלְתֹּל:

---

v. 1. בכתב היד שלנו, צורת השירה ב־37 שורות, ולפי
ההלכה של כתיבת ספר התורה, היא ב־70 שורות

6Do you thus requite the LORD,
O dull and witless people?
Is not He the Father who created you,
Fashioned you and made you endure!

7Remember the days of old,
Consider the years of ages past;
Ask your father, he will inform you,
Your elders, they will tell you:
8When the Most High gave nations their
   homes
And set the divisions of man,
He fixed the boundaries of peoples
In relation to Israel's numbers.
9For the LORD's portion is His people,
Jacob His own allotment.

10He found him in a desert region,
In an empty howling waste.
He engirded him, watched over him,
Guarded him as the pupil of His eye.
11Like an eagle who rouses his nestlings,
Gliding down to his young,
So did He spread His wings and take him,
Bear him along on His pinions;
12The LORD alone did guide him,
No alien god at His side.

13He set him atop the highlands,
To feast on the yield of the earth;
He fed him honey from the crag,
And oil from the flinty rock,
14Curd of kine and milk of flocks;
With the bestc of lambs,
And rams of Bashan, and he-goats;
With the d-very finest-d wheat—
And foaming grape-blood was your drink.

15So Jeshurun grew fat and kicked—
You grew fat and gross and coarsee—
He forsook the God who made him

הֲ־לַיהֹוָה* תִּגְמְלוּ־זֹאת
עַם נָבָל וְלֹא חָכָם
הֲלוֹא־הוּא אָבִיךָ קָּנֶךָ
הוּא עָשְׂךָ וַיְכֹנְנֶךָ:
7 זְכֹר יְמוֹת עוֹלָם
בִּינוּ שְׁנוֹת דּוֹר־וָדוֹר
שְׁאַל אָבִיךָ וְיַגֵּדְךָ
זְקֵנֶיךָ וְיֹאמְרוּ לָךְ:
8 בְּהַנְחֵל עֶלְיוֹן גּוֹיִם
בְּהַפְרִידוֹ בְּנֵי אָדָם
יַצֵּב גְּבֻלֹת עַמִּים
לְמִסְפַּר בְּנֵי יִשְׂרָאֵל:
9 כִּי חֵלֶק יְהֹוָה עַמּוֹ
יַעֲקֹב חֶבֶל נַחֲלָתוֹ:
10 יִמְצָאֵהוּ בְּאֶרֶץ מִדְבָּר
וּבְתֹהוּ יְלֵל יְשִׁמֹן
יְסֹבְבֶנְהוּ יְבוֹנְנֵהוּ
יִצְּרֶנְהוּ כְּאִישׁוֹן עֵינוֹ:
11 כְּנֶשֶׁר יָעִיר קִנּוֹ
עַל־גּוֹזָלָיו יְרַחֵף
יִפְרֹשׂ כְּנָפָיו יִקָּחֵהוּ
יִשָּׂאֵהוּ עַל־אֶבְרָתוֹ:
12 יְהֹוָה בָּדָד יַנְחֶנּוּ
וְאֵין עִמּוֹ אֵל נֵכָר:
13 יַרְכִּבֵהוּ עַל־במותי בָּמֳתֵי אָרֶץ
וַיֹּאכַל תְּנוּבֹת שָׂדָי
וַיֵּנִקֵהוּ דְבַשׁ מִסֶּלַע
וְשֶׁמֶן מֵחַלְמִישׁ צוּר:
14 חֶמְאַת בָּקָר וַחֲלֵב צֹאן
עִם־חֵלֶב כָּרִים
וְאֵילִים בְּנֵי־בָשָׁן וְעַתּוּדִים
עִם־חֵלֶב כִּלְיוֹת חִטָּה
וְדַם־עֵנָב תִּשְׁתֶּה־חָמֶר:
15 וַיִּשְׁמַן יְשֻׁרוּן וַיִּבְעָט
שָׁמַנְתָּ עָבִיתָ כָּשִׂיתָ
וַיִּטֹּשׁ אֱלוֹהַּ עָשָׂהוּ

c   Lit. "fat."
d-d   "kidney fat of."
e   Meaning of Heb. uncertain.

446

And spurned the Rock of his support.
16They incensed Him with alien things,
Vexed Him with abominations.
17They sacrificed to demons, no-gods,
Gods they had never known,
New ones, who came but lately,
f-Who stirred not your fathers' fears.-f
18You neglected the Rock that begot you,
Forgot the God who brought you forth.

19The Lord saw and was vexed
And spurned His sons and His daughters.
20He said:
I will hide My countenance from them,
And see how they fare in the end.
For they are a treacherous breed,
Children with no loyalty in them.
21They incensed Me with no-gods,
Vexed Me with their futilities;g
I'll incense them with a no-folk,
Vex them with a nation of fools.
22For a fire has flared in My wrath
And burned to the bottom of Sheol,
Has consumed the earth and its increase,
Eaten down to the base of the hills.
23I will sweepe misfortunes on them,
Use up My arrows on them:
24Wasting famine, ravaging plague,
Deadly pestilence, and fanged beasts
Will I let loose against them,
With venomous creepers in dust.
25The sword shall deal death without,
As shall the terror within,
To youth and maiden alike,
The suckling as well as the aged.
26h-I might have reduced them to naught,-h
Made their memory cease among men,
27But for fear of the taunts of the foe,

וַיְנַבֵּל צוּר יְשֻׁעָתֽוֹ׃
16 יַקְנִאֻהוּ בְּזָרִים
בְּתוֹעֵבֹת יַכְעִיסֻֽהוּ׃
17 יִזְבְּחוּ לַשֵּׁדִים לֹא אֱלֹהַ
אֱלֹהִים לֹא יְדָעוּם
חֲדָשִׁים מִקָּרֹב בָּאוּ
לֹא שְׂעָרוּם אֲבֹתֵיכֶֽם׃
18 צוּר יְלָדְךָ תֶּֽשִׁי*
וַתִּשְׁכַּח אֵל מְחֹלְלֶֽךָ׃
19 וַיַּרְא יְהֹוָה וַיִּנְאָץ
מִכַּעַס בָּנָיו וּבְנֹתָֽיו׃
20 וַיֹּאמֶר אַסְתִּירָה פָנַי מֵהֶם
אֶרְאֶה מָה אַחֲרִיתָם
כִּי דוֹר תַּהְפֻּכֹת הֵמָּה
בָּנִים לֹא־אֵמֻן בָּֽם׃
21 הֵם קִנְאוּנִי בְלֹא־אֵל
כִּעֲסוּנִי בְּהַבְלֵיהֶם
וַאֲנִי אַקְנִיאֵם בְּלֹא־עָם
בְּגוֹי נָבָל אַכְעִיסֵֽם׃
22 כִּי־אֵשׁ קָדְחָה בְאַפִּי
וַתִּיקַד עַד־שְׁאוֹל תַּחְתִּית
וַתֹּאכַל אֶרֶץ וִיבֻלָהּ
וַתְּלַהֵט מוֹסְדֵי הָרִֽים׃
23 אַסְפֶּה עָלֵימוֹ רָעוֹת
חִצַּי אֲכַלֶּה־בָּֽם׃
24 מְזֵי רָעָב וּלְחֻמֵי רֶשֶׁף
וְקֶטֶב מְרִירִי
וְשֶׁן־בְּהֵמֹת אֲשַׁלַּח־בָּם
עִם־חֲמַת זֹחֲלֵי עָפָֽר׃
25 מִחוּץ תְּשַׁכֶּל־חֶרֶב
וּמֵחֲדָרִים אֵימָה
גַּם־בָּחוּר גַּם־בְּתוּלָה
יוֹנֵק עִם־אִישׁ שֵׂיבָֽה׃
26 אָמַרְתִּי אַפְאֵיהֶם
אַשְׁבִּיתָה מֵאֱנוֹשׁ זִכְרָֽם׃
27 לוּלֵי כַּעַס אוֹיֵב אָגוּר

---

f-f Meaning of Heb. uncertain; Arabic sha'ara suggests the
     rendering "Whom your fathers did not know."
g I.e., idols.
h-h Lit. "I said, I will reduce…"; meaning of Heb. 'aph'ehem
     uncertain.

447

Their enemies who might misjudge
And say, "Our own hand has prevailed;
None of this was wrought by the LORD!"

28[i]For they are a folk void of sense,
Lacking in all discernment.

29Were they wise, they would think upon this,
Gain insight into their future:

30"How could one have routed a thousand,
Or two put ten thousand to flight,
Unless their Rock had sold them,
The LORD had given them up?"

31For their rock is not like our Rock,
[j]-In our enemies' own[k] estimation.-[j]

32Ah! The vine for them is from Sodom,
From the vineyards of Gomorrah;
The grapes for them are poison,
A bitter growth their clusters.

33Their wine is the venom of asps,
The pitiless poison of vipers.

34Lo, I have it all put away,
Sealed up in My storehouses,

35To be My vengeance and recompense,
At the time that their foot falters.
Yea, their day of disaster is near,
And destiny rushes upon them.

36For the LORD will vindicate His people
[l]-And take revenge for-[l] His servants,
When He sees that their might is gone,
And neither bond nor free is left.

37He will say: Where are their gods,
The rock in whom they sought refuge,

38Who ate the fat of their offerings
And drank their libation wine?
Let them rise up to your help,
And let them be a shield unto you!

39See, then, that I, I am He;

פֶּן־יְנַכְּרוּ צָרֵימוֹ

פֶּן־יֹאמְרוּ יָדֵנוּ רָמָה

וְלֹא יְהוָה פָּעַל כָּל־זֹאת:

28 כִּי־גוֹי אֹבַד עֵצוֹת הֵמָּה

וְאֵין בָּהֶם תְּבוּנָה:

29 לוּ חָכְמוּ יַשְׂכִּילוּ זֹאת

יָבִינוּ לְאַחֲרִיתָם:

30 אֵיכָה יִרְדֹּף אֶחָד אֶלֶף

וּשְׁנַיִם יָנִיסוּ רְבָבָה

אִם־לֹא כִּי־צוּרָם מְכָרָם

וַיהוָה הִסְגִּירָם:

31 כִּי לֹא כְצוּרֵנוּ צוּרָם

וְאֹיְבֵינוּ פְּלִילִים:

32 כִּי־מִגֶּפֶן סְדֹם גַּפְנָם

וּמִשַּׁדְמֹת עֲמֹרָה

עֲנָבֵמוֹ עִנְּבֵי־רוֹשׁ

אַשְׁכְּלֹת מְרֹרֹת לָמוֹ:

33 חֲמַת תַּנִּינִם יֵינָם

וְרֹאשׁ פְּתָנִים אַכְזָר:

34 הֲלֹא־הוּא כָּמֻס עִמָּדִי

חָתֻם בְּאוֹצְרֹתָי:

35 לִי נָקָם וְשִׁלֵּם

לְעֵת תָּמוּט רַגְלָם

כִּי קָרוֹב יוֹם אֵידָם

וְחָשׁ עֲתִדֹת לָמוֹ:

36 כִּי־יָדִין יְהוָה עַמּוֹ

וְעַל־עֲבָדָיו יִתְנֶחָם

כִּי יִרְאֶה כִּי־אָזְלַת יָד

וְאֶפֶס עָצוּר וְעָזוּב:

37 וְאָמַר אֵי אֱלֹהֵימוֹ

צוּר חָסָיוּ בוֹ:

38 אֲשֶׁר חֵלֶב זְבָחֵימוֹ יֹאכֵלוּ

יִשְׁתּוּ יֵין נְסִיכָם

יָקוּמוּ וְיַעְזְרֻכֶם

יְהִי עֲלֵיכֶם סִתְרָה:

39 רְאוּ | עַתָּה כִּי אֲנִי אֲנִי הוּא

---

i   Here, apparently, Moses is the speaker; God resumes in v. 32.

j-j   I.e., as everyone must admit.

k   For Heb. pelilim see Exod. 21.22; cf. Gen. 48.11.

l-l   Cf. Isa. 1.24. Others "and repent Himself concerning."

There is no god beside Me.
I deal death and give life;
I wounded and I will heal:
None can deliver from My hand.
[40]Lo, I raise My hand to heaven
And say: As I live forever,
[41]When I whet My flashing blade
And My hand lays hold on judgment,
Vengeance will I wreak on My foes,
Will I deal to those who reject Me.
[42]I will make My arrows drunk with blood—
As My sword devours flesh—
Blood of the slain and the captive
From the long-haired enemy chiefs.

[43]O nations, acclaim His people!
For He'll avenge the blood of His servants,
Wreak vengeance on His foes,
And cleanse the land of His people.*m*

[44]Moses came, together with Hosea son of Nun, and recited all the words of this poem in the hearing of the people.

[45]And when Moses finished reciting all these words to all Israel, [46]he said to them: Take to heart all the words with which I have warned you this day. Enjoin them upon your children, that they may observe faithfully all the terms of this Teaching. [47]For this is not a trifling thing for you: it is your very life; through it you shall long endure on the land that you are to possess upon crossing the Jordan.

[48]That very day the LORD spoke to Moses: [49]Ascend these heights of Abarim to Mount Nebo, which is in the land of Moab facing Jericho, and view the land of Canaan, which I am giving the Israelites as their holding. [50]You shall die on the mountain that you are about to ascend, and shall be gathered to your kin, as your brother Aaron died on Mount Hor and was

וְאֵ֥ין אֱלֹהִ֖ים עִמָּדִ֑י
אֲנִ֧י אָמִ֣ית וַאֲחַיֶּ֗ה
מָחַ֙צְתִּי֙ וַאֲנִ֣י אֶרְפָּ֔א
וְאֵ֥ין מִיָּדִ֖י מַצִּֽיל׃
40 כִּֽי־אֶשָּׂ֥א אֶל־שָׁמַ֖יִם יָדִ֑י
וְאָמַ֕רְתִּי חַ֥י אָנֹכִ֖י לְעֹלָֽם׃
41 אִם־שַׁנּוֹתִי֙ בְּרַ֣ק חַרְבִּ֔י
וְתֹאחֵ֥ז בְּמִשְׁפָּ֖ט יָדִ֑י
אָשִׁ֤יב נָקָם֙ לְצָרָ֔י
וְלִמְשַׂנְאַ֖י אֲשַׁלֵּֽם׃
42 אַשְׁכִּ֤יר חִצַּי֙ מִדָּ֔ם
וְחַרְבִּ֖י תֹּ֣אכַל בָּשָׂ֑ר
מִדַּ֤ם חָלָל֙ וְשִׁבְיָ֔ה
מֵרֹ֖אשׁ פַּרְע֥וֹת אוֹיֵֽב׃
43 הַרְנִ֤ינוּ גוֹיִם֙ עַמּ֔וֹ
כִּ֥י דַם־עֲבָדָ֖יו יִקּ֑וֹם
וְנָקָם֙ יָשִׁ֣יב לְצָרָ֔יו
וְכִפֶּ֥ר אַדְמָת֖וֹ עַמּֽוֹ׃ פ

44 וַיָּבֹ֣א מֹשֶׁ֗ה וַיְדַבֵּ֛ר אֶת־כָּל־דִּבְרֵ֥י הַשִּׁירָֽה־הַזֹּ֖את בְּאָזְנֵ֣י הָעָ֑ם ה֥וּא וְהוֹשֵׁ֖עַ בִּן־נֽוּן׃
45 וַיְכַ֣ל מֹשֶׁ֗ה לְדַבֵּ֛ר אֶת־כָּל־הַדְּבָרִ֥ים הָאֵ֖לֶּה אֶל־כָּל־יִשְׂרָאֵֽל׃ 46 וַיֹּ֤אמֶר אֲלֵהֶם֙ שִׂ֣ימוּ לְבַבְכֶ֔ם לְכָל־הַדְּבָרִ֔ים אֲשֶׁ֧ר אָנֹכִ֛י מֵעִ֥יד בָּכֶ֖ם הַיּ֑וֹם אֲשֶׁ֣ר תְּצַוֻּם֙ אֶת־בְּנֵיכֶ֔ם לִשְׁמֹ֣ר לַעֲשׂ֔וֹת אֶת־כָּל־דִּבְרֵ֖י הַתּוֹרָ֥ה הַזֹּֽאת׃ 47 כִּ֠י לֹֽא־דָבָ֨ר רֵ֥ק הוּא֙ מִכֶּ֔ם כִּי־ה֖וּא חַיֵּיכֶ֑ם וּבַדָּבָ֣ר הַזֶּ֗ה תַּאֲרִ֤יכוּ יָמִים֙ עַל־הָ֣אֲדָמָ֔ה אֲשֶׁ֨ר אַתֶּ֜ם עֹבְרִ֧ים אֶת־הַיַּרְדֵּ֛ן שָׁ֖מָּה לְרִשְׁתָּֽהּ׃ פ
48 וַיְדַבֵּ֤ר יְהֹוָה֙ אֶל־מֹשֶׁ֔ה בְּעֶ֛צֶם הַיּ֥וֹם הַזֶּ֖ה לֵאמֹֽר׃ 49 עֲלֵ֡ה אֶל־הַר֩ הָעֲבָרִ֨ים הַזֶּ֜ה הַר־נְב֗וֹ אֲשֶׁר֙ בְּאֶ֣רֶץ מוֹאָ֔ב אֲשֶׁ֖ר עַל־פְּנֵ֣י יְרֵח֑וֹ וּרְאֵה֙ אֶת־אֶ֣רֶץ כְּנַ֔עַן אֲשֶׁ֨ר אֲנִ֥י נֹתֵ֛ן לִבְנֵ֥י יִשְׂרָאֵ֖ל לַאֲחֻזָּֽה׃ 50 וּמֻ֗ת בָּהָר֙ אֲשֶׁ֤ר אַתָּה֙ עֹלֶ֣ה שָׁ֔מָּה וְהֵאָסֵ֖ף אֶל־עַמֶּ֑יךָ

---

m Cf. Num. 35.33. Meaning of Heb. uncertain; Ugaritic 'udm't "tears" suggests the rendering "And wipe away His people's tears." Cf. Isa. 25.8.

gathered to his kin; ⁵¹for you both broke faith with Me among the Israelite people, at the waters of Meribath-kadesh in the wilderness of Zin, by failing to uphold My sanctity among the Israelite people. ⁵²You may view the land from a distance, but you shall not enter it—the land that I am giving to the Israelite people.

33 VE-ZO'T HA-BERAKHAH

This is the blessing with which Moses, the man of God, bade the Israelites farewell before he died. ²He said:

The LORD came from Sinai;
He shone upon them from Seir;
He appeared from Mount Paran,
And approached from Ribeboth-kodesh,ᵃ
Lightning flashing at them from His right.ᵇ
³ᶜLover, indeed, of the people,
Their hallowed are all in Your hand.
They followed in Your steps,
Accepting Your pronouncements,
⁴When Moses charged us with the Teaching
As the heritage of the congregation of Jacob.
⁵Then He became King in Jeshurun,
When the heads of the people assembled,
The tribes of Israel together.

⁶May Reuben live and not die,
Though few be his numbers.

⁷And this he said of Judah:
Hear, O LORD the voice of Judah
And restore him to his people.
ᵈ-Though his own hands strive for him,-ᵈ
Help him against his foes.

---

a   Cf. Meribath-kadesh, 32.51.
b   Meaning of Heb. mimino 'eshdath uncertain, perhaps a place name.
c   The meaning of vv. 3–5 is uncertain. An alternative rendering, with v. 3 apostrophizing Moses, is: ³Then were, O lover of the people, / All His worshipers in your care; / They followed your lead, / Accepted your precepts. / ⁴Moses charged us with the Teaching / As the heritage of the congregation of Jacob. / ⁵Thus was he king in Jeshurun…
d-d   Better (vocalizing rab with pathaḥ) "Make his hands strong for him." Cf. rabbeh, Judg. 9.29.

כַּאֲשֶׁר־מֵּת אַהֲרֹן אָחִיךָ בְּהֹר הָהָר וַיֵּאָסֶף אֶל־עַמָּיו: 51 עַל אֲשֶׁר מְעַלְתֶּם בִּי בְּתוֹךְ בְּנֵי יִשְׂרָאֵל בְּמֵי־מְרִיבַת קָדֵשׁ מִדְבַּר־צִן עַל אֲשֶׁר לֹא־קִדַּשְׁתֶּם אוֹתִי בְּתוֹךְ בְּנֵי יִשְׂרָאֵל: 52 כִּי מִנֶּגֶד תִּרְאֶה אֶת־הָאָרֶץ וְשָׁמָּה לֹא תָבוֹא אֶל־הָאָרֶץ אֲשֶׁר־אֲנִי נֹתֵן לִבְנֵי יִשְׂרָאֵל: פ

לג וזאת הברכה

וְזֹאת הַבְּרָכָה אֲשֶׁר בֵּרַךְ מֹשֶׁה אִישׁ הָאֱלֹהִים אֶת־בְּנֵי יִשְׂרָאֵל לִפְנֵי מוֹתוֹ: 2 וַיֹּאמַר

יְהֹוָה מִסִּינַי בָּא
וְזָרַח מִשֵּׂעִיר לָמוֹ
הוֹפִיעַ מֵהַר פָּארָן
וְאָתָה מֵרִבְבֹת קֹדֶשׁ
מִימִינוֹ אשׁדת אֵשׁ דָּת לָמוֹ:
3 אַף חֹבֵב עַמִּים
כָּל־קְדֹשָׁיו בְּיָדֶךָ
וְהֵם תֻּכּוּ לְרַגְלֶךָ
יִשָּׂא מִדַּבְּרֹתֶיךָ:
4 תּוֹרָה צִוָּה־לָנוּ מֹשֶׁה
מוֹרָשָׁה קְהִלַּת יַעֲקֹב:
5 וַיְהִי בִישֻׁרוּן מֶלֶךְ
בְּהִתְאַסֵּף רָאשֵׁי עָם
יַחַד שִׁבְטֵי יִשְׂרָאֵל:

6 יְחִי רְאוּבֵן וְאַל־יָמֹת
וִיהִי מְתָיו מִסְפָּר: ס

7 וְזֹאת לִיהוּדָה וַיֹּאמַר
שְׁמַע יְהֹוָה קוֹל יְהוּדָה
וְאֶל־עַמּוֹ תְּבִיאֶנּוּ
יָדָיו רָב לוֹ
וְעֵזֶר מִצָּרָיו תִּהְיֶה: ס

8And of Levi he said:

Let Your Thummim and Urim
Be with Your faithful one,
Whom You tested at Massah,
Challenged at the waters of Meribah;
9Who said of his father and mother,
"I consider them not."
His brothers he disregarded,
Ignored his own children.
Your precepts alone they observed,
And kept Your covenant.
10They shall teach Your laws to Jacob
And Your instructions to Israel.
e-They shall offer You incense to savor-e
And whole-offerings on Your altar.
11Bless, O LORD, his substance,
And favor his undertakings.
Smite the loins of his foes;
Let his enemies rise no more.

12Of Benjamin he said:
Beloved of the LORD,
He rests securely beside Him;
Ever does He protect him,
f-As he rests between His shoulders.-f

13And of Joseph he said:
Blessed of the LORD be his land
With the bounty of dew^g from heaven,
And of the deep that couches below;
14With the bounteous yield of the sun,
And the bounteous crop of the moons;
15With the best from the ancient mountains,
And the bounty of hills immemorial;
16With the bounty of earth and its fullness,
And the favor of the Presence^h in the Bush.
May these rest on the head of Joseph,

8 וּלְלֵוִי אָמַר
תֻּמֶּיךָ וְאוּרֶיךָ
לְאִישׁ חֲסִידֶךָ
אֲשֶׁר נִסִּיתוֹ בְּמַסָּה
תְּרִיבֵהוּ עַל־מֵי מְרִיבָה:
9 הָאֹמֵר לְאָבִיו וּלְאִמּוֹ
לֹא רְאִיתִיו
וְאֶת־אֶחָיו לֹא הִכִּיר
וְאֶת־בָּנָו לֹא יָדָע
כִּי שָׁמְרוּ אִמְרָתֶךָ
וּבְרִיתְךָ יִנְצֹרוּ:
10 יוֹרוּ מִשְׁפָּטֶיךָ לְיַעֲקֹב
וְתוֹרָתְךָ לְיִשְׂרָאֵל
יָשִׂימוּ קְטוֹרָה בְּאַפֶּךָ
וְכָלִיל עַל־מִזְבְּחֶךָ:
11 בָּרֵךְ יְהוָה חֵילוֹ
וּפֹעַל יָדָיו תִּרְצֶה
מְחַץ מָתְנַיִם קָמָיו
וּמְשַׂנְאָיו מִן־יְקוּמוּן: ס

12 לְבִנְיָמִן אָמַר
יְדִיד יְהוָה
יִשְׁכֹּן לָבֶטַח עָלָיו
חֹפֵף עָלָיו כָּל־הַיּוֹם
וּבֵין כְּתֵיפָיו שָׁכֵן: ס

13 וּלְיוֹסֵף אָמַר
מְבֹרֶכֶת יְהוָה אַרְצוֹ
מִמֶּגֶד שָׁמַיִם מִטָּל
וּמִתְּהוֹם רֹבֶצֶת תָּחַת:
14 וּמִמֶּגֶד תְּבוּאֹת שָׁמֶשׁ
וּמִמֶּגֶד גֶּרֶשׁ יְרָחִים:
15 וּמֵרֹאשׁ הַרְרֵי־קֶדֶם
וּמִמֶּגֶד גִּבְעוֹת עוֹלָם:
16 וּמִמֶּגֶד אֶרֶץ וּמְלֹאָהּ
וּרְצוֹן שֹׁכְנִי סְנֶה
תָּבוֹאתָה לְרֹאשׁ יוֹסֵף

---

e-e   Lit. "They shall place incense in Your nostril."
f-f   Or "He dwells amid his slopes."
g   Targum Onkelos and two Hebrew manuscripts read: "With the bounty of heaven above" (me'al for miṭṭal, cf. Gen. 49.25).
h   Lit. "Dweller"; cf. Exod. 3.1 ff.

On the crown of the elect of his brothers.

¹⁷Like a firstling bull in his majesty,
He has horns like the horns of the wild-ox;
With them he gores the peoples,
The ends of the earth one and all.
Theseⁱ are the myriads of Ephraim,
Those^j are the thousands of Manasseh.

¹⁸And of Zebulun he said:
Rejoice, O Zebulun, on your journeys,
And Issachar, in your tents.
¹⁹They invite their kin to the mountain,
Where they offer sacrifices of success.
For they draw from the riches of the sea
And the hidden hoards of the sand.

²⁰And of Gad he said:
Blessed be He who enlarges Gad!
Poised is he like a lion
To tear off arm and scalp.
^{21k}-He chose for himself the best,
For there is the portion of the revered chief-
 tain,
Where the heads of the people come.
He executed the LORD's judgments
And His decisions for Israel.-^k

²²And of Dan he said:
Dan is a lion's whelp
That leaps forth from Bashan.

²³And of Naphtali he said:
O Naphtali, sated with favor
And full of the LORD's blessing,
Take possession on the west and south.

²⁴And of Asher he said:
Most blessed of sons be Asher;
May he be the favorite of his brothers,
May he dip his foot in oil.

---

i   I.e., the one horn.
j   I.e., the other horn.
k-k   Meaning of Heb. uncertain; cf. vv. 3–5 (with note c) above,
    and saphun "esteemed" in post-biblical Heb.

וּלְקָדְקֹד נְזִיר אֶחָיו:

17 בְּכוֹר שׁוֹרוֹ הָדָר לוֹ
וְקַרְנֵי רְאֵם קַרְנָיו
בָּהֶם עַמִּים יְנַגַּח
יַחְדָּו אַפְסֵי־אָרֶץ
וְהֵם רִבְבוֹת אֶפְרַיִם
וְהֵם אַלְפֵי מְנַשֶּׁה: ס

18 וְלִזְבוּלֻן אָמַר
שְׂמַח זְבוּלֻן בְּצֵאתֶךָ
וְיִשָּׂשכָר בְּאֹהָלֶיךָ:
19 עַמִּים הַר־יִקְרָאוּ
שָׁם יִזְבְּחוּ זִבְחֵי־צֶדֶק
כִּי שֶׁפַע יַמִּים יִינָקוּ
וּשְׂפוּנֵי טְמוּנֵי חוֹל: ס

20 וּלְגָד אָמַר
בָּרוּךְ מַרְחִיב גָּד
כְּלָבִיא שָׁכֵן
וְטָרַף זְרוֹעַ אַף־קָדְקֹד:
21 וַיַּרְא רֵאשִׁית לוֹ
כִּי־שָׁם חֶלְקַת מְחֹקֵק סָפוּן
וַיֵּתֵא רָאשֵׁי עָם
צִדְקַת יְהוָה עָשָׂה
וּמִשְׁפָּטָיו עִם־יִשְׂרָאֵל: ס

22 וּלְדָן אָמַר
דָּן גּוּר אַרְיֵה
יְזַנֵּק מִן־הַבָּשָׁן:

23 וּלְנַפְתָּלִי אָמַר
נַפְתָּלִי שְׂבַע רָצוֹן
וּמָלֵא בִּרְכַּת יְהוָה
יָם וְדָרוֹם יְרָשָׁה: ס

24 וּלְאָשֵׁר אָמַר
בָּרוּךְ מִבָּנִים אָשֵׁר
יְהִי רְצוּי אֶחָיו
וְטֹבֵל בַּשֶּׁמֶן רַגְלוֹ:

²⁵May your doorbolts be iron and copper,
And your security last all your days.

²⁶O Jeshurun, there is none like God,
Riding through the heavens to help you,
Through the skies in His majesty.
^{27l}The ancient God is a refuge,
A support are the arms everlasting.
He drove out the enemy before you
By His command: Destroy!
²⁸Thus Israel dwells in safety,
Untroubled is Jacob's abode,^m
In a land of grain and wine,
Under heavens dripping dew.
²⁹O happy Israel! Who is like you,
A people delivered by the LORD,
Your protecting Shield, your Sword triumphant!
Your enemies shall come cringing before you,
And you shall tread on their backs.

34 ²Moses went up from the steppes of Moab to Mount Nebo, to the summit of Pisgah, opposite Jericho, and the LORD showed him the whole land: Gilead as far as Dan; ²all Naphtali; the land of Ephraim and Manasseh; the whole land of Judah as far as the Western^a Sea; ³the Negeb; and the Plain—the Valley of Jericho, the city of palm trees—as far as Zoar. ⁴And the LORD said to him, "This is the land of which I swore to Abraham, Isaac, and Jacob, 'I will assign it to your offspring.' I have let you see it with your own eyes, but you shall not cross there."

⁵So Moses the servant of the LORD died there, in the land of Moab, at the command of the LORD. ⁶He buried him in the valley in the land of Moab, near Beth-peor; and no one knows his burial place to this day. ⁷Moses was a hundred

25 בַּרְזֶל וּנְחֹשֶׁת מִנְעָלֶיךָ
וּכְיָמֶיךָ דָּבְאֶךָ:

26 אֵין כָּאֵל יְשֻׁרוּן
רֹכֵב שָׁמַיִם בְּעֶזְרֶךָ
וּבְגַאֲוָתוֹ שְׁחָקִים:
27 מְעֹנָה אֱלֹהֵי קֶדֶם
וּמִתַּחַת זְרֹעֹת עוֹלָם
וַיְגָרֶשׁ מִפָּנֶיךָ אוֹיֵב
וַיֹּאמֶר הַשְׁמֵד:
28 וַיִּשְׁכֹּן יִשְׂרָאֵל בֶּטַח
בָּדָד עֵין יַעֲקֹב
אֶל־אֶרֶץ דָּגָן וְתִירוֹשׁ
אַף־שָׁמָיו יַעַרְפוּ טָל:
29 אַשְׁרֶיךָ יִשְׂרָאֵל מִי כָמוֹךָ
עַם נוֹשַׁע בַּיהוָה
מָגֵן עֶזְרֶךָ וַאֲשֶׁר־חֶרֶב גַּאֲוָתֶךָ
וְיִכָּחֲשׁוּ אֹיְבֶיךָ לָךְ
וְאַתָּה עַל־בָּמוֹתֵימוֹ תִדְרֹךְ: ס

לד וַיַּעַל מֹשֶׁה מֵעַרְבֹת מוֹאָב אֶל־
הַר נְבוֹ רֹאשׁ הַפִּסְגָּה אֲשֶׁר עַל־פְּנֵי יְרֵחוֹ
וַיַּרְאֵהוּ יְהוָה אֶת־כָּל־הָאָרֶץ אֶת־הַגִּלְעָד
עַד־דָּן: 2 וְאֵת כָּל־נַפְתָּלִי וְאֶת־אֶרֶץ
אֶפְרַיִם וּמְנַשֶּׁה וְאֵת כָּל־אֶרֶץ יְהוּדָה עַד
הַיָּם הָאַחֲרוֹן: 3 וְאֶת־הַנֶּגֶב וְאֶת־הַכִּכָּר
בִּקְעַת יְרֵחוֹ עִיר הַתְּמָרִים עַד־צֹעַר:
4 וַיֹּאמֶר יְהוָה אֵלָיו זֹאת הָאָרֶץ אֲשֶׁר
נִשְׁבַּעְתִּי לְאַבְרָהָם לְיִצְחָק וּלְיַעֲקֹב לֵאמֹר
לְזַרְעֲךָ אֶתְּנֶנָּה הֶרְאִיתִיךָ בְעֵינֶיךָ וְשָׁמָּה
לֹא תַעֲבֹר:

5 וַיָּמָת שָׁם מֹשֶׁה עֶבֶד־יְהוָה בְּאֶרֶץ מוֹאָב
עַל־פִּי יְהוָה: 6 וַיִּקְבֹּר אֹתוֹ בַגַּי בְּאֶרֶץ
מוֹאָב מוּל בֵּית פְּעוֹר וְלֹא־יָדַע אִישׁ
אֶת־קְבֻרָתוֹ עַד הַיּוֹם הַזֶּה: 7 וּמֹשֶׁה בֶּן־

---

l   *Meaning of Heb. uncertain.*
m   *Others "fountain."*

a   *I.e., Mediterranean; cf. note at 11.24.*

and twenty years old when he died; his eyes were undimmed and his vigor unabated. [8]And the Israelites bewailed Moses in the steppes of Moab for thirty days.

The period of wailing and mourning for Moses came to an end. [9]Now Joshua son of Nun was filled with the spirit of wisdom because Moses had laid his hands upon him; and the Israelites heeded him, doing as the Lord had commanded Moses.

[10]Never again did there arise in Israel a prophet like Moses—whom the Lord singled out, face to face, [11]for the various signs and portents that the Lord sent him to display in the land of Egypt, against Pharaoh and all his courtiers and his whole country, [12]and for all the great might and awesome power that Moses displayed before all Israel.

מֵאָה וְעֶשְׂרִים שָׁנָה בְּמֹתֹו לֹא־כָהֲתָה עֵינוֹ וְלֹא־נָס לֵחֹה: 8 וַיִּבְכּוּ בְנֵי יִשְׂרָאֵל אֶת־מֹשֶׁה בְּעַרְבֹת מוֹאָב שְׁלֹשִׁים יֹום וַיִּתְּמוּ יְמֵי בְכִי אֵבֶל מֹשֶׁה: 9 וִיהוֹשֻׁעַ בִּן־נוּן מָלֵא רוּחַ חָכְמָה כִּי־סָמַךְ מֹשֶׁה אֶת־יָדָיו עָלָיו וַיִּשְׁמְעוּ אֵלָיו בְּנֵי־יִשְׂרָאֵל וַיַּעֲשׂוּ כַּאֲשֶׁר צִוָּה יְהוָה אֶת־מֹשֶׁה: 10 וְלֹא־קָם נָבִיא עוֹד בְּיִשְׂרָאֵל כְּמֹשֶׁה אֲשֶׁר יְדָעוֹ יְהוָה פָּנִים אֶל־פָּנִים: 11 לְכָל־הָאֹתֹת וְהַמּוֹפְתִים אֲשֶׁר שְׁלָחוֹ יְהוָה לַעֲשֹׂות בְּאֶרֶץ מִצְרָיִם לְפַרְעֹה וּלְכָל־עֲבָדָיו וּלְכָל־אַרְצוֹ: 12 וּלְכֹל הַיָּד הַחֲזָקָה וּלְכֹל הַמּוֹרָא הַגָּדֹול אֲשֶׁר עָשָׂה מֹשֶׁה לְעֵינֵי כָּל־יִשְׂרָאֵל: **

תם ונשלם תהילה לאל בורא עולם

v. 12. למערבאי סכום הפסוקים של ספר 955 וחציו
17.10
v. 12. סכום הפסוקים של תורה 5,845

NEVI'IM THE PROPHETS

JOSHUA	יהושע
JUDGES	שופטים
1 SAMUEL	שמואל א
2 SAMUEL	שמואל ב
1 KINGS	מלכים א
2 KINGS	מלכים ב
ISAIAH	ישעיה
JEREMIAH	ירמיה
EZEKIEL	יחזקאל

The Twelve Minor Prophets

HOSEA	הושע
JOEL	יואל
AMOS	עמוס
OBADIAH	עבדיה
JONAH	יונה
MICAH	מיכה
NAHUM	נחום
HABAKKUK	חבקוק
ZEPHANIAH	צפניה
HAGGAI	חגי
ZECHARIAH	זכריה
MALACHI	מלאכי

NEVI'IM THE PROPHETS

JOSHUA

1 After the death of Moses the servant of the LORD, the LORD said to Joshua son of Nun, Moses' attendant:

2"My servant Moses is dead. Prepare to cross the Jordan, together with all this people, into the land that I am giving to the Israelites. 3Every spot on which your foot treads I give to you, as I promised Moses. 4Your territory shall extend from the wilderness and the Lebanon to the Great River, the River Euphrates [on the east]—the whole Hittite country—and up to the Mediterranean*a* Sea on the west. 5No one shall be able to resist you as long as you live. As I was with Moses, so I will be with you; I will not fail you or forsake you.

6"Be strong and resolute, for you shall apportion to this people the land that I swore to their fathers to assign to them. 7But you must be very strong and resolute to observe faithfully all the Teaching that My servant Moses enjoined upon you. Do not deviate from it to the right or to the left, that you may be successful wherever you go. 8Let not this Book of the Teaching cease from your lips, but recite it day and night, so that you may observe faithfully all that is written in it. Only then will you prosper in your undertakings and only then will you be successful.

9"I charge you: Be strong and resolute; do not be terrified or dismayed, for the LORD your God is with you wherever you go."

10Joshua thereupon gave orders to the officials of the people: 11"Go through the camp

---

a Heb. "Great."

457

א וַיְהִי אַחֲרֵי מוֹת מֹשֶׁה עֶבֶד יְהוָה וַיֹּאמֶר יְהוָה אֶל־יְהוֹשֻׁעַ בִּן־נוּן מְשָׁרֵת מֹשֶׁה לֵאמֹר: 2 מֹשֶׁה עַבְדִּי מֵת וְעַתָּה קוּם עֲבֹר אֶת־הַיַּרְדֵּן הַזֶּה אַתָּה וְכָל־הָעָם הַזֶּה אֶל־הָאָרֶץ אֲשֶׁר אָנֹכִי נֹתֵן לָהֶם לִבְנֵי יִשְׂרָאֵל: 3 כָּל־מָקוֹם אֲשֶׁר תִּדְרֹךְ כַּף־רַגְלְכֶם בּוֹ לָכֶם נְתַתִּיו כַּאֲשֶׁר דִּבַּרְתִּי אֶל־מֹשֶׁה: 4 מֵהַמִּדְבָּר וְהַלְּבָנוֹן הַזֶּה וְעַד־הַנָּהָר הַגָּדוֹל נְהַר־פְּרָת כֹּל אֶרֶץ הַחִתִּים וְעַד־הַיָּם הַגָּדוֹל מְבוֹא הַשָּׁמֶשׁ יִהְיֶה גְּבוּלְכֶם: 5 לֹא־יִתְיַצֵּב אִישׁ לְפָנֶיךָ כֹּל יְמֵי חַיֶּיךָ כַּאֲשֶׁר הָיִיתִי עִם־מֹשֶׁה אֶהְיֶה עִמָּךְ לֹא אַרְפְּךָ וְלֹא אֶעֶזְבֶךָּ: 6 חֲזַק וֶאֱמָץ כִּי אַתָּה תַּנְחִיל אֶת־הָעָם הַזֶּה אֶת־הָאָרֶץ אֲשֶׁר־נִשְׁבַּעְתִּי לַאֲבוֹתָם לָתֵת לָהֶם: 7 רַק חֲזַק וֶאֱמַץ מְאֹד לִשְׁמֹר לַעֲשׂוֹת כְּכָל־הַתּוֹרָה אֲשֶׁר צִוְּךָ מֹשֶׁה עַבְדִּי אַל־תָּסוּר מִמֶּנּוּ* יָמִין וּשְׂמֹאול* לְמַעַן תַּשְׂכִּיל בְּכֹל אֲשֶׁר תֵּלֵךְ: 8 לֹא־יָמוּשׁ סֵפֶר הַתּוֹרָה הַזֶּה מִפִּיךָ וְהָגִיתָ בּוֹ יוֹמָם וָלַיְלָה לְמַעַן תִּשְׁמֹר לַעֲשׂוֹת כְּכָל־הַכָּתוּב בּוֹ כִּי־אָז תַּצְלִיחַ אֶת־דְּרָכֶךָ וְאָז תַּשְׂכִּיל: 9 הֲלוֹא צִוִּיתִיךָ חֲזַק וֶאֱמָץ אַל־תַּעֲרֹץ וְאַל־תֵּחָת כִּי עִמְּךָ יְהוָה אֱלֹהֶיךָ בְּכֹל אֲשֶׁר תֵּלֵךְ: פ

10 וַיְצַו יְהוֹשֻׁעַ אֶת־שֹׁטְרֵי הָעָם לֵאמֹר: 11 עִבְרוּ ׀ בְּקֶרֶב הַמַּחֲנֶה וְצַוּוּ אֶת־הָעָם

v. 7. סבירין ומטעין "ממנה"
v. 7. מלא ו'

and charge the people thus: Get provisions ready, for in three days' time you are to cross the Jordan, in order to enter and possess the land that the LORD your God is giving you as a possession."

¹²Then Joshua said to the Reubenites, the Gadites, and the half-tribe of Manasseh, ¹³"Remember what Moses the servant of the LORD enjoined upon you, when he said: 'The LORD your God is granting you a haven; He has assigned this territory to you.' ¹⁴Let your wives, children, and livestock remain in the land that Moses assigned to you ᵇ-on this side of-ᵇ the Jordan; but every one of your fighting men shall go across armedᶜ in the van of your kinsmen. And you shall assist them ¹⁵until the LORD has given your kinsmen a haven, such as you have, and they too have gained possession of the land that the LORD your God has assigned to them. Then you may return to the land on the east side of the Jordan, which Moses the servant of the LORD assigned to you as your possession, and you may possess it."

¹⁶They answered Joshua, "We will do everything you have commanded us and we will go wherever you send us. ¹⁷We will obey you just as we obeyed Moses; let but the LORD your God be with you as He was with Moses! ¹⁸Any man who flouts your commands and does not obey every order you give him shall be put to death. Only be strong and resolute!"

2 Joshua son of Nun secretly sent two spies from Shittim, saying, "Go, reconnoiter the region of Jericho." So they set out, and they came to the house of a harlot named Rahab and lodged there. ²The king of Jericho was told, "Some men have come here tonight, Israelites, to spy out the country." ³The king of Jericho

לֵאמֹר הָכִ֣ינוּ לָכֶ֖ם צֵידָ֑ה כִּ֣י בְּע֣וֹד ׀ שְׁלֹ֣שֶׁת יָמִ֗ים אַתֶּם֙ עֹֽבְרִים֙ אֶת־הַיַּרְדֵּ֣ן הַזֶּ֔ה לָבוֹא֙ לָרֶ֣שֶׁת אֶת־הָאָ֔רֶץ אֲשֶׁר֙ יְהוָ֣ה אֱלֹֽהֵיכֶ֔ם נֹתֵ֥ן לָכֶ֖ם לְרִשְׁתָּֽהּ׃ ס

¹²וְלָרֽאוּבֵנִי֙ וְלַגָּדִ֔י וְלַֽחֲצִ֖י שֵׁ֣בֶט הַֽמְנַשֶּׁ֑ה אָמַ֥ר יְהוֹשֻׁ֖עַ לֵאמֹֽר׃ ¹³זָכוֹר֙ אֶת־הַדָּבָ֔ר אֲשֶׁ֨ר צִוָּ֥ה אֶתְכֶ֛ם מֹשֶׁ֥ה עֶֽבֶד־יְהוָ֖ה לֵאמֹ֑ר יְהוָ֤ה אֱלֹהֵיכֶם֙ מֵנִ֣יחַ לָכֶ֔ם וְנָתַ֥ן לָכֶ֖ם אֶת־הָאָ֥רֶץ הַזֹּֽאת׃ ¹⁴נְשֵׁיכֶ֣ם טַפְּכֶם֮ וּמִקְנֵיכֶם֒ יֵֽשְׁבוּ֙ בָּאָ֔רֶץ אֲשֶׁ֨ר נָתַ֥ן לָכֶ֛ם מֹשֶׁ֖ה בְּעֵ֣בֶר הַיַּרְדֵּ֑ן וְאַתֶּם֩ תַּֽעַבְר֨וּ חֲמֻשִׁ֜ים לִפְנֵ֣י אֲחֵיכֶ֗ם כֹּ֚ל גִּבּוֹרֵ֣י הַחַ֔יִל וַֽעֲזַרְתֶּ֖ם אוֹתָֽם׃ ¹⁵עַ֠ד אֲשֶׁר־יָנִ֨יחַ יְהוָ֥ה ׀ לַֽאֲחֵיכֶם֮ כָּכֶם֒ וְיָֽרְשׁ֣וּ גַם־הֵ֔מָּה אֶת־הָאָ֕רֶץ אֲשֶׁר־ יְהוָ֥ה אֱלֹֽהֵיכֶ֖ם נֹתֵ֣ן לָהֶ֑ם וְשַׁבְתֶּ֞ם לְאֶ֣רֶץ יְרֻשַּׁתְכֶ֗ם וִֽירִשְׁתֶּ֤ם אוֹתָהּ֙ אֲשֶׁ֣ר ׀ נָתַ֣ן לָכֶ֗ם מֹשֶׁה֙ עֶ֣בֶד יְהוָ֔ה בְּעֵ֥בֶר הַיַּרְדֵּ֖ן מִזְרַ֥ח הַשָּֽׁמֶשׁ׃

¹⁶וַֽיַּֽעֲנ֔וּ אֶת־יְהוֹשֻׁ֖עַ לֵאמֹ֑ר כֹּ֤ל אֲשֶׁר־ צִוִּיתָ֨נוּ֙ נַֽעֲשֶׂ֔ה וְאֶֽל־כָּל־אֲשֶׁ֥ר תִּשְׁלָחֵ֖נוּ נֵלֵֽךְ׃ ¹⁷כְּכֹ֤ל אֲשֶׁר־שָׁמַ֨עְנוּ֙ אֶל־מֹשֶׁ֔ה כֵּ֥ן נִשְׁמַ֖ע אֵלֶ֑יךָ רַ֠ק יִֽהְיֶ֞ה יְהוָ֤ה אֱלֹהֶ֨יךָ֙ עִמָּ֔ךְ כַּֽאֲשֶׁ֥ר הָיָ֖ה עִם־מֹשֶֽׁה׃ ¹⁸כָּל־אִ֞ישׁ אֲשֶׁר־ יַמְרֶ֣ה אֶת־פִּ֗יךָ וְלֹֽא־יִשְׁמַ֧ע אֶת־דְּבָרֶ֛יךָ לְכֹ֥ל אֲשֶׁר־תְּצַוֶּ֖נּוּ יוּמָ֑ת רַ֖ק חֲזַ֥ק וֶֽאֱמָֽץ׃ פ

ב ¹וַיִּשְׁלַ֣ח יְהוֹשֻׁ֣עַ־בִּן־נ֠וּן מִן־הַשִּׁטִּ֞ים שְׁנַֽיִם־אֲנָשִׁ֤ים מְרַגְּלִים֙ חֶ֣רֶשׁ לֵאמֹ֔ר לְכ֛וּ רְא֥וּ אֶת־הָאָ֖רֶץ וְאֶת־יְרִיח֑וֹ וַיֵּ֨לְכ֜וּ וַיָּבֹ֜אוּ בֵּית־אִשָּׁ֥ה זוֹנָ֛ה וּשְׁמָ֥הּ רָחָ֖ב וַיִּשְׁכְּבוּ־ שָֽׁמָּה׃ ²וַיֵּֽאָמַ֗ר לְמֶ֤לֶךְ יְרִיחוֹ֙ לֵאמֹ֔ר הִנֵּ֣ה אֲנָשִׁ֗ים בָּ֣אוּ הֵ֧נָּה הַלַּ֛יְלָה מִבְּנֵ֥י יִשְׂרָאֵ֖ל

ᵇ⁻ᵇ Lit. "across."
ᶜ Meaning of Heb. uncertain.

458

thereupon sent orders to Rahab: "Produce the men who came to you and entered your house, for they have come to spy out the whole country." [4]The woman, however, had taken the two men and hidden them. "It is true," she said, "the men did come to me, but I didn't know where they were from. [5]And at dark, when the gate was about to be closed, the men left; and I don't know where the men went. Quick, go after them, for you can overtake them."—[6]Now she had taken them up to the roof and hidden them under some stalks of flax which she had lying on the roof.—[7]So the men pursued them in the direction of the Jordan down to the fords; and no sooner had the pursuers gone out than the gate was shut behind them.

[8a]-The spies-[a] had not yet gone to sleep when she came up to them on the roof. [9]She said to the men, "I know that the LORD has given the country to you, because dread of you has fallen upon us, and all the inhabitants of the land are quaking before you. [10]For we have heard how the LORD dried up the waters of the Sea of Reeds for you when you left Egypt, and what you did to Sihon and Og, the two Amorite kings across the Jordan, whom you doomed.[b] [11]When we heard about it, we lost heart, and no man had any more spirit left because of you; for the LORD your God is the only God in heaven above and on earth below. [12]Now, since I have shown loyalty to you, swear to me by the LORD that you in turn will show loyalty to my family. Provide me with a reliable sign [13]that you will spare the lives of my father and mother, my brothers and sisters, and all who belong to them, and save us from death." [14]The men answered her, "Our persons are pledged for yours, even to death! If you do not disclose this mission of ours, we will show you true loyalty when the LORD gives us the land."

לַחְפֹּר אֶת־הָאָרֶץ: 3 וַיִּשְׁלַח מֶלֶךְ יְרִיחוֹ
אֶל־רָחָב לֵאמֹר הוֹצִיאִי הָאֲנָשִׁים הַבָּאִים
אֵלַיִךְ אֲשֶׁר־בָּאוּ לְבֵיתֵךְ כִּי לַחְפֹּר אֶת־
כָּל־הָאָרֶץ בָּאוּ: 4 וַתִּקַּח הָאִשָּׁה אֶת־שְׁנֵי
הָאֲנָשִׁים וַתִּצְפְּנוֹ וַתֹּאמֶר ׀ כֵּן בָּאוּ אֵלַי
הָאֲנָשִׁים וְלֹא יָדַעְתִּי מֵאַיִן הֵמָּה: 5 וַיְהִי
הַשַּׁעַר לִסְגּוֹר בַּחֹשֶׁךְ וְהָאֲנָשִׁים יָצָאוּ לֹא
יָדַעְתִּי אָנָה הָלְכוּ הָאֲנָשִׁים רִדְפוּ מַהֵר
אַחֲרֵיהֶם כִּי תַשִּׂיגוּם: 6 וְהִיא הֶעֱלָתַם
הַגָּגָה וַתִּטְמְנֵם בְּפִשְׁתֵּי הָעֵץ הָעֲרֻכוֹת
לָהּ עַל־הַגָּג: 7 וְהָאֲנָשִׁים רָדְפוּ אַחֲרֵיהֶם
דֶּרֶךְ הַיַּרְדֵּן עַל הַמַּעְבְּרוֹת וְהַשַּׁעַר סָגָרוּ
אַחֲרֵי כַּאֲשֶׁר יָצְאוּ הָרֹדְפִים אַחֲרֵיהֶם:
8 וְהֵמָּה טֶרֶם יִשְׁכָּבוּן וְהִיא עָלְתָה עֲלֵיהֶם
עַל־הַגָּג: 9 וַתֹּאמֶר אֶל־הָאֲנָשִׁים יָדַעְתִּי
כִּי־נָתַן יְהוָה לָכֶם אֶת־הָאָרֶץ וְכִי־נָפְלָה
אֵימַתְכֶם עָלֵינוּ וְכִי נָמֹגוּ כָּל־יֹשְׁבֵי הָאָרֶץ
מִפְּנֵיכֶם: 10 כִּי שָׁמַעְנוּ אֵת אֲשֶׁר־הוֹבִישׁ
יְהוָה אֶת־מֵי יַם־סוּף מִפְּנֵיכֶם בְּצֵאתְכֶם
מִמִּצְרָיִם וַאֲשֶׁר עֲשִׂיתֶם לִשְׁנֵי מַלְכֵי
הָאֱמֹרִי אֲשֶׁר בְּעֵבֶר הַיַּרְדֵּן לְסִיחֹן וּלְעוֹג
אֲשֶׁר הֶחֱרַמְתֶּם אוֹתָם: 11 וַנִּשְׁמַע וַיִּמַּס
לְבָבֵנוּ וְלֹא־קָמָה עוֹד רוּחַ בְּאִישׁ מִפְּנֵיכֶם
כִּי יְהוָה אֱלֹהֵיכֶם הוּא אֱלֹהִים בַּשָּׁמַיִם
מִמַּעַל וְעַל־הָאָרֶץ מִתָּחַת: 12 וְעַתָּה
הִשָּׁבְעוּ־נָא לִי בַּיהוָה כִּי־עָשִׂיתִי עִמָּכֶם
חָסֶד וַעֲשִׂיתֶם גַּם־אַתֶּם עִם־בֵּית אָבִי
חֶסֶד וּנְתַתֶּם לִי אוֹת אֱמֶת: 13 וְהַחֲיִתֶם
אֶת־אָבִי וְאֶת־אִמִּי וְאֶת־אַחַי וְאֶת־אַחְיוֹתַי
אַחְיוֹתַי וְאֵת כָּל־אֲשֶׁר לָהֶם וְהִצַּלְתֶּם
אֶת־נַפְשֹׁתֵינוּ מִמָּוֶת: 14 וַיֹּאמְרוּ לָהּ
הָאֲנָשִׁים נַפְשֵׁנוּ תַחְתֵּיכֶם לָמוּת אִם לֹא
תַגִּידוּ אֶת־דְּבָרֵנוּ זֶה וְהָיָה בְּתֵת־יְהוָה
לָנוּ אֶת־הָאָרֶץ וְעָשִׂינוּ עִמָּךְ חֶסֶד וֶאֱמֶת:

---

a-a   Heb. "They."
b   I.e., placed under ḥerem, which meant the annihilation of the inhabitants. Cf. Deut. 2.34 ff.

15She let them down by a rope through the window—for her dwelling was at the outer side of the city wall and she lived in the actual wall. 16She said to them, "Make for the hills, so that the pursuers may not come upon you. Stay there in hiding three days, until the pursuers return; then go your way."

17But the men warned her, "We will be released from this oath which you have made us take 18[unless,] when we invade the country, you tie this length of crimson cord to the window through which you let us down. Bring your father, your mother, your brothers, and all your family together in your house; 19and if anyone ventures outside the doors of your house, his blood will be on his head, and we shall be clear. But if a hand is laid on anyone who remains in the house with you, his blood shall be on our heads. 20And if you disclose this mission of ours, we shall likewise be released from the oath which you made us take." 21She replied, "Let it be as you say."

She sent them on their way, and they left; and she tied the crimson cord to the window.

22They went straight to the hills and stayed there three days, until the pursuers turned back. And so the pursuers, searching all along the road, did not find them.

23Then the two men came down again from the hills and crossed over. They came to Joshua son of Nun and reported to him all that had happened to them. 24They said to Joshua, "The Lord has delivered the whole land into our power; in fact, all the inhabitants of the land are quaking before us."

3 Early next morning, Joshua and all the Israelites set out from Shittim and marched to the Jordan. They did not cross immediately, but spent the night there. 2Three days later, the

15 וַתּוֹרִדֵ֥ם בַּחֶ֖בֶל בְּעַ֣ד הַֽחַלּ֑וֹן כִּ֤י בֵיתָהּ֙ בְּקִ֣יר הַֽחוֹמָ֔ה וּבַֽחוֹמָ֖ה הִ֥יא יוֹשָֽׁבֶת׃ 16 וַתֹּ֤אמֶר לָהֶם֙ הָהָ֣רָה לֵּ֔כוּ פֶּֽן־יִפְגְּע֥וּ בָכֶ֖ם הָרֹֽדְפִ֑ים וְנַחְבֵּתֶ֨ם שָׁ֜מָּה שְׁלֹ֣שֶׁת יָמִ֗ים עַ֚ד שׁ֣וֹב הָרֹֽדְפִ֔ים וְאַחַ֖ר תֵּֽלְכ֥וּ לְדַרְכְּכֶֽם׃ 17 וַיֹּֽאמְר֥וּ אֵלֶ֖יהָ הָֽאֲנָשִׁ֑ים נְקִיִּ֣ם אֲנַ֔חְנוּ מִשְּׁבֻעָתֵ֥ךְ הַזֶּ֖ה אֲשֶׁ֥ר הִשְׁבַּעְתָּֽנוּ׃ 18 הִנֵּ֛ה אֲנַ֥חְנוּ בָאִ֖ים בָּאָ֑רֶץ אֶת־תִּקְוַ֡ת חוּט֩ הַשָּׁנִ֨י הַזֶּ֜ה תִּקְשְׁרִ֗י בַּֽחַלּוֹן֙ אֲשֶׁ֣ר הֽוֹרַדְתֵּ֣נוּ ב֔וֹ וְאֶת־אָבִ֨יךְ וְאֶת־אִמֵּ֜ךְ וְאֶת־אַחַ֗יִךְ וְאֵת֙ כָּל־בֵּ֣ית אָבִ֔יךְ תַּֽאַסְפִ֥י אֵלַ֖יִךְ הַבָּֽיְתָה׃ 19 וְהָיָ֡ה כֹּ֣ל אֲשֶׁר־יֵצֵא֩ מִדַּלְתֵ֨י בֵיתֵ֤ךְ ׀ הַח֨וּצָה֙ דָּמ֣וֹ בְרֹאשׁ֔וֹ וַֽאֲנַ֖חְנוּ נְקִיִּ֑ם וְ֠כֹל אֲשֶׁ֨ר יִֽהְיֶ֤ה אִתָּךְ֙ בַּבַּ֔יִת דָּמ֣וֹ בְרֹאשֵׁ֔נוּ אִם־יָ֖ד תִּֽהְיֶה־בּֽוֹ׃ 20 וְאִם־תַּגִּ֖ידִי אֶת־דְּבָרֵ֣נוּ זֶ֑ה וְהָיִ֣ינוּ נְקִיִּ֔ם מִשְּׁבֻעָתֵ֖ךְ אֲשֶׁ֥ר הִשְׁבַּעְתָּֽנוּ׃ 21 וַתֹּ֨אמֶר֙ כְּדִבְרֵיכֶ֣ם כֶּן־ה֔וּא וַֽתְּשַׁלְּחֵ֖ם וַיֵּלֵ֑כוּ וַתִּקְשֹׁ֛ר אֶת־תִּקְוַ֥ת הַשָּׁנִ֖י בַּֽחַלּֽוֹן׃ 22 וַיֵּֽלְכוּ֙ וַיָּבֹ֣אוּ הָהָ֔רָה וַיֵּ֤שְׁבוּ שָׁם֙ שְׁלֹ֣שֶׁת יָמִ֔ים עַד־שָׁ֖בוּ הָרֹֽדְפִ֑ים וַיְבַקְשׁ֧וּ הָרֹֽדְפִ֛ים בְּכָל־הַדֶּ֖רֶךְ וְלֹ֥א מָצָֽאוּ׃ 23 וַיָּשֻׁ֜בוּ שְׁנֵ֤י הָֽאֲנָשִׁים֙ וַיֵּֽרְד֣וּ מֵֽהָהָ֔ר וַיַּֽעַבְרוּ֙ וַיָּבֹ֔אוּ אֶל־יְהוֹשֻׁ֖עַ בִּן־נ֑וּן וַיְסַפְּרוּ־ל֕וֹ אֵ֥ת כָּל־הַמֹּֽצְא֖וֹת אוֹתָֽם׃ 24 וַיֹּֽאמְרוּ֙ אֶל־יְהוֹשֻׁ֔עַ כִּֽי־נָתַ֧ן יְהוָ֛ה בְּיָדֵ֖נוּ אֶת־כָּל־הָאָ֑רֶץ וְגַם־נָמֹ֛גוּ כָּל־יֹֽשְׁבֵ֥י הָאָ֖רֶץ מִפָּנֵֽינוּ׃ ס

ג וַיַּשְׁכֵּם֩ יְהוֹשֻׁ֨עַ בַּבֹּ֜קֶר וַיִּסְע֣וּ מֵֽהַשִּׁטִּ֗ים וַיָּבֹ֙אוּ֙ עַד־הַיַּרְדֵּ֔ן ה֖וּא וְכָל־בְּנֵ֣י יִשְׂרָאֵ֑ל וַיָּלִ֥נוּ שָׁ֖ם טֶ֥רֶם יַֽעֲבֹֽרוּ׃ 2 וַיְהִ֕י מִקְצֵ֖ה

officials went through the camp ³and charged the people as follows: "When you see the Ark of the Covenant of the Lord your God being borne by the levitical priests, you shall move forward. Follow it—⁴but keep a distance of some two thousand cubits from it, never coming any closer to it—so that you may know by what route to march, since it is a road you have not traveled before." ⁵And Joshua said to the people, "Purify yourselves,ᵃ for tomorrow the Lord will perform wonders in your midst."

⁶Then Joshua ordered the priests, "Take up the Ark of the Covenant and advance to the head of the people." And they took up the Ark of the Covenant and marched at the head of the people.

⁷The Lord said to Joshua, "This day, for the first time, I will exalt you in the sight of all Israel, so that they shall know that I will be with you as I was with Moses. ⁸For your part, command the priests who carry the Ark of the Covenant as follows: When you reach the edge of the waters of the Jordan, make a halt in the Jordan."

⁹And Joshua said to the Israelites, "Come closer and listen to the words of the Lord your God. ¹⁰By this," Joshua continued, "you shall know that a living God is among you, and that He will dispossess for you the Canaanites, Hittites, Hivites, Perizzites, Girgashites, Amorites, and Jebusites: ¹¹the Ark of the Covenant of the Sovereign of all the earth is advancing before you into the Jordan. ¹²Now select twelve men from the tribes of Israel, one man from each tribe. ¹³When the feet of the priests bearing the Ark of the Lord, the Sovereign of all the earth, come to rest in the waters of the Jordan, the waters of the Jordan—the water coming from upstream—will be cut off and will stand in a single heap."

¹⁴When the people set out from their en-

ᵃ See Exod. 19.10, 15.

שְׁלֹ֣שֶׁת יָמִ֑ים וַיַּעַבְר֤וּ הַשֹּֽׁטְרִים֙ בְּקֶ֣רֶב הַֽמַּחֲנֶֽה׃ 3 וַיְצַוּוּ֙ אֶת־הָעָ֣ם לֵאמֹ֔ר כִּרְאֽוֹתְכֶ֗ם אֵ֣ת אֲר֤וֹן בְּרִית־יְהוָה֙ אֱלֹ֣הֵיכֶ֔ם וְהַכֹּֽהֲנִים֙ הַלְוִיִּ֔ם נֹשְׂאִ֖ים אֹת֑וֹ וְאַתֶּ֗ם תִּסְע֙וּ מִמְּק֣וֹמְכֶ֔ם וַהֲלַכְתֶּ֖ם אַחֲרָֽיו׃ 4 אַ֣ךְ ׀ רָח֣וֹק יִהְיֶ֗ה בֵּֽינֵיכֶם֙ ובינו *וּבֵינָ֔יו כְּאַלְפַּ֥יִם אַמָּ֖ה בַּמִּדָּ֑ה אַל־תִּקְרְב֣וּ אֵלָ֗יו לְמַ֨עַן֙ אֲשֶׁר־תֵּֽדְעוּ֙ אֶת־הַדֶּ֙רֶךְ֙ אֲשֶׁ֣ר תֵּֽלְכוּ־בָ֔הּ כִּ֣י לֹ֧א עֲבַרְתֶּ֛ם בַּדֶּ֖רֶךְ מִתְּמ֥וֹל שִׁלְשֽׁוֹם׃ ס 5 וַיֹּ֧אמֶר יְהוֹשֻׁ֛עַ אֶל־הָעָ֖ם הִתְקַדָּ֑שׁוּ כִּ֣י מָחָ֗ר יַעֲשֶׂ֧ה יְהוָ֛ה בְּקִרְבְּכֶ֖ם נִפְלָאֽוֹת׃ 6 וַיֹּ֤אמֶר יְהוֹשֻׁ֙עַ֙ אֶל־הַכֹּֽהֲנִ֣ים לֵאמֹ֔ר שְׂאוּ֙ אֶת־אֲר֣וֹן הַבְּרִ֔ית וְעִבְר֖וּ לִפְנֵ֣י הָעָ֑ם וַיִּשְׂאוּ֙ אֶת־אֲר֣וֹן הַבְּרִ֔ית וַיֵּֽלְכ֖וּ לִפְנֵ֥י הָעָֽם׃ ס 7 וַיֹּ֣אמֶר יְהוָה֮ אֶל־יְהוֹשֻׁעַ֒ הַיּ֣וֹם הַזֶּ֗ה אָחֵל֙ גַּדֶּלְךָ֔ בְּעֵינֵ֖י כָּל־יִשְׂרָאֵ֑ל אֲשֶׁר֙ יֵֽדְע֔וּן כִּ֗י כַּאֲשֶׁ֥ר הָיִ֛יתִי עִם־מֹשֶׁ֖ה אֶהְיֶ֥ה עִמָּֽךְ׃ 8 וְאַתָּ֞ה תְּצַוֶּ֣ה אֶת־הַכֹּֽהֲנִ֗ים נֹשְׂאֵ֣י אֲרֽוֹן־ הַבְּרִ֖ית לֵאמֹ֑ר כְּבֹאֲכֶ֗ם עַד־קְצֵה֙ מֵ֣י הַיַּרְדֵּ֔ן בַּיַּרְדֵּ֖ן תַּֽעֲמֹֽדוּ׃ פ 9 וַיֹּ֣אמֶר יְהוֹשֻׁ֔עַ אֶל־בְּנֵ֖י יִשְׂרָאֵ֑ל גֹּ֣שׁוּ הֵ֔נָּה וְשִׁמְע֕וּ אֶת־דִּבְרֵ֖י יְהוָ֥ה אֱלֹֽהֵיכֶֽם׃ 10 וַיֹּ֣אמֶר יְהוֹשֻׁ֔עַ בְּזֹאת֙ תֵּֽדְע֔וּן כִּ֛י אֵ֥ל חַ֖י בְּקִרְבְּכֶ֑ם וְהוֹרֵ֣שׁ יוֹרִ֣ישׁ מִפְּנֵיכֶ֡ם אֶת־ הַכְּנַעֲנִ֡י וְאֶת־הַֽחִתִּי֩ וְאֶת־הַֽחִוִּ֨י וְאֶת־ הַפְּרִזִּ֜י וְאֶת־הַגִּרְגָּשִׁ֗י וְהָֽאֱמֹרִ֖י וְהַיְבוּסִֽי׃ 11 הִנֵּה֙ אֲר֣וֹן הַבְּרִ֔ית אֲד֖וֹן כָּל־הָאָ֑רֶץ עֹבֵ֥ר לִפְנֵיכֶ֖ם בַּיַּרְדֵּֽן׃ 12 וְעַתָּ֗ה קְח֤וּ לָכֶם֙ שְׁנֵ֣י עָשָׂ֣ר אִ֔ישׁ מִשִּׁבְטֵ֖י יִשְׂרָאֵ֑ל אִישׁ־אֶחָ֥ד אִישׁ־אֶחָ֖ד לַשָּֽׁבֶט׃ 13 וְהָיָ֡ה כְּנ֣וֹחַ כַּפּ֣וֹת רַגְלֵ֣י הַכֹּהֲנִ֡ים נֹשְׂאֵי֩ אֲר֨וֹן יְהוָ֜ה אֲד֣וֹן כָּל־הָאָ֗רֶץ בְּמֵי֙ הַיַּרְדֵּ֔ן מֵ֤י הַיַּרְדֵּן֙ יִכָּ֣רֵת֔וּן הַמַּ֣יִם הַיֹּרְדִ֣ים מִלְמָ֑עְלָה וְיַעַמְד֖וּ נֵ֥ד אֶחָֽד׃ 14 וַיְהִ֗י בִּנְסֹ֤עַ הָעָם֙ מֵאָ֣הֳלֵיהֶ֔ם לַעֲבֹ֖ר

campment to cross the Jordan, the priests bearing the Ark of the Covenant were at the head of the people. [15]Now the Jordan keeps flowing over its entire bed throughout the harvest season. But as soon as the bearers of the Ark reached the Jordan, and the feet of the priests bearing the Ark dipped into the water at its edge, [16]the waters coming down from upstream piled up in a single heap a great way off, at[b] Adam, the town next to Zarethan; and those flowing away downstream to the Sea of the Arabah (the Dead Sea) ran out completely. So the people crossed near Jericho. [17]The priests who bore the Ark of the Lord's Covenant stood on dry land exactly in the middle of the Jordan, while all Israel crossed over on dry land, until the entire nation had finished crossing the Jordan.

4 When the entire nation had finished crossing the Jordan, the Lord said to Joshua, [2]"Select twelve men from among the people, one from each tribe, [3]and instruct them as follows: Pick up twelve stones from the spot exactly in the middle of the Jordan, where the priests' feet are standing; take them along with you and deposit them in the place where you will spend the night."

[4]Joshua summoned the twelve men whom he had designated among the Israelites, one from each tribe; [5]and Joshua said to them, "Walk up to the Ark of the Lord your God, in the middle of the Jordan, and each of you lift a stone onto his shoulder—corresponding to the number of the tribes of Israel. [6]This shall serve as a symbol among you: in time to come, when your children ask, 'What is the meaning of these stones for you?' [7]you shall tell them, 'The waters of the Jordan were cut off because of the Ark of the Lord's Covenant; when it passed through the

אֶת־הַיַּרְדֵּן וְהַכֹּהֲנִים נֹשְׂאֵי הָאָרוֹן הַבְּרִית לִפְנֵי הָעָם: 15 וּכְבוֹא נֹשְׂאֵי הָאָרוֹן עַד־הַיַּרְדֵּן וְרַגְלֵי הַכֹּהֲנִים נֹשְׂאֵי הָאָרוֹן נִטְבְּלוּ בִּקְצֵה הַמָּיִם וְהַיַּרְדֵּן מָלֵא עַל־כָּל־גְּדוֹתָיו כֹּל יְמֵי קָצִיר: 16 וַיַּעַמְדוּ הַמַּיִם הַיֹּרְדִים מִלְמַעְלָה קָמוּ נֵד־אֶחָד הַרְחֵק מְאֹד באדם מֵאָדָם הָעִיר אֲשֶׁר מִצַּד צָרְתָן וְהַיֹּרְדִים עַל יָם הָעֲרָבָה יָם־הַמֶּלַח תַּמּוּ נִכְרָתוּ וְהָעָם עָבְרוּ נֶגֶד יְרִיחוֹ: 17 וַיַּעַמְדוּ הַכֹּהֲנִים נֹשְׂאֵי הָאָרוֹן בְּרִית־יְהֹוָה בֶּחָרָבָה בְּתוֹךְ הַיַּרְדֵּן הָכֵן וְכָל־יִשְׂרָאֵל עֹבְרִים בֶּחָרָבָה עַד אֲשֶׁר־תַּמּוּ כָּל־הַגּוֹי לַעֲבֹר אֶת־הַיַּרְדֵּן:

ד וַיְהִי כַּאֲשֶׁר־תַּמּוּ כָל־הַגּוֹי לַעֲבוֹר אֶת־הַיַּרְדֵּן ס וַיֹּאמֶר יְהֹוָה אֶל־יְהוֹשֻׁעַ לֵאמֹר: 2 קְחוּ לָכֶם מִן־הָעָם שְׁנֵים עָשָׂר אֲנָשִׁים אִישׁ־אֶחָד אִישׁ־אֶחָד מִשָּׁבֶט: 3 וְצַוּוּ אוֹתָם לֵאמֹר שְׂאוּ־לָכֶם מִזֶּה מִתּוֹךְ הַיַּרְדֵּן מִמַּצַּב רַגְלֵי הַכֹּהֲנִים הָכִין שְׁתֵּים־עֶשְׂרֵה אֲבָנִים וְהַעֲבַרְתֶּם אוֹתָם עִמָּכֶם וְהִנַּחְתֶּם אוֹתָם בַּמָּלוֹן אֲשֶׁר־תָּלִינוּ בוֹ הַלָּיְלָה: ס

4 וַיִּקְרָא יְהוֹשֻׁעַ אֶל־שְׁנֵים הֶעָשָׂר אִישׁ אֲשֶׁר הֵכִין מִבְּנֵי יִשְׂרָאֵל אִישׁ־אֶחָד אִישׁ־אֶחָד מִשָּׁבֶט: 5 וַיֹּאמֶר לָהֶם יְהוֹשֻׁעַ עִבְרוּ לִפְנֵי אֲרוֹן יְהֹוָה אֱלֹהֵיכֶם אֶל־תּוֹךְ הַיַּרְדֵּן וְהָרִימוּ לָכֶם אִישׁ אֶבֶן אַחַת עַל־שִׁכְמוֹ לְמִסְפַּר שִׁבְטֵי בְנֵי־יִשְׂרָאֵל: 6 לְמַעַן תִּהְיֶה זֹאת אוֹת בְּקִרְבְּכֶם כִּי־יִשְׁאָלוּן בְּנֵיכֶם מָחָר לֵאמֹר מָה הָאֲבָנִים הָאֵלֶּה לָכֶם: 7 וַאֲמַרְתֶּם לָהֶם אֲשֶׁר נִכְרְתוּ מֵימֵי הַיַּרְדֵּן

Jordan, the waters of the Jordan were cut off.'
And so these stones shall serve the people of
Israel as a memorial for all time."

8The Israelites did as Joshua ordered. They
picked up twelve stones, corresponding to the
number of the tribes of Israel, from the middle of the Jordan—as the LORD had charged
Joshua—and they took them along with them
to their night encampment and deposited them
there.

9Joshua also set up twelve stones in the middle
of the Jordan, at the spot where the feet of the
priests bearing the Ark of the Covenant had
stood; and they have remained there to this day.

10The priests who bore the Ark remained
standing in the middle of the Jordan until all
the instructions that the LORD had ordered
Joshua to convey to the people had been carried
out. And so the people speedily crossed over,
a-just as Moses had assured Joshua in his charge
to him.-a 11And when all the people finished
crossing, the Ark of the LORD and the priests
advanced to the head of the people.

12The Reubenites, the Gadites, and the
half-tribe of Manasseh went across armedb in
the van of the Israelites, as Moses had charged
them.c 13About forty thousand shock troops
went across, at the instance of the LORD, to the
steppes of Jericho for battle.

14On that day the LORD exalted Joshua in the
sight of all Israel, so that they revered him all
his days as they had revered Moses.

15The LORD said to Joshua, 16"Command the
priests who bear the Ark of the Pact to come
up out of the Jordan." 17So Joshua commanded
the priests, "Come up out of the Jordan." 18As
soon as the priests who bore the Ark of the
LORD's Covenant came up out of the Jordan,
and the feet of the priests stepped onto the dry

מִפְּנֵי אֲרוֹן בְּרִית־יְהֹוָה בְּעׇבְרוֹ בַּיַּרְדֵּן
נִכְרְתוּ מֵי הַיַּרְדֵּן וְהָיוּ הָאֲבָנִים הָאֵלֶּה
לְזִכָּרוֹן לִבְנֵי יִשְׂרָאֵל עַד־עוֹלָם:
8 וַיַּעֲשׂוּ־כֵן בְּנֵי־יִשְׂרָאֵל כַּאֲשֶׁר צִוָּה
יְהוֹשֻׁעַ וַיִּשְׂאוּ שְׁתֵּי־עֶשְׂרֵה אֲבָנִים מִתּוֹךְ
הַיַּרְדֵּן כַּאֲשֶׁר דִּבֶּר יְהֹוָה אֶל־יְהוֹשֻׁעַ
לְמִסְפַּר שִׁבְטֵי בְנֵי־יִשְׂרָאֵל וַיַּעֲבִרוּם עִמָּם
אֶל־הַמָּלוֹן וַיַּנִּחוּם שָׁם:
9 וּשְׁתֵּים עֶשְׂרֵה אֲבָנִים הֵקִים יְהוֹשֻׁעַ
בְּתוֹךְ הַיַּרְדֵּן תַּחַת מַצַּב רַגְלֵי הַכֹּהֲנִים
נֹשְׂאֵי אֲרוֹן הַבְּרִית וַיִּהְיוּ שָׁם עַד הַיּוֹם
הַזֶּה:
10 וְהַכֹּהֲנִים נֹשְׂאֵי הָאָרוֹן עֹמְדִים בְּתוֹךְ
הַיַּרְדֵּן עַד תֹּם כׇּל־הַדָּבָר אֲשֶׁר־צִוָּה יְהֹוָה
אֶת־יְהוֹשֻׁעַ לְדַבֵּר אֶל־הָעָם כְּכֹל אֲשֶׁר־
צִוָּה מֹשֶׁה אֶת־יְהוֹשֻׁעַ וַיְמַהֲרוּ הָעָם
וַיַּעֲבֹרוּ: 11 וַיְהִי כַּאֲשֶׁר־תַּם כׇּל־הָעָם
לַעֲבוֹר וַיַּעֲבֹר אֲרוֹן־יְהֹוָה וְהַכֹּהֲנִים לִפְנֵי
הָעָם:
12 וַיַּעַבְרוּ בְּנֵי־רְאוּבֵן וּבְנֵי־גָד וַחֲצִי שֵׁבֶט
הַמְנַשֶּׁה חֲמֻשִׁים לִפְנֵי בְּנֵי יִשְׂרָאֵל כַּאֲשֶׁר
דִּבֶּר אֲלֵיהֶם מֹשֶׁה: 13 כְּאַרְבָּעִים אֶלֶף
חֲלוּצֵי הַצָּבָא עָבְרוּ לִפְנֵי יְהֹוָה לַמִּלְחָמָה
אֶל עַרְבוֹת יְרִיחוֹ: ס
14 בַּיּוֹם הַהוּא גִּדַּל יְהֹוָה אֶת־יְהוֹשֻׁעַ
בְּעֵינֵי כׇּל־יִשְׂרָאֵל וַיִּרְאוּ אֹתוֹ כַּאֲשֶׁר יָרְאוּ
אֶת־מֹשֶׁה כׇּל־יְמֵי חַיָּיו: פ
15 וַיֹּאמֶר יְהֹוָה אֶל־יְהוֹשֻׁעַ לֵאמֹר: 16 צַוֵּה
אֶת־הַכֹּהֲנִים נֹשְׂאֵי אֲרוֹן הָעֵדוּת וְיַעֲלוּ
מִן־הַיַּרְדֵּן: 17 וַיְצַו יְהוֹשֻׁעַ אֶת־הַכֹּהֲנִים
לֵאמֹר עֲלוּ מִן־הַיַּרְדֵּן: 18 וַיְהִי בַּעֲלוֹת
כַּעֲלוֹת הַכֹּהֲנִים נֹשְׂאֵי אֲרוֹן בְּרִית־יְהֹוָה
מִתּוֹךְ הַיַּרְדֵּן נִתְּקוּ כַּפּוֹת רַגְלֵי הַכֹּהֲנִים

---

a-a Connection of clause uncertain; cf. Deut. 31.7–8.
b Meaning of Heb. uncertain.
c See Num. 32.20–22.

ground, the waters of the Jordan resumed their course, flowing over its entire bed as before.

¹⁹The people came up from the Jordan on the tenth day of the first month, and encamped at Gilgal on the eastern border of Jericho. ²⁰And Joshua set up in Gilgal the twelve stones they had taken from the Jordan. ²¹He charged the Israelites as follows: "In time to come, when your children ask their fathers, 'What is the meaning of those stones?' ²²tell your children: 'Here the Israelites crossed the Jordan on dry land.' ²³For the Lᴏʀᴅ your God dried up the waters of the Jordan before you until you crossed, just as the Lᴏʀᴅ your God did to the Sea of Reeds, which He dried up before us until we crossed. ²⁴Thus all the peoples of the earth shall know how mighty is the hand of the Lᴏʀᴅ, and you shall fear the Lᴏʀᴅ your God always."

5 When all the kings of the Amorites on the western side of the Jordan, and all the kings of the Canaanites near the Sea, heard how the Lᴏʀᴅ had dried up the waters of the Jordan for the sake of the Israelites until they crossed over, they lost heart, and no spirit was left in them because of the Israelites.

²At that time the Lᴏʀᴅ said to Joshua, "Make flint knives and proceed with a second circumcision of the Israelites." ³So Joshua had flint knives made, and the Israelites were circumcised at Gibeath-haaraloth.ᵃ

⁴This is the reason why Joshua had the circumcision performed: All the people who had come out of Egypt, all the males of military age, had died during the desert wanderings after leaving Egypt. ⁵Now, whereas all the people who came out of Egypt had been circumcised, none

---

אֶל הֶחָרָבָ֔ה וַיָּשֻׁ֤בוּ מֵֽי־הַיַּרְדֵּן֙ לִמְקוֹמָ֔ם וַיֵּלְכ֥וּ כִתְמוֹל־שִׁלְשׁ֖וֹם עַל־כָּל־גְּדוֹתָֽיו:

¹⁹ וְהָעָ֗ם עָלוּ֙ מִן־הַיַּרְדֵּ֔ן בֶּעָשׂ֖וֹר לַחֹ֣דֶשׁ הָרִאשׁ֑וֹן וַֽיַּחֲנוּ֙ בַּגִּלְגָּ֔ל בִּקְצֵ֖ה מִזְרַ֥ח יְרִיחֽוֹ: ²⁰ וְאֵת֩ שְׁתֵּ֨ים עֶשְׂרֵ֤ה הָֽאֲבָנִים֙ הָאֵ֔לֶּה אֲשֶׁ֥ר לָקְח֖וּ מִן־הַיַּרְדֵּ֑ן הֵקִ֥ים יְהוֹשֻׁ֖עַ בַּגִּלְגָּֽל: ²¹ וַיֹּ֛אמֶר אֶל־בְּנֵ֥י יִשְׂרָאֵ֖ל לֵאמֹ֑ר אֲשֶׁר֩ יִשְׁאָל֨וּן בְּנֵיכֶ֤ם מָחָר֙ אֶת־אֲבוֹתָ֣ם לֵאמֹ֔ר מָ֖ה הָאֲבָנִ֥ים הָאֵֽלֶּה: ²² וְהוֹדַעְתֶּ֖ם אֶת־בְּנֵיכֶ֣ם לֵאמֹ֑ר בַּיַּבָּשָׁה֙ עָבַ֣ר יִשְׂרָאֵ֔ל אֶת־הַיַּרְדֵּ֖ן הַזֶּֽה: ²³ אֲשֶׁר־הוֹבִ֣ישׁ יְהוָ֪ה אֱלֹֽהֵיכֶ֡ם אֶת־מֵי֩ הַיַּרְדֵּ֨ן מִפְּנֵיכֶ֜ם עַד־עָבְרְכֶ֗ם כַּאֲשֶׁ֣ר עָשָׂה֩ יְהוָ֨ה אֱלֹהֵיכֶ֤ם לְיַם־ס֔וּף אֲשֶׁר־הוֹבִ֥ישׁ מִפָּנֵ֖ינוּ עַד־עָבְרֵֽנוּ: ²⁴ לְמַ֗עַן דַּ֙עַת֙ כָּל־עַמֵּ֣י הָאָ֔רֶץ אֶת־יַ֣ד יְהוָ֔ה כִּ֥י חֲזָקָ֖ה הִ֑יא לְמַ֧עַן יְרָאתֶ֛ם אֶת־יְהוָ֥ה אֱלֹהֵיכֶ֖ם כָּל־הַיָּמִֽים: ס

ה וַיְהִ֣י כִשְׁמֹ֣עַ כָּל־מַלְכֵ֣י הָאֱמֹרִ֗י אֲשֶׁ֞ר בְּעֵ֤בֶר הַיַּרְדֵּן֙ יָ֔מָּה וְכָל־מַלְכֵ֤י הַֽכְּנַעֲנִי֙ אֲשֶׁ֣ר עַל־הַיָּ֔ם אֵ֠ת אֲשֶׁר־הוֹבִ֨ישׁ יְהוָ֜ה אֶת־מֵ֧י הַיַּרְדֵּ֛ן מִפְּנֵ֥י בְנֵֽי־יִשְׂרָאֵ֖ל עַד־עברנו [עָבְרָ֑ם] וַיִּמַּ֣ס לְבָבָ֗ם וְלֹא־הָ֨יָה בָ֥ם עוֹד֙ ר֔וּחַ מִפְּנֵ֖י בְּנֵֽי־יִשְׂרָאֵֽל: ס

² בָּעֵ֣ת הַהִ֗יא אָמַ֤ר יְהוָה֙ אֶל־יְהוֹשֻׁ֔עַ עֲשֵׂ֥ה לְךָ֖ חַֽרְב֣וֹת צֻרִ֑ים וְשׁ֛וּב מֹ֥ל אֶת־בְּנֵֽי־יִשְׂרָאֵ֖ל שֵׁנִֽית: ³ וַיַּֽעַשׂ־ל֥וֹ יְהוֹשֻׁ֖עַ חַֽרְב֣וֹת צֻרִ֑ים וַיָּ֙מָל֙ אֶת־בְּנֵ֣י יִשְׂרָאֵ֔ל אֶל־גִּבְעַ֖ת הָעֲרָלֽוֹת: ⁴ וְזֶ֥ה הַדָּבָ֖ר אֲשֶׁר־מָ֣ל יְהוֹשֻׁ֑עַ כָּל־הָעָ֣ם הַיֹּצֵ֣א מִמִּצְרַ֗יִם הַזְּכָרִ֞ים כֹּ֣ל ׀ אַנְשֵׁ֣י הַמִּלְחָמָ֗ה מֵ֤תוּ בַמִּדְבָּר֙ בַּדֶּ֔רֶךְ בְּצֵאתָ֖ם מִמִּצְרָֽיִם: ⁵ כִּי־מֻלִ֗ים הָיוּ֙ כָּל־הָעָ֣ם הַיֹּֽצְאִ֔ים וְכָל־הָעָ֗ם הַיִּלֹּדִ֛ים בַּמִּדְבָּ֥ר

ᵃ   *I.e., "the Hill of Foreskins."*

of the people born after the exodus, during the desert wanderings, had been circumcised. ⁶For the Israelites had traveled in the wilderness forty years, until the entire nation—the men of military age who had left Egypt—had perished; because they had not obeyed the LORD, and the LORD had sworn never to let them see the land that the LORD had sworn to their fathers to assign to us, a land flowing with milk and honey. ⁷But He had raised up their sons in their stead; and it was these that Joshua circumcised, for they were uncircumcised, not having been circumcised on the way. ⁸After the circumcising of the whole nation was completed, they remained where they were, in the camp, until they recovered.

⁹And the LORD said to Joshua, "Today I have rolled away from you the disgrace of Egypt."^b So that place was called Gilgal,^c as it still is.

¹⁰Encamped at Gilgal, in the steppes of Jericho, the Israelites offered the passover sacrifice on the fourteenth day of the month, toward evening.

¹¹On the day after the passover offering, on that very day, they ate of the produce of the country, unleavened bread and parched grain. ¹²On that same day,^d when they ate of the produce of the land, the manna ceased. The Israelites got no more manna; that year they ate of the yield of the land of Canaan.

¹³Once, when Joshua was near Jericho, he looked up and saw a man standing before him, drawn sword in hand. Joshua went up to him and asked him, "Are you one of us or of our enemies?" ¹⁴He replied, "No, I am captain of the LORD's host. Now I have come!" Joshua threw himself face down to the ground and, prostrating himself, said to him, "What does my lord command his servant?" ¹⁵The captain of

בַּדֶּרֶךְ בְּצֵאתָם מִמִּצְרַיִם לֹא־מָֽלוּ׃ 6 כִּ֣י ׀ אַרְבָּעִ֣ים שָׁנָ֗ה הָלְכ֣וּ בְנֵֽי־יִשְׂרָאֵל֮ בַּמִּדְבָּר֒ עַד־תֹּ֨ם כָּל־הַגּ֜וֹי אַנְשֵׁ֤י הַמִּלְחָמָה֙ הַיֹּצְאִ֣ים מִמִּצְרַ֔יִם אֲשֶׁ֥ר לֹֽא־שָׁמְע֖וּ בְּק֣וֹל יְהֹוָ֑ה אֲשֶׁ֨ר נִשְׁבַּ֤ע יְהֹוָה֙ לָהֶ֔ם לְבִלְתִּ֞י הַרְאוֹתָ֣ם אֶת־הָאָ֗רֶץ אֲשֶׁר֩ נִשְׁבַּ֨ע יְהֹוָ֤ה לַֽאֲבוֹתָם֙ לָ֣תֶת לָ֔נוּ אֶ֛רֶץ זָבַ֥ת חָלָ֖ב וּדְבָֽשׁ׃ 7 וְאֶת־בְּנֵיהֶם֙ הֵקִ֣ים תַּחְתָּ֔ם אֹתָ֖ם מָ֣ל יְהוֹשֻׁ֑עַ כִּֽי־עֲרֵלִ֣ים הָי֔וּ כִּ֛י לֹא־מָ֥לוּ אוֹתָ֖ם בַּדָּֽרֶךְ׃ 8 וַיְהִ֛י כַּאֲשֶׁר־תַּ֥מּוּ כָל־הַגּ֖וֹי לְהִמּ֑וֹל וַיֵּשְׁב֥וּ תַחְתָּ֛ם בַּֽמַּחֲנֶ֖ה עַ֥ד חֲיוֹתָֽם׃ פ

9 וַיֹּ֤אמֶר יְהֹוָה֙ אֶל־יְהוֹשֻׁ֔עַ הַיּ֗וֹם גַּלּ֨וֹתִי֙ אֶת־חֶרְפַּ֤ת מִצְרַ֨יִם֙ מֵעֲלֵיכֶ֔ם וַיִּקְרָ֞א שֵׁ֣ם הַמָּק֤וֹם הַהוּא֙ גִּלְגָּ֔ל עַ֖ד הַיּ֥וֹם הַזֶּֽה׃ 10 וַיַּחֲנ֥וּ בְנֵֽי־יִשְׂרָאֵ֖ל בַּגִּלְגָּ֑ל וַיַּעֲשׂ֣וּ אֶת־הַפֶּ֡סַח בְּאַרְבָּעָה֩ עָשָׂ֨ר י֥וֹם לַחֹ֛דֶשׁ בָּעֶ֖רֶב בְּעַֽרְב֥וֹת יְרִיחֽוֹ׃ 11 וַיֹּ֨אכְל֜וּ מֵעֲב֤וּר הָאָ֨רֶץ֙ מִמׇּחֳרַ֣ת הַפֶּ֔סַח מַצּ֖וֹת וְקָל֑וּי בְּעֶ֖צֶם הַיּ֥וֹם הַזֶּֽה׃ 12 וַיִּשְׁבֹּ֣ת הַמָּ֗ן מִֽמׇּחֳרָת֙ בְּאׇכְלָם֙ מֵעֲב֣וּר הָאָ֔רֶץ וְלֹא־הָ֥יָה ע֖וֹד לִבְנֵ֣י יִשְׂרָאֵ֑ל מָ֑ן וַיֹּֽאכְל֗וּ מִתְּבוּאַת֙ אֶ֣רֶץ כְּנַ֔עַן בַּשָּׁנָ֖ה הַהִֽיא׃ ס

13 וַֽיְהִ֗י בִּֽהְי֣וֹת יְהוֹשֻׁעַ֮ בִּֽירִיחוֹ֒ וַיִּשָּׂ֤א עֵינָיו֙ וַיַּ֔רְא וְהִנֵּה־אִישׁ֙ עֹמֵ֣ד לְנֶגְדּ֔וֹ וְחַרְבּ֥וֹ שְׁלוּפָ֖ה בְּיָד֑וֹ וַיֵּ֨לֶךְ יְהוֹשֻׁ֤עַ אֵלָיו֙ וַיֹּ֣אמֶר ל֔וֹ הֲלָ֥נוּ אַתָּ֖ה אִם־לְצָרֵֽינוּ׃ 14 וַיֹּ֣אמֶר ׀ לֹ֗א כִּ֠י אֲנִ֞י שַׂר־צְבָֽא־יְהֹוָ֛ה עַתָּ֣ה בָ֑אתִי וַיִּפֹּל֩ יְהוֹשֻׁ֨עַ אֶל־פָּנָ֥יו אַ֨רְצָה֙ וַיִּשְׁתָּ֔חוּ וַיֹּ֣אמֶר ל֔וֹ מָ֥ה אֲדֹנִ֖י מְדַבֵּ֥ר אֶל־עַבְדּֽוֹ׃

---

b　I.e., of the Egyptian bondage.

c　Interpreted as "rolling."

d　Lit. "on the day after."

465

the LORD's host answered Joshua, "Remove your sandals from your feet, for the place where you stand is holy." And Joshua did so.

6 Now Jericho was shut up tight because of the Israelites; no one could leave or enter.

2The LORD said to Joshua, "See, I will deliver Jericho and her king [and her] warriors into your hands. 3Let all your troops march around the city and complete one circuit of the city. Do this six days, 4with seven priests carrying seven ram's horns preceding the Ark. On the seventh day, march around the city seven times, with the priests blowing the horns. 5And when a long blast is sounded on the horn—as soon as you hear that sound of the horn—all the people shall give a mighty shout. Thereupon the city wall will collapse, and the people shall advance, every man straight ahead."

6Joshua son of Nun summoned the priests and said to them, "Take up the Ark of the Covenant, and let seven priests carrying seven ram's horns precede the Ark of the LORD." 7And he instructed the people, "Go forward, march around the city, with the vanguard marching in front of the Ark of the LORD." 8When Joshua had instructed the people, the seven priests carrying seven ram's horns advanced before the LORD, blowing their horns; and the Ark of the LORD's Covenant followed them. 9The vanguard marched in front of the priests who were blowing the horns, and the rear guard marched behind the Ark, with the horns sounding all the time. 10But Joshua's orders to the rest of the people were, "Do not shout, do not let your voices be heard, and do not let a sound issue from your lips until the moment that I command you, 'Shout!' Then you shall shout."

11So he had the Ark of the LORD go around

15 וַיֹּאמֶר֩ שַׂר־צְבָ֨א יְהוָ֜ה אֶל־יְהוֹשֻׁ֗עַ שַׁל־
נַעַלְךָ֙ מֵעַ֣ל רַגְלֶ֔ךָ* כִּ֣י הַמָּק֗וֹם אֲשֶׁ֤ר אַתָּה֙
עֹמֵ֣ד עָלָ֔יו קֹ֖דֶשׁ ה֑וּא וַיַּ֥עַשׂ יְהוֹשֻׁ֖עַ כֵּֽן׃

ו וִֽירִיח֗וֹ סֹגֶ֙רֶת֙ וּמְסֻגֶּ֔רֶת מִפְּנֵ֖י בְּנֵ֣י
יִשְׂרָאֵ֑ל אֵ֥ין יוֹצֵ֖א וְאֵ֥ין בָּֽא׃ ס 2 וַיֹּ֤אמֶר
יְהוָה֙ אֶל־יְהוֹשֻׁ֔עַ רְאֵה֙ נָתַ֣תִּי בְיָֽדְךָ֔ אֶת־יְרִיח֖וֹ
וְאֶת־מַלְכָּ֑הּ גִּבּוֹרֵ֖י הֶחָֽיִל׃ 3 וְסַבֹּתֶ֣ם אֶת־הָעִ֗יר
כֹּ֚ל אַנְשֵׁ֣י הַמִּלְחָמָ֔ה הַקֵּ֥יף אֶת־הָעִ֖יר פַּ֣עַם אֶחָ֑ת
כֹּ֥ה תַעֲשֶׂ֖ה שֵׁ֥שֶׁת יָמִֽים׃ 4 וְשִׁבְעָ֣ה כֹהֲנִ֡ים
יִשְׂאוּ֩ שִׁבְעָ֨ה שֽׁוֹפְר֤וֹת הַיּֽוֹבְלִים֙ לִפְנֵ֣י הָֽאָר֔וֹן
וּבַיּוֹם֙ הַשְּׁבִיעִ֔י תָּסֹ֥בּוּ אֶת־הָעִ֖יר שֶׁ֣בַע פְּעָמִ֑ים
וְהַכֹּ֣הֲנִ֔ים יִתְקְע֖וּ בַּשּׁוֹפָרֽוֹת׃ 5 וְהָיָ֞ה בִּמְשֹׁ֣ךְ ׀
בְּקֶ֣רֶן הַיּוֹבֵ֗ל בשמעכם כְּשָׁמְעֲכֶם֙ אֶת־ק֣וֹל הַשּׁוֹפָ֔ר
יָרִ֥יעוּ כָל־הָעָ֖ם תְּרוּעָ֣ה גְדוֹלָ֑ה וְנָ֤פְלָה חוֹמַ֤ת
הָעִיר֙ תַּחְתֶּ֔יהָ וְעָל֥וּ הָעָ֖ם אִ֥ישׁ נֶגְדּֽוֹ׃
6 וַיִּקְרָ֞א יְהוֹשֻׁ֤עַ בִּן־נוּן֙ אֶל־הַכֹּ֣הֲנִ֔ים וַיֹּ֣אמֶר
אֲלֵהֶ֔ם שְׂא֖וּ אֶת־אֲר֣וֹן הַבְּרִ֑ית וְשִׁבְעָ֣ה כֹֽהֲנִ֗ים
יִשְׂאוּ֙ שִׁבְעָ֤ה שֽׁוֹפְרוֹת֙ יוֹבְלִ֔ים לִפְנֵ֖י אֲר֥וֹן
יְהוָֽה׃ 7 ויאמרו וַיֹּ֙אמֶר֙ אֶל־הָעָ֔ם עִבְר֖וּ וְסֹ֣בּוּ
אֶת־הָעִ֑יר וְהֶ֣חָל֔וּץ יַעֲבֹ֕ר לִפְנֵ֖י אֲר֥וֹן יְהוָֽה׃
8 וַיְהִ֗י כֶּאֱמֹ֤ר יְהוֹשֻׁ֙עַ֙ אֶל־הָעָ֔ם וְשִׁבְעָ֣ה
הַכֹּהֲנִ֡ים נֹשְׂאִים֩ שִׁבְעָ֨ה שֽׁוֹפְר֤וֹת הַיּֽוֹבְלִים֙
לִפְנֵ֣י יְהוָ֔ה עָבְר֕וּ וְתָקְע֖וּ בַּשּֽׁוֹפָר֑וֹת וַאֲרוֹן֙
בְּרִ֣ית יְהוָ֔ה הֹלֵ֖ךְ אַחֲרֵיהֶֽם׃ 9 וְהֶחָל֣וּץ הֹלֵ֔ךְ
לִפְנֵי֙ הַכֹּ֣הֲנִ֔ים תֹּקְעֵ֖י הַשּֽׁוֹפָר֑וֹת וְהַֽמְאַסֵּ֗ף
הֹלֵךְ֙ אַחֲרֵ֣י הָֽאָר֔וֹן הָל֖וֹךְ וְתָק֣וֹעַ
בַּשּׁוֹפָרֽוֹת׃ 10 וְאֶת־הָעָם֩ צִוָּ֨ה יְהוֹשֻׁ֤עַ
לֵאמֹר֙ לֹ֣א תָרִ֔יעוּ וְלֹֽא־תַשְׁמִ֙יעוּ֙ אֶת־
קוֹלְכֶ֔ם וְלֹא־יֵצֵ֥א מִפִּיכֶ֖ם דָּבָ֑ר עַ֠ד י֣וֹם
אָמְרִ֧י אֲלֵיכֶ֛ם הָרִ֖יעוּ וַהֲרִיעֹתֶֽם׃
11 וַיַּסֵּ֤ב אֲרוֹן־יְהוָה֙ אֶת־הָעִ֔יר הַקֵּ֖ף פַּ֥עַם

the city and complete one circuit; then they returned to camp and spent the night in camp. [12]Joshua rose early the next day; and the priests took up the Ark of the LORD, [13]while the seven priests bearing the seven ram's horns marched in front of the Ark of the LORD, blowing the horns as they marched. The vanguard marched in front of them, and the rear guard marched behind the Ark of the LORD, with the horns sounding all the time. [14]And so they marched around the city once on the second day and returned to the camp. They did this six days.

[15]On the seventh day, they rose at daybreak and marched around the city, in the same manner, seven times; that was the only day that they marched around the city seven times. [16]On the seventh round, as the priests blew the horns, Joshua commanded the people, "Shout! For the LORD has given you the city. [17]The city and everything in it are to be proscribed for the LORD; only Rahab the harlot is to be spared, and all who are with her in the house, because she hid the messengers we sent. [18]But you must beware of that which is proscribed, or else you will be proscribed:[a] if you take anything from that which is proscribed, you will cause the camp of Israel to be proscribed; you will bring calamity upon it. [19]All the silver and gold and objects of copper and iron are consecrated to the LORD; they must go into the treasury of the LORD."

[20]So the people shouted when the horns were sounded. When the people heard the sound of the horns, the people raised a mighty shout and the wall collapsed. The people rushed into the city, every man straight in front of him, and they captured the city. [21]They exterminated everything in the city with the sword: man and woman, young and old, ox and sheep and ass. [22]But Joshua bade the two men who had spied out the land, "Go into the harlot's house and

---

a *I.e., be put to death; cf. Lev. 27.28–29.*

אַחַת וַיָּבֹ֙אוּ֙ הַֽמַּחֲנֶ֔ה וַיָּלִ֖ינוּ בַּֽמַּחֲנֶֽה׃ פ
12 וַיַּשְׁכֵּ֥ם יְהוֹשֻׁ֖עַ בַּבֹּ֑קֶר וַיִּשְׂא֥וּ הַכֹּהֲנִ֖ים
אֶת־אֲר֥וֹן יְהוָֽה׃ 13 וְשִׁבְעָ֣ה הַכֹּהֲנִ֡ים
נֹשְׂאִים֩ שִׁבְעָ֨ה שֽׁוֹפְר֜וֹת הַיֹּבְלִ֗ים לִפְנֵי֙
אֲר֣וֹן יְהוָ֔ה הֹלְכִ֥ים הָל֖וֹךְ וְתָקְע֣וּ בַּשּׁוֹפָר֑וֹת
וְהֶחָלוּץ֙ הֹלֵ֣ךְ לִפְנֵיהֶ֔ם וְהַֽמְאַסֵּף֙ הֹלֵ֣ךְ
אַחֲרֵי֙ אֲר֣וֹן יְהוָ֔ה הָל֖וֹךְ וְתָק֥וֹעַ
בַּשּׁוֹפָרֽוֹת׃ 14 וַיָּסֹ֧בּוּ אֶת־הָעִ֛יר בַּיּ֥וֹם הַשֵּׁנִ֖י
פַּ֣עַם אַחַ֔ת וַיָּשֻׁ֖בוּ הַֽמַּחֲנֶ֑ה כֹּ֥ה עָשׂ֖וּ שֵׁ֥שֶׁת
יָמִֽים׃
15 וַיְהִ֣י ׀ בַּיּ֣וֹם הַשְּׁבִיעִ֗י וַיַּשְׁכִּ֙מוּ֙ כַּעֲל֣וֹת
הַשַּׁ֔חַר וַיָּסֹ֧בּוּ אֶת־הָעִ֛יר כַּמִּשְׁפָּ֥ט הַזֶּ֖ה
שֶׁ֣בַע פְּעָמִ֑ים רַ֚ק בַּיּ֣וֹם הַה֔וּא סָבְב֥וּ
אֶת־הָעִ֖יר שֶׁ֥בַע פְּעָמִֽים׃ 16 וַֽיְהִי֙ בַּפַּ֣עַם
הַשְּׁבִיעִ֔ית תָּקְע֥וּ הַכֹּהֲנִ֖ים בַּשּׁוֹפָר֑וֹת
וַיֹּ֨אמֶר יְהוֹשֻׁ֤עַ אֶל־הָעָם֙ הָרִ֔יעוּ כִּֽי־נָתַ֧ן
יְהוָ֛ה לָכֶ֖ם אֶת־הָעִֽיר׃ 17 וְהָיְתָ֨ה הָעִ֥יר
חֵ֛רֶם הִ֥יא וְכָל־אֲשֶׁר־בָּ֖הּ לַֽיהוָ֑ה רַק֩
רָחָ֨ב הַזּוֹנָ֜ה תִּֽחְיֶ֗ה הִ֤יא וְכָל־אֲשֶׁ֣ר אִתָּהּ֙
בַּבַּ֔יִת כִּ֣י הֶחְבְּאַ֔תָה אֶת־הַמַּלְאָכִ֖ים אֲשֶׁ֥ר
שָׁלָֽחְנוּ׃ 18 וְרַק־אַתֶּם֙ שִׁמְר֣וּ מִן־הַחֵ֔רֶם
פֶּֽן־תַּחֲרִ֖ימוּ וּלְקַחְתֶּ֣ם מִן־הַחֵ֑רֶם וְשַׂמְתֶּ֞ם
אֶת־מַחֲנֵ֤ה יִשְׂרָאֵל֙ לְחֵ֔רֶם וַעֲכַרְתֶּ֖ם אוֹתֽוֹ׃
19 וְכֹ֣ל ׀ כֶּ֣סֶף וְזָהָ֗ב וּכְלֵ֤י נְחֹ֙שֶׁת֙ וּבַרְזֶ֔ל
קֹ֥דֶשׁ ה֖וּא לַֽיהוָ֑ה אוֹצַ֥ר יְהוָ֖ה יָבֽוֹא׃
20 וַיָּ֣רַע הָעָ֔ם וַֽיִּתְקְע֖וּ בַּשֹּֽׁפָר֑וֹת וַיְהִ֣י
כִשְׁמֹ֣עַ הָעָם֩ אֶת־ק֨וֹל הַשּׁוֹפָ֜ר וַיָּרִ֧יעוּ
הָעָ֣ם תְּרוּעָ֣ה גְדוֹלָ֗ה וַתִּפֹּ֤ל הַֽחוֹמָה֙
תַּחְתֶּ֔יהָ וַיַּ֨עַל הָעָ֤ם הָעִ֙ירָה֙ אִ֣ישׁ נֶגְדּ֔וֹ
וַֽיִּלְכְּד֖וּ אֶת־הָעִֽיר׃ 21 וַֽיַּחֲרִ֙ימוּ֙ אֶת־כָּל־
אֲשֶׁ֣ר בָּעִ֔יר מֵאִישׁ֙ וְעַד־אִשָּׁ֔ה מִנַּ֖עַר וְעַד־
זָקֵ֑ן וְעַ֨ד שׁ֥וֹר וָשֶׂ֛ה וַחֲמ֖וֹר לְפִי־חָֽרֶב׃
22 וְלִשְׁנַ֨יִם הָאֲנָשִׁ֜ים הַֽמְרַגְּלִ֤ים אֶת־
הָאָ֙רֶץ֙ אָמַ֣ר יְהוֹשֻׁ֔עַ בֹּ֖אוּ בֵּית־הָאִשָּׁ֣ה

bring out the woman and all that belong to her, as you swore to her." [23]So the young spies went in and brought out Rahab, her father and her mother, her brothers and all that belonged to her—they brought out her whole family and left them outside the camp of Israel.

[24]They burned down the city and everything in it. But the silver and gold and the objects of copper and iron were deposited in the treasury of the House of the LORD. [25]Only Rahab the harlot and her father's family were spared by Joshua, along with all that belonged to her, and she dwelt among the Israelites—as is still the case. For she had hidden the messengers that Joshua sent to spy out Jericho.

[26]At that time Joshua pronounced this oath: "Cursed of the LORD be the man who shall undertake to fortify this city of Jericho: he shall lay its foundations at the cost of his first-born, and set up its gates at the cost of his youngest."

[27]The LORD was with Joshua, and his fame spread throughout the land.

7

The Israelites, however, violated the proscription: Achan son of Carmi son of Zabdi son of Zerah, of the tribe of Judah, took of that which was proscribed, and the LORD was incensed with the Israelites.

[2]Joshua sent men from Jericho to Ai, which lies close to Beth-aven—east of Bethel—with orders to go up and spy out the country. So the men went up and spied out Ai. [3]They returned to Joshua and reported to him, "Not all the troops need go up. Let two or three thousand men go and attack Ai; do not trouble all the troops to go up there, for [the people] there are few." [4]So about three thousand of the troops marched up there; but they were routed by the men of Ai. [5]The men of Ai killed about thirty-six of them, pursuing them outside the gate as far

הַזּוֹנָה וְהוֹצִיאוּ מִשָּׁם אֶת־הָאִשָּׁה וְאֶת־כׇּל־אֲשֶׁר־לָהּ כַּאֲשֶׁר נִשְׁבַּעְתֶּם לָהּ: [23] וַיָּבֹאוּ הַנְּעָרִים הַמְרַגְּלִים וַיֹּצִיאוּ אֶת־רָחָב וְאֶת־אָבִיהָ וְאֶת־אִמָּהּ וְאֶת־אַחֶיהָ וְאֶת־כׇּל־אֲשֶׁר־לָהּ וְאֵת כׇּל־מִשְׁפְּחוֹתֶיהָ הוֹצִיאוּ וַיַּנִּיחוּם מִחוּץ לְמַחֲנֵה יִשְׂרָאֵל: [24] וְהָעִיר שָׂרְפוּ בָאֵשׁ וְכׇל־אֲשֶׁר־בָּהּ רַק ׀ הַכֶּסֶף וְהַזָּהָב וּכְלֵי הַנְּחֹשֶׁת וְהַבַּרְזֶל נָתְנוּ אוֹצַר בֵּית־יְהֹוָה: [25] וְאֶת־רָחָב הַזּוֹנָה וְאֶת־בֵּית אָבִיהָ וְאֶת־כׇּל־אֲשֶׁר־לָהּ הֶחֱיָה יְהוֹשֻׁעַ וַתֵּשֶׁב בְּקֶרֶב יִשְׂרָאֵל עַד הַיּוֹם הַזֶּה כִּי הֶחְבִּיאָה אֶת־הַמַּלְאָכִים אֲשֶׁר שָׁלַח יְהוֹשֻׁעַ לְרַגֵּל אֶת־יְרִיחוֹ: פ [26] וַיַּשְׁבַּע יְהוֹשֻׁעַ בָּעֵת הַהִיא לֵאמֹר אָרוּר הָאִישׁ לִפְנֵי יְהֹוָה אֲשֶׁר יָקוּם וּבָנָה אֶת־הָעִיר הַזֹּאת אֶת־יְרִיחוֹ בִּבְכֹרוֹ יְיַסְּדֶנָּה וּבִצְעִירוֹ יַצִּיב דְּלָתֶיהָ: [27] וַיְהִי יְהֹוָה אֶת־יְהוֹשֻׁעַ וַיְהִי שׇׁמְעוֹ בְּכׇל־הָאָרֶץ:

ז וַיִּמְעֲלוּ בְנֵי־יִשְׂרָאֵל מַעַל בַּחֵרֶם וַיִּקַּח עָכָן בֶּן־כַּרְמִי בֶן־זַבְדִּי בֶן־זֶרַח לְמַטֵּה יְהוּדָה מִן־הַחֵרֶם וַיִּחַר־אַף יְהֹוָה בִּבְנֵי יִשְׂרָאֵל: [2] וַיִּשְׁלַח יְהוֹשֻׁעַ אֲנָשִׁים מִירִיחוֹ הָעַי אֲשֶׁר עִם־בֵּית אָוֶן מִקֶּדֶם לְבֵית־אֵל וַיֹּאמֶר אֲלֵיהֶם לֵאמֹר עֲלוּ וְרַגְּלוּ אֶת־הָאָרֶץ וַיַּעֲלוּ הָאֲנָשִׁים וַיְרַגְּלוּ אֶת־הָעָי: [3] וַיָּשֻׁבוּ אֶל־יְהוֹשֻׁעַ וַיֹּאמְרוּ אֵלָיו אַל־יַעַל כׇּל־הָעָם כְּאַלְפַּיִם אִישׁ אוֹ כִּשְׁלֹשֶׁת אֲלָפִים אִישׁ יַעֲלוּ וְיַכּוּ אֶת־הָעָי אַל־תְּיַגַּע־שָׁמָּה אֶת־כׇּל־הָעָם כִּי מְעַט הֵמָּה: [4] וַיַּעֲלוּ מִן־הָעָם שָׁמָּה כִּשְׁלֹשֶׁת אֲלָפִים אִישׁ וַיָּנֻסוּ לִפְנֵי אַנְשֵׁי הָעָי: [5] וַיַּכּוּ מֵהֶם אַנְשֵׁי הָעַי כִּשְׁלֹשִׁים וְשִׁשָּׁה אִישׁ וַיִּרְדְּפוּם

as Shebarim, and cutting them down along the descent. And the heart of the troops ^a-sank in utter dismay.-^a

⁶Joshua thereupon rent his clothes. He and the elders of Israel lay until evening with their faces to the ground in front of the Ark of the LORD; and they strewed earth on their heads. ⁷"Ah, Lord GOD!" cried Joshua. "Why did You lead this people across the Jordan only to deliver us into the hands of the Amorites, to be destroyed by them? If only we had been content to remain on the other side of the Jordan! ⁸O Lord, what can I say after Israel has turned tail before its enemies? ⁹When the Canaanites and all the inhabitants of the land hear of this, they will turn upon us and wipe out our very name from the earth. And what will You do about Your great name?"

¹⁰But the LORD answered Joshua: "Arise! Why do you lie prostrate? ¹¹Israel has sinned! They have broken the covenant by which I bound them. They have taken of the proscribed and put it in their vessels; they have stolen; they have broken faith! ¹²Therefore, the Israelites will not be able to hold their ground against their enemies; they will have to turn tail before their enemies, for they have become proscribed. I will not be with you any more unless you root out from among you what is proscribed. ¹³Go and purify the people. Order them: Purify yourselves for tomorrow. For thus says the LORD, the God of Israel: Something proscribed is in your midst, O Israel, and you will not be able to stand up to your enemies until you have purged the proscribed from among you. ¹⁴Tomorrow morning you shall present yourselves by tribes. Whichever tribe the LORD indicates^b shall come forward by clans; the clan that the LORD indicates shall come forward by ancestral houses, and the ancestral house that the LORD indicates

לִפְנֵי הַשַּׁעַר עַד־הַשְּׁבָרִים וַיַּכּוּם בַּמּוֹרָד וַיִּמַּס לְבַב־הָעָם וַיְהִי לְמָיִם: ⁶וַיִּקְרַע יְהוֹשֻׁעַ שִׂמְלֹתָיו וַיִּפֹּל עַל־פָּנָיו אַרְצָה לִפְנֵי אֲרוֹן יְהוָה עַד־הָעֶרֶב הוּא וְזִקְנֵי יִשְׂרָאֵל וַיַּעֲלוּ עָפָר עַל־רֹאשָׁם: ⁷וַיֹּאמֶר יְהוֹשֻׁעַ אֲהָהּ ׀ אֲדֹנָי יְהוִֹה לָמָה הֵעֲבַרְתָּ הַעֲבִיר אֶת־הָעָם הַזֶּה אֶת־הַיַּרְדֵּן לָתֵת אֹתָנוּ בְּיַד הָאֱמֹרִי לְהַאֲבִידֵנוּ וְלוּ הוֹאַלְנוּ וַנֵּשֶׁב בְּעֵבֶר הַיַּרְדֵּן: ⁸בִּי אֲדֹנָי מָה אֹמַר אַחֲרֵי אֲשֶׁר הָפַךְ יִשְׂרָאֵל עֹרֶף לִפְנֵי אֹיְבָיו: ⁹וְיִשְׁמְעוּ הַכְּנַעֲנִי וְכֹל יֹשְׁבֵי הָאָרֶץ וְנָסַבּוּ עָלֵינוּ וְהִכְרִיתוּ אֶת־שְׁמֵנוּ מִן־הָאָרֶץ וּמַה־תַּעֲשֵׂה לְשִׁמְךָ הַגָּדוֹל: ס ¹⁰וַיֹּאמֶר יְהוָה אֶל־יְהוֹשֻׁעַ קֻם לָךְ לָמָּה זֶּה אַתָּה נֹפֵל עַל־פָּנֶיךָ: ¹¹חָטָא יִשְׂרָאֵל וְגַם עָבְרוּ אֶת־בְּרִיתִי אֲשֶׁר צִוִּיתִי אוֹתָם וְגַם לָקְחוּ מִן־הַחֵרֶם וְגַם גָּנְבוּ וְגַם כִּחֲשׁוּ וְגַם שָׂמוּ בִכְלֵיהֶם: ¹²וְלֹא יֻכְלוּ בְּנֵי יִשְׂרָאֵל לָקוּם לִפְנֵי אֹיְבֵיהֶם עֹרֶף יִפְנוּ לִפְנֵי אֹיְבֵיהֶם כִּי הָיוּ לְחֵרֶם לֹא אוֹסִיף לִהְיוֹת עִמָּכֶם אִם־לֹא תַשְׁמִידוּ הַחֵרֶם מִקִּרְבְּכֶם: ¹³קֻם קַדֵּשׁ אֶת־הָעָם וְאָמַרְתָּ הִתְקַדְּשׁוּ לְמָחָר כִּי כֹה אָמַר יְהוָה אֱלֹהֵי יִשְׂרָאֵל חֵרֶם בְּקִרְבְּךָ יִשְׂרָאֵל לֹא תוּכַל לָקוּם לִפְנֵי אֹיְבֶיךָ עַד־הֲסִירְכֶם הַחֵרֶם מִקִּרְבְּכֶם: ¹⁴וְנִקְרַבְתֶּם בַּבֹּקֶר לְשִׁבְטֵיכֶם וְהָיָה הַשֵּׁבֶט אֲשֶׁר־יִלְכְּדֶנּוּ יְהוָה יִקְרַב לַמִּשְׁפָּחוֹת וְהַמִּשְׁפָּחָה אֲשֶׁר־יִלְכְּדֶנָּה יְהוָה תִּקְרַב לַבָּתִּים וְהַבַּיִת אֲשֶׁר יִלְכְּדֶנּוּ

---

a-a Lit. "melted and turned to water."
b Lit. "catches."

shall come forward man by man. ¹⁵Then he who is ᶜ-indicated for proscription,-ᶜ and all that is his, shall be put to the fire, because he broke the Covenant of the LORD and because he committed an outrage in Israel."

¹⁶Early next morning, Joshua had Israel come forward by tribes; and the tribe of Judah was indicated. ¹⁷He then had the clans of Judah come forward, and the clan of Zerah was indicated. Then he had the clan of Zerah come forward by ᵈ-ancestral houses,-ᵈ and Zabdi was indicated. ¹⁸Finally he had his ancestral house come forward man by man, and Achan son of Carmi, son of Zabdi, son of Zerah, of the tribe of Judah, was indicated.

¹⁹Then Joshua said to Achan, "My son, pay honor to the LORD, the God of Israel, and make confession to Him. Tell me what you have done; do not hold anything back from me." ²⁰Achan answered Joshua, "It is true, I have sinned against the LORD, the God of Israel. This is what I did: ²¹I saw among the spoil a fine Shinar mantle, two hundred shekels of silver, and a wedge of gold weighing fifty shekels, and I coveted them and took them. They are buried in the ground in my tent, with the silver under it."ᵉ

²²Joshua sent messengers, who hurried to the tent; and there itᵉ was, buried in his tent, with the silver underneath. ²³They took them from the tent and brought them to Joshua and all the Israelites, and displayedᶠ them before the LORD. ²⁴Then Joshua, and all Israel with him, took Achan son of Zerah—and the silver, the mantle, and the wedge of gold—his sons and daughters, and his ox, his ass, and his flock, and his tent, and all his belongings, and brought them up to the Valley of Achor. ²⁵And Joshua said, "What calamity you have brought upon us! The LORD will bring calamity upon you this day." And all

---

15 יְהוָה יִקְרַב לַגְּבָרִים: וְהָיָה הַנִּלְכָּד
בַּחֵרֶם יִשָּׂרֵף בָּאֵשׁ אֹתוֹ וְאֶת־כָּל־אֲשֶׁר־לוֹ
כִּי עָבַר אֶת־בְּרִית יְהוָה וְכִי־עָשָׂה נְבָלָה
בְּיִשְׂרָאֵל:
16 וַיַּשְׁכֵּם יְהוֹשֻׁעַ בַּבֹּקֶר וַיַּקְרֵב אֶת־
יִשְׂרָאֵל לִשְׁבָטָיו וַיִּלָּכֵד שֵׁבֶט יְהוּדָה:
17 וַיַּקְרֵב אֶת־מִשְׁפַּחַת יְהוּדָה וַיִּלְכֹּד אֵת
מִשְׁפַּחַת הַזַּרְחִי וַיַּקְרֵב אֶת־מִשְׁפַּחַת
הַזַּרְחִי לַגְּבָרִים וַיִּלָּכֵד זַבְדִּי: 18 וַיַּקְרֵב
אֶת־בֵּיתוֹ לַגְּבָרִים וַיִּלָּכֵד עָכָן בֶּן־כַּרְמִי
בֶן־זַבְדִּי בֶּן־זֶרַח לְמַטֵּה יְהוּדָה:
19 וַיֹּאמֶר יְהוֹשֻׁעַ אֶל־עָכָן בְּנִי שִׂים־נָא
כָבוֹד לַיהוָה אֱלֹהֵי יִשְׂרָאֵל וְתֶן־לוֹ תוֹדָה
וְהַגֶּד־נָא לִי מֶה עָשִׂיתָ אַל־תְּכַחֵד מִמֶּנִּי:
20 וַיַּעַן עָכָן אֶת־יְהוֹשֻׁעַ וַיֹּאמַר אָמְנָה
אָנֹכִי חָטָאתִי לַיהוָה אֱלֹהֵי יִשְׂרָאֵל וְכָזֹאת
וְכָזֹאת עָשִׂיתִי: 21 ואראה וָאֵרֶא בַשָּׁלָל
אַדֶּרֶת שִׁנְעָר אַחַת טוֹבָה וּמָאתַיִם
שְׁקָלִים כֶּסֶף וּלְשׁוֹן זָהָב אֶחָד חֲמִשִּׁים
שְׁקָלִים מִשְׁקָלוֹ וָאֶחְמְדֵם וָאֶקָּחֵם וְהִנָּם
טְמוּנִים בָּאָרֶץ בְּתוֹךְ הָאָהֳלִי וְהַכֶּסֶף
תַּחְתֶּיהָ:
22 וַיִּשְׁלַח יְהוֹשֻׁעַ מַלְאָכִים וַיָּרֻצוּ הָאֹהֱלָה
וְהִנֵּה טְמוּנָה בְּאָהֳלוֹ וְהַכֶּסֶף תַּחְתֶּיהָ:
23 וַיִּקָּחוּם מִתּוֹךְ הָאֹהֶל וַיְבִאוּם אֶל־
יְהוֹשֻׁעַ וְאֶל כָּל־בְּנֵי יִשְׂרָאֵל וַיַּצִּקֻם לִפְנֵי
יְהוָה: 24 וַיִּקַּח יְהוֹשֻׁעַ אֶת־עָכָן בֶּן־זֶרַח
וְאֶת־הַכֶּסֶף וְאֶת־הָאַדֶּרֶת וְאֶת־לְשׁוֹן
הַזָּהָב וְאֶת־בָּנָיו וְאֶת־בְּנֹתָיו וְאֶת־שׁוֹרוֹ
וְאֶת־חֲמֹרוֹ וְאֶת־צֹאנוֹ וְאֶת־אָהֳלוֹ וְאֶת־
כָּל־אֲשֶׁר־לוֹ וְכָל־יִשְׂרָאֵל עִמּוֹ וַיַּעֲלוּ אֹתָם
עֵמֶק עָכוֹר: 25 וַיֹּאמֶר יְהוֹשֻׁעַ מֶה עֲכַרְתָּנוּ
יַעְכָּרְךָ יְהוָה בַּיּוֹם הַזֶּה וַיִּרְגְּמוּ אֹתוֹ
כָל־יִשְׂרָאֵל אֶבֶן וַיִּשְׂרְפוּ אֹתָם בָּאֵשׁ

---

c-c   Or "caught in the net."

d-d   So some Heb. mss. and some ancient versions; most mss. and editions have "men."

e   I.e., the mantle.

f   Meaning of Heb. uncertain.

Israel pelted him with stones. They put them to the fire and stoned them. 26They raised a huge mound of stones over him, which is still there. Then the anger of the LORD subsided. That is why that place was named the Valley of Achor*g*—as is still the case.

8 The LORD said to Joshua, "Do not be frightened or dismayed. Take all the fighting troops with you, go and march against Ai. See, I will deliver the king of Ai, his people, his city, and his land into your hands. 2You shall treat Ai and her king as you treated Jericho and her king; however, you may take the spoil and the cattle as booty for yourselves. Now set an ambush against the city behind it."

3So Joshua and all the fighting troops prepared for the march on Ai. Joshua chose thirty thousand men, valiant warriors, and sent them ahead by night. 4He instructed them as follows: "Mind, you are to lie in ambush behind the city; don't stay too far from the city, and all of you be on the alert. 5I and all the troops with me will approach the city; and when they come out against us, as they did the first time, we will flee from them. 6They will come rushing after us until we have drawn them away from the city. They will think, 'They are fleeing from us the same as last time'; but while we are fleeing before them, 7you will dash out from your ambush and seize the city, and the LORD your God will deliver it into your hands. 8And when you take the city, set it on fire. Do as the LORD has commanded. Mind, I have given you your orders."

9Joshua then sent them off, and they proceeded to the ambush; they took up a position between Ai and Bethel—west of Ai—while Joshua spent the night with the rest of the troops.

---

g   *Connected with 'akhar "to bring calamity upon"; cf. v. 25.*

---

26 וַיִּסְקְלוּ אֹתָם בָּאֲבָנִים: וַיָּקִימוּ עָלָיו
גַּל־אֲבָנִים גָּדוֹל עַד הַיּוֹם הַזֶּה וַיָּשָׁב יְהוָה
מֵחֲרוֹן אַפּוֹ עַל־כֵּן קָרָא שֵׁם הַמָּקוֹם
הַהוּא עֵמֶק עָכוֹר עַד הַיּוֹם הַזֶּה: פ

ח וַיֹּאמֶר יְהוָה אֶל־יְהוֹשֻׁעַ אַל־תִּירָא
וְאַל־תֵּחָת קַח עִמְּךָ אֵת כָּל־עַם
הַמִּלְחָמָה וְקוּם עֲלֵה הָעָי רְאֵה ׀ נָתַתִּי
בְיָדְךָ אֶת־מֶלֶךְ הָעַי וְאֶת־עַמּוֹ וְאֶת־עִירוֹ
וְאֶת־אַרְצוֹ: 2 וְעָשִׂיתָ לָעַי וּלְמַלְכָּהּ כַּאֲשֶׁר
עָשִׂיתָ לִירִיחוֹ וּלְמַלְכָּהּ רַק־שְׁלָלָהּ
וּבְהֶמְתָּהּ תָּבֹזּוּ לָכֶם שִׂים־לְךָ אֹרֵב לָעִיר
מֵאַחֲרֶיהָ:
3 וַיָּקָם יְהוֹשֻׁעַ וְכָל־עַם הַמִּלְחָמָה לַעֲלוֹת
הָעָי וַיִּבְחַר יְהוֹשֻׁעַ שְׁלֹשִׁים אֶלֶף אִישׁ
גִּבּוֹרֵי הַחַיִל וַיִּשְׁלָחֵם לָיְלָה: 4 וַיְצַו
אֹתָם לֵאמֹר רְאוּ אַתֶּם אֹרְבִים לָעִיר
מֵאַחֲרֵי הָעִיר אַל־תִּרְחִיקוּ מִן־הָעִיר
מְאֹד וִהְיִיתֶם כֻּלְּכֶם נְכֹנִים: 5 וַאֲנִי וְכָל־
הָעָם אֲשֶׁר אִתִּי נִקְרַב אֶל־הָעִיר וְהָיָה
כִּי־יֵצְאוּ לִקְרָאתֵנוּ כַּאֲשֶׁר בָּרִאשֹׁנָה וְנַסְנוּ
לִפְנֵיהֶם: 6 וְיָצְאוּ אַחֲרֵינוּ עַד הַתִּיקֵנוּ
אוֹתָם מִן־הָעִיר כִּי יֹאמְרוּ נָסִים לְפָנֵינוּ
כַּאֲשֶׁר בָּרִאשֹׁנָה וְנַסְנוּ לִפְנֵיהֶם: 7 וְאַתֶּם
תָּקֻמוּ מֵהָאוֹרֵב וְהוֹרַשְׁתֶּם אֶת־הָעִיר
וּנְתָנָהּ יְהוָה אֱלֹהֵיכֶם בְּיֶדְכֶם: 8 וְהָיָה
כְּתָפְשְׂכֶם אֶת־הָעִיר תַּצִּיתוּ אֶת־הָעִיר
בָּאֵשׁ כִּדְבַר יְהוָה תַּעֲשׂוּ רְאוּ צִוִּיתִי
אֶתְכֶם:
9 וַיִּשְׁלָחֵם יְהוֹשֻׁעַ וַיֵּלְכוּ אֶל־הַמַּאְרָב
וַיֵּשְׁבוּ בֵּין בֵּית־אֵל וּבֵין הָעַי מִיָּם לָעָי
וַיָּלֶן יְהוֹשֻׁעַ בַּלַּיְלָה הַהוּא בְּתוֹךְ הָעָם:

10Early in the morning, Joshua mustered the troops; then he and the elders of Israel marched upon Ai at the head of the troops. 11All the fighting force that was with him advanced near the city and encamped to the north of Ai, with a hollow between them and Ai.—12He selected about five thousand men and stationed them as an ambush between Bethel and Ai, west of the city. 13Thus the main body of the army was disposed on the north of the city, but the far end of it was on the west. (This was after Joshua had a-spent the night-a in the valley.b)—14When the king of Ai saw them, he and all his people, the inhabitants of the city, rushed out in the early morning to the c-meeting place,-c facing the Arabah, to engage the Israelites in battle; for he was unaware that a force was lying in ambush behind the city. 15Joshua and all Israel fled in the direction of the wilderness, as though routed by them. 16All the troops in the city gathered to pursue them; pursuing Joshua, they were drawn out of the city. 17Not a man was left in Ai or in Bethel who did not go out after Israel; they left the city open while they pursued Israel.

18The LORD then said to Joshua, "Hold out the javelin in your hand toward Ai, for I will deliver it into your hands." So Joshua held out the javelin in his hand toward the city. 19As soon as he held out his hand, the ambush came rushing out of their station. They entered the city and captured it; and they swiftly set fire to the city. 20The men of Ai looked back and saw the smoke of the city rising to the sky; they had no room for flight in any direction.

The people who had been fleeing to the wilderness now became the pursuers. 21For when Joshua and all Israel saw that the ambush had captured the city, and that smoke was rising from the city, they turned around and attacked the men of Ai. 22Now the other [Israelites] were

10 וַיַּשְׁכֵּם יְהוֹשֻׁעַ בַּבֹּקֶר וַיִּפְקֹד אֶת־הָעָם וַיַּעַל הוּא וְזִקְנֵי יִשְׂרָאֵל לִפְנֵי הָעָם הָעָי: 11 וְכָל־הָעָם הַמִּלְחָמָה אֲשֶׁר אִתּוֹ עָלוּ וַיִּגְּשׁוּ וַיָּבֹאוּ נֶגֶד הָעִיר וַיַּחֲנוּ מִצְּפוֹן לָעַי וְהַגַּי בֵּינוֹ וּבֵין־הָעָי: 12 וַיִּקַּח כַּחֲמֵשֶׁת אֲלָפִים אִישׁ וַיָּשֶׂם אוֹתָם אֹרֵב בֵּין בֵּית־אֵל וּבֵין הָעַי מִיָּם לָעִיר: 13 וַיָּשִׂימוּ הָעָם אֶת־כָּל־הַמַּחֲנֶה אֲשֶׁר מִצְּפוֹן לָעִיר וְאֶת־עֲקֵבוֹ מִיָּם לָעִיר* וַיֵּלֶךְ יְהוֹשֻׁעַ בַּלַּיְלָה הַהוּא בְּתוֹךְ הָעֵמֶק: 14 וַיְהִי כִּרְאוֹת מֶלֶךְ־הָעַי וַיְמַהֲרוּ וַיַּשְׁכִּימוּ וַיֵּצְאוּ אַנְשֵׁי־הָעִיר לִקְרַאת־יִשְׂרָאֵל לַמִּלְחָמָה הוּא וְכָל־עַמּוֹ לַמּוֹעֵד לִפְנֵי הָעֲרָבָה וְהוּא לֹא יָדַע כִּי־אֹרֵב לוֹ מֵאַחֲרֵי הָעִיר: 15 וַיִּנָּגְעוּ יְהוֹשֻׁעַ וְכָל־יִשְׂרָאֵל לִפְנֵיהֶם וַיָּנֻסוּ דֶּרֶךְ הַמִּדְבָּר: 16 וַיִּזָּעֲקוּ כָּל־הָעָם אֲשֶׁר בעיר בָּעַי לִרְדֹּף אַחֲרֵיהֶם וַיִּרְדְּפוּ אַחֲרֵי יְהוֹשֻׁעַ וַיִּנָּתְקוּ מִן־הָעִיר: 17 וְלֹא־נִשְׁאַר אִישׁ בָּעַי וּבֵית* אֵל אֲשֶׁר לֹא־יָצְאוּ אַחֲרֵי יִשְׂרָאֵל וַיַּעַזְבוּ אֶת־הָעִיר פְּתוּחָה וַיִּרְדְּפוּ אַחֲרֵי יִשְׂרָאֵל: פ

18 וַיֹּאמֶר יְהוָה אֶל־יְהוֹשֻׁעַ נְטֵה בַכִּידוֹן אֲשֶׁר־בְּיָדְךָ אֶל־הָעַי כִּי בְיָדְךָ אֶתְּנֶנָּה וַיֵּט יְהוֹשֻׁעַ בַּכִּידוֹן אֲשֶׁר־בְּיָדוֹ אֶל־הָעִיר: 19 וְהָאוֹרֵב קָם מְהֵרָה מִמְּקוֹמוֹ וַיָּרוּצוּ כִּנְטוֹת יָדוֹ וַיָּבֹאוּ הָעִיר וַיִּלְכְּדוּהָ וַיְמַהֲרוּ וַיַּצִּיתוּ אֶת־הָעִיר בָּאֵשׁ: 20 וַיִּפְנוּ אַנְשֵׁי הָעַי אַחֲרֵיהֶם וַיִּרְאוּ וְהִנֵּה עָלָה עֲשַׁן הָעִיר הַשָּׁמַיְמָה וְלֹא־הָיָה בָהֶם יָדַיִם לָנוּס הֵנָּה וָהֵנָּה וְהָעָם הַנָּס הַמִּדְבָּר נֶהְפַּךְ אֶל־הָרוֹדֵף: 21 וִיהוֹשֻׁעַ וְכָל־יִשְׂרָאֵל רָאוּ כִּי־לָכַד הָאֹרֵב אֶת־הָעִיר וְכִי עָלָה עֲשַׁן הָעִיר וַיָּשֻׁבוּ וַיַּכּוּ אֶת־אַנְשֵׁי הָעָי: 22 וְאֵלֶּה יָצְאוּ

---

a-a   *So with some mss. (cf. v. 9); most mss. and editions read "marched."*

b   *Syriac reads "with the troops"; cf. v. 9.*

c-c   *Emendation yields "descent"; cf. 7.5.*

v. 13.   בנוסח אחר "וילן"

v. 17.   סבירין ומטעין "ובבית"

coming out of the city against them, so that they were between two bodies of Israelites, one on each side of them. They were slaughtered, so that no one escaped or got away. 23The king of Ai was taken alive and brought to Joshua.

24When Israel had killed all the inhabitants of Ai who had pursued them into the open wilderness, and all of them, to the last man, had fallen by the sword, all the Israelites turned back to Ai and put it to the sword.

25The total of those who fell that day, men and women, the entire population of Ai, came to twelve thousand.

26Joshua did not draw back the hand with which he held out his javelin until all the inhabitants of Ai had been exterminated. 27However, the Israelites took the cattle and the spoil of the city as their booty, in accordance with the instructions that the LORD had given to Joshua.

28Then Joshua burned down Ai, and turned it into a mound of ruins for all time, a desolation to this day. 29And the king of Ai was impaled on a stake until the evening. At sunset, Joshua had the corpse taken down from the stake and it was left lying at the entrance to the city gate. They raised a great heap of stones over it, which is there to this day.

30At that time Joshua built an altar to the LORD, the God of Israel, on Mount Ebal, 31as Moses, the servant of the LORD, had commanded the Israelites—as is written in the Book of the Teaching of Moses[d]—an altar of unhewn stone upon which no iron had been wielded. They offered on it burnt offerings to the LORD, and brought sacrifices of well-being. 32And there, on the stones, he inscribed a copy of the Teaching that Moses had written for the Israelites. 33All Israel—stranger and citizen alike—with their elders, officials, and magistrates,

---

d *See Deut. 27.3–8.*

מִן־הָעִיר לִקְרָאתָם וַיִּהְיוּ לְיִשְׂרָאֵל בַּתָּוֶךְ אֵלֶּה מִזֶּה וְאֵלֶּה מִזֶּה וַיַּכּוּ אוֹתָם עַד־בִּלְתִּי הִשְׁאִיר־לוֹ שָׂרִיד וּפָלִיט: 23 וְאֶת־מֶלֶךְ הָעַי תָּפְשׂוּ חָי וַיַּקְרִבוּ אֹתוֹ אֶל־יְהוֹשֻׁעַ:

24 וַיְהִי כְּכַלּוֹת יִשְׂרָאֵל לַהֲרֹג אֶת־כָּל־יֹשְׁבֵי הָעַי בַּשָּׂדֶה בַּמִּדְבָּר אֲשֶׁר רְדָפוּם בּוֹ וַיִּפְּלוּ כֻלָּם לְפִי־חֶרֶב עַד־תֻּמָּם וַיָּשֻׁבוּ כָל־יִשְׂרָאֵל הָעַי וַיַּכּוּ אֹתָהּ לְפִי־חָרֶב: 25 וַיְהִי כָל־הַנֹּפְלִים בַּיּוֹם הַהוּא מֵאִישׁ וְעַד־אִשָּׁה שְׁנֵים עָשָׂר אָלֶף כֹּל אַנְשֵׁי הָעָי:

26 וִיהוֹשֻׁעַ לֹא־הֵשִׁיב יָדוֹ אֲשֶׁר נָטָה בַּכִּידוֹן עַד אֲשֶׁר הֶחֱרִים אֵת כָּל־יֹשְׁבֵי הָעָי: 27 רַק הַבְּהֵמָה וּשְׁלַל הָעִיר הַהִיא בָּזְזוּ לָהֶם יִשְׂרָאֵל כִּדְבַר יְהֹוָה אֲשֶׁר צִוָּה אֶת־יְהוֹשֻׁעַ:

28 וַיִּשְׂרֹף יְהוֹשֻׁעַ אֶת־הָעָי וַיְשִׂימֶהָ תֵּל־עוֹלָם שְׁמָמָה עַד הַיּוֹם הַזֶּה: 29 וְאֶת־מֶלֶךְ הָעַי תָּלָה עַל־הָעֵץ עַד־עֵת הָעָרֶב וּכְבוֹא הַשֶּׁמֶשׁ צִוָּה יְהוֹשֻׁעַ וַיֹּרִידוּ אֶת־נִבְלָתוֹ מִן־הָעֵץ וַיַּשְׁלִיכוּ אוֹתָהּ אֶל־פֶּתַח שַׁעַר הָעִיר וַיָּקִימוּ עָלָיו גַּל־אֲבָנִים גָּדוֹל עַד הַיּוֹם הַזֶּה: פ

30 אָז יִבְנֶה יְהוֹשֻׁעַ מִזְבֵּחַ לַיהֹוָה אֱלֹהֵי יִשְׂרָאֵל בְּהַר עֵיבָל: 31 כַּאֲשֶׁר צִוָּה מֹשֶׁה עֶבֶד־יְהֹוָה אֶת־בְּנֵי יִשְׂרָאֵל כַּכָּתוּב בְּסֵפֶר תּוֹרַת מֹשֶׁה מִזְבַּח אֲבָנִים שְׁלֵמוֹת אֲשֶׁר לֹא־הֵנִיף עֲלֵיהֶן בַּרְזֶל וַיַּעֲלוּ עָלָיו עֹלוֹת לַיהֹוָה וַיִּזְבְּחוּ שְׁלָמִים: 32 וַיִּכְתָּב־שָׁם עַל־הָאֲבָנִים אֵת מִשְׁנֵה תּוֹרַת מֹשֶׁה אֲשֶׁר כָּתַב לִפְנֵי בְּנֵי יִשְׂרָאֵל: 33 וְכָל־יִשְׂרָאֵל וּזְקֵנָיו וְשֹׁטְרִים | וְשֹׁפְטָיו עֹמְדִים מִזֶּה |

stood on either side of the Ark, facing the levitical priests who carried the Ark of the LORD's Covenant. Half of them faced Mount Gerizim and half of them faced Mount Ebal, as Moses the servant of the LORD had commanded them of old, in order to bless the people of Israel. [34]After that, he read all the words of the Teaching, the blessing and the curse, just as is written in the Book of the Teaching.[e] [35]There was not a word of all that Moses had commanded that Joshua failed to read in the presence of the entire assembly of Israel, including the women and children and the strangers who accompanied them.

9 When all the kings [a]west of-[a] the Jordan—in the hill country, in the Shephelah, and along the entire coast of the Mediterranean Sea up to the vicinity of Lebanon, the [land of the] Hittites, Amorites, Canaanites, Perizzites, Hivites, and Jebusites—learned of this, [2]they gathered with one accord to fight against Joshua and Israel.

[3]But when the inhabitants of Gibeon learned how Joshua had treated Jericho and Ai, [4]they for their part resorted to cunning. They set out [b]in disguise:-[b] they took worn-out sacks for their asses, and worn-out waterskins that were cracked and patched; [5]they had worn-out, patched sandals on their feet, and threadbare clothes on their bodies; and all the bread they took as provision was dry and crumbly. [6]And so they went to Joshua in the camp at Gilgal and said to him and to the men of Israel, "We come from a distant land; we propose that you make a pact with us." [7]The men of Israel replied to the Hivites, "But perhaps you live among us; how then can we make a pact with you?"[c]

---

e   See Deut. 27.11–28.68.

a-a   Lit. "across."
b-b   Meaning of Heb. uncertain.
c   Cf. Deut. 7.2.

וּמִזֶּה ׀ לָאָרֹון נֶגֶד הַכֹּהֲנִים הַלְוִיִּם נֹשְׂאֵי ׀ אֲרֹון בְּרִית־יְהוָה כַּגֵּר כָּאֶזְרָח חֶצְיֹו אֶל־מוּל הַר־גְּרִזִים וְהַחֶצְיֹו אֶל־מוּל הַר־עֵיבָל כַּאֲשֶׁר צִוָּה מֹשֶׁה עֶבֶד־יְהוָה לְבָרֵךְ אֶת־הָעָם יִשְׂרָאֵל בָּרִאשֹׁנָה: 34 וְאַחֲרֵי־כֵן קָרָא אֶת־כָּל־דִּבְרֵי הַתֹּורָה הַבְּרָכָה וְהַקְּלָלָה כְּכָל־הַכָּתוּב בְּסֵפֶר הַתֹּורָה: 35 לֹא־הָיָה דָבָר מִכֹּל אֲשֶׁר־צִוָּה מֹשֶׁה אֲשֶׁר לֹא־קָרָא יְהֹושֻׁעַ נֶגֶד כָּל־קְהַל יִשְׂרָאֵל וְהַנָּשִׁים וְהַטַּף וְהַגֵּר הַהֹלֵךְ בְּקִרְבָּם: פ

ט וַיְהִי כִשְׁמֹעַ כָּל־הַמְּלָכִים אֲשֶׁר בְּעֵבֶר הַיַּרְדֵּן בָּהָר וּבַשְּׁפֵלָה וּבְכֹל חֹוף הַיָּם הַגָּדֹול אֶל־מוּל הַלְּבָנֹון הַחִתִּי וְהָאֱמֹרִי הַכְּנַעֲנִי הַפְּרִזִּי הַחִוִּי וְהַיְבוּסִי: 2 וַיִּתְקַבְּצוּ יַחְדָּו לְהִלָּחֵם עִם־יְהֹושֻׁעַ וְעִם־יִשְׂרָאֵל פֶּה אֶחָד: פ 3 וְיֹשְׁבֵי גִבְעֹון שָׁמְעוּ אֵת אֲשֶׁר עָשָׂה יְהֹושֻׁעַ לִירִיחֹו וְלָעָי: 4 וַיַּעֲשׂוּ גַם־הֵמָּה בְּעָרְמָה וַיֵּלְכוּ וַיִּצְטַיָּרוּ וַיִּקְחוּ שַׂקִּים בָּלִים לַחֲמֹורֵיהֶם וְנֹאדֹות יַיִן בָּלִים וּמְבֻקָּעִים וּמְצֹרָרִים: 5 וּנְעָלֹות בָּלֹות וּמְטֻלָּאֹות בְּרַגְלֵיהֶם וּשְׂלָמֹות בָּלֹות עֲלֵיהֶם וְכֹל לֶחֶם צֵידָם יָבֵשׁ הָיָה נִקֻּדִים: 6 וַיֵּלְכוּ אֶל־יְהֹושֻׁעַ אֶל־הַמַּחֲנֶה הַגִּלְגָּל וַיֹּאמְרוּ אֵלָיו וְאֶל־אִישׁ יִשְׂרָאֵל מֵאֶרֶץ רְחֹוקָה בָּאנוּ וְעַתָּה כִּרְתוּ־לָנוּ בְרִית: 7 וַיֹּאמרו וַיֹּאמֶר אִישׁ־יִשְׂרָאֵל אֶל־הַחִוִּי אוּלַי בְּקִרְבִּי אַתָּה יֹושֵׁב וְאֵיךְ אֶכְרָת־לְךָ בְרִית:

8They said to Joshua, "We will be your subjects." But Joshua asked them, "Who are you and where do you come from?" 9They replied, "Your servants have come from a very distant country, because of the fame of the LORD your God. For we heard the report of Him: of all that He did in Egypt, 10and of all that He did to the two Amorite kings on the other side of the Jordan, King Sihon of Heshbon and King Og of Bashan who lived in Ashtaroth. 11So our elders and all the inhabitants of our country instructed us as follows, 'Take along provisions for a trip, and go to them and say: We will be your subjects; come make a pact with us.' 12This bread of ours, which we took from our houses as provision, was still hot when we set out to come to you; and see how dry and crumbly it has become. 13These wineskins were new when we filled them, and see how they have cracked. These clothes and sandals of ours are worn out from the very long journey." 14The men *b*-took [their word] because of-*b* their provisions, and did not inquire of the LORD. 15Joshua established friendship with them; he made a pact with them to spare their lives, and the chieftains of the community gave them their oath.

16But when three days had passed after they made this pact with them, they learned that they were neighbors, living among them. 17So the Israelites set out, and on the third day they came to their towns; these towns were Gibeon, Chephirah, Beeroth, and Kiriath-jearim. 18But the Israelites did not attack them, since the chieftains of the community had sworn to them by the LORD, the God of Israel. The whole community muttered against the chieftains, 19but all the chieftains answered the whole community, "We swore to them by the LORD, the God of Israel; therefore we cannot touch them. 20This is what we will do to them: We will spare their

8 וַיֹּאמְר֤וּ אֶל־יְהוֹשֻׁ֙עַ֙ עֲבָדֶ֣יךָ אֲנַ֔חְנוּ וַיֹּ֤אמֶר אֲלֵהֶם֙ יְהוֹשֻׁ֔עַ מִ֥י אַתֶּ֖ם וּמֵאַ֥יִן תָּבֹֽאוּ: 9 וַיֹּאמְר֣וּ אֵלָ֗יו מֵאֶ֨רֶץ רְחוֹקָ֤ה מְאֹד֙ בָּ֣אוּ עֲבָדֶ֔יךָ לְשֵׁ֖ם יְהוָ֣ה אֱלֹהֶ֑יךָ כִּֽי־שָׁמַ֣עְנוּ שָׁמְע֔וֹ וְאֵ֛ת כָּל־אֲשֶׁ֥ר עָשָׂ֖ה בְּמִצְרָֽיִם: 10 וְאֵ֣ת ׀ כָּל־אֲשֶׁ֣ר עָשָׂ֗ה לִשְׁנֵי֙ מַלְכֵ֣י הָאֱמֹרִ֔י אֲשֶׁ֖ר בְּעֵ֣בֶר הַיַּרְדֵּ֑ן לְסִיחוֹן֙ מֶ֣לֶךְ חֶשְׁבּ֔וֹן וּלְע֥וֹג מֶֽלֶךְ־הַבָּשָׁ֖ן אֲשֶׁ֥ר בְּעַשְׁתָּרֽוֹת: 11 וַיֹּאמְר֣וּ אֵלֵ֡ינוּ זְקֵינֵ֩ינוּ֩ וְכָל־יֹשְׁבֵ֨י אַרְצֵ֜נוּ לֵאמֹ֗ר קְח֨וּ בְיֶדְכֶ֤ם צֵידָה֙ לַדֶּ֔רֶךְ וּלְכ֖וּ לִקְרָאתָ֑ם וַאֲמַרְתֶּ֤ם אֲלֵיהֶם֙ עַבְדֵיכֶ֣ם אֲנַ֔חְנוּ וְעַתָּ֖ה כִּרְתוּ־לָ֥נוּ בְרִֽית: 12 זֶ֣ה ׀ לַחְמֵ֗נוּ חָ֞ם הִצְטַיַּ֤דְנוּ אֹתוֹ֙ מִבָּ֣תֵּ֔ינוּ בְּי֥וֹם צֵאתֵ֖נוּ לָלֶ֣כֶת אֲלֵיכֶ֑ם וְעַתָּה֙ הִנֵּ֣ה יָבֵ֔שׁ וְהָיָ֖ה נִקֻּדִֽים: 13 וְאֵ֨לֶּה נֹאד֤וֹת הַיַּ֙יִן֙ אֲשֶׁ֣ר מִלֵּ֣אנוּ חֲדָשִׁ֔ים וְהִנֵּ֖ה הִתְבַּקָּ֑עוּ וְאֵ֤לֶּה שַׂלְמוֹתֵ֙ינוּ֙ וּנְעָלֵ֔ינוּ בָּל֕וּ מֵרֹ֥ב הַדֶּ֖רֶךְ מְאֹֽד: 14 וַיִּקְח֥וּ הָֽאֲנָשִׁ֖ים מִצֵּידָ֑ם וְאֶת־פִּ֥י יְהוָ֖ה לֹ֥א שָׁאָֽלוּ: 15 וַיַּ֨עַשׂ לָהֶ֤ם יְהוֹשֻׁ֙עַ֙ שָׁל֔וֹם וַיִּכְרֹ֥ת לָהֶ֛ם בְּרִ֖ית לְחַיּוֹתָ֑ם וַיִּשָּׁבְע֣וּ לָהֶ֔ם נְשִׂיאֵ֖י הָעֵדָֽה:

16 וַיְהִ֗י מִקְצֵה֙ שְׁלֹ֣שֶׁת יָמִ֔ים אַחֲרֵ֕י אֲשֶׁר־כָּרְת֥וּ לָהֶ֖ם בְּרִ֑ית וַֽיִּשְׁמְע֗וּ כִּֽי־קְרֹבִ֥ים הֵם֙ אֵלָ֔יו וּבְקִרְבּ֖וֹ הֵ֥ם יֹשְׁבִֽים: 17 וַיִּסְע֣וּ בְנֵֽי־יִשְׂרָאֵ֗ל וַיָּבֹ֛אוּ אֶל־עָרֵיהֶ֖ם בַּיּ֣וֹם הַשְּׁלִישִׁ֑י וְעָרֵיהֶם֙ גִּבְע֣וֹן וְהַכְּפִירָ֔ה וּבְאֵר֖וֹת וְקִרְיַ֥ת יְעָרִֽים: 18 וְלֹ֤א הִכּוּם֙ בְּנֵ֣י יִשְׂרָאֵ֔ל כִּֽי־נִשְׁבְּע֤וּ לָהֶם֙ נְשִׂיאֵ֣י הָֽעֵדָ֔ה בַּֽיהוָ֖ה אֱלֹהֵ֣י יִשְׂרָאֵ֑ל וַיִּלֹּ֥נוּ כָל־הָעֵדָ֖ה עַל־הַנְּשִׂיאִֽים: 19 וַיֹּאמְר֤וּ כָל־הַנְּשִׂיאִים֙ אֶל־כָּל־הָ֣עֵדָ֔ה אֲנַ֙חְנוּ֙ נִשְׁבַּ֣עְנוּ לָהֶ֔ם בַּֽיהוָ֖ה אֱלֹהֵ֣י יִשְׂרָאֵ֑ל וְעַתָּ֕ה לֹ֥א נוּכַ֖ל לִנְגֹּ֥עַ בָּהֶֽם: 20 זֹ֖את נַעֲשֶׂ֣ה לָהֶ֑ם וְהַחֲיֵ֣ה אוֹתָ֔ם וְלֹֽא־יִֽהְיֶ֥ה עָלֵ֙ינוּ֙

---

lives, so that there may be no wrath against us because of the oath that we swore to them." [21]And the chieftains declared concerning them, "They shall live!" And they became hewers of wood and drawers of water for the whole community, as the chieftains had decreed concerning them.

[22]Joshua summoned them and spoke to them thus: "Why did you deceive us and tell us you lived very far from us, when in fact you live among us? [23]Therefore, be accursed! Never shall your descendants cease to be slaves, hewers of wood and drawers of water for the House of my God." [24]But they replied to Joshua, "You see, your servants had heard that the LORD your God had promised His servant Moses to give you the whole land and to wipe out all the inhabitants of the country on your account; so we were in great fear for our lives on your account. That is why we did this thing. [25]And now we are at your mercy; do with us what you consider right and proper." [26]And he did so; he saved them from being killed by the Israelites. [27]That day Joshua made them hewers of wood and drawers of water—as they still are—for the community and for the altar of the LORD, in the place that He would choose.

10

When King Adoni-zedek of Jerusalem learned that Joshua had captured Ai and proscribed it, treating Ai and its king as he had treated Jericho and its king, and that, moreover, the people of Gibeon had come to terms with Israel and remained among them, [2]a-he was-a very frightened. For Gibeon was a large city, like one of the royal cities—in fact, larger than Ai—and all its men were warriors. [3]So King Adoni-zedek of Jerusalem sent this message to King Hoham of Hebron, King Piram of

---

קֶצֶף עַל־הַשְּׁבוּעָה אֲשֶׁר־נִשְׁבַּ֫עְנוּ לָהֶֽם׃ 21 וַיֹּאמְר֧וּ אֲלֵיהֶ֛ם הַנְּשִׂיאִ֖ים יִֽחְי֑וּ וַ֠יִּהְי֠וּ חֹטְבֵ֨י עֵצִ֤ים וְשֹׁאֲבֵי־מַ֙יִם֙ לְכָל־הָ֣עֵדָ֔ה כַּֽאֲשֶׁ֛ר דִּבְּר֥וּ לָהֶ֖ם הַנְּשִׂיאִֽים׃ 22 וַיִּקְרָ֤א לָהֶם֙ יְהוֹשֻׁ֔עַ וַיְדַבֵּ֥ר אֲלֵיהֶ֖ם לֵאמֹ֑ר לָ֣מָּה רִמִּיתֶ֤ם אֹתָ֙נוּ֙ לֵאמֹ֔ר רְחוֹקִ֨ים אֲנַ֤חְנוּ מִכֶּם֙ מְאֹ֔ד וְאַתֶּ֖ם בְּקִרְבֵּ֥נוּ יֹשְׁבִֽים׃ 23 וְעַתָּ֖ה אֲרוּרִ֣ים אַתֶּ֑ם וְלֹֽא־יִכָּרֵ֨ת מִכֶּ֜ם עֶ֗בֶד וְחֹטְבֵ֥י עֵצִ֛ים וְשֹׁאֲבֵי־מַ֖יִם לְבֵ֥ית אֱלֹהָֽי׃ 24 וַיַּעֲנ֣וּ אֶת־יְהוֹשֻׁ֗עַ וַיֹּאמְרוּ֮ כִּי֩ הֻגֵּ֨ד הֻגַּ֜ד לַעֲבָדֶ֗יךָ אֵת֩ אֲשֶׁ֨ר צִוָּ֜ה יְהוָ֤ה אֱלֹהֶ֙יךָ֙ אֶת־מֹשֶׁ֣ה עַבְדּ֔וֹ לָתֵ֤ת לָכֶם֙ אֶת־כָּל־הָאָ֔רֶץ וּלְהַשְׁמִ֛יד אֶת־כָּל־יֹשְׁבֵ֥י הָאָ֖רֶץ מִפְּנֵיכֶ֑ם וַנִּירָ֨א מְאֹ֤ד לְנַפְשֹׁתֵ֙ינוּ֙ מִפְּנֵיכֶ֔ם וַֽנַּעֲשֵׂ֖ה אֶת־הַדָּבָ֥ר הַזֶּֽה׃ 25 וְעַתָּ֖ה הִנְנ֣וּ בְיָדֶ֑ךָ כַּטּ֨וֹב וְכַיָּשָׁ֧ר בְּעֵינֶ֛יךָ לַעֲשׂ֥וֹת לָ֖נוּ עֲשֵֽׂה׃ 26 וַיַּ֥עַשׂ לָהֶ֖ם כֵּ֑ן וַיַּצֵּ֤ל אוֹתָם֙ מִיַּ֣ד בְּנֵֽי־יִשְׂרָאֵ֔ל וְלֹ֖א הֲרָגֽוּם׃ 27 וַיִּתְּנֵ֨ם יְהוֹשֻׁ֜עַ בַּיּ֤וֹם הַהוּא֙ חֹטְבֵ֣י עֵצִ֔ים וְשֹׁאֲבֵי־מַ֖יִם לָֽעֵדָ֑ה וּֽלְמִזְבַּ֤ח יְהוָה֙ עַד־הַיּ֣וֹם הַזֶּ֔ה אֶל־הַמָּק֖וֹם אֲשֶׁ֥ר יִבְחָֽר׃ פ

ל וַיְהִ֣י כִשְׁמֹ֣עַ אֲדֹֽנִי־צֶ֩דֶק֩ מֶ֨לֶךְ יְרוּשָׁלַ֜͏ִם כִּֽי־לָכַ֣ד יְהוֹשֻׁ֣עַ אֶת־הָעַי֮ וַיַּחֲרִימָהּ֒ כַּאֲשֶׁ֨ר עָשָׂ֤ה לִֽירִיחוֹ֙ וּלְמַלְכָּ֔הּ כֵּן־עָשָׂ֥ה לָעַ֖י וּלְמַלְכָּ֑הּ וְכִ֣י הִשְׁלִ֜ימוּ יֹשְׁבֵ֤י גִבְעוֹן֙ אֶת־יִשְׂרָאֵ֔ל וַיִּהְי֖וּ בְּקִרְבָּֽם׃ 2 וַיִּֽירְא֣וּ מְאֹ֔ד כִּ֣י עִ֤יר גְּדוֹלָה֙ גִּבְע֔וֹן כְּאַחַ֖ת עָרֵ֣י הַמַּמְלָכָ֑ה וְכִ֨י הִ֤יא גְדוֹלָה֙ מִן־הָעַ֔י וְכָל־אֲנָשֶׁ֖יהָ גִּבֹּרִֽים׃ 3 וַיִּשְׁלַ֡ח אֲדֹֽנִי־צֶ֩דֶק֩ מֶ֨לֶךְ יְרוּשָׁלַ֜͏ִם אֶל־הוֹהָ֣ם מֶֽלֶךְ־חֶבְר֗וֹן וְאֶל־פִּרְאָ֤ם מֶֽלֶךְ־

---

a-a Heb. "they were."

Jarmuth, King Japhia of Lachish, and King De-bir of Eglon: ⁴"Come up and help me defeat Gibeon; for it has come to terms with Joshua and the Israelites."

⁵The five Amorite kings—the king of Jeru-salem, the king of Hebron, the king of Jarmuth, the king of Lachish, and the king of Eglon, with all their armies—joined forces and marched on Gibeon, and encamped against it and attacked it. ⁶The people of Gibeon thereupon sent this message to Joshua in the camp at Gilgal: "Do not fail your servants; come up quickly and aid us and deliver us, for all the Amorite kings of the hill country have gathered against us." ⁷So Joshua marched up from Gilgal with his whole fighting force, all the trained warriors.

⁸The LORD said to Joshua, "Do not be afraid of them, for I will deliver them into your hands; not one of them shall withstand you." ⁹Joshua took them by surprise, marching all night from Gilgal. ¹⁰The LORD threw them into a panic be-fore Israel: [Joshua] inflicted a crushing defeat on them at Gibeon, pursued them in the direc-tion of the Beth-horon ascent, and harried them all the way to Azekah and Makkedah. ¹¹While they were fleeing before Israel down the descent from Beth-horon, the LORD hurled huge stones on them from the sky, all the way to Azekah, and they perished; more perished from the hail-stones than were killed by the Israelite weapons.

¹²On that occasion, when the LORD routed the Amorites before the Israelites, Joshua ad-dressed the LORD; he said in the presence of the Israelites:

"Stand still, O sun, at Gibeon,
O moon, in the Valley of Aijalon!"

¹³And the sun stood still
And the moon halted,
While a nation wreaked judgment on its foes
—as is written in the Book of Jashar.ᵇ Thus

ᵇ Presumably a collection of war songs.

477

נביאים יהושע י

יַרְמוּת֙ וְאֶל־יָפִ֣יעַ מֶֽלֶךְ־לָכִ֔ישׁ וְאֶל־דְּבִ֖יר מֶֽלֶךְ־עֶגְל֥וֹן לֵאמֹֽר׃ ⁴ עֲלֽוּ־אֵלַ֣י וְעִזְרֻ֔נִי וְנַכֶּ֖ה אֶת־גִּבְע֑וֹן כִּֽי־הִשְׁלִ֥ימָה אֶת־יְהוֹשֻׁ֖עַ וְאֶת־בְּנֵ֥י יִשְׂרָאֵֽל׃ ⁵ וַיֵּאָסְפ֨וּ וַֽיַּעֲל֜וּ חֲמֵ֣שֶׁת ׀ מַלְכֵ֣י הָאֱמֹרִ֗י מֶ֣לֶךְ יְרוּשָׁלַ֜͏ִם מֶֽלֶךְ־חֶבְר֤וֹן מֶֽלֶךְ־יַרְמוּת֙ מֶֽלֶךְ־לָכִ֣ישׁ מֶֽלֶךְ־עֶגְל֔וֹן הֵ֖ם וְכָל־מַֽחֲנֵיהֶ֑ם וַֽיַּחֲנוּ֙ עַל־גִּבְע֔וֹן וַיִּֽלָּחֲמ֖וּ עָלֶֽיהָ׃ ⁶ וַיִּשְׁלְח֣וּ אַנְשֵׁי֩ גִבְע֨וֹן אֶל־יְהוֹשֻׁ֤עַ אֶל־הַֽמַּחֲנֶה֙ הַגִּלְגָּ֣לָה לֵאמֹ֔ר אַל־תֶּ֥רֶף יָדֶ֖יךָ מֵֽעֲבָדֶ֑יךָ עֲלֵ֧ה אֵלֵ֣ינוּ מְהֵרָ֗ה וְהוֹשִׁ֤יעָה לָּ֨נוּ֙ וְעָזְרֵ֔נוּ כִּ֚י נִקְבְּצ֣וּ אֵלֵ֔ינוּ כָּל־מַלְכֵ֥י הָֽאֱמֹרִ֖י יֹשְׁבֵ֥י הָהָֽר׃ ⁷ וַיַּ֨עַל יְהוֹשֻׁ֜עַ מִן־הַגִּלְגָּ֗ל ה֚וּא וְכָל־עַ֤ם הַמִּלְחָמָה֙ עִמּ֔וֹ וְכֹ֖ל גִּבּוֹרֵ֥י הֶחָֽיִל׃ פ ⁸ וַיֹּ֨אמֶר יְהֹוָ֤ה אֶל־יְהוֹשֻׁ֙עַ֙ אַל־תִּירָ֣א מֵהֶ֔ם כִּ֥י בְיָֽדְךָ֖ נְתַתִּ֑ים לֹא־יַעֲמֹ֥ד אִ֛ישׁ מֵהֶ֖ם בְּפָנֶֽיךָ׃ ⁹ וַיָּבֹ֧א אֲלֵיהֶ֛ם יְהוֹשֻׁ֖עַ פִּתְאֹ֑ם כָּל־הַלַּ֕יְלָה עָלָ֖ה מִן־הַגִּלְגָּֽל׃ ¹⁰ וַיְהֻמֵּ֧ם יְהֹוָ֣ה לִפְנֵ֣י יִשְׂרָאֵ֗ל וַיַּכֵּ֥ם מַכָּֽה־גְדוֹלָ֖ה בְּגִבְע֑וֹן וַֽיִּרְדְּפֵ֗ם דֶּ֚רֶךְ מַעֲלֵ֣ה בֵית־חוֹרֹ֔ן וַיַּכֵּ֥ם עַד־עֲזֵקָ֖ה וְעַד־מַקֵּדָֽה׃ ¹¹ וַיְהִ֞י בְּנֻסָ֣ם ׀ מִפְּנֵ֣י יִשְׂרָאֵ֗ל הֵ֞ם בְּמוֹרַ֤ד בֵּֽית־חוֹרֹן֙ וַֽיהֹוָ֡ה הִשְׁלִ֣יךְ עֲלֵיהֶם֩ אֲבָנִ֨ים גְּדֹל֧וֹת מִן־הַשָּׁמַ֛יִם עַד־עֲזֵקָ֖ה וַיָּמֻ֑תוּ רַבִּ֗ים אֲשֶׁר־מֵ֙תוּ֙ בְּאַבְנֵ֣י הַבָּרָ֔ד מֵאֲשֶׁ֥ר הָרְג֛וּ בְּנֵ֥י יִשְׂרָאֵ֖ל בֶּחָֽרֶב׃ ס ¹² אָ֣ז יְדַבֵּ֤ר יְהוֹשֻׁעַ֙ לַֽיהֹוָ֔ה בְּי֗וֹם תֵּ֤ת יְהֹוָה֙ אֶת־הָ֣אֱמֹרִ֔י לִפְנֵ֖י בְּנֵ֣י יִשְׂרָאֵ֑ל וַיֹּ֣אמֶר ׀ לְעֵינֵ֣י יִשְׂרָאֵ֗ל שֶׁ֚מֶשׁ בְּגִבְע֣וֹן דּ֔וֹם וְיָרֵ֖חַ בְּעֵ֥מֶק אַיָּלֽוֹן׃ ¹³ וַיִּדֹּ֨ם הַשֶּׁ֜מֶשׁ וְיָרֵ֣חַ עָמָ֗ד עַד־יִקֹּ֥ם גּוֹי֙ אֹֽיְבָ֔יו הֲלֹא־הִ֥יא כְתוּבָ֖ה עַל־סֵ֣פֶר הַיָּשָׁ֑ר וַיַּעֲמֹ֤ד

the sun halted in midheaven, and did not press on to set, for a whole day; [14]for the LORD fought for Israel. Neither before nor since has there ever been such a day, when the LORD acted on words spoken by a man. [15]Then Joshua together with all Israel returned to the camp at Gilgal.

[16]Meanwhile, those five kings fled and hid in a cave at Makkedah. [17]When it was reported to Joshua that the five kings had been found hiding in a cave at Makkedah, [18]Joshua ordered, "Roll large stones up against the mouth of the cave, and post men over it to keep guard over them. [19]But as for the rest of you, don't stop, but press on the heels of your enemies and harass them from the rear. Don't let them reach their towns, for the LORD your God has delivered them into your hands." [20]When Joshua and the Israelites had finished dealing them a deadly blow, they were wiped out, except for some fugitives who escaped into the fortified towns. [21]The whole army returned in safety to Joshua in the camp at Makkedah; no one so much as snarled[c] at the Israelites. [22]And now Joshua ordered, "Open the mouth of the cave, and bring those five kings out of the cave to me." [23]This was done. Those five kings—the king of Jerusalem, the king of Hebron, the king of Jarmuth, the king of Lachish, and the king of Eglon—were brought out to him from the cave. [24]And when the kings were brought out to Joshua, Joshua summoned all the men of Israel and ordered the army officers who had accompanied him, "Come forward and place your feet on the necks of these kings." They came forward and placed their feet on their necks. [25]Joshua said to them, "Do not be frightened or dismayed; be firm and resolute. For this is what the LORD is going to do to all the enemies with whom you are at war." [26]After that, Joshua had them put to death and impaled on five stakes, and they remained impaled on

c Cf. Exod. 11.7.

הַשֶּׁמֶשׁ בַּחֲצִי הַשָּׁמַיִם וְלֹא־אָץ לָבוֹא
כְּיוֹם תָּמִים׃ 14 וְלֹא הָיָה כַּיּוֹם הַהוּא
לְפָנָיו וְאַחֲרָיו לִשְׁמֹעַ יְהוָה בְּקוֹל אִישׁ
כִּי יְהוָה נִלְחָם לְיִשְׂרָאֵל׃ פ 15 וַיָּשָׁב
יְהוֹשֻׁעַ וְכָל־יִשְׂרָאֵל עִמּוֹ אֶל־הַמַּחֲנֶה
הַגִּלְגָּלָה׃
16 וַיָּנֻסוּ חֲמֵשֶׁת הַמְּלָכִים הָאֵלֶּה וַיֵּחָבְאוּ
בַמְּעָרָה בְּמַקֵּדָה׃ 17 וַיֻּגַּד לִיהוֹשֻׁעַ לֵאמֹר
נִמְצְאוּ חֲמֵשֶׁת הַמְּלָכִים נֶחְבָּאִים בַּמְּעָרָה
בְּמַקֵּדָה׃ 18 וַיֹּאמֶר יְהוֹשֻׁעַ גֹּלּוּ אֲבָנִים
גְּדֹלוֹת אֶל־פִּי הַמְּעָרָה וְהַפְקִידוּ עָלֶיהָ
אֲנָשִׁים לְשָׁמְרָם׃ 19 וְאַתֶּם אַל־תַּעֲמֹדוּ
רִדְפוּ אַחֲרֵי אֹיְבֵיכֶם וְזִנַּבְתֶּם אוֹתָם אַל־
תִּתְּנוּם לָבוֹא אֶל־עָרֵיהֶם כִּי נְתָנָם יְהוָה
אֱלֹהֵיכֶם בְּיֶדְכֶם׃ 20 וַיְהִי כְּכַלּוֹת יְהוֹשֻׁעַ
וּבְנֵי יִשְׂרָאֵל לְהַכּוֹתָם מַכָּה גְדוֹלָה־מְאֹד
עַד־תֻּמָּם וְהַשְּׂרִידִים שָׂרְדוּ מֵהֶם וַיָּבֹאוּ
אֶל־עָרֵי הַמִּבְצָר׃ 21 וַיָּשֻׁבוּ כָל־הָעָם אֶל־
הַמַּחֲנֶה אֶל־יְהוֹשֻׁעַ מַקֵּדָה בְּשָׁלוֹם לֹא־
חָרַץ לִבְנֵי יִשְׂרָאֵל לְאִישׁ אֶת־לְשֹׁנוֹ׃
22 וַיֹּאמֶר יְהוֹשֻׁעַ פִּתְחוּ אֶת־פִּי הַמְּעָרָה
וְהוֹצִיאוּ אֵלַי אֶת־חֲמֵשֶׁת הַמְּלָכִים
הָאֵלֶּה מִן־הַמְּעָרָה׃ 23 וַיַּעֲשׂוּ כֵן וַיֹּצִיאוּ
אֵלָיו אֶת־חֲמֵשֶׁת הַמְּלָכִים הָאֵלֶּה מִן־
הַמְּעָרָה אֵת ׀ מֶלֶךְ יְרוּשָׁלַם אֶת־מֶלֶךְ
חֶבְרוֹן אֶת־מֶלֶךְ יַרְמוּת אֶת־מֶלֶךְ לָכִישׁ
אֶת־מֶלֶךְ עֶגְלוֹן׃ 24 וַיְהִי כְּהוֹצִיאָם אֶת־
הַמְּלָכִים הָאֵלֶּה אֶל־יְהוֹשֻׁעַ וַיִּקְרָא
יְהוֹשֻׁעַ אֶל־כָּל־אִישׁ יִשְׂרָאֵל וַיֹּאמֶר אֶל־
קְצִינֵי אַנְשֵׁי הַמִּלְחָמָה הֶהָלְכוּא אִתּוֹ
קִרְבוּ שִׂימוּ אֶת־רַגְלֵיכֶם עַל־צַוְּארֵי*
הַמְּלָכִים הָאֵלֶּה וַיִּקְרְבוּ וַיָּשִׂימוּ אֶת־
רַגְלֵיהֶם עַל־צַוְּארֵיהֶם׃ 25 וַיֹּאמֶר אֲלֵיהֶם
יְהוֹשֻׁעַ אַל־תִּירְאוּ וְאַל־תֵּחָתּוּ חִזְקוּ
וְאִמְצוּ כִּי כָכָה יַעֲשֶׂה יְהוָה לְכָל־אֹיְבֵיכֶם
אֲשֶׁר אַתֶּם נִלְחָמִים אוֹתָם׃ 26 וַיַּכֵּם

the stakes until evening. [27]At sunset Joshua ordered them taken down from the poles and thrown into the cave in which they had hidden. Large stones were placed over the mouth of the cave, [and there they are] to this very day.

[28]At that time Joshua captured Makkedah and put it and its king to the sword, proscribing it[d] and every person in it and leaving none that escaped. And he treated the king of Makkedah as he had treated the king of Jericho.

[29]From Makkedah, Joshua proceeded with all Israel to Libnah, and he attacked it. [30]The LORD delivered it and its king into the hands of Israel; they put it and all the people in it to the sword, letting none escape. And he treated its king as he had treated the king of Jericho.

[31]From Libnah, Joshua proceeded with all Israel to Lachish; he encamped against it and attacked it. [32]The LORD delivered Lachish into the hands of Israel. They captured it on the second day and put it and all the people in it to the sword, just as they had done to Libnah.

[33]At that time King Horam of Gezer marched to the help of Lachish; but Joshua defeated him and his army, letting none of them escape.

[34]From Lachish, Joshua proceeded with all Israel to Eglon; they encamped against it and attacked it. [35]They captured it on the same day and put it to the sword, proscribing all the people that were in it, as they had done to Lachish.

[36]From Eglon, Joshua marched with all Israel to Hebron and attacked it. [37]They captured it and put it, its king, and all its towns, and all the people that were in it, to the sword. He let none escape, proscribing it and all the people in it, just as he had done in the case of Eglon.

יְהוֹשֻׁעַ אַחֲרֵי־כֵן וַיְמִיתֵם וַיִּתְלֵם עַל
חֲמִשָּׁה עֵצִים וַיִּהְיוּ תְּלוּיִם עַל־הָעֵצִים
עַד־הָעָרֶב: [27] וַיְהִי לְעֵת ׀ בּוֹא הַשֶּׁמֶשׁ
צִוָּה יְהוֹשֻׁעַ וַיֹּרִידוּם מֵעַל הָעֵצִים
וַיַּשְׁלִכֻם אֶל־הַמְּעָרָה אֲשֶׁר נֶחְבְּאוּ־שָׁם
וַיָּשִׂמוּ אֲבָנִים גְּדֹלוֹת עַל־פִּי הַמְּעָרָה
עַד־עֶצֶם הַיּוֹם הַזֶּה: פ

[28] וְאֶת־מַקֵּדָה לָכַד יְהוֹשֻׁעַ בַּיּוֹם הַהוּא
וַיַּכֶּהָ לְפִי־חֶרֶב וְאֶת־מַלְכָּהּ הֶחֱרִם
אוֹתָם* וְאֶת־כָּל־הַנֶּפֶשׁ אֲשֶׁר־בָּהּ לֹא
הִשְׁאִיר שָׂרִיד וַיַּעַשׂ לְמֶלֶךְ מַקֵּדָה כַּאֲשֶׁר
עָשָׂה לְמֶלֶךְ יְרִיחוֹ:

[29] וַיַּעֲבֹר יְהוֹשֻׁעַ וְכָל־יִשְׂרָאֵל עִמּוֹ
מִמַּקֵּדָה לִבְנָה וַיִּלָּחֶם עִם־לִבְנָה: [30] וַיִּתֵּן
יְהוָה גַּם־אוֹתָהּ בְּיַד יִשְׂרָאֵל וְאֶת־מַלְכָּהּ
וַיַּכֶּהָ לְפִי־חֶרֶב וְאֶת־כָּל־הַנֶּפֶשׁ אֲשֶׁר־בָּהּ
לֹא־הִשְׁאִיר בָּהּ שָׂרִיד וַיַּעַשׂ לְמַלְכָּהּ
כַּאֲשֶׁר עָשָׂה לְמֶלֶךְ יְרִיחוֹ: ס

[31] וַיַּעֲבֹר יְהוֹשֻׁעַ וְכָל־יִשְׂרָאֵל עִמּוֹ מִלִּבְנָה
לָכִישָׁה וַיִּחַן עָלֶיהָ וַיִּלָּחֶם בָּהּ: [32] וַיִּתֵּן
יְהוָה אֶת־לָכִישׁ בְּיַד יִשְׂרָאֵל וַיִּלְכְּדָהּ
בַּיּוֹם הַשֵּׁנִי וַיַּכֶּהָ לְפִי־חֶרֶב וְאֶת־כָּל־
הַנֶּפֶשׁ אֲשֶׁר־בָּהּ כְּכֹל אֲשֶׁר־עָשָׂה
לְלִבְנָה: פ

[33] אָז עָלָה הֹרָם מֶלֶךְ גֶּזֶר לַעְזֹר אֶת־
לָכִישׁ וַיַּכֵּהוּ יְהוֹשֻׁעַ וְאֶת־עַמּוֹ עַד־בִּלְתִּי
הִשְׁאִיר־לוֹ שָׂרִיד:

[34] וַיַּעֲבֹר יְהוֹשֻׁעַ וְכָל־יִשְׂרָאֵל עִמּוֹ מִלָּכִישׁ
עֶגְלֹנָה וַיַּחֲנוּ עָלֶיהָ וַיִּלָּחֲמוּ עָלֶיהָ:
[35] וַיִּלְכְּדוּהָ בַּיּוֹם הַהוּא וַיַּכּוּהָ לְפִי־חֶרֶב
וְאֵת כָּל־הַנֶּפֶשׁ אֲשֶׁר־בָּהּ בַּיּוֹם הַהוּא
הֶחֱרִים כְּכֹל אֲשֶׁר־עָשָׂה לְלָכִישׁ: פ

[36] וַיַּעַל יְהוֹשֻׁעַ וְכָל־יִשְׂרָאֵל עִמּוֹ
מֵעֶגְלוֹנָה חֶבְרוֹנָה וַיִּלָּחֲמוּ עָלֶיהָ:
[37] וַיִּלְכְּדוּהָ וַיַּכּוּהָ־לְפִי־חֶרֶב וְאֶת־מַלְכָּהּ
וְאֶת־כָּל־עָרֶיהָ וְאֶת־כָּל־הַנֶּפֶשׁ אֲשֶׁר־בָּהּ

---

d   *So several mss.; most mss. and the editions read "them."*   בנוסח אחר "אֹתָהּ"   v. 28.

38Joshua and all Israel with him then turned back to Debir and attacked it. 39He captured it and its king and all its towns. They put them to the sword and proscribed all the people in it. They let none escape; just as they had done to Hebron, and as they had done to Libnah and its king, so they did to Debir and its king.

40Thus Joshua conquered the whole country:e the hill country, the Negeb, the Shephelah, and the slopes, with all their kings; he let none escape, but proscribed everything that breathed—as the LORD, the God of Israel, had commanded. 41Joshua conquered them from Kadesh-barnea to Gaza, all the land of Goshen, and up to Gibeon. 42All those kings and their lands were conquered by Joshua at a single stroke, for the LORD, the God of Israel, fought for Israel. 43Then Joshua, with all Israel, returned to the camp at Gilgal.

11

When the news reached King Jabin of Hazor, he sent messages to King Jobab of Madon, to the king of Shimron, to the king of Achshaph, 2and to the other kings in the north—in the hill country, in the Arabah south of Chinnereth, in the lowlands, and in the districta of Dor on the west; 3to the Canaanites in the east and in the west; to the Amorites, Hittites, Perizzites, and Jebusites in the hill country; and to the Hivites at the foot of Hermon, in the land of Mizpah. 4They took the field with all their armies—an enormous host, as numerous as the sands on the seashore—and a vast multitude of horses and chariots. 5All these kings joined forces; they came and encamped to-

---

e I.e., the whole southern part of Canaan.

a Meaning of Heb. uncertain.

לֹא־הִשְׁאִיר שָׂרִיד כְּכֹל אֲשֶׁר־עָשָׂה לְעֶגְלוֹן וַיַּחֲרֵם אוֹתָהּ וְאֶת־כָּל־הַנֶּפֶשׁ אֲשֶׁר־בָּהּ: ס 38 וַיָּשָׁב יְהוֹשֻׁעַ וְכָל־יִשְׂרָאֵל עִמּוֹ דְּבִרָה וַיִּלָּחֶם עָלֶיהָ: 39 וַיִּלְכְּדָהּ וְאֶת־מַלְכָּהּ וְאֶת־כָּל־עָרֶיהָ וַיַּכּוּם לְפִי־חֶרֶב וַיַּחֲרִימוּ אֶת־כָּל־נֶפֶשׁ אֲשֶׁר־בָּהּ לֹא הִשְׁאִיר שָׂרִיד כַּאֲשֶׁר עָשָׂה לְחֶבְרוֹן כֵּן־עָשָׂה לִדְבִרָה וּלְמַלְכָּהּ וְכַאֲשֶׁר עָשָׂה לְלִבְנָה וּלְמַלְכָּהּ: 40 וַיַּכֶּה יְהוֹשֻׁעַ אֶת־כָּל־הָאָרֶץ הָהָר וְהַנֶּגֶב וְהַשְּׁפֵלָה וְהָאֲשֵׁדוֹת וְאֵת כָּל־מַלְכֵיהֶם לֹא הִשְׁאִיר שָׂרִיד וְאֵת כָּל־הַנְּשָׁמָה הֶחֱרִים כַּאֲשֶׁר צִוָּה יְהוָה אֱלֹהֵי יִשְׂרָאֵל: 41 וַיַּכֵּם יְהוֹשֻׁעַ מִקָּדֵשׁ בַּרְנֵעַ וְעַד־עַזָּה וְאֵת כָּל־אֶרֶץ גֹּשֶׁן וְעַד־גִּבְעוֹן: 42 וְאֵת כָּל־הַמְּלָכִים הָאֵלֶּה וְאֶת־אַרְצָם לָכַד יְהוֹשֻׁעַ פַּעַם אֶחָת כִּי יְהוָה אֱלֹהֵי יִשְׂרָאֵל נִלְחָם לְיִשְׂרָאֵל: 43 וַיָּשָׁב יְהוֹשֻׁעַ וְכָל־יִשְׂרָאֵל עִמּוֹ אֶל־הַמַּחֲנֶה הַגִּלְגָּלָה: פ

יא וַיְהִי כִּשְׁמֹעַ יָבִין מֶלֶךְ־חָצוֹר וַיִּשְׁלַח אֶל־יוֹבָב מֶלֶךְ מָדוֹן וְאֶל־מֶלֶךְ שִׁמְרוֹן וְאֶל־מֶלֶךְ אַכְשָׁף: 2 וְאֶל־הַמְּלָכִים אֲשֶׁר מִצְּפוֹן בָּהָר וּבָעֲרָבָה נֶגֶב כִּנֲרוֹת וּבַשְּׁפֵלָה וּבְנָפוֹת דּוֹר מִיָּם: 3 הַכְּנַעֲנִי מִמִּזְרָח וּמִיָּם וְהָאֱמֹרִי וְהַחִתִּי וְהַפְּרִזִּי וְהַיְבוּסִי בָּהָר וְהַחִוִּי תַּחַת חֶרְמוֹן בְּאֶרֶץ הַמִּצְפָּה: 4 וַיֵּצְאוּ הֵם וְכָל־מַחֲנֵיהֶם עִמָּם עַם־רָב כַּחוֹל אֲשֶׁר עַל־שְׂפַת־הַיָּם לָרֹב וְסוּס וָרֶכֶב רַב־מְאֹד: 5 וַיִּוָּעֲדוּ כֹּל הַמְּלָכִים הָאֵלֶּה וַיָּבֹאוּ וַיַּחֲנוּ יַחְדָּו אֶל־מֵי מֵרוֹם לְהִלָּחֵם עִם־יִשְׂרָאֵל: פ

gether at the Waters of Merom to give battle to Israel.

6But the Lord said to Joshua, "Do not be afraid of them; tomorrow at this time I will have them all lying slain before Israel. You shall hamstring their horses and burn their chariots." 7So Joshua, with all his fighting men, came upon them suddenly at the Waters of Merom, and pounced upon them. 8The Lord delivered them into the hands of Israel, and they defeated them and pursued them all the way to Great Sidon b-and Misrephothmaim,-b and all the way to the Valley of Mizpehc on the east; they crushed them, letting none escape. 9And Joshua dealt with them as the Lord had ordered him; he hamstrung their horses and burned their chariots.

10Joshua then turned back and captured Hazor and put her king to the sword.—Hazor was formerly the head of all those kingdoms.—11They proscribed and put to the sword every person in it. Not a soul survived, and Hazor itself was burned down. 12Joshua captured all those royal cities and their kings. He put them to the sword; he proscribed them in accordance with the charge of Moses, the servant of the Lord. 13However, all those towns that are still standing on their mounds were not burned down by Israel; it was Hazor alone that Joshua burned down. 14The Israelites kept all the spoil and cattle of the rest of those cities as booty. But they cut down their populations with the sword until they exterminated them; they did not spare a soul. 15Just as the Lord had commanded His servant Moses, so Moses had charged Joshua, and so Joshua did; he left nothing undone of all that the Lord had commanded Moses.

16Joshua conquered the whole of this region: the hill country [of Judah], the Negeb, the whole

6 וַיֹּאמֶר יְהוָה אֶל־יְהוֹשֻׁעַ אַל־תִּירָא מִפְּנֵיהֶם כִּי־מָחָר כָּעֵת הַזֹּאת אָנֹכִי נֹתֵן אֶת־כֻּלָּם חֲלָלִים לִפְנֵי יִשְׂרָאֵל אֶת־סוּסֵיהֶם תְּעַקֵּר וְאֶת־מַרְכְּבֹתֵיהֶם תִּשְׂרֹף בָּאֵשׁ׃ 7 וַיָּבֹא יְהוֹשֻׁעַ וְכָל־עַם הַמִּלְחָמָה עִמּוֹ עֲלֵיהֶם עַל־מֵי מֵרוֹם פִּתְאֹם וַיִּפְּלוּ בָּהֶם׃ 8 וַיִּתְּנֵם יְהוָה בְּיַד־יִשְׂרָאֵל וַיַּכּוּם וַיִּרְדְּפוּם עַד־צִידוֹן רַבָּה וְעַד מִשְׂרְפוֹת מַיִם וְעַד־בִּקְעַת מִצְפֶּה מִזְרָחָה וַיַּכֻּם עַד־בִּלְתִּי הִשְׁאִיר־לָהֶם שָׂרִיד׃ 9 וַיַּעַשׂ לָהֶם יְהוֹשֻׁעַ כַּאֲשֶׁר אָמַר־לוֹ יְהוָה אֶת־סוּסֵיהֶם עִקֵּר וְאֶת־מַרְכְּבֹתֵיהֶם שָׂרַף בָּאֵשׁ׃ ס

10 וַיָּשָׁב יְהוֹשֻׁעַ בָּעֵת הַהִיא וַיִּלְכֹּד אֶת־חָצוֹר וְאֶת־מַלְכָּהּ הִכָּה בֶחָרֶב כִּי־חָצוֹר לְפָנִים הִיא רֹאשׁ כָּל־הַמַּמְלָכוֹת הָאֵלֶּה׃ 11 וַיַּכּוּ אֶת־כָּל־הַנֶּפֶשׁ אֲשֶׁר־בָּהּ לְפִי־חֶרֶב הַחֲרֵם לֹא נוֹתַר כָּל־נְשָׁמָה וְאֶת־חָצוֹר שָׂרַף בָּאֵשׁ׃ 12 וְאֶת־כָּל־עָרֵי הַמְּלָכִים־הָאֵלֶּה וְאֶת־כָּל־מַלְכֵיהֶם לָכַד יְהוֹשֻׁעַ וַיַּכֵּם לְפִי־חֶרֶב הֶחֱרִים אוֹתָם כַּאֲשֶׁר צִוָּה מֹשֶׁה עֶבֶד יְהוָה׃ 13 רַק כָּל־הֶעָרִים הָעֹמְדוֹת עַל־תִּלָּם לֹא שְׂרָפָם יִשְׂרָאֵל זוּלָתִי אֶת־חָצוֹר לְבַדָּהּ שָׂרַף יְהוֹשֻׁעַ׃ 14 וְכֹל שְׁלַל הֶעָרִים הָאֵלֶּה וְהַבְּהֵמָה בָּזְזוּ לָהֶם בְּנֵי יִשְׂרָאֵל רַק אֶת־כָּל־הָאָדָם הִכּוּ לְפִי־חֶרֶב עַד־הִשְׁמִדָם אוֹתָם לֹא הִשְׁאִירוּ כָּל־נְשָׁמָה׃ 15 כַּאֲשֶׁר צִוָּה יְהוָה אֶת־מֹשֶׁה עַבְדּוֹ כֵּן־צִוָּה מֹשֶׁה אֶת־יְהוֹשֻׁעַ וְכֵן עָשָׂה יְהוֹשֻׁעַ לֹא־הֵסִיר דָּבָר מִכֹּל אֲשֶׁר־צִוָּה יְהוָה אֶת־מֹשֶׁה׃ 16 וַיִּקַּח יְהוֹשֻׁעַ אֶת־כָּל־הָאָרֶץ הַזֹּאת הָהָר וְאֶת־כָּל־הַנֶּגֶב וְאֵת כָּל־אֶרֶץ הַגֹּשֶׁן וְאֶת־הַשְּׁפֵלָה וְאֶת־הָעֲרָבָה וְאֶת־הַר

---

b-b Change of vocalization yields "and Misrephoth on the west."
c Apparently identical with Mizpah in v. 3.

land of Goshen, the Shephelah, the Arabah, and the hill country and coastal plain of Israel— [17][everything] from Mount Halak, which ascends to Seir, all the way to Baal-gad in [d]-the Valley of the Lebanon-[d] at the foot of Mount Hermon; and he captured all the kings there and executed them.

[18]Joshua waged war with all those kings over a long period. [19]Apart from the Hivites who dwelt in Gibeon, not a single city made terms with the Israelites; all were taken in battle. [20]For it was the Lord's doing to stiffen their hearts to give battle to Israel, in order that they might be proscribed without quarter and wiped out, as the Lord had commanded Moses.

[21]At that time, Joshua went and wiped out the Anakites from the hill country, from Hebron, Debir, and Anab, from the entire hill country of Judah, and from the entire hill country of Israel; Joshua proscribed them and their towns. [22]No Anakites remained in the land of the Israelites; but some remained in Gaza, Gath, and Ashdod.

[23]Thus Joshua conquered the whole country, just as the Lord had promised Moses; and Joshua assigned it to Israel to share according to their tribal divisions. And the land had rest from war.

12

The following are the local kings whom the Israelites defeated and whose territories they took possession of:

East of the Jordan, from the Wadi Arnon to Mount Hermon, including the eastern half of the Arabah: [2a]King Sihon of the Amorites, who resided in Heshbon and ruled over part of Gilead—from Aroer on the bank of the Wadi Arnon and the wadi proper up to the Wadi

יִשְׂרָאֵל וּשְׁפֵלָתָהּ: 17 מִן־הָהָר הֶחָלָק הָעוֹלֶה שֵׂעִיר וְעַד־בַּעַל גָּד בְּבִקְעַת הַלְּבָנוֹן תַּחַת הַר־חֶרְמוֹן וְאֵת כָּל־מַלְכֵיהֶם לָכַד וַיַּכֵּם וַיְמִיתֵם: 18 יָמִים רַבִּים עָשָׂה יְהוֹשֻׁעַ אֶת־כָּל־הַמְּלָכִים הָאֵלֶּה מִלְחָמָה: 19 לֹא־הָיְתָה עִיר אֲשֶׁר הִשְׁלִימָה אֶל־בְּנֵי יִשְׂרָאֵל בִּלְתִּי הַחִוִּי יֹשְׁבֵי גִבְעוֹן אֶת־הַכֹּל לָקְחוּ בַמִּלְחָמָה: 20 כִּי מֵאֵת יְהוָה ׀ הָיְתָה לְחַזֵּק אֶת־לִבָּם לִקְרַאת הַמִּלְחָמָה אֶת־יִשְׂרָאֵל לְמַעַן הַחֲרִימָם לְבִלְתִּי הֱיוֹת־לָהֶם תְּחִנָּה כִּי לְמַעַן הַשְׁמִידָם כַּאֲשֶׁר צִוָּה יְהוָה אֶת־מֹשֶׁה: ס 21 וַיָּבֹא יְהוֹשֻׁעַ בָּעֵת הַהִיא וַיַּכְרֵת אֶת־הָעֲנָקִים מִן־הָהָר מִן־חֶבְרוֹן מִן־דְּבִר מִן־עֲנָב וּמִכֹּל הַר יְהוּדָה וּמִכֹּל הַר יִשְׂרָאֵל עִם־עָרֵיהֶם הֶחֱרִימָם יְהוֹשֻׁעַ: 22 לֹא־נוֹתַר עֲנָקִים בְּאֶרֶץ בְּנֵי יִשְׂרָאֵל רַק בְּעַזָּה בְּגַת וּבְאַשְׁדּוֹד נִשְׁאָרוּ: 23 וַיִּקַּח יְהוֹשֻׁעַ אֶת־כָּל־הָאָרֶץ כְּכֹל אֲשֶׁר דִּבֶּר יְהוָה אֶל־מֹשֶׁה וַיִּתְּנָהּ יְהוֹשֻׁעַ לְנַחֲלָה לְיִשְׂרָאֵל כְּמַחְלְקֹתָם לְשִׁבְטֵיהֶם וְהָאָרֶץ שָׁקְטָה מִמִּלְחָמָה: פ

יב וְאֵלֶּה ׀ מַלְכֵי הָאָרֶץ אֲשֶׁר הִכּוּ בְנֵי־יִשְׂרָאֵל וַיִּרְשׁוּ אֶת־אַרְצָם בְּעֵבֶר הַיַּרְדֵּן מִזְרְחָה הַשָּׁמֶשׁ מִנַּחַל אַרְנוֹן עַד־הַר חֶרְמוֹן וְכָל־הָעֲרָבָה מִזְרָחָה: 2 סִיחוֹן מֶלֶךְ הָאֱמֹרִי הַיּוֹשֵׁב בְּחֶשְׁבּוֹן מֹשֵׁל מֵעֲרוֹעֵר אֲשֶׁר עַל־שְׂפַת־נַחַל אַרְנוֹן וְתוֹךְ הַנַּחַל וַחֲצִי הַגִּלְעָד וְעַד יַבֹּק הַנַּחַל גְּבוּל בְּנֵי עַמּוֹן: 3 וְהָעֲרָבָה עַד־יָם כִּנְרוֹת

---

d-d   I.e., the valley between the Lebanon and Anti-Lebanon ranges.

a   Meaning of vv. 2 and 3 uncertain.

Jabbok [and] the border of the Ammonites—
³and over the eastern Arabah up to the Sea of
Chinnereth and, southward by way of Beth-
jeshimoth at the foot of the slopes of Pisgah
on the east, down to the Sea of the Arabah,
that is, the Dead Sea. ⁴Also the territory of
King Og of Bashan—one of the last of the
Rephaim—who resided in Ashtaroth and in
Edrei ⁵and ruled over Mount Hermon, Salcah,
and all of Bashan up to the border of the
Geshurites and the Maacathites, as also over
part of Gilead [down to] the border of King
Sihon of Heshbon. ⁶These were vanquished by
Moses, the servant of the LORD, and the Isra-
elites; and Moses, the servant of the LORD, as-
signed *b-that territory-b* as a possession to the
Reubenites, the Gadites, and the half-tribe of
Manasseh.

⁷And the following are the local kings whom
Joshua and the Israelites defeated on the west
side of the Jordan—from Baal-gad in the Valley
of the Lebanon to Mount Halak, which ascends
to Seir—which Joshua assigned as a possession
to the tribal divisions of Israel: ⁸in the hill country, in the lowlands, in the Arabah, in the slopes,ᶜ
in the wilderness, and in the Negeb—[in the
land of] the Hittites, the Amorites, the Canaanites, the Perizzites, the Hivites, and the Jebusites.
⁹They were:

the king of Jericho	1
the king of Ai, near Bethel,	1
¹⁰the king of Jerusalem	1
the king of Hebron	1
¹¹the king of Jarmuth	1
the king of Lachish	1
¹²the king of Eglon	1
the king of Gezer	1
¹³the king of Debir	1
the king of Geder	1
¹⁴the king of Hormah	1

מִזְרָ֣חָה וְעַ֣ד יָ֤ם הָֽעֲרָבָה֙ יָ֣ם הַמֶּ֔לַח
מִזְרָ֔חָה דֶּ֖רֶךְ בֵּ֣ית הַיְשִׁמ֑וֹת וּמִ֨תֵּימָ֔ן תַּ֖חַת
אַשְׁדּ֥וֹת הַפִּסְגָּֽה: ⁴ וּגְבוּל֙ ע֣וֹג מֶ֣לֶךְ הַבָּשָׁ֔ן
מִיֶּ֖תֶר הָרְפָאִ֑ים הַיּוֹשֵׁ֥ב בְּעַשְׁתָּר֖וֹת
וּבְאֶדְרֶֽעִי: ⁵ וּמֹשֵׁ֤ל בְּהַ֣ר חֶרְמוֹן֙ וּבְסַלְכָ֔ה
וּבְכָל־הַבָּשָׁ֗ן עַד־גְּב֤וּל הַגְּשׁוּרִי֙ וְהַמַּ֣עֲכָתִ֔י
וַחֲצִי֙ הַגִּלְעָ֔ד גְּב֖וּל סִיח֥וֹן מֶֽלֶךְ־חֶשְׁבּֽוֹן:
⁶ מֹשֶׁ֧ה עֶֽבֶד־יְהֹוָ֛ה וּבְנֵ֥י יִשְׂרָאֵ֖ל הִכּ֑וּם
וַֽיִּתְּנָ֞הּ מֹשֶׁ֨ה עֶֽבֶד־יְהֹוָ֤ה יְרֻשָּׁה֙ לָרֽאוּבֵנִ֣י
וְלַגָּדִ֔י וְלַחֲצִ֖י שֵׁ֥בֶט הַֽמְנַשֶּֽׁה: ס
⁷ וְאֵ֣לֶּה מַלְכֵ֣י הָאָ֗רֶץ אֲשֶׁ֨ר הִכָּ֤ה יְהוֹשֻׁ֙עַ֙
וּבְנֵ֣י יִשְׂרָאֵ֔ל בְּעֵ֥בֶר הַיַּרְדֵּ֖ן יָ֑מָּה מִבַּ֤עַל גָּד֙
בְּבִקְעַ֣ת הַלְּבָנ֔וֹן וְעַד־הָהָ֥ר הֶֽחָלָ֖ק הָעֹלֶ֣ה
שֵׂעִ֑ירָה וַיִּתְּנָ֨הּ יְהוֹשֻׁ֜עַ לְשִׁבְטֵ֧י יִשְׂרָאֵ֛ל
יְרֻשָּׁ֖ה כְּמַחְלְקֹתָֽם: ⁸ בָּהָ֣ר וּבַשְּׁפֵלָ֗ה
וּבָֽעֲרָבָה֙ וּבָ֣אֲשֵׁד֔וֹת וּבַמִּדְבָּ֖ר וּבַנֶּ֑גֶב הַֽחִתִּי֙
הָֽאֱמֹרִ֔י וְהַֽכְּנַעֲנִי֙ הַפְּרִזִּ֔י הַֽחִוִּ֖י וְהַיְבוּסִֽי:
⁹ מֶ֥לֶךְ יְרִיח֖וֹ   אֶחָ֑ד
מֶ֛לֶךְ הָעַ֥י אֲשֶׁר־מִצַּ֛ד בֵּֽית־אֵ֖ל אֶחָֽד:
¹⁰ מֶ֥לֶךְ יְרֽוּשָׁלִַ֖ם   אֶחָ֑ד
מֶ֥לֶךְ חֶבְר֖וֹן   אֶחָֽד:
¹¹ מֶ֥לֶךְ יַרְמוּת֙   אֶחָ֔ד
מֶ֥לֶךְ לָכִ֖ישׁ   אֶחָֽד:
¹² מֶ֥לֶךְ עֶגְלוֹן֙   אֶחָ֔ד
מֶ֥לֶךְ גֶּ֖זֶר   אֶחָֽד:
¹³ מֶ֥לֶךְ דְּבִר֙   אֶחָ֔ד
מֶ֥לֶךְ גֶּ֖דֶר   אֶחָֽד:
¹⁴ מֶ֥לֶךְ חָרְמָה֙   אֶחָ֔ד
מֶ֥לֶךְ עֲרָ֖ד   אֶחָֽד:
¹⁵ מֶ֥לֶךְ לִבְנָה֙   אֶחָ֔ד
מֶ֥לֶךְ עֲדֻלָּ֖ם   אֶחָֽד:

---

b-b   Lit. "it."
ᶜ   I.e., the slopes of Pisgah; cf. 13.20.

the king of Arad	1	אֶחָ֖ד	16 מֶ֤לֶךְ מַקֵּדָה֙
15the king of Libnah	1	אֶחָֽד׃	מֶ֥לֶךְ בֵּֽית־אֵ֖ל
the king of Adullam	1	אֶחָ֖ד	17 מֶ֤לֶךְ תַּפּ֙וּחַ֙
16the king of Makkedah	1	אֶחָ֖ד	מֶ֤לֶךְ חֵ֖פֶר
the king of Bethel	1	אֶחָ֖ד	18 מֶ֤לֶךְ אֲפֵ֖ק
17the king of Tappuah	1	אֶחָֽד׃	מֶ֥לֶךְ לַשָּׁר֖וֹן
the king of Hepher	1	אֶחָ֖ד	19 מֶ֤לֶךְ מָד֖וֹן
18the king of Aphek	1	אֶחָֽד׃	מֶ֥לֶךְ חָצ֖וֹר
the king of Sharon	1	אֶחָ֖ד	20 מֶ֤לֶךְ שִׁמְר֤וֹן מְראוֹן֙*
19the king of Madon	1	אֶחָֽד׃	מֶ֥לֶךְ אַכְשָׁ֖ף
the king of Hazor	1	אֶחָ֖ד	21 מֶ֤לֶךְ תַּעְנַךְ֙
20the king of Shimron-meron	1	אֶחָֽד׃	מֶ֥לֶךְ מְגִדּ֖וֹ
the king of Achshaph	1	אֶחָ֖ד	22 מֶ֤לֶךְ קֶ֖דֶשׁ
21the king of Taanach	1	אֶחָֽד׃	מֶֽלֶךְ־יׇקְנְעָ֖ם לַכַּרְמֶ֖ל
the king of Megiddo	1	אֶחָ֖ד	23 מֶ֤לֶךְ דּ֤וֹר לְנָ֖פַת דּ֖וֹר
22the king of Kedesh	1	אֶחָֽד׃	מֶֽלֶךְ־גּוֹיִ֖ם לְגִלְגָּ֖ל
the king of Jokneam in the Carmel	1	אֶחָ֖ד	24 מֶ֤לֶךְ תִּרְצָ֖ה
23the king of Dor in the district*d* of Dor	1	אֶחָֽד׃	כׇּל־מְלָכִ֖ים שְׁלֹשִׁ֥ים וְאֶחָֽד׃ פ
the king of Goiim in Gilgal	1		
24the king of Tirzah	1		
Total number of kings	31.		

13

Joshua was now old, advanced in years. The Lord said to him, "You have grown old, you are advanced in years; and very much of the land still remains to be taken possession of. ²This is the territory that remains: all the districts of the Philistines and all [those of] the Geshurites, ³from the Shihor, which is close to Egypt, to the territory of Ekron on the north, are accounted Canaanite, namely, those of the five lords of the Philistines—the Gazites, the Ashdodites, the Ashkelonites, the Gittites, and the Ekronites—and those of the Avvim ⁴on the south; further, all the Canaanite country from Mearah of the Sidonians to Aphek at the Amorite border ⁵and the land of the Gebalites, with the whole [Valley of the] Lebanon, from

יג וִֽיהוֹשֻׁ֙עַ֙ זָקֵ֔ן בָּ֖א בַּיָּמִ֑ים וַיֹּ֨אמֶר יְהֹוָ֜ה אֵלָ֗יו אַתָּ֤ה זָקַ֙נְתָּה֙ בָּ֖אתָ בַיָּמִ֔ים וְהָאָ֛רֶץ נִשְׁאֲרָ֥ה הַרְבֵּה־מְאֹ֖ד לְרִשְׁתָּֽהּ׃ 2 זֹ֥את הָאָ֖רֶץ הַנִּשְׁאָ֑רֶת כׇּל־גְּלִיל֥וֹת הַפְּלִשְׁתִּ֖ים וְכׇל־הַגְּשׁוּרִֽי׃ 3 מִֽן־הַשִּׁיח֞וֹר אֲשֶׁ֣ר ׀ עַל־פְּנֵ֣י מִצְרַ֗יִם וְעַ֛ד גְּב֥וּל עֶקְר֖וֹן צָפ֑וֹנָה לַֽכְּנַעֲנִ֖י תֵּחָשֵׁ֑ב חֲמֵ֣שֶׁת ׀ סַרְנֵ֣י פְלִשְׁתִּ֗ים הָעַזָּתִ֤י וְהָאַשְׁדּוֹדִי֙ הָאֶשְׁקְלוֹנִ֔י הַגִּתִּ֖י וְהָעֶקְרוֹנִ֑י וְהָעַוִּֽים׃ 4 מִתֵּימָ֗ן כׇּל־אֶ֤רֶץ הַֽכְּנַעֲנִי֙ וּמְעָרָ֗ה אֲשֶׁ֣ר לַצִּֽידֹנִ֔ים עַד־אֲפֵ֖קָה עַ֖ד גְּב֥וּל הָאֱמֹרִֽי׃ 5 וְהָאָ֥רֶץ הַגִּבְלִ֖י וְכׇל־הַלְּבָנ֗וֹן מִזְרַ֤ח הַשֶּׁ֙מֶשׁ֙ מִבַּ֣עַל גָּ֔ד

יתיר א' v. 20.

---

d Meaning of Heb. uncertain.

Baal-gad at the foot of Mount Hermon to Lebo-hamath on the east, [6]with all the inhabitants of the hill country from the [Valley of the] Lebanon to *a*-Misrephoth-maim,-*a* namely, all the Sidonians. I Myself will dispossess *b*-those nations-*b* for the Israelites; you have only to apportion *c*-their lands-*c* by lot among Israel, as I have commanded you. [7]Therefore, divide this territory into hereditary portions for the nine tribes and the half-tribe of Manasseh."

[8]Now the Reubenites and the Gadites, along with *c*-the other half-tribe,-*c* had already received the shares which Moses assigned to them on the east side of the Jordan—as assigned to them by Moses the servant of the LORD: [9]from Aroer on the edge of the Wadi Arnon and the town in the middle of the wadi, the entire Tableland [from] Medeba to Dibon, [10]embracing all the towns of King Sihon of the Amorites, who had reigned in Heshbon, up to the border of the Ammonites; [11]further, Gilead, the territories of the Geshurites and the Maacathites, and all of Mount Hermon, and the whole of Bashan up to Salcah—[12]the entire kingdom of Og, who had reigned over Bashan at Ashtaroth and at Edrei. (He was the last of the remaining Rephaim.) These were defeated and dispossessed by Moses; [13]but the Israelites failed to dispossess the Geshurites and the Maacathites, and Geshur and Maacath remain among Israel to this day. [14]No hereditary portion, however, was assigned to the tribe of Levi, their portion being the fire offerings of the LORD, the God of Israel, as He spoke concerning them.*d*

[15]And so Moses assigned [the following] to the tribe of the Reubenites, for their various clans, [16]and it became theirs: The territory from Aroer, on the edge of the Wadi Arnon and the town in the middle of the wadi, up to Medeba—

תַּחַת הַר־חֶרְמוֹן עַד לְבוֹא חֲמָת: 6 כָּל־יֹשְׁבֵי הָהָר מִן־הַלְּבָנוֹן עַד־מִשְׂרְפֹת מַיִם כָּל־צִידֹנִים אָנֹכִי אוֹרִישֵׁם מִפְּנֵי בְּנֵי יִשְׂרָאֵל רַק הַפִּלֶהָ לְיִשְׂרָאֵל בְּנַחֲלָה כַּאֲשֶׁר צִוִּיתִיךָ: 7 וְעַתָּה חַלֵּק אֶת־הָאָרֶץ הַזֹּאת בְּנַחֲלָה לְתִשְׁעַת הַשְּׁבָטִים וַחֲצִי הַשֵּׁבֶט הַמְנַשֶּׁה: 8 עִמּוֹ הָרֵאוּבֵנִי וְהַגָּדִי לָקְחוּ נַחֲלָתָם אֲשֶׁר נָתַן לָהֶם מֹשֶׁה בְּעֵבֶר הַיַּרְדֵּן מִזְרָחָה כַּאֲשֶׁר נָתַן לָהֶם מֹשֶׁה עֶבֶד יְהוָה: 9 מֵעֲרוֹעֵר אֲשֶׁר עַל־שְׂפַת־נַחַל אַרְנוֹן וְהָעִיר אֲשֶׁר בְּתוֹךְ־הַנַּחַל וְכָל־הַמִּישֹׁר מֵידְבָא עַד־דִּיבוֹן: 10 וְכֹל עָרֵי סִיחוֹן מֶלֶךְ הָאֱמֹרִי אֲשֶׁר מָלַךְ בְּחֶשְׁבּוֹן עַד־גְּבוּל בְּנֵי עַמּוֹן: 11 וְהַגִּלְעָד וּגְבוּל הַגְּשׁוּרִי וְהַמַּעֲכָתִי וְכֹל הַר חֶרְמוֹן וְכָל־הַבָּשָׁן עַד־סַלְכָה: 12 כָּל־מַמְלְכוּת עוֹג בַּבָּשָׁן אֲשֶׁר־מָלַךְ בְּעַשְׁתָּרוֹת וּבְאֶדְרֶעִי הוּא נִשְׁאַר מִיֶּתֶר הָרְפָאִים וַיַּכֵּם מֹשֶׁה וַיֹּרִשֵׁם: 13 וְלֹא הוֹרִישׁוּ בְּנֵי יִשְׂרָאֵל אֶת־הַגְּשׁוּרִי וְאֶת־הַמַּעֲכָתִי וַיֵּשֶׁב גְּשׁוּר וּמַעֲכָת בְּקֶרֶב יִשְׂרָאֵל עַד הַיּוֹם הַזֶּה: 14 רַק לְשֵׁבֶט הַלֵּוִי לֹא נָתַן נַחֲלָה אִשֵּׁי יְהוָה אֱלֹהֵי יִשְׂרָאֵל הוּא נַחֲלָתוֹ כַּאֲשֶׁר דִּבֶּר־לוֹ: ס 15 וַיִּתֵּן מֹשֶׁה לְמַטֵּה בְנֵי־רְאוּבֵן לְמִשְׁפְּחֹתָם: 16 וַיְהִי לָהֶם הַגְּבוּל מֵעֲרוֹעֵר אֲשֶׁר עַל־שְׂפַת־נַחַל אַרְנוֹן וְהָעִיר אֲשֶׁר בְּתוֹךְ־הַנַּחַל וְכָל־הַמִּישֹׁר עַל־מֵידְבָא: 17 חֶשְׁבּוֹן וְכָל־עָרֶיהָ אֲשֶׁר

---

a-a   See note on 11.8.
b-b   Lit. "them."
c-c   Lit. "it."
d   See Deut. 18.1.

the entire Tableland—¹⁷Heshbon and all its towns in the Tableland: Dibon, Bamoth-baal, Beth-baal-meon, ¹⁸Jahaz, Kedemoth, Mepha-ath, ¹⁹Kiriathaim, Sibmah, and Zereth-shahar ᵉ-in the hill of the valley,-ᵉ ²⁰Beth-peor, the slopes of Pisgah, and Beth-jeshimoth—²¹all the towns of the Tableland and the entire kingdom of Sihon, the king of the Amorites, who had reigned in Heshbon. (For Moses defeated him and the Midianite chiefs Evi, Rekem, Zur, Hur, and Reba, who had dwelt in the land as princes of Sihon. ²²Together with the others that they slew, the Israelites put Balaam son of Beor, the augur, to the sword.) ²³The boundary of the Reubenites was the edge of the Jordan. That was the portion of the Reubenites for their various clans—those towns with their villages.

²⁴To the tribe of Gad, for the various Gadite clans, Moses assigned [the following], ²⁵and it became their territory: Jazer, all the towns of Gilead, part of the country of the Ammon-ites up to Aroer, which is close to Rabbah, ²⁶and from Heshbon to Ramath-mizpeh and Betonim, and from Mahanaim to the border of Lidbir;ᶠ ²⁷and in the Valley, Beth-haram, Beth-nimrah, Succoth, and Zaphon—the rest of the kingdom of Sihon, the king of Heshbon—down to the edge of the Jordan and up to the tip of the Sea of Chinnereth on the east side of the Jordan. ²⁸That was the portion of the Gadites, for their various clans—those towns with their villages.

²⁹And to the half-tribe of Manasseh Moses assigned [the following], so that it went to the half-tribe of Manasseh, for its various clans, ³⁰and became their territory: Mahanaim,ᵍ all of Bashan, the entire kingdom of Og, king of Ba-shan, and all of Havvoth-jairʰ in Bashan, sixty towns; ³¹and part of Gilead, and Ashtaroth and

בַּמִּישֹׁר דִּיבוֹן וּבָמוֹת בַּעַל וּבֵית בַּעַל
מְעוֹן: 18 וְיַהְצָה וּקְדֵמֹת וּמֵפָעַת:
19 וְקִרְיָתַיִם וְשִׂבְמָה וְצֶרֶת הַשַּׁחַר בְּהַר
הָעֵמֶק: 20 וּבֵית פְּעוֹר וְאַשְׁדּוֹת הַפִּסְגָּה
וּבֵית הַיְשִׁמוֹת: 21 וְכֹל עָרֵי הַמִּישֹׁר וְכָל־
מַמְלְכוּת סִיחוֹן מֶלֶךְ הָאֱמֹרִי אֲשֶׁר מָלַךְ
בְּחֶשְׁבּוֹן אֲשֶׁר הִכָּה מֹשֶׁה אֹתוֹ וְאֶת־
נְשִׂיאֵי מִדְיָן אֶת־אֱוִי וְאֶת־רֶקֶם וְאֶת־צוּר
וְאֶת־חוּר וְאֶת־רֶבַע נְסִיכֵי סִיחוֹן יֹשְׁבֵי
הָאָרֶץ: 22 וְאֶת־בִּלְעָם בֶּן־בְּעוֹר הַקּוֹסֵם
הָרְגוּ בְנֵי־יִשְׂרָאֵל בַּחֶרֶב אֶל־חַלְלֵיהֶם:
23 וַיְהִי גְּבוּל בְּנֵי רְאוּבֵן הַיַּרְדֵּן וּגְבוּל זֹאת
נַחֲלַת בְּנֵי־רְאוּבֵן לְמִשְׁפְּחֹתָם הֶעָרִים
וְחַצְרֵיהֶן: פ
24 וַיִּתֵּן מֹשֶׁה לְמַטֵּה־גָד לִבְנֵי־גָד
לְמִשְׁפְּחֹתָם: 25 וַיְהִי לָהֶם הַגְּבוּל יַעְזֵר
וְכָל־עָרֵי הַגִּלְעָד וַחֲצִי אֶרֶץ בְּנֵי
עַמּוֹן עַד־עֲרוֹעֵר אֲשֶׁר עַל־פְּנֵי רַבָּה:
26 *וּמֵחֶשְׁבּוֹן עַד־רָמַת הַמִּצְפֶּה וּבְטֹנִים
וּמִמַּחֲנַיִם עַד־גְּבוּל לִדְבִר: 27 וּבָעֵמֶק בֵּית
הָרָם וּבֵית נִמְרָה וְסֻכּוֹת וְצָפוֹן יֶתֶר
מַמְלְכוּת סִיחוֹן מֶלֶךְ חֶשְׁבּוֹן הַיַּרְדֵּן וּגְבֻל
עַד־קְצֵה יָם־כִּנֶּרֶת עֵבֶר הַיַּרְדֵּן מִזְרָחָה:
28 זֹאת נַחֲלַת בְּנֵי־גָד לְמִשְׁפְּחֹתָם הֶעָרִים
וְחַצְרֵיהֶם:
29 וַיִּתֵּן מֹשֶׁה לַחֲצִי שֵׁבֶט מְנַשֶּׁה וַיְהִי
לַחֲצִי מַטֵּה בְנֵי־מְנַשֶּׁה לְמִשְׁפְּחוֹתָם:
30 וַיְהִי גְבוּלָם מִמַּחֲנַיִם כָּל־הַבָּשָׁן
כָּל־מַמְלְכוּת עוֹג מֶלֶךְ־הַבָּשָׁן וְכָל־חַוֹּת
יָאִיר אֲשֶׁר בַּבָּשָׁן שִׁשִּׁים עִיר: 31 וַחֲצִי
הַגִּלְעָד וְעַשְׁתָּרוֹת וְאֶדְרֶעִי עָרֵי מַמְלְכוּת

---

e-e   Emendation yields "in the hill country; and in the Valley..."
f   Change of vocalization yields "Lo-debar"; cf. 2 Sam. 9.4, 5; 17.27.
g   Lit. "from Mahanaim."
h   See note on Num. 32.41.

Edrei, the royal cities of Og in Bashan, were assigned to the descendants of Machir son of Manasseh—to a part of the descendants of Machir—for their various clans.

³²Those, then, were the portions that Moses assigned in the steppes of Moab, on the east side of the Jordan. ³³But no portion was assigned by Moses to the tribe of Levi; the Lord, the God of Israel, is their portion, as He spoke concerning them.*d*

14 And these are the allotments of the Israelites in the land of Canaan, that were apportioned to them by the priest Eleazar, by Joshua son of Nun, and by the heads of the ancestral houses of the Israelite tribes, ²the portions that fell to them by lot, as the Lord had commanded through Moses for the nine and a half tribes. ³For the portion of the other two and a half tribes had been assigned to them by Moses on the other side of the Jordan. He had not assigned any portion among them to the Levites; ⁴for whereas the descendants of Joseph constituted two tribes, Manasseh and Ephraim, the Levites were assigned no share in the land, but only some towns to live in, with the pastures for their livestock and cattle. ⁵Just as the Lord had commanded Moses, so the Israelites did when they apportioned the land.

⁶The Judites approached Joshua at Gilgal, and Caleb son of Jephunneh the Kenizzite said to him: "You know what instructions the Lord gave at Kadesh-barnea to Moses, the man of God, concerning you and me. ⁷I was forty years old when Moses the servant of the Lord sent me from Kadesh-barnea to spy out the land, and I gave him a forthright report. ⁸While my companions who went up with me took the heart out of the people, I was loyal to the Lord my God. ⁹On that day, Moses promised on oath,

עֹ֣וג בַּבָּשָׁ֗ן לִבְנֵ֤י מָכִיר֙ בֶּן־מְנַשֶּׁ֔ה לַחֲצִ֖י בְנֵֽי־מָכִ֑יר לְמִשְׁפְּחוֹתָֽם׃

³² אֵ֗לֶּה אֲשֶׁר־נִחַ֤ל מֹשֶׁה֙ בְּעַֽרְב֣וֹת מוֹאָ֔ב מֵעֵ֛בֶר לְיַרְדֵּ֥ן יְרִיח֖וֹ מִזְרָֽחָה׃ ס

³³ וּלְשֵׁ֙בֶט֙ הַלֵּוִ֔י לֹֽא־נָתַ֥ן מֹשֶׁ֖ה נַחֲלָ֑ה יְהֹוָ֞ה אֱלֹהֵ֤י יִשְׂרָאֵל֙ ה֣וּא נַחֲלָתָ֔ם כַּאֲשֶׁ֖ר דִּבֶּ֥ר לָהֶֽם׃

יד וְאֵ֛לֶּה אֲשֶׁר־נָחֲל֥וּ בְנֵֽי־יִשְׂרָאֵ֖ל בְּאֶ֣רֶץ כְּנָ֑עַן אֲשֶׁ֨ר נִֽחֲל֜וּ אוֹתָ֗ם אֶלְעָזָ֤ר הַכֹּהֵן֙ וִיהוֹשֻׁ֣עַ בִּן־נ֔וּן וְרָאשֵׁ֛י אֲב֥וֹת הַמַּטּ֖וֹת לִבְנֵ֥י יִשְׂרָאֵֽל׃ ² בְּגוֹרַ֖ל נַחֲלָתָ֑ם כַּאֲשֶׁ֨ר צִוָּ֤ה יְהֹוָה֙ בְּיַד־מֹשֶׁ֔ה לְתִשְׁעַ֥ת הַמַּטּ֖וֹת וַחֲצִ֥י הַמַּטֶּֽה׃ ³ כִּֽי־נָתַ֨ן מֹשֶׁ֜ה נַחֲלַ֣ת שְׁנֵ֣י הַמַּטּ֗וֹת וַחֲצִ֤י הַמַּטֶּה֙ מֵעֵ֣בֶר לַיַּרְדֵּ֔ן וְלַ֨לְוִיִּ֔ם לֹֽא־נָתַ֥ן נַחֲלָ֖ה בְּתוֹכָֽם׃ ⁴ כִּֽי־הָי֤וּ בְנֵֽי־יוֹסֵף֙ שְׁנֵ֣י מַטּ֔וֹת מְנַשֶּׁ֖ה וְאֶפְרָ֑יִם וְלֹֽא־נָתְנ֩וּ חֵ֨לֶק לַלְוִיִּ֜ם בָּאָ֗רֶץ כִּ֤י אִם־עָרִים֙ לָשֶׁ֔בֶת וּמִ֨גְרְשֵׁיהֶ֔ם לְמִקְנֵיהֶ֖ם וּלְקִנְיָנָֽם׃ ⁵ כַּאֲשֶׁ֨ר צִוָּ֤ה יְהֹוָה֙ אֶת־מֹשֶׁ֔ה כֵּ֥ן עָשׂ֖וּ בְּנֵ֣י יִשְׂרָאֵ֑ל וַֽיַּחְלְק֖וּ אֶת־הָאָֽרֶץ׃ פ

⁶ וַיִּגְּשׁ֨וּ בְנֵֽי־יְהוּדָ֤ה אֶל־יְהוֹשֻׁ֙עַ֙ בַּגִּלְגָּ֔ל וַיֹּ֣אמֶר אֵלָ֗יו כָּלֵ֤ב בֶּן־יְפֻנֶּה֙ הַקְּנִזִּ֔י אַתָּ֣ה יָדַ֗עְתָּ אֶֽת־הַדָּבָר֙ אֲשֶׁר־דִּבֶּ֣ר יְהֹוָ֗ה אֶל־מֹשֶׁ֤ה אִישׁ־הָֽאֱלֹהִים֙ עַ֣ל אֹדוֹתַ֔י וְעַ֖ל אֹדוֹתֶ֑יךָ בְּקָדֵ֖שׁ בַּרְנֵֽעַ׃ ⁷ בֶּן־אַרְבָּעִ֨ים שָׁנָ֜ה אָנֹכִ֗י בִּ֠שְׁלֹ֠חַ מֹשֶׁ֨ה עֶֽבֶד־יְהֹוָ֥ה אֹתִ֛י מִקָּדֵ֥שׁ בַּרְנֵ֖עַ לְרַגֵּ֣ל אֶת־הָאָ֑רֶץ וָאָשֵׁ֤ב אֹתוֹ֙ דָּבָ֔ר כַּאֲשֶׁ֖ר עִם־לְבָבִֽי׃ ⁸ וְאַחַי֙ אֲשֶׁ֣ר עָל֣וּ עִמִּ֔י הִמְסִ֖יו אֶת־לֵ֣ב הָעָ֑ם וְאָנֹכִ֣י מִלֵּ֔אתִי אַחֲרֵ֖י יְהֹוָ֥ה אֱלֹהָֽי׃ ⁹ וַיִּשָּׁבַ֣ע מֹשֶׁ֗ה בַּיּ֣וֹם הַהוּא֮

'The land on which your foot trod shall be a portion for you and your descendants forever, because you were loyal to the LORD my God.' [10]Now the LORD has preserved me, as He promised. It is forty-five years since the LORD made this promise to Moses, when Israel was journeying through the wilderness; and here I am today, eighty-five years old. [11]I am still as strong today as on the day that Moses sent me; my strength is the same now as it was then, for battle and for activity.[a] [12]So assign to me this hill country as the LORD promised on that day. Though you too heard on that day that Anakites are there and great fortified cities, if only the LORD is with me, I will dispossess them, as the LORD promised."

[13]So Joshua blessed Caleb son of Jephunneh and assigned Hebron to him as his portion. [14]Thus Hebron became the portion of Caleb son of Jephunneh the Kenizzite, as it still is, because he was loyal to the LORD, the God of Israel.— [15]The name of Hebron was formerly Kiriath-arba: [Arba] was the great man among the Anakites.

And the land had rest from war.

15 The portion that fell by lot to the various clans of the tribe of Judah lay farthest south, down to the border of Edom, which is the Wilderness of Zin. [2]Their southern boundary began from the tip of the Dead Sea, from the tongue that projects southward. [3]It proceeded to the south of the Ascent of Akrabbim, passed on to Zin, ascended to the south of Kadesh-barnea, passed on to Hezron, ascended to Addar, and made a turn to Karka. [4]From there it passed on to Azmon and proceeded to the Wadi of Egypt; and the boundary ran on to the Sea. That shall be your southern boundary.

---

[a] Lit. "and to go out and come in."

לֵאמֹר אִם־לֹא הָאָרֶץ אֲשֶׁר דָּרְכָה רַגְלְךָ
בָּהּ לְךָ תִהְיֶה לְנַחֲלָה וּלְבָנֶיךָ עַד־עוֹלָם
כִּי מִלֵּאתָ אַחֲרֵי יְהוָה אֱלֹהָי: 10 וְעַתָּה
הִנֵּה הֶחֱיָה יְהוָה ׀ אוֹתִי כַּאֲשֶׁר דִּבֵּר זֶה
אַרְבָּעִים וְחָמֵשׁ שָׁנָה מֵאָז דִּבֶּר יְהוָה
אֶת־הַדָּבָר הַזֶּה אֶל־מֹשֶׁה אֲשֶׁר־הָלַךְ
יִשְׂרָאֵל בַּמִּדְבָּר וְעַתָּה הִנֵּה אָנֹכִי הַיּוֹם
בֶּן־חָמֵשׁ וּשְׁמוֹנִים שָׁנָה: 11 עוֹדֶנִּי הַיּוֹם
חָזָק כַּאֲשֶׁר בְּיוֹם שְׁלֹחַ אוֹתִי מֹשֶׁה כְּכֹחִי
אָז וּכְכֹחִי עָתָּה לַמִּלְחָמָה וְלָצֵאת וְלָבוֹא:
12 וְעַתָּה תְּנָה־לִּי אֶת־הָהָר הַזֶּה אֲשֶׁר־
דִּבֶּר יְהוָה בַּיּוֹם הַהוּא כִּי אַתָּה־שָׁמַעְתָּ
בַיּוֹם הַהוּא כִּי־עֲנָקִים שָׁם וְעָרִים גְּדֹלוֹת
בְּצֻרוֹת אוּלַי יְהוָה אוֹתִי וְהוֹרַשְׁתִּים
כַּאֲשֶׁר דִּבֶּר יְהוָה:

13 וַיְבָרְכֵהוּ יְהוֹשֻׁעַ וַיִּתֵּן אֶת־חֶבְרוֹן לְכָלֵב
בֶּן־יְפֻנֶּה לְנַחֲלָה: 14 עַל־כֵּן הָיְתָה־חֶבְרוֹן
לְכָלֵב בֶּן־יְפֻנֶּה הַקְּנִזִּי לְנַחֲלָה עַד הַיּוֹם
הַזֶּה יַעַן אֲשֶׁר מִלֵּא אַחֲרֵי יְהוָה אֱלֹהֵי
יִשְׂרָאֵל: 15 וְשֵׁם חֶבְרוֹן לְפָנִים קִרְיַת
אַרְבַּע הָאָדָם הַגָּדוֹל בָּעֲנָקִים הוּא
וְהָאָרֶץ שָׁקְטָה מִמִּלְחָמָה: פ

טו וַיְהִי הַגּוֹרָל לְמַטֵּה בְּנֵי יְהוּדָה
לְמִשְׁפְּחֹתָם אֶל־גְּבוּל אֱדוֹם מִדְבַּר־צִן
נֶגְבָּה מִקְצֵה תֵימָן: 2 וַיְהִי לָהֶם גְּבוּל נֶגֶב
מִקְצֵה יָם הַמֶּלַח מִן־הַלָּשֹׁן הַפֹּנֶה נֶגְבָּה:
3 וְיָצָא אֶל־מִנֶּגֶב לְמַעֲלֵה עַקְרַבִּים וְעָבַר
צִנָה וְעָלָה מִנֶּגֶב לְקָדֵשׁ בַּרְנֵעַ וְעָבַר חֶצְרוֹן
וְעָלָה אַדָּרָה וְנָסַב הַקַּרְקָעָה: 4 וְעָבַר
עַצְמוֹנָה וְיָצָא נַחַל מִצְרַיִם וְהָיָה וְהָיוּ
תֹצְאוֹת הַגְּבוּל יָמָּה זֶה־יִהְיֶה לָכֶם גְּבוּל
נֶגֶב:

5The boundary on the east was the Dead Sea up to the mouth of the Jordan. On the northern side, the boundary began at the tongue of the Sea at the mouth of the Jordan. 6The boundary ascended to Beth-hoglah and passed north of Beth-arabah; then the boundary ascended to the Stone of Bohan son of Reuben. 7The boundary ascended *-from the Valley of Achor to Debir and turned north-* to Gilgal,*b* facing the Ascent of Adummim which is south of the wadi; from there the boundary continued to the waters of En-shemesh and ran on to En-rogel. 8Then the boundary ascended into the Valley of Ben-hinnom, along the southern flank of the Jebusites—that is, Jerusalem. The boundary then ran up to the top of the hill which flanks the Valley of Hinnom on the west, at the northern end of the Valley of Rephaim. 9From that hilltop the boundary curved to the fountain of the Waters of Nephtoah and ran on to the towns of Mount Ephron; then the boundary curved to Baalah—that is, Kiriath-jearim. 10From Baalah the boundary turned westward to Mount Seir,*c* passed north of the slope of Mount Jearim—that is, Chesalon—descended to Beth-shemesh, and passed on to Timnah. 11The boundary then proceeded to the northern flank of Ekron; the boundary curved to Shikkeron, passed on to Mount Baalah, and proceeded to Jabneel; and the boundary ran on to the Sea. 12And the western boundary was the edge of the Mediterranean Sea. Those were the boundaries of the various clans of the Judites on all sides.

13In accordance with the LORD's command to Joshua, Caleb son of Jephunneh was given a portion among the Judites, namely, Kiriath-arba—that is, Hebron. ([Arba] was the father of Anak.) 14Caleb dislodged from there the three Anakites: Sheshai, Ahiman, and Talmai, descendants of Anak. 15From there he marched

5 וּגְב֞וּל קֵ֤דְמָה יָ֣ם הַמֶּ֔לַח עַד־קְצֵ֖ה הַיַּרְדֵּ֑ן וּגְב֞וּל לִפְאַ֤ת צָפ֙וֹנָה֙ מִלְּשׁ֣וֹן הַיָּ֔ם מִקְצֵ֖ה הַיַּרְדֵּֽן׃ 6 וְעָלָ֤ה הַגְּבוּל֙ בֵּ֣ית חׇגְלָ֔ה וְעָבַ֕ר מִצְּפ֖וֹן לְבֵ֣ית הָעֲרָבָ֑ה וְעָלָ֣ה הַגְּב֔וּל אֶ֥בֶן בֹּ֖הַן בֶּן־רְאוּבֵֽן׃ 7 וְעָלָ֨ה הַגְּב֥וּל ׀ דְּבִ֘רָה֮ מֵעֵ֣מֶק עָכוֹר֒ וְצָפ֜וֹנָה פֹּנֶ֣ה אֶל־הַגִּלְגָּ֗ל אֲשֶׁר־נֹ֙כַח֙ לְמַעֲלֵ֣ה אֲדֻמִּ֔ים אֲשֶׁ֥ר מִנֶּ֖גֶב לַנָּ֑חַל וְעָבַ֤ר הַגְּבוּל֙ אֶל־מֵי־עֵ֣ין שֶׁ֔מֶשׁ וְהָי֥וּ תֹצְאֹתָ֖יו אֶל־עֵ֥ין רֹגֵֽל׃ 8 וְעָלָ֣ה הַגְּבוּל֩ גֵּ֨י בֶן־הִנֹּ֜ם אֶל־כֶּ֤תֶף הַיְבוּסִי֙ מִנֶּ֔גֶב הִ֖יא יְרֽוּשָׁלָ֑͏ִם וְעָלָ֨ה הַגְּב֜וּל אֶל־רֹ֣אשׁ הָהָ֗ר אֲשֶׁ֨ר עַל־פְּנֵ֤י גֵֽי־הִנֹּם֙ יָ֔מָּה אֲשֶׁ֛ר בִּקְצֵ֥ה עֵֽמֶק־רְפָאִ֖ים צָפֹֽנָה׃ 9 וְתָאַ֨ר הַגְּב֜וּל מֵרֹ֣אשׁ הָהָ֗ר אֶל־מַעְיַן֙ מֵ֣י נֶפְתּ֔וֹחַ וְיָצָ֖א אֶל־עָרֵ֣י הַר־עֶפְר֑וֹן וְתָאַ֤ר הַגְּבוּל֙ בַּעֲלָ֔ה הִ֖יא קִרְיַ֥ת יְעָרִֽים׃ 10 וְנָסַב֩ הַגְּב֨וּל מִבַּעֲלָ֥ה יָ֙מָּה֙ אֶל־הַ֣ר שֵׂעִ֔יר וְעָבַ֕ר אֶל־כֶּ֧תֶף הַר־יְעָרִ֛ים מִצָּפ֖וֹנָה הִ֣יא כְסָל֑וֹן וְיָרַ֥ד בֵּֽית־שֶׁ֖מֶשׁ וְעָבַ֥ר תִּמְנָֽה׃ 11 וְיָצָ֨א הַגְּב֜וּל אֶל־כֶּ֣תֶף עֶקְרוֹן֮ צָפוֹנָה֒ וְתָאַ֤ר הַגְּבוּל֙ שִׁכְּר֔וֹנָה וְעָבַ֥ר הַר־הַבַּעֲלָ֖ה וְיָצָ֣א יַבְנְאֵ֑ל וְהָי֛וּ תֹּצְא֥וֹת הַגְּב֖וּל יָֽמָּה׃ 12 וּגְב֣וּל יָ֔ם הַיָּ֥מָּה הַגָּד֖וֹל וּגְב֑וּל זֶ֠ה גְּב֧וּל בְּנֵֽי־יְהוּדָ֛ה סָבִ֖יב לְמִשְׁפְּחֹתָֽם׃ 13 וּלְכָלֵ֣ב בֶּן־יְפֻנֶּ֗ה נָ֤תַן חֵ֙לֶק֙ בְּת֣וֹךְ בְּנֵֽי־יְהוּדָ֔ה אֶל־פִּ֥י יְהֹוָ֖ה לִיהוֹשֻׁ֑עַ אֶת־קִרְיַ֥ת אַרְבַּ֛ע אֲבִ֥י הָעֲנָ֖ק הִ֥יא חֶבְרֽוֹן׃ 14 וַיֹּ֤רֶשׁ מִשָּׁם֙ כָּלֵ֔ב אֶת־שְׁלוֹשָׁ֖ה בְּנֵ֣י הָעֲנָ֑ק אֶת־שֵׁשַׁ֤י וְאֶת־אֲחִימַן֙ וְאֶת־תַּלְמַ֔י יְלִידֵ֖י הָעֲנָֽק׃ 15 וַיַּ֣עַל מִשָּׁ֔ם אֶל־יֹשְׁבֵ֖י דְּבִ֑ר וְשֵׁם־

---

a-a   *Meaning of Heb. uncertain.*
b   *Apparently identical with Geliloth, 18.17.*
c   *Not the Seir of Edom.*

489

against the inhabitants of Debir—the name of Debir was formerly Kiriath-sepher—[16]and Caleb announced, "I will give my daughter Achsah in marriage to the man who attacks and captures Kiriath-sepher." [17]His kinsman Othniel the Kenizzite[d] captured it; and Caleb gave him his daughter Achsah in marriage.

[18][e]-When she came [to him], she induced him-[e] to ask her father for some property. She dismounted from her donkey, and Caleb asked her, "What is the matter?" [19]She replied, "Give me a present; for you have given me away as Negeb-land;[f] so give me springs of water." And he gave her Upper and Lower Gulloth.[g]

[20]This was the portion of the tribe of the Judites by their clans:

[21]The towns at the far end of the tribe of Judah, near the border of Edom, in the Negeb, were: Kabzeel, Eder, Jagur, [22]Kinah, Dimonah, Adadah, [23]Kedesh, Hazor, Ithnan, [24]Ziph, Telem, Bealoth, [25]Hazor-hadattah, Kerioth-hezron—that is, Hazor—[26]Amam, Shema, Moladah, [27]Hazar-gaddah, Heshmon, Beth-pelet, [28]Hazar-shual, Beer-sheba, Biziothiah, [29]Baalah, Iim, Ezem, [30]Eltolad, Chesil, Hormah, [31]Ziklag, Madmannah, Sansannah, [32][h]-Lebaoth, Shilhim,-[h] Ain and Rimmon.[i] Total: 29[j] towns, with their villages.

[33]In the Lowland: Eshtaol, Zorah, Ashnah, [34]Zanoah, En-gannim, Tappuah, Enam, [35]Jarmuth, Adullam, Socoh, Azekah, [36]Shaaraim, Adithaim, Gederah, and Gederothaim—14[k] towns, with their villages.

[37]Zenan, Hadashah, Migdal-gad, [38]Dilan, Mizpeh, Joktheel, [39]Lachish, Bozkath, Eglon,

דִּבֶּר לְפָנִים קִרְיַת־סֵפֶר: 16 וַיֹּאמֶר כָּלֵב אֲשֶׁר־יַכֶּה אֶת־קִרְיַת־סֵפֶר וּלְכָדָהּ וְנָתַתִּי לוֹ אֶת־עַכְסָה בִתִּי לְאִשָּׁה: 17 וַיִּלְכְּדָהּ עָתְנִיאֵל בֶּן־קְנַז אֲחִי כָלֵב וַיִּתֶּן־לוֹ אֶת־עַכְסָה בִתּוֹ לְאִשָּׁה:

18 וַיְהִי בְּבוֹאָהּ וַתְּסִיתֵהוּ לִשְׁאוֹל מֵאֵת־אָבִיהָ שָׂדֶה וַתִּצְנַח מֵעַל הַחֲמוֹר וַיֹּאמֶר־לָהּ כָּלֵב מַה־לָּךְ: 19 וַתֹּאמֶר תְּנָה־לִּי בְרָכָה כִּי אֶרֶץ הַנֶּגֶב נְתַתָּנִי וְנָתַתָּה לִי גֻּלֹּת מָיִם וַיִּתֶּן־לָהּ אֵת גֻּלֹּת עִלִּיּוֹת וְאֵת גֻּלֹּת תַּחְתִּיּוֹת: פ

20 זֹאת נַחֲלַת מַטֵּה בְנֵי־יְהוּדָה לְמִשְׁפְּחֹתָם:

21 וַיִּהְיוּ הֶעָרִים מִקְצֵה לְמַטֵּה בְנֵי־יְהוּדָה אֶל־גְּבוּל אֱדוֹם בַּנֶּגְבָּה קַבְצְאֵל וְעֵדֶר וְיָגוּר: 22 וְקִינָה וְדִימוֹנָה וְעַדְעָדָה: 23 וְקֶדֶשׁ וְחָצוֹר וְיִתְנָן: 24 זִיף וָטֶלֶם וּבְעָלוֹת: 25 וְחָצוֹר ׀ חֲדַתָּה וּקְרִיּוֹת חֶצְרוֹן הִיא חָצוֹר: 26 אֲמָם וּשְׁמַע וּמוֹלָדָה: 27 וַחֲצַר גַּדָּה וְחֶשְׁמוֹן וּבֵית פָּלֶט: 28 וַחֲצַר שׁוּעָל וּבְאֵר שֶׁבַע וּבִזְיוֹתְיָה: 29 בַּעֲלָה וְעִיִּים וָעָצֶם: 30 וְאֶלְתּוֹלַד וּכְסִיל וְחָרְמָה: 31 וְצִקְלַג וּמַדְמַנָּה וְסַנְסַנָּה: 32 וּלְבָאוֹת וְשִׁלְחִים וְעַיִן וְרִמּוֹן כָּל־עָרִים עֶשְׂרִים וָתֵשַׁע וְחַצְרֵיהֶן: ס

33 בַּשְּׁפֵלָה אֶשְׁתָּאוֹל וְצָרְעָה וְאַשְׁנָה: 34 וְזָנוֹחַ וְעֵין גַּנִּים תַּפּוּחַ וְהָעֵינָם: 35 יַרְמוּת וַעֲדֻלָּם שׂוֹכֹה וַעֲזֵקָה: 36 וְשַׁעֲרַיִם וַעֲדִיתַיִם וְהַגְּדֵרָה וּגְדֵרֹתָיִם עָרִים אַרְבַּע־עֶשְׂרֵה וְחַצְרֵיהֶן: 37 צְנָן וַחֲדָשָׁה וּמִגְדַּל־גָּד: 38 וְדִלְעָן

---

d   Cf. 14.6, 14.

e-e   Meaning of Heb. uncertain. Some Greek mss. read "he induced her"; cf. Judg. 1.14.

f   I.e., as a dry land, that is, without a dowry.

g   I.e., "springs."

h-h   Cf. below 19.6.

i   Cf. Ain, Rimmon, 19.7 below, and 1 Chron. 4.32; En-rimmon, Neh. 11.29.

j   The number is uncertain. Some of the same towns are listed under Simeon, cf. 19.1–9; so Rashi.

k   The number is uncertain. Tappuah and Enam may have been one place; so Rashi on basis of 17.7.

40Cabbon, Lahmas, Chithlish, 41Gederoth, Beth-dagon, Naamah, and Makkedah: 16 towns, with their villages.

42Libnah, Ether, Ashan, 43Iphtah, Ashnah, Nezib, 44Keilah, Achzib, and Mareshah: 9 towns, with their villages.

45Ekron, with its dependencies and villages. 46From Ekron westward, all the towns in the vicinity of Ashdod, with their villages—47Ashdod, its dependencies and its villages—Gaza, its dependencies and its villages, all the way to the Wadi of Egypt and the edge of the Mediterranean Sea.

48And in the hill country: Shamir, Jattir, Socoh, 49Dannah, Kiriath-sannah*l*—that is, Debir—50Anab, Eshtemoh, Anim, 51Goshen, Holon, and Giloh: 11 towns, with their villages.

52Arab, Dumah, Eshan, 53Janum, Beth-tappuah, Aphekah, 54Humtah, Kiriath-arba—that is, Hebron—and Zior: 9 towns, with their villages.

55Maon, Carmel, Ziph, Juttah, 56Jezreel, Jokdeam, Zanoah, 57Kain, Gibeah, and Timnah: 10 towns, with their villages.

58Halhul, Beth-zur, Gedor, 59Maarath, Beth-anoth, and Eltekon: 6 towns, with their villages.*m*

60Kiriath-baal—that is, Kiriath-jearim—and Rabbah: 2 towns, with their villages.

61In the wilderness: Beth-arabah, Middin, Secacah, 62Nibshan, Ir-melah,*n* and En-gedi: 6 towns, with their villages.

63But the Judites could not dispossess the Jebusites, the inhabitants of Jerusalem; so the Judites dwell with the Jebusites in Jerusalem to this day.

---

l   Emendation yields "Kiriath-sepher"; cf. Septuagint.
m   Septuagint adds: Tekoa, Ephrathah—that is, Bethlehem—Peor, Etam, Kulon, Tatam, Sores, Karem, Gallim, Bether, and Manach—11 towns, with their villages.
n   Or "the City of Salt."

39 לָכִישׁ וּבָצְקַת וְהַמִּצְפֶּה וְיָקְתְאֵל: 40 וְכַבּוֹן וְלַחְמַס וְכִתְלִישׁ וְעֶגְלוֹן: 41 וּגְדֵרוֹת בֵּית־דָּגוֹן וְנַעֲמָה וּמַקֵּדָה עָרִים שֵׁשׁ־עֶשְׂרֵה וְחַצְרֵיהֶן: ס 42 לִבְנָה וָעֶתֶר וְעָשָׁן: 43 וְיִפְתָּח וְאַשְׁנָה וּנְצִיב: 44 וּקְעִילָה וְאַכְזִיב וּמָרֵאשָׁה עָרִים תֵּשַׁע וְחַצְרֵיהֶן: 45 עֶקְרוֹן וּבְנֹתֶיהָ וַחֲצֵרֶיהָ: 46 מֵעֶקְרוֹן וָיָמָּה כֹּל אֲשֶׁר־עַל־יַד אַשְׁדּוֹד וְחַצְרֵיהֶן: 47 אַשְׁדּוֹד בְּנוֹתֶיהָ וַחֲצֵרֶיהָ עַזָּה בְּנוֹתֶיהָ וַחֲצֵרֶיהָ עַד־נַחַל מִצְרָיִם וְהַיָּם הַגָּדוֹל וּגְבוּל: ס 48 וּבָהָר שָׁמִיר וְיַתִּיר וְשׂוֹכֹה: 49 וְדַנָּה וְקִרְיַת־סַנָּה הִיא דְבִר: 50 וַעֲנָב וְאֶשְׁתְּמֹה וְעָנִים: 51 וְגֹשֶׁן וְחֹלֹן וְגִלֹה עָרִים אַחַת־עֶשְׂרֵה וְחַצְרֵיהֶן: 52 אֲרַב וְרוּמָה* וְאֶשְׁעָן: 53 וְיָנִים וּבֵית־תַּפּוּחַ וַאֲפֵקָה: 54 וְחֻמְטָה וְקִרְיַת אַרְבַּע הִיא חֶבְרוֹן וְצִיעֹר עָרִים תֵּשַׁע וְחַצְרֵיהֶן: ס 55 מָעוֹן כַּרְמֶל וָזִיף וְיוּטָּה: 56 וְיִזְרְעֶאל וְיָקְדְעָם וְזָנוֹחַ: 57 הַקַּיִן גִּבְעָה וְתִמְנָה עָרִים עֶשֶׂר וְחַצְרֵיהֶן: 58 חַלְחוּל בֵּית־צוּר וּגְדוֹר: 59 וּמַעֲרָת וּבֵית־עֲנוֹת וְאֶלְתְּקֹן עָרִים שֵׁשׁ וְחַצְרֵיהֶן: 60 קִרְיַת־בַּעַל הִיא קִרְיַת יְעָרִים וְהָרַבָּה עָרִים שְׁתַּיִם וְחַצְרֵיהֶן: ס 61 בַּמִּדְבָּר בֵּית הָעֲרָבָה מִדִּין וּסְכָכָה: 62 וְהַנִּבְשָׁן וְעִיר־הַמֶּלַח וְעֵין גֶּדִי עָרִים שֵׁשׁ וְחַצְרֵיהֶן: 63 וְאֶת־הַיְבוּסִי יוֹשְׁבֵי יְרוּשָׁלַ͏ִם לֹא־יוּכְלוּ יָכְלוּ בְנֵי־יְהוּדָה לְהוֹרִישָׁם וַיֵּשֶׁב הַיְבוּסִי אֶת־בְּנֵי יְהוּדָה בִּירוּשָׁלַ͏ִם עַד הַיּוֹם הַזֶּה: פ

v. 52. בְּנֻסַח אַחֵר "וְדוּמָה"

16 The portion that fell by lot to the Josephites ran from the Jordan at Jericho— from the waters of Jericho east of the wilderness. From Jericho it ascended through the hill country to Bethel. [2]From Bethel it ran to Luz and passed on to the territory of the Archites at Ataroth, [3]descended westward to the territory of the Japhletites as far as the border of Lower Beth-horon and Gezer, and ran on to the Sea. [4]Thus the Josephites—that is, Manasseh and Ephraim—received their portion.

[5]The territory of the Ephraimites, by their clans, was as follows: The boundary of their portion ran from Atroth-addar on the east to Upper Beth-horon, [6]and the boundary ran on to the Sea. And on the north, the boundary proceeded from Michmethath to the east of Taanath-shiloh and passed beyond it up to the east of Janoah; [7]from Janoah it descended to Ataroth and Naarath, touched on Jericho, and ran on to the Jordan. [8]Westward, the boundary proceeded from Tappuah to the Wadi Kanah and ran on to the Sea. This was the portion of the tribe of the Ephraimites, by their clans, [9]together with the towns marked off[a] for the Ephraimites within the territory of the Manassites—all those towns with their villages. [10]However, they failed to dispossess the Canaanites who dwelt in Gezer; so the Canaanites remained in the midst of Ephraim, as is still the case. But they had to perform forced labor.

17 And this is the portion that fell by lot to the tribe of Manasseh—for he was Joseph's first-born. Since Machir, the first-born of Manasseh and the father of Gilead, was a valiant warrior, Gilead and Bashan were assigned to him. [2]And now assignments were made to the

---

a Meaning of Heb. uncertain.

טז וַיֵּצֵא הַגּוֹרָל לִבְנֵי יוֹסֵף מִיַּרְדֵּן יְרִיחוֹ לְמֵי יְרִיחוֹ מִזְרָחָה הַמִּדְבָּר עֹלֶה מִירִיחוֹ בָּהָר בֵּית־אֵל: 2 וְיָצָא מִבֵּית־אֵל לוּזָה וְעָבַר אֶל־גְּבוּל הָאַרְכִּי עֲטָרוֹת: 3 וְיָרַד־יָמָּה אֶל־גְּבוּל הַיַּפְלֵטִי עַד גְּבוּל בֵּית־חוֹרֹן תַּחְתּוֹן וְעַד־גָּזֶר וְהָיוּ תֹצְאֹתָו יָמָּה: 4 וַיִּנְחֲלוּ בְנֵי־יוֹסֵף מְנַשֶּׁה וְאֶפְרָיִם:

5 וַיְהִי גְּבוּל בְּנֵי־אֶפְרַיִם לְמִשְׁפְּחֹתָם וַיְהִי גְּבוּל נַחֲלָתָם מִזְרָחָה עַטְרוֹת אַדָּר עַד־בֵּית חוֹרֹן עֶלְיוֹן: 6 וְיָצָא הַגְּבוּל הַיָּמָּה הַמִּכְמְתָת מִצָּפוֹן וְנָסַב הַגְּבוּל מִזְרָחָה תַּאֲנַת שִׁלֹה וְעָבַר אוֹתוֹ מִמִּזְרַח יָנוֹחָה: 7 וְיָרַד מִיָּנוֹחָה עֲטָרוֹת וְנַעֲרָתָה וּפָגַע בִּירִיחוֹ וְיָצָא הַיַּרְדֵּן: 8 מִתַּפּוּחַ יֵלֵךְ הַגְּבוּל יָמָּה נַחַל קָנָה וְהָיוּ תֹצְאֹתָיו הַיָּמָּה זֹאת נַחֲלַת מַטֵּה בְנֵי־אֶפְרַיִם לְמִשְׁפְּחֹתָם: 9 וְהֶעָרִים הַמִּבְדָּלוֹת לִבְנֵי אֶפְרַיִם בְּתוֹךְ נַחֲלַת בְּנֵי־מְנַשֶּׁה כָּל־הֶעָרִים וְחַצְרֵיהֶן: 10 וְלֹא הוֹרִישׁוּ אֶת־הַכְּנַעֲנִי הַיּוֹשֵׁב בְּגָזֶר וַיֵּשֶׁב הַכְּנַעֲנִי בְּקֶרֶב אֶפְרַיִם עַד־הַיּוֹם הַזֶּה וַיְהִי לְמַס־עֹבֵד: פ

יז וַיְהִי הַגּוֹרָל לְמַטֵּה מְנַשֶּׁה כִּי־הוּא בְּכוֹר יוֹסֵף לְמָכִיר בְּכוֹר מְנַשֶּׁה אֲבִי הַגִּלְעָד כִּי הוּא הָיָה אִישׁ מִלְחָמָה וַיְהִי־לוֹ הַגִּלְעָד וְהַבָּשָׁן: 2 וַיְהִי לִבְנֵי מְנַשֶּׁה

remaining Manassites, by their clans: the descendants of Abiezer, Helek, Asriel, Shechem, Hepher, and Shemida. Those were the male descendants of Manasseh son of Joseph, by their clans.

3aNow Zelophehad son of Hepher son of Gilead son of Machir son of Manasseh had no sons, but only daughters. The names of his daughters were Mahlah, Noah, Hoglah, Milcah, and Tirzah. 4They appeared before the priest Eleazer, Joshua son of Nun, and the chieftains, saying: "The Lord commanded Moses to grant us a portion among our male kinsmen." So, in accordance with the Lord's instructions, they were granted a portion among their father's kinsmen. 5Ten districts fell to Manasseh, apart from the lands of Gilead and Bashan, which are across the Jordan. 6Manasseh's daughters inherited a portion in these together with his sons, while the land of Gilead was assigned to the rest of Manasseh's descendants.

7The boundary of Manasseh ran from Asher to Michmethath, which lies near Shechem. The boundary continued to the right, toward the inhabitants of En-tappuah.—8The region of Tappuah belonged to Manasseh; but Tappuah, on the border of Manasseh, belonged to the Ephraimites.—9Then the boundary descended to the Wadi Kanah. Those towns to the south of the wadi belonged to Ephraim as an enclave among the towns of Manasseh. The boundary of Manasseh lay north of the wadi and ran on to the Sea. 10What lay to the south belonged to Ephraim, and what lay to the north belonged to Manasseh, with the Sea as its boundary. [This territory] was contiguous with Asher on the north and with Issachar on the east. 11Within Issachar and Asher, Manasseh possessed Bethshean and its dependencies, Ibleam and its dependencies, the inhabitants of Dor and its

---

a   Cf. Num. 27.1–11.

הַנּוֹתָרִים֙ לְמִשְׁפְּחֹתָ֔ם לִבְנֵ֣י אֲבִיעֶ֗זֶר וְלִבְנֵי־חֵ֙לֶק֙ וְלִבְנֵ֣י אַשְׂרִיאֵ֔ל וְלִבְנֵי־שֶׁ֖כֶם וְלִבְנֵי־חֵ֑פֶר וְלִבְנֵ֖י שְׁמִידָ֑ע אֵ֠לֶּה בְּנֵ֨י מְנַשֶּׁ֧ה בֶּן־יוֹסֵ֛ף הַזְּכָרִ֖ים לְמִשְׁפְּחֹתָֽם׃ 3 וְלִצְלָפְחָד֩ בֶּן־חֵ֨פֶר בֶּן־גִּלְעָ֜ד בֶּן־מָכִ֣יר בֶּן־מְנַשֶּׁ֗ה לֹא־הָ֥יוּ ל֛וֹ בָּנִ֖ים כִּ֣י אִם־בָּנ֑וֹת וְאֵ֙לֶּה֙ שְׁמ֣וֹת בְּנֹתָ֔יו מַחְלָ֣ה וְנֹעָ֔ה חָגְלָ֖ה מִלְכָּ֥ה וְתִרְצָֽה׃ 4 וַתִּקְרַ֡בְנָה לִפְנֵי֩ אֶלְעָזָ֨ר הַכֹּהֵ֜ן וְלִפְנֵ֣י ׀ יְהוֹשֻׁ֣עַ בִּן־נ֗וּן וְלִפְנֵ֣י הַנְּשִׂיאִים֮ לֵאמֹר֒ יְהוָה֙ צִוָּ֣ה אֶת־מֹשֶׁ֔ה לָֽתֶת־לָ֥נוּ נַחֲלָ֖ה בְּת֣וֹךְ אַחֵ֑ינוּ וַיִּתֵּ֨ן לָהֶ֜ם אֶל־פִּ֣י יְהוָ֗ה נַחֲלָ֖ה בְּת֥וֹךְ אֲחֵ֥י אֲבִיהֶֽן׃ 5 וַיִּפְּל֥וּ חַבְלֵֽי־מְנַשֶּׁ֖ה עֲשָׂרָ֑ה לְבַ֞ד מֵאֶ֤רֶץ הַגִּלְעָד֙ וְהַבָּשָׁ֔ן אֲשֶׁ֖ר מֵעֵ֥בֶר לַיַּרְדֵּֽן׃ 6 כִּ֚י בְּנ֣וֹת מְנַשֶּׁ֔ה נָחֲל֥וּ נַחֲלָ֖ה בְּת֣וֹךְ בָּנָ֑יו וְאֶ֙רֶץ֙ הַגִּלְעָ֔ד הָיְתָ֥ה לִבְנֵֽי־מְנַשֶּׁ֖ה הַנּֽוֹתָרִֽים׃ 7 וַיְהִ֤י גְבוּל־מְנַשֶּׁה֙ מֵֽאָשֵׁ֔ר הַֽמִּכְמְתָ֔ת אֲשֶׁ֖ר עַל־פְּנֵ֣י שְׁכֶ֑ם וְהָלַ֤ךְ הַגְּבוּל֙ אֶל־הַיָּמִ֔ין אֶל־יֹשְׁבֵ֖י עֵ֥ין תַּפּֽוּחַ׃ 8 לִמְנַשֶּׁ֕ה הָיְתָ֖ה אֶ֣רֶץ תַּפּ֑וּחַ וְתַפּ֛וּחַ אֶל־גְּב֥וּל מְנַשֶּׁ֖ה לִבְנֵ֥י אֶפְרָֽיִם׃ 9 וְיָרַ֣ד הַגְּבוּל֩ נַ֨חַל קָנָ֜ה נֶ֣גְבָּה לַנַּ֗חַל עָרִ֤ים הָאֵ֙לֶּה֙ לְאֶפְרַ֔יִם בְּת֖וֹךְ עָרֵ֣י מְנַשֶּׁ֑ה וּגְב֤וּל מְנַשֶּׁה֙ מִצְּפ֣וֹן לַנַּ֔חַל וַיְהִ֥י תֹצְאֹתָ֖יו הַיָּֽמָּה׃ 10 נֶ֣גְבָּה לְאֶפְרַ֗יִם וְצָפ֙וֹנָה֙ לִמְנַשֶּׁ֔ה וַיְהִ֥י הַיָּ֖ם גְּבוּל֑וֹ וּבְאָשֵׁר֙ יִפְגְּע֣וּן מִצָּפ֔וֹן וּבְיִשָּׂשכָ֖ר מִמִּזְרָֽח׃ 11 וַיְהִ֨י לִמְנַשֶּׁ֜ה בְּיִשָּׂשכָ֣ר וּבְאָשֵׁ֗ר בֵּֽית־שְׁאָ֣ן וּבְנוֹתֶ֣יהָ וְיִבְלְעָ֣ם וּבְנוֹתֶ֡יהָ וְֽאֶת־יֹשְׁבֵ֣י דֹאר֩ וּבְנוֹתֶ֨יהָ וְיֹשְׁבֵ֤י עֵֽין־דֹּר֙ וּבְנֹתֶ֔יהָ

dependencies, the inhabitants of En-dor and its dependencies, the inhabitants of Taanach and its dependencies, and the inhabitants of Me-giddo and its dependencies: *b*-these constituted three regions.-*b*

12The Manassites could not dispossess [the inhabitants of] these towns, and the Canaanites stubbornly remained in this region. 13When the Israelites became stronger, they imposed trib-ute on the Canaanites; but they did not dispos-sess them.

14The Josephites complained to Joshua, say-ing, "Why have you assigned as our portion a single allotment and a single district, seeing that we are a numerous people whom the LORD has blessed so greatly?" 15"If you are a numerous people," Joshua answered them, "go up to the forest country and clear an area for yourselves there, in the territory of the Perizzites and the Rephaim, seeing that you are cramped in the hill country of Ephraim." 16"The hill country is not enough for us," the Josephites replied, "and all the Canaanites who live in the valley area have iron chariots, both those in Beth-shean and its dependencies and those in the Valley of Jezreel." 17But Joshua declared to the House of Joseph, to Ephraim and Manasseh, "You are indeed a numerous people, possessed of great strength; you shall not have one allot-ment only. 18The hill country shall be yours as well; true, it is forest land, but you will clear it and possess it to its farthest limits. And you shall also dispossess the Canaanites, even though they have iron chariots and even though they are strong."

18 The whole community of the Israelite people assembled at Shiloh, and set up the Tent

וְיֹשְׁבֵי תַעְנַךְ וּבְנֹתֶיהָ וְיֹשְׁבֵי מְגִדּוֹ וּבְנוֹתֶיהָ שְׁלֹשֶׁת הַנָּפֶת:

12 וְלֹא יָכְלוּ בְּנֵי מְנַשֶּׁה לְהוֹרִישׁ אֶת־הֶעָרִים הָאֵלֶּה וַיּוֹאֶל הַכְּנַעֲנִי לָשֶׁבֶת בָּאָרֶץ הַזֹּאת: 13 וַיְהִי כִּי חָזְקוּ בְּנֵי יִשְׂרָאֵל וַיִּתְּנוּ אֶת־הַכְּנַעֲנִי לָמַס וְהוֹרֵשׁ לֹא הוֹרִישׁוֹ: ס

14 וַיְדַבְּרוּ בְּנֵי יוֹסֵף אֶת־יְהוֹשֻׁעַ לֵאמֹר מַדּוּעַ נָתַתָּה לִּי נַחֲלָה גּוֹרָל אֶחָד וְחֶבֶל אֶחָד וַאֲנִי עַם־רָב עַד אֲשֶׁר־עַד־כֹּה בֵּרְכַנִי יְהוָה: 15 וַיֹּאמֶר אֲלֵיהֶם יְהוֹשֻׁעַ אִם־עַם־רָב אַתָּה עֲלֵה לְךָ הַיַּעְרָה וּבֵרֵאתָ לְךָ שָׁם בְּאֶרֶץ הַפְּרִזִּי וְהָרְפָאִים כִּי־אָץ לְךָ הַר־אֶפְרָיִם: 16 וַיֹּאמְרוּ בְּנֵי יוֹסֵף לֹא־יִמָּצֵא לָנוּ הָהָר וְרֶכֶב בַּרְזֶל בְּכָל־הַכְּנַעֲנִי הַיֹּשֵׁב בְּאֶרֶץ־הָעֵמֶק לַאֲשֶׁר בְּבֵית־שְׁאָן וּבְנוֹתֶיהָ וְלַאֲשֶׁר בְּעֵמֶק יִזְרְעֶאל: 17 וַיֹּאמֶר יְהוֹשֻׁעַ אֶל־בֵּית יוֹסֵף לְאֶפְרַיִם וְלִמְנַשֶּׁה לֵאמֹר עַם־רָב אַתָּה וְכֹחַ גָּדוֹל לָךְ לֹא־יִהְיֶה לְךָ גּוֹרָל אֶחָד: 18 כִּי הַר יִהְיֶה־לָּךְ כִּי־יַעַר הוּא וּבֵרֵאתוֹ וְהָיָה לְךָ תֹּצְאֹתָיו כִּי־תוֹרִישׁ אֶת־הַכְּנַעֲנִי כִּי רֶכֶב בַּרְזֶל לוֹ כִּי חָזָק הוּא: פ

יח וַיִּקָּהֲלוּ כָּל־עֲדַת בְּנֵי־יִשְׂרָאֵל שִׁלֹה וַיַּשְׁכִּינוּ שָׁם אֶת־אֹהֶל מוֹעֵד

---

b-b   Meaning of Heb. uncertain.

of Meeting there. The land was now under their control; [2]but there remained seven tribes of the Israelites which had not yet received their portions. [3]So Joshua said to the Israelites, "How long will you be slack about going and taking possession of the land which the LORD, the God of your fathers, has assigned to you? [4]Appoint three men of each tribe; I will send them out to go through the country and write down a description of it for purposes of apportionment, and then come back to me. [5]They shall divide it into seven parts—Judah shall remain by its territory in the south, and the house of Joseph shall remain by its territory in the north.— [6]When you have written down the description of the land in seven parts, bring it here to me. Then I will cast lots for you here before the LORD our God. [7]For the Levites have no share among you, since the priesthood of the LORD is their portion; and Gad and Reuben and the half-tribe of Manasseh have received the portions which were assigned to them by Moses the servant of the LORD, on the eastern side of the Jordan."

[8]The men set out on their journeys. Joshua ordered the men who were leaving to write down a description of the land—"Go, traverse the country and write down a description of it. Then return to me, and I will cast lots for you here at Shiloh before the LORD."

[9]So the men went and traversed the land; they described it in a document, town by town, in seven parts, and they returned to Joshua in the camp at Shiloh. [10]Joshua cast lots for them at Shiloh before the LORD, and there Joshua apportioned the land among the Israelites according to their divisions.

[11]The lot of the tribe of the Benjaminites, by their clans, came out first. The territory which fell to their lot lay between the Judites and the Josephites. [12]The boundary on their northern rim began at the Jordan; the boundary ascended

וְהָאָרֶץ נִכְבְּשָׁה לִפְנֵיהֶם: [2] וַיִּתְחַלְקוּ בְנֵי־
יִשְׂרָאֵל אֲשֶׁר לֹא־חָלְקוּ אֶת־נַחֲלָתָם
שִׁבְעָה שְׁבָטִים: [3] וַיֹּאמֶר יְהוֹשֻׁעַ אֶל־בְּנֵי
יִשְׂרָאֵל עַד־אָנָה אַתֶּם מִתְרַפִּים לָבוֹא
לָרֶשֶׁת אֶת־הָאָרֶץ אֲשֶׁר נָתַן לָכֶם יְהוָה
אֱלֹהֵי אֲבוֹתֵיכֶם: [4] הָבוּ לָכֶם שְׁלֹשָׁה
אֲנָשִׁים לַשָּׁבֶט וְאֶשְׁלָחֵם וְיָקֻמוּ וְיִתְהַלְּכוּ
בָאָרֶץ וְיִכְתְּבוּ אוֹתָהּ לְפִי נַחֲלָתָם וְיָבֹאוּ
אֵלָי: [5] וְהִתְחַלְּקוּ אֹתָהּ לְשִׁבְעָה חֲלָקִים
יְהוּדָה יַעֲמֹד עַל־גְּבוּלוֹ מִנֶּגֶב וּבֵית
יוֹסֵף יַעַמְדוּ עַל־גְּבוּלָם מִצָּפוֹן: [6] וְאַתֶּם
תִּכְתְּבוּ אֶת־הָאָרֶץ שִׁבְעָה חֲלָקִים
וַהֲבֵאתֶם אֵלַי הֵנָּה וְיָרִיתִי לָכֶם גּוֹרָל פֹּה
לִפְנֵי יְהוָה אֱלֹהֵינוּ: [7] כִּי אֵין־חֵלֶק לַלְוִיִּם
בְּקִרְבְּכֶם כִּי־כְהֻנַּת יְהוָה נַחֲלָתוֹ וְגָד
וּרְאוּבֵן וַחֲצִי שֵׁבֶט הַמְנַשֶּׁה לָקְחוּ נַחֲלָתָם
מֵעֵבֶר לַיַּרְדֵּן מִזְרָחָה אֲשֶׁר נָתַן לָהֶם
מֹשֶׁה עֶבֶד יְהוָה:

[8] וַיָּקֻמוּ הָאֲנָשִׁים וַיֵּלֵכוּ וַיְצַו יְהוֹשֻׁעַ אֶת־
הַהֹלְכִים לִכְתֹּב אֶת־הָאָרֶץ לֵאמֹר לְכוּ
וְהִתְהַלְּכוּ בָאָרֶץ וְכִתְבוּ אוֹתָהּ וְשׁוּבוּ
אֵלַי וּפֹה אַשְׁלִיךְ לָכֶם גּוֹרָל לִפְנֵי יְהוָה
בְּשִׁלֹה:

[9] וַיֵּלְכוּ הָאֲנָשִׁים וַיַּעַבְרוּ בָאָרֶץ וַיִּכְתְּבוּהָ
לֶעָרִים לְשִׁבְעָה חֲלָקִים עַל־סֵפֶר וַיָּבֹאוּ
אֶל־יְהוֹשֻׁעַ אֶל־הַמַּחֲנֶה שִׁלֹה: [10] וַיַּשְׁלֵךְ
לָהֶם יְהוֹשֻׁעַ גּוֹרָל בְּשִׁלֹה לִפְנֵי יְהוָה
וַיְחַלֶּק־שָׁם יְהוֹשֻׁעַ אֶת־הָאָרֶץ לִבְנֵי
יִשְׂרָאֵל כְּמַחְלְקֹתָם: פ

[11] וַיַּעַל גּוֹרַל מַטֵּה בְנֵי־בִנְיָמִן לְמִשְׁפְּחֹתָם
וַיֵּצֵא גְּבוּל גּוֹרָלָם בֵּין בְּנֵי יְהוּדָה וּבֵין
בְּנֵי יוֹסֵף: [12] וַיְהִי לָהֶם הַגְּבוּל לִפְאַת
צָפוֹנָה מִן־הַיַּרְדֵּן וְעָלָה הַגְּבוּל אֶל־כֶּתֶף

to the northern flank of Jericho, ascended westward into the hill country and ran on to the Wilderness of Beth-aven. [13]From there the boundary passed on southward to Luz, to the flank of Luz—that is, Bethel; then the boundary descended to Atroth-addar [and] to the hill south of Lower Beth-horon. [14]The boundary now turned and curved onto the western rim; and the boundary ran southward from the hill on the south side of Beth-horon till it ended at Kiriath-baal—that is, Kiriath-jearim—a town of the Judites. That was the western rim. [15]The southern rim: From the outskirts of Kiriath-jearim, the boundary passed westward*a* and ran on to the fountain of the Waters of Nephtoah. [16]Then the boundary descended to the foot of the hill by the Valley of Ben-hinnom at the northern end of the Valley of Rephaim; then it ran down the Valley of Hinnom along the southern flank of the Jebusites to En-rogel. [17]Curving northward, it ran on to En-shemesh and ran on to Geliloth, facing the Ascent of Adummim, and descended to the Stone of Bohan son of Reuben. [18]It continued northward to the edge of the Arabah and descended into the Arabah. [19]The boundary passed on to the northern flank of Beth-hoglah, and the boundary ended at the northern tongue of the Dead Sea, at the southern end of the Jordan. That was the southern boundary. [20]On their eastern rim, finally, the Jordan was their boundary. That was the portion of the Benjaminites, by their clans, according to its boundaries on all sides.

[21]And the towns of the tribe of the Benjaminites, by its clans, were: Jericho, Beth-hoglah, Emek-keziz, [22]Beth-arabah, Zemaraim, Bethel, [23]Avvim, Parah, Ophrah, [24]Chephar-ammonah, Ophni, and Geba—12 towns, with their villages. [25]Also Gibeon, Ramah, Beeroth, [26]Mizpeh, Chephirah, Mozah, [27]Rekem, Irpeel,

a *Emendation yields "eastward."*

יְרִיחוֹ֙ מִצָּפ֔וֹן וְעָלָ֤ה בָהָר֙ יָ֔מָּה והיה וְהָי֖וּ תֹצְאֹתָ֔יו מִדְבַּ֖רָה בֵּ֥ית אָֽוֶן׃ 13 וְעָבַ֨ר מִשָּׁ֜ם הַגְּב֗וּל ל֚וּזָה אֶל־כֶּ֣תֶף ל֔וּזָה נֶ֖גְבָּה הִ֣יא בֵּֽית־אֵ֑ל וְיָרַ֤ד הַגְּבוּל֙ עַטְר֣וֹת אַדָּ֔ר עַל־הָהָ֕ר אֲשֶׁ֛ר מִנֶּ֥גֶב לְבֵית־חֹר֖וֹן תַּחְתּֽוֹן׃ 14 וְתָאַ֣ר הַגְּבוּל֩ וְנָסַ֨ב לִפְאַת־יָ֜ם נֶ֗גְבָּה מִן־הָהָר֙ אֲשֶׁ֣ר עַל־פְּנֵ֤י בֵית־חֹרוֹן֙ נֶ֔גְבָּה וְהָיֽוּ־תֹצְאֹתָ֔יו אֶל־קִרְיַת־בַּ֙עַל֙ הִ֣יא קִרְיַ֣ת יְעָרִ֔ים עִ֖יר בְּנֵ֣י יְהוּדָ֑ה זֹ֖את פְּאַת־יָֽם׃ 15 וּפְאַת־נֶ֕גְבָּה מִקְצֵ֖ה קִרְיַ֣ת יְעָרִ֑ים וְיָצָ֤א הַגְּבוּל֙ יָ֔מָּה וְיָצָ֕א אֶל־מַעְיַ֖ן מֵ֥י נֶפְתּֽוֹחַ׃ 16 וְיָרַ֨ד הַגְּב֜וּל אֶל־קְצֵ֣ה הָהָ֗ר אֲשֶׁר֙ עַל־פְּנֵי֙ גֵּ֣י בֶן־הִנֹּ֔ם אֲשֶׁ֛ר בְּעֵ֥מֶק רְפָאִ֖ים צָפ֑וֹנָה וְיָרַד֩ גֵּ֨י הִנֹּ֜ם אֶל־כֶּ֤תֶף הַיְבוּסִי֙ נֶ֔גְבָּה וְיָרַ֖ד עֵ֥ין רֹגֵֽל׃ 17 וְתָאַ֣ר מִצָּפ֗וֹן וְיָצָא֙ עֵ֣ין שֶׁ֔מֶשׁ וְיָצָא֙ אֶל־גְּלִיל֔וֹת אֲשֶׁר־נֹ֖כַח מַעֲלֵ֣ה אֲדֻמִּ֑ים וְיָרַ֕ד אֶ֥בֶן בֹּ֖הַן בֶּן־רְאוּבֵֽן׃ 18 וְעָבַ֛ר אֶל־כֶּ֥תֶף מוּל־הָעֲרָבָ֖ה צָפ֑וֹנָה וְיָרַ֖ד הָעֲרָבָֽתָה׃ 19 וְעָבַ֣ר הַגְּב֗וּל אֶל־כֶּ֤תֶף בֵּית־חָגְלָה֙ צָפ֔וֹנָה והיה ׀ וְהָי֣וּ תֹצְאוֹתָ֣יו הַגְּב֗וּל אֶל־לְשׁ֤וֹן יָם־הַמֶּ֙לַח֙ צָפ֔וֹנָה אֶל־קְצֵ֥ה הַיַּרְדֵּ֖ן נֶ֑גְבָּה זֶ֖ה גְּב֥וּל נֶֽגֶב׃ 20 וְהַיַּרְדֵּ֥ן יִגְבֹּל־אֹת֖וֹ לִפְאַת־קֵ֑דְמָה זֹ֣את נַחֲלַ֞ת בְּנֵ֧י בִנְיָמִ֛ן לִגְבֽוּלֹתֶ֖יהָ סָבִ֑יב לְמִשְׁפְּחֹתָֽם׃ 21 וְהָי֣וּ הֶעָרִ֗ים לְמַטֵּ֛ה בְּנֵ֥י בִנְיָמִ֖ן לְמִשְׁפְּחֽוֹתֵיהֶ֑ם יְרִיח֥וֹ וּבֵית־חָגְלָ֖ה וְעֵ֥מֶק קְצִֽיץ׃ 22 וּבֵ֧ית הָעֲרָבָ֛ה וּצְמָרַ֖יִם וּבֵֽית־אֵֽל׃ 23 וְהָעַוִּ֥ים וְהַפָּרָ֖ה וְעָפְרָֽה׃ 24 וּכְפַ֣ר הָֽעַמֹּנִ֗י וְהָֽעָפְנִ֛י וָגָ֖בַע עָרִ֣ים שְׁתֵּים־עֶשְׂרֵ֖ה וְחַצְרֵיהֶֽן׃ 25 גִּבְע֥וֹן וְהָֽרָמָ֖ה וּבְאֵרֽוֹת׃ 26 וְהַמִּצְפֶּ֥ה וְהַכְּפִירָ֖ה וְהַמֹּצָֽה׃ 27 וְרֶ֥קֶם וְיִרְפְּאֵ֖ל וְתַרְאֲלָֽה׃ 28 וְצֵלַ֡ע הָאֶ֡לֶף

Taralah, [28]Zela, Eleph, and Jebus[b]—that is, Jerusalem—Gibeath [and] Kiriath:[c] 14 towns, with their villages. That was the portion of the Benjaminites, by their clans.

19

The second lot fell to Simeon. The portion of the tribe of the Simeonites, by their clans, lay inside the portion of the Judites. [2]Their portion comprised: Beer-sheba—or Sheba—Moladah, [3]Hazar-shual, Balah, Ezem, [4]Eltolad, Bethul,[a] Hormah, [5]Ziklag, Beth-marcaboth, Hazar-susah, [6b]-Beth-lebaoth, and Sharuhen-[b]—13 towns, with their villages. [7]Ain, Rimmon, Ether, and Ashan: 4 towns, with their villages—[8]together with all the villages in the vicinity of those towns, down to Baalath-beer [and] Ramath-negeb. That was the portion of the tribe of the Simeonites, by their clans. [9]The portion of the Simeonites was part of the territory of the Judites; since the share of the Judites was larger than they needed, the Simeonites received a portion inside their portion.

[10]The third lot emerged for the Zebulunites, by their clans. The boundary of their portion: Starting at Sarid, [11]their boundary[c] ascended westward to Maralah, touching Dabbesheth and touching the wadi alongside Jokneam. [12]And it also ran from Sarid along the eastern side, where the sun rises, past the territory of Chisloth-tabor and on to Daberath and ascended to Japhia. [13]From there it ran [back] to the east, toward the sunrise, to Gath-hepher, to Eth-kazin, and on to Rimmon, where it curved to Neah. [14]Then it turned—that is, the boundary on the north—to Hannathon. Its extreme limits[d] were the Valley of Iphtah-el, [15]Kattath, Nahalal, Shimron, Idalah, and Bethlehem: 12

וְהַיְבוּסִ֗י הִ֤יא יְרֽוּשָׁלִַ֙ם֙ גִּבְעַ֣ת קִרְיַ֣ת עָרִ֔ים אַרְבַּֽע־עֶשְׂרֵ֖ה וְחַצְרֵיהֶ֑ן זֹ֛את נַחֲלַ֥ת בְּנֵֽי־בִנְיָמִ֖ן לְמִשְׁפְּחֹתָֽם׃ פ

יט וַיֵּצֵ֞א הַגּוֹרָ֤ל הַשֵּׁנִי֙ לְשִׁמְע֔וֹן לְמַטֵּ֥ה בְנֵֽי־שִׁמְע֖וֹן לְמִשְׁפְּחוֹתָ֑ם וַיְהִי֙ נַחֲלָתָ֔ם בְּת֖וֹךְ נַחֲלַ֥ת בְּנֵֽי־יְהוּדָֽה׃ [2]וַיְהִ֥י לָהֶ֖ם בְּנַֽחֲלָתָ֑ם בְּאֵֽר־שֶׁ֥בַע וְשֶׁ֖בַע וּמוֹלָדָֽה׃ [3]וַחֲצַ֥ר שׁוּעָ֛ל וּבָלָ֖ה וָעָֽצֶם׃ [4]וְאֶלְתּוֹלַ֥ד וּבְת֖וּל וְחָרְמָֽה׃ [5]וְצִֽקְלַג֙ וּבֵֽית־הַמַּרְכָּב֔וֹת וַחֲצַ֖ר סוּסָֽה׃ [6]וּבֵ֥ית לְבָא֖וֹת וְשָֽׁרוּחֶ֑ן עָרִ֥ים שְׁלֹֽשׁ־עֶשְׂרֵ֖ה וְחַצְרֵיהֶֽן׃ [7]עַ֥יִן ׀ רִמּ֛וֹן וָעֶ֥תֶר וְעָשָׁ֖ן עָרִ֣ים אַרְבַּ֑ע וְחַצְרֵיהֶֽן׃ [8]וְכָל־הַחֲצֵרִ֗ים אֲשֶׁ֤ר סְבִיבוֹת֙ הֶֽעָרִ֣ים הָאֵ֔לֶּה עַד־בַּֽעֲלַ֥ת בְּאֵ֖ר רָ֣אמַת* נֶ֑גֶב זֹ֗את נַחֲלַ֛ת מַטֵּ֥ה בְנֵֽי־שִׁמְע֖וֹן לְמִשְׁפְּחֹתָֽם׃ [9]מֵחֶ֙בֶל֙ בְּנֵ֣י יְהוּדָ֔ה נַחֲלַ֖ת בְּנֵ֣י שִׁמְע֑וֹן כִּֽי־הָיָ֞ה חֵ֤לֶק בְּנֵֽי־יְהוּדָה֙ רַ֣ב מֵהֶ֔ם וַיִּנְחֲל֥וּ בְנֵֽי־שִׁמְע֖וֹן בְּת֥וֹךְ נַחֲלָתָֽם׃ [10]וַיַּ֙עַל֙ הַגּוֹרָ֣ל הַשְּׁלִישִׁ֔י לִבְנֵ֥י זְבוּלֻ֖ן לְמִשְׁפְּחֹתָ֑ם וַיְהִ֛י גְּב֥וּל נַחֲלָתָ֖ם עַד־שָׂרִֽיד׃ [11]וְעָלָ֨ה גְבוּלָ֥ם ׀ לַיָּ֙מָּה֙ וּמַרְעֲלָ֔ה וּפָגַ֖ע בְּדַבָּ֑שֶׁת וּפָגַע֙ אֶל־הַנַּ֔חַל אֲשֶׁ֖ר עַל־פְּנֵ֥י יָקְנְעָֽם׃ [12]וְשָׁ֣ב מִשָּׂרִ֗יד קֵ֚דְמָה מִזְרַ֣ח הַשֶּׁ֔מֶשׁ עַל־גְּב֥וּל כִּסְלֹ֖ת תָּבֹ֑ר וְיָצָ֥א אֶל־הַדָּֽבְרַ֖ת וְעָלָ֥ה יָפִֽיעַ׃ [13]וּמִשָּׁ֤ם עָבַר֙ קֵ֣דְמָה מִזְרָ֔חָה גִּתָּ֥ה חֵ֖פֶר עִתָּ֣ה קָצִ֑ין וְיָצָ֛א רִמּ֥וֹן הַמְּתֹאָ֖ר הַנֵּעָֽה׃ [14]וְנָסַ֤ב אֹתוֹ֙ הַגְּב֔וּל מִצְּפ֖וֹן חַנָּתֹ֑ן וְהָיוּ֙ תֹּֽצְאֹתָ֔יו גֵּ֖י יִפְתַּח־אֵֽל׃ [15]וְקַטָּ֤ת וְנַֽהֲלָל֙ וְשִׁמְר֔וֹן וְיִדְאֲלָ֖ה וּבֵ֣ית לָ֑חֶם עָרִ֥ים שְׁתֵּֽים־עֶשְׂרֵ֖ה וְחַצְרֵיהֶֽן׃ [16]זֹ֛את נַחֲלַ֥ת

יתיר א׳ v. 8.

---

b Heb. "the Jebusite."
c Emendation yields "and Kiriath-jearim."

a 15.30 reads "Chesil."
b-b 15.32 reads "Shilhim."
c I.e., the southern one.
d I.e., the northwest corner, opposite the starting point, Sarid.

towns, with their villages. 16That was the portion of the Zebulunites by their clans—those towns, with their villages.

17The fourth lot fell to Issachar, the Issacharites by their clans. 18Their territory comprised: Jezreel, Chesulloth, Shunem, 19Hapharaim, Shion, Anaharath, 20Rabbith, Kishion, Ebez, 21Remeth, En-gannim, En-haddah, and Beth-pazzez. 22The boundary touched Tabor, Shahazimah, and Beth-shemesh; and their boundary ran to the Jordan: 16 towns, with their villages. 23That was the portion of the tribe of the Issacharites, by their clans—the towns with their villages.

24The fifth lot fell to the tribe of the Asherites, by their clans. 25Their boundary^c ran along Helkath, Hali, Beten, Achshaph, 26Allammelech, Amad, and Mishal; and it touched Carmel on the west, and Shihor-libnath. 27It also ran^e along the east side to Beth-dagon, and touched Zebulun and the Valley of Iphtah-el to the north, [as also] Beth-emek and Neiel; ^fthen it ran to Cabul on the north,^f 28Ebron,^g Rehob, Hammon, and Kanah, up to Great Sidon. 29The boundary turned to Ramah and on to the fortified city of Tyre; then the boundary turned to Hosah ^fand it ran on westward to Mehebel,^f Achzib, 30Ummah, Aphek, and Rehob: 22 towns, with their villages. 31That was the portion of the tribe of the Asherites, by their clans—those towns, with their villages.

32The sixth lot fell to the Naphtalites, the Naphtalites by their clans. 33^hTheir boundary ran from Heleph, Elon-bezaanannim, Adami-nekeb, and Jabneel to Lakkum, and it ended at the Jordan. 34The boundary then turned westward to Aznoth-tabor and ran from there to Hukok. It touched Zebulun on the south, and it touched Asher on the west, and Judah at the

בְּנֵי־זְבוּלֻן לְמִשְׁפְּחוֹתָם הֶעָרִים הָאֵלֶּה וְחַצְרֵיהֶן: פ 17 לְיִשָּׂשכָר יָצָא הַגּוֹרָל הָרְבִיעִי לִבְנֵי יִשָּׂשכָר לְמִשְׁפְּחוֹתָם: 18 וַיְהִי גְבוּלָם יִזְרְעֶאלָה וְהַכְּסֻלֹּת וְשׁוּנֵם: 19 וַחֲפָרַיִם וְשִׁיאֹן וַאֲנָחֲרַת: 20 וְהָרַבִּית וְקִשְׁיוֹן וָאָבֶץ: 21 וְרֶמֶת וְעֵין־גַּנִּים וְעֵין חַדָּה וּבֵית פַּצֵּץ: 22 וּפָגַע הַגְּבוּל בְּתָבוֹר ושחצומה [וְשַׁחֲצִימָה] וּבֵית שֶׁמֶשׁ וְהָיוּ תֹצְאוֹת גְּבוּלָם הַיַּרְדֵּן עָרִים שֵׁשׁ־עֶשְׂרֵה וְחַצְרֵיהֶן: 23 זֹאת נַחֲלַת מַטֵּה בְנֵי־יִשָּׂשכָר לְמִשְׁפְּחֹתָם הֶעָרִים וְחַצְרֵיהֶן: פ 24 וַיֵּצֵא הַגּוֹרָל הַחֲמִישִׁי לְמַטֵּה בְנֵי־אָשֵׁר לְמִשְׁפְּחוֹתָם: 25 וַיְהִי גְּבוּלָם חֶלְקַת וַחֲלִי וָבֶטֶן וְאַכְשָׁף: 26 וְאַלַּמֶּלֶךְ וְעַמְעָד וּמִשְׁאָל וּפָגַע בְּכַרְמֶל הַיָּמָּה וּבְשִׁיחוֹר לִבְנָת: 27 וְשָׁב מִזְרַח הַשֶּׁמֶשׁ בֵּית דָּגֹן וּפָגַע בִּזְבֻלוּן וּבְגֵי יִפְתַּח־אֵל צָפוֹנָה בֵּית הָעֵמֶק וּנְעִיאֵל וְיָצָא אֶל־כָּבוּל מִשְּׂמֹאל: 28 וְעֶבְרֹן וּרְחֹב וְחַמּוֹן וְקָנָה עַד צִידוֹן רַבָּה: 29 וְשָׁב הַגְּבוּל הָרָמָה וְעַד־עִיר מִבְצַר־צֹר וְשָׁב הַגְּבוּל חֹסָה ויהיו [וְהָיוּ] תֹצְאֹתָיו הַיָּמָּה מֵחֶבֶל אַכְזִיבָה: 30 וְעֻמָה וַאֲפֵק וּרְחֹב עָרִים עֶשְׂרִים וּשְׁתַּיִם וְחַצְרֵיהֶן: 31 זֹאת נַחֲלַת מַטֵּה בְנֵי־אָשֵׁר לְמִשְׁפְּחֹתָם הֶעָרִים הָאֵלֶּה וְחַצְרֵיהֶן: פ 32 לִבְנֵי נַפְתָּלִי יָצָא הַגּוֹרָל הַשִּׁשִּׁי לִבְנֵי נַפְתָּלִי לְמִשְׁפְּחֹתָם: 33 וַיְהִי גְבוּלָם מֵחֵלֶף מֵאֵלוֹן בְּצַעֲנַנִּים וַאֲדָמִי הַנֶּקֶב וְיַבְנְאֵל עַד־לַקּוּם וַיְהִי תֹצְאֹתָיו הַיַּרְדֵּן: 34 וְשָׁב הַגְּבוּל יָמָּה אַזְנוֹת תָּבוֹר וְיָצָא מִשָּׁם חוּקֹקָה וּפָגַע בִּזְבֻלוּן מִנֶּגֶב וּבְאָשֵׁר פָּגַע מִיָּם וּבִיהוּדָה הַיַּרְדֵּן מִזְרַח הַשָּׁמֶשׁ:

---

e   I.e., from Helkath, v. 25.

f-f   Meaning of Heb. uncertain.

g   Some Heb. mss., as well as Josh. 21.30 and 1 Chron. 6.59, read "Abdon."

h   The geography of vv. 33–35 is unclear in part.

Jordan on the east. ³⁵Its fortified towns were Ziddim, Zer, Hammath, Rakkath, Chinnereth, ³⁶Adamah, Ramah, Hazor, ³⁷Kedesh, Edrei, En-hazor, ³⁸Iron, Migdal-el, Horem, Beth-anath, and Beth-shemesh: 19 towns, with their villages. ³⁹That was the portion of the tribe of the Naphtalites, by their clans—the towns, with their villages.

⁴⁰The seventh lot fell to the tribe of the Danites, by their clans. ⁴¹Their allotted territory comprised: Zorah, Eshtaol, Ir-shemesh, ⁴²Shaalabbin, Aijalon, Ithlah, ⁴³Elon, Timnah, Ekron, ⁴⁴Eltekeh, Gibbethon, Baalath, ⁴⁵Jehud, Bene-berak, Gath-rimmon, ⁴⁶Me-jarkon, and Rakkon, at the border near Joppa. ⁴⁷But the territory of the Danites slipped from their grasp. So the Danites migrated and made war on Leshem.^i They captured it and put it to the sword; they took possession of it and settled in it. And they changed the name of Leshem to Dan, after their ancestor Dan. ⁴⁸That was the portion of the tribe of the Danites, by their clans—those towns, with their villages.

⁴⁹When they had finished allotting the land by its boundaries, the Israelites gave a portion in their midst to Joshua son of Nun. ⁵⁰At the command of the LORD they gave him the town that he asked for, Timnath-serah in the hill country of Ephraim; he fortified the town and settled in it.

⁵¹These are the portions assigned by lot to the tribes of Israel by the priest Eleazar, Joshua son of Nun, and the heads of the ancestral houses, before the LORD at Shiloh, at the entrance of the Tent of Meeting.

20

When they had finished dividing the land, ¹the LORD said to Joshua: ²"Speak to the Israelites: Designate the cities of refuge—about

---

וְעָרֵי מִבְצָר הַצִּדִּים צֵר וְחַמַּת רַקַּת ³⁵
וְכִנָּֽרֶת: ³⁶ וַאֲדָמָה וְהָרָמָה וְחָצֽוֹר:
³⁷ וְקֶדֶשׁ וְאֶדְרֶעִי וְעֵין חָצֽוֹר: ³⁸ וְיִרְאוֹן
וּמִגְדַּל־אֵל חֳרֵם וּבֵית־עֲנָת וּבֵית שָׁמֶשׁ
עָרִים תְּשַׁע־עֶשְׂרֵה וְחַצְרֵיהֶֽן: ³⁹ זֹאת
נַחֲלַת מַטֵּה בְנֵי־נַפְתָּלִי לְמִשְׁפְּחֹתָם
הֶעָרִים וְחַצְרֵיהֶֽן: פ
⁴⁰ לְמַטֵּה בְנֵי־דָן לְמִשְׁפְּחֹתָם יָצָא הַגּוֹרָל
הַשְּׁבִיעִֽי: ⁴¹ וַיְהִי גְּבוּל נַחֲלָתָם צָרְעָה
וְאֶשְׁתָּאוֹל וְעִיר שָֽׁמֶשׁ: ⁴² וְשַֽׁעֲלַבִּין
וְאַיָּלוֹן וְיִתְלָֽה: ⁴³ וְאֵילוֹן וְתִמְנָתָה
וְעֶקְרֽוֹן: ⁴⁴ וְאֶלְתְּקֵה וְגִבְּתוֹן וּבַעֲלָֽת:
⁴⁵ וִיהֻד וּבְנֵי־בְרַק וְגַת־רִמּֽוֹן: ⁴⁶ וּמֵי
הַיַּרְקוֹן וְהָרַקּוֹן עִם־הַגְּבוּל מוּל יָפֽוֹ:
⁴⁷ וַיֵּצֵא גְבוּל־בְּנֵי־דָן מֵהֶם וַיַּעֲלוּ בְנֵי־דָן
וַיִּלָּחֲמוּ עִם־לֶשֶׁם וַיִּלְכְּדוּ אוֹתָהּ ׀ וַיַּכּוּ
אוֹתָהּ לְפִי־חֶרֶב וַיִּרְשׁוּ אוֹתָהּ וַיֵּשְׁבוּ בָהּ
וַיִּקְרְאוּ לְלֶשֶׁם דָּן כְּשֵׁם דָּן אֲבִיהֶֽם:
⁴⁸ זֹאת נַחֲלַת מַטֵּה בְנֵי־דָן לְמִשְׁפְּחֹתָם
הֶעָרִים הָאֵלֶּה וְחַצְרֵיהֶֽן: פ
⁴⁹ וַיְכַלּוּ לִנְחֹל־אֶת־הָאָרֶץ לִגְבֽוּלֹתֶיהָ
וַיִּתְּנוּ בְנֵי־יִשְׂרָאֵל נַחֲלָה לִיהוֹשֻׁעַ בִּן־נוּן
בְּתוֹכָֽם: ⁵⁰ עַל־פִּי יְהוָה נָתְנוּ לוֹ אֶת־
הָעִיר אֲשֶׁר שָׁאָל אֶת־תִּמְנַת־סֶרַח בְּהַר
אֶפְרָיִם וַיִּבְנֶה אֶת־הָעִיר וַיֵּשֶׁב בָּֽהּ:
⁵¹ אֵלֶּה הַנְּחָלֹת אֲשֶׁר נִחֲלוּ אֶלְעָזָר הַכֹּהֵן ׀
וִיהוֹשֻׁעַ בִּן־נוּן וְרָאשֵׁי הָאָבוֹת לְמַטּוֹת
בְּנֵי־יִשְׂרָאֵל ׀ בְּגוֹרָל ׀ בְּשִׁלֹה לִפְנֵי יְהוָה
פֶּתַח אֹהֶל מוֹעֵד

וַיְכַלּוּ מֵחַלֵּק אֶת־הָאָֽרֶץ: פ

כ

¹ וַיְדַבֵּר יְהוָה אֶל־יְהוֹשֻׁעַ לֵאמֹֽר: ² דַּבֵּר
אֶל־בְּנֵי יִשְׂרָאֵל לֵאמֹר תְּנוּ לָכֶם אֶת־עָרֵי

which I commanded you through Moses—³to which a manslayer who kills a person by mistake, unintentionally, may flee. They shall serve you as a refuge from the blood avenger. ⁴He shall flee to one of those cities, present himself at the entrance to the city gate, and plead his case before the elders of that city; and they shall admit him into the city and give him a place in which to live among them. ⁵Should the blood avenger pursue him, they shall not hand the manslayer over to him, since he killed the other person without intent and had not been his enemy in the past. ⁶He shall live in that city until he can stand trial before the assembly, [and remain there] until the death of the high priest who is in office at that time. Thereafter, the manslayer may go back to his home in his own town, to the town from which he fled."

⁷So they set aside Kedesh in the hill country of Naphtali in Galilee, Shechem in the hill country of Ephraim, and Kiriath-arba—that is, Hebron—in the hill country of Judah. ⁸And across the Jordan, east of Jericho, they assigned Bezer in the wilderness, in the Tableland, from the tribe of Reuben; Ramoth in Gilead from the tribe of Gad; and Golan in Bashan from the tribe of Manasseh. ⁹Those were the towns designated[a] for all the Israelites and for aliens residing among them, to which anyone who killed a person unintentionally might flee, and not die by the hand of the blood avenger before standing trial by the assembly.

21
The heads of the ancestral houses of the Levites approached the priest Eleazer, Joshua son of Nun, and the heads of the ancestral houses of the Israelite tribes, ²and spoke to them at Shiloh in the land of Canaan, as follows: "The LORD commanded through Moses that we be

---

הַמִּקְלָט אֲשֶׁר־דִּבַּרְתִּי אֲלֵיכֶם בְּיַד־מֹשֶׁה:
3 לָנוּס שָׁמָּה רוֹצֵחַ מַכֵּה־נֶפֶשׁ בִּשְׁגָגָה
בִּבְלִי־דָעַת וְהָיוּ לָכֶם לְמִקְלָט מִגֹּאֵל
הַדָּם: 4 וְנָס אֶל־אַחַת ׀ מֵהֶעָרִים הָאֵלֶּה
וְעָמַד פֶּתַח שַׁעַר הָעִיר וְדִבֶּר בְּאָזְנֵי זִקְנֵי
הָעִיר־הַהִיא אֶת־דְּבָרָיו וְאָסְפוּ אֹתוֹ
הָעִירָה אֲלֵיהֶם וְנָתְנוּ־לוֹ מָקוֹם וְיָשַׁב
עִמָּם: 5 וְכִי יִרְדֹּף גֹּאֵל הַדָּם אַחֲרָיו וְלֹא־
יַסְגִּרוּ אֶת־הָרֹצֵחַ בְּיָדוֹ כִּי בִבְלִי־דַעַת
הִכָּה אֶת־רֵעֵהוּ וְלֹא־שֹׂנֵא הוּא לוֹ
מִתְּמוֹל שִׁלְשׁוֹם: 6 וְיָשַׁב ׀ בָּעִיר הַהִיא
עַד־עָמְדוֹ לִפְנֵי הָעֵדָה לַמִּשְׁפָּט עַד־מוֹת
הַכֹּהֵן הַגָּדוֹל אֲשֶׁר יִהְיֶה בַּיָּמִים הָהֵם
אָז ׀ יָשׁוּב הָרוֹצֵחַ וּבָא אֶל־עִירוֹ וְאֶל־בֵּיתוֹ
אֶל־הָעִיר אֲשֶׁר־נָס מִשָּׁם:
7 וַיַּקְדִּשׁוּ אֶת־קֶדֶשׁ בַּגָּלִיל בְּהַר נַפְתָּלִי
וְאֶת־שְׁכֶם בְּהַר אֶפְרָיִם וְאֶת־קִרְיַת
אַרְבַּע הִיא חֶבְרוֹן בְּהַר יְהוּדָה: 8 וּמֵעֵבֶר
לְיַרְדֵּן יְרִיחוֹ מִזְרָחָה נָתְנוּ אֶת־בֶּצֶר
בַּמִּדְבָּר בַּמִּישֹׁר מִמַּטֵּה רְאוּבֵן וְאֶת־
רָאמֹת בַּגִּלְעָד מִמַּטֵּה־גָד וְאֶת־גֹלָן גּוֹלָן
בַּבָּשָׁן מִמַּטֵּה מְנַשֶּׁה: 9 אֵלֶּה הָיוּ עָרֵי
הַמּוּעָדָה לְכֹל ׀ בְּנֵי יִשְׂרָאֵל וְלַגֵּר הַגָּר
בְּתוֹכָם לָנוּס שָׁמָּה כָּל־מַכֵּה־נֶפֶשׁ בִּשְׁגָגָה
וְלֹא יָמוּת בְּיַד גֹּאֵל הַדָּם עַד־עָמְדוֹ לִפְנֵי
הָעֵדָה: פ

כא וַיִּגְּשׁוּ רָאשֵׁי אֲבוֹת הַלְוִיִּם
אֶל־אֶלְעָזָר הַכֹּהֵן וְאֶל־יְהוֹשֻׁעַ בִּן־נוּן
וְאֶל־רָאשֵׁי אֲבוֹת הַמַּטּוֹת לִבְנֵי יִשְׂרָאֵל:
2 וַיְדַבְּרוּ אֲלֵיהֶם בְּשִׁלֹה בְּאֶרֶץ כְּנַעַן
לֵאמֹר יְהוָה צִוָּה בְיַד־מֹשֶׁה לָתֶת־לָנוּ

---

a Meaning of Heb. uncertain.

given towns to live in, along with their pastures for our livestock." ³So the Israelites, in accordance with the LORD's command, assigned to the Levites, out of their own portions, the following towns with their pastures:

⁴The [first] lot among the Levites fell to the Kohathite clans. To the descendants of the priest Aaron, there fell by lot 13 towns from the tribe of Judah, the tribe of Simeon, and the tribe of Benjamin; ⁵and to the remaining Kohathites [there fell] by lot 10 towns from the clans of the tribe of Ephraim, the tribe of Dan, and the half-tribe of Manasseh.

⁶To the Gershonites [there fell] by lot 13 towns from the clans of the tribe of Issachar, the tribe of Asher, the tribe of Naphtali, and the half-tribe of Manasseh in Bashan.

⁷[And] to the Merarites, by their clans—12 towns from the tribe of Reuben, the tribe of Gad, and the tribe of Zebulun. ⁸The Israelites assigned those towns with their pastures by lot to the Levites—as the LORD had commanded through Moses.

⁹From the tribe of the Judites and the tribe of the Simeonites were assigned the following towns, which will be listed by name; ¹⁰they went to the descendants of Aaron among the Kohathite clans of the Levites, for the first lot had fallen to them. ¹¹To them were assigned in the hill country of Judah Kiriath-arba—that is, Hebron—together with the pastures around it. [Arba was] the father of the Anokites.ᵃ ¹²They gave the fields and the villages of the town to Caleb son of Jephunneh as his holding. ¹³But to the descendants of Aaron the priest they assigned Hebron—the city of refuge for manslayers—together with its pastures, Libnah with its pastures, ¹⁴Jattir with its pastures, Eshtemoa with its pastures, ¹⁵Holon with its

---

ᵃ *Elsewhere Anakites; cf. Num. 13.22; Deut. 9.2.*

עָרִים לָשֶׁבֶת וּמִגְרְשֵׁיהֶן לִבְהֶמְתֵּנוּ: 3 וַיִּתְּנוּ בְנֵי־יִשְׂרָאֵל לַלְוִיִּם מִנַּחֲלָתָם אֶל־פִּי יְהוָה אֶת־הֶעָרִים הָאֵלֶּה וְאֶת־מִגְרְשֵׁיהֶן:

4 וַיֵּצֵא הַגּוֹרָל לְמִשְׁפְּחֹת הַקְּהָתִי וַיְהִי לִבְנֵי אַהֲרֹן הַכֹּהֵן מִן־הַלְוִיִּם מִמַּטֵּה יְהוּדָה וּמִמַּטֵּה הַשִּׁמְעֹנִי וּמִמַּטֵּה בִנְיָמִן בַּגּוֹרָל עָרִים שְׁלֹשׁ עֶשְׂרֵה: ס 5 וְלִבְנֵי קְהָת הַנּוֹתָרִים מִמִּשְׁפְּחֹת מַטֵּה־אֶפְרַיִם וּמִמַּטֵּה־דָן וּמֵחֲצִי מַטֵּה מְנַשֶּׁה בַּגּוֹרָל עָרִים עָשֶׂר: ס

6 וְלִבְנֵי גֵרְשׁוֹן מִמִּשְׁפְּחוֹת מַטֵּה־יִשָּׂשכָר וּמִמַּטֵּה־אָשֵׁר וּמִמַּטֵּה נַפְתָּלִי וּמֵחֲצִי מַטֵּה מְנַשֶּׁה בַבָּשָׁן בַּגּוֹרָל עָרִים שְׁלֹשׁ עֶשְׂרֵה: ס

7 לִבְנֵי מְרָרִי לְמִשְׁפְּחֹתָם מִמַּטֵּה רְאוּבֵן וּמִמַּטֵּה־גָד וּמִמַּטֵּה זְבוּלֻן עָרִים שְׁתֵּים עֶשְׂרֵה: 8 וַיִּתְּנוּ בְנֵי־יִשְׂרָאֵל לַלְוִיִּם אֶת־הֶעָרִים הָאֵלֶּה וְאֶת־מִגְרְשֵׁיהֶן כַּאֲשֶׁר צִוָּה יְהוָה בְּיַד־מֹשֶׁה בַּגּוֹרָל: פ

9 וַיִּתְּנוּ מִמַּטֵּה בְּנֵי יְהוּדָה וּמִמַּטֵּה בְּנֵי שִׁמְעוֹן אֵת הֶעָרִים הָאֵלֶּה אֲשֶׁר־יִקְרָא אֶתְהֶן בְּשֵׁם: 10 וַיְהִי לִבְנֵי אַהֲרֹן מִמִּשְׁפְּחוֹת הַקְּהָתִי מִבְּנֵי לֵוִי כִּי לָהֶם הָיָה הַגּוֹרָל רִיאשֹׁנָה: 11 וַיִּתְּנוּ לָהֶם אֶת־קִרְיַת אַרְבַּע אֲבִי הָעֲנוֹק הִיא חֶבְרוֹן בְּהַר יְהוּדָה וְאֶת־מִגְרָשֶׁהָ סְבִיבֹתֶיהָ: 12 וְאֶת־שְׂדֵה הָעִיר וְאֶת־חֲצֵרֶיהָ נָתְנוּ לְכָלֵב בֶּן־יְפֻנֶּה בַּאֲחֻזָּתוֹ: ס 13 וְלִבְנֵי | אַהֲרֹן הַכֹּהֵן נָתְנוּ אֶת־עִיר מִקְלַט הָרֹצֵחַ אֶת־חֶבְרוֹן וְאֶת־מִגְרָשֶׁהָ וְאֶת־לִבְנָה וְאֶת־מִגְרָשֶׁהָ: 14 וְאֶת־יַתִּר וְאֶת־מִגְרָשֶׁהָ וְאֶת־אֶשְׁתְּמֹעַ וְאֶת־מִגְרָשֶׁהָ: 15 וְאֶת־חֹלֹן

pastures, Debir with its pastures, ¹⁶Ain with its pastures, Juttah with its pastures, and Beth-shemesh with its pastures—9 towns from those two tribes. ¹⁷And from the tribe of Benjamin: Gibeon with its pastures, Geba with its pastures, ¹⁸Anathoth with its pastures, and Almon with its pastures—4 towns. ¹⁹All the towns of the descendants of the priest Aaron, 13 towns with their pastures.

^{20b}As for the other clans of the Kohathites, the remaining Levites descended from Kohath, the towns in their lot were: From the tribe of Ephraim ²¹they were given, in the hill country of Ephraim, Shechem—the city of refuge for manslayers—with its pastures, Gezer with its pastures, ²²Kibzaim with its pastures, and Beth-horon with its pastures—4 towns. ²³From the tribe of Dan, Elteke with its pastures, Gibbethon with its pastures, ²⁴Aijalon with its pastures, and Gath-rimmon with its pastures—4 towns. ²⁵And from the half-tribe of Manasseh, Taanach with its pastures, and Gath-rimmon with its pastures—2 towns. ²⁶All the towns for the remaining clans of the Kohathites came to 10, with their pastures.

²⁷To the Gershonites of the levitical clans: From the half-tribe of Manasseh, Golan in Bashan—the city of refuge for manslayers—with its pastures, and Beeshterah with its pastures—2 towns. ²⁸From the tribe of Issachar: Kishion with its pastures, Dobrath with its pastures, ²⁹Jarmuth with its pastures, and Engannim with its pastures—4 towns. ³⁰From the tribe of Asher: Mishal with its pastures, Abdon with its pastures, ³¹Helkath with its pastures, and Rehob with its pastures—4 towns. ³²From the tribe of Naphtali, Kedesh in Galilee—the city of refuge for manslayers—with its pastures, Hammoth-dor with its pastures, and Kartan

---

b   *Explicating v. 5.*

וְאֶת־מִגְרָשֶׁהָ וְאֶת־דְּבִר וְאֶת־מִגְרָשֶׁהָ:
16 וְאֶת־עַיִן וְאֶת־מִגְרָשֶׁהָ וְאֶת־יֻטָּה וְאֶת־
מִגְרָשֶׁהָ אֶת־בֵּית שֶׁמֶשׁ וְאֶת־מִגְרָשֶׁהָ
עָרִים תֵּשַׁע מֵאֵת שְׁנֵי הַשְּׁבָטִים
הָאֵלֶּה: פ 17 וּמִמַּטֵּה בִנְיָמִן אֶת־גִּבְעוֹן
וְאֶת־מִגְרָשֶׁהָ אֶת־גֶּבַע וְאֶת־מִגְרָשֶׁהָ:
18 אֶת־עֲנָתוֹת וְאֶת־מִגְרָשֶׁהָ וְאֶת־עַלְמוֹן
וְאֶת־מִגְרָשֶׁהָ עָרִים אַרְבַּע: 19 כָּל־עָרֵי
בְנֵי־אַהֲרֹן הַכֹּהֲנִים שְׁלֹשׁ־עֶשְׂרֵה עָרִים
וּמִגְרְשֵׁיהֶן: ס
20 וּלְמִשְׁפְּחוֹת בְּנֵי־קְהָת הַלְוִיִּם הַנּוֹתָרִים
מִבְּנֵי קְהָת וַיְהִי עָרֵי גוֹרָלָם מִמַּטֵּה
אֶפְרָיִם: 21 וַיִּתְּנוּ לָהֶם אֶת־עִיר
מִקְלַט הָרֹצֵחַ אֶת־שְׁכֶם וְאֶת־מִגְרָשֶׁהָ
בְּהַר אֶפְרָיִם וְאֶת־גֶּזֶר וְאֶת־מִגְרָשֶׁהָ:
22 וְאֶת־קִבְצַיִם וְאֶת־מִגְרָשֶׁהָ וְאֶת־בֵּית
חוֹרֹן וְאֶת־מִגְרָשֶׁהָ עָרִים אַרְבַּע: ס
23 וּמִמַּטֵּה־דָן אֶת־אֶלְתְּקֵא וְאֶת־מִגְרָשֶׁהָ
אֶת־גִּבְּתוֹן וְאֶת־מִגְרָשֶׁהָ: 24 אֶת־אַיָּלוֹן
וְאֶת־מִגְרָשֶׁהָ אֶת־גַּת־רִמּוֹן וְאֶת־מִגְרָשֶׁהָ
עָרִים אַרְבַּע: ס 25 וּמִמַּחֲצִית מַטֵּה
מְנַשֶּׁה אֶת־תַּעְנַךְ וְאֶת־מִגְרָשֶׁהָ וְאֶת־גַּת־
רִמּוֹן וְאֶת־מִגְרָשֶׁהָ עָרִים שְׁתָּיִם: 26 כָּל־
עָרִים עֶשֶׂר וּמִגְרְשֵׁיהֶן לְמִשְׁפְּחוֹת בְּנֵי־
קְהָת הַנּוֹתָרִים: ס
27 וְלִבְנֵי גֵרְשׁוֹן מִמִּשְׁפְּחֹת הַלְוִיִּם מֵחֲצִי
מַטֵּה מְנַשֶּׁה אֶת־עִיר מִקְלַט הָרֹצֵחַ אֶת־
גֹּלָן בַּבָּשָׁן וְאֶת־מִגְרָשֶׁהָ וְאֶת־
בְּעֶשְׁתְּרָה וְאֶת־מִגְרָשֶׁהָ עָרִים שְׁתָּיִם: ס
28 וּמִמַּטֵּה יִשָּׂשכָר אֶת־קִשְׁיוֹן וְאֶת־
מִגְרָשֶׁהָ אֶת־דָּבְרַת וְאֶת־מִגְרָשֶׁהָ: 29 אֶת־
יַרְמוּת וְאֶת־מִגְרָשֶׁהָ אֶת־עֵין גַּנִּים וְאֶת־
מִגְרָשֶׁהָ עָרִים אַרְבַּע: ס 30 וּמִמַּטֵּה
אָשֵׁר אֶת־מִשְׁאָל וְאֶת־מִגְרָשֶׁהָ אֶת־עַבְדּוֹן
וְאֶת־מִגְרָשֶׁהָ: 31 אֶת־חֶלְקָת וְאֶת־
מִגְרָשֶׁהָ וְאֶת־רְחֹב וְאֶת־מִגְרָשֶׁהָ עָרִים

with its pastures—3 towns. ³³All the towns of the Gershonites, by their clans, came to 13 towns, with their pastures.

³⁴To the remaining Levites, the clans of the Merarites: From the tribe of Zebulun, Jokneam with its pastures, Kartah with its pastures, ³⁵Dimnah with its pastures, and Nahalal with its pastures—4 towns.ᶜ ³⁶From the tribe of Gad, Ramoth in Gilead—the city of refuge for manslayers—with its pastures, Mahanaim with its pastures, ³⁷Heshbon with its pastures, and Jazer with its pastures—4 towns in all. ³⁸All the towns which went by lot to the Merarites, by their clans—the rest of the levitical clans—came to 12 towns. ³⁹All the towns of the Levites within the holdings of the Israelites came to 48 towns, with their pastures. ⁴⁰ᵈ Thus those towns were assigned, every town with its surrounding pasture; and so it was with all those towns.

⁴¹The Lᴏʀᴅ gave to Israel the whole country which He had sworn to their fathers that He would assign to them; they took possession of it and settled in it. ⁴²The Lᴏʀᴅ gave them rest on all sides, just as He had promised to their fathers on oath. Not one man of all their enemies withstood them; the Lᴏʀᴅ delivered all their enemies into their hands. ⁴³Not one of the good things which the Lᴏʀᴅ had promised to the House of Israel was lacking. Everything was fulfilled.

22

Then Joshua summoned the Reubenites, the Gadites, and the half-tribe of Manasseh, ²and said to them, "You have observed all that

אַרְבַּע: ס 32 וּמִמַּטֵּה נַפְתָּלִי אֶת־עִיר ׀ מִקְלַט הָרֹצֵחַ אֶת־קֶדֶשׁ בַּגָּלִיל וְאֶת־מִגְרָשֶׁהָ וְאֶת־חַמֹּת דֹּאר וְאֶת־מִגְרָשֶׁהָ וְאֶת־קַרְתָּן וְאֶת־מִגְרָשֶׁהָ עָרִים שָׁלֹשׁ: 33 כָּל־עָרֵי הַגֵּרְשֻׁנִּי לְמִשְׁפְּחֹתָם שְׁלֹשׁ עֶשְׂרֵה עִיר וּמִגְרְשֵׁיהֶן: ס 34 וּלְמִשְׁפְּחוֹת בְּנֵי־מְרָרִי הַלְוִיִּם הַנּוֹתָרִים מֵאֵת מַטֵּה זְבוּלֻן אֶת־יָקְנְעָם וְאֶת־מִגְרָשֶׁהָ אֶת־קַרְתָּה וְאֶת־מִגְרָשֶׁהָ: 35 אֶת־דִּמְנָה וְאֶת־מִגְרָשֶׁהָ אֶת־נַהֲלָל וְאֶת־מִגְרָשֶׁהָ עָרִים אַרְבַּע: ס 36 *וּמִמַּטֵּה־גָד אֶת־עִיר מִקְלַט הָרֹצֵחַ אֶת־רָמֹת בַּגִּלְעָד וְאֶת־מִגְרָשֶׁהָ וְאֶת־מַחֲנַיִם וְאֶת־מִגְרָשֶׁהָ: 37 אֶת־חֶשְׁבּוֹן וְאֶת־מִגְרָשֶׁהָ אֶת־יַעְזֵר וְאֶת־מִגְרָשֶׁהָ כָּל־עָרִים אַרְבַּע: 38 כָּל־הֶעָרִים לִבְנֵי מְרָרִי לְמִשְׁפְּחֹתָם הַנּוֹתָרִים מִמִּשְׁפְּחוֹת הַלְוִיִּם וַיְהִי גּוֹרָלָם עָרִים שְׁתֵּים עֶשְׂרֵה: 39 כֹּל עָרֵי הַלְוִיִּם בְּתוֹךְ אֲחֻזַּת בְּנֵי־יִשְׂרָאֵל עָרִים אַרְבָּעִים וּשְׁמֹנֶה וּמִגְרְשֵׁיהֶן: 40 תִּהְיֶינָה הֶעָרִים הָאֵלֶּה עִיר עִיר וּמִגְרָשֶׁיהָ סְבִיבֹתֶיהָ כֵּן לְכָל־הֶעָרִים הָאֵלֶּה: ס 41 וַיִּתֵּן יְהֹוָה לְיִשְׂרָאֵל אֶת־כָּל־הָאָרֶץ אֲשֶׁר נִשְׁבַּע לָתֵת לַאֲבוֹתָם וַיִּרָשׁוּהָ וַיֵּשְׁבוּ בָהּ: 42 וַיָּנַח יְהֹוָה לָהֶם מִסָּבִיב כְּכֹל אֲשֶׁר־נִשְׁבַּע לַאֲבוֹתָם וְלֹא־עָמַד אִישׁ בִּפְנֵיהֶם מִכָּל־אֹיְבֵיהֶם אֵת כָּל־אֹיְבֵיהֶם נָתַן יְהֹוָה בְּיָדָם: 43 לֹא־נָפַל דָּבָר מִכֹּל הַדָּבָר הַטּוֹב אֲשֶׁר־דִּבֶּר יְהֹוָה אֶל־בֵּית יִשְׂרָאֵל הַכֹּל בָּא: פ

כב

אָז יִקְרָא יְהוֹשֻׁעַ לָרְאוּבֵנִי וְלַגָּדִי וְלַחֲצִי מַטֵּה מְנַשֶּׁה: 2 וַיֹּאמֶר אֲלֵיהֶם אַתֶּם שְׁמַרְתֶּם אֵת כָּל־אֲשֶׁר צִוָּה אֶתְכֶם

ᶜ Some mss. and editions add the following (cf. 1 Chron. 6.63–64): "And from the tribe of Reuben: Bezer with its pastures, Jahaz with its pastures, Kedemoth with its pastures, and Mephaath with its pastures—4 towns."

ᵈ Meaning of verse uncertain.

v. 36. כאן נתחבר שני פסוקים במהדורת שטוטגארט על פי נוסח אחר, אז בשאר הפרק גורמים לשינוי פסוקים כנסֿפר

Moses the servant of the Lord commanded you, and have obeyed me in everything that I commanded you. [3]You have not forsaken your kinsmen through the long years down to this day, but have faithfully observed the Instruction of the Lord your God. [4]Now the Lord your God has given your kinsmen rest, as He promised them. Therefore turn and go to your homes, to the land of your holdings beyond the Jordan that Moses the servant of the Lord assigned to you. [5]But be very careful to fulfill the Instruction and the Teaching that Moses the servant of the Lord enjoined upon you, to love the Lord your God and to walk in all His ways, and to keep His commandments and hold fast to Him, and to serve Him with all your heart and soul." [6]Then Joshua blessed them and dismissed them, and they went to their homes.

[7]To the one half-tribe of Manasseh Moses had assigned territory in Bashan, and to the other Joshua assigned [territory] on the west side of the Jordan, with their kinsmen.[a]

Furthermore, when Joshua sent them[b] off to their homes, he blessed them [8]and said to them, "Return to your homes with great wealth—with very much livestock, with silver and gold, with copper and iron, and with a great quantity of clothing. Share the spoil of your enemies with your kinsmen." [9]So the Reubenites, the Gadites, and the half-tribe of Manasseh left the Israelites at Shiloh, in the land of Canaan, and made their way back to the land of Gilead, the land of their own holding, which they had acquired by the command of the Lord through Moses. [10]When they came to the region of the Jordan in the land of Canaan, the Reubenites and the Gadites and the half-tribe of Manasseh built an altar there by the Jordan, a great conspicuous altar.

[11]A report reached the Israelites: "The Reubenites, the Gadites, and the half-tribe of

מֹשֶׁ֛ה עֶ֥בֶד יְהֹוָ֖ה וַתִּשְׁמְע֣וּ בְקוֹלִ֔י לְכֹ֥ל
אֲשֶׁר־צִוִּ֖יתִי אֶתְכֶֽם: 3 לֹֽא־עֲזַבְתֶּ֣ם אֶת־
אֲחֵיכֶ֗ם זֶ֚ה יָמִ֣ים רַבִּ֔ים עַ֖ד הַיּ֣וֹם הַזֶּ֑ה
וּשְׁמַרְתֶּ֕ם אֶת־מִשְׁמֶ֕רֶת מִצְוַ֖ת יְהֹוָ֥ה
אֱלֹהֵיכֶֽם: 4 וְעַתָּ֗ה הֵנִ֨יחַ יְהֹוָ֤ה אֱלֹֽהֵיכֶם֙
לַֽאֲחֵיכֶ֔ם כַּֽאֲשֶׁ֖ר דִּבֶּ֣ר לָהֶ֑ם וְעַתָּ֡ה פְּנ֣וּ
וּלְכ֣וּ לָכֶ֣ם לְאָהֳלֵיכֶ֗ם אֶל־אֶ֙רֶץ֙ אֲחֻזַּתְכֶ֔ם
אֲשֶׁ֣ר ׀ נָתַ֣ן לָכֶ֗ם מֹשֶׁה֙ עֶ֣בֶד יְהֹוָ֔ה בְּעֵ֖בֶר
הַיַּרְדֵּֽן: 5 רַ֣ק ׀ שִׁמְר֣וּ מְאֹ֗ד לַֽעֲשׂ֣וֹת אֶת־
הַמִּצְוָ֣ה וְאֶת־הַתּוֹרָה֮ אֲשֶׁ֣ר צִוָּ֣ה אֶתְכֶם֒
מֹשֶׁה֙ עֶֽבֶד־יְהֹוָ֔ה לְאַֽהֲבָ֞ה אֶת־יְהֹוָ֣ה
אֱלֹֽהֵיכֶ֗ם וְלָלֶ֤כֶת בְּכָל־דְּרָכָיו֙ וְלִשְׁמֹ֣ר
מִצְוֺתָ֔יו וּלְדָבְקָה־ב֑וֹ וּלְעָבְד֕וֹ בְּכָל־לְבַבְכֶ֖ם
וּבְכָל־נַפְשְׁכֶֽם: 6 וַיְבָרֲכֵ֖ם יְהוֹשֻׁ֑עַ וַֽיְשַׁלְּחֵ֔ם
וַיֵּלְכ֖וּ אֶל־אָהֳלֵיהֶֽם: ס
7 וְלַֽחֲצִ֣י ׀ שֵׁ֣בֶט הַֽמְנַשֶּׁ֗ה נָתַ֣ן מֹשֶׁה֮ בַּבָּשָׁן֒
וּלְחֶצְי֗וֹ נָתַ֤ן יְהוֹשֻׁ֙עַ֙ עִם־אֲחֵיהֶ֔ם מֵעֵ֥בֶר
בְּעֵ֖בֶר הַיַּרְדֵּ֣ן יָ֑מָּה
וְגַ֣ם כִּ֣י שִׁלְּחָ֧ם יְהוֹשֻׁ֛עַ אֶל־אָֽהֳלֵיהֶ֖ם
וַֽיְבָרֲכֵֽם: 8 וַיֹּ֨אמֶר אֲלֵיהֶ֜ם לֵאמֹ֗ר בִּנְכָסִ֨ים
רַבִּ֜ים שׁ֣וּבוּ אֶל־אָֽהֳלֵיכֶ֗ם וּבְמִקְנֶ֣ה רַב־
מְאֹ֣ד בְּכֶ֤סֶף וּבְזָהָב֙ וּבִנְחֹ֣שֶׁת וּבְבַרְזֶ֔ל
וּבִשְׂלָמ֖וֹת הַרְבֵּ֣ה מְאֹ֑ד חִלְק֥וּ שְׁלַל־
אֹֽיְבֵיכֶ֖ם עִם־אֲחֵיכֶֽם: פ 9 וַיָּשֻׁ֣בוּ וַיֵּֽלְכ֡וּ
בְּנֵֽי־רְאוּבֵ֨ן וּבְנֵי־גָ֜ד וַֽחֲצִ֣י ׀ שֵׁ֣בֶט הַֽמְנַשֶּׁ֗ה
מֵאֵת֙ בְּנֵ֣י יִשְׂרָאֵ֔ל מִשִּׁלֹ֖ה אֲשֶׁ֣ר בְּאֶֽרֶץ־
כְּנָ֑עַן לָלֶ֜כֶת אֶל־אֶ֤רֶץ הַגִּלְעָד֙ אֶל־אֶ֣רֶץ
אֲחֻזָּתָ֔ם אֲשֶׁ֥ר נֹֽאחֲזוּ־בָ֖הּ עַל־פִּ֥י יְהֹוָ֖ה
בְּיַד־מֹשֶֽׁה: 10 וַיָּבֹ֙אוּ֙ אֶל־גְּלִיל֣וֹת הַיַּרְדֵּ֔ן
אֲשֶׁ֖ר בְּאֶ֣רֶץ כְּנָ֑עַן וַיִּבְנ֣וּ בְנֵֽי־רְאוּבֵ֣ן וּבְנֵי־
גָ֡ד וַֽחֲצִי֩ שֵׁ֨בֶט הַֽמְנַשֶּׁ֜ה שָׁ֤ם מִזְבֵּ֙חַ֙ עַל־
הַיַּרְדֵּ֔ן מִזְבֵּ֥חַ גָּד֖וֹל לְמַרְאֶֽה:
11 וַיִּשְׁמְע֥וּ בְנֵֽי־יִשְׂרָאֵ֖ל לֵאמֹ֑ר הִנֵּ֣ה בָנ֣וּ
בְנֵֽי־רְאוּבֵ֣ן וּבְנֵי־גָ֗ד וַֽחֲצִי֙ שֵׁ֣בֶט הַֽמְנַשֶּׁ֔ה

---

a   I.e., the other nine tribes.
b   I.e., the two and a half tribes.

Manasseh have built an altar opposite the land of Canaan, in the region of the Jordan, across from the Israelites." [12]When the Israelites heard this, the whole community of the Israelites assembled at Shiloh to make war on them. [13]But [first] the Israelites sent the priest Phinehas son of Eleazar to the Reubenites, the Gadites, and the half-tribe of Manasseh in the land of Gilead, [14]accompanied by ten chieftains, one chieftain from each ancestral house of each of the tribes of Israel; they were every one of them heads of ancestral houses of the contingents of Israel. [15]When they came to the Reubenites, the Gadites, and the half-tribe of Manasseh in the land of Gilead, they spoke to them as follows:

[16]"Thus said the whole community of the Lord: What is this treachery that you have committed this day against the God of Israel, turning away from the Lord, building yourselves an altar and rebelling this day against the Lord! [17]Is the sin of Peor, which brought a plague upon the community of the Lord, such a small thing to us? We have not cleansed ourselves from it to this very day; [18]and now you would turn away from the Lord! If you rebel against the Lord today, tomorrow He will be angry with the whole community of Israel. [19]If it is because the land of your holding is unclean, cross over into the land of the Lord's own holding, where the Tabernacle of the Lord abides, and acquire holdings among us. But do not rebel against the Lord, and do not rebel against us by building for yourselves an altar other than the altar of the Lord our God. [20]When Achan son of Zerah violated the proscription, anger struck the whole community of Israel; he was not the only one who perished for that sin."

[21]The Reubenites, the Gadites, and the half-tribe of Manasseh replied to the heads of the contingents of Israel: They said, [22]"God, the Lord God! God, the Lord God! He knows, and

אֶת־הַמִּזְבֵּחַ אֶל־מוּל אֶרֶץ כְּנַעַן אֶל־ גְּלִילוֹת הַיַּרְדֵּן אֶל־עֵבֶר בְּנֵי יִשְׂרָאֵל: [12]וַיִּשְׁמְעוּ בְּנֵי יִשְׂרָאֵל וַיִּקָּהֲלוּ כָּל־ עֲדַת בְּנֵי־יִשְׂרָאֵל שִׁלֹה לַעֲלוֹת עֲלֵיהֶם לַצָּבָא: פ [13]וַיִּשְׁלְחוּ בְנֵי־יִשְׂרָאֵל אֶל־ בְּנֵי־רְאוּבֵן וְאֶל־בְּנֵי־גָד וְאֶל־חֲצִי שֵׁבֶט־ מְנַשֶּׁה אֶל־אֶרֶץ הַגִּלְעָד אֶת־פִּינְחָס בֶּן־ אֶלְעָזָר הַכֹּהֵן: [14]וַעֲשָׂרָה נְשִׂאִים עִמּוֹ נָשִׂיא אֶחָד נָשִׂיא אֶחָד לְבֵית אָב לְכֹל מַטּוֹת יִשְׂרָאֵל וְאִישׁ רֹאשׁ בֵּית־אֲבוֹתָם הֵמָּה לְאַלְפֵי יִשְׂרָאֵל: [15]וַיָּבֹאוּ אֶל־בְּנֵי־ רְאוּבֵן וְאֶל־בְּנֵי־גָד וְאֶל־חֲצִי שֵׁבֶט־מְנַשֶּׁה אֶל־אֶרֶץ הַגִּלְעָד וַיְדַבְּרוּ אִתָּם לֵאמֹר: [16]כֹּה אָמְרוּ כֹּל ׀ עֲדַת יְהוָה מָה־הַמַּעַל הַזֶּה אֲשֶׁר מְעַלְתֶּם בֵּאלֹהֵי יִשְׂרָאֵל לָשׁוּב הַיּוֹם מֵאַחֲרֵי יְהוָה בִּבְנוֹתְכֶם לָכֶם מִזְבֵּחַ לִמְרָדְכֶם הַיּוֹם בַּיהוָה: [17]הַמְעַט־לָנוּ אֶת־עֲוֹן פְּעוֹר אֲשֶׁר לֹא־הִטַּהַרְנוּ מִמֶּנּוּ עַד הַיּוֹם הַזֶּה וַיְהִי הַנֶּגֶף בַּעֲדַת יְהוָה: [18]וְאַתֶּם תָּשֻׁבוּ הַיּוֹם מֵאַחֲרֵי יְהוָה וְהָיָה אַתֶּם תִּמְרְדוּ הַיּוֹם בַּיהוָה וּמָחָר אֶל־כָּל־ עֲדַת יִשְׂרָאֵל יִקְצֹף: [19]וְאַךְ אִם־טְמֵאָה אֶרֶץ אֲחֻזַּתְכֶם עִבְרוּ לָכֶם אֶל־אֶרֶץ אֲחֻזַּת יְהוָה אֲשֶׁר שָׁכַן־שָׁם מִשְׁכַּן יְהוָה וְהֵאָחֲזוּ בְּתוֹכֵנוּ וּבַיהוָה אַל־תִּמְרֹדוּ וְאֹתָנוּ אַל־ תִּמְרֹדוּ בִּבְנֹתְכֶם לָכֶם מִזְבֵּחַ מִבַּלְעֲדֵי מִזְבַּח יְהוָה אֱלֹהֵינוּ: [20]הֲלוֹא ׀ עָכָן בֶּן־זֶרַח מָעַל מַעַל בַּחֵרֶם וְעַל־כָּל־עֲדַת יִשְׂרָאֵל הָיָה קָצֶף וְהוּא אִישׁ אֶחָד לֹא גָוַע בַּעֲוֹנוֹ: פ [21]וַיַּעֲנוּ בְּנֵי־רְאוּבֵן וּבְנֵי־גָד וַחֲצִי שֵׁבֶט הַמְנַשֶּׁה וַיְדַבְּרוּ אֶת־רָאשֵׁי אַלְפֵי יִשְׂרָאֵל: [22]אֵל ׀ אֱלֹהִים ׀ יְהוָה אֵל ׀ אֱלֹהִים ׀ יְהוָה הוּא יֹדֵעַ וְיִשְׂרָאֵל הוּא יֵדָע אִם־

Israel too shall know! If we acted in rebellion or in treachery against the Lord, do not vindicate us this day! 23If we built an altar to turn away from the Lord, if it was to offer burnt offerings or meal offerings upon it, or to present sacrifices of well-being upon it, may the Lord Himself demand [a reckoning]. 24We did this thing only out of our concern that, in time to come, your children might say to our children, 'What have you to do with the Lord, the God of Israel? 25The Lord has made the Jordan a boundary between you and us, O Reubenites and Gadites; you have no share in the Lord!' Thus your children might prevent our children from worshiping the Lord. 26So we decided to provide [a witness] for ourselves by building an altar—not for burnt offerings or [other] sacrifices, 27but as a witness between you and us, and between the generations to come—that we may perform the service of the Lord before Him[c] with our burnt offerings, our sacrifices, and our offerings of well-being; and that your children should not say to our children in time to come, 'You have no share in the Lord.' 28We reasoned: should they speak thus to us and to our children in time to come, we would reply, 'See the replica of the Lord's altar,[c] which our fathers made—not for burnt offerings or sacrifices, but as a witness between you and us.' 29Far be it from us to rebel against the Lord, or to turn away this day from the Lord and build an altar for burnt offerings, meal offerings, and sacrifices other than the altar of the Lord our God which stands before His Tabernacle."

30When the priest Phinehas and the chieftains of the community—the heads of the contingents of Israel—who were with him heard the explanation given by the Reubenites, the Gadites, and the Manassites, they approved. 31The priest Phinehas son of Eleazar said to the

---

c *I.e., at Shiloh.*

בְּמֶ֣רֶד וְאִם־בְּמַ֘עַל֮ בַּֽיהוָה֒ אַל־תּוֹשִׁיעֵ֖נוּ הַיּ֣וֹם הַזֶּֽה׃ 23 לִבְנ֥וֹת לָ֙נוּ֙ מִזְבֵּ֔חַ לָשׁ֖וּב מֵאַחֲרֵ֣י יְהוָ֑ה וְאִם־לְהַעֲל֨וֹת עָלָ֜יו עוֹלָ֣ה וּמִנְחָ֗ה וְאִם־לַעֲשׂ֤וֹת עָלָיו֙ זִבְחֵ֣י שְׁלָמִ֔ים יְהוָ֖ה ה֥וּא יְבַקֵּֽשׁ׃ 24 וְאִם־לֹ֤א מִדְּאָגָ֨ה מִדָּבָ֜ר עָשִׂ֤ינוּ אֶת־זֹאת֙ לֵאמֹ֔ר מָחָ֗ר יֹאמְר֤וּ בְנֵיכֶם֙ לְבָנֵ֔ינוּ לֵאמֹ֕ר מַה־לָּכֶ֖ם וְלַֽיהוָ֥ה אֱלֹהֵ֥י יִשְׂרָאֵֽל׃ 25 וּגְב֣וּל נָֽתַן־יְ֠הוָה בֵּינֵ֙נוּ וּבֵינֵיכֶ֜ם בְּנֵי־רְאוּבֵ֤ן וּבְנֵי־גָד֙ אֶת־הַיַּרְדֵּ֔ן אֵין־לָכֶ֥ם חֵ֖לֶק בַּֽיהוָ֑ה וְהִשְׁבִּ֤יתוּ בְנֵיכֶם֙ אֶת־בָּנֵ֔ינוּ לְבִלְתִּ֖י יְרֹ֥א אֶת־יְהוָֽה׃ 26 וַנֹּ֕אמֶר נַעֲשֶׂה־נָּ֣א לָ֔נוּ לִבְנ֖וֹת אֶת־הַמִּזְבֵּ֑חַ לֹ֥א לְעוֹלָ֖ה וְלֹ֥א לְזָֽבַח׃ 27 כִּי֩ עֵ֨ד ה֜וּא בֵּינֵ֣ינוּ וּבֵינֵיכֶ֗ם וּבֵ֣ין דֹּרוֹתֵ֘ינוּ֮ אַחֲרֵ֒ינוּ֒ לַעֲבֹ֞ד אֶת־עֲבֹדַ֤ת יְהוָה֙ לְפָנָ֔יו בְּעֹלוֹתֵ֥ינוּ וּבִזְבָחֵ֖ינוּ וּבִשְׁלָמֵ֑ינוּ וְלֹא־יֹאמְר֨וּ בְנֵיכֶ֤ם מָחָר֙ לְבָנֵ֔ינוּ אֵין־לָכֶ֥ם חֵ֖לֶק בַּֽיהוָֽה׃ 28 וַנֹּ֕אמֶר וְהָיָ֗ה כִּֽי־יֹאמְר֥וּ אֵלֵ֖ינוּ וְאֶל־דֹּרֹתֵ֑ינוּ מָחָ֒ר וְאָמַ֗רְנוּ רְא֣וּ אֶת־תַּבְנִית֙ מִזְבַּ֣ח יְהוָ֗ה אֲשֶׁר־עָשׂ֣וּ אֲבוֹתֵ֔ינוּ לֹ֤א לְעוֹלָה֙ וְלֹ֣א לְזֶ֔בַח כִּי־עֵ֣ד ה֔וּא בֵּינֵ֖ינוּ וּבֵינֵיכֶֽם׃ 29 חָלִ֩ילָה֩ לָּ֨נוּ מִמֶּ֜נּוּ לִמְרֹ֣ד בַּֽיהוָ֗ה וְלָשׁ֤וּב הַיּוֹם֙ מֵאַחֲרֵ֣י יְהוָ֔ה לִבְנ֣וֹת מִזְבֵּ֔חַ לְעֹלָ֖ה לְמִנְחָ֣ה וּלְזָ֑בַח מִלְּבַ֗ד מִזְבַּח֙ יְהוָ֣ה אֱלֹהֵ֔ינוּ אֲשֶׁ֖ר לִפְנֵ֥י מִשְׁכָּנֽוֹ׃ פ 30 וַיִּשְׁמַ֞ע פִּֽינְחָ֣ס הַכֹּהֵ֗ן וּנְשִׂיאֵ֤י הָֽעֵדָה֙ וְרָאשֵׁ֞י אַלְפֵ֤י יִשְׂרָאֵל֙ אֲשֶׁ֣ר אִתּ֔וֹ אֶת־הַדְּבָרִ֔ים אֲשֶׁ֥ר דִּבְּר֖וּ בְּנֵי־רְאוּבֵ֣ן וּבְנֵי־גָ֑ד וּבְנֵ֥י מְנַשֶּׁ֖ה וַיִּיטַ֥ב בְּעֵינֵיהֶֽם׃ 31 וַיֹּ֣אמֶר פִּֽינְחָ֣ס בֶּן־אֶלְעָזָ֣ר הַכֹּהֵ֗ן אֶל־בְּנֵי־רְאוּבֵ֣ן

Reubenites, the Gadites, and the Manassites, "Now we know that the LORD is in our midst, since you have not committed such treachery against the LORD. You have indeed saved the Israelites from punishment by the LORD."

32Then the priest Phinehas son of Eleazar and the chieftains returned from the Reubenites and the Gadites in the land of Gilead to the Israelites in the land of Canaan, and gave them their report. 33The Israelites were pleased, and the Israelites praised God; and they spoke no more of going to war against them, to ravage the land in which the Reubenites and Gadites dwelt.

34The Reubenites and the Gadites named the altar ["Witness"], meaning, "It is a witness between us and them that the LORD is [our] God."

23 Much later, after the LORD had given Israel rest from all the enemies around them, and when Joshua was old and well advanced in years, 2Joshua summoned all Israel, their elders and commanders, their magistrates and officials, and said to them: "I have grown old and am advanced in years. 3You have seen all that the LORD your God has done to all those nations on your account, for it was the LORD your God who fought for you. 4See, I have allotted to you, by your tribes, [the territory of] these nations that still remain, and that of all the nations that I have destroyed, from the Jordan to the Mediterranean Sea in the west. 5The LORD your God Himself will thrust them out on your account and drive them out to make way for you, and you shall possess their land as the LORD your God promised you.

6"But be most resolute to observe faithfully all that is written in the Book of the Teaching of Moses, without ever deviating from it to the right or to the left, 7and without intermingling

וְאֶל־בְּנֵי־גָד וְאֶל־בְּנֵי מְנַשֶּׁה הַיּוֹם ׀ יָדַעְנוּ
כִּי־בְתוֹכֵנוּ יְהֹוָה אֲשֶׁר לֹא־מְעַלְתֶּם
בַּיהֹוָה הַמַּעַל הַזֶּה אָז הִצַּלְתֶּם אֶת־בְּנֵי
יִשְׂרָאֵל מִיַּד יְהֹוָה:

32 וַיָּשָׁב פִּינְחָס בֶּן־אֶלְעָזָר הַכֹּהֵן ׀
וְהַנְּשִׂיאִים מֵאֵת בְּנֵי־רְאוּבֵן וּמֵאֵת בְּנֵי־
גָד מֵאֶרֶץ הַגִּלְעָד אֶל־אֶרֶץ כְּנַעַן אֶל־בְּנֵי
יִשְׂרָאֵל וַיָּשִׁבוּ אוֹתָם דָּבָר: 33 וַיִּיטַב הַדָּבָר
בְּעֵינֵי בְּנֵי יִשְׂרָאֵל וַיְבָרְכוּ אֱלֹהִים בְּנֵי
יִשְׂרָאֵל וְלֹא אָמְרוּ לַעֲלוֹת עֲלֵיהֶם לַצָּבָא
לְשַׁחֵת אֶת־הָאָרֶץ אֲשֶׁר בְּנֵי־רְאוּבֵן וּבְנֵי־
גָד יֹשְׁבִים בָּהּ:

34 וַיִּקְרְאוּ בְּנֵי־רְאוּבֵן וּבְנֵי־גָד לַמִּזְבֵּחַ כִּי
עֵד הוּא בֵּינֹתֵינוּ כִּי יְהֹוָה הָאֱלֹהִים: פ

כג וַיְהִי מִיָּמִים רַבִּים אַחֲרֵי אֲשֶׁר־
הֵנִיחַ יְהֹוָה לְיִשְׂרָאֵל מִכָּל־אֹיְבֵיהֶם
מִסָּבִיב וִיהוֹשֻׁעַ זָקֵן בָּא בַּיָּמִים: 2 וַיִּקְרָא
יְהוֹשֻׁעַ לְכָל־יִשְׂרָאֵל לִזְקֵנָיו וּלְרָאשָׁיו
וּלְשֹׁפְטָיו וּלְשֹׁטְרָיו וַיֹּאמֶר אֲלֵהֶם אֲנִי
זָקַנְתִּי בָּאתִי בַּיָּמִים: 3 וְאַתֶּם רְאִיתֶם אֵת
כָּל־אֲשֶׁר עָשָׂה יְהֹוָה אֱלֹהֵיכֶם לְכָל־
הַגּוֹיִם הָאֵלֶּה מִפְּנֵיכֶם כִּי יְהֹוָה אֱלֹהֵיכֶם
הוּא הַנִּלְחָם לָכֶם: 4 רְאוּ הִפַּלְתִּי לָכֶם
אֶת־הַגּוֹיִם הַנִּשְׁאָרִים הָאֵלֶּה בְּנַחֲלָה
לְשִׁבְטֵיכֶם מִן־הַיַּרְדֵּן וְכָל־הַגּוֹיִם אֲשֶׁר
הִכְרַתִּי וְהַיָּם הַגָּדוֹל מְבוֹא הַשָּׁמֶשׁ:
5 וַיהֹוָה אֱלֹהֵיכֶם הוּא יֶהְדֳּפֵם מִפְּנֵיכֶם
וְהוֹרִישׁ אֹתָם מִלִּפְנֵיכֶם וִירִשְׁתֶּם אֶת־
אַרְצָם כַּאֲשֶׁר דִּבֶּר יְהֹוָה אֱלֹהֵיכֶם לָכֶם:
6 וַחֲזַקְתֶּם מְאֹד לִשְׁמֹר וְלַעֲשׂוֹת אֵת
כָּל־הַכָּתוּב בְּסֵפֶר תּוֹרַת מֹשֶׁה לְבִלְתִּי
סוּר־מִמֶּנּוּ יָמִין וּשְׂמֹאול*: 7 לְבִלְתִּי־בוֹא*
בַּגּוֹיִם הָאֵלֶּה הַנִּשְׁאָרִים הָאֵלֶּה אִתְּכֶם

with these nations that are left among you. Do not utter the names of their gods or swear by them; do not serve them or bow down to them. 8But hold fast to the LORD your God as you have done to this day.

9"The LORD has driven out great, powerful nations on your account, and not a man has withstood you to this day. 10A single man of you would put a thousand to flight, for the LORD your God Himself has been fighting for you, as He promised you. 11For your own sakes, therefore, be most mindful to love the LORD your God. 12For should you turn away and attach yourselves to the remnant of those nations—to those that are left among you—and intermarry with them, you joining them and they joining you, 13know for certain that the LORD your God will not continue to drive these nations out before you; they shall become a snare and a trap for you, a scourge to your sides and thorns in your eyes, until you perish from this good land that the LORD your God has given you.

14"I am now going the way of all the earth. Acknowledge with all your heart and soul that not one of the good things that the LORD your God promised you has failed to happen; they have all come true for you, not a single one has failed. 15But just as every good thing that the LORD your God promised you has been fulfilled for you, so the LORD can bring upon you every evil thing until He has wiped you off this good land that the LORD your God has given you. 16If you break the covenant that the LORD your God enjoined upon you, and go and serve other gods and bow down to them, then the LORD's anger will burn against you, and you shall quickly perish from the good land that He has given you."

וּבְשֵׁם אֱלֹהֵיהֶם לֹא־תַזְכִּירוּ וְלֹא תַשְׁבִּיעוּ
וְלֹא תַעַבְדוּם וְלֹא תִשְׁתַּחֲווּ לָהֶם: 8 כִּי
אִם־בַּיהוָה אֱלֹהֵיכֶם תִּדְבָּקוּ כַּאֲשֶׁר
עֲשִׂיתֶם עַד הַיּוֹם הַזֶּה:
9 וַיּוֹרֶשׁ יְהוָה מִפְּנֵיכֶם גּוֹיִם גְּדֹלִים
וַעֲצוּמִים וְאַתֶּם לֹא־עָמַד אִישׁ בִּפְנֵיכֶם
עַד הַיּוֹם הַזֶּה: 10 אִישׁ־אֶחָד מִכֶּם יִרְדָּף־
אֶלֶף כִּי ׀ יְהוָה אֱלֹהֵיכֶם הוּא הַנִּלְחָם
לָכֶם כַּאֲשֶׁר דִּבֶּר לָכֶם: 11 וְנִשְׁמַרְתֶּם מְאֹד
לְנַפְשֹׁתֵיכֶם לְאַהֲבָה אֶת־יְהוָה אֱלֹהֵיכֶם:
12 כִּי ׀ אִם־שׁוֹב תָּשׁוּבוּ וּדְבַקְתֶּם בְּיֶתֶר
הַגּוֹיִם הָאֵלֶּה הַנִּשְׁאָרִים הָאֵלֶּה אִתְּכֶם
וְהִתְחַתַּנְתֶּם בָּהֶם וּבָאתֶם בָּהֶם וְהֵם
בָּכֶם: 13 יָדוֹעַ תֵּדְעוּ כִּי לֹא יוֹסִיף יְהוָה
אֱלֹהֵיכֶם לְהוֹרִישׁ אֶת־הַגּוֹיִם הָאֵלֶּה
מִלִּפְנֵיכֶם וְהָיוּ לָכֶם לְפַח וּלְמוֹקֵשׁ
וּלְשֹׁטֵט בְּצִדֵּיכֶם וְלִצְנִנִים בְּעֵינֵיכֶם עַד־
אֲבָדְכֶם מֵעַל הָאֲדָמָה הַטּוֹבָה הַזֹּאת
אֲשֶׁר נָתַן לָכֶם יְהוָה אֱלֹהֵיכֶם:
14 וְהִנֵּה אָנֹכִי הוֹלֵךְ הַיּוֹם בְּדֶרֶךְ כָּל־
הָאָרֶץ וִידַעְתֶּם בְּכָל־לְבַבְכֶם וּבְכָל־
נַפְשְׁכֶם כִּי לֹא־נָפַל דָּבָר אֶחָד מִכֹּל ׀
הַדְּבָרִים הַטּוֹבִים אֲשֶׁר דִּבֶּר יְהוָה
אֱלֹהֵיכֶם עֲלֵיכֶם הַכֹּל בָּאוּ לָכֶם לֹא־נָפַל
מִמֶּנּוּ דָּבָר אֶחָד: 15 וְהָיָה כַּאֲשֶׁר־בָּא
עֲלֵיכֶם כָּל־הַדָּבָר הַטּוֹב אֲשֶׁר דִּבֶּר יְהוָה
אֱלֹהֵיכֶם אֲלֵיכֶם כֵּן יָבִיא יְהוָה עֲלֵיכֶם
אֵת כָּל־הַדָּבָר הָרָע עַד־הַשְׁמִידוֹ אוֹתְכֶם
מֵעַל הָאֲדָמָה הַטּוֹבָה הַזֹּאת אֲשֶׁר נָתַן
לָכֶם יְהוָה אֱלֹהֵיכֶם: 16 בְּעָבְרְכֶם אֶת־
בְּרִית יְהוָה אֱלֹהֵיכֶם אֲשֶׁר צִוָּה אֶתְכֶם
וַהֲלַכְתֶּם וַעֲבַדְתֶּם אֱלֹהִים אֲחֵרִים
וְהִשְׁתַּחֲוִיתֶם לָהֶם וְחָרָה אַף־יְהוָה בָּכֶם
וַאֲבַדְתֶּם מְהֵרָה מֵעַל הָאָרֶץ הַטּוֹבָה
אֲשֶׁר נָתַן לָכֶם: פ

24

Joshua assembled all the tribes of Israel at Schechem. He summoned Israel's elders and commanders, magistrates and officers; and they presented themselves before God. ²Then Joshua said to all the people, "Thus said the LORD, the God of Israel: In olden times, your forefathers—Terah, father of Abraham and father of Nahor—lived beyond the Euphrates and worshiped other gods. ³But I took your father Abraham from beyond the Euphrates and led him through the whole land of Canaan and multiplied his offspring. I gave him Isaac, ⁴and to Isaac I gave Jacob and Esau. I gave Esau the hill country of Seir as his possession, while Jacob and his children went down to Egypt.

⁵"Then I sent Moses and Aaron, and I plagued Egypt with [the wonders] that I wrought in their midst, after which I freed you—⁶I freed your fathers—from Egypt, and you came to the Sea. But the Egyptians pursued your fathers to the Sea of Reeds with chariots and horsemen. ⁷They cried out to the LORD, and He put darkness between you and the Egyptians; then He brought the Sea upon them, and it covered them. Your own eyes saw what I did to the Egyptians.

"After you had lived a long time in the wilderness, ⁸I brought you to the land of the Amorites who lived beyond the Jordan. They gave battle to you, but I delivered them into your hands; I annihilated them for you, and you took possession of their land. ⁹Thereupon Balak son of Zippor, the king of Moab, made ready to attack Israel. He sent for Balaam son of Beor to curse you, ¹⁰but I refused to listen to Balaam; he had to bless you, and thus I saved you from him.

¹¹"Then you crossed the Jordan and you came to Jericho. The citizens of Jericho and the Amorites, Perizzites, Canaanites, Hittites, Girgashites, Hivites, and Jebusites fought you,

כד וַיֶּאֶסֹף יְהוֹשֻׁעַ אֶת־כָּל־שִׁבְטֵי יִשְׂרָאֵל שְׁכֶמָה וַיִּקְרָא לְזִקְנֵי יִשְׂרָאֵל וּלְרָאשָׁיו וּלְשֹׁפְטָיו וּלְשֹׁטְרָיו וַיִּתְיַצְּבוּ לִפְנֵי הָאֱלֹהִים: ² וַיֹּאמֶר יְהוֹשֻׁעַ אֶל־כָּל־הָעָם כֹּה־אָמַר יְהוָה אֱלֹהֵי יִשְׂרָאֵל בְּעֵבֶר הַנָּהָר יָשְׁבוּ אֲבוֹתֵיכֶם מֵעוֹלָם תֶּרַח אֲבִי אַבְרָהָם וַאֲבִי נָחוֹר וַיַּעַבְדוּ אֱלֹהִים אֲחֵרִים: ³ וָאֶקַּח אֶת־אֲבִיכֶם אֶת־אַבְרָהָם מֵעֵבֶר הַנָּהָר וָאוֹלֵךְ אוֹתוֹ בְּכָל־אֶרֶץ כְּנָעַן וארב וָאַרְבֶּה אֶת־זַרְעוֹ וָאֶתֶּן לוֹ אֶת־יִצְחָק: ⁴ וָאֶתֵּן לְיִצְחָק אֶת־יַעֲקֹב וְאֶת־עֵשָׂו וָאֶתֵּן לְעֵשָׂו אֶת־הַר שֵׂעִיר לָרֶשֶׁת אוֹתוֹ וְיַעֲקֹב וּבָנָיו יָרְדוּ מִצְרָיִם: ⁵ וָאֶשְׁלַח אֶת־מֹשֶׁה וְאֶת־אַהֲרֹן וָאֶגֹּף אֶת־מִצְרַיִם כַּאֲשֶׁר עָשִׂיתִי בְּקִרְבּוֹ וְאַחַר הוֹצֵאתִי אֶתְכֶם: ⁶ וָאוֹצִיא אֶת־אֲבוֹתֵיכֶם מִמִּצְרַיִם וַתָּבֹאוּ הַיָּמָּה וַיִּרְדְּפוּ מִצְרַיִם אַחֲרֵי אֲבוֹתֵיכֶם בְּרֶכֶב וּבְפָרָשִׁים יַם־סוּף: ⁷ וַיִּצְעֲקוּ אֶל־יְהוָה וַיָּשֶׂם מַאֲפֵל בֵּינֵיכֶם | וּבֵין הַמִּצְרִים וַיָּבֵא עָלָיו אֶת־הַיָּם וַיְכַסֵּהוּ וַתִּרְאֶינָה עֵינֵיכֶם אֵת אֲשֶׁר־עָשִׂיתִי בְּמִצְרָיִם וַתֵּשְׁבוּ בַמִּדְבָּר יָמִים רַבִּים: ⁸ ואבאה וָאָבִיא אֶתְכֶם אֶל־אֶרֶץ הָאֱמֹרִי הַיּוֹשֵׁב בְּעֵבֶר הַיַּרְדֵּן וַיִּלָּחֲמוּ אִתְּכֶם וָאֶתֵּן אוֹתָם בְּיֶדְכֶם וַתִּירְשׁוּ אֶת־אַרְצָם וָאַשְׁמִידֵם מִפְּנֵיכֶם: ⁹ וַיָּקָם בָּלָק בֶּן־צִפּוֹר מֶלֶךְ מוֹאָב וַיִּלָּחֶם בְּיִשְׂרָאֵל וַיִּשְׁלַח וַיִּקְרָא לְבִלְעָם בֶּן־בְּעוֹר לְקַלֵּל אֶתְכֶם: ¹⁰ וְלֹא אָבִיתִי לִשְׁמֹעַ לְבִלְעָם וַיְבָרֶךְ בָּרוֹךְ אֶתְכֶם וָאַצִּל אֶתְכֶם מִיָּדוֹ: ¹¹ וַתַּעַבְרוּ אֶת־הַיַּרְדֵּן וַתָּבֹאוּ אֶל־יְרִיחוֹ וַיִּלָּחֲמוּ בָכֶם בַּעֲלֵי־יְרִיחוֹ הָאֱמֹרִי וְהַפְּרִזִּי וְהַכְּנַעֲנִי וְהַחִתִּי וְהַגִּרְגָּשִׁי הַחִוִּי וְהַיְבוּסִי וָאֶתֵּן אוֹתָם בְּיֶדְכֶם: ¹² וָאֶשְׁלַח לִפְנֵיכֶם

but I delivered them into your hands. [12]I sent a plague[a] ahead of you, and it drove them out before you—[just like] the two Amorite kings—not by your sword or by your bow. [13]I have given you a land for which you did not labor and towns which you did not build, and you have settled in them; you are enjoying vineyards and olive groves which you did not plant.

[14]"Now, therefore, revere the Lord and serve Him with undivided loyalty; put away the gods that your forefathers served beyond the Euphrates and in Egypt, and serve the Lord. [15]Or, if you are loath to serve the Lord, choose this day which ones you are going to serve—the gods that your forefathers served beyond the Euphrates, or those of the Amorites in whose land you are settled; but I and my household will serve the Lord."

[16]In reply, the people declared, "Far be it from us to forsake the Lord and serve other gods! [17]For it was the Lord our God who brought us and our fathers up from the land of Egypt, the house of bondage, and who wrought those wondrous signs before our very eyes, and guarded us all along the way that we traveled and among all the peoples through whose midst we passed. [18]And then the Lord drove out before us all the peoples—the Amorites—that inhabited the country. We too will serve the Lord, for He is our God."

[19]Joshua, however, said to the people, "You will not be able to serve the Lord, for He is a holy God. He is a jealous God; He will not forgive your transgressions and your sins. [20]If you forsake the Lord and serve alien gods, He will turn and deal harshly with you and make an end of you, after having been gracious to you." [21]But the people replied to Joshua, "No, we will serve the Lord!" [22]Thereupon Joshua said to the people, "You are witnesses against yourselves that

אֶת־הַצִּרְעָ֗ה וַתְּגָ֤רֶשׁ אוֹתָם֙ מִפְּנֵיכֶ֔ם שְׁנֵ֖י
מַלְכֵ֣י הָאֱמֹרִ֑י לֹ֥א בְחַרְבְּךָ֖ וְלֹ֥א בְקַשְׁתֶּֽךָ׃
[13] וָאֶתֵּ֨ן לָכֶ֜ם אֶ֣רֶץ ׀ אֲשֶׁ֧ר לֹֽא־יָגַ֣עְתָּ בָּ֗הּ
וְעָרִים֙ אֲשֶׁ֣ר לֹא־בְנִיתֶ֔ם וַתֵּשְׁב֖וּ בָּהֶ֑ם
כְּרָמִ֤ים וְזֵיתִים֙ אֲשֶׁ֣ר לֹֽא־נְטַעְתֶּ֔ם אַתֶּ֖ם
אֹכְלִֽים׃
[14] וְעַתָּ֞ה יְר֧אוּ אֶת־יְהֹוָ֛ה וְעִבְד֥וּ אֹת֖וֹ
בְּתָמִ֣ים וּבֶֽאֱמֶ֑ת וְהָסִ֣ירוּ אֶת־אֱלֹהִ֗ים אֲשֶׁר֩
עָבְד֨וּ אֲבֽוֹתֵיכֶ֜ם בְּעֵ֤בֶר הַנָּהָר֙ וּבְמִצְרַ֔יִם
וְעִבְד֖וּ אֶת־יְהֹוָֽה׃ [15] וְאִם֩ רַ֨ע בְּעֵֽינֵיכֶ֜ם
לַעֲבֹ֣ד אֶת־יְהֹוָ֗ה בַּחֲר֨וּ לָכֶ֣ם הַיּוֹם֮ אֶת־
מִ֣י תַעֲבֹדוּן֒ אִ֣ם אֶת־אֱלֹהִ֞ים אֲשֶׁר־עָבְד֣וּ
אֲבֽוֹתֵיכֶ֗ם אֲשֶׁר֙ בעבר מֵעֵ֣בֶר הַנָּהָ֔ר
וְאִם֙ אֶת־אֱלֹהֵ֣י הָאֱמֹרִ֔י אֲשֶׁ֥ר אַתֶּ֖ם
יֹשְׁבִ֣ים בְּאַרְצָ֑ם וְאָנֹכִ֣י וּבֵיתִ֔י נַעֲבֹ֖ד אֶת־
יְהֹוָֽה׃ פ
[16] וַיַּ֤עַן הָעָם֙ וַיֹּ֔אמֶר חָלִ֣ילָה לָּ֔נוּ מֵעֲזֹ֖ב
אֶת־יְהֹוָ֑ה לַעֲבֹ֖ד אֱלֹהִ֥ים אֲחֵרִֽים׃ [17] כִּ֚י
יְהֹוָ֣ה אֱלֹהֵ֔ינוּ הוּא֩ הַמַּעֲלֶ֨ה אֹתָ֧נוּ וְאֶת־
אֲבוֹתֵ֛ינוּ מֵאֶ֥רֶץ מִצְרַ֖יִם מִבֵּ֣ית עֲבָדִ֑ים
וַאֲשֶׁ֧ר עָשָׂ֣ה לְעֵינֵ֗ינוּ אֶת־הָאֹת֤וֹת הַגְּדֹלוֹת֙
הָאֵ֔לֶּה וַֽיִּשְׁמְרֵ֗נוּ בְּכׇל־הַדֶּ֙רֶךְ֙ אֲשֶׁ֣ר הָלַ֣כְנוּ
בָ֔הּ וּבְכֹל֙ הָֽעַמִּ֔ים אֲשֶׁ֥ר עָבַ֖רְנוּ בְּקִרְבָּֽם׃
[18] וַיְגָ֨רֶשׁ יְהֹוָ֜ה אֶת־כׇּל־הָעַמִּ֗ים וְאֶת־
הָאֱמֹרִ֛י יֹשֵׁ֥ב הָאָ֖רֶץ מִפָּנֵ֑ינוּ גַּם־אֲנַ֙חְנוּ֙
נַעֲבֹ֣ד אֶת־יְהֹוָ֔ה כִּי־ה֖וּא אֱלֹהֵֽינוּ׃ ס
[19] וַיֹּ֤אמֶר יְהוֹשֻׁ֙עַ֙ אֶל־הָעָ֔ם לֹ֥א תֽוּכְלוּ֙
לַעֲבֹ֣ד אֶת־יְהֹוָ֔ה כִּֽי־אֱלֹהִ֥ים קְדֹשִׁ֖ים ה֑וּא
אֵֽל־קַנּ֣וֹא ה֔וּא לֹֽא־יִשָּׂ֥א לְפִשְׁעֲכֶ֖ם
וּלְחַטֹּאותֵיכֶֽם*׃ [20] כִּ֤י תַֽעַזְבוּ֙ אֶת־יְהֹוָ֔ה
וַעֲבַדְתֶּ֖ם אֱלֹהֵ֣י נֵכָ֑ר וְשָׁ֨ב וְהֵרַ֤ע לָכֶם֙
וְכִלָּ֣ה אֶתְכֶ֔ם אַחֲרֵ֖י אֲשֶׁר־הֵיטִ֥יב לָכֶֽם׃
[21] וַיֹּ֧אמֶר* הָעָ֛ם אֶל־יְהוֹשֻׁ֖עַ לֹ֑א כִּ֥י אֶת־
יְהֹוָ֖ה נַעֲבֹֽד׃ [22] וַיֹּ֤אמֶר יְהוֹשֻׁ֙עַ֙ אֶל־הָעָ֔ם
עֵדִ֤ים אַתֶּם֙ בָּכֶ֔ם כִּֽי־אַתֶּ֞ם בְּחַרְתֶּ֥ם לָכֶ֛ם

---

a   *See note at Exod. 23.28.*

you have by your own act chosen to serve the
LORD." "Yes, we are!" they responded. [23]"Then
put away the alien gods that you have among
you and direct your hearts to the LORD, the God
of Israel." [24]And the people declared to Joshua,
"We will serve none but the LORD our God, and
we will obey none but Him."

[25]On that day at Shechem, Joshua made a covenant for the people and he made a fixed rule
for them. [26]Joshua recorded all this in a book
of divine instruction. He took a great stone and
set it up at the foot of the oak in the sacred precinct of the LORD; [27]and Joshua said to all the
people, "See, this very stone shall be a witness
against us, for it heard all the words that the
LORD spoke to us; it shall be a witness against
you, lest you break faith with your God."
[28]Joshua then dismissed the people to their allotted portions.

[29]After these events, Joshua son of Nun, the
servant of the LORD, died at the age of one hundred and ten years. [30]They buried him on his
own property, at Timnath-serah in the hill
country of Ephraim, north of Mount Gaash.
[31]Israel served the LORD during the lifetime of
Joshua and the lifetime of the elders who lived
on after Joshua, and who had experienced all
the deeds that the LORD had wrought for Israel.

[32]The bones of Joseph, which the Israelites
had brought up from Egypt, were buried at Shechem, in the piece of ground which Jacob had
bought for a hundred *kesitahs*[b] from the children of Hamor, Shechem's father, and which
had become a heritage of the Josephites.

[33]Eleazar son of Aaron also died, and they
buried him on the hill of his son Phinehas,
which had been assigned to him in the hill country of Ephraim.

אֶת־יְהֹוָה לַעֲבֹד אוֹתוֹ וַיֹּאמְרוּ עֵדִים: [23] וְעַתָּה הָסִירוּ אֶת־אֱלֹהֵי הַנֵּכָר אֲשֶׁר בְּקִרְבְּכֶם וְהַטּוּ אֶת־לְבַבְכֶם אֶל־יְהֹוָה אֱלֹהֵי יִשְׂרָאֵל: [24] וַיֹּאמְרוּ הָעָם אֶל־יְהוֹשֻׁעַ אֶת־יְהֹוָה אֱלֹהֵינוּ נַעֲבֹד וּבְקוֹלוֹ נִשְׁמָע:

[25] וַיִּכְרֹת יְהוֹשֻׁעַ בְּרִית לָעָם בַּיּוֹם הַהוּא וַיָּשֶׂם לוֹ חֹק וּמִשְׁפָּט בִּשְׁכֶם: [26] וַיִּכְתֹּב יְהוֹשֻׁעַ אֶת־הַדְּבָרִים הָאֵלֶּה בְּסֵפֶר תּוֹרַת אֱלֹהִים וַיִּקַּח אֶבֶן גְּדוֹלָה וַיְקִימֶהָ שָּׁם תַּחַת הָאַלָּה אֲשֶׁר בְּמִקְדַּשׁ יְהֹוָה: ס [27] וַיֹּאמֶר יְהוֹשֻׁעַ אֶל־כָּל־הָעָם הִנֵּה הָאֶבֶן הַזֹּאת תִּהְיֶה־בָּנוּ לְעֵדָה כִּי־הִיא שָׁמְעָה אֵת כָּל־אִמְרֵי יְהֹוָה אֲשֶׁר דִּבֶּר עִמָּנוּ וְהָיְתָה בָכֶם לְעֵדָה פֶּן־תְּכַחֲשׁוּן בֵּאלֹהֵיכֶם: [28] וַיְשַׁלַּח יְהוֹשֻׁעַ אֶת־הָעָם אִישׁ לְנַחֲלָתוֹ: פ

[29] וַיְהִי אַחֲרֵי הַדְּבָרִים הָאֵלֶּה וַיָּמָת יְהוֹשֻׁעַ בִּן־נוּן עֶבֶד יְהֹוָה בֶּן־מֵאָה וָעֶשֶׂר שָׁנִים: [30] וַיִּקְבְּרוּ אֹתוֹ בִּגְבוּל נַחֲלָתוֹ בְּתִמְנַת־סֶרַח אֲשֶׁר בְּהַר־אֶפְרָיִם מִצְּפוֹן לְהַר־גָּעַשׁ: [31] וַיַּעֲבֹד יִשְׂרָאֵל אֶת־יְהֹוָה כֹּל יְמֵי יְהוֹשֻׁעַ וְכֹל | יְמֵי הַזְּקֵנִים אֲשֶׁר הֶאֱרִיכוּ יָמִים אַחֲרֵי יְהוֹשֻׁעַ וַאֲשֶׁר יָדְעוּ אֵת כָּל־מַעֲשֵׂה יְהֹוָה אֲשֶׁר עָשָׂה לְיִשְׂרָאֵל:

[32] וְאֶת־עַצְמוֹת יוֹסֵף אֲשֶׁר־הֶעֱלוּ בְנֵי־יִשְׂרָאֵל | מִמִּצְרַיִם קָבְרוּ בִשְׁכֶם בְּחֶלְקַת הַשָּׂדֶה אֲשֶׁר קָנָה יַעֲקֹב מֵאֵת בְּנֵי־חֲמוֹר אֲבִי־שְׁכֶם בְּמֵאָה קְשִׂיטָה וַיִּהְיוּ לִבְנֵי־יוֹסֵף לְנַחֲלָה:

[33] וְאֶלְעָזָר בֶּן־אַהֲרֹן מֵת וַיִּקְבְּרוּ אֹתוֹ בְּגִבְעַת פִּינְחָס בְּנוֹ אֲשֶׁר נִתַּן־לוֹ בְּהַר אֶפְרָיִם: *

תם ונשלם תהילה לאל בורא עולם

JUDGES*

1 After the death of Joshua, the Israelites inquired of the LORD, "Which of us shall be the first to go up against the Canaanites and attack them?" ²The LORD replied, "Let [the tribe of] Judah go up. I now deliver the land into their hands." ³Judah then said to their brother-tribe Simeon, "Come up with us to our allotted territory and let us attack the Canaanites, and then we will go with you to your allotted territory." So Simeon joined them.

⁴When Judah advanced, the LORD delivered the Canaanites and the Perizzites into their hands, and they defeated ten thousand of them at Bezek. ⁵At Bezek, they encountered Adoni-bezek, engaged him in battle, and defeated the Canaanites and the Perizzites. ⁶Adoni-bezek fled, but they pursued him and captured him; and they cut off his thumbs and his big toes. ⁷And Adoni-bezek said, "Seventy kings, with thumbs and big toes cut off, used to pick up scraps under my table; as I have done, so God has requited me." They brought him to Jerusalem and he died there.

⁸The Judites attacked Jerusalem and captured it; they put it to the sword and set the city on fire. ⁹After that the Judites went down to attack the Canaanites who inhabited the hill country, the Negeb, and the Shephelah.

¹⁰The Judites marched against the Canaanites who dwelt in Hebron, and they defeated Sheshai, Ahiman, and Talmai. (The name of Hebron was formerly Kiriath-arba.) ¹¹From there they marched against the inhabitants of Debir (the name of Debir was formerly Kiriath-

א וַיְהִי אַחֲרֵי מוֹת יְהוֹשֻׁעַ וַיִּשְׁאֲלוּ
בְּנֵי יִשְׂרָאֵל בַּיהוָה לֵאמֹר מִי יַעֲלֶה־לָּנוּ
אֶל־הַכְּנַעֲנִי בַּתְּחִלָּה לְהִלָּחֶם בּוֹ: 2 וַיֹּאמֶר
יְהוָה יְהוּדָה יַעֲלֶה הִנֵּה נָתַתִּי אֶת־הָאָרֶץ
בְּיָדוֹ: 3 וַיֹּאמֶר יְהוּדָה לְשִׁמְעוֹן אָחִיו עֲלֵה
אִתִּי בְגוֹרָלִי וְנִלָּחֲמָה בַּכְּנַעֲנִי וְהָלַכְתִּי
גַם־אֲנִי אִתְּךָ בְּגוֹרָלֶךָ וַיֵּלֶךְ אִתּוֹ שִׁמְעוֹן:
4 וַיַּעַל יְהוּדָה וַיִּתֵּן יְהוָה אֶת־הַכְּנַעֲנִי
וְהַפְּרִזִּי בְּיָדָם וַיַּכּוּם בְּבֶזֶק עֲשֶׂרֶת אֲלָפִים
אִישׁ: 5 וַיִּמְצְאוּ אֶת־אֲדֹנִי בֶזֶק בְּבֶזֶק
וַיִּלָּחֲמוּ בּוֹ וַיַּכּוּ אֶת־הַכְּנַעֲנִי וְאֶת־הַפְּרִזִּי:
6 וַיָּנָס אֲדֹנִי בֶזֶק וַיִּרְדְּפוּ אַחֲרָיו וַיֹּאחֲזוּ
אֹתוֹ וַיְקַצְּצוּ אֶת־בְּהֹנוֹת יָדָיו וְרַגְלָיו:
7 וַיֹּאמֶר אֲדֹנִי־בֶזֶק שִׁבְעִים ׀ מְלָכִים
בְּהֹנוֹת יְדֵיהֶם וְרַגְלֵיהֶם מְקֻצָּצִים הָיוּ
מְלַקְּטִים תַּחַת שֻׁלְחָנִי כַּאֲשֶׁר עָשִׂיתִי כֵּן
שִׁלַּם־לִי אֱלֹהִים וַיְבִיאֻהוּ יְרוּשָׁלַ͏ִם וַיָּמָת
שָׁם: פ
8 וַיִּלָּחֲמוּ בְנֵי־יְהוּדָה בִּירוּשָׁלַ͏ִם וַיִּלְכְּדוּ
אוֹתָהּ וַיַּכּוּהָ לְפִי־חָרֶב וְאֶת־הָעִיר שִׁלְּחוּ
בָאֵשׁ: 9 וְאַחַר יָרְדוּ בְּנֵי יְהוּדָה לְהִלָּחֵם
בַּכְּנַעֲנִי יוֹשֵׁב הָהָר וְהַנֶּגֶב וְהַשְּׁפֵלָה:
10 וַיֵּלֶךְ יְהוּדָה אֶל־הַכְּנַעֲנִי הַיּוֹשֵׁב
בְּחֶבְרוֹן וְשֵׁם־חֶבְרוֹן לְפָנִים קִרְיַת אַרְבַּע
וַיַּכּוּ אֶת־שֵׁשַׁי וְאֶת־אֲחִימַן וְאֶת־תַּלְמָי:
11 וַיֵּלֶךְ מִשָּׁם אֶל־יוֹשְׁבֵי דְּבִיר וְשֵׁם־דְּבִיר

---

* *This is the traditional rendering of* shopheṭim, *which, however, in the text is rendered "chieftains." The corresponding verb* shaphaṭ *is usually translated not "judged" but "ruled" or "led."*

sepher). [12]And Caleb announced, "I will give my daughter Achsah in marriage to the man who attacks and captures Kiriath-sepher." [13]His younger kinsman, Othniel the Kenizzite,[a] captured it; and Caleb gave him his daughter Achsah in marriage. [14b]When she came [to him], she induced him to ask her father for some property. She dismounted from her donkey, and Caleb asked her, "What is the matter?" [15]She replied, "Give me a present, for you have given me away as Negeb-land; give me springs of water." And Caleb gave her Upper and Lower Gulloth.[-b]

[16]The descendants of the Kenite, the father-in-law of Moses, went up with the Judites from the City of Palms to the wilderness of Judah; and they went and settled among the people[c] in the Negeb of Arad. [17]And Judah with its brother-tribe Simeon went on and defeated the Canaanites who dwelt in Zephath. They proscribed it, and so the town was named Hormah.[d] [18]And Judah captured[e] Gaza and its territory, Ashkelon and its territory, and Ekron and its territory.

[19]The LORD was with Judah, so that they took possession of the hill country; but they were not able to dispossess the inhabitants of the plain, for they had iron chariots. [20]They gave Hebron to Caleb, as Moses had promised; and he drove the three Anakites out of there. [21]The Benjaminites did not dispossess the Jebusite inhabitants of Jerusalem; so the Jebusites have dwelt with the Benjaminites in Jerusalem to this day.

[22]The House of Joseph, for their part, advanced against Bethel, and the LORD was with them. [23]While the House of Joseph were scouting at Bethel (the name of the town was formerly Luz), [24]their patrols[f] saw a man leaving the town. They said to him, "Just show us how to get into

לְפָנִים קִרְיַת־סֵפֶר: 12 וַיֹּאמֶר כָּלֵב אֲשֶׁר־ יַכֶּה אֶת־קִרְיַת־סֵפֶר וּלְכָדָהּ וְנָתַתִּי לוֹ אֶת־עַכְסָה בִתִּי לְאִשָּׁה: 13 וַיִּלְכְּדָהּ עָתְנִיאֵל בֶּן־קְנַז אֲחִי כָלֵב הַקָּטֹן מִמֶּנּוּ וַיִּתֶּן־לוֹ אֶת־עַכְסָה בִתּוֹ לְאִשָּׁה: 14 וַיְהִי בְּבוֹאָהּ וַתְּסִיתֵהוּ לִשְׁאוֹל מֵאֵת־אָבִיהָ הַשָּׂדֶה וַתִּצְנַח מֵעַל הַחֲמוֹר וַיֹּאמֶר־לָהּ כָּלֵב מַה־לָּךְ: 15 וַתֹּאמֶר לוֹ הָבָה־לִּי בְרָכָה כִּי אֶרֶץ הַנֶּגֶב נְתַתָּנִי וְנָתַתָּה לִי גֻּלֹּת מָיִם וַיִּתֶּן־לָהּ כָּלֵב אֵת גֻּלֹּת עִלִּית וְאֵת גֻּלֹּת תַּחְתִּית: פ

16 וּבְנֵי קֵינִי חֹתֵן מֹשֶׁה עָלוּ מֵעִיר הַתְּמָרִים אֶת־בְּנֵי יְהוּדָה מִדְבַּר יְהוּדָה אֲשֶׁר בְּנֶגֶב עֲרָד וַיֵּלֶךְ וַיֵּשֶׁב אֶת־הָעָם: 17 וַיֵּלֶךְ יְהוּדָה אֶת־שִׁמְעוֹן אָחִיו וַיַּכּוּ אֶת־הַכְּנַעֲנִי יוֹשֵׁב צְפַת וַיַּחֲרִימוּ אוֹתָהּ וַיִּקְרָא אֶת־שֵׁם־הָעִיר חָרְמָה: 18 וַיִּלְכֹּד יְהוּדָה אֶת־עַזָּה וְאֶת־גְּבוּלָהּ וְאֶת־ אַשְׁקְלוֹן וְאֶת־גְּבוּלָהּ וְאֶת־עֶקְרוֹן וְאֶת־ גְּבוּלָהּ:

19 וַיְהִי יְהוָה אֶת־יְהוּדָה וַיֹּרֶשׁ אֶת־הָהָר כִּי לֹא לְהוֹרִישׁ אֶת־יֹשְׁבֵי הָעֵמֶק כִּי־רֶכֶב בַּרְזֶל לָהֶם: 20 וַיִּתְּנוּ לְכָלֵב אֶת־חֶבְרוֹן כַּאֲשֶׁר דִּבֶּר מֹשֶׁה וַיּוֹרֶשׁ מִשָּׁם אֶת־ שְׁלֹשָׁה בְּנֵי הָעֲנָק: 21 וְאֶת־הַיְבוּסִי יֹשֵׁב יְרוּשָׁלַ͏ִם לֹא הוֹרִישׁוּ בְּנֵי בִנְיָמִן וַיֵּשֶׁב הַיְבוּסִי אֶת־בְּנֵי בִנְיָמִן בִּירוּשָׁלַ͏ִם עַד הַיּוֹם הַזֶּה: ס

22 וַיַּעֲלוּ בֵית־יוֹסֵף גַּם־הֵם בֵּית־אֵל וַיהוָה עִמָּם: 23 וַיָּתִירוּ בֵית־יוֹסֵף בְּבֵית־אֵל וְשֵׁם־הָעִיר לְפָנִים לוּז: 24 וַיִּרְאוּ הַשֹּׁמְרִים אִישׁ יוֹצֵא מִן־הָעִיר וַיֹּאמְרוּ לוֹ הַרְאֵנוּ נָא אֶת־מְבוֹא הָעִיר וְעָשִׂינוּ עִמְּךָ חָסֶד:

---

a   Cf. Josh. 14.6, 14.
b-b   Cf. Josh. 15.18–19 and notes.
c   Meaning of Heb. uncertain. Emendation yields "Amalekites"; cf. 1 Sam. 15.6.
d   I.e., "Proscribed." Cf. notes at Num. 21.2–3.
e   Septuagint reads "But Judah did not capture Gaza…" Gaza is in the coastal plain referred to in v. 19.
f   Lit. "watchmen."

the town, and we will treat you kindly." 25He showed them how to get into the town; they put the town to the sword, but they let the man and all his relatives go free. 26The man went to the Hittite country. He founded a city and named it Luz, and that has been its name to this day.

27Manasseh did not dispossess [the inhabitants of] Beth-shean and its dependencies, or [of] Taanach and its dependencies, or the inhabitants of Dor and its dependencies, or the inhabitants of Ibleam and its dependencies, or the inhabitants of Megiddo and its dependencies. The Canaanites persisted in dwelling in this region. 28And when Israel gained the upper hand, they subjected the Canaanites to forced labor; but they did not dispossess them. 29Nor did Ephraim dispossess the Canaanites who inhabited Gezer; so the Canaanites dwelt in their midst at Gezer.

30Zebulun did not dispossess the inhabitants of Kitron or the inhabitants of Nahalol; so the Canaanites dwelt in their midst, but they were subjected to forced labor. 31Asher did not dispossess the inhabitants of Acco or the inhabitants of Sidon, Ahlab, Achzib, Helbah, Aphik, and Rehob. 32So the Asherites dwelt in the midst of the Canaanites, the inhabitants of the land, for they did not dispossess them. 33Naphtali did not dispossess the inhabitants of Beth-shemesh or the inhabitants of Beth-anath. But they settled in the midst of the Canaanite inhabitants of the land, and the inhabitants of Beth-shemesh and Beth-anath had to perform forced labor for them.

34The Amorites pressed the Danites into the hill country; they would not let them come down to the plain. 35The Amorites also persisted in dwelling in Har-heres, in Aijalon, and in Shaalbim. But the hand of the House of Joseph bore heavily on them and they had to perform forced labor. 36The territory of the Amoritesᵍ extended from the Ascent of Akrabbim—from Sela—onward.

25 וַיַּרְאֵם אֶת־מְבוֹא הָעִיר וַיַּכּוּ אֶת־הָעִיר לְפִי־חָרֶב וְאֶת־הָאִישׁ וְאֶת־כָּל־מִשְׁפַּחְתּוֹ שִׁלֵּחוּ׃ 26 וַיֵּלֶךְ הָאִישׁ אֶרֶץ הַחִתִּים וַיִּבֶן עִיר וַיִּקְרָא שְׁמָהּ לוּז הוּא שְׁמָהּ עַד הַיּוֹם הַזֶּה׃ פ

27 וְלֹא־הוֹרִישׁ מְנַשֶּׁה אֶת־בֵּית־שְׁאָן וְאֶת־בְּנוֹתֶיהָ וְאֶת־תַּעְנַךְ וְאֶת־בְּנֹתֶיהָ וְאֶת־יֹשֵׁב דוֹר וְאֶת־בְּנוֹתֶיהָ וְאֶת־יוֹשְׁבֵי יִבְלְעָם וְאֶת־בְּנֹתֶיהָ וְאֶת־יוֹשְׁבֵי מְגִדּוֹ וְאֶת־בְּנוֹתֶיהָ וַיּוֹאֶל הַכְּנַעֲנִי לָשֶׁבֶת בָּאָרֶץ הַזֹּאת׃ 28 וַיְהִי כִּי־חָזַק יִשְׂרָאֵל וַיָּשֶׂם אֶת־הַכְּנַעֲנִי לָמַס וְהוֹרֵישׁ לֹא הוֹרִישׁוֹ׃ ס 29 וְאֶפְרַיִם לֹא הוֹרִישׁ אֶת־הַכְּנַעֲנִי הַיּוֹשֵׁב בְּגָזֶר וַיֵּשֶׁב הַכְּנַעֲנִי בְּקִרְבּוֹ בְּגָזֶר׃ פ

30 זְבוּלֻן לֹא הוֹרִישׁ אֶת־יוֹשְׁבֵי קִטְרוֹן וְאֶת־יוֹשְׁבֵי נַהֲלֹל וַיֵּשֶׁב הַכְּנַעֲנִי בְּקִרְבּוֹ וַיִּהְיוּ לָמַס׃ ס 31 אָשֵׁר לֹא הוֹרִישׁ אֶת־יֹשְׁבֵי עַכּוֹ וְאֶת־יוֹשְׁבֵי צִידוֹן וְאֶת־אַחְלָב וְאֶת־אַכְזִיב וְאֶת־חֶלְבָּה וְאֶת־אֲפִיק וְאֶת־רְחֹב׃ 32 וַיֵּשֶׁב הָאָשֵׁרִי בְּקֶרֶב הַכְּנַעֲנִי יֹשְׁבֵי הָאָרֶץ כִּי לֹא הוֹרִישׁוֹ׃ ס 33 נַפְתָּלִי לֹא־הוֹרִישׁ אֶת־יֹשְׁבֵי בֵית־שֶׁמֶשׁ וְאֶת־יֹשְׁבֵי בֵית־עֲנָת וַיֵּשֶׁב בְּקֶרֶב הַכְּנַעֲנִי יֹשְׁבֵי הָאָרֶץ וְיֹשְׁבֵי בֵית־שֶׁמֶשׁ וּבֵית עֲנָת הָיוּ לָהֶם לָמַס׃ ס

34 וַיִּלְחֲצוּ הָאֱמֹרִי אֶת־בְּנֵי־דָן הָהָרָה כִּי־לֹא נְתָנוֹ לָרֶדֶת לָעֵמֶק׃ 35 וַיּוֹאֶל הָאֱמֹרִי לָשֶׁבֶת בְּהַר־חֶרֶס בְּאַיָּלוֹן וּבְשַׁעַלְבִים וַתִּכְבַּד יַד בֵּית־יוֹסֵף וַיִּהְיוּ לָמַס׃ 36 וּגְבוּל הָאֱמֹרִי מִמַּעֲלֵה עַקְרַבִּים מֵהַסֶּלַע וָמָעְלָה׃ פ

g Some Septuagint mss. read "Edomites."

2 An angel of the Lord came up from Gilgal to Bochim and said, "I brought you up from Egypt and I took you into the land which I had promised on oath to your fathers. And I said, 'I will never break My covenant with you. [2]And you, for your part, must make no covenant with the inhabitants of this land; you must tear down their altars.' But you have not obeyed Me—look what you have done! [3]Therefore, I have resolved not to drive them out before you; they shall become your oppressors,[a] and their gods shall be a snare to you." [4]As the angel of the Lord spoke these words to all the Israelites, the people broke into weeping. [5]So they named that place Bochim,[b] and they offered sacrifices there to the Lord.

[6]When Joshua dismissed the people, the Israelites went to their allotted territories and took possession of the land. [7]The people served the Lord during the lifetime of Joshua and the lifetime of the older people who lived on after Joshua and who had witnessed all the marvelous deeds that the Lord had wrought for Israel. [8]Joshua son of Nun, the servant of the Lord, died at the age of one hundred and ten years, [9]and was buried on his own property, at Timnath-heres[c] in the hill country of Ephraim, north of Mount Gaash. [10]And all that generation were likewise gathered to their fathers.

Another generation arose after them, which had not experienced [the deliverance of] the Lord or the deeds that He had wrought for Israel. [11]And the Israelites did what was offensive to the Lord. They worshiped the Baalim [12]and forsook the Lord, the God of their fathers, who had brought them out of the land of Egypt. They followed other gods, from among the gods of the peoples around them, and bowed

ב וַיַּ֧עַל מַלְאַךְ־יְהֹוָ֛ה מִן־הַגִּלְגָּ֖ל אֶל־הַבֹּכִ֑ים פ וַיֹּ֙אמֶר֙ אַעֲלֶ֣ה אֶתְכֶ֜ם מִמִּצְרַ֗יִם וָאָבִ֤יא אֶתְכֶם֙ אֶל־הָאָ֔רֶץ אֲשֶׁ֥ר נִשְׁבַּ֖עְתִּי לַאֲבֹֽתֵיכֶ֑ם וָאֹמַ֕ר לֹא־אָפֵ֧ר בְּרִיתִ֛י אִתְּכֶ֖ם לְעוֹלָֽם׃ [2]וְאַתֶּ֗ם לֹֽא־תִכְרְת֤וּ בְרִית֙ לְיֽוֹשְׁבֵי֙ הָאָ֣רֶץ הַזֹּ֔את מִזְבְּחוֹתֵיהֶ֖ם תִּתֹּצ֑וּן וְלֹֽא־שְׁמַעְתֶּ֣ם בְּקֹלִ֔י מַה־זֹּ֖את עֲשִׂיתֶֽם׃ [3]וְגַ֣ם אָמַ֔רְתִּי לֹֽא־אֲגָרֵ֥שׁ אוֹתָ֖ם מִפְּנֵיכֶ֑ם וְהָי֤וּ לָכֶם֙ לְצִדִּ֔ים וֵאלֹ֣הֵיהֶ֔ם יִהְי֥וּ לָכֶ֖ם לְמוֹקֵֽשׁ׃ [4]וַיְהִ֗י כְּדַבֵּ֞ר מַלְאַ֤ךְ יְהֹוָה֙ אֶת־הַדְּבָרִ֣ים הָאֵ֔לֶּה אֶֽל־כׇּל־בְּנֵ֖י יִשְׂרָאֵ֑ל וַיִּשְׂא֥וּ הָעָ֛ם אֶת־קוֹלָ֖ם וַיִּבְכּֽוּ׃ [5]וַֽיִּקְרְא֛וּ שֵֽׁם־הַמָּק֥וֹם הַה֖וּא בֹּכִ֑ים וַיִּזְבְּחוּ־שָׁ֖ם לַֽיהֹוָֽה׃ פ

[6]וַיְשַׁלַּ֥ח יְהוֹשֻׁ֖עַ אֶת־הָעָ֑ם וַיֵּלְכ֧וּ בְנֵֽי־יִשְׂרָאֵ֛ל אִ֥ישׁ לְנַחֲלָת֖וֹ לָרֶ֥שֶׁת אֶת־הָאָֽרֶץ׃ [7]וַיַּעַבְד֤וּ הָעָם֙ אֶת־יְהֹוָ֔ה כֹּ֖ל יְמֵ֣י יְהוֹשֻׁ֑עַ וְכֹ֣ל ׀ יְמֵ֣י הַזְּקֵנִ֗ים אֲשֶׁ֨ר הֶאֱרִ֤יכוּ יָמִים֙ אַחֲרֵ֣י יְהוֹשׁ֔וּעַ אֲשֶׁ֣ר רָא֗וּ אֵ֣ת כׇּל־מַעֲשֵׂ֤ה יְהֹוָה֙ הַגָּד֔וֹל אֲשֶׁ֥ר עָשָׂ֖ה לְיִשְׂרָאֵֽל׃ [8]וַיָּ֛מׇת יְהוֹשֻׁ֥עַ בִּן־נ֖וּן עֶ֣בֶד יְהֹוָ֑ה בֶּן־מֵאָ֥ה וָעֶ֖שֶׂר שָׁנִֽים׃ [9]וַיִּקְבְּר֤וּ אוֹתוֹ֙ בִּגְב֣וּל נַחֲלָת֔וֹ בְּתִמְנַת־חֶ֖רֶס בְּהַ֣ר אֶפְרָ֑יִם מִצְּפ֖וֹן לְהַר־גָּֽעַשׁ׃ [10]וְגַם֙ כׇּל־הַדּ֣וֹר הַה֔וּא נֶאֶסְפ֖וּ אֶל־אֲבוֹתָ֑יו וַיָּ֩קׇם֩ דּ֨וֹר אַחֵ֜ר אַחֲרֵיהֶ֗ם אֲשֶׁ֤ר לֹא־יָֽדְעוּ֙ אֶת־יְהֹוָ֔ה וְגַם֙ אֶת־הַֽמַּעֲשֶׂ֔ה אֲשֶׁ֥ר עָשָׂ֖ה לְיִשְׂרָאֵֽל׃ ס [11]וַיַּעֲשׂ֧וּ בְנֵֽי־יִשְׂרָאֵ֛ל אֶת־הָרַ֖ע בְּעֵינֵ֣י יְהֹוָ֑ה וַיַּעַבְד֖וּ אֶת־הַבְּעָלִֽים׃ [12]וַיַּעַזְב֞וּ אֶת־יְהֹוָ֣ה ׀ אֱלֹהֵ֣י אֲבוֹתָ֗ם הַמּוֹצִ֣יא אוֹתָם֮ מֵאֶ֣רֶץ מִצְרַיִם֒ וַיֵּלְכ֞וּ אַחֲרֵ֣י ׀ אֱלֹהִ֣ים אֲחֵרִ֗ים מֵאֱלֹהֵ֤י הָֽעַמִּים֙

a   *So Targum and other ancient versions. Meaning of Heb. uncertain.*

b   *I.e., "weepers."*

c   *Some mss. read "Timnath-serah"; cf. Josh. 24.30.*

down to them; they provoked the LORD. 13They forsook the LORD and worshiped Baal and the Ashtaroth.*d* 14Then the LORD was incensed at Israel, and He handed them over to foes*e* who plundered them. He surrendered them to their enemies on all sides, and they could no longer hold their own against their enemies. 15In all their campaigns, the hand of the LORD was against them to their undoing, as the LORD had declared and as the LORD had sworn to them; and they were in great distress. 16Then the LORD raised up chieftains who delivered them from those who plundered them. 17But they did not heed their chieftains either; they went astray after other gods and bowed down to them. They were quick to turn aside from the way their fathers had followed in obedience to the commandments of the LORD; they did not do right. 18When the LORD raised up chieftains for them, the LORD would be with the chieftain and would save them from their enemies during the chieftain's lifetime; for the LORD would be moved to pity by their moanings because of those who oppressed and crushed them. 19But when the chieftain died, they would again act basely, even more than *f*-the preceding generation-*f*— following other gods, worshiping them, and bowing down to them; they omitted none of their practices and stubborn ways.

20Then the LORD became incensed against Israel, and He said, "Since that nation has transgressed the covenant that I enjoined upon their fathers and has not obeyed Me, 21I for My part will no longer drive out before them any of the nations that Joshua left when he died." 22For it was in order to test Israel by them—[to see] whether or not they would faithfully walk in the ways of the LORD, as their fathers had done— 23that the LORD had left those nations, instead of driving them out at once, and had not delivered them into the hands of Joshua.

---

d Canaanite female deities.
e Lit. "plunderers."
f-f Lit. "their fathers."

אֲשֶׁר֙ סְבִיבֽוֹתֵיהֶ֔ם וַיִּֽשְׁתַּחֲו֖וּ לָהֶ֑ם וַיַּכְעִ֖סוּ אֶת־יְהוָֽה: 13 וַיַּעַזְב֖וּ אֶת־יְהוָ֑ה וַיַּעַבְד֥וּ לַבַּ֖עַל וְלָעַשְׁתָּרֽוֹת: 14 וַיִּֽחַר־אַ֤ף יְהוָה֙ בְּיִשְׂרָאֵ֔ל וַֽיִּתְּנֵם֙ בְּיַד־שֹׁסִ֔ים וַיָּשֹׁ֖סּוּ אֹתָ֑ם וַֽיִּמְכְּרֵ֞ם בְּיַ֤ד אֽוֹיְבֵיהֶם֙ מִסָּבִ֔יב וְלֹֽא־יָכְל֣וּ ע֔וֹד לַעֲמֹ֖ד לִפְנֵ֥י אֽוֹיְבֵיהֶֽם: 15 בְּכֹ֣ל ׀ אֲשֶׁ֣ר יָֽצְא֗וּ יַד־יְהוָה֙ הָיְתָה־בָּ֣ם לְרָעָ֔ה כַּֽאֲשֶׁר֙ דִּבֶּ֣ר יְהוָ֔ה וְכַאֲשֶׁ֛ר נִשְׁבַּ֥ע יְהוָ֖ה לָהֶ֑ם וַיֵּ֥צֶר לָהֶ֖ם מְאֹֽד: 16 וַיָּ֥קֶם יְהוָ֖ה שֹֽׁפְטִ֑ים וַיּ֣וֹשִׁיע֔וּם מִיַּ֖ד שֹׁסֵיהֶֽם: 17 וְגַ֤ם אֶל־שֹֽׁפְטֵיהֶם֙ לֹ֣א שָׁמֵ֔עוּ כִּ֣י זָנ֗וּ אַֽחֲרֵי֙ אֱלֹהִ֣ים אֲחֵרִ֔ים וַיִּֽשְׁתַּחֲו֖וּ לָהֶ֑ם סָ֣רוּ מַהֵ֗ר מִן־הַדֶּ֜רֶךְ אֲשֶׁ֨ר הָלְכ֧וּ אֲבוֹתָ֛ם לִשְׁמֹ֥עַ מִצְוֺת־יְהוָ֖ה לֹא־עָ֥שׂוּ כֵֽן: 18 וְכִֽי־הֵקִ֣ים יְהוָ֣ה ׀ לָהֶם֮ שֹֽׁפְטִים֒ וְהָיָ֤ה יְהוָה֙ עִם־הַשֹּׁפֵ֔ט וְהֽוֹשִׁיעָם֙ מִיַּ֣ד אֹֽיְבֵיהֶ֔ם כֹּ֖ל יְמֵ֣י הַשּׁוֹפֵ֑ט כִּֽי־יִנָּחֵ֤ם יְהוָה֙ מִנַּֽאֲקָתָ֔ם מִפְּנֵ֥י לֹֽחֲצֵיהֶ֖ם וְדֹֽחֲקֵיהֶֽם: 19 וְהָיָ֣ה ׀ בְּמ֣וֹת הַשּׁוֹפֵ֗ט יָשֻׁ֙בוּ֙ וְהִשְׁחִ֤יתוּ מֵֽאֲבוֹתָם֙ לָלֶ֗כֶת אַֽחֲרֵי֙ אֱלֹהִ֣ים אֲחֵרִ֔ים לְעָבְדָ֖ם וּלְהִשְׁתַּחֲוֺ֣ת לָהֶ֑ם לֹ֤א הִפִּ֙ילוּ֙ מִמַּ֣עַלְלֵיהֶ֔ם וּמִדַּרְכָּ֖ם הַקָּשָֽׁה: 20 וַיִּֽחַר־אַ֥ף יְהוָ֖ה בְּיִשְׂרָאֵ֑ל וַיֹּ֗אמֶר יַ֩עַן֩ אֲשֶׁ֨ר עָֽבְר֜וּ הַגּ֣וֹי הַזֶּ֗ה אֶת־בְּרִיתִי֙ אֲשֶׁ֣ר צִוִּ֣יתִי אֶת־אֲבוֹתָ֔ם וְלֹ֥א שָׁמְע֖וּ לְקוֹלִֽי: 21 גַּם־אֲנִי֙ לֹ֣א אוֹסִ֔יף לְהוֹרִ֥ישׁ אִ֖ישׁ מִפְּנֵיהֶ֑ם מִן־הַגּוֹיִ֛ם אֲשֶׁר־עָזַ֥ב יְהוֹשֻׁ֖עַ וַיָּמֹֽת: 22 לְמַ֛עַן נַסּ֥וֹת בָּ֖ם אֶת־יִשְׂרָאֵ֑ל הֲשֹׁמְרִ֣ים הֵם֩ אֶת־דֶּ֨רֶךְ יְהוָ֜ה לָלֶ֤כֶת בָּם֙* כַּֽאֲשֶׁ֛ר שָׁמְר֥וּ אֲבוֹתָ֖ם אִם־לֹֽא: 23 וַיַּנַּ֤ח יְהוָה֙ אֶת־הַגּוֹיִ֣ם הָאֵ֔לֶּה לְבִלְתִּ֥י הֽוֹרִישָׁ֖ם מַהֵ֑ר וְלֹ֥א נְתָנָ֖ם בְּיַד־יְהוֹשֻֽׁעַ: פ

3 ^aThese are the nations that the Lord left so that He might test by them all the Israelites who had not known any of the wars of Canaan, ²so that succeeding generations of Israelites might be made to experience war—but only those who had not known the ^b-former wars:-^b ³the five principalities^c of the Philistines and all the Canaanites, Sidonians, and Hivites who inhabited the hill country of the Lebanon from Mount Baal-hermon to Lebo-hamath.^d ⁴These served as a means of testing Israel, to learn whether they would obey the commandments which the Lord had enjoined upon their fathers through Moses.

⁵The Israelites settled among the Canaanites, Hittites, Amorites, Perizzites, Hivites, and Jebusites; ⁶they took their daughters to wife and gave their own daughters to their sons, and they worshiped their gods. ⁷The Israelites did what was offensive to the Lord; they ignored the Lord their God and worshiped the Baalim and the Asheroth. ⁸The Lord became incensed at Israel and surrendered them to King Cushan-rishathaim of Aram-naharaim; and the Israelites were subject to Cushan-rishathaim for eight years. ⁹The Israelites cried out to the Lord, and the Lord raised a champion for the Israelites to deliver them: Othniel the Kenizzite, a younger kinsman of Caleb. ¹⁰The spirit of the Lord descended upon him and he became Israel's chieftain. He went out to war, and the Lord delivered King Cushan-rishathaim of Aram into his hands. He prevailed over Cushan-rishathaim, ¹¹and the land had peace for forty years.

When Othniel the Kenizzite died, ¹²the Israelites again did what was offensive to the Lord. And because they did what was offensive to the Lord, the Lord let King Eglon of Moab prevail over Israel. ¹³[Eglon] brought the Ammonites and the Amalekites together under his command, and went and defeated Israel and occu-

---

a　The sentence structure of vv. 1–2 is uncertain.
b-b　Lit. "them formerly."
c　Lit. "lords."
d　See note at Num. 13.21.

ג וְאֵ֣לֶּה הַגּוֹיִ֗ם אֲשֶׁ֤ר הִנִּ֙יחַ֙ יְהוָ֔ה לְנַסּ֥וֹת בָּ֖ם אֶת־יִשְׂרָאֵ֑ל אֵ֚ת כָּל־אֲשֶׁ֣ר לֹֽא־יָֽדְע֔וּ אֵ֖ת כָּל־מִלְחֲמ֥וֹת כְּנָֽעַן׃ 2 רַ֗ק לְמַ֙עַן֙ דַּ֣עַת דֹּר֣וֹת בְּנֵֽי־יִשְׂרָאֵ֔ל לְלַמְּדָ֖ם מִלְחָמָ֑ה רַ֥ק אֲשֶׁר־לְפָנִ֖ים לֹ֥א יְדָעֽוּם׃ 3 חֲמֵ֣שֶׁת ׀ סַרְנֵ֣י פְלִשְׁתִּ֗ים וְכָל־הַֽכְּנַעֲנִי֙ וְהַצִּ֣ידֹנִ֔י וְהַ֣חִוִּ֔י יֹשֵׁ֖ב הַ֣ר הַלְּבָנ֑וֹן מֵהַ֣ר בַּ֣עַל חֶרְמ֔וֹן עַ֖ד לְב֥וֹא חֲמָֽת׃ 4 וַֽיִּהְי֗וּ לְנַסּ֤וֹת בָּם֙ אֶת־יִשְׂרָאֵ֔ל לָדַ֗עַת הֲיִשְׁמְעוּ֙ אֶת־מִצְוֺ֣ת יְהוָ֔ה אֲשֶׁר־צִוָּ֥ה אֶת־אֲבוֹתָ֖ם בְּיַד־מֹשֶֽׁה׃

5 וּבְנֵ֣י יִשְׂרָאֵ֔ל יָשְׁב֖וּ בְּקֶ֣רֶב הַֽכְּנַעֲנִ֑י הַחִתִּ֤י וְהָֽאֱמֹרִי֙ וְהַפְּרִזִּ֔י וְהַֽחִוִּ֖י וְהַיְבוּסִֽי׃ 6 וַיִּקְח֨וּ אֶת־בְּנוֹתֵיהֶ֤ם לָהֶם֙ לְנָשִׁ֔ים וְאֶת־בְּנֽוֹתֵיהֶ֖ם נָתְנ֣וּ לִבְנֵיהֶ֑ם וַיַּעַבְד֖וּ אֶת־אֱלֹהֵיהֶֽם׃ פ 7 וַיַּעֲשׂ֨וּ בְנֵֽי־יִשְׂרָאֵ֤ל אֶת־הָרַע֙ בְּעֵינֵ֣י יְהוָ֔ה וַֽיִּשְׁכְּח֖וּ אֶת־יְהוָ֣ה אֱלֹֽהֵיהֶ֑ם וַיַּעַבְד֥וּ אֶת־הַבְּעָלִ֖ים וְאֶת־הָאֲשֵׁרֽוֹת׃ 8 וַיִּֽחַר־אַ֤ף יְהוָה֙ בְּיִשְׂרָאֵ֔ל וַֽיִּמְכְּרֵ֗ם בְּיַד֙ כּוּשַׁ֣ן רִשְׁעָתַ֔יִם מֶ֖לֶךְ אֲרַ֣ם נַהֲרָ֑יִם וַיַּעַבְד֧וּ בְנֵֽי־יִשְׂרָאֵ֛ל אֶת־כּוּשַׁ֥ן רִשְׁעָתַ֖יִם שְׁמֹנֶ֥ה שָׁנִֽים׃ 9 וַיִּזְעֲק֤וּ בְנֵֽי־יִשְׂרָאֵל֙ אֶל־יְהוָ֔ה וַיָּ֨קֶם יְהוָ֥ה מוֹשִׁ֛יעַ לִבְנֵ֥י יִשְׂרָאֵ֖ל וַיּֽוֹשִׁיעֵ֑ם אֵ֚ת עָתְנִיאֵ֣ל בֶּן־קְנַ֔ז אֲחִ֥י כָלֵ֖ב הַקָּטֹ֥ן מִמֶּֽנּוּ׃ 10 וַתְּהִ֨י עָלָ֥יו רֽוּחַ־יְהוָה֮ וַיִּשְׁפֹּ֣ט אֶת־יִשְׂרָאֵל֒ וַיֵּצֵא֙ לַמִּלְחָמָ֔ה וַיִּתֵּ֤ן יְהוָה֙ בְּיָד֔וֹ אֶת־כּוּשַׁ֥ן רִשְׁעָתַ֖יִם מֶ֣לֶךְ אֲרָ֑ם וַתָּ֣עָז יָד֔וֹ עַ֖ל כּוּשַׁ֥ן רִשְׁעָתָֽיִם׃ 11 וַתִּשְׁקֹ֥ט הָאָ֖רֶץ אַרְבָּעִ֣ים שָׁנָ֑ה וַיָּ֖מָת עָתְנִיאֵ֥ל בֶּן־קְנַֽז׃ פ 12 וַיֹּסִ֙פוּ֙ בְּנֵ֣י יִשְׂרָאֵ֔ל לַעֲשׂ֥וֹת הָרַ֖ע בְּעֵינֵ֣י יְהוָ֑ה וַיְחַזֵּ֨ק יְהוָ֜ה אֶת־עֶגְל֤וֹן מֶֽלֶךְ־מוֹאָב֙ עַל־יִשְׂרָאֵ֔ל עַ֛ל כִּֽי־עָשׂ֥וּ אֶת־הָרַ֖ע בְּעֵינֵ֥י יְהוָֽה׃ 13 וַיֶּאֱסֹ֣ף אֵלָ֔יו אֶת־בְּנֵ֥י עַמּ֖וֹן וַעֲמָלֵ֑ק וַיֵּ֗לֶךְ וַיַּךְ֙ אֶת־יִשְׂרָאֵ֔ל וַיִּֽירְשׁ֖וּ אֶת־עִ֥יר

pied the City of Palms. 14The Israelites were subject to King Eglon of Moab for eighteen years.

15Then the Israelites cried out to the LORD, and the LORD raised up a champion for them: the Benjaminite Ehud son of Gera, a left-handed man. It happened that the Israelites sent tribute to King Eglon of Moab through him. 16So Ehud made for himself a two-edged dagger, a *gomed* in length, which he girded on his right side under his cloak. 17He presented the tribute to King Eglon of Moab. Now Eglon was a very stout man. 18When [Ehud] had finished presenting the tribute, he dismissed the people who had conveyed the tribute. 19But he himself returned from Pesilim, near Gilgal, and said, "Your Majesty, I have a secret message for you." [Eglon] thereupon commanded, "Silence!" So all those in attendance left his presence; 20and when Ehud approached him, he was sitting alone in his cool upper chamber. Ehud said, "I have a message for you from God"; whereupon he rose from his seat. 21Reaching with his left hand, Ehud drew the dagger from his right side and drove it into [Eglon's]ᵉ belly. 22The fat closed over the blade and the hilt went in after the blade—for he did not pull the dagger out of his belly—and the filthᶠ came out.

23Stepping out into the vestibule,ᶠ Ehud shut the doors of the upper chamber on him and locked them. 24After he left, the courtiers returned. When they saw that the doors of the upper chamber were locked, they thought, "He must be relieving himself in the cool chamber." 25They waited a long time; and when he did not open the doors of the chamber, they took the key and opened them—and there their master was lying dead on the floor! 26But Ehud had made good his escape while they delayed; he had passed Pesilim and escaped to Seirah. 27When he got there, he had the ram's horn sounded through the hill country of Ephraim, and all the Israelites descended with him from the hill

---

e Heb. "his."
f Meaning of Heb. uncertain.

הַתְּמָרִים׃ 14 וַיַּעַבְד֤וּ בְנֵֽי־יִשְׂרָאֵל֙ אֶת־עֶגְל֣וֹן מֶֽלֶךְ־מוֹאָ֔ב שְׁמֹנֶ֥ה עֶשְׂרֵ֖ה שָׁנָֽה׃ ס

15 וַיִּזְעֲק֣וּ בְנֵֽי־יִשְׂרָאֵל֮ אֶל־יְהוָה֒ וַיָּקֶם֩ יְהוָ֨ה לָהֶ֜ם מוֹשִׁ֗יעַ אֶת־אֵה֤וּד בֶּן־גֵּרָא֙ בֶּן־הַיְמִינִ֔י אִ֥ישׁ אִטֵּ֖ר יַד־יְמִינ֑וֹ וַיִּשְׁלְח֨וּ בְנֵי־יִשְׂרָאֵ֤ל בְּיָדוֹ֙ מִנְחָ֔ה לְעֶגְל֖וֹן מֶ֥לֶךְ מוֹאָֽב׃ 16 וַיַּ֩עַשׂ֩ ל֨וֹ אֵה֜וּד חֶ֗רֶב וְלָ֛הּ שְׁנֵ֥י פֵי֖וֹת גֹּ֣מֶד אָרְכָּ֑הּ וַיַּחְגֹּ֤ר אוֹתָהּ֙ מִתַּ֣חַת לְמַדָּ֔יו עַ֖ל יֶ֥רֶךְ יְמִינֽוֹ׃ 17 וַיַּקְרֵב֙ אֶת־הַמִּנְחָ֔ה לְעֶגְל֖וֹן מֶ֣לֶךְ מוֹאָ֑ב וְעֶגְל֕וֹן אִ֥ישׁ בָּרִ֖יא מְאֹֽד׃ 18 וַֽיְהִ֗י כַּאֲשֶׁ֤ר כִּלָּה֙ לְהַקְרִ֣יב אֶת־הַמִּנְחָ֔ה וַיְשַׁלַּח֙ אֶת־הָעָ֔ם נֹשְׂאֵ֖י הַמִּנְחָֽה׃ 19 וְה֣וּא שָׁ֗ב מִן־הַפְּסִילִים֮ אֲשֶׁ֣ר אֶת־הַגִּלְגָּל֒ וַיֹּ֕אמֶר דְּבַר־סֵ֥תֶר לִ֛י אֵלֶ֖יךָ הַמֶּ֑לֶךְ וַיֹּ֣אמֶר הָ֔ס וַיֵּֽצְאוּ֙ מֵֽעָלָ֔יו כָּל־הָעֹמְדִ֖ים עָלָֽיו׃ 20 וְאֵה֣וּד ׀ בָּ֣א אֵלָ֗יו וְהֽוּא־יֹ֠שֵׁב בַּעֲלִיַּ֨ת הַמְּקֵרָ֤ה אֲשֶׁר־לוֹ֙ לְבַדּ֔וֹ וַיֹּ֣אמֶר אֵה֗וּד דְּבַר־אֱלֹהִ֥ים לִ֛י אֵלֶ֖יךָ וַיָּ֥קָם מֵעַ֥ל הַכִּסֵּֽא׃ 21 וַיִּשְׁלַ֤ח אֵהוּד֙ אֶת־יַ֣ד שְׂמֹאל֔וֹ וַיִּקַּח֙ אֶת־הַחֶ֔רֶב מֵעַ֖ל יֶ֣רֶךְ יְמִינ֑וֹ וַיִּתְקָעֶ֖הָ בְּבִטְנֽוֹ׃ 22 וַיָּבֹ֨א גַֽם־הַנִּצָּ֜ב אַחַ֣ר הַלַּ֗הַב וַיִּסְגֹּ֤ר הַחֵ֙לֶב֙ בְּעַ֣ד הַלַּ֔הַב כִּ֣י לֹ֥א שָׁלַ֛ף הַחֶ֖רֶב מִבִּטְנ֑וֹ וַיֵּצֵ֖א הַֽפַּרְשְׁדֹֽנָה׃ 23 וַיֵּצֵ֥א אֵה֖וּד הַֽמִּסְדְּר֑וֹנָה וַיִּסְגֹּ֞ר דַּלְת֧וֹת הָעֲלִיָּ֛ה בַּעֲד֖וֹ וְנָעָֽל׃ 24 וְה֤וּא יָצָא֙ וַעֲבָדָ֣יו בָּ֔אוּ וַיִּרְא֕וּ וְהִנֵּ֛ה דַּלְת֥וֹת הָעֲלִיָּ֖ה נְעֻל֑וֹת וַיֹּ֣אמְר֔וּ אַ֣ךְ מֵסִ֥יךְ ה֛וּא אֶת־רַגְלָ֖יו בַּחֲדַ֥ר הַמְּקֵרָֽה׃ 25 וַיָּחִ֣ילוּ עַד־בּ֔וֹשׁ וְהִנֵּ֛ה אֵינֶ֥נּוּ פֹתֵ֖חַ דַּלְת֣וֹת הָעֲלִיָּ֑ה וַיִּקְח֤וּ אֶת־הַמַּפְתֵּ֙חַ֙ וַיִּפְתָּ֔חוּ וְהִנֵּה֙ אֲדֹ֣נֵיהֶ֔ם נֹפֵ֥ל אַ֖רְצָה מֵֽת׃ 26 וְאֵה֥וּד נִמְלַ֖ט עַ֣ד הִֽתְמַהְמְהָ֑ם וְהוּא֙ עָבַ֣ר אֶת־הַפְּסִילִ֔ים וַיִּמָּלֵ֖ט הַשְּׂעִירָֽתָה׃ 27 וַיְהִ֣י בְּבוֹא֔וֹ וַיִּתְקַ֥ע בַּשּׁוֹפָ֖ר בְּהַ֣ר אֶפְרָ֑יִם וַיֵּרְד֧וּ עִמּ֛וֹ בְנֵֽי־יִשְׂרָאֵ֖ל מִן־הָהָ֑ר וְה֖וּא לִפְנֵיהֶֽם׃ 28 וַיֹּ֤אמֶר אֲלֵהֶם֙ רִדְפ֣וּ אַחֲרַ֔י

country; and he took the lead. 28"Follow me closely," he said, "for the LORD has delivered your enemies, the Moabites, into your hands." They followed him down and seized the fords of the Jordan against the Moabites; they let no one cross. 29On that occasion they slew about 10,000 Moabites; they were all robust and brave men, yet not one of them escaped. 30On that day, Moab submitted to Israel; and the land was tranquil for eighty years.

31After him came Shamgar *g*-son of Anath,-*g* who slew six hundred Philistines with an ox-goad. He too was a champion of Israel.

4 The Israelites again did what was offensive to the LORD—Ehud now being dead. 2And the LORD surrendered them to King Jabin of Canaan, who reigned in Hazor. His army commander was Sisera, whose base was Harosheth-goiim. 3The Israelites cried out to the LORD; for he had nine hundred iron chariots, and he had oppressed Israel ruthlessly for twenty years.

4Deborah, wife of Lappidoth, was a prophetess; she led Israel at that time. 5She used to sit under the Palm of Deborah, between Ramah and Bethel in the hill country of Ephraim, and the Israelites would come to her for decisions.

6She summoned Barak son of Abinoam, of Kedesh in Naphtali, and said to him, "The LORD, the God of Israel, has commanded: Go, march up to Mount Tabor, and take with you ten thousand men of Naphtali and Zebulun. 7And I will draw Sisera, Jabin's army commander, with his chariots and his troops, toward you up to the Wadi Kishon; and I will deliver him into your hands." 8But Barak said to her, "If you will go with me, I will go; if not, I will not go." 9"Very well, I will go with you," she answered. "However, there will be no glory for you in the course you are taking, for then the LORD will deliver Sisera into the hands of a woman." So Deborah went with Barak to Kedesh. 10Barak then mus-

כִּי־נָתַ֨ן יְהוָ֧ה אֶת־אֹֽיְבֵיכֶ֛ם אֶת־מוֹאָ֖ב בְּיֶדְכֶ֑ם וַיֵּרְד֣וּ אַֽחֲרָ֗יו וַֽיִּלְכְּד֞וּ אֶת־מַעְבְּר֤וֹת הַיַּרְדֵּן֙ לְמוֹאָ֔ב וְלֹֽא־נָֽתְנ֥וּ אִ֖ישׁ לַֽעֲבֹֽר׃ 29 וַיַּכּ֨וּ אֶת־מוֹאָ֜ב בָּעֵ֣ת הַהִ֗יא כַּֽעֲשֶׂ֤רֶת אֲלָפִים֙ אִ֔ישׁ כָּל־שָׁמֵ֖ן וְכָל־אִ֣ישׁ חָ֑יִל וְלֹ֥א נִמְלַ֖ט אִֽישׁ׃ 30 וַתִּכָּנַ֤ע מוֹאָב֙ בַּיּ֣וֹם הַה֔וּא תַּ֖חַת יַ֣ד יִשְׂרָאֵ֑ל וַתִּשְׁקֹ֥ט הָאָ֖רֶץ שְׁמוֹנִ֥ים שָׁנָֽה׃ ס

31 וְאַֽחֲרָ֤יו הָיָה֙ שַׁמְגַּ֣ר בֶּן־עֲנָ֔ת וַיַּ֤ךְ אֶת־פְּלִשְׁתִּים֙ שֵֽׁשׁ־מֵא֣וֹת אִ֔ישׁ בְּמַלְמַ֖ד הַבָּקָ֑ר וַיֹּ֥שַׁע גַּם־ה֖וּא אֶת־יִשְׂרָאֵֽל׃ ס

ד וַיֹּסִ֙פוּ֙ בְּנֵ֣י יִשְׂרָאֵ֔ל לַֽעֲשׂ֥וֹת הָרַ֖ע בְּעֵינֵ֣י יְהוָ֑ה וְאֵה֖וּד מֵֽת׃ 2 וַיִּמְכְּרֵ֣ם יְהוָ֗ה בְּיַד֙ יָבִ֣ין מֶֽלֶךְ־כְּנַ֔עַן אֲשֶׁ֥ר מָלַ֖ךְ בְּחָצ֑וֹר וְשַׂר־צְבָאוֹ֙ סִֽיסְרָ֔א וְה֥וּא יוֹשֵׁ֖ב בַּֽחֲרֹ֥שֶׁת הַגּוֹיִֽם׃ 3 וַיִּצְעֲק֥וּ בְנֵֽי־יִשְׂרָאֵ֖ל אֶל־יְהוָ֑ה כִּ֠י תְּשַׁ֤ע מֵאוֹת֙ רֶֽכֶב־בַּרְזֶל֙ ל֔וֹ וְה֗וּא לָחַ֞ץ אֶת־בְּנֵ֧י יִשְׂרָאֵ֛ל בְּחָזְקָ֖ה עֶשְׂרִ֥ים שָׁנָֽה׃ ס

4 וּדְבוֹרָה֙ אִשָּׁ֣ה נְבִיאָ֔ה אֵ֖שֶׁת לַפִּיד֑וֹת הִ֛יא שֹֽׁפְטָ֥ה אֶת־יִשְׂרָאֵ֖ל בָּעֵ֥ת הַהִֽיא׃ 5 וְ֠הִיא יוֹשֶׁ֨בֶת תַּֽחַת־תֹּ֜מֶר דְּבוֹרָ֗ה בֵּ֧ין הָֽרָמָ֛ה וּבֵ֥ין בֵּֽית־אֵ֖ל בְּהַ֣ר אֶפְרָ֑יִם וַיַּֽעֲל֥וּ אֵלֶ֛יהָ בְּנֵ֥י יִשְׂרָאֵ֖ל לַמִּשְׁפָּֽט׃

6 וַתִּשְׁלַ֗ח וַתִּקְרָא֙ לְבָרָ֣ק בֶּן־אֲבִינֹ֔עַם מִקֶּ֖דֶשׁ נַפְתָּלִ֑י וַתֹּ֨אמֶר אֵלָ֜יו הֲלֹ֥א צִוָּ֣ה ׀ יְהוָ֣ה אֱלֹֽהֵֽי־יִשְׂרָאֵ֗ל לֵ֤ךְ וּמָֽשַׁכְתָּ֙ בְּהַ֣ר תָּב֔וֹר וְלָֽקַחְתָּ֣ עִמְּךָ֗ עֲשֶׂ֤רֶת אֲלָפִים֙ אִ֔ישׁ מִבְּנֵ֥י נַפְתָּלִ֖י וּמִבְּנֵ֣י זְבֻל֑וּן׃ 7 וּמָֽשַׁכְתִּ֨י אֵלֶ֜יךָ אֶל־נַ֣חַל קִישׁ֗וֹן אֶת־סִֽיסְרָא֙ שַׂר־צְבָ֣א יָבִ֔ין וְאֶת־רִכְבּ֖וֹ וְאֶת־הֲמוֹנ֑וֹ וּנְתַתִּ֖יהוּ בְּיָדֶֽךָ׃ 8 וַיֹּ֤אמֶר אֵלֶ֨יהָ֙ בָּרָ֔ק אִם־תֵּֽלְכִ֥י עִמִּ֖י וְהָלָ֑כְתִּי וְאִם־לֹ֥א תֵֽלְכִ֛י עִמִּ֖י לֹ֥א אֵלֵֽךְ׃ 9 וַתֹּ֜אמֶר הָלֹ֧ךְ אֵלֵ֣ךְ עִמָּ֗ךְ אֶ֚פֶס כִּי֩ לֹ֨א תִֽהְיֶ֜ה תִּֽפְאַרְתְּךָ֗ עַל־הַדֶּ֨רֶךְ֙ אֲשֶׁ֣ר אַתָּ֣ה הוֹלֵ֔ךְ כִּ֣י בְיַד־אִשָּׁ֔ה יִמְכֹּ֥ר יְהוָ֖ה

tered Zebulun and Naphtali at Kedesh; ten thousand men marched up a-after him;-a and Deborah also went up with him.

11Now Heber the Kenite had separated b-from the other Kenites,-b descendants of Hobab, father-in-law of Moses, and had pitched his tent at Elon-bezaanannim, which is near Kedesh.

12Sisera was informed that Barak son of Abinoam had gone up to Mount Tabor. 13So Sisera ordered all his chariots—nine hundred iron chariots—and all the troops he had to move from Harosheth-goiim to the Wadi Kishon. 14Then Deborah said to Barak, "Up! This is the day on which the LORD will deliver Sisera into your hands: the LORD is marching before you." Barak charged down Mount Tabor, followed by the ten thousand men, 15and the LORD threw Sisera and all his chariots and army into a panic c-before the onslaught of Barak.-c Sisera leaped from his chariot and fled on foot 16as Barak pursued the chariots and the soldiers as far as Harosheth-goiim. All of Sisera's soldiers fell by the sword; not a man was left.

17Sisera, meanwhile, had fled on foot to the tent of Jael, wife of Heber the Kenite; for there was friendship between King Jabin of Hazor and the family of Heber the Kenite. 18Jael came out to greet Sisera and said to him, "Come in, my lord, come in here, do not be afraid." So he entered her tent, and she covered him with a blanket. 19He said to her, "Please let me have some water; I am thirsty." She opened a skin of milk and gave him some to drink; and she covered him again. 20He said to her, "Stand at the entrance of the tent. If anybody comes and asks you if there is anybody here, say 'No.'" 21Then Jael wife of Heber took a tent pin and grasped the mallet. When he was fast asleep from exhaustion, she approached him stealthily and drove the pin through his temple till it went down to the ground. Thus he died.

22Now Barak appeared in pursuit of Sisera.

אֶת־סִיסְרָא וַתָּקָם דְּבוֹרָה וַתֵּלֶךְ עִם־בָּרָק קֵדְשָׁה: 10 וַיַּזְעֵק בָּרָק אֶת־זְבוּלֻן וְאֶת־נַפְתָּלִי קֶדְשָׁה וַיַּעַל בְּרַגְלָיו עֲשֶׂרֶת אַלְפֵי אִישׁ וַתַּעַל עִמּוֹ דְּבוֹרָה:

11 וְחֶבֶר הַקֵּינִי נִפְרָד מִקַּיִן מִבְּנֵי חֹבָב חֹתֵן מֹשֶׁה וַיֵּט אָהֳלוֹ עַד־אֵלוֹן בצענים בְּצַעֲנַנִּים אֲשֶׁר אֶת־קֶדֶשׁ:

12 וַיַּגִּדוּ לְסִיסְרָא כִּי עָלָה בָּרָק בֶּן־אֲבִינֹעַם הַר־תָּבוֹר: ס 13 וַיַּזְעֵק סִיסְרָא אֶת־כָּל־רִכְבּוֹ תְּשַׁע מֵאוֹת רֶכֶב בַּרְזֶל וְאֶת־כָּל־הָעָם אֲשֶׁר אִתּוֹ מֵחֲרֹשֶׁת הַגּוֹיִם אֶל־נַחַל קִישׁוֹן: 14 וַתֹּאמֶר דְּבֹרָה אֶל־בָּרָק קוּם כִּי זֶה הַיּוֹם אֲשֶׁר נָתַן יְהוָה אֶת־סִיסְרָא בְּיָדֶךָ הֲלֹא יְהוָה יָצָא לְפָנֶיךָ וַיֵּרֶד בָּרָק מֵהַר תָּבוֹר וַעֲשֶׂרֶת אֲלָפִים אִישׁ אַחֲרָיו: 15 וַיָּהָם יְהוָה אֶת־סִיסְרָא וְאֶת־כָּל־הָרֶכֶב וְאֶת־כָּל־הַמַּחֲנֶה לְפִי־חֶרֶב לִפְנֵי בָרָק וַיֵּרֶד סִיסְרָא מֵעַל הַמֶּרְכָּבָה וַיָּנָס בְּרַגְלָיו: 16 וּבָרָק רָדַף אַחֲרֵי הָרֶכֶב וְאַחֲרֵי הַמַּחֲנֶה עַד חֲרֹשֶׁת הַגּוֹיִם וַיִּפֹּל כָּל־מַחֲנֵה סִיסְרָא לְפִי־חֶרֶב לֹא נִשְׁאַר עַד־אֶחָד: 17 וְסִיסְרָא נָס בְּרַגְלָיו אֶל־אֹהֶל יָעֵל אֵשֶׁת חֶבֶר הַקֵּינִי כִּי שָׁלוֹם בֵּין יָבִין מֶלֶךְ־חָצוֹר וּבֵין בֵּית חֶבֶר הַקֵּינִי: 18 וַתֵּצֵא יָעֵל לִקְרַאת סִיסְרָא וַתֹּאמֶר אֵלָיו סוּרָה אֲדֹנִי סוּרָה אֵלַי אַל־תִּירָא וַיָּסַר אֵלֶיהָ הָאֹהֱלָה וַתְּכַסֵּהוּ בַּשְּׂמִיכָה: 19 וַיֹּאמֶר אֵלֶיהָ הַשְׁקִינִי־נָא מְעַט־מַיִם כִּי צָמֵאתִי וַתִּפְתַּח אֶת־נֹאוד הֶחָלָב וַתַּשְׁקֵהוּ וַתְּכַסֵּהוּ: 20 וַיֹּאמֶר אֵלֶיהָ עֲמֹד פֶּתַח הָאֹהֶל וְהָיָה אִם־אִישׁ יָבוֹא וּשְׁאֵלֵךְ וְאָמַר הֲיֵשׁ־פֹּה אִישׁ וְאָמַרְתְּ אָיִן: 21 וַתִּקַּח יָעֵל אֵשֶׁת־חֶבֶר אֶת־יְתַד הָאֹהֶל וַתָּשֶׂם אֶת־הַמַּקֶּבֶת בְּיָדָהּ וַתָּבוֹא אֵלָיו בַּלָּאט וַתִּתְקַע אֶת־הַיָּתֵד בְּרַקָּתוֹ וַתִּצְנַח בָּאָרֶץ וְהוּא־נִרְדָּם וַיָּעַף וַיָּמֹת: 22 וְהִנֵּה בָרָק רֹדֵף אֶת־סִיסְרָא וַתֵּצֵא יָעֵל

a-a   Lit. "at his feet."
b-b   Lit. "from Cain"; cf. 1.16.
521   c-c   Lit. "at the edge of the sword before Barak."   א׳ נחה   v. 21.

Jael went out to greet him and said, "Come, I will show you the man you are looking for." He went inside with her, and there Sisera was lying dead, with the pin in his temple.

23On that day God subdued King Jabin of Canaan before the Israelites. 24The hand of the Israelites bore harder and harder on King Jabin of Canaan, until they destroyed King Jabin of Canaan.

לִקְרָאתוֹ וַתֹּאמֶר לוֹ לֵךְ וְאַרְאֶךָּ אֶת־
הָאִישׁ אֲשֶׁר־אַתָּה מְבַקֵּשׁ וַיָּבֹא אֵלֶיהָ
וְהִנֵּה סִיסְרָא נֹפֵל מֵת וְהַיָּתֵד בְּרַקָּתוֹ:

23 וַיַּכְנַע אֱלֹהִים בַּיּוֹם הַהוּא אֵת יָבִין
מֶלֶךְ־כְּנָעַן לִפְנֵי בְּנֵי יִשְׂרָאֵל: 24 וַתֵּלֶךְ יַד
בְּנֵי־יִשְׂרָאֵל הָלוֹךְ וְקָשָׁה עַל יָבִין מֶלֶךְ־
כְּנָעַן עַד אֲשֶׁר הִכְרִיתוּ אֵת יָבִין מֶלֶךְ־
כְּנָעַן: פ

ה

בַּיּוֹם הַהוּא	*וַתָּשַׁר דְּבוֹרָה וּבָרָק בֶּן־אֲבִינֹעַם
בְּהִתְנַדֵּב	לֵאמֹר: 2 בִּפְרֹעַ פְּרָעוֹת בְּיִשְׂרָאֵל
שִׁמְעוּ מְלָכִים הַאֲזִינוּ	עַם בָּרֲכוּ יְהוָה: 3
אֲזַמֵּר	אָנֹכִי לַיהוָה אָנֹכִי אָשִׁירָה רֹזְנִים
יְהוָה בְּצֵאתְךָ 4	לַיהוָה אֱלֹהֵי יִשְׂרָאֵל:
אֶרֶץ	בְּצַעְדְּךָ מִשְּׂדֵה אֱדוֹם מִשֵּׂעִיר
גַּם־עָבִים נָטְפוּ	רָעָשָׁה גַּם־שָׁמַיִם נָטְפוּ
זֶה	מָיִם: 5 הָרִים נָזְלוּ מִפְּנֵי יְהוָה
בִּימֵי שַׁמְגַּר בֶּן־ 6	סִינַי מִפְּנֵי יְהוָה אֱלֹהֵי יִשְׂרָאֵל:
וְהֹלְכֵי	עֲנָת בִּימֵי יָעֵל חָדְלוּ אֳרָחוֹת
חָדְלוּ פְרָזוֹן בְּיִשְׂרָאֵל 7	נְתִיבוֹת יֵלְכוּ אֳרָחוֹת עֲקַלְקַלּוֹת:
יִבְחַר 8	חָדֵלּוּ עַד שַׁקַּמְתִּי דְּבוֹרָה שַׁקַּמְתִּי אֵם בְּיִשְׂרָאֵל:
מָגֵן אִם־יֵרָאֶה	אֱלֹהִים חֲדָשִׁים אָז לָחֶם שְׁעָרִים
וְרֹמַח 9 לִבִּי	בְּאַרְבָּעִים אֶלֶף בְּיִשְׂרָאֵל:

5 On that day Deborah and Barak son of Abinoam sang:

2*a*When *b*-locks go untrimmed-*b* in Israel,
When people dedicate themselves—
Bless the Lord!

3Hear, O kings! Give ear, O potentates!
I will sing, will sing to the Lord,
Will hymn the Lord, the God of Israel.

4O Lord, when You came forth from Seir,
Advanced from the country of Edom,
The earth trembled;
The heavens dripped,
Yea, the clouds dripped water,
5The mountains quaked*c*—
Before the Lord, Him of Sinai,
Before the Lord, God of Israel.

6In the days of Shamgar *d*-son of Anath,-*d*
In the days of Jael, caravans*e* ceased,
And wayfarers went
By roundabout paths.
7Deliverance ceased,
Ceased in Israel,
Till you*f* arose, O Deborah,
Arose, O mother, in Israel!
8When they chose new gods,
g-Was there a fighter then in the gates?-*g*
No shield or spear was seen
Among forty thousand in Israel!

---

a   In many parts of this poem the meaning is uncertain.
b-b   Apparently an expression of dedication; cf. Num. 6.5.
c   Taking nazelu as a by-form of nazollu; cf. Targum.
d-d   Or "the Beth-anathite."

e   Or "roads."
f   Heb. qamti, archaic second-person singular feminine.
g-g   Meaning of Heb. uncertain; others "then was war in the gates."

לְחוֹקְקֵי יִשְׂרָאֵל הַמִּתְנַדְּבִים בָּעָם בָּרֲכוּ

יְהוָה: ¹⁰ רֹכְבֵי אֲתֹנוֹת צְחֹרוֹת יֹשְׁבֵי

עַל־מִדִּין וְהֹלְכֵי עַל־דֶּרֶךְ שִׂיחוּ: ¹¹ מִקּוֹל מְחַצְצִים בֵּין

מַשְׁאַבִּים שָׁם יְתַנּוּ צִדְקוֹת יְהוָה צִדְקֹת

פִּרְזֹנוֹ בְּיִשְׂרָאֵל אָז יָרְדוּ לַשְּׁעָרִים עַם־

יְהוָה: ¹² עוּרִי עוּרִי דְּבוֹרָה עוּרִי

עוּרִי דַּבְּרִי־שִׁיר קוּם בָּרָק וּשֲׁבֵה שֶׁבְיְךָ בֶּן־

אֲבִינֹעַם: ¹³ אָז יְרַד שָׂרִיד לְאַדִּירִים עָם יְהוָה

יְרַד־לִי בַּגִּבּוֹרִים: ¹⁴ מִנִּי אֶפְרַיִם שָׁרְשָׁם

בַּעֲמָלֵק אַחֲרֶיךָ בִנְיָמִין בַּעֲמָמֶיךָ מִנִּי

מָכִיר יָרְדוּ מְחֹקְקִים וּמִזְּבוּלֻן מֹשְׁכִים בְּשֵׁבֶט

סֹפֵר: ¹⁵ וְשָׂרַי בְּיִשָּׂשכָר עִם־דְּבֹרָה וְיִשָּׂשכָר

כֵּן בָּרָק בָּעֵמֶק שֻׁלַּח בְּרַגְלָיו בִּפְלַגּוֹת רְאוּבֵן גְּדֹלִים חִקְקֵי־

לֵב: ¹⁶ לָמָּה יָשַׁבְתָּ בֵּין הַמִּשְׁפְּתַיִם לִשְׁמֹעַ

שְׁרִקוֹת עֲדָרִים לִפְלַגּוֹת רְאוּבֵן גְּדוֹלִים חִקְרֵי־

לֵב: ¹⁷ גִּלְעָד בְּעֵבֶר הַיַּרְדֵּן שָׁכֵן וְדָן

לָמָּה יָגוּר אֳנִיּוֹת אָשֵׁר יָשַׁב לְחוֹף

יַמִּים וְעַל מִפְרָצָיו יִשְׁכּוֹן: ¹⁸ זְבֻלוּן

עַם חֵרֵף נַפְשׁוֹ לָמוּת וְנַפְתָּלִי עַל מְרוֹמֵי

שָׂדֶה: ¹⁹ בָּאוּ מְלָכִים נִלְחָמוּ אָז

נִלְחֲמוּ מַלְכֵי כְנַעַן בְּתַעְנַךְ עַל־מֵי

9My heart is with Israel's leaders,
With the dedicated of the people—
Bless the LORD!
10You riders on tawny she-asses,
You who sit on saddle rugs,
And you wayfarers, declare it!
11Louder than the *h*-sound of archers,-*h*
There among the watering places
Let them chant the gracious acts of the LORD,
His gracious deliverance of Israel.
Then did the people of the LORD
March down to the gates!
12Awake, awake, O Deborah!
Awake, awake, strike up the chant!
Arise, O Barak;
Take your captives, O son of Abinoam!

13Then was the remnant made victor over the mighty,
The LORD's people*i* won my victory over the warriors.

14From Ephraim came they whose roots are in Amalek;
After you, your kin Benjamin;
From Machir came down leaders,
From Zebulun such as hold the marshal's staff.
15And Issachar's chiefs were with Deborah;
As Barak, so was Issachar—
Rushing after him into the valley.

Among the clans of Reuben
Were great decisions of heart.
16Why then did you stay among the sheepfolds
And listen as they pipe for the flocks?
Among the clans of Reuben
Were great searchings of heart!
17Gilead tarried beyond the Jordan;
And Dan—why did he linger *j*-by the ships?-*j*
Asher remained at the seacoast
And tarried at his landings.
18Zebulun is a people *k*-that mocked at death,-*k*
Naphtali—on the open heights.

19Then the kings came, they fought:
The kings of Canaan fought
At Taanach, by Megiddo's waters—

---

h-h Or "thunder peals"; meaning of Heb. uncertain.
i   Reading 'am (with pataḥ) Adonai; so many Heb. mss.

j-j Or "at Onioth," a presumed designation of Dan's region.
k-k Lit. "belittled its life to die."

מְגִדּוֹ בֶּצַע כֶּסֶף לֹא לָקָחוּ:

20 מִן־שָׁמַיִם נִלְחָמוּ הַכּוֹכָבִים מִמְּסִלּוֹתָם נִלְחֲמוּ עִם־סִיסְרָא:

21 נַחַל קִישׁוֹן גְּרָפָם נַחַל קְדוּמִים נַחַל קִישׁוֹן תִּדְרְכִי נַפְשִׁי עֹז:

22 אָז הָלְמוּ עִקְּבֵי־סוּס מִדַּהֲרוֹת דַּהֲרוֹת אַבִּירָיו:

23 אוֹרוּ מֵרוֹז אָמַר מַלְאַךְ יְהוָה אֹרוּ אָרוֹר יֹשְׁבֶיהָ כִּי לֹא־בָאוּ לְעֶזְרַת יְהוָה לְעֶזְרַת יְהוָה בַּגִּבּוֹרִים:

24 תְּבֹרַךְ מִנָּשִׁים יָעֵל אֵשֶׁת חֶבֶר הַקֵּינִי מִנָּשִׁים בָּאֹהֶל תְּבֹרָךְ:

25 מַיִם שָׁאַל חָלָב נָתָנָה בְּסֵפֶל אַדִּירִים הִקְרִיבָה חֶמְאָה:

26 יָדָהּ לַיָּתֵד תִּשְׁלַחְנָה וִימִינָהּ לְהַלְמוּת עֲמֵלִים וְהָלְמָה סִיסְרָא מָחֲקָה רֹאשׁוֹ וּמָחֲצָה וְחָלְפָה רַקָּתוֹ:

27 בֵּין רַגְלֶיהָ כָּרַע נָפַל שָׁכָב בֵּין רַגְלֶיהָ כָּרַע נָפָל בַּאֲשֶׁר כָּרַע שָׁם נָפַל שָׁדוּד:

28 בְּעַד הַחַלּוֹן נִשְׁקְפָה וַתְּיַבֵּב אֵם סִיסְרָא בְּעַד הָאֶשְׁנָב מַדּוּעַ בֹּשֵׁשׁ רִכְבּוֹ לָבוֹא מַדּוּעַ אֶחֱרוּ פַּעֲמֵי מַרְכְּבוֹתָיו:

29 חַכְמוֹת שָׂרוֹתֶיהָ תַּעֲנֶינָּה אַף־הִיא תָּשִׁיב אֲמָרֶיהָ לָהּ:

30 הֲלֹא יִמְצְאוּ יְחַלְּקוּ שָׁלָל רַחַם רַחֲמָתַיִם לְרֹאשׁ גֶּבֶר שְׁלַל צְבָעִים לְסִיסְרָא שְׁלַל צְבָעִים רִקְמָה צֶבַע רִקְמָתַיִם לְצַוְּארֵי שָׁלָל:

31 כֵּן יֹאבְדוּ כָל־אוֹיְבֶיךָ יְהוָה וְאֹהֲבָיו כְּצֵאת הַשֶּׁמֶשׁ בִּגְבֻרָתוֹ וַתִּשְׁקֹט הָאָרֶץ אַרְבָּעִים שָׁנָה: פ

They got no spoil of silver.
20The stars fought from heaven,
From their courses they fought against Sisera.
21The torrent Kishon swept them*l* away,
The raging torrent, the torrent Kishon.

March on, my soul, with courage!

22Then the horses' hoofs pounded
m-As headlong galloped the steeds.-*m*
23"Curse Meroz!" said the angel of the LORD.
"Bitterly curse its inhabitants,
Because they came not to the aid of the LORD,
To the aid of the LORD among*n* the warriors."

24Most blessed of women be Jael,
Wife of Heber the Kenite,
Most blessed of women in tents.
25He asked for water, she offered milk;
In a princely bowl she brought him curds.
26Her [left] hand reached for the tent pin,
Her right for the workmen's hammer.
She struck Sisera, crushed his head,
Smashed and pierced his temple.
27At her feet he sank, lay outstretched,
At her feet he sank, lay still;
Where he sank, there he lay——destroyed.

28Through the window peered Sisera's mother,
Behind the lattice she whined:*o*
"Why is his chariot so long in coming?
Why so late the clatter of his wheels?"
29The wisest of her ladies give answer;
She, too, replies to herself:
30"They must be dividing the spoil they have found:
A damsel or two for each man,
Spoil of dyed cloths for Sisera,
Spoil of embroidered cloths,
A couple of embroidered cloths
Round every neck as spoil."

31So may all Your enemies perish, O LORD!
But may His friends be as the sun rising in might!

And the land was tranquil forty years.

---

l I.e., the kings of Canaan (v. 19).
m-m Lit. "From the gallopings, the gallopings of his steeds."

n Or "against."
o Or "gazed"; meaning of Heb. uncertain.

6 Then the Israelites did what was offensive to the LORD, and the LORD delivered them into the hands of the Midianites for seven years. [2]The hand of the Midianites prevailed over Israel; and because of Midian, the Israelites a-provided themselves with refuges in the caves and strongholds of the mountains.-a [3]After the Israelites had done their sowing, Midian, Amalek, and the Kedemites would come up and raid them; [4]they would attack them, destroyb the produce of the land all the way to Gaza, and leave no means of sustenance in Israel, not a sheep or an ox or an ass. [5]For they would come up with their livestock and their tents, swarming as thick as locusts; they and their camels were innumerable. Thus they would invade the land and ravage it. [6]Israel was reduced to utter misery by the Midianites, and the Israelites cried out to the LORD.

[7]When the Israelites cried to the LORD on account of Midian, [8]the LORD sent a prophet to the Israelites who said to them, "Thus said the LORD, the God of Israel: I brought you up out of Egypt and freed you from the house of bondage. [9]I rescued you from the Egyptians and from all your oppressors; I drove them out before you, and gave you their land. [10]And I said to you, 'I the LORD am your God. You must not worship the gods of the Amorites in whose land you dwell.' But you did not obey Me."

[11]An angel of the LORD came and sat under the terebinth at Ophrah, which belonged to Joash the Abiezrite. His son Gideon was then beating out wheat inside a winepress in order to keep it safe from the Midianites. [12]The angel of the LORD appeared to him and said to him, "The LORD is with you, valiant warrior!" [13]Gideon said to him, "Please, my lord, if the LORD is with us, why has all this befallen us? Where are all

---

a-a   *Meaning of Heb. uncertain.*
b   *I.e., by grazing their livestock.*

ו וַיַּעֲשׂ֧וּ בְנֵֽי־יִשְׂרָאֵ֛ל הָרַ֖ע בְּעֵינֵ֣י יְהֹוָ֑ה וַיִּתְּנֵ֧ם יְהֹוָ֛ה בְּיַד־מִדְיָ֖ן שֶׁ֥בַע שָׁנִֽים: 2 וַתָּ֤עׇז יַד־מִדְיָ֖ן עַל־יִשְׂרָאֵ֑ל מִפְּנֵ֨י מִדְיָ֜ן עָשׂ֣וּ לָהֶ֣ם ׀ בְּנֵ֣י יִשְׂרָאֵ֗ל אֶת־הַמִּנְהָרוֹת֙ אֲשֶׁ֣ר בֶּֽהָרִ֔ים וְאֶת־הַמְּעָר֖וֹת וְאֶת־הַמְּצָדֽוֹת: 3 וְהָיָ֖ה אִם־זָרַ֣ע יִשְׂרָאֵ֑ל וְעָלָ֨ה מִדְיָ֧ן וַֽעֲמָלֵ֛ק וּבְנֵי־קֶ֖דֶם וְעָל֥וּ עָלָֽיו: 4 וַיַּֽחֲנ֣וּ עֲלֵיהֶ֗ם וַיַּשְׁחִ֨יתוּ֙ אֶת־יְב֣וּל הָאָ֔רֶץ עַד־בּוֹאֲךָ֖ עַזָּ֑ה וְלֹא־יַשְׁאִ֤ירוּ מִֽחְיָה֙ בְּיִשְׂרָאֵ֔ל וְשֶׂ֥ה וָשׁ֖וֹר וַֽחֲמֽוֹר: 5 כִּ֡י הֵם֩ וּמִקְנֵיהֶ֨ם יַֽעֲל֜וּ וְאׇהֳלֵיהֶ֗ם יבאו וּבָ֤אוּ כְדֵֽי־אַרְבֶּה֙ לָרֹ֔ב וְלָהֶ֥ם וְלִגְמַלֵּיהֶ֖ם אֵ֣ין מִסְפָּ֑ר וַיָּבֹ֥אוּ בָאָ֖רֶץ לְשַֽׁחֲתָֽהּ: 6 וַיִּדַּ֧ל יִשְׂרָאֵ֛ל מְאֹ֖ד מִפְּנֵ֣י מִדְיָ֑ן וַיִּזְעֲק֥וּ בְנֵֽי־יִשְׂרָאֵ֖ל אֶל־יְהֹוָֽה: פ

7 וַיְהִ֕י כִּֽי־זָֽעֲק֥וּ בְנֵֽי־יִשְׂרָאֵ֖ל אֶל־יְהֹוָ֑ה עַ֖ל אֹד֥וֹת מִדְיָֽן: 8 וַיִּשְׁלַ֧ח יְהֹוָ֛ה אִ֥ישׁ נָבִ֖יא אֶל־בְּנֵ֣י יִשְׂרָאֵ֑ל וַיֹּ֨אמֶר לָהֶ֜ם כֹּה־אָמַ֥ר יְהֹוָ֣ה ׀ אֱלֹהֵ֣י יִשְׂרָאֵ֗ל אָֽנֹכִ֞י הֶֽעֱלֵ֤יתִי אֶתְכֶם֙ מִמִּצְרַ֔יִם וָֽאֹצִ֥יא אֶתְכֶ֖ם מִבֵּ֥ית עֲבָדִֽים: 9 וָֽאַצִּ֤ל אֶתְכֶם֙ מִיַּ֣ד מִצְרַ֔יִם וּמִיַּ֖ד כׇּל־לֹֽחֲצֵיכֶ֑ם וָֽאֲגָרֵ֤שׁ אוֹתָם֙ מִפְּנֵיכֶ֔ם וָֽאֶתְּנָ֥ה לָכֶ֖ם אֶת־אַרְצָֽם: 10 וָֽאֹמְרָ֣ה לָכֶ֗ם אֲנִי֙ יְהֹוָ֣ה אֱלֹֽהֵיכֶ֔ם לֹ֤א תִֽירְאוּ֙ אֶת־אֱלֹהֵ֣י הָֽאֱמֹרִ֔י אֲשֶׁ֥ר אַתֶּ֖ם יֽוֹשְׁבִ֣ים בְּאַרְצָ֑ם וְלֹ֥א שְׁמַעְתֶּ֖ם בְּקוֹלִֽי: פ

11 וַיָּבֹ֞א מַלְאַ֣ךְ יְהֹוָ֗ה וַיֵּ֙שֶׁב֙ תַּ֣חַת הָֽאֵלָ֔ה אֲשֶׁ֣ר בְּעׇפְרָ֔ה אֲשֶׁ֥ר לְיוֹאָ֖שׁ אֲבִ֣י הָֽעֶזְרִ֑י וְגִדְע֣וֹן בְּנ֗וֹ חֹבֵ֤ט חִטִּים֙ בַּגַּ֔ת לְהָנִ֖יס מִפְּנֵ֥י מִדְיָֽן: 12 וַיֵּרָ֥א אֵלָ֖יו מַלְאַ֣ךְ יְהֹוָ֑ה וַיֹּ֣אמֶר אֵלָ֔יו יְהֹוָ֥ה עִמְּךָ֖ גִּבּ֥וֹר הֶחָֽיִל: 13 וַיֹּ֨אמֶר אֵלָ֜יו גִּדְע֗וֹן בִּ֣י אֲדֹנִי֮ וְיֵ֣שׁ יְהֹוָ֣ה עִמָּ֒נוּ֒ וְלָ֤מָּה מְצָאַ֙תְנוּ֙ כׇּל־זֹ֔את וְאַיֵּ֤ה כׇל־נִפְלְאֹתָ֙יו

528

His wondrous deeds about which our fathers told us, saying, 'Truly the Lord brought us up from Egypt'? Now the Lord has abandoned us and delivered us into the hands of Midian!" [14]The Lord turned to him and said, "Go in this strength of yours and deliver Israel from the Midianites. I herewith make you My messenger." [15]He said to Him, "Please, my lord, how can I deliver Israel? Why, my clan is the humblest in Manasseh, and I am the youngest in my father's household." [16]The Lord replied, "I will be with you, and you shall defeat Midian to a man." [17]And he said to Him, "If I have gained Your favor, give me a sign that it is You who are speaking to me: [18]do not leave this place until I come back to You and bring out my offering and place it before You." And He answered, "I will stay until you return."

[19]So Gideon went in and prepared a kid, and [baked] unleavened bread from an ephah of flour. He put the meat in a basket and poured the broth into a pot, and he brought them out to Him under the terebinth. As he presented them, [20]the angel of God said to him, "Take the meat and the unleavened bread, put them on yonder rock, and spill out the broth." He did so. [21]The angel of the Lord held out the staff that he carried, and touched the meat and the unleavened bread with its tip. A fire sprang up from the rock and consumed the meat and the unleavened bread. And the angel of the Lord vanished from his sight. [22]Then Gideon realized that it was an angel of the Lord; and Gideon said, "Alas, O Lord God! For I have seen an angel of the Lord face to face."

[23]But the Lord said to him, "All is well; have no fear, you shall not die." [24]So Gideon built there an altar to the Lord and called it ᶜ-Adonai-shalom.-ᶜ To this day it stands in Ophrah of the Abiezrites.

---

c-c   *I.e., "The Lord, 'All-is-well.'"*

אֲשֶׁ֣ר סִפְּרוּ־לָ֣נוּ אֲבוֹתֵ֗ינוּ לֵאמֹר֙ הֲלֹ֤א מִמִּצְרַ֙יִם֙ הֶעֱלָ֣נוּ יְהֹוָ֔ה וְעַתָּה֙ נְטָשָׁ֣נוּ יְהֹוָ֔ה וַֽיִּתְּנֵ֖נוּ בְּכַף־מִדְיָֽן׃ 14 וַיִּ֤פֶן אֵלָיו֙ יְהֹוָ֔ה וַיֹּ֗אמֶר לֵ֚ךְ בְּכֹחֲךָ֣ זֶ֔ה וְהוֹשַׁעְתָּ֥ אֶת־יִשְׂרָאֵ֖ל מִכַּ֣ף מִדְיָ֑ן הֲלֹ֖א שְׁלַחְתִּֽיךָ׃ 15 וַיֹּ֣אמֶר אֵלָ֗יו בִּ֣י אֲדֹנָ֔י בַּמָּ֥ה אוֹשִׁ֖יעַ אֶת־יִשְׂרָאֵ֑ל הִנֵּ֤ה אַלְפִּי֙ הַדַּ֣ל בִּמְנַשֶּׁ֔ה וְאָנֹכִ֥י הַצָּעִ֖יר בְּבֵ֥ית אָבִֽי׃ 16 וַיֹּ֤אמֶר אֵלָיו֙ יְהֹוָ֔ה כִּ֥י אֶהְיֶ֖ה עִמָּ֑ךְ וְהִכִּיתָ֥ אֶת־מִדְיָ֖ן כְּאִ֥ישׁ אֶחָֽד׃ 17 וַיֹּ֣אמֶר אֵלָ֔יו אִם־נָ֛א מָצָ֥אתִי חֵ֖ן בְּעֵינֶ֑יךָ וְעָשִׂ֤יתָ לִּי֙ א֔וֹת שָׁאַתָּ֖ה מְדַבֵּ֥ר עִמִּֽי׃ 18 אַל־נָ֨א תָמֻ֤שׁ מִזֶּה֙ עַד־בֹּאִ֣י אֵלֶ֔יךָ וְהֹֽצֵאתִי֙ אֶת־מִנְחָתִ֔י וְהִנַּחְתִּ֖י לְפָנֶ֑יךָ וַיֹּאמַ֕ר אָנֹכִ֥י אֵשֵׁ֖ב עַ֥ד שׁוּבֶֽךָ׃

19 וְגִדְע֣וֹן בָּ֗א וַיַּ֤עַשׂ גְּדִֽי־עִזִּים֙ וְאֵיפַת־קֶ֣מַח מַצּ֔וֹת הַבָּשָׂר֙ שָׂ֣ם בַּסַּ֔ל וְהַמָּרַ֖ק שָׂ֣ם בַּפָּר֑וּר וַיּוֹצֵ֥א אֵלָ֛יו אֶל־תַּ֥חַת הָאֵלָ֖ה וַיַּגַּֽשׁ׃ ס 20 וַיֹּ֨אמֶר אֵלָ֜יו מַלְאַ֣ךְ הָאֱלֹהִ֗ים קַ֣ח אֶת־הַבָּשָׂ֤ר וְאֶת־הַמַּצּוֹת֙ וְהַנַּח֙ אֶל־הַסֶּ֣לַע הַלָּ֔ז וְאֶת־הַמָּרַ֖ק שְׁפ֑וֹךְ וַיַּ֖עַשׂ כֵּֽן׃ 21 וַיִּשְׁלַ֞ח מַלְאַ֣ךְ יְהֹוָ֗ה אֶת־קְצֵ֤ה הַמִּשְׁעֶ֙נֶת֙ אֲשֶׁ֣ר בְּיָד֔וֹ וַיִּגַּ֥ע בַּבָּשָׂ֖ר וּבַמַּצּ֑וֹת וַתַּ֨עַל הָאֵ֜שׁ מִן־הַצּ֗וּר וַתֹּ֤אכַל אֶת־הַבָּשָׂר֙ וְאֶת־הַמַּצּ֔וֹת וּמַלְאַ֣ךְ יְהֹוָ֔ה הָלַ֖ךְ מֵעֵינָֽיו׃ 22 וַיַּ֣רְא גִּדְע֔וֹן כִּֽי־מַלְאַ֥ךְ יְהֹוָ֖ה ה֑וּא ס וַיֹּ֣אמֶר גִּדְע֗וֹן אֲהָהּ֙ אֲדֹנָ֣י יְהֹוִ֔ה כִּֽי־עַל־כֵּ֤ן רָאִ֙יתִי֙ מַלְאַ֣ךְ יְהֹוָ֔ה פָּנִ֖ים אֶל־פָּנִֽים׃ 23 וַיֹּ֨אמֶר ל֤וֹ יְהֹוָה֙ שָׁל֣וֹם לְךָ֔ אַל־תִּירָ֖א לֹ֣א תָמֽוּת׃ 24 וַיִּ֩בֶן֩ שָׁ֨ם גִּדְע֤וֹן מִזְבֵּ֙חַ֙ לַֽיהֹוָ֔ה וַיִּקְרָא־ל֖וֹ יְהֹוָ֣ה שָׁל֑וֹם עַ֚ד הַיּ֣וֹם הַזֶּ֔ה עוֹדֶ֕נּוּ בְּעָפְרָ֖ת אֲבִ֥י הָעֶזְרִֽי׃ פ

25That night the Lord said to him: "Take the *a*-young bull-*a* belonging to your father and another bull seven years old; pull down the altar of Baal which belongs to your father, and cut down the sacred post which is beside it. 26Then build an altar to the Lord your God, on *a*-the level ground-*a* on top of this stronghold. Take the other bull and offer it as a burnt offering, using the wood of the sacred post that you have cut down." 27So Gideon took ten of his servants and did as the Lord had told him; but as he was afraid to do it by day, on account of his father's household and the townspeople, he did it by night. 28Early the next morning, the townspeople found that the altar of Baal had been torn down and the sacred post beside it had been cut down, and that the second bull had been offered on the newly built altar. 29They said to one another, "Who did this thing?" Upon inquiry and investigation, they were told, "Gideon son of Joash did this thing!" 30The townspeople said to Joash, "Bring out your son, for he must die: he has torn down the altar of Baal and cut down the sacred post beside it!" 31But Joash said to all who had risen against him, "Do you have to contend for Baal? Do you have to vindicate him? Whoever fights his battles shall be dead by morning! If he is a god, let him fight his own battles, since it is his altar that has been torn down!" 32That day they named him*d* Jerubbaal, meaning "Let Baal contend with him, since he tore down his altar."

33All Midian, Amalek, and the Kedemites joined forces; they crossed over and encamped in the Valley of Jezreel. 34The spirit of the Lord enveloped Gideon; he sounded the horn, and the Abiezrites rallied behind him. 35And he sent messengers throughout Manasseh, and they too rallied behind him. He then sent messengers through Asher, Zebulun, and Naphtali, and they came up to meet the Manassites.*e*

---

d I.e., Gideon.
e Heb. "them."

25 וַיְהִי֮ בַּלַּ֣יְלָה הַהוּא֒ וַיֹּ֧אמֶר ל֣וֹ יְהוָ֗ה קַ֤ח אֶת־פַּר־הַשּׁוֹר֙ אֲשֶׁ֣ר לְאָבִ֔יךָ וּפַ֥ר הַשֵּׁנִ֖י שֶׁ֣בַע שָׁנִ֑ים וְהָרַסְתָּ֗ אֶת־מִזְבַּ֤ח הַבַּ֙עַל֙ אֲשֶׁ֣ר לְאָבִ֔יךָ וְאֶת־הָאֲשֵׁרָ֥ה אֲשֶׁר־עָלָ֖יו תִּכְרֹֽת׃ 26 וּבָנִ֨יתָ מִזְבֵּ֜חַ לַיהוָ֣ה אֱלֹהֶ֗יךָ עַ֣ל רֹ֤אשׁ הַמָּעוֹז֙ הַזֶּ֔ה בַּמַּעֲרָכָ֑ה וְלָקַחְתָּ֙ אֶת־הַפָּ֣ר הַשֵּׁנִ֔י וְהַעֲלִ֣יתָ עוֹלָ֔ה בַּעֲצֵ֥י הָאֲשֵׁרָ֖ה אֲשֶׁ֥ר תִּכְרֹֽת׃ 27 וַיִּקַּ֨ח גִּדְע֜וֹן עֲשָׂרָ֤ה אֲנָשִׁים֙ מֵֽעֲבָדָ֔יו וַיַּ֕עַשׂ כַּאֲשֶׁ֛ר דִּבֶּ֥ר אֵלָ֖יו יְהוָ֑ה וַיְהִ֡י כַּאֲשֶׁ֣ר יָרֵא֩ אֶת־בֵּ֨ית אָבִ֜יו וְאֶת־אַנְשֵׁ֥י הָעִ֛יר מֵעֲשׂ֥וֹת יוֹמָ֖ם וַיַּ֥עַשׂ לָֽיְלָה׃ 28 וַיַּשְׁכִּ֜ימוּ אַנְשֵׁ֤י הָעִיר֙ בַּבֹּ֔קֶר וְהִנֵּ֤ה נֻתַּץ֙ מִזְבַּ֣ח הַבַּ֔עַל וְהָאֲשֵׁרָ֥ה אֲשֶׁר־עָלָ֖יו כֹּרָ֑תָה וְאֵת֙ הַפָּ֣ר הַשֵּׁנִ֔י הֹֽעֲלָ֔ה עַל־הַמִּזְבֵּ֖חַ הַבָּנֽוּי׃ 29 וַיֹּֽאמְרוּ֙ אִ֣ישׁ אֶל־רֵעֵ֔הוּ מִ֥י עָשָׂ֖ה הַדָּבָ֣ר הַזֶּ֑ה וַֽיִּדְרְשׁוּ֙ וַיְבַקְשׁ֔וּ וַיֹּ֣אמְר֔וּ גִּדְע֖וֹן בֶּן־יוֹאָ֔שׁ עָשָׂ֖ה הַדָּבָ֥ר הַזֶּֽה׃ 30 וַיֹּ֨אמְר֜וּ אַנְשֵׁ֤י הָעִיר֙ אֶל־יוֹאָ֔שׁ הוֹצֵ֥א אֶת־בִּנְךָ֖ וְיָמֹ֑ת כִּ֤י נָתַץ֙ אֶת־מִזְבַּ֣ח הַבַּ֔עַל וְכִ֥י כָרַ֖ת הָאֲשֵׁרָ֥ה אֲשֶׁר־עָלָֽיו׃ 31 וַיֹּ֣אמֶר יוֹאָ֡שׁ לְכֹל֩ אֲשֶׁר־עָמְד֨וּ עָלָ֜יו הַאַתֶּ֣ם ׀ תְּרִיב֣וּן לַבַּ֗עַל אִם־אַתֶּם֙ תּוֹשִׁיע֣וּן אוֹת֔וֹ אֲשֶׁ֨ר יָרִ֥יב ל֛וֹ יוּמַ֖ת עַד־הַבֹּ֑קֶר אִם־אֱלֹהִ֥ים הוּא֙ יָ֣רֶב ל֔וֹ כִּ֥י נָתַ֖ץ אֶת־מִזְבְּחֽוֹ׃ 32 וַיִּקְרָא־ל֥וֹ בַיּוֹם־הַה֖וּא יְרֻבַּ֣עַל לֵאמֹ֑ר יָ֤רֶב בּוֹ֙ הַבַּ֔עַל כִּ֥י נָתַ֖ץ אֶת־מִזְבְּחֽוֹ׃ פ

33 וְכָל־מִדְיָ֧ן וַעֲמָלֵ֛ק וּבְנֵי־קֶ֖דֶם נֶאֶסְפ֣וּ יַחְדָּ֑ו וַיַּעַבְר֖וּ וַיַּחֲנ֥וּ בְּעֵ֥מֶק יִזְרְעֶֽאל׃ 34 וְר֣וּחַ יְהוָ֔ה לָבְשָׁ֖ה אֶת־גִּדְע֑וֹן וַיִּתְקַע֙ בַּשּׁוֹפָ֔ר וַיִּזָּעֵ֥ק אֲבִיעֶ֖זֶר אַחֲרָֽיו׃ 35 וּמַלְאָכִים֙ שָׁלַ֣ח בְּכָל־מְנַשֶּׁ֔ה וַיִּזָּעֵ֥ק גַּם־ה֖וּא אַחֲרָ֑יו וּמַלְאָכִ֣ים שָׁלַ֗ח בְּאָשֵׁ֤ר וּבִזְבֻלוּן֙ וּבְנַפְתָּלִ֔י וַיַּעֲל֖וּ לִקְרָאתָֽם׃

530

³⁶And Gideon said to God, "If You really intend to deliver Israel through me as You have said—³⁷here I place a fleece of wool on the threshing floor. If dew falls only on the fleece and all the ground remains dry, I shall know that You will deliver Israel through me, as You have said." ³⁸And that is what happened. Early the next day, he squeezed the fleece and wrung out the dew from the fleece, a bowlful of water. ³⁹Then Gideon said to God, "Do not be angry with me if I speak just once more. Let me make just one more test with the fleece: let the fleece alone be dry, while there is dew all over the ground." ⁴⁰God did so that night: only the fleece was dry, while there was dew all over the ground.

7 Early next day, Jerubbaal—that is, Gideon—and all the troops with him encamped above En-harod,^a while the camp of Midian was in the plain to the north of him, at Gibeath-moreh.^b ²The LORD said to Gideon, "You have too many troops with you for Me to deliver Midian into their hands; Israel might claim for themselves the glory due to Me, thinking, 'Our own hand has brought us victory.' ³Therefore, announce to the men, 'Let anybody who is timid and fearful turn back, ^{c-}as a bird flies from Mount Gilead.'"^{-c} Thereupon, 22,000 of the troops turned back and 10,000 remained.

⁴"There are still too many troops," the LORD said to Gideon. "Take them down to the water and I will sift^d them for you there. Anyone of whom I tell you, 'This one is to go with you,' that one shall go with you; and anyone of whom I tell you, 'This one is not to go with you,' that one shall not go." ⁵So he took the troops down to the water. Then the LORD said to Gideon, "Set apart all those who ^{e-}lap up the water with their

וַיֹּ֤אמֶר גִּדְעוֹן֙ אֶל־הָ֣אֱלֹהִ֔ים אִם־יֶשְׁךָ֛ ³⁶
מוֹשִׁ֥יעַ בְּיָדִ֖י אֶת־יִשְׂרָאֵ֑ל כַּאֲשֶׁ֖ר דִּבַּֽרְתָּ׃
הִנֵּ֣ה אָנֹכִ֗י מַצִּ֛יג אֶת־גִּזַּ֥ת הַצֶּ֖מֶר בַּגֹּ֑רֶן ³⁷
אִם־טַ֡ל יִהְיֶה֩ עַֽל־הַגִּזָּ֨ה לְבַדָּ֜הּ וְעַל־כָּל־
הָאָ֣רֶץ חֹ֗רֶב וְיָדַעְתִּ֕י כִּֽי־תוֹשִׁ֥יעַ בְּיָדִ֖י
אֶת־יִשְׂרָאֵ֖ל כַּאֲשֶׁ֥ר דִּבַּֽרְתָּ׃ וַיְהִי־כֵ֑ן ³⁸
וַיַּשְׁכֵּ֣ם מִֽמָּחֳרָ֗ת וַיָּ֙זַר֙ אֶת־הַגִּזָּ֔ה וַיִּ֥מֶץ טַ֖ל
מִן־הַגִּזָּ֑ה מְל֖וֹא הַסֵּ֥פֶל מָֽיִם׃ וַיֹּ֤אמֶר ³⁹
גִּדְעוֹן֙ אֶל־הָ֣אֱלֹהִ֔ים אַל־יִ֤חַר אַפְּךָ֙ בִּ֔י
וַאֲדַבְּרָ֖ה אַ֣ךְ הַפָּ֑עַם אֲנַסֶּ֤ה נָּא־רַק־הַפַּ֙עַם֙
בַּגִּזָּ֔ה יְהִי־נָ֨א חֹ֤רֶב אֶל־הַגִּזָּה֙ לְבַדָּ֔הּ וְעַל־
כָּל־הָאָ֖רֶץ יִהְיֶה־טָּֽל׃ וַיַּ֧עַשׂ אֱלֹהִ֛ים כֵּ֖ן ⁴⁰
בַּלַּ֣יְלָה הַה֑וּא וַיְהִי־חֹ֤רֶב אֶל־הַגִּזָּה֙ לְבַדָּ֔הּ
וְעַל־כָּל־הָאָ֖רֶץ הָ֥יָה טָֽל׃ פ

וַיַּשְׁכֵּ֨ם יְרֻבַּ֜עַל ה֤וּא גִדְעוֹן֙ וְכָל־הָעָ֣ם **ז**
אֲשֶׁ֣ר אִתּ֔וֹ וַֽיַּחֲנ֖וּ עַל־עֵ֣ין חֲרֹ֑ד וּמַחֲנֵ֤ה
מִדְיָן֙ הָֽיָה־ל֣וֹ מִצָּפ֔וֹן מִגִּבְעַ֥ת הַמּוֹרֶ֖ה
בָּעֵֽמֶק׃ וַיֹּ֤אמֶר יְהוָה֙ אֶל־גִּדְע֔וֹן רַ֣ב הָעָ֗ם ²
אֲשֶׁ֣ר אִתָּ֔ךְ מִתִּתִּ֥י אֶת־מִדְיָ֖ן בְּיָדָ֑ם פֶּן־
יִתְפָּאֵ֨ר עָלַ֤י יִשְׂרָאֵל֙ לֵאמֹ֔ר יָדִ֖י הוֹשִׁ֥יעָה
לִּֽי׃ וְעַתָּ֗ה קְרָ֤א נָא֙ בְּאָזְנֵ֣י הָעָ֣ם לֵאמֹ֔ר ³
מִֽי־יָרֵ֣א וְחָרֵ֔ד יָשֹׁ֥ב וְיִצְפֹּ֖ר מֵהַ֣ר הַגִּלְעָ֑ד
וַיָּ֣שָׁב מִן־הָעָ֗ם עֶשְׂרִ֤ים וּשְׁנַ֙יִם֙ אֶ֔לֶף
וַעֲשֶׂ֥רֶת אֲלָפִ֖ים נִשְׁאָֽרוּ׃ ס
וַיֹּ֨אמֶר יְהוָ֜ה אֶל־גִּדְע֗וֹן עוֹד֮ הָעָ֣ם רָב֒ ⁴
הוֹרֵ֤ד אוֹתָם֙ אֶל־הַמַּ֔יִם וְאֶצְרְפֶ֥נּוּ לְךָ֖ שָׁ֑ם
וְהָיָ֡ה אֲשֶׁר֩ אֹמַ֨ר אֵלֶ֜יךָ זֶ֣ה ׀ יֵלֵ֣ךְ אִתָּ֗ךְ
ה֚וּא יֵלֵ֣ךְ אִתָּ֔ךְ וְכֹ֨ל אֲשֶׁר־אֹמַ֜ר אֵלֶ֗יךָ זֶ֚ה
לֹא־יֵלֵ֣ךְ עִמָּ֔ךְ ה֖וּא לֹ֥א יֵלֵֽךְ׃ וַיּ֥וֹרֶד ⁵
אֶת־הָעָ֖ם אֶל־הַמָּ֑יִם ס וַיֹּ֨אמֶר יְהוָ֜ה
אֶל־גִּדְע֗וֹן כֹּ֣ל אֲשֶׁר־יָלֹק֩ בִּלְשׁוֹנ֨וֹ מִן־
הַמַּ֜יִם כַּאֲשֶׁ֧ר יָלֹ֣ק הַכֶּ֗לֶב תַּצִּ֤יג אוֹתוֹ֙ לְבָ֔ד
וְכֹ֛ל אֲשֶׁר־יִכְרַ֥ע עַל־בִּרְכָּ֖יו לִשְׁתּֽוֹת׃

---

^a Or "the Spring of Harod."
^b Or "the Hill of Moreh."
^{c-c} Meaning of Heb. uncertain.
^d Lit. "smelt."
^{e-e} Actually, using their hands as a dog uses its tongue; see v. 6.

tongues like dogs-e from all those who get down on their knees to drink." 6Now those who "lapped" the water into their mouths by hand numbered three hundred; all the rest of the troops got down on their knees to drink. 7Then the Lord said to Gideon, "I will deliver you and I will put Midian into your hands through the three hundred 'lappers'; let the rest of the troops go home." 8c-So [the lappers] took the provisions and horns that the other men had with them,-c and he sent the rest of the men of Israel back to their homes, retaining only the three hundred men.

The Midianite camp was below him, in the plain. 9That night the Lord said to him, "Come, attack/the camp, for I have delivered it into your hands. 10And if you are afraid to attack, first go down to the camp with your attendant Purah 11and listen to what they say; after that you will have the courage to attack the camp." So he went down with his attendant Purah to the outposts of the warriors who were in the camp.—12Now Midian, Amalek, and all the Kedemites were spread over the plain, as thick as locusts; and their camels were countless, as numerous as the sands on the seashore.—13Gideon came there just as one man was narrating a dream to another. "Listen," he was saying, "I had this dream: There was a commotionc—a loaf of barley bread was whirling through the Midianite camp. It came to a tent and struck it, and it fell; it turned it upside down, and the tent collapsed." 14To this the other responded, "That can only mean the sword of the Israelite Gideon son of Joash. God is delivering Midian and the entire camp into his hands."g

15When Gideon heard the dream told and interpreted, he bowed low. Returning to the camp of Israel, he shouted, "Come on! The Lord has delivered the Midianite camp into your hands!"

6 וַיְהִ֣י מִסְפַּ֣ר הַֽמֲלַקְקִ֗ים בְּיָדָם֙ אֶל־פִּיהֶ֔ם שְׁלֹ֥שׁ מֵא֖וֹת אִ֑ישׁ וְכֹל֙ יֶ֣תֶר הָעָ֔ם כָּרְע֥וּ עַל־בִּרְכֵיהֶ֖ם לִשְׁתּ֥וֹת מָֽיִם׃ ס 7 וַיֹּ֣אמֶר יְהֹוָ֣ה אֶל־גִּדְע֗וֹן בִּשְׁלֹשׁ֩ מֵא֨וֹת הָאִ֤ישׁ הַֽמֲלַקְקִים֙ אוֹשִׁ֣יעַ אֶתְכֶ֔ם וְנָתַתִּ֥י אֶת־מִדְיָ֖ן בְּיָדֶ֑ךָ וְכׇל־הָעָ֔ם יֵלְכ֖וּ אִ֥ישׁ לִמְקֹמֽוֹ׃ 8 וַיִּקְח֣וּ אֶת־צֵדָה֩ הָעָ֨ם בְּיָדָ֜ם וְאֵ֣ת שֽׁוֹפְרֹֽתֵיהֶ֗ם וְאֵ֨ת כׇּל־אִ֤ישׁ יִשְׂרָאֵל֙ שִׁלַּח֙ אִ֣ישׁ לְאֹֽהָלָ֔יו וּבִשְׁלֹשׁ־מֵא֥וֹת הָאִ֖ישׁ הֶחֱזִ֑יק וּמַחֲנֵ֣ה מִדְיָ֔ן הָ֥יָה ל֖וֹ מִתַּ֥חַת בָּעֵֽמֶק׃ פ

9 וַֽיְהִי֙ בַּלַּ֣יְלָה הַה֔וּא וַיֹּ֤אמֶר אֵלָיו֙ יְהֹוָ֔ה ק֖וּם רֵ֣ד בַּֽמַּחֲנֶ֑ה כִּ֥י נְתַתִּ֖יו בְּיָדֶֽךָ׃ 10 וְאִם־יָרֵ֥א אַתָּ֖ה לָרֶ֑דֶת רֵ֥ד אַתָּ֛ה וּפֻרָ֥ה נַעַרְךָ֖ אֶל־הַֽמַּחֲנֶֽה׃ 11 וְשָֽׁמַעְתָּ֙ מַה־יְדַבֵּ֔רוּ וְאַחַר֙ תֶּחֱזַ֣קְנָה יָדֶ֔יךָ וְיָרַדְתָּ֖ בַּֽמַּחֲנֶ֑ה וַיֵּ֤רֶד הוּא֙ וּפֻרָ֣ה נַעֲר֔וֹ אֶל־קְצֵ֥ה הַֽחֲמֻשִׁ֖ים אֲשֶׁ֥ר בַּֽמַּחֲנֶֽה׃ 12 וּמִדְיָ֨ן וַֽעֲמָלֵ֤ק וְכׇל־בְּנֵי־קֶ֙דֶם֙ נֹפְלִ֣ים בָּעֵ֔מֶק כָּאַרְבֶּ֖ה לָרֹ֑ב וְלִגְמַלֵּיהֶ֗ם אֵ֣ין מִסְפָּ֔ר כַּח֛וֹל שֶׁעַל־שְׂפַ֥ת הַיָּ֖ם לָרֹֽב׃ 13 וַיָּבֹ֣א גִדְע֔וֹן וְהִנֵּה־אִ֕ישׁ מְסַפֵּ֥ר לְרֵעֵ֖הוּ חֲל֑וֹם וַיֹּ֜אמֶר הִנֵּ֧ה חֲל֣וֹם חָלַ֗מְתִּי וְהִנֵּ֨ה צְלִ֤יל לֶ֙חֶם֙ שְׂעֹרִים֙ מִתְהַפֵּךְ֙ בְּמַחֲנֵ֣ה מִדְיָ֔ן וַיָּבֹ֣א עַד־הָאֹ֗הֶל וַיַּכֵּ֧הוּ וַיִּפֹּ֛ל וַיַּהַפְכֵ֥הוּ לְמַ֖עְלָה וְנָפַ֥ל הָאֹֽהֶל׃ 14 וַיַּ֨עַן רֵעֵ֤הוּ וַיֹּ֙אמֶר֙ אֵ֣ין זֹ֔את בִּלְתִּ֗י אִם־חֶ֙רֶב֙ גִּדְע֣וֹן בֶּן־יוֹאָ֖שׁ אִ֣ישׁ יִשְׂרָאֵ֑ל נָתַ֤ן הָֽאֱלֹהִים֙ בְּיָד֔וֹ אֶת־מִדְיָ֖ן וְאֶת־כׇּל־הַֽמַּחֲנֶֽה׃ פ 15 וַיְהִי֩ כִשְׁמֹ֨עַ גִּדְע֜וֹן אֶת־מִסְפַּ֧ר הַֽחֲל֛וֹם וְאֶת־שִׁבְר֖וֹ וַיִּשְׁתָּ֑חוּ וַיָּ֙שׇׁב֙ אֶל־מַחֲנֵ֣ה יִשְׂרָאֵ֔ל וַיֹּ֣אמֶר ק֔וּמוּ כִּֽי־נָתַ֧ן יְהֹוָ֛ה בְּיֶדְכֶ֖ם אֶת־מַחֲנֵ֥ה מִדְיָֽן׃ 16 וַיַּ֧חַץ אֶת־שְׁלֹשׁ־

---

f   Lit. "descend upon"; so in vv. 10 and 11.

g   The loaf of bread symbolizes the agricultural Israelites; the tent, the nomadic Midianites.

¹⁶He divided the three hundred men into three columns and equipped every man with a ram's horn and an empty jar, with a torch in each jar. ¹⁷"Watch me," he said, "and do the same. When I get to the outposts of the camp, do exactly as I do. ¹⁸When I and all those with me blow our horns, you too, all around the camp, will blow your horns and shout, 'For the Lord and for Gideon!'"

¹⁹Gideon and the hundred men with him arrived at the outposts of the camp, at the beginning of the middle watch, just after the sentries were posted. ^{h-}They sounded the horns and smashed the jars that they had with them,^{-h} ²⁰and the three columns blew their horns and broke their jars. Holding the torches in their left hands and the horns for blowing in their right hands, they shouted, "A sword for the Lord and for Gideon!" ²¹They remained standing where they were, surrounding the camp; but the entire camp ran about yelling, and took to flight. ²²For when the three hundred horns were sounded, the Lord turned every man's sword against his fellow, throughout the camp, and the entire host fled as far as Beth-shittah and on to Zererah—as far as the outskirts of Abel-meholah near Tabbath.

²³And now the men of Israel from Naphtali and Asher and from all of Manasseh rallied for the pursuit of the Midianites. ²⁴Gideon also sent messengers all through the hill country of Ephraim with this order: ⁱ"Go down ahead of the Midianites and seize their access to the water all along the Jordan down to Beth-barah." So all the men of Ephraim rallied and seized the waterside down to Beth-barah by the Jordan. ²⁵They pursued the Midianites and captured Midian's two generals, Oreb and Zeeb. They killed Oreb at the Rock of Oreb and they killed Zeeb at the Winepress of Zeeb; and they brought

מֵא֣וֹת הָאִ֗ישׁ שְׁלֹשָׁ֖ה רָאשִׁ֑ים וַיִּתֵּ֨ן שׁוֹפָר֤וֹת בְּיַד־כֻּלָּם֙ וְכַדִּ֣ים רֵקִ֔ים וְלַפִּדִ֖ים בְּת֥וֹךְ הַכַּדִּֽים׃ ¹⁷ וַיֹּ֣אמֶר אֲלֵיהֶ֔ם מִמֶּ֥נִּי תִרְא֖וּ וְכֵ֣ן תַּעֲשׂ֑וּ וְהִנֵּ֨ה אָנֹכִ֥י בָא֙ בִּקְצֵ֣ה הַֽמַּחֲנֶ֔ה וְהָיָ֥ה כַאֲשֶׁר־אֶעֱשֶׂ֖ה כֵּ֥ן תַּעֲשֽׂוּן׃ ¹⁸ וְתָקַעְתִּי֙ בַּשּׁוֹפָ֔ר אָנֹכִ֖י וְכָל־אֲשֶׁ֣ר אִתִּ֑י וּתְקַעְתֶּ֨ם בַּשּׁוֹפָר֜וֹת גַּם־אַתֶּ֗ם סְבִיבוֹת֙ כָּל־הַֽמַּחֲנֶ֔ה וַאֲמַרְתֶּ֖ם לַיהֹוָ֥ה וּלְגִדְעֽוֹן׃ פ

¹⁹ וַיָּבֹ֣א גִ֠דְע֠וֹן וּמֵאָה־אִ֣ישׁ אֲשֶׁר־אִתּ֗וֹ בִּקְצֵה֙ הַֽמַּחֲנֶ֔ה רֹ֖אשׁ הָאַשְׁמֹ֣רֶת הַתִּֽיכוֹנָ֑ה אַ֖ךְ הָקֵ֣ם הֵקִ֣ימוּ אֶת־הַשֹּֽׁמְרִ֑ים וַֽיִּתְקְעוּ֙ בַּשּׁ֣וֹפָר֔וֹת וְנָפ֖וֹץ הַכַּדִּ֥ים אֲשֶׁ֥ר בְּיָדָֽם׃ ²⁰ וַֽ֠יִּתְקְע֠וּ שְׁלֹ֨שֶׁת הָרָאשִׁ֥ים בַּשּֽׁוֹפָרוֹת֮ וַיִּשְׁבְּר֣וּ הַכַּדִּים֒ וַיַּחֲזִ֤יקוּ בְיַד־שְׂמאֹולָם֙ בַּלַּפִּדִ֔ים וּבְיַ֣ד־יְמִינָ֔ם הַשּׁוֹפָר֖וֹת לִתְק֑וֹעַ וַיִּקְרְא֕וּ חֶ֥רֶב לַֽיהֹוָ֖ה וּלְגִדְעֽוֹן׃ ²¹ וַיַּֽעַמְדוּ֙ אִ֣ישׁ תַּחְתָּ֔יו סָבִ֖יב לַֽמַּחֲנֶ֑ה וַיָּ֧רׇץ כָּל־הַֽמַּחֲנֶ֛ה וַיָּרִ֥יעוּ ויניסו וַיָּנֽוּסוּ׃ ²² וַֽיִּתְקְעוּ֮ שְׁלֹשׁ־מֵא֣וֹת הַשּׁוֹפָרוֹת֒ וַיָּ֣שֶׂם יְהֹוָ֗ה אֵ֣ת חֶ֥רֶב אִ֛ישׁ בְּרֵעֵ֖הוּ וּבְכָל־הַֽמַּחֲנֶ֑ה וַיָּ֨נׇס הַֽמַּחֲנֶ֜ה עַד־בֵּ֤ית הַשִּׁטָּה֙ צְרֵרָ֔תָה עַ֛ד שְׂפַת־אָבֵ֥ל מְחוֹלָ֖ה עַל־טַבָּֽת׃

²³ וַיִּצָּעֵ֧ק אִֽישׁ־יִשְׂרָאֵ֛ל מִנַּפְתָּלִ֥י וּמִן־אָשֵׁ֖ר וּמִן־כָּל־מְנַשֶּׁ֑ה וַֽיִּרְדְּפ֖וּ אַחֲרֵ֥י מִדְיָֽן׃ ²⁴ וּמַלְאָכִ֡ים שָׁלַ֣ח גִּדְעוֹן֩ בְּכָל־הַ֨ר אֶפְרַ֜יִם לֵאמֹ֗ר רְד֞וּ לִקְרַ֤את מִדְיָן֙ וְלִכְדּ֤וּ לָהֶם֙ אֶת־הַמַּ֔יִם עַ֛ד בֵּ֥ית בָּרָ֖ה וְאֶת־הַיַּרְדֵּ֑ן וַיִּצָּעֵ֞ק כָּל־אִ֤ישׁ אֶפְרַ֙יִם֙ וַיִּלְכְּד֣וּ אֶת־הַמַּ֔יִם עַ֛ד בֵּ֥ית בָּרָ֖ה וְאֶת־הַיַּרְדֵּֽן׃ ²⁵ וַֽיִּלְכְּד֡וּ שְׁנֵֽי־שָׂרֵ֨י מִדְיָ֜ן אֶת־עֹרֵ֣ב וְאֶת־זְאֵ֗ב וַיַּהַרְג֨וּ אֶת־עוֹרֵ֤ב בְּצוּר־עוֹרֵב֙ וְאֶת־זְאֵ֣ב הָרְג֣וּ בְיֶֽקֶב־זְאֵ֔ב וַֽיִּרְדְּפ֖וּ אֶל־מִדְיָ֑ן

---

^{h-h} *Emendation yields* "He sounded the horn and smashed the jar that he had with him."
ⁱ *Meaning of rest of verse uncertain.*

the heads of Oreb and Zeeb from the other side of the Jordan to Gideon.

8 And the men of Ephraim said to him, "Why did you do that to us—not calling us when you went to fight the Midianites?" And they rebuked him severely. ²But he answered them, "After all, what have I accomplished compared to you? Why, Ephraim's gleanings are better than Abiezer's vintage! ³God has delivered the Midianite generals Oreb and Zeeb into your hands, and what was I able to do compared to you?" And when he spoke in this fashion, their anger against him abated.

⁴Gideon came to the Jordan and crossed it. The three hundred men with him were famished, but still in pursuit. ⁵He said to the people of Succoth, "Please give some loaves of bread to the men who are following me, for they are famished, and I am pursuing Zebah and Zalmunna, the kings of Midian." ⁶But the officials of Succoth replied, *a*-"Are Zebah and Zalmunna already in your hands,-*a* that we should give bread to your troops?" ⁷"I swear," declared Gideon, "when the Lᴏʀᴅ delivers Zebah and Zalmunna into my hands, I'll thresh*b* your bodies upon desert thorns and briers!" ⁸From there he went up to Penuel and made the same request of them; but the people of Penuel gave him the same reply as the people of Succoth. ⁹So he also threatened the people of Penuel: "When I come back safe, I'll tear down this tower!"

¹⁰Now Zebah and Zalmunna were at Karkor with their army of about 15,000; these were all that remained of the entire host of the Kedemites, for the slain numbered 120,000 fighting men.*c* ¹¹Gideon marched up the road of the tent dwellers, up to east of Nobah and

וְרֹאשׁ־עֹרֵב וּזְאֵב הֵבִיאוּ אֶל־גִּדְעוֹן מֵעֵבֶר לַיַּרְדֵּן:

ח וַיֹּאמְרוּ אֵלָיו אִישׁ אֶפְרַיִם מָה־הַדָּבָר הַזֶּה עָשִׂיתָ לָּנוּ לְבִלְתִּי קְרֹאות לָנוּ כִּי הָלַכְתָּ לְהִלָּחֵם בְּמִדְיָן וַיְרִיבוּן אִתּוֹ בְּחָזְקָה: ² וַיֹּאמֶר אֲלֵיהֶם מֶה־עָשִׂיתִי עַתָּה כָּכֶם הֲלוֹא טוֹב עֹלְלוֹת אֶפְרַיִם מִבְצִיר אֲבִיעֶזֶר: ³ בְּיֶדְכֶם נָתַן אֱלֹהִים אֶת־שָׂרֵי מִדְיָן אֶת־עֹרֵב וְאֶת־זְאֵב וּמַה־יָּכֹלְתִּי עֲשׂוֹת כָּכֶם אָז רָפְתָה רוּחָם מֵעָלָיו בְּדַבְּרוֹ הַדָּבָר הַזֶּה: ⁴ וַיָּבֹא גִדְעוֹן הַיַּרְדֵּנָה עֹבֵר הוּא וּשְׁלֹשׁ מֵאוֹת הָאִישׁ אֲשֶׁר אִתּוֹ עֲיֵפִים וְרֹדְפִים: ⁵ וַיֹּאמֶר לְאַנְשֵׁי סֻכּוֹת תְּנוּ־נָא כִּכְּרוֹת לֶחֶם לָעָם אֲשֶׁר בְּרַגְלָי כִּי־עֲיֵפִים הֵם וְאָנֹכִי רֹדֵף אַחֲרֵי זֶבַח וְצַלְמֻנָּע מַלְכֵי מִדְיָן: ⁶ וַיֹּאמֶר* שָׂרֵי סֻכּוֹת הֲכַף זֶבַח וְצַלְמֻנָּע עַתָּה בְּיָדֶךָ כִּי־נִתֵּן לִצְבָאֲךָ לָחֶם: ⁷ וַיֹּאמֶר גִּדְעוֹן לָכֵן בְּתֵת יְהֹוָה אֶת־זֶבַח וְאֶת־צַלְמֻנָּע בְּיָדִי וְדַשְׁתִּי אֶת־בְּשַׂרְכֶם אֶת־קוֹצֵי הַמִּדְבָּר וְאֶת־הַבַּרְקֳנִים: ⁸ וַיַּעַל מִשָּׁם פְּנוּאֵל וַיְדַבֵּר אֲלֵיהֶם כָּזֹאת וַיַּעֲנוּ אוֹתוֹ אַנְשֵׁי פְנוּאֵל כַּאֲשֶׁר עָנוּ אַנְשֵׁי סֻכּוֹת: ⁹ וַיֹּאמֶר גַּם־לְאַנְשֵׁי פְנוּאֵל לֵאמֹר בְּשׁוּבִי בְשָׁלוֹם אֶתֹּץ אֶת־הַמִּגְדָּל הַזֶּה: פ

¹⁰ וְזֶבַח וְצַלְמֻנָּע בַּקַּרְקֹר וּמַחֲנֵיהֶם עִמָּם כַּחֲמֵשֶׁת עָשָׂר אֶלֶף כֹּל הַנּוֹתָרִים מִכֹּל מַחֲנֵה בְנֵי־קֶדֶם וְהַנֹּפְלִים מֵאָה וְעֶשְׂרִים אֶלֶף אִישׁ שֹׁלֵף חָרֶב: ¹¹ וַיַּעַל גִּדְעוֹן דֶּרֶךְ הַשְּׁכוּנֵי בָאֳהָלִים מִקֶּדֶם לְנֹבַח וְיָגְבְּהָה

---

a-a Lit. "Is the palm of Zebah and Zalmunna in your hand."
b I.e., throw them naked in a bed of thorns and trample them; but exact meaning uncertain.
c Lit. "men who drew the sword."

סבירין ומטעין לשון רבים   v. 6.

534

Jogbehah, and routed the camp, which was off guard. [12]Zebah and Zalmunna took to flight, with Gideon[d] in pursuit. He captured Zebah and Zalmunna, the two kings of Midian, and threw the whole army into panic.

[13]On his way back from the battle at the Ascent of Heres, Gideon son of Joash [14]captured a boy from among the people of Succoth and interrogated him. The latter drew up for him a list of the officials and elders of Succoth, seventy-seven in number. [15]Then he came to the people of Succoth and said, "Here are Zebah and Zalmunna, about whom you mocked me, saying, [a]-'Are Zebah and Zalmunna already in your hands,-[a] that we should give your famished men bread?'" [16]And he took the elders of the city and, [bringing] desert thorns and briers, he punished[e] the people of Succoth with them. [17]As for Penuel, he tore down its tower and killed the townspeople.

[18]Then he asked Zebah and Zalmunna, "Those men you killed at Tabor, [f]-what were they like?"-[f] "They looked just like you," they replied, "like sons of a king." [19]"They were my brothers," he declared, "the sons of my mother. As the LORD lives, if you had spared them, I would not kill you." [20]And he commanded his oldest son Jether, "Go kill them!" But the boy did not draw his sword, for he was timid, being still a boy. [21]Then Zebah and Zalmunna said, "Come, you slay us; for strength comes with manhood." So Gideon went over and killed Zebah and Zalmunna, and he took the crescents that were on the necks of their camels.

[22]Then the men of Israel said to Gideon, "Rule over us—you, your son, and your grandson as well; for you have saved us from the Midianites." [23]But Gideon replied, "I will not rule over you myself, nor shall my son rule over you; the

וַיַּ֣ךְ אֶת־הַֽמַּחֲנֶ֔ה וְהַֽמַּחֲנֶ֖ה הָיָ֥ה בֶֽטַח׃
12 וַיָּנ֗וּסוּ זֶ֚בַח וְצַלְמֻנָּ֔ע וַיִּרְדֹּ֖ף אַחֲרֵיהֶ֑ם וַיִּלְכֹּ֞ד אֶת־שְׁנֵ֣י ׀ מַלְכֵ֣י מִדְיָ֗ן אֶת־זֶ֙בַח֙ וְאֶת־צַלְמֻנָּ֔ע וְכׇל־הַֽמַּחֲנֶ֖ה הֶחֱרִֽיד׃ 13 וַיָּ֛שׇׁב גִּדְע֥וֹן בֶּן־יוֹאָ֖שׁ מִן־הַמִּלְחָמָ֑ה מִֽלְמַעֲלֵ֖ה הֶחָֽרֶס׃ 14 וַיִּלְכׇּד־נַ֛עַר מֵאַנְשֵׁ֥י סֻכּ֖וֹת וַיִּשְׁאָלֵ֑הוּ וַיִּכְתֹּ֨ב אֵלָ֜יו אֶת־שָׂרֵ֤י סֻכּוֹת֙ וְאֶת־זְקֵנֶ֔יהָ שִׁבְעִ֥ים וְשִׁבְעָ֖ה אִֽישׁ׃ 15 וַיָּבֹא֮ אֶל־אַנְשֵׁ֣י סֻכּוֹת֒ וַיֹּ֕אמֶר הִנֵּ֖ה זֶ֣בַח וְצַלְמֻנָּ֑ע אֲשֶׁר֩ חֵרַפְתֶּ֨ם אוֹתִ֜י לֵאמֹ֗ר הֲ֠כַ֠ף זֶ֣בַח וְצַלְמֻנָּ֤ע עַתָּה֙ בְּיָדֶ֔ךָ כִּ֥י נִתֵּ֖ן לַאֲנָשֶׁ֥יךָ הַיְעֵפִ֖ים לָֽחֶם׃ 16 וַיִּקַּח֙ אֶת־זִקְנֵ֣י הָעִ֔יר וְאֶת־קוֹצֵ֥י הַמִּדְבָּ֖ר וְאֶת־הַֽבַּרְקֳנִ֑ים וַיֹּ֣דַע בָּהֶ֔ם אֵ֖ת אַנְשֵׁ֥י סֻכּֽוֹת׃ 17 וְאֶת־מִגְדַּ֥ל פְּנוּאֵ֖ל נָתָ֑ץ וַֽיַּהֲרֹ֖ג אֶת־אַנְשֵׁ֥י הָעִֽיר׃ 18 וַיֹּ֗אמֶר אֶל־זֶ֙בַח֙ וְאֶל־צַלְמֻנָּ֔ע אֵיפֹה֙ הָאֲנָשִׁ֔ים אֲשֶׁ֥ר הֲרַגְתֶּ֖ם בְּתָב֑וֹר וַיֹּאמְרוּ֙ כָּמ֔וֹךָ כְּמוֹהֶ֣ם אֶחָ֔ד כְּתֹ֖אַר בְּנֵ֥י הַמֶּֽלֶךְ׃ 19 וַיֹּאמַ֕ר אַחַ֥י בְּנֵֽי־אִמִּ֖י הֵ֑ם חַי־יְהֹוָ֗ה ל֚וּ הַחֲיִתֶ֣ם אוֹתָ֔ם לֹ֥א הָרַ֖גְתִּי אֶתְכֶֽם׃ 20 וַיֹּ֙אמֶר֙ לְיֶ֣תֶר בְּכוֹר֔וֹ ק֖וּם הֲרֹ֣ג אוֹתָ֑ם וְלֹא־שָׁלַ֨ף הַנַּ֤עַר חַרְבּוֹ֙ כִּ֣י יָרֵ֔א כִּ֥י עוֹדֶ֖נּוּ נָֽעַר׃ 21 וַיֹּ֜אמֶר זֶ֣בַח וְצַלְמֻנָּ֗ע ק֤וּם אַתָּה֙ וּפְגַע־בָּ֔נוּ כִּ֥י כָאִ֖ישׁ גְּבוּרָת֑וֹ וַיָּ֣קׇם גִּדְע֗וֹן וַֽיַּהֲרֹג֙ אֶת־זֶ֣בַח וְאֶת־צַלְמֻנָּ֔ע וַיִּקַּח֙ אֶת־הַשַּׂ֣הֲרֹנִ֔ים אֲשֶׁ֖ר בְּצַוְּארֵ֥י גְמַלֵּיהֶֽם׃ 22 וַיֹּאמְר֤וּ אִֽישׁ־יִשְׂרָאֵל֙ אֶל־גִּדְע֔וֹן מְשׇׁל־בָּ֙נוּ֙ גַּם־אַתָּ֔ה גַּם־בִּנְךָ֖ גַּ֣ם בֶּן־בְּנֶ֑ךָ כִּ֥י הוֹשַׁעְתָּ֖נוּ מִיַּ֥ד מִדְיָֽן׃ 23 וַיֹּ֤אמֶר אֲלֵהֶם֙ גִּדְע֔וֹן לֹֽא־אֶמְשֹׁ֤ל אֲנִי֙ בָּכֶ֔ם וְלֹֽא־יִמְשֹׁ֥ל

---

d   Heb. "him."
e   Meaning of Heb. uncertain; emendation yields "threshed"; cf. v. 7.
f-f   Others "Where are they?"

LORD alone shall rule over you." [24]And Gideon said to them, "I have a request to make of you: Each of you give me the earring he received as booty." (They[g] had golden earrings, for they were Ishmaelites.) [25]"Certainly!" they replied. And they spread out a cloth, and everyone threw onto it the earring he had received as booty. [26]The weight of the golden earrings that he had requested came to 1,700 shekels of gold; this was in addition to the crescents and the pendants and the purple robes worn by the kings of Midian and in addition to the collars on the necks of their camels. [27]Gideon made an ephod of [h]-this gold-[h] and set it up in his own town of Ophrah. There all Israel went astray after it, and it became a snare to Gideon and his household.

[28]Thus Midian submitted to the Israelites and did not raise its head again; and the land was tranquil for forty years in Gideon's time.

[29]So Jerubbaal son of Joash retired to his own house. [30]Gideon had seventy sons of his own issue, for he had many wives. [31]A son was also born to him by his concubine in Shechem, and he named him Abimelech. [32]Gideon son of Joash died at a ripe old age, and was buried in the tomb of his father Joash at Ophrah of the Abiezrites.

[33]After Gideon died, the Israelites again went astray after the Baalim, and they adopted Baal-berith as a god. [34]The Israelites gave no thought to the LORD their God, who saved them from all the enemies around them. [35]Nor did they show loyalty to the house of Jerubbaal-Gideon in return for all the good that he had done for Israel.

9 Abimelech son of Jerubbaal went to his mother's brothers in Shechem and spoke to

בְּנִי בָכֶם יְהוָה יִמְשֹׁל בָּכֶם: [24] וַיֹּאמֶר אֲלֵהֶם גִּדְעוֹן אֶשְׁאֲלָה מִכֶּם שְׁאֵלָה וּתְנוּ־לִי אִישׁ נֶזֶם שְׁלָלוֹ כִּי־נִזְמֵי זָהָב לָהֶם כִּי יִשְׁמְעֵאלִים הֵם: [25] וַיֹּאמְרוּ נָתוֹן נִתֵּן וַיִּפְרְשׂוּ אֶת־הַשִּׂמְלָה וַיַּשְׁלִיכוּ שָׁמָּה אִישׁ נֶזֶם שְׁלָלוֹ: [26] וַיְהִי מִשְׁקַל נִזְמֵי הַזָּהָב אֲשֶׁר שָׁאָל אֶלֶף וּשְׁבַע־מֵאוֹת זָהָב לְבַד מִן־הַשַּׂהֲרֹנִים וְהַנְּטִפוֹת וּבִגְדֵי הָאַרְגָּמָן שֶׁעַל מַלְכֵי מִדְיָן וּלְבַד מִן־הָעֲנָקוֹת אֲשֶׁר בְּצַוְּארֵי גְמַלֵּיהֶם: [27] וַיַּעַשׂ אוֹתוֹ גִדְעוֹן לְאֵפוֹד וַיַּצֵּג אוֹתוֹ בְעִירוֹ בְּעָפְרָה וַיִּזְנוּ כָל־יִשְׂרָאֵל אַחֲרָיו שָׁם וַיְהִי לְגִדְעוֹן וּלְבֵיתוֹ לְמוֹקֵשׁ: [28] וַיִּכָּנַע מִדְיָן לִפְנֵי בְּנֵי יִשְׂרָאֵל וְלֹא יָסְפוּ לָשֵׂאת רֹאשָׁם וַתִּשְׁקֹט הָאָרֶץ אַרְבָּעִים שָׁנָה בִּימֵי גִדְעוֹן: פ

[29] וַיֵּלֶךְ יְרֻבַּעַל בֶּן־יוֹאָשׁ וַיֵּשֶׁב בְּבֵיתוֹ: [30] וּלְגִדְעוֹן הָיוּ שִׁבְעִים בָּנִים יֹצְאֵי יְרֵכוֹ כִּי־נָשִׁים רַבּוֹת הָיוּ לוֹ: [31] וּפִילַגְשׁוֹ אֲשֶׁר בִּשְׁכֶם יָלְדָה־לּוֹ גַם־הִיא בֵּן וַיָּשֶׂם אֶת־שְׁמוֹ אֲבִימֶלֶךְ: [32] וַיָּמָת גִּדְעוֹן בֶּן־יוֹאָשׁ בְּשֵׂיבָה טוֹבָה וַיִּקָּבֵר בְּקֶבֶר יוֹאָשׁ אָבִיו בְּעָפְרָה אֲבִי הָעֶזְרִי: פ

[33] וַיְהִי כַּאֲשֶׁר מֵת גִּדְעוֹן וַיָּשׁוּבוּ בְּנֵי יִשְׂרָאֵל וַיִּזְנוּ אַחֲרֵי הַבְּעָלִים וַיָּשִׂימוּ לָהֶם בַּעַל בְּרִית לֵאלֹהִים: [34] וְלֹא זָכְרוּ בְּנֵי יִשְׂרָאֵל אֶת־יְהוָה אֱלֹהֵיהֶם הַמַּצִּיל אוֹתָם מִיַּד כָּל־אֹיְבֵיהֶם מִסָּבִיב: [35] וְלֹא־עָשׂוּ חֶסֶד עִם־בֵּית יְרֻבַּעַל גִּדְעוֹן כְּכָל־הַטּוֹבָה אֲשֶׁר עָשָׂה עִם־יִשְׂרָאֵל: פ

ט וַיֵּלֶךְ אֲבִימֶלֶךְ בֶּן־יְרֻבַּעַל שְׁכֶמָה אֶל־אֲחֵי אִמּוֹ וַיְדַבֵּר אֲלֵיהֶם וְאֶל־כָּל־

---

g   *I.e., the Midianites. The author explains that the Midianites wore earrings like the Ishmaelites, who were better known to his contemporaries.*

h-h   *Heb. "it."*

them and to the whole clan of his mother's family. He said, 2"Put this question to all the citizens of Shechem: Which is better for you, to be ruled by seventy men—by all the sons of Jerubbaal—or to be ruled by one man? And remember, I am your own *a-flesh and blood."-a* 3His mother's brothers said all this in his behalf to all the citizens of Shechem, and they were won over to Abimelech; for they thought, "He is our kinsman." 4They gave him seventy shekels from the temple of Baal-berith; and with this Abimelech hired some worthless and reckless fellows, and they followed him. 5Then he went to his father's house in Ophrah and killed his brothers, the sons of Jerubbaal, seventy men on one stone. Only Jotham, the youngest son of Jerubbaal, survived, because he went into hiding.

6All the citizens of Shechem and all Bethmillo convened, and they proclaimed Abimelech king at the terebinth of the pillar*b* at Shechem. 7When Jotham was informed, he went and stood on top of Mount Gerizim and called out to them in a loud voice. "Citizens of Shechem!" he cried, "listen to me, that God may listen to you.

8"Once the trees went to anoint a king over themselves. They said to the olive tree, 'Reign over us.' 9But the olive tree replied, 'Have I, through whom God and men are honored, stopped yielding my rich oil, that I should go and wave above the trees?' 10So the trees said to the fig tree, 'You come and reign over us.' 11But the fig tree replied, 'Have I stopped yielding my sweetness, my delicious fruit, that I should go and wave above the trees?' 12So the trees said to the vine, 'You come and reign over us.' 13But the vine replied, 'Have I stopped yielding my new wine, which gladdens God and men, that I should go and wave above the trees?' 14Then all the trees said to the thornbush, 'You come and reign over us.' 15And the thornbush

---

מִשְׁפַּ֣חַת בֵּית־אֲבִ֣י אִמּ֑וֹ לֵאמֹֽר׃ 2 דַּבְּרוּ־ נָ֞א בְּאׇזְנֵ֤י כׇל־בַּעֲלֵ֣י שְׁכֶם֙ מַה־טּ֣וֹב לָכֶ֔ם הַמְשֹׁ֨ל בָּכֶ֜ם שִׁבְעִ֣ים אִ֗ישׁ כֹּ֚ל בְּנֵ֣י יְרֻבַּ֔עַל אִם־מְשֹׁ֥ל בָּכֶ֖ם אִ֣ישׁ אֶחָ֑ד וּזְכַרְתֶּ֕ם כִּֽי־ עַצְמְכֶ֥ם וּבְשַׂרְכֶ֖ם אָֽנִי׃ 3 וַיְדַבְּר֨וּ אֲחֵֽי־אִמּ֜וֹ עָלָ֗יו בְּאׇזְנֵי֙ כׇּל־בַּעֲלֵ֣י שְׁכֶ֔ם אֵ֥ת כׇּל־ הַדְּבָרִ֖ים הָאֵ֑לֶּה וַיֵּ֤ט לִבָּם֙ אַחֲרֵ֣י אֲבִימֶ֔לֶךְ כִּ֥י אָמְר֖וּ אָחִ֥ינוּ הֽוּא׃ 4 וַיִּתְּנוּ־לוֹ֙ שִׁבְעִ֣ים כֶּ֔סֶף מִבֵּ֖ית בַּ֣עַל בְּרִ֑ית וַיִּשְׂכֹּ֨ר בָּהֶ֜ם אֲבִימֶ֗לֶךְ אֲנָשִׁ֤ים רֵיקִים֙ וּפֹ֣חֲזִ֔ים וַיֵּלְכ֖וּ אַחֲרָֽיו׃ 5 וַיָּבֹ֤א בֵית־אָבִיו֙ עׇפְרָ֔תָה וַֽיַּהֲרֹ֞ג אֶת־אֶחָ֧יו בְּנֵֽי־יְרֻבַּ֛עַל שִׁבְעִ֥ים אִ֖ישׁ עַל־ אֶ֣בֶן אֶחָ֑ת וַיִּוָּתֵ֞ר יוֹתָ֧ם בֶּן־יְרֻבַּ֛עַל הַקָּטֹ֖ן כִּ֥י נֶחְבָּֽא׃ ס

6 וַיֵּאָ֨סְפ֜וּ כׇּל־בַּעֲלֵ֤י שְׁכֶם֙ וְכׇל־בֵּ֣ית מִלּ֔וֹא וַיֵּ֣לְכ֔וּ וַיַּמְלִ֥יכוּ אֶת־אֲבִימֶ֖לֶךְ לְמֶ֑לֶךְ עִם־ אֵל֥וֹן מֻצָּ֖ב אֲשֶׁ֥ר בִּשְׁכֶֽם׃ 7 וַיַּגִּ֣דוּ לְיוֹתָ֗ם וַיֵּ֙לֶךְ֙ וַיַּעֲמֹד֙ בְּרֹ֣אשׁ הַר־גְּרִזִ֔ים וַיִּשָּׂ֥א קוֹל֖וֹ וַיִּקְרָ֑א וַיֹּ֣אמֶר לָהֶ֗ם שִׁמְע֤וּ אֵלַי֙ בַּעֲלֵ֣י שְׁכֶ֔ם וְיִשְׁמַ֥ע אֲלֵיכֶ֖ם אֱלֹהִֽים׃

8 הָל֤וֹךְ הָֽלְכוּ֙ הָעֵצִ֔ים לִמְשֹׁ֥חַ עֲלֵיהֶ֖ם מֶ֑לֶךְ וַיֹּאמְר֥וּ לַזַּ֖יִת מׇלְכָ֥ה עָלֵֽינוּ׃ 9 וַיֹּ֤אמֶר לָהֶם֙ הַזַּ֔יִת הֶחֳדַ֙לְתִּי֙ אֶת־דִּשְׁנִ֔י אֲשֶׁר־בִּ֛י יְכַבְּד֥וּ אֱלֹהִ֖ים וַאֲנָשִׁ֑ים וְהָ֣לַכְתִּ֔י לָנ֖וּעַ עַל־הָעֵצִֽים׃ 10 וַיֹּאמְר֥וּ הָעֵצִ֖ים לַתְּאֵנָ֑ה לְכִי־אַ֖תְּ מׇלְכִ֥י עָלֵֽינוּ׃ 11 וַתֹּ֤אמֶר לָהֶם֙ הַתְּאֵנָ֔ה הֶחֳדַ֙לְתִּי֙ אֶת־מׇתְקִ֔י וְאֶת־ תְּנוּבָתִ֖י הַטּוֹבָ֑ה וְהָ֣לַכְתִּ֔י לָנ֖וּעַ עַל־ הָעֵצִֽים׃ 12 וַיֹּאמְר֥וּ הָעֵצִ֖ים לַגָּ֑פֶן לְכִי־אַ֖תְּ מׇלְכִ֥י עָלֵֽינוּ׃ 13 וַתֹּ֤אמֶר לָהֶם֙ הַגֶּ֔פֶן הֶחֳדַ֙לְתִּי֙ אֶת־תִּ֣ירוֹשִׁ֔י הַמְשַׂמֵּ֥חַ אֱלֹהִ֖ים וַאֲנָשִׁ֑ים וְהָ֣לַכְתִּ֔י לָנ֖וּעַ עַל־הָעֵצִֽים׃ 14 וַיֹּאמְר֥וּ כׇל־הָעֵצִ֖ים אֶל־הָאָטָ֑ד לֵ֥ךְ אַתָּ֖ה מְלׇךְ־עָלֵֽינוּ׃ 15 וַיֹּ֤אמֶר הָֽאָטָד֙ אֶל־

---

a-a   Lit. "bone and flesh."
b   Meaning of Heb. uncertain.

said to the trees, 'If you are acting honorably in anointing me king over you, come and take shelter in my shade; but if not, may fire issue from the thornbush and consume the cedars of Lebanon!'

16"Now then, if you acted honorably and loyally in making Abimelech king, if you have done right by Jerubbaal and his house and have requited him according to his deserts—17considering that my father fought for you and saved you from the Midianites at the risk of his life, 18and now you have turned on my father's household, killed his sons, seventy men on one stone, and set up Abimelech, the son of his handmaid, as king over the citizens of Shechem just because he is your kinsman—19if, I say, you have this day acted honorably and loyally toward Jerubbaal and his house, have joy in Abimelech and may he likewise have joy in you. 20But if not, may fire issue from Abimelech and consume the citizens of Shechem and Beth-millo, and may fire issue from the citizens of Shechem and Beth-millo and consume Abimelech!"

21With that, Jotham fled. He ran to Beer and stayed there, because of his brother Abimelech.

22Abimelech held sway over Israel for three years. 23Then God sent a spirit of discord between Abimelech and the citizens of Shechem, and the citizens of Shechem broke faith with Abimelech—24to the end that the crime committed against the seventy sons of Jerubbaal might be avenged, and their blood recoil upon their brother Abimelech, who had slain them, and upon the citizens of Shechem, who had abetted him in the slaying of his brothers. 25The citizens of Shechem planted ambuscades against him on the hilltops; and they robbed whoever passed by them on the road. Word of this reached Abimelech.

26Then Gaal son of Ebed and his companions came passing through Shechem, and the citi-

הָעֵצִ֗ים אִם־בֶּאֱמֶ֞ת אַתֶּ֣ם מֹשְׁחִ֥ים אֹתִ֛י לְמֶ֙לֶךְ֙ עֲלֵיכֶ֔ם בֹּ֖אוּ חֲס֣וּ בְצִלִּ֑י וְאִם־אַ֗יִן תֵּ֤צֵא אֵשׁ֙ מִן־הָ֣אָטָ֔ד וְתֹאכַ֖ל אֶת־אַרְזֵ֥י הַלְּבָנֽוֹן׃ 16 וְעַתָּ֗ה אִם־בֶּאֱמֶ֤ת וּבְתָמִים֙ עֲשִׂיתֶ֔ם וַתַּמְלִ֖יכוּ אֶת־אֲבִימֶ֑לֶךְ וְאִם־טוֹבָ֤ה עֲשִׂיתֶם֙ עִם־יְרֻבַּ֣עַל וְעִם־בֵּית֔וֹ וְאִם־ כִּגְמ֥וּל יָדָ֖יו עֲשִׂ֥יתֶם לֽוֹ׃ 17 אֲשֶׁר־נִלְחַ֥ם אָבִ֖י עֲלֵיכֶ֑ם וַיַּשְׁלֵ֤ךְ אֶת־נַפְשׁוֹ֙ מִנֶּ֔גֶד וַיַּצֵּ֥ל אֶתְכֶ֖ם מִיַּ֥ד מִדְיָֽן׃ 18 וְאַתֶּ֞ם קַמְתֶּ֨ם עַל־ בֵּ֤ית אָבִי֙ הַיּ֔וֹם וַתַּהַרְג֧וּ אֶת־בָּנָ֛יו שִׁבְעִ֥ים אִ֖ישׁ עַל־אֶ֣בֶן אֶחָ֑ת וַתַּמְלִ֜יכוּ אֶת־ אֲבִימֶ֤לֶךְ בֶּן־אֲמָתוֹ֙ עַל־בַּעֲלֵ֣י שְׁכֶ֔ם כִּ֥י אֲחִיכֶ֖ם הֽוּא׃ 19 וְאִם־בֶּאֱמֶ֨ת וּבְתָמִ֜ים עֲשִׂיתֶ֧ם עִם־יְרֻבַּ֛עַל וְעִם־בֵּית֖וֹ הַיּ֣וֹם הַזֶּ֑ה שִׂמְחוּ֙ בַּאֲבִימֶ֔לֶךְ וְיִשְׂמַ֥ח גַּם־ה֖וּא בָּכֶֽם׃ 20 וְאִם־אַ֕יִן תֵּ֤צֵא אֵשׁ֙ מֵאֲבִימֶ֔לֶךְ וְתֹאכַ֛ל אֶת־בַּעֲלֵ֥י שְׁכֶ֖ם וְאֶת־בֵּ֣ית מִלּ֑וֹא וְתֵצֵ֨א אֵ֜שׁ מִבַּעֲלֵ֤י שְׁכֶם֙ וּמִבֵּ֣ית מִלּ֔וֹא וְתֹאכַ֖ל אֶת־אֲבִימֶֽלֶךְ׃ 21 וַיָּ֣נָס יוֹתָ֔ם וַיִּבְרַ֖ח וַיֵּ֣לֶךְ בְּאֵ֑רָה וַיֵּ֣שֶׁב שָׁ֔ם מִפְּנֵ֖י אֲבִימֶ֥לֶךְ אָחִֽיו׃ פ 22 וַיָּ֧שַׂר אֲבִימֶ֛לֶךְ עַל־יִשְׂרָאֵ֖ל שָׁלֹ֥שׁ שָׁנִֽים׃ 23 וַיִּשְׁלַ֤ח אֱלֹהִים֙ ר֣וּחַ רָעָ֔ה בֵּ֚ין אֲבִימֶ֔לֶךְ וּבֵ֖ין בַּעֲלֵ֣י שְׁכֶ֑ם וַיִּבְגְּד֥וּ בַעֲלֵי־שְׁכֶ֖ם בַּאֲבִימֶֽלֶךְ׃ 24 לָב֕וֹא חֲמַ֛ס שִׁבְעִ֥ים בְּנֵֽי־ יְרֻבָּ֑עַל וְדָמָ֗ם לָשׂ֞וּם עַל־אֲבִימֶ֤לֶךְ אֲחִיהֶם֙ אֲשֶׁ֣ר הָרַ֣ג אוֹתָ֔ם וְעַל֙ בַּעֲלֵ֣י שְׁכֶ֔ם אֲשֶׁר־ חִזְּק֥וּ אֶת־יָדָ֖יו לַהֲרֹ֥ג אֶת־אֶחָֽיו׃ 25 וַיָּשִׂ֣ימוּ ל֣וֹ בַעֲלֵ֣י שְׁכֶ֗ם מְאָֽרְבִים֙ עַ֚ל רָאשֵׁ֣י הֶהָרִ֔ים וַיִּגְזְל֗וּ אֵ֛ת כָּל־אֲשֶׁר־יַעֲבֹ֥ר עֲלֵיהֶ֖ם בַּדָּ֑רֶךְ וַיֻּגַּ֖ד לַאֲבִימֶֽלֶךְ׃ פ 26 וַיָּבֹ֞א גַּ֤עַל בֶּן־עֶ֙בֶד֙ וְאֶחָ֔יו וַיַּעַבְר֖וּ בִּשְׁכֶ֑ם וַיִּבְטְחוּ־ב֖וֹ בַּעֲלֵ֥י שְׁכֶֽם׃ 27 וַיֵּצְאוּ֩ הַשָּׂדֶ֨ה

zens of Shechem gave him their confidence. [27]They went out into the fields, gathered and trod out the vintage of their vineyards, and made a festival. They entered the temple of their god, and as they ate and drank they reviled Abimelech. [28]Gaal son of Ebed said, "Who is Abimelech and who are [we] Shechemites, that we should serve him? *b*-This same son of Jerubbaal and his lieutenant Zebul once served the men of Hamor, the father of Shechem;-*b* so why should we serve him? [29]Oh, if only this people were under my command, I would get rid of Abimelech! One*c* would challenge Abimelech, 'Fill up your ranks and come out here!'"

[30]When Zebul, the governor of the city, heard the words of Gaal son of Ebed, he was furious. [31]He sent messages to Abimelech at Tormah*d* to say, "Gaal son of Ebed and his companions have come to Shechem and they are inciting*b* the city against you. [32]Therefore, set out at night with the forces you have with you and conceal yourself in the fields. [33]Early next morning, as the sun rises, advance on the city. He and his men will thereupon come out against you, and you will do to him whatever you find possible."

[34]Abimelech and all the men with him set out at night and disposed themselves against Shechem in four hiding places. [35]When Gaal son of Ebed came out and stood at the entrance to the city gate, Abimelech and the army with him emerged from concealment. [36]Gaal saw the army and said to Zebul, "That's an army marching down from the hilltops!" But Zebul said to him, "The shadows of the hills look to you like men." [37]Gaal spoke up again, "Look, an army is marching down from Tabbur-erez, and another column is coming from the direction of Elon-meonenim." [38]"Well," replied Zebul, "where is your boast, 'Who is Abimelech that we should serve him'? There is the army you sneered at; now go out and fight it!"

וַיִּבְצְר֤וּ אֶת־כַּרְמֵיהֶם֙ וַיִּדְרְכ֔וּ וַיַּֽעֲשׂ֖וּ הִלּוּלִ֑ים וַיָּבֹ֙אוּ֙ בֵּ֣ית אֱלֹֽהֵיהֶ֔ם וַיֹּֽאכְלוּ֙ וַיִּשְׁתּ֔וּ וַֽיְקַֽלְל֖וּ אֶת־אֲבִימֶֽלֶךְ׃ 28 וַיֹּ֣אמֶר ׀ גַּ֣עַל בֶּן־עֶ֗בֶד מִֽי־אֲבִימֶ֤לֶךְ וּמִֽי־שְׁכֶם֙ כִּ֣י נַֽעַבְדֶ֔נּוּ הֲלֹ֥א בֶן־יְרֻבַּ֖עַל וּזְבֻ֣ל פְּקִיד֑וֹ עִבְד֗וּ אֶת־אַנְשֵׁ֤י חֲמוֹר֙ אֲבִ֣י שְׁכֶ֔ם וּמַדּ֖וּעַ נַֽעַבְדֶ֥נּוּ אֲנָֽחְנוּ׃ 29 וּמִ֣י יִתֵּ֞ן אֶת־הָעָ֤ם הַזֶּה֙ בְּיָדִ֔י וְאָסִ֖ירָה אֶת־אֲבִימֶ֑לֶךְ וַיֹּ֙אמֶר֙ לַֽאֲבִימֶ֔לֶךְ רַבֶּ֥ה צְבָֽאֲךָ֖ וָצֵֽאָה׃

30 וַיִּשְׁמַ֗ע זְבֻל֙ שַׂר־הָעִ֔יר אֶת־דִּבְרֵ֖י גַּ֣עַל בֶּן־עָ֑בֶד וַיִּ֖חַר אַפּֽוֹ׃ 31 וַיִּשְׁלַ֧ח מַלְאָכִ֛ים אֶל־אֲבִימֶ֖לֶךְ בְּתׇרְמָ֣ה לֵאמֹ֑ר הִנֵּה֩ גַ֨עַל בֶּן־עֶ֤בֶד וְאֶחָיו֙ בָּאִ֣ים שְׁכֶ֔מָה וְהִנָּ֛ם צָרִ֥ים אֶת־הָעִ֖יר עָלֶֽיךָ׃ 32 וְעַתָּה֙ ק֣וּם לַ֔יְלָה אַתָּ֖ה וְהָעָ֣ם אֲשֶׁר־אִתָּ֑ךְ וֶֽאֱרֹ֖ב בַּשָּׂדֶֽה׃ 33 וְהָיָ֤ה בַבֹּ֙קֶר֙ כִּזְרֹ֣חַ הַשֶּׁ֔מֶשׁ תַּשְׁכִּ֖ים וּפָֽשַׁטְתָּ֣ עַל־הָעִ֑יר וְהִנֵּה־ה֞וּא וְהָעָ֤ם אֲשֶׁר־אִתּוֹ֙ יֹֽצְאִ֣ים אֵלֶ֔יךָ וְעָשִׂ֣יתָ לּ֔וֹ כַּֽאֲשֶׁ֖ר תִּמְצָ֥א יָדֶֽךָ׃ ס

34 וַיָּ֧קׇם אֲבִימֶ֛לֶךְ וְכׇל־הָעָ֥ם אֲשֶׁר־עִמּ֖וֹ לָ֑יְלָה וַיֶּֽאֶרְב֣וּ עַל־שְׁכֶ֔ם אַרְבָּעָ֖ה רָאשִֽׁים׃ 35 וַיֵּצֵא֙ גַּ֣עַל בֶּן־עֶ֔בֶד וַֽיַּעֲמֹ֔ד פֶּ֖תַח שַׁ֣עַר הָעִ֑יר וַיָּ֧קׇם אֲבִימֶ֛לֶךְ וְהָעָ֥ם אֲשֶׁר־אִתּ֖וֹ מִן־הַמַּאְרָֽב׃ 36 וַיַּרְא־גַּ֘עַל֮ אֶת־הָעָם֒ וַיֹּ֣אמֶר אֶל־זְבֻ֔ל הִנֵּה־עָ֣ם יוֹרֵ֔ד מֵֽרָאשֵׁ֖י הֶֽהָרִ֑ים וַיֹּ֤אמֶר אֵלָיו֙ זְבֻ֔ל אֵ֣ת צֵ֧ל הֶֽהָרִ֛ים אַתָּ֥ה רֹאֶ֖ה כָּֽאֲנָשִֽׁים׃ ס 37 וַיֹּ֨סֶף ע֣וֹד גַּעַל֮ לְדַבֵּר֒ וַיֹּ֕אמֶר הִנֵּה־עָם֙ יֽוֹרְדִ֔ים מֵעִ֖ם טַבּ֣וּר הָאָ֑רֶץ וְרֹאשׁ־אֶחָ֣ד בָּ֔א מִדֶּ֖רֶךְ אֵל֥וֹן מְעֽוֹנְנִֽים׃ 38 וַיֹּ֨אמֶר אֵלָ֜יו זְבֻ֗ל אַיֵּ֨ה אֵפ֥וֹא פִ֙יךָ֙ אֲשֶׁ֣ר תֹּאמַ֔ר מִ֥י אֲבִימֶ֖לֶךְ כִּ֣י נַֽעַבְדֶ֑נּוּ הֲלֹ֨א זֶ֤ה הָעָם֙ אֲשֶׁ֣ר מָאַ֣סְתָּה בּ֔וֹ צֵא־נָ֥א עַתָּ֖ה וְהִלָּ֥חֶם בּֽוֹ׃ ס

c   Septuagint reads "I."
d   Called "Arumah" in v. 41.

39So Gaal went out at the head of the citizens of Shechem and gave battle to Abimelech. 40But he had to flee before him, and Abimelech pursued him, and many fell slain, all the way to the entrance of the gate. 41Then Abimelech stayed in Arumah,*e* while Zebul expelled Gaal and his companions and kept them out of Shechem.

42The next day, when people went out into the fields, Abimelech was informed. 43Taking the army, he divided it into three columns and lay in ambush in the fields; and when he saw the people coming out of the city, he pounced upon them and struck them down. 44While Abimelech and the column*f* that followed him dashed ahead and took up a position at the entrance of the city gate, the other two columns rushed upon all that were in the open and struck them down. 45Abimelech fought against the city all that day. He captured the city and massacred the people in it; he razed the town and sowed it with salt.

46When all the citizens of the Tower of Shechem*g* learned of this, they went into the tunnel*h* of the temple of El-berith.*i* 47When Abimelech was informed that all the citizens of the Tower of Shechem had gathered [there], 48Abimelech and all the troops he had with him went up on Mount Zalmon. Taking an ax*j* in his hand, Abimelech lopped off a tree limb and lifted it onto his shoulder. Then he said to the troops that accompanied him, "What you saw me do—quick, do the same!" 49So each of the troops also lopped off a bough; then they marched behind Abimelech and laid them against the tunnel, and set fire to the tunnel over their heads. Thus all the people of the Tower of Shechem also perished, about a thousand men and women.

39 וַיֵּצֵא גַּעַל לִפְנֵי בַּעֲלֵי שְׁכֶם וַיִּלָּחֶם בַּאֲבִימֶלֶךְ: 40 וַיִּרְדְּפֵהוּ אֲבִימֶלֶךְ וַיָּנָס מִפָּנָיו וַיִּפְּלוּ חֲלָלִים רַבִּים עַד־פֶּתַח הַשָּׁעַר: 41 וַיֵּשֶׁב אֲבִימֶלֶךְ בָּארוּמָה* וַיְגָרֶשׁ זְבֻל אֶת־גַּעַל וְאֶת־אֶחָיו מִשֶּׁבֶת בִּשְׁכֶם:

42 וַיְהִי מִמָּחֳרָת וַיֵּצֵא הָעָם הַשָּׂדֶה וַיַּגִּדוּ לַאֲבִימֶלֶךְ: 43 וַיִּקַּח אֶת־הָעָם וַיֶּחֱצֵם לִשְׁלֹשָׁה רָאשִׁים וַיֶּאֱרֹב בַּשָּׂדֶה וַיַּרְא וְהִנֵּה הָעָם יֹצֵא מִן־הָעִיר וַיָּקָם עֲלֵיהֶם וַיַּכֵּם: 44 וַאֲבִימֶלֶךְ וְהָרָאשִׁים אֲשֶׁר עִמּוֹ פָּשְׁטוּ וַיַּעַמְדוּ פֶּתַח שַׁעַר הָעִיר וּשְׁנֵי הָרָאשִׁים פָּשְׁטוּ עַל־כָּל־אֲשֶׁר בַּשָּׂדֶה וַיַּכּוּם: 45 וַאֲבִימֶלֶךְ נִלְחָם בָּעִיר כֹּל הַיּוֹם הַהוּא וַיִּלְכֹּד אֶת־הָעִיר וְאֶת־הָעָם אֲשֶׁר־בָּהּ הָרָג וַיִּתֹּץ אֶת־הָעִיר וַיִּזְרָעֶהָ מֶלַח: פ

46 וַיִּשְׁמְעוּ כָּל־בַּעֲלֵי מִגְדַּל־שְׁכֶם וַיָּבֹאוּ אֶל־צְרִיחַ בֵּית אֵל בְּרִית: 47 וַיֻּגַּד לַאֲבִימֶלֶךְ כִּי הִתְקַבְּצוּ כָּל־בַּעֲלֵי מִגְדַּל־שְׁכֶם: 48 וַיַּעַל אֲבִימֶלֶךְ הַר־צַלְמוֹן הוּא וְכָל־הָעָם אֲשֶׁר־אִתּוֹ וַיִּקַּח אֲבִימֶלֶךְ אֶת־הַקַּרְדֻּמּוֹת בְּיָדוֹ וַיִּכְרֹת שׂוֹכַת עֵצִים וַיִּשָּׂאֶהָ וַיָּשֶׂם עַל־שִׁכְמוֹ וַיֹּאמֶר אֶל־הָעָם אֲשֶׁר־עִמּוֹ מָה רְאִיתֶם עָשִׂיתִי מַהֲרוּ עֲשׂוּ כָמוֹנִי: 49 וַיִּכְרְתוּ גַם־כָּל־הָעָם אִישׁ שׂוֹכֹה וַיֵּלְכוּ אַחֲרֵי אֲבִימֶלֶךְ וַיָּשִׂימוּ עַל־הַצְּרִיחַ וַיַּצִּיתוּ עֲלֵיהֶם אֶת־הַצְּרִיחַ בָּאֵשׁ וַיָּמֻתוּ גַּם כָּל־אַנְשֵׁי מִגְדַּל־שְׁכֶם כְּאֶלֶף אִישׁ וְאִשָּׁה: פ

---

e   Cf. "Tormah" in v. 31.
f   Heb. "columns."
g   Perhaps identical with Beth-millo of vv. 6 and 20.
h   Cf. 1 Sam. 13.6; others "citadel."
i   Called "Baal-berith" in v. 4.
j   Heb. plural.

⁵⁰Abimelech proceeded to Thebez; he encamped at Thebez and occupied it. ⁵¹Within the town was a fortified tower; and all the citizens of the town, men and women, took refuge there. They shut themselves in, and went up on the roof of the tower. ⁵²Abimelech pressed forward to the tower and attacked it. He approached the door of the tower to set it on fire. ⁵³But a woman dropped an upper millstone on Abimelech's head and cracked his skull. ⁵⁴He immediately cried out to his attendant, his arms-bearer, "Draw your dagger and finish me off, that they may not say of me, 'A woman killed him!'" So his attendant stabbed him, and he died. ⁵⁵When the men of Israel saw that Abimelech was dead, everyone went home.

⁵⁶Thus God repaid Abimelech for the evil he had done to his father by slaying his seventy brothers; ⁵⁷and God likewise repaid the men of Shechem for all their wickedness. And so the curse of Jotham son of Jerubbaal was fulfilled upon them.

10

After Abimelech, Tola son of Puah son of Dodo, a man of Issachar, arose to deliver Israel. He lived at Shamir in the hill country of Ephraim. ²He led Israel for twenty-three years; then he died and was buried at Shamir.

³After him arose Jair the Gileadite, and he led Israel for twenty-two years. (⁴He had thirty sons, who rode on thirty burros and owned thirty boroughs[a] in the region of Gilead; these are called Havvoth-jair[b] to this day.) ⁵Then Jair died and was buried at Kamon.

⁶The Israelites again did what was offensive to the Lord. They served the Baalim and the Ashtaroth, and the gods of Aram, the gods of Sidon, the gods of Moab, the gods of the Ammonites, and the gods of the Philistines; they

---

⁵⁰ וַיֵּ֤לֶךְ אֲבִימֶ֙לֶךְ֙ אֶל־תֵּבֵ֔ץ וַיִּ֥חַן בְּתֵבֵ֖ץ
וַֽיִּלְכְּדָֽהּ׃ ⁵¹ וּמִגְדַּל־עֹז֩ הָיָ֨ה בְתֽוֹךְ־הָעִ֜יר
וַיָּנֻ֣סוּ שָׁ֗מָּה כָּל־הָאֲנָשִׁ֤ים וְהַנָּשִׁים֙ וְכֹל֙
בַּעֲלֵ֣י הָעִ֔יר וַֽיִּסְגְּר֖וּ בַּעֲדָ֑ם וַֽיַּעֲל֖וּ עַל־גַּ֥ג
הַמִּגְדָּֽל׃ ⁵² וַיָּבֹ֤א אֲבִימֶ֙לֶךְ֙ עַד־הַמִּגְדָּ֔ל
וַיִּלָּ֖חֶם בּ֑וֹ וַיִּגַּ֞שׁ עַד־פֶּ֤תַח הַמִּגְדָּל֙ לְשָׂרְפ֣וֹ
בָאֵֽשׁ׃ ⁵³ וַתַּשְׁלֵ֞ךְ אִשָּׁ֥ה אַחַ֛ת פֶּ֥לַח רֶ֖כֶב
עַל־רֹ֣אשׁ אֲבִימֶ֑לֶךְ וַתָּ֖רִץ אֶת־גֻּלְגָּלְתּֽוֹ׃
⁵⁴ וַיִּקְרָ֨א מְהֵרָ֜ה אֶל־הַנַּ֣עַר ׀ נֹשֵׂ֣א כֵלָ֗יו
וַיֹּ֤אמֶר לוֹ֙ שְׁלֹ֤ף חַרְבְּךָ֙ וּמ֣וֹתְתֵ֔נִי פֶּן־יֹ֥אמְרוּ
לִ֖י אִשָּׁ֣ה הֲרָגָ֑תְהוּ וַיִּדְקְרֵ֥הוּ נַעֲר֖וֹ וַיָּמֹֽת׃
⁵⁵ וַיִּרְא֥וּ אִֽישׁ־יִשְׂרָאֵ֖ל כִּ֣י מֵ֣ת אֲבִימֶ֑לֶךְ
וַיֵּלְכ֖וּ אִ֥ישׁ לִמְקֹמֽוֹ׃
⁵⁶ וַיָּ֣שֶׁב אֱלֹהִ֗ים אֵ֚ת רָעַ֣ת אֲבִימֶ֔לֶךְ אֲשֶׁ֤ר
עָשָׂה֙ לְאָבִ֔יו לַהֲרֹ֖ג אֶת־שִׁבְעִ֥ים אֶחָֽיו׃
⁵⁷ וְאֵ֗ת כָּל־רָעַת֙ אַנְשֵׁ֣י שְׁכֶ֔ם הֵשִׁ֥יב
אֱלֹהִ֖ים בְּרֹאשָׁ֑ם וַתָּבֹ֣א אֲלֵיהֶ֔ם קִֽלֲלַ֖ת
יוֹתָ֥ם בֶּן־יְרֻבָּֽעַל׃ פ

ל

וַיָּקָם֩ אַחֲרֵ֨י אֲבִימֶ֜לֶךְ לְהוֹשִׁ֣יעַ אֶת־
יִשְׂרָאֵ֗ל תּוֹלָ֧ע בֶּן־פּוּאָ֛ה בֶּן־דּוֹד֖וֹ אִ֣ישׁ
יִשָּׂשכָ֑ר וְהֽוּא־יֹשֵׁ֥ב בְּשָׁמִ֖יר בְּהַ֥ר אֶפְרָֽיִם׃
² וַיִּשְׁפֹּט֙ אֶת־יִשְׂרָאֵ֔ל עֶשְׂרִ֥ים וְשָׁלֹ֖שׁ שָׁנָ֑ה
וַיָּ֖מָת וַיִּקָּבֵ֥ר בְּשָׁמִֽיר׃ פ
³ וַיָּ֣קָם אַחֲרָ֔יו יָאִ֖יר הַגִּלְעָדִ֑י וַיִּשְׁפֹּט֙ אֶת־
יִשְׂרָאֵ֔ל עֶשְׂרִ֥ים וּשְׁתַּ֖יִם שָׁנָֽה׃ ⁴ וַֽיְהִי־ל֗וֹ
שְׁלֹשִׁ֣ים בָּנִ֗ים רֹֽכְבִים֙ עַל־שְׁלֹשִׁ֣ים עֲיָרִ֔ים
וּשְׁלֹשִׁ֥ים עֲיָרִ֖ים לָהֶ֑ם לָהֶ֞ם יִקְרְא֣וּ ׀ חַוֺּ֣ת
יָאִ֗יר עַ֚ד הַיּ֣וֹם הַזֶּ֔ה אֲשֶׁ֖ר בְּאֶ֥רֶץ הַגִּלְעָֽד׃
⁵ וַיָּ֣מָת יָאִ֔יר וַיִּקָּבֵ֖ר בְּקָמֽוֹן׃ פ
⁶ וַיֹּסִ֣פוּ ׀ בְּנֵ֣י יִשְׂרָאֵ֗ל לַעֲשׂ֣וֹת הָרַע֮
בְּעֵינֵ֣י יְהוָה֒ וַיַּעַבְד֣וּ אֶת־הַבְּעָלִ֣ים וְאֶת־
הָעַשְׁתָּר֡וֹת וְאֶת־אֱלֹהֵ֣י אֲרָם֩ וְאֶת־אֱלֹהֵ֨י
צִיד֜וֹן וְאֵ֣ת ׀ אֱלֹהֵ֣י מוֹאָ֗ב וְאֵת֙ אֱלֹהֵ֣י

---

a   Imitating the pun in the Heb., which employs 'ayarim first in the sense of "donkeys" and then in the sense of "towns."
b   I.e., "the villages of Jair"; cf. Num. 32.41.

541

forsook the LORD and did not serve Him. 7And the LORD, incensed with Israel, surrendered them to the Philistines and to the Ammonites. 8That year they battered and shattered the Israelites—for‹ eighteen years—all the Israelites beyond the Jordan, in [what had been] the land of the Amorites in Gilead. 9The Ammonites also crossed the Jordan to make war on Judah, Benjamin, and the House of Ephraim. Israel was in great distress.

10Then the Israelites cried out to the LORD, "We stand guilty before You, for we have forsaken our God and served the Baalim." 11But the LORD said to the Israelites, "[I have rescued you] from the Egyptians, from the Amorites, from the Ammonites, and from the Philistines. 12The Sidonians, Amalek, and Maon‹ᵈ› also oppressed you; and when you cried out to Me, I saved you from them. 13Yet you have forsaken Me and have served other gods. No, I will not deliver you again. 14Go cry to the gods you have chosen; let them deliver you in your time of distress!" 15But the Israelites implored the LORD: "We stand guilty. Do to us as You see fit; only save us this day!" 16They removed the alien gods from among them and served the LORD; and He could not bear the miseries of Israel.

17The Ammonites mustered and they encamped in Gilead; and the Israelites massed and they encamped at Mizpah. 18The troops—the officers of Gilead—said to one another, "Let the man who is the first to fight the Ammonites be chieftain over all the inhabitants of Gilead."

11

Jephthah the Gileadite was an able warrior, who was the son of a prostitute. Jephthah's father was Gilead; 2but Gilead also had sons by his wife, and when the wife's sons grew up, they

---

בְּנֵי־עַמּוֹן וְאֵת אֱלֹהֵי פְלִשְׁתִּים וַיַּעַזְבוּ אֶת־יְהוָה וְלֹא עֲבָדוּהוּ: 7 וַיִּחַר־אַף יְהוָה בְּיִשְׂרָאֵל וַיִּמְכְּרֵם בְּיַד־פְּלִשְׁתִּים וּבְיַד בְּנֵי עַמּוֹן: 8 *וַיִּרְעֲצוּ וַיְרֹצְצוּ אֶת־בְּנֵי יִשְׂרָאֵל בַּשָּׁנָה הַהִיא שְׁמֹנֶה עֶשְׂרֵה שָׁנָה אֶת־כָּל־בְּנֵי יִשְׂרָאֵל אֲשֶׁר בְּעֵבֶר הַיַּרְדֵּן בְּאֶרֶץ הָאֱמֹרִי אֲשֶׁר בַּגִּלְעָד: 9 וַיַּעַבְרוּ בְנֵי־עַמּוֹן אֶת־הַיַּרְדֵּן לְהִלָּחֵם גַּם־בִּיהוּדָה וּבְבִנְיָמִין וּבְבֵית אֶפְרָיִם וַתֵּצֶר לְיִשְׂרָאֵל מְאֹד: 10 וַיִּזְעֲקוּ בְּנֵי יִשְׂרָאֵל אֶל־יְהוָה לֵאמֹר חָטָאנוּ לָךְ וְכִי עָזַבְנוּ אֶת־אֱלֹהֵינוּ וַנַּעֲבֹד אֶת־הַבְּעָלִים: פ 11 וַיֹּאמֶר יְהוָה אֶל־בְּנֵי יִשְׂרָאֵל הֲלֹא מִמִּצְרַיִם וּמִן־הָאֱמֹרִי וּמִן־בְּנֵי עַמּוֹן וּמִן־פְּלִשְׁתִּים: 12 וְצִידוֹנִים וַעֲמָלֵק וּמָעוֹן לָחֲצוּ אֶתְכֶם וַתִּצְעֲקוּ אֵלַי וָאוֹשִׁיעָה אֶתְכֶם מִיָּדָם: 13 וְאַתֶּם עֲזַבְתֶּם אוֹתִי וַתַּעַבְדוּ אֱלֹהִים אֲחֵרִים לָכֵן לֹא־אוֹסִיף לְהוֹשִׁיעַ אֶתְכֶם: 14 לְכוּ וְזַעֲקוּ אֶל־הָאֱלֹהִים אֲשֶׁר בְּחַרְתֶּם בָּם הֵמָּה יוֹשִׁיעוּ לָכֶם בְּעֵת צָרַתְכֶם: 15 וַיֹּאמְרוּ בְנֵי־יִשְׂרָאֵל אֶל־יְהוָה חָטָאנוּ עֲשֵׂה־אַתָּה לָנוּ כְּכָל־הַטּוֹב בְּעֵינֶיךָ אַךְ הַצִּילֵנוּ נָא הַיּוֹם הַזֶּה: 16 וַיָּסִירוּ אֶת־אֱלֹהֵי הַנֵּכָר מִקִּרְבָּם וַיַּעַבְדוּ אֶת־יְהוָה וַתִּקְצַר נַפְשׁוֹ בַּעֲמַל יִשְׂרָאֵל: פ

17 וַיִּצָּעֲקוּ בְּנֵי עַמּוֹן וַיַּחֲנוּ בַּגִּלְעָד וַיֵּאָסְפוּ בְּנֵי יִשְׂרָאֵל וַיַּחֲנוּ בַּמִּצְפָּה: 18 וַיֹּאמְרוּ הָעָם שָׂרֵי גִלְעָד אִישׁ אֶל־רֵעֵהוּ מִי הָאִישׁ אֲשֶׁר יָחֵל לְהִלָּחֵם בִּבְנֵי עַמּוֹן יִהְיֶה לְרֹאשׁ לְכֹל יֹשְׁבֵי גִלְעָד: ס

יא

וְיִפְתָּח הַגִּלְעָדִי הָיָה גִּבּוֹר חַיִל וְהוּא בֶּן־אִשָּׁה זוֹנָה וַיּוֹלֶד גִּלְעָד אֶת־יִפְתָּח: 2 וַתֵּלֶד אֵשֶׁת־גִּלְעָד לוֹ בָּנִים וַיִּגְדְּלוּ בְנֵי־הָאִשָּׁה וַיְגָרְשׁוּ אֶת־יִפְתָּח

---

c   *Meaning of Heb. uncertain; perhaps "enough for" or "continuing for."*
d   *Septuagint reads "Midian."*

חצי הספר בפסוקים   v. 8.

drove Jephthah out. They said to him, "You shall have no share in our father's property, for you are the son of an outsider."[a] [3]So Jephthah fled from his brothers and settled in the Tob country. Men of low character gathered about Jephthah and went out raiding with him.

[4]Some time later, the Ammonites went to war against Israel. [5]And when the Ammonites attacked Israel, the elders of Gilead went to bring Jephthah back from the Tob country. [6]They said to Jephthah, "Come be our chief, so that we can fight the Ammonites." [7]Jephthah replied to the elders of Gilead, "You are the very people who rejected me and drove me out of my father's house. How can you come to me now when you are in trouble?" [8]The elders of Gilead said to Jephthah, "Honestly, we have now turned back to you. If you come with us and fight the Ammonites, you shall be our commander over all the inhabitants of Gilead." [9]Jephthah said to the elders of Gilead, "[Very well,] if you bring me back to fight the Ammonites and the Lord delivers them to me, I am to be your commander." [10]And the elders of Gilead answered Jephthah, "The Lord Himself shall be witness between us: we will do just as you have said."

[11]Jephthah went with the elders of Gilead, and the people made him their commander and chief. And Jephthah repeated all these terms before the Lord at Mizpah.

[12]Jephthah then sent messengers to the king of the Ammonites, saying, "What have you against me that you have come to make war on my country?" [13]The king of the Ammonites replied to Jephthah's messengers, "When Israel came from Egypt, they seized the land which is mine, from the Arnon to the Jabbok as far as the Jordan. Now, then, restore it peaceably." [14]Jephthah again sent messengers to the king of the Ammonites. [15]He said to him, "Thus said

---

a Lit. "another woman."

וַיֹּאמְרוּ לוֹ לֹא־תִנְחַל בְּבֵית־אָבִינוּ כִּי בֶן־אִשָּׁה אַחֶרֶת אָתָּה: 3 וַיִּבְרַח יִפְתָּח מִפְּנֵי אֶחָיו וַיֵּשֶׁב בְּאֶרֶץ טוֹב וַיִּתְלַקְּטוּ אֶל־יִפְתָּח אֲנָשִׁים רֵיקִים וַיֵּצְאוּ עִמּוֹ: פ

4 וַיְהִי מִיָּמִים וַיִּלָּחֲמוּ בְנֵי־עַמּוֹן עִם־יִשְׂרָאֵל: 5 וַיְהִי כַּאֲשֶׁר־נִלְחֲמוּ בְנֵי־עַמּוֹן עִם־יִשְׂרָאֵל וַיֵּלְכוּ זִקְנֵי גִלְעָד לָקַחַת אֶת־יִפְתָּח מֵאֶרֶץ טוֹב: 6 וַיֹּאמְרוּ לְיִפְתָּח לְכָה וְהָיִיתָה לָּנוּ לְקָצִין וְנִלָּחֲמָה בִּבְנֵי עַמּוֹן: 7 וַיֹּאמֶר יִפְתָּח לְזִקְנֵי גִלְעָד הֲלֹא אַתֶּם שְׂנֵאתֶם אוֹתִי וַתְּגָרְשׁוּנִי מִבֵּית אָבִי וּמַדּוּעַ בָּאתֶם אֵלַי עַתָּה כַּאֲשֶׁר צַר לָכֶם: 8 וַיֹּאמְרוּ זִקְנֵי גִלְעָד אֶל־יִפְתָּח לָכֵן עַתָּה שַׁבְנוּ אֵלֶיךָ וְהָלַכְתָּ עִמָּנוּ וְנִלְחַמְתָּ בִּבְנֵי עַמּוֹן וְהָיִיתָ לָּנוּ לְרֹאשׁ לְכֹל יֹשְׁבֵי גִלְעָד: 9 וַיֹּאמֶר יִפְתָּח אֶל־זִקְנֵי גִלְעָד אִם־מְשִׁיבִים אַתֶּם אוֹתִי לְהִלָּחֵם בִּבְנֵי עַמּוֹן וְנָתַן יְהוָה אוֹתָם לְפָנָי אָנֹכִי אֶהְיֶה לָכֶם לְרֹאשׁ: 10 וַיֹּאמְרוּ זִקְנֵי־גִלְעָד אֶל־יִפְתָּח יְהוָה יִהְיֶה שֹׁמֵעַ בֵּינוֹתֵינוּ אִם־לֹא כִדְבָרְךָ כֵּן נַעֲשֶׂה:

11 וַיֵּלֶךְ יִפְתָּח עִם־זִקְנֵי גִלְעָד וַיָּשִׂימוּ הָעָם אוֹתוֹ עֲלֵיהֶם לְרֹאשׁ וּלְקָצִין וַיְדַבֵּר יִפְתָּח אֶת־כָּל־דְּבָרָיו לִפְנֵי יְהוָה בַּמִּצְפָּה: פ

12 וַיִּשְׁלַח יִפְתָּח מַלְאָכִים אֶל־מֶלֶךְ בְּנֵי־עַמּוֹן לֵאמֹר מַה־לִּי וָלָךְ כִּי־בָאתָ אֵלַי לְהִלָּחֵם בְּאַרְצִי: 13 וַיֹּאמֶר מֶלֶךְ בְּנֵי־עַמּוֹן אֶל־מַלְאֲכֵי יִפְתָּח כִּי־לָקַח יִשְׂרָאֵל אֶת־אַרְצִי בַּעֲלוֹתוֹ מִמִּצְרַיִם מֵאַרְנוֹן וְעַד־הַיַּבֹּק וְעַד־הַיַּרְדֵּן וְעַתָּה הָשִׁיבָה אֶתְהֶן בְּשָׁלוֹם: 14 וַיּוֹסֶף עוֹד יִפְתָּח וַיִּשְׁלַח מַלְאָכִים

Jephthah: Israel did not seize the land of Moab or the land of the Ammonites. [16]When they left Egypt, Israel traveled through the wilderness to the Sea of Reeds and went on to Kadesh. [17]Israel then sent messengers to the king of Edom, saying, 'Allow us to cross your country.' But the king of Edom would not consent. They also sent a mission to the king of Moab, and he refused. So Israel, after staying at Kadesh, [18]traveled on through the wilderness, skirting the land of Edom and the land of Moab. They kept to the east of the land of Moab until they encamped on the other side of the Arnon; and, since Moab ends at the Arnon, they never entered Moabite territory.

[19]"Then Israel sent messengers to Sihon king of the Amorites, the king of Heshbon. Israel said to him, 'Allow us to cross through your country to our homeland.' [20]But Sihon would not trust Israel to pass through his territory. Sihon mustered all his troops, and they encamped at Jahaz; he engaged Israel in battle. [21]But the Lord, the God of Israel, delivered Sihon and all his troops into Israel's hands, and they defeated them; and Israel took possession of all the land of the Amorites, the inhabitants of that land. [22]Thus they possessed all the territory of the Amorites from the Arnon to the Jabbok and from the wilderness to the Jordan.

[23]"Now, then, the Lord, the God of Israel, dispossessed the Amorites before His people Israel; and should you possess their land? [24]Do you not hold what Chemosh your god gives you to possess? So we will hold on to everything that the Lord our God has given us to possess.

[25]"Besides, are you any better than Balak son of Zippor, king of Moab? Did he start a quarrel with Israel or go to war with them?

[26]"While Israel has been inhabiting Heshbon and its dependencies, and Aroer and its dependencies, and all the towns along the Arnon for

אֶל־מֶלֶךְ בְּנֵי עַמּוֹן 15 וַיֹּאמֶר* לוֹ כֹּה אָמַר יִפְתָּח לֹא־לָקַח יִשְׂרָאֵל אֶת־אֶרֶץ מוֹאָב וְאֶת־אֶרֶץ בְּנֵי עַמּוֹן: 16 כִּי בַּעֲלוֹתָם מִמִּצְרָיִם וַיֵּלֶךְ יִשְׂרָאֵל בַּמִּדְבָּר עַד־יַם־ סוּף וַיָּבֹא קָדֵשָׁה: 17 וַיִּשְׁלַח יִשְׂרָאֵל מַלְאָכִים ׀ אֶל־מֶלֶךְ ׀ אֱדוֹם ׀ לֵאמֹר אֶעְבְּרָה־נָּא בְאַרְצֶךָ וְלֹא שָׁמַע מֶלֶךְ אֱדוֹם וְגַם אֶל־מֶלֶךְ מוֹאָב שָׁלַח וְלֹא אָבָה וַיֵּשֶׁב יִשְׂרָאֵל בְּקָדֵשׁ: 18 וַיֵּלֶךְ בַּמִּדְבָּר וַיָּסָב אֶת־אֶרֶץ אֱדוֹם וְאֶת־אֶרֶץ מוֹאָב וַיָּבֹא מִמִּזְרַח־שֶׁמֶשׁ לְאֶרֶץ מוֹאָב וַיַּחֲנוּן בְּעֵבֶר אַרְנוֹן וְלֹא־בָאוּ בִּגְבוּל מוֹאָב כִּי אַרְנוֹן גְּבוּל מוֹאָב:

19 וַיִּשְׁלַח יִשְׂרָאֵל מַלְאָכִים אֶל־סִיחוֹן מֶלֶךְ־הָאֱמֹרִי מֶלֶךְ חֶשְׁבּוֹן וַיֹּאמֶר לוֹ יִשְׂרָאֵל נַעְבְּרָה־נָּא בְאַרְצְךָ עַד־מְקוֹמִי: 20 וְלֹא־הֶאֱמִין סִיחוֹן אֶת־יִשְׂרָאֵל עֲבֹר בִּגְבֻלוֹ וַיֶּאֱסֹף סִיחוֹן אֶת־כָּל־עַמּוֹ וַיַּחֲנוּ בְּיָהְצָה וַיִּלָּחֶם עִם־יִשְׂרָאֵל: 21 וַיִּתֵּן יְהוָה אֱלֹהֵי־יִשְׂרָאֵל אֶת־סִיחוֹן וְאֶת־כָּל־עַמּוֹ בְּיַד יִשְׂרָאֵל וַיַּכּוּם וַיִּירַשׁ יִשְׂרָאֵל אֵת כָּל־אֶרֶץ הָאֱמֹרִי יוֹשֵׁב הָאָרֶץ הַהִיא: 22 וַיִּירְשׁוּ אֵת כָּל־גְּבוּל הָאֱמֹרִי מֵאַרְנוֹן וְעַד־הַיַּבֹּק וּמִן־הַמִּדְבָּר וְעַד־הַיַּרְדֵּן: 23 וְעַתָּה יְהוָה ׀ אֱלֹהֵי יִשְׂרָאֵל הוֹרִישׁ אֶת־הָאֱמֹרִי מִפְּנֵי עַמּוֹ יִשְׂרָאֵל וְאַתָּה תִּירָשֶׁנּוּ: 24 הֲלֹא אֵת אֲשֶׁר יוֹרִישְׁךָ כְּמוֹשׁ אֱלֹהֶיךָ אוֹתוֹ תִירָשׁ וְאֵת כָּל־אֲשֶׁר הוֹרִישׁ יְהוָה אֱלֹהֵינוּ מִפָּנֵינוּ אוֹתוֹ נִירָשׁ: 25 וְעַתָּה הֲטוֹב טוֹב אַתָּה מִבָּלָק בֶּן־צִפּוֹר מֶלֶךְ מוֹאָב הֲרוֹב רָב עִם־יִשְׂרָאֵל אִם־ נִלְחֹם נִלְחַם בָּם: 26 בְּשֶׁבֶת יִשְׂרָאֵל בְּחֶשְׁבּוֹן וּבִבְנוֹתֶיהָ וּבְעַרְעוֹר וּבִבְנוֹתֶיהָ וּבְכָל־הֶעָרִים אֲשֶׁר עַל־יְדֵי אַרְנוֹן שְׁלֹשׁ מֵאוֹת שָׁנָה וּמַדּוּעַ

three hundred years, why have you not tried to recover them all this time? 27I have done you no wrong; yet you are doing me harm and making war on me. May the LORD, who judges, decide today between the Israelites and the Ammonites!"

28But the king of the Ammonites paid no heed to the message that Jephthah sent him.

29Then the spirit of the LORD came upon Jephthah. He marched through Gilead and Manasseh, passing Mizpeh of Gilead; and from Mizpeh of Gilead he crossed over [to] the Ammonites. 30And Jephthah made the following vow to the LORD: "If you deliver the Ammonites into my hands, 31then whatever comes out of the door of my house to meet me on my safe return from the Ammonites shall be the LORD's and shall be offered by me as a burnt offering."

32Jephthah crossed over to the Ammonites and attacked them, and the LORD delivered them into his hands. 33He utterly routed them—from Aroer as far as Minnith, twenty towns—all the way to Abel-cheramim. So the Ammonites submitted to the Israelites.

34When Jephthah arrived at his home in Mizpah, there was his daughter coming out to meet him, with timbrel and dance! She was an only child; he had no other son or daughter. 35On seeing her, he rent his clothes and said, "Alas, daughter! You have brought me low; you have become my troubler! For I have *b*-uttered a vow-*b* to the LORD and I cannot retract." 36"Father," she said, "you have uttered a vow to the LORD; do to me as you have vowed, seeing that the LORD has vindicated you against your enemies, the Ammonites." 37She further said to her father, "Let this be done for me: let me be for two months, and I will go with my companions and lament*c* upon the hills and there

כז וְאָנֹכִי לֹא־חָטָאתִי לָךְ וְאַתָּה עֹשֶׂה אִתִּי רָעָה לְהִלָּחֶם בִּי יִשְׁפֹּט יְהֹוָה הַשֹּׁפֵט הַיּוֹם בֵּין בְּנֵי יִשְׂרָאֵל וּבֵין בְּנֵי עַמּוֹן: כח וְלֹא שָׁמַע מֶלֶךְ בְּנֵי עַמּוֹן אֶל־דִּבְרֵי יִפְתָּח אֲשֶׁר שָׁלַח אֵלָיו: פ כט וַתְּהִי עַל־יִפְתָּח רוּחַ יְהֹוָה וַיַּעֲבֹר אֶת־הַגִּלְעָד וְאֶת־מְנַשֶּׁה וַיַּעֲבֹר אֶת־מִצְפֵּה גִלְעָד וּמִמִּצְפֵּה גִלְעָד עָבַר בְּנֵי עַמּוֹן: ל וַיִּדַּר יִפְתָּח נֶדֶר לַיהֹוָה וַיֹּאמַר אִם־נָתוֹן תִּתֵּן אֶת־בְּנֵי עַמּוֹן בְּיָדִי: לא וְהָיָה הַיּוֹצֵא אֲשֶׁר יֵצֵא מִדַּלְתֵי בֵיתִי לִקְרָאתִי בְּשׁוּבִי בְשָׁלוֹם מִבְּנֵי עַמּוֹן וְהָיָה לַיהֹוָה וְהַעֲלִיתִהוּ עֹלָה: פ לב וַיַּעֲבֹר יִפְתָּח אֶל־בְּנֵי עַמּוֹן לְהִלָּחֶם בָּם וַיִּתְּנֵם יְהֹוָה בְּיָדוֹ: לג וַיַּכֵּם מֵעֲרוֹעֵר וְעַד־בּוֹאֲךָ מִנִּית עֶשְׂרִים עִיר וְעַד אָבֵל כְּרָמִים מַכָּה גְּדוֹלָה מְאֹד וַיִּכָּנְעוּ בְּנֵי עַמּוֹן מִפְּנֵי בְּנֵי יִשְׂרָאֵל: פ

לד וַיָּבֹא יִפְתָּח הַמִּצְפָּה אֶל־בֵּיתוֹ וְהִנֵּה בִתּוֹ יֹצֵאת לִקְרָאתוֹ בְתֻפִּים וּבִמְחֹלוֹת וְרַק הִיא יְחִידָה אֵין־לוֹ מִמֶּנּוּ* בֵּן אוֹ־בַת: לה וַיְהִי כִרְאוֹתוֹ אוֹתָהּ וַיִּקְרַע אֶת־בְּגָדָיו וַיֹּאמֶר אֲהָהּ בִּתִּי הַכְרֵעַ הִכְרַעְתִּנִי וְאַתְּ הָיִית בְּעֹכְרָי וְאָנֹכִי פָּצִיתִי־פִי אֶל־יְהֹוָה וְלֹא אוּכַל לָשׁוּב: לו וַתֹּאמֶר אֵלָיו אָבִי פָּצִיתָה אֶת־פִּיךָ אֶל־יְהֹוָה עֲשֵׂה לִי כַּאֲשֶׁר יָצָא מִפִּיךָ אַחֲרֵי אֲשֶׁר עָשָׂה לְךָ יְהֹוָה נְקָמוֹת מֵאֹיְבֶיךָ מִבְּנֵי עַמּוֹן: לז וַתֹּאמֶר אֶל־אָבִיהָ יֵעָשֶׂה לִּי הַדָּבָר הַזֶּה הַרְפֵּה מִמֶּנִּי שְׁנַיִם חֳדָשִׁים וְאֵלְכָה וְיָרַדְתִּי עַל־הֶהָרִים וְאֶבְכֶּה עַל־בְּתוּלַי אָנֹכִי וְרֵעוֹתַי

---

b-b Lit. "opened my mouth."
c Lit. "descend," i.e., with weeping; cf. Isa. 15.3.

סבירין ומטעין "מִמֶּנָּה"   v. 34.

bewail my maidenhood." 38"Go," he replied. He let her go for two months, and she and her companions went and bewailed her maidenhood upon the hills. 39After two months' time, she returned to her father, and he did to her as he had vowed. She had never known a man. So it became a custom in Israel 40for the maidens of Israel to go every year, for four days in the year, and chant dirges for the daughter of Jephthah the Gileadite.

12

The men of Ephraim mustered and crossed [the Jordan] to Zaphon. They said to Jephthah, "Why did you march to fight the Ammonites without calling us to go with you? We'll burn your house down over you!" 2Jephthah answered them, "I and my people were in a bitter conflict with the Ammonites; and I summoned you, but you did not save me from them. 3When I saw that you were no saviors, I risked my life and advanced against the Ammonites; and the LORD delivered them into my hands. Why have you come here now to fight against me?" 4And Jephthah gathered all the men of Gilead and fought the Ephraimites. The men of Gilead defeated the Ephraimites; for ^athey had said, "You Gileadites are nothing but fugitives from Ephraim—being in Manasseh is like being in Ephraim."-^a 5The Gileadites held the fords of the Jordan against the Ephraimites. And when any fugitive from Ephraim said, "Let me cross," the men of Gilead would ask him, "Are you an Ephraimite?"; if he said "No," 6they would say to him, "Then say *shibboleth*"; but he would say *"sibboleth,"* not being able to pronounce it correctly. Thereupon they would seize him and slay him by the fords of the Jordan. Forty-two thousand Ephraimites fell at that time.

a-a Meaning of Heb. uncertain.

וּרְעוֹתָֽי׃ 38וַיֹּ֣אמֶר לֵ֔כִי וַיִּשְׁלַ֥ח אוֹתָ֖הּ שְׁנֵ֣י חֳדָשִׁ֑ים וַתֵּ֤לֶךְ הִיא֙ וְרֵ֣עוֹתֶ֔יהָ וַתֵּ֥בְךְּ עַל־ בְּתוּלֶ֖יהָ עַל־הֶהָרִֽים׃ 39וַֽיְהִ֞י מִקֵּ֣ץ ׀ שְׁנַ֣יִם חֳדָשִׁ֗ים וַתָּ֙שָׁב֙ אֶל־אָבִ֔יהָ וַיַּ֣עַשׂ לָ֔הּ אֶת־ נִדְר֖וֹ אֲשֶׁ֣ר נָדָ֑ר וְהִיא֙ לֹא־יָדְעָ֣ה אִ֔ישׁ וַתְּהִי־חֹ֖ק בְּיִשְׂרָאֵֽל׃ 40מִיָּמִ֣ים ׀ יָמִ֗ימָה תֵּלַ֙כְנָה֙ בְּנ֣וֹת יִשְׂרָאֵ֔ל לְתַנּ֕וֹת לְבַת־יִפְתָּ֖ח הַגִּלְעָדִ֑י אַרְבַּ֥עַת יָמִ֖ים בַּשָּׁנָֽה׃ ס

יב

וַיִּצָּעֵק֙ אִ֣ישׁ אֶפְרַ֔יִם וַֽיַּעֲבֹ֖ר צָפ֑וֹנָה וַיֹּאמְר֣וּ לְיִפְתָּ֗ח מַדּ֣וּעַ ׀ עָבַ֣רְתָּ ׀ לְהִלָּחֵ֣ם בִּבְנֵֽי־עַמּ֗וֹן וְלָ֙נוּ֙ לֹ֤א קָרָ֙אתָ֙ לָלֶ֣כֶת עִמָּ֔ךְ בֵּיתְךָ֕ נִשְׂרֹ֥ף עָלֶ֖יךָ בָּאֵֽשׁ׃ 2וַיֹּ֤אמֶר יִפְתָּח֙ אֲלֵיהֶ֔ם אִ֣ישׁ רִ֗יב הָיִ֛יתִי אֲנִ֛י וְעַמִּ֥י וּבְנֵֽי־ עַמּ֖וֹן מְאֹ֑ד וָאֶזְעַ֣ק אֶתְכֶ֔ם וְלֹֽא־הוֹשַׁעְתֶּ֥ם אוֹתִ֖י מִיָּדָֽם׃ 3וָֽאֶרְאֶ֞ה כִּֽי־אֵינְךָ֣ מוֹשִׁ֗יעַ וָאָשִׂ֨ימָה נַפְשִׁ֤י בְכַפִּי֙ וָֽאֶעְבְּרָה֙ אֶל־בְּנֵ֣י עַמּ֔וֹן וַיִּתְּנֵ֥ם יְהֹוָ֖ה בְּיָדִ֑י וְלָמָ֞ה עֲלִיתֶ֥ם אֵלַ֛י הַיּ֥וֹם הַזֶּ֖ה לְהִלָּ֥חֶם בִּֽי׃ 4וַיִּקְבֹּ֤ץ יִפְתָּח֙ אֶת־כָּל־אַנְשֵׁ֣י גִלְעָ֔ד וַיִּלָּ֖חֶם אֶת־אֶפְרָ֑יִם וַיַּכּוּ֩ אַנְשֵׁ֨י גִלְעָ֜ד אֶת־אֶפְרַ֗יִם כִּ֣י אָמְר֤וּ פְּלִיטֵ֤י אֶפְרַ֙יִם֙ אַתֶּ֔ם גִּלְעָ֕ד בְּת֥וֹךְ אֶפְרַ֖יִם בְּת֣וֹךְ מְנַשֶּֽׁה׃ 5וַיִּלְכֹּ֥ד גִּלְעָ֛ד אֶת־מַעְבְּר֥וֹת הַיַּרְדֵּ֖ן לְאֶפְרָ֑יִם וְֽהָיָ֡ה כִּ֣י יֹאמְרוּ֩ פְּלִיטֵ֨י אֶפְרַ֜יִם אֶעֱבֹ֗רָה וַיֹּ֨אמְרוּ ל֧וֹ אַנְשֵׁי־גִלְעָ֛ד הַֽאֶפְרָתִ֥י אַ֖תָּה וַיֹּ֥אמֶר ׀ לֹֽא׃ 6וַיֹּ֣אמְרוּ לוֹ֩ אֱמָר־נָ֨א שִׁבֹּ֜לֶת וַיֹּ֣אמֶר סִבֹּ֗לֶת וְלֹ֤א יָכִין֙ לְדַבֵּ֣ר כֵּ֔ן וַיֹּאחֲז֣וּ אוֹת֔וֹ וַֽיִּשְׁחָט֖וּהוּ אֶל־ מַעְבְּר֣וֹת הַיַּרְדֵּ֑ן וַיִּפֹּ֞ל בָּעֵ֤ת הַהִיא֙ מֵֽאֶפְרַ֔יִם אַרְבָּעִ֥ים וּשְׁנַ֖יִם אָֽלֶף׃ 7וַיִּשְׁפֹּ֥ט יִפְתָּ֛ח אֶת־יִשְׂרָאֵ֖ל שֵׁ֥שׁ שָׁנִ֑ים

7Jephthah led Israel six years. Then Jephthah the Gileadite died and he was buried in one of the towns of Gilead.

8After him, Ibzan of Bethlehem*b* led Israel. 9He had thirty sons, and he married off thirty daughters outside the clan and brought in thirty girls from outside the clan for his sons. He led Israel seven years. 10Then Ibzan died and was buried in Bethlehem.

11After him, Elon the Zebulunite led Israel; he led Israel for ten years. 12Then Elon the Zebulunite died and was buried in Aijalon, in the territory of Zebulun.

13After him, Abdon son of Hillel the Pirathonite led Israel. 14He had forty sons and thirty grandsons, who rode on seventy jackasses. He led Israel for eight years. 15Then Abdon son of Hillel the Pirathonite died. He was buried in Pirathon, in the territory of Ephraim, on the hill of the Amalekites.

13

The Israelites again did what was offensive to the Lord, and the Lord delivered them into the hands of the Philistines for forty years. 2There was a certain man from Zorah, of the stock of Dan, whose name was Manoah. His wife was barren and had borne no children. 3An angel of the Lord appeared to the woman and said to her, "You are barren and have borne no children; but you shall conceive and bear a son. 4Now be careful not to drink wine or other intoxicant, or to eat anything unclean. 5For you are going to conceive and bear a son; let no razor touch his head, for the boy is to be a nazirite to God from the womb on. He shall be the first to deliver Israel from the Philistines." 6The woman went and told her husband, "A

וַיָּ֧מָת יִפְתָּ֣ח הַגִּלְעָדִ֑י וַיִּקָּבֵ֖ר בְּעָרֵ֥י גִלְעָֽד׃ פ

8 וַיִּשְׁפֹּ֤ט אַֽחֲרָיו֙ אֶת־יִשְׂרָאֵ֔ל אִבְצָ֖ן מִבֵּ֥ית לָֽחֶם׃ 9 וַיְהִי־ל֞וֹ שְׁלֹשִׁ֣ים בָּנִ֗ים וּשְׁלֹשִׁ֤ים בָּנוֹת֙ שִׁלַּ֣ח הַח֔וּצָה וּשְׁלֹשִׁ֣ים בָּנ֔וֹת הֵבִ֥יא לְבָנָ֖יו מִן־הַח֑וּץ וַיִּשְׁפֹּ֥ט אֶת־יִשְׂרָאֵ֖ל שֶׁ֥בַע שָׁנִֽים׃ 10 וַיָּ֣מָת אִבְצָ֔ן וַיִּקָּבֵ֖ר בְּבֵ֥ית לָֽחֶם׃ פ

11 וַיִּשְׁפֹּ֤ט אַֽחֲרָיו֙ אֶת־יִשְׂרָאֵ֔ל אֵיל֖וֹן הַזְּבֽוּלֹנִ֑י וַיִּשְׁפֹּ֤ט אֶת־יִשְׂרָאֵל֙ עֶ֥שֶׂר שָׁנִֽים׃ 12 וַיָּ֛מָת אֵל֥וֹן* הַזְּבֽוּלֹנִ֖י וַיִּקָּבֵ֣ר בְּאַיָּל֑וֹן בְּאֶ֖רֶץ זְבוּלֻֽן׃ פ

13 וַיִּשְׁפֹּ֤ט אַֽחֲרָיו֙ אֶת־יִשְׂרָאֵ֔ל עַבְדּ֥וֹן בֶּן־הִלֵּ֖ל הַפִּרְעָתוֹנִֽי׃ 14 וַֽיְהִי־ל֞וֹ אַרְבָּעִ֣ים בָּנִ֗ים וּשְׁלֹשִׁים֙ בְּנֵ֣י בָנִ֔ים רֹכְבִ֖ים עַל־שִׁבְעִ֣ים עֲיָרִ֑ם וַיִּשְׁפֹּ֥ט אֶת־יִשְׂרָאֵ֖ל שְׁמֹנֶ֥ה שָׁנִֽים׃ 15 וַיָּ֛מָת עַבְדּ֥וֹן בֶּן־הִלֵּ֖ל הַפִּרְעָתוֹנִ֑י וַיִּקָּבֵ֤ר בְּפִרְעָתוֹן֙ בְּאֶ֣רֶץ אֶפְרַ֔יִם בְּהַ֖ר הָעֲמָלֵקִֽי׃ פ

יג וַיֹּסִ֙פוּ֙ בְּנֵ֣י יִשְׂרָאֵ֔ל לַעֲשׂ֥וֹת הָרַ֖ע בְּעֵינֵ֣י יְהֹוָ֑ה וַיִּתְּנֵ֧ם יְהֹוָ֛ה בְּיַד־פְּלִשְׁתִּ֖ים אַרְבָּעִ֥ים שָׁנָֽה׃ פ 2 וַיְהִי֩ אִ֨ישׁ אֶחָ֤ד מִצׇּרְעָה֙ מִמִּשְׁפַּ֣חַת הַדָּנִ֔י וּשְׁמ֖וֹ מָנ֑וֹחַ וְאִשְׁתּ֥וֹ עֲקָרָ֖ה וְלֹ֥א יָלָֽדָה׃ 3 וַיֵּרָ֥א מַלְאַךְ־יְהֹוָ֖ה אֶל־הָאִשָּׁ֑ה וַיֹּ֣אמֶר אֵלֶ֗יהָ הִנֵּה־נָ֤א אַתְּ־עֲקָרָה֙ וְלֹ֣א יָלַ֔דְתְּ וְהָרִ֖ית וְיָלַ֥דְתְּ בֵּֽן׃ 4 וְעַתָּה֙ הִשָּׁ֣מְרִי נָ֔א וְאַל־תִּשְׁתִּ֥י יַ֖יִן וְשֵׁכָ֑ר וְאַל־תֹּאכְלִ֖י כׇּל־טָמֵֽא׃ 5 כִּי֩ הִנָּ֨ךְ הָרָ֜ה וְיֹלַ֣דְתְּ בֵּ֗ן וּמוֹרָה֙ לֹא־יַעֲלֶ֣ה עַל־רֹאשׁ֔וֹ כִּֽי־נְזִ֧יר אֱלֹהִ֛ים יִהְיֶ֥ה הַנַּ֖עַר מִן־הַבָּ֑טֶן וְה֗וּא יָחֵ֛ל לְהוֹשִׁ֥יעַ אֶת־יִשְׂרָאֵ֖ל מִיַּ֥ד פְּלִשְׁתִּֽים׃ 6 וַתָּבֹ֣א הָאִשָּׁ֗ה וַתֹּ֤אמֶר לְאִישָׁהּ֙ לֵאמֹ֔ר

---

b I.e., Bethlehem in Zebulun; cf. Josh. 19.15.

    v. 12. חסר י׳ בכתב היד שלנו

man of God came to me; he looked like an angel of God, very frightening. I did not ask him where he was from, nor did he tell me his name. [7]He said to me, 'You are going to conceive and bear a son. Drink no wine or other intoxicant, and eat nothing unclean, for the boy is to be a nazirite to God from the womb to the day of his death!'"

[8]Manoah pleaded with the LORD. "Oh, my Lord!" he said, "please let the man of God that You sent come to us again, and let him instruct us how to act with the child that is to be born." [9]God heeded Manoah's plea, and the angel of God came to the woman again. She was sitting in the field and her husband Manoah was not with her. [10]The woman ran in haste to tell her husband. She said to him, "The man who came to me before[a] has just appeared to me." [11]Manoah promptly followed his wife. He came to the man and asked him: "Are you the man who spoke to my wife?" "Yes," he answered. [12]Then Manoah said, "May your words soon come true! What rules shall be observed for the boy?" [13]The angel of the LORD said to Manoah, "The woman must abstain from all the things against which I warned her. [14]She must not eat anything that comes from the grapevine, or drink wine or other intoxicant, or eat anything unclean. She must observe all that I commanded her."

[15]Manoah said to the angel of the LORD, "Let us detain you and prepare a kid for you." [16]But the angel of the LORD said to Manoah, "If you detain me, I shall not eat your food; and if you present a burnt offering, offer it to LORD."—For Manoah did not know that he was an angel of the LORD. [17]So Manoah said to the angel of the LORD, "What is your name? We should like to honor you when your words come true." [18]The angel said to him, "You must not ask for my name; it is unknowable!"

---

a Lit. "in the day."

אִישׁ הָאֱלֹהִים בָּא אֵלַי וּמַרְאֵהוּ כְּמַרְאֵה
מַלְאַךְ הָאֱלֹהִים נוֹרָא מְאֹד וְלֹא
שְׁאִלְתִּיהוּ אֵי־מִזֶּה הוּא וְאֶת־שְׁמוֹ לֹא־
הִגִּיד לִי: [7] וַיֹּאמֶר לִי הִנָּךְ הָרָה וְיֹלַדְתְּ
בֵּן וְעַתָּה אַל־תִּשְׁתִּי ׀ יַיִן וְשֵׁכָר וְאַל־
תֹּאכְלִי כָּל־טֻמְאָה כִּי־נְזִיר אֱלֹהִים יִהְיֶה
הַנַּעַר מִן־הַבֶּטֶן עַד־יוֹם מוֹתוֹ: פ
[8] וַיֶּעְתַּר מָנוֹחַ אֶל־יְהוָה וַיֹּאמַר בִּי אֲדוֹנָי
אִישׁ הָאֱלֹהִים אֲשֶׁר שָׁלַחְתָּ יָבוֹא־נָא עוֹד
אֵלֵינוּ וְיוֹרֵנוּ מַה־נַּעֲשֶׂה לַנַּעַר הַיּוּלָּד:
[9] וַיִּשְׁמַע הָאֱלֹהִים בְּקוֹל מָנוֹחַ וַיָּבֹא
מַלְאַךְ הָאֱלֹהִים עוֹד אֶל־הָאִשָּׁה וְהִיא
יוֹשֶׁבֶת בַּשָּׂדֶה וּמָנוֹחַ אִישָׁהּ אֵין עִמָּהּ:
[10] וַתְּמַהֵר הָאִשָּׁה וַתָּרָץ וַתַּגֵּד לְאִישָׁהּ
וַתֹּאמֶר אֵלָיו הִנֵּה נִרְאָה אֵלַי הָאִישׁ
אֲשֶׁר־בָּא בַיּוֹם אֵלָי: [11] וַיָּקָם וַיֵּלֶךְ מָנוֹחַ
אַחֲרֵי אִשְׁתּוֹ וַיָּבֹא אֶל־הָאִישׁ וַיֹּאמֶר לוֹ
הַאַתָּה הָאִישׁ אֲשֶׁר־דִּבַּרְתָּ אֶל־הָאִשָּׁה
וַיֹּאמֶר אָנִי: [12] וַיֹּאמֶר מָנוֹחַ עַתָּה יָבֹא
דְבָרֶיךָ מַה־יִּהְיֶה מִשְׁפַּט־הַנַּעַר וּמַעֲשֵׂהוּ:
[13] וַיֹּאמֶר מַלְאַךְ יְהוָה אֶל־מָנוֹחַ מִכֹּל
אֲשֶׁר־אָמַרְתִּי אֶל־הָאִשָּׁה תִּשָּׁמֵר: [14] מִכֹּל
אֲשֶׁר־יֵצֵא מִגֶּפֶן הַיַּיִן לֹא תֹאכַל וְיַיִן וְשֵׁכָר
אַל־תֵּשְׁתְּ וְכָל־טֻמְאָה אַל־תֹּאכַל כֹּל
אֲשֶׁר־צִוִּיתִיהָ תִּשְׁמֹר:
[15] וַיֹּאמֶר מָנוֹחַ אֶל־מַלְאַךְ יְהוָה נַעְצְרָה־
נָּא אוֹתָךְ וְנַעֲשֶׂה לְפָנֶיךָ גְּדִי עִזִּים:
[16] וַיֹּאמֶר מַלְאַךְ יְהוָה אֶל־מָנוֹחַ אִם־
תַּעְצְרֵנִי לֹא־אֹכַל בְּלַחְמֶךָ וְאִם־תַּעֲשֶׂה
עֹלָה לַיהוָה תַּעֲלֶנָּה כִּי לֹא־יָדַע מָנוֹחַ
כִּי־מַלְאַךְ יְהוָה הוּא: [17] וַיֹּאמֶר מָנוֹחַ
אֶל־מַלְאַךְ יְהוָה מִי שְׁמֶךָ כִּי־יָבֹא דבריך
דְבָרְךָ וְכִבַּדְנוּךָ: [18] וַיֹּאמֶר לוֹ מַלְאַךְ יְהוָה
לָמָּה זֶּה תִּשְׁאַל לִשְׁמִי וְהוּא־פֶלִאי: ס

¹⁹Manoah took the kid and the meal offering and offered them up on the rock to the Lord; ᵇ-and a marvelous thing happened-ᵇ while Manoah and his wife looked on. ²⁰As the flames leaped up from the altar toward the sky, the angel of the Lord ascended in the flames of the altar, while Manoah and his wife looked on; and they flung themselves on their faces to the ground.—²¹The angel of the Lord never appeared again to Manoah and his wife.—Manoah then realized that it had been an angel of the Lord. ²²And Manoah said to his wife, "We shall surely die, for we have seen a divine being." ²³But his wife said to him, "Had the Lord meant to take our lives, He would not have accepted a burnt offering and meal offering from us, nor let us see all these things; and He would not have made such an announcement to us."

²⁴The woman bore a son, and she named him Samson. The boy grew up, and the Lord blessed him. ²⁵The spirit of the Lord first moved him in the encampment of Dan, between Zorah and Eshtaol.

14 Once Samson went down to Timnah; and while in Timnah, he noticed a girl among the Philistine women. ²On his return, he told his father and mother, "I noticed one of the Philistine women in Timnah; please get her for me as a wife." ³His father and mother said to him, "Is there no one among the daughters of your own kinsmen and among all ourᵃ people, that you must go and take a wife from the uncircumcised Philistines?" But Samson answered his father, "Get me that one, for she is the one that pleases me." ⁴His father and mother did not realize that this was the Lord's doing: He was seeking a pretext against the Philistines, for the Philistines were ruling over Israel at that time.

ᵇ⁻ᵇ   *Meaning of Heb. uncertain.*

ᵃ   *Heb.* "my."

549

יט וַיִּקַּ֨ח מָנ֜וֹחַ אֶת־גְּדִ֤י הָעִזִּים֙ וְאֶת־הַמִּנְחָ֗ה וַיַּ֛עַל עַל־הַצּ֖וּר לַֽיהוָ֑ה וּמַפְלִ֣א לַעֲשׂ֔וֹת וּמָנ֥וֹחַ וְאִשְׁתּ֖וֹ רֹאִֽים: כ וַיְהִ֗י בַּעֲל֤וֹת הַלַּ֙הַב֙ מֵעַ֣ל הַמִּזְבֵּ֔חַ הַשָּׁמַ֔יְמָה וַיַּ֥עַל מַלְאַךְ־יְהוָ֖ה בְּלַ֣הַב הַמִּזְבֵּ֑חַ וּמָנ֤וֹחַ וְאִשְׁתּוֹ֙ רֹאִ֔ים וַיִּפְּל֥וּ עַל־פְּנֵיהֶ֖ם אָֽרְצָה: כא וְלֹא־יָ֤סַף עוֹד֙ מַלְאַ֣ךְ יְהוָ֔ה לְהֵרָאֹ֖ה אֶל־מָנ֣וֹחַ וְאֶל־אִשְׁתּ֑וֹ אָ֚ז יָדַ֣ע מָנ֔וֹחַ כִּֽי־מַלְאַ֥ךְ יְהוָ֖ה הֽוּא: כב וַיֹּ֧אמֶר מָנ֛וֹחַ אֶל־אִשְׁתּ֖וֹ מ֣וֹת נָמ֑וּת כִּ֥י אֱלֹהִ֖ים רָאִֽינוּ: כג וַתֹּ֧אמֶר ל֣וֹ אִשְׁתּ֗וֹ לוּ֩ חָפֵ֨ץ יְהוָ֤ה לַהֲמִיתֵ֙נוּ֙ לֹֽא־לָקַ֤ח מִיָּדֵ֙נוּ֙ עֹלָ֣ה וּמִנְחָ֔ה וְלֹ֥א הֶרְאָ֖נוּ אֶת־כָּל־אֵ֑לֶּה וְכָעֵ֕ת לֹ֥א הִשְׁמִיעָ֖נוּ כָּזֹֽאת: כד וַתֵּ֤לֶד הָֽאִשָּׁה֙ בֵּ֔ן וַתִּקְרָ֥א אֶת־שְׁמ֖וֹ שִׁמְשׁ֑וֹן וַיִּגְדַּ֤ל הַנַּ֙עַר֙ וַֽיְבָרְכֵ֖הוּ יְהוָֽה: כה וַתָּ֙חֶל֙ ר֣וּחַ יְהוָ֔ה לְפַעֲמ֖וֹ בְּמַחֲנֵה־דָ֑ן בֵּ֥ין צָרְעָ֖ה וּבֵ֥ין אֶשְׁתָּאֹֽל: פ

יד א וַיֵּ֥רֶד שִׁמְשׁ֖וֹן תִּמְנָ֑תָה וַיַּ֥רְא אִשָּׁ֛ה בְּתִמְנָ֖תָה מִבְּנ֥וֹת פְּלִשְׁתִּֽים: ב וַיַּ֗עַל וַיַּגֵּד֙ לְאָבִ֣יו וּלְאִמּ֔וֹ וַיֹּ֗אמֶר אִשָּׁ֤ה רָאִ֙יתִי֙ בְתִמְנָ֔תָה מִבְּנ֖וֹת פְּלִשְׁתִּ֑ים וְעַתָּ֕ה קְחוּ־אוֹתָ֥הּ לִּ֖י לְאִשָּֽׁה: ג וַיֹּ֨אמֶר ל֜וֹ אָבִ֣יו וְאִמּ֗וֹ הַאֵין֩ בִּבְנ֨וֹת אַחֶ֜יךָ וּבְכָל־עַמִּי֙ אִשָּׁ֔ה כִּֽי־אַתָּ֤ה הוֹלֵךְ֙ לָקַ֣חַת אִשָּׁ֔ה מִפְּלִשְׁתִּ֖ים הָעֲרֵלִ֑ים וַיֹּ֨אמֶר שִׁמְשׁ֤וֹן אֶל־אָבִיו֙ אוֹתָ֣הּ קַֽח־לִ֔י כִּֽי־הִ֖יא יָשְׁרָ֥ה בְעֵינָֽי: ד וְאָבִ֨יו וְאִמּ֜וֹ לֹ֣א יָדְע֗וּ כִּ֤י מֵֽיהוָה֙ הִ֔יא כִּֽי־תֹאֲנָ֥ה הֽוּא־מְבַקֵּ֖שׁ מִפְּלִשְׁתִּ֑ים וּבָעֵ֤ת הַהִ֙יא

5So Samson and his father and mother went down to Timnah.

When he[b] came to the vineyards of Timnah [for the first time], a full-grown lion came roaring at him. 6The spirit of the LORD gripped him, and he tore him asunder with his bare hands as one might tear a kid asunder; but he did not tell his father and mother what he had done. 7Then he went down and spoke to the woman, and she pleased Samson.

8Returning the following year to marry her, he turned aside to look at the remains of the lion; and in the lion's skeleton he found a swarm of bees, and honey. 9He scooped it into his palms and ate it as he went along. When he rejoined his father and mother, he gave them some and they ate it; but he did not tell them that he had scooped the honey out of a lion's skeleton.

10So his father came down to the woman, and Samson made a feast there, as young men used to do. 11When they[c] saw him, they designated thirty companions to be with him. 12Then Samson said to them, "Let me propound a riddle to you. If you can give me the right answer during the seven days of the feast, I shall give you thirty linen tunics and thirty sets of clothing; 13but if you are not able to tell it to me, you must give me thirty linen tunics and thirty sets of clothing." And they said to him, "Ask your riddle and we will listen." 14So he said to them:

"Out of the eater came something to eat,
Out of the strong came something sweet."

For three days they could not answer the riddle.

15On the seventh[d] day, they said to Samson's wife, "Coax your husband to provide us with the answer to the riddle; else we shall put you and your father's household to the fire; have you invited us here[e] in order to impoverish us?"

פְּלִשְׁתִּים מֹשְׁלִים בְּיִשְׂרָאֵל׃ פ 5 וַיֵּ֣רֶד
שִׁמְשׁוֹן וְאָבִ֥יו וְאִמּ֖וֹ תִּמְנָ֑תָה
וַיָּבֹ֙אוּ֙ עַד־כַּרְמֵ֣י תִמְנָ֔תָה וְהִנֵּה֙ כְּפִ֣יר
אֲרָי֔וֹת שֹׁאֵ֖ג לִקְרָאתֽוֹ׃ 6 וַתִּצְלַ֨ח עָלָ֜יו ר֣וּחַ
יְהֹוָ֗ה וַֽיְשַׁסְּעֵ֙הוּ֙ כְּשַׁסַּ֣ע הַגְּדִ֔י וּמְא֖וּמָה אֵ֣ין
בְּיָד֑וֹ וְלֹ֤א הִגִּיד֙ לְאָבִ֣יו וּלְאִמּ֔וֹ אֵ֖ת אֲשֶׁ֥ר
עָשָֽׂה׃ 7 וַיֵּ֖רֶד וַיְדַבֵּ֣ר לָאִשָּׁ֑ה וַתִּישַׁ֖ר בְּעֵינֵ֥י
שִׁמְשֽׁוֹן׃

8 וַיָּ֤שׇׁב מִיָּמִים֙ לְקַחְתָּ֔הּ וַיָּ֣סַר לִרְא֔וֹת אֵ֖ת
מַפֶּ֣לֶת הָאַרְיֵ֑ה וְהִנֵּ֨ה עֲדַ֧ת דְּבוֹרִ֛ים בִּגְוִיַּ֥ת
הָאַרְיֵ֖ה וּדְבָֽשׁ׃ 9 וַיִּרְדֵּ֣הוּ אֶל־כַּפָּ֗יו וַיֵּ֤לֶךְ
הָלוֹךְ֙ וְאָכֹ֔ל וַיֵּ֙לֶךְ֙ אֶל־אָבִ֣יו וְאֶל־אִמּ֔וֹ וַיִּתֵּ֥ן
לָהֶ֖ם וַיֹּאכֵ֑לוּ וְלֹא־הִגִּ֣יד לָהֶ֔ם כִּ֛י מִגְּוִיַּ֥ת
הָאַרְיֵ֖ה רָדָ֥ה הַדְּבָֽשׁ׃

10 וַיֵּ֥רֶד אָבִ֖יהוּ אֶל־הָאִשָּׁ֑ה וַיַּ֨עַשׂ שָׁ֤ם
שִׁמְשׁוֹן֙ מִשְׁתֶּ֔ה כִּ֛י כֵּ֥ן יַעֲשׂ֖וּ הַבַּחוּרִֽים׃
11 וַיְהִ֥י כִּרְאוֹתָ֖ם אוֹת֑וֹ וַיִּקְח֙וּ֙ שְׁלֹשִׁ֣ים
מֵֽרֵעִ֔ים וַיִּהְי֖וּ אִתּֽוֹ׃ 12 וַיֹּ֤אמֶר לָהֶם֙
שִׁמְשׁ֔וֹן אָחֽוּדָה־נָּ֥א לָכֶ֖ם חִידָ֑ה אִם־הַגֵּ֣ד
תַּגִּ֩ידוּ֩ אוֹתָ֨הּ לִ֜י שִׁבְעַ֤ת יְמֵ֣י הַמִּשְׁתֶּ֔ה
וּמְצָאתֶ֔ם וְנָתַתִּ֤י לָכֶם֙ שְׁלֹשִׁ֣ים סְדִינִ֔ים
וּשְׁלֹשִׁ֖ים חֲלִפֹ֥ת בְּגָדִֽים׃ 13 וְאִם־לֹ֣א
תוּכְלוּ֮ לְהַגִּ֣יד לִי֒ וּנְתַתֶּ֥ם אַתֶּ֛ם לִ֖י שְׁלֹשִׁ֣ים
סְדִינִ֔ים וּשְׁלֹשִׁ֖ים חֲלִיפ֣וֹת בְּגָדִ֑ים וַיֹּ֣אמְרוּ
ל֔וֹ ח֥וּדָה חִידָתְךָ֖ וְנִשְׁמָעֶֽנָּה׃ 14 וַיֹּ֣אמֶר
לָהֶ֗ם

מֵהָֽאֹכֵל֙ יָצָ֣א מַאֲכָ֔ל

וּמֵעַ֖ז יָצָ֣א מָת֑וֹק

וְלֹ֥א יָכְל֛וּ לְהַגִּ֥יד הַחִידָ֖ה שְׁלֹ֥שֶׁת יָמִֽים׃
15 וַיְהִ֣י ׀ בַּיּ֣וֹם הַשְּׁבִיעִ֗י וַיֹּאמְר֤וּ לְאֵֽשֶׁת־
שִׁמְשׁוֹן֙ פַּתִּ֣י אֶת־אִישֵׁ֗ךְ וְיַגֶּד־לָ֙נוּ֙ אֶת־
הַ֣חִידָ֔ה פֶּן־נִשְׂרֹ֣ף אוֹתָ֥ךְ וְאֶת־בֵּ֣ית אָבִ֖יךְ
בָּאֵ֑שׁ הַלְיׇרְשֵׁ֙נוּ֙ קְרָאתֶ֣ם לָ֔נוּ הֲלֹֽא׃*

v. 15. בנוסח אחר "הלם"

---

b   Heb. "they."
c   I.e., the people of Timnah.
d   Septuagint and Syriac read "fourth."
e   Reading halom, with some Heb. mss. and Targum.

16Then Samson's wife harassed him with tears, and she said, "You really hate me, you don't love me. You asked my countrymen a riddle, and you didn't tell me the answer." He replied, "I haven't even told my father and mother; shall I tell you?" 17During the rest of the seven days of the feast she continued to harass him with her tears, and on the seventh day he told her, because she nagged him so. And she explained the riddle to her countrymen. 18On the seventh day, before the sunset, the townsmen said to him:

"What is sweeter than honey,
And what is stronger than a lion?"
He responded:

"Had you not plowed with my heifer,
You would not have guessed my riddle!"

19The spirit of the LORD gripped him. He went down to Ashkelon and killed thirty of its men. He stripped them and gave the sets of clothing to those who had answered the riddle. And he left in a rage for his father's house.

20Samson's wife then married one of those who had been his wedding companions.

15 Some time later, in the season of the wheat harvest, Samson came to visit his wife, bringing a kid as a gift. He said, "Let me go into the chamber to my wife." But her father would not let him go in. 2"I was sure," said her father, "that you had taken a dislike to her, so I gave her to your wedding companion. But her younger sister is more beautiful than she; let her become your wife instead." 3Thereupon Samson declared, "Now the Philistines can have no claim against me for the harm I shall do them."

4Samson went and caught three hundred foxes. He took torches and, turning [the foxes] tail to tail, he placed a torch between each pair of tails. 5He lit the torches and turned [the foxes]

16 וַתֵּבְךְּ אֵשֶׁת שִׁמְשׁוֹן עָלָיו וַתֹּאמֶר רַק־שְׂנֵאתַנִי וְלֹא אֲהַבְתָּנִי הַחִידָה חַדְתָּ לִבְנֵי עַמִּי וְלִי לֹא הִגַּדְתָּה וַיֹּאמֶר לָהּ הִנֵּה לְאָבִי וּלְאִמִּי לֹא הִגַּדְתִּי וְלָךְ אַגִּיד: 17 וַתֵּבְךְּ עָלָיו שִׁבְעַת הַיָּמִים אֲשֶׁר־הָיָה לָהֶם הַמִּשְׁתֶּה וַיְהִי ׀ בַּיּוֹם הַשְּׁבִיעִי וַיַּגֶּד־לָהּ כִּי הֱצִיקַתְהוּ וַתַּגֵּד הַחִידָה לִבְנֵי עַמָּהּ: 18 וַיֹּאמְרוּ לוֹ אַנְשֵׁי הָעִיר בַּיּוֹם הַשְּׁבִיעִי בְּטֶרֶם יָבֹא הַחַרְסָה

מַה־מָּתוֹק מִדְּבַשׁ

וּמֶה עַז מֵאֲרִי

וַיֹּאמֶר לָהֶם

לוּלֵא חֲרַשְׁתֶּם בְּעֶגְלָתִי

לֹא מְצָאתֶם חִידָתִי:

19 וַתִּצְלַח עָלָיו רוּחַ יְהוָה וַיֵּרֶד אַשְׁקְלוֹן וַיַּךְ מֵהֶם ׀ שְׁלֹשִׁים אִישׁ וַיִּקַּח אֶת־חֲלִיצוֹתָם וַיִּתֵּן הַחֲלִיפוֹת לְמַגִּידֵי הַחִידָה וַיִּחַר אַפּוֹ וַיַּעַל בֵּית אָבִיהוּ: פ 20 וַתְּהִי אֵשֶׁת שִׁמְשׁוֹן לְמֵרֵעֵהוּ אֲשֶׁר רֵעָה לוֹ:

טו וַיְהִי מִיָּמִים בִּימֵי קְצִיר־חִטִּים וַיִּפְקֹד שִׁמְשׁוֹן אֶת־אִשְׁתּוֹ בִּגְדִי עִזִּים וַיֹּאמֶר אָבֹאָה אֶל־אִשְׁתִּי הֶחָדְרָה וְלֹא־נְתָנוֹ אָבִיהָ לָבוֹא: 2 וַיֹּאמֶר אָבִיהָ אָמֹר אָמַרְתִּי כִּי־שָׂנֹא שְׂנֵאתָהּ וָאֶתְּנֶנָּה לְמֵרֵעֶךָ הֲלֹא אֲחֹתָהּ הַקְּטַנָּה טוֹבָה מִמֶּנָּה תְּהִי־נָא לְךָ תַּחְתֶּיהָ: 3 וַיֹּאמֶר לָהֶם שִׁמְשׁוֹן נִקֵּיתִי הַפַּעַם מִפְּלִשְׁתִּים כִּי־עֹשֶׂה אֲנִי עִמָּם רָעָה:

4 וַיֵּלֶךְ שִׁמְשׁוֹן וַיִּלְכֹּד שְׁלֹשׁ־מֵאוֹת שׁוּעָלִים וַיִּקַּח לַפִּדִים וַיֶּפֶן זָנָב אֶל־זָנָב וַיָּשֶׂם לַפִּיד אֶחָד בֵּין־שְׁנֵי הַזְּנָבוֹת בַּתָּוֶךְ: 5 וַיַּבְעֶר־אֵשׁ בַּלַּפִּידִים וַיְשַׁלַּח בְּקָמוֹת

loose among the standing grain of the Philis-tines, setting fire to stacked grain, standing grain, vineyards, [and]*a* olive trees.

⁶The Philistines asked, "Who did this?" And they were told, "It was Samson, the son-in-law of the Timnite, who took Samson's*b* wife and gave her to his wedding companion." There-upon the Philistines came up and put her and her father*c* to the fire. ⁷Samson said to them, "If that is how you act, I will not rest until I have taken revenge on you." ⁸*d*-He gave them a sound and thorough thrashing.-*d* Then he went down and stayed in the cave of the rock of Etam.

⁹The Philistines came up, pitched camp in Ju-dah and spread out over Lehi. ¹⁰The men of Ju-dah asked, "Why have you come up against us?" They answered, "We have come to take Samson prisoner, and to do to him as he did to us." ¹¹Thereupon three thousand men of Judah went down to the cave of the rock of Etam, and they said to Samson, "You knew that the Phi-listines rule over us; why have you done this to us?" He replied, "As they did to me, so I did to them." ¹²"We have come down," they told him, "to take you prisoner and to hand you over to the Philistines." "But swear to me," said Sam-son to them, "that you yourselves will not at-tack me." ¹³"We won't," they replied. "We will only take you prisoner and hand you over to them; we will not slay you." So they bound him with two new ropes and brought him up from the rock.

¹⁴When he reached Lehi, the Philistines came shouting to meet him. Thereupon the spirit of the Lᴏʀᴅ gripped him, and the ropes on his arms became like flax that catches fire; the bonds melted off his hands. ¹⁵He came upon a fresh jawbone of an ass and he picked it up; and with it he killed a thousand men. ¹⁶Then Samson said:

פְּלִשְׁתִּים וַיַּבְעֵר מִגָּדִישׁ וְעַד־קָמָה וְעַד־
כֶּרֶם זָיִת׃
⁶ וַיֹּאמְרוּ פְלִשְׁתִּים מִי עָשָׂה זֹאת וַיֹּאמְרוּ
שִׁמְשׁוֹן חֲתַן הַתִּמְנִי כִּי לָקַח אֶת־אִשְׁתּוֹ
וַיִּתְּנָהּ לְמֵרֵעֵהוּ וַיַּעֲלוּ פְלִשְׁתִּים וַיִּשְׂרְפוּ
אוֹתָהּ וְאֶת־אָבִיהָ בָּאֵשׁ׃ ⁷ וַיֹּאמֶר לָהֶם
שִׁמְשׁוֹן אִם־תַּעֲשׂוּן כָּזֹאת כִּי אִם־נִקַּמְתִּי
בָכֶם וְאַחַר אֶחְדָּל׃ ⁸ וַיַּךְ אוֹתָם שׁוֹק
עַל־יָרֵךְ מַכָּה גְדוֹלָה וַיֵּרֶד וַיֵּשֶׁב בִּסְעִיף
סֶלַע עֵיטָם׃ ס
⁹ וַיַּעֲלוּ פְלִשְׁתִּים וַיַּחֲנוּ בִּיהוּדָה וַיִּנָּטְשׁוּ
בַּלֶּחִי׃ ¹⁰ וַיֹּאמְרוּ אִישׁ יְהוּדָה לָמָה
עֲלִיתֶם עָלֵינוּ וַיֹּאמְרוּ לֶאֱסוֹר אֶת־
שִׁמְשׁוֹן עָלִינוּ לַעֲשׂוֹת לוֹ כַּאֲשֶׁר עָשָׂה
לָנוּ׃ ¹¹ וַיֵּרְדוּ שְׁלֹשֶׁת אֲלָפִים אִישׁ
מִיהוּדָה אֶל־סְעִיף סֶלַע עֵיטָם וַיֹּאמְרוּ
לְשִׁמְשׁוֹן הֲלֹא יָדַעְתָּ כִּי־מֹשְׁלִים בָּנוּ
פְלִשְׁתִּים וּמַה־זֹּאת עָשִׂיתָ לָּנוּ וַיֹּאמֶר
לָהֶם כַּאֲשֶׁר עָשׂוּ לִי כֵּן עָשִׂיתִי לָהֶם׃
¹² וַיֹּאמְרוּ לוֹ לֶאֱסָרְךָ יָרַדְנוּ לְתִתְּךָ בְּיַד־
פְּלִשְׁתִּים וַיֹּאמֶר לָהֶם שִׁמְשׁוֹן הִשָּׁבְעוּ
לִי פֶּן־תִּפְגְּעוּן בִּי אַתֶּם׃ ¹³ וַיֹּאמְרוּ לוֹ
לֵאמֹר לֹא כִּי־אָסֹר נֶאֱסָרְךָ וּנְתַנּוּךָ בְיָדָם
וְהָמֵת לֹא נְמִיתֶךָ וַיַּאַסְרֻהוּ בִּשְׁנַיִם
עֲבֹתִים חֲדָשִׁים וַיַּעֲלוּהוּ מִן־הַסָּלַע׃
¹⁴ הוּא־בָא עַד־לֶחִי וּפְלִשְׁתִּים הֵרִיעוּ
לִקְרָאתוֹ וַתִּצְלַח עָלָיו רוּחַ יְהֹוָה וַתִּהְיֶינָה
הָעֲבֹתִים אֲשֶׁר עַל־זְרוֹעוֹתָיו כַּפִּשְׁתִּים
אֲשֶׁר בָּעֲרוּ בָאֵשׁ וַיִּמַּסּוּ אֱסוּרָיו מֵעַל יָדָיו׃
¹⁵ וַיִּמְצָא לְחִי־חֲמוֹר טְרִיָּה וַיִּשְׁלַח יָדוֹ
וַיִּקָּחֶהָ וַיַּךְ־בָּהּ אֶלֶף אִישׁ׃ ¹⁶ וַיֹּאמֶר
שִׁמְשׁוֹן

---

a   So Targum.
b   Heb. "his."
c   Many mss. read "her father's household"; cf. 14.15.
d-d Lit. "He smote them leg as well as thigh, a great smiting."

"With the jaw of an ass,
Mass upon mass!
With the jaw of an ass
I have slain a thousand men."

[17]As he finished speaking, he threw the jaw-bone away; hence that place was called Ramath-lehi.[e]

[18]He was very thirsty and he called to the LORD, "You Yourself have granted this great victory through Your servant; and must I now die of thirst and fall into the hands of the uncircumcised?" [19]So God split open the hollow which is at Lehi, and the water gushed out of it; he drank, regained his strength, and revived. That is why it is called to this day "En-hakkore[f] of Lehi."

[20]He led Israel in the days of the Philistines for twenty years.

16

Once Samson went to Gaza; there he met a whore and slept with her. [2][a]The Gazites [learned][b] that Samson had come there, so they gathered and lay in ambush for him in the town gate the whole night; and all night long they kept whispering to each other, "When day-light comes, we'll kill him." [3]But Samson lay in bed only till midnight. At midnight he got up, grasped the doors of the town gate together with the two gateposts, and pulled them out along with the bar. He placed them on his shoulders and carried them off to the top of the hill that is near Hebron.

[4]After that, he fell in love with a woman in the Wadi Sorek, named Delilah. [5]The lords of the Philistines went up to her and said, "Coax him and find out what makes him so strong, and how we can overpower him, tie him up, and

בִּלְחִי הַחֲמוֹר
חֲמוֹר חֲמֹרָתָיִם
בִּלְחִי הַחֲמוֹר
הִכֵּיתִי אֶלֶף אִישׁ:

17 וַיְהִי כְּכַלֹּתוֹ לְדַבֵּר וַיַּשְׁלֵךְ הַלְּחִי מִיָּדוֹ
וַיִּקְרָא לַמָּקוֹם הַהוּא רָמַת לֶחִי:
18 וַיִּצְמָא מְאֹד וַיִּקְרָא אֶל־יְהוָה וַיֹּאמַר
אַתָּה נָתַתָּ בְיַד־עַבְדְּךָ אֶת־הַתְּשׁוּעָה
הַגְּדֹלָה הַזֹּאת וְעַתָּה אָמוּת בַּצָּמָא
וְנָפַלְתִּי בְּיַד הָעֲרֵלִים: 19 וַיִּבְקַע אֱלֹהִים
אֶת־הַמַּכְתֵּשׁ אֲשֶׁר־בַּלֶּחִי וַיֵּצְאוּ מִמֶּנּוּ
מַיִם וַיֵּשְׁתְּ וַתָּשָׁב רוּחוֹ וַיֶּחִי עַל־כֵּן | קָרָא
שְׁמָהּ עֵין הַקּוֹרֵא אֲשֶׁר בַּלֶּחִי עַד הַיּוֹם
הַזֶּה:
20 וַיִּשְׁפֹּט אֶת־יִשְׂרָאֵל בִּימֵי פְלִשְׁתִּים
עֶשְׂרִים שָׁנָה: פ

טז וַיֵּלֶךְ שִׁמְשׁוֹן עַזָּתָה וַיַּרְא־שָׁם
אִשָּׁה זוֹנָה וַיָּבֹא אֵלֶיהָ: 2 לַעַזָּתִים | לֵאמֹר
בָּא שִׁמְשׁוֹן הֵנָּה וַיָּסֹבּוּ וַיֶּאֶרְבוּ־לוֹ כָל־
הַלַּיְלָה בְּשַׁעַר הָעִיר וַיִּתְחָרְשׁוּ כָל־
הַלַּיְלָה לֵאמֹר עַד־אוֹר הַבֹּקֶר וַהֲרַגְנֻהוּ:
3 וַיִּשְׁכַּב שִׁמְשׁוֹן עַד־חֲצִי הַלַּיְלָה וַיָּקָם |
בַּחֲצִי הַלַּיְלָה וַיֶּאֱחֹז בְּדַלְתוֹת שַׁעַר־הָעִיר
וּבִשְׁתֵּי הַמְּזוּזוֹת וַיִּסָּעֵם עִם־הַבְּרִיחַ וַיָּשֶׂם
עַל־כְּתֵפָיו וַיַּעֲלֵם אֶל־רֹאשׁ הָהָר אֲשֶׁר
עַל־פְּנֵי חֶבְרוֹן: פ

4 וַיְהִי אַחֲרֵי־כֵן וַיֶּאֱהַב אִשָּׁה בְּנַחַל שֹׂרֵק
וּשְׁמָהּ דְּלִילָה: 5 וַיַּעֲלוּ אֵלֶיהָ סַרְנֵי
פְלִשְׁתִּים וַיֹּאמְרוּ לָהּ פַּתִּי אוֹתוֹ וּרְאִי
בַּמֶּה כֹּחוֹ גָדוֹל וּבַמֶּה נוּכַל לוֹ וַאֲסַרְנֻהוּ

---

e   I.e., "Jawbone Heights."
f   Understood as "The Spring of the Caller."

a   Meaning of parts of verse uncertain.
b   Septuagint reads "were told."

make him helpless; and we'll each give you eleven hundred shekels of silver."

⁶So Delilah said to Samson, "Tell me, what makes you so strong? And how could you be tied up and made helpless?" ⁷Samson replied, "If I were to be tied with seven fresh tendons that had not been dried,ᶜ I should become as weak as an ordinary man." ⁸So the lords of the Philistines brought up to her seven fresh tendons that had not been dried. She bound him with them, ⁹while an ambush was waiting in her room. Then she called out to him, "Samson, the Philistines are upon you!" Whereat he pulled the tendons apart, as a strand of tow comes apart at the touch of fire. So the secret of his strength remained unknown.

¹⁰Then Delilah said to Samson, "Oh, you deceived me; you lied to me! Do tell me now how you could be tied up." ¹¹He said, "If I were to be bound with new ropes that had never been used, I would become as weak as an ordinary man." ¹²So Delilah took new ropes and bound him with them, while an ambush was waiting in a room. And she cried, "Samson, the Philistines are upon you!" But he tore them off his arms like a thread. ¹³Then Delilah said to Samson, "You have been deceiving me all along; you have been lying to me! Tell me, how could you be tied up?" He answered her, "If you weave seven locks of my head into the web."ᵈ ¹⁴And she pinned it with a pegᵉ and cried to him, "Samson, the Philistines are upon you!" Awaking from his sleep, he pulled out the peg, the loom,ᶠ and the web.

¹⁵Then she said to him, "How can you say you love me, when you don't confide in me? This makes three times that you've deceived me and haven't told me what makes you so strong."

ᶜ For use as bowstrings.
ᵈ Septuagint adds "and pin it with a peg to the wall, I shall become as weak as an ordinary man. So Delilah put him to sleep and wove the seven locks of his head into the web."
ᵉ Septuagint adds "to the wall."
ᶠ Meaning of Heb. uncertain.

לְעַנּוֹתוֹ וַאֲנַ֗חְנוּ נִתַּן־לְךָ֗ אִ֛ישׁ אֶ֥לֶף וּמֵאָ֖ה כָּֽסֶף:

⁶ וַתֹּ֤אמֶר דְּלִילָה֙ אֶל־שִׁמְשׁ֔וֹן הַגִּֽידָה־נָּ֣א לִ֔י בַּמֶּ֖ה כֹּחֲךָ֣ גָד֑וֹל וּבַמֶּ֥ה תֵֽאָסֵ֖ר לְעַנּוֹתֶֽךָ: ⁷ וַיֹּ֤אמֶר אֵלֶ֙יהָ֙ שִׁמְשׁ֔וֹן אִם־יַאַסְרֻ֗נִי בְּשִׁבְעָ֛ה יְתָרִ֥ים לַחִ֖ים אֲשֶׁ֣ר לֹא־חֹרָ֑בוּ וְחָלִ֥יתִי וְהָיִ֖יתִי כְּאַחַ֥ד הָאָדָֽם: ⁸ וַיַּעֲלוּ־לָ֞הּ סַרְנֵ֣י פְלִשְׁתִּ֗ים שִׁבְעָ֛ה יְתָרִ֥ים לַחִ֖ים אֲשֶׁ֣ר לֹא־חֹרָ֑בוּ וַתַּֽאַסְרֵ֖הוּ בָּהֶֽם: ⁹ וְהָאֹרֵ֗ב יֹשֵׁ֥ב לָהּ֙ בַּחֶ֔דֶר וַתֹּ֣אמֶר אֵלָ֔יו פְּלִשְׁתִּ֥ים עָלֶ֖יךָ שִׁמְשׁ֑וֹן וַיְנַתֵּ֣ק אֶת־הַיְתָרִ֗ים כַּאֲשֶׁ֨ר יִנָּתֵ֤ק פְּתִֽיל־הַנְּעֹ֙רֶת֙ בַּהֲרִיח֣וֹ אֵ֔שׁ וְלֹ֥א נוֹדַ֖ע כֹּחֽוֹ:

¹⁰ וַתֹּ֤אמֶר דְּלִילָה֙ אֶל־שִׁמְשׁ֔וֹן הִנֵּה֙ הֵתַ֣לְתָּ בִּ֔י וַתְּדַבֵּ֥ר אֵלַ֖י כְּזָבִ֑ים עַתָּה֙ הַגִּֽידָה־נָּ֣א לִ֔י בַּמֶּ֖ה תֵּאָסֵֽר: ¹¹ וַיֹּ֣אמֶר אֵלֶ֔יהָ אִם־אָס֤וֹר יַֽאַסְר֙וּנִי֙ בַּעֲבֹתִ֣ים חֲדָשִׁ֔ים אֲשֶׁ֛ר לֹֽא־נַעֲשָׂ֥ה בָהֶ֖ם מְלָאכָ֑ה וְחָלִ֥יתִי וְהָיִ֖יתִי כְּאַחַ֥ד הָאָדָֽם: ¹² וַתִּקַּ֣ח דְּלִילָה֩ עֲבֹתִ֨ים חֲדָשִׁ֜ים וַתַּאַסְרֵ֣הוּ בָהֶ֗ם וַתֹּ֤אמֶר אֵלָיו֙ פְּלִשְׁתִּ֤ים עָלֶ֙יךָ֙ שִׁמְשׁ֔וֹן וְהָאֹרֵ֖ב יֹשֵׁ֣ב בֶּחָ֑דֶר וַֽיְנַתְּקֵ֛ם מֵעַ֥ל זְרֹעֹתָ֖יו כַּחֽוּט: ¹³ וַתֹּ֨אמֶר דְּלִילָ֜ה אֶל־שִׁמְשׁ֗וֹן עַד־הֵ֜נָּה הֵתַ֤לְתָּ בִּי֙ וַתְּדַבֵּ֤ר אֵלַי֙ כְּזָבִ֔ים הַגִּ֣ידָה לִּ֔י בַּמֶּ֖ה תֵּאָסֵ֑ר וַיֹּ֣אמֶר אֵלֶ֔יהָ אִם־תַּאַרְגִ֗י אֶת־שֶׁ֛בַע מַחְלְפ֥וֹת רֹאשִׁ֖י עִם־הַמַּסָּֽכֶת: ¹⁴ וַתִּתְקַע֙ בַּיָּתֵ֔ד וַתֹּ֣אמֶר אֵלָ֔יו פְּלִשְׁתִּ֥ים עָלֶ֖יךָ שִׁמְשׁ֑וֹן וַיִּיקַץ֙ מִשְּׁנָת֔וֹ וַיִּסַּ֛ע אֶת־הַיְתַ֥ד הָאֶ֖רֶג וְאֶת־הַמַּסָּֽכֶת: ¹⁵ וַתֹּ֣אמֶר אֵלָ֗יו אֵ֚יךְ תֹּאמַ֣ר אֲהַבְתִּ֔יךְ וְלִבְּךָ֖ אֵ֣ין אִתִּ֑י זֶ֣ה שָׁלֹ֤שׁ פְּעָמִים֙ הֵתַ֣לְתָּ בִּ֔י וְלֹא־הִגַּ֣דְתָּ לִּ֔י בַּמֶּ֖ה כֹּחֲךָ֣ גָד֑וֹל: ¹⁶ וַֽיְהִי֙

16Finally, after she had nagged him and pressed him constantly, he was wearied to death 17and he confided everything to her. He said to her, "No razor has ever touched my head, for I have been a nazirite to God since I was in my mother's womb. If my hair were cut, my strength would leave me and I should become as weak as an ordinary man."

18Sensing that he had confided everything to her, Delilah sent for the lords of the Philistines, with this message: "Come up once more, for he has confided everything to me." And the lords of the Philistines came up and brought the money with them. 19She lulled him to sleep on her lap. Then she called in a man, and she had him cut off the seven locks of his head; thus she weakened him*g* and made him helpless: his strength slipped away from him. 20She cried, "Samson, the Philistines are upon you!" And he awoke from his sleep, thinking he would break loose*f* and shake himself free as he had the other times. For he did not know that the Lord had departed from him. 21The Philistines seized him and gouged out his eyes. They brought him down to Gaza and shackled him in bronze fetters, and he became a mill slave in the prison. 22After his hair was cut off, it began to grow back.

23Now the lords of the Philistines gathered to offer a great sacrifice to their god Dagon and to make merry. They chanted,

"Our god has delivered into our hands
Our enemy Samson."

24*h*When the people saw him, they sang praises to their god, chanting,

"Our god has delivered into our hands
The enemy who devastated our land,
And who slew so many of us."

25As their spirits rose, they said, "Call Samson here and let him dance for us." Samson was fetched from the prison, and he danced for

כִּי־הֵצִיקָה לּוֹ בִּדְבָרֶ֫יהָ כָּל־הַיָּמִים וַתְּאַלְצֵהוּ וַתִּקְצַר נַפְשׁוֹ לָמוּת: 17 וַיַּגֶּד־ לָהּ אֶת־כָּל־לִבּוֹ וַיֹּאמֶר לָהּ מוֹרָה֙ לֹא־ עָלָה עַל־רֹאשִׁי כִּי־נְזִיר אֱלֹהִים אֲנִי מִבֶּ֣טֶן אִמִּי אִם־גֻּלַּחְתִּי וְסָר מִמֶּנִּי כֹחִי וְחָלִיתִי וְהָיִ֫יתִי כְּכָל־הָאָדָם: 18 וַתֵּרֶא דְּלִילָה כִּי־הִגִּיד לָהּ אֶת־כָּל־לִבּוֹ וַתִּשְׁלַ֫ח וַתִּקְרָא לְסַרְנֵי פְלִשְׁתִּים לֵאמֹר עֲלוּ הַפַּעַם כִּי־הִגִּיד לה לִי אֶת־כָּל־ לִבּוֹ וְעָלוּ אֵלֶ֫יהָ סַרְנֵי פְלִשְׁתִּים וַיַּעֲלוּ הַכֶּסֶף בְּיָדָם: 19 וַתְּיַשְּׁנֵהוּ עַל־בִּרְכֶּ֫יהָ וַתִּקְרָא לָאִישׁ וַתְּגַלַּח אֶת־שֶׁ֫בַע מַחְלְפוֹת רֹאשׁוֹ וַתָּ֫חֶל לְעַנּוֹתוֹ וַיָּסַר כֹּחוֹ מֵעָלָיו: 20 וַתֹּאמֶר פְּלִשְׁתִּים עָלֶ֫יךָ שִׁמְשׁוֹן וַיִּקַ֫ץ* מִשְּׁנָתוֹ וַיֹּאמֶר אֵצֵא כְּפַ֫עַם בְּפַ֫עַם וְאִנָּעֵר וְהוּא לֹא יָדַע כִּי יְהוָה סָר מֵעָלָיו: 21 וַיֹּאחֲזוּ֫הוּ פְלִשְׁתִּים וַיְנַקְּרוּ אֶת־עֵינָיו וַיּוֹרִ֫ידוּ אוֹתוֹ עַזָּ֫תָה וַיַּאַסְרוּ֫הוּ בַּנְחֻשְׁתַּ֫יִם וַיְהִי טוֹחֵן בְּבֵית הָאֲסִירִים הָאֲסוּרִים: 22 וַיָּ֫חֶל שְׂעַר־רֹאשׁוֹ לְצַמֵּחַ כַּאֲשֶׁר גֻּלָּח: פ 23 וְסַרְנֵי פְלִשְׁתִּים נֶאֶסְפוּ לִזְבֹּחַ זֶבַח־גָּדוֹל לְדָגוֹן אֱלֹהֵיהֶם וּלְשִׂמְחָה וַיֹּאמְרוּ נָתַן אֱלֹהֵינוּ בְּיָדֵ֫נוּ אֵת שִׁמְשׁוֹן אוֹיְבֵ֫ינוּ: 24 וַיִּרְאוּ אֹתוֹ הָעָם וַיְהַלְלוּ אֶת־אֱלֹהֵיהֶם כִּי אָמְרוּ נָתַן אֱלֹהֵ֫ינוּ בְיָדֵ֫נוּ אֶת־אוֹיְבֵ֫נוּ וְאֵת מַחֲרִיב אַרְצֵ֫נוּ וַאֲשֶׁר הִרְבָּה אֶת־חֲלָלֵ֫ינוּ: 25 וַיְהִי כִּי טוֹב כְּטוֹב לִבָּם וַיֹּאמְרוּ קִרְאוּ לְשִׁמְשׁוֹן וִישַׂחֶק־לָ֫נוּ וַיִּקְרְאוּ לְשִׁמְשׁוֹן מִבֵּית הָאֲסִירִים הָאֲסוּרִים וַיְצַחֵק לִפְנֵיהֶם

---

g   Taking *wattaḥel* as equivalent to *wattaḥal*; cf. vv. 7, 11, and 17.
h   This verse would read well after v. 25.

them. Then they put him between the pillars.
[26]And Samson said to the boy who was leading
him by the hand, "Let go of me and let me feel
the pillars that the temple rests upon, that I may
lean on them." [27]Now the temple was full of men
and women; all the lords of the Philistines were
there, and there were some three thousand men
and women on the roof watching Samson
dance. [28]Then Samson called to the Lord, "O
Lord God! Please remember me, and give me
strength just this once, O God, to take revenge
of the Philistines, if only for one of my two eyes."
[29]He embraced the two middle pillars that the
temple rested upon, one with his right arm and
one with his left, and leaned against them;
[30]Samson cried, "Let me die with the Philistines!" and he pulled with all his might. The
temple came crashing down on the lords and
on all the people in it. Those who were slain by
him as he died outnumbered those who had
been slain by him when he lived.

[31]His brothers and all his father's household
came down and carried him up and buried him
in the tomb of his father Manoah, between
Zorah and Eshtaol. He had led Israel for twenty
years.

17 There was a man in the hill country of
Ephraim whose name was Micah.[a] [2]He said to
his mother, "The eleven hundred shekels of silver that were taken from you, so that you uttered
an imprecation[b] which you repeated in my
hearing—I have that silver; I took it." "Blessed
of the Lord be my son," said his mother.[c] [3]He
returned the eleven hundred shekels of silver to
his mother; but his mother said, "I herewith
consecrate the silver to the Lord, transferring
it to my son to make a sculptured image and
a molten image. I now return it to you." [4]So

וַיַּעֲמִ֥ידוּ אוֹת֖וֹ בֵּ֣ין הָעַמּוּדִֽים׃ 26 וַיֹּ֣אמֶר
שִׁמְשׁ֜וֹן אֶל־הַנַּ֣עַר הַמַּחֲזִ֣יק בְּיָדוֹ֮ הַנִּ֣יחָה
אוֹתִי֒ וַהֲמִישֵׁ֙נִי֙ אֶת־הָ֣עַמֻּדִ֔ים אֲשֶׁ֥ר
הַבַּ֖יִת נָכ֣וֹן עֲלֵיהֶ֑ם וְאֶשָּׁעֵ֖ן עֲלֵיהֶֽם׃
27 וְהַבַּ֗יִת מָלֵ֤א הָֽאֲנָשִׁים֙ וְהַנָּשִׁ֔ים וְשָׁ֕מָּה
כֹּ֖ל סַרְנֵ֣י פְלִשְׁתִּ֑ים וְעַל־הַגָּ֗ג כִּשְׁלֹ֤שֶׁת
אֲלָפִים֙ אִ֣ישׁ וְאִשָּׁ֔ה הָרֹאִ֖ים בִּשְׂח֥וֹק
שִׁמְשֽׁוֹן׃ 28 וַיִּקְרָ֥א שִׁמְשׁ֛וֹן אֶל־יְהֹוָ֖ה
וַיֹּאמַ֑ר אֲדֹנָ֣י יֱהֹוִ֡ה זׇכְרֵ֣נִי נָא֩ וְחַזְּקֵ֨נִי נָ֜א
אַ֣ךְ הַפַּ֤עַם הַזֶּה֙ הָֽאֱלֹהִ֔ים וְאִנָּקְמָ֧ה נְקַם־
אַחַ֛ת מִשְּׁתֵ֥י עֵינַ֖י מִפְּלִשְׁתִּֽים׃ 29 וַיִּלְפֹּ֨ת
שִׁמְשׁ֜וֹן אֶת־שְׁנֵ֣י ׀ עַמּוּדֵ֣י הַתָּ֗וֶךְ אֲשֶׁ֤ר
הַבַּ֨יִת֙ נָכ֣וֹן עֲלֵיהֶ֔ם וַיִּסָּמֵ֖ךְ עֲלֵיהֶ֑ם אֶחָ֥ד
בִּימִינ֖וֹ וְאֶחָ֥ד בִּשְׂמֹאלֽוֹ׃ 30 וַיֹּ֣אמֶר שִׁמְשׁ֗וֹן
תָּמ֣וֹת נַפְשִׁי֮ עִם־פְּלִשְׁתִּים֒ וַיֵּ֣ט בְּכֹ֔חַ וַיִּפֹּ֤ל
הַבַּ֨יִת֙ עַל־הַסְּרָנִ֔ים וְעַל־כׇּל־הָעָ֖ם אֲשֶׁר־בּ֑וֹ
וַיִּהְי֤וּ הַמֵּתִים֙ אֲשֶׁ֣ר הֵמִ֣ית בְּמוֹת֔וֹ רַבִּ֕ים
מֵאֲשֶׁ֥ר הֵמִ֖ית בְּחַיָּֽיו׃
31 וַיֵּרְד֣וּ אֶחָיו֮ וְכׇל־בֵּ֣ית אָבִיהוּ֒ וַיִּשְׂא֣וּ אֹת֗וֹ
וַֽיַּעֲל֣וּ ׀ וַיִּקְבְּר֣וּ אוֹת֗וֹ בֵּ֤ין צׇרְעָה֙ וּבֵ֣ין
אֶשְׁתָּאֹ֔ל בְּקֶ֖בֶר מָנ֣וֹחַ אָבִ֑יו וְה֛וּא שָׁפַ֥ט
אֶת־יִשְׂרָאֵ֖ל עֶשְׂרִ֥ים שָׁנָֽה׃ פ

רז וַיְהִי־אִ֥ישׁ מֵֽהַר־אֶפְרָ֖יִם וּשְׁמ֥וֹ
מִיכָֽיְהוּ׃ 2 וַיֹּ֣אמֶר לְאִמּ֡וֹ אֶ֩לֶף֩ וּמֵאָ֨ה הַכֶּ֜סֶף
אֲשֶׁ֣ר לֻֽקַּֽח־לָ֗ךְ וְאַ֤תְּ אָלִית֙ וְגַם֙ אָמַ֣רְתְּ
בְּאׇזְנַ֔י הִנֵּֽה־הַכֶּ֥סֶף אִתִּ֖י אֲנִ֣י לְקַחְתִּ֑יו
וַתֹּ֣אמֶר אִמּ֔וֹ בָּר֥וּךְ בְּנִ֖י לַיהֹוָֽה׃ 3 וַיָּ֛שֶׁב
אֶת־אֶֽלֶף־וּמֵאָ֥ה הַכֶּ֖סֶף לְאִמּ֑וֹ וַתֹּ֣אמֶר
אִמּ֗וֹ הַקְדֵּ֣שׁ הִקְדַּ֣שְׁתִּי אֶת־הַכֶּ֣סֶף לַֽיהֹוָ֩ה
מִיָּדִ֙י לִבְנִ֜י לַעֲשׂוֹת֙ פֶּ֣סֶל וּמַסֵּכָ֔ה וְעַתָּ֖ה
אֲשִׁיבֶ֥נּוּ לָֽךְ׃ 4 וַיָּ֥שֶׁב אֶת־הַכֶּ֖סֶף לְאִמּֽוֹ

---

a "Micaihu" here and in v. 4.
b Cursing anyone who knew the whereabouts of the silver and did
   not disclose it; cf. Lev. 5.1; 1 Kings 8.31.
c In order to nullify the imprecation.

when he gave the silver back to his mother, his mother took two hundred shekels of silver and gave it to a smith. He made of it a sculptured image and a molten image, which were kept in the house of Micah.

⁵Now the man Micah had a house of God; he had made an ephod and teraphim and he had inducted one of his sons to be his priest. ⁶In those days there was no king in Israel; every man did as he pleased.

⁷There was a young man from Bethlehem of Judah, from the clan seat of Judah; he was a Levite and had resided there as a sojourner. ⁸This man had left the town of Bethlehem of Judah to take up residence wherever he could find a place. On his way, he came to the house of Micah in the hill country of Ephraim. ⁹"Where do you come from?" Micah asked him. He replied, "I am a Levite from Bethlehem of Judah, and I am traveling to take up residence wherever I can find a place." ¹⁰"Stay with me," Micah said to him, "and be a father and a priest to me, and I will pay you ten shekels of silver a year, an allowance of clothing, and your food." ᵈ-The Levite went.-ᵈ ¹¹The Levite agreed to stay with the man, and the youth became like one of his own sons. ¹²Micah inducted the Levite, and the young man became his priest and remained in Micah's shrine. ¹³"Now I know," Micah told himself, "that the Lord will prosper me, since the Levite has become my priest."

18

In those days there was no king in Israel, and in those days the tribe of Dan was seeking a territory in which to settle; for to that day no territory had fallen to their lot among the tribes of Israel. ²The Danites sent out five of their number, from their clan seat at Zorah and Eshtaol—valiant men—to spy out the land and

וַתִּקַּ֨ח אִמּ֜וֹ מָאתַ֣יִם כֶּ֗סֶף וַתִּתְּנֵ֣הוּ לַצּוֹרֵ֔ף
וַיַּעֲשֵׂ֙הוּ֙ פֶּ֣סֶל וּמַסֵּכָ֔ה וַיְהִ֖י בְּבֵ֥ית מִיכָֽיְהוּ׃
⁵ וְהָאִ֣ישׁ מִיכָ֔ה ל֥וֹ בֵּ֣ית אֱלֹהִ֑ים וַיַּ֤עַשׂ
אֵפוֹד֙ וּתְרָפִ֔ים וַיְמַלֵּ֗א אֶת־יַ֤ד אַחַד֙ מִבָּנָ֔יו
וַיְהִי־ל֖וֹ לְכֹהֵֽן׃ ⁶ בַּיָּמִ֣ים הָהֵ֔ם אֵ֥ין מֶ֖לֶךְ
בְּיִשְׂרָאֵ֑ל אִ֛ישׁ הַיָּשָׁ֥ר בְּעֵינָ֖יו יַעֲשֶֽׂה׃ פ
⁷ וַֽיְהִי־נַ֗עַר מִבֵּ֥ית לֶ֙חֶם֙ יְהוּדָ֔ה מִמִּשְׁפַּ֖חַת
יְהוּדָ֑ה וְה֥וּא לֵוִ֖י וְה֥וּא גָֽר־שָֽׁם׃ ⁸ וַיֵּ֣לֶךְ
הָאִ֗ישׁ מֵהָעִיר֙ מִבֵּ֣ית לֶ֣חֶם יְהוּדָ֔ה לָג֖וּר
בַּאֲשֶׁ֣ר יִמְצָ֑א וַיָּבֹ֧א הַר־אֶפְרַ֛יִם עַד־בֵּ֥ית
מִיכָ֖ה לַעֲשׂ֥וֹת דַּרְכּֽוֹ׃ ⁹ וַיֹּֽאמֶר־ל֥וֹ מִיכָ֖ה
מֵאַ֣יִן תָּב֑וֹא וַיֹּ֨אמֶר אֵלָ֜יו לֵוִ֣י אָנֹ֗כִי מִבֵּ֥ית
לֶ֙חֶם֙ יְהוּדָ֔ה וְאָנֹכִ֣י הֹלֵ֔ךְ לָג֖וּר בַּאֲשֶׁ֣ר
אֶמְצָֽא׃ ¹⁰ וַיֹּֽאמֶר־ל֣וֹ מִיכָה֮ שְׁבָ֣ה עִמָּדִי֒
וֶֽהְיֵה־לִ֙י לְאָ֣ב וּלְכֹהֵ֔ן וְאָנֹכִ֣י אֶֽתֶּן־לְךָ֗
עֲשֶׂ֤רֶת כֶּ֙סֶף֙ לַיָּמִ֔ים וְעֵ֥רֶךְ בְּגָדִ֖ים וּמִחְיָתֶ֑ךָ
וַיֵּ֖לֶךְ הַלֵּוִֽי׃ ¹¹ וַיּ֥וֹאֶל הַלֵּוִ֖י לָשֶׁ֣בֶת אֶת־
הָאִ֑ישׁ וַיְהִ֤י הַנַּ֙עַר֙ ל֔וֹ כְּאַחַ֖ד מִבָּנָֽיו׃
¹² וַיְמַלֵּ֤א מִיכָה֙ אֶת־יַ֣ד הַלֵּוִ֔י וַיְהִי־ל֥וֹ
הַנַּ֖עַר לְכֹהֵ֑ן וַיְהִ֖י בְּבֵ֥ית מִיכָֽה׃ ¹³ וַיֹּ֣אמֶר
מִיכָ֔ה עַתָּ֣ה יָדַ֔עְתִּי כִּֽי־יֵיטִ֥יב יְהוָֹ֖ה לִ֑י כִּ֛י
הָיָה־לִ֥י הַלֵּוִ֖י לְכֹהֵֽן׃

יח בַּיָּמִ֣ים הָהֵ֔ם אֵ֥ין מֶ֖לֶךְ בְּיִשְׂרָאֵ֑ל
וּבַיָּמִ֣ים הָהֵ֔ם שֵׁ֣בֶט הַדָּנִ֗י מְבַקֶּשׁ־ל֤וֹ
נַחֲלָה֙ לָשֶׁ֔בֶת כִּי֩ לֹֽא־נָ֨פְלָה לּ֜וֹ עַד־הַיּ֣וֹם
הַה֗וּא בְּתוֹךְ־שִׁבְטֵ֥י יִשְׂרָאֵ֖ל בְּנַחֲלָֽה׃ ס
² וַיִּשְׁלְח֣וּ בְנֵי־דָ֣ן ׀ מִמִּשְׁפַּחְתָּ֡ם חֲמִשָּׁ֣ה
אֲנָשִׁ֣ים מִקְצוֹתָם֩ אֲנָשִׁ֨ים בְּנֵי־חַ֜יִל

ᵈ-ᵈ Force of Heb. uncertain.

explore it. "Go," they told them, "and explore the land." When they had advanced into the hill country of Ephraim as far as the house of Micah, they stopped there for the night. ³While in the vicinity of Micah's house, they recognized the speech[a] of the young Levite, so they went over and asked him, "Who brought you to these parts? What are you doing in this place? What is your business here?" ⁴He replied, "Thus and thus Micah did for me—he hired me and I became his priest." ⁵They said to him, "Please, inquire of God; we would like to know if the mission on which we are going will be successful." ⁶"Go in peace," the priest said to them, "the LORD views with favor the mission you are going on." ⁷The five men went on and came to Laish. They observed the people in it dwelling carefree, after the manner of the Sidonians, a tranquil and unsuspecting people, with no one in the land to molest them and [b]with no hereditary ruler.[b] Moreover, they were distant from the Sidonians and had no dealings with anybody.

⁸When [the men] came back to their kinsmen at Zorah and Eshtaol, their kinsmen asked them, "How did you fare?" ⁹They replied, "Let us go at once and attack them! For we found that the land was very good, and you are sitting idle! Don't delay; go and invade the land and take possession of it, ¹⁰for God has delivered it into your hand. When you come, you will come to an unsuspecting people; and the land is spacious and nothing on earth is lacking there."

¹¹They departed from there, from the clan seat of the Danites, from Zorah and Eshtaol, six hundred strong, girt with weapons of war. ¹²They went up and encamped at Kiriath-jearim in Judah. That is why that place is called "the Camp of Dan" to this day; it lies west of Kiriath-jearim. ¹³From there they passed on to the hill

---

מִצְרָעָה וּמֵאֶשְׁתָּאֹל לְרַגֵּל אֶת־הָאָרֶץ
וּלְחָקְרָהּ וַיֹּאמְרוּ אֲלֵהֶם לְכוּ חִקְרוּ אֶת־
הָאָרֶץ וַיָּבֹאוּ הַר־אֶפְרַיִם עַד־בֵּית מִיכָה
וַיָּלִינוּ שָׁם׃ 3 הֵמָּה עִם־בֵּית מִיכָה וְהֵמָּה
הִכִּירוּ אֶת־קוֹל הַנַּעַר הַלֵּוִי וַיָּסוּרוּ שָׁם
וַיֹּאמְרוּ לוֹ מִי־הֱבִיאֲךָ הֲלֹם וּמָה־אַתָּה
עֹשֶׂה בָּזֶה וּמַה־לְּךָ פֹּה׃ 4 וַיֹּאמֶר אֲלֵהֶם
כָּזֹה וְכָזֶה עָשָׂה לִי מִיכָה וַיִּשְׂכְּרֵנִי וָאֱהִי־
לוֹ לְכֹהֵן׃ 5 וַיֹּאמְרוּ לוֹ שְׁאַל־נָא בֵאלֹהִים
וְנֵדְעָה הֲתַצְלִיחַ דַּרְכֵּנוּ אֲשֶׁר אֲנַחְנוּ
הֹלְכִים עָלֶיהָ׃ 6 וַיֹּאמֶר לָהֶם הַכֹּהֵן לְכוּ
לְשָׁלוֹם נֹכַח יְהֹוָה דַּרְכְּכֶם אֲשֶׁר תֵּלְכוּ־
בָהּ׃ פ 7 וַיֵּלְכוּ חֲמֵשֶׁת הָאֲנָשִׁים וַיָּבֹאוּ
לַיְשָׁה וַיִּרְאוּ אֶת־הָעָם אֲשֶׁר־בְּקִרְבָּהּ
יוֹשֶׁבֶת־לָבֶטַח כְּמִשְׁפַּט צִדֹנִים שֹׁקֵט ׀
וּבֹטֵחַ וְאֵין־מַכְלִים דָּבָר בָּאָרֶץ יוֹרֵשׁ עֶצֶר
וּרְחֹקִים הֵמָּה מִצִּדֹנִים וְדָבָר אֵין־לָהֶם
עִם־אָדָם׃ 8 וַיָּבֹאוּ אֶל־אֲחֵיהֶם צָרְעָה וְאֶשְׁתָּאֹל
וַיֹּאמְרוּ לָהֶם אֲחֵיהֶם מָה אַתֶּם׃ 9 וַיֹּאמְרוּ
קוּמָה וְנַעֲלֶה עֲלֵיהֶם כִּי רָאִינוּ אֶת־הָאָרֶץ
וְהִנֵּה טוֹבָה מְאֹד וְאַתֶּם מַחְשִׁים אַל־
תֵּעָצְלוּ לָלֶכֶת לָבֹא לָרֶשֶׁת אֶת־הָאָרֶץ׃
10 כְּבֹאֲכֶם תָּבֹאוּ ׀ אֶל־עַם בֹּטֵחַ וְהָאָרֶץ
רַחֲבַת יָדַיִם כִּי־נְתָנָהּ אֱלֹהִים בְּיֶדְכֶם
מָקוֹם אֲשֶׁר אֵין־שָׁם מַחְסוֹר כָּל־דָּבָר
אֲשֶׁר בָּאָרֶץ׃ 11 וַיִּסְעוּ מִשָּׁם מִמִּשְׁפַּחַת הַדָּנִי מִצָּרְעָה
וּמֵאֶשְׁתָּאֹל שֵׁשׁ־מֵאוֹת אִישׁ חָגוּר כְּלֵי
מִלְחָמָה׃ 12 וַיַּעֲלוּ וַיַּחֲנוּ בְּקִרְיַת יְעָרִים
בִּיהוּדָה עַל־כֵּן קָרְאוּ לַמָּקוֹם הַהוּא
מַחֲנֵה־דָן עַד הַיּוֹם הַזֶּה הִנֵּה אַחֲרֵי קִרְיַת
יְעָרִים׃ 13 וַיַּעַבְרוּ מִשָּׁם הַר־אֶפְרַיִם וַיָּבֹאוּ

---

a   Lit. "voice." The men could tell by his dialect that he came from Judah and was therefore a former neighbor of the Danites; cf. vv. 11–12.

b-b   Meaning of Heb. uncertain.

country of Ephraim and arrived at the house of Micah. [14]Here the five men who had gone to spy out the Laish region remarked to their kinsmen, "Do you know, there is an ephod in these houses, and teraphim, and a sculptured image and a molten image? Now you know what you have to do." [15]So they turned off there and entered the home of the young Levite at Micah's house and greeted him. [16]The six hundred Danite men, girt with their weapons of war, stood at the entrance of the gate, [17]while the five men who had gone to spy out the land went inside and took the sculptured image, the ephod, the teraphim, and the molten image. The priest was standing at the entrance of the gate, and the six hundred men girt with their weapons of war, [18]while those men entered Micah's house and took c-the sculptured image, the molten image, the ephod, and the household gods.-c The priest said to them, "What are you doing?" [19]But they said to him, "Be quiet; put your hand on your mouth! Come with us and be our father and priest. Would you rather be priest to one man's household or be priest to a tribe and clan in Israel?" [20]The priest was delighted. He took the ephod, the household gods, and the sculptured image, and he joined the people.

[21]They set out again, placing the children, the cattle, and their household goods in front. [22]They had already gone some distance from Micah's house, when the men in the houses near Micah's mustered and caught up with the Danites. [23]They called out to the Danites, who turned around and said to Micah, "What's the matter? Why have you mustered?" [24]He said, "You have taken my priest and the gods that I made, and walked off! What do I have left? How can you ask, 'What's the matter'?" [25]But the Danites replied, "Don't do any shouting at us, or some desperate men might attack you, and

עַד־בֵּית מִיכָה: [14] וַיַּעֲנ֡וּ חֲמֵ֣שֶׁת הָאֲנָשִׁ֣ים הַהֹלְכִים֩ לְרַגֵּ֨ל אֶת־הָאָ֜רֶץ לַ֗יִשׁ וַיֹּֽאמְרוּ֙ אֶל־אֲחֵיהֶ֔ם הַיְדַעְתֶּ֗ם כִּ֣י יֵ֣שׁ בַּבָּתִּ֣ים הָאֵ֗לֶּה אֵפ֤וֹד וּתְרָפִים֙ וּפֶ֣סֶל וּמַסֵּכָ֔ה וְעַתָּ֖ה דְּע֥וּ מַֽה־תַּעֲשֽׂוּ: [15] וַיָּסֻ֣רוּ שָׁ֗מָּה וַיָּבֹ֛אוּ אֶל־בֵּֽית־הַנַּ֥עַר הַלֵּוִ֖י בֵּ֣ית מִיכָ֑ה וַיִּשְׁאֲלוּ־ ל֖וֹ לְשָׁלֽוֹם: [16] וְשֵֽׁשׁ־מֵא֣וֹת אִ֗ישׁ חֲגוּרִים֙ כְּלֵ֣י מִלְחַמְתָּ֔ם נִצָּבִ֖ים פֶּ֣תַח הַשָּׁ֑עַר אֲשֶׁ֖ר מִבְּנֵי־דָֽן: [17] וַֽיַּעֲל֡וּ חֲמֵ֣שֶׁת הָאֲנָשִׁ֣ים הַהֹלְכִים֩ לְרַגֵּ֨ל אֶת־הָאָ֜רֶץ בָּ֣אוּ שָׁ֗מָּה לָקְח֗וּ אֶת־הַפֶּ֙סֶל֙ וְאֶת־הָ֣אֵפ֔וֹד וְאֶת־ הַתְּרָפִ֖ים וְאֶת־הַמַּסֵּכָ֑ה וְהַכֹּהֵ֗ן נִצָּב֙ פֶּ֣תַח הַשַּׁ֔עַר וְשֵֽׁשׁ־מֵא֣וֹת הָאִ֔ישׁ הֶחָג֖וּר כְּלֵ֥י הַמִּלְחָמָֽה: [18] וְאֵ֗לֶּה בָּ֚אוּ בֵּ֣ית מִיכָ֔ה וַיִּקְחוּ֙ אֶת־פֶּ֣סֶל הָאֵפ֔וֹד וְאֶת־הַתְּרָפִ֖ים וְאֶת־ הַמַּסֵּכָ֑ה וַיֹּ֤אמֶר אֲלֵיהֶם֙ הַכֹּהֵ֔ן מָ֥ה אַתֶּ֖ם עֹשִֽׂים: [19] וַיֹּאמְרוּ֩ ל֨וֹ הַחֲרֵ֜שׁ שִֽׂים־יָדְךָ֣ עַל־פִּ֗יךָ וְלֵ֣ךְ עִמָּ֔נוּ וֶהְיֵה־לָ֖נוּ לְאָ֣ב וּלְכֹהֵ֑ן הֲט֣וֹב | הֱיוֹתְךָ֣ כֹהֵ֗ן לְבֵית֙ אִ֣ישׁ אֶחָ֔ד א֚וֹ הֱיוֹתְךָ֣ כֹהֵ֔ן לְשֵׁ֥בֶט וּלְמִשְׁפָּחָ֖ה בְּיִשְׂרָאֵֽל: [20] וַיִּיטַב֙ לֵ֣ב הַכֹּהֵ֔ן וַיִּקַּח֙ אֶת־הָ֣אֵפ֔וֹד וְאֶת־הַתְּרָפִ֖ים וְאֶת־הַפָּ֑סֶל וַיָּבֹ֖א בְּקֶ֥רֶב הָעָֽם:

[21] וַיִּפְנ֖וּ וַיֵּלֵ֑כוּ וַיָּשִׂ֨ימוּ אֶת־הַטַּ֧ף וְאֶת־ הַמִּקְנֶ֛ה וְאֶת־הַכְּבוּדָּ֖ה לִפְנֵיהֶֽם: [22] הֵ֗מָּה הִרְחִ֙יקוּ֙ מִבֵּ֣ית מִיכָ֔ה וְהָאֲנָשִׁ֗ים אֲשֶׁ֤ר בַּבָּתִּים֙ אֲשֶׁר֙ עִם־בֵּ֣ית מִיכָ֔ה נִֽזְעֲק֔וּ וַיַּדְבִּ֖יקוּ אֶת־בְּנֵי־דָֽן: [23] וַֽיִּקְרְאוּ֙ אֶל־בְּנֵי־דָ֔ן וַיַּסֵּ֖בּוּ פְּנֵיהֶ֑ם וַיֹּאמְר֣וּ לְמִיכָ֔ה מַה־לְּךָ֖ כִּ֥י נִזְעָֽקְתָּ: [24] וַיֹּ֡אמֶר אֶת־אֱלֹהַי֩ אֲשֶׁר־עָשִׂ֨יתִי לְקַחְתֶּ֧ם וְאֶת־הַכֹּהֵ֛ן וַתֵּלְכ֖וּ וּמַה־לִּ֣י ע֑וֹד וּמַה־זֶּ֛ה תֹּאמְר֥וּ אֵלַ֖י מַה־לָּֽךְ: [25] וַיֹּאמְר֤וּ אֵלָיו֙ בְּנֵי־דָ֔ן אַל־תַּשְׁמַ֥ע קוֹלְךָ֖ עִמָּ֑נוּ פֶּֽן־ יִפְגְּע֣וּ בָכֶ֗ם אֲנָשִׁים֙ מָ֣רֵי נֶ֔פֶשׁ וְאָסַפְתָּ֥ה

---

c-c Lit. "the sculptured image of the ephod, and the household gods, and the molten image."

you and your family would lose your lives." ²⁶So Micah, realizing that they were stronger than he, turned back and went home; and the Danites went on their way, ²⁷taking the things Micah had made and the priest he had acquired. They proceeded to Laish, a people tranquil and unsuspecting, and they put them to the sword and burned down the town. ²⁸There was none to come to the rescue, for it was distant from Sidon and they had no dealings with anyone; it lay in the valley of Beth-rehob.

They rebuilt the town and settled there, ²⁹and they named the town Dan, after their ancestor Dan who was Israel's son. Originally, however, the name of the town was Laish. ³⁰The Danites set up the sculptured image for themselves; and Jonathan son of Gershom son of Manasseh,ᵈ and his descendants, served as priests to the Danite tribe until the land went into exile. ³¹They maintainedᵇ the sculptured image that Micah had made throughout the time that the House of God stood at Shiloh.

19

In those days, when there was no king in Israel, a Levite residing at the other end of the hill country of Ephraim took to himself a concubine from Bethlehem in Judah. ²Once his concubine desertedᵃ him, leaving him for her father's house in Bethlehem in Judah; and she stayed there a full four months. ³Then her husband set out, with an attendant and a pair of donkeys, and went after her to woo her and to win her back. She admitted him into her father's house; and when the girl's father saw him, he received him warmly. ⁴His father-in-law, the girl's father, pressed him, and he stayed with him three days; they ate and drank and lodged there. ⁵Early in the morning of the fourth day,

---

נַפְשְׁךָ֖ וְנֶ֣פֶשׁ בֵּיתֶֽךָ׃ 26 וַיֵּלְכ֥וּ בְנֵי־דָ֖ן לְדַרְכָּ֑ם וַיַּ֣רְא מִיכָ֗ה כִּֽי־חֲזָקִ֥ים הֵ֙מָּה֙ מִמֶּ֔נּוּ וַיִּ֖פֶן וַיָּ֥שָׁב אֶל־בֵּיתֽוֹ׃ 27 וְהֵ֡מָּה לָקְחוּ֩ אֵ֨ת אֲשֶׁר־עָשָׂ֜ה מִיכָ֗ה וְאֶֽת־הַכֹּהֵן֮ אֲשֶׁ֣ר הָיָה־ל֒וֹ וַיָּבֹ֣אוּ עַל־לַ֗יִשׁ עַל־עַם֙ שֹׁקֵ֣ט וּבֹטֵ֔חַ וַיַּכּ֥וּ אוֹתָ֖ם לְפִי־חָ֑רֶב וְאֶת־הָעִ֖יר שָׂרְפ֥וּ בָאֵֽשׁ׃ 28 וְאֵ֨ין מַצִּ֜יל כִּ֧י רְחֽוֹקָה־הִ֣יא מִצִּידֹ֗ון וְדָבָ֤ר אֵין־לָהֶם֙ עִם־אָדָ֔ם וְהִ֖יא בָּעֵ֕מֶק אֲשֶׁ֖ר לְבֵית־רְחֹ֑וב וַיִּבְנ֥וּ אֶת־הָעִ֖יר וַיֵּ֥שְׁבוּ בָֽהּ׃ 29 וַיִּקְרְא֤וּ שֵׁם־הָעִיר֙ דָּ֔ן בְּשֵׁם֙ דָּ֣ן אֲבִיהֶ֔ם אֲשֶׁ֥ר יוּלַּ֖ד לְיִשְׂרָאֵ֑ל וְאוּלָ֛ם לַ֥יִשׁ שֵׁם־הָעִ֖יר לָרִאשֹׁנָֽה׃ 30 וַיָּקִ֧ימוּ לָהֶ֛ם בְּנֵי־דָ֖ן אֶת־הַפָּ֑סֶל וִ֠יהוֹנָתָן בֶּן־גֵּרְשֹׁ֨ם בֶּן־מְנַשֶּׁ֜ה* ה֗וּא וּבָנָיו֙ הָי֣וּ כֹהֲנִ֔ים לְשֵׁ֖בֶט הַדָּנִ֑י עַד־יֹ֖ום גְּלֹ֥ות הָאָֽרֶץ׃ 31 וַיָּשִׂ֣ימוּ לָהֶ֔ם אֶת־פֶּ֖סֶל מִיכָ֑ה אֲשֶׁ֣ר עָשָׂ֔ה כָּל־יְמֵ֛י הֱיֹ֥ות בֵּית־הָאֱלֹהִ֖ים בְּשִׁלֹֽה׃ פ

יט וַיְהִי֙ בַּיָּמִ֣ים הָהֵ֔ם וּמֶ֖לֶךְ אֵ֣ין בְּיִשְׂרָאֵ֑ל וַיְהִ֣י ׀ אִ֣ישׁ לֵוִ֗י גָּ֚ר בְּיַרְכְּתֵ֣י הַר־אֶפְרַ֔יִם וַיִּֽקַּֽח־לֹו֙ אִשָּׁ֣ה פִילֶ֔גֶשׁ מִבֵּ֥ית לֶ֖חֶם יְהוּדָֽה׃ 2 וַתִּזְנֶ֤ה עָלָיו֙ פִּֽילַגְשֹׁ֔ו וַתֵּ֤לֶךְ מֵֽאִתֹּו֙ אֶל־בֵּ֣ית אָבִ֔יהָ אֶל־בֵּ֥ית לֶ֖חֶם יְהוּדָ֑ה וַתְּהִי־שָׁ֕ם יָמִ֖ים אַרְבָּעָ֥ה חֳדָשִֽׁים׃ 3 וַיָּ֨קָם אִישָׁ֜הּ וַיֵּ֣לֶךְ אַחֲרֶ֗יהָ לְדַבֵּ֤ר עַל־לִבָּהּ֙ לַהֲשִׁיבָ֔הּ וְנַעֲרֹ֥ו עִמֹּ֖ו וְצֶ֣מֶד חֲמֹרִ֑ים וַתְּבִיאֵ֙הוּ֙ בֵּ֣ית אָבִ֔יהָ וַיִּרְאֵ֙הוּ֙ אֲבִ֣י הַֽנַּעֲרָ֔ה וַיִּשְׂמַ֖ח לִקְרָאתֹֽו׃ 4 וַיֶּחֱזַק־בֹּ֤ו חֹֽתְנֹו֙ אֲבִ֣י הַֽנַּעֲרָ֔ה וַיֵּ֥שֶׁב אִתֹּ֖ו שְׁלֹ֣שֶׁת יָמִ֑ים וַיֹּאכְלוּ֙ וַיִּשְׁתּ֔וּ וַיָּלִ֖ינוּ שָֽׁם׃ 5 וַֽיְהִי֙ בַּיֹּ֣ום הָרְבִיעִ֔י וַיַּשְׁכִּ֣ימוּ בַבֹּ֔קֶר וַיָּ֖קָם לָלֶ֑כֶת

נ' תלויה   v. 30.

ᵈ   Heb. מנשה with נ suspended, indicating an earlier reading "Moses"; cf. Exod. 2.22.

ᵃ   Lit. "played the harlot."

he started to leave; but the girl's father said to his son-in-law, "Eat something to give you strength, then you can leave." [6]So the two of them sat down and they feasted together. Then the girl's father said to the man, "Won't you stay overnight and enjoy yourself?" [7]The man started to leave, but his father-in-law kept urging him until he turned back and spent the night there. [8]Early in the morning of the fifth day, he was about to leave, when the girl's father said, "Come, have a bite." The two of them ate, dawdling until past noon. [9]Then the man, his concubine, and his attendant started to leave. His father-in-law, the girl's father, said to him, "Look, the day is waning toward evening; do stop for the night. See, the day is declining; spend the night here and enjoy yourself. You can start early tomorrow on your journey and head for home."

[10]But the man refused to stay for the night. He set out and traveled as far as the vicinity of Jebus—that is, Jerusalem; he had with him a pair of laden donkeys, and his concubine [b]was with him.[b] [11]Since they were close to Jebus, and the day was very far spent, the attendant said to his master, "Let us turn aside to this town of the Jebusites and spend the night in it." [12]But his master said to him, "We will not turn aside to a town of aliens who are not of Israel, but will continue to Gibeah. [13]Come," he said to his attendant, "let us approach one of those places and spend the night either in Gibeah or in Ramah." [14]So they traveled on, and the sun set when they were near Gibeah of Benjamin.

[15]They turned off there and went in to spend the night in Gibeah. He went and sat down in the town square, but nobody took them indoors to spend the night. [16]In the evening, an old man came along from his property [c]outside the town.[c] (This man hailed from the hill country

וַיֹּ֨אמֶר֙ אֲבִ֣י הַֽנַּעֲרָ֔ה אֶל־חֲתָנ֔וֹ סְעָ֥ד לִבְּךָ֖ פַּת־לֶ֔חֶם וְאַחַ֖ר תֵּלֵֽכוּ׃ 6וַיֵּשְׁב֗וּ וַיֹּאכְל֤וּ שְׁנֵיהֶם֙ יַחְדָּ֔ו וַיִּשְׁתּ֑וּ וַיֹּ֨אמֶר֙ אֲבִ֣י הַֽנַּעֲרָ֔ה אֶל־הָאִ֔ישׁ הֽוֹאֶל־נָ֥א וְלִ֖ין וְיִטַ֥ב לִבֶּֽךָ׃ 7וַיָּ֥קָם הָאִ֖ישׁ לָלֶ֑כֶת וַיִּפְצַר־בּ֣וֹ חֹתְנ֔וֹ וַיָּ֥שָׁב וַיָּ֖לֶן שָֽׁם׃ 8וַיַּשְׁכֵּ֨ם בַּבֹּ֜קֶר בַּיּ֣וֹם הַחֲמִישִׁי֮ לָלֶכֶת֒ וַיֹּ֣אמֶר ׀ אֲבִ֣י הַֽנַּעֲרָ֗ה סְעָד־נָ֤א לְבָֽבְךָ֙ וְהִֽתְמַהְמְה֔וּ עַד־נְט֣וֹת הַיּ֑וֹם וַיֹּאכְל֖וּ שְׁנֵיהֶֽם׃ 9וַיָּ֤קָם הָאִישׁ֙ לָלֶ֣כֶת ה֔וּא וּפִֽילַגְשׁ֖וֹ וְנַעֲר֑וֹ וַיֹּ֣אמֶר ל֣וֹ חֹתְנ֣וֹ אֲבִ֣י הַֽנַּעֲרָ֡ה הִנֵּ֣ה נָא֩ רָפָ֨ה הַיּ֜וֹם לַעֲרֹ֗ב לִֽינוּ־נָ֞א הִנֵּ֨ה חֲנ֤וֹת הַיּוֹם֙ לִ֣ין פֹּ֔ה וְיִיטַ֖ב לְבָבֶ֑ךָ וְהִשְׁכַּמְתֶּ֤ם מָחָר֙ לְדַרְכְּכֶ֔ם וְהָלַכְתָּ֖ לְאֹהָלֶֽךָ׃ 10וְלֹֽא־אָבָ֤ה הָאִישׁ֙ לָל֔וּן וַיָּ֣קָם וַיֵּ֗לֶךְ וַיָּבֹא֙ עַד־נֹ֣כַח יְב֔וּס הִ֖יא יְרוּשָׁלָ֑͏ִם וְעִמּ֗וֹ צֶ֚מֶד חֲמוֹרִים֙ חֲבוּשִׁ֔ים וּפִילַגְשׁ֖וֹ עִמּֽוֹ׃ 11הֵ֣ם עִם־יְב֔וּס וְהַיּ֖וֹם רַ֣ד מְאֹ֑ד וַיֹּ֨אמֶר הַנַּ֜עַר אֶל־אֲדֹנָ֗יו לְכָה־נָּ֛א וְנָס֥וּרָה אֶל־עִֽיר־הַיְבוּסִ֥י הַזֹּ֖את וְנָלִ֥ין בָּֽהּ׃ 12וַיֹּ֤אמֶר אֵלָיו֙ אֲדֹנָ֔יו לֹ֤א נָסוּר֙ אֶל־עִ֣יר נָכְרִ֔י אֲשֶׁ֛ר לֹֽא־מִבְּנֵ֥י יִשְׂרָאֵ֖ל הֵ֑נָּה וְעָבַ֖רְנוּ עַד־גִּבְעָֽה׃ 13וַיֹּ֣אמֶר לְנַעֲר֔וֹ לֵ֥ךְ וְנִקְרְבָ֖ה בְּאַחַ֣ד הַמְּקֹמ֑וֹת וְלַ֥נּוּ בַגִּבְעָ֖ה א֥וֹ בָרָמָֽה׃ 14וַיַּעַבְר֖וּ וַיֵּלֵ֑כוּ וַתָּבֹ֤א לָהֶם֙ הַשֶּׁ֔מֶשׁ אֵ֥צֶל הַגִּבְעָ֖ה אֲשֶׁ֥ר לְבִנְיָמִֽן׃ 15וַיָּסֻ֣רוּ שָׁ֔ם לָב֖וֹא לָל֣וּן בַּגִּבְעָ֑ה וַיָּבֹ֗א וַיֵּ֙שֶׁב֙ בִּרְח֣וֹב הָעִ֔יר וְאֵ֥ין אִ֛ישׁ מְאַסֵּֽף־אוֹתָ֥ם הַבַּ֖יְתָה לָלֽוּן׃ 16וְהִנֵּ֣ה ׀ אִ֣ישׁ זָקֵ֗ן בָּ֣א מִֽן־מַעֲשֵׂ֤הוּ מִן־הַשָּׂדֶה֙ בָּעֶ֔רֶב וְהָאִישׁ֙ מֵהַ֣ר אֶפְרַ֔יִם וְהוּא־גָ֖ר בַּגִּבְעָ֑ה וְאַנְשֵׁ֥י

b-b Emendation yields "and his attendant."
c-c Lit. "in the field."

of Ephraim and resided at Gibeah, where the townspeople were Benjaminites.) [17]He happened to see the wayfarer in the town square. "Where," the old man inquired, "are you going to, and where do you come from?" [18]He replied, "We are traveling from Bethlehem in Judah to the other end of the hill country of Ephraim. That is where I live. I made a journey to Bethlehem of Judah, and now I am on my way d-to the House of the LORD,-d and nobody has taken me indoors. [19]We have both bruised straw and feed for our donkeys, and bread and wine for me and your handmaid,e and for the attendant f-with your servants.-f We lack nothing." [20]"Rest easy," said the old man. "Let me take care of all your needs. Do not on any account spend the night in the square." [21]And he took him into his house. He mixed fodder for the donkeys; then they bathed their feet and ate and drank.

[22]While they were enjoying themselves, the men of the town, a depraved lot, had gathered about the house and were pounding on the door. They called to the aged owner of the house, "Bring out the man who has come into your house, so that we can be intimate with him." [23]The owner of the house went out and said to them, "Please, my friends, do not commit such a wrong. Since this man has entered my house, do not perpetrate this outrage. [24]Look, here is my virgin daughter, and his concubine. Let me bring them out to you. Have your pleasure of them, do what you like with them; but don't do that outrageous thing to this man." [25]But the men would not listen to him, so the man seized his concubine and pushed her out to them. They raped her and abused her all night long until morning; and they let her go when dawn broke.

[26]Toward morning the woman came back; and as it was growing light, she collapsed at the

הַמָּק֖וֹם בְּנֵ֥י יְמִינִֽי׃ 17 וַיִּשָּׂ֣א עֵינָ֗יו וַיַּ֛רְא אֶת־הָאִ֥ישׁ הָאֹרֵ֖חַ בִּרְחֹ֣ב הָעִ֑יר וַיֹּ֨אמֶר הָאִ֤ישׁ הַזָּקֵן֙ אָ֣נָה תֵלֵ֔ךְ וּמֵאַ֖יִן תָּבֽוֹא׃ 18 וַיֹּ֣אמֶר אֵלָ֗יו עֹבְרִ֨ים אֲנַ֜חְנוּ מִבֵּֽית־לֶ֣חֶם יְהוּדָה֮ עַד־יַרְכְּתֵ֣י הַר־אֶפְרַיִם֒ מִשָּׁ֣ם אָנֹ֔כִי וָאֵלֵ֕ךְ עַד־בֵּ֥ית לֶ֖חֶם יְהוּדָ֑ה וְאֶת־בֵּ֤ית יְהוָה֙ אֲנִ֣י הֹלֵ֔ךְ וְאֵ֣ין אִ֔ישׁ מְאַסֵּ֥ף אוֹתִ֖י הַבָּֽיְתָה׃ 19 וְגַם־תֶּ֤בֶן גַּם־מִסְפּוֹא֙ יֵ֣שׁ לַחֲמוֹרֵ֔ינוּ וְ֠גַם לֶ֣חֶם וָיַ֤יִן יֶשׁ־לִי֙ וְלַֽאֲמָתֶ֔ךָ וְלַנַּ֖עַר עִם־עֲבָדֶ֑יךָ אֵ֥ין מַחְס֖וֹר כָּל־דָּבָֽר׃ 20 וַיֹּ֨אמֶר הָאִ֤ישׁ הַזָּקֵן֙ שָׁל֣וֹם לָ֔ךְ רַ֥ק כָּל־מַחְסוֹרְךָ֖ עָלָ֑י רַ֥ק בָּרְח֖וֹב אַל־תָּלַֽן׃ 21 וַיְבִיאֵ֣הוּ לְבֵית֔וֹ וַיָּ֖בָל לַחֲמוֹרִ֑ים וַֽיִּרְחֲצוּ֙ רַגְלֵיהֶ֔ם וַיֹּאכְל֖וּ וַיִּשְׁתּֽוּ׃ 22 הֵמָּה֮ מֵיטִיבִ֣ים אֶת־לִבָּם֒ וְהִנֵּה֩ אַנְשֵׁ֨י הָעִ֜יר אַנְשֵׁ֣י בְנֵֽי־בְלִיַּ֗עַל נָסַ֙בּוּ֙ אֶת־הַבַּ֔יִת מִֽתְדַּפְּקִ֖ים עַל־הַדָּ֑לֶת וַיֹּאמְר֗וּ אֶל־הָאִ֜ישׁ בַּ֤עַל הַבַּ֙יִת֙ הַזָּקֵ֣ן לֵאמֹ֔ר הוֹצֵ֗א אֶת־הָאִ֛ישׁ אֲשֶׁר־בָּ֥א אֶל־בֵּיתְךָ֖ וְנֵדָעֶֽנּוּ׃ 23 וַיֵּצֵ֣א אֲלֵיהֶ֗ם הָאִישׁ֙ בַּ֣עַל הַבַּ֔יִת וַיֹּ֣אמֶר אֲלֵהֶ֔ם אַל־אַחַ֖י אַל־תָּרֵ֣עוּ נָ֑א אַ֠חֲרֵי אֲשֶׁר־בָּ֞א הָאִ֤ישׁ הַזֶּה֙ אֶל־בֵּיתִ֔י אַֽל־תַּעֲשׂ֖וּ אֶת־הַנְּבָלָ֥ה הַזֹּֽאת׃ 24 הִנֵּה֩ בִתִּ֨י הַבְּתוּלָ֜ה וּפִֽילַגְשֵׁ֗הוּ אוֹצִֽיאָה־נָּ֤א אוֹתָם֙ וְעַנּ֣וּ אוֹתָ֔ם וַעֲשׂ֣וּ לָהֶ֔ם הַטּ֖וֹב בְּעֵינֵיכֶ֑ם וְלָאִ֤ישׁ הַזֶּה֙ לֹ֣א תַעֲשׂ֔וּ דְּבַ֖ר הַנְּבָלָ֥ה הַזֹּֽאת׃ 25 וְלֹֽא־אָב֤וּ הָאֲנָשִׁים֙ לִשְׁמֹ֣עַֽ ל֔וֹ וַיַּחֲזֵ֤ק הָאִישׁ֙ בְּפִ֣ילַגְשׁ֔וֹ וַיֹּצֵ֥א אֲלֵיהֶ֖ם הַח֑וּץ וַיֵּדְע֣וּ א֠וֹתָהּ וַיִּֽתְעַלְּלוּ־בָ֤הּ כָּל־הַלַּ֙יְלָה֙ עַד־הַבֹּ֔קֶר וַֽיְשַׁלְּח֖וּהָ בעלות כַּעֲל֥וֹת הַשָּֽׁחַר׃ 26 וַתָּבֹ֣א הָאִשָּׁ֔ה לִפְנ֖וֹת הַבֹּ֑קֶר וַתִּפֹּ֞ל פֶּ֧תַח בֵּית־הָאִ֛ישׁ אֲשֶׁר־אֲדוֹנֶ֥יהָ שָּׁ֖ם עַד־הָאֽוֹר׃

---

d-d Meaning of Heb. uncertain; emendation yields "to my home"; cf. v. 29.
e I.e., the concubine.
f-f I.e., "with us."

entrance of the man's house where her husband was. ²⁷When her husband arose in the morning, he opened the doors of the house and went out to continue his journey; and there was the woman, his concubine, lying at the entrance of the house, with her hands on the threshold. ²⁸"Get up," he said to her, "let us go." But there was no reply. So the man placed her on the donkey and set out for home. ²⁹When he came home, he picked up a knife, and took hold of his concubine and cut her up limb by limb into twelve parts. He sent them throughout the territory of Israel. ³⁰And everyone who saw it cried out, "Never has such a thing happened or been seen from the day the Israelites came out of the land of Egypt to this day! Put your mind to this; take counsel and decide."

20

Thereupon all the Israelites—from Dan to Beer-sheba and [from] the land of Gilead—marched forth, and the community assembled to a man before the Lord at Mizpah. ²All the leaders of the people [and] all the tribes of Israel presented themselves in the assembly of God's people, 400,000 fighting men on foot.—³The Benjaminites heard that the Israelites had come up to Mizpah.ᵃ—The Israelites said, "Tell us, how did this evil thing happen?" ⁴And the Levite, the husband of the murdered woman, replied, "My concubine and I came to Gibeah of Benjamin to spend the night. ⁵The citizens of Gibeah set out to harm me. They gathered against me around the house in the night; they meant to kill me, and they ravished my concubine until she died. ⁶So I took hold of my concubine and I cut her in pieces and sent them through every part of Israel's territory. For an outrageous act of depravity had been committed in Israel. ⁷Now you are all Israelites; produce a plan of action here and now!"

---

a   *This sentence is continued at v. 14 below.*

²⁷ וַיָּ֤קָם אֲדֹנֶ֙יהָ֙ בַּבֹּ֔קֶר וַיִּפְתַּח֙ דַּלְת֣וֹת הַבַּ֔יִת וַיֵּצֵ֖א לָלֶ֣כֶת לְדַרְכּ֑וֹ וְהִנֵּ֧ה הָאִשָּׁ֣ה פִֽילַגְשׁ֗וֹ נֹפֶ֙לֶת֙ פֶּ֣תַח הַבַּ֔יִת וְיָדֶ֖יהָ עַל־הַסַּֽף׃ ²⁸ וַיֹּ֧אמֶר אֵלֶ֛יהָ ק֥וּמִי וְנֵלֵ֖כָה וְאֵ֣ין עֹנֶ֑ה וַיִּקָּחֶ֙הָ֙ עַֽל־הַחֲמ֔וֹר וַיָּ֣קׇם הָאִ֔ישׁ וַיֵּ֖לֶךְ לִמְקֹמֽוֹ׃ ²⁹ וַיָּבֹ֣א אֶל־בֵּית֗וֹ וַיִּקַּ֤ח אֶת־הַֽמַּאֲכֶ֙לֶת֙ וַיַּחֲזֵ֣ק בְּפִֽילַגְשׁ֔וֹ וַֽיְנַתְּחֶ֙הָ֙ לַֽעֲצָמֶ֔יהָ לִשְׁנֵ֥ים עָשָׂ֖ר נְתָחִ֑ים וַֽיְשַׁלְּחֶ֔הָ בְּכֹ֖ל גְּב֥וּל יִשְׂרָאֵֽל׃ ³⁰ וְהָיָ֣ה כׇל־הָֽרֹאֶ֗ה וְאָמַר֙ לֹֽא־נִהְיְתָ֤ה וְלֹֽא־נִרְאֲתָה֙ כָּזֹ֔את לְמִיּ֞וֹם עֲל֤וֹת בְּנֵֽי־יִשְׂרָאֵל֙ מֵאֶ֣רֶץ מִצְרַ֔יִם עַ֖ד הַיּ֣וֹם הַזֶּ֑ה שִֽׂימוּ־לָכֶ֥ם עָלֶ֖יהָ עֻ֥צוּ וְדַבֵּֽרוּ׃ פ

כ

וַיֵּֽצְאוּ֮ כׇּל־בְּנֵ֣י יִשְׂרָאֵל֒ וַתִּקָּהֵ֣ל הָעֵדָ֗ה כְּאִ֣ישׁ אֶחָ֔ד לְמִדָּ֥ן וְעַד־בְּאֵ֖ר שֶׁ֑בַע וְאֶ֣רֶץ הַגִּלְעָ֔ד אֶל־יְהֹוָ֖ה הַמִּצְפָּֽה׃ ² וַיִּֽתְיַצְּב֞וּ פִּנּ֣וֹת כׇּל־הָעָ֗ם כֹּ֚ל שִׁבְטֵ֣י יִשְׂרָאֵ֔ל בִּקְהַ֖ל עַ֣ם הָאֱלֹהִ֑ים אַרְבַּ֨ע מֵא֥וֹת אֶ֛לֶף אִ֥ישׁ רַגְלִ֖י שֹׁ֥לֵֽף חָֽרֶב׃ פ ³ וַֽיִּשְׁמְעוּ֙ בְּנֵ֣י בִנְיָמִ֔ן כִּֽי־עָל֥וּ בְנֵֽי־יִשְׂרָאֵ֖ל הַמִּצְפָּ֑ה וַיֹּֽאמְרוּ֙ בְּנֵ֣י יִשְׂרָאֵ֔ל דַּבְּר֕וּ אֵיכָ֥ה נִהְיְתָ֖ה הָרָעָ֥ה הַזֹּֽאת׃ ⁴ וַיַּ֜עַן הָאִ֣ישׁ הַלֵּוִ֗י אִ֛ישׁ הָאִשָּׁ֥ה הַנִּרְצָחָ֖ה וַיֹּאמַ֑ר הַגִּבְעָ֙תָה֙ אֲשֶׁ֣ר לְבִנְיָמִ֔ן בָּ֛אתִי אֲנִ֥י וּפִֽילַגְשִׁ֖י לָלֽוּן׃ ⁵ וַיָּקֻ֤מוּ עָלַי֙ בַּעֲלֵ֣י הַגִּבְעָ֔ה וַיָּסֹ֧בּוּ עָלַ֛י אֶת־הַבַּ֖יִת לָ֑יְלָה אוֹתִ֣י דִּמּ֣וּ לַהֲרֹ֔ג וְאֶת־פִּילַגְשִׁ֥י עִנּ֖וּ וַתָּמֹֽת׃ ⁶ וָֽאֹחֵ֣ז בְּפִֽילַגְשִׁ֗י וָֽאֲנַתְּחֶ֙הָ֙ וָֽאֲשַׁלְּחֶ֔הָ בְּכׇל־שְׂדֵ֖ה נַחֲלַ֣ת יִשְׂרָאֵ֑ל כִּ֥י עָשׂ֛וּ זִמָּ֥ה וּנְבָלָ֖ה בְּיִשְׂרָאֵֽל׃ ⁷ הִנֵּ֥ה כֻלְּכֶ֖ם בְּנֵ֣י יִשְׂרָאֵ֑ל הָב֥וּ לָכֶ֛ם דָּבָ֥ר וְעֵצָ֖ה הֲלֹֽם׃

⁸Then all the people rose, as one man, and declared, "We will not go back to our homes, we will not enter our houses! ⁹But this is what we will do to Gibeah: [we will wage war] against it according to lot. ¹⁰We will take from all the tribes of Israel ten men to the hundred, a hundred to the thousand, and a thousand to the ten thousand to supply provisions for the troops—^bto prepare for their going to Geba in Benjamin-^b for all the outrage it has committed in Israel." ¹¹So all the men of Israel, united as one man, massed against the town. ¹²And the tribes of Israel sent men through the whole tribe^c of Benjamin, saying, "What is this evil thing that has happened among you? ¹³Come, hand over those scoundrels in Gibeah so that we may put them to death and stamp out the evil from Israel." But the Benjaminites would not yield to the demand of their fellow Israelites.

¹⁴So the Benjaminites gathered from their towns to Gibeah in order to take the field against the Israelites. ^{15d}On that day the Benjaminites mustered from the towns 26,000 fighting men, mustered apart from the inhabitants of Gibeah; 700 picked men ¹⁶of all this force—700 picked men—were left-handed. Every one of them could sling a stone at a hair and not miss. ¹⁷The men of Israel other than Benjamin mustered 400,000 fighting men, warriors to a man. ¹⁸They proceeded to Bethel and inquired of God; the Israelites asked, "Who of us shall advance first to fight the Benjaminites?" And the LORD replied, "Judah first." ¹⁹So the Israelites arose in the morning and encamped against Gibeah.

²⁰The men of Israel took the field against the Benjaminites; the men of Israel drew up in battle order against them at Gibeah. ²¹But the Benjaminites issued from Gibeah, and that day they struck down 22,000 men of Israel.

---

b-b Emendation yields "for those who go to requite Gibeah."
c   Heb. plural.
d   Meaning of parts of vv. 15 and 16 uncertain.

8 וַיָּ֣קָם כָּל־הָעָם֮ כְּאִ֣ישׁ אֶחָד֮ לֵאמֹר֒ לֹ֣א נֵלֵ֗ךְ אִ֣ישׁ לְאָהֳל֔וֹ וְלֹ֥א נָס֖וּר אִ֥ישׁ לְבֵיתֽוֹ: 9 וְעַתָּ֕ה זֶ֣ה הַדָּבָ֔ר אֲשֶׁ֥ר נַעֲשֶׂ֖ה לַגִּבְעָ֑ה עָלֶ֖יהָ בְּגוֹרָֽל: 10 וְלָקַ֣חְנוּ עֲשָׂרָה֩ אֲנָשִׁ֨ים לַמֵּאָ֜ה לְכֹ֣ל ׀ שִׁבְטֵ֣י יִשְׂרָאֵ֗ל וּמֵאָ֤ה לָאֶ֙לֶף֙ וְאֶ֣לֶף לָרְבָבָ֔ה לָקַ֥חַת צֵדָ֖ה לָעָ֑ם לַעֲשׂ֗וֹת לְבוֹאָם֙ לְגֶ֣בַע בִּנְיָמִ֔ן כְּכָל־הַנְּבָלָ֕ה אֲשֶׁ֥ר עָשָׂ֖ה בְּיִשְׂרָאֵֽל: 11 וַיֵּֽאָסֵ֞ף כָּל־אִ֤ישׁ יִשְׂרָאֵל֙ אֶל־הָעִ֔יר כְּאִ֥ישׁ אֶחָ֖ד חֲבֵרִֽים: פ 12 וַֽיִּשְׁלְח֞וּ שִׁבְטֵ֤י יִשְׂרָאֵל֙ אֲנָשִׁ֔ים בְּכָל־שִׁבְטֵ֖י בִנְיָמִ֣ן לֵאמֹ֑ר מָ֚ה הָרָעָ֣ה הַזֹּ֔את אֲשֶׁ֥ר נִהְיְתָ֖ה בָּכֶֽם: 13 וְעַתָּ֡ה תְּנוּ֩ אֶת־הָאֲנָשִׁ֨ים בְּנֵֽי־בְלִיַּ֜עַל אֲשֶׁ֤ר בַּגִּבְעָה֙ וּנְמִיתֵ֔ם וּנְבַעֲרָ֥ה רָעָ֖ה מִיִּשְׂרָאֵ֑ל וְלֹ֤א אָבוּ֙ [בְּנֵ֣י*] בִּנְיָמִ֔ן לִשְׁמֹ֕עַ בְּק֖וֹל אֲחֵיהֶ֥ם בְּנֵֽי־יִשְׂרָאֵֽל:

14 וַיֵּאָסְפ֧וּ בְנֵֽי־בִנְיָמִ֛ן מִן־הֶעָרִ֖ים הַגִּבְעָ֑תָה לָצֵ֥את לַמִּלְחָמָ֖ה עִם־בְּנֵ֥י יִשְׂרָאֵֽל: 15 וַיִּתְפָּֽקְד֞וּ בְנֵ֤י בִנְיָמִן֙ בַּיּ֣וֹם הַה֔וּא מֵהֶ֣עָרִ֔ים עֶשְׂרִ֧ים וְשִׁשָּׁ֛ה אֶ֥לֶף אִ֖ישׁ שֹׁ֣לֵֽף חָ֑רֶב לְבַ֗ד מִיֹּשְׁבֵ֤י הַגִּבְעָה֙ הִתְפָּ֣קְד֔וּ שְׁבַ֥ע מֵא֖וֹת אִ֥ישׁ בָּחֽוּר: 16 מִכֹּ֣ל ׀ הָעָ֣ם הַזֶּ֗ה שְׁבַ֤ע מֵאוֹת֙ אִ֣ישׁ בָּח֔וּר אִטֵּ֖ר יַד־יְמִינ֑וֹ כָּל־זֶ֗ה קֹלֵ֧עַ בָּאֶ֛בֶן אֶל־הַֽשַּׂעֲרָ֖ה וְלֹ֥א יַחֲטִֽא: פ 17 וְאִ֨ישׁ יִשְׂרָאֵ֜ל הִתְפָּ֣קְד֗וּ לְבַד֙ מִבִּנְיָמִ֔ן אַרְבַּ֥ע מֵא֛וֹת אֶ֖לֶף אִ֣ישׁ שֹׁ֣לֵֽף חָ֑רֶב כָּל־זֶ֖ה אִ֥ישׁ מִלְחָמָֽה: 18 וַיָּקֻ֜מוּ וַיַּעֲל֣וּ בֵית־אֵל֮ וַיִּשְׁאֲל֣וּ בֵאלֹהִים֒ וַיֹּֽאמְרוּ֙ בְּנֵ֣י יִשְׂרָאֵ֔ל מִ֚י יַעֲלֶה־לָּ֣נוּ בַתְּחִלָּ֔ה לַמִּלְחָמָ֖ה עִם־בְּנֵ֣י בִנְיָמִ֑ן וַיֹּ֥אמֶר יְהוָ֖ה יְהוּדָ֥ה בַתְּחִלָּֽה: 19 וַיָּק֥וּמוּ בְנֵֽי־יִשְׂרָאֵ֖ל בַּבֹּ֑קֶר וַיַּחֲנ֖וּ עַל־הַגִּבְעָֽה: פ

20 וַיֵּצֵא֙ אִ֣ישׁ יִשְׂרָאֵ֔ל לַמִּלְחָמָ֖ה עִם־בִּנְיָמִ֑ן וַיַּעַרְכ֨וּ אִתָּ֧ם אִֽישׁ־יִשְׂרָאֵ֛ל מִלְחָמָ֖ה אֶל־הַגִּבְעָֽה: 21 וַיֵּצְא֥וּ בְנֵֽי־בִנְיָמִ֖ן מִן־הַגִּבְעָ֑ה וַיַּשְׁחִ֩יתוּ֩ בְיִשְׂרָאֵ֨ל בַּיּ֤וֹם הַהוּא֙ שְׁנַ֣יִם וְעֶשְׂרִ֥ים אֶ֖לֶף אִ֥ישׁ אָֽרְצָה:

22Now the army—the men of Israel—rallied and again drew up in battle order at the same place as they had on the first day. 23For the Israelites had gone up and wept before the LORD until evening. They had inquired of the LORD, "Shall we again join battle with our kinsmen the Benjaminites?" And the LORD had replied, "March against them." 24The Israelites advanced against the Benjaminites on the second day. 25But the Benjaminites came out from Gibeah against them on the second day and struck down 18,000 more of the Israelites, all of them fighting men.

26Then all the Israelites, all the army, went up and came to Bethel and they sat there, weeping before the LORD. They fasted that day until evening, and presented burnt offerings and offerings of well-being to the LORD. 27The Israelites inquired of the LORD (for the Ark of God's Covenant was there in those days, 28and Phinehas son of Eleazar son of Aaron the priest ministered before Him in those days), "Shall we again take the field against our kinsmen the Benjaminites, or shall we not?" The LORD answered, "Go up, for tomorrow I will deliver them into your hands."

29Israel put men in ambush against Gibeah on all sides. 30And on the third day, the Israelites went up against the Benjaminites, as before, and engaged them in battle at Gibeah. 31The Benjaminites dashed out to meet the army and were drawn away from the town onto the roads, of which one runs to Bethel and the other to Gibeah. As before, they started out by striking some of the men dead in the open field, about 30 men of Israel.

32The Benjaminites thought, "They are being routed before us as previously." But the Israelites had planned: "We will take to flight and draw them away from the town to the roads." 33And while the main body of the Israelites had

22 וַיִּתְחַזֵּ֤ק הָעָם֙ אִ֣ישׁ יִשְׂרָאֵ֔ל וַיֹּסִ֖פוּ לַעֲרֹ֣ךְ מִלְחָמָ֑ה בַּמָּק֕וֹם אֲשֶׁר־עָ֥רְכוּ שָׁ֖ם בַּיּ֥וֹם הָרִאשֽׁוֹן׃ 23 וַיַּעֲל֣וּ בְנֵֽי־יִשְׂרָאֵ֗ל וַיִּבְכּ֣וּ לִפְנֵֽי־יְהֹוָה֮ עַד־הָעֶרֶב֒ וַיִּשְׁאֲל֤וּ בַֽיהֹוָה֙ לֵאמֹ֔ר הַאוֹסִ֗יף לָגֶ֙שֶׁת֙ לַמִּלְחָמָ֔ה עִם־בְּנֵ֥י בִנְיָמִ֖ן אָחִ֑י וַיֹּ֥אמֶר יְהֹוָ֖ה עֲל֥וּ אֵלָֽיו׃ פ 24 וַיִּקְרְב֧וּ בְנֵֽי־יִשְׂרָאֵ֛ל אֶל־בְּנֵ֥י בִנְיָמִ֖ן בַּיּ֥וֹם הַשֵּׁנִֽי׃ 25 וַיֵּצֵא֩ בִנְיָמִ֨ן ׀ לִקְרָאתָ֥ם ׀ מִן־הַגִּבְעָה֮ בַּיּ֣וֹם הַשֵּׁנִי֒ וַיַּשְׁחִ֩יתוּ֩ בִבְנֵ֨י יִשְׂרָאֵ֜ל ע֗וֹד שְׁמֹנַ֨ת עָשָׂ֥ר אֶ֛לֶף אִ֖ישׁ אָ֑רְצָה כׇּל־אֵ֖לֶּה שֹׁ֥לְפֵי חָֽרֶב׃ 26 וַיַּעֲל֣וּ כׇל־בְּנֵי֩ יִשְׂרָאֵ֨ל וְכׇל־הָעָ֜ם וַיָּבֹ֣אוּ בֵֽית־אֵ֗ל וַיִּבְכּוּ֙ וַיֵּ֤שְׁבוּ שָׁם֙ לִפְנֵ֣י יְהֹוָ֔ה וַיָּצ֥וּמוּ בַיּוֹם־הַה֖וּא עַד־הָעָ֑רֶב וַֽיַּעֲל֛וּ עֹל֥וֹת וּשְׁלָמִ֖ים לִפְנֵ֥י יְהֹוָֽה׃ 27 וַיִּשְׁאֲל֥וּ בְנֵֽי־יִשְׂרָאֵ֖ל בַּֽיהֹוָ֑ה וְשָׁ֗ם אֲרוֹן֙ בְּרִ֣ית הָֽאֱלֹהִ֔ים בַּיָּמִ֖ים הָהֵֽם׃ 28 וּ֠פִֽינְחָ֠ס בֶּן־אֶלְעָזָ֨ר בֶּֽן־אַהֲרֹ֜ן עֹמֵ֣ד ׀ לְפָנָ֗יו בַּיָּמִ֣ים הָהֵם֮ לֵאמֹר֒ הַאוֹסִ֨ף ע֜וֹד לָצֵ֤את לַמִּלְחָמָה֙ עִם־בְּנֵֽי־בִנְיָמִ֣ן אָחִ֔י אִם־אֶחְדָּ֑ל וַיֹּ֤אמֶר יְהֹוָה֙ עֲל֔וּ כִּ֥י מָחָ֖ר אֶתְּנֶ֥נּוּ בְיָדֶֽךָ׃ 29 וַיָּ֤שֶׂם יִשְׂרָאֵל֙ אֹֽרְבִ֔ים אֶל־הַגִּבְעָ֖ה סָבִֽיב׃ פ 30 וַיַּעֲל֧וּ בְנֵֽי־יִשְׂרָאֵ֛ל אֶל־בְּנֵ֥י בִנְיָמִ֖ן בַּיּ֣וֹם הַשְּׁלִישִׁ֑י וַיַּעַרְכ֥וּ אֶל־הַגִּבְעָ֖ה כְּפַ֥עַם בְּפָֽעַם׃ 31 וַיֵּצְא֤וּ בְנֵֽי־בִנְיָמִן֙ לִקְרַ֣את הָעָ֔ם הׇנְתְּק֖וּ מִן־הָעִ֑יר וַיָּחֵ֡לּוּ לְהַכּוֹת֩ מֵהָעָ֨ם חֲלָלִ֜ים כְּפַ֣עַם ׀ בְּפַ֗עַם בַּֽמְסִלּוֹת֙ אֲשֶׁ֨ר אַחַ֜ת עֹלָ֣ה בֵֽית־אֵ֗ל וְאַחַ֤ת גִּבְעָ֙תָה֙ בַּשָּׂדֶ֔ה כִּשְׁלֹשִׁ֥ים אִ֖ישׁ בְּיִשְׂרָאֵֽל׃ 32 וַיֹּֽאמְרוּ֙ בְּנֵ֣י בִנְיָמִ֔ן נִגָּפִ֥ים הֵ֖ם לְפָנֵ֑ינוּ כְּבָרִ֣אשֹׁנָ֑ה וּבְנֵ֧י יִשְׂרָאֵ֣ל אָמְר֗וּ נָנ֙וּסָה֙ וּֽנְתַקְּנֻ֔הוּ מִן־הָעִ֖יר אֶל־הַֽמְסִלּֽוֹת׃ 33 וְכֹ֣ל ׀ אִ֣ישׁ יִשְׂרָאֵ֗ל קָ֚מוּ מִמְּק֔וֹמוֹ וַיַּעַרְכ֖וּ בְּבַ֣עַל

moved away from their positions and had drawn up in battle order at Baal-tamar, the Israelite ambush was rushing out from its position at Maareh-geba.*e* *34*Thus 10,000 picked men of all Israel came to a point south of*f* Gibeah, and the battle was furious. Before they realized that disaster was approaching, *35*the LORD routed the Benjaminites before Israel. That day the Israelites slew 25,100 men of Benjamin, all of them fighting men. *36*Then the Benjaminites realized that they were routed.*g* Now the Israelites had yielded ground to the Benjaminites, for they relied on the ambush which they had laid against Gibeah. *37*One ambush quickly deployed against Gibeah, and the other ambush advanced and put the whole town to the sword.

*38*A time had been agreed upon by the Israelite men with those in ambush: When a huge column of smoke was sent up from the town, *39*the Israelite men were to turn about in battle. Benjamin had begun by striking dead about 30 Israelite men, and they thought, "They are being routed before us as in the previous fighting." *40*But when the column, the pillar of smoke, began to rise from the city, the Benjaminites looked behind them, and there was the whole town going up in smoke to the sky! *41*And now the Israelites turned about, and the men of Benjamin were thrown into panic, for they realized that disaster had overtaken them. *42*They retreated before the men of Israel along the road to the wilderness, where the fighting caught up with them; meanwhile those *h*-from the towns-*h* were massacring them in it. *43i*They encircled the Benjaminites, pursued them, and trod them down [from] Menuhah to a point opposite

תָּמָ֑ר וְאֹרֵ֣ב יִשְׂרָאֵ֗ל מֵגִ֛יחַ מִמְּקֹמ֖וֹ מִֽמַּעֲרֵה־גָֽבַע: 34 וַיָּבֹ֩אוּ֩ מִנֶּ֨גֶד* לַגִּבְעָ֜ה עֲשֶׂ֤רֶת אֲלָפִים֙ אִ֣ישׁ בָּח֔וּר מִכָּל־יִשְׂרָאֵ֔ל וְהַמִּלְחָמָ֖ה כָּבֵ֑דָה וְהֵ֣ם לֹ֣א יָדְע֔וּ כִּֽי־נֹגַ֥עַת עֲלֵיהֶ֖ם הָרָעָֽה: פ 35 וַיִּגֹּ֨ף יְהֹוָ֣ה ׀ אֶֽת־בִּנְיָמִן֮ לִפְנֵ֣י יִשְׂרָאֵל֒ וַיַּשְׁחִ֩יתוּ֩ בְנֵ֨י יִשְׂרָאֵ֤ל בְּבִנְיָמִן֙ בַּיּ֣וֹם הַה֔וּא עֶשְׂרִ֨ים וַחֲמִשָּׁ֥ה אֶ֛לֶף וּמֵאָ֖ה אִ֑ישׁ כָּל־אֵ֖לֶּה שֹׁ֥לֵֽף חָֽרֶב: 36 וַיִּרְא֥וּ בְנֵֽי־בִנְיָמִ֖ן כִּ֣י נִגָּ֑פוּ וַיִּתְּנ֨וּ אִֽישׁ־יִשְׂרָאֵ֤ל מָקוֹם֙ לְבִנְיָמִ֔ן כִּ֤י בָֽטְחוּ֙ אֶל־הָ֣אֹרֵ֔ב אֲשֶׁ֣ר שָׂ֔מוּ אֶל־הַגִּבְעָֽה: 37 וְהָֽאֹרֵ֣ב הֵחִ֔ישׁוּ וַֽיִּפְשְׁט֖וּ אֶל־הַגִּבְעָ֑ה וַיִּמְשֹׁךְ֙ הָאֹרֵ֔ב וַיַּ֥ךְ אֶת־כָּל־הָעִ֖יר לְפִי־חָֽרֶב:

38 וְהַמּוֹעֵ֗ד הָיָ֛ה לְאִ֥ישׁ יִשְׂרָאֵ֖ל עִם־הָאֹרֵ֑ב הֶ֕רֶב לְהַעֲלוֹתָ֛ם מַשְׂאַ֥ת הֶעָשָׁ֖ן מִן־הָעִֽיר: 39 וַיַּהֲפֹ֥ךְ אִֽישׁ־יִשְׂרָאֵ֖ל בַּמִּלְחָמָ֑ה וּבִנְיָמִ֡ן הֵחֵל֩ לְהַכּ֨וֹת חֲלָלִ֤ים בְּאִֽישׁ־יִשְׂרָאֵל֙ כִּשְׁלֹשִׁ֣ים אִ֔ישׁ כִּ֣י אָֽמְר֔וּ אַךְ֙ נִגּ֤וֹף נִגָּף֙ ה֔וּא לְפָנֵ֔ינוּ כַּמִּלְחָמָ֖ה הָרִֽאשֹׁנָֽה: 40 וְהַמַּשְׂאֵ֗ת הֵחֵ֛לָּה לַעֲל֥וֹת מִן־הָעִ֖יר עַמּ֣וּד עָשָׁ֑ן וַיִּ֤פֶן בִּנְיָמִן֙ אַחֲרָ֔יו וְהִנֵּ֛ה עָלָ֥ה כְלִֽיל־הָעִ֖יר הַשָּׁמָֽיְמָה: 41 וְאִ֤ישׁ יִשְׂרָאֵל֙ הָפַ֔ךְ וַיִּבָּהֵ֖ל אִ֣ישׁ בִּנְיָמִ֑ן כִּ֣י רָאָ֔ה כִּֽי־נָגְעָ֥ה עָלָ֖יו הָרָעָֽה: 42 וַיִּפְנ֞וּ לִפְנֵ֨י אִ֤ישׁ יִשְׂרָאֵל֙ אֶל־דֶּ֣רֶךְ הַמִּדְבָּ֔ר וְהַמִּלְחָמָ֖ה הִדְבִּיקָ֑תְהוּ וַאֲשֶׁר֙ מֵהֶ֣עָרִ֔ים מַשְׁחִיתִ֥ים אוֹת֖וֹ בְּתוֹכֽוֹ: 43 כִּתְּר֣וּ אֶת־בִּנְיָמִ֗ן הִרְדִיפֻ֙הוּ֙ מְנוּחָ֔ה הִדְרִיכֻ֕הוּ עַ֖ד נֹ֣כַח הַגִּבְעָ֑ה מִמִּזְרַח־שָֽׁמֶשׁ:

---

e   *Emendation yields "west of Gibeah."*
f   *So many Heb. mss. and Targum; most mss. and the editions read "opposite."*
g   *This sentence is continued by v. 45.*
h-h   *Meaning of Heb. uncertain; emendation yields "in the town" (i.e., Gibeah).*
i   *Meaning of verse uncertain.*

v. 34. בנוסח אחר "מנגב"

Gibeah on the east. 44That day 18,000 men of Benjamin fell, all of them brave men. 45They turned and fled to the wilderness, to the Rock of Rimmon; but [the Israelites] picked off another 5,000 on the roads and, continuing in hot pursuit of them up to Gidom, they slew 2,000 more. 46Thus the total number of Benjaminites who fell that day came to 25,000 fighting men, all of them brave. 47But 600 men turned and fled to the wilderness, to the Rock of Rimmon; they remained at the Rock of Rimmon four months. 48The men of Israel, meanwhile, turned back to the rest of the Benjaminites and put them to the sword—towns, people, cattle—everything that remained. Finally, they set fire to all the towns that were left.

21

Now the men of Israel had taken an oath at Mizpah: "None of us will give his daughter in marriage to a Benjaminite."

2The people came to Bethel and sat there before God until evening. They wailed and wept bitterly, 3and they said, "O Lord God of Israel, why has this happened in Israel, that one tribe must now be missing from Israel?" 4Early the next day, the people built an altar there, and they brought burnt offerings and offerings of well-being.

5The Israelites asked, "Is there anyone from all the tribes of Israel who failed to come up to the assembly before the Lord?" For a solemn oath had been taken concerning anyone who did not go up to the Lord at Mizpah: "He shall be put to death." 6The Israelites now relented toward their kinsmen the Benjaminites, and they said, "This day one tribe has been cut off from Israel! 7What can we do to provide wives for those who are left, seeing that we have sworn by the Lord not to give any of our daughters to them in marriage?"

44 וַיִּפְּל֣וּ מִבִּנְיָמִ֔ן שְׁמֹנָֽה־עָשָׂ֥ר אֶ֖לֶף אִ֑ישׁ אֶת־כָּל־אֵ֖לֶּה אַנְשֵׁי־חָֽיִל׃ 45 וַיִּפְנ֞וּ וַיָּנֻ֤סוּ הַמִּדְבָּ֙רָה֙ אֶל־סֶ֣לַע הָֽרִמּ֔וֹן וַיְעֹֽלְלֻ֙הוּ֙ בַּֽמְסִלּ֔וֹת חֲמֵ֥שֶׁת אֲלָפִ֖ים אִ֑ישׁ וַיַּדְבִּ֤יקוּ אַֽחֲרָיו֙ עַד־גִּדְעֹ֔ם וַיַּכּ֥וּ מִמֶּ֖נּוּ אַלְפַּ֥יִם אִֽישׁ׃ 46 וַיְהִ֞י כָל־הַנֹּֽפְלִ֤ים מִבִּנְיָמִן֙ עֶשְׂרִ֤ים וַֽחֲמִשָּׁ֣ה אֶ֣לֶף אִ֗ישׁ שֹׁ֚לֵֽף חֶ֔רֶב בַּיּ֖וֹם הַה֑וּא אֶת־כָּל־אֵ֖לֶּה אַנְשֵׁי־חָֽיִל׃ 47 וַיִּפְנ֞וּ וַיָּנֻ֤סוּ הַמִּדְבָּ֙רָה֙ אֶל־סֶ֣לַע הָֽרִמּ֔וֹן שֵׁ֥שׁ מֵא֖וֹת אִ֑ישׁ וַיֵּֽשְׁבוּ֙ בְּסֶ֣לַע רִמּ֔וֹן אַרְבָּעָ֥ה חֳדָשִֽׁים׃ 48 וְאִ֨ישׁ יִשְׂרָאֵ֜ל שָׁ֣בוּ אֶל־בְּנֵ֤י בִנְיָמִן֙ וַיַּכּ֣וּם לְפִי־חֶ֔רֶב מֵעִ֤יר מְתֹם֙ עַד־בְּהֵמָ֔ה עַ֖ד כָּל־הַנִּמְצָ֑א גַּ֛ם כָּל־הֶֽעָרִ֥ים הַנִּמְצָא֖וֹת שִׁלְּח֥וּ בָאֵֽשׁ׃ פ

כא וְאִ֣ישׁ יִשְׂרָאֵ֗ל נִשְׁבַּ֛ע בַּמִּצְפָּ֖ה לֵאמֹ֑ר אִ֣ישׁ מִמֶּ֔נּוּ לֹֽא־יִתֵּ֥ן בִּתּ֛וֹ לְבִנְיָמִ֖ן לְאִשָּֽׁה׃ 2 וַיָּבֹ֤א הָעָם֙ בֵּֽית־אֵ֔ל וַיֵּ֤שְׁבוּ שָׁם֙ עַד־הָעֶ֔רֶב לִפְנֵ֖י הָֽאֱלֹהִ֑ים וַיִּשְׂא֣וּ קוֹלָ֔ם וַיִּבְכּ֖וּ בְּכִ֥י גָדֽוֹל׃ 3 וַיֹּ֣אמְר֔וּ לָמָ֗ה יְהֹוָה֙ אֱלֹהֵ֣י יִשְׂרָאֵ֔ל הָ֥יְתָה זֹּ֖את בְּיִשְׂרָאֵ֑ל לְהִפָּקֵ֥ד הַיּ֛וֹם מִיִּשְׂרָאֵ֖ל שֵׁ֥בֶט אֶחָֽד׃ 4 וַיְהִי֙ מִֽמָּֽחֳרָ֔ת וַיַּשְׁכִּ֣ימוּ הָעָ֔ם וַיִּבְנוּ־שָׁ֖ם מִזְבֵּ֑חַ וַיַּֽעֲל֥וּ עֹל֖וֹת וּשְׁלָמִֽים׃ פ 5 וַיֹּֽאמְרוּ֙ בְּנֵ֣י יִשְׂרָאֵ֔ל מִ֗י אֲשֶׁ֧ר לֹֽא־עָלָ֛ה בַקָּהָ֖ל מִכָּל־שִׁבְטֵ֣י יִשְׂרָאֵ֑ל אֶל־יְהֹוָ֔ה כִּי֩ הַשְּׁבוּעָ֨ה הַגְּדוֹלָ֜ה הָֽיְתָ֗ה לַֽאֲשֶׁ֤ר לֹֽא־עָלָה֙ אֶל־יְהֹוָ֣ה הַמִּצְפָּ֔ה לֵאמֹ֖ר מ֥וֹת יוּמָֽת׃ 6 וַיִּנָּֽחֲמוּ֙ בְּנֵ֣י יִשְׂרָאֵ֔ל אֶל־בִּנְיָמִ֖ן אָחִ֑יו וַיֹּ֣אמְר֔וּ נִגְדַּ֥ע הַיּ֛וֹם שֵׁ֥בֶט אֶחָ֖ד מִיִּשְׂרָאֵֽל׃ 7 מַה־נַּֽעֲשֶׂ֥ה לָהֶ֛ם לַנּֽוֹתָרִ֖ים לְנָשִׁ֑ים וַֽאֲנַ֙חְנוּ֙ נִשְׁבַּ֣עְנוּ בַֽיהֹוָ֔ה לְבִלְתִּ֛י תֵּת־לָהֶ֥ם מִבְּנוֹתֵ֖ינוּ לְנָשִֽׁים׃

8They inquired, "Is there anyone from the tribes of Israel who did not go up to the Lord at Mizpah?" Now no one from Jabesh-gilead had come to the camp, to the assembly. 9For, when the roll of the troops was taken, not one of the inhabitants of Jabesh-gilead was present. 10So the assemblage dispatched 12,000 of the warriors, instructing them as follows: "Go and put the inhabitants of Jabesh-gilead to the sword, women and children included. 11This is what you are to do: Proscribe every man, and every woman who has known a man carnally." 12They found among the inhabitants of Jabesh-gilead 400 maidens who had not known a man carnally; and they brought them to the camp at Shiloh, which is in the land of Canaan.a

13Then the whole community sent word to the Benjaminites who were at the Rock of Rimmon, and offered them terms of peace. 14Thereupon the Benjaminites returned, and they gave them the girls who had been spared from the women of Jabesh-gilead. b-But there were not enough of them.-b

15Now the people had relented toward Benjamin, for the Lord had made a breach in the tribes of Israel. 16So the elders of the community asked, "What can we do about wives for those who are left, since the women of Benjamin have been killed off?" 17For they said, "There must be a saving remnant for Benjamin, that a tribe may not be blotted out of Israel; 18yet we cannot give them any of our daughters as wives," since the Israelites had taken an oath: "Cursed be anyone who gives a wife to Benjamin!"

19They said, "The annual feast of the Lord is now being held at Shiloh." (It lies north of Bethel, east of the highway that runs from Bethel to Shechem, and south of Lebonah.)

20So they instructed the Benjaminites as follows: "Go and lie in wait in the vineyards. 21As

8 וַיֹּאמְרוּ מִי אֶחָד מִשִּׁבְטֵי יִשְׂרָאֵל אֲשֶׁר לֹא־עָלָה אֶל־יְהוָה הַמִּצְפָּה וְהִנֵּה לֹא בָא־אִישׁ אֶל־הַמַּחֲנֶה מִיָּבֵישׁ גִּלְעָד אֶל־הַקָּהָל׃ 9 וַיִּתְפָּקֵד הָעָם וְהִנֵּה אֵין־שָׁם אִישׁ מִיּוֹשְׁבֵי יָבֵישׁ גִּלְעָד׃ 10 וַיִּשְׁלְחוּ־שָׁם הָעֵדָה שְׁנֵים־עָשָׂר אֶלֶף אִישׁ מִבְּנֵי הֶחָיִל וַיְצַוּוּ אוֹתָם לֵאמֹר לְכוּ וְהִכִּיתֶם אֶת־יוֹשְׁבֵי יָבֵישׁ גִּלְעָד לְפִי־חֶרֶב וְהַנָּשִׁים וְהַטָּף׃ 11 וְזֶה הַדָּבָר אֲשֶׁר תַּעֲשׂוּ כָּל־זָכָר וְכָל־אִשָּׁה יֹדַעַת מִשְׁכַּב־זָכָר תַּחֲרִימוּ׃ 12 וַיִּמְצְאוּ מִיּוֹשְׁבֵי ׀ יָבֵישׁ גִּלְעָד אַרְבַּע מֵאוֹת נַעֲרָה בְתוּלָה אֲשֶׁר לֹא־יָדְעָה אִישׁ לְמִשְׁכַּב זָכָר וַיָּבִיאוּ אוֹתָם אֶל־הַמַּחֲנֶה שִׁלֹה אֲשֶׁר בְּאֶרֶץ כְּנָעַן׃ ס

13 וַיִּשְׁלְחוּ כָּל־הָעֵדָה וַיְדַבְּרוּ אֶל־בְּנֵי בִנְיָמִן אֲשֶׁר בְּסֶלַע רִמּוֹן וַיִּקְרְאוּ לָהֶם שָׁלוֹם׃ 14 וַיָּשָׁב בִּנְיָמִן בָּעֵת הַהִיא וַיִּתְּנוּ לָהֶם הַנָּשִׁים אֲשֶׁר חִיּוּ מִנְּשֵׁי יָבֵישׁ גִּלְעָד וְלֹא־מָצְאוּ לָהֶם כֵּן׃

15 וְהָעָם נִחָם לְבִנְיָמִן כִּי־עָשָׂה יְהוָה פֶּרֶץ בְּשִׁבְטֵי יִשְׂרָאֵל׃ 16 וַיֹּאמְרוּ זִקְנֵי הָעֵדָה מַה־נַּעֲשֶׂה לַנּוֹתָרִים לְנָשִׁים כִּי־נִשְׁמְדָה מִבִּנְיָמִן אִשָּׁה׃ 17 וַיֹּאמְרוּ יְרֻשַּׁת פְּלֵיטָה לְבִנְיָמִן וְלֹא־יִמָּחֶה שֵׁבֶט מִיִּשְׂרָאֵל׃ 18 וַאֲנַחְנוּ לֹא נוּכַל לָתֵת־לָהֶם נָשִׁים מִבְּנוֹתֵינוּ כִּי־נִשְׁבְּעוּ בְנֵי־יִשְׂרָאֵל לֵאמֹר אָרוּר נֹתֵן אִשָּׁה לְבִנְיָמִן׃ ס 19 וַיֹּאמְרוּ הִנֵּה חַג־יְהוָה בְּשִׁלוֹ מִיָּמִים ׀ יָמִימָה אֲשֶׁר מִצְּפוֹנָה לְבֵית־אֵל מִזְרְחָה הַשֶּׁמֶשׁ לִמְסִלָּה הָעֹלָה מִבֵּית־אֵל שְׁכֶמָה וּמִנֶּגֶב לִלְבוֹנָה׃ 20 ויצו וַיְצַוּוּ אֶת־בְּנֵי בִנְיָמִן לֵאמֹר לְכוּ וַאֲרַבְתֶּם בַּכְּרָמִים׃ 21 וּרְאִיתֶם וְהִנֵּה אִם־

---

a   I.e., west of the Jordan, while Jabesh-gilead is east of the Jordan.
b-b   Meaning of Heb. uncertain.

soon as you see the girls of Shiloh coming out to join in the dances, come out from the vineyards; let each of you seize a wife from among the girls of Shiloh, and be off for the land of Benjamin. 22And if their fathers or brothers come to us to complain, we shall say to them, *b*-'Be generous to them for our sake! We could not provide any of them with a wife on account of the war, and you would have incurred guilt if you yourselves had given them [wives].'"-*b*

23The Benjaminites did so. They took to wife, from the dancers whom they carried off, as many as they themselves numbered. Then they went back to their own territory, and rebuilt their towns and settled in them. 24Thereupon the Israelites dispersed, each to his own tribe and clan; everyone departed for his own territory.

25In those days there was no king in Israel; everyone did as he pleased.

יֵצְאוּ בְנוֹת־שִׁילוֹ לָחוּל בַּמְּחֹלֹת וִיצָאתֶם מִן־הַכְּרָמִים וַחֲטַפְתֶּם לָכֶם אִישׁ אִשְׁתּוֹ מִבְּנוֹת שִׁילוֹ וַהֲלַכְתֶּם אֶרֶץ בִּנְיָמִן: 22 וְהָיָה כִּי־יָבֹאוּ אֲבוֹתָם אוֹ אֲחֵיהֶם לָרוֹב אֵלֵינוּ וְאָמַרְנוּ אֲלֵיהֶם חָנּוּנוּ אוֹתָם כִּי לֹא לָקַחְנוּ אִישׁ אִשְׁתּוֹ בַּמִּלְחָמָה כִּי לֹא אַתֶּם נְתַתֶּם לָהֶם כָּעֵת תֶּאְשָׁמוּ: ס

23 וַיַּעֲשׂוּ־כֵן בְּנֵי בִנְיָמִן וַיִּשְׂאוּ נָשִׁים לְמִסְפָּרָם מִן־הַמְּחֹלְלוֹת אֲשֶׁר גָּזָלוּ וַיֵּלְכוּ וַיָּשׁוּבוּ אֶל־נַחֲלָתָם וַיִּבְנוּ אֶת־הֶעָרִים וַיֵּשְׁבוּ בָּהֶם: 24 וַיִּתְהַלְּכוּ מִשָּׁם בְּנֵי־ יִשְׂרָאֵל בָּעֵת הַהִיא אִישׁ לְשִׁבְטוֹ וּלְמִשְׁפַּחְתּוֹ וַיֵּצְאוּ מִשָּׁם אִישׁ לְנַחֲלָתוֹ: 25 בַּיָּמִים הָהֵם אֵין מֶלֶךְ בְּיִשְׂרָאֵל אִישׁ הַיָּשָׁר בְּעֵינָיו יַעֲשֶׂה: *

תם ונשלם תהילה לאל בורא עולם

1 SAMUEL

1 There was a man from [a]-Ramathaim of the Zuphites,-[a] in the hill country of Ephraim, whose name was Elkanah son of Jeroham son of Elihu son of Tohu son of Zuph, an Ephraimite. [2]He had two wives, one named Hannah and the other Peninnah; Peninnah had children, but Hannah was childless. [3]This man used to go up from his town every year to worship and to offer sacrifice to the Lord of Hosts at Shiloh.—Hophni and Phinehas, the two sons of Eli, were priests of the Lord there.

[4]One such day, Elkanah offered a sacrifice. He used to give portions to his wife Peninnah and to all her sons and daughters; [5]but to Hannah he would give one portion [b]-only—though-[b] Hannah was his favorite—for the Lord had closed her womb. [6]Moreover, her rival, to make her miserable, would taunt her that the Lord had closed her womb. [7c]-This happened-[c] year after year: Every time she went up to the House of the Lord, the other would taunt her, so that she wept and would not eat. [8]Her husband Elkanah said to her, "Hannah, why are you crying and why aren't you eating? Why are you so sad? Am I not more devoted to you than ten sons?"

[9]After they had eaten and drunk at Shiloh, Hannah rose.[d]—The priest Eli was sitting on the seat near the doorpost of the temple of the Lord.—[10]In her wretchedness, she prayed to the Lord, weeping all the while. [11]And she made

א וַיְהִי֩ אִ֨ישׁ אֶחָ֜ד מִן־הָרָמָתַ֛יִם צוֹפִ֖ים מֵהַ֣ר אֶפְרָ֑יִם וּשְׁמ֡וֹ אֶ֠לְקָנָה בֶּן־יְרֹחָ֧ם בֶּן־אֱלִיה֛וּא בֶּן־תֹּ֥חוּ בֶן־צ֖וּף אֶפְרָתִֽי׃ 2 וְלוֹ֙ שְׁתֵּ֣י נָשִׁ֔ים שֵׁ֤ם אַחַת֙ חַנָּ֔ה וְשֵׁ֥ם הַשֵּׁנִ֖ית פְּנִנָּ֑ה וַיְהִ֤י לִפְנִנָּה֙ יְלָדִ֔ים וּלְחַנָּ֖ה אֵ֥ין יְלָדִֽים׃ 3 וְעָלָה֩ הָאִ֨ישׁ הַה֤וּא מֵֽעִירוֹ֙ מִיָּמִ֣ים ׀ יָמִ֔ימָה לְהִֽשְׁתַּחֲוֺ֧ת וְלִזְבֹּ֛חַ לַיהֹוָ֥ה צְבָא֖וֹת בְּשִׁלֹ֑ה וְשָׁ֞ם שְׁנֵ֣י בְנֵֽי־עֵלִ֗י חׇפְנִי֙ וּפִ֣נְחָ֔ס כֹּהֲנִ֖ים לַיהֹוָֽה׃ 4 וַיְהִ֣י הַיּ֔וֹם וַיִּזְבַּ֖ח אֶלְקָנָ֑ה וְנָתַ֞ן לִפְנִנָּ֣ה אִשְׁתּ֗וֹ וּֽלְכׇל־בָּנֶ֛יהָ וּבְנוֹתֶ֖יהָ מָנֽוֹת׃ 5 וּלְחַנָּ֕ה יִתֵּ֛ן מָנָ֥ה אַחַ֖ת אַפָּ֑יִם כִּ֤י אֶת־חַנָּה֙ אָהֵ֔ב וַֽיהֹוָ֖ה סָגַ֥ר רַחְמָֽהּ׃ 6 וְכִעֲסַ֤תָּה צָֽרָתָהּ֙ גַּם־כַּ֔עַס בַּעֲב֖וּר הַרְּעִמָ֑הּ* כִּֽי־סָגַ֥ר יְהֹוָ֖ה בְּעַ֥ד רַחְמָֽהּ׃ 7 וְכֵ֨ן יַעֲשֶׂ֜ה שָׁנָ֣ה בְשָׁנָ֗ה מִדֵּ֤י עֲלֹתָהּ֙ בְּבֵ֣ית יְהֹוָ֔ה כֵּ֖ן תַּכְעִסֶ֑נָּה וַתִּבְכֶּ֖ה וְלֹ֥א תֹאכַֽל׃ 8 וַיֹּ֨אמֶר לָ֜הּ אֶלְקָנָ֣ה אִישָׁ֗הּ חַנָּה֙ לָ֣מֶה תִבְכִּ֗י וְלָ֙מֶה֙ לֹ֣א תֹֽאכְלִ֔י וְלָ֖מֶה יֵרַ֣ע לְבָבֵ֑ךְ הֲל֤וֹא אָֽנֹכִי֙ ט֣וֹב לָ֔ךְ מֵעֲשָׂרָ֖ה בָּנִֽים׃ 9 וַתָּ֣קׇם חַנָּ֔ה אַחֲרֵ֛י אׇכְלָ֥ה בְשִׁלֹ֖ה וְאַחֲרֵ֣י שָׁתֹ֑ה וְעֵלִ֣י הַכֹּהֵ֗ן יֹשֵׁב֙ עַל־הַכִּסֵּ֔א עַל־מְזוּזַ֖ת הֵיכַ֥ל יְהֹוָֽה׃ 10 וְהִ֖יא מָ֣רַת נָ֑פֶשׁ וַתִּתְפַּלֵּ֥ל עַל־יְהֹוָ֖ה וּבָכֹ֥ה תִבְכֶּֽה׃ 11 וַתִּדֹּ֨ר נֶ֜דֶר וַתֹּאמַ֗ר יְהֹוָ֤ה צְבָאוֹת֙ אִם־רָאֹ֣ה תִרְאֶ֣ה ׀ בׇּעֳנִ֣י אֲמָתֶ֗ךָ וּזְכַרְתַּ֙נִי֙ וְלֹֽא־

a-a   Heb. "Ramathaim-zophim." In 1.19, 2.11, 7.17, 15.34, 19.18, etc., the town is called Ramah; and 9.5 ff. shows that it was in the district of Zuph.
b-b   Meaning of Heb. uncertain.
c-c   Lit. "Thus he did."
d   Septuagint adds "and stood before the Lord."

571

this vow: "O LORD of Hosts, if You will look upon the suffering of Your maidservant and will remember me and not forget Your maidservant, and if You will grant Your maidservant a male child, I will dedicate him to the LORD for all the days of his life; and no razor shall ever touch his head."

12As she kept on praying before the LORD, Eli watched her mouth. 13Now Hannah was praying in her heart; only her lips moved, but her voice could not be heard. So Eli thought she was drunk. 14Eli said to her, "How long will you make a drunken spectacle of yourself? e-Sober up!"-e 15And Hannah replied, "Oh no, my lord! I am a very unhappy woman. I have drunk no wine or other strong drink, but I have been pouring out my heart to the LORD. 16Do not take your maidservant for a worthless woman; I have only been speaking all this time out of my great anguish and distress." 17"Then go in peace," said Eli, "and may the God of Israel grant you what you have asked of Him." 18She answered, "You are most kind to your handmaid." So the woman left, and she ate, and was no longer downcast. 19Early next morning they bowed low before the LORD, and they went back home to Ramah.

Elkanah knewf his wife Hannah and the LORD remembered her. 20Hannah conceived, and at the turn of the year bore a son. She named him Samuel,g meaning, "I asked the LORD for him." 21And when the man Elkanah and all his household were going up to offer to the LORD the annual sacrifice and his votive sacrifice, 22Hannah did not go up. She said to her husband, "When the child is weaned, I will bring him. For when he has appeared before the LORD, he must remain there for good." 23Her husband Elkanah said to her, "Do as you think best. Stay home until you have weaned him. May the LORD fulfill

תִּשְׁכַּח אֶת־אֲמָתֶךָ וְנָתַתָּה לַאֲמָתְךָ זֶרַע אֲנָשִׁים וּנְתַתִּיו לַיהוָה כָּל־יְמֵי חַיָּיו וּמוֹרָה לֹא־יַעֲלֶה עַל־רֹאשׁוֹ: 12וְהָיָה כִּי הִרְבְּתָה לְהִתְפַּלֵּל לִפְנֵי יְהוָה וְעֵלִי שֹׁמֵר אֶת־פִּיהָ: 13וְחַנָּה הִיא מְדַבֶּרֶת עַל־לִבָּהּ רַק שְׂפָתֶיהָ נָּעוֹת וְקוֹלָהּ לֹא יִשָּׁמֵעַ וַיַּחְשְׁבֶהָ עֵלִי לְשִׁכֹּרָה: 14וַיֹּאמֶר אֵלֶיהָ עֵלִי עַד־מָתַי תִּשְׁתַּכָּרִין הָסִירִי אֶת־יֵינֵךְ מֵעָלָיִךְ: 15וַתַּעַן חַנָּה וַתֹּאמֶר לֹא אֲדֹנִי אִשָּׁה קְשַׁת־רוּחַ אָנֹכִי וְיַיִן וְשֵׁכָר לֹא שָׁתִיתִי וָאֶשְׁפֹּךְ אֶת־נַפְשִׁי לִפְנֵי יְהוָה: 16אַל־תִּתֵּן אֶת־אֲמָתְךָ לִפְנֵי בַּת־בְּלִיָּעַל כִּי־מֵרֹב שִׂיחִי וְכַעְסִי דִּבַּרְתִּי עַד־הֵנָּה: 17וַיַּעַן עֵלִי וַיֹּאמֶר לְכִי לְשָׁלוֹם וֵאלֹהֵי יִשְׂרָאֵל יִתֵּן אֶת־שֵׁלָתֵךְ* אֲשֶׁר שָׁאַלְתְּ מֵעִמּוֹ: 18וַתֹּאמֶר תִּמְצָא שִׁפְחָתְךָ חֵן בְּעֵינֶיךָ וַתֵּלֶךְ הָאִשָּׁה לְדַרְכָּהּ וַתֹּאכַל וּפָנֶיהָ לֹא־הָיוּ־לָהּ עוֹד: 19וַיַּשְׁכִּמוּ בַבֹּקֶר וַיִּשְׁתַּחֲווּ לִפְנֵי יְהוָה וַיָּשֻׁבוּ וַיָּבֹאוּ אֶל־בֵּיתָם הָרָמָתָה וַיֵּדַע אֶלְקָנָה אֶת־חַנָּה אִשְׁתּוֹ וַיִּזְכְּרֶהָ יְהוָה: 20וַיְהִי לִתְקֻפוֹת הַיָּמִים וַתַּהַר חַנָּה וַתֵּלֶד בֵּן וַתִּקְרָא אֶת־שְׁמוֹ שְׁמוּאֵל כִּי מֵיְהוָה שְׁאִלְתִּיו: 21וַיַּעַל הָאִישׁ אֶלְקָנָה וְכָל־בֵּיתוֹ לִזְבֹּחַ לַיהוָה אֶת־זֶבַח הַיָּמִים וְאֶת־נִדְרוֹ: 22וְחַנָּה לֹא עָלָתָה כִּי־אָמְרָה לְאִישָׁהּ עַד יִגָּמֵל הַנַּעַר וַהֲבִאֹתִיו וְנִרְאָה אֶת־פְּנֵי יְהוָה וְיָשַׁב שָׁם עַד־עוֹלָם: 23וַיֹּאמֶר לָהּ אֶלְקָנָה אִישָׁהּ עֲשִׂי הַטּוֹב בְּעֵינַיִךְ שְׁבִי עַד־גָּמְלֵךְ אֹתוֹ אַךְ יָקֵם יְהוָה

---

e-e   Lit. "Remove your wine from you."
f   Cf. note at Gen. 4.1.
g   Connected with sha'ul me'el "asked of God"; cf. vv. 17, 27–28.

v. 17.   חסר א'

572

h-His word."-*h* So the woman stayed home and nursed her son until she weaned him.

24When she had weaned him, she took him up with her, along with *i*-three bulls,-*i* one ephah of flour, and a jar of wine. And *b*-though the boy was still very young,-*b* she brought him to the House of the LORD at Shiloh. 25After slaughtering the bull, they brought the boy to Eli. 26She said, "Please, my lord! As you live, my lord, I am the woman who stood here beside you and prayed to the LORD. 27It was this boy I prayed for; and the LORD has granted me what I asked of Him. 28I, in turn, hereby lend*j* him to the LORD. For as long as he lives he is lent to the LORD." And they*k* bowed low there before the LORD.

2

And Hannah prayed:

My heart exults in the LORD;
a-I have triumphed-*a* through the LORD.
b-I gloat-*b* over my enemies;
I rejoice in Your deliverance.

2There is no holy one like the LORD,
Truly, there is none beside You;
There is no rock like our God.

3Talk no more with lofty pride,
Let no arrogance cross your lips!
For the LORD is an all-knowing God;
By Him actions are measured.

4The bows of the mighty are broken,
And the faltering are girded with strength.

---

h-h   Septuagint and 4QSam^a (a Samuel fragment from Qumran) read "the utterance of your mouth." The translators express their thanks to Professor Frank M. Cross, Jr., for graciously making available to them copies of his unpublished Samuel fragments.

i-i   Septuagint and 4QSam^a read "a three-year-old [cf. Gen. 15.9] bull and bread"; cf. v. 25.

j   From the same root as that of the verb rendered "asked for" in v. 20.

k   Heb. "he"; cf. 2.11. A reading in the Talmud (Berakhot 61a) implies that Elkanah was there.

a-a   Lit. "My horn is high."
b-b   Lit. "My mouth is wide."

אֶת־דְּבָרוֹ וַתֵּשֶׁב הָאִשָּׁה וַתֵּינֶק אֶת־בְּנָהּ
עַד־גָּמְלָהּ אֹתוֹ:

24 וַתַּעֲלֵהוּ עִמָּהּ כַּאֲשֶׁר גְּמָלַתּוּ בְּפָרִים
שְׁלֹשָׁה וְאֵיפָה אַחַת קֶמַח וְנֵבֶל יַיִן
וַתְּבִאֵהוּ בֵית־יְהוָה שִׁלוֹ וְהַנַּעַר נָעַר:
25 וַיִּשְׁחֲטוּ אֶת־הַפָּר וַיָּבִיאוּ אֶת־הַנַּעַר
אֶל־עֵלִי: 26 וַתֹּאמֶר בִּי אֲדֹנִי חֵי נַפְשְׁךָ
אֲדֹנִי אֲנִי הָאִשָּׁה הַנִּצֶּבֶת עִמְּכָה בָּזֶה
לְהִתְפַּלֵּל אֶל־יְהוָה: 27 אֶל־הַנַּעַר הַזֶּה
הִתְפַּלָּלְתִּי וַיִּתֵּן יְהוָה לִי אֶת־שְׁאֵלָתִי
אֲשֶׁר שָׁאַלְתִּי מֵעִמּוֹ: 28 וְגַם אָנֹכִי
הִשְׁאִלְתִּהוּ לַיהוָה כָּל־הַיָּמִים אֲשֶׁר הָיָה
הוּא שָׁאוּל לַיהוָה וַיִּשְׁתַּחוּ שָׁם
לַיהוָה: פ

ב

וַתִּתְפַּלֵּל חַנָּה וַתֹּאמַר

עָלַץ לִבִּי בַּיהוָה
רָמָה קַרְנִי בַּיהוָה
רָחַב פִּי עַל־אוֹיְבַי
כִּי שָׂמַחְתִּי בִּישׁוּעָתֶךָ:

2 אֵין־קָדוֹשׁ כַּיהוָה
כִּי אֵין בִּלְתֶּךָ
וְאֵין צוּר כֵּאלֹהֵינוּ:

3 אַל־תַּרְבּוּ תְדַבְּרוּ גְּבֹהָה גְבֹהָה
יֵצֵא עָתָק מִפִּיכֶם
כִּי אֵל דֵּעוֹת יְהוָה
וְלֹא נִתְכְּנוּ עֲלִלוֹת:

4 קֶשֶׁת גִּבֹּרִים חַתִּים
וְנִכְשָׁלִים אָזְרוּ חָיִל:

5Men once sated must hire out for bread;
Men once hungry hunger no more.
While the barren woman bears seven,
The mother of many is forlorn.
6The LORD deals death and gives life,
Casts down into Sheol and raises up.
7The LORD makes poor and makes rich;
He casts down, He also lifts high.
8He raises the poor from the dust,
Lifts up the needy from the dunghill,
Setting them with nobles,
Granting them seats of honor.
For the pillars of the earth are the LORD's;
He has set the world upon them.
9He guards the steps of His faithful,
But the wicked perish in darkness—
For not by strength shall man prevail.

10The foes of the LORD shall be shattered;
He will thunder against them in the heavens.
The LORD will judge the ends of the earth.
He will give power to His king,
c-And triumph to-c His anointed one.

11Then Elkanahd [and Hannah] went home to Ramah; and the boy entered the service of the LORD under the priest Eli.

12Now Eli's sons were scoundrels; they paid no heed to the LORD. 13This is how the priests used to deal with the people: When anyone brought a sacrifice, the priest's boy would come along with a three-pronged fork while the meat was boiling, 14and he would thrust it into e-the cauldron, or the kettle, or the great pot, or the small cooking-pot;-e and whatever the fork brought up, the priest would take away f-on it.-f This was the practice at Shiloh with all the Israelites who came there. 15[But now] even before the suet was turned into smoke, the priest's boy would come and say to the man who was

שְׁבֵעִ֤ים בַּלֶּ֙חֶם֙ נִשְׂכָּ֔רוּ 5
וּרְעֵבִ֖ים חָדֵ֑לּוּ
עַד־עֲקָרָה֙ יָלְדָ֣ה שִׁבְעָ֔ה
וְרַבַּ֥ת בָּנִ֖ים אֻמְלָֽלָה׃
יְהוָ֖ה מֵמִ֣ית וּמְחַיֶּ֑ה 6
מוֹרִ֥יד שְׁא֖וֹל וַיָּֽעַל׃
יְהוָ֖ה מוֹרִ֣ישׁ וּמַעֲשִׁ֑יר 7
מַשְׁפִּ֖יל אַף־מְרוֹמֵֽם׃
מֵקִ֤ים מֵֽעָפָר֙ דָּ֔ל 8
מֵֽאַשְׁפֹּת֙ יָרִ֣ים אֶבְי֔וֹן
לְהוֹשִׁיב֙ עִם־נְדִיבִ֔ים
וְכִסֵּ֥א כָב֖וֹד יַנְחִלֵ֑ם
כִּ֤י לַֽיהוָה֙ מְצֻ֣קֵי אֶ֔רֶץ
וַיָּ֥שֶׁת עֲלֵיהֶ֖ם תֵּבֵֽל׃
רַגְלֵ֤י חֲסִידָו֙ יִשְׁמֹ֔ר 9
וּרְשָׁעִ֖ים בַּחֹ֣שֶׁךְ יִדָּ֑מּוּ
כִּֽי־לֹ֥א בְכֹ֖חַ יִגְבַּר־אִֽישׁ׃

יְהוָ֞ה יֵחַ֣תּוּ מְרִיבָ֗ו 10
עָלָו֙ בַּשָּׁמַ֣יִם יַרְעֵ֔ם
יְהוָ֖ה יָדִ֣ין אַפְסֵי־אָ֑רֶץ
וְיִתֶּן־עֹ֣ז לְמַלְכּ֔וֹ
וְיָרֵ֖ם קֶ֥רֶן מְשִׁיחֽוֹ׃ פ

וַיֵּ֧לֶךְ אֶלְקָנָ֛ה הָרָמָ֖תָה עַל־בֵּית֑וֹ וְהַנַּ֗עַר 11
הָיָ֤ה מְשָׁרֵת֙ אֶת־יְהוָ֔ה אֶת־פְּנֵ֖י עֵלִ֥י
הַכֹּהֵֽן׃
וּבְנֵ֥י עֵלִ֖י בְּנֵ֣י בְלִיָּ֑עַל לֹ֥א יָדְע֖וּ אֶת־ 12
יְהוָֽה׃ וּמִשְׁפַּ֣ט הַכֹּֽהֲנִים֮ אֶת־הָעָם֒ כָּל־ 13
אִ֨ישׁ זֹבֵ֜חַ זֶ֗בַח וּבָ֨א נַ֤עַר הַכֹּהֵן֙ כְּבַשֵּׁ֣ל
הַבָּשָׂ֔ר וְהַמַּזְלֵ֛ג שְׁלֹשׁ־הַשִּׁנַּ֖יִם בְּיָדֽוֹ׃
וְהִכָּ֨ה בַכִּיּ֜וֹר א֣וֹ בַדּ֗וּד א֤וֹ בַקַּלַּ֙חַת֙ א֣וֹ 14
בַפָּר֔וּר כֹּ֚ל אֲשֶׁ֣ר יַעֲלֶ֣ה הַמַּזְלֵ֔ג יִקַּ֥ח הַכֹּהֵ֖ן
בּ֑וֹ כָּ֚כָה יַעֲשׂ֣וּ לְכָל־יִשְׂרָאֵ֔ל הַבָּאִ֥ים שָׁ֖ם
בְּשִׁלֹֽה׃ גַּם֮ בְּטֶרֶם֮ יַקְטִר֣וּן אֶת־הַחֵלֶב֒ 15

c-c   Lit. "And will raise the horn of."
d   See note k at 1.28.
e-e   These vessels have not been distinguished precisely.
f-f   Targum and Septuagint add "for himself."

574

sacrificing, "Hand over some meat to roast for the priest; for he won't accept boiled meat from you, only raw." [16]And if the man said to him, "Let them first turn the suet into smoke, and then take as much as you want," he would reply, "No, hand it over at once or I'll take it by force." [17]The sin of the young men against the LORD was very great, for the men treated the LORD's offerings impiously.

[18]Samuel was engaged in the service of the LORD as an attendant, girded with a linen ephod. [19]His mother would also make a little robe for him and bring it up to him every year, when she made the pilgrimage with her husband to offer the annual sacrifice. [20]Eli would bless Elkanah and his wife, and say, "May the LORD grant*g* you offspring by this woman in place of the loan she made to the LORD." Then they would return home. [21]For*h* the LORD took note of Hannah; she conceived and bore three sons and two daughters. Young Samuel meanwhile grew up in the service of the LORD.

[22]Now Eli was very old. When he heard all that his sons were doing to all Israel, and how they lay with the women who *i*-performed tasks-*i* at the entrance of the Tent of Meeting, [23]he said to them, "Why do you do such things? I get evil reports about you from the people on all hands. [24]Don't, my sons! It is no favorable report I hear the people of the LORD spreading about. [25]If a man sins against a man, the LORD may pardon*i* him; but if a man offends against God, who can *i*-obtain pardon-*i* for him?" But they ignored their father's plea; for the LORD was resolved that they should die. [26]Young Samuel, meanwhile, grew in esteem and favor both with God and with men.

[27]A man of God came to Eli and said to him, "Thus said the LORD: Lo, I revealed Myself to

וּבָא ׀ נַעַר הַכֹּהֵן וְאָמַר לָאִישׁ הַזֹּבֵחַ תְּנָה בָשָׂר לִצְלוֹת לַכֹּהֵן וְלֹא־יִקַּח מִמְּךָ בָּשָׂר מְבֻשָּׁל כִּי אִם־חָי: 16 וַיֹּאמֶר אֵלָיו הָאִישׁ קַטֵּר יַקְטִירוּן כַּיּוֹם הַחֵלֶב וְקַח־לְךָ כַּאֲשֶׁר תְּאַוֶּה נַפְשֶׁךָ וְאָמַר ׀ לוֹ לֹא כִּי עַתָּה תִתֵּן וְאִם־לֹא לָקַחְתִּי בְחָזְקָה: 17 וַתְּהִי חַטַּאת הַנְּעָרִים גְּדוֹלָה מְאֹד אֶת־פְּנֵי יְהוָה כִּי נִאֲצוּ הָאֲנָשִׁים אֵת מִנְחַת יְהוָה:

18 וּשְׁמוּאֵל מְשָׁרֵת אֶת־פְּנֵי יְהוָה נַעַר חָגוּר אֵפוֹד בָּד: 19 וּמְעִיל קָטֹן תַּעֲשֶׂה־לּוֹ אִמּוֹ וְהַעַלְתָה לוֹ מִיָּמִים ׀ יָמִימָה בַּעֲלוֹתָהּ אֶת־אִישָׁהּ לִזְבֹּחַ אֶת־זֶבַח הַיָּמִים: 20 וּבֵרַךְ עֵלִי אֶת־אֶלְקָנָה וְאֶת־אִשְׁתּוֹ וְאָמַר יָשֵׂם יְהוָה לְךָ זֶרַע מִן־הָאִשָּׁה הַזֹּאת תַּחַת הַשְּׁאֵלָה אֲשֶׁר שָׁאַל לַיהוָה וְהָלְכוּ לִמְקֹמוֹ: 21 כִּי־פָקַד יְהוָה אֶת־חַנָּה וַתַּהַר וַתֵּלֶד שְׁלֹשָׁה־בָנִים וּשְׁתֵּי בָנוֹת וַיִּגְדַּל הַנַּעַר שְׁמוּאֵל עִם־יְהוָה: ס

22 וְעֵלִי זָקֵן מְאֹד וְשָׁמַע אֵת כָּל־אֲשֶׁר יַעֲשׂוּן בָּנָיו לְכָל־יִשְׂרָאֵל וְאֵת אֲשֶׁר־יִשְׁכְּבוּן אֶת־הַנָּשִׁים הַצֹּבְאוֹת פֶּתַח אֹהֶל מוֹעֵד: 23 וַיֹּאמֶר לָהֶם לָמָּה תַעֲשׂוּן כַּדְּבָרִים הָאֵלֶּה אֲשֶׁר אָנֹכִי שֹׁמֵעַ אֶת־דִּבְרֵיכֶם רָעִים מֵאֵת כָּל־הָעָם אֵלֶּה: 24 אַל בָּנָי כִּי לוֹא־טוֹבָה הַשְּׁמֻעָה אֲשֶׁר אָנֹכִי שֹׁמֵעַ מַעֲבִרִים עַם־יְהוָה: 25 אִם־יֶחֱטָא אִישׁ לְאִישׁ וּפִלְלוֹ אֱלֹהִים וְאִם לַיהוָה יֶחֱטָא־אִישׁ מִי יִתְפַּלֶּל־לוֹ וְלֹא יִשְׁמְעוּ לְקוֹל אֲבִיהֶם כִּי־חָפֵץ יְהוָה לַהֲמִיתָם: 26 וְהַנַּעַר שְׁמוּאֵל הֹלֵךְ וְגָדֵל וָטוֹב גַּם עִם־יְהוָה וְגַם עִם־אֲנָשִׁים: ס 27 וַיָּבֹא אִישׁ־אֱלֹהִים אֶל־עֵלִי וַיֹּאמֶר אֵלָיו כֹּה אָמַר יְהוָה הֲנִגְלֹה נִגְלֵיתִי אֶל־בֵּית

---

g *4QSamᵃ and Septuagint read "repay."*
h *4QSamᵃ reads "And."*
i *Meaning of Heb. uncertain.*

your father's house in Egypt when they were subject to the House of Pharaoh, 28and I chose them from among all the tribes of Israel to be My priests—to ascend My altar, to burn incense, [and] to carry an ephod*j* before Me—and I assigned to your father's house all offerings by fire of the Israelites. 29Why, then, do you *k*-maliciously trample upon the sacrifices and offerings that I have commanded?-*k* You have honored your sons more than Me, feeding on the first portions of every offering of My people Israel.*l* 30Assuredly—declares the LORD, the God of Israel—I intended for you and your father's house to remain in My service forever. But now—declares the LORD—far be it from Me! For I honor those who honor Me, but those who spurn Me shall be dishonored. 31A time is coming when I will break your power and that of your father's house, and there shall be no elder in your house. 32You will gaze grudgingly*m* at all the bounty that will be bestowed on Israel, but there shall never be an elder in your house. 33*i*-I shall not cut off all your offspring from My altar; [but,] to make your eyes pine and your spirit languish, all the increase in your house shall die as [ordinary] men.-*i* 34And this shall be a sign for you: The fate of your two sons Hophni and Phinehas—they shall both die on the same day. 35And I will raise up for Myself a faithful priest, who will act in accordance with My wishes and My purposes. I will build for him an enduring house, and he shall walk before My anointed evermore. 36And all the survivors of your house shall come and bow low to him for the sake of a money fee and a loaf of bread, and shall say, 'Please, assign me to one of the priestly duties, that I may have a morsel of bread to eat.'"

אָבִ֫יךָ בִּהְיוֹתָ֥ם בְּמִצְרַ֖יִם לְבֵ֥ית פַּרְעֹֽה׃ 28 וּבָחֹ֨ר אֹת֜וֹ מִכָּל־שִׁבְטֵ֣י יִשְׂרָאֵל֮ לִי֮ לְכֹהֵן֒ לַעֲל֣וֹת עַֽל־מִזְבְּחִ֗י לְהַקְטִ֥יר קְטֹ֛רֶת לָשֵׂ֥את אֵפ֖וֹד לְפָנָ֑י וָֽאֶתְּנָה֙ לְבֵ֣ית אָבִ֔יךָ אֶת־כָּל־אִשֵּׁ֖י בְּנֵ֥י יִשְׂרָאֵֽל׃ 29 לָ֣מָּה תִבְעֲט֗וּ בְּזִבְחִי֙ וּבְמִנְחָתִ֔י אֲשֶׁ֥ר צִוִּ֖יתִי מָע֑וֹן וַתְּכַבֵּ֤ד אֶת־בָּנֶ֨יךָ֙ מִמֶּ֔נִּי לְהַבְרִֽיאֲכֶ֗ם מֵרֵאשִׁ֛ית כָּל־מִנְחַ֥ת יִשְׂרָאֵ֖ל לְעַמִּֽי׃ 30 לָכֵ֗ן נְאֻם־יְהוָה֮ אֱלֹהֵ֣י יִשְׂרָאֵל֒ אָמ֣וֹר אָמַ֔רְתִּי בֵּֽיתְךָ֙ וּבֵ֣ית אָבִ֔יךָ יִתְהַלְּכ֥וּ לְפָנַ֖י עַד־עוֹלָ֑ם וְעַתָּ֤ה נְאֻם־יְהוָה֙ חָלִ֣ילָה לִּ֔י כִּֽי־מְכַבְּדַ֥י אֲכַבֵּ֖ד וּבֹזַ֥י יֵקָֽלּוּ׃ 31 הִנֵּה֙ יָמִ֣ים בָּאִ֔ים וְגָֽדַעְתִּי֙ אֶת־זְרֹ֣עֲךָ֔ וְאֶת־זְרֹ֖עַ בֵּ֣ית אָבִ֑יךָ מִֽהְי֥וֹת זָקֵ֖ן בְּבֵיתֶֽךָ׃ 32 וְהִבַּטְתָּ֞ צַ֣ר מָע֗וֹן בְּכֹ֤ל אֲשֶׁר־יֵיטִיב֙ אֶת־יִשְׂרָאֵ֔ל וְלֹֽא־יִהְיֶ֥ה זָקֵ֖ן בְּבֵֽיתְךָ֖ כָּל־הַיָּמִֽים׃ 33 וְאִ֗ישׁ לֹֽא־אַכְרִ֤ית לְךָ֙ מֵעִ֣ם מִזְבְּחִ֔י לְכַלּ֥וֹת אֶת־עֵינֶ֖יךָ וְלַאֲדִ֣יב אֶת־נַפְשֶׁ֑ךָ וְכָל־מַרְבִּ֥ית בֵּיתְךָ֖ יָמ֥וּתוּ אֲנָשִֽׁים׃ 34 וְזֶה־לְּךָ֣ הָא֗וֹת אֲשֶׁ֤ר יָבֹא֙ אֶל־שְׁנֵ֣י בָנֶ֔יךָ אֶל־חָפְנִ֖י וּפִֽינְחָ֑ס בְּי֥וֹם אֶחָ֖ד יָמ֥וּתוּ שְׁנֵיהֶֽם׃ 35 וַהֲקִֽימֹתִ֥י לִ֨י כֹּהֵ֜ן נֶאֱמָ֗ן כַּאֲשֶׁ֧ר בִּלְבָבִ֛י וּבְנַפְשִׁ֖י יַעֲשֶׂ֑ה וּבָנִ֤יתִי לוֹ֙ בַּ֣יִת נֶאֱמָ֔ן וְהִתְהַלֵּ֥ךְ לִפְנֵֽי־מְשִׁיחִ֖י כָּל־הַיָּמִֽים׃ 36 וְהָיָ֗ה כָּל־הַנּוֹתָר֙ בְּבֵ֣יתְךָ֔ יָבוֹא֙ לְהִשְׁתַּחֲוֺ֣ת ל֔וֹ לַאֲג֥וֹרַת כֶּ֖סֶף וְכִכַּר־לָ֑חֶם וְאָמַ֗ר סְפָחֵ֥נִי נָ֛א אֶל־אַחַ֥ת הַכְּהֻנּ֖וֹת לֶאֱכֹ֥ל פַּת־לָֽחֶם׃ ס

---

j　Here a device for obtaining oracles (cf. 14.3; 23.6, 9–12), not a garment as in v. 18 above.

k-k　Meaning of Heb. uncertain. Emendation yields "gaze [cf. Septuagint] grudgingly upon the sacrifices and offerings which I have commanded" (connecting ma'on with 'oyen, "keeping a jealous eye"; see 1 Sam. 18.9); cf. v. 32 and note m below.

l　See vv. 15–16.

m　Cf. note k-k above.

3 Young Samuel was in the service of the Lord under Eli. In those days the word of the Lord was rare; prophecy was not widespread. ²One day, Eli was asleep in his usual place; his eyes had begun to fail and he could barely see. ³The lamp of God had not yet gone out, and Samuel was sleeping in the temple of the Lord where the Ark of God was. ⁴The Lord called out to Samuel, and he answered, "I'm coming." ⁵He ran to Eli and said, "Here I am; you called me." But he replied, "I didn't call you; go back to sleep." So he went back and lay down. ⁶Again the Lord called, "Samuel!" Samuel rose and went to Eli and said, "Here I am; you called me." But he replied, "I didn't call, my son; go back to sleep."—⁷Now Samuel had not yet experienced the Lord; the word of the Lord had not yet been revealed to him.—⁸The Lord called Samuel again, a third time, and he rose and went to Eli and said, "Here I am; you called me." Then Eli understood that the Lord was calling the boy. ⁹And Eli said to Samuel, "Go lie down. If you are called again, say, 'Speak, Lord, for Your servant is listening.'" And Samuel went to his place and lay down.

¹⁰The Lord came, and stood there, and He called as before: "Samuel! Samuel!" And Samuel answered, "Speak, for Your servant is listening." ¹¹The Lord said to Samuel: "I am going to do in Israel such a thing that both ears of anyone who hears about it will tingle. ¹²In that day I will fulfill against Eli all that I spoke concerning his house, from beginning to end. ¹³And I declare to him that I sentence his house to endless punishment for the iniquity he knew about— how his sons committed sacrilege ᵃ-at will-ᵃ— and he did not rebuke them. ¹⁴Assuredly, I swear concerning the house of Eli that the iniquity of the house of Eli will never be expiated by sacrifice or offering."

---

a-a   Meaning of Heb. uncertain. Septuagint reads "against God."

ג וְהַנַּ֗עַר שְׁמוּאֵ֛ל מְשָׁרֵ֥ת אֶת־יְהֹוָ֖ה לִפְנֵ֣י עֵלִ֑י וּדְבַר־יְהֹוָ֗ה הָיָ֤ה יָקָר֙ בַּיָּמִ֣ים הָהֵ֔ם אֵ֥ין חָז֖וֹן נִפְרָֽץ׃ ס ²וַיְהִי֙ בַּיּ֣וֹם הַה֔וּא וְעֵלִ֖י שֹׁכֵ֣ב בִּמְקוֹמ֑וֹ וְעֵינָו֙ הֵחֵ֣לּוּ כֵה֔וֹת לֹ֥א יוּכַ֖ל לִרְאֽוֹת׃ ³וְנֵ֤ר אֱלֹהִים֙ טֶ֣רֶם יִכְבֶּ֔ה וּשְׁמוּאֵ֖ל שֹׁכֵ֑ב בְּהֵיכַ֣ל יְהֹוָ֔ה אֲשֶׁר־שָׁ֖ם אֲר֥וֹן אֱלֹהִֽים׃ פ ⁴וַיִּקְרָ֧א יְהֹוָ֛ה אֶל־שְׁמוּאֵ֖ל וַיֹּ֥אמֶר הִנֵּֽנִי׃ ⁵וַיָּ֣רׇץ אֶל־עֵלִ֗י וַיֹּ֤אמֶר הִנְנִי֙ כִּֽי־קָרָ֣אתָ לִּ֔י וַיֹּ֥אמֶר לֹֽא־קָרָ֖אתִי שׁ֣וּב שְׁכָ֑ב וַיֵּ֖לֶךְ וַיִּשְׁכָּֽב׃ ס ⁶וַיֹּ֨סֶף יְהֹוָ֥ה קְרֹ֛א עוֹד֙ שְׁמוּאֵ֔ל וַיָּ֤קׇם שְׁמוּאֵל֙ וַיֵּ֣לֶךְ אֶל־עֵלִ֔י וַיֹּ֥אמֶר הִנְנִ֖י כִּ֣י קָרָ֣אתָ לִ֑י וַיֹּ֛אמֶר לֹֽא־קָרָ֥אתִי בְנִ֖י שׁ֥וּב שְׁכָֽב׃ ⁷וּשְׁמוּאֵ֕ל טֶ֖רֶם יָדַ֣ע אֶת־יְהֹוָ֑ה וְטֶ֛רֶם יִגָּלֶ֥ה אֵלָ֖יו דְּבַר־יְהֹוָֽה׃ ⁸וַיֹּ֨סֶף יְהֹוָ֥ה קְרֹֽא־שְׁמוּאֵל֮ בַּשְּׁלִשִׁית֒ וַיָּ֙קׇם֙ וַיֵּ֣לֶךְ אֶל־עֵלִ֔י וַיֹּ֥אמֶר הִנְנִ֖י כִּ֣י קָרָ֣אתָ לִ֑י וַיָּ֣בֶן עֵלִ֔י כִּ֥י יְהֹוָ֖ה קֹרֵ֥א לַנָּֽעַר׃ ⁹וַיֹּ֨אמֶר עֵלִ֜י לִשְׁמוּאֵ֗ל לֵ֣ךְ שְׁכָ֔ב וְהָיָה֙ אִם־יִקְרָ֣א אֵלֶ֔יךָ וְאָֽמַרְתָּ֙ דַּבֵּ֣ר יְהֹוָ֔ה כִּ֥י שֹׁמֵ֖עַ עַבְדֶּ֑ךָ וַיֵּ֣לֶךְ שְׁמוּאֵ֔ל וַיִּשְׁכַּ֖ב בִּמְקוֹמֽוֹ׃ ¹⁰וַיָּבֹ֤א יְהֹוָה֙ וַיִּתְיַצַּ֔ב וַיִּקְרָ֥א כְפַֽעַם־בְּפַ֖עַם שְׁמוּאֵ֣ל ׀ שְׁמוּאֵ֑ל וַיֹּ֤אמֶר שְׁמוּאֵל֙ דַּבֵּ֔ר כִּ֥י שֹׁמֵ֖עַ עַבְדֶּֽךָ׃ פ ¹¹וַיֹּ֤אמֶר יְהֹוָה֙ אֶל־שְׁמוּאֵ֔ל הִנֵּ֧ה אָנֹכִ֛י עֹשֶׂ֥ה דָבָ֖ר בְּיִשְׂרָאֵ֑ל אֲשֶׁר֙ כׇּל־שֹׁ֣מְע֔וֹ תְּצִלֶּ֖ינָה שְׁתֵּ֥י אׇזְנָֽיו׃ ¹²בַּיּ֤וֹם הַהוּא֙ אָקִ֣ים אֶל־עֵלִ֔י אֵ֛ת כׇּל־אֲשֶׁ֥ר דִּבַּ֖רְתִּי אֶל־בֵּית֑וֹ הָחֵ֖ל וְכַלֵּֽה׃ ¹³וְהִגַּ֣דְתִּי ל֔וֹ כִּֽי־שֹׁפֵ֥ט אֲנִ֛י אֶת־בֵּית֖וֹ עַד־עוֹלָ֑ם בַּעֲוֺ֣ן אֲשֶׁר־יָדַ֗ע כִּֽי־מְקַֽלְלִ֤ים לָהֶם֙ בָּנָ֔יו וְלֹ֥א כִהָ֖ה בָּֽם׃ ¹⁴וְלָכֵ֥ן נִשְׁבַּ֖עְתִּי לְבֵ֣ית עֵלִ֑י אִֽם־יִתְכַּפֵּ֞ר עֲוֺ֧ן בֵּית־עֵלִ֛י בְּזֶ֥בַח וּבְמִנְחָ֖ה עַד־עוֹלָֽם׃

15Samuel lay there until morning; and then he opened the doors of the House of the Lord. Samuel was afraid to report the vision to Eli, 16but Eli summoned Samuel and said, "Samuel, my son"; and he answered, "Here." 17And [Eli] asked, "What did He say to you? Keep nothing from me. b-Thus and more may God do to you-b if you keep from me a single word of all that He said to you!" 18Samuel then told him everything, withholding nothing from him. And [Eli] said, "He is the Lord; He will do what He deems right."

19Samuel grew up and the Lord was with him: He did not leave any of Samuel'sc predictions unfulfilled. 20All Israel, from Dan to Beer-sheba, knew that Samuel was trustworthy as a prophet of the Lord. 21And the Lord continued to appear at Shiloh: the Lord revealed Himself to Samuel at Shiloh with the word of the Lord; 1and Samuel's word went forth to all Israel.

aIsrael marched out to engage the Philistines in battle; they encamped near Eben-ezer, while the Philistines encamped at Aphek. 2The Philistines arrayed themselves against Israel; and when the battle was fought,b Israel was routed by the Philistines, who slew about four thousand men on the field of battle. 3When the [Israelite] troops returned to the camp, the elders of Israel asked, "Why did the Lord put us to rout today before the Philistines? Let us fetch the Ark of the Covenant of the Lord from Shiloh; thus He will be present among us and will deliver us from the hands of our enemies." 4So the troops sent men to Shiloh; there Eli's two sons, Hophni and Phinehas, were in charge of the Ark of the Covenant of God, and they brought down from there the Ark of the Cov-

---

b-b   A formula of adjuration.
c   Heb. "his."

a   Preceding this, Septuagint has "In those days, the Philistines gathered for war against Israel."
b   Meaning of Heb. uncertain.

15 וַיִּשְׁכַּ֤ב שְׁמוּאֵל֙ עַד־הַבֹּ֔קֶר וַיִּפְתַּ֖ח אֶת־דַּלְת֣וֹת בֵּית־יְהוָ֑ה וּשְׁמוּאֵ֣ל יָרֵ֔א מֵהַגִּ֥יד אֶת־הַמַּרְאָ֖ה אֶל־עֵלִֽי׃ 16 וַיִּקְרָ֤א עֵלִי֙ אֶת־שְׁמוּאֵ֔ל וַיֹּ֥אמֶר שְׁמוּאֵ֖ל בְּנִ֑י וַיֹּ֖אמֶר הִנֵּֽנִי׃ 17 וַיֹּ֗אמֶר מָ֤ה הַדָּבָר֙ אֲשֶׁ֣ר דִּבֶּ֣ר אֵלֶ֔יךָ אַל־נָ֥א תְכַחֵ֖ד מִמֶּ֑נִּי כֹּ֣ה יַעֲשֶׂה־לְּךָ֤ אֱלֹהִים֙ וְכֹ֣ה יוֹסִ֔יף אִם־תְּכַחֵ֤ד מִמֶּ֙נִּי֙ דָּבָ֔ר מִכָּל־הַדָּבָ֖ר אֲשֶׁר־דִּבֶּ֥ר אֵלֶֽיךָ׃ 18 וַיַּגֶּד־ל֨וֹ שְׁמוּאֵ֜ל אֶת־כָּל־הַדְּבָרִ֗ים וְלֹ֤א כִחֵ֖ד מִמֶּ֑נּוּ וַיֹּאמַ֕ר יְהוָ֣ה ה֔וּא הַטּ֥וֹב בְּעֵינָ֖ו יַעֲשֶֽׂה׃ פ

19 וַיִּגְדַּ֖ל שְׁמוּאֵ֑ל וַֽיהוָה֙ הָיָ֣ה עִמּ֔וֹ וְלֹֽא־הִפִּ֥יל מִכָּל־דְּבָרָ֖יו אָֽרְצָה׃ 20 וַיֵּ֙דַע֙ כָּל־יִשְׂרָאֵ֔ל מִדָּ֖ן וְעַד־בְּאֵ֣ר שָׁ֑בַע כִּ֚י נֶאֱמָ֣ן שְׁמוּאֵ֔ל לְנָבִ֖יא לַיהוָֽה׃ 21 וַיֹּ֤סֶף יְהוָה֙ לְהֵרָאֹ֣ה בְשִׁלֹ֔ה כִּֽי־נִגְלָ֤ה יְהוָה֙ אֶל־שְׁמוּאֵ֔ל בְּשִׁלֹ֖ו בִּדְבַ֥ר יְהוָֽה׃ פ

1 וַֽיְהִ֥י דְבַר־שְׁמוּאֵ֖ל לְכָל־יִשְׂרָאֵ֑ל וַיֵּצֵ֣א יִשְׂרָאֵ֗ל לִקְרַ֤את פְּלִשְׁתִּים֙ לַמִּלְחָמָ֔ה וַֽיַּחֲנוּ֙ עַל־הָאֶ֣בֶן הָעֵ֔זֶר וּפְלִשְׁתִּ֖ים חָנ֥וּ בַאֲפֵֽק׃ 2 וַיַּעַרְכ֨וּ פְלִשְׁתִּ֜ים לִקְרַ֣את יִשְׂרָאֵ֗ל וַתִּטֹּשׁ֙ הַמִּלְחָמָ֔ה וַיִּנָּ֥גֶף יִשְׂרָאֵ֖ל לִפְנֵ֣י פְלִשְׁתִּ֑ים וַיַּכּ֤וּ בַמַּֽעֲרָכָה֙ בַּשָּׂדֶ֔ה כְּאַרְבַּ֥עַת אֲלָפִ֖ים אִֽישׁ׃ 3 וַיָּבֹ֣א הָעָם֮ אֶל־הַֽמַּחֲנֶה֒ וַיֹּֽאמְרוּ֙ זִקְנֵ֣י יִשְׂרָאֵ֔ל לָ֣מָּה נְגָפָ֧נוּ יְהוָ֛ה הַיּ֖וֹם לִפְנֵ֣י פְלִשְׁתִּ֑ים נִקְחָ֧ה אֵלֵ֣ינוּ מִשִּׁלֹ֗ה אֶת־אֲרוֹן֙ בְּרִ֣ית יְהוָ֔ה וְיָבֹ֣א בְקִרְבֵּ֔נוּ וְיֹשִׁעֵ֖נוּ מִכַּ֥ף אֹיְבֵֽינוּ׃ 4 וַיִּשְׁלַ֤ח הָעָם֙ שִׁלֹ֔ה וַיִּשְׂא֣וּ מִשָּׁ֗ם אֵ֣ת אֲר֧וֹן בְּרִית־יְהוָ֛ה צְבָא֖וֹת יֹשֵׁ֣ב הַכְּרֻבִ֑ים וְשָׁ֞ם שְׁנֵ֣י

enant of the LORD of Hosts Enthroned on the Cherubim.

⁵When the Ark of the Covenant of the LORD entered the camp, all Israel burst into a great shout, so that the earth resounded. ⁶The Philistines heard the noise of the shouting and they wondered, "Why is there such a loud shouting in the camp of the Hebrews?" And when they learned that the Ark of the LORD had come to the camp, ⁷the Philistines were frightened; for they said, "God has come to the camp." And they cried, "Woe to us! Nothing like this has ever happened before. ⁸Woe to us! Who will save us from the power of this mighty God? He is the same God who struck the Egyptians with every kind of plague in the wilderness! ⁹Brace yourselves and be men, O Philistines! Or you will become slaves to the Hebrews as they were slaves to you. Be men and fight!" ¹⁰The Philistines fought; Israel was routed, and they all fled to their homes. The defeat was very great, thirty thousand foot soldiers of Israel fell there. ¹¹The Ark of God was captured, and Eli's two sons, Hophni and Phinehas, were slain.

¹²A Benjaminite ran from the battlefield and reached Shiloh the same day; his clothes were rent and there was earth on his head.ᶜ ¹³When he arrived, he found Eli sitting on a seat, waiting beside the road—his heart trembling for the Ark of God. The man entered the city to spread the news, and the whole city broke out in a cry. ¹⁴And when Eli heard the sound of the outcry and asked, "What is the meaning of this uproar?" the man rushed over to tell Eli. ¹⁵Now Eli was ninety-eight years old; his eyes were fixed in a blind stare. ¹⁶The man said to Eli, "I am the one who came from the battlefield; I have just fled from the battlefield." [Eli] asked, "What happened, my son?" ¹⁷The bearer of the news replied, "Israel fled before the Philistines

---

בְּנֵי־עֵלִ֗י עִם־אֲרוֹן֙ בְּרִ֣ית הָֽאֱלֹהִ֔ים חׇפְנִ֖י וּפִֽינְחָֽס׃

⁵ וַיְהִ֗י כְּב֨וֹא אֲר֤וֹן בְּרִית־יְהֹוָה֙ אֶל־הַֽמַּחֲנֶ֔ה וַיָּרִ֥עוּ כׇל־יִשְׂרָאֵ֖ל תְּרוּעָ֣ה גְדוֹלָ֑ה וַתֵּהֹ֖ם הָאָֽרֶץ׃ ⁶ וַיִּשְׁמְע֤וּ פְלִשְׁתִּים֙ אֶת־ק֣וֹל הַתְּרוּעָ֔ה וַיֹּ֣אמְר֔וּ מֶ֠ה ק֣וֹל הַתְּרוּעָ֧ה הַגְּדוֹלָ֛ה הַזֹּ֖את בְּמַחֲנֵ֣ה הָעִבְרִ֑ים וַיֵּ֣דְע֔וּ כִּ֚י אֲר֣וֹן יְהֹוָ֔ה בָּ֖א אֶל־הַֽמַּחֲנֶֽה׃ ⁷ וַיִּֽרְאוּ֙ הַפְּלִשְׁתִּ֔ים כִּ֣י אָֽמְר֔וּ בָּ֥א אֱלֹהִ֖ים אֶל־הַֽמַּחֲנֶ֑ה וַיֹּֽאמְרוּ֙ א֣וֹי לָ֔נוּ כִּ֣י לֹ֤א הָֽיְתָה֙ כָּזֹ֔את אֶתְמ֖וֹל שִׁלְשֹֽׁם׃ ⁸ א֣וֹי לָ֔נוּ מִ֣י יַצִּילֵ֔נוּ מִיַּ֛ד הָאֱלֹהִ֥ים הָאַדִּירִ֖ים הָאֵ֑לֶּה אֵ֧לֶּה הֵ֣ם הָאֱלֹהִ֗ים הַמַּכִּ֧ים אֶת־מִצְרַ֛יִם בְּכׇל־מַכָּ֖ה בַּמִּדְבָּֽר׃ ⁹ הִֽתְחַזְּק֞וּ וִֽהְי֤וּ לַֽאֲנָשִׁים֙ פְּלִשְׁתִּ֔ים פֶּ֚ן תַּעַבְד֣וּ לָֽעִבְרִ֔ים כַּאֲשֶׁ֥ר עָבְד֖וּ לָכֶ֑ם וִהְיִיתֶ֥ם לַֽאֲנָשִׁ֖ים וְנִלְחַמְתֶּֽם׃ ¹⁰ וַיִּלָּֽחֲמ֣וּ פְלִשְׁתִּ֗ים וַיִּנָּ֤גֶף יִשְׂרָאֵל֙ וַיָּנֻ֙סוּ֙ אִ֣ישׁ לְאֹֽהָלָ֔יו וַתְּהִ֥י הַמַּכָּ֖ה גְּדוֹלָ֣ה מְאֹ֑ד וַיִּפֹּל֙ מִיִּשְׂרָאֵ֔ל שְׁלֹשִׁ֥ים אֶ֖לֶף רַגְלִֽי׃ ¹¹ וַֽאֲר֥וֹן אֱלֹהִ֖ים נִלְקָ֑ח וּשְׁנֵ֤י בְנֵֽי־עֵלִי֙ מֵ֔תוּ חׇפְנִ֖י וּפִֽינְחָֽס׃

¹² וַיָּ֤רׇץ אִישׁ־בִּנְיָמִן֙ מֵֽהַמַּ֣עֲרָכָ֔ה וַיָּבֹ֥א שִׁלֹ֖ה בַּיּ֣וֹם הַה֑וּא וּמַדָּ֣יו קְרֻעִ֔ים וַאֲדָמָ֖ה עַל־רֹאשֽׁוֹ׃ ¹³ וַיָּב֗וֹא וְהִנֵּ֣ה עֵלִ֡י יֹשֵׁ֣ב עַֽל־הַ֠כִּסֵּ֠א יׇ֨ד דֶּ֜רֶךְ מְצַפֶּ֗ה כִּֽי־הָיָ֤ה לִבּוֹ֙ חָרֵ֔ד עַ֖ל אֲר֣וֹן הָאֱלֹהִ֑ים וְהָאִ֗ישׁ בָּ֚א לְהַגִּ֣יד בָּעִ֔יר וַתִּזְעַ֖ק כׇּל־הָעִֽיר׃ ¹⁴ וַיִּשְׁמַ֤ע עֵלִי֙ אֶת־ק֣וֹל הַצְּעָקָ֔ה וַיֹּ֕אמֶר מֶ֛ה ק֥וֹל הֶהָמ֖וֹן הַזֶּ֑ה וְהָאִ֣ישׁ מִהַ֔ר וַיָּבֹ֖א וַיַּגֵּ֥ד לְעֵלִֽי׃ ¹⁵ וְעֵלִ֕י בֶּן־תִּשְׁעִ֥ים וּשְׁמֹנֶ֖ה שָׁנָ֑ה וְעֵינָ֣יו קָ֔מָה וְלֹ֥א יָכ֖וֹל לִרְאֽוֹת׃ ¹⁶ וַיֹּ֨אמֶר הָאִ֜ישׁ אֶל־עֵלִ֗י אָֽנֹכִי֙ הַבָּ֣א מִן־הַמַּ֣עֲרָכָ֔ה וַֽאֲנִ֕י מִן־הַמַּעֲרָכָ֖ה נַ֣סְתִּי הַיּ֑וֹם וַיֹּ֛אמֶר מֶֽה־הָיָ֥ה הַדָּבָ֖ר בְּנִֽי׃ ¹⁷ וַיַּ֣עַן הַֽמְבַשֵּׂר֮ וַיֹּ֒אמֶר֒ נָ֤ס יִשְׂרָאֵל֙ לִפְנֵ֣י פְלִשְׁתִּ֔ים וְגַ֛ם מַגֵּפָ֥ה

---

and the troops also suffered a great slaughter. Your two sons, Hophni and Phinehas, are dead, and the Ark of God has been captured." [18]When he mentioned the Ark of God, [Eli] fell backward off the seat beside[b] the gate, broke his neck and died; for he was an old man and heavy. He had been a chieftain of Israel for forty years.

[19]His daughter-in-law, the wife of Phinehas, was with child, about to give birth. When she heard the report that the Ark of God was captured and that her father-in-law and her husband were dead, she was seized with labor pains, and she crouched down and gave birth. [20]As she lay dying, the women attending her said, "Do not be afraid, for you have borne a son." But she did not respond or pay heed. [21]She named the boy Ichabod, meaning, "The glory has departed from Israel"—referring to the capture of the Ark of God and to [the death of] her father-in-law and her husband. [22]"The glory is gone from Israel," she said, "for the Ark of God has been captured."

5 When the Philistines captured the Ark of God, they brought it from Eben-ezer to Ashdod. [2]The Philistines took the Ark of God and brought it into the temple of Dagon and they set it up beside Dagon. [3]Early the next day, the Ashdodites found Dagon lying face down on the ground in front of the Ark of the LORD. They picked Dagon up and put him back in his place; [4]but early the next morning, Dagon was again lying prone on the ground in front of the Ark of the LORD. The head and both hands of Dagon were cut off, lying on the threshold; only [a-]Dagon's trunk was left intact.[-a] [5]That is why, to this day, the priests of Dagon and all who enter the temple of Dagon do not tread on the threshold of Dagon in Ashdod.

---

a-a Meaning of Heb. uncertain.

גְדוֹלָ֖ה הָיְתָ֣ה בָעָ֑ם וְגַם־שְׁנֵ֨י בָנֶ֤יךָ מֵ֙תוּ֙ חׇפְנִ֣י וּפִ֣ינְחָ֔ס וַאֲר֥וֹן הָאֱלֹהִ֖ים נִלְקָֽחָה׃ פ
18 וַיְהִ֞י כְּהַזְכִּיר֣וֹ ׀ אֶת־אֲר֣וֹן הָאֱלֹהִ֗ים וַיִּפֹּ֣ל מֵעַֽל־הַ֠כִּסֵּ֠א אֲחֹרַנִּ֜ית בְּעַ֣ד ׀ יַ֣ד הַשַּׁ֗עַר וַתִּשָּׁבֵ֤ר מַפְרַקְתּוֹ֙ וַיָּמֹ֔ת כִּֽי־זָקֵ֥ן הָאִ֖ישׁ וְכָבֵ֑ד וְה֛וּא שָׁפַ֥ט אֶת־יִשְׂרָאֵ֖ל אַרְבָּעִ֥ים שָׁנָֽה׃
19 וְכַלָּת֣וֹ אֵֽשֶׁת־פִּֽינְחָס֮ הָרָ֣ה לָלַת֒ וַתִּשְׁמַ֣ע אֶת־הַשְּׁמֻעָ֔ה אֶל־הִלָּקַח֙ אֲר֣וֹן הָאֱלֹהִ֔ים וּמֵ֥ת חָמִ֖יהָ וְאִישָׁ֑הּ וַתִּכְרַ֣ע וַתֵּ֔לֶד כִּֽי־נֶהֶפְכ֥וּ עָלֶ֖יהָ צִרֶֽיהָ׃ 20 וּכְעֵ֣ת מוּתָ֗הּ וַתְּדַבֵּ֙רְנָה֙ הַנִּצָּב֣וֹת עָלֶ֔יהָ אַל־תִּֽירְאִ֖י כִּ֣י בֵ֣ן יָלָ֑דְתְּ וְלֹ֥א עָֽנְתָ֖ה וְלֹא־שָׁ֥תָה לִבָּֽהּ׃
21 וַתִּקְרָ֣א לַנַּ֗עַר אִֽי־כָבוֹד֙ לֵאמֹ֔ר גָּלָ֥ה כָב֖וֹד מִיִּשְׂרָאֵ֑ל אֶל־הִלָּקַח֙ אֲר֣וֹן הָאֱלֹהִ֔ים וְאֶל־חָמִ֖יהָ וְאִישָֽׁהּ׃ 22 וַתֹּ֕אמֶר גָּלָ֥ה כָב֖וֹד מִיִּשְׂרָאֵ֑ל כִּ֥י נִלְקַ֖ח אֲר֥וֹן הָאֱלֹהִֽים׃ פ

ה וּפְלִשְׁתִּים֙ לָֽקְח֔וּ אֵ֖ת אֲר֣וֹן הָאֱלֹהִ֑ים וַיְבִאֻ֛הוּ מֵאֶ֥בֶן הָעֵ֖זֶר אַשְׁדּֽוֹדָה׃ 2 וַיִּקְח֣וּ פְלִשְׁתִּים֮ אֶת־אֲר֣וֹן הָאֱלֹהִים֒ וַיָּבִ֣יאוּ אֹת֔וֹ בֵּ֣ית דָּג֑וֹן וַיַּצִּ֥יגוּ אֹת֖וֹ אֵ֥צֶל דָּגֽוֹן׃ 3 וַיַּשְׁכִּ֤מוּ אַשְׁדּוֹדִים֙ מִֽמׇּחֳרָ֔ת וְהִנֵּ֣ה דָג֗וֹן נֹפֵ֤ל לְפָנָיו֙ אַ֔רְצָה לִפְנֵ֖י אֲר֣וֹן יְהֹוָ֑ה וַיִּקְחוּ֙ אֶת־דָּג֔וֹן וַיָּשִׁ֥בוּ אֹת֖וֹ לִמְקוֹמֽוֹ׃ 4 וַיַּשְׁכִּ֣מוּ בַבֹּ֩קֶר֩ מִֽמׇּחֳרָ֜ת וְהִנֵּ֣ה דָג֗וֹן נֹפֵ֤ל לְפָנָיו֙ אַ֔רְצָה לִפְנֵ֖י אֲר֣וֹן יְהֹוָ֑ה וְרֹ֨אשׁ דָּג֜וֹן וּשְׁתֵּ֣י ׀ כַּפּ֣וֹת יָדָ֗יו כְּרֻתוֹת֙ אֶל־הַמִּפְתָּ֔ן רַ֥ק דָּג֖וֹן נִשְׁאַ֥ר עָלָֽיו׃ 5 עַל־כֵּ֡ן לֹֽא־יִדְרְכוּ֩ כֹהֲנֵ֨י דָג֜וֹן וְכׇֽל־הַבָּאִ֧ים בֵּית־דָּג֛וֹן עַל־מִפְתַּ֥ן דָּג֖וֹן בְּאַשְׁדּ֑וֹד עַ֖ד הַיּ֥וֹם הַזֶּֽה׃ ס

6The hand of the Lord lay heavy upon the Ashdodites, and He wrought havoc among them: He struck b-Ashdod and its territory-b with hemorrhoids. 7When the men of Ashdod saw how matters stood, they said, "The Ark of the God of Israel must not remain with us, for His hand has dealt harshly with us and with our god Dagon." 8They sent messengers and assembled all the lords of the Philistines and asked, "What shall we do with the Ark of the God of Israel?" They answered, "Let the Ark of the God of Israel be removed to Gath." So they moved the Ark of the God of Israel [to Gath]. 9And after they had moved it, the hand of the Lord came against the city, causing great panic; He struck the people of the city, young and old, so that hemorrhoids a-broke out-a among them. 10Then they sent the Ark of God to Ekron. But when the Ark of God came to Ekron, the Ekronites cried out, "They have moved the Ark of the God of Israel to us to slay us and our kindred." 11They too sent messengers and assembled all the lords of the Philistines and said, "Send the Ark of the God of Israel away, and let it return to its own place, that it may not slay us and our kindred." For the panic of death pervaded the whole city, so heavily had the hand of God fallen there; 12and the men who did not die were stricken with hemorrhoids. The outcry of the city went up to heaven.

6 The Ark of the Lord remained in the territory of the Philistines seven months.a 2Then the Philistines summoned the priests and the diviners and asked, "What shall we do about the Ark of the Lord? Tell us with what we shall send it off to its own place." 3They answered, "If you

6 וַתִּכְבַּ֧ד יַד־יְהוָ֛ה אֶל־הָאַשְׁדּוֹדִ֖ים וַיְשִׁמֵּ֑ם וַיַּ֤ךְ אֹתָם֙ בעפלים בַּטְּחֹרִ֔ים אֶת־אַשְׁדּ֖וֹד וְאֶת־גְּבוּלֶֽיהָ׃ 7 וַיִּרְא֥וּ אַנְשֵֽׁי־אַשְׁדּ֖וֹד כִּי־כֵ֑ן וְאָמְר֗וּ לֹֽא־יֵשֵׁ֞ב אֲר֨וֹן אֱלֹהֵ֤י יִשְׂרָאֵל֙ עִמָּ֔נוּ כִּֽי־קָשְׁתָ֤ה יָדוֹ֙ עָלֵ֔ינוּ וְעַ֖ל דָּג֥וֹן אֱלֹהֵֽינוּ׃ 8 וַיִּשְׁלְח֡וּ וַיַּאַסְפוּ֩ אֶת־כָּל־סַרְנֵ֨י פְלִשְׁתִּ֜ים אֲלֵיהֶ֗ם וַיֹּֽאמְרוּ֙ מַֽה־נַּעֲשֶׂ֔ה לַֽאֲרוֹן֙ אֱלֹהֵ֣י יִשְׂרָאֵ֔ל וַיֹּ֣אמְר֔וּ גַּ֣ת יִסֹּ֔ב אֲר֖וֹן אֱלֹהֵ֣י יִשְׂרָאֵ֑ל וַיַּסֵּ֕בּוּ אֶת־אֲר֖וֹן אֱלֹהֵ֥י יִשְׂרָאֵֽל׃ ס 9 וַיְהִ֞י אַחֲרֵ֣י ׀ הֵסַ֣בּוּ אֹת֗וֹ וַתְּהִ֨י יַד־יְהוָ֤ה ׀ בָּעִיר֙ מְהוּמָה֙ גְּדוֹלָ֣ה מְאֹ֔ד וַיַּךְ֙ אֶת־אַנְשֵׁ֣י הָעִ֔יר מִקָּטֹ֖ן וְעַד־גָּד֑וֹל וַיִּשָּׂתְר֥וּ לָהֶ֖ם עפלים טְחֹרִֽים׃ 10 וַֽיְשַׁלְּח֛וּ אֶת־אֲר֥וֹן הָאֱלֹהִ֖ים עֶקְר֑וֹן וַיְהִ֗י כְּב֨וֹא אֲר֤וֹן הָֽאֱלֹהִים֙ עֶקְר֔וֹן וַיִּזְעֲק֤וּ הָעֶקְרֹנִים֙ לֵאמֹ֔ר הֵסַ֧בּוּ אֵלַ֛י אֶת־אֲר֛וֹן אֱלֹהֵ֥י יִשְׂרָאֵ֖ל לַהֲמִיתֵ֥נִי וְאֶת־עַמִּֽי׃ 11 וַיִּשְׁלְח֗וּ וַיַּֽאַסְפוּ֙ אֶת־כָּל־סַרְנֵ֣י פְלִשְׁתִּ֔ים וַיֹּֽאמְרוּ֙ שַׁלְּח֞וּ אֶת־אֲר֨וֹן אֱלֹהֵ֤י יִשְׂרָאֵל֙ וְיָשֹׁ֣ב לִמְקֹמ֔וֹ וְלֹֽא־יָמִ֥ית אֹתִ֖י וְאֶת־עַמִּ֑י כִּֽי־הָיְתָ֤ה מְהֽוּמַת־מָ֙וֶת֙ בְּכָל־הָעִ֔יר כָּבְדָ֥ה מְאֹ֖ד יַ֣ד הָאֱלֹהִ֖ים שָֽׁם׃ 12 וְהָֽאֲנָשִׁים֙ אֲשֶׁ֣ר לֹא־מֵ֔תוּ הֻכּ֖וּ בעפלים בַּטְּחֹרִ֑ים וַתַּ֛עַל שַֽׁוְעַ֥ת הָעִ֖יר הַשָּׁמָֽיִם׃

ו וַיְהִ֧י אֲרוֹן־יְהוָ֛ה בִּשְׂדֵ֥ה פְלִשְׁתִּ֖ים שִׁבְעָ֥ה חֳדָשִֽׁים׃ 2 וַיִּקְרְא֣וּ פְלִשְׁתִּ֗ים לַכֹּהֲנִ֤ים וְלַקֹּֽסְמִים֙ לֵאמֹ֔ר מַה־נַּעֲשֶׂ֖ה לַֽאֲר֣וֹן יְהוָ֑ה הוֹדִעֻ֕נוּ בַּמֶּ֖ה נְשַׁלְּחֶ֥נּוּ לִמְקוֹמֽוֹ׃ 3 וַיֹּאמְר֗וּ אִֽם־מְשַׁלְּחִ֞ים אֶת־

---

b-b   Meaning of Heb. uncertain. Septuagint reads differently from our Heb. text; it also mentions mice swarming in the Philistine ships and invading their fields. Cf. the mention of "mice" in 6.4, 18; and the note at 6.1.

a   Septuagint continues "and mice invaded their fields"; cf. vv. 4, 5, 18, and note at 5.6.

are going to send the Ark of the God of Israel away, do not send it away without anything; you must also pay an indemnity to Him. Then you will be healed, and b-He will make Himself known to you; otherwise His hand will not turn away from you."-b 4They asked, "What is the indemnity that we should pay to Him?" They answered, "Five golden hemorrhoids and five golden mice, corresponding to the number of lords of the Philistines; for the same plague struck all of youᶜ and your lords. 5You shall make figures of your hemorrhoids and of the mice that are ravaging your land; thus you shall honor the God of Israel, and perhaps He will lighten the weight of His hand upon you and your gods and your land. 6Don't harden your hearts as the Egyptians and Pharaoh hardened their hearts. As you know, when He made a mockery of them, they had to let Israelᶜ go, and they departed. 7Therefore, get a new cart ready and two milch cows that have not borne a yoke; harness the cows to the cart, but take back indoors the calves that follow them. 8Take the Ark of the Lord and place it on the cart; and put next to it in a chest the gold objects you are paying Him as indemnity. Send it off, and let it go its own way. 9Then watch: If it goes up the road to Beth-shemesh, to His own territory, it was He who has inflicted this great harm on us. But if not, we shall know that it was not His hand that struck us; it just happened to us by chance."

10The men did so. They took two milch cows and harnessed them to the cart, and shut up their calves indoors. 11They placed the Ark of the Lord on the cart together with the chest, the golden mice, and the figures of their hemorrhoids. 12The cows went straight ahead along the road to Beth-shemesh. They went along a single highroad, lowing as they went, and turning off neither to the right nor to the left; and

אֲרוֹן אֱלֹהֵי יִשְׂרָאֵל אַל־תְּשַׁלְּחוּ אֹתוֹ רֵיקָם כִּי־הָשֵׁב תָּשִׁיבוּ לוֹ אָשָׁם אָז תֵּרָפְאוּ וְנוֹדַע לָכֶם לָמָּה לֹא־תָסוּר יָדוֹ מִכֶּם: 4 וַיֹּאמְרוּ מָה הָאָשָׁם אֲשֶׁר נָשִׁיב לוֹ וַיֹּאמְרוּ מִסְפַּר סַרְנֵי פְלִשְׁתִּים חֲמִשָּׁה עׇפְלֵי זָהָב וַחֲמִשָּׁה עַכְבְּרֵי זָהָב כִּי־מַגֵּפָה אַחַת לְכֻלָּם וּלְסַרְנֵיכֶם: 5 וַעֲשִׂיתֶם צַלְמֵי עׇפְלֵיכֶם וְצַלְמֵי עַכְבְּרֵיכֶם הַמַּשְׁחִיתִם אֶת־הָאָרֶץ וּנְתַתֶּם לֵאלֹהֵי יִשְׂרָאֵל כָּבוֹד אוּלַי יָקֵל אֶת־יָדוֹ מֵעֲלֵיכֶם וּמֵעַל אֱלֹהֵיכֶם וּמֵעַל אַרְצְכֶם: 6 וְלָמָּה תְכַבְּדוּ אֶת־לְבַבְכֶם כַּאֲשֶׁר כִּבְּדוּ מִצְרַיִם וּפַרְעֹה אֶת־לִבָּם הֲלוֹא כַּאֲשֶׁר הִתְעַלֵּל בָּהֶם וַיְשַׁלְּחוּם וַיֵּלֵכוּ: 7 וְעַתָּה קְחוּ וַעֲשׂוּ עֲגָלָה חֲדָשָׁה אֶחָת וּשְׁתֵּי פָרוֹת עָלוֹת אֲשֶׁר לֹא־עָלָה עֲלֵיהֶם עֹל וַאֲסַרְתֶּם אֶת־הַפָּרוֹת בָּעֲגָלָה וַהֲשֵׁיבֹתֶם בְּנֵיהֶם מֵאַחֲרֵיהֶם הַבָּיְתָה: 8 וּלְקַחְתֶּם אֶת־אֲרוֹן יְהֹוָה וּנְתַתֶּם אֹתוֹ אֶל־הָעֲגָלָה וְאֵת ׀ כְּלֵי הַזָּהָב אֲשֶׁר הֲשֵׁבֹתֶם לוֹ אָשָׁם תָּשִׂימוּ בָאַרְגַּז מִצִּדּוֹ וְשִׁלַּחְתֶּם אֹתוֹ וְהָלָךְ: 9 וּרְאִיתֶם אִם־דֶּרֶךְ גְּבוּלוֹ יַעֲלֶה בֵּית שֶׁמֶשׁ הוּא עָשָׂה לָנוּ אֶת־הָרָעָה הַגְּדוֹלָה הַזֹּאת וְאִם־לֹא וְיָדַעְנוּ כִּי לֹא יָדוֹ נָגְעָה בָּנוּ מִקְרֶה הוּא הָיָה לָנוּ: 10 וַיַּעֲשׂוּ הָאֲנָשִׁים כֵּן וַיִּקְחוּ שְׁתֵּי פָרוֹת עָלוֹת וַיַּאַסְרוּם בָּעֲגָלָה וְאֶת־בְּנֵיהֶם כָּלוּ בַבָּיִת: 11 וַיָּשִׂמוּ אֶת־אֲרוֹן יְהֹוָה אֶל־הָעֲגָלָה וְאֵת הָאַרְגַּז וְאֵת עַכְבְּרֵי הַזָּהָב וְאֵת צַלְמֵי טְחֹרֵיהֶם: 12 וַיִּשַּׁרְנָה הַפָּרוֹת בַּדֶּרֶךְ עַל־דֶּרֶךְ בֵּית שֶׁמֶשׁ בִּמְסִלָּה אַחַת הָלְכוּ הָלֹךְ וְגָעוֹ וְלֹא־סָרוּ יָמִין וּשְׂמֹאול*

b-b Or "and you will know why His hand would not turn away from you." Meaning of Heb. uncertain.
c Heb. "them."

מלא ו׳ v. 12.

the lords of the Philistines walked behind them as far as the border of Beth-shemesh.

13The people of Beth-shemesh were reaping their wheat harvest in the valley. They looked up and saw the Ark, and they rejoiced d-when they saw [it].-d 14The cart came into the field of Joshua of Beth-shemesh and it stopped there. They split up the wood of the cart and presented the cows as a burnt offering to the LORD. A large stone was there; 15and the Levites took down the Ark of the LORD and the chest beside it containing the gold objects and placed them on the large stone. Then the men of Beth-shemesh presented burnt offerings and other sacrifices to the LORD that day. 16The five lords of the Philistines saw this and returned the same day to Ekron.

17The following were the golden hemorrhoids that the Philistines paid as an indemnity to the LORD: For Ashdod, one; for Gaza, one; for Ashkelon, one; for Gath, one; for Ekron, one. 18eAs for the golden mice, their number accorded with all the Philistine towns that belonged to the five lords—both fortified towns and unwalled f-villages, as far as-f the great stoneg on which the Ark of the LORD was set down, to this day, in the field of Joshua of Beth-shemesh.

19[The LORD] struck at the men of Beth-shemesh because h-they looked into the Ark of the LORD; He struck down seventy men among the people [and] fifty thousand men.-h The people mourned, for He had inflicted a great slaughter upon the population. 20And the men of Beth-shemesh asked, "Who can stand in attendance on the LORD, this holy God? And to whom shall He go up from us?" 21They sent messengers to the inhabitants of Kiriath-jearim to say, "The Philistines have sent back the Ark

וְסַרְנֵי פְלִשְׁתִּים הָלְכִים אַחֲרֵיהֶם עַד־גְּבוּל בֵּית שָׁמֶשׁ: 13 וּבֵית שֶׁמֶשׁ קֹצְרִים קְצִיר־חִטִּים בָּעֵמֶק וַיִּשְׂאוּ אֶת־עֵינֵיהֶם וַיִּרְאוּ אֶת־הָאָרוֹן וַיִּשְׂמְחוּ לִרְאוֹת: 14 וְהָעֲגָלָה בָּאָה אֶל־שְׂדֵה יְהוֹשֻׁעַ בֵּית־הַשִּׁמְשִׁי וַתַּעֲמֹד שָׁם וְשָׁם אֶבֶן גְּדוֹלָה וַיְבַקְּעוּ אֶת־עֲצֵי הָעֲגָלָה וְאֶת־הַפָּרוֹת הֶעֱלוּ עֹלָה לַיהוָה: ס 15 וְהַלְוִיִּם הוֹרִידוּ | אֶת־אֲרוֹן יְהוָה וְאֶת־הָאַרְגַּז אֲשֶׁר־אִתּוֹ אֲשֶׁר־בּוֹ כְלֵי־זָהָב וַיָּשִׂמוּ אֶל־הָאֶבֶן הַגְּדוֹלָה וְאַנְשֵׁי בֵית־שֶׁמֶשׁ הֶעֱלוּ עֹלוֹת וַיִּזְבְּחוּ זְבָחִים בַּיּוֹם הַהוּא לַיהוָה: 16 וַחֲמִשָּׁה סַרְנֵי־פְלִשְׁתִּים רָאוּ וַיָּשֻׁבוּ עֶקְרוֹן בַּיּוֹם הַהוּא: ס 17 וְאֵלֶּה טְחֹרֵי הַזָּהָב אֲשֶׁר הֵשִׁיבוּ פְלִשְׁתִּים אָשָׁם לַיהוָה *לְאַשְׁדּוֹד אֶחָד לְעַזָּה אֶחָד לְאַשְׁקְלוֹן אֶחָד לְגַת אֶחָד לְעֶקְרוֹן אֶחָד: ס 18 וְעַכְבְּרֵי הַזָּהָב מִסְפַּר כָּל־עָרֵי פְלִשְׁתִּים לַחֲמֵשֶׁת הַסְּרָנִים מֵעִיר מִבְצָר וְעַד כֹּפֶר הַפְּרָזִי וְעַד | אָבֵל* הַגְּדוֹלָה אֲשֶׁר הִנִּיחוּ עָלֶיהָ אֵת אֲרוֹן יְהוָה עַד הַיּוֹם הַזֶּה בִּשְׂדֵה יְהוֹשֻׁעַ בֵּית־הַשִּׁמְשִׁי: 19 וַיַּךְ בְּאַנְשֵׁי בֵית־שֶׁמֶשׁ כִּי רָאוּ בַּאֲרוֹן יְהוָה וַיַּךְ בָּעָם שִׁבְעִים אִישׁ חֲמִשִּׁים אֶלֶף אִישׁ וַיִּתְאַבְּלוּ הָעָם כִּי־הִכָּה יְהוָה בָּעָם מַכָּה גְדוֹלָה: 20 וַיֹּאמְרוּ אַנְשֵׁי בֵית־שֶׁמֶשׁ מִי יוּכַל לַעֲמֹד לִפְנֵי יְהוָה הָאֱלֹהִים הַקָּדוֹשׁ הַזֶּה וְאֶל־מִי יַעֲלֶה מֵעָלֵינוּ: ס 21 וַיִּשְׁלְחוּ מַלְאָכִים אֶל־יוֹשְׁבֵי קִרְיַת־יְעָרִים לֵאמֹר הֵשִׁבוּ

d-d Septuagint reads "As they met it."
e Meaning of vv. 18 and 19 uncertain in part.
f-f Emendation yields "villages, as witness there is."
g Reading 'eben with some Heb. mss., Septuagint, and Targum, most mss. and editions 'abel, "meadow [?]."
h-h Force of Heb. uncertain.

583

of the LORD. Come down and take it into your keeping."

7 ¹The men of Kiriath-jearim came and took up the Ark of the LORD and brought it into the house of Abinadab on the hill; and they consecrated his son Eleazar to have charge of the Ark of the LORD.

²A long time elapsed from the day that the Ark was housed in Kiriath-jearim, twenty years in all; and all the House of Israel *a*-yearned after-*a* the LORD. ³And Samuel said to all the House of Israel, "If you mean to return to the LORD with all your heart, you must remove the alien gods and the Ashtaroth from your midst and direct your heart to the LORD and serve Him alone. Then He will deliver you from the hands of the Philistines." ⁴And the Israelites removed the Baalim and Ashtaroth and they served the LORD alone.

⁵Samuel said, "Assemble all Israel at Mizpah, and I will pray to the LORD for you." ⁶They assembled at Mizpah, and they drew water and poured it out before the LORD; they fasted that day, and there they confessed that they had sinned against the LORD. And Samuel acted as chieftain of the Israelites at Mizpah.

⁷When the Philistines heard that the Israelites had assembled at Mizpah, the lords of the Philistines marched out against Israel. Hearing of this, the Israelites were terrified of the Philistines ⁸and they implored Samuel, "Do not neglect us and do not refrain from crying out to the LORD our God to save us from the hands of the Philistines." ⁹Thereupon Samuel took a suckling lamb and sacrificed it as a whole burnt offering to the LORD; and Samuel cried out to the LORD in behalf of Israel, and the LORD responded to him. ¹⁰For as Samuel was presenting the burnt offering and the Philistines advanced to attack Israel, the LORD thundered mightily against the Philistines that day. He threw them into confusion, and they were routed by Israel.

---

a-a Meaning of Heb. uncertain.

פְּלִשְׁתִּים אֶת־אֲרוֹן יְהוָה רְדוּ הַעֲלוּ אֹתוֹ
אֲלֵיכֶם: ¹ וַיָּבֹאוּ אַנְשֵׁי ׀ קִרְיַת יְעָרִים
וַיַּעֲלוּ אֶת־אֲרוֹן יְהוָה וַיָּבִאוּ אֹתוֹ
אֶל־בֵּית אֲבִינָדָב בַּגִּבְעָה וְאֶת־אֶלְעָזָר בְּנוֹ
קִדְּשׁוּ לִשְׁמֹר אֶת־אֲרוֹן יְהוָה: פ
² וַיְהִי מִיּוֹם שֶׁבֶת הָאָרוֹן בְּקִרְיַת יְעָרִים
וַיִּרְבּוּ הַיָּמִים וַיִּהְיוּ עֶשְׂרִים שָׁנָה
וַיִּנָּהוּ כָּל־בֵּית יִשְׂרָאֵל אַחֲרֵי יְהוָה: ס
³ וַיֹּאמֶר שְׁמוּאֵל אֶל־כָּל־בֵּית יִשְׂרָאֵל
לֵאמֹר אִם־בְּכָל־לְבַבְכֶם אַתֶּם שָׁבִים אֶל־
יְהוָה הָסִירוּ אֶת־אֱלֹהֵי הַנֵּכָר מִתּוֹכְכֶם
וְהָעַשְׁתָּרוֹת וְהָכִינוּ לְבַבְכֶם אֶל־יְהוָה
וְעִבְדֻהוּ לְבַדּוֹ וְיַצֵּל אֶתְכֶם מִיַּד פְּלִשְׁתִּים:
⁴ וַיָּסִירוּ בְּנֵי יִשְׂרָאֵל אֶת־הַבְּעָלִים וְאֶת־
הָעַשְׁתָּרֹת וַיַּעַבְדוּ אֶת־יְהוָה לְבַדּוֹ: פ
⁵ וַיֹּאמֶר שְׁמוּאֵל קִבְצוּ אֶת־כָּל־יִשְׂרָאֵל
הַמִּצְפָּתָה וְאֶתְפַּלֵּל בַּעַדְכֶם אֶל־יְהוָה:
⁶ וַיִּקָּבְצוּ הַמִּצְפָּתָה וַיִּשְׁאֲבוּ־מַיִם
וַיִּשְׁפְּכוּ ׀ לִפְנֵי יְהוָה וַיָּצוּמוּ בַּיּוֹם הַהוּא
וַיֹּאמְרוּ שָׁם חָטָאנוּ לַיהוָה וַיִּשְׁפֹּט
שְׁמוּאֵל אֶת־בְּנֵי יִשְׂרָאֵל בַּמִּצְפָּה:
⁷ וַיִּשְׁמְעוּ פְלִשְׁתִּים כִּי־הִתְקַבְּצוּ בְנֵי־
יִשְׂרָאֵל הַמִּצְפָּתָה וַיַּעֲלוּ סַרְנֵי־פְלִשְׁתִּים
אֶל־יִשְׂרָאֵל וַיִּשְׁמְעוּ בְּנֵי יִשְׂרָאֵל וַיִּרְאוּ
מִפְּנֵי פְלִשְׁתִּים: ⁸ וַיֹּאמְרוּ בְנֵי־יִשְׂרָאֵל
אֶל־שְׁמוּאֵל אַל־תַּחֲרֵשׁ מִמֶּנּוּ מִזְּעֹק אֶל־
יְהוָה אֱלֹהֵינוּ וְיֹשִׁעֵנוּ מִיַּד פְּלִשְׁתִּים:
⁹ וַיִּקַּח שְׁמוּאֵל טְלֵה חָלָב אֶחָד וַיַּעֲלֵהוּ
וַיַּעֲלֵהוּ עוֹלָה כָּלִיל לַיהוָה וַיִּזְעַק שְׁמוּאֵל
אֶל־יְהוָה בְּעַד יִשְׂרָאֵל וַיַּעֲנֵהוּ יְהוָה:
¹⁰ וַיְהִי שְׁמוּאֵל מַעֲלֶה הָעוֹלָה וּפְלִשְׁתִּים
נִגְּשׁוּ לַמִּלְחָמָה בְּיִשְׂרָאֵל וַיַּרְעֵם יְהוָה ׀
בְּקוֹל־גָּדוֹל בַּיּוֹם הַהוּא עַל־פְּלִשְׁתִּים
וַיְהֻמֵּם וַיִּנָּגְפוּ לִפְנֵי יִשְׂרָאֵל: ¹¹ וַיֵּצְאוּ

11The men of Israel sallied out of Mizpah and pursued the Philistines, striking them down to a point below Beth-car.

12Samuel took a stone and set it up between Mizpah and Shen,*b* and named it Eben-ezer:*c* "For up to now," he said, "the LORD has helped us." 13The Philistines were humbled and did not invade the territory of Israel again; and the hand of the LORD was set against the Philistines as long as Samuel lived. 14The towns which the Philistines had taken from Israel, from Ekron to Gath, were restored to Israel; Israel recovered all her territory from the Philistines. There was also peace between Israel and the Amorites.

15Samuel judged Israel as long as he lived. 16Each year he made the rounds of Bethel, Gilgal, and Mizpah, and acted as judge over Israel at all those places. 17Then he would return to Ramah, for his home was there, and there too he would judge Israel. He built an altar there to the LORD.

8 When Samuel grew old, he appointed his sons judges over Israel. 2The name of his firstborn son was Joel, and his second son's name was Abijah; they sat as judges in Beer-sheba. 3But his sons did not follow in his ways; they were bent on gain, they accepted bribes, and they subverted justice.

4All the elders of Israel assembled and came to Samuel at Ramah, 5and they said to him, "You have grown old, and your sons have not followed your ways. Therefore appoint a king for us, to govern us like all other nations." 6Samuel was displeased that they said "Give us a king to govern us." Samuel prayed to the LORD, 7and the LORD replied to Samuel, "Heed the demand of the people in everything they say to you. For it is not you that they have rejected; it is Me they

אַנְשֵׁי יִשְׂרָאֵל מִן־הַמִּצְפָּה וַיִּרְדְּפוּ אֶת־פְּלִשְׁתִּים וַיַּכּוּם עַד־מִתַּחַת לְבֵית כָּר: 12וַיִּקַּח שְׁמוּאֵל אֶבֶן אַחַת וַיָּשֶׂם בֵּין־הַמִּצְפָּה וּבֵין הַשֵּׁן וַיִּקְרָא אֶת־שְׁמָהּ אֶבֶן הָעָזֶר וַיֹּאמַר עַד־הֵנָּה עֲזָרָנוּ יְהוָה: 13וַיִּכָּנְעוּ הַפְּלִשְׁתִּים וְלֹא־יָסְפוּ עוֹד לָבוֹא בִּגְבוּל יִשְׂרָאֵל וַתְּהִי יַד־יְהוָה בַּפְּלִשְׁתִּים כֹּל יְמֵי שְׁמוּאֵל: 14וַתָּשֹׁבְנָה הֶעָרִים אֲשֶׁר לָקְחוּ־פְלִשְׁתִּים מֵאֵת יִשְׂרָאֵל | לְיִשְׂרָאֵל מֵעֶקְרוֹן וְעַד־גַּת וְאֶת־גְּבוּלָן הִצִּיל יִשְׂרָאֵל מִיַּד פְּלִשְׁתִּים וַיְהִי שָׁלוֹם בֵּין יִשְׂרָאֵל וּבֵין הָאֱמֹרִי: 15וַיִּשְׁפֹּט שְׁמוּאֵל אֶת־יִשְׂרָאֵל כֹּל יְמֵי חַיָּיו: 16וְהָלַךְ מִדֵּי שָׁנָה בְּשָׁנָה וְסָבַב בֵּית־אֵל וְהַגִּלְגָּל וְהַמִּצְפָּה וְשָׁפַט אֶת־יִשְׂרָאֵל אֵת כָּל־הַמְּקוֹמוֹת הָאֵלֶּה: 17וּתְשֻׁבָתוֹ הָרָמָתָה כִּי־שָׁם בֵּיתוֹ וְשָׁם שָׁפַט אֶת־יִשְׂרָאֵל וַיִּבֶן־שָׁם מִזְבֵּחַ לַיהוָה: פ

ח וַיְהִי כַּאֲשֶׁר זָקֵן שְׁמוּאֵל וַיָּשֶׂם אֶת־בָּנָיו שֹׁפְטִים לְיִשְׂרָאֵל: 2וַיְהִי שֶׁם־בְּנוֹ הַבְּכוֹר יוֹאֵל וְשֵׁם מִשְׁנֵהוּ אֲבִיָּה שֹׁפְטִים בִּבְאֵר שָׁבַע: 3וְלֹא־הָלְכוּ בָנָיו בִּדְרָכָו וַיִּטּוּ אַחֲרֵי הַבָּצַע וַיִּקְחוּ־שֹׁחַד וַיַּטּוּ מִשְׁפָּט: פ 4וַיִּתְקַבְּצוּ כֹּל זִקְנֵי יִשְׂרָאֵל וַיָּבֹאוּ אֶל־שְׁמוּאֵל הָרָמָתָה: 5וַיֹּאמְרוּ אֵלָיו הִנֵּה אַתָּה זָקַנְתָּ וּבָנֶיךָ לֹא הָלְכוּ בִּדְרָכֶיךָ עַתָּה שִׂימָה־לָּנוּ מֶלֶךְ לְשָׁפְטֵנוּ כְּכָל־הַגּוֹיִם: 6וַיֵּרַע הַדָּבָר בְּעֵינֵי שְׁמוּאֵל כַּאֲשֶׁר אָמְרוּ תְּנָה־לָּנוּ מֶלֶךְ לְשָׁפְטֵנוּ וַיִּתְפַּלֵּל שְׁמוּאֵל אֶל־יְהוָה: פ 7וַיֹּאמֶר יְהוָה אֶל־שְׁמוּאֵל שְׁמַע בְּקוֹל הָעָם לְכֹל אֲשֶׁר־

---

b Otherwise unknown; perhaps identical with "Jeshanah"; cf. Septuagint; also 2 Chron. 13.19.

c I.e., "Stone of Help."

have rejected as their king. ⁸Like everything else they have done ever since I brought them out of Egypt to this day—forsaking Me and worshiping other gods—so they are doing to you. ⁹Heed their demand; but warn them solemnly, and tell them about the practices of any king who will rule over them."

¹⁰Samuel reported all the words of the LORD to the people, who were asking him for a king. ¹¹He said, "This will be the practice of the king who will rule over you: He will take your sons and appoint them as his charioteers and horsemen, and they will serve as outrunners for his chariots. ¹²He will appoint them as his chiefs of thousands and of fifties; or they will have to plow his fields, reap his harvest, and make his weapons and the equipment for his chariots. ¹³He will take your daughters as perfumers, cooks, and bakers. ¹⁴He will seize your choice fields, vineyards, and olive groves, and give them to his courtiers. ¹⁵He will take a tenth part of your grain and vintage and give it to his eunuchs and courtiers. ¹⁶He will take your male and female slaves, your choice ᵃ-young men,-ᵃ and your asses, and put them to work for him. ¹⁷He will take a tenth part of your flocks, and you shall become his slaves. ¹⁸The day will come when you cry out because of the king whom you yourselves have chosen; and the LORD will not answer you on that day."

¹⁹But the people would not listen to Samuel's warning. "No," they said. "We must have a king over us, ²⁰that we may be like all the other nations: Let our king rule over us and go out at our head and fight our battles." ²¹When Samuel heard all that the people said, he reported it to the LORD. ²²And the LORD said to Samuel, "Heed their demands and appoint a king for them." Samuel then said to the men of Israel, "All of you go home."

ᵃ⁻ᵃ *Septuagint reads "cattle."*

יֹּאמְר֣וּ אֵלֶ֗יךָ כִּ֣י לֹ֤א אֹֽתְךָ֙ מָאָ֔סוּ כִּי־אֹתִ֥י מָאֲס֖וּ מִמְּלֹ֥ךְ עֲלֵיהֶֽם׃ 8 כְּכָֽל־הַֽמַּעֲשִׂ֣ים אֲשֶׁר־עָשׂ֗וּ מִיּוֹם֩ הַעֲלֹתִ֨י אֹתָ֜ם מִמִּצְרַ֗יִם וְעַד־הַיּ֣וֹם הַזֶּ֔ה וַיַּ֣עַזְבֻ֔נִי וַיַּעַבְד֖וּ אֱלֹהִ֣ים אֲחֵרִ֑ים כֵּ֛ן הֵ֥מָּה עֹשִׂ֖ים גַּם־לָֽךְ׃ 9 וְעַתָּ֖ה שְׁמַ֣ע בְּקוֹלָ֑ם אַ֗ךְ כִּֽי־הָעֵ֤ד תָּעִיד֙ בָּהֶ֔ם וְהִגַּדְתָּ֣ לָהֶ֔ם מִשְׁפַּ֣ט הַמֶּ֔לֶךְ אֲשֶׁ֥ר יִמְלֹ֖ךְ עֲלֵיהֶֽם׃ ס

10 וַיֹּ֣אמֶר שְׁמוּאֵ֗ל אֵ֚ת כָּל־דִּבְרֵ֣י יְהֹוָ֔ה אֶל־הָעָ֕ם הַשֹּׁאֲלִ֥ים מֵאִתּ֖וֹ מֶֽלֶךְ׃ ס 11 וַיֹּ֕אמֶר זֶ֗ה יִֽהְיֶה֙ מִשְׁפַּ֣ט הַמֶּ֔לֶךְ אֲשֶׁ֥ר יִמְלֹ֖ךְ עֲלֵיכֶ֑ם אֶת־בְּנֵיכֶ֣ם יִקָּ֗ח וְשָׂ֥ם לוֹ֙ בְּמֶרְכַּבְתּ֣וֹ וּבְפָרָשָׁ֔יו וְרָצ֖וּ לִפְנֵ֥י מֶרְכַּבְתּֽוֹ׃ 12 וְלָשׂ֣וּם ל֗וֹ שָׂרֵ֤י אֲלָפִים֙ וְשָׂרֵ֣י חֲמִשִּׁ֔ים וְלַחֲרֹ֤שׁ חֲרִישׁוֹ֙ וְלִקְצֹ֣ר קְצִיר֔וֹ וְלַעֲשׂ֥וֹת כְּלֵֽי־מִלְחַמְתּ֖וֹ וּכְלֵ֥י רִכְבּֽוֹ׃ 13 וְאֶת־בְּנוֹתֵיכֶ֖ם יִקָּ֑ח לְרַקָּח֥וֹת וּלְטַבָּח֖וֹת וּלְאֹפֽוֹת׃ 14 וְאֶת־שְׂדֽוֹתֵיכֶ֞ם וְאֶת־כַּרְמֵיכֶ֧ם וְזֵיתֵיכֶ֛ם הַטּוֹבִ֖ים יִקָּ֑ח וְנָתַ֖ן לַעֲבָדָֽיו׃ 15 וְזַרְעֵיכֶ֥ם וְכַרְמֵיכֶ֖ם יַעְשֹׂ֑ר וְנָתַ֥ן לְסָרִיסָ֖יו וְלַעֲבָדָֽיו׃ 16 וְאֶת־עַבְדֵיכֶם֩ וְֽאֶת־שִׁפְחֽוֹתֵיכֶ֨ם וְאֶת־בַּחוּרֵיכֶ֧ם הַטּוֹבִ֛ים וְאֶת־חֲמוֹרֵיכֶ֖ם יִקָּ֑ח וְעָשָׂ֥ה לִמְלַאכְתּֽוֹ׃ 17 צֹאנְכֶ֖ם יַעְשֹׂ֑ר וְאַתֶּ֖ם תִּֽהְיוּ־ל֥וֹ לַעֲבָדִֽים׃ 18 וּזְעַקְתֶּם֙ בַּיּ֣וֹם הַה֔וּא מִלִּפְנֵ֣י מַלְכְּכֶ֔ם אֲשֶׁ֥ר בְּחַרְתֶּ֖ם לָכֶ֑ם וְלֹֽא־יַעֲנֶ֧ה יְהֹוָ֛ה אֶתְכֶ֖ם בַּיּ֥וֹם הַהֽוּא׃

19 וַיְמָאֲנ֣וּ הָעָ֔ם לִשְׁמֹ֖עַ בְּק֣וֹל שְׁמוּאֵ֑ל וַיֹּאמְר֣וּ לֹּ֔א כִּ֥י אִם־מֶ֖לֶךְ יִֽהְיֶ֥ה עָלֵֽינוּ׃ 20 וְהָיִ֥ינוּ גַם־אֲנַ֖חְנוּ כְּכָל־הַגּוֹיִ֑ם וּשְׁפָטָ֤נוּ מַלְכֵּ֙נוּ֙ וְיָצָ֣א לְפָנֵ֔ינוּ וְנִלְחַ֖ם אֶת־מִלְחֲמֹתֵֽנוּ׃ 21 וַיִּשְׁמַ֣ע שְׁמוּאֵ֔ל אֵ֖ת כָּל־דִּבְרֵ֣י הָעָ֑ם וַֽיְדַבְּרֵ֖ם בְּאָזְנֵ֥י יְהֹוָֽה׃ פ 22 וַיֹּ֨אמֶר יְהֹוָ֤ה אֶל־שְׁמוּאֵל֙ שְׁמַ֣ע בְּקוֹלָ֔ם וְהִמְלַכְתָּ֥ לָהֶ֖ם מֶ֑לֶךְ וַיֹּ֤אמֶר שְׁמוּאֵל֙ אֶל־אַנְשֵׁ֣י יִשְׂרָאֵ֔ל לְכ֖וּ אִ֥ישׁ לְעִירֽוֹ׃ פ

586

9 There was a man of Benjamin whose name was Kish son of Abiel son of Zeror son of Becorath son of Aphiah, a Benjaminite, a man of substance. ²He had a son whose name was Saul, an excellent young man; no one among the Israelites was handsomer than he; *a*-he was a head taller-*a* than any of the people.

³Once the asses of Saul's father Kish went astray, and Kish said to his son Saul, "Take along one of the servants and go out and look for the asses." ⁴He passed into the hill country of Ephraim. He crossed the district of Shalishah, but they did not find them. They passed through the district of Shaalim, but they were not there. They traversed the [entire] territory of Benjamin, and still they did not find them. ⁵When they reached the district of Zuph, Saul said to the servant who was with him, "Let us turn back, or my father will stop worrying about the asses and begin to worry about us." ⁶But he replied, "There is a man of God in that town, and the man is highly esteemed; everything that he says comes true. Let us go there; perhaps he will tell us about the errand on which we set out." ⁷"But if we go," Saul said to his servant, "what can we bring the man? For the food in our bags is all gone, and there is nothing we can bring to the man of God as a present. What have we got?" ⁸The servant answered Saul again, "I happen to have a quarter-shekel of silver. I can give that to the man of God and he will tell us about our errand."—⁹*b*Formerly in Israel, when a man went to inquire of God, he would say, "Come, let us go to the seer," for the prophet of today was formerly called a seer.—¹⁰Saul said to his servant, "A good idea; let us go." And they went to the town where the man of God lived.

¹¹As they were climbing the ascent to the town, they met some girls coming out to draw

ט וַיְהִי־אִ֗ישׁ מִבֶּן־יָמִין֙ וּשְׁמ֔וֹ
קִ֡ישׁ בֶּן־אֲבִיאֵ֣ל בֶּן־צְר֞וֹר בֶּן־בְּכוֹרַ֣ת בֶּן־
אֲפִ֗יחַ בֶּן־אִ֥ישׁ יְמִינִ֖י גִּבּ֥וֹר חָֽיִל׃ ² וְלוֹ־הָיָ֨ה
בֵ֜ן וּשְׁמ֤וֹ שָׁאוּל֙ בָּח֣וּר וָט֔וֹב וְאֵ֥ין אִ֛ישׁ
מִבְּנֵ֥י יִשְׂרָאֵ֖ל ט֣וֹב מִמֶּ֑נּוּ מִשִּׁכְמ֣וֹ וָמַ֔עְלָה
גָּבֹ֖הַּ מִכָּל־הָעָֽם׃ ³ וַתֹּאבַ֗דְנָה הָאֲתֹנוֹת֙ לְקִ֣ישׁ אֲבִ֣י שָׁא֔וּל
וַיֹּ֨אמֶר קִ֜ישׁ אֶל־שָׁא֣וּל בְּנ֗וֹ קַח־נָ֤א אִתְּךָ֙
אֶת־אַחַ֣ד מֵֽהַנְּעָרִ֔ים וְק֣וּם לֵ֔ךְ בַּקֵּ֖שׁ אֶת־
הָאֲתֹנֹֽת׃ ⁴ וַֽיַּעֲבֹ֧ר בְּהַר־אֶפְרַ֛יִם וַֽיַּעֲבֹ֥ר
בְּאֶֽרֶץ־שָׁלִ֖שָׁה וְלֹ֣א מָצָ֑אוּ וַיַּעַבְר֤וּ בְאֶֽרֶץ־
שַׁעֲלִים֙ וָאַ֔יִן וַיַּעֲבֹ֥ר בְּאֶֽרֶץ־יְמִינִ֖י וְלֹ֥א
מָצָֽאוּ׃ ⁵ הֵ֗מָּה בָּ֚אוּ בְּאֶ֣רֶץ צ֔וּף וְשָׁא֥וּל
אָמַ֛ר לְנַעֲר֥וֹ אֲשֶׁר־עִמּ֖וֹ לְכָ֣ה וְנָשׁ֑וּבָה
פֶּן־יֶחְדַּ֥ל אָבִ֛י מִן־הָאֲתֹנ֖וֹת וְדָ֥אַג לָֽנוּ׃ ⁶ וַיֹּ֣אמֶר ל֗וֹ הִנֵּה־נָ֤א אִישׁ־אֱלֹהִים֙ בָּעִ֣יר
הַזֹּ֔את וְהָאִ֣ישׁ נִכְבָּ֔ד כֹּ֥ל אֲשֶׁר־יְדַבֵּ֖ר בּ֣וֹא
יָב֑וֹא עַתָּה֙ נֵ֣לְכָה שָּׁ֔ם אוּלַ֗י יַגִּ֤יד לָ֨נוּ֙
אֶת־דַּרְכֵּ֔נוּ אֲשֶׁר־הָלַ֖כְנוּ עָלֶֽיהָ׃ ⁷ וַיֹּ֨אמֶר
שָׁא֜וּל לְנַעֲר֗וֹ וְהִנֵּ֣ה נֵלֵךְ֮ וּמַה־נָּבִ֣יא לָאִישׁ֒
כִּ֤י הַלֶּ֨חֶם֙ אָזַ֣ל מִכֵּלֵ֔ינוּ וּתְשׁוּרָ֥ה אֵֽין־
לְהָבִ֖יא לְאִ֣ישׁ הָאֱלֹהִ֑ים מָ֖ה אִתָּֽנוּ׃ ⁸ וַיֹּ֨סֶף
הַנַּ֜עַר לַעֲנ֣וֹת אֶת־שָׁא֗וּל וַיֹּ֨אמֶר֙ הִנֵּה֙
נִמְצָ֣א בְיָדִ֔י רֶ֖בַע שֶׁ֣קֶל כָּ֑סֶף וְנָֽתַתִּי֙ לְאִ֣ישׁ
הָאֱלֹהִ֔ים וְהִגִּ֥יד לָ֖נוּ אֶת־דַּרְכֵּֽנוּ׃ ⁹ לְפָנִ֣ים ׀
בְּיִשְׂרָאֵ֗ל כֹּֽה־אָמַ֤ר הָאִישׁ֙ בְּלֶכְתּוֹ֙ לִדְר֣וֹשׁ
אֱלֹהִ֔ים לְכ֥וּ וְנֵלְכָ֖ה עַד־הָרֹאֶ֑ה כִּ֤י
לַנָּבִיא֙ הַיּ֔וֹם יִקָּרֵ֥א לְפָנִ֖ים הָרֹאֶֽה׃ ¹⁰ וַיֹּ֨אמֶר שָׁא֧וּל לְנַעֲר֛וֹ ט֥וֹב דְּבָרְךָ֖ לְכָ֣ה ׀
נֵלֵ֑כָה וַיֵּֽלְכוּ֙ אֶל־הָעִ֔יר אֲשֶׁר־שָׁ֖ם אִ֥ישׁ
הָאֱלֹהִֽים׃ ¹¹ הֵ֗מָּה עֹלִים֙ בְּמַעֲלֵ֣ה הָעִ֔יר וְהֵ֨מָּה֙ מָצְא֣וּ
נְעָר֔וֹת יֹצְא֖וֹת לִשְׁאֹ֣ב מָ֑יִם וַיֹּאמְר֣וּ לָהֶ֔ן

---

water, and they asked them, "Is the seer in town?" [12]"Yes," they replied. "He is up there ahead of you. *c*-Hurry, for he has just come to the town-*c* because the people have a sacrifice at the shrine today. [13]As soon as you enter the town, you will find him before he goes up to the shrine to eat; the people will not eat until he comes; for he must first bless the sacrifice and only then will the guests eat. Go up at once, for you will find him right away." [14]So they went up to the town; and as they were entering the town,*d* Samuel came out toward them, on his way up to the shrine.

[15]Now the day before Saul came, the LORD had revealed the following to Samuel: [16]"At this time tomorrow, I will send a man to you from the territory of Benjamin, and you shall anoint him ruler of My people Israel. He will deliver My people from the hands of the Philistines; for I have taken note of *e*-My people,-*e* their outcry has come to Me."

[17]As soon as Samuel saw Saul, the LORD declared to him, "This is the man that I told you would govern My people." [18]Saul approached Samuel inside the gate and said to him, "Tell me, please, where is the house of the seer?" [19]And Samuel answered Saul, "I am the seer. Go up ahead of me to the shrine, for you shall eat with me today; and in the morning I will let you go, after telling you whatever may be on your mind. [20]As for your asses that strayed three days ago, do not concern yourself about them, for they have been found. And for whom is all Israel yearning, if not for you and all your ancestral house?" [21]Saul replied, "But I am only a Benjaminite, from the smallest of the tribes of Israel, and my clan is the least of all the clans of the tribe*f* of Benjamin! Why do you say such things to me?"

הָאִישׁ בָּזֶה הָרֹאֶה: [12] וַתַּעֲנֶינָה אוֹתָם וַתֹּאמַרְנָה יֵשׁ הִנֵּה לְפָנֶיךָ מַהֵר | עַתָּה כִּי הַיּוֹם בָּא לָעִיר כִּי זֶבַח הַיּוֹם לָעָם בַּבָּמָה: [13] כְּבֹאֲכֶם הָעִיר כֵּן תִּמְצְאוּן אֹתוֹ בְּטֶרֶם יַעֲלֶה הַבָּמָתָה לֶאֱכֹל כִּי לֹא־יֹאכַל הָעָם עַד־בֹּאוֹ כִּי־הוּא יְבָרֵךְ הַזֶּבַח אַחֲרֵי־כֵן יֹאכְלוּ הַקְּרֻאִים וְעַתָּה עֲלוּ כִּי־אֹתוֹ כְהַיּוֹם תִּמְצְאוּן אֹתוֹ: [14] וַיַּעֲלוּ הָעִיר הֵמָּה בָּאִים בְּתוֹךְ הָעִיר וְהִנֵּה שְׁמוּאֵל יֹצֵא לִקְרָאתָם לַעֲלוֹת הַבָּמָה: ס

[15] וַיהוָה גָּלָה אֶת־אֹזֶן שְׁמוּאֵל יוֹם אֶחָד לִפְנֵי בוֹא־שָׁאוּל לֵאמֹר: [16] כָּעֵת | מָחָר אֶשְׁלַח אֵלֶיךָ אִישׁ מֵאֶרֶץ בִּנְיָמִן וּמְשַׁחְתּוֹ לְנָגִיד עַל־עַמִּי יִשְׂרָאֵל וְהוֹשִׁיעַ אֶת־עַמִּי מִיַּד פְּלִשְׁתִּים כִּי רָאִיתִי אֶת־עַמִּי כִּי בָּאָה צַעֲקָתוֹ אֵלָי:

[17] וּשְׁמוּאֵל רָאָה אֶת־שָׁאוּל וַיהוָה עָנָהוּ הִנֵּה הָאִישׁ אֲשֶׁר אָמַרְתִּי אֵלֶיךָ זֶה יַעְצֹר בְּעַמִּי: [18] וַיִּגַּשׁ שָׁאוּל אֶת־שְׁמוּאֵל בְּתוֹךְ הַשָּׁעַר וַיֹּאמֶר הַגִּידָה־נָּא לִי אֵי־זֶה בֵּית הָרֹאֶה: [19] וַיַּעַן שְׁמוּאֵל אֶת־שָׁאוּל וַיֹּאמֶר אָנֹכִי הָרֹאֶה עֲלֵה לְפָנַי הַבָּמָה וַאֲכַלְתֶּם עִמִּי הַיּוֹם וְשִׁלַּחְתִּיךָ בַבֹּקֶר וְכֹל אֲשֶׁר בִּלְבָבְךָ אַגִּיד לָךְ: [20] וְלָאֲתֹנוֹת הָאֹבְדוֹת לְךָ הַיּוֹם שְׁלֹשֶׁת הַיָּמִים אַל־תָּשֶׂם אֶת־לִבְּךָ לָהֶם כִּי נִמְצָאוּ וּלְמִי כָּל־חֶמְדַּת יִשְׂרָאֵל הֲלוֹא לְךָ וּלְכֹל בֵּית אָבִיךָ: ס [21] וַיַּעַן שָׁאוּל וַיֹּאמֶר הֲלוֹא בֶן־יְמִינִי אָנֹכִי מִקַּטַנֵּי שִׁבְטֵי יִשְׂרָאֵל וּמִשְׁפַּחְתִּי הַצְּעִרָה מִכָּל־מִשְׁפְּחוֹת שִׁבְטֵי בִנְיָמִן וְלָמָּה דִּבַּרְתָּ אֵלַי כַּדָּבָר הַזֶּה: ס

---

c-c Emendation yields "Hurry, for he has just reached ('attah kayyom ba, so Septuagint) the gate"; cf. v. 18.
d Emendation yields "gate"; cf. v. 18.
e-e Septuagint and Targum read "the plight of My people"; cf. Exod. 3.7.
f Heb. plural.

²²Samuel took Saul and his servant and brought them into the hall, and gave them a place at the head of the guests, who numbered about thirty. ²³And Samuel said to the cook, "Bring the portion which I gave you and told you to set aside." ²⁴The cook lifted up the thigh and ^{g-}what was on it,^{-g} and set it before Saul. And [Samuel] said, ^{h-}"What has been reserved is set before you. Eat; it has been kept for you for this occasion, when I said I was inviting the people."^{-h} So Saul ate with Samuel that day. ²⁵They then descended from the shrine to the town, and ⁱ⁻[Samuel] talked with Saul on the roof.

²⁶Early, at⁻ⁱ the break of day, Samuel called to Saul on the roof. He said, "Get up, and I will send you off." Saul arose, and the two of them, Samuel and he, went outside. ²⁷As they were walking toward the end of the town, Samuel said to Saul, "Tell the servant to walk ahead of us"—and he walked ahead—"but you stop here a moment and I will make known to you the word of God."

10

Samuel took a flask of oil and poured some on Saul's^a head and kissed him, and said, "The Lord herewith ^{b-}anoints you ruler^{-b} over His own people. ²When you leave me today, you will meet two men near the tomb of Rachel in the territory of Benjamin, ^{c-}at Zelzah,^{-c} and they will tell you that the asses you set out to look for have been found, and that your father has stopped being concerned about the asses and is worrying about you, saying: 'What shall I do

---

g-g   *Meaning of Heb. uncertain. Emendation yields "the broad tail."*

h-h   *Meaning of Heb. uncertain.*

i-i   *Meaning of Heb. uncertain. Septuagint reads "They spread a bed for Saul on the roof, and he lay down. At..."*

a   *Heb. "his."*

b-b   *Septuagint and Vulgate read "anoints you ruler over His people Israel, and you will govern the people of the Lord and deliver them from the hands of their foes roundabout. And this is the sign for you that the Lord anoints you."*

c-c   *Meaning of Heb. uncertain.*

---

²²וַיִּקַּ֣ח שְׁמוּאֵ֗ל אֶת־שָׁאוּל֙ וְאֶֽת־נַעֲר֔וֹ וַיְבִיאֵ֖ם לִשְׁכָּ֑תָה וַיִּתֵּ֨ן לָהֶ֤ם מָקוֹם֙ בְּרֹ֣אשׁ הַקְּרוּאִ֔ים וְהֵ֖מָּה כִּשְׁלֹשִׁ֥ים אִֽישׁ׃ ²³וַיֹּ֤אמֶר שְׁמוּאֵל֙ לַטַּבָּ֔ח תְּנָה֙ אֶת־הַמָּנָ֔ה אֲשֶׁ֥ר נָתַ֖תִּי לָ֑ךְ אֲשֶׁר֙ אָמַ֣רְתִּי אֵלֶ֔יךָ שִׂ֥ים אֹתָ֖הּ עִמָּֽךְ׃ ²⁴וַיָּ֣רֶם הַטַּבָּ֗ח אֶת־הַשּׁ֤וֹק וְהֶעָלֶ֙יהָ֙ וַיָּ֣שֶׂם ׀ לִפְנֵ֣י שָׁא֔וּל וַיֹּ֙אמֶר֙ הִנֵּ֣ה הַנִּשְׁאָ֔ר שִׂים־לְפָנֶ֖יךָ אֱכֹ֑ל כִּ֧י לַמּוֹעֵ֛ד שָֽׁמוּר־לְךָ֥ לֵאמֹ֖ר הָעָ֣ם ׀ קָרָ֑אתִי וַיֹּ֧אכַל שָׁא֛וּל עִם־שְׁמוּאֵ֖ל בַּיּ֥וֹם הַהֽוּא׃ ²⁵וַיֵּרְד֥וּ מֵהַבָּמָ֖ה הָעִ֑יר וַיְדַבֵּ֥ר עִם־שָׁא֖וּל עַל־הַגָּֽג׃

²⁶וַיַּשְׁכִּ֗מוּ וַיְהִ֞י כַּעֲל֤וֹת הַשַּׁ֙חַר֙ וַיִּקְרָ֨א שְׁמוּאֵ֤ל אֶל־שָׁאוּל֙ הַגָּ֣גָה לֵאמֹ֔ר ק֖וּמָה וַאֲשַׁלְּחֶ֑ךָּ וַיָּ֣קׇם שָׁא֗וּל וַיֵּצְא֧וּ שְׁנֵיהֶ֛ם ה֥וּא וּשְׁמוּאֵ֖ל הַחֽוּצָה׃ ²⁷הֵ֗מָּה יֽוֹרְדִים֙ בִּקְצֵ֣ה הָעִ֔יר וּשְׁמוּאֵ֞ל אָמַ֣ר אֶל־שָׁא֗וּל אֱמֹ֥ר לַנַּ֛עַר וְיַעֲבֹ֥ר לְפָנֵ֖ינוּ וַֽיַּעֲבֹ֑ר וְאַתָּה֙ עֲמֹ֣ד כַּיּ֔וֹם וְאַשְׁמִיעֲךָ֖ אֶת־דְּבַ֥ר אֱלֹהִֽים׃ פ

י

וַיִּקַּ֨ח שְׁמוּאֵ֜ל אֶת־פַּ֥ךְ הַשֶּׁ֛מֶן וַיִּצֹ֥ק עַל־רֹאשׁ֖וֹ וַיִּשָּׁקֵ֑הוּ וַיֹּ֕אמֶר הֲל֗וֹא כִּֽי־מְשָׁחֲךָ֧ יְהֹוָ֛ה עַל־נַחֲלָת֖וֹ לְנָגִֽיד׃ ²בְּלֶכְתְּךָ֤ הַיּוֹם֙ מֵעִמָּדִ֔י וּמָצָאתָ֩ שְׁנֵ֨י אֲנָשִׁ֜ים עִם־קְבֻרַ֥ת רָחֵ֛ל בִּגְב֥וּל בִּנְיָמִ֖ן בְּצֶלְצַ֑ח וְאָמְר֣וּ אֵלֶ֗יךָ נִמְצְא֤וּ הָאֲתֹנוֹת֙ אֲשֶׁ֣ר הָלַ֣כְתָּ לְבַקֵּ֔שׁ וְהִנֵּ֨ה נָטַ֤שׁ אָבִ֙יךָ֙ אֶת־דִּבְרֵ֣י הָאֲתֹנ֔וֹת וְדָאַ֥ג לָכֶ֖ם לֵאמֹ֑ר מָ֥ה אֶעֱשֶׂ֖ה לִבְנִֽי׃ ³וְחָלַפְתָּ֨

about my son?' ³You shall pass on from there until you come to the terebinth of Tabor. There you will be met by three men making a pilgrimage to God at Bethel. One will be carrying three kids, another will be carrying three loaves of bread, and the third will be carrying a jar of wine. ⁴They will greet you and offer you two loaves of bread, which you shall accept. ⁵After that, you are to go on to ᵈ-the Hill-ᵈ of God, where the Philistine prefects reside. There, as you enter the town, you will encounter a band of prophets coming down from the shrine, preceded by lyres, timbrels, flutes, and harps, and they will be ᵉ-speaking in ecstasy.-ᵉ ⁶The spirit of the LORD will grip you, and you will speak in ecstasy along with them; you will become another man. ⁷And once these signs have happened to you, ᶠ-act when the occasion arises,-ᶠ for God is with you. ⁸After that, you are to go down to Gilgal ahead of me, and I will come down to you to present burnt offerings and offer sacrifices of well-being. Wait seven days until I come to you and instruct you what you are to do next."

⁹As [Saul] turned around to leave Samuel, God gave him another heart; and all those signs were fulfilled that same day. ¹⁰And when they came there, to ᵈ-the Hill,-ᵈ he saw a band of prophets coming toward him. Thereupon the spirit of God gripped him, and he spoke in ecstasy among them. ¹¹When all who knew him previously saw him speaking in ecstasy together with the prophets, the people said to one another, "What's happened to ᵍ-the son of Kish?-ᵍ Is Saul too among the prophets?" ¹²But another person there spoke up and said, "And who are their fathers?" Thus the proverb arose: "Is Saul too among the prophets?" ¹³And when he

---

מִשָּׁם וָהָלְאָה וּבָאתָ עַד־אֵלוֹן תָּבוֹר וּמְצָאוּךָ שָּׁם שְׁלֹשָׁה אֲנָשִׁים עֹלִים אֶל־הָאֱלֹהִים בֵּית־אֵל אֶחָד נֹשֵׂא ׀ שְׁלֹשָׁה גְדָיִים וְאֶחָד נֹשֵׂא שְׁלֹשֶׁת כִּכְּרוֹת לֶחֶם וְאֶחָד נֹשֵׂא נֵבֶל־יָיִן: 4וְשָׁאֲלוּ לְךָ לְשָׁלוֹם וְנָתְנוּ לְךָ שְׁתֵּי־לֶחֶם וְלָקַחְתָּ מִיָּדָם: 5אַחַר כֵּן תָּבוֹא גִּבְעַת הָאֱלֹהִים אֲשֶׁר־שָׁם נְצִבֵי פְלִשְׁתִּים וִיהִי כְבֹאֲךָ שָׁם הָעִיר וּפָגַעְתָּ חֶבֶל נְבִיאִים יֹרְדִים מֵהַבָּמָה וְלִפְנֵיהֶם נֵבֶל וְתֹף וְחָלִיל וְכִנּוֹר וְהֵמָּה מִתְנַבְּאִים: 6וְצָלְחָה עָלֶיךָ רוּחַ יְהוָה וְהִתְנַבִּיתָ עִמָּם וְנֶהְפַּכְתָּ לְאִישׁ אַחֵר: 7וְהָיָה כִּי תבאינה תָבֹאנָה הָאֹתוֹת הָאֵלֶּה לָךְ עֲשֵׂה לְךָ אֲשֶׁר תִּמְצָא יָדֶךָ כִּי הָאֱלֹהִים עִמָּךְ: 8וְיָרַדְתָּ לְפָנַי הַגִּלְגָּל וְהִנֵּה אָנֹכִי יֹרֵד אֵלֶיךָ לְהַעֲלוֹת עֹלוֹת לִזְבֹּחַ זִבְחֵי שְׁלָמִים שִׁבְעַת יָמִים תּוֹחֵל עַד־בּוֹאִי אֵלֶיךָ וְהוֹדַעְתִּי לְךָ אֵת אֲשֶׁר תַּעֲשֶׂה: 9וְהָיָה כְּהַפְנֹתוֹ שִׁכְמוֹ לָלֶכֶת מֵעִם שְׁמוּאֵל וַיַּהֲפָךְ־לוֹ אֱלֹהִים לֵב אַחֵר וַיָּבֹאוּ כָּל־הָאֹתוֹת הָאֵלֶּה בַּיּוֹם הַהוּא: ס 10וַיָּבֹאוּ שָׁם הַגִּבְעָתָה וְהִנֵּה חֶבֶל־נְבִיאִים לִקְרָאתוֹ וַתִּצְלַח עָלָיו רוּחַ אֱלֹהִים וַיִּתְנַבֵּא בְּתוֹכָם: 11וַיְהִי כָּל־יוֹדְעוֹ מֵאִתְּמוֹל שִׁלְשׁוֹם וַיִּרְאוּ וְהִנֵּה עִם־נְבִאִים נִבָּא וַיֹּאמֶר הָעָם אִישׁ אֶל־רֵעֵהוּ מַה־זֶּה הָיָה לְבֶן־קִישׁ הֲגַם שָׁאוּל בַּנְּבִיאִים: 12וַיַּעַן אִישׁ מִשָּׁם וַיֹּאמֶר וּמִי אֲבִיהֶם עַל־כֵּן הָיְתָה לְמָשָׁל הֲגַם שָׁאוּל בַּנְּבִאִים: 13וַיְכַל מֵהִתְנַבּוֹת וַיָּבֹא הַבָּמָה:

---

d-d Or "Gibeah."
e-e Others "prophesying"; cf. Num. 11.25 and note.
f-f See 11.5–13.
g-g To refer to a person merely as "the son (ben) of…" is slighting; cf. 20, 27, 30, 31; Isa. 7.4.

stopped speaking in ecstasy, he entered the shrine.

¹⁴Saul's uncle asked him and his servant, "Where did you go?" "To look for the asses," he replied. "And when we saw that they were not to be found, we went to Samuel." ¹⁵"Tell me," said Saul's uncle, "what did Samuel say to you?" ¹⁶Saul answered his uncle, "He just told us that the asses had been found." But he did not tell him anything of what Samuel had said about the kingship.

¹⁷Samuel summoned the people to the Lord at Mizpah ¹⁸and said to them, "Thus said the Lord, the God of Israel: 'I brought Israel out of Egypt, and I delivered you from the hands of the Egyptians and of all the kingdoms that oppressed you.' ¹⁹But today you have rejected your God who delivered you from all your troubles and calamities. For you said, 'No,ʰ set up a king over us!' Now station yourselves before the Lord, by your tribes and clans."

²⁰Samuel brought forward each of the tribes of Israel, and the lot indicated the tribe of Benjamin. ²¹Then Samuel brought forward the tribe of Benjamin by its clans, and the clan of the Matrites was indicated; and thenⁱ Saul son of Kish was indicated. But when they looked for him, he was not to be found. ²²They inquired of the Lord again, ʲ-"Has anyone else come here?"⁻ʲ And the Lord replied, "Yes; he is hiding among the baggage." ²³So they ran over and brought him from there; and when he took his place among the people, he stood a head taller than all the people. ²⁴And Samuel said to the people, "Do you see the one whom the Lord has chosen? There is none like him among all the people." And all the people acclaimed him, shouting, "Long live the king!"

14 וַיֹּאמֶר דּוֹד שָׁאוּל אֵלָיו וְאֶל־נַעֲרוֹ אָן הֲלַכְתֶּם וַיֹּאמֶר לְבַקֵּשׁ אֶת־הָאֲתֹנוֹת וַנִּרְאֶה כִי־אַיִן וַנָּבוֹא אֶל־שְׁמוּאֵל: 15 וַיֹּאמֶר דּוֹד שָׁאוּל הַגִּידָה־נָּא לִי מֶה־אָמַר לָכֶם שְׁמוּאֵל: 16 וַיֹּאמֶר שָׁאוּל אֶל־דּוֹדוֹ הַגֵּד הִגִּיד לָנוּ כִּי נִמְצְאוּ הָאֲתֹנוֹת וְאֶת־דְּבַר הַמְּלוּכָה לֹא־הִגִּיד לוֹ אֲשֶׁר אָמַר שְׁמוּאֵל: פ

17 וַיַּצְעֵק שְׁמוּאֵל אֶת־הָעָם אֶל־יְהוָה הַמִּצְפָּה: 18 וַיֹּאמֶר ׀ אֶל־בְּנֵי יִשְׂרָאֵל פ כֹּה־אָמַר יְהוָה אֱלֹהֵי יִשְׂרָאֵל אָנֹכִי הֶעֱלֵיתִי אֶת־יִשְׂרָאֵל מִמִּצְרָיִם וָאַצִּיל אֶתְכֶם מִיַּד מִצְרַיִם וּמִיַּד כָּל־הַמַּמְלָכוֹת הַלֹּחֲצִים אֶתְכֶם: 19 וְאַתֶּם הַיּוֹם מְאַסְתֶּם אֶת־אֱלֹהֵיכֶם אֲשֶׁר־הוּא מוֹשִׁיעַ לָכֶם מִכָּל־רָעוֹתֵיכֶם וְצָרֹתֵיכֶם וַתֹּאמְרוּ לוֹ* כִּי־מֶלֶךְ תָּשִׂים עָלֵינוּ וְעַתָּה הִתְיַצְּבוּ לִפְנֵי יְהוָה לְשִׁבְטֵיכֶם וּלְאַלְפֵיכֶם: 20 וַיַּקְרֵב שְׁמוּאֵל אֵת כָּל־שִׁבְטֵי יִשְׂרָאֵל וַיִּלָּכֵד שֵׁבֶט בִּנְיָמִן: 21 וַיַּקְרֵב אֶת־שֵׁבֶט בִּנְיָמִן לְמִשְׁפְּחֹתָיו וַתִּלָּכֵד מִשְׁפַּחַת הַמַּטְרִי וַיִּלָּכֵד שָׁאוּל בֶּן־קִישׁ וַיְבַקְשֻׁהוּ וְלֹא נִמְצָא: 22 וַיִּשְׁאֲלוּ־עוֹד בַּיהוָה הֲבָא עוֹד הֲלֹם אִישׁ ס וַיֹּאמֶר יְהוָה הִנֵּה־הוּא נֶחְבָּא אֶל־הַכֵּלִים: 23 וַיָּרֻצוּ וַיִּקָּחֻהוּ מִשָּׁם וַיִּתְיַצֵּב בְּתוֹךְ הָעָם וַיִּגְבַּהּ מִכָּל־הָעָם מִשִּׁכְמוֹ וָמָעְלָה: 24 וַיֹּאמֶר שְׁמוּאֵל אֶל־כָּל־הָעָם הַרְּאִיתֶם* אֲשֶׁר בָּחַר־בּוֹ יְהוָה כִּי אֵין כָּמֹהוּ בְּכָל־הָעָם וַיָּרִעוּ כָל־הָעָם וַיֹּאמְרוּ יְחִי הַמֶּלֶךְ: פ

v. 19. בְּנֻסַח אַחֵר ״לֹא״
v. 24. רִי דְגוּשָׁה

---

h   *So many Heb. mss. and ancient versions. Other mss. and editions read "to Him."*

i   *Septuagint reads "then he brought up the family of the Matrites by their men and…"*

   j-j   *Septuagint reads "Has the man come here?"*

25Samuel expounded to the people the rules of the monarchy, and recorded them in a document which he deposited before the LORD. Samuel then sent the people back to their homes. 26Saul also went home to Gibeah, accompanied by k-upstanding men-k whose hearts God had touched. 27But some scoundrels said, "How can this fellow save us?" So they scorned him and brought him no gift. l-But he pretended not to mind.-l

11 Nahash the Ammonite marched up and besieged Jabesh-gilead. All the men of Jabesh-gilead said to Nahash, "Make a pact with us, and we will serve you." 2But Nahash the Ammonite answered them, "I will make a pact with you on this condition, that everyone's right eye be gouged out; I will make this a humiliation for all Israel." 3The elders of Jabesh said to him, "Give us seven days' respite, so that we may send messengers throughout the territory of Israel; if no one comes to our aid, we will surrender to you." 4When the messengers came to Gibeah of Saul and gave this report in the hearing of the people, all the people broke into weeping.

5Saul was just coming from the field driving the cattle; and Saul asked, "Why are the people crying?" And they told him about the situation of the men of Jabesh. 6When he heard these things, the spirit of God gripped Saul and his anger blazed up. 7He took a yoke of oxen and cut them into pieces, which he sent by messengers throughout the territory of Israel, with the warning, "Thus shall be done to the cattle of anyone who does not follow Saul and Samuel into battle!" Terror from the LORD fell upon the people, and they came out as one man. 8[Saul] mustered them in Bezek, and the Israelites num-

25 וַיְדַבֵּ֨ר שְׁמוּאֵ֜ל אֶל־הָעָ֗ם אֵ֚ת מִשְׁפַּ֣ט הַמְּלֻכָ֔ה וַיִּכְתֹּ֣ב בַּסֵּ֔פֶר וַיַּנַּ֖ח לִפְנֵ֣י יְהוָ֑ה וַיְשַׁלַּ֧ח שְׁמוּאֵ֛ל אֶת־כָּל־הָעָ֖ם אִ֥ישׁ לְבֵיתֽוֹ׃ 26 וְגַם־שָׁא֗וּל הָלַ֥ךְ לְבֵית֖וֹ גִּבְעָ֑תָה וַיֵּלְכ֣וּ עִמּ֔וֹ הַחַ֕יִל אֲשֶׁר־נָגַ֥ע אֱלֹהִ֖ים בְּלִבָּֽם׃ 27 וּבְנֵ֧י בְלִיַּ֣עַל אָמְר֗וּ מַה־יֹּשִׁעֵ֙נוּ֙ זֶ֔ה וַיִּבְזֻ֕הוּ וְלֹֽא־הֵבִ֥יאוּ ל֖וֹ מִנְחָ֑ה וַיְהִ֖י כְּמַחֲרִֽישׁ׃ פ

יא וַיַּ֗עַל נָחָשׁ֙ הָֽעַמּוֹנִ֔י וַיִּ֖חַן עַל־יָבֵ֣שׁ גִּלְעָ֑ד וַיֹּ֨אמְר֜וּ כָּל־אַנְשֵׁ֤י יָבֵישׁ֙ אֶל־נָחָ֔שׁ כְּרָת־לָ֥נוּ בְרִ֖ית וְנַֽעַבְדֶֽךָּ׃ 2 וַיֹּ֣אמֶר אֲלֵיהֶ֗ם נָחָשׁ֙ הָעַמּוֹנִ֔י בְּזֹאת֙ אֶכְרֹ֣ת לָכֶ֔ם בִּנְק֥וֹר לָכֶ֖ם כָּל־עֵ֣ין יָמִ֑ין וְשַׂמְתִּ֥יהָ חֶרְפָּ֖ה עַל־כָּל־יִשְׂרָאֵֽל׃ 3 וַיֹּאמְר֨וּ אֵלָ֜יו זִקְנֵ֣י יָבֵ֗ישׁ הֶ֣רֶף לָ֜נוּ שִׁבְעַ֣ת יָמִ֗ים וְנִשְׁלְחָה֙ מַלְאָכִ֔ים בְּכֹ֖ל גְּב֣וּל יִשְׂרָאֵ֑ל וְאִם־אֵ֥ין מוֹשִׁ֛יעַ אֹתָ֖נוּ וְיָצָ֥אנוּ אֵלֶֽיךָ׃ 4 וַיָּבֹ֣אוּ הַמַּלְאָכִ֗ים גִּבְעַ֤ת שָׁאוּל֙ וַיְדַבְּר֥וּ הַדְּבָרִ֖ים בְּאָזְנֵ֣י הָעָ֑ם וַיִּשְׂא֧וּ כָל־הָעָ֛ם אֶת־קוֹלָ֖ם וַיִּבְכּֽוּ׃

5 וְהִנֵּ֣ה שָׁא֗וּל בָּ֣א אַחֲרֵ֤י הַבָּקָר֙ מִן־הַשָּׂדֶ֔ה וַיֹּ֣אמֶר שָׁא֔וּל מַה־לָּעָ֖ם כִּ֣י יִבְכּ֑וּ וַיְסַ֨פְּרוּ־ל֔וֹ אֶת־דִּבְרֵ֖י אַנְשֵׁ֥י יָבֵֽישׁ׃ 6 וַתִּצְלַ֣ח רֽוּחַ־אֱלֹהִ֤ים עַל־שָׁאוּל֙ בְּשָׁמְע֖וֹ אֶת־הַדְּבָרִ֣ים הָאֵ֑לֶּה וַיִּ֥חַר אַפּ֖וֹ מְאֹֽד׃ 7 וַיִּקַּח֩ צֶ֨מֶד בָּקָ֜ר וַֽיְנַתְּחֵ֗הוּ וַיְשַׁלַּ֞ח בְּכָל־גְּב֣וּל יִשְׂרָאֵל֮ בְּיַ֣ד הַמַּלְאָכִים֮ לֵאמֹר֒ אֲשֶׁר֩ אֵינֶ֨נּוּ יֹצֵ֜א אַחֲרֵ֤י שָׁאוּל֙ וְאַחַ֣ר שְׁמוּאֵ֔ל כֹּ֥ה יֵעָשֶׂ֖ה לִבְקָר֑וֹ וַיִּפֹּ֤ל פַּֽחַד־יְהוָה֙ עַל־הָעָ֔ם וַיֵּצְא֖וּ כְּאִ֥ישׁ אֶחָֽד׃ 8 וַֽיִּפְקְדֵ֖ם בְּבָ֑זֶק וַיִּהְי֤וּ בְנֵֽי־יִשְׂרָאֵל֙ שְׁלֹ֣שׁ מֵא֣וֹת אֶ֔לֶף וְאִ֥ישׁ יְהוּדָ֖ה שְׁלֹשִׁ֥ים אָֽלֶף׃ 9 וַיֹּאמְר֣וּ לַמַּלְאָכִ֣ים הַבָּאִ֗ים כֹּ֤ה תֹֽאמְרוּן֙ לְאִישׁ֙ יָבֵ֣ישׁ גִּלְעָ֔ד

---

k-k   *In contrast to "scoundrels" (v. 27); understanding Heb.* ḥayil *as the equivalent of* bene ḥayil, *as read by Septuagint and 4QSamᵃ.*

l-l   *Lit. "But he was as one who holds his peace." Septuagint and 4QSamᵃ read "About a month later," connecting with what follows.*

bered 300,000, the men of Judah 30,000. 9The messengers who had come were told, "Thus shall you speak to the men of Jabesh-gilead: Tomorrow, when the sun grows hot, you shall be saved." When the messengers came and told this to the men of Jabesh-gilead, they rejoiced. 10The men of Jabesh then told [the Ammonites], "Tomorrow we will surrender to you, and you can do to us whatever you please."

11The next day, Saul divided the troops into three columns; at the morning watch they entered the camp and struck down the Ammonites until the day grew hot. The survivors scattered; no two were left together.

12The people then said to Samuel, "Who was it said, 'Shall Saul be king over us?' Hand the men over and we will put them to death!" 13But Saul replied, "No man shall be put to death this day! For this day the Lord has brought victory to Israel."

14Samuel said to the people, "Come, let us go to Gilgal and there inaugurate the monarchy." 15So all the people went to Gilgal, and there at Gilgal they declared Saul king before the Lord. They offered sacrifices of well-being there before the Lord; and Saul and all the men of Israel held a great celebration there.

12

Then Samuel said to all Israel, "I have yielded to you in all you have asked of me and have set a king over you. 2Henceforth the king will be your leader.

"As for me, I have grown old and gray—but my sons are still with you—and I have been your leader from my youth to this day. 3Here I am! Testify against me, in the presence of the Lord and in the presence of His anointed one: Whose ox have I taken, or whose ass have I taken? Whom have I defrauded or whom have

מָחָר תִּהְיֶה־לָכֶם תְּשׁוּעָה בחם כְּחֹם הַשֶּׁמֶשׁ וַיָּבֹאוּ הַמַּלְאָכִים וַיַּגִּידוּ לְאַנְשֵׁי יָבֵישׁ וַיִּשְׂמָחוּ: 10 וַיֹּאמְרוּ אַנְשֵׁי יָבֵישׁ מָחָר נֵצֵא אֲלֵיכֶם וַעֲשִׂיתֶם לָנוּ כְּכָל־ הַטּוֹב בְּעֵינֵיכֶם: ס

11 וַיְהִי מִמָּחֳרָת וַיָּשֶׂם שָׁאוּל אֶת־הָעָם שְׁלֹשָׁה רָאשִׁים וַיָּבֹאוּ בְתוֹךְ־הַמַּחֲנֶה בְּאַשְׁמֹרֶת הַבֹּקֶר וַיַּכּוּ אֶת־עַמּוֹן עַד־חֹם הַיּוֹם וַיְהִי הַנִּשְׁאָרִים וַיָּפֻצוּ וְלֹא נִשְׁאֲרוּ־ בָם שְׁנַיִם יָחַד:

12 וַיֹּאמֶר הָעָם אֶל־שְׁמוּאֵל מִי הָאֹמֵר שָׁאוּל יִמְלֹךְ עָלֵינוּ תְּנוּ הָאֲנָשִׁים וּנְמִיתֵם: 13 וַיֹּאמֶר שָׁאוּל לֹא־יוּמַת אִישׁ בַּיּוֹם הַזֶּה כִּי הַיּוֹם עָשָׂה־יְהוָה תְּשׁוּעָה בְּיִשְׂרָאֵל: ס

14 וַיֹּאמֶר שְׁמוּאֵל אֶל־הָעָם לְכוּ וְנֵלְכָה הַגִּלְגָּל וּנְחַדֵּשׁ שָׁם הַמְּלוּכָה: 15 וַיֵּלְכוּ כָל־הָעָם הַגִּלְגָּל וַיַּמְלִכוּ שָׁם אֶת־שָׁאוּל לִפְנֵי יְהוָה בַּגִּלְגָּל וַיִּזְבְּחוּ־שָׁם זְבָחִים שְׁלָמִים לִפְנֵי יְהוָה וַיִּשְׂמַח שָׁם שָׁאוּל וְכָל־אַנְשֵׁי יִשְׂרָאֵל עַד־מְאֹד: פ

יב וַיֹּאמֶר שְׁמוּאֵל אֶל־כָּל־יִשְׂרָאֵל הִנֵּה שָׁמַעְתִּי בְקֹלְכֶם לְכֹל אֲשֶׁר־אֲמַרְתֶּם לִי וָאַמְלִיךְ עֲלֵיכֶם מֶלֶךְ: 2 וְעַתָּה הִנֵּה הַמֶּלֶךְ ׀ מִתְהַלֵּךְ לִפְנֵיכֶם וַאֲנִי זָקַנְתִּי וָשַׂבְתִּי וּבָנַי הִנָּם אִתְּכֶם וַאֲנִי הִתְהַלַּכְתִּי לִפְנֵיכֶם מִנְּעֻרַי עַד־הַיּוֹם הַזֶּה: 3 הִנְנִי עֲנוּ בִי נֶגֶד יְהוָה וְנֶגֶד מְשִׁיחוֹ אֶת־שׁוֹר ׀ מִי לָקַחְתִּי וַחֲמוֹר מִי לָקַחְתִּי וְאֶת־מִי עָשַׁקְתִּי אֶת־מִי רַצּוֹתִי וּמִיַּד־מִי לָקַחְתִּי כֹפֶר וְאַעְלִים עֵינַי בּוֹ וְאָשִׁיב

I robbed? From whom have I taken a bribe *a-*to look the other way?-*a* I will return it to you." ⁴They responded, "You have not defrauded us, and you have not robbed us, and you have taken nothing from anyone." ⁵He said to them, "The LORD then is witness, and His anointed is witness, *b-*to your admission-*b* this day that you have found nothing in my possession." They*c* responded, "He is!"

⁶Samuel said to the people, *d-*"The LORD [is witness], He who appointed-*d* Moses and Aaron and who brought your fathers out of the land of Egypt. ⁷Come, stand before the LORD while I cite against you all the kindnesses that the LORD has done to you and your fathers.

⁸"When Jacob came to Egypt,*e*...your fathers cried out to the LORD, and the LORD sent Moses and Aaron, who brought your fathers out of Egypt and settled them in this place. ⁹But they forgot the LORD their God; so He delivered them into the hands of Sisera the military commander of Hazor, into the hands of the Philistines, and into the hands of the kind of Moab; and these made war upon them. ¹⁰They cried to the LORD, 'We are guilty, for we have forsaken the LORD and worshiped the Baalim and Ashtaroth. Oh, deliver us from our enemies and we will serve You.' ¹¹And the LORD sent Jerubbaal and Bedan*f* and Jephthah and Samuel, and delivered you from the enemies around you; and you dwelt in security. ¹²But when you saw that Nahash king of the Ammonites was advancing against you, you said to me, 'No, we must have a king reigning over us'—though the LORD your God is your King.

¹³"Well, the LORD has set a king over you! Here is the king that you have chosen, that you have asked for.

לָכֶם: 4 וַיֹּאמְרוּ לֹא עֲשַׁקְתָּנוּ וְלֹא רַצּוֹתָנוּ וְלֹא־לָקַחְתָּ מִיַּד־אִישׁ מְאוּמָה: 5 וַיֹּאמֶר אֲלֵיהֶם עֵד יְהֹוָה בָּכֶם וְעֵד מְשִׁיחוֹ הַיּוֹם הַזֶּה כִּי לֹא מְצָאתֶם בְּיָדִי מְאוּמָה וַיֹּאמֶר* עֵד: פ

6 וַיֹּאמֶר שְׁמוּאֵל אֶל־הָעָם יְהֹוָה אֲשֶׁר עָשָׂה אֶת־מֹשֶׁה וְאֶת־אַהֲרֹן וַאֲשֶׁר הֶעֱלָה אֶת־אֲבֹתֵיכֶם מֵאֶרֶץ מִצְרָיִם: 7 וְעַתָּה הִתְיַצְּבוּ וְאִשָּׁפְטָה אִתְּכֶם לִפְנֵי יְהֹוָה אֵת כָּל־צִדְקוֹת יְהֹוָה אֲשֶׁר־עָשָׂה אִתְּכֶם וְאֶת־אֲבוֹתֵיכֶם:

8 כַּאֲשֶׁר־בָּא יַעֲקֹב מִצְרָיִם וַיִּזְעֲקוּ אֲבוֹתֵיכֶם אֶל־יְהֹוָה וַיִּשְׁלַח יְהֹוָה אֶת־מֹשֶׁה וְאֶת־אַהֲרֹן וַיּוֹצִיאוּ אֶת־אֲבֹתֵיכֶם מִמִּצְרַיִם וַיֹּשִׁבוּם בַּמָּקוֹם הַזֶּה: 9 וַיִּשְׁכְּחוּ אֶת־יְהֹוָה אֱלֹהֵיהֶם וַיִּמְכֹּר אֹתָם בְּיַד סִיסְרָא שַׂר־צְבָא חָצוֹר וּבְיַד־פְּלִשְׁתִּים וּבְיַד מֶלֶךְ מוֹאָב וַיִּלָּחֲמוּ בָּם: 10 וַיִּזְעֲקוּ אֶל־יְהֹוָה וַיֹּאמֶר חָטָאנוּ כִּי עָזַבְנוּ אֶת־יְהֹוָה וַנַּעֲבֹד אֶת־הַבְּעָלִים וְאֶת־הָעַשְׁתָּרוֹת וְעַתָּה הַצִּילֵנוּ מִיַּד אֹיְבֵינוּ וְנַעַבְדֶךָ: 11 וַיִּשְׁלַח יְהֹוָה אֶת־יְרֻבַּעַל וְאֶת־בְּדָן וְאֶת־יִפְתָּח וְאֶת־שְׁמוּאֵל וַיַּצֵּל אֶתְכֶם מִיַּד אֹיְבֵיכֶם מִסָּבִיב וַתֵּשְׁבוּ בֶּטַח: 12 וַתִּרְאוּ כִּי־נָחָשׁ מֶלֶךְ בְּנֵי־עַמּוֹן בָּא עֲלֵיכֶם וַתֹּאמְרוּ לִי לֹא כִּי־מֶלֶךְ יִמְלֹךְ עָלֵינוּ וַיהֹוָה אֱלֹהֵיכֶם מַלְכְּכֶם: 13 וְעַתָּה הִנֵּה הַמֶּלֶךְ אֲשֶׁר בְּחַרְתֶּם אֲשֶׁר שְׁאֶלְתֶּם וְהִנֵּה נָתַן יְהֹוָה עֲלֵיכֶם מֶלֶךְ:

---

a-a   Septuagint reads "or a pair of sandals? [cf. Amos 2.6]. Testify against me."
b-b   Lit. "against you."
c   Heb. "he."
d-d   Meaning of Heb. uncertain.
e   Septuagint adds "the Egyptians oppressed them."
f   Septuagint "Barak."

סְבִירִין וּמַטְעִין לְשׁוֹן רַבִּים   v. 5.

¹⁴"If you will revere the LORD, worship Him, and obey Him, and will not flout the LORD's command, if both you and the king who reigns over you will follow the LORD your God, [well and good]. ¹⁵But if you do not obey the LORD and you flout the LORD's command, the hand of the LORD will strike you *d*-as it did your fathers.-*d*

¹⁶"Now stand by and see the marvelous thing that the LORD will do before your eyes. ¹⁷It is the season of the wheat harvest.*g* I will pray to the LORD and He will send thunder and rain; then you will take thought and realize what a wicked thing you did in the sight of the LORD when you asked for a king."

¹⁸Samuel prayed to the LORD, and the LORD sent thunder and rain that day, and the people stood in awe of the LORD and of Samuel. ¹⁹The people all said to Samuel, "Intercede for your servants with the LORD your God that we may not die, for we have added to all our sins the wickedness of asking for a king." ²⁰But Samuel said to the people, "Have no fear. You have, indeed, done all those wicked things. Do not, however, turn away from the LORD, but serve the LORD with all your heart. ²¹Do not turn away to follow worthless things, which can neither profit nor save but are worthless. ²²For the sake of His great name, the LORD will never abandon His people, seeing that the LORD undertook to make you His people.

²³"As for me, far be it from me to sin against the LORD and refrain from praying for you; and I will continue to instruct you in the practice of what is good and right. ²⁴Above all, you must revere the LORD and serve Him faithfully with all your heart; and consider how grandly He has dealt with you. ²⁵For if you persist in your wrongdoing, both you and your king shall be swept away."

---

g   *When thunderstorms do not occur in the land of Israel.*

14 אִם־תִּירְא֣וּ אֶת־יְהֹוָ֗ה וַעֲבַדְתֶּ֤ם אֹתוֹ֙ וּשְׁמַעְתֶּ֣ם בְּקֹל֔וֹ וְלֹ֥א תַמְר֖וּ אֶת־פִּ֣י יְהֹוָ֑ה וִהְיִתֶ֣ם גַּם־אַתֶּ֗ם וְגַם־הַמֶּ֙לֶךְ֙ אֲשֶׁ֣ר מָלַ֣ךְ עֲלֵיכֶ֔ם אַחַ֖ר יְהֹוָ֥ה אֱלֹהֵיכֶֽם׃ 15 וְאִם־לֹ֤א תִשְׁמְעוּ֙ בְּק֣וֹל יְהֹוָ֔ה וּמְרִיתֶ֖ם אֶת־פִּ֣י יְהֹוָ֑ה וְהָיְתָ֧ה יַד־יְהֹוָ֛ה בָּכֶ֖ם וּבַאֲבֹתֵיכֶֽם׃

16 גַּם־עַתָּ֣ה הִֽתְיַצְּב֗וּ וּרְאוּ֙ אֶת־הַדָּבָ֣ר הַגָּד֣וֹל הַזֶּ֔ה אֲשֶׁ֥ר יְהֹוָ֖ה עֹשֶׂ֥ה לְעֵינֵיכֶֽם׃ 17 הֲל֤וֹא קְצִיר־חִטִּים֙ הַיּ֔וֹם אֶקְרָא֙ אֶל־יְהֹוָ֔ה וְיִתֵּ֥ן קֹל֖וֹת וּמָטָ֑ר וּדְע֣וּ וּרְא֗וּ כִּֽי־רָעַתְכֶ֤ם רַבָּה֙ אֲשֶׁ֣ר עֲשִׂיתֶ�zֶם בְּעֵינֵ֣י יְהֹוָ֔ה לִשְׁא֥וֹל לָכֶ֖ם מֶֽלֶךְ׃ ס

18 וַיִּקְרָ֤א שְׁמוּאֵל֙ אֶל־יְהֹוָ֔ה וַיִּתֵּ֧ן יְהֹוָ֛ה קֹלֹ֥ת וּמָטָ֖ר בַּיּ֣וֹם הַה֑וּא וַיִּירָ֨א כׇל־הָעָ֥ם מְאֹ֛ד אֶת־יְהֹוָ֖ה וְאֶת־שְׁמוּאֵֽל׃ 19 וַיֹּאמְר֨וּ כׇל־הָעָ֜ם אֶל־שְׁמוּאֵ֗ל הִתְפַּלֵּ֧ל בְּעַד־עֲבָדֶ֛יךָ אֶל־יְהֹוָ֥ה אֱלֹהֶ֖יךָ וְאַל־נָמ֑וּת כִּֽי־יָסַ֤פְנוּ עַל־כׇּל־חַטֹּאתֵ֙ינוּ֙ רָעָ֔ה לִשְׁאֹ֥ל לָ֖נוּ מֶֽלֶךְ׃ ס 20 וַיֹּ֨אמֶר שְׁמוּאֵ֤ל אֶל־הָעָם֙ אַל־תִּירָ֔אוּ אַתֶּ֣ם עֲשִׂיתֶ֔ם אֵ֥ת כׇּל־הָרָעָ֖ה הַזֹּ֑את אַ֗ךְ אַל־תָּס֙וּרוּ֙ מֵאַחֲרֵ֣י יְהֹוָ֔ה וַעֲבַדְתֶּ֥ם אֶת־יְהֹוָ֖ה בְּכׇל־לְבַבְכֶֽם׃ 21 וְלֹ֖א תָּס֑וּרוּ כִּ֣י ׀ אַחֲרֵ֣י הַתֹּ֗הוּ אֲשֶׁ֧ר לֹֽא־יוֹעִ֛ילוּ וְלֹ֥א יַצִּ֖ילוּ כִּי־תֹ֥הוּ הֵֽמָּה׃ 22 כִּ֠י לֹֽא־יִטֹּ֤שׁ יְהֹוָה֙ אֶת־עַמּ֔וֹ בַּעֲב֖וּר שְׁמ֣וֹ הַגָּד֑וֹל כִּ֚י הוֹאִ֣יל יְהֹוָ֔ה לַעֲשׂ֥וֹת אֶתְכֶ֛ם ל֖וֹ לְעָֽם׃ 23 גַּ֣ם אָנֹכִ֗י חָלִ֤ילָה לִּי֙ מֵחֲטֹ֣א לַֽיהֹוָ֔ה מֵחֲדֹ֖ל לְהִתְפַּלֵּ֣ל בַּעַדְכֶ֑ם וְהוֹרֵיתִ֣י אֶתְכֶ֔ם בְּדֶ֥רֶךְ הַטּוֹבָ֖ה וְהַיְשָׁרָֽה׃ 24 אַ֣ךְ ׀ יְר֣אוּ אֶת־יְהֹוָ֗ה וַעֲבַדְתֶּ֥ם אֹת֛וֹ בֶּאֱמֶ֖ת בְּכׇל־לְבַבְכֶ֑ם כִּ֣י רְא֔וּ אֵ֥ת אֲשֶׁר־הִגְדִּ֖ל עִמָּכֶֽם׃ 25 וְאִם־הָרֵ֣עַ תָּרֵ֑עוּ גַּם־אַתֶּ֥ם גַּם־מַלְכְּכֶ֖ם תִּסָּפֽוּ׃ פ

13

Saul was…*a* years old when he became king, and he reigned over Israel two years. [2]Saul picked 3,000 Israelites, of whom 2,000 were with Saul in Michmas*b* and in the hill country of Bethel, and 1,000 with Jonathan in Gibeah of Benjamin; the rest of the troops he sent back to their homes. [3]Jonathan struck down the Philistine prefect in Geba;*c* and the Philistines heard about it. *d*-Saul had the ram's horn sounded throughout the land, saying, "Let the Hebrews hear."-*d*

[4]When all Israel heard that Saul had struck down the Philistine prefect, and that Israel had *e*-incurred the wrath of-*e* the Philistines, all the people rallied to Saul at Gilgal. [5]The Philistines, in turn, gathered to attack Israel: 30,000*f* chariots and 6,000 horsemen, and troops as numerous as the sands of the seashore. They marched up and encamped at Michmas, east of Beth-aven.

[6]*d*-When the men of Israel saw that they were in trouble—for the troops were hard pressed—the people hid in caves, among thorns, among rocks, in tunnels, and in cisterns. [7]Some Hebrews crossed the Jordan, [to] the territory of Gad and Gilead. Saul was still at Gilgal, and the rest of the people rallied to him in alarm.-*d*

[8]He waited seven days, the time that Samuel [had set].*g* But when Samuel failed to come to Gilgal, and the people began to scatter, [9]Saul said, "Bring me the burnt offering and the sacrifice of well-being"; and he presented the burnt offering. [10]He had just finished presenting the burnt offering when Samuel arrived; and

יג בֶּן־שָׁנָ֖ה שָׁא֣וּל בְּמָלְכ֑וֹ וּשְׁתֵּ֥י שָׁנִ֖ים מָלַ֖ךְ עַל־יִשְׂרָאֵֽל: 2וַיִּבְחַר־ל֨וֹ שָׁא֜וּל שְׁלֹ֣שֶׁת אֲלָפִים֮ מִיִּשְׂרָאֵל֒ וַיִּהְי֣וּ עִם־שָׁא֗וּל אַלְפַּ֙יִם֙ בְּמִכְמָ֣שׂ* וּבְהַ֣ר בֵּֽית־אֵ֔ל וְאֶ֤לֶף הָיוּ֙ עִם־י֣וֹנָתָ֔ן בְּגִבְעַ֖ת בִּנְיָמִ֑ין וְיֶ֣תֶר הָעָ֔ם שִׁלַּ֖ח אִ֥ישׁ לְאֹהָלָֽיו: 3וַיַּ֣ךְ יוֹנָתָ֗ן אֵ֣ת נְצִ֤יב פְּלִשְׁתִּים֙ אֲשֶׁ֣ר בְּגֶ֔בַע וַֽיִּשְׁמְע֖וּ פְּלִשְׁתִּ֑ים וְשָׁאוּל֩ תָּקַ֨ע בַּשּׁוֹפָ֜ר בְּכָל־הָאָ֣רֶץ לֵאמֹ֔ר יִשְׁמְע֖וּ הָעִבְרִֽים: 4וְכָל־יִשְׂרָאֵ֞ל שָׁמְע֣וּ לֵאמֹ֗ר הִכָּ֤ה שָׁאוּל֙ אֶת־נְצִ֣יב פְּלִשְׁתִּ֔ים וְגַם־נִבְאַ֥שׁ יִשְׂרָאֵ֖ל בַּפְּלִשְׁתִּ֑ים וַיִּצָּעֲק֥וּ הָעָ֛ם אַחֲרֵ֥י שָׁא֖וּל הַגִּלְגָּֽל: 5וּפְלִשְׁתִּ֞ים נֶאֶסְפ֣וּ ׀ לְהִלָּחֵ֣ם עִם־יִשְׂרָאֵ֗ל שְׁלֹשִׁ֨ים אֶ֜לֶף רֶ֗כֶב וְשֵׁ֤שֶׁת אֲלָפִים֙ פָּ֣רָשִׁ֔ים וְעָ֕ם כַּח֛וֹל אֲשֶׁ֥ר עַל־שְׂפַֽת־הַיָּ֖ם לָרֹ֑ב וַֽיַּעֲלוּ֙ וַיַּחֲנ֣וּ בְמִכְמָ֔שׂ קִדְמַ֖ת בֵּ֥ית אָֽוֶן: 6וְאִ֨ישׁ יִשְׂרָאֵ֤ל רָאוּ֙ כִּ֣י צַר־ל֔וֹ כִּ֥י נִגַּ֖שׂ הָעָ֑ם וַיִּֽתְחַבְּא֣וּ הָעָ֗ם בַּמְּעָר֤וֹת וּבַֽחֲוָחִים֙ וּבַסְּלָעִ֔ים וּבַצְּרִחִ֖ים וּבַבֹּרֽוֹת: 7וְעִבְרִ֗ים עָֽבְרוּ֙ אֶת־הַיַּרְדֵּ֔ן אֶ֥רֶץ גָּ֖ד וְגִלְעָ֑ד וְשָׁאוּל֙ עוֹדֶ֣נּוּ בַגִּלְגָּ֔ל וְכָל־הָעָ֖ם חָרְד֥וּ אַחֲרָֽיו: 8וַיּ֣וֹחֶל ׀ שִׁבְעַ֣ת יָמִ֗ים לַמּוֹעֵד֙ אֲשֶׁ֣ר שְׁמוּאֵ֔ל* וְלֹא־בָ֥א שְׁמוּאֵ֖ל הַגִּלְגָּ֑ל וַיָּ֥פֶץ הָעָ֖ם מֵעָלָֽיו: 9וַיֹּ֣אמֶר שָׁא֔וּל הַגִּ֣שׁוּ אֵלַ֔י הָעֹלָ֖ה וְהַשְּׁלָמִ֑ים וַיַּ֖עַל הָעֹלָֽה: 10וַיְהִ֗י כְּכַלֹּתוֹ֙ לְהַעֲל֣וֹת הָעֹלָ֔ה וְהִנֵּ֥ה שְׁמוּאֵ֖ל בָּ֑א וַיֵּצֵ֥א שָׁא֛וּל לִקְרָאת֖וֹ לְבָרֲכֽוֹ:

v. 2.   בנוסח אחר "מכמש", כלומר בסימן ימנית, וכן בכל הפרק

v. 8.   בנוסח אחר "אשר שמואל אמר" וגם בנוסח אחר "אשר שמואל שם"

---

a   The number is lacking in the Heb. text; also, the precise context of the "two years" is uncertain. The verse is lacking in the Septuagint.

b   So in oldest mss.; other mss. and editions read "Michmash" throughout the chapter.

c   Apparently identical with Gibeah in v. 2.

d-d   Meaning of Heb. uncertain.

e-e   Lit. "became malodorous to."

f   Septuagint and other versions read "three thousand."

g   So some Heb. mss.; other mss., Septuagint, and Targum read "said." Cf. 10.8.

Saul went out to meet him and welcome him. [11]But Samuel said, "What have you done?" Saul replied, "I saw the people leaving me and scattering; you had not come at the appointed time, and the Philistines had gathered at Michmas. [12]I thought the Philistines would march down against me at Gilgal before I had entreated the LORD, so I [d]forced myself[d] to present the burnt offering." [13]Samuel answered Saul, [h]"You acted foolishly in not keeping the commandments that the LORD your God laid upon you! Otherwise[h] the LORD would have established your dynasty over Israel forever. [14]But now your dynasty will not endure. The LORD will seek out a man after His own heart, and the LORD will appoint him ruler over His people, because you did not abide by what the LORD had commanded you."

[15] [i]Samuel arose and went up from Gilgal[i] to Gibeah[j] of Benjamin. Saul numbered the troops who remained with him—about 600 strong. [16]Saul and his son Jonathan, and the troops who remained with them, stayed in Geba of Benjamin, while the Philistines were encamped at Michmas. [17]The raiders came out of the Philistine camp in three columns: One column headed for the Ophrah road that leads to the district of Shual, [18]another column headed for the Beth-horon road, and the third column headed for the border[k] road that overlooks the valley of Zeboim toward the desert.

[19]No smith was to be found in all the land of Israel, for the Philistines were afraid that the Hebrews would make swords or spears. [20]So all the Israelites had to go down to the Philistines to have their plowshares, their mattocks, axes, and colters[l] sharpened. [21][m]The charge for

11 וַיֹּאמֶר שְׁמוּאֵל מֶה עָשִׂיתָ וַיֹּאמֶר שָׁאוּל כִּי־רָאִיתִי כִי־נָפַץ הָעָם מֵעָלַי וְאַתָּה לֹא־בָאתָ לְמוֹעֵד הַיָּמִים וּפְלִשְׁתִּים נֶאֱסָפִים מִכְמָשׂ: 12 וָאֹמַר עַתָּה יֵרְדוּ פְלִשְׁתִּים אֵלַי הַגִּלְגָּל וּפְנֵי יְהוָה לֹא חִלִּיתִי וָאֶתְאַפַּק וָאַעֲלֶה הָעֹלָה: ס 13 וַיֹּאמֶר שְׁמוּאֵל אֶל־שָׁאוּל נִסְכָּלְתָּ לֹא שָׁמַרְתָּ אֶת־מִצְוַת יְהוָה אֱלֹהֶיךָ אֲשֶׁר צִוָּךְ כִּי עַתָּה הֵכִין יְהוָה אֶת־מַמְלַכְתְּךָ אֶל־יִשְׂרָאֵל עַד־עוֹלָם: 14 וְעַתָּה מַמְלַכְתְּךָ לֹא־תָקוּם בִּקֵּשׁ יְהוָה לוֹ אִישׁ כִּלְבָבוֹ וַיְצַוֵּהוּ יְהוָה לְנָגִיד עַל־עַמּוֹ כִּי לֹא שָׁמַרְתָּ אֵת אֲשֶׁר־צִוְּךָ יְהוָה: פ 15 וַיָּקָם שְׁמוּאֵל וַיַּעַל מִן־הַגִּלְגָּל גִּבְעַת בִּנְיָמִן וַיִּפְקֹד שָׁאוּל אֶת־הָעָם הַנִּמְצְאִים עִמּוֹ כְּשֵׁשׁ מֵאוֹת אִישׁ: 16 וְשָׁאוּל וְיוֹנָתָן בְּנוֹ וְהָעָם הַנִּמְצָא עִמָּם יֹשְׁבִים בְּגֶבַע בִּנְיָמִן וּפְלִשְׁתִּים חָנוּ בְמִכְמָשׂ: 17 וַיֵּצֵא הַמַּשְׁחִית מִמַּחֲנֵה פְלִשְׁתִּים שְׁלֹשָׁה רָאשִׁים הָרֹאשׁ אֶחָד יִפְנֶה אֶל־דֶּרֶךְ עָפְרָה אֶל־אֶרֶץ שׁוּעָל: 18 וְהָרֹאשׁ אֶחָד יִפְנֶה דֶּרֶךְ בֵּית חֹרוֹן וְהָרֹאשׁ אֶחָד יִפְנֶה דֶּרֶךְ הַגְּבוּל הַנִּשְׁקָף עַל־גֵּי הַצְּבֹעִים הַמִּדְבָּרָה: ס 19 וְחָרָשׁ לֹא יִמָּצֵא בְּכֹל אֶרֶץ יִשְׂרָאֵל כִּי־אָמְרוּ פְלִשְׁתִּים פֶּן יַעֲשׂוּ הָעִבְרִים חֶרֶב אוֹ חֲנִית: 20 וַיֵּרְדוּ כָל־יִשְׂרָאֵל הַפְּלִשְׁתִּים לִלְטוֹשׁ אִישׁ אֶת־מַחֲרַשְׁתּוֹ וְאֶת־אֵתוֹ וְאֶת־קַרְדֻּמּוֹ וְאֵת מַחֲרֵשָׁתוֹ: 21 וְהָיְתָה הַפְּצִירָה פִים לַמַּחֲרֵשֹׁת

---

h-h Change of vocalization yields, "You acted foolishly. If you had kept the commandment the LORD your God laid upon you…"
i-i Septuagint reads here, "Samuel rose and left Gilgal and went his way. The rest of the people followed Saul to meet the soldiers, and they went from Gilgal."
j Sometimes called Geba; cf. vv. 3, 16; 14.5.
k Septuagint reads "Geba."
l Meaning of Heb. uncertain. Septuagint reads "sickle."
m Meaning of several terms in this verse uncertain.

sharpening was a *pim*[n] for plowshares, mattocks, three-pronged forks, and axes, and for setting the goads. [22]Thus on the day of the battle, no sword or spear was to be found in the possession of any of the troops with Saul and Jonathan; only Saul and Jonathan had them.

[23]Now the Philistine garrison had marched out to the pass of Michmas.

14

One day, Jonathan son of Saul said to the attendant who carried his arms, "Come, let us cross over to the Philistine garrison on the other side"; but he did not tell his father. [2]Now Saul was staying on the outskirts of Gibeah,[a] under the pomegranate tree at Migron, and the troops with him numbered about 600. [3]Ahijah son of Ahitub brother of Ichabod son of Phinehas son of Eli, the priest of the LORD at Shiloh, was there bearing an ephod.—The troops did not know that Jonathan had gone. [4]b-At the crossing-[b] by which Jonathan sought to reach the Philistine garrison, there was a rocky crag on one side, and another rocky crag on the other, the one called Bozez and the other Seneh. [5]One crag was located on the north, near Michmas, and the other on the south, near Geba.

[6]Jonathan said to the attendant who carried his arms, "Come, let us cross over to the outpost of those uncircumcised fellows. Perhaps the LORD will act in our behalf, for nothing prevents the LORD from winning a victory by many or by few." [7]His arms-bearer answered him, "Do whatever c-you like. You go first,-[c] I am d-with you, whatever you decide."-[d] [8]Jonathan said, "We'll cross over to those men and let them see

וְלָאֵתִים וְלִשְׁלֹשׁ קִלְּשׁוֹן וּלְהַקַּרְדֻּמִּים וּלְהַצִּיב הַדָּרְבָן: 22 וְהָיָה בְּיוֹם מִלְחֶמֶת וְלֹא נִמְצָא חֶרֶב וַחֲנִית בְּיַד כָּל־הָעָם אֲשֶׁר אֶת־שָׁאוּל וְאֶת־יוֹנָתָן וַתִּמָּצֵא לְשָׁאוּל וּלְיוֹנָתָן בְּנוֹ: 23 וַיֵּצֵא מַצַּב פְּלִשְׁתִּים אֶל־מַעֲבַר מִכְמָשׂ: ס

יד וַיְהִי הַיּוֹם וַיֹּאמֶר יוֹנָתָן בֶּן־שָׁאוּל אֶל־הַנַּעַר נֹשֵׂא כֵלָיו לְכָה וְנַעְבְּרָה אֶל־מַצַּב פְּלִשְׁתִּים אֲשֶׁר מֵעֵבֶר הַלָּז וּלְאָבִיו לֹא הִגִּיד: 2 וְשָׁאוּל יוֹשֵׁב בִּקְצֵה הַגִּבְעָה תַּחַת הָרִמּוֹן אֲשֶׁר בְּמִגְרוֹן וְהָעָם אֲשֶׁר עִמּוֹ כְּשֵׁשׁ מֵאוֹת אִישׁ: 3 וַאֲחִיָּה בֶן־אֲחִטוּב אֲחִי אִיכָבוֹד ׀ בֶּן־פִּינְחָס בֶּן־עֵלִי כֹּהֵן ׀ יְהוָה בְּשִׁלוֹ נֹשֵׂא אֵפוֹד וְהָעָם לֹא יָדַע כִּי הָלַךְ יוֹנָתָן: 4 וּבֵין הַמַּעְבְּרוֹת אֲשֶׁר בִּקֵּשׁ יוֹנָתָן לַעֲבֹר עַל־מַצַּב פְּלִשְׁתִּים שֵׁן־הַסֶּלַע מֵהָעֵבֶר מִזֶּה וְשֵׁן־ הַסֶּלַע מֵהָעֵבֶר מִזֶּה וְשֵׁם הָאֶחָד בּוֹצֵץ וְשֵׁם הָאֶחָד סֶנֶּה: 5 הַשֵּׁן הָאֶחָד מָצוּק מִצָּפוֹן מוּל מִכְמָשׂ וְהָאֶחָד מִנֶּגֶב מוּל גָּבַע: ס

6 וַיֹּאמֶר יְהוֹנָתָן אֶל־הַנַּעַר ׀ נֹשֵׂא כֵלָיו לְכָה וְנַעְבְּרָה אֶל־מַצַּב הָעֲרֵלִים הָאֵלֶּה אוּלַי יַעֲשֶׂה יְהוָה לָנוּ כִּי אֵין לַיהוָה מַעְצוֹר לְהוֹשִׁיעַ בְּרַב אוֹ בִמְעָט: 7 וַיֹּאמֶר לוֹ נֹשֵׂא כֵלָיו עֲשֵׂה כָּל־אֲשֶׁר בִּלְבָבֶךָ נְטֵה לָךְ הִנְנִי עִמְּךָ כִּלְבָבֶךָ: ס 8 וַיֹּאמֶר יְהוֹנָתָן הִנֵּה אֲנַחְנוּ עֹבְרִים אֶל־הָאֲנָשִׁים

---

n   I.e., two-thirds of a shekel.

a   See note j at 13.15.

b-b   Meaning of Heb. uncertain.

c-c   Lit. "is in your heart. Incline yourself." Septuagint reads "your heart inclines to."

d-d   Lit. "with you, according to your heart." Septuagint reads "with you; my heart is like your heart."

us. 9If they say to us, 'Wait until we get to you,' then we'll stay where we are, and not go up to them. 10But if they say, 'Come up to us,' then we will go up, for the LORD is delivering them into our hands. That shall be our sign." 11They both showed themselves to the Philistine outpost and the Philistines said, "Look, some Hebrews are coming out of the holes where they have been hiding." 12The men of the outpost shouted to Jonathan and his arms-bearer, "Come up to us, and we'll teach you a lesson." Then Jonathan said to his arms-bearer, "Follow me, for the LORD will deliver them into the hands of Israel." 13And Jonathan clambered up on his hands and feet, his arms-bearer behind him; [the Philistines] fell before Jonathan, and his arms-bearer finished them off behind him. 14The initial attack that Jonathan and his arms-bearer made accounted for some twenty men, *b*-within a space about half a furrow long [in] an acre of land.-*b* 15Terror broke out among all the troops both in the camp [and] in the field; the outposts and the raiders were also terrified. The very earth quaked, and a terror from God ensued.

16Saul's scouts in Gibeah of Benjamin saw that the multitude was *e*-scattering in all directions.-*e* 17And Saul said to the troops with him, "Take a count and see who has left us." They took a count and found that Jonathan and his arms-bearer were missing. 18Thereupon Saul said to Ahijah, "Bring the Ark*f* of God here"; for the Ark*f* of God was at the time among*g* the Israelites. 19But while Saul was speaking to the priest, the confusion in the Philistine camp kept increasing; and Saul said to the priest, "Withdraw your hand." 20Saul and the troops with him assembled and rushed into battle; they found [the Philistines] in very great confusion, every man's sword turned against his fellow.

וְנִגְלֵינוּ אֲלֵיהֶֽם׃ 9 אִם־כֹּ֤ה יֹֽאמְרוּ֙ אֵלֵ֔ינוּ דֹּ֕מּוּ עַד־הַגִּיעֵ֖נוּ אֲלֵיכֶ֑ם וְעָמַ֣דְנוּ תַחְתֵּ֔ינוּ וְלֹ֥א נַעֲלֶ֖ה אֲלֵיהֶֽם׃ 10 וְאִם־כֹּ֨ה יֹאמְר֜וּ עֲלֵ֤ה עָלֵ֙ינוּ֙ וְעָלִ֔ינוּ כִּֽי־נְתָנָ֥ם יְהֹוָ֖ה בְּיָדֵ֑נוּ וְזֶה־לָּ֖נוּ הָאֽוֹת׃ 11 וַיִּגָּל֣וּ שְׁנֵיהֶ֔ם אֶל־מַצַּ֖ב פְּלִשְׁתִּ֑ים וַיֹּאמְר֣וּ פְלִשְׁתִּ֗ים הִנֵּ֤ה עִבְרִים֙ יֹֽצְאִ֔ים מִן־הַחֹרִ֖ים אֲשֶׁ֥ר הִתְחַבְּאוּ־שָֽׁם׃ 12 וַיַּעֲנוּ֩ אַנְשֵׁ֨י הַמַּצָּבָ֜ה אֶת־יוֹנָתָ֣ן ׀ וְאֶת־נֹשֵׂ֣א כֵלָ֗יו וַיֹּֽאמְרוּ֙ עֲל֣וּ אֵלֵ֔ינוּ וְנוֹדִ֥יעָה אֶתְכֶ֖ם דָּבָ֑ר פ וַיֹּ֨אמֶר יוֹנָתָ֜ן אֶל־נֹשֵׂ֤א כֵלָיו֙ עֲלֵ֣ה אַחֲרַ֔י כִּֽי־נְתָנָ֥ם יְהֹוָ֖ה בְּיַ֥ד יִשְׂרָאֵֽל׃ 13 וַיַּ֣עַל יוֹנָתָ֗ן עַל־יָדָיו֙ וְעַל־רַגְלָ֔יו וְנֹשֵׂ֥א כֵלָ֖יו אַחֲרָ֑יו וַֽיִּפְּלוּ֙ לִפְנֵ֣י יוֹנָתָ֔ן וְנֹשֵׂ֥א כֵלָ֖יו מְמוֹתֵ֥ת אַחֲרָֽיו׃ 14 וַתְּהִ֞י הַמַּכָּ֣ה הָרִֽאשֹׁנָ֗ה אֲשֶׁ֨ר הִכָּ֧ה יוֹנָתָ֛ן וְנֹשֵׂ֥א כֵלָ֖יו כְּעֶשְׂרִ֣ים אִ֑ישׁ כְּבַחֲצִ֥י מַעֲנָ֖ה צֶ֥מֶד שָׂדֶֽה׃ 15 וַתְּהִי֩ חֲרָדָ֨ה בַמַּחֲנֶ֤ה בַשָּׂדֶה֙ וּבְכָל־הָעָ֔ם הַמַּצָּב֙ וְהַמַּשְׁחִ֔ית חָרְד֖וּ גַּם־הֵ֑מָּה וַתִּרְגַּ֣ז הָאָ֔רֶץ וַתְּהִ֖י לְחֶרְדַּ֥ת אֱלֹהִֽים׃ 16 וַיִּרְא֤וּ הַצֹּפִים֙ לְשָׁא֔וּל בְּגִבְעַ֖ת בִּנְיָמִ֑ן וְהִנֵּ֧ה הֶהָמ֛וֹן נָמ֖וֹג וַיֵּ֥לֶךְ וַהֲלֹֽם׃ פ 17 וַיֹּ֣אמֶר שָׁא֗וּל לָעָם֙ אֲשֶׁ֣ר אִתּ֔וֹ פִּקְדוּ־נָ֣א וּרְא֔וּ מִ֖י הָלַ֣ךְ מֵעִמָּ֑נוּ וַֽיִּפְקְד֔וּ וְהִנֵּ֛ה אֵ֥ין יוֹנָתָ֖ן וְנֹשֵׂ֥א כֵלָֽיו׃ 18 וַיֹּ֤אמֶר שָׁאוּל֙ לַֽאֲחִיָּ֔ה הַגִּ֖ישָׁה אֲר֣וֹן הָאֱלֹהִ֑ים כִּֽי־הָיָ֞ה אֲר֧וֹן הָאֱלֹהִ֛ים בַּיּ֥וֹם הַה֖וּא וּבְנֵ֥י יִשְׂרָאֵֽל׃ 19 וַיְהִ֗י עַ֣ד דִּבֶּ֤ר שָׁאוּל֙ אֶל־הַכֹּהֵ֔ן וְהֶהָמ֗וֹן אֲשֶׁר֙ בְּמַחֲנֵ֣ה פְלִשְׁתִּ֔ים וַיֵּ֥לֶךְ הָל֖וֹךְ וָרָ֑ב פ וַיֹּ֧אמֶר שָׁא֛וּל אֶל־הַכֹּהֵ֖ן אֱסֹ֥ף יָדֶֽךָ׃ 20 וַיִּזָּעֵ֣ק שָׁא֗וּל וְכָל־הָעָם֙ אֲשֶׁ֣ר אִתּ֔וֹ וַיָּבֹ֖אוּ עַד־הַמִּלְחָמָ֑ה וְהִנֵּ֨ה הָיְתָ֜ה חֶ֤רֶב אִישׁ֙ בְּרֵעֵ֔הוּ מְהוּמָ֖ה גְּדוֹלָ֥ה מְאֹֽד׃

---

e-e   Lit. "shaken and going thither." Meaning of Heb. uncertain.
f   Septuagint reads "ephod," and cf. vv. 3, 23.9, 30.7.
g   Heb. "and."

21*b*-And the Hebrews who had previously sided with the Philistines, who had come up with them in the army [from] round about—they too joined the Israelites-*b* who were with Saul and Jonathan. 22When all the men of Israel who were hiding in the hill country of Ephraim heard that the Philistines were fleeing, they too pursued them in battle. 23Thus the LORD brought victory to Israel that day.

The fighting passed beyond Beth-aven. 24*h*-The men of Israel were distressed-*h* that day. For Saul had laid an oath upon the troops: "Cursed be the man who eats any food before night falls and I take revenge on my enemies." So none of the troops ate anything. 25Everybody came to a -*i*-stack of beehives-*i* where some honey had spilled on the ground. 26When the troops came to the beehives*i* and found the flow of honey there, no one put*b* his hand to his mouth, for the troops feared the oath. 27Jonathan, however, had not heard his father adjure the troops. So he put out the stick he had with him, dipped it into the beehive of honey, and brought his hand back to his mouth; and his eyes lit up. 28At this one of the soldiers spoke up, "Your father adjured the troops: 'Cursed be the man who eats anything this day.' And so the troops are faint." 29Jonathan answered, "My father has brought trouble on the people. See for yourselves how my eyes lit up when I tasted that bit of honey. 30If only the troops had eaten today of spoil captured from the enemy, the defeat of the Philistines would have been greater still!"

31They struck down the Philistines that day from Michmas to Aijalon, and the troops were famished. 32The troops pounced on the spoil; they took the sheep and cows and calves and slaughtered them on the ground, and the troops

21 וְהָעִבְרִ֗ים הָי֤וּ לַפְּלִשְׁתִּים֙ כְּאֶתְמ֣וֹל שִׁלְשׁ֔וֹם אֲשֶׁ֨ר עָל֥וּ עִמָּ֛ם בַּמַּחֲנֶ֖ה סָבִ֑יב וְגַם־הֵ֗מָּה לִהְיוֹת֙ עִם־יִשְׂרָאֵ֔ל אֲשֶׁ֥ר עִם־שָׁא֖וּל וְיוֹנָתָֽן׃ 22 וְכֹל֩ אִ֨ישׁ יִשְׂרָאֵ֜ל הַמִּֽתְחַבְּאִ֤ים בְּהַר־אֶפְרַ֙יִם֙ שָֽׁמְע֔וּ כִּי־נָ֖סוּ פְּלִשְׁתִּ֑ים וַיַּדְבְּק֥וּ גַם־הֵ֛מָּה אַחֲרֵיהֶ֖ם בַּמִּלְחָמָֽה׃ 23 וַיּ֧וֹשַׁע יְהֹוָ֛ה בַּיּ֥וֹם הַה֖וּא אֶת־יִשְׂרָאֵ֑ל

וְהַ֨מִּלְחָמָ֔ה עָֽבְרָ֖ה אֶת־בֵּ֥ית אָֽוֶן׃ 24 וְאִֽישׁ־יִשְׂרָאֵ֥ל נִגַּ֖שׂ בַּיּ֣וֹם הַה֑וּא וַיֹּ֩אֶל֩ שָׁא֨וּל אֶת־הָעָ֜ם לֵאמֹ֗ר אָר֣וּר הָאִ֡ישׁ אֲשֶׁר־יֹ֩אכַל֩ לֶ֨חֶם עַד־הָעֶ֜רֶב וְנִקַּמְתִּי֙ מֵאֹ֣יְבַ֔י וְלֹ֥א טָעַ֛ם כׇּל־הָעָ֖ם לָֽחֶם׃ ס 25 וְכׇל־הָאָ֖רֶץ בָּ֣אוּ בַיָּ֑עַר וַיְהִ֥י דְבַ֖שׁ עַל־פְּנֵ֥י הַשָּׂדֶֽה׃ 26 וַיָּבֹ֤א הָעָם֙ אֶל־הַיַּ֔עַר וְהִנֵּ֖ה הֵ֣לֶךְ דְּבָ֑שׁ וְאֵין־מַשִּׂ֤יג יָדוֹ֙ אֶל־פִּ֔יו כִּֽי־יָרֵ֥א הָעָ֖ם אֶת־הַשְּׁבֻעָֽה׃ 27 וְיוֹנָתָ֣ן לֹֽא־שָׁמַ֗ע בְּהַשְׁבִּ֤יעַ אָבִיו֙ אֶת־הָעָ֔ם וַיִּשְׁלַ֗ח אֶת־קְצֵ֤ה הַמַּטֶּה֙ אֲשֶׁ֣ר בְּיָד֔וֹ וַיִּטְבֹּ֥ל אוֹתָ֖הּ בְּיַעְרַ֣ת הַדְּבָ֑שׁ וַיָּ֤שֶׁב יָדוֹ֙ אֶל־פִּ֔יו וַתָּרֹ֖אנָה עֵינָֽיו׃ 28 וַיַּ֩עַן֩ אִ֨ישׁ מֵהָעָ֜ם וַיֹּ֗אמֶר הַשְׁבֵּ֩עַ֩ הִשְׁבִּ֨יעַ אָבִ֤יךָ אֶת־הָעָם֙ לֵאמֹ֔ר אָר֧וּר הָאִ֛ישׁ אֲשֶׁר־יֹ֥אכַל לֶ֖חֶם הַיּ֑וֹם וַיָּ֖עַף הָעָֽם׃ 29 וַיֹּ֙אמֶר֙ יֽוֹנָתָ֔ן עָכַ֥ר אָבִ֖י אֶת־הָאָ֑רֶץ רְאוּ־נָא֙ כִּֽי־אֹ֣רוּ עֵינַ֔י כִּ֣י טָעַ֔מְתִּי מְעַ֖ט דְּבַ֥שׁ הַזֶּֽה׃ 30 אַ֗ף כִּ֡י לוּא֩ אָכֹ֨ל אָכַ֤ל הַיּוֹם֙ הָעָ֔ם מִשְּׁלַ֥ל אֹֽיְבָ֖יו אֲשֶׁ֣ר מָצָ֑א כִּ֥י עַתָּ֛ה לֹֽא־רָבְתָ֥ה מַכָּ֖ה בַּפְּלִשְׁתִּֽים׃ 31 וַיַּכּ֞וּ בַּיּ֤וֹם הַהוּא֙ בַּפְּלִשְׁתִּ֔ים מִמִּכְמָ֖שׂ אַיָּלֹ֑נָה וַיָּ֥עַף הָעָ֖ם מְאֹֽד׃ 32 ויעש וַיַּ֤עַט הָעָם֙ אֶל־שלל הַשָּׁלָ֔ל וַיִּקְח֨וּ צֹ֧אן וּבָקָ֛ר וּבְנֵ֥י בָקָ֖ר וַיִּשְׁחֲטוּ־אָ֑רְצָה וַיֹּ֥אכַל הָעָ֖ם

---

h-h   *Meaning of Heb. uncertain. Septuagint reads "And all the troops, about 10,000 men, were with Saul; and the battle spread into the hill country of Ephraim. Now Saul committed a rash act."*

i-i   *Meaning of Heb. uncertain; cf. Song of Songs 5.1.*

ate with the blood.*j* ³³When it was reported to Saul that the troops were sinning against the LORD, eating with the blood, he said, "You have acted faithlessly. Roll a large stone over to me today."*k* ³⁴And Saul ordered, "Spread out among the troops and tell them that everyone must bring me his ox or his sheep and slaughter it here, and then eat. You must not sin against the LORD and eat with the blood." Every one of the troops brought *l*his own ox with him*-l* that night and slaughtered it there. ³⁵Thus Saul set up an altar to the LORD; it was the first altar he erected to the LORD.

³⁶Saul said, "Let us go down after the Philistines by night and plunder among them until the light of morning; and let us not leave a single survivor among them." "Do whatever you please," they replied. But the priest said, "Let us approach God here." ³⁷So Saul inquired of God, "Shall I go down after the Philistines? Will You deliver them into the hands of Israel?" But this time He did not respond to him. ³⁸Then Saul said, "Come forward, all chief officers of the troops, and find out how this guilt was incurred today. ³⁹For as the LORD lives who brings victory to Israel, even if it was through my son Jonathan, he shall be put to death!" Not one soldier answered him. ⁴⁰And he said to all the Israelites, "You stand on one side, and my son Jonathan and I shall stand on the other." The troops said to Saul, "Do as you please." ⁴¹Saul then said to the LORD, the God of Israel, *m*-"Show Thammim."-*m* Jonathan and Saul were indicated by lot, and the troops were cleared. ⁴²And Saul said, "Cast the lots between my son and me"; and Jonathan was indicated.

⁴³Saul said to Jonathan, "Tell me, what have

---

j   *I.e., without the proper rites.*
k   *Septuagint reads "here."*
l-l   *Septuagint reads "whatever he had in his possession."*
m-m   *Meaning of Heb. uncertain. Septuagint reads "Why have You not responded to Your servant today? If this iniquity was due to my son Jonathan or to me, O LORD, God of Israel, show Urim; and if You say it was due to Your people Israel, show Thummim."*

עַל־הַדָּם: 33 וַיַּגִּידוּ לְשָׁאוּל לֵאמֹר הִנֵּה הָעָם חֹטִאים לַיהוָה לֶאֱכֹל עַל־הַדָּם וַיֹּאמֶר בְּגַדְתֶּם גֹּלּוּ־אֵלַי הַיּוֹם אֶבֶן גְּדוֹלָה: 34 וַיֹּאמֶר שָׁאוּל פֻּצוּ בָעָם וַאֲמַרְתֶּם לָהֶם הַגִּישׁוּ אֵלַי אִישׁ שׁוֹרוֹ וְאִישׁ שְׂיֵהוּ וּשְׁחַטְתֶּם בָּזֶה וַאֲכַלְתֶּם וְלֹא־תֶחֶטְאוּ לַיהוָה לֶאֱכֹל אֶל־הַדָּם וַיַּגִּשׁוּ כָל־הָעָם אִישׁ שׁוֹרוֹ בְיָדוֹ הַלַּיְלָה וַיִּשְׁחֲטוּ־שָׁם: 35 וַיִּבֶן שָׁאוּל מִזְבֵּחַ לַיהוָה אֹתוֹ הֵחֵל לִבְנוֹת מִזְבֵּחַ לַיהוָה: פ

36 וַיֹּאמֶר שָׁאוּל נֵרְדָה אַחֲרֵי פְלִשְׁתִּים ׀ לַיְלָה וְנָבֹזָה בָהֶם ׀ עַד־אוֹר הַבֹּקֶר וְלֹא־נַשְׁאֵר בָּהֶם אִישׁ וַיֹּאמְרוּ כָּל־הַטּוֹב בְּעֵינֶיךָ עֲשֵׂה ס וַיֹּאמֶר הַכֹּהֵן נִקְרְבָה הֲלֹם אֶל־הָאֱלֹהִים: 37 וַיִּשְׁאַל שָׁאוּל בֵּאלֹהִים הַאֵרֵד אַחֲרֵי פְלִשְׁתִּים הֲתִתְּנֵם בְּיַד יִשְׂרָאֵל וְלֹא עָנָהוּ בַּיּוֹם הַהוּא: 38 וַיֹּאמֶר שָׁאוּל גֹּשׁוּ הֲלֹם כֹּל פִּנּוֹת הָעָם וּדְעוּ וּרְאוּ בַּמָּה הָיְתָה הַחַטָּאת הַזֹּאת הַיּוֹם: 39 כִּי חַי־יְהוָה הַמּוֹשִׁיעַ אֶת־יִשְׂרָאֵל כִּי אִם־יֶשְׁנוֹ בְּיוֹנָתָן בְּנִי כִּי מוֹת יָמוּת וְאֵין עֹנֵהוּ מִכָּל־הָעָם: 40 וַיֹּאמֶר אֶל־כָּל־יִשְׂרָאֵל אַתֶּם תִּהְיוּ לְעֵבֶר אֶחָד וַאֲנִי וְיוֹנָתָן בְּנִי נִהְיֶה לְעֵבֶר אֶחָד וַיֹּאמְרוּ הָעָם אֶל־שָׁאוּל הַטּוֹב בְּעֵינֶיךָ עֲשֵׂה: ס 41 וַיֹּאמֶר שָׁאוּל אֶל־יְהוָה אֱלֹהֵי יִשְׂרָאֵל הָבָה תָמִים וַיִּלָּכֵד יוֹנָתָן וְשָׁאוּל וְהָעָם יָצָאוּ: 42 וַיֹּאמֶר שָׁאוּל הַפִּילוּ בֵּינִי וּבֵין יוֹנָתָן בְּנִי וַיִּלָּכֵד יוֹנָתָן: 43 וַיֹּאמֶר שָׁאוּל אֶל־יוֹנָתָן הַגִּידָה לִּי מֶה

you done?" And Jonathan told him, "I only tasted a bit of honey with the tip of the stick in my hand. I am ready to die." [44]Saul said, "Thus and more may God do:[n] You shall be put to death, Jonathan!" [45]But the troops said to Saul, "Shall Jonathan die, after bringing this great victory to Israel? Never! As the Lord lives, not a hair of his head shall fall to the ground! For he brought this day to pass with the help of God." Thus the troops saved Jonathan and he did not die. [46]Saul broke off his pursuit of the Philistines, and the Philistines returned to their homes.

[47]After Saul had secured his kingship over Israel, he waged on every side against all his enemies: against the Moabites, Ammonites, Edomites, the Philistines, and the kings[o] of Zobah; and wherever he turned he worsted [them]. [48]He was triumphant, defeating the Amalekites and saving Israel from those who plundered it.

[49]Saul's sons were: Jonathan, Ishvi,[p] and Malchishua; and the names of his two daughters were Merab, the older, and Michal, the younger. [50]The name of Saul's wife was Ahinoam daughter of Ahimaaz; and the name of his army commander was Abiner[q] son of Saul's uncle Ner. [51]Kish, Saul's father, and Ner, Abner's father, were sons of Abiel.

[52]There was bitter war against the Philistines all the days of Saul; and whenever Saul noticed any stalwart man or warrior, he would take him into his service.

15 Samuel said to Saul, "I am the one the Lord sent to anoint you king over His people Israel. Therefore, listen to the Lord's command!

עָשִׂיתָ וַיַּגֶּד־לוֹ יוֹנָתָן וַיֹּאמֶר טָעֹם
טָעַמְתִּי בִּקְצֵה הַמַּטֶּה אֲשֶׁר־בְּיָדִי מְעַט
דְּבַשׁ הִנְנִי אָמוּת: [44] וַיֹּאמֶר שָׁאוּל כֹּה־
יַעֲשֶׂה אֱלֹהִים וְכֹה יוֹסִף כִּי־מוֹת תָּמוּת
יוֹנָתָן: [45] וַיֹּאמֶר הָעָם אֶל־שָׁאוּל הֲיוֹנָתָן ׀
יָמוּת אֲשֶׁר עָשָׂה הַיְשׁוּעָה הַגְּדוֹלָה הַזֹּאת
בְּיִשְׂרָאֵל חָלִילָה חַי־יְהֹוָה אִם־יִפֹּל
מִשַּׂעֲרַת רֹאשׁוֹ אַרְצָה כִּי־עִם־אֱלֹהִים
עָשָׂה הַיּוֹם הַזֶּה וַיִּפְדּוּ הָעָם אֶת־יוֹנָתָן
וְלֹא־מֵת: ס [46] וַיַּעַל שָׁאוּל מֵאַחֲרֵי
פְלִשְׁתִּים וּפְלִשְׁתִּים הָלְכוּ לִמְקוֹמָם:
[47] וְשָׁאוּל לָכַד הַמְּלוּכָה עַל־יִשְׂרָאֵל
וַיִּלָּחֶם סָבִיב ׀ בְּכָל־אֹיְבָיו בְּמוֹאָב ׀
וּבִבְנֵי־עַמּוֹן וּבֶאֱדוֹם וּבְמַלְכֵי צוֹבָה
וּבַפְּלִשְׁתִּים וּבְכֹל אֲשֶׁר־יִפְנֶה יַרְשִׁיעַ:
[48] וַיַּעַשׂ חַיִל וַיַּךְ אֶת־עֲמָלֵק וַיַּצֵּל אֶת־
יִשְׂרָאֵל מִיַּד שֹׁסֵהוּ: ס
[49] וַיִּהְיוּ בְּנֵי שָׁאוּל יוֹנָתָן וְיִשְׁוִי וּמַלְכִּי־
שׁוּעַ וְשֵׁם שְׁתֵּי בְנֹתָיו שֵׁם הַבְּכִירָה מֵרַב
וְשֵׁם הַקְּטַנָּה מִיכַל: [50] וְשֵׁם אֵשֶׁת שָׁאוּל
אֲחִינֹעַם בַּת־אֲחִימָעַץ וְשֵׁם שַׂר־צְבָאוֹ
אֲבִינֵר בֶּן־נֵר דּוֹד שָׁאוּל: [51] וְקִישׁ אֲבִי־
שָׁאוּל וְנֵר אֲבִי־אַבְנֵר בֶּן־אֲבִיאֵל: ס
[52] וַתְּהִי הַמִּלְחָמָה חֲזָקָה עַל־פְּלִשְׁתִּים
כֹּל יְמֵי שָׁאוּל וְרָאָה שָׁאוּל כָּל־אִישׁ גִּבּוֹר
וְכָל־בֶּן־חַיִל וַיַּאַסְפֵהוּ אֵלָיו: ס

טו וַיֹּאמֶר שְׁמוּאֵל אֶל־שָׁאוּל אֹתִי
שָׁלַח יְהֹוָה לִמְשָׁחֲךָ לְמֶלֶךְ עַל־עַמּוֹ
עַל־יִשְׂרָאֵל וְעַתָּה שְׁמַע לְקוֹל דִּבְרֵי
יְהֹוָה: ס

---

n   Many mss. and Septuagint add "to me."
o   Septuagint and 4QSamᵃ read "king."
p   The same as Ishbosheth (2 Sam. 2.8) and Eshbaal (1 Chron. 8.33).
q   Usually "Abner."

2"Thus said the LORD of Hosts: I am exacting the penalty for what Amalek did to Israel, for the assault he made upon them on the road, on their way up from Egypt. 3Now go, attack Amalek, and proscribe*a* all that belongs to him. Spare no one, but kill alike men and women, infants and sucklings, oxen and sheep, camels and asses!"

4Saul mustered the troops and enrolled them at Telaim: 200,000 men on foot, and 10,000 men of Judah. 5Then Saul advanced as far as the city of Amalek and *b*-lay in wait-*b* in the wadi. 6Saul said to the Kenites, "Come, withdraw at once from among the Amalekites, that I may not destroy you along with them; for you showed kindness to all the Israelites when they left Egypt." So the Kenites withdrew from among the Amalekites.

7Saul destroyed Amalek from Havilah all the way to Shur, which is close to Egypt, 8and he captured King Agag of Amalek alive. He proscribed all the people, putting them to the sword; 9but Saul and the troops spared Agag and the best of the sheep, the oxen, the second-born,*c* the lambs, and all else that was of value. They would not proscribe them; they proscribed only *b*-what was cheap and worthless.-*b*

10The word of the LORD then came to Samuel: 11"I regret that I made Saul king, for he has turned away from Me and has not carried out My commands." Samuel was distressed and he entreated the LORD all night long. 12Early in the morning Samuel went to meet Saul. Samuel was told, "Saul went to Carmel, where he erected a monument for himself; then he left and went on down to Gilgal."

13When Samuel came to Saul, Saul said to him, "Blessed are you of the LORD! I have fulfilled the LORD's command." 14"Then what,"

2 כֹּה אָמַר יְהוָה צְבָא֔וֹת פָּקַ֙דְתִּי֙ אֵ֣ת
אֲשֶׁר־עָשָׂ֧ה עֲמָלֵ֛ק לְיִשְׂרָאֵ֖ל אֲשֶׁר־שָׂ֣ם ל֑וֹ
בַּדֶּ֖רֶךְ בַּעֲלֹת֥וֹ מִמִּצְרָֽיִם׃ 3 עַתָּה֩ לֵ֨ךְ
וְהִכִּיתָ֜ה אֶת־עֲמָלֵ֗ק וְהַחֲרַמְתֶּם֙ אֶת־כָּל־
אֲשֶׁר־ל֔וֹ וְלֹ֥א תַחְמֹ֖ל עָלָ֑יו וְהֵמַתָּ֞ה מֵאִ֣ישׁ
עַד־אִשָּׁ֗ה מֵֽעֹלֵל֙ וְעַד־יוֹנֵ֔ק מִשּׁ֣וֹר וְעַד־שֶׂ֔ה
מִגָּמָ֖ל וְעַד־חֲמֽוֹר׃ ס

4 וַיְשַׁמַּ֤ע שָׁאוּל֙ אֶת־הָעָ֔ם וַֽיִּפְקְדֵם֙
בַּטְּלָאִ֔ים מָאתַ֥יִם אֶ֖לֶף רַגְלִ֑י וַעֲשֶׂ֥רֶת
אֲלָפִ֖ים אֶת־אִ֥ישׁ יְהוּדָֽה׃ 5 וַיָּבֹ֥א שָׁא֖וּל
עַד־עִ֣יר עֲמָלֵ֑ק וַיָּ֖רֶב בַּנָּֽחַל׃ 6 וַיֹּ֣אמֶר
שָׁא֣וּל אֶל־הַקֵּינִ֡י לְכוּ֩ סֻּ֨רוּ רְד֜וּ מִתּ֣וֹךְ
עֲמָֽלֵקִ֗י פֶּן־אֹֽסִפְךָ֙ עִמּ֔וֹ וְאַתָּ֞ה עָשִׂ֤יתָה
חֶ֙סֶד֙ עִם־כָּל־בְּנֵ֣י יִשְׂרָאֵ֔ל בַּעֲלוֹתָ֖ם
מִמִּצְרָ֑יִם וַיָּ֥סַר קֵינִ֖י מִתּ֥וֹךְ עֲמָלֵֽק׃
7 וַיַּ֥ךְ שָׁא֖וּל אֶת־עֲמָלֵ֑ק מֵֽחֲוִילָ֙ה בּוֹאֲךָ֣
שׁ֔וּר אֲשֶׁ֖ר עַל־פְּנֵ֥י מִצְרָֽיִם׃ 8 וַיִּתְפֹּ֛שׂ אֶת־
אֲגַ֥ג מֶֽלֶךְ־עֲמָלֵ֖ק חָ֑י וְאֶת־כָּל־הָעָ֖ם
הֶחֱרִ֥ים לְפִי־חָֽרֶב׃ 9 וַיַּחְמֹל֩ שָׁא֨וּל וְהָעָ֜ם
עַל־אֲגָ֗ג וְעַל־מֵיטַ֤ב הַצֹּאן֙ וְהַבָּקָ֔ר
וְהַמִּשְׁנִ֣ים וְעַל־הַכָּרִ֗ים וְעַֽל־כָּל־הַטּ֔וֹב
וְלֹ֥א אָב֖וּ הַחֲרִימָ֑ם וְכָל־הַמְּלָאכָ֛ה נְמִבְזָ֥ה
וְנָמֵ֖ס אֹתָ֥הּ הֶחֱרִֽימוּ׃ פ

10 וַֽיְהִי֙ דְּבַר־יְהוָ֔ה אֶל־שְׁמוּאֵ֖ל לֵאמֹֽר׃
11 נִחַ֗מְתִּי כִּֽי־הִמְלַ֤כְתִּי אֶת־שָׁאוּל֙ לְמֶ֔לֶךְ
כִּֽי־שָׁ֤ב מֵאַֽחֲרַי֙ וְאֶת־דְּבָרַ֔י לֹ֥א הֵקִ֖ים וַיִּ֣חַר
לִשְׁמוּאֵ֔ל וַיִּזְעַ֥ק אֶל־יְהוָ֖ה כָּל־הַלָּֽיְלָה׃
12 וַיַּשְׁכֵּ֧ם שְׁמוּאֵ֛ל לִקְרַ֥את שָׁא֖וּל בַּבֹּ֑קֶר
וַיֻּגַּ֨ד לִשְׁמוּאֵ֜ל לֵאמֹ֗ר בָּֽא־שָׁא֤וּל הַכַּרְמֶ֙לָה֙
וְהִנֵּ֙ה מַצִּ֥יב לוֹ֙ יָ֔ד וַיִּסֹּב֙ וַֽיַּעֲבֹ֔ר וַיֵּ֖רֶד
הַגִּלְגָּֽל׃

13 וַיָּבֹ֥א שְׁמוּאֵ֖ל אֶל־שָׁא֑וּל וַיֹּ֧אמֶר ל֣וֹ
שָׁא֗וּל בָּר֤וּךְ אַתָּה֙ לַֽיהוָ֔ה הֲקִימֹ֖תִי אֶת־
דְּבַ֥ר יְהוָֽה׃ 14 וַיֹּ֙אמֶר֙ שְׁמוּאֵ֔ל וּמֶ֣ה ק֖וֹל

---

a   *See note at Josh. 6.18.*
b-b *Meaning of Heb. uncertain.*
c   *Targum and Syriac read "fatlings."*

demanded Samuel, "is this bleating of sheep in my ears, and the lowing of oxen that I hear?" ¹⁵Saul answered, "They were brought from the Amalekites, for the troops spared the choicest of the sheep and oxen for sacrificing to the Lord your God. And we proscribed the rest." ¹⁶Samuel said to Saul, "Stop! Let me tell you what the Lord said to me last night!" "Speak," he replied. ¹⁷And Samuel said, "You may look small to yourself, but you are the head of the tribes of Israel. The Lord anointed you king over Israel, ¹⁸and the Lord sent you on a mission, saying, 'Go and proscribe the sinful Amalekites; make war on them until you have exterminated them.' ¹⁹Why did you disobey the Lord and swoop down on the spoil ^d-in defiance of the Lord's will?"-^d ²⁰Saul said to Samuel, "But I did obey the Lord! I performed the mission on which the Lord sent me: I captured King Agag of Amalek, and I proscribed Amalek, ²¹and the troops took from the spoil some sheep and oxen—the best of what had been proscribed— to sacrifice to the Lord your God at Gilgal." ²²But Samuel said:

"Does the Lord delight in burnt offerings and
    sacrifices
As much as in obedience to the Lord's com-
    mand?
Surely, obedience is better than sacrifice,
Compliance than the fat of rams.
²³For rebellion is like the sin of divination,
Defiance, like the iniquity of teraphim.^e
Because you rejected the Lord's command,
He has rejected you as king."

²⁴Saul said to Samuel, "I did wrong to transgress the Lord's command and your instructions; but I was afraid of the troops and I yielded to them. ²⁵Please, forgive my offense and come back with me, and I will bow low to the Lord." ²⁶But Samuel said to Saul, "I will not go back

הַצֹּאן הַזֶּה בְּאָזְנָי וְקוֹל הַבָּקָר אֲשֶׁר אָנֹכִי
שֹׁמֵעַ: 15 וַיֹּאמֶר שָׁאוּל מֵעֲמָלֵקִי הֱבִיאוּם
אֲשֶׁר חָמַל הָעָם עַל־מֵיטַב הַצֹּאן וְהַבָּקָר
לְמַעַן זְבֹחַ לַיהוָה אֱלֹהֶיךָ וְאֶת־הַיּוֹתֵר
הֶחֱרַמְנוּ: ס 16 וַיֹּאמֶר שְׁמוּאֵל אֶל־
שָׁאוּל הֶרֶף וְאַגִּידָה לְּךָ אֵת אֲשֶׁר דִּבֶּר
יְהוָה אֵלַי הַלָּיְלָה וַיֹּאמְרוּ ‪[‬וַיֹּאמֶר‪]‬ לוֹ
דַּבֵּר: ס 17 וַיֹּאמֶר שְׁמוּאֵל הֲלוֹא אִם־
קָטֹן אַתָּה בְּעֵינֶיךָ רֹאשׁ שִׁבְטֵי יִשְׂרָאֵל
אָתָּה וַיִּמְשָׁחֲךָ יְהוָה לְמֶלֶךְ עַל־יִשְׂרָאֵל:
18 וַיִּשְׁלָחֲךָ יְהוָה בְּדָרֶךְ וַיֹּאמֶר לֵךְ
וְהַחֲרַמְתָּה אֶת־הַחַטָּאִים אֶת־עֲמָלֵק
וְנִלְחַמְתָּ בוֹ עַד כַּלּוֹתָם אֹתָם: 19 וְלָמָּה
לֹא־שָׁמַעְתָּ בְּקוֹל יְהוָה וַתַּעַט אֶל־הַשָּׁלָל
וַתַּעַשׂ הָרַע בְּעֵינֵי יְהוָה: ס 20 וַיֹּאמֶר
שָׁאוּל אֶל־שְׁמוּאֵל אֲשֶׁר שָׁמַעְתִּי בְּקוֹל
יְהוָה וָאֵלֵךְ בַּדֶּרֶךְ אֲשֶׁר־שְׁלָחַנִי יְהוָה
וָאָבִיא אֶת־אֲגַג מֶלֶךְ עֲמָלֵק וְאֶת־עֲמָלֵק
הֶחֱרַמְתִּי: 21 וַיִּקַּח הָעָם מֵהַשָּׁלָל צֹאן
וּבָקָר רֵאשִׁית הַחֵרֶם לִזְבֹּחַ לַיהוָה אֱלֹהֶיךָ
בַּגִּלְגָּל: 22 וַיֹּאמֶר שְׁמוּאֵל
הַחֵפֶץ לַיהוָה בְּעֹלוֹת וּזְבָחִים
כִּשְׁמֹעַ בְּקוֹל יְהוָה
הִנֵּה שְׁמֹעַ מִזֶּבַח טוֹב
לְהַקְשִׁיב מֵחֵלֶב אֵילִים:
23 כִּי חַטַּאת־קֶסֶם מֶרִי
וְאָוֶן וּתְרָפִים הַפְצַר
יַעַן מָאַסְתָּ אֶת־דְּבַר יְהוָה
וַיִּמְאָסְךָ מִמֶּלֶךְ: ס
24 וַיֹּאמֶר שָׁאוּל אֶל־שְׁמוּאֵל חָטָאתִי כִּי־
עָבַרְתִּי אֶת־פִּי־יְהוָה וְאֶת־דְּבָרֶיךָ כִּי
יָרֵאתִי אֶת־הָעָם וָאֶשְׁמַע בְּקוֹלָם:
25 וְעַתָּה שָׂא נָא אֶת־חַטָּאתִי וְשׁוּב עִמִּי

d-d Lit. "and do what was evil in the sight of the Lord."
e   Idols consulted for oracles; see Ezek. 21.26; Zech. 10.2.

with you; for you have rejected the Lord's command, and the Lord has rejected you as king over Israel."

²⁷As Samuel turned to leave, Saul seized the corner of his robe, and it tore. ²⁸And Samuel said to him, "The Lord has this day torn the kingship over Israel away from you and has given it to another who is worthier than you. ²⁹Moreover, the Glory^b of Israel does not deceive or change His mind, for He is not human that He should change His mind." ³⁰But [Saul] pleaded, "I did wrong. Please, honor me in the presence of the elders of my people and in the presence of Israel, and come back with me until I have bowed low to the Lord your God." ³¹So Samuel followed Saul back, and Saul bowed low to the Lord.

³²Samuel said, "Bring forward to me King Agag of Amalek." Agag approached him *f*-with faltering steps;-*f* and Agag said, "Ah, bitter death is at hand!"^b

³³Samuel said:

"As your sword has bereaved women,
So shall your mother be bereaved among
    women."

And Samuel *b*-cut Agag down-*b* before the Lord at Gilgal.

³⁴Samuel then departed for Ramah, and Saul went up to his home at Gibeah of Saul.

³⁵Samuel never saw Saul again to the day of his death. But Samuel grieved over Saul, because the Lord regretted that He had made Saul king

16 over Israel. ¹And the Lord said to Samuel, "How long will you grieve over Saul, since I have rejected him as king over Israel? Fill your horn with oil and set out; I am sending you to Jesse the Bethlehemite, for I have decided on one of his sons to be king." ²Samuel replied, "How can I go? If Saul hears of it, he will kill me." The Lord answered, "Take a heifer

---

f-f From root ma'ad, "to falter"; cf. Septuagint.

וְאֶשְׁתַּחֲוֶה לַיהֹוָה: ²⁶ וַיֹּאמֶר שְׁמוּאֵל' אֶל־שָׁאוּל לֹא אָשׁוּב עִמָּךְ כִּי מָאַסְתָּה אֶת־דְּבַר יְהֹוָה וַיִּמְאָסְךָ יְהֹוָה מִהְיוֹת מֶלֶךְ עַל־יִשְׂרָאֵל: ס

²⁷ וַיִּסֹּב שְׁמוּאֵל לָלֶכֶת וַיַּחֲזֵק בִּכְנַף־מְעִילוֹ וַיִּקָּרַע: ²⁸ וַיֹּאמֶר אֵלָיו שְׁמוּאֵל קָרַע יְהֹוָה אֶת־מַמְלְכוּת יִשְׂרָאֵל מֵעָלֶיךָ הַיּוֹם וּנְתָנָהּ לְרֵעֲךָ הַטּוֹב מִמֶּךָ: ²⁹ וְגַם' נֵצַח יִשְׂרָאֵל לֹא יְשַׁקֵּר וְלֹא יִנָּחֵם כִּי לֹא אָדָם הוּא לְהִנָּחֵם: ³⁰ וַיֹּאמֶר חָטָאתִי עַתָּה כַּבְּדֵנִי נָא נֶגֶד זִקְנֵי־עַמִּי וְנֶגֶד יִשְׂרָאֵל וְשׁוּב עִמִּי וְהִשְׁתַּחֲוֵיתִי לַיהֹוָה אֱלֹהֶיךָ: ³¹ וַיָּשָׁב שְׁמוּאֵל אַחֲרֵי שָׁאוּל וַיִּשְׁתַּחוּ שָׁאוּל לַיהֹוָה: ס

³² וַיֹּאמֶר שְׁמוּאֵל הַגִּישׁוּ אֵלַי אֶת־אֲגַג מֶלֶךְ עֲמָלֵק וַיֵּלֶךְ אֵלָיו אֲגַג מַעֲדַנֹּת וַיֹּאמֶר אֲגָג אָכֵן סָר מַר־הַמָּוֶת: ס ³³ וַיֹּאמֶר שְׁמוּאֵל

כַּאֲשֶׁר שִׁכְּלָה' נָשִׁים חַרְבֶּךָ

כֵּן־תִּשְׁכַּל מִנָּשִׁים אִמֶּךָ

וַיְשַׁסֵּף שְׁמוּאֵל אֶת־אֲגַג לִפְנֵי יְהֹוָה בַּגִּלְגָּל: ס

³⁴ וַיֵּלֶךְ שְׁמוּאֵל הָרָמָתָה וְשָׁאוּל עָלָה אֶל־בֵּיתוֹ גִּבְעַת שָׁאוּל: ³⁵ וְלֹא־יָסַף שְׁמוּאֵל לִרְאוֹת אֶת־שָׁאוּל עַד־יוֹם מוֹתוֹ כִּי־הִתְאַבֵּל שְׁמוּאֵל אֶל־שָׁאוּל וַיהֹוָה נִחָם כִּי־הִמְלִיךְ אֶת־שָׁאוּל עַל־יִשְׂרָאֵל: פ

טז ¹ וַיֹּאמֶר יְהֹוָה אֶל־שְׁמוּאֵל עַד־מָתַי אַתָּה' מִתְאַבֵּל אֶל־שָׁאוּל וַאֲנִי מְאַסְתִּיו מִמְּלֹךְ עַל־יִשְׂרָאֵל מַלֵּא קַרְנְךָ שֶׁמֶן וְלֵךְ אֶשְׁלָחֲךָ אֶל־יִשַׁי בֵּית־הַלַּחְמִי כִּי־רָאִיתִי בְּבָנָיו לִי מֶלֶךְ: ² וַיֹּאמֶר שְׁמוּאֵל אֵיךְ אֵלֵךְ וְשָׁמַע שָׁאוּל וַהֲרָגָנִי ס וַיֹּאמֶר יְהֹוָה עֶגְלַת

with you, and say, 'I have come to sacrifice to the LORD.' ³Invite Jesse to the sacrificial feast, and then I will make known to you what you shall do; you shall anoint for Me the one I point out to you." ⁴Samuel did what the LORD commanded. When he came to Bethlehem, the elders of the city went out in alarm to meet him and said, "Do you come on a peaceful errand?" ⁵"Yes," he replied, "I have come to sacrifice to the LORD. Purify yourselves and join me in the sacrificial feast." He also instructed Jesse and his sons to purify themselves and invited them to the sacrificial feast.

⁶When they arrived and he saw Eliab, he thought: "Surely the LORD's anointed stands before Him." ⁷But the LORD said to Samuel, "Pay no attention to his appearance or his stature, for I have rejected him. For not as man sees [does the LORD see];ᵃ man sees only what is visible, but the LORD sees into the heart." ⁸Then Jesse called Abinadab and had him pass before Samuel; but he said, "The LORD has not chosen this one either." ⁹Next Jesse presented Shammah; and again he said, "The LORD has not chosen this one either." ¹⁰Thus Jesse presented seven of his sons before Samuel, and Samuel said to Jesse, "The LORD has not chosen any of these."

¹¹Then Samuel asked Jesse, "Are these all the boys you have?" He replied, "There is still the youngest; he is tending the flock." And Samuel said to Jesse, "Send someone to bring him, for we will not ᵇ-sit down to eat-ᵇ until he gets here." ¹²So they sent and brought him. He was ᵇ-ruddy-cheeked, bright-eyed,-ᵇ and handsome. And the LORD said, "Rise and anoint him, for this is the one." ¹³Samuel took the horn of oil and anointed him in the presence of his brothers; and the spirit of the LORD gripped David from that day on. Samuel then set out for Ramah.

בָּקָ֤ר תִּקַּח֙ בְּיָדֶ֔ךָ וְאָ֣מַרְתָּ֔ לִזְבֹּ֥חַ לַיהֹוָ֖ה בָּֽאתִי: ³ וְקָרָ֥אתָ לְיִשַׁ֖י בַּזָּ֑בַח וְאָ֣נֹכִ֗י אוֹדִֽיעֲךָ֙ אֵ֣ת אֲשֶֽׁר־תַּעֲשֶׂ֔ה וּמָשַׁחְתָּ֣ לִ֔י אֵ֥ת אֲשֶׁר־אֹמַ֖ר אֵלֶֽיךָ: ⁴ וַיַּ֣עַשׂ שְׁמוּאֵ֗ל אֵ֤ת אֲשֶׁ֣ר דִּבֶּ֣ר יְהֹוָ֔ה וַיָּבֹ֖א בֵּ֣ית לָ֑חֶם וַיֶּחֶרְד֞וּ זִקְנֵ֤י הָעִיר֙ לִקְרָאת֔וֹ וַיֹּ֖אמֶר שָׁלֹ֥ם בּוֹאֶֽךָ: ⁵ וַיֹּ֣אמֶר ׀ שָׁל֗וֹם לִזְבֹּ֤חַ לַֽיהֹוָה֙ בָּ֔אתִי הִֽתְקַדְּשׁ֔וּ וּבָאתֶ֥ם אִתִּ֖י בַּזָּ֑בַח וַיְקַדֵּ֤שׁ אֶת־יִשַׁי֙ וְאֶת־בָּנָ֔יו וַיִּקְרָ֥א לָהֶ֖ם לַזָּֽבַח: ⁶ וַיְהִ֣י בְּבוֹאָ֔ם וַיַּ֖רְא אֶת־אֱלִיאָ֑ב וַיֹּ֕אמֶר אַ֛ךְ נֶ֥גֶד יְהֹוָ֖ה מְשִׁיחֽוֹ: ⁷ וַיֹּ֨אמֶר יְהֹוָ֜ה אֶל־שְׁמוּאֵ֗ל אַל־תַּבֵּ֧ט אֶל־מַרְאֵ֛הוּ וְאֶל־גְּבֹ֥הַּ קֽוֹמָת֖וֹ כִּ֣י מְאַסְתִּ֑יהוּ כִּ֣י ׀ לֹ֗א אֲשֶׁ֤ר יִרְאֶ֣ה הָֽאָדָ֔ם כִּ֤י הָֽאָדָם֙ יִרְאֶ֣ה לַעֵינַ֔יִם וַֽיהֹוָ֖ה יִרְאֶ֥ה לַלֵּבָֽב: ⁸ וַיִּקְרָ֣א יִשַׁי֮ אֶל־אֲבִ֣ינָדָב֒ וַיַּֽעֲבִרֵ֖הוּ לִפְנֵ֣י שְׁמוּאֵ֑ל וַיֹּ֕אמֶר גַּם־בָּזֶ֖ה לֹֽא־בָחַ֥ר יְהֹוָֽה: ⁹ וַיַּעֲבֵ֥ר יִשַׁ֖י שַׁמָּ֑ה וַיֹּ֕אמֶר גַּם־בָּזֶ֖ה לֹֽא־בָחַ֥ר יְהֹוָֽה: ¹⁰ וַיַּעֲבֵ֥ר יִשַׁ֛י שִׁבְעַ֥ת בָּנָ֖יו לִפְנֵ֣י שְׁמוּאֵ֑ל וַיֹּ֤אמֶר שְׁמוּאֵל֙ אֶל־יִשַׁ֔י לֹֽא־בָחַ֥ר יְהֹוָ֖ה בָּאֵֽלֶּה: ¹¹ וַיֹּ֨אמֶר שְׁמוּאֵ֣ל אֶל־יִשַׁי֮ הֲתַ֣מּוּ הַנְּעָרִים֒ וַיֹּ֗אמֶר ע֚וֹד שָׁאַ֣ר הַקָּטָ֔ן וְהִנֵּ֥ה רֹעֶ֖ה בַּצֹּ֑אן וַיֹּ֨אמֶר שְׁמוּאֵ֤ל אֶל־יִשַׁי֙ שִׁלְחָ֣ה וְקָחֶ֔נּוּ כִּ֥י לֹֽא־נָסֹ֖ב עַד־בֹּא֥וֹ פֹֽה: ¹² וַיִּשְׁלַ֣ח וַיְבִיאֵ֗הוּ וְה֤וּא אַדְמוֹנִי֙ עִם־יְפֵ֣ה עֵינַ֔יִם וְט֣וֹב רֹ֑אִי פ וַיֹּ֧אמֶר יְהֹוָ֛ה ק֥וּם מְשָׁחֵ֖הוּ כִּֽי־זֶ֥ה הֽוּא: ¹³ וַיִּקַּ֨ח שְׁמוּאֵ֜ל אֶת־קֶ֣רֶן הַשֶּׁ֗מֶן וַיִּמְשַׁ֣ח אֹתוֹ֮ בְּקֶ֣רֶב אֶחָיו֒ וַתִּצְלַ֤ח רֽוּחַ־יְהֹוָה֙ אֶל־דָּוִ֔ד מֵהַיּ֥וֹם הַה֖וּא וָמָ֑עְלָה וַיָּ֣קָם שְׁמוּאֵ֔ל וַיֵּ֖לֶךְ הָרָמָֽתָה: ס

ᵃ   *These words are preserved in the Septuagint.*
ᵇ⁻ᵇ *Meaning of Heb. uncertain.*

14Now the spirit of the Lord had departed from Saul, and an evil spirit from the Lord began to terrify him. 15Saul's courtiers said to him, "An evil spirit of God is terrifying you. 16Let our lord give the order [and] the courtiers in attendance on you will look for someone who is skilled at playing the lyre; whenever the evil spirit of God comes over you, he will play it[b] and you will feel better." 17So Saul said to his courtiers, "Find me someone who can play well and bring him to me." 18One of the attendants spoke up, "I have observed a son of Jesse the Bethlehemite who is skilled in music; he is a stalwart fellow and a warrior, sensible in speech, and handsome in appearance, and the Lord is with him." 19Whereupon Saul sent messengers to Jesse to say, "Send me your son David, who is with the flock." 20Jesse took [b-]an ass [laden with]-[b] bread, a skin of wine, and a kid, and sent them to Saul by his son David. 21So David came to Saul and entered his service; [Saul] took a strong liking to him and made him one of his arms-bearers. 22Saul sent word to Jesse, "Let David remain in my service, for I am pleased with him." 23Whenever the [evil] spirit of God came upon Saul, David would take the lyre and play it;[b] Saul would find relief and feel better, and the evil spirit would leave him.

17

The Philistines assembled their forces for battle; they massed at Socoh of Judah, and encamped at Ephes-dammim, between Socoh and Azekah. 2Saul and the men of Israel massed and encamped in the valley of Elah. They drew up their line of battle against the Philistines, 3with the Philistines stationed on one hill and Israel stationed on the opposite hill; the ravine was between them. 4A champion[a] of the Philistine forces stepped forward; his name was Go-

---

14 וְר֧וּחַ יְהוָ֛ה סָ֥רָה מֵעִ֖ם שָׁא֑וּל וּבִֽעֲתַ֥תּוּ רֽוּחַ־רָעָ֖ה מֵאֵ֥ת יְהוָֽה׃ 15 וַיֹּאמְר֥וּ עַבְדֵֽי־שָׁא֖וּל אֵלָ֑יו הִנֵּה־נָ֧א רֽוּחַ־אֱלֹהִ֛ים רָעָ֖ה מְבַֽעִתֶּֽךָ׃ 16 יֹֽאמַר־נָ֤א אֲדֹנֵ֙נוּ֙ עֲבָדֶ֣יךָ לְפָנֶ֔יךָ יְבַקְשׁ֕וּ אִ֕ישׁ יֹדֵ֖עַ מְנַגֵּ֣ן בַּכִּנּ֑וֹר וְהָיָ֗ה בִּֽהְי֨וֹת עָלֶ֜יךָ רֽוּחַ־אֱלֹהִ֤ים רָעָה֙ וְנִגֵּ֣ן בְּיָד֔וֹ וְט֥וֹב לָֽךְ׃ פ 17 וַיֹּ֥אמֶר שָׁא֖וּל אֶל־עֲבָדָ֑יו רְאוּ־נָ֣א לִ֗י אִ֚ישׁ מֵיטִ֣יב לְנַגֵּ֔ן וַהֲבִֽיאוֹתֶ֖ם אֵלָֽי׃ 18 וַיַּ֨עַן אֶחָ֜ד מֵהַנְּעָרִ֗ים וַיֹּ֙אמֶר֙ הִנֵּ֤ה רָאִ֙יתִי֙ בֵּ֣ן לְיִשַׁי֙ בֵּ֣ית הַלַּחְמִ֔י יֹדֵ֣עַ נַ֠גֵּן וְגִבּ֨וֹר חַ֜יִל וְאִ֧ישׁ מִלְחָמָ֛ה וּנְב֥וֹן דָּבָ֖ר וְאִ֣ישׁ תֹּ֑אַר וַֽיהוָ֖ה עִמּֽוֹ׃ 19 וַיִּשְׁלַ֥ח שָׁא֛וּל מַלְאָכִ֖ים אֶל־יִשָׁ֑י וַיֹּ֕אמֶר שִׁלְחָ֥ה אֵלַ֛י אֶת־דָּוִ֥ד בִּנְךָ֖ אֲשֶׁ֥ר בַּצֹּֽאן׃ 20 וַיִּקַּ֨ח יִשַׁ֜י חֲמ֥וֹר לֶ֙חֶם֙ וְנֹ֣אד יַ֔יִן וּגְדִ֥י עִזִּ֖ים אֶחָ֑ד וַיִּשְׁלַ֛ח בְּיַד־דָּוִ֥ד בְּנ֖וֹ אֶל־שָׁאֽוּל׃ 21 וַיָּבֹ֤א דָוִד֙ אֶל־שָׁא֔וּל וַיַּֽעֲמֹ֖ד לְפָנָ֑יו וַיֶּאֱהָבֵ֣הֽוּ מְאֹ֔ד וַֽיְהִי־ל֖וֹ נֹשֵׂ֥א כֵלִֽים׃ 22 וַיִּשְׁלַ֣ח שָׁא֔וּל אֶל־יִשַׁ֖י לֵאמֹ֑ר יַעֲמָד־נָ֤א דָוִד֙ לְפָנַ֔י כִּֽי־מָ֥צָא חֵ֖ן בְּעֵינָֽי׃ 23 וְהָיָ֗ה בִּֽהְי֤וֹת רֽוּחַ־אֱלֹהִים֙ אֶל־שָׁא֔וּל וְלָקַ֥ח דָּוִ֛ד אֶת־הַכִּנּ֖וֹר וְנִגֵּ֣ן בְּיָד֑וֹ וְרָוַ֤ח לְשָׁאוּל֙ וְט֣וֹב ל֔וֹ וְסָ֥רָה מֵעָלָ֖יו ר֥וּחַ הָרָעָֽה׃ פ

יז וַיַּאַסְפ֨וּ פְלִשְׁתִּ֤ים אֶת־מַֽחֲנֵיהֶם֙ לַמִּלְחָמָ֔ה וַיֵּאָ֣סְפ֔וּ שֹׂכֹ֖ה אֲשֶׁ֣ר לִיהוּדָ֑ה וַֽיַּחֲנ֛וּ בֵּֽין־שׂוֹכֹ֥ה וּבֵין־עֲזֵקָ֖ה בְּאֶ֥פֶס דַּמִּֽים׃ 2 וְשָׁא֤וּל וְאִֽישׁ־יִשְׂרָאֵל֙ נֶאֶסְפ֔וּ וַֽיַּחֲנ֖וּ בְּעֵ֣מֶק הָאֵלָ֑ה וַיַּֽעַרְכ֥וּ מִלְחָמָ֖ה לִקְרַ֥את פְּלִשְׁתִּֽים׃ 3 וּפְלִשְׁתִּ֞ים עֹמְדִ֤ים אֶל־הָהָר֙ מִזֶּ֔ה וְיִשְׂרָאֵ֛ל עֹמְדִ֥ים אֶל־הָהָ֖ר מִזֶּ֑ה וְהַגַּ֖יְא בֵּינֵיהֶֽם׃ 4 וַיֵּצֵ֤א אִֽישׁ־הַבֵּנַ֙יִם֙ מִמַּחֲנ֣וֹת פְּלִשְׁתִּ֔ים גָּלְיָ֥ת שְׁמ֖וֹ מִגַּ֑ת גָּבְה֕וֹ

---

a   Lit. "the man of the space between," i.e., between the armies.

liath of Gath, and he was six cubits and a span tall. [5]He had a bronze helmet on his head, and wore a breastplate of scale armor, a bronze breastplate weighing five thousand shekels. [6]He had bronze greaves on his legs, and a bronze javelin [slung] from his shoulders. [7]The shaft of his spear was like a weaver's bar, and the iron head of his spear weighed six hundred shekels; and the shield-bearer marched in front of him.

[8]He stopped and called out to the ranks of Israel and he said to them, "Why should you come out to engage in battle? I am the Philistine [champion], and you are Saul's servants. Choose[b] one of your men and let him come down against me. [9]If he bests me in combat and kills me, we will become your slaves; but if I best him and kill him, you shall be our slaves and serve us." [10]And the Philistine ended, "I here-with defy the ranks of Israel. Get me a man and let's fight it out!" [11]When Saul and all Israel heard these words of the Philistine, they were dismayed and terror-stricken.

[12]David was the son of a certain Ephrathite of Bethlehem in Judah whose name was Jesse. He had eight sons, and in the days of Saul the man was already old, advanced in years.[b] [13]The three oldest sons of Jesse had left and gone with Saul to the war. The names of his three sons who had gone to the war were Eliab the first-born, the next Abinadab, and the third Shammah; [14]and David was the youngest. The three oldest had followed Saul, [15]and David would go back and forth from attending on Saul to shepherd his father's flock at Bethlehem.

[16]The Philistine stepped forward morning and evening and took his stand for forty days.

[17]Jesse said to his son David, "Take an ephah of this parched corn and these ten loaves of bread for your brothers, and carry them quickly to your brothers in camp. [18]Take these ten

שֵׁשׁ אַמּוֹת וָזָרֶת: 5 וְכוֹבַע נְחֹשֶׁת עַל־
רֹאשׁוֹ וְשִׁרְיוֹן קַשְׂקַשִּׂים הוּא לָבוּשׁ
וּמִשְׁקַל הַשִּׁרְיוֹן חֲמֵשֶׁת־אֲלָפִים שְׁקָלִים
נְחֹשֶׁת: 6 וּמִצְחַת נְחֹשֶׁת עַל־רַגְלָיו וְכִידוֹן
נְחֹשֶׁת בֵּין כְּתֵפָיו: 7 וְחָץ וְעֵץ חֲנִיתוֹ
כִּמְנוֹר אֹרְגִים וְלַהֶבֶת חֲנִיתוֹ שֵׁשׁ־מֵאוֹת
שְׁקָלִים בַּרְזֶל וְנֹשֵׂא הַצִּנָּה הֹלֵךְ לְפָנָיו:
8 וַיַּעֲמֹד וַיִּקְרָא אֶל־מַעַרְכֹת יִשְׂרָאֵל
וַיֹּאמֶר לָהֶם לָמָּה תֵצְאוּ לַעֲרֹךְ מִלְחָמָה
הֲלוֹא אָנֹכִי הַפְּלִשְׁתִּי וְאַתֶּם עֲבָדִים
לְשָׁאוּל בְּרוּ־לָכֶם אִישׁ וְיֵרֵד אֵלָי: 9 אִם־
יוּכַל לְהִלָּחֵם אִתִּי וְהִכָּנִי וְהָיִינוּ לָכֶם
לַעֲבָדִים וְאִם־אֲנִי אוּכַל־לוֹ וְהִכִּיתִיו
וִהְיִיתֶם לָנוּ לַעֲבָדִים וַעֲבַדְתֶּם אֹתָנוּ:
10 וַיֹּאמֶר הַפְּלִשְׁתִּי אֲנִי חֵרַפְתִּי אֶת־
מַעַרְכוֹת יִשְׂרָאֵל הַיּוֹם הַזֶּה תְּנוּ־לִי אִישׁ
וְנִלָּחֲמָה יָחַד: 11 וַיִּשְׁמַע שָׁאוּל וְכָל־
יִשְׂרָאֵל אֶת־דִּבְרֵי הַפְּלִשְׁתִּי הָאֵלֶּה וַיֵּחַתּוּ
וַיִּרְאוּ מְאֹד: פ
12 וְדָוִד בֶּן־אִישׁ אֶפְרָתִי הַזֶּה מִבֵּית לֶחֶם
יְהוּדָה וּשְׁמוֹ יִשַׁי וְלוֹ שְׁמֹנָה בָנִים וְהָאִישׁ
בִּימֵי שָׁאוּל זָקֵן בָּא בָאֲנָשִׁים: 13 וַיֵּלְכוּ
שְׁלֹשֶׁת בְּנֵי־יִשַׁי הַגְּדֹלִים הָלְכוּ אַחֲרֵי־
שָׁאוּל לַמִּלְחָמָה וְשֵׁם ׀ שְׁלֹשֶׁת בָּנָיו אֲשֶׁר
הָלְכוּ בַּמִּלְחָמָה אֱלִיאָב הַבְּכוֹר וּמִשְׁנֵהוּ
אֲבִינָדָב וְהַשְּׁלִשִׁי שַׁמָּה: 14 וְדָוִד הוּא
הַקָּטָן וּשְׁלֹשָׁה הַגְּדֹלִים הָלְכוּ אַחֲרֵי
שָׁאוּל: ס 15 וְדָוִד הֹלֵךְ וָשָׁב מֵעַל שָׁאוּל
לִרְעוֹת אֶת־צֹאן אָבִיו בֵּית־לָחֶם:
16 וַיִּגַּשׁ הַפְּלִשְׁתִּי הַשְׁכֵּם וְהַעֲרֵב וַיִּתְיַצֵּב
אַרְבָּעִים יוֹם: פ
17 וַיֹּאמֶר יִשַׁי לְדָוִד בְּנוֹ קַח־נָא לְאַחֶיךָ
אֵיפַת הַקָּלִיא* הַזֶּה וַעֲשָׂרָה לֶחֶם הַזֶּה
וְהָרֵץ הַמַּחֲנֶה לְאַחֶיךָ: 18 וְאֵת עֲשֶׂרֶת

---

[b] *Meaning of Heb. uncertain.*

cheeses[b] to the captain of their thousand. Find out how your brothers are and bring some token[b] from them." [19]Saul and [c]the brothers[c] and all the men of Israel were in the valley of Elah, in the war against the Philistines.

[20]Early next morning, David left someone in charge of the flock, took [the provisions], and set out, as his father Jesse had instructed him. He reached the barricade[b] as the army was going out to the battle lines shouting the war cry. [21]Israel and the Philistines drew up their battle lines opposite each other. [22]David left his baggage with the man in charge of the baggage and ran toward the battle line and went to greet his brothers. [23]While he was talking to them, the champion, whose name was Goliath, the Philistine of Gath, stepped forward from the Philistine ranks and spoke the same words as before; and David heard him.

[24]When the men of Israel saw the man, they fled in terror. [25]And the men of Israel were saying [among themselves], "Do you see that man coming out? He comes out to defy Israel! The man who kills him will be rewarded by the king with great riches; he will also give him his daughter in marriage and grant exemption[d] to his father's house in Israel." [26]David asked the men standing near him, "What will be done for the man who kills that Philistine and removes the disgrace from Israel? Who is that uncircumcised Philistine that he dares defy the ranks of the living God?" [27]The troops told him in the same words what would be done for the man who killed him.

[28]When Eliab, his oldest brother, heard him speaking to the men, Eliab became angry with David and said, "Why did you come down here, and with whom did you leave those few sheep in the wilderness? I know your impudence and your impertinence:[e] you came down to watch

חָרִצֵי הֶחָלָב הָאֵלֶּה תָּבִיא לְשַׂר־הָאָלֶף וְאֶת־אַחֶיךָ תִּפְקֹד לְשָׁלוֹם וְאֶת־עֲרֻבָּתָם תִּקָּח: 19 וְשָׁאוּל וְהֵמָּה וְכָל־אִישׁ יִשְׂרָאֵל בְּעֵמֶק הָאֵלָה נִלְחָמִים עִם־פְּלִשְׁתִּים: 20 וַיַּשְׁכֵּם דָּוִד בַּבֹּקֶר וַיִּטֹּשׁ אֶת־הַצֹּאן עַל־שֹׁמֵר וַיִּשָּׂא וַיֵּלֶךְ כַּאֲשֶׁר צִוָּהוּ יִשָׁי וַיָּבֹא הַמַּעְגָּלָה וְהַחַיִל הַיֹּצֵא אֶל־הַמַּעֲרָכָה וְהֵרֵעוּ בַּמִּלְחָמָה: 21 וַתַּעֲרֹךְ יִשְׂרָאֵל וּפְלִשְׁתִּים מַעֲרָכָה לִקְרַאת מַעֲרָכָה: 22 וַיִּטֹּשׁ דָּוִד אֶת־הַכֵּלִים מֵעָלָיו עַל־יַד שׁוֹמֵר הַכֵּלִים וַיָּרָץ הַמַּעֲרָכָה וַיָּבֹא וַיִּשְׁאַל לְאֶחָיו לְשָׁלוֹם: 23 וְהוּא ׀ מְדַבֵּר עִמָּם וְהִנֵּה אִישׁ הַבֵּנַיִם עוֹלֶה גָּלְיָת הַפְּלִשְׁתִּי שְׁמוֹ מִגַּת ממערות מִמַּעַרְכוֹת פְּלִשְׁתִּים וַיְדַבֵּר כַּדְּבָרִים הָאֵלֶּה וַיִּשְׁמַע דָּוִד: 24 וְכֹל אִישׁ יִשְׂרָאֵל בִּרְאוֹתָם אֶת־הָאִישׁ וַיָּנֻסוּ מִפָּנָיו וַיִּירְאוּ מְאֹד: 25 וַיֹּאמֶר ׀ אִישׁ יִשְׂרָאֵל הַרְאִיתֶם* הָאִישׁ הָעֹלֶה הַזֶּה כִּי לְחָרֵף אֶת־יִשְׂרָאֵל עֹלֶה וְהָיָה הָאִישׁ אֲשֶׁר־יַכֶּנּוּ יַעְשְׁרֶנּוּ הַמֶּלֶךְ ׀ עֹשֶׁר גָּדוֹל וְאֶת־בִּתּוֹ יִתֶּן־לוֹ וְאֵת בֵּית אָבִיו יַעֲשֶׂה חָפְשִׁי בְּיִשְׂרָאֵל: 26 וַיֹּאמֶר דָּוִד אֶל־הָאֲנָשִׁים הָעֹמְדִים עִמּוֹ לֵאמֹר מַה־יֵּעָשֶׂה לָאִישׁ אֲשֶׁר יַכֶּה אֶת־הַפְּלִשְׁתִּי הַלָּז וְהֵסִיר חֶרְפָּה מֵעַל יִשְׂרָאֵל כִּי מִי הַפְּלִשְׁתִּי הֶעָרֵל הַזֶּה כִּי חֵרֵף מַעַרְכוֹת אֱלֹהִים חַיִּים: 27 וַיֹּאמֶר לוֹ הָעָם כַּדָּבָר הַזֶּה לֵאמֹר כֹּה יֵעָשֶׂה לָאִישׁ אֲשֶׁר יַכֶּנּוּ: 28 וַיִּשְׁמַע אֱלִיאָב אָחִיו הַגָּדוֹל בְּדַבְּרוֹ אֶל־הָאֲנָשִׁים וַיִּחַר־אַף אֱלִיאָב בְּדָוִד וַיֹּאמֶר ׀ לָמָּה־זֶּה יָרַדְתָּ וְעַל־מִי נָטַשְׁתָּ מְעַט הַצֹּאן הָהֵנָּה בַּמִּדְבָּר אֲנִי יָדַעְתִּי אֶת־זְדֹנְךָ וְאֵת רֹעַ לְבָבֶךָ כִּי לְמַעַן רְאוֹת הַמִּלְחָמָה יָרָדְתָּ: 29 וַיֹּאמֶר דָּוִד מֶה

---

c-c   Heb. "they."
d   I.e., freedom from royal levies.
e   Lit. "badness of heart."

ר׳ דגושה   v. 25.

the fighting!" ²⁹But David replied, "What have I done now? I was only asking!" ³⁰And he turned away from him toward someone else; he asked the same question, and the troops gave him the same answer as before.

³¹The things David said were overheard and were reported to Saul, who had him brought over. ³²David said to Saul, "Let f-no man's-f courage fail him. Your servant will go and fight that Philistine!" ³³But Saul said to David, "You cannot go to that Philistine and fight him; you are only a boy, and he has been a warrior from his youth!" ³⁴David replied to Saul, "Your servant has been tending his father's sheep, and if a lion or^b a bear came and carried off an animal from the flock, ³⁵I would go after it and fight it and rescue it from its mouth. And if it attacked me, I would seize it by the beard and strike it down and kill it. ³⁶Your servant has killed both lion and bear; and that uncircumcised Philistine shall end up like one of them, for he has defied the ranks of the living God. ³⁷The Lord," David went on, "who saved me from lion and bear will also save me from that Philistine." "Then go," Saul said to David, "and may the Lord be with you!"

³⁸Saul clothed David in his own garment; he placed a bronze helmet on his head and fastened g-a breastplate on him.-g ³⁹David girded his sword over his garment. Then he ^h-tried to walk; but-^h he was not used to it. And David said to Saul, "I cannot walk in these, for I am not used to them." So David took them off. ⁴⁰He took his stick, picked a fewⁱ smooth stones from the wadi, put them in the pocket^b of his shepherd's bag and, sling in hand, he went toward the Philistine.

⁴¹The Philistine, meanwhile, was coming closer to David, preceded by his shield-bearer.

עָשִׂיתִי עַתָּה הֲלוֹא דָבָר הוּא: ³⁰ וַיִּסֹּב מֵאֶצְלוֹ אֶל־מוּל אַחֵר וַיֹּאמֶר כַּדָּבָר הַזֶּה וַיְשִׁבֻהוּ הָעָם דָּבָר כַּדָּבָר הָרִאשׁוֹן: ³¹ וַיִּשָּׁמְעוּ הַדְּבָרִים אֲשֶׁר דִּבֶּר דָּוִד וַיַּגִּדוּ לִפְנֵי־שָׁאוּל וַיִּקָּחֵהוּ: ³² וַיֹּאמֶר דָּוִד אֶל־שָׁאוּל אַל־יִפֹּל לֵב־אָדָם עָלָיו עַבְדְּךָ יֵלֵךְ וְנִלְחַם עִם־הַפְּלִשְׁתִּי הַזֶּה: ³³ וַיֹּאמֶר שָׁאוּל אֶל־דָּוִד לֹא תוּכַל לָלֶכֶת אֶל־הַפְּלִשְׁתִּי הַזֶּה לְהִלָּחֵם עִמּוֹ כִּי־נַעַר אַתָּה וְהוּא אִישׁ מִלְחָמָה מִנְּעֻרָיו: ס ³⁴ וַיֹּאמֶר דָּוִד אֶל־שָׁאוּל רֹעֶה הָיָה עַבְדְּךָ לְאָבִיו בַּצֹּאן וּבָא הָאֲרִי וְאֶת־הַדּוֹב וְנָשָׂא שֶׂה מֵהָעֵדֶר: ³⁵ וְיָצָאתִי אַחֲרָיו וְהִכִּתִיו וְהִצַּלְתִּי מִפִּיו וַיָּקָם עָלַי וְהֶחֱזַקְתִּי בִּזְקָנוֹ וְהִכִּתִיו וַהֲמִיתִּיו: ³⁶ גַּם אֶת־הָאֲרִי גַּם הַדּוֹב הִכָּה עַבְדֶּךָ וְהָיָה הַפְּלִשְׁתִּי הֶעָרֵל הַזֶּה כְּאַחַד מֵהֶם כִּי חֵרֵף מַעַרְכֹת אֱלֹהִים חַיִּים: ס ³⁷ וַיֹּאמֶר דָּוִד יְהוָה אֲשֶׁר הִצִּלַנִי מִיַּד הָאֲרִי וּמִיַּד הַדֹּב הוּא יַצִּילֵנִי מִיַּד הַפְּלִשְׁתִּי הַזֶּה ס וַיֹּאמֶר שָׁאוּל אֶל־דָּוִד לֵךְ וַיהוָה יִהְיֶה עִמָּךְ: ³⁸ וַיַּלְבֵּשׁ שָׁאוּל אֶת־דָּוִד מַדָּיו וְנָתַן קוֹבַע נְחֹשֶׁת עַל־רֹאשׁוֹ וַיַּלְבֵּשׁ אֹתוֹ שִׁרְיוֹן: ³⁹ וַיַּחְגֹּר דָּוִד אֶת־חַרְבּוֹ מֵעַל לְמַדָּיו וַיֹּאֶל לָלֶכֶת כִּי לֹא־נִסָּה וַיֹּאמֶר דָּוִד אֶל־שָׁאוּל לֹא אוּכַל לָלֶכֶת בָּאֵלֶּה כִּי לֹא נִסִּיתִי וַיְסִרֵם דָּוִד מֵעָלָיו: ⁴⁰ וַיִּקַּח מַקְלוֹ בְּיָדוֹ וַיִּבְחַר־לוֹ חֲמִשָּׁה חַלֻּקֵי־אֲבָנִים מִן־הַנַּחַל וַיָּשֶׂם אֹתָם בִּכְלִי הָרֹעִים אֲשֶׁר־לוֹ וּבַיַּלְקוּט וְקַלְעוֹ בְיָדוֹ וַיִּגַּשׁ אֶל־הַפְּלִשְׁתִּי: ⁴¹ וַיֵּלֶךְ הַפְּלִשְׁתִּי הֹלֵךְ וְקָרֵב אֶל־דָּוִד וְהָאִישׁ נֹשֵׂא הַצִּנָּה לְפָנָיו: ⁴² וַיַּבֵּט

---

f-f Septuagint reads "not my lord's."
g-g Heb. "clothed him in a breastplate" (cf. v. 5), because a breastplate was combined with a leather jerkin.
h-h Septuagint reads "was unable to walk, for…"
i Lit. "five."

42When the Philistine caught sight of David, he scorned him, for he was but a boy, ruddy and handsome. 43And the Philistine called out to David, "Am I a dog that you come against me with sticks?" The Philistine cursed David by his gods; 44and the Philistine said to David, "Come here, and I will give your flesh to the birds of the sky and the beasts of the field."

45David replied to the Philistine, "You come against me with sword and spear and javelin; but I come against you in the name of the LORD of Hosts, the God of the ranks of Israel, whom you have defied. 46This very day the LORD will deliver you into my hands. I will kill you and cut off your head; and I will give j-the carcasses-j of the Philistine camp to the birds of the sky and the beasts of the earth. All the earth shall know that there is a God ink Israel. 47And this whole assembly shall know that the LORD can give victory without sword or spear. For the battle is the LORD's, and He will deliver you into our hands."

48When the Philistine began to advance toward him again, David quickly ran up to the battle line to face the Philistine. 49David put his hand into the bag; he took out a stone and slung it. It struck the Philistine in the forehead; the stone sank into his forehead, and he fell face down on the ground. 50Thus David bested the Philistine with sling and stone; he struck him down and killed him. David had no sword; 51so David ran up and stood over the Philistine, grasped his sword and pulled it from its sheath; and with it he dispatched him and cut off his head.

When the Philistines saw that their warrior was dead, they ran. 52The men of Israel and Judah rose up with a war cry and they pursued the Philistines all the way to Gail and up to the gates of Ekron; the Philistines fell mortally

הַפְּלִשְׁתִּי וַיִּרְאֶה אֶת־דָּוִד וַיִּבְזֵהוּ כִּי־הָיָה
נַעַר וְאַדְמֹנִי עִם־יְפֵה מַרְאֶה: 43 וַיֹּאמֶר
הַפְּלִשְׁתִּי אֶל־דָּוִד הֲכֶלֶב אָנֹכִי כִּי־אַתָּה
בָא־אֵלַי בַּמַּקְלוֹת וַיְקַלֵּל הַפְּלִשְׁתִּי אֶת־
דָּוִד בֵּאלֹהָיו: 44 וַיֹּאמֶר הַפְּלִשְׁתִּי אֶל־דָּוִד
לְכָה אֵלַי וְאֶתְּנָה אֶת־בְּשָׂרְךָ לְעוֹף
הַשָּׁמַיִם וּלְבֶהֱמַת הַשָּׂדֶה: ס
45 וַיֹּאמֶר דָּוִד אֶל־הַפְּלִשְׁתִּי אַתָּה בָּא אֵלַי
בְּחֶרֶב וּבַחֲנִית וּבְכִידוֹן וְאָנֹכִי בָא־אֵלֶיךָ
בְּשֵׁם יְהוָה צְבָאוֹת אֱלֹהֵי מַעַרְכוֹת
יִשְׂרָאֵל אֲשֶׁר חֵרַפְתָּ: 46 הַיּוֹם הַזֶּה יְסַגֶּרְךָ
יְהוָה בְּיָדִי וְהִכִּיתִךָ וַהֲסִרֹתִי אֶת־רֹאשְׁךָ
מֵעָלֶיךָ וְנָתַתִּי פֶּגֶר מַחֲנֵה פְלִשְׁתִּים הַיּוֹם
הַזֶּה לְעוֹף הַשָּׁמַיִם וּלְחַיַּת הָאָרֶץ וְיֵדְעוּ
כָּל־הָאָרֶץ כִּי יֵשׁ אֱלֹהִים לְיִשְׂרָאֵל*:
47 וְיֵדְעוּ כָּל־הַקָּהָל הַזֶּה כִּי־לֹא בְּחֶרֶב
וּבַחֲנִית יְהוֹשִׁיעַ יְהוָה כִּי לַיהוָה
הַמִּלְחָמָה וְנָתַן אֶתְכֶם בְּיָדֵנוּ:
48 וְהָיָה כִּי־קָם הַפְּלִשְׁתִּי וַיֵּלֶךְ וַיִּקְרַב
לִקְרַאת דָּוִד וַיְמַהֵר דָּוִד וַיָּרָץ הַמַּעֲרָכָה
לִקְרַאת הַפְּלִשְׁתִּי: 49 וַיִּשְׁלַח דָּוִד אֶת־יָדוֹ
אֶל־הַכֶּלִי וַיִּקַּח מִשָּׁם אֶבֶן וַיְקַלַּע וַיַּךְ
אֶת־הַפְּלִשְׁתִּי אֶל־מִצְחוֹ וַתִּטְבַּע הָאֶבֶן
בְּמִצְחוֹ וַיִּפֹּל עַל־פָּנָיו אָרְצָה: 50 וַיֶּחֱזַק
דָּוִד מִן־הַפְּלִשְׁתִּי בַּקֶּלַע וּבָאֶבֶן וַיַּךְ אֶת־
הַפְּלִשְׁתִּי וַיְמִיתֵהוּ וְחֶרֶב אֵין בְּיַד־דָּוִד:
51 וַיָּרָץ דָּוִד וַיַּעֲמֹד אֶל־הַפְּלִשְׁתִּי וַיִּקַּח
אֶת־חַרְבּוֹ וַיִּשְׁלְפָהּ מִתַּעְרָהּ וַיְמֹתְתֵהוּ
וַיִּכְרָת־בָּהּ אֶת־רֹאשׁוֹ
וַיִּרְאוּ הַפְּלִשְׁתִּים כִּי־מֵת גִּבּוֹרָם וַיָּנֻסוּ:
52 וַיָּקֻמוּ אַנְשֵׁי יִשְׂרָאֵל וִיהוּדָה וַיָּרִעוּ
וַיִּרְדְּפוּ אֶת־הַפְּלִשְׁתִּים עַד־בּוֹאֲךָ גַיְא וְעַד
שַׁעֲרֵי עֶקְרוֹן וַיִּפְּלוּ חַלְלֵי פְלִשְׁתִּים בְּדֶרֶךְ
שַׁעֲרַיִם וְעַד־גַּת וְעַד־עֶקְרוֹן: 53 וַיָּשֻׁבוּ בְּנֵי

בנוסח אחר "בישראל"   v. 46.

---

j-j   *Septuagint reads "your carcass and the carcasses."*
k   *So many Heb. mss. and ancient versions; other mss. and the editions read "to."*

   l   *Septuagint reads "Gath"; cf. end of verse.*

wounded along the road to Shaarim up to Gath and Ekron. 53Then the Israelites returned from chasing the Philistines and looted their camp.

54David took the head of the Philistine and brought it to Jerusalem;*m* and he put his weapons in his own tent.

55When Saul saw David going out to assault the Philistine, he asked his army commander Abner, "Whose son is that boy, Abner?" And Abner replied, "By your life, Your Majesty, I do not know." 56"Then find out whose son that young fellow is," the king ordered. 57So when David returned after killing the Philistine, Abner took him and brought him to Saul, with the head of the Philistine still in his hand. 58Saul said to him, "Whose son are you, my boy?" And David answered, "The son of your servant Jesse the Bethlehemite."

18 When [David] finished speaking with Saul, Jonathan's soul became bound up with the soul of David; Jonathan loved David as himself. 2Saul took him [into his service] that day and would not let him return to his father's house.— 3Jonathan and David made a pact, because [Jonathan] loved him as himself. 4Jonathan took off the cloak and tunic he was wearing and gave them to David, together with his sword, bow, and belt. 5David went out [with the troops], and he was successful in every mission on which Saul sent him, and Saul put him in command of all the soldiers; this pleased all the troops and Saul's courtiers as well. 6When the [troops] came home [and] David returned from killing the Philistine, *a-*the women of all the towns of Israel came out singing and dancing to greet King Saul*-a* with timbrels, shouting, and sistrums.*b* 7The women sang as they danced, and they chanted:

---

m   I.e., after David's capture of Jerusalem (2 Sam. 5).

a-a   Meaning of Heb. uncertain. Septuagint reads "the dancing women came out to meet David from all the towns of Israel."

b   Meaning of Heb. uncertain.

יִשְׂרָאֵל מִדְּלֹק אַחֲרֵי פְלִשְׁתִּים וַיָּשֹׁסּוּ אֶת־מַחֲנֵיהֶם: 54 וַיִּקַּח דָּוִד אֶת־רֹאשׁ הַפְּלִשְׁתִּי וַיְבִאֵהוּ יְרוּשָׁלָ͏ִם וְאֶת־כֵּלָיו שָׂם בְּאָהֳלוֹ: ס 55 וְכִרְאוֹת שָׁאוּל אֶת־דָּוִד יֹצֵא לִקְרַאת הַפְּלִשְׁתִּי אָמַר אֶל־אַבְנֵר שַׂר הַצָּבָא בֶּן־מִי־זֶה הַנַּעַר אַבְנֵר וַיֹּאמֶר אַבְנֵר חֵי־נַפְשְׁךָ הַמֶּלֶךְ אִם־יָדָעְתִּי: 56 וַיֹּאמֶר הַמֶּלֶךְ שְׁאַל אַתָּה בֶּן־מִי־זֶה הָעָלֶם: ס 57 וּכְשׁוּב דָּוִד מֵהַכּוֹת אֶת־הַפְּלִשְׁתִּי וַיִּקַּח אֹתוֹ אַבְנֵר וַיְבִאֵהוּ לִפְנֵי שָׁאוּל וְרֹאשׁ הַפְּלִשְׁתִּי בְּיָדוֹ: 58 וַיֹּאמֶר אֵלָיו שָׁאוּל בֶּן־מִי אַתָּה הַנַּעַר וַיֹּאמֶר דָּוִד בֶּן־עַבְדְּךָ יִשַׁי בֵּית הַלַּחְמִי:

יח וַיְהִי כְּכַלֹּתוֹ לְדַבֵּר אֶל־שָׁאוּל וְנֶפֶשׁ יְהוֹנָתָן נִקְשְׁרָה בְּנֶפֶשׁ דָּוִד וַיֶּאֱהָבוֹ יְהוֹנָתָן כְּנַפְשׁוֹ: 2 וַיִּקָּחֵהוּ שָׁאוּל בַּיּוֹם הַהוּא וְלֹא נְתָנוֹ לָשׁוּב בֵּית אָבִיו: 3 וַיִּכְרֹת יְהוֹנָתָן וְדָוִד בְּרִית בְּאַהֲבָתוֹ אֹתוֹ כְּנַפְשׁוֹ: 4 וַיִּתְפַּשֵּׁט יְהוֹנָתָן אֶת־הַמְּעִיל אֲשֶׁר עָלָיו וַיִּתְּנֵהוּ לְדָוִד וּמַדָּיו וְעַד־חַרְבּוֹ וְעַד־קַשְׁתּוֹ וְעַד־חֲגֹרוֹ: 5 וַיֵּצֵא דָוִד בְּכֹל אֲשֶׁר יִשְׁלָחֶנּוּ שָׁאוּל יַשְׂכִּיל וַיְשִׂמֵהוּ שָׁאוּל עַל אַנְשֵׁי הַמִּלְחָמָה וַיִּיטַב בְּעֵינֵי כָל־הָעָם וְגַם בְּעֵינֵי עַבְדֵי שָׁאוּל: פ 6 וַיְהִי בְּבוֹאָם בְּשׁוּב דָּוִד מֵהַכּוֹת אֶת־הַפְּלִשְׁתִּי וַתֵּצֶאנָה הַנָּשִׁים מִכָּל־עָרֵי יִשְׂרָאֵל לָשׁוּר לָשִׁיר וְהַמְּחֹלוֹת לִקְרַאת שָׁאוּל הַמֶּלֶךְ בְּתֻפִּים בְּשִׂמְחָה וּבְשָׁלִשִׁים: 7 וַתַּעֲנֶינָה הַנָּשִׁים הַמְשַׂחֲקוֹת וַתֹּאמַרְןָ

Saul has slain his thousands;

David, his tens of thousands!

8Saul was much distressed and greatly vexed about the matter. For he said, "To David they have given tens of thousands, and to me they have given thousands. All that he lacks is the kingship!" 9From that day on Saul kept a jealous eye on David. 10The next day an evil spirit of God gripped Saul and he began to rave in the house, while David was playing [the lyre], as he did daily. Saul had a spear in his hand, 11and Saul threw*c* the spear, thinking to pin David to the wall. But David eluded him twice. 12Saul was afraid of David, for the LORD was with him and had turned away from Saul. 13So Saul removed him from his presence and appointed him chief of a thousand, *d*-to march at the head of the troops.-*d* 14David was successful in all his undertakings, for the LORD was with him; 15and when Saul saw that he was successful, he dreaded him. 16All Israel and Judah loved David, for he marched at their head.

17Saul said to David, "Here is my older daughter, Merab; I will give her to you in marriage; in return, you be my warrior and fight the battles of the LORD." Saul thought: "Let not my hand strike him; let the hand of the Philistines strike him." 18David replied to Saul, "Who am I and *e*-what is my life-*e*—my father's family in Israel—that I should become Your Majesty's son-in-law?" 19But at the time that Merab, daughter of Saul, should have been given to David, she was given in marriage to Adriel the Meholathite. 20Now Michal daughter of Saul had fallen in love with David; and when this was reported to Saul, he was pleased. 21Saul thought: "I will give her to him, and she can serve as a snare for him, so that the Philistines may kill him." So Saul said to David, *b*-"You can become

הִכָּה שָׁאוּל֙ באלפו בַּאֲלָפָ֔יו
וְדָוִ֖ד בְּרִבְבֹתָֽיו׃

8 וַיִּ֨חַר לְשָׁא֜וּל מְאֹ֗ד וַיֵּ֤רַע בְּעֵינָיו֙ הַדָּבָ֣ר הַזֶּ֔ה וַיֹּ֗אמֶר נָתְנ֤וּ לְדָוִד֙ רְבָב֔וֹת וְלִ֥י נָתְנ֖וּ הָאֲלָפִ֑ים וְע֥וֹד ל֖וֹ אַ֥ךְ הַמְּלוּכָֽה׃ 9 וַיְהִ֥י שָׁא֖וּל עון עוֹיֵ֣ן אֶת־דָּוִ֑ד מֵהַיּ֥וֹם הַה֖וּא וָהָֽלְאָה׃ ס 10 וַיְהִ֣י מִֽמָּחֳרָ֗ת וַתִּצְלַ֣ח רֽוּחַ אֱלֹהִ֣ים ׀ רָעָ֣ה ׀ אֶל־שָׁא֗וּל וַיִּתְנַבֵּ֤א בְתֽוֹךְ־הַבַּ֙יִת֙ וְדָוִ֗ד מְנַגֵּ֧ן בְּיָד֛וֹ כְּי֥וֹם ׀ בְּי֑וֹם וְהַחֲנִ֖ית בְּיַד־שָׁאֽוּל׃ 11 וַיָּ֤טֶל שָׁאוּל֙ אֶת־הַ֣חֲנִ֔ית וַיֹּ֕אמֶר אַכֶּ֥ה בְדָוִ֖ד וּבַקִּ֑יר וַיִּסֹּ֥ב דָּוִ֛ד מִפָּנָ֖יו פַּעֲמָֽיִם׃ 12 וַיִּרָ֥א שָׁא֖וּל מִלִּפְנֵ֣י דָוִ֑ד כִּֽי־הָיָ֤ה יְהוָה֙ עִמּ֔וֹ וּמֵעִ֥ם שָׁא֖וּל סָֽר׃ 13 וַיְסִרֵ֤הוּ שָׁאוּל֙ מֵֽעִמּ֔וֹ וַיְשִׂמֵ֥הוּ ל֖וֹ שַׂר־אָ֑לֶף וַיֵּצֵ֥א וַיָּבֹ֖א לִפְנֵ֥י הָעָֽם׃ פ 14 וַיְהִ֥י דָוִ֛ד לְכָל־דְּרָכָ֖ו מַשְׂכִּ֑יל וַֽיהוָ֖ה עִמּֽוֹ׃ 15 וַיַּ֣רְא שָׁא֔וּל אֲשֶׁר־ה֖וּא מַשְׂכִּ֣יל מְאֹ֑ד וַיָּ֖גָר מִפָּנָֽיו׃ 16 וְכָל־יִשְׂרָאֵל֙ וִֽיהוּדָ֔ה אֹהֵ֖ב אֶת־דָּוִ֑ד כִּֽי־ה֛וּא יוֹצֵ֥א וָבָ֖א לִפְנֵיהֶֽם׃ פ

17 וַיֹּ֨אמֶר שָׁא֜וּל אֶל־דָּוִ֗ד הִנֵּה֩ בִתִּ֨י הַגְּדוֹלָ֤ה מֵרַב֙ אֹתָ֤הּ אֶתֶּן־לְךָ֙ לְאִשָּׁ֔ה אַ֚ךְ הֱיֵה־לִּ֣י לְבֶן־חַ֔יִל וְהִלָּחֵ֖ם מִלְחֲמ֣וֹת יְהוָ֑ה וְשָׁא֣וּל אָמַ֗ר אַל־תְּהִ֤י יָדִי֙ בּ֔וֹ וּתְהִי־ב֖וֹ יַד־פְּלִשְׁתִּֽים׃ ס 18 וַיֹּ֨אמֶר דָּוִ֜ד אֶל־שָׁא֗וּל מִ֤י אָֽנֹכִי֙ וּמִ֣י חַיַּ֔י מִשְׁפַּ֥חַת אָבִ֖י בְּיִשְׂרָאֵ֑ל כִּֽי־אֶהְיֶ֥ה חָתָ֖ן לַמֶּֽלֶךְ׃ 19 וַיְהִ֗י בְּעֵ֥ת תֵּ֛ת אֶת־מֵרַ֥ב בַּת־שָׁא֖וּל לְדָוִ֑ד וְהִ֧יא נִתְּנָ֛ה לְעַדְרִיאֵ֥ל הַמְּחֹלָתִ֖י לְאִשָּֽׁה׃ 20 וַתֶּאֱהַ֥ב מִיכַ֛ל בַּת־שָׁא֖וּל אֶת־דָּוִ֑ד וַיַּגִּ֣דוּ לְשָׁא֔וּל וַיִּשַׁ֥ר הַדָּבָ֖ר בְּעֵינָֽיו׃ 21 וַיֹּ֨אמֶר שָׁא֜וּל אֶתְּנֶ֤נָּה לּוֹ֙ וּתְהִי־ל֣וֹ לְמוֹקֵ֔שׁ וּתְהִי־ב֖וֹ יַד־פְּלִשְׁתִּ֑ים וַיֹּ֧אמֶר שָׁא֛וּל אֶל־דָּוִ֖ד בִּשְׁתַּ֥יִם תִּתְחַתֵּ֥ן בִּ֖י הַיּֽוֹם׃ 22 וַיְצַ֨ו שָׁא֜וּל

---

c   *Change of vocalization yields "raised."*
d-d   *Lit. "and he went out and came in before the troops."*
e-e   *Meaning of Heb. uncertain. Change of vocalization yields "who are my kin."*

my son-in-law even now through the second one."-*b* ²²And Saul instructed his courtiers to say to David privately, "The king is fond of you and all his courtiers like you. So why not become the king's son-in-law?" ²³When the king's courtiers repeated these words to David, David replied, "Do you think that becoming the son-in-law of a king is a small matter, when I am but a poor man of no consequence?" ²⁴Saul's courtiers reported to him, "This is what David answered." ²⁵And Saul said, "Say this to David: 'The king desires no other bride-price than the foreskins of a hundred Philistines, as vengeance on the king's enemies.'"—Saul intended to bring about David's death at the hands of the Philistines.—²⁶When his courtiers told this to David, David was pleased with the idea of becoming the king's son-in-law. *b*-Before the time had expired,-*b* ²⁷David went out with his men and killed two hundred*f* Philistines; David brought their foreskins and *b*-they were counted out-*b* for the king, that he might become the king's son-in-law. Saul then gave him his daughter Michal in marriage. ²⁸When Saul realized that the Lord was with David *g*-and that Michal daughter of Saul loved him,-*g* ²⁹Saul grew still more afraid of David; and Saul was David's enemy ever after.

³⁰The Philistine chiefs marched out [to battle]; and every time they marched out, David was more successful than all the other officers of Saul. His reputation soared.

19

Saul urged his son Jonathan and all his courtiers to kill David. But Saul's son Jonathan was very fond of David, ²and Jonathan told David, "My father Saul is bent on killing you. Be on your guard tomorrow morning; get to a secret place and remain in hiding. ³I will go out

אֶת־עַבְדּוֹ עֲבָדָיו דִּבְּר֣וּ אֶל־דָּוִ֗ד בַּלָּ֣ט לֵאמֹ֔ר הִנֵּ֨ה חָפֵ֤ץ בְּךָ֙ הַמֶּ֔לֶךְ וְכָל־עֲבָדָ֖יו אֲהֵב֑וּךָ וְעַתָּ֖ה הִתְחַתֵּ֥ן בַּמֶּֽלֶךְ׃ ²³ וַיְדַבְּר֞וּ עַבְדֵ֤י שָׁאוּל֙ בְּאָזְנֵ֣י דָוִ֔ד אֶת־הַדְּבָרִ֖ים הָאֵ֑לֶּה וַיֹּ֣אמֶר דָּוִ֗ד הַֽנְקַלָּ֤ה בְעֵֽינֵיכֶם֙ הִתְחַתֵּ֣ן בַּמֶּ֔לֶךְ וְאָנֹכִ֥י אִישׁ־רָ֖שׁ וְנִקְלֶֽה׃ ²⁴ וַיַּגִּ֜דוּ עַבְדֵ֥י שָׁא֛וּל ל֖וֹ לֵאמֹ֑ר כַּדְּבָרִ֥ים הָאֵ֖לֶּה דִּבֶּ֥ר דָּוִֽד׃ פ ²⁵ וַיֹּ֨אמֶר שָׁא֜וּל כֹּֽה־תֹאמְר֣וּ לְדָוִ֗ד אֵֽין־חֵ֤פֶץ לַמֶּ֙לֶךְ֙ בְּמֹ֔הַר כִּ֗י בְּמֵאָה֙ עָרְל֣וֹת פְּלִשְׁתִּ֔ים לְהִנָּקֵ֖ם בְּאֹיְבֵ֣י הַמֶּ֑לֶךְ וְשָׁא֣וּל חָשַׁ֔ב לְהַפִּ֥יל אֶת־דָּוִ֖ד בְּיַד־פְּלִשְׁתִּֽים׃ ²⁶ וַיַּגִּ֨דוּ עֲבָדָ֤יו לְדָוִד֙ אֶת־הַדְּבָרִ֣ים הָאֵ֔לֶּה וַיִּשַׁ֤ר הַדָּבָר֙ בְּעֵינֵ֣י דָוִ֔ד לְהִתְחַתֵּ֖ן בַּמֶּ֑לֶךְ וְלֹ֥א מָלְא֖וּ הַיָּמִֽים׃ ²⁷ וַיָּ֨קָם דָּוִ֜ד וַיֵּ֣לֶךְ ׀ ה֣וּא וַאֲנָשָׁ֗יו וַיַּ֣ךְ בַּפְּלִשְׁתִּים֮ מָאתַ֣יִם אִישׁ֒ וַיָּבֵ֤א דָוִד֙ אֶת־עָרְלֹ֣תֵיהֶ֔ם וַיְמַלְא֣וּם לַמֶּ֔לֶךְ לְהִתְחַתֵּ֖ן בַּמֶּ֑לֶךְ וַיִּתֶּן־ל֥וֹ שָׁא֛וּל אֶת־מִיכַ֥ל בִּתּ֖וֹ לְאִשָּֽׁה׃ ס ²⁸ וַיַּ֤רְא שָׁאוּל֙ וַיֵּ֔דַע כִּ֥י יְהֹוָ֖ה עִם־דָּוִ֑ד וּמִיכַ֥ל בַּת־שָׁא֖וּל אֲהֵבַֽתְהוּ׃ ²⁹ וַיֹּ֣אסֶף* שָׁא֗וּל לֵרֹ֥א מִפְּנֵ֛י דָוִ֖ד ע֑וֹד וַיְהִ֥י שָׁא֛וּל אֹיֵ֥ב אֶת־דָּוִ֖ד כָּל־הַיָּמִֽים׃ ס ³⁰ וַיֵּצְא֖וּ שָׂרֵ֣י פְלִשְׁתִּ֑ים וַיְהִ֣י ׀ מִדֵּ֣י צֵאתָ֗ם שָׂכַ֤ל דָּוִד֙ מִכֹּל֙ עַבְדֵ֣י שָׁא֔וּל וַיִּיקַ֥ר שְׁמ֖וֹ מְאֹֽד׃ ס

יט וַיְדַבֵּ֣ר שָׁא֗וּל אֶל־יוֹנָתָ֤ן בְּנוֹ֙ וְאֶל־כָּל־עֲבָדָ֔יו לְהָמִ֖ית אֶת־דָּוִ֑ד וִיהֽוֹנָתָן֙ בֶּן־שָׁא֔וּל חָפֵ֥ץ בְּדָוִ֖ד מְאֹֽד׃ ² וַיַּגֵּ֤ד יְהֽוֹנָתָן֙ לְדָוִ֣ד לֵאמֹ֔ר מְבַקֵּ֛שׁ שָׁא֥וּל אָבִ֖י לַהֲמִיתֶ֑ךָ וְעַתָּה֙ הִשָּֽׁמֶר־נָ֣א בַבֹּ֔קֶר וְיָשַׁבְתָּ֥ בַסֵּ֖תֶר

---

f   Septuagint reads "one hundred" and cf. 2 Sam. 3.14.
g-g   Septuagint reads "and that all Israel loved him."

יתיר א'   v. 29.

and stand next to my father in the field where you will be, and I will speak to my father about you. If I learn anything, I will tell you." [4]So Jonathan spoke well of David to his father Saul. He said to him, "Let not Your Majesty wrong his servant David, for he has not wronged you; indeed, all his actions have been very much to your advantage. [5]He took his life in his hands and killed the Philistine, and the LORD wrought a great victory for all Israel. You saw it and rejoiced. Why then should you incur the guilt of shedding the blood of an innocent man, killing David without cause?" [6]Saul heeded Jonathan's plea, and Saul swore, "As the LORD lives, he shall not be put to death!" [7]Jonathan called David, and Jonathan told him all this. Then Jonathan brought David to Saul, and he served him as before.

[8]Fighting broke out again. David went out and fought the Philistines. He inflicted a great defeat upon them and they fled before him. [9]Then an evil spirit of the LORD came upon Saul while he was sitting in his house with his spear in his hand, and David was playing [the lyre]. [10]Saul tried to pin David to the wall with the spear, but he eluded Saul, so that he drove the spear into the wall. David fled and got away.

That night [11]Saul sent messengers to David's home to keep watch on him and to kill him in the morning. But David's wife Michal told him, "Unless you run for your life tonight, you will be killed tomorrow." [12]Michal let David down from the window and he escaped and fled. [13]Michal then took the household idol, laid it on the bed, and covered it with a cloth; and at its head she put a net of goat's hair. [14]Saul sent messengers to seize David; but she said, "He is sick." [15]Saul, however, sent back the messengers to see David for themselves. "Bring him up to me in the bed," he ordered, "that he may be put to death." [16]When the messengers came, they

וְנַחְבֵּאתָ: 3 וַאֲנִ֗י אֵצֵ֞א וְעָמַדְתִּ֣י לְיַד־אָבִ֗י בַּשָּׂדֶה֙ אֲשֶׁ֣ר אַתָּ֣ה שָׁ֔ם וַאֲנִ֕י אֲדַבֵּ֥ר בְּךָ֖ אֶל־אָבִ֑י וְרָאִ֥יתִי מָ֖ה וְהִגַּ֥דְתִּי לָֽךְ: ס 4 וַיְדַבֵּ֨ר יְהוֹנָתָ֤ן בְּדָוִד֙ ט֔וֹב אֶל־שָׁא֖וּל אָבִ֑יו וַיֹּ֣אמֶר אֵלָ֗יו אַל־יֶחֱטָ֤א הַמֶּ֙לֶךְ֙ בְּעַבְדּ֣וֹ בְדָוִ֔ד כִּ֣י ל֤וֹא חָטָא֙ לָ֔ךְ וְכִ֥י מַעֲשָׂ֖יו טוֹב־לְךָ֥ מְאֹֽד: 5 וַיָּשֶׂם֩ אֶת־נַפְשׁ֨וֹ בְכַפּ֜וֹ וַיַּ֣ךְ אֶת־הַפְּלִשְׁתִּ֗י וַיַּ֨עַשׂ יְהוָ֜ה תְּשׁוּעָ֤ה גְדוֹלָה֙ לְכָל־יִשְׂרָאֵ֔ל רָאִ֖יתָ וַתִּשְׂמָ֑ח וְלָ֤מָּה תֶחֱטָא֙ בְּדָ֣ם נָקִ֔י לְהָמִ֥ית אֶת־דָּוִ֖ד חִנָּֽם: 6 וַיִּשְׁמַ֥ע שָׁא֖וּל בְּק֣וֹל יְהוֹנָתָ֑ן וַיִּשָּׁבַ֣ע שָׁא֔וּל חַי־יְהוָ֖ה אִם־יוּמָֽת: 7 וַיִּקְרָ֤א יְהוֹנָתָן֙ לְדָוִ֔ד וַיַּגֶּד־לוֹ֙ יְה֣וֹנָתָ֔ן אֵ֥ת כָּל־הַדְּבָרִ֖ים הָאֵ֑לֶּה וַיָּבֵ֨א יְהוֹנָתָ֤ן אֶת־דָּוִד֙ אֶל־שָׁא֔וּל וַיְהִ֥י לְפָנָ֖יו כְּאֶתְמ֥וֹל שִׁלְשֽׁוֹם: ס

8 וַתּ֥וֹסֶף הַמִּלְחָמָ֖ה לִֽהְי֑וֹת וַיֵּצֵ֨א דָוִ֜ד וַיִּלָּ֣חֶם בַּפְּלִשְׁתִּ֗ים וַיַּ֤ךְ בָּהֶם֙ מַכָּ֣ה גְדוֹלָ֔ה וַיָּנֻ֖סוּ מִפָּנָֽיו: 9 וַתְּהִי֩ ר֨וּחַ יְהוָ֤ה ׀ רָעָה֙ אֶל־שָׁא֔וּל וְה֤וּא בְּבֵיתוֹ֙ יוֹשֵׁ֔ב וַחֲנִית֖וֹ בְּיָד֑וֹ וְדָוִ֖ד מְנַגֵּ֥ן בְּיָֽד: 10 וַיְבַקֵּ֨שׁ שָׁא֜וּל לְהַכּ֤וֹת בַּֽחֲנִית֙ בְּדָוִ֣ד וּבַקִּ֔יר וַיִּפְטַר֙ מִפְּנֵ֣י שָׁא֔וּל וַיַּ֥ךְ אֶת־הַחֲנִ֖ית בַּקִּ֑יר וְדָוִ֣ד נָ֔ס וַיִּמָּלֵ֖ט בַּלַּ֥יְלָה הֽוּא: פ 11 וַיִּשְׁלַח֩ שָׁא֨וּל מַלְאָכִ֜ים אֶל־בֵּ֤ית דָּוִד֙ לְשָׁמְר֔וֹ וְלַהֲמִית֖וֹ בַּבֹּ֑קֶר וַתַּגֵּ֣ד לְדָוִ֗ד מִיכַ֤ל אִשְׁתּוֹ֙ לֵאמֹ֔ר אִם־אֵ֨ינְךָ֜ מְמַלֵּ֤ט אֶֽת־נַפְשְׁךָ֙ הַלַּ֔יְלָה מָחָ֖ר אַתָּ֥ה מוּמָֽת: 12 וַתֹּ֧רֶד מִיכַ֛ל אֶת־דָּוִ֖ד בְּעַ֣ד הַֽחַלּ֑וֹן וַיֵּ֥לֶךְ וַיִּבְרַ֖ח וַיִּמָּלֵֽט: 13 וַתִּקַּ֣ח מִיכַ֗ל אֶת־הַתְּרָפִים֙ וַתָּ֣שֶׂם אֶל־הַמִּטָּ֔ה וְאֵת֙ כְּבִ֣יר הָֽעִזִּ֔ים שָׂ֖מָה מְרַֽאֲשֹׁתָ֑יו וַתְּכַ֖ס בַּבָּֽגֶד: 14 וַיִּשְׁלַ֥ח שָׁא֛וּל מַלְאָכִ֖ים לָקַ֣חַת אֶת־דָּוִ֑ד וַתֹּ֖אמֶר חֹלֶ֥ה הֽוּא: פ 15 וַיִּשְׁלַ֤ח שָׁאוּל֙ אֶת־הַמַּלְאָכִ֔ים לִרְא֥וֹת אֶת־דָּוִ֖ד לֵאמֹ֑ר הַעֲל֨וּ אֹת֧וֹ בַמִּטָּ֛ה אֵלַ֖י לַהֲמִתֽוֹ: 16 וַיָּבֹ֙אוּ֙ הַמַּלְאָכִ֔ים וְהִנֵּ֥ה הַתְּרָפִ֖ים אֶל־הַמִּטָּ֑ה וּכְבִ֥יר הָעִזִּ֖ים

found the household idol in the bed, with the net of goat's hair at its head. ¹⁷Saul said to Michal, "Why did you play that trick on me and let my enemy get away safely?" "Because," Michal answered Saul, "he said to me: 'Help me get away or I'll kill you.'"

¹⁸David made good his escape, and he came to Samuel at Ramah and told him all that Saul had done to him. He and Samuel went and stayed at Naioth. ¹⁹Saul was told that David was at Naioth in Ramah, ²⁰and Saul sent messengers to seize David. They*a* saw a band of prophets *b*-speaking in ecstasy,-*b* with Samuel standing by *c*-as their leader;-*c* and the spirit of God came upon Saul's messengers and they too began to speak in ecstasy. ²¹When Saul was told about this, he sent other messengers; but they too spoke in ecstasy. Saul sent a third group of messengers; and they also spoke in ecstasy. ²²So he himself went to Ramah. When he came to *d*-the great cistern at Secu,-*d* he asked, "Where are Samuel and David?" and was told that they were at Naioth in Ramah. ²³He was on his way there, to Naioth in Ramah, when the spirit of God came upon him too; and he walked on, speaking in ecstasy, until he reached Naioth in Ramah. ²⁴Then he too stripped off his clothes and he too spoke in ecstasy before Samuel; and he lay naked all that day and all night. That is why people say, "Is Saul too among the prophets?"

20

David fled from Naioth in Ramah; he came to Jonathan and said, "What have I done, what is my crime and my guilt against your father, that he seeks my life?" ²He replied, "Heaven forbid! You shall not die. My father does not do anything, great or small, without disclosing it to me; why should my father con-

מְרַאֲשֹׁתָיו׃ 17 וַיֹּאמֶר שָׁאוּל אֶל־מִיכַל לָמָּה כָּכָה רִמִּיתִנִי וַתְּשַׁלְּחִי אֶת־אֹיְבִי וַיִּמָּלֵט וַתֹּאמֶר מִיכַל אֶל־שָׁאוּל הוּא־ אָמַר אֵלַי שַׁלְּחִנִי לָמָה אֲמִיתֵךְ׃ 18 וְדָוִד בָּרַח וַיִּמָּלֵט וַיָּבֹא אֶל־שְׁמוּאֵל הָרָמָתָה וַיַּגֶּד־לוֹ אֵת כָּל־אֲשֶׁר עָשָׂה־לוֹ שָׁאוּל וַיֵּלֶךְ הוּא וּשְׁמוּאֵל וַיֵּשְׁבוּ בְּנָיוֹת׃ 19 וַיֻּגַּד לְשָׁאוּל לֵאמֹר הִנֵּה דָוִד בְּנָיוֹת בָּרָמָה׃ 20 וַיִּשְׁלַח שָׁאוּל מַלְאָכִים לָקַחַת אֶת־דָּוִד וַיַּרְא אֶת־ לַהֲקַת הַנְּבִיאִים נִבְּאִים וּשְׁמוּאֵל עֹמֵד נִצָּב עֲלֵיהֶם וַתְּהִי עַל־מַלְאֲכֵי שָׁאוּל רוּחַ אֱלֹהִים וַיִּתְנַבְּאוּ גַּם־הֵמָּה׃ 21 וַיַּגִּדוּ לְשָׁאוּל וַיִּשְׁלַח מַלְאָכִים אֲחֵרִים וַיִּתְנַבְּאוּ גַּם־הֵמָּה וַיֹּסֶף שָׁאוּל וַיִּשְׁלַח מַלְאָכִים שְׁלִשִׁים וַיִּתְנַבְּאוּ גַּם־הֵמָּה׃ 22 וַיֵּלֶךְ גַּם־ הוּא הָרָמָתָה וַיָּבֹא עַד־בּוֹר הַגָּדוֹל אֲשֶׁר בַּשֶּׂכוּ וַיִּשְׁאַל וַיֹּאמֶר אֵיפֹה שְׁמוּאֵל וְדָוִד וַיֹּאמֶר* הִנֵּה בְּנָיוֹת בָּרָמָה׃ 23 וַיֵּלֶךְ שָׁם אֶל־נָיוֹת בָּרָמָה וַתְּהִי עָלָיו גַּם־הוּא רוּחַ אֱלֹהִים וַיֵּלֶךְ הָלוֹךְ וַיִּתְנַבֵּא עַד־בֹּאוֹ בְּנָיוֹת בָּרָמָה׃ 24 וַיִּפְשַׁט גַּם־הוּא בְּגָדָיו וַיִּתְנַבֵּא גַם־הוּא לִפְנֵי שְׁמוּאֵל וַיִּפֹּל עָרֹם כָּל־הַיּוֹם הַהוּא וְכָל־הַלָּיְלָה עַל־כֵּן יֹאמְרוּ הֲגַם שָׁאוּל בַּנְּבִיאִם׃ פ

כ וַיִּבְרַח דָּוִד מִנָּיוֹת בָּרָמָה וַיָּבֹא וַיֹּאמֶר ׀ לִפְנֵי יְהוֹנָתָן מֶה עָשִׂיתִי מֶה־עֲוֹנִי וּמֶה־חַטָּאתִי לִפְנֵי אָבִיךָ כִּי מְבַקֵּשׁ אֶת־ נַפְשִׁי׃ 2 וַיֹּאמֶר לוֹ חָלִילָה לֹא תָמוּת הִנֵּה לוֹ עשׂה לֹא־יַעֲשֶׂה אָבִי דָּבָר גָּדוֹל אוֹ דָּבָר קָטֹן וְלֹא יִגְלֶה אֶת־אָזְנִי וּמַדּוּעַ יַסְתִּיר

סבירין ומטעין לשון רבים   v. 22.

---

a   Heb. "He."
b-b   Cf. note at 10.5.
c-c   Meaning of Heb. uncertain.
d-d   Septuagint reads "the cistern of the threshing floor on the bare height."

ceal this matter from me? It cannot be!" [3]David
[a]-swore further,-[a] "Your father knows well that
you are fond of me and has decided: Jonathan
must not learn of this or he will be grieved.
But, as the LORD lives and as you live, there is
only a step between me and death." [4]Jonathan
said to David, "Whatever you want, I will do
it for you."

[5]David said to Jonathan, "Tomorrow is the
new moon, and I [b]-am to sit with the king at
the meal. Instead, let-[b] me go and I will hide in
the countryside until the third[c] evening. [6]If your
father notes my absence, you say, 'David asked
my permission to run down to his home town,
Bethlehem, for the whole family has its annual
sacrifice there.' [7]If he says 'Good,' your servant
is safe; but if his anger flares up, know that he
is resolved to do [me] harm. [8]Deal faithfully
with your servant, since you have taken your
servant into a covenant of the LORD with you.
And if I am guilty, kill me yourself, but don't
make me go back to your father." [9]Jonathan replied, "Don't talk like that! If I learn that my
father has resolved to kill you, I will surely tell
you about it." [10]David said to Jonathan, "Who
will tell me if[d] your father answers you harshly?"
[11]Jonathan said to David, "Let us go into the
open"; and they both went out into the open.

[12e]Then Jonathan said to David, "By the
LORD, the God of Israel! I will sound out my
father at this time tomorrow, [or] on the third
day; and if [his response] is favorable for David,
I will send a message to you at once and disclose
it to you. [13]But if my father intends to do you
harm, may the LORD do thus to Jonathan and
more if I do [not] disclose it to you and send
you off to escape unharmed. May the LORD be
with you, as He used to be with my father. [14]Nor

אָבִ֛י מִמֶּ֥נִּי אֶת־הַדָּבָ֖ר הַזֶּ֑ה אֵ֥ין זֹֽאת׃
3 וַיִּשָּׁבַ֨ע ע֜וֹד דָּוִ֗ד וַיֹּ֙אמֶר֙ יָדֹ֤עַ יָדַע֙ אָבִ֔יךָ
כִּֽי־מָצָ֥אתִי חֵ֖ן בְּעֵינֶ֑יךָ וַיֹּ֛אמֶר אַל־יֵֽדַע־
זֹ֤את יְהֽוֹנָתָן֙ פֶּן־יֵֽעָצֵ֔ב וְאוּלָ֗ם חַי־יְהוָה֙
וְחֵ֣י נַפְשֶׁ֔ךָ כִּ֣י כְפֶ֔שַׂע בֵּינִ֖י וּבֵ֥ין הַמָּֽוֶת׃
4 וַיֹּ֥אמֶר יְהֽוֹנָתָ֖ן אֶל־דָּוִ֑ד מַה־תֹּאמַ֥ר
נַפְשְׁךָ֖ וְאֶֽעֱשֶׂה־לָּֽךְ׃ פ

5 וַיֹּ֨אמֶר דָּוִ֜ד אֶל־יְהֽוֹנָתָ֗ן הִנֵּֽה־חֹ֙דֶשׁ֙ מָחָ֔ר
וְאָֽנֹכִ֛י יָשֹׁב־אֵשֵׁ֥ב עִם־הַמֶּ֖לֶךְ לֶֽאֱכ֑וֹל
וְשִׁלַּחְתַּ֗נִי וְנִסְתַּרְתִּ֥י בַשָּׂדֶ֖ה עַ֥ד הָעֶ֥רֶב
הַשְּׁלִשִֽׁית׃ 6 אִם־פָּקֹ֥ד יִפְקְדֵ֖נִי אָבִ֑יךָ
וְאָֽמַרְתָּ֗ נִשְׁאֹל֩ נִשְׁאַ֨ל מִמֶּ֤נִּי דָוִד֙ לָרוּץ֙
בֵּֽית־לֶ֣חֶם עִיר֔וֹ כִּ֣י זֶ֧בַח הַיָּמִ֛ים שָׁ֖ם
לְכָל־הַמִּשְׁפָּחָֽה׃ 7 אִם־כֹּ֥ה יֹאמַ֖ר ט֑וֹב
שָׁל֣וֹם לְעַבְדֶּ֑ךָ וְאִם־חָרֹ֤ה יֶֽחֱרֶה֙ ל֔וֹ דַּ֕ע
כִּֽי־כָֽלְתָ֥ה הָרָעָ֖ה מֵֽעִמּֽוֹ׃ 8 וְעָשִׂ֤יתָ חֶ֙סֶד֙
עַל־עַבְדֶּ֔ךָ כִּ֚י בִּבְרִ֣ית יְהוָ֔ה הֵבֵ֥אתָ אֶֽת־
עַבְדְּךָ֖ עִמָּ֑ךְ וְאִם־יֶשׁ־בִּ֣י עָוֹ֤ן הֲמִיתֵ֙נִי֙
אַ֔תָּה וְעַד־אָבִ֖יךָ לָ֥מָּה־זֶּ֖ה תְבִיאֵֽנִי׃ פ
9 וַיֹּ֥אמֶר יְהֽוֹנָתָ֖ן חָלִ֣ילָה לָּ֑ךְ כִּ֣י ׀ אִם־יָדֹ֣עַ
אֵדַ֗ע כִּֽי־כָֽלְתָ֤ה הָֽרָעָה֙ מֵעִ֣ם אָבִ֔י לָב֖וֹא
עָלֶ֑יךָ וְלֹ֥א אֹתָ֖הּ אַגִּ֥יד לָֽךְ׃ ס 10 וַיֹּ֤אמֶר
דָּוִד֙ אֶל־יְה֣וֹנָתָ֔ן מִ֣י יַגִּ֣יד לִ֔י א֖וֹ מַה־יַּֽעֲנְךָ֥
אָבִ֖יךָ קָשָֽׁה׃ ס 11 וַיֹּ֤אמֶר יְהֽוֹנָתָן֙ אֶל־
דָּוִ֔ד לְכָ֖ה וְנֵצֵ֣א הַשָּׂדֶ֑ה וַיֵּֽצְא֥וּ שְׁנֵיהֶ֖ם
הַשָּׂדֶֽה׃ ס

12 וַיֹּ֨אמֶר יְהֽוֹנָתָ֜ן אֶל־דָּוִ֗ד יְהוָ֞ה אֱלֹהֵ֤י
יִשְׂרָאֵל֙ כִּֽי־אֶחְקֹ֣ר אֶת־אָבִ֗י כָּעֵ֤ת ׀ מָחָר֙
הַשְּׁלִשִׁ֔ית וְהִנֵּה־ט֖וֹב אֶל־דָּוִ֑ד וְלֹֽא־אָ֗ז
אֶשְׁלַ֤ח אֵלֶ֙יךָ֙ וְגָלִ֥יתִי אֶת־אָזְנֶֽךָ׃ 13 כֹּֽה־
יַֽעֲשֶׂה֩ יְהוָ֨ה לִֽיהוֹנָתָ֜ן וְכֹ֣ה יֹסִ֗יף כִּֽי־יֵיטִ֤ב
אֶל־אָבִ֜י אֶת־הָֽרָעָה֙ עָלֶ֔יךָ וְגָלִ֙יתִי֙ אֶת־
אָזְנֶ֔ךָ וְשִׁלַּחְתִּ֖יךָ וְהָלַכְתָּ֣ לְשָׁל֑וֹם וִיהִ֤י
יְהוָה֙ עִמָּ֔ךְ כַּֽאֲשֶׁ֥ר הָיָ֖ה עִם־אָבִֽי׃ 14 וְלֹ֣א

---

a-a　Septuagint reads "replied to him."
b-b　Septuagint reads "will not sit…meal. Let…"
c　　Septuagint lacks "third."
d　　Meaning of Heb. uncertain.
e　　The meaning of several parts of vv. 12–16 is uncertain.

shall you fail to show me the *f*-LORD's faithful-ness,*-f* while I am alive; nor, when I am dead, [15]shall you ever discontinue your faithfulness to my house—not even after the LORD has wiped out every one of David's enemies from the face of the earth. [16]Thus has Jonathan covenanted with the house of David; and may the LORD requite the enemies of David!"

[17]Jonathan, out of his love for David, adjured*g* him again, for he loved him as himself. [18]Jonathan said to him, "Tomorrow will be the new moon; and you will be missed when your seat remains vacant.*h* [19]So the day after tomorrow, go down *i*-all the way-*i* to the place where you hid *j*-the other time,-*j* and stay close to the Ezel stone. [20]Now I will shoot three arrows to one side of it, as though I were shooting at a mark, [21]and I will order the boy to go and find the ar-rows. If I call to the boy, 'Hey! the arrows are on this side of you,' be reassured*k* and come, for you are safe and there is no danger—as the LORD lives! [22]But if, instead, I call to the lad, 'Hey! the arrows are beyond you,' then leave, for the LORD has sent you away. [23]As for the promise we made to each other,*l* may the LORD be [witness] between you and me forever."

[24]David hid in the field. The new moon came, and the king sat down to partake of the meal. [25]When the king took his usual place on the seat by the wall, Jonathan rose*m* and Abner sat down at Saul's side; but David's place remained va-cant. [26]That day, however, Saul said nothing. "It's accidental," he thought. *n*-"He must be un-clean and not yet cleansed."-*n* [27]But on the day after the new moon, the second day, David's place was vacant again. So Saul said to his son

אִם־עוֹדֶ֥נִּי חַ֖י וְלֹֽא־תַעֲשֶׂ֛ה עִמָּדִ֖י חֶ֥סֶד יְהֹוָ֖ה וְלֹ֥א אָמֽוּת׃ 15 וְלֹֽא־תַכְרִ֧ת אֶת־חַסְדְּךָ֛ מֵעִ֥ם בֵּיתִ֖י עַד־עוֹלָ֑ם וְלֹ֗א בְּהַכְרִ֤ת יְהֹוָה֙ אֶת־אֹ֣יְבֵ֣י דָוִ֔ד אִ֕ישׁ מֵעַ֖ל פְּנֵ֥י הָאֲדָמָֽה׃ 16 וַיִּכְרֹ֥ת יְהוֹנָתָ֖ן עִם־בֵּ֣ית דָּוִ֑ד וּבִקֵּ֣שׁ יְהֹוָ֔ה מִיַּ֖ד אֹיְבֵ֥י דָוִֽד׃ 17 וַיּ֤וֹסֶף יְהֽוֹנָתָן֙ לְהַשְׁבִּ֣יעַ אֶת־דָּוִ֔ד בְּאַהֲבָת֖וֹ אֹת֑וֹ כִּֽי־אַהֲבַ֥ת נַפְשׁ֖וֹ אֲהֵבֽוֹ׃ ס 18 וַיֹּֽאמֶר־ל֥וֹ יְהוֹנָתָ֖ן מָחָ֣ר חֹ֑דֶשׁ וְנִפְקַ֕דְתָּ כִּ֥י יִפָּקֵ֖ד מוֹשָׁבֶֽךָ׃ 19 וְשִׁלַּשְׁתָּ֙ תֵּרֵ֣ד מְאֹ֔ד וּבָאתָ֙ אֶל־הַמָּק֔וֹם אֲשֶׁר־נִסְתַּ֥רְתָּ שָּׁ֖ם בְּי֣וֹם הַֽמַּעֲשֶׂ֑ה וְיָ֣שַׁבְתָּ֔ אֵ֖צֶל הָאֶ֥בֶן הָאָֽזֶל׃ 20 וַאֲנִ֕י שְׁלֹ֥שֶׁת הַחִצִּ֖ים צִדָּ֣ה אוֹרֶ֑ה לְשַׁלַּֽח־לִ֖י לְמַטָּרָֽה׃ 21 וְהִנֵּה֙ אֶשְׁלַ֣ח אֶת־הַנַּ֔עַר לֵ֖ךְ מְצָ֣א אֶת־הַחִצִּ֑ים אִם־אָמֹר֩ אֹמַ֨ר לַנַּ֜עַר הִנֵּ֥ה הַחִצִּ֣ים ׀ מִמְּךָ֣ וָהֵ֗נָּה קָחֶ֧נּוּ ׀ וָבֹ֛אָה כִּֽי־שָׁל֥וֹם לְךָ֛ וְאֵ֥ין דָּבָ֖ר חַי־יְהֹוָֽה׃ 22 וְאִם־כֹּ֤ה אֹמַר֙ לָעֶ֔לֶם הִנֵּ֥ה הַחִצִּ֖ים מִמְּךָ֣ וָהָ֑לְאָה לֵ֕ךְ כִּ֥י שִֽׁלַּחֲךָ֖ יְהֹוָֽה׃ 23 וְהַ֨דָּבָ֔ר אֲשֶׁ֥ר דִּבַּ֖רְנוּ אֲנִ֣י וָאָ֑תָּה הִנֵּ֧ה יְהֹוָ֛ה בֵּינִ֥י וּבֵינְךָ֖ עַד־עוֹלָֽם׃ ס 24 וַיִּסָּתֵ֥ר דָּוִ֖ד בַּשָּׂדֶ֑ה וַיְהִ֣י הַחֹ֔דֶשׁ וַיֵּ֧שֶׁב הַמֶּ֛לֶךְ עַל־הַלֶּ֖חֶם אֶל־הַלֶּ֥חֶם לֶאֱכֽוֹל׃ 25 וַיֵּ֣שֶׁב הַ֠מֶּ֠לֶךְ עַל־מ֨וֹשָׁב֜וֹ כְּפַ֣עַם ׀ בְּפַ֗עַם אֶל־מוֹשַׁב֙ הַקִּ֔יר וַיָּ֙קׇם֙ יְה֣וֹנָתָ֔ן וַיֵּ֥שֶׁב אַבְנֵ֖ר מִצַּ֣ד שָׁא֑וּל וַיִּפָּקֵ֖ד מְק֥וֹם דָּוִֽד׃ 26 וְלֹֽא־דִבֶּ֥ר שָׁא֛וּל מְא֖וּמָה בַּיּ֣וֹם הַה֑וּא כִּ֤י אָמַר֙ מִקְרֶ֣ה ה֔וּא בִּלְתִּ֥י טָה֛וֹר ה֖וּא כִּֽי־לֹ֥א טָהֽוֹר׃ ס 27 וַיְהִ֗י מִֽמׇּחֳרַ֤ת הַחֹ֙דֶשׁ֙ הַשֵּׁנִ֔י וַיִּפָּקֵ֖ד מְק֣וֹם דָּוִ֑ד ס וַיֹּ֤אמֶר שָׁאוּל֙ אֶל־יְה֣וֹנָתָ֣ן בְּנ֔וֹ מַדּ֗וּעַ לֹא־בָ֤א בֶן־יִשַׁי֙ גַּם־

---

f-f   I.e., the faithfulness pledged in the covenant before the LORD.
g   Septuagint reads "swore to."
h   At the festal meal.
i-i   Lit. "very much."
j-j   Lit. "on the day of the incident"; see 19.2 ff.
k   Lit. "accept it."
l   See above, vv. 12–17.
m   Force of Heb. uncertain; Septuagint "faced him."
n-n   Heb. construction unclear.

Jonathan, "Why didn't the son of Jesse[o] come to the meal yesterday or today?" [28]Jonathan answered Saul, "David begged leave of me to go to Bethlehem. [29]He said, 'Please let me go, for we are going to have a family feast in our town and my brother has summoned me to it. Do me a favor, let me slip away to see my kinsmen.' That is why he has not come to the king's table."

[30]Saul flew into a rage against Jonathan. "You son of a perverse, rebellious woman!" he shouted. "I know that you side with the son of Jesse—to your shame, and to the shame of your mother's nakedness! [31]For as long as the son of Jesse lives on earth, neither you nor your kingship will be secure. Now then, have him brought to me, for he is marked for death." [32]But Jonathan spoke up and said to his father, "Why should he be put to death? What has he done?" [33]At that, Saul threw[p] his spear at him to strike him down; and Jonathan realized that his father was determined to do away with David. [34]Jonathan rose from the table in a rage. He ate no food on the second day of the new moon, because he was grieved about David, and because his father had humiliated him.

[35]In the morning, Jonathan went out into the open for the meeting with David, accompanied by a young boy. [36]He said to the boy, "Run ahead and find the arrows that I shoot." And as the boy ran, he shot the arrows past him. [37]When the boy came to the place where the arrows shot by Jonathan had fallen, Jonathan called out to the boy, "Hey, the arrows are beyond you!" [38]And Jonathan called after the boy, "Quick, hurry up. Don't stop!" So Jonathan's boy gathered the arrows and came back to his master.— [39]The boy suspected nothing; only Jonathan and David knew the arrangement.— [40]Jonathan handed the gear to his boy and told him, "Take these back to the town." [41]When the boy got

o *See note at 10.11.*
p *See 18.11 and note.*

---

28 וַיַּעַן אֶל־הַלָּחֶם: תְּמוֹל גַּם־הַיּוֹם
יְהוֹנָתָן אֶת־שָׁאוּל נִשְׁאֹל נִשְׁאַל דָּוִד
מֵעִמָּדִי עַד־בֵּית לָחֶם: 29 וַיֹּאמֶר שַׁלְּחֵנִי
נָא כִּי זֶבַח מִשְׁפָּחָה לָנוּ בָּעִיר וְהוּא
צִוָּה־לִי אָחִי וְעַתָּה אִם־מָצָאתִי חֵן
בְּעֵינֶיךָ אִמָּלְטָה נָּא וְאֶרְאֶה אֶת־אֶחָי
עַל־כֵּן לֹא־בָא אֶל־שֻׁלְחַן הַמֶּלֶךְ: ס
30 וַיִּחַר־אַף שָׁאוּל בִּיהוֹנָתָן וַיֹּאמֶר לוֹ
בֶּן־נַעֲוַת הַמַּרְדּוּת הֲלוֹא יָדַעְתִּי כִּי־בֹחֵר
אַתָּה לְבֶן־יִשַׁי לְבָשְׁתְּךָ וּלְבֹשֶׁת עֶרְוַת
אִמֶּךָ: 31 כִּי כָל־הַיָּמִים אֲשֶׁר בֶּן־יִשַׁי חַי
עַל־הָאֲדָמָה לֹא תִכּוֹן אַתָּה וּמַלְכוּתֶךָ
וְעַתָּה שְׁלַח וְקַח אֹתוֹ אֵלַי כִּי בֶן־מָוֶת
הוּא: ס 32 וַיַּעַן יְהוֹנָתָן אֶת־שָׁאוּל
אָבִיו וַיֹּאמֶר אֵלָיו לָמָּה יוּמַת מֶה עָשָׂה:
33 וַיָּטֶל שָׁאוּל אֶת־הַחֲנִית עָלָיו לְהַכֹּתוֹ
וַיֵּדַע יְהוֹנָתָן כִּי־כָלָה הִיא מֵעִם אָבִיו
לְהָמִית אֶת־דָּוִד: ס 34 וַיָּקָם יְהוֹנָתָן
מֵעִם הַשֻּׁלְחָן בָּחֳרִי־אָף וְלֹא־אָכַל בְּיוֹם־
הַחֹדֶשׁ הַשֵּׁנִי לֶחֶם כִּי נֶעְצַב אֶל־דָּוִד כִּי
הִכְלִמוֹ אָבִיו: ס
35 וַיְהִי בַבֹּקֶר וַיֵּצֵא יְהוֹנָתָן הַשָּׂדֶה לְמוֹעֵד
דָּוִד וְנַעַר קָטֹן עִמּוֹ: 36 וַיֹּאמֶר לְנַעֲרוֹ רֻץ
מְצָא נָא אֶת־הַחִצִּים אֲשֶׁר אָנֹכִי מוֹרֶה
הַנַּעַר רָץ וְהוּא־יָרָה הַחֵצִי לְהַעֲבִרוֹ:
37 וַיָּבֹא הַנַּעַר עַד־מְקוֹם הַחֵצִי אֲשֶׁר יָרָה
יְהוֹנָתָן וַיִּקְרָא יְהוֹנָתָן אַחֲרֵי הַנַּעַר וַיֹּאמֶר
הֲלוֹא הַחֵצִי מִמְּךָ וָהָלְאָה: 38 וַיִּקְרָא
יְהוֹנָתָן אַחֲרֵי הַנַּעַר מְהֵרָה חוּשָׁה אַל־
תַּעֲמֹד וַיְלַקֵּט נַעַר יְהוֹנָתָן אֶת־הַחֵצִי
הַחִצִּים וַיָּבֹא אֶל־אֲדֹנָיו: 39 וְהַנַּעַר לֹא־
יָדַע מְאוּמָה אַךְ יְהוֹנָתָן וְדָוִד יָדְעוּ אֶת־
הַדָּבָר: 40 וַיִּתֵּן יְהוֹנָתָן אֶת־כֵּלָיו אֶל־הַנַּעַר
אֲשֶׁר־לוֹ וַיֹּאמֶר לוֹ לֵךְ הָבֵיא הָעִיר:

there, David q-emerged from his concealment at-q the Negeb.r He flung himself face down on the ground and bowed low three times. They kissed each other and wept together; David wept the longer.

42Jonathan said to David, "Go in peace! For we two have sworn to each other in the name of the LORD: 'May the LORD be [witness] between you and me, and between your

21 offspring and mine, forever!'" 1David then went his way, and Jonathan returned to the town.

2David went to the priest Ahimelech at Nob. Ahimelech came out in alarm to meet David, and he said to him, "Why are you alone, and no one with you?" 3David answered the priest Ahimelech, "The king has ordered me on a mission, and he said to me, 'No one must know anything about the mission on which I am sending you and for which I have given you orders.' So I have a-directed [my] young men to-a such and such a place. 4Now then, what have you got on hand? Anyb loaves of bread? Let me have them—or whatever is available." 5The priest answered David, "I have no ordinary bread on hand; there is only consecrated bread— provided the young men have kept away from women." 6In reply to the priest, David said, "I assure you that women have been kept from us, as always. Whenever I went on a mission, even if the journey was a common one, the vessels of the young men were consecrated; all the more then c-may consecrated food be put into their vessels today."-c 7So the priest gave him consecrated bread, because there was none there except the bread of display, which had been removed from the presence of the LORD, to be replaced by warm bread as soon as it was taken

---

41 הַנַּעַר בָּא וְדָוִד קָם מֵאֵצֶל הַנֶּגֶב וַיִּפֹּל לְאַפָּיו אַרְצָה וַיִּשְׁתַּחוּ שָׁלֹשׁ פְּעָמִים וַיִּשְּׁקוּ ׀ אִישׁ אֶת־רֵעֵהוּ וַיִּבְכּוּ אִישׁ אֶת־רֵעֵהוּ עַד־דָּוִד הִגְדִּיל׃

42 וַיֹּאמֶר יְהוֹנָתָן לְדָוִד לֵךְ לְשָׁלוֹם אֲשֶׁר נִשְׁבַּעְנוּ שְׁנֵינוּ אֲנַחְנוּ בְּשֵׁם יְהוָה לֵאמֹר יְהוָה יִהְיֶה ׀ בֵּינִי וּבֵינֶךָ וּבֵין זַרְעִי וּבֵין זַרְעֲךָ עַד־עוֹלָם׃ פ 1וַיָּקָם

כא וַיֵּלֶךְ וִיהוֹנָתָן בָּא הָעִיר׃

2 וַיָּבֹא דָוִד נֹבֶה אֶל־אֲחִימֶלֶךְ הַכֹּהֵן וַיֶּחֱרַד אֲחִימֶלֶךְ לִקְרַאת דָּוִד וַיֹּאמֶר לוֹ מַדּוּעַ אַתָּה לְבַדֶּךָ וְאִישׁ אֵין אִתָּךְ׃ 3וַיֹּאמֶר דָּוִד לַאֲחִימֶלֶךְ הַכֹּהֵן הַמֶּלֶךְ צִוַּנִי דָבָר וַיֹּאמֶר אֵלַי אִישׁ אַל־יֵדַע מְאוּמָה אֶת־הַדָּבָר אֲשֶׁר־אָנֹכִי שֹׁלֵחֲךָ וַאֲשֶׁר צִוִּיתִךָ וְאֶת־הַנְּעָרִים יוֹדַעְתִּי אֶל־מְקוֹם פְּלֹנִי אַלְמוֹנִי׃ 4וְעַתָּה מַה־יֵּשׁ תַּחַת־יָדְךָ חֲמִשָּׁה־לֶחֶם תְּנָה בְיָדִי אוֹ הַנִּמְצָא׃ 5וַיַּעַן הַכֹּהֵן אֶת־דָּוִד וַיֹּאמֶר אֵין־לֶחֶם חֹל אֶל־תַּחַת יָדִי כִּי־אִם־לֶחֶם קֹדֶשׁ יֵשׁ אִם־נִשְׁמְרוּ הַנְּעָרִים אַךְ מֵאִשָּׁה׃ פ 6וַיַּעַן דָּוִד אֶת־הַכֹּהֵן וַיֹּאמֶר לוֹ כִּי אִם־אִשָּׁה עֲצֻרָה־לָנוּ כִּתְמוֹל שִׁלְשֹׁם בְּצֵאתִי וַיִּהְיוּ כְלֵי־הַנְּעָרִים קֹדֶשׁ וְהוּא דֶּרֶךְ חֹל וְאַף כִּי הַיּוֹם יִקְדַּשׁ בַּכֶּלִי׃ 7וַיִּתֶּן־לוֹ הַכֹּהֵן קֹדֶשׁ כִּי לֹא־הָיָה שָׁם לֶחֶם כִּי־אִם־לֶחֶם הַפָּנִים הַמּוּסָרִים מִלִּפְנֵי יְהוָה לָשׂוּם לֶחֶם חֹם בְּיוֹם הִלָּקְחוֹ׃ 8וְשָׁם אִישׁ מֵעַבְדֵי שָׁאוּל בַּיּוֹם הַהוּא נֶעְצָר

---

q-q *Lit. "rose up from beside."*
r *Identical with the "Ezel Stone," v. 19.*

a-a *Meaning of Heb. uncertain. 4QSamb (cf. Septuagint) reads "made an appointment with [my] young men at…"*
b *Lit. "five."*
c-c *Meaning of Heb. uncertain in part.*

away.—⁸Now one of Saul's officials was there that day, *d*-detained before the LORD;-*d* his name was Doeg the Edomite, Saul's *e*-chief herds-man.-*e*

⁹David said to Ahimelech, "Haven't you got a spear or sword on hand? I didn't take my sword or any of my weapons with me, because the king's 'mission was urgent." ¹⁰The priest said, "There is the sword of Goliath the Philis-tine whom you slew in the valley of Elah; it is over there, wrapped in a cloth, behind the ephod. If you want to take that one, take it, for there is none here but that one." David replied, "There is none like it; give it to me."

¹¹That day David continued on his flight from Saul and he came to King Achish of Gath. ¹²The courtiers of Achish said to him, "Why, that's David, king of the land! That's the one of whom they sing as they dance:

Saul has slain his thousands;

David, his tens of thousands."

¹³These words worried David and he became very much afraid of King Achish of Gath. ¹⁴So he concealed his good sense from them; he feigned madness *f*-for their benefit.-*f* He scratched marks on the doors of the gate and let his saliva run down his beard. ¹⁵And Achish said to his courtiers, "You see the man is raving; why bring him to me? ¹⁶Do I lack madmen that you have brought this fellow to rave for me? Should this fellow enter my house?"

22 David departed from there and escaped to the cave*a* of Adullam; and when his brothers and all his father's house heard, they joined him down there. ²Everyone who was in straits and everyone who was in debt and everyone who

לִפְנֵ֣י יְהֹוָ֔ה וּשְׁמ֖וֹ דֹּאֵ֣ג הָאֲדֹמִ֑י אַבִּ֥יר הָרֹעִ֖ים אֲשֶׁ֥ר לְשָׁאֽוּל׃

⁹ וַיֹּ֤אמֶר דָּוִד֙ לַאֲחִימֶ֔לֶךְ וְאִ֛ין יֶשׁ־פֹּ֥ה תַֽחַת־יָֽדְךָ֖ חֲנִ֣ית אוֹ־חָ֑רֶב כִּ֣י גַם־חַרְבִּ֤י וְגַם־כֵּלַי֙ לֹֽא־לָקַ֣חְתִּי בְיָדִ֔י כִּֽי־הָיָ֥ה דְבַר־הַמֶּ֖לֶךְ נָחֽוּץ׃ ס ¹⁰ וַיֹּ֣אמֶר הַכֹּהֵ֗ן חֶ֣רֶב גׇּלְיָ֣ת הַפְּלִשְׁתִּ֡י אֲשֶׁר־הִכִּ֣יתָ ׀ בְּעֵ֣מֶק הָאֵלָ֡ה הִנֵּה־הִ֞יא לוּטָ֣ה בַשִּׂמְלָה֮ אַחֲרֵ֣י הָאֵפוֹד֒ אִם־אֹתָ֤הּ תִּֽקַּֽח־לְךָ֙ קָ֔ח כִּ֣י אֵ֥ין אַחֶ֛רֶת זוּלָתָ֖הּ בָּזֶ֑ה וַיֹּ֧אמֶר דָּוִ֛ד אֵ֥ין כָּמֹ֖הָ תְּנֶ֥נָּה לִּֽי׃

¹¹ וַיָּ֣קׇם דָּוִ֔ד וַיִּבְרַ֥ח בַּיּוֹם־הַה֖וּא מִפְּנֵ֣י שָׁא֑וּל וַיָּבֹ֕א אֶל־אָכִ֖ישׁ מֶ֥לֶךְ גַּֽת׃ ¹² וַיֹּ֨אמְר֜וּ עַבְדֵ֤י אָכִישׁ֙ אֵלָ֔יו הֲלוֹא־זֶ֥ה דָוִ֖ד מֶ֣לֶךְ הָאָ֑רֶץ הֲל֣וֹא לָזֶ֗ה יַעֲנ֤וּ בַמְּחֹלוֹת֙ לֵאמֹ֔ר

הִכָּ֤ה שָׁאוּל֙ באלפו בַּֽאֲלָפָ֔יו וְדָוִ֖ד ברבבתו בְּרִֽבְבֹתָֽיו׃

¹³ וַיָּ֧שֶׂם דָּוִ֛ד אֶת־הַדְּבָרִ֥ים הָאֵ֖לֶּה בִּלְבָב֑וֹ וַיִּרָ֣א מְאֹ֔ד מִפְּנֵ֖י אָכִ֥ישׁ מֶֽלֶךְ־גַּֽת׃ ¹⁴ וַיְשַׁנּ֤וֹ אֶת־טַעְמוֹ֙ בְּעֵ֣ינֵיהֶ֔ם וַיִּתְהֹלֵ֖ל בְּיָדָ֑ם ויתו וַיְתָ֗ו עַל־דַּלְת֣וֹת הַשַּׁ֔עַר וַיּ֥וֹרֶד רִירוֹ֖ אֶל־זְקָנֽוֹ׃ ¹⁵ וַיֹּ֥אמֶר אָכִ֖ישׁ אֶל־עֲבָדָ֑יו הִנֵּ֤ה תִרְאוּ֙ אִ֣ישׁ מִשְׁתַּגֵּ֔עַ לָ֛מָּה תָּבִ֥יאוּ אֹת֖וֹ אֵלָֽי׃ ¹⁶ חֲסַ֤ר מְשֻׁגָּעִים֙ אָ֔נִי כִּי־הֲבֵאתֶ֣ם אֶת־זֶ֔ה לְהִשְׁתַּגֵּ֖עַ עָלָ֑י הֲזֶ֖ה יָב֥וֹא אֶל־בֵּיתִֽי׃ ס

כב וַיֵּ֤לֶךְ דָּוִד֙ מִשָּׁ֔ם וַיִּמָּלֵ֖ט אֶל־מְעָרַ֣ת עֲדֻלָּ֑ם וַיִּשְׁמְע֤וּ אֶחָיו֙ וְכׇל־בֵּ֣ית אָבִ֔יו וַיֵּרְד֥וּ אֵלָ֖יו שָֽׁמָּה׃ ² וַיִּֽתְקַבְּצ֣וּ אֵלָ֡יו כׇּל־אִ֣ישׁ מָצוֹק֩ וְכׇל־אִ֨ישׁ אֲשֶׁר־ל֤וֹ נֹשֶׁא֙

---

d-d   I.e., excluded from the shrine, perhaps because of ritual impurity.

e-e   Meaning of Heb. uncertain.

f-f   Lit. "in their hand"; meaning of Heb. uncertain.

a   The "cave" in v. 1 is referred to as "stronghold" in vv. 4–5; cf. the same variation in 2 Sam. 23.13–14; 1 Chron. 11.15–16.

was desperate joined him, and he became their leader; there were about four hundred men with him. [3]David went from there to Mizpeh of Moab, and he said to the king of Moab, "Let my father and mother come [and stay] with you, until I know what God will do for me." [4]So he [b]-led them to-[b] the king of Moab, and they stayed with him as long as David remained in the stronghold.[a] [5]But the prophet Gad said to David, "Do not stay in the stronghold; go at once to the territory of Judah." So David left and went to the forest of Hereth.

[6]When Saul heard that David and the men with him had been located—Saul was then in Gibeah, sitting under the tamarisk tree on the height, spear in hand, with all his courtiers in attendance upon him—[7]Saul said to the courtiers standing about him, "Listen, men of Benjamin! Will the son of Jesse[c] give fields and vineyards to every one of you? And will he make all of you captains of thousands or captains of hundreds? [8]Is that why all of you have conspired against me? For no one informs me when my own son makes a pact with the son of Jesse; no one is concerned[d] for me and no one informs me when my own son has set my servant [e]-in ambush-[e] against me, as is now the case."

[9]Doeg the Edomite, who was standing among the courtiers of Saul, spoke up: "I saw the son of Jesse come to Ahimelech son of Ahitub at Nob. [10]He inquired of the LORD on his behalf and gave him provisions; he also gave him the sword of Goliath the Philistine." [11]Thereupon the king sent for the priest Ahimelech son of Ahitub and for all the priests belonging to his father's house at Nob. They all came to the king, [12]and Saul said, "Listen to me, son[c] of Ahitub." "Yes, my lord," he replied. [13]And Saul said to him, "Why have you and the son of Jesse con-

וְכָל־אִישׁ מַר־נֶפֶשׁ וַיְהִי עֲלֵיהֶם לְשָׂר וַיִּהְיוּ עִמּוֹ כְּאַרְבַּע מֵאוֹת אִישׁ: 3 וַיֵּלֶךְ דָּוִד מִשָּׁם מִצְפֵּה מוֹאָב וַיֹּאמֶר ׀ אֶל־מֶלֶךְ מוֹאָב יֵצֵא־נָא אָבִי וְאִמִּי אִתְּכֶם עַד אֲשֶׁר אֵדַע מַה־יַּעֲשֶׂה־לִּי אֱלֹהִים: 4 וַיַּנְחֵם אֶת־פְּנֵי מֶלֶךְ מוֹאָב וַיֵּשְׁבוּ עִמּוֹ כָּל־יְמֵי הֱיוֹת־דָּוִד בַּמְּצוּדָה: ס 5 וַיֹּאמֶר גָּד הַנָּבִיא אֶל־דָּוִד לֹא תֵשֵׁב בַּמְּצוּדָה לֵךְ וּבָאתָ־לְּךָ אֶרֶץ יְהוּדָה וַיֵּלֶךְ דָּוִד וַיָּבֹא יַעַר חָרֶת: ס

6 וַיִּשְׁמַע שָׁאוּל כִּי נוֹדַע דָּוִד וַאֲנָשִׁים אֲשֶׁר אִתּוֹ וְשָׁאוּל יוֹשֵׁב בַּגִּבְעָה תַּחַת־הָאֶשֶׁל בָּרָמָה וַחֲנִיתוֹ בְיָדוֹ וְכָל־עֲבָדָיו נִצָּבִים עָלָיו: 7 וַיֹּאמֶר שָׁאוּל לַעֲבָדָיו הַנִּצָּבִים עָלָיו שִׁמְעוּ־נָא בְּנֵי יְמִינִי גַּם־לְכֻלְּכֶם יִתֵּן בֶּן־יִשַׁי שָׂדוֹת וּכְרָמִים לְכֻלְּכֶם יָשִׂים שָׂרֵי אֲלָפִים וְשָׂרֵי מֵאוֹת: 8 כִּי קְשַׁרְתֶּם כֻּלְּכֶם עָלַי וְאֵין־גֹּלֶה אֶת־אָזְנִי בִּכְרָת־בְּנִי עִם־בֶּן־יִשַׁי וְאֵין־חֹלֶה מִכֶּם עָלַי וְגֹלֶה אֶת־אָזְנִי כִּי הֵקִים בְּנִי אֶת־עַבְדִּי עָלַי לְאֹרֵב כַּיּוֹם הַזֶּה: ס

9 וַיַּעַן דֹּאֵג הָאֲדֹמִי וְהוּא נִצָּב עַל־עַבְדֵי־שָׁאוּל וַיֹּאמַר רָאִיתִי אֶת־בֶּן־יִשַׁי בָּא נֹבֶה אֶל־אֲחִימֶלֶךְ בֶּן־אֲחִטוּב: 10 וַיִּשְׁאַל־לוֹ בַּיהוָה וְצֵידָה נָתַן לוֹ וְאֵת חֶרֶב גָּלְיָת הַפְּלִשְׁתִּי נָתַן לוֹ: 11 וַיִּשְׁלַח הַמֶּלֶךְ לִקְרֹא אֶת־אֲחִימֶלֶךְ בֶּן־אֲחִיטוּב הַכֹּהֵן וְאֵת כָּל־בֵּית אָבִיו הַכֹּהֲנִים אֲשֶׁר בְּנֹב וַיָּבֹאוּ כֻלָּם אֶל־הַמֶּלֶךְ: ס 12 וַיֹּאמֶר שָׁאוּל שְׁמַע־נָא בֶּן־אֲחִיטוּב וַיֹּאמֶר הִנְנִי אֲדֹנִי: 13 וַיֹּאמֶר אֵלָו אֵלָיו שָׁאוּל לָמָּה קְשַׁרְתֶּם עָלַי אַתָּה וּבֶן־יִשַׁי בְּתִתְּךָ לוֹ לֶחֶם וְחֶרֶב

---

b-b Targum and Syriac read "left them with."
c See note at 10.11.
d For this meaning of ḥoleh, cf. Amos 6.6.
e-e Septuagint reads "as an enemy."

spired against me? You gave him food and a sword, and inquired of God for him—that he may rise *e-in ambush-e* against me, as is now the case."

14Ahimelech replied to the king, "But who is there among all your courtiers as trusted as David, son-in-law of Your Majesty and *f-obedient to your bidding,-f* and esteemed in your household? 15This is the first time that I inquired of God for him; *g-I have done no wrong.-g* Let not Your Majesty find fault with his servant [or] with any of my father's house; for your servant knew nothing whatever about all this." 16But the king said, "You shall die, Ahimelech, you and all your father's house." 17And the king commanded the guards standing by, "Turn about and kill the priests of the LORD, for they are in league with David; they knew he was running away and they did not inform me." But the king's servants would not raise a hand to strike down the priests of the LORD. 18Thereupon the king said to Doeg, "You, Doeg, go and strike down the priests." And Doeg the Edomite went and struck down the priests himself; that day, he killed eighty-five men *h-who wore the linen ephod.-h* 19He put Nob, the town of the priests, to the sword: men and women, children and infants, oxen, asses, and sheep—[all] to the sword.

20But one son of Ahimelech son of Ahitub escaped—his name was Abiathar—and he fled to David. 21When Abiathar told David that Saul had killed the priests of the LORD, 22David said to Abiathar, "I knew that day, when Doeg the Edomite was there, that he would tell Saul. I *i-am to blame for all the deaths-i* in your father's house. 23Stay with me; do not be afraid; for *i-whoever seeks your life must seek my life also.-i* It will be my care to guard you."

---

f-f Cf. Isa. 11.14; but meaning of Heb. uncertain.
g-g Lit. "Far be it from me!"
h-h Septuagint reads "bearers of the ephod"; cf. note at 2.28.
i-i Meaning of Heb. uncertain.

וְשָׁא֣וּל ל֣וֹ בֵֽאלֹהִ֗ים לָק֥וּם אֵלַ֛י לְאֹרֵ֖ב כַּיּ֥וֹם הַזֶּֽה׃ ס
14 וַיַּ֨עַן אֲחִימֶ֜לֶךְ אֶת־הַמֶּ֣לֶךְ וַיֹּאמַ֔ר וּמִ֤י בְכָל־עֲבָדֶ֙יךָ֙ כְּדָוִ֣ד נֶאֱמָ֔ן וַחֲתַ֥ן הַמֶּ֖לֶךְ וְסָ֣ר אֶל־מִשְׁמַעְתֶּ֑ךָ וְנִכְבָּ֖ד בְּבֵיתֶֽךָ׃ 15 הַיּ֧וֹם הַחִלֹּ֛תִי לִשְׁאָול־ל֥וֹ בֵאלֹהִ֖ים חָלִ֣ילָה לִּ֑י אַל־יָשֵׂם֩ הַמֶּ֨לֶךְ בְּעַבְדּ֤וֹ דָבָר֙ בְּכָל־בֵּ֣ית אָבִ֔י כִּ֠י לֹֽא־יָדַ֤ע עַבְדְּךָ֙ בְּכָל־זֹ֔את דָּבָ֥ר קָטֹ֖ן א֥וֹ גָדֽוֹל׃ 16 וַיֹּ֣אמֶר הַמֶּ֔לֶךְ מ֥וֹת תָּמ֖וּת אֲחִימֶ֑לֶךְ אַתָּ֖ה וְכָל־בֵּ֥ית אָבִֽיךָ׃ 17 וַיֹּ֣אמֶר הַמֶּ֡לֶךְ לָרָצִים֩ הַנִּצָּבִ֨ים עָלָ֜יו סֹ֥בּוּ וְהָמִ֣יתוּ ׀ כֹּהֲנֵ֣י יְהוָ֗ה כִּ֤י גַם־יָדָם֙ עִם־דָּוִ֔ד וְכִ֤י יָֽדְעוּ֙ כִּֽי־בֹרֵ֣חַ ה֔וּא וְלֹ֥א גָל֖וּ אֶת־*אזנו* אָזְנִ֑י וְלֹֽא־אָב֞וּ עַבְדֵ֤י הַמֶּ֙לֶךְ֙ לִשְׁלֹ֣חַ אֶת־יָדָ֔ם לִפְגֹ֖עַ בְּכֹהֲנֵ֥י יְהוָֽה׃ ס
18 וַיֹּ֤אמֶר הַמֶּ֙לֶךְ֙ *לדויג* לְדוֹאֵ֔ג סֹ֣ב אַתָּ֔ה וּפְגַ֖ע בַּכֹּהֲנִ֑ים וַיִּסֹּ֞ב *דויג* דּוֹאֵ֣ג הָאֲדֹמִ֗י וַיִּפְגַּע־הוּא֙ בַּכֹּ֣הֲנִ֔ים וַיָּ֣מֶת ׀ בַּיּ֣וֹם הַה֗וּא שְׁמֹנִ֤ים וַחֲמִשָּׁה֙ אִ֔ישׁ נֹשֵׂ֖א אֵפ֥וֹד בָּֽד׃ 19 וְאֵ֨ת נֹ֤ב עִיר־הַכֹּֽהֲנִים֙ הִכָּ֣ה לְפִי־חֶ֔רֶב מֵאִישׁ֙ וְעַד־אִשָּׁ֔ה מֵעֹולֵ֖ל וְעַד־יוֹנֵ֑ק וְשׁ֥וֹר וַחֲמ֖וֹר וָשֶׂ֥ה לְפִי־חָֽרֶב׃
20 וַיִּמָּלֵ֣ט בֵּן־אֶחָ֗ד לַאֲחִימֶ֙לֶךְ֙ בֶּן־אֲחִט֔וּב וּשְׁמ֖וֹ אֶבְיָתָ֑ר וַיִּבְרַ֖ח אַחֲרֵ֥י דָוִֽד׃ 21 וַיַּגֵּ֥ד אֶבְיָתָ֖ר לְדָוִ֑ד כִּ֚י הָרַ֣ג שָׁא֔וּל אֵ֖ת כֹּהֲנֵ֥י יְהוָֽה׃ 22 וַיֹּ֨אמֶר דָּוִ֜ד לְאֶבְיָתָ֗ר יָדַ֜עְתִּי בַּיּ֤וֹם הַהוּא֙ כִּֽי־שָׁ֣ם *דויג* דּוֹאֵ֣ג הָֽאֲדֹמִ֔י כִּֽי־הַגֵּ֥ד יַגִּ֖יד לְשָׁא֑וּל אָנֹכִ֣י סַבֹּ֔תִי בְּכָל־נֶ֖פֶשׁ בֵּ֥ית אָבִֽיךָ׃ 23 שְׁבָ֤ה אִתִּי֙ אַל־תִּירָ֔א כִּ֛י אֲשֶׁר־יְבַקֵּ֥שׁ אֶת־נַפְשִׁ֖י יְבַקֵּ֣שׁ אֶת־נַפְשֶׁ֑ךָ כִּֽי־מִשְׁמֶ֥רֶת אַתָּ֖ה עִמָּדִֽי׃

23

David was told: "The Philistines are raiding Keilah and plundering the threshing floors." ²David consulted the LORD, "Shall I go and attack those Philistines?" And the LORD said to David, "Go; attack the Philistines and you will save Keilah." ³But David's men said to him, "Look, we are afraid here in Judah, how much more if we go to Keilah against the forces of the Philistines!" ⁴So David consulted the LORD again, and the LORD answered him, "March down at once to Keilah, for I am going to deliver the Philistines into your hands." ⁵David and his men went to Keilah and fought against the Philistines; he drove off their cattle and inflicted a severe defeat on them. Thus David saved the inhabitants of Keilah.

⁶When Abiathar son of Ahimelech fled to David at Keilah, ᵃ-he brought down an ephod with him.-ᵃ

⁷Saul was told that David had come to Keilah, and Saul thought, "God has deliveredᵃ him into my hands, for he has shut himself in by entering a town with gates and bars." ⁸Saul summoned all the troops for war, to go down to Keilah and besiege David and his men. ⁹When David learned that Saul was planningᵃ to harm him, he told the priest Abiathar to bring the ephod forward. ¹⁰And David said, "O LORD, God of Israel, Your servant has heard that Saul intends to come to Keilah and destroy the town because of me. ¹¹Will the citizens of Keilah deliver me into his hands? Will Saul come down, as Your servant has heard? O LORD, God of Israel, tell Your servant!" And the LORD said, "He will." ¹²David continued, "Will the citizens of Keilah deliver me and my men into Saul's hands?" And the LORD answered, "They will." ¹³So David and his men, about six hundred in number, left Keilah at once and moved about wherever they

---

a-a Meaning of Heb. uncertain.

כג וַיַּגִּדוּ לְדָוִד לֵאמֹר הִנֵּה פְלִשְׁתִּים נִלְחָמִים בִּקְעִילָה וְהֵמָּה שֹׁסִים אֶת־הַגֳּרָנוֹת: 2 וַיִּשְׁאַל דָּוִד בַּיהוָה לֵאמֹר הַאֵלֵךְ וְהִכֵּיתִי בַּפְּלִשְׁתִּים הָאֵלֶּה ס וַיֹּאמֶר יְהוָה אֶל־דָּוִד לֵךְ וְהִכִּיתָ בַפְּלִשְׁתִּים וְהוֹשַׁעְתָּ אֶת־קְעִילָה: 3 וַיֹּאמְרוּ אַנְשֵׁי דָוִד אֵלָיו הִנֵּה אֲנַחְנוּ פֹה בִיהוּדָה יְרֵאִים וְאַף כִּי־נֵלֵךְ קְעִלָה אֶל־מַעַרְכוֹת פְּלִשְׁתִּים: ס 4 וַיּוֹסֶף עוֹד דָּוִד לִשְׁאֹל בַּיהוָה ס וַיַּעֲנֵהוּ יְהוָה וַיֹּאמֶר קוּם רֵד קְעִילָה כִּי־אֲנִי נֹתֵן אֶת־פְּלִשְׁתִּים בְּיָדֶךָ: 5 וַיֵּלֶךְ דָּוִד וַאֲנָשָׁו קְעִילָה וַיִּלָּחֶם בַּפְּלִשְׁתִּים וַיִּנְהַג אֶת־מִקְנֵיהֶם וַיַּךְ בָּהֶם מַכָּה גְדוֹלָה וַיֹּשַׁע דָּוִד אֵת יֹשְׁבֵי קְעִילָה: ס

6 וַיְהִי בִּבְרֹחַ אֶבְיָתָר בֶּן־אֲחִימֶלֶךְ אֶל־דָּוִד קְעִילָה אֵפוֹד יָרַד בְּיָדוֹ: 7 וַיֻּגַּד לְשָׁאוּל כִּי־בָא דָוִד קְעִילָה וַיֹּאמֶר שָׁאוּל נִכַּר אֹתוֹ אֱלֹהִים בְּיָדִי כִּי נִסְגַּר לָבוֹא בְּעִיר דְּלָתַיִם וּבְרִיחַ: 8 וַיְשַׁמַּע שָׁאוּל אֶת־כָּל־הָעָם לַמִּלְחָמָה לָרֶדֶת קְעִילָה לָצוּר אֶל־דָּוִד וְאֶל־אֲנָשָׁיו: 9 וַיֵּדַע דָּוִד כִּי עָלָיו שָׁאוּל מַחֲרִישׁ הָרָעָה וַיֹּאמֶר אֶל־אֶבְיָתָר הַכֹּהֵן הַגִּישָׁה הָאֵפוֹד: ס 10 וַיֹּאמֶר דָּוִד יְהוָה אֱלֹהֵי יִשְׂרָאֵל שָׁמֹעַ שָׁמַע עַבְדְּךָ כִּי־מְבַקֵּשׁ שָׁאוּל לָבוֹא אֶל־קְעִילָה לְשַׁחֵת לָעִיר בַּעֲבוּרִי: 11 הֲיַסְגִּרֻנִי בַעֲלֵי קְעִילָה בְיָדוֹ הֲיֵרֵד שָׁאוּל כַּאֲשֶׁר שָׁמַע עַבְדֶּךָ יְהוָה אֱלֹהֵי יִשְׂרָאֵל הַגֶּד־נָא לְעַבְדֶּךָ ס וַיֹּאמֶר יְהוָה יֵרֵד: 12 וַיֹּאמֶר דָּוִד הֲיַסְגִּרוּ בַּעֲלֵי קְעִילָה אֹתִי וְאֶת־אֲנָשַׁי בְּיַד־שָׁאוּל וַיֹּאמֶר יְהוָה יַסְגִּירוּ: ס 13 וַיָּקָם דָּוִד וַאֲנָשָׁיו כְּשֵׁשׁ־מֵאוֹת אִישׁ וַיֵּצְאוּ מִקְּעִלָה וַיִּתְהַלְּכוּ בַּאֲשֶׁר יִתְהַלָּכוּ

could. And when Saul was told that David had got away from Keilah, he did not set out.

[14] David was staying *-in the strongholds of the wilderness [of Judah];-* he stayed in the hill country, in the wilderness of Ziph. Saul searched for him constantly, but God did not deliver him into his hands. [15] David was once at Horesh in the wilderness of Ziph, when David learned that Saul had come out to seek his life. [16] And Saul's son Jonathan came to David at Horesh and encouraged him in [the name of] God. [17] He said to him, "Do not be afraid: the hand of my father Saul will never touch you. You are going to be king over Israel and I shall be second to you; and even my father Saul knows this is so." [18] And the two of them entered into a pact before the LORD. David remained in Horesh, and Jonathan went home.

[19] *b* Some Ziphites went up to Saul in Gibeah and said, "David is hiding among us in the strongholds of Horesh, at the hill of Hachilah south of Jeshimon. [20] So if Your Majesty has the desire to come down, come down, and it will be our task to deliver him into Your Majesty's hands." [21] And Saul replied, "May you be blessed of the LORD for the compassion you have shown me! [22] Go now and prepare further. Look around and learn what places he sets foot on [and] who has seen him there, for I have been told he is a very cunning fellow. [23] Look around and learn in which of all his hiding places he has been hiding, and return to me when you are certain. I will then go with you, and if he is in the region, I will search him out among all the clans of Judah."

[24] They left at once for Ziph, ahead of Saul; David and his men were then in the wilderness of Maon, in the Arabah, to the south of Jeshimon. [25] When Saul and his men came to search, David was told about it; and he went

וּלְשָׁאוּל הֻגַּד כִּי־נִמְלַט דָּוִד מִקְּעִילָה וַיֶּחְדַּל לָצֵאת: [14] וַיֵּשֶׁב דָּוִד בַּמִּדְבָּר בַּמְּצָדוֹת וַיֵּשֶׁב בָּהָר בְּמִדְבַּר־זִיף וַיְבַקְשֵׁהוּ שָׁאוּל כָּל־הַיָּמִים וְלֹא־נְתָנוֹ אֱלֹהִים בְּיָדוֹ: [15] וַיַּרְא דָּוִד כִּי־יָצָא שָׁאוּל לְבַקֵּשׁ אֶת־נַפְשׁוֹ וְדָוִד בְּמִדְבַּר־זִיף בַּחֹרְשָׁה: ס [16] וַיָּקָם יְהוֹנָתָן בֶּן־שָׁאוּל וַיֵּלֶךְ אֶל־דָּוִד חֹרְשָׁה וַיְחַזֵּק אֶת־יָדוֹ בֵּאלֹהִים: [17] וַיֹּאמֶר אֵלָיו אַל־תִּירָא כִּי לֹא תִמְצָאֲךָ יַד שָׁאוּל אָבִי וְאַתָּה תִּמְלֹךְ עַל־יִשְׂרָאֵל וְאָנֹכִי אֶהְיֶה־לְּךָ לְמִשְׁנֶה וְגַם־שָׁאוּל אָבִי יֹדֵעַ כֵּן: [18] וַיִּכְרְתוּ שְׁנֵיהֶם בְּרִית לִפְנֵי יְהוָה וַיֵּשֶׁב דָּוִד בַּחֹרְשָׁה וִיהוֹנָתָן הָלַךְ לְבֵיתוֹ: ס [19] וַיַּעֲלוּ זִפִים אֶל־שָׁאוּל הַגִּבְעָתָה לֵאמֹר הֲלוֹא דָוִד מִסְתַּתֵּר עִמָּנוּ בַמְּצָדוֹת בַּחֹרְשָׁה בְּגִבְעַת הַחֲכִילָה אֲשֶׁר מִימִין הַיְשִׁימוֹן: [20] וְעַתָּה לְכָל־אַוַּת נַפְשְׁךָ הַמֶּלֶךְ לָרֶדֶת רֵד וְלָנוּ הַסְגִּירוֹ בְּיַד הַמֶּלֶךְ: [21] וַיֹּאמֶר שָׁאוּל בְּרוּכִים אַתֶּם לַיהוָה כִּי חֲמַלְתֶּם עָלָי: [22] לְכוּ־נָא הָכִינוּ עוֹד וּדְעוּ וּרְאוּ אֶת־מְקוֹמוֹ אֲשֶׁר תִּהְיֶה רַגְלוֹ מִי רָאָהוּ שָׁם כִּי אָמַר אֵלַי עָרוֹם יַעְרִם הוּא: [23] וּרְאוּ וּדְעוּ מִכֹּל הַמַּחֲבֹאִים אֲשֶׁר יִתְחַבֵּא שָׁם וְשַׁבְתֶּם אֵלַי אֶל־נָכוֹן וְהָלַכְתִּי אִתְּכֶם וְהָיָה אִם־יֶשְׁנוֹ בָאָרֶץ וְחִפַּשְׂתִּי אֹתוֹ בְּכֹל אַלְפֵי יְהוּדָה: [24] וַיָּקוּמוּ וַיֵּלְכוּ זִיפָה לִפְנֵי שָׁאוּל וְדָוִד וַאֲנָשָׁיו בְּמִדְבַּר מָעוֹן בָּעֲרָבָה אֶל יְמִין הַיְשִׁימוֹן: [25] וַיֵּלֶךְ שָׁאוּל וַאֲנָשָׁיו לְבַקֵּשׁ וַיַּגִּדוּ לְדָוִד וַיֵּרֶד הַסֶּלַע וַיֵּשֶׁב בְּמִדְבַּר

---

b *The meaning of many parts of 23.19 ff. is uncertain. The events described in 23.19–24.22 are partly paralleled in chapter 26, with variations.*

down to *a*-the rocky region-*a* and stayed in the wilderness of Maon. On hearing this, Saul pursued David in the wilderness of Maon. 26Saul was making his way along one side of a hill, and David and his men were on the other side of the hill. *a*-David was trying hard to elude Saul, and Saul and his men were trying to encircle David and his men and capture them,-*a* 27when a messenger came and told Saul, "Come quickly, for the Philistines have invaded the land." 28Saul gave up his pursuit of David and went to meet the Philistines. That is why that place came to be called the Rock of Separation.*a*

24 David went from there and stayed in the wildernesses of En-gedi.

2When Saul returned from pursuing the Philistines, he was told that David was in the wilderness of En-gedi. 3So Saul took three thousand picked men from all Israel and went in search of David and his men *a*-in the direction of the rocks of the wild goats;-*a* 4and he came to the sheepfolds along the way. There was a cave there, and Saul went in *b*-to relieve himself.-*b* Now David and his men were sitting in the back of the cave.

5David's men said to him, "This is the day of which the LORD said to you, 'I will deliver your enemy into your hands; you can do with him as you please.'" *c*David went and stealthily cut off the corner of Saul's cloak. 6But afterward *d*-David reproached himself-*d* for cutting off *e*-the corner of Saul's cloak.-*e* 7He said to his men, "The LORD forbid that I should do such a thing to my lord—the LORD's anointed—that I should raise my hand against him; for he is the LORD's anointed." 8David rebuked*d* his men and did not permit them to attack Saul.

---

a-a Meaning of Heb. uncertain.
b-b Lit. "to cover his feet."
c Vv. 5b–6 read well after 8a.
d-d Lit. "David's heart struck him."
e-e So several mss. and ancient versions; cf. v. 5. Most mss. and editions read "Saul's corner."

מָע֑וֹן וַיִּשְׁמַ֣ע שָׁא֔וּל וַיִּרְדֹּ֥ף אַחֲרֵי־דָוִ֖ד מִדְבַּ֥ר מָעֽוֹן׃ 26 וַיֵּ֨לֶךְ שָׁא֜וּל מִצַּ֤ד הָהָר֙ מִזֶּ֔ה וְדָוִ֧ד וַאֲנָשָׁ֛יו מִצַּ֥ד הָהָ֖ר מִזֶּ֑ה וַיְהִ֣י דָוִ֗ד נֶחְפָּז֙ לָלֶ֣כֶת מִפְּנֵ֣י שָׁא֔וּל וְשָׁא֣וּל וַאֲנָשָׁ֗יו עֹֽטְרִ֛ים אֶל־דָּוִ֥ד וְאֶל־אֲנָשָׁ֖יו לְתָפְשָֽׂם׃ 27 וּמַלְאָ֣ךְ בָּ֔א אֶל־שָׁא֖וּל לֵאמֹ֑ר מַהֲרָ֣ה וְלֵ֔כָה כִּֽי־פָשְׁט֥וּ פְלִשְׁתִּ֖ים עַל־הָאָֽרֶץ׃ 28 וַיָּ֣שׇׁב שָׁא֗וּל מִרְדֹף֙ אַחֲרֵ֣י דָוִ֔ד וַיֵּ֖לֶךְ לִקְרַ֣את פְּלִשְׁתִּ֑ים עַל־כֵּ֗ן קָֽרְאוּ֙ לַמָּק֣וֹם הַה֔וּא סֶ֖לַע הַֽמַּחְלְקֽוֹת׃

כד וַיַּ֣עַל דָּוִ֔ד מִשָּׁ֑ם וַיֵּ֖שֶׁב בִּמְצָד֥וֹת עֵֽין־גֶּֽדִי׃ 2 וַיְהִ֗י כַּֽאֲשֶׁר֙ שָׁ֣ב שָׁא֔וּל מֵאַחֲרֵ֖י פְּלִשְׁתִּ֑ים וַיַּגִּ֤דוּ לוֹ֙ לֵאמֹ֔ר הִנֵּ֣ה דָוִ֔ד בְּמִדְבַּ֖ר עֵ֥ין גֶּֽדִי׃ ס 3 וַיִּקַּ֣ח שָׁא֗וּל שְׁלֹ֧שֶׁת אֲלָפִ֛ים אִ֥ישׁ בָּח֖וּר מִכׇּל־יִשְׂרָאֵ֑ל וַיֵּ֗לֶךְ לְבַקֵּ֤שׁ אֶת־דָּוִד֙ וַֽאֲנָשָׁ֔יו עַל־פְּנֵ֖י צוּרֵ֥י הַיְּעֵלִֽים׃ 4 וַ֠יָּבֹ֠א אֶל־גִּדְר֨וֹת הַצֹּ֤אן עַל־הַדֶּ֙רֶךְ֙ וְשָׁ֣ם מְעָרָ֔ה וַיָּבֹ֥א שָׁא֖וּל לְהָסֵ֣ךְ אֶת־רַגְלָ֑יו וְדָוִד֙ וַאֲנָשָׁ֔יו בְּיַרְכְּתֵ֥י הַמְּעָרָ֖ה יֹשְׁבִֽים׃

5 וַיֹּֽאמְרוּ֩ אַנְשֵׁ֨י דָוִ֜ד אֵלָ֗יו הִנֵּ֨ה הַיּ֜וֹם אֲֽשֶׁר־אָמַ֧ר יְהֹוָ֣ה אֵלֶ֗יךָ הִנֵּ֨ה אָנֹכִ֜י נֹתֵ֤ן אֶת־*אֹיִבְיךָ* בְּיָדֶ֔ךָ וְעָשִׂ֣יתָ לּ֔וֹ כַּאֲשֶׁ֖ר יִטַ֣ב בְּעֵינֶ֑יךָ וַיָּ֣קׇם דָּוִ֗ד וַיִּכְרֹ֛ת אֶת־כְּנַף־הַמְּעִ֥יל אֲשֶׁר־לְשָׁא֖וּל בַּלָּֽט׃ 6 וַֽיְהִי֙ אַֽחֲרֵי־כֵ֔ן וַיַּ֥ךְ לֵב־דָּוִ֖ד אֹת֑וֹ עַ֚ל אֲשֶׁ֣ר כָּרַ֔ת אֶת־כָּנָ֖ף* אֲשֶׁ֥ר לְשָׁאֽוּל׃ ס 7 וַיֹּ֨אמֶר לַאֲנָשָׁ֜יו חָלִ֧ילָה לִּ֣י מֵֽיהֹוָ֗ה אִם־אֶעֱשֶׂה֩ אֶת־הַדָּבָ֨ר הַזֶּ֤ה לַֽאדֹנִי֙ לִמְשִׁ֣יחַ יְהֹוָ֔ה לִשְׁלֹ֥חַ יָדִ֖י בּ֑וֹ כִּֽי־מְשִׁ֥יחַ יְהֹוָ֖ה הֽוּא׃ 8 וַיְשַׁסַּ֨ע דָּוִ֤ד אֶת־אֲנָשָׁיו֙ בַּדְּבָרִ֔ים וְלֹ֥א נְתָנָ֖ם לָק֣וּם אֶל־שָׁא֑וּל

Saul left the cave and started on his way. ⁹Then David also went out of the cave and called after Saul, "My lord king!" Saul looked around and David bowed low in homage, with his face to the ground. ¹⁰And David said to Saul, "Why do you listen to the people who say, 'David is out to do you harm?' ¹¹You can see for yourself now that the LORD delivered you into my hands in the cave today. And though *a*-I was urged-*a* to kill you, I showed you pity;*f* for I said, 'I will not raise a hand against my lord, since he is the LORD's anointed.' ¹²Please, sir,*g* take a close look at the corner of your cloak in my hand; for when I cut off the corner of your cloak, I did not kill you. You must see plainly that I have done nothing evil or rebellious, and I have never wronged you. Yet you are bent on taking my life. ¹³May the LORD judge between you and me! And may He take vengeance upon you for me, but my hand will never touch you. ¹⁴As the ancient proverb has it: 'Wicked deeds come from wicked men!' My hand will never touch you. ¹⁵Against whom has the king of Israel come out? Whom are you pursuing? A dead dog? A single flea? ¹⁶May the LORD be arbiter and may He judge between you and me! May He take note and uphold my cause, and vindicate me against you."

¹⁷When David finished saying these things to Saul, Saul said, "Is that your voice, my son David?" And Saul broke down and wept. ¹⁸He said to David, "You are right, not I; for you have treated me generously, but I have treated you badly. ¹⁹Yes, you have just revealed how generously you treated me, for the LORD delivered me into your hands and you did not kill me. ²⁰If a man meets his enemy, does he let him go his way unharmed? Surely, the LORD will reward you generously for *h*-what you have done for me

ס וְשָׁא֗וּל קָ֚ם מֵֽהַמְּעָרָ֔ה וַיֵּ֖לֶךְ בַּדָּֽרֶךְ׃
⁹וַיָּ֚קָם דָּוִד֙ אַֽחֲרֵי־כֵ֔ן וַיֵּצֵא֙ מִן־הַמְּעָרָ֔ה וַיִּקְרָ֚א אַֽחֲרֵי־שָׁאוּל֙ לֵאמֹ֔ר אֲדֹנִ֖י הַמֶּ֑לֶךְ וַיַּבֵּ֚ט שָׁאוּל֙ אַֽחֲרָ֔יו וַיִּקֹּ֨ד דָּוִ֧ד אַפַּ֛יִם אַ֖רְצָה וַיִּשְׁתָּֽחוּ׃ ס ¹⁰וַיֹּ֚אמֶר דָּוִד֙ לְשָׁא֔וּל לָ֚מָּה תִשְׁמַע֙ אֶת־דִּבְרֵ֣י אָדָ֔ם לֵאמֹ֑ר הִנֵּ֚ה דָוִד֙ מְבַקֵּ֣שׁ רָֽעָתֶ֔ךָ׃ ¹¹הִנֵּה֩ הַיּ֨וֹם הַזֶּ֜ה רָא֣וּ עֵינֶ֗יךָ אֵ֣ת אֲשֶׁר־נְתָנְךָ֩ יְהֹוָ֨ה ׀ הַיּ֚וֹם ׀ בְּיָדִי֙ בַּמְּעָרָ֔ה וְאָמַ֖ר לַהֲרָגֶ֑ךָ וַתָּ֚חָס עָלֶ֙יךָ֙ וָאֹמַ֔ר לֹא־אֶשְׁלַ֥ח יָדִ֖י בַּֽאדֹנִ֑י כִּֽי־מְשִׁ֥יחַ יְהֹוָ֖ה הֽוּא׃ ¹²וְאָבִ֣י רְאֵ֗ה גַּ֣ם רְאֵ֞ה אֶת־כְּנַ֧ף מְעִֽילְךָ֛ בְּיָדִ֖י כִּ֣י בְּכָרְתִ֗י אֶת־כְּנַ֚ף מְעִֽילְךָ֙ וְלֹ֣א הֲרַגְתִּ֔יךָ דַּ֣ע וּרְאֵ֗ה כִּ֠י אֵ֣ין בְּיָדִ֞י רָעָ֚ה וָפֶ֙שַׁע֙ וְלֹֽא־חָטָ֣אתִי לָ֔ךְ וְאַתָּ֛ה צֹדֶ֥ה אֶת־נַפְשִׁ֖י לְקַחְתָּֽהּ׃ ¹³יִשְׁפֹּ֚ט יְהֹוָה֙ בֵּינִ֣י וּבֵינֶ֔ךָ וּנְקָמַ֥נִי יְהֹוָ֖ה מִמֶּ֑ךָּ וְיָדִ֖י לֹ֥א תִֽהְיֶה־בָּֽךְ׃ ¹⁴כַּֽאֲשֶׁ֣ר יֹאמַ֗ר מְשַׁל֙ הַקַּדְמֹנִ֔י מֵרְשָׁעִ֖ים יֵ֣צֵא רֶ֑שַׁע וְיָדִ֖י לֹ֥א תִֽהְיֶה־בָּֽךְ׃ ¹⁵אַֽחֲרֵ֨י מִ֚י יָצָא֙ מֶ֣לֶךְ יִשְׂרָאֵ֔ל אַֽחֲרֵ֥י מִ֖י אַתָּ֣ה רֹדֵ֑ף אַֽחֲרֵי֙ כֶּ֣לֶב מֵ֔ת אַֽחֲרֵ֖י פַּרְעֹ֥שׁ אֶחָֽד׃ ¹⁶וְהָיָ֚ה יְהֹוָה֙ לְדַיָּ֔ן וְשָׁפַ֖ט בֵּינִ֣י וּבֵינֶ֑ךָ וְיֵ֙רֶא֙ וְיָ֣רֶב אֶת־רִיבִ֔י וְיִשְׁפְּטֵ֖נִי מִיָּדֶֽךָ׃ פ

¹⁷וַיְהִ֣י ׀ כְּכַלּ֣וֹת דָּוִ֗ד לְדַבֵּ֞ר אֶת־הַדְּבָרִ֚ים הָאֵ֙לֶּה֙ אֶל־שָׁא֔וּל וַיֹּ֣אמֶר שָׁא֔וּל הֲקֹלְךָ֥ זֶ֖ה בְּנִ֣י דָוִ֑ד וַיִּשָּׂ֥א שָׁא֛וּל קֹל֖וֹ וַיֵּֽבְךְּ׃ ¹⁸וַיֹּ֙אמֶר֙ אֶל־דָּוִ֔ד צַדִּ֥יק אַתָּ֖ה מִמֶּ֑נִּי כִּ֚י אַתָּה֙ גְּמַלְתַּ֣נִי הַטּוֹבָ֔ה וַֽאֲנִ֖י גְּמַלְתִּ֥יךָ הָֽרָעָֽה׃ ¹⁹וְאַ֗תְּ וְאַתָּ֚ה הִגַּ֣דְתָּ הַיּ֔וֹם אֵ֚ת אֲשֶׁר־עָשִׂ֥יתָה אִתִּ֖י טוֹבָ֑ה אֵת֩ אֲשֶׁ֨ר סִגְּרַ֚נִי יְהֹוָה֙ בְּיָֽדְךָ֖ וְלֹ֥א הֲרַגְתָּֽנִי׃ ²⁰וְכִֽי־יִמְצָ֚א אִישׁ֙ אֶת־אֹ֣יְב֔וֹ וְשִׁלְּח֖וֹ בְּדֶ֣רֶךְ טוֹבָ֑ה וַֽיהֹוָה֙ יְשַׁלֶּמְךָ֣ טוֹבָ֔ה תַּ֚חַת הַיּ֣וֹם הַזֶּ֔ה אֲשֶׁ֥ר עָשִׂ֖יתָה לִֽי׃ ²¹וְעַתָּה֙ הִנֵּ֣ה יָדַ֔עְתִּי כִּ֥י מָלֹ֖ךְ

---

f   Understanding the Heb. as an ellipsis of wattaḥos 'eni (cf., e.g., Deut. 7.16).
g   Lit. "[my] father," cf. 2 Kings 5.13.
h-h   Meaning of Heb. uncertain. Emendation yields "the generosity you have shown me."

this day.‑h 21I know now that you will become king, and that the kingship over Israel will remain in your hands. 22So swear to me by the LORD that you will not destroy my descendants or wipe out my name from my father's house." 23David swore to Saul, Saul went home, and David and his men went up to the strongholds.

25 Samuel died, and all Israel gathered and made lament for him; and they buried him in Ramah, his home.

David went down to the wilderness of Paran.a

2There was a man in Maon whose possessions were in Carmel. The man was very wealthy; he owned three thousand sheep and a thousand goats. At the time, he was shearing his sheep in Carmel. 3The man's name was Nabal, and his wife's name was Abigail. The woman was intelligent and beautiful, but the man, a Calebite, was a hard man and an evildoer. 4David was in the wilderness when he heard that Nabal was shearing his sheep. 5David dispatched ten young men, and David instructed the young men, "Go up to Carmel. When you come to Nabal, greet him in my name. 6Say b‑as follows: 'To life!'‑b Greetings to you and to your household and to all that is yours! 7I hear that you are now doing your shearing. As you know, your shepherds have been with us; we did not harm them, and nothing of theirs was missing all the time they were in Carmel. 8Ask your young men and they will tell you. So receive these young men graciously, for we have come on a festive occasion. Please give your servants and your son David whatever you can.'"

9David's young men went and delivered this message to Nabal in the name of David. When they stopped speaking, 10Nabal answered David's servants, "Who is David? Who is the son

תִּמְלוֹךְ וְקָ֫מָה בְּיָדְךָ֫ מַמְלֶ֫כֶת יִשְׂרָאֵל׃ 22 וְעַתָּ֫ה הִשָּׁ֫בְעָה לִּי֫ בַּיהֹוָה אִם־תַּכְרִ֫ית אֶת־זַרְעִי֫ אַחֲרָ֫י וְאִם־תַּשְׁמִ֫יד אֶת־שְׁמִ֫י מִבֵּית אָבִי׃ 23 וַיִּשָּׁבַ֫ע דָּוִ֫ד לְשָׁא֫וּל וַיֵּ֫לֶךְ שָׁאוּל֫ אֶל־בֵּית֫וֹ וְדָוִד֫ וַאֲנָשָׁיו֫ עָלוּ עַל־הַמְּצוּדָֽה׃ פ

כה וַיָּ֫מׇת שְׁמוּאֵל֫ וַיִּקׇּבְצ֫וּ כׇל־יִשְׂרָאֵל֫ וַיִּסְפְּדוּ־לוֹ֫ וַיִּקְבְּרֻ֫הוּ בְּבֵית֫וֹ בָּרָמָ֫ה וַיָּ֫קׇם דָּוִד֫ וַיֵּ֫רֶד אֶל־מִדְבַּ֫ר פָּארָֽן׃ ס 2 וְאִ֫ישׁ בְּמָע֫וֹן וּמַעֲשֵׂ֫הוּ בַכַּרְמֶל֫ וְהָאִ֫ישׁ גָּד֫וֹל מְאֹ֫ד וְל֫וֹ צֹאן֫ שְׁלֹ֫שֶׁת־אֲלָפִים֫ וְאֶ֫לֶף עִזִּ֫ים וַיְהִ֫י בִּגְזֹ֫ז אֶת־צֹאנ֫וֹ בַּכַּרְמֶֽל׃ 3 וְשֵׁ֫ם הָאִ֫ישׁ נָבָ֫ל וְשֵׁ֫ם אִשְׁתּ֫וֹ אֲבִגַ֫יִל וְהָאִשָּׁ֫ה טֽוֹבַת־שֶׂ֫כֶל וִ֫יפַת תֹּ֫אַר וְהָאִ֫ישׁ קָשֶׁ֫ה וְרַ֫ע מַעֲלָלִ֫ים וְה֫וּא כָלִבִּֽי׃ 4 וַיִּשְׁמַ֫ע דָּוִ֫ד בַּמִּדְבָּ֫ר כִּי־גֹזֵ֫ז נָבָ֫ל אֶת־צֹאנֽוֹ׃ 5 וַיִּשְׁלַ֫ח דָּוִ֫ד עֲשָׂרָ֫ה נְעָרִ֫ים וַיֹּ֫אמֶר דָּוִד֫ לַנְּעָרִ֫ים עֲל֫וּ כַרְמֶ֫לָה וּבָאתֶ֫ם אֶל־נָבָ֫ל וּשְׁאֶלְתֶּם־ל֫וֹ בִשְׁמִ֫י לְשָׁלֽוֹם׃ 6 וַאֲמַרְתֶּ֫ם כֹּ֫ה לֶחָ֫י וְאַתָּ֫ה שָׁל֫וֹם וּבֵֽיתְךָ֫ שָׁל֫וֹם וְכֹ֫ל אֲשֶׁר־לְךָ֫ שָׁלֽוֹם׃ 7 וְעַתָּ֫ה שָׁמַ֫עְתִּי כִּ֫י גֹזְזִ֫ים לָ֫ךְ עַתָּ֫ה הָרֹעִ֫ים אֲשֶׁר־לְךָ֫ הָי֫וּ עִמָּ֫נוּ לֹ֫א הֶכְלַמְנ֫וּם וְלֹא־נִפְקַ֫ד לָהֶ֫ם מְא֫וּמָה כׇּל־יְמֵ֫י הֱיוֹתָ֫ם בַּכַּרְמֶֽל׃ 8 שְׁאַ֫ל אֶת־נְעָרֶ֫יךָ וְיַגִּ֫ידוּ לָ֫ךְ וְיִמְצְא֫וּ הַנְּעָרִ֫ים חֵ֫ן בְּעֵינֶ֫יךָ כִּֽי־עַל־י֫וֹם ט֫וֹב בָּ֫נוּ* תְּנָה־נָּ֫א אֵ֫ת אֲשֶׁר֫ תִּמְצָ֫א יָֽדְךָ֫ לַעֲבָדֶ֫יךָ וּלְבִנְךָ֫ לְדָוִֽד׃ 9 וַיָּבֹ֫אוּ נַעֲרֵ֫י דָוִ֫ד וַיְדַבְּר֫וּ אֶל־נָבָ֫ל כְּכׇל־הַדְּבָרִ֫ים הָאֵ֫לֶּה בְּשֵׁ֫ם דָּוִ֫ד וַיָּנֽוּחוּ׃ 10 וַיַּ֫עַן נָבָ֫ל אֶת־עַבְדֵ֫י דָוִד֫ וַיֹּ֫אמֶר מִ֫י דָוִ֫ד וּמִ֫י

חסר א׳ v. 8.

a Septuagint reads "Maon," cf. v. 2 and 23.24, 25.
b-b Meaning of Heb. uncertain.

of Jesse? There are many slaves nowadays who run away from their masters. [11]Should I then take my bread and my water,[c] and the meat that I slaughtered for my own shearers, and give them to men who come from I don't know where?" [12]Thereupon David's young men retraced their steps; and when they got back, they told him all this. [13]And David said to his men, "Gird on your swords." Each girded on his sword; David too girded on his sword. About four hundred men went up after David, while two hundred remained with the baggage.

[14]One of [Nabal's] young men told Abigail, Nabal's wife, that David had sent messengers from the wilderness to greet their master, and that he had spurned[b] them. [15]"But the men had been very friendly to us; we were not harmed, nor did we miss anything all the time that we went about with them while we were in the open. [16]They were a wall about us both by night and by day all the time that we were with them tending the flocks. [17]So consider carefully what you should do, for harm threatens our master and all his household; he is such a nasty fellow that no one can speak to him."

[18]Abigail quickly got together two hundred loaves of bread, two jars of wine, five dressed sheep, five *seah*s of parched corn, one hundred cakes of raisin, and two hundred cakes of pressed figs. She loaded them on asses, [19]and she told her young men, "Go on ahead of me, and I'll follow you"; but she did not tell her husband Nabal. [20]She was riding on the ass and going down a trail[b] on the hill, when David and his men appeared, coming down toward her; and she met them.—[21]Now David had been saying, "It was all for nothing that I protected that fellow's possessions in the wilderness, and that nothing he owned is missing. He has paid me back evil for good. [22]May God do thus and more

c Septuagint reads "wine," and cf. v. 18.

בֶּן־יִשַׁי֒ הַיּ֗וֹם רַבּ֤וּ עֲבָדִים֙ הַמִּתְפָּ֣רְצִ֔ים אִ֖ישׁ מִפְּנֵ֣י אֲדֹנָֽיו: 11 וְלָקַחְתִּ֤י אֶת־לַחְמִי֙ וְאֶת־מֵימַ֔י וְאֵת֙ טִבְחָתִ֔י אֲשֶׁ֥ר טָבַ֖חְתִּי לְגֹֽזְזָ֑י וְנָֽתַתִּי֙ לַֽאֲנָשִׁ֔ים אֲשֶׁר֙ לֹ֣א יָדַ֔עְתִּי אֵ֥י מִזֶּ֖ה הֵֽמָּה: 12 וַיַּֽהַפְכ֥וּ נַֽעֲרֵֽי־דָוִ֖ד לְדַרְכָּ֑ם וַיָּשֻׁ֙בוּ֙ וַיָּבֹ֔אוּ וַיַּגִּ֣דוּ ל֔וֹ כְּכֹ֖ל הַדְּבָרִ֥ים הָאֵֽלֶּה: 13 וַיֹּאמֶר֩ דָּוִ֨ד לַֽאֲנָשָׁ֜יו חִגְר֣וּ ׀ אִ֣ישׁ אֶת־חַרְבּ֗וֹ וַֽיַּחְגְּרוּ֙ אִ֣ישׁ אֶת־חַרְבּ֔וֹ וַיַּחְגֹּ֥ר גַּם־דָּוִ֖ד אֶת־חַרְבּ֑וֹ וַיַּֽעֲל֣וּ ׀ אַֽחֲרֵ֣י דָוִ֗ד כְּאַרְבַּ֤ע מֵאוֹת֙ אִ֔ישׁ וּמָאתַ֖יִם יָֽשְׁב֥וּ עַל־הַכֵּלִֽים: 14 וְלַֽאֲבִיגַ֨יִל֙ אֵ֣שֶׁת נָבָ֔ל הִגִּ֥יד נַֽעַר־אֶחָ֖ד מֵֽהַנְּעָרִ֣ים לֵאמֹ֑ר הִנֵּ֣ה שָׁלַח֩ דָּוִ֨ד מַלְאָכִ֤ים ׀ מֵֽהַמִּדְבָּר֙ לְבָרֵ֣ךְ אֶת־אֲדֹנֵ֔ינוּ וַיָּ֖עַט בָּהֶֽם: 15 וְהָ֣אֲנָשִׁ֔ים טֹבִ֥ים לָ֖נוּ מְאֹ֑ד וְלֹ֤א הָכְלַ֙מְנוּ֙ וְלֹֽא־פָקַ֣דְנוּ מְא֔וּמָה כָּל־יְמֵי֙ הִתְהַלַּ֣כְנוּ אִתָּ֔ם בִּֽהְיוֹתֵ֖נוּ בַּשָּׂדֶֽה: 16 חוֹמָה֙ הָי֣וּ עָלֵ֔ינוּ גַּם־לַ֖יְלָה גַּם־יוֹמָ֑ם כָּל־יְמֵ֛י הֱיוֹתֵ֥נוּ עִמָּ֖ם רֹעִ֥ים הַצֹּֽאן: 17 וְעַתָּ֗ה דְּעִ֤י וּרְאִי֙ מַה־תַּֽעֲשִׂ֔י כִּֽי־כָֽלְתָ֧ה הָֽרָעָ֛ה אֶל־אֲדֹנֵ֖ינוּ וְעַ֣ל כָּל־בֵּית֑וֹ וְהוּא֙ בֶּן־בְּלִיַּ֔עַל מִדַּבֵּ֖ר אֵלָֽיו: 18 וַתְּמַהֵ֣ר אֲבוֹגַ֗יִל וַתִּקַּח֮ מָאתַ֣יִם לֶ֣חֶם וּשְׁנַ֣יִם נִבְלֵי־יַ֗יִן וְחָמֵ֨שׁ צֹ֤אן עֲשׂוּוֹת֙ וְחָמֵ֤שׁ סְאִים֙ קָלִ֔י וּמֵאָ֥ה צִמֻּקִ֖ים וּמָאתַ֣יִם דְּבֵלִ֑ים וַתָּ֖שֶׂם עַל־הַֽחֲמֹרִֽים: 19 וַתֹּ֤אמֶר לִנְעָרֶ֙יהָ֙ עִבְר֣וּ לְפָנַ֔י הִנְנִ֖י אַֽחֲרֵיכֶ֣ם בָּאָ֑ה וּלְאִישָׁ֥הּ נָבָ֖ל לֹ֥א הִגִּֽידָה: 20 וְהָיָ֡ה הִ֣יא ׀ רֹכֶ֣בֶת עַֽל־הַֽחֲמ֡וֹר וְיֹרֶ֩דֶת֩ בְּסֵ֨תֶר הָהָ֜ר וְהִנֵּ֤ה דָוִד֙ וַֽאֲנָשָׁ֔יו יֹֽרְדִ֖ים לִקְרָאתָ֑הּ וַתִּפְגֹּ֖שׁ אֹתָֽם: 21 וְדָוִ֣ד אָמַ֗ר אַךְ֩ לַשֶּׁ֨קֶר שָׁמַ֜רְתִּי אֶת־כָּל־אֲשֶׁ֤ר לָזֶה֙ בַּמִּדְבָּ֔ר וְלֹֽא־נִפְקַ֥ד מִכָּל־אֲשֶׁר־ל֖וֹ מְא֑וּמָה וַיָּֽשֶׁב־לִ֥י רָעָ֖ה תַּ֥חַת טוֹבָֽה: 22 כֹּֽה־יַֽעֲשֶׂ֧ה אֱלֹהִ֛ים

to *d*-the enemies of-*d* David if, by the light of morning, I leave *e*-a single male-*e* of his."— ²³When Abigail saw David, she quickly dismounted from the ass and threw herself face down before*b* David, bowing to the ground. ²⁴Prostrate at his feet, she pleaded, "Let the blame be mine, my lord, but let your handmaid speak to you; hear your maid's plea. ²⁵Please, my lord, pay no attention to that wretched fellow Nabal. For he is just what his name says: His name means 'boor' and he is a boor.

"Your handmaid did not see the young men whom my lord sent. ²⁶I swear, my lord, as the LORD lives and as you live—the LORD who has kept you from seeking redress by blood with your own hands—let your enemies and all who would harm my lord fare like Nabal! ²⁷Here is the present which your maidservant has brought to my lord; let it be given to the young men who are the followers of my lord. ²⁸Please pardon your maid's boldness. For the LORD will grant my lord an enduring house, because my lord is fighting the battles of the LORD, and no wrong is ever to be found in you. ²⁹And if anyone sets out to pursue you and seek your life, the life of my lord will be bound up in the bundle of life in the care of the LORD; but He will fling away the lives of your enemies as from the hollow of a sling. ³⁰And when the LORD has accomplished for my lord all the good He has promised you, and has appointed you ruler of Israel, ³¹do not let this be a cause of stumbling and of faltering courage to my lord that you have shed blood needlessly and that my lord sought redress with his own hands. And when the LORD has prospered my lord, remember your maid."

³²David said to Abigail, "Praised be the LORD, the God of Israel, who sent you this day to meet me! ³³And blessed be your prudence, and blessed be you yourself for restraining me from

לְאֹיְבֵי דָוִד וְכֹה יֹסִיף אִם־אַשְׁאִיר מִכָּל־
אֲשֶׁר־לוֹ עַד־הַבֹּקֶר מַשְׁתִּין בְּקִיר: ²³ וַתֵּרֶא
אֲבִיגַיִל אֶת־דָּוִד וַתְּמַהֵר וַתֵּרֶד מֵעַל הַחֲמוֹר
וַתִּפֹּל לְאַפֵּי דָוִד עַל־פָּנֶיהָ וַתִּשְׁתַּחוּ אָרֶץ:
²⁴ וַתִּפֹּל עַל־רַגְלָיו וַתֹּאמֶר בִּי־אֲנִי אֲדֹנִי
הֶעָוֹן וּתְדַבֶּר־נָא אֲמָתְךָ בְּאָזְנֶיךָ וּשְׁמַע אֵת
דִּבְרֵי אֲמָתֶךָ: ²⁵ אַל־נָא יָשִׂים אֲדֹנִי ׀ אֶת־
לִבּוֹ אֶל־אִישׁ הַבְּלִיַּעַל הַזֶּה עַל־נָבָל כִּי כִשְׁמוֹ
כֶּן־הוּא נָבָל שְׁמוֹ וּנְבָלָה עִמּוֹ וַאֲנִי אֲמָתְךָ לֹא
רָאִיתִי אֶת־נַעֲרֵי אֲדֹנִי אֲשֶׁר שָׁלָחְתָּ: ²⁶ וְעַתָּה
אֲדֹנִי חַי־יְהוָה וְחֵי־נַפְשְׁךָ אֲשֶׁר מְנָעֲךָ יְהוָה
מִבּוֹא בְדָמִים וְהוֹשֵׁעַ יָדְךָ לָךְ וְעַתָּה יִהְיוּ כְנָבָל
אֹיְבֶיךָ וְהַמְבַקְשִׁים אֶל־אֲדֹנִי רָעָה: ²⁷ וְעַתָּה
הַבְּרָכָה הַזֹּאת אֲשֶׁר־הֵבִיא שִׁפְחָתְךָ לַאדֹנִי
וְנִתְּנָה לַנְּעָרִים הַמִּתְהַלְּכִים בְּרַגְלֵי אֲדֹנִי:
²⁸ שָׂא נָא לְפֶשַׁע אֲמָתֶךָ כִּי עָשֹׂה־יַעֲשֶׂה יְהוָה
לַאדֹנִי בַּיִת נֶאֱמָן כִּי־מִלְחֲמוֹת יְהוָה אֲדֹנִי
נִלְחָם וְרָעָה לֹא־תִמָּצֵא בְךָ מִיָּמֶיךָ: ²⁹ וַיָּקָם
אָדָם לִרְדָפְךָ וּלְבַקֵּשׁ אֶת־נַפְשֶׁךָ וְהָיְתָה נֶפֶשׁ
אֲדֹנִי צְרוּרָה ׀ בִּצְרוֹר הַחַיִּים אֵת יְהוָה אֱלֹהֶיךָ
וְאֵת נֶפֶשׁ אֹיְבֶיךָ יְקַלְּעֶנָּה בְּתוֹךְ כַּף הַקָּלַע:
³⁰ וְהָיָה כִּי־יַעֲשֶׂה יְהוָה לַאדֹנִי כְּכֹל אֲשֶׁר־
דִּבֶּר אֶת־הַטּוֹבָה עָלֶיךָ וְצִוְּךָ לְנָגִיד עַל־יִשְׂרָאֵל:
³¹ וְלֹא תִהְיֶה זֹאת ׀ לְךָ לְפוּקָה וּלְמִכְשׁוֹל לֵב
לַאדֹנִי וְלִשְׁפָּךְ־דָּם חִנָּם וּלְהוֹשִׁיעַ אֲדֹנִי לוֹ
וְהֵיטִב יְהוָה לַאדֹנִי וְזָכַרְתָּ אֶת־אֲמָתֶךָ: ס
³² וַיֹּאמֶר דָּוִד לַאֲבִיגַל בָּרוּךְ יְהוָה אֱלֹהֵי
יִשְׂרָאֵל אֲשֶׁר שְׁלָחֵךְ הַיּוֹם הַזֶּה לִקְרָאתִי:
³³ וּבָרוּךְ טַעְמֵךְ וּבְרוּכָה אָתְּ אֲשֶׁר כְּלִתִנִי
הַיּוֹם הַזֶּה מִבּוֹא בְדָמִים וְהֹשֵׁעַ יָדִי לִי:

---

d-d   *The phrase is intended to avoid the imprecation of David against himself; it is lacking in the Septuagint.*
e-e   *Lit. "one who pees against a wall."*

seeking redress in blood by my own hands. ³⁴For as sure as the LORD, the God of Israel, lives—who has kept me from harming you—had you not come quickly to meet me, not *ᵉ-a single male-ᵉ* of Nabal's line would have been left by daybreak." ³⁵David then accepted from her what she had brought him, and he said to her, "Go up to your home safely. See, I have heeded your plea and respected your wish."

³⁶When Abigail came home to Nabal, he was having a feast in his house, a feast fit for a king; Nabal was in a merry mood and very drunk, so she did not tell him anything at all until daybreak. ³⁷The next morning, when Nabal had slept off the wine, his wife told him everything that had happened; and his courage died within him, and he became like a stone. ³⁸About ten days later the LORD struck Nabal and he died. ³⁹When David heard that Nabal was dead, he said, "Praised be the LORD who championed my cause against the insults of Nabal and held back His servant from wrongdoing; the LORD has brought Nabal's wrongdoing down on his own head."

David sent messengers *ᶠ-to propose marriage to-ᶠ* Abigail, to take her as his wife. ⁴⁰When David's servants came to Abigail at Carmel and told her that David had sent them to her to make her his wife, ⁴¹she immediately bowed low with her face to the ground and said, "Your handmaid is ready to be your maidservant, to wash the feet of my lord's servants." ⁴²Then Abigail rose quickly and mounted an ass, and with five of her maids in attendance she followed David's messengers; and she became his wife.

⁴³Now David had taken Ahinoam of Jezreel; so both of them became his wives. ⁴⁴Saul had given his daughter Michal, David's wife, to Palti son of Laish from Gallim.

---

f-f Lit. "and spoke for"; cf. Song of Songs 8.8.

³⁴ וְאוּלָ֗ם חַי־יְהוָה֙ אֱלֹהֵ֣י יִשְׂרָאֵ֔ל אֲשֶׁ֣ר מְנָעַ֔נִי מֵהָרַ֖ע אֹתָ֑ךְ כִּ֣י ׀ לוּלֵ֣י מִהַ֗רְתְּ וַתָּבֹאת֙ לִקְרָאתִ֔י כִּ֣י אִם־נוֹתַ֧ר לְנָבָ֛ל עַד־א֥וֹר הַבֹּ֖קֶר מַשְׁתִּ֥ין בְּקִֽיר׃

³⁵ וַיִּקַּ֤ח דָּוִד֙ מִיָּדָ֔הּ אֵ֥ת אֲשֶׁר־הֵבִ֖יאָה ל֑וֹ וְלָ֣הּ אָמַ֗ר עֲלִ֤י לְשָׁלוֹם֙ לְבֵיתֵ֔ךְ רְאִי֙ שָׁמַ֣עְתִּי בְקוֹלֵ֔ךְ וָאֶשָּׂ֖א פָּנָֽיִךְ׃

³⁶ וַתָּבֹ֣א אֲבִיגַ֣יִל ׀ אֶל־נָבָ֗ל וְהִנֵּה־לוֹ֩ מִשְׁתֶּ֨ה בְּבֵית֜וֹ כְּמִשְׁתֵּ֣ה הַמֶּ֗לֶךְ וְלֵ֤ב נָבָל֙ ט֣וֹב עָלָ֔יו וְה֥וּא שִׁכֹּ֖ר עַד־מְאֹ֑ד וְלֹֽא־הִגִּ֤ידָה לּוֹ֙ דָּבָ֣ר קָטֹ֣ן וְגָד֔וֹל עַד־א֖וֹר הַבֹּֽקֶר׃

³⁷ וַיְהִ֣י בַבֹּ֗קֶר בְּצֵ֤את הַיַּ֙יִן֙ מִנָּבָ֔ל וַתַּגֶּד־ל֣וֹ אִשְׁתּ֔וֹ אֶת־הַדְּבָרִ֖ים הָאֵ֑לֶּה וַיָּ֣מָת לִבּוֹ֙ בְּקִרְבּ֔וֹ וְה֖וּא הָיָ֥ה לְאָֽבֶן׃ ³⁸ וַיְהִ֖י כַּעֲשֶׂ֣רֶת הַיָּמִ֑ים וַיִּגֹּ֧ף יְהוָ֛ה אֶת־נָבָ֖ל וַיָּמֹֽת׃

³⁹ וַיִּשְׁמַ֣ע דָּוִד֮ כִּ֣י מֵ֣ת נָבָל֒ וַיֹּ֡אמֶר בָּר֣וּךְ יְהוָ֗ה אֲשֶׁ֣ר רָב֩ אֶת־רִ֨יב חֶרְפָּתִ֜י מִיַּ֣ד נָבָ֗ל וְאֶת־עַבְדּוֹ֙ חָשַׂ֣ךְ מֵֽרָעָ֔ה וְאֵת֙ רָעַ֣ת נָבָ֔ל הֵשִׁ֥יב יְהוָ֖ה בְּרֹאשׁ֑וֹ וַיִּשְׁלַ֤ח דָּוִד֙ וַיְדַבֵּ֣ר בַּאֲבִיגַ֔יִל לְקַחְתָּ֥הּ ל֖וֹ לְאִשָּֽׁה׃ ⁴⁰ וַיָּבֹ֜אוּ עַבְדֵ֥י דָוִ֛ד אֶל־אֲבִיגַ֖יִל הַכַּרְמֶ֑לָה וַיְדַבְּר֤וּ אֵלֶ֙יהָ֙ לֵאמֹ֔ר דָּוִד֙ שְׁלָחָ֣נוּ אֵלַ֔יִךְ לְקַחְתֵּ֥ךְ ל֖וֹ לְאִשָּֽׁה׃ ⁴¹ וַתָּ֕קָם וַתִּשְׁתַּ֥חוּ אַפַּ֖יִם אָ֑רְצָה וַתֹּ֗אמֶר הִנֵּ֤ה אֲמָֽתְךָ֙ לְשִׁפְחָ֔ה לִרְחֹ֕ץ רַגְלֵ֖י עַבְדֵ֥י אֲדֹנִֽי׃ ⁴² וַתְּמַהֵ֞ר וַתָּ֣קָם אֲבִיגַ֗יִל וַתִּרְכַּב֙ עַֽל־הַחֲמ֔וֹר וְחָמֵשׁ֙ נַעֲרֹתֶ֔יהָ הַהֹלְכ֖וֹת לְרַגְלָ֑הּ וַתֵּ֗לֶךְ אַֽחֲרֵי֙ מַלְאֲכֵ֣י דָוִ֔ד וַתְּהִי־ל֖וֹ לְאִשָּֽׁה׃

⁴³ וְאֶת־אֲחִינֹ֛עַם לָקַ֥ח דָּוִ֖ד מִֽיִּזְרְעֶ֑אל וַתִּהְיֶ֛יןָ גַּֽם־שְׁתֵּיהֶ֥ן ל֖וֹ לְנָשִֽׁים׃ ס ⁴⁴ וְשָׁא֗וּל נָתַ֛ן אֶת־מִיכַ֥ל בִּתּ֖וֹ אֵ֣שֶׁת דָּוִ֑ד לְפַלְטִ֥י בֶן־לַ֖יִשׁ אֲשֶׁ֥ר מִגַּלִּֽים׃

26 [a]The Ziphites came to Saul at Gibeah and said, "David is hiding in the hill of Hachilah facing Jeshimon." [2]Saul went down at once to the wilderness of Ziph, together with three thousand picked men of Israel, to search for David in the wilderness of Ziph, [3]and Saul encamped on the hill of Hachilah which faces Jeshimon, by the road. When David, who was then living in the wilderness, learned that Saul had come after him into the wilderness, [4]David sent out scouts and made sure that Saul had come. [5]David went at once to the place where Saul had encamped, and David saw the spot where Saul and his army commander, Abner son of Ner, lay asleep. Saul lay asleep inside the barricade[b] and the troops were posted around him.

[6]David spoke up and asked Ahimelech the Hittite and Abishai son of Zeruiah, Joab's brother, "Who will go down with me into the camp to Saul?" And Abishai answered, "I will go down with you." [7]So David and Abishai approached the troops by night, and found Saul fast asleep inside the barricade,[b] his spear stuck in the ground at his head, and Abner and the troops sleeping around him. [8]And Abishai said to David, "God has delivered your enemy into your hands today. Let me pin him to the ground with a single thrust of the spear. I will not have to strike him twice." [9]But David said to Abishai, "Don't do him violence! No one can lay hands on the LORD's anointed with impunity." [10]And David went on, "As the LORD lives, the LORD Himself will strike him down, or his time will come and he will die, or he will go down to battle and perish. [11]But the LORD forbid that I should lay a hand on the LORD's anointed! Just take the spear and the water jar at his head and let's be off." [12]So David took away the spear and the wa-

כו וַיָּבֹ֤אוּ הַזִּפִים֙ אֶל־שָׁא֔וּל הַגִּבְעָ֖תָה
לֵאמֹ֑ר הֲל֨וֹא דָוִ֤ד מִסְתַּתֵּר֙ בְּגִבְעַ֣ת
הַֽחֲכִילָ֔ה עַ֖ל פְּנֵ֥י הַיְשִׁימֹֽן׃ [2]וַיָּ֣קָם שָׁא֗וּל
וַיֵּ֨רֶד֙ אֶל־מִדְבַּר־זִ֔יף וְאִתּ֛וֹ שְׁלֹֽשֶׁת־אֲלָפִ֥ים
אִ֖ישׁ בְּחוּרֵ֣י יִשְׂרָאֵ֑ל לְבַקֵּ֥שׁ אֶת־דָּוִ֖ד
בְּמִדְבַּר־זִֽיף׃ [3]וַיִּ֨חַן שָׁא֜וּל בְּגִבְעַ֣ת
הַֽחֲכִילָ֗ה אֲשֶׁ֛ר עַל־פְּנֵ֥י הַיְשִׁימֹ֖ן עַל־הַדָּ֑רֶךְ
וְדָוִד֙ יֹשֵׁ֣ב בַּמִּדְבָּ֔ר וַיַּ֕רְא כִּ֣י בָ֥א שָׁא֖וּל
אַֽחֲרָ֥יו הַמִּדְבָּֽרָה׃ [4]וַיִּשְׁלַ֥ח דָּוִ֖ד מְרַגְּלִ֑ים
וַיֵּ֕דַע כִּֽי־בָ֥א שָׁא֖וּל אֶל־נָכֽוֹן׃ [5]וַיָּ֣קָם דָּוִ֗ד
וַיָּבֹא֮ אֶל־הַמָּקוֹם֮ אֲשֶׁ֣ר חָֽנָה־שָׁ֣ם שָׁאוּל֒
וַיַּ֣רְא דָּוִ֗ד אֶת־הַמָּקוֹם֙ אֲשֶׁ֣ר שָֽׁכַב־שָׁ֣ם
שָׁא֔וּל וְאַבְנֵ֥ר בֶּן־נֵ֖ר שַׂר־צְבָא֑וֹ וְשָׁא֗וּל
שֹׁכֵב֙ בַּמַּעְגָּ֔ל וְהָעָ֖ם חֹנִ֥ים סְבִ֥יבֹתָֽיו׃

[6]וַיַּ֨עַן דָּוִ֜ד וַיֹּ֣אמֶר ׀ אֶל־אֲחִימֶ֣לֶךְ הַֽחִתִּ֗י
וְאֶל־אֲבִישַׁ֨י בֶּן־צְרוּיָ֜ה אֲחִ֤י יוֹאָב֙ לֵאמֹ֔ר
מִֽי־יֵרֵ֥ד אִתִּ֛י אֶל־שָׁא֖וּל אֶל־הַֽמַּחֲנֶ֑ה
וַיֹּ֣אמֶר אֲבִישַׁ֔י אֲנִ֖י אֵרֵ֥ד עִמָּֽךְ׃ [7]וַיָּבֹא֩ דָוִ֨ד
וַֽאֲבִישַׁ֥י ׀ אֶל־הָעָם֮ לַיְלָה֒ וְהִנֵּ֣ה שָׁא֗וּל
שֹׁכֵ֤ב יָשֵׁן֙ בַּמַּעְגָּ֔ל וַֽחֲנִית֥וֹ מְעֽוּכָה־בָאָ֖רֶץ
מְרַֽאֲשֹׁתָ֑יו וְאַבְנֵ֣ר וְהָעָ֔ם שֹׁכְבִ֖ים
סְבִֽיבֹתָֽיו׃ ס [8]וַיֹּ֤אמֶר אֲבִישַׁי֙
אֶל־דָּוִ֔ד סִגַּ֨ר אֱלֹהִ֥ים הַיּ֛וֹם אֶת־אֽוֹיִבְךָ֖
בְּיָדֶ֑ךָ וְעַתָּה֩ אַכֶּ֨נּוּ נָ֜א בַּֽחֲנִ֤ית וּבָאָ֙רֶץ֙ פַּ֣עַם
אַחַ֔ת וְלֹ֥א אֶשְׁנֶ֖ה לֽוֹ׃ [9]וַיֹּ֨אמֶר דָּוִ֤ד אֶל־
אֲבִישַׁי֙ אַל־תַּשְׁחִיתֵ֔הוּ כִּ֠י מִ֣י שָׁלַ֥ח יָד֛וֹ
בִּמְשִׁ֥יחַ יְהֹוָ֖ה וְנִקָּֽה׃ פ [10]וַיֹּ֣אמֶר דָּוִ֔ד
חַי־יְהֹוָ֗ה כִּ֚י אִם־יְהֹוָ֣ה יִגֳּפֶ֔נּוּ אֽוֹ־יוֹמ֥וֹ יָב֖וֹא
וָמֵ֑ת א֧וֹ בַמִּלְחָמָ֛ה יֵרֵ֖ד וְנִסְפָּֽה׃ [11]חָלִ֤ילָה
לִּי֙ מֵֽיהֹוָ֔ה מִשְּׁלֹ֥חַ יָדִ֖י בִּמְשִׁ֣יחַ יְהֹוָ֑ה
וְעַתָּ֡ה קַח־נָ֣א אֶת־הַֽחֲנִ֡ית אֲשֶׁ֣ר מְרַֽאֲשֹׁתָיו֩
מְרַֽאֲשֹׁתָ֨יו וְאֶת־צַפַּ֤חַת הַמַּ֙יִם֙ וְנֵ֥לְכָה לָּֽנוּ׃
[12]וַיִּקַּח֩ דָּוִ֨ד אֶת־הַֽחֲנִ֜ית וְאֶת־צַפַּ֣חַת

a Cf. 23.19 and note.
b Meaning of Heb. uncertain; cf. 17.20.

ter jar at Saul's head, and they left. No one saw or knew or woke up; all remained asleep; a deep sleep from the Lord had fallen upon them.

13David crossed over to the other side and stood afar on top of a hill; there was considerable distance between them. 14And David shouted to the troops and to Abner son of Ner, "Abner, aren't you going to answer?" And Abner shouted back, "Who are you to shout at the king?" 15And David answered Abner, "You are a man, aren't you? And there is no one like you in Israel! So why didn't you keep watch over your lord the king? For one of [our] troops came to do violence to your lord the king. 16You have not given a good account of yourself! As the Lord lives, [all of] you deserve to die, because you did not keep watch over your lord, the Lord's anointed. Look around, where are the king's spear and the water jar that were at his head?"

17Saul recognized David's voice, and he asked, "Is that your voice, my son David?" And David replied, "It is, my lord king." 18And he went on, "But why does my lord continue to pursue his servant? What have I done, and what wrong am I guilty of? 19Now let my lord the king hear his servant out. If the Lord has incited you against me, let Him be appeased[c] by an offering; but if it is men, may they be accursed of the Lord! For they have driven me out today, so that I cannot have a share in the Lord's possession, but am told, 'Go and worship other gods.' 20Oh, let my blood not fall to the ground, away from the presence of the Lord! For the king of Israel has come out to seek a single flea—as if he were hunting a partridge in the hills."

21And Saul answered, "I am in the wrong. Come back, my son David, for I will never harm you again, seeing how you have held my life pre-

---

c   Cf. Amos 5.21.

הַמַּ֗יִם מֵרַאֲשֹׁתֵ֤י שָׁאוּל֙ וַיֵּ֣לְכוּ לָהֶ֔ם וְאֵ֣ין רֹאֶה֩ וְאֵ֨ין יוֹדֵ֜עַ וְאֵ֣ין מֵקִ֗יץ כִּ֤י כֻלָּם֙ יְשֵׁנִ֔ים כִּ֚י תַּרְדֵּמַ֣ת יְהוָ֔ה נָפְלָ֖ה עֲלֵיהֶֽם׃ 13 וַיַּעֲבֹ֤ר דָּוִד֙ הָעֵ֔בֶר וַיַּעֲמֹ֥ד עַל־רֹאשׁ־הָהָ֖ר מֵֽרָחֹ֑ק רַ֥ב הַמָּק֖וֹם בֵּינֵיהֶֽם׃ 14 וַיִּקְרָ֣א דָוִ֣ד אֶל־הָעָ֗ם וְאֶל־אַבְנֵ֤ר בֶּן־נֵר֙ לֵאמֹ֔ר הֲל֥וֹא תַעֲנֶ֖ה אַבְנֵ֑ר וַיַּ֤עַן אַבְנֵר֙ וַיֹּ֔אמֶר מִ֥י אַתָּ֖ה קָרָ֥אתָ אֶל־הַמֶּֽלֶךְ׃ פ 15 וַיֹּ֨אמֶר דָּוִ֜ד אֶל־אַבְנֵ֗ר הֲלוֹא־אִ֣ישׁ אַתָּה֮ וּמִ֣י כָמ֣וֹךָ בְּיִשְׂרָאֵל֒ וְלָ֨מָּה֙ לֹ֣א שָׁמַ֔רְתָּ אֶל־אֲדֹנֶ֖יךָ הַמֶּ֑לֶךְ כִּי־בָא֙ אַחַ֣ד הָעָ֔ם לְהַשְׁחִ֖ית אֶת־הַמֶּ֥לֶךְ אֲדֹנֶֽיךָ׃ 16 לֹא־ט֞וֹב הַדָּבָ֣ר הַזֶּה֮ אֲשֶׁ֣ר עָשִׂיתָ֒ חַי־יְהוָ֗ה כִּ֤י בְנֵי־מָ֙וֶת֙ אַתֶּ֔ם אֲשֶׁ֤ר לֹֽא־שְׁמַרְתֶּם֙ עַל־אֲדֹנֵיכֶ֔ם עַל־מְשִׁ֖יחַ יְהוָ֑ה וְעַתָּ֣ה ׀ רְאֵ֣ה אֵֽי־חֲנִ֣ית הַמֶּ֗לֶךְ וְאֶת־צַפַּ֤חַת הַמַּ֙יִם֙ אֲשֶׁ֣ר מראשתו מְרַאֲשֹׁתָֽיו׃ 17 וַיַּכֵּ֤ר שָׁאוּל֙ אֶת־ק֣וֹל דָּוִ֔ד וַיֹּ֕אמֶר הֲקוֹלְךָ֥ זֶ֖ה בְּנִ֣י דָוִ֑ד וַיֹּ֣אמֶר דָּוִ֔ד קוֹלִ֖י אֲדֹנִ֥י הַמֶּֽלֶךְ׃ 18 וַיֹּ֕אמֶר לָ֥מָּה זֶּ֛ה אֲדֹנִ֥י רֹדֵ֖ף אַחֲרֵ֣י עַבְדּ֑וֹ כִּ֚י מֶ֣ה עָשִׂ֔יתִי וּמַה־בְּיָדִ֖י רָעָֽה׃ 19 וְעַתָּ֗ה יִֽשְׁמַֽע־נָא֙ אֲדֹנִ֣י הַמֶּ֔לֶךְ אֵ֖ת דִּבְרֵ֣י עַבְדּ֑וֹ אִם־יְהוָ֞ה הֱסִֽיתְךָ֥ בִי֙ יָרַ֣ח מִנְחָ֔ה וְאִ֣ם ׀ בְּנֵ֣י הָאָדָ֗ם אֲרוּרִ֥ים הֵם֙ לִפְנֵ֣י יְהוָ֔ה כִּֽי־גֵרְשׁ֣וּנִי הַיּ֗וֹם מֵֽהִסְתַּפֵּ֜חַ בְּנַחֲלַ֣ת יְהוָ֗ה לֵאמֹ֔ר לֵ֥ךְ עֲבֹ֖ד אֱלֹהִ֥ים אֲחֵרִֽים׃ 20 וְעַתָּ֗ה אַל־יִפֹּ֤ל דָּֽמִי֙ אַ֔רְצָה מִנֶּ֖גֶד פְּנֵ֣י יְהוָ֑ה כִּֽי־יָצָ֞א מֶ֣לֶךְ יִשְׂרָאֵ֗ל לְבַקֵּשׁ֙ אֶת־פַּרְעֹ֣שׁ אֶחָ֔ד כַּאֲשֶׁ֛ר יִרְדֹּ֥ף הַקֹּרֵ֖א בֶּהָרִֽים׃ 21 וַיֹּ֩אמֶר֩ שָׁא֨וּל חָטָ֜אתִי שׁ֣וּב בְּנִֽי־דָוִ֗ד כִּ֠י לֹֽא־אָרַ֤ע לְךָ֙ ע֔וֹד תַּ֗חַת אֲשֶׁ֨ר יָקְרָ֤ה נַפְשִׁי֙

cious this day. Yes, I have been a fool, and I have erred so very much." 22David replied, "Here is Your Majesty's spear. Let one of the young men come over and get it. 23And the LORD will requite every man for his right conduct and loyalty—for this day the LORD delivered you into my*d* hands and I would not raise a hand against the LORD's anointed. 24And just as I valued your life highly this day, so may the LORD value my life and may He rescue me from all trouble." 25Saul answered David, "May you be blessed, my son David. You shall achieve, and you shall prevail."

David then went his way, and Saul returned home.

27

David said to himself, "Some day I shall certainly perish at the hands of Saul. The best thing for me is to flee to the land of the Philistines; Saul will then give up hunting me throughout the territory of Israel, and I will escape him." 2So David and the six hundred men with him went and crossed over to King Achish son of Maoch of Gath. 3David and his men stayed with Achish in Gath, each man with his family, and David with his two wives, Ahinoam the Jezreelite and Abigail wife of Nabal the Carmelite. 4And when Saul was told that David had fled to Gath, he did not pursue him any more.

5David said to Achish, "If you please, let a place be granted me in one of the country towns where I can live; why should your servant remain with you in the royal city?" 6At that time Achish granted him Ziklag; that is how Ziklag came to belong to the kings of Judah, as is still the case. 7The length of time that David lived in Philistine territory was a year and four months.

8David and his men went up and raided the Geshurites, the Gizrites, and the Amalekites—

בְּעֵינֶיךָ הַיּוֹם הַזֶּה הִנֵּה הִסְכַּלְתִּי וָאֶשְׁגֶּה הַרְבֵּה מְאֹד: 22 וַיַּעַן דָּוִד וַיֹּאמֶר הִנֵּה הַחֲנִית הַמֶּלֶךְ וְיַעֲבֹר אֶחָד מֵהַנְּעָרִים וְיִקָּחֶהָ: 23 וַיהֹוָה יָשִׁיב לָאִישׁ אֶת־צִדְקָתוֹ וְאֶת־אֱמֻנָתוֹ אֲשֶׁר נְתָנְךָ יְהֹוָה | הַיּוֹם בְּיָד* וְלֹא אָבִיתִי לִשְׁלֹחַ יָדִי בִּמְשִׁיחַ יְהֹוָה: 24 וְהִנֵּה כַּאֲשֶׁר גָּדְלָה נַפְשְׁךָ הַיּוֹם הַזֶּה בְּעֵינָי כֵּן תִּגְדַּל נַפְשִׁי בְּעֵינֵי יְהֹוָה וְיַצִּלֵנִי מִכָּל־צָרָה: פ 25 וַיֹּאמֶר שָׁאוּל אֶל־דָּוִד בָּרוּךְ אַתָּה בְּנִי דָוִד גַּם עָשֹׂה תַעֲשֶׂה וְגַם יָכֹל תּוּכָל וַיֵּלֶךְ דָּוִד לְדַרְכּוֹ וְשָׁאוּל שָׁב לִמְקוֹמוֹ: פ

כז וַיֹּאמֶר דָּוִד אֶל־לִבּוֹ עַתָּה אֶסָּפֶה יוֹם־אֶחָד בְּיַד־שָׁאוּל אֵין־לִי טוֹב כִּי הִמָּלֵט אִמָּלֵט | אֶל־אֶרֶץ פְּלִשְׁתִּים וְנוֹאַשׁ מִמֶּנִּי שָׁאוּל לְבַקְשֵׁנִי עוֹד בְּכָל־גְּבוּל יִשְׂרָאֵל וְנִמְלַטְתִּי מִיָּדוֹ: 2 וַיָּקָם דָּוִד וַיַּעֲבֹר הוּא וְשֵׁשׁ־מֵאוֹת אִישׁ אֲשֶׁר עִמּוֹ אֶל־אָכִישׁ בֶּן־מָעוֹךְ מֶלֶךְ גַּת: 3 וַיֵּשֶׁב דָּוִד עִם־אָכִישׁ בְּגַת הוּא וַאֲנָשָׁיו אִישׁ וּבֵיתוֹ דָּוִד וּשְׁתֵּי נָשָׁיו אֲחִינֹעַם הַיִּזְרְעֵאלִית וַאֲבִיגַיִל אֵשֶׁת־נָבָל הַכַּרְמְלִית: 4 וַיֻּגַּד לְשָׁאוּל כִּי־בָרַח דָּוִד גַּת וְלֹא־יוֹסַף עוֹד לְבַקְשׁוֹ: ס 5 וַיֹּאמֶר דָּוִד אֶל־אָכִישׁ אִם־נָא מָצָאתִי חֵן בְּעֵינֶיךָ יִתְּנוּ־לִי מָקוֹם בְּאַחַת עָרֵי הַשָּׂדֶה וְאֵשְׁבָה שָּׁם וְלָמָּה יֵשֵׁב עַבְדְּךָ בְּעִיר הַמַּמְלָכָה עִמָּךְ: 6 וַיִּתֶּן־לוֹ אָכִישׁ בַּיּוֹם הַהוּא אֶת־צִקְלָג לָכֵן הָיְתָה צִקְלַג לְמַלְכֵי יְהוּדָה עַד הַיּוֹם הַזֶּה: פ 7 וַיְהִי מִסְפַּר הַיָּמִים אֲשֶׁר־יָשַׁב דָּוִד בִּשְׂדֵה פְלִשְׁתִּים יָמִים וְאַרְבָּעָה חֳדָשִׁים: 8 וַיַּעַל דָּוִד וַאֲנָשָׁיו וַיִּפְשְׁטוּ אֶל־הַגְּשׁוּרִי

---

d So many mss.; other mss. and editions omit.

בנוסח אחר "בידי"   v. 23.

634

who were the inhabitants of the region of Olam,[a] all the way to Shur and to the land of Egypt.—[9]When David attacked a region, he would leave no man or woman alive; he would take flocks, herds, asses, camels, and clothing. When he returned and came[b] to Achish, [10]Achish would ask, "Where[c] did you raid today?" and David would reply, "The Negeb[d] of Judah," or "the Negeb of the Jerahmeelites," or "the Negeb of the Kenites." [11]David would leave no man or woman alive to be brought to Gath; for he thought, "They might tell about us: David did this." Such was his practice as long as he stayed in the territory of the Philistines. [12]Achish trusted David. He thought: [e-]"He has aroused the wrath of-[e] his own people Israel, and so he will be my vassal forever."

28 At that time the Philistines mustered their forces for war, to take the field against Israel. Achish said to David, "You know, of course, that you and your men must march out with my forces." [2]David answered Achish, "You surely know what your servant will do." "In that case," Achish replied to David, "I will appoint you my bodyguard for life."

[3][a]Now Samuel had died and all Israel made lament for him; and he was buried in his own town of Ramah. And Saul had forbidden [recourse to] ghosts and familiar spirits in the land.

[4]The Philistines mustered and they marched to Shunem and encamped; and Saul gathered all Israel, and they encamped at Gilboa. [5]When Saul saw the Philistine force, his heart trembled with fear. [6]And Saul inquired of the LORD, but

---

a   *Septuagint reads "Telam" (cf. "Telaim" in 15.4; and "Telem" in Josh. 15.24).*

b   *Change of vocalization yields "brought it"; cf. v. 11.*

c   *So some mss. and Targum; Septuagint and 4QSam[a] read "Whom."*

d   *I.e., the part of the Negeb occupied by these clans.*

e-e   *Cf. note at 13.4.*

a   *The rest of this chapter would read well after chapters 29 and 30.*

וְהַגִּזְרִי וְהָעֲמָלֵקִי כִּי הֵנָּה יֹשְׁבוֹת הָאָרֶץ אֲשֶׁר מֵעוֹלָם בּוֹאֲךָ שׁוּרָה וְעַד־אֶרֶץ מִצְרָיִם: 9 וְהִכָּה דָוִד אֶת־הָאָרֶץ וְלֹא יְחַיֶּה אִישׁ וְאִשָּׁה וְלָקַח צֹאן וּבָקָר וַחֲמֹרִים וּגְמַלִּים וּבְגָדִים וַיָּשָׁב וַיָּבֹא אֶל־אָכִישׁ: 10 וַיֹּאמֶר אָכִישׁ אַל־*פְּשַׁטְתֶּם הַיּוֹם וַיֹּאמֶר דָּוִד עַל־נֶגֶב יְהוּדָה וְעַל־נֶגֶב הַיְּרַחְמְאֵלִי וְאֶל־נֶגֶב הַקֵּינִי: 11 וְאִישׁ וְאִשָּׁה לֹא־יְחַיֶּה דָוִד לְהָבִיא גַת לֵאמֹר פֶּן־יַגִּדוּ עָלֵינוּ לֵאמֹר כֹּה־עָשָׂה דָוִד וְכֹה מִשְׁפָּטוֹ כָּל־הַיָּמִים אֲשֶׁר יָשַׁב בִּשְׂדֵה פְלִשְׁתִּים: 12 וַיַּאֲמֵן אָכִישׁ בְּדָוִד לֵאמֹר הַבְאֵשׁ הִבְאִישׁ בְּעַמּוֹ בְיִשְׂרָאֵל וְהָיָה לִי לְעֶבֶד עוֹלָם: פ

כח וַיְהִי בַּיָּמִים הָהֵם וַיִּקְבְּצוּ פְלִשְׁתִּים אֶת־מַחֲנֵיהֶם לַצָּבָא לְהִלָּחֵם בְּיִשְׂרָאֵל וַיֹּאמֶר אָכִישׁ אֶל־דָּוִד יָדֹעַ תֵּדַע כִּי אִתִּי תֵּצֵא בַמַּחֲנֶה אַתָּה וַאֲנָשֶׁיךָ: 2 וַיֹּאמֶר דָּוִד אֶל־אָכִישׁ לָכֵן אַתָּה תֵדַע אֵת אֲשֶׁר־יַעֲשֶׂה עַבְדֶּךָ וַיֹּאמֶר אָכִישׁ אֶל־דָּוִד לָכֵן שֹׁמֵר לְרֹאשִׁי אֲשִׂימְךָ כָּל־הַיָּמִים: פ

3 וּשְׁמוּאֵל מֵת וַיִּסְפְּדוּ־לוֹ כָּל־יִשְׂרָאֵל וַיִּקְבְּרֻהוּ בָרָמָה וּבְעִירוֹ וְשָׁאוּל הֵסִיר הָאֹבוֹת וְאֶת־הַיִּדְּעֹנִים מֵהָאָרֶץ: 4 וַיִּקָּבְצוּ פְלִשְׁתִּים וַיָּבֹאוּ וַיַּחֲנוּ בְשׁוּנֵם וַיִּקְבֹּץ שָׁאוּל אֶת־כָּל־יִשְׂרָאֵל וַיַּחֲנוּ בַגִּלְבֹּעַ: 5 וַיַּרְא שָׁאוּל אֶת־מַחֲנֵה פְלִשְׁתִּים וַיִּרָא וַיֶּחֱרַד לִבּוֹ מְאֹד: 6 וַיִּשְׁאַל שָׁאוּל בַּיהוָה וְלֹא עָנָהוּ יְהוָה גַּם בַּחֲלֹמוֹת גַּם בָּאוּרִים גַּם בַּנְּבִיאִם:

v. 10. בנוסח אחר "אָן"

the LORD did not answer him, either by dreams or by Urim[b] or by prophets. [7]Then Saul said to his courtiers, "Find me a woman who consults ghosts, so that I can go to her and inquire through her." And his courtiers told him that there was a woman in En-dor who consulted ghosts.

[8]Saul disguised himself; he put on different clothes and set out with two men. They came to the woman by night, and he said, "Please divine for me by a ghost. Bring up for me the one I shall name to you." [9]But the woman answered him, "You know what Saul has done, how he has banned [the use of] ghosts and familiar spirits in the land. So why are you laying a trap for me, to get me killed?" [10]Saul swore to her by the LORD: "As the LORD lives, you won't get into trouble over this." [11]At that, the woman asked, "Whom shall I bring up for you?" He answered, "Bring up Samuel for me." [12]Then the woman recognized Samuel,[c] and she shrieked loudly, and said to Saul, "Why have you deceived me? You are Saul!" [13]The king answered her, "Don't be afraid. What do you see?" And the woman said to Saul, "I see a divine being coming up from the earth." [14]"What does he look like?" he asked her. "It is an old man coming up," she said, "and he is wrapped in a robe." Then Saul knew that it was Samuel; and he bowed low in homage with his face to the ground.

[15]Samuel said to Saul, "Why have you disturbed me and brought me up?" And Saul answered, "I am in great trouble. The Philistines are attacking me and God has turned away from me; He no longer answers me, either by prophets or in dreams. So I have called you to tell me what I am to do." [16]Samuel said, "Why do you ask me, seeing that the LORD has turned away from you and has become your adversary?[d] [17]The LORD has done [e-for Himself-e] as He fore-

7 וַיֹּאמֶר שָׁאוּל לַעֲבָדָיו בַּקְּשׁוּ־לִי אֵשֶׁת בַּעֲלַת־אוֹב וְאֵלְכָה אֵלֶיהָ וְאֶדְרְשָׁה־בָּהּ וַיֹּאמְרוּ עֲבָדָיו אֵלָיו הִנֵּה אֵשֶׁת בַּעֲלַת־אוֹב בְּעֵין דּוֹר: 8 וַיִּתְחַפֵּשׂ שָׁאוּל וַיִּלְבַּשׁ בְּגָדִים אֲחֵרִים וַיֵּלֶךְ הוּא וּשְׁנֵי אֲנָשִׁים עִמּוֹ וַיָּבֹאוּ אֶל־הָאִשָּׁה לָיְלָה וַיֹּאמֶר קסומי קָסֳמִי־נָא לִי בָּאוֹב וְהַעֲלִי לִי אֵת אֲשֶׁר־אֹמַר אֵלָיִךְ: 9 וַתֹּאמֶר הָאִשָּׁה אֵלָיו הִנֵּה אַתָּה יָדַעְתָּ אֵת אֲשֶׁר־עָשָׂה שָׁאוּל אֲשֶׁר הִכְרִית אֶת־הָאֹבוֹת וְאֶת־הַיִּדְּעֹנִי מִן־הָאָרֶץ וְלָמָה אַתָּה מִתְנַקֵּשׁ בְּנַפְשִׁי לַהֲמִיתֵנִי: 10 וַיִּשָּׁבַע לָהּ שָׁאוּל בַּיהוָה לֵאמֹר חַי־יְהוָה אִם־יִקְּרֵךְ עָוֺן בַּדָּבָר הַזֶּה: 11 וַתֹּאמֶר הָאִשָּׁה אֶת־מִי אַעֲלֶה־לָּךְ וַיֹּאמֶר אֶת־שְׁמוּאֵל הַעֲלִי־לִי: 12 וַתֵּרֶא הָאִשָּׁה אֶת־שְׁמוּאֵל וַתִּזְעַק בְּקוֹל גָּדוֹל וַתֹּאמֶר הָאִשָּׁה אֶל־שָׁאוּל לֵאמֹר לָמָּה רִמִּיתָנִי וְאַתָּה שָׁאוּל: 13 וַיֹּאמֶר לָהּ הַמֶּלֶךְ אַל־תִּירְאִי כִּי מָה רָאִית וַתֹּאמֶר הָאִשָּׁה אֶל־שָׁאוּל אֱלֹהִים רָאִיתִי עֹלִים מִן־הָאָרֶץ: 14 וַיֹּאמֶר לָהּ מַה־תָּאֳרוֹ וַתֹּאמֶר אִישׁ זָקֵן עֹלֶה וְהוּא עֹטֶה מְעִיל וַיֵּדַע שָׁאוּל כִּי־שְׁמוּאֵל הוּא וַיִּקֹּד אַפַּיִם אַרְצָה וַיִּשְׁתָּחוּ: ס 15 וַיֹּאמֶר שְׁמוּאֵל אֶל־שָׁאוּל לָמָה הִרְגַּזְתַּנִי לְהַעֲלוֹת אֹתִי וַיֹּאמֶר שָׁאוּל צַר־לִי מְאֹד וּפְלִשְׁתִּים | נִלְחָמִים בִּי וֵאלֹהִים סָר מֵעָלַי וְלֹא־עָנָנִי עוֹד גַּם בְּיַד־הַנְּבִיאִם גַּם־בַּחֲלֹמוֹת וָאֶקְרָאֶה לְךָ לְהוֹדִיעֵנִי מָה אֶעֱשֶׂה: ס 16 וַיֹּאמֶר שְׁמוּאֵל וְלָמָּה תִּשְׁאָלֵנִי וַיהוָה סָר מֵעָלֶיךָ וַיְהִי עָרֶךָ: 17 וַיַּעַשׂ יְהוָה לוֹ כַּאֲשֶׁר דִּבֶּר

b   A kind of oracle; see note at Exod. 28.30 and 1 Sam. 14.41.
c   Some Septuagint mss. read "Saul."
d   Meaning of Heb. uncertain.
e-e Some mss. and Septuagint read "to you."

636

told through me: The LORD has torn the king-ship out of your hands and has given it to your fellow, to David, [18]because you did not obey the LORD and did not execute His wrath upon the Amalekites. That is why the LORD has done this to you today. [19]Further, the LORD will deliver the Israelites who are with you into the hands of the Philistines. Tomorrow your sons and you will be with me; and the LORD will also deliver the Israelite forces into the hands of the Philistines."

[20]At once Saul flung himself prone on the ground, terrified by Samuel's words. Besides, there was no strength in him, for he had not eaten anything all day and all night. [21]The woman went up to Saul and, seeing how greatly disturbed he was, she said to him, "Your hand-maid listened to you; I took my life in my hands and heeded the request you made of me. [22]So now you listen to me: Let me set before you a bit of food. Eat, and then you will have the strength to go on your way." [23]He refused, say-ing, "I will not eat." But when his courtiers as well as the woman urged him, he listened to them; he got up from the ground and sat on the bed. [24]The woman had a stall-fed calf in the house; she hastily slaughtered it, and took flour and kneaded it, and baked some unleavened cakes. [25]She set this before Saul and his court-iers, and they ate. Then they rose and left the same night.

29 The Philistines mustered all their forces at Aphek, while Israel was encamping at the spring in Jezreel. [2]The Philistine lords came marching, each with his units of hundreds and of thousands; and David and his men came marching last, with Achish. [3]The Philistine officers asked, "Who are those Hebrews?" "Why, that's David, the servant of King Saul of

בְּיָדֶךְ וַיִּקְרַע יְהוָה אֶת־הַמַּמְלָכָה מִיָּדֶךְ וַיִּתְּנָהּ לְרֵעֲךָ לְדָוִד: 18 כַּאֲשֶׁר לֹא־שָׁמַעְתָּ בְּקוֹל יְהוָה וְלֹא־עָשִׂיתָ חֲרוֹן־אַפּוֹ בַּעֲמָלֵק עַל־כֵּן הַדָּבָר הַזֶּה עָשָׂה־לְךָ יְהוָה הַיּוֹם הַזֶּה: 19 וְיִתֵּן יְהוָה גַּם אֶת־יִשְׂרָאֵל עִמְּךָ בְּיַד־פְּלִשְׁתִּים וּמָחָר אַתָּה וּבָנֶיךָ עִמִּי גַּם אֶת־מַחֲנֵה יִשְׂרָאֵל יִתֵּן יְהוָה בְּיַד־פְּלִשְׁתִּים:

20 וַיְמַהֵר שָׁאוּל וַיִּפֹּל מְלֹא־קוֹמָתוֹ אַרְצָה וַיִּרָא מְאֹד מִדִּבְרֵי שְׁמוּאֵל גַּם־כֹּחַ לֹא־הָיָה בוֹ כִּי לֹא אָכַל לֶחֶם כָּל־הַיּוֹם וְכָל־הַלָּיְלָה: 21 וַתָּבוֹא הָאִשָּׁה אֶל־שָׁאוּל וַתֵּרֶא כִּי־נִבְהַל מְאֹד וַתֹּאמֶר אֵלָיו הִנֵּה שָׁמְעָה שִׁפְחָתְךָ בְּקוֹלֶךָ וָאָשִׂים נַפְשִׁי בְכַפִּי וָאֶשְׁמַע אֶת־דְּבָרֶיךָ אֲשֶׁר דִּבַּרְתָּ אֵלָי: 22 וְעַתָּה שְׁמַע־נָא גַם־אַתָּה בְּקוֹל שִׁפְחָתֶךָ וְאָשִׂמָה לְפָנֶיךָ פַּת־לֶחֶם וֶאֱכוֹל וִיהִי בְךָ כֹּחַ כִּי תֵלֵךְ בַּדָּרֶךְ: 23 *וַיְמָאֵן וַיֹּאמֶר לֹא אֹכַל וַיִּפְרְצוּ־בוֹ עֲבָדָיו וְגַם־הָאִשָּׁה וַיִּשְׁמַע לְקֹלָם וַיָּקָם מֵהָאָרֶץ וַיֵּשֶׁב אֶל־הַמִּטָּה: 24 וְלָאִשָּׁה עֵגֶל־מַרְבֵּק בַּבַּיִת וַתְּמַהֵר וַתִּזְבָּחֵהוּ וַתִּקַּח־קֶמַח וַתָּלָשׁ וַתֹּפֵהוּ מַצּוֹת: 25 וַתַּגֵּשׁ לִפְנֵי־שָׁאוּל וְלִפְנֵי עֲבָדָיו וַיֹּאכֵלוּ וַיָּקֻמוּ וַיֵּלְכוּ בַּלַּיְלָה הַהוּא: פ

כט וַיִּקְבְּצוּ פְלִשְׁתִּים אֶת־כָּל־מַחֲנֵיהֶם אֲפֵקָה וְיִשְׂרָאֵל חֹנִים בַּעַיִן אֲשֶׁר בְּיִזְרְעֶאל: 2 וְסַרְנֵי פְלִשְׁתִּים עֹבְרִים לְמֵאוֹת וְלַאֲלָפִים וְדָוִד וַאֲנָשָׁיו עֹבְרִים בָּאַחֲרֹנָה עִם־אָכִישׁ: 3 וַיֹּאמְרוּ שָׂרֵי פְלִשְׁתִּים מָה הָעִבְרִים הָאֵלֶּה וַיֹּאמֶר אָכִישׁ אֶל־שָׂרֵי פְלִשְׁתִּים הֲלוֹא־זֶה דָוִד

v. 23. חֲצִי הַסֵּפֶר בִּפְסוּקִים (אַף עַל פִּי שֶׁנִּסְמַן 28.24 בִּכְתַב הַיָּד שֶׁלָּנוּ)

Israel," Achish answered the Philistine officers. "He has been with me *a*-for a year or more,-*a* and I have found no fault in him from the day he defected until now." 4But the Philistine officers were angry with him; and the Philistine officers said to him, "Send the man back; let him go back to the place you assigned him. He shall not march down with us to the battle, or else he may become our adversary in battle. For with what could that fellow appease his master if not with *b*-the heads of these men?-*b* 5Remember, he is the David of whom they sang as they danced:

Saul has slain his thousands;
David, his tens of thousands."

6Achish summoned David and said to him, "As the Lord lives, you are an honest man, and I would like to have you serve*c* in my forces; for I have found no fault with you from the day you joined me until now. But you are not acceptable to the other lords. 7So go back in peace, and do nothing to displease the Philistine lords."

8David, however, said to Achish, "But what have I done, what fault have you found in your servant from the day I appeared before you to this day, that I should not go and fight against the enemies of my lord the king?" 9Achish replied to David, "I know; you are as acceptable to me as an angel of God. But the Philistine officers have decided that you must not march out with us to the battle. 10So rise early in the morning, you and your lord's servants who came with you—*d*-rise early in the morning,-*d* and leave as soon as it is light." 11Accordingly, David and his men rose early in the morning to leave, to return to the land of the Philistines, while the Philistines marched up to Jezreel.

---

a-a   Meaning of phrase uncertain.
b-b   A euphemism for "our heads."
c   Lit. "go out and come in."
d-d   Meaning of parts of verse uncertain. Septuagint reads "and go to the place that I have assigned you; and harbor no evil thought in your heart, for you are acceptable to me."

עֶבֶד ׀ שָׁא֤וּל מֶֽלֶךְ־יִשְׂרָאֵל֙ אֲשֶׁ֣ר הָיָ֣ה אִתִּ֗י זֶ֤ה יָמִים֙ אוֹ־זֶ֣ה שָׁנִ֔ים וְלֹֽא־מָצָ֤אתִי ב֙וֹ מְא֔וּמָה מִיּ֥וֹם נׇפְל֖וֹ עַד־הַיּ֥וֹם הַזֶּֽה׃ פ 4וַיִּקְצְפ֤וּ עָלָיו֙ שָׂרֵ֣י פְלִשְׁתִּ֔ים וַיֹּ֧אמְרוּ ל֣וֹ שָׂרֵ֣י פְלִשְׁתִּ֗ים הָשֵׁ֤ב אֶת־הָאִישׁ֙ וְיָשֹׁ֣ב אֶל־מְקוֹמוֹ֙ אֲשֶׁ֣ר הִפְקַדְתּ֣וֹ שָׁ֔ם וְלֹֽא־יֵרֵ֤ד עִמָּ֙נוּ֙ בַּמִּלְחָמָ֔ה וְלֹא־יִֽהְיֶה־לָּ֥נוּ לְשָׂטָ֖ן בַּמִּלְחָמָ֑ה וּבַמֶּ֗ה יִתְרַצֶּ֤ה זֶה֙ אֶל־אֲדֹנָ֔יו הֲל֕וֹא בְּרָאשֵׁ֖י הָאֲנָשִׁ֥ים הָהֵֽם׃ 5הֲלוֹא־זֶ֣ה דָוִ֔ד אֲשֶׁ֧ר יַעֲנוּ־ל֛וֹ בַּמְּחֹל֖וֹת לֵאמֹ֑ר הִכָּ֤ה שָׁאוּל֙ בַּֽאֲלָפָ֔יו

וְדָוִ֖ד בְּרִֽבְבֹתָֽיו׃ ס

6וַיִּקְרָ֨א אָכִ֜ישׁ אֶל־דָּוִ֗ד וַיֹּ֣אמֶר אֵלָיו֮ חַי־יְהֹוָה֒ כִּֽי־יָשָׁ֣ר אַתָּ֗ה וְט֣וֹב בְּעֵינַ֤י צֵֽאתְךָ֙ וּבֹאֲךָ֤ אִתִּי֙ בַּֽמַּחֲנֶ֔ה כִּ֠י לֹֽא־מָצָ֤אתִי בְךָ֤ רָעָה֙ מִיּ֨וֹם בֹּאֲךָ֤ אֵלַי֙ עַד־הַיּ֣וֹם הַזֶּ֔ה וּבְעֵינֵ֥י הַסְּרָנִ֖ים לֹא־ט֥וֹב אָֽתָּה׃ 7וְעַתָּ֥ה שׁ֖וּב וְלֵ֣ךְ בְּשָׁל֑וֹם וְלֹֽא־תַעֲשֶׂ֣ה רָ֔ע בְּעֵינֵ֖י סַרְנֵ֥י פְלִשְׁתִּֽים׃ ס

8וַיֹּ֨אמֶר דָּוִ֜ד אֶל־אָכִ֗ישׁ כִּ֤י מֶ֤ה עָשִׂ֙יתִי֙ וּמַה־מָּצָ֣אתָ בְעַבְדְּךָ֔ מִיּוֹם֙ אֲשֶׁ֣ר הָיִ֣יתִי לְפָנֶ֔יךָ עַ֖ד הַיּ֣וֹם הַזֶּ֑ה כִּ֣י לֹ֤א אָבוֹא֙ וְנִלְחַ֔מְתִּי בְּאֹיְבֵ֖י אֲדֹנִ֥י הַמֶּֽלֶךְ׃ 9וַיַּ֣עַן אָכִישׁ֮ וַיֹּ֣אמֶר אֶל־דָּוִד֒ יָדַ֕עְתִּי כִּ֣י ט֥וֹב אַתָּ֛ה בְּעֵינַ֖י כְּמַלְאַ֣ךְ אֱלֹהִ֑ים אַ֣ךְ שָׂרֵ֤י פְלִשְׁתִּים֙ אָֽמְר֔וּ לֹֽא־יַעֲלֶ֥ה עִמָּ֖נוּ בַּמִּלְחָמָֽה׃ 10וְעַתָּה֙ הַשְׁכֵּ֣ם בַּבֹּ֔קֶר וְעַבְדֵ֥י אֲדֹנֶ֖יךָ אֲשֶׁר־בָּ֣אוּ אִתָּ֑ךְ וְהִשְׁכַּמְתֶּ֣ם בַּבֹּ֔קֶר וְא֥וֹר לָכֶ֖ם וָלֵֽכוּ׃ 11וַיַּשְׁכֵּ֨ם דָּוִ֜ד ה֤וּא וַֽאֲנָשָׁיו֙ לָלֶ֣כֶת בַּבֹּ֔קֶר לָשׁ֖וּב אֶל־אֶ֣רֶץ פְּלִשְׁתִּ֑ים וּפְלִשְׁתִּ֖ים עָל֥וּ יִזְרְעֶֽאל׃ ס

638

30

By the time David and his men arrived in Ziklag, on the third day, the Amalekites had made a raid into the Negeb and against Ziklag; they had stormed Ziklag and burned it down. ²They had taken the women in it captive, low-born and high-born alike; they did not kill any, but carried them off and went their way. ³When David and his men came to the town and found it burned down, and their wives and sons and daughters taken captive, ⁴David and the troops with him broke into tears, until they had no strength left for weeping. ⁵David's two wives had been taken captive, Ahinoam of Jezreel and Abigail wife of Nabal from Carmel. ⁶David was in great danger, for the troops threatened to stone him; for all the troops were embittered on account of their sons and daughters.

But David sought strength in the Lord his God. ⁷David said to the priest Abiathar son of Ahimelech, "Bring the ephod up to me." When Abiathar brought up the ephod[a] to David, ⁸David inquired of the Lord, "Shall I pursue those raiders? Will I overtake them?" And He answered him, "Pursue, for you shall overtake and you shall rescue."

⁹So David and the six hundred men with him set out, and they came to the Wadi Besor, where a halt was made by those who were to be left behind. ¹⁰David continued the pursuit with four hundred men; two hundred men had halted, too faint to cross the Wadi Besor. ¹¹They came upon an Egyptian in the open country and brought him to David. They gave him food to eat and water to drink; ¹²he was also given a piece of pressed fig cake and two cakes of raisins. He ate and regained his strength, for he had eaten no food and drunk no water for three days and three nights. ¹³Then David asked him, "To whom do you belong and where are you from?"

---

a *See note at 2.28.*

639

ל

וַיְהִ֞י בְּבֹ֨א דָוִ֧ד וַאֲנָשָׁ֛יו צִֽקְלַ֖ג בַּיּ֣וֹם הַשְּׁלִישִׁ֑י וַעֲמָלֵקִ֣י פָשְׁט֗וּ אֶל־נֶ֙גֶב֙ וְאֶל־צִ֣קְלַ֔ג וַיַּכּוּ֙ אֶת־צִ֣קְלַ֔ג וַיִּשְׂרְפ֥וּ אֹתָ֖הּ בָּאֵֽשׁ׃ ²וַיִּשְׁבּ֨וּ אֶת־הַנָּשִׁ֤ים אֲשֶׁר־בָּהּ֙ מִקָּטֹ֣ן וְעַד־גָּד֔וֹל לֹ֥א הֵמִ֖יתוּ אִ֑ישׁ וַיִּֽנְהֲג֔וּ וַיֵּלְכ֖וּ לְדַרְכָּֽם׃ ³וַיָּבֹ֨א דָוִ֤ד וַֽאֲנָשָׁיו֙ אֶל־הָעִ֔יר וְהִנֵּ֥ה שְׂרוּפָ֖ה בָּאֵ֑שׁ וּנְשֵׁיהֶ֧ם וּבְנֵיהֶ֛ם וּבְנֹתֵיהֶ֖ם נִשְׁבּֽוּ׃ ⁴וַיִּשָּׂ֨א דָוִ֜ד וְהָעָ֧ם אֲשֶׁר־אִתּ֛וֹ אֶת־קוֹלָ֖ם וַיִּבְכּ֑וּ עַ֣ד אֲשֶׁ֧ר אֵֽין־בָּהֶ֛ם כֹּ֖חַ לִבְכּֽוֹת׃ ⁵וּשְׁתֵּ֥י נְשֵֽׁי־דָוִ֖ד נִשְׁבּ֑וּ אֲחִינֹ֙עַם֙ הַיִּזְרְעֵלִ֔ית וַאֲבִיגַ֕יִל אֵ֖שֶׁת נָבָ֥ל הַֽכַּרְמְלִֽי׃ ⁶וַתֵּ֨צֶר לְדָוִ֜ד מְאֹ֗ד כִּֽי־אָמְר֤וּ הָעָם֙ לְסָקְל֔וֹ כִּֽי־מָ֙רָה֙ נֶ֣פֶשׁ כָּל־הָעָ֔ם אִ֥ישׁ עַל־בָּנָ֖ו וְעַל־בְּנֹתָ֑יו וַיִּתְחַזֵּ֣ק דָּוִ֔ד בַּֽיהֹוָ֖ה אֱלֹהָֽיו׃ ס ⁷וַיֹּ֣אמֶר דָּוִ֗ד אֶל־אֶבְיָתָ֤ר הַכֹּהֵן֙ בֶּן־אֲחִימֶ֔לֶךְ הַגִּֽישָׁה־נָּ֥א לִ֖י הָאֵפֹ֑ד וַיַּגֵּ֧שׁ אֶבְיָתָ֛ר אֶת־הָאֵפֹ֖ד אֶל־דָּוִֽד׃ ⁸וַיִּשְׁאַ֨ל דָּוִ֤ד בַּֽיהֹוָה֙ לֵאמֹ֔ר אֶרְדֹּ֛ף אַחֲרֵ֥י הַגְּדֽוּד־הַזֶּ֖ה הַֽאַשִּׂגֶ֑נּוּ וַיֹּ֤אמֶר לוֹ֙ רְדֹ֔ף כִּֽי־הַשֵּׂ֥ג תַּשִּׂ֖יג וְהַצֵּ֥ל תַּצִּֽיל׃

⁹וַיֵּ֣לֶךְ דָּוִ֗ד ה֚וּא וְשֵׁשׁ־מֵא֥וֹת אִישׁ֙ אֲשֶׁ֣ר אִתּ֔וֹ וַיָּבֹ֖אוּ עַד־נַ֣חַל הַבְּשׂ֑וֹר וְהַנּֽוֹתָרִ֖ים עָמָֽדוּ׃ ¹⁰וַיִּרְדֹּ֣ף דָּוִ֔ד ה֖וּא וְאַרְבַּע־מֵא֣וֹת אִ֑ישׁ וַיַּֽעַמְדוּ֙ מָאתַ֣יִם אִ֔ישׁ אֲשֶׁ֣ר פִּגְּר֔וּ מֵעֲבֹ֖ר אֶת־נַ֥חַל הַבְּשֽׂוֹר׃ ¹¹וַיִּמְצְא֤וּ אִישׁ־מִצְרִי֙ בַּשָּׂדֶ֔ה וַיִּקְח֥וּ אֹת֖וֹ אֶל־דָּוִ֑ד וַיִּתְּנוּ־ל֣וֹ לֶ֗חֶם וַיֹּ֙אכַל֙ וַיַּשְׁקֻ֣הוּ מָֽיִם׃ ¹²וַיִּתְּנוּ־לוֹ֩ פֶ֨לַח דְּבֵלָ֜ה וּשְׁנֵ֣י צִמֻּקִ֗ים וַיֹּ֙אכַל֙ וַתָּ֣שָׁב רוּח֣וֹ אֵלָ֔יו כִּ֠י לֹֽא־אָ֤כַל לֶ֙חֶם֙ וְלֹא־שָׁ֣תָה מַ֔יִם שְׁלֹשָׁ֥ה יָמִ֖ים וּשְׁלֹשָׁ֥ה לֵילֽוֹת׃ ס ¹³וַיֹּ֨אמֶר ל֤וֹ דָוִד֙ לְמִֽי־אַ֔תָּה וְאֵ֥י מִזֶּ֖ה אָֽתָּה

"I am an Egyptian boy," he answered, "the slave of an Amalekite. My master abandoned me when I fell ill three days ago. ¹⁴We had raided the Negeb of the Cherethites, and [the Negeb] of Judah, and the Negeb of Caleb; we also burned down Ziklag." ¹⁵And David said to him, "Can you lead me down to that band?" He replied, "Swear to me by God that you will not kill me or deliver me into my master's hands, and I will lead you down to that band." ¹⁶So he led him down, and there they were, scattered all over the ground, eating and drinking and making merry because of all the vast spoil they had taken from the land of the Philistines and from the land of Judah. ¹⁷David attacked them from ᵇ-before dawn until the evening of the next day;-ᵇ none of them escaped, except four hundred young men who mounted camels and got away. ¹⁸David rescued everything the Amalekites had taken; David also rescued his two wives. ¹⁹Nothing of theirs was missing—young or old, sons or daughters, spoil or anything else that had been carried off—David recovered everything. ²⁰David took all the flocks and herds, ᵇ-which [the troops] drove ahead of the other livestock;-ᵇ and they declared, "This is David's spoil."

²¹When David reached the two hundred men who were too faint to follow David and who had been left at the Wadi Besor, they came out to welcome David and the troops with him; David came forward with the troops and greeted them. ²²But all the mean and churlish fellows among the men who had accompanied David spoke up, "Since they did not accompany us,ᶜ we will not give them any of the spoil that we seized— except that each may take his wife and children and go." ²³David, however, spoke up, "You must not do that, ᵈ-my brothers, in view of-ᵈ

וַיֹּ֣אמֶר נַ֣עַר מִצְרִ֤י אָנֹ֙כִי֙ עֶ֣בֶד לְאִ֣ישׁ עֲמָלֵקִ֔י וַיַּעַזְבֵ֣נִי אֲדֹנִ֔י כִּ֥י חָלִ֖יתִי הַיּ֥וֹם שְׁלֹשָֽׁה׃ 14 אֲנַ֡חְנוּ פָּשַׁטְנוּ֩ נֶ֨גֶב הַכְּרֵתִ֜י וְעַל־אֲשֶׁ֤ר לִֽיהוּדָה֙ וְעַל־נֶ֣גֶב כָּלֵ֔ב וְאֶת־צִֽקְלַ֖ג שָׂרַ֥פְנוּ בָאֵֽשׁ׃ 15 וַיֹּ֤אמֶר אֵלָיו֙ דָּוִ֔ד הֲתוֹרִדֵ֖נִי אֶל־הַגְּד֣וּד הַזֶּ֑ה וַיֹּ֡אמֶר הִשָּׁ֩בְעָ֨ה לִּ֜י בֵֽאלֹהִ֗ים אִם־תְּמִיתֵ֙נִי֙ וְאִם־תַּסְגִּרֵ֙נִי֙ בְּיַד־אֲדֹנִ֔י וְאוֹרִֽדְךָ֖ אֶל־הַגְּד֥וּד הַזֶּֽה׃ 16 וַיֹּ֣רִדֵ֔הוּ וְהִנֵּ֥ה נְטֻשִׁ֖ים עַל־פְּנֵ֣י כָל־הָאָ֑רֶץ אֹכְלִ֤ים וְשֹׁתִים֙ וְחֹ֣גְגִ֔ים בְּכֹל֙ הַשָּׁלָ֣ל הַגָּד֔וֹל אֲשֶׁ֥ר לָקְח֖וּ מֵאֶ֣רֶץ פְּלִשְׁתִּ֑ים וּמֵאֶ֖רֶץ יְהוּדָֽה׃ 17 וַיַּכֵּ֥ם דָּוִ֛ד מֵהַנֶּ֖שֶׁף וְעַד־הָעֶ֣רֶב לְמׇֽחֳרָתָ֑ם וְלֹֽא־נִמְלַ֤ט מֵהֶם֙ אִ֔ישׁ כִּ֠י אִם־אַרְבַּ֤ע מֵא֥וֹת אִֽישׁ־נַ֙עַר֙ אֲשֶׁר־רָכְב֣וּ עַל־הַגְּמַלִּ֔ים וַיָּנֻֽסוּ׃ 18 וַיַּצֵּ֣ל דָּוִ֔ד אֵ֛ת כׇּל־אֲשֶׁ֥ר לָקְח֖וּ עֲמָלֵ֑ק וְאֶת־שְׁתֵּ֥י נָשָׁ֖יו הִצִּ֥יל דָּוִֽד׃ 19 וְלֹ֣א נֶעְדַּר־לָהֶ֗ם מִן־הַקָּטֹן֙ וְעַד־הַגָּד֔וֹל וְעַד־בָּנִ֣ים וּבָנ֔וֹת וּמִשָּׁלָ֕ל וְעַ֥ד כׇּל־אֲשֶׁ֖ר לָקְח֣וּ לָהֶ֑ם הַכֹּ֖ל הֵשִׁ֥יב דָּוִֽד׃ 20 וַיִּקַּ֣ח דָּוִ֔ד אֶת־כׇּל־הַצֹּ֖אן וְהַבָּקָ֑ר נָהֲג֗וּ לִפְנֵי֙ הַמִּקְנֶ֣ה הַה֔וּא וַיֹּ֣אמְר֔וּ זֶ֖ה שְׁלַ֥ל דָּוִֽד׃

21 וַיָּבֹ֣א דָוִ֗ד אֶל־מָאתַ֣יִם הָאֲנָשִׁ֡ים אֲשֶֽׁר־פִּגְּר֣וּ ׀ מִלֶּ֣כֶת ׀ אַחֲרֵ֣י דָוִ֡ד וַיֹּֽשִׁיבֻם֩ בְּנַ֨חַל הַבְּשׂ֜וֹר וַיֵּֽצְאוּ֙ לִקְרַ֣את דָּוִ֔ד וְלִקְרַ֖את הָעָ֣ם אֲשֶׁר־אִתּ֑וֹ וַיִּגַּ֤שׁ דָּוִד֙ אֶת־הָעָ֔ם וַיִּשְׁאַ֥ל לָהֶ֖ם לְשָׁלֽוֹם׃ ס 22 וַיַּ֜עַן כׇּל־אִֽישׁ־רָ֣ע וּבְלִיַּ֗עַל מֵֽהָאֲנָשִׁים֮ אֲשֶׁ֣ר הָלְכ֣וּ עִם־דָּוִד֒ וַיֹּֽאמְר֗וּ יַ֚עַן אֲשֶׁ֣ר לֹא־הָלְכ֣וּ עִמִּ֔י* לֹֽא־נִתֵּ֣ן לָהֶ֗ם מֵהַשָּׁלָל֙ אֲשֶׁ֣ר הִצַּ֔לְנוּ כִּֽי־אִם־אִ֤ישׁ אֶת־אִשְׁתּוֹ֙ וְאֶת־בָּנָ֔יו וְיִנְהֲג֖וּ וְיֵלֵֽכוּ׃ ס 23 וַיֹּ֣אמֶר דָּוִ֔ד לֹא־תַעֲשׂ֥וּ כֵ֖ן אֶחָ֑י אֵ֠ת אֲשֶׁר־נָתַ֨ן יְהֹוָ֥ה לָ֙נוּ֙ וַיִּשְׁמֹ֣ר אֹתָ֔נוּ וַיִּתֵּ֣ן אֶֽת־הַגְּד֔וּד הַבָּ֥א עָלֵ֖ינוּ בְּיָדֵֽנוּ׃ 24 וּמִ֣י

v. 22. בנוסח אחר ״עמנו״

---

b-b   *Meaning of Heb. uncertain.*
c   *So some mss. and versions; most mss. and editions read "me."*
d-d   *Meaning of Heb. uncertain. Septuagint reads "after."*

what the LORD has granted us, guarding us and delivering into our hands the band that attacked us. 24How could anyone agree with you in this matter? The share of those who remain with the baggage shall be the same as the share of those who go down to battle; they shall share alike." 25So from that day on it was made a fixed rule for Israel, continuing to the present day.

26When David reached Ziklag, he sent some of the spoil to the elders of Judah b-[and] to his friends,-b saying, "This is a present for you from our spoil of the enemies of the LORD." 27[He sent the spoil to the elders] in Bethel,e Ramoth-negeb, and Jattir; 28in Aroer, Siphmoth, and Eshtemoa; 29in Racal, in the towns of the Jerahmeelites, and in the towns of the Kenites; 30in Hormah, Bor-ashan, and Athach; 31and to those in Hebron—all the places where David and his men had roamed.

31

31 aThe Philistines attacked Israel, and the men of Israel fled before the Philistines and [many] fell on Mount Gilboa. 2The Philistines pursued Saul and his sons, and the Philistines struck down Jonathan, Abinadab, and Malchishua, sons of Saul. 3The battle raged around Saul, and b-some of the archers-b hit him, and he c-was severely wounded-c by the archers. 4Saul said to his arms-bearer, "Draw your sword and run me through, so that the uncircumcised may not run me through and make sport of me." But his arms-bearer, in his great awe, refused; whereupon Saul grasped the sword and fell upon it. 5When his arms-bearer saw that Saul was dead, he too fell on his sword and died with him. 6Thus Saul and his three sons and his arms-bearer, d-as well as all his men,-d

יִשְׁמַ֤ע לָכֶם֙ לַדָּבָ֣ר הַזֶּ֔ה כִּ֖י כְּחֵ֣לֶק ׀ הַיֹּרֵ֣ד בַּמִּלְחָמָ֗ה וּֽכְחֵ֛לֶק הַיֹּשֵׁ֥ב עַל־הַכֵּלִ֖ים יַחְדָּ֣ו יַחֲלֹֽקוּ׃ ס 25 וַֽיְהִ֞י מֵהַיּ֤וֹם הַהוּא֙ וָמָ֔עְלָה וַיְשִׂמֶ֛הָ לְחֹ֥ק וּלְמִשְׁפָּ֖ט לְיִשְׂרָאֵ֑ל עַ֖ד הַיּ֥וֹם הַזֶּֽה׃ פ

26 וַיָּבֹ֤א דָוִד֙ אֶל־צִ֣קְלַ֔ג וַיְשַׁלַּ֧ח מֵֽהַשָּׁלָ֛ל לְזִקְנֵ֥י יְהוּדָ֖ה לְרֵעֵ֣הוּ לֵאמֹ֑ר הִנֵּ֤ה לָכֶם֙ בְּרָכָ֔ה מִשְּׁלַ֖ל אֹיְבֵ֥י יְהוָֽה׃ 27 *לַאֲשֶׁ֣ר בְּבֵֽית־אֵ֗ל וְלַאֲשֶׁ֤ר בְּרָמֽוֹת־נֶ֨גֶב֙ וְלַאֲשֶׁ֣ר בְּיַתִּֽר׃ 28 וְלַאֲשֶׁ֣ר בַּעֲרֹעֵ֗ר וְלַאֲשֶׁ֤ר בְּשִׂפְמ֨וֹת֙ וְלַאֲשֶׁ֣ר בְּאֶשְׁתְּמֹ֔עַ׃ ס 29 וְלַאֲשֶׁ֣ר בְּרָכָ֗ל וְלַֽאֲשֶׁר֙ בְּעָרֵ֣י הַיְּרַחְמְאֵלִ֔י וְלַאֲשֶׁ֖ר בְּעָרֵ֥י הַקֵּינִֽי׃ 30 וְלַאֲשֶׁ֣ר בְּחָרְמָ֗ה וְלַֽאֲשֶׁר֙ בְּבֽוֹר־עָשָׁ֔ן וְלַאֲשֶׁ֖ר בַּעֲתָֽךְ׃ 31 וְלַאֲשֶׁ֖ר בְּחֶבְר֑וֹן וּֽלְכָל־הַמְּקֹמ֗וֹת אֲשֶֽׁר־הִתְהַלֶּךְ־שָׁ֥ם דָּוִ֛ד ה֥וּא וַאֲנָשָֽׁיו׃ פ

לא

וּפְלִשְׁתִּ֖ים נִלְחָמִ֣ים בְּיִשְׂרָאֵ֑ל וַיָּנֻ֜סוּ אַנְשֵׁ֤י יִשְׂרָאֵל֙ מִפְּנֵ֣י פְלִשְׁתִּ֔ים וַיִּפְּל֥וּ חֲלָלִ֖ים בְּהַ֥ר הַגִּלְבֹּֽעַ׃ 2 וַיַּדְבְּק֣וּ פְלִשְׁתִּ֔ים אֶת־שָׁא֖וּל וְאֶת־בָּנָ֑יו וַיַּכּ֣וּ פְלִשְׁתִּ֗ים אֶת־יְהוֹנָתָ֧ן וְאֶת־אֲבִינָדָ֛ב וְאֶת־מַלְכִּי־שׁ֖וּעַ בְּנֵ֥י שָׁאֽוּל׃ 3 וַתִּכְבַּ֤ד הַמִּלְחָמָה֙ אֶל־שָׁא֔וּל וַיִּמְצָאֻ֥הוּ הַמּוֹרִ֖ים אֲנָשִׁ֣ים בַּקָּ֑שֶׁת וַיָּ֥חֶל מְאֹ֖ד מֵהַמּוֹרִֽים׃ 4 וַיֹּ֣אמֶר שָׁאוּל֩ לְנֹשֵׂ֨א כֵלָ֜יו שְׁלֹ֥ף חַרְבְּךָ֣ ׀ וְדָקְרֵ֣נִי בָ֗הּ פֶּן־יָב֜וֹאוּ הָעֲרֵלִ֤ים הָאֵ֨לֶּה֙ וּדְקָרֻ֨נִי֙ וְהִתְעַלְּלוּ־בִ֔י וְלֹ֤א אָבָה֙ נֹשֵׂ֣א כֵלָ֔יו כִּ֥י יָרֵ֖א מְאֹ֑ד וַיִּקַּ֤ח שָׁאוּל֙ אֶת־הַחֶ֔רֶב וַיִּפֹּ֖ל עָלֶֽיהָ׃ 5 וַיַּ֥רְא נֹשֵֽׂא־כֵלָ֖יו כִּ֣י מֵ֣ת שָׁא֑וּל וַיִּפֹּ֥ל גַּם־ה֛וּא עַל־חַרְבּ֖וֹ וַיָּ֥מָת עִמּֽוֹ׃ 6 וַיָּ֣מָת שָׁא֗וּל וּשְׁלֹ֧שֶׁת בָּנָ֛יו וְנֹשֵׂ֥א כֵלָ֖יו גַּ֣ם כָּל־אֲנָשָׁ֑יו בַּיּ֥וֹם הַה֖וּא

---

e   Called Bethul in Josh. 19.4.

a   1 Chron. 10 reproduces this chapter, with minor variations.
b-b   Meaning of Heb. uncertain. Lit. "the archers, men with the bow."
c-c   Construed as hophal form; cf. 1 Kings 2.34.
d-d   Lacking in the Septuagint; 1 Chron. 10.6 reads "all his house."

v. 27.   בכתב היד שלנו הרשימה בצורת שירה

died together on that day. [7]And when the men of Israel e-on the other side of the valley and on the other side of the Jordan-e saw that the men of Israel had fled and that Saul and his sons were dead, they abandoned the towns and fled; the Philistines then came and occupied them.

[8]The next day the Philistines came to strip the slain, and they found Saul and his three sons lying on Mount Gilboa. [9]They cut off his head and stripped him of his armor, and they sent them throughout the land of the Philistines, to spread the news f-in the temples of their idols-f and among the people. [10]They placed his armor in the temple of Ashtaroth, and they impaled his body on the wall of Beth-shan. [11]When g-the inhabitants of Jabesh-gilead heard about it— what-g the Philistines had done to Saul—[12]all their stalwart men set out and marched all night; they removed the bodies of Saul and his sons from the wall of Beth-shan and came[h] to Jabesh and burned them there. [13]Then they took the bones and buried them under the tamarisk tree in Jabesh, and they fasted for seven days.

יַחְדָּו: 7 וַיִּרְאוּ אַנְשֵׁי־יִשְׂרָאֵל אֲשֶׁר־בְּעֵבֶר הָעֵמֶק וַאֲשֶׁר ׀ בְּעֵבֶר הַיַּרְדֵּן כִּי־נָסוּ אַנְשֵׁי יִשְׂרָאֵל וְכִי־מֵתוּ שָׁאוּל וּבָנָיו וַיַּעַזְבוּ אֶת־הֶעָרִים וַיָּנֻסוּ וַיָּבֹאוּ פְלִשְׁתִּים וַיֵּשְׁבוּ בָּהֶן: ס 8 וַיְהִי מִמָּחֳרָת וַיָּבֹאוּ פְלִשְׁתִּים לְפַשֵּׁט אֶת־הַחֲלָלִים וַיִּמְצְאוּ אֶת־שָׁאוּל וְאֶת־שְׁלֹשֶׁת בָּנָיו נֹפְלִים בְּהַר הַגִּלְבֹּעַ: 9 וַיִּכְרְתוּ אֶת־רֹאשׁוֹ וַיַּפְשִׁיטוּ אֶת־כֵּלָיו וַיְשַׁלְּחוּ בְאֶרֶץ־פְּלִשְׁתִּים סָבִיב לְבַשֵּׂר בֵּית עֲצַבֵּיהֶם וְאֶת־הָעָם: 10 וַיָּשִׂמוּ אֶת־כֵּלָיו בֵּית עַשְׁתָּרוֹת וְאֶת־גְּוִיָּתוֹ תָּקְעוּ בְּחוֹמַת בֵּית שָׁן: 11 וַיִּשְׁמְעוּ אֵלָיו יֹשְׁבֵי יָבֵישׁ גִּלְעָד אֵת אֲשֶׁר־עָשׂוּ פְלִשְׁתִּים לְשָׁאוּל: 12 וַיָּקוּמוּ כָּל־אִישׁ חַיִל וַיֵּלְכוּ כָל־הַלַּיְלָה וַיִּקְחוּ אֶת־גְּוִיַּת שָׁאוּל וְאֵת גְּוִיֹּת בָּנָיו מֵחוֹמַת בֵּית שָׁן וַיָּבֹאוּ יָבֵשָׁה וַיִּשְׂרְפוּ אֹתָם שָׁם: 13 וַיִּקְחוּ אֶת־עַצְמֹתֵיהֶם וַיִּקְבְּרוּ תַחַת־הָאֶשֶׁל בְּיָבֵשָׁה וַיָּצֻמוּ שִׁבְעַת יָמִים: פ

---

e-e   Meaning of Heb. uncertain. 1 Chron. 10.7 reads "in the valley."
f-f   Septuagint and 1 Chron. 10.9 read "among their idols."
g-g   1 Chron. 10.11 reads "all [the inhabitants of] Jabesh-gilead heard all that."
h   1 Chron. 10.12 reads "brought them."

642

2 SAMUEL

1 After the death of Saul—David had already returned from defeating the Amalekites—David stayed two days in Ziklag. ²On the third day, a man came from Saul's camp, with his clothes rent and earth on his head; and as he approached David, he flung himself to the ground and bowed low. ³David said to him, "Where are you coming from?" He answered, "I have just escaped from the camp of Israel." ⁴"What happened?" asked David. "Tell me!" And he told him how the troops had fled the battlefield, and that, moreover, many of the troops had fallen and died; also that Saul and his son Jonathan were dead. ⁵"How do you know," David asked the young man who brought him the news, "that Saul and his son Jonathan are dead?" ⁶The young man who brought him the news answered, "I happened to be at Mount Gilboa, and I saw Saul leaning on his spear, and the chariots and horsemen closing in on him. ⁷He looked around and saw me, and he called to me. When I responded, 'At your service,' ⁸he asked me, 'Who are you?' And I told him that I was an Amalekite. ⁹Then he said to me, 'Stand over me, and finish me off, ᵃ-for I am in agony and am barely alive.'-ᵃ ¹⁰So I stood over him and finished him off, for I knew that ᵃ-he would never rise from where he was lying.-ᵃ Then I took the crown from his head and the armlet from his arm, and I have brought them here to my lord."

¹¹David took hold of his clothes and rent them, and so did all the men with him. ¹²They

---

ᵃ-ᵃ *Meaning of Heb. uncertain.*

א וַיְהִי אַחֲרֵי מוֹת שָׁאוּל וְדָוִד שָׁב מֵהַכּוֹת אֶת־הָעֲמָלֵק וַיֵּשֶׁב דָּוִד בְּצִקְלָג יָמִים שְׁנָיִם: 2 וַיְהִי | בַּיּוֹם הַשְּׁלִישִׁי וְהִנֵּה אִישׁ בָּא מִן־הַמַּחֲנֶה מֵעִם שָׁאוּל וּבְגָדָיו קְרֻעִים וַאֲדָמָה עַל־רֹאשׁוֹ וַיְהִי בְּבֹאוֹ אֶל־דָּוִד וַיִּפֹּל אַרְצָה וַיִּשְׁתָּחוּ: 3 וַיֹּאמֶר לוֹ דָּוִד אֵי מִזֶּה תָּבוֹא וַיֹּאמֶר אֵלָיו מִמַּחֲנֵה יִשְׂרָאֵל נִמְלָטְתִּי: 4 וַיֹּאמֶר אֵלָיו דָּוִד מֶה־הָיָה הַדָּבָר הַגֶּד־נָא לִי וַיֹּאמֶר אֲשֶׁר־נָס הָעָם מִן־הַמִּלְחָמָה וְגַם־הַרְבֵּה נָפַל מִן־הָעָם וַיָּמֻתוּ וְגַם שָׁאוּל וִיהוֹנָתָן בְּנוֹ מֵתוּ: 5 וַיֹּאמֶר דָּוִד אֶל־הַנַּעַר הַמַּגִּיד לוֹ אֵיךְ יָדַעְתָּ כִּי־מֵת שָׁאוּל וִיהוֹנָתָן בְּנוֹ: 6 וַיֹּאמֶר הַנַּעַר | הַמַּגִּיד לוֹ נִקְרֹא נִקְרֵיתִי בְּהַר הַגִּלְבֹּעַ וְהִנֵּה שָׁאוּל נִשְׁעָן עַל־חֲנִיתוֹ וְהִנֵּה הָרֶכֶב וּבַעֲלֵי הַפָּרָשִׁים הִדְבִּקֻהוּ: 7 וַיִּפֶן אַחֲרָיו וַיִּרְאֵנִי וַיִּקְרָא אֵלָי וָאֹמַר הִנֵּנִי: 8 וַיֹּאמֶר לִי מִי־אָתָּה וָאֹמַר אֵלָיו עֲמָלֵקִי אָנֹכִי: 9 וַיֹּאמֶר אֵלַי עֲמָד־נָא עָלַי וּמֹתְתֵנִי כִּי אֲחָזַנִי הַשָּׁבָץ כִּי־כָל־עוֹד נַפְשִׁי בִּי: 10 וָאֶעֱמֹד עָלָיו וַאֲמֹתְתֵהוּ כִּי יָדַעְתִּי כִּי לֹא יִחְיֶה אַחֲרֵי נִפְלוֹ וָאֶקַּח הַנֵּזֶר | אֲשֶׁר עַל־רֹאשׁוֹ וְאֶצְעָדָה אֲשֶׁר עַל־זְרֹעוֹ וָאֲבִיאֵם אֶל־אֲדֹנִי הֵנָּה: 11 וַיַּחֲזֵק דָּוִד בִּבְגָדָו וַיִּקְרָעֵם וְגַם כָּל־הָאֲנָשִׁים אֲשֶׁר אִתּוֹ: 12 וַיִּסְפְּדוּ וַיִּבְכּוּ

lamented and wept, and they fasted until evening for Saul and his son Jonathan, and for the
soldiers of the Lord[b] and the House of Israel
who had fallen by the sword. [13]David said to
the young man who had brought him the news,
"Where are you from?" He replied, "I am the
son of a resident alien, an Amalekite." [14]"How
did you dare," David said to him, "to lift your
hand and kill the Lord's anointed?" [15]There-
upon David called one of the attendants and
said to him, "Come over and strike him!" He
struck him down and he died. [16]And David said
to him, "Your blood be on your own head! Your
own mouth testified against you when you said,
'I put the Lord's anointed to death.'"

[17]And David intoned this dirge over Saul and
his son Jonathan—[18a]He ordered the Judites
to be taught [The Song of the] Bow.[-a] It is recorded in the Book of Jashar.[c]

[19]Your glory, O Israel,
Lies slain on your heights;
How have the mighty fallen!
[20]Tell it not in Gath,
Do not proclaim it in the streets of Ashkelon,
Lest the daughters of the Philistine rejoice,
Lest the daughters of the uncircumcised
   exult.

[21]O hills of Gilboa—
Let there be no dew or rain on you,
[d]-Or bountiful fields,[-d]
For there the shield of warriors lay rejected,
The shield of Saul,
Polished with oil no more.

[22]From the blood of slain,
From the fat of warriors—
The bow of Jonathan

וַיִּסְפְּדוּ֙ עַד־הָעֶ֔רֶב עַל־שָׁא֖וּל וְעַל־יְהוֹנָתָ֣ן
בְּנ֑וֹ וְעַל־עַ֤ם יְהֹוָה֙ וְעַל־בֵּ֣ית יִשְׂרָאֵ֔ל כִּ֥י
נָפְל֖וּ בֶּחָֽרֶב׃ ס 13 וַיֹּ֣אמֶר דָּוִ֗ד אֶל־הַנַּ֙עַר֙
הַמַּגִּ֣יד ל֔וֹ אֵ֥י מִזֶּ֖ה אָ֑תָּה וַיֹּ֕אמֶר בֶּן־אִ֛ישׁ
גֵּ֥ר עֲמָלֵקִ֖י אָנֹֽכִי׃ 14 וַיֹּ֤אמֶר אֵלָיו֙ דָּוִ֔ד אֵ֚יךְ
לֹ֣א יָרֵ֔אתָ לִשְׁלֹ֙חַ֙ יָֽדְךָ֔ לְשַׁחֵ֖ת אֶת־מְשִׁ֥יחַ
יְהֹוָֽה׃ 15 וַיִּקְרָ֣א דָוִ֗ד לְאַחַד֙ מֵֽהַנְּעָרִ֔ים
וַיֹּ֖אמֶר גַּ֣שׁ פְּגַע־בּ֑וֹ וַיַּכֵּ֖הוּ וַיָּמֹֽת׃ 16 וַיֹּ֤אמֶר
אֵלָיו֙ דָּוִ֔ד דָּמְךָ֖ עַל־רֹאשֶׁ֑ךָ כִּ֣י פִ֗יךָ
עָנָ֤ה בְךָ֙ לֵאמֹ֔ר אָנֹכִ֥י מֹתַ֖תִּי אֶת־מְשִׁ֥יחַ
יְהֹוָֽה׃ ס

17 וַיְקֹנֵ֣ן דָּוִ֔ד אֶת־הַקִּינָ֖ה הַזֹּ֑את עַל־שָׁא֖וּל
וְעַל־יְהוֹנָתָ֥ן בְּנֽוֹ׃ 18 וַיֹּ֕אמֶר לְלַמֵּ֥ד בְּנֵֽי־
יְהוּדָ֖ה קָ֑שֶׁת הִנֵּ֥ה כְתוּבָ֖ה עַל־סֵ֥פֶר
הַיָּשָֽׁר׃

19 הַצְּבִי֙ יִשְׂרָאֵ֔ל
עַל־בָּמוֹתֶ֖יךָ חָלָ֑ל
אֵ֖יךְ נָפְל֥וּ גִבּוֹרִֽים׃
20 אַל־תַּגִּ֣ידוּ בְגַ֔ת
אַֽל־תְּבַשְּׂר֖וּ בְּחוּצֹ֣ת אַשְׁקְל֑וֹן
פֶּן־תִּשְׂמַ֙חְנָה֙ בְּנ֣וֹת פְּלִשְׁתִּ֔ים
פֶּֽן־תַּעֲלֹ֖זְנָה בְּנ֥וֹת הָעֲרֵלִֽים׃

21 הָרֵ֣י בַגִּלְבֹּ֗עַ
אַל־טַ֧ל וְאַל־מָטָ֛ר עֲלֵיכֶ֖ם
וּשְׂדֵ֣י תְרוּמֹ֑ת
כִּ֣י שָׁ֤ם נִגְעַל֙ מָגֵ֣ן גִּבּוֹרִ֔ים
מָגֵ֣ן שָׁא֔וּל
בְּלִ֖י מָשִׁ֥יחַ בַּשָּֽׁמֶן׃
22 מִדַּ֣ם חֲלָלִ֗ים
מֵחֵ֙לֶב֙ גִּבּוֹרִ֔ים
קֶ֚שֶׁת יְהֹ֣ונָתָ֔ן

---

b   *Septuagint reads "Judah."*
c   *See note at Josh. 10.13.*
d-d   *Meaning of Heb. uncertain. Emendation yields "springs from*
        the deep" (cf. Ugaritic shr'thmtm, and Gen. 7.11; 8.2).

Never turned back;
The sword of Saul
Never withdrew empty.

²³Saul and Jonathan,
Beloved and cherished,
Never parted
In life or in death!
They were swifter than eagles,
They were stronger than lions!

²⁴Daughters of Israel,
Weep over Saul,
Who clothed you in crimson and finery,
Who decked your robes with jewels of gold.

²⁵How have the mighty fallen
In the thick of battle—
Jonathan, slain on your heights!
²⁶I grieve for you,
My brother Jonathan,
You were most dear to me.
Your love was wonderful to me
More than the love of women.

²⁷How have the mighty fallen,
The *e*-weapons of war-*e* perished!

לֹא נָשׂוֹג אָחֹ֑ור
וְחֶ֣רֶב שָׁא֔וּל
לֹ֥א תָשׁ֖וּב רֵיקָֽם׃

²³ שָׁא֣וּל וִיהֽוֹנָתָ֗ן
הַנֶּאֱהָבִ֤ים וְהַנְּעִימִם֙
בְּחַיֵּיהֶ֣ם וּבְמוֹתָ֔ם
לֹ֖א נִפְרָ֑דוּ
מִנְּשָׁרִ֣ים קַ֔לּוּ
מֵאֲרָי֖וֹת גָּבֵֽרוּ׃

²⁴ בְּנוֹת֙ יִשְׂרָאֵ֔ל
אֶל־שָׁא֖וּל בְּכֶ֑ינָה
הַמַּלְבִּֽשְׁכֶ֤ם שָׁנִי֙ עִם־עֲדָנִ֔ים
הַֽמַּעֲלֶה֙ עֲדִ֣י זָהָ֔ב עַ֖ל לְבוּשְׁכֶֽן׃

²⁵ אֵ֚יךְ נָפְל֣וּ גִבֹּרִ֔ים
בְּת֖וֹךְ הַמִּלְחָמָ֑ה
יְה֣וֹנָתָ֔ן עַל־בָּמוֹתֶ֖יךָ חָלָֽל׃

²⁶ צַר־לִ֣י עָלֶ֗יךָ
אָחִי֙ יְה֣וֹנָתָ֔ן
נָעַ֥מְתָּ לִּ֖י מְאֹ֑ד
נִפְלְאַ֤תָה אַהֲבָֽתְךָ֙ לִ֔י
מֵאַהֲבַ֖ת נָשִֽׁים׃

²⁷ אֵ֚יךְ נָפְל֣וּ גִבּוֹרִ֔ים
וַיֹּאבְד֖וּ כְּלֵ֥י מִלְחָמָֽה׃ פ

2 Sometime afterward, David inquired of the LORD, "Shall I go up to one of the towns of Judah?" The LORD answered, "Yes." David further asked, "Which one shall I go up to?" And the LORD replied, "To Hebron." ²So David went up there, along with his two wives, Ahinoam of Jezreel and Abigail wife of Nabal the Carmelite. ³David also took the men who were with him, each with his family, and they settled in the towns about Hebron. ⁴The men of Judah came

ב וַיְהִ֣י אַחֲרֵי־כֵ֗ן וַיִּשְׁאַל֩ דָּוִ֨ד בַּֽיהֹוָ֜ה ׀
לֵאמֹ֗ר הַאֶעֱלֶ֤ה בְּאַחַת֙ עָרֵ֣י יְהוּדָ֔ה וַיֹּ֤אמֶר
יְהֹוָה֙ אֵלָ֣יו עֲלֵ֔ה וַיֹּ֧אמֶר דָּוִ֛ד אָ֥נָה אֶעֱלֶ֖ה
וַיֹּ֣אמֶר חֶבְרֹֽנָה׃ ² וַיַּ֤עַל שָׁם֙ דָּוִ֔ד וְגַ֖ם שְׁתֵּ֣י
נָשָׁ֑יו אֲחִינֹ֙עַם֙ הַיִּזְרְעֵלִ֔ית וַאֲבִיגַ֕יִל אֵ֖שֶׁת
נָבָ֥ל הַֽכַּרְמְלִֽי׃ ³ וַאֲנָשָׁ֧יו אֲשֶׁר־עִמּ֛וֹ הֶעֱלָ֥ה
דָוִ֖ד אִ֣ישׁ וּבֵית֑וֹ וַיֵּשְׁב֖וּ בְּעָרֵ֥י חֶבְרֽוֹן׃
⁴ וַיָּבֹ֙אוּ֙ אַנְשֵׁ֣י יְהוּדָ֔ה וַיִּמְשְׁחוּ־שָׁ֥ם אֶת־
דָּוִ֖ד לְמֶ֖לֶךְ עַל־בֵּ֥ית יְהוּדָ֑ה

e-e I.e., Saul and Jonathan.

645

and there they anointed David king over the House of Judah.

David was told about the men of Jabesh-gilead who buried Saul. [5]So David sent messengers to the men of Jabesh-gilead and said to them, "May you be blessed of the LORD because you performed this act of faithfulness to your lord Saul and buried him. [6]May the LORD in turn show you true faithfulness; and I too will reward you generously because you performed this act. [7]Now take courage and be brave men; for your lord Saul is dead and the House of Judah have already anointed me king over them."

[8]But Abner son of Ner, Saul's army commander, had taken Ish-bosheth[a] son of Saul and brought him across to Mahanaim [9]and made him king over Gilead, the Ashurites,[b] Jezreel, Ephraim, and Benjamin—over all Israel. [10]Ish-bosheth[a] son of Saul was forty years old when he became king of Israel, and he reigned two years. But the House of Judah supported David. [11]The length of time that David reigned in Hebron over the House of Judah was seven years and six months.

[12]Once Abner son of Ner and the soldiers of Ish-bosheth son of Saul marched out from Mahanaim to Gibeon, [13]and Joab son of Zeruiah and the soldiers of David [also] came out.[c] They confronted one another at the pool of Gibeon: one group sat on one side of the pool, and the other group on the other side of the pool. [14]Abner said to Joab, "Let the young men come forward and sport[d] before us." "Yes, let them," Joab answered. [15]They came forward and were counted off, twelve for Benjamin and Ish-bosheth son of Saul, and twelve of David's soldiers. [16]Each one grasped his opponent's head[e] [and thrust] his dagger into his

---

a   *Meaning "Man of Shame," deliberately altered from* Ish-baal, "man of Baal"; *cf.* 1 Chron. 8.33; 9.39, *and note at* 2 Sam. 4.4.
b   *Meaning of Heb. uncertain.*
c   *Septuagint adds "from Hebron."*
d   *I.e., engage in single combat.*
e   *Septuagint adds "with his hand."*

וַיַּגִּ֣דוּ לְדָוִ֔ד לֵאמֹ֕ר אַנְשֵׁ֖י יָבֵ֣ישׁ גִּלְעָ֑ד אֲשֶׁ֥ר קָבְר֖וּ אֶת־שָׁאֽוּל׃ ס 5 וַיִּשְׁלַ֤ח דָּוִד֙ מַלְאָכִ֔ים אֶל־אַנְשֵׁ֖י יָבֵ֣ישׁ גִּלְעָ֑ד וַיֹּ֣אמֶר אֲלֵיהֶ֗ם בְּרֻכִ֤ים אַתֶּם֙ לַֽיהֹוָ֔ה אֲשֶׁ֨ר עֲשִׂיתֶ֜ם הַחֶ֣סֶד הַזֶּ֗ה עִם־אֲדֹֽנֵיכֶם֙ עִם־שָׁא֔וּל וַֽתִּקְבְּר֖וּ אֹתֽוֹ׃ 6 וְעַתָּ֕ה יַֽעַשׂ־יְהֹוָ֧ה עִמָּכֶ֛ם חֶ֣סֶד וֶֽאֱמֶ֑ת וְגַ֣ם אָנֹכִ֗י אֶעֱשֶׂ֤ה אִתְּכֶם֙ הַטּוֹבָ֣ה הַזֹּ֔את אֲשֶׁ֥ר עֲשִׂיתֶ֖ם הַדָּבָ֥ר הַזֶּֽה׃ 7 וְעַתָּ֣ה ׀ תֶּחֱזַ֣קְנָה יְדֵיכֶ֗ם וִֽהְיוּ֙ לִבְנֵי־חַ֔יִל כִּי־מֵ֖ת אֲדֹֽנֵיכֶ֣ם שָׁא֑וּל וְגַם־אֹתִ֗י מָֽשְׁח֧וּ בֵית־יְהוּדָ֛ה לְמֶ֖לֶךְ עֲלֵיהֶֽם׃ פ

8 וְאַבְנֵ֣ר בֶּן־נֵ֗ר שַׂר־צָבָ֛א אֲשֶׁ֥ר לְשָׁא֑וּל לָקַ֗ח אֶת־אִ֥ישׁ בֹּ֙שֶׁת֙ בֶּן־שָׁא֔וּל וַיַּֽעֲבִרֵ֖הוּ מַֽחֲנָֽיִם׃ 9 וַיַּמְלִכֵ֙הוּ֙ אֶל־הַגִּלְעָ֔ד וְאֶל־הָאֲשׁוּרִ֖י וְאֶל־יִזְרְעֶ֑אל וְעַל־אֶפְרַ֙יִם֙ וְעַל־בִּנְיָמִ֔ן וְעַל־יִשְׂרָאֵ֖ל כֻּלֹּֽה׃ פ 10 בֶּן־אַרְבָּעִ֨ים שָׁנָ֜ה אִֽישׁ־בֹּ֣שֶׁת בֶּן־שָׁא֗וּל בְּמׇלְכוֹ֙ עַל־יִשְׂרָאֵ֔ל וּשְׁתַּ֥יִם שָׁנִ֖ים מָלָ֑ךְ אַ֚ךְ בֵּ֣ית יְהוּדָ֔ה הָי֖וּ אַחֲרֵ֥י דָוִֽד׃ 11 וַֽיְהִי֙ מִסְפַּ֣ר הַיָּמִ֔ים אֲשֶׁר֩ הָיָ֨ה דָוִ֥ד מֶ֛לֶךְ בְּחֶבְר֖וֹן עַל־בֵּ֣ית יְהוּדָ֑ה שֶׁ֥בַע שָׁנִ֖ים וְשִׁשָּׁ֥ה חֳדָשִֽׁים׃ ס

12 וַיֵּצֵא֙ אַבְנֵ֣ר בֶּן־נֵ֔ר וְעַבְדֵ֖י אִֽישׁ־בֹּ֑שֶׁת בֶּן־שָׁא֖וּל מִֽמַּחֲנַ֖יִם גִּבְעֽוֹנָה׃ 13 וְיוֹאָ֨ב בֶּן־צְרוּיָ֜ה וְעַבְדֵ֥י דָוִד֙ יָֽצְא֔וּ וַֽיִּפְגְּשׁ֛וּם עַל־בְּרֵכַ֥ת גִּבְע֖וֹן יַחְדָּ֑ו וַיֵּ֨שְׁב֜וּ אֵ֤לֶּה עַל־הַבְּרֵכָה֙ מִזֶּ֔ה וְאֵ֥לֶּה עַל־הַבְּרֵכָ֖ה מִזֶּֽה׃ 14 וַיֹּ֤אמֶר אַבְנֵר֙ אֶל־יוֹאָ֔ב יָק֤וּמוּ נָא֙ הַנְּעָרִ֔ים וִֽישַׂחֲק֖וּ לְפָנֵ֑ינוּ וַיֹּ֥אמֶר יוֹאָ֖ב יָקֻֽמוּ׃ 15 וַיָּקֻ֖מוּ וַיַּֽעַבְר֣וּ בְמִסְפָּ֑ר שְׁנֵ֧ים עָשָׂ֣ר לְבִנְיָמִ֗ן וּלְאִ֥ישׁ בֹּ֙שֶׁת֙ בֶּן־שָׁא֔וּל וּשְׁנֵ֧ים עָשָׂ֛ר מֵעַבְדֵ֥י דָוִֽד׃ 16 וַיַּֽחֲזִ֜קוּ אִ֣ישׁ ׀ בְּרֹ֣אשׁ רֵעֵ֗הוּ וְחַרְבּוֹ֙ בְּצַ֣ד רֵעֵ֔הוּ וַיִּפְּל֖וּ

opponent's side; thus they fell together. That place, which is in Gibeon, was called Helkath-hazzurim.*

17A fierce battle ensued that day, and Abner and the men of Israel were routed by David's soldiers. 18The three sons of Zeruiah*g* were there—Joab, Abishai, and Asahel. Asahel was swift of foot, like a gazelle in the open field. 19And Asahel ran after Abner, swerving neither right nor left in his pursuit of Abner. 20Abner looked back and shouted, "Is that you, Asahel?" "Yes, it is," he called back. 21Abner said to him, "Turn to the right or to the left, and seize one of our boys and strip off his tunic." But Asahel would not leave off. 22Abner again begged Asahel, "Stop pursuing me, or I'll have to strike you down. How will I look your brother Joab in the face?" 23When he refused to desist, Abner struck him in the belly with *b*-a backward thrust-*b* of his spear and the spear protruded from his back. He fell there and died on the spot. And all who came to the place where Asahel fell and died halted; 24but Joab and Abishai continued to pursue Abner. And the sun was setting as they reached the hill of Ammah, *b*-which faces Giah on the road to the wilderness of Gibeon.-*b*

25The Benjaminites rallied behind Abner, forming a single company; and they took up a position on the top of a hill. 26Abner then called out to Joab, "Must the sword devour forever? You know how bitterly it's going to end! How long will you delay ordering your troops to stop the pursuit of their kinsmen?" 27And Joab replied, "As God lives, *h*-if you hadn't spoken up, the troops would have given up the pursuit of their kinsmen only the next morning."-*h* 28Joab then sounded the horn, and all the troops halted; they ceased their pursuit of Israel and stopped the fighting. 29Abner and his men

יַחְדָּ֑ו וַיִּקְרָא֙ לַמָּק֣וֹם הַה֔וּא חֶלְקַ֖ת הַצֻּרִ֑ים אֲשֶׁ֖ר בְּגִבְעֽוֹן׃ 17 וַתְּהִ֧י הַמִּלְחָמָ֛ה קָשָׁ֥ה עַד־מְאֹ֖ד בַּיּ֣וֹם הַה֑וּא וַיִּנָּ֤גֶף אַבְנֵר֙ וְאַנְשֵׁ֣י יִשְׂרָאֵ֔ל לִפְנֵ֖י עַבְדֵ֥י דָוִֽד׃ 18 וַיִּֽהְיוּ־שָׁ֗ם שְׁלֹשָׁה֙ בְּנֵ֣י צְרוּיָ֔ה יוֹאָ֥ב וַֽאֲבִישַׁ֖י וַעֲשָׂהאֵ֑ל וַעֲשָׂהאֵל֙ קַ֣ל בְּרַגְלָ֔יו כְּאַחַ֥ד הַצְּבָיִ֖ם אֲשֶׁ֥ר בַּשָּׂדֶֽה׃ 19 וַיִּרְדֹּ֥ף עֲשָׂהאֵ֖ל אַחֲרֵ֣י אַבְנֵ֑ר וְלֹֽא־נָטָ֣ה לָלֶ֗כֶת עַל־הַיָּמִין֙ וְעַל־הַשְּׂמֹ֔אול* מֵאַחֲרֵ֖י אַבְנֵֽר׃ 20 וַיִּ֤פֶן אַבְנֵר֙ אַֽחֲרָ֔יו וַיֹּ֕אמֶר הַאַתָּ֥ה זֶ֖ה עֲשָׂהאֵ֑ל וַיֹּ֖אמֶר אָנֹֽכִי׃ 21 וַיֹּ֧אמֶר ל֣וֹ אַבְנֵ֗ר נְטֵ֤ה לְךָ֙ עַל־יְמִֽינְךָ֙ א֣וֹ עַל־שְׂמֹאלֶ֔ךָ וֶאֱחֹ֣ז לְךָ֗ אֶחָד֙ מֵֽהַנְּעָרִ֔ים וְקַח־לְךָ֖ אֶת־חֲלִצָת֑וֹ וְלֹֽא־אָבָ֣ה עֲשָׂהאֵ֔ל לָס֖וּר מֵאַחֲרָֽיו׃ 22 וַיֹּ֨סֶף ע֤וֹד אַבְנֵר֙ לֵאמֹ֣ר אֶל־עֲשָׂהאֵ֔ל ס֥וּר לְךָ֖ מֵאַֽחֲרָ֑י לָ֤מָּה אַכֶּ֙כָּה֙ אַ֔רְצָה וְאֵיךְ֙ אֶשָּׂ֣א פָנַ֔י אֶל־יוֹאָ֖ב אָחִֽיךָ׃ 23 וַיְמָאֵ֣ן לָס֗וּר וַיַּכֵּ֣הוּ אַבְנֵר֩ בְּאַֽחֲרֵ֨י הַחֲנִ֜ית אֶל־הַחֹ֗מֶשׁ וַתֵּצֵ֤א הַֽחֲנִית֙ מֵאַ֣חֲרָ֔יו וַיִּפָּל־שָׁ֖ם וַיָּ֣מָת תַּחְתָּ֑ו וַיְהִ֡י כָּל־הַבָּ֣א אֶֽל־הַמָּקוֹם֩ אֲשֶׁר־נָ֨פַל שָׁ֧ם עֲשָׂהאֵ֛ל וַיָּמֹ֖ת וַֽיַּעֲמֹֽדוּ׃ 24 וַיִּרְדְּפ֤וּ יוֹאָב֙ וַֽאֲבִישַׁי֙ אַֽחֲרֵ֣י אַבְנֵ֔ר וְהַשֶּׁ֣מֶשׁ בָּ֔אָה וְהֵ֗מָּה בָּ֚אוּ עַד־גִּבְעַ֣ת אַמָּ֔ה אֲשֶׁר֙ עַל־פְּנֵי־גִ֔יחַ דֶּ֖רֶךְ מִדְבַּ֥ר גִּבְעֽוֹן׃ 25 וַיִּֽתְקַבְּצ֤וּ בְנֵֽי־בִנְיָמִן֙ אַֽחֲרֵ֣י אַבְנֵ֔ר וַיִּֽהְי֖וּ לַֽאֲגֻדָּ֣ה אֶחָ֑ת וַיַּ֣עַמְד֔וּ עַ֥ל רֹאשׁ־גִּבְעָ֖ה אֶחָֽת׃ 26 וַיִּקְרָ֨א אַבְנֵ֜ר אֶל־יוֹאָ֗ב וַיֹּ֙אמֶר֙ הֲלָנֶ֙צַח֙ תֹּ֣אכַל חֶ֔רֶב הֲל֣וֹא יָדַ֔עְתָּ כִּֽי־מָרָ֥ה תִֽהְיֶ֖ה בָּאַֽחֲרוֹנָ֑ה וְעַד־מָתַי֙ לֹֽא־תֹאמַ֣ר לָעָ֔ם לָשׁ֖וּב מֵאַחֲרֵ֥י אֲחֵיהֶֽם׃ 27 וַיֹּ֣אמֶר יוֹאָ֗ב חַ֚י הָֽאֱלֹהִ֔ים כִּ֥י לוּלֵ֖א דִּבַּ֑רְתָּ כִּ֣י אָ֤ז מֵֽהַבֹּ֙קֶר֙ נַֽעֲלָ֣ה הָעָ֔ם אִ֖ישׁ מֵֽאַחֲרֵ֥י אָחִֽיו׃ 28 וַיִּתְקַ֤ע יוֹאָב֙ בַּשּׁוֹפָ֔ר וַיַּֽעַמְד֖וּ כָּל־הָעָ֑ם וְלֹֽא־יִרְדְּפ֥וּ ע֛וֹד אַחֲרֵ֥י

---

f Meaning perhaps "the Field of the Flints (or Blades)."
g A sister of David, 1 Chron. 2.16.
h-h Emendation yields "If you had only spoken up, the troops would already have given up the pursuit of their kinsmen this morning."

מלא ו׳   *v.* 19.

marched through the Arabah all that night and, after crossing the Jordan, they marched *b*-through all of Bithron-*b* until they came to Mahanaim. 30After Joab gave up the pursuit of Abner, he assembled all the troops and found nineteen of David's soldiers missing, besides Asahel. 31David's soldiers, on the other hand, *b*-defeated the Benjaminites and the men under Abner and killed three hundred and sixty men.-*b* 32They bore Asahel away and buried him in his father's tomb in Bethlehem. Then Joab and his men marched all night; day broke upon them in Hebron.

3 The war between the House of Saul and the House of David was long-drawn-out; but David kept growing stronger, while the House of Saul grew weaker.

2*a*Sons were born to David in Hebron: His first-born was Amnon, by Ahinoam of Jezreel; 3his second was Chileab, by Abigail wife of Nabal the Carmelite; the third was Absalom son of Maacah, daughter of King Talmai of Geshur; 4the fourth was Adonijah son of Haggith; the fifth was Shephatiah son of Abital; 5and the sixth was Ithream, by David's wife Eglah. These were born to David in Hebron.

6During the war between the House of Saul and the House of David, Abner supported the House of Saul. 7Now Saul had a concubine named Rizpah, daughter of Aiah; and [Ish-bo-sheth] said to Abner, "Why have you lain with my father's concubine?" 8Abner was very upset by what Ish-bosheth said, and he replied, "Am I a dog's head *b*-from Judah?-*b* Here I have been loyally serving the House of your father Saul and his kinsfolk and friends, and I have not betrayed you into the hands of David; yet this day you reproach me over a woman! 9May God do thus

יִשְׂרָאֵל וְלֹא־יָסְפוּ עוֹד לְהִלָּחֵם: 29 וְאַבְנֵר וַאֲנָשָׁיו הָלְכוּ בָּעֲרָבָה כֹּל הַלַּיְלָה הַהוּא וַיַּעַבְרוּ אֶת־הַיַּרְדֵּן וַיֵּלְכוּ כָּל־הַבִּתְרוֹן וַיָּבֹאוּ מַחֲנָיִם: 30 וְיוֹאָב שָׁב מֵאַחֲרֵי אַבְנֵר וַיִּקְבֹּץ אֶת־כָּל־הָעָם וַיִּפָּקְדוּ מֵעַבְדֵי דָוִד תִּשְׁעָה־עָשָׂר אִישׁ וַעֲשָׂה־אֵל: 31 וְעַבְדֵי דָוִד הִכּוּ מִבִּנְיָמִן וּבְאַנְשֵׁי אַבְנֵר שְׁלֹשׁ־מֵאוֹת וְשִׁשִּׁים אִישׁ מֵתוּ: 32 וַיִּשְׂאוּ אֶת־עֲשָׂהאֵל וַיִּקְבְּרֻהוּ בְּקֶבֶר אָבִיו אֲשֶׁר בֵּית לָחֶם וַיֵּלְכוּ כָל־הַלַּיְלָה יוֹאָב וַאֲנָשָׁיו וַיֵּאֹר לָהֶם בְּחֶבְרוֹן:

ג וַתְּהִי הַמִּלְחָמָה אֲרֻכָּה בֵּין בֵּית שָׁאוּל וּבֵין בֵּית דָּוִד וְדָוִד הֹלֵךְ וְחָזֵק וּבֵית שָׁאוּל הֹלְכִים וְדַלִּים: ס 2 וילדו וַיִּוָּלְדוּ לְדָוִד בָּנִים בְּחֶבְרוֹן וַיְהִי בְכוֹרוֹ אַמְנוֹן לַאֲחִינֹעַם הַיִּזְרְעֵאלִת: 3 וּמִשְׁנֵהוּ כִלְאָב לאביגל לַאֲבִיגַיִל אֵשֶׁת נָבָל הַכַּרְמְלִי וְהַשְּׁלִשִׁי אַבְשָׁלוֹם בֶּן־מַעֲכָה בַּת־תַּלְמַי מֶלֶךְ גְּשׁוּר: 4 וְהָרְבִיעִי אֲדֹנִיָּה בֶן־חַגִּית וְהַחֲמִישִׁי שְׁפַטְיָה בֶן־אֲבִיטָל: 5 וְהַשִּׁשִּׁי יִתְרְעָם לְעֶגְלָה אֵשֶׁת דָּוִד אֵלֶּה יֻלְּדוּ לְדָוִד בְּחֶבְרוֹן: פ 6 וַיְהִי בִּהְיוֹת הַמִּלְחָמָה בֵּין בֵּית שָׁאוּל וּבֵין בֵּית דָּוִד וְאַבְנֵר הָיָה מִתְחַזֵּק בְּבֵית שָׁאוּל: 7 וּלְשָׁאוּל פִּלֶגֶשׁ וּשְׁמָהּ רִצְפָּה בַת־אַיָּה וַיֹּאמֶר אֶל־אַבְנֵר מַדּוּעַ בָּאתָה אֶל־פִּילֶגֶשׁ אָבִי: 8 וַיִּחַר לְאַבְנֵר מְאֹד עַל־דִּבְרֵי אִישׁ־בֹּשֶׁת וַיֹּאמֶר הֲרֹאשׁ כֶּלֶב אָנֹכִי אֲשֶׁר לִיהוּדָה הַיּוֹם אֶעֱשֶׂה־חֶסֶד עִם־בֵּית שָׁאוּל אָבִיךָ אֶל־אֶחָיו וְאֶל־מֵרֵעֵהוּ וְלֹא הִמְצִיתִךָ בְּיַד־דָּוִד וַתִּפְקֹד עָלַי עֲוֹן הָאִשָּׁה הַיּוֹם: 9 כֹּה־יַעֲשֶׂה אֱלֹהִים לְאַבְנֵר וְכֹה יֹסִיף לוֹ כִּי כַּאֲשֶׁר

---

a The list of David's wives and sons in vv. 2–5 differs somewhat from the parallel list in 1 Chron. 3.1–3. The narrative in v. 1 is resumed in v. 6.

b-b Meaning of Heb. uncertain.

and more to Abner if I do not do for David as the LORD swore to him—[10]to transfer the kingship from the House of Saul, and to establish the throne of David over Israel and Judah from Dan to Beer-sheba." [11][Ish-bosheth] could say nothing more in reply to Abner, because he was afraid of him.

[12]Abner immediately[b] sent messengers to David, saying, [b]-"To whom shall the land belong?" and to say [further],-[b] "Make a pact with me, and I will help you and bring all Israel over to your side." [13]He replied, "Good; I will make a pact with you. But I make one demand upon you: Do not appear before me unless you bring Michal daughter of Saul when you come before me." [14]David also sent messengers to Ishbosheth son of Saul, to say, "Give me my wife Michal, for whom I paid the bride-price[c] of one hundred Philistine foreskins."[d] [15]So Ishbosheth sent and had her taken away from [her] husband, Paltiel son of Laish. [16]Her husband walked with her as far as Bahurim, weeping as he followed her; then Abner ordered him to turn back, and he went back.

[17]Abner had conferred with the elders of Israel, saying, "You have wanted David to be king over you all along. [18]Now act! For the LORD has said concerning David: [e]-I will deliver-[e] My people Israel from the hands of the Philistines and all its other enemies through My servant David." [19]Abner also talked with the Benjaminites; then Abner went and informed David in Hebron of all the wishes of Israel and of the whole House of Benjamin.

[20]When Abner came to David in Hebron, accompanied by twenty men, David made a feast for Abner and the men with him. [21]Abner said to David, "Now I will go and rally all Israel to Your Majesty. They will make a pact with you, and you can reign over all that your heart de-

נִשְׁבַּ֤ע יְהוָה֙ לְדָוִ֔ד כִּי־כֵ֖ן אֶעֱשֶׂה־לּֽוֹ:
10 לְהַעֲבִ֥יר הַמַּמְלָכָ֖ה מִבֵּ֣ית שָׁא֑וּל וּלְהָקִ֞ים אֶת־כִּסֵּ֣א דָוִ֗ד עַל־יִשְׂרָאֵל֙ וְעַל־יְהוּדָ֔ה מִדָּ֖ן וְעַד־בְּאֵ֥ר שָֽׁבַע: 11 וְלֹֽא־יָכֹ֣ל ע֗וֹד לְהָשִׁ֤יב אֶת־אַבְנֵר֙ דָּבָ֔ר מִיִּרְאָת֖וֹ אֹתֽוֹ: ס

12 וַיִּשְׁלַח֩ אַבְנֵ֨ר מַלְאָכִ֤ים ׀ אֶל־דָּוִד֙ תַּחְתָּ֣ו תַּחְתָּ֗יו לֵאמֹ֔ר לְמִי־אָ֑רֶץ לֵאמֹ֗ר כָּרְתָ֤ה בְרִֽיתְךָ֙ אִתִּ֔י וְהִנֵּ֤ה יָדִי֙ עִמָּ֔ךְ לְהָסֵ֥ב אֵלֶ֖יךָ אֶת־כָּל־יִשְׂרָאֵֽל: 13 וַיֹּ֣אמֶר ט֔וֹב אֲנִ֕י אֶכְרֹ֥ת אִתְּךָ֖ בְּרִ֑ית אַ֣ךְ דָּבָ֣ר אֶחָ֡ד אָנֹכִי֩ שֹׁאֵ֨ל מֵאִתְּךָ֤ לֵאמֹר֙ לֹא־תִרְאֶ֣ה אֶת־פָּנַ֔י כִּ֣י ׀ אִם־לִפְנֵ֣י הֱבִיאֲךָ֗ אֵ֚ת מִיכַ֣ל בַּת־שָׁא֔וּל בְּבֹאֲךָ֖ לִרְא֥וֹת אֶת־פָּנָֽי: ס 14 וַיִּשְׁלַ֤ח דָּוִד֙ מַלְאָכִ֔ים אֶל־אִֽישׁ־בֹּ֥שֶׁת בֶּן־שָׁא֖וּל לֵאמֹ֑ר תְּנָ֤ה אֶת־אִשְׁתִּי֙ אֶת־מִיכַ֔ל אֲשֶׁר֙ אֵרַ֣שְׂתִּי לִ֔י בְּמֵאָ֖ה עָרְל֥וֹת פְּלִשְׁתִּֽים: 15 וַיִּשְׁלַח֙ אִ֣ישׁ בֹּ֔שֶׁת וַיִּקָּחֶ֖הָ מֵעִ֣ם אִ֑ישׁ מֵעִ֖ם פַּלְטִיאֵ֥ל בֶּן־לָֽוִשׁ לָֽיִשׁ: 16 וַיֵּ֨לֶךְ אִתָּ֜הּ אִישָׁ֗הּ הָל֧וֹךְ וּבָכֹ֛ה אַחֲרֶ֖יהָ עַד־בַּֽחֻרִ֑ים וַיֹּ֧אמֶר אֵלָ֛יו אַבְנֵ֖ר לֵ֥ךְ שׁ֑וּב וַיָּשֹֽׁב:

17 וּדְבַר־אַבְנֵ֣ר הָיָ֔ה עִם־זִקְנֵ֥י יִשְׂרָאֵ֖ל לֵאמֹ֑ר גַּם־תְּמוֹל֙ גַּם־שִׁלְשֹׁ֔ם הֱיִיתֶ֛ם מְבַקְשִׁ֥ים אֶת־דָּוִ֖ד לְמֶ֥לֶךְ עֲלֵיכֶֽם: 18 וְעַתָּ֖ה עֲשׂ֑וּ כִּ֣י יְהוָ֗ה אָמַ֤ר אֶל־דָּוִד֙ לֵאמֹ֔ר בְּיַ֣ד ׀ דָּוִ֣ד עַבְדִּ֗י הוֹשִׁ֣יעַ* אֶת־עַמִּ֤י יִשְׂרָאֵל֙ מִיַּ֣ד פְּלִשְׁתִּ֔ים וּמִיַּ֖ד כָּל־אֹיְבֵיהֶֽם: 19 וַיְדַבֵּ֥ר גַּם־אַבְנֵ֖ר בְּאָזְנֵ֣י בִנְיָמִ֑ין וַיֵּ֣לֶךְ גַּם־אַבְנֵ֗ר לְדַבֵּ֞ר בְּאָזְנֵ֤י דָוִד֙ בְּחֶבְר֔וֹן אֵ֣ת כָּל־אֲשֶׁר־טוֹב֙ בְּעֵינֵ֣י יִשְׂרָאֵ֔ל וּבְעֵינֵ֖י כָּל־בֵּ֥ית בִּנְיָמִֽן:

20 וַיָּבֹ֨א אַבְנֵ֤ר אֶל־דָּוִד֙ חֶבְר֔וֹן וְאִתּ֖וֹ עֶשְׂרִ֣ים אֲנָשִׁ֑ים וַיַּ֨עַשׂ דָּוִ֧ד לְאַבְנֵ֛ר וְלַאֲנָשִׁ֥ים אֲשֶׁר־אִתּ֖וֹ מִשְׁתֶּֽה: 21 וַיֹּ֣אמֶר אַבְנֵ֣ר אֶל־דָּוִד֮ אָק֣וּמָה ׀ וְאֵלֵ֗כָה וְאֶקְבְּצָ֞ה

---

c   Cf. Exod. 22.15; Deut. 20.7; 22.23–29.
d   Cf. 1 Sam. 18.27 (where the number is given as "two hundred").
e-e So many mss. and versions; most mss. and editions have "He has delivered."

sires." And David dismissed Abner, who went away unharmed.

22Just then David's soldiers and Joab returned from a raid, bringing much plunder with them; Abner was no longer with David in Hebron, for he had been dismissed and had gone away unharmed. 23When Joab and the whole force with him arrived, Joab was told that Abner son of Ner had come to the king, had been dismissed by him, and had gone away unharmed. 24Joab went to the king and said, "What have you done? Here Abner came to you; why did you let him go? Now he has gotten away! 25Don't you know that Abner son of Ner came only to deceive you, to learn your comings and goings and to find out all that you are planning?" 26Joab left David and sent messengers after Abner, and they brought him back from the cistern of Sirah; but David knew nothing about it. 27When Abner returned to Hebron, Joab took him aside within the gate to talk to him privately;b there he struck him in the belly. Thus [Abner] died for shedding the blood of Asahel, Joab'sf brother.

28Afterward, when David heard of it, he said, "Both I and my kingdom are forever innocent before the Lord of shedding the blood of Abner son of Ner. 29May [the guilt] fall upon the head of Joab and all his father's house. May the house of Joab never be without someone suffering from a discharge or an eruption, or g-a male who handles the spindle,-g or one slain by the sword, or one lacking bread."—30Now Joab and his brother Abishai had killed Abner because he had killed their brother Asahel during the battle at Gibeon.—31David then ordered Joab and all the troops with him to rend their clothes, gird on sackcloth, and make lament beforeh Abner; and King David himself walked behind the bier. 32And so they buried Abner at Hebron; the king wept aloud by Abner's grave, and all the troops

אֶל־אֲדֹנִי הַמֶּלֶךְ אֶת־כָּל־יִשְׂרָאֵל וְיִכְרְתוּ
אִתְּךָ בְּרִית וּמָלַכְתָּ בְּכֹל אֲשֶׁר־תְּאַוֶּה
נַפְשֶׁךָ וַיְשַׁלַּח דָּוִד אֶת־אַבְנֵר וַיֵּלֶךְ
בְּשָׁלוֹם:
22 וְהִנֵּה עַבְדֵי דָוִד וְיוֹאָב בָּא* מֵהַגְּדוּד
וְשָׁלָל רָב עִמָּם הֵבִיאוּ וְאַבְנֵר אֵינֶנּוּ
עִם־דָּוִד בְּחֶבְרוֹן כִּי שִׁלְּחוֹ וַיֵּלֶךְ בְּשָׁלוֹם:
23 וְיוֹאָב וְכָל־הַצָּבָא אֲשֶׁר־אִתּוֹ בָּאוּ וַיַּגִּדוּ
לְיוֹאָב לֵאמֹר בָּא־אַבְנֵר בֶּן־נֵר אֶל־הַמֶּלֶךְ
וַיְשַׁלְּחֵהוּ וַיֵּלֶךְ בְּשָׁלוֹם: 24 וַיָּבֹא יוֹאָב
אֶל־הַמֶּלֶךְ וַיֹּאמֶר מֶה עָשִׂיתָה הִנֵּה־בָא
אַבְנֵר אֵלֶיךָ לָמָּה־זֶּה שִׁלַּחְתּוֹ וַיֵּלֶךְ הָלוֹךְ:
25 יָדַעְתָּ אֶת־אַבְנֵר בֶּן־נֵר כִּי לְפַתֹּתְךָ בָּא
וְלָדַעַת אֶת־מוֹצָאֲךָ וְאֶת־מִבוֹאֶךָ מוֹבָאֶךָ
וְלָדַעַת אֵת כָּל־אֲשֶׁר אַתָּה עֹשֶׂה: 26 וַיֵּצֵא
יוֹאָב מֵעִם דָּוִד וַיִּשְׁלַח מַלְאָכִים אַחֲרֵי
אַבְנֵר וַיָּשִׁבוּ אֹתוֹ מִבּוֹר הַסִּרָה וְדָוִד
לֹא יָדָע: 27 וַיָּשָׁב אַבְנֵר חֶבְרוֹן וַיַּטֵּהוּ
יוֹאָב אֶל־תּוֹךְ הַשַּׁעַר לְדַבֵּר אִתּוֹ בַּשֶּׁלִי
וַיַּכֵּהוּ שָׁם הַחֹמֶשׁ וַיָּמָת בְּדַם עֲשָׂה־אֵל
אָחִיו:
28 וַיִּשְׁמַע דָּוִד מֵאַחֲרֵי כֵן וַיֹּאמֶר נָקִי אָנֹכִי
וּמַמְלַכְתִּי מֵעִם יְהוָה עַד־עוֹלָם מִדְּמֵי
אַבְנֵר בֶּן־נֵר: 29 יָחֻלוּ עַל־רֹאשׁ יוֹאָב וְאֶל
כָּל־בֵּית אָבִיו וְאַל־יִכָּרֵת מִבֵּית יוֹאָב זָב
וּמְצֹרָע וּמַחֲזִיק בַּפֶּלֶךְ וְנֹפֵל בַּחֶרֶב וַחֲסַר־
לָחֶם: 30 וְיוֹאָב וַאֲבִישַׁי אָחִיו הָרְגוּ
לְאַבְנֵר עַל אֲשֶׁר הֵמִית אֶת־עֲשָׂהאֵל
אֲחִיהֶם בְּגִבְעוֹן בַּמִּלְחָמָה: פ 31 וַיֹּאמֶר
דָּוִד אֶל־יוֹאָב וְאֶל־כָּל־הָעָם אֲשֶׁר־אִתּוֹ
קִרְעוּ בִגְדֵיכֶם וְחִגְרוּ שַׂקִּים וְסִפְדוּ לִפְנֵי
אַבְנֵר וְהַמֶּלֶךְ דָּוִד הֹלֵךְ אַחֲרֵי הַמִּטָּה:
32 וַיִּקְבְּרוּ אֶת־אַבְנֵר בְּחֶבְרוֹן וַיִּשָּׂא הַמֶּלֶךְ
אֶת־קוֹלוֹ וַיֵּבְךְּ אֶל־קֶבֶר אַבְנֵר וַיִּבְכּוּ כָּל־

f Heb. "his."
g-g I.e., a man fit only for woman's work.
h I.e., in the procession.

wept. [33]And the king intoned this dirge over Abner,

> "Should Abner have died the death of a churl?
> [34]Your hands were not bound,
> Your feet were not put in fetters;
> But you fell as one falls
> Before treacherous men!"

And all the troops continued to weep over him. [35]All the troops came to urge David to eat something while it was still day; but David swore, "May God do thus to me and more if I eat bread or anything else before sundown." [36]All the troops *b*-took note of it-*b* and approved, *b*-just as all the troops approved everything else the king did.-*b* [37]That day all the troops and all Israel knew that it was not by the king's will that Abner son of Ner was killed. [38]And the king said to his soldiers, "You well know that a prince, a great man in Israel, has fallen this day. [39]And today I am weak, even though anointed king; those men, the sons of Zeruiah, are too savage for me. May the Lord requite the wicked for their wickedness!"

4 When [Ish-bosheth] son of Saul heard that Abner had died in Hebron, *a*-he lost heart-*a* and all Israel was alarmed. [2]The son of Saul [had] two company commanders, one named Baanah and the other Rechab, sons of Rimmon the Beerothite—Benjaminites, since Beeroth too was considered part of Benjamin. [3]The Beerothites had fled to Gittaim,*b* where they have sojourned to this day. ([4]Jonathan son of Saul had a son whose feet were crippled. He was five years old when the news about Saul and Jonathan came from Jezreel, and his nurse picked him up and fled; but as she was fleeing in haste, he fell and was lamed. His name was

---

33 פ וַיְקֹנֵ֥ן הַמֶּ֖לֶךְ אֶל־אַבְנֵ֑ר הָעָֽם׃
וַיֹּאמַ֕ר
הַכְּמ֥וֹת נָבָ֖ל יָמ֥וּת אַבְנֵֽר׃
34 יָדֶ֣ךָ* לֹא־אֲסֻר֗וֹת
וְרַגְלֶ֙יךָ֙ לֹא־לִנְחֻשְׁתַּ֣יִם הֻגָּ֔שׁוּ כִּנְפ֛וֹל
לִפְנֵ֥י בְנֵֽי־עַוְלָ֖ה נָפָ֑לְתָּ
וַיֹּסִ֛פוּ כׇל־הָעָ֖ם לִבְכּ֥וֹת עָלָֽיו׃
35 וַיָּבֹ֣א כׇל־הָעָ֗ם לְהַבְר֧וֹת אֶת־דָּוִ֛ד לֶ֖חֶם בְּע֣וֹד הַיּ֑וֹם וַיִּשָּׁבַ֙ע דָּוִ֜ד לֵאמֹ֗ר כֹּ֣ה יַעֲשֶׂה־לִּ֤י אֱלֹהִים֙ וְכֹ֣ה יֹסִ֔יף כִּ֣י אִם־לִפְנֵ֣י בֽוֹא־הַשֶּׁ֗מֶשׁ אֶטְעַם־לֶ֖חֶם א֥וֹ כׇל־מְאֽוּמָה׃
36 וְכׇל־הָעָ֣ם הִכִּ֔ירוּ וַיִּיטַ֖ב בְּעֵֽינֵיהֶ֑ם כְּכֹל֙ אֲשֶׁ֣ר עָשָׂ֣ה הַמֶּ֔לֶךְ בְּעֵינֵ֥י כׇל־הָעָ֖ם טֽוֹב׃
37 וַיֵּדְע֧וּ כׇל־הָעָ֛ם וְכׇל־יִשְׂרָאֵ֖ל בַּיּ֣וֹם הַה֑וּא כִּ֣י לֹ֤א הָֽיְתָה֙ מֵֽהַמֶּ֔לֶךְ לְהָמִ֖ית אֶת־אַבְנֵ֥ר בֶּן־נֵֽר׃
38 פ וַיֹּ֥אמֶר הַמֶּ֖לֶךְ אֶל־עֲבָדָ֑יו הֲל֣וֹא תֵֽדְע֔וּ כִּי־שַׂ֣ר וְגָד֗וֹל נָפַ֛ל הַיּ֥וֹם הַזֶּ֖ה בְּיִשְׂרָאֵֽל׃
39 וְאָנֹכִ֨י הַיּ֤וֹם רַךְ֙ וּמָשׁ֣וּחַ מֶ֔לֶךְ וְהָאֲנָשִׁ֥ים הָאֵ֛לֶּה בְּנֵ֥י צְרוּיָ֖ה קָשִׁ֣ים מִמֶּ֑נִּי יְשַׁלֵּ֧ם יְהֹוָ֛ה לְעֹשֵׂ֥ה הָרָעָ֖ה כְּרָעָתֽוֹ׃ פ

ד וַיִּשְׁמַ֣ע בֶּן־שָׁא֗וּל כִּ֣י מֵ֤ת אַבְנֵר֙ בְּחֶבְר֔וֹן וַיִּרְפּ֖וּ יָדָ֑יו וְכׇל־יִשְׂרָאֵ֖ל נִבְהָֽלוּ׃
2 וּשְׁנֵ֣י אֲנָשִׁ֣ים שָׂרֵֽי־גְדוּדִ֗ים הָי֣וּ בֶן־שָׁא֔וּל שֵׁם֩ הָאֶחָ֨ד בַּעֲנָ֜ה וְשֵׁ֧ם הַשֵּׁנִ֣י רֵכָ֗ב בְּנֵ֤י רִמּוֹן֙ הַבְּאֵ֣רֹתִ֔י מִבְּנֵ֖י בִנְיָמִ֑ן כִּ֚י גַּם־בְּאֵר֔וֹת תֵּחָשֵׁ֖ב עַל־בִּנְיָמִֽן׃
3 וַיִּבְרְח֥וּ הַבְּאֵרֹתִ֖ים גִּתָּ֑יְמָה וַיִּֽהְיוּ־שָׁ֣ם גָּרִ֔ים עַ֖ד הַיּ֥וֹם הַזֶּֽה׃ ס
4 וְלִיהֽוֹנָתָן֙ בֶּן־שָׁא֔וּל בֵּ֖ן נְכֵ֣ה רַגְלָ֑יִם בֶּן־חָמֵ֣שׁ שָׁנִ֣ים הָיָ֡ה בְּבֹ֣א שְׁמֻעַת֩ שָׁא֨וּל וִיהֽוֹנָתָ֜ן מִֽיִּזְרְעֶ֗אל וַתִּשָּׂאֵ֤הוּ אֹמַנְתּוֹ֙ וַתָּנֹ֔ס וַיְהִ֞י בְּחׇפְזָ֥הּ לָנ֛וּס וַיִּפֹּ֥ל וַיִּפָּסֵ֖חַ וּשְׁמ֥וֹ מְפִיבֹֽשֶׁת׃
5 וַיֵּ֣לְכ֗וּ בְּנֵֽי־רִמּ֣וֹן

---

a-a Lit. "his hands weakened"; and so frequently.
b Gittaim was likewise in Benjamin; cf. Neh. 11.31 ff.

Mephibosheth.[c] [5]Rechab and Baanah, sons of Rimmon the Beerothite, started out, and they reached the home of Ish-bosheth at the heat of the day, when he was taking his midday rest. [6d]-So they went inside the house, as though fetching wheat, and struck him in the belly.-[d] Rechab and his brother Baanah slipped by, [7]and entered the house while he was asleep on his bed in his bedchamber; and they stabbed him to death. They cut off his head and took his head and made their way all night through the Arabah. [8]They brought the head of Ish-bosheth to David in Hebron. "Here," they said to the king, "is the head of your enemy, Ish-bosheth son of Saul, who sought your life. This day the LORD has avenged my lord the king upon Saul and his offspring."

[9]But David answered Rechab and his brother Baanah, the sons of Rimmon the Beerothite, and said to them, "As the LORD lives, who has rescued me from every trouble: [10]The man who told me in Ziklag that Saul was dead thought he was bringing good news. But instead of rewarding him for the news, I seized and killed him. [11]How much more, then, when wicked men have killed a blameless man in bed in his own house! I will certainly avenge his blood on you, and I will rid the earth of you." [12]David gave orders to the young men, who killed them; they cut off their hands and feet and hung them up by the pool in Hebron. And they took the head of Ish-bosheth and buried it in the grave of Abner at Hebron.

5

[a]All the tribes of Israel came to David at Hebron and said, "We are your own flesh and

---

הַבְּאֵרֹתִ֛י רֵכָ֥ב וּבַעֲנָ֖ה וַיָּבֹ֣אוּ כְּחֹ֣ם הַיּ֑וֹם אֶל־בֵּ֣ית אִ֣ישׁ בֹּ֔שֶׁת וְה֣וּא שֹׁכֵ֔ב אֵ֖ת מִשְׁכַּ֥ב הַֽצָּהֳרָֽיִם׃ [6]וְ֠הֵנָּה בָּ֜אוּ עַד־תּ֤וֹךְ הַבַּ֙יִת֙ לֹקְחֵ֣י חִטִּ֔ים וַיַּכֻּ֖הוּ אֶל־הַחֹ֑מֶשׁ וְרֵכָ֛ב וּבַעֲנָ֥ה אָחִ֖יו נִמְלָֽטוּ׃ [7]וַיָּבֹ֣אוּ הַבַּ֗יִת וְהֽוּא־שֹׁכֵ֤ב עַל־מִטָּתוֹ֙ בַּחֲדַ֣ר מִשְׁכָּב֔וֹ וַיַּכֻּ֙הוּ֙ וַיְמִתֻ֔הוּ וַיָּסִ֖ירוּ אֶת־רֹאשׁ֑וֹ וַיִּקְחוּ֙ אֶת־רֹאשׁ֔וֹ וַיֵּ֛לְכ֥וּ דֶּֽרֶךְ הָעֲרָבָ֖ה כׇּל־הַלָּֽיְלָה׃ [8]וַ֠יָּבִ֠אוּ אֶת־רֹ֨אשׁ אִֽישׁ־בֹּ֥שֶׁת אֶל־דָּוִד֮ חֶבְרוֹן֒ וַיֹּֽאמְרוּ֙ אֶל־הַמֶּ֔לֶךְ הִנֵּֽה־רֹ֤אשׁ אִֽישׁ־בֹּ֙שֶׁת֙ בֶּן־שָׁא֣וּל אֹֽיִבְךָ֔ אֲשֶׁ֥ר בִּקֵּ֖שׁ אֶת־נַפְשֶׁ֑ךָ וַיִּתֵּ֣ן יְ֠הֹוָ֠ה לַֽאדֹנִ֨י הַמֶּ֤לֶךְ נְקָמוֹת֙ הַיּ֣וֹם הַזֶּ֔ה מִשָּׁא֖וּל וּמִזַּרְעֽוֹ׃ ס [9]וַיַּ֨עַן דָּוִ֜ד אֶת־רֵכָ֣ב ׀ וְאֶת־בַּעֲנָ֣ה אָחִ֗יו בְּנֵ֛י רִמּ֥וֹן הַבְּאֵרֹתִ֖י וַיֹּ֣אמֶר לָהֶ֑ם חַי־יְהֹוָ֕ה אֲשֶׁר־פָּדָ֥ה אֶת־נַפְשִׁ֖י מִכׇּל־צָרָֽה׃ [10]כִּ֣י הַמַּגִּיד֩ לִ֨י לֵאמֹ֜ר הִנֵּה־מֵ֣ת שָׁא֗וּל וְהֽוּא־הָיָ֤ה כִמְבַשֵּׂר֙ בְּעֵינָ֔יו וָאֹֽחֲזָ֣ה ב֔וֹ וָאֶהְרְגֵ֖הוּ בְּצִֽקְלָ֑ג אֲשֶׁ֥ר לְתִתִּי־ל֖וֹ בְּשֹׂרָֽה׃ [11]אַ֞ף כִּֽי־אֲנָשִׁ֣ים רְשָׁעִ֗ים הָרְג֧וּ אֶת־אִֽישׁ־צַדִּ֛יק בְּבֵית֖וֹ עַל־מִשְׁכָּב֑וֹ וְעַתָּ֗ה הֲל֨וֹא אֲבַקֵּ֤שׁ אֶת־דָּמוֹ֙ מִיֶּדְכֶ֔ם וּבִעַרְתִּ֥י אֶתְכֶ֖ם מִן־הָאָֽרֶץ׃ [12]וַיְצַו֩ דָּוִ֨ד אֶת־הַנְּעָרִ֜ים וַיַּֽהַרְג֗וּם וַֽיְקַצְּצ֤וּ אֶת־יְדֵיהֶם֙ וְאֶת־רַגְלֵיהֶ֔ם וַיִּתְל֥וּ עַל־הַבְּרֵכָ֖ה בְּחֶבְר֑וֹן וְאֵ֨ת רֹ֤אשׁ אִֽישׁ־בֹּ֙שֶׁת֙ לָקָ֔חוּ וַיִּקְבְּר֥וּ בְקֶֽבֶר־אַבְנֵ֖ר בְּחֶבְרֽוֹן׃ פ

ה

[1]וַיָּבֹ֜אוּ כׇּל־שִׁבְטֵ֧י יִשְׂרָאֵ֛ל אֶל־דָּוִ֖ד חֶבְר֑וֹנָה וַיֹּאמְר֣וּ לֵאמֹ֔ר הִנְנ֛וּ עַצְמְךָ֥

---

c   The original form of the name, Merib-baal, is preserved in
     1 Chron. 8.34; 9.40. Cf. Ish-bosheth (Eshbaal) in 2 Sam. 2.8,
     note a. This subject is resumed in chapter 9.
d-d Meaning of Heb. uncertain. Septuagint reads, "And behold,
     the woman who kept the door of the house was cleaning wheat.
     She became drowsy and fell asleep."

a   The account in vv. 1–3 and 6–10 is to be found also, with
     variations, in 1 Chron. 11.1–9.

blood. 2Long before now, when Saul was king over us, it was you who b-led Israel in war;-b and the Lord said to you: You shall shepherd My people Israel; you shall be ruler of Israel." 3All the elders of Israel came to the king at Hebron, and King David made a pact with them in Hebron before the Lord. And they anointed David king over Israel.

4David was thirty years old when he became king, and he reigned forty years. 5In Hebron he reigned over Judah seven years and six months, and in Jerusalem he reigned over all Israel and Judah thirty-three years.

6The king and his men set out for Jerusalem against the Jebusites who inhabited the region. David was told, "You will never get in here! c-Even the blind and the lame will turn you back." (They meant: David will never enter here.)-c 7But David captured the stronghold of Zion; it is now the City of David. 8On that occasion David said, "Those who attack the Jebusites c-shall reach the water channel and [strike down] the lame and the blind, who are hateful to David." That is why they say: "No one who is blind or lame may enter the House."-c

9David occupied the stronghold and renamed it the City of David; David also fortified the surrounding area, from the Millod inward. 10David kept growing stronger, for the Lord, the God of Hosts, was with him.

11eKing Hiram of Tyre sent envoys to David with cedar logs, carpenters, and stonemasons; and they built a palace for David. 12Thus David knew that the Lord had established him as king over Israel and had exalted his kingship for the sake of His people Israel.

---

b-b   Lit. "led Israel out and in."
c-c   Meaning of Heb. uncertain.
d   A citadel.
e   The account in vv. 11–25 is to be found also, with variations, in 1 Chron. 14.1–16.

וּבְשָׂרְךָ אֲנָחְנוּ: 2 גַּם־אֶתְמוֹל גַּם־שִׁלְשׁוֹם בִּהְיוֹת שָׁאוּל מֶלֶךְ עָלֵינוּ אַתָּה הָיִיתָה הָיִיתָ מוֹצִיא הַמּוֹצִיא והמבי וְהַמֵּבִיא אֶת־יִשְׂרָאֵל וַיֹּאמֶר יְהֹוָה לְךָ אַתָּה תִרְעֶה אֶת־עַמִּי אֶת־יִשְׂרָאֵל וְאַתָּה תִּהְיֶה לְנָגִיד עַל־יִשְׂרָאֵל: 3 וַיָּבֹאוּ כָּל־זִקְנֵי יִשְׂרָאֵל אֶל־הַמֶּלֶךְ חֶבְרוֹנָה וַיִּכְרֹת לָהֶם הַמֶּלֶךְ דָּוִד בְּרִית בְּחֶבְרוֹן לִפְנֵי יְהֹוָה וַיִּמְשְׁחוּ אֶת־דָּוִד לְמֶלֶךְ עַל־יִשְׂרָאֵל: פ

4 בֶּן־שְׁלֹשִׁים שָׁנָה דָּוִד בְּמָלְכוֹ אַרְבָּעִים שָׁנָה מָלָךְ: 5 בְּחֶבְרוֹן מָלַךְ עַל־יְהוּדָה שֶׁבַע שָׁנִים וְשִׁשָּׁה חֳדָשִׁים וּבִירוּשָׁלַ͏ִם מָלַךְ שְׁלֹשִׁים וְשָׁלֹשׁ שָׁנָה עַל כָּל־יִשְׂרָאֵל וִיהוּדָה:

6 וַיֵּלֶךְ הַמֶּלֶךְ וַאֲנָשָׁיו יְרוּשָׁלַ͏ִם אֶל־הַיְבֻסִי יוֹשֵׁב הָאָרֶץ וַיֹּאמֶר לְדָוִד לֵאמֹר לֹא־תָבוֹא הֵנָּה כִּי אִם־הֱסִירְךָ הַעִוְרִים וְהַפִּסְחִים לֵאמֹר לֹא־יָבוֹא דָוִד הֵנָּה: 7 וַיִּלְכֹּד דָּוִד אֵת מְצֻדַת צִיּוֹן הִיא עִיר דָּוִד: 8 וַיֹּאמֶר דָּוִד בַּיּוֹם הַהוּא כָּל־מַכֵּה יְבֻסִי וְיִגַּע בַּצִּנּוֹר וְאֶת־הַפִּסְחִים וְאֶת־הָעִוְרִים שנאו שְׂנֻאֵי נֶפֶשׁ דָּוִד עַל־כֵּן יֹאמְרוּ עִוֵּר וּפִסֵּחַ לֹא יָבוֹא אֶל־הַבָּיִת: 9 וַיֵּשֶׁב דָּוִד בַּמְּצֻדָה וַיִּקְרָא־לָהּ עִיר דָּוִד וַיִּבֶן דָּוִד סָבִיב מִן־הַמִּלּוֹא וָבָיְתָה: 10 וַיֵּלֶךְ דָּוִד הָלוֹךְ וְגָדוֹל וַיהֹוָה אֱלֹהֵי צְבָאוֹת עִמּוֹ: פ

11 וַיִּשְׁלַח חִירָם מֶלֶךְ־צֹר מַלְאָכִים אֶל־דָּוִד וַעֲצֵי אֲרָזִים וְחָרָשֵׁי עֵץ וְחָרָשֵׁי אֶבֶן קִיר וַיִּבְנוּ־בַיִת לְדָוִד: 12 וַיֵּדַע דָּוִד כִּי־הֱכִינוֹ יְהֹוָה לְמֶלֶךְ עַל־יִשְׂרָאֵל וְכִי נִשֵּׂא מַמְלַכְתּוֹ בַּעֲבוּר עַמּוֹ יִשְׂרָאֵל: ס

¹³After he left Hebron, David took more concubines and wives in Jerusalem, and more sons and daughters were born to David. ¹⁴These are the names of the children born to him in Jerusalem: ᶠShammua, Shobab, Nathan, and Solomon; ¹⁵Ibhar, Elishua, Nepheg, and Japhia; ¹⁶Elishama, Eliada, and Eliphelet.

¹⁷ᵍWhen the Philistines heard that David had been anointed king over Israel, the Philistines marched up in search of David; but David heard of it, and he went down to the fastness.ʰ ¹⁸The Philistines came and spread out over the Valley of Rephaim. ¹⁹David inquired of the LORD, "Shall I go up against the Philistines? Will You deliver them into my hands?" And the LORD answered David, "Go up, and I will deliver the Philistines into your hands." ²⁰Thereupon David marched to Baal-perazim, and David defeated them there. And he said, "The LORD has broken through my enemies before me as waters break through [a dam]." That is why that place was named Baal-perazim.ⁱ ²¹The Philistines abandoned their idols there, and David and his men carried them off.

²²Once again the Philistines marched up and spread out over the Valley of Rephaim. ²³David inquired of the LORD, and He answered, "Do not go up, but circle around behind them and confront them at the *bacaʲ* trees. ²⁴And when you hear the sound of marching in the tops of the *baca* trees, then go into action, for the LORD will be going in front of you to attack the Philistine forces." ²⁵David did as the LORD had commanded him; and he routed the Philistines from Geba all the way to Gezer.

---

f The list in vv. 14–16 is found, in addition to 1 Chron. 14.4–7, in 1 Chron. 3.5–8, with variations.
g Vv. 17–25 continue the narrative of v. 3.
h Probably the stronghold of Adullam (cf. 1 Sam. 22.4–5).
i Interpreted as "Baal of Breaches." Cf. 6.8 below, and the name Perez in Gen. 38.29 and note.
j Meaning of Heb. uncertain.

13 וַיִּקַּח֩ דָּוִ֨ד ע֜וֹד פִּֽלַגְשִׁ֣ים וְנָשִׁ֗ים מִירֽוּשָׁלִַ֙ם֙ אַחֲרֵ֣י בֹּא֣וֹ מֵחֶבְר֔וֹן וַיִּוָּ֥לְדוּ ע֛וֹד לְדָוִ֖ד בָּנִ֥ים וּבָנֽוֹת׃ 14 וְאֵ֗לֶּה שְׁמ֛וֹת הַיִּלֹּדִ֥ים ל֖וֹ בִּירוּשָׁלִָ֑ם שַׁמּ֣וּעַ וְשׁוֹבָ֔ב וְנָתָ֖ן וּשְׁלֹמֹֽה׃ 15 וְיִבְחָ֥ר וֶאֱלִישׁ֖וּעַ וְנֶ֥פֶג וְיָפִֽיעַ׃ 16 וֶאֱלִישָׁמָ֥ע וְאֶלְיָדָ֖ע וֶאֱלִיפָֽלֶט׃ פ

17 וַיִּשְׁמְע֣וּ פְלִשְׁתִּ֗ים כִּֽי־מָשְׁח֨וּ אֶת־דָּוִ֤ד לְמֶ֙לֶךְ֙ עַל־יִשְׂרָאֵ֔ל וַיַּעֲל֥וּ כָל־פְּלִשְׁתִּ֖ים לְבַקֵּ֣שׁ אֶת־דָּוִ֑ד וַיִּשְׁמַ֣ע דָּוִ֔ד וַיֵּ֖רֶד אֶל־הַמְּצוּדָֽה׃ 18 וּפְלִשְׁתִּ֖ים בָּ֑אוּ וַיִּנָּטְשׁ֖וּ בְּעֵ֥מֶק רְפָאִֽים׃ 19 וַיִּשְׁאַ֨ל דָּוִ֤ד בַּֽיהוָה֙ לֵאמֹ֔ר הַאֶֽעֱלֶה֙ אֶל־פְּלִשְׁתִּ֔ים הֲתִתְּנֵ֖ם בְּיָדִ֑י וַיֹּ֨אמֶר יְהוָ֤ה אֶל־דָּוִד֙ עֲלֵ֔ה כִּֽי־נָתֹ֥ן אֶתֵּ֛ן אֶת־הַפְּלִשְׁתִּ֖ים בְּיָדֶֽךָ׃ 20 וַיָּבֹ֨א דָוִ֜ד בְּבַֽעַל־פְּרָצִ֗ים וַיַּכֵּ֨ם שָׁ֤ם דָּוִד֙ וַיֹּ֔אמֶר פָּרַ֨ץ יְהוָ֤ה אֶת־אֹיְבַי֙ לְפָנַ֔י כְּפֶ֖רֶץ מָ֑יִם עַל־כֵּ֗ן קָרָ֛א שֵֽׁם־הַמָּק֥וֹם הַה֖וּא בַּ֥עַל פְּרָצִֽים׃ 21 וַיַּעַזְבוּ־שָׁ֖ם אֶת־עֲצַבֵּיהֶ֑ם וַיִּשָּׂאֵ֥ם דָּוִ֖ד וַאֲנָשָֽׁיו׃ פ

22 וַיֹּסִ֥פוּ ע֛וֹד פְּלִשְׁתִּ֖ים לַֽעֲל֑וֹת וַיִּנָּטְשׁ֖וּ בְּעֵ֥מֶק רְפָאִֽים׃ 23 וַיִּשְׁאַ֤ל דָּוִד֙ בַּֽיהוָ֔ה וַיֹּ֕אמֶר לֹ֖א תַעֲלֶ֑ה הָסֵב֙ אֶל־אַחֲרֵיהֶ֔ם וּבָאתָ֥ לָהֶ֖ם מִמּ֥וּל בְּכָאִֽים׃ 24 וִ֠יהִי בְּשָׁמְעֲךָ֙ אֶת־ק֤וֹל צְעָדָה֙ בְּרָאשֵׁ֣י הַבְּכָאִ֔ים אָ֖ז תֶּחֱרָ֑ץ כִּ֣י אָ֗ז יָצָ֤א יְהוָה֙ לְפָנֶ֔יךָ לְהַכּ֖וֹת בְּמַחֲנֵ֥ה פְלִשְׁתִּֽים׃ 25 וַיַּ֤עַשׂ דָּוִד֙ כֵּ֔ן כַּֽאֲשֶׁ֥ר צִוָּ֖הוּ יְהוָ֑ה וַיַּךְ֙ אֶת־פְּלִשְׁתִּ֔ים מִגֶּ֖בַע עַד־בֹּאֲךָ֥ גָֽזֶר׃ פ

6 David again assembled all the picked men of Israel, thirty thousand strong. [2a]Then David and all the troops that were with him set out from Baalim[b] of Judah to bring up from there the Ark of God to which the Name was attached, the name LORD of Hosts Enthroned on the Cherubim.

[3]They loaded the Ark of God onto a new cart and conveyed it from the house of Abinadab, which was on the hill; and Abinadab's sons, Uzza and Ahio, guided the [c]new cart. [4]They conveyed it from Abinadab's house on the hill, [Uzzah walking][d] alongside[-c] the Ark of God and Ahio walking in front of the Ark. [5]Meanwhile, David and all the House of Israel danced before the LORD to [e]-[the sound of] all kinds of cypress wood [instruments],[-e] with lyres, harps, timbrels, sistrums, and cymbals.

[6]But when they came to the threshing floor of Nacon, Uzzah reached out for the Ark of God and grasped it, for the oxen had stumbled.[f] [7]The LORD was incensed at Uzzah. And God struck him down on the spot [g]-for his indiscretion,[-g] and he died there beside the Ark of God. [8]David was distressed because the LORD had inflicted a breach upon Uzzah; and that place was named Perez-uzzah,[h] as it is still called.

[9]David was afraid of the LORD that day; he said, "How can I let the Ark of the LORD come to me?" [10]So David would not bring the Ark of the LORD to his place in the City of David; instead, David diverted it to the house of Obed-edom the Gittite. [11]The Ark of the LORD remained in the house of Obed-edom the

ו וַיֹּ֨סֶף ע֥וֹד דָּוִ֛ד אֶת־כָּל־בָּח֖וּר בְּיִשְׂרָאֵ֑ל שְׁלֹשִׁ֖ים אָֽלֶף׃ 2 וַיָּ֣קָם ׀ וַיֵּ֣לֶךְ דָּוִ֗ד וְכָל־הָעָם֙ אֲשֶׁ֣ר אִתּ֔וֹ מִֽבַּעֲלֵ֖י יְהוּדָ֑ה לְהַעֲל֣וֹת מִשָּׁ֗ם אֵ֚ת אֲר֣וֹן הָאֱלֹהִ֔ים אֲשֶׁר־נִקְרָ֣א שֵׁ֗ם שֵׁ֣ם יְהֹוָ֧ה צְבָא֛וֹת יֹשֵׁ֥ב הַכְּרֻבִ֖ים עָלָֽיו׃ 3 וַיַּרְכִּ֜בוּ אֶת־אֲר֤וֹן הָֽאֱלֹהִים֙ אֶל־עֲגָלָ֣ה חֲדָשָׁ֔ה וַיִּשָּׂאֻ֔הוּ מִבֵּ֥ית אֲבִינָדָ֖ב אֲשֶׁ֣ר בַּגִּבְעָ֑ה וְעֻזָּ֣א וְאַחְי֗וֹ בְּנֵי֙ אֲבִ֣ינָדָ֔ב נֹהֲגִ֖ים אֶת־הָעֲגָלָ֥ה חֲדָשָֽׁה׃ 4 וַיִּשָּׂאֻ֗הוּ מִבֵּ֤ית אֲבִֽינָדָב֙ אֲשֶׁ֣ר בַּגִּבְעָ֔ה עִ֖ם אֲר֣וֹן הָאֱלֹהִ֑ים וְאַחְי֕וֹ הֹלֵ֖ךְ לִפְנֵ֥י הָאָרֽוֹן׃ 5 וְדָוִ֣ד ׀ וְכָל־בֵּ֣ית יִשְׂרָאֵ֗ל מְשַֽׂחֲקִים֙ לִפְנֵ֣י יְהֹוָ֔ה בְּכֹ֖ל עֲצֵ֣י בְרוֹשִׁ֑ים וּבְכִנֹּר֤וֹת וּבִנְבָלִים֙ וּבְתֻפִּ֔ים וּבִמְנַֽעַנְעִ֖ים וּֽבְצֶלְצֶלִֽים׃ 6 וַיָּבֹ֖אוּ עַד־גֹּ֣רֶן נָכ֑וֹן וַיִּשְׁלַ֨ח עֻזָּ֜א אֶל־אֲר֤וֹן הָֽאֱלֹהִים֙ וַיֹּ֣אחֶז בּ֔וֹ כִּ֥י שָׁמְט֖וּ הַבָּקָֽר׃ 7 וַיִּֽחַר־אַ֤ף יְהֹוָה֙ בְּעֻזָּ֔ה וַיַּכֵּ֥הוּ שָׁ֛ם הָאֱלֹהִ֖ים עַל־הַשַּׁ֑ל וַיָּ֤מָת שָׁם֙ עִ֖ם אֲר֥וֹן הָאֱלֹהִֽים׃ 8 וַיִּ֣חַר לְדָוִ֔ד עַל֩ אֲשֶׁ֨ר פָּרַ֤ץ יְהֹוָה֙ פֶּ֣רֶץ בְּעֻזָּ֔ה וַיִּקְרָ֞א לַמָּק֤וֹם הַהוּא֙ פֶּ֣רֶץ עֻזָּ֔ה עַ֖ד הַיּ֥וֹם הַזֶּֽה׃ 9 וַיִּרָ֥א דָוִ֛ד אֶת־יְהֹוָ֖ה בַּיּ֣וֹם הַה֑וּא וַיֹּ֕אמֶר אֵ֛יךְ יָב֥וֹא אֵלַ֖י אֲר֥וֹן יְהֹוָֽה׃ 10 וְלֹֽא־אָבָ֣ה דָוִ֗ד לְהָסִ֥יר אֵלָ֛יו אֶת־אֲר֥וֹן יְהֹוָ֖ה עַל־עִ֣יר דָּוִ֑ד וַיַּטֵּ֣הוּ דָוִ֔ד בֵּ֥ית עֹבֵֽד־אֱד֖וֹם הַגִּתִּֽי׃ 11 וַיֵּ֩שֶׁב֩ אֲר֨וֹן יְהֹוָ֜ה בֵּ֣ית עֹבֵ֥ד אֱדֹ֛ם הַגִּתִּ֖י

---

a   Vv. 2–12 are found also in 1 Chron. 13.5–14, with variations.
b   Identical with Baalah, another name for Kiriath-jearim, where the Ark had been kept (cf. 1 Sam. 6.21; 1 Chron. 13.6; Josh. 15.9).
c-c Septuagint and 4QSam[a] read "cart alongside."
d   Cf. vv. 6–7.
e-e Cf. Kimhi; the parallel passage 1 Chron. 13.8 reads "with all their might and with songs."
f   Meaning of Heb. uncertain.
g-g So Targum; 1 Chron. 13.10 reads "because he had laid a hand on the Ark."
h   I.e., "the Breach of Uzzah"; cf. 5.20 and note.

Gittite three months, and the LORD blessed Obed-edom and his whole household.

¹²It was reported to King David: "The LORD has blessed Obed-edom's house and all that belongs to him because of the Ark of God." *ⁱThereupon David went and brought up the Ark of God from the house of Obed-edom to the City of David, amid rejoicing.* ¹³When the bearers of the Ark of the LORD had moved forward six paces, he sacrificed *^jan ox and a fatling.^j* ¹⁴David whirled with all his might before the LORD; David was girt with a linen ephod. ¹⁵Thus David and all the House of Israel brought up the Ark of the LORD with shouts and with blasts of the horn.

¹⁶As the Ark of the LORD entered the City of David, Michal daughter of Saul looked out of the window and saw King David leaping and whirling before the LORD; and she despised him for it.

¹⁷They brought in the Ark of the LORD and set it up in its place inside the tent which David had pitched for it, and David sacrificed burnt offerings and offerings of well-being before the LORD. ¹⁸When David finished sacrificing the burnt offerings and the offerings of well-being, he blessed the people in the name of the LORD of Hosts. ¹⁹And he distributed among all the people—the entire multitude of Israel, man and woman alike—to each a loaf of bread, *^fa cake made in a pan, and a raisin cake.^f* Then all the people left for their homes.

²⁰David went home to greet his household. And Michal daughter of Saul came out to meet David and said, "Didn't the king of Israel do himself honor today—exposing himself today in the sight of the slavegirls of his subjects, as one of the riffraff might expose himself!" ²¹Da-

שְׁלֹשָׁ֣ה חֳדָשִׁ֑ים וַיְבָ֧רֶךְ יְהֹוָ֛ה אֶת־עֹבֵ֥ד
אֱדֹ֖ם וְאֶת־כָּל־בֵּיתֽוֹ: ¹² וַיֻּגַּ֣ד לַמֶּ֣לֶךְ דָּוִד֮ לֵאמֹר֒ בֵּרַ֣ךְ יְהֹוָ֗ה
אֶת־בֵּ֨ית עֹבֵ֤ד אֱדֹם֙ וְאֶת־כָּל־אֲשֶׁר־ל֔וֹ
בַּֽעֲב֖וּר אֲר֣וֹן הָאֱלֹהִ֑ים וַיֵּ֣לֶךְ דָּוִ֗ד וַיַּ֩עַל֩
אֶת־אֲר֨וֹן הָאֱלֹהִ֜ים מִבֵּ֨ית עֹבֵ֥ד אֱדֹ֛ם עִ֥יר
דָּוִ֖ד בְּשִׂמְחָֽה: ¹³ וַֽיְהִ֗י כִּ֧י צָֽעֲד֛וּ נֹֽשְׂאֵ֥י
אֲרוֹן־יְהֹוָ֖ה שִׁשָּׁ֣ה צְעָדִ֑ים וַיִּזְבַּ֥ח שׁ֖וֹר
וּמְרִֽיא: ¹⁴ וְדָוִ֛ד מְכַרְכֵּ֥ר בְּכָל־עֹ֖ז לִפְנֵ֣י
יְהֹוָ֑ה וְדָוִ֕ד חָג֖וּר אֵפ֥וֹד בָּֽד: ¹⁵ וְדָוִד֙ וְכָל־
בֵּ֣ית יִשְׂרָאֵ֔ל מַֽעֲלִ֖ים אֶת־אֲר֣וֹן יְהֹוָ֑ה
בִּתְרוּעָ֖ה וּבְק֥וֹל שׁוֹפָֽר:

¹⁶ וְהָיָה֙ אֲר֣וֹן יְהֹוָ֔ה בָּ֖א עִ֣יר דָּוִ֑ד וּמִיכַ֨ל
בַּת־שָׁא֜וּל נִשְׁקְפָ֣ה ׀ בְּעַ֣ד הַחַלּ֗וֹן וַתֵּ֨רֶא
אֶת־הַמֶּ֤לֶךְ דָּוִד֙ מְפַזֵּ֣ז וּמְכַרְכֵּר֙ לִפְנֵ֣י יְהֹוָ֔ה
וַתִּ֥בֶז ל֖וֹ בְּלִבָּֽהּ: ¹⁷ וַיָּבִ֜אוּ אֶת־אֲר֤וֹן יְהֹוָה֙ וַיַּצִּ֣גוּ אֹת֔וֹ
בִּמְקוֹמ֔וֹ בְּת֣וֹךְ הָאֹ֔הֶל אֲשֶׁ֥ר נָטָה־ל֖וֹ דָּוִ֑ד
וַיַּ֨עַל דָּוִ֥ד עֹל֛וֹת לִפְנֵ֥י יְהֹוָ֖ה וּשְׁלָמִֽים:
¹⁸ וַיְכַ֣ל דָּוִ֔ד מֵהַֽעֲל֥וֹת הָֽעוֹלָ֖ה וְהַשְּׁלָמִ֑ים
וַיְבָ֣רֶךְ אֶת־הָעָ֔ם בְּשֵׁ֖ם יְהֹוָ֥ה צְבָאֽוֹת:
¹⁹ וַיְחַלֵּ֨ק לְכָל־הָעָ֜ם לְכָל־הֲמ֣וֹן יִשְׂרָאֵ֗ל
לְמֵאִישׁ֙ וְעַד־אִשָּׁ֔ה לְאִ֣ישׁ חַלַּ֥ת לֶ֨חֶם֙
אַחַ֔ת וְאֶשְׁפָּ֣ר אֶחָ֔ד וַֽאֲשִׁישָׁ֖ה אֶחָ֑ת וַיֵּ֥לֶךְ
כָּל־הָעָ֖ם אִ֥ישׁ לְבֵיתֽוֹ:

²⁰ וַיָּ֥שָׁב דָּוִ֖ד לְבָרֵ֣ךְ אֶת־בֵּית֑וֹ וַתֵּצֵ֣א מִיכַ֣ל
בַּת־שָׁא֗וּל לִקְרַ֣את דָּוִד֮ וַתֹּ֒אמֶר֒ מַה־נִּכְבַּ֨ד
הַיּ֜וֹם מֶ֣לֶךְ יִשְׂרָאֵ֗ל אֲשֶׁ֨ר נִגְלָ֤ה הַיּוֹם֙ לְעֵינֵ֣י
אַמְה֣וֹת עֲבָדָ֔יו כְּהִגָּל֥וֹת נִגְל֖וֹת אַחַ֥ד
הָֽרֵקִֽים: ²¹ וַיֹּ֣אמֶר דָּוִד֮ אֶל־מִיכַל֒ לִפְנֵ֣י

---

i   Vv. 12b–14 are found, with variations, in 1 Chron. 15.25–27; vv. 15–19a, with variations, in 1 Chron. 15.28–16.3; vv. 19b–20a, with variations, in 1 Chron. 16.43.

j-j 4QSam^a reads "seven oxen and seven [rams]"; cf. 1 Chron. 15.26.

vid answered Michal, "It was before the Lord who chose me instead of your father and all his family and appointed me ruler over the Lord's people Israel! I will dance before the Lord [22]and dishonor myself even more, and be low in [k-]my own[-k] esteem; but among the slavegirls that you speak of I will be honored." [23]So to her dying day Michal daughter of Saul had no children.

7

[a]When the king was settled in his palace and the Lord had granted him safety from all the enemies around him, [2]the king said to the prophet Nathan: "Here I am dwelling in a house of cedar, while the Ark of the Lord abides in a tent!" [3]Nathan said to the king, "Go and do whatever you have in mind, for the Lord is with you."

[4]But that same night the word of the Lord came to Nathan: [5]"Go and say to My servant David: Thus said the Lord: Are you the one to build a house for Me to dwell in? [6]From the day that I brought the people of Israel out of Egypt to this day I have not dwelt in a house, but have moved about in Tent and Tabernacle. [7]As I moved about wherever the Israelites went, did I ever reproach any of the tribal leaders[b] whom I appointed to care for My people Israel: Why have you not built Me a house of cedar?

[8]"Further, say thus to My servant David: Thus said the Lord of Hosts: I took you from the pasture, from following the flock, to be ruler of My people Israel, [9]and I have been with you wherever you went, and have cut down all your enemies before you. Moreover, I will give you great renown like that of the greatest men on earth. [10]I will establish a home for My people Israel and will plant them firm, so that they shall dwell secure and shall tremble no more. Evil men shall

יְהֹוָה אֲשֶׁר בָּחַר־בִּי מֵאָבִיךְ וּמִכָּל־בֵּיתוֹ לְצַוֹּת אֹתִי נָגִיד עַל־עַם יְהֹוָה עַל־יִשְׂרָאֵל וְשִׂחַקְתִּי לִפְנֵי יְהֹוָה: [22] וּנְקַלֹּתִי עוֹד מִזֹּאת וְהָיִיתִי שָׁפָל בְּעֵינָי וְעִם־הָאֲמָהוֹת אֲשֶׁר אָמַרְתְּ עִמָּם אִכָּבֵדָה: [23] וּלְמִיכַל בַּת־שָׁאוּל לֹא־הָיָה לָהּ יָלֶד עַד יוֹם מוֹתָהּ: פ

[ז] [1] וַיְהִי כִּי־יָשַׁב הַמֶּלֶךְ בְּבֵיתוֹ וַיהֹוָה הֵנִיחַ־לוֹ מִסָּבִיב מִכָּל־אֹיְבָיו: [2] וַיֹּאמֶר הַמֶּלֶךְ אֶל־נָתָן הַנָּבִיא רְאֵה נָא אָנֹכִי יוֹשֵׁב בְּבֵית אֲרָזִים וַאֲרוֹן הָאֱלֹהִים יֹשֵׁב בְּתוֹךְ הַיְרִיעָה: [3] וַיֹּאמֶר נָתָן אֶל־הַמֶּלֶךְ כֹּל אֲשֶׁר בִּלְבָבְךָ לֵךְ עֲשֵׂה כִּי יְהֹוָה עִמָּךְ: ס

[4] וַיְהִי בַּלַּיְלָה הַהוּא וַיְהִי דְּבַר־יְהֹוָה אֶל־נָתָן לֵאמֹר: [5] לֵךְ וְאָמַרְתָּ אֶל־עַבְדִּי אֶל־דָּוִד כֹּה אָמַר יְהֹוָה הַאַתָּה תִּבְנֶה־לִּי בַיִת לְשִׁבְתִּי: [6] כִּי לֹא יָשַׁבְתִּי בְּבַיִת לְמִיּוֹם הַעֲלֹתִי אֶת־בְּנֵי יִשְׂרָאֵל מִמִּצְרַיִם וְעַד הַיּוֹם הַזֶּה וָאֶהְיֶה מִתְהַלֵּךְ בְּאֹהֶל וּבְמִשְׁכָּן: [7] בְּכֹל אֲשֶׁר־הִתְהַלַּכְתִּי בְּכָל־בְּנֵי יִשְׂרָאֵל הֲדָבָר דִּבַּרְתִּי אֶת־אַחַד שִׁבְטֵי יִשְׂרָאֵל אֲשֶׁר צִוִּיתִי לִרְעוֹת אֶת־עַמִּי אֶת־יִשְׂרָאֵל לֵאמֹר לָמָּה לֹא־בְנִיתֶם לִי בֵּית אֲרָזִים:

[8] וְעַתָּה כֹּה־תֹאמַר לְעַבְדִּי לְדָוִד כֹּה אָמַר יְהֹוָה צְבָאוֹת אֲנִי לְקַחְתִּיךָ מִן־הַנָּוֶה מֵאַחַר הַצֹּאן לִהְיוֹת נָגִיד עַל־עַמִּי עַל־יִשְׂרָאֵל: [9] וָאֶהְיֶה עִמְּךָ בְּכֹל אֲשֶׁר הָלַכְתָּ וָאַכְרִתָה אֶת־כָּל־אֹיְבֶיךָ מִפָּנֶיךָ וְעָשִׂתִי לְךָ שֵׁם גָּדוֹל כְּשֵׁם הַגְּדֹלִים אֲשֶׁר בָּאָרֶץ: [10] וְשַׂמְתִּי מָקוֹם לְעַמִּי לְיִשְׂרָאֵל וּנְטַעְתִּיו וְשָׁכַן תַּחְתָּיו וְלֹא יִרְגַּז עוֹד וְלֹא־יֹסִיפוּ

---

k-k   Septuagint reads "your."

a   This chapter is found, with variations, also in 1 Chron. 17.

b   Understanding shibte as "scepters"; so Kimhi. 1 Chron. 17.6 reads "chieftains"; cf. below, v. 11.

not oppress them any more as in the past, [11]ever since I appointed chieftains over My people Israel. I will give you safety from all your enemies.

"The LORD declares to you that He, the LORD, will establish a house[c] for you. [12]When your days are done and you lie with your fathers, I will raise up your offspring after you, one of your own issue, and I will establish his kingship. [13]He shall build a house for My name, and I will establish his royal throne forever. [14]I will be a father to him, and he shall be a son to Me. When he does wrong, I will chastise him [d]with the rod of men and the affliction of mortals;[-d] [15]but I will never withdraw My favor from him as I withdrew it from Saul, whom I removed [e]to make room for you.[-e] [16]Your house and your kingship shall ever be secure before you;[f] your throne shall be established forever."

[17]Nathan spoke to David in accordance with all these words and all this prophecy. [18]Then King David came and sat before the LORD, and he said, "What am I, O Lord GOD, and what is my family, that You have brought me thus far? [19]Yet even this, O Lord GOD, has seemed too little to You; for You have spoken of Your servant's house also for the future. [g]May that be the law for the people,[-g] O Lord GOD. [20]What more can David say to You? You know Your servant, O Lord GOD. [21][g]For Your word's sake and of Your own accord[-g] You have wrought this great thing, and made it known to Your servant. [22]You are great indeed, O Lord GOD! There is none like You and there is no other God but You, as we have always heard. [23]And who is like Your people Israel, a unique nation on earth, whom God went and redeemed as His people, winning renown for Himself and doing great and marvelous deeds for them[h] [and] for

בְּנֵי־עַוְלָה לְעַנּוֹתוֹ כַּאֲשֶׁר בָּרִאשׁוֹנָה:
11 וּלְמִן־הַיּוֹם אֲשֶׁר צִוִּיתִי שֹׁפְטִים עַל־
עַמִּי יִשְׂרָאֵל וַהֲנִיחֹתִי לְךָ מִכָּל־אֹיְבֶיךָ
וְהִגִּיד לְךָ יְהֹוָה כִּי־בַיִת יַעֲשֶׂה־לְּךָ יְהֹוָה:
12 כִּי | יִמְלְאוּ יָמֶיךָ וְשָׁכַבְתָּ אֶת־אֲבֹתֶיךָ
וַהֲקִימֹתִי אֶת־זַרְעֲךָ אַחֲרֶיךָ אֲשֶׁר יֵצֵא
מִמֵּעֶיךָ וַהֲכִינֹתִי אֶת־מַמְלַכְתּוֹ: 13 הוּא
יִבְנֶה־בַּיִת לִשְׁמִי וְכֹנַנְתִּי אֶת־כִּסֵּא
מַמְלַכְתּוֹ עַד־עוֹלָם: 14 אֲנִי אֶהְיֶה־לּוֹ
לְאָב וְהוּא יִהְיֶה־לִּי לְבֵן אֲשֶׁר בְּהַעֲוֹתוֹ
וְהֹכַחְתִּיו בְּשֵׁבֶט אֲנָשִׁים וּבְנִגְעֵי בְּנֵי
אָדָם: 15 וְחַסְדִּי לֹא־יָסוּר מִמֶּנּוּ כַּאֲשֶׁר
הֲסִרֹתִי מֵעִם שָׁאוּל אֲשֶׁר הֲסִרֹתִי
מִלְּפָנֶיךָ: 16 וְנֶאְמַן בֵּיתְךָ וּמַמְלַכְתְּךָ עַד־
עוֹלָם לְפָנֶיךָ כִּסְאֲךָ יִהְיֶה נָכוֹן עַד־
עוֹלָם:
17 כְּכֹל הַדְּבָרִים הָאֵלֶּה וּכְכֹל הַחִזָּיוֹן הַזֶּה
כֵּן דִּבֶּר נָתָן אֶל־דָּוִד: ס 18 וַיָּבֹא הַמֶּלֶךְ
דָּוִד וַיֵּשֶׁב לִפְנֵי יְהֹוָה וַיֹּאמֶר מִי אָנֹכִי
אֲדֹנָי יְהֹוִה וּמִי בֵיתִי כִּי הֲבִיאֹתַנִי עַד־
הֲלֹם: 19 וַתִּקְטַן עוֹד זֹאת בְּעֵינֶיךָ אֲדֹנָי
יְהֹוִה וַתְּדַבֵּר גַּם אֶל־בֵּית־עַבְדְּךָ לְמֵרָחוֹק
וְזֹאת תּוֹרַת הָאָדָם אֲדֹנָי יְהֹוִה: 20 וּמַה־
יּוֹסִיף דָּוִד עוֹד לְדַבֵּר אֵלֶיךָ וְאַתָּה יָדַעְתָּ
אֶת־עַבְדְּךָ אֲדֹנָי יְהֹוִה: 21 בַּעֲבוּר דְּבָרְךָ
וּכְלִבְּךָ עָשִׂיתָ אֵת כָּל־הַגְּדוּלָּה הַזֹּאת
לְהוֹדִיעַ אֶת־עַבְדֶּךָ: 22 עַל־כֵּן גָּדַלְתָּ אֲדֹנָי
יְהֹוִה כִּי־אֵין כָּמוֹךָ וְאֵין אֱלֹהִים זוּלָתֶךָ
בְּכֹל אֲשֶׁר־שָׁמַעְנוּ בְּאָזְנֵינוּ: 23 וּמִי כְעַמְּךָ
כְּיִשְׂרָאֵל גּוֹי אֶחָד בָּאָרֶץ אֲשֶׁר הָלְכוּ־
אֱלֹהִים לִפְדּוֹת־לוֹ לְעָם וְלָשׂוּם לוֹ שֵׁם
וְלַעֲשׂוֹת לָכֶם הַגְּדוּלָּה וְנֹרָאוֹת לְאַרְצְךָ

---

c   I.e., a dynasty; play on "house" (i.e., Temple) in v. 5.
d-d   I.e., only as a human father would.
e-e   Lit. "from before you."
f   Septuagint reads "before Me," i.e., "by My favor."
g-g   Meaning of Heb. uncertain.
h   Heb. "you," apparently denoting Israel.

Your land—[driving out][i] nations and their gods before Your people, whom You redeemed for Yourself from Egypt. [24]You have established Your people Israel as Your very own people forever; and You, O LORD, have become their God.

[25]"And now, O Lord GOD, fulfill Your promise to Your servant and his house forever; and do as You have promised. [26]And may Your name be glorified forever, in that men will say, 'The LORD of Hosts is God over Israel'; and may the house of Your servant David be established before You. [27]Because You, O LORD of Hosts, the God of Israel, have revealed to Your servant that You will build a house for him, Your servant has ventured to offer this prayer to You. [28]And now, O Lord GOD, You are God and Your words will surely come true, and You have made this gracious promise to Your servant. [29]Be pleased, therefore, to bless Your servant's house, that it abide before You forever; for You, O Lord GOD, have spoken. May Your servant's house be blessed forever by Your blessing."

8 [a]Some time afterward, David attacked the Philistines and subdued them; and David took Metheg-ammah[b] from the Philistines. [2]He also defeated the Moabites. He made them lie down on the ground and he measured them off with a cord; he measured out two lengths of cord for those who were to be put to death, and one length for those to be spared.[c] And the Moabites became tributary vassals of David.

[3]David defeated Hadadezer son of Rehob, king of Zobah, who was then on his way to restore his monument[d] at the Euphrates River. [4]David captured 1,700 horsemen and 20,000 foot soldiers of his force; and David hamstrung

מִפְּנֵי עַמְּךָ אֲשֶׁר פָּדִיתָ לְּךָ מִמִּצְרַיִם גּוֹיִם וֵאלֹהָיו: 24 וַתְּכוֹנֵן לְךָ אֶת־עַמְּךָ יִשְׂרָאֵל ׀ לְךָ לְעָם עַד־עוֹלָם וְאַתָּה יְהוָה הָיִיתָ לָהֶם לֵאלֹהִים: ס

25 וְעַתָּה יְהוָה אֱלֹהִים הַדָּבָר אֲשֶׁר דִּבַּרְתָּ עַל־עַבְדְּךָ וְעַל־בֵּיתוֹ הָקֵם עַד־עוֹלָם וַעֲשֵׂה כַּאֲשֶׁר דִּבַּרְתָּ: 26 וְיִגְדַּל שִׁמְךָ עַד־עוֹלָם לֵאמֹר יְהוָה צְבָאוֹת אֱלֹהִים עַל־יִשְׂרָאֵל וּבֵית עַבְדְּךָ דָוִד יִהְיֶה נָכוֹן לְפָנֶיךָ: 27 כִּי־אַתָּה יְהוָה צְבָאוֹת אֱלֹהֵי יִשְׂרָאֵל גָּלִיתָה אֶת־אֹזֶן עַבְדְּךָ לֵאמֹר בַּיִת אֶבְנֶה־לָּךְ עַל־כֵּן מָצָא עַבְדְּךָ אֶת־לִבּוֹ לְהִתְפַּלֵּל אֵלֶיךָ אֶת־הַתְּפִלָּה הַזֹּאת: 28 וְעַתָּה ׀ אֲדֹנָי יְהוִה אַתָּה־הוּא הָאֱלֹהִים וּדְבָרֶיךָ יִהְיוּ אֱמֶת וַתְּדַבֵּר אֶל־עַבְדְּךָ אֶת־הַטּוֹבָה הַזֹּאת: 29 וְעַתָּה הוֹאֵל וּבָרֵךְ אֶת־בֵּית עַבְדְּךָ לִהְיוֹת לְעוֹלָם לְפָנֶיךָ כִּי־אַתָּה אֲדֹנָי יְהוִה דִּבַּרְתָּ וּמִבִּרְכָתְךָ יְבֹרַךְ בֵּית־עַבְדְּךָ לְעוֹלָם: פ

ח וַיְהִי אַחֲרֵי־כֵן וַיַּךְ דָּוִד אֶת־פְּלִשְׁתִּים וַיַּכְנִיעֵם וַיִּקַּח דָּוִד אֶת־מֶתֶג הָאַמָּה מִיַּד פְּלִשְׁתִּים: 2 וַיַּךְ אֶת־מוֹאָב וַיְמַדְּדֵם בַּחֶבֶל הַשְׁכֵּב אוֹתָם אַרְצָה וַיְמַדֵּד שְׁנֵי־חֲבָלִים לְהָמִית וּמְלֹא הַחֶבֶל לְהַחֲיוֹת וַתְּהִי מוֹאָב לְדָוִד לַעֲבָדִים נֹשְׂאֵי מִנְחָה:

3 וַיַּךְ דָּוִד אֶת־הֲדַדְעֶזֶר בֶּן־רְחֹב מֶלֶךְ צוֹבָה בְּלֶכְתּוֹ לְהָשִׁיב יָדוֹ בִּנְהַר־*פְּרָת[*]: 4 וַיִּלְכֹּד דָּוִד מִמֶּנּוּ אֶלֶף וּשְׁבַע־מֵאוֹת פָּרָשִׁים וְעֶשְׂרִים אֶלֶף אִישׁ רַגְלִי וַיְעַקֵּר דָּוִד אֶת־כָּל־הָרֶכֶב וַיּוֹתֵר מִמֶּנּוּ מֵאָה

v. 3. קְרִיא וְלֹא כְּתִיב

---

i   *So 1 Chron. 17.21.*

a   *This chapter is reproduced, with some variations, in 1 Chron. 18.*
b   *If not a place name, meaning of Heb. uncertain.*
c   *I.e., he repeatedly doomed twice the number he spared.*
d   *On yad in this sense, cf. 18.18; 1 Chron. 18.3; 1 Sam. 15.12. Others "dominion."*

all the chariot horses, except for 100 which he retained. 5And when the Arameans of Damascus came to the aid of King Hadadezer of Zobah, David struck down 22,000 of the Arameans. 6David stationed garrisons in Aram of Damascus, and the Arameans became tributary vassals of David. The Lord gave David victory wherever he went. 7David took the gold shields[e] carried by Hadadezer's retinue and brought them to Jerusalem; 8and from Betah and Berothai, towns of Hadadezer, King David took a vast amount of copper.

9When King Toi of Hamath heard that David had defeated the entire army of Hadadezer, 10Toi sent his son Joram to King David to greet him and to congratulate him on his military victory over Hadadezer—for Hadadezer had been at war with Toi. [Joram] brought with him objects of silver, gold, and copper. 11King David dedicated these to the Lord, along with the other silver and gold that he dedicated, [taken] from all the nations he had conquered: 12from Edom,[f] Moab, and Ammon; from the Philistines and the Amalekites, and from the plunder of Hadadezer son of Rehob, king of Zobah.

13David gained fame[g] when he returned from defeating[g] Edom[f] in the Valley of Salt, 18,000 in all. 14He stationed garrisons in Edom—[h]he stationed garrisons in all of Edom[h]—and all the Edomites became vassals of David. The Lord gave David victory wherever he went.

15David reigned over all Israel, and David executed true justice among all his people. 16Joab son of Zeruiah was commander of the army; Jehoshaphat son of Ahilud was recorder; 17Zadok son of Ahitub and [i]Ahimelech son of Abiathar[i] were priests; Seraiah[j] was scribe; 18Benaiah

רֶכֶב: 5 וַתָּבֹא אֲרַם דַּמֶּשֶׂק לַעְזֹר לַהֲדַדְעֶזֶר מֶלֶךְ צוֹבָה וַיַּךְ דָּוִד בַּאֲרָם עֶשְׂרִים־וּשְׁנַיִם אֶלֶף אִישׁ: 6 וַיָּשֶׂם דָּוִד נְצִבִים בַּאֲרַם דַּמֶּשֶׂק וַתְּהִי אֲרָם לְדָוִד לַעֲבָדִים נוֹשְׂאֵי מִנְחָה וַיֹּשַׁע יְהוָה אֶת־דָּוִד בְּכֹל אֲשֶׁר הָלָךְ: 7 וַיִּקַּח דָּוִד אֵת שִׁלְטֵי הַזָּהָב אֲשֶׁר הָיוּ אֶל עַבְדֵי הֲדַדְעֶזֶר וַיְבִיאֵם יְרוּשָׁלָ‍ִם: 8 וּמִבֶּטַח וּמִבֵּרֹתַי עָרֵי הֲדַדְעֶזֶר לָקַח הַמֶּלֶךְ דָּוִד נְחֹשֶׁת הַרְבֵּה מְאֹד: ס

9 וַיִּשְׁמַע תֹּעִי מֶלֶךְ חֲמָת כִּי הִכָּה דָוִד אֵת כָּל־חֵיל הֲדַדְעָזֶר: 10 וַיִּשְׁלַח תֹּעִי אֶת־יוֹרָם־בְּנוֹ אֶל־הַמֶּלֶךְ־דָּוִד לִשְׁאָל־לוֹ לְשָׁלוֹם וּלְבָרֲכוֹ עַל אֲשֶׁר נִלְחַם בַּהֲדַדְעֶזֶר וַיַּכֵּהוּ כִּי־אִישׁ מִלְחֲמוֹת תֹּעִי הָיָה הֲדַדְעָזֶר וּבְיָדוֹ הָיוּ כְּלֵי־כֶסֶף וּכְלֵי־זָהָב וּכְלֵי נְחֹשֶׁת: 11 גַּם־אֹתָם הִקְדִּישׁ הַמֶּלֶךְ דָּוִד לַיהוָה עִם־הַכֶּסֶף וְהַזָּהָב אֲשֶׁר הִקְדִּישׁ מִכָּל־הַגּוֹיִם אֲשֶׁר כִּבֵּשׁ: 12 מֵאֲרָם וּמִמּוֹאָב וּמִבְּנֵי עַמּוֹן וּמִפְּלִשְׁתִּים וּמֵעֲמָלֵק וּמִשְּׁלַל הֲדַדְעֶזֶר בֶּן־רְחֹב מֶלֶךְ צוֹבָה:

13 וַיַּעַשׂ דָּוִד שֵׁם בְּשֻׁבוֹ מֵהַכּוֹתוֹ אֶת־אֲרָם* בְּגֵיא־מֶלַח שְׁמוֹנָה עָשָׂר אָלֶף: 14 וַיָּשֶׂם בֶּאֱדוֹם נְצִבִים בְּכָל־אֱדוֹם שָׂם נְצִבִים וַיְהִי כָל־אֱדוֹם עֲבָדִים לְדָוִד וַיּוֹשַׁע יְהוָה אֶת־דָּוִד בְּכֹל אֲשֶׁר הָלָךְ: 15 וַיִּמְלֹךְ דָּוִד עַל־כָּל־יִשְׂרָאֵל וַיְהִי דָוִד עֹשֶׂה מִשְׁפָּט וּצְדָקָה לְכָל־עַמּוֹ: 16 וְיוֹאָב בֶּן־צְרוּיָה עַל־הַצָּבָא וִיהוֹשָׁפָט בֶּן־אֲחִילוּד מַזְכִּיר: 17 וְצָדוֹק בֶּן־אֲחִיטוּב וַאֲחִימֶלֶךְ בֶּן־אֶבְיָתָר כֹּהֲנִים וּשְׂרָיָה

v. 13. בנוסח אחר "אד(ו)ם"

---

e   Or "quivers."
f   So several mss., Septuagint, and 1 Chron. 18.11–13; and cf. v. 14 below. Printed editions and most mss. read "Aram."
g-g 1 Chron. 18.12 and Ps. 60.1 read differently.
h-h This phrase is lacking in 1 Chron. 18.13.
i-i Emendation yields "Abiathar son of Ahimelech," cf., e.g., 20.25; 1 Sam. 22.20.
j   "Sheva" in 20.25; "Shavsha" in 1 Chron. 18.16.

son of Jehoiada was *k*-commander of-*k* the Cherethites and the Pelethites; and David's sons were priests.

9 David inquired, "Is there anyone still left of the House of Saul with whom I can keep faith for the sake of Jonathan?" ²There was a servant of the House of Saul named Ziba, and they summoned him to David. "Are you Ziba?" the king asked him. *a*-"Yes, sir,"-*a* he replied. ³The king continued, "Is there anyone at all left of the House of Saul with whom I can keep faith as pledged before God?"*b* Ziba answered the king, "Yes, there is still a son of Jonathan whose feet are crippled." ⁴"Where is he?" the king asked, and Ziba said to the king, "He is in the house of Machir son of Ammiel, in Lo-debar." ⁵King David had him brought from the house of Machir son of Ammiel, at Lo-debar; ⁶and when Mephibosheth son of Jonathan son of Saul came to David, he flung himself on his face and prostrated himself. David said, "Mephibosheth!" and he replied, "At your service, sir." ⁷David said to him, "Don't be afraid, for I will keep faith with you for the sake of your father Jonathan. I will give you back all the land of your grandfather Saul; moreover, you shall always eat at my table." ⁸[Mephibosheth] prostrated himself again, and said, "What is your servant, that you should show regard for a dead dog like me?"

⁹The king summoned Ziba, Saul's steward, and said to him, "I give to your master's grandson everything that belonged to Saul and to his entire family. ¹⁰You and your sons and your slaves shall farm the land for him and shall bring in [its yield] to provide food for your master's grandson*c* to live on; but Mephibosheth, your master's grandson, shall always eat at my

סוֹפֵֽר׃ 18 וּבְנָיָ֙הוּ֙ בֶּן־יְה֣וֹיָדָ֔ע וְהַכְּרֵתִ֖י וְהַפְּלֵתִ֑י וּבְנֵ֥י דָוִ֖ד כֹּהֲנִ֥ים הָיֽוּ׃ פ

ט וַיֹּ֣אמֶר דָּוִ֔ד הֲכִ֣י יֶשׁ־ע֔וֹד אֲשֶׁ֥ר נוֹתַ֖ר לְבֵ֣ית שָׁא֑וּל וְאֶעֱשֶׂ֤ה עִמּוֹ֙ חֶ֔סֶד בַּעֲב֖וּר יְהוֹנָתָֽן׃ 2 וּלְבֵ֨ית שָׁא֥וּל עֶ֙בֶד֙ וּשְׁמ֣וֹ צִיבָ֔א וַיִּקְרְאוּ־ל֖וֹ אֶל־דָּוִ֑ד וַיֹּ֨אמֶר הַמֶּ֜לֶךְ אֵלָ֗יו הַאַתָּ֥ה צִיבָ֛א וַיֹּ֖אמֶר עַבְדֶּֽךָ׃ 3 וַיֹּ֣אמֶר הַמֶּ֗לֶךְ הַאֶ֨פֶס ע֥וֹד אִישׁ֙ לְבֵ֣ית שָׁא֔וּל וְאֶעֱשֶׂ֥ה עִמּ֖וֹ חֶ֣סֶד אֱלֹהִ֑ים וַיֹּ֤אמֶר צִיבָא֙ אֶל־הַמֶּ֔לֶךְ ע֛וֹד בֵּ֥ן לִיהוֹנָתָ֖ן נְכֵ֥ה רַגְלָֽיִם׃ 4 וַיֹּֽאמֶר־ל֥וֹ הַמֶּ֖לֶךְ אֵיפֹ֣ה ה֑וּא וַיֹּ֤אמֶר צִיבָא֙ אֶל־הַמֶּ֔לֶךְ הִנֵּה־ה֗וּא בֵּ֛ית מָכִ֥יר בֶּן־עַמִּיאֵ֖ל בְּל֥וֹ דְבָֽר׃ 5 וַיִּשְׁלַ֖ח הַמֶּ֣לֶךְ דָּוִ֑ד וַיִּקָּחֵ֗הוּ מִבֵּ֛ית מָכִ֥יר בֶּן־עַמִּיאֵ֖ל מִלּ֥וֹ דְבָֽר׃ 6 וַ֠יָּבֹ֠א מְפִיבֹ֨שֶׁת בֶּן־יְהוֹנָתָ֤ן בֶּן־שָׁאוּל֙ אֶל־דָּוִ֔ד וַיִּפֹּ֥ל עַל־פָּנָ֖יו וַיִּשְׁתָּ֑חוּ וַיֹּ֤אמֶר דָּוִד֙ מְפִיבֹ֔שֶׁת וַיֹּ֖אמֶר הִנֵּ֥ה עַבְדֶּֽךָ׃ 7 וַיֹּ֩אמֶר ל֨וֹ דָוִ֜ד אַל־תִּירָ֗א כִּ֣י עָשֹׂ֤ה אֶעֱשֶׂה֙ עִמְּךָ֣ חֶ֔סֶד בַּֽעֲבוּר֙ יְהוֹנָתָ֣ן אָבִ֔יךָ וַהֲשִׁבֹתִ֣י לְךָ֗ אֶֽת־כָּל־שְׂדֵ֖ה שָׁא֣וּל אָבִ֑יךָ וְאַתָּ֗ה תֹּ֥אכַל לֶ֛חֶם עַל־שֻׁלְחָנִ֖י תָּמִֽיד׃ 8 וַיִּשְׁתַּ֖חוּ וַיֹּ֑אמֶר מֶ֣ה עַבְדֶּ֔ךָ כִּ֥י פָנִ֖יתָ אֶל־הַכֶּ֥לֶב הַמֵּ֖ת אֲשֶׁ֥ר כָּמֽוֹנִי׃

9 וַיִּקְרָ֨א הַמֶּ֜לֶךְ אֶל־צִיבָ֗א נַ֣עַר שָׁא֑וּל וַיֹּ֣אמֶר אֵלָ֔יו כֹּל֩ אֲשֶׁ֨ר הָיָ֤ה לְשָׁאוּל֙ וּלְכָל־בֵּית֔וֹ נָתַ֖תִּי לְבֶן־אֲדֹנֶֽיךָ׃ 10 וְעָבַ֣דְתָּ לּ֣וֹ אֶֽת־הָאֲדָמָ֡ה אַתָּה֩ וּבָנֶ֨יךָ וַעֲבָדֶ֜יךָ וְהֵבֵ֗אתָ וְהָיָ֨ה לְבֶן־אֲדֹנֶ֤יךָ לֶּ֙חֶם֙ וַאֲכָל֔וֹ וּמְפִיבֹ֙שֶׁת֙ בֶּן־אֲדֹנֶ֔יךָ יֹאכַ֥ל תָּמִ֛יד לֶ֖חֶם עַל־שֻׁלְחָנִ֑י וּלְצִיבָ֗א חֲמִשָּׁ֥ה עָשָׂ֛ר בָּנִ֖ים וְעֶשְׂרִ֥ים

---

k-k So Targum (cf. 20.23; 1 Chron. 18.17); Heb. "and."

a-a Lit. "Your servant is."
b See 1 Sam. 20.14 and note.
c Septuagint reads "household."

table."—Ziba had fifteen sons and twenty slaves.—[11]Ziba said to the king, "Your servant will do just as my lord the king has commanded him." [d-]"Mephibosheth shall eat at my table[-d] like one of the king's sons."

[12]Mephibosheth had a young son named Mica; and all the members of Ziba's household worked for Mephibosheth. [13]Mephibosheth lived in Jerusalem, for he ate regularly at the king's table. He was lame in both feet.

10

[a]Some time afterward, the king of Ammon died, and his son Hanun succeeded him as king. [2]David said, "I will keep faith with Hanun son of Nahash, just as his father kept faith with me." He sent his courtiers with a message of condolence to him over his father. But when David's courtiers came to the land of Ammon, [3]the Ammonite officials said to their lord Hanun, "Do you think David is really honoring your father just because he sent you men with condolences? Why, David has sent his courtiers to you to explore and spy out the city, and to overthrow[b] it." [4]So Hanun seized David's courtiers, clipped off one side of their beards and cut away half of their garments at the buttocks, and sent them off. [5]When David was told of it, he dispatched men to meet them, for the men were greatly embarrassed. And the king gave orders: "Stop in Jericho until your beards grow back; then you can return."

[6]The Ammonites realized that they had [c-]incurred the wrath of[-c] David; so the Ammonites sent agents and hired Arameans of Beth-rehob and Arameans of Zobah—20,000 foot soldiers—the king of Maacah [with] 1,000 men, and 12,000 men from Tob. [7]On learning this, David sent out Joab and the whole army—

עֲבָדִֽים: 11 וַיֹּ֨אמֶר צִיבָא֙ אֶל־הַמֶּ֔לֶךְ כְּכֹל֩ אֲשֶׁ֨ר יְצַוֶּ֜ה אֲדֹנִ֤י הַמֶּ֙לֶךְ֙ אֶת־עַבְדּ֔וֹ כֵּ֖ן יַעֲשֶׂ֣ה עַבְדֶּ֑ךָ וּמְפִיבֹ֗שֶׁת אֹכֵל֙ עַל־שֻׁלְחָנִ֔י כְּאַחַ֖ד מִבְּנֵ֥י הַמֶּֽלֶךְ: 12 וְלִמְפִיבֹ֥שֶׁת בֵּֽן־קָטָ֖ן וּשְׁמ֣וֹ מִיכָ֑א וְכֹל֙ מוֹשַׁ֣ב בֵּֽית־צִיבָ֔א עֲבָדִ֖ים לִמְפִיבֹֽשֶׁת: 13 וּמְפִיבֹ֗שֶׁת יֹשֵׁב֙ בִּיר֣וּשָׁלִַ֔ם כִּ֣י עַל־שֻׁלְחַ֥ן הַמֶּ֛לֶךְ תָּמִ֖יד ה֣וּא אֹכֵ֑ל וְה֥וּא פִּסֵּ֖חַ שְׁתֵּ֥י רַגְלָֽיו: פ

י

וַיְהִי֙ אַֽחֲרֵי־כֵ֔ן וַיָּ֕מָת מֶ֖לֶךְ בְּנֵ֣י עַמּ֑וֹן וַיִּמְלֹ֛ךְ חָנ֥וּן בְּנ֖וֹ תַּחְתָּֽיו: 2 וַיֹּ֨אמֶר דָּוִ֜ד אֶֽעֱשֶׂה־חֶ֣סֶד ׀ עִם־חָנ֣וּן בֶּן־נָחָ֗שׁ כַּאֲשֶׁר֩ עָשָׂ֨ה אָבִ֤יו עִמָּדִי֙ חֶ֔סֶד וַיִּשְׁלַ֨ח דָּוִ֧ד לְנַחֲמ֛וֹ בְּיַד־עֲבָדָ֖יו אֶל־אָבִ֑יו וַיָּבֹ֙אוּ֙ עַבְדֵ֣י דָוִ֔ד אֶ֖רֶץ בְּנֵ֥י עַמּֽוֹן: 3 וַיֹּֽאמְרוּ֩ שָׂרֵ֨י בְנֵֽי־עַמּ֜וֹן אֶל־חָנ֣וּן אֲדֹֽנֵיהֶ֗ם הַֽמְכַבֵּ֨ד דָּוִ֤ד אֶת־אָבִ֙יךָ֙ בְּעֵינֶ֔יךָ כִּֽי־שָׁלַ֥ח לְךָ֖ מְנַֽחֲמִ֑ים הֲל֡וֹא בַּעֲב֣וּר חֲק֣וֹר אֶת־הָ֠עִיר וּלְרַגְּלָ֤הּ וּלְהָפְכָהּ֙ שָׁלַ֨ח דָּוִ֧ד אֶת־עֲבָדָ֖יו אֵלֶֽיךָ: 4 וַיִּקַּ֨ח חָנ֜וּן אֶת־עַבְדֵ֣י דָוִ֗ד וַיְגַלַּח֙ אֶת־חֲצִ֣י זְקָנָ֔ם וַיִּכְרֹ֧ת אֶת־מַדְוֵיהֶ֛ם בַּחֵ֖צִי עַ֣ד שְׁתֽוֹתֵיהֶ֑ם וַֽיְשַׁלְּחֵֽם: 5 וַיַּגִּ֣דוּ לְדָוִד֮ וַיִּשְׁלַ֣ח לִקְרָאתָם֒ כִּֽי־הָי֤וּ הָֽאֲנָשִׁים֙ נִכְלָמִ֣ים מְאֹ֔ד וַיֹּ֤אמֶר הַמֶּ֙לֶךְ֙ שְׁב֣וּ בִֽירֵח֔וֹ עַד־יְצַמַּ֥ח זְקַנְכֶ֖ם וְשַׁבְתֶּֽם: 6 וַיִּרְאוּ֙ בְּנֵ֣י עַמּ֔וֹן כִּ֥י נִבְאֲשׁ֖וּ בְּדָוִ֑ד וַיִּשְׁלְח֣וּ בְנֵֽי־עַמּ֡וֹן וַיִּשְׂכְּרוּ֩ אֶת־אֲרַ֨ם בֵּֽית־רְח֜וֹב וְאֶת־אֲרַ֣ם צוֹבָ֗א עֶשְׂרִ֥ים אֶ֙לֶף֙ רַגְלִ֔י וְאֶת־מֶ֤לֶךְ מַֽעֲכָה֙ אֶ֣לֶף אִ֔ישׁ וְאִ֣ישׁ ט֔וֹב שְׁנֵֽים־עָשָׂ֥ר אֶ֖לֶף אִֽישׁ: 7 וַיִּשְׁמַ֖ע דָּוִ֑ד וַיִּשְׁלַח֙ אֶת־יוֹאָ֔ב וְאֵ֥ת כָּל־הַצָּבָ֖א הַגִּבֹּרִֽים:

---

d-d   Septuagint reads "And Mephibosheth ate at David's table."

a   This chapter is found also in 1 Chron. 19.
b   Emendation yields "reconnoiter"; cf. Deut. 1.22; Josh. 2.2–3.
c-c   See note at 1 Sam. 13.4.

[including] the professional fighters. 8The Ammonites marched out and took up their battle position at the entrance of the gate, while the Arameans of Zobah and Rehob and the men of Tob and Maacah took their stand separately in the open. 9Joab saw that there was a battle line against him both front and rear. So he made a selection from all the picked men of Israel and arrayed them against the Arameans, 10and the rest of the troops he put under the command of his brother Abishai*d* and arrayed them against the Ammonites. 11[Joab] said, "If the Arameans prove too strong for me, you come to my aid; and if the Ammonites prove too strong for you, I will come to your aid. 12Let us be strong and resolute for the sake of our people and the land*e* of our God; and the LORD will do what He deems right."

13Joab and the troops with him marched into battle against the Arameans, who fled before him. 14And when the Ammonites saw that the Arameans had fled, they fled before Abishai and withdrew into the city. So Joab broke off the attack against the Ammonites, and went to Jerusalem.

15When the Arameans saw that they had been routed by Israel, they regrouped their forces. 16Hadadezer*f* sent for and brought out the Arameans from across the Euphrates; they came to Helam, led by Shobach, Hadadezer's*f* army commander. 17David was informed of it; he assembled all Israel, crossed the Jordan, and came to Helam. The Arameans drew up their forces against David and attacked him; 18but the Arameans were put to flight by Israel. David killed 700 Aramean charioteers and 40,000 horsemen;*g* he also struck down Shobach, Hadadezer's*h* army commander, who died there. 19And when all the vassal kings of Hadadezer*f*

ח וַיֵּצְאוּ בְּנֵי עַמּוֹן וַיַּעַרְכוּ מִלְחָמָה פֶּתַח הַשַּׁעַר וַאֲרַם צוֹבָא וּרְחוֹב וְאִישׁ־טוֹב וּמַעֲכָה לְבַדָּם בַּשָּׂדֶה: ט וַיַּרְא יוֹאָב כִּי־הָיְתָה אֵלָיו פְּנֵי הַמִּלְחָמָה מִפָּנִים וּמֵאָחוֹר וַיִּבְחַר מִכֹּל בְּחוּרֵי בְיִשְׂרָאֵל וַיַּעֲרֹךְ לִקְרַאת אֲרָם: י וְאֵת יֶתֶר הָעָם נָתַן בְּיַד אַבְשַׁי אָחִיו וַיַּעֲרֹךְ לִקְרַאת בְּנֵי עַמּוֹן: יא וַיֹּאמֶר אִם־תֶּחֱזַק אֲרָם מִמֶּנִּי וְהָיְתָה לִּי לִישׁוּעָה וְאִם־בְּנֵי עַמּוֹן יֶחֱזְקוּ מִמְּךָ וְהָלַכְתִּי לְהוֹשִׁיעַ לָךְ: יב חֲזַק וְנִתְחַזַּק בְּעַד־עַמֵּנוּ וּבְעַד עָרֵי אֱלֹהֵינוּ וַיהוָה יַעֲשֶׂה הַטּוֹב בְּעֵינָיו:

יג וַיִּגַּשׁ יוֹאָב וְהָעָם אֲשֶׁר עִמּוֹ לַמִּלְחָמָה בַּאֲרָם וַיָּנֻסוּ מִפָּנָיו: יד וּבְנֵי עַמּוֹן רָאוּ כִּי־נָס אֲרָם וַיָּנֻסוּ מִפְּנֵי אֲבִישַׁי וַיָּבֹאוּ הָעִיר וַיָּשָׁב יוֹאָב מֵעַל בְּנֵי עַמּוֹן וַיָּבֹא יְרוּשָׁלָ͏ִם:

טו וַיַּרְא אֲרָם כִּי נִגַּף לִפְנֵי יִשְׂרָאֵל וַיֵּאָסְפוּ יָחַד: טז וַיִּשְׁלַח הֲדַדְעֶזֶר וַיֹּצֵא אֶת־אֲרָם אֲשֶׁר מֵעֵבֶר הַנָּהָר וַיָּבֹאוּ חֵילָם וְשׁוֹבַךְ שַׂר־צְבָא הֲדַדְעֶזֶר לִפְנֵיהֶם: יז וַיֻּגַּד לְדָוִד ס וַיֶּאֱסֹף אֶת־כָּל־יִשְׂרָאֵל וַיַּעֲבֹר אֶת־הַיַּרְדֵּן וַיָּבֹא חֵלָאמָה* וַיַּעַרְכוּ אֲרָם לִקְרַאת דָּוִד וַיִּלָּחֲמוּ עִמּוֹ: יח וַיָּנָס אֲרָם מִפְּנֵי יִשְׂרָאֵל וַיַּהֲרֹג דָּוִד מֵאֲרָם שְׁבַע מֵאוֹת רֶכֶב וְאַרְבָּעִים אֶלֶף פָּרָשִׁים וְאֵת שׁוֹבַךְ שַׂר־צְבָאוֹ הִכָּה וַיָּמָת שָׁם: יט וַיִּרְאוּ כָל־הַמְּלָכִים עַבְדֵי הֲדַדְעֶזֶר כִּי נִגְּפוּ לִפְנֵי

v. 17. ׳יתיר א

---

d   *Heb. "Abshai."*
e   *Lit. "towns."*
f   *Many editions read "Hadarezer…Hadarezer's."*
g   *1 Chron. 19.18 reads "foot soldiers."*
h   *Heb. "his."*

saw that they had been routed by Israel, they submitted to Israel and became their vassals. And the Arameans were afraid to help the Ammonites any more.

11 At the turn of the year, the season when kings go out [to battle], David sent Joab with his officers and all Israel with him, and they devastated Ammon and besieged Rabbah; David remained in Jerusalem. ²Late one afternoon, David rose from his couch and strolled on the roof of the royal palace; and from the roof he saw a woman bathing. The woman was very beautiful, ³and the king sent someone to make inquiries about the woman. He reported, "She is Bathsheba daughter of Eliam [and] wife of Uriah the Hittite." ⁴David sent messengers to fetch her; she came to him and he lay with her—she had just purified herself after her period—and she went back home. ⁵The woman conceived, and she sent word to David, "I am pregnant." ⁶Thereupon David sent a message to Joab, "Send Uriah the Hittite to me"; and Joab sent Uriah to David.

⁷When Uriah came to him, David asked him how Joab and the troops were faring and how the war was going. ⁸Then David said to Uriah, "Go down to your house and bathe your feet." When Uriah left the royal palace, a present from the king followed him. ⁹But Uriah slept at the entrance of the royal palace, along with the other officers of his lord, and did not go down to his house. ¹⁰When David was told that Uriah had not gone down to his house, he said to Uriah, "You just came from a journey; why didn't you go down to your house?" ¹¹Uriah answered David, "The Ark and Israel and Judah are located at Succoth, and my master Joab and Your Majesty's men are camped in the open; how can I go home and eat and drink and sleep

יִשְׂרָאֵ֔ל וַיַּשְׁלִ֙מוּ֙ אֶת־יִשְׂרָאֵ֖ל וַיַּֽעַבְד֑וּם וַיִּֽרְא֣וּ אֲרָ֔ם לְהוֹשִׁ֥יעַ ע֖וֹד אֶת־בְּנֵ֥י עַמּֽוֹן׃ פ

יא וַיְהִי֩ לִתְשׁוּבַ֨ת הַשָּׁנָ֜ה לְעֵ֣ת ׀ צֵ֣את הַמַּלְאכִ֗ים* וַיִּשְׁלַ֣ח דָּוִ֡ד אֶת־יוֹאָב֩ וְאֶת־עֲבָדָ֨יו עִמּ֜וֹ וְאֶת־כָּל־יִשְׂרָאֵ֗ל וַיַּשְׁחִ֙תוּ֙ אֶת־בְּנֵ֣י עַמּ֔וֹן וַיָּצֻ֖רוּ עַל־רַבָּ֑ה וְדָוִ֖ד יוֹשֵׁ֥ב בִּירוּשָׁלָֽ͏ִם׃ ס ²וַיְהִ֣י ׀ לְעֵ֣ת הָעֶ֗רֶב וַיָּ֨קָם דָּוִ֜ד מֵעַ֤ל מִשְׁכָּבוֹ֙ וַיִּתְהַלֵּךְ֙ עַל־גַּ֣ג בֵּית־הַמֶּ֔לֶךְ וַיַּ֥רְא אִשָּׁ֛ה רֹחֶ֖צֶת מֵעַ֣ל הַגָּ֑ג וְהָ֣אִשָּׁ֔ה טוֹבַ֥ת מַרְאֶ֖ה מְאֹֽד׃ ³וַיִּשְׁלַ֣ח דָּוִ֔ד וַיִּדְרֹ֖שׁ לָאִשָּׁ֑ה וַיֹּ֗אמֶר הֲלוֹא־זֹאת֙ בַּת־שֶׁ֣בַע בַּת־אֱלִיעָ֔ם אֵ֖שֶׁת אוּרִיָּ֥ה הַֽחִתִּֽי׃ ⁴וַיִּשְׁלַח֩ דָּוִ֨ד מַלְאָכִ֜ים וַיִּקָּחֶ֗הָ וַתָּב֤וֹא אֵלָיו֙ וַיִּשְׁכַּ֣ב עִמָּ֔הּ וְהִ֥יא מִתְקַדֶּ֖שֶׁת מִטֻּמְאָתָ֑הּ וַתָּ֖שָׁב אֶל־בֵּיתָֽהּ׃ ⁵וַתַּ֖הַר הָֽאִשָּׁ֑ה וַתִּשְׁלַח֙ וַתַּגֵּ֣ד לְדָוִ֔ד וַתֹּ֖אמֶר הָרָ֥ה אָנֹֽכִי׃ ⁶וַיִּשְׁלַ֤ח דָּוִד֙ אֶל־יוֹאָ֔ב שְׁלַ֣ח אֵלַ֔י אֶת־אֽוּרִיָּ֖ה הַֽחִתִּ֑י וַיִּשְׁלַ֥ח יוֹאָ֛ב אֶת־אוּרִיָּ֖ה אֶל־דָּוִֽד׃

⁷וַיָּבֹ֥א אוּרִיָּ֖ה אֵלָ֑יו וַיִּשְׁאַ֣ל דָּוִ֗ד לִשְׁל֤וֹם יוֹאָב֙ וְלִשְׁל֣וֹם הָעָ֔ם וְלִשְׁל֖וֹם הַמִּלְחָמָֽה׃ ⁸וַיֹּ֤אמֶר דָּוִד֙ לְא֣וּרִיָּ֔ה רֵ֥ד לְבֵיתְךָ֖ וּרְחַ֣ץ רַגְלֶ֑יךָ וַיֵּצֵ֤א אֽוּרִיָּה֙ מִבֵּ֣ית הַמֶּ֔לֶךְ וַתֵּצֵ֥א אַחֲרָ֖יו מַשְׂאַ֥ת הַמֶּֽלֶךְ׃ ⁹וַיִּשְׁכַּ֣ב אוּרִיָּ֗ה פֶּ֚תַח בֵּ֣ית הַמֶּ֔לֶךְ אֵ֖ת כָּל־עַבְדֵ֣י אֲדֹנָ֑יו וְלֹ֥א יָרַ֖ד אֶל־בֵּיתֽוֹ׃ ¹⁰וַיַּגִּ֤דוּ לְדָוִד֙ לֵאמֹ֔ר לֹא־יָרַ֥ד אוּרִיָּ֖ה אֶל־בֵּית֑וֹ וַיֹּ֨אמֶר דָּוִ֜ד אֶל־אוּרִיָּ֗ה הֲל֤וֹא מִדֶּ֙רֶךְ֙ אַתָּ֣ה בָ֔א מַדּ֖וּעַ לֹֽא־יָרַ֥דְתָּ אֶל־בֵּיתֶֽךָ׃ ¹¹וַיֹּ֨אמֶר אוּרִיָּ֜ה אֶל־דָּוִ֗ד הָֽאָר֞וֹן וְיִשְׂרָאֵ֤ל וִֽיהוּדָה֙ יֹשְׁבִ֣ים בַּסֻּכּ֔וֹת וַֽאדֹנִ֨י יוֹאָ֜ב וְעַבְדֵ֤י אֲדֹנִי֙ עַל־פְּנֵ֤י הַשָּׂדֶה֙ חֹנִ֔ים וַאֲנִ֞י אָב֧וֹא אֶל־בֵּיתִ֛י לֶאֱכֹ֥ל וְלִשְׁתּ֖וֹת וְלִשְׁכַּ֣ב עִם־אִשְׁתִּ֑י חַיֶּ֙ךָ֙* וְחֵ֣י

with my wife? *a-As you live, by your very life,-a* I will not do this!" 12David said to Uriah, "Stay here today also, and tomorrow I will send you off." So Uriah remained in Jerusalem that day. The next day, 13David summoned him, and he ate and drank with him until he got him drunk; but in the evening, [Uriah] went out to sleep in the same place, with his lord's officers; he did not go down to his home.

14In the morning, David wrote a letter to Joab, which he sent with Uriah. 15He wrote in the letter as follows: "Place Uriah in the front line where the fighting is fiercest; then fall back so that he may be killed." 16So when Joab was besieging the city, he stationed Uriah at the point where he knew that there were able warriors. 17The men of the city sallied out and attacked Joab, and some of David's officers among the troops fell; Uriah the Hittite was among those who died.

18Joab sent a full report of the battle to David. 19He instructed the messenger as follows: "When you finish reporting to the king all about the battle, 20the king may get angry and say to you, 'Why did you come so close to the city to attack it? Didn't you know that they would shoot from the wall? 21Who struck down Abimelech son of Jerubbesheth?*b* Was it not a woman who dropped an upper millstone on him from the wall at Thebez, from which he died? Why did you come so close to the wall?' Then say: 'Your servant Uriah the Hittite was among those killed.'"

22The messenger set out; he came and told David all that Joab had sent him to say.*c* 23The messenger said to David, "First the men prevailed against us and sallied out against us into the open; then we drove them back up to the

נַפְשֶׁ֔ךָ אִם־אֶעֱשֶׂ֖ה אֶת־הַדָּבָ֥ר הַזֶּֽה׃
12 וַיֹּ֨אמֶר דָּוִ֜ד אֶל־אוּרִיָּ֗ה שֵׁ֥ב בָּזֶ֛ה גַּם־
הַיּ֖וֹם וּמָחָ֣ר אֲשַׁלְּחֶ֑ךָ וַיֵּ֨שֶׁב אוּרִיָּ֧ה
בִירוּשָׁלַ֛͏ִם בַּיּ֥וֹם הַה֖וּא וּמִֽמָּחֳרָֽת׃
13 וַיִּקְרָא־ל֣וֹ דָוִ֗ד וַיֹּ֧אכַל לְפָנָ֛יו וַיֵּ֖שְׁתְּ
וַֽיְשַׁכְּרֵ֑הוּ וַיֵּצֵ֣א בָעֶ֗רֶב לִשְׁכַּ֤ב בְּמִשְׁכָּבוֹ֙
עִם־עַבְדֵ֣י אֲדֹנָ֔יו וְאֶל־בֵּית֖וֹ לֹ֥א יָרָֽד׃
14 וַיְהִ֣י בַבֹּ֔קֶר וַיִּכְתֹּ֥ב דָּוִ֛ד סֵ֖פֶר אֶל־יוֹאָ֑ב
וַיִּשְׁלַ֖ח בְּיַ֥ד אוּרִיָּֽה׃ 15 וַיִּכְתֹּ֥ב בַּסֵּ֖פֶר
לֵאמֹ֑ר הָב֣וּ אֶת־אֽוּרִיָּ֗ה אֶל־מוּל֙ פְּנֵ֤י
הַמִּלְחָמָה֙ הַֽחֲזָקָ֔ה וְשַׁבְתֶּ֥ם מֵאַֽחֲרָ֖יו וְנִכָּ֥ה
וָמֵֽת׃ ס 16 וַיְהִ֕י בִּשְׁמ֥וֹר יוֹאָ֖ב אֶל־הָעִ֑יר
וַיִּתֵּן֙ אֶת־א֣וּרִיָּ֔ה אֶל־הַמָּק֖וֹם אֲשֶׁ֣ר יָדַ֔ע
כִּ֥י אַנְשֵׁי־חַ֖יִל שָֽׁם׃ 17 וַיֵּ֨צְא֜וּ אַנְשֵׁ֤י הָעִיר֙
וַיִּלָּֽחֲמ֣וּ אֶת־יוֹאָ֔ב וַיִּפֹּ֥ל מִן־הָעָ֖ם מֵעַבְדֵ֣י
דָוִ֑ד וַיָּ֕מׇת גַּ֖ם אוּרִיָּ֥ה הַחִתִּֽי׃
18 וַיִּשְׁלַ֖ח יוֹאָ֑ב וַיַּגֵּ֣ד לְדָוִ֔ד אֶת־כׇּל־דִּבְרֵ֖י
הַמִּלְחָמָֽה׃ 19 וַיְצַ֥ו אֶת־הַמַּלְאָ֖ךְ לֵאמֹ֑ר
כְּכַלּֽוֹתְךָ֗ אֵ֛ת כׇּל־דִּבְרֵ֥י הַמִּלְחָמָ֖ה לְדַבֵּ֥ר
אֶל־הַמֶּֽלֶךְ׃ 20 וְהָיָ֗ה אִֽם־תַּעֲלֶה֙ חֲמַ֣ת
הַמֶּ֔לֶךְ וְאָמַ֣ר לְךָ֔ מַדּ֛וּעַ נִגַּשְׁתֶּ֥ם אֶל־הָעִ֖יר
לְהִלָּחֵ֑ם הֲל֣וֹא יְדַעְתֶּ֔ם אֵ֥ת אֲשֶׁר־יֹר֖וּ מֵעַ֥ל
הַחוֹמָֽה׃ 21 מִֽי־הִכָּ֞ה אֶת־אֲבִימֶ֣לֶךְ בֶּן־
יְרֻבֶּ֗שֶׁת הֲלֽוֹא־אִשָּׁ֡ה הִשְׁלִ֣יכָה עָלָיו֩ פֶּ֨לַח
רֶ֜כֶב מֵעַ֤ל הַֽחוֹמָה֙ וַיָּ֣מׇת בְּתֵבֵ֔ץ לָ֥מָּה
נִגַּשְׁתֶּ֖ם אֶל־הַֽחוֹמָ֑ה וְאָ֣מַרְתָּ֔ גַּ֗ם עַבְדְּךָ֛
אוּרִיָּ֥ה הַחִתִּ֖י מֵֽת׃
22 וַיֵּ֖לֶךְ הַמַּלְאָ֑ךְ וַיָּבֹא֙ וַיַּגֵּ֣ד לְדָוִ֔ד אֵ֛ת
כׇּל־אֲשֶׁ֥ר שְׁלָח֖וֹ יוֹאָֽב׃ 23 וַיֹּ֤אמֶר הַמַּלְאָךְ֙
אֶל־דָּוִ֔ד כִּֽי־גָבְר֤וּ עָלֵ֙ינוּ֙ הָ֣אֲנָשִׁ֔ים וַיֵּצְא֥וּ
אֵלֵ֖ינוּ הַשָּׂדֶ֑ה וַנִּהְיֶ֥ה עֲלֵיהֶ֖ם עַד־פֶּ֥תַח
הַשָּֽׁעַר׃ 24 וַיֹּר֨וּ הַמּוֹרִ֤אים הַמּוֹרִ֥ים

---

a-a *Meaning of Heb. uncertain. Emendation yields "As the Lord lives and as you live" (cf. 1 Sam. 20.3; 25.26; etc.). Lit. "as you live and as your being lives."*

b *The earlier form is Jerubbaal (another name for Gideon), Judg. 7.1; on -bosheth/besheth for -baal, see note at 2 Sam. 4.4. For the event at Thebez described here, see Judg. 9.35 ff.*

c *Septuagint continues with a recapitulation of vv. 19–21.*

entrance to the gate. 24But the archers shot at your men from the wall and some of Your Majesty's men fell; your servant Uriah the Hittite also fell." 25Whereupon David said to the messenger, "Give Joab this message: 'Do not be distressed about the matter. The sword *d*-always takes its toll.-*d* Press your attack on the city and destroy it!' Encourage him!"

26When Uriah's wife heard that her husband Uriah was dead, she lamented over her husband. 27After the period of mourning was over, David sent and had her brought into his palace; she became his wife and she bore him a son.

12 But the LORD was displeased with what David had done, 1and the LORD sent Nathan to David. He came to him and said, "There were two men in the same city, one rich and one poor. 2The rich man had very large flocks and herds, 3but the poor man had only one little ewe lamb that he had bought. He tended it and it grew up together with him and his children: it used to share his morsel of bread, drink from his cup, and nestle in his bosom; it was like a daughter to him. 4One day, a traveler came to the rich man, but he was loath to take anything from his own flocks or herds to prepare a meal for the guest who had come to him; so he took the poor man's lamb and prepared it for the man who had come to him."

5David flew into a rage against the man, and said to Nathan, "As the LORD lives, the man who did this deserves to die! 6He shall pay for the lamb four times over, because he did such a thing and showed no pity." 7And Nathan said to David, "That man is you! Thus said the LORD, the God of Israel: 'It was I who anointed you king over Israel and it was I who rescued you from the hand of Saul. 8I gave you your master's house and possession of your master's wives; and I gave you the House of Israel and Judah;

אֶל־עֲבָדֶ֙יךָ֙ מֵעַ֣ל הַחוֹמָ֔ה וַיָּמ֖וּתוּ מֵעַבְדֵ֣י הַמֶּ֑לֶךְ וְגַ֗ם עַבְדְּךָ֛ אוּרִיָּ֥ה הַחִתִּ֖י מֵֽת׃ ס 25 וַיֹּ֨אמֶר דָּוִ֜ד אֶל־הַמַּלְאָ֗ךְ כֹּֽה־תֹאמַ֣ר אֶל־יוֹאָ֔ב אַל־יֵרַ֤ע בְּעֵינֶ֙יךָ֙ אֶת־הַדָּבָ֣ר הַזֶּ֔ה כִּֽי־כָזֹ֥ה וְכָזֶ֖ה תֹּאכַ֣ל הֶחָ֑רֶב הַחֲזֵ֨ק מִלְחַמְתְּךָ֧ אֶל־הָעִ֛יר וְהָרְסָ֖הּ וְחַזְּקֵֽהוּ׃ 26 וַתִּשְׁמַע֙ אֵ֣שֶׁת אֽוּרִיָּ֔ה כִּי־מֵ֖ת אוּרִיָּ֣ה אִישָׁ֑הּ וַתִּסְפֹּ֖ד עַל־בַּעְלָֽהּ׃ 27 וַיַּעֲבֹ֣ר הָאֵ֗בֶל וַיִּשְׁלַ֨ח דָּוִ֜ד וַיַּאַסְפָ֣הּ אֶל־בֵּית֗וֹ וַתְּהִי־ל֤וֹ לְאִשָּׁה֙ וַתֵּ֣לֶד ל֣וֹ בֵּ֔ן

יב וַיֵּ֧רַע הַדָּבָ֛ר אֲשֶׁר־עָשָׂ֥ה דָוִ֖ד בְּעֵינֵ֥י יְהֹוָֽה׃ פ 1 וַיִּשְׁלַ֧ח יְהֹוָ֛ה אֶת־נָתָ֖ן אֶל־דָּוִ֑ד וַיָּבֹ֣א אֵלָ֗יו וַיֹּ֣אמֶר ל֜וֹ שְׁנֵ֣י אֲנָשִׁ֗ים הָיוּ֙ בְּעִ֣יר אֶחָ֔ת אֶחָ֥ד עָשִׁ֖יר וְאֶחָ֥ד רָֽאשׁ׃* 2 לֶֽעָשִׁ֗יר הָיָ֛ה צֹ֥אן וּבָקָ֖ר הַרְבֵּ֥ה מְאֹֽד׃ 3 וְלָרָ֣שׁ אֵֽין־כֹּ֗ל כִּ֩י אִם־כִּבְשָׂ֨ה אַחַ֤ת קְטַנָּה֙ אֲשֶׁ֣ר קָנָ֔ה וַֽיְחַיֶּ֔הָ וַתִּגְדַּ֥ל עִמּ֛וֹ וְעִם־בָּנָ֖יו יַחְדָּ֑ו מִפִּתּ֨וֹ תֹאכַ֜ל וּמִכֹּס֤וֹ תִשְׁתֶּה֙ וּבְחֵיק֣וֹ תִשְׁכָּ֔ב וַתְּהִי־ל֖וֹ כְּבַֽת׃ 4 וַיָּ֣בֹא הֵ֘לֶךְ֮ לְאִ֣ישׁ הֶֽעָשִׁיר֒ וַיַּחְמֹ֗ל לָקַ֤חַת מִצֹּאנוֹ֙ וּמִבְּקָר֔וֹ לַֽעֲשׂ֔וֹת לָאֹרֵ֖חַ הַבָּא־ל֑וֹ וַיִּקַּ֗ח אֶת־כִּבְשַׂת֙ הָאִ֣ישׁ הָרָ֔אשׁ* וַֽיַּעֲשֶׂ֔הָ לָאִ֖ישׁ הַבָּ֥א אֵלָֽיו׃ 5 וַיִּֽחַר־אַ֥ף דָּוִ֛ד בָּאִ֖ישׁ מְאֹ֑ד וַיֹּ֙אמֶר֙ אֶל־נָתָ֔ן חַי־יְהֹוָ֕ה כִּ֣י בֶן־מָ֔וֶת הָאִ֖ישׁ הָעֹשֶׂ֥ה זֹֽאת׃ 6 וְאֶת־הַכִּבְשָׂ֖ה יְשַׁלֵּ֣ם אַרְבַּעְתָּ֑יִם עֵ֗קֶב אֲשֶׁ֤ר עָשָׂה֙ אֶת־הַדָּבָ֣ר הַזֶּ֔ה וְעַ֖ל אֲשֶׁ֥ר לֹֽא־חָמָֽל׃ 7 וַיֹּ֧אמֶר נָתָ֛ן אֶל־דָּוִ֖ד אַתָּ֣ה הָאִ֑ישׁ כֹּֽה־אָמַ֤ר יְהֹוָה֙ אֱלֹהֵ֣י יִשְׂרָאֵ֔ל אָנֹכִ֞י מְשַׁחְתִּ֤יךָֽ לְמֶ֙לֶךְ֙ עַל־יִשְׂרָאֵ֔ל וְאָנֹכִ֥י הִצַּלְתִּ֖יךָ מִיַּ֥ד שָׁאֽוּל׃ 8 וָאֶתְּנָ֨ה לְךָ֜ אֶת־בֵּ֣ית אֲדֹנֶ֗יךָ וְאֶת־נְשֵׁ֤י אֲדֹנֶ֙יךָ֙ בְּחֵיקֶ֔ךָ וָאֶתְּנָ֣ה לְךָ֔ אֶת־בֵּ֥ית יִשְׂרָאֵ֖ל וִֽיהוּדָ֑ה וְאִם־

v. 1. ‎יתיר א׳

v. 4. ‎יתיר א׳

d-d Lit. "consumes the like and the like."

and if that were not enough, I would give you twice as much more. 9Why then have you flouted the command of the LORD and done what displeases Him? You have put Uriah the Hittite to the sword; you took his wife and made her your wife and had him killed by the sword of the Ammonites. 10Therefore the sword shall never depart from your House—because you spurned Me by taking the wife of Uriah the Hittite and making her your wife.' 11Thus said the LORD: 'I will make a calamity rise against you from within your own house; I will take your wives and give them to another man before your very eyes and he shall sleep with your wives under this very sun. 12You acted in secret, but I will make this happen in the sight of all Israel and in broad daylight.'"

13David said to Nathan, "I stand guilty before the LORD!" And Nathan replied to David, "The LORD has remitted your sin; you shall not die. 14However, since you have spurned ^a-the enemies of-^a the LORD by this deed, even the child about to be born to you shall die."

15Nathan went home, and the LORD afflicted the child that Uriah's wife had borne to David, and it became critically ill. 16David entreated God for the boy; David fasted, and he went in and spent the night lying^b on the ground. 17The senior servants of his household tried to induce him to get up from the ground; but he refused, nor would he partake of food with them. 18On the seventh day the child died. David's servants were afraid to tell David that the child was dead; for they said, "We spoke to him when the child was alive and he wouldn't listen to us; how can we tell him that the child is dead? He might do something terrible." 19When David saw his servants talking in whispers, David understood that the child was dead; David asked his servants, "Is the child dead?" "Yes," they replied.

מְעָט וְאֹסִ֫פָה לְּךָ֥ כָּהֵ֖נָּה וְכָהֵֽנָּה׃ 9 מַדּ֜וּעַ בָּזִ֗יתָ ׀ אֶת־דְּבַ֤ר יְהֹוָה֙ לַעֲשׂ֣וֹת הָרַע֙ בְּעֵינַ֔י אֵ֣ת אוּרִיָּ֣ה הַחִתִּ֗י הִכִּ֣יתָ בַחֶ֔רֶב וְאֶת־אִשְׁתּ֖וֹ לָקַ֣חְתָּ לְּךָ֣ לְאִשָּׁ֑ה וְאֹת֣וֹ הָרַ֔גְתָּ בְּחֶ֖רֶב בְּנֵ֥י עַמּֽוֹן׃ 10 וְעַתָּ֗ה לֹֽא־תָס֤וּר חֶ֨רֶב֙ מִבֵּֽיתְךָ֖ עַד־עוֹלָ֑ם עֵ֕קֶב כִּ֣י בְזִתָ֔נִי וַתִּקַּ֗ח אֶת־אֵ֨שֶׁת֙ אוּרִיָּ֣ה הַֽחִתִּ֔י לִהְי֥וֹת לְךָ֖ לְאִשָּֽׁה׃ ס 11 כֹּ֣ה ׀ אָמַ֣ר יְהֹוָ֡ה הִנְנִי֩ מֵקִ֨ים עָלֶ֤יךָ רָעָה֙ מִבֵּיתֶ֔ךָ וְלָקַחְתִּ֤י אֶת־נָשֶׁ֨יךָ֙ לְעֵינֶ֔יךָ וְנָתַתִּ֖י לְרֵעֶ֑יךָ וְשָׁכַב֙ עִם־נָשֶׁ֔יךָ לְעֵינֵ֖י הַשֶּׁ֥מֶשׁ הַזֹּֽאת׃ 12 כִּ֥י אַתָּ֖ה עָשִׂ֣יתָ בַסָּ֑תֶר וַאֲנִ֗י אֶעֱשֶׂה֙ אֶת־הַדָּבָ֣ר הַזֶּ֔ה נֶ֥גֶד כָּל־יִשְׂרָאֵ֖ל וְנֶ֥גֶד הַשָּֽׁמֶשׁ׃ ס

13 וַיֹּ֤אמֶר דָּוִד֙ אֶל־נָתָ֔ן חָטָ֖אתִי לַֽיהֹוָ֑ה ס וַיֹּ֨אמֶר נָתָ֜ן אֶל־דָּוִ֗ד גַּם־יְהֹוָ֛ה הֶעֱבִ֥יר חַטָּֽאתְךָ֖ לֹ֥א תָמֽוּת׃ 14 אֶ֗פֶס כִּֽי־נִאֵ֤ץ נִאַ֨צְתָּ֙ אֶת־אֹֽיְבֵ֣י יְהֹוָ֔ה בַּדָּבָ֖ר הַזֶּ֑ה גַּ֗ם הַבֵּ֛ן הַיִּלּ֥וֹד לְךָ֖ מ֥וֹת יָמֽוּת׃ 15 וַיֵּ֥לֶךְ נָתָ֖ן אֶל־בֵּית֑וֹ וַיִּגֹּ֣ף יְהֹוָ֗ה אֶת־הַיֶּ֜לֶד אֲשֶׁ֨ר יָלְדָ֧ה אֵֽשֶׁת־אוּרִיָּ֛ה לְדָוִ֖ד וַיֵּאָנַֽשׁ׃ 16 וַיְבַקֵּ֥שׁ דָּוִ֛ד אֶת־הָאֱלֹהִ֖ים בְּעַ֣ד הַנָּ֑עַר וַיָּ֤צׇם דָּוִד֙ צ֔וֹם וּבָ֣א וְלָ֔ן וְשָׁכַ֖ב אָֽרְצָה׃ 17 וַיָּקֻ֜מוּ זִקְנֵ֤י בֵיתוֹ֙ עָלָ֔יו לַהֲקִימ֖וֹ מִן־הָאָ֑רֶץ וְלֹ֣א אָבָ֔ה וְלֹא־בָרָ֥א אִתָּ֖ם לָֽחֶם׃ 18 וַיְהִ֣י בַּיּ֣וֹם הַשְּׁבִיעִ֗י וַיָּ֣מׇת הַיָּ֑לֶד וַיִּֽרְאוּ֩ עַבְדֵ֨י דָוִ֜ד לְהַגִּ֥יד ל֣וֹ ׀ כִּי־מֵ֣ת הַיֶּ֗לֶד כִּ֤י אָֽמְרוּ֙ הִנֵּה֩ בִֽהְי֨וֹת הַיֶּ֤לֶד חַי֙ דִּבַּ֣רְנוּ אֵלָ֔יו וְלֹא־שָׁמַ֖ע בְּקוֹלֵ֑נוּ וְאֵ֨יךְ נֹאמַ֥ר אֵלָ֛יו מֵ֥ת הַיֶּ֖לֶד וְעָשָׂ֥ה רָעָֽה׃ 19 וַיַּ֣רְא דָּוִ֗ד כִּ֤י עֲבָדָיו֙ מִֽתְלַחֲשִׁ֔ים וַיָּ֥בֶן דָּוִ֖ד כִּ֣י מֵ֣ת הַיָּ֑לֶד וַיֹּ֨אמֶר דָּוִ֤ד אֶל־עֲבָדָיו֙ הֲמֵ֣ת הַיֶּ֔לֶד וַיֹּ֖אמְרוּ מֵֽת׃

---

a-a   *The phrase is intended to avoid saying "spurned the* LORD*"; cf. note d-d at 1 Sam. 25.22.*
b   *Some Septuagint mss. and 4QSam^a add "in sackcloth"; cf. 1 Kings 21.27.*

20Thereupon David rose from the ground; he bathed and anointed himself, and he changed his clothes. He went into the House of the LORD and prostrated himself. Then he went home and asked for food, which they set before him, and he ate. 21His courtiers asked him, "Why have you acted in this manner? While the child was alive, you fasted and wept; but now that the child is dead, you rise and take food!" 22He replied, "While the child was still alive, I fasted and wept because I thought: 'Who knows? The LORD may have pity on me, and the child may live.' 23But now that he is dead, why should I fast? Can I bring him back again? I shall go to him, but he will never come back to me."

24David consoled his wife Bathsheba; he went to her and lay with her. She bore a son and she named him Solomon. The LORD favored him, 25and He sent a message through the prophet Nathan; and he was named Jedidiahc at the instance of the LORD.

26dJoab attacked Rabbah of Ammon and captured the royal city. 27Joab sent messengers to David and said, "I have attacked Rabbah and I have already captured e-the water city.-e 28Now muster the rest of the troops and besiege the city and capture it; otherwise I will capture the city myself, and my name will be connected with it." 29David mustered all the troops and marched on Rabbah, and he attacked it and captured it. 30fThe crown was taken from the head of their kingg and it was placed on David's head—it weighed a talent of gold, and [on it]h were precious stones. He also carried off a vast amount of booty from the city. 31He led out the people who lived there and set them to work with saws,

20 וַיָּ֩קָם֩ דָּוִ֨ד מֵהָאָ֜רֶץ וַיִּרְחַ֣ץ וַיָּ֗סֶךְ וַיְחַלֵּף֙ שִׂמְלֹתָ֔יו וַיָּבֹ֥א בֵית־יְהוָ֖ה וַיִּשְׁתָּ֑חוּ וַיָּבֹא֙ אֶל־בֵּית֔וֹ וַיִּשְׁאַ֕ל וַיָּשִׂ֥ימוּ ל֛וֹ לֶ֖חֶם וַיֹּאכַֽל׃ 21 וַיֹּאמְר֤וּ עֲבָדָיו֙ אֵלָ֔יו מָֽה־הַדָּבָ֥ר הַזֶּ֖ה אֲשֶׁ֣ר עָשִׂ֑יתָה בַּעֲב֞וּר הַיֶּ֤לֶד חַי֙ צַ֣מְתָּ וַתֵּ֔בְךְּ וְכַֽאֲשֶׁר֙ מֵ֣ת הַיֶּ֔לֶד קַ֖מְתָּ וַתֹּ֥אכַל לָֽחֶם׃ 22 וַיֹּ֕אמֶר בְּעוֹד֙ הַיֶּ֣לֶד חַ֔י צַ֥מְתִּי וָֽאֶבְכֶּ֑ה כִּ֤י אָמַ֙רְתִּי֙ מִ֣י יוֹדֵ֔עַ יְחָנַּ֖נִי יְהוָ֑ה וְחַ֥י הַיָּֽלֶד׃ 23 וְעַתָּ֣ה ׀ מֵ֗ת לָ֤מָּה זֶּה֙ אֲנִ֣י צָ֔ם הַאוּכַ֥ל לַהֲשִׁיב֖וֹ ע֑וֹד אֲנִי֙ הֹלֵ֣ךְ אֵלָ֔יו וְה֖וּא לֹֽא־יָשׁ֥וּב אֵלָֽי׃

24 וַיְנַחֵ֣ם דָּוִ֗ד אֵ֚ת בַּת־שֶׁ֣בַע אִשְׁתּ֔וֹ וַיָּבֹ֥א אֵלֶ֖יהָ וַיִּשְׁכַּ֣ב עִמָּ֑הּ וַתֵּ֣לֶד בֵּ֗ן ויקרא וַתִּקְרָ֤א אֶת־שְׁמוֹ֙ שְׁלֹמֹ֔ה וַיהוָ֖ה אֲהֵבֽוֹ׃ 25 וַיִּשְׁלַ֗ח בְּיַד֙ נָתָ֣ן הַנָּבִ֔יא וַיִּקְרָ֥א אֶת־שְׁמ֖וֹ יְדִ֣ידְיָ֑הּ בַּעֲב֖וּר יְהוָֽה׃ פ

26 וַיִּלָּ֣חֶם יוֹאָ֔ב בְּרַבַּ֖ת בְּנֵ֣י עַמּ֑וֹן וַיִּלְכֹּ֖ד אֶת־עִ֥יר הַמְּלוּכָֽה׃ 27 וַיִּשְׁלַ֥ח יוֹאָ֛ב מַלְאָכִ֖ים אֶל־דָּוִ֑ד וַיֹּ֙אמֶר֙ נִלְחַ֣מְתִּי בְרַבָּ֔ה גַּם־לָכַ֖דְתִּי אֶת־עִ֥יר הַמָּֽיִם׃ 28 וְעַתָּ֗ה אֱסֹף֙ אֶת־יֶ֣תֶר הָעָ֔ם וַחֲנֵ֥ה עַל־הָעִ֖יר וְלָכְדָ֑הּ פֶּן־אֶלְכֹּ֤ד אֲנִי֙ אֶת־הָעִ֔יר וְנִקְרָ֥א שְׁמִ֖י עָלֶֽיהָ׃ 29 וַיֶּאֱסֹ֥ף דָּוִ֛ד אֶת־כָּל־הָעָ֖ם וַיֵּ֣לֶךְ רַבָּ֑תָה וַיִּלָּ֥חֶם בָּ֖הּ וַֽיִּלְכְּדָֽהּ׃ 30 וַיִּקַּ֣ח אֶת־עֲטֶרֶת־מַלְכָּם֩* מֵעַ֨ל רֹאשׁ֜וֹ וּמִשְׁקָלָ֨הּ כִּכַּ֣ר זָהָ֗ב וְאֶ֙בֶן֙ יְקָרָ֔ה וַתְּהִ֖י עַל־רֹ֣אשׁ דָּוִ֑ד וּשְׁלַ֥ל הָעִ֛יר הוֹצִ֥יא הַרְבֵּ֖ה מְאֹֽד׃ 31 וְאֶת־הָעָ֣ם אֲשֶׁר־בָּ֡הּ הוֹצִ֣יא וַיָּ֣שֶׂם בַּ֠מְּגֵרָ֠ה וּבַחֲרִצֵ֨י הַבַּרְזֶ֜ל וּֽבְמַגְזְרֹ֣ת הַבַּרְזֶ֗ל וְהֶעֱבִ֤יר אוֹתָם֙

v. 30. סבירין ומטעין "מלכה"

---

c   I.e., "Beloved of the LORD."
d   Vv. 26–29 are abridged in 1 Chron. 20.1b.
e-e   Meaning of Heb. uncertain; perhaps the source of the water supply.
f   Vv. 30–31 are found also in 1 Chron. 20.2–3.
g   Heb. "malkam," perhaps equivalent to "Milcom," the Ammonite deity; cf. 1 Kings 11.5.
h   So Targum and 1 Chron. 20.2.

iron threshing boards, and iron axes, or as-signed them to brickmaking; David did this to all the towns of Ammon. Then David and all the troops returned to Jerusalem.

13 This happened sometime afterward: Absalom son of David had a beautiful sister named Tamar, and Amnon son of David became infatuated with her. [2]Amnon was so distraught because of his [half-]sister Tamar that he became sick; for she was a virgin, and it seemed impossible to Amnon to do anything to her. [3]Amnon had a friend named Jonadab, the son of David's brother Shimah; Jonadab was a very clever man. [4]He asked him, "Why are you so dejected, O prince, morning after morning? Tell me!" Amnon replied, "I am in love with Tamar, the sister of my brother Absalom!" [5]Jonadab said to him, "Lie down in your bed and pretend you are sick. When your father comes to see you, say to him, 'Let my sister Tamar come and give me something to eat. Let her prepare the food in front of me, so that I may look on, and let her serve it to me.'"

[6]Amnon lay down and pretended to be sick. The king came to see him, and Amnon said to the king, "Let my sister Tamar come and prepare a couple of cakes in front of me, and let her bring them to me." [7]David sent a message to Tamar in the palace, "Please go to the house of your brother Amnon and prepare some food for him." [8]Tamar went to the house of her brother Amnon, who was in bed. She took dough and kneaded it into cakes in front of him, and cooked the cakes. [9]She took the *a-*pan and set out [the cakes],*-a* but Amnon refused to eat and ordered everyone to withdraw. After everyone had withdrawn, [10]Amnon said to Tamar,

---

a-a Meaning of Heb. uncertain.

בְמַלְבֵּן וְכֵן יַעֲשֶׂה לְכֹל עָרֵי בְנֵי־עַמּוֹן וַיָּשָׁב דָּוִד וְכָל־הָעָם יְרוּשָׁלָםִ׃ פ

יג וַיְהִי אַחֲרֵי־כֵן וּלְאַבְשָׁלוֹם בֶּן־דָּוִד אָחוֹת יָפָה וּשְׁמָהּ תָּמָר וַיֶּאֱהָבֶהָ אַמְנוֹן בֶּן־דָּוִד׃ [2]וַיֵּצֶר לְאַמְנוֹן לְהִתְחַלּוֹת בַּעֲבוּר תָּמָר אֲחֹתוֹ כִּי בְתוּלָה הִיא וַיִּפָּלֵא בְּעֵינֵי אַמְנוֹן לַעֲשׂוֹת לָהּ מְאוּמָה׃ [3]וּלְאַמְנוֹן רֵעַ וּשְׁמוֹ יוֹנָדָב בֶּן־שִׁמְעָה אֲחִי דָוִד וְיוֹנָדָב אִישׁ חָכָם מְאֹד׃ [4]וַיֹּאמֶר לוֹ מַדּוּעַ אַתָּה כָּכָה דַּל בֶּן־הַמֶּלֶךְ בַּבֹּקֶר בַּבֹּקֶר הֲלוֹא תַּגִּיד לִי וַיֹּאמֶר לוֹ אַמְנוֹן אֶת־תָּמָר אֲחוֹת אַבְשָׁלֹם אָחִי אֲנִי אֹהֵב׃ [5]וַיֹּאמֶר לוֹ יְהוֹנָדָב שְׁכַב עַל־מִשְׁכָּבְךָ וְהִתְחָל וּבָא אָבִיךָ לִרְאוֹתֶךָ וְאָמַרְתָּ אֵלָיו תָּבֹא נָא תָמָר אֲחוֹתִי וְתַבְרֵנִי לֶחֶם וְעָשְׂתָה לְעֵינַי אֶת־הַבִּרְיָה לְמַעַן אֲשֶׁר אֶרְאֶה וְאָכַלְתִּי מִיָּדָהּ׃ [6]וַיִּשְׁכַּב אַמְנוֹן וַיִּתְחָל וַיָּבֹא הַמֶּלֶךְ לִרְאֹתוֹ וַיֹּאמֶר אַמְנוֹן אֶל־הַמֶּלֶךְ תָּבוֹא־נָא תָּמָר אֲחֹתִי וּתְלַבֵּב לְעֵינַי שְׁתֵּי לְבִבוֹת וְאֶבְרֶה מִיָּדָהּ׃ [7]וַיִּשְׁלַח דָּוִד אֶל־תָּמָר הַבַּיְתָה לֵאמֹר לְכִי נָא בֵּית אַמְנוֹן אָחִיךְ וַעֲשִׂי־לוֹ הַבִּרְיָה׃ [8]וַתֵּלֶךְ תָּמָר בֵּית אַמְנוֹן אָחִיהָ וְהוּא שֹׁכֵב וַתִּקַּח אֶת־הַבָּצֵק ותלוש וַתָּלָשׁ וַתְּלַבֵּב לְעֵינָיו וַתְּבַשֵּׁל אֶת־הַלְּבִבוֹת׃ [9]וַתִּקַּח אֶת־הַמַּשְׂרֵת וַתִּצֹק לְפָנָיו וַיְמָאֵן לֶאֱכוֹל וַיֹּאמֶר אַמְנוֹן הוֹצִיאוּ כָל־אִישׁ מֵעָלַי וַיֵּצְאוּ כָל־אִישׁ מֵעָלָיו׃ [10]וַיֹּאמֶר אַמְנוֹן

"Bring the food inside and feed me." Tamar took the cakes she had made and brought them to her brother inside. 11But when she served them to him, he caught hold of her and said to her, "Come lie with me, sister." 12But she said to him, "Don't, brother. Don't force me. Such things are not done in Israel! Don't do such a vile thing! 13Where will I carry my shame? And you, you will be like any of the scoundrels in Israel! Please, speak to the king; he will not refuse me to you." 14But he would not listen to her; he overpowered her and lay with her by force.

15Then Amnon felt a very great loathing for her; indeed, his loathing for her was greater than the passion he had felt for her. And Amnon said to her, "Get out!" 16She pleaded with him, "Please don't *a*-commit this wrong; to send me away would be even worse-*a* than the first wrong you committed against me." But he would not listen to her. 17He summoned his young attendant and said, "Get that woman out of my presence, and bar the door behind her."—18She was wearing an ornamented tunic,*b* for maiden princesses were customarily dressed *c*-in such garments.-*c*—His attendant took her outside and barred the door after her. 19Tamar put dust on her head and rent the ornamented tunic she was wearing; she put her hands on her head,*d* and walked away, screaming loudly as she went. 20Her brother Absalom said to her, "Was it your brother Amnon*e* who did this to you? For the present, sister, keep quiet about it; he is your brother. Don't brood over the matter." And Tamar remained in her brother Absalom's house, forlorn. 21When King David heard about all this, he was greatly upset.*f* 22Absalom didn't utter a word to Amnon, good or bad; but Absalom

אֶל־תָּמָר הָבִיאִי הַבִּרְיָה הַחֶדֶר וְאֶבְרֶה
מִיָּדֵךְ וַתִּקַּח תָּמָר אֶת־הַלְּבִבוֹת אֲשֶׁר
עָשָׂתָה וַתָּבֵא לְאַמְנוֹן אָחִיהָ הֶחָדְרָה:
11 וַתַּגֵּשׁ אֵלָיו לֶאֱכֹל וַיַּחֲזֶק־בָּהּ וַיֹּאמֶר לָהּ
בּוֹאִי שִׁכְבִי עִמִּי אֲחוֹתִי: 12 וַתֹּאמֶר לוֹ
אַל־אָחִי אַל־תְּעַנֵּנִי כִּי לֹא־יֵעָשֶׂה כֵן
בְּיִשְׂרָאֵל אַל־תַּעֲשֵׂה אֶת־הַנְּבָלָה הַזֹּאת:
13 וַאֲנִי אָנָה אוֹלִיךְ אֶת־חֶרְפָּתִי וְאַתָּה
תִּהְיֶה כְּאַחַד הַנְּבָלִים בְּיִשְׂרָאֵל וְעַתָּה
דַּבֶּר־נָא אֶל־הַמֶּלֶךְ כִּי לֹא יִמְנָעֵנִי מִמֶּךָּ:
14 וְלֹא אָבָה לִשְׁמֹעַ בְּקוֹלָהּ וַיֶּחֱזַק מִמֶּנָּה
וַיְעַנֶּהָ וַיִּשְׁכַּב אֹתָהּ:
15 וַיִּשְׂנָאֶהָ אַמְנוֹן שִׂנְאָה גְּדוֹלָה מְאֹד כִּי
גְדוֹלָה הַשִּׂנְאָה אֲשֶׁר שְׂנֵאָהּ מֵאַהֲבָה
אֲשֶׁר אֲהֵבָהּ וַיֹּאמֶר־לָהּ אַמְנוֹן קוּמִי לֵכִי:
16 וַתֹּאמֶר לוֹ אַל־אוֹדֹת הָרָעָה הַגְּדוֹלָה
הַזֹּאת מֵאַחֶרֶת אֲשֶׁר־עָשִׂיתָ עִמִּי לְשַׁלְּחֵנִי
וְלֹא אָבָה לִשְׁמֹעַ לָהּ: 17 וַיִּקְרָא אֶת־נַעֲרוֹ
מְשָׁרְתוֹ וַיֹּאמֶר שִׁלְחוּ־נָא אֶת־זֹאת מֵעָלַי
הַחוּצָה וּנְעֹל הַדֶּלֶת אַחֲרֶיהָ: 18 וְעָלֶיהָ
כְּתֹנֶת פַּסִּים כִּי כֵן תִּלְבַּשְׁןָ בְנוֹת־הַמֶּלֶךְ
הַבְּתוּלֹת מְעִילִים וַיֹּצֵא אוֹתָהּ מְשָׁרְתוֹ
הַחוּץ וְנָעַל הַדֶּלֶת אַחֲרֶיהָ: 19 וַתִּקַּח תָּמָר
אֵפֶר עַל־רֹאשָׁהּ וּכְתֹנֶת הַפַּסִּים אֲשֶׁר
עָלֶיהָ קָרָעָה וַתָּשֶׂם יָדָהּ עַל־רֹאשָׁהּ וַתֵּלֶךְ
הָלוֹךְ וְזָעָקָה: 20 וַיֹּאמֶר אֵלֶיהָ אַבְשָׁלוֹם
אָחִיהָ הַאֲמִינוֹן אָחִיךְ הָיָה עִמָּךְ וְעַתָּה
אֲחוֹתִי הַחֲרִישִׁי אָחִיךְ הוּא אַל־תָּשִׁיתִי
אֶת־לִבֵּךְ לַדָּבָר הַזֶּה וַתֵּשֶׁב תָּמָר וְשֹׁמֵמָה
בֵּית אַבְשָׁלוֹם אָחִיהָ: 21 וְהַמֶּלֶךְ דָּוִד שָׁמַע
אֵת כָּל־הַדְּבָרִים הָאֵלֶּה וַיִּחַר לוֹ מְאֹד:
22 וְלֹא־דִבֶּר אַבְשָׁלוֹם עִם־אַמְנוֹן לְמֵרָע

---

b   See Gen. 37.3 and note.
c-c   Meaning of Heb. uncertain. Emendation yields "(thus) in olden times," me'olam.
d   A gesture of wild grief; cf. Jer. 2.37.
e   Heb. "Aminon."
f   Septuagint adds "but he did not rebuke his son Amnon, for he favored him, since he was his first-born"; cf. 1 Kings 1.6.

hated Amnon because he had violated his sister Tamar.

23Two years later, when Absalom was having his flocks sheared at Baal-hazor near Ephraim, Absalom invited all the king's sons. 24And Absalom came to the king and said, "Your servant is having his flocks sheared. Would Your Majesty and your retinue accompany your servant?" 25But the king answered Absalom, "No, my son. We must not all come, or we'll be a burden to you." He urged him, but he would not go, and he said good-bye to him. 26Thereupon Absalom said, "In that case, let my brother Amnon come with us," to which the king replied, "He shall not go with you." 27But Absalom urged him, and he sent with him Amnon and all the other princes.g

28Now Absalom gave his attendants these orders: "Watch, and when Amnon is merry with wine and I tell you to strike down Amnon, kill him! Don't be afraid, for it is I who give you the order. Act with determination, like brave men!" 29Absalom's attendants did to Amnon as Absalom had ordered; whereupon all the other princes mounted their mules and fled. 30They were still on the road when a rumor reached David that Absalom had killed all the princes, and that not one of them had survived. 31At this, David rent his garment and lay down on the ground, h-and all his courtiers stood by with their clothes rent.-h 32But Jonadab, the son of David's brother Shimah, said, "My lord must not think that all the young princes have been killed. Only Amnon is dead; for this has been i-decided by-i Absalom ever since his sister Tamar was violated. 33So my lord the king must not think for a moment that all the princes are dead; Amnon alone is dead."

34Meanwhile Absalom had fled.

The watchman on duty looked up and saw

וְעַד־ט֔וֹב כִּֽי־שָׂנֵ֥א אַבְשָׁל֖וֹם אֶת־אַמְנ֑וֹן
עַל־דְּבַר֙ אֲשֶׁ֣ר עִנָּ֔ה אֵ֖ת תָּמָ֥ר אֲחֹתֽוֹ׃ פ
23 וַֽיְהִי֙ לִשְׁנָתַ֣יִם יָמִ֔ים וַיִּהְי֤וּ גֹֽזְזִים֙
לְאַבְשָׁל֔וֹם בְּבַ֥עַל חָצ֖וֹר אֲשֶׁ֣ר עִם־אֶפְרָ֑יִם
וַיִּקְרָ֣א אַבְשָׁל֔וֹם לְכָל־בְּנֵ֖י הַמֶּֽלֶךְ׃ 24 וַיָּבֹ֤א
אַבְשָׁלוֹם֙ אֶל־הַמֶּ֔לֶךְ וַיֹּ֕אמֶר הִנֵּה־נָ֥א
גֹֽזְזִים֙ לְעַבְדֶּ֔ךָ יֵֽלֶךְ־נָ֥א הַמֶּ֛לֶךְ וַעֲבָדָ֖יו
עִם־עַבְדֶּֽךָ׃ 25 וַיֹּ֨אמֶר הַמֶּ֜לֶךְ אֶל־אַבְשָׁל֗וֹם
אַל־בְּנִי֙ אַל־נָ֤א נֵלֵךְ֙ כֻּלָּ֔נוּ וְלֹ֥א נִכְבַּ֖ד עָלֶ֑יךָ
וַיִּפְרָץ־בּ֛וֹ וְלֹֽא־אָבָ֥ה לָלֶ֖כֶת וַֽיְבָרֲכֵֽהוּ׃
26 וַיֹּ֨אמֶר֙ אַבְשָׁל֔וֹם וָלֹ֕א יֵֽלֶךְ־נָ֥א אִתָּ֖נוּ
אַמְנ֣וֹן אָחִ֑י וַיֹּ֤אמֶר לוֹ֙ הַמֶּ֔לֶךְ לָ֥מָּה יֵלֵ֖ךְ
עִמָּֽךְ׃ 27 וַיִּפְרָץ־בּ֖וֹ אַבְשָׁל֑וֹם וַיִּשְׁלַ֤ח אִתּוֹ֙
אֶת־אַמְנ֔וֹן וְאֵ֖ת כָּל־בְּנֵ֥י הַמֶּֽלֶךְ׃ ס
28 וַיְצַ֣ו אַבְשָׁל֣וֹם אֶת־נְעָרָיו֮ לֵאמֹר֒ רְא֣וּ
נָ֠א כְּט֨וֹב לֵב־אַמְנ֤וֹן בַּיַּ֙יִן֙ וְאָמַרְתִּ֣י אֲלֵיכֶ֔ם
הַכּ֧וּ אֶת־אַמְנ֛וֹן וַהֲמִתֶּ֥ם אֹת֖וֹ אַל־תִּירָ֑אוּ
הֲל֗וֹא כִּ֤י אָֽנֹכִי֙ צִוִּ֣יתִי אֶתְכֶ֔ם חִזְק֖וּ וִהְי֥וּ
לִבְנֵי־חָֽיִל׃ 29 וַיַּֽעֲשׂ֞וּ נַעֲרֵ֤י אַבְשָׁלוֹם֙
לְאַמְנ֔וֹן כַּאֲשֶׁ֥ר צִוָּ֖ה אַבְשָׁל֑וֹם וַיָּקֻ֣מוּ ׀
כָּל־בְּנֵ֣י הַמֶּ֗לֶךְ וַֽיִּרְכְּב֛וּ אִ֥ישׁ עַל־פִּרְדּ֖וֹ
וַיָּנֻֽסוּ׃ 30 וַֽיְהִ֣י הֵ֣מָּה בַדֶּ֔רֶךְ וְהַשְּׁמֻעָ֣ה
בָ֔אָה אֶל־דָּוִ֖ד לֵאמֹ֑ר הִכָּ֤ה אַבְשָׁלוֹם֙ אֶת־
כָּל־בְּנֵ֣י הַמֶּ֔לֶךְ וְלֹֽא־נוֹתַ֥ר מֵהֶ֖ם אֶחָֽד׃ ס
31 וַיָּ֧קָם הַמֶּ֛לֶךְ וַיִּקְרַ֥ע אֶת־בְּגָדָ֖יו וַיִּשְׁכַּ֣ב
אָ֑רְצָה וְכָל־עֲבָדָ֥יו נִצָּבִ֖ים קְרֻעֵ֥י
בְגָדִֽים׃ ס 32 וַיַּ֡עַן יוֹנָדָ֣ב ׀ בֶּן־שִׁמְעָ֨ה
אֲחִֽי־דָוִ֜ד וַיֹּ֗אמֶר אַל־יֹאמַ֤ר אֲדֹנִי֙ אֵ֣ת
כָּל־הַנְּעָרִ֞ים בְּנֵֽי־הַמֶּ֤לֶךְ הֵמִ֙יתוּ֙ כִּֽי־אַמְנ֤וֹן
לְבַדּ֣וֹ מֵ֔ת כִּֽי־עַל־פִּ֤י אַבְשָׁלוֹם֙ הָֽיְתָ֣ה
שׂוּמָ֔ה מִיּוֹם֙ עַנֹּת֔וֹ אֵ֖ת תָּמָ֥ר אֲחֹתֽוֹ׃
33 וְעַתָּ֡ה אַל־יָשֵׂם֩ אֲדֹנִ֨י הַמֶּ֤לֶךְ אֶל־לִבּוֹ֙
דָּבָ֣ר לֵאמֹ֔ר כָּל־בְּנֵ֥י הַמֶּ֖לֶךְ מֵ֑תוּ כִּֽי־אִם־*
אַמְנ֥וֹן לְבַדּ֖וֹ מֵֽת׃ פ
34 וַיִּבְרַ֖ח אַבְשָׁל֑וֹם
וַיִּשָּׂ֞א הַנַּ֤עַר הַצֹּפֶה֙ אֶת־עֵינָ֔ו וַיַּ֗רְא

g   Septuagint adds "and Absalom made a feast fit for a king."
h-h Septuagint reads "and all his courtiers who were standing by him rent their clothes."
i-i Lit. "determined by the command of."

כתיב ולא קריא   v. 33.

a large crowd coming *j*-from the road to his rear,-*j* from the side of the hill. ³⁵Jonadab said to the king, "See, the princes have come! It is just as your servant said." ³⁶As he finished speaking, the princes came in and broke into weeping; and David and all his courtiers wept bitterly, too.

³⁷Absalom had fled, and he came to Talmai son of Ammihud, king of Geshur. And [King David] mourned over his son a long time. ³⁸Absalom, who had fled to Geshur, remained there three years. ³⁹And *k*-King David-*k* was pining away for Absalom, for [the king] had gotten over Amnon's death.

14 Joab son of Zeruiah could see that the king's mind was on Absalom; ²so Joab sent to Tekoa and brought a clever woman from there. He said to her, "Pretend you are in mourning; put on mourning clothes and don't anoint yourself with oil; and act like a woman who has grieved a long time over a departed one. ³Go to the king and say to him thus and thus." And Joab told her what to say.ᵃ

⁴The woman of Tekoa cameᵇ to the king, flung herself face down to the ground, and prostrated herself. She cried out, "Help, O king!" ⁵The king asked her, "What troubles you?" And she answered, "Alas, I am a widow, my husband is dead. ⁶Your maidservant had two sons. The two of them came to blows out in the fields where there was no one to stop them, and one of them struck the other and killed him. ⁷Then the whole clan confronted your maidservant and said, 'Hand over the one who killed his brother, that we may put him to death for the

וְהִנֵּה עַם־רָב הֹלְכִים מִדֶּרֶךְ אַחֲרָיו מִצַּד הָהָר: 35 וַיֹּאמֶר יוֹנָדָב אֶל־הַמֶּלֶךְ הִנֵּה בְנֵי־הַמֶּלֶךְ בָּאוּ כִּדְבַר עַבְדְּךָ כֵּן הָיָה: 36 וַיְהִי ׀ כְּכַלֹּתוֹ לְדַבֵּר וְהִנֵּה בְנֵי־הַמֶּלֶךְ בָּאוּ וַיִּשְׂאוּ קוֹלָם וַיִּבְכּוּ וְגַם־הַמֶּלֶךְ וְכָל־עֲבָדָיו בָּכוּ בְּכִי גָּדוֹל מְאֹד: 37 וְאַבְשָׁלוֹם בָּרַח וַיֵּלֶךְ אֶל־תַּלְמַי בֶּן־עמיחור עַמִּיהוּד מֶלֶךְ גְּשׁוּר וַיִּתְאַבֵּל עַל־בְּנוֹ כָּל־הַיָּמִים: 38 וְאַבְשָׁלוֹם בָּרַח וַיֵּלֶךְ גְּשׁוּר וַיְהִי־שָׁם שָׁלֹשׁ שָׁנִים: 39 וַתְּכַל דָּוִד הַמֶּלֶךְ לָצֵאת אֶל־אַבְשָׁלוֹם כִּי־נִחַם עַל־אַמְנוֹן כִּי־מֵת: ס

יד וַיֵּדַע יוֹאָב בֶּן־צְרֻיָה כִּי־לֵב הַמֶּלֶךְ עַל־אַבְשָׁלוֹם: 2 וַיִּשְׁלַח יוֹאָב תְּקוֹעָה וַיִּקַּח מִשָּׁם אִשָּׁה חֲכָמָה וַיֹּאמֶר אֵלֶיהָ הִתְאַבְּלִי־נָא וְלִבְשִׁי־נָא בִגְדֵי־אֵבֶל וְאַל־תָּסוּכִי שֶׁמֶן וְהָיִית כְּאִשָּׁה זֶה יָמִים רַבִּים מִתְאַבֶּלֶת עַל־מֵת: 3 וּבָאת אֶל־הַמֶּלֶךְ וְדִבַּרְתְּ אֵלָיו כַּדָּבָר הַזֶּה וַיָּשֶׂם יוֹאָב אֶת־הַדְּבָרִים בְּפִיהָ: 4 וַתֹּאמֶר* הָאִשָּׁה הַתְּקֹעִית אֶל־הַמֶּלֶךְ וַתִּפֹּל עַל־אַפֶּיהָ אַרְצָה וַתִּשְׁתָּחוּ וַתֹּאמֶר הוֹשִׁעָה הַמֶּלֶךְ: ס 5 וַיֹּאמֶר־לָהּ הַמֶּלֶךְ מַה־לָּךְ וַתֹּאמֶר אֲבָל אִשָּׁה־אַלְמָנָה אָנִי וַיָּמָת אִישִׁי: 6 וּלְשִׁפְחָתְךָ שְׁנֵי בָנִים וַיִּנָּצוּ שְׁנֵיהֶם בַּשָּׂדֶה וְאֵין מַצִּיל בֵּינֵיהֶם וַיַּכּוֹ הָאֶחָד אֶת־הָאֶחָד וַיָּמֶת אֹתוֹ: 7 וְהִנֵּה קָמָה כָל־הַמִּשְׁפָּחָה עַל־שִׁפְחָתֶךָ וַיֹּאמְרוּ תְּנִי ׀ אֶת־מַכֵּה אָחִיו וּנְמִתֵהוּ בְּנֶפֶשׁ אָחִיו אֲשֶׁר הָרָג וְנַשְׁמִידָה גַּם אֶת־הַיּוֹרֵשׁ

---

j-j   Emendation yields "down the slope of the Horonaim road. The watchman came and told the king 'I see men coming from the Horonaim road.'" Cf. Septuagint.

k-k   Some Septuagint mss. and 4QSamᵃ read "the spirit [ruah] of the king."

a   Lit. "and he put words into her mouth."

b   So many mss. and printed editions. Most mss. and printed editions read "said."

slaying of his brother, c-even though we wipe out the heir.'-c Thus they would quench the last ember remaining to me, and leave my husband without name or remnant upon the earth." 8The king said to the woman, "Go home. I will issue an order in your behalf." 9And the woman of Tekoa said to the king, "My lord king, may the guilt be on me and on my ancestral house; Your Majesty and his throne are guiltless." 10The king said, "If anyone says anything more to you, have him brought to me, and he will never trouble you again." 11She replied, "Let Your Majesty be mindful of the LORD your God and restrain the blood avenger bent on destruction, so that my son may not be killed." And he said, "As the LORD lives, not a hair of your son shall fall to the ground."

12Then the woman said, "Please let your maidservant say another word to my lord the king." "Speak on," said the king. 13And the woman said, "Why then have you planned the like against God's people? In making this pronouncement, Your Majesty condemns himself in that Your Majesty does not bring back his own banished one. 14We must all die; we are like water that is poured out on the ground and cannot be gathered up. d-God will not take away the life of one who makes plans so that no one may be kept banished.-d 15And the reason I have come to say these things to the king, my lord, is that the people have frightened me. Your maidservant thought I would speak to Your Majesty; perhaps Your Majesty would act on his handmaid's plea. 16For Your Majesty would surely agree to deliver his handmaid from the hands of anyone [who would seek to] cut off both me and my son from the heritagee of God. 17Your maidservant thought, 'Let the word of my lord the king provide comfort; for my lord

וְכִבּוּ אֶת־גַּחַלְתִּי אֲשֶׁר נִשְׁאָרָה לְבִלְתִּי שׂים־לְאִישִׁי שֵׁם וּשְׁאֵרִית עַל־פְּנֵי הָאֲדָמָה: פ 8 וַיֹּאמֶר הַמֶּלֶךְ אֶל־הָאִשָּׁה לְכִי לְבֵיתֵךְ וַאֲנִי אֲצַוֶּה עָלָיִךְ: 9 וַתֹּאמֶר הָאִשָּׁה הַתְּקוֹעִית אֶל־הַמֶּלֶךְ עָלַי אֲדֹנִי הַמֶּלֶךְ הֶעָוֺן וְעַל־בֵּית אָבִי וְהַמֶּלֶךְ וְכִסְאוֹ נָקִי: ס 10 וַיֹּאמֶר הַמֶּלֶךְ הַמְדַבֵּר אֵלַיִךְ וַהֲבֵאתוֹ אֵלַי וְלֹא־יֹסִיף עוֹד לָגַעַת בָּךְ: 11 וַתֹּאמֶר יִזְכָּר־נָא הַמֶּלֶךְ אֶת־יְהוָה אֱלֹהֶיךָ מֵהַרְבִּית מֵהַרְבַּת גֹּאֵל הַדָּם לְשַׁחֵת וְלֹא יַשְׁמִידוּ אֶת־בְּנִי וַיֹּאמֶר חַי־יְהוָה אִם־יִפֹּל מִשַּׂעֲרַת בְּנֵךְ אָרְצָה: 12 וַתֹּאמֶר הָאִשָּׁה תְּדַבֶּר־נָא שִׁפְחָתְךָ אֶל־אֲדֹנִי הַמֶּלֶךְ דָּבָר וַיֹּאמֶר דַּבֵּרִי: ס 13 וַתֹּאמֶר הָאִשָּׁה וְלָמָּה חָשַׁבְתָּה כָּזֹאת עַל־עַם אֱלֹהִים וּמִדַּבֵּר הַמֶּלֶךְ הַדָּבָר הַזֶּה כְּאָשֵׁם לְבִלְתִּי הָשִׁיב הַמֶּלֶךְ אֶת־נִדְּחוֹ: 14 כִּי־מוֹת נָמוּת וְכַמַּיִם הַנִּגָּרִים אַרְצָה אֲשֶׁר לֹא יֵאָסֵפוּ וְלֹא־יִשָּׂא אֱלֹהִים נֶפֶשׁ וְחָשַׁב מַחֲשָׁבוֹת לְבִלְתִּי יִדַּח מִמֶּנּוּ נִדָּח: 15 וְעַתָּה אֲשֶׁר־בָּאתִי לְדַבֵּר אֶל־הַמֶּלֶךְ אֲדֹנִי אֶת־הַדָּבָר הַזֶּה כִּי יֵרְאֻנִי הָעָם וַתֹּאמֶר שִׁפְחָתְךָ אֲדַבְּרָה־נָּא אֶל־הַמֶּלֶךְ אוּלַי יַעֲשֶׂה הַמֶּלֶךְ אֶת־דְּבַר אֲמָתוֹ: 16 כִּי יִשְׁמַע הַמֶּלֶךְ לְהַצִּיל אֶת־אֲמָתוֹ מִכַּף הָאִישׁ לְהַשְׁמִיד אֹתִי וְאֶת־בְּנִי יַחַד מִנַּחֲלַת אֱלֹהִים: 17 וַתֹּאמֶר שִׁפְחָתְךָ יִהְיֶה־נָּא דְּבַר־אֲדֹנִי הַמֶּלֶךְ לִמְנוּחָה כִּי ׀ כְּמַלְאַךְ הָאֱלֹהִים כֵּן אֲדֹנִי הַמֶּלֶךְ לִשְׁמֹעַ הַטּוֹב וְהָרָע וַיהוָה אֱלֹהֶיךָ יְהִי עִמָּךְ: פ

---

c-c   *Emendation yields "Thus they would destroy the [last] heir and…"*

d-d   *Meaning of Heb. uncertain. The apparent sense is: God will not punish you for bringing back the banished Absalom.*

e   *I.e., people.*

673

the king is like an angel of God, understanding everything, good and bad.' May the LORD your God be with you."

18In reply, the king said to the woman, "Do not withhold from me anything I ask you!" The woman answered, "Let my lord the king speak." 19The king asked, "Is Joab in league with you in all this?" The woman replied, "As you live, my lord the king, *f*-it is just as my lord the king says.-*f* Yes, your servant Joab was the one who instructed me, and it was he who *g*-told your maidservant everything she was to say.-*g* 20It was to conceal the real purpose of the matter that your servant Joab did this thing. My lord is as wise as an angel of God, and he knows all that goes on in the land."

21Then the king said to Joab, "I will do this thing. Go and bring back my boy Absalom." 22Joab flung himself face down on the ground and prostrated himself. Joab blessed the king and said, "Today your servant knows that he has found favor with you, my lord king, for Your Majesty has granted his servant's request." 23And Joab went at once to Geshur and brought Absalom to Jerusalem. 24But the king said, "Let him go directly to his house and not present himself to me." So Absalom went directly to his house and did not present himself to the king.

25No one in all Israel was so admired for his beauty as Absalom; from the sole of his foot to the crown of his head he was without blemish. 26When he cut his hair—he had to have it cut every year, for it grew too heavy for him—the hair of his head weighed two hundred shekels by the royal weight. 27Absalom had three sons and a daughter whose name was Tamar; she was a beautiful woman.

28Absalom lived in Jerusalem two years without appearing before the king. 29Then Absalom

18 וַיַּ֨עַן הַמֶּ֜לֶךְ וַיֹּ֤אמֶר אֶל־הָֽאִשָּׁה֙ אַל־נָ֣א תְכַחֲדִ֣י מִמֶּ֔נִּי דָּבָ֕ר אֲשֶׁ֥ר אָנֹכִ֖י שֹׁאֵ֣ל אֹתָ֑ךְ וַתֹּ֙אמֶר֙ הָֽאִשָּׁ֔ה יְדַבֶּר־נָ֖א אֲדֹנִ֥י הַמֶּֽלֶךְ׃ 19 וַיֹּ֣אמֶר הַמֶּ֔לֶךְ הֲיַ֥ד יוֹאָ֛ב אִתָּ֖ךְ בְּכָל־זֹ֑את וַתַּ֣עַן הָאִשָּׁ֣ה וַתֹּ֡אמֶר חֵֽי־נַפְשְׁךָ֩ אֲדֹנִ֨י הַמֶּ֜לֶךְ אִם־אִ֣שׁ ׀ לְהֵמִ֣ין וּלְהַשְׂמִ֗יל מִכֹּ֤ל אֲשֶׁר־דִּבֶּר֙ אֲדֹנִ֣י הַמֶּ֔לֶךְ כִּֽי־עַבְדְּךָ֤ יוֹאָב֙ ה֣וּא צִוָּ֔נִי וְה֗וּא שָׂ֚ם בְּפִ֣י שִׁפְחָֽתְךָ֔ אֵ֥ת כָּל־הַדְּבָרִ֖ים הָאֵֽלֶּה׃ 20 לְבַעֲב֤וּר סַבֵּב֙ אֶת־פְּנֵ֣י הַדָּבָ֔ר עָשָׂ֛ה עַבְדְּךָ֥ יוֹאָ֖ב אֶת־הַדָּבָ֣ר הַזֶּ֑ה וַאדֹנִ֣י חָכָ֗ם כְּחָכְמַת֙ מַלְאַ֣ךְ הָֽאֱלֹהִ֔ים לָדַ֖עַת אֶֽת־כָּל־אֲשֶׁ֥ר בָּאָֽרֶץ׃ ס

21 וַיֹּ֤אמֶר הַמֶּ֙לֶךְ֙ אֶל־יוֹאָ֔ב הִנֵּה־נָ֥א עָשִׂ֖יתִי אֶת־הַדָּבָ֣ר הַזֶּ֑ה וְלֵ֛ךְ הָשֵׁ֥ב אֶת־הַנַּ֖עַר אֶת־אַבְשָׁלֽוֹם׃ 22 וַיִּפֹּל֩ יוֹאָ֨ב אֶל־פָּנָ֤יו אַ֙רְצָה֙ וַיִּשְׁתַּ֔חוּ וַיְבָ֖רֶךְ אֶת־הַמֶּ֑לֶךְ וַיֹּ֣אמֶר יוֹאָ֡ב הַיּוֹם֩ יָדַ֨ע עַבְדְּךָ֜ כִּֽי־מָצָ֨אתִי חֵ֤ן בְּעֵינֶ֙יךָ֙ אֲדֹנִ֣י הַמֶּ֔לֶךְ אֲשֶׁר־עָשָׂ֥ה הַמֶּ֖לֶךְ אֶת־דְּבַ֥ר עַבְדֶּֽךָ׃ 23 וַיָּ֥קָם יוֹאָ֖ב וַיֵּ֣לֶךְ גְּשׁ֑וּרָה וַיָּבֵ֥א אֶת־אַבְשָׁל֖וֹם יְרוּשָׁלָֽ͏ִם׃ פ 24 וַיֹּ֣אמֶר הַמֶּ֗לֶךְ יִסֹּ֤ב אֶל־בֵּיתוֹ֙ וּפָנַ֣י לֹ֣א יִרְאֶ֔ה וַיִּסֹּ֥ב אַבְשָׁל֖וֹם אֶל־בֵּית֑וֹ וּפְנֵ֥י הַמֶּ֖לֶךְ לֹ֥א רָאָֽה׃ ס 25 וּכְאַבְשָׁל֗וֹם לֹא־הָיָ֧ה אִישׁ־יָפֶ֛ה בְּכָל־יִשְׂרָאֵ֖ל לְהַלֵּ֣ל מְאֹ֑ד מִכַּ֤ף רַגְלוֹ֙ וְעַ֣ד קָדְקֳד֔וֹ לֹא־הָ֥יָה ב֖וֹ מֽוּם׃ 26 וּֽבְגַלְּחוֹ֮ אֶת־רֹאשׁוֹ֒ וְֽהָיָ֗ה מִקֵּ֤ץ יָמִים֙ ׀ לַיָּמִ֔ים אֲשֶׁ֣ר יְגַלֵּ֔חַ כִּֽי־כָבֵ֥ד עָלָ֖יו וְגִלְּח֑וֹ וְשָׁקַל֙ אֶת־שְׂעַ֣ר רֹאשׁ֔וֹ מָאתַ֥יִם שְׁקָלִ֖ים בְּאֶ֥בֶן הַמֶּֽלֶךְ׃ 27 וַיִּוָּלְד֤וּ לְאַבְשָׁלוֹם֙ שְׁלוֹשָׁ֣ה בָנִ֔ים וּבַ֥ת אַחַ֖ת וּשְׁמָ֣הּ תָּמָ֑ר הִ֤יא הָֽיְתָה֙ אִשָּׁ֔ה יְפַ֖ת מַרְאֶֽה׃ פ

28 וַיֵּ֧שֶׁב אַבְשָׁל֛וֹם בִּירוּשָׁלַ֖͏ִם שְׁנָתַ֣יִם יָמִ֑ים וּפְנֵ֥י הַמֶּ֖לֶךְ לֹ֥א רָאָֽה׃ 29 וַיִּשְׁלַ֤ח אַבְשָׁלוֹם֙

---

f-f Lit. "there is no turning to the right or to the left of what my lord the king says."
g-g See note a above.

v. 19.   סבירין ומטעין "יש"

sent for Joab, in order to send him to the king; but Joab would not come to him. He sent for him a second time, but he would not come. [30]So [Absalom] said to his servants, "Look, Joab's field is next to mine, and he has barley there. Go and set it on fire." And Absalom's servants set the field on fire. [31]Joab came at once to Absalom's house and said to him, "Why did your servants set fire to my field?" [32]Absalom replied to Joab, "I sent for you to come here; I wanted to send you to the king to say [on my behalf]: 'Why did I leave Geshur? I would be better off if I were still there. Now let me appear before the king; and if I am guilty of anything, let him put me to death!'" [33]Joab went to the king and reported to him; whereupon he summoned Absalom. He came to the king and flung himself face down to the ground before the king. And the king kissed Absalom.

15

Sometime afterward, Absalom provided himself with a chariot, horses, and fifty outrunners. [2]Absalom used to rise early and stand by the road to the city gates; and whenever a man had a case that was to come before the king for judgment, Absalom would call out to him, "What town are you from?" And when he answered, "Your servant is from a-such and such a tribe-a in Israel," [3]Absalom would say to him, "It is clear that your claim is right and just, but there is no one assigned to you by the king to hear it." [4]And Absalom went on, "If only I were appointed judge in the land and everyone with a legal dispute came before me, I would see that he got his rights." [5]And if a man approached to bow to him, [Absalom] would extend his hand and take hold of him and kiss him. [6]Absalom did this to every Israelite who came to the king for judgment. Thus Absalom won away the hearts of the men of Israel.

אֶל־יוֹאָב לִשְׁלֹחַ אֹתוֹ אֶל־הַמֶּ֫לֶךְ וְלֹא
אָבָה לָבוֹא אֵלָיו וַיִּשְׁלַח עוֹד שֵׁנִית וְלֹא
אָבָה לָבוֹא: 30 וַיֹּאמֶר אֶל־עֲבָדָיו רְאוּ
חֶלְקַת יוֹאָב אֶל־יָדִי וְלוֹ־שָׁם שְׂעֹרִים לְכוּ
וְהוֹצִתִּיהָ וְהַצִּיתוּהָ בָאֵשׁ וַיַּצִּתוּ עַבְדֵי
אַבְשָׁלוֹם אֶת־הַחֶלְקָה בָּאֵשׁ: פ 31 וַיָּקָם
יוֹאָב וַיָּבֹא אֶל־אַבְשָׁלוֹם הַבָּיְתָה וַיֹּאמֶר
אֵלָיו לָמָּה הִצִּיתוּ עֲבָדֶיךָ אֶת־הַחֶלְקָה
אֲשֶׁר־לִי בָּאֵשׁ: 32 וַיֹּאמֶר אַבְשָׁלוֹם אֶל־
יוֹאָב הִנֵּה שָׁלַחְתִּי אֵלֶיךָ | לֵאמֹר בֹּא
הֵנָּה וְאֶשְׁלְחָה אֹתְךָ אֶל־הַמֶּ֫לֶךְ לֵאמֹר
לָמָּה בָּאתִי מִגְּשׁוּר טוֹב לִי עֹד אֲנִי־שָׁם
וְעַתָּה אֶרְאֶה פְּנֵי הַמֶּ֫לֶךְ וְאִם־יֶשׁ־בִּי עָוֹן
וֶהֱמִתָנִי: 33 וַיָּבֹא יוֹאָב אֶל־הַמֶּ֫לֶךְ וַיַּגֶּד־לוֹ
וַיִּקְרָא אֶל־אַבְשָׁלוֹם וַיָּבֹא אֶל־הַמֶּ֫לֶךְ
וַיִּשְׁתַּחוּ לוֹ עַל־אַפָּיו אַרְצָה לִפְנֵי הַמֶּ֫לֶךְ
וַיִּשַּׁק הַמֶּ֫לֶךְ לְאַבְשָׁלוֹם: פ

טו

וַיְהִי מֵאַחֲרֵי כֵן וַיַּעַשׂ לוֹ אַבְשָׁלוֹם
מֶרְכָּבָה וְסֻסִים וַחֲמִשִּׁים אִישׁ רָצִים
לְפָנָיו: 2 וְהִשְׁכִּים אַבְשָׁלוֹם וְעָמַד עַל־יַד
דֶּרֶךְ הַשָּׁעַר וַיְהִי כָּל־הָאִישׁ אֲשֶׁר־יִהְיֶה־
לּוֹ־רִיב לָבוֹא אֶל־הַמֶּ֫לֶךְ לַמִּשְׁפָּט וַיִּקְרָא
אַבְשָׁלוֹם אֵלָיו וַיֹּאמֶר אֵי־מִזֶּה עִיר אַתָּה
וַיֹּאמֶר מֵאַחַד שִׁבְטֵי־יִשְׂרָאֵל עַבְדֶּךָ:
3 וַיֹּאמֶר אֵלָיו אַבְשָׁלוֹם רְאֵה דְבָרֶךָ טוֹבִים
וּנְכֹחִים וְשֹׁמֵעַ אֵין־לְךָ מֵאֵת הַמֶּ֫לֶךְ:
4 וַיֹּאמֶר אַבְשָׁלוֹם מִי־יְשִׂמֵנִי שֹׁפֵט בָּאָרֶץ
וְעָלַי יָבוֹא כָּל־אִישׁ אֲשֶׁר־יִהְיֶה־לּוֹ־רִיב
וּמִשְׁפָּט וְהִצְדַּקְתִּיו: 5 וְהָיָה בִּקְרָב־אִישׁ
לְהִשְׁתַּחֲוֹת לוֹ וְשָׁלַח אֶת־יָדוֹ וְהֶחֱזִיק לוֹ
וְנָשַׁק לוֹ: 6 וַיַּעַשׂ אַבְשָׁלוֹם כַּדָּבָר הַזֶּה
לְכָל־יִשְׂרָאֵל אֲשֶׁר־יָבֹאוּ לַמִּשְׁפָּט אֶל־
הַמֶּ֫לֶךְ וַיְגַנֵּב אַבְשָׁלוֹם אֶת־לֵב אַנְשֵׁי
יִשְׂרָאֵל: פ

---

a-a Lit. "one of the tribes."

7After a period of forty[b] years had gone by, Absalom said to the king, "Let me go to Hebron and fulfill a vow that I made to the Lord. 8For your servant made a vow when I lived in Geshur of Aram: If the Lord ever brings me back to Jerusalem, I will worship the Lord."[c] 9The king said to him, "Go in peace"; and so he set out for Hebron.

10But Absalom sent agents to all the tribes of Israel to say, "When you hear the blast of the horn, announce that Absalom has become king in Hebron." 11Two hundred men of Jerusalem accompanied Absalom; they were invited and went in good faith, suspecting nothing. 12Absalom also [d]sent [to fetch][d] Ahithophel the Gilonite, David's counselor, from his town, Giloh, when the sacrifices were to be offered. The conspiracy gained strength, and the people supported Absalom in increasing numbers.

13Someone came and told David, "The loyalty of the men of Israel has veered toward Absalom." 14Whereupon David said to all the courtiers who were with him in Jerusalem, "Let us flee at once, or none of us will escape from Absalom. We must get away quickly, or he will soon overtake us and bring down disaster upon us and put the city to the sword." 15The king's courtiers said to the king, "Whatever our lord the king decides, your servants are ready." 16So the king left, followed by his entire household, except for ten concubines whom the king left to mind the palace.

17The king left, followed by [e]all the people,[e] and they stopped at [f]the last house.[f] 18All [g]his followers[g] marched past him, including all the Cherethites and all the Pelethites; and[h] all the Gittites, six hundred men who had accompa-

7 וַיְהִ֕י מִקֵּ֖ץ אַרְבָּעִ֣ים שָׁנָ֑ה וַיֹּ֤אמֶר אַבְשָׁלוֹם֙ אֶל־הַמֶּ֔לֶךְ אֵ֣לְכָה נָּ֗א וַאֲשַׁלֵּ֛ם אֶת־נִדְרִ֥י אֲשֶׁר־נָדַ֖רְתִּי לַיהֹוָ֥ה בְּחֶבְרֽוֹן׃ 8 כִּי־נֵ֙דֶר֙ נָדַ֣ר עַבְדְּךָ֔ בְּשִׁבְתִּ֥י בִגְשׁ֖וּר בַּאֲרָ֣ם לֵאמֹ֑ר אִם־יָשׁ֨וֹב יְשִׁיבֵ֤נִי יְהֹוָה֙ יְר֣וּשָׁלַ֔͏ִם וְעָבַדְתִּ֖י אֶת־יְהֹוָֽה׃ 9 וַיֹּֽאמֶר־ל֥וֹ הַמֶּ֛לֶךְ לֵ֥ךְ בְּשָׁל֖וֹם וַיָּ֣קׇם וַיֵּ֥לֶךְ חֶבְרֽוֹנָה׃ פ

10 וַיִּשְׁלַ֤ח אַבְשָׁלוֹם֙ מְרַגְּלִ֔ים בְּכׇל־שִׁבְטֵ֥י יִשְׂרָאֵ֖ל לֵאמֹ֑ר כְּשׇׁמְעֲכֶם֙ אֶת־ק֣וֹל הַשֹּׁפָ֔ר וַאֲמַרְתֶּ֕ם מָלַ֥ךְ אַבְשָׁל֖וֹם בְּחֶבְרֽוֹן׃ 11 וְאֶת־אַבְשָׁל֗וֹם הָלְכ֞וּ מָאתַ֤יִם אִישׁ֙ מִיר֣וּשָׁלַ֔͏ִם קְרֻאִ֖ים וְהֹלְכִ֣ים לְתֻמָּ֑ם וְלֹ֥א יָדְע֖וּ כׇּל־דָּבָֽר׃ 12 וַיִּשְׁלַ֣ח אַ֠בְשָׁל֠וֹם אֶת־אֲחִיתֹ֨פֶל הַגִּֽילֹנִ֜י יוֹעֵ֣ץ דָּוִ֗ד מֵֽעִירוֹ֙ מִגִּלֹ֔ה בְּזׇבְח֖וֹ אֶת־הַזְּבָחִ֑ים וַיְהִ֤י הַקֶּ֙שֶׁר֙ אַמִּ֔ץ וְהָעָ֛ם הֹלֵ֥ךְ וָרָ֖ב אֶת־אַבְשָׁלֽוֹם׃

13 וַיָּבֹא֙ הַמַּגִּ֔יד אֶל־דָּוִ֖ד לֵאמֹ֑ר הָיָ֛ה לֶב־אִ֥ישׁ יִשְׂרָאֵ֖ל אַחֲרֵ֥י אַבְשָׁלֽוֹם׃ 14 וַיֹּ֣אמֶר דָּ֠וִ֠ד לְכׇל־עֲבָדָ֨יו אֲשֶׁר־אִתּ֤וֹ בִירֽוּשָׁלַ֙͏ִם֙ ק֣וּמוּ וְנִבְרָ֔חָה כִּ֛י לֹא־תִֽהְיֶה־לָּ֥נוּ פְלֵיטָ֖ה מִפְּנֵ֣י אַבְשָׁל֑וֹם מַהֲר֣וּ לָלֶ֗כֶת פֶּן־יְמַהֵ֤ר וְהִשִּׂגָ֙נוּ֙ וְהִדִּ֤יחַ עָלֵ֙ינוּ֙ אֶת־הָ֣רָעָ֔ה וְהִכָּ֥ה הָעִ֖יר לְפִי־חָֽרֶב׃ 15 וַיֹּאמְר֥וּ עַבְדֵֽי־הַמֶּ֖לֶךְ אֶל־הַמֶּ֑לֶךְ כְּכֹ֧ל אֲשֶׁר־יִבְחַ֛ר אֲדֹנִ֥י הַמֶּ֖לֶךְ הִנֵּ֥ה עֲבָדֶֽיךָ׃ 16 וַיֵּצֵ֥א הַמֶּ֛לֶךְ וְכׇל־בֵּית֖וֹ בְּרַגְלָ֑יו וַיַּעֲזֹ֣ב הַמֶּ֗לֶךְ אֵ֣ת עֶ֧שֶׂר נָשִׁ֛ים פִּֽלַגְשִׁ֖ים לִשְׁמֹ֥ר הַבָּֽיִת׃

17 וַיֵּצֵ֥א הַמֶּ֛לֶךְ וְכׇל־הָעָ֖ם בְּרַגְלָ֑יו וַיַּעַמְד֖וּ בֵּ֥ית הַמֶּרְחָֽק׃ 18 וְכׇל־עֲבָדָיו֙ עֹבְרִ֣ים עַל־יָד֔וֹ וְכׇל־הַכְּרֵתִ֖י וְכׇל־הַפְּלֵתִ֑י וְכׇֽל־הַגִּתִּ֞ים שֵׁשׁ־מֵא֣וֹת אִ֗ישׁ אֲשֶׁר־בָּ֤אוּ בְרַגְלוֹ֙ מִגַּ֔ת

---

b   *Some Septuagint mss. and Syriac read "four."*

c   *Some Septuagint mss. add "in Hebron."*

d-d   *Some Septuagint mss. and 4QSam[a] read "sent and summoned."*

e-e   *Septuagint reads "his courtiers."*

f-f   *Meaning of Heb. uncertain.*

g-g   *Septuagint reads "the people."*

h   *Emendation yields "and Ittai and."*

nied him from Gath, also marched by the king. [19]And the king said to Ittai the Gittite, "Why should you too go with us? Go back and stay with the [new] king, for you are a foreigner and you are also an exile from[i] your country. [20]You came only yesterday; should I make you wander about with us today, when I myself must go wherever I can? Go back, and take your kinsmen with you, [in][j] true faithfulness." [21]Ittai replied to the king, "As the LORD lives and as my lord the king lives, wherever my lord the king may be, there your servant will be, whether for death or for life!" [22]And David said to Ittai, "Then march by." And Ittai the Gittite and all his men and all the children who were with him marched by.

[23]The whole countryside wept aloud as the troops marched by. The king [k]crossed the Kidron Valley, and all the troops crossed by the road to-[k] the wilderness. [24]Then Zadok appeared, with all the Levites carrying the Ark of the Covenant of God; and they set down the Ark of God until all the people had finished marching out of the city. [f]Abiathar also came up.[f] [25]But the king said to Zadok, "Take the Ark of God back to the city. If I find favor with the LORD, He will bring me back and let me see it and its abode. [26]And if He should say, 'I do not want you,' I am ready; let Him do with me as He pleases." [27]And the king said to the priest Zadok, [l]"Do you understand? You return[l] to the safety of the city with your two sons, your own son Ahimaaz and Abiathar's son Jonathan. [28]Look, I shall linger in the steppes of the wilderness until word comes from you to inform me." [29]Zadok and Abiathar brought the Ark of God back to Jerusalem, and they stayed there.

---

19 וַיֹּ֤אמֶר הַמֶּ֙לֶךְ֙ עֹבְרִ֖ים עַל־פְּנֵ֥י הַמֶּֽלֶךְ׃
אֶל־אִתַּ֣י הַגִּתִּ֔י לָ֧מָּה תֵלֵ֛ךְ גַּם־אַתָּ֖ה אִתָּ֑נוּ
שׁ֣וּב וְשֵׁ֤ב עִם־הַמֶּ֙לֶךְ֙ כִּֽי־נָכְרִ֣י אַ֔תָּה וְגַם־
גֹּלֶ֥ה אַתָּ֖ה לִמְקוֹמֶֽךָ׃* 20 תְּמ֣וֹל ׀ בּוֹאֶ֗ךָ
וְהַיּ֞וֹם אֲנוֹעֲךָ֤* עִמָּ֙נוּ֙ לָלֶ֔כֶת וַאֲנִ֣י
הוֹלֵ֔ךְ עַ֥ל אֲשֶׁר־אֲנִ֖י הוֹלֵ֑ךְ שׁ֣וּב וְהָשֵׁ֤ב
אֶת־אַחֶ֙יךָ֙ עִמָּ֔ךְ חֶ֖סֶד וֶאֱמֶֽת׃ 21 וַיַּ֤עַן אִתַּי֙
אֶת־הַמֶּ֣לֶךְ וַיֹּאמַ֔ר חַי־יְהֹוָ֖ה וְחֵ֣י אֲדֹנִ֣י
הַמֶּ֗לֶךְ כִּ֠י אִם־*בִּמְק֞וֹם אֲשֶׁ֥ר יִֽהְיֶה־שָּׁ֣ם ׀
אֲדֹנִ֣י הַמֶּ֗לֶךְ אִם־לְמָ֙וֶת֙ אִם־לְחַיִּ֔ים כִּי־
שָׁ֖ם יִהְיֶ֥ה עַבְדֶּֽךָ׃ 22 וַיֹּ֤אמֶר דָּוִד֙ אֶל־אִתַּ֔י
לֵ֖ךְ וַעֲבֹ֑ר וַֽיַּעֲבֹ֞ר אִתַּ֤י הַגִּתִּי֙ וְכׇל־אֲנָשָׁ֔יו
וְכׇל־הַטַּ֖ף אֲשֶׁ֥ר אִתּֽוֹ׃
23 וְכׇל־הָאָ֗רֶץ בּוֹכִים֙ ק֣וֹל גָּד֔וֹל וְכׇל־הָעָ֖ם
עֹֽבְרִ֑ים וְהַמֶּ֗לֶךְ עֹבֵר֙ בְּנַ֣חַל קִדְר֔וֹן וְכׇל־
הָעָם֙ עֹבְרִ֔ים עַל־פְּנֵי־דֶ֖רֶךְ אֶת־הַמִּדְבָּֽר׃
24 וְהִנֵּ֨ה גַם־צָד֜וֹק וְכׇל־הַלְוִיִּ֣ם אִתּ֗וֹ
נֹֽשְׂאִים֙ אֶת־אֲרוֹן֙ בְּרִ֣ית הָאֱלֹהִ֔ים וַיַּצִּ֙קוּ֙
אֶת־אֲר֣וֹן הָאֱלֹהִ֔ים וַיַּ֖עַל אֶבְיָתָ֑ר עַד־תֹּ֥ם
כׇּל־הָעָ֖ם לַעֲב֥וֹר מִן־הָעִֽיר׃ 25 וַיֹּ֤אמֶר
הַמֶּ֙לֶךְ֙ לְצָד֔וֹק הָשֵׁ֛ב אֶת־אֲר֥וֹן הָאֱלֹהִ֖ים
הָעִ֑יר אִם־אֶמְצָ֥א חֵן֙ בְּעֵינֵ֣י יְהֹוָ֔ה וֶהֱשִׁבַ֔נִי
וְהִרְאַ֥נִי אֹת֖וֹ וְאֶת־נָוֵֽהוּ׃ 26 וְאִם֙ כֹּ֣ה יֹאמַ֔ר
לֹ֥א חָפַ֖צְתִּי בָּ֑ךְ הִנְנִ֕י יַעֲשֶׂה־לִּ֕י כַּאֲשֶׁ֥ר ט֖וֹב
בְּעֵינָֽיו׃ 27 וַיֹּ֤אמֶר הַמֶּ֙לֶךְ֙ אֶל־צָד֣וֹק
הַכֹּהֵ֔ן הֲרוֹאֶ֣ה אַתָּ֔ה שֻׁ֥בָה הָעִ֖יר בְּשָׁל֑וֹם
וַאֲחִימַ֤עַץ בִּנְךָ֙ וִיהוֹנָתָ֣ן בֶּן־אֶבְיָתָ֔ר שְׁנֵ֥י
בְנֵיכֶ֖ם אִתְּכֶֽם׃ 28 רְאוּ֙ אָנֹכִ֣י מִתְמַהְמֵ֔הַּ
בְּעַבְר֖וֹת הַמִּדְבָּ֑ר עַ֣ד בּ֥וֹא דָבָ֛ר
מֵעִמָּכֶ֖ם לְהַגִּ֥יד לִֽי׃ 29 וַיָּ֤שֶׁב צָדוֹק֙ וְאֶבְיָתָ֔ר
אֶת־אֲר֥וֹן הָאֱלֹהִ֖ים יְרוּשָׁלָ֑͏ִם וַיֵּשְׁב֖וּ שָֽׁם׃

---

i   *So one Heb. ms. and several ancient versions; most mss. and editions read "to."*

j   *Meaning of Heb. uncertain. Septuagint reads "and may the LORD show you" (cf., e.g., 2.6).*

k-k   *Meaning of Heb. uncertain. Emendation yields "stopped in the Kidron Valley, while all the people marched on before him by way of the Mount of Olives to…"*

l-l   *Meaning of Heb. uncertain. Emendation yields "Look, you and Abiathar return."*

³⁰David meanwhile went up the slope of the [Mount of] Olives, weeping as he went; his head was covered and he walked barefoot. And all the people who were with him covered their heads and wept as they went up. ³¹David [was] told that Ahithophel was among the conspirators with Absalom, and he prayed, "Please, O LORD, frustrate Ahithophel's counsel!"

³²When David reached the top, where people would prostrate themselves to God, Hushai the Archite was there to meet him, with his robe torn and with earth on his head. ³³David said to him, "If you march on with me, you will be a burden to me. ³⁴But if you go back to the city and say to Absalom, 'I will be your servant, O king; I was your father's servant formerly, and now I will be yours,' then you can nullify Ahithophel's counsel for me. ³⁵You will have the priests Zadok and Abiathar there, and you can report everything that you hear in the king's palace to the priests Zadok and Abiathar. ³⁶Also, their two sons are there with them, Zadok's son Ahimaaz and Abiathar's son Jonathan; and through them you can report to me everything you hear." ³⁷And so Hushai, the friend of David, reached the city as Absalom was entering Jerusalem.

16 David had passed a little beyond the summit when Ziba the servant of Mephibosheth came toward him with a pair of saddled asses carrying two hundred loaves of bread, one hundred cakes of raisin, one hundred cakes of figs,^a and a jar of wine. ²The king asked Ziba, "What are you doing with these?" Ziba answered, "The asses are for Your Majesty's family to ride on, the bread and figs are for the attendants to eat, and the wine is to be drunk by any who are exhausted in the wilderness." ³"And where is your master's son?" the king asked. "He

---

^a Lit. "summer fruit."

---

³⁰ וְדָוִ֞ד עֹלֶ֣ה בְמַעֲלֵ֣ה הַזֵּיתִ֗ים עֹלֶ֤ה ׀ וּבוֹכֶה֙ וְרֹ֣אשׁ לוֹ֙ חָפ֔וּי וְה֖וּא הֹלֵ֣ךְ יָחֵ֑ף וְכָל־הָעָ֣ם אֲשֶׁר־אִתּ֗וֹ חָפוּ֙ אִ֣ישׁ רֹאשׁ֔וֹ וְעָל֥וּ עָלֹ֖ה וּבָכֹֽה׃ ³¹ וְדָוִד֙ הִגִּ֣יד לֵאמֹ֔ר אֲחִיתֹ֥פֶל בַּקֹּשְׁרִ֖ים עִם־אַבְשָׁל֑וֹם וַיֹּ֣אמֶר דָּוִ֔ד סַכֶּל־נָ֛א אֶת־עֲצַ֥ת אֲחִיתֹ֖פֶל יְהֹוָֽה׃ ³² וַיְהִ֤י דָוִד֙ בָּ֣א עַד־הָרֹ֔אשׁ אֲשֶֽׁר־יִשְׁתַּחֲוֶ֥ה שָׁ֖ם לֵאלֹהִ֑ים וְהִנֵּ֤ה לִקְרָאתוֹ֙ חוּשַׁ֣י הָאַרְכִּ֔י קָר֙וּעַ֙ כֻּתׇּנְתּ֔וֹ וַאֲדָמָ֖ה עַל־רֹאשֽׁוֹ׃ ³³ וַיֹּ֥אמֶר ל֖וֹ דָּוִ֑ד אִ֤ם עָבַ֙רְתָּ֙ אִתִּ֔י וְהָיִ֥תָ עָלַ֖י לְמַשָּֽׂא׃ ³⁴ וְאִם־הָעִ֣יר תָּשׁ֗וּב וְאָמַרְתָּ֣ לְאַבְשָׁל֡וֹם עַבְדְּךָ֩ אֲנִ֨י הַמֶּ֜לֶךְ אֶהְיֶ֗ה עֶ֤בֶד אָבִ֙יךָ֙ וַֽאֲנִי֙ מֵאָ֔ז וְעַתָּ֖ה וַאֲנִ֣י עַבְדֶּ֑ךָ וְהֵפַרְתָּ֣ה לִ֔י אֵ֖ת עֲצַ֥ת אֲחִיתֹֽפֶל׃ ³⁵ וַהֲל֤וֹא עִמְּךָ֙ שָׁ֔ם צָד֥וֹק וְאֶבְיָתָ֖ר הַכֹּהֲנִ֑ים וְהָיָ֗ה כׇּל־הַדָּבָר֙ אֲשֶׁ֣ר תִּשְׁמַ֔ע מִבֵּ֣ית הַמֶּ֔לֶךְ תַּגִּ֕יד לְצָד֥וֹק וּלְאֶבְיָתָ֖ר הַכֹּהֲנִֽים׃ ³⁶ הִנֵּה־שָׁ֤ם עִמָּם֙ שְׁנֵ֣י בְנֵיהֶ֔ם אֲחִימַ֣עַץ לְצָד֔וֹק וִיהוֹנָתָ֖ן לְאֶבְיָתָ֑ר וּשְׁלַחְתֶּ֤ם בְּיָדָם֙ אֵלַ֔י כׇּל־דָּבָ֖ר אֲשֶׁ֥ר תִּשְׁמָֽעוּ׃ ³⁷ וַיָּבֹ֥א חוּשַׁ֛י רֵעֶ֥ה דָוִ֖ד הָעִ֑יר וְאַבְשָׁלֹ֔ם יָבֹ֖א יְרוּשָׁלָֽ͏ִם׃

טז וְדָוִ֗ד עָבַ֤ר מְעַט֙ מֵֽהָרֹ֔אשׁ וְהִנֵּ֥ה צִיבָ֛א נַ֥עַר מְפִי־בֹ֖שֶׁת לִקְרָאת֑וֹ וְצֶ֨מֶד חֲמֹרִ֣ים חֲבֻשִׁ֗ים וַעֲלֵיהֶם֩ מָאתַ֨יִם לֶ֜חֶם וּמֵאָ֧ה צִמּוּקִ֛ים וּמֵ֥אָה קַ֖יִץ וְנֵ֥בֶל יָֽיִן׃ ² וַיֹּ֧אמֶר הַמֶּ֛לֶךְ אֶל־צִיבָ֖א מָה־אֵ֣לֶּה לָּ֑ךְ וַיֹּ֣אמֶר צִ֠יבָ֠א הַחֲמוֹרִ֨ים לְבֵית־הַמֶּ֜לֶךְ לִרְכֹּ֗ב וְהַלֶּ֤חֶם וְהַקַּ֙יִץ֙ לֶאֱכ֣וֹל הַנְּעָרִ֔ים וְהַיַּ֕יִן לִשְׁתּ֥וֹת הַיָּעֵ֖ף בַּמִּדְבָּֽר׃ ³ וַיֹּ֣אמֶר הַמֶּ֔לֶךְ וְאַיֵּ֖ה בֶּן־אֲדֹנֶ֑יךָ וַיֹּ֣אמֶר

is staying in Jerusalem," Ziba replied to the king, "for he thinks that the House of Israel will now give him back the throne of his grandfather." [4]The king said to Ziba, "Then all that belongs to Mephibosheth is now yours!" And Ziba replied, "I bow low. Your Majesty is most gracious to me."

[5]As King David was approaching Bahurim, a member of Saul's clan—a man named Shimei son of Gera—came out from there, hurling insults as he came. [6]He threw stones at David and all King David's courtiers, while all the troops and all the warriors were at his right and his left. [7]And these are the insults that Shimei hurled: "Get out, get out, you criminal, you villain! [8]The LORD is paying you back for all your crimes against the family of Saul, whose throne you seized. The LORD is handing over the throne to your son Absalom; you are in trouble because you are a criminal!"

[9]Abishai son of Zeruiah said to the king, "Why let that dead dog abuse my lord the king? Let me go over and cut off his head!" [10]But the king said, [b]-"What has this to do with you,[-b] you sons of Zeruiah? He is abusing [me] only because the LORD told him to abuse David; and who is to say, 'Why did You do that?'" [11]David said further to Abishai and all the courtiers, "If my son, my own issue, seeks to kill me, how much more the Benjaminite! Let him go on hurling abuse, for the LORD has told him to. [12]Perhaps the LORD will look upon my punishment[c] and recompense me for the abuse [Shimei] has uttered today." [13]David and his men continued on their way, while Shimei walked alongside on the slope of the hill, insulting him as he walked, and throwing stones at him and flinging dirt. [14]The king and all who accompanied him arrived[d] exhausted, and he rested there.

---

b-b   Lit. "What have I and you."

c   So kethib; qere "eye." Ancient versions read "suffering."

d   Some Septuagint mss. add "at the Jordan."

צִיבָא אֶל־הַמֶּלֶךְ הִנֵּה יוֹשֵׁב בִּירוּשָׁלִַם כִּי אָמַר הַיּוֹם יָשִׁיבוּ לִי בֵּית יִשְׂרָאֵל אֵת מַמְלְכוּת אָבִי: 4 וַיֹּאמֶר הַמֶּלֶךְ לְצִבָא הִנֵּה לְךָ כֹּל אֲשֶׁר לִמְפִי־בֹשֶׁת וַיֹּאמֶר צִיבָא הִשְׁתַּחֲוֵיתִי אֶמְצָא־חֵן בְּעֵינֶיךָ אֲדֹנִי הַמֶּלֶךְ:

5 וּבָא הַמֶּלֶךְ דָּוִד עַד־בַּחוּרִים וְהִנֵּה מִשָּׁם אִישׁ יוֹצֵא מִמִּשְׁפַּחַת בֵּית־שָׁאוּל וּשְׁמוֹ שִׁמְעִי בֶן־גֵּרָא יֹצֵא יָצוֹא וּמְקַלֵּל: 6 וַיְסַקֵּל בָּאֲבָנִים אֶת־דָּוִד וְאֶת־כָּל־עַבְדֵי הַמֶּלֶךְ דָּוִד וְכָל־הָעָם וְכָל־הַגִּבֹּרִים מִימִינוֹ וּמִשְּׂמֹאלוֹ: 7 וְכֹה־אָמַר שִׁמְעִי בְּקַלְלוֹ צֵא צֵא אִישׁ הַדָּמִים וְאִישׁ הַבְּלִיָּעַל: 8 הֵשִׁיב עָלֶיךָ יְהוָה כֹּל | דְּמֵי בֵית־שָׁאוּל אֲשֶׁר מָלַכְתָּ תחתו תַּחְתָּיו וַיִּתֵּן יְהוָה אֶת־הַמְּלוּכָה בְּיַד אַבְשָׁלוֹם בְּנֶךָ וְהִנְּךָ בְּרָעָתֶךָ כִּי אִישׁ דָּמִים אָתָּה:

9 וַיֹּאמֶר אֲבִישַׁי בֶּן־צְרוּיָה אֶל־הַמֶּלֶךְ לָמָּה יְקַלֵּל הַכֶּלֶב הַמֵּת הַזֶּה אֶת־אֲדֹנִי הַמֶּלֶךְ אֶעְבְּרָה־נָּא וְאָסִירָה אֶת־רֹאשׁוֹ: ס 10 וַיֹּאמֶר הַמֶּלֶךְ מַה־לִּי וְלָכֶם בְּנֵי צְרֻיָה כִּי כֹה יְקַלֵּל וכי כִּי יְהוָה אָמַר לוֹ קַלֵּל אֶת־דָּוִד וּמִי יֹאמַר מַדּוּעַ עָשִׂיתָה כֵּן: ס 11 וַיֹּאמֶר דָּוִד אֶל־אֲבִישַׁי וְאֶל־כָּל־עֲבָדָיו הִנֵּה בְנִי אֲשֶׁר־יָצָא מִמֵּעַי מְבַקֵּשׁ אֶת־נַפְשִׁי וְאַף כִּי־עַתָּה בֶּן־הַיְמִינִי הַנִּחוּ לוֹ וִיקַלֵּל כִּי אָמַר־לוֹ יְהוָה: 12 אוּלַי יִרְאֶה יְהוָה בעוני בְּעֵינִי וְהֵשִׁיב יְהוָה לִי טוֹבָה תַּחַת קִלְלָתוֹ הַיּוֹם הַזֶּה: 13 וַיֵּלֶךְ דָּוִד וַאֲנָשָׁיו בַּדָּרֶךְ ס וְשִׁמְעִי הֹלֵךְ בְּצֵלַע הָהָר לְעֻמָּתוֹ הָלוֹךְ וַיְקַלֵּל וַיְסַקֵּל בָּאֲבָנִים לְעֻמָּתוֹ וְעִפַּר בֶּעָפָר: פ 14 וַיָּבֹא הַמֶּלֶךְ וְכָל־הָעָם אֲשֶׁר־אִתּוֹ עֲיֵפִים וַיִּנָּפֵשׁ שָׁם:

¹⁵Meanwhile Absalom and all the people, the men of Israel, arrived in Jerusalem, together with Ahithophel. ¹⁶When Hushai the Archite, David's friend, came before Absalom, Hushai said to Absalom, "Long live the king! Long live the king!" ¹⁷But Absalom said to Hushai, "Is this your loyalty to your friend? Why didn't you go with your friend?" ¹⁸"Not at all!" Hushai replied. "I am for the one whom the LORD and this people and all the men of Israel have chosen, and I will stay with him. ¹⁹Furthermore, whom should I serve, if not David's^e son? As I was in your father's service, so I will be in yours."

²⁰Absalom then said to Ahithophel, "What do you advise us to do?" ²¹And Ahithophel said to Absalom, "Have intercourse with your father's concubines, whom he left to mind the palace; and when all Israel hears that you have dared the wrath of your father, all who support you will be encouraged." ²²So they pitched a tent for Absalom on the roof, and Absalom lay with his father's concubines *f-with the full knowledge-f* of all Israel.—²³In those days, the advice which Ahithophel gave was accepted like an oracle sought from God; that is how all the advice of Ahithophel was esteemed both by David and by Absalom.

17

And Ahithophel said to Absalom, "Let me pick twelve thousand men and set out tonight in pursuit of David. ²I will come upon him when he is weary and disheartened, and I will throw him into a panic; and when all the troops with him flee, I will kill the king alone. ³And I will bring back all the people *a-to you; when all have come back [except] the man you are after,-a* all the people will be at peace." ⁴The advice pleased Absalom and all the elders of Israel.

---

^e   Heb. "his."

^{f-f}   Lit. "before the eyes."

^{a-a}   Meaning of Heb. uncertain. Septuagint reads "to you as a bride comes back to her husband; you seek the life of but one man, and…"

---

15 וְאַבְשָׁלוֹם וְכָל־הָעָם אִישׁ יִשְׂרָאֵל בָּאוּ יְרוּשָׁלָ͏ִם וַאֲחִיתֹפֶל אִתּוֹ׃ 16 וַיְהִי כַּאֲשֶׁר־בָּא חוּשַׁי הָאַרְכִּי רֵעֶה דָוִד אֶל־אַבְשָׁלוֹם וַיֹּאמֶר חוּשַׁי אֶל־אַבְשָׁלֹם יְחִי הַמֶּלֶךְ יְחִי הַמֶּלֶךְ׃ 17 וַיֹּאמֶר אַבְשָׁלוֹם אֶל־חוּשַׁי זֶה חַסְדְּךָ אֶת־רֵעֶךָ לָמָּה לֹא־הָלַכְתָּ אֶת־רֵעֶךָ׃ 18 וַיֹּאמֶר חוּשַׁי אֶל־אַבְשָׁלֹם לֹא כִּי אֲשֶׁר בָּחַר יְהוָה וְהָעָם הַזֶּה וְכָל־אִישׁ יִשְׂרָאֵל לֹא לוֹ אֶהְיֶה וְאִתּוֹ אֵשֵׁב׃ 19 וְהַשֵּׁנִית לְמִי אֲנִי אֶעֱבֹד הֲלוֹא לִפְנֵי בְנוֹ כַּאֲשֶׁר עָבַדְתִּי לִפְנֵי אָבִיךָ כֵּן אֶהְיֶה לְפָנֶיךָ׃ פ 20 וַיֹּאמֶר אַבְשָׁלוֹם אֶל־אֲחִיתֹפֶל הָבוּ לָכֶם עֵצָה מַה־נַּעֲשֶׂה׃ 21 וַיֹּאמֶר אֲחִיתֹפֶל אֶל־אַבְשָׁלֹם בּוֹא אֶל־פִּלַגְשֵׁי אָבִיךָ אֲשֶׁר הִנִּיחַ לִשְׁמוֹר הַבָּיִת וְשָׁמַע כָּל־יִשְׂרָאֵל כִּי־נִבְאַשְׁתָּ אֶת־אָבִיךָ וְחָזְקוּ יְדֵי כָּל־אֲשֶׁר אִתָּךְ׃ 22 וַיַּטּוּ לְאַבְשָׁלוֹם הָאֹהֶל עַל־הַגָּג וַיָּבֹא אַבְשָׁלוֹם אֶל־פִּלַגְשֵׁי אָבִיו לְעֵינֵי כָּל־יִשְׂרָאֵל׃ 23 וַעֲצַת אֲחִיתֹפֶל אֲשֶׁר יָעַץ בַּיָּמִים הָהֵם כַּאֲשֶׁר יִשְׁאַל־[אִישׁ*] בִּדְבַר הָאֱלֹהִים כֵּן כָּל־עֲצַת אֲחִיתֹפֶל גַּם־לְדָוִד גַּם לְאַבְשָׁלֹם׃ ס

רז

וַיֹּאמֶר אֲחִיתֹפֶל אֶל־אַבְשָׁלֹם אֶבְחֲרָה נָּא שְׁנֵים־עָשָׂר אֶלֶף אִישׁ וְאָקוּמָה וְאֶרְדְּפָה אַחֲרֵי־דָוִד הַלָּיְלָה׃ 2 וְאָבוֹא עָלָיו וְהוּא יָגֵעַ וּרְפֵה יָדַיִם וְהַחֲרַדְתִּי אֹתוֹ וְנָס כָּל־הָעָם אֲשֶׁר־אִתּוֹ וְהִכֵּיתִי אֶת־הַמֶּלֶךְ לְבַדּוֹ׃ 3 וְאָשִׁיבָה כָל־הָעָם אֵלֶיךָ כְּשׁוּב הַכֹּל הָאִישׁ אֲשֶׁר אַתָּה מְבַקֵּשׁ כָּל־הָעָם יִהְיֶה שָׁלוֹם׃ 4 וַיִּישַׁר הַדָּבָר בְּעֵינֵי אַבְשָׁלֹם וּבְעֵינֵי כָּל־זִקְנֵי

v. 23. קְרֵי וְלֹא כְּתִיב *

5But Absalom said, "Summon Hushai the Archite as well, so we can hear what he too has to say." 6Hushai came to Absalom, and Absalom said to him, "This is what Ahithophel has advised. Shall we follow his advice? If not, what do you say?"

7Hushai said to Absalom, "This time the advice that Ahithophel has given is not good. 8You know," Hushai continued, "that your father and his men are courageous fighters, and they are as desperate as a bear in the wild robbed of her whelps. Your father is an experienced soldier, and he will not spend the night with the troops; 9even now he must be hiding in one of the pits or in some other place. And if any of them*b* fall at the first attack, whoever hears of it will say, 'A disaster has struck the troops that follow Absalom'; 10and even if he is a brave man with the heart of a lion, he will be shaken—for all Israel knows that your father and the soldiers with him are courageous fighters. 11So I advise that all Israel from Dan to Beer-sheba—as numerous as the sands of the sea—be called up to join you, and that you yourself march *c-*into battle.*-c* 12When we come upon him in whatever place he may be, we'll descend on him [as thick] as dew falling on the ground; and no one will survive, neither he nor any of the men with him. 13And if he withdraws into a city, all Israel will bring ropes to that city and drag *d-*its stones*-d* as far as the riverbed, until not even a pebble of it is left." 14Absalom and all Israel agreed that the advice of Hushai the Archite was better than that of Ahithophel.—The Lord had decreed that Ahithophel's sound advice be nullified, in order that the Lord might bring ruin upon Absalom.

15Then Hushai told the priests Zadok and Abiathar, "This is what Ahithophel advised Absalom and the elders of Israel; this is what I ad-

---

b   *Some Septuagint mss. read "the troops" (i.e., Absalom's).*
c-c   *Ancient versions read "among them."*
d-d   *Heb. "it."*

681

5 וַיֹּ֙אמֶר֙ אַבְשָׁל֔וֹם קְרָ֣א נָ֔א גַּ֖ם לְחוּשַׁ֣י הָאַרְכִּ֑י וְנִשְׁמְעָ֥ה מַה־בְּפִ֖יו גַּם־הֽוּא׃ 6 וַיָּבֹ֣א חוּשַׁי֮ אֶל־אַבְשָׁלוֹם֒ וַיֹּ֩אמֶר֩ אַבְשָׁל֨וֹם אֵלָ֜יו לֵאמֹ֗ר כַּדָּבָ֤ר הַזֶּה֙ דִּבֶּ֣ר אֲחִיתֹ֔פֶל הֲנַעֲשֶׂ֖ה אֶת־דְּבָר֑וֹ אִם־אַ֖יִן אַתָּ֥ה דַבֵּֽר׃ ס

7 וַיֹּ֥אמֶר חוּשַׁ֖י אֶל־אַבְשָׁל֑וֹם לֹֽא־טוֹבָ֧ה הָעֵצָ֛ה אֲשֶׁר־יָעַ֥ץ אֲחִיתֹ֖פֶל בַּפַּ֥עַם הַזֹּֽאת׃ 8 וַיֹּ֣אמֶר חוּשַׁ֗י אַתָּ֣ה יָדַ֜עְתָּ אֶת־אָבִ֣יךָ וְאֶת־אֲנָשָׁיו֮ כִּ֣י גִבֹּרִ֣ים הֵ֗מָּה וּמָרֵ֥י נֶ֙פֶשׁ֙ הֵ֔מָּה כְּדֹ֥ב שַׁכּ֖וּל בַּשָּׂדֶ֑ה וְאָבִ֙יךָ֙ אִ֣ישׁ מִלְחָמָ֔ה וְלֹ֥א יָלִ֖ין אֶת־הָעָֽם׃ 9 הִנֵּ֨ה עַתָּ֤ה הֽוּא־נֶחְבָּא֙ בְּאַחַ֣ת הַפְּחָתִ֔ים א֖וֹ בְּאַחַ֣ד הַמְּקוֹמֹ֑ת וְהָיָ֗ה כִּנְפֹ֤ל בָּהֶם֙ בַּתְּחִלָּ֔ה וְשָׁמַ֤ע הַשֹּׁמֵ֙עַ֙ וְאָמַ֔ר הָֽיְתָה֙ מַגֵּפָ֔ה בָּעָ֕ם אֲשֶׁ֖ר אַחֲרֵ֥י אַבְשָׁלֹֽם׃ 10 וְה֣וּא גַם־בֶּן־חַ֗יִל אֲשֶׁ֤ר לִבּוֹ֙ כְּלֵ֣ב הָאַרְיֵ֔ה הִמֵּ֖ס יִמָּ֑ס כִּֽי־יֹדֵ֤עַ כָּל־יִשְׂרָאֵל֙ כִּֽי־גִבּ֣וֹר אָבִ֔יךָ וּבְנֵי־חַ֖יִל אֲשֶׁ֥ר אִתּֽוֹ׃ 11 כִּ֣י יָעַ֗צְתִּי הֵ֠אָסֹף יֵאָסֵ֨ף עָלֶ֤יךָ כָל־יִשְׂרָאֵל֙ מִדָּן֙ וְעַד־בְּאֵ֣ר שֶׁ֔בַע כַּח֥וֹל אֲשֶׁר־עַל־הַיָּ֖ם לָרֹ֑ב וּפָנֶ֥יךָ הֹלְכִ֖ים בַּקְרָֽב׃ 12 וּבָ֣אנוּ אֵלָ֗יו באחת בְּאַחַ֤ד הַמְּקוֹמֹת֙ אֲשֶׁ֣ר נִמְצָ֣א שָׁ֔ם וְנַ֣חְנוּ עָלָ֔יו כַּאֲשֶׁ֛ר יִפֹּ֥ל הַטַּ֖ל עַל־הָאֲדָמָ֑ה וְלֹֽא־נ֤וֹתַר בּוֹ֙ וּבְכָל־הָאֲנָשִׁ֥ים אֲשֶׁר־אִתּ֖וֹ גַּם־אֶחָֽד׃ 13 וְאִם־אֶל־עִיר֙ יֵֽאָסֵ֔ף וְהִשִּׂ֧יאוּ כָֽל־יִשְׂרָאֵ֛ל אֶל־הָעִ֥יר הַהִ֖יא חֲבָלִ֑ים וְסָחַ֤בְנוּ אֹתוֹ֙ עַד־הַנַּ֔חַל עַ֛ד אֲשֶֽׁר־לֹא־נִמְצָ֥א שָׁ֖ם גַּם־צְרֽוֹר׃ פ 14 וַיֹּ֤אמֶר אַבְשָׁלוֹם֙ וְכָל־אִ֣ישׁ יִשְׂרָאֵ֔ל טוֹבָ֗ה עֲצַ֛ת חוּשַׁ֥י הָאַרְכִּ֖י מֵעֲצַ֣ת אֲחִיתֹ֑פֶל וַֽיהוָ֣ה צִוָּ֗ה לְהָפֵ֞ר אֶת־עֲצַ֤ת אֲחִיתֹ֙פֶל֙ הַטּוֹבָ֔ה לְבַעֲב֗וּר הָבִ֤יא יְהוָה֙ אֶל־אַבְשָׁל֖וֹם אֶת־הָרָעָֽה׃ ס

15 וַיֹּ֣אמֶר חוּשַׁ֗י אֶל־צָד֤וֹק וְאֶל־אֶבְיָתָר֙ הַכֹּ֣הֲנִ֔ים כָּזֹ֤את וְכָזֹאת֙ יָעַ֣ץ אֲחִיתֹ֔פֶל

vised. 16Now send at once and tell David, 'Do not spend the night at the fords of the wilderness, but cross over at once; otherwise the king and all the troops with him will be annihilated.'" 17Jonathan and Ahimaaz were staying at En-rogel, and a slave girl would go and bring them word and they in turn would go and inform King David. For they themselves dared not be seen entering the city. 18But a boy saw them and informed Absalom. They left at once and came to the house of a man in Bahurim who had a well in his courtyard. They got down into it, 19and the wife took a cloth, spread it over the mouth of the well, and scattered groats on top of it, so that nothing would be noticed. 20When Absalom's servants came to the woman at the house and asked where Ahimaaz and Jonathan were, the woman told them that they had crossed e-a bit beyond the water.-e They searched, but found nothing; and they returned to Jerusalem.

21After they were gone, [Ahimaaz and Jonathan] came up from the well and went and informed King David. They said to David, "Go and cross the water quickly, for Ahithophel has advised thus and thus concerning you." 22David and all the troops with him promptly crossed the Jordan, and by daybreak not one was left who had not crossed the Jordan.

23When Ahithophel saw that his advice had not been followed, he saddled his ass and went home to his native town. He set his affairs in order, and then he hanged himself. He was buried in his ancestral tomb.

24David had reached Mahanaim when Absalom and all the men of Israel with him crossed the Jordan. 25Absalom had appointed Amasa army commander in place of Joab; Amasa was the son of a man named Ithra the f-Israelite, who had married Abigal, daughter of Nahash and

---

e-e Meaning of Heb. uncertain. Targum reads "the Jordan."
f-f Some Septuagint mss. and 1 Chron. 2.12–17 read "Ishmaelite" and give a somewhat different genealogy.

אֶת־אַבְשָׁלֹ֖ם וְאֵ֥ת זִקְנֵ֣י יִשְׂרָאֵ֑ל וְכָזֹ֛את וְכָזֹ֖את יָעַ֥צְתִּי אָֽנִי׃ 16 וְעַתָּ֡ה שִׁלְח֣וּ מְהֵרָה֩ וְהַגִּ֨ידוּ לְדָוִ֜ד לֵאמֹ֗ר אַל־תָּ֤לֶן הַלַּ֙יְלָה֙ בְּעַֽרְב֣וֹת הַמִּדְבָּ֔ר וְגַ֖ם עָב֣וֹר תַּֽעֲב֑וֹר פֶּ֚ן יְבֻלַּ֣ע לַמֶּ֔לֶךְ וּלְכָל־הָעָ֖ם אֲשֶׁ֥ר אִתּֽוֹ׃ 17 וִיהֽוֹנָתָ֨ן וַאֲחִימַ֜עַץ עֹמְדִ֣ים בְּעֵין־רֹגֵ֗ל וְהָלְכָ֤ה הַשִּׁפְחָה֙ וְהִגִּ֣ידָה לָהֶ֔ם וְהֵם֙ יֵֽלְכ֔וּ וְהִגִּ֖ידוּ לַמֶּ֣לֶךְ דָּוִ֑ד כִּ֣י לֹ֤א יוּכְלוּ֙ לְהֵ֣רָא֔וֹת לָב֖וֹא הָעִֽירָה׃ 18 וַיַּ֤רְא אֹתָם֙ נַ֔עַר וַיַּגֵּ֖ד לְאַבְשָׁלֹ֑ם וַיֵּלְכוּ֩ שְׁנֵיהֶ֨ם מְהֵרָ֜ה וַיָּבֹ֣אוּ ׀ אֶל־בֵּֽית־אִ֣ישׁ בְּבַחוּרִ֗ים וְל֥וֹ בְאֵ֛ר בַּחֲצֵר֖וֹ וַיֵּ֥רְדוּ שָֽׁם׃ 19 וַתִּקַּ֣ח הָאִשָּׁ֗ה וַתִּפְרֹ֤שׂ אֶת־הַמָּסָךְ֙ עַל־פְּנֵ֣י* הַבְּאֵ֔ר וַתִּשְׁטַ֥ח עָלָ֖יו הָרִפ֑וֹת וְלֹ֥א נוֹדַ֖ע דָּבָֽר׃ 20 וַיָּבֹ֣אוּ עַבְדֵי֩ אַבְשָׁל֨וֹם אֶל־הָֽאִשָּׁ֜ה הַבַּ֗יְתָה וַיֹּֽאמְרוּ֙ אַיֵּ֗ה אֲחִימַ֙עַץ֙ וִיה֣וֹנָתָ֔ן וַתֹּ֤אמֶר לָהֶם֙ הָֽאִשָּׁ֔ה עָבְר֖וּ מִיכַ֣ל הַמָּ֑יִם וַיְבַקְשׁוּ֙ וְלֹ֣א מָצָ֔אוּ וַיָּשֻׁ֖בוּ יְרוּשָׁלָֽ͏ִם׃ ס 21 וַיְהִ֣י ׀ אַחֲרֵ֣י לֶכְתָּ֗ם וַֽיַּעֲלוּ֙ מֵֽהַבְּאֵ֔ר וַיֵּ֣לְכ֔וּ וַיַּגִּ֖דוּ לַמֶּ֣לֶךְ דָּוִ֑ד וַיֹּאמְר֣וּ אֶל־דָּוִ֗ד ק֣וּמוּ וְעִבְר֤וּ מְהֵרָה֙ אֶת־הַמַּ֔יִם כִּי־כָ֛כָה יָעַ֥ץ עֲלֵיכֶ֖ם אֲחִיתֹֽפֶל׃ 22 וַיָּ֣קׇם דָּוִ֗ד וְכָל־הָעָם֙ אֲשֶׁ֣ר אִתּ֔וֹ וַיַּעַבְר֖וּ אֶת־הַיַּרְדֵּ֑ן עַד־א֣וֹר הַבֹּ֗קֶר עַד־אַחַד֙ לֹ֣א נֶעְדָּ֔ר אֲשֶׁ֥ר לֹא־עָבַ֖ר אֶת־הַיַּרְדֵּֽן׃ 23 וַאֲחִיתֹ֣פֶל רָאָ֗ה כִּ֣י לֹ֤א נֶֽעֶשְׂתָה֙ עֲצָת֔וֹ וַיַּחֲבֹ֣שׁ אֶֽת־הַחֲמ֗וֹר וַיָּ֜קׇם וַיֵּ֤לֶךְ אֶל־בֵּיתוֹ֙ אֶל־עִיר֔וֹ וַיְצַ֥ו אֶל־בֵּית֖וֹ וַיֵּחָנַ֑ק וַיָּ֕מׇת וַיִּקָּבֵ֖ר בְּקֶ֥בֶר אָבִֽיו׃ ס 24 וְדָוִ֖ד בָּ֣א מַחֲנָ֑יְמָה וְאַבְשָׁלֹ֗ם עָבַר֙ אֶת־הַיַּרְדֵּ֔ן ה֕וּא וְכָל־אִ֥ישׁ יִשְׂרָאֵ֖ל עִמּֽוֹ׃ 25 וְאֶת־עֲמָשָׂ֗א שָׂ֣ם אַבְשָׁלֹ֛ם תַּ֥חַת יוֹאָ֖ב עַל־הַצָּבָ֑א וַעֲמָשָׂ֣א בֶן־אִ֗ישׁ וּשְׁמוֹ֙ יִתְרָ֣א הַיִּשְׂרְאֵלִ֔י אֲשֶׁר־בָּא֙ אֶל־אֲבִיגַ֣ל בַּת־נָחָ֔שׁ

sister of Joab's mother Zeruiah.-*f* 26The Israelites and Absalom encamped in the district of Gilead. 27When David reached Mahanaim, Shobi son of Nahash from Rabbath-ammon, Machir son of Ammiel from Lo-debar, and Barzillai the Gileadite from Rogelim 28presented*g* couches, basins, and earthenware; also wheat, barley, flour, parched grain, beans, lentils, *h*-parched grain,-*h* 29honey, *i*-curds, a flock,-*i* and cheese*j* from the herd for David and the troops with him to eat. For they knew that the troops must have grown hungry, faint, and thirsty in the wilderness.

18 David mustered the troops who were with him and set over them captains of thousands and captains of hundreds. 2David *a*-sent out the troops,-*a* one-third under the command of Joab, one-third under the command of Joab's brother Abishai son of Zeruiah, and one-third under the command of Ittai the Gittite. And David said to the troops, "I myself will march out with you." 3But the troops replied, "No! For if some of us flee, the rest will not be concerned about us; even if half of us should die, the others will not be concerned about us. But *b*-you are worth ten thousand of us.-*b* Therefore, it is better for you to support us from the town." 4And the king said to them, "I will do whatever you think best."

So the king stood beside the gate as all the troops marched out by their hundreds and thousands. 5The king gave orders to Joab, Abishai, and Ittai: "Deal gently with my boy Absalom, for my sake." All the troops heard the

אֲחוֹת צְרוּיָ֖ה אֵ֥ם יוֹאָֽב׃ 26 וַיִּ֧חַן יִשְׂרָאֵ֛ל וְאַבְשָׁלֹ֖ם אֶ֥רֶץ הַגִּלְעָֽד׃ ס 27 וַיְהִ֗י כְּב֣וֹא דָוִד֮ מַחֲנַ֒יְמָה֒ וְשֹׁבִ֨י בֶן־נָחָ֜שׁ מֵרַבַּ֣ת בְּנֵֽי־עַמּ֗וֹן וּמָכִ֤יר בֶּן־עַמִּיאֵל֙ מִלֹּ֣א דְבָ֔ר וּבַרְזִלַּ֥י הַגִּלְעָדִ֖י מֵרֹגְלִֽים׃ 28 מִשְׁכָּ֤ב וְסַפּוֹת֙ וּכְלִ֣י יוֹצֵ֔ר וְחִטִּ֥ים וּשְׂעֹרִ֖ים וְקֶ֣מַח וְקָלִ֑י וּפ֥וֹל וַעֲדָשִׁ֖ים וְקָלִֽי׃ 29 וּדְבַ֣שׁ וְחֶמְאָ֗ה וְצֹאן֙ וּשְׁפ֣וֹת בָּקָ֔ר הִגִּ֖ישׁוּ לְדָוִ֑ד וְלָעָ֣ם אֲשֶׁר־אִתּ֖וֹ לֶאֱכ֑וֹל כִּ֣י אָמְר֔וּ הָעָ֗ם רָעֵ֧ב וְעָיֵ֛ף וְצָמֵ֖א בַּמִּדְבָּֽר׃

יח וַיִּפְקֹ֣ד דָּוִ֗ד אֶת־הָעָ֖ם אֲשֶׁ֣ר אִתּ֑וֹ וַיָּ֣שֶׂם עֲלֵיהֶ֗ם שָׂרֵ֥י אֲלָפִ֖ים וְשָׂרֵ֥י מֵאֽוֹת׃ 2 וַיְשַׁלַּ֣ח דָּוִ֣ד אֶת־הָעָ֗ם הַשְּׁלִשִׁ֞ית בְּיַד־יוֹאָ֗ב וְֽהַשְּׁלִשִׁ֞ית בְּיַ֨ד אֲבִישַׁ֤י בֶּן־צְרוּיָה֙ אֲחִ֣י יוֹאָ֔ב וְֽהַשְּׁלִשִׁ֔ת בְּיַ֖ד אִתַּ֣י הַגִּתִּ֑י ס וַיֹּ֤אמֶר הַמֶּ֙לֶךְ֙ אֶל־הָעָ֔ם יָצֹ֥א אֵצֵ֖א גַּם־אֲנִ֥י עִמָּכֶֽם׃ 3 וַיֹּ֨אמֶר הָעָ֜ם לֹ֣א תֵצֵ֗א כִּי֩ אִם־נֹ֨ס נָנ֜וּס לֹא־יָשִׂ֧ימוּ אֵלֵ֣ינוּ לֵ֗ב וְאִם־יָמֻ֤תוּ חֶצְיֵ֙נוּ֙ לֹֽא־יָשִׂ֤ימוּ אֵלֵ֙ינוּ֙ לֵ֔ב כִּֽי־עַתָּ֗ה* כָּמֹ֛נוּ עֲשָׂרָ֥ה אֲלָפִ֑ים וְעַתָּ֣ה ט֗וֹב כִּֽי־תִהְיֶה־לָּ֥נוּ מֵעִ֖יר לַעְז֑וֹר ס 4 וַיֹּ֧אמֶר אֲלֵיהֶ֣ם הַמֶּ֗לֶךְ אֲשֶׁר־יִיטַ֥ב בְּעֵֽינֵיכֶ֖ם אֶעֱשֶׂ֑ה וַיַּעֲמֹ֤ד הַמֶּ֙לֶךְ֙ אֶל־יַ֣ד הַשַּׁ֔עַר וְכָל־הָעָם֙ יָֽצְא֔וּ לְמֵא֖וֹת וְלַאֲלָפִֽים׃ 5 וַיְצַ֣ו הַמֶּ֡לֶךְ אֶת־י֠וֹאָב וְאֶת־אֲבִישַׁ֨י וְאֶת־אִתַּ֜י לֵאמֹ֗ר לְאַט־לִ֛י לַנַּ֥עַר לְאַבְשָׁל֖וֹם וְכָל־הָעָ֣ם

---

g   Brought up from v. 29 for clarity.
h-h Lacking in the Septuagint and Syriac.
i-i Emendation yields "curds from the flock."
j   Meaning of Heb. uncertain.

a-a Some Septuagint mss. read "divided the troops into three."
b-b So two Heb. mss., Septuagint, and Vulgate; cf. 1 Kings 1.18 and note. Most mss. and the editions read "Now there are ten thousand like us."

king give the order about Absalom to all the officers.

[6] The troops marched out into the open to confront the Israelites,[c] and the battle was fought in the forest of Ephraim.[d] [7] The Israelite troops were routed by David's followers, and a great slaughter took place there that day— twenty thousand men. [8] The battle spread out over that whole region, and the forest devoured more troops that day than the sword.

[9] Absalom encountered some of David's followers. Absalom was riding on a mule, and as the mule passed under the tangled branches of a great terebinth, his hair got caught in the terebinth; he [e-was held-e] between heaven and earth as the mule under him kept going. [10] One of the men saw it and told Joab, "I have just seen Absalom hanging from a terebinth." [11] Joab said to the man who told him, "You saw it! Why didn't you kill him [f-then and there?-f] I would have owed you ten[g] shekels of silver and a belt." [12] But the man answered Joab, "Even if I had a thousand shekels of silver in my hands, I would not raise a hand against the king's son. For the king charged you and Abishai and Ittai in our hearing, 'Watch over my boy Absalom, [h-for my sake.'-h] [13] If I betrayed myself[i]—and nothing is hidden from the king—you would have stood aloof." [14] Joab replied, [j-"Then I will not wait for you."-j] He took three darts in his hand and drove them into Absalom's chest. [Absalom] was still alive in the thick growth of the terebinth, [15] when ten of Joab's young arms-bearers closed in and struck at Absalom until he died. [16] Then Joab sounded the horn, and the troops gave up

שָׁמְעוּ בְּצַוֺּת הַמֶּלֶךְ אֶת־כָּל־הַשָּׂרִים עַל־
דְּבַר אַבְשָׁלוֹם:
6 וַיֵּצֵא הָעָם הַשָּׂדֶה לִקְרַאת יִשְׂרָאֵל וַתְּהִי
הַמִּלְחָמָה בְּיַעַר אֶפְרָיִם: 7 וַיִּנָּגְפוּ שָׁם עַם
יִשְׂרָאֵל לִפְנֵי עַבְדֵי דָוִד וַתְּהִי־שָׁם הַמַּגֵּפָה
גְדוֹלָה בַּיּוֹם הַהוּא עֶשְׂרִים אָלֶף: 8 וַתְּהִי־
שָׁם הַמִּלְחָמָה נפצית נָפֹצֶת עַל־פְּנֵי
כָל־הָאָרֶץ וַיֶּרֶב הַיַּעַר לֶאֱכֹל בָּעָם מֵאֲשֶׁר
אָכְלָה הַחֶרֶב בַּיּוֹם הַהוּא:
9 וַיִּקָּרֵא אַבְשָׁלוֹם לִפְנֵי עַבְדֵי דָוִד
וְאַבְשָׁלוֹם רֹכֵב עַל־הַפֶּרֶד וַיָּבֹא הַפֶּרֶד
תַּחַת שׂוֹבֶךְ הָאֵלָה הַגְּדוֹלָה וַיֶּחֱזַק רֹאשׁוֹ
בָאֵלָה וַיֻּתַּן בֵּין הַשָּׁמַיִם וּבֵין הָאָרֶץ
וְהַפֶּרֶד אֲשֶׁר־תַּחְתָּיו עָבָר: 10 וַיַּרְא אִישׁ
אֶחָד וַיַּגֵּד לְיוֹאָב וַיֹּאמֶר הִנֵּה רָאִיתִי
אֶת־אַבְשָׁלֹם תָּלוּי בָּאֵלָה: 11 וַיֹּאמֶר יוֹאָב
לָאִישׁ הַמַּגִּיד לוֹ וְהִנֵּה רָאִיתָ וּמַדּוּעַ
לֹא־הִכִּיתוֹ שָׁם אָרְצָה וְעָלַי לָתֶת לְךָ
עֲשָׂרָה כֶסֶף וַחֲגֹרָה אֶחָת: 12 וַיֹּאמֶר
הָאִישׁ אֶל־יוֹאָב ולא וְלוּ אָנֹכִי שֹׁקֵל
עַל־כַּפַּי אֶלֶף כֶּסֶף לֹא־אֶשְׁלַח יָדִי אֶל־
בֶּן־הַמֶּלֶךְ כִּי בְאָזְנֵינוּ צִוָּה הַמֶּלֶךְ אֹתְךָ
וְאֶת־אֲבִישַׁי וְאֶת־אִתַּי לֵאמֹר שִׁמְרוּ־מִי*
בַנַּעַר בְּאַבְשָׁלוֹם: 13 אוֹ־עָשִׂיתִי בנפשו
בְנַפְשִׁי שֶׁקֶר וְכָל־דָּבָר לֹא־יִכָּחֵד מִן־
הַמֶּלֶךְ וְאַתָּה תִּתְיַצֵּב מִנֶּגֶד: 14 וַיֹּאמֶר
יוֹאָב לֹא־כֵן אֹחִילָה לְפָנֶיךָ וַיִּקַּח שְׁלֹשָׁה
שְׁבָטִים בְּכַפּוֹ וַיִּתְקָעֵם בְּלֵב אַבְשָׁלוֹם
עוֹדֶנּוּ חַי בְּלֵב הָאֵלָה: 15 וַיָּסֹבּוּ עֲשָׂרָה
נְעָרִים נֹשְׂאֵי כְּלֵי יוֹאָב וַיַּכּוּ אֶת־אַבְשָׁלוֹם
וַיְמִיתֻהוּ: 16 וַיִּתְקַע יוֹאָב בַּשֹּׁפָר וַיָּשָׁב

---

c   The usual term in this narrative for the supporters of Absalom.
d   Some Septuagint mss. read "Mahanaim"; cf. 17.24.
e-e Meaning of Heb. uncertain. Ancient versions and 4QSam[a] read "was left hanging"; cf. v. 10.
f-f Lit. "to the ground."
g   Some Septuagint mss. and 4QSam[a] read "fifty."
h-h So some Heb. mss. and ancient versions. Most mss. and editions read "who"—perhaps meaning "whoever you are."
i   I.e., by killing Absalom.
j-j Some Septuagint mss. and Targum read "Therefore, I will begin before you."

their pursuit of the Israelites; for Joab held the troops in check. [17]They took Absalom and flung him into a large pit in the forest, and they piled up a very great heap of stones over it. Then all the Israelites fled to their homes.—[18]Now Absalom, in his lifetime, had taken the pillar which is in the Valley of the King and set it up for himself; for he said, "I have no son to keep my name alive." He had named the pillar after himself, and it has been called Absalom's Monument to this day.

[19]Ahimaaz son of Zadok said, "Let me run and report to the king that the LORD has vindicated him against his enemies." [20]But Joab said to him, "You shall not be the one to bring tidings today. You may bring tidings some other day, but you'll not bring any today; for the king's son is dead!" [21]And Joab said to a Cushite, "Go tell the king what you have seen." The Cushite bowed to Joab and ran off. [22]But Ahimaaz son of Zadok again said to Joab, "No matter what, let me run, too, behind the Cushite." Joab asked, "Why should you run, my boy, when you have no news *k-worth telling?"-k* [23]"I am going to run anyway." "Then run," he said. So Ahimaaz ran by way of the Plain, and he passed the Cushite.

[24]David was sitting between the two gates.*l* The watchman on the roof of the gate walked over to the city wall. He looked up and saw a man running alone. [25]The watchman called down and told the king; and the king said, "If he is alone, he has news to report." As he was coming nearer, [26]the watchman saw another man running; and he called out to the gate-keeper, "There is another man running alone." And the king said, "That one, too, brings news." [27]The watchman said, "I can see that the first one runs like Ahimaaz son of Zadok"; to which the king replied, "He is a good man, and he comes with good news." [28]Ahimaaz called out and said to the king, "All is well!" He bowed low

הָעָ֖ם מֵרְדֹ֣ף אַחֲרֵ֣י יִשְׂרָאֵ֑ל כִּֽי־חָשַׂ֥ךְ יוֹאָ֖ב אֶת־הָעָֽם׃ 17 וַיִּקְח֣וּ אֶת־אַבְשָׁל֗וֹם וַיַּשְׁלִ֨כוּ אֹת֤וֹ בַיַּ֙עַר֙ אֶל־הַפַּ֣חַת הַגָּד֔וֹל וַיַּצִּ֧בוּ עָלָ֛יו גַּל־אֲבָנִ֖ים גָּד֣וֹל מְאֹ֑ד וְכָל־יִשְׂרָאֵ֔ל נָ֖סוּ אִ֥ישׁ לְאֹהָלָֽו׃ ס

18 וְאַבְשָׁלֹ֣ם לָקַ֗ח וַיַּצֶּב־ל֤וֹ בְחַיָּו֙ אֶת־מַצֶּ֣בֶת אֲשֶׁ֣ר בְּעֵֽמֶק־הַמֶּ֗לֶךְ כִּ֤י אָמַר֙ אֵֽין־לִ֣י בֵ֔ן בַּעֲב֖וּר הַזְכִּ֣יר שְׁמִ֑י וַיִּקְרָ֤א לַמַּצֶּ֙בֶת֙ עַל־שְׁמ֔וֹ וַיִּקָּ֤רֵא לָהּ֙ יַ֣ד אַבְשָׁל֔וֹם עַ֖ד הַיּ֥וֹם הַזֶּֽה׃ ס

19 וַאֲחִימַ֣עַץ בֶּן־צָד֗וֹק אָמַר֙ אָר֤וּצָה נָּא֙ וַאֲבַשְּׂרָ֣ה אֶת־הַמֶּ֔לֶךְ כִּֽי־שְׁפָט֥וֹ יְהוָ֖ה מִיַּ֥ד אֹיְבָֽיו׃ 20 וַיֹּ֧אמֶר ל֣וֹ יוֹאָ֗ב לֹא֩ אִ֨ישׁ בְּשֹׂרָ֤ה אַתָּה֙ הַיּ֣וֹם הַזֶּ֔ה וּבִשַּׂרְתָּ֖ בְּי֣וֹם אַחֵ֑ר וְהַיּ֤וֹם הַזֶּה֙ לֹ֣א תְבַשֵּׂ֔ר כִּֽי־עַל־[כֵּֽן־]*בֶּן־הַמֶּ֥לֶךְ מֵֽת׃ 21 וַיֹּ֤אמֶר יוֹאָב֙ לַכּוּשִׁ֔י לֵ֛ךְ הַגֵּ֥ד לַמֶּ֖לֶךְ אֲשֶׁ֣ר רָאִ֑יתָה וַיִּשְׁתַּ֧חוּ כוּשִׁ֛י לְיוֹאָ֖ב וַיָּרֹֽץ׃ 22 וַיֹּ֨סֶף ע֜וֹד אֲחִימַ֣עַץ בֶּן־צָד֗וֹק וַיֹּ֣אמֶר אֶל־יוֹאָ֔ב וִ֣יהִי מָ֔ה אָרֻֽצָה־נָּ֥א גַם־אָ֖נִי אַחֲרֵ֣י הַכּוּשִׁ֑י וַיֹּ֣אמֶר יוֹאָ֗ב לָֽמָּה־זֶּ֞ה אַתָּ֥ה רָץ֙ בְּנִ֔י וּלְכָ֖ה* אֵֽין־בְּשׂוֹרָ֥ה מֹצֵֽאת׃ 23 וִיהִי־מָ֣ה אָר֔וּץ וַיֹּ֥אמֶר ל֖וֹ ר֑וּץ וַיָּ֤רָץ אֲחִימַ֙עַץ֙ דֶּ֣רֶךְ הַכִּכָּ֔ר וַֽיַּעֲבֹ֖ר אֶת־הַכּוּשִֽׁי׃

24 וְדָוִ֥ד יוֹשֵׁ֖ב בֵּֽין־שְׁנֵ֣י הַשְּׁעָרִ֑ים וַיֵּ֙לֶךְ֙ הַצֹּפֶ֜ה אֶל־גַּ֤ג הַשַּׁ֙עַר֙ אֶל־הַ֣חוֹמָ֔ה וַיִּשָּׂ֤א אֶת־עֵינָיו֙ וַיַּ֔רְא וְהִנֵּה־אִ֖ישׁ רָ֥ץ לְבַדּֽוֹ׃ 25 וַיִּקְרָ֤א הַצֹּפֶה֙ וַיַּגֵּ֣ד לַמֶּ֔לֶךְ וַיֹּ֣אמֶר הַמֶּ֔לֶךְ אִם־לְבַדּ֖וֹ בְּשׂוֹרָ֣ה בְּפִ֑יו וַיֵּ֥לֶךְ הָל֖וֹךְ וְקָרֵֽב׃ 26 וַיַּ֣רְא הַצֹּפֶה֮ אִישׁ־אַחֵ֣ר רָץ֒ וַיִּקְרָ֤א הַצֹּפֶה֙ אֶל־הַשֹּׁעֵ֔ר וַיֹּ֕אמֶר הִנֵּה־אִ֖ישׁ רָ֣ץ לְבַדּ֑וֹ וַיֹּ֥אמֶר הַמֶּ֖לֶךְ גַּם־זֶ֥ה מְבַשֵּֽׂר׃ 27 וַיֹּ֙אמֶר֙ הַצֹּפֶ֔ה אֲנִ֤י רֹאֶה֙ אֶת־מְרוּצַ֣ת הָרִאשׁ֔וֹן כִּמְרֻצַ֖ת אֲחִימַ֣עַץ בֶּן־צָד֑וֹק וַיֹּ֤אמֶר הַמֶּ֙לֶךְ֙ אִֽישׁ־ט֣וֹב זֶ֔ה וְאֶל־בְּשׂוֹרָ֥ה טוֹבָ֖ה יָבֽוֹא׃ 28 וַיִּקְרָ֣א אֲחִימַ֔עַץ וַיֹּ֥אמֶר

with his face to the ground and said, "Praised be the LORD your God, who has delivered up the men who raised their hand against my lord the king." 29The king asked, "Is my boy Absalom safe?" And Ahimaaz answered, "I saw *k-a large crowd when Your Majesty's servant Joab was sending your servant off,-k* but I don't know what it was about." 30The king said, "Step aside and stand over there"; he stepped aside and waited.

31Just then the Cushite came up; and the Cushite said, "Let my lord the king be informed that the LORD has vindicated you today against all who rebelled against you!" 32The king asked the Cushite, "Is my boy Absalom safe?" And the Cushite replied, "May the enemies of my lord the king and all who rose against you to do you

19 harm fare like that young man!" 1aThe king was shaken. He went up to the upper chamber of the gateway and wept, moaning these words as he went,b "My son Absalom! O my son, my son Absalom! If only I had died instead of you! O Absalom, my son, my son!"

2Joab was told that the king was weeping and mourning over Absalom. 3And the victory that day was turned into mourning for all the troops, for that day the troops heard that the king was grieving over his son. 4The troops stole into town that day like troops ashamed after running away in battle. 5The king covered his face and the king kept crying aloud, "O my son Absalom! O Absalom, my son, my son!"

6Joab came to the king in his quarters and said, "Today you have humiliated all your followers, who this day saved your life, and the lives of your sons and daughters, and the lives of your wives and concubines, 7by showing love for those who hate you and hate for those who love you. For you have made clear today that the

---

a   *Counted as 18.33 in some versions.*
b   *Some Septuagint mss. read "wept."*

אֶל־הַמֶּ֙לֶךְ֙ שָׁל֔וֹם וַיִּשְׁתַּ֧חוּ לַמֶּ֛לֶךְ לְאַפָּ֖יו אָ֑רְצָה ס וַיֹּ֕אמֶר בָּר֖וּךְ יְהֹוָ֣ה אֱלֹהֶ֑יךָ אֲשֶׁ֤ר סִגַּר֙ אֶת־הָ֣אֲנָשִׁ֔ים אֲשֶׁר־נָשְׂא֥וּ אֶת־יָדָ֖ם בַּֽאדֹנִ֥י הַמֶּֽלֶךְ׃ 29 וַיֹּ֣אמֶר הַמֶּ֗לֶךְ שָׁל֥וֹם לַנַּ֖עַר לְאַבְשָׁל֑וֹם וַיֹּ֣אמֶר אֲחִימַ֡עַץ רָאִ֩יתִי֩ הֶהָמ֨וֹן הַגָּד֜וֹל לִ֠שְׁלֹחַ אֶת־עֶ֤בֶד הַמֶּ֙לֶךְ֙ יוֹאָב֙ וְאֶת־עַבְדֶּ֔ךָ וְלֹ֥א יָדַ֖עְתִּי מָֽה׃ 30 וַיֹּ֣אמֶר הַמֶּ֗לֶךְ סֹ֥ב הִתְיַצֵּ֛ב כֹּ֖ה וַיִּסֹּ֥ב וַֽיַּעֲמֹֽד׃

31 וְהִנֵּ֥ה הַכּוּשִׁ֖י בָּ֑א וַיֹּ֣אמֶר הַכּוּשִׁ֗י יִתְבַּשֵּׂר֙ אֲדֹנִ֣י הַמֶּ֔לֶךְ כִּֽי־שְׁפָטְךָ֤ יְהֹוָה֙ הַיּ֔וֹם מִיַּ֖ד כׇּל־הַקָּמִ֥ים עָלֶֽיךָ׃ ס 32 וַיֹּ֤אמֶר הַמֶּ֙לֶךְ֙ אֶל־הַכּוּשִׁ֔י הֲשָׁל֥וֹם לַנַּ֖עַר לְאַבְשָׁל֑וֹם וַיֹּ֣אמֶר הַכּוּשִׁ֗י יִהְי֤וּ כַנַּ֙עַר֙ אֹֽיְבֵ֣י אֲדֹנִ֣י

יט הַמֶּ֔לֶךְ וְכֹ֛ל אֲשֶׁר־קָ֥מוּ עָלֶ֖יךָ לְרָעָֽה׃ ס 1 וַיִּרְגַּ֣ז הַמֶּ֗לֶךְ וַיַּ֛עַל עַל־עֲלִיַּ֥ת הַשַּׁ֖עַר וַיֵּ֑בְךְּ וְכֹ֣ה ׀ אָמַ֣ר בְּלֶכְתּ֗וֹ בְּנִ֤י אַבְשָׁל֙וֹם֙ בְּנִ֤י בְנִי֙ אַבְשָׁל֔וֹם מִֽי־יִתֵּ֤ן מוּתִ֙י אֲנִ֣י תַחְתֶּ֔יךָ אַבְשָׁל֖וֹם בְּנִ֥י בְנִֽי׃

2 וַיֻּגַּ֖ד לְיוֹאָ֑ב הִנֵּ֙ה הַמֶּ֧לֶךְ בֹּכֶ֛ה וַיִּתְאַבֵּ֖ל עַל־אַבְשָׁלֹֽם׃ 3 וַתְּהִ֨י הַתְּשֻׁעָ֜ה בַּיּ֥וֹם הַה֛וּא לְאֵ֖בֶל לְכׇל־הָעָ֑ם כִּֽי־שָׁמַ֣ע הָעָ֗ם בַּיּ֤וֹם הַהוּא֙ לֵאמֹ֔ר נֶעֱצַ֥ב הַמֶּ֖לֶךְ עַל־בְּנֽוֹ׃ 4 וַיִּתְגַּנֵּ֥ב הָעָ֛ם בַּיּ֥וֹם הַה֖וּא לָב֣וֹא הָעִ֑יר כַּאֲשֶׁ֣ר יִתְגַּנֵּ֗ב הָעָם֙ הַנִּכְלָמִ֔ים בְּנוּסָ֖ם בַּמִּלְחָמָֽה׃ 5 וְהַמֶּ֙לֶךְ֙ לָאַ֣ט אֶת־פָּנָ֔יו וַיִּזְעַ֥ק הַמֶּ֖לֶךְ ק֣וֹל גָּד֑וֹל בְּנִי֙ אַבְשָׁל֔וֹם אַבְשָׁל֖וֹם בְּנִ֥י בְנִֽי׃ ס

6 וַיָּבֹ֥א יוֹאָ֛ב אֶל־הַמֶּ֖לֶךְ הַבָּ֑יִת וַיֹּאמֶר֩ הֹבַ֨שְׁתָּ הַיּ֜וֹם אֶת־פְּנֵ֣י כׇל־עֲבָדֶ֗יךָ הַֽמְמַלְּטִ֤ים אֶֽת־נַפְשְׁךָ֙ הַיּ֔וֹם וְאֵ֡ת נֶ֩פֶשׁ֩ בָּנֶ֨יךָ וּבְנֹתֶ֜יךָ וְנֶ֤פֶשׁ נָשֶׁ֙יךָ֙ וְנֶ֣פֶשׁ פִּלַגְשֶׁ֔יךָ׃ 7 לְאַֽהֲבָה֙ אֶת־שֹׂ֣נְאֶ֔יךָ וְלִשְׂנֹ֖א אֶת־אֹֽהֲבֶ֑יךָ כִּ֣י ׀ הִגַּ֣דְתָּ הַיּ֗וֹם כִּ֣י אֵ֤ין לְךָ֙ שָׂרִ֣ים וַעֲבָדִ֔ים

officers and men mean nothing to you. I am sure that if Absalom were alive today and the rest of us dead, you would have preferred it. [8]Now arise, come out and placate your followers! For I swear by the LORD that if[c] you do not come out, not a single man will remain with you overnight; and that would be a greater disaster for you than any disaster that has befallen you from your youth until now." [9]So the king arose and sat down in the gateway; and when all the troops were told that the king was sitting in the gateway, all the troops presented themselves to the king.

Now the Israelites had fled to their homes. [10]All the people throughout the tribes of Israel were arguing: Some said, "The king saved us from the hands of our enemies, and he delivered us from the hands of the Philistines; and just now he had to flee the country because of Absalom. [11]But Absalom, whom we anointed over us, has died in battle; why then do you sit idle instead of escorting the king back?" [12]The talk of all Israel reached the king in his quarters. So King David sent this message to the priests Zadok and Abiathar: "Speak to the elders of Judah and say, 'Why should you be the last to bring the king back to his palace? [13]You are my kinsmen, my own flesh and blood! Why should you be the last to escort the king back?' [14]And to Amasa say this, 'You are my own flesh and blood. May God do thus and more to me if you do not become my army commander permanently in place of Joab!'" [15]So [Amasa] swayed the hearts of all the Judites as one man; and they sent a message to the king: "Come back with all your followers."

[16]The king started back and arrived at the Jordan; and the Judites went to Gilgal to meet the king and to conduct the king across the Jordan. [17]Shimei son of Gera, the Benjaminite from

כִּי | יָדַ֨עְתִּי הַיּ֜וֹם כִּ֣י לֹ֣א לֽוּ־אַבְשָׁל֥וֹם חַי֙ וְכֻלָּ֤נוּ הַיּוֹם֙ מֵתִ֔ים כִּי־אָ֖ז יָשָׁ֥ר בְּעֵינֶֽיךָ׃ [8]וְעַתָּ֤ה ק֙וּם צֵ֔א וְדַבֵּ֖ר עַל־לֵ֣ב עֲבָדֶ֑יךָ כִּי֩ בַיהֹוָ֨ה נִשְׁבַּ֜עְתִּי כִּֽי־אֵינְךָ֣ יוֹצֵ֗א אִם־יָלִ֨ין אִ֤ישׁ אִתְּךָ֙ הַלַּ֔יְלָה וְרָעָ֧ה לְךָ֣ זֹ֗את מִכׇּל־הָרָעָה֙ אֲשֶׁר־בָּ֣אָה עָלֶ֔יךָ מִנְּעֻרֶ֖יךָ עַד־עָֽתָּה׃ ס [9]וַיָּ֥קׇם הַמֶּ֖לֶךְ וַיֵּ֣שֶׁב בַּשָּׁ֑עַר וּֽלְכׇל־הָעָ֞ם הִגִּ֣ידוּ לֵאמֹ֗ר הִנֵּ֤ה הַמֶּ֙לֶךְ֙ יוֹשֵׁ֣ב בַּשַּׁ֔עַר וַיָּבֹ֤א כׇל־הָעָם֙ לִפְנֵ֣י הַמֶּ֔לֶךְ וְיִשְׂרָאֵ֔ל נָ֖ס אִ֥ישׁ לְאֹהָלָֽיו׃ ס [10]וַיְהִ֤י כׇל־הָעָם֙ נָד֔וֹן בְּכׇל־שִׁבְטֵ֥י יִשְׂרָאֵ֖ל לֵאמֹ֑ר הַמֶּ֜לֶךְ הִצִּילָ֣נוּ | מִכַּ֣ף אֹיְבֵ֗ינוּ וְה֤וּא מִלְּטָ֙נוּ֙ מִכַּ֣ף פְּלִשְׁתִּ֔ים וְעַתָּ֛ה בָּרַ֥ח מִן־הָאָ֖רֶץ מֵעַ֥ל אַבְשָׁלֽוֹם׃ [11]וְאַבְשָׁלוֹם֙ אֲשֶׁ֣ר מָשַׁ֣חְנוּ עָלֵ֔ינוּ מֵ֖ת בַּמִּלְחָמָ֑ה וְעַתָּ֗ה לָמָ֥ה אַתֶּ֛ם מַחֲרִשִׁ֖ים לְהָשִׁ֥יב אֶת־הַמֶּֽלֶךְ׃ ס [12]וְהַמֶּ֣לֶךְ דָּוִ֗ד שָׁ֠לַ֠ח אֶל־צָד֨וֹק וְאֶל־אֶבְיָתָ֥ר הַכֹּהֲנִים֮ לֵאמֹר֒ דַּבְּר֞וּ אֶל־זִקְנֵ֤י יְהוּדָה֙ לֵאמֹ֔ר לָ֤מָּה תִֽהְיוּ֙ אַחֲרֹנִ֔ים לְהָשִׁ֥יב אֶת־הַמֶּ֖לֶךְ אֶל־בֵּית֑וֹ וּדְבַר֙ כׇּל־יִשְׂרָאֵ֔ל בָּ֥א אֶל־הַמֶּ֖לֶךְ אֶל־בֵּיתֽוֹ׃ [13]אַחַ֣י אַתֶּ֔ם עַצְמִ֥י וּבְשָׂרִ֖י אַתֶּ֑ם וְלָ֧מָּה תִֽהְי֛וּ אַחֲרֹנִ֖ים לְהָשִׁ֥יב אֶת־הַמֶּֽלֶךְ׃ [14]וְלַֽעֲמָשָׂא֙ תֹּֽמְרוּ֙ הֲל֨וֹא עַצְמִ֥י וּבְשָׂרִ֖י אָ֑תָּה כֹּ֣ה יַעֲשֶׂה־לִּ֤י אֱלֹהִים֙ וְכֹ֣ה יוֹסִ֔יף אִם־לֹ֥א שַׂר־צָבָ֛א תִּֽהְיֶ֥ה לְפָנַ֖י כׇּל־הַיָּמִ֑ים תַּ֖חַת יוֹאָֽב׃ [15]וַיַּ֛ט אֶת־לְבַ֥ב כׇּל־אִישׁ־יְהוּדָ֖ה כְּאִ֣ישׁ אֶחָ֑ד וַֽיִּשְׁלְחוּ֙ אֶל־הַמֶּ֔לֶךְ שׁ֖וּב אַתָּ֥ה וְכׇל־עֲבָדֶֽיךָ׃ [16]וַיָּ֣שׇׁב הַמֶּ֔לֶךְ וַיָּבֹ֖א עַד־הַיַּרְדֵּ֑ן וִיהוּדָ֞ה בָּ֣א הַגִּלְגָּ֗לָה לָלֶ֙כֶת֙ לִקְרַ֣את הַמֶּ֔לֶךְ לְהַעֲבִ֥יר אֶת־הַמֶּ֖לֶךְ אֶת־הַיַּרְדֵּֽן׃ [17]וַיְמַהֵ֗ר שִׁמְעִ֤י בֶן־גֵּרָא֙ בֶּן־הַיְמִינִ֔י אֲשֶׁ֖ר מִבַּחוּרִ֑ים

c   So Septuagint, 4QSam[a], and some other Heb. mss., and an ancient masoretic tradition; ordinary texts omit "if."

Bahurim, hurried down with the Judites to meet King David, [18]accompanied by a thousand Benjaminites. [d]And Ziba, the servant of the House of Saul, together with his fifteen sons and twenty slaves, rushed down to the Jordan ahead of the king [19]while the crossing was being made, to escort the king's family over, and to do whatever he wished. Shimei son of Gera flung himself before the king as he was about to cross the Jordan. [20]He said to the king, "Let not my lord hold me guilty, and do not remember the wrong your servant committed on the day my lord the king left Jerusalem; let Your Majesty give it no thought. [21]For your servant knows that he has sinned; so here I have come down today, the first of all the House of Joseph, to meet my lord the king." [22]Thereupon Abishai son of Zeruiah spoke up, "Shouldn't Shimei be put to death for that—insulting the Lord's anointed?" [23]But David said, [e-]"What has this to do with you,[-e] you sons of Zeruiah, that you should cross me today? Should a single Israelite be put to death today? Don't I[f] know that today I am again king over Israel?" [24]Then the king said to Shimei, "You shall not die"; and the king gave him his oath.

[25]Mephibosheth, the grandson of Saul, also came down to meet the king. He had not pared his toenails, or trimmed his mustache, or washed his clothes from the day that the king left until the day he returned safe. [26]When he [g-]came [from][-g] Jerusalem to meet the king, the king asked him, "Why didn't you come with me, Mephibosheth?" [27]He replied, "My lord the king, my own servant[h] deceived me. [i-]Your servant planned to saddle his ass and ride[-i] on it and go with Your Majesty—for your servant is lame. [28][Ziba] has slandered your servant to my

וַיֵּרֶד עִם־אִישׁ יְהוּדָה לִקְרַאת הַמֶּלֶךְ דָּוִד׃
18 וְאֶלֶף אִישׁ עִמּוֹ מִבִּנְיָמִן וְצִיבָא נַעַר בֵּית שָׁאוּל וַחֲמֵשֶׁת עָשָׂר בָּנָיו וְעֶשְׂרִים עֲבָדָיו אִתּוֹ וְצָלְחוּ הַיַּרְדֵּן לִפְנֵי הַמֶּלֶךְ׃
19 וְעָבְרָה הָעֲבָרָה לַעֲבִיר אֶת־בֵּית הַמֶּלֶךְ וְלַעֲשׂוֹת הַטּוֹב בעיניו וְשִׁמְעִי בֶן־גֵּרָא נָפַל לִפְנֵי הַמֶּלֶךְ בְּעָבְרוֹ בַּיַּרְדֵּן׃
20 וַיֹּאמֶר אֶל־הַמֶּלֶךְ אַל־יַחֲשָׁב־לִי אֲדֹנִי עָוֹן וְאַל־תִּזְכֹּר אֵת אֲשֶׁר הֶעֱוָה עַבְדְּךָ בַּיּוֹם אֲשֶׁר־יָצָא* אֲדֹנִי־הַמֶּלֶךְ מִירוּשָׁלָ͏ִם לָשׂוּם הַמֶּלֶךְ אֶל־לִבּוֹ׃ 21 כִּי יָדַע עַבְדְּךָ כִּי אֲנִי חָטָאתִי וְהִנֵּה־בָאתִי הַיּוֹם רִאשׁוֹן לְכָל־בֵּית יוֹסֵף לָרֶדֶת לִקְרַאת אֲדֹנִי הַמֶּלֶךְ׃ ס 22 וַיַּעַן אֲבִישַׁי בֶּן־צְרוּיָה וַיֹּאמֶר הֲתַחַת זֹאת לֹא יוּמַת שִׁמְעִי כִּי קִלֵּל אֶת־מְשִׁיחַ יְהוָה׃ ס 23 וַיֹּאמֶר דָּוִד מַה־לִּי וְלָכֶם בְּנֵי צְרוּיָה כִּי־תִהְיוּ־לִי הַיּוֹם לְשָׂטָן הַיּוֹם יוּמַת אִישׁ בְּיִשְׂרָאֵל כִּי הֲלוֹא יָדַעְתִּי כִּי הַיּוֹם אֲנִי־מֶלֶךְ עַל־יִשְׂרָאֵל׃ 24 וַיֹּאמֶר הַמֶּלֶךְ אֶל־שִׁמְעִי לֹא תָמוּת וַיִּשָּׁבַע לוֹ הַמֶּלֶךְ׃ ס
25 וּמְפִבֹשֶׁת בֶּן־שָׁאוּל יָרַד לִקְרַאת הַמֶּלֶךְ וְלֹא־עָשָׂה רַגְלָיו וְלֹא־עָשָׂה שְׂפָמוֹ וְאֶת־בְּגָדָיו לֹא כִבֵּס לְמִן־הַיּוֹם לֶכֶת הַמֶּלֶךְ עַד־הַיּוֹם אֲשֶׁר־בָּא בְשָׁלוֹם׃ 26 וַיְהִי כִּי־בָא יְרוּשָׁלַ͏ִם לִקְרַאת הַמֶּלֶךְ וַיֹּאמֶר לוֹ הַמֶּלֶךְ לָמָּה לֹא־הָלַכְתָּ עִמִּי מְפִיבֹשֶׁת׃ 27 וַיֹּאמַר אֲדֹנִי הַמֶּלֶךְ עַבְדִּי רִמָּנִי כִּי־אָמַר עַבְדְּךָ אֶחְבְּשָׁה־לִּי הַחֲמוֹר וְאֶרְכַּב עָלֶיהָ וְאֵלֵךְ אֶת־הַמֶּלֶךְ כִּי פִסֵּחַ עַבְדֶּךָ׃ 28 וַיְרַגֵּל בְּעַבְדְּךָ אֶל־אֲדֹנִי הַמֶּלֶךְ וַאדֹנִי הַמֶּלֶךְ

v. 20. נקוד על י׳ צ׳ א׳

---

d   Meaning of parts of the rest of vv. 18 and 19 uncertain.
e-e   See note at 16.10.
f   Some Septuagint mss. read "you."
g-g   So Septuagint. Heb. "entered."
h   I.e., Ziba (cf. v. 30 and 9.2 ff.).
i-i   Ancient versions read "Your servant said to him, 'Saddle my ass, that I may ride…'"

lord the king. But my lord the king is like an angel of the Lord; do as you see fit. ²⁹For all the members of my father's family deserved only death from my lord the king; yet you set your servant among those who ate at your table. What right have I to appeal further to Your Majesty?" ³⁰The king said to him, "You need not speak further. I decree that you and Ziba shall divide the property." ³¹And Mephibosheth said to the king, "Let him take it all, as long as my lord the king has come home safe."

³²Barzillai the Gileadite had come down from Rogelin and *j*-passed on to the Jordan with the king, to see him off at-*j* the Jordan. ³³Barzillai was very old, eighty years of age; and he had provided the king with food during his stay at Mahanaim, for he was a very wealthy man. ³⁴The king said to Barzillai, "Cross over with me, and I will provide for you in Jerusalem at my side." ³⁵But Barzillai said to the king, "How many years are left to me that I should go up with Your Majesty to Jerusalem? ³⁶I am now eighty years old. Can I tell the difference between good and bad? Can your servant taste what he eats and drinks? Can I still listen to the singing of men and women? Why then should your servant continue to be a burden to my lord the king? ³⁷*j*-Your servant could barely cross the Jordan-*j* with your Majesty! Why should Your Majesty reward me so generously? ³⁸Let your servant go back, and let me die in my own town, near the graves of my father and mother. But here is your servant Chimham; let him cross with my lord the king, and do for him as you see fit." ³⁹And the king said, "Chimham shall cross with me, and I will do for him as you see fit; and anything you want me to do, I will do for you."

^{40k}All the troops crossed the Jordan; and when the king was ready to cross, the king kissed

כְּמַלְאַ֥ךְ הָאֱלֹהִ֖ים וַעֲשֵׂ֥ה הַטּ֖וֹב בְּעֵינֶֽיךָ׃ ²⁹ כִּ֣י לֹא֩ הָיָ֨ה כָּל־בֵּ֤ית אָבִי֙ כִּ֣י אִם־אַנְשֵׁי־מָ֙וֶת֙ לַאדֹנִ֣י הַמֶּ֔לֶךְ וַתָּ֙שֶׁת֙ אֶֽת־עַבְדְּךָ֔ בְּאֹכְלֵ֖י שֻׁלְחָנֶ֑ךָ וּמַה־יֶּשׁ־לִ֥י עוֹד֙ צְדָקָ֔ה וְלִזְעֹ֥ק ע֖וֹד אֶל־הַמֶּֽלֶךְ׃ פ ³⁰ וַיֹּ֤אמֶר לוֹ֙ הַמֶּ֔לֶךְ לָ֛מָּה תְּדַבֵּ֥ר ע֖וֹד דְּבָרֶ֑יךָ אָמַ֔רְתִּי אַתָּ֣ה וְצִיבָ֔א תַּחְלְק֖וּ אֶת־הַשָּׂדֶֽה׃ ³¹ וַיֹּ֤אמֶר מְפִיבֹ֙שֶׁת֙ אֶל־הַמֶּ֔לֶךְ גַּ֥ם אֶת־הַכֹּ֖ל יִקָּ֑ח אַ֠חֲרֵי אֲשֶׁר־בָּ֞א אֲדֹנִ֥י הַמֶּ֛לֶךְ בְּשָׁל֖וֹם אֶל־בֵּיתֽוֹ׃ ס

³² וּבַרְזִלַּי֙ הַגִּלְעָדִ֔י יָרַ֖ד מֵרֹגְלִ֑ים וַיַּעֲבֹ֤ר אֶת־הַמֶּ֙לֶךְ֙ הַיַּרְדֵּ֔ן לְשַׁלְּח֖וֹ אֶת־הַיַּרְדֵּֽן׃ ³³ וּבַרְזִלַּי֙ זָקֵ֣ן מְאֹ֔ד בֶּן־שְׁמֹנִ֖ים שָׁנָ֑ה וְהֽוּא־כִלְכַּ֤ל אֶת־הַמֶּ֙לֶךְ֙ בְשִׁיבָת֣וֹ בְמַחֲנַ֔יִם כִּֽי־אִ֥ישׁ גָּד֛וֹל ה֖וּא מְאֹֽד׃ ³⁴ וַיֹּ֥אמֶר הַמֶּ֖לֶךְ אֶל־בַּרְזִלָּ֑י אַתָּה֙ עֲבֹ֣ר אִתִּ֔י וְכִלְכַּלְתִּ֥י אֹתְךָ֛ עִמָּדִ֖י בִּירוּשָׁלָֽ͏ִם׃ ³⁵ וַיֹּ֥אמֶר בַּרְזִלַּ֖י אֶל־הַמֶּ֑לֶךְ כַּמָּ֗ה יְמֵי֙ שְׁנֵ֣י חַיַּ֔י כִּֽי־אֶעֱלֶ֥ה אֶת־הַמֶּ֖לֶךְ יְרוּשָׁלָֽ͏ִם׃ ³⁶ בֶּן־שְׁמֹנִ֣ים שָׁנָה֩ אָנֹכִ֨י הַיּ֜וֹם הַאֵדַ֣ע ׀ בֵּֽין־ט֣וֹב לְרָ֗ע אִם־יִטְעַ֤ם עַבְדְּךָ֙ אֶת־אֲשֶׁ֤ר אֹכַל֙ וְאֶת־אֲשֶׁ֣ר אֶשְׁתֶּ֔ה אִם־אֶשְׁמַ֣ע ע֔וֹד בְּק֖וֹל שָׁרִ֣ים וְשָׁר֑וֹת וְלָ֧מָּה יִֽהְיֶ֣ה עַבְדְּךָ֗ עוֹד֙ לְמַשָּׂ֔א אֶל־אֲדֹנִ֖י הַמֶּֽלֶךְ׃ ³⁷ כִּמְעַ֞ט יַעֲבֹ֤ר עַבְדְּךָ֙ אֶת־הַיַּרְדֵּ֔ן אֶת־הַמֶּ֑לֶךְ וְלָ֙מָּה֙ יִגְמְלֵ֣נִי הַמֶּ֔לֶךְ הַגְּמוּלָ֖ה הַזֹּֽאת׃ ³⁸ יָֽשָׁב־נָ֤א עַבְדְּךָ֙ וְאָמֻ֣ת בְּעִירִ֔י עִ֛ם קֶ֥בֶר אָבִ֖י וְאִמִּ֑י וְהִנֵּ֣ה ׀ עַבְדְּךָ֣ כִמְהָ֗ם יַֽעֲבֹר֙ עִם־אֲדֹנִ֣י הַמֶּ֔לֶךְ וַעֲשֵׂה־ל֕וֹ אֵ֥ת אֲשֶׁר־ט֖וֹב בְּעֵינֶֽיךָ׃ ³⁹ וַיֹּ֣אמֶר הַמֶּ֗לֶךְ אִתִּי֙ יַעֲבֹ֣ר כִּמְהָ֔ם וַאֲנִי֙ אֶעֱשֶׂה־לּ֔וֹ אֶת־הַטּ֖וֹב בְּעֵינֶ֑יךָ וְכֹ֛ל אֲשֶׁר־תִּבְחַ֥ר עָלַ֖י אֶֽעֱשֶׂה־לָּֽךְ׃ ⁴⁰ וַיַּעֲבֹ֧ר כָּל־הָעָ֛ם אֶת־הַיַּרְדֵּ֖ן וְהַמֶּ֣לֶךְ עָבָ֑ר וַיִּשַּׁ֨ק הַמֶּ֤לֶךְ לְבַרְזִלַּי֙ וַיְבָ֣רֲכֵ֔הוּ

---

j-j Meaning of Heb. uncertain.
k Meaning of parts of vv. 40–44 uncertain.

689

Barzillai and bade him farewell; and [Barzillai] returned to his home. ⁴¹The king passed on to Gilgal, with Chimham*l* accompanying him; and all the Judite soldiers and part of the Israelite army escorted the king across.

⁴²Then all the men of Israel came to the king and said to the king, "Why did our kinsmen, the men of Judah, steal you away and escort the king and his family across the Jordan, along with all David's men?" ⁴³All the men of Judah replied to the men of Israel, "Because the king is our relative! Why should this upset you? Have we consumed anything that belongs to the king? Has he given us any gifts?" ⁴⁴But the men of Israel answered the men of Judah, "We have ten shares in the king, and *m*-in David, too, we have more than you.*-m* Why then have you slighted us? Were we not the first to propose that our king be brought back?" However, the men of Judah prevailed over the men of Israel.

20

A scoundrel named Sheba son of Bichri, a Benjaminite, happened to be there. He sounded the horn and proclaimed:

"We have no portion in David,
No share in Jesse's son!
Every man to his tent, O Israel!"

²All the men of Israel left David and followed Sheba son of Bichri; but the men of Judah accompanied their king from the Jordan to Jerusalem. ³David went to his palace in Jerusalem, and the king took the ten concubines he had left to mind the palace and put them in a guarded place; he provided for them, but he did not cohabit with them. They remained in seclusion until the day they died, in living widowhood.

⁴The king said to Amasa, "Call up the men of Judah to my standard, and report here three days from now." ⁵Amasa went to call up Judah,

וַיֵּשֶׁב לִמְקֹמוֹ: ס ⁴¹וַיַּעֲבֹר הַמֶּלֶךְ
הַגִּלְגָּלָה וְכִמְהָן עָבַר עִמּוֹ וְכָל־עַם יְהוּדָה
וַיַּעֲבִרוּ אֶת־הַמֶּלֶךְ וְגַם חֲצִי עַם
יִשְׂרָאֵל:

⁴²וְהִנֵּה כָּל־אִישׁ יִשְׂרָאֵל בָּאִים אֶל־הַמֶּלֶךְ
וַיֹּאמְרוּ אֶל־הַמֶּלֶךְ מַדּוּעַ גְּנָבוּךָ אַחֵינוּ
אִישׁ יְהוּדָה וַיַּעֲבִרוּ אֶת־הַמֶּלֶךְ וְאֶת־
בֵּיתוֹ אֶת־הַיַּרְדֵּן וְכָל־אַנְשֵׁי דָוִד עִמּוֹ: ס ⁴³וַיַּעַן כָּל־אִישׁ יְהוּדָה עַל־אִישׁ יִשְׂרָאֵל
כִּי־קָרוֹב הַמֶּלֶךְ אֵלַי וְלָמָּה זֶּה חָרָה לְךָ
עַל־הַדָּבָר הַזֶּה הֶאָכוֹל אָכַלְנוּ מִן־הַמֶּלֶךְ
אִם־נִשֵּׂאת נִשָּׂא לָנוּ: ס ⁴⁴וַיַּעַן אִישׁ־
יִשְׂרָאֵל אֶת־אִישׁ יְהוּדָה וַיֹּאמֶר עֶשֶׂר
יָדוֹת לִי בַמֶּלֶךְ וְגַם־בְּדָוִד אֲנִי מִמְּךָ
וּמַדּוּעַ הֱקִלֹּתַנִי וְלֹא־הָיָה דְבָרִי רִאשׁוֹן
לִי לְהָשִׁיב אֶת־מַלְכִּי וַיִּקֶשׁ דְּבַר־אִישׁ
יְהוּדָה מִדְּבַר אִישׁ יִשְׂרָאֵל: ס

כ ¹וְשָׁם נִקְרָא אִישׁ בְּלִיַּעַל וּשְׁמוֹ שֶׁבַע
בֶּן־בִּכְרִי אִישׁ יְמִינִי וַיִּתְקַע בַּשֹּׁפָר וַיֹּאמֶר
אֵין־לָנוּ חֵלֶק בְּדָוִד
וְלֹא נַחֲלָה־לָנוּ בְּבֶן־יִשַׁי
אִישׁ לְאֹהָלָיו יִשְׂרָאֵל:

²וַיַּעַל כָּל־אִישׁ יִשְׂרָאֵל מֵאַחֲרֵי דָוִד
אַחֲרֵי שֶׁבַע בֶּן־בִּכְרִי וְאִישׁ יְהוּדָה דָּבְקוּ
בְמַלְכָּם מִן־הַיַּרְדֵּן וְעַד־יְרוּשָׁלָםִ: ³וַיָּבֹא
דָוִד אֶל־בֵּיתוֹ יְרוּשָׁלַםִ וַיִּקַּח הַמֶּלֶךְ אֵת
עֶשֶׂר־נָשִׁים ׀ פִּלַגְשִׁים אֲשֶׁר הִנִּיחַ לִשְׁמֹר
הַבַּיִת וַיִּתְּנֵם בֵּית־מִשְׁמֶרֶת וַיְכַלְכְּלֵם
וַאֲלֵיהֶם לֹא־בָא וַתִּהְיֶינָה צְרֻרוֹת עַד־יוֹם
מֻתָן אַלְמְנוּת חַיּוּת: ס

⁴וַיֹּאמֶר הַמֶּלֶךְ אֶל־עֲמָשָׂא הַזְעֶק־לִי אֶת־
אִישׁ־יְהוּדָה שְׁלֹשֶׁת יָמִים וְאַתָּה פֹּה
עֲמֹד: ⁵וַיֵּלֶךְ עֲמָשָׂא לְהַזְעִיק אֶת־יְהוּדָה

---

l Heb. Chimham.
m-m Septuagint reads "we are the first-born, rather than you."

but he took longer than the time set for him.
⁶And David said to Abishai, "Now Sheba son of Bichri will cause us more trouble than Absalom. So take your lord's servants and pursue him, before he finds fortified towns and ᵃ-eludes us."-ᵃ ⁷ᵇ-Joab's men, the Cherethites and Pelethites, and all the warriors, marched out behind him.-ᵇ They left Jerusalem in pursuit of Sheba son of Bichri. ⁸They were near the great stone in Gibeon when Amasa appeared before them. ᵃ-Joab was wearing his military dress, with his sword girded over it and fastened around his waist in its sheath; and, as he stepped forward, it fell out.-ᵃ ⁹Joab said to Amasa, "How are you, brother?" and with his right hand Joab took hold of Amasa's beard as if to kiss him. ¹⁰Amasa was not on his guard against the sword in Joab's [left] hand, and [Joab] drove it into his belly so that his entrails poured out on the ground and he died; he did not need to strike him a second time.

Joab and his brother Abishai then set off in pursuit of Sheba son of Bichri, ¹¹while one of Joab's henchmen stood by ᶜ-the corpse-ᶜ and called out, "Whoever favors Joab, and whoever is on David's side, follow Joab!" ¹²Amasa lay in the middle of the road, drenched in his blood; and the man saw that everyone stopped. And when he saw that all the people were stopping, he dragged Amasa from the road into the field and covered him with a garment. ¹³Once he was removed from the road, everybody continued to follow Joab in pursuit of Sheba son of Bichri. ¹⁴[Sheba] had passed through all the tribes of Israel up to Abel ofᵈ Beth-maacah; and all the Beeritesᵉ assembled and followed him inside. ¹⁵[Joab's men] came and besieged him in Abel of Beth-maacah; they threw up a siegemound

---

ס וַיִּיחַר וַיּ֨וֹחֶר֙ מִן־הַמּוֹעֵ֔ד אֲשֶׁ֖ר יְעָדֽוֹ׃
⁶ וַיֹּ֤אמֶר דָּוִד֙ אֶל־אֲבִישַׁ֔י עַתָּ֗ה יֵ֧רַֽע לָ֛נוּ שֶׁ֥בַע בֶּן־בִּכְרִ֖י מִן־אַבְשָׁל֑וֹם אַתָּ֡ה קַ֣ח אֶת־עַבְדֵ֣י אֲדֹנֶיךָ֩ וּרְדֹ֨ף אַחֲרָ֜יו פֶּן־מָ֥צָא ל֛וֹ עָרִ֥ים בְּצֻר֖וֹת וְהִצִּ֥יל עֵינֵֽנוּ׃ ⁷ וַיֵּצְא֣וּ אַחֲרָ֗יו אַנְשֵׁ֤י יוֹאָב֙ וְהַכְּרֵתִ֣י וְהַפְּלֵתִ֔י וְכָל־הַגִּבֹּרִ֑ים וַיֵּֽצְאוּ֙ מִיר֣וּשָׁלִַ֔ם לִרְדֹּ֕ף אַחֲרֵ֖י שֶׁ֥בַע בֶּן־בִּכְרִֽי׃ ⁸ הֵ֗ם עִם־הָאֶ֤בֶן הַגְּדוֹלָה֙ אֲשֶׁ֣ר בְּגִבְע֔וֹן וַעֲמָשָׂ֖א בָּ֣א לִפְנֵיהֶ֑ם וְיוֹאָ֞ב חָג֣וּר ׀ מִדּ֣וֹ לְבֻשׁ֗וֹ וְעָלָ֞יו חֲג֣וֹר חֶ֨רֶב֙ מְצֻמֶּ֤דֶת עַל־מָתְנָיו֙ בְּתַעְרָ֔הּ וְה֥וּא יָצָ֖א וַתִּפֹּֽל׃ ס ⁹ וַיֹּ֤אמֶר יוֹאָב֙ לַעֲמָשָׂ֔א הֲשָׁל֥וֹם אַתָּ֖ה אָחִ֑י וַתֹּ֜חֶז* יַד־יְמִ֥ין יוֹאָ֛ב בִּזְקַ֥ן עֲמָשָׂ֖א לִנְשָׁק־לֽוֹ׃ ¹⁰ וַעֲמָשָׂ֡א לֹֽא־נִשְׁמַ֣ר בַּחֶ֣רֶב ׀ אֲשֶׁ֣ר בְּיַד־יוֹאָ֡ב וַיַּכֵּהוּ֩ בָ֨הּ אֶל־הַחֹ֜מֶשׁ וַיִּשְׁפֹּ֤ךְ מֵעָיו֙ אַ֔רְצָה וְלֹא־שָׁ֥נָה ל֖וֹ וַיָּמֹ֑ת ס וְיוֹאָב֙ וַאֲבִישַׁ֣י אָחִ֔יו רָדַ֕ף אַחֲרֵ֖י שֶׁ֥בַע בֶּן־בִּכְרִֽי׃ ¹¹ וְאִישׁ֙ עָמַ֣ד עָלָ֔יו מִנַּעֲרֵ֖י יוֹאָ֑ב וַיֹּ֗אמֶר מִ֣י אֲשֶׁ֤ר חָפֵץ֙ בְּיוֹאָ֔ב וּמִ֥י אֲשֶׁר־לְדָוִ֖ד אַחֲרֵ֥י יוֹאָֽב׃ ¹² וַעֲמָשָׂ֤א מִתְגֹּלֵל֙ בַּדָּ֔ם בְּת֖וֹךְ הַֽמְסִלָּ֑ה וַיַּ֨רְא הָאִ֜ישׁ כִּֽי־עָמַ֣ד כָּל־הָעָ֗ם וַיַּסֵּב֩ אֶת־עֲמָשָׂ֨א מִן־הַֽמְסִלָּ֤ה הַשָּׂדֶה֙ וַיַּשְׁלֵ֤ךְ עָלָיו֙ בֶּ֔גֶד כַּאֲשֶׁ֣ר רָאָ֔ה כָּֽל־הַבָּ֥א עָלָ֖יו וְעָמָֽד׃ ¹³ כַּאֲשֶׁ֤ר הֹגָה֙ מִן־הַֽמְסִלָּ֔ה עָבַ֧ר כָּל־אִ֛ישׁ אַחֲרֵ֥י יוֹאָ֖ב לִרְדֹּ֕ף אַחֲרֵ֖י שֶׁ֥בַע בֶּן־בִּכְרִֽי׃ ¹⁴ וַֽיַּעֲבֹ֞ר בְּכָל־שִׁבְטֵ֣י יִשְׂרָאֵ֗ל אָבֵ֛לָה וּבֵ֥ית מַעֲכָ֖ה וְכָל־הַבֵּרִ֑ים ס ויקלהו וַיִּקָּ֣הֲל֔וּ וַיָּבֹ֖אוּ אַף־אַחֲרָֽיו׃ ¹⁵ וַיָּבֹ֗אוּ וַיָּצֻ֤רוּ עָלָיו֙ בְּאָבֵ֙לָה֙

חסר א׳   v. 9.

---

a-a Meaning of Heb. uncertain.
b-b Emendation yields "Joab, the Cherethites and Pelethites, and all the warriors marched out behind Abishai."
c-c Heb. "him."
d Heb. "and." Cf. v. 15 (and "Abel-beth-maacah" in 1 Kings 15.20 and 2 Kings 15.29).
e Emendation yields "Bichrites"; cf. Septuagint.

against the city *f*-and it stood against the rampart.-*f*

All the troops with Joab were *g*-engaged in battering the wall,-*g* 16when a clever woman shouted from the city, "Listen! Listen! Tell Joab to come over here so I can talk to him." 17He approached her, and the woman asked, "Are you Joab?" "Yes," he answered; and she said to him, "Listen to what your handmaid has to say." "I'm listening," he replied. 18And she continued, "In olden times people used to say, *a*-'Let them inquire of Abel,'-*a* and that was the end of the matter. 19I am one of those who seek the welfare of the faithful in Israel. But you seek to bring death upon a mother city in Israel! Why should you destroy the LORD's possession?" 20Joab replied, "Far be it, far be it from me to destroy or to ruin! 21Not at all! But a certain man from the hill country of Ephraim, named Sheba son of Bichri, has rebelled against King David. Just hand him alone over to us, and I will withdraw from the city." The woman assured Joab, "His head shall be thrown over the wall to you." 22The woman came to all the people with her clever plan; and they cut off the head of Sheba son of Bichri and threw it down to Joab. He then sounded the horn; all the men dispersed to their homes, and Joab returned to the king in Jerusalem.

23Joab was commander of the whole army [of] Israel; Benaiah son of Jehoiada was commander of the Cherethites and the Pelethites; 24Adoram*h* was in charge of forced labor; Jehoshaphat son of Ahilud was recorder; 25Sheva*i* was scribe; and Zadok and Abiathar were priests. 26Ira the Jairite also served David as priest.

בֵּית הַמַּעֲכָה וַיִּשְׁפְּכוּ סֹלְלָה אֶל־הָעִיר וַתַּעֲמֹד בַּחֵל וְכָל־הָעָם אֲשֶׁר אֶת־יוֹאָב מַשְׁחִיתִם לְהַפִּיל הַחוֹמָה: 16 וַתִּקְרָא אִשָּׁה חֲכָמָה מִן־הָעִיר שִׁמְעוּ שִׁמְעוּ אִמְרוּ־נָא אֶל־יוֹאָב קְרַב עַד־הֵנָּה וַאֲדַבְּרָה אֵלֶיךָ: 17 וַיִּקְרַב אֵלֶיהָ וַתֹּאמֶר הָאִשָּׁה הַאַתָּה יוֹאָב וַיֹּאמֶר אָנִי וַתֹּאמֶר לוֹ שְׁמַע דִּבְרֵי אֲמָתֶךָ וַיֹּאמֶר שֹׁמֵעַ אָנֹכִי: 18 וַתֹּאמֶר לֵאמֹר דַּבֵּר יְדַבְּרוּ בָרִאשֹׁנָה לֵאמֹר שָׁאֹל יְשָׁאֲלוּ בְּאָבֵל וְכֵן הֵתַמּוּ: 19 אָנֹכִי שְׁלֻמֵי אֱמוּנֵי יִשְׂרָאֵל אַתָּה מְבַקֵּשׁ לְהָמִית עִיר וְאֵם בְּיִשְׂרָאֵל לָמָּה תְבַלַּע נַחֲלַת יְהוָה: פ 20 וַיַּעַן יוֹאָב וַיֹּאמַר חָלִילָה חָלִילָה לִי אִם־אֲבַלַּע וְאִם־אַשְׁחִית: 21 לֹא־כֵן הַדָּבָר כִּי אִישׁ מֵהַר אֶפְרַיִם שֶׁבַע בֶּן־בִּכְרִי שְׁמוֹ נָשָׂא יָדוֹ בַּמֶּלֶךְ בְּדָוִד תְּנוּ־אֹתוֹ לְבַדּוֹ וְאֵלְכָה מֵעַל הָעִיר וַתֹּאמֶר הָאִשָּׁה אֶל־יוֹאָב הִנֵּה רֹאשׁוֹ מֻשְׁלָךְ אֵלֶיךָ בְּעַד הַחוֹמָה: 22 וַתָּבוֹא הָאִשָּׁה אֶל־כָּל־הָעָם בְּחָכְמָתָהּ וַיִּכְרְתוּ אֶת־רֹאשׁ שֶׁבַע בֶּן־בִּכְרִי וַיַּשְׁלִכוּ אֶל־יוֹאָב וַיִּתְקַע בַּשּׁוֹפָר וַיָּפֻצוּ מֵעַל־הָעִיר אִישׁ לְאֹהָלָיו וְיוֹאָב שָׁב יְרוּשָׁלִַם אֶל־הַמֶּלֶךְ: ס

23 וְיוֹאָב אֶל כָּל־הַצָּבָא יִשְׂרָאֵל וּבְנָיָה בֶן־יְהוֹיָדָע עַל־הכרי הַכְּרֵתִי וְעַל־הַפְּלֵתִי: 24 וַאֲדֹרָם עַל־הַמַּס וִיהוֹשָׁפָט בֶּן־אֲחִילוּד הַמַּזְכִּיר: 25 ושיא וּשְׁוָא סֹפֵר וְצָדוֹק וְאֶבְיָתָר כֹּהֲנִים: 26 וְגַם עִירָא הַיָּאִרִי הָיָה כֹהֵן לְדָוִד: ס

---

f-f Meaning of Heb. uncertain. The phrase would read well in the next verse ("…a clever woman stood on the rampart and shouted…").

g-g Lit. "destroying, to topple the wall." Septuagint and Targum read "were planning to topple the wall."

h So in 1 Kings 12.18 and 2 Chron. 10.18 ("Hadoram"); elsewhere "Adoniram."

i See note *j* at 8.17.

21

There was a famine during the reign of David, year after year for three years. David inquired of the LORD, and the LORD replied, "It is because of the bloodguilt of Saul and [his] house, for he put some Gibeonites to death." [2]The king summoned the Gibeonites and spoke to them.—Now the Gibeonites were not of Israelite stock, but a remnant of the Amorites, to whom the Israelites had given an oath; and Saul had tried to wipe them out in his zeal for the people of Israel and Judah.—[3]David asked the Gibeonites, "What shall I do for you? How shall I make expiation, so that you may bless the LORD's own people?" [4]The Gibeonites answered him, "We have no claim for silver or gold against Saul and his household; and we have no claim on the life of any other man in Israel." And [David] responded, "Whatever you say I will do for you." [5]Thereupon they said to the king, "The man who massacred us and planned to *a*-exterminate us, so that we-*a* should not survive in all the territory of Israel—[6]let seven of his male issue be handed over to us, and we will impale them before the LORD in *b*-Gibeah of Saul, the chosen of the LORD."-*b* And the king replied, "I will do so."

[7]The king spared Mephibosheth son of Jonathan son of Saul, because of the oath before the LORD between the two, between David and Jonathan son of Saul. [8]Instead, the king took Armoni and Mephibosheth, the two sons that Rizpah daughter of Aiah bore to Saul, and the five sons that Merab*c* daughter of Saul bore to Adriel son of Barzillai the Meholathite, [9]and he handed them over to the Gibeonites. They impaled them on the mountain before the LORD; all seven of them perished at the same time.

כא וַיְהִ֣י רָעָב֩ בִּימֵ֨י דָוִ֜ד שָׁלֹ֣שׁ שָׁנִ֗ים שָׁנָה֙ אַחֲרֵ֣י שָׁנָ֔ה וַיְבַקֵּ֥שׁ דָּוִ֖ד אֶת־פְּנֵ֣י יְהֹוָ֑ה ס וַיֹּ֣אמֶר יְהֹוָ֗ה אֶל־שָׁאוּל֙ וְאֶל־בֵּ֣ית הַדָּמִ֔ים עַל־אֲשֶׁר־הֵמִ֖ית אֶת־הַגִּבְעֹנִֽים: [2]וַיִּקְרָ֣א הַמֶּ֘לֶךְ֮ לַגִּבְעֹנִים֒ וַיֹּ֣אמֶר אֲלֵיהֶ֔ם וְהַגִּבְעֹנִ֗ים לֹ֤א מִבְּנֵ֤י יִשְׂרָאֵל֙ הֵ֔מָּה כִּ֚י אִם־מִיֶּ֣תֶר הָאֱמֹרִ֔י וּבְנֵ֣י יִשְׂרָאֵל֙ נִשְׁבְּע֣וּ לָהֶ֔ם וַיְבַקֵּ֤שׁ שָׁאוּל֙ לְהַכֹּתָ֔ם בְּקַנֹּאת֥וֹ לִבְנֵֽי־יִשְׂרָאֵ֖ל וִיהוּדָֽה: [3]וַיֹּ֤אמֶר דָּוִד֙ אֶל־הַגִּבְעֹנִ֔ים מָ֥ה אֶעֱשֶׂ֖ה לָכֶ֑ם וּבַמָּ֣ה אֲכַפֵּ֔ר וּבָרְכ֖וּ אֶת־נַחֲלַ֥ת יְהֹוָֽה: [4]וַיֹּ֧אמְרוּ ל֣וֹ הַגִּבְעֹנִ֗ים אֵֽין־לִ֤י כֶּ֤סֶף וְזָהָב֙ עִם־שָׁא֣וּל וְעִם־בֵּית֔וֹ וְאֵֽין־לָ֥נוּ אִ֖ישׁ לְהָמִ֣ית בְּיִשְׂרָאֵ֑ל וַיֹּ֛אמֶר מָֽה־אַתֶּ֥ם אֹמְרִ֖ים אֶעֱשֶׂ֥ה לָכֶֽם: [5]וַיֹּֽאמְרוּ֙ אֶל־הַמֶּ֔לֶךְ הָאִישׁ֙ אֲשֶׁ֣ר כִּלָּ֔נוּ וַאֲשֶׁ֖ר דִּמָּה־לָ֑נוּ נִשְׁמַ֕דְנוּ מֵֽהִתְיַצֵּ֖ב בְּכָל־גְּבֻ֥ל יִשְׂרָאֵֽל: [6]יֻתַּן־לָ֜נוּ שִׁבְעָ֤ה אֲנָשִׁים֙ מִבָּנָ֔יו וְהוֹקַֽעֲנוּם֙ לַֽיהֹוָ֔ה בְּגִבְעַ֥ת שָׁא֖וּל בְּחִ֣יר יְהֹוָ֑ה ס וַיֹּ֥אמֶר הַמֶּ֖לֶךְ אֲנִ֥י אֶתֵּֽן: [7]וַיַּחְמֹ֣ל הַמֶּ֔לֶךְ עַל־מְפִי־בֹ֖שֶׁת בֶּן־יְהוֹנָתָ֣ן בֶּן־שָׁא֑וּל עַל־שְׁבֻעַ֤ת יְהֹוָה֙ אֲשֶׁ֣ר בֵּֽינֹתָ֔ם בֵּ֣ין דָּוִ֔ד וּבֵ֖ין יְהוֹנָתָ֥ן בֶּן־שָׁאֽוּל: [8]וַיִּקַּ֣ח הַמֶּ֡לֶךְ אֶת־שְׁ֠נֵ֠י בְּנֵ֨י רִצְפָּ֤ה בַת־אַיָּה֙ אֲשֶׁ֣ר יָֽלְדָ֣ה לְשָׁא֔וּל אֶת־אַרְמֹנִ֖י וְאֶת־מְפִבֹ֑שֶׁת וְאֶת־חֲמֵ֗שֶׁת בְּנֵ֤י מִיכַל֙* בַּת־שָׁא֔וּל אֲשֶׁ֥ר יָלְדָ֛ה לְעַדְרִיאֵ֥ל בֶּן־בַּרְזִלַּ֖י הַמְּחֹלָתִֽי: [9]וַֽיִּתְּנֵ֞ם בְּיַ֣ד הַגִּבְעֹנִ֗ים וַיֹּקִיעֻ֤ם בָּהָר֙ לִפְנֵ֣י יְהֹוָ֔ה וַיִּפְּל֥וּ שְׁבַעְתָּ֖ם יָ֑חַד וְהֵ֨ם

---

a-a   *Meaning of Heb. uncertain.*
b-b   *Emendation yields "at Gibeon, on the mountain of the LORD"*
    (cf. Septuagint and v. 9).
c   *So two Heb. mss., many Septuagint mss., and Peshitta; and cf.*
    Targum, Sanhedrin 19b, and 1 Sam. 18.19. Most mss. and the
    printed editions read "Michal."

v. 8.   בנוסח אחר "מירב"

They were put to death in the first days of the harvest, the beginning of the barley harvest.

[10]Then Rizpah daughter of Aiah took sackcloth and spread it on a rock for herself, and she stayed there from the beginning of the harvest until rain from the sky fell on [d]-the bodies;-[d] she did not let the birds of the sky settle on them by day or the wild beasts [approach] by night. [11]David was told what Saul's concubine Rizpah daughter of Aiah had done. [12]And David went and took the bones of Saul and of his son Jonathan from the citizens of Jabesh-gilead, who had made off with them from the public square of Beth-shan, where the Philistines had hung them up on the day the Philistines killed Saul at Gilboa. [13]He brought up the bones of Saul and of his son Jonathan from there; and he gathered the bones of those who had been impaled. [14]And they buried the bones of Saul and of his son Jonathan[e] in Zela, in the territory of Benjamin, in the tomb of his father Kish. And when all that the king had commanded was done, God responded to the plea of the land thereafter.

[15]Again war broke out between the Philistines and Israel, and David and the men with him went down and fought the Philistines; David grew weary, [16]and [a]-Ishbi-benob-[a] tried to kill David.—He was a descendant of the Raphah;[f] his bronze spear weighed three hundred shekels and he wore new armor.—[17]But Abishai son of Zeruiah came to his aid; he attacked the Philistine and killed him. It was then that David's men declared to him on oath, "You shall not go with us into battle any more, lest you extinguish the lamp of Israel!"

[18g]After this, fighting broke out again with the Philistines, at Gob; that was when Sibbecai the Hushathite killed Saph, a descendant of the

וְהֵ֙מָּה֙ הֻמְת֔וּ בִּימֵ֥י קָצִ֖יר בָּרִֽאשֹׁנִ֑ים תְּחִלַּ֖ת תְּחִלַּ֖ת קְצִ֥יר שְׂעֹרִֽים׃

10 וַתִּקַּ֣ח רִצְפָּה֩ בַת־אַיָּ֨ה אֶת־הַשַּׂ֜ק וַתַּטֵּ֨הוּ לָ֤הּ אֶל־הַצּוּר֙ מִתְּחִלַּ֣ת קָצִ֔יר עַ֛ד נִתַּךְ־מַ֥יִם עֲלֵיהֶ֖ם מִן־הַשָּׁמָ֑יִם וְלֹֽא־נָתְנָ֞ה ע֤וֹף הַשָּׁמַ֙יִם֙ לָנ֣וּחַ עֲלֵיהֶ֣ם יוֹמָ֔ם וְאֶת־חַיַּ֥ת הַשָּׂדֶ֖ה לָֽיְלָה׃ 11 וַיֻּגַּ֖ד לְדָוִ֑ד אֵ֛ת אֲשֶׁר־עָשְׂתָ֥ה רִצְפָּ֖ה בַת־אַיָּ֖ה פִּלֶ֥גֶשׁ שָׁאֽוּל׃ 12 וַיֵּ֣לֶךְ דָּוִ֗ד וַיִּקַּ֞ח אֶת־עַצְמ֤וֹת שָׁאוּל֙ וְאֶת־עַצְמוֹת֙ יְהוֹנָתָ֣ן בְּנ֔וֹ מֵאֵ֕ת בַּעֲלֵ֖י יָבֵ֣ישׁ גִּלְעָ֑ד אֲשֶׁר֩ גָּנְב֨וּ אֹתָ֜ם מֵרְחֹ֣ב בֵּֽית־שַׁ֗ן* אֲשֶׁ֨ר תלום תְּלָא֥וּם שם שָׁ֛מָּה הַפְּלִשְׁתִּ֔ים בְּי֨וֹם הַכּ֧וֹת פְּלִשְׁתִּ֛ים אֶת־שָׁא֖וּל בַּגִּלְבֹּֽעַ׃ 13 וַיַּ֥עַל מִשָּׁ֖ם אֶת־עַצְמ֣וֹת שָׁא֔וּל וְאֶת־עַצְמ֖וֹת יְהוֹנָתָ֣ן בְּנ֑וֹ וַיַּ֣אַסְפ֔וּ אֶת־עַצְמ֥וֹת הַמּוּקָעִֽים׃ 14 וַיִּקְבְּר֣וּ אֶת־עַצְמוֹת־שָׁא֣וּל וִיהוֹנָתָן־בְּנ֡וֹ בְּאֶ֣רֶץ בִּנְיָמִן֩ בְּצֵלָ֨ע בְּקֶ֜בֶר קִ֣ישׁ אָבִ֗יו וַֽיַּעֲשׂ֔וּ כֹּ֥ל אֲשֶׁר־צִוָּ֖ה הַמֶּ֑לֶךְ וַיֵּעָתֵ֧ר אֱלֹהִ֛ים לָאָ֖רֶץ אַחֲרֵי־כֵֽן׃ פ

15 וַתְּהִי־ע֧וֹד מִלְחָמָ֛ה לַפְּלִשְׁתִּ֖ים אֶת־יִשְׂרָאֵ֑ל וַיֵּ֣רֶד דָּ֠וִד וַעֲבָדָ֤יו עִמּוֹ֙ וַיִּלָּחֲמ֣וּ אֶת־פְּלִשְׁתִּ֔ים וַיָּ֖עַף דָּוִֽד׃ 16 וישבו וְיִשְׁבּ֨וֹ בְּנֹ֜ב אֲשֶׁ֣ר ׀ בִּילִידֵ֣י הָרָפָ֗ה וּמִשְׁקַ֤ל קֵֽינוֹ֙ שְׁלֹ֤שׁ מֵאוֹת֙ מִשְׁקַ֣ל נְחֹ֔שֶׁת וְה֖וּא חָג֣וּר חֲדָשָׁ֑ה וַיֹּ֖אמֶר לְהַכּ֥וֹת אֶת־דָּוִֽד׃ 17 וַיַּֽעֲזָר־ל֞וֹ אֲבִישַׁ֣י בֶּן־צְרוּיָ֗ה וַיַּ֤ךְ אֶת־הַפְּלִשְׁתִּי֙ וַיְמִיתֵ֑הוּ אָ֣ז נִשְׁבְּע֞וּ אַנְשֵׁי־דָוִ֤ד ל֣וֹ לֵאמֹ֔ר לֹא־תֵצֵ֨א ע֤וֹד אִתָּ֙נוּ֙ לַמִּלְחָמָ֔ה וְלֹ֥א תְכַבֶּ֖ה אֶת־נֵ֥ר יִשְׂרָאֵֽל׃ פ

18 וַֽיְהִי֙ אַֽחֲרֵי־כֵ֔ן וַתְּהִי־ע֥וֹד הַמִּלְחָמָ֖ה בְּג֣וֹב עִם־פְּלִשְׁתִּ֑ים אָ֣ז הִכָּ֗ה סִבְּכַ֤י הַחֻֽשָׁתִי֙ אֶת־סַ֔ף אֲשֶׁ֖ר בִּילִדֵ֥י הָרָפָֽה׃ פ

---

d-d Heb. "them."
e Septuagint adds "and the bones of those impaled."
f Apparently a race of giants.
g This paragraph is found also in 1 Chron. 20.4–8; in part, also in 1QSamᵃ, with some variations.

Raphah.*f* ¹⁹Again there was fighting with the Philistines at Gob; and Elhanan son of Jaare-oregim*h* the Bethlehemite killed Goliath the Gittite, whose spear had a shaft like a weaver's bar. ²⁰Once again there was fighting, at Gath. There was a *ᵃ*-giant of a man,-*ᵃ* who had six fingers on each hand and six toes on each foot, twenty-four in all; he too was descended from the Raphah. ²¹When he taunted Israel, Jonathan, the son of David's brother Shimei, killed him. ²²Those four were descended from the Raphah in Gath, and they fell by the hands of David and his men.

22

*ᵃ*David addressed the words of this song to the LORD, after the LORD had saved him from the hands of all his enemies and from the hands of Saul. ²He said:

O LORD, my crag, my fastness, my deliverer!
³O *ᵇ*-God, the rock-*ᵇ* wherein I take shelter:
My shield, my *ᶜ*-mighty champion,-*ᶜ* my fortress and refuge!
My savior, You who rescue me from violence!

⁴*ᵈ*-All praise! I called on the LORD,-*ᵈ*
And I was delivered from my enemies.

⁵For the breakers of Death encompassed me,
The torrents of Belial*ᵉ* terrified me;
⁶The snares of Sheol encircled me,
The coils of Death engulfed me.

⁷In my anguish I called on the LORD,
Cried out to my God;
In His Abode*f* He heard my voice,
My cry entered His ears.

---

h   Perhaps a duplicate of 'oregim ("weavers") at the end of the verse; meaning of Heb. uncertain. 1 Chron. 20.5 reads "And Elhanan son of Jair killed Lahmi, the brother of Goliath the Gittite."

a   This poem occurs again as Ps. 18, with a number of variations, some of which are cited in the following notes.
b-b   Lit. "the God of my rock"; Ps. 18.3 "my God, my rock."
c-c   Lit. "horn of rescue."
d-d   Construction of Heb. uncertain.
e   I.e., the netherworld, like "Death" and "Sheol."
f   Lit. "Temple."

695

---

¹⁹ וַתְּהִי־עוֹד הַמִּלְחָמָה בְּגוֹב עִם־
פְּלִשְׁתִּים וַיַּךְ אֶלְחָנָן בֶּן־יַעְרֵי אֹרְגִים בֵּית
הַלַּחְמִי אֵת גָּלְיָת הַגִּתִּי וְעֵץ חֲנִיתוֹ כִּמְנוֹר
אֹרְגִים׃ ס ²⁰ וַתְּהִי־עוֹד מִלְחָמָה בְּגַת
וַיְהִי ׀ אִישׁ מדין מָדוֹן וְאֶצְבְּעֹת יָדָיו
וְאֶצְבְּעֹת רַגְלָיו שֵׁשׁ וָשֵׁשׁ עֶשְׂרִים וְאַרְבַּע
מִסְפָּר וְגַם־הוּא יֻלַּד לְהָרָפָה׃ ²¹ וַיְחָרֵף
אֶת־יִשְׂרָאֵל וַיַּכֵּהוּ יְהוֹנָתָן בֶּן־שִׁמְעִי
שָׁמְעָה אֲחִי דָוִד׃ ²² אֶת־אַרְבַּעַת אֵלֶּה
יֻלְּדוּ לְהָרָפָה בְּגַת וַיִּפְּלוּ בְיַד־דָּוִד וּבְיַד
עֲבָדָיו׃ פ

כב

*וַיְדַבֵּר דָּוִד לַיהוָה אֶת־דִּבְרֵי
הַשִּׁירָה הַזֹּאת בְּיוֹם הִצִּיל יְהוָה אֹתוֹ
מִכַּף כָּל־אֹיְבָיו וּמִכַּף שָׁאוּל׃ ² וַיֹּאמַר

יְהוָה סַלְעִי וּמְצֻדָתִי וּמְפַלְטִי־לִי׃
³ אֱלֹהֵי צוּרִי אֶחֱסֶה־בּוֹ
מָגִנִּי וְקֶרֶן יִשְׁעִי מִשְׂגַּבִּי וּמְנוּסִי
מֹשִׁעִי מֵחָמָס תֹּשִׁעֵנִי׃

⁴ מְהֻלָּל אֶקְרָא יְהוָה
וּמֵאֹיְבַי אִוָּשֵׁעַ׃

⁵ כִּי אֲפָפֻנִי מִשְׁבְּרֵי־מָוֶת
נַחֲלֵי בְלִיַּעַל יְבַעֲתֻנִי׃
⁶ חֶבְלֵי שְׁאוֹל סַבֻּנִי
קִדְּמֻנִי מֹקְשֵׁי־מָוֶת׃

⁷ בַּצַּר־לִי אֶקְרָא יְהוָה
וְאֶל־אֱלֹהַי אֶקְרָא
וַיִּשְׁמַע מֵהֵיכָלוֹ קוֹלִי
וְשַׁוְעָתִי בְּאָזְנָיו׃

v. 1. בכתב היד שלנו כתוב בצורת שירה

⁸Then the earth rocked and quaked,
The foundations of heaven*g* shook—
Rocked by His indignation.
⁹Smoke went up from His nostrils,
From His mouth came devouring fire;
Live coals blazed forth from Him.
¹⁰He bent the sky and came down,
Thick cloud beneath His feet.
¹¹He mounted a cherub and flew;
h-He was seen-*h* on the wings of the wind.
¹²He made pavilions of darkness about Him,
Dripping clouds, huge thunderheads;
¹³In the brilliance before Him
Blazed fiery coals.
¹⁴The Lord thundered forth from heaven,
The Most High sent forth His voice;
¹⁵He let loose bolts, and scattered them;*i*
Lightning, and put them to rout.
¹⁶The bed of the sea was exposed,
The foundations of the world were laid bare
By the mighty roaring of the Lord,
At the blast of the breath of His nostrils.
¹⁷He reached down from on high, He took me,
Drew me out of the mighty waters;*j*
¹⁸He rescued me from my enemy so strong,
From foes too mighty for me.
¹⁹They attacked me on my day of calamity,
But the Lord was my stay.
²⁰He brought me out to freedom,
He rescued me because He was pleased with me.
²¹The Lord rewarded me according to my merit,
He requited the cleanness of my hands.

²²For I have kept the ways of the Lord
And have not been guilty before my God;
²³I am mindful of all His rules
And have not departed from His laws.

ותגעש ויתגעש ותרעש הארץ 8
מוסדות השמים ירגזו
ויתגעשו כי־חרה לו:
עלה עשן באפו 9
ואש מפיו תאכל
גחלים בערו ממנו:
ויט שמים וירד 10
וערפל תחת רגליו:
וירכב על־כרוב ויעף 11
וירא על־כנפי־רוח:
וישת חשך סביבתיו סכות 12
חשרת־מים עבי שחקים:
מנגה נגדו 13
בערו גחלי־אש:
ירעם מן־שמים יהוה 14
ועליון יתן קולו:
וישלח חצים ויפיצם 15
ברק ויהמם ויהם:
ויראו אפקי ים 16
יגלו מסדות תבל
בגערת יהוה
מנשמת רוח אפו:
ישלח ממרום יקחני 17
ימשני ממים רבים:
יצילני מאיבי עז 18
משנאי כי אמצו ממני:
יקדמני ביום אידי 19
ויהי יהוה משען לי:
ויצא למרחב אתי 20
יחלצני כי־חפץ בי:
יגמלני יהוה כצדקתי 21
כבר ידי ישיב לי:

כי שמרתי דרכי יהוה 22
ולא רשעתי מאלהי:
כי כל־משפטו משפטיו לנגדי 23
וחקתיו לא־אסור ממנה:

---

g   *Ps. 18.8 "mountains."*
h-h *Ps. 18.11 "Gliding."*
i   *I.e., the enemies in v. 4.*
j   *Cf. v. 5.*

696

24I have been blameless before Him,
And have guarded myself against sinning—
25And the LORD has requited my merit,
According to my purity in His sight.
26With the loyal You deal loyally;
With the blameless hero,[k] blamelessly.
27With the pure You act in purity,
And with the perverse You are wily.
28To humble folk You give victory,
[l]-And You look with scorn on the haughty.-[l]

29You, O LORD, are my lamp;
The LORD lights up my darkness.
30With You, I can rush a barrier,[m]
With my God, I can scale a wall.
31The way of God is perfect,
The word of the LORD is pure.
He is a shield to all who take refuge in Him.
32Yea, who is a god except the LORD,
Who is a rock except God—
33The God, [n]-my mighty stronghold,-[n]
Who kept[o] my path secure;
34Who made my legs like a deer's,
And set me firm on the[p] heights;
35Who trained my hands for battle,
So that my arms can bend a bow of bronze!
36You have granted me the shield of Your
protection
[q]-And Your providence has made me great.-[q]
37You have let me stride on freely,
And my feet have not slipped.
38I pursued my enemies and wiped them out,
I did not turn back till I destroyed them.
39I destroyed them, I struck them down;
They rose no more, they lay at my feet.
40You have girt me with strength for battle,
Brought low my foes before me,

---

24 וָאֶהְיֶה תָמִים לֹו
וָאֶשְׁתַּמְּרָה מֵעֲוֹנִי:
25 וַיָּשֶׁב יְהוָה לִי כְּצִדְקָתִי
כְּבֹרִי לְנֶגֶד עֵינָיו:
26 עִם־חָסִיד תִּתְחַסָּד
עִם־גִּבֹּור תָּמִים תִּתַּמָּם:
27 עִם־נָבָר תִּתָּבָר
וְעִם־עִקֵּשׁ תִּתַּפָּל:
28 וְאֶת־עַם עָנִי תֹּושִׁיעַ
וְעֵינֶיךָ עַל־רָמִים תַּשְׁפִּיל:
29 כִּי־אַתָּה נֵירִי יְהוָה
וַיהוָה יַגִּיהַּ חָשְׁכִּי:
30 כִּי בְכָה* אָרוּץ גְּדוּד
בֵּאלֹהַי אֲדַלֶּג־שׁוּר:
31 הָאֵל תָּמִים דַּרְכֹּו
אִמְרַת יְהוָה צְרוּפָה
מָגֵן הוּא לְכֹל הַחֹסִים בֹּו:
32 כִּי מִי־אֵל מִבַּלְעֲדֵי יְהוָה
וּמִי צוּר מִבַּלְעֲדֵי אֱלֹהֵינוּ:
33 הָאֵל מָעוּזִּי חָיִל
וַיַּתֵּר תָּמִים דרכו דַּרְכִּי:
34 מְשַׁוֶּה רַגְלָיו כָּאַיָּלֹות
וְעַל בָּמֹותַי יַעֲמִדֵנִי:
35 מְלַמֵּד יָדַי לַמִּלְחָמָה
וְנִחַת קֶשֶׁת־נְחוּשָׁה זְרֹעֹתָי:
36 וַתִּתֶּן־לִי מָגֵן יִשְׁעֶךָ
וַעֲנֹתְךָ תַּרְבֵּנִי:
37 תַּרְחִיב צַעֲדִי תַּחְתֵּנִי
וְלֹא מָעֲדוּ קַרְסֻלָּי:
38 אֶרְדְּפָה אֹיְבַי וָאַשְׁמִידֵם
וְלֹא אָשׁוּב עַד־כַּלֹּותָם:
39 וָאֲכַלֵּם וָאֶמְחָצֵם
וְלֹא יְקוּמוּן וַיִּפְּלוּ תַּחַת רַגְלָי:
40 וַתַּזְרֵנִי* חַיִל לַמִּלְחָמָה
תַּכְרִיעַ קָמַי תַּחְתֵּנִי:

---

k   Ps. 18.26 "man."
l-l   Lit. "And lower Your eyes on the haughty"; Ps. 18.28 "But
        haughty eyes You humble."
m   Cf. postbiblical gedudiyyoth "walls," Aramaic gudda, "wall."
n-n   Ps. 18.33 "who girded me with might."
o   Meaning of Heb. uncertain; Ps. 18.33 "made."
p   Taking bamothai as a poetic form of bamoth; cf. Hab. 3.19;
        others "my."
q-q   Meaning of Heb. uncertain.

v. 30.   יתיר ה'
v. 40.   חסר א'

41Made my enemies turn tail before me,
My foes—and I wiped them out.
42They looked,ʳ but there was none to deliver;
To the Lᴏʀᴅ, but He answered them not.
43I pounded them like dust of the earth,
Stamped, crushed them like dirt of the streets.
44You have rescued me from the strife of peoples,ˢ
ᵗ-Kept me to be-ᵗ a ruler of nations;
Peoples I knew not must serve me.
45Aliens have cringed before me,
Paid me homage at the mere report of me.
46Aliens have lost courage
�q-And come trembling out of their fast-
nesses.-q

47The Lᴏʀᴅ lives! Blessed is my rock!
Exalted be God, the rock
Who gives me victory;
48The God who has vindicated me
And made peoples subject to me,
49Rescued me from my enemies,
Raised me clear of my foes,
Saved me from lawless men!
50For this I sing Your praise among the na-
tions
And hymn Your name:
51ᵘ-Tower of victory-ᵘ to His king,
Who deals graciously with His anointed,
With David and his offspring evermore.

23 These are the last words of David:

ᵃThe utterance of David son of Jesse,
The utterance of the man ᵇ-set on high,-ᵇ
The anointed of the God of Jacob,

41 וְאֹיְבַי תַּתָּה לִּי עֹרֶף
מְשַׂנְאַי וָאַצְמִיתֵם:
42 יִשְׁעוּ וְאֵין מֹשִׁיעַ
אֶל־יְהוָה וְלֹא עָנָם:
43 וְאֶשְׁחָקֵם כַּעֲפַר־אָרֶץ
כְּטִיט־חוּצוֹת אֲדִקֵּם אֶרְקָעֵם:
44 וַתְּפַלְּטֵנִי מֵרִיבֵי עַמִּי*
תִּשְׁמְרֵנִי לְרֹאשׁ גּוֹיִם
עַם לֹא־יָדַעְתִּי יַעַבְדֻנִי:
45 בְּנֵי נֵכָר יִתְכַּחֲשׁוּ־לִי
לִשְׁמוֹעַ אֹזֶן יִשָּׁמְעוּ לִי:
46 בְּנֵי נֵכָר יִבֹּלוּ
וְיַחְגְּרוּ מִמִּסְגְּרוֹתָם:
47 חַי־יְהוָה וּבָרוּךְ צוּרִי
וְיָרֻם אֱלֹהֵי צוּר
יִשְׁעִי:
48 הָאֵל הַנֹּתֵן נְקָמֹת לִי
וּמוֹרִיד עַמִּים תַּחְתֵּנִי:
49 וּמוֹצִיאִי מֵאֹיְבָי
וּמִקָּמַי תְּרוֹמְמֵנִי
מֵאִישׁ חֲמָסִים תַּצִּילֵנִי:
50 עַל־כֵּן אוֹדְךָ יְהוָה בַּגּוֹיִם
וּלְשִׁמְךָ אֲזַמֵּר:
51 מִגְדִּיל מַגְדּוֹל יְשׁוּעוֹת מַלְכּוֹ
וְעֹשֶׂה־חֶסֶד לִמְשִׁיחוֹ
לְדָוִד וּלְזַרְעוֹ עַד־עוֹלָם: פ

כג וְאֵלֶּה דִּבְרֵי דָוִד הָאַחֲרֹנִים

נְאֻם דָּוִד בֶּן־יִשַׁי
וּנְאֻם הַגֶּבֶר הֻקַם עַל
מְשִׁיחַ אֱלֹהֵי יַעֲקֹב

ʳ   Ps. 18.42 "cried."
ˢ   So some mss. and the Septuagint; most mss. and the printed
     editions "my people."
ᵗ⁻ᵗ Ps. 18.44 "made me."
ᵘ⁻ᵘ Kethib and Ps. 18.51 read "He accords wondrous victories."

ᵃ   Meaning of much of this poem (vv. 1–7) uncertain.
ᵇ⁻ᵇ 4QSamᵃ reads "God raised up."

v. 44.   סבירין ומטעין "עמים", ובנוסחא אחר "עם" וגם
בנוסח אחר "עמים"

c-The favorite of the songs of Israel:-*c*

2The spirit of the LORD has spoken through me,

His message is on my tongue;

3The God of Israel has spoken,

The Rock of Israel said concerning me:

"He who rules men justly,

He who rules in*d* awe of God

4Is like the light of morning at sunrise,

A morning without clouds—

e-Through sunshine and rain

[Bringing]-*e* vegetation out of the earth."

5Is not my House established before God?

For He has granted me an eternal pact,

Drawn up in full and secured.

Will He not cause all my success

And [my] every desire to blossom?

6But the wicked shall all

Be raked aside like thorns;

For no one will take them in his hand.

7Whoever touches them

Must arm himself with iron

And the shaft of a spear;

And they must be burned up on the spot.

8These are the names*f* of David's warriors: Josheb-basshebeth, a Tahchemonite, the chief officer—he is Adino the Eznite; *g*-[he wielded his spear]-*g* against eight hundred *h*-and slew them-*h* on one occasion.

9Next to him was Eleazar son of Dodo son of Ahohi. He was one of the three warriors with David when they defied the Philistines gathered there for battle. The Israelite soldiers retreated, 10but he held his ground. He struck down Philistines until his arm grew tired and his hand stuck to his sword; and the LORD wrought a

וּנְעִים זְמִרוֹת יִשְׂרָאֵל:

2 רוּחַ יְהוָה דִּבֶּר־בִּי

וּמִלָּתוֹ עַל־לְשׁוֹנִי:

3 אָמַר אֱלֹהֵי יִשְׂרָאֵל

לִי דִבֶּר צוּר יִשְׂרָאֵל

מוֹשֵׁל בָּאָדָם צַדִּיק

מוֹשֵׁל יִרְאַת* אֱלֹהִים:

4 וּכְאוֹר בֹּקֶר יִזְרַח־שָׁמֶשׁ

בֹּקֶר לֹא עָבוֹת

מִנֹּגַהּ מִמָּטָר

דֶּשֶׁא מֵאָרֶץ:

5 כִּי־לֹא־כֵן בֵּיתִי עִם־אֵל

כִּי בְרִית עוֹלָם שָׂם לִי

עֲרוּכָה בַכֹּל וּשְׁמֻרָה

כִּי־כָל־יִשְׁעִי וְכָל־חֵפֶץ

כִּי־לֹא יַצְמִיחַ:

6 וּבְלִיַּעַל כְּקוֹץ

מֻנָד כֻּלָּהַם

כִּי־לֹא בְיָד יִקָּחוּ:

7 וְאִישׁ יִגַּע בָּהֶם

יִמָּלֵא בַרְזֶל

וְעֵץ חֲנִית

וּבָאֵשׁ שָׂרוֹף יִשָּׂרְפוּ בַּשָּׁבֶת: פ

8 אֵלֶּה שְׁמוֹת הַגִּבֹּרִים אֲשֶׁר לְדָוִד יֹשֵׁב בַּשֶּׁבֶת תַּחְכְּמֹנִי ׀ רֹאשׁ הַשָּׁלִשִׁי הוּא עֲדִינוֹ העצנו הָעֶצְנִי עַל־שְׁמֹנֶה מֵאוֹת חָלָל בְּפַעַם אֶחָד: ס

9 וְאַחֲרָו אֶלְעָזָר בֶּן־דֹּדִי דֹדוֹ בֶּן־אֲחֹחִי בִּשְׁלֹשָׁה גברים הַגִּבֹּרִים עִם־דָּוִד בְּחָרְפָם בַּפְּלִשְׁתִּים נֶאֶסְפוּ־שָׁם לַמִּלְחָמָה וַיַּעֲלוּ אִישׁ יִשְׂרָאֵל: 10 הוּא קָם וַיַּךְ בַּפְּלִשְׁתִּים עַד ׀ כִּי־יָגְעָה יָדוֹ וַתִּדְבַּק יָדוֹ אֶל־הַחֶרֶב וַיַּעַשׂ יְהוָה תְּשׁוּעָה גְדוֹלָה

---

c-c Or "The favorite of the Mighty One of Israel"; cf. Exod. 15.2. Others "The sweet singer of Israel."

d So many Heb. mss. Most mss. and the printed editions lack "in."

e-e Meaning of Heb. uncertain.

f A number of these names, with variations, are found in 1 Chron. 11 and 27.

g-g Preserved in 1 Chron. 11.11; similarly some Septuagint mss. of 2 Sam.

h-h Lit. "slain."

v. 3. בנוסח אחר "בִּירְאַת"

great victory that day. Then the troops came back to him—but only to strip [the slain].

¹¹Next to him was Shammah son of Age the Ararite. The Philistines had gathered ^e-in force-^e where there was a plot of ground full of lentils; and the troops fled from the Philistines. ¹²But [Shammah] took his stand in the middle of the plot and defended it, and he routed the Philistines. Thus the Lord wrought a great victory.

¹³^e-Once, during the harvest,-^e three of the thirty chiefs went down to David at the caveⁱ of Adullam, while a force of Philistines was encamped in the Valley of Rephaim. ¹⁴David was then in the stronghold,ⁱ and a Philistine garrison was then at Bethlehem. ¹⁵David felt a craving and said, "If only I could get a drink of water from the cistern which is by the gate of Bethlehem!" ¹⁶So the three warriors got through the Philistine camp and drew water from the cistern which is by the gate of Bethlehem, and they carried it back. But when they brought it to David he would not drink it, and he poured it out as a libation to the Lord. ¹⁷For he said, "The Lord forbid that I should do this! Can [I drink]^j the blood of the men who went at the risk of their lives?" So he would not drink it. Such were the exploits of the three warriors.

¹⁸Abishai, the brother of Joab son of Zeruiah, was head of ^k-another three.-^k He once wielded his spear against three hundred ^h-and slew them.-^h ¹⁹He won a name among the three;^l since he was the most highly regarded among the three,^l he became their leader. However, he did not attain to the three.

²⁰Benaiah son of Jehoiada, from Kabzeel, was ^m-a brave soldier-^m who performed great deeds. He killed the two ^e-[sons] of Ariel of Moab.-^e Once, on a snowy day, he went down into a pit and killed a lion. ²¹He also killed an Egyptian,

---

בַּיּ֣וֹם הַה֔וּא וְהָעָ֛ם יָשֻׁ֥בוּ אַחֲרָ֖יו אַךְ־
לְפַשֵּֽׁט׃ ס

¹¹ וְאַחֲרָ֞יו שַׁמָּ֣א בֶן־אָגֵ֗א הָרָרִ֔י וַיֵּאָסְפ֨וּ
פְלִשְׁתִּ֜ים לַחַיָּ֗ה וַתְּהִי־שָׁ֞ם חֶלְקַ֤ת הַשָּׂדֶה֙
מְלֵאָ֣ה עֲדָשִׁ֔ים וְהָעָ֥ם נָ֖ס מִפְּנֵ֥י פְלִשְׁתִּֽים׃

¹² וַיִּתְיַצֵּ֤ב בְּתוֹךְ־הַֽחֶלְקָה֙ וַיַּצִּילֶ֔הָ וַיַּ֖ךְ
אֶת־פְּלִשְׁתִּ֑ים וַיַּ֥עַשׂ יְהוָ֖ה תְּשׁוּעָ֥ה
גְדוֹלָֽה׃ ס

¹³ וַיֵּרְד֨וּ שְׁלֹשָׁ֜ה מֵהַשְּׁלֹשִׁ֣ים רֹ֗אשׁ
וַיָּבֹ֤אוּ אֶל־קָצִיר֙ אֶל־דָּוִ֔ד אֶל־מְעָרַ֖ת עֲדֻלָּ֑ם
וְחַיַּ֣ת פְּלִשְׁתִּ֔ים חֹנָ֖ה בְּעֵ֥מֶק רְפָאִֽים׃

¹⁴ וְדָוִ֖ד אָ֣ז בַּמְּצוּדָ֑ה וּמַצַּ֣ב פְּלִשְׁתִּ֔ים אָ֖ז
בֵּ֥ית לָֽחֶם׃ ¹⁵ וַיִּתְאַוֶּ֥ה דָוִ֖ד וַיֹּאמַ֑ר מִ֚י
יַשְׁקֵ֣נִי מַ֔יִם מִבֹּ֥אר בֵּֽית־לֶ֖חֶם אֲשֶׁ֥ר
בַּשָּֽׁעַר׃ ¹⁶ וַיִּבְקְע֞וּ שְׁלֹ֣שֶׁת הַגִּבֹּרִ֗ים
בְּמַחֲנֵ֣ה פְלִשְׁתִּ֗ים וַיִּֽשְׁאֲבוּ־מַ֙יִם֙ מִבֹּ֤אר
בֵּֽית־לֶ֙חֶם֙ אֲשֶׁ֣ר בַּשַּׁ֔עַר וַיִּשְׂא֖וּ וַיָּבִ֣אוּ
אֶל־דָּוִ֑ד וְלֹ֤א אָבָה֙ לִשְׁתּוֹתָ֔ם וַיַּסֵּ֥ךְ אֹתָ֖ם
לַֽיהוָֽה׃ ¹⁷ וַיֹּ֡אמֶר חָלִ֩ילָה֩ לִּ֨י יְהוָ֜ה
מֵעֲשֹׂ֣תִי זֹ֗את הֲדַ֤ם הָֽאֲנָשִׁים֙ הַהֹלְכִ֣ים
בְּנַפְשׁוֹתָ֔ם וְלֹ֥א אָבָ֖ה לִשְׁתּוֹתָ֑ם אֵ֣לֶּה עָשׂ֔וּ
שְׁלֹ֖שֶׁת הַגִּבֹּרִֽים׃ ס

¹⁸ וַאֲבִישַׁ֞י אֲחִ֣י ׀ יוֹאָ֣ב בֶּן־צְרוּיָ֗ה ה֚וּא
רֹ֣אשׁ הַשְּׁלֹשָׁ֔ה וְהוּא֙ עוֹרֵ֣ר אֶת־
חֲנִית֔וֹ עַל־שְׁלֹ֥שׁ מֵא֖וֹת חָלָ֑ל וְלוֹ־שֵׁ֖ם
בַּשְּׁלֹשָֽׁה׃ ¹⁹ מִן־הַשְּׁלֹשָׁה֙ הֲכִ֣י נִכְבָּ֔ד וַֽיְהִ֥י
לָהֶ֖ם לְשָׂ֑ר וְעַד־הַשְּׁלֹשָׁ֖ה לֹא־בָֽא׃ ס

²⁰ וּבְנָיָ֨הוּ בֶן־יְהוֹיָדָ֧ע בֶּן־אִֽישׁ־חַ֛י רַב־
פְּעָלִ֖ים מִֽקַּבְצְאֵ֑ל ה֣וּא הִכָּ֗ה אֵ֣ת שְׁנֵ֣י
אֲרִאֵ֣ל מוֹאָ֔ב וְ֠הוּא יָרַ֞ד וְהִכָּ֧ה אֶֽת־הָאֲרִי
בְּת֥וֹךְ הַבֹּ֖אר בְּי֥וֹם הַשָּֽׁלֶג׃ ²¹ וְהוּא־
הִכָּה֩ אֶת־אִ֨ישׁ מִצְרִ֜י אֲשֶׁ֥ר אִ֣ישׁ מַרְאֶ֗ה

---

i   See note at 1 Sam. 22.1.
j   So Septuagint and 1 Chron. 11.19.
k-k   Two Heb. mss. and Syriac read "the thirty"; cf. vv. 23–24.
l   Emendation yields "thirty."
m-m   Heb. "the son of a brave soldier."

a huge[n] man. The Egyptian had a spear in his hand, yet [Benaiah] went down against him with a club, wrenched the spear out of the Egyptian's hand, and killed him with his own spear. [22]Such were the exploits of Benaiah son of Jehoiada; and he won a name among the three[l] warriors. [23]He was highly regarded among the thirty, but he did not attain to the three. David put him in charge of his bodyguard.[e]

[24]Among the thirty were Asahel, the brother of Joab; Elhanan son of Dodo [from] Bethlehem, [25]Shammah the Harodite, Elika the Harodite, [26]Helez the Paltite, Ira son of Ikkesh from Tekoa, [27]Abiezer of Anathoth, Mebunnai the Hushathite, [28]Zalmon the Ahohite, Maharai the Netophathite, [29]Heleb son of Baanah the Netophathite, Ittai son of Ribai from Gibeah of the Benjaminites, [30]Benaiah of Pirathon, Hiddai of Nahale-gaash, [31]Abi-albon the Arbathite, Azmaveth the Barhumite, [32]Eliahba of Shaalbon, sons of [e-]Jashen, Jonathan,[-e] [33]Shammah the Ararite, Ahiam son of Sharar the Ararite, [34]Eliphelet son of Ahasbai son of the Maacathite, Eliam son of Ahithophel the Gilonite, [35]Hezrai the Carmelite, Paarai the Arbite, [36]Igal son of Nathan from Zobah, Bani the Gadite, [37]Zelek the Ammonite, Naharai the Beerothite—the arms-bearer of Joab son of Zeruiah—[38]Ira the Ithrite, Gareb the Ithrite, [39]Uriah the Hittite: thirty-seven in all.[o]

24

[a]The anger of the Lord again[b] flared up against Israel; and He incited David against them, saying, "Go and number Israel and Judah." [2]The king said to Joab, [c-]his army com-

---

וּבְיַ֤ד הַמִּצְרִי֙ חֲנִ֔ית וַיֵּ֥רֶד אֵלָ֖יו בַּשָּׁ֑בֶט וַיִּגְזֹ֤ל אֶֽת־הַחֲנִית֙ מִיַּ֣ד הַמִּצְרִ֔י וַיַּהַרְגֵ֖הוּ בַּחֲנִיתֽוֹ׃ [22] אֵ֣לֶּה עָשָׂ֔ה בְּנָיָ֖הוּ בֶּן־יְהוֹיָדָ֑ע וְלוֹ־שֵׁ֖ם בִּשְׁלֹשָׁ֥ה הַגִּבֹּרִֽים׃ [23] מִן־הַשְּׁלֹשִׁ֣ים נִכְבָּ֔ד וְאֶל־הַשְּׁלֹשָׁ֖ה לֹא־בָ֑א וַיְשִׂמֵ֥הוּ דָוִ֖ד אֶל־מִשְׁמַעְתּֽוֹ׃ ס

[24] עֲשָׂה־אֵ֥ל אֲחִֽי־יוֹאָ֖ב בַּשְּׁלֹשִׁ֑ים אֶלְחָנָ֥ן בֶּן־דֹּד֖וֹ בֵּ֥ית לָֽחֶם׃ [25] שַׁמָּה֙ הַֽחֲרֹדִ֔י אֱלִיקָ֖א הַֽחֲרֹדִֽי׃ ס [26] חֶ֙לֶץ֙ הַפַּלְטִ֔י עִירָ֥א בֶן־עִקֵּ֖שׁ הַתְּקוֹעִֽי׃ ס [27] אֲבִיעֶ֙זֶר֙ הָֽעַנְּתֹתִ֔י מְבֻנַּ֖י הַחֻֽשָׁתִֽי׃ ס [28] צַלְמוֹן֙ הָֽאֲחֹחִ֔י מַהְרַ֖י הַנְּטֹֽפָתִֽי׃ ס [29] חֵ֥לֶב בֶּֽן־בַּֽעֲנָ֖ה הַנְּטֹֽפָתִ֑י ס אִתַּי֙ בֶּן־רִיבַ֔י מִגִּבְעַ֖ת בְּנֵ֥י בִנְיָמִֽן׃ ס [30] בְּנָיָ֙הוּ֙ פִּרְעָ֣תֹנִ֔י הִדַּ֖י מִנַּ֥חֲלֵי גָֽעַשׁ׃ ס [31] אֲבִֽי־עַלְבוֹן֙ הָֽעַרְבָתִ֔י עַזְמָ֖וֶת הַבַּרְחֻמִֽי׃ ס [32] אֶלְיַחְבָּא֙ הַשַּׁ֣עַלְבֹנִ֔י בְּנֵ֥י יָשֵׁ֖ן יְהוֹנָתָֽן׃ [33] שַׁמָּה֙ הַֽהֲרָרִ֔י אֲחִיאָ֥ם בֶּן־שָׁרָ֖ר הָאֲרָרִֽי׃ ס [34] אֱלִיפֶ֥לֶט בֶּן־אֲחַסְבַּ֖י בֶּן־הַמַּֽעֲכָתִ֑י ס אֱלִיעָ֣ם בֶּן־אֲחִיתֹ֖פֶל הַגִּֽלֹנִֽי׃ ס [35] חֶצְרַי֙ הַֽכַּרְמְלִ֔י פַּֽעֲרַ֖י הָאַרְבִּֽי׃ ס [36] יִגְאָ֤ל בֶּן־נָתָן֙ מִצֹּבָ֔ה ס בָּנִ֖י הַגָּדִֽי׃ ס [37] צֶ֖לֶק הָעַמֹּנִ֑י ס נַחְרַי֙ הַבְּאֵ֣רֹתִ֔י נֹשֵׂ֕א כְּלֵ֖י יוֹאָ֥ב בֶּן־צְרֻיָֽה׃ ס [38] עִירָא֙ הַיִּתְרִ֔י גָּרֵ֖ב הַיִּתְרִֽי׃ ס [39] אֽוּרִיָּ֖ה הַֽחִתִּ֑י ס כֹּ֖ל שְׁלֹשִׁ֥ים וְשִׁבְעָֽה׃ פ

כד

וַיֹּ֙סֶף֙ אַף־יְהֹוָ֔ה לַחֲר֖וֹת בְּיִשְׂרָאֵ֑ל וַיָּ֙סֶת֙ אֶת־דָּוִ֤ד בָּהֶם֙ לֵאמֹ֔ר לֵ֣ךְ מְנֵ֔ה אֶת־יִשְׂרָאֵ֖ל וְאֶת־יְהוּדָֽה׃ [2] וַיֹּ֣אמֶר הַמֶּ֡לֶךְ

---

n   *Meaning of Heb. uncertain. 1 Chron. 11.23 reads "a giant of a man."*

o   *Septuagint and 1 Chron. 11 differ from the foregoing lists in vv. 8–38, and from each other in the number and forms of the names.*

a   *This chapter is also found, with some variations, in 1 Chron. 21.1–7.*

b   *Cf. above 21.1–14.*

mander,-c "Make the rounds of all the tribes of Israel, from Dan to Beer-sheba, and take a census of the people, so that I may know the size of the population." [3]Joab answered the king, "May the LORD your God increase the number of the people a hundredfold, while your own eyes see it! But why should my lord king want this?" [4]However, the king's command to Joab and to the officers of the army remained firm; and Joab and the officers of the army set out, at the instance of the king, to take a census of the people of Israel.

[5]They crossed the Jordan and d-encamped at Aroer, on the right side of the town, which is in the middle of the wadi of Gad, and-d [went on] to Jazer. [6]They continued to Gilead and to the region of e-Tahtim-hodshi, and they came to Dan-jaan and around to-e Sidon. [7]They went onto the fortress of Tyre and all the towns of the Hivites and Canaanites, and finished at Beer-sheba in southern Judah. [8]They traversed the whole country, and then they came back to Jerusalem at the end of nine months and twenty days. [9]Joab reported to the king the number of the people that had been recorded: in Israel there were 800,000 soldiers ready to draw the sword, and the men of Judah numbered 500,000.

[10]But afterward David f-reproached himself-f for having numbered the people. And David said to the LORD, "I have sinned grievously in what I have done. Please, O LORD, remit the guilt of Your servant, for I have acted foolishly." [11]When David rose in the morning, the word of the LORD had come to the prophet Gad, David's seer: [12]"Go and tell David, 'Thus said the LORD: I hold three things over you; choose one of them, and I will bring it upon you.'" [13]Gad

אֶל־יוֹאָב ׀ שַׂר־הַחַ֫יִל אֲשֶׁר־אִתּוֹ שׁוּט־נָ֫א בְּכָל־שִׁבְטֵ֣י יִשְׂרָאֵל֙ מִדָּן֙ וְעַד־בְּאֵ֣ר שֶׁ֔בַע וּפִקְד֖וּ אֶת־הָעָ֑ם וְיָ֣דַעְתִּ֔י אֵ֖ת מִסְפַּ֥ר הָעָֽם׃ ס [3] וַיֹּ֨אמֶר יוֹאָ֜ב אֶל־הַמֶּ֗לֶךְ וְיוֹסֵ֣ף יְהוָה֩ אֱלֹהֶ֨יךָ אֶל־הָעָ֜ם כָּהֵ֤ם ׀ וְכָהֵם֙ מֵאָ֣ה פְעָמִ֔ים וְעֵינֵ֥י אֲדֹנִֽי־הַמֶּ֖לֶךְ רֹא֑וֹת וַֽאדֹנִ֣י הַמֶּ֔לֶךְ לָ֥מָּה חָפֵ֖ץ בַּדָּבָ֥ר הַזֶּֽה׃ [4] וַיֶּחֱזַ֤ק דְּבַר־הַמֶּ֙לֶךְ֙ אֶל־יוֹאָ֔ב וְעַ֖ל שָׂרֵ֣י הֶחָ֑יִל וַיֵּצֵ֨א יוֹאָ֜ב וְשָׂרֵ֤י הַחַ֙יִל֙ לִפְנֵ֣י הַמֶּ֔לֶךְ לִפְקֹ֖ד אֶת־הָעָ֥ם אֶת־יִשְׂרָאֵֽל׃ [5] וַיַּעַבְר֖וּ אֶת־הַיַּרְדֵּ֑ן וַיַּחֲנ֣וּ בַעֲרוֹעֵ֗ר יְמִ֤ין הָעִיר֙ אֲשֶׁ֤ר בְּתוֹךְ־הַנַּ֙חַל֙ הַגָּ֔ד וְאֶֽל־יַעְזֵֽר׃ [6] וַיָּבֹ֙אוּ֙ הַגִּלְעָ֔דָה וְאֶל־אֶ֥רֶץ תַּחְתִּ֖ים חָדְשִׁ֑י וַיָּבֹ֙אוּ֙ דָּ֣נָה יַּ֔עַן וְסָבִ֖יב אֶל־צִידֽוֹן׃ [7] וַיָּבֹ֙אוּ֙ מִבְצַר־צֹ֔ר וְכָל־עָרֵ֥י הַחִוִּ֖י וְהַֽכְּנַעֲנִ֑י וַיֵּֽצְא֛וּ אֶל־נֶ֥גֶב יְהוּדָ֖ה בְּאֵ֥ר שָֽׁבַע׃ [8] וַיָּשֻׁ֖טוּ בְּכָל־הָאָ֑רֶץ וַיָּבֹ֜אוּ מִקְצֵ֨ה תִשְׁעָ֧ה חֳדָשִׁ֛ים וְעֶשְׂרִ֥ים י֖וֹם יְרוּשָׁלָֽ͏ִם׃ [9] וַיִּתֵּ֥ן יוֹאָ֛ב אֶת־מִסְפַּ֥ר מִפְקַד־הָעָ֖ם אֶל־הַמֶּ֑לֶךְ וַתְּהִ֣י יִשְׂרָאֵ֗ל שְׁמֹנֶ֨ה מֵא֤וֹת אֶ֙לֶף֙ אִֽישׁ־חַ֙יִל֙ שֹׁ֣לֵֽף חֶ֔רֶב וְאִ֣ישׁ יְהוּדָ֔ה חֲמֵ֥שׁ מֵא֖וֹת אֶ֥לֶף אִֽישׁ׃ [10] וַיַּ֤ךְ לֵב־דָּוִד֙ אֹת֔וֹ אַחֲרֵי־כֵ֖ן סָפַ֣ר אֶת־הָעָ֑ם ס וַיֹּ֨אמֶר דָּוִ֜ד אֶל־יְהוָ֗ה חָטָ֤אתִי מְאֹד֙ אֲשֶׁ֣ר עָשִׂ֔יתִי וְעַתָּ֣ה יְהוָ֔ה הַֽעֲבֶר־נָא֙ אֶת־עֲוֺ֣ן עַבְדְּךָ֔ כִּ֥י נִסְכַּ֖לְתִּי מְאֹֽד׃ [11] וַיָּ֥קָם דָּוִ֖ד בַּבֹּ֑קֶר פ וּדְבַר־יְהוָ֗ה הָיָה֙ אֶל־גָּ֣ד הַנָּבִ֔יא חֹזֵ֥ה דָוִ֖ד לֵאמֹֽר׃ [12] הָל֞וֹךְ וְדִבַּרְתָּ֣ אֶל־דָּוִ֗ד כֹּ֚ה אָמַ֣ר יְהוָ֔ה שָׁלֹ֕שׁ אָנֹכִ֖י נוֹטֵ֣ל עָלֶ֑יךָ בְּחַר־לְךָ֥ אַֽחַת־מֵהֶ֖ם וְאֶעֱשֶׂה־לָּֽךְ׃

---

c-c   1 Chron. 21.2 reads "and to the officers of the army"; cf. below v. 4.

d-d   Some Septuagint mss. read "began at Aroer, and from the town, which is...Gad, they."

e-e   Meaning of Heb. uncertain.

f-f   See note at 1 Sam. 24.6.

came to David and told him; he asked, "Shall a seven-year famine come upon you in the land, or shall you be in flight from your adversaries for three months while they pursue you, or shall there be three days of pestilence in your land? Now consider carefully what reply I shall take back to Him who sent me." [14]David said to Gad, "I am in great distress. Let us fall into the hands of the Lord, for His compassion is great; and let me not fall into the hands of men."[g]

[15]The Lord sent a pestilence upon Israel from morning [e]until the set time;[-e] and 70,000 of the people died, from Dan to Beer-sheba. [16]But when the angel extended his hand against Jerusalem to destroy it, the Lord renounced further punishment and said to the angel who was destroying the people, "Enough! Stay your hand!" The angel of the Lord was then by the threshing floor of Araunah the Jebusite. [17]When David saw the angel who was striking down the people, he said to the Lord, "I alone am guilty, I alone have done wrong; but these poor sheep, what have they done? Let Your hand fall upon me and my father's house!"

[18]Gad came to David the same day and said to him, "Go and set up an altar to the Lord on the threshing floor of Araunah the Jebusite." [19]David went up, following Gad's instructions, as the Lord had commanded. [20]Araunah looked out and saw the king and his courtiers approaching him.[h] So Araunah went out and bowed low to the king, with his face to the ground. [21]And Araunah asked, "Why has my lord the king come to his servant?" David replied, "To buy the threshing floor from you, that I may build an altar to the Lord and that the plague against the people may be checked." [22]And Araunah said to David, "Let my lord the king take it and offer up whatever he sees fit.

---

g   Septuagint adds "So David chose the pestilence. It was the time of the wheat harvest."
h   4QSamᵃ and 1 Chron. 21.20 add "Araunah (Ornan) was threshing wheat."

13 וַיָּבֹא־גָד אֶל־דָּוִד וַיַּגֶּד־לוֹ וַיֹּאמֶר לוֹ הֲתָבוֹא לְךָ שֶׁבַע שָׁנִים ׀ רָעָב ׀ בְּאַרְצֶךָ אִם־שְׁלֹשָׁה חֳדָשִׁים נֻסְךָ לִפְנֵי־צָרֶיךָ וְהוּא רֹדְפֶךָ וְאִם־הֱיוֹת שְׁלֹשֶׁת יָמִים דֶּבֶר בְּאַרְצֶךָ עַתָּה דַּע וּרְאֵה מָה־אָשִׁיב שֹׁלְחִי דָּבָר: ס 14 וַיֹּאמֶר דָּוִד אֶל־גָּד צַר־לִי מְאֹד נִפְּלָה־נָּא בְיַד־יְהֹוָה כִּי־רַבִּים רחמו רַחֲמָיו וּבְיַד־אָדָם אַל־אֶפֹּלָה:

15 וַיִּתֵּן יְהֹוָה דֶּבֶר בְּיִשְׂרָאֵל מֵהַבֹּקֶר וְעַד־עֵת מוֹעֵד וַיָּמׇת מִן־הָעָם מִדָּן וְעַד־בְּאֵר שֶׁבַע שִׁבְעִים אֶלֶף אִישׁ: 16 וַיִּשְׁלַח יָדוֹ הַמַּלְאָךְ ׀ יְרוּשָׁלַ͏ִם לְשַׁחֲתָהּ וַיִּנָּחֶם יְהֹוָה אֶל־הָרָעָה וַיֹּאמֶר לַמַּלְאָךְ הַמַּשְׁחִית בָּעָם רַב עַתָּה הֶרֶף יָדֶךָ וּמַלְאַךְ יְהֹוָה הָיָה עִם־גֹּרֶן האורנה הָאֲרַוְנָה הַיְבֻסִי: ס 17 וַיֹּאמֶר דָּוִד אֶל־יְהֹוָה בִּרְאֹתוֹ ׀ אֶת־הַמַּלְאָךְ ׀ הַמַּכֶּה בָעָם וַיֹּאמֶר הִנֵּה אָנֹכִי חָטָאתִי וְאָנֹכִי הֶעֱוֵיתִי וְאֵלֶּה הַצֹּאן מֶה עָשׂוּ תְּהִי נָא יָדְךָ בִּי וּבְבֵית אָבִי: פ 18 וַיָּבֹא־גָד אֶל־דָּוִד בַּיּוֹם הַהוּא וַיֹּאמֶר לוֹ עֲלֵה הָקֵם לַיהֹוָה מִזְבֵּחַ בְּגֹרֶן ארניה אֲרַוְנָה הַיְבֻסִי: 19 וַיַּעַל דָּוִד כִּדְבַר־גָּד כַּאֲשֶׁר צִוָּה יְהֹוָה: 20 וַיַּשְׁקֵף אֲרַוְנָה וַיַּרְא אֶת־הַמֶּלֶךְ וְאֶת־עֲבָדָיו עֹבְרִים עָלָיו וַיֵּצֵא אֲרַוְנָה וַיִּשְׁתַּחוּ לַמֶּלֶךְ אַפָּיו אָרְצָה: 21 וַיֹּאמֶר אֲרַוְנָה מַדּוּעַ בָּא אֲדֹנִי־הַמֶּלֶךְ אֶל־עַבְדּוֹ וַיֹּאמֶר דָּוִד לִקְנוֹת מֵעִמְּךָ אֶת־הַגֹּרֶן לִבְנוֹת מִזְבֵּחַ לַיהֹוָה וְתֵעָצַר הַמַּגֵּפָה מֵעַל הָעָם: 22 וַיֹּאמֶר אֲרַוְנָה אֶל־דָּוִד יִקַּח וְיַעַל אֲדֹנִי הַמֶּלֶךְ הַטּוֹב בעינו בְּעֵינָיו

Here are oxen for a burnt offering, and the threshing boards and the gear of the oxen for wood. [23]All this, [e-]O king,[-e] Araunah gives to Your Majesty. And may the LORD your God," Araunah added, "respond to you with favor!"

[24]But the king replied to Araunah, "No, I will buy them from you at a price. I cannot sacrifice to the LORD my God burnt offerings that have cost me nothing." So David bought the threshing floor and the oxen for fifty shekels of silver. [25]And David built there an altar to the LORD and sacrificed burnt offerings and offerings of well-being. The LORD responded to the plea for the land, and the plague against Israel was checked.

רְאֵה הַבָּקָר לָעֹלָה וְהַמֹּרִגִּים וּכְלֵי הַבָּקָר
לָעֵצִים: 23 הַכֹּל נָתַן אֲרַוְנָה הַמֶּלֶךְ
לַמֶּלֶךְ ס וַיֹּאמֶר אֲרַוְנָה אֶל־הַמֶּלֶךְ
יְהוָה אֱלֹהֶיךָ יִרְצֶךָ: 24 וַיֹּאמֶר הַמֶּלֶךְ אֶל־אֲרַוְנָה לֹא כִּי־קָנוֹ
אֶקְנֶה מֵאוֹתְךָ בִּמְחִיר וְלֹא אַעֲלֶה לַיהוָה
אֱלֹהַי עֹלוֹת חִנָּם וַיִּקֶן דָּוִד אֶת־הַגֹּרֶן
וְאֶת־הַבָּקָר בְּכֶסֶף שְׁקָלִים חֲמִשִּׁים:
25 וַיִּבֶן שָׁם דָּוִד מִזְבֵּחַ לַיהוָה וַיַּעַל עֹלוֹת
וּשְׁלָמִים וַיֵּעָתֵר יְהוָה לָאָרֶץ וַתֵּעָצַר
הַמַּגֵּפָה מֵעַל יִשְׂרָאֵל: *

תם ונשלם תהילה לאל בורא עולם

v. 25. סכום הפסוקים של ספר 1,506 וחציו 28.23 בחלק
הראשון (אף על פי שנסמן 28.24 בכתב היד שלנו)

1 KINGS

1 King David was now old, advanced in years; and though they covered him with bedclothes, he never felt warm. ²His courtiers said to him, "Let a young virgin be sought for my lord the king, to wait upon Your Majesty and be his attendant;*a* and let her lie in your bosom, and my lord the king will be warm." ³So they looked for a beautiful girl throughout the territory of Israel. They found Abishag the Shunammite and brought her to the king. ⁴The girl was exceedingly beautiful. She became the king's attendant*a* and waited upon him; but the king was not intimate with her.

⁵Now Adonijah son of Haggith *b*-went about boasting,-*b* "I will be king!" He provided himself with chariots and horses,*c* and an escort of fifty outrunners. ⁶His father had never scolded him: "Why did you do that?" He was the one born after Absalom*d* and, like him, was very handsome.

⁷He conferred with Joab son of Zeruiah and with the priest Abiathar, and they supported Adonijah; ⁸but the priest Zadok, Benaiah son of Jehoiada, the prophet Nathan, Shimei and Rei, and David's own fighting men did not side with Adonijah. ⁹Adonijah made a sacrificial feast of sheep, oxen, and fatlings at the Zoheleth stone which is near En-rogel; he invited all his brother princes*e* and all the king's courtiers of

א וְהַמֶּ֤לֶךְ דָּוִד֙ זָקֵ֔ן בָּ֖א בַּיָּמִ֑ים וַיְכַסֻּ֙הוּ֙ בַּבְּגָדִ֔ים וְלֹ֥א יִחַ֖ם לֽוֹ׃ 2 וַיֹּ֧אמְרוּ ל֣וֹ עֲבָדָ֗יו יְבַקְשׁ֞וּ לַאדֹנִ֤י הַמֶּ֙לֶךְ֙ נַעֲרָ֣ה בְתוּלָ֔ה וְעָֽמְדָה֙ לִפְנֵ֣י הַמֶּ֔לֶךְ וּתְהִי־ל֖וֹ סֹכֶ֑נֶת וְשָׁכְבָ֣ה בְחֵיקֶ֔ךָ וְחַ֖ם לַאדֹנִ֥י הַמֶּֽלֶךְ׃ 3 וַיְבַקְשׁוּ֙ נַעֲרָ֣ה יָפָ֔ה בְּכֹ֖ל גְּב֣וּל יִשְׂרָאֵ֑ל וַֽיִּמְצְא֗וּ אֶת־אֲבִישַׁג֙ הַשּׁ֣וּנַמִּ֔ית וַיָּבִ֥אוּ אֹתָ֖הּ לַמֶּֽלֶךְ׃ 4 וְהַֽנַּעֲרָ֖ה יָפָ֣ה עַד־מְאֹ֑ד וַתְּהִ֨י לַמֶּ֤לֶךְ סֹכֶ֙נֶת֙ וַתְּשָׁ֣רְתֵ֔הוּ וְהַמֶּ֖לֶךְ לֹ֥א יְדָעָֽהּ׃

5 וַאֲדֹנִיָּ֧ה בֶן־חַגִּ֛ית מִתְנַשֵּׂ֥א לֵאמֹ֖ר אֲנִ֣י אֶמְלֹ֑ךְ וַיַּ֣עַשׂ ל֗וֹ רֶ֚כֶב וּפָ֣רָשִׁ֔ים וַחֲמִשִּׁ֥ים אִ֖ישׁ רָצִ֥ים לְפָנָֽיו׃ 6 וְלֹֽא־עֲצָב֨וֹ אָבִ֤יו מִיָּמָיו֙ לֵאמֹ֔ר מַדּ֖וּעַ כָּ֣כָה עָשִׂ֑יתָ וְגַם־ה֗וּא טֽוֹב־תֹּ֙אַר֙ מְאֹ֔ד וְאֹת֥וֹ יָֽלְדָ֖ה אַחֲרֵ֥י אַבְשָׁלֽוֹם׃ 7 וַיִּהְי֣וּ דְבָרָ֔יו עִ֚ם יוֹאָ֣ב בֶּן־צְרוּיָ֔ה וְעִ֖ם אֶבְיָתָ֣ר הַכֹּהֵ֑ן וַֽיַּעְזְר֔וּ אַחֲרֵ֖י אֲדֹנִיָּֽה׃ 8 וְצָד֣וֹק הַ֠כֹּהֵן וּבְנָיָ֨הוּ בֶן־יְהוֹיָדָ֤ע וְנָתָ֤ן הַנָּבִיא֙ וְשִׁמְעִ֣י וְרֵעִ֔י וְהַגִּבּוֹרִ֖ים אֲשֶׁ֣ר לְדָוִ֑ד לֹ֥א הָי֖וּ עִם־אֲדֹנִיָּֽהוּ׃ 9 וַיִּזְבַּ֣ח אֲדֹנִיָּ֗הוּ צֹ֤אן וּבָקָר֙ וּמְרִ֔יא עִ֚ם אֶ֣בֶן הַזֹּחֶ֔לֶת אֲשֶׁר־אֵ֖צֶל עֵ֣ין רֹגֵ֑ל וַיִּקְרָ֗א אֶת־כָּל־אֶחָיו֙ בְּנֵ֣י הַמֶּ֔לֶךְ וּלְכָל־אַנְשֵׁ֥י יְהוּדָ֖ה עַבְדֵ֥י הַמֶּֽלֶךְ׃ 10 וְאֶת־

---

a Meaning of Heb. uncertain.
b-b Or "presumed to think."
c Others "horsemen"; meaning of Heb. parash(im) not always certain.
d Thus, Absalom having died, Adonijah was David's oldest living son.
e Lit. "all his brothers sons of the king."

the tribe of Judah; 10but he did not invite the prophet Nathan, or Benaiah, or the fighting men, or his brother Solomon.

11Then Nathan said to Bathsheba, Solomon's mother, "You must have heard that Adonijah son of Haggith has assumed the kingship without the knowledge of our lord David. 12Now take my advice, so that you may save your life and the life of your son Solomon. 13Go immediately to King David and say to him, 'Did not you, O lord king, swear to your maidservant: "Your son Solomon shall succeed me as king, and he shall sit upon my throne"? Then why has Adonijah become king?' 14While you are still there talking with the king, I will come in after you and confirm your words."

15So Bathsheba went to the king in his chamber.—The king was very old, and Abishag the Shunammite was waiting on the king.—16Bathsheba bowed low in homage to the king; and the king asked, "What troubles you?" 17She answered him, "My lord, you yourself swore to your maidservant by the LORD your God: 'Your son Solomon shall succeed me as king, and he shall sit upon my throne.' 18Yet now Adonijah has become king, and you, *f* my lord the king, know nothing about it. 19He has prepared a sacrificial feast of a great many oxen, fatlings, and sheep, and he has invited all the king's sons and Abiathar the priest and Joab commander of the army; but he has not invited your servant Solomon. 20And so the eyes of all Israel are upon you, O lord king, to tell them who shall succeed my lord the king on the throne. 21Otherwise, when my lord the king lies down with his fathers, my son Solomon and I will be regarded as traitors."

22She was still talking to the king when the prophet Nathan arrived. 23They announced to the king, "The prophet Nathan is here," and he

נָתָן הַנָּבִיא וּבְנָיָהוּ וְאֶת־הַגִּבּוֹרִים וְאֶת־שְׁלֹמֹה אָחִיו לֹא קָרָא: 11 וַיֹּאמֶר נָתָן אֶל־בַּת־שֶׁבַע אֵם־שְׁלֹמֹה לֵאמֹר הֲלוֹא שָׁמַעַתְּ כִּי מָלַךְ אֲדֹנִיָּהוּ בֶן־חַגִּית וַאֲדֹנֵינוּ דָוִד לֹא יָדָע: 12 וְעַתָּה לְכִי אִיעָצֵךְ נָא עֵצָה וּמַלְּטִי אֶת־נַפְשֵׁךְ וְאֶת־נֶפֶשׁ בְּנֵךְ שְׁלֹמֹה: 13 לְכִי וּבֹאִי אֶל־הַמֶּלֶךְ דָּוִד וְאָמַרְתְּ אֵלָיו הֲלֹא־אַתָּה אֲדֹנִי הַמֶּלֶךְ נִשְׁבַּעְתָּ לַאֲמָתְךָ לֵאמֹר כִּי־שְׁלֹמֹה בְנֵךְ יִמְלֹךְ אַחֲרַי וְהוּא יֵשֵׁב עַל־כִּסְאִי וּמַדּוּעַ מָלַךְ אֲדֹנִיָּהוּ: 14 הִנֵּה עוֹדֵךְ מְדַבֶּרֶת שָׁם עִם־הַמֶּלֶךְ וַאֲנִי אָבוֹא אַחֲרַיִךְ וּמִלֵּאתִי אֶת־דְּבָרָיִךְ: 15 וַתָּבֹא בַת־שֶׁבַע אֶל־הַמֶּלֶךְ הַחַדְרָה וְהַמֶּלֶךְ זָקֵן מְאֹד וַאֲבִישַׁג הַשּׁוּנַמִּית מְשָׁרַת אֶת־הַמֶּלֶךְ: 16 וַתִּקֹּד בַּת־שֶׁבַע וַתִּשְׁתַּחוּ לַמֶּלֶךְ וַיֹּאמֶר הַמֶּלֶךְ מַה־לָּךְ: 17 וַתֹּאמֶר לוֹ אֲדֹנִי אַתָּה נִשְׁבַּעְתָּ בַּיהוָה אֱלֹהֶיךָ לַאֲמָתֶךָ כִּי־שְׁלֹמֹה בְנֵךְ יִמְלֹךְ אַחֲרָי וְהוּא יֵשֵׁב עַל־כִּסְאִי: 18 וְעַתָּה הִנֵּה אֲדֹנִיָּה מָלָךְ וְעַתָּה* אֲדֹנִי הַמֶּלֶךְ לֹא יָדָעְתָּ: 19 וַיִּזְבַּח שׁוֹר וּמְרִיא־וְצֹאן לָרֹב וַיִּקְרָא לְכָל־בְּנֵי הַמֶּלֶךְ וּלְאֶבְיָתָר הַכֹּהֵן וּלְיֹאָב שַׂר הַצָּבָא וְלִשְׁלֹמֹה עַבְדְּךָ לֹא קָרָא: 20 וְאַתָּה אֲדֹנִי הַמֶּלֶךְ עֵינֵי כָל־יִשְׂרָאֵל עָלֶיךָ לְהַגִּיד לָהֶם מִי יֵשֵׁב עַל־כִּסֵּא אֲדֹנִי־הַמֶּלֶךְ אַחֲרָיו: 21 וְהָיָה כִּשְׁכַב אֲדֹנִי־הַמֶּלֶךְ עִם־אֲבֹתָיו וְהָיִיתִי אֲנִי וּבְנִי שְׁלֹמֹה חַטָּאִים: 22 וְהִנֵּה עוֹדֶנָּה מְדַבֶּרֶת עִם־הַמֶּלֶךְ וְנָתָן הַנָּבִיא בָּא: 23 וַיַּגִּידוּ לַמֶּלֶךְ לֵאמֹר הִנֵּה

f So many mss. and ancient versions; usual editions "now."

בנוסח אחר "אתה" *v.* 18.

entered the king's presence. Bowing low to the king with his face to the ground, 24Nathan said, "O lord king, g-you must have said,-g 'Adonijah shall succeed me as king and he shall sit upon my throne.' 25For he has gone down today and prepared a sacrificial feast of a great many oxen, fatlings, and sheep. He invited all the king's sons and the army officers and Abiathar the priest. At this very moment they are eating and drinking with him, and they are shouting, 'Long live King Adonijah!' 26But he did not invite me your servant, or the priest Zadok, or Benaiah son of Jehoiada, or your servant Solomon. 27Can this decision have come from my lord the king, without your telling your servant who is to succeed to the throne of my lord the king?"

28King David's response was: "Summon Bathsheba!" She entered the king's presence and stood before the king. 29And the king took an oath, saying, "As the LORD lives, who has rescued me from every trouble: 30The oath I swore to you by the LORD, the God of Israel, that your son Solomon should succeed me as king and that he should sit upon my throne in my stead, I will fulfill this very day!" 31Bathsheba bowed low in homage to the king with her face to the ground, and she said, "May my lord King David live forever!"

32Then King David said, "Summon to me the priest Zadok, the prophet Nathan, and Benaiah son of Jehoiada." When they came before the king, 33the king said to them, "Take h-my loyal soldiers,-h and have my son Solomon ride on my mule and bring him down to Gihon. 34Let the priest Zadok and the prophet Nathan anoint him there king over Israel, whereupon you shall sound the horn and shout, 'Long live King Solomon!' 35Then march up after him, and let him come in and sit on my throne. For he shall succeed me as king; him I designate to be ruler of

נָתָן הַנָּבִיא וַיָּבֹא לִפְנֵי הַמֶּלֶךְ וַיִּשְׁתַּחוּ
לַמֶּלֶךְ עַל־אַפָּיו אָרְצָה: 24 וַיֹּאמֶר נָתָן
אֲדֹנִי הַמֶּלֶךְ אַתָּה אָמַרְתָּ אֲדֹנִיָּהוּ יִמְלֹךְ
אַחֲרָי וְהוּא יֵשֵׁב עַל־כִּסְאִי: 25 כִּי | יָרַד
הַיּוֹם וַיִּזְבַּח שׁוֹר וּמְרִיא־וְצֹאן לָרֹב וַיִּקְרָא
לְכָל־בְּנֵי הַמֶּלֶךְ וּלְשָׂרֵי הַצָּבָא וּלְאֶבְיָתָר
הַכֹּהֵן וְהִנָּם אֹכְלִים וְשֹׁתִים לְפָנָיו וַיֹּאמְרוּ
יְחִי הַמֶּלֶךְ אֲדֹנִיָּהוּ: 26 וְלִי אֲנִי־עַבְדֶּךָ
וּלְצָדֹק הַכֹּהֵן וְלִבְנָיָהוּ בֶן־יְהוֹיָדָע
וְלִשְׁלֹמֹה עַבְדְּךָ לֹא קָרָא: 27 אִם מֵאֵת
אֲדֹנִי הַמֶּלֶךְ נִהְיָה הַדָּבָר הַזֶּה וְלֹא הוֹדַעְתָּ
אֶת־עֲבָדְךָ מִי יֵשֵׁב עַל־כִּסֵּא אֲדֹנִי־
הַמֶּלֶךְ אַחֲרָיו: ס
28 וַיַּעַן הַמֶּלֶךְ דָּוִד וַיֹּאמֶר קִרְאוּ־לִי לְבַת־
שֶׁבַע וַתָּבֹא לִפְנֵי הַמֶּלֶךְ וַתַּעֲמֹד לִפְנֵי
הַמֶּלֶךְ: 29 וַיִּשָּׁבַע הַמֶּלֶךְ וַיֹּאמַר חַי־יְהוָה
אֲשֶׁר־פָּדָה אֶת־נַפְשִׁי מִכָּל־צָרָה: 30 כִּי
כַּאֲשֶׁר נִשְׁבַּעְתִּי לָךְ בַּיהוָה אֱלֹהֵי יִשְׂרָאֵל
לֵאמֹר כִּי־שְׁלֹמֹה בְנֵךְ יִמְלֹךְ אַחֲרַי וְהוּא
יֵשֵׁב עַל־כִּסְאִי תַּחְתָּי כִּי כֵּן אֶעֱשֶׂה הַיּוֹם
הַזֶּה: 31 וַתִּקֹּד בַּת־שֶׁבַע אַפַּיִם אֶרֶץ*
וַתִּשְׁתַּחוּ לַמֶּלֶךְ וַתֹּאמֶר יְחִי אֲדֹנִי הַמֶּלֶךְ
דָּוִד לְעֹלָם: פ
32 וַיֹּאמֶר | הַמֶּלֶךְ דָּוִד קִרְאוּ־לִי לְצָדוֹק
הַכֹּהֵן וּלְנָתָן הַנָּבִיא וְלִבְנָיָהוּ בֶּן־יְהוֹיָדָע
וַיָּבֹאוּ לִפְנֵי הַמֶּלֶךְ: 33 וַיֹּאמֶר הַמֶּלֶךְ לָהֶם
קְחוּ עִמָּכֶם אֶת־עַבְדֵי אֲדֹנֵיכֶם וְהִרְכַּבְתֶּם
אֶת־שְׁלֹמֹה בְנִי עַל־הַפִּרְדָּה אֲשֶׁר־לִי
וְהוֹרַדְתֶּם אֹתוֹ אֶל־גִּחוֹן: 34 וּמָשַׁח אֹתוֹ
שָׁם צָדוֹק הַכֹּהֵן וְנָתָן הַנָּבִיא לְמֶלֶךְ
עַל־יִשְׂרָאֵל וּתְקַעְתֶּם בַּשּׁוֹפָר וַאֲמַרְתֶּם
יְחִי הַמֶּלֶךְ שְׁלֹמֹה: 35 וַעֲלִיתֶם אַחֲרָיו וּבָא
וְיָשַׁב עַל־כִּסְאִי וְהוּא יִמְלֹךְ תַּחְתָּי וְאֹתוֹ
צִוִּיתִי לִהְיוֹת נָגִיד עַל־יִשְׂרָאֵל וְעַל־

v. 31. סבירין ומטעין "ארצה"

g-g Or (cf. Rashi, Ralbag, Radak) "have you said…?"
h-h Lit. "your lord's men."

Israel and Judah." ³⁶Benaiah son of Jehoiada spoke up and said to the king, "Amen! And may the LORD, the God of my lord the king, so ordain. ³⁷As the LORD was with my lord the king, so may He be with Solomon; and may He exalt his throne even higher than the throne of my lord King David."

³⁸Then the priest Zadok, and the prophet Nathan, and Benaiah son of Jehoiada went down with the Cherethites and the Pelethites. They had Solomon ride on King David's mule and they led him to Gihon. ³⁹The priest Zadok took the horn of oil from the Tent and anointed Solomon. They sounded the horn and all the people shouted, "Long live King Solomon!" ⁴⁰All the people then marched up behind him, playing on flutes and making merry till the earth was split open by the uproar.

⁴¹Adonijah and all the guests who were with him, who had just finished eating, heard it. When Joab heard the sound of the horn, he said, "Why is the city in such an uproar?" ⁴²He was still speaking when the priest Jonathan son of Abiathar arrived. "Come in," said Adonijah. "You are a worthy man, and you surely bring good news." ⁴³But Jonathan replied to Adonijah, "Alas, our lord King David has made Solomon king! ⁴⁴The king sent with him the priest Zadok and the prophet Nathan and Benaiah son of Jehoiada, and the Cherethites and Pelethites. They had him ride on the king's mule, ⁴⁵and the priest Zadok and the prophet Nathan anointed him king at Gihon. Then they came up from there making merry, and the city went into an uproar. That's the noise you heard. ⁴⁶Further, Solomon seated himself on the royal throne; ⁴⁷further, the king's courtiers came to congratulate our lord King David, saying, 'May God make the renown of Solomon even greater

יְהוּדָֽה׃ ³⁶ וַיַּ֨עַן בְּנָיָ֤הוּ בֶן־יְהֽוֹיָדָע֙ אֶת־הַמֶּ֔לֶךְ וַיֹּ֖אמֶר ׀ אָמֵ֑ן כֵּ֚ן יֹאמַ֣ר יְהֹוָ֔ה אֱלֹהֵ֖י אֲדֹנִ֥י הַמֶּֽלֶךְ׃ ³⁷ כַּאֲשֶׁ֨ר הָיָ֤ה יְהֹוָה֙ עִם־אֲדֹנִ֣י הַמֶּ֔לֶךְ כֵּ֖ן יִֽהְיֶ֣ה עִם־שְׁלֹמֹ֑ה וִֽיגַדֵּל֙ אֶת־כִּסְא֔וֹ מִכִּסֵּ֖א אֲדֹנִ֥י הַמֶּ֥לֶךְ דָּוִֽד׃

³⁸ וַיֵּ֣רֶד צָד֣וֹק הַ֠כֹּהֵ֠ן וְנָתָ֨ן הַנָּבִ֜יא וּבְנָיָ֣הֽוּ בֶן־יְהוֹיָדָ֗ע וְהַכְּרֵתִי֙ וְהַפְּלֵתִ֔י וַיַּרְכִּ֙בוּ֙ אֶת־שְׁלֹמֹ֔ה עַל־פִּרְדַּ֖ת הַמֶּ֣לֶךְ דָּוִ֑ד וַיֹּלִ֥כוּ אֹת֖וֹ עַל־גִּחֽוֹן׃ ³⁹ וַיִּקַּח֩ צָד֨וֹק הַכֹּהֵ֜ן אֶת־קֶ֤רֶן הַשֶּׁ֙מֶן֙ מִן־הָאֹ֔הֶל וַיִּמְשַׁ֖ח אֶת־שְׁלֹמֹ֑ה וַֽיִּתְקְעוּ֙ בַּשּׁוֹפָ֔ר וַיֹּֽאמְרוּ֙ כָּל־הָעָ֔ם יְחִ֖י הַמֶּ֥לֶךְ שְׁלֹמֹֽה׃ ⁴⁰ וַיַּעֲל֤וּ כָל־הָעָם֙ אַֽחֲרָ֔יו וְהָעָם֙ מְחַלְּלִ֣ים בַּֽחֲלִלִ֔ים וּשְׂמֵחִ֖ים שִׂמְחָ֣ה גְדוֹלָ֑ה וַתִּבָּקַ֥ע הָאָ֖רֶץ בְּקוֹלָֽם׃

⁴¹ וַיִּשְׁמַ֣ע אֲדֹ֣נִיָּ֗הוּ וְכָל־הַקְּרֻאִים֙ אֲשֶׁ֣ר אִתּ֔וֹ וְהֵ֖ם כִּלּ֣וּ לֶאֱכֹ֑ל וַיִּשְׁמַ֤ע יוֹאָב֙ אֶת־ק֣וֹל הַשּׁוֹפָ֔ר וַיֹּ֕אמֶר מַדּ֥וּעַ קֽוֹל־הַקִּרְיָ֖ה הוֹמָֽה׃ ⁴² עוֹדֶ֣נּוּ מְדַבֵּ֔ר וְהִנֵּ֛ה יֽוֹנָתָ֥ן בֶּן־אֶבְיָתָ֥ר הַכֹּהֵ֖ן בָּ֑א וַיֹּ֤אמֶר אֲדֹֽנִיָּ֙הוּ֙ בֹּ֔א כִּ֣י אִ֥ישׁ חַ֛יִל אַ֖תָּה וְט֥וֹב תְּבַשֵּֽׂר׃ ⁴³ וַיַּ֙עַן֙ יֽוֹנָתָ֔ן וַיֹּ֖אמֶר לַאֲדֹֽנִיָּ֑הוּ אֲבָ֕ל אֲדֹנֵ֥ינוּ הַמֶּֽלֶךְ־דָּוִ֖ד הִמְלִ֥יךְ אֶת־שְׁלֹמֹֽה׃ ⁴⁴ וַיִּשְׁלַ֣ח אִתּֽוֹ־הַמֶּ֡לֶךְ אֶת־צָד֣וֹק הַכֹּהֵ֣ן וְאֶת־נָתָ֣ן הַנָּבִ֡יא וּ֠בְנָיָ֠הוּ בֶּן־יְהֽוֹיָדָ֞ע וְהַכְּרֵתִ֣י וְהַפְּלֵתִ֗י וַיַּרְכִּ֥בוּ אֹת֖וֹ עַ֥ל פִּרְדַּ֥ת הַמֶּֽלֶךְ׃ ⁴⁵ וַיִּמְשְׁח֣וּ אֹת֡וֹ צָד֣וֹק הַכֹּהֵ֣ן וְנָתָן֩ הַנָּבִ֨יא לְמֶ֜לֶךְ בְּגִח֗וֹן וַיַּעֲל֤וּ מִשָּׁם֙ שְׂמֵחִ֔ים וַתֵּהֹ֖ם הַקִּרְיָ֑ה ה֥וּא הַקּ֖וֹל אֲשֶׁ֥ר שְׁמַעְתֶּֽם׃ ⁴⁶ וְגַ֛ם יָשַׁ֥ב שְׁלֹמֹ֖ה עַ֥ל כִּסֵּ֥א הַמְּלוּכָֽה׃ ⁴⁷ וְגַם־בָּ֜אוּ עַבְדֵ֣י הַמֶּ֗לֶךְ לְ֠בָרֵ֠ךְ אֶת־אֲדֹנֵ֜ינוּ הַמֶּ֣לֶךְ דָּוִד֮ לֵאמֹר֒ יֵיטֵ֨ב אֱלֹהֶ֤יךָ אֶת־שֵׁם֙ שְׁלֹמֹה֙ מִשְּׁמֶ֔ךָ וִֽיגַדֵּ֥ל אֶת־כִּסְא֖וֹ מִכִּסְאֶ֑ךָ

than yours, and may He exalt his throne even higher than yours!' And the king bowed low on his couch. [48]And further, this is what the king said, 'Praised be the LORD, the God of Israel who has this day provided a successor to my throne, while my own eyes can see it.'" [49]Thereupon, all of Adonijah's guests rose in alarm and each went his own way.

[50]Adonijah, in fear of Solomon, went at once [to the Tent] and grasped the horns of the altar. [51]It was reported to Solomon: "Adonijah is in fear of King Solomon and has grasped the horns of the altar, saying, 'Let King Solomon first swear to me that he will not put his servant to the sword.'" [52]Solomon said, "If he behaves worthily, not a hair of his head shall fall to the ground; but if he is caught in any offense, he shall die." [53]So King Solomon sent and had him taken down from the altar. He came and bowed before King Solomon, and Solomon said to him, "Go home."

2 When David's life was drawing to a close, he instructed his son Solomon as follows: [2]"I am going the way of all the earth; be strong and show yourself a man. [3]Keep the charge of the LORD your God, walking in His ways and following His laws, His commandments, His rules, and His admonitions as recorded in the Teaching of Moses, in order that you may succeed in whatever you undertake and wherever you turn. [4]Then the LORD will fulfill the promise that He made concerning me: 'If your descendants are scrupulous in their conduct, and walk before Me faithfully, with all their heart and soul, [a]-your line on the throne of Israel shall never end!'-[a]

[5]"Further, you know what Joab son of Zeruiah did to me, what he did to the two com-

וַיִּשְׁתַּ֥חוּ הַמֶּ֖לֶךְ עַל־הַמִּשְׁכָּֽב׃ 48 וְגַם־כָּ֙כָה֙ אָמַ֣ר הַמֶּ֔לֶךְ בָּר֥וּךְ יְהֹוָ֖ה אֱלֹהֵ֣י יִשְׂרָאֵ֑ל אֲשֶׁ֣ר נָתַ֣ן הַיּ֗וֹם יֹשֵׁ֛ב עַל־כִּסְאִ֖י וְעֵינַ֥י רֹאֽוֹת׃ 49 וַיֶּחֶרְדוּ֙ וַיָּקֻ֔מוּ כׇּל־הַקְּרֻאִ֖ים אֲשֶׁ֣ר לַאֲדֹנִיָּ֑הוּ וַיֵּלְכ֖וּ אִ֥ישׁ לְדַרְכּֽוֹ׃ 50 וַאֲדֹ֣נִיָּ֔הוּ יָרֵ֖א מִפְּנֵ֣י שְׁלֹמֹ֑ה וַיָּ֣קׇם וַיֵּ֔לֶךְ וַֽיַּחֲזֵ֖ק בְּקַרְנ֥וֹת הַמִּזְבֵּֽחַ׃ 51 וַיֻּגַּ֣ד לִשְׁלֹמֹ֣ה לֵאמֹ֗ר הִנֵּה֙ אֲדֹ֣נִיָּ֔הוּ יָרֵ֖א אֶת־הַמֶּ֣לֶךְ שְׁלֹמֹ֑ה וְ֠הִנֵּ֠ה אָחַ֞ז בְּקַרְנ֤וֹת הַמִּזְבֵּ֙חַ֙ לֵאמֹ֔ר יִשָּֽׁבַֽע־לִ֤י כַיּוֹם֙ הַמֶּ֣לֶךְ שְׁלֹמֹ֔ה אִם־יָמִ֥ית אֶת־עַבְדּ֖וֹ בֶּחָֽרֶב׃ 52 וַיֹּ֣אמֶר שְׁלֹמֹ֔ה אִ֚ם יִֽהְיֶ֣ה לְבֶן־חַ֔יִל לֹֽא־יִפֹּ֥ל מִשַּׂעֲרָת֖וֹ אָ֑רְצָה וְאִם־רָעָ֥ה תִמָּצֵא־ב֖וֹ וָמֵֽת׃ 53 וַיִּשְׁלַ֞ח הַמֶּ֣לֶךְ שְׁלֹמֹ֗ה וַיֹּרִדֻ֙הוּ֙ מֵעַ֣ל הַמִּזְבֵּ֔חַ וַיָּבֹ֕א וַיִּשְׁתַּ֖חוּ לַמֶּ֣לֶךְ שְׁלֹמֹ֑ה וַיֹּֽאמֶר־ל֥וֹ שְׁלֹמֹ֖ה לֵ֥ךְ לְבֵיתֶֽךָ׃ פ

ב וַיִּקְרְב֥וּ יְמֵֽי־דָוִ֖ד לָמ֑וּת וַיְצַ֛ו אֶת־שְׁלֹמֹ֥ה בְנ֖וֹ לֵאמֹֽר׃ 2 אָנֹכִ֣י הֹלֵ֔ךְ בְּדֶ֖רֶךְ כׇּל־הָאָ֑רֶץ וְחָזַקְתָּ֖ וְהָיִ֥יתָֽ לְאִֽישׁ׃ 3 וְשָׁמַרְתָּ֞ אֶת־מִשְׁמֶ֣רֶת ׀ יְהֹוָ֣ה אֱלֹהֶ֗יךָ לָלֶ֤כֶת בִּדְרָכָיו֙ לִשְׁמֹ֨ר חֻקֹּתָ֤יו מִצְוֺתָיו֙ וּמִשְׁפָּטָ֣יו וְעֵדְוֺתָ֔יו כַּכָּת֖וּב בְּתוֹרַ֣ת מֹשֶׁ֑ה לְמַ֣עַן תַּשְׂכִּ֗יל אֵ֤ת כׇּל־אֲשֶׁר֙ תַּעֲשֶׂ֔ה וְאֵ֛ת כׇּל־אֲשֶׁ֥ר תִּפְנֶ֖ה שָֽׁם׃ 4 לְמַ֩עַן֩ יָקִ֨ים יְהֹוָ֜ה אֶת־דְּבָר֗וֹ אֲשֶׁ֨ר דִּבֶּ֣ר עָלַי֮ לֵאמֹר֒ אִם־יִשְׁמְר֣וּ בָנֶ֣יךָ אֶת־דַּרְכָּ֗ם לָלֶ֤כֶת לְפָנַי֙ בֶּאֱמֶ֔ת בְּכׇל־לְבָבָ֖ם וּבְכׇל־נַפְשָׁ֑ם לֵאמֹ֕ר לֹא־יִכָּרֵ֤ת לְךָ֙ אִ֔ישׁ מֵעַ֖ל כִּסֵּ֥א יִשְׂרָאֵֽל׃ 5 וְגַ֣ם אַתָּ֣ה יָדַ֗עְתָּ אֵת֩ אֲשֶׁר־עָ֨שָׂה לִ֜י יוֹאָ֣ב בֶּן־צְרוּיָ֗ה אֲשֶׁ֣ר עָשָׂ֣ה לִשְׁנֵֽי־שָׂרֵ֣י צִבְא֣וֹת

---

[a]-[a] Lit. "there shall never cease to be a man of yours on the throne of Israel." Cf. 2 Sam. 7.12–16.

manders of Israel's forces, Abner son of Ner and Amasa son of Jether: he killed them, shedding[b] blood of war in peacetime, staining the girdle of his loins and the sandals on his feet with blood of war.[c] 6So act in accordance with your wisdom, and see that his white hair does not go down to Sheol in peace.

7"But deal graciously with the sons of Barzillai the Gileadite, for they befriended me when I fled from your brother Absalom; let them be among those that eat at your table.[d]

8"You must also deal with Shimei son of Gera, the Benjaminite from Bahurim. He insulted me outrageously when I was on my way to Mahanaim; but he came down to meet me at the Jordan,[e] and I swore to him by the LORD: 'I will not put you to the sword.' 9So do not let him go unpunished; for you are a wise man and you will know how to deal with him and send his gray hair down to Sheol in blood."

10So David slept with his fathers, and he was buried in the City of David. 11The length of David's reign over Israel was forty years: he reigned seven years in Hebron, and he reigned thirty-three years in Jerusalem. 12And Solomon sat upon the throne of his father David, and his rule was firmly established.

13Adonijah son of Haggith came to see Bath-sheba, Solomon's mother. She said, "Do you come with friendly intent?" "Yes," he replied; 14and he continued, "I would like to have a word with you." "Speak up," she said. 15Then he said, "You know that the kingship was rightly mine and that all Israel wanted me to reign. But the kingship passed on to my brother; it came to him by the will of the LORD. 16And now I have one request to make of you; do not refuse me." She said, "Speak up." 17He replied, "Please ask

יִשְׂרָאֵל לְאַבְנֵר בֶּן־נֵר וְלַעֲמָשָׂא בֶן־יֶתֶר
וַיַּהַרְגֵם וַיָּשֶׂם דְּמֵי־מִלְחָמָה בְּשָׁלֹם וַיִּתֵּן
דְּמֵי מִלְחָמָה בַּחֲגֹרָתוֹ אֲשֶׁר בְּמָתְנָיו
וּבְנַעֲלוֹ אֲשֶׁר בְּרַגְלָיו: 6 וְעָשִׂיתָ כְּחָכְמָתֶךָ
וְלֹא־תוֹרֵד שֵׂיבָתוֹ בְּשָׁלֹם שְׁאֹל: ס
7 וְלִבְנֵי בַרְזִלַּי הַגִּלְעָדִי תַּעֲשֶׂה־חֶסֶד וְהָיוּ
בְּאֹכְלֵי שֻׁלְחָנֶךָ כִּי־כֵן קָרְבוּ אֵלַי בְּבָרְחִי
מִפְּנֵי אַבְשָׁלוֹם אָחִיךָ:
8 וְהִנֵּה עִמְּךָ שִׁמְעִי בֶן־גֵּרָא בֶן־הַיְמִינִי
מִבַּחֻרִים וְהוּא קִלְלַנִי קְלָלָה נִמְרֶצֶת בְּיוֹם
לֶכְתִּי מַחֲנָיִם וְהוּא־יָרַד לִקְרָאתִי הַיַּרְדֵּן
וָאֶשָּׁבַע לוֹ בַיהוָה לֵאמֹר אִם־אֲמִיתְךָ
בֶּחָרֶב: 9 וְעַתָּה אַל־תְּנַקֵּהוּ כִּי אִישׁ חָכָם
אָתָּה וְיָדַעְתָּ אֵת אֲשֶׁר תַּעֲשֶׂה־לּוֹ וְהוֹרַדְתָּ
אֶת־שֵׂיבָתוֹ בְּדָם שְׁאוֹל:
10 וַיִּשְׁכַּב דָּוִד עִם־אֲבֹתָיו וַיִּקָּבֵר בְּעִיר
דָּוִד: פ 11 וְהַיָּמִים אֲשֶׁר מָלַךְ דָּוִד עַל־
יִשְׂרָאֵל אַרְבָּעִים שָׁנָה בְּחֶבְרוֹן מָלַךְ שֶׁבַע
שָׁנִים וּבִירוּשָׁלַ͏ִם מָלַךְ שְׁלֹשִׁים וְשָׁלֹשׁ
שָׁנִים: 12 וּשְׁלֹמֹה יָשַׁב עַל־כִּסֵּא דָּוִד אָבִיו
וַתִּכֹּן מַלְכֻתוֹ מְאֹד:
13 וַיָּבֹא אֲדֹנִיָּהוּ בֶן־חַגֵּית אֶל־בַּת־שֶׁבַע
אֵם־שְׁלֹמֹה וַתֹּאמֶר הֲשָׁלוֹם בֹּאֶךָ וַיֹּאמֶר
שָׁלוֹם: 14 וַיֹּאמֶר דָּבָר לִי אֵלָיִךְ וַתֹּאמֶר
דַּבֵּר: 15 וַיֹּאמֶר אַתְּ יָדַעַתְּ כִּי־לִי הָיְתָה
הַמְּלוּכָה וְעָלַי שָׂמוּ כָל־יִשְׂרָאֵל פְּנֵיהֶם
לִמְלֹךְ וַתִּסֹּב הַמְּלוּכָה וַתְּהִי לְאָחִי כִּי
מֵיהוָה הָיְתָה לּוֹ: 16 וְעַתָּה שְׁאֵלָה אַחַת
אָנֹכִי שֹׁאֵל מֵאִתָּךְ אַל־תָּשִׁבִי אֶת־פָּנָי
וַתֹּאמֶר אֵלָיו דַּבֵּר: 17 וַיֹּאמֶר אִמְרִי־נָא

---

b   Meaning of Heb. uncertain.
c   I.e., Joab had thus brought bloodguilt on David's house; see 2 Sam. 3.27 and 20.10.
d   I.e., for whose maintenance you provide; see 2 Sam. 19.32 ff.
e   See 2 Sam. 16.5 ff; 19.17 ff.

King Solomon—for he won't refuse you—to give me Abishag the Shunammite as wife." [18]"Very well," said Bathsheba, "I will speak to the king in your behalf."

[19]So Bathsheba went to King Solomon to speak to him about Adonijah. The king rose to greet her and bowed down to her. He sat on his throne; and he had a throne placed for the queen mother, and she sat on his right. [20]She said, "I have one small request to make of you, do not refuse me." He responded, "Ask, Mother; I shall not refuse you." [21]Then she said, "Let Abishag the Shunammite be given to your brother Adonijah as wife." [22]The king replied to his mother, "Why request Abishag the Shunammite for Adonijah? Request the kingship for him! For he is my older brother, *f-and the priest Abiathar and Joab son of Zeruiah are on his side."-f*

[23]Thereupon, King Solomon swore by the LORD, saying, "So may God do to me and even more, if broaching this matter does not cost Adonijah his life! [24]Now, as the LORD lives, who has established me and set me on the throne of my father David and who has provided him*g* with a house, as he promised, Adonijah shall be put to death this very day!" [25]And Solomon instructed Benaiah son of Jehoiada, who struck Adonijah*h* down; and so he died.

[26]To the priest Abiathar, the king said, "Go to your estate at Anathoth! You deserve to die, but I shall not put you to death at this time, because you carried the Ark of my Lord GOD before my father David and because you shared all the hardships that my father endured." [27]So Solomon dismissed Abiathar from his office of priest of the LORD—thus fulfilling what the LORD had spoken at Shiloh*i* regarding the house of Eli.

לִשְׁלֹמֹה הַמֶּלֶךְ כִּי לֹא־יָשִׁיב אֶת־פָּנָיִךְ וְיִתֶּן־לִי אֶת־אֲבִישַׁג הַשּׁוּנַמִּית לְאִשָּׁה: [18] וַתֹּאמֶר בַּת־שֶׁבַע טוֹב אָנֹכִי אֲדַבֵּר עָלַיִךְ אֶל־הַמֶּלֶךְ: [19] וַתָּבֹא בַת־שֶׁבַע אֶל־הַמֶּלֶךְ שְׁלֹמֹה לְדַבֶּר־לוֹ עַל־אֲדֹנִיָּהוּ וַיָּקָם הַמֶּלֶךְ לִקְרָאתָהּ וַיִּשְׁתַּחוּ לָהּ וַיֵּשֶׁב עַל־כִּסְאוֹ וַיָּשֶׂם כִּסֵּא לְאֵם הַמֶּלֶךְ וַתֵּשֶׁב לִימִינוֹ: [20] וַתֹּאמֶר שְׁאֵלָה אַחַת קְטַנָּה אָנֹכִי שֹׁאֶלֶת מֵאִתָּךְ אַל־תָּשֶׁב אֶת־פָּנָי וַיֹּאמֶר־לָהּ הַמֶּלֶךְ שַׁאֲלִי אִמִּי כִּי לֹא־אָשִׁיב אֶת־פָּנָיִךְ: [21] וַתֹּאמֶר יֻתַּן אֶת־אֲבִישַׁג הַשֻּׁנַמִּית לַאֲדֹנִיָּהוּ אָחִיךָ לְאִשָּׁה: [22] וַיַּעַן הַמֶּלֶךְ שְׁלֹמֹה וַיֹּאמֶר לְאִמּוֹ וְלָמָה אַתְּ שֹׁאֶלֶת אֶת־אֲבִישַׁג הַשֻּׁנַמִּית לַאֲדֹנִיָּהוּ וְשַׁאֲלִי־לוֹ אֶת־הַמְּלוּכָה כִּי הוּא אָחִי הַגָּדוֹל מִמֶּנִּי וְלוֹ וּלְאֶבְיָתָר הַכֹּהֵן וּלְיוֹאָב בֶּן־צְרוּיָה: פ [23] וַיִּשָּׁבַע הַמֶּלֶךְ שְׁלֹמֹה בַּיהוָה לֵאמֹר כֹּה יַעֲשֶׂה־לִּי אֱלֹהִים וְכֹה יוֹסִיף כִּי בְנַפְשׁוֹ דִּבֶּר אֲדֹנִיָּהוּ אֶת־הַדָּבָר הַזֶּה: [24] וְעַתָּה חַי־יְהוָה אֲשֶׁר הֱכִינַנִי וַיּוֹשִׁיבַנִי עַל־כִּסֵּא דָּוִד אָבִי וַאֲשֶׁר עָשָׂה־לִי בַּיִת כַּאֲשֶׁר דִּבֵּר כִּי הַיּוֹם יוּמַת אֲדֹנִיָּהוּ: [25] וַיִּשְׁלַח הַמֶּלֶךְ שְׁלֹמֹה בְּיַד בְּנָיָהוּ בֶן־יְהוֹיָדָע וַיִּפְגַּע־בּוֹ וַיָּמֹת: ס [26] וּלְאֶבְיָתָר הַכֹּהֵן אָמַר הַמֶּלֶךְ עֲנָתֹת לֵךְ עַל־שָׂדֶיךָ כִּי אִישׁ מָוֶת אָתָּה וּבַיּוֹם הַזֶּה לֹא אֲמִיתֶךָ כִּי־נָשָׂאתָ אֶת־אֲרוֹן אֲדֹנָי יְהוִֹה לִפְנֵי דָּוִד אָבִי וְכִי הִתְעַנִּיתָ בְּכֹל אֲשֶׁר־הִתְעַנָּה אָבִי: [27] וַיְגָרֶשׁ שְׁלֹמֹה אֶת־אֶבְיָתָר מִהְיוֹת כֹּהֵן לַיהוָה לְמַלֵּא אֶת־דְּבַר יְהוָה אֲשֶׁר דִּבֶּר עַל־בֵּית עֵלִי בְּשִׁלֹה: פ

---

f-f   Lit. "And for him and for Abiathar and for Joab son of Zeruiah."
       Meaning of Heb. uncertain.
g   Heb. "me."
h   Heb. "him."
i   Cf. 1 Sam. 3.14.

²⁸When the news reached Joab, he fled to the Tent of the Lᴏʀᴅ and grasped the horns of the altar—for Joab had sided with Adonijah, though he had not sided with Absalom. ²⁹King Solomon was told that Joab had fled to the Tent of the Lᴏʀᴅ and that he was there by the altar; so Solomon sent Benaiah son of Jehoiada, saying, "Go and strike him down." ³⁰Benaiah went to the Tent of the Lᴏʀᴅ and said to him, "Thus said the king: Come out!" "No!" he replied; "I will die here." Benaiah reported back to the king that Joab had answered thus and thus, ³¹and the king said, "Do just as he said; strike him down and bury him, and remove guilt from me and my father's house for the blood of the innocent that Joab has shed. ³²Thus the Lᴏʀᴅ will bring his blood guilt down upon his own head, because, unbeknown to my father, he struck down with the sword two men more righteous and honorable than he—Abner son of Ner, the army commander of Israel, and Amasa son of Jether, the army commander of Judah. ³³May the guilt for their blood come down upon the head of Joab and his descendants forever, and may good fortune from the Lᴏʀᴅ be granted forever to David and his descendants, his house and his throne." ³⁴So Benaiah son of Jehoiada went up and struck him down. And he was buried at his home in the wilderness. ³⁵In his place, the king appointed Benaiah son of Jehoiada over the army, and in place of Abiathar, the king appointed the priest Zadok.

³⁶Then the king summoned Shimei and said to him, "Build yourself a house in Jerusalem and stay there—do not ever go out from there anywhere else. ³⁷On the very day that you go out and cross the Wadi Kidron, you can be sure that you will die; your blood shall be on your own head." ³⁸"That is fair," said Shimei to the king, "your servant will do just as my lord the king has spoken." And for a long time, Shimei remained in Jerusalem.

וְהַשְּׁמֻעָה בָּאָה עַד־יוֹאָב כִּי יוֹאָב נָטָה 28
אַחֲרֵי אֲדֹנִיָּה וְאַחֲרֵי אַבְשָׁלוֹם לֹא נָטָה
וַיָּנָס יוֹאָב אֶל־אֹהֶל יְהֹוָה וַיַּחֲזֵק בְּקַרְנוֹת
הַמִּזְבֵּחַ: 29 וַיֻּגַּד לַמֶּלֶךְ שְׁלֹמֹה כִּי נָס יוֹאָב
אֶל־אֹהֶל יְהֹוָה וְהִנֵּה אֵצֶל הַמִּזְבֵּחַ וַיִּשְׁלַח
שְׁלֹמֹה אֶת־בְּנָיָהוּ בֶן־יְהוֹיָדָע לֵאמֹר לֵךְ
פְּגַע־בּוֹ: 30 וַיָּבֹא בְנָיָהוּ אֶל־אֹהֶל יְהֹוָה
וַיֹּאמֶר אֵלָיו כֹּה־אָמַר הַמֶּלֶךְ צֵא וַיֹּאמֶר
לֹא כִּי פֹה אָמוּת וַיָּשֶׁב בְּנָיָהוּ אֶת־הַמֶּלֶךְ
דָּבָר לֵאמֹר כֹּה־דִבֶּר יוֹאָב וְכֹה עָנָנִי:
31 וַיֹּאמֶר לוֹ הַמֶּלֶךְ עֲשֵׂה כַּאֲשֶׁר דִּבֶּר
וּפְגַע־בּוֹ וּקְבַרְתּוֹ וַהֲסִירֹתָ ׀ דְּמֵי חִנָּם אֲשֶׁר
שָׁפַךְ יוֹאָב מֵעָלַי וּמֵעַל בֵּית אָבִי:
32 וְהֵשִׁיב יְהֹוָה אֶת־דָּמוֹ עַל־רֹאשׁוֹ אֲשֶׁר
פָּגַע בִּשְׁנֵי־אֲנָשִׁים צַדִּקִים וְטֹבִים מִמֶּנּוּ
וַיַּהַרְגֵם בַּחֶרֶב וְאָבִי דָוִד לֹא יָדָע אֶת־
אַבְנֵר בֶּן־נֵר שַׂר־צְבָא יִשְׂרָאֵל וְאֶת־
עֲמָשָׂא בֶן־יֶתֶר שַׂר־צְבָא יְהוּדָה: 33 וְשָׁבוּ
דְמֵיהֶם בְּרֹאשׁ יוֹאָב וּבְרֹאשׁ זַרְעוֹ לְעֹלָם
וּלְדָוִד וּלְזַרְעוֹ וּלְבֵיתוֹ וּלְכִסְאוֹ יִהְיֶה
שָׁלוֹם עַד־עוֹלָם מֵעִם יְהֹוָה: 34 וַיַּעַל
בְּנָיָהוּ בֶּן־יְהוֹיָדָע וַיִּפְגַּע־בּוֹ וַיְמִתֵהוּ וַיִּקָּבֵר
בְּבֵיתוֹ בַּמִּדְבָּר: 35 וַיִּתֵּן הַמֶּלֶךְ אֶת־בְּנָיָהוּ
בֶן־יְהוֹיָדָע תַּחְתָּיו עַל־הַצָּבָא וְאֶת־צָדוֹק
הַכֹּהֵן נָתַן הַמֶּלֶךְ תַּחַת אֶבְיָתָר:
36 וַיִּשְׁלַח הַמֶּלֶךְ וַיִּקְרָא לְשִׁמְעִי וַיֹּאמֶר
לוֹ בְּנֵה־לְךָ בַיִת בִּירוּשָׁלַ͏ִם וְיָשַׁבְתָּ שָׁם
וְלֹא־תֵצֵא מִשָּׁם אָנֶה וָאָנָה: 37 וְהָיָה ׀
בְּיוֹם צֵאתְךָ וְעָבַרְתָּ אֶת־נַחַל קִדְרוֹן יָדֹעַ
תֵּדַע כִּי מוֹת תָּמוּת דָּמְךָ יִהְיֶה בְרֹאשֶׁךָ:
38 וַיֹּאמֶר שִׁמְעִי לַמֶּלֶךְ טוֹב הַדָּבָר כַּאֲשֶׁר
דִּבֶּר אֲדֹנִי הַמֶּלֶךְ כֵּן יַעֲשֶׂה עַבְדֶּךָ וַיֵּשֶׁב
שִׁמְעִי בִּירוּשָׁלַ͏ִם יָמִים רַבִּים: ס

39Three years later, two slaves of Shimei ran away to King Achish son of Maacah of Gath. Shimei was told, "Your slaves are in Gath." 40Shimei thereupon saddled his ass and went to Achish in Gath to claim his slaves; and Shimei returned from Gath with his slaves. 41Solomon was told that Shimei had gone from Jerusalem to Gath and back, 42and the king summoned Shimei and said to him, "Did I not adjure you by the LORD and warn you, 'On the very day that you leave and go anywhere else, you can be sure that you will die,' and did you not say to me, 'It is fair; I accept'? 43Why did you not abide by the oath before the LORD and by the orders which I gave you?" 44The king said further to Shimei, "You know all the wrong, which you remember very well, that you did to my father David. Now the LORD brings down your wrongdoing upon your own head. 45But King Solomon shall be blessed, and the throne of David shall be established before the LORD forever."

46The king gave orders to Benaiah son of Jehoiada and he went out and struck Shimei[h] down; and so he died.

Thus the kingdom was secured in Solomon's hands.

3 Solomon allied himself by marriage with Pharaoh king of Egypt. He married Pharaoh's daughter and brought her to the City of David [to live there] until he had finished building his palace, and the House of the LORD, and the walls around Jerusalem.

2The people, however, continued to offer sacrifices at the open shrines, because up to that time no house had been built for the name of the LORD. 3And Solomon, though he loved the LORD and followed the practices of his father David, also sacrificed and offered at the shrines.

39 וַיְהִי מִקֵּץ שָׁלֹשׁ שָׁנִים וַיִּבְרְחוּ שְׁנֵי־
עֲבָדִים לְשִׁמְעִי אֶל־אָכִישׁ בֶּן־מַעֲכָה מֶלֶךְ
גַּת וַיַּגִּידוּ לְשִׁמְעִי לֵאמֹר הִנֵּה עֲבָדֶיךָ
בְּגַת: 40 וַיָּקָם שִׁמְעִי וַיַּחֲבֹשׁ אֶת־חֲמֹרוֹ
וַיֵּלֶךְ גַּתָה אֶל־אָכִישׁ לְבַקֵּשׁ אֶת־עֲבָדָיו
וַיֵּלֶךְ שִׁמְעִי וַיָּבֵא אֶת־עֲבָדָיו מִגַּת: 41 וַיֻּגַּד
לִשְׁלֹמֹה כִּי־הָלַךְ שִׁמְעִי מִירוּשָׁלַ͏ִם גַּת
וַיָּשֹׁב: 42 וַיִּשְׁלַח הַמֶּלֶךְ וַיִּקְרָא לְשִׁמְעִי
וַיֹּאמֶר אֵלָיו הֲלוֹא הִשְׁבַּעְתִּיךָ בַיהוָה
וָאָעִד בְּךָ לֵאמֹר בְּיוֹם צֵאתְךָ וְהָלַכְתָּ אָנֶה
וָאָנָה יָדֹעַ תֵּדַע כִּי מוֹת תָּמוּת וַתֹּאמֶר
אֵלַי טוֹב הַדָּבָר שָׁמָעְתִּי: 43 וּמַדּוּעַ לֹא
שָׁמַרְתָּ אֵת שְׁבֻעַת יְהוָה וְאֶת־הַמִּצְוָה
אֲשֶׁר־צִוִּיתִי עָלֶיךָ: 44 וַיֹּאמֶר הַמֶּלֶךְ אֶל־
שִׁמְעִי אַתָּה יָדַעְתָּ אֵת כָּל־הָרָעָה אֲשֶׁר
יָדַע לְבָבְךָ אֲשֶׁר עָשִׂיתָ לְדָוִד אָבִי וְהֵשִׁיב
יְהוָה אֶת־רָעָתְךָ בְּרֹאשֶׁךָ: 45 וְהַמֶּלֶךְ
שְׁלֹמֹה בָּרוּךְ וְכִסֵּא דָוִד יִהְיֶה נָכוֹן לִפְנֵי
יְהוָה עַד־עוֹלָם:
46 וַיְצַו הַמֶּלֶךְ אֶת־בְּנָיָהוּ בֶּן־יְהוֹיָדָע וַיֵּצֵא
וַיִּפְגַּע־בּוֹ וַיָּמֹת
וְהַמַּמְלָכָה נָכוֹנָה בְּיַד־שְׁלֹמֹה:

ג וַיִּתְחַתֵּן שְׁלֹמֹה אֶת־פַּרְעֹה מֶלֶךְ
מִצְרָיִם וַיִּקַּח אֶת־בַּת־פַּרְעֹה וַיְבִיאֶהָ אֶל־
עִיר דָּוִד עַד כַּלֹּתוֹ לִבְנוֹת אֶת־בֵּיתוֹ
וְאֶת־בֵּית יְהוָה וְאֶת־חוֹמַת יְרוּשָׁלַ͏ִם
סָבִיב:
2 רַק הָעָם מְזַבְּחִים בַּבָּמוֹת כִּי לֹא־נִבְנָה
בַיִת לְשֵׁם יְהוָה עַד הַיָּמִים הָהֵם: פ
3 וַיֶּאֱהַב שְׁלֹמֹה אֶת־יְהוָה לָלֶכֶת בְּחֻקּוֹת
דָּוִד אָבִיו רַק בַּבָּמוֹת הוּא מְזַבֵּחַ וּמַקְטִיר:

⁴The king went to Gibeon to sacrifice there, for that was the largest shrine; on that altar Solomon presented a thousand burnt offerings. ⁵At Gibeon the Lᴏʀᴅ appeared to Solomon in a dream by night; and God said, "Ask, what shall I grant you?" ⁶Solomon said, "You dealt most graciously with Your servant my father David, because he walked before You in faithfulness and righteousness and in integrity of heart. You have continued this great kindness to him by giving him a son to occupy his throne, as is now the case. ⁷And now, O Lᴏʀᴅ my God, You have made Your servant king in place of my father David; but I am a young lad, ᵃ-with no experience in leadership.-ᵃ ⁸Your servant finds himself in the midst of the people You have chosen, a people too numerous to be numbered or counted. ⁹Grant, then, Your servant an understanding mind to judge Your people, to distinguish between good and bad; for who can judge this vast people of Yours?"

¹⁰The Lord was pleased that Solomon had asked for this. ¹¹And God said to him, "Because you asked for this—you did not ask for long life, you did not ask for riches, you did not ask for the life of your enemies, but you asked for discernment in dispensing justice—¹²I now do as you have spoken. I grant you a wise and discerning mind; there has never been anyone like you before, nor will anyone like you arise again. ¹³And I also grant you what you did not ask for—both riches and glory all your life—the like of which no king has ever had. ¹⁴And I will further grant you long life, if you will walk in My ways and observe My laws and commandments, as did your father David."

¹⁵Then Solomon awoke: it was a dream! He went to Jerusalem, stood before the Ark of the Covenant of the Lord, and sacrificed burnt offerings and presented offerings of well-being; and he made a banquet for all his courtiers.

4 וַיֵּ֨לֶךְ הַמֶּ֤לֶךְ גִּבְעֹ֨נָה֙ לִזְבֹּ֣חַ שָׁ֔ם כִּ֥י הִ֖יא הַבָּמָ֣ה הַגְּדוֹלָ֑ה אֶ֤לֶף עֹלוֹת֙ יַעֲלֶ֣ה שְׁלֹמֹ֔ה עַ֖ל הַמִּזְבֵּ֥חַ הַהֽוּא: 5 בְּגִבְע֗וֹן נִרְאָ֧ה יְהֹוָ֛ה אֶל־שְׁלֹמֹ֖ה בַּחֲל֣וֹם הַלָּ֑יְלָה וַיֹּ֣אמֶר אֱלֹהִ֔ים שְׁאַ֖ל מָ֥ה אֶתֶּן־לָֽךְ: 6 וַיֹּ֣אמֶר שְׁלֹמֹ֗ה אַתָּ֨ה עָשִׂ֜יתָ עִם־עַבְדְּךָ֩ דָוִ֨ד אָבִ֜י חֶ֣סֶד גָּד֗וֹל כַּאֲשֶׁר֩ הָלַ֨ךְ לְפָנֶ֜יךָ בֶּאֱמֶ֤ת וּבִצְדָקָה֙ וּבְיִשְׁרַ֤ת לֵבָב֙ עִמָּ֔ךְ וַתִּשְׁמׇר־ל֗וֹ אֶת־הַחֶ֤סֶד הַגָּדוֹל֙ הַזֶּ֔ה וַתִּתֶּן־ל֥וֹ בֵ֛ן יֹשֵׁ֥ב עַל־כִּסְא֖וֹ כַּיּ֥וֹם הַזֶּֽה: 7 וְעַתָּה֙ יְהֹוָ֣ה אֱלֹהָ֔י אַתָּה֙ הִמְלַ֣כְתָּ אֶֽת־עַבְדְּךָ֔ תַּ֖חַת דָּוִ֣ד אָבִ֑י וְאָֽנֹכִי֙ נַ֣עַר קָטֹ֔ן לֹ֥א אֵדַ֖ע צֵ֥את וָבֹֽא: 8 וְעַ֨בְדְּךָ֜ בְּת֣וֹךְ עַמְּךָ֗ אֲשֶׁ֣ר בָּחָ֑רְתָּ עַם־רָ֕ב אֲשֶׁ֧ר לֹֽא־יִמָּנֶ֛ה וְלֹ֥א יִסָּפֵ֖ר מֵרֹֽב: 9 וְנָתַתָּ֨ לְעַבְדְּךָ֜ לֵ֤ב שֹׁמֵ֙עַ֙ לִשְׁפֹּ֣ט אֶֽת־עַמְּךָ֔ לְהָבִ֖ין בֵּֽין־ט֣וֹב לְרָ֑ע כִּ֣י מִ֤י יוּכַל֙ לִשְׁפֹּ֔ט אֶת־עַמְּךָ֥ הַכָּבֵ֖ד הַזֶּֽה: 10 וַיִּיטַ֥ב הַדָּבָ֖ר בְּעֵינֵ֣י אֲדֹנָ֑י כִּ֚י שָׁאַ֣ל שְׁלֹמֹ֔ה אֶת־הַדָּבָ֖ר הַזֶּֽה: 11 וַיֹּ֨אמֶר אֱלֹהִ֜ים אֵלָ֗יו יַ֨עַן֩ אֲשֶׁ֨ר שָׁאַ֜לְתָּ אֶת־הַדָּבָ֣ר הַזֶּ֗ה וְלֹֽא־שָׁאַ֨לְתָּ לְּךָ֜ יָמִ֣ים רַבִּ֗ים וְלֹֽא־שָׁאַ֤לְתָּ לְּךָ֙ עֹ֔שֶׁר וְלֹ֥א שָׁאַ֖לְתָּ נֶ֣פֶשׁ אֹיְבֶ֑יךָ וְשָׁאַ֥לְתָּ לְּךָ֛ הָבִ֖ין לִשְׁמֹ֥עַ מִשְׁפָּֽט: 12 הִנֵּ֥ה עָשִׂ֖יתִי כִּדְבָרֶ֑יךָ הִנֵּ֣ה ׀ נָתַ֣תִּי לְךָ֗ לֵ֚ב חָכָ֣ם וְנָב֔וֹן אֲשֶׁ֤ר כָּמ֙וֹךָ֙ לֹא־הָיָ֣ה לְפָנֶ֔יךָ וְאַחֲרֶ֖יךָ לֹֽא־יָק֥וּם כָּמֽוֹךָ: 13 וְגַ֨ם אֲשֶׁ֤ר לֹֽא־שָׁאַ֙לְתָּ֙ נָתַ֣תִּי לָ֔ךְ גַּם־עֹ֖שֶׁר גַּם־כָּב֑וֹד אֲשֶׁ֨ר לֹא־הָיָ֥ה כָמ֛וֹךָ אִ֖ישׁ בַּמְּלָכִ֖ים כׇּל־יָמֶֽיךָ: 14 וְאִ֣ם ׀ תֵּלֵ֣ךְ בִּדְרָכַ֗י לִשְׁמֹ֤ר חֻקַּי֙ וּמִצְוֺתַ֔י כַּאֲשֶׁ֥ר הָלַ֖ךְ דָּוִ֣יד אָבִ֑יךָ וְהַאֲרַכְתִּ֖י אֶת־יָמֶֽיךָ: ס 15 וַיִּקַ֤ץ* שְׁלֹמֹה֙ וְהִנֵּ֣ה חֲל֑וֹם וַיָּב֣וֹא יְרוּשָׁלַ֗͏ִם וַֽיַּעֲמֹ֞ד ׀ לִפְנֵ֣י ׀ אֲר֣וֹן בְּרִית־אֲדֹנָ֗י וַיַּ֤עַל עֹלוֹת֙ וַיַּ֣עַשׂ שְׁלָמִ֔ים וַיַּ֥עַשׂ מִשְׁתֶּ֖ה לְכׇל־עֲבָדָֽיו: פ

ᵃ⁻ᵃ Lit. "do not know to go out and come in"; cf. Num. 27.17.

16Later two prostitutes came to the king and stood before him. 17The first woman said, "Please, my lord! This woman and I live in the same house; and I gave birth to a child while she was in the house. 18On the third day after I was delivered, this woman also gave birth to a child. We were alone; there was no one else with us in the house, just the two of us in the house. 19During the night this woman's child died, because she lay on it. 20She arose in the night and took my son from my side while your maidservant was asleep, and laid him in her bosom; and she laid her dead son in my bosom. 21When I arose in the morning to nurse my son, there he was, dead; but when I looked at him closely in the morning, it was not the son I had borne."

22The other woman spoke up, "No, the live one is my son, and the dead one is yours!" But the first insisted, "No, the dead boy is yours; mine is the live one!" And they went on arguing before the king.

23The king said, "One says, 'This is my son, the live one, and the dead one is yours'; and the other says, 'No, the dead boy is yours, mine is the live one.' 24So the king gave the order, "Fetch me a sword." A sword was brought before the king, 25and the king said, "Cut the live child in two, and give half to one and half to the other."

26But the woman whose son was the live one pleaded with the king, for she was overcome with compassion for her son. "Please, my lord," she cried, "give her the live child; only don't kill it!" The other insisted, "It shall be neither yours nor mine; cut it in two!" 27Then the king spoke up. "Give the live child to her," he said, "and do not put it to death; she is its mother."

28When all Israel heard the decision that the king had rendered, they stood in awe of the king; for they saw that he possessed divine wisdom to execute justice.

16 אָ֣ז תָּבֹ֗אנָה שְׁתַּ֛יִם נָשִׁ֥ים זֹנ֖וֹת אֶל־הַמֶּ֑לֶךְ וַֽתַּעֲמֹ֖דְנָה לְפָנָֽיו׃ 17 וַתֹּ֜אמֶר הָאִשָּׁ֤ה הָֽאַחַת֙ בִּ֣י אֲדֹנִ֔י אֲנִי֙ וְהָאִשָּׁ֣ה הַזֹּ֔את יֹשְׁבֹ֖ת בְּבַ֣יִת אֶחָ֑ד וָאֵלֵ֥ד עִמָּ֖הּ בַּבָּֽיִת׃ 18 וַיְהִ֞י בַּיּ֤וֹם הַשְּׁלִישִׁי֙ לְלִדְתִּ֔י וַתֵּ֖לֶד גַּם־הָאִשָּׁ֣ה הַזֹּ֑את וַאֲנַ֣חְנוּ יַחְדָּ֗ו אֵין־זָ֤ר אִתָּ֙נוּ֙ בַּבַּ֔יִת זוּלָתִ֥י שְׁתַּֽיִם־אֲנַ֖חְנוּ בַּבָּֽיִת׃ 19 וַיָּ֛מָת בֶּן־הָאִשָּׁ֥ה הַזֹּ֖את לָ֑יְלָה אֲשֶׁ֥ר שָׁכְבָ֖ה עָלָֽיו׃ 20 וַתָּ֞קָם בְּת֣וֹךְ הַלַּ֗יְלָה וַתִּקַּ֤ח אֶת־בְּנִי֙ מֵֽאֶצְלִ֔י וַאֲמָֽתְךָ֖ יְשֵׁנָ֑ה וַתַּשְׁכִּיבֵ֣הוּ בְחֵיקָ֔הּ וְאֶת־בְּנָ֥הּ הַמֵּ֖ת הִשְׁכִּ֥יבָה בְחֵיקִֽי׃ 21 וָאָקֻ֥ם בַּבֹּ֛קֶר לְהֵינִ֥יק אֶת־בְּנִ֖י וְהִנֵּה־מֵ֑ת וָאֶתְבּוֹנֵ֤ן אֵלָיו֙ בַּבֹּ֔קֶר וְהִנֵּ֕ה לֹֽא־הָיָ֥ה בְנִ֖י אֲשֶׁ֥ר יָלָֽדְתִּי׃

22 וַתֹּאמֶר֩ הָאִשָּׁ֨ה הָאַחֶ֜רֶת לֹ֣א כִ֗י בְּנִ֤י הַחַי֙ וּבְנֵ֣ךְ הַמֵּ֔ת וְזֹ֤את אֹמֶ֙רֶת֙ לֹ֣א כִ֔י בְּנֵ֥ךְ הַמֵּ֖ת וּבְנִ֣י הֶחָ֑י וַתְּדַבֵּ֖רְנָה לִפְנֵ֥י הַמֶּֽלֶךְ׃

23 וַיֹּ֣אמֶר הַמֶּ֗לֶךְ זֹ֤את אֹמֶ֙רֶת֙ זֶה־בְּנִ֤י הַחַי֙ וּבְנֵ֣ךְ הַמֵּ֔ת וְזֹ֤את אֹמֶ֙רֶת֙ לֹ֣א כִ֔י בְּנֵ֥ךְ הַמֵּ֖ת וּבְנִ֥י הֶחָֽי׃ פ 24 וַיֹּ֖אמֶר הַמֶּ֑לֶךְ קְח֥וּ לִי־חָ֑רֶב וַיָּבִ֥אוּ הַחֶ֖רֶב לִפְנֵ֥י הַמֶּֽלֶךְ׃ 25 וַיֹּ֣אמֶר הַמֶּ֗לֶךְ גִּזְר֛וּ אֶת־הַיֶּ֥לֶד הַחַ֖י לִשְׁנָ֑יִם וּתְנ֤וּ אֶת־הַחֲצִי֙ לְאַחַ֔ת וְאֶת־הַחֲצִ֖י לְאֶחָֽת׃ 26 וַתֹּ֣אמֶר הָאִשָּׁה֩ אֲשֶׁר־בְּנָ֨הּ הַחַ֜י אֶל־הַמֶּ֗לֶךְ כִּֽי־נִכְמְר֣וּ רַחֲמֶיהָ֮ עַל־בְּנָהּ֒ וַתֹּ֣אמֶר ׀ בִּ֣י אֲדֹנִ֗י תְּנוּ־לָהּ֙ אֶת־הַיָּל֣וּד הַחַ֔י וְהָמֵ֖ת אַל־תְּמִיתֻ֑הוּ וְזֹ֣את אֹמֶ֗רֶת גַּם־לִ֥י גַם־לָ֖ךְ לֹ֣א יִהְיֶ֑ה גְּזֹֽרוּ׃ 27 וַיַּ֨עַן הַמֶּ֜לֶךְ וַיֹּ֗אמֶר תְּנוּ־לָהּ֙ אֶת־הַיָּל֣וּד הַחַ֔י וְהָמֵ֖ת לֹ֣א תְמִיתֻ֑הוּ הִ֖יא אִמּֽוֹ׃ 28 וַיִּשְׁמְע֣וּ כָל־יִשְׂרָאֵ֗ל אֶת־הַמִּשְׁפָּט֙ אֲשֶׁ֣ר שָׁפַ֣ט הַמֶּ֔לֶךְ וַיִּֽרְא֖וּ מִפְּנֵ֣י הַמֶּ֑לֶךְ כִּ֣י רָא֔וּ כִּֽי־חָכְמַ֧ת אֱלֹהִ֛ים בְּקִרְבּ֖וֹ לַעֲשׂ֥וֹת מִשְׁפָּֽט׃ ס

4 King Solomon was now king over all Israel.
²These were his officials:

Azariah son of Zadok—the priest;

³Elihoreph and Ahijah sons of Shisha—scribes;

Jehoshaphat son of Ahilud—recorder;

⁴Benaiah son of Jehoiada—over the army;

Zadok and Abiathar—priests;

⁵Azariah son of Nathan—in charge of the prefects;

Zabud son of Nathan the priest—companion of the king;

⁶Ahishar—in charge of the palace; and

Adoniram son of Abda—in charge of the forced labor.

⁷Solomon had twelve prefects governing all Israel, who provided food for the king and his household; each had to provide food for one month in the year. ⁸And these were their names: Ben-hur, in the hill country of Ephraim; ⁹Ben-deker, in Makaz, Shaalbim, Beth-shemesh, and Elon-beth-hanan; ¹⁰Ben-hesed in Arubboth—he governed Socho and all the Hepher area; ¹¹Ben-abinadab, [in] all of Naphath-dor (Solomon's daughter Taphath was his wife); ¹²Baana son of Ahilud [in] Taanach and Megiddo and all Beth-shean, which is beside Zarethan, below Jezreel—from Beth-shean to Abel-meholah as far as the other side of Jokmeam; ¹³Ben-geber, in Ramoth-gilead—he governed the villages of Jair son of Manasseh which are in Gilead, and he also governed the district of Argob which is in Bashan, sixty large towns with walls and bronze bars; ¹⁴Ahinadab son of Iddo, in Mahanaim; ¹⁵Ahimaaz, in Naphtali (he too took a daughter of Solomon—Basemath—to wife); ¹⁶Baanah son of Hushi, in Asher and Bealoth;ᵃ ¹⁷Jehoshaphat son of Paruah, in Issachar; ¹⁸Shimei son of Ela, in Ben-

---

ᵃ Or "in Aloth."

ד וַיְהִי֙ הַמֶּ֣לֶךְ שְׁלֹמֹ֔ה מֶ֖לֶךְ עַל־כָּל־
יִשְׂרָאֵֽל׃ ס ² וְאֵ֥לֶּה הַשָּׂרִ֖ים אֲשֶׁר־ל֑וֹ
עֲזַרְיָ֥הוּ בֶן־צָד֖וֹק הַכֹּהֵֽן׃ ס
³ אֱלִיחֹ֧רֶף וַאֲחִיָּ֛ה בְּנֵ֥י שִׁישָׁ֖א סֹפְרִ֑ים
יְהוֹשָׁפָ֥ט בֶּן־אֲחִיל֖וּד הַמַּזְכִּֽיר׃
⁴ וּבְנָיָ֥הוּ בֶן־יְהוֹיָדָ֖ע עַל־הַצָּבָ֑א
וְצָד֥וֹק וְאֶבְיָתָ֖ר כֹּהֲנִֽים׃ ס
⁵ וַעֲזַרְיָ֥הוּ בֶן־נָתָ֖ן עַל־הַנִּצָּבִ֑ים
וְזָב֧וּד בֶּן־נָתָ֛ן כֹּהֵ֖ן רֵעֶ֥ה הַמֶּֽלֶךְ׃
⁶ וַאֲחִישָׁ֖ר עַל־הַבָּ֑יִת
וַאֲדֹנִירָ֥ם בֶּן־עַבְדָּ֖א עַל־הַמַּֽס׃ ס
⁷ וְלִשְׁלֹמֹ֞ה שְׁנֵים־עָשָׂ֤ר נִצָּבִים֙ עַל־כָּל־
יִשְׂרָאֵ֔ל וְכִלְכְּל֥וּ אֶת־הַמֶּ֖לֶךְ וְאֶת־בֵּית֑וֹ
חֹ֧דֶשׁ בַּשָּׁנָ֛ה יִהְיֶ֥ה עַל־אֶחָ֖ד הָאֶחָ֑ד
לְכַלְכֵּֽל׃ ס ⁸ וְאֵ֣לֶּה שְׁמוֹתָ֔ם בֶּן־ח֖וּר
בְּהַ֥ר אֶפְרָֽיִם׃ ס ⁹ בֶּן־דֶּ֛קֶר בְּמָקַ֥ץ
וּבְשַֽׁעַלְבִ֖ים וּבֵ֣ית שָׁ֑מֶשׁ וְאֵיל֖וֹן בֵּ֥ית
חָנָֽן׃ ס ¹⁰ בֶּן־חֶ֖סֶד בָּֽאֲרֻבּ֑וֹת ל֥וֹ שֹׂכֹ֖ה
וְכָל־אֶ֥רֶץ חֵֽפֶר׃ ¹¹ בֶּן־אֲבִֽינָדָ֖ב כָּל־
נָ֣פַת דֹּ֑אר טָפַ֤ת בַּת־שְׁלֹמֹה֙ הָ֣יְתָה לּ֖וֹ
לְאִשָּֽׁה׃ ס ¹² בַּֽעֲנָא֙ בֶּן־אֲחִיל֔וּד תַּעְנַ֖ךְ
וּמְגִדּ֗וֹ וְכָל־בֵּ֣ית שְׁאָן֩ אֲשֶׁ֨ר אֵ֤צֶל צָֽרְתַ֙נָה֙
מִתַּ֣חַת לְיִזְרְעֶ֔אל מִבֵּ֣ית שְׁאָ֔ן עַ֖ד אָבֵ֣ל
מְחוֹלָ֔ה עַ֖ד מֵעֵ֥בֶר לְיָקְמֳעָֽם׃ ס ¹³ בֶּן־
גֶּ֖בֶר בְּרָמֹ֣ת גִּלְעָ֑ד ל֞וֹ חַוֺּ֣ת יָאִ֣יר בֶּן־
מְנַשֶּׁה֙ אֲשֶׁ֣ר בַּגִּלְעָ֔ד ל֗וֹ חֶ֤בֶל אַרְגֹּב֙ אֲשֶׁ֣ר
בַּבָּשָׁ֔ן שִׁשִּׁים֙ עָרִ֣ים גְּדֹל֔וֹת חוֹמָ֖ה
וּבְרִ֣יחַ נְחֹֽשֶׁת׃ ס ¹⁴ אֲחִֽינָדָ֥ב בֶּן־עִדֹּ֖א
מַחֲנָֽיְמָה׃ ¹⁵ אֲחִימַ֖עַץ בְּנַפְתָּלִ֑י גַּם־ה֗וּא
לָקַ֛ח אֶת־בָּשְׂמַ֥ת בַּת־שְׁלֹמֹ֖ה לְאִשָּֽׁה׃
¹⁶ בַּֽעֲנָא֙ בֶּן־חוּשָׁ֔י בְּאָשֵׁ֖ר וּבְעָלֽוֹת׃ ס
¹⁷ יְהוֹשָׁפָ֥ט בֶּן־פָּר֖וּחַ בְּיִשָּׂשכָֽר׃ ס
¹⁸ שִׁמְעִ֥י בֶן־אֵלָ֖א בְּבִנְיָמִֽן׃ ס ¹⁹ גֶּ֥בֶר בֶּן־

jamin; [19]Geber son of Uri, in the region of Gilead, the country of Sihon, king of the Amorites, and Og, king of Bashan; [b]-and one prefect who was in the land.[-b]

[20]Judah and Israel were as numerous as the sands of the sea; they ate and drank and were content.

5 Solomon's rule extended over all the kingdoms from the Euphrates to the land of the Philistines and the boundary of Egypt. They brought Solomon tribute and were subject to him all his life. [2]Solomon's daily provisions consisted of 30 *kors* of semolina, and 60 *kors* of [ordinary] flour, [3]10 fattened oxen, 20 pasture-fed oxen, and 100 sheep and goats, besides deer and gazelles, roebucks and [a]-fatted geese.[-a] [4]For he controlled the whole region west of the Euphrates—all the kings west of the Euphrates, from Tiphsah to Gaza—and he had peace on all his borders roundabout. [5]All the days of Solomon, Judah and Israel from Dan to Beer-sheba dwelt in safety, everyone under his own vine and under his own fig tree. [6]Solomon had 40,000 stalls of horses for his chariotry and 12,000 horsemen.

[7b]All those prefects, each during his month, would furnish provisions for King Solomon and for all who were admitted to King Solomon's table; they did not fall short in anything. [8]They would also, each in his turn, deliver barley and straw for the horses and the swift steeds to the places where they were stationed.

[9]God endowed Solomon with wisdom and discernment in great measure, with understanding as vast as the sands on the seashore. [10]Solomon's wisdom was greater than the wisdom of all the Kedemites and than all the wis-

אֲרִי בְּאֶרֶץ גִּלְעָד אֶרֶץ סִיחוֹן ׀ מֶלֶךְ הָאֱמֹרִי וְעֹג מֶלֶךְ הַבָּשָׁן וּנְצִיב אֶחָד אֲשֶׁר בָּאָרֶץ: [20]יְהוּדָה וְיִשְׂרָאֵל רַבִּים כַּחוֹל אֲשֶׁר־עַל־הַיָּם לָרֹב אֹכְלִים וְשֹׁתִים וּשְׂמֵחִים:

ה [1] וּשְׁלֹמֹה הָיָה מוֹשֵׁל בְּכָל־הַמַּמְלָכוֹת מִן־הַנָּהָר אֶרֶץ פְּלִשְׁתִּים וְעַד גְּבוּל מִצְרָיִם מַגִּשִׁים מִנְחָה וְעֹבְדִים אֶת־שְׁלֹמֹה כָּל־יְמֵי חַיָּיו: פ [2]וַיְהִי לֶחֶם־שְׁלֹמֹה לְיוֹם אֶחָד שְׁלֹשִׁים כֹּר סֹלֶת וְשִׁשִּׁים כֹּר קָמַח: [3]עֲשָׂרָה בָקָר בְּרִאִים וְעֶשְׂרִים בָּקָר רְעִי וּמֵאָה צֹאן לְבַד מֵאַיָּל וּצְבִי וְיַחְמוּר וּבַרְבֻּרִים אֲבוּסִים: [4]כִּי־הוּא רֹדֶה ׀ בְּכָל־עֵבֶר הַנָּהָר מִתִּפְסַח וְעַד־עַזָּה בְּכָל־מַלְכֵי עֵבֶר הַנָּהָר וְשָׁלוֹם הָיָה לוֹ מִכָּל־עֲבָרָיו מִסָּבִיב: [5]וַיֵּשֶׁב יְהוּדָה וְיִשְׂרָאֵל לָבֶטַח אִישׁ תַּחַת גַּפְנוֹ וְתַחַת תְּאֵנָתוֹ מִדָּן וְעַד־בְּאֵר שָׁבַע כֹּל יְמֵי שְׁלֹמֹה: ס [6]וַיְהִי לִשְׁלֹמֹה אַרְבָּעִים אֶלֶף אֻרְוֺת סוּסִים לְמֶרְכָּבוֹ וּשְׁנֵים־עָשָׂר אֶלֶף פָּרָשִׁים: [7]וְכִלְכְּלוּ הַנִּצָּבִים הָאֵלֶּה אֶת־הַמֶּלֶךְ שְׁלֹמֹה וְאֵת כָּל־הַקָּרֵב אֶל־שֻׁלְחַן הַמֶּלֶךְ־שְׁלֹמֹה אִישׁ חָדְשׁוֹ לֹא יְעַדְּרוּ דָּבָר: [8]וְהַשְּׂעֹרִים וְהַתֶּבֶן לַסּוּסִים וְלָרָכֶשׁ יָבִאוּ אֶל־הַמָּקוֹם אֲשֶׁר יִהְיֶה־שָּׁם אִישׁ כְּמִשְׁפָּטוֹ: ס

[9]וַיִּתֵּן אֱלֹהִים חָכְמָה לִשְׁלֹמֹה וּתְבוּנָה הַרְבֵּה מְאֹד וְרֹחַב לֵב כַּחוֹל אֲשֶׁר עַל־שְׂפַת הַיָּם: [10]וַתֵּרֶב חָכְמַת שְׁלֹמֹה מֵחָכְמַת כָּל־בְּנֵי־קֶדֶם וּמִכֹּל חָכְמַת

---

b-b   Meaning of Heb. uncertain.

a-a   Exact meaning of Heb. uncertain.

b   Resuming the account begun in 4.2.

dom of the Egyptians. [11]He was the wisest of all men: [wiser] than Ethan the Ezrahite, and Heman, Chalkol, and Darda the sons of Mahol. His fame spread among all the surrounding nations. [12]He composed three thousand proverbs, and his songs numbered one thousand and five. [13]He discoursed about trees, from the cedar in Lebanon to the hyssop that grows out of the wall; and he discoursed about beasts, birds, creeping things, and fishes. [14]Men of all peoples came to hear Solomon's wisdom, [sent] by all the kings of the earth who had heard of his wisdom.

[15]King Hiram of Tyre sent his officials to Solomon when he heard that he had been anointed king in place of his father; for Hiram had always been a friend of David. [16]Solomon sent this message to Hiram: [17]"You know that my father David could not build a house for the name of the LORD his God because of the enemies[c] that encompassed him, until the LORD had placed them under the soles of his feet. [18]But now the LORD my God has given me respite all around; there is no adversary and no mischance. [19]And so I propose to build a house for the name of the LORD my God, as the LORD promised my father David, saying, 'Your son, whom I will set on your throne in your place, shall build the house for My name.' [20]Please, then, give orders for cedars to be cut for me in the Lebanon. My servants will work with yours, and I will pay you any wages you may ask for your servants; for as you know, there is none among us who knows how to cut timber like the Sidonians."

[21]When Hiram heard Solomon's message, he was overjoyed. "Praised be the LORD this day," he said, "for granting David a wise son to govern this great people." [22]So Hiram sent word to Solomon: "I have your message; I will supply all the cedar and cypress logs you require. [23]My ser-

---

c   Heb. "war"; cf. Targum.

מִצְרָיִם: 11 וַיֶּחְכַּם֙ מִכָּל־הָ֣אָדָ֔ם מֵאֵיתָ֣ן
הָאֶזְרָחִ֗י וְהֵימָ֤ן וְכַלְכֹּל֙ וְדַרְדַּ֣ע בְּנֵ֣י מָח֔וֹל
וַֽיְהִי־שְׁמ֖וֹ בְכָל־הַגּוֹיִ֥ם סָבִֽיב: 12 וַיְדַבֵּ֗ר
שְׁלֹ֤שֶׁת אֲלָפִים֙ מָשָׁ֔ל וַיְהִ֥י שִׁיר֖וֹ חֲמִשָּׁ֥ה
וָאָֽלֶף: 13 וַיְדַבֵּר֮ עַל־הָ֣עֵצִים֒ מִן־הָאֶ֗רֶז
אֲשֶׁ֣ר בַּלְּבָנ֔וֹן וְעַד֙ הָאֵז֔וֹב אֲשֶׁ֥ר יֹצֵ֖א בַּקִּ֑יר
וַיְדַבֵּר֙ עַל־הַבְּהֵמָ֣ה וְעַל־הָע֔וֹף וְעַל־
הָרֶ֖מֶשׂ וְעַל־הַדָּגִֽים: 14 וַיָּבֹ֙אוּ֙ מִכָּל־
הָ֣עַמִּ֔ים לִשְׁמֹ֕עַ אֵ֖ת חָכְמַ֣ת שְׁלֹמֹ֑ה מֵאֵת֙
כָּל־מַלְכֵ֣י הָאָ֔רֶץ אֲשֶׁ֥ר שָׁמְע֖וּ אֶת־
חָכְמָתֽוֹ: ס

15 וַיִּשְׁלַ֞ח חִירָ֤ם מֶֽלֶךְ־צֹר֙ אֶת־עֲבָדָ֔יו אֶל־
שְׁלֹמֹ֔ה כִּ֣י שָׁמַ֔ע כִּ֥י אֹת֛וֹ מָשְׁח֥וּ לְמֶ֖לֶךְ
תַּ֣חַת אָבִ֑יהוּ כִּ֣י אֹהֵ֗ב הָיָ֧ה חִירָ֛ם לְדָוִ֖ד
כָּל־הַיָּמִֽים: ס 16 וַיִּשְׁלַ֣ח שְׁלֹמֹ֔ה אֶל־
חִירָ֖ם לֵאמֹֽר: 17 אַתָּ֨ה יָדַ֜עְתָּ אֶת־דָּוִ֣ד אָבִ֗י
כִּ֣י לֹ֤א יָכֹל֙ לִבְנ֣וֹת בַּ֗יִת לְשֵׁם֙ יְהוָ֣ה אֱלֹהָ֔יו
מִפְּנֵ֤י הַמִּלְחָמָה֙ אֲשֶׁ֣ר סְבָבֻ֔הוּ עַ֠ד תֵּת־
יְהוָ֤ה אֹתָם֙ תַּ֔חַת כַּפּ֖וֹת רגלו רַגְלָֽי:
18 וְעַתָּ֕ה הֵנִ֨יחַ יְהוָ֧ה אֱלֹהַ֛י לִ֖י מִסָּבִ֑יב אֵ֣ין
שָׂטָ֔ן וְאֵ֖ין פֶּ֥גַע רָֽע: 19 וְהִנְנִ֣י אֹמֵ֔ר לִבְנ֣וֹת
בַּ֔יִת לְשֵׁ֖ם יְהוָ֣ה אֱלֹהָ֑י כַּֽאֲשֶׁ֣ר | דִּבֶּ֣ר
יְהוָ֗ה אֶל־דָּוִ֤ד אָבִי֙ לֵאמֹ֔ר בִּנְךָ֗ אֲשֶׁ֨ר אֶתֵּ֤ן
תַּחְתֶּ֙יךָ֙ עַל־כִּסְאֶ֔ךָ הֽוּא־יִבְנֶ֥ה הַבַּ֖יִת
לִשְׁמִֽי: 20 וְעַתָּ֡ה צַוֵּה֩ וְיִכְרְתוּ־לִ֨י אֲרָזִ֜ים
מִן־הַלְּבָנ֗וֹן וַֽעֲבָדַי֙ יִֽהְי֣וּ עִם־עֲבָדֶ֔יךָ וּשְׂכַ֣ר
עֲבָדֶ֗יךָ אֶתֵּ֤ן לְךָ֙ כְּכֹ֣ל אֲשֶׁ֣ר תֹּאמֵ֔ר כִּ֣י |
אַתָּ֣ה יָדַ֔עְתָּ כִּ֣י אֵ֣ין בָּ֗נוּ אִ֛ישׁ יֹדֵ֥עַ לִכְרָת־
עֵצִ֖ים כַּצִּֽדֹנִֽים:
21 וַיְהִ֞י כִּשְׁמֹ֤עַ חִירָם֙ אֶת־דִּבְרֵ֣י שְׁלֹמֹ֔ה
וַיִּשְׂמַ֖ח מְאֹ֑ד וַיֹּ֕אמֶר בָּר֤וּךְ יְהוָה֙ הַיּ֔וֹם
אֲשֶׁ֨ר נָתַ֤ן לְדָוִד֙ בֵּ֣ן חָכָ֔ם עַל־הָעָ֥ם הָרָ֖ב
הַזֶּֽה: 22 וַיִּשְׁלַ֤ח חִירָם֙ אֶל־שְׁלֹמֹ֣ה לֵאמֹ֔ר
שָׁמַ֕עְתִּי אֵ֥ת אֲשֶׁר־שָׁלַ֖חְתָּ אֵלָ֑י אֲנִ֣י אֶֽעֱשֶׂ֗ה
אֶת־כָּל־חֶפְצְךָ֛ בַּעֲצֵ֥י אֲרָזִ֖ים וּבַעֲצֵ֥י

vants will bring them down to the sea from the Lebanon; and at the sea I will make them into floats and [deliver them] to any place that you designate to me. There I shall break them up for you to carry away. You, in turn, will supply the food I require for my household." [24]So Hiram kept Solomon provided with all the cedar and cypress wood he required, [25]and Solomon delivered to Hiram 20,000 *kors* of wheat as provisions for his household and *d*-20 *kors*-*d* of beaten oil. Such was Solomon's annual payment to Hiram.

[26]The Lord had given Solomon wisdom, as He had promised him. There was friendship between Hiram and Solomon, and the two of them made a treaty.

[27]King Solomon imposed forced labor on all Israel; the levy came to 30,000 men. [28]He sent them to the Lebanon in shifts of 10,000 a month: they would spend one month in the Lebanon and two months at home. Adoniram was in charge of the forced labor. [29]Solomon also had 70,000 porters and 80,000 quarriers in the hills, [30]apart from Solomon's 3,300 officials who were in charge of the work and supervised the gangs doing the work.

[31]The king ordered huge blocks of choice stone to be quarried, so that the foundations of the house might be laid with hewn stones. [32]Solomon's masons, Hiram's masons, and the men of Gebal shaped them. Thus the timber and the stones for building the house were made ready.

6 In the four hundred and eightieth year after the Israelites left the land of Egypt, in the month of Ziv—that is, the second month—in the fourth year of his reign over Israel, Solomon be-

בְּרוֹשִׁים: 23 עֲבָדַי יֹרִדוּ מִן־הַלְּבָנוֹן יָמָּה וַאֲנִי אֲשִׂימֵם דֹּבְרוֹת בַּיָּם עַד־הַמָּקוֹם אֲשֶׁר־תִּשְׁלַח אֵלַי וְנִפַּצְתִּים שָׁם וְאַתָּה תִשָּׂא וְאַתָּה תַּעֲשֶׂה אֶת־חֶפְצִי לָתֵת לֶחֶם בֵּיתִי: 24 וַיְהִי חִירוֹם נֹתֵן לִשְׁלֹמֹה עֲצֵי אֲרָזִים וַעֲצֵי בְרוֹשִׁים כָּל־חֶפְצוֹ: 25 וּשְׁלֹמֹה נָתַן לְחִירָם עֶשְׂרִים אֶלֶף כֹּר חִטִּים מַכֹּלֶת לְבֵיתוֹ וְעֶשְׂרִים כֹּר שֶׁמֶן כָּתִית כֹּה־יִתֵּן שְׁלֹמֹה לְחִירָם שָׁנָה בְשָׁנָה: פ

26 וַיהֹוָה נָתַן חָכְמָה לִשְׁלֹמֹה כַּאֲשֶׁר דִּבֶּר־לוֹ וַיְהִי שָׁלֹם בֵּין חִירָם וּבֵין שְׁלֹמֹה וַיִּכְרְתוּ בְרִית שְׁנֵיהֶם:

27 וַיַּעַל הַמֶּלֶךְ שְׁלֹמֹה מַס מִכָּל־יִשְׂרָאֵל וַיְהִי הַמַּס שְׁלֹשִׁים אֶלֶף אִישׁ: 28 וַיִּשְׁלָחֵם לְבָנוֹנָה עֲשֶׂרֶת אֲלָפִים בַּחֹדֶשׁ חֲלִיפוֹת חֹדֶשׁ יִהְיוּ בַלְּבָנוֹן שְׁנַיִם חֳדָשִׁים בְּבֵיתוֹ וַאֲדֹנִירָם עַל־הַמַּס: ס 29 וַיְהִי לִשְׁלֹמֹה שִׁבְעִים אֶלֶף נֹשֵׂא סַבָּל וּשְׁמֹנִים אֶלֶף חֹצֵב בָּהָר: 30 לְבַד מִשָּׂרֵי הַנִּצָּבִים לִשְׁלֹמֹה אֲשֶׁר עַל־הַמְּלָאכָה שְׁלֹשֶׁת אֲלָפִים וּשְׁלֹשׁ מֵאוֹת הָרֹדִים בָּעָם הָעֹשִׂים בַּמְּלָאכָה: 31 וַיְצַו הַמֶּלֶךְ וַיַּסִּעוּ אֲבָנִים גְּדֹלוֹת אֲבָנִים יְקָרוֹת לְיַסֵּד הַבָּיִת אַבְנֵי גָזִית: 32 וַיִּפְסְלוּ בֹּנֵי שְׁלֹמֹה וּבֹנֵי חִירוֹם וְהַגִּבְלִים וַיָּכִינוּ הָעֵצִים וְהָאֲבָנִים לִבְנוֹת הַבָּיִת: פ

ו וַיְהִי בִשְׁמוֹנִים שָׁנָה וְאַרְבַּע מֵאוֹת שָׁנָה לְצֵאת בְּנֵי־יִשְׂרָאֵל מֵאֶרֶץ־מִצְרַיִם בַּשָּׁנָה הָרְבִיעִית בְּחֹדֶשׁ זִו הוּא הַחֹדֶשׁ הַשֵּׁנִי לִמְלֹךְ שְׁלֹמֹה עַל־יִשְׂרָאֵל וַיִּבֶן

---

d-d Septuagint reads, "20,000 baths."

gan to build the House of the Lord. ²The House which King Solomon built for the Lord was 60 cubits long, 20 cubits wide, and 30 cubits high. ³The portico in front of the Great Hall of the House was 20 cubits long—along the width of the House—and 10 cubits deep to the front of the House. ⁴*a*He made windows for the House, recessed and latticed. ⁵Against the outside wall of the House—the outside walls of the House enclosing the Great Hall and the Shrine*b*—he built a storied structure; and he made side chambers all around. ⁶The lowest story was 5 cubits wide, the middle one 6 cubits wide, and the third 7 cubits wide; for he had provided recesses around the outside of the House so as not to penetrate the walls of the House.

⁷When the House was built, only finished stones cut at the quarry were used, so that no hammer or ax or any iron tool was heard in the House while it was being built.

⁸The entrance to the middle*c* [story of] the side chambers was on the right side of the House; and winding stairs led up to the middle chambers, and from the middle chambers to the third story. ⁹When he finished building the House, *d*-he paneled the House with beams and planks of cedar.-*d* ¹⁰He built the storied structure against the entire House—each story 5 cubits high, so that it encased the House with timbers of cedar.

¹¹Then the word of the Lord came to Solomon, ¹²"With regard to this House you are building—if you follow My laws and observe My rules and faithfully keep My commandments, I will fulfill for you the promise that I gave to your father David: ¹³I will abide among the children of Israel, and I will never forsake My people Israel."

¹⁴When Solomon had completed the con-

הַבַּ֖יִת לַיהוָֽה׃ 2 וְהַבַּ֗יִת אֲשֶׁ֨ר בָּנָ֜ה הַמֶּ֤לֶךְ שְׁלֹמֹה֙ לַֽיהוָ֔ה שִׁשִּֽׁים־אַמָּ֥ה אָרְכּ֖וֹ וְעֶשְׂרִ֣ים רָחְבּ֑וֹ וּשְׁלֹשִׁ֥ים אַמָּ֖ה קוֹמָתֽוֹ׃ 3 וְהָאוּלָ֗ם עַל־פְּנֵי֙ הֵיכַ֣ל הַבַּ֔יִת עֶשְׂרִ֤ים אַמָּה֙ אָרְכּ֔וֹ עַל־פְּנֵ֖י רֹ֣חַב הַבָּ֑יִת עֶ֧שֶׂר בָּאַמָּ֛ה רָחְבּ֖וֹ עַל־פְּנֵ֥י הַבָּֽיִת׃ 4 וַיַּ֣עַשׂ לַבָּ֔יִת חַלּוֹנֵ֖י שְׁקֻפִ֥ים אֲטֻמִֽים׃ 5 וַיִּבֶן֩ עַל־קִ֨יר הַבַּ֤יִת יָצִ֙יעַ֙ סָבִ֔יב אֶת־קִיר֥וֹת הַבַּ֖יִת סָבִ֑יב לַהֵיכָ֣ל וְלַדְּבִ֔יר וַיַּ֥עַשׂ צְלָע֖וֹת סָבִֽיב׃ 6 הַיָּצ֨יעַ הַתַּחְתֹּנָ֜ה חָמֵ֧שׁ בָּאַמָּ֣ה רָחְבָּ֗הּ וְהַתִּיכֹנָה֙ שֵׁ֤שׁ בָּֽאַמָּה֙ רָחְבָּ֔הּ וְהַ֨שְּׁלִישִׁ֔ית שֶׁ֥בַע בָּאַמָּ֖ה רָחְבָּ֑הּ כִּ֡י מִגְרָע֞וֹת נָתַ֤ן לַבַּ֙יִת֙ סָבִ֣יב ח֔וּצָה לְבִלְתִּ֖י אֲחֹ֥ז בְּקִירֽוֹת־הַבָּֽיִת׃ 7 וְהַבַּ֙יִת֙ בְּהִבָּ֣נֹת֔וֹ אֶֽבֶן־שְׁלֵמָ֥ה מַסָּ֖ע נִבְנָ֑ה וּמַקָּב֤וֹת וְהַגַּרְזֶן֙ כָּל־כְּלִ֣י בַרְזֶ֔ל לֹֽא־נִשְׁמַ֥ע בַּבַּ֖יִת בְּהִבָּנֹתֽוֹ׃ 8 פֶּ֗תַח הַצֵּלָע֙ הַתִּ֣יכֹנָ֔ה אֶל־כֶּ֥תֶף הַבַּ֖יִת הַיְמָנִ֑ית וּבְלוּלִּ֗ים יַֽעֲלוּ֙ עַל־הַתִּ֣יכֹנָ֔ה וּמִן־הַתִּֽיכֹנָ֖ה אֶל־הַשְּׁלִשִֽׁים׃ 9 וַיִּ֥בֶן אֶת־הַבַּ֖יִת וַיְכַלֵּ֑הוּ וַיִּסְפֹּ֤ן אֶת־הַבַּ֙יִת֙ גֵּבִ֔ים וּשְׂדֵרֹ֖ת בָּאֲרָזִֽים׃ 10 וַיִּ֤בֶן אֶת־הַיָּצ֙יעַ֙ עַל־כָּל־הַבַּ֔יִת חָמֵ֥שׁ אַמּ֖וֹת קֽוֹמָת֑וֹ וַיֶּאֱחֹ֥ז אֶת־הַבַּ֖יִת בַּעֲצֵ֥י אֲרָזִֽים׃ פ 11 וַֽיְהִי֙ דְּבַר־יְהוָ֔ה אֶל־שְׁלֹמֹ֖ה לֵאמֹֽר׃ 12 הַבַּ֨יִת הַזֶּ֜ה אֲשֶׁר־אַתָּ֣ה בֹנֶ֗ה אִם־תֵּלֵ֤ךְ בְּחֻקֹּתַי֙ וְאֶת־מִשְׁפָּטַ֣י תַּֽעֲשֶׂ֔ה וְשָׁמַרְתָּ֤ אֶת־כָּל־מִצְוֺתַי֙ לָלֶ֣כֶת בָּהֶ֔ם וַהֲקִמֹתִ֤י אֶת־דְּבָרִי֙ אִתָּ֔ךְ אֲשֶׁ֥ר דִּבַּ֖רְתִּי אֶל־דָּוִ֥ד אָבִֽיךָ׃ 13 וְשָׁ֣כַנְתִּ֔י בְּת֖וֹךְ בְּנֵ֣י יִשְׂרָאֵ֑ל וְלֹ֥א אֶעֱזֹ֖ב אֶת־עַמִּ֥י יִשְׂרָאֵֽל׃ ס 14 וַיִּ֧בֶן שְׁלֹמֹ֛ה אֶת־הַבַּ֖יִת וַיְכַלֵּֽהוּ׃ 15 וַיִּ֤בֶן

---

a   *Meaning of parts of vv. 4–6 uncertain.*
b   *I.e., the inner sanctuary, designated in v. 16 and elsewhere as the "Holy of Holies."*
c   *Septuagint and Targum read "lowest."*
d-d   *Meaning of Heb. uncertain.*

struction of the House, [15]he paneled the walls of the House on the inside with planks of cedar. He also overlaid the walls on the inside with wood, from the floor of the House to the ceiling. And he overlaid the floor of the House with planks of cypress. [16]Twenty cubits from the rear of the House, he built [a partition] of cedar planks from the floor to the walls;[e] he furnished its interior to serve as a shrine, as the Holy of Holies. [17][f]The front part of the House, that is, the Great Hall, measured 40 cubits. [18]The cedar of the interior of the House had carvings of gourds and calyxes; it was all cedar, no stone was exposed. [19]In the innermost part of the House, he fixed a Shrine in which to place the Ark of the LORD's Covenant. [20][b-]The interior of the-[b] Shrine was 20 cubits long, 20 cubits wide, and 20 cubits high. He overlaid it with solid gold; he similarly overlaid [its] cedar altar. [21]Solomon overlaid the interior of the House with solid gold; and he inserted golden chains [g-]into the door of-[g] the Shrine. He overlaid [the Shrine] with gold, [22]so that the entire House was overlaid with gold; he even overlaid with gold the entire altar of the Shrine. And so the entire House was completed.

[23]In the Shrine he made two cherubim of olive wood, each 10 cubits high. [24][One] had a wing measuring 5 cubits and another wing measuring 5 cubits, so that the spread from wingtip to wingtip was 10 cubits; [25]and the wingspread of the other cherub was also 10 cubits. The two cherubim had the same measurements and proportions: [26]the height of the one cherub was 10 cubits, and so was that of the other cherub.

[27]He placed the cherubim inside the [h-]inner chamber.-[h] Since the wings of the cherubim were extended, a wing of the one touched one wall and a wing of the other touched the other

אֶת־קִירֹות הַבַּ֫יִת מִבַּ֫יְתָה בְּצַלָעֹות אֲרָזִים מִקַּרְקַע הַבַּ֫יִת עַד־קִירֹות הַסִּפֻּן צִפָּה עֵץ מִבָּ֫יִת וַיְצַף אֶת־קַרְקַע הַבַּ֫יִת בְּצַלְעֹות בְּרֹושִׁים: [16]וַיִּ֫בֶן אֶת־עֶשְׂרִים אַמָּה מירכותי מִיַּרְכְּתֵי הַבַּ֫יִת בְּצַלְעֹות אֲרָזִים מִן־הַקַּרְקַע עַד־הַקִּירֹות וַיִּ֫בֶן לֹו מִבַּ֫יִת לִדְבִיר לְקֹ֫דֶשׁ הַקֳּדָשִׁים: [17]וְאַרְבָּעִים בָּאַמָּה הָיָה הַבָּ֫יִת הוּא הַהֵיכָל לִפְנָֽי: [18]וְאֶ֫רֶז אֶל־הַבַּ֫יִת פְּנִ֫ימָה מִקְלַעַת פְּקָעִים וּפְטוּרֵי צִצִּים הַכֹּל אֶ֫רֶז אֵין אֶ֫בֶן נִרְאָֽה: [19]וּדְבִיר בְּתֹוךְ־הַבַּ֫יִת מִפְּנִ֫ימָה הֵכִין לְתִתֵּן שָׁם אֶת־אֲרֹון בְּרִית יְהוָֽה: [20]וְלִפְנֵי הַדְּבִיר עֶשְׂרִים אַמָּה אֹ֫רֶךְ וְעֶשְׂרִים אַמָּה רֹ֫חַב וְעֶשְׂרִים אַמָּה קֹומָתֹו וַיְצַפֵּהוּ זָהָב סָגוּר וַיְצַף מִזְבֵּחַ אָֽרֶז: [21]וַיְצַף שְׁלֹמֹה אֶת־הַבַּ֫יִת מִפְּנִ֫ימָה זָהָב סָגוּר וַיְעַבֵּר בְּרַתִּיקֹות זָהָב לִפְנֵי הַדְּבִיר וַיְצַפֵּהוּ זָהָב: [22]וְאֶת־כָּל־הַבַּ֫יִת צִפָּה זָהָב עַד־תֹּם כָּל־הַבָּ֫יִת וְכָל־הַמִּזְבֵּחַ אֲשֶׁר־לַדְּבִיר צִפָּה זָהָֽב:

[23]וַיַּ֫עַשׂ בַּדְּבִיר שְׁנֵי כְרוּבִים עֲצֵי־שָׁ֫מֶן עֶ֫שֶׂר אַמֹּות קֹומָתֹֽו: [24]וְחָמֵשׁ אַמֹּות כְּנַף הַכְּרוּב הָֽאֶחָת וְחָמֵשׁ אַמֹּות כְּנַף הַכְּרֹוב הַשֵּׁנִית עֶ֫שֶׂר אַמֹּות מִקְצֹות כְּנָפָיו וְעַד־קְצֹות כְּנָפָיו: [25]וְעֶ֫שֶׂר בָּֽאַמָּה הַכְּרוּב הַשֵּׁנִי מִדָּה אַחַת וְקֶ֫צֶב אֶחָד לִשְׁנֵי הַכְּרֻבִים: [26]קֹומַת הַכְּרוּב הָאֶחָד עֶ֫שֶׂר בָּאַמָּה וְכֵן הַכְּרוּב הַשֵּׁנִֽי: [27]וַיִּתֵּן אֶת־הַכְּרוּבִים בְּתֹוךְ | הַבַּ֫יִת הַפְּנִימִי וַֽיִּפְרְשׂוּ אֶת־כַּנְפֵי הַכְּרֻבִים וַתִּגַּע כְּנַף־הָֽאֶחָד בַּקִּיר וּכְנַף הַכְּרוּב הַשֵּׁנִי נֹגַעַת בַּקִּיר הַשֵּׁנִי וְכַנְפֵיהֶם אֶל־תֹּוךְ

e   Septuagint reads "rafters."
f   Meaning of vv. 17–22 is unclear in part.
g-g   Heb. "in front of."
h-h   I.e., the Shrine.

wall, while their wings in the center of the chamber touched each other. 28He overlaid the cherubim with gold. 29All over the walls of the House, of both the inner area and the outer area, he carved reliefs of cherubim, palms, and calyxes, 30and he overlaid the floor of the House with gold, both the inner and the outer areas.

31For the entrance of the Shrine he made doors of olive wood, d-the pilasters and the doorposts having five sides.-d 32The double doors were of olive wood, and on them he carved reliefs of cherubim, palms, and calyxes. He overlaid them with gold, hammering the gold onto the cherubim and the palms. 33For the entrance of the Great Hall, too, he made doorposts of oleaster wood, d-having four sides,-d 34and the double doors of cypress wood, each door consisting of two rounded planks. 35On them he carved cherubim, palms, and calyxes, overlaying them with gold applied evenly over the carvings. 36He built the inner enclosure of three courses of hewn stones and one course of cedar beams.

37In the fourth year, in the month of Ziv, the foundations of the House were laid; 38and in the eleventh year, in the month of Bul—that is, the eighth month—the House was completed according to all its details and all its specifications. It took him seven years to build it.

7 1And it took Solomon thirteen years to build his palace, until his whole palace was completed.

2He built the a-Lebanon Forest House with four rows-a of cedar columns, and with hewn cedar beams above the columns. Its length was 100 cubits, its breadth 50 cubits, and its height 30 cubits. 3It was paneled above with cedar, with the planksb that were above on the 45 columns—15 in each row. 4And there were three

---

a-a   So called because of the rows of cedar columns. Septuagint reads "three rows" instead of "four rows"; cf. v. 3.

b   Apparently the "planks" connected the columns longitudinally, and the "beams" (v. 2) connected the planks transversely.

הַבַּ֫יִת נֹגְעֹת כָּנָ֖ף אֶל־כָּנָֽף׃ 28 וַיְצַ֥ף אֶת־הַכְּרוּבִ֖ים זָהָֽב׃ 29 וְאֵת֩ כָּל־קִיר֨וֹת הַבַּ֜יִת מֵסַ֣ב ׀ קָלַ֗ע פִּתּוּחֵי֙ מִקְלְעוֹת֙ כְּרוּבִ֣ים וְתִֽמֹרֹ֔ת וּפְטוּרֵ֖י צִצִּ֑ים מִלִּפְנִ֖ים וְלַחִיצֽוֹן׃ 30 וְאֶת־קַרְקַ֧ע הַבַּ֛יִת צִפָּ֥ה זָהָ֖ב לִפְנִ֥ימָה וְלַחִיצֽוֹן׃

31 וְאֵת֙ פֶּ֣תַח הַדְּבִ֔יר עָשָׂ֖ה דַּלְת֣וֹת עֲצֵי־שָׁ֑מֶן הָאַ֥יִל מְזוּז֖וֹת חֲמִשִֽׁית׃ 32 וּשְׁתֵּי֙ דַּלְת֣וֹת עֲצֵי־שֶׁ֔מֶן וְקָלַ֣ע עֲלֵיהֶ֗ם מִקְלְעוֹת֩ כְּרוּבִ֨ים וְתִמֹר֜וֹת וּפְטוּרֵ֣י צִצִּ֗ים וְצִפָּ֣ה זָהָ֔ב וַיָּ֛רֶד עַל־הַכְּרוּבִ֥ים וְעַל־הַתִּֽמֹר֖וֹת אֶת־הַזָּהָֽב׃ 33 וְכֵ֥ן עָשָׂ֛ה לְפֶ֥תַח הַֽהֵיכָ֖ל מְזוּז֣וֹת עֲצֵי־שָׁ֑מֶן מֵאֵ֖ת רְבִעִֽית׃ 34 וּשְׁתֵּ֥י דַלְת֖וֹת עֲצֵ֣י בְרוֹשִׁ֑ים שְׁנֵ֤י צְלָעִים֙ הַדֶּ֣לֶת הָֽאַחַ֔ת גְּלִילִ֔ים וּשְׁנֵ֥י קְלָעִ֛ים הַדֶּ֥לֶת הַשֵּׁנִ֖ית גְּלִילִֽים׃ 35 וְקָלַ֤ע כְּרוּבִים֙ וְתִֽמֹר֔וֹת וּפְטֻרֵ֖י צִצִּ֑ים וְצִפָּ֣ה זָהָ֔ב מְיֻשָּׁ֖ר עַל־הַמְּחֻקֶּֽה׃ 36 וַיִּ֙בֶן֙ אֶת־הֶחָצֵ֣ר הַפְּנִימִ֔ית שְׁלֹשָׁ֖ה טוּרֵ֣י גָזִ֑ית וְט֖וּר כְּרֻתֹ֥ת אֲרָזִֽים׃

37 בַּשָּׁנָה֙ הָֽרְבִיעִ֔ית יֻסַּ֖ד בֵּ֣ית יְהֹוָ֑ה בְּיֶ֖רַח זִֽו׃ 38 וּבַשָּׁנָ֣ה הָֽאַחַ֣ת עֶשְׂרֵ֡ה בְּיֶרַח֩ בּ֨וּל ה֜וּא הַחֹ֣דֶשׁ הַשְּׁמִינִ֗י כָּלָ֤ה הַבַּ֙יִת֙ לְכָל־דְּבָרָ֔יו וּלְכָל־מִשְׁפָּטָ֑יו וַיִּבְנֵ֖הוּ שֶׁ֥בַע שָׁנִֽים׃

7 1 וְאֶת־בֵּיתוֹ֙ בָּנָ֣ה שְׁלֹמֹ֔ה שְׁלֹ֥שׁ עֶשְׂרֵ֖ה שָׁנָ֑ה וַיְכַ֖ל אֶת־כָּל־בֵּיתֽוֹ׃ 2 וַיִּ֜בֶן אֶת־בֵּ֣ית ׀ יַ֣עַר הַלְּבָנ֗וֹן מֵאָ֨ה אַמָּ֤ה אָרְכּוֹ֙ וַחֲמִשִּׁ֤ים אַמָּה֙ רׇחְבּ֔וֹ וּשְׁלֹשִׁ֥ים אַמָּ֖ה קוֹמָת֑וֹ עַ֗ל אַרְבָּעָה֙ טוּרֵ֣י עַמּוּדֵ֣י אֲרָזִ֔ים וּכְרֻת֥וֹת אֲרָזִ֖ים עַל־הָעַמּוּדִֽים׃ 3 וְסָפֻ֣ן בָּאֶ֗רֶז מִמַּ֙עַל֙ עַל־הַצְּלָעֹת֙ אֲשֶׁ֣ר עַל־הָעַמּוּדִ֔ים אַרְבָּעִ֖ים וַחֲמִשָּׁ֑ה חֲמִשָּׁ֥ה עָשָׂ֖ר הַטּֽוּר׃ 4 וּשְׁקֻפִ֥ים שְׁלֹשָׁ֖ה טוּרִ֑ים

rows of window frames, with three tiers of windows facing each other. [5]All the doorways and doorposts[c] had square frames—with three tiers of windows facing each other.

[6]He made the portico of columns 50 cubits long and 30 cubits wide; [d]-the portico was in front of [the columns], and there were columns with a canopy in front of them.-[d] [7]He made the throne portico, where he was to pronounce judgment—the Hall of Judgment. It was paneled with cedar from floor to floor.[e]

[8]The house that he used as a residence, in the rear courtyard, back of the portico, was of the same construction. Solomon also constructed a palace like that portico for the daughter of Pharaoh, whom he had married.

[9]All these buildings, from foundation to coping and all the way out to the great courtyard, were of choice stones, hewn according to measure, smooth on all sides.[f] [10]The foundations were huge blocks of choice stone, stones of 10 cubits and stones of 8 cubits; [11]and above were choice stones, hewn according to measure, and cedar wood. [12]The large surrounding courtyard had three tiers of hewn stone and a row of cedar beams, the same as for the inner court of the House of the LORD, and for the portico of the House.

[13]King Solomon sent for Hiram and brought him down from Tyre. [14]He was the son of a widow of the tribe of Naphtali, and his father had been a Tyrian, a coppersmith. He was endowed with skill, ability, and talent for executing all work in bronze.[g] He came to King Solomon and executed all his work. [15]He cast two columns of bronze; one column was 18 cubits high and measured 12 cubits in circumference,

וּמֶחֱזָה אֶל־מֶחֱזָה שָׁלֹשׁ פְּעָמִים: 5 וְכָל־
הַפְּתָחִים וְהַמְּזוּזוֹת רְבֻעִים שָׁקֶף וּמוּל
מֶחֱזָה אֶל־מֶחֱזָה שָׁלֹשׁ פְּעָמִים:
6 וְאֵת אוּלָם הָעַמּוּדִים עָשָׂה חֲמִשִּׁים
אַמָּה אָרְכּוֹ וּשְׁלֹשִׁים אַמָּה רָחְבּוֹ וְאוּלָם
עַל־פְּנֵיהֶם וְעַמֻּדִים וְעָב עַל־פְּנֵיהֶם:
7 וְאוּלָם הַכִּסֵּא אֲשֶׁר יִשְׁפָּט־שָׁם אֻלָם
הַמִּשְׁפָּט עָשָׂה וְסָפוּן בָּאֶרֶז מֵהַקַּרְקַע
עַד־הַקַּרְקָע:
8 וּבֵיתוֹ אֲשֶׁר־יֵשֶׁב שָׁם חָצֵר הָאַחֶרֶת
מִבֵּית לָאוּלָם כַּמַּעֲשֶׂה הַזֶּה הָיָה וּבַיִת
יַעֲשֶׂה לְבַת־פַּרְעֹה אֲשֶׁר לָקַח שְׁלֹמֹה
כָּאוּלָם הַזֶּה:
9 כָּל־אֵלֶּה אֲבָנִים יְקָרֹת כְּמִדֹּת גָּזִית
מְגֹרָרוֹת בַּמְּגֵרָה מִבַּיִת וּמִחוּץ וּמִמַּסָּד
עַד־הַטְּפָחוֹת וּמִחוּץ עַד־הֶחָצֵר הַגְּדוֹלָה:
10 וּמְיֻסָּד אֲבָנִים יְקָרוֹת אֲבָנִים גְּדֹלוֹת
אַבְנֵי עֶשֶׂר אַמּוֹת וְאַבְנֵי שְׁמֹנֶה אַמּוֹת:
11 וּמִלְמַעְלָה אֲבָנִים יְקָרוֹת כְּמִדּוֹת גָּזִית
וָאָרֶז: 12 וְחָצֵר הַגְּדוֹלָה סָבִיב שְׁלֹשָׁה
טוּרִים גָּזִית וְטוּר כְּרֻתֹת אֲרָזִים וְלַחֲצַר
בֵּית־יְהֹוָה הַפְּנִימִית וּלְאֻלָם הַבָּיִת: פ

13 וַיִּשְׁלַח הַמֶּלֶךְ שְׁלֹמֹה וַיִּקַּח אֶת־חִירָם
מִצֹּר: 14 בֶּן־אִשָּׁה אַלְמָנָה הוּא מִמַּטֵּה
נַפְתָּלִי וְאָבִיו אִישׁ־צֹרִי חֹרֵשׁ נְחֹשֶׁת
וַיִּמָּלֵא אֶת־הַחָכְמָה וְאֶת־הַתְּבוּנָה וְאֶת־
הַדַּעַת לַעֲשׂוֹת כָּל־מְלָאכָה בַּנְּחֹשֶׁת
וַיָּבוֹא אֶל־הַמֶּלֶךְ שְׁלֹמֹה וַיַּעַשׂ אֶת־כָּל־
מְלַאכְתּוֹ: 15 וַיָּצַר אֶת־שְׁנֵי הָעַמּוּדִים
נְחֹשֶׁת שְׁמֹנֶה עֶשְׂרֵה אַמָּה קוֹמַת הָעַמּוּד
הָאֶחָד וְחוּט שְׁתֵּים־עֶשְׂרֵה אַמָּה יָסֹב
אֶת־הָעַמּוּד הַשֵּׁנִי: 16 וּשְׁתֵּי כֹתָרֹת עָשָׂה

---

c   *Septuagint reads "windows."*
d-d   *Meaning of Heb. uncertain.*
e   *Syriac reads "rafters."*
f   *Lit. "sawed with a saw in the inside and outside."*
g   *Heb.* nehosheth *means both copper and bronze. In the translation "copper" is ordinarily used to denote the natural product and "bronze" for the artifacts.*

[and similarly] the other column. ¹⁶He made two capitals, cast in bronze, to be set upon the two columns, the height of each of the two capitals being 5 cubits; ¹⁷also nets of meshwork with festoons of chainwork for the capitals that were on the top of the columns, seven for each of the two capitals. ¹⁸He made the columns*ʰ* so that there were two rows [of pomegranates] encircling the top of the one network, to cover the capitals that were on the top of the pomegranates;*ⁱ* and he did the same for [the network on] the second capital. ¹⁹The capitals upon the columns of the portico were of lily design, 4 cubits high; ²⁰so also the capitals upon the two columns extended above and next to the bulge*ʲ* that was beside the network. There were 200 pomegranates in rows around the top of the second capital.*ᵏ*

²¹He set up the columns at the portico of the Great Hall; he set up one column on the right and named it Jachin, and he set up the other column on the left and named it Boaz. ²²Upon the top of the columns there was a lily design. Thus the work of the columns was completed.

²³Then he made the tank*ˡ* of cast metal, 10 cubits across from brim to brim, completely round; it was 5 cubits high, and it measured 30 cubits in circumference. ²⁴There were gourds below the brim completely encircling it—ten to a cubit, encircling the tank; the gourds were in two rows, cast in one piece with it. ²⁵It stood upon twelve oxen: three facing north, three facing west, three facing south, and three facing east, with the tank resting upon them; their haunches were all turned inward. ²⁶It was a handbreadth thick, and its brim was made like that of a cup, like the petals of a lily. Its capacity was 2,000 *baths*.

²⁷He made the ten laver stands of bronze. The

---

h   Two Heb. mss. read "pomegranates."
i   About fifty Heb. mss. read "columns."
j   Lit. "belly"; exact force of Heb. uncertain.
k   I.e., each of the two capitals.
l   Lit. "sea."

לָתֵ֗ת עַל־רָאשֵׁ֤י הָֽעַמּוּדִים֙ מֻצַ֣ק נְחֹ֔שֶׁת חָמֵ֣שׁ אַמּ֗וֹת קוֹמַת֙ הַכֹּתֶ֣רֶת הָֽאֶחָ֔ת וְחָמֵ֣שׁ אַמּ֔וֹת קוֹמַ֖ת הַכֹּתֶ֥רֶת הַשֵּׁנִֽית:

¹⁷ שְׂבָכִ֞ים מַֽעֲשֵׂ֣ה שְׂבָכָ֗ה גְּדִלִים֙ מַֽעֲשֵׂ֣ה שַׁרְשְׁר֔וֹת לַכֹּ֣תָרֹ֔ת אֲשֶׁ֖ר עַל־רֹ֣אשׁ הָֽעַמּוּדִ֑ים שִׁבְעָה֙ לַכֹּתֶ֣רֶת הָֽאֶחָ֔ת וְשִׁבְעָ֖ה לַכֹּתֶ֥רֶת הַשֵּׁנִֽית: ¹⁸ וַיַּ֖עַשׂ אֶת־הָעַמּוּדִ֑ים וּשְׁנֵי֩ טוּרִ֨ים סָבִ֜יב עַל־הַשְּׂבָכָ֣ה הָֽאֶחָ֗ת לְכַסּ֞וֹת אֶת־הַכֹּֽתָרֹת֙ אֲשֶׁ֣ר עַל־רֹ֣אשׁ הָֽרִמֹּנִ֔ים וְכֵ֣ן עָשָׂ֔ה לַכֹּתֶ֖רֶת הַשֵּׁנִֽית: ¹⁹ וְכֹֽתָרֹ֗ת אֲשֶׁר֙ עַל־רֹ֣אשׁ הָֽעַמּוּדִ֔ים מַֽעֲשֵׂ֥ה שׁוּשַׁ֖ן בָּֽאוּלָ֑ם אַרְבַּ֖ע אַמּֽוֹת: ²⁰ וְכֹֽתָרֹ֗ת עַל־שְׁנֵי֙ הָ֣עַמּוּדִ֔ים גַּם־מִמַּ֗עַל מִלְּעֻמַּ֣ת הַבֶּ֔טֶן אֲשֶׁ֖ר לְעֵ֣בֶר שבכה הַשְּׂבָכָ֑ה וְהָֽרִמּוֹנִ֤ים מָאתַ֙יִם֙ טֻרִ֣ים סָבִ֔יב עַ֖ל הַכֹּתֶ֥רֶת הַשֵּׁנִֽית: ²¹ וַיָּ֙קֶם֙ אֶת־הָ֣עַמֻּדִ֔ים לְאֻלָ֖ם הַֽהֵיכָ֑ל וַיָּ֜קֶם אֶת־הָֽעַמּ֣וּד הַיְמָנִ֗י וַיִּקְרָ֤א אֶת־שְׁמוֹ֙ יָכִ֔ין וַיָּ֙קֶם֙ אֶת־הָֽעַמּ֣וּד הַשְּׂמָאלִ֔י וַיִּקְרָ֥א אֶת־שְׁמ֖וֹ בֹּֽעַז: ²² וְעַ֛ל רֹ֥אשׁ הָֽעַמּוּדִ֖ים מַֽעֲשֵׂ֣ה שׁוֹשָׁ֑ן וַתִּתֹּ֖ם מְלֶ֥אכֶת הָֽעַמּוּדִֽים: ²³ וַיַּ֥עַשׂ אֶת־הַיָּ֖ם מוּצָ֑ק עֶ֣שֶׂר בָּֽאַמָּ֣ה מִשְּׂפָת֣וֹ עַד־שְׂפָתוֹ֩ עָגֹ֨ל ׀ סָבִ֜יב וְחָמֵ֧שׁ בָּֽאַמָּ֣ה קֽוֹמָת֗וֹ וקוה וְקָו֙ שְׁלֹשִׁ֣ים בָּֽאַמָּ֔ה יָסֹ֥ב אֹת֖וֹ סָבִֽיב: ²⁴ וּפְקָעִים֩ מִתַּ֨חַת לִשְׂפָת֤וֹ ׀ סָבִיב֙ סֹבְבִ֣ים אֹת֔וֹ עֶ֛שֶׂר בָּֽאַמָּ֗ה מַקִּפִ֥ים אֶת־הַיָּ֖ם סָבִ֑יב שְׁנֵ֤י טוּרִים֙ הַפְּקָעִ֔ים יְצֻקִ֖ים בִּיצֻֽקָתֽוֹ: ²⁵ עֹמֵ֞ד עַל־שְׁנֵ֧י עָשָׂ֣ר בָּקָ֗ר שְׁלֹשָׁ֣ה פֹנִ֣ים ׀ צָפ֡וֹנָה וּשְׁלֹשָׁה֩ פֹנִ֨ים ׀ יָ֜מָּה וּשְׁלֹשָׁ֣ה ׀ פֹּנִ֣ים נֶ֗גְבָּה וּשְׁלֹשָׁה֙ פֹּנִ֣ים מִזְרָ֔חָה וְהַיָּ֥ם עֲלֵיהֶ֖ם מִלְמָ֑עְלָה וְכָל־אֲחֹֽרֵיהֶ֖ם בָּֽיְתָה: ²⁶ וְעָבְי֣וֹ טֶ֔פַח וּשְׂפָת֛וֹ כְּמַֽעֲשֵׂ֥ה שְׂפַת־כּ֖וֹס פֶּ֣רַח שׁוֹשָׁ֑ן אַלְפַּ֥יִם בַּ֖ת יָכִֽיל: פ ²⁷ וַיַּ֧עַשׂ אֶת־הַמְּכֹנ֛וֹת עֶ֖שֶׂר נְחֹ֑שֶׁת אַרְבַּ֣ע

length of each laver stand was 4 cubits and the width 4 cubits, and the height was 3 cubits. 28The structure of the laver stands was as follows: They had insets,^m and there were insets within the frames; 29and on the insets within the frames were lions, oxen, and cherubim. Above the frames was a stand; and both above and below the lions and the oxen were spirals of hammered metal. 30Each laver stand had four bronze wheels and [two] bronze axletrees. Its four legs had brackets; the brackets were under the laver, cast ᵈ-with spirals beyond each.-ᵈ 31Its funnel, within the crown, rose a cubit above it; this funnel was round, in the fashion of a stand, a cubit and a half in diameter. On the funnel too there were carvings.

But the insets were square, not round. 32And below the insets were the four wheels. The axletrees of the wheels were [fixed] in the laver stand, and the height of each wheel was a cubit and a half. 33The structure of the wheels was like the structure of chariot wheels; and their axletrees, their rims, their spokes, and their hubs were all of cast metal. 34Four brackets ran to the four corners of each laver stand; the brackets were of a piece with the laver stand. 35At the top of the laver stand was a round band half a cubit high, and together with the top of the laver stand; its sides and its insets were of one piece with it. 36ᵈ-On its surface—on its sides—and on its insets [Hiram] engraved cherubim, lions, and palms, as the clear space on each allowed,-ᵈ with spirals roundabout. 37It was after this manner that he made the ten laver stands, all of them cast alike, of the same measure and the same form. 38Then he made ten bronze lavers, one laver on each of the ten laver stands, each laver measuring 4 cubits and each laver containing forty *baths*.

39He disposed the laver stands, five at the right

---

m *Emendation yields "frames."*

בָּאַמָּה אֹרֶךְ הַמְּכוֹנָה הָאֶחָת וְאַרְבַּע
בָּאַמָּה רָחְבָּהּ וְשָׁלֹשׁ בָּאַמָּה קוֹמָתָהּ: 28וְזֶה מַעֲשֵׂה הַמְּכוֹנָה מִסְגֶּרֶת לָהֶם
וּמִסְגְּרֹת בֵּין הַשְׁלַבִּים: 29וְעַל־הַמִּסְגְּרוֹת
אֲשֶׁר ׀ בֵּין הַשְׁלַבִּים אֲרָיוֹת ׀ בָּקָר
וּכְרוּבִים וְעַל־הַשְׁלַבִּים כֵּן מִמָּעַל
וּמִתַּחַת לַאֲרָיוֹת וְלַבָּקָר לֹיוֹת מַעֲשֵׂה
מוֹרָד: 30וְאַרְבָּעָה אוֹפַנֵּי נְחֹשֶׁת לַמְּכוֹנָה
הָאַחַת וְסַרְנֵי נְחֹשֶׁת וְאַרְבָּעָה פַעֲמֹתָיו
כְּתֵפֹת לָהֶם מִתַּחַת לַכִּיֹּר הַכְּתֵפֹת יְצֻקוֹת
מֵעֵבֶר אִישׁ לֹיוֹת: 31וּפִיהוּ מִבֵּית לַכֹּתֶרֶת
וָמַעְלָה בָּאַמָּה וּפִיהָ עָגֹל מַעֲשֵׂה־כֵן אַמָּה
וַחֲצִי הָאַמָּה וְגַם־עַל־פִּיהָ מִקְלָעוֹת
וּמִסְגְּרֹתֵיהֶם מְרֻבָּעוֹת לֹא עֲגֻלּוֹת:
32וְאַרְבַּעַת הָאוֹפַנִּים לְמִתַּחַת לַמִּסְגְּרוֹת
וִידוֹת הָאוֹפַנִּים בַּמְּכוֹנָה וְקוֹמַת הָאוֹפַן
הָאֶחָד אַמָּה וַחֲצִי הָאַמָּה: 33וּמַעֲשֵׂה
הָאוֹפַנִּים כְּמַעֲשֵׂה אוֹפַן הַמֶּרְכָּבָה יְדוֹתָם
וְגַבֵּיהֶם וְחִשֻּׁקֵיהֶם וְחִשֻּׁרֵיהֶם הַכֹּל
מוּצָק: 34וְאַרְבַּע כְּתֵפוֹת אֶל אַרְבַּע פִּנּוֹת
הַמְּכֹנָה הָאֶחָת מִן־הַמְּכֹנָה כְּתֵפֶיהָ:
35וּבְרֹאשׁ הַמְּכוֹנָה חֲצִי הָאַמָּה קוֹמָה
עָגֹל ׀ סָבִיב וְעַל רֹאשׁ הַמְּכֹנָה יְדֹתֶיהָ
וּמִסְגְּרֹתֶיהָ מִמֶּנָּה: 36וַיְפַתַּח עַל־הַלֻּחֹת
יְדֹתֶיהָ וְעַל ומסגרתיה מִסְגְּרֹתֶיהָ כְּרוּבִים
אֲרָיוֹת וְתִמֹרֹת כְּמַעַר־אִישׁ וְלֹיוֹת סָבִיב:
37כָּזֹאת עָשָׂה אֵת עֶשֶׂר הַמְּכֹנוֹת מוּצָק
אֶחָד מִדָּה אַחַת קֶצֶב אֶחָד לְכֻלָּהְנָה: ס
38וַיַּעַשׂ עֲשָׂרָה כִיֹּרוֹת נְחֹשֶׁת אַרְבָּעִים
בַּת יָכִיל ׀ הַכִּיּוֹר הָאֶחָד אַרְבַּע בָּאַמָּה
הַכִּיּוֹר הָאֶחָד כִּיּוֹר אֶחָד עַל־הַמְּכֹנָה
הָאַחַת לְעֶשֶׂר הַמְּכֹנוֹת:
39וַיִּתֵּן אֶת־הַמְּכֹנוֹת חָמֵשׁ עַל־כֶּתֶף
הַבַּיִת מִיָּמִין וְחָמֵשׁ עַל־כֶּתֶף הַבַּיִת

side of the House and five at its left side; and the tank he placed on the right side of the House, at the southeast [corner].

40Hiram also made the lavers, the scrapers, and the sprinkling bowls.

So Hiram finished all the work that he had been doing for King Solomon on the House of the Lord: 41the two columns, the two globes of the capitals upon the columns; and the two pieces of network to cover the two globes of the capitals upon the columns; 42the four hundred pomegranates for the two pieces of network, two rows of pomegranates for each network, to cover the two globes of the capitals upon the columns; 43the ten stands and the ten lavers upon the stands; 44the one tank with the twelve oxen underneath the tank; 45the pails, the scrapers, and the sprinkling bowls. All those vessels in the House of the Lord that Hiram made for King Solomon were of burnished bronze. 46The king had them cast n-in earthen molds,-n in the plain of the Jordan between Succoth and Zarethan. 47Solomon left all the vessels [unweighed] because of their very great quantity; the weight of the bronze was not reckoned.

48And Solomon made all the furnishings that were in the House of the Lord: the altar, of gold; the table for the bread of display, of gold; 49the lampstands—five on the right side and five on the left—in front of the Shrine, of solid gold; and the petals, lamps, and tongs, of gold; 50the basins, snuffers, sprinkling bowls, ladles, and fire pans, of solid gold; and the hinge sockets for the doors of the innermost part of the House, the Holy of Holies, and for the doors of the Great Hall of the House, of gold.

n-n Lit. "in the thick of the earth."

מִשְּׂמֹאלֹו וְאֶת־הַיָּם נָתַן מִכֶּתֶף הַבַּיִת הַיְמָנִית קֵדְמָה מִמּוּל נֶגֶב: ס 40 וַיַּעַשׂ חִירֹום אֶת־הַכִּיֹּרֹות וְאֶת־הַיָּעִים וְאֶת־הַמִּזְרָקֹות

וַיְכַל חִירָם לַעֲשֹׂות אֶת־כָּל־הַמְּלָאכָה אֲשֶׁר עָשָׂה לַמֶּלֶךְ שְׁלֹמֹה בֵּית יְהוָה: 41 עַמֻּדִים שְׁנַיִם וְגֻלֹּת הַכֹּתָרֹת אֲשֶׁר־עַל־רֹאשׁ הָעַמֻּדִים שְׁתָּיִם וְהַשְּׂבָכֹות שְׁתַּיִם לְכַסֹּות אֶת־שְׁתֵּי גֻּלֹּת הַכֹּתָרֹת אֲשֶׁר עַל־רֹאשׁ הָעַמּוּדִים: 42 וְאֶת־הָרִמֹּנִים אַרְבַּע מֵאֹות לִשְׁתֵּי הַשְּׂבָכֹות שְׁנֵי־טוּרִים רִמֹּנִים לַשְּׂבָכָה הָאֶחָת לְכַסֹּות אֶת־שְׁתֵּי גֻּלֹּת הַכֹּתָרֹת אֲשֶׁר עַל־פְּנֵי הָעַמּוּדִים: 43 וְאֶת־הַמְּכֹנֹות עָשֶׂר וְאֶת־הַכִּיֹּרֹת עֲשָׂרָה עַל־הַמְּכֹנֹות: 44 וְאֶת־הַיָּם הָאֶחָד וְאֶת־הַבָּקָר שְׁנֵים־עָשָׂר תַּחַת הַיָּם: 45 וְאֶת־הַסִּירֹות וְאֶת־הַיָּעִים וְאֶת־הַמִּזְרָקֹות וְאֵת כָּל־הַכֵּלִים הָאֵהֶל הָאֵלֶּה אֲשֶׁר עָשָׂה חִירָם לַמֶּלֶךְ שְׁלֹמֹה בֵּית יְהוָה נְחֹשֶׁת מְמֹרָט: 46 בְּכִכַּר הַיַּרְדֵּן יְצָקָם הַמֶּלֶךְ בְּמַעֲבֵה הָאֲדָמָה בֵּין סֻכֹּות וּבֵין צָרְתָן: 47 וַיַּנַּח שְׁלֹמֹה אֶת־כָּל־הַכֵּלִים מֵרֹב מְאֹד מְאֹד לֹא נֶחְקַר מִשְׁקַל הַנְּחֹשֶׁת:

48 וַיַּעַשׂ שְׁלֹמֹה אֵת כָּל־הַכֵּלִים אֲשֶׁר בֵּית יְהוָה אֵת מִזְבַּח הַזָּהָב וְאֶת־הַשֻּׁלְחָן אֲשֶׁר עָלָיו לֶחֶם הַפָּנִים זָהָב: 49 וְאֶת־הַמְּנֹרֹות חָמֵשׁ מִיָּמִין וְחָמֵשׁ מִשְּׂמֹאול לִפְנֵי הַדְּבִיר זָהָב סָגוּר וְהַפֶּרַח וְהַנֵּרֹת וְהַמֶּלְקַחַיִם זָהָב: 50 וְהַסִּפֹּות וְהַמְזַמְּרֹות וְהַמִּזְרָקֹות וְהַכַּפֹּות וְהַמַּחְתֹּות זָהָב סָגוּר וְהַפֹּתֹות לְדַלְתֹות הַבַּיִת הַפְּנִימִי לְקֹדֶשׁ הַקֳּדָשִׁים לְדַלְתֵי הַבַּיִת לַהֵיכָל זָהָב: פ

51When all the work that King Solomon had done in the House of the LORD was completed, Solomon brought in the sacred donations of his father David—the silver, the gold, and the vessels—and deposited them in the treasury of the House of the LORD.

8 Then Solomon convoked the elders of Israel—all the heads of the tribes and the ancestral chieftains of the Israelites—before King Solomon in Jerusalem, to bring up the Ark of the Covenant of the LORD from the City of David, that is, Zion.

2All the men of Israel gathered before King Solomon at the Feast,*a* in the month of Ethanim—that is, the seventh month. 3When all the elders of Israel had come, the priests lifted the Ark 4and carried up the Ark of the LORD. Then the priests and the Levites brought the Tent of Meeting and all the holy vessels that were in the Tent. 5Meanwhile, King Solomon and the whole community of Israel, who were assembled with him before the Ark, were sacrificing sheep and oxen in such abundance that they could not be numbered or counted.

6The priests brought the Ark of the LORD's Covenant to its place underneath the wings of the cherubim, in the Shrine of the House, in the Holy of Holies; 7for the cherubim had their wings spread out over the place of the Ark, so that the cherubim shielded the Ark and its poles from above. 8The poles projected so that the ends of the poles were visible in the sanctuary in front of the Shrine, but they could not be seen outside; and there they remain to this day. 9There was nothing inside the Ark but the two tablets of stone which Moses placed there at Horeb, when the LORD made [a covenant] with the Israelites after their departure from the land of Egypt.

51וַתִּשְׁלַם כָּל־הַמְּלָאכָה אֲשֶׁר עָשָׂה הַמֶּלֶךְ שְׁלֹמֹה בֵּית יְהֹוָה וַיָּבֵא שְׁלֹמֹה אֶת־קָדְשֵׁי ׀ דָּוִד אָבִיו אֶת־הַכֶּסֶף וְאֶת־הַזָּהָב וְאֶת־הַכֵּלִים נָתַן בְּאֹצְרוֹת בֵּית יְהֹוָה: פ

ח אָז יַקְהֵל שְׁלֹמֹה אֶת־זִקְנֵי יִשְׂרָאֵל אֶת־כָּל־רָאשֵׁי הַמַּטּוֹת נְשִׂיאֵי הָאָבוֹת לִבְנֵי יִשְׂרָאֵל אֶל־הַמֶּלֶךְ שְׁלֹמֹה יְרוּשָׁלָ͏ִם לְהַעֲלוֹת אֶת־אֲרוֹן בְּרִית־יְהֹוָה מֵעִיר דָּוִד הִיא צִיּוֹן: 2וַיִּקָּהֲלוּ אֶל־הַמֶּלֶךְ שְׁלֹמֹה כָּל־אִישׁ יִשְׂרָאֵל בְּיֶרַח הָאֵתָנִים בֶּחָג הוּא הַחֹדֶשׁ הַשְּׁבִיעִי: 3וַיָּבֹאוּ כֹּל זִקְנֵי יִשְׂרָאֵל וַיִּשְׂאוּ הַכֹּהֲנִים אֶת־הָאָרוֹן: 4וַיַּעֲלוּ אֶת־אֲרוֹן יְהֹוָה וְאֶת־אֹהֶל מוֹעֵד וְאֶת־כָּל־כְּלֵי הַקֹּדֶשׁ אֲשֶׁר בָּאֹהֶל וַיַּעֲלוּ אֹתָם הַכֹּהֲנִים וְהַלְוִיִּם: 5וְהַמֶּלֶךְ שְׁלֹמֹה וְכָל־עֲדַת יִשְׂרָאֵל הַנּוֹעָדִים עָלָיו אִתּוֹ לִפְנֵי הָאָרוֹן מְזַבְּחִים צֹאן וּבָקָר אֲשֶׁר לֹא־יִסָּפְרוּ וְלֹא יִמָּנוּ מֵרֹב: 6וַיָּבִאוּ הַכֹּהֲנִים אֶת־אֲרוֹן בְּרִית־יְהֹוָה אֶל־מְקוֹמוֹ אֶל־דְּבִיר הַבַּיִת אֶל־קֹדֶשׁ הַקֳּדָשִׁים אֶל־תַּחַת כַּנְפֵי הַכְּרוּבִים: 7כִּי הַכְּרוּבִים פֹּרְשִׂים כְּנָפַיִם אֶל־מְקוֹם הָאָרוֹן וַיָּסֹכּוּ הַכְּרֻבִים עַל־הָאָרוֹן וְעַל־בַּדָּיו מִלְמָעְלָה: 8וַיַּאֲרִכוּ הַבַּדִּים וַיֵּרָאוּ רָאשֵׁי הַבַּדִּים מִן־הַקֹּדֶשׁ עַל־פְּנֵי הַדְּבִיר וְלֹא יֵרָאוּ הַחוּצָה וַיִּהְיוּ שָׁם עַד הַיּוֹם הַזֶּה: 9אֵין בָּאָרוֹן רַק שְׁנֵי לֻחוֹת הָאֲבָנִים אֲשֶׁר הִנִּחַ שָׁם מֹשֶׁה בְּחֹרֵב אֲשֶׁר כָּרַת יְהֹוָה עִם־בְּנֵי יִשְׂרָאֵל בְּצֵאתָם מֵאֶרֶץ מִצְרָיִם:

---

a I.e., of Booths. Cf. Lev. 23.34.

10When the priests came out of the sanctuary—for the cloud had filled the House of the LORD 11and the priests were not able to remain and perform the service because of the cloud, for the Presence of the LORD filled the House of the LORD—12then Solomon declared:

"The LORD has chosen
To abide in a thick cloud:
13I have now built for You
A stately House,
A place where You
May dwell forever."

14Then, with the whole congregation of Israel standing, the king faced about and blessed the whole congregation of Israel. 15He said:

"Praised be the LORD, the God of Israel, b-who has fulfilled with deeds the promise He made-b to my father David. For He said, 16'Ever since I brought My people Israel out of Egypt, I have not chosen a city among all the tribes of Israel for building a House where My name might abide; but I have chosen David to rule My people Israel.'

17"Now my father David had intended to build a House for the name of the LORD, the God of Israel. 18But the LORD said to my father David, 'As regards your intention to build a House for My name, you did right to have that intention. 19However, you shall not build the House yourself; instead, your son, the issue of your loins, shall build the House for My name.'

20"And the LORD has fulfilled the promise that He made: I have succeeded c my father David and have ascended the throne of Israel, as the LORD promised. I have built the House for the name of the LORD, the God of Israel; 21and I have set a place there for the Ark, containing the covenant which the LORD made with our fathers when He brought them out from the land of Egypt."

10 וַיְהִי בְּצֵאת הַכֹּהֲנִים מִן־הַקֹּדֶשׁ וְהֶעָנָן מָלֵא אֶת־בֵּית יְהוָה: 11 וְלֹא־יָכְלוּ הַכֹּהֲנִים לַעֲמֹד לְשָׁרֵת מִפְּנֵי הֶעָנָן כִּי־מָלֵא כְבוֹד־יְהוָה אֶת־בֵּית יְהוָה: פ 12 אָז אָמַר שְׁלֹמֹה

יְהוָה אָמַר
לִשְׁכֹּן בָּעֲרָפֶל:
13 בָּנֹה בָנִיתִי
בֵּית זְבֻל לָךְ
מָכוֹן לְשִׁבְתְּךָ
עוֹלָמִים:

14 וַיַּסֵּב הַמֶּלֶךְ אֶת־פָּנָיו וַיְבָרֶךְ אֵת כָּל־קְהַל יִשְׂרָאֵל וְכָל־קְהַל יִשְׂרָאֵל עֹמֵד: 15 וַיֹּאמֶר בָּרוּךְ יְהוָה אֱלֹהֵי יִשְׂרָאֵל אֲשֶׁר דִּבֶּר בְּפִיו אֵת דָּוִד אָבִי וּבְיָדוֹ מִלֵּא לֵאמֹר: 16 מִן־הַיּוֹם אֲשֶׁר הוֹצֵאתִי אֶת־עַמִּי אֶת־יִשְׂרָאֵל מִמִּצְרַיִם לֹא־בָחַרְתִּי בְעִיר מִכֹּל שִׁבְטֵי יִשְׂרָאֵל לִבְנוֹת בַּיִת לִהְיוֹת שְׁמִי שָׁם וָאֶבְחַר בְּדָוִד לִהְיוֹת עַל־עַמִּי יִשְׂרָאֵל: 17 וַיְהִי עִם־לְבַב דָּוִד אָבִי לִבְנוֹת בַּיִת לְשֵׁם יְהוָה אֱלֹהֵי יִשְׂרָאֵל: 18 וַיֹּאמֶר יְהוָה אֶל־דָּוִד אָבִי יַעַן אֲשֶׁר הָיָה עִם־לְבָבְךָ לִבְנוֹת בַּיִת לִשְׁמִי הֱטִיבֹתָ כִּי הָיָה עִם־לְבָבֶךָ: 19 רַק אַתָּה לֹא תִבְנֶה הַבָּיִת כִּי אִם־בִּנְךָ הַיֹּצֵא מֵחֲלָצֶיךָ הוּא־יִבְנֶה הַבַּיִת לִשְׁמִי: 20 וַיָּקֶם יְהוָה אֶת־דְּבָרוֹ אֲשֶׁר דִּבֵּר וָאָקֻם תַּחַת דָּוִד אָבִי וָאֵשֵׁב עַל־כִּסֵּא יִשְׂרָאֵל כַּאֲשֶׁר דִּבֶּר יְהוָה וָאֶבְנֶה הַבַּיִת לְשֵׁם יְהוָה אֱלֹהֵי יִשְׂרָאֵל: 21 וָאָשִׂם שָׁם מָקוֹם לָאָרוֹן אֲשֶׁר־שָׁם בְּרִית יְהוָה אֲשֶׁר כָּרַת עִם־אֲבֹתֵינוּ בְּהוֹצִיאוֹ אֹתָם מֵאֶרֶץ מִצְרָיִם: ס

---

b-b Lit. "who spoke with His own mouth … and has fulfilled with His own hand."
c Lit. "risen in place of."

22Then Solomon stood before the altar of the LORD in the presence of the whole community of Israel; he spread the palms of his hands toward heaven 23and said, "O LORD God of Israel, in the heavens above and on the earth below there is no god like You, who keep Your gracious covenant with Your servants when they walk before You in wholehearted devotion; 24You who have kept the promises You made to Your servant, my father David, fulfilling with deeds the promise You made—as is now the case. 25And now, O LORD God of Israel, keep the further promise that You made to Your servant, my father David: 'Your line on the throne of Israel shall never end, if only your descendants will look to their way and walk before Me as you have walked before Me.' 26Now, therefore, O God of Israel, let the promise that You made to Your servant my father David be fulfilled.

27"But will God really dwell^d on earth? Even the heavens to their uttermost reaches cannot contain You, how much less this House that I have built! 28Yet turn, O LORD my God, to the prayer and supplication of Your servant, and hear the cry and prayer which Your servant offers before You this day. 29May Your eyes be open day and night toward this House, toward the place of which You have said, 'My name shall abide there'; may You heed the prayers which Your servant will offer toward this place. 30And when You hear the supplications which Your servant and Your people Israel offer toward this place, give heed in Your heavenly abode—give heed and pardon.

31"Whenever one man commits an offense against another, and the latter utters an imprecation to bring a curse upon him, and comes with his imprecation before Your altar in this House, 32oh, hear in heaven and take action to judge Your servants, condemning him who is

---

d   2 Chron. 6.18 adds "with man."

22 וַיַּעֲמֹד שְׁלֹמֹה לִפְנֵי מִזְבַּח יְהֹוָה נֶגֶד כָּל־קְהַל יִשְׂרָאֵל וַיִּפְרֹשׂ כַּפָּיו הַשָּׁמָיִם: 23 וַיֹּאמַר יְהֹוָה אֱלֹהֵי יִשְׂרָאֵל אֵין־כָּמוֹךָ אֱלֹהִים בַּשָּׁמַיִם מִמַּעַל וְעַל־הָאָרֶץ מִתָּחַת שֹׁמֵר הַבְּרִית וְהַחֶסֶד לַעֲבָדֶיךָ הַהֹלְכִים לְפָנֶיךָ בְּכָל־לִבָּם: 24 אֲשֶׁר שָׁמַרְתָּ לְעַבְדְּךָ דָּוִד אָבִי אֵת אֲשֶׁר־דִּבַּרְתָּ לוֹ וַתְּדַבֵּר בְּפִיךָ וּבְיָדְךָ מִלֵּאתָ כַּיּוֹם הַזֶּה: 25 וְעַתָּה יְהֹוָה ׀ אֱלֹהֵי יִשְׂרָאֵל שְׁמֹר לְעַבְדְּךָ דָוִד אָבִי אֵת אֲשֶׁר דִּבַּרְתָּ לּוֹ לֵאמֹר לֹא־יִכָּרֵת לְךָ אִישׁ מִלְּפָנַי יֹשֵׁב עַל־כִּסֵּא יִשְׂרָאֵל רַק אִם־יִשְׁמְרוּ בָנֶיךָ אֶת־דַּרְכָּם לָלֶכֶת לְפָנַי כַּאֲשֶׁר הָלַכְתָּ לְפָנָי: 26 וְעַתָּה אֱלֹהֵי יִשְׂרָאֵל יֵאָמֶן נָא דבריך דְּבָרְךָ אֲשֶׁר דִּבַּרְתָּ לְעַבְדְּךָ דָּוִד אָבִי:

27 כִּי הַאֻמְנָם יֵשֵׁב אֱלֹהִים עַל־הָאָרֶץ הִנֵּה הַשָּׁמַיִם וּשְׁמֵי הַשָּׁמַיִם לֹא יְכַלְכְּלוּךָ אַף כִּי־הַבַּיִת הַזֶּה אֲשֶׁר בָּנִיתִי: 28 וּפָנִיתָ אֶל־תְּפִלַּת עַבְדְּךָ וְאֶל־תְּחִנָּתוֹ יְהֹוָה אֱלֹהָי לִשְׁמֹעַ אֶל־הָרִנָּה וְאֶל־הַתְּפִלָּה אֲשֶׁר עַבְדְּךָ מִתְפַּלֵּל לְפָנֶיךָ הַיּוֹם: 29 לִהְיוֹת עֵינֶךָ פְתֻחֹת אֶל־הַבַּיִת הַזֶּה לַיְלָה וָיוֹם אֶל־הַמָּקוֹם אֲשֶׁר אָמַרְתָּ יִהְיֶה שְׁמִי שָׁם לִשְׁמֹעַ אֶל־הַתְּפִלָּה אֲשֶׁר יִתְפַּלֵּל עַבְדְּךָ אֶל־הַמָּקוֹם הַזֶּה: 30 וְשָׁמַעְתָּ אֶל־תְּחִנַּת עַבְדְּךָ וְעַמְּךָ יִשְׂרָאֵל אֲשֶׁר יִתְפַּלְלוּ אֶל־הַמָּקוֹם הַזֶּה וְאַתָּה תִּשְׁמַע אֶל־מְקוֹם שִׁבְתְּךָ אֶל־הַשָּׁמַיִם וְשָׁמַעְתָּ וְסָלָחְתָּ: 31 אֵת אֲשֶׁר יֶחֱטָא אִישׁ לְרֵעֵהוּ וְנָשָׁא־בוֹ אָלָה לְהַאֲלֹתוֹ וּבָא אָלָה לִפְנֵי מִזְבַּחֲךָ בַּבַּיִת הַזֶּה: 32 וְאַתָּה ׀ תִּשְׁמַע הַשָּׁמַיִם וְעָשִׂיתָ וְשָׁפַטְתָּ אֶת־עֲבָדֶיךָ לְהַרְשִׁיעַ

in the wrong and bringing down the punishment of his conduct on his head, vindicating him who is in the right by rewarding him according to his righteousness.

33"Should Your people Israel be routed by an enemy because they have sinned against You, and then turn back to You and acknowledge Your name, and they offer prayer and supplication to You in this House, 34oh, hear in heaven and pardon the sin of Your people Israel, and restore them to the land that You gave to their fathers.

35"Should the heavens be shut up and there be no rain, because they have sinned against You, and then they pray toward this place and acknowledge Your name and repent of their sins, when You answer[e] them, 36oh, hear in heaven and pardon the sin of Your servants, Your people Israel, after You have shown them the proper way in which they are to walk; and send down rain upon the land which You gave to Your people as their heritage. 37So, too, if there is a famine in the land, if there is pestilence, blight, mildew, locusts or caterpillars, or if an enemy oppresses them in any of the settlements of the land.

"In any plague and in any disease, 38in any prayer or supplication offered by any person among all Your people Israel—each of whom knows his own affliction—when he spreads his palms toward this House, 39oh, hear in Your heavenly abode, and pardon and take action! Render to each man according to his ways as You know his heart to be—for You alone know the hearts of all men—40so that they may revere You all the days that they live on the land that You gave to our fathers.

41"Or if a foreigner who is not of Your people Israel comes from a distant land for the sake of Your name—42for they shall hear about Your

רָשָׁע לָתֵת דַּרְכּוֹ בְּרֹאשׁוֹ וּלְהַצְדִּיק צַדִּיק לָתֶת לוֹ כְּצִדְקָתוֹ׃ ס

33 בְּהִנָּגֵף עַמְּךָ יִשְׂרָאֵל לִפְנֵי אוֹיֵב אֲשֶׁר יֶחֶטְאוּ־לָךְ וְשָׁבוּ אֵלֶיךָ וְהוֹדוּ אֶת־שְׁמֶךָ וְהִתְפַּלְלוּ וְהִתְחַנְּנוּ אֵלֶיךָ בַּבַּיִת הַזֶּה׃ 34 וְאַתָּה תִּשְׁמַע הַשָּׁמַיִם וְסָלַחְתָּ לְחַטַּאת עַמְּךָ יִשְׂרָאֵל וַהֲשֵׁבֹתָם אֶל־הָאֲדָמָה אֲשֶׁר נָתַתָּ לַאֲבוֹתָם׃ ס

35 בְּהֵעָצֵר שָׁמַיִם וְלֹא־יִהְיֶה מָטָר כִּי יֶחֶטְאוּ־לָךְ וְהִתְפַּלְלוּ אֶל־הַמָּקוֹם הַזֶּה וְהוֹדוּ אֶת־שְׁמֶךָ וּמֵחַטָּאתָם יְשׁוּבוּן כִּי תַעֲנֵם׃ 36 וְאַתָּה ׀ תִּשְׁמַע הַשָּׁמַיִם וְסָלַחְתָּ לְחַטַּאת עֲבָדֶיךָ וְעַמְּךָ יִשְׂרָאֵל כִּי תוֹרֵם אֶת־הַדֶּרֶךְ הַטּוֹבָה אֲשֶׁר יֵלְכוּ־בָהּ וְנָתַתָּה מָטָר עַל־אַרְצְךָ אֲשֶׁר־נָתַתָּה לְעַמְּךָ לְנַחֲלָה׃ 37 רָעָב כִּי־יִהְיֶה בָאָרֶץ דֶּבֶר כִּי־יִהְיֶה שִׁדָּפוֹן יֵרָקוֹן אַרְבֶּה חָסִיל כִּי יִהְיֶה כִּי יָצַר־לוֹ אֹיְבוֹ בְּאֶרֶץ שְׁעָרָיו כָּל־נֶגַע כָּל־מַחֲלָה׃ 38 כָּל־תְּפִלָּה כָל־תְּחִנָּה אֲשֶׁר תִּהְיֶה לְכָל־הָאָדָם לְכֹל עַמְּךָ יִשְׂרָאֵל אֲשֶׁר יֵדְעוּן אִישׁ נֶגַע לְבָבוֹ וּפָרַשׂ כַּפָּיו אֶל־הַבַּיִת הַזֶּה׃ 39 וְאַתָּה תִּשְׁמַע הַשָּׁמַיִם מְכוֹן שִׁבְתֶּךָ וְסָלַחְתָּ וְעָשִׂיתָ וְנָתַתָּ לָאִישׁ כְּכָל־דְּרָכָיו אֲשֶׁר תֵּדַע אֶת־לְבָבוֹ כִּי־אַתָּה יָדַעְתָּ לְבַדְּךָ אֶת־לְבַב כָּל־בְּנֵי הָאָדָם׃ 40 לְמַעַן יִרָאוּךָ כָּל־הַיָּמִים אֲשֶׁר־הֵם חַיִּים עַל־פְּנֵי הָאֲדָמָה אֲשֶׁר נָתַתָּה לַאֲבֹתֵינוּ׃ 41 וְגַם אֶל־הַנָּכְרִי אֲשֶׁר לֹא־מֵעַמְּךָ יִשְׂרָאֵל הוּא וּבָא מֵאֶרֶץ רְחוֹקָה לְמַעַן שְׁמֶךָ׃ 42 כִּי יִשְׁמְעוּן אֶת־שִׁמְךָ הַגָּדוֹל וְאֶת־יָדְךָ

---

e The Septuagint, with a different vocalization, reads "chastise."

great name and Your mighty hand and Your outstretched arm—when he comes to pray toward this House, ⁴³oh, hear in Your heavenly abode and grant all that the foreigner asks You for. Thus all the peoples of the earth will know Your name and revere You, as does Your people Israel; and they will recognize that Your name is attached to this House that I have built.

⁴⁴"When Your people take the field against their enemy by whatever way You send them, and they pray to the Lord in the direction of the city which You have chosen, and of the House which I have built to Your name, ⁴⁵oh, hear in heaven their prayer and supplication and uphold their cause.

⁴⁶"When they sin against You—for there is no man who does not sin—and You are angry with them and deliver them to the enemy, and their captors carry them off to an enemy land, near or far; ⁴⁷and then they take it to heart in the land to which they have been carried off, and they repent and make supplication to You in the land of their captors, saying: 'We have sinned, we have acted perversely, we have acted wickedly,' ⁴⁸and they turn back to You with all their heart and soul, in the land of the enemies who have carried them off, and they pray to You in the direction of their land which You gave to their fathers, of the city which You have chosen, and of the House which I have built to Your name—⁴⁹oh, give heed in Your heavenly abode to their prayer and supplication, uphold their cause, ⁵⁰and pardon Your people who have sinned against You for all the transgressions that they have committed against You. Grant them mercy in the sight of their captors that they may be merciful to them. ⁵¹For they are Your very own people that You freed from Egypt, from the midst of the iron furnace. ⁵²May Your eyes be open to the supplication of Your servant and the supplication of Your people Israel, and may

הַחֲזָקָ֔ה וּֽזְרֹֽעֲךָ֖ הַנְּטוּיָ֑ה וּבָ֥א וְהִתְפַּלֵּ֖ל אֶל־הַבַּ֥יִת הַזֶּֽה׃ 43 אַתָּ֞ה תִּשְׁמַ֤ע הַשָּׁמַ֙יִם֙ מְכ֣וֹן שִׁבְתֶּ֔ךָ וְעָשִׂ֕יתָ כְּכֹ֛ל אֲשֶׁר־יִקְרָ֥א אֵלֶ֖יךָ הַנָּכְרִ֑י לְמַ֣עַן יֵדְע֩וּן כָּל־עַמֵּ֨י הָאָ֜רֶץ אֶת־שְׁמֶ֗ךָ לְיִרְאָ֤ה אֹֽתְךָ֙ כְּעַמְּךָ֣ יִשְׂרָאֵ֔ל וְלָדַ֕עַת כִּֽי־שִׁמְךָ֣ נִקְרָ֔א עַל־הַבַּ֥יִת הַזֶּ֖ה אֲשֶׁ֥ר בָּנִֽיתִי׃ 44 כִּֽי־יֵצֵ֨א עַמְּךָ֤ לַמִּלְחָמָה֙ עַל־אֹ֣יְב֔וֹ בַּדֶּ֖רֶךְ אֲשֶׁ֣ר תִּשְׁלָחֵ֑ם וְהִתְפַּֽלְל֣וּ אֶל־יְהֹוָ֗ה דֶּ֤רֶךְ הָעִיר֙ אֲשֶׁ֣ר בָּחַ֣רְתָּ בָּ֔הּ וְהַבַּ֖יִת אֲשֶׁר־בָּנִ֥תִי לִשְׁמֶֽךָ׃ 45 וְשָׁמַעְתָּ֙ הַשָּׁמַ֔יִם אֶת־תְּפִלָּתָ֖ם וְאֶת־תְּחִנָּתָ֑ם וְעָשִׂ֖יתָ מִשְׁפָּטָֽם׃ 46 כִּ֣י יֶֽחֶטְאוּ־לָ֗ךְ כִּ֣י אֵ֤ין אָדָם֙ אֲשֶׁ֣ר לֹא־יֶחֱטָ֔א וְאָנַפְתָּ֣ בָ֔ם וּנְתַתָּ֖ם לִפְנֵ֣י אוֹיֵ֑ב וְשָׁב֤וּם שֹֽׁבֵיהֶם֙ אֶל־אֶ֣רֶץ הָאוֹיֵ֔ב רְחוֹקָ֖ה א֥וֹ קְרוֹבָֽה׃ 47 וְהֵשִׁ֣יבוּ אֶל־לִבָּ֔ם בָּאָ֖רֶץ אֲשֶׁ֣ר נִשְׁבּוּ־שָׁ֑ם וְשָׁ֣בוּ ׀ וְהִֽתְחַנְּנ֣וּ אֵלֶ֗יךָ בְּאֶ֤רֶץ שֹֽׁבֵיהֶם֙ לֵאמֹ֔ר חָטָ֥אנוּ וְהֶעֱוִ֖ינוּ רָשָֽׁעְנוּ׃ 48 וְשָׁ֣בוּ אֵלֶ֗יךָ בְּכָל־לְבָבָם֙ וּבְכָל־נַפְשָׁ֔ם בְּאֶ֥רֶץ אֹֽיְבֵיהֶ֖ם אֲשֶׁר־שָׁב֣וּ אֹתָ֑ם וְהִֽתְפַּֽלְל֣וּ אֵלֶ֗יךָ דֶּ֤רֶךְ אַרְצָם֙ אֲשֶׁ֣ר נָתַ֣תָּה לַֽאֲבוֹתָ֔ם הָעִיר֙ אֲשֶׁ֣ר בָּחַ֔רְתָּ וְהַבַּ֖יִת אֲשֶׁר־בָּנִ֣יתִי לִשְׁמֶֽךָ׃ 49 וְשָׁמַעְתָּ֤ הַשָּׁמַ֙יִם֙ מְכ֣וֹן שִׁבְתְּךָ֔ אֶת־תְּפִלָּתָ֖ם וְאֶת־תְּחִנָּתָ֑ם וְעָשִׂ֖יתָ מִשְׁפָּטָֽם׃ 50 וְסָֽלַחְתָּ֣ לְעַמְּךָ֗ אֲשֶׁ֤ר חָֽטְאוּ־לָךְ֙ וּלְכָל־פִּשְׁעֵיהֶ֔ם אֲשֶׁ֖ר פָּ֣שְׁעוּ־בָ֑ךְ וּנְתַתָּ֧ם לְרַחֲמִ֛ים לִפְנֵ֥י שֹׁבֵיהֶ֖ם וְרִֽחֲמֽוּם׃ 51 כִּֽי־עַמְּךָ֥ וְנַֽחֲלָתְךָ֖ הֵ֑ם אֲשֶׁ֤ר הוֹצֵ֙אתָ֙ מִמִּצְרַ֔יִם מִתּ֖וֹךְ כּ֥וּר הַבַּרְזֶֽל׃ 52 לִֽהְי֧וֹת עֵינֶ֣יךָ פְתֻחֹ֗ת אֶל־תְּחִנַּ֤ת עַבְדְּךָ֙ וְאֶל־

You heed them whenever they call upon You. ⁵³For You, O Lord GOD, have set them apart for Yourself from all the peoples of the earth as Your very own, as You promised through Moses Your servant when You freed our fathers from Egypt."

⁵⁴When Solomon finished offering to the LORD all this prayer and supplication, he rose from where he had been kneeling, in front of the altar of the LORD, his hands spread out toward heaven. ⁵⁵He stood, and in a loud voice blessed the whole congregation of Israel:

⁵⁶"Praised be the LORD who has granted a haven to His people Israel, just as He promised; not a single word has failed of all the gracious promises that He made through His servant Moses. ⁵⁷May the LORD our God be with us, as He was with our fathers. May He never abandon or forsake us. ⁵⁸May He incline our hearts to Him, that we may walk in all His ways and keep the commandments, the laws, and the rules, which He enjoined upon our fathers. ⁵⁹And may these words of mine, which I have offered in supplication before the LORD, be close to the LORD our God day and night, that He may provide for His servant and for His people Israel, according to each day's needs—⁶⁰to the end that all the peoples of the earth may know that the LORD alone is God, there is no other. ⁶¹And may you be wholehearted with the LORD our God, to walk in His ways and keep His commandments, even as now."

⁶²The king and all Israel with him offered sacrifices before the LORD. ⁶³Solomon offered 22,000 oxen and 120,000 sheep as sacrifices of well-being to the LORD. Thus the king and all the Israelites dedicated the House of the LORD. ⁶⁴That day the king consecrated the center of the court that was in front of the House of the LORD. For it was there that he presented the

תְּחִנַּת עַמְּךָ יִשְׂרָאֵל לִשְׁמֹעַ אֲלֵיהֶם בְּכֹל קָרְאָם אֵלֶיךָ: 53 כִּי־אַתָּה הִבְדַּלְתָּם לְךָ לְנַחֲלָה מִכֹּל עַמֵּי הָאָרֶץ כַּאֲשֶׁר דִּבַּרְתָּ בְּיַד | מֹשֶׁה עַבְדֶּךָ בְּהוֹצִיאֲךָ אֶת־אֲבֹתֵינוּ מִמִּצְרַיִם אֲדֹנָי יְהוִה: פ

54 וַיְהִי | כְּכַלּוֹת שְׁלֹמֹה לְהִתְפַּלֵּל אֶל־ יְהוָה אֵת כָּל־הַתְּפִלָּה וְהַתְּחִנָּה הַזֹּאת קָם מִלִּפְנֵי מִזְבַּח יְהוָה מִכְּרֹעַ עַל־בִּרְכָּיו וְכַפָּיו פְּרֻשׂוֹת הַשָּׁמָיִם: 55 וַיַּעֲמֹד וַיְבָרֶךְ אֵת כָּל־קְהַל יִשְׂרָאֵל קוֹל גָּדוֹל לֵאמֹר: 56 בָּרוּךְ יְהוָה אֲשֶׁר נָתַן מְנוּחָה לְעַמּוֹ יִשְׂרָאֵל כְּכֹל אֲשֶׁר דִּבֵּר לֹא־נָפַל דָּבָר אֶחָד מִכֹּל דְּבָרוֹ הַטּוֹב אֲשֶׁר דִּבֶּר בְּיַד מֹשֶׁה עַבְדּוֹ: 57 יְהִי יְהוָה אֱלֹהֵינוּ עִמָּנוּ כַּאֲשֶׁר הָיָה עִם־אֲבֹתֵינוּ אַל־יַעַזְבֵנוּ וְאַל־יִטְּשֵׁנוּ: 58 לְהַטּוֹת לְבָבֵנוּ אֵלָיו לָלֶכֶת בְּכָל־דְּרָכָיו וְלִשְׁמֹר מִצְוֹתָיו וְחֻקָּיו וּמִשְׁפָּטָיו אֲשֶׁר צִוָּה אֶת־אֲבֹתֵינוּ: 59 וְיִהְיוּ דְבָרַי אֵלֶּה אֲשֶׁר הִתְחַנַּנְתִּי לִפְנֵי יְהוָה קְרֹבִים אֶל־ יְהוָה אֱלֹהֵינוּ יוֹמָם וָלָיְלָה לַעֲשׂוֹת | מִשְׁפַּט עַבְדּוֹ וּמִשְׁפַּט עַמּוֹ יִשְׂרָאֵל דְּבַר־ יוֹם בְּיוֹמוֹ: 60 לְמַעַן דַּעַת כָּל־עַמֵּי הָאָרֶץ כִּי יְהוָה הוּא הָאֱלֹהִים אֵין עוֹד: 61 וְהָיָה לְבַבְכֶם שָׁלֵם עִם יְהוָה אֱלֹהֵינוּ לָלֶכֶת בְּחֻקָּיו וְלִשְׁמֹר מִצְוֹתָיו כַּיּוֹם הַזֶּה: 62 וְהַמֶּלֶךְ וְכָל־יִשְׂרָאֵל עִמּוֹ זֹבְחִים זֶבַח לִפְנֵי יְהוָה: 63 וַיִּזְבַּח שְׁלֹמֹה אֵת זֶבַח הַשְּׁלָמִים אֲשֶׁר זָבַח לַיהוָה בָּקָר עֶשְׂרִים וּשְׁנַיִם אֶלֶף וְצֹאן מֵאָה וְעֶשְׂרִים אֶלֶף וַיַּחְנְכוּ אֶת־בֵּית יְהוָה הַמֶּלֶךְ וְכָל־בְּנֵי יִשְׂרָאֵל: 64 בַּיּוֹם הַהוּא קִדַּשׁ הַמֶּלֶךְ אֶת־ תּוֹךְ הֶחָצֵר אֲשֶׁר לִפְנֵי בֵית־יְהוָה כִּי־ עָשָׂה שָׁם אֶת־הָעֹלָה וְאֶת־הַמִּנְחָה וְאֵת

burnt offerings, the meal offerings, and the fat parts of the offerings of well-being, because the bronze altar that was before the Lord was too small to hold the burnt offerings, the meal offerings, and the fat parts of the offerings of well-being.

65So Solomon and all Israel with him—a great assemblage, [coming] from Lebo-hamath to the Wadi of Egypt*f*—observed the Feast*a* at that time before the Lord our God, seven days and again seven days, fourteen days in all. 66On the eighth day*g* he let the people go. They bade the king good-bye and went to their homes, joyful and glad of heart over all the goodness that the Lord had shown to His servant David and His people Israel.

9 When Solomon had finished building the House of the Lord and the royal palace and everything that Solomon had set his heart on constructing, 2the Lord appeared to Solomon a second time, as He had appeared to him at Gibeon. 3The Lord said to him, "I have heard the prayer and the supplication which you have offered to Me. I consecrate this House which you have built and I set My name there forever. My eyes and My heart shall ever be there. 4As for you, if you walk before Me as your father David walked before Me, wholeheartedly and with uprightness, doing all that I have commanded you [and] keeping My laws and My rules, 5then I will establish your throne of kingship over Israel forever, as I promised your father David, saying, 'Your line on the throne of Israel shall never end.' 6[But] if you and your descendants turn away from Me and do not keep the commandments [and] the laws which I have set before you, and go and serve other gods and worship them, 7then I will sweep*a* Is-

חֶלְבֵי הַשְּׁלָמִים כִּי־מִזְבַּח הַנְּחֹשֶׁת אֲשֶׁר לִפְנֵי יְהוָה קָטֹן מֵהָכִיל אֶת־הָעֹלָה וְאֶת־הַמִּנְחָה וְאֵת חֶלְבֵי הַשְּׁלָמִים: 65וַיַּעַשׂ שְׁלֹמֹה בָעֵת־הַהִיא | אֶת־הֶחָג וְכָל־יִשְׂרָאֵל עִמּוֹ קָהָל גָּדוֹל מִלְּבוֹא חֲמָת | עַד־נַחַל מִצְרַיִם לִפְנֵי יְהוָה אֱלֹהֵינוּ שִׁבְעַת יָמִים וְשִׁבְעַת יָמִים אַרְבָּעָה עָשָׂר יוֹם: 66בַּיּוֹם הַשְּׁמִינִי שִׁלַּח אֶת־הָעָם וַיְבָרֲכוּ אֶת־הַמֶּלֶךְ וַיֵּלְכוּ לְאָהֳלֵיהֶם שְׂמֵחִים וְטוֹבֵי לֵב עַל כָּל־הַטּוֹבָה אֲשֶׁר עָשָׂה יְהוָה לְדָוִד עַבְדּוֹ וּלְיִשְׂרָאֵל עַמּוֹ:

ט וַיְהִי כְּכַלּוֹת שְׁלֹמֹה לִבְנוֹת אֶת־בֵּית־יְהוָה וְאֶת־בֵּית הַמֶּלֶךְ וְאֵת כָּל־חֵשֶׁק שְׁלֹמֹה אֲשֶׁר חָפֵץ לַעֲשׂוֹת: פ 2וַיֵּרָא יְהוָה אֶל־שְׁלֹמֹה שֵׁנִית כַּאֲשֶׁר נִרְאָה אֵלָיו בְּגִבְעוֹן: 3וַיֹּאמֶר יְהוָה אֵלָיו שָׁמַעְתִּי אֶת־תְּפִלָּתְךָ וְאֶת־תְּחִנָּתְךָ אֲשֶׁר הִתְחַנַּנְתָּה לְפָנַי הִקְדַּשְׁתִּי אֶת־הַבַּיִת הַזֶּה אֲשֶׁר בָּנִתָה לָשׂוּם־שְׁמִי שָׁם עַד־עוֹלָם וְהָיוּ עֵינַי וְלִבִּי שָׁם כָּל־הַיָּמִים: 4וְאַתָּה אִם־תֵּלֵךְ לְפָנַי כַּאֲשֶׁר הָלַךְ דָּוִד אָבִיךָ בְּתָם־לֵבָב וּבְיֹשֶׁר לַעֲשׂוֹת כְּכֹל אֲשֶׁר צִוִּיתִיךָ חֻקַּי וּמִשְׁפָּטַי תִּשְׁמֹר: 5וַהֲקִמֹתִי אֶת־כִּסֵּא מַמְלַכְתְּךָ עַל־יִשְׂרָאֵל לְעֹלָם כַּאֲשֶׁר דִּבַּרְתִּי עַל־דָּוִד אָבִיךָ לֵאמֹר לֹא־יִכָּרֵת לְךָ אִישׁ מֵעַל כִּסֵּא יִשְׂרָאֵל: 6אִם־שׁוֹב תְּשֻׁבוּן אַתֶּם וּבְנֵיכֶם מֵאַחֲרַי וְלֹא תִשְׁמְרוּ מִצְוֹתַי חֻקֹּתַי אֲשֶׁר נָתַתִּי לִפְנֵיכֶם וַהֲלַכְתֶּם וַעֲבַדְתֶּם אֱלֹהִים אֲחֵרִים וְהִשְׁתַּחֲוִיתֶם לָהֶם: 7וְהִכְרַתִּי

---

f I.e., coming from one end of the country to the other.
g I.e., of the second seven-day feast; cf. 2 Chron. 7.8–10.
a Lit. "cut."

rael off the land which I gave them; I will reject[b] the House which I have consecrated to My name; and Israel shall become a proverb and a byword among all peoples. [8]And [c-as for this House, once so exalted,-c] everyone passing by it shall be appalled and shall hiss.[d] And when they ask, 'Why did the LORD do thus to the land and to this House?' [9]they shall be told, 'It is because they forsook the LORD their God who freed them from the land of Egypt, and they embraced other gods and worshiped them and served them; therefore the LORD has brought all this calamity upon them.'"

[10]At the end of the twenty years[e] during which Solomon constructed the two buildings, the LORD's House and the royal palace—[11]since King Hiram of Tyre had supplied Solomon with all the cedar and cypress timber and gold that he required—King Solomon in turn gave Hiram twenty towns in the region of Galilee. [12]But when Hiram came from Tyre to inspect the towns that Solomon had given him, he was not pleased with them. [13]"My brother," he said, "what sort of towns are these you have given me?" So they were named the land of Cabul,[f] as is still the case. [14]However, Hiram sent the king one hundred and twenty talents of gold.

[15]This was the purpose of the forced labor which Solomon imposed: It was to build the House of the LORD, his own palace, the Millo,[g] and the wall of Jerusalem, and [to fortify] Hazor, Megiddo, and Gezer. ([16]Pharaoh king of Egypt had come up and captured Gezer; he destroyed it by fire, killed the Canaanites who dwelt in the town, and gave it as dowry to his daughter, Solomon's wife.) [17]So Solomon

אֶת־יִשְׂרָאֵל מֵעַל פְּנֵי הָאֲדָמָה אֲשֶׁר נָתַתִּי לָהֶם וְאֶת־הַבַּיִת אֲשֶׁר הִקְדַּשְׁתִּי לִשְׁמִי אֲשַׁלַּח מֵעַל פָּנָי וְהָיָה יִשְׂרָאֵל לְמָשָׁל וְלִשְׁנִינָה בְּכָל־הָעַמִּים: [8]וְהַבַּיִת הַזֶּה יִהְיֶה עֶלְיוֹן כָּל־עֹבֵר עָלָיו יִשֹּׁם וְשָׁרָק וְאָמְרוּ עַל־מֶה עָשָׂה יְהוָה כָּכָה לָאָרֶץ הַזֹּאת וְלַבַּיִת הַזֶּה: [9]וְאָמְרוּ עַל אֲשֶׁר עָזְבוּ אֶת־יְהוָה אֱלֹהֵיהֶם אֲשֶׁר הוֹצִיא אֶת־אֲבֹתָם מֵאֶרֶץ מִצְרַיִם וַיַּחֲזִקוּ בֵּאלֹהִים אֲחֵרִים וַיִּשְׁתַּחוּ לָהֶם וַיַּעַבְדֻם עַל־כֵּן הֵבִיא יְהוָֹה עֲלֵיהֶם אֵת כָּל־הָרָעָה הַזֹּאת: פ

[10]וַיְהִי מִקְצֵה עֶשְׂרִים שָׁנָה אֲשֶׁר־בָּנָה שְׁלֹמֹה אֶת־שְׁנֵי הַבָּתִּים אֶת־בֵּית יְהוָה וְאֶת־בֵּית הַמֶּלֶךְ: [11]חִירָם מֶלֶךְ־צֹר נִשָּׂא אֶת־שְׁלֹמֹה בַּעֲצֵי אֲרָזִים וּבַעֲצֵי בְרוֹשִׁים וּבַזָּהָב לְכָל־חֶפְצוֹ אָז יִתֵּן הַמֶּלֶךְ שְׁלֹמֹה לְחִירָם עֶשְׂרִים עִיר בְּאֶרֶץ הַגָּלִיל: [12]וַיֵּצֵא חִירָם מִצֹּר לִרְאוֹת אֶת־הֶעָרִים אֲשֶׁר נָתַן־לוֹ שְׁלֹמֹה וְלֹא יָשְׁרוּ בְּעֵינָיו: [13]וַיֹּאמֶר מָה הֶעָרִים הָאֵלֶּה אֲשֶׁר־נָתַתָּה לִּי אָחִי וַיִּקְרָא לָהֶם אֶרֶץ כָּבוּל עַד הַיּוֹם הַזֶּה: פ [14]וַיִּשְׁלַח חִירָם לַמֶּלֶךְ מֵאָה וְעֶשְׂרִים כִּכַּר זָהָב:

[15]וְזֶה דְבַר־הַמַּס אֲשֶׁר־הֶעֱלָה | הַמֶּלֶךְ שְׁלֹמֹה לִבְנוֹת אֶת־בֵּית יְהוָה וְאֶת־בֵּיתוֹ וְאֶת־הַמִּלּוֹא וְאֵת חוֹמַת יְרוּשָׁלָ͏ִם וְאֶת־חָצֹר וְאֶת־מְגִדּוֹ וְאֶת־גָּזֶר: [16]פַּרְעֹה מֶלֶךְ־מִצְרַיִם עָלָה וַיִּלְכֹּד אֶת־גֶּזֶר וַיִּשְׂרְפָהּ בָּאֵשׁ וְאֶת־הַכְּנַעֲנִי הַיֹּשֵׁב בָּעִיר הָרָג וַיִּתְּנָהּ שִׁלֻּחִים לְבִתּוֹ אֵשֶׁת שְׁלֹמֹה: [17]וַיִּבֶן שְׁלֹמֹה אֶת־גָּזֶר וְאֶת־בֵּית חֹרֹן

---

b Lit. "dismiss from My presence."
c-c Targum and some other ancient versions read "and this House shall become a ruin."
d An action performed at the sight of ruin to ward off a like fate from the observer; cf. note at Jer. 18.16.
e See 6.38–7.1.
f Perhaps taken to mean "as nothing."
g A citadel.

fortified Gezer, lower Beth-horon, [18]Baalith, and Tamar*h* in the wilderness, in the land [of Judah], [19]and all of Solomon's garrison towns, chariot towns, and cavalry towns—everything that Solomon set his heart on building in Jerusalem and in the Lebanon, and throughout the territory that he ruled. [20]All the people that were left of the Amorites, Hittites, Perizzites, Hivites, and Jebusites who were not of the Israelite stock—[21]those of their descendants who remained in the land and whom the Israelites were not able to annihilate—of these Solomon made a slave force, as is still the case. [22]But he did not reduce any Israelites to slavery; they served, rather, as warriors and as his attendants, officials, and officers, and as commanders of his chariotry and cavalry.

[23]These were the prefects that were in charge of Solomon's works and were foremen over the people engaged in the work, who numbered 550.*i*

[24]As soon as Pharaoh's daughter went up from the City of David to the palace that he had built for her, he built the Millo.*g*

[25]Solomon used to offer burnt offerings and sacrifices of well-being three times a year on the altar that he had built for the Lord, and *j*-he used to offer incense on the one that was before the Lord. And he kept the House in repair.-*j*

[26]King Solomon also built a fleet of ships at Ezion-geber, which is near Eloth*k* on the shore of the Sea of Reeds in the land of Edom. [27]Hiram sent servants of his with the fleet, mariners who were experienced on the sea, to serve with Solomon's men. [28]They came to Ophir; there they obtained gold in the amount of four hundred and twenty talents, which they delivered to King Solomon.

תַּחְתּֽוֹן: 18 וְאֶת־בַּעֲלָת וְאֶת־תָּמֹר תַּדְמֹר בַּמִּדְבָּר בָּאָֽרֶץ: 19 וְאֵת כׇּל־עָרֵי הַֽמִּסְכְּנוֹת אֲשֶׁר הָיוּ לִשְׁלֹמֹה וְאֵת עָרֵי הָרֶכֶב וְאֵת עָרֵי הַפָּֽרָשִׁים וְאֵת ׀ חֵשֶׁק שְׁלֹמֹה אֲשֶׁר חָשַׁק לִבְנוֹת בִּירֽוּשָׁלַ͏ִם וּבַלְּבָנוֹן וּבְכֹל אֶרֶץ מֶמְשַׁלְתּֽוֹ: 20 כׇּל־הָעָם הַנּוֹתָר מִן־ הָאֱמֹרִי הַֽחִתִּי הַפְּרִזִּי הַחִוִּי וְהַיְבוּסִי אֲשֶׁר לֹֽא־מִבְּנֵי יִשְׂרָאֵל הֵֽמָּה: 21 בְּנֵיהֶם אֲשֶׁר נֹתְרוּ אַחֲרֵיהֶם בָּאָרֶץ אֲשֶׁר לֹֽא־יָכְלוּ בְּנֵי יִשְׂרָאֵל לְהַֽחֲרִימָם וַיַּעֲלֵם שְׁלֹמֹה לְמַס־ עֹבֵד עַד הַיּוֹם הַזֶּֽה: 22 וּמִבְּנֵי יִשְׂרָאֵל לֹֽא־נָתַן שְׁלֹמֹה עָבֶד כִּי־הֵם אַנְשֵׁי הַמִּלְחָמָה וַעֲבָדָיו וְשָׂרָיו וְשָׁלִשָׁיו וְשָׂרֵי רִכְבּוֹ וּפָרָשָֽׁיו: ס

23 אֵלֶּה ׀ שָׂרֵי הַנִּצָּבִים אֲשֶׁר עַל־הַמְּלָאכָה לִשְׁלֹמֹה חֲמִשִּׁים וַחֲמֵשׁ מֵאוֹת הָרֹדִים בָּעָם הָעֹשִׂים בַּמְּלָאכָֽה: 24 אַךְ בַּת־פַּרְעֹה עָֽלְתָה מֵעִיר דָּוִד אֶל־ בֵּיתָהּ אֲשֶׁר בָּֽנָה־לָהּ אָז בָּנָה אֶת־ הַמִּלּֽוֹא: 25 וְהֶעֱלָה שְׁלֹמֹה שָׁלֹשׁ פְּעָמִים בַּשָּׁנָה עֹלוֹת וּשְׁלָמִים עַל־הַמִּזְבֵּחַ אֲשֶׁר בָּנָה לַֽיהֹוָה וְהַקְטֵיר אִתּוֹ אֲשֶׁר לִפְנֵי יְהֹוָה וְשִׁלַּם אֶת־הַבָּֽיִת: 26 וָֽאֳנִי עָשָׂה הַמֶּלֶךְ שְׁלֹמֹה בְּעֶצְיֽוֹן־גֶּבֶר אֲשֶׁר אֶת־אֵלוֹת עַל־שְׂפַת יַם־סוּף בְּאֶרֶץ אֱדֽוֹם: 27 וַיִּשְׁלַח חִירָם בׇּאֳנִי אֶת־עֲבָדָיו אַנְשֵׁי אֳנִיּוֹת יֹדְעֵי הַיָּם עִם עַבְדֵי שְׁלֹמֹֽה: 28 וַיָּבֹאוּ אוֹפִירָה וַיִּקְחוּ מִשָּׁם זָהָב אַרְבַּע־ מֵאוֹת וְעֶשְׂרִים כִּכָּר וַיָּבִאוּ אֶל־הַמֶּלֶךְ שְׁלֹמֹֽה: פ

---

h So kethib, cf. Ezek. 47.19, 48.28; qere *Tadmor.*
i Their names are not listed in the text.
j-j Meaning of Heb. uncertain.
k Elsewhere called Elath.

10

The queen of Sheba heard of Solomon's fame, *a*-through the name of the LORD,-*a* and she came to test him with hard questions. ²She arrived in Jerusalem with a very large retinue, with camels bearing spices, a great quantity of gold, and precious stones. When she came to Solomon, she asked him all that she had in mind. ³Solomon had answers for all her questions; there was nothing that the king did not know, [nothing] to which he could not give her an answer. ⁴When the queen of Sheba observed all of Solomon's wisdom, and the palace he had built, ⁵the fare of his table, the seating of his courtiers, the service and attire of his attendants, and his wine service, *b*-and the burnt offerings that he offered at-*b* the House of the LORD, she was left breathless.

⁶She said to the king, "The report I heard in my own land about you and your wisdom was true. ⁷But I did not believe the reports until I came and saw with my own eyes that not even the half had been told me; your wisdom and wealth surpass the reports that I heard. ⁸How fortunate are your men and how fortunate are these your courtiers, who are always in attendance on you and can hear your wisdom! ⁹Praised be the LORD your God, who delighted in you and set you on the throne of Israel. It is because of the LORD's everlasting love for Israel that He made you king to administer justice and righteousness."

¹⁰She presented the king with one hundred and twenty talents of gold, and a large quantity of spices, and precious stones. Never again did such a vast quantity of spices arrive as that which the queen of Sheba gave to King Solomon.—¹¹Moreover, Hiram's fleet, which carried gold from Ophir, brought in from Ophir a huge quantity of *almug* wood*c* and precious stones.

ל וּמַלְכַּת־שְׁבָא שֹׁמַעַת אֶת־שֵׁמַע
שְׁלֹמֹה לְשֵׁם יְהוָה וַתָּבֹא לְנַסֹּתוֹ
בְּחִידֽוֹת: ²וַתָּבֹא יְרוּשָׁלְַמָה בְּחַיִל כָּבֵד
מְאֹד גְּמַלִּים נֹשְׂאִים בְּשָׂמִים וְזָהָב רַב־
מְאֹד וְאֶבֶן יְקָרָה וַתָּבֹא אֶל־שְׁלֹמֹה
וַתְּדַבֵּר אֵלָיו אֵת כָּל־אֲשֶׁר הָיָה עִם־
לְבָבָֽהּ: ³וַיַּגֶּד־לָהּ שְׁלֹמֹה אֶת־כָּל־דְּבָרֶיהָ
לֹא־הָיָה דָּבָר נֶעְלָם מִן־הַמֶּלֶךְ אֲשֶׁר לֹא
הִגִּיד לָֽהּ: ⁴וַתֵּרֶא מַלְכַּת־שְׁבָא אֵת כָּל־
חָכְמַת שְׁלֹמֹה וְהַבַּיִת אֲשֶׁר בָּנָֽה:
⁵וּמַאֲכַל שֻׁלְחָנוֹ וּמוֹשַׁב עֲבָדָיו וּמַעֲמַד
מְשָׁרְתָו וּמַלְבֻּשֵׁיהֶם וּמַשְׁקָיו
וְעֹלָתוֹ אֲשֶׁר יַעֲלֶה בֵּית יְהוָה וְלֹא־הָיָה
בָהּ עוֹד רֽוּחַ:
⁶וַתֹּאמֶר אֶל־הַמֶּלֶךְ אֱמֶת הָיָה הַדָּבָר
אֲשֶׁר שָׁמַעְתִּי בְּאַרְצִי עַל־דְּבָרֶיךָ וְעַל־
חָכְמָתֶֽךָ: ⁷וְלֹא־הֶאֱמַנְתִּי לַדְּבָרִים עַד
אֲשֶׁר־בָּאתִי וַתִּרְאֶינָה עֵינַי וְהִנֵּה לֹֽא־
הֻגַּד־לִי הַחֵצִי הוֹסַפְתָּ חָכְמָה וָטוֹב אֶל־
הַשְּׁמוּעָה אֲשֶׁר שָׁמָֽעְתִּי: ⁸אַשְׁרֵי אֲנָשֶׁיךָ
אַשְׁרֵי עֲבָדֶיךָ אֵלֶּה הָעֹמְדִים לְפָנֶיךָ תָּמִיד
הַשֹּׁמְעִים אֶת־חָכְמָתֶֽךָ: ⁹יְהִי יְהוָה
אֱלֹהֶיךָ בָּרוּךְ אֲשֶׁר חָפֵץ בְּךָ לְתִתְּךָ עַל־
כִּסֵּא יִשְׂרָאֵל בְּאַהֲבַת יְהוָה אֶת־יִשְׂרָאֵל
לְעֹלָם וַיְשִׂימְךָ לְמֶלֶךְ לַעֲשׂוֹת מִשְׁפָּט
וּצְדָקָֽה:
¹⁰וַתִּתֵּן לַמֶּלֶךְ מֵאָה וְעֶשְׂרִים ׀ כִּכַּר זָהָב
וּבְשָׂמִים הַרְבֵּה מְאֹד וְאֶבֶן יְקָרָה לֹא־בָא
כַבֹּשֶׂם הַהוּא עוֹד לָרֹב אֲשֶׁר־נָתְנָה
מַלְכַּת־שְׁבָא לַמֶּלֶךְ שְׁלֹמֹֽה: ¹¹וְגַם אֳנִי
חִירָם אֲשֶׁר־נָשָׂא זָהָב מֵאוֹפִיר הֵבִיא
מֵאֹפִיר עֲצֵי אַלְמֻגִּים הַרְבֵּה מְאֹד וְאֶבֶן

a-a The force of the phrase is uncertain.
b-b 2 Chron. 9.4 reads "…and the procession with which he went
     up to…"
c   Others "sandalwood."

¹²The king used the *almug* wood for decorations in the House of the Lord and in the royal palace, and for harps and lyres for the musicians. Such a quantity of *almug* wood has never arrived or been seen to this day.—¹³King Solomon, in turn, gave the queen of Sheba everything she wanted and asked for, in addition to what King Solomon gave her out of his royal bounty. Then she and her attendants left and returned to her own land.

¹⁴The weight of the gold which Solomon received every year was 666 talents of gold, ¹⁵besides what came from tradesmen, from the traffic of the merchants, and from all the kings of Arabia and the governors of the regions. ¹⁶King Solomon made 200 shields of beaten gold—600 shekels of gold to each shield—¹⁷and 300 bucklers of beaten gold—three *mina*s of gold to each buckler. The king placed them in the Lebanon Forest House.

¹⁸The king also made a large throne of ivory, and he overlaid it with refined gold. ¹⁹Six steps led up to the throne, and the throne had a back with a rounded top, and arms on either side of the seat. Two lions stood beside the arms, ²⁰and twelve lions stood on the six steps, six on either side. No such throne was ever made for any other kingdom.*d*

²¹All King Solomon's drinking cups were of gold, and all the utensils of the Lebanon Forest House were of pure gold: silver did not count for anything in Solomon's days. ²²For the king had a Tarshish*e* fleet on the sea, along with Hiram's fleet. Once every three years, the Tarshish fleet came in, bearing gold and silver, ivory, apes, and peacocks.

²³King Solomon excelled all the kings on earth in wealth and in wisdom. ²⁴All the world came to pay homage to Solomon and to listen to the wisdom with which God had endowed

---

d   Or "prince"; like Phoenician *mamlakt.*
e   Probably a fleet of large ships.

12 וַיַּעַשׂ הַמֶּלֶךְ אֶת־עֲצֵי הָאַלְמֻגִּים מִסְעָד לְבֵית־יְהוָה וּלְבֵית הַמֶּלֶךְ וְכִנֹּרוֹת וּנְבָלִים לַשָּׁרִים לֹא בָא־כֵן עֲצֵי אַלְמֻגִּים וְלֹא נִרְאָה עַד הַיּוֹם הַזֶּה: 13 וְהַמֶּלֶךְ שְׁלֹמֹה נָתַן לְמַלְכַּת־שְׁבָא אֶת־כָּל־חֶפְצָהּ אֲשֶׁר שָׁאָלָה מִלְּבַד אֲשֶׁר נָתַן־לָהּ כְּיַד הַמֶּלֶךְ שְׁלֹמֹה וַתֵּפֶן וַתֵּלֶךְ לְאַרְצָהּ הִיא וַעֲבָדֶיהָ: ס

14 וַיְהִי מִשְׁקַל הַזָּהָב אֲשֶׁר־בָּא לִשְׁלֹמֹה בְּשָׁנָה אֶחָת שֵׁשׁ מֵאוֹת שִׁשִּׁים וָשֵׁשׁ כִּכַּר זָהָב: 15 לְבַד מֵאַנְשֵׁי הַתָּרִים וּמִסְחַר הָרֹכְלִים וְכָל־מַלְכֵי הָעֶרֶב וּפַחוֹת הָאָרֶץ: 16 וַיַּעַשׂ הַמֶּלֶךְ שְׁלֹמֹה מָאתַיִם צִנָּה זָהָב שָׁחוּט שֵׁשׁ־מֵאוֹת זָהָב יַעֲלֶה עַל־הַצִּנָּה הָאֶחָת: 17 וּשְׁלֹשׁ־מֵאוֹת מָגִנִּים זָהָב שָׁחוּט שְׁלֹשֶׁת מָנִים זָהָב יַעֲלֶה עַל־הַמָּגֵן הָאֶחָת וַיִּתְּנֵם הַמֶּלֶךְ בֵּית יַעַר הַלְּבָנוֹן: פ

18 וַיַּעַשׂ הַמֶּלֶךְ כִּסֵּא־שֵׁן גָּדוֹל וַיְצַפֵּהוּ זָהָב מוּפָז: 19 שֵׁשׁ מַעֲלוֹת לַכִּסֵּה וְרֹאשׁ־עָגֹל לַכִּסֵּה מֵאַחֲרָיו וְיָדֹת מִזֶּה וּמִזֶּה אֶל־מְקוֹם הַשָּׁבֶת וּשְׁנַיִם אֲרָיוֹת עֹמְדִים אֵצֶל הַיָּדוֹת: 20 וּשְׁנֵים עָשָׂר אֲרָיִים עֹמְדִים שָׁם עַל־שֵׁשׁ הַמַּעֲלוֹת מִזֶּה וּמִזֶּה לֹא־נַעֲשָׂה כֵן לְכָל־מַמְלָכוֹת:

21 וְכֹל כְּלֵי מַשְׁקֵה הַמֶּלֶךְ שְׁלֹמֹה זָהָב וְכֹל כְּלֵי בֵּית־יַעַר הַלְּבָנוֹן זָהָב סָגוּר אֵין כֶּסֶף לֹא נֶחְשָׁב בִּימֵי שְׁלֹמֹה לִמְאוּמָה: 22 כִּי אֳנִי תַרְשִׁישׁ לַמֶּלֶךְ בַּיָּם עִם אֳנִי חִירָם אַחַת לְשָׁלֹשׁ שָׁנִים תָּבוֹא | אֳנִי תַרְשִׁישׁ נֹשְׂאֵת זָהָב וָכֶסֶף שֶׁנְהַבִּים וְקֹפִים וְתֻכִּיִּים:

23 וַיִּגְדַּל הַמֶּלֶךְ שְׁלֹמֹה מִכֹּל מַלְכֵי הָאָרֶץ לְעֹשֶׁר וּלְחָכְמָה: 24 וְכָל־הָאָרֶץ מְבַקְשִׁים אֶת־פְּנֵי שְׁלֹמֹה לִשְׁמֹעַ אֶת־חָכְמָתוֹ אֲשֶׁר־נָתַן אֱלֹהִים בְּלִבּוֹ: 25 וְהֵמָּה מְבִאִים

him; 25and each one would bring his tribute—silver and gold objects, robes, weapons and spices, horses and mules—in the amount due each year.

26Solomon assembled chariots and horses. He had 1,400 chariots and 12,000 horses, which he stationed *f* in the chariot towns and with the king in Jerusalem. 27The king made silver as plentiful in Jerusalem as stones, and cedars as plentiful as sycamores in the Shephelah. 28Solomon's horses were procured from Mizraim*g* and Kue. The king's dealers would buy them from Kue at a fixed price. 29A chariot imported from Mizraim*g* cost 600 shekels of silver, and a horse 150; these in turn were exported by them*h* to all the kings of the Hittites and the kings of the Arameans.

11

King Solomon loved many foreign women in addition to Pharaoh's daughter—Moabite, Ammonite, Edomite, Phoenician, and Hittite women, 2from the nations of which the Lord had said to the Israelites, "None of you shall join them and none of them shall join you,*a* lest they turn your heart away to follow their gods." Such Solomon clung to and loved. 3He had seven hundred royal wives and three hundred concubines; and his wives turned his heart away. 4In his old age, his wives turned away Solomon's heart after other gods, and he was not as wholeheartedly devoted to the Lord his God as his father David had been. 5Solomon followed Ashtoreth the goddess of the Phoenicians, and Milcom the abomination of the Ammonites.

6Solomon did what was displeasing to the Lord and did not remain loyal to the Lord like his father David. 7At that time, Solomon built

אִישׁ מִנְחָתוֹ כְּלֵי כֶסֶף וּכְלֵי זָהָב וּשְׂלָמוֹת וְנֵשֶׁק וּבְשָׂמִים סוּסִים וּפְרָדִים דְּבַר־שָׁנָה בְּשָׁנָה: ס

26 וַיֶּאֱסֹף שְׁלֹמֹה רֶכֶב וּפָרָשִׁים וַיְהִי־לוֹ אֶלֶף וְאַרְבַּע־מֵאוֹת רֶכֶב וּשְׁנֵים־עָשָׂר אֶלֶף פָּרָשִׁים וַיַּנְחֵם* בְּעָרֵי הָרֶכֶב וְעִם־הַמֶּלֶךְ בִּירוּשָׁלָ͏ִם: 27 וַיִּתֵּן הַמֶּלֶךְ אֶת־הַכֶּסֶף בִּירוּשָׁלַ͏ִם כָּאֲבָנִים וְאֵת הָאֲרָזִים נָתַן כַּשִּׁקְמִים אֲשֶׁר־בַּשְּׁפֵלָה לָרֹב: 28 וּמוֹצָא הַסּוּסִים אֲשֶׁר לִשְׁלֹמֹה מִמִּצְרָיִם וּמִקְוֵה סֹחֲרֵי הַמֶּלֶךְ יִקְחוּ מִקְוֵה בִּמְחִיר: 29 וַתַּעֲלֶה וַתֵּצֵא מֶרְכָּבָה מִמִּצְרַיִם בְּשֵׁשׁ מֵאוֹת כֶּסֶף וְסוּס בַּחֲמִשִּׁים וּמֵאָה וְכֵן לְכָל־מַלְכֵי הַחִתִּים וּלְמַלְכֵי אֲרָם בְּיָדָם יֹצִאוּ: פ

יא וְהַמֶּלֶךְ שְׁלֹמֹה אָהַב נָשִׁים נָכְרִיּוֹת רַבּוֹת וְאֶת־בַּת־פַּרְעֹה מוֹאֲבִיּוֹת עַמֳּנִיּוֹת אֲדֹמִיֹּת צֵדְנִיֹּת חִתִּיֹּת: 2 מִן־הַגּוֹיִם אֲשֶׁר אָמַר־יְהֹוָה אֶל־בְּנֵי יִשְׂרָאֵל לֹא־תָבֹאוּ בָהֶם וְהֵם לֹא־יָבֹאוּ בָכֶם אָכֵן יַטּוּ אֶת־לְבַבְכֶם אַחֲרֵי אֱלֹהֵיהֶם בָּהֶם דָּבַק שְׁלֹמֹה לְאַהֲבָה: 3 וַיְהִי־לוֹ נָשִׁים שָׂרוֹת שְׁבַע מֵאוֹת וּפִלַגְשִׁים שְׁלֹשׁ מֵאוֹת וַיַּטּוּ נָשָׁיו אֶת־לִבּוֹ: 4 וַיְהִי לְעֵת זִקְנַת שְׁלֹמֹה נָשָׁיו הִטּוּ אֶת־לְבָבוֹ אַחֲרֵי אֱלֹהִים אֲחֵרִים וְלֹא־הָיָה לְבָבוֹ שָׁלֵם עִם־יְהֹוָה אֱלֹהָיו כִּלְבַב דָּוִיד אָבִיו: 5 וַיֵּלֶךְ שְׁלֹמֹה אַחֲרֵי עַשְׁתֹּרֶת אֱלֹהֵי צִדֹנִים וְאַחֲרֵי מִלְכֹּם שִׁקֻּץ עַמֹּנִים: 6 וַיַּעַשׂ שְׁלֹמֹה הָרַע בְּעֵינֵי יְהֹוָה וְלֹא מִלֵּא אַחֲרֵי יְהֹוָה כְּדָוִד אָבִיו: ס 7 אָז יִבְנֶה שְׁלֹמֹה בָּמָה לִכְמוֹשׁ שִׁקֻּץ מוֹאָב בָּהָר

בדברי הימים "ויניחם" *v. 26.*

---

f So 2 Chron. 1.14; 9.25; Heb. here "led."
g Usually Egypt, here perhaps Muṣru, a neighbor of Kue (Cilicia).
h I.e., Solomon's dealers.
a I.e., in marriage; cf. Deut. 7.3–4; 23.4, 8–9.

a shrine for Chemosh the abomination of Moab on the hill near Jerusalem, and one for Molech the abomination of the Ammonites. [8]And he did the same for all his foreign wives who offered and sacrificed to their gods.

[9]The Lord was angry with Solomon, because his heart turned away from the Lord, the God of Israel, who had appeared to him twice [10]and had commanded him about this matter, not to follow other gods; he did not obey what the Lord had commanded. [11]And the Lord said to Solomon, b-"Because you are guilty of this-b— you have not kept My covenant and the laws which I enjoined upon you—I will tear the kingdom away from you and give it to one of your servants. [12]But, for the sake of your father David, I will not do it in your lifetime; I will tear it away from your son. [13]However, I will not tear away the whole kingdom; I will give your son one tribe, for the sake of My servant David and for the sake of Jerusalem which I have chosen."

[14]So the Lord raised up an adversary against Solomon, the Edomite Hadad, who was of the royal family of Edom. [15]When David c-was in-c Edom, Joab the army commander went up to bury the slain, and he killed every male in Edom; [16]for Joab and all Israel stayed there for six months until he had killed off every male in Edom. [17]But Hadad,[d] together with some Edomite men, servants of his father, escaped and headed for Egypt; Hadad was then a young boy. [18]Setting out from Midian, they came to Paran and took along with them men from Paran. Thus they came to Egypt, to Pharaoh king of Egypt, who gave him a house, assigned a food allowance to him, and granted him an estate. [19]Pharaoh took a great liking to Hadad and gave him his sister-in-law, the sister of Queen Tahpenes, as wife. [20]The sister of Tahpenes bore him a son, Genubath. Tahpenes

אֲשֶׁ֣ר עַל־פְּנֵ֣י יְרוּשָׁלִַ֔ם וּלְמֹ֕לֶךְ שִׁקֻּ֖ץ בְּנֵ֥י עַמּֽוֹן׃ [8]וְכֵ֣ן עָשָׂ֔ה לְכָל־נָשָׁ֖יו הַנָּכְרִיּ֑וֹת מַקְטִיר֥וֹת וּֽמְזַבְּח֖וֹת לֵאלֹהֵיהֶֽן׃ [9]וַיִּתְאַנַּ֥ף יְהֹוָ֖ה בִּשְׁלֹמֹ֑ה כִּֽי־נָטָ֣ה לְבָב֗וֹ מֵעִ֤ם יְהֹוָה֙ אֱלֹהֵ֣י יִשְׂרָאֵ֔ל הַנִּרְאָ֥ה אֵלָ֖יו פַּעֲמָֽיִם׃ [10]וְצִוָּ֤ה אֵלָיו֙ עַל־הַדָּבָ֣ר הַזֶּ֔ה לְבִלְתִּי־לֶ֕כֶת אַחֲרֵ֖י אֱלֹהִ֣ים אֲחֵרִ֑ים וְלֹ֣א שָׁמַ֔ר אֵ֥ת אֲשֶׁר־צִוָּ֖ה יְהֹוָֽה׃ פ [11]וַיֹּ֨אמֶר יְהֹוָ֜ה לִשְׁלֹמֹ֗ה יַ֚עַן אֲשֶׁ֣ר הָֽיְתָה־זֹּ֣את עִמָּ֔ךְ וְלֹ֤א שָׁמַ֙רְתָּ֙ בְּרִיתִ֣י וְחֻקֹּתַ֔י אֲשֶׁ֥ר צִוִּ֖יתִי עָלֶ֑יךָ קָרֹ֨עַ אֶקְרַ֤ע אֶת־הַמַּמְלָכָה֙ מֵֽעָלֶ֔יךָ וּנְתַתִּ֖יהָ לְעַבְדֶּֽךָ׃ [12]אַךְ־בְּיָמֶ֙יךָ֙ לֹ֣א אֶעֱשֶׂ֔נָּה לְמַ֖עַן דָּוִ֣ד אָבִ֑יךָ מִיַּ֥ד בִּנְךָ֖ אֶקְרָעֶֽנָּה׃ [13]רַ֣ק אֶת־כׇּל־הַמַּמְלָכָה֮ לֹ֣א אֶקְרָע֒ שֵׁ֥בֶט אֶחָ֖ד אֶתֵּ֣ן לִבְנֶ֑ךָ לְמַ֙עַן֙ דָּוִ֣ד עַבְדִּ֔י וּלְמַ֥עַן יְרוּשָׁלִַ֖ם אֲשֶׁ֥ר בָּחָֽרְתִּי׃

[14]וַיָּ֨קֶם יְהֹוָ֤ה שָׂטָן֙ לִשְׁלֹמֹ֔ה אֵ֖ת הֲדַ֣ד הָאֲדֹמִ֑י מִזֶּ֧רַע הַמֶּ֛לֶךְ ה֖וּא בֶּאֱדֽוֹם׃ [15]וַיְהִ֗י בִּֽהְי֤וֹת דָּוִד֙ אֶת־אֱד֔וֹם בַּעֲל֗וֹת יוֹאָב֙ שַׂ֣ר הַצָּבָ֔א לְקַבֵּ֖ר אֶת־הַחֲלָלִ֑ים וַיַּ֥ךְ כׇּל־זָכָ֖ר בֶּאֱדֽוֹם׃ [16]כִּ֣י שֵׁ֧שֶׁת חֳדָשִׁ֛ים יָשַׁב־שָׁ֥ם יוֹאָ֖ב וְכׇל־יִשְׂרָאֵ֑ל עַד־הִכְרִ֥ית כׇּל־זָכָ֖ר בֶּאֱדֽוֹם׃ [17]וַיִּבְרַ֣ח אֲדַ֡ד הוּא֩ וַאֲנָשִׁ֨ים אֲדֹמִיִּ֜ים מֵעַבְדֵ֥י אָבִ֛יו אִתּ֖וֹ לָב֣וֹא מִצְרָ֑יִם וַהֲדַ֖ד נַ֥עַר קָטָֽן׃ [18]וַיָּקֻ֙מוּ֙ מִמִּדְיָ֔ן וַיָּבֹ֖אוּ פָּארָ֑ן וַיִּקְחוּ֩ אֲנָשִׁ֨ים עִמָּ֜ם מִפָּארָ֗ן וַיָּבֹ֤אוּ מִצְרַ֙יִם֙ אֶל־פַּרְעֹ֣ה מֶֽלֶךְ־מִצְרַ֔יִם וַיִּתֶּן־ל֣וֹ בַ֔יִת וְלֶ֖חֶם אָ֣מַר ל֑וֹ וְאֶ֖רֶץ נָ֥תַן לֽוֹ׃ [19]וַיִּמְצָא֩ הֲדַ֨ד חֵ֤ן בְּעֵינֵ֣י פַרְעֹה֙ מְאֹ֔ד וַיִּתֶּן־ל֣וֹ אִשָּׁ֗ה אֶת־אֲח֤וֹת אִשְׁתּוֹ֙ אֲח֖וֹת תַּחְפְּנֵ֣יס הַגְּבִירָֽה׃ [20]וַתֵּ֨לֶד ל֜וֹ אֲח֣וֹת תַּחְפְּנֵ֗יס אֶת־גְּנֻבַ֣ת בְּנ֔וֹ וַתִּגְמְלֵ֣הוּ תַחְפְּנֵ֗ס

---

b-b   Lit. "This is with you."
c-c   Emendation yields "defeated"; cf. 2 Sam. 8.13.
d   Heb. Adad.

weaned[e] him in Pharaoh's palace, and Genubath remained in Pharaoh's palace among the sons of Pharaoh. [21]When Hadad heard in Egypt that David had been laid to rest with his fathers and that Joab the army commander was dead, Hadad said to Pharaoh, "Give me leave to go to my own country." [22]Pharaoh replied, "What do you lack with me, that you want to go to your own country?" But he said, "Nevertheless, give me leave to go."

[23]Another adversary that God raised up against Solomon[f] was Rezon son of Eliada, who had fled from his lord, King Hadadezer of Zobah, [24]when David was slaughtering them. He gathered men about him and became captain over a troop; they went to Damascus and settled there, and they established a kingdom in Damascus. [25]He was an adversary of Israel all the days of Solomon, adding to the trouble [caused by] Hadad; he repudiated [the authority of] Israel and reigned over Aram.

[26]Jeroboam son of Nebat, an Ephraimite of Zeredah, the son of a widow whose name was Zeruah, was in Solomon's service; he raised his hand against the king. [27]The circumstances under which he raised his hand against the king were as follows: Solomon built the Millo and repaired the breach of the city of his father, David. [28]This Jeroboam was an able man, and when Solomon saw that the young man was a capable worker, he appointed him over all the forced labor of the House of Joseph.

[29]During that time Jeroboam went out of Jerusalem and the prophet Ahijah of Shiloh met him on the way. He had put on a new robe; and when the two were alone in the open country, [30]Ahijah took hold of the new robe he was wearing and tore it into twelve pieces. [31]"Take ten pieces," he said to Jeroboam. "For thus said the LORD, the God of Israel: I am about to tear the

בְּתֹ֖וךְ בֵּ֣ית פַּרְעֹ֑ה וַיְהִ֤י גְנֻבַת֙ בֵּ֣ית פַּרְעֹ֔ה בְּת֖וֹךְ בְּנֵ֥י פַרְעֹֽה: 21 וַהֲדַ֗ד שָׁמַ֣ע בְּמִצְרַ֔יִם כִּֽי־שָׁכַ֤ב דָּוִד֙ עִם־אֲבֹתָ֔יו וְכִי־מֵ֖ת יוֹאָ֣ב שַׂר־הַצָּבָ֑א וַיֹּ֤אמֶר הֲדַד֙ אֶל־פַּרְעֹ֔ה שַׁלְּחֵ֖נִי וְאֵלֵ֥ךְ אֶל־אַרְצִֽי: 22 וַיֹּ֧אמֶר ל֣וֹ פַרְעֹ֗ה כִּ֠י מָה־אַתָּ֤ה חָסֵר֙ עִמִּ֔י וְהִנְּךָ֥ מְבַקֵּ֖שׁ לָלֶ֣כֶת אֶל־אַרְצֶ֑ךָ וַיֹּ֣אמֶר ׀ לֹ֔א כִּ֥י שַׁלֵּ֖חַ תְּשַׁלְּחֵֽנִי:

23 וַיָּ֨קֶם אֱלֹהִ֥ים לוֹ֙ שָׂטָ֔ן אֶת־רְז֖וֹן בֶּן־ אֶלְיָדָ֑ע אֲשֶׁ֣ר בָּרַ֗ח מֵאֵ֛ת הֲדַדְעֶ֥זֶר מֶֽלֶךְ־ צוֹבָ֖ה אֲדֹנָֽיו: 24 וַיִּקְבֹּ֤ץ עָלָיו֙ אֲנָשִׁ֔ים וַיְהִ֣י שַׂר־גְּד֔וּד בַּהֲרֹ֥ג דָּוִ֖ד אֹתָ֑ם וַיֵּלְכ֤וּ דַמֶּ֙שֶׂק֙ וַיֵּ֣שְׁבוּ בָ֔הּ וַֽיִּמְלְכ֖וּ בְּדַמָּֽשֶׂק: 25 וַיְהִ֣י שָׂטָ֣ן לְיִשְׂרָאֵל֮ כָּל־יְמֵ֣י שְׁלֹמֹה֒ וְאֶת־הָרָעָ֖ה אֲשֶׁ֣ר הֲדָ֑ד וַיָּ֙קָץ֙ בְּיִשְׂרָאֵ֔ל וַיִּמְלֹ֖ךְ עַל־ אֲרָֽם: פ

26 וְיָרָבְעָם֩ בֶּן־נְבָ֨ט אֶפְרָתִ֜י מִן־הַצְּרֵדָ֗ה וְשֵׁ֤ם אִמּוֹ֙ צְרוּעָ֔ה אִשָּׁ֣ה אַלְמָנָ֔ה עֶ֖בֶד לִשְׁלֹמֹ֑ה וַיָּ֥רֶם יָ֖ד בַּמֶּֽלֶךְ: 27 וְזֶ֣ה הַדָּבָ֔ר אֲשֶׁר־הֵרִ֥ים יָ֖ד בַּמֶּ֑לֶךְ שְׁלֹמֹה֙ בָּנָ֣ה אֶת־ הַמִּלּ֔וֹא סָגַ֕ר אֶת־פֶּ֕רֶץ עִ֖יר דָּוִ֥ד אָבִֽיו: 28 וְהָאִ֥ישׁ יָרָבְעָ֖ם גִּבּ֣וֹר חָ֑יִל וַיַּ֨רְא שְׁלֹמֹ֜ה אֶת־הַנַּ֗עַר כִּֽי־עֹשֵׂ֤ה מְלָאכָה֙ ה֔וּא וַיַּפְקֵ֣ד אֹת֔וֹ לְכָל־סֵ֖בֶל בֵּ֥ית יוֹסֵֽף: ס

29 וַֽיְהִי֙ בָּעֵ֣ת הַהִ֔יא וְיָרָבְעָ֖ם יָצָ֣א מִירֽוּשָׁלָ֑͏ִם וַיִּמְצָ֣א אֹת֡וֹ אֲחִיָּה֩ הַשִּׁילֹנִ֨י הַנָּבִ֜יא בַּדֶּ֗רֶךְ וְה֤וּא מִתְכַּסֶּה֙ בְּשַׂלְמָ֣ה חֲדָשָׁ֔ה וּשְׁנֵיהֶ֥ם לְבַדָּ֖ם בַּשָּׂדֶֽה: 30 וַיִּתְפֹּ֣שׂ אֲחִיָּ֔ה בַּשַּׂלְמָ֥ה הַחֲדָשָׁ֖ה אֲשֶׁ֣ר עָלָ֑יו וַיִּ֨קְרָעֶ֔הָ שְׁנֵ֥ים עָשָׂ֖ר קְרָעִֽים: 31 וַיֹּ֙אמֶר֙ לְיָ֣רָבְעָ֔ם קַח־לְךָ֖ עֲשָׂרָ֣ה קְרָעִ֑ים כִּ֣י כֹ֗ה אָמַ֤ר יְהוָה֙ אֱלֹהֵ֣י יִשְׂרָאֵ֔ל הִנְנִ֣י קֹרֵ֗עַ

---

kingdom out of Solomon's hands, and I will give you ten tribes. ³²But one tribe shall remain his—for the sake of My servant David and for the sake of Jerusalem, the city that I have chosen out of all the tribes of Israel. ³³For they have forsaken Me; they have worshiped Ashtoreth the goddess of the Phoenicians, Chemosh the god of Moab, and Milcom the god of the Ammonites; they have not walked in My ways, or done what is pleasing to Me, or [kept] My laws and rules, as his father David did. ³⁴However, I will not take the entire kingdom away from him, but will keep him as ruler as long as he lives for the sake of My servant David whom I chose, and who kept My commandments and My laws. ³⁵But I will take the kingship out of the hands of his son and give it to you—the ten tribes. ³⁶To his son I will give one tribe, so that there may be a lamp for My servant David forever before Me in Jerusalem—the city where I have chosen to establish My name. ³⁷But you have been chosen by Me; reign wherever you wish, and you shall be king over Israel. ³⁸If you heed all that I command you, and walk in My ways, and do what is right in My sight, keeping My laws and commandments as My servant David did, then I will be with you and I will build for you a lasting dynasty as I did for David. I hereby give Israel to you; ³⁹and I will chastise David's descendants for that [sin], though not forever."

⁴⁰Solomon sought to put Jeroboam to death, but Jeroboam promptly fled to King Shishak of Egypt; and he remained in Egypt till the death of Solomon.

⁴¹The other events of Solomon's reign, and all his actions and his wisdom, are recorded in the book of the Annals of Solomon. ⁴²The length of Solomon's reign in Jerusalem, over all Israel, was forty years. ⁴³Solomon slept with his fathers and was buried in the city of his father David; and his son Rehoboam succeeded him as king.

---

g *I.e., establish your residence.*

אֶת־הַמַּמְלָכָה מִיַּד שְׁלֹמֹה וְנָתַתִּי לְךָ
אֵת עֲשָׂרָה הַשְּׁבָטִים: 32 וְהַשֵּׁבֶט הָאֶחָד
יִהְיֶה־לּוֹ לְמַעַן ׀ עַבְדִּי דָוִד וּלְמַעַן
יְרוּשָׁלַ͏ִם הָעִיר אֲשֶׁר בָּחַרְתִּי בָהּ מִכֹּל
שִׁבְטֵי יִשְׂרָאֵל: 33 יַעַן ׀ אֲשֶׁר עֲזָבוּנִי
וַיִּשְׁתַּחֲווּ לְעַשְׁתֹּרֶת אֱלֹהֵי צִדֹנִין לִכְמוֹשׁ
אֱלֹהֵי מוֹאָב וּלְמִלְכֹּם אֱלֹהֵי בְנֵי־עַמּוֹן
וְלֹא־הָלְכוּ בִדְרָכַי לַעֲשׂוֹת הַיָּשָׁר בְּעֵינַי
וְחֻקֹּתַי וּמִשְׁפָּטַי כְּדָוִד אָבִיו: 34 וְלֹא־אֶקַּח
אֶת־כָּל־הַמַּמְלָכָה מִיָּדוֹ כִּי ׀ נָשִׂיא אֲשִׁתֶנּוּ
כֹּל יְמֵי חַיָּיו לְמַעַן דָּוִד עַבְדִּי אֲשֶׁר
בָּחַרְתִּי אֹתוֹ אֲשֶׁר שָׁמַר מִצְוֺתַי וְחֻקֹּתָי:
35 וְלָקַחְתִּי הַמְּלוּכָה מִיַּד בְּנוֹ וּנְתַתִּיהָ
לְּךָ אֵת עֲשֶׂרֶת הַשְּׁבָטִים: 36 וְלִבְנוֹ אֶתֵּן
שֵׁבֶט־אֶחָד לְמַעַן הֱיוֹת־נִיר לְדָוִיד־עַבְדִּי
כָּל־הַיָּמִים ׀ לְפָנַי בִּירוּשָׁלַ͏ִם הָעִיר אֲשֶׁר
בָּחַרְתִּי לִי לָשׂוּם שְׁמִי שָׁם: 37 וְאֹתְךָ אֶקַּח
וּמָלַכְתָּ בְּכֹל אֲשֶׁר־תְּאַוֶּה נַפְשֶׁךָ וְהָיִיתָ
מֶּלֶךְ עַל־יִשְׂרָאֵל: 38 וְהָיָה אִם־תִּשְׁמַע
אֶת־כָּל־אֲשֶׁר אֲצַוֶּךָ וְהָלַכְתָּ בִדְרָכַי
וְעָשִׂיתָ הַיָּשָׁר בְּעֵינַי לִשְׁמוֹר חֻקּוֹתַי
וּמִצְוֺתַי כַּאֲשֶׁר עָשָׂה דָּוִד עַבְדִּי וְהָיִיתִי
עִמָּךְ וּבָנִיתִי לְךָ בַיִת־נֶאֱמָן כַּאֲשֶׁר בָּנִיתִי
לְדָוִד וְנָתַתִּי לְךָ אֶת־יִשְׂרָאֵל: 39 וַאֲעַנֶּה*
אֶת־זֶרַע דָּוִד לְמַעַן זֹאת אַךְ לֹא כָל־
הַיָּמִים: ס

40 וַיְבַקֵּשׁ שְׁלֹמֹה לְהָמִית אֶת־יָרָבְעָם
וַיָּקָם יָרָבְעָם וַיִּבְרַח מִצְרַיִם אֶל־שִׁישַׁק
מֶלֶךְ־מִצְרַיִם וַיְהִי בְמִצְרַיִם עַד־מוֹת
שְׁלֹמֹה:

41 וְיֶתֶר דִּבְרֵי שְׁלֹמֹה וְכָל־אֲשֶׁר עָשָׂה
וְחָכְמָתוֹ הֲלֹא־הֵם כְּתֻבִים עַל־סֵפֶר
דִּבְרֵי שְׁלֹמֹה: 42 וְהַיָּמִים אֲשֶׁר מָלַךְ
שְׁלֹמֹה בִירוּשָׁלַ͏ִם עַל־כָּל־יִשְׂרָאֵל
אַרְבָּעִים שָׁנָה: 43 וַיִּשְׁכַּב שְׁלֹמֹה עִם־
אֲבֹתָיו וַיִּקָּבֵר בְּעִיר דָּוִד אָבִיו וַיִּמְלֹךְ
רְחַבְעָם בְּנוֹ תַּחְתָּיו: ס

12 Rehoboam went to Shechem, for all Is-rael had come to Shechem to acclaim him as king. ²Jeroboam son of Nebat learned of it while he was still in Egypt; for Jeroboam had fled from King Solomon, ᵃ-and had settled in Egypt.-ᵃ ³They sent for him; and Jeroboam and all the assembly of Israel came and spoke to Rehoboam as follows: ⁴"Your father made our yoke heavy. Now lighten the harsh labor and the heavy yoke which your father laid on us, and we will serve you." ⁵He answered them, "Go away for three days and then come back to me." So the people went away.

⁶King Rehoboam took counsel with the elders who had served his father Solomon during his lifetime. He said, "What answer do you advise [me] to give to this people?" ⁷They answered him, "If you will be a servant to those people today and serve them, and if you respond to them with kind words, they will be your servants always." ⁸But he ignored the advice that the el-ders gave him, and took counsel with the young men who had grown up with him and were serv-ing him. ⁹"What," he asked, "do you advise that we reply to the people who said to me, 'Lighten the yoke that your father placed upon us'?" ¹⁰And the young men who had grown up with him answered, "Speak thus to the people who said to you, 'Your father made our yoke heavy, now you make it lighter for us.' Say to them, 'My little finger is thicker than my father's loins. ¹¹My father imposed a heavy yoke on you, and I will add to your yoke; my father flogged you with whips, but I will flog you with scorpions.'"

¹²Jeroboam and all the people came to Re-hoboam on the third day, since the king had told them: "Come back on the third day." ¹³The king answered the people harshly, ignoring the ad-

a-a   2 Chron. 10.2 reads "So Jeroboam returned from Egypt."

יב וַיֵּ֥לֶךְ רְחַבְעָ֖ם שְׁכֶ֑ם כִּ֥י שְׁכֶ֛ם בָּ֥א
כׇל־יִשְׂרָאֵ֖ל לְהַמְלִ֥יךְ אֹתֽוֹ: 2 וַיְהִ֞י כִּשְׁמֹ֣עַ ׀
יָרׇבְעָ֣ם בֶּן־נְבָ֗ט וְה֤וּא עוֹדֶ֙נּוּ֙ בְמִצְרַ֔יִם אֲשֶׁ֣ר
בָּרַ֔ח מִפְּנֵ֖י הַמֶּ֣לֶךְ שְׁלֹמֹ֑ה וַיֵּ֥שֶׁב יָרׇבְעָ֖ם
בְּמִצְרָֽיִם: 3 וַֽיִּשְׁלְחוּ֙ וַיִּקְרְאוּ־ל֔וֹ ויבאו וַיָּבֹ֨א
יָרׇבְעָ֜ם וְכׇל־קְהַ֣ל יִשְׂרָאֵ֗ל וַֽיְדַבְּר֔וּ אֶל־
רְחַבְעָ֖ם לֵאמֹֽר: 4 אָבִ֖יךָ הִקְשָׁ֣ה אֶת־עֻלֵּ֑נוּ
וְאַתָּ֡ה עַתָּ֣ה הָקֵל֩ מֵעֲבֹדַ֨ת אָבִ֜יךָ הַקָּשָׁ֗ה
וּמֵעֻלּ֧וֹ הַכָּבֵ֛ד אֲשֶׁר־נָתַ֥ן עָלֵ֖ינוּ וְנַעַבְדֶֽךָּ:
5 וַיֹּ֣אמֶר אֲלֵיהֶ֗ם לְכ֥וּ עֹ֛ד שְׁלֹשָׁ֥ה יָמִ֖ים
וְשׁ֣וּבוּ אֵלָ֑י וַיֵּלְכ֖וּ הָעָֽם:

6 וַיִּוָּעַ֞ץ הַמֶּ֣לֶךְ רְחַבְעָ֗ם אֶת־הַזְּקֵנִים֙
אֲשֶׁר־הָי֣וּ עֹמְדִ֗ים אֶת־פְּנֵי֙ שְׁלֹמֹ֣ה אָבִ֔יו
בִּֽהְיֹת֥וֹ חַ֖י לֵאמֹ֑ר אֵ֚יךְ אַתֶּ֣ם נֽוֹעָצִ֔ים
לְהָשִׁ֥יב אֶת־הָֽעָם־הַזֶּ֖ה דָּבָֽר: 7 וידבר
וַיְדַבְּר֨וּ אֵלָ֜יו לֵאמֹ֗ר אִם־הַ֠יּ֠וֹם תִּֽהְיֶה־עֶ֜בֶד
לָעָ֤ם הַזֶּה֙ וַעֲבַדְתָּ֔ם וַעֲנִיתָ֕ם וְדִבַּרְתָּ֧
אֲלֵיהֶ֛ם דְּבָרִ֥ים טוֹבִ֖ים וְהָי֥וּ לְךָ֖ עֲבָדִ֥ים
כׇּל־הַיָּמִֽים: 8 וַֽיַּעֲזֹ֛ב אֶת־עֲצַ֥ת הַזְּקֵנִ֖ים
אֲשֶׁ֣ר יְעָצֻ֑הוּ וַיִּוָּעַ֗ץ אֶת־הַיְלָדִים֙ אֲשֶׁ֣ר
גָּדְל֣וּ אִתּ֔וֹ אֲשֶׁ֥ר הָעֹמְדִ֖ים לְפָנָֽיו: 9 וַיֹּ֣אמֶר
אֲלֵיהֶ֗ם מָ֚ה אַתֶּ֣ם נֽוֹעָצִ֔ים וְנָשִׁ֥יב דָּבָ֖ר
אֶת־הָעָ֣ם הַזֶּ֑ה אֲשֶׁ֨ר דִּבְּר֤וּ אֵלַי֙ לֵאמֹ֔ר
הָקֵל֙ מִן־הָעֹ֔ל אֲשֶׁר־נָתַ֥ן אָבִ֖יךָ עָלֵֽינוּ:
10 וַיְדַבְּר֣וּ אֵלָ֗יו הַיְלָדִים֙ אֲשֶׁ֨ר גָּדְל֣וּ אִתּוֹ֒
לֵאמֹ֗ר כֹּֽה־תֹאמַ֤ר לָעָ֤ם הַזֶּה֙ אֲשֶׁ֨ר דִּבְּר֤וּ
אֵלֶ֙יךָ֙ לֵאמֹ֔ר אָבִ֙יךָ֙ הִכְבִּ֣יד אֶת־עֻלֵּ֔נוּ
וְאַתָּ֖ה הָקֵ֣ל מֵעָלֵ֑ינוּ כֹּ֚ה תְּדַבֵּ֣ר אֲלֵיהֶ֔ם
קׇטׇנִּ֥י עָבָ֖ה מִמׇּתְנֵ֥י אָבִֽי: 11 וְעַתָּ֕ה אָבִי֙
הֶעְמִ֤יס עֲלֵיכֶם֙ עֹ֣ל כָּבֵ֔ד וַאֲנִ֖י אוֹסִ֣יף
עַֽל־עֻלְּכֶ֑ם אָבִ֗י יִסַּ֤ר אֶתְכֶם֙ בַּשּׁוֹטִ֔ים וַאֲנִ֕י
אֲיַסֵּ֥ר אֶתְכֶ֖ם בָּֽעַקְרַבִּֽים:

12 ויבו וַיָּבֹ֨א יָרׇבְעָ֧ם וְכׇל־הָעָ֛ם אֶל־
רְחַבְעָ֖ם בַּיּ֣וֹם הַשְּׁלִישִׁ֑י כַּאֲשֶׁ֨ר דִּבֶּ֤ר הַמֶּ֙לֶךְ֙
לֵאמֹ֔ר שׁ֥וּבוּ אֵלַ֖י בַּיּ֥וֹם הַשְּׁלִישִֽׁי: 13 וַיַּ֧עַן

742

vice that the elders had given him. ¹⁴He spoke to them in accordance with the advice of the young men, and said, "My father made your yoke heavy, but I will add to your yoke; my father flogged you with whips, but I will flog you with scorpions." ¹⁵(The king did not listen to the people; for the LORD had brought it about in order to fulfill the promise that the LORD had made through Ahijah the Shilonite to Jeroboam son of Nebat.) ¹⁶When all Israel saw that the king had not listened to them, the people answered the king:

"We have no portion in David,
No share in Jesse's son!
To your tents, O Israel!
Now look to your own House, O David."

So the Israelites returned to their homes.*b* ¹⁷But Rehoboam continued to reign over the Israelites who lived in the towns of Judah.

¹⁸King Rehoboam sent Adoram,*c* who was in charge of the forced labor, but all Israel pelted him to death with stones. Thereupon King Rehoboam hurriedly mounted his chariot and fled to Jerusalem. ¹⁹Thus Israel revolted against the House of David, as is still the case.

²⁰When all Israel heard that Jeroboam had returned, they sent messengers and summoned him to the assembly and made him king over all Israel. Only the tribe of Judah remained loyal to the House of David.

²¹On his return to Jerusalem, Rehoboam mustered all the House of Judah and the tribe of Benjamin, 180,000 picked warriors, to fight against the House of Israel, in order to restore the kingship to Rehoboam son of Solomon. ²²But the word of God came to Shemaiah, the man of God: ²³"Say to King Rehoboam son of Solomon of Judah, and to all the House of Judah and Benjamin and the rest of the people: ²⁴Thus said the LORD: You shall not set out to make

הַמֶּלֶךְ אֶת־הָעָם קָשָׁה וַיַּעֲזֹב אֶת־עֲצַת
הַזְּקֵנִים אֲשֶׁר יְעָצֻהוּ: 14 וַיְדַבֵּר אֲלֵיהֶם
כַּעֲצַת הַיְלָדִים לֵאמֹר אָבִי הִכְבִּיד אֶת־
עֻלְּכֶם וַאֲנִי אֹסִיף עַל־עֻלְּכֶם אָבִי יִסַּר
אֶתְכֶם בַּשּׁוֹטִים וַאֲנִי אֲיַסֵּר אֶתְכֶם
בָּעַקְרַבִּים: 15 וְלֹא־שָׁמַע הַמֶּלֶךְ אֶל־הָעָם
כִּי־הָיְתָה סִבָּה מֵעִם יְהֹוָה לְמַעַן הָקִים
אֶת־דְּבָרוֹ אֲשֶׁר דִּבֶּר יְהֹוָה בְּיַד אֲחִיָּה
הַשִּׁילֹנִי אֶל־יָרָבְעָם בֶּן־נְבָט: 16 וַיַּרְא כָּל־
יִשְׂרָאֵל כִּי לֹא־שָׁמַע הַמֶּלֶךְ אֲלֵיהֶם וַיָּשִׁבוּ
הָעָם אֶת־הַמֶּלֶךְ דָּבָר ׀ לֵאמֹר

מַה־לָּנוּ חֵלֶק בְּדָוִד
וְלֹא־נַחֲלָה בְּבֶן־יִשַׁי
לְאֹהָלֶיךָ יִשְׂרָאֵל
עַתָּה רְאֵה בֵיתְךָ דָּוִד

וַיֵּלֶךְ יִשְׂרָאֵל לְאֹהָלָיו: 17 וּבְנֵי יִשְׂרָאֵל
הַיֹּשְׁבִים בְּעָרֵי יְהוּדָה וַיִּמְלֹךְ עֲלֵיהֶם
רְחַבְעָם: פ

18 וַיִּשְׁלַח הַמֶּלֶךְ רְחַבְעָם אֶת־אֲדֹרָם אֲשֶׁר
עַל־הַמַּס וַיִּרְגְּמוּ כָל־יִשְׂרָאֵל בּוֹ אֶבֶן
וַיָּמֹת וְהַמֶּלֶךְ רְחַבְעָם הִתְאַמֵּץ לַעֲלוֹת
בַּמֶּרְכָּבָה לָנוּס יְרוּשָׁלָ͏ִם: 19 וַיִּפְשְׁעוּ
יִשְׂרָאֵל בְּבֵית דָּוִד עַד הַיּוֹם הַזֶּה: ס
20 וַיְהִי כִּשְׁמֹעַ כָּל־יִשְׂרָאֵל כִּי־שָׁב יָרָבְעָם
וַיִּשְׁלְחוּ וַיִּקְרְאוּ אֹתוֹ אֶל־הָעֵדָה וַיַּמְלִיכוּ
אֹתוֹ עַל־כָּל־יִשְׂרָאֵל לֹא הָיָה אַחֲרֵי בֵית־
דָּוִד זוּלָתִי שֵׁבֶט־יְהוּדָה לְבַדּוֹ:
21 וַיָּבֹאוּ וַיָּבֹא רְחַבְעָם יְרוּשָׁלַ͏ִם וַיַּקְהֵל
אֶת־כָּל־בֵּית יְהוּדָה וְאֶת־שֵׁבֶט בִּנְיָמִן
מֵאָה וּשְׁמֹנִים אֶלֶף בָּחוּר עֹשֵׂה מִלְחָמָה
לְהִלָּחֵם עִם־בֵּית יִשְׂרָאֵל לְהָשִׁיב אֶת־
הַמְּלוּכָה לִרְחַבְעָם בֶּן־שְׁלֹמֹה: פ
22 וַיְהִי דְּבַר הָאֱלֹהִים אֶל־שְׁמַעְיָה אִישׁ־
הָאֱלֹהִים לֵאמֹר: 23 אֱמֹר אֶל־רְחַבְעָם
בֶּן־שְׁלֹמֹה מֶלֶךְ יְהוּדָה וְאֶל־כָּל־בֵּית

---

b   Lit. "tents."
c   Elsewhere called Adoniram; cf. 2 Sam. 20.24 and note.

war on your kinsmen the Israelites. Let every man return to his home, for this thing has been brought about by Me." They heeded the word of the LORD and turned back, in accordance with the word of the LORD.

²⁵Jeroboam fortified Shechem in the hill country of Ephraim and resided there; he moved out from there and fortified Penuel. ²⁶Jeroboam said to himself, "Now the kingdom may well return to the House of David. ²⁷If these people still go up to offer sacrifices at the House of the LORD in Jerusalem, the heart of these people will turn back to their master, King Rehoboam of Judah; they will kill me and go back to King Rehoboam of Judah." ²⁸So the king took counsel and made two golden calves. He said to ^d-the people,-^d "You have been going up to Jerusalem long enough. This is your god, O Israel, who brought you up from the land of Egypt!" ²⁹He set up one in Bethel and placed the other in Dan. ³⁰That proved to be a cause of guilt, for the people went to worship [the calf at Bethel and] the one at Dan. ³¹He also made cult places and appointed priests from the ranks of the people who were not of Levite descent.

³²He stationed at Bethel the priests of the shrines that he had appointed to sacrifice to the calves that he had made. And Jeroboam established a festival on the fifteenth day of the eighth month; in imitation of the festival in Judah, he established one at Bethel, and he ascended the altar [there]. ³³On the fifteenth day of the eighth month—the month in which he had contrived of his own mind to establish a festival for the Israelites—Jeroboam ascended the altar that he had made in Bethel.

13 As he ascended the altar to present an offering, ¹a man of God arrived at Bethel from Judah at the command of the LORD.

יְהוּדָה וּבִנְיָמִן וְיֶתֶר הָעָם לֵאמֹר: 24 כֹּה אָמַר יְהוָה לֹא־תַעֲלוּ וְלֹא־תִלָּחֲמוּן עִם־אֲחֵיכֶם בְּנֵי־יִשְׂרָאֵל שׁוּבוּ אִישׁ לְבֵיתוֹ כִּי מֵאִתִּי נִהְיָה הַדָּבָר הַזֶּה וַיִּשְׁמְעוּ אֶת־דְּבַר יְהוָה וַיָּשֻׁבוּ לָלֶכֶת כִּדְבַר יְהוָה: ס

25 וַיִּבֶן יָרָבְעָם אֶת־שְׁכֶם בְּהַר אֶפְרַיִם וַיֵּשֶׁב בָּהּ וַיֵּצֵא מִשָּׁם וַיִּבֶן אֶת־פְּנוּאֵל: 26 וַיֹּאמֶר יָרָבְעָם בְּלִבּוֹ עַתָּה תָּשׁוּב הַמַּמְלָכָה לְבֵית דָּוִד: 27 אִם־יַעֲלֶה ׀ הָעָם הַזֶּה לַעֲשׂוֹת זְבָחִים בְּבֵית־יְהוָה בִּירוּשָׁלִַם וְשָׁב לֵב הָעָם הַזֶּה אֶל־אֲדֹנֵיהֶם אֶל־רְחַבְעָם מֶלֶךְ יְהוּדָה וַהֲרָגֻנִי וְשָׁבוּ אֶל־רְחַבְעָם מֶלֶךְ־יְהוּדָה: 28 וַיִּוָּעַץ הַמֶּלֶךְ וַיַּעַשׂ שְׁנֵי עֶגְלֵי זָהָב וַיֹּאמֶר אֲלֵהֶם רַב־לָכֶם מֵעֲלוֹת יְרוּשָׁלִַם הִנֵּה אֱלֹהֶיךָ יִשְׂרָאֵל אֲשֶׁר הֶעֱלוּךָ מֵאֶרֶץ מִצְרָיִם: 29 וַיָּשֶׂם אֶת־הָאֶחָד בְּבֵית־אֵל וְאֶת־הָאֶחָד נָתַן בְּדָן: 30 וַיְהִי הַדָּבָר הַזֶּה לְחַטָּאת וַיֵּלְכוּ הָעָם לִפְנֵי הָאֶחָד עַד־דָּן: 31 וַיַּעַשׂ אֶת־בֵּית בָּמוֹת וַיַּעַשׂ כֹּהֲנִים מִקְצוֹת הָעָם אֲשֶׁר לֹא־הָיוּ מִבְּנֵי לֵוִי: 32 וַיַּעַשׂ יָרָבְעָם ׀ חָג בַּחֹדֶשׁ הַשְּׁמִינִי בַּחֲמִשָּׁה־עָשָׂר יוֹם לַחֹדֶשׁ כֶּחָג ׀ אֲשֶׁר בִּיהוּדָה וַיַּעַל עַל־הַמִּזְבֵּחַ כֵּן עָשָׂה בְּבֵית־אֵל לְזַבֵּחַ לָעֲגָלִים אֲשֶׁר־עָשָׂה וְהֶעֱמִיד בְּבֵית אֵל אֶת־כֹּהֲנֵי הַבָּמוֹת אֲשֶׁר עָשָׂה: 33 וַיַּעַל עַל־הַמִּזְבֵּחַ ׀ אֲשֶׁר־עָשָׂה בְּבֵית־אֵל בַּחֲמִשָּׁה עָשָׂר יוֹם בַּחֹדֶשׁ הַשְּׁמִינִי בַּחֹדֶשׁ אֲשֶׁר־בָּדָא מִלִּבּוֹ מִלְּבַד וַיַּעַשׂ חָג לִבְנֵי יִשְׂרָאֵל

יג וַיַּעַל עַל־הַמִּזְבֵּחַ לְהַקְטִיר: פ 1 וְהִנֵּה ׀ אִישׁ אֱלֹהִים בָּא מִיהוּדָה בִּדְבַר יְהוָה אֶל־בֵּית־אֵל וְיָרָבְעָם עֹמֵד

---

d-d Heb. "them."

While Jeroboam was standing on the altar*a* to present the offering, the man of God, at the command of the LORD, cried out against the altar: 2"O altar, altar! Thus said the LORD: A son shall be born to the House of David, Josiah by name; and he shall slaughter upon you the priests of the shrines who bring offerings upon you. And human bones shall be burned upon you." 3He gave a portent on that day, saying, "Here is the portent that the LORD has decreed: This altar shall break apart, and the ashes on it shall be spilled." 4When the king heard what the man of God had proclaimed against the altar in Bethel, Jeroboam stretched out his arm above the altar and cried, "Seize him!" But the arm that he stretched out against him became rigid, and he could not draw it back. 5The altar broke apart and its ashes were spilled—the very portent that the man of God had announced at the LORD's command. 6Then the king spoke up and said to the man of God, "Please entreat the LORD your God and pray for me that I may be able to draw back my arm." The man of God entreated the LORD and the king was able to draw his arm back; it became as it was before.

7The king said to the man of God, "Come with me to my house and have some refreshment; and I shall give you a gift." 8But the man of God replied to the king, "Even if you give me half your wealth, I will not go in with you, nor will I eat bread or drink water in this place; 9for so I was commanded by the word of the LORD: You shall eat no bread and drink no water, nor shall you go back by the road by which you came." 10So he left by another road and did not go back by the road on which he had come to Bethel.

11There was an old prophet living in Bethel; and his sons*b* came and told him all the things that the man of God had done that day in Bethel [and] the words that he had spoken to the king.

עַל־הַמִּזְבֵּחַ לְהַקְטִיר: 2 וַיִּקְרָא עַל־הַמִּזְבֵּחַ בִּדְבַר יְהֹוָה וַיֹּאמֶר מִזְבֵּחַ מִזְבֵּחַ כֹּה אָמַר יְהֹוָה הִנֵּה־בֵן נוֹלָד לְבֵית־דָּוִד יֹאשִׁיָּהוּ שְׁמוֹ וְזָבַח עָלֶיךָ אֶת־כֹּהֲנֵי הַבָּמוֹת הַמַּקְטִרִים עָלֶיךָ וְעַצְמוֹת אָדָם יִשְׂרְפוּ עָלֶיךָ: 3 וְנָתַן בַּיּוֹם הַהוּא מוֹפֵת לֵאמֹר זֶה הַמּוֹפֵת אֲשֶׁר דִּבֶּר יְהֹוָה הִנֵּה הַמִּזְבֵּחַ נִקְרָע וְנִשְׁפַּךְ הַדֶּשֶׁן אֲשֶׁר עָלָיו: 4 וַיְהִי כִשְׁמֹעַ הַמֶּלֶךְ אֶת־דְּבַר אִישׁ־הָאֱלֹהִים אֲשֶׁר קָרָא עַל־הַמִּזְבֵּחַ בְּבֵית־אֵל וַיִּשְׁלַח יָרׇבְעָם אֶת־יָדוֹ מֵעַל הַמִּזְבֵּחַ לֵאמֹר ׀ תִּפְשֻׂהוּ וַתִּיבַשׁ יָדוֹ אֲשֶׁר שָׁלַח עָלָיו וְלֹא יָכֹל לַהֲשִׁיבָהּ אֵלָיו: 5 וְהַמִּזְבֵּחַ נִקְרָע וַיִּשָּׁפֵךְ הַדֶּשֶׁן מִן־הַמִּזְבֵּחַ כַּמּוֹפֵת אֲשֶׁר נָתַן אִישׁ הָאֱלֹהִים בִּדְבַר יְהֹוָה: 6 וַיַּעַן הַמֶּלֶךְ וַיֹּאמֶר ׀ אֶל־אִישׁ הָאֱלֹהִים חַל־נָא אֶת־פְּנֵי יְהֹוָה אֱלֹהֶיךָ וְהִתְפַּלֵּל בַּעֲדִי וְתָשֹׁב יָדִי אֵלָי וַיְחַל אִישׁ־הָאֱלֹהִים אֶת־פְּנֵי יְהֹוָה וַתָּשׇׁב יַד־הַמֶּלֶךְ אֵלָיו וַתְּהִי כְּבָרִאשֹׁנָה: 7 וַיְדַבֵּר הַמֶּלֶךְ אֶל־אִישׁ הָאֱלֹהִים בֹּאָה־אִתִּי הַבַּיְתָה וּסְעָדָה וְאֶתְּנָה לְךָ מַתָּת: 8 וַיֹּאמֶר אִישׁ־הָאֱלֹהִים אֶל־הַמֶּלֶךְ אִם־תִּתֶּן־לִי אֶת־חֲצִי בֵיתֶךָ לֹא אָבֹא עִמָּךְ וְלֹא־אֹכַל לֶחֶם וְלֹא אֶשְׁתֶּה־מַּיִם בַּמָּקוֹם הַזֶּה: 9 כִּי־כֵן ׀ צִוָּה אֹתִי בִּדְבַר יְהֹוָה לֵאמֹר לֹא־תֹאכַל לֶחֶם וְלֹא תִשְׁתֶּה־מָּיִם וְלֹא תָשׁוּב בַּדֶּרֶךְ אֲשֶׁר הָלָכְתָּ: 10 וַיֵּלֶךְ בְּדֶרֶךְ אַחֵר וְלֹא־שָׁב בַּדֶּרֶךְ אֲשֶׁר בָּא בָהּ אֶל־בֵּית־אֵל: פ

11 וְנָבִיא אֶחָד זָקֵן יֹשֵׁב בְּבֵית־אֵל וַיָּבוֹא בְנוֹ וַיְסַפֶּר־לוֹ אֶת־כׇּל־הַמַּעֲשֶׂה אֲשֶׁר־עָשָׂה אִישׁ־הָאֱלֹהִים ׀ הַיּוֹם בְּבֵית־אֵל אֶת־הַדְּבָרִים אֲשֶׁר דִּבֶּר אֶל־הַמֶּלֶךְ

---

a   I.e., at the top of the steps or ramp.
b   Heb. "son."

When they told it to their father, 12their father said to them, "Which road did he leave by?" c-His sons had seen-c the road taken by the man of God who had come from Judah. 13"Saddle the ass for me," he said to his sons. They saddled the ass for him, and he mounted it 14and rode after the man of God. He came upon him sitting under a terebinth and said to him, "Are you the man of God who came from Judah?" "Yes, I am," he answered. 15"Come home with me," he said, "and have something to eat." 16He replied, "I may not go back with you and enter your home; and I may not eat bread or drink water in this place; 17the order I received by the word of the LORD was: You shall not eat bread or drink water there; nor shall you return by the road on which you came." 18"I am a prophet, too," said the other, "and an angel said to me by command of the LORD: Bring him back with you to your house, that he may eat bread and drink water." He was lying to him. 19So he went back with him, and he ate bread and drank water in his house.

20While they were sitting at the table, the word of the LORD came to the prophet who had brought him back. 21He cried out to the man of God who had come from Judah: "Thus said the LORD: Because you have flouted the word of the LORD and have not observed what the LORD your God commanded you, 22but have gone back and eaten bread and drunk water in the place of which He said to you, 'Do not eat bread or drink water [there],' your corpse shall not come to the grave of your fathers." 23After he had eaten bread and had drunk, he saddled the ass for him—for the prophet whom he had brought back. 24He set out, and a lion came upon him on the road and killed him. His corpse lay on the road, with the ass standing beside it, and the lion also standing beside the corpse.

c-c *Septuagint reads "And his sons showed."*

וַיְסַפְּרוּם לַאֲבִיהֶם: 12 וַיְדַבֵּר אֲלֵהֶם אֲבִיהֶם אֵי־זֶה הַדֶּרֶךְ הָלָךְ וַיִּרְאוּ בָנָיו אֶת־הַדֶּרֶךְ אֲשֶׁר הָלַךְ אִישׁ הָאֱלֹהִים אֲשֶׁר־בָּא מִיהוּדָה: 13 וַיֹּאמֶר אֶל־בָּנָיו חִבְשׁוּ־לִי הַחֲמוֹר וַיַּחְבְּשׁוּ־לוֹ הַחֲמוֹר וַיִּרְכַּב עָלָיו: 14 וַיֵּלֶךְ אַחֲרֵי אִישׁ הָאֱלֹהִים וַיִּמְצָאֵהוּ יֹשֵׁב תַּחַת הָאֵלָה וַיֹּאמֶר אֵלָיו הַאַתָּה אִישׁ־הָאֱלֹהִים אֲשֶׁר־בָּאתָ מִיהוּדָה וַיֹּאמֶר אָנִי: 15 וַיֹּאמֶר אֵלָיו לֵךְ אִתִּי הַבָּיְתָה וֶאֱכֹל לָחֶם: 16 וַיֹּאמֶר לֹא אוּכַל לָשׁוּב אִתָּךְ וְלָבוֹא אִתָּךְ וְלֹא־אֹכַל לֶחֶם וְלֹא־אֶשְׁתֶּה אִתְּךָ מַיִם בַּמָּקוֹם הַזֶּה: 17 כִּי־דָבָר אֵלַי בִּדְבַר יְהוָה לֹא־תֹאכַל לֶחֶם וְלֹא־תִשְׁתֶּה שָׁם מָיִם לֹא־תָשׁוּב לָלֶכֶת בַּדֶּרֶךְ אֲשֶׁר־הָלַכְתָּ בָּהּ: 18 וַיֹּאמֶר לוֹ גַּם־אֲנִי נָבִיא כָּמוֹךָ וּמַלְאָךְ דִּבֶּר אֵלַי בִּדְבַר יְהוָה לֵאמֹר הֲשִׁבֵהוּ אִתְּךָ אֶל־בֵּיתֶךָ וְיֹאכַל לֶחֶם וְיֵשְׁתְּ מָיִם כִּחֵשׁ לוֹ: 19 וַיָּשָׁב אִתּוֹ וַיֹּאכַל לֶחֶם בְּבֵיתוֹ וַיֵּשְׁתְּ מָיִם:

20 וַיְהִי הֵם יֹשְׁבִים אֶל־הַשֻּׁלְחָן ס וַיְהִי דְּבַר־יְהוָה אֶל־הַנָּבִיא אֲשֶׁר הֱשִׁיבוֹ: 21 וַיִּקְרָא אֶל־אִישׁ הָאֱלֹהִים אֲשֶׁר־בָּא מִיהוּדָה לֵאמֹר כֹּה אָמַר יְהוָה יַעַן כִּי מָרִיתָ פִּי יְהוָה וְלֹא שָׁמַרְתָּ אֶת־הַמִּצְוָה אֲשֶׁר צִוְּךָ יְהוָה אֱלֹהֶיךָ: 22 וַתָּשָׁב וַתֹּאכַל לֶחֶם וַתֵּשְׁתְּ מַיִם בַּמָּקוֹם אֲשֶׁר דִּבֶּר אֵלֶיךָ אַל־תֹּאכַל לֶחֶם וְאַל־תֵּשְׁתְּ מָיִם לֹא־תָבוֹא נִבְלָתְךָ אֶל־קֶבֶר אֲבֹתֶיךָ: 23 וַיְהִי אַחֲרֵי אָכְלוֹ לֶחֶם וְאַחֲרֵי שְׁתוֹתוֹ וַיַּחֲבָשׁ־לוֹ הַחֲמוֹר לַנָּבִיא אֲשֶׁר הֱשִׁיבוֹ: 24 וַיֵּלֶךְ וַיִּמְצָאֵהוּ אַרְיֵה בַּדֶּרֶךְ וַיְמִיתֵהוּ וַתְּהִי נִבְלָתוֹ מֻשְׁלֶכֶת בַּדֶּרֶךְ וְהַחֲמוֹר עֹמֵד אֶצְלָהּ וְהָאַרְיֵה עֹמֵד אֵצֶל הַנְּבֵלָה: 25 וְהִנֵּה אֲנָשִׁים עֹבְרִים וַיִּרְאוּ אֶת־הַנְּבֵלָה

²⁵Some men who passed by saw the corpse lying on the road and the lion standing beside the corpse; they went and told it in the town where the old prophet lived. ²⁶And when the prophet who had brought him back from the road heard it, he said, "That is the man of God who flouted the Lord's command; the Lord gave him over to the lion, which mauled him and killed him in accordance with the word that the Lord had spoken to him." ²⁷He said to his sons, "Saddle the ass for me," and they did so. ²⁸He set out and found the corpse lying on the road, with the ass and the lion standing beside the corpse; the lion had not eaten the corpse nor had it mauled the ass. ²⁹The prophet lifted up the corpse of the man of God, laid it on the ass, and brought it back; *d*-it was brought-*d* to the town of the old prophet for lamentation and burial. ³⁰He laid the corpse in his own burial place; and they lamented over it, "Alas, my brother!" ³¹After burying him, he said to his sons, "When I die, bury me in the grave where the man of God lies buried; lay my bones beside his. ³²For what he announced by the word of the Lord against the altar in Bethel, and against all the cult places in the towns of Samaria, shall surely come true."

³³Even after this incident, Jeroboam did not turn back from his evil way, but kept on appointing priests for the shrines from the ranks of the people. He ordained as priests of the shrines any who so desired. ³⁴Thereby the House of Jeroboam incurred guilt—to their utter annihilation from the face of the earth.

14

At that time, Abijah, a son of Jeroboam, fell sick. ²Jeroboam said to his wife, "Go and disguise yourself, so that you will not be recognized as Jeroboam's wife, and go to Shiloh. The prophet Ahijah lives there, the one who pre-

---

d-d Lit. "it came."

מֻשְׁלֶכֶת בַּדֶּרֶךְ וְאֶת־הָאַרְיֵה עֹמֵד אֵצֶל הַנְּבֵלָה וַיָּבֹאוּ וַיְדַבְּרוּ בָעִיר אֲשֶׁר הַנָּבִיא הַזָּקֵן יֹשֵׁב בָּהּ׃ 26 וַיִּשְׁמַע הַנָּבִיא אֲשֶׁר הֱשִׁיבוֹ מִן־הַדֶּרֶךְ וַיֹּאמֶר אִישׁ הָאֱלֹהִים הוּא אֲשֶׁר מָרָה אֶת־פִּי יְהוָה וַיִּתְּנֵהוּ יְהוָה לָאַרְיֵה וַיִּשְׁבְּרֵהוּ וַיְמִתֵהוּ כִּדְבַר יְהוָה אֲשֶׁר דִּבֶּר־לוֹ׃ 27 וַיְדַבֵּר אֶל־בָּנָיו לֵאמֹר חִבְשׁוּ־לִי אֶת־הַחֲמוֹר וַיַּחֲבֹשׁוּ׃ 28 וַיֵּלֶךְ וַיִּמְצָא אֶת־נִבְלָתוֹ מֻשְׁלֶכֶת בַּדֶּרֶךְ וַחֲמוֹר וְהָאַרְיֵה עֹמְדִים אֵצֶל הַנְּבֵלָה לֹא־אָכַל הָאַרְיֵה אֶת־הַנְּבֵלָה וְלֹא שָׁבַר אֶת־הַחֲמוֹר׃ 29 וַיִּשָּׂא הַנָּבִיא אֶת־נִבְלַת אִישׁ־הָאֱלֹהִים וַיַּנִּחֵהוּ אֶל־הַחֲמוֹר וַיְשִׁיבֵהוּ וַיָּבֹא אֶל־עִיר הַנָּבִיא הַזָּקֵן לִסְפֹּד וּלְקָבְרוֹ׃ 30 וַיַּנַּח אֶת־נִבְלָתוֹ בְּקִבְרוֹ וַיִּסְפְּדוּ עָלָיו הוֹי אָחִי׃ 31 וַיְהִי אַחֲרֵי קָבְרוֹ אֹתוֹ וַיֹּאמֶר אֶל־בָּנָיו לֵאמֹר בְּמוֹתִי וּקְבַרְתֶּם אֹתִי בַּקֶּבֶר אֲשֶׁר אִישׁ הָאֱלֹהִים קָבוּר בּוֹ אֵצֶל עַצְמֹתָיו הַנִּיחוּ אֶת־עַצְמֹתָי׃ 32 כִּי הָיֹה יִהְיֶה הַדָּבָר אֲשֶׁר קָרָא בִּדְבַר יְהוָה עַל־הַמִּזְבֵּחַ אֲשֶׁר בְּבֵית־אֵל וְעַל כָּל־בָּתֵּי הַבָּמוֹת אֲשֶׁר בְּעָרֵי שֹׁמְרוֹן׃ פ

33 אַחַר הַדָּבָר הַזֶּה לֹא־שָׁב יָרָבְעָם מִדַּרְכּוֹ הָרָעָה וַיָּשָׁב וַיַּעַשׂ מִקְצוֹת הָעָם כֹּהֲנֵי בָמוֹת הֶחָפֵץ יְמַלֵּא אֶת־יָדוֹ וִיהִי כֹּהֲנֵי בָמוֹת׃ 34 וַיְהִי בַּדָּבָר הַזֶּה לְחַטַּאת בֵּית יָרָבְעָם וּלְהַכְחִיד וּלְהַשְׁמִיד מֵעַל פְּנֵי הָאֲדָמָה׃ פ

יד בָּעֵת הַהִיא חָלָה אֲבִיָּה בֶן־יָרָבְעָם׃ 2 וַיֹּאמֶר יָרָבְעָם לְאִשְׁתּוֹ קוּמִי נָא וְהִשְׁתַּנִּית וְלֹא יֵדְעוּ כִּי־אַתִּי אֵשֶׁת יָרָבְעָם וְהָלַכְתְּ שִׁלֹה הִנֵּה־שָׁם אֲחִיָּה

dicted that I would be king over this people. ³Take with you ten loaves, some wafers, and a jug of honey, and go to him; he will tell you what will happen to the boy." ⁴Jeroboam's wife did so; she left and went to Shiloh and came to the house of Ahijah. Now Ahijah could not see, for his eyes had become sightless with age; ⁵but the LORD had said to Ahijah, "Jeroboam's wife is coming to inquire of you concerning her son, who is sick. Speak to her thus and thus. When she arrives, she will be in disguise."

⁶Ahijah heard the sound of her feet as she came through the door, and he said, "Come in, wife of Jeroboam. Why are you disguised? I have a harsh message for you. ⁷Go tell Jeroboam: Thus said the LORD, the God of Israel: I raised you up from among the people and made you a ruler over My people Israel; ⁸I tore away the kingdom from the House of David and gave it to you. But you have not been like My servant David, who kept My commandments and followed Me with all his heart, doing only what was right in My sight. ⁹You have acted worse than all those who preceded you; you have gone and made for yourself other gods and molten images to vex Me; and Me you have cast behind your back. ¹⁰Therefore I will bring disaster upon the House of Jeroboam and will cut off from Jeroboam every male, ᵃ-bond and free,-ᵃ in Israel. I will sweep away the House of Jeroboam utterly, as dung is swept away. ¹¹Anyone belonging to Jeroboam who dies in the town shall be devoured by dogs; and anyone who dies in the open country shall be eaten by the birds of the air; for the LORD has spoken. ¹²As for you, go back home; as soon as you set foot in the town, the child will die. ¹³And all Israel shall lament over him and bury him; he alone of Jeroboam's family shall be brought to burial, for in him alone of the House of Jeroboam has some

---

הַנָּבִ֗יא ה֤וּא דִבֶּ֤ר עָלַי֙ לְמֶ֔לֶךְ עַל־הָעָ֖ם הַזֶּֽה׃ 3 וְלָקַ֣חַתְּ בְּ֠יָדֵךְ עֲשָׂרָ֨ה לֶ֜חֶם וְנִקֻּדִ֗ים וּבַקְבֻּ֤ק דְּבַשׁ֙ וּבָ֣את אֵלָ֔יו ה֖וּא יַגִּ֣יד לָ֑ךְ מַה־יִּהְיֶ֖ה לַנָּֽעַר׃ 4 וַתַּ֤עַשׂ כֵּן֙ אֵ֣שֶׁת יָרָבְעָ֔ם וַתָּ֙קָם֙ וַתֵּ֣לֶךְ שִׁלֹ֔ה וַתָּבֹ֖א בֵּ֣ית אֲחִיָּ֑ה וַאֲחִיָּ֙הוּ֙ לֹא־יָכֹ֣ל לִרְא֔וֹת כִּ֛י קָ֥מוּ עֵינָ֖יו מִשֵּׂיבֽוֹ׃ ס 5 וַֽיהֹוָ֞ה אָמַ֣ר אֶל־אֲחִיָּ֗הוּ הִנֵּ֣ה אֵ֣שֶׁת יָרָבְעָ֡ם בָּאָ֣ה לִדְרֹשׁ֩ דָּבָ֨ר מֵעִמְּךָ֤ אֶל־בְּנָהּ֙ כִּֽי־חֹלֶ֣ה ה֔וּא כָּזֹ֥ה וְכָזֶ֖ה תְּדַבֵּ֣ר אֵלֶ֑יהָ וִיהִ֣י כְבֹאָ֔הּ וְהִ֖יא מִתְנַכֵּרָֽה׃

6 וַיְהִי֩ כִשְׁמֹ֨עַ אֲחִיָּ֜הוּ אֶת־ק֤וֹל רַגְלֶ֙יהָ֙ בָּאָ֣ה בַפֶּ֔תַח וַיֹּ֕אמֶר בֹּ֖אִי אֵ֣שֶׁת יָרָבְעָ֑ם לָ֣מָּה זֶּ֗ה אַ֚תְּ מִתְנַכֵּרָ֔ה וְאָ֣נֹכִ֔י שָׁל֥וּחַ אֵלַ֖יִךְ קָשָֽׁה׃ 7 לְכִ֞י אִמְרִ֣י לְיָרָבְעָ֗ם כֹּֽה־אָמַ֤ר יְהֹוָה֙ אֱלֹהֵ֣י יִשְׂרָאֵ֔ל יַ֛עַן אֲשֶׁ֥ר הֲרִימֹתִ֖יךָ מִתּ֣וֹךְ הָעָ֑ם וָאֶתֶּנְךָ֣ נָגִ֔יד עַ֖ל עַמִּ֥י יִשְׂרָאֵֽל׃ 8 וָאֶקְרַ֤ע אֶת־הַמַּמְלָכָה֙ מִבֵּ֣ית דָּוִ֔ד וָאֶתְּנֶ֖הָ לָ֑ךְ וְלֹֽא־הָיִ֜יתָ כְּעַבְדִּ֣י דָוִ֗ד אֲשֶׁר֩ שָׁמַ֨ר מִצְוֺתַ֜י וַאֲשֶׁר־הָלַ֤ךְ אַֽחֲרַי֙ בְּכָל־לְבָב֔וֹ לַעֲשׂ֕וֹת רַ֖ק הַיָּשָׁ֥ר בְּעֵינָֽי׃ 9 וַתָּ֣רַע לַעֲשׂ֗וֹת מִכֹּ֤ל אֲשֶׁר־הָיוּ֙ לְפָנֶ֔יךָ וַתֵּ֣לֶךְ וַתַּעֲשֶׂה־לְּךָ֩ אֱלֹהִ֨ים אֲחֵרִ֤ים וּמַסֵּכוֹת֙ לְהַכְעִיסֵ֔נִי וְאֹתִ֥י הִשְׁלַ֖כְתָּ אַחֲרֵ֥י גַוֶּֽךָ׃ ס 10 לָכֵ֗ן הִנְנִ֨י מֵבִ֤יא רָעָה֙ אֶל־בֵּ֣ית יָרָבְעָ֔ם וְהִכְרַתִּ֤י לְיָֽרָבְעָם֙ מַשְׁתִּ֣ין בְּקִ֔יר עָצ֥וּר וְעָז֖וּב בְּיִשְׂרָאֵ֑ל וּבִֽעַרְתִּ֙י אַחֲרֵ֣י בֵית־יָרָבְעָ֔ם כַּֽאֲשֶׁ֛ר יְבַעֵ֥ר הַגָּלָ֖ל עַד־תֻּמּֽוֹ׃ 11 הַמֵּ֨ת לְיָֽרָבְעָ֤ם בָּעִיר֙ יֹֽאכְל֣וּ הַכְּלָבִ֔ים וְהַמֵּת֙ בַּשָּׂדֶ֔ה יֹֽאכְל֖וּ ע֣וֹף הַשָּׁמָ֑יִם כִּ֥י יְהֹוָ֖ה דִּבֵּֽר׃ 12 וְאַ֙תְּ֙ ק֣וּמִי לְכִ֣י לְבֵיתֵ֔ךְ בְּבֹאָ֥ה רַגְלַ֖יִךְ הָעִ֑ירָה וּמֵ֖ת הַיָּֽלֶד׃ 13 וְסָֽפְדוּ־ל֣וֹ כָל־יִשְׂרָאֵל֮ וְקָבְר֣וּ אֹתוֹ֒ כִּֽי־זֶ֣ה לְבַדּ֗וֹ יָבֹ֤א לְיָֽרָבְעָם֙ אֶל־קָ֔בֶר יַ֣עַן נִמְצָא־ב֞וֹ דָּבָ֣ר ט֗וֹב אֶל־יְהֹוָ֛ה אֱלֹהֵ֥י יִשְׂרָאֵ֖ל בְּבֵ֥ית יָרָבְעָֽם׃

---

a-a   *Meaning of Heb. uncertain; possibly "kinsman and friend,"*
       cf. 16.11.

devotion been found to the LORD, the God of Israel. [14]Moreover, the LORD will raise up a king over Israel who will destroy the House of Jeroboam, *b-this day and even now.-b*

[15]"The LORD will strike Israel until it sways like a reed in water. He will uproot Israel from this good land that He gave to their fathers, and will scatter them beyond the Euphrates, because they have provoked the LORD by the sacred posts that they have made for themselves. [16]He will forsake Israel because of the sins that Jeroboam committed and led Israel to commit."

[17]Jeroboam's wife got up and left, and she went to Tirzah. As soon as she stepped over the threshold of her house, the child died. [18]They buried him and all Israel lamented over him, in accordance with the word that the LORD had spoken through His servant the prophet Ahijah.

[19]The other events of Jeroboam's reign, how he fought and how he ruled, are recorded in the Annals of the Kings of Israel. [20]Jeroboam reigned twenty-two years; then he slept with his fathers, and his son Nadab succeeded him as king.

[21]Meanwhile, Rehoboam son of Solomon had become king in Judah. Rehoboam was forty-one years old when he became king, and he reigned seventeen years in Jerusalem—the city the LORD had chosen out of all the tribes of Israel to establish His name there. His mother's name was Naamah the Ammonitess. [22]Judah did what was displeasing to the LORD, and angered Him more than their fathers had done by the sins that they committed. [23]They too built for themselves shrines, pillars, and sacred posts on every high hill and under every leafy tree; [24]there were also male prostitutes in the land. [Judah] imitated all the abhorrent practices of the nations that the LORD had dispossessed before the Israelites.

14 וְהֵקִים֩ יְהֹוָ֨ה ל֥וֹ מֶ֙לֶךְ֙ עַל־יִשְׂרָאֵ֔ל אֲשֶׁ֥ר יַכְרִ֛ית אֶת־בֵּ֥ית יָרׇבְעָ֖ם זֶ֣ה הַיּ֑וֹם וּמֶ֖ה גַּם־עָֽתָּה: 15 וְהִכָּ֨ה יְהֹוָ֜ה אֶת־יִשְׂרָאֵ֗ל כַּאֲשֶׁ֨ר יָנ֣וּד הַקָּנֶה֮ בַּמַּ֒יִם֒ וְנָתַ֣שׁ אֶת־יִשְׂרָאֵ֗ל מֵעַ֨ל הָאֲדָמָ֤ה הַטּוֹבָה֙ הַזֹּ֔את אֲשֶׁ֤ר נָתַן֙ לַאֲב֣וֹתֵיהֶ֔ם וְזֵרָ֖ם מֵעֵ֣בֶר לַנָּהָ֑ר יַ֗עַן אֲשֶׁ֤ר עָשׂוּ֙ אֶת־אֲשֵׁ֣רֵיהֶ֔ם מַכְעִיסִ֖ים אֶת־יְהֹוָֽה: 16 וְיִתֵּ֖ן אֶת־יִשְׂרָאֵ֑ל בִּגְלַ֞ל חַטֹּאות֙* יָרׇבְעָ֔ם אֲשֶׁ֣ר חָטָ֔א וַאֲשֶׁ֥ר הֶחֱטִ֖יא אֶת־יִשְׂרָאֵֽל: 17 וַתָּ֙קׇם֙ אֵ֣שֶׁת יָרׇבְעָ֔ם וַתֵּ֖לֶךְ וַתָּבֹ֣א תִרְצָ֑תָה הִ֛יא בָּאָ֥ה בְסַף־הַבַּ֖יִת וְהַנַּ֥עַר מֵֽת: 18 וַיִּקְבְּר֥וּ אֹת֛וֹ וַיִּסְפְּדוּ־ל֖וֹ כׇּל־יִשְׂרָאֵ֑ל כִּדְבַ֤ר יְהֹוָה֙ אֲשֶׁ֣ר דִּבֶּ֔ר בְּיַד־עַבְדּ֖וֹ אֲחִיָּ֥הוּ הַנָּבִֽיא: 19 וְיֶ֙תֶר֙ דִּבְרֵ֣י יָרׇבְעָ֔ם אֲשֶׁ֥ר נִלְחַ֖ם וַאֲשֶׁ֣ר מָלָ֑ךְ הִנָּ֣ם כְּתוּבִ֗ים עַל־סֵ֛פֶר דִּבְרֵ֥י הַיָּמִ֖ים לְמַלְכֵ֥י יִשְׂרָאֵֽל: 20 וְהַיָּמִים֙ אֲשֶׁ֣ר מָלַ֣ךְ יָרׇבְעָ֔ם עֶשְׂרִ֥ים וּשְׁתַּ֖יִם שָׁנָ֑ה וַיִּשְׁכַּב֙ עִם־אֲבֹתָ֔יו וַיִּמְלֹ֛ךְ נָדָ֥ב בְּנ֖וֹ תַּחְתָּֽיו: פ

21 וּרְחַבְעָם֙ בֶּן־שְׁלֹמֹ֔ה מָלַ֖ךְ בִּֽיהוּדָ֑ה בֶּן־אַרְבָּעִ֣ים וְאַחַ֣ת שָׁנָה֩ רְחַבְעָ֨ם בְּמׇלְכ֜וֹ וּֽשְׁבַ֣ע עֶשְׂרֵ֣ה שָׁנָ֣ה ׀ מָלַ֣ךְ בִּירֽוּשָׁלַ֗͏ִם הָעִ֗יר אֲשֶׁר־בָּחַ֨ר יְהֹוָ֜ה לָשׂ֨וּם אֶת־שְׁמ֥וֹ שָׁם֙ מִכֹּל֙ שִׁבְטֵ֣י יִשְׂרָאֵ֔ל וְשֵׁ֣ם אִמּ֔וֹ נַעֲמָ֖ה הָעַמֹּנִֽית: 22 וַיַּ֧עַשׂ יְהוּדָ֛ה הָרַ֖ע בְּעֵינֵ֣י יְהֹוָ֑ה וַיְקַנְא֣וּ אֹת֗וֹ מִכֹּל֙ אֲשֶׁ֣ר עָשׂ֣וּ אֲבֹתָ֔ם בְּחַטֹּאתָ֖ם אֲשֶׁ֥ר חָטָֽאוּ: 23 וַיִּבְנ֨וּ גַם־הֵ֧מָּה לָהֶ֛ם בָּמ֥וֹת וּמַצֵּב֖וֹת וַאֲשֵׁרִ֑ים עַ֚ל כׇּל־גִּבְעָ֣ה גְבֹהָ֔ה וְתַ֖חַת כׇּל־עֵ֥ץ רַעֲנָֽן: 24 וְגַם־קָדֵ֖שׁ הָיָ֣ה בָאָ֑רֶץ עָשׂ֗וּ כְּכֹל֙ הַתּוֹעֲבֹ֣ת הַגּוֹיִ֔ם אֲשֶׁר֙ הוֹרִ֣ישׁ יְהֹוָ֔ה מִפְּנֵ֖י בְּנֵ֥י יִשְׂרָאֵֽל: פ

מלא ו' *v. 16.*

---

b-b *Meaning of Heb. uncertain.*

25In the fifth year of King Rehoboam, King Shishak of Egypt marched against Jerusalem 26and carried off the treasures of the House of the Lord and the treasures of the royal palace. He carried off everything; he even carried off all the golden shields that Solomon had made. 27King Rehoboam had bronze shields made instead, and he entrusted them to the officers of the guard^c who guarded the entrance to the royal palace. 28Whenever the king went into the House of the Lord, the guards would carry them and then bring them back to the armory of the guards.

29The other events of Rehoboam's reign, and all his actions, are recorded in the Annals of the Kings of Judah. 30There was continual war between Rehoboam and Jeroboam. 31Rehoboam slept with his fathers and was buried with his fathers in the City of David; his mother's name was Naamah the Ammonitess. His son Abijam succeeded him as king.

15

In the eighteenth year of King Jeroboam son of Nebat, Abijam became king over Judah. 2He reigned three years in Jerusalem; his mother's name was ᵃ⁻Maacah daughter of Abishalom.⁻ᵃ 3He continued in all the sins that his father before him had committed; he was not wholehearted with the Lord his God, like his father David. 4Yet, for the sake of David, the Lord his God gave him a lamp in Jerusalem, by raising up his descendant after him and by preserving Jerusalem. 5For David had done what was pleasing to the Lord and never turned throughout his life from all that He had commanded him, except in the matter of Uriah the Hittite. 6There was war between Abijam^b and Jeroboam all the days of his life. 7The other

---

25 וַיְהִ֞י בַּשָּׁנָ֤ה הַחֲמִישִׁית֙ לַמֶּ֣לֶךְ רְחַבְעָ֔ם עָלָ֛ה שׁוּשַׁ֥ק מֶֽלֶךְ־מִצְרַ֖יִם עַל־יְרוּשָׁלָֽ͏ִם׃ 26 וַיִּקַּ֞ח אֶת־אֹצְר֣וֹת בֵּית־יְהֹוָ֗ה וְאֶת־אֽוֹצְרוֹת֙ בֵּ֣ית הַמֶּ֔לֶךְ וְאֶת־הַכֹּ֖ל לָקָ֑ח וַיִּקַּח֙ אֶת־כׇּל־מָגִנֵּ֣י הַזָּהָ֔ב אֲשֶׁ֥ר עָשָׂ֖ה שְׁלֹמֹֽה׃ 27 וַיַּ֨עַשׂ הַמֶּ֤לֶךְ רְחַבְעָם֙ תַּחְתָּ֔ם מָגִנֵּ֖י נְחֹ֑שֶׁת וְהִפְקִ֗יד עַל־יַד֙ שָׂרֵ֣י הָרָצִ֔ים הַשֹּׁ֣מְרִ֔ים פֶּ֖תַח בֵּ֥ית הַמֶּֽלֶךְ׃ 28 וַיְהִ֛י מִדֵּי־בֹ֥א הַמֶּ֖לֶךְ בֵּ֣ית יְהֹוָ֑ה יִשָּׂאוּם֙ הָֽרָצִ֔ים וֶהֱשִׁיב֖וּם אֶל־תָּ֥א הָרָצִֽים׃ 29 וְיֶ֛תֶר דִּבְרֵ֥י רְחַבְעָ֖ם וְכׇל־אֲשֶׁ֣ר עָשָׂ֑ה הֲלֹא־הֵ֣מָּה כְתוּבִ֗ים עַל־סֵ֛פֶר דִּבְרֵ֥י הַיָּמִ֖ים לְמַלְכֵ֥י יְהוּדָֽה׃ 30 וּמִלְחָמָ֨ה הָיְתָ֧ה בֵין־רְחַבְעָ֛ם וּבֵ֥ין יָרׇבְעָ֖ם כׇּל־הַיָּמִֽים׃ 31 וַיִּשְׁכַּ֨ב רְחַבְעָ֜ם עִם־אֲבֹתָ֗יו וַיִּקָּבֵ֤ר עִם־אֲבֹתָיו֙ בְּעִ֣יר דָּוִ֔ד וְשֵׁ֣ם אִמּ֔וֹ נַעֲמָ֖ה הָעַמֹּנִ֑ית וַיִּמְלֹ֛ךְ אֲבִיָּ֥ם בְּנ֖וֹ תַּחְתָּֽיו׃ פ

טו

וּבִשְׁנַת֙ שְׁמֹנֶ֣ה עֶשְׂרֵ֔ה לַמֶּ֖לֶךְ יָרׇבְעָ֣ם בֶּן־נְבָ֑ט מָלַ֥ךְ אֲבִיָּ֖ם עַל־יְהוּדָֽה׃ 2 שָׁלֹ֣שׁ שָׁנִ֔ים מָלַ֖ךְ בִּירוּשָׁלָ֑͏ִם וְשֵׁ֣ם אִמּ֔וֹ מַעֲכָ֖ה בַּת־אֲבִישָׁלֽוֹם׃ 3 וַיֵּ֕לֶךְ בְּכׇל־חַטֹּ֥אות* אָבִ֖יו אֲשֶׁר־עָשָׂ֣ה לְפָנָ֑יו וְלֹא־הָיָ֨ה לְבָב֤וֹ שָׁלֵם֙ עִם־יְהֹוָ֣ה אֱלֹהָ֔יו כִּלְבַ֖ב דָּוִ֥ד אָבִֽיו׃ 4 כִּ֚י לְמַ֣עַן דָּוִ֔ד נָתַן֩ יְהֹוָ֨ה אֱלֹהָ֥יו ל֛וֹ נִ֖יר בִּירוּשָׁלָ֑͏ִם לְהָקִ֤ים אֶת־בְּנוֹ֙ אַחֲרָ֔יו וּֽלְהַעֲמִ֖יד אֶת־יְרוּשָׁלָֽ͏ִם׃ 5 אֲשֶׁ֨ר עָשָׂ֥ה דָוִ֛ד אֶת־הַיָּשָׁ֖ר בְּעֵינֵ֣י יְהֹוָ֑ה וְלֹא־סָ֞ר מִכֹּ֣ל אֲשֶׁר־צִוָּ֗הוּ כֹּ֚ל יְמֵ֣י חַיָּ֔יו רַ֕ק בִּדְבַ֖ר אוּרִיָּ֥ה הַחִתִּֽי׃ 6 וּמִלְחָמָ֨ה הָיְתָ֧ה בֵין־רְחַבְעָ֛ם* וּבֵ֥ין יָרׇבְעָ֖ם כׇּל־יְמֵ֥י חַיָּֽיו׃ 7 וְיֶ֨תֶר דִּבְרֵ֤י אֲבִיָּם֙ וְכׇל־אֲשֶׁ֣ר עָשָׂ֔ה הֲלֽוֹא־הֵ֣ם כְּתוּבִ֗ים

---

c   Lit. "runners."

a-a   2 Chron. 13.2 reads "Micaiah daughter of Uriel of Gibeah"; cf. v. 10 below, where Maacah, daughter of Abishalom, appears as mother of Asa.

b   So several mss.; most mss. and the editions read "Rehoboam."

events of Abijam's reign and all his actions are recorded in the Annals of the Kings of Judah; there was war between Abijam and Jeroboam. [8]Abijam slept with his fathers; he was buried in the City of David, and his son Asa succeeded him as king.

[9]In the twentieth year of King Jeroboam of Israel, Asa became king over Judah. [10]He reigned forty-one years in Jerusalem; his mother's name was Maacah daughter of Abishalom. [11]Asa did what was pleasing to the Lord, as his father David had done. [12]He expelled the male prostitutes from the land, and he removed all the idols that his ancestors had made. [13]He also deposed his mother Maacah from the rank of queen mother, because she had made *c*-an abominable thing-*c* for [the goddess] Asherah. Asa cut down her abominable thing and burnt it in the Wadi Kidron. [14]The shrines, indeed, were not abolished; however, Asa was wholehearted with the Lord his God all his life. [15]He brought into the House of the Lord all the consecrated things of his father and *d*-his own consecrated things-*d*—silver, gold, and utensils.

[16]There was war between Asa and King Baasha of Israel all their days. [17]King Baasha of Israel advanced against Judah, and he fortified Ramah to prevent anyone belonging to King Asa from going out or coming in. [18]So Asa took all the silver and gold that remained in the treasuries of the House of the Lord as well as the treasuries of the royal palace, and he entrusted them to his officials. King Asa sent them to King Ben-hadad son of Tabrimmon son of Hezion of Aram, who resided in Damascus, with this message: [19]"There is a pact between you and me, and between your father and my father. I herewith send you a gift of silver and gold: Go and break your pact with King Baasha of Israel, so that he may withdraw from me." [20]Ben-hadad

עַל־סֵ֣פֶר דִּבְרֵ֣י הַיָּמִ֔ים לְמַלְכֵ֖י יְהוּדָ֑ה וּמִלְחָמָ֥ה הָיְתָ֛ה בֵּ֥ין אֲבִיָּ֖ם וּבֵ֥ין יָרָבְעָֽם׃ [8]וַיִּשְׁכַּ֨ב אֲבִיָּ֜ם עִם־אֲבֹתָ֗יו וַיִּקְבְּר֤וּ אֹתוֹ֙ בְּעִ֣יר דָּוִ֔ד וַיִּמְלֹ֛ךְ אָסָ֥א בְנ֖וֹ תַּחְתָּֽיו׃ פ [9]וּבִשְׁנַ֣ת עֶשְׂרִ֔ים לְיָרׇבְעָ֖ם מֶ֣לֶךְ יִשְׂרָאֵ֑ל מָלַ֥ךְ אָסָ֖א מֶ֥לֶךְ יְהוּדָֽה׃ [10]וְאַרְבָּעִ֤ים וְאַחַת֙ שָׁנָ֔ה מָלַ֖ךְ בִּירוּשָׁלָ֑͏ִם וְשֵׁ֣ם אִמּ֔וֹ מַעֲכָ֖ה בַּת־אֲבִישָׁלֽוֹם׃ [11]וַיַּ֧עַשׂ אָסָ֛א הַיָּשָׁ֖ר בְּעֵינֵ֣י יְהֹוָ֑ה כְּדָוִ֖ד אָבִֽיו׃ [12]וַיַּעֲבֵ֤ר הַקְּדֵשִׁים֙ מִן־הָאָ֔רֶץ וַיָּ֙סַר֙ אֶת־כׇּל־הַגִּלֻּלִ֔ים אֲשֶׁ֥ר עָשׂ֖וּ אֲבֹתָֽיו׃ [13]וְגַ֣ם ׀ אֶת־מַעֲכָ֣ה אִמּ֗וֹ וַיְסִרֶ֙הָ֙ מִגְּבִירָ֔ה אֲשֶׁר־עָשְׂתָ֥ה מִפְלֶ֖צֶת לָאֲשֵׁרָ֑ה וַיִּכְרֹ֤ת אָסָא֙ אֶת־מִפְלַצְתָּ֔הּ וַיִּשְׂרֹ֖ף בְּנַ֥חַל קִדְרֽוֹן׃ [14]וְהַבָּמ֖וֹת לֹא־סָ֑רוּ רַ֣ק לְבַב־אָסָ֗א הָיָ֥ה שָׁלֵ֛ם עִם־יְהֹוָ֖ה כׇּל־יָמָֽיו׃ [15]וַיָּבֵ֞א אֶת־קׇדְשֵׁ֥י אָבִ֛יו וקדשו וְקׇדְשֵׁ֥י בֵּ֣ית יְהֹוָ֖ה כֶּ֥סֶף וְזָהָ֖ב וְכֵלִֽים׃ [16]וּמִלְחָמָ֣ה הָיְתָ֔ה בֵּ֥ין אָסָ֖א וּבֵ֣ין בַּעְשָׁ֣א מֶֽלֶךְ־יִשְׂרָאֵ֑ל כׇּל־יְמֵיהֶֽם׃ [17]וַיַּ֨עַל בַּעְשָׁ֤א מֶֽלֶךְ־יִשְׂרָאֵל֙ עַל־יְהוּדָ֔ה וַיִּ֖בֶן אֶת־הָרָמָ֑ה לְבִלְתִּ֗י תֵּ֚ת יֹצֵ֣א וָבָ֔א לְאָסָ֖א מֶ֥לֶךְ יְהוּדָֽה׃ [18]וַיִּקַּ֣ח אָ֠סָ֠א אֶת־כׇּל־הַכֶּ֨סֶף וְהַזָּהָ֜ב הַנּֽוֹתָרִ֣ים ׀ בְּאוֹצְר֣וֹת בֵּית־יְהֹוָ֗ה וְאֶת־אֽוֹצְרוֹת֙ בֵּ֣ית המלך הַמֶּ֔לֶךְ וַֽיִּתְּנֵ֖ם בְּיַד־עֲבָדָ֑יו וַיִּשְׁלָחֵ֞ם הַמֶּ֣לֶךְ אָסָ֗א אֶל־בֶּן־הֲדַ֡ד בֶּן־טַבְרִמֹּן֩ בֶּן־חֶזְיוֹ֨ן מֶ֤לֶךְ אֲרָם֙ הַיֹּשֵׁ֣ב בְּדַמֶּ֔שֶׂק לֵאמֹֽר׃ [19]בְּרִית֙ בֵּינִ֣י וּבֵינֶ֔ךָ בֵּ֥ין אָבִ֖י וּבֵ֣ין אָבִ֑יךָ הִנֵּה֩ שָׁלַ֨חְתִּי לְךָ֥ שֹׁ֙חַד֙ כֶּ֣סֶף וְזָהָ֔ב לֵ֣ךְ הָפֵ֗רָה אֶת־בְּרִֽיתְךָ֙ אֶת־בַּעְשָׁ֣א מֶֽלֶךְ־יִשְׂרָאֵ֔ל וְיַעֲלֶ֖ה מֵעָלָֽי׃

---

c-c Exact meaning of Heb. uncertain.
d-d So kethib and 2 Chron. 15.18.

responded to King Asa's request; he sent his army commanders against the towns of Israel and captured Ijon, Dan, Abel-beth-maacah, and all Chinneroth, as well as all the land of Naphtali. 21When Baasha heard about it, he stopped fortifying Ramah and remained in Tirzah.

22Then King Asa mustered all Judah, with no exemptions; and they carried away the stones and timber with which Baasha had fortified Ramah. With these King Asa fortified Geba of Benjamin, and Mizpah.

23All the other events of Asa's reign, and all his exploits, and all his actions, and the towns that he fortified, are recorded in the Annals of the Kings of Judah. However, in his old age he suffered from a foot ailment. 24Asa slept with his fathers and was buried with his fathers in the city of his father David. His son Jehoshaphat succeeded him as king.

25Nadab son of Jeroboam had become king over Israel in the second year of King Asa of Judah, and he reigned over Israel for two years. 26He did what was displeasing to the Lord; he continued in the ways of his father, in the sins which he caused Israel to commit. 27Then Baasha son of Ahijah, of the House of Issachar, conspired against him; and Baasha struck him down at Gibbethon of the Philistines, while Nadab and all Israel were laying siege to Gibbethon. 28Baasha killed him in the third year of King Asa of Judah and became king in his stead. 29As soon as he became king, he struck down all the House of Jeroboam; he did not spare a single soul belonging to Jeroboam until he destroyed it—in accordance with the word that the Lord had spoken through His servant, the prophet Ahijah the Shilonite—30because of the sins which Jeroboam committed and which he caused Israel to commit thereby vexing the Lord, the God of Israel.

20 וַיִּשְׁמַ֞ע בֶּן־הֲדַ֣ד אֶל־הַמֶּ֣לֶךְ אָסָ֗א וַיִּשְׁלַ֣ח אֶת־שָׂרֵ֣י הַחֲיָלִ֣ים אֲשֶׁר־ל֣וֹ עַל־עָרֵ֣י יִשְׂרָאֵל֒ וַיַּךְ֙ אֶת־עִיּ֣וֹן וְאֶת־דָּ֔ן וְאֵ֖ת אָבֵ֣ל בֵּֽית־מַעֲכָ֑ה וְאֵת֙ כָּל־כִּנְר֔וֹת עַ֖ל כָּל־אֶ֥רֶץ נַפְתָּלִֽי: 21 וַיְהִי֙ כִּשְׁמֹ֣עַ בַּעְשָׁ֔א וַיֶּחְדַּ֕ל מִבְּנ֖וֹת אֶת־הָֽרָמָ֑ה וַיֵּ֖שֶׁב בְּתִרְצָֽה: 22 וְהַמֶּ֤לֶךְ אָסָא֙ הִשְׁמִ֣יעַ אֶת־כָּל־יְהוּדָ֔ה אֵ֣ין נָקִ֔י וַיִּשְׂא֞וּ אֶת־אַבְנֵ֤י הָֽרָמָה֙ וְאֶת־עֵצֶ֔יהָ אֲשֶׁ֥ר בָּנָ֖ה בַּעְשָׁ֑א וַיִּ֤בֶן בָּם֙ הַמֶּ֣לֶךְ אָסָ֔א אֶת־גֶּ֣בַע בִּנְיָמִ֔ן וְאֶת־הַמִּצְפָּֽה: 23 וְיֶ֨תֶר כָּל־דִּבְרֵֽי־אָ֜סָא וְכָל־גְּב֣וּרָת֗וֹ וְכָל־אֲשֶׁ֤ר עָשָׂה֙ וְהֶ֣עָרִ֔ים אֲשֶׁ֣ר בָּנָ֔ה הֲלֹֽא־הֵ֣מָּה כְתוּבִ֗ים עַל־סֵ֛פֶר דִּבְרֵ֥י הַיָּמִ֖ים לְמַלְכֵ֣י יְהוּדָ֑ה רַ֚ק לְעֵ֣ת זִקְנָת֔וֹ חָלָ֖ה אֶת־רַגְלָֽיו: 24 וַיִּשְׁכַּ֤ב אָסָא֙ עִם־אֲבֹתָ֔יו וַיִּקָּבֵר֙ עִם־אֲבֹתָ֔יו בְּעִ֖יר דָּוִ֣ד אָבִ֑יו וַיִּמְלֹ֛ךְ יְהוֹשָׁפָ֥ט בְּנ֖וֹ תַּחְתָּֽיו: פ 25 וְנָדָ֣ב בֶּן־יָֽרָבְעָ֗ם מָלַךְ֙ עַל־יִשְׂרָאֵ֔ל בִּשְׁנַ֣ת שְׁתַּ֔יִם לְאָסָ֖א מֶ֣לֶךְ יְהוּדָ֑ה וַיִּמְלֹ֥ךְ עַל־יִשְׂרָאֵ֖ל שְׁנָתָֽיִם: 26 וַיַּ֥עַשׂ הָרַ֖ע בְּעֵינֵ֣י יְהוָ֑ה וַיֵּ֙לֶךְ֙ בְּדֶ֣רֶךְ אָבִ֔יו וּבְ֨חַטָּאת֔וֹ אֲשֶׁ֥ר הֶחֱטִ֖יא אֶת־יִשְׂרָאֵֽל: 27 וַיִּקְשֹׁ֨ר עָלָ֜יו בַּעְשָׁ֣א בֶן־אֲחִיָּ֗ה לְבֵ֣ית יִשָּׂשכָ֔ר וַיַּכֵּ֣הוּ בַעְשָׁ֗א בְּגִבְּת֙וֹן֙ אֲשֶׁ֣ר לַפְּלִשְׁתִּ֔ים וְנָדָב֙ וְכָל־יִשְׂרָאֵ֔ל צָרִ֖ים עַל־גִּבְּתֽוֹן: 28 וַיְמִתֵ֣הוּ בַעְשָׁ֔א בִּשְׁנַ֣ת שָׁלֹ֔שׁ לְאָסָ֖א מֶ֣לֶךְ יְהוּדָ֑ה וַיִּמְלֹ֖ךְ תַּחְתָּֽיו: 29 וַיְהִ֣י כְמָלְכ֗וֹ הִכָּה֙ אֶת־כָּל־בֵּ֣ית יָֽרָבְעָ֔ם לֹֽא־הִשְׁאִ֧יר כָּל־נְשָׁמָ֛ה לְיָרָבְעָ֖ם עַד־הִשְׁמִד֑וֹ כִּדְבַ֤ר יְהוָה֙ אֲשֶׁ֣ר דִּבֶּ֔ר בְּיַד־עַבְדּ֖וֹ אֲחִיָּ֥ה הַשִּׁילֹנִֽי: 30 עַל־חַטֹּ֤אות* יָֽרָבְעָם֙ אֲשֶׁ֣ר חָטָ֔א וַאֲשֶׁ֥ר הֶחֱטִ֖יא אֶת־יִשְׂרָאֵ֑ל בְּכַעְס֕וֹ אֲשֶׁ֣ר הִכְעִ֔יס אֶת־יְהוָ֖ה אֱלֹהֵ֥י יִשְׂרָאֵֽל: 31 וְיֶ֛תֶר דִּבְרֵ֥י נָדָ֖ב וְכָל־אֲשֶׁ֣ר עָשָׂ֑ה הֲלֹא־

31The other events of Nadab's reign and all his actions are recorded in the Annals of the Kings of Israel.

32There was war between Asa and King Baasha of Israel all their days. 33In the third year of King Asa of Judah, Baasha son of Ahijah became king in Tirzah over all Israel—for twenty-four years. 34He did what was displeasing to the Lord; he followed the ways of Jeroboam and the sins which he caused Israel to commit.

16 The word of the Lord came to Jehu son of Hanani against Baasha: 2"Because I lifted you up from the dust and made you a ruler over My people Israel, but you followed the way of Jeroboam and caused My people Israel to sin, vexing Me with their sins—3I am going to sweep away Baasha and his house. I will make your house like the House of Jeroboam son of Nebat. 4Anyone belonging to Baasha who dies in the town shall be devoured by dogs, and anyone belonging to him who dies in the open country shall be devoured by the birds of the sky."

5The other events of Baasha's reign and his actions and his exploits are recorded in the Annals of the Kings of Israel. 6Baasha slept with his fathers and was buried in Tirzah. His son Elah succeeded him as king.

7But the word of the Lord had come through the prophet Jehu son of Hanani against Baasha and against his house, that it would fare like the House of Jeroboam, *a*-which he himself had struck down,-*a* because of all the evil he did which was displeasing to the Lord, vexing him with his deeds.

8In the twenty-sixth year of King Asa of Judah, Elah son of Baasha became king over Israel, at Tirzah—for two years. 9His officer Zimri, commander of half the chariotry, committed

---

a-a Syntax of Heb. unclear.

הֵם כְּתוּבִים עַל־סֵפֶר דִּבְרֵי הַיָּמִים לְמַלְכֵי יִשְׂרָאֵל: 32וּמִלְחָמָה הָיְתָה בֵּין אָסָא וּבֵין בַּעְשָׁא מֶלֶךְ־יִשְׂרָאֵל כָּל־יְמֵיהֶם: פ 33בִּשְׁנַת שָׁלֹשׁ לְאָסָא מֶלֶךְ יְהוּדָה מָלַךְ בַּעְשָׁא בֶן־אֲחִיָּה עַל־כָּל־יִשְׂרָאֵל בְּתִרְצָה עֶשְׂרִים וְאַרְבַּע שָׁנָה: 34וַיַּעַשׂ הָרַע בְּעֵינֵי יְהוָה וַיֵּלֶךְ בְּדֶרֶךְ יָרָבְעָם וּבְחַטָּאתוֹ אֲשֶׁר הֶחֱטִיא אֶת־יִשְׂרָאֵל: ס

טז וַיְהִי דְבַר־יְהוָה אֶל־יֵהוּא בֶן־חֲנָנִי עַל־בַּעְשָׁא לֵאמֹר: 2יַעַן אֲשֶׁר הֲרִימֹתִיךָ מִן־הֶעָפָר וָאֶתֶּנְךָ נָגִיד עַל עַמִּי יִשְׂרָאֵל וַתֵּלֶךְ ׀ בְּדֶרֶךְ יָרָבְעָם וַתַּחֲטִא אֶת־עַמִּי יִשְׂרָאֵל לְהַכְעִיסֵנִי בְּחַטֹּאתָם: 3הִנְנִי מַבְעִיר אַחֲרֵי בַעְשָׁא וְאַחֲרֵי בֵיתוֹ וְנָתַתִּי אֶת־בֵּיתְךָ כְּבֵית יָרָבְעָם בֶּן־נְבָט: 4הַמֵּת לְבַעְשָׁא בָּעִיר יֹאכְלוּ הַכְּלָבִים וְהַמֵּת לוֹ בַּשָּׂדֶה יֹאכְלוּ עוֹף הַשָּׁמָיִם: 5וְיֶתֶר דִּבְרֵי בַעְשָׁא וַאֲשֶׁר עָשָׂה וּגְבוּרָתוֹ הֲלֹא־הֵם כְּתוּבִים עַל־סֵפֶר דִּבְרֵי הַיָּמִים לְמַלְכֵי יִשְׂרָאֵל: 6וַיִּשְׁכַּב בַּעְשָׁא עִם־אֲבֹתָיו וַיִּקָּבֵר בְּתִרְצָה וַיִּמְלֹךְ אֵלָה בְנוֹ תַּחְתָּיו: 7וְגַם בְּיַד־יֵהוּא בֶן־חֲנָנִי הַנָּבִיא דְּבַר־יְהוָה הָיָה אֶל־בַּעְשָׁא וְאֶל־בֵּיתוֹ וְעַל כָּל־הָרָעָה ׀ אֲשֶׁר־עָשָׂה ׀ בְּעֵינֵי יְהוָה לְהַכְעִיסוֹ בְּמַעֲשֵׂה יָדָיו לִהְיוֹת כְּבֵית יָרָבְעָם וְעַל אֲשֶׁר־הִכָּה אֹתוֹ: פ 8בִּשְׁנַת עֶשְׂרִים וָשֵׁשׁ שָׁנָה לְאָסָא מֶלֶךְ יְהוּדָה מָלַךְ אֵלָה בֶן־בַּעְשָׁא עַל־יִשְׂרָאֵל בְּתִרְצָה שְׁנָתָיִם: 9וַיִּקְשֹׁר עָלָיו עַבְדּוֹ זִמְרִי שַׂר מַחֲצִית הָרָכֶב וְהוּא בְתִרְצָה

treason against him while he was at Tirzah drinking himself drunk in the house of Arza, who was in charge of the palace at Tirzah. [10]Zimri entered, struck him down, and killed him; he succeeded him as king in the twenty-seventh year of King Asa of Judah. [11]No sooner had he become king and ascended the throne than he struck down all the House of Baasha; he did not leave a single male of his, nor any kinsman or friend. [12]Thus Zimri destroyed all the House of Baasha, in accordance with the word that the Lord had spoken through the prophet Jehu—[13]because of the sinful acts which Baasha and his son Elah committed, and which they caused Israel to commit, vexing the Lord, the God of Israel, with their false gods. [14]The other events of Elah's reign and all his actions are recorded in the Annals of the Kings of Israel.

[15]During the twenty-seventh year of King Asa of Judah, Zimri reigned in Tirzah for seven days. At the time, the troops were encamped at Gibbethon of the Philistines. [16]When the troops who were encamped there learned that Zimri had committed treason and had struck down the king, that very day, in the camp, all Israel acclaimed the army commander Omri king over Israel. [17]Omri and all Israel then withdrew from Gibbethon and laid siege to Tirzah. [18]When Zimri saw that the town was taken, he went into the citadel of the royal palace and burned down the royal palace over himself. And so he died—[19]because of the sins which he committed and caused Israel to commit, doing what was displeasing to the Lord and following the ways of Jeroboam. [20]The other events of Zimri's reign, and the treason which he committed, are recorded in the Annals of the Kings of Israel.

[21]Then the people of Israel split into two factions: a part of the people followed Tibni son of Ginath to make him king, and the other

שֹׁתֶה שִׁכּוֹר בֵּית אַרְצָא אֲשֶׁר עַל־הַבַּיִת בְּתִרְצָה: 10 וַיָּבֹא זִמְרִי וַיַּכֵּהוּ וַיְמִיתֵהוּ בִּשְׁנַת עֶשְׂרִים וָשֶׁבַע לְאָסָא מֶלֶךְ יְהוּדָה וַיִּמְלֹךְ תַּחְתָּיו: 11 וַיְהִי בְמָלְכוֹ כְּשִׁבְתּוֹ עַל־כִּסְאוֹ הִכָּה אֶת־כָּל־בֵּית בַּעְשָׁא לֹא־הִשְׁאִיר לוֹ מַשְׁתִּין בְּקִיר וְגֹאֲלָיו וְרֵעֵהוּ: 12 וַיַּשְׁמֵד זִמְרִי אֵת כָּל־בֵּית בַּעְשָׁא כִּדְבַר יְהוָה אֲשֶׁר דִּבֶּר אֶל־בַּעְשָׁא בְּיַד יֵהוּא הַנָּבִיא: 13 אֶל כָּל־חַטֹּאות* בַּעְשָׁא וְחַטֹּאות אֵלָה בְנוֹ אֲשֶׁר חָטְאוּ וַאֲשֶׁר הֶחֱטִיאוּ אֶת־יִשְׂרָאֵל לְהַכְעִיס אֶת־יְהוָה אֱלֹהֵי יִשְׂרָאֵל בְּהַבְלֵיהֶם: 14 וְיֶתֶר דִּבְרֵי אֵלָה וְכָל־אֲשֶׁר עָשָׂה הֲלוֹא־הֵם כְּתוּבִים עַל־סֵפֶר דִּבְרֵי הַיָּמִים לְמַלְכֵי יִשְׂרָאֵל: פ

15 בִּשְׁנַת עֶשְׂרִים וָשֶׁבַע שָׁנָה לְאָסָא מֶלֶךְ יְהוּדָה מָלַךְ זִמְרִי שִׁבְעַת יָמִים בְּתִרְצָה וְהָעָם חֹנִים עַל־גִּבְּתוֹן אֲשֶׁר לַפְּלִשְׁתִּים: 16 וַיִּשְׁמַע הָעָם הַחֹנִים לֵאמֹר קָשַׁר זִמְרִי וְגַם הִכָּה אֶת־הַמֶּלֶךְ וַיַּמְלִכוּ כָל־יִשְׂרָאֵל אֶת־עָמְרִי שַׂר־צָבָא עַל־יִשְׂרָאֵל בַּיּוֹם הַהוּא בַּמַּחֲנֶה: 17 וַיַּעֲלֶה עָמְרִי וְכָל־יִשְׂרָאֵל עִמּוֹ מִגִּבְּתוֹן וַיָּצֻרוּ עַל־תִּרְצָה: 18 וַיְהִי כִּרְאוֹת זִמְרִי כִּי־נִלְכְּדָה הָעִיר וַיָּבֹא אֶל־אַרְמוֹן בֵּית־הַמֶּלֶךְ וַיִּשְׂרֹף עָלָיו אֶת־בֵּית־מֶלֶךְ בָּאֵשׁ וַיָּמֹת: 19 עַל־חטאתו חַטֹּאתָיו אֲשֶׁר חָטָא לַעֲשׂוֹת הָרַע בְּעֵינֵי יְהוָה לָלֶכֶת בְּדֶרֶךְ יָרָבְעָם וּבְחַטָּאתוֹ אֲשֶׁר עָשָׂה לְהַחֲטִיא אֶת־יִשְׂרָאֵל: 20 וְיֶתֶר דִּבְרֵי זִמְרִי וְקִשְׁרוֹ אֲשֶׁר קָשָׁר הֲלֹא־הֵם כְּתוּבִים עַל־סֵפֶר דִּבְרֵי הַיָּמִים לְמַלְכֵי יִשְׂרָאֵל: פ

21 אָז יֵחָלֵק הָעָם יִשְׂרָאֵל לַחֵצִי חֲצִי הָעָם הָיָה אַחֲרֵי תִבְנִי בֶן־גִּינַת לְהַמְלִיכוֹ

v. 13. מלא ו'

754

part followed Omri. 22Those who followed Omri proved stronger than those who followed Tibni son of Ginath; Tibni died and Omri became king.

23In the thirty-first year of King Asa of Judah, Omri became king over Israel—for twelve years. He reigned in Tirzah six years. 24Then he bought the hill of Samaria from Shemer for two talents of silver; he built [a town] on the hill and named the town which he built Samaria, after Shemer, the owner of the hill.

25Omri did what was displeasing to the LORD; he was worse than all who preceded him. 26He followed all the ways of Jeroboam son of Nebat and the sins which he committed and caused Israel to commit, vexing the LORD, the God of Israel, with their futilities. 27The other events of Omri's reign, [and] his actions, and the exploits he performed, are recorded in the Annals of the Kings of Israel. 28Omri slept with his fathers and was buried in Samaria; and his son Ahab succeeded him as king.

29Ahab son of Omri became king over Israel in the thirty-eighth year of King Asa of Judah, and Ahab son of Omri reigned over Israel in Samaria for twenty-two years. 30Ahab son of Omri did what was displeasing to the LORD, more than all who preceded him. 31Not content to follow the sins of Jeroboam son of Nebat, he took as wife Jezebel daughter of King Ethbaal of the Phoenicians, and he went and served Baal and worshiped him. 32He erected an altar to Baal in the temple of Baal which he built in Samaria. 33Ahab also made a sacred post. Ahab did more to vex the LORD, the God of Israel, than all the kings of Israel who preceded him.

וְהַחֲצִי אַחֲרֵי עָמְרִי: 22 וַיֶּחֱזַק הָעָם אֲשֶׁר אַחֲרֵי עָמְרִי אֶת־הָעָם אֲשֶׁר אַחֲרֵי תִּבְנִי בֶן־גִּינַת וַיָּמָת תִּבְנִי וַיִּמְלֹךְ עָמְרִי: פ

23 בִּשְׁנַת שְׁלֹשִׁים וְאַחַת שָׁנָה לְאָסָא מֶלֶךְ יְהוּדָה מָלַךְ עָמְרִי עַל־יִשְׂרָאֵל שְׁתֵּים עֶשְׂרֵה שָׁנָה בְּתִרְצָה מָלַךְ שֵׁשׁ־שָׁנִים: 24 וַיִּקֶן אֶת־הָהָר שֹׁמְרוֹן מֵאֵת שֶׁמֶר בְּכִכְּרַיִם כָּסֶף וַיִּבֶן אֶת־הָהָר וַיִּקְרָא אֶת־שֵׁם הָעִיר אֲשֶׁר בָּנָה עַל שֶׁם־שֶׁמֶר אֲדֹנֵי הָהָר שֹׁמְרוֹן: 25 וַיַּעֲשֶׂה עָמְרִי הָרַע בְּעֵינֵי יְהוָה וַיָּרַע מִכֹּל אֲשֶׁר לְפָנָיו: 26 וַיֵּלֶךְ בְּכָל־דֶּרֶךְ יָרָבְעָם בֶּן־נְבָט וּבְחַטֹּאתָיו אֲשֶׁר הֶחֱטִיא אֶת־יִשְׂרָאֵל לְהַכְעִיס אֶת־יְהוָה אֱלֹהֵי יִשְׂרָאֵל בְּהַבְלֵיהֶם: 27 וְיֶתֶר דִּבְרֵי עָמְרִי אֲשֶׁר עָשָׂה וּגְבוּרָתוֹ אֲשֶׁר עָשָׂה הֲלֹא־הֵם כְּתוּבִים עַל־סֵפֶר דִּבְרֵי הַיָּמִים לְמַלְכֵי יִשְׂרָאֵל: 28 וַיִּשְׁכַּב עָמְרִי עִם־אֲבֹתָיו וַיִּקָּבֵר בְּשֹׁמְרוֹן וַיִּמְלֹךְ אַחְאָב בְּנוֹ תַּחְתָּיו: פ

29 וְאַחְאָב בֶּן־עָמְרִי מָלַךְ עַל־יִשְׂרָאֵל בִּשְׁנַת שְׁלֹשִׁים וּשְׁמֹנֶה שָׁנָה לְאָסָא מֶלֶךְ יְהוּדָה וַיִּמְלֹךְ אַחְאָב בֶּן־עָמְרִי עַל־יִשְׂרָאֵל בְּשֹׁמְרוֹן עֶשְׂרִים וּשְׁתַּיִם שָׁנָה: 30 וַיַּעַשׂ אַחְאָב בֶּן־עָמְרִי הָרַע בְּעֵינֵי יְהוָה מִכֹּל אֲשֶׁר לְפָנָיו: 31 וַיְהִי הֲנָקֵל לֶכְתּוֹ בְּחַטֹּאות* יָרָבְעָם בֶּן־נְבָט וַיִּקַּח אִשָּׁה אֶת־אִיזֶבֶל בַּת־אֶתְבַּעַל מֶלֶךְ צִידֹנִים וַיֵּלֶךְ וַיַּעֲבֹד אֶת־הַבַּעַל וַיִּשְׁתַּחוּ לוֹ: 32 וַיָּקֶם מִזְבֵּחַ לַבָּעַל בֵּית הַבַּעַל אֲשֶׁר בָּנָה בְּשֹׁמְרוֹן: 33 וַיַּעַשׂ אַחְאָב אֶת־הָאֲשֵׁרָה וַיּוֹסֶף אַחְאָב לַעֲשׂוֹת לְהַכְעִיס אֶת־יְהוָה אֱלֹהֵי יִשְׂרָאֵל מִכֹּל מַלְכֵי יִשְׂרָאֵל אֲשֶׁר הָיוּ לְפָנָיו:

34During his reign, Hiel the Bethelite fortified Jericho. He laid its foundations at the cost of Abiram his first-born, and set its gates in place at the cost of Segub his youngest, in accordance with the words that the LORD had spoken through Joshua son of Nun.b

17 Elijah the Tishbite, an inhabitant of Gilead, said to Ahab, "As the LORD lives, the God of Israel whom I serve, there will be no dew or rain except at my bidding."

2 The word of the LORD came to him: 3"Leave this place; turn eastward and go into hiding by the Wadi Cherith, which is east of the Jordan. 4You will drink from the wadi, and I have commanded the ravens to feed you there." 5He proceeded to do as the LORD had bidden: he went, and he stayed by the Wadi Cherith, which is east of the Jordan. 6The ravens brought him bread and meat every morning and every evening, and he drank from the wadi.

7After some time the wadi dried up, because there was no rain in the land. 8And the word of the LORD came to him: 9"Go at once to Zarephath of Sidon, and stay there; I have designated a widow there to feed you." 10So he went at once to Zarephath. When he came to the entrance of the town, a widow was there gathering wood. He called out to her, "Please bring me a little water in your pitcher, and let me drink." 11As she went to fetch it, he called out to her, "Please bring along a piece of bread for me." 12"As the LORD your God lives," she replied, "I have nothing baked, nothing but a handful of flour in a jar and a little oil in a jug. I am just gathering a couple of sticks, so that I can go home and prepare it for me and my son; we shall eat it and then we shall die." 13"Don't be afraid," said Elijah to her. "Go and do as you have said;

b Cf. Josh. 6.26.

34 בְּיָמָ֞יו בָּנָ֥ה חִיאֵ֛ל בֵּ֥ית הָאֱלִ֖י אֶת־יְרִיחֹ֑ה בַּאֲבִירָ֤ם בְּכֹרוֹ֙ יִסְּדָ֔הּ וּבִשְׂג֤וּב צְעִירוֹ֙ הִצִּ֣יב דְּלָתֶ֔יהָ כִּדְבַ֣ר יְהֹוָ֔ה אֲשֶׁ֣ר דִּבֶּ֔ר בְּיַ֖ד יְהוֹשֻׁ֥עַ בִּן־נֽוּן׃ ס

יז וַיֹּאמֶר֩ אֵלִיָּ֨הוּ הַתִּשְׁבִּ֜י מִתֹּשָׁבֵ֣י גִלְעָד֮ אֶל־אַחְאָב֒ חַי־יְהֹוָ֞ה אֱלֹהֵ֤י יִשְׂרָאֵל֙ אֲשֶׁ֣ר עָמַ֣דְתִּי לְפָנָ֔יו אִם־יִהְיֶ֛ה הַשָּׁנִ֥ים הָאֵ֖לֶּה טַ֣ל וּמָטָ֑ר כִּ֖י אִם־לְפִ֥י דְבָרִֽי׃ ס 2 וַיְהִ֥י דְבַר־יְהֹוָ֖ה אֵלָ֥יו לֵאמֹֽר׃ 3 לֵ֣ךְ מִזֶּ֔ה וּפָנִ֥יתָ לְּךָ֖ קֵ֑דְמָה וְנִסְתַּרְתָּ֙ בְּנַ֣חַל כְּרִ֔ית אֲשֶׁ֖ר עַל־פְּנֵ֥י הַיַּרְדֵּֽן׃ 4 וְהָיָ֛ה מֵהַנַּ֥חַל תִּשְׁתֶּ֑ה וְאֶת־הָעֹרְבִ֣ים צִוִּ֔יתִי לְכַלְכֶּלְךָ֖ שָֽׁם׃ 5 וַיֵּ֙לֶךְ֙ וַיַּ֣עַשׂ כִּדְבַ֣ר יְהֹוָ֔ה וַיֵּ֗לֶךְ וַיֵּ֙שֶׁב֙ בְּנַ֣חַל כְּרִ֔ית אֲשֶׁ֖ר עַל־פְּנֵ֥י הַיַּרְדֵּֽן׃ 6 וְהָעֹרְבִ֗ים מְבִיאִ֥ים לוֹ֙ לֶ֣חֶם וּבָשָׂ֣ר בַּבֹּ֔קֶר וְלֶ֥חֶם וּבָשָׂ֖ר בָּעָ֑רֶב וּמִן־הַנַּ֖חַל יִשְׁתֶּֽה׃ 7 וַיְהִ֛י מִקֵּ֥ץ יָמִ֖ים וַיִּיבַ֣שׁ הַנָּ֑חַל כִּ֛י לֹא־הָיָ֥ה גֶ֖שֶׁם בָּאָֽרֶץ׃ ס 8 וַיְהִ֥י דְבַר־יְהֹוָ֖ה אֵלָ֥יו לֵאמֹֽר׃ 9 ק֞וּם לֵ֤ךְ צָרְפַ֙תָה֙ אֲשֶׁ֣ר לְצִיד֔וֹן וְיָשַׁבְתָּ֖ שָׁ֑ם הִנֵּ֨ה צִוִּ֥יתִי שָׁ֛ם אִשָּׁ֥ה אַלְמָנָ֖ה לְכַלְכְּלֶֽךָ׃ 10 וַיָּ֣קׇם ׀ וַיֵּ֣לֶךְ צָרְפַ֗תָה וַיָּבֹא֙ אֶל־פֶּ֣תַח הָעִ֔יר וְהִנֵּֽה־שָׁ֛ם אִשָּׁ֥ה אַלְמָנָ֖ה מְקֹשֶׁ֣שֶׁת עֵצִ֑ים וַיִּקְרָ֤א אֵלֶ֙יהָ֙ וַיֹּאמַ֔ר קְחִי־נָ֨א לִ֧י מְעַט־מַ֛יִם בַּכְּלִ֖י וְאֶשְׁתֶּֽה׃ 11 וַתֵּ֖לֶךְ לָקַ֑חַת וַיִּקְרָ֤א אֵלֶ֙יהָ֙ וַיֹּאמַ֔ר לִֽקְחִי־נָ֥א לִ֛י פַּת־לֶ֖חֶם בְּיָדֵֽךְ׃ 12 וַתֹּ֗אמֶר חַי־יְהֹוָ֤ה אֱלֹהֶ֙יךָ֙ אִם־יֶשׁ־לִ֣י מָע֔וֹג כִּ֣י אִם־מְלֹ֤א כַף־קֶ֙מַח֙ בַּכַּ֔ד וּמְעַט־שֶׁ֖מֶן בַּצַּפָּ֑חַת וְהִנְנִ֨י מְקֹשֶׁ֜שֶׁת שְׁנַ֣יִם עֵצִ֗ים וּבָ֙אתִי֙ וַעֲשִׂיתִ֙יהוּ֙ לִ֣י וְלִבְנִ֔י וַאֲכַלְנֻ֖הוּ וָמָֽתְנוּ׃ 13 וַיֹּ֨אמֶר אֵלֶ֤יהָ אֵלִיָּ֙הוּ֙ אַל־תִּ֣ירְאִ֔י בֹּ֖אִי עֲשִׂ֣י כִדְבָרֵ֑ךְ אַ֣ךְ עֲשִׂי־לִ֣י מִשָּׁ֞ם עֻגָ֣ה

756

but first make me a small cake from what you have there, and bring it out to me; then make some for yourself and your son. ¹⁴For thus said the LORD, the God of Israel: The jar of flour shall not give out and the jug of oil shall not fail until the day that the LORD sends rain upon the ground." ¹⁵She went and did as Elijah had spoken, and she and he and her household had food for a long time. ¹⁶The jar of flour did not give out, nor did the jug of oil fail, just as the LORD had spoken through Elijah.

¹⁷After a while, the son of the mistress of the house fell sick, and his illness grew worse, until he had no breath left in him. ¹⁸She said to Elijah, "What harm have I done you, O man of God, that you should come here to recall my sin and cause the death of my son?" ¹⁹"Give me the boy," he said to her; and taking him from her arms, he carried him to the upper chamber where he was staying, and laid him down on his own bed. ²⁰He cried out to the LORD and said, "O LORD my God, will You bring calamity upon this widow whose guest I am, and let her son die?" ²¹Then he stretched out over the child three times, and cried out to the LORD, saying, "O LORD my God, let this child's life return to his body!" ²²The LORD heard Elijah's plea; the child's life returned to his body, and he revived. ²³Elijah picked up the child and brought him down from the upper room into the main room, and gave him to his mother. "See," said Elijah, "your son is alive." ²⁴And the woman answered Elijah, "Now I know that you are a man of God and that the word of the LORD is truly in your mouth."

18 Much later, in the third year,ᵃ the word of the LORD came to Elijah: "Go, appear before Ahab; then I will send rain upon the earth."

ᵃ   I.e., of the drought; see 17.1.

קְטַנָּה בָרִאשֹׁנָה וְהוֹצֵאתְ לִי וְלָךְ וְלִבְנֵךְ תַּעֲשִׂי בָּאַחֲרֹנָה: ס 14 כִּי כֹה אָמַר יְהוָה אֱלֹהֵי יִשְׂרָאֵל כַּד הַקֶּמַח לֹא תִכְלָה וְצַפַּחַת הַשֶּׁמֶן לֹא תֶחְסָר עַד יוֹם תֵּת־יְהוָה גֶּשֶׁם עַל־פְּנֵי הָאֲדָמָה: 15 וַתֵּלֶךְ וַתַּעֲשֶׂה כִּדְבַר אֵלִיָּהוּ וַתֹּאכַל הוא־הִיא וָהִיא וְהוּא וּבֵיתָהּ יָמִים: 16 כַּד הַקֶּמַח לֹא כָלָתָה וְצַפַּחַת הַשֶּׁמֶן לֹא חָסֵר כִּדְבַר יְהוָה אֲשֶׁר דִּבֶּר בְּיַד אֵלִיָּהוּ: פ

17 וַיְהִי אַחַר הַדְּבָרִים הָאֵלֶּה חָלָה בֶּן־הָאִשָּׁה בַּעֲלַת הַבָּיִת וַיְהִי חָלְיוֹ חָזָק מְאֹד עַד אֲשֶׁר לֹא־נוֹתְרָה־בּוֹ נְשָׁמָה: 18 וַתֹּאמֶר אֶל־אֵלִיָּהוּ מַה־לִּי וָלָךְ אִישׁ הָאֱלֹהִים בָּאתָ אֵלַי לְהַזְכִּיר אֶת־עֲוֺנִי וּלְהָמִית אֶת־בְּנִי: 19 וַיֹּאמֶר אֵלֶיהָ תְּנִי־לִי אֶת־בְּנֵךְ וַיִּקָּחֵהוּ מֵחֵיקָהּ וַיַּעֲלֵהוּ אֶל־הָעֲלִיָּה אֲשֶׁר־הוּא יֹשֵׁב שָׁם וַיַּשְׁכִּבֵהוּ עַל־מִטָּתוֹ: 20 וַיִּקְרָא אֶל־יְהוָה וַיֹּאמַר יְהוָה אֱלֹהָי הֲגַם עַל־הָאַלְמָנָה אֲשֶׁר־אֲנִי מִתְגּוֹרֵר עִמָּהּ הֲרֵעוֹתָ לְהָמִית אֶת־בְּנָהּ: 21 וַיִּתְמֹדֵד עַל־הַיֶּלֶד שָׁלֹשׁ פְּעָמִים וַיִּקְרָא אֶל־יְהוָה וַיֹּאמַר יְהוָה אֱלֹהָי תָּשָׁב נָא נֶפֶשׁ־הַיֶּלֶד הַזֶּה עַל־קִרְבּוֹ: 22 וַיִּשְׁמַע יְהוָה בְּקוֹל אֵלִיָּהוּ וַתָּשָׁב נֶפֶשׁ־הַיֶּלֶד עַל־קִרְבּוֹ וַיֶּחִי: 23 וַיִּקַּח אֵלִיָּהוּ אֶת־הַיֶּלֶד וַיֹּרִדֵהוּ מִן־הָעֲלִיָּה הַבַּיְתָה וַיִּתְּנֵהוּ לְאִמּוֹ וַיֹּאמֶר אֵלִיָּהוּ רְאִי חַי בְּנֵךְ: 24 וַתֹּאמֶר הָאִשָּׁה אֶל־אֵלִיָּהוּ זֶה עַתָּה יָדַעְתִּי כִּי אִישׁ אֱלֹהִים אָתָּה וּדְבַר־יְהוָה בְּפִיךָ אֱמֶת: פ

יח וַיְהִי יָמִים רַבִּים וּדְבַר־יְהוָה הָיָה אֶל־אֵלִיָּהוּ בַּשָּׁנָה הַשְּׁלִישִׁית לֵאמֹר לֵךְ הֵרָאֵה אֶל־אַחְאָב וְאֶתְּנָה מָטָר עַל־פְּנֵי

2Thereupon Elijah set out to appear before Ahab.

The famine was severe in Samaria. 3Ahab had summoned Obadiah, the steward of the palace. (Obadiah revered the LORD greatly. 4When Jezebel was killing off the prophets of the LORD, Obadiah had taken a hundred prophets and hidden them, fifty to a cave, and provided them with food and drink.) 5And Ahab had said to Obadiah, "Go through the land, to all the springs of water and to all the wadis. Perhaps we shall find some grass to keep horses and mules alive, so that we are not left without beasts."

6They divided the country between them to explore it, Ahab going alone in one direction and Obadiah going alone in another direction. 7Obadiah was on the road, when Elijah suddenly confronted him. [Obadiah] recognized him and flung himself on his face, saying, "Is that you, my lord Elijah?" 8"Yes, it is I," he answered. "Go tell your lord: Elijah is here!" 9But he said, "What wrong have I done, that you should hand your servant over to Ahab to be killed? 10As the LORD your God lives, there is no nation or kingdom to which my lord has not sent to look for you; and when they said, 'He is not here,' he made that kingdom or nation swear that you could not be found. 11And now you say, 'Go tell your lord: Elijah is here!' 12When I leave you, the spirit of the LORD will carry you off I don't know where; and when I come and tell Ahab and he does not find you, he will kill me. Yet your servant has revered the LORD from my youth. 13My lord has surely been told what I did when Jezebel was killing the prophets of the LORD, how I hid a hundred of the prophets of the LORD, fifty men to a cave, and provided them with food and drink. 14And now you say, 'Go tell your lord: Elijah is here.' Why, he will kill me!"

הָאֲדָמָֽה׃ 2וַיֵּ֙לֶךְ֙ אֵ֣לִיָּ֔הוּ לְהֵרָא֖וֹת אֶל־
אַחְאָ֑ב
וְהָרָעָ֖ב חָזָ֥ק בְּשֹׁמְרֽוֹן׃ 3וַיִּקְרָ֤א אַחְאָב֙
אֶל־עֹבַדְיָ֔הוּ אֲשֶׁ֖ר עַל־הַבָּ֑יִת וְעֹבַדְיָ֗הוּ
הָיָ֥ה יָרֵ֛א אֶת־יְהֹוָ֖ה מְאֹֽד׃ 4וַיְהִי֙ בְּהַכְרִ֣ית
אִיזֶ֔בֶל אֵ֖ת נְבִיאֵ֣י יְהֹוָ֑ה וַיִּקַּ֨ח עֹבַדְיָ֜הוּ
מֵאָ֣ה נְבִאִ֗ים וַֽיַּחְבִּיאֵ֞ם חֲמִשִּׁ֥ים אִישׁ֙
בַּמְּעָרָ֔ה וְכִלְכְּלָ֖ם לֶ֥חֶם וָמָֽיִם׃ 5וַיֹּ֤אמֶר
אַחְאָב֙ אֶל־עֹ֣בַדְיָ֔הוּ לֵ֥ךְ בָּאָ֖רֶץ אֶל־כׇּל־
מַעְיְנֵ֣י הַמַּ֗יִם וְאֶ֖ל כׇּל־הַנְּחָלִ֑ים אוּלַ֣י ׀
נִמְצָ֣א חָצִ֗יר וּנְחַיֶּה֙ ס֣וּס וָפֶ֔רֶד וְל֥וֹא נַכְרִ֖ית
מֵהַבְּהֵמָֽה׃
6וַֽיְחַלְּק֥וּ לָהֶ֛ם אֶת־הָאָ֖רֶץ לַֽעֲבׇר־בָּ֑הּ
אַחְאָ֞ב הָלַ֨ךְ בְּדֶ֤רֶךְ אֶחָד֙ לְבַדּ֔וֹ וְעֹבַדְיָ֗הוּ
הָלַ֛ךְ בְּדֶֽרֶךְ־אֶחָ֖ד לְבַדּֽוֹ׃ 7וַיְהִ֤י עֹבַדְיָ֙הוּ֙
בַּדֶּ֔רֶךְ וְהִנֵּ֥ה אֵלִיָּ֖הוּ לִקְרָאת֑וֹ וַיַּכִּרֵ֙הוּ֙ וַיִּפֹּ֣ל
עַל־פָּנָ֔יו וַיֹּ֕אמֶר הַֽאַתָּ֥ה זֶ֖ה אֲדֹנִ֥י אֵלִיָּֽהוּ׃
8וַיֹּ֣אמֶר ל֖וֹ אָ֑נִי לֵ֛ךְ אֱמֹ֥ר לַאדֹנֶ֖יךָ הִנֵּ֥ה
אֵלִיָּֽהוּ׃ 9וַיֹּ֖אמֶר מֶ֣ה חָטָ֑אתִי כִּֽי־אַתָּ֞ה
נֹתֵ֧ן אֶֽת־עַבְדְּךָ֛ בְּיַד־אַחְאָ֖ב לַהֲמִיתֵֽנִי׃
10חַ֣י ׀ יְהֹוָ֣ה אֱלֹהֶ֗יךָ אִם־יֶשׁ־גּ֤וֹי וּמַמְלָכָה֙
אֲשֶׁ֨ר לֹא־שָׁלַ֜ח אֲדֹנִ֥י שָׁם֙ לְבַקֶּשְׁךָ֔ וְאָמְר֖וּ
אָ֑יִן וְהִשְׁבִּ֤יעַ אֶת־הַמַּמְלָכָה֙ וְאֶת־הַגּ֔וֹי כִּ֖י
לֹ֥א יִמְצָאֶֽכָּה*׃ 11וְעַתָּ֖ה אַתָּ֣ה אֹמֵ֑ר לֵ֛ךְ
אֱמֹ֥ר לַֽאדֹנֶ֖יךָ הִנֵּ֥ה אֵלִיָּֽהוּ׃ 12וְהָיָ֞ה אֲנִ֣י ׀
אֵלֵ֣ךְ מֵֽאִתָּ֗ךְ וְר֣וּחַ יְהֹוָ֣ה ׀ יִֽשָּׂאֲךָ֮ עַ֣ל אֲשֶׁ֣ר
לֹֽא־אֵדָע֒ וּבָ֤אתִי לְהַגִּ֣יד לְאַחְאָ֔ב וְלֹ֥א
יִמְצָֽאֲךָ֖ וַהֲרָגָ֑נִי וְעַבְדְּךָ֛ יָרֵ֥א אֶת־יְהֹוָ֖ה
מִנְּעֻרָֽי׃ 13הֲלֹֽא־הֻגַּ֣ד לַֽאדֹנִ֔י אֵ֖ת אֲשֶׁר־
עָשִׂ֑יתִי בַּהֲרֹ֣ג אִיזֶ֗בֶל אֵ֚ת נְבִיאֵ֣י יְהֹוָ֔ה
וָאַחְבִּא֩ מִנְּבִיאֵ֨י יְהֹוָ֜ה מֵאָ֣ה אִ֗ישׁ חֲמִשִּׁ֨ים
חֲמִשִּׁ֥ים אִישׁ֙ בַּמְּעָרָ֔ה וָאֲכַלְכְּלֵ֖ם לֶ֥חֶם
וָמָֽיִם׃ 14וְעַתָּה֙ אַתָּ֣ה אֹמֵ֔ר לֵ֛ךְ אֱמֹ֥ר
לַֽאדֹנֶ֖יךָ הִנֵּ֣ה אֵלִיָּ֑הוּ וַהֲרָגָֽנִי׃ ס

758

[15]Elijah replied, "As the LORD of Hosts lives, whom I serve, I will appear before him this very day."

[16]Obadiah went to find Ahab, and informed him; and Ahab went to meet Elijah. [17]When Ahab caught sight of Elijah, Ahab said to him, "Is that you, you troubler of Israel?" [18]He retorted, "It is not I who have brought trouble on Israel, but you and your father's House, by forsaking the commandments of the LORD and going after the Baalim. [19]Now summon all Israel to join me at Mount Carmel, together with the four hundred and fifty prophets of Baal and the four hundred prophets of Asherah, b-who eat at Jezebel's table."-b

[20]Ahab sent orders to all the Israelites and gathered the prophets at Mount Carmel. [21]Elijah approached all the people and said, "How long will you keep hopping c-between two opinions?-c If the LORD is God, follow Him; and if Baal, follow him!" But the people answered him not a word. [22]Then Elijah said to the people, "I am the only prophet of the LORD left, while the prophets of Baal are four hundred and fifty men. [23]Let two young bulls be given to us. Let them choose one bull, cut it up, and lay it on the wood, but let them not apply fire; I will prepare the other bull, and lay it on the wood, and will not apply fire. [24]You will then invoke your god by name, and I will invoke the LORD by name; d-and let us agree:-d the god who responds with fire, that one is God." And all the people answered, "Very good!"

[25]Elijah said to the prophets of Baal, "Choose one bull and prepare it first, for you are the majority; invoke your god by name, but apply no fire." [26]They took the bull that was given them; they prepared it, and invoked Baal by name from morning until noon, shouting, "O Baal,

15 וַיֹּ֙אמֶר֙ אֵ֣לִיָּ֔הוּ חַ֤י יְהֹוָ֣ה צְבָאוֹת֙ אֲשֶׁ֣ר עָמַ֣דְתִּי לְפָנָ֔יו כִּ֥י הַיּ֖וֹם אֵרָאֶ֥ה אֵלָֽיו׃ 16 וַיֵּ֧לֶךְ עֹבַדְיָ֛הוּ לִקְרַ֥את אַחְאָ֖ב וַיַּגֶּד־ל֑וֹ וַיֵּ֥לֶךְ אַחְאָ֖ב לִקְרַ֥את אֵלִיָּֽהוּ׃ 17 וַיְהִ֗י כִּרְא֤וֹת אַחְאָב֙ אֶת־אֵ֣לִיָּ֔הוּ וַיֹּ֤אמֶר אַחְאָב֙ אֵלָ֔יו הַאַתָּ֥ה זֶ֖ה עֹכֵ֥ר יִשְׂרָאֵֽל׃ 18 וַיֹּ֗אמֶר לֹ֤א עָכַ֙רְתִּי֙ אֶת־יִשְׂרָאֵ֔ל כִּ֥י אִם־אַתָּ֖ה וּבֵ֣ית אָבִ֑יךָ בַּֽעֲזׇבְכֶם֙ אֶת־מִצְוֺ֣ת יְהֹוָ֔ה וַתֵּ֖לֶךְ אַחֲרֵ֥י הַבְּעָלִֽים׃ 19 וְעַתָּ֗ה שְׁלַ֣ח קְבֹ֥ץ אֵלַ֛י אֶת־כׇּל־יִשְׂרָאֵ֖ל אֶל־הַ֣ר הַכַּרְמֶ֑ל וְאֶת־נְבִיאֵ֣י הַבַּ֗עַל אַרְבַּ֤ע מֵאוֹת֙ וַחֲמִשִּׁ֔ים וּנְבִיאֵ֤י הָאֲשֵׁרָה֙ אַרְבַּ֣ע מֵא֔וֹת אֹכְלֵ֖י שֻׁלְחַ֥ן אִיזָֽבֶל׃

20 וַיִּשְׁלַ֥ח אַחְאָ֖ב בְּכׇל־בְּנֵ֣י יִשְׂרָאֵ֑ל וַיִּקְבֹּ֥ץ אֶת־הַנְּבִיאִ֖ים אֶל־הַ֥ר הַכַּרְמֶֽל׃ 21 וַיִּגַּ֨שׁ אֵ֣לִיָּ֣הוּ אֶל־כׇּל־הָעָ֗ם וַיֹּ֙אמֶר֙ עַד־מָתַ֞י אַתֶּ֣ם פֹּסְחִים֮ עַל־שְׁתֵּ֣י הַסְּעִפִּים֒ אִם־יְהֹוָ֤ה הָֽאֱלֹהִים֙ לְכ֣וּ אַחֲרָ֔יו וְאִם־הַבַּ֖עַל לְכ֣וּ אַחֲרָ֑יו וְלֹא־עָנ֥וּ הָעָ֛ם אֹת֖וֹ דָּבָֽר׃ 22 וַיֹּ֤אמֶר אֵ֣לִיָּ֙הוּ֙ אֶל־הָעָ֔ם אֲנִ֞י נוֹתַ֧רְתִּי נָבִ֛יא לַיהֹוָ֖ה לְבַדִּ֑י וּנְבִיאֵ֣י הַבַּ֔עַל אַרְבַּע־מֵא֥וֹת וַחֲמִשִּׁ֖ים אִֽישׁ׃ 23 וְיִתְּנוּ־לָ֜נוּ שְׁנַ֣יִם פָּרִ֗ים וְיִבְחֲר֣וּ לָהֶם֩ הַפָּ֨ר הָאֶחָ֜ד וִינַתְּחֻ֗הוּ וְיָשִׂ֙ימוּ֙ עַל־הָ֣עֵצִ֔ים וְאֵ֖שׁ לֹ֣א יָשִׂ֑ימוּ וַאֲנִ֞י אֶֽעֱשֶׂ֣ה ׀ אֶת־הַפָּ֣ר הָאֶחָ֗ד וְנָֽתַתִּי֙ עַל־הָ֣עֵצִ֔ים וְאֵ֖שׁ לֹ֥א אָשִֽׂים׃ 24 וּקְרָאתֶ֞ם בְּשֵׁ֣ם אֱלֹֽהֵיכֶ֗ם וַֽאֲנִי֙ אֶקְרָ֣א בְשֵׁם־יְהֹוָ֔ה וְהָיָ֧ה הָאֱלֹהִ֛ים אֲשֶׁר־יַעֲנֶ֥ה בָאֵ֖שׁ ה֣וּא הָאֱלֹהִ֑ים וַיַּ֧עַן כׇּל־הָעָ֛ם וַיֹּאמְר֖וּ ט֥וֹב הַדָּבָֽר׃ 25 וַיֹּ֙אמֶר אֵלִיָּ֜הוּ לִנְבִיאֵ֣י הַבַּ֗עַל בַּחֲר֨וּ לָכֶ֜ם הַפָּ֤ר הָֽאֶחָד֙ וַעֲשׂ֣וּ רִֽאשֹׁנָ֔ה כִּ֥י אַתֶּ֖ם הָרַבִּ֑ים וְקִרְאוּ֙ בְּשֵׁ֣ם אֱלֹהֵיכֶ֔ם וְאֵ֖שׁ לֹ֥א תָשִֽׂימוּ׃ 26 וַ֠יִּקְח֠וּ אֶת־הַפָּ֨ר אֲשֶׁר־נָתַ֣ן לָהֶם֮ וַֽיַּעֲשׂוּ֒ וַיִּקְרְא֣וּ בְשֵׁם־הַ֠בַּ֠עַל מֵהַבֹּ֙קֶר֙

---

b-b   *I.e., who are maintained by Jezebel.*
c-c   *Lit. "on the two boughs."*
d-d   *Lit. "and it shall be."*

answer us!" But there was no sound, and none who responded; so they performed a hopping dance about the altar that had been set up. 27When noon came, Elijah mocked them, saying, "Shout louder! After all, he is a god. *e-But he may be in conversation, he may be detained, or he may be on a journey,-e* or perhaps he is asleep and will wake up." 28So they shouted louder, and gashed themselves with knives and spears, according to their practice, until the blood streamed over them. 29When noon passed, they *f-kept raving-f* until the hour of presenting the meal offering. Still there was no sound, and none who responded or heeded.

30Then Elijah said to all the people, "Come closer to me"; and all the people came closer to him. He repaired the damaged altar of the LORD. 31Then Elijah took twelve stones, corresponding to the number of the tribes of the sons of Jacob—to whom the word of the LORD had come: "Israel shall be your name"*g*—32and with the stones he built an altar in the name of the LORD. Around the altar he made a trench large enough for two *seahs* of seed.*h* 33He laid out the wood, and he cut up the bull and laid it on the wood. 34And he said, "Fill four jars with water and pour it over the burnt offering and the wood." Then he said, "Do it a second time"; and they did it a second time. "Do it a third time," he said; and they did it a third time. 35The water ran down around the altar, and even the trench was filled with water.

36When it was time to present the meal offering, the prophet Elijah came forward and said, "O LORD, God of Abraham, Isaac, and Israel! Let it be known today that You are God in Israel and that I am Your servant, and that I have done all these things at Your bidding. 37Answer me, O LORD, answer me, that this peo-

וְעַד־הַצָּהֳרַיִם לֵאמֹר הַבַּעַל עֲנֵנוּ וְאֵין קוֹל וְאֵין עֹנֶה וַיְפַסְּחוּ עַל־הַמִּזְבֵּחַ אֲשֶׁר עָשָׂה: 27 וַיְהִי בַצָּהֳרַיִם וַיְהַתֵּל בָּהֶם אֵלִיָּהוּ וַיֹּאמֶר קִרְאוּ בְקוֹל־גָּדוֹל כִּי־אֱלֹהִים הוּא כִּי שִׂיחַ וְכִי־שִׂיג לוֹ וְכִי־דֶרֶךְ לוֹ אוּלַי יָשֵׁן הוּא וְיִקָץ*: 28 וַיִּקְרְאוּ בְּקוֹל גָּדוֹל וַיִּתְגֹּדְדוּ כְּמִשְׁפָּטָם בַּחֲרָבוֹת וּבָרְמָחִים עַד־שְׁפָךְ־דָּם עֲלֵיהֶם: 29 וַיְהִי כַּעֲבֹר הַצָּהֳרַיִם וַיִּתְנַבְּאוּ עַד לַעֲלוֹת הַמִּנְחָה וְאֵין־קוֹל וְאֵין־עֹנֶה וְאֵין קָשֶׁב: 30 וַיֹּאמֶר אֵלִיָּהוּ לְכָל־הָעָם גְּשׁוּ אֵלַי וַיִּגְּשׁוּ כָל־הָעָם אֵלָיו וַיְרַפֵּא אֶת־מִזְבַּח יְהוָה הֶהָרוּס: 31 וַיִּקַּח אֵלִיָּהוּ שְׁתֵּים עֶשְׂרֵה אֲבָנִים כְּמִסְפַּר שִׁבְטֵי בְנֵי־יַעֲקֹב אֲשֶׁר הָיָה דְבַר־יְהוָה אֵלָיו לֵאמֹר יִשְׂרָאֵל יִהְיֶה שְׁמֶךָ: 32 וַיִּבְנֶה אֶת־הָאֲבָנִים מִזְבֵּחַ בְּשֵׁם יְהוָה וַיַּעַשׂ תְּעָלָה כְּבֵית סָאתַיִם זֶרַע סָבִיב לַמִּזְבֵּחַ: 33 וַיַּעֲרֹךְ אֶת־הָעֵצִים וַיְנַתַּח אֶת־הַפָּר וַיָּשֶׂם עַל־הָעֵצִים: 34 וַיֹּאמֶר מִלְאוּ אַרְבָּעָה כַדִּים מַיִם וְיִצְקוּ עַל־הָעֹלָה וְעַל־הָעֵצִים וַיֹּאמֶר שְׁנוּ וַיִּשְׁנוּ וַיֹּאמֶר שַׁלֵּשׁוּ וַיְשַׁלֵּשׁוּ: 35 וַיֵּלְכוּ הַמַּיִם סָבִיב לַמִּזְבֵּחַ וְגַם אֶת־הַתְּעָלָה מִלֵּא־מָיִם: 36 וַיְהִי ׀ בַּעֲלוֹת הַמִּנְחָה וַיִּגַּשׁ אֵלִיָּהוּ הַנָּבִיא וַיֹּאמַר יְהוָה אֱלֹהֵי אַבְרָהָם יִצְחָק וְיִשְׂרָאֵל הַיּוֹם יִוָּדַע כִּי־אַתָּה אֱלֹהִים בְּיִשְׂרָאֵל וַאֲנִי עַבְדֶּךָ וּבִדְבָרְךָ עָשִׂיתִי אֵת כָּל־הַדְּבָרִים הָאֵלֶּה: 37 עֲנֵנִי

---

e-e *Meaning of Heb. uncertain.*
f-f *Others "prophesied"; see Num. 11.25–26.*
g *See Gen. 35.10.*
h *I.e., of an area which would require two seahs of seed if sown. Cf. Lev. 27.16; Isa. 5.10.*

ple may know that You, O LORD, are God; e-for You have turned their hearts backward."-e

38Then fire from the LORD descended and consumed the burnt offering, the wood, the stones, and the earth; and it licked up the water that was in the trench. 39When they saw this, all the people flung themselves on their faces and cried out: "The LORD alone is God, The LORD alone is God!"

40Then Elijah said to them, "Seize the prophets of Baal, let not a single one of them get away." They seized them, and Elijah took them down to the Wadi Kishon and slaughtered them there.

41Elijah said to Ahab, "Go up, eat and drink, for there is a rumbling of [approaching] rain," 42and Ahab went up to eat and drink. Elijah meanwhile climbed to the top of Mount Carmel, crouched on the ground, and put his face between his knees. 43And he said to his servant, "Go up and look toward the Sea." He went up and looked and reported, "There is nothing." Seven times [Elijah] said, "Go back," 44and the seventh time, [the servant] reported, "A cloud as small as a man's hand is rising in the west." Then [Elijah] said, "Go say to Ahab, 'Hitch up [your chariot] and go down before the rain stops you.'" 45Meanwhile the sky grew black with clouds; there was wind, and a heavy downpour fell; Ahab mounted his chariot and drove off to Jezreel. 46The hand of the LORD had come upon Elijah. i-He tied up his skirts-i and ran in front of Ahab all the way to Jezreel.

19 When Ahab told Jezebel all that Elijah had done and how he had put all the prophetsa to the sword, 2Jezebel sent a messenger to Elijah, saying, b-"Thus and more may the gods do-b if

---

i-i Lit. "He bound up his loins."

a Of Baal; see 18.40.
b-b A formula of imprecation. Many Heb. mss. and Septuagint
    add "to me."

יְהֹוָה֙ עֲנֵ֔נִי וְיֵ֣דְעוּ הָעָ֥ם הַזֶּ֖ה כִּֽי־אַתָּ֥ה יְהֹוָ֖ה הָאֱלֹהִ֑ים וְאַתָּ֛ה הֲסִבֹּ֥תָ אֶת־לִבָּ֖ם אֲחֹרַנִּֽית׃

38 וַתִּפֹּ֣ל אֵשׁ־יְהֹוָ֗ה וַתֹּ֤אכַל אֶת־הָֽעֹלָה֙ וְאֶת־הָ֣עֵצִ֔ים וְאֶת־הָֽאֲבָנִ֖ים וְאֶת־הֶֽעָפָ֑ר וְאֶת־הַמַּ֥יִם אֲשֶׁר־בַּתְּעָלָ֖ה לִחֵֽכָה׃ 39 וַיַּרְא֙ כׇּל־הָעָ֔ם וַֽיִּפְּל֖וּ עַל־פְּנֵיהֶ֑ם וַיֹּ֣אמְר֔וּ יְהֹוָה֙ ה֣וּא הָאֱלֹהִ֔ים יְהֹוָ֖ה ה֥וּא הָאֱלֹהִֽים׃

40 וַיֹּ֩אמֶר֩ אֵלִיָּ֨הוּ לָהֶ֜ם תִּפְשׂ֣וּ ׀ אֶת־נְבִיאֵ֣י הַבַּ֗עַל אִ֛ישׁ אַל־יִמָּלֵ֥ט מֵהֶ֖ם וַֽיִּתְפְּשׂ֑וּם וַיּוֹרִדֵ֤ם אֵלִיָּ֙הוּ֙ אֶל־נַ֣חַל קִישׁ֔וֹן וַיִּשְׁחָטֵ֖ם שָֽׁם׃

41 וַיֹּ֤אמֶר אֵלִיָּ֙הוּ֙ לְאַחְאָ֔ב עֲלֵ֖ה אֱכֹ֣ל וּשְׁתֵ֑ה כִּי־ק֖וֹל הֲמ֥וֹן הַגָּֽשֶׁם׃ 42 וַיַּעֲלֶ֥ה אַחְאָ֖ב לֶאֱכֹ֣ל וְלִשְׁתּ֑וֹת וְאֵ֨לִיָּ֜הוּ עָלָ֨ה אֶל־רֹ֤אשׁ הַכַּרְמֶל֙ וַיִּגְהַ֣ר אַ֔רְצָה וַיָּ֥שֶׂם פָּנָ֖יו בֵּ֥ין בִּרְכָּֽו׃ 43 וַיֹּ֣אמֶר אֶֽל־נַעֲר֗וֹ עֲלֵֽה־נָ֣א הַבֵּ֤ט דֶּֽרֶךְ־יָ֔ם וַיַּ֙עַל֙ וַיַּבֵּ֔ט וַיֹּ֖אמֶר אֵ֣ין מְא֑וּמָה וַיֹּ֕אמֶר שֻׁ֖ב שֶׁ֥בַע פְּעָמִֽים׃ 44 וַֽיְהִי֙ בַּשְּׁבִעִ֔ית וַיֹּ֕אמֶר הִנֵּה־עָ֛ב קְטַנָּ֥ה כְּכַף־אִ֖ישׁ עֹלָ֣ה מִיָּ֑ם וַיֹּ֗אמֶר עֲלֵ֞ה אֱמֹ֤ר אֶל־אַחְאָב֙ אֱסֹ֣ר וָרֵ֔ד וְלֹ֥א יַעַצׇרְכָ֖ה* הַגָּֽשֶׁם׃ 45 וַֽיְהִ֣י ׀ עַד־כֹּ֣ה וְעַד־כֹּ֗ה וְהַשָּׁמַ֙יִם֙ הִֽתְקַדְּרוּ֙ עָבִ֣ים וְר֔וּחַ וַיְהִ֖י גֶּ֣שֶׁם גָּד֑וֹל וַיִּרְכַּ֥ב אַחְאָ֖ב וַיֵּ֥לֶךְ יִזְרְעֶֽאלָה׃ 46 וְיַד־יְהֹוָ֗ה הָֽיְתָה֙ אֶל־אֵ֣לִיָּ֔הוּ וַיְשַׁנֵּ֖ס מׇתְנָ֑יו וַיָּ֙רׇץ֙ לִפְנֵ֣י אַחְאָ֔ב עַד־בֹּאֲכָ֖ה יִזְרְעֶֽאלָה׃

יט וַיַּגֵּ֤ד אַחְאָב֙ לְאִיזֶ֔בֶל אֵ֛ת כׇּל־אֲשֶׁ֥ר עָשָׂ֖ה אֵלִיָּ֑הוּ וְאֵ֨ת כׇּל־אֲשֶׁ֥ר הָרַ֛ג אֶת־כׇּל־הַנְּבִיאִ֖ים בֶּחָֽרֶב׃ 2 וַתִּשְׁלַ֤ח אִיזֶ֙בֶל֙ מַלְאָ֔ךְ אֶל־אֵלִיָּ֖הוּ לֵאמֹ֑ר כֹּֽה־יַעֲשׂ֤וּן אֱלֹהִים֙ וְכֹ֣ה

by this time tomorrow I have not made you like one of them."

³Frightened,ᶜ he fled at once for his life. He came to Beer-sheba, which is in Judah, and left his servant there; ⁴he himself went a day's journey into the wilderness. He came to a broom bush and sat down under it, and prayed that he might die. "Enough!" he cried. "Now, O LORD, take my life, for I am no better than my fathers."

⁵He lay down and fell asleep under a broom bush. Suddenly an angel touched him and said to him, "Arise and eat." ⁶He looked about; and there, beside his head, was a cake baked on hot stones and a jar of water! He ate and drank, and lay down again. ⁷The angel of the LORD came a second time and touched him and said, "Arise and eat, or the journey will be too much for you." ⁸He arose and ate and drank; and with the strength from that meal he walked forty days and forty nights as far as the mountain of God at Horeb. ⁹There he went into a cave, and there he spent the night.

Then the word of the LORD came to him. He said to him, "Why are you here, Elijah?" ¹⁰He replied, "I am moved by zeal for the LORD, the God of Hosts, for the Israelites have forsaken Your covenant, torn down Your altars, and put Your prophets to the sword. I alone am left, and they are out to take my life." ¹¹"Come out," He called, "and stand on the mountain before the LORD."

And lo, the LORD passed by. There was a great and mighty wind, splitting mountains and shattering rocks by the power of the LORD; but the LORD was not in the wind. After the wind—an earthquake; but the LORD was not in the earthquake. ¹²After the earthquake—fire; but the LORD was not in the fire. And after the fire—a soft murmuring sound.ᵈ ¹³When Elijah heard

יוֹסִפ֑וּן כִּי־כָעֵ֤ת מָחָר֙ אָשִׂ֣ים אֶֽת־נַפְשְׁךָ֔ כְּנֶ֖פֶשׁ אַחַ֥ד מֵהֶֽם׃

3 וַיַּרְא֙* וַיָּ֣קָם וַיֵּ֣לֶךְ אֶל־נַפְשׁ֔וֹ וַיָּבֹ֖א בְּאֵ֣ר שֶׁ֑בַע אֲשֶׁ֣ר לִֽיהוּדָ֔ה וַיַּנַּ֥ח אֶֽת־נַעֲר֖וֹ שָֽׁם׃ 4 וְהֽוּא־הָלַ֤ךְ בַּמִּדְבָּר֙ דֶּ֣רֶךְ י֔וֹם וַיָּבֹ֕א וַיֵּ֕שֶׁב תַּ֥חַת רֹ֖תֶם אֶחָ֑ת וַיִּשְׁאַ֤ל אֶת־נַפְשׁוֹ֙ לָמ֔וּת וַיֹּ֣אמֶר ׀ רַ֗ב עַתָּ֤ה יְהוָה֙ קַ֣ח נַפְשִׁ֔י כִּֽי־לֹא־ט֥וֹב אָנֹכִ֖י מֵֽאֲבֹתָֽי׃ 5 וַיִּשְׁכַּב֙ וַיִּישַׁ֔ן תַּ֖חַת רֹ֣תֶם אֶחָ֑ד וְהִנֵּֽה־זֶ֤ה מַלְאָךְ֙ נֹגֵ֣עַ בּ֔וֹ וַיֹּ֥אמֶר ל֖וֹ ק֥וּם אֱכֽוֹל׃ 6 וַיַּבֵּ֕ט וְהִנֵּ֤ה מְרַֽאֲשֹׁתָיו֙ עֻגַ֣ת רְצָפִ֔ים וְצַפַּ֣חַת מָ֑יִם וַיֹּ֣אכַל וַיֵּ֔שְׁתְּ וַיָּ֖שָׁב וַיִּשְׁכָּֽב׃ 7 וַיָּ֩שָׁב֩ מַלְאַ֨ךְ יְהוָ֤ה ׀ שֵׁנִית֙ וַיִּגַּע־בּ֔וֹ וַיֹּ֖אמֶר ק֣וּם אֱכֹ֑ל כִּ֛י רַ֥ב מִמְּךָ֖ הַדָּֽרֶךְ׃ 8 וַיָּ֖קָם וַיֹּ֣אכַל וַיִּשְׁתֶּ֑ה וַיֵּ֜לֶךְ בְּכֹ֣חַ ׀ הָאֲכִילָ֣ה הַהִ֗יא אַרְבָּעִ֥ים יוֹם֙ וְאַרְבָּעִ֣ים לַ֔יְלָה עַ֛ד הַ֥ר הָאֱלֹהִ֖ים חֹרֵֽב׃ 9 וַיָּבֹא־שָׁ֥ם אֶל־הַמְּעָרָ֖ה וַיָּ֣לֶן שָׁ֑ם וְהִנֵּ֤ה דְבַר־יְהוָה֙ אֵלָ֔יו וַיֹּ֣אמֶר ל֔וֹ מַה־לְּךָ֥ פֹ֖ה אֵלִיָּֽהוּ׃ 10 וַיֹּאמֶר֩ קַנֹּ֨א קִנֵּ֜אתִי לַיהוָ֣ה ׀ אֱלֹהֵ֣י צְבָא֗וֹת כִּֽי־עָזְב֤וּ בְרִֽיתְךָ֙ בְּנֵ֣י יִשְׂרָאֵ֔ל אֶת־מִזְבְּחֹתֶ֣יךָ הָרָ֔סוּ וְאֶת־נְבִיאֶ֖יךָ הָרְג֣וּ בֶחָ֑רֶב וָאִוָּתֵ֤ר אֲנִי֙ לְבַדִּ֔י וַיְבַקְשׁ֥וּ אֶת־נַפְשִׁ֖י לְקַחְתָּֽהּ׃ 11 וַיֹּ֗אמֶר צֵ֣א וְעָמַדְתָּ֤ בָהָר֙ לִפְנֵ֣י יְהוָ֔ה וְהִנֵּ֧ה יְהוָ֣ה עֹבֵ֗ר וְר֣וּחַ גְּדוֹלָ֡ה וְחָזָ֞ק מְפָרֵק֩ הָרִ֨ים וּמְשַׁבֵּ֤ר סְלָעִים֙ לִפְנֵ֣י יְהוָ֔ה לֹ֥א בָר֖וּחַ יְהוָ֑ה וְאַחַ֤ר הָר֨וּחַ֙ רַ֔עַשׁ לֹ֥א בָרַ֖עַשׁ יְהוָֽה׃ 12 וְאַחַ֤ר הָרַ֨עַשׁ֙ אֵ֔שׁ לֹ֥א בָאֵ֖שׁ יְהוָ֑ה וְאַחַ֣ר הָאֵ֔שׁ ק֖וֹל דְּמָמָ֥ה דַקָּֽה׃ 13 וַיְהִ֣י ׀ כִּשְׁמֹ֣עַ אֵלִיָּ֗הוּ וַיָּ֤לֶט פָּנָיו֙ בְּאַדַּרְתּ֔וֹ וַיֵּצֵא֙

---

c   So many Heb. mss. and Septuagint; most mss., and the editions, read "And he saw, and."

d   Others "a still, small voice."

it, he wrapped his mantle about his face and went out and stood at the entrance of the cave. Then a voice addressed him: "Why are you here, Elijah?" [14]He answered, "I am moved by zeal for the LORD, the God of Hosts; for the Israelites have forsaken Your covenant, torn down Your altars, and have put Your prophets to the sword. I alone am left, and they are out to take my life."

[15]The LORD said to him, "Go back by the way you came, [and] on to the wilderness of Damascus. When you get there, anoint Hazael as king of Aram. [16]Also anoint Jehu son of Nimshi as king of Israel, and anoint Elisha son of Shaphat of Abel-meholah to succeed you as prophet. [17]Whoever escapes the sword of Hazael shall be slain by Jehu, and whoever escapes the sword of Jehu shall be slain by Elisha. [18]I will leave in Israel only seven thousand— every knee that has not knelt to Baal and every mouth that has not kissed him."

[19]He set out from there and came upon Elisha son of Shaphat as he was plowing. There were twelve yoke of oxen ahead of him, and he was with the twelfth. Elijah came over to him and threw his mantle over him. [20]He left the oxen and ran after Elijah, saying: "Let me kiss my father and mother good-by, and I will follow you." And he answered him, "Go back. What have I done to you?"*e* [21]He turned back from him and took the yoke of oxen and slaughtered them; he boiled *f*their meat*f* with the gear*g* of the oxen and gave it to the people, and they ate. Then he arose and followed Elijah and became his attendant.

20

King Ben-hadad of Aram gathered his whole army; thirty-two kings accompanied him with horses and chariots. He advanced against Samaria, laid siege to it, and attacked it. [2]And

וַיַּעֲמֹד פֶּתַח הַמְּעָרָה וְהִנֵּה אֵלָיו קוֹל וַיֹּאמֶר מַה־לְּךָ פֹה אֵלִיָּהוּ: 14 וַיֹּאמֶר קַנֹּא קִנֵּאתִי לַיהוָה ׀ אֱלֹהֵי צְבָאוֹת כִּי־עָזְבוּ בְרִיתְךָ בְּנֵי יִשְׂרָאֵל אֶת־מִזְבְּחֹתֶיךָ הָרָסוּ וְאֶת־נְבִיאֶיךָ הָרְגוּ בֶחָרֶב וָאִוָּתֵר אֲנִי לְבַדִּי וַיְבַקְשׁוּ אֶת־נַפְשִׁי לְקַחְתָּהּ: ס
15 וַיֹּאמֶר יְהוָה אֵלָיו לֵךְ שׁוּב לְדַרְכְּךָ מִדְבַּרָה דַמָּשֶׂק וּבָאתָ וּמָשַׁחְתָּ אֶת־חֲזָאֵל לְמֶלֶךְ עַל־אֲרָם: 16 וְאֵת יֵהוּא בֶן־נִמְשִׁי תִּמְשַׁח לְמֶלֶךְ עַל־יִשְׂרָאֵל וְאֶת־אֱלִישָׁע בֶּן־שָׁפָט מֵאָבֵל מְחוֹלָה תִּמְשַׁח לְנָבִיא תַּחְתֶּיךָ: 17 וְהָיָה הַנִּמְלָט מֵחֶרֶב חֲזָאֵל יָמִית יֵהוּא וְהַנִּמְלָט מֵחֶרֶב יֵהוּא יָמִית אֱלִישָׁע: 18 וְהִשְׁאַרְתִּי בְיִשְׂרָאֵל שִׁבְעַת אֲלָפִים כָּל־הַבִּרְכַּיִם אֲשֶׁר לֹא־כָרְעוּ לַבַּעַל וְכָל־הַפֶּה אֲשֶׁר לֹא־נָשַׁק לוֹ: 19 וַיֵּלֶךְ מִשָּׁם וַיִּמְצָא אֶת־אֱלִישָׁע בֶּן־שָׁפָט וְהוּא חֹרֵשׁ שְׁנֵים־עָשָׂר צְמָדִים לְפָנָיו וְהוּא בִּשְׁנֵים הֶעָשָׂר וַיַּעֲבֹר אֵלִיָּהוּ אֵלָיו וַיַּשְׁלֵךְ אַדַּרְתּוֹ אֵלָיו: 20 וַיַּעֲזֹב אֶת־הַבָּקָר וַיָּרָץ אַחֲרֵי אֵלִיָּהוּ וַיֹּאמֶר אֶשְּׁקָה־נָּא לְאָבִי וּלְאִמִּי וְאֵלְכָה אַחֲרֶיךָ וַיֹּאמֶר לוֹ לֵךְ שׁוּב כִּי מֶה־עָשִׂיתִי לָךְ: 21 וַיָּשָׁב מֵאַחֲרָיו וַיִּקַּח אֶת־צֶמֶד הַבָּקָר וַיִּזְבָּחֵהוּ וּבִכְלִי הַבָּקָר בִּשְּׁלָם הַבָּשָׂר וַיִּתֵּן לָעָם וַיֹּאכֵלוּ וַיָּקָם וַיֵּלֶךְ אַחֲרֵי אֵלִיָּהוּ וַיְשָׁרְתֵהוּ: פ

כ וּבֶן־הֲדַד מֶלֶךְ־אֲרָם קָבַץ אֶת־כָּל־ חֵילוֹ וּשְׁלֹשִׁים וּשְׁנַיִם מֶלֶךְ אִתּוֹ וְסוּס וָרָכֶב וַיַּעַל וַיָּצַר עַל־שֹׁמְרוֹן וַיִּלָּחֶם בָּהּ:

---

e   *I.e., I am not stopping you.*
f-f   *Lit. "them, the flesh."*
g   *I.e., using it as firewood; cf. 2 Sam. 24.22.*

he sent messengers to Ahab inside the city ³to say to him, "Thus said Ben-hadad: Your silver and gold are mine, and your beautiful wives and children are mine." ⁴The king of Israel replied, "As you say, my lord king: I and all I have are yours." ⁵Then the messengers came again and said, "Thus said Ben-hadad: When I sent you the order to give me your silver and gold, and your wives and children, ⁶I meant that tomorrow at this time I will send my servants to you and they will search your house and the houses of your courtiers and seize everything youᵃ prize and take it away."

⁷Then the king of Israel summoned all the elders of the land, and he said, "See for yourselves how that man is bent on evil! For when he demanded my wives and my children, my silver and my gold, I did not refuse him." ⁸All the elders and all the people said, "Do not obey and do not submit!" ⁹So he said to Ben-hadad's messengers, "Tell my lord the king: All that you first demanded of your servant I shall do, but this thing I cannot do." The messengers went and reported this to him. ¹⁰Thereupon Ben-hadad sent him this message: ᵇ-"May the gods do thus to me and even more,-ᵇ if the dust of Samaria will provide even a handful for each of the men who follow me!"

¹¹The king of Israel replied, "Tell him: Let not him who girds on his sword boast like him who ungirds it!"

¹²On hearing this reply—while he and the other kings were drinking together at Succoth—heᶜ commanded his followers, "Advance!" And they advanced against the city. ¹³Then a certain prophet went up to King Ahab of Israel and said, "Thus said the LORD: Do you see that great host? I will deliver it into your hands today, and you shall know that I am the LORD." ¹⁴"Through whom?" asked Ahab. He

---

a   *Several ancient versions read "they."*
b-b   *See note at 19.2.*
c   *I.e., Ben-hadad.*

---

2 וַיִּשְׁלַ֧ח מַלְאָכִ֛ים אֶל־אַחְאָ֥ב מֶֽלֶךְ־
יִשְׂרָאֵ֖ל הָעִֽירָה: 3 וַיֹּ֣אמֶר* ל֗וֹ כֹּ֚ה אָמַ֣ר
בֶּן־הֲדַ֔ד כַּסְפְּךָ֥ וּזְהָבְךָ֖ לִי־ה֑וּא וְנָשֶׁ֧יךָ
וּבָנֶ֛יךָ הַטּוֹבִ֖ים לִי־הֵֽם: 4 וַיַּ֣עַן מֶֽלֶךְ־
יִשְׂרָאֵל֙ וַיֹּ֔אמֶר כִּדְבָרְךָ֖ אֲדֹנִ֣י הַמֶּ֑לֶךְ לְךָ֣
אֲנִ֔י וְכָל־אֲשֶׁר־לִֽי: 5 וַיָּשֻׁ֙בוּ֙ הַמַּלְאָכִ֔ים
וַיֹּ֣אמְר֔וּ כֹּֽה־אָמַ֥ר בֶּן־הֲדַ֖ד לֵאמֹ֑ר כִּֽי־
שָׁלַ֤חְתִּי אֵלֶ֙יךָ֙ לֵאמֹ֔ר כַּסְפְּךָ֧ וּזְהָבְךָ֛ וְנָשֶׁ֥יךָ
וּבָנֶ֖יךָ לִ֥י תִתֵּֽן: 6 כִּ֣י | אִם־כָּעֵ֣ת מָחָ֗ר
אֶשְׁלַ֤ח אֶת־עֲבָדַי֙ אֵלֶ֔יךָ וְחִפְּשׂוּ֙ אֶת־בֵּ֣יתְךָ֔
וְאֵ֖ת בָּתֵּ֣י עֲבָדֶ֑יךָ וְהָיָה֙ כָּל־מַחְמַ֣ד עֵינֶ֔יךָ
יָשִׂ֥ימוּ בְיָדָ֖ם וְלָקָֽחוּ:

7 וַיִּקְרָ֤א מֶֽלֶךְ־יִשְׂרָאֵל֙ לְכָל־זִקְנֵ֣י הָאָ֔רֶץ
וַיֹּ֙אמֶר֙ דְּעֽוּ־נָ֣א וּרְא֔וּ כִּ֥י רָעָ֖ה זֶ֣ה מְבַקֵּ֑שׁ
כִּֽי־שָׁלַ֨ח אֵלַ֜י לְנָשַׁ֤י וּלְבָנַי֙ וּלְכַסְפִּ֣י וְלִזְהָבִ֔י
וְלֹ֥א מָנַ֖עְתִּי מִמֶּֽנּוּ: 8 וַיֹּאמְר֤וּ אֵלָיו֙ כָּל־
הַזְּקֵנִ֔ים וְכָל־הָעָ֖ם אַל־תִּשְׁמַ֣ע וְל֣וֹא
תֹאבֶֽה: 9 וַיֹּ֜אמֶר לְמַלְאֲכֵ֣י בֶן־הֲדַ֗ד אִמְר֞וּ
לַֽאדֹנִ֤י הַמֶּ֙לֶךְ֙ כֹּ֣ל אֲשֶׁר־שָׁלַ֤חְתָּ אֶל־
עַבְדְּךָ֨ בָרִֽאשֹׁנָ֜ה אֶעֱשֶׂ֗ה וְהַדָּבָ֤ר הַזֶּה֙ לֹ֣א
אוּכַ֣ל לַעֲשׂ֔וֹת וַיֵּֽלְכוּ֙ הַמַּלְאָכִ֔ים וַיְשִׁבֻ֖הוּ
דָּבָֽר: 10 וַיִּשְׁלַ֤ח אֵלָיו֙ בֶּן־הֲדַ֔ד וַיֹּ֕אמֶר כֹּֽה־
יַעֲשׂ֥וּן לִ֛י אֱלֹהִ֖ים וְכֹ֣ה יוֹסִ֑פוּ אִם־יִשְׂפֹּק֙
עֲפַ֣ר שֹׁמְר֔וֹן לִשְׁעָלִ֕ים לְכָל־הָעָ֖ם אֲשֶׁ֥ר
בְּרַגְלָֽי:

11 וַיַּ֙עַן֙ מֶֽלֶךְ־יִשְׂרָאֵ֔ל וַיֹּ֖אמֶר דַּבְּר֑וּ אַל־
יִתְהַלֵּ֥ל חֹגֵ֖ר כִּמְפַתֵּֽחַ:

12 וַיְהִ֗י כִּשְׁמֹ֙עַ֙ אֶת־הַדָּבָ֣ר הַזֶּ֔ה וְה֥וּא שֹׁתֶ֛ה
ה֥וּא וְהַמְּלָכִ֖ים בַּסֻּכּ֑וֹת וַיֹּ֤אמֶר אֶל־עֲבָדָיו֙
שִׂ֔ימוּ וַיָּשִׂ֖ימוּ עַל־הָעִֽיר: 13 וְהִנֵּ֣ה | נָבִ֣יא
אֶחָ֗ד נִגַּשׁ֙ אֶל־אַחְאָ֣ב מֶֽלֶךְ־יִשְׂרָאֵ֔ל וַיֹּ֗אמֶר
כֹּ֚ה אָמַ֣ר יְהֹוָ֔ה הֲרָאִ֕יתָ אֵ֛ת כָּל־הֶהָמ֥וֹן
הַגָּד֖וֹל הַזֶּ֑ה הִנְנִ֨י נֹתְנ֤וֹ בְיָֽדְךָ֙ הַיּ֔וֹם
וְיָדַעְתָּ֖ כִּֽי־אֲנִ֥י יְהֹוָֽה: 14 וַיֹּ֤אמֶר אַחְאָב֙

v. 3. ‏סבירין ומטעין לשון רבים‏

764

answered, "Thus said the Lᴏʀᴅ: Through the aides of the provincial governors." He asked, "Who shall begin the battle?" And he answered, "You."

¹⁵So he mustered the aides of the provincial governors, 232 strong, and then he mustered all the troops—all the Israelites—7,000 strong. ¹⁶They marched out at noon, while Ben-hadad was drinking himself drunk at Succoth together with the thirty-two kings allied with him. ¹⁷The aides of the provincial governors rushed out first. Ben-hadad sent [scouts], who told him, "Some men have come out from Samaria." ¹⁸He said, "If they have come out to surrender, take them alive; and if they have come out for battle, take them alive anyhow." ¹⁹But the others—the aides of the provincial governors, with the army behind them—had already rushed out of the city, ²⁰and each of them struck down his opponent. The Arameans fled, and Israel pursued them; but King Ben-hadad of Aram escaped on a horse with other horsemen. ²¹The king of Israel came out and attacked the horses and chariots, and inflicted a great defeat on the Arameans. ²²Then the prophet approached the king of Israel and said to him, "Go, keep up your efforts, and consider well what you must do; for the king of Aram will attack you at the turn of the year."

²³Now the ministers of the king of Aram said to him, "Their God is a God of mountains; that is why they got the better of us. But if we fight them in the plain, we will surely get the better of them. ²⁴Do this: Remove all the kings from their posts and appoint governors in their place. ²⁵Then muster for yourself an army equal to the army you lost, horse for horse and chariot for chariot. And let us fight them in the plain, and we will surely get the better of them." He took their advice and acted accordingly.

²⁶At the turn of the year, Ben-hadad mustered

בְּמִי וַיֹּאמֶר כֹּה־אָמַר יְהֹוָה בְּנַעֲרֵי שָׂרֵי הַמְּדִינוֹת וַיֹּאמֶר מִי־יֶאְסֹר הַמִּלְחָמָה וַיֹּאמֶר אָתָּה:
¹⁵ וַיִּפְקֹד אֶת־נַעֲרֵי שָׂרֵי הַמְּדִינוֹת וַיִּהְיוּ מָאתַיִם שְׁנַיִם וּשְׁלֹשִׁים וְאַחֲרֵיהֶם פָּקַד אֶת־כָּל־הָעָם כָּל־בְּנֵי יִשְׂרָאֵל שִׁבְעַת אֲלָפִים: ¹⁶ וַיֵּצְאוּ בַּצָּהֳרָיִם וּבֶן־הֲדַד שֹׁתֶה שִׁכּוֹר בַּסֻּכּוֹת הוּא וְהַמְּלָכִים שְׁלֹשִׁים־וּשְׁנַיִם מֶלֶךְ עֹזֵר אֹתוֹ: ¹⁷ וַיֵּצְאוּ נַעֲרֵי שָׂרֵי הַמְּדִינוֹת בָּרִאשֹׁנָה וַיִּשְׁלַח בֶּן־הֲדַד וַיַּגִּידוּ לוֹ לֵאמֹר אֲנָשִׁים יָצְאוּ מִשֹּׁמְרוֹן: ¹⁸ וַיֹּאמֶר אִם־לְשָׁלוֹם יָצָאוּ תִּפְשׂוּם חַיִּים וְאִם לְמִלְחָמָה יָצָאוּ חַיִּים תִּפְשׂוּם: ¹⁹ וְאֵלֶּה יָצְאוּ מִן־הָעִיר נַעֲרֵי שָׂרֵי הַמְּדִינוֹת וְהַחַיִל אֲשֶׁר אַחֲרֵיהֶם: ²⁰ וַיַּכּוּ אִישׁ אִישׁוֹ וַיָּנֻסוּ אֲרָם וַיִּרְדְּפֵם יִשְׂרָאֵל וַיִּמָּלֵט בֶּן־הֲדַד מֶלֶךְ אֲרָם עַל־סוּס וּפָרָשִׁים: ²¹ וַיֵּצֵא מֶלֶךְ יִשְׂרָאֵל וַיַּךְ אֶת־הַסּוּס וְאֶת־הָרָכֶב וְהִכָּה בַאֲרָם מַכָּה גְדוֹלָה: ²² וַיִּגַּשׁ הַנָּבִיא אֶל־מֶלֶךְ יִשְׂרָאֵל וַיֹּאמֶר לוֹ לֵךְ הִתְחַזַּק וְדַע וּרְאֵה אֵת אֲשֶׁר־תַּעֲשֶׂה כִּי לִתְשׁוּבַת הַשָּׁנָה מֶלֶךְ אֲרָם עֹלֶה עָלֶיךָ: ס
²³ וְעַבְדֵי מֶלֶךְ־אֲרָם אָמְרוּ אֵלָיו אֱלֹהֵי הָרִים אֱלֹהֵיהֶם עַל־כֵּן חָזְקוּ מִמֶּנּוּ וְאוּלָם נִלָּחֵם אִתָּם בַּמִּישׁוֹר אִם־לֹא נֶחֱזַק מֵהֶם: ²⁴ וְאֶת־הַדָּבָר הַזֶּה עֲשֵׂה הָסֵר הַמְּלָכִים אִישׁ מִמְּקֹמוֹ וְשִׂים פַּחוֹת תַּחְתֵּיהֶם: ²⁵ וְאַתָּה תִמְנֶה־לְךָ | חַיִל כַּחַיִל הַנֹּפֵל מֵאוֹתָךְ וְסוּס כַּסּוּס | וְרֶכֶב כָּרֶכֶב וְנִלָּחֲמָה אוֹתָם בַּמִּישׁוֹר אִם־לֹא נֶחֱזַק מֵהֶם וַיִּשְׁמַע לְקֹלָם וַיַּעַשׂ כֵּן: פ
²⁶ וַיְהִי לִתְשׁוּבַת הַשָּׁנָה וַיִּפְקֹד בֶּן־הֲדַד

the Arameans and advanced on Aphek to fight Israel. 27Now the Israelites had been mustered and provisioned, and they went out against them; but when the Israelites encamped against them, they looked like two flocks[d] of goats, while the Arameans covered the land. 28Then the man of God approached and spoke to the king of Israel, "Thus said the LORD: Because the Arameans have said, 'The LORD is a God of mountains, but He is not a God of lowlands,' I will deliver that great host into your hands; and you shall know that I am the LORD."

29For seven days they were encamped opposite each other. On the seventh day, the battle was joined and the Israelites struck down 100,000 Aramean foot soldiers in one day. 30The survivors fled to Aphek, inside the town, and the wall fell on the 27,000 survivors.

Ben-hadad also fled and took refuge inside the town, in an inner chamber. 31His ministers said to him, "We have heard that the kings of the House of Israel are magnanimous kings. Let us put sackcloth on our loins and ropes on our heads, and surrender to the king of Israel; perhaps he will spare your life." 32So they girded sackcloth on their loins and wound ropes around their heads, and came to the king of Israel and said, "Your servant Ben-hadad says, 'I beg you, spare my life.'" He replied, "Is he still alive? He is my brother." 33The men divined his meaning and quickly [d]caught the word from him,[d] saying, "Yes, Ben-hadad is your brother." "Go, bring him," he said. Ben-hadad came out to him, and he invited him into his chariot. 34Ben-hadad said to him, "I will give back the towns that my father took from your father, and you may set up bazaars for yourself in Damascus as my father did in Samaria." "And I, for my part," [said Ahab,] "will let you go home under these terms." So he made a treaty with him and dismissed him.

---

d Meaning of Heb. uncertain.

אֶת־אֲרָם וַיַּעַל אֲפֵקָה לַמִּלְחָמָה עִם־
יִשְׂרָאֵל: 27 וּבְנֵי יִשְׂרָאֵל הָתְפָּקְדוּ וְכָלְכְּלוּ
וַיֵּלְכוּ לִקְרָאתָם וַיַּחֲנוּ בְנֵי־יִשְׂרָאֵל נֶגְדָּם
כִּשְׁנֵי חֲשִׂפֵי עִזִּים וַאֲרָם מִלְאוּ אֶת־
הָאָרֶץ: 28 וַיִּגַּשׁ אִישׁ הָאֱלֹהִים וַיֹּאמֶר
אֶל־מֶלֶךְ יִשְׂרָאֵל וַיֹּאמֶר כֹּה־אָמַר יְהֹוָה
יַעַן אֲשֶׁר אָמְרוּ אֲרָם אֱלֹהֵי הָרִים יְהֹוָה
וְלֹא־אֱלֹהֵי עֲמָקִים הוּא וְנָתַתִּי אֶת־כָּל־
הֶהָמוֹן הַגָּדוֹל הַזֶּה בְּיָדֶךָ וִידַעְתֶּם כִּי־אֲנִי
יְהֹוָה:

29 וַיַּחֲנוּ אֵלֶּה נֹכַח אֵלֶּה שִׁבְעַת יָמִים
וַיְהִי ׀ בַּיּוֹם הַשְּׁבִיעִי וַתִּקְרַב הַמִּלְחָמָה
וַיַּכּוּ בְנֵי־יִשְׂרָאֵל אֶת־אֲרָם מֵאָה־אֶלֶף
רַגְלִי בְּיוֹם אֶחָד: 30 וַיָּנֻסוּ הַנּוֹתָרִים ׀
אֲפֵקָה אֶל־הָעִיר וַתִּפֹּל הַחוֹמָה עַל־
עֶשְׂרִים וְשִׁבְעָה אֶלֶף אִישׁ הַנּוֹתָרִים
וּבֶן־הֲדַד נָס וַיָּבֹא אֶל־הָעִיר חֶדֶר
בְּחָדֶר: ס 31 וַיֹּאמְרוּ אֵלָיו עֲבָדָיו הִנֵּה־
נָא שָׁמַעְנוּ כִּי מַלְכֵי בֵּית יִשְׂרָאֵל כִּי־מַלְכֵי
חֶסֶד הֵם נָשִׂימָה נָּא שַׂקִּים בְּמָתְנֵינוּ
וַחֲבָלִים בְּרֹאשֵׁנוּ וְנֵצֵא אֶל־מֶלֶךְ יִשְׂרָאֵל
אוּלַי יְחַיֶּה אֶת־נַפְשֶׁךָ: 32 וַיַּחְגְּרוּ שַׂקִּים
בְּמָתְנֵיהֶם וַחֲבָלִים בְּרָאשֵׁיהֶם וַיָּבֹאוּ אֶל־
מֶלֶךְ יִשְׂרָאֵל וַיֹּאמְרוּ עַבְדְּךָ בֶן־הֲדַד אָמַר
תְּחִי־נָא נַפְשִׁי וַיֹּאמֶר הַעוֹדֶנּוּ חַי אָחִי
הוּא: 33 וְהָאֲנָשִׁים יְנַחֲשׁוּ וַיְמַהֲרוּ וַיַּחְלְטוּ
הֲמִמֶּנּוּ וַיֹּאמְרוּ אָחִיךָ בֶן־הֲדַד וַיֹּאמֶר בֹּאוּ
קָחֻהוּ וַיֵּצֵא אֵלָיו בֶּן־הֲדַד וַיַּעֲלֵהוּ עַל־
הַמֶּרְכָּבָה: 34 וַיֹּאמֶר אֵלָיו הֶעָרִים אֲשֶׁר־
לָקַח־אָבִי מֵאֵת אָבִיךָ אָשִׁיב וְחוּצוֹת
תָּשִׂים לְךָ בְדַמֶּשֶׂק כַּאֲשֶׁר־שָׂם אָבִי
בְּשֹׁמְרוֹן וַאֲנִי בַּבְּרִית אֲשַׁלְּחֶךָ וַיִּכְרָת־לוֹ
בְרִית וַיְשַׁלְּחֵהוּ: ס

35A certain man, a disciple of the prophets, said to another, at the word of the LORD, "Strike me"; but the man refused to strike him. 36He said to him, "Because you have not obeyed the LORD, a lion will strike you dead as soon as you leave me." And when he left, a lion came upon him and killed him. 37Then he met another man and said, "Come, strike me." So the man struck him and wounded him. 38Then the prophet, disguised by a cloth over his eyes, went and waited for the king by the road. 39As the king passed by, he cried out to the king and said, "Your servant went out into the thick of the battle. Suddenly a man came over and brought a man to me, saying, 'Guard this man! If he is missing, it will be your life for his, or you will have to pay a talent of silver.' 40While your servant was busy here and there, [the man] got away." The king of Israel responded, "You have your verdict; you pronounced it yourself." 41Quickly he removed the cloth from his eyes, and the king recognized him as one of the prophets. 42He said to him, "Thus said the LORD: Because you have set free the man whom I doomed, your life shall be forfeit for his life and your people for his people." 43Dispirited and sullen, the king left for home and came to Samaria.

21 [The following events] occurred sometime afterward: Naboth the Jezreelite owned a vineyard in Jezreel, adjoining the palace of King Ahab of Samaria. 2Ahab said to Naboth, "Give me your vineyard, so that I may have it as a vegetable garden, since it is right next to my palace. I will give you a better vineyard in exchange; or, if you prefer, I will pay you the price in money." 3But Naboth replied, "The LORD forbid that I should give up to you what I have inherited from my fathers!" 4Ahab went home dispirited and sullen because of the answer that

35 וְאִ֣ישׁ אֶחָ֞ד מִבְּנֵ֣י הַנְּבִיאִ֗ים אָמַ֧ר אֶל־רֵעֵ֛הוּ בִּדְבַ֥ר יְהֹוָ֖ה הַכֵּ֣ינִי נָ֑א וַיְמָאֵ֥ן הָאִ֖ישׁ לְהַכֹּתֽוֹ׃ 36 וַיֹּ֣אמֶר ל֗וֹ יַ֚עַן אֲשֶׁ֣ר לֹֽא־שָׁמַ֣עְתָּ בְּקוֹל֘ יְהֹוָה֒ הִנְּךָ֤ הוֹלֵךְ֙ מֵֽאִתִּ֔י וְהִכְּךָ֣ הָאַרְיֵ֔ה וַיֵּ֙לֶךְ֙ מֵֽאֶצְל֔וֹ וַיִּמְצָאֵ֥הוּ הָאַרְיֵ֖ה וַיַּכֵּֽהוּ׃ 37 וַיִּמְצָא֙ אִ֣ישׁ אַחֵ֔ר וַיֹּ֖אמֶר הַכֵּ֣ינִי נָ֑א וַיַּכֵּ֥הוּ הָאִ֖ישׁ הַכֵּ֥ה וּפָצֹֽעַ׃ 38 וַיֵּ֙לֶךְ֙ הַנָּבִ֔יא וַיַּעֲמֹ֥ד לַמֶּ֖לֶךְ עַל־הַדָּ֑רֶךְ וַיִּתְחַפֵּ֥שׂ בָּאֲפֵ֖ר עַל־עֵינָֽיו׃ 39 וַיְהִ֤י הַמֶּ֙לֶךְ֙ עֹבֵ֔ר וְה֖וּא צָעַ֣ק אֶל־הַמֶּ֑לֶךְ וַיֹּ֜אמֶר עַבְדְּךָ֣ ׀ יָצָ֣א בְקֶֽרֶב־הַמִּלְחָמָ֗ה וְהִנֵּֽה־אִ֣ישׁ סָ֗ר וַיָּבֵ֨א אֵלַ֤י אִישׁ֙ וַיֹּ֙אמֶר֙ שְׁמֹר֙ אֶת־הָאִ֣ישׁ הַזֶּ֔ה אִם־הִפָּקֵד֙ יִפָּקֵ֔ד וְהָיְתָ֤ה נַפְשְׁךָ֙ תַּ֣חַת נַפְשׁ֔וֹ א֥וֹ כִכַּר־כֶּ֖סֶף תִּשְׁקֽוֹל׃ 40 וַיְהִ֣י עַבְדְּךָ֗ עֹשֵׂ֥ה הֵ֙נָּה֙ וָהֵ֔נָּה וְה֖וּא אֵינֶ֑נּוּ וַיֹּ֨אמֶר אֵלָ֧יו מֶֽלֶךְ־יִשְׂרָאֵ֛ל כֵּ֥ן מִשְׁפָּטֶ֖ךָ אַתָּ֥ה חָרָֽצְתָּ׃ 41 וַיְמַהֵ֕ר וַיָּ֙סַר֙ אֶת־הָ֣אֲפֵ֔ר מֵעֲלֵ֖י עֵינָ֑יו וַיַּכֵּ֤ר אֹתוֹ֙ מֶ֣לֶךְ יִשְׂרָאֵ֔ל כִּ֥י מֵֽהַנְּבִיאִ֖ים הֽוּא׃ 42 וַיֹּ֣אמֶר אֵלָ֗יו כֹּ֚ה אָמַ֣ר יְהֹוָ֔ה יַ֛עַן שִׁלַּ֥חְתָּ אֶת־אִישׁ־חֶרְמִ֖י מִיָּ֑ד וְהָיְתָ֤ה נַפְשְׁךָ֙ תַּ֣חַת נַפְשׁ֔וֹ וְעַמְּךָ֖ תַּ֥חַת עַמּֽוֹ׃ 43 וַיֵּ֧לֶךְ מֶֽלֶךְ־יִשְׂרָאֵ֛ל עַל־בֵּית֖וֹ סַ֣ר וְזָעֵ֑ף וַיָּבֹ֖א שֹׁמְרֽוֹנָה׃ פ

כא וַיְהִ֗י אַחַר֙ הַדְּבָרִ֣ים הָאֵ֔לֶּה כֶּ֧רֶם הָיָ֛ה לְנָב֥וֹת הַיִּזְרְעֵאלִ֖י אֲשֶׁ֣ר בְּיִזְרְעֶ֑אל אֵ֚צֶל הֵיכַ֣ל אַחְאָ֔ב מֶ֖לֶךְ שֹׁמְרֽוֹן׃ 2 וַיְדַבֵּ֣ר אַחְאָ֣ב אֶל־נָב֣וֹת ׀ לֵאמֹר֩ ׀ תְּנָה־לִּ֨י אֶֽת־כַּרְמְךָ֜ וִיהִי־לִ֣י לְגַן־יָרָ֗ק כִּ֣י ה֤וּא קָרוֹב֙ אֵ֣צֶל בֵּיתִ֔י וְאֶתְּנָ֤ה לְךָ֙ תַּחְתָּ֔יו כֶּ֖רֶם ט֣וֹב מִמֶּ֑נּוּ אִ֣ם ט֣וֹב בְּעֵינֶ֗יךָ אֶתְּנָה־לְּךָ֥ כֶ֖סֶף מְחִ֥יר זֶֽה׃ 3 וַיֹּ֥אמֶר נָב֖וֹת אֶל־אַחְאָ֑ב חָלִ֤ילָה לִּי֙ מֵֽיהֹוָ֔ה מִתִּתִּ֛י אֶת־נַחֲלַ֥ת אֲבֹתַ֖י לָֽךְ׃ 4 וַיָּבֹא֩ אַחְאָ֨ב אֶל־בֵּית֜וֹ סַ֣ר

Naboth the Jezreelite had given him: "I will not give up to you what I have inherited from my fathers!" He lay down on his bed and turned away his face, and he would not eat. 5His wife Jezebel came to him and asked him, "Why are you so dispirited that you won't eat?" 6So he told her, "I spoke to Naboth the Jezreelite and proposed to him, 'Sell me your vineyard for money, or if you prefer, I'll give you another vineyard in exchange'; but he answered, 'I will not give my vineyard to you.'" 7His wife Jezebel said to him, "Now is the time to show yourself king over Israel. Rise and eat something, and be cheerful; I will get the vineyard of Naboth the Jezreelite for you."

8So she wrote letters in Ahab's name and sealed them with his seal, and sent the letters to the elders and the nobles who lived in the same town with Naboth. 9In the letters she wrote as follows: "Proclaim a fast and seat Naboth at the front of the assembly. 10And seat two scoundrels opposite him, and let them testify against him: 'You have reviled God and king!' Then take him out and stone him to death."

11His townsmen—the elders and nobles who lived in his town—did as Jezebel had instructed them, just as was written in the letters she had sent them: 12They proclaimed a fast and seated Naboth at the front of the assembly. 13Then the two scoundrels came and sat down opposite him; and the scoundrels testified against Naboth publicly as follows: "Naboth has reviled God and king." Then they took him outside the town and stoned him to death. 14Word was sent to Jezebel: "Naboth has been stoned to death." 15As soon as Jezebel heard that Naboth had been stoned to death, she said to Ahab, "Go and take possession of the vineyard which Naboth the Jezreelite refused to sell you for money; for Naboth is no longer alive, he is dead." 16When

וְזָעֵף עַל־הַדָּבָר אֲשֶׁר־דִּבֶּר אֵלָיו נָבוֹת הַיִּזְרְעֵאלִי וַיֹּאמֶר לֹא־אֶתֵּן לְךָ אֶת־נַחֲלַת אֲבוֹתָי וַיִּשְׁכַּב עַל־מִטָּתוֹ וַיַּסֵּב אֶת־פָּנָיו וְלֹא־אָכַל לָחֶם: 5 וַתָּבֹא אֵלָיו אִיזֶבֶל אִשְׁתּוֹ וַתְּדַבֵּר אֵלָיו מַה־זֶּה רוּחֲךָ סָרָה וְאֵינְךָ אֹכֵל לָחֶם: 6 וַיְדַבֵּר אֵלֶיהָ כִּי־אֲדַבֵּר אֶל־נָבוֹת הַיִּזְרְעֵאלִי וָאֹמַר לוֹ תְּנָה־לִּי אֶת־כַּרְמְךָ בְּכֶסֶף אוֹ אִם־חָפֵץ אַתָּה אֶתְּנָה־לְךָ כֶרֶם תַּחְתָּיו וַיֹּאמֶר לֹא־אֶתֵּן לְךָ אֶת־כַּרְמִי: 7 וַתֹּאמֶר אֵלָיו אִיזֶבֶל אִשְׁתּוֹ אַתָּה עַתָּה תַּעֲשֶׂה מְלוּכָה עַל־יִשְׂרָאֵל קוּם אֱכָל־לֶחֶם וְיִטַב לִבֶּךָ אֲנִי אֶתֵּן לְךָ אֶת־כֶּרֶם נָבוֹת הַיִּזְרְעֵאלִי: 8 וַתִּכְתֹּב סְפָרִים בְּשֵׁם אַחְאָב וַתַּחְתֹּם בְּחֹתָמוֹ וַתִּשְׁלַח הספרים סְפָרִים אֶל־הַזְּקֵנִים וְאֶל־הַחֹרִים אֲשֶׁר בְּעִירוֹ הַיֹּשְׁבִים אֶת־נָבוֹת: 9 וַתִּכְתֹּב בַּסְּפָרִים לֵאמֹר קִרְאוּ־צוֹם וְהוֹשִׁיבוּ אֶת־נָבוֹת בְּרֹאשׁ הָעָם: 10 וְהוֹשִׁיבוּ שְׁנַיִם אֲנָשִׁים בְּנֵי־בְלִיַּעַל נֶגְדּוֹ וִיעִדֻהוּ לֵאמֹר בֵּרַכְתָּ אֱלֹהִים וָמֶלֶךְ וְהוֹצִיאֻהוּ וְסִקְלֻהוּ וְיָמֹת: 11 וַיַּעֲשׂוּ אַנְשֵׁי עִירוֹ הַזְּקֵנִים וְהַחֹרִים אֲשֶׁר הַיֹּשְׁבִים בְּעִירוֹ כַּאֲשֶׁר שָׁלְחָה אֲלֵיהֶם אִיזָבֶל כַּאֲשֶׁר כָּתוּב בַּסְּפָרִים אֲשֶׁר שָׁלְחָה אֲלֵיהֶם: 12 קָרְאוּ צוֹם וְהוֹשִׁיבוּ אֶת־נָבוֹת בְּרֹאשׁ הָעָם: 13 וַיָּבֹאוּ שְׁנֵי הָאֲנָשִׁים בְּנֵי־בְלִיַּעַל וַיֵּשְׁבוּ נֶגְדּוֹ וַיְעִדֻהוּ אַנְשֵׁי הַבְּלִיַּעַל אֶת־נָבוֹת נֶגֶד הָעָם לֵאמֹר בֵּרַךְ נָבוֹת אֱלֹהִים וָמֶלֶךְ וַיֹּצִאֻהוּ מִחוּץ לָעִיר וַיִּסְקְלֻהוּ בָאֲבָנִים וַיָּמֹת: 14 וַיִּשְׁלְחוּ אֶל־אִיזֶבֶל לֵאמֹר סֻקַּל נָבוֹת וַיָּמֹת: 15 וַיְהִי כִּשְׁמֹעַ אִיזֶבֶל כִּי־סֻקַּל נָבוֹת וַיָּמֹת וַתֹּאמֶר אִיזֶבֶל אֶל־אַחְאָב קוּם רֵשׁ אֶת־כֶּרֶם | נָבוֹת הַיִּזְרְעֵאלִי אֲשֶׁר מֵאֵן לָתֶת־לְךָ בְכֶסֶף כִּי אֵין נָבוֹת חַי כִּי־מֵת: 16 וַיְהִי כִּשְׁמֹעַ

Ahab heard that Naboth was dead, Ahab set out for the vineyard of Naboth the Jezreelite to take possession of it.

¹⁷Then the word of the LORD came to Elijah the Tishbite: ¹⁸"Go down and confront King Ahab of Israel who [resides] in Samaria. He is now in Naboth's vineyard; he has gone down there to take possession of it. ¹⁹Say to him, 'Thus said the LORD: Would you murder and take possession? Thus said the LORD: In the very place where the dogs lapped up Naboth's blood, the dogs will lap up your blood too.'"

²⁰Ahab said to Elijah, "So you have found me, my enemy?" "Yes, I have found you," he replied. "Because you have committed yourself to doing what is evil in the sight of the LORD, ²¹I will bring disaster upon you. I will make a clean sweep of you, I will cut off from Israel every male belonging to Ahab,^{-a}bond and free.^{-a} ²²And I will make your house like the House of Jeroboam son of Nebat and like the House of Baasha son of Ahijah, because of the provocation you have caused by leading Israel to sin. ²³And the LORD has also spoken concerning Jezebel: 'The dogs shall devour Jezebel in the field^b of Jezreel. ²⁴All of Ahab's line who die in the town shall be devoured by dogs, and all who die in the open country shall be devoured by the birds of the sky.'"

(²⁵Indeed, there never was anyone like Ahab, who committed himself to doing what was displeasing to the LORD, at the instigation of his wife Jezebel. ²⁶He acted most abominably, straying after the fetishes just like the Amorites, whom the LORD had dispossessed before the Israelites.)

²⁷When Ahab heard these words, he rent his clothes and put sackcloth on his body. He fasted and lay in sackcloth and walked about subdued. ²⁸Then the word of the LORD came to Elijah the

אַחְאָב כִּי מֵת נָבוֹת וַיָּקָם אַחְאָב לָרֶדֶת אֶל־כֶּרֶם נָבוֹת הַיִּזְרְעֵאלִי לְרִשְׁתּוֹ: ס ¹⁷ וַיְהִי דְּבַר־יְהֹוָה אֶל־אֵלִיָּהוּ הַתִּשְׁבִּי לֵאמֹר: ¹⁸ קוּם רֵד לִקְרַאת אַחְאָב מֶלֶךְ־יִשְׂרָאֵל אֲשֶׁר בְּשֹׁמְרוֹן הִנֵּה בְּכֶרֶם נָבוֹת אֲשֶׁר־יָרַד שָׁם לְרִשְׁתּוֹ: ¹⁹ וְדִבַּרְתָּ אֵלָיו לֵאמֹר כֹּה אָמַר יְהֹוָה הֲרָצַחְתָּ וְגַם־יָרָשְׁתָּ וְדִבַּרְתָּ אֵלָיו לֵאמֹר כֹּה אָמַר יְהֹוָה בִּמְקוֹם אֲשֶׁר לָקְקוּ הַכְּלָבִים אֶת־דַּם נָבוֹת יָלֹקּוּ הַכְּלָבִים אֶת־דָּמְךָ גַּם־אָתָּה: ²⁰ וַיֹּאמֶר אַחְאָב אֶל־אֵלִיָּהוּ הַמְצָאתַנִי אֹיְבִי וַיֹּאמֶר מָצָאתִי יַעַן הִתְמַכֶּרְךָ לַעֲשׂוֹת הָרַע בְּעֵינֵי יְהֹוָה: ²¹ הִנְנִי מבי מֵבִיא אֵלֶיךָ רָעָה וּבִעַרְתִּי אַחֲרֶיךָ וְהִכְרַתִּי לְאַחְאָב מַשְׁתִּין בְּקִיר וְעָצוּר וְעָזוּב בְּיִשְׂרָאֵל: ²² וְנָתַתִּי אֶת־בֵּיתְךָ כְּבֵית יָרָבְעָם בֶּן־נְבָט וּכְבֵית בַּעְשָׁא בֶן־אֲחִיָּה אֶל־הַכַּעַס אֲשֶׁר הִכְעַסְתָּ וַתַּחֲטִא אֶת־יִשְׂרָאֵל: ²³ וְגַם־לְאִיזֶבֶל דִּבֶּר יְהֹוָה לֵאמֹר הַכְּלָבִים יֹאכְלוּ אֶת־אִיזֶבֶל בְּחֵל*־יִזְרְעֶאל: ²⁴ הַמֵּת לְאַחְאָב בָּעִיר יֹאכְלוּ הַכְּלָבִים וְהַמֵּת בַּשָּׂדֶה יֹאכְלוּ עוֹף הַשָּׁמָיִם: ²⁵ רַק לֹא־הָיָה כְאַחְאָב אֲשֶׁר הִתְמַכֵּר לַעֲשׂוֹת הָרַע בְּעֵינֵי יְהֹוָה אֲשֶׁר־הֵסַתָּה אֹתוֹ אִיזֶבֶל אִשְׁתּוֹ: ²⁶ וַיַּתְעֵב מְאֹד לָלֶכֶת אַחֲרֵי הַגִּלֻּלִים כְּכֹל אֲשֶׁר עָשׂוּ הָאֱמֹרִי אֲשֶׁר הוֹרִישׁ יְהֹוָה מִפְּנֵי בְּנֵי יִשְׂרָאֵל: ס ²⁷ וַיְהִי כִשְׁמֹעַ אַחְאָב אֶת־הַדְּבָרִים הָאֵלֶּה וַיִּקְרַע בְּגָדָיו וַיָּשֶׂם־שַׂק עַל־בְּשָׂרוֹ וַיָּצוֹם וַיִּשְׁכַּב בַּשָּׂק וַיְהַלֵּךְ אַט: ס ²⁸ וַיְהִי דְּבַר־יְהֹוָה אֶל־אֵלִיָּהוּ הַתִּשְׁבִּי

v. 23. בנוסח אחר "בחלק".

---

a-a   See note at 14.10.
b   So nine Heb. mss. and the parallel 2 Kings 9.36, as well as Targum and other ancient versions. Most texts read here "rampart."

Tishbite: [29]"Have you seen how Ahab has humbled himself before Me? Because he has humbled himself before Me, I will not bring the disaster in his lifetime; I will bring the disaster upon his house in his son's time."

22 [a]There was a lull of [a] three years, with no war between Aram and Israel. [2]In the third year, King Jehoshaphat of Judah came to visit the king of Israel. [3]The king of Israel said to his courtiers, "You know that Ramoth-gilead belongs to us, and yet we do nothing to recover it from the hands of the king of Aram." [4]And he said to Jehoshaphat, "Will you come with me to battle at Ramoth-gilead?" Jehoshaphat answered the king of Israel, "I will do what you do; my troops shall be your troops, my horses shall be your horses." [5]But Jehoshaphat said further to the king of Israel, "Please, first inquire of the LORD."

[6]So the king of Israel gathered the prophets, about four hundred men, and asked them, "Shall I march upon Ramoth-gilead for battle, or shall I not?" "March," they said, "and the Lord will deliver [it] into Your Majesty's hands." [7]Then Jehoshaphat asked, "Isn't there another prophet of the LORD here through whom we can inquire?" [8]And the king of Israel answered Jehoshaphat, "There is one more man through whom we can inquire of the LORD; but I hate him, because he never prophesies anything good for me, but only misfortune—Micaiah son of Imlah." But King Jehoshaphat said, "Don't say that, Your Majesty." [9]So the king of Israel summoned an officer and said, "Bring Micaiah son of Imlah at once."

[10]The king of Israel and King Jehoshaphat of Judah were seated on their thrones, arrayed in their robes, on the threshing floor at the en-

a-a Lit. "They remained."

לֵאמֹֽר: [29] הֲרָאִיתָ כִּֽי־נִכְנַע אַחְאָב מִלְּפָנָי יַעַן כִּֽי־נִכְנַע מִפָּנַי לֹֽא־אָבִיא הָֽרָעָה בְּיָמָיו בִּימֵי בְנוֹ אָבִיא הָרָעָה עַל־בֵּיתֽוֹ:

כב וַיֵּשְׁבוּ שָׁלֹשׁ שָׁנִים אֵין מִלְחָמָה בֵּין אֲרָם וּבֵין יִשְׂרָאֵֽל: פ [2] וַֽיְהִי בַּשָּׁנָה הַשְּׁלִישִׁית וַיֵּרֶד יְהוֹשָׁפָט מֶֽלֶךְ־יְהוּדָה אֶל־מֶלֶךְ יִשְׂרָאֵֽל: [3] וַיֹּאמֶר מֶֽלֶךְ־יִשְׂרָאֵל אֶל־עֲבָדָיו הַיְדַעְתֶּם כִּֽי־לָנוּ רָמֹת גִּלְעָד וַאֲנַחְנוּ מַחְשִׁים מִקַּחַת אֹתָהּ מִיַּד מֶלֶךְ אֲרָֽם: [4] וַיֹּאמֶר אֶל־יְהוֹשָׁפָט הֲתֵלֵךְ אִתִּי לַמִּלְחָמָה רָמֹת גִּלְעָד וַיֹּאמֶר יְהוֹשָׁפָט אֶל־מֶלֶךְ יִשְׂרָאֵל כָּמוֹנִי כָמוֹךָ כְּעַמִּי כְעַמֶּךָ כְּסוּסַי כְּסוּסֶֽיךָ: [5] וַיֹּאמֶר יְהוֹשָׁפָט אֶל־מֶלֶךְ יִשְׂרָאֵל דְּרָשׁ־נָא כַיּוֹם אֶת־דְּבַר יְהוָֽה:

*[6] וַיִּקְבֹּץ מֶֽלֶךְ־יִשְׂרָאֵל אֶת־הַנְּבִיאִים כְּאַרְבַּע מֵאוֹת אִישׁ וַיֹּאמֶר אֲלֵהֶם הַאֵלֵךְ עַל־רָמֹת גִּלְעָד לַמִּלְחָמָה אִם־אֶחְדָּל וַיֹּאמְרוּ עֲלֵה וְיִתֵּן אֲדֹנָי בְּיַד הַמֶּֽלֶךְ: [7] וַיֹּאמֶר יְהוֹשָׁפָט הַאֵין פֹּה נָבִיא לַיהוָה עוֹד וְנִדְרְשָׁה מֵֽאוֹתֽוֹ: [8] וַיֹּאמֶר מֶֽלֶךְ־יִשְׂרָאֵל ׀ אֶל־יְהוֹשָׁפָט עוֹד אִישׁ־אֶחָד לִדְרֹשׁ אֶת־יְהוָה מֵאֹתוֹ וַאֲנִי שְׂנֵאתִיו כִּי לֹֽא־יִתְנַבֵּא עָלַי טוֹב כִּי אִם־רָע מִיכָיְהוּ בֶּן־יִמְלָה וַיֹּאמֶר יְהוֹשָׁפָט אַל־יֹאמַר הַמֶּלֶךְ כֵּֽן: [9] וַיִּקְרָא מֶלֶךְ יִשְׂרָאֵל אֶל־סָרִיס אֶחָד וַיֹּאמֶר מַהֲרָה מִיכָיְהוּ בֶן־יִמְלָֽה: [10] וּמֶלֶךְ יִשְׂרָאֵל וִֽיהוֹשָׁפָט מֶֽלֶךְ־יְהוּדָה יֹשְׁבִים אִישׁ עַל־כִּסְאוֹ מְלֻבָּשִׁים בְּגָדִים בְּגֹרֶן פֶּתַח שַׁעַר שֹׁמְרוֹן וְכָל־הַנְּבִיאִים

חֲצִי הַסֵּפֶר בִּפְסוּקִים v. 6.

770

trance of the gate of Samaria; and all the prophets were prophesying before them. [11]Zedekiah son of Chenaanah had provided himself with iron horns; and he said, "Thus said the LORD: With these you shall gore the Arameans till you make an end of them." [12]And all the other prophets were prophesying similarly, "March upon Ramoth-gilead and triumph! The LORD will deliver it into Your Majesty's hands."

[13]The messenger who had gone to summon Micaiah said to him: "Look, the words of the prophets are with one accord favorable to the king. Let your word be like that of the rest of them; speak a favorable word." [14]"As the LORD lives," Micaiah answered, "I will speak only what the LORD tells me." [15]When he came before the king, the king said to him, "Micaiah, shall we march upon Ramoth-gilead for battle, or shall we not?" He answered him, "March and triumph! The LORD will deliver [it] into Your Majesty's hands." [16]The king said to him, "How many times must I adjure you to tell me nothing but the truth in the name of the LORD?" [17]Then he said, "I saw all Israel scattered over the hills like sheep without a shepherd; and the LORD said, 'These have no master; let everyone return to his home in safety.'" [18]"Didn't I tell you," said the king of Israel to Jehoshaphat, "that he would not prophesy good fortune for me, but only misfortune?" [19]But [Micaiah] said, "I call upon you to hear the word of the LORD! I saw the LORD seated upon His throne, with all the host of heaven standing in attendance to the right and to the left of Him. [20]The LORD asked, 'Who will entice Ahab so that he will march and fall at Ramoth-gilead?' Then one said thus and another said thus, [21]until a certain spirit came forward and stood before the LORD and said, 'I will entice him.' 'How?' the LORD asked him. [22]And he replied, 'I will go out and be a lying spirit in the mouth of all his prophets.' Then He said,

מִתְנַבְּאִים לִפְנֵיהֶם׃ 11 וַיַּ֤עַשׂ לוֹ֙ צִדְקִיָּ֣ה בֶן־כְּנַעֲנָ֔ה קַרְנֵ֖י בַרְזֶ֑ל וַיֹּ֙אמֶר֙ כֹּֽה־אָמַ֣ר יְהוָ֔ה בְּאֵ֛לֶּה תְּנַגַּ֥ח אֶת־אֲרָ֖ם עַד־כַּלֹּתָֽם׃ 12 וְכָל־הַנְּבִאִ֔ים נִבְּאִ֥ים כֵּ֖ן לֵאמֹ֑ר עֲלֵ֞ה רָמֹ֤ת גִּלְעָד֙ וְהַצְלַ֔ח וְנָתַ֥ן יְהוָ֖ה בְּיַ֥ד הַמֶּֽלֶךְ׃ 13 וְהַמַּלְאָ֞ךְ אֲשֶׁר־הָלַ֣ךְ ׀ לִקְרֹ֣א מִיכָ֗יְהוּ דִּבֶּ֣ר אֵלָיו֮ לֵאמֹר֒ הִנֵּה־נָ֞א דִּבְרֵ֤י הַנְּבִיאִים֙ פֶּֽה־אֶחָ֥ד ט֖וֹב אֶל־הַמֶּ֑לֶךְ יְהִֽי־נָ֣א דְבָרְךָ֗ כִּדְבַ֛ר אַחַ֥ד מֵהֶ֖ם וְדִבַּ֥רְתָּ טּֽוֹב׃ 14 וַיֹּ֖אמֶר מִיכָ֑יְהוּ חַי־יְהוָ֕ה כִּ֠י אֶת־אֲשֶׁ֨ר יֹאמַ֧ר יְהוָ֛ה אֵלַ֖י אֹת֥וֹ אֲדַבֵּֽר׃ 15 וַיָּבוֹא֮ אֶל־הַמֶּלֶךְ֒ וַיֹּ֨אמֶר הַמֶּ֜לֶךְ אֵלָ֗יו מִיכָ֙יְהוּ֙ הֲנֵלֵ֞ךְ אֶל־רָמֹ֥ת גִּלְעָ֛ד לַמִּלְחָמָ֖ה אִם־נֶחְדָּ֑ל וַיֹּ֤אמֶר אֵלָיו֙ עֲלֵ֣ה וְהַצְלַ֔ח וְנָתַ֥ן יְהוָ֖ה בְּיַ֥ד הַמֶּֽלֶךְ׃ 16 וַיֹּ֤אמֶר אֵלָיו֙ הַמֶּ֔לֶךְ עַד־כַּמֶּ֥ה פְעָמִ֖ים אֲנִ֣י מַשְׁבִּעֶ֑ךָ אֲ֠שֶׁר לֹֽא־תְדַבֵּ֥ר אֵלַ֛י רַק־אֱמֶ֖ת בְּשֵׁ֥ם יְהוָֽה׃ 17 וַיֹּ֗אמֶר רָאִ֤יתִי אֶת־כָּל־יִשְׂרָאֵל֙ נְפֹצִ֣ים אֶל־הֶֽהָרִ֔ים כַּצֹּ֕אן אֲשֶׁ֥ר אֵין־לָהֶ֖ם רֹעֶ֑ה וַיֹּ֤אמֶר יְהוָה֙ לֹֽא־אֲדֹנִ֣ים לָאֵ֔לֶּה יָשׁ֥וּבוּ אִישׁ־לְבֵית֖וֹ בְּשָׁלֽוֹם׃ 18 וַיֹּ֙אמֶר֙ מֶֽלֶךְ־יִשְׂרָאֵ֔ל אֶל־יְהוֹשָׁפָ֑ט הֲל֚וֹא אָמַ֣רְתִּי אֵלֶ֔יךָ לֽוֹא־יִתְנַבֵּ֥א עָלַ֛י ט֖וֹב כִּ֥י אִם־רָֽע׃ 19 וַיֹּ֕אמֶר לָכֵ֖ן שְׁמַ֣ע דְּבַר־יְהוָ֑ה רָאִ֤יתִי אֶת־יְהוָה֙ יֹשֵׁ֣ב עַל־כִּסְא֔וֹ וְכָל־צְבָ֤א הַשָּׁמַ֙יִם֙ עֹמֵ֣ד עָלָ֔יו מִימִינ֖וֹ וּמִשְּׂמֹאלֽוֹ׃ 20 וַיֹּ֣אמֶר יְהוָ֗ה מִ֤י יְפַתֶּה֙ אֶת־אַחְאָ֔ב וְיַ֕עַל וְיִפֹּ֖ל בְּרָמֹ֣ת גִּלְעָ֑ד וַיֹּ֤אמֶר זֶה֙ בְּכֹ֔ה וְזֶ֥ה אֹמֵ֖ר בְּכֹֽה׃ 21 וַיֵּצֵ֣א הָר֗וּחַ וַֽיַּעֲמֹד֙ לִפְנֵ֣י יְהוָ֔ה וַיֹּ֖אמֶר אֲנִ֣י אֲפַתֶּ֑נּוּ וַיֹּ֧אמֶר יְהוָ֛ה אֵלָ֖יו בַּמָּֽה׃ 22 וַיֹּ֗אמֶר אֵצֵא֙ וְהָיִ֙יתִי֙ ר֣וּחַ שֶׁ֔קֶר בְּפִ֖י כָּל־נְבִיאָ֑יו וַיֹּ֙אמֶר֙ תְּפַתֶּ֣ה וְגַם־

'You will entice and you will prevail. Go out and do it.' [23]So the Lord has put a lying spirit in the mouth of all these prophets of yours; for the Lord has decreed disaster upon you."

[24]Thereupon Zedekiah son of Chenaanah stepped up and struck Micaiah on the cheek, and demanded, "Which way did the spirit of the Lord pass from me to speak with you?" [25]And Micaiah replied, "You'll find out on the day when you try to hide in the innermost room." [26]Then the king of Israel said, "Take Micaiah and turn him over to Amon, the city's governor, and to Prince Joash, [27]and say, 'The king's orders are: Put this fellow in prison, and let his fare be scant bread and scant water until I come home safe.'" [28]To which Micaiah retorted, "If you ever come home safe, the Lord has not spoken through me." b-He said further, "Listen, all you peoples!"-b

[29]So the king of Israel and King Jehoshaphat of Judah marched upon Ramoth-gilead. [30]The king of Israel said to Jehoshaphat, c-"Disguise yourself and go-c into the battle; but you, wear your robes." So the king of Israel went into the battle disguised. [31]Now the king of Aram had instructed his thirty-two chariot officers: "Don't attack anyone, small or great, except the king of Israel." [32]So when the chariot officers saw Jehoshaphat, whom they took for the king of Israel, they turned upon him to attack him, and Jehoshaphat cried out. [33]And when the chariot officers became aware that he was not the king of Israel, they turned back from pursuing him. [34]Then a man drew his bow at random and he hit the king of Israel between d-the plates of-d the armor; and he said to his charioteer, "Turn e-the horses-e around and get me

תּוּכַ֥ל צֵ֖א וַעֲשֵׂה־כֵֽן: 23 וְעַתָּ֗ה הִנֵּ֨ה נָתַ֤ן יְהוָה֙ ר֣וּחַ שֶׁ֔קֶר בְּפִ֖י כָּל־נְבִיאֶ֣יךָ אֵ֑לֶּה וַֽיהוָ֔ה דִּבֶּ֥ר עָלֶ֖יךָ רָעָֽה: 24 וַיִּגַּשׁ֙ צִדְקִיָּ֣הוּ בֶֽן־כְּנַעֲנָ֔ה וַיַּכֶּ֥ה אֶת־מִיכָ֖יְהוּ עַל־הַלֶּ֑חִי וַיֹּ֕אמֶר אֵי־זֶ֨ה עָבַ֧ר רֽוּחַ־יְהוָ֛ה מֵאִתִּ֖י לְדַבֵּ֥ר אוֹתָֽךְ: 25 וַיֹּ֣אמֶר מִיכָ֔יְהוּ הִנְּךָ֥ רֹאֶ֖ה בַּיּ֣וֹם הַה֑וּא אֲשֶׁ֥ר תָּבֹ֛א חֶ֥דֶר בְּחֶ֖דֶר לְהֵחָבֵֽה: 26 וַיֹּ֙אמֶר֙ מֶ֣לֶךְ יִשְׂרָאֵ֔ל קַ֣ח אֶת־מִיכָ֔יְהוּ וַהֲשִׁיבֵ֖הוּ אֶל־אָמֹ֣ן שַׂר־הָעִ֑יר וְאֶל־יוֹאָ֖שׁ בֶּן־הַמֶּֽלֶךְ: 27 וְאָמַרְתָּ֗ כֹּ֚ה אָמַ֣ר הַמֶּ֔לֶךְ שִׂ֥ימוּ אֶת־זֶ֖ה בֵּ֣ית הַכֶּ֑לֶא וְהַאֲכִילֻ֜הוּ לֶ֤חֶם לַ֙חַץ֙ וּמַ֣יִם לַ֔חַץ עַ֖ד בֹּאִ֥י בְשָׁלֽוֹם: 28 וַיֹּ֣אמֶר מִיכָ֔יְהוּ אִם־שׁ֤וֹב תָּשׁוּב֙ בְּשָׁל֔וֹם לֹא־דִבֶּ֥ר יְהוָ֖ה בִּ֑י וַיֹּ֕אמֶר שִׁמְע֖וּ עַמִּ֥ים כֻּלָּֽם: 29 וַיַּ֧עַל מֶֽלֶךְ־יִשְׂרָאֵ֛ל וִֽיהוֹשָׁפָ֥ט מֶֽלֶךְ־יְהוּדָ֖ה רָמֹ֣ת גִּלְעָ֑ד: 30 וַיֹּ֩אמֶר֩ מֶ֨לֶךְ יִשְׂרָאֵ֜ל אֶל־יְהוֹשָׁפָ֗ט הִתְחַפֵּשׂ֙ וָבֹ֣א בַמִּלְחָמָ֔ה וְאַתָּ֖ה לְבַ֣שׁ בְּגָדֶ֑יךָ וַיִּתְחַפֵּשׂ֙ מֶ֣לֶךְ יִשְׂרָאֵ֔ל וַיָּב֖וֹא בַּמִּלְחָמָֽה: 31 וּמֶ֣לֶךְ אֲרָ֡ם צִוָּה֩ אֶת־שָׂרֵ֨י הָרֶ֜כֶב אֲשֶׁר־ל֗וֹ שְׁלֹשִׁ֤ים וּשְׁנַ֙יִם֙ לֵאמֹ֔ר לֹ֚א תִּלָּ֣חֲמ֔וּ אֶת־קָטֹ֖ן וְאֶת־גָּד֑וֹל כִּ֛י אִֽם־אֶת־מֶ֥לֶךְ יִשְׂרָאֵ֖ל לְבַדּֽוֹ: 32 וַיְהִ֡י כִּרְאוֹת֩ שָׂרֵ֨י הָרֶ֜כֶב אֶת־יְהוֹשָׁפָ֗ט וְהֵ֤מָּה אָֽמְרוּ֙ אַ֣ךְ מֶֽלֶךְ־יִשְׂרָאֵ֥ל ה֔וּא וַיָּסֻ֥רוּ עָלָ֖יו לְהִלָּחֵ֑ם וַיִּזְעַ֖ק יְהוֹשָׁפָֽט: 33 וַיְהִ֗י כִּרְאוֹת֙ שָׂרֵ֣י הָרֶ֔כֶב כִּֽי־לֹא־מֶ֥לֶךְ יִשְׂרָאֵ֖ל ה֑וּא וַיָּשׁ֖וּבוּ מֵאַחֲרָֽיו: 34 וְאִ֗ישׁ מָשַׁ֤ךְ בַּקֶּ֙שֶׁת֙ לְתֻמּ֔וֹ וַיַּכֶּה֙ אֶת־מֶ֣לֶךְ יִשְׂרָאֵ֔ל בֵּ֥ין הַדְּבָקִ֖ים וּבֵ֣ין הַשִּׁרְיָ֑ן וַיֹּ֣אמֶר לְרַכָּב֗וֹ הֲפֹ֥ךְ יָדְךָ֛ וְהוֹצִיאֵ֥נִי מִן־הַֽמַּחֲנֶ֖ה כִּ֥י הָחֳלֵֽיתִי:

---

b-b   *Perhaps a notation suggesting that Micaiah was identical with Micah, whose prophecies begin, "Listen, all you peoples," Mic. 1.2.*

c-c   *Targum and Septuagint read, "I will disguise myself and go."*

d-d   *Meaning of Heb. uncertain.*

e-e   *Lit. "your hand," because horses are guided by a pull on the appropriate rein; cf. 2 Kings 9.23.*

f-behind the lines;-*f* I'm wounded." ³⁵The battle
d-raged all day long,-*d* and the king remained
propped up in the chariot facing Aram; the
blood from the wound ran down into the hollow of the chariot, and at dusk he died. ³⁶As the
sun was going down, a shout went through the
army: "Every man to his own town! Every man
to his own district."

³⁷So the king died *g*-and was brought-*g* to Samaria. They buried the king in Samaria, ³⁸and
they flushed out the chariot at the pool of Samaria. Thus the dogs lapped up his blood and
the whores bathed [in it], in accordance with
the word that the LORD had spoken.*h*

³⁹The other events of Ahab's reign, and all his
actions—the ivory palace that he built and all
the towns that he fortified—are all recorded in
the Annals of the Kings of Israel. ⁴⁰Ahab slept
with his fathers, and his son Ahaziah succeeded
him as king.

⁴¹Jehoshaphat son of Asa had become king
of Judah in the fourth year of King Ahab of Israel. ⁴²Jehoshaphat was thirty-five years old
when he became king, and he reigned in Jerusalem for twenty-five years. His mother's name
was Azubah daughter of Shilhi. ⁴³He followed
closely the course of his father Asa and did not
deviate from it, doing what was pleasing to the
LORD. ⁴⁴However, the shrines did not cease to
function; the people still sacrificed and offered
at the shrines. ⁴⁵And further, Jehoshaphat submitted to the king of Israel. ⁴⁶As for the other
events of Jehoshaphat's reign and the valor he
displayed in battle, they are recorded in the Annals of the Kings of Judah. (⁴⁷He also stamped
out the remaining male prostitutes who had
survived in the land from the time of his father Asa.)

³⁵ וַתַּעֲלֶ֤ה הַמִּלְחָמָה֙ בַּיּ֣וֹם הַה֔וּא וְהַמֶּ֗לֶךְ
הָיָ֧ה מׇעֳמָ֛ד בַּמֶּרְכָּבָ֖ה נֹ֣כַח אֲרָ֑ם וַיָּ֣מׇת
בָּעֶ֗רֶב וַיִּ֙צֶק֙ דַּֽם־הַמַּכָּ֔ה אֶל־חֵ֖יק הָרָֽכֶב׃
³⁶ וַיַּעֲבֹ֤ר הָרִנָּה֙ בַּֽמַּחֲנֶ֔ה כְּבֹ֥א הַשֶּׁ֖מֶשׁ
לֵאמֹ֑ר אִ֥ישׁ אֶל־עִיר֖וֹ וְאִ֥ישׁ אֶל־אַרְצֽוֹ׃
³⁷ וַיָּ֣מׇת הַמֶּ֔לֶךְ וַיָּב֖וֹא שֹׁמְר֑וֹן וַיִּקְבְּר֥וּ
אֶת־הַמֶּ֖לֶךְ בְּשֹׁמְרֽוֹן׃ ³⁸ וַיִּשְׁטֹ֣ף אֶת־הָרֶ֗כֶב
עַ֣ל ׀ בְּרֵכַ֣ת שֹׁמְר֗וֹן וַיָּלֹ֤קּוּ הַכְּלָבִים֙
אֶת־דָּמ֔וֹ וְהַזֹּנ֖וֹת רָחָ֑צוּ כִּדְבַ֥ר יְהֹוָ֖ה אֲשֶׁ֥ר
דִּבֵּֽר׃
³⁹ וְיֶ֩תֶר֩ דִּבְרֵ֨י אַחְאָ֜ב וְכׇל־אֲשֶׁ֣ר עָשָׂ֗ה וּבֵ֤ית
הַשֵּׁן֙ אֲשֶׁ֣ר בָּנָ֔ה וְכׇל־הֶעָרִ֖ים אֲשֶׁ֣ר בָּנָ֑ה
הֲלֽוֹא־הֵ֣ם כְּתוּבִ֗ים עַל־סֵ֛פֶר דִּבְרֵ֥י הַיָּמִ֖ים
לְמַלְכֵ֥י יִשְׂרָאֵֽל׃ ⁴⁰ וַיִּשְׁכַּ֤ב אַחְאָב֙ עִם־
אֲבֹתָ֔יו וַיִּמְלֹ֛ךְ אֲחַזְיָ֥הוּ בְנ֖וֹ תַּחְתָּֽיו׃ פ

⁴¹ וִיהֽוֹשָׁפָט֙ בֶּן־אָסָ֔א מָלַ֖ךְ עַל־יְהוּדָ֑ה
בִּשְׁנַ֣ת אַרְבַּ֔ע לְאַחְאָ֖ב מֶ֥לֶךְ יִשְׂרָאֵֽל׃
⁴² יְהוֹשָׁפָ֗ט בֶּן־שְׁלֹשִׁ֨ים וְחָמֵ֤שׁ שָׁנָה֙
בְּמׇלְכ֔וֹ וְעֶשְׂרִ֣ים וְחָמֵ֤שׁ שָׁנָה֙ מָלַ֖ךְ
בִּירֽוּשָׁלָ֑͏ִם וְשֵׁ֣ם אִמּ֔וֹ עֲזוּבָ֖ה בַּת־שִׁלְחִֽי׃
⁴³ וַיֵּ֗לֶךְ בְּכׇל־דֶּ֛רֶךְ אָסָ֥א אָבִ֖יו לֹא־סָ֣ר
מִמֶּ֑נּוּ* לַעֲשׂ֥וֹת הַיָּשָׁ֖ר בְּעֵינֵ֥י יְהֹוָֽה׃ ⁴⁴ אַ֥ךְ
הַבָּמ֖וֹת לֹא־סָ֑רוּ ע֥וֹד הָעָ֛ם מְזַבְּחִ֥ים
וּֽמְקַטְּרִ֖ים בַּבָּמֽוֹת׃ ⁴⁵ וַיַּשְׁלֵ֥ם יְהוֹשָׁפָ֖ט
עִם־מֶ֥לֶךְ יִשְׂרָאֵֽל׃ ⁴⁶ וְיֶ֩תֶר֩ דִּבְרֵ֨י יְהוֹשָׁפָ֜ט
וּגְבֽוּרָת֤וֹ אֲשֶׁר־עָשָׂה֙ וַאֲשֶׁ֣ר נִלְחָ֔ם הֲלֹא־
הֵ֣ם כְּתוּבִ֗ים עַל־סֵ֛פֶר דִּבְרֵ֥י הַיָּמִ֖ים
לְמַלְכֵ֥י יְהוּדָֽה׃ ⁴⁷ וְיֶ֙תֶר֙ הַקָּדֵ֔שׁ אֲשֶׁ֣ר
נִשְׁאַ֔ר בִּימֵ֖י אָסָ֣א אָבִ֑יו בִּעֵ֖ר מִן־הָאָֽרֶץ׃

f-f Lit. "outside the camp."
g-g Lit. "he came."
h Cf. 21.19.

 v. 43.   סְבִירִין וּמְטֻעַ͏ְ "מִמֶּנָּה"

⁴⁸There was no king in Edom; ⁱ-a viceroy acted as king. ⁴⁹Jehoshaphat-ⁱ constructed Tarshish^j ships to sail to Ophir for gold. But he did not sail because the ships were wrecked at Ezion-geber. ⁵⁰Then Ahaziah son of Ahab proposed to Jehoshaphat, "Let my servants sail on the ships with your servants"; but Jehoshaphat would not agree. ⁵¹Jehoshaphat slept with his fathers and was buried with his fathers in the city of his father David, and his son Jehoram succeeded him as king.

⁵²[Meanwhile,] Ahaziah son of Ahab had become king of Israel, in Samaria, in the seventeenth year of King Jehoshaphat of Judah; he reigned over Israel two years. ⁵³He did what was displeasing to the LORD, following in the footsteps of his father and his mother, and in those of Jeroboam son of Nebat who had caused Israel to sin. ⁵⁴He worshiped Baal and bowed down to him; he vexed the LORD, the God of Israel, just as his father had done.

וּמֶ֥לֶךְ אֵ֛ין בֶּאֱד֖וֹם נִצָּ֣ב מֶ֑לֶךְ: ⁴⁹ יְהוֹשָׁפָ֡ט עָשָׂה֩ אֳנִיּ֨וֹת תַּרְשִׁ֜ישׁ לָלֶ֧כֶת אוֹפִ֛ירָה לַזָּהָ֖ב וְלֹ֣א הָלָ֑ךְ כִּֽי־נִשְׁבְּר֥ה נִשְׁבְּר֛וּ אֳנִיּ֖וֹת בְּעֶצְי֥וֹן גָּֽבֶר: ⁵⁰ אָ֣ז אָמַ֗ר אֲחַזְיָ֤הוּ בֶן־אַחְאָב֙ אֶל־יְה֣וֹשָׁפָ֔ט יֵלְכ֧וּ עֲבָדַ֛י עִם־עֲבָדֶ֖יךָ בָּאֳנִיּ֑וֹת וְלֹ֥א אָבָ֖ה יְהוֹשָׁפָֽט: ⁵¹ וַיִּשְׁכַּ֣ב יְהוֹשָׁפָט֮ עִם־אֲבֹתָיו֒ וַיִּקָּבֵר֙ עִם־אֲבֹתָ֔יו בְּעִ֖יר דָּוִ֣ד אָבִ֑יו וַיִּמְלֹ֛ךְ יְהוֹרָ֥ם בְּנ֖וֹ תַּחְתָּֽיו: ס

⁵² אֲחַזְיָ֤הוּ בֶן־אַחְאָב֙ מָלַ֣ךְ עַל־יִשְׂרָאֵ֔ל בְּשֹׁ֣מְר֔וֹן בִּשְׁנַת֙ שְׁבַ֣ע עֶשְׂרֵ֔ה לִיהוֹשָׁפָ֖ט מֶ֣לֶךְ יְהוּדָ֑ה וַיִּמְלֹ֥ךְ עַל־יִשְׂרָאֵ֖ל שְׁנָתָֽיִם: ⁵³ וַיַּ֥עַשׂ הָרַ֖ע בְּעֵינֵ֣י יְהוָ֑ה וַיֵּ֗לֶךְ בְּדֶ֣רֶךְ אָבִ֞יו וּבְדֶ֣רֶךְ אִמּ֗וֹ וּבְדֶ֙רֶךְ֙ יָרָבְעָ֣ם בֶּן־נְבָ֔ט אֲשֶׁ֥ר הֶחֱטִ֖יא אֶת־יִשְׂרָאֵֽל: ⁵⁴ וַֽיַּעֲבֹד֙ אֶת־הַבַּ֔עַל וַיִּשְׁתַּחֲוֶ֖ה ל֑וֹ וַיַּכְעֵ֗ס אֶת־יְהוָה֙ אֱלֹהֵ֣י יִשְׂרָאֵ֔ל כְּכֹ֥ל אֲשֶׁר־עָשָׂ֖ה אָבִֽיו:

מלכים ב

2 KINGS

1 After Ahab's death, Moab rebelled against Israel.

²Ahaziah fell through the lattice in his upper chamber at Samaria and was injured. So he sent messengers, whom he instructed: "Go inquire of Baal-zebub, the god of Ekron, whether I shall recover from this injury." ³But an angel of the LORD said to Elijah the Tishbite, "Go and confront the messengers of the king of Samaria and say to them, 'Is there no God in Israel that you go to inquire of Baal-zebub, the god of Ekron? ⁴Assuredly, thus said the LORD: You shall not *a*-rise from the bed you are lying on,-*a* but you shall die.'" And Elijah went.

⁵The messengers returned to Ahaziah;*b* and he asked, "Why have you come back?" ⁶They answered him, "A man came toward us and said to us, 'Go back to the king who sent you, and say to him: Thus said the LORD: Is there no God in Israel that you must send to inquire of Baal-zebub, the god of Ekron? Assuredly, you shall not rise from the bed you are lying on, but shall die.'" ⁷"What sort of man was it," he asked them, "who came toward you and said these things to you?" ⁸"A hairy man," they replied, "with a leather belt tied around his waist." "That's Elijah the Tishbite!" he said.

⁹Then he sent to him a captain of fifty with his fifty men. He climbed up to him, and found him sitting at the top of a hill. "Man of God," he said to him, "by order of the king, come down!" ¹⁰Elijah replied to the captain of the fifty, "If I am a man of God, let fire come down

א וַיִּפְשַׁ֤ע מוֹאָב֙ בְּיִשְׂרָאֵ֔ל אַחֲרֵ֖י מ֥וֹת אַחְאָֽב:

2 וַיִּפֹּ֨ל אֲחַזְיָ֜ה בְּעַ֣ד הַשְּׂבָכָ֗ה בַּעֲלִיָּת֛וֹ אֲשֶׁ֥ר בְּשֹׁמְר֖וֹן וַיָּ֑חַל וַיִּשְׁלַ֣ח מַלְאָכִ֔ים וַיֹּ֤אמֶר אֲלֵהֶם֙ לְכ֣וּ דִרְשׁ֗וּ בְּבַ֤עַל זְבוּב֙ אֱלֹהֵ֣י עֶקְר֔וֹן אִם־אֶחְיֶ֖ה מֵחֳלִ֥י זֶֽה: ס 3 וּמַלְאַ֣ךְ יְהוָ֗ה דִּבֶּר֙ אֶל־אֵלִיָּ֣ה הַתִּשְׁבִּ֔י ק֣וּם עֲלֵ֔ה לִקְרַ֖את מַלְאֲכֵ֣י מֶֽלֶךְ־שֹׁמְר֑וֹן וְדַבֵּ֣ר אֲלֵהֶ֔ם הֲֽמִבְּלִ֤י אֵין־אֱלֹהִים֙ בְּיִשְׂרָאֵ֔ל אַתֶּם֙ הֹֽלְכִ֔ים לִדְרֹ֕שׁ בְּבַ֥עַל זְב֖וּב אֱלֹהֵ֥י עֶקְרֽוֹן: 4 וְלָכֵ֞ן כֹּֽה־אָמַ֣ר יְהוָ֗ה הַמִּטָּ֞ה אֲשֶׁר־עָלִ֤יתָ שָּׁם֙ לֹֽא־תֵרֵ֣ד מִמֶּ֔נָּה כִּ֥י מ֖וֹת תָּמ֑וּת וַיֵּ֖לֶךְ אֵלִיָּֽה:

5 וַיָּשׁ֥וּבוּ הַמַּלְאָכִ֖ים אֵלָ֑יו וַיֹּ֥אמֶר אֲלֵיהֶ֖ם מַה־זֶּ֥ה שַׁבְתֶּֽם: 6 וַיֹּאמְר֣וּ אֵלָ֗יו אִ֣ישׁ ׀ עָלָ֣ה לִקְרָאתֵ֗נוּ וַיֹּ֣אמֶר אֵלֵ֘ינוּ֮ לְכ֣וּ שׁוּבוּ֮ אֶל־הַמֶּ֣לֶךְ אֲשֶׁר־שָׁלַ֣ח אֶתְכֶם֒ וְדִבַּרְתֶּ֣ם אֵלָ֗יו כֹּ֚ה אָמַ֣ר יְהוָ֔ה הֲֽמִבְּלִ֤י אֵין־אֱלֹהִים֙ בְּיִשְׂרָאֵ֔ל אַתָּ֣ה שֹׁלֵ֔חַ לִדְרֹ֕שׁ בְּבַ֥עַל זְב֖וּב אֱלֹהֵ֣י עֶקְר֑וֹן לָ֠כֵן הַמִּטָּ֞ה אֲשֶׁר־עָלִ֥יתָ שָּׁ֛ם לֹֽא־תֵרֵ֥ד מִמֶּ֖נָּה כִּֽי־מ֥וֹת תָּמֽוּת: 7 וַיְדַבֵּ֣ר אֲלֵהֶ֔ם מֶ֚ה מִשְׁפַּ֣ט הָאִ֔ישׁ אֲשֶׁ֥ר עָלָ֖ה לִקְרַאתְכֶ֑ם וַיְדַבֵּ֣ר אֲלֵיכֶ֔ם אֶת־הַדְּבָרִ֖ים הָאֵֽלֶּה: 8 וַיֹּאמְר֣וּ אֵלָ֗יו אִ֚ישׁ בַּ֣עַל שֵׂעָ֔ר וְאֵז֥וֹר ע֖וֹר אָז֣וּר בְּמָתְנָ֑יו וַיֹּאמַ֕ר אֵלִיָּ֥ה הַתִּשְׁבִּ֖י הֽוּא:

9 וַיִּשְׁלַ֥ח אֵלָ֛יו שַׂר־חֲמִשִּׁ֖ים וַחֲמִשָּׁ֑יו וַיַּ֣עַל אֵלָ֗יו וְהִנֵּה֙ יֹשֵׁב֙ עַל־רֹ֣אשׁ הָהָ֔ר וַיְדַבֵּ֣ר אֵלָ֔יו אִ֣ישׁ הָאֱלֹהִ֔ים הַמֶּ֖לֶךְ דִּבֶּ֥ר רֵֽדָה: 10 וַיַּעֲנֶ֣ה אֵלִיָּ֗הוּ וַיְדַבֵּר֮ אֶל־שַׂ֣ר הַחֲמִשִּׁים֒

---

a-a Lit. "descend from the bed you have mounted."
b Heb. "him."

775

from heaven and consume you with your fifty men!" And fire came down from heaven and consumed him and his fifty men. ¹¹The king then sent to him another captain with his fifty men; and he ᶜ-addressed him-ᶜ as follows: "Man of God, by order of the king, come down at once!" ¹²But Elijah answered him, "If I am a man of God, let fire come down from heaven and consume you with your fifty men!" And fire of God came down from heaven and consumed him and his fifty men. ¹³Then he sent a third captain of fifty with his fifty men. The third captain of fifty climbed to the top, knelt before Elijah, and implored him, saying, "Oh, man of God, please have regard for my life and the lives of these fifty servants of yours! ¹⁴Already fire has come from heaven and consumed the first two captains of fifty and their men;ᵈ I beg you, have regard for my life!"

¹⁵Then the angel of the LORD said to Elijah, "Go down with him, do not be afraid of him." So he rose and went down with him to the king. ¹⁶He said to him, "Because you sent messengers to inquire of Baal-zebub the god of Ekron— as if there were no God in Israel whose word you could seek—assuredly, you shall not rise from the bed which you are lying on; but you shall die."

¹⁷And [Ahaziah] died, according to the word of the LORD that Elijah had spoken. Jehoramᵉ succeeded him as king, in the second year of King Jehoram son of Jehoshaphat of Judah, for he had no son. ¹⁸The other events of Ahaziah's reign [and] his actions are recorded in the Annals of the Kings of Israel.

2 When the LORD was about to take Elijah up to heaven in a whirlwind, Elijah and Elisha

וְאִם־אִישׁ אֱלֹהִים אָנִי תֵּרֶד אֵשׁ מִן־
הַשָּׁמַ֫יִם וְתֹאכַל אֹתְךָ֖ וְאֶת־חֲמִשֶּׁ֑יךָ וַתֵּ֣רֶד
אֵשׁ מִן־הַשָּׁמַ֫יִם וַתֹּ֥אכַל אֹת֖וֹ וְאֶת־
חֲמִשָּֽׁיו: ¹¹ וַיָּ֗שָׁב וַיִּשְׁלַ֣ח אֵלָ֔יו שַׂר־
חֲמִשִּׁ֥ים אַחֵ֖ר וַחֲמִשָּׁ֑יו וַיַּ֡עַן וַיְדַבֵּ֣ר אֵלָ֗יו
אִ֣ישׁ הָאֱלֹהִ֗ים כֹּֽה־אָמַ֤ר הַמֶּ֙לֶךְ֙ מְהֵרָ֣ה
רֵֽדָה: ¹² וַיַּ֣עַן אֵלִיָּ֗ה וַיְדַבֵּר֮ אֲלֵיהֶם֒ אִם־
אִ֤ישׁ הָֽאֱלֹהִים֙ אָ֔נִי תֵּ֤רֶד אֵשׁ֙ מִן־הַשָּׁמַ֔יִם
וְתֹאכַ֣ל אֹֽתְךָ֔ וְאֶת־חֲמִשֶּׁ֑יךָ וַתֵּ֤רֶד אֵשׁ־
אֱלֹהִים֙ מִן־הַשָּׁמַ֔יִם וַתֹּ֥אכַל אֹת֖וֹ וְאֶת־
חֲמִשָּֽׁיו: ¹³ וַיָּ֗שָׁב וַיִּשְׁלַ֞ח שַׂר־חֲמִשִּׁ֤ים
שְׁלִשִׁים֙ וַחֲמִשָּׁ֔יו וַיַּ֗עַל וַיָּבֹא֙ שַׂר־
הַחֲמִשִּׁ֣ים הַשְּׁלִישִׁ֔י וַיִּכְרַ֥ע עַל־בִּרְכָּ֣יו ׀
לְנֶ֣גֶד אֵלִיָּ֗הוּ וַיִּתְחַנֵּ֤ן אֵלָיו֙ וַיְדַבֵּ֣ר אֵלָ֔יו
אִ֣ישׁ הָאֱלֹהִ֗ים תִּֽיקַר־נָ֣א נַפְשִׁ֗י וְנֶ֨פֶשׁ
עֲבָדֶ֥יךָ אֵ֛לֶּה חֲמִשִּׁ֖ים בְּעֵינֶֽיךָ: ¹⁴ הִנֵּ֡ה
יָ֣רְדָה אֵ֣שׁ מִן־הַשָּׁמַ֗יִם וַ֠תֹּאכַל אֶת־שְׁנֵ֞י
שָׂרֵ֨י הַחֲמִשִּׁ֤ים הָרִֽאשֹׁנִים֙ וְאֶת־חֲמִשֵּׁיהֶ֔ם
וְעַתָּ֕ה תִּיקַ֥ר נַפְשִׁ֖י בְּעֵינֶֽיךָ: ס

¹⁵ וַיְדַבֵּ֞ר מַלְאַ֤ךְ יְהוָה֙ אֶל־אֵ֣לִיָּ֔הוּ רֵ֥ד אוֹת֖וֹ
אַל־תִּירָ֣א מִפָּנָ֑יו וַיָּ֛קָם וַיֵּ֥רֶד אוֹת֖וֹ אֶל־
הַמֶּֽלֶךְ: ¹⁶ וַיְדַבֵּ֨ר אֵלָ֜יו כֹּֽה־אָמַ֣ר יְהוָ֗ה יַ֜עַן
אֲשֶׁר־שָׁלַ֣חְתָּ מַלְאָכִים֮ לִדְרֹשׁ֮ בְּבַ֣עַל זְבוּב֒
אֱלֹהֵ֣י עֶקְר֔וֹן הַֽמִבְּלִ֥י אֵין־אֱלֹהִים֙ בְּיִשְׂרָאֵ֔ל
לִדְרֹ֖שׁ בִּדְבָר֑וֹ לָכֵן֩ הַמִּטָּ֨ה אֲשֶׁר־עָלִ֧יתָ שָּׁ֛ם
לֹֽא־תֵרֵ֥ד מִמֶּ֖נָּה כִּֽי־מ֥וֹת תָּמֽוּת:

¹⁷ וַיָּ֜מָת כִּדְבַ֥ר יְהוָ֣ה ׀ אֲשֶׁר־דִּבֶּ֣ר אֵֽלִיָּ֗הוּ
וַיִּמְלֹ֤ךְ יְהוֹרָם֙ תַּחְתָּ֔יו פ בִּשְׁנַ֣ת שְׁתַּ֔יִם
לִיהוֹרָ֥ם בֶּן־יְהוֹשָׁפָ֖ט מֶ֣לֶךְ יְהוּדָ֑ה כִּ֥י
לֹֽא־הָ֥יָה ל֖וֹ בֵּֽן: ¹⁸ וְיֶ֛תֶר דִּבְרֵ֥י אֲחַזְיָ֖הוּ
אֲשֶׁ֣ר עָשָׂ֑ה הֲלֹֽא־הֵ֣מָּה כְתוּבִ֗ים עַל־סֵ֛פֶר
דִּבְרֵ֥י הַיָּמִ֖ים לְמַלְכֵ֥י יִשְׂרָאֵֽל: פ

ב וַיְהִ֗י בְּהַעֲל֤וֹת יְהוָה֙ אֶת־אֵ֣לִיָּ֔הוּ
בַּֽסְעָרָ֖ה הַשָּׁמָ֑יִם וַיֵּ֧לֶךְ אֵלִיָּ֛הוּ וֶאֱלִישָׁ֖ע

ᶜ-ᶜ   *Emendation yields "went up and said to him," cf. v. 9.*
ᵈ   *Lit. "fifties."*
ᵉ   *Brother of Ahaziah.*

had set out from Gilgal. ²Elijah said to Elisha, "Stay here, for the LORD has sent me on to Bethel." "As the LORD lives and as you live," said Elisha, "I will not leave you." So they went down to Bethel. ³Disciples of the prophets at Bethel came out to Elisha and said to him, "Do you know that the LORD will take your master ᵃ-away from you-ᵃ today?" He replied, "I know it, too; be silent."

⁴Then Elijah said to him, "Elisha, stay here, for the LORD has sent me on to Jericho." "As the LORD lives and as you live," said Elisha, "I will not leave you." So they went on to Jericho. ⁵The disciples of the prophets who were at Jericho came over to Elisha and said to him, "Do you know that the LORD will take your master ᵃ-away from you-ᵃ today?" He replied, "I know it, too; be silent."

⁶Elijah said to him, "Stay here, for the LORD has sent me on to the Jordan." "As the LORD lives and as you live, I will not leave you," he said, and the two of them went on. ⁷Fifty men of the disciples of the prophets followed and stood by at a distance from them as the two of them stopped at the Jordan. ⁸Thereupon Elijah took his mantle and, rolling it up, he struck the water; it divided to the right and left, so that the two of them crossed over on dry land. ⁹As they were crossing, Elijah said to Elisha, "Tell me, what can I do for you before I am taken from you?" Elisha answered, "Let a ᵇ-double portion-ᵇ of your spirit pass on to me." ¹⁰"You have asked a difficult thing," he said. "If you see me as I am being taken from you, this will be granted to you; if not, it will not." ¹¹As they kept on walking and talking, a fiery chariot with fiery horses suddenly appeared and separated one from the other; and Elijah went up to heaven in a whirlwind. ¹²Elisha saw it, and he cried out, "Oh, father, father! Israel's chariots and horse-

מִן־הַגִּלְגָּל׃ 2 וַיֹּאמֶר אֵלִיָּהוּ אֶל־אֱלִישָׁע שֵׁב־נָא פֹה כִּי יְהוָה שְׁלָחַנִי עַד־בֵּית־אֵל וַיֹּאמֶר אֱלִישָׁע חַי־יְהוָה וְחֵי־נַפְשְׁךָ אִם־אֶעֶזְבֶךָ וַיֵּרְדוּ בֵּית־אֵל׃ 3 וַיֵּצְאוּ בְנֵי־הַנְּבִיאִים אֲשֶׁר־בֵּית־אֵל* אֶל־אֱלִישָׁע וַיֹּאמְרוּ אֵלָיו הֲיָדַעְתָּ כִּי הַיּוֹם יְהוָה לֹקֵחַ אֶת־אֲדֹנֶיךָ מֵעַל רֹאשֶׁךָ וַיֹּאמֶר גַּם־אֲנִי יָדַעְתִּי הֶחֱשׁוּ׃ 4 וַיֹּאמֶר לוֹ אֵלִיָּהוּ אֱלִישָׁע ׀ שֵׁב־נָא פֹה כִּי יְהוָה שְׁלָחַנִי יְרִיחוֹ וַיֹּאמֶר חַי־יְהוָה וְחֵי־נַפְשְׁךָ אִם־אֶעֶזְבֶךָ וַיָּבֹאוּ יְרִיחוֹ׃ 5 וַיִּגְּשׁוּ בְנֵי־הַנְּבִיאִים אֲשֶׁר־בִּירִיחוֹ אֶל־אֱלִישָׁע וַיֹּאמְרוּ אֵלָיו הֲיָדַעְתָּ כִּי הַיּוֹם יְהוָה לֹקֵחַ אֶת־אֲדֹנֶיךָ מֵעַל רֹאשֶׁךָ וַיֹּאמֶר גַּם־אֲנִי יָדַעְתִּי הֶחֱשׁוּ׃ 6 וַיֹּאמֶר לוֹ אֵלִיָּהוּ שֵׁב־נָא פֹה כִּי יְהוָה שְׁלָחַנִי הַיַּרְדֵּנָה וַיֹּאמֶר חַי־יְהוָה וְחֵי־נַפְשְׁךָ אִם־אֶעֶזְבֶךָ וַיֵּלְכוּ שְׁנֵיהֶם׃ 7 וַחֲמִשִּׁים אִישׁ מִבְּנֵי הַנְּבִיאִים הָלְכוּ וַיַּעַמְדוּ מִנֶּגֶד מֵרָחוֹק וּשְׁנֵיהֶם עָמְדוּ עַל־הַיַּרְדֵּן׃ 8 וַיִּקַּח אֵלִיָּהוּ אֶת־אַדַּרְתּוֹ וַיִּגְלֹם וַיַּכֶּה אֶת־הַמַּיִם וַיֵּחָצוּ הֵנָּה וָהֵנָּה וַיַּעַבְרוּ שְׁנֵיהֶם בֶּחָרָבָה׃ 9 וַיְהִי כְעָבְרָם וְאֵלִיָּהוּ אָמַר אֶל־אֱלִישָׁע שְׁאַל מָה אֶעֱשֶׂה־לָּךְ בְּטֶרֶם אֶלָּקַח מֵעִמָּךְ וַיֹּאמֶר אֱלִישָׁע וִיהִי־נָא פִּי־שְׁנַיִם בְּרוּחֲךָ אֵלָי׃ 10 וַיֹּאמֶר הִקְשִׁיתָ לִשְׁאוֹל אִם־תִּרְאֶה אֹתִי לֻקָּח מֵאִתָּךְ יְהִי־לְךָ כֵן וְאִם־אַיִן לֹא יִהְיֶה׃ 11 וַיְהִי הֵמָּה הֹלְכִים הָלוֹךְ וְדַבֵּר וְהִנֵּה רֶכֶב־אֵשׁ וְסוּסֵי אֵשׁ וַיַּפְרִדוּ בֵּין שְׁנֵיהֶם וַיַּעַל אֵלִיָּהוּ בַּסְעָרָה הַשָּׁמָיִם׃ 12 וֶאֱלִישָׁע רֹאֶה וְהוּא מְצַעֵק אָבִי ׀ אָבִי רֶכֶב יִשְׂרָאֵל

---

v. 3. סבירין ומטעין "בבית"

men!" When he could no longer see him, he grasped his garments and rent them in two.

¹³He picked up Elijah's mantle, which had dropped from him; and he went back and stood on the bank of the Jordan. ¹⁴Taking the mantle which had dropped from Elijah, he struck the water and said, "Where is the LORD, the God of Elijah?" As he too struck the water, it parted to the right and to the left, and Elisha crossed over. ¹⁵When the disciples of the prophets at Jericho saw him from a distance, they exclaimed, "The spirit of Elijah has settled on Elisha!" And they went to meet him and bowed low before him to the ground.

¹⁶They said to him, "Your servants have fifty able men with them. Let them go and look for your master; perhaps the spirit of the LORD has carried him off and cast him upon some mountain or into some valley." "Do not send them," he replied. ¹⁷But they kept pressing him for a long time, until he said, "Send them." So they sent out fifty men, who searched for three days but did not find him. ¹⁸They came back to him while he was still in Jericho; and he said to them, "I told you not to go."

¹⁹The men of the town said to Elisha, "Look, the town is a pleasant place to live in, as my lord can see; but the water is bad and the land causes bereavement." ²⁰He responded, "Bring me a new dish and put salt in it." They brought it to him; ²¹he went to the spring and threw salt into it. And he said, "Thus said the LORD: I heal this water; no longer shall death and bereavement come from it!" ²²The water has remained wholesome to this day, in accordance with the word spoken by Elisha.

²³From there he went up to Bethel. As he was going up the road, some little boys came out of the town and jeered at him, saying, "Go away, baldhead! Go away, baldhead!" ²⁴He turned

וּפָרָשָׁיו וְלֹא רָאָהוּ עוֹד וַיַּחֲזֵק בִּבְגָדָיו
וַיִּקְרָעֵם לִשְׁנַיִם קְרָעִים:

¹³ וַיָּרֶם אֶת־אַדֶּרֶת אֵלִיָּהוּ אֲשֶׁר נָפְלָה
מֵעָלָיו וַיָּשָׁב וַיַּעֲמֹד עַל־שְׂפַת הַיַּרְדֵּן:

¹⁴ וַיִּקַּח אֶת־אַדֶּרֶת אֵלִיָּהוּ אֲשֶׁר־נָפְלָה
מֵעָלָיו וַיַּכֶּה אֶת־הַמַּיִם וַיֹּאמַר אַיֵּה יְהוָה
אֱלֹהֵי אֵלִיָּהוּ אַף־הוּא ׀ וַיַּכֶּה אֶת־הַמַּיִם
וַיֵּחָצוּ הֵנָּה וָהֵנָּה וַיַּעֲבֹר אֱלִישָׁע:

¹⁵ וַיִּרְאֻהוּ בְנֵי־הַנְּבִיאִים אֲשֶׁר־בִּירִיחוֹ
מִנֶּגֶד וַיֹּאמְרוּ נָחָה רוּחַ אֵלִיָּהוּ עַל־אֱלִישָׁע
וַיָּבֹאוּ לִקְרָאתוֹ וַיִּשְׁתַּחֲווּ־לוֹ אָרְצָה:

¹⁶ וַיֹּאמְרוּ אֵלָיו הִנֵּה־נָא יֵשׁ־אֶת־עֲבָדֶיךָ
חֲמִשִּׁים אֲנָשִׁים בְּנֵי־חַיִל יֵלְכוּ נָא וִיבַקְשׁוּ
אֶת־אֲדֹנֶיךָ פֶּן־נְשָׂאוֹ רוּחַ יְהוָה וַיַּשְׁלִכֵהוּ
בְּאַחַד הֶהָרִים אוֹ בְּאַחַת הַגֵּאָיוֹת
וַיֹּאמֶר לֹא תִשְׁלָחוּ: ¹⁷ וַיִּפְצְרוּ־בוֹ עַד־
בֹּשׁ וַיֹּאמֶר שְׁלָחוּ וַיִּשְׁלְחוּ חֲמִשִּׁים אִישׁ
וַיְבַקְשׁוּ שְׁלֹשָׁה־יָמִים וְלֹא מְצָאֻהוּ:

¹⁸ וַיָּשֻׁבוּ אֵלָיו וְהוּא יֹשֵׁב בִּירִיחוֹ וַיֹּאמֶר
אֲלֵהֶם הֲלוֹא־אָמַרְתִּי אֲלֵיכֶם אַל־תֵּלֵכוּ:

¹⁹ וַיֹּאמְרוּ אַנְשֵׁי הָעִיר אֶל־אֱלִישָׁע הִנֵּה־
נָא מוֹשַׁב הָעִיר טוֹב כַּאֲשֶׁר אֲדֹנִי רֹאֶה
וְהַמַּיִם רָעִים וְהָאָרֶץ מְשַׁכָּלֶת: ²⁰ וַיֹּאמֶר
קְחוּ־לִי צְלֹחִית חֲדָשָׁה וְשִׂימוּ שָׁם מֶלַח
וַיִּקְחוּ אֵלָיו: ²¹ וַיֵּצֵא אֶל־מוֹצָא הַמַּיִם
וַיַּשְׁלֶךְ־שָׁם מֶלַח וַיֹּאמֶר כֹּה־אָמַר יְהוָה
רִפִּאתִי לַמַּיִם הָאֵלֶּה לֹא־יִהְיֶה מִשָּׁם עוֹד
מָוֶת וּמְשַׁכָּלֶת: ²² וַיֵּרָפוּ* הַמַּיִם עַד הַיּוֹם
הַזֶּה כִּדְבַר אֱלִישָׁע אֲשֶׁר דִּבֵּר: פ

²³ וַיַּעַל מִשָּׁם בֵּית־אֵל וְהוּא ׀ עֹלֶה בַדֶּרֶךְ
וּנְעָרִים קְטַנִּים יָצְאוּ מִן־הָעִיר וַיִּתְקַלְּסוּ־
בוֹ וַיֹּאמְרוּ לוֹ עֲלֵה קֵרֵחַ עֲלֵה קֵרֵחַ:

²⁴ וַיִּפֶן אַחֲרָיו וַיִּרְאֵם וַיְקַלְלֵם בְּשֵׁם

around and looked at them and cursed them in the name of the Lord. Thereupon, two she-bears came out of the woods and mangled forty-two of the children. 25He went on from there to Mount Carmel, and from there he returned to Samaria.

3 Jehoram son of Ahab became king of Israel in Samaria in the eighteenth year of King Jehoshaphat of Judah; and he reigned twelve years. 2He did what was displeasing to the Lord, yet not like his father and mother, for he removed the pillars of Baal that his father had made. 3However, he clung to the sins which Jeroboam son of Nebat caused Israel to commit; he did not depart from them.

4Now King Mesha of Moab was a sheep breeder; and he used to pay as tribute to the king of Israel *a*-a hundred thousand lambs and the wool of a hundred thousand rams.-*a* 5But when Ahab died, the king of Moab rebelled against the king of Israel. 6So King Jehoram promptly set out from Samaria and mustered all Israel. 7At the same time, he sent this message to King Jehoshaphat of Judah: "The king of Moab has rebelled against me; will you come with me to make war on Moab?" He replied, "I will go. I will do what you do: my troops shall be your troops, my horses shall be your horses." 8And he asked, "Which route shall we take?" [Jehoram] replied, "The road through the wilderness of Edom."

9So the king of Israel, the king of Judah, and the king of Edom set out, and they marched for seven days until they rounded [the tip of the Dead Sea]; and there was no water left for the army or for the animals that were with them. 10"Alas!" cried the king of Israel. "The Lord has

יְהֹוָה וַתֵּצֶ֫אנָה שְׁתַּ֫יִם דֻּבִּים֙ מִן־הַיַּ֔עַר וַתְּבַקַּ֣עְנָה מֵהֶ֔ם אַרְבָּעִ֥ים וּשְׁנֵ֖י יְלָדִֽים׃ 25וַיֵּ֥לֶךְ מִשָּׁ֖ם אֶל־הַ֣ר הַכַּרְמֶ֑ל וּמִשָּׁ֖ם שָׁ֥ב שֹׁמְרֽוֹן׃ פ

ג וִֽיהוֹרָ֣ם בֶּן־אַחְאָ֗ב מָלַ֤ךְ עַל־יִשְׂרָאֵל֙ בְּשֹׁ֣מְר֔וֹן בִּשְׁנַת֙ שְׁמֹנֶ֣ה עֶשְׂרֵ֔ה לִיהוֹשָׁפָ֖ט מֶ֣לֶךְ יְהוּדָ֑ה וַיִּמְלֹ֖ךְ שְׁתֵּים־עֶשְׂרֵ֥ה שָׁנָֽה׃ 2וַיַּֽעֲשֶׂ֤ה הָרַע֙ בְּעֵינֵ֣י יְהֹוָ֔ה רַ֕ק לֹ֥א כְאָבִ֖יו וּכְאִמּ֑וֹ וַיָּ֕סַר אֶת־מַצְּבַ֣ת הַבַּ֔עַל אֲשֶׁ֥ר עָשָׂ֖ה אָבִֽיו׃ 3רַ֠ק בְּחַטֹּאות֩* יָרׇבְעָ֨ם בֶּן־נְבָ֜ט אֲשֶׁר־הֶחֱטִ֤יא אֶת־יִשְׂרָאֵל֙ דָּבֵ֔ק לֹא־סָ֖ר מִמֶּֽנָּה׃ ס

4וּמֵישַׁ֤ע מֶֽלֶךְ־מוֹאָב֙ הָיָ֣ה נֹקֵ֔ד וְהֵשִׁ֥יב לְמֶֽלֶךְ־יִשְׂרָאֵ֖ל מֵאָה־אֶ֥לֶף כָּרִ֑ים וּמֵ֥אָה אֶ֖לֶף אֵילִ֥ים צָֽמֶר׃ 5וַיְהִ֖י כְּמ֣וֹת אַחְאָ֑ב וַיִּפְשַׁ֥ע מֶֽלֶךְ־מוֹאָ֖ב בְּמֶ֥לֶךְ יִשְׂרָאֵֽל׃ 6וַיֵּצֵ֞א הַמֶּ֧לֶךְ יְהוֹרָ֛ם בַּיּ֥וֹם הַה֖וּא מִשֹּׁמְר֑וֹן וַיִּפְקֹ֖ד אֶת־כׇּל־יִשְׂרָאֵֽל׃ 7וַיֵּ֡לֶךְ וַיִּשְׁלַח֩ אֶל־יְהוֹשָׁפָ֨ט מֶֽלֶךְ־יְהוּדָ֜ה לֵאמֹ֗ר מֶ֤לֶךְ מוֹאָב֙ פָּשַׁ֣ע בִּ֔י הֲתֵלֵ֥ךְ אִתִּ֛י אֶל־מוֹאָ֖ב לַמִּלְחָמָ֑ה וַיֹּ֣אמֶר אֶעֱלֶ֔ה כָּמ֧וֹנִי כָמ֛וֹךָ כְּעַמִּ֥י כְעַמֶּ֖ךָ כְּסוּסַ֥י כְּסוּסֶֽיךָ׃ 8וַיֹּ֕אמֶר אֵי־זֶ֥ה הַדֶּ֖רֶךְ נַעֲלֶ֑ה וַיֹּ֕אמֶר דֶּ֖רֶךְ מִדְבַּ֥ר אֱדֽוֹם׃ 9וַיֵּ֩לֶךְ֩ מֶ֨לֶךְ יִשְׂרָאֵ֤ל וּמֶֽלֶךְ־יְהוּדָה֙ וּמֶ֣לֶךְ אֱד֔וֹם וַיָּסֹ֙בּוּ֙ דֶּ֚רֶךְ שִׁבְעַ֣ת יָמִ֔ים וְלֹא־הָיָ֨ה מַ֜יִם לַֽמַּחֲנֶ֗ה וְלַבְּהֵמָ֖ה אֲשֶׁ֥ר בְּרַגְלֵיהֶֽם׃ 10וַיֹּ֖אמֶר מֶ֣לֶךְ יִשְׂרָאֵ֑ל אֲהָ֕הּ כִּֽי־קָרָ֣א יְהֹוָ֗ה

---

a-a Or *"the wool of 100,000 lambs and of 100,000 rams."*

brought these three kings together only to deliver them into the hands of Moab." ¹¹But Jehoshaphat said, "Isn't there a prophet of the LORD here, through whom we may inquire of the LORD?" One of the courtiers of the king of Israel spoke up and said, "Elisha son of Shaphat, who ᵇ-poured water on the hands of-ᵇ Elijah, is here." ¹²"The word of the LORD is with him," said Jehoshaphat. So the king of Israel and Jehoshaphat and the king of Edom went down to him. ¹³Elisha said to the king of Israel, "What have you to do with me? Go to your father's prophets or your mother's prophets." But the king of Israel said, "Don't [say that], for the LORD has brought these three kings together only to deliver them into the hands of Moab." ¹⁴"As the LORD of Hosts lives, whom I serve," Elisha answered, "were it not that I respect King Jehoshaphat of Judah, I wouldn't look at you or notice you. ¹⁵Now then, get me a musician."

As the musician played, the hand of the LORD came upon him, ¹⁶and he said, "Thus said the LORD: This wadi shall be full of pools. ¹⁷For thus said the LORD: You shall see no wind, you shall see no rain, and yet the wadi shall be filled with water; and you and your cattle and your pack animals shall drink. ¹⁸And this is but a slight thing in the sight of the LORD, for He will also deliver Moab into your hands. ¹⁹You shall conquer every fortified town and every splendid city; you shall fell every good tree and stop up all wells of water; and every fertile field you shall ruin with stones." ²⁰And in the morning, when it was time to present the meal offering, water suddenly came from the direction of Edom and the land was covered by the water.

²¹Meanwhile, all the Moabites had heard that the kings were advancing to make war on them; ᶜ-every man old enough to bear arms-ᶜ rallied, and they stationed themselves at the border.

לִשְׁלֹ֨שֶׁת הַמְּלָכִ֤ים הָאֵ֙לֶּה֙ לָתֵ֣ת אוֹתָ֔ם בְּיַד־מוֹאָֽב׃ ¹¹ וַיֹּ֣אמֶר יְהוֹשָׁפָ֗ט הַאֵ֨ין פֹּ֤ה נָבִיא֙ לַֽיהוָ֔ה וְנִדְרְשָׁ֥ה אֶת־יְהוָ֖ה מֵאוֹת֑וֹ וַ֠יַּעַן אֶחָ֞ד מֵעַבְדֵ֤י מֶֽלֶךְ־יִשְׂרָאֵל֙ וַיֹּ֔אמֶר פֹּ֚ה אֱלִישָׁ֣ע בֶּן־שָׁפָ֔ט אֲשֶׁר־יָ֥צַק מַ֖יִם עַל־יְדֵ֥י אֵלִיָּֽהוּ׃ ¹² וַיֹּ֙אמֶר֙ יְה֣וֹשָׁפָ֔ט יֵ֥שׁ אוֹת֖וֹ דְּבַר־יְהוָ֑ה וַיֵּרְד֣וּ אֵלָ֗יו מֶ֤לֶךְ יִשְׂרָאֵל֙ וִיהוֹשָׁפָ֖ט וּמֶ֥לֶךְ אֱדֽוֹם׃ ¹³ וַיֹּ֙אמֶר֙ אֱלִישָׁ֜ע אֶל־מֶ֤לֶךְ יִשְׂרָאֵל֙ מַה־לִּ֣י וָלָ֔ךְ לֵ֚ךְ אֶל־נְבִיאֵ֣י אָבִ֔יךָ וְאֶל־נְבִיאֵ֖י אִמֶּ֑ךָ וַיֹּ֤אמֶר לוֹ֙ מֶ֣לֶךְ יִשְׂרָאֵ֔ל אַ֗ל כִּֽי־קָרָ֤א יְהוָה֙ לִשְׁלֹ֣שֶׁת הַמְּלָכִ֣ים הָאֵ֔לֶּה לָתֵ֥ת אוֹתָ֖ם בְּיַד־מוֹאָֽב׃ ¹⁴ וַיֹּ֣אמֶר אֱלִישָׁ֗ע חַי־יְהוָ֤ה צְבָאוֹת֙ אֲשֶׁ֣ר עָמַ֣דְתִּי לְפָנָ֔יו כִּ֗י לוּלֵ֛י פְּנֵ֛י יְהוֹשָׁפָ֥ט מֶֽלֶךְ־יְהוּדָ֖ה אֲנִ֣י נֹשֵׂ֑א אִם־אַבִּ֥יט אֵלֶ֖יךָ וְאִם־אֶרְאֶֽךָּ׃ ¹⁵ וְעַתָּ֖ה קְחוּ־לִ֣י מְנַגֵּ֑ן וְהָיָה֙ כְּנַגֵּ֣ן הַֽמְנַגֵּ֔ן וַתְּהִ֥י עָלָ֖יו יַד־יְהוָֽה׃ ¹⁶ וַיֹּ֕אמֶר כֹּ֖ה אָמַ֣ר יְהוָ֑ה עָשֹׂ֛ה הַנַּ֥חַל הַזֶּ֖ה גֵּבִ֥ים ׀ גֵּבִֽים׃ ¹⁷ כִּֽי־כֹ֣ה ׀ אָמַ֣ר יְהֹוָ֗ה לֹֽא־תִרְא֥וּ ר֙וּחַ֙ וְלֹֽא־תִרְא֣וּ גֶ֔שֶׁם וְהַנַּ֥חַל הַה֖וּא יִמָּ֣לֵא מָ֑יִם וּשְׁתִיתֶ֛ם אַתֶּ֥ם וּמִקְנֵיכֶ֖ם וּֽבְהֶמְתְּכֶֽם׃ ¹⁸ וְנָקַ֥ל זֹ֖את בְּעֵינֵ֣י יְהוָ֑ה וְנָתַ֥ן אֶת־מוֹאָ֖ב בְּיֶדְכֶֽם׃ ¹⁹ וְהִכִּיתֶ֞ם כָּל־עִ֤יר מִבְצָר֙ וְכָל־עִ֣יר מִבְח֔וֹר וְכָל־עֵ֥ץ טוֹב֙ תַּפִּ֔ילוּ וְכָל־מַעְיְנֵי־מַ֖יִם תִּסְתֹּ֑מוּ וְכֹל֙ הַחֶלְקָ֣ה הַטּוֹבָ֔ה תַּכְאִ֖בוּ בָּאֲבָנִֽים׃ ²⁰ וַיְהִ֤י בַבֹּ֙קֶר֙ כַּעֲל֣וֹת הַמִּנְחָ֔ה וְהִנֵּה־מַ֥יִם בָּאִ֖ים מִדֶּ֣רֶךְ אֱד֑וֹם וַתִּמָּלֵ֥א הָאָ֖רֶץ אֶת־הַמָּֽיִם׃ ²¹ וְכָל־מוֹאָב֙ שָֽׁמְע֔וּ כִּֽי־עָל֥וּ הַמְּלָכִ֖ים לְהִלָּ֣חֶם בָּ֑ם וַיִּצָּעֲק֗וּ מִכֹּ֤ל חֹגֵ֤ר חֲגֹרָה֙ וָמַ֔עְלָה וַיַּעַמְד֖וּ עַל־הַגְּבֽוּל׃ ²² וַיַּשְׁכִּ֣ימוּ

---

b-b   I.e., personally attended.
c-c   Lit. "from all those old enough to gird on a sword."

780

22Next morning, when they rose, the sun was shining over the water, and from the distance the water appeared to the Moabites as red as blood. 23"That's blood!" they said. "The kings must have fought among themselves and killed each other. Now to the spoil, Moab!"

24They entered the Israelite camp, and the Israelites arose and attacked the Moabites, who fled before them. d-They advanced, constantly attacking-d the Moabites, 25and they destroyed the towns. Every man threw a stone into each fertile field, so that it was covered over; and they stopped up every spring and felled every fruit tree. e-Only the walls of-e Kir-hareseth were left, and then the slingers surrounded it and attacked it. 26Seeing that the battle was going against him, the king of Moab led an attempt of seven hundred swordsmen to break a way through to the king of Edom;f but they failed. 27So he took his first-born son, who was to succeed him as king, and offered him up on the wall as a burnt offering. A great wrath came upon Israel, so they withdrew from him and went back to [their own] land.

4 A certain woman, the wife of one of the disciples of the prophets, cried out to Elisha: "Your servant my husband is dead, and you know how your servant revered the LORD. And now a creditor is coming to seize my two children as slaves." 2Elisha said to her, "What can I do for you? Tell me, what have you in the house?" She replied, "Your maidservant has nothing at all in the house, except a jug of oil." 3"Go," he said, "and borrow vessels outside, from all your neighbors, empty vessels, as many as you can. 4Then go in and shut the door behind you and your children, and pour [oil] into all those vessels, removing each one as it is filled."

בַּבֹּ֣קֶר וְהַשֶּׁ֖מֶשׁ זָרְחָ֣ה עַל־הַמָּ֑יִם וַיִּרְא֨וּ מוֹאָ֧ב מִנֶּ֛גֶד אֶת־הַמַּ֖יִם אֲדֻמִּ֥ים כַּדָּֽם׃ 23 וַיֹּֽאמְרוּ֙ דָּ֣ם זֶ֔ה הׇחֳרֵ֤ב נֶחֶרְבוּ֙ הַמְּלָכִ֔ים וַיַּכּ֖וּ אִ֣ישׁ אֶת־רֵעֵ֑הוּ וְעַתָּ֥ה לַשָּׁלָ֖ל מוֹאָֽב׃

24 וַיָּבֹ֘אוּ֮ אֶל־מַחֲנֵ֣ה יִשְׂרָאֵל֒ וַיָּקֻ֤מוּ יִשְׂרָאֵל֙ וַיַּכּ֣וּ אֶת־מוֹאָ֔ב וַיָּנֻ֖סוּ מִפְּנֵיהֶ֑ם וַיָּבוֹ־בָ֔הּ* וְהַכּ֖וֹת אֶת־מוֹאָֽב׃ 25 וְהֶעָרִ֣ים יַהֲרֹ֡סוּ וְכׇל־חֶלְקָ֣ה ט֠וֹבָ֠ה יַשְׁלִ֨יכוּ אִישׁ־אַבְנ֜וֹ וּמִלְא֗וּהָ וְכׇל־מַעְיַן־מַ֤יִם יִסְתֹּ֙מוּ֙ וְכׇל־עֵֽץ־ט֣וֹב יַפִּ֔ילוּ עַד־הִשְׁאִ֧יר אֲבָנֶ֛יהָ בַּקִּ֖יר חֲרָ֑שֶׂת וַיָּסֹ֥בּוּ הַקַּלָּעִ֖ים וַיַּכּֽוּהָ׃ 26 וַיַּ֗רְא מֶ֚לֶךְ מוֹאָ֔ב כִּֽי־חָזַ֥ק מִמֶּ֖נּוּ הַמִּלְחָמָ֑ה וַיִּקַּ֣ח א֠וֹת֠וֹ שְׁבַע־מֵא֨וֹת אִ֜ישׁ שֹׁ֣לֵֽף חֶ֗רֶב לְהַבְקִ֛יעַ אֶל־מֶ֥לֶךְ אֱד֖וֹם וְלֹ֥א יָכֹֽלוּ׃ 27 וַיִּקַּח֩ אֶת־בְּנ֨וֹ הַבְּכ֜וֹר אֲשֶׁר־יִמְלֹ֣ךְ תַּחְתָּ֗יו וַיַּעֲלֵ֤הוּ עֹלָה֙ עַל־הַ֣חֹמָ֔ה וַיְהִ֥י קֶֽצֶף־גָּד֖וֹל עַל־יִשְׂרָאֵ֑ל וַיִּסְעוּ֙ מֵֽעָלָ֔יו וַיָּשֻׁ֖בוּ לָאָֽרֶץ׃ פ

ד וְאִשָּׁ֣ה אַחַ֣ת מִנְּשֵׁ֣י בְנֵֽי־הַנְּבִיאִ֡ים צָעֲקָ֣ה אֶל־אֱלִישָׁ֣ע לֵאמֹר֒ עַבְדְּךָ֣ אִישִׁ֣י מֵ֔ת וְאַתָּ֣ה יָדַ֔עְתָּ כִּ֣י עַבְדְּךָ֔ הָיָ֥ה יָרֵ֖א אֶת־יְהֹוָ֑ה וְהַ֨נֹּשֶׁ֔ה בָּ֚א לָקַ֣חַת אֶת־שְׁנֵ֧י יְלָדַ֛י ל֖וֹ לַעֲבָדִֽים׃ 2 וַיֹּ֨אמֶר אֵלֶ֤יהָ אֱלִישָׁע֙ מָ֣ה אֶֽעֱשֶׂה־לָּ֔ךְ הַגִּ֣ידִי לִ֔י מַה־יֶּשׁ־[לָ֖ךְ] בַּבָּ֑יִת וַתֹּ֗אמֶר אֵ֣ין לְשִׁפְחָֽתְךָ֥ כֹל֙ בַּבַּ֔יִת כִּ֖י אִם־אָס֥וּךְ שָֽׁמֶן׃ 3 וַיֹּ֗אמֶר לְכִ֞י שַׁאֲלִי־לָ֤ךְ כֵּלִים֙ מִן־הַח֔וּץ מֵאֵ֖ת כׇּל־[שְׁכֵנָ֑יִךְ] שְׁכֵנָ֔יִךְ כֵּלִ֥ים רֵקִ֖ים אַל־תַּמְעִֽיטִי׃ 4 וּבָ֗את וְסָגַ֤רְתְּ הַדֶּ֙לֶת֙ בַּעֲדֵ֣ךְ וּבְעַד־בָּנַ֔יִךְ וְיָצַ֕קְתְּ עַ֥ל כׇּל־הַכֵּלִ֖ים הָאֵ֑לֶּה וְהַמָּלֵ֖א תַּסִּֽיעִי׃

v. 24. סבירין ומטעין "בם"

d-d Meaning of Heb. uncertain.
e-e Lit. "Until the stones in"; meaning of Heb. uncertain.
f Emendation yields "Aram."

5She went away and shut the door behind her and her children. They kept bringing [vessels] to her and she kept pouring. 6When the vessels were full, she said to her son, "Bring me another vessel." He answered her, "There are no more vessels"; and the oil stopped. 7She came and told the man of God, and he said, "Go sell the oil and pay your debt, and you and your children can live on the rest."

8One day Elisha visited Shunem. A wealthy woman lived there, and she urged him to have a meal; and whenever he passed by, he would stop there for a meal. 9Once she said to her husband, "I am sure it is a holy man of God who comes this way regularly. 10Let us make a small a-enclosed upper chamber-a and place a bed, a table, a chair, and a lampstand there for him, so that he can stop there whenever he comes to us." 11One day he came there; he retired to the upper chamber and lay down there. 12He said to his servant Gehazi, "Call that Shunammite woman." He called her, and she stood before him. 13He said to him, "Tell her, 'You have gone to all this trouble for us. What can we do for you? Can we speak in your behalf to the king or to the army commander?'" She replied, "I live among my own people." 14"What then can be done for her?" he asked. "The fact is," said Gehazi, "she has no son, and her husband is old." 15"Call her," he said. He called her, and she stood in the doorway. 16And Elisha said, "At this season next year, you will be embracing a son." She replied, "Please, my lord, man of God, do not delude your maidservant."

17The woman conceived and bore a son at the same season the following year, as Elisha had assured her. 18The child grew up. One day, he went out to his father among the reapers. 19[Suddenly] he cried to his father, "Oh, my head, my head!" He said to a servant, "Carry

5 וַתֵּ֙לֶךְ֙ מֵֽאִתּ֔וֹ וַתִּסְגֹּ֣ר הַדֶּ֔לֶת בַּעֲדָ֖הּ וּבְעַ֣ד בָּנֶ֑יהָ הֵ֚ם מַגִּשִׁ֣ים אֵלֶ֔יהָ וְהִ֖יא מיצקת מוֹצָֽקֶת׃ 6 וַיְהִ֣י ׀ כִּמְלֹ֣את הַכֵּלִ֗ים וַתֹּ֤אמֶר אֶל־בְּנָהּ֙ הַגִּ֨ישָׁה אֵלַ֥י עוֹד֙ כֶּ֔לִי וַיֹּ֣אמֶר אֵלֶ֔יהָ אֵ֥ין ע֖וֹד כֶּ֑לִי וַֽיַּעֲמֹ֖ד הַשָּֽׁמֶן׃ 7 וַתָּבֹ֗א וַתַּגֵּד֙ לְאִ֣ישׁ הָֽאֱלֹהִ֔ים וַיֹּ֗אמֶר לְכִי֙ מִכְרִ֣י אֶת־הַשֶּׁ֔מֶן וְשַׁלְּמִ֖י אֶת־נשיכי נִשְׁיֵ֑ךְ וְאַ֣תְּ בָּנַ֔יךְ תִּֽחְיִ֖י בַּנּוֹתָֽר׃ פ

8 וַיְהִ֣י הַיּ֗וֹם וַיַּעֲבֹ֤ר אֱלִישָׁע֙ אֶל־שׁוּנֵ֔ם וְשָׁ֛ם אִשָּׁ֥ה גְדוֹלָ֖ה וַתַּחֲזֶק־בּ֣וֹ לֶאֱכָל־לָ֑חֶם וַיְהִ֣י מִדֵּ֣י עָבְר֔וֹ יָסֻ֥ר שָׁ֖מָּה לֶאֱכָל־לָֽחֶם׃ 9 וַתֹּ֙אמֶר֙ אֶל־אִישָׁ֔הּ הִנֵּה־נָ֣א יָדַ֔עְתִּי כִּ֛י אִ֥ישׁ אֱלֹהִ֖ים קָד֣וֹשׁ ה֑וּא עֹבֵ֥ר עָלֵ֖ינוּ תָּמִֽיד׃ 10 נַעֲשֶׂה־נָּ֤א עֲלִיַּת־קִיר֙ קְטַנָּ֔ה וְנָשִׂ֧ים ל֣וֹ שָׁ֗ם מִטָּ֤ה וְשֻׁלְחָן֙ וְכִסֵּ֣א וּמְנוֹרָ֔ה וְהָיָ֛ה בְּבֹא֥וֹ אֵלֵ֖ינוּ יָס֥וּר שָֽׁמָּה׃ 11 וַיְהִ֣י הַיּ֔וֹם וַיָּ֖בֹא שָׁ֑מָּה וַיָּ֥סַר אֶל־הָעֲלִיָּ֖ה וַיִּשְׁכַּב־שָֽׁמָּה׃ 12 וַיֹּ֙אמֶר֙ אֶל־גֵּחֲזִ֣י נַעֲר֔וֹ קְרָ֖א לַשּׁוּנַמִּ֣ית הַזֹּ֑את וַיִּקְרָא־לָ֔הּ וַֽתַּעֲמֹ֖ד לְפָנָֽיו׃ 13 וַיֹּ֣אמֶר ל֗וֹ אֱמָר־נָ֣א אֵלֶיהָ֮ הִנֵּ֣ה חָרַ֣דְתְּ ׀ אֵלֵינוּ֮ אֶת־כָּל־הַחֲרָדָ֣ה הַזֹּאת֒ מֶ֚ה לַעֲשׂ֣וֹת לָ֔ךְ הֲיֵ֤שׁ לְדַבֶּר־לָךְ֙ אֶל־הַמֶּ֔לֶךְ א֖וֹ אֶל־שַׂ֣ר הַצָּבָ֑א וַתֹּ֕אמֶר בְּת֥וֹךְ עַמִּ֖י אָנֹכִ֥י יֹשָֽׁבֶת׃ 14 וַיֹּ֕אמֶר וּמֶ֖ה לַעֲשׂ֣וֹת לָ֑הּ וַיֹּ֣אמֶר גֵּיחֲזִ֗י אֲבָ֛ל בֵּ֥ן אֵֽין־לָ֖הּ וְאִישָׁ֥הּ זָקֵֽן׃ 15 וַיֹּ֖אמֶר קְרָא־לָ֑הּ וַיִּקְרָא־לָ֔הּ וַֽתַּעֲמֹ֖ד בַּפָּֽתַח׃ 16 וַיֹּ֗אמֶר לַמּוֹעֵ֤ד הַזֶּה֙ כָּעֵ֣ת חַיָּ֔ה אַ֖תְּ חֹבֶ֣קֶת בֵּ֑ן וַתֹּ֗אמֶר אַל־אֲדֹנִי֙ אִ֣ישׁ הָאֱלֹהִ֔ים אַל־תְּכַזֵּ֖ב בְּשִׁפְחָתֶֽךָ׃ 17 וַתַּ֥הַר הָאִשָּׁ֖ה וַתֵּ֣לֶד בֵּ֑ן לַמּוֹעֵ֤ד הַזֶּה֙ כָּעֵ֣ת חַיָּ֔ה אֲשֶׁר־דִּבֶּ֥ר אֵלֶ֖יהָ אֱלִישָֽׁע׃ 18 וַיִּגְדַּ֖ל הַיָּ֑לֶד וַיְהִ֣י הַיּ֔וֹם וַיֵּצֵ֥א אֶל־אָבִ֖יו אֶל־הַקֹּצְרִֽים׃ 19 וַיֹּ֥אמֶר אֶל־אָבִ֖יו רֹאשִׁ֣י ׀ רֹאשִׁ֑י וַיֹּ֙אמֶר֙ אֶל־הַנַּ֔עַר שָׂאֵ֖הוּ אֶל־אִמּֽוֹ׃

---

a-a   Or "upper wall-chamber"; lit. "an upper chamber of wall(s)."

him to his mother." [20]He picked him up and brought him to his mother. And the child sat on her lap until noon; and he died. [21]She took him up and laid him on the bed of the man of God, and left him and closed the door. [22]Then she called to her husband: "Please, send me one of the servants and one of the she-asses, so I can hurry to the man of God and back." [23]But he said, "Why are you going to him today? It is neither new moon nor sabbath." She answered, b-"It's all right."-b

[24]She had the ass saddled, and said to her servant, "Urge [the beast] on;c see that I don't slow down unless I tell you." [25]She went on until she came to the man of God on Mount Carmel. When the man of God saw her from afar, he said to his servant Gehazi, "There is that Shunammite woman. [26]Go, hurry toward her and ask her, 'How are you? How is your husband? How is the child?'" "We are well," she replied. [27]But when she came up to the man of God on the mountain, she clasped his feet. Gehazi stepped forward to push her away; but the man of God said, "Let her alone, for she is in bitter distress; and the LORD has hidden it from me and has not told me." [28]Then she said, "Did I ask my lord for a son? Didn't I say: 'Don't mislead me'?"

[29]He said to Gehazi, d-"Tie up your skirts,-d take my staff in your hand, and go. If you meet anyone, do not greet him; and if anyone greets you, do not answer him. And place my staff on the face of the boy." [30]But the boy's mother said, "As the LORD lives and as you live, I will not leave you!" So he arose and followed her.

[31]Gehazi had gone on before them and had placed the staff on the boy's face; but there was no sound or response. He turned back to meet him and told him, "The boy has not awakened." [32]Elisha came into the house, and there was the

20 וַיִּשָּׂאֵהוּ וַיְבִיאֵהוּ אֶל־אִמּוֹ וַיֵּשֶׁב עַל־בִּרְכֶּיהָ עַד־הַצָּהֳרַיִם וַיָּמֹת: 21 וַתַּעַל וַתַּשְׁכִּבֵהוּ עַל־מִטַּת אִישׁ הָאֱלֹהִים וַתִּסְגֹּר בַּעֲדוֹ וַתֵּצֵא: 22 וַתִּקְרָא אֶל־אִישָׁהּ וַתֹּאמֶר שִׁלְחָה נָא לִי אֶחָד מִן־הַנְּעָרִים וְאַחַת הָאֲתֹנוֹת וְאָרוּצָה עַד־אִישׁ הָאֱלֹהִים וְאָשׁוּבָה: 23 וַיֹּאמֶר מַדּוּעַ אַתְּי אַתְּ הֹלַכְתִּי הֹלֶכֶת אֵלָיו הַיּוֹם לֹא־חֹדֶשׁ וְלֹא שַׁבָּת וַתֹּאמֶר שָׁלוֹם: 24 וַתַּחֲבֹשׁ הָאָתוֹן וַתֹּאמֶר אֶל־נַעֲרָהּ נְהַג וָלֵךְ אַל־תַּעֲצָר־לִי לִרְכֹּב כִּי אִם־אָמַרְתִּי לָךְ: 25 וַתֵּלֶךְ וַתָּבוֹא אֶל־אִישׁ הָאֱלֹהִים אֶל־הַר הַכַּרְמֶל וַיְהִי כִּרְאוֹת אִישׁ־הָאֱלֹהִים אֹתָהּ מִנֶּגֶד וַיֹּאמֶר אֶל־גֵּיחֲזִי נַעֲרוֹ הִנֵּה הַשּׁוּנַמִּית הַלָּז: 26 עַתָּה רוּץ־נָא לִקְרָאתָהּ וֶאֱמָר־לָהּ הֲשָׁלוֹם לָךְ הֲשָׁלוֹם לְאִישֵׁךְ הֲשָׁלוֹם לַיָּלֶד וַתֹּאמֶר שָׁלוֹם: 27 וַתָּבֹא אֶל־אִישׁ הָאֱלֹהִים אֶל־הָהָר וַתַּחֲזֵק בְּרַגְלָיו וַיִּגַּשׁ גֵּיחֲזִי לְהָדְפָהּ וַיֹּאמֶר אִישׁ הָאֱלֹהִים הַרְפֵּה־לָהּ כִּי־נַפְשָׁהּ מָרָה־לָהּ וַיהוָה הֶעְלִים מִמֶּנִּי וְלֹא הִגִּיד לִי: 28 וַתֹּאמֶר הֲשָׁאַלְתִּי בֵן מֵאֵת אֲדֹנִי הֲלֹא אָמַרְתִּי לֹא תַשְׁלֶה אֹתִי: 29 וַיֹּאמֶר לְגֵיחֲזִי חֲגֹר מָתְנֶיךָ וְקַח מִשְׁעַנְתִּי בְיָדְךָ וָלֵךְ כִּי־תִמְצָא אִישׁ לֹא תְבָרְכֶנּוּ וְכִי־יְבָרֶכְךָ אִישׁ לֹא תַעֲנֶנּוּ וְשַׂמְתָּ מִשְׁעַנְתִּי עַל־פְּנֵי הַנָּעַר: 30 וַתֹּאמֶר אֵם הַנַּעַר חַי־יְהוָה וְחֵי־נַפְשְׁךָ אִם־אֶעֶזְבֶךָּ וַיָּקָם וַיֵּלֶךְ אַחֲרֶיהָ: 31 וְגֵחֲזִי עָבַר לִפְנֵיהֶם וַיָּשֶׂם אֶת־הַמִּשְׁעֶנֶת עַל־פְּנֵי הַנַּעַר וְאֵין קוֹל וְאֵין קָשֶׁב וַיָּשָׁב לִקְרָאתוֹ וַיַּגֶּד־לוֹ לֵאמֹר לֹא הֵקִיץ הַנָּעַר: 32 וַיָּבֹא אֱלִישָׁע הַבָּיְתָה וְהִנֵּה הַנַּעַר מֵת מֻשְׁכָּב עַל־מִטָּתוֹ:

---

b-b Heb. Shalom.
c   The servant runs behind the donkey and urges it on with a stick.
d-d Lit. "Gird your loins"; cf. 1 Kings 18.46.

boy, laid out dead on his couch. 33He went in, shut the door behind the two of them, and prayed to the LORD. 34Then he mounted [the bed] and placed himself over the child. He put his mouth on its mouth, his eyes on its eyes, and his hands on its hands, as he bent over it. And the body of the child became warm. 35He stepped down, walked once up and down the room, then mounted and bent over him. Thereupon, the boy sneezed seven times, and the boy opened his eyes. 36[Elisha] called Gehazi and said, "Call the Shunammite woman," and he called her. When she came to him, he said, "Pick up your son." 37She came and fell at his feet and bowed low to the ground; then she picked up her son and left.

38Elisha returned to Gilgal. There was a famine in the land, and the disciples of the prophets were sitting before him. He said to his servant, "Set the large pot [on the fire] and cook a stew for the disciples of the prophets." 39So one of them went out into the fields to gather sprouts. He came across a wild vine and picked from it wild gourds, as many as his garment would hold. Then he came back and sliced them into the pot of stew, for they did not know [what they were]; 40and they served it for the men to eat. While they were still eating of the stew, they began to cry out: "O man of God, there is death in the pot!"e And they could not eat it. 41"Fetch some flour," [Elisha] said. He threw it into the pot and said, "Serve it to the people and let them eat." And there was no longer anything harmful in the pot.

42A man came from Baal-shalishah and he brought the man of God some bread of the first reaping—twenty loaves of barley bread, and some fresh grain f-in his sack.-f And [Elisha]

33 וַיָּבֹא וַיִּסְגֹּר הַדֶּלֶת בְּעַד שְׁנֵיהֶם וַיִּתְפַּלֵּל אֶל־יְהֹוָה: 34 וַיַּעַל וַיִּשְׁכַּב עַל־הַיֶּלֶד וַיָּשֶׂם פִּיו עַל־פִּיו וְעֵינָיו עַל־עֵינָיו וְכַפָּיו עַל־כַּפָּיו כַּפָּיו וַיִּגְהַר עָלָיו וַיָּחׇם בְּשַׂר הַיָּלֶד: 35 וַיָּשׇׁב וַיֵּלֶךְ בַּבַּיִת אַחַת הֵנָּה וְאַחַת הֵנָּה וַיַּעַל וַיִּגְהַר עָלָיו וַיְזוֹרֵר הַנַּעַר עַד־שֶׁבַע פְּעָמִים וַיִּפְקַח הַנַּעַר אֶת־עֵינָיו: 36 וַיִּקְרָא אֶל־גֵּיחֲזִי וַיֹּאמֶר קְרָא אֶל־הַשֻּׁנַמִּית הַזֹּאת וַיִּקְרָאֶהָ וַתָּבוֹא אֵלָיו וַיֹּאמֶר שְׂאִי בְנֵךְ: 37 וַתָּבֹא וַתִּפֹּל עַל־רַגְלָיו וַתִּשְׁתַּחוּ אָרְצָה וַתִּשָּׂא אֶת־בְּנָהּ וַתֵּצֵא: פ

38 וֶאֱלִישָׁע שָׁב הַגִּלְגָּלָה וְהָרָעָב בָּאָרֶץ וּבְנֵי הַנְּבִיאִים יֹשְׁבִים לְפָנָיו וַיֹּאמֶר לְנַעֲרוֹ שְׁפֹת הַסִּיר הַגְּדוֹלָה וּבַשֵּׁל נָזִיד לִבְנֵי הַנְּבִיאִים: 39 וַיֵּצֵא אֶחָד אֶל־הַשָּׂדֶה לְלַקֵּט אֹרֹת וַיִּמְצָא גֶּפֶן שָׂדֶה וַיְלַקֵּט מִמֶּנּוּ* פַּקֻּעֹת שָׂדֶה מְלֹא בִגְדוֹ וַיָּבֹא וַיְפַלַּח אֶל־סִיר הַנָּזִיד כִּי־לֹא יָדָעוּ: 40 וַיִּצְקוּ לַאֲנָשִׁים לֶאֱכוֹל וַיְהִי כְּאׇכְלָם מֵהַנָּזִיד וְהֵמָּה צָעָקוּ וַיֹּאמְרוּ מָוֶת בַּסִּיר אִישׁ הָאֱלֹהִים וְלֹא יָכְלוּ לֶאֱכֹל: 41 וַיֹּאמֶר וּקְחוּ־קֶמַח וַיַּשְׁלֵךְ אֶל־הַסִּיר וַיֹּאמֶר צַק לָעָם וְיֹאכֵלוּ וְלֹא הָיָה דָּבָר רָע בַּסִּיר: ס

42 וְאִישׁ בָּא מִבַּעַל שָׁלִשָׁה וַיָּבֵא לְאִישׁ הָאֱלֹהִים לֶחֶם בִּכּוּרִים עֶשְׂרִים־לֶחֶם שְׂעֹרִים וְכַרְמֶל בְּצִקְלֹנוֹ וַיֹּאמֶר תֵּן לָעָם

---

e   The wild gourds cause severe cramps.
f-f   Or "on the stalk"; perhaps connected with Ugaritic bṣql.

said, "Give it to the people and let them eat."
⁴³His attendant replied, "How can I set this before a hundred men?" But he said, "Give it to
the people and let them eat. For thus said the
LORD: They shall eat and have some left over."
⁴⁴So he set it before them; and when they
had eaten, they had some left over, as the LORD
had said.

5 Naaman, commander of the army of the
king of Aram, was important to his lord and
high in his favor, for through him the LORD had
granted victory to Aram. But the man, though
a great warrior, was a leper.ᵃ ²Once, when the
Arameans were out raiding, they carried off a
young girl from the land of Israel, and she became an attendant to Naaman's wife. ³She said
to her mistress, "I wish Master could come before the prophet in Samaria; he would cure him
of his leprosy." ⁴[Naaman] went and told his
lord just what the girl from the land of Israel
had said. ⁵And the king of Aram said, "Go to
the king of Israel, and I will send along a letter."

He set out, taking with him ten talents of
silver, six thousand shekels of gold, and ten
changes of clothing. ⁶He brought the letter to
the king of Israel. It read: "Now, when this letter
reaches you, know that I have sent my courtier
Naaman to you, that you may cure him of his
leprosy." ⁷When the king of Israel read the letter, he rent his clothes and cried, "Am I God,
to deal death or give life, that this fellow writes
to me to cure a man of leprosy? Just see for yourselves that he is seeking a pretext against me!"

⁸When Elisha, the man of God, heard that the
king of Israel had rent his clothes, he sent a message to the king: "Why have you rent your
clothes? Let him come to me, and he will learn
that there is a prophet in Israel."

ᵃ Cf. note on Lev. 13.3.

וַיֹּאכֵלוּ: ⁴³וַיֹּאמֶר מְשָׁרְתוֹ מָה אֶתֵּן
זֶה לִפְנֵי מֵאָה אִישׁ וַיֹּאמֶר תֵּן לָעָם
וְיֹאכֵלוּ כִּי כֹה אָמַר יְהוָה אָכֹל וְהוֹתֵר:
⁴⁴וַיִּתֵּן לִפְנֵיהֶם וַיֹּאכְלוּ וַיּוֹתִרוּ כִּדְבַר
יְהוָה: פ

ה וְנַעֲמָן שַׂר־צְבָא מֶלֶךְ־אֲרָם הָיָה
אִישׁ גָּדוֹל לִפְנֵי אֲדֹנָיו וּנְשֻׂא פָנִים כִּי־בוֹ
נָתַן־יְהוָה תְּשׁוּעָה לַאֲרָם וְהָאִישׁ הָיָה
גִּבּוֹר חַיִל מְצֹרָע: ²וַאֲרָם יָצְאוּ גְדוּדִים
וַיִּשְׁבּוּ מֵאֶרֶץ יִשְׂרָאֵל נַעֲרָה קְטַנָּה וַתְּהִי
לִפְנֵי אֵשֶׁת נַעֲמָן: ³וַתֹּאמֶר אֶל־גְּבִרְתָּהּ
אַחֲלֵי אֲדֹנִי לִפְנֵי הַנָּבִיא אֲשֶׁר בְּשֹׁמְרוֹן
אָז יֶאֱסֹף אֹתוֹ מִצָּרַעְתּוֹ: ⁴וַיָּבֹא וַיַּגֵּד
לַאדֹנָיו לֵאמֹר כָּזֹאת וְכָזֹאת דִּבְּרָה
הַנַּעֲרָה אֲשֶׁר מֵאֶרֶץ יִשְׂרָאֵל: ⁵וַיֹּאמֶר
מֶלֶךְ־אֲרָם לֶךְ־בֹּא וְאֶשְׁלְחָה סֵפֶר אֶל־
מֶלֶךְ יִשְׂרָאֵל
וַיֵּלֶךְ וַיִּקַּח בְּיָדוֹ עֶשֶׂר כִּכְּרֵי־כֶסֶף וְשֵׁשֶׁת
אֲלָפִים זָהָב וְעֶשֶׂר חֲלִיפוֹת בְּגָדִים: ⁶וַיָּבֵא
הַסֵּפֶר אֶל־מֶלֶךְ יִשְׂרָאֵל לֵאמֹר וְעַתָּה
כְּבוֹא הַסֵּפֶר הַזֶּה אֵלֶיךָ הִנֵּה שָׁלַחְתִּי
אֵלֶיךָ אֶת־נַעֲמָן עַבְדִּי וַאֲסַפְתּוֹ מִצָּרַעְתּוֹ:
⁷וַיְהִי כִּקְרֹא מֶלֶךְ־יִשְׂרָאֵל אֶת־הַסֵּפֶר
וַיִּקְרַע בְּגָדָיו וַיֹּאמֶר הַאֱלֹהִים אָנִי לְהָמִית
וּלְהַחֲיוֹת כִּי־זֶה שֹׁלֵחַ אֵלַי לֶאֱסֹף אִישׁ
מִצָּרַעְתּוֹ כִּי אַךְ־דְּעוּ־נָא וּרְאוּ כִּי־מִתְאַנֶּה
הוּא לִי:
⁸וַיְהִי כִּשְׁמֹעַ אֱלִישָׁע אִישׁ־הָאֱלֹהִים
כִּי־קָרַע מֶלֶךְ־יִשְׂרָאֵל אֶת־בְּגָדָיו וַיִּשְׁלַח
אֶל־הַמֶּלֶךְ לֵאמֹר לָמָּה קָרַעְתָּ בְּגָדֶיךָ
יָבֹא־נָא אֵלַי וְיֵדַע כִּי יֵשׁ נָבִיא בְּיִשְׂרָאֵל:

9So Naaman came with his horses and chariots and halted at the door of Elisha's house. 10Elisha sent a messenger to say to him, "Go and bathe seven times in the Jordan, and your flesh shall be restored and you shall be clean." 11But Naaman was angered and walked away. "I thought," he said, "he would surely come out to me, and would stand and invoke the LORD his God by name, and would wave his hand toward the spot, and cure the affected part. 12Are not the Amanah and the Pharpar, the rivers of Damascus, better than all the waters of Israel? I could bathe in them and be clean!" And he stalked off in a rage.

13But his servants came forward and spoke to him. "Sir,"[b] they said, "if the prophet told you to do something difficult, would you not do it? How much more when he has only said to you, 'Bathe and be clean.'" 14So he went down and immersed himself in the Jordan seven times, as the man of God had bidden; and his flesh became like a little boy's, and he was clean. 15Returning with his entire retinue to the man of God, he stood before him and exclaimed, "Now I know that there is no God in the whole world except in Israel! So please accept a gift from your servant." 16But he replied, "As the LORD lives, whom I serve, I will not accept anything." He pressed him to accept, but he refused. 17And Naaman said, "Then at least let your servant be given two mule-loads of earth; for your servant will never again offer up burnt offering or sacrifice to any god, except the LORD. 18But may the LORD pardon your servant for this: When my master enters the temple of Rimmon to bow low in worship there, and he is leaning on my arm so that I must bow low in the temple of Rimmon—when I bow low in the temple of Rimmon, may the LORD pardon your servant in this." 19And he said to him, "Go in peace."

---

9 וַיָּבֹא נַעֲמָן בְּסוּסָו וּבְרִכְבּוֹ וַיַּעֲמֹד פֶּתַח־הַבַּיִת לֶאֱלִישָׁע: 10 וַיִּשְׁלַח אֵלָיו אֱלִישָׁע מַלְאָךְ לֵאמֹר הָלוֹךְ וְרָחַצְתָּ שֶׁבַע־פְּעָמִים בַּיַּרְדֵּן וְיָשֹׁב בְּשָׂרְךָ לְךָ וּטְהָר: 11 וַיִּקְצֹף נַעֲמָן וַיֵּלַךְ וַיֹּאמֶר הִנֵּה אָמַרְתִּי אֵלַי ׀ יֵצֵא יָצוֹא וְעָמַד וְקָרָא בְּשֵׁם־יְהוָה אֱלֹהָיו וְהֵנִיף יָדוֹ אֶל־הַמָּקוֹם וְאָסַף הַמְּצֹרָע: 12 הֲלֹא טוֹב אבנה אֲמָנָה וּפַרְפַּר נַהֲרוֹת דַּמֶּשֶׂק מִכֹּל מֵימֵי יִשְׂרָאֵל הֲלֹא־אֶרְחַץ בָּהֶם וְטָהָרְתִּי וַיִּפֶן וַיֵּלֶךְ בְּחֵמָה:

13 וַיִּגְּשׁוּ עֲבָדָיו וַיְדַבְּרוּ אֵלָיו וַיֹּאמְרוּ אָבִי דָּבָר גָּדוֹל הַנָּבִיא דִּבֶּר אֵלֶיךָ הֲלוֹא תַעֲשֶׂה וְאַף כִּי־אָמַר אֵלֶיךָ רְחַץ וּטְהָר: 14 וַיֵּרֶד וַיִּטְבֹּל בַּיַּרְדֵּן שֶׁבַע פְּעָמִים כִּדְבַר אִישׁ הָאֱלֹהִים וַיָּשָׁב בְּשָׂרוֹ כִּבְשַׂר נַעַר קָטֹן וַיִּטְהָר: 15 וַיָּשָׁב אֶל־אִישׁ הָאֱלֹהִים הוּא וְכָל־מַחֲנֵהוּ וַיָּבֹא וַיַּעֲמֹד לְפָנָיו וַיֹּאמֶר הִנֵּה־נָא יָדַעְתִּי כִּי אֵין אֱלֹהִים בְּכָל־הָאָרֶץ כִּי אִם־בְּיִשְׂרָאֵל וְעַתָּה קַח־נָא בְרָכָה מֵאֵת עַבְדֶּךָ: 16 וַיֹּאמֶר חַי־יְהוָה אֲשֶׁר־עָמַדְתִּי לְפָנָיו אִם־אֶקָּח וַיִּפְצַר־בּוֹ לָקַחַת וַיְמָאֵן: 17 וַיֹּאמֶר נַעֲמָן וָלֹא יֻתַּן־נָא לְעַבְדְּךָ מַשָּׂא צֶמֶד־פְּרָדִים אֲדָמָה כִּי לוֹא־יַעֲשֶׂה עוֹד עַבְדְּךָ עֹלָה וָזֶבַח לֵאלֹהִים אֲחֵרִים כִּי אִם־לַיהוָה: 18 לַדָּבָר הַזֶּה יִסְלַח יְהוָה לְעַבְדֶּךָ בְּבוֹא אֲדֹנִי בֵית־רִמּוֹן לְהִשְׁתַּחֲוֹת שָׁמָּה וְהוּא ׀ נִשְׁעָן עַל־יָדִי וְהִשְׁתַּחֲוֵיתִי בֵּית רִמֹּן בְּהִשְׁתַּחֲוָיָתִי בֵּית רִמֹּן יִסְלַח־נא* יְהוָה לְעַבְדְּךָ בַּדָּבָר הַזֶּה: 19 וַיֹּאמֶר לוֹ לֵךְ לְשָׁלוֹם

When he had gone some distance from him, ²⁰Gehazi, the attendant of Elisha the man of God, thought: "My master ᶜhas let that Aramean Naaman off without accepting what he brought!⁻ᶜ As the Lᴏʀᴅ lives, I will run after him and get something from him." ²¹So Gehazi hurried after Naaman. When Naaman saw someone running after him, he alighted from his chariot to meet him and said, "Is all well?" ²²"All is well," he replied. "My master has sent me to say: Two youths, disciples of the prophets, have just come to me from the hill country of Ephraim. Please give them a talent of silver and two changes of clothing." ²³Naaman said, "Please take two talents." He urged him, and he wrapped the two talents of silver in two bags and gave them, along with two changes of clothes, to two of his servants, who carried them ahead of him. ²⁴When [Gehazi] arrived at the citadel, he took [the things] from them and deposited them in the house. Then he dismissed the men and they went their way.

²⁵He entered and stood before his master; and Elisha said to him, "Where have you been, Gehazi?" He replied, "Your servant has not gone anywhere." ²⁶Then [Elisha] said to him, "Did not my spiritᵈ go along when a man got down from his chariot to meet you? Is this a time to take money in order to buy clothing and olive groves and vineyards, sheep and oxen, and male and female slaves? ²⁷Surely, the leprosy of Naaman shall cling to you and to your descendants forever." And as [Gehazi] left his presence, he was snow-white with leprosy.

6 The disciples of the prophets said to Elisha, "See, the place where we live under your direction is too cramped for us. ²Let us go to the Jordan, and let us each get a log there and build

c-c   *Lit. "has prevented that Aramean Naaman from having what he brought accepted."*
d   *Lit. "heart."*

וַיֵּ֥לֶךְ מֵאִתּ֖וֹ כִּבְרַת־אָֽרֶץ׃ ס 20 וַיֹּ֨אמֶר גֵּיחֲזִ֜י נַ֣עַר ׀ אֱלִישָׁ֣ע אִישׁ־הָאֱלֹהִ֗ים הִנֵּ֣ה ׀ חָשַׂ֣ךְ אֲדֹנִ֡י אֶֽת־נַעֲמָן֩ הָאֲרַמִּ֨י הַזֶּ֜ה מִקַּ֤חַת מִיָּדוֹ֙ אֵ֣ת אֲשֶׁר־הֵבִ֔יא חַי־יְהֹוָה֙ כִּֽי־אִם־רַ֣צְתִּי אַחֲרָ֔יו וְלָקַחְתִּ֥י מֵאִתּ֖וֹ מְאֽוּמָה׃ 21 וַיִּרְדֹּ֥ף גֵּיחֲזִ֖י אַחֲרֵ֣י נַֽעֲמָ֑ן וַיִּרְאֶ֤ה נַֽעֲמָן֙ רָ֣ץ אַחֲרָ֔יו וַיִּפֹּ֛ל מֵעַ֥ל הַמֶּרְכָּבָ֖ה לִקְרָאת֑וֹ וַיֹּ֖אמֶר הֲשָׁלֽוֹם׃ 22 וַיֹּ֣אמֶר ׀ שָׁל֗וֹם אֲדֹנִי֮ שְׁלָחַ֣נִי לֵאמֹר֒ הִנֵּ֣ה עַתָּ֡ה זֶ֠ה בָּ֣אוּ אֵלַ֞י שְׁנֵֽי־נְעָרִ֤ים מֵהַ֤ר אֶפְרַ֙יִם֙ מִבְּנֵ֣י הַנְּבִיאִ֑ים תְּנָה־נָּ֤א לָהֶם֙ כִּכַּר־כֶּ֔סֶף וּשְׁתֵּ֖י חֲלִפ֥וֹת בְּגָדִֽים׃ 23 וַיֹּ֣אמֶר נַעֲמָ֔ן הוֹאֵ֖ל קַ֣ח כִּכָּרָ֑יִם וַיִּפְרׇץ־בּ֗וֹ וַיָּצַר֩ כִּכְּרַ֨יִם כֶּ֜סֶף בִּשְׁנֵ֣י חֲרִטִ֗ים וּשְׁתֵּי֙ חֲלִפ֣וֹת בְּגָדִ֔ים וַיִּתֵּן֙ אֶל־שְׁנֵ֣י נְעָרָ֔יו וַיִּשְׂא֖וּ לְפָנָֽיו׃ 24 וַיָּבֹא֙ אֶל־הָעֹ֔פֶל וַיִּקַּ֥ח מִיָּדָ֖ם וַיִּפְקֹ֣ד בַּבָּ֑יִת וַיְשַׁלַּ֥ח אֶת־הָאֲנָשִׁ֖ים וַיֵּלֵֽכוּ׃

25 וְהוּא־בָ֗א וַיַּֽעֲמֹד֙ אֶל־אֲדֹנָ֔יו וַיֹּ֤אמֶר אֵלָיו֙ אֱלִישָׁ֔ע מֵ֥אַ֖יִן גֵּֽחֲזִ֑י וַיֹּ֕אמֶר לֹֽא־הָלַ֥ךְ עַבְדְּךָ֖ אָ֥נֶה וָאָֽנָה׃ 26 וַיֹּ֤אמֶר אֵלָיו֙ לֹא־לִבִּ֣י הָלַ֔ךְ כַּאֲשֶׁ֧ר הָֽפַךְ־אִ֛ישׁ מֵעַ֥ל מֶרְכַּבְתּ֖וֹ לִקְרָאתֶ֑ךָ הַעֵ֞ת לָקַ֤חַת אֶת־הַכֶּ֙סֶף֙ וְלָקַ֣חַת בְּגָדִ֔ים וְזֵיתִ֤ים וּכְרָמִים֙ וְצֹ֣אן וּבָקָ֔ר וַעֲבָדִ֖ים וּשְׁפָחֽוֹת׃ 27 וְצָרַ֤עַת נַֽעֲמָן֙ תִּֽדְבַּק־בְּךָ֔ וּֽבְזַרְעֲךָ֖ לְעוֹלָ֑ם וַיֵּצֵ֥א מִלְּפָנָ֖יו מְצֹרָ֥ע כַּשָּֽׁלֶג׃ ס

ו וַיֹּאמְר֥וּ בְנֵֽי־הַנְּבִיאִ֖ים אֶל־אֱלִישָׁ֑ע הִנֵּֽה־נָ֣א הַמָּק֗וֹם אֲשֶׁ֨ר אֲנַ֜חְנוּ יֹשְׁבִ֥ים שָׁ֛ם לְפָנֶ֖יךָ צַ֥ר מִמֶּֽנּוּ׃ 2 נֵֽלְכָה־נָּ֣א עַד־הַיַּרְדֵּ֗ן וְנִקְחָ֤ה מִשָּׁם֙ אִ֣ישׁ קוֹרָ֣ה אֶחָ֔ת וְנַעֲשֶׂה־לָּ֥נוּ

quarters there for ourselves to live in." "Do so," he replied. [3]Then one of them said, "Will you please come along with your servants?" "Yes, I will come," he said; [4]and he accompanied them. So they went to the Jordan and cut timber. [5]As one of them was felling a trunk, the iron ax head fell into the water. And he cried aloud, "Alas, master, it was a borrowed one!" [6]"Where did it fall?" asked the man of God. He showed him the spot; and he cut off a stick and threw it in, and he made the ax head float. [7]"Pick it up," he said; so he reached out and took it.

[8]While the king of Aram was waging war against Israel, he took counsel with his officers and said, [a]-"I will encamp-[a] in such and such a place." [9]But the man of God sent word to the king of Israel, "Take care not to pass through that place, for the Arameans are encamped there." [10]So the king of Israel sent word to the place of which the man of God had told him. [b]-Time and again-[b] he alerted [c]-such a place-[c] and took precautions there. [11]Greatly agitated about this matter, the king of Aram summoned his officers and said to them, "Tell me! Who of us is on the side of the king of Israel?" [12]"No one, my lord king," said one of the officers. "Elisha, that prophet in Israel, tells the king of Israel the very words you speak in your bedroom." [13]"Go find out where he is," he said, "so that I can have him seized." It was reported to him that [Elisha] was in Dothan; [14]so he sent horses and chariots there and a strong force. They arrived at night and encircled the town.

[15]When the attendant of the man of God rose early and went outside, he saw a force, with horses and chariots, surrounding the town. "Alas, master, what shall we do?" his servant asked him. [16]"Have no fear," he replied. "There

שָׁם מָקוֹם לָשֶׁבֶת שָׁם וַיֹּאמֶר לֵכוּ: [3] וַיֹּאמֶר הָאֶחָד הוֹאֶל נָא וְלֵךְ אֶת־עֲבָדֶיךָ וַיֹּאמֶר אֲנִי אֵלֵךְ: [4] וַיֵּלֶךְ אִתָּם וַיָּבֹאוּ הַיַּרְדֵּנָה וַיִּגְזְרוּ הָעֵצִים: [5] וַיְהִי הָאֶחָד מַפִּיל הַקּוֹרָה וְאֶת־הַבַּרְזֶל נָפַל אֶל־הַמָּיִם וַיִּצְעַק וַיֹּאמֶר אֲהָהּ אֲדֹנִי וְהוּא שָׁאוּל: [6] וַיֹּאמֶר אִישׁ־הָאֱלֹהִים אָנָה נָפָל וַיַּרְאֵהוּ אֶת־הַמָּקוֹם וַיִּקְצָב־עֵץ וַיַּשְׁלֶךְ־שָׁמָּה וַיָּצֶף הַבַּרְזֶל: [7] וַיֹּאמֶר הָרֶם לָךְ וַיִּשְׁלַח יָדוֹ וַיִּקָּחֵהוּ: פ

[8] וּמֶלֶךְ אֲרָם הָיָה נִלְחָם בְּיִשְׂרָאֵל וַיִּוָּעַץ אֶל־עֲבָדָיו לֵאמֹר אֶל־מְקוֹם פְּלֹנִי אַלְמֹנִי תַּחֲנֹתִי: [9] וַיִּשְׁלַח אִישׁ הָאֱלֹהִים אֶל־מֶלֶךְ יִשְׂרָאֵל לֵאמֹר הִשָּׁמֶר מֵעֲבֹר הַמָּקוֹם הַזֶּה כִּי־שָׁם אֲרָם נְחִתִּים: [10] וַיִּשְׁלַח מֶלֶךְ יִשְׂרָאֵל אֶל־הַמָּקוֹם אֲשֶׁר אָמַר־לוֹ אִישׁ־הָאֱלֹהִים וְהִזְהִירוֹ וְנִשְׁמַר שָׁם לֹא אַחַת וְלֹא שְׁתָּיִם: [11] וַיִּסָּעֵר לֵב מֶלֶךְ־אֲרָם עַל־הַדָּבָר הַזֶּה וַיִּקְרָא אֶל־עֲבָדָיו וַיֹּאמֶר אֲלֵיהֶם הֲלוֹא תַּגִּידוּ לִי מִי מִשֶּׁלָּנוּ אֶל־מֶלֶךְ יִשְׂרָאֵל: [12] וַיֹּאמֶר אַחַד מֵעֲבָדָיו לוֹא אֲדֹנִי הַמֶּלֶךְ כִּי־אֱלִישָׁע הַנָּבִיא אֲשֶׁר בְּיִשְׂרָאֵל יַגִּיד לְמֶלֶךְ יִשְׂרָאֵל אֶת־הַדְּבָרִים אֲשֶׁר תְּדַבֵּר בַּחֲדַר מִשְׁכָּבֶךָ: [13] וַיֹּאמֶר לְכוּ וּרְאוּ אֵיכֹה הוּא וְאֶשְׁלַח וְאֶקָּחֵהוּ וַיֻּגַּד־לוֹ לֵאמֹר הִנֵּה בְדֹתָן: [14] וַיִּשְׁלַח־שָׁמָּה סוּסִים וְרֶכֶב וְחַיִל כָּבֵד וַיָּבֹאוּ לַיְלָה וַיַּקִּפוּ עַל־הָעִיר: [15] וַיַּשְׁכֵּם מְשָׁרֵת אִישׁ הָאֱלֹהִים לָקוּם וַיֵּצֵא וְהִנֵּה־חַיִל סוֹבֵב אֶת־הָעִיר וְסוּס וָרֶכֶב וַיֹּאמֶר נַעֲרוֹ אֵלָיו אֲהָהּ אֲדֹנִי אֵיכָה נַעֲשֶׂה: [16] וַיֹּאמֶר אַל־תִּירָא כִּי רַבִּים אֲשֶׁר

a-a   Meaning of Heb. uncertain.
b-b   Lit. "not once or twice."
c-c   Heb. "it."

788

are more on our side than on theirs." [17]Then Elisha prayed: "Lord, open his eyes and let him see." And the Lord opened the servant's eyes and he saw the hills all around Elisha covered with horses and chariots of fire. [18][The Arameans] came down against him, and Elisha prayed to the Lord: "Please strike this people with a blinding light." And He struck them with a blinding light, as Elisha had asked.

[19]Elisha said to them, "This is not the road, and that is not the town; follow me, and I will lead you to the man you want." And he led them to Samaria. [20]When they entered Samaria, Elisha said, "O Lord, open the eyes of these men so that they may see." The Lord opened their eyes and they saw that they were inside Samaria. [21]When the king of Israel saw them, he said to Elisha, "Father, shall I strike them down?" [22]"No, do not," he replied. "Did you take them captive with your sword and bow that you would strike them down? Rather, set food and drink before them, and let them eat and drink and return to their master." [23]So he prepared a lavish feast for them and, after they had eaten and drunk, he let them go, and they returned to their master. And the Aramean bands stopped invading the land of Israel.

[24]Sometime later, King Ben-hadad of Aram mustered his entire army and marched upon Samaria and besieged it. [25]There was a great famine in Samaria, and the siege continued until a donkey's head sold for eighty [shekels] of silver and a quarter of a *kab* of *d*-doves' dung-*d* for five shekels. [26]Once, when the king of Israel was walking on the city wall, a woman cried out to him: "Help me, Your Majesty!" [27]"Don't [ask me]," he replied. "Let the Lord help you! Where could I get help for you, from the threshing floor or from the winepress? [28]But what troubles

---

אֹתָ֫נוּ מֵאֲשֶׁ֥ר אוֹתָֽם׃ 17 וַיִּתְפַּלֵּ֣ל אֱלִישָׁ֗ע וַיֹּאמַ֔ר יְהוָ֕ה פְּקַח־נָ֥א אֶת־עֵינָ֖יו וְיִרְאֶ֑ה וַיִּפְקַ֤ח יְהוָה֙ אֶת־עֵינֵ֣י הַנַּ֔עַר וַיַּ֕רְא וְהִנֵּ֣ה הָהָ֗ר מָלֵ֛א סוּסִ֥ים וְרֶ֛כֶב אֵ֖שׁ סְבִיבֹ֥ת אֱלִישָֽׁע׃ 18 וַיֵּרְדוּ֮ אֵלָיו֒ וַיִּתְפַּלֵּ֣ל אֱלִישָׁ֣ע אֶל־יְהוָה֮ וַיֹּאמַר֒ הַךְ־נָ֥א אֶת־הַגּוֹי־הַזֶּ֖ה בַּסַּנְוֵרִ֑ים וַיַּכֵּ֥ם בַּסַּנְוֵרִ֖ים כִּדְבַ֥ר אֱלִישָֽׁע׃ 19 וַיֹּ֨אמֶר אֲלֵהֶ֜ם אֱלִישָׁ֗ע לֹ֣א זֶ֣ה הַדֶּרֶךְ֮ וְלֹ֣א זֹ֣ה הָעִיר֒ לְכ֣וּ אַחֲרַ֔י וְאוֹלִ֣יכָה אֶתְכֶ֔ם אֶל־הָאִ֖ישׁ אֲשֶׁ֣ר תְּבַקֵּשׁ֑וּן וַיֹּ֥לֶךְ אוֹתָ֖ם שֹׁמְרֽוֹנָה׃ 20 וַיְהִ֞י כְּבֹאָ֣ם שֹׁמְר֗וֹן וַיֹּ֣אמֶר אֱלִישָׁ֔ע יְהוָ֕ה פְּקַ֥ח אֶת־עֵינֵֽי־אֵ֖לֶּה וְיִרְא֑וּ וַיִּפְקַ֤ח יְהוָה֙ אֶת־עֵ֣ינֵיהֶ֔ם וַיִּרְא֕וּ וְהִנֵּ֖ה בְּת֥וֹךְ שֹׁמְרֽוֹן׃ 21 וַיֹּ֤אמֶר מֶֽלֶךְ־יִשְׂרָאֵל֙ אֶל־אֱלִישָׁ֔ע כִּרְאֹת֖וֹ אוֹתָ֑ם הַאַכֶּ֥ה אַכֶּ֖ה אָבִֽי׃ 22 וַיֹּ֗אמֶר לֹ֣א תַכֶּה֒ הַאֲשֶׁ֣ר שָׁבִ֗יתָ בְּחַרְבְּךָ֤ וּֽבְקַשְׁתְּךָ֙ אַתָּ֣ה מַכֶּ֔ה שִׂ֚ים לֶ֣חֶם וָמַ֔יִם לִפְנֵיהֶ֖ם וְיֹֽאכְלוּ֙ וְיִשְׁתּ֔וּ וְיֵלְכ֖וּ אֶל־אֲדֹֽנֵיהֶֽם׃ 23 וַיִּכְרֶ֨ה לָהֶ֜ם כֵּרָ֣ה גְדוֹלָ֗ה וַיֹּֽאכְלוּ֙ וַיִּשְׁתּ֔וּ וַֽיְשַׁלְּחֵ֔ם וַיֵּלְכ֖וּ אֶל־אֲדֹֽנֵיהֶ֑ם וְלֹא־יָ֨סְפ֥וּ עוֹד֙ גְּדוּדֵ֣י אֲרָ֔ם לָב֖וֹא בְּאֶ֥רֶץ יִשְׂרָאֵֽל׃ פ

24 וַיְהִ֣י אַחֲרֵי־כֵ֗ן וַיִּקְבֹּ֞ץ בֶּן־הֲדַ֤ד מֶֽלֶךְ־אֲרָם֙ אֶת־כָּל־מַחֲנֵ֔הוּ וַיַּ֖עַל וַיָּ֥צַר עַל־שֹׁמְרֽוֹן׃ 25 וַיְהִ֨י רָעָ֤ב גָּדוֹל֙ בְּשֹׁ֣מְר֔וֹן וְהִנֵּ֖ה צָרִ֣ים עָלֶ֑יהָ עַ֣ד הֱי֤וֹת רֹאשׁ־חֲמוֹר֙ בִּשְׁמֹנִ֣ים כֶּ֔סֶף וְרֹ֛בַע הַקַּ֥ב חֲרֵייוֹנִ֖ים בַּחֲמִשָּׁה־כָֽסֶף׃ 26 וַיְהִי֙ מֶ֣לֶךְ יִשְׂרָאֵ֔ל עֹבֵ֖ר עַל־הַחֹמָ֑ה וְאִשָּׁ֗ה צָעֲקָ֤ה אֵלָיו֙ לֵאמֹ֔ר הוֹשִׁ֖יעָה אֲדֹנִ֥י הַמֶּֽלֶךְ׃ 27 וַיֹּ֨אמֶר֙ אַל־יוֹשִׁעֵ֣ךְ יְהוָ֔ה מֵאַ֖יִן אֽוֹשִׁיעֵ֑ךְ הֲמִן־הַגֹּ֖רֶן א֥וֹ מִן־הַיָּֽקֶב׃ 28 וַיֹּֽאמֶר־לָ֥הּ

---

d-d   Apparently a popular term for "carob pods," as in Akkadian.

you?" the king asked her. The woman answered, "That woman said to me, 'Give up your son and we will eat him today; and tomorrow we'll eat my son.' ²⁹So we cooked my son and we ate him. The next day I said to her, 'Give up your son and let's eat him'; but she hid her son." ³⁰When the king heard what the woman said, he rent his clothes; and as he walked along the wall, the people could see that he was wearing sackcloth underneath.

³¹He said, "Thus and more may God do to me if the head of Elisha son of Shaphat remains on *e*-his shoulders-*e* today." ³²Now Elisha was sitting at home and the elders were sitting with him. The king had sent ahead one of his men; but before the messenger arrived, [Elisha] said to the elders, "Do you see—that murderer has sent someone to cut off my head! Watch when the messenger comes, and shut the door and hold the door fast against him. No doubt the sound of his master's footsteps will follow."

³³While he was still talking to them, the messenger*f* came to him and said, "This calamity is from the Lord. What more can I hope for from the Lord?" ¹And Elisha replied, "Hear the word of the Lord. Thus said the Lord: This time tomorrow, a *seah* of choice flour shall sell for a shekel at the gate of Samaria, and two *seahs* of barley for a shekel." ²The aide on whose arm the king was leaning spoke up and said to the man of God, "Even if the Lord were to make windows in the sky, could this come to pass?" And he retorted, "You shall see it with your own eyes, but you shall not eat of it."

³There were four men, lepers, outside the gate. They said to one another, "Why should we sit here waiting for death? ⁴If we decide to go into the town, what with the famine in the

---

הַמֶּ֫לֶךְ מַה־לָּ֖ךְ וַתֹּ֑אמֶר הָאִשָּׁ֤ה הַזֹּאת֙ אָמְרָ֣ה אֵלַ֗י תְּנִ֤י אֶת־בְּנֵךְ֙ וְנֹאכְלֶ֣נּוּ הַיּ֔וֹם וְאֶת־בְּנִ֖י נֹאכַ֥ל מָחָֽר: ²⁹ וַנְּבַשֵּׁ֤ל אֶת־בְּנִי֙ וַנֹּ֣אכְלֵ֔הוּ וָאֹמַ֤ר אֵלֶ֙יהָ֙ בַּיּ֣וֹם הָאַחֵ֔ר תְּנִ֥י אֶת־בְּנֵ֖ךְ וְנֹאכְלֶ֑נּוּ וַתַּחְבִּ֖א אֶת־בְּנָֽהּ: ³⁰ וַיְהִי֩ כִשְׁמֹ֨עַ הַמֶּ֜לֶךְ אֶת־דִּבְרֵ֣י הָאִשָּׁ֗ה וַיִּקְרַ֖ע אֶת־בְּגָדָ֑יו וְה֛וּא עֹבֵ֥ר עַל־הַחֹמָ֖ה וַיַּ֣רְא הָעָ֔ם וְהִנֵּ֥ה הַשַּׂ֛ק עַל־בְּשָׂר֖וֹ מִבָּֽיִת: ³¹ וַיֹּ֕אמֶר כֹּֽה־יַעֲשֶׂה־לִּ֥י אֱלֹהִ֖ים וְכֹ֣ה יוֹסִ֑ף אִֽם־יַעֲמֹ֞ד רֹ֣אשׁ אֱלִישָׁ֧ע בֶּן־שָׁפָ֛ט עָלָ֖יו הַיּֽוֹם: ³² וֶאֱלִישָׁע֙ יֹשֵׁ֣ב בְּבֵית֔וֹ וְהַזְּקֵנִ֖ים יֹשְׁבִ֣ים אִתּ֑וֹ וַיִּשְׁלַ֨ח אִ֜ישׁ מִלְּפָנָ֗יו בְּטֶ֣רֶם יָבֹ֣א הַמַּלְאָךְ֮ אֵלָיו֒ וְה֣וּא ׀ אָמַ֣ר אֶל־הַזְּקֵנִ֗ים הַרְּאִיתֶם֙* כִּֽי־שָׁלַ֞ח בֶּן־הַֽמְרַצֵּ֤חַ הַזֶּה֙ לְהָסִ֣יר אֶת־רֹאשִׁ֔י רְא֣וּ ׀ כְּבֹ֣א הַמַּלְאָ֗ךְ סִגְר֤וּ הַדֶּ֙לֶת֙ וּלְחַצְתֶּ֤ם אֹתוֹ֙ בַּדֶּ֔לֶת הֲל֗וֹא ק֛וֹל רַגְלֵ֥י אֲדֹנָ֖יו אַחֲרָֽיו: ³³ עוֹדֶ֙נּוּ֙ מְדַבֵּ֣ר עִמָּ֔ם וְהִנֵּ֥ה הַמַּלְאָ֖ךְ יֹרֵ֣ד אֵלָ֑יו וַיֹּ֗אמֶר הִנֵּֽה־זֹ֤את הָֽרָעָה֙ מֵאֵ֣ת יְהֹוָ֔ה מָֽה־אוֹחִ֥יל לַֽיהֹוָ֖ה עֽוֹד: ס ¹ וַיֹּ֣אמֶר אֱלִישָׁ֗ע שִׁמְע֖וּ דְּבַר־יְהֹוָ֑ה כֹּ֣ה ׀ אָמַ֣ר יְהֹוָ֗ה כָּעֵ֤ת ׀ מָחָר֙ סְאָֽה־סֹ֣לֶת בְּשֶׁ֔קֶל וְסָאתַ֧יִם שְׂעֹרִ֛ים בְּשֶׁ֖קֶל בְּשַׁ֥עַר שֹׁמְרֽוֹן: ² וַיַּ֣עַן הַשָּׁלִ֡ישׁ אֲשֶׁר־לַמֶּלֶךְ֩ נִשְׁעָ֨ן עַל־יָד֜וֹ אֶת־אִ֣ישׁ הָאֱלֹהִים֮ וַיֹּאמַר֒ הִנֵּ֣ה יְהֹוָ֗ה עֹשֶׂ֤ה אֲרֻבּוֹת֙ בַּשָּׁמַ֔יִם הֲיִהְיֶ֖ה הַדָּבָ֣ר הַזֶּ֑ה וַיֹּ֗אמֶר הִנְּכָ֤ה* רֹאֶה֙ בְּעֵינֶ֔יךָ וּמִשָּׁ֖ם לֹ֥א תֹאכֵֽל: ס

³ וְאַרְבָּעָ֧ה אֲנָשִׁ֛ים הָי֥וּ מְצֹרָעִ֖ים פֶּ֣תַח הַשָּׁ֑עַר וַיֹּֽאמְרוּ֙ אִ֣ישׁ אֶל־רֵעֵ֔הוּ מָ֗ה אֲנַ֛חְנוּ יֹשְׁבִ֥ים פֹּ֖ה עַד־מָֽתְנוּ: ⁴ אִם־אָמַרְנוּ֩ נָב֨וֹא הָעִ֜יר וְהָרָעָ֣ב בָּעִ֗יר וָמַ֙תְנוּ֙ שָׁ֔ם וְאִם־

---

e-e Lit. "him."
f Emendation yields "king."

town, we shall die there; and if we just sit here, still we die. Come, let us desert to the Aramean camp. If they let us live, we shall live; and if they put us to death, we shall but die."

⁵They set out at twilight for the Aramean camp; but when they came to the edge of the Aramean camp, there was no one there. ⁶For the Lord had caused the Aramean camp to hear a sound of chariots, a sound of horses—the din of a huge army. They said to one another, "The king of Israel must have hired the kings of the Hittites and the kings of Mizraim*ᵃ* to attack us!" ⁷And they fled headlong in the twilight, abandoning their tents and horses and asses—the [entire] camp just as it was—as they fled for their lives.

⁸When those lepers came to the edge of the camp, they went into one of the tents and ate and drank; then they carried off silver and gold and clothing from there and buried it. They came back and went into another tent, and they carried off what was there and buried it. ⁹Then they said to one another, "We are not doing right. This is a day of good news, and we are keeping silent! If we wait until the light of morning, we shall incur guilt. Come, let us go and inform the king's palace." ¹⁰They went and called out to the gatekeepers of the city and told them, "We have been to the Aramean camp. There is not a soul there, nor any human sound; but the horses are tethered and the asses are tethered and the tents are undisturbed."

¹¹The gatekeepers called out, and the news was passed on into the king's palace. ¹²The king rose in the night and said to his courtiers, "I will tell you what the Arameans have done to us. They know that we are starving, so they have gone out of camp and hidden in the fields, thinking: When they come out of the town, we will take them alive and get into the town." ¹³But

---

a Cf. 1 Kings 10.28 and note g there.

יֹשְׁבֵנוּ פֹה וָמַתְנוּ וְעַתָּה לְכוּ וְנִפְּלָה אֶל־מַחֲנֵה אֲרָם אִם־יְחַיֻּנוּ נִחְיֶה וְאִם־יְמִיתֻנוּ וָמָתְנוּ׃

⁵וַיָּקוּמוּ בַנֶּשֶׁף לָבוֹא אֶל־מַחֲנֵה אֲרָם וַיָּבֹאוּ עַד־קְצֵה מַחֲנֵה אֲרָם וְהִנֵּה אֵין־שָׁם אִישׁ׃ ⁶וַאדֹנָי הִשְׁמִיעַ ׀ אֶת־מַחֲנֵה אֲרָם קוֹל רֶכֶב קוֹל סוּס קוֹל חַיִל גָּדוֹל וַיֹּאמְרוּ אִישׁ אֶל־אָחִיו הִנֵּה שָׂכַר־עָלֵינוּ מֶלֶךְ יִשְׂרָאֵל אֶת־מַלְכֵי הַחִתִּים וְאֶת־מַלְכֵי מִצְרַיִם לָבוֹא עָלֵינוּ׃ ⁷וַיָּקוּמוּ וַיָּנוּסוּ בַנֶּשֶׁף וַיַּעַזְבוּ אֶת־אָהֳלֵיהֶם וְאֶת־סוּסֵיהֶם וְאֶת־חֲמֹרֵיהֶם הַמַּחֲנֶה כַּאֲשֶׁר־הִיא וַיָּנֻסוּ אֶל־נַפְשָׁם׃ ⁸וַיָּבֹאוּ הַמְצֹרָעִים הָאֵלֶּה עַד־קְצֵה הַמַּחֲנֶה וַיָּבֹאוּ אֶל־אֹהֶל אֶחָד וַיֹּאכְלוּ וַיִּשְׁתּוּ וַיִּשְׂאוּ מִשָּׁם כֶּסֶף וְזָהָב וּבְגָדִים וַיֵּלְכוּ וַיַּטְמִנוּ וַיָּשֻׁבוּ וַיָּבֹאוּ אֶל־אֹהֶל אַחֵר וַיִּשְׂאוּ מִשָּׁם וַיֵּלְכוּ וַיַּטְמִנוּ׃ ⁹וַיֹּאמְרוּ אִישׁ אֶל־רֵעֵהוּ לֹא־כֵן ׀ אֲנַחְנוּ עֹשִׂים הַיּוֹם הַזֶּה יוֹם־בְּשֹׂרָה הוּא וַאֲנַחְנוּ מַחְשִׁים וְחִכִּינוּ עַד־אוֹר הַבֹּקֶר וּמְצָאָנוּ עָוֹן וְעַתָּה לְכוּ וְנָבֹאָה וְנַגִּידָה בֵּית הַמֶּלֶךְ׃ ¹⁰וַיָּבֹאוּ וַיִּקְרְאוּ אֶל־שֹׁעֵר הָעִיר וַיַּגִּידוּ לָהֶם לֵאמֹר בָּאנוּ אֶל־מַחֲנֵה אֲרָם וְהִנֵּה אֵין־שָׁם אִישׁ וְקוֹל אָדָם כִּי אִם־הַסּוּס אָסוּר וְהַחֲמוֹר אָסוּר וְאֹהָלִים כַּאֲשֶׁר־הֵמָּה׃ ¹¹וַיִּקְרָא הַשֹּׁעֲרִים וַיַּגִּידוּ בֵּית הַמֶּלֶךְ פְּנִימָה׃ ¹²וַיָּקָם הַמֶּלֶךְ לַיְלָה וַיֹּאמֶר אֶל־עֲבָדָיו אַגִּידָה־נָּא לָכֶם אֵת אֲשֶׁר־עָשׂוּ לָנוּ אֲרָם יָדְעוּ כִּי־רְעֵבִים אֲנַחְנוּ וַיֵּצְאוּ מִן־הַמַּחֲנֶה לְהֵחָבֵה בהשדה בַשָּׂדֶה לֵאמֹר כִּי־יֵצְאוּ מִן־הָעִיר וְנִתְפְּשֵׂם חַיִּים וְאֶל־הָעִיר נָבֹא׃ ¹³וַיַּעַן אֶחָד מֵעֲבָדָיו

one of the courtiers spoke up, "Let a few[b] of the remaining horses that are still here be taken— [c]they are like those that are left here of the whole multitude of Israel, out of the whole multitude of Israel that have perished[-c]—and let us send and find out."

[14]They took two teams[c] of horses and the king sent them after the Aramean army, saying, "Go and find out." [15]They followed them as far as the Jordan, and found the entire road full of clothing and gear which the Arameans had thrown away in their haste; and the messengers returned and told the king. [16]The people then went out and plundered the Aramean camp. So a *seah* of choice flour sold for a shekel, and two *seah*s of barley for a shekel—as the LORD had spoken.

[17]Now the king had put the aide on whose arm he leaned in charge of the gate; and he was trampled to death in the gate by the people— just as the man of God had spoken, as he had spoken when the king came down to him. [18]For when the man of God said to the king, "This time tomorrow two *seah*s of barley shall sell at the gate of Samaria for a shekel, and a *seah* of choice flour for a shekel," [19]the aide answered the man of God and said, "Even if the LORD made windows in the sky, could this come to pass?" And he retorted, "You shall see it with your own eyes, but you shall not eat of it." [20]That is exactly what happened to him: The people trampled him to death in the gate.

8 Elisha had said to the woman whose son he revived, "Leave immediately with your family and go sojourn [a]somewhere else;[-a] for the LORD has decreed a seven-year famine upon the land, and it has already begun." [2]The woman

וַיֹּאמֶר וְיִקְחוּ־נָ֠א חֲמִשָּׁה מִן־הַסּוּסִים֙ הַנִּשְׁאָרִים֙ אֲשֶׁ֣ר נִשְׁאֲרוּ־בָ֔הּ הִנָּ֗ם כְּכָל־ הֶהָמוֹן֙ יִשְׂרָאֵל֙ אֲשֶׁ֣ר נִשְׁאֲרוּ־בָ֔הּ הִנָּ֗ם כְּכָל־הֲמ֥וֹן יִשְׂרָאֵ֖ל אֲשֶׁר־תָּ֑מּוּ וְנִשְׁלְחָ֖ה וְנִרְאֶֽה׃

14 וַיִּקְח֕וּ שְׁנֵ֖י רֶ֣כֶב סוּסִ֑ים וַיִּשְׁלַ֨ח הַמֶּ֜לֶךְ אַחֲרֵ֧י מַחֲנֵֽה־אֲרָ֛ם לֵאמֹ֖ר לְכ֥וּ וּרְאֽוּ׃

15 וַיֵּלְכ֣וּ אַחֲרֵיהֶם֮ עַד־הַיַּרְדֵּן֒ וְהִנֵּ֣ה כָל־הַדֶּ֗רֶךְ מְלֵאָ֤ה בְגָדִים֙ וְכֵלִ֔ים אֲשֶׁר־ הִשְׁלִ֥יכוּ אֲרָ֖ם בְּהֵחָפְזָ֑ם וַיָּשֻׁ֨בוּ֙ הַמַּלְאָכִ֔ים וַיַּגִּ֖דוּ לַמֶּֽלֶךְ׃ 16 וַיֵּצֵ֣א הָעָ֔ם וַיָּבֹ֕זּוּ אֵ֖ת מַחֲנֵ֣ה אֲרָ֑ם וַיְהִ֨י סְאָה־סֹ֜לֶת בְּשֶׁ֗קֶל וְסָאתַ֧יִם שְׂעֹרִ֛ים בְּשֶׁ֖קֶל כִּדְבַ֥ר יְהוָֽה׃

17 וְהַמֶּ֣לֶךְ הִפְקִ֣יד אֶת־הַשָּׁלִ֞ישׁ אֲשֶׁר־ נִשְׁעָ֤ן עַל־יָדוֹ֙ עַל־הַשַּׁ֔עַר וַיִּרְמְסֻ֧הוּ הָעָ֛ם בַּשַּׁ֖עַר וַיָּמֹ֑ת כַּאֲשֶׁ֤ר דִּבֶּר֙ אִ֣ישׁ הָאֱלֹהִ֔ים אֲשֶׁ֣ר דִּבֶּ֔ר בְּרֶ֥דֶת הַמֶּ֖לֶךְ אֵלָֽיו׃ 18 וַיְהִ֗י כְּדַבֵּ֞ר אִ֤ישׁ הָאֱלֹהִים֙ אֶל־הַמֶּ֣לֶךְ לֵאמֹ֔ר סָאתַ֨יִם שְׂעֹרִ֜ים בְּשֶׁ֗קֶל וּסְאָה־סֹ֨לֶת֙ בְּשֶׁ֔קֶל יִהְיֶה֙ כָּעֵ֣ת מָחָ֔ר בְּשַׁ֖עַר שֹׁמְרֽוֹן׃ 19 וַיַּ֨עַן הַשָּׁלִ֜ישׁ אֶת־אִ֣ישׁ הָאֱלֹהִים֮ וַיֹּאמַר֒ וְהִנֵּ֣ה יְהוָ֗ה עֹשֶׂ֤ה אֲרֻבּוֹת֙ בַּשָּׁמַ֔יִם הֲיִהְיֶ֖ה כַּדָּבָ֣ר הַזֶּ֑ה וַיֹּ֗אמֶר הִנְּךָ֤ רֹאֶה֙ בְּעֵינֶ֔יךָ וּמִשָּׁ֖ם לֹ֥א תֹאכֵֽל׃ 20 וַיְהִי־ל֖וֹ כֵּ֑ן וַיִּרְמְס֨וּ אֹת֥וֹ הָעָ֛ם בַּשַּׁ֖עַר וַיָּמֹֽת׃ ס

ח וֶאֱלִישָׁ֡ע דִּבֶּ֣ר אֶל־הָאִשָּׁה֩ אֲשֶׁר־ הֶחֱיָ֨ה אֶת־בְּנָ֜הּ לֵאמֹ֗ר ק֤וּמִי וּלְכִי֙ אתי [אַ֣תְּ] וּבֵיתֵ֔ךְ וְג֖וּרִי בַּאֲשֶׁ֣ר תָּג֑וּרִי כִּֽי־קָרָ֤א יְהוָה֙ לָֽרָעָ֔ב וְגַם־בָּ֥א אֶל־הָאָ֖רֶץ שֶׁ֥בַע

792

had done as the man of God had spoken; she left with her family and sojourned in the land of the Philistines for seven years. ³At the end of the seven years, the woman returned from the land of the Philistines and went to the king to complain about her house and farm. ⁴Now the king was talking to Gehazi, the servant of the man of God, and he said, "Tell me all the wonderful things that Elisha has done." ⁵While he was telling the king how [Elisha] had revived a dead person, in came the woman whose son he had revived, complaining to the king about her house and farm. "My lord king," said Gehazi, "this is the woman and this is her son whom Elisha revived." ⁶The king questioned the woman, and she told him [the story]; so the king assigned a eunuch to her and instructed him: "Restore all her property, and all the revenue from her farm from the time she left the country until now."

⁷Elisha arrived in Damascus at a time when King Ben-hadad of Aram was ill. ᵇ⁻The kingᵇ was told, "The man of God is on his way here," ⁸and he said to Hazael, "Take a gift with you and go meet the man of God, and through him inquire of the LORD: Will I recover from this illness?" ⁹Hazael went to meet him, taking with him as a gift forty camel-loads of all the bounty of Damascus. He came and stood before him and said, "Your son, King Ben-hadad of Aram, has sent me to you to ask: Will I recover from this illness?" ¹⁰Elisha said to him, "Go and say to him, 'You will recover.' However, the LORD has revealed to me that he will die." ¹¹The man of God ᶜ⁻kept his face expressionlessᶜ for a long time; and then he wept. ¹²"Why does my lord weep?" asked Hazael. "Because I know," he replied, "what harm you will do to the Israelite people: you will set their fortresses on fire, put

שָׁנִֽים: ²וַתָּ֤קָם הָֽאִשָּׁה֙ וַתַּ֔עַשׂ כִּדְבַ֖ר אִ֣ישׁ הָאֱלֹהִ֑ים וַתֵּ֤לֶךְ הִיא֙ וּבֵיתָ֔הּ וַתָּ֥גָר בְּאֶֽרֶץ־פְּלִשְׁתִּ֖ים שֶׁ֥בַע שָׁנִֽים: ³וַיְהִ֗י מִקְצֵה֙ שֶׁ֣בַע שָׁנִ֔ים וַתָּ֥שָׁב הָאִשָּׁ֖ה מֵאֶ֣רֶץ פְּלִשְׁתִּ֑ים וַתֵּצֵא֙ לִצְעֹ֣ק אֶל־הַמֶּ֔לֶךְ אֶל־בֵּיתָ֖הּ וְאֶל־שָׂדָֽהּ: ⁴וְהַמֶּ֗לֶךְ מְדַבֵּר֙ אֶל־גֵּ֣חֲזִ֔י נַ֥עַר אִישׁ־הָאֱלֹהִ֖ים לֵאמֹ֑ר סַפְּרָה־נָּ֣א לִ֗י אֵ֥ת כָּל־הַגְּדֹל֖וֹת אֲשֶׁר־עָשָׂ֥ה אֱלִישָֽׁע: ⁵וַיְהִ֗י ה֣וּא מְסַפֵּ֣ר לַמֶּ֡לֶךְ אֵת֩ אֲשֶׁר־הֶחֱיָ֨ה אֶת־הַמֵּ֜ת וְהִנֵּ֣ה הָאִשָּׁ֡ה אֲשֶׁר־הֶחֱיָ֣ה אֶת־בְּנָהּ֩ צֹעֶ֨קֶת אֶל־הַמֶּ֜לֶךְ עַל־בֵּיתָ֣הּ וְעַל־שָׂדָ֗הּ וַיֹּ֤אמֶר גֵּֽחֲזִי֙ אֲדֹנִ֣י הַמֶּ֔לֶךְ זֹ֚את הָֽאִשָּׁ֔ה וְזֶה־בְּנָ֖הּ אֲשֶׁר־הֶחֱיָ֥ה אֱלִישָֽׁע: ⁶וַיִּשְׁאַ֥ל הַמֶּ֛לֶךְ לָאִשָּׁ֖ה וַתְּסַפֶּר־ל֑וֹ וַיִּתֶּן־לָ֣הּ הַמֶּלֶךְ֩ סָרִ֨יס אֶחָ֜ד לֵאמֹ֗ר הָשֵׁ֤יב אֶת־כָּל־אֲשֶׁר־לָהּ֙ וְאֵת֙ כָּל־תְּבוּאֹ֣ת הַשָּׂדֶ֔ה מִיּ֛וֹם עָזְבָ֥ה אֶת־הָאָ֖רֶץ וְעַד־עָֽתָּה: פ

⁷וַיָּבֹ֤א אֱלִישָׁע֙ דַּמֶּ֔שֶׂק וּבֶן־הֲדַ֥ד מֶֽלֶךְ־אֲרָ֖ם חֹלֶ֑ה וַיֻּגַּד־ל֣וֹ לֵאמֹ֔ר בָּ֛א אִ֥ישׁ הָאֱלֹהִ֖ים עַד־הֵֽנָּה: ⁸וַיֹּ֣אמֶר הַמֶּ֣לֶךְ אֶל־חֲזָהאֵ֗ל קַ֤ח בְּיָֽדְךָ֙ מִנְחָ֔ה וְלֵ֕ךְ לִקְרַ֖את אִ֣ישׁ הָאֱלֹהִ֑ים וְדָרַשְׁתָּ֨ אֶת־יְהֹוָ֤ה מֵֽאוֹתוֹ֙ לֵאמֹ֔ר הַאֶחְיֶ֖ה מֵחֳלִ֥י זֶֽה: ⁹וַיֵּ֣לֶךְ חֲזָאֵ֣ל לִקְרָאתוֹ֒ וַיִּקַּ֨ח מִנְחָ֤ה בְיָדוֹ֙ וְכָל־ט֣וּב דַּמֶּ֔שֶׂק מַשָּׂ֖א אַרְבָּעִ֣ים גָּמָ֑ל וַיָּבֹא֙ וַיַּעֲמֹ֣ד לְפָנָ֔יו וַיֹּ֕אמֶר בִּנְךָ֨ בֶן־הֲדַ֧ד מֶֽלֶךְ־אֲרָ֛ם שְׁלָחַ֥נִי אֵלֶ֖יךָ לֵאמֹ֑ר הַאֶחְיֶ֖ה מֵחֳלִ֥י זֶֽה: ¹⁰וַיֹּ֤אמֶר אֵלָיו֙ אֱלִישָׁ֔ע לֵ֥ךְ אֱמָר־ל֖וֹ חָיֹ֣ה תִחְיֶ֑ה וְהִרְאַ֥נִי יְהֹוָ֖ה כִּֽי־מ֥וֹת יָמֽוּת: ¹¹וַֽיַּעֲמֵ֥ד אֶת־פָּנָ֛יו וַיָּ֖שֶׂם עַד־בֹּ֑שׁ וַיֵּ֖בְךְּ אִ֥ישׁ הָאֱלֹהִֽים: ¹²וַיֹּ֣אמֶר חֲזָאֵ֔ל מַדּ֖וּעַ אֲדֹנִ֣י בֹכֶ֑ה וַיֹּ֡אמֶר כִּֽי־יָדַ֡עְתִּי אֵ֣ת אֲשֶׁר־תַּעֲשֶׂה֩ לִבְנֵ֨י יִשְׂרָאֵ֜ל רָעָ֗ה מִבְצְרֵיהֶ֞ם תְּשַׁלַּ֤ח בָּאֵשׁ֙ וּבַחֻרֵיהֶם֙ בַּחֶ֣רֶב תַּהֲרֹ֔ג וְעֹלְלֵיהֶ֣ם

ᵇ⁻ᵇ Brought up from v. 8 for clarity.
ᶜ⁻ᶜ Meaning of Heb. uncertain.

their young men to the sword, dash their little ones in pieces, and rip open their pregnant women." [13]"But how," asked Hazael, "can your servant, who is a mere dog, perform such a mighty deed?" Elisha replied, "The LORD has shown me a vision of you as king of Aram." [14]He left Elisha and returned to his master, who asked him, "What did Elisha say to you?" He replied, "He told me that you would recover." [15]The next day, [Hazael] took c-a piece of netting,-c dipped it in water, and spread it over his face. So [Ben-hadad] died, and Hazael succeeded him as king.

[16]In the fifth year of King Joramᵈ son of Ahab of Israel—Jehoshaphat had been king of Judah—Joram son of King Jehoshaphat of Judah became king. [17]He was thirty-two years old when he became king, and he reigned in Jerusalem eight years. [18]He followed the practices of the kings of Israel—whatever the House of Ahab did, for he had married a daughterᵉ of Ahab—and he did what was displeasing to the LORD. [19]However, the LORD refrained from destroying Judah, for the sake of His servant David, in accordance with His promise to maintain a lamp for his descendants for all time. [20]During his reign, the Edomites rebelled against Judah's rule and set up a king of their own. [21]Joram crossed over to Zair with all his chariotry. c-He arose by night and attacked the Edomites, who were surrounding him and the chariot commanders; but-c his troops fled to their homes. [22]Thus Edom fell away from Judah, as is still the case. Libnah likewise fell away at that time.

[23]The other events of Joram's reign, and all his actions, are recorded in the Annals of the Kings of Judah. [24]Joram slept with his fathers and was buried with his fathers in the City of David; his son Ahaziah succeeded him as king.

תְּרֹטֵשׁ וְהָרֹתֵיהֶם תְּבַקֵּעַ: 13 וַיֹּאמֶר חֲזָהאֵל כִּי מָה עַבְדְּךָ הַכֶּלֶב כִּי יַעֲשֶׂה הַדָּבָר הַגָּדוֹל הַזֶּה וַיֹּאמֶר אֱלִישָׁע הִרְאַנִי יְהוָה אֹתְךָ מֶלֶךְ עַל־אֲרָם: 14 וַיֵּלֶךְ ׀ מֵאֵת אֱלִישָׁע וַיָּבֹא אֶל־אֲדֹנָיו וַיֹּאמֶר לוֹ מָה־אָמַר לְךָ אֱלִישָׁע וַיֹּאמֶר אָמַר לִי חָיֹה תִחְיֶה: 15 וַיְהִי מִמָּחֳרָת וַיִּקַּח הַמַּכְבֵּר וַיִּטְבֹּל בַּמַּיִם וַיִּפְרֹשׂ עַל־פָּנָיו וַיָּמֹת וַיִּמְלֹךְ חֲזָהאֵל תַּחְתָּיו: פ

16 וּבִשְׁנַת חָמֵשׁ לְיוֹרָם בֶּן־אַחְאָב מֶלֶךְ יִשְׂרָאֵל וִיהוֹשָׁפָט מֶלֶךְ יְהוּדָה מָלַךְ יְהוֹרָם בֶּן־יְהוֹשָׁפָט מֶלֶךְ יְהוּדָה: 17 בֶּן־שְׁלֹשִׁים וּשְׁתַּיִם שָׁנָה הָיָה בְמָלְכוֹ וּשְׁמֹנֶה שָׁנָה שָׁנִים מָלַךְ בִּירוּשָׁלָםִ: 18 וַיֵּלֶךְ בְּדֶרֶךְ ׀ מַלְכֵי יִשְׂרָאֵל כַּאֲשֶׁר עָשׂוּ בֵּית אַחְאָב כִּי בַּת־אַחְאָב הָיְתָה־לּוֹ לְאִשָּׁה וַיַּעַשׂ הָרַע בְּעֵינֵי יְהוָה: 19 וְלֹא־אָבָה יְהוָה לְהַשְׁחִית אֶת־יְהוּדָה לְמַעַן דָּוִד עַבְדּוֹ כַּאֲשֶׁר אָמַר לוֹ לָתֵת לוֹ נִיר לְבָנָיו כָּל־הַיָּמִים: 20 בְּיָמָיו פָּשַׁע אֱדוֹם מִתַּחַת יַד־יְהוּדָה וַיַּמְלִכוּ עֲלֵיהֶם מֶלֶךְ: 21 וַיַּעֲבֹר יוֹרָם צָעִירָה וְכָל־הָרֶכֶב עִמּוֹ וַיְהִי־הוּא קָם לַיְלָה וַיַּכֶּה אֶת־אֱדוֹם הַסֹּבֵיב אֵלָיו וְאֵת שָׂרֵי הָרֶכֶב וַיָּנָס הָעָם לְאֹהָלָיו: 22 וַיִּפְשַׁע אֱדוֹם מִתַּחַת יַד־יְהוּדָה עַד הַיּוֹם הַזֶּה אָז תִּפְשַׁע לִבְנָה בָּעֵת הַהִיא: 23 וְיֶתֶר דִּבְרֵי יוֹרָם וְכָל־אֲשֶׁר עָשָׂה הֲלוֹא־הֵם כְּתוּבִים עַל־סֵפֶר דִּבְרֵי הַיָּמִים לְמַלְכֵי יְהוּדָה: 24 וַיִּשְׁכַּב יוֹרָם עִם־אֲבֹתָיו וַיִּקָּבֵר עִם־אֲבֹתָיו בְּעִיר דָּוִד וַיִּמְלֹךְ אֲחַזְיָהוּ בְנוֹ תַּחְתָּיו: פ

---

d   Throughout this chapter, the name Joram is sometimes written Jehoram.

e   Emendation yields "sister"; cf. v. 26.

25In the twelfth year of King Joram son of Ahab of Israel, Ahaziah son of Joram became king of Judah. 26Ahaziah was twenty-two years old when he became king, and he reigned in Jerusalem one year; his mother's name was Athaliah daughter of King Omri of Israel. 27He walked in the ways of the House of Ahab and did what was displeasing to the LORD, like the House of Ahab, for he was related by marriage to the House of Ahab. 28He marched with Joram son of Ahab to battle against King Hazael of Aram at Ramoth-gilead, but the Arameans wounded Joram. 29King Joram retired to Jezreel to recover from the wounds which the Arameans had inflicted upon him at Ramah, when he fought against King Hazael of Aram. And King Ahaziah son of Joram of Judah went down to Jezreel to visit Joram son of Ahab while he was ill.

9 Then the prophet Elisha summoned one of the disciples of the prophets and said to him, "Tie up your skirts,ᵃ and take along this flask of oil, and go to Ramoth-gilead. 2When you arrive there, go and see Jehu son of Jehoshaphat son of Nimshi; get him to leave his comrades, and take him into an inner room. 3Then take the flask of oil and pour some on his head, and say, 'Thus said the LORD: I anoint you king over Israel.' Then open the door and flee without delay."

4The young man, the servant of the prophet, went to Ramoth-gilead. 5When he arrived, the army commanders were sitting together. He said, "Commander, I have a message for you." "For which one of us?" Jehu asked. He answered, "For you, commander." 6So [Jehu] arose and went inside; and [the disciple] poured the oil on his head, and said to him, "Thus said

---

בִּשְׁנַת֩ שְׁתֵּים־עֶשְׂרֵ֨ה שָׁנָ֜ה לְיוֹרָ֣ם בֶּן־25 אַחְאָב֙ מֶ֣לֶךְ יִשְׂרָאֵ֔ל מָלַ֖ךְ אֲחַזְיָ֣הוּ בֶן־יְהוֹרָ֖ם מֶ֥לֶךְ יְהוּדָֽה׃ 26 בֶּן־עֶשְׂרִ֨ים וּשְׁתַּ֜יִם שָׁנָ֗ה אֲחַזְיָ֙הוּ֙ בְּמָלְכ֔וֹ וְשָׁנָ֣ה אַחַ֔ת מָלַ֖ךְ בִּירֽוּשָׁלִָ֑ם וְשֵׁ֤ם אִמּוֹ֙ עֲתַלְיָ֔הוּ בַּת־עׇמְרִ֖י מֶ֥לֶךְ יִשְׂרָאֵֽל׃ 27 וַיֵּ֜לֶךְ בְּדֶ֣רֶךְ בֵּ֣ית אַחְאָ֗ב וַיַּ֨עַשׂ הָרַ֜ע בְּעֵינֵ֤י יְהֹוָה֙ כְּבֵ֣ית אַחְאָ֔ב כִּ֛י חֲתַ֥ן בֵּית־אַחְאָ֖ב הֽוּא׃ 28 וַיֵּ֤לֶךְ אֶת־יוֹרָם֙ בֶּן־אַחְאָ֔ב לַמִּלְחָמָ֛ה עִם־חֲזָהאֵ֥ל מֶֽלֶךְ־אֲרָ֖ם בְּרָמֹ֣ת גִּלְעָ֑ד וַיַּכּ֥וּ אֲרַמִּ֖ים אֶת־יוֹרָֽם׃ 29 וַיָּ֩שׇׁב֩ יוֹרָ֨ם הַמֶּ֜לֶךְ לְהִתְרַפֵּ֣א בְיִזְרְעֶ֗אל מִן־הַמַּכִּים֙ אֲשֶׁ֣ר יַכֻּ֣הוּ אֲרַמִּ֔ים בָּרָמָ֕ה בְּהִלָּ֣חֲמ֔וֹ אֶת־חֲזָהאֵ֖ל מֶ֣לֶךְ אֲרָ֑ם וַאֲחַזְיָ֙הוּ בֶן־יְהוֹרָ֜ם מֶ֣לֶךְ יְהוּדָ֗ה יָרַ֡ד לִרְא֞וֹת אֶת־יוֹרָ֧ם בֶּן־אַחְאָ֛ב בְּיִזְרְעֶ֖אל כִּֽי־חֹלֶ֥ה הֽוּא׃ פ

ט וֶאֱלִישָׁע֙ הַנָּבִ֔יא קָרָ֕א לְאַחַ֖ד מִבְּנֵ֣י הַנְּבִיאִ֑ים וַיֹּ֣אמֶר ל֗וֹ חֲגֹ֤ר מׇתְנֶ֙יךָ֙ וְ֠קַ֠ח פַּ֣ךְ הַשֶּׁ֤מֶן הַזֶּה֙ בְּיָדֶ֔ךָ וְלֵ֖ךְ רָמֹ֥ת גִּלְעָֽד׃ 2 וּבָ֣אתָ שָׁ֔מָּה וּרְאֵֽה־שָׁ֠ם יֵה֣וּא בֶן־יְהוֹשָׁפָ֖ט בֶּן־נִמְשִׁ֑י וּבָ֙אתָ֙ וַהֲקֵֽמֹת֣וֹ מִתּ֣וֹךְ אֶחָ֔יו וְהֵבֵיאתָ֥* אֹת֖וֹ חֶ֥דֶר בְּחָֽדֶר׃ 3 וְלָקַחְתָּ֤ פַךְ־הַשֶּׁ֙מֶן֙ וְיָצַקְתָּ֣ עַל־רֹאשׁ֔וֹ וְאָ֣מַרְתָּ֔ כֹּֽה־אָמַ֣ר יְהֹוָ֔ה מְשַׁחְתִּ֥יךָ לְמֶ֖לֶךְ אֶל־יִשְׂרָאֵ֑ל וּפָתַחְתָּ֥ הַדֶּ֛לֶת וְנַ֖סְתָּה וְלֹ֥א תְחַכֶּֽה׃ 4 וַיֵּ֙לֶךְ֙ הַנַּ֣עַר הַנָּבִ֔יא רָמֹ֖ת גִּלְעָֽד׃ 5 וַיָּבֹ֗א וְהִנֵּ֨ה שָׂרֵ֤י הַחַ֙יִל֙ יֹֽשְׁבִ֔ים וַיֹּ֙אמֶר֙ דָּבָ֥ר לִ֛י אֵלֶ֖יךָ הַשָּׂ֑ר וַיֹּ֤אמֶר יֵהוּא֙ אֶל־מִ֣י מִכֻּלָּ֔נוּ וַיֹּ֖אמֶר אֵלֶ֥יךָ הַשָּֽׂר׃ 6 וַיָּ֙קׇם֙ וַיָּבֹ֣א הַבַּ֔יְתָה וַיִּצֹ֥ק הַשֶּׁ֖מֶן אֶל־רֹאשׁ֑וֹ וַיֹּ֣אמֶר ל֗וֹ

the LORD, the God of Israel: I anoint you king over the people of the LORD, over Israel. 7You shall strike down the House of Ahab your master; thus will I avenge on Jezebel the blood of My servants the prophets, and the blood of the other servants of the LORD. 8The whole House of Ahab shall perish, and I will cut off every male belonging to Ahab, b-bond and free-b in Israel. 9I will make the House of Ahab like the House of Jeroboam son of Nebat, and like the House of Baasha son of Ahijah. 10The dogs shall devour Jezebel in the field of Jezreel, with none to bury her." Then he opened the door and fled.

11Jehu went out to the other officers of his master, and they asked him, "Is all well? What did that madman come to you for?" He said to them, "You know the man and his ranting!" 12"You're lying," they said. "Tell us [the truth]." Then he replied, "Thus and thus he said: Thus said the LORD: I anoint you king over Israel!" 13Quickly each man took his cloak and placed it under him,c on d-the top step.-d They sounded the horn and proclaimed, "Jehu is king!" 14Thus Jehu son of Jehoshaphat son of Nimshi conspired against Joram.

Joram and all Israel had been defending Ramoth-gilead against King Hazael of Aram, 15but King Joram had gone back to Jezreel to recover from the wounds which the Arameans had inflicted on him in his battle with King Hazael of Aram.

Jehu said, "If such is your wish, allow no one to slip out of the town to go and report this in Jezreel." 16Then Jehu mounted his chariot and drove to Jezreel; for Joram was lying ill there, and King Ahaziah of Judah had gone down to visit Joram. 17The lookout was stationed on the tower in Jezreel, and he saw the troop of Jehu

כֹּה־אָמַ֞ר יְהוָ֤ה אֱלֹהֵ֣י יִשְׂרָאֵ֔ל מְשַׁחְתִּ֥יךָ לְמֶ֖לֶךְ אֶל־עַ֣ם יְהוָ֑ה אֶל־יִשְׂרָאֵֽל׃ 7 וְהִ֨כִּיתָ֔ה אֶת־בֵּ֥ית אַחְאָ֖ב אֲדֹנֶ֑יךָ וְנִקַּמְתִּ֞י דְּמֵ֣י ׀ עֲבָדַ֣י הַנְּבִיאִ֗ים וּדְמֵ֛י כָּל־עַבְדֵ֥י יְהוָ֖ה מִיַּ֥ד אִיזָֽבֶל׃ 8 וְאָבַ֖ד כָּל־בֵּ֣ית אַחְאָ֑ב וְהִכְרַתִּ֤י לְאַחְאָב֙ מַשְׁתִּ֣ין בְּקִ֔יר וְעָצ֥וּר וְעָז֖וּב בְּיִשְׂרָאֵֽל׃ 9 וְנָתַתִּי֙ אֶת־בֵּ֣ית אַחְאָ֔ב כְּבֵ֖ית יָרָבְעָ֣ם בֶּן־נְבָ֑ט וּכְבֵ֖ית בַּעְשָׁ֥א בֶן־אֲחִיָּֽה׃ 10 וְאֶת־אִיזֶ֜בֶל יֹאכְל֧וּ הַכְּלָבִ֛ים בְּחֵ֥לֶק יִזְרְעֶ֖אל וְאֵ֣ין קֹבֵ֑ר וַיִּפְתַּ֥ח הַדֶּ֖לֶת וַיָּנֹֽס׃

11 וְיֵה֗וּא יָצָא֙ אֶל־עַבְדֵ֣י אֲדֹנָ֔יו וַיֹּ֤אמֶר* ל֣וֹ הֲשָׁל֔וֹם מַדּ֛וּעַ בָּֽא־הַמְשֻׁגָּ֥ע הַזֶּ֖ה אֵלֶ֑יךָ וַיֹּ֣אמֶר אֲלֵיהֶ֔ם אַתֶּ֛ם יְדַעְתֶּ֥ם אֶת־הָאִ֖ישׁ וְאֶת־שִׂיחֽוֹ׃ 12 וַיֹּאמְר֣וּ שֶׁ֔קֶר הַגֶּד־נָ֖א לָ֑נוּ וַיֹּ֗אמֶר כָּזֹ֤את וְכָזֹאת֙ אָמַ֤ר אֵלַי֙ לֵאמֹ֔ר כֹּ֚ה אָמַ֣ר יְהוָ֔ה מְשַׁחְתִּ֥יךָ לְמֶ֖לֶךְ אֶל־יִשְׂרָאֵֽל׃ 13 וַֽיְמַהֲר֗וּ וַיִּקְחוּ֙ אִ֣ישׁ בִּגְד֔וֹ וַיָּשִׂ֥ימוּ תַחְתָּ֖יו אֶל־גֶּ֣רֶם הַֽמַּעֲל֑וֹת וַֽיִּתְקְעוּ֙ בַּשּׁוֹפָ֔ר וַיֹּאמְר֖וּ מָלַ֥ךְ יֵהֽוּא׃ 14 וַיִּתְקַשֵּׁ֗ר יֵה֛וּא בֶּן־יְהוֹשָׁפָ֥ט בֶּן־נִמְשִׁ֖י אֶל־יוֹרָ֑ם

וְיוֹרָם֩ הָיָ֨ה שֹׁמֵ֜ר בְּרָמֹ֤ת גִּלְעָד֙ ה֣וּא וְכָל־יִשְׂרָאֵ֔ל מִפְּנֵ֖י חֲזָאֵ֥ל מֶֽלֶךְ־אֲרָֽם׃ 15 וַיָּשָׁב֩ יְהוֹרָ֨ם הַמֶּ֜לֶךְ לְהִתְרַפֵּ֣א בְיִזְרְעֶ֗אל מִן־הַמַּכִּים֙ אֲשֶׁ֣ר יַכֻּ֣הוּ אֲרַמִּ֔ים בְּהִלָּ֣חֲמ֔וֹ אֶת־חֲזָאֵ֖ל מֶ֥לֶךְ אֲרָ֑ם

וַיֹּ֤אמֶר יֵהוּא֙ אִם־יֵ֣שׁ נַפְשְׁכֶ֔ם אַל־יֵצֵ֤א פָלִיט֙ מִן־הָעִ֔יר לָלֶ֖כֶת לגיד לְהַגִּ֣יד בְּיִזְרְעֶֽאל׃ 16 וַיִּרְכַּ֤ב יֵהוּא֙ וַיֵּ֣לֶךְ יִזְרְעֶ֔אלָה כִּ֥י יוֹרָ֖ם שֹׁכֵ֣ב שָׁ֑מָּה וַֽאֲחַזְיָה֙ מֶ֣לֶךְ יְהוּדָ֔ה יָרַ֖ד לִרְא֥וֹת אֶת־יוֹרָֽם׃ 17 וְהַצֹּפֶה֩ עֹמֵ֨ד עַֽל־הַמִּגְדָּ֜ל בְּיִזְרְעֶ֗אל וַיַּ֛רְא אֶת־שִׁפְעַ֥ת

v. 11. סבירין ומטעין לשון רבים

b-b   See note at 1 Kings 14.10.
c   I.e., Jehu.
d-d   Meaning of Heb. uncertain.

as he approached. He called out, "I see a troop!" Joram said, "Dispatch a horseman to meet them and let him ask: Is all well?" 18The horseman went to meet him, and he said, "The king inquires: Is all well?" Jehu replied, "What concern of yours is it whether all is well? Fall in behind me." The lookout reported: "The messenger has reached them, but has not turned back." 19So he sent out a second horseman. He came to them and said, "Thus says the king: Is all well?" Jehu answered, "What concern of yours is it whether all is well? Fall in behind me." 20And the lookout reported, "The messenger has reached them, but has not turned back. And it looks like the driving of Jehu son of Nimshi, who drives wildly."

21Joram ordered, "Hitch up [the chariot]!" They hitched up his chariot; and King Joram of Israel and King Ahaziah of Judah went out, each in his own chariot, to meet Jehu. They met him at the field of Naboth the Jezreelite. 22When Joram saw Jehu, he asked, "Is all well, Jehu?" But Jehu replied, "How can all be well as long as your mother Jezebel carries on her countless harlotries and sorceries?" 23Thereupon Joram turned his horses^e around and fled, crying out to Ahaziah, "Treason, Ahaziah!" 24But Jehu drew his bow and hit Joram between the shoulders,^f so that the arrow pierced his heart; and he collapsed in his chariot.

25Jehu thereupon ordered his officer Bidkar, "Pick him up and throw him into the field of Naboth the Jezreelite. Remember how you and I were riding side by side behind his father Ahab, when the Lord made this pronouncement about him: 26'I swear, I have taken note of the blood of Naboth and the blood of his sons yesterday—declares the Lord. And I will requite you in this plot—declares the Lord.' So pick him up and throw him unto the plot in accordance with the word of the Lord."

יֵה֖וּא בְּבֹא֑וֹ וַיֹּ֕אמֶר שִׁפְעַ֣ת אֲנִ֣י רֹאֶ֔ה
וַיֹּ֤אמֶר יְהוֹרָם֙ קַ֣ח רַכָּ֔ב וּֽשְׁלַ֖ח לִקְרָאתָ֑ם
וַיֹּ֖אמֶר הֲשָׁלֽוֹם׃ 18 וַיֵּ֩לֶךְ֩ רֹכֵ֨ב הַסּ֜וּס
לִקְרָאת֗וֹ וַיֹּ֙אמֶר֙ כֹּֽה־אָמַ֣ר הַמֶּ֔לֶךְ הֲשָׁל֔וֹם
וַיֹּ֧אמֶר יֵה֛וּא מַה־לְּךָ֥ וּלְשָׁל֖וֹם סֹ֣ב אֶל־
אַחֲרָ֑י וַיַּגֵּ֤ד הַצֹּפֶה֙ לֵאמֹ֔ר בָּֽא־הַמַּלְאָ֥ךְ
עַד־הֶ֖ם וְלֹא־שָֽׁב׃ 19 וַיִּשְׁלַ֗ח רֹכֵ֣ב ס֣וּס שֵׁנִ֔י
וַיָּבֹ֣א אֲלֵהֶ֗ם וַיֹּ֙אמֶר֙ כֹּֽה־אָמַ֣ר הַמֶּ֔לֶךְ
שָׁל֑וֹם וַיֹּ֧אמֶר יֵה֛וּא מַה־לְּךָ֥ וּלְשָׁל֖וֹם סֹ֥ב
אֶל־אַחֲרָֽי׃ 20 וַיַּגֵּ֤ד הַצֹּפֶה֙ לֵאמֹ֔ר בָּ֥א עַד־
אֲלֵיהֶ֖ם וְלֹא־שָׁ֑ב וְהַמִּנְהָג֙ כְּמִנְהַג֙ יֵה֣וּא
בֶן־נִמְשִׁ֔י כִּ֥י בְשִׁגָּע֖וֹן יִנְהָֽג׃
21 וַיֹּ֤אמֶר יְהוֹרָם֙ אֱסֹ֔ר וַיֶּאְסֹ֖ר רִכְבּ֑וֹ וַיֵּצֵ֣א
יְהוֹרָ֣ם מֶֽלֶךְ־יִשְׂרָאֵ֗ל וַאֲחַזְיָ֤הוּ מֶֽלֶךְ־
יְהוּדָה֙ אִ֣ישׁ בְּרִכְבּ֔וֹ וַיֵּצְא֖וּ לִקְרַ֣את יֵה֑וּא
וַיִּמְצָאֻ֔הוּ בְּחֶלְקַ֖ת נָב֥וֹת הַיִּזְרְעֵאלִֽי׃ 22 וַיְהִ֗י כִּרְא֤וֹת יְהוֹרָם֙ אֶת־יֵה֔וּא וַיֹּ֖אמֶר
הֲשָׁל֣וֹם יֵה֑וּא וַיֹּ֙אמֶר֙ מָ֣ה הַשָּׁל֔וֹם עַד־
זְנוּנֵ֞י אִיזֶ֧בֶל אִמְּךָ֛ וּכְשָׁפֶ֖יהָ הָרַבִּֽים׃
23 וַיַּהֲפֹ֧ךְ יְהוֹרָ֛ם יָדָ֖יו וַיָּנֹ֑ס וַיֹּ֥אמֶר אֶל־
אֲחַזְיָ֖הוּ מִרְמָ֥ה אֲחַזְיָֽה׃ 24 וְיֵה֞וּא מִלֵּ֣א
יָד֣וֹ בַקֶּ֗שֶׁת וַיַּ֤ךְ אֶת־יְהוֹרָם֙ בֵּ֣ין זְרֹעָ֔יו וַיֵּצֵ֤א
הַחֵ֙צִי֙ מִלִּבּ֔וֹ וַיִּכְרַ֖ע בְּרִכְבּֽוֹ׃
25 וַיֹּ֗אמֶר אֶל־בִּדְקַר֙ שָֽׁלִשֹׁ֔ה שָׂ֚א
הַשְׁלִכֵ֔הוּ בְּחֶלְקַ֕ת שְׂדֵ֖ה נָב֣וֹת הַיִּזְרְעֵאלִ֑י
כִּֽי־זְכֹ֞ר אֲנִ֣י וָאַ֗תָּה אֵ֣ת רֹכְבִ֤ים צְמָדִים֙
אַֽחֲרֵי֙ אַחְאָ֣ב אָבִ֔יו וַֽיהוָה֙ נָשָׂ֣א עָלָ֔יו
אֶת־הַמַּשָּׂ֖א הַזֶּֽה׃ 26 אִם־לֹ֡א אֶת־דְּמֵ֣י
נָב֣וֹת וְאֶת־דְּמֵ֣י בָנָיו֩ רָאִ֨יתִי אֶ֜מֶשׁ נְאֻם־
יְהוָ֗ה וְשִׁלַּמְתִּ֤י לְךָ֙ בַּחֶלְקָ֣ה הַזֹּ֔את נְאֻם־
יְהוָ֑ה וְעַתָּ֗ה שָׂ֧א הַשְׁלִכֵ֛הוּ בַּחֶלְקָ֖ה כִּדְבַ֥ר
יְהוָֽה׃

e   Lit. "hands"; see note at 1 Kings 22.34.
f   Lit. "arms."

27On seeing this, King Ahaziah of Judah fled along the road to Beth-haggan. Jehu pursued him and said, "Shoot him down too!" [And they shot him] in his chariot at the ascent of Gur, which is near Ibleam. He fled to Megiddo and died there. 28His servants conveyed him in a chariot to Jerusalem, and they buried him in his grave with his fathers, in the City of David. (29Ahaziah had become king over Judah in the eleventh year of Joram son of Ahab.)

30Jehu went on to Jezreel. When Jezebel heard of it, she painted her eyes with kohl and dressed her hair, and she looked out of the window. 31As Jehu entered the gate, she called out, "Is all well, Zimri, murderer of your master?"g 32He looked up toward the window and said, "Who is on my side, who?" And two or three eunuchs leaned out toward him. 33"Throw her down," he said. They threw her down; and her blood spattered on the wall and on the horses, and they trampled her.

34Then he went inside and ate and drank. And he said, "Attend to that cursed woman and bury her, for she was a king's daughter." 35So they went to bury her; but all they found of her were the skull, the feet, and the hands. 36They came back and reported to him; and he said, "It is just as the LORD spoke through His servant Elijah the Tishbite: The dogs shall devour the flesh of Jezebel in the field of Jezreel; 37and the carcass of Jezebel shall be like dung on the ground, in the field of Jezreel, so that none will be able to say: 'This was Jezebel.'"

10
Ahab had seventy descendants in Samaria. Jehu wrote letters and sent them to Samaria, to the elders and officials of Jezreela and to the guardians of [the children] of Ahab, as

27 וַאֲחַזְיָה מֶלֶךְ־יְהוּדָה רָאָה וַיָּנָס דֶּרֶךְ בֵּית הַגָּן וַיִּרְדֹּף אַחֲרָיו יֵהוּא וַיֹּאמֶר גַּם־אֹתוֹ הַכֻּהוּ אֶל־הַמֶּרְכָּבָה בְּמַעֲלֵה־גוּר אֲשֶׁר אֶת־יִבְלְעָם וַיָּנָס מְגִדּוֹ וַיָּמָת שָׁם: 28 וַיַּרְכִּבוּ אֹתוֹ עֲבָדָיו יְרוּשָׁלְָמָה וַיִּקְבְּרוּ אֹתוֹ בִקְבֻרָתוֹ עִם־אֲבֹתָיו בְּעִיר דָּוִד: פ 29 וּבִשְׁנַת אַחַת עֶשְׂרֵה שָׁנָה לְיוֹרָם בֶּן־אַחְאָב מָלַךְ אֲחַזְיָה עַל־יְהוּדָה:

30 וַיָּבוֹא יֵהוּא יִזְרְעֶאלָה וְאִיזֶבֶל שָׁמְעָה וַתָּשֶׂם בַּפּוּךְ עֵינֶיהָ וַתֵּיטֶב אֶת־רֹאשָׁהּ וַתַּשְׁקֵף בְּעַד הַחַלּוֹן: 31 וְיֵהוּא בָּא בַשָּׁעַר וַתֹּאמֶר הֲשָׁלוֹם זִמְרִי הֹרֵג אֲדֹנָיו: 32 וַיִּשָּׂא פָנָיו אֶל־הַחַלּוֹן וַיֹּאמֶר מִי אִתִּי מִי וַיַּשְׁקִיפוּ אֵלָיו שְׁנַיִם שְׁלֹשָׁה סָרִיסִים: 33 וַיֹּאמֶר שִׁמְטֻהוּ וַיִּשְׁמְטוּהָ וַיִּז מִדָּמָהּ אֶל־הַקִּיר וְאֶל־הַסּוּסִים וַיִּרְמְסֶנָּה: 34 וַיָּבֹא וַיֹּאכַל וַיֵּשְׁתְּ וַיֹּאמֶר פִּקְדוּ־נָא אֶת־הָאֲרוּרָה הַזֹּאת וְקִבְרוּהָ כִּי בַת־מֶלֶךְ הִיא: 35 וַיֵּלְכוּ לְקָבְרָהּ וְלֹא־מָצְאוּ בָהּ כִּי אִם־הַגֻּלְגֹּלֶת וְהָרַגְלַיִם וְכַפּוֹת הַיָּדָיִם: 36 וַיָּשֻׁבוּ וַיַּגִּידוּ לוֹ וַיֹּאמֶר דְּבַר־יְהוָה הוּא אֲשֶׁר דִּבֶּר בְּיַד־עַבְדּוֹ אֵלִיָּהוּ הַתִּשְׁבִּי לֵאמֹר בְּחֵלֶק יִזְרְעֶאל יֹאכְלוּ הַכְּלָבִים אֶת־בְּשַׂר אִיזָבֶל: 37 והית וְהָיְתָה נִבְלַת אִיזֶבֶל כְּדֹמֶן עַל־פְּנֵי הַשָּׂדֶה בְּחֵלֶק יִזְרְעֶאל אֲשֶׁר לֹא־יֹאמְרוּ זֹאת אִיזָבֶל: פ

ל וּלְאַחְאָב שִׁבְעִים בָּנִים בְּשֹׁמְרוֹן וַיִּכְתֹּב יֵהוּא סְפָרִים וַיִּשְׁלַח שֹׁמְרוֹן אֶל־שָׂרֵי יִזְרְעֶאל הַזְּקֵנִים וְאֶל־הָאֹמְנִים

---

g   See 1 Kings 16.8–10.

a   Emendation yields "of the city."

798

follows: 2"Now, when this letter reaches you—since your master's sons are with you and you also have chariots and horses, and a fortified city and weapons—3select the best and the most suitable of your master's sons and set him on his father's throne, and fight for your master's house." 4But they were overcome by fear, for they thought, "If the two kings could not stand up to him, how can we?" 5The steward of the palace and the governor of the city and the elders and the guardians sent this message to Jehu: "We are your subjects, and we shall do whatever you tell us to. We shall not proclaim anyone king; do whatever you like."

6He wrote them a second time: "If you are on my side and are ready to obey me, take the heads of the attendants of your master's sons and come[b] to me in Jezreel tomorrow at this time." Now the princes, seventy in number, were with the notables of the town, who were rearing them. 7But when the letter reached them, they took the princes and slaughtered all seventy of them; they put their heads in baskets and sent them to him in Jezreel. 8A messenger came and reported to him: "They have brought the heads of the princes." He said, "Pile them up in two heaps at the entrance of the gate before morning." 9In the morning he went out and stood there; and he said to all the people, "Are you blameless?[c] True, I conspired against my master and killed him; but who struck down all of these? 10Know, then, that nothing that the Lord has spoken concerning the House of Ahab shall remain unfulfilled, for the Lord has done what he announced through His servant Elijah." 11And Jehu struck down all that were left of the House of Ahab in Jezreel—and all his notables, intimates, and priests—till he left him no survivor.

12He then set out for Samaria. On the way,

אַחְאָ֖ב לֵאמֹֽר׃ 2וְעַתָּ֗ה כְּבֹ֨א הַסֵּ֤פֶר הַזֶּה֙ אֲלֵיכֶ֔ם וְאִתְּכֶ֖ם בְּנֵ֣י אֲדֹנֵיכֶ֑ם וְאִתְּכֶ֞ם הָרֶ֤כֶב וְהַסּוּסִים֙ וְעִ֣יר מִבְצָ֔ר וְהַנָּֽשֶׁק׃ 3וּרְאִיתֶ֞ם הַטּ֤וֹב וְהַיָּשָׁר֙ מִבְּנֵ֣י אֲדֹֽנֵיכֶ֔ם וְשַׂמְתֶּ֖ם עַל־כִּסֵּ֣א אָבִ֑יו וְהִֽלָּחֲמ֖וּ עַל־בֵּ֥ית אֲדֹנֵיכֶֽם׃ 4וַיִּֽרְאוּ֙ מְאֹ֣ד מְאֹ֔ד וַיֹּ֣אמְר֔וּ הִנֵּ֞ה שְׁנֵ֤י הַמְּלָכִים֙ לֹ֣א עָֽמְד֣וּ לְפָנָ֔יו וְאֵ֖יךְ נַעֲמֹ֥ד אֲנָֽחְנוּ׃ 5וַיִּשְׁלַ֣ח אֲשֶׁר־עַל־הַבַּ֣יִת וַאֲשֶׁ֪ר עַל־הָעִ֡יר וְהַזְּקֵנִים֩ וְהָאֹמְנִ֨ים אֶל־יֵה֤וּא ׀ לֵאמֹר֙ עֲבָדֶ֣יךָ אֲנַ֔חְנוּ וְכֹ֛ל אֲשֶׁר־תֹּאמַ֥ר אֵלֵ֖ינוּ נַעֲשֶׂ֑ה לֹֽא־נַמְלִ֣יךְ אִ֔ישׁ הַטּ֥וֹב בְּעֵינֶ֖יךָ עֲשֵֽׂה׃

6וַיִּכְתֹּ֣ב אֲלֵיהֶ֣ם סֵ֣פֶר ׀ שֵׁנִית֮ לֵאמֹר֒ אִם־לִ֨י אַתֶּ֜ם וּלְקֹלִ֣י ׀ אַתֶּ֣ם שֹֽׁמְעִים֮ קְחוּ֙ אֶת־רָאשֵׁי֙ אַנְשֵׁ֣י בְנֵֽי־אֲדֹנֵיכֶ֔ם וּבֹ֧אוּ אֵלַ֛י כָּעֵ֥ת מָחָ֖ר יִזְרְעֶ֑אלָה וּבְנֵ֤י הַמֶּ֙לֶךְ֙ שִׁבְעִ֣ים אִ֔ישׁ אֶת־גְּדֹלֵ֥י הָעִ֖יר מְגַדְּלִ֥ים אוֹתָֽם׃ 7וַיְהִ֗י כְּבֹ֤א הַסֵּ֙פֶר֙ אֲלֵיהֶ֔ם וַיִּקְחוּ֙ אֶת־בְּנֵ֣י הַמֶּ֔לֶךְ וַֽיִּשְׁחֲט֖וּ שִׁבְעִ֣ים אִ֑ישׁ וַיָּשִׂ֤ימוּ אֶת־רָֽאשֵׁיהֶם֙ בַּדּוּדִ֔ים וַיִּשְׁלְח֥וּ אֵלָ֖יו יִזְרְעֶֽאלָה׃ 8וַיָּבֹ֤א הַמַּלְאָךְ֙ וַיַּגֶּד־ל֣וֹ לֵאמֹ֔ר הֵבִ֖יאוּ רָאשֵׁ֣י בְנֵֽי־הַמֶּ֑לֶךְ וַיֹּ֗אמֶר שִׂ֣ימוּ אֹתָ֞ם שְׁנֵ֧י צִבֻּרִ֛ים פֶּ֥תַח הַשַּׁ֖עַר עַד־הַבֹּֽקֶר׃ 9וַיְהִ֤י בַבֹּ֙קֶר֙ וַיֵּצֵ֣א וַֽיַּעֲמֹ֔ד וַיֹּ֙אמֶר֙ אֶל־כָּל־הָעָ֔ם צַדִּקִ֖ים אַתֶּ֑ם הִנֵּ֨ה אֲנִ֜י קָשַׁ֣רְתִּי עַל־אֲדֹנִ֗י וָאֶהְרְגֵ֔הוּ וּמִ֥י הִכָּ֖ה אֶת־כָּל־אֵֽלֶּה׃ 10דְּע֣וּ אֵפ֗וֹא כִּ֠י לֹ֣א יִפֹּ֤ל מִדְּבַ֤ר יְהוָה֙ אַ֔רְצָה אֲשֶׁר־דִּבֶּ֥ר יְהוָ֖ה עַל־בֵּ֣ית אַחְאָ֑ב וַֽיהוָ֣ה עָשָׂ֔ה אֵ֚ת אֲשֶׁ֣ר דִּבֶּ֔ר בְּיַ֖ד עַבְדּ֥וֹ אֵלִיָּֽהוּ׃ 11וַיַּ֣ךְ יֵה֗וּא אֵ֣ת כָּל־הַנִּשְׁאָרִ֤ים לְבֵית־אַחְאָב֙ בְּיִזְרְעֶ֔אל וְכָל־גְּדֹלָ֧יו וּמְיֻדָּעָ֛יו וְכֹהֲנָ֖יו עַד־בִּלְתִּ֥י הִשְׁאִֽיר־ל֖וֹ שָׂרִֽיד׃ 12וַיָּ֙קָם֙ וַיָּבֹ֔א וַיֵּ֖לֶךְ שֹׁמְר֑וֹן ה֛וּא בֵּֽית־עֵ֥קֶד

---

b   *Targum and Septuagint read "and bring them."*

c   *Or "You are blameless."*

when he was at Beth-eked of the shepherds, [13]Jehu came upon the kinsmen of King Ahaziah of Judah. "Who are you?" he asked. They replied, "We are the kinsmen of Ahaziah, and we have come to pay our respects to the sons of the king and the sons of the queen mother." [14]"Take them alive!" he said. They took them alive and then slaughtered them at the pit of Beth-eked, forty-two of them; he did not spare a single one.

[15]He went on from there, and he met Jehonadab son of Rechab coming toward him. He greeted him and said to him, "Are you as wholehearted with me as I am with you?" "I am," Jehonadab replied. "If so," [said Jehu,] "give me your hand." He gave him his hand and [Jehu] helped him into the chariot. [16]"Come with me," he said, "and see my zeal for the Lord." And he was taken along in the chariot. [17]Arriving in Samaria, [Jehu] struck down all the survivors of [the House of] Ahab in Samaria, until he wiped it out, fulfilling the word that the Lord had spoken to Elijah.

[18]Jehu assembled all the people and said to them, "Ahab served Baal little; Jehu shall serve him much! [19]Therefore, summon to me all the prophets of Baal, all his worshipers, and all his priests: let no one fail to come, for I am going to hold a great sacrifice for Baal. Whoever fails to come shall forfeit his life." Jehu was acting with guile in order to exterminate the worshipers of Baal. [20]Jehu gave orders to convoke a solemn assembly for Baal, and one was proclaimed. [21]Jehu sent word throughout Israel, and all the worshipers of Baal came, not a single one remained behind. They came into the temple of Baal, and the temple of Baal was filled from end to end. [22]He said to the man in charge of the wardrobe,[d] "Bring out the vestments for all the worshipers of Baal"; and he brought vest-

הָרֹעִֽים בַּדָּֽרֶךְ׃ 13 וְיֵהוּא מָצָא אֶת־אֲחֵי אֲחַזְיָהוּ מֶֽלֶךְ־יְהוּדָה וַיֹּאמֶר מִי אַתֶּם וַיֹּאמְרוּ אֲחֵי אֲחַזְיָהוּ אֲנַחְנוּ וַנֵּרֶד לִשְׁלוֹם בְּנֵֽי־הַמֶּלֶךְ וּבְנֵי הַגְּבִירָֽה׃ 14 וַיֹּאמֶר תִּפְשׂוּם חַיִּים וַֽיִּתְפְּשׂוּם חַיִּים וַיִּשְׁחָטוּם אֶל־בּוֹר בֵּֽית־עֵקֶד אַרְבָּעִים וּשְׁנַיִם אִישׁ וְלֹֽא־הִשְׁאִיר אִישׁ מֵהֶֽם׃ ס 15 וַיֵּלֶךְ מִשָּׁם וַיִּמְצָא אֶת־יְהוֹנָדָב בֶּן־רֵכָב לִקְרָאתוֹ וַֽיְבָרְכֵהוּ וַיֹּאמֶר אֵלָיו הֲיֵשׁ אֶת־לְבָבְךָ יָשָׁר כַּאֲשֶׁר לְבָבִי עִם־לְבָבֶךָ וַיֹּאמֶר יְהוֹנָדָב יֵשׁ וָיֵשׁ תְּנָה אֶת־יָדֶךָ וַיִּתֵּן יָדוֹ וַיַּעֲלֵהוּ אֵלָיו אֶל־הַמֶּרְכָּבָֽה׃ 16 וַיֹּאמֶר לְכָה אִתִּי וּרְאֵה בְּקִנְאָתִי לַֽיהוָה וַיַּרְכִּבוּ אֹתוֹ בְּרִכְבּֽוֹ׃ 17 וַיָּבֹא שֹֽׁמְרוֹן וַיַּךְ אֶת־כָּל־ הַנִּשְׁאָרִים לְאַחְאָב בְּשֹֽׁמְרוֹן עַד־הִשְׁמִידֽוֹ כִּדְבַר יְהוָה אֲשֶׁר דִּבֶּר אֶל־אֵלִיָּֽהוּ׃ פ 18 וַיִּקְבֹּץ יֵהוּא אֶת־כָּל־הָעָם וַיֹּאמֶר אֲלֵהֶם אַחְאָב עָבַד אֶת־הַבַּעַל מְעָט יֵהוּא יַעַבְדֶנּוּ הַרְבֵּֽה׃ 19 וְעַתָּה כָל־נְבִיאֵי הַבַּעַל כָּל־עֹבְדָיו וְכָל־כֹּהֲנָיו קִרְאוּ אֵלַי אִישׁ אַל־יִפָּקֵד כִּי זֶבַח גָּדוֹל לִי לַבַּעַל כֹּל אֲשֶׁר־יִפָּקֵד לֹא יִֽחְיֶה וְיֵהוּא עָשָׂה בְעָקְבָּה* לְמַעַן הַאֲבִיד אֶת־עֹבְדֵי הַבָּֽעַל׃ 20 וַיֹּאמֶר יֵהוּא קַדְּשׁוּ עֲצָרָה לַבַּעַל וַיִּקְרָֽאוּ׃ 21 וַיִּשְׁלַח יֵהוּא בְּכָל־יִשְׂרָאֵל וַיָּבֹאוּ כָּל־עֹבְדֵי הַבַּעַל וְלֹא־נִשְׁאַר אִישׁ אֲשֶׁר לֹֽא־בָא וַיָּבֹאוּ בֵּית הַבַּעַל וַיִּמָּלֵא בֵֽית־הַבַּעַל פֶּה לָפֶֽה׃ 22 וַיֹּאמֶר לַֽאֲשֶׁר עַל־הַמֶּלְתָּחָה הוֹצֵא לְבוּשׁ לְכָל עֹבְדֵי

---

d *Meaning of Heb. uncertain.*

ments out for them. [23] Then Jehu and Jehonadab son of Rechab came into the temple of Baal, and they said to the worshipers of Baal, "Search and make sure that there are no worshipers of the LORD among you, but only worshipers of Baal." [24] So they went in to offer sacrifices and burnt offerings. But Jehu had stationed eighty of his men outside and had said, "Whoever permits the escape of a single one of the men I commit to your charge shall forfeit life for life."

[25] When Jehu had finished presenting the burnt offering, he said to the guards and to the officers, "Come in and strike them down; let no man get away!" The guards and the officers struck them down with the sword and left them lying where they were; then they proceeded to the interior[e] of the temple of Baal. [26] They brought out the pillars[f] of the temple of Baal and burned them. [27] They destroyed the pillar[g] of Baal, and they tore down the temple of Baal and turned it into latrines, as is still the case. [28] Thus Jehu eradicated the Baal from Israel. [29] However, Jehu did not turn away from the sinful objects by which Jeroboam son of Nebat had caused Israel to sin, namely, the golden calves at Bethel and at Dan.

[30] The LORD said to Jehu, "Because you have acted well and done what was pleasing to Me, having carried out all that I desired upon the House of Ahab, four generations of your descendants shall occupy the throne of Israel." [31] But Jehu was not careful to follow the Teaching of the LORD, the God of Israel, with all his heart; he did not turn away from the sins that Jeroboam had caused Israel to commit.

[32] In those days the LORD began to reduce Israel; and Hazael harassed them throughout the territory of Israel [33] east of the Jordan, all the

הַבַּעַל וַיֹּצֵא לָהֶם הַמַּלְבּֽוּשׁ׃ [23] וַיָּבֹא יֵהוּא וִיהוֹנָדָב בֶּן־רֵכָב בֵּית הַבָּעַל וַיֹּאמֶר לְעֹבְדֵי הַבַּעַל חַפְּשׂוּ וּרְאוּ פֶּן־יֶשׁ־פֹּה עִמָּכֶם מֵעַבְדֵי יְהֹוָה כִּי אִם־עֹבְדֵי הַבַּעַל לְבַדָּם׃ [24] וַיָּבֹאוּ לַעֲשׂוֹת זְבָחִים וְעֹלוֹת וְיֵהוּא שָׂם־לוֹ בַחוּץ שְׁמֹנִים אִישׁ וַיֹּאמֶר הָאִישׁ אֲשֶׁר־יִמָּלֵט מִן־הָאֲנָשִׁים אֲשֶׁר אֲנִי מֵבִיא עַל־יְדֵיכֶם נַפְשׁוֹ תַּחַת נַפְשֽׁוֹ׃ [25] וַיְהִי כְּכַלֹּתוֹ ׀ לַעֲשׂוֹת הָעֹלָה וַיֹּאמֶר יֵהוּא לָרָצִים וְלַשָּׁלִשִׁים בֹּאוּ הַכּוּם אִישׁ אַל־יֵצֵא וַיַּכּוּם לְפִי־חָרֶב וַיַּשְׁלִכוּ הָרָצִים וְהַשָּׁלִשִׁים וַיֵּלְכוּ עַד־עִיר בֵּית־הַבָּעַל׃ [26] וַיֹּצִאוּ אֶת־מַצְּבוֹת בֵּית־הַבַּעַל וַיִּשְׂרְפֽוּהָ׃ [27] וַיִּתְּצוּ אֵת מַצְּבַת הַבָּעַל וַיִּתְּצוּ אֶת־בֵּית הַבַּעַל וַיְשִׂמֻהוּ למחראות לְמוֹצָאוֹת עַד־הַיּֽוֹם׃ [28] וַיַּשְׁמֵד יֵהוּא אֶת־הַבַּעַל מִיִּשְׂרָאֵֽל׃ [29] רַק חֲטָאֵי יָרָבְעָם בֶּן־נְבָט אֲשֶׁר הֶחֱטִיא אֶת־יִשְׂרָאֵל לֹא־סָר יֵהוּא מֵאַחֲרֵיהֶם עֶגְלֵי הַזָּהָב אֲשֶׁר בֵּית־*אֵל וַאֲשֶׁר בְּדָֽן׃ ס [30] וַיֹּאמֶר יְהֹוָה אֶל־יֵהוּא יַעַן אֲשֶׁר־הֱטִיבֹתָ לַעֲשׂוֹת הַיָּשָׁר בְּעֵינַי כְּכֹל אֲשֶׁר בִּלְבָבִי עָשִׂיתָ לְבֵית אַחְאָב בְּנֵי רְבִעִים יֵשְׁבוּ לְךָ עַל־כִּסֵּא יִשְׂרָאֵֽל׃ [31] וְיֵהוּא לֹא שָׁמַר לָלֶכֶת בְּתוֹרַת־יְהֹוָה אֱלֹהֵי־יִשְׂרָאֵל בְּכָל־לְבָבוֹ לֹא סָר מֵעַל חַטֹּאות יָרָבְעָם אֲשֶׁר הֶחֱטִיא אֶת־יִשְׂרָאֵֽל׃ [32] בַּיָּמִים הָהֵם הֵחֵל יְהֹוָה לְקַצּוֹת בְּיִשְׂרָאֵל וַיַּכֵּם חֲזָאֵל בְּכָל־גְּבוּל יִשְׂרָאֵֽל׃ [33] מִן־הַיַּרְדֵּן מִזְרַח הַשֶּׁמֶשׁ אֵת כָּל־אֶרֶץ

---

e   Lit. "city."
f   Emendation yields "sacred posts"; cf. Deut. 12.3.
g   Emendation yields "altar."

v. 29. סבירין ומטעין "בבית"

land of Gilead—the Gadites, the Reubenites, and the Manassites—from Aroer, by the Wadi Arnon, up to Gilead and Bashan.

³⁴The other events of Jehu's reign, and all his actions, and all his exploits, are recorded in the Annals of the Kings of Israel. ³⁵Jehu slept with his fathers and he was buried in Samaria; he was succeeded as king by his son Jehoahaz. ³⁶Jehu reigned over Israel for twenty-eight years in Samaria.

11 When Athaliah, the mother of Ahaziah, learned that her son was dead, she promptly killed off all who were of royal stock. ²But Jehosheba, daughter of King Joram and sister of Ahaziah, secretly took Ahaziah's son Joash away from among the princes who were being slain, and [put]ᵃ him and his nurse in a bedroom. And theyᵇ kept him hidden from Athaliah so that he was not put to death. ³He stayed with her for six years, hidden in the House of the Lord,ᶜ while Athaliah reigned over the land.

⁴In the seventh year, Jehoiada sent for the chiefs of the hundreds of the Caritesᵈ and of the guards, and had them come to him in the House of the Lord. He made a pact with them, exacting an oath from them in the House of the Lord, and he showed them the king's son. ⁵He instructed them: "This is what you must do: One-third of those who are on duty for the week ᵉ-shall maintain guard-ᵉ over the royal palace; ⁶another third shall be [stationed] at the ᶠ-Sur Gate;ᶠ and the other third shall be at the gate behind ᵍ-the guards; you shall keep guard over the House on every side.-ᵍ ⁷The two divisions

הַגִּלְעָד הַגָּדִי וְהָראוּבֵנִי וְהַמְנַשִּׁי מֵעֲרֹעֵר אֲשֶׁר עַל־נַחַל אַרְנֹן וְהַגִּלְעָד וְהַבָּשָׁן: ³⁴ וְיֶתֶר דִּבְרֵי יֵהוּא וְכָל־אֲשֶׁר עָשָׂה וְכָל־גְּבוּרָתוֹ הֲלוֹא־הֵם כְּתוּבִים עַל־סֵפֶר דִּבְרֵי הַיָּמִים לְמַלְכֵי יִשְׂרָאֵל: ³⁵ וַיִּשְׁכַּב יֵהוּא עִם־אֲבֹתָיו וַיִּקְבְּרוּ אֹתוֹ בְּשֹׁמְרוֹן וַיִּמְלֹךְ יְהוֹאָחָז בְּנוֹ תַּחְתָּיו: ³⁶ וְהַיָּמִים אֲשֶׁר מָלַךְ יֵהוּא עַל־יִשְׂרָאֵל עֶשְׂרִים וּשְׁמֹנֶה־שָׁנָה בְּשֹׁמְרוֹן: פ

יא וַעֲתַלְיָה אֵם אֲחַזְיָהוּ וראתה רָאֲתָה כִּי מֵת בְּנָהּ וַתָּקָם וַתְּאַבֵּד אֵת כָּל־זֶרַע הַמַּמְלָכָה: ² וַתִּקַּח יְהוֹשֶׁבַע בַּת־הַמֶּלֶךְ־יוֹרָם אֲחוֹת אֲחַזְיָהוּ אֶת־יוֹאָשׁ בֶּן־אֲחַזְיָה וַתִּגְנֹב אֹתוֹ מִתּוֹךְ בְּנֵי־הַמֶּלֶךְ הממותתים הַמּוּמָתִים אֹתוֹ וְאֶת־מֵינִקְתּוֹ בַּחֲדַר הַמִּטּוֹת וַיַּסְתִּרוּ אֹתוֹ מִפְּנֵי עֲתַלְיָהוּ וְלֹא הוּמָת: ³ וַיְהִי אִתָּהּ בֵּית יְהֹוָה מִתְחַבֵּא שֵׁשׁ שָׁנִים וַעֲתַלְיָה מֹלֶכֶת עַל־הָאָרֶץ: פ ⁴ וּבַשָּׁנָה הַשְּׁבִיעִית שָׁלַח יְהוֹיָדָע וַיִּקַּח אֶת־שָׂרֵי הַמֵּאיוֹת לַכָּרִי וְלָרָצִים וַיָּבֵא אֹתָם אֵלָיו בֵּית יְהֹוָה וַיִּכְרֹת לָהֶם בְּרִית וַיַּשְׁבַּע אֹתָם בְּבֵית יְהֹוָה וַיַּרְא אֹתָם אֶת־בֶּן־הַמֶּלֶךְ: ⁵ וַיְצַוֵּם לֵאמֹר זֶה הַדָּבָר אֲשֶׁר תַּעֲשׂוּן הַשְּׁלִשִׁית מִכֶּם בָּאֵי הַשַּׁבָּת וְשֹׁמְרֵי מִשְׁמֶרֶת בֵּית הַמֶּלֶךְ: ⁶ וְהַשְּׁלִשִׁית בְּשַׁעַר סוּר וְהַשְּׁלִשִׁית בַּשַּׁעַר אַחַר הָרָצִים וּשְׁמַרְתֶּם אֶת־מִשְׁמֶרֶת הַבַּיִת מַסָּח: ⁷ וּשְׁתֵּי הַיָּדוֹת בָּכֶם כֹּל יֹצְאֵי הַשַּׁבָּת וְשָׁמְרוּ אֶת־מִשְׁמֶרֶת בֵּית־יְהֹוָה

---

a Cf. 2 Chron. 22.11.
b 2 Chron. 22.11 reads "she."
c Jehosheba was the wife of the high priest Jehoiada; cf. 2 Chron. 22.11.
d Perhaps the Cherethites (cf. 2 Sam. 20.23) or the Carians. They were members of the king's bodyguard.
e-e Heb. "and who keep guard."
f-f 2 Chron. 23.5 reads "Foundation Gate."
g-g Meaning of Heb. uncertain.

of yours who are off duty this week shall keep guard over the House of the LORD for the protection of the king. [8]You shall surround the king on every side, every man with his weapons at the ready; and whoever breaks through the ranks shall be killed. Stay close to the king in his comings and goings."

[9]The chiefs of hundreds did just as Jehoiada ordered: Each took his men—those who were on duty that week and those who were off duty that week—and they presented themselves to Jehoiada the priest. [10]The priest gave the chiefs of hundreds King David's spears[h] and quivers that were kept in the House of the LORD. [11]The guards, each with his weapons at the ready, stationed themselves—from the south end of the House to the north end of the House, at the altar and the House—to guard the king on every side. [12][Jehoiada] then brought out the king's son, and placed upon him the crown and the insignia.[g] They anointed him and proclaimed him king; they clapped their hands and shouted, "Long live the king!"

[13]When Athaliah heard the shouting of the guards [and] the people, she came out to the people in the House of the LORD. [14]She looked about and saw the king standing by the pillar, as was the custom, the chiefs with their trumpets beside the king, and all the people of the land rejoicing and blowing trumpets. Athaliah rent her garments and cried out, "Treason, treason!" [15]Then the priest Jehoiada gave the command to the army officers, the chiefs of hundreds, and said to them, "Take her out [g-]between the ranks[-g] and, if anyone follows her, put him to the sword." For the priest thought: "Let her not be put to death in the House of the LORD." [16]They cleared a passageway for her and she entered the royal palace through the horses' entrance: there she was put to death.

אֶל־הַמֶּֽלֶךְ: 8 וְהִקַּפְתֶּ֨ם עַל־הַמֶּ֥לֶךְ סָבִ֖יב אִ֣ישׁ וְכֵלָ֣יו בְּיָד֑וֹ וְהַבָּ֥א אֶל־הַשְּׂדֵר֖וֹת יוּמָ֑ת וִהְי֥וּ אֶת־הַמֶּ֖לֶךְ בְּצֵאת֥וֹ וּבְבֹאֽוֹ: 9 וַיַּעֲשׂ֜וּ שָׂרֵ֣י הַמֵּא֗וֹת כְּכֹ֣ל אֲשֶׁר־צִוָּה֮ יְהוֹיָדָ֣ע הַכֹּהֵן֒ וַיִּקְחוּ֙ אִ֣ישׁ אֶת־אֲנָשָׁ֔יו בָּאֵ֣י הַשַּׁבָּ֔ת עִ֖ם יֹצְאֵ֣י הַשַּׁבָּ֑ת וַיָּבֹ֖אוּ אֶל־יְהוֹיָדָ֥ע הַכֹּהֵֽן: 10 וַיִּתֵּ֨ן הַכֹּהֵ֜ן לְשָׂרֵ֣י הַמֵּא֗וֹת אֶת־הַחֲנִית֙ וְאֶת־הַשְּׁלָטִ֔ים אֲשֶׁ֖ר לַמֶּ֣לֶךְ דָּוִ֑ד אֲשֶׁ֖ר בְּבֵ֥ית יְהוָֽה: 11 וַיַּֽעַמְד֨וּ הָרָצִ֜ים אִ֣ישׁ ׀ וְכֵלָ֣יו בְּיָד֗וֹ מִכֶּ֨תֶף הַבַּ֤יִת הַיְמָנִית֙ עַד־כֶּ֤תֶף הַבַּ֨יִת֙ הַשְּׂמָאלִ֔ית לַמִּזְבֵּ֖חַ וְלַבָּ֑יִת עַל־הַמֶּ֖לֶךְ סָבִֽיב: 12 וַיּוֹצִ֣א אֶת־בֶּן־הַמֶּ֗לֶךְ וַיִּתֵּ֤ן עָלָיו֙ אֶת־הַנֵּ֨זֶר֙ וְאֶת־הָ֣עֵד֔וּת וַיַּמְלִ֣כוּ אֹת֔וֹ וַיִּמְשָׁחֻ֑הוּ וַיַּכּוּ־כָ֔ף וַיֹּאמְר֖וּ יְחִ֥י הַמֶּֽלֶךְ: ס

13 וַתִּשְׁמַ֣ע עֲתַלְיָ֔ה אֶת־ק֥וֹל הָֽרָצִ֖ין הָעָ֑ם וַתָּבֹ֥א אֶל־הָעָ֖ם בֵּ֥ית יְהוָֽה: 14 וַתֵּ֡רֶא וְהִנֵּ֣ה הַמֶּ֩לֶךְ֩ עֹמֵ֨ד עַֽל־הָעַמּ֜וּד כַּמִּשְׁפָּ֗ט וְהַשָּׂרִ֤ים וְהַחֲצֹֽצְרוֹת֙ אֶל־הַמֶּ֔לֶךְ וְכָל־עַ֤ם הָאָ֨רֶץ֙ שָׂמֵ֔חַ וְתֹקֵ֖עַ בַּחֲצֹֽצְר֑וֹת וַתִּקְרַ֤ע עֲתַלְיָה֙ אֶת־בְּגָדֶ֔יהָ וַתִּקְרָ֖א קֶ֥שֶׁר קָֽשֶׁר: ס 15 וַיְצַ֣ו יְהוֹיָדָ֣ע הַכֹּהֵ֡ן אֶת־שָׂרֵ֣י הַמֵּא֣וֹת ׀ פְּקֻדֵ֣י הַחַ֗יִל וַיֹּ֤אמֶר אֲלֵיהֶם֙ הוֹצִ֤יאוּ אֹתָהּ֙ אֶל־מִבֵּ֣ית לַשְּׂדֵרֹ֔ת וְהַבָּ֥א אַחֲרֶ֖יהָ הָמֵ֣ת בֶּחָ֑רֶב כִּ֚י אָמַ֣ר הַכֹּהֵ֔ן אַל־תּוּמַ֖ת בֵּ֥ית יְהוָֽה: 16 וַיָּשִׂ֤מוּ לָהּ֙ יָדַ֔יִם וַתָּב֛וֹא דֶּֽרֶךְ־מְב֥וֹא הַסּוּסִ֖ים בֵּ֣ית הַמֶּ֑לֶךְ וַתּוּמַ֖ת שָֽׁם: ס

---

h   2 Chron. 23.9 adds "and shields."

17And Jehoiada solemnized the covenant between the LORD, on the one hand, and the king
and the people, on the other—as well as between
the king and the people—that they should be
the people of the LORD. 18Thereupon all the people of the land went to the temple of Baal. They
tore it down and smashed its altars and images
to bits, and they slew Mattan, the priest of Baal,
in front of the altars. [Jehoiada] the priest then
placed guards over the House of the LORD. 19He
took the chiefs of hundreds, the Carites,d the
guards, and all the people of the land, and they
escorted the king from the House of the LORD
into the royal palace by the gate of the guards.
And he ascended the royal throne. 20All the people of the land rejoiced, and the city was quiet.
As for Athaliah, she had been put to the sword
in the royal palace.

12 Jehoash was seven years old when he

became king. 2Jehoash began his reign in the
seventh year of Jehu, and he reigned in Jerusalem forty years. His mother's name was Zibiah
of Beer-sheba. 3All his days Jehoash did what
was pleasing to the LORD, as the priest Jehoiada
instructed him. 4The shrines, however, were not
removed; the people continued to sacrifice and
offer at the shrines.

5Jehoash said to the priests, "All the money,
current money, brought into the House of the
LORD as sacred donations—a-any money a man
may pay as the money equivalent of persons,-a
or any other money that a man may be minded
to bring to the House of the LORD—6let the
priests receive it, each from his benefactor; they,
in turn, shall make repairs on the House, wherever damage may be found."

7But in the twenty-third year of King Jehoash,

17 וַיִּכְרֹת יְהוֹיָדָע אֶת־הַבְּרִית בֵּין יְהֹוָה
וּבֵין הַמֶּלֶךְ וּבֵין הָעָם לִהְיוֹת לְעָם לַיהֹוָה
וּבֵין הַמֶּלֶךְ וּבֵין הָעָם: 18 וַיָּבֹאוּ כָל־עַם
הָאָרֶץ בֵּית־הַבַּעַל וַיִּתְּצֻהוּ אֶת־מִזְבְּחֹתָו
מִזְבְּחֹתָיו וְאֶת־צְלָמָיו שִׁבְּרוּ הֵיטֵב וְאֵת
מַתָּן כֹּהֵן הַבַּעַל הָרְגוּ לִפְנֵי הַמִּזְבְּחוֹת
וַיָּשֶׂם הַכֹּהֵן פְּקֻדּוֹת עַל־בֵּית יְהֹוָה:
19 וַיִּקַּח אֶת־שָׂרֵי הַמֵּאוֹת וְאֶת־הַכָּרִי
וְאֶת־הָרָצִים וְאֵת ׀ כָּל־עַם הָאָרֶץ וַיֹּרִידוּ
אֶת־הַמֶּלֶךְ מִבֵּית יְהֹוָה וַיָּבוֹאוּ דֶּרֶךְ־
שַׁעַר הָרָצִים בֵּית הַמֶּלֶךְ וַיֵּשֶׁב עַל־כִּסֵּא
הַמְּלָכִים: 20 וַיִּשְׂמַח כָּל־עַם־הָאָרֶץ
וְהָעִיר שָׁקָטָה וְאֶת־עֲתַלְיָהוּ הֵמִיתוּ
בַחֶרֶב בֵּית מֶלֶךְ הַמֶּלֶךְ: ס

יב בֶּן־שֶׁבַע שָׁנִים יְהוֹאָשׁ בְּמָלְכוֹ:
2 פ בִּשְׁנַת־שֶׁבַע לְיֵהוּא מָלַךְ יְהוֹאָשׁ
וְאַרְבָּעִים שָׁנָה מָלַךְ בִּירוּשָׁלָיִם וְשֵׁם אִמּוֹ
צִבְיָה מִבְּאֵר שָׁבַע: 3 וַיַּעַשׂ יְהוֹאָשׁ הַיָּשָׁר
בְּעֵינֵי יְהֹוָה כָּל־יָמָיו אֲשֶׁר הוֹרָהוּ יְהוֹיָדָע
הַכֹּהֵן: 4 רַק הַבָּמוֹת לֹא־סָרוּ עוֹד הָעָם
מְזַבְּחִים וּמְקַטְּרִים בַּבָּמוֹת:

5 וַיֹּאמֶר יְהוֹאָשׁ אֶל־הַכֹּהֲנִים כֹּל כֶּסֶף
הַקֳּדָשִׁים אֲשֶׁר־יוּבָא בֵית־יְהֹוָה כֶּסֶף
עוֹבֵר אִישׁ כֶּסֶף נַפְשׁוֹת עֶרְכּוֹ כָּל־כֶּסֶף
אֲשֶׁר יַעֲלֶה עַל לֶב־אִישׁ לְהָבִיא בֵּית
יְהֹוָה: 6 יִקְחוּ לָהֶם הַכֹּהֲנִים אִישׁ מֵאֵת
מַכָּרוֹ וְהֵם יְחַזְּקוּ אֶת־בֶּדֶק הַבַּיִת לְכֹל
אֲשֶׁר־יִמָּצֵא שָׁם בָּדֶק: פ
7 וַיְהִי בִּשְׁנַת עֶשְׂרִים וְשָׁלֹשׁ שָׁנָה לַמֶּלֶךְ

a-a See Lev. 27.2–8.

[it was found that] the priests had not made the repairs on the House. 8So King Jehoash summoned the priest Jehoiada and the other priests and said to them, "Why have you not kept the House in repair? Now do not accept money from your benefactors any more, but have it donated for the repair of the House." 9The priests agreed that they would neither accept money from the people nor make repairs on the House.

10And the priest Jehoiada took a chest and bored a hole in its lid. He placed it at the right side of the altar as one entered the House of the LORD, and the priestly guards of the threshold deposited there all the money that was brought into the House of the LORD. 11Whenever they saw that there was much money in the chest, the royal scribe and the high priest would come up and put the money accumulated in the House of the LORD into bags, and they would count it. 12Then they would deliver the money b-that was weighed out-b to the overseers of the work, who were in charge of the House of the LORD. These, in turn, used to pay the carpenters and the laborers who worked on the House of the LORD, 13and the masons and the stone-cutters. They also paid for wood and for quarried stone with which to make the repairs on the House of the LORD, and for every other expenditure that had to be made in repairing the House. 14However, no silver bowls and no snuffers, basins, or trumpets—no vessels of gold or silver—were made at the House of the LORD from the money brought into the House of the LORD; 15this was given only to the overseers of the work for the repair of the House of the LORD. 16No check was kept on the men to whom the money was delivered to pay the workers; for they dealt honestly.

17Money brought c-as a guilt offering or as a sin offering-c was not deposited in the House of the LORD; it went to the priests.

יְהוֹאָ֑שׁ לֹא־חִזְּק֥וּ הַכֹּהֲנִ֖ים אֶת־בֶּ֥דֶק הַבָּֽיִת: 8וַיִּקְרָא֩ הַמֶּ֨לֶךְ יְהוֹאָ֜שׁ לִֽיהוֹיָדָ֣ע הַכֹּהֵ֗ן וְלַכֹּֽהֲנִים֙ וַיֹּ֣אמֶר אֲלֵהֶ֔ם מַדּ֛וּעַ אֵינְכֶ֥ם מְחַזְּקִ֖ים אֶת־בֶּ֣דֶק הַבָּ֑יִת וְעַתָּ֗ה אַל־תִּקְחוּ־כֶ֙סֶף֙ מֵאֵ֣ת מַכָּֽרֵיכֶ֔ם כִּֽי־לְבֶ֥דֶק הַבַּ֖יִת תִּתְּנֻֽהוּ: 9וַיֵּאֹ֖תוּ הַכֹּֽהֲנִ֑ים לְבִלְתִּ֤י קְחַת־כֶּ֙סֶף֙ מֵאֵ֣ת הָעָ֔ם וּלְבִלְתִּ֥י חַזֵּ֖ק אֶת־בֶּ֥דֶק הַבָּֽיִת:

10וַיִּקַּ֞ח יְהוֹיָדָ֤ע הַכֹּהֵן֙ אֲר֣וֹן אֶחָ֔ד וַיִּקֹּ֥ב חֹ֖ר בְּדַלְתּ֑וֹ וַיִּתֵּ֣ן אֹת֣וֹ אֵ֣צֶל הַמִּזְבֵּ֗חַ בַּיָּמִין֙ בְּבוֹא־אִישׁ֙ בֵּ֣ית יְהֹוָ֔ה וְנָֽתְנוּ־שָׁ֤מָּה הַכֹּֽהֲנִים֙ שֹֽׁמְרֵ֣י הַסַּ֔ף אֶת־כָּל־הַכֶּ֖סֶף הַמּוּבָ֥א בֵית־יְהוָֽה: 11וַיְהִ֗י כִּרְאוֹתָם֙ כִּי־רַ֤ב הַכֶּ֙סֶף֙ בָּֽאָר֔וֹן וַיַּ֨עַל סֹפֵ֤ר הַמֶּ֙לֶךְ֙ וְהַכֹּהֵ֣ן הַגָּד֔וֹל וַיָּצֻ֙רוּ֙ וַיִּמְנ֔וּ אֶת־הַכֶּ֖סֶף הַנִּמְצָ֥א בֵית־יְהֹוָֽה: 12וְנָתְנוּ֙ אֶת־הַכֶּ֣סֶף הַֽמְתֻכָּ֔ן עַל־יְ֯דֵ֯ עֹשֵׂ֣י הַמְּלָאכָ֔ה הַפְּקֻדִ֖ים הַמֻּפְקָדִ֑ים בֵּ֣ית יְהֹוָ֔ה וַיּֽוֹצִיאֻ֗הוּ לְחָרָשֵׁ֤י הָעֵץ֙ וְלַבֹּנִ֔ים הָעֹשִׂ֖ים בֵּ֥ית יְהֹוָֽה: 13וְלַגֹּֽדְרִ֗ים וּלְחֹצְבֵ֤י הָאֶ֙בֶן֙ וְלִקְנ֤וֹת עֵצִים֙ וְאַבְנֵ֣י מַחְצֵ֔ב לְחַזֵּ֖ק אֶת־בֶּ֣דֶק בֵּית־יְהֹוָ֑ה וּלְכֹ֛ל אֲשֶׁר־יֵצֵ֥א עַל־הַבַּ֖יִת לְחָזְקָֽה: 14אַ֣ךְ לֹ֣א יֵעָשֶׂ֞ה בֵּ֣ית יְהֹוָ֗ה סִפּ֥וֹת כֶּ֙סֶף֙ מְזַמְּר֤וֹת מִזְרָקוֹת֙ חֲצֹ֣צְר֔וֹת כָּל־כְּלִ֥י זָהָ֖ב וּכְלִי־כָ֑סֶף מִן־הַכֶּ֖סֶף הַמּוּבָ֥א בֵית־יְהֹוָֽה: 15כִּֽי־לְעֹשֵׂ֥י הַמְּלָאכָ֖ה יִתְּנֻ֑הוּ וְחִזְּקוּ־ב֖וֹ אֶת־בֵּ֥ית יְהֹוָֽה: 16וְלֹ֧א יְחַשְּׁב֣וּ אֶת־הָ֣אֲנָשִׁ֗ים אֲשֶׁ֨ר יִתְּנ֤וּ אֶת־הַכֶּ֙סֶף֙ עַל־יָדָ֔ם לָתֵ֖ת לְעֹשֵׂ֣י הַמְּלָאכָ֑ה כִּ֥י בֶאֱמֻנָ֖ה הֵ֥ם עֹשִֽׂים: 17כֶּ֤סֶף אָשָׁם֙ וְכֶ֣סֶף חַטָּא֔וֹת לֹ֥א יוּבָ֖א בֵּ֣ית יְהֹוָ֑ה לַכֹּהֲנִ֖ים יִהְיֽוּ: פ

b-b	Meaning of Heb. uncertain.
c-c	See Lev. 5.15.

18At that time, King Hazael of Aram came up and attacked Gath and captured it; and Hazael proceeded to march on Jerusalem. 19Thereupon King Joash of Judah took all the objects that had been consecrated by his fathers, Kings Jehoshaphat, Jehoram, and Ahaziah of Judah, and by himself, and all the gold that there was in the treasuries of the Temple of the Lord and in the royal palace, and he sent them to King Hazael of Aram, who then turned back from his march on Jerusalem.

20The other events of Joash's reign, and all his actions, are recorded in the Annals of the Kings of Judah. 21His courtiers formed a conspiracy against Joash and assassinated him at Beth-millo b-that leads down to Silla.-b 22The courtiers who assassinated him were Jozacar son of Shimeath and Jehozabad son of Shomer. He died and was buried with his fathers in the City of David; and his son Amaziah succeeded him as king.

13

In the twenty-third year of King Joash son of Ahaziah of Judah, Jehoahaz son of Jehu became king over Israel in Samaria—for seventeen years. 2He did what was displeasing to the Lord. He persisted in the sins which Jeroboam son of Nebat had caused Israel to commit; he did not depart from them. 3The Lord was angry with Israel and He repeatedly delivered them into the hands of King Hazael of Aram and into the hands of Ben-hadad son of Hazael. 4But Jehoahaz pleaded with the Lord; and the Lord listened to him, for He saw the suffering that the king of Aram inflicted upon Israel. 5So the Lord granted Israel a deliverer, and they gained their freedom from Aram; and Israel dwelt in its homes as before. 6However, they did not depart from the sins which the House of Jer-

b-b Meaning of Heb. uncertain.

18 אָז יַעֲלֶה חֲזָאֵל מֶלֶךְ אֲרָם וַיִּלָּחֶם עַל־גַּת וַיִּלְכְּדָהּ וַיָּשֶׂם חֲזָאֵל פָּנָיו לַעֲלוֹת עַל־יְרוּשָׁלָ͏ִם: 19 וַיִּקַּח יְהוֹאָשׁ מֶלֶךְ־יְהוּדָה אֵת כָּל־הַקֳּדָשִׁים אֲשֶׁר־הִקְדִּישׁוּ יְהוֹשָׁפָט וִיהוֹרָם וַאֲחַזְיָהוּ אֲבֹתָיו מַלְכֵי יְהוּדָה וְאֶת־קֳדָשָׁיו וְאֵת כָּל־הַזָּהָב הַנִּמְצָא בְּאֹצְרוֹת בֵּית־יְהוָה וּבֵית הַמֶּלֶךְ וַיִּשְׁלַח לַחֲזָאֵל מֶלֶךְ אֲרָם וַיַּעַל מֵעַל יְרוּשָׁלָ͏ִם: 20 וְיֶתֶר דִּבְרֵי יוֹאָשׁ וְכָל־אֲשֶׁר עָשָׂה הֲלֹא־הֵם כְּתוּבִים עַל־סֵפֶר דִּבְרֵי הַיָּמִים לְמַלְכֵי יְהוּדָה: 21 וַיָּקֻמוּ עֲבָדָיו וַיִּקְשְׁרוּ־קָשֶׁר וַיַּכּוּ אֶת־יוֹאָשׁ בֵּית מִלֹּא הַיּוֹרֵד סִלָּא: 22 וְיוֹזָבָד בֶּן־שִׁמְעָת וִיהוֹזָבָד בֶּן־שֹׁמֵר ׀ עֲבָדָיו הִכֻּהוּ וַיָּמֹת וַיִּקְבְּרוּ אֹתוֹ עִם־אֲבֹתָיו בְּעִיר דָּוִד וַיִּמְלֹךְ אֲמַצְיָה בְנוֹ תַּחְתָּיו: פ

יג בִּשְׁנַת עֶשְׂרִים וְשָׁלֹשׁ שָׁנָה לְיוֹאָשׁ בֶּן־אֲחַזְיָהוּ מֶלֶךְ יְהוּדָה מָלַךְ יְהוֹאָחָז בֶּן־יֵהוּא עַל־יִשְׂרָאֵל בְּשֹׁמְרוֹן שְׁבַע עֶשְׂרֵה שָׁנָה: 2 וַיַּעַשׂ הָרַע בְּעֵינֵי יְהוָה וַיֵּלֶךְ אַחַר חַטֹּאת יָרָבְעָם בֶּן־נְבָט אֲשֶׁר־הֶחֱטִיא אֶת־יִשְׂרָאֵל לֹא־סָר מִמֶּנָּה: 3 וַיִּחַר־אַף יְהוָה בְּיִשְׂרָאֵל וַיִּתְּנֵם בְּיַד ׀ חֲזָאֵל מֶלֶךְ־אֲרָם וּבְיַד בֶּן־הֲדַד בֶּן־חֲזָאֵל כָּל־הַיָּמִים: 4 וַיְחַל יְהוֹאָחָז אֶת־פְּנֵי יְהוָה וַיִּשְׁמַע אֵלָיו יְהוָה כִּי רָאָה אֶת־לַחַץ יִשְׂרָאֵל כִּי־לָחַץ אֹתָם מֶלֶךְ אֲרָם: 5 וַיִּתֵּן יְהוָה לְיִשְׂרָאֵל מוֹשִׁיעַ וַיֵּצְאוּ מִתַּחַת יַד־אֲרָם וַיֵּשְׁבוּ בְנֵי־יִשְׂרָאֵל בְּאָהֳלֵיהֶם כִּתְמוֹל שִׁלְשׁוֹם: 6 אַךְ לֹא־סָרוּ מֵחַטֹּאות בֵּית־יָרָבְעָם אֲשֶׁר־הֶחֱטִי הֶחֱטִיא אֶת־

oboam had caused Israel to commit; they persisted in them. Even the sacred post stood in Samaria. [a]7In fact, Jehoahaz was left with a force of only fifty horsemen, ten chariots, and ten thousand foot soldiers; for the king of Aram had decimated them and trampled them like the dust under his feet.

8The other events of Jehoahaz's reign, and all his actions and his exploits, are recorded in the Annals of the Kings of Israel. 9Jehoahaz slept with his fathers and he was buried in Samaria; his son Joash succeeded him as king.

10In the thirty-seventh year of King Joash of Judah, Jehoash son of Jehoahaz became king of Israel in Samaria—for sixteen years. 11He did what was displeasing to the LORD; he did not depart from any of the sins which Jeroboam son of Nebat had caused Israel to commit; he persisted in them.

12The other events of Joash's reign, and all his actions, and his exploits in his war with King Amaziah of Judah, are recorded in the Annals of the Kings of Israel. 13Joash slept with his fathers and Jeroboam occupied his throne; Joash was buried in Samaria with the kings of Israel.

14Elisha had been stricken with the illness of which he was to die, and King Joash of Israel went down to see him. He wept over him and cried, "Father, father! [b]Israel's chariots and horsemen!"[b] 15Elisha said to him, "Get a bow and arrows"; and he brought him a bow and arrows. 16Then he said to the king of Israel, "Grasp the bow!" And when he had grasped it, Elisha put his hands over the king's hands. 17"Open the window toward the east," he said; and he opened it. Elisha said, "Shoot!" and he shot. Then he said, "An arrow of victory for the LORD! An arrow of victory over Aram! You shall

יִשְׂרָאֵ֖ל בָּ֣הּ הָלָ֑ךְ וְגַ֛ם הָאֲשֵׁרָ֖ה עָמְדָ֥ה בְּשֹׁמְרֽוֹן׃ 7 כִּ֣י לֹא֩ הִשְׁאִ֨יר לִיהֽוֹאָחָ֜ז עָ֗ם כִּ֣י אִם־חֲמִשִּׁ֤ים פָּֽרָשִׁים֙ וַעֲשָׂ֣רָה רֶ֔כֶב וַעֲשֶׂ֥רֶת אֲלָפִ֖ים רַגְלִ֑י כִּ֤י אִבְּדָם֙ מֶ֣לֶךְ אֲרָ֔ם וַיְשִׂמֵ֖ם כֶּעָפָ֥ר לָדֻֽשׁ׃ 8 וְיֶ֩תֶר֩ דִּבְרֵ֨י יְהֽוֹאָחָ֜ז וְכׇל־אֲשֶׁ֤ר עָשָׂה֙ וּגְבֽוּרָת֔וֹ הֲלֹא־הֵ֣ם כְּתוּבִ֗ים עַל־סֵ֛פֶר דִּבְרֵ֥י הַיָּמִ֖ים לְמַלְכֵ֥י יִשְׂרָאֵֽל׃ 9 וַיִּשְׁכַּ֤ב יְהֽוֹאָחָז֙ עִם־אֲבֹתָ֔יו וַֽיִּקְבְּרֻ֖הוּ בְּשֹׁמְר֑וֹן וַיִּמְלֹ֛ךְ יוֹאָ֥שׁ בְּנ֖וֹ תַּחְתָּֽיו׃ פ

10 בִּשְׁנַ֨ת שְׁלֹשִׁ֤ים וָשֶׁ֙בַע֙ שָׁנָ֔ה לְיוֹאָ֖שׁ מֶ֣לֶךְ יְהוּדָ֑ה מָלַ֞ךְ יְהוֹאָ֤שׁ בֶּן־יְהֽוֹאָחָז֙ עַל־יִשְׂרָאֵל֙ בְּשֹׁ֣מְר֔וֹן שֵׁ֥שׁ עֶשְׂרֵ֖ה שָׁנָֽה׃ 11 וַיַּעֲשֶׂ֤ה הָרַע֙ בְּעֵינֵ֣י יְהֹוָ֔ה לֹ֣א סָ֔ר מִכׇּל־חַטֹּאות*‏ יָרׇבְעָ֥ם בֶּן־נְבָ֖ט אֲשֶׁ֣ר הֶחֱטִ֣יא אֶת־יִשְׂרָאֵ֑ל בָּ֥הּ הָלָֽךְ׃ 12 וְיֶ֩תֶר֩ דִּבְרֵ֨י יוֹאָ֜שׁ וְכׇל־אֲשֶׁ֣ר עָשָׂ֗ה וּגְב֣וּרָת֔וֹ אֲשֶׁ֣ר נִלְחַ֔ם עִ֖ם אֲמַצְיָ֣ה מֶֽלֶךְ־יְהוּדָ֑ה הֲלֹא־הֵ֣ם כְּתוּבִ֗ים עַל־סֵ֛פֶר דִּבְרֵ֥י הַיָּמִ֖ים לְמַלְכֵ֥י יִשְׂרָאֵֽל׃ 13 וַיִּשְׁכַּ֤ב יוֹאָשׁ֙ עִם־אֲבֹתָ֔יו וְיָרׇבְעָ֖ם יָשַׁ֣ב עַל־כִּסְא֑וֹ וַיִּקָּבֵ֤ר יוֹאָשׁ֙ בְּשֹׁ֣מְר֔וֹן עִ֖ם מַלְכֵ֥י יִשְׂרָאֵֽל׃ פ

14 וֶֽאֱלִישָׁע֙ חָלָ֣ה אֶת־חׇלְי֔וֹ אֲשֶׁ֥ר יָמ֖וּת בּ֑וֹ וַיֵּ֨רֶד אֵלָ֜יו יוֹאָ֣שׁ מֶֽלֶךְ־יִשְׂרָאֵ֗ל וַיֵּ֤בְךְּ עַל־פָּנָיו֙ וַיֹּאמַ֔ר אָבִ֣י ׀ אָבִ֔י רֶ֥כֶב יִשְׂרָאֵ֖ל וּפָרָשָֽׁיו׃ 15 וַיֹּ֤אמֶר לוֹ֙ אֱלִישָׁ֔ע קַ֖ח קֶ֣שֶׁת וְחִצִּ֑ים וַיִּקַּ֥ח אֵלָ֖יו קֶ֥שֶׁת וְחִצִּֽים׃ 16 וַיֹּ֣אמֶר ׀ לְמֶ֣לֶךְ יִשְׂרָאֵ֗ל הַרְכֵּ֤ב יָֽדְךָ֙ עַל־הַקֶּ֔שֶׁת וַיַּרְכֵּ֖ב יָד֑וֹ וַיָּ֧שֶׂם אֱלִישָׁ֛ע יָדָ֖יו עַל־יְדֵ֥י הַמֶּֽלֶךְ׃ 17 וַיֹּ֗אמֶר פְּתַ֤ח הַֽחַלּוֹן֙ קֵ֔דְמָה וַיִּפְתָּ֑ח וַיֹּ֧אמֶר אֱלִישָׁ֛ע יְרֵ֖ה וַיּ֑וֹר וַיֹּ֗אמֶר חֵץ־תְּשׁוּעָ֤ה לַֽיהֹוָה֙ וְחֵ֣ץ תְּשׁוּעָ֣ה בַֽאֲרָ֔ם וְהִכִּיתָ֧ אֶת־אֲרָ֛ם בַּאֲפֵ֖ק עַד־כַּלֵּֽה׃

a   This verse would read well after v. 3.
b-b   On Elisha as defender of Israel, see chapters 6–8.

rout Aram completely at Aphek." [18]He said,
"Now pick up the arrows." And he picked them
up. "Strike the ground!" he said to the king of
Israel; and he struck three times and stopped.
[19]The man of God was angry with him and said
to him, c-"If only you had struck-c five or six
times! Then you would have annihilated Aram;
as it is, you shall defeat Aram only three times."

[20]Elisha died and he was buried. Now bands
of Moabites used to invade the land d-at the
coming of every year.-d [21]Once a man was being
buried, when the people caught sight of such
a band; so they threw the corpse[e] into Elisha's
grave and f-made off.-f When the [dead] man
came in contact with Elisha's bones, he came
to life and stood up.

[22]King Hazael of Aram had oppressed the Israelites throughout the reign of Jehoahaz. [23]But
the Lord was gracious and merciful to them,
and He turned back to them for the sake of His
covenant with Abraham, Isaac, and Jacob. He
refrained from destroying them, and He still did
not cast them out from His presence. [24]When
King Hazael of Aram died, his son Ben-hadad
succeeded him as king; [25]and then Jehoash son
of Jehoahaz recovered from Ben-hadad son of
Hazael the towns which had been taken from
his father Jehoahaz in war. Three times Joash
defeated him, and he recovered the towns of
Israel.

14

In the second year of King Joash son
of Joahaz of Israel, Amaziah son of King Joash
of Judah became king. [2]He was twenty-five years
old when he became king, and he reigned twenty-nine years in Jerusalem; his mother's name
was Jehoaddan of Jerusalem. [3]He did what was

18 וַיֹּאמֶר קַח הַחִצִּים וַיִּקָּח וַיֹּאמֶר לְמֶלֶךְ
יִשְׂרָאֵל הַךְ־אַרְצָה וַיַּךְ שָׁלֹשׁ־פְּעָמִים
וַיַּעֲמֹד׃ 19 וַיִּקְצֹף עָלָיו אִישׁ הָאֱלֹהִים
וַיֹּאמֶר לְהַכּוֹת חָמֵשׁ אוֹ־שֵׁשׁ פְּעָמִים אָז
הִכִּיתָ אֶת־אֲרָם עַד־כַּלֵּה וְעַתָּה שָׁלֹשׁ
פְּעָמִים תַּכֶּה אֶת־אֲרָם׃ ס
20 וַיָּמָת אֱלִישָׁע וַיִּקְבְּרֻהוּ וּגְדוּדֵי מוֹאָב
יָבֹאוּ בָאָרֶץ בָּא שָׁנָה׃ 21 וַיְהִי הֵם ׀ קֹבְרִים
אִישׁ וְהִנֵּה רָאוּ אֶת־הַגְּדוּד וַיַּשְׁלִיכוּ אֶת־
הָאִישׁ בְּקֶבֶר אֱלִישָׁע וַיֵּלֶךְ וַיִּגַּע הָאִישׁ
בְּעַצְמוֹת אֱלִישָׁע וַיְחִי וַיָּקָם עַל־
רַגְלָיו׃ פ

22 וַחֲזָאֵל מֶלֶךְ אֲרָם לָחַץ אֶת־יִשְׂרָאֵל כֹּל
יְמֵי יְהוֹאָחָז׃ 23 וַיָּחָן יְהוָה אֹתָם וַיְרַחֲמֵם
וַיִּפֶן אֲלֵיהֶם לְמַעַן בְּרִיתוֹ אֶת־אַבְרָהָם
יִצְחָק וְיַעֲקֹב וְלֹא אָבָה הַשְׁחִיתָם וְלֹא־
הִשְׁלִיכָם מֵעַל־פָּנָיו עַד־עָתָּה׃ 24 וַיָּמָת
חֲזָאֵל מֶלֶךְ־אֲרָם וַיִּמְלֹךְ בֶּן־הֲדַד בְּנוֹ
תַּחְתָּיו׃ 25 וַיָּשָׁב יְהוֹאָשׁ בֶּן־יְהוֹאָחָז וַיִּקַּח
אֶת־הֶעָרִים מִיַּד בֶּן־הֲדַד בֶּן־חֲזָאֵל אֲשֶׁר
לָקַח מִיַּד יְהוֹאָחָז אָבִיו בַּמִּלְחָמָה שָׁלֹשׁ
פְּעָמִים הִכָּהוּ יוֹאָשׁ וַיָּשֶׁב אֶת־עָרֵי
יִשְׂרָאֵל׃ פ

יד בִּשְׁנַת שְׁתַּיִם לְיוֹאָשׁ בֶּן־יוֹאָחָז
מֶלֶךְ יִשְׂרָאֵל מָלַךְ אֲמַצְיָהוּ בֶן־יוֹאָשׁ מֶלֶךְ
יְהוּדָה׃ 2 בֶּן־עֶשְׂרִים וְחָמֵשׁ שָׁנָה הָיָה
בְמָלְכוֹ וְעֶשְׂרִים וָתֵשַׁע שָׁנָה מָלַךְ
בִּירוּשָׁלִָם וְשֵׁם אִמּוֹ יְהוֹעַדִּין מִן־

---

c-c   Lit. "to strike."
d-d   Meaning of Heb. uncertain; emendation yields "year by year."
e   Heb. "the man."
f-f   Heb. "he made off."

pleasing to the LORD, but not like his ancestor David; he did just as his father Joash had done. [4]However, the shrines were not removed; the people continued to sacrifice and make offerings at the shrines. [5]Once he had the kingdom firmly in his grasp, he put to death the courtiers who had assassinated his father the king. [6]But he did not put to death the children of the assassins, in accordance with what is written in the Book of the Teaching of Moses, where the LORD commanded, "Parents shall not be put to death for children, nor children be put to death for parents; a person shall be put to death only for his own crime."[a]

[7]He defeated ten thousand Edomites in the Valley of Salt, and he captured Sela in battle and renamed it Joktheel, as is still the case. [8]Then Amaziah sent envoys to King Jehoash son of Jehoahaz son of Jehu of Israel, with this message: "Come, let us confront[b] each other." [9]King Jehoash of Israel sent back this message to King Amaziah of Judah: "The thistle in Lebanon sent this message to the cedar in Lebanon, 'Give your daughter to my son in marriage.' But a wild beast in Lebanon went by and trampled down the thistle. [10]Because you have defeated Edom, you have become arrogant. Stay home and enjoy your glory, rather than provoke disaster and fall, dragging Judah down with you."

[11]But Amaziah paid no heed; so King Jehoash of Israel advanced, and he and King Amaziah of Judah confronted each other at Beth-shemesh in Judah. [12]The Judites were routed by Israel, and they all fled to their homes. [13]King Jehoash of Israel captured King Amaziah son of Jehoash son of Ahaziah of Judah at Beth-shemesh. He marched on Jerusalem, and he made a breach of four hundred cubits in the wall of Jerusalem, from[c] the Ephraim Gate to the Corner Gate. [14]He carried off all the gold

---

a Deut. 24.16.
b I.e., in battle.
c Heb. "at."

809

יְרוּשָׁלָ͏ִם: 3 וַיַּ֥עַשׂ הַיָּשָׁ֖ר בְּעֵינֵ֣י יְהֹוָ֑ה רַ֕ק לֹ֣א כְּדָוִ֣ד אָבִ֔יו כְּכֹ֧ל אֲשֶׁר־עָשָׂ֛ה יוֹאָ֥שׁ אָבִ֖יו עָשָֽׂה: 4 רַ֥ק הַבָּמ֖וֹת לֹא־סָ֑רוּ ע֥וֹד הָעָ֛ם מְזַבְּחִ֥ים וּֽמְקַטְּרִ֖ים בַּבָּמֽוֹת: 5 וַיְהִ֕י כַּאֲשֶׁ֛ר חׇזְקָ֥ה הַמַּמְלָכָ֖ה בְּיָד֑וֹ וַיַּךְ֙ אֶת־עֲבָדָ֔יו הַמַּכִּ֖ים אֶת־הַמֶּ֥לֶךְ אָבִֽיו: 6 וְאֶת־בְּנֵ֥י הַמַּכִּ֖ים לֹ֣א הֵמִ֑ית כַּכָּת֣וּב בְּסֵ֣פֶר תּֽוֹרַת־מֹ֠שֶׁ֠ה אֲשֶׁר־צִוָּ֨ה יְהֹוָ֜ה לֵאמֹ֗ר לֹא־יוּמְת֨וּ אָב֤וֹת עַל־בָּנִים֙ וּבָנִים֙ לֹא־יוּמְת֣וּ עַל־אָב֔וֹת כִּ֛י אִם־אִ֥ישׁ בְּחֶטְא֖וֹ ימות יוּמָֽת:

7 הוּא־הִכָּ֨ה אֶת־אֱד֤וֹם בְּגֵיא־[ה]מֶּ֙לַח֙ עֲשֶׂ֣רֶת אֲלָפִ֔ים וְתָפַ֥שׂ אֶת־הַסֶּ֖לַע בַּמִּלְחָמָ֑ה וַיִּקְרָ֤א אֶת־שְׁמָהּ֙ יׇקְתְאֵ֔ל עַ֖ד הַיּ֥וֹם הַזֶּֽה: פ 8 אָ֣ז שָׁלַ֤ח אֲמַצְיָה֙ מַלְאָכִ֗ים אֶל־יְהוֹאָ֤שׁ בֶּן־יְהֽוֹאָחָז֙ בֶּן־יֵה֔וּא מֶ֥לֶךְ יִשְׂרָאֵ֖ל לֵאמֹ֑ר לְכָ֖ה נִתְרָאֶ֥ה פָנִֽים: 9 וַיִּשְׁלַ֞ח יְהוֹאָ֣שׁ מֶֽלֶךְ־יִשְׂרָאֵ֗ל אֶל־אֲמַצְיָ֣הוּ מֶלֶךְ־יְהוּדָה֮ לֵאמֹר֒ הַח֜וֹחַ אֲשֶׁ֣ר בַּלְּבָנ֗וֹן שָׁ֠לַ֠ח אֶל־הָאֶ֜רֶז אֲשֶׁ֤ר בַּלְּבָנוֹן֙ לֵאמֹ֔ר תְּנָֽה־אֶת־בִּתְּךָ֥ לִבְנִ֖י לְאִשָּׁ֑ה וַֽתַּעֲבֹ֞ר חַיַּ֤ת הַשָּׂדֶה֙ אֲשֶׁ֣ר בַּלְּבָנ֔וֹן וַתִּרְמֹ֖ס אֶת־הַחֽוֹחַ: 10 הַכֵּ֤ה הִכִּ֙יתָ֙ אֶת־אֱד֔וֹם וּֽנְשָׂאֲךָ֖ לִבֶּ֑ךָ הִכָּבֵד֙ וְשֵׁ֣ב בְּבֵיתֶ֔ךָ וְלָ֤מָּה תִתְגָּרֶה֙ בְּרָעָ֔ה וְנָ֣פַלְתָּ֔ה אַתָּ֖ה וִיהוּדָ֥ה עִמָּֽךְ:

11 וְלֹא־שָׁמַ֣ע אֲמַצְיָ֔הוּ וַיַּ֨עַל יְהוֹאָ֤שׁ מֶֽלֶךְ־יִשְׂרָאֵל֙ וַיִּתְרָא֣וּ פָנִ֔ים ה֖וּא וַאֲמַצְיָ֣הוּ מֶלֶךְ־יְהוּדָ֑ה בְּבֵ֥ית שֶׁ֖מֶשׁ אֲשֶׁ֥ר לִיהוּדָֽה: 12 וַיִּנָּ֥גֶף יְהוּדָ֖ה לִפְנֵ֣י יִשְׂרָאֵ֑ל וַיָּנֻ֖סוּ אִ֥ישׁ לְאֹהָלָֽיו: 13 וְאֵת֩ אֲמַצְיָ֨הוּ מֶֽלֶךְ־יְהוּדָ֜ה בֶּן־יְהוֹאָ֣שׁ בֶּן־אֲחַזְיָ֗הוּ תָּפַ֛שׂ יְהוֹאָ֥שׁ מֶֽלֶךְ־יִשְׂרָאֵ֖ל בְּבֵ֣ית שָׁ֑מֶשׁ ויבאו וַיָּבֹ֣א יְרוּשָׁלַ֗͏ִם וַיִּפְרֹץ֩ בְּחוֹמַ֨ת יְרוּשָׁלַ֜͏ִם בְּשַׁ֤עַר אֶפְרַ֙יִם֙ עַד־שַׁ֣עַר הַפִּנָּ֔ה אַרְבַּ֥ע

and silver and all the vessels that there were in the House of the Lord and in the treasuries of the royal palace, as well as hostages; and he returned to Samaria.

[15]The other events of Jehoash's reign, and all his actions and exploits, and his war with King Amaziah of Judah, are recorded in the Annals of the Kings of Israel. [16]Jehoash slept with his fathers, and was buried in Samaria with the kings of Israel; his son Jeroboam succeeded him as king.

[17]King Amaziah son of Joash of Judah lived fifteen years after the death of King Jehoash son of Jehoahaz of Israel. [18]The other events of Amaziah's reign are recorded in the Annals of the Kings of Judah. [19]A conspiracy was formed against him in Jerusalem and he fled to Lachish; but they sent men after him to Lachish, and they killed him there. [20]They brought back his body on horses, and he was buried with his fathers in Jerusalem, in the City of David.

[21]Then all the people of Judah took Azariah, who was sixteen years old, and proclaimed him king to succeed his father Amaziah. [22]It was he who rebuilt Elath and restored it to Judah, after King [Amaziah] slept with his fathers.

[23]In the fifteenth year of King Amaziah son of Joash of Judah, King Jeroboam son of Joash of Israel became king in Samaria—for forty-one years. [24]He did what was displeasing to the Lord; he did not depart from all the sins that Jeroboam son of Nebat had caused Israel to commit. [25]It was he who restored the territory of Israel from Lebo-hamath to the sea of the Arabah, in accordance with the promise that the Lord, the God of Israel, had made through His servant, the prophet Jonah son of Amittai from Gath-hepher. [26]For the Lord saw the very bitter plight of Israel, with neither d-bond nor free-d

מֵא֖וֹת אַמָּ֑ה: 14 וְלָקַ֣ח אֶת־כָּל־הַזָּהָ֣ב וְהַכֶּ֗סֶף וְאֵ֤ת כָּל־הַכֵּלִים֙ הַנִּמְצְאִ֣ים בֵּית־ יְהֹוָ֔ה וּבְאֹצְר֖וֹת בֵּ֣ית הַמֶּ֑לֶךְ וְאֵ֖ת בְּנֵ֣י הַתַּעֲרֻב֑וֹת וַיָּ֖שָׁב שֹׁמְרֽוֹנָה: 15 וְיֶ֨תֶר דִּבְרֵ֤י יְהוֹאָשׁ֙ אֲשֶׁ֣ר עָשָׂ֔ה וּגְבֽוּרָת֔וֹ וַאֲשֶׁ֣ר נִלְחַ֔ם עִ֖ם אֲמַצְיָ֣הוּ מֶֽלֶךְ־יְהוּדָ֑ה הֲלֹא־הֵ֣ם כְּתוּבִ֗ים עַל־סֵ֛פֶר דִּבְרֵ֥י הַיָּמִ֖ים לְמַלְכֵ֥י יִשְׂרָאֵֽל: 16 וַיִּשְׁכַּ֤ב יְהֽוֹאָשׁ֙ עִם־ אֲבֹתָ֔יו וַיִּקָּבֵ֤ר בְּשֹֽׁמְרוֹן֙ עִ֚ם מַלְכֵ֣י יִשְׂרָאֵ֔ל וַיִּמְלֹ֛ךְ יָרָבְעָ֥ם בְּנ֖וֹ תַּחְתָּֽיו: פ

17 וַיְחִ֣י אֲמַצְיָ֣הוּ בֶן־יוֹאָ֗שׁ מֶ֚לֶךְ יְהוּדָ֔ה אַחֲרֵ֣י מ֔וֹת יְהוֹאָ֥שׁ בֶּן־יְהֽוֹאָחָ֖ז מֶ֣לֶךְ יִשְׂרָאֵ֑ל חֲמֵ֥שׁ עֶשְׂרֵ֖ה שָׁנָֽה: 18 וְיֶ֛תֶר דִּבְרֵ֥י אֲמַצְיָ֖הוּ הֲלֹא־הֵ֣ם כְּתוּבִ֗ים עַל־סֵ֛פֶר דִּבְרֵ֥י הַיָּמִ֖ים לְמַלְכֵ֥י יְהוּדָֽה: 19 וַיִּקְשְׁר֨וּ עָלָ֥יו קֶ֛שֶׁר בִּירוּשָׁלִַ֖ם וַיָּ֣נׇס לָכִ֑ישָׁה וַיִּשְׁלְח֤וּ אַחֲרָיו֙ לָכִ֔ישָׁה וַיְמִתֻ֖הוּ שָֽׁם: 20 וַיִּשְׂא֣וּ אֹתוֹ֙ עַל־הַסּוּסִ֔ים וַיִּקָּבֵ֧ר בִּירֽוּשָׁלִַ֛ם עִם־ אֲבֹתָ֖יו בְּעִ֥יר דָּוִֽד:

21 וַיִּקְח֞וּ כָּל־עַ֤ם יְהוּדָה֙ אֶת־עֲזַרְיָ֔ה וְה֕וּא בֶּן־שֵׁ֥שׁ עֶשְׂרֵ֖ה שָׁנָ֑ה וַיַּמְלִ֤כוּ אֹתוֹ֙ תַּ֣חַת אָבִ֖יו אֲמַצְיָֽהוּ: 22 ה֚וּא בָּנָ֣ה אֶת־אֵילַ֔ת וַיְשִׁבֶ֖הָ לִֽיהוּדָ֑ה אַחֲרֵ֥י שְׁכַב־הַמֶּ֖לֶךְ עִם־ אֲבֹתָֽיו: פ

23 בִּשְׁנַ֨ת חֲמֵשׁ־עֶשְׂרֵ֜ה שָׁנָ֗ה לַאֲמַצְיָ֤הוּ בֶן־יוֹאָשׁ֙ מֶ֣לֶךְ יְהוּדָ֔ה מָ֠לַ֠ךְ יָרׇבְעָ֨ם בֶּן־ יוֹאָ֧שׁ מֶֽלֶךְ־יִשְׂרָאֵ֛ל בְּשֹׁמְר֖וֹן אַרְבָּעִ֥ים וְאַחַ֖ת שָׁנָֽה: 24 וַיַּ֥עַשׂ הָרַ֖ע בְּעֵינֵ֣י יְהֹוָ֑ה לֹ֣א סָ֗ר מִכָּל־חַטֹּאות֙* יָרׇבְעָ֣ם בֶּן־נְבָ֔ט אֲשֶׁ֥ר הֶחֱטִ֖יא אֶת־יִשְׂרָאֵֽל: 25 ה֣וּא הֵשִׁ֗יב אֶת־גְּב֤וּל יִשְׂרָאֵל֙ מִלְּב֣וֹא חֲמָ֔ת עַד־יָ֣ם הָעֲרָבָ֑ה כִּדְבַ֤ר יְהֹוָה֙ אֱלֹהֵ֣י יִשְׂרָאֵ֔ל אֲשֶׁ֣ר דִּבֶּ֔ר בְּיַד־עַבְדּ֛וֹ יוֹנָ֥ה בֶן־אֲמִתַּ֖י הַנָּבִ֑יא אֲשֶׁ֖ר מִגַּ֥ת הַחֵֽפֶר: 26 כִּי־רָאָ֤ה יְהֹוָה֙ אֶת־

מלא ו'   v. 24.

left, and with none to help Israel. 27And the
LORD resolved not to blot out the name of Israel
from under heaven; and he delivered them
through Jeroboam son of Joash.

28The other events of Jeroboam's reign, and
all his actions and exploits, how he fought and
recovered Damascus and Hamath e-for Judah
in Israel,-e are recorded in the Annals of the
Kings of Israel. 29Jeroboam slept with his fathers, the kings of Israel, and his son Zechariah
succeeded him as king.

15

In the twenty-seventh year of King Jeroboam of Israel, Azariah son of King Amaziah
of Judah became king. 2He was sixteen years old
when he became king, and he reigned fifty-two
years in Jerusalem; his mother's name was Jecoliah of Jerusalem. 3He did what was pleasing to
the LORD, just as his father Amaziah had done.
4However, the shrines were not removed; the
people continued to sacrifice and make offerings at the shrines. 5The LORD struck the king
with a plague, and he was a leper until the day
of his death; he lived a-in isolated quarters,-a
while Jotham, the king's son, was in charge of
the palace and governed the people of the land.

6The other events of Azariah's reign, and all
his actions, are recorded in the Annals of the
Kings of Judah. 7Azariah slept with his fathers,
and he was buried with his fathers in the City
of David; his son Jotham succeeded him as king.

8In the thirty-eighth year of King Azariah of
Judah, Zechariah son of Jeroboam became king
over Israel in Samaria—for six months. 9He did
what was displeasing to the LORD, as his fathers
had done; he did not depart from the sins which

---

e-e   *Emendation yields "for Israel."*

a-a   *Meaning of Heb. uncertain.*

עֲנִי יִשְׂרָאֵל מֹרֶה מְאֹד וְאֶפֶס עָצוּר וְאֶפֶס
עָזוּב וְאֵין עֹזֵר לְיִשְׂרָאֵל: 27 וְלֹא־דִבֶּר
יְהֹוָה לִמְחוֹת אֶת־שֵׁם יִשְׂרָאֵל מִתַּחַת
הַשָּׁמָיִם וַיּוֹשִׁיעֵם בְּיַד יָרָבְעָם בֶּן־יוֹאָשׁ:
28 וְיֶתֶר דִּבְרֵי יָרָבְעָם וְכָל־אֲשֶׁר עָשָׂה
וּגְבוּרָתוֹ אֲשֶׁר־נִלְחָם וַאֲשֶׁר הֵשִׁיב אֶת־
דַּמֶּשֶׂק וְאֶת־חֲמָת לִיהוּדָה בְּיִשְׂרָאֵל
הֲלֹא־הֵם כְּתוּבִים עַל־סֵפֶר דִּבְרֵי הַיָּמִים
לְמַלְכֵי יִשְׂרָאֵל: 29 וַיִּשְׁכַּב יָרָבְעָם עִם־
אֲבֹתָיו עִם מַלְכֵי יִשְׂרָאֵל וַיִּמְלֹךְ זְכַרְיָה
בְנוֹ תַּחְתָּיו: פ

טו

בִּשְׁנַת עֶשְׂרִים וְשֶׁבַע שָׁנָה
לְיָרָבְעָם מֶלֶךְ יִשְׂרָאֵל מָלַךְ עֲזַרְיָה בֶן־
אֲמַצְיָה מֶלֶךְ יְהוּדָה: 2 בֶּן־שֵׁשׁ עֶשְׂרֵה
שָׁנָה הָיָה בְמָלְכוֹ וַחֲמִשִּׁים וּשְׁתַּיִם שָׁנָה
מָלַךְ בִּירוּשָׁלָ͏ִם וְשֵׁם אִמּוֹ יְכָלְיָהוּ
מִירוּשָׁלָ͏ִם: 3 וַיַּעַשׂ הַיָּשָׁר בְּעֵינֵי יְהֹוָה
כְּכֹל אֲשֶׁר־עָשָׂה אֲמַצְיָהוּ אָבִיו: 4 רַק
הַבָּמוֹת לֹא־סָרוּ עוֹד הָעָם מְזַבְּחִים
וּמְקַטְּרִים בַּבָּמוֹת: 5 וַיְנַגַּע יְהֹוָה אֶת־
הַמֶּלֶךְ וַיְהִי מְצֹרָע עַד־יוֹם מֹתוֹ וַיֵּשֶׁב
בְּבֵית הַחָפְשִׁית וְיוֹתָם בֶּן־הַמֶּלֶךְ עַל־
הַבַּיִת שֹׁפֵט אֶת־עַם הָאָרֶץ:
6 וְיֶתֶר דִּבְרֵי עֲזַרְיָהוּ וְכָל־אֲשֶׁר עָשָׂה
הֲלֹא־הֵם כְּתוּבִים עַל־סֵפֶר דִּבְרֵי הַיָּמִים
לְמַלְכֵי יְהוּדָה: 7 וַיִּשְׁכַּב עֲזַרְיָה עִם־
אֲבֹתָיו וַיִּקְבְּרוּ אֹתוֹ עִם־אֲבֹתָיו בְּעִיר דָּוִד
וַיִּמְלֹךְ יוֹתָם בְּנוֹ תַּחְתָּיו: פ

8 בִּשְׁנַת שְׁלֹשִׁים וּשְׁמֹנֶה שָׁנָה לַעֲזַרְיָהוּ
מֶלֶךְ יְהוּדָה מָלַךְ זְכַרְיָהוּ בֶן־יָרָבְעָם
עַל־יִשְׂרָאֵל בְּשֹׁמְרוֹן שִׁשָּׁה חֳדָשִׁים:
9 וַיַּעַשׂ הָרַע בְּעֵינֵי יְהֹוָה כַּאֲשֶׁר עָשׂוּ

Jeroboam son of Nebat had caused Israel to commit. [10]Shallum son of Jabesh conspired against him and struck him down [b]-before the people-[b] and killed him, and succeeded him as king. [11]The other events of Zechariah's reign are recorded in the Annals of the Kings of Israel. [12]This was in accord with the word that the LORD had spoken to Jehu: "Four generations of your descendants shall occupy the throne of Israel." And so it came about.[c]

[13]Shallum son of Jabesh became king in the thirty-ninth year of King Uzziah of Judah, and he reigned in Samaria one month. [14]Then Menahem son of Gadi set out from Tirzah and came to Samaria; he attacked Shallum son of Jabesh in Samaria and killed him, and he succeeded him as king. [15]The other events of Shallum's reign, and the conspiracy that he formed, are recorded in the Annals of the Kings of Israel.

[16]At that time, [a]-[marching] from Tirzah,-[a] Menahem subdued Tiphsah and all who were in it, and its territory; and because it did not surrender, he massacred [its people] and ripped open all its pregnant women.

[17]In the thirty-ninth year of King Azariah of Judah, Menahem son of Gadi became king over Israel in Samaria—for ten years. [18]He did what was displeasing to the LORD; throughout his days he did not depart from the sins which Jeroboam son of Nebat had caused Israel to commit. [19]King Pul of Assyria invaded the land, and Menahem gave Pul a thousand talents of silver that he might support him and strengthen his hold on the kingdom. [20]Menahem exacted the money from Israel: every man of means had to pay fifty shekels of silver for the king of Assyria. The king of Assyria withdrew and did not remain in the land. [21]The other events of

אֲבוֹתָיו לֹא סָר מֵחַטֹּאות* יָרָבְעָם בֶּן־נְבָט
אֲשֶׁר הֶחֱטִיא אֶת־יִשְׂרָאֵל׃ 10 וַיִּקְשֹׁר עָלָיו
שַׁלֻּם בֶּן־יָבֵשׁ וַיַּכֵּהוּ קָבָל־עָם וַיְמִיתֵהוּ
וַיִּמְלֹךְ תַּחְתָּיו׃ 11 וְיֶתֶר דִּבְרֵי זְכַרְיָה הִנָּם
כְּתוּבִים עַל־סֵפֶר דִּבְרֵי הַיָּמִים לְמַלְכֵי
יִשְׂרָאֵל׃ 12 הוּא דְבַר־יְהוָה אֲשֶׁר דִּבֶּר
אֶל־יֵהוּא לֵאמֹר בְּנֵי רְבִיעִים יֵשְׁבוּ לְךָ
עַל־כִּסֵּא יִשְׂרָאֵל וַיְהִי־כֵן׃ פ

13 שַׁלֻּם בֶּן־יָבֵישׁ מָלַךְ בִּשְׁנַת שְׁלֹשִׁים
וָתֵשַׁע שָׁנָה לְעֻזִיָּה מֶלֶךְ יְהוּדָה וַיִּמְלֹךְ
יֶרַח־יָמִים בְּשֹׁמְרוֹן׃ 14 וַיַּעַל מְנַחֵם בֶּן־גָּדִי
מִתִּרְצָה וַיָּבֹא שֹׁמְרוֹן וַיַּךְ אֶת־שַׁלֻּם
בֶּן־יָבֵישׁ בְּשֹׁמְרוֹן וַיְמִיתֵהוּ וַיִּמְלֹךְ
תַּחְתָּיו׃ 15 וְיֶתֶר דִּבְרֵי שַׁלּוּם וְקִשְׁרוֹ אֲשֶׁר
קָשָׁר הִנָּם כְּתֻבִים עַל־סֵפֶר דִּבְרֵי הַיָּמִים
לְמַלְכֵי יִשְׂרָאֵל׃ ס

16 אָז יַכֶּה־מְנַחֵם אֶת־תִּפְסַח וְאֶת־כָּל־
אֲשֶׁר־בָּהּ וְאֶת־גְּבוּלֶיהָ מִתִּרְצָה כִּי לֹא
פָתַח וַיַּךְ אֵת כָּל־הֶהָרוֹתֶיהָ בִּקֵּעַ׃ פ
17 בִּשְׁנַת שְׁלֹשִׁים וָתֵשַׁע שָׁנָה לַעֲזַרְיָה
מֶלֶךְ יְהוּדָה מָלַךְ מְנַחֵם בֶּן־גָּדִי עַל־
יִשְׂרָאֵל עֶשֶׂר שָׁנִים בְּשֹׁמְרוֹן׃ 18 וַיַּעַשׂ
הָרַע בְּעֵינֵי יְהוָה לֹא סָר מֵעַל חַטֹּאות*
יָרָבְעָם בֶּן־נְבָט אֲשֶׁר־הֶחֱטִיא אֶת־יִשְׂרָאֵל
כָּל־יָמָיו׃ 19 בָּא פוּל מֶלֶךְ־אַשּׁוּר עַל־
הָאָרֶץ וַיִּתֵּן מְנַחֵם לְפוּל אֶלֶף כִּכַּר־כָּסֶף
לִהְיוֹת יָדָיו אִתּוֹ לְהַחֲזִיק הַמַּמְלָכָה בְּיָדוֹ׃
20 וַיֹּצֵא מְנַחֵם אֶת־הַכֶּסֶף עַל־יִשְׂרָאֵל עַל
כָּל־גִּבּוֹרֵי הַחַיִל לָתֵת לְמֶלֶךְ אַשּׁוּר
חֲמִשִּׁים שְׁקָלִים כֶּסֶף לְאִישׁ אֶחָד וַיָּשָׁב
מֶלֶךְ אַשּׁוּר וְלֹא־עָמַד שָׁם בָּאָרֶץ׃ 21 וְיֶתֶר
דִּבְרֵי מְנַחֵם וְכָל־אֲשֶׁר עָשָׂה הֲלוֹא־הֵם
כְּתוּבִים עַל־סֵפֶר דִּבְרֵי הַיָּמִים לְמַלְכֵי

b-b   Some Septuagint mss. read "at Ibleam."
c   Cf. 10.30.

812

Menahem's reign, and all his actions, are recorded in the Annals of the Kings of Israel.
²²Menahem slept with his fathers, and his son
Pekahiah succeeded him as king.

²³In the fiftieth year of King Azariah of Judah,
Pekahiah son of Menahem became king over Israel in Samaria—for two years. ²⁴He did what
was displeasing to the LORD; he did not depart
from the sins which Jeroboam son of Nebat had
caused Israel to commit. ²⁵His aide, Pekah son
of Remaliah, conspired against him and struck
him down in the royal palace in Samaria; with
him were fifty Gileadites, ᵃ-with men from
Argob and Arieh;-ᵃ and he killed him and succeeded him as king.

²⁶The other events of Pekahiah's reign, and
all his actions, are recorded in the Annals of the
Kings of Israel.

²⁷In the fifty-second year of King Azariah of
Judah, Pekah son of Remaliah became king over
Israel and Samaria—for twenty years. ²⁸He did
what was displeasing to the LORD; he did not
depart from the sins which Jeroboam son of
Nebat had caused Israel to commit. ²⁹In the days
of King Pekah of Israel, King Tiglath-pileser of
Assyria came and captured Ijon, Abel-beth-
maacah, Janoah, Kedesh, Hazor—Gilead, Galilee, the entire region of Naphtali; and he deported ᵈ-the inhabitants-ᵈ to Assyria.
³⁰Hoshea son of Elah conspired against Pekah
son of Remaliah, attacked him, and killed him.
He succeeded him as king in the twentieth year
of Jotham son of Uzziah. ³¹The other events of
Pekah's reign, and all his actions, are recorded
in the Annals of the Kings of Israel.

³²In the second year of King Pekah son of
Remaliah of Israel, Jotham son of King Uzziah

---

²² יִשְׂרָאֵל: וַיִּשְׁכַּ֤ב מְנַחֵם֙ עִם־אֲבֹתָ֔יו
וַיִּמְלֹ֛ךְ פְּקַחְיָ֥ה בְנ֖וֹ תַּחְתָּֽיו: פ

²³ בִּשְׁנַת֙ חֲמִשִּׁ֣ים שָׁנָ֔ה לַעֲזַרְיָ֖ה מֶ֣לֶךְ
יְהוּדָ֑ה מָלַ֡ךְ פְּקַחְיָה֩ בֶן־מְנַחֵ֨ם עַל־יִשְׂרָאֵ֧ל
בְּשֹׁמְר֖וֹן שְׁנָתָֽיִם: ²⁴ וַיַּ֥עַשׂ הָרַ֖ע בְּעֵינֵ֣י
יְהוָ֑ה לֹ֣א סָ֗ר מֵֽחַטֹּאות֙* יָרָבְעָ֣ם בֶּן־נְבָ֔ט
אֲשֶׁ֥ר הֶחֱטִ֖יא אֶת־יִשְׂרָאֵֽל: ²⁵ וַיִּקְשֹׁ֣ר עָלָ֡יו
פֶּ֣קַח בֶּן־רְמַלְיָ֣הוּ שָׁלִישׁוֹ֩ וַיַּכֵּ֨הוּ בְשֹׁמְר֜וֹן
בְּאַרְמ֣וֹן בֵּֽית־מֶ֗לֶךְ אֶת־אַרְגֹּ֤ב וְאֶת־
הָֽאַרְיֵ֔ה וְעִמּ֛וֹ חֲמִשִּׁ֥ים אִ֖ישׁ מִבְּנֵ֣י גִלְעָדִ֑ים
וַיְמִיתֵ֖הוּ וַיִּמְלֹ֥ךְ תַּחְתָּֽיו: ²⁶ וְיֶ֛תֶר דִּבְרֵ֥י פְקַחְיָ֖ה וְכָל־אֲשֶׁ֣ר עָשָׂ֑ה הִנָּ֣ם
כְּתוּבִ֗ים עַל־סֵ֛פֶר דִּבְרֵ֥י הַיָּמִ֖ים לְמַלְכֵ֥י
יִשְׂרָאֵֽל: פ

²⁷ בִּשְׁנַ֨ת חֲמִשִּׁ֤ים וּשְׁתַּ֨יִם֙ שָׁנָ֔ה לַעֲזַרְיָ֖ה
מֶ֣לֶךְ יְהוּדָ֑ה מָלַ֡ךְ פֶּ֣קַח בֶּן־רְמַלְיָ֣הוּ עַל־
יִשְׂרָאֵ֤ל בְּשֹׁמְרוֹן֙ עֶשְׂרִ֣ים שָׁנָֽה: ²⁸ וַיַּ֥עַשׂ
הָרַ֖ע בְּעֵינֵ֣י יְהוָ֑ה לֹ֣א סָ֗ר מִן־חַטֹּאות֙*
יָרָבְעָ֣ם בֶּן־נְבָ֔ט אֲשֶׁ֥ר הֶחֱטִ֖יא אֶת־
יִשְׂרָאֵֽל: ²⁹ בִּימֵ֞י פֶּ֣קַח מֶֽלֶךְ־יִשְׂרָאֵ֗ל בָּ֣א
תִּגְלַ֣ת פִּלְאֶסֶר֮ מֶ֣לֶךְ אַשּׁוּר֒ וַיִּקַּ֣ח אֶת־
עִיּ֡וֹן וְאֶת־אָבֵ֣ל בֵּֽית־מַעֲכָ֣ה וְאֶת־יָנ֡וֹחַ
וְאֶת־קֶ֣דֶשׁ וְאֶת־חָצ֣וֹר וְאֶת־הַגִּלְעָ֣ד וְאֶת־
הַגָּלִ֗ילָה כֹּ֚ל אֶ֣רֶץ נַפְתָּלִ֔י וַיַּגְלֵ֖ם אַשּֽׁוּרָה: ³⁰ וַיִּקְשָׁר־קֶ֣שֶׁר הוֹשֵׁ֣עַ בֶּן־אֵלָ֗ה עַל־
פֶּ֣קַח בֶּן־רְמַלְיָ֔הוּ וַיַּכֵּ֨הוּ֙ וַיְמִיתֵ֔הוּ וַיִּמְלֹ֖ךְ
תַּחְתָּ֑יו בִּשְׁנַ֣ת עֶשְׂרִ֔ים לְיוֹתָ֖ם בֶּן־עֻזִּיָּֽה:
³¹ וְיֶ֛תֶר דִּבְרֵי־פֶ֖קַח וְכָל־אֲשֶׁ֣ר עָשָׂ֑ה הִנָּ֣ם
כְּתוּבִ֗ים עַל־סֵ֛פֶר דִּבְרֵ֥י הַיָּמִ֖ים לְמַלְכֵ֥י
יִשְׂרָאֵֽל: פ

³² בִּשְׁנַ֣ת שְׁתַּ֔יִם לְפֶ֖קַח בֶּן־רְמַלְיָ֣הוּ מֶ֣לֶךְ
יִשְׂרָאֵ֑ל מָלַ֛ךְ יוֹתָ֥ם בֶּן־עֻזִּיָּ֖הוּ מֶ֥לֶךְ יְהוּדָֽה:

ᵈ⁻ᵈ Heb. "them."

מלא ו' v. 24.
מלא ו' v. 28.

of Judah became king. ³³He was twenty-five years old when he became king, and he reigned sixteen years in Jerusalem; his mother's name was Jerusha daughter of Zadok. ³⁴He did what was pleasing to the Lord, just as his father Uzziah had done. ³⁵However, the shrines were not removed; the people continued to sacrifice and make offerings at the shrines. It was he who built the Upper Gate of the House of the Lord. ³⁶The other events of Jotham's reign, and all his actions, are recorded in the Annals of the Kings of Judah. ³⁷In those days, the Lord began to incite King Rezin of Aram and Pekah son of Remaliah against Judah. ³⁸Jotham slept with his fathers, and he was buried with his fathers in the city of his ancestor David; his son Ahaz succeeded him as king.

16

In the seventeenth year of Pekah son of Remaliah, Ahaz son of King Jotham of Judah became king. ²Ahaz was twenty years old when he became king, and he reigned sixteen years in Jerusalem. He did not do what was pleasing to the Lord his God, as his ancestor David had done, ³but followed the ways of the kings of Israel. He even consigned his son to the fire, in the abhorrent fashion of the nations which the Lord had dispossessed before the Israelites. ⁴He sacrificed and made offerings at the shrines, on the hills, and under every leafy tree.

⁵Then King Rezin of Aram and King Pekah son of Remaliah of Israel advanced on Jerusalem for battle. They besieged Ahaz, but could not overcome [him]. ⁶At that time King Rezin of Aram recovered Elath for Aram;^a he drove out the Judites from Elath, and Edomites came to Elath and settled there, as is still the case.

⁷Ahaz sent messengers to King Tiglath-pileser of Assyria to say, "I am your servant and your

---

a Emendation yields "Edom."

---

³³ בֶּן־עֶשְׂרִ֨ים וְחָמֵ֤שׁ שָׁנָה֙ הָיָ֣ה בְמָלְכ֔וֹ וְשֵׁשׁ־עֶשְׂרֵ֥ה שָׁנָ֖ה מָלַ֣ךְ בִּירוּשָׁלָ֑͏ִם וְשֵׁ֣ם אִמּ֔וֹ יְרוּשָׁ֖א בַּת־צָדֽוֹק׃ ³⁴ וַיַּ֥עַשׂ הַיָּשָׁ֖ר בְּעֵינֵ֣י יְהֹוָ֑ה כְּכֹ֧ל אֲשֶׁר־עָשָׂ֛ה עֻזִּיָּ֥הוּ אָבִ֖יו עָשָֽׂה׃ ³⁵ רַ֤ק הַבָּמוֹת֙ לֹא־סָ֔רוּ ע֥וֹד הָעָ֛ם מְזַבְּחִ֥ים וּֽמְקַטְּרִ֖ים בַּבָּמ֑וֹת ה֗וּא בָּנָ֛ה אֶת־שַׁ֥עַר בֵּית־יְהֹוָ֖ה הָעֶלְיֽוֹן׃ ³⁶ וְיֶ֛תֶר דִּבְרֵ֥י יוֹתָ֖ם אֲשֶׁ֣ר עָשָׂ֑ה הֲלֹא־הֵ֣ם כְּתוּבִ֗ים עַל־סֵ֛פֶר דִּבְרֵ֥י הַיָּמִ֖ים לְמַלְכֵ֥י יְהוּדָֽה׃ ³⁷ בַּיָּמִ֣ים הָהֵ֔ם הֵחֵ֣ל יְהֹוָ֗ה לְהַשְׁלִ֙יחַ֙ בִּֽיהוּדָ֔ה רְצִ֖ין מֶ֣לֶךְ אֲרָ֑ם וְאֵ֖ת פֶּ֥קַח בֶּן־רְמַלְיָֽהוּ׃ ³⁸ וַיִּשְׁכַּ֨ב יוֹתָ֜ם עִם־אֲבֹתָ֗יו וַיִּקָּבֵר֙ עִם־אֲבֹתָ֔יו בְּעִ֖יר דָּוִ֣ד אָבִ֑יו וַיִּמְלֹ֛ךְ אָחָ֥ז בְּנ֖וֹ תַּחְתָּֽיו׃ פ

טז בִּשְׁנַת֙ שְׁבַֽע־עֶשְׂרֵ֣ה שָׁנָ֔ה לְפֶ֖קַח בֶּן־רְמַלְיָ֑הוּ מָלַ֛ךְ אָחָ֥ז בֶּן־יוֹתָ֖ם מֶ֥לֶךְ יְהוּדָֽה׃ ² בֶּן־עֶשְׂרִ֤ים שָׁנָה֙ אָחָ֣ז בְּמׇלְכ֔וֹ וְשֵׁשׁ־עֶשְׂרֵ֣ה שָׁנָ֔ה מָלַ֖ךְ בִּירוּשָׁלָ֑͏ִם וְלֹא־עָשָׂ֣ה הַיָּשָׁ֗ר בְּעֵינֵ֛י יְהֹוָ֥ה אֱלֹהָ֖יו כְּדָוִ֥ד אָבִֽיו׃ ³ וַיֵּ֕לֶךְ בְּדֶ֖רֶךְ מַלְכֵ֣י יִשְׂרָאֵ֑ל וְגַ֤ם אֶת־בְּנוֹ֙ הֶעֱבִ֣יר בָּאֵ֔שׁ כְּתֹֽעֲבוֹת֙ הַגּוֹיִ֔ם אֲשֶׁ֨ר הוֹרִ֤ישׁ יְהֹוָה֙ אֹתָ֔ם מִפְּנֵ֖י בְּנֵ֥י יִשְׂרָאֵֽל׃ ⁴ וַיְזַבֵּ֧חַ וַיְקַטֵּ֛ר בַּבָּמ֖וֹת וְעַל־הַגְּבָע֑וֹת וְתַ֖חַת כׇּל־עֵ֥ץ רַעֲנָֽן׃

⁵ אָ֣ז יַעֲלֶ֣ה רְצִ֣ין מֶלֶךְ־אֲ֠רָ֠ם וּפֶ֨קַח בֶּן־רְמַלְיָ֤הוּ מֶֽלֶךְ־יִשְׂרָאֵל֙ יְר֣וּשָׁלַ֔͏ִם לַמִּלְחָמָ֑ה וַיָּצֻ֙רוּ֙ עַל־אָחָ֔ז וְלֹ֥א יָכְל֖וּ לְהִלָּחֵֽם׃ ⁶ בָּעֵ֣ת הַהִ֗יא הֵ֠שִׁ֠יב רְצִ֨ין מֶלֶךְ־אֲרָ֤ם אֶת־אֵילַת֙ לַֽאֲרָ֔ם וַיְנַשֵּׁ֥ל אֶת־הַיְהוּדִ֖ים מֵֽאֵיל֑וֹת וַֽאֲרַמִּים֙ בָּ֣אוּ אֵילַ֔ת וַיֵּ֣שְׁבוּ שָׁ֔ם עַ֖ד הַיּ֥וֹם הַזֶּֽה׃ פ

⁷ וַיִּשְׁלַ֨ח אָחָ֜ז מַלְאָכִ֗ים אֶל־תִּגְלַ֨ת פְּלֶ֤סֶר* מֶֽלֶךְ־אַשּׁוּר֙ לֵאמֹ֔ר עַבְדְּךָ֥ וּבִנְךָ֖ אָ֑נִי עֲלֵ֨ה

son; come and deliver me from the hands of the king of Aram and from the hands of the king of Israel, who are attacking me." [8]Ahaz took the gold and silver that were on hand in the House of the LORD and in the treasuries of the royal palace and sent them as a gift to the king of Assyria. [9]The king of Assyria responded to his request; the king of Assyria marched against Damascus and captured it. He deported [b]-its inhabitants-[b] to Kir and put Rezin to death.

[10]When King Ahaz went to Damascus to greet King Tiglath-pileser of Assyria, he saw the altar in Damascus. King Ahaz sent the priest Uriah a sketch of the altar and a detailed plan of its construction. [11]The priest Uriah did just as King Ahaz had instructed him from Damascus; the priest Uriah built the altar before King Ahaz returned from Damascus. [12]When the king returned from Damascus, and when the king saw the altar, the king drew near the altar, ascended it, [13]and offered his burnt offering and meal offering; he poured his libation, and he dashed the blood of his offering of well-being against the altar. [14]As for the bronze altar which had been before the LORD, he moved it from its place in front of the Temple, [c]-between the [new] altar and the House of the LORD,-[c] and placed it on the north side of the [new] altar. [15]And King Ahaz commanded the priest Uriah: "On the great[d] altar you shall offer the morning burnt offering and the evening meal offering and the king's burnt offering and his meal offering, with the burnt offerings of all the people of the land, their meal offerings and their libations. And against it you shall dash the blood of all the burnt offerings and all the blood of the sacrifices. And I will decide[e] about the bronze altar." [e][16]Uriah did just as King Ahaz commanded.

וְהוֹשִׁעֵנִי מִכַּף מֶֽלֶךְ־אֲרָם וּמִכַּף מֶ֥לֶךְ יִשְׂרָאֵ֖ל הַקּוֹמִ֥ים עָלָֽי׃ [8]וַיִּקַּ֨ח אָחָ֜ז אֶת־הַכֶּ֣סֶף וְאֶת־הַזָּהָ֗ב הַנִּמְצָא֙ בֵּ֣ית יְהֹוָ֔ה וּבְאֹֽצְר֖וֹת בֵּ֣ית הַמֶּ֑לֶךְ וַיִּשְׁלַ֥ח לְמֶֽלֶךְ־אַשּׁ֖וּר שֹֽׁחַד׃ [9]וַיִּשְׁמַ֤ע אֵלָיו֙ מֶ֣לֶךְ אַשּׁ֔וּר וַיַּ֩עַל֩ מֶ֨לֶךְ אַשּׁ֤וּר אֶל־דַּמֶּ֙שֶׂק֙ וַֽיִּתְפְּשֶׂ֔הָ וַיַּגְלֶ֖הָ קִ֑ירָה וְאֶת־רְצִ֖ין הֵמִֽית׃

[10]וַיֵּ֣לֶךְ הַמֶּ֣לֶךְ אָחָ֡ז לִ֠קְרַ֠את תִּגְלַ֨ת פִּלְאֶ֤סֶר מֶֽלֶךְ־אַשּׁוּר֙ דּוּמֶּ֔שֶׂק וַיַּ֖רְא אֶת־הַמִּזְבֵּ֣חַ אֲשֶׁ֣ר בְּדַמָּ֑שֶׂק וַיִּשְׁלַח֩ הַמֶּ֨לֶךְ אָחָ֜ז אֶל־אוּרִיָּ֤ה הַכֹּהֵן֙ אֶת־דְּמ֣וּת הַמִּזְבֵּ֔חַ וְאֶת־תַּבְנִית֖וֹ לְכׇֽל־מַעֲשֵֽׂהוּ׃ [11]וַיִּ֜בֶן אוּרִיָּ֤ה הַכֹּהֵן֙ אֶת־הַמִּזְבֵּ֔חַ כְּכֹ֣ל אֲשֶׁר־שָׁלַח֩ הַמֶּ֨לֶךְ אָחָ֜ז מִדַּמֶּ֗שֶׂק כֵּ֤ן עָשָׂה֙ אוּרִיָּ֣ה הַכֹּהֵ֔ן עַד־בּ֥וֹא הַמֶּֽלֶךְ־אָחָ֖ז מִדַּמָּֽשֶׂק׃ [12]וַיָּבֹ֤א הַמֶּ֙לֶךְ֙ מִדַּמֶּ֔שֶׂק וַיַּ֥רְא הַמֶּ֖לֶךְ אֶת־הַמִּזְבֵּ֑חַ וַיִּקְרַ֥ב הַמֶּ֛לֶךְ עַל־הַמִּזְבֵּ֖חַ וַיַּ֥עַל עָלָֽיו׃ [13]וַיַּקְטֵ֤ר אֶת־עֹֽלָתוֹ֙ וְאֶת־מִנְחָת֔וֹ וַיַּסֵּ֖ךְ אֶת־נִסְכּ֑וֹ וַיִּזְרֹ֛ק אֶת־דַּֽם־הַשְּׁלָמִ֥ים אֲשֶׁר־ל֖וֹ עַל־הַמִּזְבֵּֽחַ׃ [14]וְאֵ֨ת הַמִּזְבַּ֣ח הַנְּחֹ֗שֶׁת אֲשֶׁ֤ר לִפְנֵ֣י יְהֹוָ֔ה וַיַּקְרֵ֖ב מֵאֵ֣ת פְּנֵ֣י הַבַּ֗יִת מִבֵּין֙ הַמִּזְבֵּ֔חַ וּמִבֵּ֖ין בֵּ֣ית יְהֹוָ֑ה וַיִּתֵּ֥ן אֹת֛וֹ עַל־יֶ֥רֶךְ הַמִּזְבֵּ֖חַ צָפֽוֹנָה׃ [15]וַיְצַוֵּ֣הוּ הַמֶּֽלֶךְ־אָ֠חָ֠ז אֶת־אוּרִיָּ֨ה הַכֹּהֵ֜ן לֵאמֹ֗ר עַ֣ל הַמִּזְבֵּ֣חַ הַגָּד֡וֹל הַקְטֵ֣ר אֶת־עֹֽלַת־הַבֹּ֩קֶר֩ וְאֶת־מִנְחַ֨ת הָעֶ֜רֶב וְֽאֶת־עֹלַ֧ת הַמֶּ֣לֶךְ וְאֶת־מִנְחָת֗וֹ וְ֠אֵ֠ת עֹלַ֤ת כׇּל־עַ֤ם הָאָ֙רֶץ֙ וּמִנְחָתָ֣ם וְנִסְכֵּיהֶ֔ם וְכׇל־דַּ֥ם עֹלָ֛ה וְכׇל־דַּם־זֶ֖בַח עָלָ֣יו תִּזְרֹ֑ק וּמִזְבַּ֧ח הַנְּחֹ֛שֶׁת יִֽהְיֶה־לִּ֖י לְבַקֵּֽר׃ [16]וַיַּ֖עַשׂ אוּרִיָּ֣ה הַכֹּהֵ֑ן כְּכֹ֥ל אֲשֶׁר־צִוָּ֖ה הַמֶּ֥לֶךְ אָחָֽז׃

---

b-b   Heb. "it."
c-c   Meaning of Heb. uncertain.
d   I.e., the new one.
e   I.e., the old one, cf. v. 14.

17King Ahaz cut off the insets—the laver stands—and removed the lavers from them. He also removed the tank from the bronze oxen that supported it and set it on a stone pavement—18on account of the king of Assyria.*f* He also extended to the House of the LORD *-c*the sabbath passage that had been built in the palace and the king's outer entrance.*-c*

19The other events of Ahaz's reign, and his actions, are recorded in the Annals of the Kings of Judah. 20Ahaz slept with his fathers and was buried with his fathers in the City of David; his son Hezekiah succeeded him as king.

17 In the twelfth year of King Ahaz of Judah, Hoshea son of Elah became king over Israel in Samaria—for nine years. 2He did what was displeasing to the LORD, though not as much as the kings of Israel who preceded him. 3King Shalmaneser marched against him, and Hoshea became his vassal and paid him tribute. 4But the king of Assyria caught Hoshea in an act of treachery: he had sent envoys to King So of Egypt, and he had not paid the tribute to the king of Assyria, as in previous years. And the king of Assyria arrested him and put him in prison. 5Then the king of Assyria marched against the whole land; he came to Samaria and besieged it for three years. 6In the ninth year of Hoshea, the king of Assyria captured Samaria. He deported the Israelites to Assyria and settled them in Halah, at the [River] Habor, at the River Gozan, and in the towns of Media.

7This happened because the Israelites sinned against the LORD their God, who had freed them from the land of Egypt, from the hand of Pharaoh king of Egypt. They worshiped other gods 8and followed the customs of the nations which the LORD had dispossessed before the Israelites

---

f I.e., because of the metal given him in tribute.

17 וַיְקַצֵּץ֩ הַמֶּ֨לֶךְ אָחָ֜ז אֶת־הַמִּסְגְּר֣וֹת הַמְּכֹנ֗וֹת וַיָּ֤סַר מֵֽעֲלֵיהֶם֙ וְאֶת־הַכִּיֹּ֔ר וְאֶת־הַיָּ֣ם הוֹרִ֗ד מֵעַ֛ל הַבָּקָ֥ר הַנְּחֹ֖שֶׁת אֲשֶׁ֣ר תַּחְתֶּ֑יהָ וַיִּתֵּ֣ן אֹת֔וֹ עַ֖ל מַרְצֶ֥פֶת אֲבָנִֽים: 18 וְאֶת־מֵיסַ֣ךְ מוּסַ֣ךְ הַשַּׁבָּת֩ אֲשֶׁר־בָּנ֨וּ בַבַּ֜יִת וְאֶת־מְב֤וֹא הַמֶּ֨לֶךְ֙ הַחִ֣יצ֔וֹנָה הֵסֵ֥ב בֵּ֖ית יְהֹוָ֑ה מִפְּנֵ֖י מֶ֥לֶךְ אַשּֽׁוּר: 19 וְיֶ֛תֶר דִּבְרֵ֥י אָחָ֖ז אֲשֶׁ֣ר עָשָׂ֑ה הֲלֹא־הֵ֣ם כְּתוּבִ֗ים עַל־סֵ֛פֶר דִּבְרֵ֥י הַיָּמִ֖ים לְמַלְכֵ֥י יְהוּדָֽה: 20 וַיִּשְׁכַּ֤ב אָחָז֙ עִם־אֲבֹתָ֔יו וַיִּקָּבֵ֥ר עִם־אֲבֹתָ֖יו בְּעִ֣יר דָּוִ֑ד וַיִּמְלֹ֛ךְ חִזְקִיָּ֥הוּ בְנ֖וֹ תַּחְתָּֽיו: פ

לז בִּשְׁנַת֩ שְׁתֵּ֨ים עֶשְׂרֵ֜ה לְאָחָ֣ז מֶ֣לֶךְ יְהוּדָ֗ה מָלַ֞ךְ הוֹשֵׁ֨עַ בֶּן־אֵלָ֧ה בְשֹׁמְר֛וֹן עַל־יִשְׂרָאֵ֖ל תֵּ֥שַׁע שָׁנִֽים: 2 וַיַּ֥עַשׂ הָרַ֖ע בְּעֵינֵ֣י יְהֹוָ֑ה רַ֗ק לֹ֚א כְּמַלְכֵ֣י יִשְׂרָאֵ֔ל אֲשֶׁ֥ר הָי֖וּ לְפָנָֽיו: 3 עָלָ֣יו עָלָ֔ה שַׁלְמַנְאֶ֖סֶר מֶ֣לֶךְ אַשּׁ֑וּר וַֽיְהִי־ל֤וֹ הוֹשֵׁ֨עַ֙ עֶ֔בֶד וַיָּ֥שֶׁב ל֖וֹ מִנְחָֽה: 4 וַיִּמְצָא֩ מֶ֨לֶךְ־אַשּׁ֜וּר בְּהוֹשֵׁ֣עַ קֶ֗שֶׁר אֲשֶׁ֨ר שָׁלַ֤ח מַלְאָכִים֙ אֶל־ס֤וֹא מֶ֨לֶךְ־מִצְרַ֔יִם וְלֹא־הֶעֱלָ֥ה מִנְחָ֛ה לְמֶ֥לֶךְ אַשּׁ֖וּר כְּשָׁנָ֣ה בְשָׁנָ֑ה וַֽיַּעַצְרֵ֨הוּ֙ מֶ֣לֶךְ אַשּׁ֔וּר וַיַּאַסְרֵ֖הוּ בֵּ֥ית כֶּֽלֶא: 5 וַיַּ֥עַל מֶֽלֶךְ־אַשּׁ֖וּר בְּכָל־הָאָ֑רֶץ וַיַּ֨עַל֙ שֹׁמְר֔וֹן וַיָּ֥צַר עָלֶ֖יהָ שָׁלֹ֥שׁ שָׁנִֽים: 6 בִּשְׁנַ֨ת הַתְּשִׁיעִ֜ית לְהוֹשֵׁ֗עַ לָכַ֤ד מֶֽלֶךְ־אַשּׁוּר֙ אֶת־שֹׁ֣מְר֔וֹן וַיֶּ֥גֶל אֶת־יִשְׂרָאֵ֖ל אַשּׁ֑וּרָה וַיֹּ֤שֶׁב אֹתָם֙ בַּחְלַ֣ח וּבְחָב֗וֹר נְהַ֤ר גּוֹזָן֙ וְעָרֵ֥י מָדָֽי: פ 7 וַיְהִ֗י כִּֽי־חָטְא֤וּ בְנֵֽי־יִשְׂרָאֵל֙ לַיהֹוָ֣ה אֱלֹֽהֵיהֶ֔ם הַמַּעֲלֶ֤ה אֹתָם֙ מֵאֶ֣רֶץ מִצְרַ֔יִם מִתַּ֕חַת יַ֖ד פַּרְעֹ֣ה מֶֽלֶךְ־מִצְרָ֑יִם וַיִּֽירְא֖וּ אֱלֹהִ֥ים אֲחֵרִֽים: 8 וַיֵּֽלְכוּ֙ בְּחֻקּ֣וֹת הַגּוֹיִ֔ם אֲשֶׁ֤ר הוֹרִישׁ֙ יְהֹוָ֔ה מִפְּנֵ֖י בְּנֵ֣י יִשְׂרָאֵ֑ל

and the customs which the kings of Israel had practiced. [9]The Israelites committed[a] against the LORD their God acts which were not right: They built for themselves shrines in all their settlements, from watchtowers to fortified cities; [10]they set up pillars and sacred posts for themselves on every lofty hill and under every leafy tree; [11]and they offered sacrifices there, at all the shrines, like the nations whom the LORD had driven into exile before them. They committed wicked acts to vex the LORD, [12]and they worshiped fetishes concerning which the LORD had said to them, "You must not do this thing."

[13]The LORD warned Israel and Judah by every prophet [and] every seer, saying: "Turn back from your wicked ways, and observe My commandments and My laws, according to all the Teaching that I commanded your fathers and that I transmitted to you through My servants the prophets." [14]But they did not obey; they stiffened their necks, like their fathers who did not have faith in the LORD their God; [15]they spurned His laws and the covenant that He had made with their fathers, and the warnings He had given them. They went after delusion and were deluded; [they imitated] the nations that were about them, which the LORD had forbidden them to emulate. [16]They rejected all the commandments of the LORD their God; they made molten idols for themselves—two calves—and they made a sacred post and they bowed down to all the host of heaven, and they worshiped Baal. [17]They consigned their sons and daughters to the fire; they practiced augury and divination, and gave themselves over to what was displeasing to the LORD and vexed Him. [18]The LORD was incensed at Israel and He banished them from His presence; none was left but the tribe of Judah alone.

[19]Nor did Judah keep the commandments of

---

a Meaning of Heb. uncertain.

וּמַלְכֵי יִשְׂרָאֵל אֲשֶׁר עָשׂוּ: 9 וַיְחַפְּאוּ בְנֵי־
יִשְׂרָאֵל דְּבָרִים אֲשֶׁר לֹא־כֵן עַל־יְהוָה
אֱלֹהֵיהֶם וַיִּבְנוּ לָהֶם בָּמוֹת בְּכָל־עָרֵיהֶם
מִמִּגְדַּל נוֹצְרִים עַד־עִיר מִבְצָר: 10 וַיַּצִּבוּ
לָהֶם מַצֵּבוֹת וַאֲשֵׁרִים עַל כָּל־גִּבְעָה
גְבֹהָה וְתַחַת כָּל־עֵץ רַעֲנָן: 11 וַיְקַטְּרוּ־שָׁם
בְּכָל־בָּמוֹת כַּגּוֹיִם אֲשֶׁר־הֶגְלָה יְהוָה
מִפְּנֵיהֶם וַיַּעֲשׂוּ דְּבָרִים רָעִים לְהַכְעִיס
אֶת־יְהוָה: 12 וַיַּעַבְדוּ הַגִּלֻּלִים אֲשֶׁר אָמַר
יְהוָה לָהֶם לֹא תַעֲשׂוּ אֶת־הַדָּבָר הַזֶּה:
13 וַיָּעַד יְהוָה בְּיִשְׂרָאֵל וּבִיהוּדָה בְּיַד
כָּל־נביאו נְבִיאֵי כָל־חֹזֶה לֵאמֹר שֻׁבוּ*
מִדַּרְכֵיכֶם הָרָעִים וְשִׁמְרוּ מִצְוֹתַי חֻקּוֹתַי
כְּכָל־הַתּוֹרָה אֲשֶׁר צִוִּיתִי אֶת־אֲבֹתֵיכֶם
וַאֲשֶׁר שָׁלַחְתִּי אֲלֵיכֶם בְּיַד עֲבָדַי
הַנְּבִיאִים: 14 וְלֹא שָׁמֵעוּ וַיַּקְשׁוּ אֶת־
עָרְפָּם כְּעֹרֶף אֲבוֹתָם אֲשֶׁר לֹא הֶאֱמִינוּ
בַּיהוָה אֱלֹהֵיהֶם: 15 וַיִּמְאֲסוּ אֶת־חֻקָּיו
וְאֶת־בְּרִיתוֹ אֲשֶׁר כָּרַת אֶת־אֲבוֹתָם וְאֵת
עֵדְוֹתָיו אֲשֶׁר הֵעִיד בָּם וַיֵּלְכוּ אַחֲרֵי
הַהֶבֶל וַיֶּהְבָּלוּ וְאַחֲרֵי הַגּוֹיִם אֲשֶׁר
סְבִיבֹתָם אֲשֶׁר צִוָּה יְהוָה אֹתָם לְבִלְתִּי
עֲשׂוֹת כָּהֶם: 16 וַיַּעַזְבוּ אֶת־כָּל־מִצְוֹת
יְהוָה אֱלֹהֵיהֶם וַיַּעֲשׂוּ לָהֶם מַסֵּכָה שְׁנֵים
שְׁנֵי עֲגָלִים וַיַּעֲשׂוּ אֲשֵׁרָה וַיִּשְׁתַּחֲווּ
לְכָל־צְבָא הַשָּׁמַיִם וַיַּעַבְדוּ אֶת־הַבָּעַל:
17 וַיַּעֲבִירוּ אֶת־בְּנֵיהֶם וְאֶת־בְּנוֹתֵיהֶם
בָּאֵשׁ וַיִּקְסְמוּ קְסָמִים וַיְנַחֵשׁוּ וַיִּתְמַכְּרוּ
לַעֲשׂוֹת הָרַע בְּעֵינֵי יְהוָה לְהַכְעִיסוֹ:
18 וַיִּתְאַנַּף יְהוָה מְאֹד בְּיִשְׂרָאֵל וַיְסִרֵם
מֵעַל פָּנָיו לֹא נִשְׁאַר רַק שֵׁבֶט יְהוּדָה
לְבַדּוֹ:
19 גַּם־יְהוּדָה לֹא שָׁמַר אֶת־מִצְוֹת יְהוָה
אֱלֹהֵיהֶם וַיֵּלְכוּ בְּחֻקּוֹת יִשְׂרָאֵל אֲשֶׁר

שני טעמים .v 13.

the LORD their God; they followed the customs that Israel had practiced. ²⁰So the LORD spurned all the offspring of Israel, and He afflicted them and delivered them into the hands of plunderers, and finally He cast them out from His presence.

²¹For Israel broke away from the House of David, and they made Jeroboam son of Nebat king. Jeroboam caused Israel to stray from the LORD and to commit great sin, ²²and the Israelites persisted in all the sins which Jeroboam had committed; they did not depart from them. ²³In the end, the LORD removed Israel from His presence, as He had warned them through all His servants the prophets. So the Israelites were deported from their land to Assyria, as is still the case.

²⁴The king of Assyria brought [people] from Babylon, Cuthah, Avva, Hamath, and Sepharvaim, and he settled them in the towns of Samaria in place of the Israelites; they took possession of Samaria and dwelt in its towns. ²⁵When they first settled there, they did not worship the LORD; so the LORD sent lions against them which killed some of them. ²⁶They said to the king of Assyria: "The nations which you deported and resettled in the towns of Samaria do not know the rules of the God of the land; therefore He has let lions loose against them which are killing them—for they do not know the rules of the God of the land." ²⁷The king of Assyria gave an order: "Send there one of the priests whom you have deported; let him[b] go and dwell there, and let him teach them the practices of the God of the land." ²⁸So one of the priests whom they had exiled from Samaria came and settled in Bethel; he taught them how to worship the LORD. ²⁹However, each nation continued to make its own

עָשֽׂוּ׃ 20 וַיִּמְאַ֨ס יְהֹוָ֜ה בְּכׇל־זֶ֣רַע יִשְׂרָאֵ֗ל וַיְעַנֵּם֙ וַֽיִּתְּנֵם֙ בְּיַד־שֹׁסִ֔ים עַ֥ד אֲשֶׁ֖ר הִשְׁלִיכָ֥ם מִפָּנָֽיו׃

21 כִּֽי־קָרַ֣ע יִשְׂרָאֵ֗ל מֵעַל֙ בֵּ֣ית דָּוִ֔ד וַיַּמְלִ֖יכוּ אֶת־יָרׇבְעָ֣ם בֶּן־נְבָ֑ט ויד וַיַּדַּ֨ח יָרׇבְעָ֤ם אֶת־יִשְׂרָאֵל֙ מֵאַחֲרֵ֣י יְהֹוָ֔ה וְהֶחֱטִיאָ֖ם חֲטָאָ֥ה גְדוֹלָֽה׃ 22 וַיֵּֽלְכוּ֙ בְּנֵ֣י יִשְׂרָאֵ֔ל בְּכׇל־ חַטֹּאות*֙ יָרׇבְעָ֖ם אֲשֶׁ֣ר עָשָׂ֑ה לֹא־סָ֖רוּ מִמֶּֽנָּה׃ 23 עַ֠ד אֲשֶׁר־הֵסִ֨יר יְהֹוָ֤ה אֶת־ יִשְׂרָאֵל֙ מֵעַ֣ל פָּנָ֔יו כַּֽאֲשֶׁ֣ר דִּבֶּ֔ר בְּיַ֖ד כׇּל־ עֲבָדָ֣יו הַנְּבִיאִ֑ים וַיִּ֧גֶל יִשְׂרָאֵ֛ל מֵעַ֥ל אַדְמָת֖וֹ אַשּׁ֑וּרָה עַ֖ד הַיּ֥וֹם הַזֶּֽה׃ פ

24 וַיָּבֵ֣א מֶֽלֶךְ־אַשּׁ֡וּר מִבָּבֶ֡ל וּמִ֠כּ֠וּתָה וּמֵֽעַוָּ֤א וּמֵֽחֲמָת֙ וּסְפַרְוַ֔יִם וַיֹּ֙שֶׁב֙ בְּעָרֵ֣י שֹׁמְר֔וֹן תַּ֖חַת בְּנֵ֣י יִשְׂרָאֵ֑ל וַיִּֽרְשׁוּ֙ אֶת־ שֹׁ֣מְר֔וֹן וַיֵּֽשְׁב֖וּ בְּעָרֶֽיהָ׃ 25 וַיְהִ֗י בִּתְחִלַּת֙ שִׁבְתָּ֣ם שָׁ֔ם לֹ֥א יָֽרְא֖וּ אֶת־יְהֹוָ֑ה וַיְשַׁלַּ֨ח יְהֹוָ֤ה בָּהֶם֙ אֶת־הָ֣אֲרָי֔וֹת וַיִּֽהְי֥וּ הֹרְגִ֖ים בָּהֶֽם׃ 26 וַיֹּֽאמְר֗וּ לְמֶ֤לֶךְ אַשּׁוּר֙ לֵאמֹ֔ר הַגּוֹיִ֡ם אֲשֶׁ֣ר הִגְלִ֩יתָ֩ וַתּ֨וֹשֶׁב֙ בְּעָרֵ֣י שֹֽׁמְר֔וֹן לֹ֣א יָֽדְע֔וּ אֶת־מִשְׁפַּ֖ט אֱלֹהֵ֣י הָאָ֑רֶץ וַיְשַׁלַּח־ בָּ֣ם אֶת־הָֽאֲרָי֗וֹת וְהִנָּם֙ מְמִיתִ֣ים אוֹתָ֔ם כַּֽאֲשֶׁר֙ אֵינָ֣ם יֹֽדְעִ֔ים אֶת־מִשְׁפַּ֖ט אֱלֹהֵ֥י הָאָֽרֶץ׃ 27 וַיְצַ֨ו מֶֽלֶךְ־אַשּׁ֜וּר לֵאמֹ֗ר הֹלִ֤יכוּ שָׁ֙מָּה֙ אֶחָ֣ד מֵהַכֹּ֣הֲנִ֔ים אֲשֶׁ֥ר הִגְלִיתֶ֖ם מִשָּׁ֑ם וְיֵֽלְכ֣וּ וְיֵ֣שְׁבוּ שָׁ֔ם וְיֹרֵ֕ם אֶת־מִשְׁפַּ֖ט אֱלֹהֵ֥י הָאָֽרֶץ׃ 28 וַיָּבֹ֞א אֶחָ֣ד מֵהַכֹּהֲנִ֗ים אֲשֶׁ֤ר הִגְלוּ֙ מִשֹּׁ֣מְר֔וֹן וַיֵּ֖שֶׁב בְּבֵֽית־אֵ֑ל וַֽיְהִי֙ מוֹרֶ֣ה אֹתָ֔ם אֵ֖יךְ יִֽירְא֥וּ אֶת־יְהֹוָֽה׃ 29 וַיִּֽהְי֣וּ עֹשִׂ֔ים גּ֥וֹי גּ֖וֹי אֱלֹהָ֑יו וַיַּנִּ֣יחוּ ׀ בְּבֵ֣ית

---

b Heb. "them."

gods and to set them up in the cult places which had been made by the people of Samaria; each nation [set them up] in the towns in which it lived. [30]The Babylonians made Succoth-benoth, and the men of Cuth made Nergal, and the men of Hamath made Ashima, [31]and the Avvites made Nibhaz and Tartak; and the Sepharvites burned their children [as offerings] to Adrammelech and Anamelech, the gods of Sepharvaim. [32]They worshiped the LORD, but they also appointed from their own ranks priests of the shrines, who officiated for them in the cult places. [33]They worshiped the LORD, while serving their own gods according to the practices of the nations from which they had been deported. [34]To this day, they follow their former practices. They do not worship the LORD [properly]. They do not follow the laws and practices, the Teaching and Instruction that the LORD enjoined upon the descendants of Jacob—who was given the name Israel—[35]with whom He made a covenant and whom He commanded: "You shall worship no other gods; you shall not bow down to them nor serve them nor sacrifice to them. [36]You must worship only the LORD your God, who brought you out of the land of Egypt with great might and with an outstretched arm: to Him alone shall you bow down and to Him alone shall you sacrifice. [37]You shall observe faithfully, all your days, the laws and the practices; the Teaching and Instruction that I[c] wrote down for you; do not worship other gods. [38]Do not forget the covenant that I made with you; do not worship other gods. [39]Worship only the LORD your God, and He will save you from the hands of all your enemies." [40]But they did not obey; they continued their former practices. [41]Those nations worshiped the LORD, but they also served their idols. To this day their children and their children's children do as their ancestors did.

---

c Heb. "He."

הַבָּמוֹת אֲשֶׁר עָשׂוּ הַשֹּׁמְרֹנִים גּוֹי גּוֹי בְּעָרֵיהֶם אֲשֶׁר הֵם יֹשְׁבִים שָׁם: [30] וְאַנְשֵׁי בָבֶל עָשׂוּ אֶת־סֻכּוֹת בְּנוֹת וְאַנְשֵׁי־כוּת עָשׂוּ אֶת־נֵרְגַּל וְאַנְשֵׁי חֲמָת עָשׂוּ אֶת־אֲשִׁימָא: [31] וְהָעַוִּים עָשׂוּ נִבְחַז וְאֶת־תַּרְתָּק וְהַסְפַרְוִים שֹׂרְפִים אֶת־בְּנֵיהֶם בָּאֵשׁ לְאַדְרַמֶּלֶךְ וַעֲנַמֶּלֶךְ אֱלֹהֵי סְפַרְוָיִם: [32] וַיִּהְיוּ יְרֵאִים אֶת־יְהוָה וַיַּעֲשׂוּ לָהֶם מִקְצוֹתָם כֹּהֲנֵי בָמוֹת וַיִּהְיוּ עֹשִׂים לָהֶם בְּבֵית הַבָּמוֹת: [33] אֶת־יְהוָה הָיוּ יְרֵאִים וְאֶת־אֱלֹהֵיהֶם הָיוּ עֹבְדִים כְּמִשְׁפַּט הַגּוֹיִם אֲשֶׁר־הִגְלוּ אֹתָם מִשָּׁם: [34] עַד הַיּוֹם הַזֶּה הֵם עֹשִׂים כַּמִּשְׁפָּטִים הָרִאשֹׁנִים אֵינָם יְרֵאִים אֶת־יְהוָה וְאֵינָם עֹשִׂים כְּחֻקֹּתָם וּכְמִשְׁפָּטָם וְכַתּוֹרָה וְכַמִּצְוָה אֲשֶׁר צִוָּה יְהוָה אֶת־בְּנֵי יַעֲקֹב אֲשֶׁר־שָׂם שְׁמוֹ יִשְׂרָאֵל: [35] וַיִּכְרֹת יְהוָה אִתָּם בְּרִית וַיְצַוֵּם לֵאמֹר לֹא תִירְאוּ אֱלֹהִים אֲחֵרִים וְלֹא־תִשְׁתַּחֲווּ לָהֶם וְלֹא תַעַבְדוּם וְלֹא תִזְבְּחוּ לָהֶם: [36] כִּי אִם־אֶת־יְהוָה אֲשֶׁר הֶעֱלָה אֶתְכֶם מֵאֶרֶץ מִצְרַיִם בְּכֹחַ גָּדוֹל וּבִזְרוֹעַ נְטוּיָה אֹתוֹ תִירָאוּ וְלוֹ תִשְׁתַּחֲווּ וְלוֹ תִזְבָּחוּ: [37] וְאֶת־הַחֻקִּים וְאֶת־הַמִּשְׁפָּטִים וְהַתּוֹרָה וְהַמִּצְוָה אֲשֶׁר כָּתַב לָכֶם תִּשְׁמְרוּן לַעֲשׂוֹת כָּל־הַיָּמִים וְלֹא תִירְאוּ אֱלֹהִים אֲחֵרִים: [38] וְהַבְּרִית אֲשֶׁר־כָּרַתִּי אִתְּכֶם לֹא תִשְׁכָּחוּ וְלֹא תִירְאוּ אֱלֹהִים אֲחֵרִים: [39] כִּי אִם־אֶת־יְהוָה אֱלֹהֵיכֶם תִּירָאוּ וְהוּא יַצִּיל אֶתְכֶם מִיַּד כָּל־אֹיְבֵיכֶם: [40] וְלֹא שָׁמֵעוּ כִּי אִם־כְּמִשְׁפָּטָם הָרִאשׁוֹן הֵם עֹשִׂים: [41] וַיִּהְיוּ | הַגּוֹיִם הָאֵלֶּה יְרֵאִים אֶת־יְהוָה וְאֶת־פְּסִילֵיהֶם הָיוּ עֹבְדִים גַּם־בְּנֵיהֶם | וּבְנֵי בְנֵיהֶם כַּאֲשֶׁר עָשׂוּ אֲבֹתָם הֵם עֹשִׂים עַד הַיּוֹם הַזֶּה: פ

18

In the third year of King Hoshea son of Elah of Israel, Hezekiah son of King Ahaz of Judah became king. [2]He was twenty-five years old when he became king, and he reigned in Jerusalem twenty-nine years; his mother's name was Abi[a] daughter of Zechariah. [3]He did what was pleasing to the Lord, just as his father David had done. [4]He abolished the shrines and smashed the pillars and cut down the sacred post. He also broke into pieces the bronze serpent that Moses had made, for until that time the Israelites had been offering sacrifices to it; it was called Nehushtan. [5]He trusted only in the Lord the God of Israel; there was none like him among all the kings of Judah after him, nor among those before him. [6]He clung to the Lord; he did not turn away from following Him, but kept the commandments that the Lord had given to Moses. [7]And the Lord was always with him; he was successful wherever he turned. He rebelled against the king of Assyria and would not serve him. [8]He overran Philistia as far as Gaza and its border areas, from watchtower to fortified town.

[9]In the fourth year of King Hezekiah, which was the seventh year of King Hoshea son of Elah of Israel, King Shalmaneser of Assyria marched against Samaria and besieged it, [10]and he[b] captured it at the end of three years. In the sixth year of Hezekiah, which was the ninth year of King Hoshea of Israel, Samaria was captured; [11]and the king of Assyria deported the Israelites to Assyria. He [c]settled them in-[c] Halah, along the Habor [and] the River Gozan, and in the towns of Media. [12][This happened] because they did not obey the Lord their God; they transgressed His covenant—all that Moses the servant of the Lord had commanded. They did not obey and they did not fulfill it.

---

a   2 Chron. 29.1 reads "Abijah."
b   So some mss. and ancient versions; most mss. and editions read "they."
c-c   Lit. "led them to."

יח וַיְהִי בִּשְׁנַת שָׁלֹשׁ לְהוֹשֵׁעַ בֶּן־אֵלָה מֶלֶךְ יִשְׂרָאֵל מָלַךְ חִזְקִיָּה בֶן־אָחָז מֶלֶךְ יְהוּדָה: 2 בֶּן־עֶשְׂרִים וְחָמֵשׁ שָׁנָה הָיָה בְמָלְכוֹ וְעֶשְׂרִים וָתֵשַׁע שָׁנָה מָלַךְ בִּירוּשָׁלָ͏ִם וְשֵׁם אִמּוֹ אֲבִי בַּת־זְכַרְיָה: 3 וַיַּעַשׂ הַיָּשָׁר בְּעֵינֵי יְהוָה כְּכֹל אֲשֶׁר־עָשָׂה דָּוִד אָבִיו: 4 הוּא ׀ הֵסִיר אֶת־הַבָּמוֹת וְשִׁבַּר אֶת־הַמַּצֵּבֹת וְכָרַת אֶת־הָאֲשֵׁרָה וְכִתַּת נְחַשׁ הַנְּחֹשֶׁת אֲשֶׁר־עָשָׂה מֹשֶׁה כִּי עַד־הַיָּמִים הָהֵמָּה הָיוּ בְנֵי־יִשְׂרָאֵל מְקַטְּרִים לוֹ וַיִּקְרָא־לוֹ נְחֻשְׁתָּן: 5 בַּיהוָה אֱלֹהֵי־יִשְׂרָאֵל בָּטָח וְאַחֲרָיו לֹא־הָיָה כָמֹהוּ בְּכֹל מַלְכֵי יְהוּדָה וַאֲשֶׁר הָיוּ לְפָנָיו: 6 וַיִּדְבַּק בַּיהוָה לֹא־סָר מֵאַחֲרָיו וַיִּשְׁמֹר מִצְוֹתָיו אֲשֶׁר־צִוָּה יְהוָה אֶת־מֹשֶׁה: 7 וְהָיָה יְהוָה עִמּוֹ בְּכֹל אֲשֶׁר־יֵצֵא יַשְׂכִּיל וַיִּמְרֹד בְּמֶלֶךְ־אַשּׁוּר וְלֹא עֲבָדוֹ: 8 הוּא־הִכָּה אֶת־פְּלִשְׁתִּים עַד־עַזָּה וְאֶת־גְּבוּלֶיהָ מִמִּגְדַּל נוֹצְרִים עַד־עִיר מִבְצָר: פ 9 וַיְהִי בַּשָּׁנָה הָרְבִיעִית לַמֶּלֶךְ חִזְקִיָּהוּ הִיא הַשָּׁנָה הַשְּׁבִיעִית לְהוֹשֵׁעַ בֶּן־אֵלָה מֶלֶךְ יִשְׂרָאֵל עָלָה שַׁלְמַנְאֶסֶר מֶלֶךְ־אַשּׁוּר עַל־שֹׁמְרוֹן וַיָּצַר עָלֶיהָ: 10 וַיִּלְכְּדֻהָ* מִקְצֵה שָׁלֹשׁ שָׁנִים בִּשְׁנַת־שֵׁשׁ לְחִזְקִיָּה הִיא שְׁנַת־תֵּשַׁע לְהוֹשֵׁעַ מֶלֶךְ יִשְׂרָאֵל נִלְכְּדָה שֹׁמְרוֹן: 11 וַיֶּגֶל מֶלֶךְ־אַשּׁוּר אֶת־יִשְׂרָאֵל אַשּׁוּרָה וַיַּנְחֵם בַּחְלַח וּבְחָבוֹר נְהַר גּוֹזָן וְעָרֵי מָדָי: 12 עַל ׀ אֲשֶׁר לֹא־שָׁמְעוּ בְּקוֹל יְהוָה אֱלֹהֵיהֶם וַיַּעַבְרוּ אֶת־בְּרִיתוֹ אֵת כָּל־אֲשֶׁר צִוָּה מֹשֶׁה עֶבֶד יְהוָה וְלֹא שָׁמְעוּ וְלֹא עָשׂוּ: פ

v. 10. בנוסח אחר מנוקדת לשון יחיד

13In the fourteenth year of King Hezekiah, King Sennacherib of Assyria marched against all the fortified towns of Judah and seized them. 14King Hezekiah sent this message to the king of Assyria at Lachish: "I have done wrong; withdraw from me; and I shall bear whatever you impose on me." So the king of Assyria imposed upon King Hezekiah of Judah a payment of three hundred talents of silver and thirty talents of gold. 15Hezekiah gave him all the silver that was on hand in the House of the Lord and in the treasuries of the palace. 16At that time Hezekiah cut down the doors and the doorposts*d* of the Temple of the Lord, which King Hezekiah had overlaid [with gold], and gave them to the king of Assyria.

17But the king of Assyria sent *e-the Tartan, the Rabsaris, and the Rabshakeh-e* from Lachish with a large force to King Hezekiah in Jerusalem. They marched up to Jerusalem; and when they arrived, they took up a position near the conduit of the Upper Pool, by the road of the Fuller's Field. 18They summoned the king; and Eliakim son of Hilkiah, who was in charge of the palace, Shebna the scribe, and Joah son of Asaph the recorder went out to them.

19The Rabshakeh said to them, "You tell Hezekiah: Thus said the Great King, the King of Assyria: What makes you so confident? 20You must think that mere talk is counsel and valor for war! Look, on whom are you relying, that you have rebelled against me? 21You rely, of all things, on Egypt, that splintered reed of a staff, which enters and punctures the palm of anyone who leans on it! That's what Pharaoh king of Egypt is like to all who rely on him. 22And if you tell me that you are relying on the Lord your God, He is the very one whose shrines and altars Hezekiah did away with, telling Judah and Jerusalem, 'You must worship only at this altar

---

---

13 וּבְאַרְבַּע֩ עֶשְׂרֵ֨ה שָׁנָ֜ה לַמֶּ֣לֶךְ חִזְקִיָּ֗ה עָלָ֞ה סַנְחֵרִ֤יב מֶֽלֶךְ־אַשּׁוּר֙ עַ֚ל כָּל־עָרֵ֣י יְהוּדָ֔ה הַבְּצֻר֖וֹת וַֽיִּתְפְּשֵֽׂם׃ 14 וַיִּשְׁלַ֣ח חִזְקִיָּ֣ה מֶֽלֶךְ־יְהוּדָ֣ה אֶל־מֶֽלֶךְ־אַשּׁ֣וּר ׀ לָכִ֣ישָׁה ׀ לֵאמֹ֣ר ׀ חָטָ֗אתִי שׁ֚וּב מֵֽעָלַ֔י אֵ֛ת אֲשֶׁר־תִּתֵּ֥ן עָלַ֖י אֶשָּׂ֑א וַיָּ֨שֶׂם מֶֽלֶךְ־אַשּׁ֜וּר עַל־חִזְקִיָּ֣ה מֶֽלֶךְ־יְהוּדָ֗ה שְׁלֹ֤שׁ מֵאוֹת֙ כִּכַּר־כֶּ֔סֶף וּשְׁלֹשִׁ֖ים כִּכַּ֥ר זָהָֽב׃ 15 וַיִּתֵּן֙ חִזְקִיָּ֔ה אֶת־כָּל־הַכֶּ֖סֶף הַנִּמְצָ֣א בֵית־יְהוָ֑ה וּבְאֹצְר֖וֹת בֵּ֥ית הַמֶּֽלֶךְ׃ 16 בָּעֵ֣ת הַהִ֗יא קִצַּ֨ץ חִזְקִיָּ֜ה אֶת־דַּלְת֨וֹת הֵיכַ֤ל יְהוָה֙ וְאֶת־הָאֹ֣מְנ֔וֹת אֲשֶׁ֣ר צִפָּ֔ה חִזְקִיָּ֖ה מֶ֣לֶךְ יְהוּדָ֑ה וַֽיִּתְּנֵ֖ם לְמֶ֥לֶךְ אַשּֽׁוּר׃ פ

17 וַיִּשְׁלַ֣ח מֶֽלֶךְ־אַשּׁ֡וּר אֶת־תַּרְתָּ֣ן וְאֶת־רַב־סָרִ֣יס ׀ וְאֶת־רַב־שָׁקֵ֨ה מִן־לָכִ֜ישׁ אֶל־הַמֶּ֧לֶךְ חִזְקִיָּ֛הוּ בְּחֵ֥יל כָּבֵ֖ד יְרוּשָׁלָ֑͏ִם וַֽיַּעֲלוּ֙ וַיָּבֹ֣אוּ יְרוּשָׁלַ֔͏ִם וַיַּעֲלוּ֙ וַיָּבֹ֔אוּ וַיַּ֣עַמְד֔וּ בִּתְעָלַת֙ הַבְּרֵכָ֣ה הָעֶלְיוֹנָ֔ה אֲשֶׁ֕ר בִּמְסִלַּ֖ת שְׂדֵ֥ה כוֹבֵֽס׃ 18 וַֽיִּקְרְאוּ֙ אֶל־הַמֶּ֔לֶךְ וַיֵּצֵ֧א אֲלֵהֶ֛ם אֶלְיָקִ֥ים בֶּן־חִלְקִיָּ֖הוּ אֲשֶׁ֣ר עַל־הַבָּ֑יִת וְשֶׁבְנָה֙ הַסֹּפֵ֔ר וְיוֹאָ֥ח בֶּן־אָסָ֖ף הַמַּזְכִּֽיר׃

19 וַיֹּ֤אמֶר אֲלֵהֶם֙ רַב־שָׁקֵ֔ה אִמְרוּ־נָ֖א אֶל־חִזְקִיָּ֑הוּ כֹּֽה־אָמַ֞ר הַמֶּ֤לֶךְ הַגָּדוֹל֙ מֶ֣לֶךְ אַשּׁ֔וּר מָ֧ה הַבִּטָּח֛וֹן הַזֶּ֖ה אֲשֶׁ֥ר בָּטָֽחְתָּ׃ 20 אָמַ֙רְתָּ֙ אַךְ־דְּבַר־שְׂפָתַ֔יִם עֵצָ֥ה וּגְבוּרָ֖ה לַמִּלְחָמָ֑ה עַתָּה֙ עַל־מִ֣י בָטַ֔חְתָּ כִּ֥י מָרַ֖דְתָּ בִּֽי׃ 21 עַתָּ֡ה הִנֵּ֣ה בָטַ֣חְתָּ לְּךָ֡ עַל־מִשְׁעֶנֶת֩ הַקָּנֶ֨ה הָרָצ֤וּץ הַזֶּה֙ עַל־מִצְרַ֔יִם אֲשֶׁ֨ר יִסָּמֵ֥ךְ אִישׁ֙ עָלָ֔יו וּבָ֥א בְכַפּ֖וֹ וּנְקָבָ֑הּ כֵּ֚ן פַּרְעֹ֣ה מֶֽלֶךְ־מִצְרַ֔יִם לְכָל־הַבֹּטְחִ֖ים עָלָֽיו׃ 22 וְכִֽי־תֹאמְר֣וּן אֵלַ֔י אֶל־יְהוָ֥ה אֱלֹהֵ֖ינוּ בָּטָ֑חְנוּ הֲלוֹא־ה֗וּא אֲשֶׁ֨ר הֵסִ֤יר חִזְקִיָּ֙הוּ֙ אֶת־בָּמֹתָ֣יו וְאֶת־מִזְבְּחֹתָ֔יו וַיֹּ֤אמֶר לִֽיהוּדָה֙ וְלִיר֣וּשָׁלַ֔͏ִם לִפְנֵי֙ הַמִּזְבֵּ֣חַ הַזֶּ֔ה תִּֽשְׁתַּחֲוֽוּ

in Jerusalem.' 23Come now, make this wager with my master, the king of Assyria: I'll give you two thousand horses if you can produce riders to mount them. 24So how could you refuse anything even to the deputy of one of my master's lesser servants, relying on Egypt for chariots and horsemen? 25And do you think I have marched against this land to destroy it without the Lord? The Lord Himself told me: Go up against that land and destroy it."

26Eliakim son of Hilkiah, Shebna, and Joah replied to the Rabshakeh, "Please, speak to your servants in Aramaic, for we understand it; do not speak to us in Judean in the hearing of the people on the wall." 27But the Rabshakeh answered them, "Was it to your master and to you that my master sent me to speak those words? It was precisely to the men who are sitting on the wall—who will have to eat their dung and drink their urine with you." 28And the Rabshakeh stood and called out in a loud voice in Judean: "Hear the words of the Great King, the King of Assyria. 29Thus said the king: Don't let Hezekiah deceive you, for he will not be able to deliver you from my*f* hands. 30Don't let Hezekiah make you rely on the Lord, saying: The Lord will surely save us: this city will not fall into the hands of the king of Assyria. 31Don't listen to Hezekiah. For thus said the king of Assyria: Make your peace with me and come out to me,*g* so that you may all eat from your vines and your fig trees and drink water from your cisterns, 32until I come and take you away to a land like your own, a land of grain [fields] and vineyards, of bread and wine, of olive oil and honey, so that you may live and not die. Don't listen to Hezekiah, who misleads you by saying, 'The Lord will save us.' 33Did any of the gods of other nations save his land from the king of Assyria? 34Where were the gods of Hamath and

---

23 בִּירוּשָׁלָ͏ִם: וְעַתָּה֙ הִתְעָ֣רֶב נָ֔א אֶת־אֲדֹנִ֖י אֶת־מֶ֣לֶךְ אַשּׁ֑וּר וְאֶתְּנָ֤ה לְךָ֙ אַלְפַּ֣יִם סוּסִ֔ים אִם־תּוּכַ֕ל לָ֥תֶת לְךָ֖ רֹכְבִ֥ים עֲלֵיהֶֽם: 24 וְאֵ֣יךְ תָּשִׁ֗יב אֵ֠ת פְּנֵ֨י פַחַ֥ת אַחַ֛ד עַבְדֵ֥י אֲדֹנִ֖י הַקְּטַנִּ֑ים וַתִּבְטַ֤ח לְךָ֙ עַל־מִצְרַ֔יִם לְרֶ֖כֶב וּלְפָרָשִֽׁים: 25 עַתָּה֙ הֲמִבַּלְעֲדֵ֣י יְהֹוָ֔ה עָלִ֛יתִי עַל־הַמָּק֥וֹם הַזֶּ֖ה לְהַשְׁחִת֑וֹ יְהֹוָה֙ אָמַ֣ר אֵלַ֔י עֲלֵ֛ה עַל־הָאָ֥רֶץ הַזֹּ֖את וְהַשְׁחִיתָֽהּ:

26 וַיֹּ֣אמֶר אֶלְיָקִ֣ים בֶּן־חִ֠לְקִיָּ֠הוּ וְשֶׁבְנָ֨ה וְיוֹאָ֜ח אֶל־רַב־שָׁקֵ֗ה דַּבֶּר־נָ֤א אֶל־עֲבָדֶ֙יךָ֙ אֲרָמִ֔ית כִּ֥י שֹׁמְעִ֖ים אֲנָ֑חְנוּ וְאַל־תְּדַבֵּ֤ר עִמָּ֙נוּ֙ יְהוּדִ֔ית בְּאׇזְנֵ֣י הָעָ֔ם אֲשֶׁ֖ר עַל־הַחֹמָֽה: 27 וַיֹּ֨אמֶר אֲלֵיהֶ֜ם רַב־שָׁקֵ֗ה הַעַ֨ל אֲדֹנֶ֤יךָ וְאֵלֶ֙יךָ֙ שְׁלָחַ֣נִי אֲדֹנִ֔י לְדַבֵּ֖ר אֶת־הַדְּבָרִ֣ים הָאֵ֑לֶּה הֲלֹ֣א עַל־הָאֲנָשִׁ֗ים הַיֹּֽשְׁבִים֙ עַל־הַ֣חֹמָ֔ה לֶאֱכֹ֣ל אֶת־חריהם [צוֹאָתָ֗ם] וְלִשְׁתּ֛וֹת אֶת־שיניהם [מֵימֵ֥י] רַגְלֵיהֶ֖ם עִמָּכֶֽם: 28 וַֽיַּעֲמֹד֙ רַב־שָׁקֵ֔ה וַיִּקְרָ֥א בְקוֹל־גָּד֖וֹל יְהוּדִ֑ית וַיְדַבֵּ֣ר וַיֹּ֔אמֶר שִׁמְע֛וּ דְּבַר־הַמֶּ֥לֶךְ הַגָּד֖וֹל מֶ֥לֶךְ אַשּֽׁוּר: 29 כֹּ֚ה אָמַ֣ר הַמֶּ֔לֶךְ אַל־יַשִּׁ֥יא לָכֶ֖ם חִזְקִיָּ֑הוּ כִּי־לֹ֣א יוּכַ֔ל לְהַצִּ֥יל אֶתְכֶ֖ם מִיָּדֽוֹ*: 30 וְאַל־יַבְטַ֨ח אֶתְכֶ֤ם חִזְקִיָּ֙הוּ֙ אֶל־יְהֹוָ֣ה לֵאמֹ֔ר הַצֵּ֥ל יַצִּילֵ֖נוּ יְהֹוָ֑ה וְלֹ֤א תִנָּתֵן֙ אֶת־הָעִ֣יר הַזֹּ֔את בְּיַ֖ד מֶ֥לֶךְ אַשּֽׁוּר: 31 אַל־תִּשְׁמְע֖וּ אֶל־חִזְקִיָּ֑הוּ כִּי֩ כֹ֨ה אָמַ֜ר מֶ֣לֶךְ אַשּׁ֗וּר עֲשֽׂוּ־אִתִּ֤י בְרָכָה֙ וּצְא֣וּ אֵלַ֔י וְאִכְל֤וּ אִישׁ־גַּפְנוֹ֙ וְאִ֣ישׁ תְּאֵֽנָת֔וֹ וּשְׁת֖וּ אִ֣ישׁ מֵֽי־בוֹרֽוֹ: 32 עַד־בֹּאִ֡י וְלָקַחְתִּ֣י אֶתְכֶם֩ אֶל־אֶ֨רֶץ כְּאַרְצְכֶ֜ם אֶ֧רֶץ דָּגָ֣ן וְתִיר֗וֹשׁ אֶ֤רֶץ לֶ֙חֶם֙ וּכְרָמִ֔ים אֶ֗רֶץ זֵ֤ית יִצְהָר֙ וּדְבַ֔שׁ וִֽחְי֖וּ וְלֹ֣א תָמֻ֑תוּ וְאַֽל־תִּשְׁמְעוּ֙ אֶל־חִזְקִיָּ֔הוּ כִּֽי־יַסִּ֤ית אֶתְכֶם֙ לֵאמֹ֔ר יְהֹוָ֖ה יַצִּילֵֽנוּ: 33 הַהַצֵּ֥ל הִצִּ֛ילוּ אֱלֹהֵ֥י הַגּוֹיִ֖ם אִ֣ישׁ אֶת־אַרְצ֑וֹ מִיַּ֖ד

---

f So several mss. and ancient versions; most mss. and editions read "his."

g I.e., to my representative the Rabshakeh.

Arpad? Where were the gods of Sepharvaim, Hena, and Ivvah? [And] did they[h] save Samaria from me? [35]Which among all the gods of [those] countries saved their countries from me, that the Lord should save Jerusalem from me?" [36]But the people were silent and did not say a word in reply; for the king's order was: "Do not answer him." [37]And so Eliakim son of Hilkiah, who was in charge of the palace, Shebna the scribe, and Joah son of Asaph the recorder came to Hezekiah with their clothes rent, and they reported to him what the Rabshakeh had said.

19

When King Hezekiah heard this, he rent his clothes, and covered himself with sackcloth, and went into the House of the Lord. [2]He also sent Eliakim, who was in charge of the palace, Shebna the scribe, and the senior priests, covered with sackcloth, to the prophet Isaiah son of Amoz. [3]They said to him, "Thus said Hezekiah: This day is a day of distress, of chastisement, and of disgrace. [a-]The babes have reached the birthstool, but the strength to give birth is lacking.[-a] [4]Perhaps the Lord your God will take note of all the words of the Rabshakeh, whom his master the king of Assyria has sent to blaspheme the living God, and will mete out judgment for the words that the Lord your God has heard—if you will offer up prayer for the surviving remnant."

[5]When King Hezekiah's ministers came to Isaiah, [6]Isaiah said to them, "Tell your master as follows: Thus said the Lord: Do not be frightened by the words of blasphemy against Me that you have heard from the minions of the king of Assyria. [7]I will delude[b] him; he will hear a rumor and return to his land, and I will make him fall by the sword in his land."

מֶ֖לֶךְ אַשּֽׁוּר׃ 34 אַיֵּ֞ה אֱלֹהֵ֤י חֲמָת֙ וְאַרְפָּ֔ד אַיֵּ֖ה אֱלֹהֵ֣י סְפַרְוַ֑יִם הֵנַ֥ע וְעִוָּ֖ה כִּֽי־הִצִּ֥ילוּ אֶת־שֹׁמְר֖וֹן מִיָּדִֽי׃ 35 מִ֗י בְּכָל־אֱלֹהֵ֤י הָֽאֲרָצוֹת֙ אֲשֶׁר־הִצִּ֥ילוּ אֶת־אַרְצָ֖ם מִיָּדִ֑י כִּֽי־יַצִּ֧יל יְהוָ֛ה אֶת־יְרוּשָׁלַ֖͏ִם מִיָּדִֽי׃ 36 וְהֶחֱרִ֣ישׁוּ הָעָ֔ם וְלֹֽא־עָנ֥וּ אֹת֖וֹ דָּבָ֑ר כִּֽי־מִצְוַ֥ת הַמֶּ֛לֶךְ הִ֖יא לֵאמֹ֥ר לֹ֥א תַעֲנֻֽהוּ׃ 37 וַיָּבֹ֣א אֶלְיָקִ֣ים בֶּן־חִלְקִיָּ֣ה אֲשֶׁר־עַל־הַבַּ֡יִת וְשֶׁבְנָ֣א הַסֹּפֵר֩ וְיוֹאָ֨ח בֶּן־אָסָ֧ף הַמַּזְכִּ֛יר אֶל־חִזְקִיָּ֖הוּ קְרוּעֵ֣י בְגָדִ֑ים וַיַּגִּ֣דוּ ל֔וֹ דִּבְרֵ֖י רַב־שָׁקֵֽה׃

יט

וַיְהִ֗י כִּשְׁמֹ֙עַ֙ הַמֶּ֣לֶךְ חִזְקִיָּ֔הוּ וַיִּקְרַ֖ע אֶת־בְּגָדָ֑יו וַיִּתְכַּ֣ס בַּשָּׂ֔ק וַיָּבֹ֖א בֵּ֥ית יְהוָֽה׃ 2 וַ֠יִּשְׁלַח אֶת־אֶלְיָקִ֨ים אֲשֶׁר־עַל־הַבַּ֜יִת וְשֶׁבְנָ֣א הַסֹּפֵ֗ר וְאֵת֙ זִקְנֵ֣י הַכֹּֽהֲנִ֔ים מִתְכַּסִּ֖ים בַּשַּׂקִּ֑ים אֶל־יְשַֽׁעְיָ֥הוּ הַנָּבִ֖יא בֶּן־אָמֽוֹץ׃ 3 וַיֹּאמְר֣וּ אֵלָ֗יו כֹּ֚ה אָמַ֣ר חִזְקִיָּ֔הוּ יוֹם־צָרָ֧ה וְתוֹכֵחָ֛ה וּנְאָצָ֖ה הַיּ֣וֹם הַזֶּ֑ה כִּ֣י בָ֤אוּ בָנִים֙ עַד־מַשְׁבֵּ֔ר וְכֹ֥חַ אַ֖יִן לְלֵדָֽה׃ 4 אוּלַ֡י יִשְׁמַע֩ יְהוָ֨ה אֱלֹהֶ֜יךָ אֵ֣ת ׀ כָּל־דִּבְרֵ֣י רַב־שָׁקֵ֗ה אֲשֶׁר֩ שְׁלָח֨וֹ מֶֽלֶךְ־אַשּׁ֤וּר ׀ אֲדֹנָיו֙ לְחָרֵף֙ אֱלֹהִ֣ים חַ֔י וְהוֹכִ֙יחַ֙ בַּדְּבָרִ֔ים אֲשֶׁ֥ר שָׁמַ֖ע יְהוָ֣ה אֱלֹהֶ֑יךָ וְנָשָׂ֣אתָ תְפִלָּ֔ה בְּעַ֖ד הַשְּׁאֵרִ֥ית הַנִּמְצָאָֽה׃ 5 וַיָּבֹ֗אוּ עַבְדֵ֛י הַמֶּ֥לֶךְ חִזְקִיָּ֖הוּ אֶל־יְשַֽׁעְיָֽהוּ׃ 6 וַיֹּ֤אמֶר לָהֶם֙ יְשַֽׁעְיָ֔הוּ כֹּ֥ה תֹאמְר֖וּן אֶל־אֲדֹֽנֵיכֶ֑ם כֹּ֣ה ׀ אָמַ֣ר יְהוָ֗ה אַל־תִּירָא֙ מִפְּנֵ֤י הַדְּבָרִים֙ אֲשֶׁ֣ר שָׁמַ֔עְתָּ אֲשֶׁ֧ר גִּדְּפ֛וּ נַעֲרֵ֥י מֶֽלֶךְ־אַשּׁ֖וּר אֹתִֽי׃ 7 הִנְנִ֨י נֹתֵ֥ן בּוֹ֙ ר֔וּחַ וְשָׁמַ֥ע שְׁמוּעָ֖ה וְשָׁ֣ב לְאַרְצ֑וֹ וְהִפַּלְתִּ֥יו בַּחֶ֖רֶב בְּאַרְצֽוֹ׃

---

h   I.e., the gods of Samaria.

a-a   I.e., the situation is desperate and we are at a loss.
b   Lit. "put a spirit in."

8The Rabshakeh, meanwhile, heard that [the king] had left Lachish; he turned back and found the king of Assyria attacking Libnah. 9But [the king of Assyria] learned that King Tirhakah of Nubia had come out to fight him; so he again sent messengers to Hezekiah, saying, 10"Tell this to King Hezekiah of Judah: Do not let your God, on whom you are relying, mislead you into thinking that Jerusalem will not be delivered into the hands of the king of Assyria. 11You yourself have heard what the kings of Assyria have done to all the lands, how they have annihilated them; and can you escape? 12Were the nations that my predecessorsc destroyed—Gozan, Haran, Rezeph, and the Beth-edenites in Telassar—saved by their gods? 13Where is the king of Hamath? And the king of Arpad? And the kings of Lair, Sepharvaim, Hena, and Ivvah?"

14Hezekiah took the letter from the messengers and read it. Hezekiah then went up to the House of the Lord and spread it out before the Lord. 15And Hezekiah prayed to the Lord and said, "O Lord of Hosts, Enthroned on the Cherubim! You alone are God of all the kingdoms of the earth. You made the heavens and the earth. 16O Lord, incline Your ear and hear; open Your eyes and see. Hear the words that Sennacherib has sent to blaspheme the living God! 17True, O Lord, the kings of Assyria have annihilated the nations and their lands, 18and have committed their gods to the flames and have destroyed them; for they are not gods, but man's handiwork of wood and stone. 19But now, O Lord our God, deliver us from his hands, and let all the kingdoms of the earth know that You alone, O Lord, are God."

20Then Isaiah son of Amoz sent this message to Hezekiah: "Thus said the Lord, the God of Israel: I have heard the prayer you have offered

c Lit. "fathers."

8 וַיָּ֙שָׁב֙ רַב־שָׁקֵ֔ה וַיִּמְצָא֙ אֶת־מֶ֣לֶךְ אַשּׁ֔וּר נִלְחָ֖ם עַל־לִבְנָ֑ה כִּ֣י שָׁמַ֔ע כִּ֥י נָסַ֖ע מִלָּכִֽישׁ׃ 9 וַיִּשְׁמַ֗ע אֶל־תִּרְהָ֤קָה מֶֽלֶךְ־כּוּשׁ֙ לֵאמֹ֔ר הִנֵּ֥ה יָצָ֖א לְהִלָּחֵ֣ם אִתָּ֑ךְ וַיָּ֙שָׁב֙ וַיִּשְׁלַ֣ח מַלְאָכִ֔ים אֶל־חִזְקִיָּ֖הוּ לֵאמֹֽר׃ 10 כֹּ֣ה תֹאמְר֗וּן אֶל־חִזְקִיָּ֤הוּ מֶֽלֶךְ־יְהוּדָה֙ לֵאמֹ֔ר אַל־יַשִּׁאֲךָ֣ אֱלֹהֶ֔יךָ אֲשֶׁ֥ר אַתָּ֖ה בֹּטֵ֣חַ בּ֑וֹ לֵאמֹ֔ר לֹ֤א תִנָּתֵן֙ יְר֣וּשָׁלִַ֔ם בְּיַ֖ד מֶ֥לֶךְ אַשּֽׁוּר׃ 11 הִנֵּ֣ה ׀ אַתָּ֣ה שָׁמַ֗עְתָּ אֵת֩ אֲשֶׁ֙ר עָשׂ֜וּ מַלְכֵ֤י אַשּׁוּר֙ לְכָל־הָ֣אֲרָצ֔וֹת לְהַחֲרִימָ֑ם וְאַתָּ֖ה תִּנָּצֵֽל׃ 12 הַהִצִּ֙ילוּ אֹתָ֜ם אֱלֹהֵ֣י הַגּוֹיִ֗ם אֲשֶׁ֙ר שִׁחֲת֣וּ אֲבוֹתַ֔י אֶת־גּוֹזָ֥ן וְאֶת־חָרָ֖ן וְרֶ֣צֶף וּבְנֵי־עֶ֔דֶן אֲשֶׁ֥ר בִּתְלַאשָּֽׂר׃ 13 אַיּ֖וֹ מֶֽלֶךְ־חֲמָת֙ וּמֶ֣לֶךְ אַרְפָּ֔ד וּמֶ֖לֶךְ לָעִ֣יר סְפַרְוָ֑יִם הֵנַ֖ע וְעִוָּֽה׃ 14 וַיִּקַּ֙ח חִזְקִיָּ֧הוּ אֶת־הַסְּפָרִ֛ים מִיַּ֥ד הַמַּלְאָכִ֖ים וַיִּקְרָאֵ֑ם וַיַּ֙עַל֙ בֵּ֣ית יְהֹוָ֔ה וַיִּפְרְשֵׂ֥הוּ חִזְקִיָּ֖הוּ לִפְנֵ֥י יְהֹוָֽה׃ פ 15 וַיִּתְפַּלֵּ֤ל חִזְקִיָּ֙הוּ֙ לִפְנֵ֣י יְהֹוָ֔ה וַיֹּאמַ֗ר יְהֹוָ֞ה אֱלֹהֵ֤י יִשְׂרָאֵל֙ יֹשֵׁ֣ב הַכְּרֻבִ֔ים אַתָּה־ה֤וּא הָֽאֱלֹהִים֙ לְבַדְּךָ֔ לְכֹ֖ל מַמְלְכ֣וֹת הָאָ֑רֶץ אַתָּ֣ה עָשִׂ֔יתָ אֶת־הַשָּׁמַ֖יִם וְאֶת־הָאָֽרֶץ׃ 16 הַטֵּ֙ה יְהֹוָ֤ה ׀ אָזְנְךָ֙ וּֽשְׁמָ֔ע פְּקַ֧ח יְהֹוָ֛ה עֵינֶ֖יךָ וּרְאֵ֑ה וּשְׁמַ֗ע אֵ֚ת דִּבְרֵ֣י סַנְחֵרִ֔יב אֲשֶׁ֣ר שְׁלָח֔וֹ לְחָרֵ֖ף אֱלֹהִ֥ים חָֽי׃ 17 אׇמְנָ֖ם יְהֹוָ֑ה הֶחֱרִ֜יבוּ מַלְכֵ֥י אַשּׁ֛וּר אֶת־הַגּוֹיִ֖ם וְאֶת־אַרְצָֽם׃ 18 וְנָתְנ֥וּ אֶת־אֱלֹהֵיהֶ֖ם בָּאֵ֑שׁ כִּי֩ לֹ֙א אֱלֹהִ֜ים הֵ֗מָּה כִּ֣י אִם־מַעֲשֵׂ֧ה יְדֵֽי־אָדָ֛ם עֵ֥ץ וָאֶ֖בֶן וַֽיְאַבְּדֽוּם׃ 19 וְעַתָּה֙ יְהֹוָ֣ה אֱלֹהֵ֔ינוּ הוֹשִׁיעֵ֥נוּ נָ֖א מִיָּד֑וֹ וְיֵֽדְעוּ֙ כׇּל־מַמְלְכ֣וֹת הָאָ֔רֶץ כִּ֥י אַתָּ֛ה יְהֹוָ֥ה אֱלֹהִ֖ים לְבַדֶּֽךָ׃ ס 20 וַיִּשְׁלַח֙ יְשַׁעְיָ֣הוּ בֶן־אָמ֔וֹץ אֶל־חִזְקִיָּ֖הוּ לֵאמֹ֑ר כֹּֽה־אָמַ֤ר יְהֹוָה֙ אֱלֹהֵ֣י יִשְׂרָאֵ֔ל אֲשֶׁ֙ר הִתְפַּלַּ֜לְתָּ אֵלַ֗י אֶל־סַנְחֵרִ֖ב מֶ֥לֶךְ־אַשּֽׁוּר

to Me concerning King Sennacherib of Assyria.
²¹This is the word that the Lᴏʀᴅ has spoken concerning him:

"Fair Maiden Zion despises you,
She mocks at you;
Fair Jerusalem shakes
Her head at you.
²²Whom have you blasphemed and reviled?
Against whom made loud your voice
And haughtily raised your eyes?
Against the Holy One of Israel!
²³Through your envoys you have blasphemed
    my Lord.
Because you thought,
'Thanks to my vast chariotry,
It is I who have climbed the highest moun-
    tains,
To the remotest parts of the Lebanon,
And have cut down its loftiest cedars,
Its choicest cypresses,
And have reached its ᵈ-remotest lodge,-ᵈ
ᵉ-Its densest forest.-ᵉ
²⁴It is I who have drawnᶠ and drunk the waters
    of strangers;
I have dried up with the soles of my feet
All the streams of Egypt.'
²⁵Have you not heard? Of old
I planned that very thing,
I designed it long ago,
And now have fulfilled it.
And it has come to pass,
Laying waste fortified towns
In desolate heaps.
²⁶Their inhabitants are helpless,
Dismayed and shamed.
They were but grass of the field
And green herbage,
Grass of the roofs that is blasted
Before the ᵍ-standing grain.-ᵍ

שְׁמָעְתִּי: ‏²¹ זֶה הַדָּבָר אֲשֶׁר־דִּבֶּר יְהוָה
עָלָיו

בָּזָה לְךָ לָעֲגָה לְךָ
בְּתוּלַת בַּת־צִיּוֹן
אַחֲרֶיךָ רֹאשׁ הֵנִיעָה
בַּת יְרוּשָׁלָ͏ִם:
‏²² אֶת־מִי חֵרַפְתָּ וְגִדַּפְתָּ
וְעַל־מִי הֲרִימוֹתָ קּוֹל
וַתִּשָּׂא מָרוֹם עֵינֶיךָ
עַל־קְדוֹשׁ יִשְׂרָאֵל:
‏²³ בְּיַד מַלְאָכֶיךָ חֵרַפְתָּ ׀ אֲדֹנָי
וַתֹּאמֶר
ברכב בְּרֹב רִכְבִּי
אֲנִי עָלִיתִי מְרוֹם הָרִים
יַרְכְּתֵי לְבָנוֹן
וְאֶכְרֹת קוֹמַת אֲרָזָיו
מִבְחוֹר בְּרֹשָׁיו
וְאָבוֹאָה מְלוֹן קִצֹּה
יַעַר כַּרְמִלּוֹ:
‏²⁴ אֲנִי קַרְתִּי וְשָׁתִיתִי מַיִם זָרִים
וְאַחְרִב בְּכַף־פְּעָמַי
כֹּל יְאֹרֵי מָצוֹר:
‏²⁵ הֲלֹא־שָׁמַעְתָּ לְמֵרָחוֹק
אֹתָהּ עָשִׂיתִי
לְמִימֵי קֶדֶם וִיצַרְתִּיהָ
עַתָּה הֲבֵיאתִיהָ
וּתְהִי
לַהְשׁוֹת* גַּלִּים נִצִּים
עָרִים בְּצֻרוֹת:
‏²⁶ וְיֹשְׁבֵיהֶן קִצְרֵי־יָד
חַתּוּ וַיֵּבֹשׁוּ
הָיוּ עֵשֶׂב שָׂדֶה
וִירַק דֶּשֶׁא
חֲצִיר גַּגּוֹת וּשְׁדֵפָה
לִפְנֵי קָמָה:

ᵈ-ᵈ Isa. 37.24 reads "highest peak."
ᵉ-ᵉ Lit. "Its farmland forest"; exact meaning of Heb. uncertain.
ᶠ   Or "dug"; meaning of Heb. uncertain.
ᵍ-ᵍ Emendation yields "east wind"; see note at Isa. 37.27.

חסר א' v. 25.

²⁷I know your stayings
And your goings and comings,
And how you have raged against Me.
²⁸Because you have raged against Me,
And your tumult has reached My ears,
I will place My hook in your nose
And My bit between your jaws;
And I will make you go back by the road
By which you came.

²⁹"And this is the sign for you:^h This year you eat what grows of itself, and the next year what springs from that; and in the third year, sow and reap, and plant vineyards and eat their fruit. ³⁰And the survivors of the House of Judah that have escaped shall regenerate its stock below and produce boughs above.

³¹For a remnant shall come forth from Jeru-
    salem,
Survivors from Mount Zion.
The zeal of the Lord of Hosts
Shall bring this to pass.

³²Assuredly, thus said the Lord concerning the king of Assyria:

He shall not enter this city:
He shall not shoot an arrow at it,
Or advance upon it with a shield,
Or pile up a siege mound against it.
³³He shall go back
By the way he came;
He shall not enter this city
                —declares the Lord.
³⁴I will protect and save this city for My sake,
And for the sake of My servant David."

³⁵That night an angel of the Lord went out and struck down one hundred and eighty-five thousand in the Assyrian camp, and the following morning they were all dead corpses. ³⁶So King Sennacherib of Assyria broke camp and retreated, and stayed in Nineveh. ³⁷While

---

^h I.e., Hezekiah.

וְשִׁבְתְּךָ֛ 27

וְצֵאתְךָ֥ וּבוֹאֲךָ֖ יָדָ֑עְתִּי
וְאֵ֖ת הִֽתְרַגֶּזְךָ֥ אֵלָֽי׃
יַ֚עַן הִתְרַגֶּזְךָ֣ אֵלַ֔י 28
וְשַׁאֲנַנְךָ֖ עָלָ֣ה בְאָזְנָ֑י
וְשַׂמְתִּ֨י חַחִ֜י בְּאַפֶּ֗ךָ
וּמִתְגִּי֙ בִּשְׂפָתֶ֔יךָ
וַהֲשִֽׁבֹתִ֕יךָ בַּדֶּ֖רֶךְ
אֲשֶׁר־בָּ֥אתָ בָּֽהּ׃
וְזֶה־לְּךָ֣ הָא֔וֹת אָכ֤וֹל הַשָּׁנָה֙ סָפִ֔יחַ 29
וּבַשָּׁנָ֥ה הַשֵּׁנִ֖ית סָחִ֑ישׁ וּבַשָּׁנָ֣ה הַשְּׁלִישִׁ֗ית
זִרְע֧וּ וְקִצְר֛וּ וְנִטְע֥וּ כְרָמִ֖ים וְאִכְל֥וּ פִרְיָֽם׃
וְיָסְפָ֞ה פְּלֵיטַ֣ת בֵּית־יְהוּדָ֛ה הַנִּשְׁאָרָ֖ה 30
שֹׁ֣רֶשׁ לְמָ֑טָּה וְעָשָׂ֥ה פְרִ֖י לְמָֽעְלָה׃
כִּ֤י מִירֽוּשָׁלַ֙͏ִם֙ תֵּצֵ֣א שְׁאֵרִ֔ית 31
וּפְלֵיטָ֖ה מֵהַ֣ר צִיּ֑וֹן
קִנְאַ֛ת יְהוָ֥ה [צְבָא֖וֹת*]
תַּעֲשֶׂה־זֹּֽאת׃ ס
לָכֵ֗ן כֹּֽה־אָמַ֤ר יְהוָה֙ אֶל־מֶ֣לֶךְ אַשּׁ֔וּר 32

לֹ֤א יָבֹא֙ אֶל־הָעִ֣יר הַזֹּ֔את
וְלֹֽא־יוֹרֶ֥ה שָׁ֖ם חֵ֑ץ
וְלֹֽא־יְקַדְּמֶ֣נָּה מָגֵ֔ן
וְלֹֽא־יִשְׁפֹּ֥ךְ עָלֶ֖יהָ סֹלְלָֽה׃
בַּדֶּ֥רֶךְ אֲשֶׁר־יָבֹ֖א 33
בָּ֣הּ יָשׁ֑וּב
וְאֶל־הָעִ֥יר הַזֹּ֛את לֹ֥א יָבֹ֖א
נְאֻם־יְהוָֽה׃
וְגַנּוֹתִ֛י אֶל־הָעִ֥יר הַזֹּ֖את לְהֽוֹשִׁיעָ֑הּ 34
לְמַ֣עֲנִ֔י
וּלְמַ֖עַן דָּוִ֥ד עַבְדִּֽי׃
וַיְהִ֣י׀ בַּלַּ֣יְלָה הַה֗וּא וַיֵּצֵ֣א׀ מַלְאַ֣ךְ יְהוָ֡ה 35
וַיַּךְ֩ בְּמַחֲנֵ֨ה אַשּׁ֜וּר מֵאָ֨ה שְׁמוֹנִ֤ים וַחֲמִשָּׁה֙
אֶ֔לֶף וַיַּשְׁכִּ֣ימוּ בַבֹּ֔קֶר וְהִנֵּ֥ה כֻלָּ֖ם פְּגָרִ֥ים
מֵתִֽים׃
וַיִּסַּ֣ע וַיֵּ֔לֶךְ וַיָּ֖שָׁב סַנְחֵרִ֣יב מֶֽלֶךְ־אַשּׁ֑וּר 36

he was worshiping in the temple of his god Nisroch, his sons Adrammelech and Sarezer struck him down with the sword. They fled to the land of Ararat, and his son Esarhaddon succeeded him as king.

20 In those days Hezekiah fell dangerously ill. The prophet Isaiah son of Amoz came and said to him, "Thus said the Lord: Set your affairs in order, for you are going to die; you will not get well." ²Thereupon Hezekiah turned his face to the wall and prayed to the Lord. He said, ³"Please, O Lord, remember how I have walked before You sincerely and wholeheartedly, and have done what is pleasing to You." And Hezekiah wept profusely.

⁴Before Isaiah had gone out of the middle court, the word of the Lord came to him: ⁵"Go back and say to Hezekiah, the ruler of My people: Thus said the Lord, the God of your father David: I have heard your prayer, I have seen your tears. I am going to heal you; on the third day you shall go up to the House of the Lord. ⁶And I will add fifteen years to your life. I will also rescue you and this city from the hands of the king of Assyria. I will protect this city for My sake and for the sake of My servant David."—⁷Then Isaiah said, "Get a cake of figs." And they got one, and they applied it to the rash, and he recovered.—⁸Hezekiah asked Isaiah, "What is the sign that the Lord will heal me and that I shall go up to the House of the Lord on the third day?" ⁹Isaiah replied, "This is the sign for you from the Lord that the Lord will do the thing that He has promised: Shall[a] the shadow advance ten steps or recede ten steps?" ¹⁰Hezekiah said, "It is easy for the shadow to lengthen ten steps, but not for the shadow to recede ten steps." ¹¹So the prophet Isaiah called to the Lord, and He made the shadow which

---

a Cf. Targum.

וַיֵּ֖שֶׁב בְּנִֽינְוֵֽה׃ 37 וַיְהִי֩ ה֨וּא מִֽשְׁתַּחֲוֶ֜ה בֵּ֣ית ׀ נִסְרֹ֣ךְ אֱלֹהָ֗יו וְֽאַדְרַמֶּ֣לֶךְ וְשַׂרְאֶ֤צֶר [בָּנָיו֙*] הִכֻּ֣הוּ בַחֶ֔רֶב וְהֵ֥מָּה נִמְלְט֖וּ אֶ֣רֶץ אֲרָרָ֑ט וַיִּמְלֹ֛ךְ אֵֽסַר־חַדֹּ֥ן בְּנ֖וֹ תַּחְתָּֽיו׃ פ

כ בַּיָּמִ֣ים הָהֵ֔ם חָלָ֥ה חִזְקִיָּ֖הוּ לָמ֑וּת וַיָּבֹ֣א אֵלָ֡יו יְשַׁעְיָ֣הוּ בֶן־אָמוֹץ֮ הַנָּבִיא֒ וַיֹּ֨אמֶר אֵלָ֜יו כֹּֽה־אָמַ֤ר יְהֹוָה֙ צַ֣ו לְבֵיתֶ֔ךָ כִּ֛י מֵ֥ת אַתָּ֖ה וְלֹ֥א תִֽחְיֶֽה׃ 2 וַיַּסֵּ֥ב אֶת־פָּנָ֖יו אֶל־הַקִּ֑יר וַיִּתְפַּלֵּ֥ל אֶל־יְהֹוָ֖ה לֵאמֹֽר׃ 3 אָנָּ֣ה יְהֹוָ֗ה זְכׇר־נָ֞א אֵ֣ת אֲשֶׁ֣ר הִתְהַלַּ֣כְתִּי לְפָנֶ֗יךָ בֶּאֱמֶת֙ וּבְלֵבָ֣ב שָׁלֵ֔ם וְהַטּ֥וֹב בְּעֵינֶ֖יךָ עָשִׂ֑יתִי וַיֵּ֥בְךְּ חִזְקִיָּ֖הוּ בְּכִ֥י גָדֽוֹל׃ ס 4 וַיְהִ֣י יְשַׁעְיָ֔הוּ לֹ֣א יָצָ֔א הָעִ֖יר הַתִּֽיכֹנָ֑ה וּדְבַר־יְהֹוָ֔ה הָיָ֥ה אֵלָ֖יו לֵאמֹֽר׃ 5 שׁ֣וּב וְאָמַרְתָּ֞ אֶל־חִזְקִיָּ֣הוּ נְגִֽיד־עַמִּ֗י כֹּֽה־אָמַ֤ר יְהֹוָה֙ אֱלֹהֵי֙ דָּוִ֣ד אָבִ֔יךָ שָׁמַ֙עְתִּי֙ אֶת־תְּפִלָּתֶ֔ךָ רָאִ֖יתִי אֶת־דִּמְעָתֶ֑ךָ הִנְנִי֙ רֹ֣פֶא לָ֔ךְ בַּיּוֹם֙ הַשְּׁלִישִׁ֔י תַּעֲלֶ֖ה בֵּ֥ית יְהֹוָֽה׃ 6 וְהֹסַפְתִּ֣י עַל־יָמֶ֗יךָ חֲמֵ֤שׁ עֶשְׂרֵה֙ שָׁנָ֔ה וּמִכַּ֤ף מֶֽלֶךְ־אַשּׁוּר֙ אַצִּ֣ילְךָ֔ וְאֵ֖ת הָעִ֣יר הַזֹּ֑את וְגַנּוֹתִי֙ עַל־הָעִ֣יר הַזֹּ֔את לְמַ֣עֲנִ֔י וּלְמַ֖עַן דָּוִ֥ד עַבְדִּֽי׃ 7 וַיֹּ֣אמֶר יְשַֽׁעְיָ֔הוּ קְח֖וּ דְּבֶ֣לֶת תְּאֵנִ֑ים וַיִּקְח֛וּ וַיָּשִׂ֥ימוּ עַֽל־הַשְּׁחִ֖ין וַיֶּֽחִי׃ 8 וַיֹּ֤אמֶר חִזְקִיָּ֙הוּ֙ אֶל־יְשַׁ֣עְיָ֔הוּ מָ֣ה א֔וֹת כִּֽי־יִרְפָּ֥א יְהֹוָ֖ה לִ֑י וְעָלִ֛יתִי בַּיּ֥וֹם הַשְּׁלִישִׁ֖י בֵּ֥ית יְהֹוָֽה׃ 9 וַיֹּ֣אמֶר יְשַׁעְיָ֗הוּ זֶה־לְּךָ֤ הָאוֹת֙ מֵאֵ֣ת יְהֹוָ֔ה כִּ֚י יַעֲשֶׂ֣ה יְהֹוָ֔ה אֶת־הַדָּבָ֖ר אֲשֶׁ֣ר דִּבֵּ֑ר הָלַ֤ךְ הַצֵּל֙ עֶ֣שֶׂר מַֽעֲל֔וֹת אִם־יָשׁ֖וּב עֶ֥שֶׂר מַעֲלֽוֹת׃ 10 וַיֹּ֙אמֶר֙ יְחִזְקִיָּ֔הוּ נָקֵ֣ל לַצֵּ֔ל לִנְט֖וֹת עֶ֣שֶׂר מַעֲל֑וֹת לֹ֣א כִ֔י יָשׁ֥וּב הַצֵּ֛ל אֲחֹרַנִּ֖ית עֶ֥שֶׂר מַעֲלֽוֹת׃ 11 וַיִּקְרָ֛א יְשַׁעְיָ֥הוּ הַנָּבִ֖יא אֶל־יְהֹוָ֑ה וַיָּ֜שֶׁב

קרי ולא כתיב .v 37

827

had descended on the dial[b] of Ahaz recede ten steps.

¹²At that time, King Berodach-[c]baladan son of Baladan of Babylon sent [envoys with] a letter and a gift to Hezekiah, for he had heard about Hezekiah's illness. ¹³[d]-Hezekiah heard about them-[d] and he showed them all his treasure-house—the silver, the gold, the spices, and the fragrant oil—and his armory, and everything that was to be found in his storehouses. There was nothing in his palace or in all his realm that Hezekiah did not show them. ¹⁴Then the prophet Isaiah came to King Hezekiah. "What," he demanded of him, "did those men say to you? Where have they come to you from?" "They have come," Hezekiah replied, "from a far country, from Babylon." ¹⁵Next he asked, "What have they seen in your palace?" And Hezekiah replied, "They have seen everything that is in my palace. There was nothing in my store-houses that I did not show them."

¹⁶Then Isaiah said to Hezekiah, "Hear the word of the Lord: ¹⁷A time is coming when everything in your palace which your ancestors have stored up to this day will be carried off to Babylon; nothing will remain behind, said the Lord. ¹⁸And some of your sons, your own issue, whom you will have fathered, will be taken to serve as eunuchs in the palace of the king of Babylon." ¹⁹Hezekiah declared to Isaiah, "The word of the Lord that you have spoken is good." For he thought, "It means that [e]-safety is assured for-[e] my time."

²⁰The other events of Hezekiah's reign, and all his exploits, and how he made the pool and the conduit and brought the water into the city, are recorded in the Annals of the Kings of Judah. ²¹Hezekiah slept with his fathers, and his son Manasseh succeeded him as king.

אֶת־הַצֵּל בַּמַּעֲלוֹת אֲשֶׁר יָרְדָה בְּמַעֲלוֹת אָחָז אֲחֹרַנִּית עֶשֶׂר מַעֲלוֹת: פ

¹² בָּעֵת הַהִיא שָׁלַח בְּרֹאדַךְ* בַּלְאֲדָן בֶּן־בַּלְאֲדָן מֶלֶךְ־בָּבֶל סְפָרִים וּמִנְחָה אֶל־חִזְקִיָּהוּ כִּי שָׁמַע כִּי חָלָה חִזְקִיָּהוּ: ¹³ וַיִּשְׁמַע עֲלֵיהֶם חִזְקִיָּהוּ וַיַּרְאֵם אֶת־כָּל־בֵּית נְכֹתֹה אֶת־הַכֶּסֶף וְאֶת־הַזָּהָב וְאֶת־הַבְּשָׂמִים וְאֵת שֶׁמֶן הַטּוֹב וְאֵת בֵּית כֵּלָיו וְאֵת כָּל־אֲשֶׁר נִמְצָא בְּאֽוֹצְרֹתָיו לֹא־הָיָה דָבָר אֲשֶׁר לֹא־הֶרְאָם חִזְקִיָּהוּ בְּבֵיתוֹ וּבְכָל־מֶמְשַׁלְתּוֹ: ¹⁴ וַיָּבֹא יְשַׁעְיָהוּ הַנָּבִיא אֶל־הַמֶּלֶךְ חִזְקִיָּהוּ וַיֹּאמֶר אֵלָיו מָה אָמְרוּ ׀ הָאֲנָשִׁים הָאֵלֶּה וּמֵאַיִן יָבֹאוּ אֵלֶיךָ וַיֹּאמֶר חִזְקִיָּהוּ מֵאֶרֶץ רְחוֹקָה בָּאוּ מִבָּבֶל: ¹⁵ וַיֹּאמֶר מָה רָאוּ בְּבֵיתֶךָ וַיֹּאמֶר חִזְקִיָּהוּ אֵת כָּל־אֲשֶׁר בְּבֵיתִי רָאוּ לֹא־הָיָה דָבָר אֲשֶׁר לֹא־הִרְאִיתִם בְּאֹצְרֹתָי:

¹⁶ וַיֹּאמֶר יְשַׁעְיָהוּ אֶל־חִזְקִיָּהוּ שְׁמַע דְּבַר־יְהוָה: ¹⁷ הִנֵּה יָמִים בָּאִים וְנִשָּׂא ׀ כָּל־אֲשֶׁר בְּבֵיתֶךָ וַאֲשֶׁר אָצְרוּ אֲבֹתֶיךָ עַד־הַיּוֹם הַזֶּה בָּבֶלָה לֹא־יִוָּתֵר דָּבָר אָמַר יְהוָה: ¹⁸ וּמִבָּנֶיךָ אֲשֶׁר יֵצְאוּ מִמְּךָ אֲשֶׁר תּוֹלִיד יקח וְהָיוּ סָרִיסִים בְּהֵיכַל מֶלֶךְ בָּבֶל: ¹⁹ וַיֹּאמֶר חִזְקִיָּהוּ אֶל־יְשַׁעְיָהוּ טוֹב דְּבַר־יְהוָה אֲשֶׁר דִּבַּרְתָּ וַיֹּאמֶר הֲלוֹא אִם־שָׁלוֹם וֶאֱמֶת יִהְיֶה בְיָמָי:

²⁰ וְיֶתֶר דִּבְרֵי חִזְקִיָּהוּ וְכָל־גְּבוּרָתוֹ וַאֲשֶׁר עָשָׂה אֶת־הַבְּרֵכָה וְאֶת־הַתְּעָלָה וַיָּבֵא אֶת־הַמַּיִם הָעִירָה הֲלֹא־הֵם כְּתוּבִים עַל־סֵפֶר דִּבְרֵי הַיָּמִים לְמַלְכֵי יְהוּדָה: ²¹ וַיִּשְׁכַּב חִזְקִיָּהוּ עִם־אֲבֹתָיו וַיִּמְלֹךְ מְנַשֶּׁה בְנוֹ תַּחְתָּיו: פ

א׳ נחה   v. 12.

---

b   *Heb. "steps." A model of a dial with steps has been discovered in Egypt.*
c   *Several mss. and the parallel Isa. 39.1 read "Merodach."*
d-d   *Isa. 39.2 reads "Hezekiah was pleased by their coming."*
e-e   *Lit. "there shall be safety and faithfulness in."*

21

Manasseh was twelve years old when he became king, and he reigned fifty-five years in Jerusalem; his mother's name was Hephzibah. [2]He did what was displeasing to the LORD, following the abhorrent practices of the nations that the LORD had dispossessed before the Israelites. [3]He rebuilt the shrines that his father Hezekiah had destroyed; he erected altars for Baal and made a sacred post, as King Ahab of Israel had done. He bowed down to all the host of heaven and worshiped them, [4]and he built altars for them in the House of the LORD, of which the LORD had said, "I will establish My name in Jerusalem." [5]He built altars for all the hosts of heaven in the two courts of the House of the LORD. [6]He consigned his son to the fire; he practiced soothsaying and divination, and consulted ghosts and familiar spirits; he did much that was displeasing to the LORD, to vex Him. [7]The sculptured image of Asherah that he made he placed in the House concerning which the LORD had said to David and to his son Solomon, "In this House and in Jerusalem, which I chose out of all the tribes of Israel, I will establish My name forever. [8]And I will not again cause the feet of Israel to wander from the land that I gave to their fathers, if they will but faithfully observe all that I have commanded them—all the Teachings with which My servant Moses charged them." [9]But they did not obey, and Manasseh led them astray to do greater evil than the nations that the LORD had destroyed before the Israelites. [10]Therefore the LORD spoke through His servants the prophets: [11]"Because King Manasseh of Judah has done these abhorrent things—he has outdone in wickedness all that the Amorites did before his time—and because he led Judah to sin with his fetishes, [12]assuredly, thus said the LORD, the God of Israel: I am going to bring such a disas-

כא בֶּן־שְׁתֵּים עֶשְׂרֵה שָׁנָה֙ מְנַשֶּׁה בְמָלְכֹ֔ו וַחֲמִשִּׁים וְחָמֵשׁ שָׁנָ֔ה מָלַ֖ךְ בִּירוּשָׁלִָ֑ם וְשֵׁ֥ם אִמֹּ֖ו חֶפְצִי־בָֽהּ׃ 2 וַיַּ֥עַשׂ הָרַ֖ע בְּעֵינֵ֣י יְהוָ֑ה כְּתֹֽועֲבֹת֙ הַגֹּויִ֔ם אֲשֶׁר֙ הֹורִ֣ישׁ יְהוָ֔ה מִפְּנֵ֖י בְּנֵ֥י יִשְׂרָאֵֽל׃ 3 וַיָּ֗שָׁב וַיִּ֙בֶן֙ אֶת־הַבָּמֹ֔ות אֲשֶׁ֥ר אִבַּ֖ד חִזְקִיָּ֣הוּ אָבִ֑יו וַיָּ֩קֶם֩ מִזְבְּחֹ֨ת לַבַּ֜עַל וַיַּ֣עַשׂ אֲשֵׁרָ֗ה כַּאֲשֶׁ֤ר עָשָׂה֙ אַחְאָב֙ מֶ֣לֶךְ יִשְׂרָאֵ֔ל וַיִּשְׁתַּ֙חוּ֙ לְכָל־צְבָ֣א הַשָּׁמַ֔יִם וַיַּעֲבֹ֖ד אֹתָֽם׃ 4 וּבָנָ֥ה מִזְבְּחֹ֖ת בְּבֵ֣ית יְהוָ֑ה אֲשֶׁר֙ אָמַ֣ר יְהוָ֔ה בִּירוּשָׁלִַ֖ם אָשִׂ֥ים אֶת־שְׁמִֽי׃ 5 וַיִּ֥בֶן מִזְבְּחֹ֖ות לְכָל־צְבָ֣א הַשָּׁמָ֑יִם בִּשְׁתֵּ֖י חַצְרֹ֥ות בֵּית־יְהוָֽה׃ 6 וְהֶעֱבִ֤יר אֶת־בְּנֹו֙ בָּאֵ֔שׁ וְעֹונֵ֣ן וְנִחֵ֔שׁ וְעָ֥שָׂה אֹ֖וב וְיִדְּעֹנִ֑ים הִרְבָּ֗ה לַעֲשֹׂ֥ות הָרַ֛ע בְּעֵינֵ֥י יְהוָ֖ה לְהַכְעִֽיס׃ 7 וַיָּ֕שֶׂם אֶת־פֶּ֥סֶל הָאֲשֵׁרָ֖ה אֲשֶׁ֣ר עָשָׂ֑ה בַּבַּ֗יִת אֲשֶׁ֨ר אָמַ֤ר יְהוָה֙ אֶל־דָּוִ֗ד וְאֶל־שְׁלֹמֹ֣ה בְנֹ֔ו בַּבַּ֤יִת הַזֶּה֙ וּבִ֣ירוּשָׁלִַ֔ם אֲשֶׁ֤ר בָּחַ֙רְתִּי֙ מִכֹּל֙ שִׁבְטֵ֣י יִשְׂרָאֵ֔ל אָשִׂ֥ים אֶת־שְׁמִ֖י לְעֹולָֽם׃ 8 וְלֹ֣א אֹסִ֗יף לְהָנִ֙יד֙ רֶ֣גֶל יִשְׂרָאֵ֔ל מִן־הָ֣אֲדָמָ֔ה אֲשֶׁ֥ר נָתַ֖תִּי לַאֲבֹותָ֑ם רַ֣ק ׀ אִם־יִשְׁמְר֣וּ לַעֲשֹׂ֗ות כְּכֹל֙ אֲשֶׁ֣ר צִוִּיתִ֔ים וּלְכָל־הַתֹּורָ֕ה אֲשֶׁר־צִוָּ֥ה אֹתָ֖ם עַבְדִּ֣י מֹשֶֽׁה׃ 9 וְלֹ֖א שָׁמֵ֑עוּ וַיַּתְעֵ֣ם מְנַשֶּׁ֗ה לַעֲשֹׂ֥ות אֶת־הָרַ֛ע מִן־הַגֹּויִ֔ם אֲשֶׁר֙ הִשְׁמִ֣יד יְהוָ֔ה מִפְּנֵ֖י בְּנֵ֥י יִשְׂרָאֵֽל׃ 10 וַיְדַבֵּ֧ר יְהוָ֛ה בְּיַד־עֲבָדָ֥יו הַנְּבִיאִ֖ים לֵאמֹֽר׃ 11 יַ֡עַן אֲשֶׁר֩ עָשָׂ֨ה מְנַשֶּׁ֤ה מֶֽלֶךְ־יְהוּדָה֙ הַתֹּעֵבֹ֣ות הָאֵ֔לֶּה הֵרַ֕ע מִכֹּ֛ל אֲשֶׁר־עָשׂ֥וּ הָאֱמֹרִ֖י אֲשֶׁ֣ר לְפָנָ֑יו וַיַּחֲטִ֥א גַֽם־אֶת־יְהוּדָ֖ה בְּגִלּוּלָֽיו׃ פ 12 לָכֵ֗ן כֹּֽה־אָמַ֤ר יְהוָה֙ אֱלֹהֵ֣י יִשְׂרָאֵ֔ל הִנְנִ֥י מֵבִ֛יא רָעָ֖ה עַל־יְרוּשָׁלִַ֣ם וִֽיהוּדָ֑ה אֲשֶׁ֣ר

ter on Jerusalem and Judah that both ears of everyone who hears about it will tingle. [13] I will *a*-apply to Jerusalem the measuring line of Samaria and the weights of the House of Ahab;-*a* I will wipe Jerusalem clean as one wipes a dish and turns it upside down. [14] And I will cast off the remnant of My own people and deliver them into the hands of their enemies. They shall be plunder and prey to all their enemies [15] because they have done what is displeasing to Me and have been vexing Me from the day that their fathers came out of Egypt to this day."

[16] Moreover, Manasseh put so many innocent persons to death that he filled Jerusalem [with blood] from end to end—besides the sin he committed in causing Judah to do what was displeasing to the LORD.

[17] The other events of Manasseh's reign, and all his actions, and the sins he committed, are recorded in the Annals of the Kings of Judah. [18] Manasseh slept with his fathers and was buried in the garden of his palace, in the garden of Uzza; and his son Amon succeeded him as king.

[19] Amon was twenty-two years old when he became king, and he reigned two years in Jerusalem; his mother's name was Meshullemeth daughter of Haruz of Jotbah. [20] He did what was displeasing to the LORD, as his father Manasseh had done. [21] He walked in all the ways of his father, worshiping the fetishes which his father had worshiped and bowing down to them. [22] He forsook the LORD, the God of his fathers, and did not follow the way of the LORD.

[23] Amon's courtiers conspired against him; and they killed the king in his palace. [24] But the people of the land put to death all who had conspired against King Amon, and the people of the land made his son Josiah king in his stead.

a-a *I.e., I will bring the same fate upon it.*

כָּל־שֹׁמְעָיו תִּצַּלְנָה שְׁתֵּי אָזְנָיו:
13 וְנָטִיתִי עַל־יְרוּשָׁלִַם אֵת קָו שֹׁמְרוֹן וְאֶת־מִשְׁקֹלֶת בֵּית אַחְאָב וּמָחִיתִי אֶת־יְרוּשָׁלִַם כַּאֲשֶׁר־יִמְחֶה אֶת־הַצַּלַּחַת מָחָה וְהָפַךְ עַל־פָּנֶיהָ: 14 וְנָטַשְׁתִּי אֵת שְׁאֵרִית נַחֲלָתִי וּנְתַתִּים בְּיַד אֹיְבֵיהֶם וְהָיוּ לְבַז וְלִמְשִׁסָּה לְכָל־אֹיְבֵיהֶם: 15 יַעַן אֲשֶׁר עָשׂוּ אֶת־הָרַע בְּעֵינַי וַיִּהְיוּ מַכְעִסִים אֹתִי מִן־הַיּוֹם אֲשֶׁר יָצְאוּ אֲבוֹתָם מִמִּצְרַיִם וְעַד הַיּוֹם הַזֶּה:
16 וְגַם דָּם נָקִי שָׁפַךְ מְנַשֶּׁה הַרְבֵּה מְאֹד עַד אֲשֶׁר־מִלֵּא אֶת־יְרוּשָׁלִַם פֶּה לָפֶה לְבַד מֵחַטָּאתוֹ אֲשֶׁר הֶחֱטִיא אֶת־יְהוּדָה לַעֲשׂוֹת הָרַע בְּעֵינֵי יְהוָה:
17 וְיֶתֶר דִּבְרֵי מְנַשֶּׁה וְכָל־אֲשֶׁר עָשָׂה וְחַטָּאתוֹ אֲשֶׁר חָטָא הֲלֹא־הֵם כְּתוּבִים עַל־סֵפֶר דִּבְרֵי הַיָּמִים לְמַלְכֵי יְהוּדָה: 18 וַיִּשְׁכַּב מְנַשֶּׁה עִם־אֲבֹתָיו וַיִּקָּבֵר בְּגַן־בֵּיתוֹ בְּגַן־עֻזָּא וַיִּמְלֹךְ אָמוֹן בְּנוֹ תַּחְתָּיו: פ

19 בֶּן־עֶשְׂרִים וּשְׁתַּיִם שָׁנָה אָמוֹן בְּמָלְכוֹ וּשְׁתַּיִם שָׁנִים מָלַךְ בִּירוּשָׁלִָם וְשֵׁם אִמּוֹ מְשֻׁלֶּמֶת בַּת־חָרוּץ מִן־יָטְבָה: 20 וַיַּעַשׂ הָרַע בְּעֵינֵי יְהוָה כַּאֲשֶׁר עָשָׂה מְנַשֶּׁה אָבִיו: 21 וַיֵּלֶךְ בְּכָל־הַדֶּרֶךְ אֲשֶׁר־הָלַךְ אָבִיו וַיַּעֲבֹד אֶת־הַגִּלֻּלִים אֲשֶׁר עָבַד אָבִיו וַיִּשְׁתַּחוּ לָהֶם: 22 וַיַּעֲזֹב אֶת־יְהוָה אֱלֹהֵי אֲבֹתָיו וְלֹא הָלַךְ בְּדֶרֶךְ יְהוָה:
23 וַיִּקְשְׁרוּ עַבְדֵי־אָמוֹן עָלָיו וַיָּמִיתוּ אֶת־הַמֶּלֶךְ בְּבֵיתוֹ: 24 וַיַּךְ עַם־הָאָרֶץ אֶת כָּל־הַקֹּשְׁרִים עַל־הַמֶּלֶךְ אָמוֹן וַיַּמְלִיכוּ עַם־הָאָרֶץ אֶת־יֹאשִׁיָּהוּ בְנוֹ תַּחְתָּיו:

25The other events of Amon's reign [and] his actions are recorded in the Annals of the Kings of Judah. 26He was buried in his tomb in the garden of Uzza; and his son Josiah succeeded him as king.

22 Josiah was eight years old when he became king, and he reigned thirty-one years in Jerusalem. His mother's name was Jedidah daughter of Adaiah of Bozkath. 2He did what was pleasing to the LORD and he followed all the ways of his ancestor David; he did not deviate to the right or to the left.

3In the eighteenth year of King Josiah, the king sent the scribe Shaphan son of Azaliah son of Meshullam to the House of the LORD, saying, 4"Go to the high priest Hilkiah and let him weigh[a] the silver that has been deposited in the House of the LORD, which the guards of the threshold have collected from the people. 5And let it be delivered to the overseers of the work who are in charge at the House of the LORD, that they in turn may pay it out to the workmen that are in the House of the LORD, for the repair of the House: 6to the carpenters, the laborers, and the masons, and for the purchase of wood and quarried stones for repairing the House. 7However, no check is to be kept on them for the silver that is delivered to them, for they deal honestly."

8Then the high priest Hilkiah said to the scribe Shaphan, "I have found a scroll of the Teaching in the House of the LORD." And Hilkiah gave the scroll to Shaphan, who read it. 9The scribe Shaphan then went to the king and reported to the king: "Your servants have melted down the silver that was deposited in the House, and they have delivered it to the overseers of the work who are in charge at the House of the LORD." 10The scribe Shaphan also told the

25 וְיֶ֛תֶר דִּבְרֵ֥י אָמ֖וֹן אֲשֶׁ֣ר עָשָׂ֑ה הֲלֹא־הֵ֣ם כְּתוּבִ֗ים עַל־סֵ֛פֶר דִּבְרֵ֥י הַיָּמִ֖ים לְמַלְכֵ֣י יְהוּדָֽה: 26 וַיִּקְבֹּ֥ר אֹת֛וֹ בִּקְבֻרָת֖וֹ בְּגַן־עֻזָּ֑א וַיִּמְלֹ֛ךְ יֹאשִׁיָּ֥הוּ בְנ֖וֹ תַּחְתָּֽיו: פ

כב בֶּן־שְׁמֹנֶ֤ה שָׁנָה֙ יֹאשִׁיָּ֣הוּ בְמָלְכ֔וֹ וּשְׁלֹשִׁ֤ים וְאַחַת֙ שָׁנָ֔ה מָלַ֖ךְ בִּירֽוּשָׁלִָ֑ם וְשֵׁ֣ם אִמּ֔וֹ יְדִידָ֥ה בַת־עֲדָ֖יָה מִבָּצְקַֽת: 2 וַיַּ֗עַשׂ הַיָּשָׁר֙ בְּעֵינֵ֣י יְהֹוָ֔ה וַיֵּ֕לֶךְ בְּכָל־דֶּ֖רֶךְ דָּוִ֣ד אָבִ֑יו וְלֹא־סָ֖ר יָמִ֥ין וּשְׂמֹֽאול*: פ

3 וַיְהִ֗י בִּשְׁמֹנֶ֤ה עֶשְׂרֵה֙ שָׁנָ֔ה לַמֶּ֖לֶךְ יֹאשִׁיָּ֑הוּ שָׁלַ֣ח הַ֠מֶּ֠לֶךְ אֶת־שָׁפָ֨ן בֶּן־אֲצַלְיָ֤הוּ בֶן־מְשֻׁלָּם֙ הַסֹּפֵ֔ר בֵּ֥ית יְהֹוָ֖ה לֵאמֹֽר: 4 עֲלֵ֗ה אֶל־חִלְקִיָּ֨הוּ֙ הַכֹּהֵ֣ן הַגָּד֔וֹל וְיַתֵּ֣ם אֶת־הַכֶּ֔סֶף הַמּוּבָ֖א בֵּ֣ית יְהֹוָ֑ה אֲשֶׁ֥ר אָסְפ֛וּ שֹׁמְרֵ֥י הַסַּ֖ף מֵאֵ֥ת הָעָֽם: 5 וְיִתְּנֻ֗הוּ עַל־יַד֙ עֹשֵׂ֣י הַמְּלָאכָ֔ה הַמֻּפְקָדִ֖ים בֵּ֣ית בֵּ֣ית יְהֹוָ֑ה וְיִתְּנ֣וּ אֹת֗וֹ לְעֹשֵׂ֤י הַמְּלָאכָה֙ אֲשֶׁר֙ בְּבֵ֣ית יְהֹוָ֔ה לְחַזֵּ֖ק בֶּ֥דֶק הַבָּֽיִת: 6 לֶחָֽרָשִׁים֙ וְלַבֹּנִ֔ים וְלַגֹּֽדְרִ֑ים וְלִקְנ֤וֹת עֵצִים֙ וְאַבְנֵ֣י מַחְצֵ֔ב לְחַזֵּ֖ק אֶת־הַבָּֽיִת: 7 אַ֚ךְ לֹֽא־יֵֽחָשֵׁ֣ב אִתָּ֔ם הַכֶּ֖סֶף הַנִּתָּ֣ן עַל־יָדָ֑ם כִּ֥י בֶאֱמוּנָ֖ה הֵ֥ם עֹשִֽׂים: 8 וַ֠יֹּ֠אמֶר חִלְקִיָּ֨הוּ הַכֹּהֵ֤ן הַגָּדוֹל֙ עַל־שָׁפָ֣ן הַסֹּפֵ֔ר סֵ֧פֶר הַתּוֹרָ֛ה מָצָ֖אתִי בְּבֵ֣ית יְהֹוָ֑ה וַיִּתֵּ֨ן חִלְקִיָּ֧ה אֶת־הַסֵּ֛פֶר אֶל־שָׁפָ֖ן וַיִּקְרָאֵֽהוּ: 9 וַיָּבֹ֞א שָׁפָ֤ן הַסֹּפֵר֙ אֶל־הַמֶּ֔לֶךְ וַיָּ֥שֶׁב אֶת־הַמֶּ֖לֶךְ דָּבָ֑ר וַיֹּ֗אמֶר הִתִּ֤יכוּ עֲבָדֶ֨יךָ֙ אֶת־הַכֶּ֨סֶף֙ הַנִּמְצָ֣א בַבַּ֔יִת וַֽיִּתְּנֻ֗הוּ עַל־יַד֙ עֹשֵׂ֣י הַמְּלָאכָ֔ה הַמֻּפְקָדִ֖ים בֵּ֥ית יְהֹוָֽה: 10 וַיַּגֵּ֞ד שָׁפָ֤ן הַסֹּפֵר֙ לַמֶּ֣לֶךְ לֵאמֹ֔ר

---

a Meaning of Heb. uncertain. Emendation yields "melt down," cf. v. 9.

מלא ו'   v. 2.

king, "The high priest Hilkiah has given me a scroll"; and Shaphan read it to the king.

[11]When the king heard the words of the scroll of the Teaching, he rent his clothes. [12]And the king gave orders to the priest Hilkiah, and to Ahikam son of Shaphan, Achbor son of Michaiah, the scribe Shaphan, and Asaiah the king's minister: [13]"Go, inquire of the LORD on my behalf, and on behalf of the people, and on behalf of all Judah, concerning the words of this scroll that has been found. For great indeed must be the wrath of the LORD that has been kindled against us, because our fathers did not obey the words of this scroll to do all that has been prescribed for us."

[14]So the priest Hilkiah, and Ahikam, Achbor, Shaphan, and Asaiah went to the prophetess Huldah—the wife of Shallum son of Tikvah son of Harhas, the keeper of the wardrobe—who was living in Jerusalem in the Mishneh,[b] and they spoke to her. [15]She responded: "Thus said the LORD, the God of Israel: Say to the man who sent you to me: [16]Thus said the LORD: I am going to bring disaster upon this place and its inhabitants, in accordance with all the words of the scroll which the king of Judah has read. [17]Because they have forsaken Me and have made offerings to other gods and vexed Me with all their deeds, My wrath is kindled against this place and it shall not be quenched. [18]But say this to the king of Judah, who sent you to inquire of the LORD: Thus said the LORD, the God of Israel: As for the words which you have heard—[19]because your heart was softened and you humbled yourself before the LORD when you heard what I decreed against this place and its inhabitants—that it will become a desolation and a curse—and because you rent your clothes and wept before Me, I for My part have listened—declares the LORD. [20]Assuredly, I will

---

b   *A quarter in Jerusalem; cf. Zeph. 1.10.*

סֵ֤פֶר נָֽתַן־לִי֙ חִלְקִיָּ֣ה הַכֹּהֵ֔ן וַיִּקְרָאֵ֥הוּ שָׁפָ֖ן לִפְנֵ֥י הַמֶּֽלֶךְ׃ 11 וַֽיְהִי֙ כִּשְׁמֹ֣עַ הַמֶּ֔לֶךְ אֶת־דִּבְרֵ֖י סֵ֣פֶר הַתּוֹרָ֑ה וַיִּקְרַ֖ע אֶת־בְּגָדָֽיו׃ 12 וַיְצַ֣ו הַמֶּ֡לֶךְ אֶת־חִלְקִיָּ֣ה הַכֹּהֵ֡ן וְאֶת־אֲחִיקָ֣ם בֶּן־שָׁפָ֡ן וְאֶת־עַכְבּ֣וֹר בֶּן־מִיכָיָ֡ה וְאֵת֩ ׀ שָׁפָ֨ן הַסֹּפֵ֜ר וְאֵ֛ת עֲשָׂיָ֥ה עֶֽבֶד־הַמֶּ֖לֶךְ לֵאמֹֽר׃ 13 לְכוּ֩ דִרְשׁ֨וּ אֶת־יְהֹוָ֜ה בַּעֲדִ֣י וּבְעַד־הָעָ֗ם וּבְעַד֙ כׇּל־יְהוּדָ֔ה עַל־דִּבְרֵ֛י הַסֵּ֥פֶר הַנִּמְצָ֖א הַזֶּ֑ה כִּֽי־גְדוֹלָ֞ה חֲמַ֣ת יְהֹוָ֗ה אֲשֶׁר־הִיא֙ נִצְּתָ֣ה בָ֔נוּ עַ֠ל אֲשֶׁ֨ר לֹֽא־שָׁמְע֤וּ אֲבֹתֵ֙ינוּ֙ עַל־דִּבְרֵ֣י הַסֵּ֣פֶר הַזֶּ֔ה לַעֲשׂ֖וֹת כְּכׇל־הַכָּת֥וּב עָלֵֽינוּ׃ 14 וַיֵּ֣לֶךְ חִלְקִיָּ֣הוּ הַ֠כֹּהֵ֠ן וַאֲחִיקָ֨ם וְעַכְבּ֜וֹר וְשָׁפָ֣ן וַעֲשָׂיָ֗ה אֶל־חֻלְדָּ֨ה הַנְּבִיאָ֜ה אֵ֣שֶׁת ׀ שַׁלֻּ֣ם בֶּן־תִּקְוָ֗ה בֶּן־חַרְחַס֙ שֹׁמֵ֣ר הַבְּגָדִ֔ים וְהִ֛יא יֹשֶׁ֥בֶת בִּירוּשָׁלַ֖͏ִם בַּמִּשְׁנֶ֑ה וַֽיְדַבְּר֖וּ אֵלֶֽיהָ׃ 15 וַתֹּ֣אמֶר אֲלֵיהֶ֔ם כֹּֽה־אָמַ֥ר יְהֹוָ֖ה אֱלֹהֵ֣י יִשְׂרָאֵ֑ל אִמְר֣וּ לָאִ֔ישׁ אֲשֶׁר־שָׁלַ֥ח אֶתְכֶ֖ם אֵלָֽי׃ 16 כֹּ֚ה אָמַ֣ר יְהֹוָ֔ה הִנְנִ֨י מֵבִ֥יא רָעָ֛ה אֶל־הַמָּק֥וֹם הַזֶּ֖ה וְעַל־יֹשְׁבָ֑יו אֵ֚ת כׇּל־דִּבְרֵ֣י הַסֵּ֔פֶר אֲשֶׁ֥ר קָרָ֖א מֶ֥לֶךְ יְהוּדָֽה׃ 17 תַּ֗חַת ׀ אֲשֶׁ֤ר עֲזָב֙וּנִי֙ וַֽיְקַטְּרוּ֙ לֵאלֹהִ֣ים אֲחֵרִ֔ים לְמַ֙עַן֙ הַכְעִיסֵ֔נִי בְּכֹ֖ל מַעֲשֵׂ֣ה יְדֵיהֶ֑ם וְנִצְּתָ֧ה חֲמָתִ֛י בַּמָּק֥וֹם הַזֶּ֖ה וְלֹ֥א תִכְבֶּֽה׃ 18 וְאֶל־מֶ֣לֶךְ יְהוּדָ֗ה הַשֹּׁלֵ֤חַ אֶתְכֶם֙ לִדְרֹ֣שׁ אֶת־יְהֹוָ֔ה כֹּ֥ה תֹאמְר֖וּ אֵלָ֑יו כֹּֽה־אָמַ֤ר יְהֹוָה֙ אֱלֹהֵ֣י יִשְׂרָאֵ֔ל הַדְּבָרִ֖ים אֲשֶׁ֥ר שָׁמָֽעְתָּ׃ 19 יַ֠עַן רַךְ־לְבָֽבְךָ֞ וַתִּכָּנַ֣ע ׀ מִפְּנֵ֣י יְהֹוָ֗ה בְּשׇׁמְעֲךָ֡ אֲשֶׁ֣ר דִּבַּ֩רְתִּי֩ עַל־הַמָּק֨וֹם הַזֶּ֜ה וְעַל־יֹשְׁבָ֗יו לִהְי֤וֹת לְשַׁמָּה֙ וְלִקְלָלָ֔ה וַתִּקְרַע֙ אֶת־בְּגָדֶ֔יךָ וַתִּבְכֶּ֖ה לְפָנָ֑י וְגַ֧ם אָנֹכִ֛י שָׁמַ֖עְתִּי נְאֻם־יְהֹוָֽה׃ 20 לָכֵן֩ הִנְנִ֨י אֹֽסִפְךָ֜

gather you to your fathers and you will be laid in your tomb in peace. Your eyes shall not see all the disaster which I will bring upon this place." So they brought back the reply to the king.

23 At the king's summons, all the elders of Judah and Jerusalem assembled before him. [2]The king went up to the House of the Lord, together with all the men of Judah and all the inhabitants of Jerusalem, and the priests and prophets—all the people, young and old. And he read to them the entire text of the covenant scroll which had been found in the House of the Lord. [3]The king stood *a*-by the pillar-*a* and solemnized the covenant before the Lord: that they would follow the Lord and observe His commandments, His injunctions, and His laws with all their heart and soul; that they would fulfill all the terms of this covenant as inscribed upon the scroll. And all the people *b*-entered into-*b* the covenant.

[4]Then the king ordered the high priest Hilkiah, the priests of the second rank, and the guards of the threshold to bring out of the Temple of the Lord all the objects made for Baal and Asherah*c* and all the host of heaven. He burned them outside Jerusalem in the fields*d* of Kidron, and he removed the ashes to Bethel. [5]He suppressed the idolatrous priests whom the kings of Judah had appointed *e*-to make offerings-*e* at the shrines in the towns of Judah and in the environs of Jerusalem, and those who made offerings to Baal, to the sun and moon and constellations—all the host of heaven. [6]He brought out the [image of] Asherah from the House of the Lord to the Kidron Valley outside Jerusalem, and burned it in the Kidron Valley;

כג וַיִּשְׁלַ֣ח הַמֶּ֔לֶךְ וַיַּאַסְפ֣וּ אֵלָ֔יו כָּל־זִקְנֵ֥י יְהוּדָ֖ה וִירוּשָׁלָ֑͏ִם: 2 וַיַּ֣עַל הַמֶּ֣לֶךְ בֵּית־יְהֹוָ֡ה וְכָל־אִ֣ישׁ יְהוּדָה֩ וְכָל־יֹשְׁבֵ֨י יְרוּשָׁלַ֜͏ִם אִתּ֗וֹ וְהַכֹּֽהֲנִים֙ וְהַנְּבִיאִ֔ים וְכָל־הָעָ֖ם לְמִקָּטֹ֣ן וְעַד־גָּד֑וֹל וַיִּקְרָ֣א בְאָזְנֵיהֶ֗ם אֶת־כָּל־דִּבְרֵי֙ סֵ֣פֶר הַבְּרִ֔ית הַנִּמְצָ֖א בְּבֵ֥ית יְהֹוָֽה: 3 וַיַּעֲמֹ֣ד הַמֶּ֣לֶךְ עַל־הָֽעַמּ֗וּד וַיִּכְרֹ֣ת אֶֽת־הַבְּרִ֣ית | לִפְנֵ֣י יְהֹוָ֗ה לָלֶ֜כֶת אַחַ֤ר יְהֹוָה֙ וְלִשְׁמֹ֤ר מִצְוֺתָיו֙ וְאֶת־עֵֽדְוֺתָ֣יו וְאֶת־חֻקֹּתָ֔יו בְּכָל־לֵ֖ב וּבְכָל־נֶ֑פֶשׁ לְהָקִ֗ים אֶת־דִּבְרֵי֙ הַבְּרִ֣ית הַזֹּ֔את הַכְּתֻבִ֖ים עַל־הַסֵּ֣פֶר הַזֶּ֑ה וַיַּעֲמֹ֥ד כָּל־הָעָ֖ם בַּבְּרִֽית: 4 וַיְצַ֣ו הַמֶּ֡לֶךְ אֶת־חִלְקִיָּ֩הוּ֩ הַכֹּהֵ֨ן הַגָּד֜וֹל וְאֶת־כֹּֽהֲנֵ֣י הַמִּשְׁנֶה֮ וְאֶת־שֹׁמְרֵ֣י הַסַּף֒ לְהוֹצִ֣יא מֵהֵיכַ֣ל יְהֹוָ֗ה אֵ֣ת כָּל־הַכֵּלִים֙ הָעֲשׂוּיִם֙ לַבַּ֣עַל וְלָאֲשֵׁרָ֔ה וּלְכֹ֖ל צְבָ֣א הַשָּׁמָ֑יִם וַֽיִּשְׂרְפֵ֞ם מִח֤וּץ לִירוּשָׁלַ֙͏ִם֙ בְּשַׁדְמ֣וֹת קִדְר֔וֹן וְנָשָׂ֥א אֶת־עֲפָרָ֖ם בֵּֽית־אֵֽל: 5 וְהִשְׁבִּ֣ית אֶת־הַכְּמָרִ֗ים אֲשֶׁ֤ר נָֽתְנוּ֙ מַלְכֵ֣י יְהוּדָ֔ה וַיְקַטֵּ֤ר בַּבָּמוֹת֙ בְּעָרֵ֣י יְהוּדָ֔ה וּמְסִבֵּ֖י יְרוּשָׁלָ֑͏ִם וְאֶת־הַֽמְקַטְּרִ֣ים לַבַּ֗עַל לַשֶּׁ֤מֶשׁ וְלַיָּרֵ֙חַ֙ וְלַמַּזָּל֔וֹת וּלְכֹ֖ל צְבָ֥א הַשָּׁמָֽיִם: 6 וַיֹּצֵ֣א אֶת־הָאֲשֵׁרָ֩ה מִבֵּ֨ית יְהֹוָ֜ה

---

a-a   Or "on a platform," *cf.* Targum.
b-b   Cf. Targum.
c   For this goddess, cf. 1 Kings 18.19; ordinarily *asherah is rendered* "sacred post," e.g., 2 Kings 17.16.
d   *Meaning of Heb. uncertain.*
e-e   Lit. "and he offered."

he beat it to dust and scattered its dust over the burial ground of the common people. [7]He tore down the cubicles of the male prostitutes in the House of the LORD, at the place where the women wove coverings[d] for Asherah.

[8]He brought all the priests from the towns of Judah [to Jerusalem] and defiled the shrines where the priests had been making offerings— from Geba to Beer-sheba. He also demolished the shrines of the gates, which were at the entrance of the gate of Joshua, the city prefect— [d]-which were on a person's left [as he entered] the city gate.-[d] [9][f]-The priests of the shrines, however, did not ascend the altar of the LORD in Jerusalem, but they ate unleavened bread along with their kinsmen.-[f] [10]He also defiled Topheth, which is in the Valley of Ben-hinnom, so that no one might consign his son or daughter to the fire of Molech. [11]He did away with the horses that the kings of Judah had dedicated to the sun, [g]-at the entrance-[g] of the House of the LORD, near the chamber of the eunuch Nathanmelech, which was in the precincts.[d] He burned the chariots of the sun. [12]And the king tore down the altars made by the kings of Judah on the roof by the upper chamber of Ahaz, and the altars made by Manasseh in the two courts of the House of the LORD. He [h]-removed them quickly from there-[h] and scattered their rubble in the Kidron Valley. [13]The king also defiled the shrines facing Jerusalem, to the south of the [i]-Mount of the Destroyer,-[i] which King Solomon of Israel had built for Ashtoreth, the abomination of the Sidonians, for Chemosh, the abomination of Moab, and for Milcom, the detestable thing of the Ammonites.[j] [14]He shattered their pillars and cut down their sacred posts and covered their sites with human bones.

מִחוּץ לִירוּשָׁלִַם אֶל־נַחַל קִדְרוֹן וַיִּשְׂרֹף אֹתָהּ בְּנַחַל קִדְרוֹן וַיָּדֶק לְעָפָר וַיַּשְׁלֵךְ אֶת־עֲפָרָהּ עַל־קֶבֶר בְּנֵי הָעָם: [7] וַיִּתֹּץ אֶת־בָּתֵּי הַקְּדֵשִׁים אֲשֶׁר בְּבֵית יְהוָה אֲשֶׁר הַנָּשִׁים אֹרְגוֹת שָׁם בָּתִּים לָאֲשֵׁרָה: [8] וַיָּבֵא אֶת־כָּל־הַכֹּהֲנִים מֵעָרֵי יְהוּדָה וַיְטַמֵּא אֶת־הַבָּמוֹת אֲשֶׁר קִטְּרוּ־שָׁמָּה הַכֹּהֲנִים מִגֶּבַע עַד־בְּאֵר שָׁבַע וְנָתַץ אֶת־בָּמוֹת הַשְּׁעָרִים אֲשֶׁר־פֶּתַח שַׁעַר יְהוֹשֻׁעַ שַׂר־הָעִיר אֲשֶׁר־עַל־שְׂמֹאול* אִישׁ בְּשַׁעַר הָעִיר: [9] אַךְ לֹא יַעֲלוּ כֹּהֲנֵי הַבָּמוֹת אֶל־מִזְבַּח יְהוָה בִּירוּשָׁלִָם כִּי אִם־אָכְלוּ מַצּוֹת בְּתוֹךְ אֲחֵיהֶם: [10] וְטִמֵּא אֶת־הַתֹּפֶת אֲשֶׁר בְּגֵי בְנֵי־הִנֹּם לְבִלְתִּי לְהַעֲבִיר אִישׁ אֶת־בְּנוֹ וְאֶת־בִּתּוֹ בָּאֵשׁ לַמֹּלֶךְ: [11] וַיַּשְׁבֵּת אֶת־הַסּוּסִים אֲשֶׁר נָתְנוּ מַלְכֵי יְהוּדָה לַשֶּׁמֶשׁ מִבֹּא בֵית־יְהוָה אֶל־לִשְׁכַּת נְתַן־מֶלֶךְ הַסָּרִיס אֲשֶׁר בַּפַּרְוָרִים וְאֶת־מַרְכְּבוֹת הַשֶּׁמֶשׁ שָׂרַף בָּאֵשׁ: [12] וְאֶת־הַמִּזְבְּחוֹת אֲשֶׁר עַל־הַגָּג עֲלִיַּת אָחָז אֲשֶׁר־עָשׂוּ ׀ מַלְכֵי יְהוּדָה וְאֶת־הַמִּזְבְּחוֹת אֲשֶׁר־עָשָׂה מְנַשֶּׁה בִּשְׁתֵּי חַצְרוֹת בֵּית־יְהוָה נָתַץ הַמֶּלֶךְ וַיָּרָץ מִשָּׁם וְהִשְׁלִיךְ אֶת־עֲפָרָם אֶל־נַחַל קִדְרוֹן: [13] וְאֶת־הַבָּמוֹת אֲשֶׁר ׀ עַל־פְּנֵי יְרוּשָׁלִַם אֲשֶׁר מִימִין לְהַר־הַמַּשְׁחִית אֲשֶׁר בָּנָה שְׁלֹמֹה מֶלֶךְ־יִשְׂרָאֵל לְעַשְׁתֹּרֶת ׀ שִׁקֻּץ צִידֹנִים וְלִכְמוֹשׁ שִׁקֻּץ מוֹאָב וּלְמִלְכֹּם תּוֹעֲבַת בְּנֵי־עַמּוֹן טִמֵּא הַמֶּלֶךְ: [14] וְשִׁבַּר אֶת־הַמַּצֵּבוֹת וַיִּכְרֹת אֶת־הָאֲשֵׁרִים וַיְמַלֵּא אֶת־מְקוֹמָם עַצְמוֹת אָדָם:

מלא ו׳ v. 8.

---

f-f This verse may be understood in connection with vv. 21–23.
g-g Heb. "from entering."
h-h Heb. "ran from there." Emendation yields "smashed them there."
i-i Heb. har ha-mashhith: a derogatory play on har ha-mishhah ("Mount of Ointment"); Mishnah Middoth 2.4.
j Cf. 1 Kings 11.5, 7.

15As for the altar in Bethel [and] the shrine made by Jeroboam son of Nebat who caused Israel to sin—that altar, too, and the shrine as well, he tore down. He burned down the shrine and beat it to dust, and he burned the sacred post.

16Josiah turned and saw the graves that were there on the hill; and he had the bones taken out of the graves and burned on the altar. Thus he defiled it, in fulfillment of the word of the Lord foretold by the man of God who foretold these happenings. 17He asked, "What is the marker I see there?" And the men of the town replied, "That is the grave of the man of God who came from Judah and foretold these things that you have done to the altar of Bethel."k 18"Let him be," he said, "let no one disturb his bones." So they left his bones undisturbed together with the bones of the prophetl who came from Samaria.m

19Josiah also abolished all the cult places in the towns of Samaria, which the kings of Israel had built, vexing [the Lord]. He dealt with them just as he had done to Bethel: 20He slew on the altars all the priests of the shrines who were there, and he burned human bones on them. Then he returned to Jerusalem.

21The king commanded all the people, "Offer the passover sacrifice to the Lord your God as prescribed in this scroll of the covenant." 22Now the passover sacrifice had not been offered in that manner in the days of the chieftains who ruled Israel, or during the days of the kings of Israel and the kings of Judah. 23Only in the eighteenth year of King Josiah was such a passover sacrifice offered in that manner to the Lord in Jerusalem. 24Josiah also did away with n-the necromancers and the mediums,-n the idols and

15 וְגַ֣ם אֶת־הַמִּזְבֵּ֣חַ אֲשֶׁ֣ר בְּבֵֽית־אֵל֮ הַבָּמָה֒ אֲשֶׁ֨ר עָשָׂ֜ה יָרׇבְעָ֤ם בֶּן־נְבָט֙ אֲשֶׁ֣ר הֶחֱטִ֣יא אֶת־יִשְׂרָאֵ֔ל גַּ֣ם אֶת־הַמִּזְבֵּ֧חַ הַה֛וּא וְאֶת־הַבָּמָ֖ה נָתָ֑ץ וַיִּשְׂרֹ֧ף אֶת־הַבָּמָ֛ה הֵדַ֥ק לְעָפָ֖ר וְשָׂרַ֥ף אֲשֵׁרָֽה׃ 16 וַיִּ֣פֶן יֹֽאשִׁיָּ֗הוּ וַיַּ֨רְא אֶת־הַקְּבָרִ֤ים אֲשֶׁר־שָׁם֙ בָּהָ֔ר וַיִּשְׁלַ֗ח וַיִּקַּ֤ח אֶת־הָֽעֲצָמוֹת֙ מִן־הַקְּבָרִ֔ים וַיִּשְׂרֹ֖ף עַל־הַמִּזְבֵּ֑חַ וַֽיְטַמְּאֵ֔הוּ כִּדְבַ֣ר יְהֹוָ֗ה אֲשֶׁ֤ר קָרָא֙ אִ֣ישׁ הָֽאֱלֹהִ֔ים אֲשֶׁ֣ר קָרָ֔א אֶת־הַדְּבָרִ֖ים הָאֵֽלֶּה׃ 17 וַיֹּ֕אמֶר מָ֚ה הַצִּיּ֣וּן הַלָּ֔ז אֲשֶׁ֖ר אֲנִ֣י רֹאֶ֑ה וַיֹּאמְר֨וּ אֵלָ֜יו אַנְשֵׁ֣י הָעִ֗יר הַקֶּ֤בֶר אִישׁ־הָֽאֱלֹהִים֙ אֲשֶׁר־בָּ֣א מִֽיהוּדָ֔ה וַיִּקְרָ֗א אֶת־הַדְּבָרִ֤ים הָאֵ֙לֶּה֙ אֲשֶׁ֣ר עָשִׂ֔יתָ עַ֖ל הַמִּזְבַּ֥ח בֵּֽית־אֵֽל׃ 18 וַיֹּ֙אמֶר֙ הַנִּ֣יחוּ ל֔וֹ אִ֖ישׁ אַל־יָנַ֣ע עַצְמֹתָ֑יו וַֽיְמַלְּטוּ֙ עַצְמֹתָ֔יו אֵ֚ת עַצְמ֣וֹת הַנָּבִ֔יא אֲשֶׁר־בָּ֖א מִשֹּׁמְרֽוֹן׃

19 וְגַם֩ אֶת־כׇּל־בָּתֵּ֨י הַבָּמ֜וֹת אֲשֶׁ֣ר ׀ בְּעָרֵ֣י שֹֽׁמְר֗וֹן אֲשֶׁ֨ר עָשׂ֜וּ מַלְכֵ֤י יִשְׂרָאֵל֙ לְהַכְעִ֔יס הֵסִ֖יר יֹֽאשִׁיָּ֑הוּ וַיַּ֣עַשׂ לָהֶ֔ם כְּכׇל־הַֽמַּעֲשִׂ֔ים אֲשֶׁ֥ר עָשָׂ֖ה בְּבֵֽית־אֵֽל׃ 20 וַ֠יִּזְבַּ֠ח אֶת־כׇּל־כֹּהֲנֵ֨י הַבָּמ֤וֹת אֲשֶׁר־שָׁם֙ עַל־הַֽמִּזְבְּח֔וֹת וַיִּשְׂרֹ֛ף אֶת־עַצְמ֥וֹת אָדָ֖ם עֲלֵיהֶ֑ם וַיָּ֖שׇׁב יְרוּשָׁלָֽ͏ִם׃

21 וַיְצַ֤ו הַמֶּ֙לֶךְ֙ אֶת־כׇּל־הָעָ֣ם לֵאמֹ֔ר עֲשׂ֣וּ פֶ֔סַח לַֽיהֹוָ֖ה אֱלֹֽהֵיכֶ֑ם כַּכָּת֕וּב עַ֛ל סֵ֥פֶר הַבְּרִ֖ית הַזֶּֽה׃ 22 כִּ֣י לֹ֤א נַֽעֲשָׂה֙ כַּפֶּ֣סַח הַזֶּ֔ה מִימֵי֙ הַשֹּׁ֣פְטִ֔ים אֲשֶׁ֥ר שָׁפְט֖וּ אֶת־יִשְׂרָאֵ֑ל וְכֹ֗ל יְמֵ֛י מַלְכֵ֥י יִשְׂרָאֵ֖ל וּמַלְכֵ֥י יְהוּדָֽה׃ 23 כִּ֗י אִם־בִּשְׁמֹנֶ֤ה עֶשְׂרֵה֙ שָׁנָ֔ה לַמֶּ֖לֶךְ יֹֽאשִׁיָּ֑הוּ נַעֲשָׂ֞ה הַפֶּ֧סַח הַזֶּ֛ה לַיהֹוָ֖ה בִּירוּשָׁלָֽ͏ִם׃ 24 וְגַ֣ם אֶת־הָאֹב֣וֹת וְאֶת־הַ֠יִּדְּעֹנִ֠ים וְאֶת־הַתְּרָפִ֤ים וְאֶת־הַגִּלֻּלִים֙

---

k   *Cf. 1 Kings 13.2–3.*

l   *See 1 Kings 13.31–32 and note m below.*

m   *The prophet lived in Bethel, which, in Josiah's time, was part of the Assyrian province of Samaria.*

n-n   *Lit. "the ghosts and the familiar spirits."*

the fetishes—all the detestable things that were to be seen in the land of Judah and Jerusalem. Thus he fulfilled the terms of the Teaching recorded in the scroll that the priest Hilkiah had found in the House of the LORD. [25]There was no king like him before who turned back to the LORD with all his heart and soul and might, in full accord with the Teaching of Moses; nor did any like him arise after him.

[26]However, the LORD did not turn away from His awesome wrath which had blazed up against Judah because of all the things Manasseh did to vex Him. [27]The LORD said, "I will also banish Judah from My presence as I banished Israel; and I will reject the city of Jerusalem which I chose and the House where I said My name would abide."

[28]The other events of Josiah's reign, and all his actions, are recorded in the Annals of the Kings of Judah. [29]In his days, Pharaoh Neco, king of Egypt, marched against the king of Assyria[o] to the River Euphrates; King Josiah marched toward him, but when he confronted him at Megiddo, [Pharaoh Neco] slew him. [30]His servants conveyed his body in a chariot from Megiddo to Jerusalem, and they buried him in his tomb. Then the people of the land took Jehoahaz; they anointed him and made him king in place of his father.

[31]Jehoahaz was twenty-three years old when he became king, and he reigned three months in Jerusalem; his mother's name was Hamutal daughter of Jeremiah of Libnah. [32]He did what was displeasing to the LORD, just as his fathers had done. [33]Pharaoh Neco imprisoned him in Riblah in the region of Hamath, to keep him from reigning in Jerusalem. And he imposed on the land an indemnity of one hundred talents of silver and a talent of gold. [34]Then Pharaoh

---

o   *I.e., the Chaldean Empire; cf. Isa. 52.4 and note.*

וְאֵת כָּל־הַשִּׁקֻּצִים אֲשֶׁר נִרְאוּ בְּאֶרֶץ יְהוּדָה וּבִירוּשָׁלַ͏ִם בִּעֵר יֹאשִׁיָּהוּ לְמַעַן הָקִים אֶת־דִּבְרֵי הַתּוֹרָה הַכְּתֻבִים עַל־הַסֵּפֶר אֲשֶׁר מָצָא חִלְקִיָּהוּ הַכֹּהֵן בֵּית יְהוָה: [25] וְכָמֹהוּ לֹא־הָיָה לְפָנָיו מֶלֶךְ אֲשֶׁר־שָׁב אֶל־יְהוָה בְּכָל־לְבָבוֹ וּבְכָל־נַפְשׁוֹ וּבְכָל־מְאֹדוֹ כְּכֹל תּוֹרַת מֹשֶׁה וְאַחֲרָיו לֹא־קָם כָּמֹהוּ:

[26] אַךְ ׀ לֹא־שָׁב יְהוָה מֵחֲרוֹן אַפּוֹ הַגָּדוֹל אֲשֶׁר־חָרָה אַפּוֹ בִּיהוּדָה עַל כָּל־הַכְּעָסִים אֲשֶׁר הִכְעִיסוֹ מְנַשֶּׁה: [27] וַיֹּאמֶר יְהוָה גַּם אֶת־יְהוּדָה אָסִיר מֵעַל פָּנַי כַּאֲשֶׁר הֲסִרֹתִי אֶת־יִשְׂרָאֵל וּמָאַסְתִּי אֶת־הָעִיר הַזֹּאת אֲשֶׁר־בָּחַרְתִּי אֶת־יְרוּשָׁלַ͏ִם וְאֶת־הַבַּיִת אֲשֶׁר אָמַרְתִּי יִהְיֶה שְׁמִי שָׁם:

[28] וְיֶתֶר דִּבְרֵי יֹאשִׁיָּהוּ וְכָל־אֲשֶׁר עָשָׂה הֲלֹא־הֵם כְּתוּבִים עַל־סֵפֶר דִּבְרֵי הַיָּמִים לְמַלְכֵי יְהוּדָה: [29] בְּיָמָיו עָלָה פַרְעֹה נְכֹה מֶלֶךְ־מִצְרַיִם עַל־מֶלֶךְ אַשּׁוּר עַל־נְהַר־פְּרָת וַיֵּלֶךְ הַמֶּלֶךְ יֹאשִׁיָּהוּ לִקְרָאתוֹ וַיְמִיתֵהוּ בִּמְגִדּוֹ כִּרְאֹתוֹ אֹתוֹ: [30] וַיַּרְכִּבֻהוּ עֲבָדָיו מֵת מִמְּגִדּוֹ וַיְבִאֻהוּ יְרוּשָׁלַ͏ִם וַיִּקְבְּרֻהוּ בִּקְבֻרָתוֹ וַיִּקַּח עַם־הָאָרֶץ אֶת־יְהוֹאָחָז בֶּן־יֹאשִׁיָּהוּ וַיִּמְשְׁחוּ אֹתוֹ וַיַּמְלִיכוּ אֹתוֹ תַּחַת אָבִיו: פ

[31] בֶּן־עֶשְׂרִים וְשָׁלֹשׁ שָׁנָה יְהוֹאָחָז בְּמָלְכוֹ וּשְׁלֹשָׁה חֳדָשִׁים מָלַךְ בִּירוּשָׁלָ͏ִם וְשֵׁם אִמּוֹ חֲמוּטַל בַּת־יִרְמְיָהוּ מִלִּבְנָה: [32] וַיַּעַשׂ הָרַע בְּעֵינֵי יְהוָה כְּכֹל אֲשֶׁר־עָשׂוּ אֲבֹתָיו: [33] וַיַּאַסְרֵהוּ פַרְעֹה נְכֹה בְרִבְלָה בְּאֶרֶץ חֲמָת בִּמְלֹךְ בִּירוּשָׁלָ͏ִם וַיִּתֶּן־עֹנֶשׁ עַל־הָאָרֶץ מֵאָה כִכַּר־כֶּסֶף וְכִכַּר זָהָב: [34] וַיַּמְלֵךְ פַּרְעֹה נְכֹה אֶת־אֶלְיָקִים בֶּן־

Neco appointed Eliakim son of Josiah king in place of his father Josiah, changing his name to Jehoiakim. He took Jehoahaz and *P-brought him-P* to Egypt, where he died. 35Jehoiakim gave Pharaoh the silver and the gold, and he made an assessment on the land to pay the money demanded by Pharaoh. He exacted from the people of the land the silver and gold to be paid Pharaoh Neco, according to each man's assessment.

36Jehoiakim was twenty-five years old when he became king, and he reigned eleven years in Jerusalem; his mother's name was Zebudah daughter of Pedaiah of Rumah. 37He did what was displeasing to the LORD, just as his ancestors had done.

24

In his days, King Nebuchadnezzar of Babylon came up, and Jehoiakim became his vassal for three years. Then he turned and rebelled against him. 2The LORD let loose against him the raiding bands of the Chaldeans, Arameans, Moabites, and Ammonites; He let them loose against Judah to destroy it, in accordance with the word that the LORD had spoken through His servants the prophets. 3All this befell Judah at the command of the LORD, who banished [them] from His presence because of all the sins that Manasseh had committed, 4and also because of the blood of the innocent that he shed. For he filled Jerusalem with the blood of the innocent, and the LORD would not forgive.

5The other events of Jehoiakim's reign, and all of his actions, are recorded in the Annals of the Kings of Judah. 6Jehoiakim slept with his fathers, and his son Jehoiachin succeeded him as king. 7The king of Egypt did not venture out of his country again, for the king of Babylon

יֹֽאשִׁיָּ֙הוּ֙ תַּ֣חַת יֹֽאשִׁיָּ֣הוּ אָבִ֔יו וַיַּסֵּ֖ב אֶת־שְׁמ֣וֹ יְהוֹיָקִ֑ים וְאֶת־יְהוֹאָחָ֣ז לָקָ֔ח וַיָּבֹ֥א מִצְרַ֖יִם וַיָּ֥מָת שָֽׁם׃ 35 וְהַכֶּ֣סֶף וְהַזָּהָ֗ב נָתַ֤ן יְהוֹיָקִים֙ לְפַרְעֹ֔ה אַ֚ךְ הֶעֱרִ֣יךְ אֶת־הָאָ֔רֶץ לָתֵ֥ת אֶת־הַכֶּ֖סֶף עַל־פִּ֣י פַרְעֹ֑ה אִ֣ישׁ כְּעֶרְכּ֗וֹ נָגַ֞שׂ אֶת־הַכֶּ֤סֶף וְאֶת־הַזָּהָב֙ אֶת־עַ֣ם הָאָ֔רֶץ לָתֵ֖ת לְפַרְעֹ֥ה נְכֹֽה׃ ס 36 בֶּן־עֶשְׂרִ֨ים וְחָמֵ֤שׁ שָׁנָה֙ יְהוֹיָקִ֣ים בְּמָלְכ֔וֹ וְאַחַ֤ת עֶשְׂרֵה֙ שָׁנָ֔ה מָלַ֖ךְ בִּירוּשָׁלָ֑͏ִם וְשֵׁ֣ם אִמּ֗וֹ זבידה זְבוּדָּ֛ה בַת־פְּדָיָ֖ה מִן־רוּמָֽה׃ 37 וַיַּ֥עַשׂ הָרַ֖ע בְּעֵינֵ֣י יְהוָ֑ה כְּכֹ֥ל אֲשֶׁר־עָשׂ֖וּ אֲבֹתָֽיו׃

כד בְּיָמָ֣יו עָלָ֔ה נְבֻכַדְנֶאצַּ֖ר מֶ֣לֶךְ בָּבֶ֑ל וַיְהִי־ל֤וֹ יְהוֹיָקִים֙ עֶ֙בֶד֙ שָׁלֹ֣שׁ שָׁנִ֔ים וַיָּ֖שָׁב וַיִּמְרָד־בּֽוֹ׃ 2 וַיְשַׁלַּ֣ח יְהוָ֣ה ׀ בּ֡וֹ אֶת־גְּדוּדֵ֣י כַשְׂדִּים֩ וְאֶת־גְּדוּדֵ֨י אֲרָ֜ם וְאֵ֣ת ׀ גְּדוּדֵ֣י מוֹאָ֗ב וְאֵת֙ גְּדוּדֵ֣י בְנֵֽי־עַמּ֔וֹן וַיְשַׁלְּחֵ֥ם בִּֽיהוּדָ֖ה לְהַֽאֲבִיד֑וֹ כִּדְבַ֣ר יְהוָ֔ה אֲשֶׁ֣ר דִּבֶּ֔ר בְּיַ֖ד עֲבָדָ֥יו הַנְּבִיאִֽים׃ 3 אַ֣ךְ ׀ עַל־פִּ֣י יְהוָ֗ה הָֽיְתָה֙ בִּֽיהוּדָ֔ה לְהָסִ֖יר מֵעַ֣ל פָּנָ֑יו בְּחַטֹּ֣אות מְנַשֶּׁ֔ה כְּכֹ֖ל אֲשֶׁ֥ר עָשָֽׂה׃ 4 וְגַ֤ם דַּֽם־הַנָּקִי֙ אֲשֶׁ֣ר שָׁפָ֔ךְ וַיְמַלֵּ֥א אֶת־יְרוּשָׁלַ֖͏ִם דָּ֣ם נָקִ֑י וְלֹֽא־אָבָ֥ה יְהוָ֖ה לִסְלֹֽחַ׃ 5 וְיֶ֛תֶר דִּבְרֵ֥י יְהוֹיָקִ֖ים וְכָל־אֲשֶׁ֣ר עָשָׂ֑ה הֲלֹא־הֵ֣ם כְּתוּבִ֗ים עַל־סֵ֛פֶר דִּבְרֵ֥י הַיָּמִ֖ים לְמַלְכֵ֥י יְהוּדָֽה׃ 6 וַיִּשְׁכַּ֤ב יְהוֹיָקִים֙ עִם־אֲבֹתָ֔יו וַיִּמְלֹ֛ךְ יְהוֹיָכִ֥ין בְּנ֖וֹ תַּחְתָּֽיו׃ 7 וְלֹֽא־הֹסִ֥יף עוֹד֙ מֶ֣לֶךְ מִצְרַ֔יִם לָצֵ֖את מֵֽאַרְצ֑וֹ

---

p-p So 2 Chron. 36.4; Heb. here "he came."

had seized all the land that had belonged to the king of Egypt, from the Wadi of Egypt to the River Euphrates.

⁸Jehoiachin was eighteen years old when he became king, and he reigned three months in Jerusalem; his mother's name was Nehushta daughter of Elnathan of Jerusalem. ⁹He did what was displeasing to the LORD, just as his father had done. ¹⁰At that time, the troops[a] of King Nebuchadnezzar of Babylon marched against Jerusalem, and the city came under siege. ¹¹King Nebuchadnezzar of Babylon advanced against the city while his troops were besieging it. ¹²Thereupon King Jehoiachin of Judah, along with his mother, and his courtiers, commanders, and officers, surrendered to the king of Babylon. The king of Babylon took him captive in the eighth year of his reign. ¹³He carried off [b]-from Jerusalem-[b] all the treasures of the House of the LORD and the treasures of the royal palace; he stripped off all the golden decorations in the Temple of the LORD—which King Solomon of Israel had made—as the LORD had warned. ¹⁴He exiled all of Jerusalem: all the commanders and all the warriors—ten thousand exiles—as well as all the craftsmen and smiths; only the poorest people in the land were left. ¹⁵He deported Jehoiachin to Babylon; and the king's wives and officers and the notables of the land were brought as exiles from Jerusalem to Babylon. ¹⁶All the able men, to the number of seven thousand—all of them warriors, trained for battle—and a thousand craftsmen and smiths were brought to Babylon as exiles by the king of Babylon. ¹⁷And the king of Babylon appointed Mattaniah, Jehoiachin's[c] uncle, king in his place, changing his name to Zedekiah.

---

a Heb. "servants."
b-b Heb. "from there."
c Heb. "his."

כִּי־לָקַ֞ח מֶ֣לֶךְ בָּבֶ֗ל מִנַּ֙חַל֙ מִצְרַ֔יִם עַד־
נְהַר־פְּרָ֔ת כֹּ֛ל אֲשֶׁ֥ר הָיְתָ֖ה לְמֶ֣לֶךְ
מִצְרָֽיִם: פ

⁸ בֶּן־שְׁמֹנֶ֨ה עֶשְׂרֵ֤ה שָׁנָה֙ יְהוֹיָכִ֣ין בְּמָלְכ֔וֹ
וּשְׁלֹשָׁ֣ה חֳדָשִׁ֔ים מָלַ֖ךְ בִּירוּשָׁלִָ֑ם וְשֵׁ֣ם
אִמּ֔וֹ נְחֻשְׁתָּ֥א בַת־אֶלְנָתָ֖ן מִירוּשָׁלָֽיִם:
⁹ וַיַּ֥עַשׂ הָרַ֖ע בְּעֵינֵ֣י יְהוָ֑ה כְּכֹ֥ל אֲשֶׁר־עָשָׂ֖ה
אָבִֽיו: ¹⁰ בָּעֵ֣ת הַהִ֔יא עלה עָל֗וּ עַבְדֵ֛י
נְבֻכַדְנֶאצַּ֥ר מֶֽלֶךְ־בָּבֶ֖ל יְרוּשָׁלִָ֑ם וַתָּבֹ֥א
הָעִ֖יר בַּמָּצֽוֹר: ¹¹ וַיָּבֹ֛א נְבוּכַדְנֶאצַּ֥ר מֶֽלֶךְ־
בָּבֶ֖ל עַל־הָעִ֑יר וַעֲבָדָ֖יו צָרִ֥ים עָלֶֽיהָ:
¹² וַיֵּצֵ֞א יְהוֹיָכִ֤ין מֶֽלֶךְ־יְהוּדָה֙ עַל־מֶ֣לֶךְ
בָּבֶ֔ל ה֣וּא וְאִמּ֔וֹ וַעֲבָדָ֖יו וְשָׂרָ֣יו וְסָרִיסָ֑יו
וַיִּקַּ֤ח אֹתוֹ֙ מֶ֣לֶךְ בָּבֶ֔ל בִּשְׁנַ֥ת שְׁמֹנֶ֖ה
לְמָלְכֽוֹ: ¹³ וַיּוֹצֵ֣א מִשָּׁ֗ם אֶת־כָּל־אוֹצְרוֹת֙
בֵּ֣ית יְהוָ֔ה וְאֽוֹצְר֖וֹת בֵּ֣ית הַמֶּ֑לֶךְ וַיְקַצֵּ֣ץ
אֶת־כָּל־כְּלֵ֣י הַזָּהָ֗ב אֲשֶׁ֨ר עָשָׂ֜ה שְׁלֹמֹ֣ה
מֶֽלֶךְ־יִשְׂרָאֵל֙ בְּהֵיכַ֣ל יְהוָ֔ה כַּאֲשֶׁ֖ר דִּבֶּ֥ר
יְהוָֽה: ¹⁴ וְהִגְלָ֣ה אֶת־כָּל־יְרוּשָׁלִַ֡ם וְאֶת־
כָּל־הַשָּׂרִים֩ וְאֵ֨ת ׀ כָּל־גִּבּוֹרֵ֣י הַחַ֗יִל עשרה
עֲשֶׂ֤רֶת אֲלָפִים֙ גּוֹלֶ֔ה וְכָל־הֶחָרָ֖שׁ וְהַמַּסְגֵּ֑ר
לֹ֣א נִשְׁאַ֔ר זוּלַ֖ת דַּלַּ֥ת עַם־הָאָֽרֶץ: ¹⁵ וַיֶּ֥גֶל
אֶת־יְהוֹיָכִ֖ין בָּבֶ֑לָה וְאֶת־אֵ֣ם הַמֶּ֡לֶךְ וְאֶת־
נְשֵׁ֣י הַמֶּלֶךְ֩ וְאֶת־סָרִיסָ֨יו וְאֵ֤ת אולי אֵילֵ֣י
הָאָ֔רֶץ הוֹלִ֛יךְ גּוֹלָ֥ה מִירוּשָׁלִַ֖ם בָּבֶֽלָה:
¹⁶ וְאֵת֩ כָּל־אַנְשֵׁ֨י הַחַ֜יִל שִׁבְעַ֣ת אֲלָפִ֗ים
וְהֶחָרָ֤שׁ וְהַמַּסְגֵּר֙ אֶ֔לֶף הַכֹּ֕ל גִּבּוֹרִ֖ים עֹשֵׂ֣י
מִלְחָמָ֑ה וַיְבִיאֵ֧ם מֶֽלֶךְ־בָּבֶ֛ל גּוֹלָ֖ה בָּבֶֽלָה:
¹⁷ וַיַּמְלֵ֧ךְ מֶֽלֶךְ־בָּבֶ֛ל אֶת־מַתַּנְיָ֥ה דֹד֖וֹ
תַּחְתָּ֑יו וַיַּסֵּ֥ב אֶת־שְׁמ֖וֹ צִדְקִיָּֽהוּ: פ

18dZedekiah was twenty-one years old when he became king, and he reigned eleven years in Jerusalem; his mother's name was Hamutal daughter of Jeremiah of Libnah. 19He did what was displeasing to the LORD, just as Jehoiakim had done. 20Indeed, Jerusalem and Judah e-were a cause of anger for the LORD, so that-e He cast them out of His presence.

25 Zedekiah rebelled against the king of Babylon. 1And in the ninth year of hisa reign, on the tenth day of the tenth month, Nebuchadnezzar moved against Jerusalem with his whole army. He besieged it; and they built towers against it all around. 2The city continued in a state of siege until the eleventh year of King Zedekiah. 3By the ninth day [of the fourth month]b the famine had become acute in the city; there was no food left for the common people.

4Then [the wall of] the city was breached. All the soldiers [left the city] by night through the gate between the double walls, which is near the king's garden—the Chaldeans were all around the city; and [the king] set out for the Arabah.c 5But the Chaldean troops pursued the king, and they overtook him in the steppes of Jericho as his entire force left him and scattered. 6They captured the king and brought him before the king of Babylon at Riblah; and they put him on trial. 7They slaughtered Zedekiah's sons before his eyes; then Zedekiah's eyes were put out. He was chained in bronze fetters and he was brought to Babylon.

8On the seventh day of the fifth month—that was the nineteenth year of King Nebuchadnezzar of Babylon—Nebuzaradan, the chief of the guards, an officer of the king of Babylon, came to Jerusalem. 9He burned the House of the

יח בֶּן־עֶשְׂרִ֨ים וְאַחַ֤ת שָׁנָה֙ צִדְקִיָּ֣הוּ בְמָלְכ֔וֹ וְאַחַ֤ת עֶשְׂרֵה֙ שָׁנָ֔ה מָלַ֖ךְ בִּירוּשָׁלִָ֑ם וְשֵׁ֣ם אִמּ֔וֹ חֲמוּטַ֥ל בַּת־יִרְמְיָ֖הוּ מִלִּבְנָֽה׃ יט וַיַּ֥עַשׂ הָרַ֖ע בְּעֵינֵ֣י יְהֹוָ֑ה כְּכֹ֥ל אֲשֶׁר־עָשָׂ֖ה יְהוֹיָקִֽים׃ כ כִּ֣י ׀ עַל־אַ֣ף יְהֹוָ֗ה הָֽיְתָה֙ בִּירֽוּשָׁלִַ֙ם֙ וּבִ֣יהוּדָ֔ה עַד־הִשְׁלִכ֥וֹ אֹתָ֖ם מֵעַ֥ל פָּנָֽיו׃

כה וַיִּמְרֹ֥ד צִדְקִיָּ֖הוּ בְּמֶ֥לֶךְ בָּבֶֽל׃ ס א וַיְהִי֩ בִשְׁנַ֨ת הַתְּשִׁיעִ֜ית לְמׇלְכ֗וֹ בַּחֹ֤דֶשׁ הָעֲשִׂירִי֙ בֶּעָשׂ֣וֹר לַחֹ֔דֶשׁ בָּ֠א נְבֻכַדְנֶאצַּ֨ר מֶֽלֶךְ־בָּבֶ֜ל ה֧וּא וְכׇל־חֵיל֛וֹ עַל־יְרוּשָׁלַ֖͏ִם וַיִּ֣חַן עָלֶ֑יהָ וַיִּבְנ֥וּ עָלֶ֛יהָ דָּיֵ֖ק סָבִֽיב׃ ב וַתָּבֹ֥א הָעִ֖יר בַּמָּצ֑וֹר עַ֚ד עַשְׁתֵּ֣י עֶשְׂרֵ֣ה שָׁנָ֔ה לַמֶּ֖לֶךְ צִדְקִיָּֽהוּ׃ ג בְּתִשְׁעָ֣ה לַחֹ֔דֶשׁ וַיֶּחֱזַ֥ק הָרָעָ֖ב בָּעִ֑יר וְלֹא־הָ֥יָה לֶ֖חֶם לְעַ֥ם הָאָֽרֶץ׃ ד וַתִּבָּקַ֣ע הָעִ֗יר וְכׇל־אַנְשֵׁ֨י הַמִּלְחָמָ֣ה ׀ הַלַּ֜יְלָה דֶּ֣רֶךְ שַׁ֗עַר ׀ בֵּ֤ין הַחֹמֹתַ֙יִם֙ אֲשֶׁר֙ עַל־גַּ֣ן הַמֶּ֔לֶךְ וְכַשְׂדִּ֥ים עַל־הָעִ֖יר סָבִ֑יב וַיֵּ֖לֶךְ דֶּ֥רֶךְ הָעֲרָבָֽה׃ ה וַיִּרְדְּפ֤וּ חֵיל־כַּשְׂדִּים֙ אַחַ֣ר הַמֶּ֔לֶךְ וַיַּשִּׂ֥גוּ אֹת֖וֹ בְּעַרְב֣וֹת יְרֵח֑וֹ וְכׇל־חֵיל֔וֹ נָפֹ֖צוּ מֵעָלָֽיו׃ ו וַֽיִּתְפְּשׂוּ֙ אֶת־הַמֶּ֔לֶךְ וַיַּעֲל֥וּ אֹת֛וֹ אֶל־מֶ֥לֶךְ בָּבֶ֖ל רִבְלָ֑תָה וַיְדַבְּר֥וּ אִתּ֖וֹ מִשְׁפָּֽט׃ ז וְאֶת־בְּנֵי֙ צִדְקִיָּ֔הוּ שָׁחֲט֖וּ לְעֵינָ֑יו וְאֶת־עֵינֵ֤י צִדְקִיָּ֙הוּ֙ עִוֵּ֔ר וַיַּאַסְרֵ֙הוּ֙ בַֽנְחֻשְׁתַּ֔יִם וַיְבִאֵ֖הוּ בָּבֶֽל׃ ס ח וּבַחֹ֤דֶשׁ הַחֲמִישִׁי֙ בְּשִׁבְעָ֣ה לַחֹ֔דֶשׁ הִ֗יא שְׁנַת֙ תְּשַֽׁע־עֶשְׂרֵ֣ה שָׁנָ֔ה לַמֶּ֖לֶךְ נְבֻכַדְנֶאצַּ֣ר מֶֽלֶךְ־בָּבֶ֑ל בָּ֞א נְבוּזַרְאֲדָ֧ן רַב־טַבָּחִ֛ים עֶ֥בֶד מֶֽלֶךְ־בָּבֶ֖ל יְרוּשָׁלָֽͅם׃ ט וַיִּשְׂרֹ֥ף אֶת־בֵּית־יְהֹוָ֖ה וְאֶת־בֵּ֣ית הַמֶּ֑לֶךְ וְאֵ֧ת כׇּל־בָּתֵּ֣י

d For the rest of this book cf. Jer. 39 and 52.
e-e Meaning of Heb. uncertain.

a I.e., Zedekiah's.
b Cf. Jer. 52.6.
c Hoping to escape across the Jordan.

839

LORD, the king's palace, and all the houses of Jerusalem; he burned down *d*-the house of every notable person.-*d* 10The entire Chaldean force that was with the chief of the guard tore down the walls of Jerusalem on every side. 11The remnant of the people that was left in the city, the defectors who had gone over to the king of Babylon—and the remnant of the population—were taken into exile by Nebuzaradan, the chief of the guards. 12But some of the poorest in the land were left by the chief of the guards, to be vinedressers and field hands.

13The Chaldeans broke up the bronze columns of the House of the LORD, the stands, and the bronze tank that was in the House of the LORD; and they carried the bronze away to Babylon. 14They also took all the pails, scrapers, snuffers, ladles, and all the other bronze vessels used in the service. 15The chief of the guards took whatever was of gold and whatever was of silver: firepans and sprinkling bowls. 16The two columns, the one tank, and the stands that Solomon provided for the House of the LORD—all these objects contained bronze beyond weighing. 17The one column was eighteen cubits high. It had a bronze capital above it; the height of the capital was three cubits, and there was a meshwork [decorated] with pomegranates about the capital, all made of bronze. And the like was true of the other column with its meshwork.

18The chief of the guards also took Seraiah, the chief priest, Zephaniah, the deputy priest, and the three guardians of the threshold. 19And from the city he took a eunuch who was in command of the soldiers; five royal privy councillors who were present in the city; the scribe of the army commander, who was in charge of mustering the people of the land; and sixty of the

יְרוּשָׁלַ֖͏ִם וְאֶת־כָּל־בֵּ֣ית גָּד֑וֹל שָׂרַ֥ף בָּאֵֽשׁ׃ 10 וְאֶת־חוֹמֹ֥ת יְרוּשָׁלַ֖͏ִם סָבִ֑יב נָֽתְצוּ֙ כָּל־חֵ֣יל כַּשְׂדִּ֔ים אֲשֶׁ֖ר רַב־טַבָּחִֽים׃ 11 וְאֵת֩ יֶ֨תֶר הָעָ֜ם הַנִּשְׁאָרִ֣ים בָּעִ֗יר וְאֶת־הַנֹּֽפְלִים֙ אֲשֶׁ֤ר נָֽפְלוּ֙ עַל־הַמֶּ֣לֶךְ בָּבֶ֔ל וְאֵ֖ת יֶ֣תֶר הֶהָמ֑וֹן הֶגְלָ֕ה נְבֽוּזַרְאֲדָ֖ן רַב־טַבָּחִֽים׃ 12 וּמִדַּלַּ֣ת הָאָ֔רֶץ הִשְׁאִ֖יר רַב־טַבָּחִ֑ים לְכֹֽרְמִ֖ים וּלְיֹֽגְבִֽים׃

13 וְאֶת־עַמּוּדֵ֣י הַנְּחֹ֜שֶׁת אֲשֶׁ֣ר בֵּֽית־יְהֹוָ֗ה וְאֶת־הַמְּכֹנ֞וֹת וְאֶת־יָ֧ם הַנְּחֹ֛שֶׁת אֲשֶׁ֥ר בְּבֵית־יְהֹוָ֖ה שִׁבְּר֣וּ כַשְׂדִּ֑ים וַיִּשְׂא֥וּ אֶת־נְחֻשְׁתָּ֖ם בָּבֶֽלָה׃ 14 וְאֶת־הַסִּירֹ֨ת וְאֶת־הַיָּעִ֜ים וְאֶת־הַֽמְזַמְּר֣וֹת וְאֶת־הַכַּפּ֗וֹת וְאֵ֨ת כָּל־כְּלֵ֧י הַנְּחֹ֛שֶׁת אֲשֶׁ֥ר יְשָֽׁרְתוּ־בָ֖ם לָקָֽחוּ׃ 15 וְאֶת־הַמַּחְתּ֣וֹת וְאֶת־הַמִּזְרָק֗וֹת אֲשֶׁ֤ר זָהָב֙ זָהָ֔ב וַאֲשֶׁר־כֶּ֣סֶף כֶּ֔סֶף לָקַ֖ח רַב־טַבָּחִֽים׃ 16 הָעַמּוּדִ֣ים ׀ שְׁנַ֗יִם הַיָּ֤ם הָֽאֶחָד֙ וְהַמְּכֹנ֔וֹת אֲשֶׁר־עָשָׂ֥ה שְׁלֹמֹ֖ה לְבֵ֣ית יְהֹוָ֑ה לֹא־הָיָ֣ה מִשְׁקָ֔ל לִנְחֹ֖שֶׁת כָּל־הַכֵּלִ֥ים הָאֵֽלֶּה׃ 17 שְׁמֹנֶ֨ה עֶשְׂרֵ֜ה אַמָּ֣ה קוֹמַ֣ת ׀ הָעַמּ֣וּד הָֽאֶחָ֗ד וְכֹתֶ֨רֶת עָלָ֥יו ׀ נְחֹ֘שֶׁת֮ וְקוֹמַ֣ת הַכֹּתֶ֣רֶת שָׁלֹשׁ֒ אמה אַמּוֹת֙ וּשְׂבָכָ֤ה וְרִמֹּנִ֨ים עַל־הַכֹּתֶ֧רֶת סָבִ֛יב הַכֹּ֖ל נְחֹ֑שֶׁת וְכָאֵ֛לֶּה לָעַמּ֥וּד הַשֵּׁנִ֖י עַל־הַשְּׂבָכָֽה׃

18 וַיִּקַּ֣ח רַב־טַבָּחִ֗ים אֶת־שְׂרָיָה֙ כֹּהֵ֣ן הָרֹ֔אשׁ וְאֶת־צְפַנְיָ֖הוּ כֹּהֵ֣ן מִשְׁנֶ֑ה וְאֶת־שְׁלֹ֖שֶׁת שֹׁמְרֵ֥י הַסַּֽף׃ 19 וּמִן־הָעִ֡יר לָקַח֩ סָרִ֨יס אֶחָ֜ד אֲֽשֶׁר־ה֥וּא פָקִ֣יד ׀ עַל־אַנְשֵׁ֣י הַמִּלְחָמָ֗ה וַחֲמִשָּׁ֨ה אֲנָשִׁ֜ים מֵרֹאֵ֤י פְנֵֽי־הַמֶּ֙לֶךְ֙ אֲשֶׁ֣ר נִמְצְא֣וּ בָעִ֔יר וְאֵ֗ת הַסֹּפֵר֙ שַׂ֣ר הַצָּבָ֔א הַמַּצְבִּ֖א אֶת־עַ֣ם הָאָ֑רֶץ וְשִׁשִּׁ֥ים

---

d-d *Meaning of Heb. uncertain.*

common people who were inside the city.
²⁰Nebuzaradan, the chief of the guards, took
them and brought them to the king of Babylon
at Riblah. ²¹The king of Babylon had them
struck down and put to death at Riblah, in the
region of Hamath.

Thus Judah was exiled from its land. ²²King
Nebuchadnezzar of Babylon put Gedaliah son
of Ahikam son of Shaphan in charge of the people whom he left in the land of Judah. ²³When
the officers of the troops and their men heard
that the king of Babylon had put Gedaliah in
charge, they came to Gedaliah at Mizpah with
Ishmael son of Nethaniah, Johanan son of
Kareah, Seraiah son of Tanhumeth the Netophathite, and Jaazaniah son of the Maachite, together with their men. ²⁴Gedaliah reassured*
them and their men, saying, "Do not be afraid
ᶠof the servants of the Chaldeans.ᶠ Stay in the
land and serve the king of Babylon, and it will
go well with you."

²⁵In the seventh month, Ishmael son of
Nethaniah son of Elishama, who was of royal
descent, came with ten men, and they struck
down Gedaliah and he died; [they also killed]
the Judeans and the Chaldeans who were present with him at Mizpah. ²⁶And all the people,
young and old, and the officers of the troops
set out and went to Egypt because they were
afraid of the Chaldeans.

²⁷In the thirty-seventh year of the exile
of King Jehoiachin of Judah, on the twenty-
seventh day of the twelfth month, King Evil-
merodach of Babylon, in the year he became
king, ᵍtook note ofᵍ King Jehoiachin of Judah
and released him from prison. ²⁸He spoke
kindly to him, and gave him a throne above
those of other kings who were with him in Babylon. ²⁹His prison garments were removed, and

אִ֣ישׁ מֵעַ֥ם הָאָ֖רֶץ הַֽנִּמְצָאִ֥ים בָּעִֽיר׃
²⁰ וַיִּקַּ֣ח אֹתָ֗ם נְבוּזַרְאֲדָ֛ן רַב־טַבָּחִ֖ים וַיֹּ֥לֶךְ
אֹתָ֛ם עַל־מֶ֥לֶךְ בָּבֶ֖ל רִבְלָֽתָה׃ ²¹ וַיַּ֣ךְ
אֹתָם֩ מֶ֨לֶךְ בָּבֶ֤ל וַיְמִיתֵם֙ בְּרִבְלָ֣ה בְּאֶ֣רֶץ
חֲמָ֑ת

וַיִּ֥גֶל יְהוּדָ֖ה מֵעַ֥ל אַדְמָתֽוֹ׃ ²² וְהָעָ֗ם
הַנִּשְׁאָר֙ בְּאֶ֣רֶץ יְהוּדָ֔ה אֲשֶׁ֣ר הִשְׁאִ֔יר
נְבֽוּכַדְנֶאצַּ֖ר מֶ֣לֶךְ בָּבֶ֑ל וַיַּפְקֵ֣ד עֲלֵיהֶ֗ם
אֶת־גְּדַלְיָ֖הוּ בֶּן־אֲחִיקָ֥ם בֶּן־שָׁפָֽן׃ פ
²³ וַיִּשְׁמְע֣וּ כָל־שָׂרֵ֣י הַחֲיָלִים֮ הֵ֣מָּה
וְהָאֲנָשִׁים֒ כִּֽי־הִפְקִ֞יד מֶֽלֶךְ־בָּבֶל֮ אֶת־
גְּדַלְיָהוּ֒ וַיָּבֹ֣אוּ אֶל־גְּדַלְיָ֖הוּ הַמִּצְפָּ֑ה
וְיִשְׁמָעֵ֣אל בֶּן־נְתַנְיָ֡ה וְיוֹחָנָ֣ן בֶּן־קָרֵ֡חַ
וּשְׂרָיָ֣ה בֶן־תַּנְחֻ֩מֶת֩ הַנְּטֹֽפָתִ֨י וְיַאֲזַנְיָ֜הוּ
בֶּן־הַמַּֽעֲכָתִ֗י הֵ֖מָּה וְאַנְשֵׁיהֶֽם׃ ²⁴ וַיִּשָּׁבַ֨ע
לָהֶ֤ם גְּדַלְיָ֙הוּ֙ וּלְאַנְשֵׁיהֶ֔ם וַיֹּ֣אמֶר לָהֶ֗ם
אַל־תִּֽירְאוּ֙ מֵעַבְדֵ֣י הַכַּשְׂדִּ֔ים שְׁב֣וּ בָאָ֗רֶץ
וְעִבְד֛וּ אֶת־מֶ֥לֶךְ בָּבֶ֖ל וְיִטַ֥ב לָכֶֽם׃ ס
²⁵ וַיְהִ֣י ׀ בַּחֹ֣דֶשׁ הַשְּׁבִיעִ֗י בָּ֣א יִשְׁמָעֵ֣אל
בֶּן־נְתַנְיָ֣ה בֶן־אֱלִֽישָׁמָ֗ע מִזֶּ֣רַע הַמְּלוּכָ֡ה
וַעֲשָׂרָ֨ה אֲנָשִׁ֤ים אִתּוֹ֙ וַיַּכּ֣וּ אֶת־גְּדַלְיָ֖הוּ
וַיָּמֹ֑ת וְאֶת־הַיְּהוּדִים֙ וְאֶת־הַכַּשְׂדִּ֔ים
אֲשֶׁר־הָי֥וּ אִתּ֖וֹ בַּמִּצְפָּֽה׃ ²⁶ וַיָּקֻ֨מוּ כָל־
הָעָ֜ם מִקָּטֹ֤ן וְעַד־גָּדוֹל֙ וְשָׂרֵ֣י הַחֲיָלִ֔ים
וַיָּבֹ֖אוּ מִצְרָ֑יִם כִּ֥י יָרְא֖וּ מִפְּנֵ֥י כַשְׂדִּֽים׃ פ

²⁷ וַיְהִי֩ בִשְׁלֹשִׁ֨ים וָשֶׁ֜בַע שָׁנָ֗ה לְגָלוּת֙
יְהוֹיָכִ֣ין מֶֽלֶךְ־יְהוּדָ֔ה בִּשְׁנֵ֤ים עָשָׂר֙ חֹ֔דֶשׁ
בְּעֶשְׂרִ֥ים וְשִׁבְעָ֖ה לַחֹ֑דֶשׁ נָשָׂ֡א אֱוִ֣יל מְרֹדַ֣ךְ
מֶ֩לֶךְ֩ בָּבֶ֨ל בִּשְׁנַ֤ת מָלְכוֹ֙ אֶת־רֹ֙אשׁ֙ יְהוֹיָכִ֣ין
מֶֽלֶךְ־יְהוּדָ֔ה מִבֵּ֖ית כֶּֽלֶא׃ ²⁸ וַיְדַבֵּ֥ר אִתּ֖וֹ
טֹב֑וֹת וַיִּתֵּן֙ אֶת־כִּסְא֔וֹ מֵעַ֗ל כִּסֵּ֤א הַמְּלָכִים֙
אֲשֶׁ֥ר אִתּ֖וֹ בְּבָבֶֽל׃ ²⁹ וְשִׁנָּ֕א אֵ֖ת בִּגְדֵ֣י כִלְאֽוֹ

ᵉ Lit. "took an oath to them."
ᶠ⁻ᶠ Jer. 40.9 reads "to serve the Chaldeans."
ᵍ⁻ᵍ Lit. "raised the head of."

[Jehoiachin] received regular rations by his favor for the rest of his life. ³⁰A regular allotment
of food was given him at the instance of the
king—an allotment for each day—all the days
of his life.

וְאָכַל לֶחֶם תָּמִיד לְפָנָיו כָּל־יְמֵי חַיָּיו:
³⁰ וַאֲרֻחָתוֹ אֲרֻחַת תָּמִיד נִתְּנָה־לּוֹ מֵאֵת
הַמֶּלֶךְ דְּבַר־יוֹם בְּיוֹמוֹ כֹּל יְמֵי חַיָּיו:*

תם ונשלם תהילה לאל בורא עולם

v. 30.   סכום הפסוקים של ספר 1,536 (אף על פי שכתוב
1,534 בכתב היד שלנו) וחציו 22.6 בחלק הראשון

ISAIAH

1 The prophecies of Isaiah son of Amoz, who prophesied concerning Judah and Jerusalem in the reigns of Uzziah, Jotham, Ahaz, and Hezekiah, kings of Judah.

א חֲזוֹן יְשַׁעְיָהוּ בֶן־אָמוֹץ אֲשֶׁר חָזָה
עַל־יְהוּדָה וִירוּשָׁלֶָם בִּימֵי עֻזִּיָּהוּ יוֹתָם
אָחָז יְחִזְקִיָּהוּ מַלְכֵי יְהוּדָה׃

2Hear, O heavens, and give ear, O earth,
For the LORD has spoken:
"I reared children and brought them up—
And they have rebelled against Me!
3An ox knows its owner,
An ass its master's crib:
Israel does not know,
My people takes no thought."

2 שִׁמְעוּ שָׁמַיִם וְהַאֲזִינִי אֶרֶץ
כִּי יְהוָה דִּבֵּר
בָּנִים גִּדַּלְתִּי וְרוֹמַמְתִּי
וְהֵם פָּשְׁעוּ בִי׃
3 יָדַע שׁוֹר קֹנֵהוּ
וַחֲמוֹר אֵבוּס בְּעָלָיו
יִשְׂרָאֵל לֹא יָדַע
עַמִּי לֹא הִתְבּוֹנָן׃

4Ah, sinful nation!
People laden with iniquity!
Brood of evildoers!
Depraved children!
They have forsaken the LORD,
Spurned the Holy One of Israel,
Turned their backs [on Him].

4 הוֹי ׀ גּוֹי חֹטֵא
עַם כֶּבֶד עָוֹן
זֶרַע מְרֵעִים
בָּנִים מַשְׁחִיתִים
עָזְבוּ אֶת־יְהוָה
נִאֲצוּ אֶת־קְדוֹשׁ יִשְׂרָאֵל
נָזֹרוּ אָחוֹר׃

5Why do you seek further beatings,
That you continue to offend?
Every head is ailing,
And every heart is sick.
6From head to foot
No spot is sound:
All bruises, and welts,
And festering sores—
Not pressed out, not bound up,
Not softened with oil.

5 עַל מֶה תֻכּוּ עוֹד
תּוֹסִיפוּ סָרָה
כָּל־רֹאשׁ לָחֳלִי
וְכָל־לֵבָב דַּוָּי׃
6 מִכַּף־רֶגֶל וְעַד־רֹאשׁ
אֵין־בּוֹ מְתֹם
פֶּצַע וְחַבּוּרָה
וּמַכָּה טְרִיָּה
לֹא־זֹרוּ וְלֹא חֻבָּשׁוּ
וְלֹא רֻכְּכָה בַּשָּׁמֶן׃

7Your land is a waste,
Your cities burnt down;
Before your eyes, the yield of your soil
Is consumed by strangers—
A wasteland *a-as overthrown by strangers!-a*
8Fair*b* Zion is left
Like a booth in a vineyard,
Like a hut in a cucumber field,
Like a city beleaguered.
9Had not the LORD of Hosts
Left us some survivors,
We should be like Sodom,
Another Gomorrah.

10Hear the word of the LORD,
You chieftains of Sodom;
Give ear to our God's instruction,
You folk of Gomorrah!
11"What need have I of all your sacrifices?"
Says the LORD.
"I am sated with burnt offerings of rams,
And suet of fatlings,
And blood of bulls;
And I have no delight
In lambs and he-goats.
12That you come to appear before Me—
Who asked that *c-of you?*
Trample My courts
13no more;
Bringing oblations is futile,-*c*
Incense is offensive to Me.
New moon and sabbath,
Proclaiming of solemnities,
*d-*Assemblies with iniquity-*d*
I cannot abide.
14Your new moons and fixed seasons
Fill Me with loathing;

7 אַרְצְכֶ֣ם שְׁמָמָ֔ה
עָרֵיכֶ֖ם שְׂרֻפ֣וֹת אֵ֑שׁ
אַדְמַתְכֶ֗ם לְנֶגְדְּכֶם֙
זָרִים֙ אֹכְלִ֣ים אֹתָ֔הּ
וּשְׁמָמָ֖ה כְּמַהְפֵּכַ֥ת זָרִֽים׃
8 וְנוֹתְרָ֥ה בַת־צִיּ֖וֹן
כְּסֻכָּ֣ה בְכָ֑רֶם
כִּמְלוּנָ֥ה בְמִקְשָׁ֖ה
כְּעִ֥יר נְצוּרָֽה׃
9 לוּלֵי֙ יְהוָ֣ה צְבָא֔וֹת
הוֹתִ֥יר לָ֛נוּ שָׂרִ֖יד כִּמְעָ֑ט
כִּסְדֹ֣ם הָיִ֔ינוּ
לַעֲמֹרָ֖ה דָּמִֽינוּ׃ ס

10 שִׁמְע֥וּ דְבַר־יְהוָ֖ה
קְצִינֵ֣י סְדֹ֑ם
הַאֲזִ֛ינוּ תּוֹרַ֥ת אֱלֹהֵ֖ינוּ
עַ֥ם עֲמֹרָֽה׃
11 לָמָּה־לִּ֤י רֹב־זִבְחֵיכֶם֙
יֹאמַ֣ר* יְהוָ֔ה
שָׂבַ֛עְתִּי עֹל֥וֹת אֵילִ֖ים
וְחֵ֣לֶב מְרִיאִ֑ים
וְדַ֨ם פָּרִ֧ים
וּכְבָשִׂ֛ים וְעַתּוּדִ֖ים
לֹ֥א חָפָֽצְתִּי׃
12 כִּ֣י תָבֹ֔אוּ לֵרָא֣וֹת פָּנָ֑י
מִי־בִקֵּ֥שׁ זֹ֛את מִיֶּדְכֶ֖ם
רְמֹ֥ס חֲצֵרָֽי׃
13 לֹ֣א תוֹסִ֗יפוּ
הָבִיא֙ מִנְחַת־שָׁ֔וְא
קְטֹ֧רֶת תּוֹעֵבָ֛ה הִ֖יא לִ֑י
חֹ֤דֶשׁ וְשַׁבָּת֙
קְרֹ֣א מִקְרָ֔א
לֹא־אוּכַ֥ל
אָ֖וֶן וַעֲצָרָֽה׃
14 חָדְשֵׁיכֶ֤ם וּמוֹעֲדֵיכֶם֙
שָׂנְאָ֣ה נַפְשִׁ֔י

---

a-a Emendation yields "like Sodom overthrown."
b Lit. "Daughter."
c-c Others "To trample My courts? / 13Bring no more vain oblations."
d-d Septuagint "Fast and assembly"; cf. Joel 1.14.

v. 11. סבירין ומטעין "אמר"

They are become a burden to Me,
I cannot endure them.
¹⁵And when you lift up your hands,
I will turn My eyes away from you;
Though you pray at length,
I will not listen.
Your hands are stained with crime—
¹⁶Wash yourselves clean;
Put your evil doings
Away from My sight.
Cease to do evil;
¹⁷Learn to do good.
Devote yourselves to justice;
^e-Aid the wronged.-^e
Uphold the rights of the orphan;
Defend the cause of the widow.

¹⁸"Come, ^e-let us reach an understanding,-^e
     —says the Lord.
Be your sins like crimson,
They can turn snow-white;
Be they red as dyed wool,
They can become like fleece."
¹⁹If, then, you agree and give heed,
You will eat the good things of the earth;
²⁰But if you refuse and disobey,
^f-You will be devoured [by] the sword.-^f—
For it was the Lord who spoke.

²¹Alas, she has become a harlot,
The faithful city
That was filled with justice,
Where righteousness dwelt—
But now murderers.
²²Your^g silver has turned to dross;
^e-Your wine is cut with water.-^e
²³Your rulers are rogues

הָיוּ עָלַי לָטֹרַח
נִלְאֵיתִי נְשֹׂא:
15 וּבְפָרִשְׂכֶם כַּפֵּיכֶם
אַעְלִים עֵינַי מִכֶּם
גַּם כִּי־תַרְבּוּ תְפִלָּה
אֵינֶנִּי שֹׁמֵעַ
יְדֵיכֶם דָּמִים מָלֵאוּ:
16 רַחֲצוּ הִזַּכּוּ
הָסִירוּ רֹעַ מַעַלְלֵיכֶם
מִנֶּגֶד עֵינָי
חִדְלוּ הָרֵעַ:
17 לִמְדוּ הֵיטֵב
דִּרְשׁוּ מִשְׁפָּט
אַשְּׁרוּ חָמוֹץ
שִׁפְטוּ יָתוֹם
רִיבוּ אַלְמָנָה: ס

18 לְכוּ־נָא וְנִוָּכְחָה
יֹאמַר* יְהוָה
אִם־יִהְיוּ חֲטָאֵיכֶם כַּשָּׁנִים
כַּשֶּׁלֶג יַלְבִּינוּ
אִם־יַאְדִּימוּ כַתּוֹלָע
כַּצֶּמֶר יִהְיוּ:
19 אִם־תֹּאבוּ וּשְׁמַעְתֶּם
טוּב הָאָרֶץ תֹּאכֵלוּ:
20 וְאִם־תְּמָאֲנוּ וּמְרִיתֶם
חֶרֶב תְּאֻכְּלוּ
כִּי פִּי יְהוָה דִּבֵּר: ס

21 אֵיכָה הָיְתָה לְזוֹנָה
קִרְיָה נֶאֱמָנָה
מְלֵאֲתִי מִשְׁפָּט
צֶדֶק יָלִין בָּהּ
וְעַתָּה מְרַצְּחִים:
22 כַּסְפֵּךְ הָיָה לְסִיגִים
סָבְאֵךְ מָהוּל בַּמָּיִם:
23 שָׂרַיִךְ סוֹרְרִים

---

^{e-e} Meaning of Heb. uncertain.
^{f-f} Or "you will be fed the sword."
^g I.e., Jerusalem's.

And cronies of thieves,
Every one avid for presents
And greedy for gifts;
They do not judge the case of the orphan,
And the widow's cause never reaches them.

²⁴Assuredly, this is the declaration
Of the Sovereign, the LORD of Hosts,
The Mighty One of Israel:
"Ah, I will get satisfaction from My foes;
I will wreak vengeance on My enemies!
²⁵I will turn My hand against you,
And smelt out your dross ʰ-as with lye,-ʰ
And remove all your slag:
²⁶I will restore your magistrates as of old,
And your counselors as of yore.
After that you shall be called
City of Righteousness, Faithful City."

²⁷ⁱZion shall be saved in the judgment;
Her repentant ones, in the retribution.ʲ
²⁸But rebels and sinners shall all be crushed,
And those who forsake the LORD shall perish.

²⁹Truly, youᵏ shall be shamed
Because of the terebinths you desired,
And you shall be confounded
Because of the gardens you coveted.
³⁰For you shall be like a terebinth
Wilted of leaf,
And like a garden
That has no water,
³¹ˡ-Stored wealth-ˡ shall become as tow,
And he who amassed it a spark;
And the two shall burn together,
With none to quench.

וְחַבְרֵי גַּנָּבִים
כֻּלּוֹ אֹהֵב שֹׁחַד
וְרֹדֵף שַׁלְמֹנִים
יָתוֹם לֹא יִשְׁפֹּטוּ
וְרִיב אַלְמָנָה לֹא־יָבוֹא אֲלֵיהֶם: פ

24 לָכֵן נְאֻם
הָאָדוֹן יְהוָה צְבָאוֹת
אֲבִיר יִשְׂרָאֵל
הוֹי אֶנָּחֵם מִצָּרַי
וְאִנָּקְמָה מֵאוֹיְבָי:
25 וְאָשִׁיבָה יָדִי עָלַיִךְ
וְאֶצְרֹף כַּבֹּר סִיגָיִךְ
וְאָסִירָה כָּל־בְּדִילָיִךְ:
26 וְאָשִׁיבָה שֹׁפְטַיִךְ כְּבָרִאשֹׁנָה
וְיֹעֲצַיִךְ כְּבַתְּחִלָּה
אַחֲרֵי־כֵן יִקָּרֵא לָךְ
עִיר הַצֶּדֶק קִרְיָה נֶאֱמָנָה:

27 צִיּוֹן בְּמִשְׁפָּט תִּפָּדֶה
וְשָׁבֶיהָ בִּצְדָקָה:
28 וְשֶׁבֶר פֹּשְׁעִים וְחַטָּאִים יַחְדָּו
וְעֹזְבֵי יְהוָה יִכְלוּ:

29 כִּי יֵבֹשׁוּ
מֵאֵילִים אֲשֶׁר חֲמַדְתֶּם
וְתַחְפְּרוּ
מֵהַגַּנּוֹת אֲשֶׁר בְּחַרְתֶּם:
30 כִּי תִהְיוּ כְּאֵלָה
נֹבֶלֶת עָלֶהָ
וּכְגַנָּה
אֲשֶׁר־מַיִם אֵין לָהּ:
31 וְהָיָה הֶחָסֹן לִנְעֹרֶת
וּפֹעֲלוֹ לְנִיצוֹץ
וּבָעֲרוּ שְׁנֵיהֶם יַחְדָּו
וְאֵין מְכַבֶּה: ס

---

h-h   *Emendation yields "in a crucible"; cf. 48.10.*
i   *Others "Zion shall be saved by justice, / Her repentant ones by righteousness."*
j   *For this meaning cf. 5.16; 10.22.*
k   *Heb. "they."*
l-l   *Connecting ḥason with ḥasan, "to store" (23.18), and ḥosen, "treasure" (33.6).*

ב הַדָּבָר אֲשֶׁר חָזָה יְשַׁעְיָהוּ בֶּן־אָמֵוֹץ
עַל־יְהוּדָה וִירוּשָׁלָֽם:

2 **The word** that Isaiah son of Amoz prophesied concerning Judah and Jerusalem.

2In the days to come,
The Mount of the LORD's House
Shall stand firm above the mountains
And tower above the hills;
And all the nations
Shall gaze on it with joy.
3And the many peoples shall go and say:
"Come,
Let us go up to the Mount of the LORD,
To the House of the God of Jacob;
That He may instruct us in His ways,
And that we may walk in His paths."
For instruction shall come forth[a] from Zion,
The word of the LORD from Jerusalem.
4Thus He will judge among the nations
And arbitrate for the many peoples,
And they shall beat their swords into
   plowshares[b]
And their spears into pruning hooks:
Nation shall not take up
Sword against nation;
They shall never again know[c] war.

5O House of Jacob!
Come, let us walk
By the light of the LORD.
6For you have forsaken [the ways of] your
   people,
O House of Jacob!
[d]-For they are full [of practices] from the East,
And of soothsaying like the Philistines;
They abound in customs[e] of the aliens.-[d]

2 וְהָיָה | בְּאַחֲרִית הַיָּמִים
נָכוֹן יְהְיֶה הַר בֵּית־יְהוָֹה
בְּרֹאשׁ הֶהָרִים
וְנִשָּׂא מִגְּבָעֵוֹת
וְנָהֲרוּ אֵלָיו
כָּל־הַגּוֹיִֽם:
3 וְהָלְכוּ עַמִּים רַבִּים וְאָמְרוּ
לְכוּ |
וְנַעֲלֶה אֶל־הַר־יְהוָֹה
אֶל־בֵּית אֱלֹהֵי יַעֲקֹב
וְיֹרֵנוּ מִדְּרָכָיו
וְנֵלְכָה בְּאֹרְחֹתָיו
כִּי מִצִּיּוֹן תֵּצֵא תוֹרָה
וּדְבַר־יְהוָֹה מִירוּשָׁלָֽם:
4 וְשָׁפַט בֵּין הַגּוֹיִם
וְהוֹכִיחַ לְעַמִּים רַבִּים
וְכִתְּתוּ חַרְבוֹתָם לְאִתִּים
וַחֲנִיתֹתֵיהֶם לְמַזְמֵרוֹת
לֹא־יִשָּׂא גוֹי
אֶל־גּוֹי חֶרֶב
וְלֹא־יִלְמְדוּ עוֹד מִלְחָמָֽה: פ

5 בֵּית יַעֲקֹב
לְכוּ וְנֵלְכָה
בְּאוֹר יְהוָֹה:
6 כִּי נָטַשְׁתָּה עַמְּךָ
בֵּית יַעֲקֹב
כִּי מָלְאוּ מִקֶּדֶם
וְעֹנְנִים כַּפְּלִשְׁתִּים
וּבְיַלְדֵי נָכְרִים יַשְׂפִּֽיקוּ:

a   *I.e., oracles will be obtainable.*
b   *More exactly, the iron points with which wooden plows were
    tipped.*
c   *Cf. Judg. 3.2.*
d-d *Emendation yields "For they are full of divination / and have
    abundance of soothsaying, / Like Philistines / And like alien
    folk."*
e   *Cf. Targum; lit. "children."*

7Their land is full of silver and gold,
There is no limit to their treasures;
Their land is full of horses,
There is no limit to their chariots.
8And their land is full of idols;
They bow down to the work of their hands,
To what their own fingers have wrought.
9But man shall be humbled,
And mortal brought low—
f-Oh, do not forgive them!-*f*

10Go deep into the rock,
Bury yourselves in the ground,
Before the terror of the LORD
And His dread majesty!
11Man's haughty look shall be brought low,
And the pride of mortals shall be humbled.
None but the LORD shall be
Exalted in that day.

12For the LORD of Hosts has ready a day
Against all that is proud and arrogant,
Against all that is lofty—so that it is brought
  low:
13Against all the cedars of Lebanon,
Tall and stately,
And all the oaks of Bashan;
14Against all the high mountains
And all the lofty hills;
15Against every soaring tower
And every mighty wall;
16Against all the *g*-ships of Tarshish-*g*
And all the gallant barks.
17Then man's haughtiness shall be humbled
And the pride of man brought low.
None but the LORD shall be
Exalted in that day.

7 וַתִּמָּלֵא אַרְצוֹ כֶּסֶף וְזָהָב
וְאֵין קֵצֶה לְאֹצְרֹתָיו
וַתִּמָּלֵא אַרְצוֹ סוּסִים
וְאֵין קֵצֶה לְמַרְכְּבֹתָיו:
8 וַתִּמָּלֵא אַרְצוֹ אֱלִילִים
לְמַעֲשֵׂה יָדָיו יִשְׁתַּחֲווּ
לַאֲשֶׁר עָשׂוּ אֶצְבְּעֹתָיו:
9 וַיִּשַּׁח אָדָם
וַיִּשְׁפַּל־אִישׁ
וְאַל־תִּשָּׂא לָהֶם:

10 בּוֹא בַצּוּר
וְהִטָּמֵן בֶּעָפָר
מִפְּנֵי פַּחַד יְהֹוָה
וּמֵהֲדַר גְּאֹנוֹ:
11 עֵינֵי גַּבְהוּת אָדָם שָׁפֵל
וְשַׁח רוּם אֲנָשִׁים
וְנִשְׂגַּב יְהֹוָה לְבַדּוֹ
בַּיּוֹם הַהוּא: ס

12 כִּי יוֹם לַיהֹוָה צְבָאוֹת
עַל כָּל־גֵּאֶה וָרָם
וְעַל כָּל־נִשָּׂא וְשָׁפֵל:
13 וְעַל כָּל־אַרְזֵי הַלְּבָנוֹן
הָרָמִים וְהַנִּשָּׂאִים
וְעַל כָּל־אַלּוֹנֵי הַבָּשָׁן:
14 וְעַל כָּל־הֶהָרִים הָרָמִים
וְעַל כָּל־הַגְּבָעוֹת הַנִּשָּׂאוֹת:
15 וְעַל כָּל־מִגְדָּל גָּבֹהַּ
וְעַל כָּל־חוֹמָה בְצוּרָה:
16 וְעַל כָּל־אֳנִיּוֹת תַּרְשִׁישׁ
וְעַל כָּל־שְׂכִיּוֹת הַחֶמְדָּה:
17 וְשַׁח גַּבְהוּת הָאָדָם
וְשָׁפֵל רוּם אֲנָשִׁים
וְנִשְׂגַּב יְהֹוָה לְבַדּוֹ
בַּיּוֹם הַהוּא:

---

f-f Meaning of Heb. uncertain. Emendation yields "And their idols
  with them"; cf. vv. 17–21.
g-g Probably a type of large ship.

18As for idols, they shall vanish completely.

19And men shall enter caverns in the rock
And hollows in the ground—
Before the terror of the LORD
And His dread majesty,
When He comes forth to overawe the earth.

20On that day, men shall fling away,
To the *h*-flying foxes-*h* and the bats,
The idols of silver
And the idols of gold
Which they made for worshiping.

21And they shall enter the clefts in the rocks
And the crevices in the cliffs,
Before the terror of the LORD
And His dread majesty,
When He comes forth to overawe the earth.

22Oh, cease to glorify man,
Who has only a breath in his nostrils!
For by what does he merit esteem?

3 For lo!
The Sovereign LORD of Hosts
Will remove from Jerusalem and from Judah
Prop and stay,
Every prop of food
And every prop of water:*a*

2Soldier and warrior,
Magistrate and prophet,
Augur and elder;

3Captain of fifty,
Magnate and counselor,
Skilled artisan and expert enchanter;*b*

4And He*c* will make boys their rulers,
And babes shall govern them.

5So the people shall oppress one another—

יח וְהָאֱלִילִים כָּלִיל יַחֲלֹף:

יט וּבָאוּ בִּמְעָרוֹת צֻרִים
וּבִמְחִלּוֹת עָפָר
מִפְּנֵי פַּחַד יְהוָה
וּמֵהֲדַר גְּאוֹנוֹ
בְּקוּמוֹ לַעֲרֹץ הָאָרֶץ:

כ בַּיּוֹם הַהוּא יַשְׁלִיךְ הָאָדָם
אֵת אֱלִילֵי כַסְפּוֹ
וְאֵת אֱלִילֵי זְהָבוֹ
אֲשֶׁר עָשׂוּ־לוֹ לְהִשְׁתַּחֲוֺת
לַחְפֹּר פֵּרוֹת וְלָעֲטַלֵּפִים:

כא לָבוֹא בְּנִקְרוֹת הַצֻּרִים
וּבִסְעִפֵי הַסְּלָעִים
מִפְּנֵי פַּחַד יְהוָה
וּמֵהֲדַר גְּאוֹנוֹ
בְּקוּמוֹ לַעֲרֹץ הָאָרֶץ:

כב חִדְלוּ לָכֶם מִן־הָאָדָם
אֲשֶׁר נְשָׁמָה בְּאַפּוֹ
כִּי־בַמֶּה נֶחְשָׁב הוּא: פ

ג כִּי הִנֵּה
הָאָדוֹן יְהוָה צְבָאוֹת
מֵסִיר מִירוּשָׁלִַם וּמִיהוּדָה
מַשְׁעֵן וּמַשְׁעֵנָה
כֹּל מִשְׁעַן־לֶחֶם
וְכֹל מִשְׁעַן־מָיִם:

ב גִּבּוֹר וְאִישׁ מִלְחָמָה
שׁוֹפֵט וְנָבִיא
וְקֹסֵם וְזָקֵן:

ג שַׂר־חֲמִשִּׁים
וּנְשׂוּא פָנִים וְיוֹעֵץ
וַחֲכַם חֲרָשִׁים וּנְבוֹן לָחַשׁ:

ד וְנָתַתִּי נְעָרִים שָׂרֵיהֶם
וְתַעֲלוּלִים יִמְשְׁלוּ־בָם:

ה וְנִגַּשׂ הָעָם אִישׁ בְּאִישׁ

---

h-h   Exact meaning of Heb. uncertain.

a   Emendation yields "clothing"; cf. v. 7; 4.1.
b   Emendation yields "craftsman."
c   Heb. "I."

Each oppressing his fellow: וְאִישׁ בְּרֵעֵהוּ

The young shall bully the old;   יִרְהֲבוּ הַנַּעַר בַּזָּקֵן

And the despised [shall bully] the honored.   וְהַנִּקְלֶה בַּנִּכְבָּד׃

6For should a man seize his brother,   6 כִּי־יִתְפֹּשׂ אִישׁ בְּאָחִיו

d-In whose father's house there is clothing:-d   בֵּית אָבִיו שִׂמְלָה

"Come, be a chief over us,   לְכָה קָצִין תִּהְיֶה־לָּנוּ

And let this ruine be under your care,"   וְהַמַּכְשֵׁלָה הַזֹּאת תַּחַת יָדֶךָ׃

7The other will thereupon protest,   7 יִשָּׂא בַיּוֹם הַהוּא ׀ לֵאמֹר

"I will not be a dresser of wounds,   לֹא־אֶהְיֶה חֹבֵשׁ

With no food or clothing in my own house.   וּבְבֵיתִי אֵין לֶחֶם וְאֵין שִׂמְלָה

You shall not make me chief of a people!"   לֹא תְשִׂימֻנִי קְצִין עָם׃

8Ah, Jerusalem has stumbled,   8 כִּי כָשְׁלָה יְרוּשָׁלַ͏ִם

And Judah has fallen,   וִיהוּדָה נָפָל

Because by word and deed   כִּי־לְשׁוֹנָם וּמַעַלְלֵיהֶם

They insult the LORD,   אֶל־יְהֹוָה לַמְרוֹת

Defying His majestic glance.   עֵנֵי* כְבוֹדוֹ׃

9Their partiality in judgmentf accuses them;   9 הַכָּרַת פְּנֵיהֶם עָנְתָה בָּם

They avow their sins like Sodom,   וְחַטָּאתָם כִּסְדֹם הִגִּידוּ

They do not conceal them.   לֹא כִחֵדוּ

Woe to them! For ill   אוֹי לְנַפְשָׁם כִּי־

Have they served themselves.   גָמְלוּ לָהֶם רָעָה׃

10(Hailg the just man, for he shall fare well;   10 אִמְרוּ צַדִּיק כִּי־טוֹב

He shall eat the fruit of his works.   כִּי־פְרִי מַעַלְלֵיהֶם יֹאכֵלוּ׃

11Woe to the wicked man, for he shall fare ill;   11 אוֹי לְרָשָׁע רָע

As his hands have dealt, so shall it be done to him.)   כִּי־גְמוּל יָדָיו יֵעָשֶׂה לּוֹ׃

12My people's rulers are babes,   12 עַמִּי נֹגְשָׂיו מְעוֹלֵל

It is governed by women.h   וְנָשִׁים מָשְׁלוּ בוֹ

O my people!   עַמִּי

Your leaders are misleaders;   מְאַשְּׁרֶיךָ מַתְעִים

They have confused the course of your paths.   וְדֶרֶךְ אֹרְחֹתֶיךָ בִּלֵּעוּ׃ ס

13The LORD stands up to plead a cause,   13 נִצָּב לָרִיב יְהֹוָה

He rises to champion peoples.i   וְעֹמֵד לָדִין עַמִּים׃

---

d-d   *Emendation yields "His father's son, saying..."*   חסר י' בשורש   v. 8.

e   *Meaning of Heb. uncertain. Emendation yields "wound."*

f   *So Targum; cf. Deut. 1.17; 16.19.*

g   *Emendation yields "Happy is."*

h   *Emendation yields "boys"; cf. v. 4 (and v. 5).*

i   *Septuagint "His people"; cf. vv. 14, 15.*

14The LORD will bring this charge
Against the elders and officers of His people:
"It is you who have ravaged the vineyard;
That which was robbed from the poor is in
   your houses.
15How dare you crush My people
And grind the faces of the poor?"
               —says my Lord GOD of Hosts.

16The LORD said:
"Because the daughters of Zion
Are so vain
And walk with j-heads thrown back,-j
With roving eyes,
And with mincing gait,
Making a tinkling with their feet"—
17My Lord will barek the pates
Of the daughters of Zion,
The LORD will uncover their heads.

18In that day, my LORD will strip off the fineryl
of the anklets, the fillets, and the crescents; 19of
the eardrops, the bracelets, and the veils; 20the
turbans, the armlets, and the sashes; of the tal-
ismans and the amulets; 21the signet rings and
the nose rings; 22of the festive robes, the man-
tles, and the shawls; the purses, 23the lace gowns,
and the linen vests; and the kerchiefs and the
capes.

24And then—
Instead of perfume, there shall be rot;
And instead of an apron, a rope;
Instead of a diadem of beaten-work,
A shorn head;
Instead of a rich robe,
A girding of sackcloth;
m-A burn instead of beauty.-m

---

14 יְהוָה֙ בְּמִשְׁפָּ֣ט יָב֔וֹא
עִם־זִקְנֵ֥י עַמּ֖וֹ וְשָׂרָ֑יו
וְאַתֶּם֙ בִּֽעַרְתֶּ֣ם הַכֶּ֔רֶם
גְּזֵלַ֥ת הֶֽעָנִ֖י בְּבָתֵּיכֶֽם:
15 מַלָּכֶ֛ם מַה־לָּכֶ֥ם תְּדַכְּא֖וּ עַמִּ֑י
וּפְנֵ֥י עֲנִיִּ֖ים תִּטְחָ֑נוּ
נְאֻם־אֲדֹנָ֥י יְהוִ֖ה צְבָאֽוֹת: ס

16 וַיֹּ֣אמֶר יְהוָ֔ה
יַ֚עַן כִּ֣י
גָֽבְהוּ֙ בְּנ֣וֹת צִיּ֔וֹן
וַתֵּלַ֙כְנָה֙ נְטוּי֣וֹת גָּר֔וֹן
וּֽמְשַׂקְּר֖וֹת עֵינָ֑יִם
הָל֤וֹךְ וְטָפֹף֙ תֵּלַ֔כְנָה
וּבְרַגְלֵיהֶ֖ם תְּעַכַּֽסְנָה:
17 וְשִׂפַּ֣ח אֲדֹנָ֔י קָדְקֹ֖ד
בְּנ֣וֹת צִיּ֑וֹן
וַיהוָ֖ה פָּתְהֵ֥ן יְעָרֶֽה: ס

18 בַּיּ֨וֹם הַה֜וּא יָסִ֣יר אֲדֹנָ֗י אֵ֣ת תִּפְאֶ֣רֶת
הָעֲכָסִ֛ים וְהַשְּׁבִיסִ֖ים וְהַשַּׂהֲרֹנִֽים:
19 הַנְּטִיפ֥וֹת וְהַשֵּׁיר֖וֹת וְהָרְעָלֽוֹת:
20 הַפְּאֵרִ֤ים וְהַצְּעָדוֹת֙ וְהַקִּשֻּׁרִ֔ים וּבָתֵּ֥י
הַנֶּ֖פֶשׁ וְהַלְּחָשִֽׁים: 21 הַטַּבָּע֖וֹת וְנִזְמֵ֥י
הָאָֽף: 22 הַמַּֽחֲלָצוֹת֙ וְהַמַּ֣עֲטָפ֔וֹת
וְהַמִּטְפָּח֖וֹת וְהָחֲרִיטִֽים: 23 וְהַגִּלְיֹנִ֥ים
וְהַסְּדִינִ֖ים וְהַצְּנִיפ֥וֹת וְהָרְדִידִֽים:

24 וְהָיָה֩
תַ֨חַת בֹּ֜שֶׂם מַ֣ק יִֽהְיֶ֗ה
וְתַ֨חַת חֲגוֹרָ֤ה נִקְפָּה֙
וְתַ֣חַת מַעֲשֶׂ֣ה מִקְשֶׁ֔ה
קָרְחָ֕ה
וְתַ֥חַת פְּתִיגִ֖יל
מַחֲגֹ֣רֶת שָׂ֑ק
כִּי־תַ֖חַת יֹֽפִי:

---

j-j Lit. "throats bent back."
k So Saadia. To bare a woman's head in public was an intolerable
    humiliation; cf. Mishnah Baba Kamma 8.6.
l Many of the articles named in vv. 18–24 cannot be identified with
    certainty.
m-m The complete Isaiah scroll from Qumran, hereafter 1QIsᵃ,
    reads "For shame shall take the place of beauty"; cf. note k.

[25]Her[n] men shall fall by the sword,
Her fighting manhood in battle;
[26]And her gates shall lament and mourn,
And [o-]she shall be emptied,[-o]
Shall sit on the ground.

4 In that day, seven women shall take hold of one man, saying,
"We will eat our own food
And wear our own clothes;
Only let us be called by your name—
Take away our disgrace!"
[2][a]In that day,
The radiance of the LORD
Will lend beauty and glory,
And the splendor of [b-]the land[-b]
[Will give] dignity and majesty,
To the survivors of Israel.
[3]And those who remain in Zion
And are left in Jerusalem—
All who are inscribed for life in Jerusalem—
Shall be called holy.

[4]When my Lord has washed away
The filth of [c-]the daughters of Zion,[-c]
And from Jerusalem's midst
Has rinsed out her infamy—
In a spirit of judgment
And in a spirit of purging—

[5]the LORD will create[d] over the whole shrine and meeting place of Mount Zion cloud by day and smoke with a glow of flaming fire by night.

---

25 מְתַ֖יִךְ בַּחֶ֣רֶב יִפֹּ֑לוּ
וּגְבוּרָתֵ֖ךְ בַּמִּלְחָמָֽה׃
26 וְאָנ֥וּ וְאָבְל֖וּ פְּתָחֶ֑יהָ
וְנִקָּ֖תָה
לָאָ֥רֶץ תֵּשֵֽׁב׃

ד וְהֶחֱזִ֩יקוּ֩ שֶׁ֨בַע נָשִׁ֜ים בְּאִ֣ישׁ אֶחָ֗ד
בַּיּ֤וֹם הַהוּא֙ לֵאמֹ֔ר
לַחְמֵ֣נוּ נֹאכֵ֔ל
וְשִׂמְלָתֵ֖נוּ נִלְבָּ֑שׁ
רַ֗ק יִקָּרֵ֤א שִׁמְךָ֙ עָלֵ֔ינוּ
אֱסֹ֖ף חֶרְפָּתֵֽנוּ׃ ס
2 בַּיּ֣וֹם הַה֗וּא
יִהְיֶה֙ צֶ֣מַח יְהֹוָ֔ה
לִצְבִ֖י וּלְכָב֑וֹד
וּפְרִ֣י הָאָ֔רֶץ
לְגָא֖וֹן וּלְתִפְאֶ֑רֶת
לִפְלֵיטַ֖ת יִשְׂרָאֵֽל׃
3 וְהָיָ֣ה ׀ הַנִּשְׁאָ֣ר בְּצִיּ֗וֹן
וְהַנּוֹתָר֙ בִּיר֣וּשָׁלַ֔ם
קָד֖וֹשׁ יֵאָ֣מֶר ל֑וֹ
כׇּל־הַכָּת֥וּב לַחַיִּ֖ים בִּירוּשָׁלָֽ͏ִם׃

4 אִ֣ם ׀ רָחַ֣ץ אֲדֹנָ֗י
אֵ֚ת צֹאַ֣ת בְּנוֹת־צִיּ֔וֹן
וְאֶת־דְּמֵ֥י יְרוּשָׁלַ֖͏ִם
יָדִ֣יחַ מִקִּרְבָּ֑הּ
בְּר֥וּחַ מִשְׁפָּ֖ט
וּבְר֥וּחַ בָּעֵֽר׃

5 וּבָרָ֣א יְהֹוָ֡ה עַל֩ כׇּל־מְכ֨וֹן הַר־צִיּ֜וֹן וְעַֽל־
מִקְרָאֶ֗הָ עָנָ֤ן ׀ יוֹמָם֙ וְעָשָׁ֔ן וְנֹ֛גַהּ אֵ֥שׁ לֶהָבָ֖ה

---

n   *I.e., Zion's; cf. vv. 16, 17; Heb. "your."*
o-o   *Meaning of Heb. uncertain. Emendation yields "her wall"; cf. Lam. 2.8.*

a   *For the interpretation of this verse, cf. 28.5. For "radiance," cf. Septuagint and the Syriac* semḥa, *and for "splendor," cf. the meaning of* peri *in 10.12.*
b-b   *Emendation yields "my Lord"; cf. the parallelism (in reverse order) in 3.17.*
c-c   *Emendation yields "Daughter Zion," i.e., Zion personified; cf. 1.8 and note.*
d   *Emendation yields "spread"; cf. Ps. 105.39.*

Indeed, over *e*-all the glory-*e* shall hang a canopy,
⁶which shall serve as a pavilion for shade from
heat by day and as a shelter for protection
against drenching rain.

5 Let me sing for my beloved
A song of my lover about his vineyard.

My beloved had a vineyard
a-On a fruitful hill.-*a*
²He broke the ground, cleared it of stones,
And planted it with choice vines.
He built a watchtower inside it,
He even hewed a wine press in it;
For he hoped it would yield grapes.
Instead, it yielded wild grapes.
³"Now, then,
Dwellers of Jerusalem
And men of Judah,
You be the judges
Between Me and My vineyard:
⁴What more could have been done for My
   vineyard
That I failed to do in it?
Why, when I hoped it would yield grapes,
Did it yield wild grapes?

⁵"Now I am going to tell you
What I will do to My vineyard:
I will remove its hedge,
That it may be ravaged;
I will break down its wall,
That it may be trampled.
⁶And I will *a*-make it a desolation;-*a*
It shall not be pruned or hoed,
And it shall be overgrown with briers and
   thistles.

לַיְלָה כִּי עַל־כָּל־כָּבוֹד חֻפָּה: ⁶ וְסֻכָּה
תִּהְיֶה לְצֵל־יוֹמָם מֵחֹרֶב וּלְמַחְסֶה
וּלְמִסְתּוֹר מִזֶּרֶם וּמִמָּטָר: פ

ה ¹ אָשִׁירָה נָּא לִידִידִי
שִׁירַת דּוֹדִי לְכַרְמוֹ

כֶּרֶם הָיָה לִידִידִי
בְּקֶרֶן בֶּן־שָׁמֶן:
² וַיְעַזְּקֵהוּ וַיְסַקְּלֵהוּ
וַיִּטָּעֵהוּ שֹׂרֵק
וַיִּבֶן מִגְדָּל בְּתוֹכוֹ
וְגַם־יֶקֶב חָצֵב בּוֹ
וַיְקַו לַעֲשׂוֹת עֲנָבִים
וַיַּעַשׂ בְּאֻשִׁים:
³ וְעַתָּה
יוֹשֵׁב יְרוּשָׁלַם
וְאִישׁ יְהוּדָה
שִׁפְטוּ־נָא
בֵּינִי וּבֵין כַּרְמִי:
⁴ מַה־לַּעֲשׂוֹת עוֹד לְכַרְמִי
וְלֹא עָשִׂיתִי בּוֹ
מַדּוּעַ קִוֵּיתִי לַעֲשׂוֹת עֲנָבִים
וַיַּעַשׂ בְּאֻשִׁים:

⁵ וְעַתָּה אוֹדִיעָה־נָּא אֶתְכֶם
אֵת אֲשֶׁר־אֲנִי עֹשֶׂה לְכַרְמִי
הָסֵר מְשׂוּכָּתוֹ*
וְהָיָה לְבָעֵר
פָּרֹץ גְּדֵרוֹ
וְהָיָה לְמִרְמָס:
⁶ וַאֲשִׁיתֵהוּ בָתָה
לֹא יִזָּמֵר וְלֹא יֵעָדֵר
וְעָלָה שָׁמִיר וָשָׁיִת

---

e-e   Emendation yields "His whole shrine."

a-a   Meaning of Heb. uncertain.

v. 5. כ' דגשה

And I will command the clouds	וְעַל הֶעָבִים אֲצַוֶּה
To drop no rain on it."	מֵהַמְטִיר עָלָיו מָטָר:

7For the vineyard of the LORD of Hosts	7 כִּי כֶרֶם יְהוָה צְבָאוֹת
Is the House of Israel,	בֵּית יִשְׂרָאֵל
And the seedlings he lovingly tended	וְאִישׁ יְהוּדָה
Are the men of Judah.	נְטַע שַׁעֲשׁוּעָיו
bAnd He hoped for justice,	וַיְקַו לְמִשְׁפָּט
But behold, injustice;	וְהִנֵּה מִשְׂפָּח
For equity,	לִצְדָקָה
But behold, iniquity!	וְהִנֵּה צְעָקָה: ס

8Ah,	8 הוֹי
Those who add house to house	מַגִּיעֵי בַיִת בְּבַיִת
And join field to field,	שָׂדֶה בְשָׂדֶה יַקְרִיבוּ
Till there is room for none but you	עַד אֶפֶס מָקוֹם וְהוּשַׁבְתֶּם לְבַדְּכֶם
To dwell in the land!	בְּקֶרֶב הָאָרֶץ:
9In my hearing [said] the LORD of Hosts:	9 בְּאָזְנָי יְהוָה צְבָאוֹת
Surely, great houses	אִם־לֹא בָּתִּים רַבִּים
Shall lie forlorn,	לְשַׁמָּה יִהְיוּ
Spacious and splendid ones	גְּדֹלִים וְטוֹבִים
Without occupants.	מֵאֵין יוֹשֵׁב:
10For ten acres of vineyard	10 כִּי עֲשֶׂרֶת צִמְדֵּי־כֶרֶם
Shall yield just one bath,c	יַעֲשׂוּ בַּת אֶחָת
And a field sown with a ḥomer of seed	וְזֶרַע חֹמֶר
Shall yield a mere ephah.	יַעֲשֶׂה אֵיפָה: פ

11Ah,	11 הוֹי
Those who chase liquor	מַשְׁכִּימֵי בַבֹּקֶר
From early in the morning,	שֵׁכָר יִרְדֹּפוּ
And till late in the evening	מְאַחֲרֵי בַנֶּשֶׁף
Are inflamed by wine!	יַיִן יַדְלִיקֵם:
12d-Who, at their banquets,	12 וְהָיָה כִנּוֹר וָנֶבֶל
Have-d lyre and lute,	תֹּף וְחָלִיל
Timbrel, flute, and wine;	וָיַיִן מִשְׁתֵּיהֶם
But who never give a thought	וְאֵת פֹּעַל יְהוָה

b   This sentence contains two word-plays: "And He hoped for
    mishpaṭ, And there is mispaḥ [exact meaning uncertain]; / For
    ṣedaqah, But there is ṣe'aqah [lit. 'outcry']."

c   I.e., of wine. The bath was the liquid equivalent of the ephah;
    and the ḥomer was ten baths or ephahs (Ezek. 45.11).

d-d   Emendation yields "whose interests are" (mish'ehem, from
    sha'ah "to turn to," 17.7, 8; 31.1).

To the plan of the LORD,	לֹא יַבִּיטוּ
And take no note	וּמַעֲשֵׂה יָדָיו
Of what He is designing.	לֹא רָאוּ:
¹³Assuredly,	13 לָכֵן
My people will suffer exile	גָּלָה עַמִּי
For not giving heed,	מִבְּלִי־דָעַת
Its multitude victims of hunger	וּכְבוֹדוֹ מְתֵי רָעָב
And its masses parched with thirst.	וַהֲמוֹנוֹ צִחֵה צָמָא:
¹⁴Assuredly,	14 לָכֵן
Sheol has opened wide its gullet	הִרְחִיבָה שְּׁאוֹל נַפְשָׁהּ
And parted its jaws in a measureless gape;	וּפָעֲרָה פִיהָ לִבְלִי־חֹק
And down into it shall go,	וְיָרַד הֲדָרָהּ
That splendor and tumult,	וַהֲמוֹנָהּ וּשְׁאוֹנָהּ
That din and revelry.	וְעָלֵז בָּהּ:

¹⁵Yea, man is bowed,	15 וַיִּשַּׁח אָדָם
And mortal brought low;	וַיִּשְׁפַּל־אִישׁ
Brought low is the pride of the haughty.	וְעֵינֵי גְבֹהִים תִּשְׁפַּלְנָה:
¹⁶And the LORD of Hosts is exalted by judg-ment,	16 וַיִּגְבַּה יְהוָה צְבָאוֹת בַּמִּשְׁפָּט
The Holy God proved holy by retribution.	וְהָאֵל הַקָּדוֹשׁ נִקְדָּשׁ בִּצְדָקָה:
¹⁷^eThen lambs shall graze	17 וְרָעוּ כְבָשִׂים
As in their meadows,	כְּדָבְרָם
And strangers shall feed	וְחָרְבוֹת מֵחִים
On the ruins of the stout.	גָּרִים יֹאכֵלוּ:

¹⁸Ah,	18 הוֹי
Those who haul sin with cords of falsehood	מֹשְׁכֵי הֶעָוֹן בְּחַבְלֵי הַשָּׁוְא
And iniquity as with cart ropes!	וְכַעֲבוֹת הָעֲגָלָה חַטָּאָה:
¹⁹Who say,^f	19 הָאֹמְרִים
"Let Him speed, let Him hasten His purpose,	יְמַהֵר | יָחִישָׁה מַעֲשֵׂהוּ
If we are to give thought;	לְמַעַן נִרְאֶה
Let the plans of the Holy One of Israel	וְתִקְרַב וְתָבוֹאָה
Be quickly fulfilled,	עֲצַת קְדוֹשׁ יִשְׂרָאֵל
If we are to give heed."	וְנֵדָעָה: ס

²⁰Ah,	20 הוֹי
Those who call evil good	הָאֹמְרִים לָרַע טוֹב

---

e *Meaning of verse uncertain. Emendation yields "The lambs shall graze / In the pasture of the fat [rams], / And the kids shall feed / On the ranges of the stout [bucks]." The lambs and the kids are the poor and the rams and bucks are the rich oppressors (cf. Ezek. 34.17–22).*

f *By way of retort to v. 12.*

And good evil;
Who present darkness as light
And light as darkness;
Who present bitter as sweet
And sweet as bitter!
21Ah,
Those who are so wise—
In their own opinion;
So clever—
In their own judgment!

22Ah,
Those who are so doughty—
As drinkers of wine,
And so valiant—
As mixers of drink!
23Who vindicate him who is in the wrong
In return for a bribe,
And withhold vindication
From him who is in the right.
24Assuredly,
As straw is consumed by a tongue of fire
And hay g-shrivels as it burns,-g
Their stock shall become like rot,
And their buds shall blow away like dust.
For they have rejected the instruction of the
   Lord of Hosts,
Spurned the word of the Holy One of Israel.

25That is why
The Lord's anger was roused
Against His people,
Why He stretched out His arm against it
And struck it,
So that the mountains quaked,h
And its corpses lay
Like refuse in the streets.
Yet his anger has not turned back,
And His arm is outstretched still.

וְלַטּ֣וֹב רָ֑ע
שָׂמִ֥ים חֹ֙שֶׁךְ֙ לְא֔וֹר
וְא֣וֹר לְחֹ֑שֶׁךְ
שָׂמִ֥ים מַ֛ר לְמָת֖וֹק
וּמָת֥וֹק לְמָֽר׃ ס
21 ה֣וֹי
חֲכָמִ֖ים
בְּעֵֽינֵיהֶ֑ם
וְנֶ֥גֶד פְּנֵיהֶ֖ם
נְבֹנִֽים׃
22 ה֕וֹי
גִּבּוֹרִ֖ים
לִשְׁתּ֣וֹת יָ֑יִן
וְאַנְשֵׁי־חַ֖יִל
לִמְסֹ֥ךְ שֵׁכָֽר׃
23 מַצְדִּיקֵ֥י רָשָׁ֖ע
עֵ֣קֶב שֹׁ֑חַד
וְצִדְקַ֥ת צַדִּיקִ֖ים
יָסִ֥ירוּ מִמֶּֽנּוּ׃ ס
24 לָכֵן֩
כֶּאֱכֹ֨ל קַ֜שׁ לְשׁ֣וֹן אֵ֗שׁ
וַחֲשַׁ֤שׁ לֶֽהָבָה֙ יִרְפֶּ֔ה
שָׁרְשָׁם֙ כַּמָּ֣ק יִֽהְיֶ֔ה
וּפִרְחָ֖ם כָּאָבָ֣ק יַעֲלֶ֑ה
כִּ֣י מָאֲס֗וּ אֵ֚ת תּוֹרַת֙ יְהוָ֣ה צְבָא֔וֹת
וְאֵ֛ת אִמְרַ֥ת קְדֽוֹשׁ־יִשְׂרָאֵ֖ל נִאֵֽצוּ׃
25 עַל־כֵּ֡ן
חָרָה֩ אַף־יְהוָ֨ה
בְּעַמּ֜וֹ
וַיֵּ֣ט יָד֤וֹ עָלָיו֙
וַיַּכֵּ֔הוּ
וַיִּרְגְּזוּ֙ הֶֽהָרִ֔ים
וַתְּהִ֧י נִבְלָתָ֛ם
כַּסּוּחָ֖ה בְּקֶ֣רֶב חוּצ֑וֹת
בְּכָל־זֹאת֙ לֹא־שָׁ֣ב אַפּ֔וֹ
וְע֖וֹד יָד֥וֹ נְטוּיָֽה׃

---

g-g   Emendation yields "is burned by flame"; cf. 33.11–12; 47.14.
h   An allusion to the destructive earthquake in the reign of King
    Uzziah: Amos 1.1; Zech. 14.5; cf. Isa. 9.18a.

26He will raise an ensign to a nation[i] afar,
Whistle to one at the end of the earth.
There it comes with lightning speed!
27In its ranks, none is weary or stumbles,
They never sleep or slumber;
The belts on their waists do not come loose,
Nor do the thongs of their sandals break.
28Their arrows are sharpened,
And all their bows are drawn.
Their horses' hoofs are like flint,
Their chariot wheels like the whirlwind.
29Their roaring is like a lion's,
They roar like the great beasts;
When they growl and seize a prey,
They carry it off and none can recover it.

30But in that day, a roaring shall resound over
him like that of the sea;[j] and then he shall look
below and, behold,
Distressing darkness, with light;
Darkness, [a]-in its lowering clouds.-[a]

6 In the year that King Uzziah died, I beheld
my Lord seated on a high and lofty throne; and
the skirts of His robe filled the Temple. 2Seraphs
stood in attendance on Him. Each of them had
six wings: with two he covered his face, with two
he covered his legs, and with two he would fly.

3And one would call to the other,
"Holy, holy, holy!
The Lord of Hosts!
His presence fills all the earth!"

4The doorposts[a] would shake at the sound of
the one who called, and the House kept filling
with smoke. 5I cried,

26 וְנָשָׂא־נֵ֣ס לַגּוֹיִם֮ מֵרָח֒וֹק
וְשָׁ֥רַק ל֖וֹ מִקְצֵ֣ה הָאָ֑רֶץ
וְהִנֵּ֥ה מְהֵרָ֖ה קַ֥ל יָבֽוֹא׃
27 אֵין־עָיֵ֤ף וְאֵין־כּוֹשֵׁל֙ בּ֔וֹ
לֹ֥א יָנ֖וּם וְלֹ֣א יִישָׁ֑ן
וְלֹ֤א נִפְתַּח֙ אֵז֣וֹר חֲלָצָ֔יו
וְלֹ֥א נִתַּ֖ק שְׂר֥וֹךְ נְעָלָֽיו׃
28 אֲשֶׁ֤ר חִצָּיו֙ שְׁנוּנִ֔ים
וְכָל־קַשְּׁתֹתָ֖יו דְּרֻכ֑וֹת
פַּרְס֤וֹת סוּסָיו֙ כַּצַּ֣ר נֶחְשָׁ֔בוּ
וְגַלְגִּלָּ֖יו כַּסּוּפָֽה׃
29 שְׁאָגָ֥ה ל֖וֹ כַּלָּבִ֑יא
ושאג [וְשָׁאַ֤ג] כַּכְּפִירִים֙
וְיִנְהֹ֤ם וְיֹאחֵ֣ז טֶ֔רֶף
וְיַפְלִ֖יט וְאֵ֥ין מַצִּֽיל׃

30 וְיִנְהֹ֥ם עָלָ֛יו בַּיּ֥וֹם הַה֖וּא כְּנַהֲמַת־יָ֑ם
וְנִבַּ֤ט לָאָ֨רֶץ֙ וְהִנֵּה־
חֹ֔שֶׁךְ צַ֖ר וָא֑וֹר
חָשַׁ֖ךְ בַּעֲרִיפֶֽיהָ׃ פ

א 6 בִּשְׁנַת־מוֹת֙ הַמֶּ֣לֶךְ עֻזִּיָּ֔הוּ וָאֶרְאֶ֧ה
אֶת־אֲדֹנָ֛י יֹשֵׁ֥ב עַל־כִּסֵּ֖א רָ֣ם וְנִשָּׂ֑א וְשׁוּלָ֖יו
מְלֵאִ֥ים אֶת־הַהֵיכָֽל׃ 2 שְׂרָפִ֨ים עֹמְדִ֤ים ׀
מִמַּ֨עַל֙ ל֔וֹ שֵׁ֣שׁ כְּנָפַ֛יִם שֵׁ֥שׁ כְּנָפַ֖יִם לְאֶחָ֑ד
בִּשְׁתַּ֣יִם ׀ יְכַסֶּ֣ה פָנָ֗יו וּבִשְׁתַּ֛יִם יְכַסֶּ֥ה רַגְלָ֖יו
וּבִשְׁתַּ֥יִם יְעוֹפֵֽף׃

3 וְקָרָ֨א זֶ֤ה אֶל־זֶה֙ וְאָמַ֔ר
קָד֧וֹשׁ ׀ קָד֛וֹשׁ קָד֖וֹשׁ
יְהוָ֣ה צְבָא֑וֹת
מְלֹ֥א כָל־הָאָ֖רֶץ כְּבוֹדֽוֹ׃

4 וַיָּנֻ֙עוּ֙ אַמּ֣וֹת הַסִּפִּ֔ים מִקּ֖וֹל הַקּוֹרֵ֑א
וְהַבַּ֖יִת יִמָּלֵ֥א עָשָֽׁן׃ 5 וָאֹמַ֞ר

---

i   Heb. "nations."
j   I.e., the Lord will intervene and come to his aid. Cf. 29.6–7; 30.27.
    This verse may constitute a transition between chaps. 8 and 9.

a   Meaning of Heb. uncertain.

"Woe is me; I am lost!
For I am a man *b*-of unclean lips-*b*
And I live among a people
Of unclean lips;
Yet my own eyes have beheld
The King LORD of Hosts."

⁶Then one of the seraphs flew over to me with
a live coal, which he had taken from the altar
with a pair of tongs. ⁷He touched it to my lips
and declared,

"Now that this has touched your lips,
Your guilt shall depart
And your sin be purged away."

⁸Then I heard the voice of my Lord saying,
"Whom shall I send? Who will go for us?" And
I said, "Here am I; send me." ⁹And He said, "Go,
say to that people:

'Hear, indeed, but do not understand;
See, indeed, but do not grasp.'
¹⁰Dull that people's mind,
Stop its ears,
And seal its eyes—
Lest, seeing with its eyes
And hearing with its ears,
It also grasp with its mind,
And repent and save^c itself."

¹¹I asked, "How long, my Lord?" And He re-
plied:

"Till towns lie waste without inhabitants
And houses without people,
And the ground lies waste and desolate—
¹²For the LORD will banish the population—
And deserted sites are many
In the midst of the land.
¹³"But while a tenth part yet remains in it, it
shall repent. It shall be ravaged like the terebinth

אֽוֹי־לִ֣י כִּֽי־נִדְמֵ֗יתִי
כִּ֣י אִ֤ישׁ טְמֵֽא־שְׂפָתַ֙יִם֙ אָנֹ֔כִי
וּבְתוֹךְ֙ עַם־טְמֵ֣א שְׂפָתַ֔יִם
אָנֹכִ֖י יוֹשֵׁ֑ב
כִּ֗י אֶת־הַמֶּ֛לֶךְ יְהוָ֥ה צְבָא֖וֹת
רָא֥וּ עֵינָֽי׃

6 וַיָּ֣עָף אֵלַ֗י אֶחָד֙ מִן־הַשְּׂרָפִ֔ים וּבְיָד֖וֹ
רִצְפָּ֑ה בְּמֶ֨לְקַחַ֔יִם לָקַ֖ח מֵעַ֥ל הַמִּזְבֵּֽחַ׃
7 וַיַּגַּ֣ע עַל־פִּ֔י וַיֹּ֕אמֶר

הִנֵּ֛ה נָגַ֥ע זֶ֖ה עַל־שְׂפָתֶ֑יךָ
וְסָ֣ר עֲוֺנֶ֔ךָ
וְחַטָּאתְךָ֖ תְּכֻפָּֽר׃

8 וָאֶשְׁמַ֞ע אֶת־ק֤וֹל אֲדֹנָי֙ אֹמֵ֔ר אֶת־מִ֥י
אֶשְׁלַ֖ח וּמִ֣י יֵֽלֶךְ־לָ֑נוּ וָאֹמַ֖ר הִנְנִ֥י שְׁלָחֵֽנִי׃
9 וַיֹּ֕אמֶר לֵ֥ךְ וְאָמַרְתָּ֖ לָעָ֣ם הַזֶּ֑ה
שִׁמְע֤וּ שָׁמ֨וֹעַ֙ וְאַל־תָּבִ֔ינוּ
וּרְא֥וּ רָא֖וֹ וְאַל־תֵּדָֽעוּ׃
10 הַשְׁמֵן֙ לֵב־הָעָ֣ם הַזֶּ֔ה
וְאָזְנָ֥יו הַכְבֵּ֖ד
וְעֵינָ֣יו הָשַׁ֑ע
פֶּן־יִרְאֶ֣ה בְעֵינָ֡יו
וּבְאָזְנָ֣יו יִשְׁמָ֗ע
וּלְבָב֥וֹ יָבִ֛ין
וָשָׁ֖ב וְרָ֥פָא לֽוֹ׃

11 וָאֹמַ֕ר עַד־מָתַ֖י אֲדֹנָ֑י וַיֹּ֡אמֶר
עַ֣ד אֲשֶׁר֩ אִם־שָׁא֨וּ עָרִ֜ים מֵאֵ֣ין יוֹשֵׁ֗ב
וּבָתִּים֙ מֵאֵ֣ין אָדָ֔ם
וְהָאֲדָמָ֖ה תִּשָּׁאֶ֥ה שְׁמָמָֽה׃
12 וְרִחַ֥ק יְהוָ֖ה אֶת־הָאָדָ֑ם
וְרַבָּ֥ה הָעֲזוּבָ֖ה
בְּקֶ֥רֶב הָאָֽרֶץ׃
13 וְע֥וֹד בָּהּ֙ עֲשִׂ֣רִיָּ֔ה וְשָׁ֖בָה וְהָיְתָ֣ה לְבָעֵ֑ר

---

b-b I.e., speaking impiety; cf. 9.16, and contrast "pure of speech
[lit. 'lip']" in Zeph. 3.9.
c Lit. "heal."

and the oak, of which stumps are left even when they are felled: its stump shall be a holy seed."

7 In the reign of Ahaz son of Jotham son of Uzziah, king of Judah, King Rezin of Aram and King Pekah son of Remaliah of Israel marched upon Jerusalem to attack it; but they were not able to attack it.

2Now, when it was reported to the House of David that Aram had allied itself with Ephraim, their hearts and the hearts of their people trembled as trees of the forest sway before a wind. 3But the Lord said to Isaiah, "Go out with your son Shear-jashub[a] to meet Ahaz at the end of the conduit of the Upper Pool, by the road of the Fuller's Field. 4And say to him: Be firm and be calm. Do not be afraid and do not lose heart on account of those two smoking stubs of firebrands, on account of the raging of Rezin and his Arameans and the son of Remaliah.[b] 5Because the Arameans—with Ephraim and the son of Remaliah—have plotted against you, saying, 6'We will march against Judah and invade and conquer it, and we will set up as king in it the son of Tabeel,'[b] 7thus said my Lord God:

It shall not succeed,
It shall not come to pass.
8For the chief city of Aram is Damascus,
And the chief of Damascus is Rezin;
9The chief city of Ephraim is Samaria,
And the chief of Samaria is the son of Remaliah.[c]
[d-]And in another sixty-five years,
Ephraim shall be shattered as a people.[-d]
If you will not believe, for you [e-]cannot be trusted[-e]..."

כָּאֵלָה וְכָאַלּוֹן אֲשֶׁר בְּשַׁלֶּ֫כֶת מַצֶּ֫בֶת בָּם֑*
זֶ֥רַע קֹ֖דֶשׁ מַצַּבְתָּֽהּ׃ פ

ז וַיְהִ֡י בִּימֵ֣י אָ֠חָז בֶּן־יוֹתָ֨ם בֶּן־עֻזִּיָּ֜הוּ
מֶ֣לֶךְ יְהוּדָ֗ה עָלָ֣ה רְצִ֣ין מֶֽלֶךְ־אֲ֠רָם
וּפֶ֣קַח בֶּן־רְמַלְיָ֣הוּ מֶֽלֶךְ־יִשְׂרָאֵל֩ יְרוּשָׁלַ֨ם
לַמִּלְחָמָ֖ה עָלֶ֑יהָ וְלֹ֥א יָכֹ֖ל לְהִלָּחֵ֥ם
עָלֶֽיהָ׃

2 וַיֻּגַּ֗ד לְבֵ֤ית דָּוִד֙ לֵאמֹ֔ר נָ֥חָה אֲרָ֖ם עַל־
אֶפְרָ֑יִם וַיָּ֤נַע לְבָבוֹ֙ וּלְבַ֣ב עַמּ֔וֹ כְּנ֥וֹעַ עֲצֵי־
יַ֖עַר מִפְּנֵי־רֽוּחַ׃ 3 וַיֹּ֣אמֶר יְהוָה֮ אֶל־
יְשַֽׁעְיָהוּ֒ צֵא־נָ֗א לִקְרַ֣את אָחָ֔ז אַתָּ֕ה וּשְׁאָ֖ר
יָשׁ֣וּב בְּנֶ֑ךָ אֶל־קְצֵ֗ה תְּעָלַת֙ הַבְּרֵכָ֣ה
הָעֶלְיוֹנָ֔ה אֶל־מְסִלַּ֖ת שְׂדֵ֥ה כוֹבֵֽס׃
4 וְאָמַרְתָּ֣ אֵ֠לָיו הִשָּׁמֵ֨ר וְהַשְׁקֵ֜ט אַל־תִּירָ֗א
וּלְבָבְךָ֙ אַל־יֵרַ֔ךְ מִשְּׁנֵ֨י זַנְב֧וֹת הָאוּדִ֛ים
הָעֲשֵׁנִ֖ים הָאֵ֑לֶּה בָּחֳרִי־אַ֛ף רְצִ֥ין וַֽאֲרָ֖ם
וּבֶן־רְמַלְיָֽהוּ׃ 5 יַ֗עַן כִּֽי־יָעַ֥ץ עָלֶ֛יךָ אֲרָ֖ם
רָעָ֑ה אֶפְרַ֖יִם וּבֶן־רְמַלְיָ֥הוּ לֵאמֹֽר׃ 6 נַעֲלֶ֤ה
בִֽיהוּדָה֙ וּנְקִיצֶ֔נָּה וְנַבְקִעֶ֖נָּה אֵלֵ֑ינוּ וְנַמְלִ֥יךְ
מֶ֨לֶךְ֙ בְּתוֹכָ֔הּ אֵ֖ת בֶּן־טָֽבְאַֽל׃ ס 7 כֹּ֥ה
אָמַ֖ר אֲדֹנָ֣י יְהוִ֑ה
לֹ֥א תָק֖וּם וְלֹ֥א תִֽהְיֶֽה׃
8 כִּ֣י רֹ֤אשׁ אֲרָם֙ דַּמֶּ֔שֶׂק
וְרֹ֥אשׁ דַּמֶּ֖שֶׂק רְצִ֑ין
וּבְע֨וֹד שִׁשִּׁ֤ים וְחָמֵשׁ֙ שָׁנָ֔ה
יֵחַ֥ת אֶפְרַ֖יִם מֵעָֽם׃
9 וְרֹ֤אשׁ אֶפְרַ֨יִם֙ שֹׁמְר֔וֹן
וְרֹ֥אשׁ שֹׁמְר֖וֹן בֶּן־רְמַלְיָ֑הוּ
אִ֚ם לֹ֣א תַאֲמִ֔ינוּ כִּ֖י לֹ֥א תֵאָמֵֽנוּ׃ ס

---

a   Meaning "[only] a remnant will turn back," i.e., repent; cf. 6.13; 10.21.
b   To refer to a person only as "the son of—" is slighting; cf. note at 1 Sam. 10.11.
c   The thought is continued by 8.8b–10; cf. 2 Chron. 13.8–12.
d-d Brought down from v. 8 for clarity.
e-e Others "surely, you shall not be established."

סבירין ומטעין "בה"   v. 13.

[10]The Lord spoke further to Ahaz: [11]"Ask for a sign from the Lord your God, anywhere down to Sheol or up to the sky." [12]But Ahaz replied, "I will not ask, and I will not test the Lord." [13]"Listen, House of David," [Isaiah] retorted, "is it not enough for you to treat men as helpless that you also treat my God as helpless?[f] [14]Assuredly, my Lord will give you a sign of His own accord! Look, the young woman is with child and about to give birth to a son. Let her name him Immanuel.[g] [15](By the time he learns to reject the bad and choose the good, people will be feeding on curds and honey.) [16]For before the lad knows to reject the bad and choose the good, the ground whose two kings you dread shall be abandoned. [17]The Lord will cause to come upon you and your people and your ancestral house such days as never have come since Ephraim turned away from Judah—that selfsame king of Assyria![h]

[18]"In that day, the Lord will whistle to the flies at the ends of the water channels of Egypt and to the bees in the land of Assyria; [19]and they shall all come and alight in the rugged wadis, and in the clefts of the rocks, and in all the thornbrakes, and in all the watering places.

[20]"In that day, my Lord will cut away with the razor that is hired beyond the Euphrates—with the king of Assyria[i]—the hair of the head and [j]the hair of the legs,[j] and it shall clip off the beard as well. [21]And in that day, each man shall save alive a heifer of the herd and two animals of the flock. [22](And he shall obtain so much milk that he shall eat curds.) Thus everyone who is left in the land shall feed on curds and honey.

[23]"For in that day, every spot where there could stand a thousand vines worth a thousand

10 וַיּ֣וֹסֶף יְהֹוָ֔ה דַּבֵּ֥ר אֶל־אָחָ֖ז לֵאמֹֽר: 11 שְׁאַל־לְךָ֣ א֗וֹת מֵעִם֙ יְהֹוָ֣ה אֱלֹהֶ֔יךָ הַעְמֵ֣ק שְׁאָ֔לָה א֖וֹ הַגְבֵּ֥הַּ לְמָֽעְלָה: 12 וַיֹּ֖אמֶר אָחָ֑ז לֹא־אֶשְׁאַ֥ל וְלֹֽא־אֲנַסֶּ֖ה אֶת־יְהֹוָֽה: 13 וַיֹּ֕אמֶר שִׁמְעוּ־נָ֖א בֵּ֣ית דָּוִ֑ד הַמְעַ֤ט מִכֶּם֙ הַלְא֣וֹת אֲנָשִׁ֔ים כִּ֥י תַלְא֖וּ גַּ֥ם אֶת־אֱלֹהָֽי: 14 לָ֠כֵ֠ן יִתֵּ֨ן אֲדֹנָ֥י ה֛וּא לָכֶ֖ם א֑וֹת הִנֵּ֣ה הָעַלְמָ֗ה הָרָה֙ וְיֹלֶ֣דֶת בֵּ֔ן וְקָרָ֥את שְׁמ֖וֹ עִמָּ֥נוּ אֵֽל*: 15 חֶמְאָ֥ה וּדְבַ֖שׁ יֹאכֵ֑ל לְדַעְתּ֛וֹ מָא֥וֹס בָּרָ֖ע וּבָח֥וֹר בַּטּֽוֹב: 16 כִּ֠י בְּטֶ֨רֶם יֵדַ֥ע הַנַּ֛עַר מָאֹ֥ס בָּרָ֖ע וּבָ֣חֹר בַּטּ֑וֹב תֵּעָזֵ֤ב הָאֲדָמָה֙ אֲשֶׁ֣ר אַתָּ֣ה קָ֔ץ מִפְּנֵ֖י שְׁנֵ֥י מְלָכֶֽיהָ: 17 יָבִ֨יא יְהֹוָ֜ה עָלֶ֗יךָ וְעַֽל־עַמְּךָ֮ וְעַל־בֵּ֣ית אָבִ֒יךָ֒ יָמִים֙ אֲשֶׁ֣ר לֹא־בָ֔אוּ לְמִיּ֥וֹם סוּר־אֶפְרַ֖יִם מֵעַ֣ל יְהוּדָ֑ה אֵ֖ת מֶ֥לֶךְ אַשּֽׁוּר: ס

18 וְהָיָ֣ה | בַּיּ֣וֹם הַה֗וּא יִשְׁרֹ֤ק יְהֹוָה֙ לַזְּב֔וּב אֲשֶׁ֥ר בִּקְצֵ֖ה יְאֹרֵ֣י מִצְרָ֑יִם וְלַ֨דְּבוֹרָ֔ה אֲשֶׁ֖ר בְּאֶ֥רֶץ אַשּֽׁוּר: 19 וּבָ֖אוּ וְנָח֣וּ כֻלָּ֑ם בְּנַחֲלֵ֤י הַבַּתּוֹת֙ וּבִנְקִיקֵ֣י הַסְּלָעִ֔ים וּבְכֹל֙ הַנַּ֣עֲצוּצִ֔ים וּבְכֹ֖ל הַנַּהֲלֹלִֽים:

20 בַּיּ֣וֹם הַה֡וּא יְגַלַּ֣ח אֲדֹנָי֩ בְּתַ֨עַר הַשְּׂכִירָ֜ה בְּעֶבְרֵ֤י נָהָר֙ בְּמֶ֣לֶךְ אַשּׁ֔וּר אֶת־הָרֹ֖אשׁ וְשַׂ֣עַר הָרַגְלָ֑יִם וְגַ֥ם אֶת־הַזָּקָ֖ן תִּסְפֶּֽה: ס 21 וְהָיָ֖ה בַּיּ֣וֹם הַה֑וּא יְחַיֶּה־אִ֛ישׁ עֶגְלַ֥ת בָּקָ֖ר וּשְׁתֵּי־צֹֽאן: 22 וְהָיָ֗ה מֵרֹ֛ב עֲשׂ֥וֹת חָלָ֖ב יֹאכַ֣ל חֶמְאָ֑ה כִּֽי־חֶמְאָ֤ה וּדְבַשׁ֙ יֹאכֵ֔ל כָּל־הַנּוֹתָ֖ר בְּקֶ֥רֶב הָאָֽרֶץ:

23 וְהָיָה֙ בַּיּ֣וֹם הַה֔וּא יִֽהְיֶ֣ה כָל־מָק֗וֹם אֲשֶׁ֧ר יִֽהְיֶה־שָּׁ֛ם אֶ֥לֶף גֶּ֖פֶן בְּאֶ֣לֶף כָּ֑סֶף לַשָּׁמִ֥יר

---

f   *By insisting on soliciting the aid of Assyria (see 2 Kings 16.7 ff.; cf. below, v. 20). "Treat as helpless" follows the translation of Saadia; cf. Gen. 19.11.*

g   *Meaning "with us is God."*

h   *Cf. note on v. 13.*

i   *Who was hired by Ahaz; cf. notes on vv. 13 and 17.*

j-j   *I.e., the pubic hair.*

860

shekels of silver[k] shall become a wilderness of thornbush and thistle. [24]One will have to go there with bow and arrows,[l] for the country shall be all thornbushes and thistles. [25]But the perils of thornbush and thistle shall not spread to any of the hills that could only be tilled with a hoe;[m] and here cattle shall be let loose, and [n]-sheep and goats-[n] shall tramp about."

8 The Lord said to me, "Get yourself a large sheet and write on it [a]-in common script-[a] 'For Maher-shalal-hash-baz';[b] [2]and call reliable witnesses, the priest Uriah and Zechariah son of Jeberechiah, to witness for Me." [3]I was intimate with the prophetess,[c] and she conceived and bore a son; and the Lord said to me, "Name him Maher-shalal-hash-baz.[b] [4]For before the boy learns to call 'Father' and 'Mother,' the wealth of Damascus and the spoils of Samaria, [d]-and the delights of Rezin and of the son of Remaliah,-[d] shall be carried off before the king of Assyria."

[5]Again the Lord spoke to me, thus:
[6]"Because that people has spurned
The gently flowing waters of Siloam"[e]—
[7]Assuredly,
My Lord will bring up against them
The mighty, massive waters of the Euphrates,
The king of Assyria and all his multitude.

וְלַשַּׁ֖יִת יִֽהְיֶֽה׃ 24 בַּחִצִּ֥ים וּבַקֶּ֖שֶׁת יָ֣בוֹא שָׁ֑מָּה כִּֽי־שָׁמִ֥יר וָשַׁ֖יִת תִּֽהְיֶ֥ה כָל־הָאָֽרֶץ׃ 25 וְכֹ֣ל הֶהָרִ֗ים אֲשֶׁ֤ר בַּמַּעְדֵּר֙ יֵעָ֣דֵר֔וּן לֹא־תָב֣וֹא שָׁ֔מָּה יִרְאַ֖ת שָׁמִ֣יר וָשָׁ֑יִת וְהָיָה֙ לְמִשְׁלַ֣ח שׁ֔וֹר וּלְמִרְמַ֖ס שֶֽׂה׃ פ

ח וַיֹּ֤אמֶר יְהוָה֙ אֵלַ֔י קַח־לְךָ֖ גִּלָּי֣וֹן גָּד֑וֹל וּכְתֹ֤ב עָלָיו֙ בְּחֶ֣רֶט אֱנ֔וֹשׁ לְמַהֵ֥ר שָׁלָ֖ל חָ֥שׁ בַּֽז׃ 2 וְאָעִ֣ידָה לִּ֔י עֵדִ֖ים נֶאֱמָנִ֑ים אֵ֚ת אוּרִיָּ֣ה הַכֹּהֵ֔ן וְאֶת־זְכַרְיָ֖הוּ בֶּ֥ן יְבֶרֶכְיָֽהוּ׃ 3 וָאֶקְרַב֙ אֶל־הַנְּבִיאָ֔ה וַתַּ֖הַר וַתֵּ֣לֶד בֵּ֑ן וַיֹּ֤אמֶר יְהוָה֙ אֵלַ֔י קְרָ֣א שְׁמ֔וֹ מַהֵ֥ר שָׁלָ֖ל חָ֥שׁ בַּֽז׃ 4 כִּ֗י בְּטֶ֙רֶם֙ יֵדַ֣ע הַנַּ֔עַר קְרֹ֖א אָבִ֣י וְאִמִּ֑י יִשָּׂ֣א ׀ אֶת־חֵ֣יל דַּמֶּ֗שֶׂק וְאֵת֙ שְׁלַ֣ל שֹֽׁמְר֔וֹן לִפְנֵ֖י מֶ֥לֶךְ אַשּֽׁוּר׃ ס

5 וַיֹּ֣סֶף יְהוָ֗ה דַּבֵּ֥ר אֵלַ֛י ע֖וֹד לֵאמֹֽר׃
6 יַ֗עַן כִּ֤י מָאַס֙ הָעָ֣ם הַזֶּ֔ה
אֵ֚ת מֵ֣י הַשִּׁלֹ֔חַ הַהֹלְכִ֖ים לְאַ֑ט
וּמְשׂ֥וֹשׂ אֶת־רְצִ֖ין וּבֶן־רְמַלְיָֽהוּ׃
7 וְלָכֵ֡ן
הִנֵּ֣ה אֲדֹנָי֩ מַעֲלֶ֨ה עֲלֵיהֶ֜ם
אֶת־מֵ֣י הַנָּהָ֗ר הָעֲצוּמִים֙ וְהָ֣רַבִּ֔ים
אֶת־מֶ֥לֶךְ אַשּׁ֖וּר וְאֶת־כָּל־כְּבוֹד֑וֹ
וְעָלָה֙ עַל־כָּל־אֲפִיקָ֔יו

---

k   *I.e., all the best farm land, corresponding to the hairiest parts of the body; v. 20.*

l   *Because of dangerous beasts.*

m   *Marginal farm land, too rocky for the plow, corresponding to areas of the body with scant hair.*

n-n   *See note at Exod. 12.3.*

a-a   *Meaning of Heb. uncertain.*

b   *I.e., "Pillage hastens, looting speeds," indicating that two cities are to be pillaged at an early date; see v. 4.*

c   *I.e., Isaiah's wife.*

d-d   *Brought up from v. 6 for clarity.*

e   *The conduit—and later the tunnel—of Siloam conveyed into Jerusalem the waters of Gihon, which symbolize "the Lord of Hosts who dwells on Mount Zion" (v. 18). For the nature of the rejection see note at 7.13.*

It shall rise above all its channels,

And flow over all its beds,

⁸And swirl through Judah like a flash flood

Reaching up to the neck.*f*

ᵍBut with us is God,

Whose wings are spread

As wide as your land is broad!

⁹Band together, O peoples—you shall be broken!

Listen to this, you remotest parts of the earth:

Gird yourselves—you shall be broken;

Gird yourselves—you shall be broken!

¹⁰Hatch a plot—it shall be foiled;

Agree on action—it shall not succeed.

For with us is God!

¹¹For this is what the Lᴏʀᴅ said to me, when
He took me by the hand*h* and charged me not
to walk in the path of that people:

¹²*i*"You must not call conspiracy*j*

All that that people calls conspiracy,*j*

Nor revere what it reveres,

Nor hold it in awe.

¹³None but the Lᴏʀᴅ of Hosts

Shall you account holy;

Give reverence to Him alone,

Hold Him alone in awe.

¹⁴He shall be *k*-for a sanctuary,

A stone-*k* men strike against:

A rock men stumble over

For the two Houses of Israel,

And a trap and a snare for those

Who dwell in Jerusalem.

¹⁵The masses shall trip over these

וְהָלַךְ עַל־כָּל־גְּדוֹתָיו:

⁸ וְחָלַף בִּיהוּדָה שָׁטַף וְעָבַר
עַד־צַוָּאר יַגִּיעַ

וְהָיָה מֻטּוֹת כְּנָפָיו
מְלֹא רְחַב־אַרְצְךָ
עִמָּנוּ אֵל: ס

⁹ רֹעוּ עַמִּים וָחֹתּוּ
וְהַאֲזִינוּ כֹּל מֶרְחַקֵּי־אָרֶץ
הִתְאַזְּרוּ וָחֹתּוּ
הִתְאַזְּרוּ וָחֹתּוּ:

¹⁰ עֻצוּ עֵצָה וְתֻפָר
דַּבְּרוּ דָבָר וְלֹא יָקוּם
כִּי עִמָּנוּ אֵל: ס

¹¹ כִּי כֹה אָמַר יְהוָה אֵלַי כְּחֶזְקַת* הַיָּד
וְיִסְּרֵנִי מִלֶּכֶת בְּדֶרֶךְ הָעָם־הַזֶּה לֵאמֹר:

¹² לֹא־תֹאמְרוּן קֶשֶׁר
לְכֹל אֲשֶׁר־יֹאמַר הָעָם הַזֶּה קָשֶׁר
וְאֶת־מוֹרָאוֹ לֹא־תִירְאוּ
וְלֹא תַעֲרִיצוּ:

¹³ אֶת־יְהוָה צְבָאוֹת
אֹתוֹ תַקְדִּישׁוּ
וְהוּא מוֹרַאֲכֶם
וְהוּא מַעֲרִצְכֶם:

¹⁴ וְהָיָה לְמִקְדָּשׁ
וּלְאֶבֶן נֶגֶף
וּלְצוּר מִכְשׁוֹל
לִשְׁנֵי בָתֵּי יִשְׂרָאֵל
לְפַח וּלְמוֹקֵשׁ
לְיוֹשֵׁב יְרוּשָׁלָם:

¹⁵ וְכָשְׁלוּ בָם רַבִּים

---

f *I.e., Judah shall be imperiled, but, in contrast to Aram and
Ephraim (v. 4), not destroyed.*

g *See note c at 7.9.*

h *I.e., singled me out; cf. 41.9, 13; 42.6; 45.1; Jer. 31.32 [31].*

i *The Heb. forms here and in vv. 13 and 19 are plural to include
the disciples (v. 16) and the children (v. 18).*

j *Meaning of Heb. uncertain. Emendation yields "holy"; cf. v. 13.*

k-k *Emendation yields "...for His holy domain [cf. Ps. 114.2] /
A stone..."*

And shall fall and be injured,
Shall be snared and be caught.
[16]Bind up the message,
Seal the instruction with My disciples."

[17]So I will wait for the LORD, who is hiding His face from the House of Jacob, and I will trust in Him. [18]Here stand I and the children the LORD has given me as signs and portents in Israel from the LORD of Hosts, who dwells on Mount Zion.

[19]Now, should people say to you, "Inquire of the ghosts and familiar spirits that chirp and moan; for a people may inquire of its divine beings[l]—of the dead on behalf of the living— [20]for instruction and message," surely, for one who speaks thus there shall be no dawn. [21]m-And he shall go about in it wretched and hungry; and when he is hungry, he shall rage and revolt against his king and his divine beings.-m He may turn his face upward [22]or he may look below, but behold,

Distress and darkness, n-with no daybreak;-n
Straitness and gloom, n-with no dawn.-n

[23]For o-if there were to be-o any break of day for that [land] which is in straits, only the former [king] would have brought abasement to the land of Zebulun and the land of Naphtali— while the later one would have brought honor to the Way of the Sea, the other side of the Jordan, and Galilee of the Nations.p

9

[a]The people that walked in darkness
Have seen a brilliant light;
On those who dwelt in a land of gloom

וְנָפְל֖וּ וְנִשְׁבָּ֑רוּ
וְנוֹקְשׁ֖וּ וְנִלְכָּֽדוּ׃ ס
16 צ֖וֹר תְּעוּדָ֑ה
חֲת֥וֹם תּוֹרָ֖ה בְּלִמֻּדָֽי׃

17 וְחִכִּ֙יתִי֙ לַֽיהוָ֔ה הַמַּסְתִּ֥יר פָּנָ֖יו מִבֵּ֣ית יַעֲקֹ֑ב וְקִוֵּֽיתִי־לֽוֹ׃ 18 הִנֵּ֣ה אָנֹכִ֗י וְהַיְלָדִים֙ אֲשֶׁ֣ר נָֽתַן־לִ֣י יְהוָ֔ה לְאֹת֥וֹת וּלְמֽוֹפְתִ֖ים בְּיִשְׂרָאֵ֑ל מֵעִם֙ יְהוָ֣ה צְבָא֔וֹת הַשֹּׁכֵ֖ן בְּהַ֥ר צִיּֽוֹן׃ ס

19 וְכִֽי־יֹאמְר֣וּ אֲלֵיכֶ֗ם דִּרְשׁ֤וּ אֶל־הָאֹבוֹת֙ וְאֶל־הַיִּדְּעֹנִ֔ים הַֽמְצַפְצְפִ֖ים וְהַמַּהְגִּ֑ים הֲלוֹא־עַם֙ אֶל־אֱלֹהָ֣יו יִדְרֹ֔שׁ בְּעַ֥ד הַחַיִּ֖ים אֶל־הַמֵּתִֽים׃ 20 לְתוֹרָ֖ה וְלִתְעוּדָ֑ה אִם־לֹ֤א יֹֽאמְרוּ֙ כַּדָּבָ֣ר הַזֶּ֔ה אֲשֶׁ֥ר אֵֽין־ל֖וֹ שָֽׁחַר׃ 21 וְעָ֥בַר בָּ֖הּ נִקְשֶׁ֣ה וְרָעֵ֑ב וְהָיָ֨ה כִֽי־יִרְעַ֜ב וְהִתְקַצַּ֗ף וְקִלֵּ֧ל בְּמַלְכּ֛וֹ וּבֵֽאלֹהָ֖יו וּפָנָ֥ה לְמָֽעְלָה׃ 22 וְאֶל־אֶ֖רֶץ יַבִּ֑יט וְהִנֵּ֤ה צָרָה֙ וַחֲשֵׁכָ֣ה מְע֔וּף צוּקָ֖ה וַאֲפֵלָ֥ה מְנֻדָּֽח׃

23 כִּ֣י לֹ֣א* מוּעָף֮ לַאֲשֶׁ֣ר מוּצָ֣ק לָהּ֒ כָּעֵ֣ת הָרִאשׁ֗וֹן הֵקַ֞ל אַ֤רְצָה זְבֻלוּן֙ וְאַ֣רְצָה נַפְתָּלִ֔י וְהָאַחֲר֖וֹן הִכְבִּ֑יד דֶּ֤רֶךְ הַיָּם֙ עֵ֣בֶר הַיַּרְדֵּ֔ן גְּלִ֖יל הַגּוֹיִֽם׃

ט הָעָם֙ הַהֹלְכִ֣ים בַּחֹ֔שֶׁךְ
רָא֖וּ א֣וֹר גָּד֑וֹל
יֹשְׁבֵי֙ בְּאֶ֣רֶץ צַלְמָ֔וֶת

---

l   *I.e., the shades of the dead; cf. 1 Sam. 28.13.*
m-m   *This sentence would read well after v. 22.*
n-n   *Meaning of Heb. uncertain.*
o-o   *So 1QIsᵃ; the others have "there is not."*
p   *Meaning of verse uncertain. The rendering here assumes that "the former [king]" refers to Pekah (cf. 2 Kings 15.29) and "the later" to Hoshea (ibid. 30). For the construction lu...ka'eth, see Judg. 13–23.*
a   *See note j at 5.30.*

v. 23. בנוסח אחר "לו"

Light has dawned.
²You have magnified that nation,
Have given it great joy;
They have rejoiced before You
As they rejoice at reaping time,
As they exult
When dividing spoil.

³For the yoke that they bore
And the stick on their back—
The rod of their taskmaster—
You have broken as on the day of Midian.[b]
⁴Truly, all the boots put on [c]to stamp with[c]
And all the garments donned in infamy
Have been fed to the flames,
Devoured by fire.
⁵For a child has been born to us,
A son has been given us.
And authority has settled on his shoulders.
He has been named
"The Mighty God is planning grace;[d]
The Eternal Father, a peaceable ruler"—
⁶In token of abundant authority
And of peace without limit
Upon David's throne and kingdom,
That it may be firmly established
In justice and in equity
Now and evermore.
The zeal of the LORD of Hosts
Shall bring this to pass.

⁷My Lord
[e]Let loose a word[e] against Jacob
And it fell upon Israel.
⁸But all the people noted[f]—
Ephraim and the inhabitants of Samaria—
In arrogance and haughtiness:

אֽוֹר נָגַהּ עֲלֵיהֶֽם׃
2 הִרְבִּיתָ הַגּוֹי
לא לוֹ הִגְדַּלְתָּ הַשִּׂמְחָה
שָׂמְחוּ לְפָנֶיךָ
כְּשִׂמְחַת בַּקָּצִיר
כַּאֲשֶׁר יָגִילוּ
בְּחַלְּקָם שָׁלָֽל׃

3 כִּי ׀ אֶת־עֹל סֻבֳּלוֹ
וְאֵת מַטֵּה שִׁכְמוֹ
שֵׁבֶט הַנֹּגֵשׂ בּוֹ
הַחִתֹּתָ כְּיוֹם מִדְיָֽן׃
4 כִּי כׇל־סְאוֹן סֹאֵן בְּרַעַשׁ
וְשִׂמְלָה מְגוֹלָלָה בְדָמִים
וְהָיְתָה לִשְׂרֵפָה
מַאֲכֹלֶת אֵֽשׁ׃
5 כִּי־יֶלֶד יֻלַּד־לָנוּ
בֵּן נִתַּן־לָנוּ
וַתְּהִי הַמִּשְׂרָה עַל־שִׁכְמוֹ
וַיִּקְרָא שְׁמוֹ
פֶּלֶא יוֹעֵץ אֵל גִּבּוֹר
אֲבִיעַד שַׂר־שָׁלֽוֹם׃
6 לם̇רבה לְמַרְבֵּה הַמִּשְׂרָה
וּלְשָׁלוֹם אֵֽין־קֵץ
עַל־כִּסֵּא דָוִד וְעַל־מַמְלַכְתּוֹ
לְהָכִין אֹתָהּ וּֽלְסַעֲדָהּ
בְּמִשְׁפָּט וּבִצְדָקָה
מֵעַתָּה וְעַד־עוֹלָם
קִנְאַת יְהֹוָה צְבָאוֹת
תַּעֲשֶׂה־זֹּֽאת׃ ס

7 דָּבָר שָׁלַח אֲדֹנָי
בְּיַעֲקֹב
וְנָפַל בְּיִשְׂרָאֵֽל׃
8 וְיָֽדְעוּ הָעָם כֻּלּוֹ
אֶפְרַיִם וְיוֹשֵׁב שֹׁמְרוֹן
בְּגַאֲוָה וּבְגֹדֶל לֵבָב לֵאמֹֽר׃

---

b   See Judg. 7–8.
c-c   Meaning of Heb. uncertain; emendation yields "in wickedness";
     cf. Targum.
d   As in 25.1.
e-e   Septuagint reads "Let loose pestilence"; cf. Amos 4.10. In
     vv. 7–20 Isaiah alludes to and builds upon Amos 4.10–12.
f   1QIsᵃ reads "shouted."

9"Bricks have fallen—
We'll rebuild with dressed stone;
Sycamores have been felled—
We'll grow cedars instead!"
10So the Lord let g-the enemies of Rezin-g
Triumph over it
And stirred up its foes—
11Aram from the east
And Philistia from the west—
Who devoured Israel
With greedy mouths.

    Yet His anger has not turned back,
    And His arm is outstretched still.

12For the people has not turned back
To Him who struck it
And has not sought
The Lord of Hosts.
13So the Lord will cut off from Israel
Head and tail,
Palm branch and reed,
In a single day.
14Elders h-and magnates-h—
Such are the heads;
Prophets who give false instruction,
Such are the tailsi
15That people's leaders have been misleaders,
So they that are led have been confused.
16That is why my Lord
Will not sparej their youths,
Nor show compassion
To their orphans and widows;
For all are ungodly and wicked,
And every mouth speaks impiety.

17Already wickedness has blazed forth like a
    fire

לְבֵנִים נָפָלוּ 9
וְגָזִית נִבְנֶה
שִׁקְמִים גֻּדָּעוּ
וַאֲרָזִים נַחֲלִיף:
וַיְשַׂגֵּב יְהוָה אֶת־צָרֵי רְצִין 10
עָלָיו
וְאֶת־אֹיְבָיו יְסַכְסֵךְ:
אֲרָם מִקֶּדֶם 11
וּפְלִשְׁתִּים מֵאָחוֹר
וַיֹּאכְלוּ אֶת־יִשְׂרָאֵל
בְּכָל־פֶּה

בְּכָל־זֹאת לֹא־שָׁב אַפּוֹ
וְעוֹד יָדוֹ נְטוּיָה:

וְהָעָם לֹא־שָׁב 12
עַד־הַמַּכֵּהוּ
וְאֶת־יְהוָה צְבָאוֹת
לֹא דָרָשׁוּ: ס
וַיַּכְרֵת יְהוָה מִיִּשְׂרָאֵל 13
רֹאשׁ וְזָנָב
כִּפָּה וְאַגְמוֹן
יוֹם אֶחָד:
זָקֵן וּנְשׂוּא־פָנִים 14
הוּא הָרֹאשׁ
וְנָבִיא מוֹרֶה־שֶּׁקֶר
הוּא הַזָּנָב:
וַיִּהְיוּ מְאַשְּׁרֵי הָעָם־הַזֶּה מַתְעִים 15
וּמְאֻשָּׁרָיו מְבֻלָּעִים:
עַל־כֵּן עַל־בַּחוּרָיו 16
לֹא־יִשְׂמַח | אֲדֹנָי
וְאֶת־יְתֹמָיו וְאֶת־אַלְמְנֹתָיו
לֹא יְרַחֵם
כִּי כֻלּוֹ חָנֵף וּמֵרַע
וְכָל־פֶּה דֹּבֵר נְבָלָה

---

g-g   Emendation yields "its enemies."
h-h   Emendation yields "who practice partiality."
i   Emendation yields "palm branches"; the elders and the prophets
    are the leaders, the people are the led; cf. 3.1–2, 12.
j   Cf. Arabic samuḥa. 1QIsᵃ reads yḥmw.

Devouring thorn and thistle.
It has kindled the thickets of the wood,
k-Which have turned into billowing smoke.-k

l-Yet His anger has not turned back,
And His arm is outstretched still.-l

18By the fury of the Lord of Hosts,
The earth was shaken.m
Next, the people became like devouring fire:
No man spared his countryman.
19They snatched on the right, but remained
hungry,
And consumed on the left without being
sated.
Each devoured the flesh of his n-own kin-
dred-n—
20Manasseh Ephraim's, and Ephraim Manasseh's,o
And both of them against Judah!p

Yet His anger has not turned back,
And His arm is outstretched still.

10 Ha!
Those who write out evil writs
And compose iniquitous documents,
2To subvert the cause of the poor,
To rob of their rights the needy of My people;
That widows may be their spoil,
And fatherless children their booty!
3What will you do on the day of punishment,
When the calamity comes from afar?
To whom will you flee for help,
And how will you save your carcassesa

בְּכָל־זֹאת לֹא־שָׁב אַפּוֹ
וְעוֹד יָדוֹ נְטוּיָה׃

17 כִּי־בָעֲרָה כָאֵשׁ רִשְׁעָה
שָׁמִיר וָשַׁיִת תֹּאכֵל
וַתִּצַּת בְּסִבְכֵי הַיַּעַר
וַיִּתְאַבְּכוּ גֵּאוּת עָשָׁן׃

18 בְּעֶבְרַת יְהוָה צְבָאוֹת
נֶעְתַּם אָרֶץ
וַיְהִי הָעָם כְּמַאֲכֹלֶת אֵשׁ
אִישׁ אֶל־אָחִיו לֹא יַחְמֹלוּ׃
19 וַיִּגְזֹר עַל־יָמִין וְרָעֵב
וַיֹּאכַל עַל־שְׂמֹאול וְלֹא שָׂבֵעוּ
אִישׁ בְּשַׂר־זְרֹעוֹ יֹאכֵלוּ׃
20 מְנַשֶּׁה אֶת־אֶפְרַיִם וְאֶפְרַיִם אֶת־
מְנַשֶּׁה
יַחְדָּו הֵמָּה עַל־יְהוּדָה

בְּכָל־זֹאת לֹא־שָׁב אַפּוֹ
וְעוֹד יָדוֹ נְטוּיָה׃ ס

ל הוֹי
הַחֹקְקִים חִקְקֵי־אָוֶן
וּמְכַתְּבִים עָמָל כִּתֵּבוּ׃
2 לְהַטּוֹת מִדִּין דַּלִּים
וְלִגְזֹל מִשְׁפַּט עֲנִיֵּי עַמִּי
לִהְיוֹת אַלְמָנוֹת שְׁלָלָם
וְאֶת־יְתוֹמִים יָבֹזּוּ׃
3 וּמַה־תַּעֲשׂוּ לְיוֹם פְּקֻדָּה
וּלְשׁוֹאָה מִמֶּרְחָק תָּבוֹא
עַל־מִי תָּנוּסוּ לְעֶזְרָה
וְאָנָה תַעַזְבוּ כְּבוֹדְכֶם׃

k-k   Meaning of Heb. uncertain.
l-l   Moved down from v. 16 for clarity.
m   Cf. note at 5.25.
n-n   Meaning of Heb. uncertain. Emendation yields "fellow"; cf.
    Targum.
o   Alludes to the civil wars of 2 Kings 15.10, 14–16, 25.
p   Cf. 7.1–9.

a   Meaning of Heb. uncertain; for "carcasses," compare the
    rendering of kabod in v. 16; 22.18.

⁴From collapsing under [fellow] prisoners,
From falling beneath the slain?

Yet His anger has not turned back,
And his arm is outstretched still.

⁵Ha!
Assyria, rod of My anger,
^{b-}In whose hand, as a staff, is My fury!^{-b}
⁶I send him against an ungodly nation,
I charge him against a people that provokes
    Me,
To take its spoil and to seize its booty
And to make it a thing trampled
Like the mire of the streets.
⁷But he has evil plans,
His mind harbors evil designs;
For he means to destroy,
To wipe out nations, not a few.
⁸For he thinks,
"After all, ^{c-}I have kings as my captains!^{-c}
⁹Was Calno any different from Carchemish?
Or Hamath from Arpad?
Or Samaria from Damascus?
^{10d-}Since I was able to seize
The insignificant kingdoms,
Whose images exceeded
Jerusalem's and Samaria's,^{-d}
¹¹Shall I not do to Jerusalem and her images
What I did to Samaria and her idols?"

¹²But when my Lord has carried out all his purpose on Mount Zion and in Jerusalem, He^e will punish the majestic pride and overbearing arrogance of the king of Assyria. ¹³For he thought,

"By the might of my hand have I wrought it,
By my skill, for I am clever:

אֲשׁ֤וּר שֵׁ֣בֶט אַפִּ֔י

⁴ בִּלְתִּ֤י כָרַע֙ תַּ֣חַת אַסִּ֔יר
וְתַ֥חַת הֲרוּגִ֖ים יִפֹּ֑לוּ

בְּכָל־זֹאת֙ לֹא־שָׁ֣ב אַפּ֔וֹ
וְע֖וֹד יָד֥וֹ נְטוּיָֽה׃ ס

⁵ ה֥וֹי
אַשּׁ֖וּר שֵׁ֣בֶט אַפִּ֑י
וּמַטֶּה־ה֥וּא בְיָדָ֖ם זַעְמִֽי׃
⁶ בְּג֤וֹי חָנֵף֙ אֲשַׁלְּחֶ֔נּוּ
וְעַל־עַ֥ם עֶבְרָתִ֖י אֲצַוֶּ֑נּוּ
לִשְׁלֹ֤ל שָׁלָל֙ וְלָבֹ֣ז בַּ֔ז
ולשימו [וּלְשׂוּמ֥וֹ] מִרְמָ֖ס
כְּחֹ֥מֶר חוּצֽוֹת׃
⁷ וְהוּא֙ לֹא־כֵ֣ן יְדַמֶּ֔ה
וּלְבָב֖וֹ לֹא־כֵ֣ן יַחְשֹׁ֑ב
כִּ֚י לְהַשְׁמִ֣יד בִּלְבָב֔וֹ
וּלְהַכְרִ֥ית גּוֹיִ֖ם לֹ֥א מְעָֽט׃
⁸ כִּ֖י יֹאמַ֑ר
הֲלֹ֥א שָׂרַ֖י יַחְדָּ֥ו מְלָכִֽים׃
⁹ הֲלֹ֥א כְּכַרְכְּמִ֖ישׁ כַּלְנ֑וֹ
אִם־לֹ֤א כְאַרְפַּד֙ חֲמָ֔ת
אִם־לֹ֥א כְדַמֶּ֖שֶׂק שֹׁמְרֽוֹן׃
¹⁰ כַּאֲשֶׁר֙ מָצְאָ֣ה יָדִ֔י
לְמַמְלְכֹ֖ת הָאֱלִ֑יל
וּפְסִ֣ילֵיהֶ֔ם
מִירֽוּשָׁלַ֖͏ִם וּמִשֹּׁמְרֽוֹן׃
¹¹ הֲלֹ֗א כַּאֲשֶׁ֥ר עָשִׂ֛יתִי לְשֹׁמְר֖וֹן
וְלֶאֱלִילֶ֑יהָ
כֵּ֛ן אֶעֱשֶׂ֥ה לִירוּשָׁלַ֖͏ִם וְלַעֲצַבֶּֽיהָ׃ ס

¹² וְהָיָ֗ה כִּֽי־יְבַצַּ֤ע אֲדֹנָי֙ אֶת־כׇּל־מַעֲשֵׂ֔הוּ
בְּהַ֥ר צִיּ֖וֹן וּבִירוּשָׁלָ֑͏ִם אֶפְקֹ֗ד עַל־פְּרִי־גֹ֙דֶל֙
לְבַ֣ב מֶֽלֶךְ־אַשּׁ֔וּר וְעַל־תִּפְאֶ֖רֶת ר֥וּם עֵינָֽיו׃
¹³ כִּ֣י אָמַ֗ר
בְּכֹ֤חַ יָדִי֙ עָשִׂ֔יתִי
וּבְחׇכְמָתִ֖י כִּ֣י נְבֻנֹ֑ותִי

---

^{b-b} *Emendation yields "Who is a staff in the hand of my fury."*
^{c-c} *Emendation yields "all the kingdoms fared alike!"*
^{d-d} *Emendation yields "Since I was able to seize / those kingdoms and their images, / Why is Jerusalem better than Samaria?"*
^e *Heb. "I."*

I have erased the borders of peoples;
I have plundered their treasures,
And exiled their vast populations.*f*

וְאָסִיר ׀ גְּבוּלֹת עַמִּים
וַעֲתִידֹתֵיהֶם שׁוֹשֵׂתִי
וְאוֹרִיד כַּאבִּיר* יוֹשְׁבִים:

14 I was able to seize, like a nest,
The wealth of peoples;
As one gathers abandoned eggs,
So *I* gathered all the earth:
Nothing so much as flapped a wing
Or opened a mouth to peep."

14 וַתִּמְצָא כַקֵּן ׀ יָדִי
לְחֵיל הָעַמִּים
וְכֶאֱסֹף בֵּיצִים עֲזֻבוֹת
כׇּל־הָאָרֶץ אֲנִי אָסָפְתִּי
וְלֹא הָיָה נֹדֵד כָּנָף
וּפֹצֶה פֶה וּמְצַפְצֵף:

15 Does an ax boast over him who hews with
　it,
Or a saw magnify itself above him who wields
　it?
As though the rod raised him who lifts it,
As though the staff lifted the man!*g*

15 הֲיִתְפָּאֵר הַגַּרְזֶן עַל הַחֹצֵב בּוֹ
אִם־יִתְגַּדֵּל הַמַּשּׂוֹר עַל־מְנִיפוֹ
כְּהָנִיף שֵׁבֶט וְאֶת־מְרִימָיו
כְּהָרִים מַטֶּה לֹא־עֵץ:

16 Assuredly,
The Sovereign LORD of Hosts will send
A wasting away in its*h* fatness;
And under its body*i* shall burn
A burning like that of fire,
*j-*Destroying frame and flesh.
It shall be like a sick man who pines away.-*j*
17 The Light of Israel will be fire
And its Holy One flame.
It will burn and consume its thorns
And its thistles in a single day,
18 And the mass of its scrub and its farm land.
19 What trees remain of its scrub
Shall be so few that a boy may record them.

16 לָכֵן
יְשַׁלַּח הָאָדוֹן יְהֹוָה צְבָאוֹת
בְּמִשְׁמַנָּיו רָזוֹן
וְתַחַת כְּבֹדוֹ יֵקַד
יְקֹד כִּיקוֹד אֵשׁ:
17 וְהָיָה אוֹר־יִשְׂרָאֵל לְאֵשׁ
וּקְדוֹשׁוֹ לְלֶהָבָה
וּבָעֲרָה וְאָכְלָה שִׁיתוֹ
וּשְׁמִירוֹ בְּיוֹם אֶחָד:
18 וּכְבוֹד יַעְרוֹ וְכַרְמִלּוֹ
מִנֶּפֶשׁ וְעַד־בָּשָׂר יְכַלֶּה
וְהָיָה כִּמְסֹס נֹסֵס:
19 וּשְׁאָר עֵץ יַעְרוֹ מִסְפָּר יִהְיוּ
וְנַעַר יִכְתְּבֵם: פ

20 And in that day,
The remnant of Israel
And the escaped of the House of Jacob
Shall lean no more upon him that beats it,*k*

20 וְהָיָה ׀ בַּיּוֹם הַהוּא
לֹא־יוֹסִיף עוֹד שְׁאָר יִשְׂרָאֵל
וּפְלֵיטַת בֵּית־יַעֲקֹב
לְהִשָּׁעֵן עַל־מַכֵּהוּ

v. 13. יתיר א'

---

f　According to vv. 6–7, Assyria was to plunder, but not to exile.
g　Lit. "not-wood."
h　Presumably Israel's. These verses would read well after 9.16.
i　Cf. note at v. 3.
j-j　Brought up from v. 18 for clarity.
k　I.e., upon Assyria (see v. 24). Ahaz's reliance on Assyria was in-
　terpreted by Isaiah as lack of faith in the LORD; see 7.13 with
　note.

But shall lean sincerely
On the LORD, the Holy One of Israel.
21Only a remnant shall return,
Only a remnant of Jacob,
To Mighty God.
22Even if your people, O Israel,
Should be as the sands of the sea,
Only a remnant of it shall return.
Destruction is decreed;
Retribution comes like a flood!
23For my Lord GOD of Hosts is carrying out
A decree of destruction upon all the land.

24Assuredly, thus said my Lord GOD of Hosts:
"O My people that dwells in Zion, have no fear
of Assyria, who beats you with a rod and wields
his staff over you as did the Egyptians. 25For very
soon My wrath will have spent itself, and *l*-My
anger that was bent on wasting them."-*l* 26The
LORD of Hosts will brandish a scourge over him
as when He beat Midian at the Rock of Oreb,*m*
and will wield His staff as He did over the Egyptians by the sea.

27And in that day,
His burden shall drop from your back,
n-And his yoke from your neck;
The yoke shall be destroyed because of fatness.

28He advanced upon Aiath,
He proceeded to Migron,
At Michmas he deposited his baggage.
29They made the crossing;
"Geba is to be our night quarters!"-*n*
Ramah was alarmed;

וְנִשְׁעַ֗ן
עַל־יְהוָ֛ה קְד֥וֹשׁ יִשְׂרָאֵ֖ל בֶּאֱמֶֽת׃
21 שְׁאָ֥ר יָשׁ֖וּב
שְׁאָ֣ר יַעֲקֹ֑ב
אֶל־אֵ֖ל גִּבּֽוֹר׃
22 כִּ֣י אִם־יִהְיֶ֞ה עַמְּךָ֤ יִשְׂרָאֵל֙
כְּח֣וֹל הַיָּ֔ם
שְׁאָ֖ר יָשׁ֣וּב בּ֑וֹ
כִּלָּי֥וֹן חָר֖וּץ
שׁוֹטֵ֥ף צְדָקָֽה׃
23 כִּ֥י כָלָ֖ה וְנֶחֱרָצָ֑ה
אֲדֹנָ֧י יְהוִ֛ה צְבָא֖וֹת עֹשֶׂ֥ה בְּקֶ֥רֶב כָּל־
הָאָֽרֶץ׃ ס

24 לָכֵ֗ן כֹּֽה־אָמַ֞ר אֲדֹנָ֤י יְהוִה֙ צְבָא֔וֹת אַל־
תִּירָ֥א עַמִּ֛י יֹשֵׁ֥ב צִיּ֖וֹן מֵאַשּׁ֑וּר בַּשֵּׁ֣בֶט יַכֶּ֔כָּה
וּמַטֵּ֥הוּ יִשָּׂא־עָלֶ֖יךָ בְּדֶ֥רֶךְ מִצְרָֽיִם׃ 25 כִּי־
ע֤וֹד מְעַ֣ט מִזְעָ֔ר וְכָ֣לָה זַ֔עַם וְאַפִּ֖י עַל־
תַּבְלִיתָֽם׃ 26 וְעוֹרֵ֨ר עָלָ֜יו יְהוָ֤ה צְבָאוֹת֙
שׁ֔וֹט כְּמַכַּ֥ת מִדְיָ֖ן בְּצ֣וּר עוֹרֵ֑ב וּמַטֵּ֙הוּ֙
עַל־הַיָּ֔ם וּנְשָׂא֖וֹ בְּדֶ֥רֶךְ מִצְרָֽיִם׃

27 וְהָיָ֣ה ׀ בַּיּ֣וֹם הַה֗וּא
יָס֤וּר סֻבֳּלוֹ֙ מֵעַ֣ל שִׁכְמֶ֔ךָ
וְעֻלּ֖וֹ מֵעַ֣ל צַוָּארֶ֑ךָ
וְחֻבַּ֥ל עֹ֖ל מִפְּנֵי־שָֽׁמֶן׃

28 בָּ֥א עַל־עַיַּ֖ת
עָבַ֣ר בְּמִגְר֑וֹן
לְמִכְמָ֖שׂ יַפְקִ֥יד כֵּלָֽיו׃
29 עָֽבְרוּ֙ מַעְבָּרָ֔ה
גֶּ֖בַע מָל֣וֹן לָ֑נוּ
חָֽרְדָה֙ הָֽרָמָ֔ה

---

l-l   Presumably Assyria; meaning of Heb. uncertain. Emendation
     yields "My anger against the world shall cease."
m   See Judg. 7.25.
n-n   Emendation yields "And his yoke shall leave your neck. / He
     came up from Jeshimon / 28By the ascent of Aiath, / He
     proceeded to Migron; / At Michmas he commanded his forces:
     / 29'Make the crossing; / Geba is to be our night quarters!'"
     Jeshimon is the southeast corner of the Jordan Valley, Num.
     21.20; 23.28; Aiath is elsewhere called Ai.

Gibeah of Saul took to flight.

30 "Give a shrill cry, O Bath-gallim!

Hearken, Laishah!

Take up the cry, Anathoth!"

31 Madmenah ran away;

The dwellers of Gebim sought refuge.

32 This same day at Nob

He shall stand and wave his hand.*o*

O mount of Fair Zion!

O hill of Jerusalem!

33 Lo! The Sovereign LORD of Hosts

Will hew off the tree-crowns with an ax:

The tall ones shall be felled,

The lofty ones cut down:

34 The thickets of the forest shall be hacked away with iron,

And the Lebanon trees shall fall *p*-in their majesty.-*p*

גִּבְעַת שָׁא֖וּל נָֽסָה׃

30 צַהֲלִ֣י קוֹלֵ֔ךְ בַּת־גַּלִּ֑ים

הַקְשִׁ֖יבִי לַ֥יְשָׁה

עֲנִיָּ֖ה עֲנָתֽוֹת׃

31 נָדְדָ֖ה מַדְמֵנָ֑ה

יֹשְׁבֵ֥י הַגֵּבִ֖ים הֵעִֽיזוּ׃

32 ע֥וֹד הַיּ֖וֹם בְּנֹ֣ב

לַעֲמֹ֑ד יְנֹפֵ֤ף יָדוֹ֙

הַ֚ר בֵּית־בַּת־צִיּ֔וֹן

גִּבְעַ֖ת יְרוּשָׁלָֽ͏ִם׃ ס

33 הִנֵּ֤ה הָאָדוֹן֙ יְהֹוָ֣ה צְבָא֔וֹת

מְסָעֵ֥ף פֻּארָ֖ה בְּמַעֲרָצָ֑ה

וְרָמֵ֤י הַקּוֹמָה֙ גְּדוּעִ֔ים

וְהַגְּבֹהִ֖ים יִשְׁפָּֽלוּ׃

34 וְנִקַּ֛ף סִֽבְכֵ֥י הַיַּ֖עַר בַּבַּרְזֶ֑ל

וְהַלְּבָנ֖וֹן בְּאַדִּ֥יר יִפּֽוֹל׃ ס

יא

11 But a shoot shall grow out of the stump of Jesse,

A twig shall sprout from his stock.

2 The spirit of the LORD shall alight upon him:

A spirit of wisdom and insight,

A spirit of counsel and valor,

A spirit of devotion and reverence for the LORD.

3*a*-He shall sense the truth-*a* by his reverence for the LORD:

He shall not judge by what his eyes behold,

Nor decide by what his ears perceive.

4 Thus he shall judge the poor with equity

And decide with justice for the lowly of the land.

וְיָצָ֥א חֹ֖טֶר מִגֵּ֣זַע יִשָׁ֑י

וְנֵ֖צֶר מִשָּׁרָשָׁ֥יו יִפְרֶֽה׃

2 וְנָחָ֥ה עָלָ֖יו ר֣וּחַ יְהֹוָ֑ה

ר֧וּחַ חׇכְמָ֣ה וּבִינָ֗ה

ר֤וּחַ עֵצָה֙ וּגְבוּרָ֔ה

ר֥וּחַ דַּ֖עַת וְיִרְאַ֥ת יְהֹוָֽה׃

3 וַהֲרִיח֖וֹ בְּיִרְאַ֣ת יְהֹוָ֑ה

וְלֹֽא־לְמַרְאֵ֤ה עֵינָיו֙ יִשְׁפּ֔וֹט

וְלֹֽא־לְמִשְׁמַ֥ע אׇזְנָ֖יו יוֹכִֽיחַ׃

4 וְשָׁפַ֤ט בְּצֶ֙דֶק֙ דַּלִּ֔ים

וְהוֹכִ֥יחַ בְּמִישׁ֖וֹר לְעַנְוֵי־אָ֑רֶץ

---

o   I.e., the Assyrian king, arriving at Nob (close to Jerusalem), shall beckon his army onward; cf. 13.2.

p-p   Or "by the bronze," connecting Heb. 'addir with Akkadian urudu, "bronze."

a-a   Lit. "His sensing [shall be]"; meaning of Heb. uncertain.

He shall strike down a land[b] with the rod of
   his mouth
And slay the wicked with the breath of his lips.
5 Justice shall be the girdle of his loins,
And faithfulness the girdle of his waist.
6 The wolf shall dwell with the lamb,
The leopard lie down with the kid;
[c]The calf, the beast of prey, and the fatling[c]
   together,
With a little boy to herd them.
7 The cow and the bear shall graze,
Their young shall lie down together;
And the lion, like the ox, shall eat straw.
8 A babe shall play
Over a viper's hole,
And an infant pass[d] his hand
Over an adder's den.
9 In all of [e]My sacred mount[e]
Nothing evil or vile shall be done;
For the land shall be filled with devotion to
   the LORD
As water covers the sea.

10 In that day,
The stock of Jesse that has remained standing
Shall become a standard to peoples—
Nations shall seek his counsel
And his abode shall be honored.

11 In that day, my Lord will apply His hand
again to redeeming the other part[f] of His people
from Assyria—as also from Egypt, Pathros, Nubia, Elam, Shinar, Hamath, and the coastlands.

12 He will hold up a signal to the nations
And assemble the banished of Israel,
And gather the dispersed of Judah
From the four corners of the earth.

וְהִכָּה־אֶ֙רֶץ֙ בְּשֵׁ֣בֶט פִּ֔יו
וּבְר֥וּחַ שְׂפָתָ֖יו יָמִ֥ית רָשָֽׁע׃
5 וְהָ֥יָה צֶ֖דֶק אֵז֣וֹר מָתְנָ֑יו
וְהָאֱמוּנָ֖ה אֵז֥וֹר חֲלָצָֽיו׃
6 וְגָ֤ר זְאֵב֙ עִם־כֶּ֔בֶשׂ
וְנָמֵ֖ר עִם־גְּדִ֣י יִרְבָּ֑ץ
וְעֵ֨גֶל וּכְפִ֤יר וּמְרִיא֙ יַחְדָּ֔ו
וְנַ֥עַר קָטֹ֖ן נֹהֵ֥ג בָּֽם׃
7 וּפָרָ֤ה וָדֹב֙ תִּרְעֶ֔ינָה
יַחְדָּ֖ו יִרְבְּצ֣וּ יַלְדֵיהֶ֑ן
וְאַרְיֵ֖ה כַּבָּקָ֥ר יֹֽאכַל־תֶּֽבֶן׃
8 וְשִֽׁעֲשַׁ֥ע יוֹנֵ֖ק
עַל־חֻ֣ר פָּ֑תֶן
וְעַ֨ל מְאוּרַ֣ת צִפְעוֹנִ֔י
גָּמ֖וּל יָד֥וֹ הָדָֽה׃
9 לֹֽא־יָרֵ֥עוּ וְלֹֽא־יַשְׁחִ֖יתוּ
בְּכָל־הַ֣ר קָדְשִׁ֑י
כִּֽי־מָלְאָ֣ה הָאָ֗רֶץ דֵּעָה֙ אֶת־יְהֹוָ֔ה
כַּמַּ֖יִם לַיָּ֥ם מְכַסִּֽים׃ פ

10 וְהָיָה֙ בַּיּ֣וֹם הַה֔וּא
שֹׁ֣רֶשׁ יִשַׁ֗י אֲשֶׁ֤ר עֹמֵד֙
לְנֵ֣ס עַמִּ֔ים
אֵלָ֖יו גּוֹיִ֣ם יִדְרֹ֑שׁוּ
וְהָיְתָ֥ה מְנֻחָת֖וֹ כָּבֽוֹד׃ פ

11 וְהָיָ֣ה ׀ בַּיּ֣וֹם הַה֗וּא יוֹסִ֨יף אֲדֹנָ֤י ׀ שֵׁנִית֙
יָד֔וֹ לִקְנ֖וֹת אֶת־שְׁאָ֣ר עַמּ֑וֹ אֲשֶׁ֣ר יִשָּׁאֵר֩
מֵֽאַשּׁ֨וּר וּמִמִּצְרַ֜יִם וּמִפַּתְר֣וֹס וּמִכּ֗וּשׁ
וּמֵֽעֵילָ֤ם וּמִשִּׁנְעָר֙ וּמֵ֣חֲמָ֔ת וּמֵאִיֵּ֖י הַיָּֽם׃

12 וְנָשָׂ֥א נֵס֙ לַגּוֹיִ֔ם
וְאָסַ֖ף נִדְחֵ֣י יִשְׂרָאֵ֑ל
וּנְפֻצ֤וֹת יְהוּדָה֙ יְקַבֵּ֔ץ
מֵֽאַרְבַּ֖ע כַּנְפ֥וֹת הָאָֽרֶץ׃

---

b   *Emendation yields "the ruthless."*
c-c *1QIs^a reads: "The calf and the beast of prey shall feed"; so too*
     the Septuagint.
d   *Meaning of Heb. uncertain.*
e-e *I.e., the Holy Land; cf. Exod. 15.17; Ps. 78.54.*
f   *I.e., the part outside the Holy Land; lit. "the rest that will remain."*

¹³Then Ephraim's envy shall cease
And Judah's harassment shall end;
Ephraim shall not envy Judah,
And Judah shall not harass Ephraim.
¹⁴They shall pounce on the back of Philistia
  to the west,
And together plunder the peoples of the east;
Edom and Moab shall be subject to them
And the children of Ammon shall obey them.

¹⁵The LORD will dry up the tongue of the
Egyptian sea.—He will raise His hand over the
Euphrates with the might*ᵈ* of His wind and
break it into seven wadis, so that it can be trodden dry-shod. ¹⁶Thus there shall be a highway
for the other part*ᶠ* of His people out of Assyria,
such as there was for Israel when it left the land
of Egypt.

12

In that day, you shall say:
"I give thanks to You, O LORD!
Although You were wroth with me,
Your wrath has turned back and You comfort
  me,
²Behold the God who gives me triumph!
I am confident, unafraid;
For Yah the LORD is my strength and might,*ᵃ*
And He has been my deliverance."

³Joyfully shall you draw water
From the fountains of triumph,
⁴And you shall say on that day:
"Praise the LORD, proclaim His name.
Make His deeds known among the peoples;
Declare that His name is exalted.
⁵Hymn the LORD,
For He has done gloriously;
Let this be made known
In all the world!

א³ וְסָ֙רָה֙ קִנְאַ֣ת אֶפְרַ֔יִם
וְצֹרְרֵ֥י יְהוּדָ֖ה יִכָּרֵ֑תוּ
אֶפְרַ֙יִם֙ לֹֽא־יְקַנֵּ֣א אֶת־יְהוּדָ֔ה
וִיהוּדָ֖ה לֹֽא־יָצֹ֥ר אֶת־אֶפְרָֽיִם׃
¹⁴ וְעָפ֨וּ בְכָתֵ֤ף פְּלִשְׁתִּים֙ יָ֔מָּה
יַחְדָּ֖ו יָבֹ֣זּוּ אֶת־בְּנֵי־קֶ֑דֶם
אֱד֤וֹם וּמוֹאָב֙ מִשְׁל֣וֹחַ יָדָ֔ם
וּבְנֵ֥י עַמּ֖וֹן מִשְׁמַעְתָּֽם׃

¹⁵ וְהֶחֱרִ֣ים יְהֹוָ֗ה אֵ֚ת לְשׁ֣וֹן יָם־מִצְרַ֔יִם
וְהֵנִ֥יף יָד֛וֹ עַל־הַנָּהָ֖ר בַּעְיָ֣ם רוּח֑וֹ וְהִכָּ֙הוּ֙
לְשִׁבְעָ֣ה נְחָלִ֔ים וְהִדְרִ֖יךְ בַּנְּעָלִֽים׃
¹⁶ וְהָיְתָ֣ה מְסִלָּ֗ה לִשְׁאָ֤ר עַמּוֹ֙ אֲשֶׁ֣ר יִשָּׁאֵ֔ר
מֵֽאַשּׁ֑וּר כַּאֲשֶׁ֤ר הָֽיְתָה֙ לְיִשְׂרָאֵ֔ל בְּי֖וֹם
עֲלֹת֥וֹ מֵאֶ֥רֶץ מִצְרָֽיִם׃

יב וְאָמַרְתָּ֙ בַּיּ֣וֹם הַה֔וּא
אוֹדְךָ֣ יְהֹוָ֔ה
כִּ֥י אָנַ֖פְתָּ בִּ֑י
יָשֹׁ֥ב אַפְּךָ֖ וּֽתְנַחֲמֵֽנִי׃
² הִנֵּ֙ה אֵ֧ל יְשׁוּעָתִ֛י
אֶבְטַ֖ח וְלֹ֣א אֶפְחָ֑ד
כִּֽי־עׇזִּ֤י וְזִמְרָת֙ יָ֣הּ יְהֹוָ֔ה
וַֽיְהִי־לִ֖י לִֽישׁוּעָֽה׃

³ וּשְׁאַבְתֶּם־מַ֖יִם בְּשָׂשׂ֑וֹן
מִמַּעַיְנֵ֖י הַיְשׁוּעָֽה׃
⁴ וַאֲמַרְתֶּ֞ם בַּיּ֣וֹם הַה֗וּא
הוֹד֤וּ לַֽיהֹוָה֙ קִרְא֣וּ בִשְׁמ֔וֹ
הוֹדִ֥יעוּ בָֽעַמִּ֖ים עֲלִילֹתָ֑יו
הַזְכִּ֕ירוּ כִּ֥י נִשְׂגָּ֖ב שְׁמֽוֹ׃
⁵ זַמְּר֣וּ יְהֹוָ֔ה
כִּ֥י גֵא֖וּת עָשָׂ֑ה
מִדַּ֥עַת מוֹדַ֖עַת זֹ֑את
בְּכׇל־הָאָֽרֶץ׃

---

a Others "song."

⁶Oh, shout for joy,
You who dwell in Zion!
For great in your midst
Is the Holy One of Israel."

6 צַהֲלִי וָרֹנִּי
יוֹשֶׁבֶת צִיּוֹן
כִּי־גָדוֹל בְּקִרְבֵּךְ
קְדוֹשׁ יִשְׂרָאֵל: פ

13 The "Babylon" Pronouncement, a prophecy of Isaiah son of Amoz.

יג מַשָּׂא בָּבֶל אֲשֶׁר חָזָה יְשַׁעְיָהוּ
בֶּן־אָמוֹץ:

²"Raise a standard upon a bare hill,
Cry aloud to them;
Wave a hand, and let them enter
The gates of the nobles!
³I have summoned My purified guests
To execute My wrath;
Behold, I have called My stalwarts,
My proudly exultant ones."^a

2 עַל הַר־נִשְׁפֶּה שְׂאוּ־נֵס
הָרִימוּ קוֹל לָהֶם
הָנִיפוּ יָד וְיָבֹאוּ
פִּתְחֵי נְדִיבִים:
3 אֲנִי צִוֵּיתִי לִמְקֻדָּשָׁי
גַּם קָרָאתִי גִבּוֹרַי
לְאַפִּי
עַלִּיזֵי גַּאֲוָתִי:

⁴Hark! a tumult on the mountains—
As of^b a mighty force;
Hark! an uproar of kingdoms,
Nations assembling!
The Lord of Hosts is mustering
A host for war.
⁵They come from a distant land,
From the end of the sky—
The Lord with the weapons of His wrath—
To ravage all the earth!

4 קוֹל הָמוֹן בֶּהָרִים
דְּמוּת עַם־רָב
קוֹל שְׁאוֹן מַמְלְכוֹת
גּוֹיִם נֶאֱסָפִים
יְהוָה צְבָאוֹת מְפַקֵּד
צְבָא מִלְחָמָה:
5 בָּאִים מֵאֶרֶץ מֶרְחָק
מִקְצֵה הַשָּׁמָיִם
יְהוָה וּכְלֵי זַעְמוֹ
לְחַבֵּל כָּל־הָאָרֶץ:

⁶Howl!
For the day of the Lord is near;
It shall come like havoc from Shaddai.^c
⁷Therefore all hands shall grow limp,
And all men's hearts shall sink;
⁸And, overcome by terror,
They shall be seized by pangs and throes,
Writhe like a woman in travail.

6 הֵילִילוּ
כִּי קָרוֹב יוֹם יְהוָה
כְּשֹׁד מִשַּׁדַּי יָבוֹא:
7 עַל־כֵּן כָּל־יָדַיִם תִּרְפֶּינָה
וְכָל־לְבַב אֱנוֹשׁ יִמָּס:
8 וְנִבְהָלוּ |
צִירִים וַחֲבָלִים יֹאחֵזוּן
כַּיּוֹלֵדָה יְחִילוּן

---

a   *The impending slaughter is spoken of as a sacrificial meal, for which the guests were notified to purify themselves ritually; cf. Zeph. 1.7.*
b   *Meaning of Heb. uncertain.*
c   *Traditionally rendered "the Almighty."*

They shall gaze at each other in horror,
Their faces *d*-livid with fright.-*d*

9Lo! The day of the LORD is coming
With pitiless fury and wrath,
To make the earth a desolation,
To wipe out the sinners upon it.
10The stars and constellations of heaven
Shall not give off their light;
The sun shall be dark when it rises,
And the moon shall diffuse no glow.

11"And I will requite to the world its evil,
And to the wicked their iniquity;
I will put an end to the pride of the arrogant
And humble the haughtiness of tyrants.
12I will make people scarcer than fine gold,
And men than gold of Ophir."

13Therefore *e*-shall heaven be shaken,-*e*
And earth leap out of its place,
At the fury of the LORD of Hosts
On the day of His burning wrath.
14Then like gazelles that are chased,
And like sheep that no man gathers,
Each man shall turn back to his people,
They shall flee every one to his land.
15All who remain shall be pierced through,
All who *f*-are caught-*f*
Shall fall by the sword.
16And their babes shall be dashed to pieces
   in their sight,
Their homes shall be plundered,
And their wives shall be raped.

17"Behold,
I stir up the Medes against them,
Who do not value silver
Or delight in gold.

אִישׁ אֶל־רֵעֵ֙הוּ֙ יִתְמָ֔הוּ
פְּנֵ֥י לְהָבִ֖ים פְּנֵיהֶֽם׃

9 הִנֵּ֤ה יוֹם־יְהוָה֙ בָּ֔א
אַכְזָרִ֥י וְעֶבְרָ֖ה וַחֲר֣וֹן אָ֑ף
לָשׂ֤וּם הָאָ֙רֶץ֙ לְשַׁמָּ֔ה
וְחַטָּאֶ֖יהָ יַשְׁמִ֥יד מִמֶּֽנָּה׃
10 כִּֽי־כוֹכְבֵ֤י הַשָּׁמַ֙יִם֙ וּכְסִ֣ילֵיהֶ֔ם
לֹ֥א יָהֵ֖לּוּ אוֹרָ֑ם
חָשַׁ֤ךְ הַשֶּׁ֙מֶשׁ֙ בְּצֵאת֔וֹ
וְיָרֵ֖חַ לֹא־יַגִּ֥יהַ אוֹרֽוֹ׃

11 וּפָקַדְתִּ֤י עַל־תֵּבֵל֙ רָעָ֔ה
וְעַל־רְשָׁעִ֖ים עֲוֺנָ֑ם
וְהִשְׁבַּתִּי֙ גְּא֣וֹן זֵדִ֔ים
וְגַאֲוַ֥ת עָרִיצִ֖ים אַשְׁפִּֽיל׃
12 אוֹקִ֥יר אֱנ֖וֹשׁ מִפָּ֑ז
וְאָדָ֖ם מִכֶּ֥תֶם אוֹפִֽיר׃

13 עַל־כֵּן֙ שָׁמַ֣יִם אַרְגִּ֔יז
וְתִרְעַ֥שׁ הָאָ֖רֶץ מִמְּקוֹמָ֑הּ
בְּעֶבְרַת֙ יְהוָ֣ה צְבָא֔וֹת
וּבְי֖וֹם חֲר֥וֹן אַפּֽוֹ׃
14 וְהָיָה֙ כִּצְבִ֣י מֻדָּ֔ח
וּכְצֹ֖אן וְאֵ֣ין מְקַבֵּ֑ץ
אִ֤ישׁ אֶל־עַמּוֹ֙ יִפְנ֔וּ
וְאִ֥ישׁ אֶל־אַרְצ֖וֹ יָנֽוּסוּ׃
15 כָּל־הַנִּמְצָ֖א יִדָּקֵ֑ר
וְכָל־הַנִּסְפֶּ֖ה
יִפּ֥וֹל בֶּחָֽרֶב׃
16 וְעֹלְלֵיהֶ֛ם יְרֻטְּשׁ֖וּ לְעֵינֵיהֶ֑ם
יִשַּׁ֙סּוּ֙ בָּתֵּיהֶ֔ם
וּנְשֵׁיהֶ֖ם תשגלנה תִּשָּׁכַֽבְנָה׃

17 הִנְנִ֛י
מֵעִ֥יר עֲלֵיהֶ֖ם אֶת־מָדָ֑י
אֲשֶׁר־כֶּ֙סֶף֙ לֹ֣א יַחְשֹׁ֔בוּ
וְזָהָ֖ב לֹ֥א יַחְפְּצוּ־בֽוֹ׃

---

d-d   Taking the root lhb as a variant of bhl: others "shall be faces
      of flame."
e-e   Lit. "I will shake heaven."
f-f   Meaning of Heb. uncertain; emendation yields "flee."

18Their bows shall shatter the young;
They shall show no pity to infants,
They shall not spare the children."

19And Babylon, glory of kingdoms,
Proud splendor of the Chaldeans,
Shall become like Sodom and Gomorrah
Overturned by God.
20Nevermore shall it be settled
Nor dwelt in through all the ages.
No Arab shall pitch his tent there,
No shepherds make flocks lie down there.
21But beasts[b] shall lie down there,
And the houses be filled with owls;[b]
There shall ostriches make their home,
And there shall satyrs dance.
22And jackals[b] shall abide in its castles
And dragons[b] in the palaces of pleasure.
Her hour is close at hand;
Her days will not be long.

14 But the LORD will pardon Jacob, and will again choose Israel, and will settle them on their own soil. And strangers shall join them and shall cleave to the House of Jacob. 2For peoples shall take them[a] and bring them to their homeland; and the House of Israel shall possess them[b] as slaves and handmaids on the soil of the LORD. They shall be captors of their captors and masters to their taskmasters.

3And when the LORD has given you rest from your sorrow and trouble, and from the hard service that you were made to serve, 4you shall recite this song of scorn over the king of Babylon:

How is the taskmaster vanished,
How is oppression[c] ended!

18 וְקַשְּׁת֖וֹת נְעָרִ֣ים תְּרַטַּ֑שְׁנָה
וּפְרִי־בֶ֙טֶן֙ לֹ֣א יְרַחֵ֔מוּ
עַל־בָּנִ֖ים לֹא־תָח֥וּס עֵינָֽם׃

19 וְהָיְתָ֨ה בָבֶ֜ל צְבִ֤י מַמְלָכוֹת֙
תִּפְאֶ֖רֶת גְּא֣וֹן כַּשְׂדִּ֑ים
כְּמַהְפֵּכַ֣ת אֱלֹהִ֔ים
אֶת־סְדֹ֖ם וְאֶת־עֲמֹרָֽה׃

20 לֹא־תֵשֵׁ֣ב לָנֶ֔צַח
וְלֹ֥א תִשְׁכֹּ֖ן עַד־דּ֣וֹר וָד֑וֹר
וְלֹֽא־יַהֵ֥ל שָׁם֙ עֲרָבִ֔י
וְרֹעִ֖ים לֹא־יַרְבִּ֥צוּ שָֽׁם׃

21 וְרָבְצוּ־שָׁ֣ם צִיִּ֔ים
וּמָלְא֥וּ בָתֵּיהֶ֖ם אֹחִ֑ים
וְשָׁ֤כְנוּ שָׁם֙ בְּנ֣וֹת יַֽעֲנָ֔ה
וּשְׂעִירִ֖ים יְרַקְּדוּ־שָֽׁם׃

22 וְעָנָ֤ה אִיִּים֙ בְּאַלְמְנוֹתָ֔יו
וְתַנִּ֖ים בְּהֵ֣יכְלֵי עֹ֑נֶג
וְקָר֤וֹב לָבוֹא֙ עִתָּ֔הּ
וְיָמֶ֖יהָ לֹ֥א יִמָּשֵֽׁכוּ׃

יד כִּֽי־יְרַחֵ֤ם יְהוָה֙ אֶֽת־יַעֲקֹ֔ב וּבָחַ֥ר ע֖וֹד בְּיִשְׂרָאֵ֑ל וְהִנִּיחָ֣ם עַל־אַדְמָתָ֗ם וְנִלְוָ֤ה הַגֵּר֙ עֲלֵיהֶ֔ם וְנִסְפְּח֖וּ עַל־בֵּ֥ית יַעֲקֹֽב׃
2 וּלְקָח֣וּם עַמִּ֗ים וֶהֱבִיא֮וּם אֶל־מְקוֹמָם֒ וְהִֽתְנַחֲל֣וּם בֵּֽית־יִשְׂרָאֵ֗ל עַ֚ל אַדְמַ֣ת יְהוָ֔ה לַעֲבָדִ֖ים וְלִשְׁפָח֑וֹת וְהָיוּ֙ שֹׁבִ֣ים לְשֹֽׁבֵיהֶ֔ם וְרָד֖וּ בְּנֹגְשֵׂיהֶֽם׃ ס
3 וְהָיָ֗ה בְּי֨וֹם הָנִ֤יחַ יְהוָה֙ לְךָ֣ מֵֽעָצְבְּךָ֔ וּמֵרָגְזֶ֑ךָ וּמִן־הָעֲבֹדָ֥ה הַקָּשָׁ֖ה אֲשֶׁ֥ר עֻבַּד־בָּֽךְ׃ 4 וְנָשָׂ֜אתָ הַמָּשָׁ֥ל הַזֶּ֛ה עַל־מֶ֥לֶךְ בָּבֶ֖ל וְאָמָ֑רְתָּ

אֵ֚יךְ שָׁבַ֣ת נֹגֵ֔שׂ
שָׁבְתָ֖ה מַדְהֵבָֽה׃*

a I.e., the House of Jacob.
b I.e., the peoples.
c Reading marhebah with 1QIsᵃ (cf. Septuagint). The traditional reading madhebah is of unknown meaning.

5The LORD has broken the staff of the wicked,
The rod of tyrants,
6That smote peoples in wrath
With stroke unceasing,
That belabored nations in fury
In relentless pursuit.

7All the earth is calm, untroubled;
Loudly it cheers.
8Even pines rejoice at your fate,
And cedars of Lebanon:
"Now that you have lain down,
None shall come up to fell us."

9Sheol below was astir
To greet your coming—
Rousing for you the shades
Of all earth's chieftains,
Raising from their thrones
All the kings of nations.
10All speak up and say to you,
"So you have been stricken as we were,
You have become like us!
11Your pomp is brought down to Sheol,
And the strains of your lutes!
Worms are to be your bed,
Maggots your blanket!"

12How are you fallen from heaven,
O Shining One, son of Dawn!d
How are you felled to earth,
O vanquisher of nations!

13Once you thought in your heart,
"I will climb to the sky;
Higher than the stars of God
I will set my throne.

d A character in some lost myth.

5 שָׁבַ֤ר יְהוָה֙ מַטֵּ֣ה רְשָׁעִ֔ים
שֵׁ֖בֶט מֹשְׁלִֽים:
6 מַכֶּ֤ה עַמִּים֙ בְּעֶבְרָ֔ה
מַכַּ֖ת בִּלְתִּ֣י סָרָ֑ה
רֹדֶ֤ה בָאַף֙ גּוֹיִ֔ם
מֻרְדָּ֖ף בְּלִ֥י חָשָֽׂךְ:

7 נָ֥חָה שָׁקְטָ֖ה כָּל־הָאָ֑רֶץ
פָּצְח֖וּ רִנָּֽה:
8 גַּם־בְּרוֹשִׁ֛ים שָׂמְח֥וּ לְךָ֖
אַרְזֵ֣י לְבָנ֑וֹן
מֵאָ֣ז שָׁכַ֔בְתָּ
לֹא־יַעֲלֶ֥ה הַכֹּרֵ֖ת עָלֵֽינוּ:

9 שְׁא֗וֹל מִתַּ֛חַת רָגְזָ֥ה לְךָ֖
לִקְרַ֣את בּוֹאֶ֑ךָ
עוֹרֵ֨ר לְךָ֤ רְפָאִים֙
כָּל־עַתּ֣וּדֵי אָ֔רֶץ
הֵקִים֙ מִכִּסְאוֹתָ֔ם
כֹּ֖ל מַלְכֵ֥י גוֹיִֽם:
10 כֻּלָּ֣ם יַֽעֲנ֔וּ וְיֹאמְר֖וּ אֵלֶ֑יךָ
גַּם־אַתָּ֛ה חֻלֵּ֥יתָ כָמ֖וֹנוּ
אֵלֵ֥ינוּ נִמְשָֽׁלְתָּ:
11 הוּרַ֥ד שְׁא֛וֹל גְּאוֹנֶ֖ךָ
הֶמְיַ֣ת נְבָלֶ֑יךָ
תַּחְתֶּ֙יךָ֙ יֻצַּ֣ע רִמָּ֔ה
וּמְכַסֶּ֖יךָ תּוֹלֵעָֽה:

12 אֵ֛יךְ נָפַ֥לְתָּ מִשָּׁמַ֖יִם
הֵילֵ֣ל בֶּן־שָׁ֑חַר
נִגְדַּ֣עְתָּ לָאָ֔רֶץ
חוֹלֵ֖שׁ עַל־גּוֹיִֽם:

13 וְאַתָּ֞ה אָמַ֤רְתָּ בִֽלְבָבְךָ֙
הַשָּׁמַ֣יִם אֶֽעֱלֶ֔ה
מִמַּ֥עַל לְכֽוֹכְבֵי־אֵ֖ל
אָרִ֣ים כִּסְאִ֑י

I will sit in the mount of assembly,[e]
On the summit of Zaphon:[f]
[14]I will mount the back of a cloud—
I will match the Most High."
[15]Instead, you are brought down to Sheol,
To [g]the bottom of the Pit.[g]
[16]They who behold you stare;
They peer at you closely:
"Is this the man
Who shook the earth,
Who made realms tremble,
[17]Who made the world like a waste
And wrecked its towns,
[h]Who never released his prisoners to their
　homes?"
[18]All the kings of nations
Were laid, every one, in honor[h]
Each in his tomb;
[19]While you were left lying unburied,
Like loathsome carrion,[i]
Like a trampled corpse
[In] the clothing of slain gashed by the sword
Who sink to the very stones of the Pit.
[20]You shall not have a burial like them;
Because you destroyed [j]your country,
Murdered your people.[j]

Let the breed of evildoers
Nevermore be named!
[21]Prepare a slaughtering block for his sons
Because of the guilt of their father.[k]
Let them not arise to possess the earth!
Then the world's face shall be covered with
　towns.

וְאֵשֵׁב בְּהַר־מוֹעֵד
בְּיַרְכְּתֵי צָפוֹן׃
14 אֶעֱלֶה עַל־בָּמֳתֵי עָב
אֶדַּמֶּה לְעֶלְיוֹן׃
15 אַךְ אֶל־שְׁאוֹל תּוּרָד
אֶל־יַרְכְּתֵי־בוֹר׃
16 רֹאֶיךָ אֵלֶיךָ יַשְׁגִּיחוּ
אֵלֶיךָ יִתְבּוֹנָנוּ
הֲזֶה הָאִישׁ
מַרְגִּיז הָאָרֶץ
מַרְעִישׁ מַמְלָכוֹת׃
17 שָׂם תֵּבֵל כַּמִּדְבָּר
וְעָרָיו הָרָס
אֲסִירָיו לֹא־פָתַח בָּיְתָה׃
18 כָּל־מַלְכֵי גוֹיִם כֻּלָּם
שָׁכְבוּ בְכָבוֹד
אִישׁ בְּבֵיתוֹ׃
19 וְאַתָּה הָשְׁלַכְתָּ מִקִּבְרְךָ
כְּנֵצֶר נִתְעָב
לְבֻשׁ הֲרֻגִים
מְטֹעֲנֵי חָרֶב
יוֹרְדֵי אֶל־אַבְנֵי־בוֹר כְּפֶגֶר מוּבָס׃
20 לֹא־תֵחַד אִתָּם בִּקְבוּרָה
כִּי־אַרְצְךָ שִׁחַתָּ
עַמְּךָ הָרָגְתָּ
לֹא־יִקָּרֵא לְעוֹלָם
זֶרַע מְרֵעִים׃
21 הָכִינוּ לְבָנָיו מַטְבֵּחַ
בַּעֲוֹן אֲבוֹתָם
בַּל־יָקֻמוּ וְיָרְשׁוּ אָרֶץ
וּמָלְאוּ פְנֵי־תֵבֵל עָרִים׃

---

e　I.e., the assembly of the gods in council.
f　The abode of the gods; cf. Ps. 48.3.
g-g　A region of the netherworld reserved for those who have not
　received decent burial; cf. Ezek. 32.21 ff.
h-h　Emendation yields "Who chained to his palace gate / All the
　kings of nations? / Yet they were all laid in honor…" The
　practice of chaining captive chieftains to gates is attested in
　Mesopotamia.
i　So several ancient versions; cf. postbiblical neṣel, "putrefying flesh
　or blood."
j-j　Emendation yields "…countries, / Murdered peoples."
k　Heb. "fathers."

22I will rise up against them—declares the LORD of Hosts—and will wipe out from Babylon name and remnant, kith and kin—declares the LORD—23and I will make it a home of bitterns,*l* pools of water. I will sweep it with a broom of extermination—declares the LORD of Hosts.

24The LORD of Hosts has sworn this oath:
"As I have designed, so shall it happen;
What I have planned, that shall come to pass:
25To break Assyria in My land,
To crush him on My mountain."*m*
And his yoke shall drop off them,
And his burden shall drop from their*n* backs.
26That is the plan that is planned
For all the earth;
That is why an arm is poised
Over all the nations.
27For the LORD of Hosts has planned,
Who then can foil it?
It is His arm that is poised,
And who can stay it?

28This pronouncement was made in the year that King Ahaz died:
29Rejoice not, all Philistia,
Because the staff of him that beat you is broken.
For from the stock of a snake there sprouts an asp,
A flying seraph*o* branches out from it.
30*p-*The first-born of the poor shall graze-*p*
And the destitute lie down secure.
*q-*I will kill your stock by famine,-*q*

כב וְקַמְתִּ֣י עֲלֵיהֶ֔ם נְאֻ֖ם יְהֹוָ֣ה צְבָא֑וֹת
וְהִכְרַתִּ֨י לְבָבֶ֜ל שֵׁ֤ם וּשְׁאָר֙ וְנִ֣ין וָנֶ֔כֶד
נְאֻם־יְהֹוָֽה: כג וְשַׂמְתִּ֛יהָ לְמוֹרַ֥שׁ קִפֹּ֖ד
וְאַגְמֵי־מָ֑יִם וְטֵֽאטֵאתִ֙יהָ֙ בְּמַטְאֲטֵ֣א הַשְׁמֵ֔ד
נְאֻ֖ם יְהֹוָ֥ה צְבָאֽוֹת: פ

כד נִשְׁבַּ֛ע יְהֹוָ֥ה צְבָא֖וֹת לֵאמֹ֑ר
אִם־לֹ֞א כַּֽאֲשֶׁ֤ר דִּמִּ֙יתִי֙ כֵּ֣ן הָיָ֔תָה
וְכַֽאֲשֶׁ֥ר יָעַ֖צְתִּי הִ֥יא תָקֽוּם:
כה לִשְׁבֹּ֤ר אַשּׁוּר֙ בְּאַרְצִ֔י
וְעַל־הָרַ֖י אֲבוּסֶ֑נּוּ
וְסָ֤ר מֵֽעֲלֵיהֶם֙ עֻלּ֔וֹ
וְסֻ֨בֳּל֔וֹ מֵעַ֥ל שִׁכְמ֖וֹ יָסֽוּר:
כו זֹ֛את הָֽעֵצָ֥ה הַיְּעוּצָ֖ה
עַל־כׇּל־הָאָ֑רֶץ
וְזֹ֛את הַיָּ֥ד הַנְּטוּיָ֖ה
עַל־כׇּל־הַגּוֹיִֽם:
כז כִּֽי־יְהֹוָ֧ה צְבָא֛וֹת יָעָ֖ץ
וּמִ֣י יָפֵ֑ר
וְיָד֥וֹ הַנְּטוּיָ֖ה
וּמִ֥י יְשִׁיבֶֽנָּה: פ

כח בִּשְׁנַת־מ֖וֹת הַמֶּ֣לֶךְ אָחָ֑ז הָיָ֖ה הַמַּשָּׂ֥א
הַזֶּֽה:
כט אַל־תִּשְׂמְחִ֤י פְלֶ֙שֶׁת֙ כֻּלֵּ֔ךְ
כִּ֥י נִשְׁבַּ֖ר שֵׁ֣בֶט מַכֵּ֑ךְ
כִּֽי־מִשֹּׁ֤רֶשׁ נָחָשׁ֙ יֵ֣צֵא צֶ֔פַע
וּפִרְי֖וֹ שָׂרָ֥ף מְעוֹפֵֽף:
ל וְרָעוּ֙ בְּכוֹרֵ֣י דַלִּ֔ים
וְאֶבְיוֹנִ֖ים לָבֶ֣טַח יִרְבָּ֑צוּ
וְהֵמַתִּ֤י בָֽרָעָב֙ שׇׁרְשֵׁ֔ךְ

---

l   *Meaning of Heb. uncertain.*
m   *Heb. "mountains"; for the designation of the entire land of Israel as the LORD's mountain, cf. 11.9.*
n   *Heb. "his." The last two lines of this verse would read well after v. 26.*
o   *Others "fiery serpent"; cf. Num. 21.6, 8.*
p-p   *Emendation yields "The poor shall graze in his pasture." This line and the next would read well after v. 32.*
q-q   *Emendation yields "It shall kill your offspring with its venom (zar'ekh berosho)."*

וּשְׁאֵרִיתֵךְ יַהֲרֹג:

And it shall slay the very last of you.

31Howl, O gate; cry out, O city;

Quake, all Philistia!

r-For a stout one is coming from the north

And there is no straggler in his ranks.-r

31 הֵילִילִי שַׁעַר זַעֲקִי־עִיר

נָמוֹג פְּלֶשֶׁת כֻּלֵּךְ

כִּי מִצָּפוֹן עָשָׁן בָּא

וְאֵין בּוֹדֵד בְּמוֹעָדָיו:

32And what will he answer the messengers of

any nation?

That Zion has been established by the Lord:

In it, the needy of His people shall find shelter.

32 וּמַה־יַּעֲנֶה מַלְאֲכֵי־גוֹי

כִּי יְהוָֹה יִסַּד צִיּוֹן

וּבָהּ יֶחֱסוּ עֲנִיֵּי עַמּוֹ: ס

15 The "Moab" Pronouncement.

טז מַשָּׂא מוֹאָב

Ah, in the night Ar was sacked,

Moab was ruined;

Ah, in the night Kir was sacked,

Moab was ruined.

כִּי בְּלֵיל שֻׁדַּד

עָר מוֹאָב נִדְמָה

כִּי בְּלֵיל שֻׁדַּד

קִיר־מוֹאָב נִדְמָה:

2He went up to the temple to weep,

Dibona [went] to the outdoor shrines.

Over Nebo and Medeba

Moab is wailing;

On every head is baldness,

Every beard is shorn.

3In its streets, they are girt with sackcloth;

On its roofs, in its squares,

Everyone is wailing,

Streaming with tears.

4Heshbon and Elealeh cry out,

Their voice carries to Jahaz.

Therefore,

b-The shock troops of Moab shout,-b

His body is convulsed.

5My heart cries out for Moab—

His fugitives flee down to Zoar,

To Eglath-shelishiyah.

For the ascent of Luhith

2 עָלָה הַבַּיִת

וְדִיבֹן הַבָּמוֹת לְבֶכִי

עַל־נְבוֹ וְעַל מֵידְבָא

מוֹאָב יְיֵלִיל

בְּכָל־רֹאשָׁיו קָרְחָה

כָּל־זָקָן גְּרוּעָה:

3 בְּחוּצֹתָיו חָגְרוּ שָׂק

עַל גַּגּוֹתֶיהָ וּבִרְחֹבֹתֶיהָ

כֻּלֹּה יְיֵלִיל

יֹרֵד בַּבֶּכִי:

4 וַתִּזְעַק חֶשְׁבּוֹן וְאֶלְעָלֵה

עַד־יַהַץ נִשְׁמַע קוֹלָם

עַל־כֵּן

חֲלֻצֵי מוֹאָב יָרִיעוּ

נַפְשׁוֹ יָרְעָה לּוֹ:

5 לִבִּי לְמוֹאָב יִזְעָק

בְּרִיחֶהָ עַד־צֹעַר

עֶגְלַת שְׁלִשִׁיָּה

כִּי ׀ מַעֲלֵה הַלּוּחִית

---

r-r   *Meaning of Heb. uncertain; the rendering "stout one" is suggested by the Syriac 'ashshīn.*

a   *Regarded as the principal city of Moab.*

b-b   *Change of vocalization yields "The loins of Moab are trembling."*

They ascend with weeping;
On the road to Horonaim
They raise a cry of anguish.

⁶Ah, the waters of Nimrim
Are become a desolation;
The grass is sear,
The herbage is gone,
Vegetation is vanished.

⁷Therefore,
The gains they have made, and their stores,
They carry to the Wadi of Willows.

⁸Ah, the cry has compassed
The country of Moab:
All the way to Eglaim her wailing,
Even at Beer-elim her wailing!

⁹Ah, the waters of Dimon are full of blood,ᶜ
For I pour added [water] on Dimon;
I drenchᵈ it—for Moab's refugees—
With soilᵉ for its remnant.

16 ᵃDispatch as messenger
The ruler of the land,
From Sela in the wilderness
To the mount of Fair Zion:
²"Like fugitive birds,
Like nestlings driven away,
Moab's villagers linger
By the fords of the Arnon.
³Give advice,
ᵇ-Offer counsel.-ᵇ
At high noon make

בִּבְכִי יַעֲלֶה־בּוֹ
כִּי דֶּרֶךְ חוֹרֹנַיִם
זַעֲקַת־שֶׁבֶר יְעֹעֵרוּ:

6 כִּי־מֵי נִמְרִים
מְשַׁמּוֹת יִהְיוּ
כִּי־יָבֵשׁ חָצִיר
כָּלָה דֶשֶׁא
יֶרֶק לֹא הָיָה:

7 עַל־כֵּן
יִתְרָה עָשָׂה וּפְקֻדָּתָם
עַל נַחַל הָעֲרָבִים יִשָּׂאוּם:

8 כִּי־הִקִּיפָה הַזְּעָקָה
אֶת־גְּבוּל מוֹאָב
עַד־אֶגְלַיִם יִלְלָתָהּ
וּבְאֵר אֵילִים יִלְלָתָהּ:

9 כִּי מֵי דִימוֹן מָלְאוּ דָם
כִּי־אָשִׁית עַל־דִּימוֹן נוֹסָפוֹת
לִפְלֵיטַת מוֹאָב אַרְיֵה
וְלִשְׁאֵרִית אֲדָמָה:

טז
שִׁלְחוּ־כַר
מֹשֵׁל־אֶרֶץ
מִסֶּלַע מִדְבָּרָה
אֶל־הַר בַּת־צִיּוֹן:
2 וְהָיָה כְעוֹף־נוֹדֵד
קֵן מְשֻׁלָּח
תִּהְיֶינָה בְּנוֹת מוֹאָב
מַעְבָּרֹת לְאַרְנוֹן:
3 הָבִיאוּ הָבִיאִי עֵצָה
עֲשׂוּ פְלִילָה
שִׁיתִי כַלַּיִל צִלֵּךְ

---

c   *Emendation yields "tears."*
d   *Cf. 16.9.*
e   *Emendation yields "tears"; cf. Ugaritic 'dm't.*

a   *Meaning of vv. 1 and 2 uncertain.*
b-b   *Meaning of Heb. uncertain.*

Your shadow like night:
Conceal the outcasts,
Betray not the fugitives.
⁴Let *c-Moab's outcasts-c*
Find asylum in you;
Be a shelter for them
Against the despoiler."

For violence has vanished,
Rapine is ended,
And marauders have perished from this land.
⁵And a throne shall be established in goodness
In the tent of David,
And on it shall sit in faithfulness
A ruler devoted to justice
And zealous for equity.*d*

⁶"We have heard of Moab's pride—
Most haughty is he—
Of his pride and haughtiness and arrogance,
And of the iniquity in him."*e*

⁷Ah, let Moab howl;
Let all in Moab howl!
For the raisin-cakes*f* of Kir-hareseth
You shall moan most pitifully.
⁸The vineyards of Heshbon are withered,
And the vines of Sibmah;
*b-*Their tendrils spread
To Baale-goiim,*-b*
And reached to Jazer,
And strayed to the desert;
Their shoots spread out
And crossed the sea.

⁹Therefore,
As I weep for Jazer,
So I weep for Sibmah's vines;

בְּתוֹךְ צָהֳרָ֑יִם
סַתְּרִי֙ נִדָּחִ֔ים
נֹדֵ֖ד אַל־תְּגַלִּֽי׃
⁴ יָג֤וּרוּ בָךְ֙
נִדָּחַ֣י מוֹאָ֔ב
הֱוִי־סֵ֤תֶר לָ֙מוֹ֙
מִפְּנֵ֣י שׁוֹדֵ֔ד

כִּֽי־אָפֵ֤ס הַמֵּץ֙
כָּ֣לָה שֹׁ֔ד
תַּ֥מּוּ רֹמֵ֖ס מִן־הָאָֽרֶץ׃
⁵ וְהוּכַ֤ן בַּחֶ֙סֶד֙ כִּסֵּ֔א
וְיָשַׁ֨ב עָלָ֤יו בֶּאֱמֶת֙
בְּאֹ֣הֶל דָּוִ֔ד
שֹׁפֵ֛ט וְדֹרֵ֥שׁ מִשְׁפָּ֖ט
וּמְהִ֥ר צֶֽדֶק׃

⁶ שָׁמַ֥עְנוּ גְאוֹן־מוֹאָ֖ב
גֵּ֣א מְאֹ֑ד
גַּאֲוָת֧וֹ וּגְאוֹנ֛וֹ וְעֶבְרָת֖וֹ
לֹא־כֵ֥ן בַּדָּֽיו׃ ס

⁷ לָכֵ֗ן יְיֵלִ֤יל מוֹאָב֙
לְמוֹאָ֔ב כֻּלֹּ֖ה יְיֵלִ֑יל
לַאֲשִׁישֵׁ֧י קִיר־חֲרֶ֛שֶׂת תֶּהְגּ֖וּ
אַךְ־נְכָאִֽים׃
⁸ כִּ֣י שַׁדְמוֹת֩ חֶשְׁבּ֨וֹן אֻמְלָ֜ל
גֶּ֣פֶן שִׂבְמָ֗ה
בַּעֲלֵ֣י גוֹיִ֔ם
הָלְמ֣וּ שְׂרוּקֶּ֔יהָ
עַד־יַעְזֵ֣ר נָגָ֔עוּ
תָּ֖עוּ מִדְבָּ֑ר
שְׁלֻ֣חוֹתֶ֔יהָ
נִטְּשׁ֖וּ עָ֥בְרוּ יָֽם׃

⁹ עַל־כֵּ֡ן
אֶבְכֶּ֞ה בִּבְכִ֣י יַעְזֵ֗ר
גֶּ֚פֶן שִׂבְמָ֔ה

---

c-c Heb. "my outcasts, Moab."
d   14.32, above, would read well here.
e   Baddaw is a suffixed form of the preposition bede: Nah. 2.13;
*   Hab. 2.13; Job 39.25; with suffixes, Job 11.3, 41.4.*
f   Jer. 48.36 has "men."

O Heshbon and Elealeh,
I drench you with my tears.
g-Ended are the shouts
Over your fig and grain harvests.-*g*
[10]Rejoicing and gladness
Are gone from the farm land;
In the vineyards no shouting
Or cheering is heard.
No more does the treader
Tread wine in the presses—
The shouts *h*-have been silenced.-*h*

[11]Therefore,
Like a lyre my heart moans for Moab,
And my very soul for Kir-heres.

[12]And when it has become apparent that Moab has gained nothing in the outdoor shrine, he shall come to pray in his temple—but to no avail.

[13]That is the word that the Lord spoke concerning Moab long ago. [14]And now the Lord has spoken: In three years, fixed like the years of a hired laborer, Moab's population, with all its huge multitude, shall shrink. Only a remnant shall be left, of no consequence.

17 The "Damascus" Pronouncement.

Behold,
Damascus shall cease to be a city;
It shall become a heap of ruins.
[2]*a*-The towns of Aroer shall be deserted;-*a*
They shall be a place for flocks
To lie down, with none disturbing.

אֲרַיָּוֶךְ דִּמְעָתִי
חֶשְׁבּוֹן וְאֶלְעָלֵה
כִּי עַל־קֵיצֵךְ וְעַל־קְצִירֵךְ
הֵידָד נָפָל׃
10 וְנֶאֱסַף שִׂמְחָה וָגִיל
מִן־הַכַּרְמֶל
וּבַכְּרָמִים לֹא־יְרֻנָּן
לֹא יְרֹעָע
יַיִן בַּיְקָבִים
לֹא־יִדְרֹךְ הַדֹּרֵךְ
הֵידָד הִשְׁבַּתִּי׃

11 עַל־כֵּן
מֵעַי לְמוֹאָב כַּכִּנּוֹר יֶהֱמוּ
וְקִרְבִּי לְקִיר חָרֶשׂ׃

12 וְהָיָה כִי־נִרְאָה כִּי־נִלְאָה מוֹאָב עַל־הַבָּמָה וּבָא אֶל־מִקְדָּשׁוֹ לְהִתְפַּלֵּל וְלֹא יוּכָל׃
13 זֶה הַדָּבָר אֲשֶׁר דִּבֶּר יְהוָה אֶל־מוֹאָב מֵאָז׃ 14 וְעַתָּה דִּבֶּר יְהוָה לֵאמֹר בְּשָׁלֹשׁ שָׁנִים כִּשְׁנֵי שָׂכִיר וְנִקְלָה כְּבוֹד מוֹאָב בְּכֹל הֶהָמוֹן הָרָב וּשְׁאָר מְעַט מִזְעָר לוֹא כַבִּיר׃ ס

יז מַשָּׂא דַּמָּשֶׂק

הִנֵּה
דַּמֶּשֶׂק מוּסָר מֵעִיר
וְהָיְתָה מְעִי מַפָּלָה׃
2 עֲזֻבוֹת עָרֵי עֲרֹעֵר
לַעֲדָרִים תִּהְיֶינָה
וְרָבְצוּ וְאֵין מַחֲרִיד׃

---

g-g   Jer. 48.32 reads "A ravager has come down / Upon your fig and grape harvests."
h-h   Lit. "I have silenced."

a-a   Emendation yields (cf. Septuagint) "Its towns shall be deserted forevermore."

3Fortresses shall cease from Ephraim,*b*

And sovereignty from Damascus;

The remnant of Aram shall become

Like the mass of Israelites

—declares the LORD of Hosts.

4In that day,

The mass of Jacob shall dwindle,

And the fatness of his body become lean:

5After being like the standing grain

Harvested by the reaper—

Who reaps ears by the armful—

He shall be like the ears that are gleaned

In the Valley of Rephaim.

6Only gleanings shall be left of him,

As when one beats an olive tree:

Two berries or three on the topmost branch,

Four or five *c-*on the boughs of the crown-*c*

—declares the LORD, the God of Israel.

7In that day, men shall turn to their Maker, their eyes look to the Holy One of Israel; 8they shall not turn to the altars that their own hands made, or look to the sacred posts and incense stands that their own fingers wrought.

9In that day, their fortress cities shall be like the deserted sites which *d-*the Horesh and the Amir-*d* abandoned because of the Israelites; and there shall be desolation.

10Truly, you have forgotten the God who

saves you

And have not remembered the Rock who

shelters you;

That is why, though you plant a delightful*e*

sapling,

What you sow proves a disappointing slip.

11On the day that you plant, you see it grow;

3* וְנִשְׁבַּת מִבְצָר מֵאֶפְרַיִם

וּמַמְלָכָה מִדַּמֶּשֶׂק

וּשְׁאָר אֲרָם

כִּכְבוֹד בְּנֵי־יִשְׂרָאֵל יִהְיוּ

נְאֻם יְהוָה צְבָאוֹת: ס

4 וְהָיָה בַּיּוֹם הַהוּא

יִדַּל כְּבוֹד יַעֲקֹב

וּמִשְׁמַן בְּשָׂרוֹ יֵרָזֶה:

5 וְהָיָה כֶּאֱסֹף

קָצִיר קָמָה

וּזְרֹעוֹ שִׁבֳּלִים יִקְצוֹר

וְהָיָה כִּמְלַקֵּט שִׁבֳּלִים

בְּעֵמֶק רְפָאִים:

6 וְנִשְׁאַר־בּוֹ עוֹלֵלֹת

כְּנֹקֶף זַיִת

שְׁנַיִם שְׁלֹשָׁה גַּרְגְּרִים בְּרֹאשׁ אָמִיר

אַרְבָּעָה חֲמִשָּׁה בִּסְעִפֶיהָ פֹּרִיָּה

נְאֻם־יְהוָה אֱלֹהֵי יִשְׂרָאֵל: ס

7 בַּיּוֹם הַהוּא יִשְׁעֶה הָאָדָם עַל־עֹשֵׂהוּ

וְעֵינָיו אֶל־קְדוֹשׁ יִשְׂרָאֵל תִּרְאֶינָה: 8 וְלֹא

יִשְׁעֶה אֶל־הַמִּזְבְּחוֹת מַעֲשֵׂה יָדָיו וַאֲשֶׁר

עָשׂוּ אֶצְבְּעֹתָיו לֹא יִרְאֶה וְהָאֲשֵׁרִים

וְהַחַמָּנִים:

9 בַּיּוֹם הַהוּא יִהְיוּ | עָרֵי מָעֻזּוֹ כַּעֲזוּבַת

הַחֹרֶשׁ וְהָאָמִיר אֲשֶׁר עָזְבוּ מִפְּנֵי בְּנֵי

יִשְׂרָאֵל וְהָיְתָה שְׁמָמָה:

10 כִּי שָׁכַחַתְּ אֱלֹהֵי יִשְׁעֵךְ

וְצוּר מָעֻזֵּךְ לֹא זָכָרְתְּ

עַל־כֵּן תִּטְּעִי נִטְעֵי נַעֲמָנִים

וּזְמֹרַת זָר תִּזְרָעֶנּוּ:

11 בְּיוֹם נִטְעֵךְ תְּשַׂגְשֵׂגִי

b Emendation yields "Aram."
c-c Lit. "on her boughs, the many-branched one."
d-d Septuagint reads "the Amorites and the Hivites."
*e Emendation yields "true." So Vulgate (cf. Septuagint); cf. Jer.
2.21.*

On the morning you sow, you see it bud—
But the branches wither away
On a day of sickness and mortal agony.

12Ah, the roar of many peoples
That roar as roars the sea,
The rage of nations that rage
As rage the mighty waters—
13Nations raging like massive waters!
But He shouts at them, and they flee far away,
Driven like chaff before winds in the hills,
And like tumbleweed before a gale.
14At eventide, lo, terror!
By morning, it is no more.
Such is the lot of our despoilers,
The portion of them that plunder us.

18 Ah,
a-land in the deep shadow of wings,-*a*
Beyond the rivers of Nubia!

2Go, swift messengers,
To a nation *b*-far and remote,
To a people thrust forth and away-*b*—
A nation of gibber and chatter*c*—
Whose land is cut off by streams;
d-Which sends out envoys by sea,
In papyrus vessels upon the water!-*d*

3[Say this:]
"All you who live in the world
And inhabit the earth,
When a flag is raised in the hills, take note!
When a ram's horn is blown, give heed!"
4For thus the LORD said to me:

וּבַבֹּקֶר זַרְעֵךְ תַּפְרִיחִי
נֵד קָצִיר
בְּיוֹם נַחֲלָה וּכְאֵב אָנוּשׁ: ס

12 הוֹי הֲמוֹן עַמִּים רַבִּים
כַּהֲמוֹת יַמִּים יֶהֱמָיוּן
וּשְׁאוֹן לְאֻמִּים
כִּשְׁאוֹן מַיִם כַּבִּירִים יִשָּׁאוּן:
13 לְאֻמִּים כִּשְׁאוֹן מַיִם רַבִּים יִשָּׁאוּן
וְגָעַר בּוֹ וְנָס מִמֶּרְחָק
וְרֻדַּף כְּמֹץ הָרִים לִפְנֵי־רוּחַ
וּכְגַלְגַּל לִפְנֵי סוּפָה:
14 לְעֵת עֶרֶב וְהִנֵּה בַלָּהָה
בְּטֶרֶם בֹּקֶר אֵינֶנּוּ
זֶה חֵלֶק שׁוֹסֵינוּ
וְגוֹרָל לְבֹזְזֵינוּ: ס

יח הוֹי
אֶרֶץ צִלְצַל כְּנָפָיִם
אֲשֶׁר מֵעֵבֶר לְנַהֲרֵי־כוּשׁ:

2 הַשֹּׁלֵחַ בַּיָּם צִירִים
וּבִכְלֵי־גֹמֶא עַל־פְּנֵי־מַיִם
לְכוּ | מַלְאָכִים קַלִּים
אֶל־גּוֹי מְמֻשָּׁךְ וּמוֹרָט
אֶל־עַם נוֹרָא מִן־הוּא וָהָלְאָה
גּוֹי קַו־קָו וּמְבוּסָה
אֲשֶׁר־בָּזְאוּ נְהָרִים אַרְצוֹ:

3 כָּל־יֹשְׁבֵי תֵבֵל
וְשֹׁכְנֵי אָרֶץ
כִּנְשֹׂא־נֵס הָרִים תִּרְאוּ
וְכִתְקֹעַ שׁוֹפָר תִּשְׁמָעוּ: ס
4 כִּי כֹה אָמַר יְהוָה אֵלַי

a-a   Or "Most sheltered land"; cf., e.g., 30.2, 3; Ps. 36.8; 57.2; 61.5.
b-b   Meaning of Heb. uncertain.
c   Meaning of Heb. uncertain; cf. 28.10. Biblical writers often char-
      acterize distant nations by their unintelligible speech; cf. 33.19;
      Deut. 28.49; Jer. 5.15.
d-d   Brought down from beginning of verse for clarity. The Hebrew
      verb for "sends" agrees in gender with "nation," not with "land."

"I rest calm and confident[e] in My habitation—
Like a scorching heat upon sprouts,
[f]Like a rain-cloud in the heat of reaping
  time."[f]

[5]For before the harvest,[g] yet after the budding,
When the blossom has hardened into berries,
He will trim away the twigs with pruning
  hooks,
And lop off the trailing branches.[h]

[6]They shall all be left
To the kites of the hills
And to the beasts of the earth;
The kites shall summer on them
And all the beasts of the earth shall winter on
  them.

[7]In that time,
Tribute shall be brought to the LORD of Hosts
[From] a people far and remote,
From a people thrust forth and away—
A nation of gibber and chatter,
Whose land is cut off by streams—
At the place where the name of the LORD of
  Hosts abides,
At Mount Zion.

19 The "Egypt" Pronouncement.

Mounted on a swift cloud,
The LORD will come to Egypt;
Egypt's idols shall tremble before Him,
And the heart of the Egyptians shall sink
  within them.

[2]"I will incite Egyptian against Egyptian:
They shall war with each other,

אֶשְׁקוֹטָה אֶשְׁקֲטָה וְאַבִּיטָה בִמְכוֹנִי
כְּחֹם צַח עֲלֵי־אוֹר
כְּעָב טַל בְּחֹם קָצִיר:
5 כִּי־לִפְנֵי קָצִיר כְּתָם־פֶּרַח
וּבֹסֶר גֹּמֵל יִהְיֶה נִצָּה
וְכָרַת הַזַּלְזַלִּים בַּמַּזְמֵרוֹת
וְאֶת־הַנְּטִישׁוֹת הֵסִיר הֵתַז:
6 יֵעָזְבוּ יַחְדָּו
לְעֵיט הָרִים
וּלְבֶהֱמַת הָאָרֶץ
וְקָץ עָלָיו הָעַיִט
וְכָל־בֶּהֱמַת הָאָרֶץ עָלָיו תֶּחֱרָף:

7 בָּעֵת הַהִיא
יוּבַל־שַׁי לַיהוָה צְבָאוֹת
עַם מְמֻשָּׁךְ וּמוֹרָט
וּמֵעַם נוֹרָא מִן־הוּא וָהָלְאָה
גּוֹי ׀ קַו־קָו וּמְבוּסָה
אֲשֶׁר בָּזְאוּ נְהָרִים אַרְצוֹ
אֶל־מְקוֹם שֵׁם־יְהוָה צְבָאוֹת
הַר־צִיּוֹן: ס

יט מַשָּׂא מִצְרָיִם

הִנֵּה יְהוָה רֹכֵב עַל־עָב קַל
וּבָא מִצְרַיִם
וְנָעוּ אֱלִילֵי מִצְרַיִם מִפָּנָיו
וּלְבַב מִצְרַיִם יִמַּס בְּקִרְבּוֹ:

2 וְסִכְסַכְתִּי מִצְרַיִם בְּמִצְרַיִם
וְנִלְחֲמוּ אִישׁ־בְּאָחִיו

---

e   *Cf.* hibbit *"to rely" (Job 6.19). The related noun* mabbaṭ *occurs
    with similar meaning in Isa. 20.5, 6.*
f-f *I.e., like a threat of disaster; cf. Eccl. 11.4.*
g   *Emendation yields "vintage."*
h   *A figure of speech for the defeated enemy.*

Every man with his fellow,
City with city
And kingdom with kingdom.*a*

³Egypt shall be drained of spirit,
And I will confound its plans;
So they will consult the idols and the shades
And the ghosts and the familiar spirits.

⁴And I will place the Egyptians
At the mercy of a harsh master,
And a ruthless king shall rule them"
—declares the Sovereign, the LORD of Hosts.

⁵Water shall fail from the seas,
Rivers dry up and be parched,
⁶Channels turn foul as they ebb,
And Egypt's canals run dry.
Reed and rush shall decay,
⁷ᵇ-And the Nile papyrus by the Nile-side-ᵇ
And everything sown by the Nile
Shall wither, blow away, and vanish.
⁸The fishermen shall lament;
All who cast lines in the Nile shall mourn,
And those who spread nets on the water shall
    languish.
⁹The flax workers, too, shall be dismayed,
Both carders and weavers chagrined.ᵇ
¹⁰ᶜHer foundations shall be crushed,
And all who make dams shall be despondent.

¹¹Utter fools are the nobles of Tanis;
The sagest of Pharaoh's advisers
[Have made] absurd predictions.
How can you say to Pharaoh,
"I am a scion of sages,
A scion of Kedemite kings"?ᵈ
¹²Where, indeed, are your sages?

וְאִישׁ בְּרֵעֵהוּ
עִיר בְּעִיר
מַמְלָכָה בְּמַמְלָכָה:
3 וְנָבְקָה רוּחַ־מִצְרַיִם בְּקִרְבּוֹ
וַעֲצָתוֹ אֲבַלֵּעַ
וְדָרְשׁוּ אֶל־הָאֱלִילִים וְאֶל־הָאִטִּים
וְאֶל־הָאֹבוֹת וְאֶל־הַיִּדְּעֹנִים:
4 וְסִכַּרְתִּי אֶת־מִצְרַיִם
בְּיַד אֲדֹנִים קָשֶׁה
וּמֶלֶךְ עַז יִמְשָׁל־בָּם
נְאֻם הָאָדוֹן יְהוָה צְבָאוֹת:

5 וְנִשְּׁתוּ־מַיִם מֵהַיָּם
וְנָהָר יֶחֱרַב וְיָבֵשׁ:
6 וְהֶאֶזְנִיחוּ נְהָרוֹת
דָּלְלוּ וְחָרְבוּ יְאֹרֵי מָצוֹר
קָנֶה וָסוּף קָמֵלוּ:
7 עָרוֹת עַל־יְאוֹר עַל־פִּי יְאוֹר
וְכֹל מִזְרַע יְאוֹר
יִיבַשׁ נִדַּף וְאֵינֶנּוּ:
8 וְאָנוּ הַדַּיָּגִים
וְאָבְלוּ כָּל־מַשְׁלִיכֵי בַיְאוֹר חַכָּה
וּפֹרְשֵׂי מִכְמֹרֶת עַל־פְּנֵי־מַיִם אֻמְלָלוּ:
9 וּבֹשׁוּ עֹבְדֵי פִשְׁתִּים שְׂרִיקוֹת
וְאֹרְגִים חוֹרָי:
10 וְהָיוּ שָׁתֹתֶיהָ מְדֻכָּאִים
כָּל־עֹשֵׂי שֶׂכֶר אַגְמֵי־נָפֶשׁ:

11 אַךְ־אֱוִלִים שָׂרֵי צֹעַן
חַכְמֵי יֹעֲצֵי פַרְעֹה
עֵצָה נִבְעָרָה
אֵיךְ תֹּאמְרוּ אֶל־פַּרְעֹה
בֶּן־חֲכָמִים אָנִי
בֶּן־מַלְכֵי־קֶדֶם:
12 אַיָּם אֵפוֹא חֲכָמֶיךָ

---

a   *I.e., the various districts of Egypt, which in Isaiah's time were governed by hereditary princes.*
b-b   *Meaning of Heb. uncertain.*
c   *Meaning of verse uncertain; emendation yields "Her drinkers shall be dejected, / And all her brewers despondent."*
d   *Or "advisers." The wisdom of the Kedemites was proverbial; cf. 1 Kings 5.10.*

Let them tell you, let them discover
What the Lord of Hosts has planned against
    Egypt.
13The nobles of Tanis have been fools,
The nobles of Memphis deluded;
Egypt has been led astray
By the chiefs of her tribes.
14The Lord has mixed within her
A spirit of distortion,
Which shall lead Egypt astray in all her un-
    dertakings
As a vomiting drunkard goes astray;
15Nothing shall be achieved in Egypt
By either head or tail,
Palm branch or reed.*e*

16In that day, the Egyptians shall be like
women, trembling and terrified because the
Lord of Hosts will raise His hand against them.
17And the land of Judah shall also be the dread
of the Egyptians; they shall quake whenever
anybody mentions it to them, because of what
the Lord of Hosts is planning against them.
18In that day, there shall be several*f* towns in the
land of Egypt speaking the language of Canaan
and swearing loyalty to the Lord of Hosts; one*g*
shall be called Town of Heres.*h*

19In that day, there shall be an altar to the
Lord inside the land of Egypt and a pillar to
the Lord at its border.*i* 20They shall serve as a
symbol and reminder of the Lord of Hosts in
the land of Egypt, so that when [the Egyptians]
cry out to the Lord against oppressors, He will
send them a savior and champion to deliver
them. 21For the Lord will make Himself known
to the Egyptians, and the Egyptians shall acknowledge the Lord in that day, and they shall

וְהִגִּ֣ידוּ נָ֤א לָךְ֙ וְיֵ֣דְע֔וּ
מַה־יָּעַ֛ץ יְהֹוָ֥ה צְבָא֖וֹת עַל־מִצְרָֽיִם׃
13 נֽוֹאֲלוּ֙ שָׂ֣רֵי צֹ֔עַן
נִשְּׁא֖וּ שָׂ֣רֵי נֹ֑ף
הִתְע֥וּ אֶת־מִצְרַ֖יִם
פִּנַּ֥ת שְׁבָטֶֽיהָ׃
14 יְהֹוָ֛ה מָסַ֥ךְ בְּקִרְבָּ֖הּ
ר֣וּחַ עִוְעִ֑ים
וְהִתְע֤וּ אֶת־מִצְרַ֙יִם֙ בְּכׇֽל־מַעֲשֵׂ֔הוּ
כְּהִתָּע֥וֹת שִׁכּ֖וֹר בְּקִיאֽוֹ׃
15 וְלֹא־יִהְיֶ֥ה לְמִצְרַ֖יִם מַעֲשֶׂ֑ה
אֲשֶׁ֧ר יַעֲשֶׂ֛ה רֹ֥אשׁ וְזָנָ֖ב
כִּפָּ֥ה וְאַגְמֽוֹן׃ ס

16 בַּיּ֣וֹם הַה֗וּא יִֽהְיֶ֤ה מִצְרַ֙יִם֙ כַּנָּשִׁ֔ים
וְחָרַ֣ד ׀ וּפָחַ֗ד מִפְּנֵי֙ תְּנוּפַת֙ יַד־יְהֹוָ֣ה
צְבָא֔וֹת אֲשֶׁר־ה֖וּא מֵנִ֥יף עָלָֽיו׃ 17 וְֽהָיְתָ֡ה
אַדְמַת֩ יְהוּדָ֨ה לְמִצְרַ֜יִם לְחׇגָּ֗א כֹּל֩ אֲשֶׁ֨ר
יַזְכִּ֥יר אֹתָ֛הּ אֵלָ֖יו יִפְחָ֑ד מִפְּנֵי֙ עֲצַ֣ת
יְהֹוָ֣ה צְבָא֔וֹת אֲשֶׁר־ה֖וּא יוֹעֵ֥ץ עָלָֽיו׃ ס
18 בַּיּ֣וֹם הַה֡וּא יִהְי֣וּ חָמֵשׁ֩ עָרִ֨ים בְּאֶ֜רֶץ
מִצְרַ֗יִם מְדַבְּרוֹת֙ שְׂפַ֣ת כְּנַ֔עַן וְנִשְׁבָּע֖וֹת
לַֽיהֹוָ֣ה צְבָא֑וֹת עִ֣יר הַהֶ֔רֶס יֵאָמֵ֖ר
לְאֶחָֽת׃ ס
19 בַּיּ֣וֹם הַה֗וּא יִֽהְיֶ֞ה מִזְבֵּ֤חַ לַֽיהֹוָה֙ בְּת֣וֹךְ
אֶ֣רֶץ מִצְרָ֑יִם וּמַצֵּבָ֥ה אֵֽצֶל־גְּבוּלָ֖הּ לַֽיהֹוָֽה׃
20 וְהָיָ֨ה לְא֥וֹת וּלְעֵ֛ד לַֽיהֹוָ֥ה צְבָא֖וֹת בְּאֶ֣רֶץ
מִצְרָ֑יִם כִּֽי־יִצְעֲק֤וּ אֶל־יְהֹוָה֙ מִפְּנֵ֣י לֹחֲצִ֔ים
וְיִשְׁלַ֨ח לָהֶ֥ם מוֹשִׁ֛יעַ וָרָ֖ב וְהִצִּילָֽם׃
21 וְנוֹדַ֤ע יְהֹוָה֙ לְמִצְרַ֔יִם וְיָדְע֥וּ מִצְרַ֖יִם
אֶת־יְהֹוָ֑ה בַּיּ֣וֹם הַה֔וּא וְעָֽבְדוּ֙ זֶ֣בַח וּמִנְחָ֔ה

---

e   *I.e., a man of either high or low station; cf. 9.13, 14.*
f   *Lit. "five."*
g   *Or "each one."*
h   *Meaning uncertain. Many Heb. mss. read ḥeres, "sun," which*
     may refer to Heliopolis, i.e., Sun City, in Egypt. Targum's "Beth
     Shemesh" (cf. Jer. 43.13) has the same meaning.
i   *As a symbol of the Lord's sovereignty over Egypt.*

887

serve [Him] with sacrifice and oblation and shall make vows to the Lord and fulfill them. [22]The Lord will first afflict and then heal the Egyptians; when they turn back to the Lord, He will respond to their entreaties and heal them.

[23]In that day, there shall be a highway from Egypt to Assyria. The Assyrians shall join with the Egyptians and Egyptians with the Assyrians, and then the Egyptians together with the Assyrians shall serve [the Lord].

[24]In that day, Israel shall be a third partner with Egypt and Assyria as a blessing[j] on earth; [25]for the Lord of Hosts will bless them, saying, "Blessed be My people Egypt, My handiwork Assyria, and My very own Israel."

20 It was the year that the Tartan[a] came to Ashdod—being sent by King Sargon of Assyria—and attacked Ashdod and took it. [2]Previously,[b] the Lord had spoken to Isaiah son of Amoz, saying, "Go, untie the sackcloth from your loins and take your sandals off your feet," which he had done, going naked and barefoot. [3]And now the Lord said, "It is a sign and a portent for Egypt and Nubia. Just as My servant Isaiah has gone naked and barefoot for three years, [4]so shall the king of Assyria drive off the captives of Egypt and the exiles of Nubia, young and old, naked and barefoot and with bared buttocks—to the shame of Egypt! [5]And they shall be dismayed and chagrined because of Nubia their hope and Egypt their boast. [6]In that day, the dwellers of this coastland shall say, 'If this could happen to those we looked to, to whom we fled for help and rescue from the king of Assyria, how can we ourselves escape?'"

---

j   I.e., a standard by which blessing is invoked; cf. Gen. 12.2 with note.

a   An Assyrian title meaning "General"; cf. 2 Kings 18.17 and note.

b   Lit. "At that time."

וְנָדְרוּ־נֵ֛דֶר לַֽיהוָ֖ה וְשִׁלֵּֽמוּ׃ 22 וְנָגַ֧ף יְהוָ֛ה אֶת־מִצְרַ֖יִם נָגֹ֣ף וְרָפ֑וֹא וְשָׁ֙בוּ֙ עַד־יְהוָ֔ה וְנֶעְתַּ֥ר לָהֶ֖ם וּרְפָאָֽם׃ 23 בַּיּ֣וֹם הַה֗וּא תִּהְיֶ֨ה מְסִלָּ֜ה מִמִּצְרַ֣יִם אַשּׁ֗וּרָה וּבָֽא־אַשּׁ֤וּר בְּמִצְרַ֙יִם֙ וּמִצְרַ֣יִם בְּאַשּׁ֔וּר וְעָבְד֥וּ מִצְרַ֖יִם אֶת־אַשּֽׁוּר׃ ס

24 בַּיּ֣וֹם הַה֗וּא יִהְיֶ֧ה יִשְׂרָאֵ֛ל שְׁלִֽישִׁיָּ֖ה לְמִצְרַ֣יִם וּלְאַשּׁ֑וּר בְּרָכָ֖ה בְּקֶ֥רֶב הָאָֽרֶץ׃ 25 אֲשֶׁ֧ר בֵּרֲכ֛וֹ יְהוָ֥ה צְבָא֖וֹת לֵאמֹ֑ר בָּר֨וּךְ עַמִּ֤י מִצְרַ֙יִם֙ וּמַעֲשֵׂ֤ה יָדַי֙ אַשּׁ֔וּר וְנַחֲלָתִ֖י יִשְׂרָאֵֽל׃ ס

כ בִּשְׁנַ֨ת בֹּ֤א תַרְתָּן֙ אַשְׁדּ֔וֹדָה בִּשְׁלֹ֣חַ אֹת֔וֹ סַרְג֖וֹן מֶ֣לֶךְ אַשּׁ֑וּר וַיִּלָּ֙חֶם֙ בְּאַשְׁדּ֔וֹד וַֽיִּלְכְּדָֽהּ׃ 2 בָּעֵ֣ת הַהִ֗יא דִּבֶּ֣ר יְהוָה֮ בְּיַ֣ד יְשַׁעְיָ֣הוּ בֶן־אָמוֹץ֮ לֵאמֹר֒ לֵ֗ךְ וּפִתַּחְתָּ֤ הַשַּׂק֙ מֵעַ֣ל מָתְנֶ֔יךָ וְנַעַלְךָ֥ תַחֲלֹ֖ץ מֵעַ֣ל רַגְלֶ֑יךָ וַיַּ֣עַשׂ כֵּ֔ן הָלֹ֖ךְ עָר֥וֹם וְיָחֵֽף׃ ס 3 וַיֹּ֣אמֶר יְהוָ֔ה כַּאֲשֶׁ֥ר הָלַ֛ךְ עַבְדִּ֥י יְשַׁעְיָ֖הוּ עָר֣וֹם וְיָחֵ֑ף שָׁלֹ֣שׁ שָׁנִ֗ים א֣וֹת וּמוֹפֵ֔ת עַל־מִצְרַ֖יִם וְעַל־כּֽוּשׁ׃ 4 כֵּ֣ן יִנְהַ֣ג מֶֽלֶךְ־אַ֠שּׁוּר אֶת־שְׁבִ֨י מִצְרַ֜יִם וְאֶת־גָּל֣וּת כּ֗וּשׁ נְעָרִ֤ים וּזְקֵנִים֙ עָר֣וֹם וְיָחֵ֔ף וַחֲשׂוּפַ֥י שֵׁ֖ת עֶרְוַ֥ת מִצְרָֽיִם׃ 5 וְחַתּ֖וּ וָבֹ֑שׁוּ מִכּוּשׁ֙ מַבָּטָ֔ם וּמִן־מִצְרַ֖יִם תִּפְאַרְתָּֽם׃ 6 וְ֠אָמַר יֹשֵׁ֨ב הָאִ֣י הַזֶּה֮ בַּיּ֣וֹם הַהוּא֒ הִנֵּה־כֹ֣ה מַבָּטֵ֗נוּ אֲשֶׁר־נַ֤סְנוּ שָׁם֙ לְעֶזְרָ֔ה לְהִ֨נָּצֵ֔ל מִפְּנֵ֖י מֶ֣לֶךְ אַשּׁ֑וּר וְאֵ֖יךְ נִמָּלֵ֥ט אֲנָֽחְנוּ׃ ס

888

21 *a*-The "Desert of the Sea" Pronouncement.-*a*

Like the gales
That race through the Negeb,
It comes from the desert,
The terrible land.
²A harsh prophecy
Has been announced to me:
"The betrayer is *b*-betraying,
The ravager ravaging.-*b*
Advance, Elam!
Lay siege, Media!
c-I have put an end
To all her sighing."-*c*

³Therefore my loins
Are seized with trembling;
I am gripped by pangs
Like a woman in travail,
Too anguished to hear,
Too frightened to see.
⁴My mind is confused,
I shudder in panic.
My night of pleasure
He has turned to terror:
⁵"Set the table!"
To "Let the watchman watch!"
"Eat and drink!"
To "Up, officers! Grease*d* the shields!"

⁶For thus my Lord said to me:
"Go, set up a sentry;
Let him announce what he sees.
⁷He will see mounted men,
Horsemen in pairs—
Riders on asses,

כא מַשָּׂא מִדְבַּר־יָם

כְּסוּפוֹת
בַּנֶּגֶב לַחֲלֹף
מִמִּדְבָּר בָּא
מֵאֶרֶץ נוֹרָאָה:
² חָזוּת קָשָׁה
הֻגַּד־לִי
הַבּוֹגֵד | בּוֹגֵד
וְהַשּׁוֹדֵד | שׁוֹדֵד
עֲלִי עֵילָם
צוּרִי מָדַי
כָּל־אַנְחָתָה*
הִשְׁבַּתִּי:

³ עַל־כֵּן
מָלְאוּ מָתְנַי חַלְחָלָה
צִירִים אֲחָזוּנִי
כְּצִירֵי יוֹלֵדָה
נַעֲוֵיתִי מִשְּׁמֹעַ
נִבְהַלְתִּי מֵרְאוֹת:
⁴ תָּעָה לְבָבִי
פַּלָּצוּת בִּעֲתָתְנִי
אֵת נֶשֶׁף חִשְׁקִי
שָׂם לִי לַחֲרָדָה:
⁵ עָרֹךְ הַשֻּׁלְחָן
צָפֹה הַצָּפִית
אָכוֹל שָׁתֹה
קוּמוּ הַשָּׂרִים מִשְׁחוּ מָגֵן: פ

⁶ כִּי כֹה אָמַר אֵלַי אֲדֹנָי
לֵךְ הַעֲמֵד הַמְצַפֶּה
אֲשֶׁר יִרְאֶה יַגִּיד:
⁷ וְרָאָה רֶכֶב
צֶמֶד פָּרָשִׁים
רֶכֶב חֲמוֹר

---

a-a *Emendation yields "The 'From the Desert' Pronouncement,"*
    agreeing with the phrase farther on in the verse.
b-b *Emendation yields "betrayed...ravaged"; cf. 33.1.*
c-c *Emendation yields "Put an end to all her merrymaking!"*
d *Emendation yields "Grasp."*

v. 2. ה' רפה

889

Riders on camels—
And he will listen closely,
Most attentively."
8And e-[like] a lion he-e called out:
f-"On my Lord's lookout-f I stand
Ever by day,
And at my post I watch
Every night.
9And there they come, mounted men—
Horsemen in pairs!"
Then he spoke up and said,
"Fallen, fallen is Babylon,
And all the images of her gods
Have crashed to the ground!"
10g-My threshing, the product of my thresh-
ing floor:-g
What I have heard from the LORD of Hosts,
The God of Israel—
That I have told to you.

11The "Dumah"h Pronouncement.

A call comes to me from Seir:
"Watchman, what of the night?
Watchman, what of the night?"
12The watchman replied,
"Morning came, and so did night.
If you would inquire, inquire.
Come back again."

13The "In the Steppe" Pronouncement.

In the scrub, in the steppe, you will lodge,
O caravans of the Dedanites!
14Meet the thirsty with water,
You who dwell in the land of Tema;
Greet the fugitive with bread.
15For they have fled before swords:

רֶכֶב גָּמָל
וְהִקְשִׁיב קֶשֶׁב
רַב־קָשֶׁב:
8 וַיִּקְרָא אַרְיֵה
עַל־מִצְפֶּה ׀ אֲדֹנָי אָנֹכִי עֹמֵד
תָּמִיד יוֹמָם
וְעַל־מִשְׁמַרְתִּי אָנֹכִי נִצָּב
כָּל־הַלֵּילוֹת:
9 וְהִנֵּה־זֶה בָא רֶכֶב אִישׁ
צֶמֶד פָּרָשִׁים
וַיַּעַן וַיֹּאמֶר
נָפְלָה נָפְלָה בָּבֶל
וְכָל־פְּסִילֵי אֱלֹהֶיהָ
שִׁבַּר לָאָרֶץ:
10 מְדֻשָׁתִי וּבֶן־גָּרְנִי
אֲשֶׁר שָׁמַעְתִּי מֵאֵת יְהֹוָה צְבָאוֹת
אֱלֹהֵי יִשְׂרָאֵל
הִגַּדְתִּי לָכֶם: ס

11 מַשָּׂא דּוּמָה

אֵלַי קֹרֵא מִשֵּׂעִיר
שֹׁמֵר מַה־מִלַּיְלָה
שֹׁמֵר מַה־מִלֵּיל:
12 אָמַר שֹׁמֵר
אָתָה בֹקֶר וְגַם־לַיְלָה
אִם־תִּבְעָיוּן בְּעָיוּ
שֻׁבוּ אֵתָיוּ: ס

13 מַשָּׂא בַּעְרָב

בַּיַּעַר בַּעְרַב תָּלִינוּ
אֹרְחוֹת דְּדָנִים:
14 לִקְרַאת צָמֵא הֵתָיוּ מָיִם
יֹשְׁבֵי אֶרֶץ תֵּימָא
בְּלַחְמוֹ קִדְּמוּ נֹדֵד:
15 כִּי־מִפְּנֵי חֲרָבוֹת נָדָדוּ

---

e-e   *1QIsª reads "The watcher."*
f-f   *Or "On a lookout, my lord."*
g-g   *Connection of Heb. uncertain.*
h   *Name of a people; cf. Gen. 25.14.*

Before the whetted sword,
Before the bow that was drawn,
Before the stress of war.

מִפְּנֵי | חֶרֶב נְטוּשָׁה
וּמִפְּנֵי קֶשֶׁת דְּרוּכָה
וּמִפְּנֵי כֹּבֶד מִלְחָמָה: ס

16For thus my Lord has said to me: "In another year, fixed like the years of a hired laborer, all the multitude of Kedar shall vanish; 17the remaining bows of Kedar's warriors shall be few in number; for the LORD, the God of Israel, has spoken.

16 כִּי־כֹה אָמַר אֲדֹנָי אֵלַי בְּעוֹד שָׁנָה כִּשְׁנֵי שָׂכִיר וְכָלָה כָּל־כְּבוֹד קֵדָר: 17 וּשְׁאָר מִסְפַּר־קֶשֶׁת גִּבּוֹרֵי בְנֵי־קֵדָר יִמְעָטוּ כִּי יְהוָה אֱלֹהֵי־יִשְׂרָאֵל דִּבֵּר: ס

22 The a-"Valley of Vision"-a Pronouncement.

כב מַשָּׂא גֵּיא חִזָּיוֹן

bWhat can have happened to you
That you have gone, all of you, up on the
    roofs,
2O you who were full of tumult,
You clamorous town,
You city so gay?
Your slain are not the slain of the sword
Nor the dead of battle.c
3Your officers have all departed,
They fled far away;
Your survivors were all taken captive,
a-Taken captive without their bows.-a
4That is why I say, "Let me be,
I will weep bitterly.
Press not to comfort me
For the ruin of d-my poor people."-d

מַה־לָּךְ אֵפוֹא
כִּי־עָלִית כֻּלָּךְ לַגַּגּוֹת:
2 תְּשֻׁאוֹת | מְלֵאָה
עִיר הוֹמִיָּה
קִרְיָה עַלִּיזָה
חֲלָלַיִךְ לֹא חַלְלֵי־חֶרֶב
וְלֹא מֵתֵי מִלְחָמָה:
3 כָּל־קְצִינַיִךְ נָדְדוּ־יַחַד
מִקֶּשֶׁת אֻסָּרוּ
כָּל־נִמְצָאַיִךְ אֻסְּרוּ יַחְדָּו
מֵרָחוֹק בָּרָחוּ:
4 עַל־כֵּן אָמַרְתִּי שְׁעוּ מִנִּי
אֲמָרֵר בַּבֶּכִי
אַל־תָּאִיצוּ לְנַחֲמֵנִי
עַל־שֹׁד בַּת־עַמִּי:

5For my Lord GOD of Hosts had a day
Of tumult and din and confusion—
e-Kir raged in the Valley of Vision,
And Shoa on the hill;-e

5 כִּי יוֹם מְהוּמָה וּמְבוּסָה וּמְבוּכָה
לַאדֹנָי יְהוָה צְבָאוֹת
בְּגֵיא חִזָּיוֹן מְקַרְקַר קִר
וְשׁוֹעַ אֶל־הָהָר:

---

a-a Meaning of Heb. uncertain.
b   Vv. 1–3 describe a scene of mourning to take place in Jerusalem
     in the near future. In the ancient Near East, public weeping took
     place on the low flat roofs as well as in the streets and squares;
     cf. above, 15.3; Jer. 48.38.
c   I.e., executed, instead of dying in battle.
d-d Lit. "the young woman, my people."
e-e Meaning of Heb. uncertain. On Kir see 2 Kings 16.9; Amos
     1.5; 9.7; on Shoa see Ezek. 23.23.

6While Elam bore the quiver

In troops of mounted men,

And Kir bared the shield—

7And your choicest lowlands

Were filled with chariots and horsemen:

They stormed at Judah's*f* gateway

8And pressed beyond its screen.*g*

You gave thought on that day

To the arms in the Forest House,*h*

9And you took note of the many breaches

In the City of David.

i-And you collected the water of the Lower
Pool;-*i* 10and you counted the houses of Jerusalem and pulled houses down to fortify the
wall; 11and you constructed a basin between the
two walls for the water of the old pool.

But you gave no thought to Him who planned
   it,

You took no note of Him who designed it
   long before.

12My Lord GOD of Hosts summoned on that
   day

To weeping and lamenting,

To tonsuring and girding with sackcloth.

13Instead, there was rejoicing and merriment,

Killing of cattle and slaughtering of sheep,

Eating of meat and drinking of wine:

"Eat and drink, for tomorrow we die!"

14Then the LORD of Hosts revealed Himself
   to my ears:

"This iniquity shall never be forgiven you

Until you die," said my Lord GOD of Hosts.

15Thus said my Lord GOD of Hosts: Go in to
see that steward, that Shebna, in charge of the
palace:

16What have you here, and whom have you
here,

---

6 וְעֵילָם֙ נָשָׂ֣א אַשְׁפָּ֔ה

בְּרֶ֥כֶב אָדָ֖ם פָּרָשִׁ֑ים

וְקִ֖יר עֵרָ֥ה מָגֵֽן׃

7 וַיְהִ֥י מִבְחַר־עֲמָקַ֖יִךְ

מָ֣לְאוּ רָ֑כֶב וְהַפָּ֣רָשִׁ֔ים

שֹׁ֥ת שָׁ֖תוּ הַשָּֽׁעְרָה׃

8 וַיְגַ֕ל אֵ֖ת מָסַ֣ךְ יְהוּדָ֑ה

וַתַּבֵּט֙ בַּיּ֣וֹם הַה֔וּא

אֶל־נֶ֖שֶׁק בֵּ֥ית הַיָּֽעַר׃

9 וְאֵ֨ת בְּקִיעֵ֧י עִיר־דָּוִ֛ד

רְאִיתֶ֖ם כִּי־רָ֑בּוּ

וַֽתְּקַבְּצ֔וּ אֶת־מֵ֖י הַבְּרֵכָ֥ה הַתַּחְתּוֹנָֽה׃

10 וְאֶת־בָּתֵּ֤י יְרוּשָׁלַ֙͏ִם֙ סְפַרְתֶּ֔ם וַתִּתְצוּ֙*

הַבָּתִּ֔ים לְבַצֵּ֖ר הַחוֹמָֽה׃ 11 וּמִקְוָ֣ה ׀

עֲשִׂיתֶ֗ם בֵּ֚ין הַחֹ֣מֹתַ֔יִם לְמֵ֖י הַבְּרֵכָ֣ה

הַיְשָׁנָ֑ה

וְלֹ֤א הִבַּטְתֶּם֙ אֶל־עֹשֶׂ֔יהָ

וְיֹצְרָ֥הּ מֵֽרָח֖וֹק לֹ֥א רְאִיתֶֽם׃

12 וַיִּקְרָ֗א אֲדֹנָ֧י יְהוִ֛ה צְבָא֖וֹת בַּיּ֣וֹם

הַה֑וּא

לִבְכִי֙ וּלְמִסְפֵּ֔ד

וּלְקָרְחָ֖ה וְלַחֲגֹ֥ר שָֽׂק׃

13 וְהִנֵּ֣ה ׀ שָׂשׂ֣וֹן וְשִׂמְחָ֗ה

הָרֹ֤ג ׀ בָּקָר֙ וְשָׁחֹ֣ט צֹ֔אן

אָכֹ֥ל בָּשָׂ֖ר וְשָׁת֣וֹת יָ֑יִן

אָכ֣וֹל וְשָׁת֔וֹ כִּ֥י מָחָ֖ר נָמֽוּת׃

14 וְנִגְלָ֥ה בְאָזְנָ֖י יְהוָ֣ה צְבָא֑וֹת

אִם־יְכֻפַּ֞ר הֶעָוֺ֤ן הַזֶּה֙ לָכֶ֔ם

עַד־תְּמֻת֔וּן אָמַ֛ר אֲדֹנָ֥י יְהוִ֖ה צְבָאֽוֹת׃ פ

15 כֹּ֥ה אָמַ֛ר אֲדֹנָ֥י יְהוִ֖ה צְבָא֑וֹת לֶךְ־בֹּא֙

אֶל־הַסֹּכֵ֣ן הַזֶּ֔ה עַל־שֶׁבְנָ֖א אֲשֶׁ֥ר עַל־

הַבָּֽיִת׃

16 מַה־לְּךָ֥ פֹה֙ וּמִ֣י לְךָ֣ פֹ֔ה

---

f   *Brought up from 8a for clarity.*

g   *Judah's gateway is the upper course of the Valley of Elah. The*
    screen is the fortress Azekah, at the mouth of the gateway, which
    was captured by the Assyrians.

h   *See 1 Kings 7.2–5; 10.16–17.*

i-i   *This clause would read well after the prose part of v. 11a.*

That you have hewn out a tomb for yourself
here?—

O you who have hewn your*j* tomb on high;

O you who have hollowed out for yourself*j*
an abode in the cliff!

17The Lord is about to shake you

k-Severely, fellow,-*k* and then wrap you
around Himself.*l*

18Indeed, He will wind you about Him *m*-as
a headdress, a turban.-*m*

Off to a broad land!

There shall you die, and there shall be the
n-chariots bearing your body,-*n*

O shame of your master's house!

19For I will hurl you from your station
And you shall be torn down from your stand.

20And in that day, I will summon My servant
Eliakim son of Hilkiah, 21and I will invest him
with your tunic, gird him with your sash, and
deliver your authority into his hand; and he
shall be a father to the inhabitants of Jerusalem
and the men of Judah. 22I will place the keys of
David's palace on his shoulders; and what he
unlocks none may shut, and what he locks none
may open. 23He shall be a seat of honor to his
father's*o* household. I will fix him as a peg in a
firm place, 24on which all the substance of his
father's*o* household shall be hung: *a*-the sprouts
and the leaves-*a*—all the small vessels, from
bowls to all sorts of jars.

25*p*In that day—declares the Lord of Hosts—
the peg fixed in a firm place shall give way: it
shall be cut down and shall fall, and the weight
it supports shall be destroyed. For it is the Lord
who has spoken.

כִּי־חָצַ֤בְתָּ לְּךָ֙ פֹּ֣ה קֶ֔בֶר
חֹצְבִ֥י מָר֖וֹם קִבְר֑וֹ
חֹקְקִ֥י בַסֶּ֖לַע מִשְׁכָּ֥ן לֽוֹ׃
17 הִנֵּ֤ה יְהוָה֙ מְטַלְטֶלְךָ֔
טַלְטֵלָ֖ה גָּ֑בֶר וְעֹטְךָ֥ עָטֹֽה׃
18 צָנ֣וֹף יִצְנָפְךָ֗ צְנֵפָה֙ כַּדּ֔וּר
אֶל־אֶ֖רֶץ רַחֲבַ֣ת יָדָ֑יִם
שָׁ֣מָּה תָמ֗וּת וְשָׁ֙מָּה֙ מַרְכְּב֣וֹת כְּבוֹדֶ֔ךָ
קְל֖וֹן בֵּ֥ית אֲדֹנֶֽיךָ׃
19 וַהֲדַפְתִּ֖יךָ מִמַּצָּבֶ֑ךָ
וּמִמַּעֲמָֽדְךָ֖ יֶהֶרְסֶֽךָ׃

20 וְהָיָ֖ה בַּיּ֣וֹם הַה֑וּא וְקָרָ֣אתִי לְעַבְדִּ֔י
לְאֶלְיָקִ֖ים בֶּן־חִלְקִיָּֽהוּ׃ 21 וְהִלְבַּשְׁתִּ֣יו
כֻּתָּנְתֶּ֗ךָ וְאַבְנֵֽטְךָ֙ אֲחַזְּקֶ֔נּוּ וּמֶֽמְשַׁלְתְּךָ֖ אֶתֵּ֣ן
בְּיָד֑וֹ וְהָיָ֥ה לְאָ֛ב לְיוֹשֵׁ֥ב יְרוּשָׁלַ֖͏ִם וּלְבֵ֥ית
יְהוּדָֽה׃ 22 וְנָתַתִּ֛י מַפְתֵּ֥חַ בֵּית־דָּוִ֖ד עַל־
שִׁכְמ֑וֹ וּפָתַח֙ וְאֵ֣ין סֹגֵ֔ר וְסָגַ֖ר וְאֵ֥ין
פֹּתֵֽחַ׃ 23 וּתְקַעְתִּ֥יו יָתֵ֖ד בְּמָק֣וֹם נֶאֱמָ֑ן
וְהָיָ֛ה לְכִסֵּ֥א כָב֖וֹד לְבֵ֥ית אָבִֽיו׃ 24 וְתָל֨וּ
עָלָ֜יו כֹּ֣ל ׀ כְּב֣וֹד בֵּית־אָבִ֗יו הַצֶּֽאֱצָאִים֙
וְהַצְּפִע֔וֹת כֹּ֚ל כְּלֵ֣י הַקָּטֹ֔ן מִכְּלֵי֙ הָאַגָּנ֔וֹת
וְעַ֖ד כָּל־כְּלֵ֥י הַנְּבָלִֽים׃
25 בַּיּ֣וֹם הַה֗וּא נְאֻם֙ יְהוָ֣ה צְבָא֔וֹת תָּמוּשׁ֙
הַיָּתֵ֔ד הַתְּקוּעָ֖ה בְּמָק֣וֹם נֶאֱמָ֑ן וְנִגְדְּעָ֣ה
וְנָֽפְלָ֗ה וְנִכְרַת֙ הַמַּשָּׂ֣א אֲשֶׁר־עָלֶ֔יהָ כִּ֥י
יְהוָ֖ה דִּבֵּֽר׃ ס

j   Heb. "his," "himself."
k-k   Emendation yields "as a garment is shaken out."
l   I.e., and walk off with you; cf. Jer. 43.12.
m-m   Emendation yields "as a turban is wound about."
n-n   Emendation yields "abode [cf. v. 16] of your body" [cf. 10.3, 16].
o   Emendation yields "master's"; cf. v. 18 end.
p   Apparently continues v. 19.

23 The "Tyre" Pronouncement.

כג מַשָּׂא צֹר

Howl, you *a*-ships of Tarshish!*-a*
For havoc has been wrought, not a house is
　left;
As they came from the land of Kittim,
This was revealed to them.

הֵילִילוּ ׀ אֳנִיּוֹת תַּרְשִׁישׁ
כִּי־שֻׁדַּד מִבַּיִת
מִבּוֹא מֵאֶרֶץ כִּתִּים
נִגְלָה־לָמוֹ:

²Moan, you coastland dwellers,
You traders of Sidon,
Once thronged by seafarers,
³Over many waters
Your*b* revenue came:
From the trade of nations,
From the grain of Shihor,
The harvest of the Nile.
⁴Be ashamed, O Sidon!
For the sea—this stronghold of the sea—
　declares,
c-"I am as one who has-*c* never labored,
Never given birth,
Never raised youths
Or reared maidens!"
⁵When the Egyptians heard it, they quailed
As when they heard about Tyre.

² דֹּמּוּ יֹשְׁבֵי אִי
סֹחֵר צִידוֹן
עֹבֵר יָם מִלְאוּךְ:
³ וּבְמַיִם רַבִּים
זֶרַע שִׁחֹר
קְצִיר יְאוֹר תְּבוּאָתָהּ
וַתְּהִי סְחַר גּוֹיִם:
⁴ בּוֹשִׁי צִידוֹן
כִּי־אָמַר יָם מָעוֹז הַיָּם לֵאמֹר
לֹא־חַלְתִּי
וְלֹא־יָלַדְתִּי
וְלֹא גִדַּלְתִּי בַּחוּרִים
רוֹמַמְתִּי בְתוּלוֹת:
⁵ כַּאֲשֶׁר־שֵׁמַע לְמִצְרָיִם
יָחִילוּ כְּשֵׁמַע צֹר:

⁶Pass on to Tarshish—
Howl, you coastland dwellers!
⁷Was such your merry city
In former times, of yore?
Did her feet carry her off
To sojourn far away?
⁸Who was it that planned this
For crown-wearing Tyre,
Whose merchants were nobles,
Whose traders the world honored?
⁹The LORD of Hosts planned it—

⁶ עִבְרוּ תַּרְשִׁישָׁה
הֵילִילוּ יֹשְׁבֵי אִי:
⁷ הֲזֹאת לָכֶם עַלִּיזָה
מִימֵי־קֶדֶם קַדְמָתָהּ
יֹבִלוּהָ רַגְלֶיהָ
מֵרָחוֹק לָגוּר:
⁸ מִי יָעַץ זֹאת
עַל־צֹר הַמַּעֲטִירָה
אֲשֶׁר סֹחֲרֶיהָ שָׂרִים
כִּנְעָנֶיהָ נִכְבַּדֵּי־אָרֶץ:
⁹ יְהֹוָה צְבָאוֹת יְעָצָהּ

---

a-a　See note at 2.16.
b　Heb. "her."
c-c　Lit. "I have."

To defile all glorious beauty,
To shame all the honored of the world.

לְחַלֵּל֙ גְּא֣וֹן כָּל־צְבִ֔י
לְהָקֵ֖ל כָּל־נִכְבַּדֵּי־אָֽרֶץ׃

10d-Traverse your land like the Nile,
Fair Tarshish;-d
This is a harbore no more.

10 עִבְרִ֥י אַרְצֵ֖ךְ כַּיְאֹ֑ר
בַּת־תַּרְשִׁ֔ישׁ
אֵ֥ין מֵ֖זַח עֽוֹד׃

11The LORD poised His arm o'er the sea
And made kingdoms quake;
It was He decreed destruction
For Phoenicia'sf strongholds,
12And said,
"You shall be gay no more,
O plundered one, Fair Maiden Sidon.
Up, cross over to Kittim—
Even there you shall have no rest."

11 יָד֙וֹ נָטָ֣ה עַל־הַיָּ֔ם
הִרְגִּ֖יז מַמְלָכ֑וֹת
יְהוָ֞ה צִוָּ֤ה אֶל־כְּנַ֙עַן֙
לַשְׁמִ֖ד מָעֻזְנֶֽיהָ׃
12 וַיֹּ֗אמֶר
לֹֽא־תוֹסִ֥יפִי ע֖וֹד לַעְל֑וֹז
הַֽמְעֻשָּׁקָ֛ה בְּתוּלַ֥ת בַּת־צִיד֖וֹן
כתִּ֣ים כֻּמִי֙ עֲבֹ֔רִי
גַּם־שָׁ֖ם לֹא־יָנ֥וּחַ לָֽךְ׃

13gBehold the land of Chaldea—
This is the people that has ceased to be.
Assyria, which founded it for ships,
Which raised its watchtowers,
Erected its ramparts,
Has turned it into a ruin.

13 הֵ֣ן ׀ אֶ֤רֶץ כַּשְׂדִּים֙
זֶ֣ה הָעָ֔ם לֹ֣א הָיָ֔ה
אַשּׁ֖וּר יְסָדָ֣הּ לְצִיִּ֑ים
הֵקִ֣ימוּ בחיניו בַחֽוּנָ֔יו
עֹֽרְרוּ֙ אַרְמְנוֹתֶ֔יהָ
שָׂמָ֖הּ לְמַפֵּלָֽה׃

14Howl, O ships of Tarshish,
For your stronghold is destroyed!

14 הֵילִ֖ילוּ אֳנִיּ֣וֹת תַּרְשִׁ֑ישׁ
כִּ֥י שֻׁדַּ֖ד מָעֻזְכֶֽן׃ ס

15In that day, Tyre shall remain forgotten for
seventy years, equaling the lifetime of one king.
After a lapse of seventy years, it shall go with
Tyre as with the harlot in the ditty:

15 וְהָיָה֙ בַּיּ֣וֹם הַה֔וּא וְנִשְׁכַּ֤חַת צֹר֙ שִׁבְעִ֣ים
שָׁנָ֔ה כִּימֵ֖י מֶ֣לֶךְ אֶחָ֑ד מִקֵּ֞ץ שִׁבְעִ֤ים שָׁנָה֙
יִהְיֶ֣ה לְצֹ֔ר כְּשִׁירַ֖ת הַזּוֹנָֽה׃

16Take a lyre, go about the town,
Harlot long forgotten;
Sweetly play, make much music,
To bring you back to mind.

16 קְחִ֥י כִנּ֛וֹר סֹ֥בִּי עִ֖יר
זוֹנָ֣ה נִשְׁכָּחָ֑ה
הֵיטִ֣יבִי נַגֵּ֗ן הַרְבִּי־שִׁ֖יר
לְמַ֥עַן תִּזָּכֵֽרִי׃

---

d-d   Meaning of Heb. uncertain. Emendation yields "Pass on to
the land of Kittim, / You ships of Tarshish."
e   Meaning of Heb. uncertain; taking mezaḥ as a by-form of maḥoz:
cf. Ps. 107.30.
f   Heb. "Canaan's."
g   Meaning of verse uncertain. Emendation yields "The land of
Kittim itself— / Which the Sidonian people founded, / Whose
watchtowers they raised, / Whose citadels they erected— / Exists
no more; / Assyria has turned it into a ruin."

¹⁷For after a lapse of seventy years, the LORD will take note of Tyre, and she shall resume her ^h-"fee-taking" and "play the harlot"-^h with all the kingdoms of the world, on the face of the earth. ¹⁸But her profits and "hire" shall be consecrated to the LORD. They shall not be treasured or stored; rather shall her profits go to those who abide before the LORD, that they may eat their fill and clothe themselves elegantly.

וְהָיָ֣ה מִקֵּ֣ץ ׀ שִׁבְעִ֣ים שָׁנָ֗ה יִפְקֹ֤ד יְהוָה֙ 17
אֶת־צֹ֔ר וְשָׁבָ֖ה לְאֶתְנַנָּ֑ה* וְזָֽנְתָ֞ה אֶת־כָּל־
מַמְלְכ֥וֹת הָאָ֛רֶץ עַל־פְּנֵ֖י הָאֲדָמָֽה׃
וְהָיָ֨ה סַחְרָ֜הּ וְאֶתְנַנָּ֗הּ קֹ֚דֶשׁ לַֽיהוָ֔ה לֹ֥א 18
יֵֽאָצֵ֖ר וְלֹ֣א יֵֽחָסֵ֑ן כִּ֣י לַיֹּשְׁבִ֞ים לִפְנֵ֤י יְהוָה֙
יִֽהְיֶ֣ה סַחְרָ֗הּ לֶֽאֱכֹ֥ל לְשָׂבְעָ֖ה וְלִמְכַסֶּ֥ה
עָתִֽיק׃ פ

24 Behold,

The LORD will strip the earth bare,
And lay it waste,
And twist its surface,
And scatter its inhabitants.
²Layman and priest shall fare alike,
Slave and master,
Handmaid and mistress,
Buyer and seller,
Lender and borrower,
Creditor and debtor.
³The earth shall be bare, bare;
It shall be plundered, plundered;
For it is the LORD who spoke this word.

כד הִנֵּ֧ה
יְהוָ֛ה בּוֹקֵ֥ק הָאָ֖רֶץ
וּבֽוֹלְקָ֑הּ
וְעִוָּ֣ה פָנֶ֔יהָ
וְהֵפִ֖יץ יֹשְׁבֶֽיהָ׃
וְהָיָ֤ה כָעָם֙ כַּכֹּהֵ֔ן 2
כַּעֶ֖בֶד כַּֽאדֹנָ֑יו
כַּשִּׁפְחָה֙ כַּגְּבִרְתָּ֔הּ
כַּקּוֹנֶה֙ כַּמּוֹכֵ֔ר
כַּמַּלְוֶ֣ה כַּלֹּוֶ֔ה
כַּנֹּשֶׁ֕ה כַּאֲשֶׁ֖ר נֹשֶׁ֥א בֽוֹ׃
הִבּ֧וֹק ׀ תִּבּ֛וֹק הָאָ֖רֶץ 3
וְהִבּ֣וֹז ׀ תִּבּ֑וֹז
כִּ֣י יְהוָ֔ה דִּבֶּ֖ר אֶת־הַדָּבָ֥ר הַזֶּֽה׃

⁴The earth is withered, sear;
The world languishes, it is sear;
^a-The most exalted people of the earth-^a languish.
⁵For the earth was defiled
Under its inhabitants;
Because they transgressed teachings,
Violated laws,
Broke the ancient covenant.^b
⁶That is why a curse consumes the earth,
And its inhabitants pay the penalty;
That is why earth's dwellers have dwindled,
And but few men are left.

אָבְלָ֤ה נָֽבְלָה֙ הָאָ֔רֶץ 4
אֻמְלְלָ֥ה נָבְלָ֖ה תֵּבֵ֑ל
אֻמְלָ֖לוּ מְר֥וֹם עַם־הָאָֽרֶץ׃
וְהָאָ֥רֶץ חָנְפָ֖ה 5
תַּ֣חַת יֹשְׁבֶ֑יהָ
כִּֽי־עָבְר֤וּ תוֹרֹת֙
חָ֣לְפוּ חֹ֔ק
הֵפֵ֖רוּ בְּרִ֥ית עוֹלָֽם׃
עַל־כֵּ֗ן אָלָה֙ אָ֣כְלָה אֶ֔רֶץ 6
וַֽיֶּאְשְׁמ֖וּ יֹ֣שְׁבֵי בָ֑הּ
עַל־כֵּ֗ן חָרוּ֙ יֹ֣שְׁבֵי אֶ֔רֶץ
וְנִשְׁאַ֥ר אֱנ֖וֹשׁ מִזְעָֽר׃

---

h-h   I.e., "trading…trade."

a-a   Change of vocalization yields "both sky and earth."
b   I.e., the moral law, which is binding on all men (cf. Gen. 9.4–6).

v. 17.   ה' רפה

7The new wine fails,

The vine languishes;

And all the merry-hearted sigh.

8Stilled is the merriment of timbrels,

Ended the clamor of revelers,

Stilled the merriment of lyres.

9They drink their wine without song;

Liquor tastes bitter to the drinker.

10Towns are broken,c empty;

Every house is shut, none enters;

11Even over wine, a cry goes up in the streets:

The sun has set on all joy,

The gladness of the earth is banished.

12Desolation is left in the town

And the gate is battered to ruins.

13For thus shall it be among the peoples

In the midst of the earth:

As when the olive tree is beaten out,

Like gleanings when the vintage is over.

14These shall lift up their voices,

Exult in the majesty of the LORD.

They shall shout from the sea:

15Therefore, honor the LORD with lights

In the coastlands of the sea—

The name of the LORD, the God of Israel.

16From the end of the earth

We hear singing:

Glory to the righteous!

d-And I said:-d

e-I waste away! I waste away! Woe is me!

The faithless have acted faithlessly;

The faithless have broken faith!-e

17f-Terror, and pit, and trap-f

Upon you who dwell on earth!

18He who flees at the report of the terror

7 אֲבַל תִּירוֹשׁ

אֻמְלְלָה־גָפֶן

נֶאֶנְחוּ כָּל־שִׂמְחֵי־לֵב:

8 שָׁבַת מְשׂוֹשׂ תֻּפִּים

חָדַל שְׁאוֹן עַלִּיזִים

שָׁבַת מְשׂוֹשׂ כִּנּוֹר:

9 בַּשִּׁיר לֹא יִשְׁתּוּ־יָיִן

יֵמַר שֵׁכָר לְשֹׁתָיו:

10 נִשְׁבְּרָה קִרְיַת־תֹּהוּ

סֻגַּר כָּל־בַּיִת מִבּוֹא:

11 צְוָחָה עַל־הַיַּיִן בַּחוּצוֹת

עָרְבָה כָּל־שִׂמְחָה

גָּלָה מְשׂוֹשׂ הָאָרֶץ:

12 נִשְׁאַר בָּעִיר שַׁמָּה

וּשְׁאִיָּה יֻכַּת־שָׁעַר:

13 כִּי כֹה יִהְיֶה בְּקֶרֶב הָאָרֶץ

בְּתוֹךְ הָעַמִּים

כְּנֹקֶף זַיִת

כְּעוֹלֵלֹת אִם־כָּלָה בָצִיר:

14 הֵמָּה יִשְׂאוּ קוֹלָם יָרֹנּוּ

בִּגְאוֹן יְהוָה

צָהֲלוּ מִיָּם:

15 עַל־כֵּן בָּאֻרִים כַּבְּדוּ יְהוָה

בְּאִיֵּי הַיָּם

שֵׁם יְהוָה אֱלֹהֵי יִשְׂרָאֵל: ס

16 מִכְּנַף הָאָרֶץ

זְמִרֹת שָׁמַעְנוּ

צְבִי לַצַּדִּיק

וָאֹמַר

רָזִי־לִי רָזִי־לִי אוֹי לִי

בֹּגְדִים בָּגָדוּ

וּבֶגֶד בּוֹגְדִים בָּגָדוּ:

17 פַּחַד וָפַחַת וָפָח

עָלֶיךָ יוֹשֵׁב הָאָרֶץ:

18 וְהָיָה הַנָּס מִקּוֹל הַפַּחַד

---

c Emendation yields "left."

d-d Change of vocalization yields "They shall say."

e-e Meaning of Heb. uncertain. Emendation yields "Villain [Arabic razil], foolish villain! / The faithless who acted faithlessly / Have been betrayed in turn."

f-f Heb. paḥad wa-paḥath, wa-paḥ.

Shall fall into the pit;
And he who climbs out of the pit
Shall be caught in the trap.
For sluices are opened on high,
And earth's foundations tremble.

19The earth is breaking, breaking;
The earth is crumbling, crumbling.
The earth is tottering, tottering;
20The earth is swaying like a drunkard;
It is rocking to and fro like a hut.
Its iniquity shall weigh it down,
And it shall fall, to rise no more.

21In that day, the Lord will punish
The host of heaven in heaven
And the kings of the earth on earth.
22They shall be gathered in a dungeon
As captives are gathered;
And shall be locked up in a prison.
But after many days they shall be remem-
    bered.

23Then the moon shall be ashamed,
And the sun shall be abashed.
For the Lord of Hosts will reign
On Mount Zion and in Jerusalem,
And the Presence will be revealed to His el-
    ders.

25 O Lord, You are my God;
I will extol You, I will praise Your name.
For You planned graciousness*a* of old,
Counsels of steadfast faithfulness.

2For You have turned a city into a stone heap,
A walled town into a ruin,
The citadel of strangers*b* into rubble,*c*

יִפֹּל אֶל־הַפַּ֔חַת
וְהָעוֹלֶה֙ מִתּ֣וֹךְ הַפַּ֔חַת
יִלָּכֵ֖ד בַּפָּ֑ח
כִּֽי־אֲרֻבּ֤וֹת מִמָּרוֹם֙ נִפְתָּ֔חוּ
וַיִּרְעֲשׁ֖וּ מ֥וֹסְדֵי אָֽרֶץ׃

19 רֹ֥עָה הִֽתְרֹעֲעָ֖ה הָאָ֑רֶץ
פּ֤וֹר הִֽתְפּוֹרְרָה֙ אֶ֔רֶץ
מ֥וֹט הִֽתְמוֹטְטָ֖ה אָֽרֶץ׃
20 נ֣וֹעַ תָּנ֤וּעַ אֶ֨רֶץ֙ כַּשִּׁכּ֔וֹר
וְהִֽתְנוֹדְדָ֖ה כַּמְּלוּנָ֑ה
וְכָבַ֤ד עָלֶ֨יהָ֙ פִּשְׁעָ֔הּ
וְנָפְלָ֖ה וְלֹא־תֹסִ֥יף קֽוּם׃ ס

21 וְהָיָה֙ בַּיּ֣וֹם הַה֔וּא יִפְקֹ֤ד יְהֹוָה֙
עַל־צְבָ֥א הַמָּר֖וֹם בַּמָּר֑וֹם
וְעַל־מַלְכֵ֥י הָאֲדָמָ֖ה עַל־הָאֲדָמָֽה׃
22 וְאֻסְּפ֨וּ אֲסֵפָ֜ה
אַסִּיר֙ עַל־בּ֔וֹר
וְסֻגְּר֖וּ עַל־מַסְגֵּ֑ר
וּמֵרֹ֥ב יָמִ֖ים יִפָּקֵֽדוּ׃

23 וְחָֽפְרָה֙ הַלְּבָנָ֔ה
וּבוֹשָׁ֖ה הַֽחַמָּ֑ה
כִּֽי־מָלַ֞ךְ יְהֹוָ֣ה צְבָא֗וֹת
בְּהַ֤ר צִיּוֹן֙ וּבִיר֣וּשָׁלַ֔͏ִם
וְנֶ֥גֶד זְקֵנָ֖יו כָּבֽוֹד׃ פ

כה יְהֹוָ֤ה אֱלֹהַי֙ אַ֔תָּה
אֲרֽוֹמִמְךָ֙ אוֹדֶ֣ה שִׁמְךָ֔
כִּ֥י עָשִׂ֖יתָ פֶּ֑לֶא
עֵצ֥וֹת מֵֽרָח֖וֹק אֱמ֥וּנָה אֹֽמֶן׃

2 כִּ֤י שַׂ֨מְתָּ֙ מֵעִ֣יר לַגָּ֔ל
קִרְיָ֥ה בְצוּרָ֖ה לְמַפֵּלָ֑ה
אַרְמ֤וֹן זָרִים֙ מֵעִ֔יר

---

a   See 9.5.
b   Emendation yields "arrogant men."
c   Meaning of Heb. uncertain.

Never to be rebuilt.

³Therefore a fierce people must honor You,

A city of cruel nations must fear You.

⁴For You have been a refuge for the poor man,

A shelter for the needy man in his distress—

Shelter from rainstorm, shade from heat.

When the fury of tyrants was like a winter[c] rainstorm,

⁵The rage of strangers[b] like heat in the desert,

You subdued the heat with the shade of clouds,

The singing[d] of the tyrants was vanquished.

לְעוֹלָ֖ם לֹ֥א יִבָּנֶֽה׃

3 עַל־כֵּ֖ן יְכַבְּד֣וּךָ עַם־עָ֑ז

קִרְיַ֛ת גּוֹיִ֥ם עָרִיצִ֖ים יִֽירָאֽוּךָ׃

4 כִּֽי־הָיִ֨יתָ מָע֥וֹז לַדָּ֛ל

מָע֥וֹז לָאֶבְי֖וֹן בַּצַּר־ל֑וֹ

מַחְסֶ֤ה מִזֶּ֙רֶם֙ צֵ֣ל מֵחֹ֔רֶב

כִּ֛י ר֥וּחַ עָרִיצִ֖ים כְּזֶ֥רֶם קִֽיר׃

5 כְּחֹ֣רֶב בְּצָי֔וֹן שְׁא֥וֹן זָרִ֖ים

תַּכְנִ֑יעַ חֹ֛רֶב בְּצֵ֥ל עָ֖ב

זְמִ֥יר עָרִיצִ֖ים יַעֲנֶֽה׃ פ

⁶The Lᴏʀᴅ of Hosts will make on this mount[e]

For all the peoples

A banquet of [c]rich viands,

A banquet of choice wines—

Of rich viands seasoned with marrow,

Of choice wines-[c] well refined.

⁷And He will destroy on this mount[e] the shroud

That is drawn over the faces of all the peoples

And the covering that is spread

Over all the nations:

⁸He will destroy death[f] forever.

My Lord Gᴏᴅ will wipe the tears away

From all faces

And will put an end to the reproach of [g]His people-[g]

Over all the earth—

For it is the Lᴏʀᴅ who has spoken.

6 וְעָשָׂה֩ יְהֹוָ֨ה צְבָא֜וֹת

לְכָל־הָֽעַמִּים֙ בָּהָ֣ר הַזֶּ֔ה

מִשְׁתֵּ֥ה שְׁמָנִ֖ים

מִשְׁתֵּ֣ה שְׁמָרִ֑ים

שְׁמָנִים֙ מְמֻחָיִ֔ם

שְׁמָרִ֖ים מְזֻקָּקִֽים׃

7 וּבִלַּע֙ בָּהָ֣ר הַזֶּ֔ה פְּנֵֽי־הַלּ֖וֹט ׀

הַלּ֥וֹט עַל־כָּל־הָעַמִּ֑ים

וְהַמַּסֵּכָ֥ה הַנְּסוּכָ֖ה

עַל־כָּל־הַגּוֹיִֽם׃

8 בִּלַּ֤ע הַמָּ֙וֶת֙ לָנֶ֔צַח

וּמָחָ֨ה אֲדֹנָ֧י יְהֹוִ֛ה דִּמְעָ֖ה

מֵעַ֣ל כָּל־פָּנִ֑ים

וְחֶרְפַּ֣ת עַמּ֗וֹ

יָסִיר֙ מֵעַ֣ל כָּל־הָאָ֔רֶץ

כִּ֥י יְהֹוָ֖ה דִּבֵּֽר׃ פ

⁹In that day they shall say:

This is our God;

We trusted in Him, and He delivered us.

This is the Lᴏʀᴅ, in whom we trusted;

Let us rejoice and exult in His deliverance!

9 וְאָמַר֙ בַּיּ֣וֹם הַה֔וּא

הִנֵּ֨ה אֱלֹהֵ֥ינוּ זֶ֛ה

קִוִּ֥ינוּ ל֖וֹ וְיֽוֹשִׁיעֵ֑נוּ

זֶ֤ה יְהֹוָה֙ קִוִּ֣ינוּ ל֔וֹ

נָגִ֥ילָה וְנִשְׂמְחָ֖ה בִּישֽׁוּעָתֽוֹ׃

---

d   *Meaning of Heb. uncertain. Emendation yields "rainstorm"; cf. 4d.*

e   *I.e., the Holy Land, as in 11.9; 14.25; 57.13.*

f   *Perhaps an allusion to the mass killings committed by the Assyrians; cf. 10.7; 14.20.*

g-g   *Emendation yields "peoples."*

10For the hand of the LORD shall descend
Upon this mount,*e*
And Moab*h* shall be trampled under Him
As straw is threshed to bits at Madmenah.*i*
11Then He will spread out His hands in their
   homeland,*j*
As a swimmer spreads his hands out to swim,
And He will humble their pride
Along with *k*-the emblems of their power.-*k*
12Yea, the secure fortification of their*l* walls
He will lay low and humble,
Will raze to the ground, to the very dust.

10 כִּי־תָנ֤וּחַ יַד־יְהוָה֙
בָּהָ֣ר הַזֶּ֔ה
וְנָ֥דוֹשׁ מוֹאָ֖ב תַּחְתָּ֑יו
כְּהִדּ֥וּשׁ מַתְבֵּ֖ן בְּמ֥וֹ מַדְמֵנָֽה׃
11 וּפֵרַ֤שׂ יָדָיו֙ בְּקִרְבּ֔וֹ
כַּאֲשֶׁ֛ר יְפָרֵ֥שׂ הַשֹּׁחֶ֖ה לִשְׂח֑וֹת
וְהִשְׁפִּיל֙ גַּֽאֲוָת֔וֹ
עִ֖ם אָרְבּ֥וֹת יָדָֽיו׃
12 וּמִבְצַ֞ר מִשְׂגַּ֣ב חוֹמֹתֶ֗יךָ
הֵשַׁ֥ח הִשְׁפִּ֛יל
הִגִּ֥יעַ לָאָ֖רֶץ עַד־עָפָֽר׃ ס

26 In that day, this song shall be sung
In the land of Judah:
Ours is a mighty city;
He makes victory our inner and outer wall.
2Open the gates, and let
A righteous nation enter,
[A nation] that keeps faith.
3The confident mind You guard in safety,
In safety because it trusts in You.

4Trust in the LORD for ever and ever,
For in Yah the LORD you have an everlasting
   Rock.
5For He has brought low those who dwelt
   high up,
Has humbled the secure city,
Humbled it to the ground,
Leveled it with the dust—
6To be trampled underfoot,
By the feet of the needy,
By the soles of the poor.
7The path is level for the righteous man;

כו בַּיּ֤וֹם הַהוּא֙ יוּשַׁ֞ר הַשִּׁיר־הַזֶּ֖ה
בְּאֶ֣רֶץ יְהוּדָ֑ה
עִ֣יר עָז־לָ֔נוּ
יְשׁוּעָ֥ה יָשִׁ֖ית חוֹמ֥וֹת וָחֵֽל׃
2 פִּתְח֖וּ שְׁעָרִ֑ים
וְיָבֹ֥א גוֹי־צַדִּ֖יק
שֹׁמֵ֥ר אֱמֻנִֽים׃
3 יֵ֣צֶר סָמ֔וּךְ תִּצֹּ֖ר שָׁל֣וֹם ׀
שָׁל֑וֹם כִּ֥י בְךָ֖ בָּטֽוּחַ׃
4 בִּטְח֥וּ בַֽיהוָ֖ה עֲדֵי־עַ֑ד
כִּ֚י בְּיָ֣הּ יְהוָ֔ה צ֖וּר עוֹלָמִֽים׃
5 כִּ֤י הֵשַׁח֙ יֹשְׁבֵ֣י מָר֔וֹם
קִרְיָ֖ה נִשְׂגָּבָ֑ה יַשְׁפִּילֶ֣נָּה
יַשְׁפִּילָ֣הּ עַד־אֶ֔רֶץ
יַגִּיעֶ֖נָּה עַד־עָפָֽר׃
6 תִּרְמְסֶ֖נָּה רָ֑גֶל
רַגְלֵ֥י עָנִ֖י
פַּעֲמֵ֥י דַלִּֽים׃

---

h   *Emendation yields "Assyria"; cf. 14.25.*
i   *A village near Jerusalem; see 10.31. Emendation yields "As straw*
    gets shredded in the threshing."
j   *Lit. "midst."*
k-k *Meaning of Heb. uncertain. Emendation yields "their cita-*
    dels"; cf. the next verse.
l   *Heb. "your."*

O Just One, You make smooth the course of
   the righteous.

8For Your just ways, O LORD, we look to You;
We long for the name by which You are called.
9At night I yearn for You with all my being,
I seek You with all ^a-the spirit within me.-^a
For when Your judgments are wrought on
   earth,
The inhabitants of the world learn righteous-
   ness.
10But when the scoundrel is spared, he learns
   not righteousness;
In a place of integrity, he does wrong—
He ignores the majesty of the LORD.

11O LORD!
They see not Your hand exalted.
Let them be shamed as they behold
Your zeal for Your people
And fire consuming Your adversaries.
12bO LORD!
May You appoint well-being for us,
Since You have also requited all our misdeeds.

13O LORD our God!
Lords other than You possessed us,
But only Your name shall we utter.
14They are dead, they can never live;
Shades, they can never rise;
Of a truth, You have dealt with them and
   wiped them out,
Have put an end to all mention of them.
15cWhen You added to the nation, O LORD,
When You added to the nation,
Extending all the boundaries of the land,
You were honored.
16O LORD! In their distress, they sought You;

---

^{a-a} Emendation yields *"my spirit in the morning."*
^b *Meaning of verse uncertain.*
^c *Meaning of vv. 15–16 uncertain.*

901

7 אֹרַח לַצַּדִּיק מֵישָׁרִים
יָשָׁר מַעְגַּל צַדִּיק תְּפַלֵּס׃

8 אַף אֹרַח מִשְׁפָּטֶיךָ יְהוָה קִוִּינוּךָ
לְשִׁמְךָ וּלְזִכְרְךָ תַּאֲוַת־נָפֶשׁ׃
9 נַפְשִׁי אִוִּיתִיךָ בַּלַּיְלָה
אַף־רוּחִי בְקִרְבִּי אֲשַׁחֲרֶךָּ
כִּי כַּאֲשֶׁר מִשְׁפָּטֶיךָ לָאָרֶץ
צֶדֶק לָמְדוּ יֹשְׁבֵי תֵבֵל׃
10 יֻחַן רָשָׁע בַּל־לָמַד צֶדֶק
בְּאֶרֶץ נְכֹחוֹת יְעַוֵּל
וּבַל־יִרְאֶה גֵּאוּת יְהוָה׃ ס

11 יְהוָה
רָמָה יָדְךָ בַּל־יֶחֱזָיוּן
יֶחֱזוּ וְיֵבֹשׁוּ
קִנְאַת־עָם
אַף־אֵשׁ צָרֶיךָ תֹאכְלֵם׃
12 יְהוָה
תִּשְׁפֹּת שָׁלוֹם לָנוּ
כִּי גַּם כָּל־מַעֲשֵׂינוּ פָּעַלְתָּ לָּנוּ׃

13 יְהוָה אֱלֹהֵינוּ
בְּעָלוּנוּ אֲדֹנִים זוּלָתֶךָ
לְבַד־בְּךָ נַזְכִּיר שְׁמֶךָ׃
14 מֵתִים בַּל־יִחְיוּ
רְפָאִים בַּל־יָקֻמוּ
לָכֵן פָּקַדְתָּ וַתַּשְׁמִידֵם
וַתְּאַבֵּד כָּל־זֵכֶר לָמוֹ׃
15 יָסַפְתָּ לַגּוֹי יְהוָה
יָסַפְתָּ לַגּוֹי
נִכְבָּדְתָּ
רִחַקְתָּ כָּל־קַצְוֵי־אָרֶץ׃
16 יְהוָה בַּצַּר פְּקָדוּךָ

Your chastisement reduced them
To anguished[d] whispered prayer.

צָק֣וּן לַ֔חַשׁ
מוּסָרְךָ֖ לָֽמוֹ׃

17Like a woman with child
Approaching childbirth,
Writhing and screaming in her pangs,
So are we become because of You, O Lord.

כְּמ֤וֹ הָרָה֙
תַּקְרִ֣יב לָלֶ֔דֶת
תָּחִ֥יל תִּזְעַ֖ק בַּחֲבָלֶ֑יהָ
כֵּ֛ן הָיִ֥ינוּ מִפָּנֶ֖יךָ יְהוָֽה׃

18We were with child, we writhed—
It is as though we had given birth to wind;
We have won no victory on earth;
The inhabitants of the world have not [e-]come
   to life![-e]

הָרִ֣ינוּ חַ֔לְנוּ
כְּמ֖וֹ יָלַ֣דְנוּ ר֑וּחַ
יְשׁוּעֹת֙ בַּל־נַ֣עֲשֶׂה אֶ֔רֶץ
וּבַל־יִפְּל֖וּ יֹשְׁבֵ֥י תֵבֵֽל׃

19Oh, let Your dead revive!
Let corpses[f] arise!
Awake and shout for joy,
You who dwell in the dust!—
For Your dew is like the dew on fresh growth;
You make the land of the shades [e-]come to
   life.[-e]

יִֽחְי֣וּ מֵתֶ֔יךָ
נְבֵלָתִ֖י יְקוּמ֑וּן
הָקִ֧יצוּ וְרַנְּנ֣וּ
שֹׁכְנֵ֣י עָפָ֗ר
כִּ֣י טַ֤ל אוֹרֹת֙ טַלֶּ֔ךָ
וָאָ֖רֶץ רְפָאִ֥ים תַּפִּֽיל׃ ס

20Go, my people, enter your chambers,
And lock your doors behind you.
Hide but a little moment,
Until the indignation passes.
21For lo!
The Lord shall come forth from His place
To punish the dwellers of the earth
For their iniquity;
And the earth shall disclose its bloodshed
And shall no longer conceal its slain.

לֵ֤ךְ עַמִּי֙ בֹּ֣א בַחֲדָרֶ֔יךָ
וּֽסְגֹ֥ר דלתיך דְּלָֽתְךָ֖ בַּֽעֲדֶ֑ךָ
חֲבִ֥י כִמְעַט־רֶ֖גַע
עַד־יַעֲבָר־זָֽעַם׃
כִּֽי־הִנֵּ֤ה
יְהוָה֙ יֹצֵ֣א מִמְּקוֹמ֔וֹ
לִפְקֹ֛ד עֲוֺ֥ן
יֹשֵֽׁב־הָאָ֖רֶץ עָלָ֑יו
וְגִלְּתָ֤ה הָאָ֙רֶץ֙ אֶת־דָּמֶ֔יהָ
וְלֹֽא־תְכַסֶּ֥ה ע֖וֹד עַל־הֲרוּגֶֽיהָ׃ ס

27 In that day the Lord will punish,
With His great, cruel, mighty sword
Leviathan the Elusive[a] Serpent—
Leviathan the Twisting[a] Serpent;
He will slay the Dragon of the sea.[b]

כז בַּיּ֣וֹם הַה֗וּא יִפְקֹ֣ד יְהוָה֮
בְּחַרְבּ֣וֹ הַקָּשָׁ֞ה וְהַגְּדוֹלָ֣ה וְהַחֲזָקָ֗ה
עַ֤ל לִוְיָתָן֙ נָחָ֣שׁ בָּרִ֔חַ
וְעַל֙ לִוְיָתָ֔ן נָחָ֖שׁ עֲקַלָּת֑וֹן
וְהָרַ֥ג אֶת־הַתַּנִּ֖ין אֲשֶׁ֥ר בַּיָּֽם׃ ס

---

d   Lit. "anguish"; taking ṣaqun as a noun formed like zadon and
    sason.
e-e Meaning of Heb. uncertain.
f   Grammar of Heb. unclear.

a   Meaning of Heb. uncertain.
b   The monster which the Lord vanquished of old (cf. 51.9; Ps.
    74.13–14) was the embodiment of chaos; here it stands for the
    forces of evil in the present world.

²In that day,
They shall sing of it:^c
"Vineyard of Delight."^d
³I the LORD keep watch over it,
I water it every moment;
^eThat no harm may befall it,^{-e}
I watch it night and day.
⁴There is no anger in Me:
^aIf one offers Me thorns and thistles,
I will march to battle against him,
And set all of them on fire.^{-a}
⁵But if he holds fast to My refuge,
^aHe makes Me his friend;
He makes Me his friend.^{-a}

⁶[In days] to come Jacob shall strike root,
Israel shall sprout and blossom,
And the face of the world
Shall be covered with fruit.

⁷Was he beaten as his beater has been?
Did he suffer such slaughter as his slayers?
⁸^fAssailing them^{-f} with fury unchained,
His pitiless blast bore them off
On a day of gale.

⁹^gAssuredly, by this alone
Shall Jacob's sin be purged away;
This is the only price
For removing his guilt:
That he make all the altar-stones
Like shattered blocks of chalk—
With no sacred post left standing,
Nor any incense altar.
¹⁰Thus fortified cities lie desolate,

בַּיּוֹם הַהוּא 2
כֶּרֶם חֶמֶד
עַנּוּ־לָהּ:
אֲנִי יְהוָה נֹצְרָהּ 3
לִרְגָעִים אַשְׁקֶנָּה
פֶּן יִפְקֹד עָלֶיהָ
לַיְלָה וָיוֹם אֶצֳּרֶנָּה:
חֵמָה אֵין לִי 4
מִי־יִתְּנֵנִי שָׁמִיר שַׁיִת
בַּמִּלְחָמָה אֶפְשְׂעָה בָהּ
אֲצִיתֶנָּה יָּחַד:
אוֹ יַחֲזֵק בְּמָעוּזִּי 5
יַעֲשֶׂה שָׁלוֹם לִי
שָׁלוֹם יַעֲשֶׂה־לִי:
הַבָּאִים יַשְׁרֵשׁ יַעֲקֹב 6
יָצִיץ וּפָרַח יִשְׂרָאֵל
וּמָלְאוּ פְנֵי־תֵבֵל
תְּנוּבָה: ס
הַכְּמַכַּת מַכֵּהוּ הִכָּהוּ 7
אִם־כְּהֶרֶג הֲרֻגָיו הֹרָג:
בְּסַאסְּאָה בְּשַׁלְחָהּ תְּרִיבֶנָּה 8
הָגָה בְּרוּחוֹ הַקָּשָׁה
בְּיוֹם קָדִים:
לָכֵן בְּזֹאת 9
יְכֻפַּר עֲוֹן־יַעֲקֹב
וְזֶה כָּל־פְּרִי
הָסִר חַטָּאתוֹ
בְּשׂוּמוֹ ׀ כָּל־אַבְנֵי מִזְבֵּחַ
כְּאַבְנֵי־גִר מְנֻפָּצוֹת
לֹא־יָקֻמוּ אֲשֵׁרִים
וְחַמָּנִים:
כִּי עִיר בְּצוּרָה בָּדָד 10

c   Apparently the earth; cf. 26.21.
d   So some mss. (cf. Amos 5.11); other mss. and the editions have
     "Wine."
e-e Meaning of Heb. uncertain; emendation yields "My eye is open
     upon it."
f-f Lit. "Striving with her"; meaning of verse uncertain.
g   This verse would read well before v. 6; the thought of vv. 7–8,
     dealing with the punishment of Israel's enemies, is continued in
     vv. 10–11.

Homesteads deserted, forsaken like a wilder-
ness;
There calves graze, there they lie down
-h-And consume its boughs.
11When its crown is withered, they break;-h
Women come and make fires with them.
For they are a people without understanding;
That is why
Their Maker will show them no mercy,
Their Creator will deny them grace.

12And in that day, the LORD will beat out [the peoples like grain] from the channel of the Euphrates to the Wadi of Egypt; and you shall be picked up one by one, O children of Israel!

13And in that day, a great ram's horn shall be sounded; and the strayed who are in the land of Assyria and the expelled who are in the land of Egypt shall come and worship the LORD on the holy mount, in Jerusalem.

28 Ah, the proud crowns of the drunkards of Ephraim,

Whose glorious beauty is but wilted flowers
On the heads of men bloated[a] with rich food,
Who are overcome by wine!

2Lo, my Lord has something strong and
mighty,
Like a storm of hail,
A shower of pestilence.
Something like a storm of massive, torrential
rain[b]
Shall be hurled with force to the ground.
3Trampled underfoot shall be
The proud crowns of the drunkards of
Ephraim,

נָוֶה מְשֻׁלָּח וְנֶעֱזָב כַּמִּדְבָּר
שָׁם יִרְעֶה עֵגֶל וְשָׁם יִרְבָּץ
וְכִלָּה סְעִפֶיהָ׃
11 בִּיבֹשׁ קְצִירָהּ תִּשָּׁבַרְנָה
נָשִׁים בָּאוֹת מְאִירוֹת אוֹתָהּ
כִּי לֹא עַם־בִּינוֹת הוּא
עַל־כֵּן
לֹא־יְרַחֲמֶנּוּ עֹשֵׂהוּ
וְיֹצְרוֹ לֹא יְחֻנֶּנּוּ׃ ס

12 וְהָיָה בַּיּוֹם הַהוּא יַחְבֹּט יְהוָה מִשִּׁבֹּלֶת
הַנָּהָר עַד־נַחַל מִצְרָיִם וְאַתֶּם תְּלֻקְּטוּ
לְאַחַד אֶחָד בְּנֵי יִשְׂרָאֵל׃ ס
13 וְהָיָה ׀ בַּיּוֹם הַהוּא יִתָּקַע בְּשׁוֹפָר גָּדוֹל
וּבָאוּ הָאֹבְדִים בְּאֶרֶץ אַשּׁוּר וְהַנִּדָּחִים
בְּאֶרֶץ מִצְרָיִם וְהִשְׁתַּחֲווּ לַיהוָה בְּהַר
הַקֹּדֶשׁ בִּירוּשָׁלָ͏ִם׃

כח הוֹי עֲטֶרֶת גֵּאוּת שִׁכֹּרֵי אֶפְרַיִם
וְצִיץ נֹבֵל צְבִי תִפְאַרְתּוֹ
אֲשֶׁר עַל־רֹאשׁ גֵּיא־שְׁמָנִים
הֲלוּמֵי יָיִן׃

2 הִנֵּה חָזָק וְאַמִּץ לַאדֹנָי
כְּזֶרֶם בָּרָד
שַׂעַר קָטֶב
כְּזֶרֶם מַיִם כַּבִּירִים שֹׁטְפִים
הִנִּיחַ לָאָרֶץ בְּיָד׃
3 בְּרַגְלַיִם תֵּרָמַסְנָה
עֲטֶרֶת גֵּאוּת שִׁכּוֹרֵי אֶפְרָיִם׃

---

h-h Meaning of Heb. uncertain. Emendation yields "Or like a
terebinth whose boughs / Break when its crown is withered."

a Ge is contracted from ge'e; cf. Ibn Ezra.
b Lit. "water."

4The wilted flowers—
On the heads of men bloated[a] with rich
    food—
That are his glorious beauty.
They shall be like an early fig
Before the fruit harvest;
Whoever sees it devours it
While it is still [c]in his hand.[-c]

5In that day, the LORD of Hosts shall become
a crown of beauty and a diadem of glory for the
remnant of His people, 6and a spirit of judgment
for him who sits in judgment and of valor for
those who repel attacks at the gate.

7But these are also muddled by wine
And dazed by liquor:
Priest and prophet
Are muddled by liquor;
They are confused by wine,
They are dazed by liquor;
They are muddled in their visions,
They stumble in judgment.
8Yea, all tables are covered
With vomit and filth,
So that no space is left.

9[d]"To whom would he give instruction?
To whom expound a message?
To those newly weaned from milk,
Just taken away from the breast?
10That same mutter upon mutter,
Murmur upon murmur,
Now here, now there!"

11Truly, as one who speaks to that people in
a stammering jargon and an alien tongue 12is
he who declares to them, "This is the resting
place, let the weary rest;[e] this is the place of re-

4 וְהָ֥יְתָה צִיצַ֣ת נֹבֵ֗ל
צְבִ֣י תִפְאַרְתּ֔וֹ
אֲשֶׁ֥ר עַל־רֹ֖אשׁ גֵּ֣יא שְׁמָנִ֑ים
כְּבִכּוּרָהּ֙ בְּטֶ֣רֶם קַ֔יִץ
אֲשֶׁ֨ר יִרְאֶ֤ה
הָֽרֹאֶה֙ אוֹתָ֔הּ
בְּעוֹדָ֥הּ בְּכַפּ֖וֹ יִבְלָעֶֽנָּה׃ ס

5 בַּיּ֣וֹם הַה֗וּא יִֽהְיֶה֙ יְהֹוָ֣ה צְבָא֔וֹת לַעֲטֶ֣רֶת
צְבִ֔י וְלִצְפִירַ֖ת תִּפְאָרָ֑ה לִשְׁאָ֖ר עַמּֽוֹ׃
6 וּלְר֖וּחַ מִשְׁפָּ֑ט לַיּוֹשֵׁב֙ עַל־הַמִּשְׁפָּ֔ט
וְלִ֨גְבוּרָ֔ה מְשִׁיבֵ֥י מִלְחָמָ֖ה שָֽׁעְרָה׃ ס

7 וְגַם־אֵ֙לֶּה֙ בַּיַּ֣יִן שָׁג֔וּ
וּבַשֵּׁכָ֖ר תָּע֑וּ
כֹּהֵ֣ן וְנָבִיא֩
שָׁג֨וּ בַשֵּׁכָ֜ר
נִבְלְע֣וּ מִן־הַיַּ֗יִן
תָּעוּ֙ מִן־הַשֵּׁכָ֔ר
שָׁג֖וּ בָּרֹאֶ֑ה
פָּק֖וּ פְּלִילִיָּֽה׃
8 כִּ֚י כָּל־שֻׁלְחָנ֔וֹת
מָלְא֖וּ קִ֣יא צֹאָ֑ה
בְּלִ֖י מָקֽוֹם׃ ס

9 אֶת־מִי֙ יוֹרֶ֣ה דֵעָ֔ה
וְאֶת־מִ֖י יָבִ֣ין שְׁמוּעָ֑ה
גְּמוּלֵי֙ מֵֽחָלָ֔ב
עַתִּיקֵ֖י מִשָּׁדָֽיִם׃
10 כִּ֣י צַ֤ו לָצָו֙ צַ֣ו לָצָ֔ו
קַ֥ו לָקָ֖ו קַ֣ו לָקָ֑ו
זְעֵ֥יר שָׁ֖ם זְעֵ֥יר שָֽׁם׃

11 כִּ֚י בְּלַעֲגֵ֣י שָׂפָ֔ה וּבְלָשׁ֖וֹן אַחֶ֑רֶת יְדַבֵּ֖ר
אֶל־הָעָ֥ם הַזֶּֽה׃ 12 אֲשֶׁ֣ר ׀ אָמַ֣ר אֲלֵיהֶ֗ם
זֹ֤את הַמְּנוּחָה֙ הָנִ֣יחוּ לֶֽעָיֵ֔ף וְזֹ֖את

---

c-c   Emendation yields "on the bough."
d   This is the drunkards' reaction to Isaiah's reproof.
e   I.e., do not embark on any political adventure at this time.

pose." They refuse to listen. ¹³To them the word
of the LORD is:

"Mutter upon mutter,
Murmur upon murmur,
Now here, now there."
And so they will march,*f*
But they shall fall backward,
And be injured and snared and captured.

¹⁴Hear now the word of the LORD,
You men of mockery,
g-Who govern that people-*g*
In Jerusalem!
¹⁵For you have said,
"We have made a covenant with Death,
Concluded a pact with Sheol.
When the sweeping flood passes through,
It shall not reach us;
For we have made falsehood our refuge,
Taken shelter in treachery."
¹⁶Assuredly,
Thus said the Lord GOD:
"Behold, I will found in Zion,
Stone by stone,
h-A tower of precious cornerstones,-*h*
Exceedingly firm;
He who trusts need not fear.
¹⁷But I will apply judgment as a measuring
line
And retribution*i* as weights;*j*
Hail shall sweep away the refuge of falsehood,
And flood-waters engulf your shelter.
¹⁸Your covenant with Death shall be an-
nulled,
Your pact with Sheol shall not endure;
When the sweeping flood passes through,
You shall be its victims.

13 וְהָיָה לָהֶם֙ דְּבַר־יְהוָ֔ה צַ֣ו לָצָ֞ו צַ֤ו לָצָו֙ קַ֤ו לָקָו֙ קַ֣ו לָקָ֔ו זְעֵ֥יר שָׁ֖ם זְעֵ֣יר שָׁ֑ם לְמַ֣עַן יֵלְכ֡וּ וְכָשְׁל֨וּ אָח֜וֹר וְנִשְׁבָּ֗רוּ וְנוֹקְשׁ֖וּ וְנִלְכָּֽדוּ׃ פ

14 לָכֵ֛ן שִׁמְע֥וּ דְבַר־יְהוָ֖ה אַנְשֵׁ֣י לָצ֑וֹן מֹֽשְׁלֵי֙ הָעָ֣ם הַזֶּ֔ה אֲשֶׁ֖ר בִּירוּשָׁלָֽ͏ִם׃

15 כִּ֣י אֲמַרְתֶּ֗ם כָּרַ֤תְנֽוּ בְרִית֙ אֶת־מָ֔וֶת וְעִם־שְׁא֖וֹל עָשִׂ֣ינוּ חֹזֶ֑ה שֹׁ֣יט שׁוֹטֵ֤ף כִּֽי־עבר יַֽעֲבֹר֙ לֹ֣א יְבוֹאֵ֔נוּ כִּ֣י שַׂ֧מְנוּ כָזָ֛ב מַחְסֵ֖נוּ וּבַשֶּׁ֥קֶר נִסְתָּֽרְנוּ׃ ס

16 לָכֵ֗ן כֹּ֤ה אָמַר֙ אֲדֹנָ֣י יְהוִ֔ה הִנְנִ֛י יִסַּ֥ד בְּצִיּ֖וֹן אָ֑בֶן אֶ֣בֶן בֹּ֜חַן פִּנַּ֤ת יִקְרַת֙ מוּסָ֣ד מוּסָּ֔ד הַֽמַּאֲמִ֖ין לֹ֥א יָחִֽישׁ׃

17 וְשַׂמְתִּ֤י מִשְׁפָּט֙ לְקָ֔ו וּצְדָקָ֖ה לְמִשְׁקָ֑לֶת וְיָעָ֤ה בָרָד֙ מַחְסֵ֣ה כָזָ֔ב וְסֵ֥תֶר מַ֖יִם יִשְׁטֹֽפוּ׃

18 וְכֻפַּ֤ר בְּרִֽיתְכֶם֙ אֶת־מָ֔וֶת וְחָזֽוּתְכֶ֥ם אֶת־שְׁא֖וֹל לֹ֣א תָק֑וּם שֹׁ֤יט שׁוֹטֵף֙ כִּ֣י יַֽעֲבֹ֔ר וִהְיִ֥יתֶם ל֖וֹ לְמִרְמָֽס׃

---

f   I.e., embark on the political adventure.
g-g   Or "composers of taunt-verses for that people."
h-h   Meaning of Heb. uncertain.
i   As in 1.27; 5.16; 10.22.
j   I.e., I will make judgment and retribution My plan of action; cf.
     34.11; 2 Kings 21.13.

v. 12. יתיר א'

906

¹⁹It shall catch you
Every time it passes through;
It shall pass through every morning,
Every day and every night.
And it shall be sheer horror
To grasp the message."

²⁰The couch is too short for stretching out,
And the cover too narrow for curling up!

²¹For the LORD will arise
As on the hill of Perazim,
He will rouse Himself
As in the vale of Gibeon,
To do His work—
Strange is His work!
And to perform His task—
Astounding is His task!^k
²²Therefore, refrain from mockery,
Lest your bonds be tightened.
For I have heard a decree of destruction
From my Lord GOD of Hosts
Against all the land.

²³Give diligent ear to my words,
Attend carefully to what I say.
²⁴Does he who plows to sow
Plow all the time,
Breaking up and furrowing his land?
²⁵When he has smoothed its surface,
Does he not rather broadcast black cumin
And scatter cumin,
Or set wheat in a row,^l
Barley in a strip,
And emmer in a patch?
²⁶For He teaches him the right manner,
His God instructs him.

19 מִדֵּי עָבְרוֹ
יִקַּח אֶתְכֶם
כִּי־בַבֹּקֶר בַּבֹּקֶר יַעֲבֹר
בַּיּוֹם וּבַלָּיְלָה
וְהָיָה רַק־זְוָעָה
הָבִין שְׁמוּעָה:

20 כִּי־קָצַר הַמַּצָּע מֵהִשְׂתָּרֵעַ
וְהַמַּסֵּכָה צָרָה כְּהִתְכַּנֵּס:

21 כִּי כְהַר־פְּרָצִים
יָקוּם יְהֹוָה
כְּעֵמֶק בְּגִבְעוֹן
יִרְגָּז
לַעֲשׂוֹת מַעֲשֵׂהוּ
זָר מַעֲשֵׂהוּ
וְלַעֲבֹד עֲבֹדָתוֹ
נָכְרִיָּה עֲבֹדָתוֹ:

22 וְעַתָּה אַל־תִּתְלוֹצָצוּ
פֶּן־יֶחְזְקוּ מוֹסְרֵיכֶם
כִּי־כָלָה וְנֶחֱרָצָה שָׁמַעְתִּי
מֵאֵת אֲדֹנָי יְהֹוִה צְבָאוֹת
עַל־כָּל־הָאָרֶץ:

23 הַאֲזִינוּ וְשִׁמְעוּ קוֹלִי
הַקְשִׁיבוּ וְשִׁמְעוּ אִמְרָתִי:
24 הֲכֹל הַיּוֹם
יַחֲרֹשׁ הַחֹרֵשׁ לִזְרֹעַ
יְפַתַּח וִישַׂדֵּד אַדְמָתוֹ:
25 הֲלוֹא אִם־שִׁוָּה פָנֶיהָ
וְהֵפִיץ קֶצַח
וְכַמֹּן יִזְרֹק
וְשָׂם חִטָּה שׂוֹרָה
וּשְׂעֹרָה נִסְמָן
וְכֻסֶּמֶת גְּבֻלָתוֹ:
26 וְיִסְּרוֹ לַמִּשְׁפָּט
אֱלֹהָיו יוֹרֶנּוּ:

---

k   *Instead of giving victory, as at Baal-perazim and Gibeon (cf.*
    2 Sam. 5.19–25; 1 Chron. 14.9–16), He will inflict punishment.
l   *In some Near Eastern countries, wheat is actually planted rather*
    than scattered.

²⁷So, too, black cumin is not threshed with
 a threshing board,
Nor is the wheel of a threshing sledge rolled
 over cumin;
But black cumin is beaten out with a stick
And cumin with a rod.
²⁸It is cereal that is crushed.^m
For ⁿ-even if-ⁿ he threshes it thoroughly,
And the wheel of his sledge ^h-and his horses
 overwhelm it,-^h
He does not crush it.
²⁹That, too, is ordered by the Lord of Hosts;
His counsel is unfathomable,
His wisdom marvelous.

כז כִּי לֹא בֶחָרוּץ יוּדַשׁ קֶצַח
וְאוֹפַן עֲגָלָה עַל־כַּמֹּן יוּסָּב
כִּי בַמַּטֶּה יֵחָבֶט קֶצַח
וְכַמֹּן בַּשָּׁבֶט:
כח לֶחֶם יוּדָק
כִּי לֹא לָנֶצַח אָדוֹשׁ יְדוּשֶׁנּוּ
וְהָמַם גִּלְגַּל עֶגְלָתוֹ וּפָרָשָׁיו
לֹא־יְדֻקֶּנּוּ:
כט גַּם־זֹאת מֵעִם יְהוָה צְבָאוֹת יָצָאָה
הִפְלִיא עֵצָה
הִגְדִּיל תּוּשִׁיָּה: ס

29

"Ah, Ariel,^a Ariel,
City where David camped!
Add year to year,
Let festivals come in their cycles!
²And I will harass Ariel,
And there shall be sorrow and sighing.
^b-She shall be to Me like Ariel.-^b
³And I will camp against you ^c-round about;-^c
I will lay siege to you ^b-with a mound,-^b
And I will set up siegeworks against you.
⁴And you shall speak from lower than the
 ground,
Your speech shall be humbler than the sod;
Your speech shall sound like a ghost's from
 the ground,
Your voice shall chirp from the sod.
⁵And like fine dust shall be
The multitude of ^d-your strangers;-^d
And like flying chaff,
The multitude of tyrants."

כט הוֹי אֲרִיאֵל אֲרִיאֵל
קִרְיַת חָנָה דָוִד
סְפוּ שָׁנָה עַל־שָׁנָה
חַגִּים יִנְקֹפוּ:
ב וַהֲצִיקוֹתִי לַאֲרִיאֵל
וְהָיְתָה תַאֲנִיָּה וַאֲנִיָּה
וְהָיְתָה לִּי כַּאֲרִיאֵל:
ג וְחָנִיתִי כַדּוּר עָלָיִךְ
וְצַרְתִּי עָלַיִךְ מֻצָּב
וַהֲקִימֹתִי עָלַיִךְ מְצֻרֹת:
ד וְשָׁפַלְתְּ מֵאֶרֶץ תְּדַבֵּרִי
וּמֵעָפָר תִּשַּׁח אִמְרָתֵךְ
וְהָיָה כְּאוֹב מֵאֶרֶץ קוֹלֵךְ
וּמֵעָפָר אִמְרָתֵךְ תְּצַפְצֵף:
ה וְהָיָה כְּאָבָק דַּק
הֲמוֹן זָרָיִךְ
וּכְמֹץ עֹבֵר
הֲמוֹן עָרִיצִים

---

m   *Emendation yields "threshed."*
n-n *Taking lo as equivalent to lu.*

a   *A poetic name of Jerusalem; cf. 33.7.*
b-b *Meaning of Heb. uncertain.*
c-c *Meaning of Heb. uncertain. Septuagint reads "like David"; cf.
     v. 1.*
d-d *Manuscript 1QIs^a reads "haughty men."*

And suddenly, in an instant,

6She shall be remembered of the LORD of
Hosts

With roaring, and shaking, and deafening
noise,

Storm, and tempest, and blaze of consuming
fire.

7Then, like a dream, a vision of the night,

Shall be the multitude of nations

That war upon Ariel,

And all her besiegers, and the siegeworks
against her,

And those who harass her.

8Like one who is hungry

And dreams he is eating,

But wakes to find himself empty;

And like one who is thirsty

And dreams he is drinking,

But wakes to find himself faint

And utterly parched—

So shall be all the multitude of nations

That war upon Mount Zion.

9Act stupid and be stupefied!

Act blind and be blinded!

(They are drunk, but not from wine,

They stagger, but not from liquor.)

10For the LORD has spread over you

A spirit of deep sleep,

And has shut your eyes, the prophets,

And covered your heads, the seers;

11So that all prophecy has been to you

Like the words of a sealed document.

If it is handed to one who can read and he
is asked to read it, he will say, "I can't, because
it is sealed"; 12and if the document is handed
to one who cannot read and he is asked to read
it, he will say, "I can't read."

וְהָיָה לְפֶתַע פִּתְאֹם׃

6 מֵעִם יְהֹוָה צְבָאוֹת תִּפָּקֵד
בְּרַעַם וּבְרַעַשׁ וְקוֹל גָּדוֹל
סוּפָה וּסְעָרָה וְלַהַב אֵשׁ אוֹכֵלָה׃

7 וְהָיָה כַּחֲלוֹם חֲזוֹן לַיְלָה
הֲמוֹן כָּל־הַגּוֹיִם
הַצֹּבְאִים עַל־אֲרִיאֵל
וְכָל־צֹבֶיהָ וּמְצֹדָתָהּ
וְהַמְּצִיקִים לָהּ׃

8 וְהָיָה כַּאֲשֶׁר יַחֲלֹם הָרָעֵב
וְהִנֵּה אוֹכֵל
וְהֵקִיץ וְרֵיקָה נַפְשׁוֹ
וְכַאֲשֶׁר יַחֲלֹם הַצָּמֵא
וְהִנֵּה שֹׁתֶה
וְהֵקִיץ וְהִנֵּה עָיֵף
וְנַפְשׁוֹ שׁוֹקֵקָה
כֵּן יִהְיֶה הֲמוֹן כָּל־הַגּוֹיִם
הַצֹּבְאִים עַל־הַר צִיּוֹן׃ ס

9 הִתְמַהְמְהוּ וּתְמָהוּ
הִשְׁתַּעַשְׁעוּ וָשֹׁעוּ
שָׁכְרוּ וְלֹא־יַיִן
נָעוּ וְלֹא שֵׁכָר׃

10 כִּי־נָסַךְ עֲלֵיכֶם יְהֹוָה
רוּחַ תַּרְדֵּמָה
וַיְעַצֵּם אֶת־עֵינֵיכֶם אֶת־הַנְּבִיאִים
וְאֶת־רָאשֵׁיכֶם הַחֹזִים כִּסָּה׃

11 וַתְּהִי לָכֶם חָזוּת הַכֹּל
כְּדִבְרֵי הַסֵּפֶר הֶחָתוּם

אֲשֶׁר־יִתְּנוּ אֹתוֹ אֶל־יוֹדֵעַ הַסֵּפֶר
לֵאמֹר קְרָא נָא־זֶה וְאָמַר לֹא אוּכַל כִּי
חָתוּם הוּא׃ 12 וְנִתַּן הַסֵּפֶר עַל אֲשֶׁר
לֹא־יָדַע סֵפֶר לֵאמֹר קְרָא נָא־זֶה וְאָמַר
לֹא יָדַעְתִּי סֵפֶר׃ ס

13My Lord said:

Because that people has approached [Me]
   with its mouth
And honored Me with its lips,
But has kept its heart far from Me,
And its worship of Me has been
A commandment of men, learned by rote—
14Truly, I shall further baffle that people
With bafflement upon bafflement;
And the wisdom of its wise shall fail,
And the prudence of its prudent shall vanish.

15Ha! Those who would hide their plans
Deep from the LORD!
Who do their work in dark places
And say, "Who sees us, who takes note of us?"
16e-How perverse of you!
Should the potter be accounted as the clay?-e
Should what is made say of its Maker,
"He did not make me,"
And what is formed say of Him who formed
   it,
f-"He did not understand"?-f
17Surely, in a little while,
Lebanon will be transformed into farm land,
And farm land accounted as mere brush.
18In that day, the deaf shall hear even written
   words,
And the eyes of the blind shall see
Even in darkness and obscurity.
19Then the humble shall have increasing joy
   through the LORD,
And the neediest of men shall exult
In the Holy One of Israel.
20For the tyrant shall be no more,
The scoffer shall cease to be;
And those diligent for evil shall be wiped out,
21Who cause men to lose their lawsuits,
Laying a snare for the arbiter at the gate,

13 וַיֹּאמֶר אֲדֹנָי
יַעַן כִּי נִגַּשׁ הָעָם הַזֶּה
בְּפִיו וּבִשְׂפָתָיו כִּבְּדוּנִי
וְלִבּוֹ רִחַק מִמֶּנִּי
וַתְּהִי יִרְאָתָם אֹתִי
מִצְוַת אֲנָשִׁים מְלֻמָּדָה: ס
14 לָכֵן הִנְנִי יוֹסִף לְהַפְלִיא אֶת־הָעָם־
הַזֶּה
הַפְלֵא וָפֶלֶא
וְאָבְדָה חָכְמַת חֲכָמָיו
וּבִינַת נְבֹנָיו תִּסְתַּתָּר: ס

15 הוֹי הַמַּעֲמִיקִים מֵיהוָה
לַסְתִּר עֵצָה
וְהָיָה בְמַחְשָׁךְ מַעֲשֵׂיהֶם
וַיֹּאמְרוּ מִי רֹאֵנוּ וּמִי יוֹדְעֵנוּ:
16 הַפְכְּכֶם
אִם־כְּחֹמֶר הַיֹּצֵר יֵחָשֵׁב
כִּי־יֹאמַר מַעֲשֶׂה לְעֹשֵׂהוּ
לֹא עָשָׂנִי
וְיֵצֶר אָמַר לְיוֹצְרוֹ
לֹא הֵבִין:
17 הֲלוֹא־עוֹד מְעַט מִזְעָר
וְשָׁב לְבָנוֹן לַכַּרְמֶל
וְהַכַּרְמֶל לַיַּעַר יֵחָשֵׁב:
18 וְשָׁמְעוּ בַיּוֹם־הַהוּא הַחֵרְשִׁים דִּבְרֵי־
סֵפֶר
וּמֵאֹפֶל וּמֵחֹשֶׁךְ
עֵינֵי עִוְרִים תִּרְאֶינָה:
19 וְיָסְפוּ עֲנָוִים בַּיהוָה שִׂמְחָה
וְאֶבְיוֹנֵי אָדָם
בִּקְדוֹשׁ יִשְׂרָאֵל יָגִילוּ:
20 כִּי־אָפֵס עָרִיץ
וְכָלָה לֵץ
וְנִכְרְתוּ כָּל־שֹׁקְדֵי אָוֶן:
21 מַחֲטִיאֵי אָדָם בְּדָבָר
וְלַמּוֹכִיחַ בַּשַּׁעַר יְקֹשׁוּן

---

e-e   Meaning of first line uncertain; emendation yields "Should the
      potter be accounted / Like the jugs or like the clay?"
f-f   Emendation yields "He did not fashion me."

And wronging by falsehood
Him who was in the right.

וַיַּטּוּ בַתֹּהוּ
צַדִּיק: ס

22Assuredly, thus said the Lᴏʀᴅ to the House
of Jacob, g-Who redeemed Abraham:-g

22 לָכֵן כֹּה־אָמַר יְהֹוָה אֶל־בֵּית יַעֲקֹב אֲשֶׁר
פָּדָה אֶת־אַבְרָהָם

No more shall Jacob be shamed,
No longer his face grow pale.

לֹא־עַתָּה יֵבוֹשׁ יַעֲקֹב
וְלֹא עַתָּה פָּנָיו יֶחֱוָרוּ:

23For when he—that is, his children—behold
what My hands have wrought in his midst, they
will hallow My name.

23 כִּי בִרְאֹתוֹ יְלָדָיו מַעֲשֵׂה יָדַי בְּקִרְבּוֹ
יַקְדִּישׁוּ שְׁמִי

Men will hallow the Holy One of Jacob
And stand in awe of the God of Israel.
24And the confused shall acquire insight
And grumblers accept instruction.

וְהִקְדִּישׁוּ אֶת־קְדוֹשׁ יַעֲקֹב
וְאֶת־אֱלֹהֵי יִשְׂרָאֵל יַעֲרִיצוּ:
24 וְיָדְעוּ תֹעֵי־רוּחַ בִּינָה
וְרוֹגְנִים יִלְמְדוּ־לֶקַח:

30 Oh, disloyal sons!
—declares the Lᴏʀᴅ—
Making plans
Against My wishes,
Weaving schemes
Against My will,
Thereby piling
Guilt on guilt—
2Who set out to go down to Egypt
Without asking Me,
To seek refuge with Pharaoh,
To seek shelter under the protection of Egypt.

ל הוֹי בָּנִים סוֹרְרִים
נְאֻם־יְהֹוָה
לַעֲשׂוֹת עֵצָה
וְלֹא מִנִּי
וְלִנְסֹךְ מַסֵּכָה
וְלֹא רוּחִי
לְמַעַן סְפוֹת
חַטָּאת עַל־חַטָּאת:
2 הַהֹלְכִים לָרֶדֶת מִצְרַיִם
וּפִי לֹא שָׁאָלוּ
לָעוֹז בְּמָעוֹז פַּרְעֹה
וְלַחְסוֹת בְּצֵל מִצְרָיִם:

3The refuge with Pharaoh shall result in your
     shame;
The shelter under Egypt's protection, in your
     chagrin.
4Though his officers are present in Zoan,a
And his messengersb reach as far as Hanes,

3 וְהָיָה לָכֶם מָעוֹז פַּרְעֹה לְבֹשֶׁת
וְהֶחָסוּת בְּצֵל־מִצְרַיִם לִכְלִמָּה:
4 כִּי־הָיוּ בְצֹעַן שָׂרָיו
וּמַלְאָכָיו חָנֵס יַגִּיעוּ:

g-g   *Emendation yields "Whose fathers He redeemed."*

a   *Or "Tanis."*

b   *Emendation yields "kings"; cf. 19.2 with note.*

5They all shall come to shame
Because of a people that does not avail them,
That is of no help or avail,
But [brings] only chagrin and disgrace.

6c-The "Beasts of the Negeb" Pronouncement.

Through a-c land of distress and hardship,
Of lion and roaringd king-beast,
Of viper and flying seraph,e
They convey their wealth on the backs of
    asses,
Their treasures on camels' humps,
To a people of no avail.
7For the help of Egypt
Shall be vain and empty.
Truly, I call this,
f-"They are a threat that has ceased."-f

8Now,
Go, write it down on a tablet
And inscribe it in a record,
That it may be with them for future days,
A witnessg forever.
9For it is a rebellious people,
Faithless children,
Children who refused to heed
The instruction of the Lord;
10Who said to the seers,
"Do not see,"
To the prophets, "Do not prophesy truth to
    us;
Speak to us falsehoods,
Prophesy delusions.
11Leave the way!
Get off the path!

5 כָּל הֹבְאִישׁ*
עַל־עַם לֹא־יוֹעִילוּ לָמוֹ
לֹא לְעֵזֶר וְלֹא לְהוֹעִיל
כִּי לְבֹשֶׁת וְגַם־לְחֶרְפָּה: ס

6 מַשָּׂא בַּהֲמוֹת נֶגֶב

בְּאֶרֶץ צָרָה וְצוּקָה
לָבִיא וָלַיִשׁ מֵהֶם
אֶפְעֶה וְשָׂרָף מְעוֹפֵף
יִשְׂאוּ עַל־כֶּתֶף עֲיָרִים חֵילֵהֶם
וְעַל־דַּבֶּשֶׁת גְּמַלִּים אוֹצְרֹתָם
עַל־עַם לֹא יוֹעִילוּ:
7 וּמִצְרַיִם
הֶבֶל וָרִיק יַעְזֹרוּ
לָכֵן קָרָאתִי לָזֹאת
רַהַב הֵם שָׁבֶת:

8 עַתָּה
בּוֹא כָתְבָהּ עַל־לוּחַ אִתָּם
וְעַל־סֵפֶר חֻקָּהּ
וּתְהִי לְיוֹם אַחֲרוֹן
לָעַד עַד־עוֹלָם:
9 כִּי עַם מְרִי הוּא
בָּנִים כֶּחָשִׁים
בָּנִים לֹא־אָבוּ שְׁמוֹעַ
תּוֹרַת יְהוָה:
10 אֲשֶׁר אָמְרוּ לָרֹאִים
לֹא תִרְאוּ
וְלַחֹזִים לֹא תֶחֱזוּ־לָנוּ נְכֹחוֹת
דַּבְּרוּ־לָנוּ חֲלָקוֹת
חֲזוּ מַהֲתַלּוֹת:
11 סוּרוּ מִנֵּי־דֶרֶךְ
הַטּוּ מִנֵּי־אֹרַח

v. 5. יתיר א'

---

c-c   *Meaning of Heb. uncertain; emendation yields "Through the*
    wasteland of the Negeb / Through a…"
d   *Meaning of Heb. uncertain.*
e   *See note on 14.29.*
f-f   *Meaning of Heb. uncertain. Emendation yields "Disgrace and*
    chagrin"; cf. v. 5.
g   *Understanding 'ad, with Targum, as a variant of 'ed.*

<table>
<tr><td>

Let us hear no more
About the Holy One of Israel!"

12Assuredly,
Thus said the Holy One of Israel:
Because you have rejected this word,
And have put your trust and reliance
In that which is fraudulent and tortuous—
13Of a surety,
This iniquity shall work on you
Like a spreading breach that occurs in a lofty
  wall,
Whose crash comes sudden and swift.
14It is smashed as one smashes an earthen jug,
Ruthlessly shattered
So that no shard is left in its breakage
To scoop coals from a brazier,
Or ladle water from a puddle.

15For thus said my Lord GOD,
The Holy One of Israel,
"You shall triumph by stillness and quiet;
Your victory shall come about
Through calm and confidence."
But you refused.
16"No," you declared.
"We shall flee on steeds"—
Therefore you shall flee!
"We shall ride on swift mounts"—
Therefore your pursuers shall prove swift!
17One thousand before the shout of one—
You shall flee at the shout of five;
Till what is left of you
Is like a mast on a hilltop,
Like a pole upon a mountain.

18Truly, the LORD is waiting to show you
  grace,
Truly, He will arise to pardon you.

</td><td>

הִשְׁבִּ֖יתוּ מִפָּנֵ֑ינוּ
אֶת־קְד֥וֹשׁ יִשְׂרָאֵֽל׃ ס

12 לָכֵ֗ן
כֹּ֤ה אָמַר֙ קְד֣וֹשׁ יִשְׂרָאֵ֔ל
יַ֥עַן מָֽאָסְכֶ֖ם בַּדָּבָ֣ר הַזֶּ֑ה
וַתִּבְטְחוּ֙ בְּעֹ֣שֶׁק וְנָל֔וֹז
וַתִּשָּׁעֲנ֖וּ עָלָֽיו׃
13 לָכֵ֗ן
יִֽהְיֶ֤ה לָכֶם֙ הֶעָוֺ֣ן הַזֶּ֔ה
כְּפֶ֣רֶץ נֹפֵ֔ל נִבְעֶ֖ה בְּחוֹמָ֣ה נִשְׂגָּבָ֑ה
אֲשֶׁר־פִּתְאֹ֥ם לְפֶ֖תַע יָב֥וֹא שִׁבְרָֽהּ׃
14 וּ֠שְׁבָרָהּ כְּשֵׁ֨בֶר נֵ֧בֶל יוֹצְרִ֛ים כָּת֖וּת
לֹ֣א יַחְמֹ֑ל
וְלֹֽא־יִמָּצֵ֤א בִמְכִתָּתוֹ֙ חֶ֔רֶשׂ
לַחְתּ֥וֹת אֵשׁ֙ מִיָּק֔וּד
וְלַחְשֹׂ֥ף מַ֖יִם מִגֶּֽבֶא׃ פ

15 כִּ֣י כֹֽה־אָמַר֩ אֲדֹנָ֨י יְהֹוִ֜ה
קְד֣וֹשׁ יִשְׂרָאֵ֗ל
בְּשׁוּבָ֤ה וָנַ֨חַת֙ תִּוָּ֣שֵׁע֔וּן
בְּהַשְׁקֵט֙ וּבְבִטְחָ֔ה
תִּהְיֶ֖ה גְּבֽוּרַתְכֶ֑ם
וְלֹ֖א אֲבִיתֶֽם׃
16 וַתֹּ֨אמְר֥וּ לֹא־
כִ֣י עַל־ס֥וּס נָנ֖וּס
עַל־כֵּ֣ן תְּנוּס֑וּן
וְעַל־קַ֣ל נִרְכָּ֔ב
עַל־כֵּ֖ן יִקַּ֥לּוּ רֹדְפֵיכֶֽם׃
17 אֶ֣לֶף אֶחָ֗ד מִפְּנֵי֙ גַּעֲרַ֣ת אֶחָ֔ד
מִפְּנֵ֛י גַּעֲרַ֥ת חֲמִשָּׁ֖ה תָּנֻ֑סוּ
עַ֣ד אִם־נוֹתַרְתֶּ֗ם
כַּתֹּ֨רֶן֙ עַל־רֹ֣אשׁ הָהָ֔ר
וְכַנֵּ֖ס עַל־הַגִּבְעָֽה׃

18 וְלָכֵ֞ן יְחַכֶּ֤ה יְהֹוָה֙ לַחֲנַנְכֶ֔ם
וְלָכֵ֥ן יָר֖וּם לְרַֽחֶמְכֶ֑ם

</td></tr>
</table>

For the Lord is a God of justice;
Happy are all who wait for Him.

19Indeed, O people in Zion, dwellers of Jerusalem, you shall not have cause to weep. He will grant you His favor at the sound of your cry; He will respond as soon as He hears it. 20My Lord will provide for you meager bread and scant water. Then your Guide will no more *d-be ignored,-d* but your eyes will watch your Guide; 21and, whenever you deviate to the right or to the left, your ears will heed the command from behind you: "This is the road; follow it!" 22And you will treat as unclean the silver overlay of your images and the golden plating of your idols. You will cast*h* them away like a menstruous woman. "Out!" you will call to them.

23So rain shall be provided for the seed with which you sow the ground, and the bread that the ground brings forth shall be rich and fat. Your livestock, in that day, shall graze in broad pastures; 24as for the cattle and the asses that till the soil, they shall partake of salted fodder that has been winnowed with shovel and fan.

25And on every high mountain and on every lofty hill, there shall appear brooks and watercourses—on a day of heavy slaughter, when towers topple. 26And the light of the moon shall become like the light of the sun, and the light of the sun shall become sevenfold, like the light of the seven days, when the Lord binds up His people's wounds and heals the injuries it has suffered.

27Behold the *i-*Lord Himself*-i*
Comes from afar
In blazing wrath,
*j-*With a heavy burden*-j*—
His lips full of fury,

כִּֽי־אֱלֹהֵ֥י מִשְׁפָּט֙ יְהֹוָ֔ה
אַשְׁרֵ֖י כָּל־ח֥וֹכֵי לֽוֹ׃ ס

19 כִּי־עַ֛ם בְּצִיּ֥וֹן יֵשֵׁ֖ב בִּירֽוּשָׁלָ֑͏ִם בָּכ֣וֹ לֹא־
תִבְכֶּ֗ה חָנ֤וֹן יׇחְנְךָ֙ לְק֣וֹל זַעֲקֶ֔ךָ כְּשׇׁמְעָת֖וֹ
עָנָֽךְ׃ 20 וְנָתַ֨ן לָכֶ֤ם אֲדֹנָי֙ לֶ֣חֶם צָ֔ר וּמַ֖יִם
לָ֑חַץ וְלֹֽא־יִכָּנֵ֥ף עוֹד֙ מוֹרֶ֔יךָ וְהָי֥וּ עֵינֶ֖יךָ
רֹא֥וֹת אֶת־מוֹרֶֽיךָ׃ 21 וְאׇזְנֶ֨יךָ֙ תִּשְׁמַ֣עְנָה
דָבָ֔ר מֵאַחֲרֶ֖יךָ לֵאמֹ֑ר זֶ֤ה הַדֶּ֙רֶךְ֙ לְכ֣וּ ב֔וֹ
כִּ֥י תַֽאֲמִ֖ינוּ וְכִ֥י תַשְׂמְאִֽילוּ׃ 22 וְטִמֵּאתֶ֗ם
אֶת־צִפּוּי֙ פְּסִילֵ֣י כַסְפֶּ֔ךָ וְאֶת־אֲפֻדַּ֖ת
מַסֵּכַ֣ת זְהָבֶ֑ךָ תִּזְרֵם֙ כְּמ֣וֹ דָוָ֔ה צֵ֖א תֹּ֥אמַר
לֽוֹ׃

23 וְנָתַן֩ מְטַ֨ר זַרְעֲךָ֜ אֲשֶׁר־תִּזְרַ֣ע אֶת־
הָאֲדָמָ֗ה וְלֶ֙חֶם֙ תְּבוּאַ֣ת הָֽאֲדָמָ֔ה וְהָיָ֥ה
דָשֵׁ֖ן וְשָׁמֵ֑ן יִרְעֶ֧ה מִקְנֶ֛יךָ בַּיּ֥וֹם הַה֖וּא כַּ֥ר
נִרְחָֽב׃ 24 וְהָאֲלָפִ֣ים וְהָֽעֲיָרִ֗ים עֹֽבְדֵי֙
הָֽאֲדָמָ֔ה בְּלִ֥יל חָמִ֖יץ יֹאכֵ֑לוּ אֲשֶׁר־זֹרֶ֥ה
בָרַ֖חַת וּבַמִּזְרֶֽה׃

25 וְהָיָ֣ה ׀ עַל־כׇּל־הַ֣ר גָּבֹ֗הַ וְעַל֙ כׇּל־גִּבְעָ֣ה
נִשָּׂאָ֔ה פְּלָגִ֖ים יִבְלֵי־מָ֑יִם בְּיוֹם֙ הֶ֣רֶג רָ֔ב
בִּנְפֹ֖ל מִגְדָּלִֽים׃ 26 וְהָיָ֤ה אֽוֹר־הַלְּבָנָה֙
כְּא֣וֹר הַֽחַמָּ֔ה וְא֤וֹר הַֽחַמָּה֙ יִהְיֶ֣ה שִׁבְעָתַ֔יִם
כְּא֖וֹר שִׁבְעַ֣ת הַיָּמִ֑ים בְּי֗וֹם חֲבֹ֤שׁ יְהֹוָה֙
אֶת־שֶׁ֣בֶר עַמּ֔וֹ וּמַ֥חַץ מַכָּת֖וֹ יִרְפָּֽא׃ ס

27 הִנֵּ֤ה שֵׁם־יְהֹוָה֙
בָּ֣א מִמֶּרְחָ֔ק
בֹּעֵ֣ר אַפּ֔וֹ
וְכֹ֖בֶד מַשָּׂאָ֑ה
שְׂפָתָיו֙ מָ֣לְאוּ זַ֔עַם

---

h   Change of vocalization yields "keep."
i-i   Lit. "The name of the Lord."
j-j   Presumably with a heavy load of punishment. Meaning of Heb. uncertain.

His tongue like devouring fire,

וּלְשׁוֹנוֹ כְּאֵשׁ אֹכֶלֶת׃

28And his breath like a raging torrent

28 וְרוּחוֹ כְּנַחַל שׁוֹטֵף

Reaching halfway up the neck—

עַד־צַוָּאר יֶחֱצֶה

To set a misguiding yokek upon nations

לַהֲנָפָה גוֹיִם בְּנָפַת שָׁוְא

And a misleading bridle upon the jaws of
    peoples,

וְרֶסֶן מַתְעֶה עַל לְחָיֵי עַמִּים׃

29For you, there shall be singing

29 הַשִּׁיר יִהְיֶה לָכֶם

As on a night when a festival is hallowed;

כְּלֵיל הִתְקַדֶּשׁ־חָג

There shall be rejoicing as when they march

וְשִׂמְחַת לֵבָב כַּהוֹלֵךְ

With flute, l-with timbrels, and with lyres-l

בֶּחָלִיל

To the Rock of Israel on the Mount of the
   LORD.

לָבוֹא בְהַר־יְהוָה אֶל־צוּר יִשְׂרָאֵל׃

30For the LORD will make His majestic voice
   heard

30 וְהִשְׁמִיעַ יְהוָה אֶת־הוֹד קוֹלוֹ

And display the sweep of His arm

וְנַחַת זְרוֹעוֹ יַרְאֶה

In raging wrath,

בְּזַעַף אָף

In a devouring blaze of fire,

וְלַהַב אֵשׁ אוֹכֵלָה

In tempest, and rainstorm, and hailstones.

נֶפֶץ וָזֶרֶם וְאֶבֶן בָּרָד׃

31Truly, Assyria, who beats with the rod,

31 כִּי־מִקּוֹל יְהוָה יֵחַת אַשּׁוּר

Shall be cowed by the voice of the LORD;

בַּשֵּׁבֶט יַכֶּה׃

32d-And each time the appointed staff passes
   by,

32 וְהָיָה כֹּל מַעֲבַר מַטֵּה מוּסָדָה

The LORD will bring down [His arm] upon
   him

אֲשֶׁר יָנִיחַ יְהוָה עָלָיו בְּתֻפִּים וּבְכִנֹּרוֹת

And will do battle with him as he waves it.-d

וּבְמִלְחֲמוֹת תְּנוּפָה נִלְחַם־בה בָּם׃*

33The Tophethm has long been ready for him;

33 כִּי־עָרוּךְ מֵאֶתְמוּל תָּפְתֶּה

He too is destined for Melechn—

גַּם־הוּא הִיא לַמֶּלֶךְ הוּכָן

His firepit has been made both wide and deep,

הֶעְמִיק הִרְחִב מְדֻרָתָהּ

With plenty of fire and firewood,

אֵשׁ וְעֵצִים הַרְבֵּה

And with the breath of the LORD

נִשְׁמַת יְהוָה

Burning in it like a stream of sulfur.

כְּנַחַל גָּפְרִית בֹּעֲרָה בָּהּ׃ ס

31 Ha!

Those who go down to Egypt for help

לא הוֹי

הַיֹּרְדִים מִצְרַיִם לְעֶזְרָה

---

k   *Interpreting* naphath *like Arabic* nāf; *meaning of line uncertain.*
l-l   *Brought from v. 32 for clarity.*
m   *A site near Jerusalem at which human beings were sacrificed*
    by fire in periods of paganizing; see 2 Kings 23.10.
n   *Cf. Molech, Lev. 18.21; 20.2–5.*

915

And rely upon horses!

They have put their trust in abundance of
   chariots,

In vast numbers of riders,

And they have not turned to the Holy One
   of Israel,

They have not sought the LORD.

²But He too is wise!

He has brought on misfortune,

And has not canceled His word.

So He shall rise against the house of evildoers,

And the allies*ᵃ* of the workers of iniquity.

³For the Egyptians are man, not God,

And their horses are flesh, not spirit;

And when the LORD stretches out His arm,

The helper shall trip

And the helped one shall fall,

And both shall perish together.

⁴For thus the LORD has said to me:

As a lion—a great beast—

Growls over its prey

And, when the shepherds gather

In force against him,

Is not dismayed by their cries

Nor cowed by their noise—

So the LORD of Hosts will descend to make
   war

Against the mount and the hill of Zion.

⁵Like the birds that fly, even so will the LORD
of Hosts shield Jerusalem, shielding and saving,
protecting and rescuing.

⁶*ᵇ*-Return, O children of Israel,-*ᵇ* to Him to
whom they have been so shamefully false; ⁷for
in that day everyone will reject his idols of silver
and idols of gold, which your hands have made
for your guilt.

עַל־סוּסִים֙ יִשָּׁעֵ֔נוּ
וַיִּבְטְח֤וּ עַל־רֶ֙כֶב֙ כִּ֣י רָ֔ב
וְעַ֣ל פָּרָשִׁ֔ים כִּֽי־עָצְמ֖וּ מְאֹ֑ד
וְלֹ֤א שָׁעוּ֙ עַל־קְד֣וֹשׁ יִשְׂרָאֵ֔ל
וְאֶת־יְהֹוָ֖ה לֹ֥א דָרָֽשׁוּ׃

2 וְגַם־ה֣וּא חָכָם֩
וַיָּ֨בֵא רָ֜ע
וְאֶת־דְּבָרָ֣יו לֹ֣א הֵסִ֔יר
וְקָם֙ עַל־בֵּ֣ית מְרֵעִ֔ים
וְעַל־עֶזְרַ֖ת פֹּ֥עֲלֵי אָֽוֶן׃

3 וּמִצְרַ֤יִם אָדָם֙ וְֽלֹא־אֵ֔ל
וְסוּסֵיהֶ֥ם בָּשָׂ֖ר וְלֹא־ר֑וּחַ
וַֽיהֹוָ֞ה יַטֶּ֣ה יָד֗וֹ
וְכָשַׁ֤ל עוֹזֵר֙
וְנָפַ֣ל עָזֻ֔ר
וְיַחְדָּ֖ו כֻּלָּ֥ם יִכְלָיֽוּן׃ ס

4 כִּ֣י כֹ֣ה אָֽמַר־יְהֹוָ֣ה ׀ אֵלַ֡י
כַּאֲשֶׁ֣ר יֶהְגֶּה֩ הָאַרְיֵ֨ה וְהַכְּפִ֜יר
עַל־טַרְפּ֗וֹ
אֲשֶׁ֨ר יִקָּרֵ֤א עָלָיו֙
מְלֹ֣א רֹעִ֔ים
מִקּוֹלָם֙ לֹ֣א יֵחָ֔ת
וּמֵהֲמוֹנָ֖ם לֹ֣א יַעֲנֶ֑ה
כֵּ֗ן יֵרֵד֙ יְהֹוָ֣ה צְבָא֔וֹת
עַל־הַר־צִיּ֖וֹן וְעַל־גִּבְעָתָֽהּ׃

5 כְּצִפֳּרִ֣ים עָפ֔וֹת כֵּ֗ן יָגֵ֛ן יְהֹוָ֥ה צְבָא֖וֹת עַל־
יְרוּשָׁלָ֑͏ִם גָּנ֥וֹן וְהִצִּ֖יל פָּסֹ֥חַ וְהִמְלִֽיט׃

6 שׁ֗וּבוּ לַאֲשֶׁ֛ר הֶעְמִ֥יקוּ סָרָ֖ה בְּנֵ֥י יִשְׂרָאֵֽל׃

7 כִּ֚י בַּיּ֣וֹם הַה֔וּא יִמְאָס֗וּן אִ֚ישׁ אֱלִילֵ֣י כַסְפּ֔וֹ
וֶאֱלִילֵ֖י זְהָב֑וֹ אֲשֶׁ֨ר עָשׂ֥וּ לָכֶ֛ם יְדֵיכֶ֖ם חֵֽטְא׃

ᵃ Lit. "help."

ᵇ⁻ᵇ Emendation yields "Then the children of Israel shall return."

⁸Then Assyria shall fall,
Not by the sword of man;
A sword not of humans shall devour him.
He shall shrivel[c] before the sword,
And his young men [d]pine away.[-d]
⁹His rock shall melt with terror,
And his officers shall [e]collapse from weakness[-e]—
Declares the LORD, who has a fire in Zion,
Who has an oven in Jerusalem.[f]

32 Behold, a king shall reign in righteousness,
And ministers shall govern with justice;
²Every one of them shall be
Like a refuge from gales,
A shelter from rainstorms;
Like brooks of water in a desert,
Like the shade of a massive rock
In a languishing land.

³Then the eyes of those who have sight shall not be sealed,
And the ears of those who have hearing shall listen;
⁴And the minds of the thoughtless shall attend and note,
And the tongues of mumblers shall speak with fluent eloquence.
⁵No more shall a villain be called noble,
Nor shall "gentleman" be said of a knave.
⁶For the villain speaks villainy
And plots treachery;
To act impiously
And to preach disloyalty against the LORD;
To leave the hungry unsatisfied
And deprive the thirsty of drink.
⁷As for the knave, his tools are knavish.

8 וְנָפַל אַשּׁוּר
בְּחֶרֶב לֹא־אִישׁ
וְחֶרֶב לֹא־אָדָם תֹּאכְלֶנּוּ
וְנָס לוֹ מִפְּנֵי־חֶרֶב
וּבַחוּרָיו לָמַס יִהְיוּ:
9 וְסַלְעוֹ מִמָּגוֹר יַעֲבוֹר
וְחַתּוּ מִנֵּס שָׂרָיו
נְאֻם־יְהוָה אֲשֶׁר־אוּר לוֹ בְּצִיּוֹן
וְתַנּוּר לוֹ בִּירוּשָׁלָ͏ִם: ס

לב הֵן לְצֶדֶק יִמְלָךְ־מֶלֶךְ
וּלְשָׂרִים לְמִשְׁפָּט יָשֹׂרוּ:
2 וְהָיָה־אִישׁ
כְּמַחֲבֵא־רוּחַ
וְסֵתֶר זָרֶם
כְּפַלְגֵי־מַיִם בְּצָיוֹן
כְּצֵל סֶלַע־כָּבֵד
בְּאֶרֶץ עֲיֵפָה:

3 וְלֹא תִשְׁעֶינָה עֵינֵי רֹאִים
וְאָזְנֵי שֹׁמְעִים תִּקְשַׁבְנָה:
4 וּלְבַב נִמְהָרִים יָבִין לָדָעַת
וּלְשׁוֹן עִלְּגִים תְּמַהֵר לְדַבֵּר צָחוֹת:
5 לֹא־יִקָּרֵא עוֹד לְנָבָל נָדִיב
וּלְכִילַי לֹא יֵאָמֵר שׁוֹעַ:
6 כִּי נָבָל נְבָלָה יְדַבֵּר
וְלִבּוֹ יַעֲשֶׂה־אָוֶן
לַעֲשׂוֹת חֹנֶף
וּלְדַבֵּר אֶל־יְהוָה תּוֹעָה
לְהָרִיק נֶפֶשׁ רָעֵב
וּמַשְׁקֶה צָמֵא יַחְסִיר:
7 וְכֵלַי כֵּלָיו רָעִים

---

c   *From root nss; cf. 10.18; others "flee."*
d-d   *From root mss; cf. 10.18; others "become tributary."*
e-e   *Cf. note c; meaning of Heb. uncertain.*

He forges plots	הוּא זִמּוֹת יָעָץ
To destroy the poor with falsehoods	לְחַבֵּל עֲנָוִים בְּאִמְרֵי־שֶׁקֶר
And the needy when they plead their cause.	וּבְדַבֵּר אֶבְיוֹן מִשְׁפָּט:
8But the noble has noble intentions	8 וְנָדִיב נְדִיבוֹת יָעָץ
And is constant in noble acts.	וְהוּא עַל־נְדִיבוֹת יָקוּם: פ
9You carefree women,	9 נָשִׁים שַׁאֲנַנּוֹת
Attend, hear my words!	קֹמְנָה שְׁמַעְנָה קוֹלִי
You confident ladies,	בָּנוֹת בֹּטְחוֹת
Give ear to my speech!	הַאֲזֵנָּה אִמְרָתִי:
10a-In little more than a year,-a	10 יָמִים עַל־שָׁנָה
You shall be troubled, O confident ones,	תִּרְגַּזְנָה בֹּטְחוֹת
When the vintage is over	כִּי כָּלָה בָצִיר
And no ingathering takes place.	אֹסֶף בְּלִי יָבוֹא:
11Tremble, you carefree ones!	11 חִרְדוּ שַׁאֲנַנּוֹת
Quake, O confident ones!	רְגָזָה בֹּטְחוֹת
Strip yourselves naked,	פְּשֹׁטָה וְעֹרָה
Put the cloth about your loins!	וַחֲגוֹרָה עַל־חֲלָצָיִם:
12Lament b-upon the breasts,-b	12 עַל־שָׁדַיִם סֹפְדִים
For the pleasant fields,	עַל־שְׂדֵי־חֶמֶד
For the spreading grapevines,	עַל־גֶּפֶן פֹּרִיָּה:
13For my people's soil—	13 עַל אַדְמַת עַמִּי
It shall be overgrown with briers and this-tles—	קוֹץ שָׁמִיר תַּעֲלֶה
Aye, and for all the houses of delight,	כִּי עַל־כָּל־בָּתֵּי מָשׂוֹשׂ
For the city of mirth.	קִרְיָה עַלִּיזָה:
14For the castle shall be abandoned,	14 כִּי־אַרְמוֹן נֻטָּשׁ
The noisy city forsaken;	הֲמוֹן עִיר עֻזָּב
Citadel and tower shall become	עֹפֶל וָבַחַן הָיָה
c-Bare places-c forever,	בְעַד מְעָרוֹת עַד־עוֹלָם
A stamping ground for wild asses,	מְשׂוֹשׂ פְּרָאִים
A pasture for flocksd—	מִרְעֵה עֲדָרִים:
15Till a spirit from on high is poured out on us,	15 עַד־יֵעָרֶה עָלֵינוּ רוּחַ מִמָּרוֹם
And wilderness is transformed into farm land,	וְהָיָה מִדְבָּר לַכַּרְמֶל
While farm land rates as mere brush.e	וכרמל וְהַכַּרְמֶל לַיַּעַר יֵחָשֵׁב:

a-a   Meaning of Heb. uncertain.
b-b   Emendation yields "for the fields."
c-c   Meaning of Heb. uncertain; emendation yields "Brushland, desert."
d   Emendation yields "onagers"; cf. Job 39.5.
e   I.e., the transformed wilderness will surpass in fertility what is now used as farm land.

16Then justice shall abide in the wilderness
And righteousness shall dwell on the farm
    land.
17For the work of righteousness shall be peace,
And the effect of righteousness, calm and
    confidence forever.
18Then my people shall dwell in peaceful
    homes,
In secure dwellings,
In untroubled places of rest.
19fAnd the brush shall sink and vanish,
Even as the city is laid low.

20Happy shall you be who sow by all waters,
Who g-send out cattle and asses to pasture.-g

33 Ha, you ravager who are not ravaged,
You betrayer who have not been betrayed!
When you have done ravaging, you shall be
    ravaged;
When you have finished betraying, you shall
    be betrayed.

2O LORD, be gracious to us!
It is to You we have looked;
a-Be their arm-a every morning,
Also our deliverance in time of stress.
3At [Your] roaring, peoples have fled,
Before Your majesty nations have scattered;
4And spoilb was gathered as locusts are gath-
    ered,
Itc was amassedd as grasshoppers are
    amassed.e

5The LORD is exalted,
He dwells on high!

16	וְשָׁכַ֥ן בַּמִּדְבָּ֖ר מִשְׁפָּ֑ט
	וּצְדָקָ֖ה בַּכַּרְמֶ֥ל תֵּשֵֽׁב:
17	וְהָיָ֛ה מַעֲשֵׂ֥ה הַצְּדָקָ֖ה שָׁל֑וֹם
	וַֽעֲבֹדַת֙ הַצְּדָקָ֔ה הַשְׁקֵ֥ט וָבֶ֖טַח עַד־
	עוֹלָֽם:
18	וְיָשַׁ֥ב עַמִּ֖י בִּנְוֵ֣ה שָׁל֑וֹם
	וּֽבְמִשְׁכְּנוֹת֙ מִבְטַחִ֔ים
	וּבִמְנוּחֹ֖ת שַׁאֲנַנּֽוֹת:
19	וּבָרַ֖ד בְּרֶ֣דֶת הַיָּ֑עַר
	וּבַשִּׁפְלָ֖ה תִּשְׁפַּ֥ל הָעִֽיר:
20	אַ֥שְׁרֵיכֶ֖ם זֹרְעֵ֣י עַל־כָּל־מָ֑יִם
	מְשַׁלְּחֵ֥י רֶֽגֶל־הַשּׁ֖וֹר וְהַֽחֲמֽוֹר: ס

לג ה֣וֹי שׁוֹדֵ֗ד וְאַתָּה֙ לֹ֣א שָׁד֔וּד
וּבוֹגֵ֖ד וְלֹא־בָ֣גְדוּ ב֑וֹ
כַּהֲתִֽמְךָ֤ שׁוֹדֵד֙ תּוּשַּׁ֔ד
כַּנְּלֹֽתְךָ֥ לִבְגֹּ֖ד יִבְגְּדוּ־בָֽךְ: ס

2 יְהוָ֥ה חָנֵּ֖נוּ
לְךָ֣ קִוִּ֑ינוּ
הֱיֵ֤ה זְרֹעָם֙ לַבְּקָרִ֔ים
אַף־יְשֽׁוּעָתֵ֖נוּ בְּעֵ֥ת צָרָֽה:
3 מִקּ֣וֹל הָמ֔וֹן נָֽדְד֖וּ עַמִּ֑ים
מֵרֹ֣מְמֻתֶ֔ךָ נָפְצ֖וּ גּוֹיִֽם:
4 וְאֻסַּ֣ף שְׁלַלְכֶ֔ם אֹ֖סֶף הֶֽחָסִ֑יל
כְּמַשַּׁ֥ק גֵּבִ֖ים שֹׁקֵ֥ק בּֽוֹ:

5 נִשְׂגָּ֤ב יְהוָה֙
כִּ֥י שֹׁכֵ֖ן מָר֑וֹם

---

f   *Meaning of verse uncertain.*
g-g   *Lit. "let loose the feet of cattle and asses"; cf. 7.25 end.*

a-a   *Emendation yields "You have been our help."*
b   *Heb. "your spoil."*
c   *Meaning of Heb. uncertain. Emendation yields "booty"; cf. v. 23.*
d   *Taking šqq as a cognate of qšš.*
e   *Apparently for food; cf. Lev. 11.22.*

[Of old] He filled Zion
With justice and righteousness.
⁶Faithfulness to *f*Your charge-*f* was [her]
   wealth,
Wisdom and devotion [her] triumph,
Reverence for the Lord—that was her*g* treasure.

⁷Hark! The Arielites*h* cry aloud;
Shalom's*i* messengers weep bitterly.
⁸Highways are desolate,
Wayfarers have ceased.
A covenant has been renounced,
Cities*j* rejected
k-Mortal man-*k* despised.
⁹The land is wilted and withered;
Lebanon disgraced and moldering,
Sharon is become like a desert,
And Bashan and Carmel are stripped bare.
¹⁰"Now I will arise," says the Lord,
"Now I will exalt Myself, now raise Myself
   high.
¹¹You shall conceive hay,
Give birth to straw;
My*l* breath will devour you like fire.
¹²Peoples shall be burnings of lime,*m*
Thorns cut down that are set on fire.
¹³Hear, you who are far, what I have done;
You who are near, note My might."

¹⁴Sinners in Zion are frightened,
The godless are seized with trembling:
"Who of us can dwell with the devouring fire:
Who of us can dwell with the never-dying
   blaze?"
¹⁵He who walks in righteousness,

מִלֵּא צִיּ֔וֹן
מִשְׁפָּ֖ט וּצְדָקָֽה׃
6 וְהָיָה֙ אֱמוּנַ֣ת עִתֶּ֔יךָ
חֹ֥סֶן יְשׁוּעֹ֖ת חָכְמַ֣ת וָדָ֑עַת
יִרְאַ֥ת יְהוָ֖ה הִ֥יא אוֹצָרֽוֹ׃ ס

7 הֵ֚ן אֶרְאֶלָּ֔ם* צָעֲק֖וּ חֻ֑צָה
מַלְאֲכֵ֣י שָׁל֔וֹם מַ֖ר יִבְכָּיֽוּן׃
8 נָשַׁ֖מּוּ מְסִלּ֑וֹת
שָׁבַ֖ת עֹבֵ֣ר אֹ֑רַח
הֵפֵ֣ר בְּרִ֗ית
מָאַ֣ס עָרִ֔ים
לֹ֥א חָשַׁ֖ב אֱנֽוֹשׁ׃
9 אָבַ֤ל אֻמְלְלָה֙ אָ֔רֶץ
הֶחְפִּ֥יר לְבָנ֖וֹן קָמַ֑ל
הָיָ֤ה הַשָּׁרוֹן֙ כָּעֲרָבָ֔ה
וְנֹעֵ֥ר בָּשָׁ֖ן וְכַרְמֶֽל׃
10 עַתָּ֣ה אָק֔וּם יֹאמַ֖ר* יְהוָ֑ה
עַתָּ֣ה אֵרוֹמָ֔ם עַתָּ֖ה אֶנָּשֵֽׂא׃
11 תַּהֲר֥וּ חֲשַׁ֖שׁ
תֵּ֣לְד֣וּ קַ֑שׁ
רוּחֲכֶ֕ם אֵ֖שׁ תֹּאכַלְכֶֽם׃
12 וְהָי֥וּ עַמִּ֖ים מִשְׂרְפ֣וֹת שִׂ֑יד
קוֹצִ֥ים כְּסוּחִ֖ים בָּאֵ֥שׁ יִצַּֽתּוּ׃ ס
13 שִׁמְע֥וּ רְחוֹקִ֖ים אֲשֶׁ֣ר עָשִׂ֑יתִי
וּדְע֥וּ קְרוֹבִ֖ים גְּבֻֽרָתִֽי׃
14 פָּחֲד֤וּ בְצִיּוֹן֙ חַטָּאִ֔ים
אָחֲזָ֥ה רְעָדָ֖ה חֲנֵפִ֑ים
מִ֣י ׀ יָג֤וּר לָ֙נוּ֙ אֵ֣שׁ אוֹכֵלָ֔ה
מִֽי־יָג֥וּר לָ֖נוּ מוֹקְדֵ֥י עוֹלָֽם׃
15 הֹלֵ֣ךְ צְדָק֔וֹת

f-f Meaning of Heb. uncertain.
g Heb. "his."
h So a few manuscripts; cf. 29.1.
i I.e., Jerusalem's; cf. Salem (Heb. Shalem), Ps. 76.3.
j 1QIsᵃ reads "A pact."
k-k Emendation yields "an obligation."
l Heb. "your."
m Emendation yields "brambles"; cf. 32.13.

Speaks uprightly,

Spurns profit from fraudulent dealings,

Waves away a bribe instead of grasping it,

Stops his ears against listening to infamy,

Shuts his eyes against looking at evil—

16Such a one shall dwell in lofty security,

With inaccessible cliffs for his stronghold,

With his food supplied

And his drink assured.

17When your eyes behold n-a king in his beauty,-n

When they contemplate the land round about,

18Your throato shall murmur in awe,

"Where is one who could count? Where is one who could weigh?

Where is one who could count [all these] towers?"

19No more shall you see the barbarian folk,

The people of speech too obscure to comprehend,

So stammering of tongue that they are not understood.

20When you gaze upon Zion, our city of assembly,

Your eyes shall behold Jerusalem

As a secure homestead,

A tent not to be transported,

Whose pegs shall never be pulled up,

And none of whose ropes shall break.

21For there the LORD in His greatness shall be for us

Like a region of rivers, of broad streams,

Where no floating vessels can sail

And no mighty craft can travel—

p-Theirq ropes are slack,

וְדֹבֵ֖ר מֵישָׁרִ֑ים

מֹאֵ֞ס בְּבֶ֣צַע מַֽעֲשַׁקּ֗וֹת

נֹעֵ֤ר כַּפָּיו֙ מִתְּמֹ֣ךְ בַּשֹּׁ֔חַד

אֹטֵ֤ם אָזְנוֹ֙ מִשְּׁמֹ֣עַ דָּמִ֔ים

וְעֹצֵ֥ם עֵינָ֖יו מֵרְא֥וֹת בְּרָֽע׃

16הוּא֙ מְרוֹמִ֣ים יִשְׁכֹּ֔ן

מְצָד֥וֹת סְלָעִ֖ים מִשְׂגַּבּ֑וֹ

לַחְמ֣וֹ נִתָּ֔ן

מֵימָ֖יו נֶאֱמָנִֽים׃

17מֶ֥לֶךְ בְּיָפְי֖וֹ תֶּחֱזֶ֣ינָה עֵינֶ֑יךָ

תִּרְאֶ֖ינָה אֶ֥רֶץ מַרְחַקִּֽים׃

18לִבְּךָ֖ יֶהְגֶּ֣ה אֵימָ֑ה

אַיֵּ֤ה סֹפֵר֙ אַיֵּ֣ה שֹׁקֵ֔ל

אַיֵּ֖ה סֹפֵ֥ר אֶת־הַמִּגְדָּלִֽים׃

19אֶת־עַ֤ם נוֹעָז֙ לֹ֣א תִרְאֶ֔ה

עַ֚ם עִמְקֵ֣י שָׂפָ֔ה מִשְּׁמ֖וֹעַ

נִלְעַ֥ג לָשׁ֖וֹן אֵ֥ין בִּינָֽה׃

20חֲזֵ֣ה צִיּ֔וֹן קִרְיַ֖ת מֽוֹעֲדֵ֑נוּ

עֵינֶ֜יךָ תִרְאֶ֣ינָה יְרוּשָׁלִַ֗ם

נָוֶ֣ה שַׁאֲנָ֔ן

אֹ֖הֶל בַּל־יִצְעָ֑ן

בַּל־יִסַּ֤ע יְתֵֽדֹתָיו֙ לָנֶ֔צַח

וְכׇל־חֲבָלָ֖יו בַּל־יִנָּתֵֽקוּ׃

21*כִּ֣י אִם־שָׁ֞ם אַדִּ֤יר יְהֹוָה֙ לָ֔נוּ

מְקוֹם־נְהָרִ֥ים יְאֹרִ֖ים רַחֲבֵ֣י יָדָ֑יִם

בַּל־תֵּ֤לֶךְ בּוֹ֙ אֳנִי־שַׁ֔יִט

וְצִ֥י אַדִּ֖יר לֹ֥א יַעַבְרֶֽנּוּ׃

---

n-n   Emendation yields "perfection of beauty"; cf. Ps. 50.2.
o   As in 59.13 and elsewhere; others "heart."
p-p   Brought up from v. 23 for clarity. The passage means that the LORD will render Jerusalem as inaccessible to enemies as if it were surrounded by an impassable sea.
q   Heb. "your."

חצי הספר בפסוקים   v. 21.

They cannot steady the sockets of their masts,
They cannot spread a sail.-ᵖ

²²For the Lᴏʀᴅ shall be our ruler,
The Lᴏʀᴅ shall be our prince,
The Lᴏʀᴅ shall be our king:
He shall deliver us.

²³Then ʳ-shall indeed much spoil be divided,-ʳ
Even the lame shall seize booty.

²⁴And none who lives there shall say, "I am
  sick";
It shall be inhabited by folk whose sin has
  been forgiven.

22 כִּ֤י יְהוָה֙ שֹׁפְטֵ֔נוּ
יְהוָ֖ה מְחֹקְקֵ֑נוּ
יְהוָ֥ה מַלְכֵּ֖נוּ
ה֥וּא יוֹשִׁיעֵֽנוּ׃
23 נִטְּשׁ֖וּ חֲבָלָ֑יִךְ
בַּל־יְחַזְּק֤וּ כֵן־תָּרְנָם֙
בַּל־פָּ֣רְשׂוּ נֵ֔ס
אָ֣ז חֻלַּ֤ק עַד־שָׁלָל֙ מַרְבֶּ֔ה
פִּסְחִ֖ים בָּ֥זְזוּ בַֽז׃
24 וּבַל־יֹאמַ֥ר שָׁכֵ֖ן חָלִ֑יתִי
הָעָ֛ם הַיֹּשֵׁ֥ב בָּ֖הּ נְשֻׂ֥א עָוֺֽן׃

34

Approach, O nations, and listen,
Give heed, O peoples!
Let the earth and those in it hear;
The world, and what it brings forth.

²For the Lᴏʀᴅ is angry at all the nations,
Furious at all their host;
He has doomed them, consigned them to
  slaughter.

³Their slain shall be left lying,
And the stench of their corpses shall mount;
And the hills shall be drenched with their
  blood,

⁴ᵃ-All the host of heaven shall molder.-ᵃ
The heavens shall be rolled up like a scroll,
And all their host shall wither
Like a leaf withering on the vine,
Or shriveled fruit on a fig tree.

לד קִרְב֤וּ גוֹיִם֙ לִשְׁמֹ֔עַ
וּלְאֻמִּ֖ים הַקְשִׁ֑יבוּ
תִּשְׁמַ֤ע הָאָ֙רֶץ֙ וּמְלֹאָ֔הּ
תֵּבֵ֖ל וְכָל־צֶאֱצָאֶֽיהָ׃
2 כִּ֣י קֶ֤צֶף לַֽיהוָה֙ עַל־כָּל־הַגּוֹיִ֔ם
וְחֵמָ֖ה עַל־כָּל־צְבָאָ֑ם
הֶחֱרִימָ֖ם נְתָנָ֥ם לַטָּֽבַח׃
3 וְחַלְלֵיהֶ֣ם יֻשְׁלָ֔כוּ
וּפִגְרֵיהֶ֖ם יַעֲלֶ֣ה בָאְשָׁ֑ם
וְנָמַ֥סּוּ הָרִ֖ים מִדָּמָֽם׃
4 וְנָמַ֙קּוּ֙ כָּל־צְבָ֣א הַשָּׁמַ֔יִם
וְנָגֹ֥לּוּ כַסֵּ֖פֶר הַשָּׁמָ֑יִם
וְכָל־צְבָאָ֣ם יִבּ֔וֹל
כִּנְבֹ֤ל עָלֶה֙ מִגֶּ֔פֶן
וּכְנֹבֶ֖לֶת מִתְּאֵנָֽה׃

⁵For My sword shall ᵇ-be drunk-ᵇ in the sky;
Lo, it shall come down upon Edom,
Upon the people I have doomed,
To wreak judgment.

⁶The Lᴏʀᴅ has a sword; it is sated with blood,
It is gorged with fat—

5 כִּֽי־רִוְּתָ֥ה בַשָּׁמַ֖יִם חַרְבִּ֑י
הִנֵּה֙ עַל־אֱד֣וֹם תֵּרֵ֔ד
וְעַל־עַ֥ם חֶרְמִ֖י
לְמִשְׁפָּֽט׃
6 חֶ֣רֶב לַיהוָ֞ה מָלְאָ֥ה דָם֙
הֻדַּ֙שְׁנָה֙ מֵחֵ֔לֶב

---

r-r   *Meaning of Heb. uncertain; emendation yields "even a blind
     man shall divide much spoil."*

a-a   *1QIsᵃ reads "And the valleys shall be cleft, / And all the host
     of heaven shall wither."*

b-b   *1QIsᵃ reads "be seen"; cf. Targum.*

The blood of lambs and he-goats,
The kidney fat of rams.
For the LORD holds a sacrifice in Bozrah,
A great slaughter in the land of Edom.
7Wild oxen shall fall c-with them,-c
Young bulls with mighty steers;
And their land shall be drunk with blood,
Their soil shall be saturated with fat.
8For it is the LORD's day of retribution,
The year of vindication for Zion's cause.
9Itsd streams shall be turned to pitch
And its soil to sulfur.
Its land shall become burning pitch,
10Night and day it shall never go out;
Its smoke shall rise for all time.
Through the ages it shall lie in ruins;
Through the aeons none shall traverse it.
11e-Jackdaws and owls-e shall possess it;
Great owls and ravens shall dwell there.
He shall measure it with a line of chaos
And with weights of emptiness.f
12e-It shall be called, "No kingdom is there,"-e
Its nobles and all its lords shall be nothing.
13Thorns shall grow up in its palaces,
Nettles and briers in its strongholds.
It shall be a home of jackals,
An abode of ostriches.
14gWildcats shall meet hyenas,
Goat-demons shall greet each other;
There too the lilithh shall repose
And find herself a resting place.
15There the arrow-snake shall nest and lay
    eggs,
And shall brood and hatch in its shade.
There too the buzzards shall gather
With one another.
16Search and read it in the scroll of the LORD:

מִדַּם כָּרִים וְעַתּוּדִים
מֵחֵלֶב כִּלְיוֹת אֵילִים
כִּי זֶבַח לַיהוָה בְּבָצְרָה
וְטֶבַח גָּדוֹל בְּאֶרֶץ אֱדוֹם:
7 וְיָרְדוּ רְאֵמִים עִמָּם
וּפָרִים עִם־אַבִּירִים
וְרִוְּתָה אַרְצָם מִדָּם
וַעֲפָרָם מֵחֵלֶב יְדֻשָּׁן:
8 כִּי יוֹם נָקָם לַיהוָה
שְׁנַת שִׁלּוּמִים לְרִיב צִיּוֹן:
9 וְנֶהֶפְכוּ נְחָלֶיהָ לְזֶפֶת
וַעֲפָרָהּ לְגָפְרִית
וְהָיְתָה אַרְצָהּ לְזֶפֶת בֹּעֵרָה:
10 לַיְלָה וְיוֹמָם לֹא תִכְבֶּה
לְעוֹלָם יַעֲלֶה עֲשָׁנָהּ
מִדּוֹר לָדוֹר תֶּחֱרָב
לְנֵצַח נְצָחִים אֵין עֹבֵר בָּהּ:
11 וִירֵשׁוּהָ קָאַת וְקִפּוֹד
וְיַנְשׁוֹף וְעֹרֵב יִשְׁכְּנוּ־בָהּ
וְנָטָה עָלֶיהָ קַו־תֹהוּ
וְאַבְנֵי־בֹהוּ:
12 חֹרֶיהָ וְאֵין־שָׁם מְלוּכָה יִקְרָאוּ
וְכָל־שָׂרֶיהָ יִהְיוּ אָפֶס:
13 וְעָלְתָה אַרְמְנֹתֶיהָ סִירִים
קִמּוֹשׂ וָחוֹחַ בְּמִבְצָרֶיהָ
וְהָיְתָה נְוֵה תַנִּים
חָצִיר לִבְנוֹת יַעֲנָה:
14 וּפָגְשׁוּ צִיִּים אֶת־אִיִּים
וְשָׂעִיר עַל־רֵעֵהוּ יִקְרָא
אַךְ־שָׁם הִרְגִּיעָה לִּילִית
וּמָצְאָה לָהּ מָנוֹחַ:
15 שָׁמָּה קִנְּנָה קִפּוֹז וַתְּמַלֵּט
וּבָקְעָה וְדָגְרָה בְצִלָּהּ
אַךְ־שָׁם נִקְבְּצוּ דַיּוֹת
אִשָּׁה רְעוּתָהּ:
16 דִּרְשׁוּ מֵעַל־סֵפֶר יְהוָה וּקְרָאוּ

---

c-c   *Emendation yields "with fatted calves."*
d   *I.e., Edom's.*
e-e   *Meaning of Heb. uncertain.*
f   *I.e., He shall plan chaos and emptiness for it; cf. 28.17; Lam. 2.8.*
g   *Most of the creatures in vv. 14–15 cannot be identified with*
        certainty.
h   *A kind of demon.*

Not one of these shall be absent,
Not one shall miss its fellow.
For His[i] mouth has spoken,
It is His spirit that has assembled them,
17And it is He who apportioned it to them by
    lot,
Whose hand divided it for them with the line.
They shall possess it for all time,
They shall dwell there through the ages.

35 The arid desert shall be glad,
The wilderness shall rejoice
And shall blossom like a rose.[a]
2It shall blossom abundantly,
It shall also exult and shout.
It shall receive the glory of Lebanon,
The splendor of Carmel and Sharon.
They shall behold the glory of the Lord,
The splendor of our God.

3Strengthen the hands that are slack;
Make firm the tottering knees!
4Say to the anxious of heart,
"Be strong, fear not;
Behold your God!
Requital is coming,
The recompense of God—
He Himself is coming to give you triumph."

5Then the eyes of the blind shall be opened,
And the ears of the deaf shall be unstopped.
6Then the lame shall leap like a deer,
And the tongue of the dumb shall shout
    aloud;
For waters shall burst forth in the desert,
Streams in the wilderness.
7Torrid earth shall become a pool;
Parched land, fountains of water;

i   Heb. "My."

a   Lit. "crocus."

אַחַת מֵהֵ֫נָּה֙ לֹ֣א נֶעְדָּ֔רָה
אִשָּׁ֥ה רְעוּתָ֖הּ לֹ֣א פָקָ֑דוּ
כִּי־פִי֙ ה֣וּא צִוָּ֔ה
וְרוּח֖וֹ ה֥וּא קִבְּצָֽן׃
17 וְהֽוּא־הִפִּ֤יל לָהֶן֙ גּוֹרָ֔ל
וְיָד֛וֹ חִלְּקַ֥תָּה לָהֶ֖ם בַּקָּ֑ו
עַד־עוֹלָם֙ יִ֣ירָשׁ֔וּהָ
לְד֥וֹר וָד֖וֹר יִשְׁכְּנוּ־בָֽהּ׃ ס

לה יְשֻׂשׂ֥וּם מִדְבָּ֖ר וְצִיָּ֑ה
וְתָגֵ֥ל עֲרָבָ֖ה
וְתִפְרַ֥ח כַּחֲבַצָּֽלֶת׃
2 פָּרֹ֨חַ תִּפְרַ֜ח וְתָגֵ֗ל
אַ֚ף גִּילַ֣ת וְרַנֵּ֔ן
כְּב֤וֹד הַלְּבָנוֹן֙ נִתַּן־לָ֔הּ
הֲדַ֥ר הַכַּרְמֶ֖ל וְהַשָּׁר֑וֹן
הֵ֛מָּה יִרְא֥וּ כְבוֹד־יְהוָ֖ה
הֲדַ֥ר אֱלֹהֵֽינוּ׃ ס

3 חַזְּק֖וּ יָדַ֣יִם רָפ֑וֹת
וּבִרְכַּ֥יִם כֹּשְׁל֖וֹת אַמֵּֽצוּ׃
4 אִמְרוּ֙ לְנִמְהֲרֵי־לֵ֔ב
חִזְק֖וּ אַל־תִּירָ֑אוּ
הִנֵּ֤ה אֱלֹֽהֵיכֶם֙
נָקָ֣ם יָב֔וֹא
גְּמ֖וּל אֱלֹהִ֑ים
ה֥וּא יָב֖וֹא וְיֹשַׁעֲכֶֽם׃

5 אָ֥ז תִּפָּקַ֖חְנָה עֵינֵ֣י עִוְרִ֑ים
וְאָזְנֵ֥י חֵרְשִׁ֖ים תִּפָּתַֽחְנָה׃
6 אָ֣ז יְדַלֵּ֤ג כָּֽאַיָּל֙ פִּסֵּ֔חַ
וְתָרֹ֖ן לְשׁ֣וֹן אִלֵּ֑ם
כִּֽי־נִבְקְע֤וּ בַמִּדְבָּר֙ מַ֔יִם
וּנְחָלִ֖ים בָּעֲרָבָֽה׃
7 וְהָיָ֤ה הַשָּׁרָב֙ לַאֲגַ֔ם
וְצִמָּא֖וֹן לְמַבּ֣וּעֵי מָ֑יִם

The home of jackals, a pasture;[b]
The abode [of ostriches],[c] reeds and rushes.

[8]And a highway shall appear there,
Which shall be called the Sacred Way.
No one unclean shall pass along it,
But it shall be for them.[d]
[e]No traveler, not even fools, shall go astray.[e]
[9]No lion shall be there,
No ferocious beast shall set foot on it—
These shall not be found there.
But the redeemed shall walk it;
[10]And the ransomed of the LORD shall return,
And come with shouting to Zion,
Crowned with joy everlasting.
They shall attain joy and gladness,
While sorrow and sighing flee.

36 [a][In the fourteenth year of King Hezekiah, King Sennacherib of Assyria marched against all the fortified towns of Judah and seized them. [2]From Lachish, the king of Assyria sent the Rabshakeh,[b] with a large force, to King Hezekiah in Jerusalem. [The Rabshakeh] took up a position near the conduit of the Upper Pool, by the road of the Fuller's Field; [3]and Eliakim son of Hilkiah who was in charge of the palace, Shebna the scribe, and Joah son of Asaph the recorder went out to him.

[4]The Rabshakeh said to them, "You tell Hezekiah: Thus said the Great King, the king of Assyria: What makes you so confident? [5]I suppose[c] mere talk makes counsel and valor for war! Look, on whom are you relying, that you have

בִּנְוֵה תַנִּים רִבְצָהּ
חָצִיר לְקָנֶה וָגֹמֶא:

8 וְהָיָה־שָׁם מַסְלוּל וָדֶרֶךְ
וְדֶרֶךְ הַקֹּדֶשׁ יִקָּרֵא לָהּ
לֹא־יַעַבְרֶנּוּ טָמֵא
וְהוּא־לָמוֹ
הֹלֵךְ דֶּרֶךְ וֶאֱוִילִים לֹא יִתְעוּ:
9 לֹא־יִהְיֶה שָׁם אַרְיֵה
וּפְרִיץ חַיּוֹת בַּל־יַעֲלֶנָּה
לֹא תִמָּצֵא שָׁם
וְהָלְכוּ גְּאוּלִים:
10 וּפְדוּיֵי יְהֹוָה יְשֻׁבוּן
וּבָאוּ צִיּוֹן בְּרִנָּה
וְשִׂמְחַת עוֹלָם עַל־רֹאשָׁם
שָׂשׂוֹן וְשִׂמְחָה יַשִּׂיגוּ
וְנָסוּ יָגוֹן וַאֲנָחָה: פ

לו וַיְהִי בְּאַרְבַּע עֶשְׂרֵה שָׁנָה לַמֶּלֶךְ חִזְקִיָּהוּ עָלָה סַנְחֵרִיב מֶלֶךְ־אַשּׁוּר עַל כָּל־עָרֵי יְהוּדָה הַבְּצֻרוֹת וַיִּתְפְּשֵׂם: 2 וַיִּשְׁלַח מֶלֶךְ־אַשּׁוּר | אֶת־רַב־שָׁקֵה מִלָּכִישׁ יְרוּשָׁלַמָה אֶל־הַמֶּלֶךְ חִזְקִיָּהוּ בְּחֵיל כָּבֵד וַיַּעֲמֹד בִּתְעָלַת הַבְּרֵכָה הָעֶלְיוֹנָה בִּמְסִלַּת שְׂדֵה כוֹבֵס: 3 וַיֵּצֵא אֵלָיו אֶלְיָקִים בֶּן־חִלְקִיָּהוּ אֲשֶׁר עַל־הַבָּיִת וְשֶׁבְנָא הַסֹּפֵר וְיוֹאָח בֶּן־אָסָף הַמַּזְכִּיר: 4 וַיֹּאמֶר אֲלֵיהֶם רַב־שָׁקֵה אִמְרוּ־נָא אֶל־חִזְקִיָּהוּ כֹּה־אָמַר הַמֶּלֶךְ הַגָּדוֹל מֶלֶךְ אַשּׁוּר מָה הַבִּטָּחוֹן הַזֶּה אֲשֶׁר בָּטָחְתָּ: 5 אָמַרְתִּי אַךְ־דְּבַר־שְׂפָתַיִם עֵצָה וּגְבוּרָה לַמִּלְחָמָה עַתָּה עַל־מִי בָטַחְתָּ כִּי מָרַדְתָּ

---

b   Meaning of Heb. uncertain; emendation yields "a marsh."
c   Cf. 34.13.
d   Emendation yields "for His people."
e-e   Meaning of Heb. uncertain.

a   Chaps. 36–39 occur also as 2 Kings 18.13–20.19, with a number
     of variants, some of which will be cited here in the footnotes.
b   An Assyrian title; cf. "Tartan," 20.1.
c   2 Kings 18.20 "You must think."

rebelled against me? 6You are relying on Egypt, that splintered reed of a staff, which enters and punctures the palm of anyone who leans on it. That's what Pharaoh king of Egypt is like to all who rely on him. 7And if you tell me that you are relying on the LORD your God, He is the very one whose shrines and altars Hezekiah did away with, telling Judah and Jerusalem, 'You must worship only at this altar!' 8Come now, make this wager with my master, the king of Assyria: I'll give you two thousand horses, if you can produce riders to mount them. 9So how could you refuse anything, even to the deputy of one of my master's lesser servants, relying on Egypt for chariots and horsemen? 10And do you think I have marched against this land to destroy it without the LORD? The LORD Himself told me: Go up against that land and destroy it."

11Eliakim, Shebna, and Joah replied to the Rabshakeh, "Please, speak to your servants in Aramaic, since we understand it; do not speak to us in Judean in the hearing of the people on the wall." 12But the Rabshakeh replied, "Was it to your master and to you that my master sent me to speak those words? It was precisely to the men who are sitting on the wall—who will have to eat their dung and drink their urine with you." 13And the Rabshakeh stood and called out in a loud voice in Judean: 14"Hear the words of the Great King, the king of Assyria! Thus said the king: Don't let Hezekiah deceive you, for he will not be able to save you. 15Don't let Hezekiah make you rely on the LORD, saying, 'The LORD will surely save us; this city will not fall into the hands of Assyria!' 16Don't listen to Hezekiah. For thus said the king of Assyria: Make your peace with me and come out to me,d so that you may all eat from your vines and your fig trees and drink water from your cisterns, 17until I come and take you away to a land like your own, a land of bread and wine, of grain [fields] and

---

בִּֽי׃ 6 הִנֵּ֣ה בָטַ֡חְתָּ עַל־מִשְׁעֶ֩נֶת֩ הַקָּנֶ֨ה הָרָצ֤וּץ הַזֶּה֙ עַל־מִצְרַ֔יִם אֲשֶׁ֨ר יִסָּמֵ֥ךְ אִישׁ֙ עָלָ֔יו וּבָ֥א בְכַפּ֖וֹ וּנְקָבָ֑הּ כֵּ֚ן פַּרְעֹ֣ה מֶֽלֶךְ־מִצְרַ֔יִם לְכָֽל־הַבֹּטְחִ֖ים עָלָֽיו׃ 7 וְכִֽי־תֹאמַ֣ר אֵלַ֔י אֶל־יְהוָ֥ה אֱלֹהֵ֖ינוּ בָּטָ֑חְנוּ הֲלוֹא־ה֗וּא אֲשֶׁ֨ר הֵסִ֤יר חִזְקִיָּ֙הוּ֙ אֶת־בָּמֹתָ֣יו וְאֶת־מִזְבְּחֹתָ֔יו וַיֹּ֤אמֶר לִֽיהוּדָה֙ וְלִיר֣וּשָׁלִַ֔ם לִפְנֵ֛י הַמִּזְבֵּ֥חַ הַזֶּ֖ה תִּֽשְׁתַּחֲו֑וּ׃ 8 וְעַתָּה֙ הִתְעָ֣רֶב נָ֔א אֶת־אֲדֹנִ֖י הַמֶּ֣לֶךְ אַשּׁ֑וּר וְאֶתְּנָ֤ה לְךָ֙ אַלְפַּ֣יִם סוּסִ֔ים אִם־תּוּכַ֕ל לָ֥תֶת לְךָ֖ רֹכְבִ֥ים עֲלֵיהֶֽם׃ 9 וְאֵ֣יךְ תָּשִׁ֗יב אֵ֠ת פְּנֵ֨י פַחַ֥ת אַחַ֛ד עַבְדֵ֥י אֲדֹנִ֖י הַקְּטַנִּ֑ים וַתִּבְטַ֤ח לְךָ֙ עַל־מִצְרַ֔יִם לְרֶ֖כֶב וּלְפָרָשִֽׁים׃ 10 וְעַתָּ֗ה הֲמִבַּלְעֲדֵ֤י יְהוָה֙ עָלִ֙יתִי֙ עַל־הָאָ֣רֶץ הַזֹּ֔את לְהַשְׁחִיתָ֑הּ יְהוָה֙ אָמַ֣ר אֵלַ֔י עֲלֵ֛ה אֶל־הָאָ֥רֶץ הַזֹּ֖את וְהַשְׁחִיתָֽהּ׃

11 וַיֹּ֣אמֶר אֶלְיָקִ֡ים וְשֶׁבְנָא֩ וְיוֹאָ֨ח אֶל־רַב־שָׁקֵ֗ה דַּבֶּר־נָ֤א אֶל־עֲבָדֶ֙יךָ֙ אֲרָמִ֔ית כִּ֥י שֹׁמְעִ֖ים אֲנָ֑חְנוּ וְאַל־תְּדַבֵּ֤ר אֵלֵ֙ינוּ֙ יְהוּדִ֔ית בְּאָזְנֵ֣י הָעָ֔ם אֲשֶׁ֖ר עַל־הַחוֹמָֽה׃ 12 וַיֹּ֣אמֶר רַב־שָׁקֵ֗ה הַאֶ֨ל אֲדֹנֶ֤יךָ וְאֵלֶ֙יךָ֙ שְׁלָחַ֣נִי אֲדֹנִ֔י לְדַבֵּ֖ר אֶת־הַדְּבָרִ֣ים הָאֵ֑לֶּה הֲלֹ֣א עַל־הָאֲנָשִׁ֗ים הַיֹּֽשְׁבִים֙ עַל־הַ֣חוֹמָ֔ה לֶאֱכֹ֣ל אֶת־חראיהם צֽוֹאָתָ֗ם וְלִשְׁתּ֛וֹת אֶת־שיניהם מֵֽימֵ֥י רַגְלֵיהֶ֖ם עִמָּכֶֽם׃ 13 וַֽיַּעֲמֹד֙ רַב־שָׁקֵ֔ה וַיִּקְרָ֔א בְּקוֹל־גָּד֖וֹל יְהוּדִ֑ית וַיֹּ֕אמֶר שִׁמְע֗וּ אֶת־דִּבְרֵ֛י הַמֶּ֥לֶךְ הַגָּד֖וֹל מֶ֥לֶךְ אַשּֽׁוּר׃ 14 כֹּ֚ה אָמַ֣ר הַמֶּ֔לֶךְ אַל־יַשִּׁ֥א לָכֶ֖ם חִזְקִיָּ֑הוּ כִּֽי־לֹ֥א יוּכַ֖ל לְהַצִּ֥יל אֶתְכֶֽם׃ 15 וְאַל־יַבְטַ֨ח אֶתְכֶ֤ם חִזְקִיָּ֙הוּ֙ אֶל־יְהוָ֣ה לֵאמֹ֔ר הַצֵּ֥ל יַצִּילֵ֖נוּ יְהוָ֑ה לֹ֤א תִנָּתֵן֙ הָעִ֣יר הַזֹּ֔את בְּיַ֖ד מֶ֥לֶךְ אַשּֽׁוּר׃ 16 אַֽל־תִּשְׁמְע֖וּ אֶל־חִזְקִיָּ֑הוּ ס כִּי֩ כֹ֨ה אָמַ֜ר הַמֶּ֣לֶךְ אַשּׁ֗וּר עֲשֽׂוּ־אִתִּ֤י בְרָכָה֙ וּצְא֣וּ אֵלַ֔י וְאִכְל֤וּ אִישׁ־גַּפְנוֹ֙ וְאִ֣ישׁ תְּאֵ֣נָת֔וֹ וּשְׁת֖וּ אִ֥ישׁ מֵֽי־בוֹרֽוֹ׃ 17 עַד־בֹּאִ֕י וְלָקַחְתִּ֥י אֶתְכֶ֖ם אֶל־אֶ֑רֶץ

---

d I.e., to my representative the Rabshakeh.

vineyards. [18]Beware of letting Hezekiah mislead you by saying, 'The LORD will save us.' Did any of the gods of the other nations save his land from the king of Assyria? [19]Where were the gods of Hamath and Arpad? Where were the gods of Sepharvaim? And did they[e] save Samaria from me? [20]Which among all the gods of those countries saved their countries from me, that the LORD should save Jerusalem from me?" [21]But they were silent and did not answer him with a single word; for the king's order was: "Do not answer him."

[22]And so Eliakim son of Hilkiah who was in charge of the palace, Shebna the scribe, and Joah son of Asaph the recorder came to Hezekiah with their clothes rent, and they reported to him what the Rabshakeh had said.

37
When King Hezekiah heard this, he rent his clothes and covered himself with sackcloth and went into the House of the LORD. [2]He also sent Eliakim, who was in charge of the palace, Shebna, the scribe, and the senior priests, covered with sackcloth, to the prophet Isaiah son of Amoz. [3]They said to him, "Thus said Hezekiah: This day is a day of distress, of chastisement, and of disgrace. [a-]The babes have reached the birthstool, but the strength to give birth is lacking.[-a] [4]Perhaps the LORD your God will take note of the words of the Rabshakeh, whom his master the king of Assyria has sent to blaspheme the living God, and will mete out judgment for the words that the LORD your God has heard— if you will offer up prayer for the surviving remnant."

[5]When King Hezekiah's ministers came to Isaiah, [6]Isaiah said to them, "Tell your master as follows: Thus said the LORD: Do not be frightened by the words of blasphemy against Me that

כְּאַרְצְכֶם אֶרֶץ דָּגָן וְתִירוֹשׁ אֶרֶץ לֶחֶם וּכְרָמִים: 18 פֶּן־יַסִּית אֶתְכֶם חִזְקִיָּהוּ לֵאמֹר יְהוָה יַצִּילֵנוּ הַהִצִּילוּ אֱלֹהֵי הַגּוֹיִם אִישׁ אֶת־אַרְצוֹ מִיַּד מֶלֶךְ אַשּׁוּר: 19 אַיֵּה אֱלֹהֵי חֲמָת וְאַרְפָּד אַיֵּה אֱלֹהֵי סְפַרְוָיִם וְכִי־הִצִּילוּ אֶת־שֹׁמְרוֹן מִיָּדִי: 20 מִי בְּכָל־ אֱלֹהֵי הָאֲרָצוֹת הָאֵלֶּה אֲשֶׁר־הִצִּילוּ אֶת־ אַרְצָם מִיָּדִי כִּי־יַצִּיל יְהוָה אֶת־יְרוּשָׁלַ͏ִם מִיָּדִי: 21 וַיַּחֲרִישׁוּ וְלֹא־עָנוּ אֹתוֹ דָּבָר כִּי־מִצְוַת הַמֶּלֶךְ הִיא לֵאמֹר לֹא תַעֲנֻהוּ: 22 וַיָּבֹא אֶלְיָקִים בֶּן־חִלְקִיָּהוּ אֲשֶׁר־עַל־ הַבַּיִת וְשֶׁבְנָא הַסּוֹפֵר וְיוֹאָח בֶּן־אָסָף הַמַּזְכִּיר אֶל־חִזְקִיָּהוּ קְרוּעֵי בְגָדִים וַיַּגִּידוּ לוֹ אֵת דִּבְרֵי רַב־שָׁקֵה: ס

לז וַיְהִי כִּשְׁמֹעַ הַמֶּלֶךְ חִזְקִיָּהוּ וַיִּקְרַע אֶת־בְּגָדָיו וַיִּתְכַּס בַּשָּׂק וַיָּבֹא בֵּית יְהוָה: 2 וַיִּשְׁלַח אֶת־אֶלְיָקִים אֲשֶׁר־עַל־הַבַּיִת וְאֵת שֶׁבְנָא הַסּוֹפֵר וְאֵת זִקְנֵי הַכֹּהֲנִים מִתְכַּסִּים בַּשַּׂקִּים אֶל־יְשַׁעְיָהוּ בֶן־אָמוֹץ הַנָּבִיא: 3 וַיֹּאמְרוּ אֵלָיו כֹּה אָמַר חִזְקִיָּהוּ יוֹם־צָרָה וְתוֹכֵחָה וּנְאָצָה הַיּוֹם הַזֶּה כִּי בָאוּ בָנִים עַד־מַשְׁבֵּר וְכֹחַ אַיִן לְלֵדָה: 4 אוּלַי יִשְׁמַע יְהוָה אֱלֹהֶיךָ אֵת ׀ דִּבְרֵי רַב־שָׁקֵה אֲשֶׁר שְׁלָחוֹ מֶלֶךְ־אַשּׁוּר ׀ אֲדֹנָיו לְחָרֵף אֱלֹהִים חַי וְהוֹכִיחַ בַּדְּבָרִים אֲשֶׁר שָׁמַע יְהוָה אֱלֹהֶיךָ וְנָשָׂאתָ תְפִלָּה בְּעַד הַשְּׁאֵרִית הַנִּמְצָאָה: 5 וַיָּבֹאוּ עַבְדֵי הַמֶּלֶךְ חִזְקִיָּהוּ אֶל־יְשַׁעְיָהוּ: 6 וַיֹּאמֶר אֲלֵיהֶם יְשַׁעְיָהוּ כֹּה תֹאמְרוּן אֶל־אֲדֹנֵיכֶם כֹּה ׀ אָמַר יְהוָה אַל־תִּירָא מִפְּנֵי הַדְּבָרִים אֲשֶׁר שָׁמַעְתָּ אֲשֶׁר גִּדְּפוּ

---

e   I.e., the gods of Samaria.

a-a   I.e., the situation is desperate, and we are at a loss.

you have heard from the minions of the king of Assyria. [7]I will delude[b] him: He will hear a rumor and return to his land, and I will make him fall by the sword in his land."

[8]The Rabshakeh, meanwhile, heard that [the King] had left Lachish; he turned back and found the king of Assyria attacking Libnah. [9]But [the king of Assyria] learned that King Tirhakah of Nubia had come out to fight him; and when he heard it, he sent messengers to Hezekiah, saying, [10]"Tell this to King Hezekiah of Judah: Do not let your God, on whom you are relying, mislead you into thinking that Jerusalem will not be delivered into the hands of the king of Assyria. [11]You yourself have heard what the kings of Assyria have done to all the lands, how they have annihilated them; and can you escape? [12]Were the nations that my predecessors[c] destroyed—Gozan, Haran, Rezeph, and the Bethedenites in Telassar—saved by their gods? [13]Where is the king of Hamath? and the king of Arpad? and the kings of Lair, Sepharvaim, Hena, and Ivvah?"

[14]Hezekiah received the letter from the messengers and read it. Hezekiah then went up to the House of the LORD and spread it out before the LORD. [15]And Hezekiah prayed to the LORD: [16]"O LORD of Hosts, enthroned on the Cherubim! You alone are God of all the kingdoms of the earth. You made the heavens and the earth. [17]O LORD, incline Your ear and hear, open Your eye and see. Hear all the words that Sennacherib has sent to blaspheme the living God! [18]True, O LORD, the kings of Assyria have annihilated all the nations[d] and their lands [19]and have committed their gods to the flames and have destroyed them; for they are not gods, but man's handwork of wood and stone. [20]But now, O LORD our God, deliver us from his hands, and

נַעֲרֵ֥י מֶֽלֶךְ־אַשּׁ֖וּר אוֹתִֽי׃ 7 הִנְנִ֨י נֹתֵ֥ן בּוֹ֙ ר֔וּחַ וְשָׁמַ֥ע שְׁמוּעָ֖ה וְשָׁ֣ב אֶל־אַרְצ֑וֹ וְהִפַּלְתִּ֥יו בַּחֶ֖רֶב בְּאַרְצֽוֹ׃ 8 וַיָּ֙שָׁב֙ רַב־שָׁקֵ֔ה וַיִּמְצָא֙ אֶת־מֶ֣לֶךְ אַשּׁ֔וּר נִלְחָ֖ם עַל־לִבְנָ֑ה כִּ֣י שָׁמַ֔ע כִּ֥י נָסַ֖ע מִלָּכִֽישׁ׃ 9 וַיִּשְׁמַ֗ע עַל־תִּרְהָ֤קָה מֶֽלֶךְ־כּוּשׁ֙ לֵאמֹ֔ר יָצָ֖א לְהִלָּחֵ֣ם אִתָּ֑ךְ וַיִּשְׁמַע֙ וַיִּשְׁלַ֣ח מַלְאָכִ֔ים אֶל־חִזְקִיָּ֖הוּ לֵאמֹֽר׃ 10 כֹּ֣ה תֹאמְר֗וּן אֶל־חִזְקִיָּ֤הוּ מֶֽלֶךְ־יְהוּדָה֙ לֵאמֹ֔ר אַל־יַשִּֽׁאֲךָ֣ אֱלֹהֶ֔יךָ אֲשֶׁ֥ר אַתָּ֖ה בּוֹטֵ֣חַ בּ֑וֹ לֵאמֹ֔ר לֹ֤א תִנָּתֵן֙ יְר֣וּשָׁלַ֔͏ִם בְּיַ֖ד מֶ֥לֶךְ אַשּֽׁוּר׃ 11 הִנֵּ֣ה ׀ אַתָּ֣ה שָׁמַ֗עְתָּ אֲשֶׁ֨ר עָשׂ֜וּ מַלְכֵ֥י אַשּׁ֛וּר לְכָל־הָאֲרָצ֖וֹת לְהַֽחֲרִימָ֑ם וְאַתָּ֖ה תִּנָּצֵֽל׃ 12 הַהִצִּ֨ילוּ אוֹתָ֜ם אֱלֹהֵ֣י הַגּוֹיִ֗ם אֲשֶׁ֣ר הִשְׁחִ֣יתוּ אֲבוֹתַ֔י אֶת־גּוֹזָ֖ן וְאֶת־חָרָ֑ן וְרֶ֥צֶף וּבְנֵי־עֶ֖דֶן אֲשֶׁ֥ר בִּתְלַשָּֽׂר׃ 13 אַיֵּ֞ה מֶ֣לֶךְ־חֲמָ֗ת וּמֶ֙לֶךְ֙ אַרְפָּ֔ד וּמֶ֖לֶךְ לָעִ֣יר סְפַרְוָ֑יִם הֵנַ֖ע וְעִוָּֽה׃ 14 וַיִּקַּ֨ח חִזְקִיָּ֧הוּ אֶת־הַסְּפָרִ֛ים מִיַּ֥ד הַמַּלְאָכִ֖ים וַיִּקְרָאֵ֑הוּ וַיַּ֙עַל֙ בֵּ֣ית יְהוָ֔ה וַיִּפְרְשֵׂ֥הוּ חִזְקִיָּ֖הוּ לִפְנֵ֥י יְהוָֽה׃ 15 וַיִּתְפַּלֵּל֙ חִזְקִיָּ֔הוּ אֶל־יְהוָ֖ה לֵאמֹֽר׃ 16 יְהוָ֨ה צְבָא֜וֹת אֱלֹהֵ֣י יִשְׂרָאֵ֗ל יֹשֵׁ֣ב הַכְּרֻבִ֔ים אַתָּה־ה֤וּא הָֽאֱלֹהִים֙ לְבַדְּךָ֔ לְכֹ֖ל מַמְלְכ֣וֹת הָאָ֑רֶץ אַתָּ֣ה עָשִׂ֔יתָ אֶת־הַשָּׁמַ֖יִם וְאֶת־הָאָֽרֶץ׃ 17 הַטֵּ֣ה יְהוָ֤ה ׀ אָזְנְךָ֙ וּֽשֲׁמָ֔ע פְּקַ֧ח יְהוָ֛ה עֵינֶ֖ךָ וּרְאֵ֑ה וּשְׁמַ֗ע אֵ֣ת כָּל־דִּבְרֵ֣י סַנְחֵרִ֔יב אֲשֶׁ֣ר שָׁלַ֔ח לְחָרֵ֖ף אֱלֹהִ֥ים חָֽי׃ 18 אָמְנָ֖ם יְהוָ֑ה הֶחֱרִ֜יבוּ מַלְכֵ֥י אַשּׁ֛וּר אֶת־כָּל־הָאֲרָצֽוֹת* וְאֶת־אַרְצָֽם׃ 19 וְנָתֹ֥ן אֶת־אֱלֹהֵיהֶ֖ם בָּאֵ֑שׁ כִּ֣י לֹ֤א אֱלֹהִים֙ הֵ֔מָּה כִּ֣י אִם־מַעֲשֵׂ֧ה יְדֵֽי־אָדָ֛ם עֵ֥ץ וָאֶ֖בֶן וַֽיְאַבְּדֽוּם׃ 20 וְעַתָּה֙ יְהוָ֣ה אֱלֹהֵ֔ינוּ הוֹשִׁיעֵ֖נוּ מִיָּד֑וֹ

---

b   Lit. "put a spirit in."
c   Lit. "fathers."
d   So 2 Kings 19.17, and 13 mss. here; most mss. and editions read "lands."

let all the kingdoms of the earth know that You, O Lᴏʀᴅ, alone [are God]."ᵉ

²¹Then Isaiah son of Amoz sent this message to Hezekiah: "Thus said the Lᴏʀᴅ, the God of Israel, to whom you have prayed, concerning King Sennacherib of Assyria—²²this is the word that the Lᴏʀᴅ has spoken concerning him:

Fair Maiden Zion despises you,
She mocks at you;
Fair Jerusalem shakes
Her head at you.
²³Whom have you blasphemed and reviled?
Against whom made loud your voice
And haughtily raised your eyes?
Against the Holy One of Israel!
²⁴Through your servants you have blas-
    phemed my Lord.
Because you thought,
'Thanks to my vast chariotry,
It is I who have climbed the highest moun-
    tains,
To the remotest parts of the Lebanon,
And have cut down its loftiest cedars,
Its choicest cypresses,
And have reached its highest peak,
f-Its densest forest.-f
²⁵It is I who have drawnᵍ
And drunk water.
I have dried up with the soles of my feet
All the streams of Egypt.'
²⁶Have you not heard? Of old
I planned that very thing,
I designed it long ago,
And now have fulfilled it.
And it has come to pass,
Laying fortified towns waste in desolate
    heaps.
²⁷Their inhabitants are helpless,

וְיֵדְעוּ כָּל־מַמְלְכ֣וֹת הָאָ֔רֶץ כִּֽי־אַתָּ֥ה יְהוָ֖ה לְבַדֶּֽךָ׃

²¹ וַיִּשְׁלַ֞ח יְשַֽׁעְיָ֣הוּ בֶן־אָמוֹץ֮ אֶל־חִזְקִיָּ֒הוּ֒ לֵאמֹ֔ר כֹּֽה־אָמַ֤ר יְהוָה֙ אֱלֹהֵ֣י יִשְׂרָאֵ֔ל אֲשֶׁ֧ר הִתְפַּלַּ֛לְתָּ אֵלַ֖י אֶל־סַנְחֵרִ֥יב מֶ֥לֶךְ אַשּֽׁוּר׃ ²² זֶ֣ה הַדָּבָ֔ר אֲשֶׁר־דִּבֶּ֥ר יְהוָ֖ה עָלָֽיו

בָּזָ֨ה לְךָ֜ לָעֲגָ֣ה לְךָ֗
בְּתוּלַת֙ בַּת־צִיּ֔וֹן
אַחֲרֶ֙יךָ֙ רֹ֣אשׁ הֵנִ֔יעָה
בַּ֖ת יְרוּשָׁלָֽ͏ִם׃
²³ אֶת־מִ֤י חֵרַ֙פְתָּ֙ וְגִדַּ֔פְתָּ
וְעַל־מִ֖י הֲרִימ֣וֹתָה קּ֑וֹל
וַתִּשָּׂ֥א מָר֛וֹם עֵינֶ֖יךָ
אֶל־קְד֥וֹשׁ יִשְׂרָאֵֽל׃
²⁴ בְּיַ֣ד עֲבָדֶיךָ֮ חֵרַ֣פְתָּ ׀ אֲדֹנָי֒
וַתֹּ֗אמֶר
בְּרֹ֥ב רִכְבִּ֛י
אֲנִ֥י עָלִ֛יתִי מְר֥וֹם הָרִ֖ים
יַרְכְּתֵ֣י לְבָנ֑וֹן
וְאֶכְרֹ֞ת קוֹמַ֤ת אֲרָזָיו֙
מִבְחַ֣ר בְּרֹשָׁ֔יו
וְאָבוֹא֙ מְר֣וֹם קִצּ֔וֹ
יַ֖עַר כַּרְמִלּֽוֹ׃
²⁵ אֲנִ֥י קַ֖רְתִּי
וְשָׁתִ֣יתִי מָ֑יִם
וְאַחְרִב֙ בְּכַף־פְּעָמַ֔י
כֹּ֖ל יְאֹרֵ֥י מָצֽוֹר׃
²⁶ הֲלֽוֹא־שָׁמַ֤עְתָּ לְמֵֽרָחוֹק֙
אוֹתָ֣הּ עָשִׂ֔יתִי
מִ֤ימֵי קֶ֙דֶם֙ וִיצַרְתִּ֔יהָ
עַתָּ֖ה הֲבֵאתִ֑יהָ
וּתְהִ֗י
לְהַשְׁא֛וֹת גַּלִּ֥ים נִצִּ֖ים עָרִ֥ים בְּצֻרֽוֹת׃
²⁷ וְיֹֽשְׁבֵיהֶן֙ קִצְרֵי־יָ֔ד

---

e   Supplied from 2 Kings 19.19.
f-f Lit. "Its farmland forest"; exact meaning of Heb. uncertain.
g   Or "dug"; meaning of Heb. uncertain.

Dismayed and shamed.
They were but grass of the field
And green herbage,
Grass of the roofs ʰ-that is blasted
Before the east wind.-ʰ

²⁸I know your stayings
And your goings and comings,
And how you have raged against Me,
²⁹Because you have raged against Me,
And your tumult has reached My ears,
I will place My hook in your nose
And My bit between your jaws;
And I will make you go back by the road
By which you came.

³⁰"And this is the sign for you:ⁱ This year you eat what grows of itself, and the next year what springs from that, and in the third year sow and reap and plant vineyards and eat their fruit. ³¹And the survivors of the House of Judah that have escaped shall renew its trunk below and produce boughs above.

³²For a remnant shall come forth from Jeru-
    salem,
Survivors from Mount Zion.
The zeal of the Lᴏʀᴅ of Hosts
Shall bring this to pass.

³³"Assuredly, thus said the Lᴏʀᴅ concerning the king of Assyria:

He shall not enter this city;
He shall not shoot an arrow at it,
Or advance upon it with a shield,
Or pile up a siegemound against it.
³⁴He shall go back
By the way he came,

חַ֫תּוּ וָבֹֽשׁוּ
הָיוּ֙ עֵ֣שֶׂב שָׂדֶ֔ה
וִ֣ירַק דֶּ֔שֶׁא
חֲצִ֣יר גַּגּ֔וֹת וּשְׁדֵמָ֖ה
לִפְנֵ֥י קָמָֽה:*
²⁸ וְשִׁבְתְּךָ֛
וְצֵאתְךָ֥ וּבוֹאֲךָ֖ יָדָ֑עְתִּי
וְאֵ֖ת הִֽתְרַגֶּזְךָ֥ אֵלָֽי:
²⁹ יַ֚עַן הִתְרַגֶּזְךָ֣ אֵלַ֔י
וְשַׁאֲנַנְךָ֖ עָלָ֣ה בְאָזְנָ֑י
וְשַׂמְתִּ֨י חַחִ֜י בְּאַפֶּ֗ךָ
וּמִתְגִּי֙ בִּשְׂפָתֶ֔יךָ
וַהֲשִֽׁיבֹתִ֙יךָ֙ בַּדֶּ֔רֶךְ
אֲשֶׁר־בָּ֥אתָ בָּֽהּ:

³⁰ וְזֶה־לְּךָ֣ הָא֔וֹת אָכ֖וֹל הַשָּׁנָ֣ה סָפִ֑יחַ
וּבַשָּׁנָ֤ה הַשֵּׁנִית֙ שָׁחִ֔יס וּבַשָּׁנָ֣ה הַשְּׁלִישִׁ֗ית
זִרְע֧וּ וְקִצְר֛וּ וְנִטְע֥וּ כְרָמִ֖ים וְאָכ֥וֹל
וְאָכְל֖וּ פִרְיָֽם: ³¹ וְיָסְפָ֞ה פְּלֵיטַ֧ת בֵּית־
יְהוּדָ֛ה הַנִּשְׁאָרָ֖ה שֹׁ֣רֶשׁ לְמָ֑טָּה וְעָשָׂ֥ה פְרִ֖י
לְמָֽעְלָה:

³² כִּ֤י מִירוּשָׁלִַ֙ם֙ תֵּצֵ֣א שְׁאֵרִ֔ית
וּפְלֵיטָ֖ה מֵהַ֣ר צִיּ֑וֹן
קִנְאַ֛ת יְהוָ֥ה צְבָא֖וֹת
תַּֽעֲשֶׂה־זֹּֽאת: ס

³³ לָכֵ֗ן כֹּֽה־אָמַ֤ר יְהוָה֙ אֶל־מֶ֣לֶךְ אַשּׁ֔וּר

לֹ֤א יָבוֹא֙ אֶל־הָעִ֣יר הַזֹּ֔את
וְלֹֽא־יוֹרֶ֥ה שָׁ֖ם חֵ֑ץ
וְלֹֽא־יְקַדְּמֶ֣נָּה מָגֵ֔ן
וְלֹֽא־יִשְׁפֹּ֥ךְ עָלֶ֖יהָ סֹלְלָֽה:
³⁴ בַּדֶּ֧רֶךְ אֲשֶׁר־בָּ֛א
בָּ֥הּ יָשׁ֖וּב

---

h-h So ms. 1QIsᵃ; cf. 2 Kings 19.26. The usual reading in our
    passage means, literally, "and a field [?] before standing grain."
i   I.e., Hezekiah.

בנוסח אחר "הנשדף לפני קדים"   v. 27.

He shall not enter this city
—declares the LORD;
35I will protect and save this city for My sake
And for the sake of My servant David."

36[That night]*j* an angel of the LORD went out and struck down one hundred and eighty-five thousand in the Assyrian camp, and the following morning they were all dead corpses.

37So King Sennacherib of Assyria broke camp and retreated, and stayed in Nineveh. 38While he was worshiping in the temple of his god Nisroch, he was struck down with the sword by his sons Adrammelech and Sarezer. They fled to the land of Ararat, and his son Esarhaddon succeeded him as king.

38

In those days Hezekiah fell dangerously ill. The prophet Isaiah son of Amoz came and said to him, "Thus said the LORD: Set your affairs in order, for you are going to die; you will not get well." 2Thereupon Hezekiah turned his face to the wall and prayed to the LORD. 3"Please, O LORD," he said, "remember how I have walked before You sincerely and wholeheartedly, and have done what is pleasing to You." And Hezekiah wept profusely.

4Then the word of the LORD came to Isaiah: 5"Go and tell Hezekiah: Thus said the LORD, the God of your father David: I have heard your prayer, I have seen your tears. I hereby add fifteen years to your life. 6I will also rescue you and this city from the hands of the king of Assyria. I will protect this city. 7And this is the sign for you from the LORD that the LORD will do the thing that He has promised: 8I am going to make the shadow on the steps, which has descended on the dial*a* of Ahaz because of the sun,

---

j Supplied from 2 Kings 19.35.

a Heb. "steps." A model of a dial with steps has been discovered in Egypt.

וְאֶל־הָעִיר הַזֹּאת לֹא יָבֹוא
נְאֻם־יְהוָה:
35 וְגַנּוֹתִי עַל־הָעִיר הַזֹּאת לְהוֹשִׁיעָהּ
לְמַעֲנִי
וּלְמַעַן דָּוִד עַבְדִּי: ס

36 וַיֵּצֵא ׀ מַלְאַךְ יְהוָה וַיַּכֶּה בְּמַחֲנֵה אַשּׁוּר מֵאָה וּשְׁמֹנִים וַחֲמִשָּׁה אָלֶף וַיַּשְׁכִּימוּ בַבֹּקֶר וְהִנֵּה כֻלָּם פְּגָרִים מֵתִים: 37 וַיִּסַּע וַיֵּלֶךְ וַיָּשָׁב סַנְחֵרִיב מֶלֶךְ־אַשּׁוּר וַיֵּשֶׁב בְּנִינְוֵה: 38 וַיְהִי הוּא מִשְׁתַּחֲוֶה בֵּית ׀ נִסְרֹךְ אֱלֹהָיו וְאַדְרַמֶּלֶךְ וְשַׂרְאֶצֶר בָּנָיו הִכֻּהוּ בַחֶרֶב וְהֵמָּה נִמְלְטוּ אֶרֶץ אֲרָרָט וַיִּמְלֹךְ אֵסַר־חַדֹּן בְּנוֹ תַּחְתָּיו: ס

לח בַּיָּמִים הָהֵם חָלָה חִזְקִיָּהוּ לָמוּת וַיָּבֹוא אֵלָיו יְשַׁעְיָהוּ בֶן־אָמוֹץ הַנָּבִיא וַיֹּאמֶר אֵלָיו כֹּה־אָמַר יְהוָה צַו לְבֵיתֶךָ כִּי מֵת אַתָּה וְלֹא תִחְיֶה: 2 וַיַּסֵּב חִזְקִיָּהוּ פָּנָיו אֶל־הַקִּיר וַיִּתְפַּלֵּל אֶל־יְהוָה: 3 וַיֹּאמַר אָנָּה יְהוָה זְכָר־נָא אֵת אֲשֶׁר הִתְהַלַּכְתִּי לְפָנֶיךָ בֶּאֱמֶת וּבְלֵב שָׁלֵם וְהַטּוֹב בְּעֵינֶיךָ עָשִׂיתִי וַיֵּבְךְּ חִזְקִיָּהוּ בְּכִי גָדוֹל: ס

4 וַיְהִי דְּבַר־יְהוָה אֶל־יְשַׁעְיָהוּ לֵאמֹר: 5 הָלוֹךְ וְאָמַרְתָּ אֶל־חִזְקִיָּהוּ כֹּה־אָמַר יְהוָה אֱלֹהֵי דָּוִד אָבִיךָ שָׁמַעְתִּי אֶת־תְּפִלָּתֶךָ רָאִיתִי אֶת־דִּמְעָתֶךָ הִנְנִי יוֹסֵף עַל־יָמֶיךָ חֲמֵשׁ עֶשְׂרֵה שָׁנָה: 6 וּמִכַּף מֶלֶךְ־אַשּׁוּר אַצִּילְךָ וְאֵת הָעִיר הַזֹּאת וְגַנּוֹתִי עַל־הָעִיר הַזֹּאת: 7 וְזֶה־לְּךָ הָאוֹת מֵאֵת יְהוָה אֲשֶׁר יַעֲשֶׂה יְהוָה אֶת־הַדָּבָר הַזֶּה אֲשֶׁר דִּבֵּר: 8 הִנְנִי מֵשִׁיב אֶת־צֵל הַמַּעֲלוֹת אֲשֶׁר יָרְדָה בְמַעֲלוֹת אָחָז

recede ten steps." And the sun['s shadow] receded ten steps, the same steps as it had descended.

⁹A poem by King Hezekiah of Judah when he recovered from the illness he had suffered:

¹⁰*ᵇ*I had thought:
I must depart in the middle of my days;
I have been consigned to the gates of Sheol
For the rest of my years.
¹¹I thought, I shall never see Yah,*ᶜ*
Yah in the land of the living,
Or ever behold men again
Among those who inhabit the earth.
¹²My dwelling is pulled up and removed from
   me
Like a tent of shepherds;
My life is rolled up like a web
And cut from the thrum.

ᵈ-Only from daybreak to nightfall
Was I kept whole,
¹³Then it was as though a lion
Were breaking all my bones;
I cried out until morning.
(Only from daybreak to nightfall
Was I kept whole.)-*ᵈ*
¹⁴I piped like a swift or a swallow,
I moaned like a dove,
As my eyes, all worn, looked to heaven:
"My Lord, I am in straits;
Be my surety!"

¹⁵What can I say? *ᵈ*-He promised me,-*ᵈ*
And He it is who has wrought it.
ᵈ-All my sleep had fled
Because of the bitterness of my soul.
¹⁶My Lord, for all that and despite it

בַּשֶּׁמֶשׁ אֲחֹרַנִּית עֶשֶׂר מַעֲלוֹת וַתָּשׇׁב
הַשֶּׁמֶשׁ עֶשֶׂר מַעֲלוֹת בַּמַּעֲלוֹת אֲשֶׁר
יָרָדָה: ס
⁹ מִכְתָּב לְחִזְקִיָּהוּ מֶלֶךְ־יְהוּדָה בַּחֲלֹתוֹ
וַיְחִי מֵחׇלְיוֹ:

¹⁰ אֲנִי אָמַרְתִּי
בִּדְמִי יָמַי אֵלֵכָה
בְּשַׁעֲרֵי שְׁאוֹל פֻּקַּדְתִּי
יֶתֶר שְׁנוֹתָי:
¹¹ אָמַרְתִּי לֹא־אֶרְאֶה יָהּ
יָהּ בְּאֶרֶץ הַחַיִּים
לֹא־אַבִּיט אָדָם עוֹד
עִם־יוֹשְׁבֵי חָדֶל:
¹² דּוֹרִי נִסַּע וְנִגְלָה מִנִּי
כְּאֹהֶל רֹעִי
קִפַּדְתִּי כָאֹרֵג חַיַּי
מִדַּלָּה יְבַצְּעֵנִי
מִיּוֹם עַד־לַיְלָה
תַּשְׁלִימֵנִי:
¹³ שִׁוִּיתִי עַד־בֹּקֶר
כָּאֲרִי כֵּן
יְשַׁבֵּר כָּל־עַצְמוֹתָי
מִיּוֹם עַד־לַיְלָה
תַּשְׁלִימֵנִי:
¹⁴ כְּסוּס עָגוּר כֵּן אֲצַפְצֵף
אֶהְגֶּה כַּיּוֹנָה
דַּלּוּ עֵינַי לַמָּרוֹם
אֲדֹנָי עָשְׁקָה־לִּי
עׇרְבֵנִי:

¹⁵ מָה־אֲדַבֵּר וְאָמַר־לִי
וְהוּא עָשָׂה
אֶדַּדֶּה כָל־שְׁנוֹתַי
עַל־מַר נַפְשִׁי:
¹⁶ אֲדֹנָי עֲלֵיהֶם יִחְיוּ וּלְכׇל־בָּהֶן

---

b   *Meaning of verse uncertain. in part.*
c   *I.e., visit His Temple. For "Yah" see 12.2; 26.4.*
d-d   *Meaning of Heb. uncertain.*

932

My life-breath is revived;‑*d*

You have restored me to health and revived
  me.

¹⁷Truly, it was for my own good

That I had such great bitterness:

You saved my life

From the pit of destruction,

For You have cast behind Your back

All my offenses.

¹⁸For it is not Sheol that praises You,

Not [the Land of] Death that extols You;

Nor do they who descend into the Pit

Hope for Your grace.

¹⁹The living, only the living

Can give thanks to You

As I do this day;

Fathers*e* relate to children

Your acts of grace:

²⁰"[It has pleased] the Lᴏʀᴅ to deliver us,*e*

That is why we offer up music*f*

All the days of our lives

At the House of the Lᴏʀᴅ."

²¹When Isaiah said, "Let them take a cake of
figs and apply it to the rash, and he will recover,"
²²Hezekiah asked, "What will be the sign that
I shall go up to the House of the Lᴏʀᴅ?"

39

At that time, Merodach-baladan son of
Baladan, the king of Babylon, sent [envoys with]
a letter and a gift to Hezekiah, for he had heard
about his illness and recovery. ²Hezekiah was
pleased by their coming, and he showed them
his treasure house—the silver, the gold, the
spices, and the fragrant oil—and all his armory,
and everything that was to be found in his storehouses. There was nothing in his palace or in
all his realm that Hezekiah did not show them.

חַיָּ֣י רוּחִ֑י

וְתַחֲלִימֵ֖נִי וְהַחֲיֵֽנִי׃

הִנֵּ֤ה לְשָׁל֙וֹם ¹⁷

מַר־לִ֖י מָ֑ר

וְאַתָּ֞ה חָשַׁ֤קְתָּ נַפְשִׁי֙

מִשַּׁ֣חַת בְּלִ֔י

כִּ֥י הִשְׁלַ֖כְתָּ אַחֲרֵ֣י גֵוְךָ֑

כָּל־חֲטָאָֽי׃

כִּ֣י לֹ֥א שְׁא֖וֹל תּוֹדֶ֑ךָּ ¹⁸

מָ֖וֶת יְהַלְלֶ֑ךָּ

לֹא־יְשַׂבְּר֥וּ יֽוֹרְדֵי־ב֖וֹר

אֶל־אֲמִתֶּֽךָ׃

חַ֥י חַ֛י ¹⁹

ה֥וּא יוֹדֶ֖ךָ

כָּמ֣וֹנִי הַיּ֑וֹם

אָ֣ב לְבָנִ֔ים

יוֹדִ֖יעַ אֶל־אֲמִתֶּֽךָ׃

יְהוָ֖ה לְהוֹשִׁיעֵ֑נִי ²⁰

וּנְגִנוֹתַ֣י נְנַגֵּ֔ן

כָּל־יְמֵ֣י חַיֵּ֑ינוּ

עַל־בֵּ֥ית יְהוָֽה׃

וַיֹּ֣אמֶר יְשַֽׁעְיָ֔הוּ יִשְׂא֖וּ דְּבֶ֣לֶת תְּאֵנִ֑ים ²¹
וְיִמְרְח֥וּ עַל־הַשְּׁחִ֖ין וְיֶֽחִי׃ וַיֹּ֣אמֶר ²²
חִזְקִיָּ֔הוּ מָ֣ה א֔וֹת כִּ֥י אֶעֱלֶ֖ה בֵּ֥ית
יְהוָֽה׃ ס

לט בָּעֵ֣ת הַהִ֗וא שָׁלַ֞ח מְרֹדַ֧ךְ בַּלְאֲדָ֛ן
בֶּֽן־בַּלְאֲדָ֥ן מֶֽלֶךְ־בָּבֶ֖ל סְפָרִ֣ים וּמִנְחָ֑ה אֶל־
חִזְקִיָּ֔הוּ וַיִּשְׁמַ֕ע כִּ֥י חָלָ֖ה וַֽיֶּחֱזָֽק׃ ² וַיִּשְׂמַ֣ח
עֲלֵיהֶם֮ חִזְקִיָּהוּ֒ וַיַּרְאֵ֣ם אֶת־בֵּ֣ית נְכֹתֹ֡ה
אֶת־הַכֶּסֶף֩ וְאֶת־הַזָּהָ֨ב וְאֶת־
הַבְּשָׂמִ֜ים וְאֵ֣ת ׀ הַשֶּׁ֣מֶן הַטּ֗וֹב וְאֵת֙ כָּל־
בֵּ֣ית כֵּלָ֔יו וְאֵ֛ת כָּל־אֲשֶׁ֥ר נִמְצָ֖א בְּאֹצְרֹתָ֑יו
לֹא־הָיָ֣ה דָבָ֗ר אֲשֶׁ֧ר לֹֽא־הֶרְאָ֛ם חִזְקִיָּֽהוּ

---

e   Heb. singular.
f   Neginothai is a poetic form of neginoth.

933

³Then the prophet Isaiah came to King Heze-kiah. "What," he demanded of him, "did those men say to you? Where have they come to you from?" "They have come to me," replied Hez-ekiah, "from a far country, from Babylon." ⁴Next he asked, "What have they seen in your palace?" And Hezekiah replied, "They have seen everything there is in my palace. There was nothing in my storehouses that I did not show them."

⁵Then Isaiah said to Hezekiah, "Hear the word of the Lord of Hosts: ⁶A time is coming when everything in your palace, which your an-cestors have stored up to this day, will be carried off to Babylon; nothing will be left behind, said the Lord. ⁷And some of your sons, your own issue, whom you will have fathered, will be taken to serve as eunuchs in the palace of the king of Babylon." ⁸Hezekiah declared to Isaiah, "The word of the Lord that you have spoken is good." For he thought, "It means that [a]-safety is assured for-[a] my time."

בְּבֵיתוֹ וּבְכָל־מֶמְשַׁלְתּוֹ׃ 3 וַיָּבֹא יְשַׁעְיָהוּ
הַנָּבִיא אֶל־הַמֶּלֶךְ חִזְקִיָּהוּ וַיֹּאמֶר אֵלָיו
מָה אָמְרוּ ׀ הָאֲנָשִׁים הָאֵלֶּה וּמֵאַיִן יָבֹאוּ
אֵלֶיךָ וַיֹּאמֶר חִזְקִיָּהוּ מֵאֶרֶץ רְחוֹקָה בָּאוּ
אֵלַי מִבָּבֶל׃ 4 וַיֹּאמֶר מָה רָאוּ בְּבֵיתֶךָ
וַיֹּאמֶר חִזְקִיָּהוּ אֵת כָּל־אֲשֶׁר בְּבֵיתִי רָאוּ
לֹא־הָיָה דָבָר אֲשֶׁר לֹא־הִרְאִיתִים
בְּאוֹצְרֹתָי׃
5 וַיֹּאמֶר יְשַׁעְיָהוּ אֶל־חִזְקִיָּהוּ שְׁמַע דְּבַר־
יְהֹוָה צְבָאוֹת׃ 6 הִנֵּה יָמִים בָּאִים וְנִשָּׂא ׀
כָּל־אֲשֶׁר בְּבֵיתֶךָ וַאֲשֶׁר אָצְרוּ אֲבֹתֶיךָ
עַד־הַיּוֹם הַזֶּה בָּבֶל לֹא־יִוָּתֵר דָּבָר אָמַר
יְהֹוָה׃ 7 וּמִבָּנֶיךָ אֲשֶׁר יֵצְאוּ מִמְּךָ אֲשֶׁר
תּוֹלִיד יִקָּחוּ וְהָיוּ סָרִיסִים בְּהֵיכַל מֶלֶךְ
בָּבֶל׃ 8 וַיֹּאמֶר חִזְקִיָּהוּ אֶל־יְשַׁעְיָהוּ טוֹב
דְּבַר־יְהֹוָה אֲשֶׁר דִּבַּרְתָּ וַיֹּאמֶר כִּי יִהְיֶה
שָׁלוֹם וֶאֱמֶת בְּיָמָי׃ פ

40 Comfort, oh comfort My people,
Says your God.
²Speak tenderly to Jerusalem,
And declare to her
That her term of service is over,
That her iniquity is expiated;
For she has received at the hand of the Lord
Double for all her sins.

³A voice rings out:
"Clear in the desert
A road for the Lord!
Level in the wilderness
A highway for our God!
⁴Let every valley be raised,
Every hill and mount made low.

מ נַחֲמוּ נַחֲמוּ עַמִּי
יֹאמַר אֱלֹהֵיכֶם׃
2 דַּבְּרוּ עַל־לֵב יְרוּשָׁלַ͏ִם
וְקִרְאוּ אֵלֶיהָ
כִּי מָלְאָה צְבָאָהּ
כִּי נִרְצָה עֲוֹנָהּ
כִּי לָקְחָה מִיַּד יְהֹוָה
כִּפְלַיִם בְּכָל־חַטֹּאתֶיהָ׃ ס

3 קוֹל קוֹרֵא
בַּמִּדְבָּר פַּנּוּ
דֶּרֶךְ יְהֹוָה
יַשְּׁרוּ בָּעֲרָבָה
מְסִלָּה לֵאלֹהֵינוּ׃
4 כָּל־גֶּיא יִנָּשֵׂא
וְכָל־הַר וְגִבְעָה יִשְׁפָּלוּ

---

a-a Lit. "there shall be safety and faithfulness in."

Let the rugged ground become level
And the ridges become a plain.
⁵The Presence of the LORD shall appear,
And all flesh, as one, shall behold—
For the LORD Himself has spoken."

⁶A voice rings out: "Proclaim!"
a-Another asks,-*a* "What shall I proclaim?"
"All flesh is grass,
All its goodness like flowers of the field:
⁷Grass withers, flowers fade
When the breath of the LORD blows on them.
Indeed, man is but grass:
⁸Grass withers, flowers fade—
But the word of our God is always fulfilled!"

⁹Ascend a lofty mountain,
O herald of joy to Zion;
Raise your voice with power,
O herald of joy to Jerusalem—
Raise it, have no fear;
Announce to the cities of Judah:
Behold your God!
¹⁰Behold, the Lord GOD comes in might,
And His arm wins triumph for Him;
See, His reward*b* is with Him,
His recompense before Him.
¹¹Like a shepherd He pastures His flock:
He gathers the lambs in His arms
And carries them in His bosom;
Gently He drives the mother sheep.

¹²Who measured the waters with the hollow
    of His hand,
And gauged the skies with a span,
And meted earth's dust with a measure,*c*
And weighed the mountains with a scale
And the hills with a balance?

וְהָיָה הֶעָקֹב לְמִישׁוֹר
וְהָרְכָסִים לְבִקְעָה:
5 וְנִגְלָה כְּבוֹד יְהֹוָה
וְרָאוּ כָל־בָּשָׂר יַחְדָּו
כִּי פִּי יְהֹוָה דִּבֵּר: ס

6 קוֹל אֹמֵר קְרָא
וְאָמַר מָה אֶקְרָא
כָּל־הַבָּשָׂר חָצִיר
וְכָל־חַסְדּוֹ כְּצִיץ הַשָּׂדֶה:
7 יָבֵשׁ חָצִיר נָבֵל צִיץ
כִּי רוּחַ יְהֹוָה נָשְׁבָה בּוֹ
אָכֵן חָצִיר הָעָם:
8 יָבֵשׁ חָצִיר נָבֵל צִיץ
וּדְבַר־אֱלֹהֵינוּ יָקוּם לְעוֹלָם: ס

9 עַל הַר־גָּבֹהַּ עֲלִי־לָךְ
מְבַשֶּׂרֶת צִיּוֹן
הָרִימִי בַכֹּחַ קוֹלֵךְ
מְבַשֶּׂרֶת יְרוּשָׁלָ͏ִם
הָרִימִי אַל־תִּירָאִי
אִמְרִי לְעָרֵי יְהוּדָה
הִנֵּה אֱלֹהֵיכֶם:
10 הִנֵּה אֲדֹנָי יֱהֹוִה בְּחָזָק יָבוֹא
וּזְרֹעוֹ מֹשְׁלָה לוֹ
הִנֵּה שְׂכָרוֹ אִתּוֹ
וּפְעֻלָּתוֹ לְפָנָיו:
11 כְּרֹעֶה עֶדְרוֹ יִרְעֶה
בִּזְרֹעוֹ יְקַבֵּץ טְלָאִים
וּבְחֵיקוֹ יִשָּׂא
עָלוֹת יְנַהֵל: ס

12 מִי־מָדַד בְּשָׁעֳלוֹ מַיִם
וְשָׁמַיִם בַּזֶּרֶת תִּכֵּן
וְכָל בַּשָּׁלִשׁ עֲפַר הָאָרֶץ
וְשָׁקַל בַּפֶּלֶס הָרִים
וּגְבָעוֹת בְּמֹאזְנָיִם:

---

a-a 1QIsᵃ and Septuagint read "And I asked."
b *The reward and recompense to the cities of Judah; cf. Jer. 31.14, 16.*
c *Heb. shalish "third," probably a third of an ephah.*

¹³Who has plumbed the mind of the Lord,
What man could tell Him His plan?
¹⁴Whom did He consult, and who taught
  Him,
Guided Him in the way of right?
Who guided Him in knowledge
And showed Him the path of wisdom?

¹⁵The nations are but a drop in a bucket,
Reckoned as dust on a balance;
The very coastlands He lifts like motes.
¹⁶Lebanon is not fuel enough,
Nor its beasts enough for sacrifice.
¹⁷All nations are as naught in His sight;
He accounts them as less than nothing.

¹⁸To whom, then, can you liken God,
What form compare to Him?
¹⁹The idol? A woodworker shaped it,
And a smith overlaid it with gold,
^{d-}Forging links of silver.^{-d}
²⁰As a gift, he chooses the mulberry^e—
A wood that does not rot—
Then seeks a skillful woodworker
To make a firm idol,
That will not topple.

²¹Do you not know?
Have you not heard?
Have you not been told
From the very first?
Have you not discerned
^{d-}How the earth was founded?^{-d}
²²It is He who is enthroned above the vault
  of the earth,
So that its inhabitants seem as grasshoppers;
Who spread out the skies like gauze,
Stretched them out like a tent to dwell in.

מִי־תִכֵּן אֶת־ר֫וּחַ יְהוָ֥ה ¹³
וְאִ֥ישׁ עֲצָת֖וֹ יוֹדִיעֶֽנּוּ:
אֶת־מִ֣י נוֹעָץ֮ וַיְבִינֵ֒הוּ֒ ¹⁴
וַיְלַמְּדֵ֖הוּ בְּאֹ֣רַח מִשְׁפָּ֑ט
וַֽיְלַמְּדֵ֣הוּ דַ֔עַת
וְדֶ֥רֶךְ תְּבוּנ֖וֹת יוֹדִיעֶֽנּוּ:

הֵ֤ן גּוֹיִם֙ כְּמַ֣ר מִדְּלִ֔י ¹⁵
וּכְשַׁ֥חַק מֹאזְנַ֖יִם נֶחְשָׁ֑בוּ
הֵ֥ן אִיִּ֖ים כַּדַּ֥ק יִטּֽוֹל:
וּלְבָנ֕וֹן אֵ֥ין דֵּ֖י בָּעֵ֑ר ¹⁶
וְחַ֨יָּת֔וֹ אֵ֥ין דֵּ֖י עוֹלָֽה: ס
כָּל־הַגּוֹיִ֥ם כְּאַ֖יִן נֶגְדּ֑וֹ ¹⁷
מֵאֶ֥פֶס וָתֹ֖הוּ נֶחְשְׁבוּ־לֽוֹ:

וְאֶל־מִ֖י תְּדַמְּי֣וּן אֵ֑ל ¹⁸
וּמַה־דְּמ֖וּת תַּ֥עַרְכוּ לֽוֹ:
הַפֶּ֗סֶל֙ נָסַ֣ךְ חָרָ֔שׁ ¹⁹
וְצֹרֵ֖ף בַּזָּהָ֣ב יְרַקְּעֶ֑נּוּ
וּרְתֻק֥וֹת כֶּ֖סֶף צוֹרֵֽף:
הַֽמְסֻכָּ֣ן תְּרוּמָ֗ה ²⁰
עֵ֤ץ לֹֽא־יִרְקַב֙ יִבְחָ֔ר
חָרָ֥שׁ חָכָם֙ יְבַקֶּשׁ־ל֔וֹ
לְהָכִ֥ין פֶּ֖סֶל
לֹ֥א יִמּֽוֹט:

הֲל֤וֹא תֵֽדְעוּ֙ ²¹
הֲל֣וֹא תִשְׁמָ֔עוּ
הֲל֛וֹא הֻגַּ֥ד
מֵרֹ֖אשׁ לָכֶ֑ם
הֲלוֹא֙ הֲבִ֣ינֹתֶ֔ם
מֽוֹסְד֖וֹת הָאָֽרֶץ:
הַיֹּשֵׁב֙ עַל־ח֣וּג הָאָ֔רֶץ ²²
וְיֹשְׁבֶ֖יהָ כַּחֲגָבִ֑ים
הַנּוֹטֶ֤ה כַדֹּק֙ שָׁמַ֔יִם
וַיִּמְתָּחֵ֥ם כָּאֹ֖הֶל לָשָֽׁבֶת:

---

^{d-d} *Meaning of Heb. uncertain.*
^e *Heb.* mesukkan; *according to a Jewish tradition, preserved by*
  Jerome, a kind of wood; a similar word denotes a kind of wood
  in Akkadian.

23He brings potentates to naught,
Makes rulers of the earth as nothing.

24Hardly are they planted,
Hardly are they sown,
Hardly has their stem
Taken root in earth,
When He blows upon them and they dry up,
And the storm bears them off like straw.

25To whom, then, can you liken Me,
To whom can I be compared?
　　　　　　　—says the Holy One.

26Lift high your eyes and see:
Who created these?
He who sends out their host by count,
Who calls them each by name:
Because of His great might and vast power,
Not one fails to appear.

27Why do you say, O Jacob,
Why declare, O Israel,
"My way is hid from the Lord,
My cause is ignored by my God"?

28Do you not know?
Have you not heard?
The Lord is God from of old,
Creator of the earth from end to end,
He never grows faint or weary,
His wisdom cannot be fathomed.

29He gives strength to the weary,
Fresh vigor to the spent.

30Youths may grow faint and weary,
And young men stumble and fall;

31But they who trust in the Lord shall renew
　their strength
As eagles grow new plumes:f
They shall run and not grow weary,
They shall march and not grow faint.

---

f   *Alluding to a popular belief that eagles regain their youth when
they molt; cf. Ps. 103.5.*

23 הַנּוֹתֵן רוֹזְנִים לְאָ֑יִן
שֹׁפְטֵי אֶ֖רֶץ כַּתֹּ֥הוּ עָשָֽׂה׃

24 אַ֣ף בַּל־נִטָּ֗עוּ
אַ֚ף בַּל־זֹרָ֔עוּ
אַ֛ף בַּל־שֹׁרֵ֥שׁ
בָּאָ֖רֶץ גִּזְעָ֑ם
וְגַם־נָשַׁ֤ף בָּהֶם֙ וַיִּבָ֔שׁוּ
וּסְעָרָ֖ה כַּקַּ֥שׁ תִּשָּׂאֵֽם׃ ס

25 וְאֶל־מִ֥י תְדַמְּי֖וּנִי
וְאֶשְׁוֶ֑ה
יֹאמַ֖ר קָדֽוֹשׁ׃

26 שְׂאוּ־מָר֨וֹם עֵינֵיכֶ֤ם וּרְאוּ֙
מִֽי־בָרָ֣א אֵ֔לֶּה
הַמּוֹצִ֥יא בְמִסְפָּ֖ר צְבָאָ֑ם
לְכֻלָּם֙ בְּשֵׁ֣ם יִקְרָ֔א
מֵרֹ֤ב אוֹנִים֙ וְאַמִּ֣יץ כֹּ֔חַ
אִ֖ישׁ לֹ֥א נֶעְדָּֽר׃ ס

27 לָ֤מָּה תֹאמַר֙ יַעֲקֹ֔ב
וּתְדַבֵּ֖ר יִשְׂרָאֵ֑ל
נִסְתְּרָ֤ה דַרְכִּי֙ מֵֽיהֹוָ֔ה
וּמֵאֱלֹהַ֖י מִשְׁפָּטִ֥י יַעֲבֽוֹר׃

28 הֲל֨וֹא יָדַ֜עְתָּ
אִם־לֹ֣א שָׁמַ֗עְתָּ
אֱלֹהֵ֨י עוֹלָ֤ם ׀ יְהֹוָה֙
בּוֹרֵא֙ קְצ֣וֹת הָאָ֔רֶץ
לֹ֥א יִיעַ֖ף וְלֹ֣א יִיגָ֑ע
אֵ֥ין חֵ֖קֶר לִתְבוּנָתֽוֹ׃

29 נֹתֵ֥ן לַיָּעֵ֖ף כֹּ֑חַ
וּלְאֵ֥ין אוֹנִ֖ים עׇצְמָ֥ה יַרְבֶּֽה׃

30 וְיִעֲפ֥וּ נְעָרִ֖ים וְיִגָ֑עוּ
וּבַחוּרִ֖ים כָּשׁ֥וֹל יִכָּשֵֽׁלוּ׃

31 וְקוֹיֵ֤ יְהֹוָה֙ יַחֲלִ֣יפוּ כֹ֔חַ
יַעֲל֥וּ אֵ֖בֶר כַּנְּשָׁרִ֑ים
יָר֙וּצוּ֙ וְלֹ֣א יִיגָ֔עוּ
יֵלְכ֖וּ וְלֹ֥א יִיעָֽפוּ׃ פ

41 Stand silent before Me, coastlands,
And let nations *a-renew their strength.-a*
Let them approach to state their case;
Let us come forward together for argument.
²Who has roused a victor*b* from the East,
Summoned him to His service?
Has delivered up nations to him,
And trodden sovereigns down?
Has rendered their*c* swords like dust,
Their*c* bows like wind-blown straw?
³He pursues them, he goes on unscathed;
No shackle*d* is placed on his feet.
⁴Who has wrought and achieved this?
He who announced the generations from the
   start—
I, the LORD, who was first
And will be with the last as well.

⁵The coastlands look on in fear,
The ends of earth tremble.

They draw near and come;
⁶Each one helps the other,
Saying to his fellow, "Take courage!"
⁷The woodworker encourages the smith;
He who flattens with the hammer
[Encourages] him who pounds the anvil.
He says of the riveting, "It is good!"
And he fixes it with nails,
That it may not topple.

⁸But you, Israel, My servant,
Jacob, whom I have chosen,
Seed of Abraham My friend—
⁹You whom I drew from the ends of the earth
And called from its far corners,
To whom I said: You are My servant;

מָא הַחֲרִישׁוּ אֵלַי אִיִּים
וּלְאֻמִּים יַחֲלִיפוּ כֹחַ
יִגְּשׁוּ אָז יְדַבֵּרוּ
יַחְדָּו לַמִּשְׁפָּט נִקְרָבָה:
2 מִי הֵעִיר מִמִּזְרָח צֶדֶק
יִקְרָאֵהוּ לְרַגְלוֹ
יִתֵּן לְפָנָיו גּוֹיִם
וּמְלָכִים יַרְדְּ
יִתֵּן כֶּעָפָר חַרְבּוֹ
כְּקַשׁ נִדָּף קַשְׁתּוֹ:
3 יִרְדְּפֵם יַעֲבוֹר שָׁלוֹם
אֹרַח בְּרַגְלָיו לֹא יָבוֹא:
4 מִי פָעַל וְעָשָׂה
קֹרֵא הַדֹּרוֹת מֵרֹאשׁ
אֲנִי יְהוָה רִאשׁוֹן
וְאֶת אַחֲרֹנִים אֲנִי הוּא:
5 רָאוּ אִיִּים וְיִירָאוּ
קְצוֹת הָאָרֶץ יֶחֱרָדוּ
קָרְבוּ וַיֶּאֱתָיוּן:
6 אִישׁ אֶת רֵעֵהוּ יַעְזֹרוּ
וּלְאָחִיו יֹאמַר חֲזָק:
7 וַיְחַזֵּק חָרָשׁ אֶת צֹרֵף
מַחֲלִיק פַּטִּישׁ
אֶת הוֹלֶם פָּעַם
אֹמֵר לַדֶּבֶק טוֹב הוּא
וַיְחַזְּקֵהוּ בְמַסְמְרִים
לֹא יִמּוֹט: ס
8 וְאַתָּה יִשְׂרָאֵל עַבְדִּי
יַעֲקֹב אֲשֶׁר בְּחַרְתִּיךָ
זֶרַע אַבְרָהָם אֹהֲבִי:
9 אֲשֶׁר הֶחֱזַקְתִּיךָ מִקְצוֹת הָאָרֶץ
וּמֵאֲצִילֶיהָ קְרָאתִיךָ
וָאֹמַר לְךָ עַבְדִּי אַתָּה

a-a   *Connection of Heb. uncertain.*
b   *Lit. "victory."*
c   *Heb. "his."*
d   *'rḥ has this meaning in Old Aramaic.*

I chose you, I have not rejected you—

¹⁰Fear not, for I am with you,

Be not frightened, for I am your God;

I strengthen you and I help you,

I uphold you with My victorious right hand.

¹¹Shamed and chagrined shall be

All who contend with you;

They who strive with you

Shall become as naught and shall perish.

¹²You may seek, but shall not find

Those who struggle with you;

Less than nothing shall be

The men who battle against you.

¹³For I the Lord am your God,

Who grasped your right hand,

Who say to you: Have no fear;

I will be your help.

¹⁴Fear not, O worm Jacob,

O ᵉ-men of-ᵉ Israel:

I will help you

            —declares the Lord—

I your Redeemer, the Holy One of Israel.

¹⁵I will make of you a threshing board,

A new thresher, with many spikes;

You shall thresh mountains to dust,

And make hills like chaff.

¹⁶You shall winnow them

And the wind shall carry them off;

The whirlwind shall scatter them.

But you shall rejoice in the Lord,

And glory in the Holy One of Israel.

¹⁷The poor and the needy

Seek water,ᶠ and there is none;

Their tongue is parched with thirst.

I the Lord will respond to them.

I, the God of Israel, will not forsake them.

¹⁸I will open up streams on the bare hills

בְּחַרְתִּ֖יךָ וְלֹ֥א מְאַסְתִּֽיךָ׃

10 אַל־תִּירָא֙ כִּ֣י עִמְּךָ־אָ֔נִי

אַל־תִּשְׁתָּ֖ע כִּֽי־אֲנִ֣י אֱלֹהֶ֑יךָ

אִמַּצְתִּ֙יךָ֙ אַף־עֲזַרְתִּ֔יךָ

אַף־תְּמַכְתִּ֖יךָ בִּימִ֥ין צִדְקִֽי׃

11 הֵ֤ן יֵבֹ֙שׁוּ֙ וְיִכָּ֣לְמ֔וּ

כֹּ֖ל הַנֶּחֱרִ֣ים בָּ֑ךְ

יִֽהְי֥וּ כְאַ֛יִן וְיֹאבְד֖וּ

אַנְשֵׁ֥י רִיבֶֽךָ׃

12 תְּבַקְשֵׁם֙ וְלֹ֣א תִמְצָאֵ֔ם

אַנְשֵׁ֖י מַצֻּתֶ֑ךָ

יִהְי֥וּ כְאַ֛יִן וּכְאֶ֖פֶס

אַנְשֵׁ֥י מִלְחַמְתֶּֽךָ׃

13 כִּ֗י אֲנִ֛י יְהוָ֥ה אֱלֹהֶ֖יךָ

מַחֲזִ֣יק יְמִינֶ֑ךָ

הָאֹמֵ֥ר לְךָ֛ אַל־תִּירָ֖א

אֲנִ֥י עֲזַרְתִּֽיךָ׃ ס

14 אַל־תִּֽירְאִי֙ תּוֹלַ֣עַת יַעֲקֹ֔ב

מְתֵ֖י יִשְׂרָאֵ֑ל

אֲנִ֤י עֲזַרְתִּיךְ֙

נְאֻם־יְהוָ֔ה

וְגֹאֲלֵ֖ךְ קְד֥וֹשׁ יִשְׂרָאֵֽל׃

15 הִנֵּ֣ה שַׂמְתִּ֗יךְ לְמוֹרַג֙

חָר֣וּץ חָדָ֔שׁ בַּ֖עַל פִּֽיפִיּ֑וֹת

תָּד֤וּשׁ הָרִים֙ וְתָדֹ֔ק

וּגְבָע֖וֹת כַּמֹּ֥ץ תָּשִֽׂים׃

16 תִּזְרֵם֙

וְר֣וּחַ תִּשָּׂאֵ֔ם

וּסְעָרָ֖ה תָּפִ֣יץ אוֹתָ֑ם

וְאַתָּה֙ תָּגִ֣יל בַּֽיהוָ֔ה

בִּקְד֥וֹשׁ יִשְׂרָאֵ֖ל תִּתְהַלָּֽל׃ פ

17 הָעֲנִיִּ֤ים וְהָאֶבְיוֹנִים֙

מְבַקְשִׁ֥ים מַ֙יִם֙ וָאַ֔יִן

לְשׁוֹנָ֖ם בַּצָּמָ֣א נָשָׁ֑תָּה

אֲנִ֤י יְהוָה֙ אֶעֱנֵ֔ם

אֱלֹהֵ֥י יִשְׂרָאֵ֖ל לֹ֥א אֶעֶזְבֵֽם׃

18 אֶפְתַּ֤ח עַל־שְׁפָיִים֙ נְהָר֔וֹת

---

e-e Emendation yields "maggot."

f I.e., on the homeward march through the desert.

And fountains amid the valleys;
I will turn the desert into ponds,
The arid land into springs of water.
19I will plant cedars in the wilderness,
Acacias and myrtles and oleasters;
I will set cypresses in the desert,
Box trees and elms as well—
20That men may see and know,
Consider and comprehend
That the LORD's hand has done this,
That the Holy One of Israel has wrought it.

21Submit your case, says the LORD;
Offer your pleas, says the King of Jacob.
22Let them approachᵍ and tell us what will happen.
Tell us what has occurred,ʰ
And we will take note of it;
Or announce to us what will occur,
That we may know the outcome.
23Foretell what is yet to happen,
That we may know that you are gods!
Do anything, good or bad,
That we may be awed and see.ⁱ
24Why, you are less than nothing,
Your effect is less than nullity;
One who chooses you is an abomination.

25I have roused him from the north, and he has come,
From the sunrise, one who invokes My name;
And he has trampled rulers like mud,
Like a potter treading clay.
26Who foretold this from the start, that we may note it;
From aforetime, that we might say, "He is right"?
Not one foretold, not one announced;
No one has heard your utterance!

וּבְתוֹךְ בְּקָעוֹת מַעְיָנוֹת
אָשִׂים מִדְבָּר לַאֲגַם־מַיִם
וְאֶרֶץ צִיָּה לְמוֹצָאֵי מָיִם:
19 אֶתֵּן בַּמִּדְבָּר אֶרֶז
שִׁטָּה וַהֲדַס וְעֵץ שָׁמֶן
אָשִׂים בָּעֲרָבָה בְּרוֹשׁ
תִּדְהָר וּתְאַשּׁוּר יַחְדָּו:
20 לְמַעַן יִרְאוּ וְיֵדְעוּ
וְיָשִׂימוּ וְיַשְׂכִּילוּ יַחְדָּו
כִּי יַד־יְהֹוָה עָשְׂתָה זֹּאת
וּקְדוֹשׁ יִשְׂרָאֵל בְּרָאָהּ: פ

21 קָרְבוּ רִיבְכֶם יֹאמַר* יְהֹוָה
הַגִּישׁוּ עֲצֻמוֹתֵיכֶם יֹאמַר מֶלֶךְ יַעֲקֹב:
22 יַגִּישׁוּ וְיַגִּידוּ לָנוּ אֵת אֲשֶׁר תִּקְרֶינָה
הָרִאשֹׁנוֹת ׀ מָה הֵנָּה הַגִּידוּ
וְנָשִׂימָה לִבֵּנוּ
וְנֵדְעָה אַחֲרִיתָן
אוֹ הַבָּאוֹת הַשְׁמִיעֻנוּ:
23 הַגִּידוּ הָאֹתִיּוֹת לְאָחוֹר
וְנֵדְעָה כִּי אֱלֹהִים אַתֶּם
אַף־תֵּיטִיבוּ וְתָרֵעוּ
וְנִשְׁתָּעֶה וְנִרְאֶה יַחְדָּו:
24 הֵן־אַתֶּם מֵאַיִן
וּפָעָלְכֶם מֵאָפַע
תּוֹעֵבָה יִבְחַר בָּכֶם:

25 הַעִירוֹתִי מִצָּפוֹן וַיַּאת
מִמִּזְרַח־שֶׁמֶשׁ יִקְרָא בִשְׁמִי
וְיָבֹא סְגָנִים כְּמוֹ־חֹמֶר
וּכְמוֹ יוֹצֵר יִרְמָס־טִיט:
26 מִי־הִגִּיד מֵרֹאשׁ וְנֵדָעָה
וּמִלְּפָנִים וְנֹאמַר צַדִּיק
אַף אֵין־מַגִּיד אַף אֵין מַשְׁמִיעַ
אַף אֵין־שֹׁמֵעַ אִמְרֵיכֶם:

v. 21. סבירין ומטעין "אמר"

---

g   *Taking yaggishu intransitively; cf. hiqriv. Exod. 14.10.*
h   *I.e., former prophecies by your gods which have been fulfilled.*
i   *Change of vocalization yields "fear"; cf. v. 10.*

940

27*j*-The things once predicted to Zion—
Behold, here they are!-*j*
And again I send a herald to Jerusalem.
28But I look and there is not a man;
Not one of them can predict
Or can respond when I question him.
29See, they are all nothingness,
Their works are nullity,
Their statues are naught and nil.

27	רִאשׁ֥וֹן לְצִיּ֖וֹן
	הִנֵּ֣ה הִנָּ֑ם
	וְלִירוּשָׁלַ֖͏ִם מְבַשֵּׂ֥ר אֶתֵּֽן׃
28	וְאֵ֙רֶא֙ וְאֵ֣ין אִ֔ישׁ
	וּמֵאֵ֖לֶּה וְאֵ֣ין יוֹעֵ֑ץ
	וְאֶשְׁאָלֵ֖ם וְיָשִׁ֥יבוּ דָבָֽר׃
29	הֵ֚ן כֻּלָּ֣ם אָ֔וֶן
	אֶ֖פֶס מַעֲשֵׂיהֶ֑ם
	ר֥וּחַ וָתֹ֖הוּ נִסְכֵּיהֶֽם׃ פ

42

This is My servant, whom I uphold,
My chosen one, in whom I delight.
I have put My spirit upon him,
He shall teach the true way to the nations.
2He shall not cry out or shout aloud,
Or make his voice heard in the streets.
3*a*-He shall not break even a bruised reed,
Or snuff out even a dim wick.-*a*
He shall bring forth the true way.
4He shall not grow dim or be bruised
Till he has established the true way on earth;
And the coastlands shall await his teaching.

5Thus said God the LORD,
Who created the heavens and stretched them
    out,
Who spread out the earth and what it brings
    forth,
Who gave breath to the people upon it
And life to those who walk thereon:
6I the LORD, in My grace, have summoned
    you,
And I have grasped you by the hand.
I created you, and appointed you
A *b*-covenant people,-*b* *c*-a light of nations-*c*—
7*d*-Opening eyes deprived of light,-*d*

	מב הֵ֤ן עַבְדִּי֙ אֶתְמָךְ־בּ֔וֹ
	בְּחִירִ֖י רָצְתָ֣ה נַפְשִׁ֑י
	נָתַ֤תִּי רוּחִי֙ עָלָ֔יו
	מִשְׁפָּ֖ט לַגּוֹיִ֥ם יוֹצִֽיא׃
2	לֹ֥א יִצְעַ֖ק וְלֹ֣א יִשָּׂ֑א
	וְלֹֽא־יַשְׁמִ֥יעַ בַּח֖וּץ קוֹלֽוֹ׃
3	קָנֶ֤ה רָצוּץ֙ לֹ֣א יִשְׁבּ֔וֹר
	וּפִשְׁתָּ֥ה כֵהָ֖ה לֹ֣א יְכַבֶּ֑נָּה
	לֶאֱמֶ֖ת יוֹצִ֥יא מִשְׁפָּֽט׃
4	לֹ֤א יִכְהֶה֙ וְלֹ֣א יָר֔וּץ
	עַד־יָשִׂ֥ים בָּאָ֖רֶץ מִשְׁפָּ֑ט
	וּלְתוֹרָת֖וֹ אִיִּ֥ים יְיַחֵֽילוּ׃ פ
5	כֹּֽה־אָמַ֞ר הָאֵ֣ל ׀ יְהוָ֗ה
	בּוֹרֵ֤א הַשָּׁמַ֙יִם֙ וְנ֣וֹטֵיהֶ֔ם
	רֹקַ֥ע הָאָ֖רֶץ וְצֶאֱצָאֶ֑יהָ
	נֹתֵ֤ן נְשָׁמָה֙ לָעָ֣ם עָלֶ֔יהָ
	וְר֖וּחַ לַהֹלְכִ֥ים בָּֽהּ׃
6	אֲנִ֧י יְהוָ֛ה קְרָאתִ֥יךָֽ בְצֶ֖דֶק
	וְאַחְזֵ֣ק בְּיָדֶ֑ךָ
	וְאֶצָּרְךָ֗ וְאֶתֶּנְךָ֛
	לִבְרִ֥ית עָ֖ם לְא֥וֹר גּוֹיִֽם׃
7	לִפְקֹ֖חַ עֵינַ֣יִם עִוְר֑וֹת

---

j-j   Meaning of Heb. uncertain.

a-a   Or "A bruised reed, he shall not be broken; / A dim wick, he
          shall not be snuffed out."

b-b   Lit. "covenants of a people"; meaning of Heb. uncertain.

c-c   See 49.6 and note.

    d-d   An idiom meaning "freeing the imprisoned"; cf. 61.1.

Rescuing prisoners from confinement,
From the dungeon those who sit in darkness.

8I am the LORD, that is My name;
I will not yield My glory to another,
Nor My renown to idols.

9See, the things once predicted have come,
And now I foretell new things,
Announce to you ere they sprout up.

10Sing to the LORD a new song,
His praise from the ends of the earth—
e-You who sail the sea and you creatures in
   it,
You coastlands-e and their inhabitants!

11Let the desert and its towns cry aloud,
The villages where Kedar dwells;
Let Sela's inhabitants shout,
Call out from the peaks of the mountains.

12Let them do honor to the LORD,
And tell His glory in the coastlands.

13The LORD goes forth like a warrior,
Like a fighter He whips up His rage.
He yells, He roars aloud,
He charges upon His enemies.

14"I have kept silent f-far too long,-f
Kept still and restrained Myself;
Now I will scream like a woman in labor,
I will pant and I will gasp.

15Hills and heights will I scorch,
Cause all their green to wither;
I will turn rivers into isles,g
And dry the marshes up.

16I will lead the blind
By a road they did not know,
And I will make them walk
By paths they never knew.
I will turn darkness before them to light,
Rough places into level ground.
These are the promises—

לְהוֹצִ֤יא מִמַּסְגֵּר֙ אַסִּ֔יר
מִבֵּ֥ית כֶּ֖לֶא יֹ֥שְׁבֵי חֹֽשֶׁךְ׃

8 אֲנִ֥י יְהוָ֖ה ה֣וּא שְׁמִ֑י
וּכְבוֹדִי֙ לְאַחֵ֣ר לֹֽא־אֶתֵּ֔ן
וּתְהִלָּתִ֖י לַפְּסִילִֽים׃

9 הָרִֽאשֹׁנ֖וֹת הִנֵּה־בָ֑אוּ
וַֽחֲדָשׁוֹת֙ אֲנִ֣י מַגִּ֔יד
בְּטֶ֥רֶם תִּצְמַ֖חְנָה אַשְׁמִ֥יעַ אֶתְכֶֽם׃ ס

10 שִׁ֤ירוּ לַֽיהוָה֙ שִׁ֣יר חָדָ֔שׁ
תְּהִלָּת֖וֹ מִקְצֵ֣ה הָאָ֑רֶץ
יֽוֹרְדֵ֥י הַיָּ֖ם וּמְלֹא֑וֹ
אִיִּ֖ים וְיֹֽשְׁבֵיהֶֽם׃

11 יִשְׂא֤וּ מִדְבָּר֙ וְעָרָ֔יו
חֲצֵרִ֖ים תֵּשֵׁ֣ב קֵדָ֑ר
יָרֹ֨נּוּ֙ יֹ֣שְׁבֵי סֶ֔לַע
מֵרֹ֥אשׁ הָרִ֖ים יִצְוָֽחוּ׃

12 יָשִׂ֥ימוּ לַֽיהוָ֖ה כָּב֑וֹד
וּתְהִלָּת֖וֹ בָּֽאִיִּ֥ים יַגִּֽידוּ׃

13 יְהוָה֙ כַּגִּבּ֣וֹר יֵצֵ֔א
כְּאִ֥ישׁ מִלְחָמ֖וֹת יָעִ֣יר קִנְאָ֑ה
יָרִ֨יעַ֙ אַף־יַצְרִ֔יחַ
עַל־אֹֽיְבָ֖יו יִתְגַּבָּֽר׃ ס

14 הֶֽחֱשֵׁ֙יתִי֙ מֵֽעוֹלָ֔ם
אַֽחֲרִ֖ישׁ אֶתְאַפָּ֑ק
כַּיּֽוֹלֵדָ֣ה אֶפְעֶ֔ה
אֶשֹּׁ֥ם וְאֶשְׁאַ֖ף יָֽחַד׃

15 אַֽחֲרִ֤יב הָרִים֙ וּגְבָע֔וֹת
וְכָל־עֶשְׂבָּ֖ם אוֹבִ֑ישׁ
וְשַׂמְתִּ֤י נְהָרוֹת֙ לָֽאִיִּ֔ים
וַֽאֲגַמִּ֖ים אוֹבִֽישׁ׃

16 וְהֽוֹלַכְתִּ֣י עִוְרִ֗ים
בְּדֶ֙רֶךְ֙ לֹ֣א יָדָ֔עוּ
בִּנְתִיב֥וֹת לֹֽא־יָדְע֖וּ
אַדְרִיכֵ֑ם
אָשִׂים֩ מַחְשָׁ֨ךְ לִפְנֵיהֶ֜ם לָא֗וֹר
וּמַֽעֲקַשִּׁים֙ לְמִישׁ֔וֹר
אֵ֚לֶּה הַדְּבָרִ֔ים

---

e-e   Emendation yields "Let the sea roar and its creatures, / The
      coastlands..." Cf. Ps. 98.7.
f-f   Lit. "from of old."
g   Emendation yields "desert."

I will keep them without fail.

¹⁷Driven back and utterly shamed
Shall be those who trust in an image,
Those who say to idols,
'You are our gods!'"

¹⁸Listen, you who are deaf;
You blind ones, look up and see!
¹⁹Who is so blind as My servant,
So deaf as the messenger I send?
Who is so blind as the chosen[h] one,
So blind as the servant of the LORD?
²⁰Seeing many things, [i-]he gives[-i] no heed;
With ears open, he hears nothing.
^{21[j]}The LORD desires His [servant's] vindica-
    tion,
That he may magnify and glorify [His] Teach-
    ing.

²²Yet it is a people plundered and despoiled:
All of them are trapped in holes,
Imprisoned in dungeons.
They are given over to plunder, with none to
    rescue them;
To despoilment, with none to say "Give
    back!"
²³If only you would listen to this,
Attend and give heed from now on!
²⁴Who was it gave Jacob over to despoilment
And Israel to plunderers?
Surely, the LORD against whom they[k] sinned
In whose ways they would not walk
And whose Teaching they would not obey.
²⁵So He poured out wrath upon them,
His anger and the fury of war.
It blazed upon them all about, but they
    heeded not;
It burned among them, but they gave it no
    thought.

עֲשִׂיתֶם וְלֹא עֲזַבְתִּים:
17 נָסֹגוּ אָחוֹר יֵבֹשׁוּ בֹשֶׁת
הַבֹּטְחִים בַּפָּסֶל
הָאֹמְרִים לְמַסֵּכָה
אַתֶּם אֱלֹהֵינוּ: ס

18 הַחֵרְשִׁים שְׁמָעוּ
וְהַעִוְרִים הַבִּיטוּ לִרְאוֹת:
19 מִי עִוֵּר כִּי אִם־עַבְדִּי
וְחֵרֵשׁ כְּמַלְאָכִי אֶשְׁלָח
מִי עִוֵּר כִּמְשֻׁלָּם
וְעִוֵּר כְּעֶבֶד יְהוָה:
20 רָאִית רָאוֹת רַבּוֹת וְלֹא תִשְׁמֹר
פָּקוֹחַ אָזְנַיִם וְלֹא יִשְׁמָע:
21 יְהוָה חָפֵץ לְמַעַן צִדְקוֹ
יַגְדִּיל תּוֹרָה וְיַאְדִּיר:

22 וְהוּא עַם־בָּזוּז וְשָׁסוּי
הָפֵחַ בַּחוּרִים כֻּלָּם
וּבְבָתֵּי כְלָאִים הָחְבָּאוּ
הָיוּ לָבַז וְאֵין מַצִּיל
מְשִׁסָּה וְאֵין־אֹמֵר הָשַׁב:
23 מִי בָכֶם יַאֲזִין זֹאת
יַקְשֵׁב וְיִשְׁמַע לְאָחוֹר:
24 מִי־נָתַן לִמְשׁוֹסָה לִמְשִׁיסָּה יַעֲקֹב
וְיִשְׂרָאֵל לְבֹזְזִים
הֲלוֹא יְהוָה זוּ חָטָאנוּ לוֹ
וְלֹא־אָבוּ בִדְרָכָיו הָלוֹךְ
וְלֹא שָׁמְעוּ בְּתוֹרָתוֹ:
25 וַיִּשְׁפֹּךְ עָלָיו חֵמָה אַפּוֹ
וֶעֱזוּז מִלְחָמָה
וַתְּלַהֲטֵהוּ מִסָּבִיב וְלֹא יָדָע
וַתִּבְעַר־בּוֹ וְלֹא־יָשִׂים עַל־לֵב: פ

---

h   Meaning of Heb. uncertain.
i-i   Heb. "you give."
j   Meaning of verse uncertain; cf. 43.9–12.
k   Heb. "we."

43 But now thus said the LORD—
Who created you, O Jacob,
Who formed you, O Israel:
Fear not, for I will redeem you;
I have singled you out by name,
You are Mine.
²When you pass through water,
I will be with you;
Through streams,
They shall not overwhelm you.
When you walk through fire,
You shall not be scorched;
Through flame,
It shall not burn you.
³For I the LORD am your God,
The Holy One of Israel, your Savior.
I give Egypt as a ransom for you,
Ethiopia and Saba in exchange for you.
⁴Because you are precious to Me,
And honored, and I love you,
I give men in exchange for you
And peoples in your stead.
⁵Fear not, for I am with you:
I will bring your folk from the East,
Will gather you out of the West;
⁶I will say to the North, "Give back!"
And to the South, "Do not withhold!
Bring My sons from afar,
And My daughters from the end of the
earth—
⁷All who are linked to My name,
Whom I have created,
Formed, and made for My glory—
⁸Setting free that people,
Blind though it has eyes
And deaf though it has ears."
⁹All the nations assemble as one,

מג וְעַתָּה כֹּה־אָמַר יְהֹוָה
בֹּרַאֲךָ יַעֲקֹב
וְיֹצֶרְךָ יִשְׂרָאֵל
אַל־תִּירָא כִּי גְאַלְתִּיךָ
קָרָאתִי בְשִׁמְךָ
לִי־אָתָּה:
2 כִּי־תַעֲבֹר בַּמַּיִם
אִתְּךָ־אָנִי
וּבַנְּהָרוֹת
לֹא יִשְׁטְפוּךָ
כִּי־תֵלֵךְ בְּמוֹ־אֵשׁ
לֹא תִכָּוֶה
וְלֶהָבָה
לֹא תִבְעַר־בָּךְ:
3 כִּי אֲנִי יְהֹוָה אֱלֹהֶיךָ
קְדוֹשׁ יִשְׂרָאֵל מוֹשִׁיעֶךָ
נָתַתִּי כָפְרְךָ מִצְרַיִם
כּוּשׁ וּסְבָא תַּחְתֶּיךָ:
4 מֵאֲשֶׁר יָקַרְתָּ בְעֵינַי
נִכְבַּדְתָּ וַאֲנִי אֲהַבְתִּיךָ
וְאֶתֵּן אָדָם תַּחְתֶּיךָ
וּלְאֻמִּים תַּחַת נַפְשֶׁךָ:
5 אַל־תִּירָא כִּי אִתְּךָ־אָנִי
מִמִּזְרָח אָבִיא זַרְעֶךָ
וּמִמַּעֲרָב אֲקַבְּצֶךָּ:
6 אֹמַר לַצָּפוֹן תֵּנִי
וּלְתֵימָן אַל־תִּכְלָאִי
הָבִיאִי בָנַי מֵרָחוֹק
וּבְנוֹתַי מִקְצֵה הָאָרֶץ:
7 כֹּל הַנִּקְרָא בִשְׁמִי
וְלִכְבוֹדִי בְּרָאתִיו
יְצַרְתִּיו אַף־עֲשִׂיתִיו:
8 הוֹצִיא עַם־עִוֵּר
וְעֵינַיִם יֵשׁ
וְחֵרְשִׁים וְאָזְנַיִם לָמוֹ:
9 כָּל־הַגּוֹיִם נִקְבְּצוּ יַחְדָּו

944

The peoples gather.
Who among them declared this,
Foretold to us the things that have happened?
Let them produce their witnesses and be vin-
dicated,
That men, hearing them, may say, "It is
true!"[a]

10My witnesses are *you*

—declares the LORD—

My servant, whom I have chosen.
To the end that you[b] may take thought,
And believe in Me,
And understand that I am He:
Before Me no god was formed,
And after Me none shall exist—
11None but me, the LORD;
Beside Me, none can grant triumph.
12I alone foretold the triumph
And I brought it to pass;
I announced it,
And no strange god was among you.
So you are My witnesses

—declares the LORD—

And I am God.
13Ever since day was, I am He;
None can deliver from My hand.
When I act, who can reverse it?

14Thus said the LORD,
Your Redeemer, the Holy One of Israel:
For your sake [c]-I send to Babylon;
I will bring down all [her] bars,
And the Chaldeans shall raise their voice in
lamentation.-[c]
15I am your Holy One, the LORD,
Your King, the Creator of Israel.

16Thus said the LORD,
Who made a road through the sea

וְיֵאָסְפוּ֙ לְאֻמִּ֔ים
מִ֣י בָהֶ֗ם יַגִּ֣יד זֹ֔את
וְרִֽאשֹׁנ֖וֹת יַשְׁמִיעֻ֑נוּ
יִתְּנ֤וּ עֵֽדֵיהֶם֙ וְיִצְדָּ֔קוּ
וְיִשְׁמְע֖וּ וְיֹאמְר֥וּ אֱמֶֽת׃
10 אַתֶּ֤ם עֵדַי֙
נְאֻם־יְהֹוָ֔ה
וְעַבְדִּ֖י אֲשֶׁ֣ר בָּחָ֑רְתִּי
לְמַ֣עַן תֵּ֠דְע֠וּ
וְתַאֲמִ֣ינוּ לִ֗י
וְתָבִ֙ינוּ֙ כִּֽי־אֲנִ֣י ה֔וּא
לְפָנַי֙ לֹא־נ֣וֹצַר אֵ֔ל
וְאַחֲרַ֖י לֹ֥א יִֽהְיֶֽה׃ ס
11 אָנֹכִ֥י אָנֹכִ֖י יְהֹוָ֑ה
וְאֵ֥ין מִבַּלְעָדַ֖י מוֹשִֽׁיעַ׃
12 אָנֹכִ֞י הִגַּ֤דְתִּי
וְהוֹשַׁ֙עְתִּי֙
וְהִשְׁמַ֔עְתִּי
וְאֵ֥ין בָּכֶ֖ם זָ֑ר
וְאַתֶּ֥ם עֵדַ֛י
נְאֻם־יְהֹוָ֖ה
וַֽאֲנִי־אֵֽל׃
13 גַּם־מִיּוֹם֙ אֲנִ֣י ה֔וּא
וְאֵ֥ין מִיָּדִ֖י מַצִּ֑יל
אֶפְעַ֖ל וּמִ֥י יְשִׁיבֶֽנָּה׃ ס
14 כֹּֽה־אָמַ֧ר יְהֹוָ֛ה
גֹּאַלְכֶ֖ם קְד֣וֹשׁ יִשְׂרָאֵ֑ל
לְמַעַנְכֶ֞ם שִׁלַּ֣חְתִּי בָבֶ֗לָה
וְהוֹרַדְתִּ֤י בָֽרִיחִים֙ כֻּלָּ֔ם
וְכַשְׂדִּ֖ים בׇּאֳנִיּ֥וֹת רִנָּתָֽם׃
15 אֲנִ֥י יְהֹוָ֖ה קְדֽוֹשְׁכֶ֑ם
בּוֹרֵ֥א יִשְׂרָאֵ֖ל מַלְכְּכֶֽם׃ ס
16 כֹּ֚ה אָמַ֣ר יְהֹוָ֔ה
הַנּוֹתֵ֥ן בַּיָּ֖ם דָּ֑רֶךְ

---

a   I.e., that the other nations' gods are real.
b   Emendation yields "they."
c-c Meaning of Heb. uncertain.

And a path through mighty waters,

17Who destroyedd chariots and horses,

And all the mighty host—

They lay down to rise no more,

They were extinguished, quenched like a
wick:

18Do not recall what happened of old,

Or ponder what happened of yore!

19I am about to do something new;

Even now it shall come to pass,

Suddenly you shall perceive it:

I will make a road through the wilderness

And riverse in the desert.

20The wild beasts shall honor Me,

Jackals and ostriches,

For I provide water in the wilderness,

Rivers in the desert,

To give drink to My chosen people,

21The people I formed for Myself

That they might declare My praise.

22But you have not worshiped Me, O Jacob,

That you should be weary of Me, O Israel.

23You have not brought Me your sheep for
burnt offerings,

Nor honored Me with your sacrifices.

I have not burdened you with meal offerings,

Nor wearied you about frankincense.

24You have not bought Me fragrant reed with
money,

Nor sated Me with the fat of your sacrifices.

Instead, you have burdened Me with your
sins,

You have wearied Me with your iniquities.

25It is I, I who—for My own sakef—

Wipe your transgressions away

And remember your sins no more.

וּבְמַ֥יִם עַזִּ֖ים נְתִיבָֽה׃

17 הַמּוֹצִ֥יא רֶֽכֶב־וָס֑וּס

חַ֣יִל וְעִזּ֑וּז

יַחְדָּ֤ו יִשְׁכְּבוּ֙ בַּל־יָק֔וּמוּ

דָּעֲכ֖וּ כַּפִּשְׁתָּ֥ה כָבֽוּ׃

18 אַֽל־תִּזְכְּר֖וּ רִֽאשֹׁנ֑וֹת

וְקַדְמֹנִיּ֖וֹת אַל־תִּתְבֹּנָֽנוּ׃

19 הִנְנִ֤י עֹשֶׂה֙ חֲדָשָׁה֙

עַתָּ֣ה תִצְמָ֔ח

הֲל֖וֹא תֵֽדָע֑וּהָ

אַ֣ף אָשִׂ֤ים בַּמִּדְבָּר֙ דֶּ֔רֶךְ

בִּֽישִׁמ֖וֹן נְהָרֽוֹת׃

20 תְּכַבְּדֵ֙נִי֙ חַיַּ֣ת הַשָּׂדֶ֔ה

תַּנִּ֖ים וּבְנ֣וֹת יַֽעֲנָ֑ה

כִּֽי־נָתַ֨תִּי בַמִּדְבָּ֥ר מַ֙יִם֙

נְהָרוֹת֙ בִּֽישִׁימֹ֔ן

לְהַשְׁק֖וֹת עַמִּ֥י בְחִירִֽי׃

21 עַם־זוּ֙ יָצַ֣רְתִּי לִ֔י

תְּהִלָּתִ֖י יְסַפֵּֽרוּ׃ ס

22 וְלֹֽא־אֹתִ֥י קָרָ֖אתָ יַֽעֲקֹ֑ב

כִּֽי־יָגַ֥עְתָּ בִּ֖י יִשְׂרָאֵֽל׃

23 לֹֽא־הֵבֵ֤יאתָ לִּי֙ שֵׂ֣ה עֹלֹתֶ֔יךָ

וּזְבָחֶ֖יךָ לֹ֣א כִבַּדְתָּ֑נִי

לֹ֤א הֶעֱבַדְתִּ֙יךָ֙ בְּמִנְחָ֔ה

וְלֹ֥א הוֹגַעְתִּ֖יךָ בִּלְבוֹנָֽה׃

24 לֹא־קָנִ֨יתָ לִּ֤י בַכֶּ֙סֶף֙ קָנֶ֔ה

וְחֵ֥לֶב זְבָחֶ֖יךָ לֹ֣א הִרְוִיתָ֑נִי

אַ֣ךְ הֶעֱבַדְתַּ֙נִי֙ בְּחַטֹּאותֶ֔יךָ*

הוֹגַעְתַּ֖נִי בַּֽעֲוֹנֹתֶֽיךָ׃ ס

25 אָֽנֹכִ֨י אָנֹכִ֥י ה֛וּא

מֹחֶ֥ה פְשָׁעֶ֖יךָ לְמַֽעֲנִ֑י

וְחַטֹּאתֶ֖יךָ לֹ֥א אֶזְכֹּֽר׃

v. 24. מלא ו׳

---

d   Understanding hoṣi, here, as equivalent to Aramaic sheṣi.

e   1QIsa reads "paths"; cf. v. 16.

f   I.e., in order to put an end to the profanation of My holy name;
cf. 48.9–11.

26Help me remember!
Let us join in argument,
Tell your version,
That you may be vindicated.
27Your earliest ancestor sinned,
And your spokesmen transgressed against
   Me.
28So I profaned g-the holy princes;-g
I abandoned Jacob to proscriptionh
And Israel to mockery.

הַזְכִּירֵ֗נִי 26
נִשָּׁפְטָ֖ה יָ֑חַד
סַפֵּ֥ר אַתָּ֖ה
לְמַ֥עַן תִּצְדָּֽק׃
אָבִ֥יךָ הָרִאשׁ֖וֹן חָטָ֑א 27
וּמְלִיצֶ֖יךָ פָּ֥שְׁעוּ בִֽי׃
וַאֲחַלֵּ֖ל שָׂ֣רֵי קֹ֑דֶשׁ 28
וְאֶתְּנָ֤ה לַחֵ֙רֶם֙ יַעֲקֹ֔ב
וְיִשְׂרָאֵ֖ל לְגִדּוּפִֽים׃ ס

44

But hear, now, O Jacob My servant,
Israel whom I have chosen!
2Thus said the Lord, your Maker,
Your Creator who has helped you since birth:
Fear not, My servant Jacob,
Jeshuruna whom I have chosen,
3Even as I pour water on thirsty soil,
And rain upon dry ground,
So will I pour My spirit on your offspring,
My blessing upon your posterity.
4And they shall sprout likeb grass,
Like willows by watercourses.
5One shall say, "I am the Lord's,"
Another shall use the name of "Jacob,"
Another shall mark his arm "of the Lord"c
And adopt the name of "Israel."

מד וְעַתָּ֥ה שְׁמַ֖ע יַעֲקֹ֣ב עַבְדִּ֑י
וְיִשְׂרָאֵ֖ל בָּחַ֥רְתִּי בֽוֹ׃
כֹּה־אָמַ֥ר יְהֹוָ֖ה עֹשֶׂ֑ךָ 2
וְיֹצֶרְךָ֥ מִבֶּ֖טֶן יַעְזְרֶ֑ךָּ
אַל־תִּירָא֙ עַבְדִּ֣י יַעֲקֹ֔ב
וִישֻׁר֖וּן בָּחַ֥רְתִּי בֽוֹ׃
כִּ֤י אֶצׇּק־מַ֙יִם֙ עַל־צָמֵ֔א 3
וְנֹזְלִ֖ים עַל־יַבָּשָׁ֑ה
אֶצֹּ֤ק רוּחִי֙ עַל־זַרְעֶ֔ךָ
וּבִרְכָתִ֖י עַל־צֶאֱצָאֶֽיךָ׃
וְצָמְח֖וּ בְּבֵ֣ין חָצִ֑יר 4
כַּעֲרָבִ֖ים עַל־יִבְלֵי־מָֽיִם׃
זֶ֤ה יֹאמַר֙ לַיהֹוָ֣ה אָ֔נִי 5
וְזֶ֖ה יִקְרָ֣א בְשֵֽׁם־יַעֲקֹ֑ב
וְזֶ֗ה יִכְתֹּ֤ב יָדוֹ֙ לַֽיהֹוָ֔ה
וּבְשֵׁ֥ם יִשְׂרָאֵ֖ל יְכַנֶּֽה׃ פ

6Thus said the Lord, the King of Israel,
Their Redeemer, the Lord of Hosts:
I am the first and I am the last,
And there is no god but Me.
7dWho like Me can announce,
Can foretell it—and match Me thereby?
Even as I told the future to an ancient people,

כֹּֽה־אָמַ֤ר יְהֹוָה֙ מֶֽלֶךְ־יִשְׂרָאֵ֔ל 6
וְגֹאֲל֖וֹ יְהֹוָ֣ה צְבָא֑וֹת
אֲנִ֤י רִאשׁוֹן֙ וַאֲנִ֣י אַחֲר֔וֹן
וּמִבַּלְעָדַ֖י אֵ֥ין אֱלֹהִֽים׃
וּמִֽי־כָמ֣וֹנִי יִקְרָ֗א 7
וְיַגִּידֶ֤הָ וְיַעְרְכֶ֙הָ֙ לִ֔י
מִשּׂוּמִ֖י עַם־עוֹלָ֑ם וְאֹתִיּ֛וֹת

---

g-g   *Emendation yields "My holy name"; see preceding note.*
h   *Emendation yields "insult."*

a   *A name for Israel; see note on Num. 23.10; cf. Deut. 32.15; 33.5,
    26.*
b   *Lit. "in among."*
c   *It was customary to mark a slave with the owner's name.*
d   *Meaning of verse uncertain.*

So let him foretell coming events to them.

⁸Do not be frightened, do not be shaken!
Have I not from of old predicted to you?
I foretold, and you are My witnesses.
Is there any god, then, but Me?
"There is no other rock; I know none!"

⁹The makers of idols
All work to no purpose;
And the things they treasure
Can do no good,
As they themselves can testify.
They neither look nor think,
And so they shall be shamed.
¹⁰Who would fashion a god
Or cast a statue
That can do no good?
¹¹Lo, all its adherents shall be shamed;
They are craftsmen, are merely human.
Let them all assemble and stand up!
They shall be cowed, and they shall be
   shamed.

¹²ᵉThe craftsman in iron, with his tools,
Works itᶠ over charcoal
And fashions it by hammering,
Working with the strength of his arm.
Should he go hungry, his strength would ebb;
Should he drink no water, he would grow
   faint.

¹³The craftsman in wood measures with a line
And marks out a shape with a stylus;
He forms it with scraping tools,
Marking it out with a compass.
He gives it a human form,
The beauty of a man, to dwell in a shrine.
¹⁴For his use he cuts down cedars;
He chooses plane trees and oaks.

וַאֲשֶׁ֥ר תָּבֹ֖אנָה יַגִּ֥ידוּ לָֽמוֹ׃
8 אַֽל־תִּפְחֲדוּ֙ וְאַל־תִּרְה֔וּ
הֲלֹ֥א מֵאָ֛ז הִשְׁמַעְתִּ֖יךָ
וְהִגַּ֥דְתִּי וְאַתֶּ֣ם עֵדָ֑י
הֲיֵ֤שׁ אֱל֙וֹהַּ֙ מִבַּלְעָדַ֔י
וְאֵ֥ין צ֖וּר בַּל־יָדָֽעְתִּי׃

9 יֹֽצְרֵי־פֶ֣סֶל
כֻּלָּ֣ם תֹּ֔הוּ
וַחֲמוּדֵיהֶ֖ם
בַּל־יוֹעִ֑ילוּ
וְעֵדֵיהֶ֣ם הֵ֗מָּה*
בַּל־יִרְא֛וּ וּבַל־יֵדְע֖וּ
לְמַ֥עַן יֵבֹֽשׁוּ׃
10 מִֽי־יָצַ֥ר אֵ֛ל
וּפֶ֖סֶל נָסָ֑ךְ
לְבִלְתִּ֖י הוֹעִֽיל׃
11 הֵ֤ן כָּל־חֲבֵרָיו֙ יֵבֹ֔שׁוּ
וְחָרָשִׁ֥ים הֵ֖מָּה מֵאָדָ֑ם
יִתְקַבְּצ֤וּ כֻלָּם֙ יַֽעֲמֹ֔דוּ
יִפְחֲד֖וּ יֵבֹ֥שׁוּ יָֽחַד׃

12 חָרַ֤שׁ בַּרְזֶל֙ מַֽעֲצָ֔ד
וּפָעַל֙ בַּפֶּחָ֔ם
וּבַמַּקָּב֖וֹת יִצְּרֵ֑הוּ
וַיִּפְעָלֵ֙הוּ֙ בִּזְר֣וֹעַ כֹּח֔וֹ
גַּם־רָעֵב֙ וְאֵ֣ין כֹּ֔חַ
לֹא־שָׁ֥תָה מַ֖יִם וַיִּיעָֽף׃

13 חָרַ֣שׁ עֵצִים֮ נָ֣טָה קָו֒
יְתָאֲרֵ֣הוּ בַשֶּׂ֔רֶד
יַֽעֲשֵׂ֙הוּ֙ בַּמַּקְצֻע֔וֹת
וּבַמְּחוּגָ֖ה יְתָאֳרֵ֑הוּ
וַיַּֽעֲשֵׂ֙הוּ֙ כְּתַבְנִ֣ית אִ֔ישׁ
כְּתִפְאֶ֥רֶת אָדָ֖ם לָשֶׁ֥בֶת בָּֽיִת׃
14 לִכְרָת־ל֣וֹ אֲרָזִ֗ים
וַיִּקַּ֤ח תִּרְזָה֙ וְאַלּ֔וֹן

---

e *The meaning of parts of vv. 12–13 is uncertain.*
f *I.e., the image he is making.*

He sets aside trees of the forest;
Or plants firs, and the rain makes them grow.
¹⁵All this serves man for fuel:
He takes some to warm himself,
And he builds a fire and bakes bread.
He also makes a god of it and worships it,
Fashions an idol and bows down to it!
¹⁶Part of it he burns in a fire:
On that part he roasts^g meat,
He eats^g the roast and is sated;
He also warms himself and cries, "Ah,
I am warm! I can feel^h the heat!"
¹⁷Of the rest he makes a god—his own carving!
He bows down to it, worships it;
He prays to it and cries,
"Save me, for you are my god!"

¹⁸They have no wit or judgment:
Their eyes are besmeared, and they see not;
Their minds, and they cannot think.
¹⁹They do not give thought,
They lack the wit and judgment to say:
"Part of it I burned in a fire;
I also baked bread on the coals,
I roasted meat and ate it—
Should I make the rest an abhorrence?
Should I bow to a block of wood?"
²⁰He pursues ashes!ⁱ
A deluded mind has led him astray,
And he cannot save himself;
He never says to himself,
"The thing in my hand is a fraud!"
²¹Remember these things, O Jacob
For you, O Israel, are My servant:
I fashioned you, you are My servant—
O Israel, never forget Me.^j

וַיַּאַמֶּץ־לוֹ בַּעֲצֵי־יָ֫עַר
נָטַע אֹרֶן* וְגֶשֶׁם יְגַדֵּל:
15 וְהָיָ֤ה לְאָדָם֙ לְבָעֵ֔ר
וַיִּקַּ֤ח מֵהֶם֙ וַיָּ֔חָם
אַף־יַשִּׂ֣יק וְאָ֣פָה לֶ֔חֶם
אַף־יִפְעַל־אֵל֙ וַיִּשְׁתָּ֔חוּ
עָשָׂ֥הוּ פֶ֖סֶל וַיִּסְגָּד־לָֽמוֹ:
16 חֶצְיוֹ֙ שָׂרַ֣ף בְּמוֹ־אֵ֔שׁ
עַל־חֶצְיוֹ֙ בָּשָׂ֣ר יֹאכֵ֔ל
יִצְלֶ֥ה צָלִ֖י וְיִשְׂבָּ֑ע
אַף־יָחֹם֙ וְיֹאמַ֣ר הֶאָ֔ח
חַמּוֹתִ֖י רָאִ֥יתִי אֽוּר:
17 וּשְׁאֵרִית֗וֹ לְאֵ֣ל עָשָׂ֔ה לְפִסְל֑וֹ
יִסְגָּד־לוֹ וְיִשְׁתַּחוּ֙
וְיִתְפַּלֵּ֤ל אֵלָיו֙ וְיֹאמַ֔ר
הַצִּילֵ֖נִי כִּ֥י אֵלִ֥י אָֽתָּה:

18 לֹ֥א יָדְע֖וּ וְלֹ֣א יָבִ֑ינוּ
כִּ֣י טַ֤ח מֵֽרְאוֹת֙ עֵֽינֵיהֶ֔ם
מֵֽהַשְׂכִּ֖יל לִבֹּתָֽם:
19 וְלֹא־יָשִׁ֣יב אֶל־לִבּ֗וֹ
וְלֹ֨א דַ֤עַת וְלֹֽא־תְבוּנָה֙ לֵאמֹ֔ר
חֶצְיוֹ֙ שָׂרַ֣פְתִּי בְמוֹ־אֵ֔שׁ
וְ֠אַף אָפִ֤יתִי עַל־גֶּֽחָלָיו֙ לֶ֔חֶם
אֶצְלֶ֥ה בָשָׂ֖ר וְאֹכֵ֑ל
וְיִתְרוֹ֙ לְתוֹעֵבָ֣ה אֶעֱשֶׂ֔ה
לְב֥וּל עֵ֖ץ אֶסְגּֽוֹד:
20 רֹעֶ֣ה אֵ֔פֶר
לֵ֥ב הוּתַ֖ל וַיַּטֵּ֑הוּ
וְלֹֽא־יַצִּ֤יל אֶת־נַפְשׁוֹ֙
וְלֹ֣א יֹאמַ֔ר
הֲל֥וֹא שֶׁ֖קֶר בִּֽימִינִֽי: ס
21 זְכָר־אֵ֣לֶּה יַֽעֲקֹ֔ב
וְיִשְׂרָאֵ֖ל כִּ֣י עַבְדִּי־אָ֑תָּה
יְצַרְתִּ֤יךָ עֶֽבֶד־לִי֙ אַ֔תָּה
יִשְׂרָאֵ֖ל לֹ֥א תִנָּשֵֽׁנִי:

g   *Transposing the Heb. verbs for clarity.*
h   *Lit. "see."*
i   *Lit. "He shepherds ashes."*
j   *Emendation yields "them," these things.*

ן' זעירא   v. 14.

²²I wipe away your sins like a cloud,
Your transgressions like mist—
Come back to Me, for I redeem you.

מָחִ֤יתִי כָעָב֙ פְּשָׁעֶ֔יךָ 22
וְכֶעָנָ֖ן חַטֹּאותֶ֑יךָ
שׁוּבָ֥ה אֵלַ֖י כִּ֥י גְאַלְתִּֽיךָ׃

²³Shout, O heavens, for the LORD has acted;
Shout aloud, O depths of the earth!
Shout for joy, O mountains,
O forests with all your trees!
For the LORD has redeemed Jacob,
Has glorified Himself through Israel.

רָנּ֨וּ שָׁמַ֜יִם כִּֽי־עָשָׂ֣ה יְהוָ֗ה 23
הָרִ֙יעוּ֙ תַּחְתִּיּ֣וֹת אָ֔רֶץ
פִּצְח֤וּ הָרִים֙ רִנָּ֔ה
יַ֖עַר וְכָל־עֵ֣ץ בּ֑וֹ
כִּֽי־גָאַ֤ל יְהוָה֙ יַעֲקֹ֔ב
וּבְיִשְׂרָאֵ֖ל יִתְפָּאָֽר׃ פ

²⁴Thus said the LORD, your Redeemer,
Who formed you in the womb:
It is I, the LORD, who made everything,
Who alone stretched out the heavens
And unaided^k spread out the earth;
²⁵Who annul the omens of diviners,
And make fools of the augurs;
Who turn sages back
And make nonsense of their knowledge;
²⁶But confirm the word of My^l servant
And fulfill the prediction of My^l messengers.
It is I who say of Jerusalem, "It shall be in-
habited,"
And of the towns of Judah, "They shall be re-
built;
And I will restore their ruined places."
²⁷[I,] who said to the deep, "Be dry;
I will dry up your floods,"
²⁸Am the same who says of Cyrus, "He is My
shepherd;^m
He shall fulfill all My purposes!
He shall say of Jerusalem, 'She shall be re-
built,'
And to the Temple: 'You shall be founded
again.'"

כֹּֽה־אָמַ֤ר יְהוָה֙ גֹּאֲלֶ֔ךָ 24
וְיֹצֶרְךָ֖ מִבָּ֑טֶן
אָנֹכִ֤י יְהוָה֙ עֹ֣שֶׂה כֹּ֔ל
נֹטֶ֤ה שָׁמַ֙יִם֙ לְבַדִּ֔י
רֹקַ֥ע הָאָ֖רֶץ מי אתי מֵאִתִּֽי מֵֽאִתִּֽי׃
מֵפֵר֙ אֹת֣וֹת בַּדִּ֔ים 25
וְקֹסְמִ֖ים יְהוֹלֵ֑ל
מֵשִׁ֧יב חֲכָמִ֛ים אָח֖וֹר
וְדַעְתָּ֥ם יְשַׂכֵּֽל׃
מֵקִים֙ דְּבַ֣ר עַבְדּ֔וֹ 26
וַעֲצַ֥ת מַלְאָכָ֖יו יַשְׁלִ֑ים
הָאֹמֵ֨ר לִירוּשָׁלַ֜͏ִם תּוּשָׁ֗ב
וּלְעָרֵ֤י יְהוּדָה֙ תִּבָּנֶ֔ינָה
וְחָרְבוֹתֶ֖יהָ אֲקוֹמֵֽם׃
הָאֹמֵ֥ר לַצּוּלָ֖ה חֳרָ֑בִי 27
וְנַהֲרֹתַ֖יִךְ אוֹבִֽישׁ׃
הָאֹמֵ֤ר לְכ֙וֹרֶשׁ֙ רֹעִ֔י 28
וְכָל־חֶפְצִ֖י יַשְׁלִ֑ם
וְלֵאמֹ֤ר לִירוּשָׁלַ֙͏ִם֙ תִּבָּנֶ֔ה
וְהֵיכָ֖ל תִּוָּסֵֽד׃ ס

---

k   Lit. "with none beside me," or (following many Heb. mss., kethib,
    and ancient versions) "who was with me?"
l   Heb. "His."
m   I.e., the king whom I have designated.

45 Thus said the LORD to Cyrus, His anointed one—

Whose right hand *a*-He has-*a* grasped,
Treading down nations before him,
b-Ungirding the loins of kings,-*b*
Opening doors before him
And letting no gate stay shut:
²I will march before you
And level *c*-the hills that loom up;-*c*
I will shatter doors of bronze
And cut down iron bars.
³I will give you treasures concealed in the dark
And secret hoards—
So that you may know that it is I the LORD,
The God of Israel, who call you by name.
⁴For the sake of My servant Jacob,
Israel My chosen one,
I call you by name,
I hail you by title, though you have not known
    Me.
⁵I am the LORD and there is none else;
Beside Me, there is no god.
I engird you, though you have not known Me,
⁶So that they may know, from east to west,
That there is none but Me.
I am the LORD and there is none else,
⁷I form light and create darkness,
I make weal and create woe—
I the LORD do all these things.
⁸Pour down, O skies, from above!
Let the heavens rain down victory!
Let the earth open up and triumph sprout,
Yes, let vindication spring up:
I the LORD have created it.

⁹Shame on him who argues with his Maker,
Though naught but a potsherd of earth!

מה כֹּה־אָמַ֨ר יְהֹוָה֙ לִמְשִׁיחוֹ֙
לְכ֣וֹרֶשׁ
אֲשֶׁר־הֶחֱזַ֣קְתִּי בִֽימִינ֗וֹ
לְרַד־לְפָנָיו֙ גּוֹיִ֔ם
וּמׇתְנֵ֥י מְלָכִ֖ים אֲפַתֵּ֑חַ
לִפְתֹּ֤חַ לְפָנָיו֙ דְּלָתַ֔יִם
וּשְׁעָרִ֖ים לֹ֥א יִסָּגֵֽרוּ׃
²אֲנִי֙ לְפָנֶ֣יךָ
אֵלֵ֔ךְ וַהֲדוּרִ֖ים אושר אֲיַשֵּׁ֑ר
דַּלְת֤וֹת נְחוּשָׁה֙ אֲשַׁבֵּ֔ר
וּבְרִיחֵ֥י בַרְזֶ֖ל אֲגַדֵּֽעַ׃
³וְנָתַתִּ֤י לְךָ֙ אוֹצְר֣וֹת חֹ֔שֶׁךְ
וּמַטְמֻנֵ֖י מִסְתָּרִ֑ים
לְמַ֣עַן תֵּדַ֗ע כִּֽי־אֲנִ֧י יְהֹוָ֛ה
הַקּוֹרֵ֥א בְשִׁמְךָ֖ אֱלֹהֵ֥י יִשְׂרָאֵֽל׃
⁴לְמַ֙עַן֙ עַבְדִּ֣י יַעֲקֹ֔ב
וְיִשְׂרָאֵ֖ל בְּחִירִ֑י
וָאֶקְרָ֤א לְךָ֙ בִּשְׁמֶ֔ךָ
אֲכַנְּךָ֖ וְלֹ֥א יְדַעְתָּֽנִי׃
⁵אֲנִ֤י יְהֹוָה֙ וְאֵ֣ין ע֔וֹד
זוּלָתִ֖י אֵ֣ין אֱלֹהִ֑ים
אֲאַזֶּרְךָ֖ וְלֹ֥א יְדַעְתָּֽנִי׃
⁶לְמַ֣עַן יֵדְע֗וּ מִמִּזְרַח־שֶׁ֙מֶשׁ֙ וּמִמַּ֣עֲרָבָ֔ה
כִּי־אֶ֖פֶס בִּלְעָדָ֑י
אֲנִ֥י יְהֹוָ֖ה וְאֵ֥ין עֽוֹד׃
⁷יוֹצֵ֥ר אוֹר֙ וּבוֹרֵ֣א חֹ֔שֶׁךְ
עֹשֶׂ֥ה שָׁל֖וֹם וּב֣וֹרֵא רָ֑ע
אֲנִ֥י יְהֹוָ֖ה עֹשֶׂ֥ה כׇל־אֵֽלֶּה׃ ס
⁸הַרְעִ֤יפוּ שָׁמַ֙יִם֙ מִמַּ֔עַל
וּשְׁחָקִ֖ים יִזְּלוּ־צֶ֑דֶק
תִּפְתַּח־אֶ֤רֶץ וְיִפְרוּ־יֶ֙שַׁע֙
וּצְדָקָ֣ה תַצְמִ֣יחַ יַ֔חַד
אֲנִ֥י יְהֹוָ֖ה בְּרָאתִֽיו׃ ס

⁹ה֗וֹי רָ֚ב אֶת־יֹ֣צְר֔וֹ
חֶ֖רֶשׂ אֶת־חַרְשֵׂ֣י אֲדָמָ֑ה

---

a-a *Heb. "I have." Cf. note at 8.11.*
b-b *I.e., I made them helpless; one who wished to move freely belted his garment around the waist; cf. "engird," v. 5.*
c-c *Meaning of Heb. uncertain.*

הֲיֹאמַ֤ר חֹ֙מֶר֙ לְיֹ֣צְר֔וֹ מַֽה־תַּעֲשֶׂ֑ה

Shall the clay say to the potter, "What are you doing?

 וּפָעָלְךָ֖ אֵין־יָדַ֥יִם לֽוֹ: ס

d-Your work has no handles"?-d

10 ה֛וֹי אֹמֵ֥ר לְאָ֖ב מַה־תּוֹלִ֑יד

10Shame on him who asks his father, "What are you begetting?"

וּלְאִשָּׁ֖ה מַה־תְּחִילִֽין: ס

Or a woman, "What are you bearing?"

11 כֹּֽה־אָמַ֤ר יְהוָה֙

11Thus said the Lord,

קְד֤וֹשׁ יִשְׂרָאֵל֙ וְיֹ֣צְר֔וֹ

Israel's Holy One and Maker:

הָאֹתִיּ֖וֹת שְׁאָל֑וּנִי עַל־בָּנַ֛י

e-Will you question Me-e on the destiny of My children,

וְעַל־פֹּ֥עַל יָדַ֖י תְּצַוֻּֽנִי:

Will you instruct Me about the work of My hands?

12 אָ֣נֹכִי֙ עָשִׂ֣יתִי אֶ֔רֶץ

12It was I who made the earth

וְאָדָ֖ם עָלֶ֣יהָ בָרָ֑אתִי

And created man upon it;

אֲנִ֗י יָדַי֙ נָט֣וּ שָׁמַ֔יִם

My own hands stretched out the heavens,

וְכָל־צְבָאָ֖ם צִוֵּֽיתִי:

And I marshaled all their host.

13 אָנֹכִ֞י הַעִירֹתִ֤הֽוּ בְצֶ֙דֶק֙

13It was I who roused himf for victory

וְכָל־דְּרָכָ֖יו אֲיַשֵּׁ֑ר

And who level all roads for him.

הֽוּא־יִבְנֶ֤ה עִירִי֙

He shall rebuild My city

וְגָל֣וּתִ֣י יְשַׁלֵּ֔חַ

And let My exiled people go

לֹ֤א בִמְחִיר֙ וְלֹ֣א בְשֹׁ֔חַד

Without price and without payment

אָמַ֖ר יְהוָ֥ה צְבָאֽוֹת: פ

—said the Lord of Hosts.

14 כֹּ֣ה ׀ אָמַ֣ר יְהוָ֗ה

14Thus said the Lord:

יְגִ֨יעַ מִצְרַ֜יִם וּֽסְחַר־כּ֣וּשׁ

Egypt's wealth and Nubia's gains

וּסְבָאִים֮ אַנְשֵׁ֣י מִדָּה֒

And Sabaites, g-long of limb,-g

עָלַ֤יִךְ יַעֲבֹ֙רוּ֙ וְלָ֣ךְ יִֽהְי֔וּ

Shall pass over to you and be yours,

אַחֲרַ֣יִךְ יֵלֵ֔כוּ בַּזִּקִּ֖ים יַעֲבֹ֑רוּ

Pass over and follow you in fetters,

וְאֵלַ֤יִךְ יִֽשְׁתַּחֲווּ֙

Bow low to you

אֵלַ֣יִךְ יִתְפַּלָּ֔לוּ

And reverently address you:

אַ֣ךְ בָּ֥ךְ אֵ֖ל

"Only among you is God,

וְאֵ֣ין ע֔וֹד אֶ֖פֶס אֱלֹהִֽים:

There is no other god at all!

15 אָכֵ֕ן אַתָּ֖ה אֵ֣ל מִסְתַּתֵּ֑ר

15You are indeed a God who concealed Him- self,

אֱלֹהֵ֥י יִשְׂרָאֵ֖ל מוֹשִֽׁיעַ:

O God of Israel, who bring victory!

16 בּ֥וֹשׁוּ וְגַֽם־נִכְלְמ֖וּ כֻּלָּ֑ם

16Those who fabricate idols,

יַחְדָּ֛ו הָלְכ֥וּ בַכְּלִמָּ֖ה

All are shamed and disgraced;

---

d-d   *Emendation yields* "To its maker, 'You have no hands'?"

e-e   *Heb. imperative.*

f   *I.e., Cyrus.*

g-g   *Emendation yields* "bearing tribute." *For* "tribute" *cf. Ezra 4.20; 6.8; Neh. 5.4.*

To a man, they slink away in disgrace.
17But Israel has won through the LORD
Triumph everlasting.
You shall not be shamed or disgraced
In all the ages to come!"

18For thus said the LORD,
The Creator of heaven who alone is God,
Who formed the earth and made it,
Who alone established it—
He did not create it a waste,
But formed it for habitation:
I am the LORD, and there is none else.
19I did not speak in secret,
At a site in a land of darkness;
I did not say to the stock of Jacob,
"Seek Me out in a wasteland"—
I the LORD, who foretell reliably,
Who announce what is true.

20Come, gather together,
Draw nigh, you remnants of the nations!
No foreknowledge had they who carry their
   wooden images
And pray to a god who cannot give success.
21Speak up, compare testimony—
Let them even take counsel together!
Who announced this aforetime,
Foretold it of old?
Was it not I the LORD?
Then there is no god beside Me,
No God exists beside Me
Who foretells truly and grants success.
22Turn to Me and gain success,
All the ends of earth!
For I am God, and there is none else.
23By Myself have I sworn,
From My mouth has issued truth,
A word that shall not turn back:

חָרָשֵׁי צִירִים:
17 יִשְׂרָאֵל נוֹשַׁע בַּיהוָה
תְּשׁוּעַת עוֹלָמִים
לֹא־תֵבֹשׁוּ וְלֹא־תִכָּלְמוּ
עַד־עוֹלְמֵי עַד: פ

18 כִּי כֹה אָמַר־יְהוָה
בּוֹרֵא הַשָּׁמַיִם הוּא הָאֱלֹהִים
יֹצֵר הָאָרֶץ וְעֹשָׂהּ
הוּא כוֹנְנָהּ
לֹא־תֹהוּ בְרָאָהּ
לָשֶׁבֶת יְצָרָהּ
אֲנִי יְהוָה וְאֵין עוֹד:
19 לֹא בַסֵּתֶר דִּבַּרְתִּי
בִּמְקוֹם אֶרֶץ חֹשֶׁךְ
לֹא אָמַרְתִּי לְזֶרַע יַעֲקֹב
תֹּהוּ בַקְּשׁוּנִי
אֲנִי יְהוָה דֹּבֵר צֶדֶק
מַגִּיד מֵישָׁרִים:

20 הִקָּבְצוּ וָבֹאוּ
הִתְנַגְּשׁוּ יַחְדָּו פְּלִיטֵי הַגּוֹיִם
לֹא יָדְעוּ הַנֹּשְׂאִים אֶת־עֵץ פִּסְלָם
וּמִתְפַּלְלִים אֶל־אֵל לֹא יוֹשִׁיעַ:
21 הַגִּידוּ וְהַגִּישׁוּ
אַף יִוָּעֲצוּ יַחְדָּו
מִי הִשְׁמִיעַ זֹאת מִקֶּדֶם
מֵאָז הִגִּידָהּ
הֲלוֹא אֲנִי יְהוָה
וְאֵין־עוֹד אֱלֹהִים מִבַּלְעָדַי
אֵל־צַדִּיק וּמוֹשִׁיעַ
אַיִן זוּלָתִי:
22 פְּנוּ־אֵלַי וְהִוָּשְׁעוּ
כָּל־אַפְסֵי־אָרֶץ
כִּי אֲנִי־אֵל וְאֵין עוֹד:
23 בִּי נִשְׁבַּעְתִּי
יָצָא מִפִּי צְדָקָה
דָּבָר וְלֹא יָשׁוּב

To Me every knee shall bend,
Every tongue swear loyalty.
24h-They shall say: "Only through the LORD
Can I find victory and might.-h
When people i-trust in-i Him,
All their adversaries are put to shame.
25It is through the LORD that all the offspring
    of Israel
Have vindication and glory."

כִּי־לִי֙ תִּכְרַ֣ע כָּל־בֶּ֔רֶךְ
תִּשָּׁבַ֖ע כָּל־לָשֽׁוֹן׃
24 אַ֣ךְ בַּיהֹוָ֗ה
לִ֤י אָמַר֙ צְדָק֣וֹת וָעֹ֔ז
עָדָ֥יו יָב֖וֹא*
וְיֵבֹ֕שׁוּ כֹּ֖ל הַנֶּחֱרִ֥ים בּֽוֹ׃
25 בַּיהֹוָ֛ה יִצְדְּק֥וּ וְיִֽתְהַלְל֖וּ
כָּל־זֶ֥רַע יִשְׂרָאֵֽל׃

46

46 Bela is bowed, Neboa is cowering,
Their images are a burden for beasts and
    cattle;
The things youb would carry [in procession]
Are now piled as a burden
On tired [beasts].
2They cowered, they bowed as well,
They could not rescue the burden,c
And they themselves went into captivity.

מו כָּרַ֥ע בֵּל֙ קֹרֵ֣ס נְב֔וֹ
הָיוּ֙ עֲצַבֵּיהֶ֔ם לַחַיָּ֖ה וְלַבְּהֵמָ֑ה
נְשֻׂאֹתֵיכֶ֣ם
עֲמוּס֔וֹת מַשָּׂ֖א
לַעֲיֵפָֽה׃
2 קָרְס֤וּ כָֽרְעוּ֙ יַחְדָּ֔ו
לֹ֥א יָֽכְל֖וּ מַלֵּ֣ט מַשָּׂ֑א
וְנַפְשָׁ֖ם בַּשְּׁבִ֥י הָלָֽכָה׃ ס

3Listen to Me, O House of Jacob,
All that are left of the House of Israel,
Who have been carried since birth,
Supported since leaving the womb:
4Till you grow old, I will still be the same;
When you turn gray, it is I who will carry;
I was the Maker, and I will be the Bearer;
And I will carry and rescue [you].

3 שִׁמְע֤וּ אֵלַי֙ בֵּ֣ית יַֽעֲקֹ֔ב
וְכָל־שְׁאֵרִ֖ית בֵּ֣ית יִשְׂרָאֵ֑ל
הַֽעֲמֻסִים֙ מִנִּי־בֶ֔טֶן
הַנְּשֻׂאִ֖ים מִנִּי־רָֽחַם׃
4 וְעַד־זִקְנָה֙ אֲנִ֣י ה֔וּא
וְעַד־שֵׂיבָ֖ה אֲנִ֣י אֶסְבֹּ֑ל
אֲנִ֤י עָשִׂ֨יתִי֙ וַאֲנִ֣י אֶשָּׂ֔א
וַאֲנִ֥י אֶסְבֹּ֖ל וַאֲמַלֵּֽט׃ ס

5To whom can you compare Me
Or declare Me similar?
To whom can you liken Me,
So that we seem comparable?
6Those who squander gold from the purse
And weigh out silver on the balance,d

5 לְמִ֥י תְדַמְי֖וּנִי
וְתַשְׁו֑וּ
וְתַמְשִׁל֖וּנִי
וְנִדְמֶֽה׃
6 הַזָּלִ֤ים זָהָב֙ מִכִּ֔יס
וְכֶ֖סֶף בַּקָּנֶ֣ה יִשְׁקֹ֑לוּ

---

h-h   *Emendation yields "Only in the LORD / Are there victory and*
     might for man."
i-i   *Lit. "come to"; for this idiom cf. Ps. 65.3; Job 6.20.*

a   *Babylonian deities.*
b   *Emendation yields "they."*
c   *Emendation yields "him who carried [them]"; cf. Targum.*
d   *Lit. "beam [of the balance]."*

v. 24. סבירין ומטעין לשון רבים

They hire a metal worker to make it into a
  god,
To which they bow down and prostrate them-
  selves.
⁷They must carry it on their backs and trans-
  port it;
When they put it down, it stands,
It does not budge from its place.
If they cry out to it, it does not answer;
It cannot save them from their distress.
⁸Keep this in mind, and ᵉ-stand firm!-ᵉ
Take this to heart, you sinners!
⁹Bear in mind what happened of old;
For I am God, and there is none else,
I am divine, and there is none like Me.
¹⁰I foretell the end from the beginning,
And from the start, things that had not oc-
  curred.
I say: My plan shall be fulfilled;
I will do all I have purposed.
¹¹I summoned that swooping bird from the
  East;ᶠ
From a distant land, the man for My purpose.
I have spoken, so I will bring it to pass;
I have designed it, so I will complete it.
¹²Listen to Me, you ᵍ-stubborn of heart,-ᵍ
Who are far from victory:
¹³I am bringing My victory close;
It shall not be far,
And My triumph shall not be delayed.
I will grant triumph in Zion
To Israel, in whom I glory.

47 Get down, sit in the dust,
Fair Maiden Babylon;
Sit, dethroned, on the ground,
O Fair Chaldea;
Nevermore shall they call you

יִשְׂכְּרוּ צוֹרֵף וְיַעֲשֵׂהוּ אֵל
יִסְגְּדוּ אַף־יִשְׁתַּחֲוּוּ׃
⁷יִשָּׂאֻהוּ עַל־כָּתֵף יִסְבְּלֻהוּ
וְיַנִּיחֻהוּ תַחְתָּיו וְיַעֲמֹד
מִמְּקוֹמוֹ לֹא יָמִישׁ
אַף־יִצְעַק אֵלָיו וְלֹא יַעֲנֶה
מִצָּרָתוֹ לֹא יוֹשִׁיעֶנּוּ׃ ס
⁸זִכְרוּ־זֹאת וְהִתְאֹשָׁשׁוּ
הָשִׁיבוּ פוֹשְׁעִים עַל־לֵב׃
⁹זִכְרוּ רִאשֹׁנוֹת מֵעוֹלָם
כִּי אָנֹכִי אֵל וְאֵין עוֹד
אֱלֹהִים וְאֶפֶס כָּמוֹנִי׃
¹⁰מַגִּיד מֵרֵאשִׁית אַחֲרִית
וּמִקֶּדֶם אֲשֶׁר לֹא־נַעֲשׂוּ
אֹמֵר עֲצָתִי תָקוּם
וְכָל־חֶפְצִי אֶעֱשֶׂה׃
¹¹קֹרֵא מִמִּזְרָח עַיִט
מֵאֶרֶץ מֶרְחָק אִישׁ עצתו עֲצָתִי
אַף־דִּבַּרְתִּי אַף־אֲבִיאֶנָּה
יָצַרְתִּי אַף־אֶעֱשֶׂנָּה׃ ס
¹²שִׁמְעוּ אֵלַי אַבִּירֵי לֵב
הָרְחוֹקִים מִצְּדָקָה׃
¹³קֵרַבְתִּי צִדְקָתִי
לֹא תִרְחָק
וּתְשׁוּעָתִי לֹא תְאַחֵר
וְנָתַתִּי בְצִיּוֹן תְּשׁוּעָה
לְיִשְׂרָאֵל תִּפְאַרְתִּי׃ ס

מז רְדִי ׀ וּשְׁבִי עַל־עָפָר
בְּתוּלַת בַּת־בָּבֶל
שְׁבִי־לָאָרֶץ אֵין־כִּסֵּא
בַּת־כַּשְׂדִּים
כִּי לֹא תוֹסִיפִי יִקְרְאוּ־לָךְ

ᵉ-ᵉ *Meaning of Heb. uncertain.*
ᶠ *I.e., Cyrus; cf. 41.2–3; 44.28–45.1.*
ᵍ-ᵍ *Septuagint reads, "who have lost heart."*

955

The tender and dainty one.
²Grasp the handmill and grind meal.
Remove your veil,
Strip off your train, bare your leg,
Wade through the rivers.
³Your nakedness shall be uncovered,
And your shame shall be exposed.
I will take vengeance,
a-And let no man intercede.
⁴Our Redeemer—LORD of Hosts is His
    name—
Is the Holy One of Israel.-*a*
⁵Sit silent; retire into darkness,
O Fair Chaldea;
Nevermore shall they call you
Mistress of Kingdoms.

⁶I was angry at My people,
I defiled My heritage;
I put them into your hands,
But you showed them no mercy.
Even upon the aged you made
Your yoke exceedingly heavy.
⁷You thought, "I shall always be
The mistress still."
You did not take these things to heart,
You gave no thought to the end of it.

⁸And now hear this, O pampered one—
Who dwell in security,
Who think to yourself,
"I am, and there is none but me;
I shall not become a widow
Or know loss of children"—
⁹These two things shall come upon you,
Suddenly, in one day:
Loss of children and widowhood
Shall come upon you in full measure,

רַכָּה וַעֲנֻגָּה:
²קְחִי רֵחַיִם וְטַחֲנִי קָמַח
גַּלִּי צַמָּתֵךְ
חֶשְׂפִּי־שֹׁבֶל גַּלִּי־שׁוֹק
עִבְרִי נְהָרוֹת:
³תִּגָּל עֶרְוָתֵךְ
גַּם תֵּרָאֶה חֶרְפָּתֵךְ
נָקָם אֶקָּח
וְלֹא אֶפְגַּע אָדָם: ס
⁴גֹּאֲלֵנוּ יְהוָה צְבָאוֹת שְׁמוֹ
קְדוֹשׁ יִשְׂרָאֵל:
⁵שְׁבִי דוּמָם וּבֹאִי בַחֹשֶׁךְ
בַּת־כַּשְׂדִּים
כִּי לֹא תוֹסִיפִי יִקְרְאוּ־לָךְ
גְּבֶרֶת מַמְלָכוֹת:

⁶קָצַפְתִּי עַל־עַמִּי
חִלַּלְתִּי נַחֲלָתִי
וָאֶתְּנֵם בְּיָדֵךְ
לֹא־שַׂמְתְּ לָהֶם רַחֲמִים
עַל־זָקֵן
הִכְבַּדְתְּ עֻלֵּךְ מְאֹד:
⁷וַתֹּאמְרִי לְעוֹלָם
אֶהְיֶה גְבָרֶת
עַד לֹא־שַׂמְתְּ אֵלֶּה עַל־לִבֵּךְ
לֹא זָכַרְתְּ אַחֲרִיתָהּ: ס

⁸וְעַתָּה שִׁמְעִי־זֹאת עֲדִינָה
הַיּוֹשֶׁבֶת לָבֶטַח
הָאֹמְרָה בִּלְבָבָהּ
אֲנִי וְאַפְסִי עוֹד
לֹא אֵשֵׁב אַלְמָנָה
וְלֹא אֵדַע שְׁכוֹל:
⁹וְתָבֹאנָה לָּךְ שְׁתֵּי־אֵלֶּה
רֶגַע בְּיוֹם אֶחָד
שְׁכוֹל וְאַלְמֹן
כְּתֻמָּם בָּאוּ עָלַיִךְ

---

a-a   *Meaning of Heb. uncertain; emendation yields "And not be*
     appeased, / Says our Redeemer, whose name is LORD *of Hosts,*
     / *The Holy One of Israel."*

Despite your many enchantments
And all your countless spells.
10You were secure in your wickedness;
You thought, "No one can see me."
It was your skill and your science
That led you astray.
And you thought to yourself,
"I am, and there is none but me."
11Evil is coming upon you
Which you will not know how to b-charm
   away;-b
Disaster is falling upon you
Which you will not be able to appease;
Coming upon you suddenly
Is ruin of which you know nothing.
12Stand up, with your spells and your many
   enchantments
On which you labored since youth!
Perhaps you'll be able to profit,
Perhaps you c-will find strength.-c
13You are helpless, despite all your art.
Let them stand up and help you now,
The scannersd of heaven, the star-gazers,
Who announce, month by month,
Whatever will come upon you.
14See, they are become like straw,
Fire consumes them;
They cannot save themselves
From the power of the flame;
This is no coal for warming oneself,
No fire to sit by!
15This is what they have profited you—
The traders you dealt with since youth—
Each has wandered off his own way,
There is none to save you.

בְּרֹב כְּשָׁפַיִךְ
בְּעָצְמַת חֲבָרַיִךְ מְאֹד׃
10 וַתִּבְטְחִי בְרָעָתֵךְ
אָמַרְתְּ אֵין רֹאָנִי
חָכְמָתֵךְ וְדַעְתֵּךְ
הִיא שׁוֹבְבָתֶךְ
וַתֹּאמְרִי בְלִבֵּךְ
אֲנִי וְאַפְסִי עוֹד׃
11 וּבָא עָלַיִךְ רָעָה
לֹא תֵדְעִי שַׁחְרָהּ
וְתִפֹּל עָלַיִךְ הֹוָה
לֹא תוּכְלִי כַּפְּרָהּ
וְתָבֹא עָלַיִךְ פִּתְאֹם
שׁוֹאָה לֹא תֵדָעִי׃
12 עִמְדִי־נָא בַחֲבָרַיִךְ וּבְרֹב כְּשָׁפַיִךְ
בַּאֲשֶׁר יָגַעַתְּ מִנְּעוּרָיִךְ
אוּלַי תּוּכְלִי הוֹעִיל
אוּלַי תַּעֲרוֹצִי׃
13 נִלְאֵית בְּרֹב עֲצָתָיִךְ
יַעַמְדוּ־נָא וְיוֹשִׁיעֻךְ
הֹבְרֵי שָׁמַיִם הַחֹזִים בַּכּוֹכָבִים
מוֹדִיעִם לֶחֳדָשִׁים
מֵאֲשֶׁר יָבֹאוּ עָלָיִךְ׃
14 הִנֵּה הָיוּ כְקַשׁ
אֵשׁ שְׂרָפָתַם
לֹא־יַצִּילוּ אֶת־נַפְשָׁם
מִיַּד לֶהָבָה
אֵין־גַּחֶלֶת לַחְמָם
אוּר לָשֶׁבֶת נֶגְדּוֹ׃
15 כֵּן הָיוּ־לָךְ אֲשֶׁר יָגָעַתְּ
סֹחֲרַיִךְ מִנְּעוּרַיִךְ
אִישׁ לְעֶבְרוֹ תָּעוּ
אֵין מוֹשִׁיעֵךְ׃ ס

48 Listen to this, O House of Jacob,
    Who bear the name Israel

מח שִׁמְעוּ־זֹאת בֵּית־יַעֲקֹב
הַנִּקְרָאִים בְּשֵׁם יִשְׂרָאֵל

b-b   Meaning of Heb. uncertain. Emendation yields "bribe."
c-c   Taking 'araṣ as a variant of 'aṣar; cf. 2 Chron. 20.37.
d   Meaning of Heb. uncertain.

And have issued from the waters[a] of Judah,
Who swear by the name of the LORD
And invoke the God of Israel—
Though not in truth and sincerity—
²For you[b] are called after [c]the Holy City[c]
And you[b] do lean on the God of Israel,
Whose name is LORD of Hosts:

³Long ago, I foretold things that happened,
From My mouth they issued, and I announced them;
Suddenly I acted, and they came to pass.
⁴Because I know how stubborn you are
(Your neck is like an iron sinew
And your forehead bronze),
⁵Therefore I told you long beforehand,
Announced things to you ere they happened—
That you might not say, "My idol caused
   them,
My carved and molten images ordained
   them."
⁶You have [d]heard all this; look, must you not
   acknowledge it?[d]
As of now, I announce to you new things,
Well-guarded secrets you did not know.
⁷Only now are they created, and not of old;
[d]Before today[d] you had not heard them;
You cannot say, "I knew them already."
⁸You had never heard, you had never known,
Your ears were not opened of old.

Though I know that you are treacherous,
That you were called a rebel from birth,
⁹For the sake of My name I control My wrath;
To My own glory, [d]I am patient[d] with you,
And I will not destroy you.
¹⁰See, I refine you, but not as silver;

וּמִמֵּ֥י יְהוּדָ֖ה יָצָ֑אוּ
הַנִּשְׁבָּעִ֣ים ׀ בְּשֵׁ֣ם יְהֹוָ֗ה
וּבֵאלֹהֵ֤י יִשְׂרָאֵל֙ יַזְכִּ֔ירוּ
לֹ֥א בֶאֱמֶ֖ת וְלֹ֥א בִצְדָקָֽה׃
2 כִּֽי־מֵעִ֤יר הַקֹּ֙דֶשׁ֙ נִקְרָ֔אוּ
וְעַל־אֱלֹהֵ֥י יִשְׂרָאֵ֖ל נִסְמָ֑כוּ
יְהֹוָ֥ה צְבָא֖וֹת שְׁמֽוֹ׃ ס

3 הָרִֽאשֹׁנוֹת֙ מֵאָ֣ז הִגַּ֔דְתִּי
וּמִפִּ֥י יָצְא֖וּ וְאַשְׁמִיעֵ֑ם
פִּתְאֹ֥ם עָשִׂ֖יתִי וַתָּבֹֽאנָה׃
4 מִדַּעְתִּ֕י כִּ֥י קָשֶׁ֖ה אָ֑תָּה
וְגִ֤יד בַּרְזֶל֙ עׇרְפֶּ֔ךָ
וּמִצְחֲךָ֖ נְחוּשָֽׁה׃
5 וָאַגִּ֤יד לְךָ֙ מֵאָ֔ז
בְּטֶ֥רֶם תָּב֖וֹא הִשְׁמַעְתִּ֑יךָ
פֶּן־תֹּאמַר֙ עׇצְבִּ֣י עָשָׂ֔ם
וּפִסְלִ֥י וְנִסְכִּ֖י צִוָּֽם׃
6 שָׁמַ֤עְתָּ חֲזֵה֙ כֻּלָּ֔הּ וְאַתֶּ֖ם הֲל֣וֹא תַגִּ֑ידוּ
הִשְׁמַעְתִּ֤יךָ חֲדָשׁוֹת֙ מֵעַ֔תָּה
וּנְצֻר֖וֹת וְלֹ֥א יְדַעְתָּֽם׃
7 עַתָּ֤ה נִבְרְאוּ֙ וְלֹ֣א מֵאָ֔ז
וְלִפְנֵי־י֖וֹם וְלֹ֣א שְׁמַעְתָּ֑ם
פֶּן־תֹּאמַ֖ר הִנֵּ֥ה יְדַעְתִּֽין׃
8 גַּ֣ם לֹֽא־שָׁמַ֗עְתָּ גַּ֚ם לֹ֣א יָדַ֔עְתָּ
גַּ֕ם מֵאָ֖ז לֹא־פִתְּחָ֣ה אׇזְנֶ֑ךָ

כִּ֤י יָדַ֙עְתִּי֙ בָּג֣וֹד תִּבְגּ֔וֹד
וּפֹשֵׁ֥עַ מִבֶּ֖טֶן קֹ֥רָא לָֽךְ׃
9 לְמַ֤עַן שְׁמִי֙ אַאֲרִ֣יךְ אַפִּ֔י
וּתְהִלָּתִ֖י אֶחֱטׇם־לָ֑ךְ
לְבִלְתִּ֖י הַכְרִיתֶֽךָ׃
10 הִנֵּ֥ה צְרַפְתִּ֖יךָ וְלֹ֣א בְכָ֑סֶף

---

a   *Emendation yields "loins."*
b   *Heb. "they."*
c-c *Emendation yields "the holy people."*
d-d *Meaning of Heb. uncertain.*

I test you in the furnace of affliction.
[11]For My sake, My own sake, do I act—
Lest [My name]e be dishonored!
I will not give My glory to another.

בְּחַרְתִּ֖יךָ בְּכ֥וּר עֹֽנִי׃
11 לְמַעֲנִ֧י לְמַעֲנִ֛י אֶעֱשֶׂ֖ה
כִּ֣י אֵ֣יךְ יֵחָ֑ל
וּכְבוֹדִ֖י לְאַחֵ֥ר לֹֽא־אֶתֵּֽן׃ ס

[12]Listen to Me, O Jacob,
Israel, whom I have called:
I am He—I am the first,
And I am the last as well.
[13]My own hand founded the earth,
My right hand spread out the skies.

12 שְׁמַ֤ע אֵלַי֙ יַֽעֲקֹ֔ב
וְיִשְׂרָאֵ֖ל מְקֹרָאִ֑י
אֲנִי־הוּא֙ אֲנִ֣י רִאשׁ֔וֹן
אַ֖ף אֲנִ֥י אַחֲרֽוֹן׃
13 אַף־יָדִי֙ יָ֣סְדָה אֶ֔רֶץ
וִֽימִינִ֖י טִפְּחָ֣ה שָׁמָ֑יִם

I call unto them, let them stand up.
[14]Assemble, all of you, and listen!
Who among youf foretold these things:
d-"He whom the LORD loves
Shall work His will against Babylon,
And, with His might, against Chaldea"?-d
[15]I, I predicted, and I called him;
I have brought him and he shall succeed in
   his mission.
[16]Draw near to Me and hear this:
From the beginning, I did not speak in secret;
From the time anything existed, I was there.g

קֹרֵ֧א אֲנִ֛י אֲלֵיהֶ֖ם יַעַמְד֥וּ יַחְדָּֽו׃
14 הִקָּבְצ֤וּ כֻלְּכֶם֙ וּֽשֲׁמָ֔עוּ
מִ֥י בָהֶ֖ם הִגִּ֣יד אֶת־אֵ֑לֶּה
יְהוָ֣ה אֲהֵב֔וֹ
יַעֲשֶׂ֤ה חֶפְצוֹ֙ בְּבָבֶ֔ל
וּזְרֹע֖וֹ כַּשְׂדִּֽים׃
15 אֲנִ֥י אֲנִ֛י דִּבַּ֖רְתִּי אַף־קְרָאתִ֑יו
הֲבִאֹתִ֖יו וְהִצְלִ֥יחַ דַּרְכּֽוֹ׃
16 קִרְב֤וּ אֵלַי֙ שִׁמְעוּ־זֹ֔את
לֹ֤א מֵרֹאשׁ֙ בַּסֵּ֣תֶר דִּבַּ֔רְתִּי
מֵעֵ֥ת הֱיוֹתָ֖הּ שָׁ֣ם אָ֑נִי

"And now the Lord GOD has sent me,
   h-endowed with His spirit."-h

וְעַתָּ֗ה אֲדֹנָ֧י יְהוִ֛ה שְׁלָחַ֖נִי וְרוּחֽוֹ׃ פ

[17]Thus said the LORD your Redeemer,
The Holy One of Israel:
I the LORD am your God,
Instructing you for your own benefit.
Guiding you in the way you should go.
[18]If only you would heed My commands!
Then your prosperity would be like a river,
Your triumph like the waves of the sea.
[19]Your offspring would be as many as the
   sand,

17 כֹּֽה־אָמַ֧ר יְהוָ֛ה גֹּאַלְךָ֖
קְד֣וֹשׁ יִשְׂרָאֵ֑ל
אֲנִ֨י יְהוָ֤ה אֱלֹהֶ֨יךָ֙
מְלַמֶּדְךָ֣ לְהוֹעִ֔יל
מַדְרִֽיכֲךָ֖ בְּדֶ֥רֶךְ תֵּלֵֽךְ׃
18 ל֥וּא הִקְשַׁ֖בְתָּ לְמִצְוֹתָ֑י
וַיְהִ֤י כַנָּהָר֙ שְׁלוֹמֶ֔ךָ
וְצִדְקָֽתְךָ֖ כְּגַלֵּ֥י הַיָּֽם׃
19 וַיְהִ֤י כַחוֹל֙ זַרְעֶ֔ךָ

---

e   These words are supplied in some ancient versions; cf. v. 9.
f   Heb. "them."
g   I.e., I foretold it through prophets.
h-h Lit. "and His spirit."

Their issue as many as its grains.*d*

Their name would never be cut off

Or obliterated from before Me.

²⁰Go forth from Babylon,

Flee from Chaldea!

Declare this with loud shouting,

Announce this,

Bring out the word to the ends of the earth!

Say: "The LORD has redeemed

His servant Jacob!"

²¹They have known no thirst,

Though He led them through parched places;

He made water flow for them from the rock;

He cleaved the rock and water gushed forth.

²²There is no safety—said the LORD—for the
wicked.

49

Listen, O coastlands, to me,

And give heed, O nations afar:

The LORD appointed me before I was born,

He named me while I was in my mother's
womb.

²He made my mouth like a sharpened blade,

He hid me in the shadow of His hand,

And He made me like a polished arrow;

He concealed me in His quiver.

³And He said to me, "You are My servant,

Israel in whom I glory."

⁴I thought, "I have labored in vain,

I have spent my strength for empty breath."

But my case rested with the LORD,

My recompense was in the hands of my God.

⁵And now the LORD has resolved—

He who formed me in the womb to be His
servant—

To bring back Jacob to Himself,

וְצֶאֱצָאֵי מֵעֶיךָ כִּמְעֹתָיו

לֹא־יִכָּרֵת וְלֹא־יִשָּׁמֵד

שְׁמוֹ מִלְּפָנָי:

20 צְאוּ מִבָּבֶל֩

בִּרְחוּ מִכַּשְׂדִּים

בְּקוֹל רִנָּה הַגִּידוּ

הַשְׁמִיעוּ זֹאת

הוֹצִיאוּהָ עַד־קְצֵה הָאָרֶץ

אִמְרוּ גָּאַל יְהוָה

עַבְדּוֹ יַעֲקֹב:

21 וְלֹא צָמְאוּ

בָּחֳרָבוֹת הוֹלִיכָם

מַיִם מִצּוּר הִזִּיל לָמוֹ

וַיִּבְקַע־צוּר וַיָּזֻבוּ מָיִם:

22 אֵין שָׁלוֹם אָמַר יְהוָה לָרְשָׁעִים: ס

מט

שִׁמְעוּ אִיִּים אֵלַי

וְהַקְשִׁיבוּ לְאֻמִּים מֵרָחוֹק

יְהוָה מִבֶּטֶן קְרָאָנִי

מִמְּעֵי אִמִּי הִזְכִּיר שְׁמִי:

2 וַיָּשֶׂם פִּי כְּחֶרֶב חַדָּה

בְּצֵל יָדוֹ הֶחְבִּיאָנִי

וַיְשִׂימֵנִי לְחֵץ בָּרוּר

בְּאַשְׁפָּתוֹ הִסְתִּירָנִי:

3 וַיֹּאמֶר לִי עַבְדִּי־אָתָּה

יִשְׂרָאֵל אֲשֶׁר־בְּךָ אֶתְפָּאָר:

4 וַאֲנִי אָמַרְתִּי לְרִיק יָגַעְתִּי

לְתֹהוּ וְהֶבֶל כֹּחִי כִלֵּיתִי

אָכֵן מִשְׁפָּטִי אֶת־יְהוָה

וּפְעֻלָּתִי אֶת־אֱלֹהָי:

5 וְעַתָּה ׀ אָמַר יְהוָה

יֹצְרִי מִבֶּטֶן לְעֶבֶד לוֹ

לְשׁוֹבֵב יַעֲקֹב אֵלָיו

וְיִשְׂרָאֵל לֹא יֵאָסֵף

That Israel may be restored to Him.
And I have been honored in the sight of the
   LORD,
My God has been my strength.
⁶For He has said:
"It is too little that you should be My servant
In that I raise up the tribes of Jacob
And restore the survivors of Israel:
I will also make you a light*ᵃ* of nations,
That My salvation may reach the ends of the
   earth."

⁷Thus said the LORD,
The Redeemer of Israel, his Holy One,
*ᵇ-*To the despised one,
To the abhorred nations,*-ᵇ*
To the slave of rulers:
Kings shall see and stand up;
Nobles, and they shall prostrate themselves—
To the honor of the LORD, who is faithful,
To the Holy One of Israel who chose you.
⁸Thus said the LORD:
In an hour of favor I answer you,
And on a day of salvation I help you—
I created you and appointed you *ᶜ-*a covenant
   people*-ᶜ*—
Restoring the land,
Allotting anew the desolate holdings,
⁹Saying to the prisoners, "Go free,"
To those who are in darkness, "Show your-
   selves."
They shall pasture along the roads,
On every bare height shall be their pasture.
¹⁰They shall not hunger or thirst,
Hot wind and sun shall not strike them;
For He who loves them will lead them,
He will guide them to springs of water.
¹¹I will make all My mountains a road,

וְאֶכָּבֵד בְּעֵינֵי יְהוָה
וֵאלֹהַי הָיָה עֻזִּי:
⁶ וַיֹּאמֶר
נָקֵל מִהְיוֹתְךָ לִי עֶבֶד
לְהָקִים אֶת־שִׁבְטֵי יַעֲקֹב
וּנְצִירֵי יִשְׂרָאֵל לְהָשִׁיב
וּנְתַתִּיךָ לְאוֹר גּוֹיִם
לִהְיוֹת יְשׁוּעָתִי עַד־קְצֵה הָאָרֶץ: ס

⁷ כֹּה אָמַר־יְהוָה
גֹּאֵל יִשְׂרָאֵל קְדוֹשׁוֹ
לִבְזֹה־נֶפֶשׁ
לִמְתָעֵב גּוֹי
לְעֶבֶד מֹשְׁלִים
מְלָכִים יִרְאוּ וָקָמוּ
שָׂרִים וְיִשְׁתַּחֲווּ
לְמַעַן יְהוָה אֲשֶׁר נֶאֱמָן
קְדֹשׁ יִשְׂרָאֵל וַיִּבְחָרֶךָ:
⁸ כֹּה ׀ אָמַר יְהוָה
בְּעֵת רָצוֹן עֲנִיתִיךָ
וּבְיוֹם יְשׁוּעָה עֲזַרְתִּיךָ
וְאֶצָּרְךָ וְאֶתֶּנְךָ לִבְרִית עָם
לְהָקִים אֶרֶץ
לְהַנְחִיל נְחָלוֹת שֹׁמֵמוֹת:
⁹ לֵאמֹר לַאֲסוּרִים צֵאוּ
לַאֲשֶׁר בַּחֹשֶׁךְ הִגָּלוּ
עַל־דְּרָכִים יִרְעוּ
וּבְכָל־שְׁפָיִים מַרְעִיתָם:
¹⁰ לֹא יִרְעָבוּ וְלֹא יִצְמָאוּ
וְלֹא־יַכֵּם שָׁרָב וָשָׁמֶשׁ
כִּי־מְרַחֲמָם יְנַהֲגֵם
וְעַל־מַבּוּעֵי מַיִם יְנַהֲלֵם:
¹¹ וְשַׂמְתִּי כָל־הָרַי לַדֶּרֶךְ

---

a   *I.e., the agent of good fortune; cf. 42.1–4; 51.4–5.*
b-b *Meaning of Heb. uncertain. Emendation yields "Whose being
    is despised, / Whose body is detested"; cf. 51.23.*
c-c *See note b-b at 42.6.*

And My highways shall be built up.

¹²Look! These are coming from afar,

These from the north and the west,

And these from the land of Sinim.ᵈ

¹³Shout, O heavens, and rejoice, O earth!

Break into shouting, O hills!

For the Lᴏʀᴅ has comforted His people,

And has taken back His afflicted ones in love.

¹⁴Zion says,

"The Lᴏʀᴅ has forsaken me,

My Lord has forgotten me."

¹⁵Can a woman forget her baby,

Or disown the child of her womb?

Though she might forget,

I never could forget you.

¹⁶See, I have engraved you

On the palms of My hands,

Your walls are ever before Me.

¹⁷Swiftly your children are coming;

Those who ravaged and ruined you shall leave you.

¹⁸Look up all around you and see:

They are all assembled, are come to you!

As I live

      —declares the Lᴏʀᴅ—

You shall don them all like jewels,

Deck yourself with them like a bride.

¹⁹As for your ruins and desolate places

And your land laid waste—

You shall soon be crowded with settlers,

While destroyers stay far from you.

²⁰The children ᵉ-you thought you had lost-ᵉ

Shall yet say in your hearing,

"The place is too crowded for me;

Make room for me to settle."

²¹And you will say to yourself,

"Who bore these for me

When I was bereaved and barren,

ד 1QIsᵃ reads "the Syenians"; cf. Ezek. 30.6.

e-e Lit. "of your bereavement."

וּמְסִלֹּתַ֖י יְרֻמֽוּן׃

12 הִנֵּה־אֵ֙לֶּה֙ מֵרָח֣וֹק יָבֹ֔אוּ

וְהִנֵּה־אֵ֖לֶּה מִצָּפ֣וֹן וּמִיָּ֑ם

וְאֵ֖לֶּה מֵאֶ֥רֶץ סִינִֽים׃

13 רָנּ֤וּ שָׁמַ֙יִם֙ וְגִ֣ילִי אָ֔רֶץ

יִפְצְח֥וּ הָרִ֖ים רִנָּ֑ה

כִּֽי־נִחַ֤ם יְהֹוָה֙ עַמּ֔וֹ

וַעֲנִיָּ֖ו יְרַחֵֽם׃ ס

14 וַתֹּ֣אמֶר צִיּ֔וֹן

עֲזָבַ֖נִי יְהֹוָ֑ה

וַאדֹנָ֖י שְׁכֵחָֽנִי׃

15 הֲתִשְׁכַּ֤ח אִשָּׁה֙ עוּלָ֔הּ

מֵרַחֵ֖ם בֶּן־בִּטְנָ֑הּ

גַּם־אֵ֣לֶּה תִשְׁכַּ֔חְנָה

וְאָנֹכִ֖י לֹ֥א אֶשְׁכָּחֵֽךְ׃

16 הֵ֥ן עַל־כַּפַּ֖יִם

חַקֹּתִ֑יךְ

חוֹמֹתַ֖יִךְ נֶגְדִּ֥י תָּמִֽיד׃

17 מִֽהֲר֖וּ בָּנָ֑יִךְ

מְהָרְסַ֥יִךְ וּמַחֲרִבַ֖יִךְ מִמֵּ֥ךְ יֵצֵֽאוּ׃

18 שְׂאִֽי־סָבִ֤יב עֵינַ֙יִךְ֙ וּרְאִ֔י

כֻּלָּ֖ם נִקְבְּצ֣וּ בָֽאוּ־לָ֑ךְ

חַי־אָ֙נִי֙

נְאֻם־יְהֹוָ֔ה

כִּ֤י כֻלָּם֙ כָּעֲדִ֣י תִלְבָּ֔שִׁי

וּֽתְקַשְּׁרִ֖ים כַּכַּלָּֽה׃

19 כִּ֤י חָרְבֹתַ֙יִךְ֙ וְשֹׁ֣מְמֹתַ֔יִךְ

וְאֶ֖רֶץ הֲרִֻסְתֵ֑ךְ

כִּ֤י עַתָּה֙ תֵּצְרִ֣י מִיּוֹשֵׁ֔ב

וְרָחֲק֖וּ מְבַלְּעָֽיִךְ׃

20 ע֚וֹד יֹאמְר֣וּ בְאָזְנַ֔יִךְ

בְּנֵ֖י שִׁכֻּלָ֑יִךְ

צַר־לִ֥י הַמָּק֖וֹם

גְּשָׁה־לִּ֥י וְאֵשֵֽׁבָה׃

21 וְאָמַ֣רְתְּ בִּלְבָבֵ֗ךְ

מִ֤י יָֽלַד־לִי֙ אֶת־אֵ֔לֶּה

וַאֲנִ֥י שְׁכוּלָ֖ה וְגַלְמוּדָ֑ה

Exiled and disdained*f*—
By whom, then, were these reared?
I was left all alone—
And where have these been?"

גָּלָ֖ה ׀ וְסוּרָ֑ה
וְאֵ֖לֶּה מִ֣י גִדֵּ֔ל

הֵ֤ן אֲנִי֙ נִשְׁאַ֣רְתִּי לְבַדִּ֔י
אֵ֖לֶּה אֵיפֹ֥ה הֵֽם׃ פ

22Thus said the Lord God:
I will raise My hand to nations
And lift up My ensign to peoples;
And they shall bring your sons in their bos-
    oms,
And carry your daughters on their backs.
23Kings shall tend your children,
Their queens shall serve you as nurses.
They shall bow to you, face to the ground,
And lick the dust of your feet.
And you shall know that I am the Lord—
Those who trust in Me shall not be shamed.

22 כֹּֽה־אָמַ֞ר אֲדֹנָ֣י יְהֹוִ֗ה
הִנֵּ֨ה אֶשָּׂ֤א אֶל־גּוֹיִם֙ יָדִ֔י
וְאֶל־עַמִּ֖ים אָרִ֣ים נִסִּ֑י
וְהֵבִ֤יאוּ בָנַ֙יִךְ֙ בְּחֹ֔צֶן
וּבְנֹתַ֖יִךְ עַל־כָּתֵ֥ף תִּנָּשֶֽׂאנָה׃
23 וְהָי֨וּ מְלָכִ֜ים אֹֽמְנַ֗יִךְ
וְשָׂרֽוֹתֵיהֶם֙ מֵינִ֣יקֹתַ֔יִךְ
אַפַּ֗יִם אֶ֚רֶץ יִשְׁתַּ֣חֲווּ לָ֔ךְ
וַעֲפַ֥ר רַגְלַ֖יִךְ יְלַחֵ֑כוּ
וְיָדַ֙עַתְּ֙ כִּֽי־אֲנִ֣י יְהֹוָ֔ה
אֲשֶׁ֖ר לֹֽא־יֵבֹ֥שׁוּ קֹוָֽי׃ ס

24Can spoil be taken from a warrior,
Or captives retrieved from a victor?
25Yet thus said the Lord:
Captives shall be taken from a warrior
And spoil shall be retrieved from a tyrant;
For *I* will contend with your adversaries,
And *I* will deliver your children.
26I will make your oppressors eat their own
    flesh,
They shall be drunk with their own blood as
    with wine.
And all mankind shall know
That I the Lord am your Savior,
The Mighty One of Jacob, your Redeemer.

24 הֲיֻקַּ֥ח מִגִּבּ֖וֹר מַלְק֑וֹחַ
וְאִם־שְׁבִ֥י צַדִּ֖יק יִמָּלֵֽט׃
25 כִּי־כֹ֣ה ׀ אָמַ֣ר יְהֹוָ֗ה
גַּם־שְׁבִ֤י גִבּוֹר֙ יֻקָּ֔ח
וּמַלְק֥וֹחַ עָרִ֖יץ יִמָּלֵ֑ט
וְאֶת־יְרִיבֵךְ֙ אָנֹכִ֣י אָרִ֔יב
וְאֶת־בָּנַ֖יִךְ אָנֹכִ֥י אוֹשִֽׁיעַ׃
26 וְהַאֲכַלְתִּ֤י אֶת־מוֹנַ֙יִךְ֙ אֶת־בְּשָׂרָ֔ם
וְכֶעָסִ֖יס דָּמָ֣ם יִשְׁכָּר֑וּן
וְיָדְע֣וּ כָל־בָּשָׂ֗ר
כִּ֣י אֲנִ֤י יְהֹוָה֙ מֽוֹשִׁיעֵ֔ךְ
וְגֹאֲלֵ֖ךְ אֲבִ֥יר יַעֲקֹֽב׃ ס

50 Thus said the Lord:

*a*Where is the bill of divorce
Of your mother whom I dismissed?
And which of My creditors was it

נ כֹּ֣ה ׀ אָמַ֣ר יְהֹוָ֗ה
אֵ֣י זֶ֠ה סֵ֣פֶר כְּרִיתֻ֤ת
אִמְּכֶם֙ אֲשֶׁ֣ר שִׁלַּחְתִּ֔יהָ
א֚וֹ מִ֣י מִנּוֹשַׁ֔י

---

f   *Meaning of Heb. uncertain.*

a   *The mother (the country) has not been formally divorced, nor*
    the children (the people) sold because of poverty. Therefore there
    is no obstacle to their restoration.

To whom I sold you off?

You were only sold off for your sins,

And your mother dismissed for your crimes.

²Why, when I came, was no one there,

Why, when I called, would none respond?

Is my arm, then, too short to rescue,

Have I not the power to save?

With a mere rebuke I dry up the sea,

And turn rivers into desert.

Their fish stink from lack of water;

They lie dead *b*-of thirst.-*b*

³I clothe the skies in blackness

And make their raiment sackcloth.

⁴*c*-The Lord GOD gave me a skilled tongue,

To know how to speak timely words to the
   weary.-*c*

Morning by morning, He rouses,

He rouses my ear

To give heed like disciples.

⁵The Lord GOD opened my ears,

And I did not disobey,

I did not run away.

⁶I offered my back to the floggers,

And my cheeks to those who tore out my hair.

I did not hide my face

From insult and spittle.

⁷But the Lord GOD will help me—

Therefore I feel no disgrace;

Therefore I have set my face like flint,

And I know I shall not be shamed.

⁸My Vindicator is at hand—

Who dares contend with me?

Let us stand up together!*d*

Who would be my opponent?

Let him approach me!

⁹Lo, the Lord GOD will help me—

Who can get a verdict against me?

אֲשֶׁר־מָכַ֣רְתִּי אֶתְכֶ֖ם ל֑וֹ

הֵ֤ן בַּעֲוֺנֹֽתֵיכֶם֙ נִמְכַּרְתֶּ֔ם

וּבְפִשְׁעֵיכֶ֖ם שֻׁלְּחָ֥ה אִמְּכֶֽם׃

² מַדּ֨וּעַ בָּ֜אתִי וְאֵ֣ין אִ֗ישׁ

קָרָ֙אתִי֙ וְאֵ֣ין עוֹנֶ֔ה

הֲקָצ֨וֹר קָצְרָ֤ה יָדִי֙ מִפְּד֔וּת

וְאִם־אֵֽין־בִּ֥י כֹ֖חַ לְהַצִּ֑יל

הֵ֣ן בְּגַעֲרָתִ֞י אַחֲרִ֣יב יָ֗ם

אָשִׂ֤ים נְהָרוֹת֙ מִדְבָּ֔ר

תִּבְאַ֤שׁ דְּגָתָם֙ מֵאֵ֣ין מַ֔יִם

וְתָמֹ֖ת בַּצָּמָֽא׃

³ אַלְבִּ֥ישׁ שָׁמַ֖יִם קַדְר֑וּת

וְשַׂ֖ק אָשִׂ֥ים כְּסוּתָֽם׃ ס

⁴ אֲדֹנָ֤י יְהֹוִה֙ נָ֤תַן לִי֙ לְשׁ֣וֹן לִמּוּדִ֔ים

לָדַ֛עַת לָע֥וּת אֶת־יָעֵ֖ף דָּבָ֑ר

יָעִ֣יר ׀ בַּבֹּ֣קֶר בַּבֹּ֗קֶר

יָעִ֥יר לִי֙ אֹ֔זֶן

לִשְׁמֹ֖עַ כַּלִּמּוּדִֽים׃

⁵ אֲדֹנָ֤י יְהֹוִה֙ פָּתַֽח־לִ֣י אֹ֔זֶן

וְאָנֹכִ֖י לֹ֣א מָרִ֑יתִי

אָח֖וֹר לֹ֥א נְסוּגֹֽתִי׃

⁶ גֵּוִי֙ נָתַ֣תִּי לְמַכִּ֔ים

וּלְחָיַ֖י לְמֹֽרְטִ֑ים

פָּנַי֙ לֹ֣א הִסְתַּ֔רְתִּי

מִכְּלִמּ֖וֹת וָרֹֽק׃

⁷ וַאדֹנָ֤י יְהֹוִה֙ יַֽעֲזָר־לִ֔י

עַל־כֵּ֖ן לֹ֣א נִכְלָ֑מְתִּי

עַל־כֵּ֞ן שַׂ֤מְתִּי פָנַי֙ כַּֽחַלָּמִ֔ישׁ

וָאֵדַ֖ע כִּי־לֹ֥א אֵבֽוֹשׁ׃

⁸ קָרוֹב֙ מַצְדִּיקִ֔י

מִֽי־יָרִ֥יב אִתִּ֖י

נַעַמְדָ֣ה יָּ֑חַד

מִֽי־בַ֥עַל מִשְׁפָּטִ֖י

יִגַּ֥שׁ אֵלָֽי׃

⁹ הֵ֣ן אֲדֹנָ֤י יְהֹוִה֙ יַֽעֲזָר־לִ֔י

מִי־ה֖וּא יַרְשִׁיעֵ֑נִי

---

b-b   *Change of vocalization yields "on the parched ground"; cf. 44.3.*

c-c   *Meaning of Heb. uncertain.*

d   *I.e., as opponents in court; cf. Num. 35.12.*

They shall all wear out like a garment,
The moth shall consume them.

¹⁰Who among you reveres the Lord
And heeds the voice of His servant?—
Though he walk in darkness
And have no light,
Let him trust in the name of the Lord
And rely upon his God.
¹¹But you are all kindlers of fire,
e-Girding on-*e* firebrands.
Walk by the blaze of your fire,
By the brands that you have lit!
This has come to you from My hand:
c-You shall lie down in pain.-*c*

הֵן כֻּלָּם כַּבֶּגֶד יִבְלוּ
עָשׁ יֹאכְלֵם׃

10 מִי בָכֶם יְרֵא יְהֹוָה
שֹׁמֵעַ בְּקוֹל עַבְדּוֹ
אֲשֶׁר ׀ הָלַךְ חֲשֵׁכִים
וְאֵין נֹגַהּ לוֹ
יִבְטַח בְּשֵׁם יְהֹוָה
וְיִשָּׁעֵן בֵּאלֹהָיו׃
11 הֵן כֻּלְּכֶם קֹדְחֵי אֵשׁ
מְאַזְּרֵי זִיקוֹת
לְכוּ ׀ בְּאוּר אֶשְׁכֶם
וּבְזִיקוֹת בִּעַרְתֶּם
מִיָּדִי הָיְתָה־זֹּאת לָכֶם
לְמַעֲצֵבָה תִּשְׁכָּבוּן׃ פ

51 Listen to Me, you who pursue justice,
You who seek the Lord:
Look to the rock you were hewn from,
To the quarry you were dug from.
²Look back to Abraham your father
And to Sarah who brought you forth.
For he was only one when I called him,
But I blessed him and made him many.

³Truly the Lord has comforted Zion,
Comforted all her ruins;
He has made her wilderness like Eden,
Her desert like the Garden of the Lord.
Gladness and joy shall abide there,
Thanksgiving and the sound of music.

⁴Hearken to Me, *a*-My people,-*a*
And give ear to Me, O *a*-My nation,-*a*
For teaching shall go forth*b* from Me,
My way for the light of peoples.

נא שִׁמְעוּ אֵלַי רֹדְפֵי צֶדֶק
מְבַקְשֵׁי יְהֹוָה
הַבִּיטוּ אֶל־צוּר חֻצַּבְתֶּם
וְאֶל־מַקֶּבֶת בּוֹר נֻקַּרְתֶּם׃
2 הַבִּיטוּ אֶל־אַבְרָהָם אֲבִיכֶם
וְאֶל־שָׂרָה תְּחוֹלֶלְכֶם
כִּי־אֶחָד קְרָאתִיו
וַאֲבָרְכֵהוּ וְאַרְבֵּהוּ׃ ס

3 כִּי־נִחַם יְהֹוָה צִיּוֹן
נִחַם כָּל־חָרְבֹתֶיהָ
וַיָּשֶׂם מִדְבָּרָהּ כְּעֵדֶן
וְעַרְבָתָהּ כְּגַן־יְהֹוָה
שָׂשׂוֹן וְשִׂמְחָה יִמָּצֵא בָהּ
תּוֹדָה וְקוֹל זִמְרָה׃ ס

4 הַקְשִׁיבוּ אֵלַי עַמִּי
וּלְאוּמִּי אֵלַי הַאֲזִינוּ
כִּי תוֹרָה מֵאִתִּי תֵצֵא
וּמִשְׁפָּטִי לְאוֹר עַמִּים

e-e   *Emendation yields "Lighters of."*

a-a   *Several mss. read "O peoples…O nations"; cf. end of this verse and v. 5.*

b   *I.e., through My servant Israel; cf. 42.1–4; 49.6.*

In a moment I will bring it:

⁵The triumph I grant is near,
The success I give has gone forth.
My arms shall ᶜprovide forᶜ the peoples;
The coastlands shall trust in Me,
They shall look to My arm.

⁶Raise your eyes to the heavens,
And look upon the earth beneath:
Though the heavens should melt away like
   smoke,
And the earth wear out like a garment,
And its inhabitants die out ᵈas well,ᵈ
My victory shall stand forever,
My triumph shall remain unbroken.

⁷Listen to Me, you who care for the right,
O people who lay My instruction to heart!
Fear not the insults of men,
And be not dismayed at their jeers;
⁸For the moth shall eat them up like a gar-
   ment,
The wormᵉ shall eat them up like wool.
But My triumph shall endure forever,
My salvation through all the ages.

⁹Awake, awake, clothe yourself with splen-
   dor.
O arm of the LORD!
Awake as in days of old,
As in former ages!
It was you that hacked Rahabᶠ in pieces,
That pierced the Dragon.ᶠ
¹⁰It was you that dried up the Sea,
The waters of the great deep;
That made the abysses of the Sea
A road the redeemed might walk.
¹¹So let the ransomed of the LORD return,

אַרְגִּיעַ׃
5 קָר֤וֹב צִדְקִי֙
יָצָ֣א יִשְׁעִ֔י
וּזְרֹעַ֖י עַמִּ֣ים יִשְׁפֹּ֑טוּ
אֵלַי֙ אִיִּ֣ים יְקַוּ֔וּ
וְאֶל־זְרֹעִ֖י יְיַחֵלֽוּן׃

6 שְׂאוּ֩ לַשָּׁמַ֨יִם עֵינֵיכֶ֜ם
וְֽהַבִּ֣יטוּ אֶל־הָאָ֣רֶץ מִתַּ֗חַת
כִּֽי־שָׁמַ֜יִם כֶּעָשָׁ֤ן נִמְלָ֙חוּ֙
וְהָאָ֙רֶץ֙ כַּבֶּ֣גֶד תִּבְלֶ֔ה
וְיֹשְׁבֶ֖יהָ כְּמוֹ־כֵ֣ן יְמוּת֑וּן
וִישֽׁוּעָתִי֙ לְעוֹלָ֣ם תִּֽהְיֶ֔ה
וְצִדְקָתִ֖י לֹ֥א תֵחָֽת׃ ס

7 שִׁמְע֤וּ אֵלַי֙ יֹ֣דְעֵי צֶ֔דֶק
עַ֖ם תּוֹרָתִ֣י בְלִבָּ֑ם
אַל־תִּֽירְאוּ֙ חֶרְפַּ֣ת אֱנ֔וֹשׁ
וּמִגִּדֻּפֹתָ֖ם אַל־תֵּחָֽתּוּ׃
8 כִּ֤י כַבֶּ֙גֶד֙ יֹאכְלֵ֣ם עָ֔שׁ
וְכַצֶּ֖מֶר יֹאכְלֵ֣ם סָ֑ס
וְצִדְקָתִי֙ לְעוֹלָ֣ם תִּֽהְיֶ֔ה
וִישֽׁוּעָתִ֖י לְד֥וֹר דּוֹרִֽים׃ ס

9 עוּרִ֤י עוּרִי֙ לִבְשִׁי־עֹ֔ז
זְר֣וֹעַ יְהֹוָ֔ה
ע֤וּרִי כִּ֣ימֵי קֶ֔דֶם
דֹּר֖וֹת עוֹלָמִ֑ים
הֲל֥וֹא אַתְּ־הִ֛יא הַמַּחְצֶ֥בֶת רַ֖הַב
מְחוֹלֶ֥לֶת תַּנִּֽין׃
10 הֲל֤וֹא אַתְּ־הִיא֙ הַמַּחֲרֶ֣בֶת יָ֔ם
מֵ֖י תְּה֣וֹם רַבָּ֑ה
הַשָּׂ֙מָה֙ מַעֲמַקֵּי־יָ֔ם
דֶּ֖רֶךְ לַעֲבֹ֥ר גְּאוּלִֽים׃
11 וּפְדוּיֵ֨י יְהֹוָ֜ה יְשׁוּב֗וּן

ᶜ⁻ᶜ Lit. "judge."
ᵈ⁻ᵈ Emendation yields "like gnats."
ᵉ Heb. sas, another word for "moth."
ᶠ Names of primeval monsters.

And come with shouting to Zion,
Crowned with joy everlasting.
Let them attain joy and gladness,
While sorrow and sighing flee.

12I, I am He who comforts you!
What ails you that you fear
Man who must die,
Mortals who fare like grass?
13You have forgotten the LORD your Maker,
Who stretched out the skies and made firm
   the earth!
And you live all day in constant dread
Because of the rage of an oppressor
Who is aiming to cut [you] down.
Yet of what account is the rage of an oppres-
   sor?
14gQuickly the crouching one is freed;
He is not cut down and slain,
And he shall not want for food.
15For I the LORD your God—
Who stir up the sea into roaring waves,
Whose name is LORD of Hosts—
16h-Have put My words in your mouth
And sheltered you with My hand;-h
I, who plantedi the skies and made firm the
   earth,
Have said to Zion: You are My people!
17Rouse, rouse yourself!
Arise, O Jerusalem,
You who from the LORD's hand
Have drunk the cup of His wrath,
You who have drained to the dregs
The bowl, the cup of reeling!
18She has none to guide her
Of all the sons she bore;
None takes her by the hand,

וּבָ֥אוּ צִיּ֖וֹן בְּרִנָּ֑ה
וְשִׂמְחַ֤ת עוֹלָם֙ עַל־רֹאשָׁ֔ם
שָׂשׂ֤וֹן וְשִׂמְחָה֙ יַשִּׂ֔יגוּן
נָ֖סוּ יָג֥וֹן וַאֲנָחָֽה׃ ס

12 אָנֹכִ֧י אָנֹכִ֛י ה֖וּא מְנַחֶמְכֶ֑ם
מִֽי־אַ֤תְּ וַתִּֽירְאִי֙
מֵאֱנ֣וֹשׁ יָמ֔וּת
וּמִבֶּן־אָדָ֖ם חָצִ֥יר יִנָּתֵֽן׃
13 וַתִּשְׁכַּ֞ח יְהוָ֣ה עֹשֶׂ֗ךָ
נוֹטֶ֤ה שָׁמַ֙יִם֙ וְיֹסֵ֣ד אָ֔רֶץ
וַתְּפַחֵ֨ד תָּמִ֤יד כָּל־הַיּוֹם֙
מִפְּנֵי֙ חֲמַ֣ת הַמֵּצִ֔יק
כַּאֲשֶׁ֥ר כּוֹנֵ֖ן לְהַשְׁחִ֑ית
וְאַיֵּ֖ה חֲמַ֥ת הַמֵּצִֽיק׃
14 מִהַ֥ר צֹעֶ֖ה לְהִפָּתֵ֑חַ
וְלֹא־יָמ֣וּת לַשַּׁ֔חַת
וְלֹ֥א יֶחְסַ֖ר לַחְמֽוֹ׃
15 וְאָֽנֹכִי֙ יְהוָ֣ה אֱלֹהֶ֔יךָ
רֹגַ֣ע הַיָּ֔ם וַיֶּהֱמ֖וּ גַּלָּ֑יו
יְהוָ֥ה צְבָא֖וֹת שְׁמֽוֹ׃
16 וָאָשִׂ֤ים דְּבָרַי֙ בְּפִ֔יךָ
וּבְצֵ֥ל יָדִ֖י כִּסִּיתִ֑יךָ
לִנְטֹ֤עַ שָׁמַ֙יִם֙ וְלִיסֹ֣ד אָ֔רֶץ
וְלֵאמֹ֥ר לְצִיּ֖וֹן עַמִּי־אָֽתָּה׃ ס
17 הִתְעוֹרְרִ֣י הִֽתְעוֹרְרִ֗י
ק֚וּמִי יְר֣וּשָׁלִַ֔ם
אֲשֶׁ֥ר שָׁתִ֛ית מִיַּ֥ד יְהוָ֖ה
אֶת־כּ֣וֹס חֲמָת֑וֹ
אֶת־קֻבַּ֜עַת כּ֧וֹס הַתַּרְעֵלָ֛ה
שָׁתִ֖ית מָצִֽית׃
18 אֵין־מְנַהֵ֣ל לָ֔הּ
מִכָּל־בָּנִ֖ים יָלָ֑דָה
וְאֵ֤ין מַחֲזִיק֙ בְּיָדָ֔הּ

---

g   *Meaning of verse uncertain. Emendation yields (cf. Jer. 11.19;*
   Job 14.7–9) "Quickly the tree buds anew; / It does not die though
   cut down, / And its sap does not fail."
h-h   *I.e., I have chosen you to be a prophet-nation; cf. 49.2; 59.21.*
i   *Emendation yields "stretched out"; cf. Syriac version and v. 13.*

Of all the sons she reared.*j*

¹⁹These two things have befallen you:
Wrack and ruin—who can console you?
Famine and sword—*k*-how shall I-*k* comfort you?
²⁰Your sons lie in a swoon
At the corner of every street—
Like an antelope caught in a net—
Drunk with the wrath of the Lord,
With the rebuke of your God.
²¹Therefore,
Listen to this, unhappy one,
Who are drunk, but not with wine!
²²Thus said the Lord, your Lord,
Your God who champions His people:
Herewith I take from your hand
The cup of reeling,*l*
The bowl, the cup of My wrath;
You shall never drink it again.
²³I will put it in the hands of your tormentors,
Who have commanded you,
"Get down, that we may walk over you"—
So that you made your back like the ground,
Like a street for passersby.

מִכָּל־בָּנִים גִּדֵּלָה:
¹⁹ שְׁתַּיִם הֵנָּה קֹרְאֹתַיִךְ
מִי יָנוּד לָךְ הַשֹּׁד וְהַשֶּׁבֶר
וְהָרָעָב וְהַחֶרֶב מִי אֲנַחֲמֵךְ:
²⁰ בָּנַיִךְ עֻלְּפוּ שָׁכְבוּ
בְּרֹאשׁ כָּל־חוּצוֹת
כְּתוֹא מִכְמָר
הַמְלֵאִים חֲמַת־יְהוָה
גַּעֲרַת אֱלֹהָיִךְ:
²¹ לָכֵן
שִׁמְעִי־נָא זֹאת עֲנִיָּה
וּשְׁכֻרַת וְלֹא מִיָּיִן: ס
²² כֹּה־אָמַר אֲדֹנַיִךְ יְהוָה
וֵאלֹהַיִךְ יָרִיב עַמּוֹ
הִנֵּה לָקַחְתִּי מִיָּדֵךְ
אֶת־כּוֹס הַתַּרְעֵלָה
אֶת־קֻבַּעַת כּוֹס חֲמָתִי
לֹא־תוֹסִיפִי לִשְׁתּוֹתָהּ עוֹד:
²³ וְשַׂמְתִּיהָ בְּיַד־מוֹגַיִךְ
אֲשֶׁר־אָמְרוּ לְנַפְשֵׁךְ
שְׁחִי וְנַעֲבֹרָה
וַתָּשִׂימִי כָאָרֶץ גֵּוֵךְ
וְכַחוּץ לַעֹבְרִים: ס

52 Awake, awake, O Zion!
Clothe yourself in splendor;
Put on your robes of majesty,
Jerusalem, holy city!
For the uncircumcised and the unclean
Shall never enter you again.
²Arise, shake off the dust,
Sit [on your throne], Jerusalem!
Loose the bonds from your neck,
O captive one, Fair Zion!

נב עוּרִי עוּרִי
לִבְשִׁי עֻזֵּךְ צִיּוֹן
לִבְשִׁי ׀ בִּגְדֵי תִפְאַרְתֵּךְ
יְרוּשָׁלַ͏ִם עִיר הַקֹּדֶשׁ
כִּי לֹא יוֹסִיף יָבֹא־בָךְ עוֹד
עָרֵל וְטָמֵא:
² הִתְנַעֲרִי מֵעָפָר קוּמִי
שְּׁבִי יְרוּשָׁלָ͏ִם
הִתְפַּתְּחוּ [הִתְפַּתְּחִי] מוֹסְרֵי צַוָּארֵךְ
שְׁבִיָּה בַּת־צִיּוֹן: ס

³For thus said the Lord:

³ כִּי־כֹה אָמַר יְהוָה

---

j   To guide a drunken parent home was a recognized filial duty in ancient Canaan and Egypt.
k-k   Several ancient versions render "who can."
l   A figure of speech for a dire fate; cf. Jer. 25.15 ff.

You were sold for no price,
And shall be redeemed without money.
⁴For thus said the Lord GOD:
Of old, My people went down
To Egypt to sojourn there;
But Assyria has robbed them,
Giving nothing in return.ᵃ
⁵What therefore do I gain here?
        —declares the LORD—
For My people has been carried off for noth-
    ing,
Their mockers howl
        —declares the LORD—
And constantly, unceasingly,
My name is reviled.
⁶Assuredly, My people shall learn My name,
Assuredly [they shall learn] on that day
That I, the One who promised,
Am now at hand.

⁷How welcome on the mountain
Are the footsteps of the herald
Announcing happiness,
Heralding good fortune,
Announcing victory,
Telling Zion, "Your God is King!"
⁸Hark!
Your watchmen raise their voices,
As one they shout for joy;
For every eye shall behold
The LORD's return to Zion.
⁹Raise a shout together,
O ruins of Jerusalem!
For the LORD will comfort His people,
Will redeem Jerusalem.
¹⁰The LORD will bare His holy arm
In the sight of all the nations,
And the very ends of earth shall see
The victory of our God.

ᵃ   *Whereas the Israelites themselves sought hospitality in Egypt,*
   Assyria (i.e., the Chaldean Empire) has exiled them by force.

חִנָּם נִמְכַּרְתֶּ֑ם
וְלֹ֥א בְכֶ֖סֶף תִּגָּאֵֽלוּ׃
4 כִּ֣י כֹ֤ה אָמַר֙ אֲדֹנָ֣י יְהֹוִ֔ה
מִצְרַ֛יִם יָֽרַד־עַמִּ֥י בָרִֽאשֹׁנָ֖ה
לָג֣וּר שָׁ֑ם
וְאַשּׁ֖וּר
בְּאֶ֥פֶס עֲשָׁקֽוֹ׃
5 וְעַתָּ֛ה מי מַה־לִּי־פֹה֙
נְאֻם־יְהֹוָ֔ה
כִּֽי־לֻקַּ֥ח עַמִּ֖י חִנָּ֑ם
משלו מֹֽשְׁלָיו֙ יְהֵילִ֔ילוּ
נְאֻם־יְהֹוָ֔ה
וְתָמִ֥יד כׇּל־הַיּ֖וֹם
שְׁמִ֥י מִנֹּאָֽץ׃
6 לָכֵ֛ן יֵדַ֥ע עַמִּ֖י שְׁמִ֑י
לָכֵן֙ בַּיּ֣וֹם הַה֔וּא
כִּֽי־אֲנִי־ה֥וּא הַֽמְדַבֵּ֖ר
הִנֵּֽנִי׃

7 מַה־נָּאו֤וּ עַל־הֶֽהָרִים֙
רַגְלֵ֣י מְבַשֵּׂ֔ר
מַשְׁמִ֧יעַ שָׁל֛וֹם מְבַשֵּׂ֥ר ט֖וֹב
מַשְׁמִ֣יעַ יְשׁוּעָ֑ה
אֹמֵ֥ר לְצִיּ֖וֹן
מָלַ֥ךְ אֱלֹהָֽיִךְ׃
8 ק֥וֹל צֹפַ֛יִךְ
נָ֥שְׂאוּ ק֖וֹל
יַחְדָּ֣ו יְרַנֵּ֑נוּ
כִּ֣י עַ֤יִן בְּעַ֙יִן֙ יִרְא֔וּ
בְּשׁ֥וּב יְהֹוָ֖ה צִיּֽוֹן׃
9 פִּצְח֤וּ רַנְּנוּ֙ יַחְדָּ֔ו
חׇרְב֖וֹת יְרוּשָׁלָ֑͏ִם
כִּֽי־נִחַ֤ם יְהֹוָה֙ עַמּ֔וֹ
גָּאַ֖ל יְרוּשָׁלָֽ͏ִם׃
10 חָשַׂ֤ף יְהֹוָה֙ אֶת־זְר֣וֹעַ קׇדְשׁ֔וֹ
לְעֵינֵ֖י כׇּל־הַגּוֹיִ֑ם
וְרָאוּ֙ כׇּל־אַפְסֵי־אָ֔רֶץ
אֵ֖ת יְשׁוּעַ֥ת אֱלֹהֵֽינוּ׃ ס

¹¹Turn, turn away, touch naught unclean
As you depart from there;
Keep pure, as you go forth from there,
You who bear the vessels of the Lord!^b
¹²For you will not depart in haste,
Nor will you leave in flight;
For the Lord is marching before you,
The God of Israel is your rear guard.

¹³"Indeed, My servant shall prosper,
Be exalted and raised to great heights.
¹⁴Just as the many were appalled at him^c—
So marred was his appearance, unlike that of
   man,
His form, beyond human semblance—
¹⁵Just so he shall startle^d many nations.
Kings shall be silenced because of him,
For they shall see what has not been told them,
Shall behold what they never have heard."

53

"Who can believe what we have heard?
Upon whom has ^a-the arm of the Lord-^a been
   revealed?
²For he has grown, by His favor, like a tree
   crown,
Like a tree trunk out of arid ground.
He had no form or beauty, that we should
   look at him:
No charm, that we should find him pleasing.
³He was despised, ^b-shunned by men,-^b
A man of suffering, familiar with disease.
^c-As one who hid his face from us,-^c
He was despised, we held him of no account.
⁴Yet it was our sickness that he was bearing,
Our suffering that he endured.
We accounted him plagued,

11 סוּרוּ סוּרוּ צְאוּ מִשָּׁם
טָמֵא אַל־תִּגָּעוּ
צְאוּ מִתּוֹכָהּ הִבָּרוּ
נֹשְׂאֵי כְּלֵי יְהוָה:
12 כִּי לֹא בְחִפָּזוֹן תֵּצֵאוּ
וּבִמְנוּסָה לֹא תֵלֵכוּן
כִּי־הֹלֵךְ לִפְנֵיכֶם יְהוָה
וּמְאַסִּפְכֶם אֱלֹהֵי יִשְׂרָאֵל: ס

13 הִנֵּה יַשְׂכִּיל עַבְדִּי
יָרוּם וְנִשָּׂא וְגָבַהּ מְאֹד:
14 כַּאֲשֶׁר שָׁמְמוּ עָלֶיךָ רַבִּים
כֵּן־מִשְׁחַת מֵאִישׁ מַרְאֵהוּ
וְתֹאֲרוֹ מִבְּנֵי אָדָם:
15 כֵּן יַזֶּה גּוֹיִם רַבִּים
עָלָיו יִקְפְּצוּ מְלָכִים פִּיהֶם
כִּי אֲשֶׁר לֹא־סֻפַּר לָהֶם רָאוּ
וַאֲשֶׁר לֹא־שָׁמְעוּ הִתְבּוֹנָנוּ:

נג מִי הֶאֱמִין לִשְׁמֻעָתֵנוּ
וּזְרוֹעַ יְהוָה עַל־מִי נִגְלָתָה:
2 וַיַּעַל כַּיּוֹנֵק לְפָנָיו
וְכַשֹּׁרֶשׁ מֵאֶרֶץ צִיָּה
לֹא־תֹאַר לוֹ וְלֹא הָדָר וְנִרְאֵהוּ
וְלֹא־מַרְאֶה וְנֶחְמְדֵהוּ:
3 נִבְזֶה וַחֲדַל אִישִׁים
אִישׁ מַכְאֹבוֹת וִידוּעַ חֹלִי
וּכְמַסְתֵּר פָּנִים מִמֶּנּוּ
נִבְזֶה וְלֹא חֲשַׁבְנֻהוּ:
4 אָכֵן חֳלָיֵנוּ הוּא נָשָׂא
וּמַכְאֹבֵינוּ סְבָלָם
וַאֲנַחְנוּ חֲשַׁבְנֻהוּ

---

b   Cf. Ezra 1.7–8; 5.14–15.
c   Heb. "you."
d   Meaning of Heb. uncertain.

a-a   I.e., the vindication which the arm of the Lord effects.
b-b   Meaning of Heb. uncertain.
c-c   I.e., as a leper; cf. Lev. 13.45 ff.

Smitten and afflicted by God;

⁵But he was wounded because of our sins,

Crushed because of our iniquities.

He bore the chastisement that made us whole,

And by his bruises we were healed.

⁶We all went astray like sheep,

Each going his own way;

And the LORD visited upon him

The guilt of all of us."

⁷He was maltreated, yet he was submissive,

He did not open his mouth;

Like a sheep being led to slaughter,

Like a ewe, dumb before those who shear her,

He did not open his mouth.

⁸By oppressive judgment he was taken away,

ᵇ-Who could describe his abode?-ᵇ

For he was cut off from the land of the living

Through the sin of my people, who deserved
the punishment.

⁹And his grave was set among the wicked,

ᵈ-And with the rich, in his death-ᵈ—

Though he had done no injustice

And had spoken no falsehood.

¹⁰But the LORD chose to crush him ᵇ-by disease,

That, if he made himself an offering for
guilt,-ᵇ

He might see offspringᵉ and have long life,

And that through him the LORD's purpose
might prosper.

¹¹Out of his anguish he shall see it;ᶠ

He shall enjoy it to the full through his
devotion.ᵍ

"My righteous servant makes the many righteous,

It is their punishment that he bears;

נָגוּעַ מֻכֵּה אֱלֹהִים וּמְעֻנֶּה׃

⁵ וְהוּא מְחֹלָל מִפְּשָׁעֵנוּ

מְדֻכָּא מֵעֲוֺנֹתֵינוּ

מוּסַר שְׁלוֹמֵנוּ עָלָיו

וּבַחֲבֻרָתוֹ נִרְפָּא־לָנוּ׃

⁶ כֻּלָּנוּ כַּצֹּאן תָּעִינוּ

אִישׁ לְדַרְכּוֹ פָּנִינוּ

וַיהוָה הִפְגִּיעַ בּוֹ

אֵת עֲוֺן כֻּלָּנוּ׃

⁷ נִגַּשׂ וְהוּא נַעֲנֶה

וְלֹא יִפְתַּח־פִּיו

כַּשֶּׂה לַטֶּבַח יוּבָל

וּכְרָחֵל לִפְנֵי גֹזְזֶיהָ נֶאֱלָמָה

וְלֹא יִפְתַּח פִּיו׃

⁸ מֵעֹצֶר וּמִמִּשְׁפָּט לֻקָּח

וְאֶת־דּוֹרוֹ מִי יְשׂוֹחֵחַ

כִּי נִגְזַר מֵאֶרֶץ חַיִּים

מִפֶּשַׁע עַמִּי נֶגַע לָמוֹ׃

⁹ וַיִּתֵּן אֶת־רְשָׁעִים קִבְרוֹ

וְאֶת־עָשִׁיר בְּמֹתָיו

עַל לֹא־חָמָס עָשָׂה

וְלֹא מִרְמָה בְּפִיו׃

¹⁰ וַיהוָה חָפֵץ דַּכְּאוֹ הֶחֱלִי

אִם־תָּשִׂים אָשָׁם נַפְשׁוֹ

יִרְאֶה זֶרַע יַאֲרִיךְ יָמִים

וְחֵפֶץ יְהוָה בְּיָדוֹ יִצְלָח׃

¹¹ מֵעֲמַל נַפְשׁוֹ יִרְאֶה יִשְׂבָּע

בְּדַעְתּוֹ יַצְדִּיק צַדִּיק

עַבְדִּי לָרַבִּים

וַעֲוֺנֹתָם הוּא יִסְבֹּל׃

ᵈ⁻ᵈ   *Emendation yields "And his tomb with evildoers."*

ᵉ   *Emendation yields "His arm," i.e., His vindication; cf. v. 1 with
note.*

ᶠ   *I.e., the arm of the LORD; see preceding note.*

ᵍ   *For this sense of da'ath see 11.2, 9.*

12Assuredly, I will give him the many as his
　portion,
He shall receive the multitude as his spoil.
For he exposed himself to death
And was numbered among the sinners,
Whereas he bore the guilt of the many
And made intercession for sinners."

לָכֵ֞ן אֲחַלֶּק־ל֣וֹ בָֽרַבִּ֗ים 12
וְאֶת־עֲצוּמִים֮ יְחַלֵּ֣ק שָׁלָל֒ תַּ֗חַת
אֲשֶׁ֨ר הֶעֱרָ֤ה לַמָּ֙וֶת֙ נַפְשׁ֔וֹ
וְאֶת־פֹּשְׁעִ֖ים נִמְנָ֑ה
וְהוּא֙ חֵטְא־רַבִּ֣ים נָשָׂ֔א
וְלַפֹּשְׁעִ֖ים יַפְגִּֽיעַ׃ ס

54 Shout, O barren one,
You who bore no child!
Shout aloud for joy,
You who did not travail!
For the children of the wife forlorn
Shall outnumber those of the espoused
　　　　　　　　—said the Lord.

נד רָנִּ֣י עֲקָרָ֔ה
לֹ֣א יָלָ֑דָה
פִּצְחִ֥י רִנָּ֛ה וְצַהֲלִ֖י
לֹא־חָ֑לָה
כִּֽי־רַבִּ֧ים בְּנֵֽי־שׁוֹמֵמָ֛ה
מִבְּנֵ֥י בְעוּלָ֖ה
אָמַ֥ר יְהֹוָֽה׃

2Enlarge the site of your tent,
a-Extend the size of your dwelling,-a
Do not stint!
Lengthen the ropes, and drive the pegs firm.
3For you shall spread out to the right and the
　left;
Your offspring shall dispossess nationsb
And shall people the desolate towns.

הַרְחִ֣יבִי ׀ מְק֣וֹם אׇהֳלֵ֗ךְ 2
וִירִיע֧וֹת מִשְׁכְּנוֹתַ֛יִךְ יַטּ֖וּ
אַל־תַּחְשֹׂ֑כִי
הַאֲרִ֙יכִי֙ מֵיתָרַ֔יִךְ וִיתֵדֹתַ֖יִךְ חַזֵּֽקִי׃
כִּי־יָמִ֥ין וּשְׂמֹ֖אול* תִּפְרֹ֑צִי 3
וְזַרְעֵךְ֙ גּוֹיִ֣ם יִירָ֔שׁ
וְעָרִ֥ים נְשַׁמּ֖וֹת יוֹשִֽׁיבוּ׃

4Fear not, you shall not be shamed;
Do not cringe, you shall not be disgraced.
For you shall forget
The reproach of your youth,
And remember no more
The shame of your widowhood.
5For He who made you will espouse you—
His name is "Lord of Hosts."
The Holy One of Israel will redeem you—
He is called "God of all the Earth."

אַל־תִּֽירְאִי֙ כִּי־לֹ֣א תֵב֔וֹשִׁי 4
וְאַל־תִּכָּלְמִ֖י כִּ֣י לֹ֣א תַחְפִּ֑ירִי
כִּ֣י בֹ֤שֶׁת עֲלוּמַ֙יִךְ֙
תִּשְׁכָּ֔חִי
וְחֶרְפַּ֥ת אַלְמְנוּתַ֖יִךְ
לֹ֥א תִזְכְּרִי־עֽוֹד׃
כִּ֤י בֹעֲלַ֙יִךְ֙ עֹשַׂ֔יִךְ 5
יְהֹוָ֥ה צְבָא֖וֹת שְׁמ֑וֹ
וְגֹֽאֲלֵךְ֙ קְד֣וֹשׁ יִשְׂרָאֵ֔ל
אֱלֹהֵ֥י כׇל־הָאָ֖רֶץ יִקָּרֵֽא׃

6The Lord has called you back
As a wife forlorn and forsaken.

כִּֽי־כְאִשָּׁ֧ה עֲזוּבָ֛ה וַעֲצ֥וּבַת ר֖וּחַ 6
קְרָאַ֣ךְ יְהֹוָ֑ה

---

a-a　Lit. "Let the cloths of your dwelling extend."
b　I.e., the foreigners who had occupied regions from which Israelites
　　had been exiled; cf. 2 Kings 17.24.

מלא ו' v. 3.

Can one cast off the wife of his youth?

           —said your God.

⁷For a little while I forsook you,

But with vast love I will bring you back.

⁸In slight anger, for a moment,

I hid My face from you;

But with kindness everlasting

I will take you back in love

          —said the Lord your Redeemer.

⁹For this to Me is like the waters[c] of Noah:

As I swore that the waters of Noah

Nevermore would flood the earth,

So I swear that I will not

Be angry with you or rebuke you.

¹⁰For the mountains may move

And the hills be shaken,

But my loyalty shall never move from you,

Nor My covenant of friendship be shaken

    —said the Lord, who takes you back in love.

¹¹Unhappy, storm-tossed one, uncomforted!

I will lay carbuncles[d] as your building stones

And make your foundations of sapphires.

¹²I will make your battlements of rubies,

Your gates of precious stones,

The whole encircling wall of gems.

¹³And all your children shall be disciples of
the Lord,

And great shall be the happiness of your children;

¹⁴You shall be established through righteousness.

You shall be safe from oppression,

And shall have no fear;

From ruin, and it shall not come near you.

¹⁵[e]Surely no harm can be done

Without My consent:

Whoever would harm you

Shall fall because of you.

וְאֵ֧שֶׁת נְעוּרִ֛ים כִּ֥י תִמָּאֵ֖ס
אָמַ֥ר אֱלֹהָֽיִךְ׃

⁷ בְּרֶ֥גַע קָטֹ֖ן עֲזַבְתִּ֑יךְ
וּבְרַחֲמִ֥ים גְּדֹלִ֖ים אֲקַבְּצֵֽךְ׃

⁸ בְּשֶׁ֣צֶף קֶ֗צֶף
הִסְתַּ֨רְתִּי פָנַ֥י רֶ֙גַע֙ מִמֵּ֔ךְ
וּבְחֶ֥סֶד עוֹלָ֖ם
רִֽחַמְתִּ֑יךְ
אָמַ֥ר גֹּאֲלֵ֖ךְ יְהוָֽה׃ ס

⁹ כִּי־מֵ֥י נֹ֙חַ֙ זֹ֣את לִ֔י
אֲשֶׁ֣ר נִשְׁבַּ֗עְתִּי מֵעֲבֹ֥ר מֵי־נֹ֛חַ
ע֖וֹד עַל־הָאָ֑רֶץ
כֵּ֥ן נִשְׁבַּ֛עְתִּי
מִקְּצֹ֥ף עָלַ֖יִךְ וּמִגְּעָר־בָּֽךְ׃

¹⁰ כִּ֤י הֶֽהָרִים֙ יָמ֔וּשׁוּ
וְהַגְּבָע֖וֹת תְּמוּטֶ֑נָה
וְחַסְדִּ֞י מֵאִתֵּ֣ךְ לֹֽא־יָמ֗וּשׁ
וּבְרִ֤ית שְׁלוֹמִי֙ לֹ֣א תָמ֔וּט
אָמַ֥ר מְרַחֲמֵ֖ךְ יְהוָֽה׃ ס

¹¹ עֲנִיָּ֥ה סֹעֲרָ֖ה לֹ֣א נֻחָ֑מָה
הִנֵּ֙ה אָנֹכִ֜י מַרְבִּ֤יץ בַּפּוּךְ֙ אֲבָנַ֔יִךְ
וִיסַדְתִּ֖יךְ בַּסַּפִּירִֽים׃

¹² וְשַׂמְתִּ֤י כַּֽדְכֹד֙ שִׁמְשֹׁתַ֔יִךְ
וּשְׁעָרַ֖יִךְ לְאַבְנֵ֣י אֶקְדָּ֑ח
וְכָל־גְּבוּלֵ֖ךְ לְאַבְנֵי־חֵֽפֶץ׃

¹³ וְכָל־בָּנַ֖יִךְ לִמּוּדֵ֣י יְהוָ֑ה
וְרַ֖ב שְׁל֥וֹם בָּנָֽיִךְ׃

¹⁴ בִּצְדָקָ֖ה תִּכּוֹנָ֑נִי
רַחֲקִ֣י מֵעֹ֗שֶׁק
כִּֽי־לֹ֣א תִירָ֔אִי
וּמִ֨מְּחִתָּ֔ה כִּ֥י לֹֽא־תִקְרַ֖ב אֵלָֽיִךְ׃

¹⁵ הֵ֣ן גּ֥וֹר יָג֛וּר
אֶ֖פֶס מֵֽאוֹתִ֑י
מִי־גָ֥ר אִתָּ֖ךְ
עָלַ֥יִךְ יִפּֽוֹל׃

---

c *Other Heb. mss. and the ancient versions read "days."*

d *Taking* pukh *as a byform of* nophekh; *so already Rashi.*

e *Meaning of verse uncertain.*

¹⁶It is I who created the smith
To fan the charcoal fire
And produce the tools for his work;
So it is I who create
The instruments of havoc.
¹⁷No weapon formed against you
Shall succeed,
And every tongue that contends with you at
   law
You shall defeat.
Such is the lot of the servants of the LORD,
Such their triumph through Me
          —declares the LORD.

55 Ho, all who are thirsty,
Come for water,
Even if you have no money;
Come, buy food and eat:
Buy food without money,
Wine and milk without cost.
²Why do you spend money for what is not
   bread,
Your earnings for what does not satisfy?
Give heed to Me,
And you shall eat choice food
And enjoy the richest viands.
³Incline your ear and come to Me;
Hearken, and you shall be revived.
And I will make with you an everlasting cov-
   enant,
The enduring loyalty promised to David.
⁴^a-As I made him a leader^b of peoples,
A prince and commander of peoples,
⁵So you shall summon a nation you did not
   know,
And a nation that did not know you
Shall come running to you-^a—

16 הֵן הִנֵּה אָנֹכִי בָּרָאתִי חָרָשׁ
נֹפֵחַ בְּאֵשׁ פֶּחָם
וּמוֹצִיא כְלִי לְמַעֲשֵׂהוּ
וְאָנֹכִי בָּרָאתִי
מַשְׁחִית לְחַבֵּל:
17 כָּל־כְּלִי יוּצַר עָלַיִךְ
לֹא יִצְלָח
וְכָל־לָשׁוֹן תָּקוּם־אִתָּךְ לַמִּשְׁפָּט
תַּרְשִׁיעִי
זֹאת נַחֲלַת עַבְדֵי יְהֹוָה
וְצִדְקָתָם מֵאִתִּי
נְאֻם־יְהֹוָה: ס

נה הוֹי כָּל־צָמֵא
לְכוּ לַמַּיִם
וַאֲשֶׁר אֵין־לוֹ כָּסֶף
לְכוּ שִׁבְרוּ וֶאֱכֹלוּ
וּלְכוּ שִׁבְרוּ בְּלוֹא־כֶסֶף
וּבְלוֹא מְחִיר יַיִן וְחָלָב:
2 לָמָּה תִשְׁקְלוּ־כֶסֶף בְּלוֹא־לֶחֶם
וִיגִיעֲכֶם בְּלוֹא לְשָׂבְעָה
שִׁמְעוּ שָׁמוֹעַ אֵלַי
וְאִכְלוּ־טוֹב
וְתִתְעַנַּג בַּדֶּשֶׁן נַפְשְׁכֶם:
3 הַטּוּ אָזְנְכֶם וּלְכוּ אֵלַי
שִׁמְעוּ וּתְחִי נַפְשְׁכֶם
וְאֶכְרְתָה לָכֶם בְּרִית עוֹלָם
חַסְדֵי דָוִד הַנֶּאֱמָנִים:
4 הֵן עֵד לְאוּמִּים נְתַתִּיו
נָגִיד וּמְצַוֵּה לְאֻמִּים:
5 הֵן גּוֹי לֹא־תֵדַע תִּקְרָא
וְגוֹי לֹא־יְדָעוּךָ
אֵלֶיךָ יָרוּצוּ

---

a-a Cf. 2 Sam. 22.44–45 (Ps. 18.44–45).
b   Cf. Targum; others "witness."

For the sake of the LORD your God,
The Holy One of Israel who has glorified you.

6Seek the LORD while He can be found,
Call to Him while He is near.
7Let the wicked give up his ways,
The sinful man his plans;
Let him turn back to the LORD,
And He will pardon him;
To our God,
For he freely forgives.
8For My plans are not your plans,
Nor are My ways[c] your ways[c]
                    —declares the LORD.
9But as the heavens are high above the earth,
So are My ways[c] high above your ways[c]
And My plans above your plans.
10For as the rain or snow drops from heaven
And returns not there,
But soaks the earth
And makes it bring forth vegetation,
Yielding [d]-seed for sowing and bread for eating,-[d]
11So is the word that issues from My mouth:
It does not come back to Me unfulfilled,
But performs what I purpose,
Achieves what I sent it to do.
12Yea, you shall leave[e] in joy and be led home secure.
Before you, mount and hill shall shout aloud,
And all the trees of the field shall clap their hands.
13Instead of the brier, a cypress shall rise;
Instead of the nettle, a myrtle shall rise.
These shall stand as a testimony to the LORD,
As an everlasting sign that shall not perish.

לְמַעַן יְהוָה אֱלֹהֶיךָ
וְלִקְדוֹשׁ יִשְׂרָאֵל כִּי פֵאֲרָךְ: ס

6 דִּרְשׁוּ יְהוָה בְּהִמָּצְאוֹ
קְרָאֻהוּ בִּהְיוֹתוֹ קָרוֹב:
7 יַעֲזֹב רָשָׁע דַּרְכּוֹ
וְאִישׁ אָוֶן מַחְשְׁבֹתָיו
וְיָשֹׁב אֶל־יְהוָה
וִירַחֲמֵהוּ
וְאֶל־אֱלֹהֵינוּ
כִּי־יַרְבֶּה לִסְלוֹחַ:
8 כִּי לֹא מַחְשְׁבוֹתַי מַחְשְׁבוֹתֵיכֶם
וְלֹא דַרְכֵיכֶם דְּרָכָי
נְאֻם יְהוָה:
9 כִּי־גָבְהוּ שָׁמַיִם מֵאָרֶץ
כֵּן גָּבְהוּ דְרָכַי מִדַּרְכֵיכֶם
וּמַחְשְׁבֹתַי מִמַּחְשְׁבֹתֵיכֶם:
10 כִּי כַּאֲשֶׁר יֵרֵד הַגֶּשֶׁם וְהַשֶּׁלֶג מִן־הַשָּׁמַיִם
וְשָׁמָּה לֹא יָשׁוּב
כִּי אִם־הִרְוָה אֶת־הָאָרֶץ
וְהוֹלִידָהּ וְהִצְמִיחָהּ
וְנָתַן זֶרַע לַזֹּרֵעַ וְלֶחֶם לָאֹכֵל:
11 כֵּן יִהְיֶה דְבָרִי אֲשֶׁר יֵצֵא מִפִּי
לֹא־יָשׁוּב אֵלַי רֵיקָם
כִּי אִם־עָשָׂה אֶת־אֲשֶׁר חָפַצְתִּי
וְהִצְלִיחַ אֲשֶׁר שְׁלַחְתִּיו:
12 כִּי־בְשִׂמְחָה תֵצֵאוּ וּבְשָׁלוֹם תּוּבָלוּן
הֶהָרִים וְהַגְּבָעוֹת יִפְצְחוּ לִפְנֵיכֶם רִנָּה
וְכָל־עֲצֵי הַשָּׂדֶה יִמְחֲאוּ־כָף:
13 תַּחַת הַנַּעֲצוּץ יַעֲלֶה בְרוֹשׁ
תחת וְתַחַת הַסִּרְפַּד יַעֲלֶה הֲדַס
וְהָיָה לַיהוָה לְשֵׁם
לְאוֹת עוֹלָם לֹא יִכָּרֵת: ס

56 Thus said the LORD:
Observe what is right and do what is just;

נו כֹּה אָמַר יְהוָה
שִׁמְרוּ מִשְׁפָּט וַעֲשׂוּ צְדָקָה

---

c   Emendation yields "words"; cf. v. 11 and 40.8.
d-d   Lit. "seed for the sower and bread for the eater."
e   I.e., leave the Babylonian exile.

For soon My salvation shall come,
And my deliverance be revealed.

כִּי־קְרוֹבָ֤ה יְשׁוּעָתִי֙ לָב֔וֹא
וְצִדְקָתִ֖י לְהִגָּלֽוֹת׃

2Happy is the man who does this,
The man who holds fast to it:
Who keeps the sabbath and does not profane
    it,
And stays his hand from doing any evil.

2 אַשְׁרֵ֤י אֱנוֹשׁ֙ יַעֲשֶׂה־זֹּ֔את
וּבֶן־אָדָ֖ם יַחֲזִ֣יק בָּ֑הּ
שֹׁמֵ֤ר שַׁבָּת֙ מֵֽחַלְּל֔וֹ
וְשֹׁמֵ֥ר יָד֖וֹ מֵעֲשׂ֥וֹת כָּל־רָֽע׃ ס

3Let not the foreigner say,
Who has attached himself to the LORD,
"The LORD will keep me apart from His peo-
    ple";
And let not the eunuch say,
"I am a withered tree."
4For thus said the LORD:
"As for the eunuchs who keep My sabbaths,
Who have chosen what I desire
And hold fast to My covenant—
5I will give them, in My House
And within My walls,
A monument and a name
Better than sons or daughters.
I will give them an everlasting name
Which shall not perish.
6As for the foreigners
Who attach themselves to the LORD,
To minister to Him,
And to love the name of the LORD,
To be His servants—
All who keep the sabbath and do not profane
    it,
And who hold fast to My covenant—
7I will bring them to My sacred mount
And let them rejoice in My house of prayer.
Their burnt offerings and sacrifices
Shall be welcome on My altar;
For My House shall be called
A house of prayer for all peoples."
8Thus declares the Lord GOD,

3 וְאַל־יֹאמַ֣ר בֶּן־הַנֵּכָ֗ר
הַנִּלְוָ֤ה אֶל־יְהֹוָה֙ לֵאמֹ֔ר
הַבְדֵּ֧ל יַבְדִּילַ֛נִי יְהֹוָ֖ה מֵעַ֣ל עַמּ֑וֹ
וְאַל־יֹאמַר֙ הַסָּרִ֔יס
הֵ֥ן אֲנִ֖י עֵ֥ץ יָבֵֽשׁ׃ ס
4 כִּי־כֹ֣ה ׀ אָמַ֣ר יְהֹוָ֗ה
לַסָּֽרִיסִים֙ אֲשֶׁ֣ר יִשְׁמְרוּ֙ אֶת־שַׁבְּתוֹתַ֔י
וּבָֽחֲר֖וּ בַּאֲשֶׁ֣ר חָפָ֑צְתִּי
וּמַחֲזִיקִ֖ים בִּבְרִיתִֽי׃
5 וְנָתַתִּ֨י לָהֶ֜ם בְּבֵיתִ֤י
וּבְחֽוֹמֹתַי֙
יָ֣ד וָשֵׁ֔ם
ט֖וֹב מִבָּנִ֣ים וּמִבָּנ֑וֹת
שֵׁ֤ם עוֹלָם֙ אֶתֶּן־ל֔וֹ
אֲשֶׁ֖ר לֹ֥א יִכָּרֵֽת׃ ס
6 וּבְנֵ֣י הַנֵּכָ֗ר
הַנִּלְוִ֤ים עַל־יְהֹוָה֙
לְשָׁ֣רְת֔וֹ
וּֽלְאַהֲבָה֙ אֶת־שֵׁ֣ם יְהֹוָ֔ה
לִהְי֥וֹת ל֖וֹ לַעֲבָדִ֑ים
כָּל־שֹׁמֵ֤ר שַׁבָּת֙ מֵֽחַלְּל֔וֹ
וּמַחֲזִיקִ֖ים בִּבְרִיתִֽי׃
7 וַהֲבִיאוֹתִ֞ים אֶל־הַ֣ר קׇדְשִׁ֗י
וְשִׂמַּחְתִּים֙ בְּבֵ֣ית תְּפִלָּתִ֔י
עוֹלֹתֵיהֶ֧ם וְזִבְחֵיהֶ֛ם
לְרָצ֖וֹן עַֽל־מִזְבְּחִ֑י
כִּ֣י בֵיתִ֔י בֵּית־תְּפִלָּ֥ה יִקָּרֵ֖א
לְכׇל־הָעַמִּֽים׃
8 נְאֻם֙ אֲדֹנָ֣י יֱהֹוִ֔ה

Who gathers the dispersed of Israel:
"I will gather still more to those already
   gathered."

מְקַבֵּץ נִדְחֵי יִשְׂרָאֵל
עֹוד אֲקַבֵּץ עָלָיו לְנִקְבָּצָיו:

⁹All you wild beasts, come and devour,
All you beasts of the forest!
¹⁰Theᵃ watchmen are blind, all of them,
They perceive nothing.
They are all dumb dogs
That cannot bark;
They lie sprawling,ᵇ
They love to drowse.
¹¹Moreover, the dogs are greedy;
They never know satiety.
ᶜ-As for the shepherds, they know not
What it is to give heed.-ᶜ
Everyone has turned his own way,
Every last one seeks his own advantage.
¹²"Come, I'll get some wine;
Let us swill liquor.
And tomorrow will be just the same,
Or even much grander!"

⁹ כָּל־חַיְתוֹ שָׂדָי אֵתָיוּ לֶאֱכֹל
כָּל־חַיְתוֹ בַּיָּעַר: ס
¹⁰ צֹפָו עִוְרִים כֻּלָּם
לֹא יָדָעוּ
כֻּלָּם כְּלָבִים אִלְּמִים
לֹא יוּכְלוּ לִנְבֹּחַ
הֹזִים שֹׁכְבִים
אֹהֲבֵי לָנוּם:
¹¹ וְהַכְּלָבִים עַזֵּי־נֶפֶשׁ
לֹא יָדְעוּ שָׂבְעָה
וְהֵמָּה רֹעִים לֹא יָדְעוּ
הָבִין
כֻּלָּם לְדַרְכָּם פָּנוּ
אִישׁ לְבִצְעוֹ מִקָּצֵהוּ:
¹² אֵתָיוּ אֶקְחָה־יַיִן
וְנִסְבְּאָה שֵׁכָר
וְהָיָה כָזֶה יוֹם מָחָר
גָּדוֹל יֶתֶר מְאֹד:

57 The righteous man perishes,
And no one considers;
Pious men are taken away,
And no one gives thought
That because of evil
The righteous was taken away.
²Yet he shall come to peace,
ᵃ-He shall have rest on his couch-ᵃ
Who walked straightforward.

³But as for you, come closer,
You sons of a sorceress,

נז הַצַּדִּיק אָבָד
וְאֵין אִישׁ שָׂם עַל־לֵב
וְאַנְשֵׁי־חֶסֶד נֶאֱסָפִים
בְּאֵין מֵבִין
כִּי־מִפְּנֵי הָרָעָה
נֶאֱסַף הַצַּדִּיק:
² יָבוֹא שָׁלוֹם
יָנוּחוּ עַל־מִשְׁכְּבוֹתָם
הֹלֵךְ נְכֹחוֹ:

³ וְאַתֶּם קִרְבוּ־הֵנָּה
בְּנֵי עֹנְנָה

---

a   Heb. "his."
b   Meaning of Heb. uncertain.
c-c   Meaning of Heb. uncertain. Emendation yields "Neither do the
    shepherds ever know sufficiency (hon)." Cf. hon in Prov. 30.15,
    16.

a-a   Heb. "They shall have rest on their couches."

You offspring of an adulterer and a harlot!*b*

⁴With whom do you act so familiarly?
At whom do you open your mouth
And stick out your tongue?
Why, you are children of iniquity,
Offspring of treachery—
⁵You who inflame*c* yourselves
Among the terebinths,
Under every verdant tree;
Who slaughter children in the wadis,
Among*d* the clefts of the rocks.
⁶*e*-With such*f* are your share and portion,-*e*
They, they are your allotment;
To them you have poured out libations,
Presented offerings.
Should I relent in the face of this?

⁷On a high and lofty hill
You have set your couch;
There, too, you have gone up
To perform sacrifices.
⁸Behind the door and doorpost
You have directed your thoughts;
e-Abandoning Me, you have gone up
On the couch you made so wide.
You have made a covenant with them,*f*
You have loved bedding with them;*g*
You have chosen lust.*h*
⁹You have approached-*e* the king*i* with oil,
You have provided many perfumes.
And you have sent your envoys afar,
Even down to the netherworld.*j*
¹⁰Though wearied by much travel,
You never said, "I give up!"
You found gratification for your lust,

זֶרַע מְנָאֵף וַתִּזְנֶה׃
4 עַל־מִי תִּתְעַנָּגוּ
עַל־מִי תַּרְחִיבוּ פֶה
תַּאֲרִיכוּ לָשׁוֹן
הֲלוֹא־אַתֶּם יִלְדֵי־פֶשַׁע
זֶרַע שָׁקֶר׃
5 הַנֵּחָמִים
בָּאֵלִים
תַּחַת כָּל־עֵץ רַעֲנָן
שֹׁחֲטֵי הַיְלָדִים בַּנְּחָלִים
תַּחַת סְעִפֵי הַסְּלָעִים׃
6 בְּחַלְּקֵי־נַחַל חֶלְקֵךְ
הֵם הֵם גּוֹרָלֵךְ
גַּם־לָהֶם שָׁפַכְתְּ נֶסֶךְ
הֶעֱלִית מִנְחָה
הַעַל אֵלֶּה אֶנָּחֵם׃
7 עַל הַר־גָּבֹהַּ וְנִשָּׂא
שַׂמְתְּ מִשְׁכָּבֵךְ
גַּם־שָׁם עָלִית
לִזְבֹּחַ זָבַח׃
8 וְאַחַר הַדֶּלֶת וְהַמְּזוּזָה
שַׂמְתְּ זִכְרוֹנֵךְ
כִּי מֵאִתִּי גִּלִּית וַתַּעֲלִי
הִרְחַבְתְּ מִשְׁכָּבֵךְ
וַתִּכְרָת־לָךְ מֵהֶם
אָהַבְתְּ מִשְׁכָּבָם
יָד חָזִית׃
9 וַתָּשֻׁרִי לַמֶּלֶךְ בַּשֶּׁמֶן
וַתַּרְבִּי רִקֻּחָיִךְ
וַתְּשַׁלְּחִי צִירַיִךְ עַד־מֵרָחֹק
וַתַּשְׁפִּילִי עַד־שְׁאוֹל׃
10 בְּרֹב דַּרְכֵּךְ יָגַעַתְּ
לֹא אָמַרְתְּ נוֹאָשׁ
חַיַּת יָדֵךְ מָצָאת

b   Lit. "she acts the harlot."
c   I.e., in some frenzied idolatrous rite.
d   Heb. "under."
e-e   Meaning of Heb. uncertain.
f   The cult-trees referred to above in v. 5.
g   I.e., with the objects behind door and doorpost.
h   Like Ugaritic yd, from root ydd, "to love."
i   Or "Molech."
j   I.e., you have brought tribute to alien cults as to a king.

And so you never cared.

11 k-Whom do you dread and fear,
That you tell lies?-k
But you gave no thought to Me,
You paid no heed.
It is because I have stood idly by l-so long-l
That you have no fear of Me.

12 I hereby pronounce m-judgment upon your
    deeds:-m
n-Your assorted [idols]-n shall not avail you,

13 Shall not save you when you cry out.
They shall all be borne off by the wind,
Snatched away by a breeze.
But those who trust in Me shall inherit the
    land
And possess My sacred mount.

14 [The Lord] says:
Build up, build up a highway!
Clear a road!
Remove all obstacles
From the road of My people!

15 For thus said He who high aloft
Forever dwells, whose name is holy:
I dwell on high, in holiness;
Yet with the contrite and the lowly in spirit—
Reviving the spirits of the lowly,
Reviving the hearts of the contrite.

16 For I will not always contend,
I will not be angry forever:
Nay, I e-who make spirits flag,-e
Also create the breath of life.

17 For their o sinful greed I was angry;
I struck them and turned away in My wrath.
p-Though stubborn, they follow the way of
    their hearts,-p

18 I note how they fare and will heal them:

עַל־כֵּ֖ן לֹ֥א חָלִֽית׃
11 וְאֶת־מִ֞י דָּאַ֤גְתְּ וַתִּֽירְאִי֙
כִּ֣י תְכַזֵּ֔בִי
וְאוֹתִי֙ לֹ֣א זָכַ֔רְתְּ
לֹא־שַׂ֖מְתְּ עַל־לִבֵּ֑ךְ
הֲלֹ֨א אֲנִ֤י מַחְשֶׁה֙ וּמֵ֣עֹלָ֔ם
וְאוֹתִ֖י לֹ֥א תִירָֽאִי׃
12 אֲנִ֥י אַגִּ֖יד צִדְקָתֵ֑ךְ
וְאֶֽת־מַעֲשַׂ֖יִךְ וְלֹ֥א יוֹעִילֽוּךְ׃
13 בְּזַֽעֲקֵךְ֙ יַצִּילֻ֣ךְ קִבּוּצַ֔יִךְ
וְאֶת־כֻּלָּ֥ם יִשָּׂא־ר֖וּחַ
יִקַּח־הָ֑בֶל
וְהַֽחוֹסֶ֥ה בִי֙ יִנְחַל־אֶ֔רֶץ
וְיִירַ֖שׁ הַר־קָדְשִֽׁי׃
14 וְאָמַ֥ר
סֹֽלּוּ־סֹ֖לּוּ
פַּנּוּ־דָ֑רֶךְ
הָרִ֥ימוּ מִכְשׁ֖וֹל
מִדֶּ֥רֶךְ עַמִּֽי׃ ס
15 כִּי֩ כֹ֨ה אָמַ֜ר רָ֣ם וְנִשָּׂ֗א
שֹׁכֵ֥ן עַד֙ וְקָד֣וֹשׁ שְׁמ֔וֹ
מָר֥וֹם וְקָד֖וֹשׁ אֶשְׁכּ֑וֹן
וְאֶת־דַּכָּא֙ וּשְׁפַל־ר֔וּחַ
לְהַֽחֲיוֹת֙ ר֣וּחַ שְׁפָלִ֔ים
וּֽלְהַחֲי֖וֹת לֵ֥ב נִדְכָּאִֽים׃
16 כִּ֣י לֹ֤א לְעוֹלָם֙ אָרִ֔יב
וְלֹ֥א לָנֶ֖צַח אֶקְּצ֑וֹף
כִּי־ר֨וּחַ֙ מִלְּפָנַ֣י יַֽעֲט֔וֹף
וּנְשָׁמ֖וֹת אֲנִ֥י עָשִֽׂיתִי׃
17 בַּֽעֲוֺ֥ן בִּצְע֛וֹ קָצַ֖פְתִּי
וְאַכֵּ֥הוּ הַסְתֵּ֖ר וְאֶקְצֹ֑ף
וַיֵּ֥לֶךְ שׁוֹבָ֖ב בְּדֶ֥רֶךְ לִבּֽוֹ׃
18 דְּרָכָ֥יו רָאִ֖יתִי וְאֶרְפָּאֵ֑הוּ

---

k-k *Emendation yields "Them you dreaded and feared, / And so
      you gave them thought."*
l-l *Emendation yields "and shut My eyes."*
m-m *Lit. "your retribution and your deeds."*
n-n *Brought up from v. 13 for clarity.*
o   *I.e., Israel's. Cf. "My people," v. 14.*
p-p *Meaning of Heb. uncertain. Emendation yields "When they
      have walked broken in the contrition of their hearts."*

I will guide them and mete out solace to them,
And to the mourners among them 19heartening,q comfortingr words:
It shall be well,
Well with the far and the near
　　　　　　　—said the LORD—
And I will heal them.
20But the wicked are like the troubled sea
Which cannot rest,
Whose waters toss up mire and mud.
21There is no safety
　　　　　　　—said my God—
For the wicked.

וְאַנְחֵהוּ וַאֲשַׁלֵּם נִחֻמִים לוֹ
וְלַאֲבֵלָיו: 19 בּוֹרֵא נוב נִיב שְׂפָתָיִם
שָׁלוֹם |
שָׁלוֹם לָרָחוֹק וְלַקָּרוֹב
אָמַר יְהוָה
וּרְפָאתִיו:
20 וְהָרְשָׁעִים כַּיָּם נִגְרָשׁ
כִּי הַשְׁקֵט לֹא יוּכָל
וַיִּגְרְשׁוּ מֵימָיו רֶפֶשׁ וָטִיט:
21 אֵין שָׁלוֹם
אָמַר אֱלֹהַי
לָרְשָׁעִים: ס

58 Cry with full throat, without restraint;
Raise your voice like a ram's horn!
Declare to My people their transgression,
To the House of Jacob their sin.

נח קְרָא בְגָרוֹן אַל־תַּחְשֹׂךְ
כַּשּׁוֹפָר הָרֵם קוֹלֶךָ
וְהַגֵּד לְעַמִּי פִּשְׁעָם
וּלְבֵית יַעֲקֹב חַטֹּאתָם:

2To be sure, they seek Me daily,
Eager to learn My ways.
Like a nation that does what is right,
That has not abandoned the laws of its God,
They ask Me for the right way,
They are eager for the nearness of God:
3"Why, when we fasted, did You not see?
When we starved our bodies, did You pay no heed?"
Because on your fast day
You see to your business
And oppress all your laborers!
4Because you fast in strife and contention,
And you strike with a wicked fist!
Your fasting today is not such
As to make your voice heard on high.
5Is such the fast I desire,
A day for men to starve their bodies?

2 וְאוֹתִי יוֹם יוֹם יִדְרֹשׁוּן
וְדַעַת דְּרָכַי יֶחְפָּצוּן
כְּגוֹי אֲשֶׁר־צְדָקָה עָשָׂה
וּמִשְׁפַּט אֱלֹהָיו לֹא עָזָב
יִשְׁאָלוּנִי מִשְׁפְּטֵי־צֶדֶק
קִרְבַת אֱלֹהִים יֶחְפָּצוּן:
3 לָמָּה צַּמְנוּ וְלֹא רָאִיתָ
עִנִּינוּ נַפְשֵׁנוּ וְלֹא תֵדָע
הֵן בְּיוֹם צֹמְכֶם
תִּמְצְאוּ־חֵפֶץ
וְכָל־עַצְּבֵיכֶם תִּנְגֹּשׂוּ:
4 הֵן לְרִיב וּמַצָּה תָּצוּמוּ
וּלְהַכּוֹת בְּאֶגְרֹף רֶשַׁע
לֹא־תָצוּמוּ כַיּוֹם
לְהַשְׁמִיעַ בַּמָּרוֹם קוֹלְכֶם:
5 הֲכָזֶה יִהְיֶה צוֹם אֶבְחָרֵהוּ
יוֹם עַנּוֹת אָדָם נַפְשׁוֹ

---

q　Lit. "the vigor of"; cf. Eccl. 12.1 and postbiblical bori.
r　The Heb. nib is otherwise unknown; its meaning is inferred from that of nid (cf. the verb nad "to condole") in the parallel expression in Job 16.5.

Is it bowing the head like a bulrush
And lying in sackcloth and ashes?
Do you call that a fast,
A day when the LORD is favorable?
⁶No, this is the fast I desire:
To unlock fetters of wickedness,
And untie the cords of *a*-the yoke-*a*
To let the oppressed go free;
To break off every yoke.
⁷It is to share your bread with the hungry,
And to take the wretched poor into your
    home;
When you see the naked, to clothe him,
And not to ignore your own kin.

⁸Then shall your light burst through like the
    dawn
And your healing spring up quickly;
Your Vindicator shall march before you,
The Presence of the LORD shall be your rear
    guard.
⁹Then, when you call, the LORD will answer;
When you cry, He will say: Here I am.
If you banish the yoke*a* from your midst,
b-The menacing hand,-*b* and evil speech,
¹⁰And you offer your compassion*c* to the
    hungry
And satisfy the famished creature—
Then shall your light shine in darkness,
And your gloom shall be like noonday.
¹¹The LORD will guide you always;
He will slake your thirst in *d*-parched places-*d*
And give strength to your bones.
You shall be like a watered garden,
Like a spring whose waters do not fail.
¹²Men from your midst shall rebuild ancient
    ruins,
You shall restore foundations laid long ago.

הֲלָכֹף כְּאַגְמֹן רֹאשׁוֹ
וְשַׂק וָאֵפֶר יַצִּיעַ
הֲלָזֶה תִּקְרָא־צוֹם
וְיוֹם רָצוֹן לַיהוָה:
6 הֲלוֹא זֶה צוֹם אֶבְחָרֵהוּ
פַּתֵּחַ חַרְצֻבּוֹת רֶשַׁע
הַתֵּר אֲגֻדּוֹת מוֹטָה
וְשַׁלַּח רְצוּצִים חָפְשִׁים
וְכָל־מוֹטָה תְּנַתֵּקוּ:
7 הֲלוֹא פָרֹס לָרָעֵב לַחְמֶךָ
וַעֲנִיִּים מְרוּדִים תָּבִיא בָיִת
כִּי־תִרְאֶה עָרֹם וְכִסִּיתוֹ
וּמִבְּשָׂרְךָ לֹא תִתְעַלָּם:

8 אָז יִבָּקַע כַּשַּׁחַר אוֹרֶךָ
וַאֲרֻכָתְךָ מְהֵרָה תִצְמָח
וְהָלַךְ לְפָנֶיךָ צִדְקֶךָ
כְּבוֹד יְהוָה יַאַסְפֶךָ:
9 אָז תִּקְרָא וַיהוָה יַעֲנֶה
תְּשַׁוַּע וְיֹאמַר הִנֵּנִי
אִם־תָּסִיר מִתּוֹכְךָ מוֹטָה
שְׁלַח אֶצְבַּע וְדַבֶּר־אָוֶן:
10 וְתָפֵק לָרָעֵב נַפְשֶׁךָ
וְנֶפֶשׁ נַעֲנָה תַּשְׂבִּיעַ
וְזָרַח בַּחֹשֶׁךְ אוֹרֶךָ
וַאֲפֵלָתְךָ כַּצָּהֳרָיִם:
11 וְנָחֲךָ יְהוָה תָּמִיד
וְהִשְׂבִּיעַ בְּצַחְצָחוֹת נַפְשֶׁךָ
וְעַצְמֹתֶיךָ יַחֲלִיץ
וְהָיִיתָ כְּגַן רָוֶה
וּכְמוֹצָא מַיִם אֲשֶׁר לֹא־יְכַזְּבוּ מֵימָיו:
12 וּבָנוּ מִמְּךָ חָרְבוֹת עוֹלָם
מוֹסְדֵי דוֹר־וָדוֹר תְּקוֹמֵם

---

a-a   *Change of vocalization yields "lawlessness"; cf.* muṭṭeh, *Ezek.*
    9.9.
b-b   *Lit. "Extending the finger."*
c   *Some Heb. mss. and ancient versions read "bread."*
d-d   *Meaning of Heb. uncertain.*

And you shall be called
"Repairer of fallen walls,
Restorer of lanes for habitation."
¹³If you ᵉ-refrain from trampling-ᵉ the sab-
bath,
From pursuing your affairs on My holy day;
If you call the sabbath "delight,"
The LORD's holy day "honored";
And if you honor it and go not your ways
Nor look to your affairs, nor strike bargains—
¹⁴Then you ᶠ-can seek the favor of the LORD.-ᶠ
I will set you astride the heights of the earth,
And let you enjoy the heritage of your father
Jacob—
For the mouth of the LORD has spoken.

59 No, the LORD's arm is not too short to
save,
Or His ear too dull to hear;
²But your iniquities have been a barrier
Between you and your God,
Your sins have made Him turn His face away
And refuse to hear you.
³For your hands are defiled with crimeᵃ
And your fingers with iniquity.
Your lips speak falsehood,
Your tongue utters treachery.
⁴No one sues justly
Or pleads honestly;
They rely on emptiness and speak falsehood,
Conceiving wrong and begetting evil.

⁵They hatch adder's eggs
And weave spider webs;
He who eats of those eggs will die,
And if one is crushed, it hatches out a viper.
⁶Their webs will not serve as a garment,
What they make cannot serve as clothing;

וְקֹרָ֤א לְךָ֙
גֹּדֵ֣ר פֶּ֔רֶץ
מְשֹׁבֵ֥ב נְתִיב֖וֹת לָשָֽׁבֶת׃
13 אִם־תָּשִׁ֤יב מִשַּׁבָּת֙ רַגְלֶ֔ךָ
עֲשׂ֥וֹת חֲפָצֶ֖יךָ בְּי֣וֹם קׇדְשִׁ֑י
וְקָרָ֨אתָ לַשַּׁבָּ֜ת עֹ֗נֶג
לִקְד֤וֹשׁ יְהֹוָה֙ מְכֻבָּ֔ד
וְכִבַּדְתּוֹ֙ מֵעֲשׂ֣וֹת דְּרָכֶ֔יךָ
מִמְּצ֥וֹא חֶפְצְךָ֖ וְדַבֵּ֥ר דָּבָֽר׃
14 אָ֗ז תִּתְעַנַּג֙ עַל־יְהֹוָ֔ה
וְהִרְכַּבְתִּ֖יךָ עַל־בָּ֣מוֹתֵי אָ֑רֶץ
וְהַאֲכַלְתִּ֗יךָ נַחֲלַת֙ יַעֲקֹ֣ב אָבִ֔יךָ
כִּ֛י פִּ֥י יְהֹוָ֖ה דִּבֵּֽר׃ ס

נט הֵ֛ן לֹֽא־קָצְרָ֥ה יַד־יְהֹוָ֖ה מֵֽהוֹשִׁ֑יעַ
וְלֹא־כָבְדָ֥ה אׇזְנ֖וֹ מִשְּׁמֽוֹעַ׃
2 כִּ֤י אִם־עֲוֺנֹֽתֵיכֶם֙ הָי֣וּ מַבְדִּלִ֔ים
בֵּינֵכֶ֕ם לְבֵ֖ין אֱלֹהֵיכֶ֑ם
וְחַטֹּאותֵיכֶ֗ם* הִסְתִּ֧ירוּ פָנִ֛ים
מִכֶּ֖ם מִשְּׁמֽוֹעַ׃
3 כִּ֤י כַפֵּיכֶם֙ נְגֹאֲל֣וּ בַדָּ֔ם
וְאֶצְבְּעוֹתֵיכֶ֖ם בֶּעָוֺ֑ן
שִׂפְתֽוֹתֵיכֶם֙ דִּבְּרוּ־שֶׁ֔קֶר
לְשׁוֹנְכֶ֖ם עַוְלָ֥ה תֶהְגֶּֽה׃
4 אֵין־קֹרֵ֣א בְצֶ֔דֶק
וְאֵ֥ין נִשְׁפָּ֖ט בֶּאֱמוּנָ֑ה
בָּט֤וֹחַ עַל־תֹּ֙הוּ֙ וְדַבֶּר־שָׁ֔וְא
הָר֥וֹ עָמָ֖ל וְהוֹלֵ֥יד אָֽוֶן׃

5 בֵּיצֵ֤י צִפְעוֹנִי֙ בִּקֵּ֔עוּ
וְקוּרֵ֥י עַכָּבִ֖ישׁ יֶאֱרֹ֑גוּ
הָאֹכֵ֤ל מִבֵּֽיצֵיהֶם֙ יָמ֔וּת
וְהַזּוּרֶ֖ה תִּבָּקַ֥ע אֶפְעֶֽה׃
6 קֽוּרֵיהֶם֙ לֹֽא־יִהְי֣וּ לְבֶ֔גֶד
וְלֹ֥א יִתְכַּסּ֖וּ בְּמַֽעֲשֵׂיהֶ֑ם

e-e   Lit. "turn back your foot from."
f-f   Cf. Ps. 37.4; Job 22.26–27; 27.10.
a   Or "blood."

מלא ו׳   v. 2.

982

Their deeds are deeds of mischief,
Their hands commit lawless acts,
7Their feet run after evil,
They hasten to shed the blood of the innocent.
Their plans are plans of mischief,
Destructiveness and injury are on their roads.
8They do not care for the way of integrity,
There is no justice on their paths.
They make their courses crooked,
No one who walks in them cares for integrity.

9"That is why redress is far from us,
And vindication does not reach us.
We hope for light, and lo! there is darkness;
For a gleam, and we must walk in gloom.
10We grope, like blind men along a wall;
Like those without eyes we grope.
We stumble at noon, as if in darkness;
b-Among the sturdy, we are-b like the dead.
11We all growl like bears
And moan like doves.
We hope for redress, and there is none;
For victory, and it is far from us.
12For our many sins are before You,
Our guilt testifies against us.
We are aware of our sins,
And we know well our iniquities:
13Rebellion, faithlessness to the LORD,
And turning away from our God,
Planning fraud and treachery,
Conceiving lies and uttering them with the
    throat.c
14And so redress is turned back
And vindication stays afar,
Because honesty stumbles in the public
    square
And uprightness cannot enter.
15Honesty has been lacking,
He who turns away from evil is despoiled."

מַעֲשֵׂיהֶם מַעֲשֵׂי־אָ֔וֶן
וּפֹ֥עַל חָמָ֖ס בְּכַפֵּיהֶֽם׃
7 רַגְלֵיהֶם לָרַ֣ע יָרֻ֔צוּ
וִֽימַהֲר֔וּ לִשְׁפֹּ֖ךְ דָּ֣ם נָקִ֑י
מַחְשְׁבֽוֹתֵיהֶם֙ מַחְשְׁב֣וֹת אָ֔וֶן
שֹׁ֥ד וָשֶׁ֖בֶר בִּמְסִלּוֹתָֽם׃
8 דֶּ֤רֶךְ שָׁלוֹם֙ לֹ֣א יָדָ֔עוּ
וְאֵ֥ין מִשְׁפָּ֖ט בְּמַעְגְּלוֹתָ֑ם
נְתִיבֽוֹתֵיהֶם֙ עִקְּשׁ֣וּ לָהֶ֔ם
כֹּ֚ל דֹּרֵ֣ךְ בָּ֔הּ לֹ֥א יָדַ֖ע שָׁלֽוֹם׃

9 עַל־כֵּ֗ן רָחַ֤ק מִשְׁפָּט֙ מִמֶּ֔נּוּ
וְלֹ֥א תַשִּׂיגֵ֖נוּ צְדָקָ֑ה
נְקַוֶּ֤ה לָאוֹר֙ וְהִנֵּה־חֹ֔שֶׁךְ
לִנְגֹה֖וֹת בָּאֲפֵל֥וֹת נְהַלֵּֽךְ׃
10 נְגַֽשְׁשָׁ֤ה כַֽעִוְרִים֙ קִ֔יר
וּכְאֵ֥ין עֵינַ֖יִם נְגַשֵּׁ֑שָׁה
כָּשַׁ֤לְנוּ בַֽצׇּהֳרַ֙יִם֙ כַּנֶּ֔שֶׁף
בָּאַשְׁמַנִּ֖ים כַּמֵּתִֽים׃
11 נֶהֱמֶ֤ה כַדֻּבִּים֙ כֻּלָּ֔נוּ
וְכַיּוֹנִ֖ים הָגֹ֣ה נֶהְגֶּ֑ה
נְקַוֶּ֤ה לַמִּשְׁפָּט֙ וָאַ֔יִן
לִֽישׁוּעָ֖ה רָחֲקָ֥ה מִמֶּֽנּוּ׃
12 כִּֽי־רַבּ֤וּ פְשָׁעֵ֙ינוּ֙ נֶגְדֶּ֔ךָ
וְחַטֹּאותֵ֖ינוּ* עָ֣נְתָה בָּ֑נוּ
כִּֽי־פְשָׁעֵ֣ינוּ אִתָּ֔נוּ
וַעֲוֺנֹתֵ֖ינוּ יְדַעֲנֽוּם׃
13 פָּשֹׁ֤עַ וְכַחֵשׁ֙ בַּֽיהֹוָ֔ה
וְנָס֖וֹג מֵאַחַ֣ר אֱלֹהֵ֑ינוּ
דַּבֶּר־עֹ֣שֶׁק וְסָרָ֔ה
הֹר֧וֹ וְהֹג֛וֹ מִלֵּ֖ב דִּבְרֵי־שָֽׁקֶר׃
14 וְהֻסַּ֤ג אָחוֹר֙ מִשְׁפָּ֔ט
וּצְדָקָ֖ה מֵרָח֣וֹק תַּעֲמֹ֑ד
כִּֽי־כָשְׁלָ֤ה בָֽרְחוֹב֙ אֱמֶ֔ת
וּנְכֹחָ֖ה לֹא־תוּכַ֥ל לָבֽוֹא׃
15 וַתְּהִ֤י הָֽאֱמֶת֙ נֶעְדֶּ֔רֶת
וְסָ֥ר מֵרָ֖ע מִשְׁתּוֹלֵ֑ל

---

b-b   *Meaning of Heb. uncertain. Emendation yields* "In the day-
      time…"
c   *Lit.* "heart"; *see note at 33.18 and frequently elsewhere.*

The Lord saw and was displeased
That there was no redress.
16He saw that there was no man,
He gazed long, but no one intervened.
Then His own arm won Him triumph,
His victorious right hand*d* supported Him.
17He donned victory like a coat of mail,
With a helmet of triumph on His head;
He clothed Himself with garments of retri-
    bution,
Wrapped himself in zeal as in a robe.
18*e*-According to their deserts,
So shall He repay-*e* fury to His foes;
He shall make requital to His enemies,
Requital to the distant lands.
19From the west, they shall revere*f* the name
    of the Lord,
And from the east, His Presence.
For He shall come like a hemmed-in stream
Which the wind of the Lord drives on;
20He shall come as redeemer to Zion,
To those in Jacob who turn back from sin
                —declares the Lord.

21And this shall be My covenant with them,
said the Lord: My spirit*g* which is upon you,
and the words which I have placed in your
mouth, shall not be absent from your mouth,
nor from the mouth of your children, nor from
the mouth of your children's children—said the
Lord—from now on, for all time.*h*

60 Arise, shine, for your light has dawned;
The Presence of the Lord has shone upon
    you!
2Behold! Darkness shall cover the earth,
And thick clouds the peoples;

וַיַּ֤רְא יְהוָה֙ וַיֵּ֣רַע בְּעֵינָ֔יו
כִּֽי־אֵ֖ין מִשְׁפָּֽט׃
16 וַיַּרְא֙ כִּֽי־אֵ֣ין אִ֔ישׁ
וַיִּשְׁתּוֹמֵ֕ם כִּ֥י אֵ֖ין מַפְגִּ֑יעַ
וַתּ֤וֹשַֽׁע לוֹ֙ זְרֹע֔וֹ
וְצִדְקָת֖וֹ הִ֥יא סְמָכָֽתְהוּ׃
17 וַיִּלְבַּ֤שׁ צְדָקָה֙ כַּשִּׁרְיָ֔ן
וְכ֥וֹבַע יְשׁוּעָ֖ה בְּרֹאשׁ֑וֹ
וַיִּלְבַּ֞שׁ בִּגְדֵ֤י נָקָם֙ תִּלְבֹּ֔שֶׁת
וַיַּ֥עַט כַּמְעִ֖יל* קִנְאָֽה׃
18 כְּעַ֣ל גְּמֻל֔וֹת
כְּעַ֣ל יְשַׁלֵּ֗ם חֵמָ֤ה לְצָרָיו֙
גְּמ֣וּל לְאֹֽיְבָ֔יו
לָאִיִּ֖ים גְּמ֥וּל יְשַׁלֵּֽם׃
19 וְיִֽירְא֤וּ מִֽמַּעֲרָב֙ אֶת־שֵׁ֣ם יְהוָ֔ה
וּמִמִּזְרַח־שֶׁ֖מֶשׁ אֶת־כְּבוֹד֑וֹ
כִּֽי־יָב֤וֹא כַנָּהָר֙ צָ֔ר
ר֥וּחַ יְהוָ֖ה נֹ֥סְסָה בֽוֹ׃
20 וּבָ֤א לְצִיּוֹן֙ גּוֹאֵ֔ל
וּלְשָׁבֵ֥י פֶ֖שַׁע בְּיַעֲקֹ֑ב
נְאֻ֖ם יְהוָֽה׃

21 וַאֲנִ֗י זֹ֤את בְּרִיתִי֙ אוֹתָ֔ם אָמַ֣ר יְהוָ֔ה
רוּחִי֙ אֲשֶׁ֣ר עָלֶ֔יךָ וּדְבָרַ֖י אֲשֶׁר־שַׂ֣מְתִּי בְּפִ֑יךָ
לֹֽא־יָמ֡וּשׁוּ מִפִּ֩יךָ֩ וּמִפִּ֨י זַרְעֲךָ֜ וּמִפִּ֨י זֶ֤רַע
זַרְעֲךָ֙ אָמַ֣ר יְהוָ֔ה מֵעַתָּ֖ה וְעַד־עוֹלָֽם׃ ס

ס קוּמִ֥י א֖וֹרִי כִּ֣י בָ֣א אוֹרֵ֑ךְ
וּכְב֥וֹד יְהוָ֖ה עָלַ֥יִךְ זָרָֽח׃
2 כִּֽי־הִנֵּ֤ה הַחֹ֙שֶׁךְ֙ יְכַסֶּה־אֶ֔רֶץ
וַעֲרָפֶ֖ל לְאֻמִּ֑ים

d Cf. Ps. 98.1–2.
e-e Meaning of Heb. uncertain.
f Or (with a number of mss. and editions) "see."
g I.e., the gift of prophecy; cf., e.g., 61.1.
h Israel is to be a prophet-nation; cf. 51.16.

But upon you the LORD will shine,
And His Presence be seen over you.
³And nations shall walk by your light,
Kings, by your shining radiance.

⁴Raise your eyes and look about:
They have all gathered and come to you.
Your sons shall be brought from afar,
Your daughters like babes on shoulders.
⁵As you behold, you will glow;
Your heart will throb and thrill—
For the wealth of the seaᵃ shall pass on to you,
The riches of nations shall flow to you.
⁶Dust clouds of camels shall cover you,
Dromedaries of Midian and Ephah.
They all shall come from Sheba;
They shall bear gold and frankincense,
And shall herald the glories of the LORD.
⁷All the flocks of Kedar shall be assembled for
   you,
The rams of Nebaioth shall serve your needs;
They shall be welcome offerings on My altar,
And I will add glory to My glorious House.

⁸Who are these that float like a cloud,
Like doves to their cotes?
⁹ᵇ-Behold, the coastlands await me,-ᵇ
With ᶜ-ships of Tarshish-ᶜ in the lead,
To bring your sons from afar,
And theirᵈ silver and gold as well—
For the name of the LORD your God,
For the Holy One of Israel, who has glorified
   you.
¹⁰Aliens shall rebuild your walls,
Their kings shall wait upon you—
For in anger I struck you down,
But in favor I take you back.
¹¹Your gates shall always stay open—

וְעָלַ֙יִךְ֙ יִזְרַ֣ח יְהוָ֔ה
וּכְבוֹד֖וֹ עָלַ֥יִךְ יֵרָאֶֽה׃
3 וְהָלְכ֥וּ גוֹיִ֖ם לְאוֹרֵ֑ךְ
וּמְלָכִ֖ים לְנֹ֥גַהּ זַרְחֵֽךְ׃

4 שְׂאִֽי־סָבִ֤יב עֵינַ֙יִךְ֙ וּרְאִ֔י
כֻּלָּ֖ם נִקְבְּצ֣וּ בָֽאוּ־לָ֑ךְ
בָּנַ֙יִךְ֙ מֵרָח֣וֹק יָבֹ֔אוּ
וּבְנֹתַ֖יִךְ עַל־צַ֥ד תֵּאָמַֽנָה׃
5 אָ֤ז תִּרְאִי֙ וְנָהַ֔רְתְּ
וּפָחַ֥ד וְרָחַ֖ב לְבָבֵ֑ךְ
כִּֽי־יֵהָפֵ֤ךְ עָלַ֙יִךְ֙ הֲמ֣וֹן יָ֔ם
חֵ֥יל גּוֹיִ֖ם יָבֹ֥אוּ לָֽךְ׃
6 שִֽׁפְעַ֨ת גְּמַלִּים֙ תְּכַסֵּ֔ךְ
בִּכְרֵ֥י מִדְיָ֖ן וְעֵיפָ֑ה
כֻּלָּם֙ מִשְּׁבָ֣א יָבֹ֔אוּ
זָהָ֥ב וּלְבוֹנָ֖ה יִשָּׂ֑אוּ
וּתְהִלֹּ֥ת יְהוָ֖ה יְבַשֵּֽׂרוּ׃
7 כָּל־צֹ֤אן קֵדָר֙ יִקָּ֣בְצוּ לָ֔ךְ
אֵילֵ֥י נְבָי֖וֹת יְשָׁרְת֑וּנֶךְ
יַעֲל֤וּ עַל־רָצוֹן֙ מִזְבְּחִ֔י
וּבֵ֥ית תִּפְאַרְתִּ֖י אֲפָאֵֽר׃

8 מִי־אֵ֖לֶּה כָּעָ֣ב תְּעוּפֶ֑ינָה
וְכַיּוֹנִ֖ים אֶל־אֲרֻבֹּתֵיהֶֽם׃
9 כִּֽי־לִ֣י ׀ אִיִּ֣ים יְקַוּ֗וּ
וָאֳנִיּ֤וֹת תַּרְשִׁישׁ֙ בָּרִ֣אשֹׁנָ֔ה
לְהָבִ֤יא בָנַ֙יִךְ֙ מֵֽרָח֔וֹק
כַּסְפָּ֥ם וּזְהָבָ֖ם אִתָּ֑ם
לְשֵׁם֙ יְהוָ֣ה אֱלֹהַ֔יִךְ
וְלִקְד֥וֹשׁ יִשְׂרָאֵ֖ל כִּ֥י פֵאֲרָֽךְ׃
10 וּבָנ֤וּ בְנֵֽי־נֵכָר֙ חֹמֹתַ֔יִךְ
וּמַלְכֵיהֶ֖ם יְשָׁרְת֑וּנֶךְ
כִּ֤י בְקִצְפִּי֙ הִכִּיתִ֔יךְ
וּבִרְצוֹנִ֖י רִֽחַמְתִּֽיךְ׃
11 וּפִתְּח֙וּ שְׁעָרַ֧יִךְ תָּמִ֛יד

Day and night they shall never be shut—
To let in the wealth of the nations,
With their kings in procession.

¹²For the nation or the kingdom
That does not serve you shall perish;
Such nations shall be destroyed.

¹³The majesty of Lebanon shall come to
   you—
Cypress and pine and box—
To adorn the site of My Sanctuary,
To glorify the place where My feet rest.

¹⁴Bowing before you, shall come
The children of those who tormented you;
Prostrate at the soles of your feet
Shall be all those who reviled you;
And you shall be called
"City of the Lord,
Zion of the Holy One of Israel."
¹⁵Whereas you have been forsaken,
Rejected, with none passing through,
I will make you a pride everlasting,
A joy for age after age.
¹⁶You shall suck the milk of the nations,
Suckle at royal breasts.ᵉ
And you shall know
That I the Lord am your Savior,
I, The Mighty One of Jacob, am your Re-
   deemer.
¹⁷Instead of copper I will bring gold,
Instead of iron I will bring silver;
Instead of wood, copper;
And instead of stone, iron.
And I will appoint Well-being as your gov-
   ernment,
Prosperity as your officials.
¹⁸The cry "Violence!"

יוֹמָ֧ם וָלַ֛יְלָה לֹ֥א יִסָּגֵ֖רוּ
לְהָבִ֤יא אֵלַ֙יִךְ֙ חֵ֣יל גּוֹיִ֔ם
וּמַלְכֵיהֶ֖ם נְהוּגִֽים׃

12 כִּֽי־הַגּ֧וֹי וְהַמַּמְלָכָ֛ה
אֲשֶׁ֥ר לֹא־יַעַבְד֖וּךְ יֹאבֵ֑דוּ
וְהַגּוֹיִ֖ם חָרֹ֥ב יֶחֱרָֽבוּ׃

13 כְּב֤וֹד הַלְּבָנוֹן֙ אֵלַ֣יִךְ יָב֔וֹא
בְּר֛וֹשׁ תִּדְהָ֥ר וּתְאַשּׁ֖וּר יַחְדָּ֑ו
לְפָאֵר֙ מְק֣וֹם מִקְדָּשִׁ֔י
וּמְק֥וֹם רַגְלַ֖י אֲכַבֵּֽד׃

14 וְהָלְכ֨וּ אֵלַ֤יִךְ שְׁח֙וֹחַ֙
בְּנֵ֣י מְעַנַּ֔יִךְ
וְהִֽשְׁתַּחֲו֛וּ עַל־כַּפּ֥וֹת רַגְלַ֖יִךְ
כָּל־מְנַאֲצָ֑יִךְ
וְקָ֤רְאוּ לָךְ֙
עִ֣יר יְהֹוָ֔ה
צִיּ֖וֹן קְד֥וֹשׁ יִשְׂרָאֵֽל׃
15 תַּ֧חַת הֱיוֹתֵ֛ךְ עֲזוּבָ֥ה
וּשְׂנוּאָ֖ה וְאֵ֣ין עוֹבֵ֑ר
וְשַׂמְתִּיךְ֙ לִגְא֣וֹן עוֹלָ֔ם
מְשׂ֖וֹשׂ דּ֥וֹר וָדֽוֹר׃
16 וְיָנַ֙קְתְּ֙ חֲלֵ֣ב גּוֹיִ֔ם
וְשֹׁ֥ד מְלָכִ֖ים תִּינָ֑קִי
וְיָדַ֗עַתְּ
כִּ֣י אֲנִ֤י יְהֹוָה֙ מֽוֹשִׁיעֵ֔ךְ
וְגֹאֲלֵ֖ךְ אֲבִ֥יר יַעֲקֹֽב׃
17 תַּ֣חַת הַנְּחֹ֜שֶׁת אָבִ֣יא זָהָ֗ב
וְתַ֤חַת הַבַּרְזֶל֙ אָבִ֣יא כֶ֔סֶף
וְתַ֤חַת הָֽעֵצִים֙ נְחֹ֔שֶׁת
וְתַ֖חַת הָאֲבָנִ֣ים בַּרְזֶ֑ל
וְשַׂמְתִּ֤י פְקֻדָּתֵךְ֙ שָׁל֔וֹם
וְנֹגְשַׂ֖יִךְ צְדָקָֽה׃
18 לֹא־יִשָּׁמַ֨ע

ᵉ Lit. "breasts of kings" or "breasts of kingdoms."

Shall no more be heard in your land,
Nor "Wrack and ruin!"
Within your borders.
And you shall name your walls "Victory"
And your gates "Renown."

19No longer shall you need the sun
For light by day,
Nor the shining of the moon
For radiance [by night*f*];
For the Lord shall be your light everlasting,
Your God shall be your glory.
20Your sun shall set no more,
Your moon no more withdraw;
For the Lord shall be a light to you forever,
And your days of mourning shall be ended.
21And your people, all of them righteous,
Shall possess the land for all time;
They are the shoot that I planted,
My handiwork in which I glory.
22The smallest shall become a clan;
The least, a mighty nation.
I the Lord will speed it in due time.

עוֹד חָמָס בְּאַרְצֵךְ
שֹׁד וָשֶׁבֶר
בִּגְבוּלָיִךְ
וְקָרָאת יְשׁוּעָה חוֹמֹתַיִךְ
וּשְׁעָרַיִךְ תְּהִלָּה:

19 לֹא־יִהְיֶה־לָּךְ עוֹד הַשֶּׁמֶשׁ
לְאוֹר יוֹמָם
וּלְנֹגַהּ הַיָּרֵחַ
לֹא־יָאִיר לָךְ
וְהָיָה־לָךְ יְהוָה לְאוֹר עוֹלָם
וֵאלֹהַיִךְ לְתִפְאַרְתֵּךְ:
20 לֹא־יָבוֹא עוֹד שִׁמְשֵׁךְ
וִירֵחֵךְ לֹא יֵאָסֵף
כִּי יְהוָה יִהְיֶה־לָּךְ לְאוֹר עוֹלָם
וְשָׁלְמוּ יְמֵי אֶבְלֵךְ:
21 וְעַמֵּךְ כֻּלָּם צַדִּיקִים
לְעוֹלָם יִירְשׁוּ אָרֶץ
נֵצֶר מַטָּעַי
מַעֲשֵׂה יָדַי לְהִתְפָּאֵר:
22 הַקָּטֹן יִהְיֶה לָאֶלֶף
וְהַצָּעִיר לְגוֹי עָצוּם
אֲנִי יְהוָה בְּעִתָּהּ אֲחִישֶׁנָּה: ס

61 The spirit of the Lord God is upon me,
Because the Lord has anointed me;
He has sent me as a herald of joy to the
   humble,
To bind up the wounded of heart,
To proclaim release to the captives,
Liberation to the imprisoned;
2To proclaim a year of the Lord's favor
And a day of vindication by our God;
To comfort all who mourn—
3*a*-To provide for-*a* the mourners in Zion—
To give them a turban instead of ashes,

סא רוּחַ אֲדֹנָי יְהוִה עָלָי
יַעַן מָשַׁח יְהוָה אֹתִי
לְבַשֵּׂר עֲנָוִים שְׁלָחַנִי
לַחֲבֹשׁ לְנִשְׁבְּרֵי־לֵב
לִקְרֹא לִשְׁבוּיִם דְּרוֹר
וְלַאֲסוּרִים פְּקַח־קוֹחַ:
2 לִקְרֹא שְׁנַת־רָצוֹן לַיהוָה
וְיוֹם נָקָם לֵאלֹהֵינוּ
לְנַחֵם כָּל־אֲבֵלִים:
3 לָשׂוּם | לַאֲבֵלֵי צִיּוֹן
לָתֵת לָהֶם פְּאֵר תַּחַת אֵפֶר

---

f   So 1QIsª, Septuagint, and Targum.

a-a   Meaning of Heb. uncertain.

The festive ointment instead of mourning,
A garment of splendor instead of a drooping
    spirit.
They shall be called terebinths of victory,
Planted by the Lord for His glory.
⁴And they shall build the ancient ruins,
Raise up the desolations of old,
And renew the ruined cities,
The desolations of many ages.
⁵Strangers shall stand and pasture your
    flocks,
Aliens shall be your plowmen and vine-
    trimmers;
⁶While you shall be called "Priests of the
    Lord,"
And termed "Servants of our God."
You shall enjoy the wealth of nations
And revel*ᵃ* in their riches.
⁷Because your shame was double—
ᵇ-Men cried, "Disgrace is their portion"-*ᵇ*—
Assuredly,
They shall have a double share in their land,
Joy shall be theirs for all time.
⁸For I the Lord love justice,
I hate *ᶜ*-robbery with a burnt offering.-*ᶜ*
I will pay them their wages faithfully,
And make a covenant with them for all time.
⁹Their offspring shall be known among the
    nations,
Their descendants in the midst of the peoples.
All who see them shall recognize
That they are a stock the Lord has blessed.

¹⁰I greatly rejoice in the Lord,
My whole being exults in my God.
For He has clothed me with garments of tri-
    umph,
Wrapped me in a robe of victory,
Like a bridegroom adorned with a turban,

שֶׁ֤מֶן שָׂשׂוֹן֙ תַּ֣חַת אֵ֔בֶל
מַעֲטֵ֤ה תְהִלָּה֙ תַּ֣חַת ר֣וּחַ כֵּהָ֑ה
וְקֹרָ֤א לָהֶם֙ אֵילֵ֣י הַצֶּ֔דֶק
מַטַּ֥ע יְהֹוָ֖ה לְהִתְפָּאֵֽר׃
⁴ וּבָנוּ֙ חָרְב֣וֹת עוֹלָ֔ם
שֹׁמְמ֥וֹת רִֽאשֹׁנִ֖ים יְקוֹמֵ֑מוּ
וְחִדְּשׁוּ֙ עָ֣רֵי חֹ֔רֶב
שֹׁמְמ֖וֹת דּ֥וֹר וָדֽוֹר׃
⁵ וְעָמְד֣וּ זָרִ֔ים וְרָע֖וּ צֹאנְכֶ֑ם
וּבְנֵ֣י נֵכָ֔ר אִכָּרֵיכֶ֖ם וְכֹרְמֵיכֶֽם׃
⁶ וְאַתֶּ֗ם כֹּהֲנֵ֤י יְהֹוָה֙ תִּקָּרֵ֔אוּ
מְשָׁרְתֵ֣י אֱלֹהֵ֔ינוּ יֵאָמֵ֖ר לָכֶ֑ם
חֵ֤יל גּוֹיִם֙ תֹּאכֵ֔לוּ
וּבִכְבוֹדָ֖ם תִּתְיַמָּֽרוּ׃
⁷ תַּ֤חַת בָּשְׁתְּכֶם֙ מִשְׁנֶ֔ה
וּכְלִמָּ֖ה יָרֹ֣נּוּ חֶלְקָ֑ם
לָכֵ֤ן
בְּאַרְצָם֙ מִשְׁנֶ֣ה יִירָ֔שׁוּ
שִׂמְחַ֥ת עוֹלָ֖ם תִּֽהְיֶ֥ה לָהֶֽם׃
⁸ כִּ֣י אֲנִ֤י יְהֹוָה֙ אֹהֵ֣ב מִשְׁפָּ֔ט
שֹׂנֵ֥א גָזֵ֖ל בְּעוֹלָ֑ה
וְנָתַתִּ֤י פְעֻלָּתָם֙ בֶּאֱמֶ֔ת
וּבְרִ֥ית עוֹלָ֖ם אֶכְר֥וֹת לָהֶֽם׃
⁹ וְנוֹדַ֤ע בַּגּוֹיִם֙ זַרְעָ֔ם
וְצֶאֱצָאֵיהֶ֖ם בְּת֣וֹךְ הָעַמִּ֑ים
כׇּל־רֹֽאֵיהֶם֙ יַכִּיר֔וּם
כִּ֛י הֵ֥ם זֶ֖רַע בֵּרַ֥ךְ יְהֹוָֽה׃ ס

¹⁰ שׂ֧וֹשׂ אָשִׂ֣ישׂ בַּֽיהֹוָ֗ה
תָּגֵ֤ל נַפְשִׁי֙ בֵּֽאלֹהַ֔י
כִּ֤י הִלְבִּישַׁ֙נִי֙ בִּגְדֵי־יֶ֔שַׁע
מְעִ֥יל צְדָקָ֖ה יְעָטָ֑נִי
כֶּֽחָתָן֙ יְכַהֵ֣ן פְּאֵ֔ר

---

b-b   Emendation yields "They inherited disgrace as their portion."
c-c   Emendation yields "the robbing of wages."

Like a bride bedecked with her finery.
11For as the earth brings forth her growth
And a garden makes the seed shoot up,
So the Lord GOD will make
Victory and renown shoot up
In the presence of all the nations.

וְכַכַּלָּה תַּעְדֶּה כֵלֶיהָ:
11 כִּי כָאָרֶץ תּוֹצִיא צִמְחָהּ
וּכְגַנָּה זֵרוּעֶיהָ תַצְמִיחַ
כֵּן ׀ אֲדֹנָי יְהֹוִה
יַצְמִיחַ צְדָקָה וּתְהִלָּה
נֶגֶד כָּל־הַגּוֹיִם:

62 For the sake of Zion I will not be silent,
For the sake of Jerusalem I will not be still,
Till her victory emerge resplendent
And her triumph like a flaming torch.
2Nations shall see your victory,
And every king your majesty;
And you shall be called by a new name
Which the LORD Himself shall bestow.
3You shall be a glorious crown
In the hand of the LORD,
And a royal diadem
In the palm of your God.

סב לְמַעַן צִיּוֹן לֹא אֶחֱשֶׁה
וּלְמַעַן יְרוּשָׁלַ͏ִם לֹא אֶשְׁקוֹט
עַד־יֵצֵא כַנֹּגַהּ צִדְקָהּ
וִישׁוּעָתָהּ כְּלַפִּיד יִבְעָר:
2 וְרָאוּ גוֹיִם צִדְקֵךְ
וְכָל־מְלָכִים כְּבוֹדֵךְ
וְקֹרָא לָךְ שֵׁם חָדָשׁ
אֲשֶׁר פִּי יְהֹוָה יִקֳּבֶנּוּ:
3 וְהָיִית עֲטֶרֶת תִּפְאֶרֶת
בְּיַד־יְהֹוָה
וּצְנִיף מְלוּכָה
בְּכַף־אֱלֹהָיִךְ:

4Nevermore shall you be called "Forsaken,"
Nor shall your land be called "Desolate";
But you shall be called "I delight in her,"
And your land "Espoused."
For the LORD takes delight in you,
And your land shall be espoused.
5As a youth espouses a maiden,
^a-Your sons-^a shall espouse you;
And as a bridegroom rejoices over his bride,
So will your God rejoice over you.

4 לֹא־יֵאָמֵר לָךְ עוֹד עֲזוּבָה
וּלְאַרְצֵךְ לֹא־יֵאָמֵר עוֹד שְׁמָמָה
כִּי לָךְ יִקָּרֵא חֶפְצִי־בָהּ
וּלְאַרְצֵךְ בְּעוּלָה
כִּי־חָפֵץ יְהֹוָה בָּךְ
וְאַרְצֵךְ תִּבָּעֵל:
5 כִּי־יִבְעַל בָּחוּר בְּתוּלָה
יִבְעָלוּךְ בָּנָיִךְ
וּמְשׂוֹשׂ חָתָן עַל־כַּלָּה
יָשִׂישׂ עָלַיִךְ אֱלֹהָיִךְ:

6Upon your walls, O Jerusalem,
I have set watchmen,
Who shall never be silent
By day or by night.
O you, the LORD's remembrancers,^b
Take no rest

6 עַל־חוֹמֹתַיִךְ יְרוּשָׁלַ͏ִם
הִפְקַדְתִּי שֹׁמְרִים
כָּל־הַיּוֹם וְכָל־הַלַּיְלָה תָּמִיד
לֹא יֶחֱשׁוּ
הַמַּזְכִּרִים אֶת־יְהֹוָה
אַל־דֳּמִי לָכֶם:

---

a-a   Change of vocalization yields "He who rebuilds you."
b   I.e., the watchmen just mentioned.

7And give no rest to Him,
   Until He establish Jerusalem
   And make her renowned on earth.

8The LORD has sworn by His right hand,
   By His mighty arm:
Nevermore will I give your new grain
   To your enemies for food,
Nor shall foreigners drink the new wine
   For which you have labored.
9But those who harvest it shall eat it
   And give praise to the LORD;
And those who gather it shall drink it
   In My sacred courts.
10Pass through, pass through the gates!
   Clear the road for the people;
Build up, build up the highway,
   Remove the rocks!
Raise an ensign over the peoples!
11See, the LORD has proclaimed
   To the end of the earth:
Announce to Fair Zion,
   Your Deliverer is coming!
See, his reward is with Him,
   His recompense before Him.c
12And they shall be called, "The Holy People,
   The Redeemed of the LORD,"
And you shall be called, "Sought Out,
   A City Not Forsaken."

63 Who is this coming from Edom,
   In crimsoned garments from Bozrah—
Who is this, majestic in attire,
   a-Pressing forward-a in His great might?
"It is I, who contend victoriously,
   Powerful to b-give triumph."-b

7 וְאַל־תִּתְּנ֥וּ דֳמִ֖י ל֑וֹ
עַד־יְכוֹנֵ֞ן וְעַד־יָשִׂ֧ים אֶת־יְרוּשָׁלַ֛͏ִם
תְּהִלָּ֖ה בָּאָֽרֶץ׃
8 נִשְׁבַּ֧ע יְהֹוָ֛ה בִּֽימִינ֖וֹ
וּבִזְר֣וֹעַ עֻזּ֑וֹ
אִם־אֶתֵּן֩ אֶת־דְּגָנֵ֨ךְ ע֤וֹד
מַֽאֲכָל֙ לְאֹ֣יְבַ֔יִךְ
וְאִם־יִשְׁתּ֤וּ בְנֵֽי־נֵכָר֙ תִּ֣ירוֹשֵׁ֔ךְ
אֲשֶׁ֖ר יָגַ֥עַתְּ בּֽוֹ׃
9 כִּ֤י מְאַסְפָיו֙ יֹֽאכְלֻ֔הוּ
וְהִֽלְל֖וּ אֶת־יְהֹוָ֑ה
וּֽמְקַבְּצָ֥יו יִשְׁתֻּ֖הוּ
בְּחַצְר֥וֹת קׇדְשִֽׁי׃ ס
10 עִבְר֤וּ עִבְרוּ֙ בַּשְּׁעָרִ֔ים
פַּנּ֖וּ דֶּ֣רֶךְ הָעָ֑ם
סֹ֥לּוּ סֹ֙לּוּ֙ הַֽמְסִלָּ֔ה
סַקְּל֣וּ מֵאֶ֔בֶן
הָרִ֥ימוּ נֵ֖ס עַל־הָֽעַמִּֽים׃
11 הִנֵּ֣ה יְהֹוָ֗ה הִשְׁמִ֙יעַ֙
אֶל־קְצֵ֣ה הָאָ֔רֶץ
אִמְרוּ֙ לְבַת־צִיּ֔וֹן
הִנֵּ֥ה יִשְׁעֵ֖ךְ בָּ֑א
הִנֵּ֤ה שְׂכָרוֹ֙ אִתּ֔וֹ
וּפְעֻלָּת֖וֹ לְפָנָֽיו׃
12 וְקָ֥רְא֛וּ לָהֶ֖ם עַם־הַקֹּ֑דֶשׁ
גְּאוּלֵ֖י יְהֹוָ֑ה
וְלָךְ֙ יִקָּרֵ֣א דְרוּשָׁ֔ה
עִ֖יר לֹ֥א נֶעֱזָֽבָה׃ ס

סג מִי־זֶ֣ה ׀ בָּ֣א מֵֽאֱד֗וֹם
חֲמ֤וּץ בְּגָדִים֙ מִבׇּצְרָ֔ה
זֶ֚ה הָד֣וּר בִּלְבוּשׁ֔וֹ
צֹעֶ֖ה בְּרֹ֣ב כֹּח֑וֹ
אֲנִ֛י מְדַבֵּ֥ר בִּצְדָקָ֖ה
רַ֥ב לְהוֹשִֽׁיעַ׃

---

c   *See note at 40.10.*

a-a   *Meaning of Heb. uncertain; emendation yields "striding."*
b-b   *Change of vocalization yields "Who contest triumphantly"; cf.*
    19.20.

2Why is your clothing so red,
Your garments like his who treads grapes?*c*

3"I trod out a vintage alone;
d-Of the peoples-*d* no man was with Me.
I trod them down in My anger,
Trampled them in My rage;
Their life-blood*e* bespattered My garments,
And all My clothing was stained.

4For I had planned a day of vengeance,
And My year of redemption arrived.

5Then I looked, but there was none to help;
I stared, but there was none to aid—
So My own arm wrought the triumph,
And *f*-My own rage-*f* was My aid.

6I trampled peoples in My anger,
g-I made them drunk with-*g* My rage,
And I hurled their glory to the ground."

7I will recount the kind acts of the LORD,
The praises of the LORD—
For all that the LORD has wrought for us,
The vast bounty to the House of Israel
That He bestowed upon them
According to His mercy and His great kind-
   ness.

8He thought: Surely they are My people,
Children who will not play false.
h-So He was their Deliverer.

9In all their troubles He was troubled,
And the angel of His Presence delivered
   them.-*h*
In His love and pity
He Himself redeemed them,
Raised them, and exalted them
All the days of old.

מַדּוּעַ אָדֹם לִלְבוּשֶׁךָ ²
וּבְגָדֶיךָ כְּדֹרֵךְ בְּגַת:
פּוּרָה | דָּרַכְתִּי לְבַדִּי ³
וּמֵעַמִּים אֵין־אִישׁ אִתִּי
וְאֶדְרְכֵם בְּאַפִּי
וְאֶרְמְסֵם בַּחֲמָתִי
וְיֵז נִצְחָם עַל־בְּגָדַי
וְכָל־מַלְבּוּשַׁי אֶגְאָלְתִּי:
כִּי יוֹם נָקָם בְּלִבִּי ⁴
וּשְׁנַת גְּאוּלַי בָּאָה:
וְאַבִּיט וְאֵין עֹזֵר ⁵
וְאֶשְׁתּוֹמֵם וְאֵין סוֹמֵךְ
וַתּוֹשַׁע לִי זְרֹעִי
וַחֲמָתִי הִיא סְמָכָתְנִי:
וְאָבוּס עַמִּים בְּאַפִּי ⁶
וַאֲשַׁכְּרֵם בַּחֲמָתִי
וְאוֹרִיד לָאָרֶץ נִצְחָם: ס

חַסְדֵי יְהוָה | אַזְכִּיר ⁷
תְּהִלֹּת יְהוָה
כְּעַל כֹּל אֲשֶׁר־גְּמָלָנוּ יְהוָה
וְרַב־טוּב לְבֵית יִשְׂרָאֵל
אֲשֶׁר־גְּמָלָם
כְּרַחֲמָיו וּכְרֹב חֲסָדָיו:
וַיֹּאמֶר אַךְ־עַמִּי הֵמָּה ⁸
בָּנִים לֹא יְשַׁקֵּרוּ
וַיְהִי לָהֶם לְמוֹשִׁיעַ:
בְּכָל־צָרָתָם | לֹא צָר ⁹
וּמַלְאַךְ פָּנָיו הוֹשִׁיעָם
בְּאַהֲבָתוֹ וּבְחֶמְלָתוֹ
הוּא גְאָלָם
וַיְנַטְּלֵם וַיְנַשְּׂאֵם
כָּל־יְמֵי עוֹלָם:

---

c   Lit. "in a press."
d-d   Emendation yields "Peoples, and…"
e   Meaning of Heb. uncertain.
f-f   Many mss. read *weṣidqathi* "My victorious [right hand]"; cf.
     59.16.
g-g   Many mss. and Targum read "I shattered them in"; cf. 14.25.
h-h   Ancient versions read "So He was their Deliverer /⁹ In all their
     troubles. / No [so kethib] angel or messenger, / His own
     Presence delivered them." Cf. Deut. 4.37 and note.

10But they rebelled, and grieved
His holy spirit;
Then He became their enemy,
And Himself made war against them.
11Then they[i] remembered the ancient days,
j-Him, who pulled His people-j out [of the
   water]:
"Where is He who brought them up from the
   Sea
Along with the shepherd[k] of His flock?
Where is He who put
In their midst His holy spirit,
12Who made His glorious arm
March at the right hand of Moses,
Who divided the waters before them
To make Himself a name for all time,
13Who led them through the deeps
So that they did not stumble—
As a horse in a desert,
14Like a beast descending to the plain?"
'Twas the spirit of the LORD l-gave them rest;-l
Thus did You shepherd Your people
To win for Yourself a glorious name.

15Look down from heaven and see,
From Your holy and glorious height!
Where is Your zeal, Your power?
Your yearning and Your love
Are being withheld from us![m]
16Surely You are our Father:
Though Abraham regard us not,
And Israel recognize us not,
You, O LORD, are our Father;
From of old, Your name is "Our Redeemer."
17Why, LORD, do You make us stray from
   Your ways,
And turn our hearts away from revering You?

10 וְהֵ֛מָּה מָר֥וּ וְעִצְּב֖וּ
אֶת־ר֣וּחַ קָדְשׁ֑וֹ
וַיֵּהָפֵ֥ךְ לָהֶ֛ם לְאוֹיֵ֖ב
ה֥וּא נִלְחַם־בָּֽם׃
11 וַיִּזְכֹּ֥ר יְמֵי־עוֹלָ֖ם
מֹשֶׁ֣ה עַמּ֑וֹ
אַיֵּ֣ה ׀ הַֽמַּעֲלֵ֣ם מִיָּ֗ם
אֵ֚ת רֹעֵ֣י* צֹאנ֔וֹ
אַיֵּ֛ה הַשָּׂ֥ם
בְּקִרְבּ֖וֹ אֶת־ר֥וּחַ קָדְשֽׁוֹ׃
12 מוֹלִיךְ֙ לִימִ֣ין מֹשֶׁ֔ה
זְר֖וֹעַ תִּפְאַרְתּ֑וֹ
בּ֤וֹקֵֽעַ מַ֙יִם֙ מִפְּנֵיהֶ֔ם
לַעֲשׂ֥וֹת ל֖וֹ שֵׁ֥ם עוֹלָֽם׃
13 מוֹלִיכָ֖ם בַּתְּהֹמ֑וֹת
כַּסּ֥וּס בַּמִּדְבָּ֖ר
לֹ֥א יִכָּשֵֽׁלוּ׃
14 כַּבְּהֵמָה֙ בַּבִּקְעָ֣ה תֵרֵ֔ד
ר֥וּחַ יְהֹוָ֖ה תְּנִיחֶ֑נּוּ
כֵּ֣ן נִהַ֣גְתָּ עַמְּךָ֔
לַעֲשׂ֥וֹת לְךָ֖ שֵׁ֥ם תִּפְאָֽרֶת׃
15 הַבֵּ֤ט מִשָּׁמַ֙יִם֙ וּרְאֵ֔ה
מִזְּבֻ֥ל קׇדְשְׁךָ֖ וְתִפְאַרְתֶּ֑ךָ
אַיֵּ֤ה קִנְאָֽתְךָ֙ וּגְב֣וּרֹתֶ֔ךָ
הֲמ֥וֹן מֵעֶ֛יךָ וְֽרַחֲמֶ֖יךָ
אֵלַ֥י הִתְאַפָּֽקוּ׃
16 כִּֽי־אַתָּ֣ה אָבִ֔ינוּ
כִּ֤י אַבְרָהָם֙ לֹ֣א יְדָעָ֔נוּ
וְיִשְׂרָאֵ֖ל לֹ֣א יַכִּירָ֑נוּ
אַתָּ֤ה יְהֹוָה֙ אָבִ֔ינוּ
גֹּאֲלֵ֥נוּ מֵעוֹלָ֖ם שְׁמֶֽךָ׃
17 לָ֣מָּה תַתְעֵ֤נוּ יְהֹוָה֙ מִדְּרָכֶ֔יךָ
תַּקְשִׁ֥יחַ לִבֵּ֖נוּ מִיִּרְאָתֶ֑ךָ

---

i   Heb. "he."
j-j Heb. moshe 'ammo, a play on the name Moshe (Moses).
k   So many mss. and ancient versions; other texts "shepherds."
l-l Emendation yields "guided them."
m   Heb. "me." Emendation yields "[Where are] Your yearning and
   Your love" / Let them not be restrained!"

Relent for the sake of Your servants,
The tribes that are Your very own!
18Our foes have trampled Your Sanctuary,
Which Your holy people *n*-possessed but a little while.-*n*
19We have become as a people You never
ruled,
To which Your name was never attached.

If You would but tear open the heavens and
come down,
So that mountains would quake before
You—

64 *a*As when fire kindles brushwood,
And fire makes water boil—
To make Your name known to Your adver-
saries
So that nations will tremble at Your Presence,
2When You did wonders we dared not hope
for,
You came down
And mountains quaked before You.
3Such things had never been heard or noted.
No eye has seen [them], O God, but You,
Who act for those who trust in You.*b*
4Yet you have struck him who would gladly
do justice,
And remember You in Your ways.
It is because You are angry that we have
sinned;
c-We have been steeped in them from of old,
And can we be saved?-*c*
5We have all become like an unclean thing,
And all our virtues like a filthy rag.
We are all withering like leaves,
And our iniquities, like a wind, carry us off.
6Yet no one invokes Your name,

שׁוּב לְמַעַן עֲבָדֶיךָ
שִׁבְטֵי נַחֲלָתֶךָ:
18 לַמִּצְעָר יָרְשׁוּ עַם־קָדְשֶׁךָ
צָרֵינוּ בּוֹסְסוּ מִקְדָּשֶׁךָ:
19 הָיִינוּ מֵעוֹלָם לֹא־מָשַׁלְתָּ בָּם
לֹא־נִקְרָא שִׁמְךָ עֲלֵיהֶם
לוּא־קָרַעְתָּ שָׁמַיִם יָרַדְתָּ
סד מִפָּנֶיךָ הָרִים נָזֹלּוּ:
כִּקְדֹחַ אֵשׁ הֲמָסִים
מַיִם תִּבְעֶה־אֵשׁ
לְהוֹדִיעַ שִׁמְךָ לְצָרֶיךָ
מִפָּנֶיךָ גּוֹיִם יִרְגָּזוּ:
2 בַּעֲשׂוֹתְךָ נוֹרָאוֹת לֹא נְקַוֶּה
יָרַדְתָּ
מִפָּנֶיךָ הָרִים נָזֹלּוּ:
3 וּמֵעוֹלָם לֹא־שָׁמְעוּ לֹא הֶאֱזִינוּ
עַיִן לֹא־רָאָתָה אֱלֹהִים זוּלָתְךָ
יַעֲשֶׂה לִמְחַכֵּה־לוֹ:
4 פָּגַעְתָּ אֶת־שָׂשׂ וְעֹשֵׂה צֶדֶק
בִּדְרָכֶיךָ יִזְכְּרוּךָ
הֵן־אַתָּה קָצַפְתָּ וַנֶּחֱטָא
בָּהֶם עוֹלָם
וְנִוָּשֵׁעַ:
5 וַנְּהִי כַטָּמֵא כֻּלָּנוּ
וּכְבֶגֶד עִדִּים כָּל־צִדְקֹתֵינוּ
וַנָּבֶל כֶּעָלֶה כֻּלָּנוּ
וַעֲוֺנֵנוּ כָּרוּחַ יִשָּׂאֻנוּ:
6 וְאֵין־קוֹרֵא בְשִׁמְךָ

---

n-n   Meaning of Heb. uncertain.

a   Meaning of vv. 1–4 uncertain.
b   Heb. "Him."
*c-c   Emendation yields "Because You have hidden Yourself we have
      offended." For the thought cf. 63.17.*

Rouses himself to cling to You.
For You have hidden Your face from us,
And ^{d}-made us melt because of-^{d} our iniquities.

מִתְעוֹרֵר לְהַחֲזִיק בָּךְ
כִּי־הִסְתַּ֤רְתָּ פָנֶ֙יךָ֙ מִמֶּ֔נּוּ
וַתְּמוּגֵ֖נוּ בְּיַד־עֲוֺנֵֽנוּ׃

7But now, O Lord, You are our Father;
We are the clay, and You are the Potter,
We are all the work of Your hands.

7 וְעַתָּ֥ה יְהֹוָ֖ה אָבִ֣ינוּ אָ֑תָּה
אֲנַ֤חְנוּ הַחֹ֙מֶר֙ וְאַתָּ֣ה יֹצְרֵ֔נוּ
וּמַעֲשֵׂ֥ה יָדְךָ֖ כֻּלָּֽנוּ׃

8Be not implacably angry, O Lord,
Do not remember iniquity forever.
Oh, look down to Your people, to us all!

8 אַל־תִּקְצֹ֤ף יְהֹוָה֙ עַד־מְאֹ֔ד
וְאַל־לָעַ֖ד תִּזְכֹּ֣ר עָוֺ֑ן
הֵ֥ן הַבֶּט־נָ֖א עַמְּךָ֥ כֻלָּֽנוּ׃

9Your holy cities have become a desert:
Zion has become a desert,
Jerusalem a desolation.

9 עָרֵ֥י קׇדְשְׁךָ֖ הָי֣וּ מִדְבָּ֑ר
צִיּוֹן֙ מִדְבָּ֣ר הָיָ֔תָה
יְרוּשָׁלַ֖͏ִם שְׁמָמָֽה׃

10Our holy Temple, our pride,
Where our fathers praised You,
Has been consumed by fire:
And all that was dear to us is ruined.

10 בֵּ֧ית קׇדְשֵׁ֣נוּ וְתִפְאַרְתֵּ֗נוּ
אֲשֶׁ֤ר הִֽלְל֙וּךָ֙ אֲבֹתֵ֔ינוּ
הָיָ֖ה לִשְׂרֵ֣פַת אֵ֑שׁ
וְכׇל־מַחֲמַדֵּ֖ינוּ הָיָ֥ה לְחׇרְבָּֽה׃

11At such things will You restrain Yourself, O Lord,
Will You stand idly by and let us suffer so heavily?

11 הַעַל־אֵ֥לֶּה תִתְאַפַּ֖ק יְהֹוָ֑ה
תֶּחֱשֶׁ֥ה וּתְעַנֵּ֖נוּ עַד־מְאֹֽד׃ ס

65

^{a}-I responded to-^{a} those who did not ask,
I was at hand to those who did not seek Me;
I said, "Here I am, here I am,"
To a nation that did not invoke My name.

סה נִדְרַ֙שְׁתִּי֙ לְל֣וֹא שָׁאָ֔לוּ
נִמְצֵ֖אתִי לְלֹ֣א בִקְשֻׁ֑נִי
אָמַ֤רְתִּי הִנֵּ֤נִי הִנֵּ֙נִי֙
אֶל־גּ֔וֹי לֹא־קֹרָ֖א בִשְׁמִֽי׃

2I constantly spread out My hands
To a disloyal people,
Who walk the way that is not good,
Following their own designs;

2 פֵּרַ֧שְׂתִּי יָדַ֛י כׇּל־הַיּ֖וֹם
אֶל־עַ֣ם סוֹרֵ֑ר
הַהֹלְכִים֙ הַדֶּ֣רֶךְ לֹא־ט֔וֹב
אַחַ֖ר מַחְשְׁבֹתֵיהֶֽם׃

3The people who provoke My anger,
Who continually, to My very face,
Sacrifice in gardens and burn incense on tiles;

3 הָעָ֗ם הַמַּכְעִיסִ֥ים אוֹתִ֛י
עַל־פָּנַ֖י תָּמִ֑יד
זֹבְחִים֙ בַּגַּנּ֔וֹת וּֽמְקַטְּרִ֖ים עַל־הַלְּבֵנִֽים׃

4Who sit inside tombs
And pass the night in secret places;
Who eat the flesh of swine,
With broth of unclean things in their bowls;

4 הַיֹּֽשְׁבִים֙ בַּקְּבָרִ֔ים
וּבַנְּצוּרִ֖ים יָלִ֑ינוּ
הָאֹֽכְלִים֙ בְּשַׂ֣ר הַחֲזִ֔יר
[וּפְרַק֙] (ופרק) וּמְרַ֥ק פִּגֻּלִ֖ים כְּלֵיהֶֽם׃

$^{d-d}$ Emendation yields "delivered us into the hands of..."

$^{a-a}$ Lit. "I let Myself be inquired of..."

⁵Who say, "Keep your distance! Don't come
    closer!

ᵇ-For I would render you consecrated."-ᵇ
Such things make My anger rage,
Like fire blazing all day long.
⁶See, this is recorded before Me;
I will not stand idly by, but will repay,
Deliver ᶜ-theirᵈ sins-ᶜ into their bosom,
⁷And the sins of their fathers as well

              —said the LORD—

For they made offerings upon the mountains
And affronted Me upon the hills.
I will count out their recompense in full,ᵉ
Into their bosoms.
⁸Thus said the LORD:
As, when new wine is present in the cluster,
One says, "Don't destroy it; there's good in
    it,"
So will I do for the sake of My servants,
And not destroy everything.
⁹I will bring forth offspring from Jacob,
From Judah heirs to My mountains;
My chosen ones shall take possession,
My servants shall dwell thereon.
¹⁰Sharonᶠ shall become a pasture for flocks,
And the Valley of Achor a place for cattle to
    lie down,
For My people who seek Me.

¹¹But as for you who forsake the LORD,
Who ignore My holy mountain,
Who set a table for Luckᵍ
And fill a mixing bowl for Destiny:ᵍ
¹²I will destine you for the sword,
You will all kneel down, to be slaughtered—

הָאֹמְרִים֙ קְרַ֣ב אֵלֶ֔יךָ אַֽל־תִּגַּשׁ־בִּ֖י ⁵
כִּ֣י קְדַשְׁתִּ֑יךָ
אֵ֚לֶּה עָשָׁ֣ן בְּאַפִּ֔י
אֵ֥שׁ יֹקֶ֖דֶת כָּל־הַיּֽוֹם׃
הִנֵּ֥ה כְתוּבָ֖ה לְפָנָ֑י ⁶
לֹ֤א אֶחֱשֶׂה֙ כִּ֣י אִם־שִׁלַּ֔מְתִּי
וְשִׁלַּמְתִּ֖י עַל־חֵיקָֽם׃
עֲוֺנֹֽתֵיכֶ֞ם וַעֲוֺנֹ֧ת אֲבֽוֹתֵיכֶ֛ם יַחְדָּ֖ו ⁷
אָמַ֣ר יְהֹוָ֑ה
אֲשֶׁ֤ר קִטְּרוּ֙ עַל־הֶ֣הָרִ֔ים
וְעַל־הַגְּבָע֖וֹת חֵרְפ֑וּנִי
וּמַדֹּתִ֧י פְעֻלָּתָ֛ם רִאשֹׁנָ֖ה
עַל־חֵיקָֽם׃ ס
כֹּ֣ה ׀ אָמַ֣ר יְהֹוָ֗ה ⁸
כַּאֲשֶׁ֨ר יִמָּצֵ֤א הַתִּירוֹשׁ֙ בָּֽאֶשְׁכּ֔וֹל
וְאָמַר֙ אַל־תַּשְׁחִיתֵ֔הוּ כִּ֥י בְרָכָ֖ה בּ֑וֹ
כֵּ֤ן אֶֽעֱשֶׂה֙ לְמַ֣עַן עֲבָדַ֔י
לְבִלְתִּ֖י הַשְׁחִ֥ית הַכֹּֽל׃
וְהוֹצֵאתִ֤י מִֽיַּעֲקֹב֙ זֶ֔רַע ⁹
וּמִיהוּדָ֖ה יוֹרֵ֣שׁ הָרָ֑י
וִירֵשׁ֣וּהָ בְחִירַ֔י
וַעֲבָדַ֖י יִשְׁכְּנוּ־שָֽׁמָּה׃
וְהָיָ֤ה הַשָּׁרוֹן֙ לִנְוֵה־צֹ֔אן ¹⁰
וְעֵ֥מֶק עָכ֖וֹר לְרֵ֣בֶץ בָּקָ֑ר
לְעַמִּ֖י אֲשֶׁ֥ר דְּרָשֽׁוּנִי׃
וְאַתֶּם֙ עֹזְבֵ֣י יְהֹוָ֔ה ¹¹
הַשְּׁכֵחִ֖ים אֶת־הַ֣ר קׇדְשִׁ֑י
הַֽעֹרְכִ֤ים לַגַּד֙ שֻׁלְחָ֔ן
וְהַֽמְמַלְאִ֖ים לַמְנִ֥י מִמְסָֽךְ׃
וּמָנִ֨יתִ֤י אֶתְכֶם֙ לַחֶ֔רֶב ¹²
וְכֻלְּכֶ֖ם לַטֶּ֣בַח תִּכְרָ֑עוּ

ᵇ-ᵇ Taking qedashtikha as equivalent to qiddashtikha, cf. Ezek.
    44.19; others "For I am holier than thou."
ᶜ-ᶜ Brought up from v. 7 for clarity.
ᵈ   Heb. "your."
ᵉ   Taking rishonah as equivalent to beroshah; cf. Lev. 5.24; Jer.
    16.18. Meaning of Heb. uncertain.
ᶠ   Emendation yields "Jeshimon," the bleak southeast corner of the
    Jordan Valley; cf. Num. 21.20; 23.8.
ᵍ   Names of heathen deities.

Because, when I called, you did not answer,
When I spoke, you would not listen.
You did what I hold evil,
And chose what I do not want.

¹³Assuredly, thus said the Lord GOD:
My servants shall eat, and you shall hunger;
My servants shall drink, and you shall thirst;
My servants shall rejoice, and you shall be
     shamed;
¹⁴My servants shall shout in gladness,
And you shall cry out in anguish,
Howling in heartbreak.
¹⁵You shall leave behind a name
By which My chosen ones shall curse:
"So may the Lord GOD slay you!"
But His servants shall be given a ^hdifferent
     name.^{-h}
¹⁶For whoever blesses himself in the land
Shall bless himself by the true God;
And whoever swears in the land
Shall swear by the true God.
The former troubles shall be forgotten,
Shall be hidden from My eyes.

¹⁷For behold! I am creating
A new heaven and a new earth;
The former things shall not be remembered,
They shall never come to mind.
¹⁸Be glad, then, and rejoice forever
In what I am creating.
For I shall create Jerusalem as a joy,
And her people as a delight;
¹⁹And I will rejoice in Jerusalem
And delight in her people.
Never again shall be heard there
The sounds of weeping and wailing.
²⁰No more shall there be an infant or gray-
     beard

יַעַן קָרָ֫אתִי וְלֹ֣א עֲנִיתֶ֔ם
דִּבַּ֖רְתִּי וְלֹ֣א שְׁמַעְתֶּ֑ם
וַתַּעֲשׂ֤וּ הָרַע֙ בְּעֵינַ֔י
וּבַאֲשֶׁ֥ר לֹֽא־חָפַ֖צְתִּי בְּחַרְתֶּֽם׃ ס

¹³ לָכֵ֞ן כֹּה־אָמַ֣ר ׀ אֲדֹנָ֣י יְהֹוִ֗ה
הִנֵּ֨ה עֲבָדַ֤י ׀ יֹאכֵ֙לוּ֙ וְאַתֶּ֣ם תִּרְעָ֔בוּ
הִנֵּ֧ה עֲבָדַ֛י יִשְׁתּ֖וּ וְאַתֶּ֣ם תִּצְמָ֑אוּ
הִנֵּ֥ה עֲבָדַ֖י יִשְׂמָ֑חוּ וְאַתֶּ֥ם תֵּבֹֽשׁוּ׃
¹⁴ הִנֵּ֧ה עֲבָדַ֛י יָרֹ֖נּוּ מִטּ֣וּב לֵ֑ב
וְאַתֶּ֤ם תִּצְעֲקוּ֙ מִכְּאֵ֣ב לֵ֔ב
וּמִשֵּׁ֥בֶר ר֖וּחַ תְּיֵלִֽילוּ׃
¹⁵ וְהִנַּחְתֶּ֥ם שִׁמְכֶ֛ם
לִשְׁבוּעָ֖ה לִבְחִירָ֑י
וֶהֱמִיתְךָ֖ אֲדֹנָ֣י יְהֹוִ֑ה
וְלַעֲבָדָ֖יו יִקְרָ֥א שֵׁ֥ם אַחֵֽר׃
¹⁶ אֲשֶׁ֣ר הַמִּתְבָּרֵ֣ךְ בָּאָ֗רֶץ
יִתְבָּרֵךְ֙ בֵּאלֹהֵ֣י אָמֵ֔ן
וְהַנִּשְׁבָּ֣ע בָּאָ֔רֶץ
יִשָּׁבַ֖ע בֵּאלֹהֵ֣י אָמֵ֑ן
כִּ֣י נִשְׁכְּח֗וּ הַצָּרוֹת֙ הָרִ֣אשֹׁנ֔וֹת
וְכִ֥י נִסְתְּר֖וּ מֵעֵינָֽי׃

¹⁷ כִּֽי־הִנְנִ֥י בוֹרֵ֖א
שָׁמַ֣יִם חֲדָשִׁ֑ים וְאָ֖רֶץ חֲדָשָׁ֑ה
וְלֹ֤א תִזָּכַ֙רְנָה֙ הָרִ֣אשֹׁנ֔וֹת
וְלֹ֥א תַעֲלֶ֖ינָה עַל־לֵֽב׃
¹⁸ כִּֽי־אִם־שִׂ֤ישׂוּ וְגִ֙ילוּ֙ עֲדֵי־עַ֔ד
אֲשֶׁ֖ר אֲנִ֣י בוֹרֵ֑א
כִּי֩ הִנְנִ֨י בוֹרֵ֤א אֶת־יְרוּשָׁלַ֙͏ִם֙
גִּילָ֖ה וְעַמָּ֥הּ מָשֽׂוֹשׂ׃
¹⁹ וְגַלְתִּ֥י בִירוּשָׁלַ֖͏ִם
וְשַׂשְׂתִּ֣י בְעַמִּ֑י
וְלֹֽא־יִשָּׁמַ֥ע בָּ֛הּ ע֖וֹד
ק֥וֹל בְּכִ֖י וְק֥וֹל זְעָקָֽה׃
²⁰ לֹא־יִֽהְיֶ֨ה מִשָּׁ֜ם ע֗וֹד ע֤וּל יָמִים֙ וְזָקֵ֔ן

---

^{h-h} I.e., a name to be used in blessing.

996

Who does not live out his days.

He who dies at a hundred years
Shall be reckoned a youth,
And he who fails to reach a hundred
Shall be reckoned accursed.

21They shall build houses and dwell in them,
They shall plant vineyards and enjoy their
    fruit.
22They shall not build for others to dwell in,
Or plant for others to enjoy.
For the days of My people shall be
As long as the days of a tree,
My chosen ones shall outlive[i]
The work of their hands.
23They shall not toil to no purpose;
They shall not bear children j-for terror,-j
But they shall be a people blessed by the LORD,
And their offspring shall remain with them.
24Before they pray, I will answer;
While they are still speaking, I will respond.
25The wolf and the lamb shall graze together,
And the lion shall eat straw like the ox,
And the serpent's food shall be earth.
In all My sacred mount[k]
Nothing evil or vile shall be done
             —said the LORD.

66 Thus said the LORD:
The heaven is My throne
And the earth is My footstool:
Where could you build a house for Me,
What place could serve as My abode?
2All this was made by My hand,
And thus it all came into being
             —declares the LORD.

Yet to such a one I look:

---

i   Lit. "wear out."
j-j Emendation yields "in vain."
k   See note at 11.9.

אֲשֶׁר לֹא־יְמַלֵּא אֶת־יָמָיו
כִּי הַנַּעַר
בֶּן־מֵאָה שָׁנָה יָמוּת
וְהַחוֹטֶא
בֶּן־מֵאָה שָׁנָה יְקֻלָּל:
21 וּבָנוּ בָתִּים וְיָשָׁבוּ
וְנָטְעוּ כְרָמִים וְאָכְלוּ פִּרְיָם:
22 לֹא יִבְנוּ וְאַחֵר יֵשֵׁב
לֹא יִטְּעוּ וְאַחֵר יֹאכֵל
כִּי־כִימֵי הָעֵץ
יְמֵי עַמִּי
וּמַעֲשֵׂה יְדֵיהֶם
יְבַלּוּ בְחִירָי:
23 לֹא יִיגְעוּ לָרִיק
וְלֹא יֵלְדוּ לַבֶּהָלָה
כִּי זֶרַע בְּרוּכֵי יְהֹוָה הֵמָּה
וְצֶאֱצָאֵיהֶם אִתָּם:
24 וְהָיָה טֶרֶם־יִקְרָאוּ וַאֲנִי אֶעֱנֶה
עוֹד הֵם מְדַבְּרִים וַאֲנִי אֶשְׁמָע:
25 זְאֵב וְטָלֶה יִרְעוּ כְאֶחָד
וְאַרְיֵה כַּבָּקָר יֹאכַל־תֶּבֶן
וְנָחָשׁ עָפָר לַחְמוֹ
לֹא־יָרֵעוּ וְלֹא־יַשְׁחִיתוּ
בְּכָל־הַר קָדְשִׁי
אָמַר יְהֹוָה: ס

סו כֹּה אָמַר יְהֹוָה
הַשָּׁמַיִם כִּסְאִי
וְהָאָרֶץ הֲדֹם רַגְלָי
אֵי־זֶה בַיִת אֲשֶׁר תִּבְנוּ־לִי
וְאֵי־זֶה מָקוֹם מְנוּחָתִי:
2 וְאֶת־כָּל־אֵלֶּה יָדִי עָשָׂתָה
וַיִּהְיוּ כָל־אֵלֶּה
נְאֻם־יְהֹוָה
וְאֶל־זֶה אַבִּיט

To the poor and brokenhearted,
Who is concerned about My word.

3ªAs for those who slaughter oxen and slay
    humans,
Who sacrifice sheep and immolateᵇ dogs,
Who present as oblation the blood of swine,
Who offerᶜ incense and worship false gods—
Just as they have chosen their ways
And take pleasure in their abominations,
4So will I choose to mock them,
To bring on them the very thing they dread.
For I called and none responded,
I spoke and none paid heed.
They did what I deem evil
And chose what I do not want.

5Hear the word of the Lᴏʀᴅ,
You who are concerned about His word!
Your kinsmen who hate you,
Who spurn you because of Me,ᵈ are saying,
"Let the Lᴏʀᴅ manifest His Presence,
So that we may look upon your joy."
But theirs shall be the shame.
6Hark, tumult from the city,
Thunder from the Temple!
It is the thunder of the Lᴏʀᴅ
As He deals retribution to His foes.

7Before she labored, she was delivered;
Before her pangs came, she bore a son.
8Who ever heard the like?
Who ever witnessed such events?
Can a land pass through travail
In a single day?
Or is a nation born
All at once?

אֶל־עָנִי וּנְכֵה־ר֔וּחַ
וְחָרֵד עַל־דְּבָרִי:

3 שׁוֹחֵט הַשּׁוֹר מַכֵּה־אִישׁ
זוֹבֵחַ הַשֶּׂה עֹרֵף כֶּ֔לֶב
מַעֲלֵה מִנְחָה֙ דַּם־חֲזִ֔יר
מַזְכִּיר לְבֹנָה֙ מְבָ֣רֵֽךְ אָ֔וֶן
גַּם־הֵ֗מָּה בָּֽחֲרוּ֙ בְּדַרְכֵיהֶ֔ם
וּבְשִׁקּוּצֵיהֶ֖ם נַפְשָׁ֥ם חָפֵֽצָה:
4 גַּם־אֲנִ֞י אֶבְחַ֣ר בְּתַעֲלֻֽלֵיהֶ֗ם
וּמְג֤וּרֹתָם֙ אָבִ֣יא לָהֶ֔ם
יַ֤עַן קָרָ֙אתִי֙ וְאֵ֣ין עוֹנֶ֔ה
דִּבַּ֖רְתִּי וְלֹ֣א שָׁמֵ֑עוּ
וַיַּעֲשׂ֤וּ הָרַע֙ בְּעֵינַ֔י
וּבַאֲשֶׁ֥ר לֹֽא־חָפַ֖צְתִּי בָּחָֽרוּ: ס

5 שִׁמְעוּ֙ דְּבַר־יְהוָ֔ה
הַחֲרֵדִ֖ים אֶל־דְּבָר֑וֹ
אָמְרוּ֩ אֲחֵיכֶ֨ם שֹׂנְאֵיכֶ֜ם
מְנַדֵּיכֶ֗ם לְמַ֤עַן שְׁמִי֙
יִכְבַּ֣ד יְהוָ֔ה
וְנִרְאֶ֥ה בְשִׂמְחַתְכֶ֖ם
וְהֵ֥ם יֵבֹֽשׁוּ:
6 ק֤וֹל שָׁאוֹן֙ מֵעִ֔יר
ק֖וֹל מֵהֵיכָ֑ל
ק֣וֹל יְהוָ֔ה
מְשַׁלֵּ֥ם גְּמ֖וּל לְאֹיְבָֽיו:

7 בְּטֶ֥רֶם תָּחִ֖יל יָלָ֑דָה
בְּטֶ֨רֶם יָב֥וֹא חֵ֛בֶל לָ֖הּ וְהִמְלִ֥יטָה זָכָֽר:
8 מִֽי־שָׁמַ֣ע כָּזֹ֗את
מִ֤י רָאָה֙ כָּאֵ֔לֶּה
הֲי֤וּחַל אֶ֙רֶץ֙
בְּי֣וֹם אֶחָ֔ד
אִם־יִוָּ֥לֵֽד גּ֖וֹי
פַּ֥עַם אֶחָ֑ת

---

a   *Vv. 3–4 refer to practitioners of idolatrous rites; cf. v. 17 and*
     57.5–8; 65.1–12.
b   *Lit. "break the necks of."*
c   *Heb.* mazkir *refers to giving the "token portion" (*'azkarah*); cf.*
     Lev. 2.2, etc.
d   *Lit. "My name."*

Yet Zion travailed
And at once bore her children!
9Shall I who bring on labor not bring about
    birth?
                   —says the Lord.
Shall I who cause birth shut the womb?
                   —said your God.

10Rejoice with Jerusalem and be glad for her,
All you who love her!
Join in her jubilation,
All you who mourned over her—
11That you may suck from her breast
Consolation to the full,
That you may draw from her bosom[e]
Glory to your delight.

12For thus said the Lord:
I will extend to her
Prosperity like a stream,
The wealth of nations
Like a wadi in flood;
And you shall drink of it.
You shall be carried on shoulders
And dandled upon knees.
13As a mother comforts her son
So I will comfort you;
You shall find comfort in Jerusalem.
14You shall see and your heart shall rejoice,
Your limbs shall flourish like grass.
The power of the Lord shall be revealed
In behalf of His servants;
But He shall rage against His foes.

15See, the Lord is coming with fire—
His chariots are like a whirlwind—
To vent His anger in fury,
His rebuke in flaming fire.
16For with fire will the Lord contend,

---

e   *Cf. Akkadiam* zīzu, *Arabic* zīzat, *"udder."*

כִּי־חָלָה גַּם־יָלְדָה צִיּוֹן
אֶת־בָּנֶיהָ:
9 הַאֲנִי אַשְׁבִּיר וְלֹא אוֹלִיד
יֹאמַר* יְהוָה
אִם־אֲנִי הַמּוֹלִיד וְעָצַרְתִּי
אָמַר אֱלֹהָיִךְ: ס
10 שִׂמְחוּ אֶת־יְרוּשָׁלַ͏ִם
וְגִילוּ בָהּ כָּל־אֹהֲבֶיהָ
שִׂישׂוּ אִתָּהּ מָשׂוֹשׂ
כָּל־הַמִּתְאַבְּלִים עָלֶיהָ:
11 לְמַעַן תִּינְקוּ וּשְׂבַעְתֶּם
מִשֹּׁד תַּנְחֻמֶיהָ
לְמַעַן תָּמֹצּוּ וְהִתְעַנַּגְתֶּם
מִזִּיז כְּבוֹדָהּ: ס
12 כִּי־כֹה ׀ אָמַר יְהוָה
הִנְנִי נֹטֶה־אֵלֶיהָ
כְּנָהָר שָׁלוֹם
וּכְנַחַל שׁוֹטֵף
כְּבוֹד גּוֹיִם וְינַקְתֶּם
עַל־צַד תִּנָּשֵׂאוּ
וְעַל־בִּרְכַּיִם תְּשָׁעֳשָׁעוּ:
13 כְּאִישׁ אֲשֶׁר אִמּוֹ תְּנַחֲמֶנּוּ
כֵּן אָנֹכִי אֲנַחֶמְכֶם
וּבִירוּשָׁלַ͏ִם תְּנֻחָמוּ:
14 וּרְאִיתֶם וְשָׂשׂ לִבְּכֶם
וְעַצְמוֹתֵיכֶם כַּדֶּשֶׁא תִפְרַחְנָה
וְנוֹדְעָה יַד־יְהוָה
אֶת־עֲבָדָיו
וְזָעַם אֶת־אֹיְבָיו:
15 כִּי־הִנֵּה יְהוָה בָּאֵשׁ יָבוֹא
וְכַסּוּפָה מַרְכְּבֹתָיו
לְהָשִׁיב בְּחֵמָה אַפּוֹ
וְגַעֲרָתוֹ בְּלַהֲבֵי־אֵשׁ:
16 כִּי בָאֵשׁ יְהוָה נִשְׁפָּט

With His sword, against all flesh;
And many shall be the slain of the LORD.

 וּבְחַרְבּ֖וֹ אֶת־כָּל־בָּשָׂ֑ר
וְרַבּ֖וּ חַֽלְלֵ֥י יְהֹוָֽה׃

17Those who sanctify and purify themselves to enter the groves, ^f-imitating one in the center,-^f eating the flesh of the swine, the reptile, and the mouse, shall one and all come to an end—declares the LORD. ^{18g}For I [know] their deeds and purposes.

17 הַמִּתְקַדְּשִׁ֨ים וְהַמִּֽטַּהֲרִ֜ים אֶל־הַגַּנּ֗וֹת אַחַ֤ר אַחַד֙ בַּתָּ֔וֶךְ אֹֽכְלֵי֙ בְּשַׂ֣ר הַחֲזִ֔יר וְהַשֶּׁ֖קֶץ וְהָעַכְבָּ֑ר יַחְדָּ֥ו יָסֻ֖פוּ נְאֻם־יְהֹוָֽה׃ 18 וְאָנֹכִ֗י מַעֲשֵׂיהֶ֣ם וּמַחְשְׁבֹֽתֵיהֶ֔ם

[The time] has come to gather all the nations and tongues; they shall come and behold My glory. ¹⁹I will set a sign among them, and send from them survivors to the nations: to Tarshish, Pul, and Lud—that draw the bow—to Tubal, Javan, and the distant coasts, that have never heard My fame nor beheld My glory. They shall declare My glory among these nations. ²⁰And out of all the nations, said the LORD, they shall bring all your brothers on horses, in chariots and drays, on mules and dromedaries, to Jerusalem My holy mountain as an offering to the LORD—just as the Israelites bring an offering in a pure vessel to the House of the LORD. ²¹And from them likewise I will take some to be ^h-levitical priests,-^h said the LORD.

בָּאָ֕ה לְקַבֵּ֥ץ אֶת־כָּל־הַגּוֹיִ֖ם וְהַלְּשֹׁנ֑וֹת וּבָ֖אוּ וְרָא֥וּ אֶת־כְּבוֹדִֽי׃ 19 וְשַׂמְתִּ֨י בָהֶ֜ם א֗וֹת וְשִׁלַּחְתִּ֣י מֵהֶ֣ם ׀ פְּלֵיטִ֣ים אֶל־הַגּוֹיִ֡ם תַּרְשִׁ֨ישׁ פּ֣וּל וְל֤וּד מֹ֣שְׁכֵי קֶ֙שֶׁת֙ תֻּבַ֣ל וְיָוָ֔ן הָאִיִּ֣ים הָרְחֹקִ֗ים אֲשֶׁ֨ר לֹא־שָׁמְע֤וּ אֶת־שִׁמְעִי֙ וְלֹֽא־רָא֣וּ אֶת־כְּבוֹדִ֔י וְהִגִּ֥ידוּ אֶת־כְּבוֹדִ֖י בַּגּוֹיִֽם׃ 20 וְהֵבִ֣יאוּ אֶת־כָּל־אֲחֵיכֶ֣ם מִכָּל־הַגּוֹיִ֣ם ׀ מִנְחָ֣ה ׀ לַֽיהֹוָ֡ה בַּסּוּסִ֡ים וּ֠בָרֶ֠כֶב וּבַצַּבִּ֨ים וּבַפְּרָדִ֜ים וּבַכִּרְכָּר֗וֹת עַ֣ל הַ֥ר קָדְשִׁ֛י יְרוּשָׁלַ֖͏ִם אָמַ֣ר יְהֹוָ֑ה כַּאֲשֶׁ֣ר יָבִ֣יאוּ בְנֵי֩ יִשְׂרָאֵ֨ל אֶת־הַמִּנְחָ֜ה בִּכְלִ֥י טָה֖וֹר בֵּ֥ית יְהֹוָֽה׃ 21 וְגַם־מֵהֶ֥ם אֶקַּ֛ח לַכֹּהֲנִ֥ים לַלְוִיִּ֖ם אָמַ֥ר יְהֹוָֽה׃

²²For as the new heaven and the new earth
Which I will make
Shall endure by My will
      —declares the LORD—
So shall your seed and your name endure.
²³And new moon after new moon,
And sabbath after sabbath,
All flesh shall come to worship Me
      —said the LORD.
²⁴They shall go out and gaze
On the corpses of the men who rebelled
   against Me:

22 כִּ֣י כַאֲשֶׁ֣ר הַשָּׁמַ֣יִם הַֽחֲדָשִׁ֗ים וְהָאָ֙רֶץ֙ הַחֲדָשָׁ֔ה אֲשֶׁ֥ר אֲנִ֛י עֹשֶׂ֖ה עֹמְדִ֣ים לְפָנַ֑י נְאֻם־יְהֹוָ֑ה כֵּ֛ן יַעֲמֹ֥ד זַרְעֲכֶ֖ם וְשִׁמְכֶֽם׃ 23 וְהָיָ֗ה מִֽדֵּי־חֹ֙דֶשׁ֙ בְּחָדְשׁ֔וֹ וּמִדֵּ֥י שַׁבָּ֖ת בְּשַׁבַּתּ֑וֹ יָב֧וֹא כָל־בָּשָׂ֛ר לְהִשְׁתַּחֲוֺ֥ת לְפָנַ֖י אָמַ֥ר יְהֹוָֽה׃ 24 וְיָצְא֣וּ וְרָא֔וּ בְּפִגְרֵי֙ הָאֲנָשִׁ֔ים הַפֹּשְׁעִ֖ים בִּ֑י

---

f-f Meaning of Heb. uncertain.
g Exact construction of this verse uncertain; for the insertions in brackets, cf. Kimhi.
h-h Some Heb. mss. read "priests and Levites."

Their worms shall not die,
Nor their fire be quenched;
They shall be a horror
To all flesh.

כִּי תוֹלַעְתָּם לֹא תָמוּת
וְאִשָּׁם לֹא תִכְבֶּה
וְהָיוּ דֵרָאוֹן
לְכָל־בָּשָׂר:*

　　And new moon after new moon,
　　And sabbath after sabbath,
　　All flesh shall come to worship Me
　　　　　　　　—said the Lord.

[וְהָיָה מִדֵּי־חֹדֶשׁ בְּחָדְשׁוֹ
וּמִדֵּי שַׁבָּת בְּשַׁבַּתּוֹ
יָבוֹא כָל־בָּשָׂר לְהִשְׁתַּחֲוֹת לְפָנַי
אָמַר יְהוָה:*]

תם ונשלם תהילה לאל בורא עולם

v. 24.　סכום הפסוקים של ספר 1,291 וחציו 33.21

end.　במסורת הקריאה נשנה הפסוק לפני האחרון

ירמיה

JEREMIAH

1 The words of Jeremiah son of Hilkiah, one of the priests at Anathoth in the territory of Benjamin. 2The word of the LORD came to him in the days of King Josiah son of Amon of Judah, in the thirteenth year of his reign, 3and throughout the days of King Jehoiakim son of Josiah of Judah, and until the end of the eleventh year of King Zedekiah son of Josiah of Judah, when Jerusalem went into exile in the fifth month.

4The word of the LORD came to me:

5Before I created you in the womb, I selected
  you;
Before you were born, I consecrated you;
I appointed you a prophet concerning the
  nations.

6I replied:
Ah, Lord GOD!
I don't know how to speak,
For I am still a boy.
7And the LORD said to me:
Do not say, "I am still a boy,"
But go wherever I send you
And speak whatever I command you.
8Have no fear of them,
For I am with you to deliver you
                              —declares the LORD.

9The LORD put out His hand and touched my mouth, and the LORD said to me: Herewith I put My words into your mouth.

א דִּבְרֵי יִרְמְיָהוּ בֶּן־חִלְקִיָּהוּ מִן־
הַכֹּהֲנִים אֲשֶׁר בַּעֲנָתוֹת בְּאֶרֶץ בִּנְיָמִן:
2 אֲשֶׁר הָיָה דְבַר־יְהוָה אֵלָיו בִּימֵי יֹאשִׁיָּהוּ
בֶן־אָמוֹן מֶלֶךְ יְהוּדָה בִּשְׁלֹשׁ־עֶשְׂרֵה שָׁנָה
לְמָלְכוֹ: 3 וַיְהִי בִּימֵי יְהוֹיָקִים בֶּן־יֹאשִׁיָּהוּ
מֶלֶךְ יְהוּדָה עַד־תֹּם עַשְׁתֵּי עֶשְׂרֵה שָׁנָה
לְצִדְקִיָּהוּ בֶן־יֹאשִׁיָּהוּ מֶלֶךְ יְהוּדָה עַד־
גְּלוֹת יְרוּשָׁלִַם בַּחֹדֶשׁ הַחֲמִישִׁי: ס

4 וַיְהִי דְבַר־יְהוָה אֵלַי לֵאמֹר:

5 בְּטֶרֶם אצורך אֶצָּרְךָ בַבֶּטֶן יְדַעְתִּיךָ
וּבְטֶרֶם תֵּצֵא מֵרֶחֶם הִקְדַּשְׁתִּיךָ
נָבִיא לַגּוֹיִם נְתַתִּיךָ:

6 וָאֹמַר
אֲהָהּ אֲדֹנָי יְהֹוִה
הִנֵּה לֹא־יָדַעְתִּי דַּבֵּר
כִּי־נַעַר אָנֹכִי: פ
7 וַיֹּאמֶר יְהוָה אֵלַי
אַל־תֹּאמַר נַעַר אָנֹכִי
כִּי עַל־כָּל־אֲשֶׁר אֶשְׁלָחֲךָ תֵּלֵךְ
וְאֵת כָּל־אֲשֶׁר אֲצַוְּךָ תְּדַבֵּר:
8 אַל־תִּירָא מִפְּנֵיהֶם
כִּי־אִתְּךָ אֲנִי לְהַצִּלֶךָ
נְאֻם־יְהוָה:

9 וַיִּשְׁלַח יְהוָה אֶת־יָדוֹ וַיַּגַּע עַל־פִּי וַיֹּאמֶר
יְהוָה אֵלַי הִנֵּה נָתַתִּי דְבָרַי בְּפִיךָ:

¹⁰See, I appoint you this day
Over nations and kingdoms:
To uproot and to pull down,
To destroy and to overthrow,
To build and to plant.

¹¹The word of the LORD came to me: What do you see, Jeremiah? I replied: I see a branch of an almond tree.^a

¹²The LORD said to me:
You have seen right,
For I am watchful^b to bring My word to pass.

¹³And the word of the LORD came to me a second time: What do you see? I replied:
I see a steaming pot,
^cTipped away from the north.^{-c}

¹⁴And the LORD said to me:
From the north shall disaster break loose
Upon all the inhabitants of the land!
¹⁵For I am summoning all the peoples
Of the kingdoms of the north
               —declares the LORD.
They shall come, and shall each set up a throne
Before the gates of Jerusalem,
Against its walls roundabout,
And against all the towns of Judah.

¹⁶And I will argue My case against them^d
For all their wickedness:
They have forsaken Me
And sacrificed to other gods
And worshiped the works of their hands.

¹⁷So you, gird up your loins,
Arise and speak to them
All that I command you.
Do not break down before them,

---

a   *Heb.* shaqed.
b   *Heb.* shoqed.
c-c *Meaning of Heb. uncertain.*
d   *I.e., against Jerusalem and Judah.*

10 רְאֵ֞ה הִפְקַדְתִּ֣יךָ ׀ הַיּ֣וֹם הַזֶּ֗ה
עַל־הַגּוֹיִם֙ וְעַל־הַמַּמְלָכ֔וֹת
לִנְת֥וֹשׁ וְלִנְת֖וֹץ
וּלְהַאֲבִ֣יד וְלַהֲר֑וֹס
לִבְנ֖וֹת וְלִנְט֖וֹעַ׃ פ

11 וַיְהִ֤י דְבַר־יְהוָה֙ אֵלַ֣י לֵאמֹ֔ר מָה־אַתָּ֥ה
רֹאֶ֖ה יִרְמְיָ֑הוּ וָאֹמַ֕ר מַקֵּ֥ל שָׁקֵ֖ד אֲנִ֥י רֹאֶֽה׃
12 וַיֹּ֧אמֶר יְהוָ֛ה אֵלַ֖י
הֵיטַ֣בְתָּ לִרְא֑וֹת
כִּֽי־שֹׁקֵ֥ד אֲנִ֛י עַל־דְּבָרִ֖י לַעֲשֹׂתֽוֹ׃ פ

13 וַיְהִ֨י דְבַר־יְהוָ֤ה ׀ אֵלַי֙ שֵׁנִ֣ית לֵאמֹ֔ר מָ֥ה
אַתָּ֖ה רֹאֶ֑ה וָאֹמַ֗ר
סִ֤יר נָפ֙וּחַ֙ אֲנִ֣י רֹאֶ֔ה
וּפָנָ֖יו מִפְּנֵ֥י צָפֽוֹנָה׃
14 וַיֹּ֥אמֶר יְהוָ֖ה אֵלָ֑י
מִצָּפוֹן֙ תִּפָּתַ֣ח הָרָעָ֔ה
עַ֥ל כָּל־יֹשְׁבֵ֖י הָאָֽרֶץ׃
15 כִּ֣י ׀ הִנְנִ֣י קֹרֵ֗א לְכָֽל־מִשְׁפְּח֛וֹת
מַמְלְכ֥וֹת צָפ֖וֹנָה
נְאֻם־יְהוָ֑ה
וּבָ֡אוּ וְֽנָתְנוּ֩ אִ֨ישׁ כִּסְא֜וֹ
פֶּ֣תַח ׀ שַׁעֲרֵ֣י יְרוּשָׁלִַ֗ם
וְעַ֤ל כָּל־חוֹמֹתֶ֙יהָ֙ סָבִ֔יב
וְעַ֖ל כָּל־עָרֵ֥י יְהוּדָֽה׃
16 וְדִבַּרְתִּ֤י מִשְׁפָּטַי֙ אוֹתָ֔ם
עַ֖ל כָּל־רָעָתָ֑ם
אֲשֶׁ֣ר עֲזָב֗וּנִי
וַֽיְקַטְּרוּ֙ לֵאלֹהִ֣ים אֲחֵרִ֔ים
וַיִּֽשְׁתַּחֲו֖וּ לְמַעֲשֵׂ֥י יְדֵיהֶֽם׃

17 וְאַתָּה֙ תֶּאְזֹ֣ר מָתְנֶ֔יךָ
וְקַמְתָּ֙ וְדִבַּרְתָּ֣ אֲלֵיהֶ֔ם
אֵ֛ת כָּל־אֲשֶׁ֥ר אָנֹכִ֖י אֲצַוֶּ֑ךָּ
אַל־תֵּחַ֣ת מִפְּנֵיהֶ֔ם

Lest I break you before them.
18I make you this day
A fortified city,
And an iron pillar,
And bronze walls
Against the whole land—
Against Judah's kings and officers,
And against its priests and citizens.e
19They will attack you,
But they shall not overcome you;
For I am with you—declares the LORD—to
    save you.

פֶּן־אֲחִתְּךָ לִפְנֵיהֶם׃
18 וַאֲנִי הִנֵּה נְתַתִּיךָ הַיּוֹם
לְעִיר מִבְצָר
וּלְעַמּוּד בַּרְזֶל וּלְחֹמוֹת נְחֹשֶׁת
עַל־כָּל־הָאָרֶץ
לְמַלְכֵי יְהוּדָה לְשָׂרֶיהָ
לְכֹהֲנֶיהָ וּלְעַם הָאָרֶץ׃
19 וְנִלְחֲמוּ אֵלֶיךָ
וְלֹא־יוּכְלוּ לָךְ
כִּי־אִתְּךָ אֲנִי נְאֻם־יְהוָה לְהַצִּילֶךָ׃ פ

2 The word of the LORD came to me, saying,
2Go proclaim to Jerusalem: Thus said the LORD:
I accounted to your favor
The devotion of your youth,
Your love as a bride—
How you followed Me in the wilderness,
In a land not sown.
3Israel was holy to the LORD,
The first fruits of His harvest.
All who ate of it were held guilty;
Disaster befell them
               —declares the LORD.

ב וַיְהִי דְבַר־יְהוָה אֵלַי לֵאמֹר׃ 2 הָלֹךְ
וְקָרָאתָ בְאָזְנֵי יְרוּשָׁלַ͏ִם לֵאמֹר כֹּה אָמַר
יְהוָה
זָכַרְתִּי לָךְ
חֶסֶד נְעוּרַיִךְ
אַהֲבַת כְּלוּלֹתָיִךְ
לֶכְתֵּךְ אַחֲרַי בַּמִּדְבָּר
בְּאֶרֶץ לֹא זְרוּעָה׃
3 קֹדֶשׁ יִשְׂרָאֵל לַיהוָה
רֵאשִׁית תְּבוּאָתֹה תְּבוּאָתוֹ
כָּל־אֹכְלָיו יֶאְשָׁמוּ
רָעָה תָּבֹא אֲלֵיהֶם
נְאֻם־יְהוָה׃ פ

4Hear the word of the LORD, O House of
    Jacob,
Every clan of the House of Israel!
5Thus said the LORD:
What wrong did your fathers find in Me
That they abandoned Me
And went after delusion and were deluded?
6They never asked themselves, "Where is the
    LORD,
Who brought us up from the land of Egypt,
Who led us through the wilderness,
A land of deserts and pits,
A land of drought and darkness,

4 שִׁמְעוּ דְבַר־יְהוָה בֵּית יַעֲקֹב
וְכָל־מִשְׁפְּחוֹת בֵּית יִשְׂרָאֵל׃
5 כֹּה ׀ אָמַר יְהוָה
מַה־מָּצְאוּ אֲבוֹתֵיכֶם בִּי עָוֶל
כִּי רָחֲקוּ מֵעָלָי
וַיֵּלְכוּ אַחֲרֵי הַהֶבֶל וַיֶּהְבָּלוּ׃
6 וְלֹא אָמְרוּ אַיֵּה יְהוָה
הַמַּעֲלֶה אֹתָנוּ מֵאֶרֶץ מִצְרָיִם
הַמּוֹלִיךְ אֹתָנוּ בַּמִּדְבָּר
בְּאֶרֶץ עֲרָבָה וְשׁוּחָה
בְּאֶרֶץ צִיָּה וְצַלְמָוֶת

e   Lit. "the people of the land."

A land no man had traversed,
Where no human being had dwelt?"
⁷I brought you to this country of farm land
To enjoy its fruit and its bounty;
But you came and defiled My land,
You made My possession abhorrent.
⁸The priests never asked themselves, "Where
   is the Lord?"
The guardians of the Teaching ignored Me;
The rulersᵃ rebelled against Me,
And the prophets prophesied by Baal
And followed what can do no good.

⁹Oh, I will go on accusing you
          —declares the Lord—
And I will accuse your children's children!
¹⁰Just cross over to the isles of the Kittim and
   look,
Send to Kedar and observe carefully;
See if aught like this has ever happened:
¹¹Has any nation changed its gods
Even though they are no-gods?
But My people has exchanged its glory
For what can do no good.
¹²Be appalled, O heavens, at this;
Be horrified, utterly dazed!
          —says the Lord.
¹³For My people have done a twofold wrong:
They have forsaken Me, the Fount of living
   waters,
And hewed them out cisterns, broken cis-
   terns,
Which cannot even hold water.

¹⁴Is Israel a bondman?
Is he a home-born slave?
Then why is he given over to plunder?
¹⁵Lions have roared over him,
Have raised their cries.
They have made his land a waste,

בְּאֶ֗רֶץ לֹא־עָ֤בַר בָּהּ֙ אִ֔ישׁ
וְלֹא־יָשַׁ֥ב אָדָ֖ם שָֽׁם׃
7 וָאָבִ֤יא אֶתְכֶם֙ אֶל־אֶ֣רֶץ הַכַּרְמֶ֔ל
לֶאֱכֹ֥ל פִּרְיָ֖הּ וְטוּבָ֑הּ
וַתָּבֹ֙אוּ֙ וַתְּטַמְּא֣וּ אֶת־אַרְצִ֔י
וְנַחֲלָתִ֥י שַׂמְתֶּ֖ם לְתוֹעֵבָֽה׃
8 הַכֹּהֲנִ֗ים לֹ֤א אָֽמְרוּ֙ אַיֵּ֣ה יְהֹוָ֔ה
וְתֹפְשֵׂ֤י הַתּוֹרָה֙ לֹ֣א יְדָע֔וּנִי
וְהָרֹעִ֖ים פָּ֣שְׁעוּ בִ֑י
וְהַנְּבִיאִים֙ נִבְּא֣וּ בַבַּ֔עַל
וְאַחֲרֵ֥י לֹֽא־יוֹעִ֖לוּ הָלָֽכוּ׃

9 לָכֵ֗ן עֹ֛ד אָרִ֥יב אִתְּכֶ֖ם
נְאֻם־יְהֹוָ֑ה
וְאֶת־בְּנֵ֥י בְנֵיכֶ֖ם אָרִֽיב׃
10 כִּ֣י עִבְר֞וּ אִיֵּ֤י כִתִּיִּים֙ וּרְא֔וּ
וְקֵדָ֛ר שִׁלְח֥וּ וְהִתְבּוֹנְנ֖וּ מְאֹ֑ד
וּרְא֕וּ הֵ֥ן הָֽיְתָ֖ה כָּזֹֽאת׃
11 הַהֵימִ֥יר גּוֹי֙ אֱלֹהִ֔ים
וְהֵ֖מָּה לֹ֣א אֱלֹהִ֑ים
וְעַמִּ֛י הֵמִ֥יר כְּבוֹד֖וֹ
בְּל֥וֹא יוֹעִֽיל׃
12 שֹׁ֥מּוּ שָׁמַ֖יִם עַל־זֹ֑את
וְשַׂעֲר֛וּ חָרְב֥וּ מְאֹ֖ד
נְאֻם־יְהֹוָֽה׃
13 כִּֽי־שְׁתַּ֥יִם רָע֖וֹת עָשָׂ֣ה עַמִּ֑י
אֹתִ֨י עָזְב֜וּ מְק֣וֹר ׀ מַ֣יִם חַיִּ֗ים
לַחְצֹ֤ב לָהֶם֙ בֹּאר֔וֹת* בֹּארֹת֙* נִשְׁבָּרִ֔ים
אֲשֶׁ֥ר לֹא־יָכִ֖לוּ הַמָּֽיִם׃

14 הַעֶ֙בֶד֙ יִשְׂרָאֵ֔ל
אִם־יְלִ֥יד בַּ֖יִת ה֑וּא
מַדּ֖וּעַ הָיָ֥ה לָבַֽז׃
15 עָלָיו֙ יִשְׁאֲג֣וּ כְפִרִ֔ים
נָתְנ֖וּ קוֹלָ֑ם
וַיָּשִׁ֤יתוּ אַרְצוֹ֙ לְשַׁמָּ֔ה

ᵃ Lit. "shepherds"; cf. 3.15; 23.1 ff.

His cities desolate, without inhabitants.

16Those, too, in Noph and Tahpanhes[b]

c-Will lay bare-c your head.

17See, d-that is the price you have paid

For forsaking the LORD your God-d

c-While He led you in the way.-c

18What, then, is the good of your going to Egypt

To drink the waters of the Nile?

And what is the good of your going to Assyria

To drink the waters of the Euphrates?

19Let your misfortune reprove you,

Let your afflictions rebuke you;

Mark well how bad and bitter it is

That you forsake the LORD your God,

That awe for Me is not in you

    —declares the Lord GOD of Hosts.

20For long ago you[e] broke your yoke,

Tore off your yoke-bands,

And said, "I will not work!"[f]

On every high hill and under every verdant tree,

You recline as a whore.

21I planted you with noble vines,

All with choicest seed;

Alas, I find you changed

Into a base, an alien vine!

22Though you wash with natron

And use much lye,

Your guilt is ingrained before Me

    —declares the Lord GOD.

23How can you say, "I am not defiled,

I have not gone after the Baalim"?

Look at your deeds in the Valley,[g]

Consider what you have done!

Like a lustful she-camel,

עָרָיו נצתה נצתו מִבְּלִי יֹשֵׁב׃

16 גַּם־בְּנֵי־נֹף וְתַחְפַּנֵס וְתַחְפַּנְחֵס

יִרְעוּךְ קָדְקֹד׃

17 הֲלוֹא־זֹאת תַּעֲשֶׂה־לָּךְ

עָזְבֵךְ אֶת־יְהוָה אֱלֹהַיִךְ

בְּעֵת מוֹלִיכֵךְ בַּדָּרֶךְ׃

18 וְעַתָּה מַה־לָּךְ לְדֶרֶךְ מִצְרַיִם

לִשְׁתּוֹת מֵי שִׁחוֹר

וּמַה־לָּךְ לְדֶרֶךְ אַשּׁוּר

לִשְׁתּוֹת מֵי נָהָר׃

19 תְּיַסְּרֵךְ רָעָתֵךְ

וּמְשֻׁבוֹתַיִךְ תּוֹכִחֻךְ

וּדְעִי וּרְאִי כִּי־רַע וָמָר

עָזְבֵךְ אֶת־יְהוָה אֱלֹהָיִךְ

וְלֹא פַחְדָּתִי אֵלַיִךְ

נְאֻם־אֲדֹנָי יְהוִה צְבָאוֹת׃

20 כִּי מֵעוֹלָם שָׁבַרְתִּי עֻלֵּךְ

נִתַּקְתִּי מוֹסְרֹתַיִךְ

וַתֹּאמְרִי לֹא אֶעֱבוֹד

כִּי עַל־כָּל־גִּבְעָה גְבֹהָה וְתַחַת כָּל־עֵץ רַעֲנָן

אַתְּ צֹעָה זֹנֶה׃

21 וְאָנֹכִי נְטַעְתִּיךְ שֹׂרֵק

כֻּלֹּה זֶרַע אֱמֶת

וְאֵיךְ נֶהְפַּכְתְּ לִי

סוּרֵי הַגֶּפֶן נָכְרִיָּה׃

22 כִּי אִם־תְּכַבְּסִי בַּנֶּתֶר

וְתַרְבִּי־לָךְ בֹּרִית

נִכְתָּם עֲוֹנֵךְ לְפָנַי

נְאֻם אֲדֹנָי יְהוִה׃

23 אֵיךְ תֹּאמְרִי לֹא נִטְמֵאתִי

אַחֲרֵי הַבְּעָלִים לֹא הָלַכְתִּי

רְאִי דַרְכֵּךְ בַּגַּיְא

דְעִי מֶה עָשִׂית

בִּכְרָה קַלָּה

---

b   Cities in Egypt. The Egyptians, like the Assyrians, will prove a disappointment; cf. v. 36.

c-c   Meaning of Heb. uncertain.

d-d   Lit. "that is what your forsaking the LORD your God is doing to you."

e   For the form, cf. shaqqamti, Judg. 5.7; others "I."

f   Following the kethib; qere "transgress."

g   I.e., of Hinnom; cf. 7.31–32; 32.35.

c-Restlessly running about,-*c*	מְשָׁרֶ֖כֶת דְּרָכֶ֑יהָ
24Or like a wild ass used to the desert,	24 פֶּ֣רֶה ׀ לִמֻּ֣ד מִדְבָּ֗ר
Snuffing the wind in her eagerness,	בְּאַוַּ֤ת נַפְשָׁהּ שָׁאֲפָ֣ה ר֔וּחַ
Whose passion none can restrain,	תַּאֲנָתָ֖הּ מִ֣י יְשִׁיבֶ֑נָּה
None that seek her need grow weary—	כׇּל־מְבַקְשֶׁ֙יהָ֙ לֹ֣א יִיעָ֔פוּ
In her season, they'll find her!	בְּחׇדְשָׁ֖הּ יִמְצָא֥וּנְהָ
25Save your foot from going bare,	25 מִנְעִ֤י רַגְלֵךְ֙ מִיָּחֵ֔ף
And your throat from thirst.	וגרונך וּגְרֹנֵ֖ךְ מִצִּמְאָ֑ה
But you say, "It is no use.	וַתֹּאמְרִ֣י נוֹאָ֗שׁ ל֚וֹא
No, I love the strangers,*h*	כִּֽי־אָהַ֥בְתִּי זָרִ֖ים
And after them I must go."	וְאַחֲרֵיהֶ֥ם אֵלֵֽךְ
26Like a thief chagrined when he is caught,	26 כְּבֹ֤שֶׁת גַּנָּב֙ כִּ֣י יִמָּצֵ֔א
So is the House of Israel chagrined—	כֵּ֥ן הֹבִ֖ישׁוּ בֵּ֣ית יִשְׂרָאֵ֑ל
They, their kings, their officers,	הֵ֤מָּה מַלְכֵיהֶם֙ שָׂרֵיהֶ֔ם
And their priests and prophets.	וְכֹהֲנֵיהֶ֖ם וּנְבִיאֵיהֶֽם
27They said to wood, "You are my father,"	27 אֹמְרִ֣ים לָעֵ֗ץ אָ֤בִי אַ֙תָּה֙
To stone, "You gave birth to me,"	וְלָאֶ֙בֶן֙ אַ֣תְּ ילדתני יְלִדְתָּ֔נוּ
While to Me they turned their backs	כִּֽי־פָנ֥וּ אֵלַ֛י עֹ֖רֶף
And not their faces.	וְלֹ֣א פָנִ֑ים
But in their hour of calamity they cry,	וּבְעֵ֤ת רָֽעָתָם֙ יֹֽאמְר֔וּ
"Arise and save us!"	ק֖וּמָה וְהוֹשִׁיעֵֽנוּ
28And where are those gods	28 וְאַיֵּ֣ה אֱלֹהֶ֗יךָ
You made for yourself?	אֲשֶׁ֣ר עָשִׂ֣יתָ לָּ֔ךְ
Let them arise and save you, if they can,	יָק֕וּמוּ אִם־יוֹשִׁיע֖וּךָ
In your hour of calamity.	בְּעֵ֣ת רָעָתֶ֑ךָ
For your gods have become, O Judah,	כִּ֚י מִסְפַּ֣ר עָרֶ֔יךָ
As many as your towns!	הָי֥וּ אֱלֹהֶ֖יךָ יְהוּדָֽה ס
29Why do you call Me to account?	29 לָ֥מָּה תָרִ֖יבוּ אֵלָ֑י
You have all rebelled against Me	כֻּלְּכֶ֛ם פְּשַׁעְתֶּ֥ם בִּ֖י
—declares the Lord.	נְאֻם־יְהֹוָֽה
30To no purpose did I smite your children;	30 לַשָּׁוְא֙ הִכֵּ֣יתִי אֶת־בְּנֵיכֶ֔ם
They would not accept correction.	מוּסָ֖ר לֹ֣א לָקָ֑חוּ
Your sword has devoured your prophets	אָכְלָ֧ה חַרְבְּכֶ֛ם נְבִיאֵיכֶ֖ם
Like a ravening lion.	כְּאַרְיֵ֥ה מַשְׁחִֽית
31*c*-O generation, behold-*c* the word of the	31 הַדּ֗וֹר אַתֶּם֙ רְא֣וּ דְבַר־יְהֹוָ֔ה
Lord!	הֲמִדְבָּ֤ר הָיִ֙יתִי֙ לְיִשְׂרָאֵ֔ל
Have I been like a desert to Israel,	

---

h   *I.e., other gods.*

1008

Or like a land of deep gloom?
Then why do My people say, "We have bro-
ken loose,
We will not come to You any more?"
32Can a maiden forget her jewels,
A bride her adornments?
Yet My people have forgotten Me—
Days without number.

33How skillfully you plan your way
To seek out love!
Why, you have even taught
The worst of women your ways.
34Moreover, on your garments is found
The lifeblood of the innocent poor—
You did not catch them breaking in.*i*
*c-*Yet, despite all these things,*-c*
35You say, "I have been acquitted;
Surely, His anger has turned away from me."
Lo, I will bring you to judgment
For saying, "I have not sinned."

36How you cheapen yourself,
By changing your course!
You shall be put to shame through Egypt,
Just as you were put to shame through As-
syria.
37From this way, too, you will come out
*j-*With your hands on your head;*-j*
For the LORD has rejected those you trust,
You will not prosper with them.

3 [The word of the LORD came to me] as follows: If a man divorces his wife, and she leaves
him and marries another man, can he ever go
back to her? Would not such a land be defiled?*a*

אִם אֶרֶץ מַאְפֵּלְיָה
מַדּוּעַ אָמְרוּ עַמִּי רַדְנוּ
לוֹא־נָבוֹא עוֹד אֵלֶיךָ:
32 הֲתִשְׁכַּח בְּתוּלָה עֶדְיָהּ
כַּלָּה קִשֻּׁרֶיהָ
וְעַמִּי שְׁכֵחוּנִי
יָמִים אֵין מִסְפָּר:

33 מַה־תֵּיטִבִי דַּרְכֵּךְ
לְבַקֵּשׁ אַהֲבָה
לָכֵן גַּם אֶת־הָרָעוֹת
למדתי לִמַּדְתְּ אֶת־דְּרָכָיִךְ:
34 גַּם בִּכְנָפַיִךְ נִמְצְאוּ
דַּם נַפְשׁוֹת אֶבְיוֹנִים נְקִיִּים
לֹא־בַמַּחְתֶּרֶת מְצָאתִים
כִּי עַל־כָּל־אֵלֶּה:
35 וַתֹּאמְרִי כִּי נִקֵּיתִי
אַךְ שָׁב אַפּוֹ מִמֶּנִּי
הִנְנִי נִשְׁפָּט אוֹתָךְ
עַל־אָמְרֵךְ לֹא חָטָאתִי:

36 מַה־תֵּזְלִי מְאֹד
לְשַׁנּוֹת אֶת־דַּרְכֵּךְ
גַּם מִמִּצְרַיִם תֵּבוֹשִׁי
כַּאֲשֶׁר־בֹּשְׁתְּ מֵאַשּׁוּר:
37 גַּם מֵאֵת זֶה תֵּצְאִי
וְיָדַיִךְ עַל־רֹאשֵׁךְ
כִּי־מָאַס יְהוָה בְּמִבְטַחַיִךְ
וְלֹא תַצְלִיחִי לָהֶם:

ג לֵאמֹר הֵן יְשַׁלַּח אִישׁ אֶת־אִשְׁתּוֹ
וְהָלְכָה מֵאִתּוֹ וְהָיְתָה לְאִישׁ־אַחֵר הֲיָשׁוּב
אֵלֶיהָ עוֹד הֲלוֹא חָנוֹף תֶּחֱנַף הָאָרֶץ

---

i In which case there might have been an excuse for killing them;
cf. Exod. 22.1.
j-j A gesture of wild grief; cf. 2 Sam. 13.19.
a Cf. Deut. 24.1–4.

Now you have whored with many lovers: can you return to Me?—says the LORD.

²Look up to the bare heights, and see:
Where have they not lain with you?
You waited for them on the roadside
Like a bandit[b] in the wilderness.
And you defiled the land
With your whoring and your debauchery.
³And when showers were withheld
And the late rains did not come,
You had the brazenness[c] of a street woman,
You refused to be ashamed.
⁴Just now you called to Me, "Father!
You are the Companion of my youth.
⁵Does one hate[d] for all time?
Does one rage[d] forever?"
That is how you spoke;
You did wrong, and [e-had your way.-e]

⁶The LORD said to me in the days of King Josiah: Have you seen what Rebel Israel did, going to every high mountain and under every leafy tree, and whoring there? ⁷I thought: After she has done all these things, she will come back to Me. But she did not come back; and her sister, Faithless Judah, saw it. ⁸I noted: Because Rebel Israel had committed adultery, I cast her off and handed her a bill of divorce; yet her sister, Faithless Judah, was not afraid—she too went and whored. ⁹Indeed, the land was defiled by her casual immorality, as she committed adultery with stone and with wood.[f] ¹⁰And after all that, her sister, Faithless Judah, did not return to Me wholeheartedly, but insincerely—declares the LORD.

¹¹And the LORD said to me: Rebel Israel has shown herself more in the right than Faithless

הַהָיא וְאַתְּ זָנִית רֵעִים רַבִּים וְשׁוֹב אֵלַי
נְאֻם־יְהֹוָה:

2 שְׂאִי־עֵינַיִךְ עַל־שְׁפָיִם וּרְאִי
אֵיפֹה לֹא שֻׁגַּלְתְּ שֻׁכַּבְתְּ
עַל־דְּרָכִים יָשַׁבְתְּ לָהֶם
כַּעֲרָבִי בַּמִּדְבָּר
וַתַּחֲנִיפִי אֶרֶץ
בִּזְנוּתַיִךְ וּבְרָעָתֵךְ:
3 וַיִּמָּנְעוּ רְבִבִים
וּמַלְקוֹשׁ לוֹא הָיָה
וּמֵצַח אִשָּׁה זוֹנָה הָיָה לָךְ
מֵאַנְתְּ הִכָּלֵם:
4 הֲלוֹא מֵעַתָּה קָרָאתי לִי אָבִי
אַלּוּף נְעֻרַי אָתָּה:
5 הֲיִנְטֹר לְעוֹלָם
אִם־יִשְׁמֹר לָנֶצַח
הִנֵּה דברתי דברת
וַתַּעֲשִׂי הָרָעוֹת וַתּוּכָל: פ

6 וַיֹּאמֶר יְהֹוָה אֵלַי בִּימֵי יֹאשִׁיָּהוּ הַמֶּלֶךְ
הֲרָאִיתָ אֲשֶׁר עָשְׂתָה מְשֻׁבָה יִשְׂרָאֵל
הֹלְכָה הִיא עַל־כָּל־הַר גָּבֹהַ וְאֶל־תַּחַת
כָּל־עֵץ רַעֲנָן וַתִּזְנִי־שָׁם: 7 וָאֹמַר אַחֲרֵי
עֲשׂוֹתָהּ אֶת־כָּל־אֵלֶּה אֵלַי תָּשׁוּב וְלֹא־
שָׁבָה ותראה וַתֵּרֶא בָּגוֹדָה אֲחוֹתָהּ
יְהוּדָה: 8 וָאֵרֶא כִּי עַל־כָּל־אֹדוֹת אֲשֶׁר
נִאֲפָה מְשֻׁבָה יִשְׂרָאֵל שִׁלַּחְתִּיהָ וָאֶתֵּן
אֶת־סֵפֶר כְּרִיתֻתֶיהָ אֵלֶיהָ וְלֹא יָרְאָה
בֹּגֵדָה יְהוּדָה אֲחוֹתָהּ וַתֵּלֶךְ וַתִּזֶן גַּם־
הִיא: 9 וְהָיָה מִקֹּל זְנוּתָהּ וַתֶּחֱנַף אֶת־
הָאָרֶץ וַתִּנְאַף אֶת־הָאֶבֶן וְאֶת־הָעֵץ:
10 וְגַם־בְּכָל־זֹאת לֹא־שָׁבָה אֵלַי בָּגוֹדָה
אֲחוֹתָהּ יְהוּדָה בְּכָל־לִבָּהּ כִּי אִם־בְּשֶׁקֶר
נְאֻם־יְהֹוָה: פ

11 וַיֹּאמֶר יְהֹוָה אֵלַי צִדְּקָה נַפְשָׁהּ מְשֻׁבָה
יִשְׂרָאֵל מִבֹּגֵדָה יְהוּדָה: 12 הָלֹךְ וְקָרָאתָ

---

b   Lit. "Arab."
c   Lit. "forehead."
d   Cf. Akkadian parallels nadāru and shamāru.
e-e   Meaning of Heb. uncertain.
f   She deserted her God for idols of stone and wood.

Judah. 12Go, make this proclamation toward the north, and say: Turn back, O Rebel Israel—declares the Lord. I will not look on you in anger, for I am compassionate—declares the Lord; I do not bear a grudge for all time. 13Only recognize your sin; for you have transgressed against the Lord your God, and scattered your favors*g* among strangers under every leafy tree, and you have not heeded Me—declares the Lord.

14Turn back, rebellious children—declares the Lord. Since I have espoused*h* you, I will take you, one from a town and two from a clan, and bring you to Zion. 15And I will give you shepherds*e* after My own heart, who will pasture you with knowledge and skill.

16And when you increase and are fertile in the land, in those days—declares the Lord—men shall no longer speak of the Ark of the Covenant of the Lord, nor shall it come to mind. They shall not mention it, or miss it, or make another. 17At that time, they shall call Jerusalem "Throne of the Lord," and all nations shall assemble there, in the name of the Lord, at Jerusalem. They*i* shall no longer follow the willfulness of their evil hearts. 18In those days, the House of Judah shall go with the House of Israel; they shall come together from the land of the north to the land I gave your fathers as a possession.

19I had resolved to adopt you as My child, and I gave you a desirable land—the fairest heritage of all the nations; and I thought you would surely call Me "Father," and never cease to be loyal to Me. 20Instead, you have broken faith with Me, as a woman breaks faith with a paramour, O House of Israel—declares the Lord.

21Hark! On the bare heights is heard
The supplicant weeping of the people of Israel,

---

g   Lit. "ways."
h   Meaning of Heb. ba'alti uncertain; compare 31.32.
i   I.e., Israel and Judah.

אֶת־הַדְּבָרִים הָאֵלֶּה צָפוֹנָה וְאָמַרְתָּ
שׁוּבָה מְשֻׁבָה יִשְׂרָאֵל נְאֻם־יְהֹוָה לוֹא־
אַפִּיל פָּנַי בָּכֶם כִּי־חָסִיד אֲנִי נְאֻם־יְהֹוָה
לֹא אֶטּוֹר לְעוֹלָם: 13 אַךְ דְּעִי עֲוֺנֵךְ כִּי
בַּיהֹוָה אֱלֹהַיִךְ פָּשָׁעַתְּ וַתְּפַזְּרִי אֶת־דְּרָכַיִךְ
לַזָּרִים תַּחַת כָּל־עֵץ רַעֲנָן וּבְקוֹלִי לֹא־
שְׁמַעְתֶּם נְאֻם־יְהֹוָה:

14 שׁוּבוּ בָנִים שׁוֹבָבִים נְאֻם־יְהֹוָה כִּי אָנֹכִי
בָּעַלְתִּי בָכֶם וְלָקַחְתִּי אֶתְכֶם אֶחָד מֵעִיר
וּשְׁנַיִם מִמִּשְׁפָּחָה וְהֵבֵאתִי אֶתְכֶם צִיּוֹן:
15 וְנָתַתִּי לָכֶם רֹעִים כְּלִבִּי וְרָעוּ אֶתְכֶם
דֵּעָה וְהַשְׂכֵּיל:

16 וְהָיָה כִּי תִרְבּוּ וּפְרִיתֶם בָּאָרֶץ בַּיָּמִים
הָהֵמָּה נְאֻם־יְהֹוָה לֹא־יֹאמְרוּ עוֹד אֲרוֹן
בְּרִית־יְהֹוָה וְלֹא יַעֲלֶה עַל־לֵב וְלֹא
יִזְכְּרוּ־בוֹ וְלֹא יִפְקֹדוּ וְלֹא יֵעָשֶׂה עוֹד:
17 בָּעֵת הַהִיא יִקְרְאוּ לִירוּשָׁלַ͏ִם כִּסֵּא
יְהֹוָה וְנִקְוּוּ אֵלֶיהָ כָל־הַגּוֹיִם לְשֵׁם יְהֹוָה
לִירוּשָׁלָ͏ִם וְלֹא־יֵלְכוּ עוֹד אַחֲרֵי שְׁרִרוּת
לִבָּם הָרָע: ס 18 בַּיָּמִים הָהֵמָּה יֵלְכוּ
בֵית־יְהוּדָה עַל־בֵּית יִשְׂרָאֵל וְיָבֹאוּ יַחְדָּו
מֵאֶרֶץ צָפוֹן עַל־הָאָרֶץ אֲשֶׁר הִנְחַלְתִּי
אֶת־אֲבוֹתֵיכֶם:

19 וְאָנֹכִי אָמַרְתִּי אֵיךְ אֲשִׁיתֵךְ בַּבָּנִים
וְאֶתֶּן־לָךְ אֶרֶץ חֶמְדָּה נַחֲלַת צְבִי צִבְאוֹת
גּוֹיִם וָאֹמַר אָבִי תִּקְרְאוּ־לִי תִּקְרְאִי־לִי
וּמֵאַחֲרַי לֹא תָשׁוּבוּ תָשׁוּבִי: 20 אָכֵן בָּגְדָה
אִשָּׁה מֵרֵעָהּ כֵּן בְּגַדְתֶּם בִּי בֵּית יִשְׂרָאֵל
נְאֻם־יְהֹוָה:

21 קוֹל עַל־שְׁפָיִים נִשְׁמָע
בְּכִי תַחֲנוּנֵי בְּנֵי יִשְׂרָאֵל

For they have gone a crooked way,
Ignoring the LORD their God.

כִּי הֶעֱוּוּ אֶת־דַּרְכָּם
שָׁכְחוּ אֶת־יְהֹוָה אֱלֹהֵיהֶם:

22Turn back, O rebellious children,
I will heal your afflictions!

22 שׁוּבוּ בָּנִים שׁוֹבָבִים
אֶרְפָּה* מְשׁוּבֹתֵיכֶם

"Here we are, we come to You,
For You, O LORD, are our God!
23j-Surely, futility comes from the hills,
Confusion from the mountains.-j
Only through the LORD our God
Is there deliverance for Israel.
24But the Shameful Thingk has consumed
The possessions of our fathers ever since our
    youth—
Their flocks and herds,
Their sons and daughters.
25Let us lie down in our shame,
Let our disgrace cover us;
For we have sinned against the LORD our God,
We and our fathers from our youth to this
    day,
And we have not heeded the LORD our God."

הִנְנוּ אָתָנוּ לָךְ
כִּי אַתָּה יְהֹוָה אֱלֹהֵינוּ:
23 אָכֵן לַשֶּׁקֶר מִגְּבָעוֹת
הָמוֹן הָרִים
אָכֵן בַּיהֹוָה אֱלֹהֵינוּ
תְּשׁוּעַת יִשְׂרָאֵל:
24 וְהַבֹּשֶׁת אָכְלָה
אֶת־יְגִיעַ אֲבוֹתֵינוּ מִנְּעוּרֵינוּ
אֶת־צֹאנָם וְאֶת־בְּקָרָם
אֶת־בְּנֵיהֶם וְאֶת־בְּנוֹתֵיהֶם:
25 נִשְׁכְּבָה בְּבָשְׁתֵּנוּ
וּתְכַסֵּנוּ כְּלִמָּתֵנוּ
כִּי לַיהֹוָה אֱלֹהֵינוּ חָטָאנוּ
אֲנַחְנוּ וַאֲבוֹתֵינוּ מִנְּעוּרֵינוּ וְעַד־הַיּוֹם
הַזֶּה
וְלֹא שָׁמַעְנוּ בְּקוֹל יְהֹוָה אֱלֹהֵינוּ: ס

4 If you return, O Israel
    —declares the LORD—
If you return to Me,
If you remove your abominations from My
    presence
And do not waver,
2And a-swear, "As the LORD lives,"-a
In sincerity, justice, and righteousness—
Nations shall bless themselves by youb
And praise themselves by you.b
3For thus said the LORD to the men of Judah
and to Jerusalem:

ד אִם־תָּשׁוּב יִשְׂרָאֵל |
נְאֻם־יְהֹוָה
אֵלַי תָּשׁוּב
וְאִם־תָּסִיר שִׁקּוּצֶיךָ מִפָּנַי
וְלֹא תָנוּד:
2 וְנִשְׁבַּעְתָּ חַי־יְהֹוָה
בֶּאֱמֶת בְּמִשְׁפָּט וּבִצְדָקָה
וְהִתְבָּרְכוּ בוֹ גּוֹיִם
וּבוֹ יִתְהַלָּלוּ: ס
3 כִּי־כֹה | אָמַר יְהֹוָה | לְאִישׁ יְהוּדָה
וְלִירוּשָׁלַ͏ִם

---

j-j   I.e., the pagan rites celebrated on the hills are futile; exact force
      of Heb. uncertain.
k   Heb. Bosheth, a contemptuous substitute for Baal.

a-a   I.e., profess the worship of the LORD.
b   Heb. "him."

v. 22. ה׳ במקום א׳.

Break up the untilled ground,
And do not sow among thorns.
4Openᶜ your hearts to the LORD,
Remove the thickening about your hearts—
O men of Judah and inhabitants of Jeru-
    salem—
Lest My wrath break forth like fire,
And burn, with none to quench it,
Because of your wicked acts.

5Proclaim in Judah,
Announce in Jerusalem,
And say:
"Blow the horn in the land!"
Shout aloud and say:
"Assemble, and let us go
Into the fortified cities!"
6Set up a signpost: To Zion.
Take refuge, do not delay!
For I bring evil from the north,
And great disaster.
7The lion has come up from his thicket:
The destroyer of nations has set out,
Has departed from his place,
To make your land a desolation;
Your cities shall be ruined,
Without inhabitants.
8For this, put on sackcloth,
Mourn and wail;
For the blazing anger of the LORD
Has not turned away from us.
9And in that day

    —declares the LORD—

The mind of the king
And the mind of the nobles shall fail,
The priests shall be appalled,
And the prophets shall stand aghast.

10ᵈ-And I said:-ᵈ Ah, Lord GOD! Surely You
have deceived this people and Jerusalem, saying:

נִ֥ירוּ לָכֶ֖ם נִ֑יר
וְאַֽל־תִּזְרְע֖וּ אֶל־קֹצִֽים׃
4 הִמֹּ֣לוּ לַֽיהֹוָ֗ה
וְהָסִ֙רוּ֙ עׇרְל֣וֹת לְבַבְכֶ֔ם
אִ֥ישׁ יְהוּדָ֖ה וְיֹשְׁבֵ֣י יְרוּשָׁלָ֑͏ִם
פֶּן־תֵּצֵ֤א כָאֵשׁ֙ חֲמָתִ֔י
וּבָֽעֲרָ֖ה וְאֵ֣ין מְכַבֶּ֑ה
מִפְּנֵ֖י רֹ֥עַ מַעַלְלֵיכֶֽם׃

5 הַגִּ֣ידוּ בִֽיהוּדָ֗ה
וּבִירוּשָׁלַ֙͏ִם֙ הַשְׁמִ֔יעוּ
וְאִמְר֔וּ
וְתִקְע֥וּ שׁוֹפָ֖ר בָּאָ֑רֶץ
קִרְא֤וּ מַלְאוּ֙ וְאִמְר֔וּ
הֵאָסְפ֖וּ וְנָב֣וֹאָה
אֶל־עָרֵ֥י הַמִּבְצָֽר׃
6 שְׂאוּ־נֵ֣ס צִיּ֔וֹנָה
הָעִ֖יזוּ אַֽל־תַּעֲמֹ֑דוּ
כִּ֣י רָעָ֗ה אָֽנֹכִ֛י מֵבִ֥יא מִצָּפ֖וֹן
וְשֶׁ֥בֶר גָּדֽוֹל׃
7 עָלָ֤ה אַרְיֵה֙ מִֽסֻּבְּכ֔וֹ
וּמַשְׁחִ֣ית גּוֹיִ֔ם נָסַ֖ע
יָצָ֣א מִמְּקֹמ֑וֹ
לָשׂ֤וּם אַרְצֵךְ֙ לְשַׁמָּ֔ה
עָרַ֥יִךְ תִּצֶּ֖ינָה
מֵאֵ֥ין יוֹשֵֽׁב׃
8 עַל־זֹ֛את חִגְר֥וּ שַׂקִּ֖ים
סִפְד֣וּ וְהֵילִ֑ילוּ
כִּ֥י לֹֽא־שָׁ֛ב
חֲר֥וֹן אַף־יְהֹוָ֖ה מִמֶּֽנּוּ׃ פ
9 וְהָיָ֤ה בַיּוֹם־הַהוּא֙
נְאֻם־יְהֹוָ֔ה
יֹאבַ֥ד לֵב־הַמֶּ֖לֶךְ
וְלֵ֣ב הַשָּׂרִ֑ים
וְנָשַׁ֙מּוּ֙ הַכֹּ֣הֲנִ֔ים
וְהַנְּבִיאִ֖ים יִתְמָֽהוּ׃

10 וָאֹמַ֞ר אֲהָ֣הּ ׀ אֲדֹנָ֣י יֱהֹוִ֗ה אָכֵן֩ הַשֵּׁ֨א
הִשֵּׁ֜אתָ לָעָ֤ם הַזֶּה֙ וְלִירוּשָׁלַ֣͏ִם לֵאמֹ֔ר

ᶜ Lit. "circumcise"; cf. Deut. 10.16 and 30.6.
ᵈ-ᵈ Septuagint reads "And they shall say."

It shall be well with you—
Yet the sword threatens the very life!

שָׁל֤וֹם יִהְיֶ֣ה לָכֶ֔ם
וְנָגְעָ֥ה חֶ֖רֶב עַד־הַנָּֽפֶשׁ׃

11At that time, it shall be said concerning this
people and Jerusalem:
The conduct of e-My poor people-e is like sear-
ing wind
From the bare heights of the desert—
It will not serve to winnow or to fan.
12A full blast from them comes against Me:
Now I in turn will bring charges against them.

11 בָּעֵ֣ת הַהִ֗יא יֵאָמֵ֤ר לָֽעָם־הַזֶּה֙ וְלִיר֣וּשָׁלִַ֔ם
ר֣וּחַ צַ֤ח שְׁפָיִים֙ בַּמִּדְבָּ֔ר
דֶּ֖רֶךְ בַּת־עַמִּ֑י
ל֥וֹא לִזְר֖וֹת וְל֥וֹא לְהָבַֽר׃
12 ר֧וּחַ מָלֵ֛א מֵאֵ֖לֶּה יָב֣וֹא לִ֑י
עַתָּ֕ה גַּם־אֲנִ֛י אֲדַבֵּ֥ר מִשְׁפָּטִ֖ים אוֹתָֽם׃

13Lo, hef ascends like clouds,
His chariots are like a whirlwind,
His horses are swifter than eagles.
Woe to us, we are ruined!
14Wash your heart clean of wickedness,
O Jerusalem, that you may be rescued.
How long will you harbor within you
Your evil designs?

13 הִנֵּ֣ה ׀ כַּעֲנָנִ֣ים יַעֲלֶ֗ה
וְכַסּוּפָה֙ מַרְכְּבוֹתָ֔יו
קַלּ֥וּ מִנְּשָׁרִ֖ים סוּסָ֑יו
א֥וֹי לָ֖נוּ כִּ֥י שֻׁדָּֽדְנוּ׃
14 כַּבְּסִ֧י מֵרָעָ֛ה לִבֵּ֖ךְ
יְר֣וּשָׁלִַ֔ם לְמַ֖עַן תִּוָּשֵׁ֑עִי
עַד־מָתַ֛י תָּלִ֥ין בְּקִרְבֵּ֖ךְ
מַחְשְׁב֥וֹת אוֹנֵֽךְ׃

15Hark, one proclaims from Dan
And announces calamity from Mount
Ephraim!
16Tell the nations: Here they are!
Announce concerning Jerusalem:
Watchersf are coming from a distant land,
They raise their voices against the towns of
Judah.
17Like guards of fields, they surround her on
every side.
For she has rebelled against Me
       —declares the LORD.
18Your conduct and your acts
Have brought this upon you;
This is your bitter punishment;
It pierces your very heart.

15 כִּ֛י ק֥וֹל מַגִּ֖יד מִדָּ֑ן
וּמַשְׁמִ֥יעַ אָ֖וֶן מֵהַ֥ר אֶפְרָֽיִם׃
16 הַזְכִּ֣ירוּ לַגּוֹיִ֗ם הִנֵּה֙
הַשְׁמִ֣יעוּ עַל־יְר֣וּשָׁלִַ֔ם
נֹצְרִ֥ים בָּאִ֖ים מֵאֶ֣רֶץ הַמֶּרְחָ֑ק
וַֽיִּתְּנ֛וּ עַל־עָרֵ֥י יְהוּדָ֖ה קוֹלָֽם׃
17 כְּשֹׁמְרֵ֣י שָׂדַ֔י הָי֥וּ עָלֶ֖יהָ מִסָּבִ֑יב
כִּֽי־אֹתִ֥י מָרָ֖תָה
נְאֻם־יְהוָֽה׃
18 דַּרְכֵּ֣ךְ וּמַֽעֲלָלַ֔יִךְ
עָשׂ֥וֹ אֵ֖לֶּה לָ֑ךְ
זֹ֤את רָעָתֵךְ֙ כִּ֣י מָ֔ר
כִּ֥י נָגַ֖ע עַד־לִבֵּֽךְ׃ ס

---

e-e Lit. "the daughter that is My people"; so, frequently, in poetry.
f I.e., the invader of v. 7.
g Lit. "entrails."

19Oh, my suffering,ᵍ my suffering!
How I writhe!
Oh, the walls of my heart!
My heart moans within me,
I cannot be silent;
For ʰ-I hear-ʰ the blare of horns,
Alarms of war.

20Disaster overtakes disaster,
For all the land has been ravaged.
Suddenly my tents have been ravaged,
In a moment, my tent cloths.

21How long must I see standards
And hear the blare of horns?

22For My people are stupid,
They give Me no heed;
They are foolish children,
They are not intelligent.
They are clever at doing wrong,
But unable to do right.

23I look at the earth,
It is unformed and void;
At the skies,
And their light is gone.

24I look at the mountains,
They are quaking;
And all the hills are rocking.

25I look: no man is left,
And all the birds of the sky have fled.

26I look: the farm land is desert,
And all its towns are in ruin—
Because of the LORD,
Because of His blazing anger.

(27For thus said the LORD:
The whole land shall be desolate,
But I will not make an end of it.)

28For this the earth mourns,

מֵעַי ׀ מֵעַ֣י ׀ 19
אֹח֙וֹלָה֙ אָחוּלָ֔ה
קִיר֣וֹת לִבִּ֗י
הֹֽמֶה־לִּ֤י לִבִּי֙
לֹ֣א אַחֲרִ֔ישׁ
כִּ֣י ק֤וֹל שׁוֹפָר֙ שמעתי שָׁמַ֣עַתְּ נַפְשִׁ֔י
תְּרוּעַ֖ת מִלְחָמָֽה׃

שֶׁ֥בֶר עַל־שֶׁ֖בֶר נִקְרָ֑א 20
כִּ֥י שֻׁדְּדָ֖ה כָּל־הָאָ֑רֶץ
פִּתְאֹם֙ שֻׁדְּד֣וּ אֹהָלַ֔י
רֶ֖גַע יְרִיעֹתָֽי׃

עַד־מָתַ֖י אֶרְאֶה־נֵּ֑ס 21
אֶשְׁמְעָ֖ה ק֥וֹל שׁוֹפָֽר׃ ס

כִּ֣י ׀ אֱוִ֣יל עַמִּ֗י 22
אוֹתִי֙ לֹ֣א יָדָ֔עוּ
בָּנִ֤ים סְכָלִים֙ הֵ֔מָּה
וְלֹ֥א נְבוֹנִ֖ים הֵ֑מָּה
חֲכָמִ֥ים הֵ֙מָּה֙ לְהָרַ֔ע
וּלְהֵיטִ֖יב לֹ֥א יָדָֽעוּ׃

רָאִ֙יתִי֙ אֶת־הָאָ֔רֶץ 23
וְהִנֵּה־תֹ֖הוּ וָבֹ֑הוּ
וְאֶל־הַשָּׁמַ֖יִם
וְאֵ֥ין אוֹרָֽם׃

רָאִ֙יתִי֙ הֶ֣הָרִ֔ים 24
וְהִנֵּ֖ה רֹעֲשִׁ֑ים
וְכָל־הַגְּבָע֖וֹת הִתְקַלְקָֽלוּ׃

רָאִ֕יתִי וְהִנֵּ֖ה אֵ֣ין הָאָדָ֑ם 25
וְכָל־ע֥וֹף הַשָּׁמַ֖יִם נָדָֽדוּ׃

רָאִ֕יתִי וְהִנֵּ֥ה הַכַּרְמֶ֖ל הַמִּדְבָּ֑ר 26
וְכָל־עָרָ֗יו נִתְּצוּ֙
מִפְּנֵ֣י יְהֹוָ֔ה
מִפְּנֵ֖י חֲר֥וֹן אַפּֽוֹ׃ ס

כִּי־כֹה֙ אָמַ֣ר יְהֹוָ֔ה 27
שְׁמָמָ֥ה תִהְיֶ֖ה כָּל־הָאָ֑רֶץ
וְכָלָ֖ה לֹ֥א אֶעֱשֶֽׂה׃

עַל־זֹאת֙ תֶּאֱבַ֣ל הָאָ֔רֶץ 28

---

h-h   Lit. "you, O my being, hear." Change of vocalization yields
      "I hear the blare of horns, / My inner being, alarms of war."

And skies are dark above—
Because I have spoken, I have planned,
And I will not relent or turn back from it.

²⁹At the shout of horseman and bowman
The whole city flees.
They enter the thickets,
They clamber up the rocks.
The whole city is deserted,
Not a man remains there.
³⁰And you, who are doomed to ruin,
What do you accomplish by wearing crim-
    son,
By decking yourself in jewels of gold,
By enlarging your eyes with kohl?
You beautify yourself in vain:
Lovers despise you,
They seek your life!
³¹I hear a voice as of one in travail,
Anguish as of a woman bearing her first child,
The voice of Fair Zion
Panting, stretching out her hands:
"Alas for me! I faint
Before the killers!"

5 Roam the streets of Jerusalem,
Search its squares,
Look about and take note:
You will not find a man,
There is none who acts justly,
Who seeks integrity—
That I should pardon her.
²Even when they say, "As the LORD lives,"
They are sure to be swearing falsely.
³O LORD, Your eyes look for integrity.
You have struck them, but they sensed no
    pain;
You have consumed them, but they would ac-
    cept no discipline.

וְקָדְרוּ הַשָּׁמַיִם מִמָּעַל
עַל כִּי־דִבַּרְתִּי זַמֹּתִי
וְלֹא נִחַמְתִּי וְלֹא־אָשׁוּב מִמֶּנָּה:

29 מִקּוֹל פָּרָשׁ וְרֹמֵה קֶשֶׁת
בֹּרַחַת כָּל־הָעִיר
בָּאוּ בֶּעָבִים
וּבַכֵּפִים עָלוּ
כָּל־הָעִיר עֲזוּבָה
וְאֵין־יוֹשֵׁב בָּהֵן אִישׁ:
30 וְאַתִּי וְאַתְּ שָׁדוּד
מַה־תַּעֲשִׂי כִּי־תִלְבְּשִׁי שָׁנִי
כִּי־תַעְדִּי עֲדִי־זָהָב
כִּי־תִקְרְעִי בַפּוּךְ עֵינַיִךְ
לַשָּׁוְא תִּתְיַפִּי
מָאֲסוּ־בָךְ עֹגְבִים
נַפְשֵׁךְ יְבַקֵּשׁוּ:
31 כִּי קוֹל כְּחוֹלָה שָׁמַעְתִּי
צָרָה כְּמַבְכִּירָה
קוֹל בַּת־צִיּוֹן
תִּתְיַפֵּחַ תְּפָרֵשׂ כַּפֶּיהָ
אוֹי־נָא לִי כִּי־עָיְפָה נַפְשִׁי
לְהֹרְגִים: פ

ה שׁוֹטְטוּ בְּחוּצוֹת יְרוּשָׁלַ͏ִם
וּרְאוּ־נָא וּדְעוּ
וּבַקְשׁוּ בִרְחוֹבוֹתֶיהָ
אִם־תִּמְצְאוּ אִישׁ
אִם־יֵשׁ עֹשֶׂה מִשְׁפָּט
מְבַקֵּשׁ אֱמוּנָה
וְאֶסְלַח לָהּ:
2 וְאִם חַי־יְהֹוָה יֹאמֵרוּ
לָכֵן לַשֶּׁקֶר יִשָּׁבֵעוּ:
3 יְהֹוָה עֵינֶיךָ הֲלוֹא לֶאֱמוּנָה
הִכִּיתָה אֹתָם וְלֹא־חָלוּ
כִּלִּיתָם מֵאֲנוּ קַחַת מוּסָר

They made their faces harder than rock,
They refused to turn back.

⁴Then I thought: These are just poor folk;
They act foolishly;
For they do not know the way of the LORD,
The rules of their God.
⁵So I will go to the wealthy
And speak with them:
Surely they know the way of the LORD,
The rules of their God.
But they as well had broken the yoke,
Had snapped the bonds.
⁶Therefore,
The lion of the forest strikes them down,
The wolf of the desert ravages them.
A leopard lies in wait by their towns;
Whoever leaves them will be torn in pieces.
For their transgressions are many,
Their rebellious acts unnumbered.

⁷Why should I forgive you?
Your children have forsaken Me
And sworn by no-gods.
When I fed them their fill,
They committed adultery
And went trooping to the harlot's house.
⁸They were ᵃ-well-fed, lusty-ᵃ stallions,
Each neighing at another's wife.
⁹Shall I not punish such deeds?
        —says the LORD—
Shall I not bring retribution
On a nation such as this?
¹⁰Go up among her vinesᵇ and destroy;
Lop off her trailing branches,
For they are not of the LORD.
(But do not make an end.)

חִזְּק֤וּ פְנֵיהֶם֙ מִסֶּ֔לַע
מֵאֲנ֖וּ לָשֽׁוּב׃

4 וַאֲנִ֣י אָמַ֔רְתִּי אַךְ־דַּלִּ֖ים הֵ֑ם
נֽוֹאֲל֗וּ
כִּ֤י לֹ֤א יָֽדְעוּ֙ דֶּ֣רֶךְ יְהֹוָ֔ה
מִשְׁפַּ֖ט אֱלֹהֵיהֶֽם׃
5 אֵֽלְכָה־לִּ֤י אֶל־הַגְּדֹלִים֙
וַאֲדַבְּרָ֣ה אוֹתָ֔ם
כִּ֣י הֵ֗מָּה יָֽדְעוּ֙ דֶּ֣רֶךְ יְהֹוָ֔ה
מִשְׁפַּ֖ט אֱלֹהֵיהֶ֑ם
אַ֣ךְ הֵ֗מָּה יַחְדָּו֙ שָֽׁבְרוּ עֹ֔ל
נִתְּק֖וּ מֽוֹסֵרֽוֹת׃
6 עַל־כֵּן֩
הִכָּ֨ם אַרְיֵ֜ה מִיַּ֗עַר
זְאֵ֤ב עֲרָבוֹת֙ יְשָׁדְדֵ֔ם
נָמֵ֣ר שֹׁקֵ֤ד עַל־עָֽרֵיהֶ֔ם
כָּל־הַיּוֹצֵ֥א מֵהֵ֖נָּה יִטָּרֵ֑ף
כִּ֤י רַבּוּ֙ פִּשְׁעֵיהֶ֔ם
עָֽצְמ֖וּ מְשֻֽׁבֽוֹתֵיהֶֽם׃

7 אֵ֤י לָזֹאת֙ אֶסְלַ֣חַ־לָ֔ךְ
בָּנַ֣יִךְ עֲזָב֔וּנִי
וַיִּשָּֽׁבְע֖וּ בְּלֹ֣א אֱלֹהִ֑ים
וָאַשְׂבִּ֤עַ אוֹתָם֙
וַיִּנְאָ֔פוּ
וּבֵ֥ית זוֹנָ֖ה יִתְגֹּדָֽדוּ׃
8 סוּסִ֥ים מְיֻזָּנִ֖ים מַשְׁכִּ֣ים הָי֑וּ
אִ֛ישׁ אֶל־אֵ֥שֶׁת רֵעֵ֖הוּ יִצְהָֽלוּ׃
9 הַֽעַל־אֵ֥לֶּה לֽוֹא־אֶפְקֹ֖ד
נְאֻם־יְהֹוָ֑ה
וְאִם֙ בְּג֣וֹי אֲשֶׁר־כָּזֶ֔ה
לֹ֥א תִתְנַקֵּ֖ם נַפְשִֽׁי׃ ס
10 עֲל֤וּ בְשָֽׁרוֹתֶ֨יהָ֙ וְשַׁחֵ֔תוּ
וְכָלָ֖ה אַל־תַּעֲשׂ֑וּ
הָסִ֨ירוּ֙ נְטִ֣ישֽׁוֹתֶ֔יהָ
כִּ֛י ל֥וֹא לַיהֹוָ֖ה הֵֽמָּה׃

ᵃ⁻ᵃ   Meaning of Heb. uncertain.
ᵇ   Lit. "rows."

11For the House of Israel and the House of
    Judah
Have betrayed Me

           —declares the LORD.

12They have been false to the LORD
And said: "c-It is not so!-c
No trouble shall come upon us,
We shall not see sword or famine.
13The prophets shall prove mere wind
For the Word is not in them;
Thus-and-thus shall be done to them!"

14Assuredly, thus said the LORD,
The God of Hosts:
Because theyd said that,
I am putting My words into your mouth as
    fire,
And this people shall be firewood,
Which it will consume.
15Lo, I am bringing against you, O House of
    Israel,
A nation from afar

           —declares the LORD;

It is an enduring nation,
It is an ancient nation;
A nation whose language you do not know—
You will not understand what they say.
16e-Their quivers-e are like a yawning grave—
They are all mighty men.
17They will devour your harvest and food,
They will devour your sons and daughters,
They will devour your flocks and herds,
They will devour your vines and fig trees.
They will batter down with the sword
The fortified towns on which you rely.

18But even in those days—declares the
LORD—I will not make an end of you. 19And
when theyd ask, "Because of what did the LORD

11 כִּי בָגוֹד בָּגְדוּ בִּי
בֵּית יִשְׂרָאֵל וּבֵית יְהוּדָה
נְאֻם־יְהֹוָה:
12 כִּחֲשׁוּ בַּיהֹוָה
וַיֹּאמְרוּ לֹא־הוּא
וְלֹא־תָבוֹא עָלֵינוּ רָעָה
וְחֶרֶב וְרָעָב לוֹא נִרְאֶה:
13 וְהַנְּבִיאִים יִהְיוּ לְרוּחַ
וְהַדִּבֵּר אֵין בָּהֶם
כֹּה יֵעָשֶׂה לָהֶם: ס
14 לָכֵן כֹּה־אָמַר יְהֹוָה
אֱלֹהֵי צְבָאוֹת
יַעַן דַּבֶּרְכֶם אֶת־הַדָּבָר הַזֶּה
הִנְנִי נֹתֵן דְּבָרַי בְּפִיךָ לְאֵשׁ
וְהָעָם הַזֶּה עֵצִים
וַאֲכָלָתַם:
15 הִנְנִי מֵבִיא עֲלֵיכֶם גּוֹי מִמֶּרְחָק
בֵּית יִשְׂרָאֵל
נְאֻם־יְהֹוָה
גּוֹי | אֵיתָן הוּא
גּוֹי מֵעוֹלָם הוּא
גּוֹי לֹא־תֵדַע לְשֹׁנוֹ
וְלֹא תִשְׁמַע מַה־יְדַבֵּר:
16 אַשְׁפָּתוֹ כְּקֶבֶר פָּתוּחַ
כֻּלָּם גִּבּוֹרִים:
17 וְאָכַל קְצִירְךָ וְלַחְמֶךָ
יֹאכְלוּ בָּנֶיךָ וּבְנוֹתֶיךָ
יֹאכַל צֹאנְךָ וּבְקָרֶךָ
יֹאכַל גַּפְנְךָ וּתְאֵנָתֶךָ
יְרֹשֵׁשׁ עָרֵי מִבְצָרֶיךָ
אֲשֶׁר אַתָּה בּוֹטֵחַ בָּהֵנָּה בֶּחָרֶב:

18 וְגַם בַּיָּמִים הָהֵמָּה נְאֻם־יְהֹוָה לֹא־
אֶעֱשֶׂה אִתְּכֶם כָּלָה: 19 וְהָיָה כִּי תֹאמְרוּ
תַּחַת מֶה עָשָׂה יְהֹוָה אֱלֹהֵינוּ לָנוּ אֶת־

c-c Or "Not He"; cf. Deut. 32.39; Isa. 43.13.
d Heb. "you."
e-e Emendation yields "Whose mouths."

our God do all these things?" you shall answer them, "Because you forsook Me and served alien gods on your own land, you will have to serve foreigners in a land not your own."

²⁰Proclaim this to the House of Jacob
And announce it in Judah:
²¹Hear this, O foolish people,
Devoid of intelligence,
That have eyes but can't see,
That have ears but can't hear!
²²Should you not revere Me
—says the LORD—
Should you not tremble before Me,
Who set the sand as a boundary to the sea,
As a limit for all time, not to be transgressed?
Though its waves toss, they cannot prevail;
Though they roar, they cannot pass it.
²³Yet this people has a wayward and defiant heart;
They have turned aside and gone their way.
²⁴They have not said to themselves,
"Let us revere the LORD our God,
Who gives the rain,
The early and late rain in season,
Who keeps for our benefit
The weeks appointed for harvest."
²⁵It is your iniquities that have diverted these things,
Your sins that have withheld the bounty from you.
²⁶For among My people are found wicked men,
ᵃ-Who lurk, like fowlers lying in wait;-ᵃ
They set up a trap to catch men.
²⁷As a cage is full of birds,
So their houses are full of guile;
That is why they have grown so wealthy.
²⁸They have become fat and sleek;

כָּל־אֵלֶּה וְאָמַרְתָּ֣ אֲלֵיהֶ֗ם כַּאֲשֶׁ֨ר עֲזַבְתֶּ֤ם אוֹתִי֙ וַתַּֽעַבְד֞וּ אֱלֹהֵ֤י נֵכָר֙ בְּאַרְצְכֶ֔ם כֵּ֚ן תַּעַבְד֣וּ זָרִ֔ים בְּאֶ֖רֶץ לֹ֥א לָכֶֽם׃ ס

²⁰ הַגִּ֥ידוּ זֹ֖את בְּבֵ֣ית יַעֲקֹ֑ב
וְהַשְׁמִיע֥וּהָ בִיהוּדָ֖ה לֵאמֹֽר׃
²¹ שִׁמְעוּ־נָ֣א זֹ֔את עַ֥ם סָכָ֖ל
וְאֵ֣ין לֵ֑ב
עֵינַ֤יִם לָהֶם֙ וְלֹ֣א יִרְא֔וּ
אָזְנַ֥יִם לָהֶ֖ם וְלֹ֥א יִשְׁמָֽעוּ׃
²² הַאוֹתִ֨י לֹא־תִירָ֜אוּ
נְאֻם־יְהֹוָ֗ה
אִ֤ם מִפָּנַי֙ לֹ֣א תָחִ֔ילוּ
אֲשֶׁר־שַׂ֤מְתִּי חוֹל֙ גְּב֣וּל לַיָּ֔ם
חָק־עוֹלָ֖ם וְלֹ֣א יַֽעַבְרֶ֑נְהוּ
וַיִּֽתְגָּעֲשׁוּ֙ וְלֹ֣א יוּכָ֔לוּ
וְהָמ֥וּ גַלָּ֖יו וְלֹ֥א יַעַבְרֻֽנְהוּ׃
²³ וְלָעָ֤ם הַזֶּה֙ הָיָ֔ה לֵ֖ב סוֹרֵ֣ר וּמוֹרֶ֑ה
סָ֖רוּ וַיֵּלֵֽכוּ׃
²⁴ וְלֹֽא־אָמְר֣וּ בִלְבָבָ֗ם
נִ֤ירָא נָא֙ אֶת־יְהֹוָ֣ה אֱלֹהֵ֔ינוּ
הַנֹּתֵ֣ן גֶּ֗שֶׁם
וירה יוֹרֶ֤ה וּמַלְקוֹשׁ֙ בְּעִתּ֔וֹ
שְׁבֻע֛וֹת חֻקּ֥וֹת קָצִ֖יר
יִשְׁמָר־לָֽנוּ׃
²⁵ עֲוֹנֽוֹתֵיכֶ֖ם הִטּוּ־אֵ֑לֶּה
וְחַטֹּ֣אותֵיכֶ֔ם* מָנְע֥וּ הַטּ֖וֹב מִכֶּֽם׃
²⁶ כִּי־נִמְצְא֥וּ בְעַמִּ֖י רְשָׁעִ֑ים
יָשׁוּר֙ כְּשַׁ֣ךְ יְקוּשִׁ֔ים
הִצִּ֥יבוּ מַשְׁחִ֖ית אֲנָשִׁ֥ים יִלְכֹּֽדוּ׃
²⁷ כִּכְלוּב֙ מָ֣לֵא ע֔וֹף
כֵּ֥ן בָּתֵּיהֶ֖ם מְלֵאִ֣ים מִרְמָ֑ה
עַל־כֵּ֥ן גָּדְל֖וּ וַֽיַּעֲשִֽׁירוּ׃
²⁸ שָׁמְנ֣וּ עָשְׁת֗וּ

v. 25. מלא ו׳

They *f*-pass beyond the bounds of wicked-
   ness,-*f*
And they prosper.
They will not judge the case of the orphan,
Nor give a hearing to the plea of the needy.
²⁹Shall I not punish such deeds
               —says the Lord—
Shall I not bring retribution
On a nation such as this?
³⁰An appalling, horrible thing
Has happened in the land:
³¹The prophets prophesy falsely,
And the priests *a*-rule accordingly;-*a*
And My people like it so.
But what will you do at the end of it?

6 Flee for refuge, O people of Benjamin,
Out of the midst of Jerusalem!
Blow the horn in Tekoa,
Set up a signal at Beth-haccerem!
For evil is appearing from the north,
And great disaster.
²*a*-Fair Zion, the lovely and delicate,
I will destroy.-*a*
³Against her come shepherds with their
   flocks,
They pitch tents all around her;
Each grazes *b*-the sheep under his care.-*b*
⁴*c*-Prepare for-*c* battle against her:
"Up! we will attack at noon."
"Alas for us! for day is declining,
The shadows of evening grow long."
⁵"Up! let us attack by night,
And wreck her fortresses."

⁶For thus said the Lord of Hosts:
Hew down her trees,

גַּם עָבְר֖וּ דִבְרֵי־רָ֑ע
דִּ֣ין לֹא־דָ֗נוּ דִּ֤ין יָתוֹם֙
וְיַצְלִ֔יחוּ
וּמִשְׁפַּ֥ט אֶבְיוֹנִ֖ים לֹ֥א שָׁפָֽטוּ׃
²⁹ הַֽעַל־אֵ֥לֶּה לֹֽא־אֶפְקֹ֖ד
נְאֻם־יְהֹוָ֑ה
אִ֚ם בְּג֣וֹי אֲשֶׁר־כָּזֶ֔ה
לֹ֥א תִתְנַקֵּ֖ם נַפְשִֽׁי׃ ס
³⁰ שַׁמָּה֙ וְשַׁ֣עֲרוּרָ֔ה
נִהְיְתָ֖ה בָּאָֽרֶץ׃
³¹ הַנְּבִיאִ֞ים נִבְּא֣וּ־בַשֶּׁ֗קֶר
וְהַכֹּֽהֲנִים֙ יִרְדּ֣וּ עַל־יְדֵיהֶ֔ם
וְעַמִּ֖י אָ֣הֲבוּ כֵ֑ן
וּמַֽה־תַּעֲשׂ֖וּ לְאַחֲרִיתָֽהּ׃

ו הָעִ֣זוּ ׀ בְּנֵ֣י בִנְיָמִ֗ן
מִקֶּ֙רֶב֙ יְר֣וּשָׁלַ֔͏ִם
וּבִתְק֙וֹעַ֙ תִּקְע֣וּ שׁוֹפָ֔ר
וְעַל־בֵּ֥ית הַכֶּ֖רֶם שְׂא֣וּ מַשְׂאֵ֑ת
כִּ֥י רָעָ֛ה נִשְׁקְפָ֥ה מִצָּפ֖וֹן
וְשֶׁ֥בֶר גָּדֽוֹל׃
² הַנָּוָה֙ וְהַמְּעֻנָּגָ֔ה
דָּמִ֖יתִי בַּת־צִיּֽוֹן׃
³ אֵלֶ֛יהָ יָבֹ֥אוּ רֹעִ֖ים וְעֶדְרֵיהֶ֑ם
תָּקְע֨וּ עָלֶ֤יהָ אֹֽהָלִים֙ סָבִ֔יב
רָע֖וּ אִ֥ישׁ אֶת־יָדֽוֹ׃
⁴ קַדְּשׁ֤וּ עָלֶ֙יהָ֙ מִלְחָמָ֔ה
ק֖וּמוּ וְנַעֲלֶ֣ה בַֽצׇּהֳרָ֑יִם
א֥וֹי לָ֖נוּ כִּי־פָנָ֣ה הַיּ֑וֹם
כִּ֥י יִנָּט֖וּ צִלְלֵי־עָֽרֶב׃
⁵ *ק֚וּמוּ וְנַעֲלֶ֣ה בַלַּ֔יְלָה
וְנַשְׁחִ֖יתָה אַרְמְנוֹתֶֽיהָ׃ ס

⁶ כִּ֣י כֹ֤ה אָמַר֙ יְהֹוָ֣ה צְבָא֔וֹת
כִּרְת֣וּ עֵצָ֗ה*

---

f-f   *Some ancient versions read "have transgressed My words for evil."*

a-a   *Meaning of Heb. uncertain.*
b-b   *Understanding yado as in Ps. 95.7.*
c-c   *Lit. "Consecrate."*

v. 5. חצי המקרא בפסוקים (אף על פי שכתוב 6.7 במסורה)
v. 6. ה' רפה

1020

And raise a siegemound against Jerusalem.
d-She is the city destined for punishment;-*d*
Only fraud is found in her midst.
7As a well flows with water,
So she flows with wickedness.
Lawlessness and rapine are heard in her;
Before Me constantly are sickness and
  wounds.
8Accept rebuke, O Jerusalem,
Lest I come to loathe you,
Lest I make you a desolation,
An uninhabited land.

9Thus said the LORD of Hosts:
e-Let them glean-*e* over and over, as a vine,
The remnant of Israel.
Pass your hand again,
Like a vintager,
Over its branches.

10*f*To whom shall I speak,
Give warning that they may hear?
Their ears are blocked
And they cannot listen.
See, the word of the LORD has become for
  them
An object of scorn; they will have none of it.
11But I am filled with the wrath of the LORD,
I cannot hold it in.

Pour it on the infant in the street,
And on the company of youths gathered to-
  gether!
Yes, men and women alike shall be captured,
Elders and those of advanced years.
12Their houses shall pass to others,
Fields and wives as well,

וְשָׁפְכ֥וּ עַל־יְרוּשָׁלַ֖͏ִם סֹלְלָ֑ה
הִ֚יא הָעִ֣יר הׇפְקַ֔ד
כֻּלָּ֖הּ עֹ֥שֶׁק בְּקִרְבָּֽהּ׃
7 כְּהָקִ֥יר בַּ֙יִר֙ מֵימֶ֔יהָ
כֵּ֖ן הֵקֵ֣רָה רָעָתָ֑הּ
חָמָ֤ס וָשֹׁד֙ יִשָּׁ֣מַע בָּ֔הּ
עַל־פָּנַ֛י תָּמִ֖יד חֳלִ֥י וּמַכָּֽה׃
8 הִוָּֽסְרִי֙ יְר֣וּשָׁלַ֔͏ִם
פֶּן־תֵּקַ֥ע נַפְשִׁ֖י מִמֵּ֑ךְ
פֶּן־אֲשִׂימֵ֣ךְ שְׁמָמָ֔ה
אֶ֖רֶץ ל֥וֹא נוֹשָֽׁבָה׃ פ

9 כֹּ֤ה אָמַר֙ יְהֹוָ֣ה צְבָא֔וֹת
עוֹלֵ֛ל יְעוֹלְל֥וּ כַגֶּ֖פֶן
שְׁאֵרִ֣ית יִשְׂרָאֵ֑ל
הָשֵׁב֙ יָֽדְךָ֔
כְּבוֹצֵ֖ר
עַל־סַלְסִלּֽוֹת׃

10 עַל־מִ֨י אֲדַבְּרָ֤ה
וְאָעִ֙ידָה֙ וְיִשְׁמָ֔עוּ
הִנֵּ֤ה עֲרֵלָה֙ אׇזְנָ֔ם
וְלֹ֥א יוּכְל֖וּ לְהַקְשִׁ֑יב
הִנֵּ֣ה דְבַר־יְהֹוָ֗ה הָיָ֥ה לָהֶ֛ם
לְחֶרְפָּ֖ה לֹ֥א יַחְפְּצוּ־בֽוֹ׃
11 וְאֵת֩ חֲמַ֨ת יְהֹוָ֤ה ׀ מָלֵ֙אתִי֙
נִלְאֵ֣יתִי הָכִ֔יל

שְׁפֹ֤ךְ עַל־עוֹלָל֙ בַּח֔וּץ
וְעַ֛ל ס֥וֹד בַּחוּרִ֖ים יַחְדָּ֑ו
כִּֽי־גַם־אִ֤ישׁ עִם־אִשָּׁה֙ יִלָּכֵ֔דוּ
זָקֵ֖ן עִם־מְלֵ֥א יָמִֽים׃
12 וְנָסַ֤בּוּ בָֽתֵּיהֶם֙ לַֽאֲחֵרִ֔ים
שָׂד֥וֹת וְנָשִׁ֖ים יַחְדָּ֑ו

---

d-d Emendation yields "She is the city of falseness."
e-e Emendation yields "Glean" (singular).
f The prophet speaks.

For I will stretch out My arm
Against the inhabitants of the country
—declares the LORD.

כִּי־אַטֶּה אֶת־יָדִי
עַל־יֹשְׁבֵי הָאָרֶץ
נְאֻם־יְהֹוָה:

13For from the smallest to the greatest,
They are all greedy for gain;
Priest and prophet alike,
They all act falsely.

13 כִּי מִקְּטַנָּם וְעַד־גְּדוֹלָם
כֻּלּוֹ בּוֹצֵעַ בָּצַע
וּמִנָּבִיא וְעַד־כֹּהֵן
כֻּלּוֹ עֹשֶׂה שָּׁקֶר:

14They offer healing offhand
For the wounds of My people,
Saying, "All is well, all is well,"
When nothing is well.

14 וַיְרַפְּאוּ
אֶת־שֶׁבֶר עַמִּי עַל־נְקַלָּה
לֵאמֹר שָׁלוֹם ׀ שָׁלוֹם
וְאֵין שָׁלוֹם:

15They have acted shamefully;
They have done abhorrent things—
Yet they do not feel shame,
And they cannot be made to blush.
Assuredly, they shall fall among the falling,
They shall stumble at the time when I punish
    them
                    —said the LORD.

15 הֹבִישׁוּ
כִּי תוֹעֵבָה עָשׂוּ
גַּם־בּוֹשׁ לֹא־יֵבוֹשׁוּ
גַּם־הַכְלִים לֹא יָדָעוּ
לָכֵן יִפְּלוּ בַנֹּפְלִים
בְּעֵת־פְּקַדְתִּים יִכָּשְׁלוּ
אָמַר יְהֹוָה: ס

16Thus said the LORD:
Stand by the roads and consider,
Inquire about ancient paths:
Which is the road to happiness?
Travel it, and find tranquillity for yourselves.
But they said, "We will not."

16 כֹּה אָמַר יְהֹוָה
עִמְדוּ עַל־דְּרָכִים וּרְאוּ
וְשַׁאֲלוּ ׀ לִנְתִבוֹת עוֹלָם
אֵי־זֶה דֶרֶךְ הַטּוֹב
וּלְכוּ־בָהּ וּמִצְאוּ מַרְגּוֹעַ לְנַפְשְׁכֶם
וַיֹּאמְרוּ לֹא נֵלֵךְ:

17And I raised up watchmen*g* for you:
"Hearken to the sound of the horn!"
But they said, "We will not."

17 וַהֲקִמֹתִי עֲלֵיכֶם צֹפִים
הַקְשִׁיבוּ לְקוֹל שׁוֹפָר
וַיֹּאמְרוּ לֹא נַקְשִׁיב:

18Hear well, O nations,
And know, *a*-O community, what is in store
    for them.-*a*

18 לָכֵן שִׁמְעוּ הַגּוֹיִם
וּדְעִי עֵדָה אֶת־אֲשֶׁר־בָּם:

19Hear, O earth!
I am going to bring disaster upon this people,
The outcome of their own schemes;
For they would not hearken to My words,
And they rejected My Instruction.

19 שִׁמְעִי הָאָרֶץ
הִנֵּה אָנֹכִי מֵבִיא רָעָה אֶל־הָעָם הַזֶּה
פְּרִי מַחְשְׁבוֹתָם
כִּי עַל־דְּבָרַי לֹא הִקְשִׁיבוּ
וְתוֹרָתִי וַיִּמְאֲסוּ־בָהּ:

20What need have I of frankincense
That comes from Sheba,
Or fragrant cane from a distant land?

20 לָמָּה־זֶּה לִּי לְבוֹנָה
מִשְּׁבָא תָבוֹא
וְקָנֶה הַטּוֹב מֵאֶרֶץ מֶרְחָק

g I.e., prophets.

Your burnt offerings are not acceptable
And your sacrifices are not pleasing to Me.

²¹Assuredly, thus said the LORD:
I shall put before this people stumbling blocks
Over which they shall stumble—
Fathers and children alike,
Neighbor and friend shall perish.

²²Thus said the LORD:
See, a people comes from the northland,
A great nation is roused
From the remotest parts of the earth.
²³They grasp the bow and javelin;
They are cruel, they show no mercy;
The sound of them is like the roaring sea.
They ride upon horses,
Accoutered like a man for battle,
Against you, O Fair Zion!

²⁴"We have heard the report of them,
Our hands fail;
Pain seizes us,
Agony like a woman in childbirth.
²⁵Do not go out into the country,
Do not walk the roads!
For the sword of the enemy is there,
Terror on every side."

²⁶ʰ⁻My poor people,⁻ʰ
Put on sackcloth
And strew dust on yourselves!
Mourn, as for an only child;
Wail bitterly,
For suddenly the destroyer
Is coming upon us.

²⁷I have made you an assayer of My people
—A refinerᵃ—

עֲלוֹתֵיכֶם֙ לֹ֣א לְרָצ֔וֹן
וְזִבְחֵיכֶ֖ם לֹא־עָ֣רְבוּ לִ֑י: ס

21 לָכֵ֗ן כֹּ֚ה אָמַ֣ר יְהֹוָ֔ה
הִנְנִ֣י נֹתֵ֡ן אֶל־הָעָ֨ם הַזֶּ֜ה מִכְשֹׁלִ֗ים
וְכָ֥שְׁלוּ בָ֖ם
אָב֧וֹת וּבָנִ֛ים יַחְדָּ֖ו
שָׁכֵ֥ן וְרֵע֖וֹ יֹאבֵ֥דוּ וְאָבָֽדוּ: פ

22 כֹּ֚ה אָמַ֣ר יְהֹוָ֔ה
הִנֵּ֣ה עַ֥ם בָּ֖א מֵאֶ֣רֶץ צָפ֑וֹן
וְג֣וֹי גָּד֔וֹל יֵע֖וֹר
מִיַּרְכְּתֵי־אָֽרֶץ:

23 קֶ֣שֶׁת וְכִיד֤וֹן יַחֲזִ֙יקוּ֙
אַכְזָרִ֥י הוּא֙ וְלֹ֣א יְרַחֵ֔מוּ
קוֹלָם֙ כַּיָּ֣ם יֶהֱמֶ֔ה
וְעַל־סוּסִ֖ים יִרְכָּ֑בוּ
עָר֗וּךְ כְּאִישׁ֙ לַמִּלְחָמָ֔ה
עָלַ֖יִךְ בַּת־צִיּֽוֹן:

24 שָׁמַ֥עְנוּ אֶת־שׇׁמְע֖וֹ
רָפ֣וּ יָדֵ֑ינוּ
צָרָה֙ הֶחֱזִיקַ֔תְנוּ
חִ֖יל כַּיּוֹלֵדָֽה:

25 אַל־תֵּצְאִי֙ הַשָּׂדֶ֔ה
וּבַדֶּ֖רֶךְ אַל־תֵּלֵ֑כִי
כִּ֚י חֶ֣רֶב לְאֹיֵ֔ב
מָג֖וֹר מִסָּבִֽיב:

26 בַּת־עַמִּ֤י
חִגְרִי־שָׂק֙
וְהִתְפַּלְּשִׁ֣י בָאֵ֔פֶר
אֵ֤בֶל יָחִיד֙ עֲשִׂ֣י לָ֔ךְ
מִסְפַּ֖ד תַּמְרוּרִ֑ים
כִּ֣י פִתְאֹ֔ם
יָבֹ֥א הַשֹּׁדֵ֖ד עָלֵֽינוּ:

27 בָּח֛וֹן נְתַתִּ֥יךָ בְעַמִּ֖י
מִבְצָ֑ר

---

h-h Lit. "Daughter that is My people"; so, frequently, in poetry.
　　See 4.11 and note.

You are to note and assay their ways.
²⁸They are copper and iron:
They are all stubbornly defiant;
They ᶦ-deal basely-ᶦ
All of them act corruptly.
²⁹ᵃ-The bellows puff;
The lead is consumed by fire.-ᵃ
Yet the smelter smelts to no purpose—
The dross ᵃ is not separated out.
³⁰They are called "rejected silver,"
For the Lord has rejected them.

7 The word which came to Jeremiah from the Lord: ²Stand at the gate of the House of the Lord, and there proclaim this word: Hear the word of the Lord, all you of Judah who enter these gates to worship the Lord! ³Thus said the Lord of Hosts, the God of Israel: Mend your ways and your actions, and I will ᵃ-let you dwell-ᵃ in this place. ⁴Don't put your trust in illusions and say, "The Temple of the Lord, the Temple of the Lord, the Temple of the Lord are these [buildings]." ⁵No, if you really mend your ways and your actions; if you execute justice between one man and another; ⁶if you do not oppress the stranger, the orphan, and the widow; if you do not shed the blood of the innocent in this place; if you do not follow other gods, to your own hurt—⁷then only will I ᵃ-let you dwell-ᵃ in this place, in the land that I gave to your fathers for all time. ⁸See, you are relying on illusions that are of no avail. ⁹Will you steal and murder and commit adultery and swear falsely, and sacrifice to Baal, and follow other gods whom you have not experienced,ᵇ ¹⁰and then come and stand before Me in this

---

ⁱ⁻ⁱ   See note at Lev. 19.16.
ᵃ⁻ᵃ   Meaning of Heb. uncertain. Change of vocalization yields
        "dwell with you"; so Aquila and Vulgate.
ᵇ   See note at Deut. 11.28.

וְתֵדַ֖ע וּבָחַנְתָּ֥ אֶת־דַּרְכָּֽם׃
²⁸ כֻּלָּם֙ סָרֵ֣י סֽוֹרְרִ֔ים
הֹלְכֵ֥י רָכִ֖יל
נְחֹ֣שֶׁת וּבַרְזֶ֑ל
כֻּלָּ֥ם מַשְׁחִיתִ֖ים הֵֽמָּה׃
²⁹ נָחַ֣ר מַפֻּ֔חַ
מֵאֵ֯שׁתַּ֯ם תַּ֣ם עֹפָ֑רֶת
לַשָּׁוְא֙ צָרַ֣ף צָר֔וֹף
וְרָעִ֖ים לֹ֥א נִתָּֽקוּ׃
³⁰ כֶּ֣סֶף נִמְאָ֔ס קָרְא֖וּ לָהֶ֑ם
כִּֽי־מָאַ֥ס יְהֹוָ֖ה בָּהֶֽם׃ פ

ז הַדָּבָר֙ אֲשֶׁ֣ר הָיָ֣ה אֶֽל־יִרְמְיָ֔הוּ מֵאֵ֥ת
יְהֹוָ֖ה לֵאמֹֽר׃ ² עֲמֹ֗ד בְּשַׁ֙עַר֙ בֵּ֣ית יְהֹוָ֔ה
וְקָרָ֣אתָ שָּׁ֗ם אֶת־הַדָּבָ֤ר הַזֶּה֙ וְאָ֣מַרְתָּ֔ שִׁמְע֣וּ
דְבַר־יְהֹוָ֗ה כׇּל־יְהוּדָ֔ה הַבָּאִים֙ בַּשְּׁעָרִ֣ים
הָאֵ֔לֶּה לְהִֽשְׁתַּחֲוֺ֖ת לַיהֹוָֽה׃ ס ³ כֹּֽה־אָמַ֞ר יְהֹוָ֤ה צְבָאוֹת֙ אֱלֹהֵ֣י יִשְׂרָאֵ֔ל
הֵיטִ֥יבוּ דַרְכֵיכֶ֖ם וּמַֽעַלְלֵיכֶ֑ם וַאֲשַׁכְּנָ֣ה
אֶתְכֶ֔ם בַּמָּק֖וֹם הַזֶּֽה׃ ⁴ אַל־תִּבְטְח֣וּ לָכֶ֔ם
אֶל־דִּבְרֵ֥י הַשֶּׁ֖קֶר לֵאמֹ֑ר הֵיכַ֤ל יְהֹוָה֙ הֵיכַ֣ל
יְהֹוָ֔ה הֵיכַ֥ל יְהֹוָ֖ה הֵֽמָּה׃ ⁵ כִּ֤י אִם־הֵיטֵב֙
תֵּיטִ֙יבוּ֙ אֶת־דַּרְכֵיכֶ֔ם וְאֶֽת־מַֽעַלְלֵיכֶ֑ם
אִם־עָשׂ֤וֹ תַֽעֲשׂוּ֙ מִשְׁפָּ֔ט בֵּ֥ין אִ֖ישׁ וּבֵ֥ין
רֵעֵֽהוּ׃ ⁶ גֵּ֣ר יָת֤וֹם וְאַלְמָנָה֙ לֹ֣א תַעֲשֹׁ֔קוּ
וְדָ֤ם נָקִי֙ אַל־תִּשְׁפְּכ֣וּ בַּמָּק֖וֹם הַזֶּ֑ה וְאַחֲרֵ֨י
אֱלֹהִ֧ים אֲחֵרִ֛ים לֹ֥א תֵלְכ֖וּ לְרַ֥ע לָכֶֽם׃
⁷ וְשִׁכַּנְתִּ֣י אֶתְכֶ֔ם בַּמָּק֖וֹם הַזֶּ֑ה בָּאָ֕רֶץ
אֲשֶׁ֥ר נָתַ֖תִּי לַאֲבֽוֹתֵיכֶ֑ם לְמִן־עוֹלָ֖ם וְעַד־
עוֹלָֽם׃ ⁸ הִנֵּ֤ה אַתֶּם֙ בֹּטְחִ֣ים לָכֶ֔ם עַל־
דִּבְרֵ֥י הַשָּׁ֖קֶר לְבִלְתִּ֥י הוֹעִֽיל׃ ⁹ הֲגָנֹ֣ב ׀ רָצֹ֣חַ
וְֽנָאֹ֗ף וְהִשָּׁבֵ֤עַ לַשֶּׁ֙קֶר֙ וְקַטֵּ֣ר לַבַּ֔עַל וְהָלֹ֗ךְ
אַחֲרֵ֛י אֱלֹהִ֥ים אֲחֵרִ֖ים אֲשֶׁ֥ר לֹֽא־יְדַעְתֶּֽם׃
¹⁰ וּבָאתֶ֞ם וַעֲמַדְתֶּ֣ם לְפָנַ֗י בַּבַּ֤יִת הַזֶּה֙ אֲשֶׁ֣ר

House which bears My name and say, "We are safe"?—[Safe] to do all these abhorrent things! 11Do you consider this House, which bears My name, to be a den of thieves? As for Me, I have been watching—declares the LORD.

12Just go to My place at Shiloh, where I had established My name formerly, and see what I did to it because of the wickedness of My people Israel. 13And now, because you do all these things—declares the LORD—and though I spoke to you persistently, you would not listen; and though I called to you, you would not respond—14therefore I will do to the House which bears My name, on which you rely, and to the place which I gave you and your fathers, just what I did to Shiloh. 15And I will cast you out of My presence as I cast out your brothers, the whole brood of Ephraim.

16As for you, do not pray for this people, do not raise a cry of prayer on their behalf, do not plead with Me; for I will not listen to you. 17Don't you see what they are doing in the towns of Judah and in the streets of Jerusalem? 18The children gather sticks, the fathers build the fire, and the mothers knead dough, to make cakes for the Queen of Heaven,*c* and they pour libations to other gods, to vex Me. 19Is it Me they are vexing?—says the LORD. It is rather themselves, to their own disgrace. 20Assuredly, thus said the Lord GOD: My wrath and My fury will be poured out upon this place, on man and on beast, on the trees of the field and the fruit of the soil. It shall burn, with none to quench it.

21Thus said the LORD of Hosts, the God of Israel: Add your burnt offerings to your other sacrifices and eat the meat! 22For when I freed

---

נִקְרָא־שְׁמִי עָלָיו וַאֲמַרְתֶּם נִצַּלְנוּ לְמַעַן עֲשׂוֹת אֵת כָּל־הַתּוֹעֵבוֹת הָאֵלֶּה: 11 הַמְעָרַת פָּרִצִים הָיָה הַבַּיִת הַזֶּה אֲשֶׁר־נִקְרָא־שְׁמִי עָלָיו בְּעֵינֵיכֶם גַּם אָנֹכִי הִנֵּה רָאִיתִי נְאֻם־יְהוָה: ס

12 כִּי לְכוּ־נָא אֶל־מְקוֹמִי אֲשֶׁר בְּשִׁילוֹ אֲשֶׁר שִׁכַּנְתִּי שְׁמִי שָׁם בָּרִאשׁוֹנָה וּרְאוּ אֵת אֲשֶׁר־עָשִׂיתִי לוֹ מִפְּנֵי רָעַת עַמִּי יִשְׂרָאֵל: 13 וְעַתָּה יַעַן עֲשׂוֹתְכֶם אֶת־כָּל־הַמַּעֲשִׂים הָאֵלֶּה נְאֻם־יְהוָה וָאֲדַבֵּר אֲלֵיכֶם הַשְׁכֵּם וְדַבֵּר וְלֹא שְׁמַעְתֶּם וָאֶקְרָא אֶתְכֶם וְלֹא עֲנִיתֶם: 14 וְעָשִׂיתִי לַבַּיִת | אֲשֶׁר נִקְרָא־שְׁמִי עָלָיו אֲשֶׁר אַתֶּם בֹּטְחִים בּוֹ וְלַמָּקוֹם אֲשֶׁר־נָתַתִּי לָכֶם וְלַאֲבוֹתֵיכֶם כַּאֲשֶׁר עָשִׂיתִי לְשִׁלוֹ: 15 וְהִשְׁלַכְתִּי אֶתְכֶם מֵעַל פָּנָי כַּאֲשֶׁר הִשְׁלַכְתִּי אֶת־כָּל־אֲחֵיכֶם אֵת כָּל־זֶרַע אֶפְרָיִם: ס

16 וְאַתָּה אַל־תִּתְפַּלֵּל | בְּעַד־הָעָם הַזֶּה וְאַל־תִּשָּׂא בַעֲדָם רִנָּה וּתְפִלָּה וְאַל־תִּפְגַּע־בִּי כִּי־אֵינֶנִּי שֹׁמֵעַ אֹתָךְ: 17 הַאֵינְךָ רֹאֶה מָה הֵמָּה עֹשִׂים בְּעָרֵי יְהוּדָה וּבְחֻצוֹת יְרוּשָׁלָ͏ִם: 18 הַבָּנִים מְלַקְּטִים עֵצִים וְהָאָבוֹת מְבַעֲרִים אֶת־הָאֵשׁ וְהַנָּשִׁים לָשׁוֹת בָּצֵק לַעֲשׂוֹת כַּוָּנִים לִמְלֶכֶת הַשָּׁמַיִם וְהַסֵּךְ נְסָכִים לֵאלֹהִים אֲחֵרִים לְמַעַן הַכְעִסֵנִי: 19 הַאֹתִי הֵם מַכְעִסִים נְאֻם־יְהוָה הֲלוֹא אֹתָם לְמַעַן בֹּשֶׁת פְּנֵיהֶם: ס 20 לָכֵן כֹּה־אָמַר | אֲדֹנָי יְהוִֹה הִנֵּה אַפִּי וַחֲמָתִי נִתֶּכֶת אֶל־הַמָּקוֹם הַזֶּה עַל־הָאָדָם וְעַל־הַבְּהֵמָה וְעַל־עֵץ הַשָּׂדֶה וְעַל־פְּרִי הָאֲדָמָה וּבָעֲרָה וְלֹא תִכְבֶּה: ס

21 כֹּה אָמַר יְהוָה צְבָאוֹת אֱלֹהֵי יִשְׂרָאֵל עֹלוֹתֵיכֶם סְפוּ עַל־זִבְחֵיכֶם וְאִכְלוּ בָשָׂר:

---

c I.e., the mother goddess (Ishtar, Astarte) in whose honor these cakes were baked.

your fathers from the land of Egypt, I did not speak with them or command them concerning burnt offerings or sacrifice. ²³But this is what I commanded them: Do My bidding, that I may be your God and you may be My people; walk only in the way that I enjoin upon you, that it may go well with you. ²⁴Yet they did not listen or give ear; they followed their own counsels, the willfulness of their evil hearts. They have gone backward, not forward, ²⁵from the day your fathers left the land of Egypt until today. And though I kept sending all My servants, the prophets, to them[d] daily and persistently, ²⁶they would not listen to Me or give ear. They stiffened their necks, they acted worse than their fathers.

²⁷You shall say all these things to them, but they will not listen to you; you shall call to them, but they will not respond to you. ²⁸Then say to them: This is the nation that would not obey the Lᴏʀᴅ their God, that would not accept rebuke. Faithfulness has perished, vanished from their mouths.

²⁹Shear your locks and cast them away,
Take up a lament on the heights,
For the Lᴏʀᴅ has spurned and cast off
The brood that provoked His wrath.

³⁰For the people of Judah have done what displeases Me—declares the Lᴏʀᴅ. They have set up their abominations in the House which is called by My name, and they have defiled it. ³¹And they have built the shrines of Topheth in the Valley of Ben-hinnom to burn their sons and daughters in fire—which I never commanded, which never came to My mind. ³²Assuredly, a time is coming—declares the Lᴏʀᴅ—when men shall no longer speak of Topheth or the Valley of Ben-hinnom, but of the

²² כִּ֠י לֹֽא־דִבַּ֤רְתִּי אֶת־אֲבֽוֹתֵיכֶם֙ וְלֹ֣א צִוִּיתִ֔ים בְּי֛וֹם הוֹצִיאִ֥י אוֹתָ֖ם מֵאֶ֣רֶץ מִצְרָ֑יִם עַל־דִּבְרֵ֥י עוֹלָ֖ה וָזָֽבַח׃ ²³ כִּ֣י אִם־אֶת־הַדָּבָ֣ר הַ֠זֶּה צִוִּ֨יתִי אוֹתָ֤ם לֵאמֹר֙ שִׁמְע֣וּ בְקוֹלִ֔י וְהָיִ֤יתִי לָכֶם֙ לֵֽאלֹהִ֔ים וְאַתֶּ֖ם תִּֽהְיוּ־לִ֣י לְעָ֑ם וַהֲלַכְתֶּ֗ם בְּכָל־הַדֶּ֙רֶךְ֙ אֲשֶׁ֣ר אֲצַוֶּ֣ה אֶתְכֶ֔ם לְמַ֖עַן יִיטַ֥ב לָכֶֽם׃ ²⁴ וְלֹ֤א שָֽׁמְעוּ֙ וְלֹא־הִטּ֣וּ אֶת־אָזְנָ֔ם וַיֵּֽלְכוּ֙ בְּמֹ֣עֵצ֔וֹת בִּשְׁרִר֖וּת לִבָּ֣ם הָרָ֑ע וַיִּהְי֥וּ לְאָח֖וֹר וְלֹ֥א לְפָנִֽים׃ ²⁵ לְמִן־הַיּ֗וֹם אֲשֶׁ֨ר יָצְא֤וּ אֲבֽוֹתֵיכֶם֙ מֵאֶ֣רֶץ מִצְרַ֔יִם עַ֖ד הַיּ֣וֹם הַזֶּ֑ה וָאֶשְׁלַ֤ח אֲלֵיכֶם֙ אֶת־כָּל־עֲבָדַ֣י הַנְּבִיאִ֔ים י֖וֹם הַשְׁכֵּ֥ם וְשָׁלֹֽחַ׃ ²⁶ וְל֤וֹא שָֽׁמְעוּ֙ אֵלַ֔י וְלֹ֥א הִטּ֖וּ אֶת־אָזְנָ֑ם וַיַּקְשׁוּ֙ אֶת־עָרְפָּ֔ם הֵרֵ֖עוּ מֵאֲבוֹתָֽם׃

²⁷ וְדִבַּרְתָּ֤ אֲלֵיהֶם֙ אֶת־כָּל־הַדְּבָרִ֣ים הָאֵ֔לֶּה וְלֹ֥א יִשְׁמְע֖וּ אֵלֶ֑יךָ וְקָרָ֥אתָ אֲלֵיהֶ֖ם וְלֹ֥א יַעֲנֽוּכָה׃* ²⁸ וְאָמַרְתָּ֣ אֲלֵיהֶ֗ם זֶ֤ה הַגּוֹי֙ אֲשֶׁ֣ר לֽוֹא־שָׁמְע֗וּ בְּקוֹל֙ יְהוָ֣ה אֱלֹהָ֔יו וְלֹ֥א לָקְח֖וּ מוּסָ֑ר אָבְדָה֙ הָֽאֱמוּנָ֔ה וְנִכְרְתָ֖ה מִפִּיהֶֽם׃ ס

²⁹ גָּזִּ֤י נִזְרֵךְ֙ וְֽהַשְׁלִ֔יכִי וּשְׂאִ֥י עַל־שְׁפָיִ֖ם קִינָ֑ה כִּ֚י מָאַ֣ס יְהוָ֔ה וַיִּטֹּ֖שׁ אֶת־דּ֥וֹר עֶבְרָתֽוֹ׃

³⁰ כִּֽי־עָשׂ֨וּ בְנֵֽי־יְהוּדָ֥ה הָרַ֛ע בְּעֵינַ֖י נְאֻם־יְהוָ֑ה שָׂ֣מוּ שִׁקּֽוּצֵיהֶ֗ם בַּבַּ֛יִת אֲשֶׁר־נִקְרָא־שְׁמִ֥י עָלָ֖יו לְטַמְּאֽוֹ׃ ³¹ וּבָנ֞וּ בָּמ֣וֹת הַתֹּ֗פֶת אֲשֶׁר֙ בְּגֵ֣יא בֶן־הִנֹּ֔ם לִשְׂרֹ֛ף אֶת־בְּנֵיהֶ֥ם וְאֶת־בְּנֹֽתֵיהֶ֖ם בָּאֵ֑שׁ אֲשֶׁר֙ לֹ֣א צִוִּ֔יתִי וְלֹ֥א עָלְתָ֖ה עַל־לִבִּֽי׃ ס ³² לָכֵ֞ן הִנֵּֽה־יָמִ֤ים בָּאִים֙ נְאֻם־יְהוָ֔ה וְלֹא־יֵאָמֵ֨ר ע֤וֹד הַתֹּ֙פֶת֙ וְגֵ֣יא בֶן־הִנֹּ֔ם כִּ֖י אִם־

---

d   Heb. "you."

Valley of Slaughter; and they shall bury in Topheth until no room is left. ³³The carcasses of
this people shall be food for the birds of the sky
and the beasts of the earth, with none to frighten
them off. ³⁴And I will silence in the towns of
Judah and the streets of Jerusalem the sound of
mirth and gladness, the voice of bridegroom
and bride. For the whole land shall fall to ruin.

8 At that time—declares the Lord—the
bones of the kings of Judah, of its officers, of
the priests, of the prophets, and of the inhabitants of Jerusalem shall be taken out of their
graves ²and exposed to the sun, the moon, and
all the host of heaven which they loved and
served and followed, to which they turned and
bowed down. They shall not be gathered for re-
burial; they shall become dung upon the face
of the earth. ³And death shall be preferable to
life for all that are left of this wicked folk, in
all the other places to which I shall banish
them—declares the Lord of Hosts.

⁴Say to them: Thus said the Lord:
When men fall, do they not get up again?
If they turn aside, do they not turn back?
⁵Why is this people—Jerusalem—rebellious
With a persistent rebellion?
They cling to deceit,
They refuse to return.
⁶I have listened and heard:
They do not speak honestly.
No one regrets his wickedness
And says, "What have I done!"
They all persist in their wayward course
Like a steed dashing forward in the fray.

גֵּיא הַהֲרֵגָה וְקָבְר֥וּ בְתֹ֖פֶת מֵאֵ֥ין מָקֽוֹם׃
33 וְֽהָיְתָ֞ה נִבְלַ֣ת הָעָ֤ם הַזֶּה֙ לְמַֽאֲכָ֔ל לְע֥וֹף
הַשָּׁמַ֖יִם וּלְבֶהֱמַ֣ת הָאָ֑רֶץ וְאֵ֖ין מַחֲרִֽיד׃
34 וְהִשְׁבַּתִּ֣י ׀ מֵעָרֵ֣י יְהוּדָ֗ה וּמֵֽחֻצוֹת֙
יְרֽוּשָׁלַ֔͏ִם ק֤וֹל שָׂשׂוֹן֙ וְק֣וֹל שִׂמְחָ֔ה ק֥וֹל חָתָ֖ן
וְק֣וֹל כַּלָּ֑ה כִּ֥י לְחׇרְבָּ֖ה תִּהְיֶ֥ה הָאָֽרֶץ׃

ח בָּעֵ֣ת הַהִ֣יא נְאֻם־יְהֹוָ֗ה ויציאו [יוֹצִ֜יאוּ]
אֶת־עַצְמ֣וֹת מַלְכֵֽי־יְהוּדָ֣ה וְאֶת־
עַצְמֽוֹת־שָׂרָיו֮ וְאֶת־עַצְמ֣וֹת הַכֹּהֲנִים֒
וְאֵ֣ת ׀ עַצְמ֣וֹת הַנְּבִיאִ֗ים וְאֵ֖ת עַצְמ֣וֹת
יוֹשְׁבֵֽי־יְרוּשָׁלָ֑͏ִם מִקִּבְרֵיהֶֽם׃ 2 וּשְׁטָחוּם֩
לַשֶּׁ֨מֶשׁ וְלַיָּרֵ֜חַ וּלְכֹ֣ל ׀ צְבָ֣א הַשָּׁמַ֗יִם אֲשֶׁ֨ר
אֲהֵב֜וּם וַאֲשֶׁ֤ר עֲבָדוּם֙ וַֽאֲשֶׁר֙ הָלְכ֣וּ
אַֽחֲרֵיהֶ֔ם וַֽאֲשֶׁ֥ר דְּרָשׁ֖וּם וַֽאֲשֶׁ֣ר הִֽשְׁתַּחֲו֣וּ
לָהֶ֑ם לֹ֤א יֵאָֽסְפוּ֙ וְלֹ֣א יִקָּבֵ֔רוּ לְדֹ֛מֶן
עַל־פְּנֵ֥י הָאֲדָמָ֖ה יִהְיֽוּ׃ 3 וְנִבְחַ֥ר מָ֙וֶת֙
מֵֽחַיִּ֔ים לְכֹ֗ל הַשְּׁאֵרִית֙ הַנִּשְׁאָרִ֔ים מִן־
הַמִּשְׁפָּחָ֥ה הָרָעָ֖ה הַזֹּ֑את בְּכׇל־הַמְּקֹמ֣וֹת
הַנִּשְׁאָרִ֗ים אֲשֶׁ֤ר הִדַּחְתִּים֙ שָׁ֔ם נְאֻ֖ם יְהֹוָ֥ה
צְבָאֽוֹת׃ ס

4 וְאָמַרְתָּ֣ אֲלֵיהֶ֗ם כֹּ֚ה אָמַ֣ר יְהֹוָ֔ה
הֲיִפְּל֖וּ וְלֹ֣א יָק֑וּמוּ
אִם־יָשׁ֖וּב וְלֹ֥א יָשֽׁוּב׃
5 מַדּ֨וּעַ שׁוֹבְבָ֜ה הָעָ֥ם הַזֶּ֛ה יְרוּשָׁלַ֖͏ִם
מְשֻׁבָ֣ה נִצַּ֑חַת
הֶחֱזִ֙יקוּ֙ בַּתַּרְמִ֔ית
מֵאֲנ֖וּ לָשֽׁוּב׃
6 הִקְשַׁ֤בְתִּי וָֽאֶשְׁמָע֙
לוֹא־כֵ֣ן יְדַבֵּ֔רוּ
אֵ֣ין אִ֗ישׁ נִחָם֙ עַל־רָ֣עָת֔וֹ
לֵאמֹ֖ר מֶ֣ה עָשִׂ֑יתִי
כֻּלֹּ֗ה שָׁב֙ במרצותם [בִּמְר֣וּצָתָ֔ם]
כְּס֥וּס שׁוֹטֵ֖ף בַּמִּלְחָמָֽה׃

⁷Even the stork in the sky knows her seasons,
And the turtledove, swift, and crane
Keep the time of their coming;
But My people pay no heed
To the law of the LORD.

⁸How can you say, "We are wise,
And we possess the Instruction of the LORD"?
Assuredly, for naught has the pen labored,
For naught the scribes!

⁹The wise shall be put to shame,
Shall be dismayed and caught;
See, they reject the word of the LORD,
So their wisdom amounts to nothing.

⁷גַּם־חֲסִידָה בַשָּׁמַיִם יָדְעָה מֽוֹעֲדֶיהָ
וְתֹר וְסוּס וְעָגוּר
שָׁמְרוּ אֶת־עֵת בֹּאָנָה
וְעַמִּי לֹא יָדְעוּ אֵת מִשְׁפַּט יְהוָֽה:
⁸אֵיכָה תֹאמְרוּ חֲכָמִים אֲנַחְנוּ
וְתוֹרַת יְהוָה אִתָּנוּ
אָכֵן הִנֵּה לַשֶּׁקֶר עָשָׂה
עֵט שֶׁקֶר סֹפְרִֽים:
⁹הֹבִשׁוּ חֲכָמִים
חַתּוּ וַיִּלָּכֵדוּ
הִנֵּה בִדְבַר־יְהוָה מָאָסוּ
וְחָכְמַת־מֶה לָהֶֽם: ס

¹⁰Assuredly, I will give their wives to others,
And their fields to dispossessors;
For from the smallest to the greatest,
They are all greedy for gain;
Priest and prophet alike,
They all act falsely.

¹¹They offer healing offhand
For the wounds of My poor people,
Saying, "All is well, all is well,"
When nothing is well.

¹²They have acted shamefully;
They have done abhorrent things—
Yet they do not feel shame,
They cannot be made to blush.
Assuredly, they shall fall among the falling,
They shall stumble at the time of their doom
         —said the LORD.

¹⁰לָכֵן אֶתֵּן אֶת־נְשֵׁיהֶם לַאֲחֵרִים
שְׂדֽוֹתֵיהֶם לְיֽוֹרְשִׁים
כִּי מִקָּטֹן וְעַד־גָּדוֹל
כֻּלֹּה בֹּצֵעַ בָּצַע
מִנָּבִיא וְעַד־כֹּהֵן
כֻּלֹּה עֹשֶׂה שָּֽׁקֶר:
¹¹וַיְרַפֹּ֗וּ*
אֶת־שֶׁבֶר בַּת־עַמִּי עַל־נְקַלָּה
לֵאמֹר שָׁלוֹם ׀ שָׁלוֹם וְאֵין שָׁלֽוֹם:
¹²הֹבִ֗שׁוּ
כִּי תוֹעֵבָה עָשׂוּ
גַּם־בּוֹשׁ לֹא־יֵבֹשׁוּ
וְהִכָּלֵם לֹא יָדָעוּ
לָכֵן יִפְּלוּ בַנֹּפְלִים
בְּעֵת פְּקֻדָּתָם יִכָּשְׁלוּ
אָמַר יְהוָֽה: ס

¹³ᵃ-I will make an end of them-ᵃ
        —declares the LORD:
No grapes left on the vine,
No figs on the fig tree,
The leaves all withered;
ᵇ-Whatever I have given them is gone.-ᵇ

¹³אָסֹף אֲסִיפֵם
נְאֻם־יְהוָ֔ה
אֵין עֲנָבִים בַּגֶּפֶן
וְאֵין תְּאֵנִים בַּתְּאֵנָה
וְהֶעָלֶה נָבֵל
וָאֶתֵּן לָהֶם יַעַבְרֽוּם:

ᵃ-ᵃ Meaning of Heb. uncertain; change of vocalization yields
    "Their fruit harvest has been gathered in."
ᵇ-ᵇ Meaning of Heb. uncertain.

        חסר א'   v. 11.

14Why are we sitting by?
Let us gather into the fortified cities
And meet our doom there.
For the LORD our God has doomed us,
He has made us drink a bitter draft,
Because we sinned against the LORD.
15We hoped for good fortune, but no hap-
    piness came;
For a time of relief—instead there is terror!
16The snorting of their horses was heard from
    Dan;
At the loud neighing of their steeds
The whole land quaked.
They came and devoured the land and what
    was in it,
The towns and those who dwelt in them.

17Lo, I will send serpents against you,
Adders that cannot be charmed,
And they shall bite you
                    —declares the LORD.

18b-When in grief I would seek comfort,-b
My heart is sick within me.

19c"Is not the LORD in Zion?
Is not her King within her?
Why then did they anger Me with their im-
    ages,
With alien futilities?"

Hark! The outcry of my poor people
From the land far and wide:
20"Harvest is past,
Summer is gone,
But we have not been saved."
21Because my people is shattered I am shat-
    tered;
I am dejected, seized by desolation.

c Here God is speaking.

14 עַל־מָה֙ אֲנַ֣חְנוּ יֹֽשְׁבִ֔ים
הֵאָסְפ֗וּ וְנָב֛וֹא אֶל־עָרֵ֥י הַמִּבְצָ֖ר וְנִדְּמָה־
שָּׁ֑ם
כִּי֩ יְהֹוָ֨ה אֱלֹהֵ֤ינוּ הֲדִמָּ֙נוּ֙
וַיַּשְׁקֵ֣נוּ מֵי־רֹ֔אשׁ
כִּ֥י חָטָ֖אנוּ לַיהֹוָֽה:
15 קַוֵּ֥ה לְשָׁל֖וֹם וְאֵ֣ין ט֑וֹב
לְעֵ֥ת מַרְפֵּ֖ה* וְהִנֵּ֥ה בְעָתָֽה:
16 מִדָּ֤ן נִשְׁמַע֙ נַחְרַ֣ת סוּסָ֔יו
מִקּוֹל֙ מִצְהֲל֣וֹת אַבִּירָ֔יו
רָעֲשָׁ֖ה כׇּל־הָאָ֑רֶץ
וַיָּב֗וֹאוּ וַיֹּֽאכְלוּ֙ אֶ֣רֶץ וּמְלוֹאָ֔הּ
עִ֖יר וְיֹ֥שְׁבֵי בָֽהּ: ס
17 כִּ֡י הִנְנִי֩ מְשַׁלֵּ֨חַ בָּכֶ֜ם נְחָשִׁים֙
צִפְעֹנִ֔ים אֲשֶׁ֥ר אֵין־לָהֶ֖ם לָ֑חַשׁ
וְנִשְּׁכ֥וּ אֶתְכֶ֖ם
נְאֻם־יְהֹוָֽה: ס
18 מַבְלִ֥יגִיתִ֖י עֲלֵ֣י יָג֑וֹן
עָלַ֖י לִבִּ֥י דַוָּֽי:
19 הִנֵּה־ק֞וֹל שַֽׁוְעַ֣ת בַּת־עַמִּ֗י
מֵאֶ֣רֶץ מַרְחַקִּ֔ים
הַיהֹוָה֙ אֵ֣ין בְּצִיּ֔וֹן
אִם־מַלְכָּ֖הּ אֵ֣ין בָּ֑הּ
מַדּ֗וּעַ הִכְעִס֛וּנִי בִּפְסִלֵיהֶ֖ם
בְּהַבְלֵ֥י נֵכָֽר:
20 עָבַ֥ר קָצִ֖יר
כָּ֣לָה קָ֑יִץ
וַאֲנַ֖חְנוּ ל֥וֹא נוֹשָֽׁעְנוּ:
21 עַל־שֶׁ֥בֶר בַּת־עַמִּ֖י הׇשְׁבָּ֑רְתִּי
קָדַ֕רְתִּי שַׁמָּ֖ה הֶחֱזִקָֽתְנִי:

ה' במקום א' v. 15.

²²Is there no balm in Gilead?
Can no physician be found?
Why has healing not yet
Come to my poor people?
²³Oh, that my head were water,
My eyes a fount of tears!
Then would I weep day and night
For the slain of my poor people.

הַצֳרִי֙ אֵ֣ין בְּגִלְעָ֔ד ²²
אִם־רֹפֵ֖א אֵ֣ין שָׁ֑ם
כִּ֗י מַדּ֙וּעַ֙ לֹ֣א עָֽלְתָ֔ה
אֲרֻכַ֖ת בַּת־עַמִּֽי׃
מִֽי־יִתֵּ֤ן רֹאשִׁי֙ מַ֔יִם ²³
וְעֵינִ֖י מְק֣וֹר דִּמְעָ֑ה
וְאֶבְכֶּה֙ יוֹמָ֣ם וָלַ֔יְלָה
אֵ֖ת חַֽלְלֵ֥י בַת־עַמִּֽי׃

9

Oh, to be in the desert,
At an encampment for wayfarers!
Oh, to leave my people,
To go away from them—
For they are all adulterers,
A band of rogues.

ט מִֽי־יִתְּנֵ֣נִי בַמִּדְבָּ֗ר
מְלוֹן֙ אֹֽרְחִ֔ים
וְאֶֽעֶזְבָה֙ אֶת־עַמִּ֔י
וְאֵלְכָ֖ה מֵֽאִתָּ֑ם
כִּ֤י כֻלָּם֙ מְנָ֣אֲפִ֔ים
עֲצֶ֖רֶת בֹּֽגְדִֽים׃

²They bend their tongues like bows;
They are valorous in the land
For treachery, not for honesty;
They advance from evil to evil.
And they do not heed Me
      —declares the LORD.
³Beware, every man of his friend!
Trust not even a brother!
For every brother takes advantage,
Every friend ^a-is base in his dealings.^{-a}
⁴One man cheats the other,
They will not speak truth;
They have trained their tongues to speak
   falsely;
^b-They wear themselves out working iniquity.
⁵You dwell in the midst of deceit.
In their deceit,^{-b} they refuse to heed Me
      —declares the LORD.

וַֽיַּדְרְכ֤וּ אֶת־לְשׁוֹנָם֙ קַשְׁתָּ֣ם ²
שֶׁ֔קֶר וְלֹ֥א לֶאֱמוּנָ֖ה
גָּבְר֣וּ בָאָ֑רֶץ
כִּ֣י מֵרָעָ֤ה אֶל־רָעָה֙ ׀ יָצָ֔אוּ
וְאֹתִ֖י לֹֽא־יָדָ֑עוּ
נְאֻם־יְהוָֽה׃ ס
אִ֤ישׁ מֵרֵעֵ֙הוּ֙ הִשָּׁמֵ֔רוּ ³
וְעַל־כָּל־אָ֖ח אַל־תִּבְטָ֑חוּ
כִּ֤י כָל־אָח֙ עָק֣וֹב יַעְקֹ֔ב
וְכָל־רֵ֖עַ רָכִ֥יל יַהֲלֹֽךְ׃
וְאִ֤ישׁ בְּרֵעֵ֙הוּ֙ יְהָתֵ֔לּוּ ⁴
וֶאֱמֶ֖ת לֹ֣א יְדַבֵּ֑רוּ
לִמְּד֧וּ לְשׁוֹנָ֛ם דַּבֶּר־שֶׁ֖קֶר
הַעֲוֵ֥ה נִלְאֽוּ׃
שִׁבְתְּךָ֖ בְּת֣וֹךְ מִרְמָ֑ה ⁵
בְּמִרְמָ֖ה מֵאֲנ֥וּ דַֽעַת־אוֹתִ֖י
נְאֻם־יְהוָֽה׃ ס

⁶Assuredly, thus said the LORD of Hosts:
Lo, I shall smelt and assay them—

לָכֵ֗ן כֹּ֤ה אָמַר֙ יְהוָ֣ה צְבָא֔וֹת ⁶
הִנְנִ֥י צוֹרְפָ֖ם וּבְחַנְתִּ֑ים

---

^{a-a} *See note at Lev. 19.16.*
^{b-b} *Meaning of Heb. uncertain.*

b-For what else can I do because of My poor
  people?-*b*

7Their tongue is a sharpened arrow,
They use their mouths to deceive.
One speaks to his fellow in friendship,
But lays an ambush for him in his heart.
8Shall I not punish them for such deeds?
                              —says the Lord—
Shall I not bring retribution
On such a nation as this?

9For the mountains I take up weeping and
  wailing,
For the pastures in the wilderness, a dirge.
They are laid waste; no man passes through,
And no sound of cattle is heard.
Birds of the sky and beasts as well
Have fled and are gone.

10I will turn Jerusalem into rubble,
Into dens for jackals;
And I will make the towns of Judah
A desolation without inhabitants.

11What man is so wise
That he understands this?
To whom has the Lord's mouth spoken,
So that he can explain it:
Why is the land in ruins,
Laid waste like a wilderness,
With none passing through?

12The Lord replied: Because they forsook the
Teaching I had set before them. They did not
obey Me and they did not follow it, 13but followed their own willful heart and followed the
Baalim, as their fathers had taught them. 14As-
suredly, thus said the Lord of Hosts, the God
of Israel: I am going to feed that people wormwood and make them drink a bitter draft. 15I

כִּי־אֵיךְ אֶעֱשֶׂה מִפְּנֵי בַּת־עַמִּי׃
7 חֵץ שׁוחט שָׁחוּט לְשׁונָם
מִרְמָה דִבֵּר
בְּפִיו שָׁלוֹם אֶת־רֵעֵהוּ יְדַבֵּר
וּבְקִרְבּוֹ יָשִׂים אָרְבּוֹ׃
8 הַעַל־אֵלֶּה לֹא־אֶפְקָד־בָּם
נְאֻם־יְהוָה
אִם בְּגוֹי אֲשֶׁר־כָּזֶה
לֹא תִתְנַקֵּם נַפְשִׁי׃ ס

9 עַל־הֶהָרִים אֶשָּׂא בְכִי וָנֶהִי
וְעַל־נְאוֹת מִדְבָּר קִינָה
כִּי נִצְּתוּ מִבְּלִי־אִישׁ עֹבֵר
וְלֹא שָׁמְעוּ קוֹל מִקְנֶה
מֵעוֹף הַשָּׁמַיִם וְעַד־בְּהֵמָה
נָדְדוּ הָלָכוּ׃

10 וְנָתַתִּי אֶת־יְרוּשָׁלַ͏ִם לְגַלִּים
מְעוֹן תַּנִּים
וְאֶת־עָרֵי יְהוּדָה אֶתֵּן
שְׁמָמָה מִבְּלִי יוֹשֵׁב׃ ס

11 מִי־הָאִישׁ הֶחָכָם
וְיָבֵן אֶת־זֹאת
וַאֲשֶׁר דִּבֶּר פִּי־יְהוָה אֵלָיו
וְיַגִּדָהּ
עַל־מָה אָבְדָה הָאָרֶץ
נִצְּתָה כַמִּדְבָּר
מִבְּלִי עֹבֵר׃ ס

12 וַיֹּאמֶר יְהוָה עַל־עָזְבָם אֶת־תּוֹרָתִי
אֲשֶׁר נָתַתִּי לִפְנֵיהֶם וְלֹא־שָׁמְעוּ בְקוֹלִי
וְלֹא־הָלְכוּ בָהּ׃ 13 וַיֵּלְכוּ אַחֲרֵי שְׁרִרוּת
לִבָּם וְאַחֲרֵי הַבְּעָלִים אֲשֶׁר לִמְּדוּם
אֲבוֹתָם׃ ס 14 לָכֵן כֹּה־אָמַר יְהוָה
צְבָאוֹת אֱלֹהֵי יִשְׂרָאֵל הִנְנִי מַאֲכִילָם
אֶת־הָעָם הַזֶּה לַעֲנָה וְהִשְׁקִיתִים מֵי־

will scatter them among nations which they and their fathers never knew; and I will dispatch the sword after them until I have consumed them.

רֹאשׁ: 15 וַהֲפִצוֹתִים בַּגּוֹיִם אֲשֶׁר לֹא יָדְעוּ הֵמָּה וַאֲבוֹתָם וְשִׁלַּחְתִּי אַחֲרֵיהֶם אֶת־ הַחֶרֶב עַד כַּלּוֹתִי אוֹתָם: פ

16Thus said the LORD of Hosts:
Listen!
Summon the dirge-singers, let them come;
Send for the skilled women, let them come.
17Let them quickly start a wailing for us,
That our eyes may run with tears,
Our pupils flow with water.

16 כֹּה אָמַר יְהֹוָה צְבָאוֹת
הִתְבּוֹנְנוּ
וְקִרְאוּ לַמְקוֹנְנוֹת וּתְבוֹאֶינָה
וְאֶל־הַחֲכָמוֹת שִׁלְחוּ וְתָבוֹאנָה:
17 וּתְמַהֵרְנָה וְתִשֶּׂנָה* עָלֵינוּ נֶהִי
וְתֵרַדְנָה עֵינֵינוּ דִּמְעָה
וְעַפְעַפֵּינוּ יִזְּלוּ־מָיִם:

18For the sound of wailing
Is heard from Zion:
How we are despoiled!
How greatly we are shamed!
Ah, we must leave our land,
Abandonc our dwellings!

18 כִּי קוֹל נְהִי
נִשְׁמַע מִצִּיּוֹן
אֵיךְ שֻׁדָּדְנוּ
בֹּשְׁנוּ מְאֹד
כִּי־עָזַבְנוּ אָרֶץ
כִּי הִשְׁלִיכוּ מִשְׁכְּנוֹתֵינוּ: ס

19Hear, O women, the word of the LORD,
Let your ears receive the word of His mouth,
And teach your daughters wailing,
And one another lamentation.
20For death has climbed through our win-
dows,
Has entered our fortresses,
To cut off babes from the streets,
Young men from the squares.

19 כִּי־שְׁמַעְנָה נָשִׁים דְּבַר־יְהֹוָה
וְתִקַּח אָזְנְכֶם דְּבַר־פִּיו
וְלַמֵּדְנָה בְנוֹתֵיכֶם נֶהִי
וְאִשָּׁה רְעוּתָהּ קִינָה:
20 כִּי־עָלָה מָוֶת בְּחַלּוֹנֵינוּ
בָּא בְּאַרְמְנוֹתֵינוּ
לְהַכְרִית עוֹלָל מִחוּץ
בַּחוּרִים מֵרְחֹבוֹת:

21Speak thus—says the LORD:
The carcasses of men shall lie
Like dung upon the fields,
Like sheaves behind the reaper,
With none to pick them up.

21 דַּבֵּר כֹּה נְאֻם־יְהֹוָה
וְנָפְלָה נִבְלַת הָאָדָם
כְּדֹמֶן עַל־פְּנֵי הַשָּׂדֶה
וּכְעָמִיר מֵאַחֲרֵי הַקֹּצֵר
וְאֵין מְאַסֵּף: ס

22Thus said the LORD:
Let not the wise man glory in his wisdom;
Let not the strong man glory in his strength;
Let not the rich man glory in his riches.

22 כֹּה ׀ אָמַר יְהֹוָה
אַל־יִתְהַלֵּל חָכָם בְּחָכְמָתוֹ
וְאַל־יִתְהַלֵּל הַגִּבּוֹר בִּגְבוּרָתוֹ
אַל־יִתְהַלֵּל עָשִׁיר בְּעָשְׁרוֹ:

c Lit. "They abandoned."

23But only in this should one glory:
In his earnest devotion to Me.
For I the Lord act with kindness,
Justice, and equity in the world;
For in these I delight

           —declares the Lord.

24Lo, days are coming—declares the Lord—
when I will take note of everyone d-circumcised
in the foreskin:-d 25of Egypt, Judah, Edom, the
Ammonites, Moab, and all the desert dwellers
who have the hair of their temples clipped. For
all these nations are uncircumcised, but all the
House of Israel are e-uncircumcised of heart.-e

10 Hear the word which the Lord has spoken to you, O House of Israel!

2Thus said the Lord:
Do not learn to go the way of the nations,
And do not be dismayed by portents in the
    sky;
Let the nations be dismayed by them!
3For a-the laws of the nations-a are delusions:
For it is the work of a craftsman's hands.
He cuts down a tree in the forest with an ax,
4He adorns it with silver and gold,
He fastens itb with nails and hammer,
So that it does not totter.
5They are like a scarecrow in a cucumber
    patch,
They cannot speak.
They have to be carried,
For they cannot walk.
Be not afraid of them, for they can do no
    harm;
Nor is it in them to do any good.

כִּי אִם־בְּזֹאת יִתְהַלֵּל הַמִּתְהַלֵּל 23
הַשְׂכֵּל וְיָדֹעַ אוֹתִי
כִּי אֲנִי יְהוָה עֹשֶׂה חֶסֶד
מִשְׁפָּט וּצְדָקָה בָּאָרֶץ
כִּי־בְאֵלֶּה חָפַצְתִּי
נְאֻם־יְהוָה: ס

הִנֵּה יָמִים בָּאִים נְאֻם־יְהוָה וּפָקַדְתִּי 24
עַל־כָּל־מוּל בְּעָרְלָה: 25 עַל־מִצְרַיִם וְעַל־
יְהוּדָה וְעַל־אֱדוֹם וְעַל־בְּנֵי עַמּוֹן וְעַל־
מוֹאָב וְעַל כָּל־קְצוּצֵי פֵאָה הַיֹּשְׁבִים
בַּמִּדְבָּר כִּי כָל־הַגּוֹיִם עֲרֵלִים וְכָל־בֵּית
יִשְׂרָאֵל עַרְלֵי־לֵב: ס

י שִׁמְעוּ אֶת־הַדָּבָר אֲשֶׁר דִּבֶּר יְהוָה
עֲלֵיכֶם בֵּית יִשְׂרָאֵל:

כֹּה ׀ אָמַר יְהוָה 2
אֶל־דֶּרֶךְ הַגּוֹיִם אַל־תִּלְמָדוּ
וּמֵאֹתוֹת הַשָּׁמַיִם אַל־תֵּחָתּוּ
כִּי־יֵחַתּוּ הַגּוֹיִם מֵהֵמָּה:
כִּי־חֻקּוֹת הָעַמִּים הֶבֶל הוּא 3
כִּי־עֵץ מִיַּעַר כְּרָתוֹ
מַעֲשֵׂה יְדֵי־חָרָשׁ בַּמַּעֲצָד:
בְּכֶסֶף וּבְזָהָב יְיַפֵּהוּ 4
בְּמַסְמְרוֹת וּבְמַקָּבוֹת יְחַזְּקוּם
וְלוֹא יָפִיק:
כְּתֹמֶר מִקְשָׁה הֵמָּה 5
וְלֹא יְדַבֵּרוּ
נָשׂוֹא יִנָּשׂוּא
כִּי לֹא יִצְעָדוּ
אַל־תִּירְאוּ מֵהֶם כִּי־לֹא יָרֵעוּ
וְגַם־הֵיטֵיב אֵין אוֹתָם: ס

---

d-d   *Force of Heb. uncertain.*
e-e   *I.e., their minds are blocked to God's commandments.*

a-a   *Emendation yields "the objects that the nations fear."*
b   *Heb. "them."*

6 O LORD, there is none like You!
You are great and Your name is great in
   power.
7 Who would not revere You, O King of the
   nations?
For that is Your due,
Since among all the wise of the nations
And among all their royalty
There is none like You.
8 But they are both dull and foolish;
c-[Their] doctrine is but delusion;-c
It is a piece of wood,
9 Silver beaten flat, that is brought from Tar-
   shish,
And gold from Uphaz,
The work of a craftsman and the goldsmith's
   hands;
Their clothing is blue and purple,
All of them are the work of skilled men.
10 But the LORD is truly God:
He is a living God,
The everlasting King.
At His wrath, the earth quakes,
And nations cannot endure His rage.

11 d Thus shall you say to them: Let the gods,
who did not make heaven and earth, perish
from the earth and from under these heavens.

12 He made the earth by His might,
Established the world by His wisdom,
And by His understanding stretched out the
   skies.
13 e-When He makes His voice heard,-e
There is a rumbling of water in the skies;
He makes vapors rise from the end of the
   earth,
He makes lightning for the rain,
And brings forth wind from His treasuries.

6 מֵאֵין כָּמוֹךָ יְהוָה
גָּדוֹל אַתָּה וְגָדוֹל שִׁמְךָ בִּגְבוּרָה:
7 מִי לֹא יִרָאֲךָ מֶלֶךְ הַגּוֹיִם
כִּי לְךָ יָאָתָה
כִּי בְכָל־חַכְמֵי הַגּוֹיִם
וּבְכָל־מַלְכוּתָם
מֵאֵין כָּמוֹךָ:
8 וּבְאַחַת יִבְעֲרוּ וְיִכְסָלוּ
מוּסַר הֲבָלִים
עֵץ הוּא:
9 כֶּסֶף מְרֻקָּע מִתַּרְשִׁישׁ יוּבָא
וְזָהָב מֵאוּפָז
מַעֲשֵׂה חָרָשׁ וִידֵי צוֹרֵף
תְּכֵלֶת וְאַרְגָּמָן לְבוּשָׁם
מַעֲשֵׂה חֲכָמִים כֻּלָּם:
10 וַיהוָה אֱלֹהִים אֱמֶת
הוּא־אֱלֹהִים חַיִּים
וּמֶלֶךְ עוֹלָם
מִקִּצְפּוֹ תִּרְעַשׁ הָאָרֶץ
וְלֹא־יָכִלוּ גוֹיִם זַעְמוֹ: ס

11 כִּדְנָה תֵּאמְרוּן לְהוֹם אֱלָהַיָּא דִּי־שְׁמַיָּא
וְאַרְקָא לָא עֲבַדוּ יֵאבַדוּ מֵאַרְעָא וּמִן־
תְּחוֹת שְׁמַיָּא אֵלֶּה: ס

12 עֹשֵׂה אֶרֶץ בְּכֹחוֹ
מֵכִין תֵּבֵל בְּחָכְמָתוֹ
וּבִתְבוּנָתוֹ נָטָה שָׁמָיִם:
13 לְקוֹל תִּתּוֹ
הֲמוֹן מַיִם בַּשָּׁמַיִם
וַיַּעֲלֶה נְשִׂאִים מִקְצֵה אָרֶץ הָאָרֶץ
בְּרָקִים לַמָּטָר עָשָׂה
וַיּוֹצֵא רוּחַ מֵאֹצְרֹתָיו:

c-c   Meaning of Heb. uncertain.
d   This verse is in Aramaic.
e-e Lit. "At the sound of His making."

14 נִבְעַ֤ר כָּל־אָדָם֙ מִדַּ֔עַת

הֹבִ֥ישׁ כָּל־צוֹרֵ֖ף מִפָּ֑סֶל

כִּ֣י שֶׁ֤קֶר נִסְכּ֔וֹ

וְלֹא־ר֖וּחַ בָּֽם׃

15 הֶ֣בֶל הֵ֔מָּה מַעֲשֵׂ֖ה תַּעְתֻּעִ֑ים

בְּעֵ֥ת פְּקֻדָּתָ֖ם יֹאבֵֽדוּ׃

16 לֹֽא־כְאֵ֜לֶּה חֵ֣לֶק יַעֲקֹ֗ב

כִּֽי־יוֹצֵ֤ר הַכֹּל֙ ה֔וּא

וְיִ֨שְׂרָאֵ֔ל שֵׁ֖בֶט נַחֲלָת֑וֹ

יְהוָ֥ה צְבָא֖וֹת שְׁמֽוֹ׃ ס

17 אִסְפִּ֥י מֵאֶ֖רֶץ כִּנְעָתֵ֑ךְ

יֹשַׁבְתִּ֖י בַּמָּצֽוֹר׃ ס

18 כִּֽי־כֹה֙ אָמַ֣ר יְהוָ֔ה הִנְנִ֥י קוֹלֵ֖עַ אֶת־

יוֹשְׁבֵ֣י הָאָ֗רֶץ בַּפַּ֙עַם֙ הַזֹּ֔את וַהֲצֵרוֹ֥תִי לָהֶ֖ם

לְמַ֥עַן יִמְצָֽאוּ׃ ס

19 א֥וֹי לִי֙ עַל־שִׁבְרִ֔י

נַחְלָ֖ה מַכָּתִ֑י

וַאֲנִ֣י אָמַ֔רְתִּי אַ֛ךְ זֶ֥ה חֳלִ֖י

וְאֶשָּׂאֶֽנּוּ׃

20 אָהֳלִ֣י שֻׁדָּ֔ד

וְכָל־מֵיתָרַ֖י נִתָּ֑קוּ

בָּנַ֤י יְצָאֻ֙נִי֙

וְאֵינָ֔ם

אֵין־נֹטֶ֥ה עוֹד֙ אָֽהֳלִ֔י

וּמֵקִ֖ים יְרִיעוֹתָֽי׃

21 כִּ֤י נִבְעֲרוּ֙ הָרֹעִ֔ים

וְאֶת־יְהוָ֖ה לֹ֣א דָרָ֑שׁוּ

עַל־כֵּן֙ לֹ֣א הִשְׂכִּ֔ילוּ

וְכָל־מַרְעִיתָ֖ם נָפֽוֹצָה׃ ס

22 ק֣וֹל שְׁמוּעָ֔ה הִנֵּ֖ה בָ֑אָה

וְרַ֥עַשׁ גָּד֖וֹל מֵאֶ֣רֶץ צָפ֑וֹן

לָשׂ֞וּם אֶת־עָרֵ֤י יְהוּדָה֙ שְׁמָמָ֔ה

מְע֖וֹן תַּנִּֽים׃ ס

14Every man is proved dull, without knowledge;

Every goldsmith is put to shame because of
the idol,

For his molten image is a deceit—
There is no breath in them.

15They are delusion, a work of mockery;
In their hour of doom, they shall perish.

16Not like these is the Portion of Jacob;
For it is He who formed all things,
And Israel is His very own tribe:
LORD of Hosts is His name.

17Gather up your bundle^c from the ground,
You who dwell under siege!

18For thus said the LORD: I will fling away the
inhabitants of the land this time: I will harass
them so that they shall *f*-feel it.-*f*

19Woe unto me for my hurt,
My wound is severe!
I thought, "This is but a sickness
And I must bear it."

20My tents are ravaged,
All my tent cords are broken.
My children have gone forth from me
And are no more;
No one is left to stretch out my tents
And hang my tent cloths.

21For the shepherds^g are dull
And did not seek the LORD;
Therefore they have not prospered
And all their flock is scattered.

22Hark, a noise! It is coming,
A great commotion out of the north,
That the towns of Judah may be made a des-
olation,
A haunt of jackals.

f-f Emendation yields "have to leave."
g I.e., rulers; cf. note at 2.8.

23I know, O Lord, that man's road is not his [to choose],

That man, as he walks, cannot direct his own steps.

24Chastise me, O Lord, but in measure;

Not in Your wrath, lest You reduce me to naught.

25Pour out Your wrath on the nations who have not heeded You,

Upon the clans that have not invoked Your name.

For they have devoured Jacob,

Have devoured and consumed him,

And have laid desolate his homesteads.

11 The word which came to Jeremiah from the Lord:

2"Hear the terms of this covenant, and recite them to the men of Judah and the inhabitants of Jerusalem! 3And say to them, Thus said the Lord, the God of Israel: Cursed be the man who will not obey the terms of this covenant, 4which I enjoined upon your fathers when I freed them from the land of Egypt, the iron crucible, saying, 'Obey Me and observe them,[a] just as I command you, that you may be My people and I may be your God'—5in order to fulfill the oath which I swore to your fathers, to give them a land flowing with milk and honey, as is now the case." And I responded, "Amen, Lord."

6And the Lord said to me, "Proclaim all these things through the towns of Judah and the streets of Jerusalem: Hear the terms of this covenant, and perform them. 7For I have repeatedly and persistently warned your fathers from[b] the time I brought them out of Egypt to this day,

a I.e., the terms of the covenant.
b Lit. "at."

23 יָדַ֣עְתִּי יְהֹוָ֔ה כִּ֛י לֹ֥א לָאָדָ֖ם דַּרְכּ֑וֹ
לֹא־לְאִ֣ישׁ הֹלֵ֔ךְ וְהָכִ֖ין אֶֽת־צַעֲדֽוֹ׃
24 יַסְּרֵ֥נִי יְהֹוָ֖ה אַךְ־בְּמִשְׁפָּ֑ט
אַל־בְּאַפְּךָ֖ פֶּן־תַּמְעִטֵֽנִי׃
25 שְׁפֹ֣ךְ חֲמָתְךָ֗ עַל־הַגּוֹיִם֙ אֲשֶׁ֣ר לֹֽא־
יְדָע֔וּךָ
וְעַ֣ל מִשְׁפָּח֔וֹת אֲשֶׁ֥ר בְּשִׁמְךָ֖ לֹ֣א קָרָ֑אוּ
כִּֽי־אָכְל֣וּ אֶֽת־יַעֲקֹ֔ב
וַאֲכָלֻ֖הוּ וַיְכַלֻּ֑הוּ
וְאֶת־נָוֵ֖הוּ הֵשַֽׁמּוּ׃ פ

יא הַדָּבָר֙ אֲשֶׁ֣ר הָיָ֣ה אֶֽל־יִרְמְיָ֔הוּ
מֵאֵ֥ת יְהֹוָ֖ה לֵאמֹֽר׃
2 שִׁמְע֕וּ אֶת־דִּבְרֵ֖י הַבְּרִ֣ית הַזֹּ֑את וְדִבַּרְתָּ֗ם
אֶל־אִ֣ישׁ יְהוּדָ֔ה וְעַל־יֹשְׁבֵ֖י יְרוּשָׁלָֽ͏ִם׃
3 וְאָמַרְתָּ֣ אֲלֵיהֶ֗ם כֹּֽה־אָמַ֤ר יְהֹוָה֙ אֱלֹהֵ֣י
יִשְׂרָאֵ֔ל אָר֣וּר הָאִ֔ישׁ אֲשֶׁר֙ לֹ֣א יִשְׁמַ֔ע
אֶת־דִּבְרֵ֖י הַבְּרִ֥ית הַזֹּֽאת׃ 4 אֲשֶׁ֣ר צִוִּ֣יתִי
אֶת־אֲבֽוֹתֵיכֶ֡ם בְּי֣וֹם הוֹצִיאִֽי־אוֹתָ֣ם
מֵאֶֽרֶץ־מִצְרַ֘יִם֮ מִכּ֣וּר הַבַּרְזֶל֒ לֵאמֹ֔ר שִׁמְע֣וּ
בְקוֹלִ֗י וַעֲשִׂיתֶ֤ם אוֹתָם֙ כְּכֹ֣ל אֲשֶׁר־אֲצַוֶּ֣ה
אֶתְכֶ֑ם וִהְיִ֤יתֶם לִי֙ לְעָ֔ם וְאָ֣נֹכִ֔י אֶהְיֶ֥ה
לָכֶ֖ם לֵֽאלֹהִֽים׃ 5 לְמַ֩עַן֩ הָקִ֨ים אֶת־
הַשְּׁבוּעָ֜ה אֲשֶׁר־נִשְׁבַּ֣עְתִּי לַאֲבֽוֹתֵיכֶ֗ם
לָתֵ֤ת לָהֶם֙ אֶ֣רֶץ זָבַ֥ת חָלָ֖ב וּדְבַ֑שׁ כַּיּ֣וֹם
הַזֶּ֔ה וָאַ֥עַן וָאֹמַ֖ר אָמֵ֥ן ׀ יְהֹוָֽה׃ ס
6 וַיֹּ֤אמֶר יְהֹוָה֙ אֵלַ֔י קְרָ֣א אֶת־כׇּל־הַדְּבָרִ֣ים
הָאֵ֗לֶּה בְּעָרֵ֤י יְהוּדָה֙ וּבְחֻצ֣וֹת יְרוּשָׁלַ֔͏ִם
לֵאמֹ֔ר שִׁמְע֗וּ אֶת־דִּבְרֵי֙ הַבְּרִ֣ית הַזֹּ֔את
וַעֲשִׂיתֶ֖ם אוֹתָֽם׃ 7 כִּי֩ הָעֵ֨ד הַעִדֹ֜תִי
בַּאֲבֽוֹתֵיכֶ֗ם בְּי֨וֹם הַעֲלוֹתִ֤י אוֹתָם֙ מֵאֶ֣רֶץ
מִצְרַ֔יִם וְעַד־הַיּ֥וֹם הַזֶּ֖ה הַשְׁכֵּ֣ם וְהָעֵ֑ד

saying: Obey My commands. [8]But they would not listen or give ear; they all followed the willfulness of their evil hearts. So I have brought upon them all the terms[c] of this covenant, because they did not do what I commanded them to do."

[9]The LORD said to me, "A conspiracy exists among the men of Judah and the inhabitants of Jerusalem. [10]They have returned to the iniquities of their fathers of old, who refused to heed My words. They, too, have followed other gods and served them. The House of Israel and the House of Judah have broken the covenant that I made with their fathers."

[11]Assuredly, thus said the LORD: I am going to bring upon them disaster from which they will not be able to escape. Then they will cry out to me, but I will not listen to them. [12]And the townsmen[d] of Judah and the inhabitants of Jerusalem will go and cry out to the gods to which they sacrifice; but they will not be able to rescue them in their time of disaster. [13]For your gods have become as many as your towns, O Judah, and you have set up as many altars to Shame[e] as there are streets in Jerusalem—altars for sacrifice to Baal.

[14]As for you, do not pray for this people, do not raise a cry of prayer on their behalf; for I will not listen when they call to Me on account of their disaster.

[15]Why should My beloved be in My House,
[f]Who executes so many vile designs?
The sacral flesh will pass away from you,
For you exult while performing your evil
    deeds.[-f]

[16]The LORD named you
"Verdant olive tree,

---

c I.e., the punishments prescribed for violation.
d Lit. "towns."
e See note at 3.24.
f-f Meaning of Heb. uncertain. Emendation yields "Who does such vile deeds? / Can your treacheries be canceled by sacral flesh / That you exult while performing your evil deeds?"

לֵאמֹ֖ר שִׁמְע֣וּ בְקוֹלִֽי׃ 8 וְלֹ֤א שָֽׁמְעוּ֙ וְלֹֽא־הִטּ֣וּ אֶת־אָזְנָ֔ם וַיֵּ֣לְכ֔וּ אִ֕ישׁ בִּשְׁרִיר֖וּת לִבָּ֣ם הָרָ֑ע וָאָבִ֨יא עֲלֵיהֶ֜ם אֶֽת־כׇּל־דִּבְרֵ֧י הַבְּרִֽית־הַזֹּ֛את אֲשֶׁר־צִוִּ֥יתִי לַעֲשׂ֖וֹת וְלֹ֥א עָשֽׂוּ׃ ס

9 וַיֹּ֤אמֶר יְהֹוָה֙ אֵלַ֔י נִמְצָא־קֶ֖שֶׁר בְּאִ֣ישׁ יְהוּדָ֑ה וּבְיֹשְׁבֵ֖י יְרוּשָׁלָֽ͏ִם׃ 10 שָׁ֩בוּ֩ עַל־עֲוֺנֹ֨ת אֲבוֹתָ֜ם הָרִֽאשֹׁנִ֗ים אֲשֶׁ֤ר מֵֽאֲנוּ֙ לִשְׁמ֣וֹעַ אֶת־דְּבָרַ֔י וְהֵ֣מָּה הָלְכ֗וּ אַחֲרֵ֛י אֱלֹהִ֥ים אֲחֵרִ֖ים לְעׇבְדָ֑ם הֵפֵ֤רוּ בֵֽית־יִשְׂרָאֵל֙ וּבֵ֣ית יְהוּדָ֔ה אֶת־בְּרִיתִ֕י אֲשֶׁ֥ר כָּרַ֖תִּי אֶת־אֲבוֹתָֽם׃ ס

11 לָכֵ֗ן כֹּ֚ה אָמַ֣ר יְהֹוָ֔ה הִנְנִ֨י מֵבִ֤יא אֲלֵיהֶם֙ רָעָ֔ה אֲשֶׁ֥ר לֹֽא־יוּכְל֖וּ לָצֵ֣את מִמֶּ֑נָּה וְזָעֲק֣וּ אֵלַ֔י וְלֹ֥א אֶשְׁמַ֖ע אֲלֵיהֶֽם׃ 12 וְהָֽלְכ֞וּ עָרֵ֣י יְהוּדָ֗ה וְיֹשְׁבֵי֙ יְר֣וּשָׁלַ֔͏ִם וְזָֽעֲקוּ֙ אֶל־הָ֣אֱלֹהִ֔ים אֲשֶׁ֛ר הֵ֥ם מְקַטְּרִ֖ים לָהֶ֑ם וְהוֹשֵׁ֛עַ לֹֽא־יוֹשִׁ֥יעוּ לָהֶ֖ם בְּעֵ֥ת רָעָתָֽם׃ 13 כִּ֚י מִסְפַּ֣ר עָרֶ֔יךָ הָי֥וּ אֱלֹהֶ֖יךָ יְהוּדָ֑ה וּמִסְפַּ֞ר חֻצ֣וֹת יְרוּשָׁלַ֗͏ִם שַׂמְתֶּ֤ם מִזְבְּחוֹת֙ לַבֹּ֔שֶׁת מִזְבְּח֖וֹת לְקַטֵּ֥ר לַבָּֽעַל׃ ס

14 וְאַתָּ֗ה אַל־תִּתְפַּלֵּל֙ בְּעַד־הָעָ֣ם הַזֶּ֔ה וְאַל־תִּשָּׂ֥א בַעֲדָ֖ם רִנָּ֣ה וּתְפִלָּ֑ה כִּ֣י אֵינֶ֣נִּי שֹׁמֵ֗עַ בְּעֵ֛ת קׇרְאָ֥ם אֵלַ֖י בְּעַ֥ד רָעָתָֽם׃ ס

15 מֶ֣ה לִֽידִידִ֞י בְּבֵיתִ֗י
עֲשׂוֹתָ֤הּ הַֽמְזִמָּ֙תָה֙ הָֽרַבִּ֔ים
וּבְשַׂר־קֹ֙דֶשׁ֙ יַעַבְר֣וּ מֵֽעָלָ֔יִךְ
כִּ֥י רָעָתֵ֖כִי אָ֥ז תַּעֲלֹֽזִי׃
16 זַ֤יִת רַֽעֲנָן֙
יְפֵ֣ה פְרִי־תֹ֔אַר
קָרָ֥א יְהֹוָ֖ה שְׁמֵ֑ךְ

Fair, with choice fruit."
But with a great roaring sound
He has set it on fire,
And its boughs are broken.*g*

17The Lord of Hosts, who planted you, has decreed disaster for you, because of the evil wrought by the House of Israel and the House of Judah, who angered Me by sacrificing to Baal.

18The Lord informed me, and I knew—
Then You let me see their deeds.
19For I was like a docile lamb
Led to the slaughter;
I did not realize
That it was against me
They fashioned their plots:
"Let us destroy the tree with its fruit,*h*
Let us cut him off from the land of the living,
That his name be remembered no more!"
20O Lord of Hosts, O just Judge,
Who test the thoughts and the mind,
Let me see Your retribution upon them,
For I lay my case before You.

21Assuredly, thus said the Lord of Hosts concerning the men of Anathoth who seek your life and say, "You must not prophesy any more in the name of the Lord, or you will die by our hand"—22Assuredly, thus said the Lord of Hosts: "I am going to deal with them: the young men shall die by the sword, their boys and girls shall die by famine. 23No remnant shall be left of them, for I will bring disaster on the men of Anathoth, the year of their doom."

12 You will win,*a* O Lord, if I make claim against You,
Yet I shall present charges against You:

לְקוֹל ׀ הֲמוּלָּה גְדֹלָה
הִצִּית אֵשׁ עָלֶיהָ
וְרָעוּ דָּלִיּוֹתָיו:
17 וַיהוָה צְבָאוֹת הַנּוֹטֵעַ אוֹתָךְ דִּבֶּר עָלַיִךְ
רָעָה בִּגְלַל רָעַת בֵּית־יִשְׂרָאֵל וּבֵית
יְהוּדָה אֲשֶׁר עָשׂוּ לָהֶם לְהַכְעִסֵנִי לְקַטֵּר
לַבָּעַל: ס

18 וַיהוָה הוֹדִיעַנִי וָאֵדָעָה
אָז הִרְאִיתַנִי מַעַלְלֵיהֶם:
19 וַאֲנִי כְּכֶבֶשׂ אַלּוּף
יוּבַל לִטְבוֹחַ
וְלֹא־יָדַעְתִּי
כִּי־עָלַי ׀
חָשְׁבוּ מַחֲשָׁבוֹת
נַשְׁחִיתָה עֵץ בְּלַחְמוֹ
וְנִכְרְתֶנּוּ מֵאֶרֶץ חַיִּים
וּשְׁמוֹ לֹא־יִזָּכֵר עוֹד:
20 וַיהוָה צְבָאוֹת שֹׁפֵט צֶדֶק
בֹּחֵן כְּלָיוֹת וָלֵב
אֶרְאֶה נִקְמָתְךָ מֵהֶם
כִּי אֵלֶיךָ גִּלִּיתִי אֶת־רִיבִי: ס

21 לָכֵן כֹּה־אָמַר יְהוָה עַל־אַנְשֵׁי עֲנָתוֹת
הַמְבַקְשִׁים אֶת־נַפְשְׁךָ לֵאמֹר לֹא תִנָּבֵא
בְּשֵׁם יְהוָה וְלֹא תָמוּת בְּיָדֵנוּ: ס 22 לָכֵן
כֹּה אָמַר יְהוָה צְבָאוֹת הִנְנִי פֹקֵד עֲלֵיהֶם
הַבַּחוּרִים יָמֻתוּ בַחֶרֶב בְּנֵיהֶם וּבְנוֹתֵיהֶם
יָמֻתוּ בָּרָעָב: 23 וּשְׁאֵרִית לֹא תִהְיֶה לָהֶם
כִּי־אָבִיא רָעָה אֶל־אַנְשֵׁי עֲנָתוֹת שְׁנַת
פְּקֻדָּתָם: ס

יב צַדִּיק אַתָּה יְהוָה כִּי אָרִיב אֵלֶיךָ
אַךְ מִשְׁפָּטִים אֲדַבֵּר אוֹתָךְ

---

g Emendation yields "burned."
h Or "sap."

a Lit. "be in the right."

Why does the way of the wicked prosper?
Why are the workers of treachery at ease?
2You have planted them, and they have taken
   root,
They spread, they even bear fruit.
You are present in their mouths,
But far from their thoughts.
3Yet You, LORD, have noted and observed me;
You have tested my heart, and found it with
   You.
Drive them out like sheep to the slaughter,
Prepare them for the day of slaying!

4How long must the land languish,
And the grass of all the countryside dry up?
Must beasts and birds perish,
Because of the evil of its inhabitants,
Who say, "He will not look upon our
   future"?b

5cIf you race with the foot-runners and they
   exhaust you,
How then can you compete with horses?
If you are d-secure only-d in a tranquil land,
How will you fare in the jungle of the Jordan?
6For even your kinsmen and your father's
   house,
Even they are treacherous toward you,
They cry after you as a mob.
Do not believe them
When they speak cordially to you.

7I have abandoned My House,
I have deserted My possession,
I have given over My dearly beloved
Into the hands of her enemies.
8My own peoplee acted toward Me
Like a lion in the forest;

מַדּ֙וּעַ֙ דֶּ֣רֶךְ רְשָׁעִ֣ים צָלֵ֔חָה
שָׁל֖וּ כָּל־בֹּ֥גְדֵי בָֽגֶד׃
2 נְטַעְתָּם֙ גַּם־שֹׁרָ֔שׁוּ
יֵלְכ֖וּ גַּם־עָ֣שׂוּ פֶ֑רִי
קָר֤וֹב אַתָּה֙ בְּפִיהֶ֔ם
וְרָח֖וֹק מִכִּלְיוֹתֵיהֶֽם׃
3 וְאַתָּ֤ה יְהֹוָה֙ יְדַעְתָּ֔נִי תִּרְאֵ֕נִי
וּבָחַנְתָּ֥ לִבִּ֖י אִתָּ֑ךְ
הַתִּקֵ֙ם֙ כְּצֹ֣אן לְטִבְחָ֔ה
וְהַקְדִּשֵׁ֖ם לְי֥וֹם הֲרֵגָֽה׃ ס

4 עַד־מָתַ֣י תֶּאֱבַ֣ל הָאָ֔רֶץ
וְעֵ֥שֶׂב כָּל־הַשָּׂדֶ֖ה יִבָ֑שׁ
מֵרָעַ֣ת יֹשְׁבֵי־בָ֗הּ
סָפְתָ֤ה בְהֵמוֹת֙ וָע֔וֹף
כִּ֣י אָמְר֔וּ לֹ֥א יִרְאֶ֖ה אֶת־אַחֲרִיתֵֽנוּ׃

5 כִּ֣י אֶת־רַגְלִ֥ים ׀ רַ֙צְתָּה֙ וַיַּלְא֔וּךָ
וְאֵ֥יךְ תְּתַחֲרֶ֖ה אֶת־הַסּוּסִ֑ים
וּבְאֶ֤רֶץ שָׁלוֹם֙ אַתָּ֣ה בוֹטֵ֔חַ
וְאֵ֥יךְ תַּעֲשֶׂ֖ה בִּגְא֥וֹן הַיַּרְדֵּֽן׃
6 כִּ֧י גַם־אַחֶ֛יךָ וּבֵית־אָבִ֖יךָ
גַּם־הֵ֙מָּה֙ בָּ֣גְדוּ בָ֔ךְ
גַּם־הֵ֛מָּה קָרְא֥וּ אַחֲרֶ֖יךָ מָלֵ֑א
אַל־תַּאֲמֵ֣ן בָּ֔ם
כִּֽי־יְדַבְּר֥וּ אֵלֶ֖יךָ טוֹבֽוֹת׃ ס

7 עָזַ֙בְתִּי֙ אֶת־בֵּיתִ֔י
נָטַ֖שְׁתִּי אֶת־נַחֲלָתִ֑י
נָתַ֛תִּי אֶת־יְדִד֥וּת נַפְשִׁ֖י
בְּכַ֥ף אֹֽיְבֶֽיהָ׃
8 הָֽיְתָה־לִּ֥י נַחֲלָתִ֖י
כְּאַרְיֵ֣ה בַיָּ֑עַר

---

b   *Septuagint reads "ways."*
c   *God here replies to Jeremiah's plea in vv. 1–3.*
d-d   *Some Septuagint mss. read "not secure."*
e   *Lit. "possession"; the land as well as the people, as is clear in*
     v. 14.

She raised her voice against Me—
Therefore I have rejected her.
⁹ᶠ-My own people acts toward Me
Like a bird of prey [or] a hyena;
Let the birds of prey surround her!-ᶠ
Go, gather all the wild beasts,
Bring them to devour!
¹⁰Many shepherds have destroyed My vine-
    yard,
Have trampled My field,
Have made My delightful field
A desolate wilderness.
¹¹ᵍ-They have-ᵍ made her a desolation;
Desolate, she pours out grief to Me.
The whole land is laid desolate,
But no man gives it thought.
¹²Spoilers have come
Upon all the bare heights of the wilderness.
For a sword of the LORD devours
From one end of the land to the other;
No flesh is safe.
¹³They have sown wheat and reaped thorns,
They have endured pain to no avail.
Be shamed, then, by your harvest—
By the blazing wrath of the LORD!

¹⁴Thus said the LORD: As for My wicked neighbors who encroach on the heritage that I gave to My people Israel—I am going to uproot them from their soil, and I will uproot the House of Judah out of the midst of them. ¹⁵Then, after I have uprooted them, I will take them back into favor, and restore them each to his own inheritance and his own land. ¹⁶And if they learn the ways of My people, to swear by My name—"As the LORD lives"—just as they once taught My people to swear by Baal, then they shall be ʰ-built up in the midst of-ʰ My people. ¹⁷But if they do not give heed, I will tear

נָתְנָה עָלַי בְּקוֹלָהּ
עַל־כֵּן שְׂנֵאתִֽיהָ׃
9 הַעַיִט צָבוּעַ
נַחֲלָתִי לִי
הַעַיִט סָבִיב עָלֶיהָ
לְכוּ אִסְפוּ כָּל־חַיַּת הַשָּׂדֶה
הֵתָיוּ לְאָכְלָֽה׃
10 רֹעִים רַבִּים שִֽׁחֲתוּ כַרְמִי
בֹּסְסוּ אֶת־חֶלְקָתִי
נָֽתְנוּ אֶת־חֶלְקַת חֶמְדָּתִי
לְמִדְבַּר שְׁמָמָֽה׃
11 שָׂמָהּ לִשְׁמָמָה
אָֽבְלָה עָלַי שְׁמֵמָה
נָשַׁמָּה כָּל־הָאָרֶץ
כִּי אֵין אִישׁ שָׂם עַל־לֵֽב׃
12 עַל־כָּל־שְׁפָיִם בַּמִּדְבָּר
בָּאוּ שֹֽׁדְדִים
כִּי חֶרֶב לַֽיהוָה אֹֽכְלָה
מִקְצֵה־אֶרֶץ וְעַד־קְצֵה הָאָרֶץ
אֵין שָׁלוֹם לְכָל־בָּשָֽׂר׃ ס
13 זָרְעוּ חִטִּים וְקֹצִים קָצָרוּ
נֶחְלוּ לֹא יוֹעִלוּ
וּבֹשׁוּ מִתְּבוּאֹֽתֵיכֶם
מֵֽחֲרוֹן אַף־יְהוָֽה׃ ס

14 כֹּה ׀ אָמַר יְהוָה עַל־כָּל־שְׁכֵנַי הָֽרָעִים הַנֹּֽגְעִים בַּֽנַּחֲלָה אֲשֶׁר־הִנְחַלְתִּי אֶת־עַמִּי אֶת־יִשְׂרָאֵל הִנְנִי נֹֽתְשָׁם מֵעַל אַדְמָתָם וְאֶת־בֵּית יְהוּדָה אֶתּוֹשׁ מִתּוֹכָֽם׃ 15 וְהָיָה אַחֲרֵי נָתְשִׁי אוֹתָם אָשׁוּב וְרִֽחַמְתִּים וַהֲשִֽׁבֹתִים אִישׁ לְנַחֲלָתוֹ וְאִישׁ לְאַרְצֽוֹ׃ 16 וְהָיָה אִם־לָמֹד יִלְמְדוּ אֶת־דַּרְכֵי עַמִּי לְהִשָּׁבֵעַ בִּשְׁמִי חַי־יְהוָה כַּֽאֲשֶׁר לִמְּדוּ אֶת־עַמִּי לְהִשָּׁבֵעַ בַּבָּעַל וְנִבְנוּ בְּתוֹךְ עַמִּֽי׃

---

f-f   *Meaning of Heb. uncertain.*
g-g   *Heb. "He has."*
h-h   *Or "incorporated into."*

out that nation, tear it out and destroy it—declares the LORD.

13

Thus the LORD said to me: "Go buy yourself a loincloth of linen, and put it around your loins, but do not dip it into water." ²So I bought the loincloth in accordance with the LORD's command, and put it about my loins. ³And the word of the LORD came to me a second time: ⁴"Take the loincloth which you bought, which is about your loins, and go at once to Perath[a] and cover it up there in a cleft of the rock." ⁵I went and buried it at Perath, as the LORD had commanded me. ⁶Then, after a long time, the LORD said to me, "Go at once to Perath and take there the loincloth which I commanded you to bury there." ⁷So I went to Perath and dug up the loincloth from the place where I had buried it; and found the loincloth ruined; it was not good for anything.

⁸The word of the LORD came to me: ⁹Thus said the LORD: Even so will I ruin the overweening pride of Judah and Jerusalem. ¹⁰This wicked people who refuse to heed My bidding, who follow the willfulness of their own hearts, who follow other gods and serve them and worship them, shall become like that loincloth, which is not good for anything. ¹¹For as the loincloth clings close to the loins of a man, so I brought close to Me the whole House of Israel and the whole House of Judah—declares the LORD—that they might be My people, for fame, and praise, and splendor. But they would not obey.

¹²And speak this word to them: Thus said the LORD, the God of Israel: "Every jar should be filled with wine." And when they say to you, "Don't we know that every jar should be filled with wine?" ¹³say to them, "Thus said the LORD: I am going to fill with drunkenness all the in-

---

a   Or "the Euphrates"; cf. "Parah," Josh. 18.23.

17 וְאִם־לֹא יִשְׁמָעוּ וְנָתַשְׁתִּי אֶת־הַגּוֹי הַהוּא נָתוֹשׁ וְאַבֵּד נְאֻם־יְהֹוָה: ס

יג כֹּה־אָמַר יְהֹוָה אֵלַי הָלוֹךְ וְקָנִיתָ לְּךָ אֵזוֹר פִּשְׁתִּים וְשַׂמְתּוֹ עַל־מָתְנֶיךָ וּבַמַּיִם לֹא תְבִאֵהוּ: 2 וָאֶקְנֶה אֶת־הָאֵזוֹר כִּדְבַר יְהֹוָה וָאָשִׂם עַל־מָתְנָי: ס 3 וַיְהִי דְבַר־יְהֹוָה אֵלַי שֵׁנִית לֵאמֹר: 4 קַח אֶת־הָאֵזוֹר אֲשֶׁר קָנִיתָ אֲשֶׁר עַל־מָתְנֶיךָ וְקוּם לֵךְ פְּרָתָה וְטָמְנֵהוּ שָׁם בִּנְקִיק הַסָּלַע: 5 וָאֵלֵךְ וָאֶטְמְנֵהוּ בִּפְרָת כַּאֲשֶׁר צִוָּה יְהֹוָה אוֹתִי: 6 וַיְהִי מִקֵּץ יָמִים רַבִּים וַיֹּאמֶר יְהֹוָה אֵלַי קוּם לֵךְ פְּרָתָה וְקַח מִשָּׁם אֶת־הָאֵזוֹר אֲשֶׁר צִוִּיתִיךָ לְטָמְנוֹ־שָׁם: 7 וָאֵלֵךְ פְּרָתָה וָאֶחְפֹּר וָאֶקַּח אֶת־הָאֵזוֹר מִן־הַמָּקוֹם אֲשֶׁר־טְמַנְתִּיו שָׁמָּה וְהִנֵּה נִשְׁחַת הָאֵזוֹר לֹא יִצְלַח לַכֹּל: פ

8 וַיְהִי דְבַר־יְהֹוָה אֵלַי לֵאמֹר: 9 כֹּה אָמַר יְהֹוָה כָּכָה אַשְׁחִית אֶת־גְּאוֹן יְהוּדָה וְאֶת־גְּאוֹן יְרוּשָׁלַ͏ִם הָרָב: 10 הָעָם הַזֶּה הָרָע הַמֵּאֲנִים ׀ לִשְׁמוֹעַ אֶת־דְּבָרַי הַהֹלְכִים בִּשְׁרִרוּת לִבָּם וַיֵּלְכוּ אַחֲרֵי אֱלֹהִים אֲחֵרִים לְעָבְדָם וּלְהִשְׁתַּחֲוֺת לָהֶם וִיהִי כָּאֵזוֹר הַזֶּה אֲשֶׁר לֹא־יִצְלַח לַכֹּל: 11 כִּי כַּאֲשֶׁר יִדְבַּק הָאֵזוֹר אֶל־מָתְנֵי־אִישׁ כֵּן הִדְבַּקְתִּי אֵלַי אֶת־כָּל־בֵּית יִשְׂרָאֵל וְאֶת־כָּל־בֵּית יְהוּדָה נְאֻם־יְהֹוָה לִהְיוֹת לִי לְעָם וּלְשֵׁם וְלִתְהִלָּה וּלְתִפְאָרֶת וְלֹא שָׁמֵעוּ:

12 וְאָמַרְתָּ אֲלֵיהֶם אֶת־הַדָּבָר הַזֶּה ס כֹּה־אָמַר יְהֹוָה אֱלֹהֵי יִשְׂרָאֵל כָּל־נֵבֶל יִמָּלֵא יָיִן וְאָמְרוּ אֵלֶיךָ הֲיָדֹעַ לֹא נֵדַע כִּי כָל־נֵבֶל יִמָּלֵא יָיִן: 13 וְאָמַרְתָּ אֲלֵיהֶם כֹּה־אָמַר יְהֹוָה הִנְנִי מְמַלֵּא אֶת־כָּל־יֹשְׁבֵי

habitants of this land, and the kings who sit on the throne of David, and the priests and the prophets, and all the inhabitants of Jerusalem. ¹⁴And I will smash them one against the other, parents and children alike—declares the LORD; no pity, compassion, or mercy will stop Me from destroying them."

הָאָ֣רֶץ הַזֹּ֗את וְאֶת־הַמְּלָכִ֣ים הַיֹּשְׁבִים֩
לְדָוִ֨ד עַל־כִּסְא֜וֹ וְאֶת־הַכֹּהֲנִ֣ים וְאֶת־
הַנְּבִיאִ֗ים וְאֵ֛ת כָּל־יֹשְׁבֵ֥י יְרוּשָׁלָ֖͏ִם שִׁכָּרֽוֹן׃
¹⁴ וְנִפַּצְתִּ֞ים אִ֣ישׁ אֶל־אָחִ֗יו וְהָאָב֤וֹת
וְהַבָּנִים֙ יַחְדָּ֔ו נְאֻם־יְהֹוָ֑ה לֹֽא־אֶחְמ֣וֹל וְלֹֽא־
אָח֛וּס וְלֹ֥א אֲרַחֵ֖ם מֵהַשְׁחִיתָֽם׃ ס

¹⁵Attend and give ear; be not haughty,
For the LORD has spoken.

¹⁵ שִׁמְע֥וּ וְהַאֲזִ֖ינוּ אַל־תִּגְבָּ֑הוּ
כִּ֥י יְהֹוָ֖ה דִּבֵּֽר׃

¹⁶Give honor to the LORD your God
Before He brings darkness,
Before your feet stumble
On the mountains in shadow—
When you hope for light,
And it is turned to darkness
And becomes deep gloom.

¹⁶ תְּנוּ֩ לַיהֹוָ֨ה אֱלֹהֵיכֶ֤ם כָּבוֹד֙
בְּטֶ֣רֶם יַחְשִׁ֔ךְ
וּבְטֶ֛רֶם יִֽתְנַגְּפ֥וּ רַגְלֵיכֶ֖ם
עַל־הָ֣רֵי נָ֑שֶׁף
וְקִוִּיתֶ֤ם לְאוֹר֙
וְשָׂמָ֣הּ לְצַלְמָ֔וֶת
יָשִׁ֖ית (ישית) לַעֲרָפֶֽל׃

¹⁷For if you will not give heed,
My inmost self must weep,
Because of your arrogance;
My eye must stream and flow
With copious tears,
Because the flock of the LORD
Is taken captive.

¹⁷ וְאִם֙ לֹ֣א תִשְׁמָע֔וּהָ
בְּמִסְתָּרִ֥ים תִּבְכֶּה־נַפְשִׁ֖י
מִפְּנֵ֣י גֵוָ֑ה
וְדָמֹ֨עַ תִּדְמַ֜ע
וְתֵרַ֤ד עֵינִי֙ דִּמְעָ֔ה
כִּ֥י נִשְׁבָּ֖ה
עֵ֥דֶר יְהֹוָֽה׃ ס

¹⁸Say to the king and the queen mother,
"Sit in a lowly spot;
For your diadems are abased,
Your glorious crowns."

¹⁸ אֱמֹ֥ר לַמֶּ֖לֶךְ וְלַגְּבִירָ֑ה
הַשְׁפִּ֣ילוּ שֵׁ֔בוּ
כִּ֤י יָרַד֙ מַרְאֲשׁ֣וֹתֵיכֶ֔ם
עֲטֶ֖רֶת תִּֽפְאַרְתְּכֶֽם׃

¹⁹The cities of the Negeb are shut,
There is no one to open them;
ᵇ-Judah is exiled completely,
All of it exiled.-ᵇ

¹⁹ עָרֵ֥י הַנֶּ֖גֶב סֻגְּר֑וּ
וְאֵ֣ין פֹּתֵ֔חַ
הׇגְלָ֧ת יְהוּדָ֛ה כֻּלָּ֖הּ
הׇגְלָ֥ת שְׁלוֹמִֽים׃ ס

²⁰Raise your eyes and behold
Those who come from the north:
Where are the sheep entrusted to you,
The flock you took pride in?

²⁰ שְׂא֤וּ (שאי) עֵֽינֵיכֶם֙ וּרְא֔וּ (וראי)
הַבָּאִ֖ים מִצָּפ֑וֹן
אַיֵּ֗ה הָעֵ֙דֶר֙ נִתַּן־לָ֔ךְ
צֹ֖אן תִּפְאַרְתֵּֽךְ׃

²¹ᶜ-What will you say when they appoint as
   your heads

²¹ מַה־תֹּֽאמְרִי֙ כִּֽי־יִפְקֹ֣ד עָלַ֔יִךְ

ᵇ⁻ᵇ I.e., most of Judah has been annexed by an alien people.
ᶜ⁻ᶜ Meaning of Heb. uncertain.

Those among you whom you trained to be
    tame?-c

וְאֵ֣ת לִמַּ֧דְתְּ אֹתָ֛ם עָלַ֖יִךְ אַלֻּפִ֣ים לְרֹ֑אשׁ

Shall not pangs seize you
Like a woman in childbirth?

הֲל֤וֹא חֲבָלִים֙ יֹֽאחֲז֔וּךְ
כְּמ֖וֹ אֵ֥שֶׁת לֵדָֽה׃

22And when you ask yourself,
"Why have these things befallen me?"
It is because of your great iniquity
That your skirts are lifted up,
Your limbs exposed.

22וְכִ֤י תֹֽאמְרִי֙ בִּלְבָבֵ֔ךְ
מַדּ֖וּעַ קְרָאֻ֣נִי אֵ֑לֶּה
בְּרֹ֤ב עֲוֺנֵךְ֙
נִגְל֣וּ שׁוּלַ֔יִךְ
נֶחְמְס֖וּ עֲקֵבָֽיִךְ׃

23Can the Cushite change his skin,
Or the leopard his spots?
Just as much can you do good,
Who are practiced in doing evil!

23הֲיַהֲפֹ֤ךְ כּוּשִׁי֙ עוֹר֔וֹ
וְנָמֵ֖ר חֲבַרְבֻּרֹתָ֑יו
גַּם־אַתֶּם֙ תּוּכְל֣וּ לְהֵיטִ֔יב
לִמֻּדֵ֖י הָרֵֽעַ׃

24So I will scatter youd like straw that flies
Before the desert wind.

24וַאֲפִיצֵ֖ם כְּקַשׁ־עוֹבֵ֑ר
לְר֖וּחַ מִדְבָּֽר׃

25This shall be your lot,
Your measured portion from Me
         —declares the LORD.
Because you forgot Me
And trusted in falsehood,

25זֶ֣ה גוֹרָלֵ֧ךְ
מְנָת־מִדַּ֛יִךְ מֵֽאִתִּ֖י
נְאֻם־יְהֹוָ֑ה
אֲשֶׁר֙ שָׁכַ֣חַתְּ אוֹתִ֔י
וַתִּבְטְחִ֖י בַּשָּֽׁקֶר׃

26I in turn will lift your skirts over your face
And your shame shall be seen.

26וְגַם־אֲנִ֛י חָשַׂ֥פְתִּי שׁוּלַ֖יִךְ עַל־פָּנָ֑יִךְ
וְנִרְאָ֖ה קְלוֹנֵֽךְ׃

27I behold your adulteries,
Your lustful neighing,
Your unbridled depravity, your vile acts
On the hills of the countryside.
Woe to you, O Jerusalem,
Who will not be clean!
How much longer shall it be?

27נִֽאֻפַ֤יִךְ וּמִצְהֲלוֹתַ֙יִךְ֙
זִמַּ֣ת זְנוּתֵ֔ךְ
עַל־גְּבָעוֹת֙ בַּשָּׂדֶ֔ה
רָאִ֖יתִי שִׁקּוּצָ֑יִךְ
א֥וֹי לָךְ֙ יְר֣וּשָׁלַ֔͏ִם
לֹ֣א תִטְהֲרִ֔י
אַחֲרֵ֥י מָתַ֖י עֹֽד׃ פ

14

The word of the LORD which came to Jeremiah concerning the droughts.

יד אֲשֶׁ֨ר הָיָ֤ה דְבַר־יְהֹוָה֙ אֶֽל־יִרְמְיָ֔הוּ
עַל־דִּבְרֵ֖י הַבַּצָּרֽוֹת׃

2Judah is in mourning,
Her settlements languish.
Men are bowed to the ground,
And the outcry of Jerusalem rises.

2אָבְלָ֣ה יְהוּדָ֔ה
וּשְׁעָרֶ֥יהָ אֻמְלְל֖וּ
קָדְר֣וּ לָאָ֑רֶץ
וְצִוְחַ֥ת יְרוּשָׁלַ֖͏ִם עָלָֽתָה׃

d Heb. "them."

³Their nobles sent their servants for water;
They came to the cisterns, they found no
    water.
They returned, their vessels empty.
They are shamed and humiliated,
They cover their heads.
⁴ᵃ-Because of the ground there is dismay,-ᵃ
For there has been no rain on the earth.
The plowmen are shamed,
They cover their heads.
⁵Even the hind in the field
Forsakes her new-born fawn,
Because there is no grass.
⁶And the wild asses stand on the bare heights,
Snuffing the air like jackals;
Their eyes pine,
Because there is no herbage.

⁷Though our iniquities testify against us,
Act, O Lord, for the sake of Your name;
Though our rebellions are many
And we have sinned against You.
⁸O Hope of Israel,
Its deliverer in time of trouble,
Why are You like a stranger in the land,
Like a traveler who stops only for the night?
⁹Why are You like a man who is stunned,
Like a warrior who cannot give victory?
Yet You are in our midst, O Lord,
And Your name is attached to us—
Do not forsake us!

¹⁰Thus said the Lord concerning this people:
"Truly, they love to stray, they have not restrained their feet; so the Lord has no pleasure
in them. Now He will recall their iniquity and
punish their sin."

¹¹And the Lord said to me, "Do not pray for
the benefit of this people. ¹²When they fast, I

³וְאַדִּרֵיהֶם שָׁלְחוּ צעוריהם צְעִירֵיהֶם
לַמָּיִם
בָּאוּ עַל־גֵּבִים לֹא־מָצְאוּ מַיִם
שָׁבוּ כְלֵיהֶם רֵיקָם
בֹּשׁוּ וְהָכְלְמוּ
וְחָפוּ רֹאשָׁם׃
⁴בַּעֲבוּר הָאֲדָמָה חַתָּה
כִּי לֹא־הָיָה גֶשֶׁם בָּאָרֶץ
בֹּשׁוּ אִכָּרִים
חָפוּ רֹאשָׁם׃
⁵כִּי גַם־אַיֶּלֶת בַּשָּׂדֶה
יָלְדָה וְעָזוֹב
כִּי לֹא־הָיָה דֶּשֶׁא׃
⁶וּפְרָאִים עָמְדוּ עַל־שְׁפָיִם
שָׁאֲפוּ רוּחַ כַּתַּנִּים
כָּלוּ עֵינֵיהֶם
כִּי־אֵין עֵשֶׂב׃

⁷אִם־עֲוֺנֵינוּ עָנוּ בָנוּ
יְהֹוָה עֲשֵׂה לְמַעַן שְׁמֶךָ
כִּי־רַבּוּ מְשׁוּבֹתֵינוּ
לְךָ חָטָאנוּ׃
⁸מִקְוֵה יִשְׂרָאֵל
מוֹשִׁיעוֹ בְּעֵת צָרָה
לָמָּה תִהְיֶה כְּגֵר בָּאָרֶץ
וּכְאֹרֵחַ נָטָה לָלוּן׃
⁹לָמָּה תִהְיֶה כְּאִישׁ נִדְהָם
כְּגִבּוֹר לֹא־יוּכַל לְהוֹשִׁיעַ
וְאַתָּה בְקִרְבֵּנוּ יְהֹוָה
וְשִׁמְךָ עָלֵינוּ נִקְרָא
אַל־תַּנִּחֵנוּ׃ ס

¹⁰כֹּה־אָמַר יְהֹוָה לָעָם הַזֶּה כֵּן אָהֲבוּ
לָנוּעַ רַגְלֵיהֶם לֹא חָשָׂכוּ וַיהֹוָה לֹא רָצָם
עַתָּה יִזְכֹּר עֲוֺנָם וְיִפְקֹד חַטֹּאתָם׃ ס
¹¹וַיֹּאמֶר יְהֹוָה אֵלָי אַל־תִּתְפַּלֵּל בְּעַד־
הָעָם הַזֶּה לְטוֹבָה׃ ¹²כִּי יָצֻמוּ אֵינֶנִּי שֹׁמֵעַ

ᵃ⁻ᵃ Meaning of Heb. uncertain.

will not listen to their outcry; and when they present burnt offering and meal offering, I will not accept them. I will exterminate them by war, famine, and disease."

13I said, "Ah, Lord GOD! The prophets are saying to them, 'You shall not see the sword, famine shall not come upon you, but I will give you unfailing security in this place.'"

14The LORD replied: It is a lie that the prophets utter in My name. I have not sent them or commanded them. I have not spoken to them. A lying vision, an empty divination, the deceit of their own contriving—that is what they prophesy to you! 15Assuredly, thus said the LORD concerning the prophets who prophesy in My name though I have not sent them, and who say, "Sword and famine shall not befall this land"; those very prophets shall perish by sword and famine. 16And the people to whom they prophesy shall be left lying in the streets of Jerusalem because of the famine and the sword, with none to bury them—they, their wives, their sons, and their daughters. I will pour out upon them [the requital of] their wickedness.

17And do you speak to them thus:
Let my eyes run with tears,
Day and night let them not cease,
For *b-my hapless people-b* has suffered
A grievous injury, a very painful wound.
18If I go out to the country—
Lo, the slain of the sword.
If I enter the city—
Lo, *c-those who are sick with-c* famine.
Both priest and prophet roam*a* the land,
They know not where.

19Have You, then, rejected Judah?
Have You spurned Zion?
Why have You smitten us

אֶל־רִנָּתָם וְכִי יַעֲלוּ עֹלָה וּמִנְחָה אֵינֶנִּי רֹצָם כִּי בַּחֶרֶב וּבָרָעָב וּבַדֶּבֶר אָנֹכִי מְכַלֶּה אוֹתָם׃ ס

13 וָאֹמַר אֲהָהּ ׀ אֲדֹנָי יְהוִה הִנֵּה הַנְּבִאִים אֹמְרִים לָהֶם לֹא־תִרְאוּ חֶרֶב וְרָעָב לֹא־יִהְיֶה לָכֶם כִּי־שְׁלוֹם אֱמֶת אֶתֵּן לָכֶם בַּמָּקוֹם הַזֶּה׃ ס

14 וַיֹּאמֶר יְהוָה אֵלַי שֶׁקֶר הַנְּבִאִים נִבְּאִים בִּשְׁמִי לֹא שְׁלַחְתִּים וְלֹא צִוִּיתִים וְלֹא דִבַּרְתִּי אֲלֵיהֶם חֲזוֹן שֶׁקֶר וְקֶסֶם וֶאֱלִיל וְתַרְמִית לִבָּם הֵמָּה מִתְנַבְּאִים לָכֶם׃ ס 15 לָכֵן כֹּה־אָמַר יְהוָה עַל־הַנְּבִאִים הַנִּבְּאִים בִּשְׁמִי וַאֲנִי לֹא־שְׁלַחְתִּים וְהֵמָּה אֹמְרִים חֶרֶב וְרָעָב לֹא יִהְיֶה בָּאָרֶץ הַזֹּאת בַּחֶרֶב וּבָרָעָב יִתַּמּוּ הַנְּבִאִים הָהֵמָּה׃ 16 וְהָעָם אֲשֶׁר־הֵמָּה נִבְּאִים לָהֶם יִהְיוּ מֻשְׁלָכִים בְּחֻצוֹת יְרוּשָׁלַ͏ִם מִפְּנֵי ׀ הָרָעָב וְהַחֶרֶב וְאֵין מְקַבֵּר לָהֵמָּה הֵמָּה נְשֵׁיהֶם וּבְנֵיהֶם וּבְנֹתֵיהֶם וְשָׁפַכְתִּי עֲלֵיהֶם אֶת־רָעָתָם׃

17 וְאָמַרְתָּ אֲלֵיהֶם אֶת־הַדָּבָר הַזֶּה
תֵּרַדְנָה עֵינַי דִּמְעָה
לַיְלָה וְיוֹמָם וְאַל־תִּדְמֶינָה
כִּי שֶׁבֶר גָּדוֹל נִשְׁבְּרָה בְּתוּלַת בַּת־עַמִּי
מַכָּה נַחְלָה מְאֹד׃
18 אִם־יָצָאתִי הַשָּׂדֶה
וְהִנֵּה חַלְלֵי־חֶרֶב
וְאִם בָּאתִי הָעִיר
וְהִנֵּה תַּחֲלוּאֵי רָעָב
כִּי־גַם־נָבִיא גַם־כֹּהֵן סָחֲרוּ אֶל־אֶרֶץ
וְלֹא יָדָעוּ׃ ס

19 הֲמָאֹס מָאַסְתָּ אֶת־יְהוּדָה
אִם־בְּצִיּוֹן גָּעֲלָה נַפְשֶׁךָ
מַדּוּעַ הִכִּיתָנוּ

b-b Lit. "the maiden daughter, My people."
c-c Lit. "the sicknesses of."

So that there is no cure?

Why do we hope for happiness,

But find no good;

For a time of healing,

And meet terror instead?

²⁰We acknowledge our wickedness, O
Lord—

The iniquity of our fathers—

For we have sinned against You.

²¹For Your name's sake, do not disown us;

Do not dishonor Your glorious throne.

Remember, do not annul Your covenant with
us.

²²Can any of the false gods of the nations give
rain?

Can the skies of themselves give showers?

Only You can, O Lord our God!

So we hope in You,

For only You made all these things.

15 The Lord said to me, "Even if Moses
and Samuel were to ᵃ-intercede with Me,-ᵃ I
would not be won over to that people. Dismiss
them from My presence, and let them go forth!
²And if they ask you, 'To what shall we go forth?'
answer them, 'Thus said the Lord:

Those destined for the plague, to the plague;

Those destined for the sword, to the sword;

Those destined for famine, to famine;

Those destined for captivity, to captivity.

³And I will appoint over them four kindsᵇ [of
punishment]—declares the Lord—the sword
to slay, the dogs to drag, the birds of the sky,
and the beasts of the earth to devour and destroy. ⁴I will make them a horror to all the kingdoms of the earth, on account of King Manasseh
son of Hezekiah of Judah, and of what he did
in Jerusalem.'"

וְאֵין לָנוּ מַרְפֵּא

קַוֵּה לְשָׁלוֹם

וְאֵין טוֹב

וּלְעֵת מַרְפֵּא

וְהִנֵּה בְעָתָה:

20 יָדַעְנוּ יְהֹוָה רִשְׁעֵנוּ

עֲוֹן אֲבוֹתֵינוּ

כִּי חָטָאנוּ לָךְ:

21 אַל־תִּנְאַץ לְמַעַן שִׁמְךָ

אַל־תְּנַבֵּל כִּסֵּא כְבוֹדֶךָ

זְכֹר אַל־תָּפֵר בְּרִיתְךָ אִתָּנוּ:

22 הֲיֵשׁ בְּהַבְלֵי הַגּוֹיִם מַגְשִׁמִים

וְאִם־הַשָּׁמַיִם יִתְּנוּ רְבִבִים

הֲלֹא אַתָּה־הוּא יְהֹוָה אֱלֹהֵינוּ

וּנְקַוֶּה־לָּךְ

כִּי־אַתָּה עָשִׂיתָ אֶת־כָּל־אֵלֶּה: פ

טו וַיֹּאמֶר יְהֹוָה אֵלַי אִם־יַעֲמֹד מֹשֶׁה
וּשְׁמוּאֵל לְפָנַי אֵין נַפְשִׁי אֶל־הָעָם הַזֶּה
שַׁלַּח מֵעַל־פָּנַי וְיֵצֵאוּ: 2 וְהָיָה כִּי־יֹאמְרוּ
אֵלֶיךָ אָנָה נֵצֵא וְאָמַרְתָּ אֲלֵיהֶם כֹּה־אָמַר
יְהֹוָה

אֲשֶׁר לַמָּוֶת לַמָּוֶת

וַאֲשֶׁר לַחֶרֶב לַחֶרֶב

וַאֲשֶׁר לָרָעָב לָרָעָב

וַאֲשֶׁר לַשְּׁבִי לַשֶּׁבִי:

3 וּפָקַדְתִּי עֲלֵיהֶם אַרְבַּע מִשְׁפָּחוֹת נְאֻם־
יְהֹוָה אֶת־הַחֶרֶב לַהֲרֹג וְאֶת־הַכְּלָבִים
לִסְחֹב וְאֶת־עוֹף הַשָּׁמַיִם וְאֶת־בֶּהֱמַת
הָאָרֶץ לֶאֱכֹל וּלְהַשְׁחִית: 4 וּנְתַתִּים לְזַעֲוָה
לְזַעֲוָה לְכֹל מַמְלְכוֹת הָאָרֶץ בִּגְלַל מְנַשֶּׁה
בֶן־יְחִזְקִיָּהוּ מֶלֶךְ יְהוּדָה עַל אֲשֶׁר־עָשָׂה
בִּירוּשָׁלָ͏ִם:

---

a-a   Lit. "stand before Me," as Jeremiah is doing now; cf. 18.20.
b   Meaning of Heb. uncertain.

⁵But who will pity you, O Jerusalem,
Who will console you?
Who will turn aside to inquire
About your welfare?
⁶You cast Me off

—declares the LORD—

You go ever backward.
So I have stretched out My hand to destroy
   you;
I cannot relent.
⁷I will scatter them as with a winnowing fork
Through the settlements of the earth.
I will bereave, I will destroy My people,
For they would not turn back from their ways.
⁸Their widows shall be more numerous
Than the sands of the seas.
I will bring against them—
ᵇ-Young men and mothers together-ᵇ—
A destroyer at noonday.
I will bring down suddenly upon them
Alarmᵇ and terror.
⁹She who bore seven is forlorn,
Utterly disconsolate;
Her sun has set while it is still day,
She is shamed and humiliated.
The remnant of them I will deliver to the
   sword,
To the power of their enemies

—declares the LORD.

¹⁰Woe is me, my mother, that you ever bore
   me—
A man of conflict and strife with all the land!
I have not lent,
And I have not borrowed;
Yet everyone curses me.

¹¹The LORD said:
ᵇ-Surely, a mere remnant of you
Will I spare for a better fate!-ᵇ

⁵כִּי מִי־יַחְמֹל עָלַיִךְ יְרוּשָׁלַ͏ִם
וּמִי יָנוּד לָךְ
וּמִי יָסוּר לִשְׁאֹל
לְשָׁלֹם לָךְ:
⁶אַתְּ נָטַשְׁתְּ אֹתִי
נְאֻם־יְהֹוָה
אָחוֹר תֵּלֵכִי
וָאַט אֶת־יָדִי עָלַיִךְ וָאַשְׁחִיתֵךְ
נִלְאֵיתִי הִנָּחֵם:
⁷וָאֶזְרֵם בְּמִזְרֶה
בְּשַׁעֲרֵי הָאָרֶץ
שִׁכַּלְתִּי אִבַּדְתִּי אֶת־עַמִּי
מִדַּרְכֵיהֶם לוֹא־שָׁבוּ:
⁸עָצְמוּ־לִי אַלְמְנֹתָו אַלְמְנוֹתָיו
מֵחוֹל יַמִּים
הֵבֵאתִי לָהֶם
עַל־אֵם בָּחוּר
שֹׁדֵד בַּצׇּהֳרָיִם
הִפַּלְתִּי עָלֶיהָ פִּתְאֹם
עִיר וּבֶהָלוֹת:
⁹אֻמְלְלָה יֹלֶדֶת הַשִּׁבְעָה
נָפְחָה נַפְשָׁהּ
באה בָּא שִׁמְשָׁהּ בְּעֹד יוֹמָם
בּוֹשָׁה וְחָפֵרָה
וּשְׁאֵרִיתָם לַחֶרֶב אֶתֵּן
לִפְנֵי אֹיְבֵיהֶם
נְאֻם־יְהֹוָה: ס

¹⁰אוֹי־לִי אִמִּי כִּי יְלִדְתִּנִי
אִישׁ רִיב וְאִישׁ מָדוֹן לְכׇל־הָאָרֶץ
לֹא־נָשִׁיתִי
וְלֹא־נָשׁוּ־בִי
כֻּלֹּה מְקַלְלַונִי*: ס

¹¹אָמַר יְהֹוָה
אִם־לֹא שרותך שֵׁרִיתִךָ
לְטוֹב

ᵛ. 10. יתיר ו׳

By the enemy c-from the north-c

In a time of distress and a time of disaster,

Surely, I will have you struck down!

12d-Can iron break iron and bronze?-d

13b-I will hand over your wealth and your

    treasures

As a spoil, free of charge,

Because of all your sins throughout your ter-

    ritory.

14And I will bring your enemies

By way of a land you have not known.-b

For a fire has flared in My wrath,

It blazes against you.

15O LORD, you know—

Remember me and take thought of me,

Avenge me on those who persecute me;

Do not yield to Your patience,

e-Do not let me perish!-e

Consider how I have borne insult

On Your account.

16When Your words were offered, I devoured

    them;

Your word brought me the delight and joy

Of knowing that Your name is attached to me,

O LORD, God of Hosts.

17I have not sat in the company of revelers

And made merry!

I have sat lonely because of Your hand upon

    me,

For You have filled me with gloom.

18Why must my pain be endless,

My wound incurable,

Resistant to healing?

You have been to me like a spring that fails,

Like waters that cannot be relied on.

19Assuredly, thus said the LORD:

If you turn back, I shall take you back

אִם־לֹ֖א ׀ הִפְגַּעְתִּ֣י בְךָ֑

בְּעֵת־רָעָ֖ה וּבְעֵ֥ת צָרָ֖ה

אֶת־הָאֹיֵֽב:

12 הֲיָרֹ֥עַ בַּרְזֶ֖ל ׀ בַּרְזֶ֛ל מִצָּפ֖וֹן וּנְחֹֽשֶׁת:

13 חֵילְךָ֧ וְאוֹצְרוֹתֶ֛יךָ לָבַ֥ז אֶתֵּ֖ן

לֹ֣א בִמְחִ֑יר

וּבְכָל־חַטֹּאותֶ֙יךָ֙* וּבְכָל־גְּבוּלֶֽיךָ:

14 וְהַעֲבַרְתִּ֖י אֶת־אֹ֣יְבֶ֑יךָ

בְּאֶ֖רֶץ לֹ֣א יָדָ֑עְתָּ

כִּי־אֵ֛שׁ קָדְחָ֥ה בְאַפִּ֖י

עֲלֵיכֶ֥ם תּוּקָֽד: ס

15 אַתָּ֤ה יָדַ֙עְתָּ֙ יְהֹוָ֔ה

זׇכְרֵ֣נִי וּפׇקְדֵ֗נִי

וְהִנָּ֤קֶם לִי֙ מֵרֹ֣דְפַ֔י

אַל־לְאֶ֥רֶךְ אַפְּךָ֖

תִּקָּחֵ֑נִי

דַּ֕ע שְׂאֵתִ֥י

עָלֶ֖יךָ חֶרְפָּֽה:

16 נִמְצְא֤וּ דְבָרֶ֙יךָ֙ וָאֹכְלֵ֔ם

וַיְהִ֤י דְבָרְךָ֙ לִ֔י לְשָׂשׂ֖וֹן וּלְשִׂמְחַ֣ת

לְבָבִ֑י

כִּי־נִקְרָ֤א שִׁמְךָ֙ עָלַ֔י

יְהֹוָ֖ה אֱלֹהֵ֥י צְבָאֽוֹת: ס

17 לֹא־יָשַׁ֥בְתִּי בְסוֹד־מְשַׂחֲקִ֖ים

וָאֶעְלֹ֑ז

מִפְּנֵ֤י יָֽדְךָ֙ בָּדָ֣ד יָשַׁ֔בְתִּי

כִּי־זַ֖עַם מִלֵּאתָֽנִי: ס

18 לָ֣מָּה הָיָ֤ה כְאֵבִי֙ נֶ֔צַח

וּמַכָּתִ֖י אֲנוּשָׁ֑ה

מֵאֲנָ֖ה הֵרָפֵ֑א

הָי֨וֹ תִֽהְיֶ֥ה לִ֛י כְּמ֥וֹ אַכְזָ֖ב

מַ֖יִם לֹ֥א נֶאֱמָֽנוּ: ס

19 לָכֵ֗ן כֹּֽה־אָמַ֣ר יְהֹוָ֔ה

אִם־תָּשׁ֖וּב וַאֲשִֽׁיבְךָ֒

c-c   *Moved up from v. 12 for clarity.*

d-d   *Emendation yields "He shall shatter iron—iron and bronze!"*

e-e   *Lit. "Do not take me away."*

And you shall stand before Me;
If you produce what is noble
Out of the worthless,
You shall be My spokesman.
They shall come back to you,
Not you to them.
20Against this people I will make you
As a fortified wall of bronze:
They will attack you,
But they shall not overcome you,
For I am with you to deliver and save you
      —declares the LORD.
21I will save you from the hands of the wicked
And rescue you from the clutches of the
    violent.

לְפָנַי תַּעֲמֹד
וְאִם־תּוֹצִיא יָקָר
מִזּוֹלֵל
כְּפִי תִהְיֶה
יָשֻׁבוּ הֵמָּה אֵלֶיךָ
וְאַתָּה לֹא־תָשׁוּב אֲלֵיהֶם׃
20 וּנְתַתִּיךָ לָעָם הַזֶּה
לְחוֹמַת נְחֹשֶׁת בְּצוּרָה
וְנִלְחֲמוּ אֵלֶיךָ
וְלֹא־יוּכְלוּ לָךְ
כִּי־אִתְּךָ אֲנִי לְהוֹשִׁיעֲךָ וּלְהַצִּילֶךָ
נְאֻם־יְהֹוָה׃
21 וְהִצַּלְתִּיךָ מִיַּד רָעִים
וּפְדִתִיךָ מִכַּף עָרִצִים׃ פ

16 The word of the LORD came to me: 2You are not to marry and not to have sons and daughters in this place. 3For thus said the LORD concerning any sons and daughters that may be born in this place, and concerning the mothers who bear them, and concerning the fathers who beget them in this land: 4They shall die gruesome deaths. They shall not be lamented or buried; they shall be like dung on the surface of the ground. They shall be consumed by the sword and by famine, and their corpses shall be food for the birds of the sky and the beasts of the earth.

טז וַיְהִי דְבַר־יְהֹוָה אֵלַי לֵאמֹר׃
2 לֹא־תִקַּח לְךָ אִשָּׁה וְלֹא־יִהְיוּ לְךָ בָּנִים וּבָנוֹת בַּמָּקוֹם הַזֶּה׃ 3 כִּי־כֹה ׀ אָמַר יְהֹוָה עַל־הַבָּנִים וְעַל־הַבָּנוֹת הַיִּלּוֹדִים בַּמָּקוֹם הַזֶּה וְעַל־אִמֹּתָם הַיֹּלְדוֹת אוֹתָם וְעַל־אֲבוֹתָם הַמּוֹלִדִים אוֹתָם בָּאָרֶץ הַזֹּאת׃ 4 מְמוֹתֵי תַחֲלֻאִים יָמֻתוּ לֹא יִסָּפְדוּ וְלֹא יִקָּבֵרוּ לְדֹמֶן עַל־פְּנֵי הָאֲדָמָה יִהְיוּ וּבַחֶרֶב וּבָרָעָב יִכְלוּ וְהָיְתָה נִבְלָתָם לְמַאֲכָל לְעוֹף הַשָּׁמַיִם וּלְבֶהֱמַת הָאָרֶץ׃ ס

5For thus said the LORD:
Do not enter a house of mourning,a
Do not go to lament and to condole with
    them;
For I have withdrawn My favor from that
    people
      —declares the LORD—
My kindness and compassion.

5 כִּי־כֹה ׀ אָמַר יְהֹוָה
אַל־תָּבוֹא בֵּית מַרְזֵחַ
וְאַל־תֵּלֵךְ לִסְפּוֹד וְאַל־תָּנֹד לָהֶם
כִּי־אָסַפְתִּי אֶת־שְׁלוֹמִי מֵאֵת הָעָם־
הַזֶּה
נְאֻם־יְהֹוָה
אֶת־הַחֶסֶד וְאֶת־הָרַחֲמִים׃

---

a Lit. "religious gathering."

⁶Great and small alike shall die in this land,
They shall not be buried; men shall not lament them,
   ment them,
Nor gash and tonsure themselves for them.
⁷They shall not break bread[b] for a mourner[c]
To comfort him for a bereavement,
Nor offer one a cup of consolation
For the loss of his father or mother.
⁸Nor shall you enter a house of feasting,
To sit down with them to eat and drink.

⁹For thus said the LORD of Hosts, the God of Israel: I am going to banish from this place, in your days and before your eyes, the sound of mirth and gladness, the voice of bridegroom and bride.

¹⁰And when you announce all these things to that people, and they ask you, "Why has the LORD decreed upon us all this fearful evil? What is the iniquity and what the sin that we have committed against the LORD our God?" ¹¹say to them, "Because your fathers deserted Me—declares the LORD—and followed other gods and served them and worshiped them; they deserted Me and did not keep My Instruction. ¹²And you have acted worse than your fathers, every one of you following the willfulness of his evil heart and paying no heed to Me. ¹³Therefore I will hurl you out of this land to a land that neither you nor your fathers have known, and there you will serve other gods, day and night; for I will show you no mercy."

¹⁴Assuredly, a time is coming—declares the LORD—when it shall no more be said, "As the LORD lives who brought the Israelites out of the land of Egypt," ¹⁵but rather, "As the LORD lives who brought the Israelites out of the northland, and out of all the lands to which He had ban-

---

⁶וּמֵתוּ גְדֹלִים וּקְטַנִּים בָּאָרֶץ הַזֹּאת
לֹא יִקָּבֵרוּ וְלֹא־יִסְפְּדוּ לָהֶם
וְלֹא יִתְגֹּדַד וְלֹא יִקָּרֵחַ לָהֶם:
⁷וְלֹא־יִפְרְסוּ לָהֶם* עַל־אֵבֶל
לְנַחֲמוֹ עַל־מֵת
וְלֹא־יַשְׁקוּ אוֹתָם כּוֹס תַּנְחוּמִים
עַל־אָבִיו וְעַל־אִמּוֹ:
⁸וּבֵית־מִשְׁתֶּה לֹא־תָבוֹא
לָשֶׁבֶת אוֹתָם לֶאֱכֹל וְלִשְׁתּוֹת: ס

⁹כִּי כֹה אָמַר יְהוָה צְבָאוֹת אֱלֹהֵי יִשְׂרָאֵל הִנְנִי מַשְׁבִּית מִן־הַמָּקוֹם הַזֶּה לְעֵינֵיכֶם וּבִימֵיכֶם קוֹל שָׂשׂוֹן וְקוֹל שִׂמְחָה קוֹל חָתָן וְקוֹל כַּלָּה:

¹⁰וְהָיָה כִּי תַגִּיד לָעָם הַזֶּה אֵת כָּל־הַדְּבָרִים הָאֵלֶּה וְאָמְרוּ אֵלֶיךָ עַל־מֶה דִבֶּר יְהוָה עָלֵינוּ אֵת כָּל־הָרָעָה הַגְּדוֹלָה הַזֹּאת וּמֶה עֲוֹנֵנוּ וּמֶה חַטָּאתֵנוּ אֲשֶׁר חָטָאנוּ לַיהוָה אֱלֹהֵינוּ: ¹¹וְאָמַרְתָּ אֲלֵיהֶם עַל אֲשֶׁר־עָזְבוּ אֲבוֹתֵיכֶם אוֹתִי נְאֻם־יְהוָה וַיֵּלְכוּ אַחֲרֵי אֱלֹהִים אֲחֵרִים וַיַּעַבְדוּם וַיִּשְׁתַּחֲווּ לָהֶם וְאֹתִי עָזָבוּ וְאֶת־תּוֹרָתִי לֹא שָׁמָרוּ: ¹²וְאַתֶּם הֲרֵעֹתֶם לַעֲשׂוֹת מֵאֲבוֹתֵיכֶם וְהִנְּכֶם הֹלְכִים אִישׁ אַחֲרֵי שְׁרִרוּת לִבּוֹ־הָרָע לְבִלְתִּי שְׁמֹעַ אֵלָי: ¹³וְהֵטַלְתִּי אֶתְכֶם מֵעַל הָאָרֶץ הַזֹּאת עַל־הָאָרֶץ אֲשֶׁר לֹא יְדַעְתֶּם אַתֶּם וַאֲבוֹתֵיכֶם וַעֲבַדְתֶּם־שָׁם אֶת־אֱלֹהִים אֲחֵרִים יוֹמָם וָלַיְלָה אֲשֶׁר לֹא־אֶתֵּן לָכֶם חֲנִינָה: ס

¹⁴לָכֵן הִנֵּה־יָמִים בָּאִים נְאֻם־יְהוָה וְלֹא־יֵאָמֵר עוֹד חַי־יְהוָה אֲשֶׁר הֶעֱלָה אֶת־בְּנֵי יִשְׂרָאֵל מֵאֶרֶץ מִצְרָיִם: ¹⁵כִּי אִם־חַי־יְהוָה אֲשֶׁר הֶעֱלָה אֶת־בְּנֵי יִשְׂרָאֵל מֵאֶרֶץ צָפוֹן וּמִכֹּל הָאֲרָצוֹת אֲשֶׁר הִדִּיחָם

---

b   So a few mss. Most mss. and editions read "to them."
c   Lit. "mourning."

ished them." For I will bring them back to their
land, which I gave to their fathers.

16Lo, I am sending for many fishermen
   —declares the LORD—
And they shall haul them out;
And after that I will send for many hunters,
And they shall hunt them
Out of every mountain and out of every hill
And out of the clefts of the rocks.
17For My eyes are on all their ways,
They are not hidden from My presence,
Their iniquity is not concealed from My sight.
18I will pay them in full^d—
Nay, doubly for their iniquity and their sins—
Because they have defiled My land
With the corpses of their abominations,^e
And have filled My own possession
With their abhorrent things.
19O LORD, my strength and my stronghold,
My refuge in a day of trouble,
To You nations shall come
From the ends of the earth and say:
Our fathers inherited utter delusions,
Things that are futile and worthless.
20Can a man make gods for himself?
No-gods are they!
21Assuredly, I will teach them,
Once and for all I will teach them
My power and My might.
And they shall learn that My name is LORD.

17 The guilt of Judah is inscribed
With a stylus of iron,
Engraved with an adamant point
On the tablet of their hearts,

שָׁמָּה וַהֲשִׁבֹתִים עַל־אַדְמָתָם אֲשֶׁר נָתַתִּי
לַאֲבוֹתָם: ס

16 הִנְנִי שֹׁלֵחַ לְדַוָּגִים רַבִּים נְאֻם־יְהוָה
וְדִיגוּם
וְאַחֲרֵי־כֵן אֶשְׁלַח לְרַבִּים צַיָּדִים וְצָדוּם
מֵעַל כָּל־הַר וּמֵעַל כָּל־גִּבְעָה
וּמִנְּקִיקֵי הַסְּלָעִים:
17 כִּי עֵינַי עַל־כָּל־דַּרְכֵיהֶם
לֹא נִסְתְּרוּ מִלְּפָנָי
וְלֹא־נִצְפַּן עֲוֹנָם מִנֶּגֶד עֵינָי:
18 וְשִׁלַּמְתִּי רִאשׁוֹנָה
מִשְׁנֵה עֲוֹנָם וְחַטָּאתָם
עַל חַלְּלָם אֶת־אַרְצִי
בְּנִבְלַת שִׁקּוּצֵיהֶם
וְתוֹעֲבוֹתֵיהֶם מָלְאוּ אֶת־נַחֲלָתִי: ס
19 יְהוָה עֻזִּי וּמָעֻזִּי
וּמְנוּסִי בְּיוֹם צָרָה
אֵלֶיךָ גּוֹיִם יָבֹאוּ
מֵאַפְסֵי־אָרֶץ וְיֹאמְרוּ
אַךְ־שֶׁקֶר נָחֲלוּ אֲבוֹתֵינוּ
הֶבֶל וְאֵין־בָּם מוֹעִיל:
20 הֲיַעֲשֶׂה־לּוֹ אָדָם אֱלֹהִים
וְהֵמָּה לֹא אֱלֹהִים:
21 לָכֵן הִנְנִי מוֹדִיעָם
בַּפַּעַם הַזֹּאת אוֹדִיעֵם
אֶת־יָדִי וְאֶת־גְּבוּרָתִי
וְיָדְעוּ כִּי־שְׁמִי יְהוָה: ס

יז חַטַּאת יְהוּדָה כְּתוּבָה
בְּעֵט בַּרְזֶל
בְּצִפֹּרֶן שָׁמִיר חֲרוּשָׁה
עַל־לוּחַ לִבָּם

---
d   See note to Isa. 65.7.
e   I.e., their lifeless idols.

ᵃ-And on the horns of their altars,

²While their children remember-*ᵃ*

Their altars and sacred posts,

By verdant trees,

Upon lofty hills.

³*ᵇ*-Because of the sin of your shrines

Throughout your borders,

I will make your rampart a heap in the field,

And all your treasures a spoil.-*ᵇ*

⁴*ᶜ*-You will forfeit,-*ᶜ* by your own act,

The inheritance I have given you;

I will make you a slave to your enemies

In a land you have never known.

For you have kindled the flame of My wrath

Which shall burn for all time.

⁵Thus said the LORD:

Cursed is he who trusts in man,

Who makes mere flesh his strength,

And turns his thoughts from the LORD.

⁶He shall be like a bush*ᵈ* in the desert,

Which does not sense the coming of good:

It is set in the scorched places of the wilder-
    ness,

In a barren land without inhabitant.

⁷Blessed is he who trusts in the LORD,

Whose trust is the LORD alone.

⁸He shall be like a tree planted by waters,

Sending forth its roots by a stream:

It does not sense the coming of heat,

Its leaves are ever fresh;

It has no care in a year of drought,

It does not cease to yield fruit.

⁹Most devious is the heart;

It is perverse—who can fathom it?

¹⁰I the LORD probe the heart,

וּלְקַרְנ֖וֹת מִזְבְּחוֹתֵיכֶֽם׃

2 כִּזְכֹּ֤ר בְּנֵיהֶם֙

מִזְבְּחוֹתָ֖ם וַאֲשֵׁרֵיהֶ֑ם

עַל־עֵ֥ץ רַעֲנָ֖ן

עַ֥ל גְּבָע֖וֹת הַגְּבֹהֽוֹת׃

3 הֲרָרִי֙ בַּשָּׂדֶ֔ה

חֵילְךָ֥ כָל־אוֹצְרוֹתֶ֖יךָ לָבַ֣ז אֶתֵּ֑ן

בָּמֹתֶ֖יךָ בְּחַטָּ֑את

בְּכָל־גְּבוּלֶֽיךָ׃

4 וְשָׁמַטְתָּ֗ה וּבְךָ֙

מִנַּחֲלָֽתְךָ֙ אֲשֶׁ֣ר נָתַ֣תִּי לָ֔ךְ

וְהַעֲבַדְתִּ֙יךָ֙ אֶת־אֹ֣יְבֶ֔יךָ

בָּאָ֖רֶץ אֲשֶׁ֣ר לֹא־יָדָ֑עְתָּ

כִּי־אֵ֛שׁ קְדַחְתֶּ֥ם בְּאַפִּ֖י

עַד־עוֹלָ֥ם תּוּקָֽד׃ ס

5 כֹּ֣ה ׀ אָמַ֣ר יְהֹוָ֗ה

אָר֤וּר הַגֶּ֙בֶר֙ אֲשֶׁ֣ר יִבְטַ֣ח בָּֽאָדָ֔ם

וְשָׂ֥ם בָּשָׂ֖ר זְרֹע֑וֹ

וּמִן־יְהֹוָ֖ה יָס֥וּר לִבּֽוֹ׃

6 וְהָיָה֙ כְּעַרְעָ֣ר בָּֽעֲרָבָ֔ה

וְלֹ֥א יִרְאֶ֖ה כִּי־יָב֣וֹא ט֑וֹב

וְשָׁכַ֤ן חֲרֵרִים֙ בַּמִּדְבָּ֔ר

אֶ֥רֶץ מְלֵחָ֖ה וְלֹ֥א תֵשֵֽׁב׃ ס

7 בָּר֣וּךְ הַגֶּ֔בֶר אֲשֶׁ֥ר יִבְטַ֖ח בַּֽיהֹוָ֑ה

וְהָיָ֥ה יְהֹוָ֖ה מִבְטַחֽוֹ׃

8 וְהָיָ֣ה כְּעֵ֣ץ ׀ שָׁת֣וּל עַל־מַ֗יִם

וְעַל־יוּבַל֙ יְשַׁלַּ֣ח שׇׁרָשָׁ֔יו

וְלֹ֤א יִרְא֙ כִּי־יָבֹ֣א חֹ֔ם

וְהָיָ֥ה עָלֵ֖הוּ רַֽעֲנָ֑ן

וּבִשְׁנַ֤ת בַּצֹּ֙רֶת֙ לֹ֣א יִדְאָ֔ג

וְלֹ֥א יָמִ֖ישׁ מֵעֲשׂ֥וֹת פֶּֽרִי׃

9 עָקֹ֥ב הַלֵּ֖ב מִכֹּ֑ל

וְאָנֻ֥שׁ ה֖וּא מִ֥י יֵדָעֶֽנּוּ׃

10 אֲנִ֧י יְהֹוָ֛ה חֹקֵ֥ר לֵ֖ב

---

a-a   Meaning of Heb. uncertain. Emendation yields "Surely the
      horns of their altars / Are as a memorial against them."

b-b   Meaning of Heb. uncertain.

c-c   Meaning of Heb. uncertain. Emendation yields "Your hand
      must let go."

d   Or "tamarisk"; exact meaning of Heb. uncertain.

Search the mind—
To repay every man according to his ways,
With the proper fruit of his deeds.

11 b-Like a partridge hatching what she did not
    lay,-b
So is one who amasses wealth by unjust
    means;
In the middle of his life it will leave him,
And in the end he will be proved a fool.

12 O Throne of Glory exalted from of old,
Our Sacred Shrine!
13 O Hope of Israel! O Lord!
All who forsake You shall be put to shame,
Those in the land who turn from You e
Shall be doomed f men,
For they have forsaken the Lord,
The Fount of living waters.

14 Heal me, O Lord, and let me be healed;
Save me, and let me be saved;
For You are my glory.
15 See, they say to me:
"Where is the prediction of the Lord?
Let it come to pass!"
16 But I have not g-evaded
Being a shepherd in your service,-g
Nor have I longed for the fatal day.
You know the utterances of my lips,
They were ever before You.
17 Do not be a cause of dismay to me;
You are my refuge in a day of calamity.
18 Let my persecutors be shamed,
And let not me be shamed;
Let them be dismayed,
And let not me be dismayed.
Bring on them the day of disaster,
And shatter them with double destruction.

בֹּחֵן כְּלָיֹות
וְלָתֵת לְאִישׁ כדרכו כִּדְרָכָ֔יו
כִּפְרִ֖י מַעֲלָלָֽיו׃ ס

11 קֹרֵא דָגַר וְלֹא יָלָ֔ד
עֹ֤שֶׂה עֹ֙שֶׁר֙ וְלֹ֣א בְמִשְׁפָּ֔ט
בַּחֲצִ֤י יָמָיו֙ יַעַזְבֶ֔נּוּ
וּבְאַחֲרִיתֹ֖ו יִהְיֶ֥ה נָבָֽל׃

12 כִּסֵּ֣א כָבֹ֔וד מָרֹ֖ום מֵֽרִאשֹׁ֑ון
מְקֹ֖ום מִקְדָּשֵֽׁנוּ׃

13 מִקְוֵ֨ה יִשְׂרָאֵ֜ל יְהוָ֗ה
כָּל־עֹזְבֶ֖יךָ יֵבֹ֑שׁוּ
יְסוּרַי֙ וְסוּרַ֣י בָּאָ֣רֶץ
יִכָּתֵ֔בוּ
כִּ֣י עָזְב֗וּ
מְקֹ֥ור מַֽיִם־חַיִּ֖ים אֶת־יְהוָֽה׃ ס

14 רְפָאֵ֤נִי יְהוָה֙ וְאֵ֣רָפֵ֔א
הֹושִׁיעֵ֖נִי וְאִוָּשֵׁ֑עָה
כִּ֥י תְהִלָּתִ֖י אָֽתָּה׃

15 הִנֵּה־הֵ֕מָּה אֹמְרִ֖ים אֵלָ֑י
אַיֵּ֥ה דְבַר־יְהוָ֖ה
יָ֥בֹוא נָֽא׃

16 וַאֲנִ֞י לֹא־אַ֣צְתִּי ׀
מֵרֹעֶ֣ה אַחֲרֶ֗יךָ
וְיֹ֥ום אָנ֛וּשׁ לֹ֥א הִתְאַוֵּ֖יתִי
אַתָּ֣ה יָדָ֑עְתָּ מֹוצָ֣א שְׂפָתַ֔י
נֹ֥כַח פָּנֶ֖יךָ הָיָֽה׃

17 אַל־תִּֽהְיֵה־לִ֖י לִמְחִתָּ֑ה
מַחֲסִי־אַ֖תָּה בְּיֹ֥ום רָעָֽה׃

18 יֵבֹ֤שׁוּ רֹֽדְפַי֙
וְאַל־אֵבֹ֣שָׁה אָ֔נִי
יֵחַ֣תּוּ הֵ֔מָּה
וְאַל־אֵחַ֖תָּה אָ֑נִי
הָבִ֤יא עֲלֵיהֶם֙ יֹ֣ום רָעָ֔ה
וּמִשְׁנֶ֥ה שִׁבָּרֹ֖ון שָׁבְרֵֽם׃ ס

---

e   Lit. "Me."
f   Lit. "inscribed"; meaning of line uncertain.
g-g   Exact force of Heb. uncertain. Emendation yields "urged you
      to [bring] misfortune."

¹⁹Thus said the LORD to me: Go and stand in the People's Gate, by which the kings of Judah enter and by which they go forth, and in all the gates of Jerusalem, ²⁰and say to them: Hear the word of the LORD, O kings of Judah, and all Judah, and all the inhabitants of Jerusalem who enter by these gates!

²¹Thus said the LORD: Guard yourselves for your own sake against carrying burdens^h on the sabbath day, and bringing them through the gates of Jerusalem. ²²Nor shall you carry out burdens from your houses on the sabbath day, or do any work, but you shall hallow the sabbath day, as I commanded your fathers. (²³But they would not listen or turn their ear; they stiffened their necks and would not pay heed or accept discipline.) ²⁴If you obey Me—declares the LORD—and do not bring in burdens through the gates of this city on the sabbath day, but hallow the sabbath day and do no work on it, ²⁵then through the gates of this city shall enter kings who sit upon the throne of David, with their officers—riding on chariots and horses, they and their officers—and the men of Judah and the inhabitants of Jerusalem. And this city shall be inhabited for all time. ²⁶And people shall come from the towns of Judah and from the environs of Jerusalem, and from the land of Benjamin, and from the Shephelah, and from the hill country, and from the Negeb, bringing burnt offerings and sacrifices, meal offerings and frankincense, and bringing offerings of thanksgiving to the House of the LORD. ²⁷But if you do not obey My command to hallow the sabbath day and to carry in no burdens through the gates of Jerusalem on the sabbath day, then I will set fire to its gates; it shall consume the fortresses of Jerusalem and it shall not be extinguished.

---

h · Or "merchandise."

---

19 כֹּה־אָמַ֨ר יְהוָ֜ה אֵלַ֗י הָלֹךְ֙ וְעָֽמַדְתָּ֙ בְּשַׁ֣עַר בְּנֵֽי־עָ֗ם אֲשֶׁ֨ר יָבֹ֤אוּ בוֹ֙ מַלְכֵ֣י יְהוּדָ֔ה וַאֲשֶׁ֖ר יֵ֣צְאוּ ב֑וֹ וּבְכֹ֖ל שַׁעֲרֵ֥י יְרוּשָׁלָֽ͏ִם׃ 20 וְאָמַרְתָּ֣ אֲלֵיהֶ֗ם שִׁמְע֤וּ דְבַר־יְהוָה֙ מַלְכֵ֣י יְהוּדָ֔ה וְכָל־יְהוּדָ֖ה וְכֹ֣ל יֹשְׁבֵ֣י יְרוּשָׁלָ֑͏ִם הַבָּאִ֖ים בַּשְּׁעָרִ֥ים הָאֵֽלֶּה׃ ס 21 כֹּ֚ה אָמַ֣ר יְהוָ֔ה הִשָּׁמְר֖וּ בְּנַפְשֽׁוֹתֵיכֶ֑ם וְאַל־תִּשְׂא֤וּ מַשָּׂא֙ בְּי֣וֹם הַשַּׁבָּ֔ת וַהֲבֵאתֶ֖ם בְּשַׁעֲרֵ֥י יְרוּשָׁלָֽ͏ִם׃ 22 וְלֹא־תוֹצִ֨יאוּ מַשָּׂ֤א מִבָּתֵּיכֶם֙ בְּי֣וֹם הַשַּׁבָּ֔ת וְכָל־מְלָאכָ֖ה לֹ֣א תַֽעֲשׂ֑וּ וְקִדַּשְׁתֶּם֙ אֶת־י֣וֹם הַשַּׁבָּ֔ת כַּאֲשֶׁ֥ר צִוִּ֖יתִי אֶת־אֲבוֹתֵיכֶֽם׃ 23 וְלֹ֤א שָֽׁמְעוּ֙ וְלֹ֣א הִטּ֣וּ אֶת־אָזְנָ֔ם וַיַּקְשׁוּ֙ אֶת־עָרְפָּ֔ם לְבִלְתִּ֣י שׁוֹמֵ֔עַ וּלְבִלְתִּ֖י קַ֥חַת מוּסָֽר׃ 24 וְ֠הָיָ֠ה אִם־שָׁמֹ֨עַ תִּשְׁמְע֤וּן אֵלַי֙ נְאֻם־יְהוָ֔ה לְבִלְתִּ֣י ׀ הָבִ֣יא מַשָּׂ֗א בְּשַׁעֲרֵ֛י הָעִ֥יר הַזֹּ֖את בְּי֣וֹם הַשַּׁבָּ֑ת וּלְקַדֵּשׁ֙ אֶת־י֣וֹם הַשַּׁבָּ֔ת לְבִלְתִּ֥י עֲשֽׂוֹת־בֹּ֖ה כָּל־מְלָאכָֽה׃ 25 וּבָ֣אוּ בְשַׁעֲרֵ֣י הָעִ֣יר הַזֹּ֡את מְלָכִ֣ים ׀ וְשָׂרִ֡ים יֹשְׁבִים֩ עַל־כִּסֵּ֨א דָוִ֜ד רֹכְבִ֣ים ׀ בָּרֶ֣כֶב וּבַסּוּסִ֗ים הֵ֚מָּה וְשָׂ֣רֵיהֶ֔ם אִ֥ישׁ יְהוּדָ֖ה וְיֹשְׁבֵ֣י יְרוּשָׁלָ֑͏ִם וְיָשְׁבָ֥ה הָעִֽיר־הַזֹּ֖את לְעוֹלָֽם׃ 26 וּבָ֣אוּ מֵעָרֵֽי־יְ֠הוּדָ֠ה וּמִסְּבִיב֨וֹת יְרוּשָׁלַ֜͏ִם וּמֵאֶ֣רֶץ בִּנְיָמִ֗ן וּמִן־הַשְּׁפֵלָ֤ה וּמִן־הָהָר֙ וּמִן־הַנֶּ֔גֶב מְבִאִ֛ים עוֹלָ֥ה וְזֶ֖בַח וּמִנְחָ֣ה וּלְבוֹנָ֑ה וּמְבִאֵ֥י תוֹדָ֖ה בֵּ֥ית יְהוָֽה׃ 27 וְאִם־לֹ֣א תִשְׁמְע֣וּ אֵלַ֗י לְקַדֵּשׁ֙ אֶת־י֣וֹם הַשַּׁבָּ֔ת וּלְבִלְתִּ֣י ׀ שְׂאֵ֣ת מַשָּׂ֗א וּבֹ֛א בְּשַׁעֲרֵ֥י יְרוּשָׁלַ֖͏ִם בְּי֣וֹם הַשַּׁבָּ֑ת וְהִצַּ֧תִּי אֵ֣שׁ בִּשְׁעָרֶ֗יהָ וְאָֽכְלָ֛ה אַרְמְנ֥וֹת יְרוּשָׁלַ֖͏ִם וְלֹ֥א תִכְבֶּֽה׃ פ

18

The word which came to Jeremiah from the LORD: [2]"Go down to the house of a potter, and there I will impart My words to you." [3]So I went down to the house of a potter, and found him working at the wheel. [4a]-And if the vessel he was making was spoiled, as happens to clay in the potter's hands,-[a] he would make it into another vessel, such as the potter saw fit to make.

[5]Then the word of the LORD came to me: [6]O House of Israel, can I not deal with you like this potter?—says the LORD. Just like clay in the hands of the potter, so are you in My hands, O House of Israel! [7]At one moment I may decree that a nation or a kingdom shall be uprooted and pulled down and destroyed; [8]but if that nation against which I made the decree turns back from its wickedness, I change My mind concerning the punishment I planned to bring on it. [9]At another moment I may decree that a nation or a kingdom shall be built and planted; [10]but if it does what is displeasing to Me and does not obey Me, then I change My mind concerning the good I planned to bestow upon it.

[11]And now, say to the men of Judah and the inhabitants of Jerusalem: Thus said the LORD: I am devising[b] disaster for you and laying plans against you. Turn back, each of you, from your wicked ways, and mend your ways and your actions! [12]But they will say, "It is no use. We will keep on following our own plans; each of us will act in the willfulness of his evil heart."

[13]Assuredly, thus said the LORD:
Inquire among the nations:
Who has heard anything like this?
Maiden Israel has done
A most horrible thing.

יח הַדָּבָר֙ אֲשֶׁ֣ר הָיָ֣ה אֶֽל־יִרְמְיָ֔הוּ מֵאֵ֥ת יְהוָ֖ה לֵאמֹֽר: [2]ק֥וּם וְיָרַדְתָּ֖ בֵּ֣ית הַיּוֹצֵ֑ר וְשָׁ֖מָּה אַשְׁמִֽיעֲךָ֥ אֶת־דְּבָרָֽי: [3]וָאֵרֵ֖ד בֵּ֣ית הַיּוֹצֵ֑ר והנהו וְהִנֵּה־ה֛וּא עֹשֶׂ֥ה מְלָאכָ֖ה עַל־הָאָבְנָֽיִם: [4]וְנִשְׁחַ֣ת הַכְּלִ֗י אֲשֶׁ֨ר ה֥וּא עֹשֶׂ֛ה בַּחֹ֖מֶר* בְּיַ֣ד הַיּוֹצֵ֑ר וְשָׁ֗ב וַֽיַּעֲשֵׂ֨הוּ֙ כְּלִ֣י אַחֵ֔ר כַּאֲשֶׁ֥ר יָשַׁ֛ר בְּעֵינֵ֥י הַיּוֹצֵ֖ר לַעֲשֽׂוֹת: פ

[5]וַיְהִ֥י דְבַר־יְהוָ֖ה אֵלַ֥י לֵאמֽוֹר*: [6]הֲכַיּוֹצֵ֨ר הַזֶּ֜ה לֹא־אוּכַ֨ל לַעֲשׂ֥וֹת לָכֶ֛ם בֵּ֥ית יִשְׂרָאֵ֖ל נְאֻם־יְהוָ֑ה הִנֵּ֤ה כַחֹ֨מֶר֙ בְּיַ֣ד הַיּוֹצֵ֔ר כֵּן־אַתֶּ֥ם בְּיָדִ֖י בֵּ֥ית יִשְׂרָאֵֽל: ס [7]רֶ֣גַע אֲדַבֵּ֗ר עַל־גּ֤וֹי וְעַל־מַמְלָכָ֔ה לִנְת֥וֹשׁ וְלִנְת֖וֹץ וּֽלְהַאֲבִֽיד: [8]וְשָׁב֙ הַגּ֣וֹי הַה֔וּא מֵרָ֣עָת֔וֹ אֲשֶׁ֥ר דִּבַּ֖רְתִּי עָלָ֑יו וְנִֽחַמְתִּי֙ עַל־הָ֣רָעָ֔ה אֲשֶׁ֥ר חָשַׁ֖בְתִּי לַעֲשׂ֥וֹת לֽוֹ: ס [9]וְרֶ֣גַע אֲדַבֵּ֗ר עַל־גּ֤וֹי וְעַל־מַמְלָכָ֔ה לִבְנֹ֖ת וְלִנְטֹֽעַ: [10]וְעָשָׂ֤ה הָרַע֙ הָרַ֔ע בְּעֵינַ֖י לְבִלְתִּ֣י שְׁמֹ֣עַ בְּקוֹלִ֑י וְנִֽחַמְתִּי֙ עַל־הַטּוֹבָ֔ה אֲשֶׁ֥ר אָמַ֖רְתִּי לְהֵיטִ֥יב אוֹתֽוֹ: ס

[11]וְעַתָּ֡ה אֱמָר־נָ֣א אֶל־אִישׁ־יְהוּדָה֩ וְעַל־יוֹשְׁבֵ֨י יְרוּשָׁלִַ֜ם לֵאמֹ֗ר כֹּ֚ה אָמַ֣ר יְהוָ֔ה הִנֵּ֨ה אָנֹכִ֜י יוֹצֵ֤ר עֲלֵיכֶם֙ רָעָ֔ה וְחֹשֵׁ֥ב עֲלֵיכֶ֖ם מַֽחֲשָׁבָ֑ה שׁ֣וּבוּ נָ֗א אִ֚ישׁ מִדַּרְכּ֣וֹ הָֽרָעָ֔ה וְהֵיטִ֥יבוּ דַרְכֵיכֶ֖ם וּמַעַלְלֵיכֶֽם: [12]וְאָמְר֖וּ נוֹאָ֑שׁ כִּֽי־אַחֲרֵ֤י מַחְשְׁבוֹתֵ֨ינוּ֙ נֵלֵ֔ךְ וְאִ֕ישׁ שְׁרִר֥וּת לִבּֽוֹ־הָרָ֖ע נַעֲשֶֽׂה: ס

[13]לָכֵ֗ן כֹּ֚ה אָמַ֣ר יְהוָ֔ה שַׁאֲלוּ־נָא֙ בַּגּוֹיִ֔ם מִ֥י שָׁמַ֖ע כָּאֵ֑לֶּה שַׁעֲרֻרִ֣ת עָשְׂתָ֥ה מְאֹ֖ד בְּתוּלַ֥ת יִשְׂרָאֵֽל:

---

a-a   *So some mss. and one early edition. Most mss. and editions read "And if the vessel that he was making with clay in the potter's hands was spoiled."*

b   *The same Hebrew word as is used above for "potter."*

v. 4.   בנוסח אחר "כחמר"

v. 5.   מלא ו׳

14cDoes one forsake Lebanon snow
From the mountainous rocks?
Does one abandon cool water
Flowing from afar?

15Yet My people have forgotten Me:
They sacrifice to a delusion:
They are made to stumble in their ways—
The ancient paths—
And to walk instead on byways,
On a road not built up.

16So their land will become a desolation,
An object of hissingd for all time.
Every passerby will be appalled
And will shake his head.d

17Like the east wind, I will scatter them
Before the enemy.
e-I will look upon their back, not their face,-e
In their day of disaster.

18They said,f "Come let us devise a plot
against Jeremiah—for instruction shall not fail
from the priest, nor counsel from the wise, nor
oracle from the prophet. Come, let us strike him
with the tongue, and we shall no longer have
to listen to all those words of his."

19Listen to me, O Lord—
And take note of g-what my enemies say!-g
20Should good be repaid with evil?
Yet they have dug a pit for me.
Remember how I stood before You
To plead in their behalf,
To turn Your anger away from them!
21Oh, give their children over to famine,
Mow them down by the sword.
Let their wives be bereaved
Of children and husbands,

14 הֲיַעֲזֹב מִצּוּר שָׂדַי
שֶׁלֶג לְבָנוֹן
אִם־יִנָּתְשׁוּ מַיִם זָרִים קָרִים
נוֹזְלִים:

15 כִּי־שְׁכֵחֻנִי עַמִּי
לַשָּׁוְא יְקַטֵּרוּ
וַיַּכְשִׁלוּם בְּדַרְכֵיהֶם
שְׁבִילֵי עוֹלָם
לָלֶכֶת נְתִיבוֹת
דֶּרֶךְ לֹא סְלוּלָה:

16 לָשׂוּם אַרְצָם לְשַׁמָּה
שְׁרוּקֹת עוֹלָם
כֹּל עוֹבֵר עָלֶיהָ יִשֹּׁם
וְיָנִיד בְּרֹאשׁוֹ:

17 כְּרוּחַ־קָדִים אֲפִיצֵם
לִפְנֵי אוֹיֵב
עֹרֶף וְלֹא־פָנִים אֶרְאֵם
בְּיוֹם אֵידָם: ס

18 וַיֹּאמְרוּ לְכוּ וְנַחְשְׁבָה עַל־יִרְמְיָהוּ
מַחֲשָׁבוֹת כִּי לֹא־תֹאבַד תּוֹרָה מִכֹּהֵן
וְעֵצָה מֵחָכָם וְדָבָר מִנָּבִיא לְכוּ וְנַכֵּהוּ
בַלָּשׁוֹן וְאַל־נַקְשִׁיבָה אֶל־כָּל־דְּבָרָיו:

19 הַקְשִׁיבָה יְהוָה אֵלָי
וּשְׁמַע לְקוֹל יְרִיבָי:

20 הַיְשֻׁלַּם תַּחַת־טוֹבָה רָעָה
כִּי־כָרוּ שׁוּחָה לְנַפְשִׁי
זְכֹר | עָמְדִי לְפָנֶיךָ
לְדַבֵּר עֲלֵיהֶם טוֹבָה
לְהָשִׁיב אֶת־חֲמָתְךָ מֵהֶם:

21 לָכֵן תֵּן אֶת־בְּנֵיהֶם לָרָעָב
וְהַגִּרֵם עַל־יְדֵי־חֶרֶב
וְתִהְיֶנָה נְשֵׁיהֶם שַׁכֻּלוֹת
וְאַלְמָנוֹת

---

c　Meaning of verse uncertain; cf. 2.13; 17.13.
d　These actions were performed at the sight of ruin to ward off a
　like fate from the observer; cf. Lam. 2.15.
e-e　Change of vocalization yields "I will show them [My] back and
　not [My] face."
f　Cf. 20.10.
g-g　Emendation yields "my case."

Let their men be struck down by the plague,
And their young men be slain in battle by the
sword.

22Let an outcry be heard from their houses
When You bring sudden marauders against
them;
For they have dug a pit to trap me,
And laid snares for my feet.

23O LORD, You know
All their plots to kill me.
Do not pardon their iniquity,
Do not blot out their guilt from Your presence.
Let them be made to stumble before You—
Act against them in Your hour of wrath!

19

Thus said the LORD: Go buy a jug of potter's ware. And [take] some of the elders of the people and the priests, 2and go out to the Valley of Ben-hinnom—a-at the entrance of the Harsith Gate-a—and proclaim there the words which I will speak to you.

3Say: "Hear the word of the LORD, O kings of Judah and inhabitants of Jerusalem! Thus said the LORD of Hosts, the God of Israel: I am going to bring such disaster upon this place that the ears of all who hear about it will tingle. 4For they and their fathers and the kings of Judah have forsaken Me, and have made this place alien [to Me]; they have sacrificed in it to other gods whom they have not experienced,b and they have filled this place with the blood of the innocent. 5They have built shrines to Baal, to put their children to the fire as burnt offerings to Baal—which I never commanded, never decreed, and which never came to My mind. 6Assuredly, a time is coming—declares the LORD—when this place shall no longer be called To-

וְאַנְשֵׁיהֶם יִהְיוּ הֲרֻגֵי מָוֶת
בַּחוּרֵיהֶם מֻכֵּי־חֶרֶב בַּמִּלְחָמָה:
22 תִּשָּׁמַע זְעָקָה מִבָּתֵּיהֶם
כִּי־תָבִיא עֲלֵיהֶם גְּדוּד פִּתְאֹם
כִּי־כָרוּ שִׁיחָה שׁוּחָה לְלָכְדֵנִי
וּפַחִים טָמְנוּ לְרַגְלָי:
23 וְאַתָּה יְהוָה יָדַעְתָּ
אֶת־כָּל־עֲצָתָם עָלַי לַמָּוֶת
אַל־תְּכַפֵּר עַל־עֲוֹנָם
וְחַטָּאתָם מִלְּפָנֶיךָ אַל־תֶּמְחִי
וְהָיוּ וְיִהְיוּ מֻכְשָׁלִים לְפָנֶיךָ
בְּעֵת אַפְּךָ עֲשֵׂה בָהֶם: ס

יט כֹּה אָמַר יְהוָה הָלוֹךְ וְקָנִיתָ בַקְבֻּק
יוֹצֵר חָרֶשׂ וּמִזִּקְנֵי הָעָם וּמִזִּקְנֵי הַכֹּהֲנִים:
2 וְיָצָאתָ אֶל־גֵּיא בֶן־הִנֹּם אֲשֶׁר פֶּתַח
שַׁעַר הַחֲרָסוּת הַחַרְסִית וְקָרָאתָ שָּׁם אֶת־
הַדְּבָרִים אֲשֶׁר־אֲדַבֵּר אֵלֶיךָ:
3 וְאָמַרְתָּ שִׁמְעוּ דְבַר־יְהוָה מַלְכֵי יְהוּדָה
וְיֹשְׁבֵי יְרוּשָׁלִָם כֹּה־אָמַר יְהוָה צְבָאוֹת
אֱלֹהֵי יִשְׂרָאֵל הִנְנִי מֵבִיא רָעָה עַל־
הַמָּקוֹם הַזֶּה אֲשֶׁר כָּל־שֹׁמְעָהּ תִּצַּלְנָה
אָזְנָיו: 4 יַעַן אֲשֶׁר עֲזָבֻנִי וַיְנַכְּרוּ אֶת־
הַמָּקוֹם הַזֶּה וַיְקַטְּרוּ־בוֹ לֵאלֹהִים אֲחֵרִים
אֲשֶׁר לֹא־יְדָעוּם הֵמָּה וַאֲבוֹתֵיהֶם וּמַלְכֵי
יְהוּדָה וּמָלְאוּ אֶת־הַמָּקוֹם הַזֶּה דַּם נְקִיִּם:
5 וּבָנוּ אֶת־בָּמוֹת הַבַּעַל לִשְׂרֹף אֶת־בְּנֵיהֶם
בָּאֵשׁ עֹלוֹת לַבָּעַל אֲשֶׁר לֹא־צִוִּיתִי וְלֹא
דִבַּרְתִּי וְלֹא עָלְתָה עַל־לִבִּי: פ 6 לָכֵן
הִנֵּה־יָמִים בָּאִים נְאֻם־יְהוָה וְלֹא־יִקָּרֵא

---

a-a Others "by way of the Potsherd Gate"; meaning of Heb.
    uncertain.
b See note at Deut. 11.28.

pheth or Valley of Ben-hinnom, but Valley of Slaughter.

7"And I will frustrate[c] the plans of Judah and Jerusalem in this place. I will cause them to fall by the sword before their enemies, by the hand of those who seek their lives; and I will give their carcasses as food to the birds of the sky and the beasts of the earth. 8And I will make this city an object of horror and hissing;[d] everyone who passes by it will be appalled and will hiss over all its wounds. 9And I will cause them to eat the flesh of their sons and the flesh of their daughters, and they shall devour one another's flesh—because of the desperate straits to which they will be reduced by their enemies, who seek their life."

10Then you shall smash the jug in the sight of the men who go with you, 11and say to them: "Thus said the LORD of Hosts: So will I smash this people and this city, as one smashes a potter's vessel, which can never be mended. And they shall bury in Topheth until no room is left for burying. 12That is what I will do to this place and its inhabitants—declares the LORD. I will make this city like Topheth: 13the houses of Jerusalem and the houses of the kings of Judah shall be unclean, like that place Topheth—all the houses on the roofs of which offerings were made to the whole host of heaven and libations were poured out to other gods."

14When Jeremiah returned from Topheth, where the LORD had sent him to prophesy, he stood in the court of the House of the LORD and said to all the people: 15"Thus said the LORD of Hosts, the God of Israel: I am going to bring upon this city and upon all its villages all the disaster which I have decreed against it, for they have stiffened their necks and refused to heed My words."

לַמָּק֣וֹם הַזֶּה֩ ע֨וֹד הַתֹּ֜פֶת וְגֵ֣יא בֶן־הִנֹּ֗ם כִּ֖י אִם־גֵּ֥יא הַהֲרֵגָֽה׃

7 וּבַקֹּתִ֗י אֶת־עֲצַ֤ת יְהוּדָה֙ וִיר֣וּשָׁלִַ֔ם בַּמָּק֖וֹם הַזֶּ֑ה וְהִפַּלְתִּ֤ים בַּחֶ֙רֶב֙ לִפְנֵ֣י אֹיְבֵיהֶ֔ם וּבְיַ֖ד מְבַקְשֵׁ֣י נַפְשָׁ֑ם וְנָתַתִּ֤י אֶת־נִבְלָתָם֙ לְמַֽאֲכָ֔ל לְע֥וֹף הַשָּׁמַ֖יִם וּלְבֶהֱמַ֥ת הָאָֽרֶץ׃ 8 וְשַׂמְתִּי֙ אֶת־הָעִ֣יר הַזֹּ֔את לְשַׁמָּ֖ה וְלִשְׁרֵקָ֑ה כֹּ֚ל עֹבֵ֣ר עָלֶ֔יהָ יִשֹּׁ֥ם וְיִשְׁרֹ֖ק עַל־כָּל־מַכֹּתֶֽהָ׃ 9 וְהַֽאֲכַלְתִּ֞ים אֶת־בְּשַׂ֣ר בְּנֵיהֶ֗ם וְאֵת֙ בְּשַׂ֣ר בְּנֹֽתֵיהֶ֔ם וְאִ֥ישׁ בְּשַׂר־רֵעֵ֖הוּ יֹאכֵ֑לוּ בְּמָצוֹר֙ וּבְמָצ֔וֹק אֲשֶׁ֨ר יָצִ֧יקוּ לָהֶ֛ם אֹיְבֵיהֶ֖ם וּמְבַקְשֵׁ֥י נַפְשָֽׁם׃

10 וְשָׁבַרְתָּ֖ הַבַּקְבֻּ֑ק לְעֵינֵי֙ הָֽאֲנָשִׁ֔ים הַהֹלְכִ֖ים אוֹתָֽךְ׃ 11 וְאָמַרְתָּ֨ אֲלֵיהֶ֜ם כֹּה־אָמַ֣ר ׀ יְהוָ֣ה צְבָא֗וֹת כָּ֣כָה אֶשְׁבֹּ֞ר אֶת־הָעָ֤ם הַזֶּה֙ וְאֶת־הָעִ֣יר הַזֹּ֔את כַּאֲשֶׁ֤ר יִשְׁבֹּר֙ אֶת־כְּלִ֣י הַיּוֹצֵ֔ר אֲשֶׁ֛ר לֹֽא־יוּכַ֥ל לְהֵרָפֵ֖ה* ע֑וֹד וּבְתֹ֣פֶת יִקְבְּר֔וּ מֵאֵ֥ין מָק֖וֹם לִקְבּֽוֹר׃ 12 כֵּֽן־אֶעֱשֶׂ֞ה לַמָּק֥וֹם הַזֶּ֛ה נְאֻם־יְהוָ֖ה וּלְיֽוֹשְׁבָ֑יו וְלָתֵ֛ת אֶת־הָעִ֥יר הַזֹּ֖את כְּתֹֽפֶת׃ 13 וְהָי֞וּ בָּתֵּ֣י יְרוּשָׁלַ֗ם וּבָתֵּי֙ מַלְכֵ֣י יְהוּדָ֔ה כִּמְק֥וֹם הַתֹּ֖פֶת הַטְּמֵאִ֑ים לְכֹ֣ל הַבָּתִּ֗ים אֲשֶׁ֨ר קִטְּר֜וּ עַל־גַּגֹּֽתֵיהֶם֙ לְכֹל֙ צְבָ֣א הַשָּׁמַ֔יִם וְהַסֵּ֥ךְ נְסָכִ֖ים לֵאלֹהִ֥ים אֲחֵרִֽים׃ פ

14 וַיָּבֹ֤א יִרְמְיָ֙הוּ֙ מֵֽהַתֹּ֔פֶת אֲשֶׁ֨ר שְׁלָח֧וֹ יְהוָ֛ה שָׁ֖ם לְהִנָּבֵ֑א וַֽיַּעֲמֹד֙ בַּֽחֲצַ֣ר בֵּית־יְהוָ֔ה וַיֹּ֖אמֶר אֶל־כָּל־הָעָֽם׃ ס 15 כֹּֽה־אָמַ֞ר יְהוָ֤ה צְבָאוֹת֙ אֱלֹהֵ֣י יִשְׂרָאֵ֔ל הִנְנִ֨י מֵבִ֤יא אֶל־הָעִיר֙ הַזֹּ֔את וְעַל־כָּל־עָרֶ֔יהָ אֵ֚ת כָּל־הָ֣רָעָ֔ה אֲשֶׁ֥ר דִּבַּ֖רְתִּי עָלֶ֑יהָ כִּ֤י הִקְשׁוּ֙ אֶת־עָרְפָּ֔ם לְבִלְתִּ֖י שְׁמ֥וֹעַ אֶת־דְּבָרָֽי׃

v. 11. ה׳ במקום א׳

---

c   Lit. "empty," Heb. u-baqqothi, a play on baqbuq, "jug" in v. 1.
d   See note at 18.16.

20 Pashhur son of Immer, the priest who was chief officer of the House of the Lord, heard Jeremiah prophesy these things. ²Pashhur thereupon had Jeremiah flogged and put in the cell*a* at the Upper Benjamin Gate in the House of the Lord. ³The next day, Pashhur released Jeremiah from the cell.

But Jeremiah said to him, "The Lord has named you not Pashhur, but Magor-missabib.*b* ⁴For thus said the Lord: I am going to deliver you and all your friends over to terror: they will fall by the sword of their enemies while you look on. I will deliver all Judah into the hands of the king of Babylon; he will exile them to Babylon or put them to the sword. ⁵And I will deliver all the wealth, all the riches, and all the prized possessions of this city, and I will also deliver all the treasures of the kings of Judah into the hands of their enemies: they shall seize them as plunder and carry them off to Babylon. ⁶As for you, Pashhur, and all who live in your house, you shall go into captivity. You shall come to Babylon; there you shall die and there you shall be buried, and so shall all your friends to whom you prophesied falsely."

⁷You enticed me, O Lord, and I was enticed;
You overpowered me and You prevailed.
I have become a constant laughingstock,
Everyone jeers at me.
⁸For every time I speak, I must cry out,
Must shout, "Lawlessness and rapine!"
For the word of the Lord causes me
Constant disgrace and contempt.
⁹I thought, "I will not mention Him,
No more will I speak in His name"—
But [His word] was like a raging fire in my
    heart,
Shut up in my bones;

כ וַיִּשְׁמַ֣ע פַּשְׁח֔וּר בֶּן־אִמֵּ֖ר הַכֹּהֵ֑ן
וְהֽוּא־פָקִ֣יד נָגִ֔יד בְּבֵ֖ית יְהֹוָ֑ה אֶֽת־יִרְמְיָ֔הוּ
נִבָּ֖א אֶת־הַדְּבָרִ֥ים הָאֵֽלֶּה׃ ² וַיַּכֶּ֣ה פַשְׁח֔וּר
אֵ֖ת יִרְמְיָ֣הוּ הַנָּבִ֑יא וַיִּתֵּ֨ן אֹת֜וֹ עַל־
הַמַּהְפֶּ֗כֶת אֲשֶׁ֛ר בְּשַׁ֧עַר בִּנְיָמִ֛ן הָעֶלְי֖וֹן
אֲשֶׁ֣ר בְּבֵ֣ית יְהֹוָ֑ה ³ וַֽיְהִי֙ מִֽמׇּחֳרָ֔ת וַיֹּצֵ֧א
פַשְׁח֛וּר אֶֽת־יִרְמְיָ֖הוּ מִן־הַמַּהְפָּ֑כֶת
וַיֹּ֨אמֶר אֵלָ֜יו יִרְמְיָ֗הוּ לֹ֤א פַשְׁחוּר֙ קָרָ֣א
יְהֹוָ֣ה שְׁמֶ֔ךָ כִּ֖י אִם־מָג֥וֹר מִסָּבִֽיב׃ פ
⁴ כִּ֣י כֹ֣ה אָמַ֣ר יְהֹוָ֗ה הִנְנִ֨י נֹֽתֶנְךָ֤ לְמָגוֹר֙
לְךָ֣ וּלְכׇל־אֹ֣הֲבֶ֔יךָ וְנָ֣פְל֔וּ בְּחֶ֖רֶב אֹיְבֵיהֶ֑ם
וְעֵינֶ֖יךָ רֹא֑וֹת וְאֶת־כׇּל־יְהוּדָ֗ה אֶתֵּן֙ בְּיַ֣ד
מֶֽלֶךְ־בָּבֶ֔ל וְהִגְלָ֥ם בָּבֶ֖לָה וְהִכָּ֥ם בֶּחָֽרֶב׃
⁵ וְנָתַתִּ֗י אֶת־כׇּל־חֹ֣סֶן הָעִ֣יר הַזֹּ֔את וְאֶת־
כׇּל־יְגִיעָ֖הּ וְאֶת־כׇּל־יְקָרָ֑הּ וְאֵ֣ת כׇּל־
אוֹצְר֞וֹת מַלְכֵ֤י יְהוּדָה֙ אֶתֵּן֙ בְּיַ֣ד אֹֽיְבֵיהֶ֔ם
וּבְזָז֕וּם וּלְקָח֖וּם וֶהֱבִיא֥וּם בָּבֶֽלָה׃ ⁶ וְאַתָּ֣ה
פַשְׁח֗וּר וְכֹל֙ יֹשְׁבֵ֣י בֵיתֶ֔ךָ תֵּלְכ֖וּ בַּשֶּׁ֑בִי
וּבָבֶ֣ל תָּב֗וֹא וְשָׁ֤ם תָּמוּת֙ וְשָׁ֣ם תִּקָּבֵ֔ר
אַתָּה֙ וְכׇל־אֹ֣הֲבֶ֔יךָ אֲשֶׁר־נִבֵּ֥אתָ לָהֶ֖ם
בַּשָּֽׁקֶר׃ ס

⁷ פִּתִּיתַ֤נִי יְהֹוָה֙ וָֽאֶפָּ֔ת
חֲזַקְתַּ֖נִי וַתּוּכָ֑ל
הָיִ֤יתִי לִשְׂחוֹק֙ כׇּל־הַיּ֔וֹם
כֻּלֹּ֖ה לֹעֵ֥ג לִֽי׃
⁸ כִּֽי־מִדֵּ֤י אֲדַבֵּר֙ אֶזְעָ֔ק
חָמָ֥ס וָשֹׁ֖ד אֶקְרָ֑א
כִּֽי־הָיָ֨ה דְבַר־יְהֹוָ֥ה לִ֛י
לְחֶרְפָּ֥ה וּלְקֶ֖לֶס כׇּל־הַיּֽוֹם׃
⁹ וְאָמַרְתִּ֣י לֹֽא־אֶזְכְּרֶ֗נּוּ
וְלֹֽא־אֲדַבֵּ֥ר עוֹד֙ בִּשְׁמ֔וֹ
וְהָיָ֤ה בְלִבִּי֙ כְּאֵ֣שׁ בֹּעֶ֔רֶת
עָצֻ֖ר בְּעַצְמֹתָ֑י

---

a Meaning of Heb. uncertain.
b I.e., "Terror all around"; cf. v. 10.

I could not hold it in, I was helpless.
10I heard the whispers of the crowd—
Terror all around:
"Inform! Let us inform against him!"
All my [supposed] friends
Are waiting for me to stumble:
"Perhaps he can be entrapped,
And we can prevail against him
And take our vengeance on him."
11But the LORD is with me like a mighty war-
rior;
Therefore my persecutors shall stumble;
They shall not prevail and shall not succeed.
They shall be utterly shamed
With a humiliation for all time,
Which shall not be forgotten.
12O LORD of Hosts, You who test the right-
eous,
Who examine the heart and the mind,
Let me see Your retribution upon them,
For I lay my case before You.
13Sing unto the LORD,
Praise the LORD,
For He has rescued the needy
From the hands of evildoers!

14Accursed be the day
That I was born!
Let not the day be blessed
When my mother bore me!
15Accursed be the man
Who brought my father the news
And said, "A boy
Is born to you,"
And gave him such joy!
16Let that manᶜ become like the cities
Which the LORD overthrew without relent-
ing!
Let him hear shrieks in the morning
And battle shouts at noontide—

וְנִלְאֵ֥יתִי כַּֽלְכֵ֖ל וְלֹ֥א אוּכָֽל׃
10 כִּ֣י שָׁמַ֜עְתִּי דִּבַּ֣ת רַבִּים֮
מָג֣וֹר מִסָּבִיב֒
הַגִּ֙ידוּ֙ וְנַגִּידֶ֔נּוּ
כֹּ֚ל אֱנ֣וֹשׁ שְׁלוֹמִ֔י
שֹׁמְרֵ֖י צַלְעִ֑י
אוּלַ֤י יְפֻתֶּה֙
וְנ֣וּכְלָה ל֔וֹ
וְנִקְחָ֥ה נִקְמָתֵ֖נוּ מִמֶּֽנּוּ׃
11 וַֽיהוָ֤ה אוֹתִי֙ כְּגִבּ֣וֹר עָרִ֔יץ
עַל־כֵּ֛ן רֹדְפַ֥י יִכָּשְׁל֖וּ
וְלֹ֣א יֻכָ֑לוּ
בֹּ֤שׁוּ מְאֹד֙ כִּֽי־לֹ֣א הִשְׂכִּ֔ילוּ
כְּלִמַּ֥ת עוֹלָ֖ם
לֹ֥א תִשָּׁכֵֽחַ׃
12 וַיהוָ֤ה צְבָאוֹת֙ בֹּחֵ֣ן צַדִּ֔יק
רֹאֶ֖ה כְלָי֣וֹת וָלֵ֑ב
אֶרְאֶ֤ה נִקְמָֽתְךָ֙ מֵהֶ֔ם
כִּ֥י אֵלֶ֖יךָ גִּלִּ֥יתִי אֶת־רִיבִֽי׃ ס
13 שִׁ֖ירוּ לַֽיהוָ֑ה
הַֽלְל֖וּ אֶת־יְהוָ֑ה
כִּ֥י הִצִּ֛יל אֶת־נֶ֥פֶשׁ אֶבְי֖וֹן
מִיַּ֥ד מְרֵעִֽים׃ ס

14 אָר֣וּר הַיּ֔וֹם
אֲשֶׁ֥ר יֻלַּ֖דְתִּי בּ֑וֹ
י֛וֹם אֲשֶׁר־יְלָדַ֥תְנִי אִמִּ֖י
אַל־יְהִ֥י בָרֽוּךְ׃
15 אָר֣וּר הָאִ֗ישׁ
אֲשֶׁ֨ר בִּשַּׂ֤ר אֶת־אָבִי֙
לֵאמֹ֔ר יֻֽלַּד־לְךָ֖
בֵּ֣ן זָכָ֑ר
שַׂמֵּ֖חַ שִׂמֳּחָֽהוּ׃
16 וְהָיָה֙ הָאִ֣ישׁ הַה֔וּא כֶּֽעָרִ֕ים
אֲשֶׁר־הָפַ֥ךְ יְהוָ֖ה וְלֹ֣א נִחָ֑ם
וְשָׁמַ֤ע זְעָקָה֙ בַּבֹּ֔קֶר
וּתְרוּעָ֖ה בְּעֵ֥ת צָהֳרָֽיִם׃

c *Emendation yields "day."*

17Because he did not kill me before birth
So that my mother might be my grave,
And her womb big [with me] for all time.
18Why did I ever issue from the womb,
To see misery and woe,
To spend all my days in shame!

17 אֲשֶׁ֥ר לֹא־מוֹתְתַ֖נִי מֵרָ֑חֶם
וַתְּהִי־לִ֤י אִמִּי֙ קִבְרִ֔י
וְרַחְמָ֖ה* הֲרַ֥ת עוֹלָֽם׃
18 לָ֤מָּה זֶּה֙ מֵרֶ֣חֶם יָצָ֔אתִי
לִרְא֥וֹת עָמָ֖ל וְיָג֑וֹן
וַיִּכְל֥וּ בְּבֹ֖שֶׁת יָמָֽי׃ פ

21 The word which came to Jeremiah from the LORD, when King Zedekiah sent to him Pashhur son of Malchiah and the priest Zephaniah, son of Maaseiah, to say, 2"Please inquire of the LORD on our behalf, for King Nebuchadrezzar of Babylon is attacking us. Perhaps the LORD will act for our sake in accordance with all His wonders, so that [Nebuchadrezzar] will withdraw from us."

3Jeremiah answered them, "Thus shall you say to Zedekiah: 4Thus said the LORD, the God of Israel: I am going to turn around the weapons in your hands with which you are battling outside the wall against those who are besieging you—the king of Babylon and the Chaldeans—and I will take them into the midst of this city; 5and I Myself will battle against you with an outstretched mighty arm, with anger and rage and great wrath. 6I will strike the inhabitants of this city, man and beast: they shall die by a terrible pestilence. 7And then—declares the LORD—I will deliver King Zedekiah of Judah and his courtiers and the people—those in this city who survive the pestilence, the sword, and the famine—into the hands of King Nebuchadrezzar of Babylon, into the hands of their enemies, into the hands of those who seek their lives. He will put them to the sword without pity, without compassion, without mercy.

8"And to this people you shall say: Thus said the LORD: I set before you the way of life and the way of death. 9Whoever remains in this city

כא הַדָּבָ֛ר אֲשֶׁר־הָיָ֥ה אֶֽל־יִרְמְיָ֖הוּ מֵאֵ֣ת יְהֹוָ֑ה בִּשְׁלֹ֨חַ אֵלָ֜יו הַמֶּ֣לֶךְ צִדְקִיָּ֗הוּ אֶת־פַּשְׁחוּר֙ בֶּן־מַלְכִּיָּ֔ה וְאֶת־צְפַנְיָ֥ה בֶן־מַעֲשֵׂיָ֖ה הַכֹּהֵ֣ן לֵאמֹֽר׃ 2 דְּרׇשׁ־נָ֤א בַעֲדֵ֙נוּ֙ אֶת־יְהֹוָ֔ה כִּ֛י נְבוּכַדְרֶאצַּ֥ר מֶלֶךְ־בָּבֶ֖ל נִלְחָ֣ם עָלֵ֑ינוּ אוּלַי֩ יַעֲשֶׂ֨ה יְהֹוָ֤ה אוֹתָ֙נוּ֙ כְּכׇל־נִפְלְאֹתָ֔יו וְיַעֲלֶ֖ה מֵעָלֵֽינוּ׃ ס 3 וַיֹּ֥אמֶר יִרְמְיָ֖הוּ אֲלֵיהֶ֑ם כֹּ֥ה תֹאמְרֻ֖ן אֶל־צִדְקִיָּֽהוּ׃ 4 כֹּֽה־אָמַ֨ר יְהֹוָ֜ה אֱלֹהֵ֣י יִשְׂרָאֵ֗ל הִנְנִ֣י מֵסֵב֮ אֶת־כְּלֵ֣י הַמִּלְחָמָה֒ אֲשֶׁ֣ר בְּיֶדְכֶ֗ם אֲשֶׁ֨ר אַתֶּ֜ם נִלְחָמִ֣ים בָּ֗ם אֶת־מֶ֤לֶךְ בָּבֶל֙ וְאֶת־הַכַּשְׂדִּ֔ים הַצָּרִ֣ים עֲלֵיכֶ֔ם מִח֖וּץ לַחוֹמָ֑ה וְאָסַפְתִּ֣י אוֹתָ֔ם אֶל־תּ֖וֹךְ הָעִ֥יר הַזֹּֽאת׃ 5 וְנִלְחַמְתִּ֤י אֲנִי֙ אִתְּכֶ֔ם בְּיָ֥ד נְטוּיָ֖ה וּבִזְר֣וֹעַ חֲזָקָ֑ה וּבְאַ֥ף וּבְחֵמָ֖ה וּבְקֶ֥צֶף גָּדֽוֹל׃ 6 וְהִכֵּיתִ֗י אֶת־יֽוֹשְׁבֵי֙ הָעִ֣יר הַזֹּ֔את וְאֶת־הָאָדָ֖ם וְאֶת־הַבְּהֵמָ֑ה בְּדֶ֥בֶר גָּד֖וֹל יָמֻֽתוּ׃ 7 וְאַחֲרֵי־כֵ֣ן נְאֻם־יְהֹוָ֡ה אֶתֵּ֣ן אֶת־צִדְקִיָּ֣הוּ מֶֽלֶךְ־יְהוּדָ֣ה וְאֶת־עֲבָדָ֣יו ׀ וְאֶת־הָעָ֡ם וְאֶת־הַנִּשְׁאָרִים֩ בָּעִ֨יר הַזֹּ֜את מִן־הַדֶּ֣בֶר ׀ מִן־הַחֶ֣רֶב וּמִן־הָרָעָ֗ב בְּיַד֙ נְבוּכַדְרֶאצַּ֣ר מֶֽלֶךְ־בָּבֶ֔ל וּבְיַד֙ אֹֽיְבֵיהֶ֔ם וּבְיַ֖ד מְבַקְשֵׁ֣י נַפְשָׁ֑ם וְהִכָּ֣ם לְפִי־חֶ֔רֶב לֹֽא־יָח֣וּס עֲלֵיהֶ֔ם וְלֹ֥א יַחְמֹ֖ל וְלֹ֥א יְרַחֵֽם׃ 8 וְאֶל־הָעָ֤ם הַזֶּה֙ תֹּאמַ֔ר כֹּ֖ה אָמַ֣ר יְהֹוָ֑ה הִנְנִ֤י נֹתֵן֙ לִפְנֵיכֶ֔ם אֶת־דֶּ֥רֶךְ הַחַיִּ֖ים וְאֶת־דֶּ֥רֶךְ הַמָּֽוֶת׃ 9 הַיֹּשֵׁב֙ בָּעִ֣יר הַזֹּ֔את יָמ֕וּת

shall die by the sword, by famine, and by pestilence; but whoever leaves and goes over to the Chaldeans who are besieging you shall live; *a-he shall at least gain his life.-a* ¹⁰For I have set My face against this city for evil and not for good—declares the LORD. It shall be delivered into the hands of the king of Babylon, who will destroy it by fire."

¹¹To the House of the king of Judah: Hear the word of the LORD! ¹²O House of David, thus said the LORD:

Render just verdicts
Morning by morning;
Rescue him who is robbed
From him who defrauded him.
Else My wrath will break forth like fire
And burn, with none to quench it,
Because of your wicked acts.

¹³I will deal with you, *b-O inhabitants of the valley,
O rock of the plain-b*—declares the LORD—
You who say, "Who can come down against us?
Who can get into our lairs?"

¹⁴I will punish you according to your deeds
           —declares the LORD.
I will set fire to its forest;*c*
It shall consume all that is around it.

22 Thus said the LORD: Go down to the palace of the king of Judah, where you shall utter this word. ²Say: "Hear the word of the LORD: O king of Judah, you who sit on the throne of David, and your courtiers and your subjects who enter these gates! ³Thus said the LORD: Do what is just and right; rescue from the defrauder him who is robbed; do not wrong the stranger,

---

בַּחֶ֖רֶב וּבָרָעָ֣ב וּבַדָּ֑בֶר וְהַיּוֹצֵ֡א וְנָפַ֣ל עַל־
הַכַּשְׂדִּ֨ים הַצָּרִ֤ים עֲלֵיכֶם֙ יחיה וְחָ֣יָה
וְהָיְתָה־לּ֥וֹ נַפְשׁ֖וֹ לְשָׁלָֽל׃ 10 כִּ֣י שַׂ֣מְתִּי פָנַ֣י
בָּעִ֨יר הַזֹּ֧את לְרָעָ֛ה וְלֹ֥א לְטוֹבָ֖ה נְאֻם־
יְהֹוָ֑ה בְּיַד־מֶ֤לֶךְ בָּבֶל֙ תִּנָּתֵ֔ן וּשְׂרָפָ֖הּ
בָּאֵֽשׁ׃ ס

11 וּלְבֵית֙ מֶ֣לֶךְ יְהוּדָ֔ה שִׁמְע֖וּ דְּבַר־יְהֹוָֽה׃
12 בֵּ֣ית דָּוִ֗ד כֹּ֚ה אָמַ֣ר יְהֹוָ֔ה
דִּ֣ינוּ
לַבֹּ֙קֶר֙ מִשְׁפָּ֔ט
וְהַצִּ֥ילוּ גָז֖וּל
מִיַּ֣ד עוֹשֵׁ֑ק
פֶּן־תֵּצֵ֨א כָאֵ֜שׁ חֲמָתִ֗י
וּבָעֲרָה֙ וְאֵ֣ין מְכַבֶּ֔ה
מִפְּנֵ֖י רֹ֣עַ מעלליהם מַעַלְלֵיכֶֽם׃
13 הִנְנִ֨י אֵלַ֜יִךְ יֹשֶׁ֤בֶת הָעֵ֙מֶק֙
צ֥וּר הַמִּישֹׁ֖ר נְאֻם־יְהֹוָ֑ה
הָאֹֽמְרִים֙ מִֽי־יֵחַ֣ת עָלֵ֔ינוּ
וּמִ֥י יָב֖וֹא בִּמְעוֹנוֹתֵֽינוּ׃
14 וּפָקַדְתִּ֧י עֲלֵיכֶ֛ם כִּפְרִ֥י מַעַלְלֵיכֶ֖ם
נְאֻם־יְהֹוָ֑ה
וְהִצַּ֥תִּי אֵ֖שׁ בְּיַעְרָ֑הּ
וְאָכְלָ֖ה כָּל־סְבִיבֶֽיהָ׃ ס

כב כֹּ֚ה אָמַ֣ר יְהֹוָ֔ה רֵ֖ד בֵּית־מֶ֣לֶךְ
יְהוּדָ֑ה וְדִבַּרְתָּ֣ שָׁ֔ם אֶת־הַדָּבָ֖ר הַזֶּֽה׃
2 וְאָֽמַרְתָּ֗ שְׁמַ֤ע דְּבַר־יְהֹוָה֙ מֶ֣לֶךְ יְהוּדָ֔ה
הַיֹּשֵׁ֖ב עַל־כִּסֵּ֣א דָוִ֑ד אַתָּ֤ה וַעֲבָדֶ֙יךָ֙ וְעַמְּךָ֔
הַבָּאִ֖ים בַּשְּׁעָרִ֥ים הָאֵֽלֶּה׃ ס 3 כֹּ֣ה ׀
אָמַ֣ר יְהֹוָ֗ה עֲשׂ֤וּ מִשְׁפָּט֙ וּצְדָקָ֔ה וְהַצִּ֥ילוּ
גָז֖וּל מִיַּ֣ד עָשׁ֑וֹק וְגֵר֩ יָת֨וֹם וְאַלְמָנָ֤ה אַל־

---

a-a Lit. "he shall have his life as booty."
b-b Force of Heb. uncertain.
c Perhaps a reference to the royal palace; cf. 1 Kings 7.2.

1062

the fatherless, and the widow; commit no law-less act, and do not shed the blood of the in-nocent in this place. 4For if you fulfill this com-mand, then through the gates of this palace shall enter kings of David's line who sit upon his throne, riding horse-drawn chariots, with their courtiers and their subjects. 5But if you do not heed these commands, I swear by Myself—declares the LORD—that this palace shall be-come a ruin."

6For thus said the LORD concerning the royal palace of Judah:

You are as Gilead to Me,
As the summit of Lebanon;
But I will make you a desert,
Uninhabited towns.

7I will appoint destroyers against you,
Each with his tools;
They shall cut down your choicest cedars
And make them fall into the fire.

8And when many nations pass by this city and one man asks another, "Why did the LORD do thus to that great city?" 9the reply will be, "Be-cause they forsook the covenant with the LORD their God and bowed down to other gods and served them."

10Do not weep for the dead*a*
And do not lament for him;
Weep rather for *b-*him who is leaving,*-b*
For he shall never come back
To see the land of his birth!

11For thus said the LORD concerning Shal-lum*b* son of King Josiah of Judah, who suc-ceeded his father Josiah as king, but who has gone forth from this place: He shall never come back. 12He shall die in the place to which he was exiled, and he shall not see this land again.

תְּנוּ אַל־תַּחְמֹסוּ וְדָם נָקִי אַל־תִּשְׁפְּכוּ
בַּמָּקוֹם הַזֶּה: 4 כִּי אִם־עָשׂוֹ תַּעֲשׂוּ אֶת־
הַדָּבָר הַזֶּה וּבָאוּ בְשַׁעֲרֵי הַבַּיִת הַזֶּה
מְלָכִים יֹשְׁבִים לְדָוִד עַל־כִּסְאוֹ רֹכְבִים
בָּרֶכֶב וּבַסּוּסִים הוּא ועבדו וַעֲבָדָיו וְעַמּוֹ:
5 וְאִם לֹא תִשְׁמְעוּ אֶת־הַדְּבָרִים הָאֵלֶּה
בִּי נִשְׁבַּעְתִּי נְאֻם־יְהוָה כִּי־לְחָרְבָּה יִהְיֶה
הַבַּיִת הַזֶּה: ס
6 כִּי־כֹה ׀ אָמַר יְהוָה עַל־בֵּית מֶלֶךְ יְהוּדָה
גִּלְעָד אַתָּה לִי
רֹאשׁ הַלְּבָנוֹן
אִם־לֹא אֲשִׁיתְךָ מִדְבָּר
עָרִים לֹא נושבה נוֹשָׁבוּ:
7 וְקִדַּשְׁתִּי עָלַיִךְ מַשְׁחִתִים
אִישׁ וְכֵלָיו
וְכָרְתוּ מִבְחַר אֲרָזַיִךְ
וְהִפִּילוּ עַל־הָאֵשׁ:
8 וְעָבְרוּ גּוֹיִם רַבִּים עַל הָעִיר הַזֹּאת
וְאָמְרוּ אִישׁ אֶל־רֵעֵהוּ עַל־מֶה עָשָׂה יְהוָה
כָּכָה לָעִיר הַגְּדוֹלָה הַזֹּאת: 9 וְאָמְרוּ עַל
אֲשֶׁר עָזְבוּ אֶת־בְּרִית יְהוָה אֱלֹהֵיהֶם
וַיִּשְׁתַּחֲווּ לֵאלֹהִים אֲחֵרִים וַיַּעַבְדוּם: ס

10 אַל־תִּבְכּוּ לְמֵת
וְאַל־תָּנֻדוּ לוֹ
בְּכוּ בָכוֹ לַהֹלֵךְ
כִּי לֹא יָשׁוּב עוֹד
וְרָאָה אֶת־אֶרֶץ מוֹלַדְתּוֹ: ס

11 כִּי כֹה אָמַר־יְהוָה אֶל־שַׁלֻּם בֶּן־יֹאשִׁיָּהוּ
מֶלֶךְ יְהוּדָה הַמֹּלֵךְ תַּחַת יֹאשִׁיָּהוּ אָבִיו
אֲשֶׁר יָצָא מִן־הַמָּקוֹם הַזֶּה לֹא־יָשׁוּב
שָׁם עוֹד: 12 כִּי בִּמְקוֹם אֲשֶׁר־הִגְלוּ אֹתוֹ
שָׁם יָמוּת וְאֶת־הָאָרֶץ הַזֹּאת לֹא־יִרְאֶה
עוֹד: ס

---

a   *I.e., Josiah; see 2 Kings 23.29–30.*
b-b   *I.e., the king called by his throne name Jehoahaz in 2 Kings 23.31 ff., and by his private name Shallum here in v. 11 and in 1 Chron. 3.15.*

¹³Ha! he who builds his house with unfairness
And his upper chambers with injustice,
Who makes his fellow man work without pay
And does not give him his wages,
¹⁴Who thinks: I will build me a vast palace
With spacious upper chambers,
Provided with windows,
Paneled in cedar,
Painted with vermilion!
¹⁵Do you think you are more a king
Because you compete in cedar?
Your father ^c-ate and drank-^c
And dispensed justice and equity—
Then all went well with him.
¹⁶He upheld the rights of the poor and
    needy—
Then all was well.
^d-That is truly heeding Me-^d
           —declares the Lord.
¹⁷But your eyes and your mind are only
On ill-gotten gains,
On shedding the blood of the innocent,
On committing fraud and violence.
¹⁸Assuredly, thus said the Lord concerning
Jehoiakim son of Josiah, king of Judah:
^e-They shall not mourn for him,
"Ah, brother! Ah, sister!"
They shall not mourn for him,
"Ah, lord! Ah, his majesty!"-^e
¹⁹He shall have the burial of an ass,
Dragged out and left lying
Outside the gates of Jerusalem.

²⁰^fClimb Lebanon and cry out,
Raise your voice in Bashan,
Cry out from Abarim,
For all your lovers are crushed.
²¹I spoke to you when you were prosperous;

13 הוֹי בֹּנֶה בֵיתוֹ בְּלֹא־צֶדֶק
וַעֲלִיּוֹתָיו בְּלֹא מִשְׁפָּט
בְּרֵעֵהוּ יַעֲבֹד חִנָּם
וּפֹעֲלוֹ לֹא יִתֶּן־לוֹ:
14 הָאֹמֵר אֶבְנֶה־לִּי בֵּית מִדּוֹת
וַעֲלִיּוֹת מְרֻוָּחִים
וְקָרַע לוֹ חַלּוֹנָי
וְסָפוּן בָּאָרֶז
וּמָשׁוֹחַ בַּשָּׁשַׁר:
15 הֲתִמְלֹךְ
כִּי אַתָּה מְתַחֲרֶה בָאָרֶז
אָבִיךָ הֲלוֹא אָכַל וְשָׁתָה
וְעָשָׂה מִשְׁפָּט וּצְדָקָה
אָז טוֹב לוֹ:
16 דָּן דִּין־עָנִי וְאֶבְיוֹן
אָז טוֹב
הֲלוֹא־הִיא הַדַּעַת אֹתִי
נְאֻם־יְהֹוָה:
17 כִּי אֵין עֵינֶיךָ וְלִבְּךָ
כִּי אִם־עַל־בִּצְעֶךָ
וְעַל דַּם־הַנָּקִי לִשְׁפּוֹךְ
וְעַל־הָעֹשֶׁק וְעַל־הַמְּרוּצָה
לַעֲשׂוֹת: ס
18 לָכֵן כֹּה־אָמַר יְהֹוָה אֶל־יְהוֹיָקִים בֶּן־
יֹאשִׁיָּהוּ מֶלֶךְ יְהוּדָה
לֹא־יִסְפְּדוּ לוֹ
הוֹי אָחִי וְהוֹי אָחוֹת
לֹא־יִסְפְּדוּ לוֹ
הוֹי אָדוֹן וְהוֹי הֹדֹה הֹדוֹ:
19 קְבוּרַת חֲמוֹר יִקָּבֵר
סָחוֹב וְהַשְׁלֵךְ
מֵהָלְאָה לְשַׁעֲרֵי יְרוּשָׁלָ͏ִם: ס
20 עֲלִי הַלְּבָנוֹן וּצְעָקִי
וּבַבָּשָׁן תְּנִי קוֹלֵךְ
וְצַעֲקִי מֵעֲבָרִים
כִּי נִשְׁבְּרוּ כָּל־מְאַהֲבָיִךְ:

---

^{c-c} *I.e., he was content with the simple necessities of life.*
^{d-d} *Or "That is the reward for heeding Me."*
^{e-e} *They shall express neither sorrow at the loss of a relative nor*
    grief at the death of a ruler.
^f *Israel is addressed.*

You said, "I will not listen."
That was your way ever since your youth,
You would not heed Me.
²²All your shepherds$g$ shall be devoured by
   the wind,
And your lovers shall go into captivity.
Then you shall be shamed and humiliated
Because of all your depravity.
²³You who dwell in Lebanon,
Nestled among the cedars,
^{h}-How much grace will you have-^{h}
When pains come upon you,
Travail as in childbirth!

²⁴As I live—declares the Lord—^{i}-if you, O
King Coniah, son of Jehoiakim, of Judah, were-^{i}
a signet on my right hand, I would tear you off
even from there. ²⁵I will deliver you into the
hands of those who seek your life, into the hands
of those you dread, into the hands of King Nebuchadrezzar of Babylon and into the hands of
the Chaldeans. ²⁶I will hurl you and the mother
who bore you into another land, where you were
not born; there you shall both die. ²⁷They shall
not return to the land that they yearn to come
back to.

²⁸Is this man Coniah
A wretched broken pot,
A vessel no one wants?
Why are he and his offspring hurled out,
And cast away in a land they knew not?
²⁹O land, land, land,
Hear the word of the Lord!
³⁰Thus said the Lord:
Record this man as without succession,
One who shall never be found acceptable;
For no man of his offspring shall be accepted
To sit on the throne of David
And to rule again in Judah.

כא דִּבַּ֤רְתִּי אֵלַ֙יִךְ֙ בְּשַׁלְוֺתַ֔יִךְ
אָמַ֖רְתְּ לֹ֣א אֶשְׁמָ֑ע
זֶ֤ה דַרְכֵּךְ֙ מִנְּעוּרַ֔יִךְ
כִּ֥י לֹא־שָׁמַ֖עַתְּ בְּקוֹלִֽי׃
כב כָּל־רֹעַ֙יִךְ֙ תִּרְעֶה־ר֔וּחַ
וּֽמְאַהֲבַ֖יִךְ בַּשְּׁבִ֣י יֵלֵ֑כוּ
כִּ֣י אָ֤ז תֵּבֹ֙שִׁי֙ וְנִכְלַ֔מְתְּ
מִכֹּ֖ל רָעָתֵֽךְ׃
כג ישבתי יֹשַׁבְתְּ֙ בַּלְּבָנ֔וֹן
מְקֻנַּ֖נְתְּ בָּֽאֲרָזִ֑ים
מַה־נֵּחַ֙נְתְּ֙
בְּבֹא־לָ֤ךְ חֲבָלִ֔ים
חִ֖יל כַּיֹּלֵדָֽה׃

כד חַי־אָ֙נִי֙ נְאֻם־יְהֹוָ֔ה כִּ֣י אִם־יִהְיֶ֞ה כָּנְיָ֤הוּ
בֶן־יְהֽוֹיָקִים֙ מֶ֣לֶךְ יְהוּדָ֔ה חוֹתָ֖ם עַל־יַ֣ד
יְמִינִ֑י כִּ֥י מִשָּׁ֖ם אֶתְּקֶֽנְךָּ׃ כה וּנְתַתִּ֗יךָ בְּיַד֙
מְבַקְשֵׁ֣י נַפְשֶׁ֔ךָ וּבְיַ֛ד אֲשֶׁר־אַתָּ֥ה יָג֖וֹר
מִפְּנֵיהֶ֑ם וּבְיַ֛ד נְבוּכַדְרֶאצַּ֥ר מֶֽלֶךְ־בָּבֶ֖ל
וּבְיַ֥ד הַכַּשְׂדִּֽים׃ כו וְהֵֽטַלְתִּ֣י אֹֽתְךָ֗ וְאֶת־
אִמְּךָ֙ אֲשֶׁ֣ר יְלָדַ֔תְךָ עַ֚ל הָאָ֣רֶץ אַחֶ֔רֶת אֲשֶׁ֥ר
לֹֽא־יֻלַּדְתֶּ֖ם שָׁ֑ם וְשָׁ֖ם תָּמֽוּתוּ׃ כז וְעַל־
הָאָ֗רֶץ אֲשֶׁר־הֵ֛ם מְנַשְּׂאִ֥ים אֶת־נַפְשָׁ֖ם
לָשׁ֣וּב שָׁ֑ם שָׁ֖מָּה לֹ֥א יָשֽׁוּבוּ׃ ס
כח הַעֶ֣צֶב נִבְזֶ֗ה נָפ֙וּץ֙
הָאִ֤ישׁ הַזֶּה֙ כָּנְיָ֔הוּ
אִם־כְּלִ֖י אֵ֣ין חֵ֣פֶץ בּ֑וֹ
מַדּ֤וּעַ הֽוּטֲלוּ֙ ה֣וּא וְזַרְע֔וֹ
וְהֻ֙שְׁלְכ֔וּ עַל־הָאָ֖רֶץ אֲשֶׁ֥ר לֹא־יָדָֽעוּ׃
כט אֶ֥רֶץ אֶ֖רֶץ אָ֑רֶץ
שִׁמְעִ֖י דְּבַר־יְהֹוָֽה׃ ס
ל כֹּ֣ה ׀ אָמַ֣ר יְהֹוָ֗ה
כִּתְב֞וּ אֶת־הָאִ֤ישׁ הַזֶּה֙ עֲרִירִ֔י
גֶּ֖בֶר לֹא־יִצְלַ֣ח בְּיָמָ֑יו
כִּי֩ לֹ֙א יִצְלַ֜ח מִזַּרְע֗וֹ אִ֚ישׁ
יֹשֵׁב֙ עַל־כִּסֵּ֣א דָוִ֔ד
וּמֹשֵׁ֥ל ע֖וֹד בִּיהוּדָֽה׃

g   *Change of vocalization yields "paramours."*
h-h *Septuagint reads "How you will groan."*
i-i *Heb. "If Coniah…were…"; Coniah (Jeconiah in 24.1) is iden-*
    tical with Jehoiachin, 2 Kings 24.8 ff.

1065

23 Ah, shepherds who let the flock of My pasture stray and scatter!—declares the LORD. [2]Assuredly, thus said the LORD, the God of Israel, concerning the shepherds who should tend My people: It is you who let My flock scatter and go astray. You gave no thought to them, but I am going to give thought to you, for your wicked acts—declares the LORD. [3]And I Myself will gather the remnant of My flock from all the lands to which I have banished them, and I will bring them back to their pasture, where they shall be fertile and increase. [4]And I will appoint over them shepherds who will tend them; they shall no longer fear or be dismayed, and none of them shall be missing—declares the LORD.

[5]See, a time is coming—declares the LORD— when I will raise up a true branch of David's line. He shall reign as king and shall prosper, and he shall do what is just and right in the land. [6]In his days Judah shall be delivered and Israel shall dwell secure. And this is the name by which he shall be called: "The LORD is our Vindicator."

[7]Assuredly, a time is coming—declares the LORD—when it shall no more be said, "As the LORD lives, who brought the Israelites out of the land of Egypt," [8]but rather, "As the LORD lives, who brought out and led the offspring of the House of Israel from the northland and from all the lands to which I have banished them." And they shall dwell upon their own soil.

[9]Concerning the prophets.

My heart is crushed within me,
All my bones are trembling;[a]
I have become like a drunken man,
Like one overcome by wine—
Because of the LORD and His holy word.
[10]For the land is full of adulterers,

כג הוֹי רֹעִים מְאַבְּדִים וּמְפִצִים אֶת־צֹאן מַרְעִיתִי נְאֻם־יְהֹוָה: [2]לָכֵן כֹּה־אָמַר יְהֹוָה אֱלֹהֵי יִשְׂרָאֵל עַל־הָרֹעִים הָרֹעִים אֶת־עַמִּי אַתֶּם הֲפִצֹתֶם אֶת־צֹאנִי וַתַּדִּחוּם וְלֹא פְקַדְתֶּם אֹתָם הִנְנִי פֹקֵד עֲלֵיכֶם אֶת־רֹעַ מַעַלְלֵיכֶם נְאֻם־יְהֹוָה: [3]וַאֲנִי אֲקַבֵּץ אֶת־שְׁאֵרִית צֹאנִי מִכֹּל הָאֲרָצוֹת אֲשֶׁר־הִדַּחְתִּי אֹתָם שָׁם וַהֲשִׁבֹתִי אֶתְהֶן עַל־נְוֵהֶן וּפָרוּ וְרָבוּ: [4]וַהֲקִמֹתִי עֲלֵיהֶם רֹעִים וְרָעוּם וְלֹא־יִירְאוּ עוֹד וְלֹא־יֵחַתּוּ וְלֹא יִפָּקֵדוּ נְאֻם־יְהֹוָה: ס

[5]הִנֵּה יָמִים בָּאִים נְאֻם־יְהֹוָה וַהֲקִמֹתִי לְדָוִד צֶמַח צַדִּיק וּמָלַךְ מֶלֶךְ וְהִשְׂכִּיל וְעָשָׂה מִשְׁפָּט וּצְדָקָה בָּאָרֶץ: [6]בְּיָמָיו תִּוָּשַׁע יְהוּדָה וְיִשְׂרָאֵל יִשְׁכֹּן לָבֶטַח וְזֶה־שְּׁמוֹ אֲשֶׁר־יִקְרְאוֹ יְהֹוָה ׀ צִדְקֵנוּ: ס

[7]לָכֵן הִנֵּה־יָמִים בָּאִים נְאֻם־יְהֹוָה וְלֹא־יֹאמְרוּ עוֹד חַי־יְהֹוָה אֲשֶׁר הֶעֱלָה אֶת־בְּנֵי יִשְׂרָאֵל מֵאֶרֶץ מִצְרָיִם: [8]כִּי אִם־חַי־יְהֹוָה אֲשֶׁר הֶעֱלָה וַאֲשֶׁר הֵבִיא אֶת־זֶרַע בֵּית יִשְׂרָאֵל מֵאֶרֶץ צָפוֹנָה וּמִכֹּל הָאֲרָצוֹת אֲשֶׁר הִדַּחְתִּים שָׁם וְיָשְׁבוּ עַל־אַדְמָתָם: ס

[9]לַנְּבִאִים

נִשְׁבַּר לִבִּי בְקִרְבִּי רָחֲפוּ כָּל־עַצְמוֹתַי הָיִיתִי כְּאִישׁ שִׁכּוֹר וּכְגֶבֶר עֲבָרוֹ יָיִן מִפְּנֵי יְהֹוָה וּמִפְּנֵי דִּבְרֵי קָדְשׁוֹ: [10]כִּי מְנָאֲפִים מָלְאָה הָאָרֶץ

---

a *Meaning of Heb. uncertain.*

The land mourns because of b-a curse;-b
The pastures of the wilderness are dried up.
c-For they run to do evil,
They strain to do wrong.-c
11For both prophet and priest are godless;
Even in My House I find their wickedness
　　　　　　—declares the LORD.

12Assuredly,
Their path shall become
Like slippery ground;
They shall be thrust into darkness
And there they shall fall;
For I will bring disaster upon them,
The year of their doom
　　　　　　—declares the LORD.

13In the prophets of Samaria
I saw a repulsive thing:
They prophesied by Baal
And led My people Israel astray.
14But what I see in the prophets of Jerusalem
Is something horrifying:
Adultery and false dealing.
They encourage evildoers,
So that no one turns back from his wicked-
　　ness.
To Me they are all like Sodom,
And [all] its inhabitants like Gomorrah.

15Assuredly, thus said the LORD of Hosts concerning the prophets:

I am going to make them eat wormwood
And drink a bitter draft;
For from the prophets of Jerusalem
Godlessness has gone forth to the whole land.

16Thus said the LORD of Hosts:
Do not listen to the words of the prophets
Who prophesy to you.

כִּי־מִפְּנֵי אָלָה֙ אָבְלָ֣ה הָאָ֔רֶץ
יָבְשׁ֖וּ נְא֣וֹת מִדְבָּ֑ר
וַתְּהִ֤י מְרֽוּצָתָם֙ רָעָ֔ה
וּגְבוּרָתָ֖ם לֹא־כֵֽן׃
11 כִּֽי־גַם־נָבִ֥יא גַם־כֹּהֵ֖ן חָנֵ֑פוּ
גַּם־בְּבֵיתִ֛י מָצָ֥אתִי רָעָתָ֖ם
נְאֻם־יְהוָֽה׃
12 לָכֵן֩ יִֽהְיֶ֨ה דַרְכָּ֜ם לָהֶ֗ם
כַּחֲלַקְלַקּוֹת֙
בָּאֲפֵלָ֣ה יִדַּ֔חוּ
וְנָ֖פְלוּ בָ֑הּ
כִּֽי־אָבִ֧יא עֲלֵיהֶ֛ם רָעָ֖ה
שְׁנַ֣ת פְּקֻדָּתָ֑ם
נְאֻם־יְהוָֽה׃
13 וּבִנְבִיאֵ֥י שֹׁמְר֖וֹן
רָאִ֣יתִי תִפְלָ֑ה
הִנַּבְּא֣וּ בַבַּ֔עַל
וַיַּתְע֥וּ אֶת־עַמִּ֖י אֶת־יִשְׂרָאֵֽל׃ ס
14 וּבִנְבִאֵ֨י יְרוּשָׁלִַ֜ם רָאִ֣יתִי
שַׁעֲרוּרָ֗ה
נָא֤וֹף וְהָלֹךְ֙ בַּשֶּׁ֔קֶר
וְחִזְּקוּ֙ יְדֵ֣י מְרֵעִ֔ים
לְבִלְתִּי־שָׁ֖בוּ אִ֣ישׁ מֵרָֽעָת֑וֹ
הָֽיוּ־לִ֤י כֻלָּם֙ כִּסְדֹ֔ם
וְיֹשְׁבֶ֖יהָ כַּעֲמֹרָֽה׃ ס
15 לָכֵ֞ן כֹּֽה־אָמַ֨ר יְהוָ֤ה צְבָאוֹת֙ עַל־
הַנְּבִאִ֔ים
הִנְנִ֨י מַאֲכִ֤יל אוֹתָם֙ לַֽעֲנָ֔ה
וְהִשְׁקִתִ֖ים מֵי־רֹ֑אשׁ
כִּ֗י מֵאֵת֙ נְבִיאֵ֣י יְרוּשָׁלִַ֔ם
יָצְאָ֥ה חֲנֻפָּ֖ה לְכָל־הָאָֽרֶץ׃ פ
16 כֹּֽה־אָמַ֞ר יְהוָ֣ה צְבָא֗וֹת
אַֽל־תִּשְׁמְע֞וּ עַל־דִּבְרֵ֤י הַנְּבִאִים֙
הַנִּבְּאִ֣ים לָכֶ֔ם

---

b-b   *A few Heb. mss. and Septuagint read "these."*
c-c   *Lit. "Their running is wickedness, / Their straining is iniquity."*

They are deluding you,

The prophecies they speak are from their own minds,

Not from the mouth of the LORD.

17They declare to men who despise Me:

The LORD has said:

"All shall be well with you";

And to all who follow their willful hearts they say:

"No evil shall befall you."

18But he who has stood in the council of the LORD,

And seen, and heard His word—

He who has listened to His word must obey.*d*

19*e*-Lo, the storm of the LORD goes forth in fury,

A whirling storm,

It shall whirl down upon the heads of the wicked.

20The anger of the LORD shall not turn back

Till it has fulfilled and completed His purposes.-*e*

In the days to come

You shall clearly perceive it.

21I did not send those prophets,

But they rushed in;

I did not speak to them,

Yet they prophesied.

22If they have stood in My council,

Let them announce My words to My people

And make them turn back

From their evil ways and wicked acts.

23Am I only a God near at hand

         —says the LORD—

And not a God far away?

24If a man enters a hiding place,

---

d   *Change of vocalization yields "announce it"; cf. vv. 22, 28.*

e-e   *This section constitutes the word of God to which Jeremiah refers.*

מַהְבִּלִים הֵמָּה אֶתְכֶם

חֲזוֹן לִבָּם יְדַבֵּרוּ

לֹא מִפִּי יְהוָה:

17 אֹמְרִים אָמוֹר לִמְנַאֲצַי

דִּבֶּר יְהוָה

שָׁלוֹם יִהְיֶה לָכֶם

וְכֹל הֹלֵךְ בִּשְׁרִרוּת לִבּוֹ אָמְרוּ

לֹא־תָבוֹא עֲלֵיכֶם רָעָה:

18 כִּי מִי עָמַד בְּסוֹד יְהוָה

וְיֵרֶא וְיִשְׁמַע אֶת־דְּבָרוֹ

מִי־הִקְשִׁיב דְּבָרִי דְּבָרוֹ וַיִּשְׁמָע: ס

19 הִנֵּה | סַעֲרַת יְהוָה חֵמָה יָצְאָה

וְסַעַר מִתְחוֹלֵל

עַל רֹאשׁ רְשָׁעִים יָחוּל:

20 לֹא יָשׁוּב אַף־יְהוָה

עַד־עֲשֹׂתוֹ וְעַד־הֲקִימוֹ מְזִמּוֹת לִבּוֹ

בְּאַחֲרִית הַיָּמִים

תִּתְבּוֹנְנוּ בָהּ בִּינָה:

21 לֹא־שָׁלַחְתִּי אֶת־הַנְּבִאִים

וְהֵם רָצוּ

לֹא־דִבַּרְתִּי אֲלֵיהֶם

וְהֵם נִבָּאוּ:

22 וְאִם־עָמְדוּ בְּסוֹדִי

וְיַשְׁמִעוּ דְבָרַי אֶת־עַמִּי

וִישִׁבוּם

מִדַּרְכָּם הָרָע וּמֵרֹעַ מַעַלְלֵיהֶם: ס

23 הַאֱלֹהֵי מִקָּרֹב אָנִי

נְאֻם־יְהוָה

וְלֹא אֱלֹהֵי מֵרָחֹק:

24 אִם־יִסָּתֵר אִישׁ בַּמִּסְתָּרִים

Do I not see him?

—says the LORD.

For I fill both heaven and earth

—declares the LORD.

25I have heard what the prophets say, who prophesy falsely in My name: "I had a dream, I had a dream." 26a-How long will there be-a in the minds of the prophets who prophesy falsehood—the prophets of their own deceitful minds—27the plan to make My people forget My name, by means of the dreams which they tell each other, just as their fathers forgot My name because of Baal? 28Let the prophet who has a dream tell the dream; and let him who has received My word report My word faithfully! How can straw be compared to grain?—says the LORD. 29Behold, My word is like fire—declares the LORD—and like a hammer that shatters rock!

30Assuredly, I am going to deal with the prophets—declares the LORD—who steal My words from one another. 31I am going to deal with the prophets—declares the LORD—who wag[a] their tongues and make oracular utterances. 32I am going to deal with those who prophesy lying dreams—declares the LORD—who relate them to lead My people astray with their reckless lies, when I did not send them or command them. They do this people no good—declares the LORD.

33And when this people—or a prophet or a priest—asks you, "What is the burden[f] of the LORD?" you shall answer them, g-"What is the burden?-g I will cast you off"—declares the LORD.

34As for the prophet or priest or layman who shall say "the burden of the LORD," I will punish that person and his house. 35Thus you shall

וַאֲנִ֥י לֹֽא־אֶרְאֶ֖נּוּ
נְאֻם־יְהוָ֑ה
הֲל֨וֹא אֶת־הַשָּׁמַ֧יִם וְאֶת־הָאָ֛רֶץ אֲנִ֥י מָלֵ֖א
נְאֻם־יְהוָֽה׃

25 שָׁמַ֗עְתִּי אֵ֤ת אֲשֶׁר־אָֽמְרוּ֙ הַנְּבִאִ֔ים הַֽנִּבְּאִ֥ים בִּשְׁמִ֛י שֶׁ֖קֶר לֵאמֹ֑ר חָלַ֖מְתִּי חָלָֽמְתִּי׃ 26 עַד־מָתַ֗י הֲיֵ֛שׁ בְּלֵ֥ב הַנְּבִאִ֖ים נִבְּאֵ֣י הַשָּׁ֑קֶר וּנְבִיאֵ֖י תַּרְמִ֥ת לִבָּֽם׃ 27 הַחֹֽשְׁבִ֗ים לְהַשְׁכִּ֤יחַ אֶת־עַמִּי֙ שְׁמִ֔י בַּחֲל֣וֹמֹתָ֔ם אֲשֶׁ֥ר יְסַפְּר֖וּ אִ֣ישׁ לְרֵעֵ֑הוּ כַּאֲשֶׁ֨ר שָׁכְח֧וּ אֲבוֹתָ֛ם אֶת־שְׁמִ֖י בַּבָּֽעַל׃ 28 הַנָּבִ֞יא אֲשֶׁר־אִתּ֤וֹ חֲלוֹם֙ יְסַפֵּ֣ר חֲל֔וֹם וַאֲשֶׁ֤ר דְּבָרִי֙ אִתּ֔וֹ יְדַבֵּ֥ר דְּבָרִ֖י אֱמֶ֑ת מַה־לַתֶּ֥בֶן אֶת־הַבָּ֖ר נְאֻם־יְהוָֽה׃ 29 הֲל֨וֹא כֹ֧ה דְבָרִ֛י כָּאֵ֖שׁ נְאֻם־יְהוָ֑ה וּכְפַטִּ֖ישׁ יְפֹ֥צֵֽץ סָֽלַע׃ ס

30 לָכֵ֛ן הִנְנִ֥י עַל־הַנְּבִאִ֖ים נְאֻם־יְהוָ֑ה מְגַנְּבֵ֣י דְבָרַ֔י אִ֖ישׁ מֵאֵ֥ת רֵעֵֽהוּ׃ 31 הִנְנִ֥י עַל־הַנְּבִיאִ֖ם נְאֻם־יְהוָ֑ה הַלֹּקְחִ֣ים לְשׁוֹנָ֔ם וַֽיִּנְאֲמ֖וּ נְאֻֽם׃ 32 הִ֠נְנִי עַֽל־נִבְּאֵ֞י חֲלֹמ֥וֹת שֶׁ֙קֶר֙ נְאֻם־יְהוָ֔ה וַֽיְסַפְּרוּם֙ וַיַּתְע֣וּ אֶת־עַמִּ֔י בְּשִׁקְרֵיהֶ֖ם וּבְפַחֲזוּתָ֑ם וְאָנֹכִ֨י לֹֽא־שְׁלַחְתִּ֜ים וְלֹ֣א צִוִּיתִ֗ים וְהוֹעֵ֛יל לֹֽא־יוֹעִ֥ילוּ לָֽעָם־הַזֶּ֖ה נְאֻם־יְהוָֽה׃ 33 וְכִי־יִשְׁאָלְךָ֩ הָעָ֨ם הַזֶּ֜ה אֽוֹ־הַנָּבִ֤יא אֽוֹ־כֹהֵן֙ לֵאמֹ֔ר מַה־מַשָּׂ֖א יְהוָ֑ה וְאָמַרְתָּ֤ אֲלֵיהֶם֙ אֶת־מַה־מַשָּׂ֔א וְנָטַשְׁתִּ֥י אֶתְכֶ֖ם נְאֻם־יְהוָֽה׃ 34 וְהַנָּבִ֤יא וְהַכֹּהֵן֙ וְהָעָ֔ם אֲשֶׁ֥ר יֹאמַ֖ר מַשָּׂ֣א יְהוָ֑ה וּפָקַדְתִּ֛י עַל־הָאִ֥ישׁ הַה֖וּא וְעַל־בֵּיתֽוֹ׃ 35 כֹּ֥ה תֹאמְר֛וּ אִ֥ישׁ עַל־רֵעֵ֖הוּ וְאִ֥ישׁ

---

f I.e., pronouncement; cf. Isa. 13.1, 15.1, etc., where the word rendered "pronouncement" can also mean "burden."

g-g Septuagint and other versions read "You are the burden!"

speak to each other, every one to his fellow, "What has the Lord answered?" or "What has the Lord spoken?" ³⁶But do not mention "the burden of the Lord" any more. ^{a-}Does a man regard his own word as a "burden,"^{-a} that you pervert the words of the living God, the Lord of Hosts, our God? ³⁷Thus you shall speak to the prophet: "What did the Lord answer you?" or "What did the Lord speak?" ³⁸But if you say "the burden of the Lord"—assuredly, thus said the Lord: Because you said this thing, "the burden of the Lord," whereas I sent word to you not to say "the burden of the Lord," ³⁹I will utterly ^{h-}forget you^{-h} and I will cast you away from My presence, together with the city that I gave to you and your fathers. ⁴⁰And I will lay upon you a disgrace for all time, shame for all time, which shall never be forgotten.

24

The Lord showed me two baskets of figs, placed in front of the Temple of the Lord. This was after King Nebuchadrezzar of Babylon had exiled King Jeconiah son of Jehoiakim of Judah, and the officials of Judah, and the craftsmen and smiths, from Jerusalem, and had brought them to Babylon. ²One basket contained very good figs, like first-ripened figs, and the other basket contained very bad figs, so bad that they could not be eaten.

³And the Lord said to me, "What do you see, Jeremiah?" I answered, "Figs—the good ones are very good, and the bad ones very bad, so bad that they cannot be eaten."

⁴Then the word of the Lord came to me:

⁵Thus said the Lord, the God of Israel: As with these good figs, so will I single out for good the Judean exiles whom I have driven out from this place to the land of the Chaldeans. ⁶I will look upon them favorably, and I will bring them

אֶל־אָחִיו מֶה־עָנָה יְהֹוָה וּמַה־דִּבֶּר יְהֹוָה:
³⁶ וּמַשָּׂא יְהֹוָה לֹא תִזְכְּרוּ־עוֹד כִּי הַמַּשָּׂא
יִהְיֶה לְאִישׁ דְּבָרוֹ וַהֲפַכְתֶּם אֶת־דִּבְרֵי
אֱלֹהִים חַיִּים יְהֹוָה צְבָאוֹת אֱלֹהֵינוּ:
³⁷ כֹּה תֹאמַר אֶל־הַנָּבִיא מֶה־עָנָךְ יְהֹוָה
וּמַה־דִּבֶּר יְהֹוָה: ³⁸ וְאִם־מַשָּׂא יְהֹוָה
תֹּאמֵרוּ לָכֵן כֹּה אָמַר יְהֹוָה יַעַן אֲמָרְכֶם
אֶת־הַדָּבָר הַזֶּה מַשָּׂא יְהֹוָה וָאֶשְׁלַח
אֲלֵיכֶם לֵאמֹר לֹא תֹאמְרוּ מַשָּׂא יְהֹוָה:
³⁹ לָכֵן הִנְנִי וְנָשִׁיתִי אֶתְכֶם נָשֹׁא וְנָטַשְׁתִּי
אֶתְכֶם וְאֶת־הָעִיר אֲשֶׁר נָתַתִּי לָכֶם
וְלַאֲבוֹתֵיכֶם מֵעַל פָּנָי: ⁴⁰ וְנָתַתִּי עֲלֵיכֶם
חֶרְפַּת עוֹלָם וּכְלִמּוּת עוֹלָם אֲשֶׁר לֹא
תִשָּׁכֵחַ: ס

כד

הִרְאַנִי יְהֹוָה וְהִנֵּה שְׁנֵי דּוּדָאֵי
תְאֵנִים מוּעָדִים לִפְנֵי הֵיכַל יְהֹוָה אַחֲרֵי
הַגְלוֹת נְבוּכַדְרֶאצַּר מֶלֶךְ־בָּבֶל אֶת־
יְכָנְיָהוּ בֶן־יְהוֹיָקִים מֶלֶךְ־יְהוּדָה וְאֶת־
שָׂרֵי יְהוּדָה וְאֶת־הֶחָרָשׁ וְאֶת־הַמַּסְגֵּר
מִירוּשָׁלַם וַיְבִאֵם בָּבֶל: ² הַדּוּד אֶחָד
תְּאֵנִים טֹבוֹת מְאֹד כִּתְאֵנֵי הַבַּכֻּרוֹת
וְהַדּוּד אֶחָד תְּאֵנִים רָעוֹת מְאֹד אֲשֶׁר
לֹא־תֵאָכַלְנָה מֵרֹעַ: ס
³ וַיֹּאמֶר יְהֹוָה אֵלַי מָה־אַתָּה רֹאֶה
יִרְמְיָהוּ וָאֹמַר תְּאֵנִים הַתְּאֵנִים הַטֹּבוֹת
טֹבוֹת מְאֹד וְהָרָעוֹת רָעוֹת מְאֹד אֲשֶׁר
לֹא־תֵאָכַלְנָה מֵרֹעַ: פ
⁴ וַיְהִי דְבַר־יְהֹוָה אֵלַי לֵאמֹר:
⁵ כֹּה־אָמַר יְהֹוָה אֱלֹהֵי יִשְׂרָאֵל כַּתְּאֵנִים
הַטֹּבוֹת הָאֵלֶּה כֵּן־אַכִּיר אֶת־גָּלוּת יְהוּדָה
אֲשֶׁר שִׁלַּחְתִּי מִן־הַמָּקוֹם הַזֶּה אֶרֶץ
כַּשְׂדִּים לְטוֹבָה: ⁶ וְשַׂמְתִּי עֵינִי עֲלֵיהֶם

---

^{h-h} *Some Heb. mss., Septuagint, and other versions read "lift you up," a word from the same root as "burden."*

back to this land; I will build them and not overthrow them; I will plant them and not uproot them. 7And I will give them the understanding to acknowledge Me, for I am the LORD. And they shall be My people and I will be their God, when they turn back to Me with all their heart.

8And like the bad figs, which are so bad that they cannot be eaten—thus said the Lord—so will I treat King Zedekiah of Judah and his officials and the remnant of Jerusalem that is left in this land, and those who are living in the land of Egypt: 9I will make them a horror—an evil—to all the kingdoms of the earth, a disgrace and a proverb, a byword and a curse*a* in all the places to which I banish them. 10I will send the sword, famine, and pestilence against them until they are exterminated from the land that I gave to them and their fathers.

25 The word which came to Jeremiah concerning all the people of Judah, in the fourth year of King Jehoiakim son of Josiah of Judah, which was the first year of King Nebuchadrezzar of Babylon. 2This is what the prophet Jeremiah said to all the people of Judah and to all the inhabitants of Jerusalem:

3From the thirteenth year of King Josiah son of Amon of Judah, to this day—these twenty-three years—the word of the LORD has come to me. I have spoken to you persistently, but you would not listen. 4Moreover, the LORD constantly sent all his servants the prophets to you, but you would not listen or incline your ears to hear 5when they said, "Turn back, every one, from your evil ways and your wicked acts, that you may remain throughout the ages on the soil which the LORD gave to you and your fathers. 6Do not follow other gods, to serve them and

לְטוֹבָ֑ה וַהֲשִֽׁבֹתִ֗ים עַל־הָאָ֨רֶץ הַזֹּ֔את
וּבְנִיתִים֙ וְלֹ֣א אֶהֱרֹ֔ס וּנְטַעְתִּ֖ים וְלֹ֥א
אֶתּֽוֹשׁ׃ 7 וְנָתַתִּ֨י לָהֶ֥ם לֵב֙ לָדַ֣עַת אֹתִ֔י כִּ֣י
אֲנִ֣י יְהֹוָ֑ה וְהָיוּ־לִ֣י לְעָ֗ם וְאָֽנֹכִ֗י אֶהְיֶ֤ה לָהֶם֙
לֵֽאלֹהִ֔ים כִּי־יָשֻׁ֥בוּ אֵלַ֖י בְּכָל־לִבָּֽם׃ ס
8 וְכַתְּאֵנִים֙ הָ֣רָע֔וֹת אֲשֶׁ֥ר לֹא־תֵֽאָכַ֖לְנָה
מֵרֹ֑עַ כִּי־כֹ֣ה ׀ אָמַ֣ר יְהֹוָ֗ה כֵּ֣ן אֶתֵּ֞ן אֶת־
צִדְקִיָּ֣הוּ מֶֽלֶךְ־יְהוּדָ֣ה וְאֶת־שָׂרָיו֮ וְאֵ֣ת ׀
שְׁאֵרִ֣ית יְרֽוּשָׁלִַ֗ם הַנִּשְׁאָרִים֙ בָּאָ֣רֶץ הַזֹּ֔את
וְהַיֹּשְׁבִ֖ים בְּאֶ֣רֶץ מִצְרָֽיִם׃ 9 וּנְתַתִּים֙ לזועה
לְזַעֲוָ֣ה לְרָעָ֔ה לְכֹ֖ל מַמְלְכ֣וֹת הָאָ֑רֶץ
לְחֶרְפָּ֤ה וּלְמָשָׁל֙ לִשְׁנִינָ֣ה וְלִקְלָלָ֔ה בְּכָל־
הַמְּקֹמ֖וֹת אֲשֶׁר־אַדִּיחֵ֥ם שָֽׁם׃ 10 וְשִׁלַּחְתִּ֣י
בָ֗ם אֶת־הַחֶ֙רֶב֙ אֶת־הָֽרָעָ֔ב וְאֶת־הַדָּ֑בֶר
עַד־תֻּמָּ֗ם מֵעַ֤ל הָֽאֲדָמָה֙ אֲשֶׁר־נָתַ֣תִּי לָהֶ֔ם
וְלַאֲבוֹתֵיהֶֽם׃ פ

כה הַדָּבָר֙ אֲשֶׁ֣ר הָיָ֔ה עַֽל־יִרְמְיָ֑הוּ
עַל־כָּל־עַ֖ם יְהוּדָ֑ה בַּשָּׁנָה֙ הָֽרְבִעִ֔ית
לִיהוֹיָקִ֥ים בֶּן־יֹֽאשִׁיָּ֖הוּ מֶ֣לֶךְ יְהוּדָ֑ה הִ֚יא
הַשָּׁנָה֙ הָרִ֣אשֹׁנִ֔ית לִנְבֽוּכַדְרֶאצַּ֖ר מֶ֥לֶךְ
בָּבֶֽל׃ 2 אֲשֶׁ֨ר דִּבֶּ֜ר יִרְמְיָ֣הוּ הַנָּבִ֗יא עַל־כָּל־
עַ֣ם יְהוּדָ֔ה וְאֶ֖ל כָּל־יֹשְׁבֵ֣י יְרוּשָׁלִָ֑ם לֵאמֹֽר׃

3 מִן־שְׁלֹ֣שׁ עֶשְׂרֵ֣ה שָׁנָ֡ה לְיֹֽאשִׁיָּ֣הוּ בֶן־
אָמ֣וֹן מֶ֣לֶךְ יְהוּדָ֗ה וְעַ֣ד ׀ הַיּ֣וֹם הַזֶּ֗ה
זֶ֣ה שָׁלֹ֤שׁ וְעֶשְׂרִים֙ שָׁנָ֔ה הָיָ֥ה דְבַר־
יְהֹוָ֖ה אֵלָ֑י וָֽאֲדַבֵּ֧ר אֲלֵיכֶ֛ם אַשְׁכֵּ֥ים וְדַבֵּ֖ר
וְלֹ֥א שְׁמַעְתֶּֽם׃ 4 וְשָׁלַ֣ח יְהֹוָ֣ה אֲלֵיכֶ֗ם
אֶת־כָּל־עֲבָדָ֣יו הַנְּבִאִים֮ הַשְׁכֵּ֣ם וְשָׁלֹ֒חַ֒
וְלֹ֤א שְׁמַעְתֶּם֙ וְלֹֽא־הִטִּיתֶ֣ם אֶֽת־אָזְנְכֶ֔ם
לִשְׁמֹֽעַ׃ 5 לֵאמֹ֗ר שֽׁוּבוּ־נָ֞א אִ֣ישׁ מִדַּרְכּ֤וֹ
הָֽרָעָה֙ וּמֵרֹ֣עַ מַעַלְלֵיכֶ֔ם וּשְׁב֣וּ עַל־
הָאֲדָמָ֗ה אֲשֶׁ֨ר נָתַ֧ן יְהֹוָ֛ה לָכֶ֖ם
וְלַאֲבֽוֹתֵיכֶ֑ם לְמִן־עוֹלָ֖ם וְעַד־עוֹלָֽם׃
6 וְאַל־תֵּֽלְכ֗וּ אַֽחֲרֵי֙ אֱלֹהִ֣ים אֲחֵרִ֔ים

---

a   *I.e., a standard by which men curse; cf. Gen. 12.2 and note; Zech.
8.13.*

worship them. Do not vex Me with what your own hands have made,[a] and I will not bring disaster upon you." [7]But you would not listen to Me—declares the LORD—but vexed Me with what your hands made, to your own hurt.

[8]Assuredly, thus said the LORD of Hosts: Because you would not listen to My words, [9]I am going to send for all the peoples of the north—declares the LORD—and for My servant, King Nebuchadrezzar of Babylon, and bring them against this land and its inhabitants, and against all those nations roundabout. I will exterminate them and make them a desolation, an object of hissing[b]—ruins for all time. [10]And I will banish from them the sound of mirth and gladness, the voice of bridegroom and bride, and the sound of the mill and the light of the lamp. [11]This whole land shall be a desolate ruin.

And those nations shall serve the king of Babylon seventy years. [12]When the seventy years are over, I will punish the king of Babylon and that nation and the land of the Chaldeans for their sins—declares the LORD—and I will make it a desolation for all time. [13]And I will bring upon that land all that I have decreed against it, all that is recorded in this book—that which Jeremiah prophesied against all the nations. [14]For they too shall be enslaved by many nations and great kings; and I will requite them according to their acts and according to their conduct.

[15]For thus said the LORD, the God of Israel, to me: "Take from My hand this cup of wine—of wrath—and make all the nations to whom I send you drink of it. [16]Let them drink and retch and act crazy, because of the sword that I am sending among them."

[17]So I took the cup from the hand of the LORD and gave drink to all the nations to whom the

---

a   I.e., idols.
b   Cf. note at 18.16.

לְעׇבְדָ֛ם וּלְהִֽשְׁתַּחֲוֺ֥ת לָהֶ֖ם וְלֹֽא־תַכְעִ֣סוּ
אוֹתִ֛י בְּמַעֲשֵׂ֥ה יְדֵיכֶ֖ם וְלֹ֥א אָרַ֖ע לָכֶֽם׃
[7] וְלֹֽא־שְׁמַעְתֶּ֥ם אֵלַ֖י נְאֻם־יְהֹוָ֑ה לְמַ֧עַן
הַכְעִסֵ֛נִי בְּמַעֲשֵׂ֥ה יְדֵיכֶ֖ם לְרַ֥ע
לָכֶֽם׃ ס

[8] לָכֵ֗ן כֹּ֤ה אָמַר֙ יְהֹוָ֣ה צְבָא֔וֹת יַ֛עַן אֲשֶׁ֥ר
לֹא־שְׁמַעְתֶּ֖ם אֶת־דְּבָרָֽי׃ [9] הִנְנִ֣י שֹׁלֵ֡חַ
וְלָקַחְתִּי֩ אֶת־כׇּל־מִשְׁפְּח֨וֹת צָפ֜וֹן נְאֻם־
יְהֹוָ֗ה וְאֶל־נְבֽוּכַדְרֶאצַּ֣ר מֶֽלֶךְ־בָּבֶל֮ עַבְדִּי֒
וַהֲבִֽאֹתִ֗ים עַל־הָאָ֤רֶץ הַזֹּאת֙ וְעַל־יֹ֣שְׁבֶ֔יהָ
וְעַ֛ל כׇּל־הַגּוֹיִ֥ם הָאֵ֖לֶּה סָבִ֑יב וְהַ֣חֲרַמְתִּ֔ים
וְשַׂמְתִּים֙ לְשַׁמָּ֣ה וְלִשְׁרֵקָ֔ה וּלְחׇרְב֖וֹת
עוֹלָֽם׃ [10] וְהַ֣אֲבַדְתִּ֣י מֵהֶ֗ם ק֤וֹל שָׂשׂוֹן֙ וְק֣וֹל
שִׂמְחָ֔ה ק֥וֹל חָתָ֖ן וְק֣וֹל כַּלָּ֑ה ק֥וֹל רֵחַ֖יִם
וְא֥וֹר נֵֽר׃ [11] וְהָֽיְתָה֙ כׇּל־הָאָ֣רֶץ הַזֹּ֔את
לְחׇרְבָּ֖ה לְשַׁמָּ֑ה

וְעָבְד֞וּ הַגּוֹיִ֣ם הָאֵ֗לֶּה אֶת־מֶ֥לֶךְ בָּבֶ֖ל
שִׁבְעִ֥ים שָׁנָֽה׃ [12] וְהָיָ֣ה כִמְלֹאות֩* שִׁבְעִ֨ים
שָׁנָ֜ה אֶפְקֹ֤ד עַל־מֶֽלֶךְ־בָּבֶל֙ וְעַל־הַגּ֣וֹי
הַה֗וּא נְאֻם־יְהֹוָ֛ה אֶת־עֲוֺנָ֖ם וְעַל־אֶ֣רֶץ
כַּשְׂדִּ֑ים וְשַׂמְתִּ֥י אֹת֖וֹ לְשִֽׁמְמ֥וֹת עוֹלָֽם׃
[13] וְהֵבֵאתִי֙ עַל־הָאָ֣רֶץ הַהִ֔יא
אֶת־כׇּל־דְּבָרַ֖י אֲשֶׁר־דִּבַּ֣רְתִּי עָלֶ֑יהָ אֵ֧ת
כׇּל־הַכָּת֣וּב בַּסֵּ֣פֶר הַזֶּ֗ה אֲשֶׁר־נִבָּ֛א יִרְמְיָ֖הוּ
עַל־כׇּל־הַגּוֹיִֽם׃ [14] כִּ֣י עָֽבְדוּ־בָ֤ם גַּם־הֵ֙מָּה֙
גּוֹיִ֣ם רַבִּ֔ים וּמְלָכִ֖ים גְּדוֹלִ֑ים וְשִׁלַּמְתִּ֧י
לָהֶ֛ם כְּפׇעֳלָ֖ם וּכְמַעֲשֵׂ֥ה יְדֵיהֶֽם׃ ס
[15] כִּ֣י כֹה֩ אָמַ֨ר יְהֹוָ֜ה אֱלֹהֵ֤י יִשְׂרָאֵל֙ אֵלַ֔י
קַ֠ח אֶת־כּ֨וֹס הַיַּ֧יִן הַחֵמָ֛ה הַזֹּ֖את מִיָּדִ֑י
וְהִשְׁקִיתָ֤ה אֹתוֹ֙ אֶת־כׇּל־הַגּוֹיִ֔ם אֲשֶׁ֧ר אָנֹכִ֛י
שֹׁלֵ֥חַ אוֹתְךָ֖ אֲלֵיהֶֽם׃ [16] וְשָׁת֥וּ וְהִֽתְגֹּעֲשׁ֖וּ
וְהִתְהֹלָ֑לוּ מִפְּנֵ֣י הַחֶ֔רֶב אֲשֶׁ֥ר אָנֹכִ֖י שֹׁלֵ֥חַ
בֵּינֹתָֽם׃
[17] וָאֶקַּ֥ח אֶת־הַכּ֖וֹס מִיַּ֣ד יְהֹוָ֑ה וָֽאַשְׁקֶה֙
אֶת־כׇּל־הַגּוֹיִ֔ם אֲשֶׁר־שְׁלָחַ֥נִי יְהֹוָֽה

מלא ר׳   v. 12.

LORD had sent me: [18]Jerusalem and the towns of Judah, and its kings and officials, to make them a desolate ruin, an object of hissing and a curse[c]—as is now the case; [19]Pharaoh king of Egypt, his courtiers, his officials, and all his people; [20]all [d]the mixed peoples;[-d] all the kings of the land of Uz; all the kings of the land of the Philistines—Ashkelon, Gaza, Ekron, and what is left of Ashdod; [21]Edom, Moab, and Ammon; [22]all the kings of Tyre and all the kings of Sidon, and all the kings of the coastland across the sea; [23]Dedan, Tema, and Buz, and all those who have their hair clipped; [24]all the kings of Arabia, and all the kings of [d]the mixed peoples[-d] who live in the desert; [25]all the kings of Zimri[d] and all the kings of Elam and all the kings of Media; [26]all the kings of the north, whether far from or close to each other—all the [d]royal lands which are on the earth.[-d] And last of all, the king of Sheshach[e] shall drink.

[27]Say to them: "Thus said the LORD of Hosts, the God of Israel: Drink and get drunk and vomit; fall and never rise again, because of the sword that I send among you." [28]And if they refuse to take the cup from your hand and drink, say to them, "Thus said the LORD of Hosts: You must drink! [29]If I am bringing the punishment first on the city that bears My name, do you expect to go unpunished? You will not go unpunished, for I am summoning the sword against all the inhabitants of the earth—declares the LORD of Hosts."

[30]You are to prophesy all those things to them, and then say to them:

The LORD roars from on high,
He makes His voice heard from His holy
   dwelling;
He roars aloud over His [earthly] abode;

---

c   Cf. note at 24.9.
d-d   Meaning of Heb. uncertain.
e   A cipher for Babel, Babylon.

1073

אֲלֵיהֶ֑ם ׃ 18 אֶת־יְרוּשָׁלִַ֙ם֙ וְאֶת־עָרֵ֣י יְהוּדָ֔ה וְאֶת־מְלָכֶ֙יהָ֙ אֶת־שָׂרֶ֔יהָ לָתֵ֥ת אֹתָ֖ם לְחָרְבָּ֛ה לְשַׁמָּ֥ה לִשְׁרֵקָ֖ה וְלִקְלָלָ֑ה כַּיּ֥וֹם הַזֶּֽה ׃ 19 אֶת־פַּרְעֹ֧ה מֶֽלֶךְ־מִצְרַ֛יִם וְאֶת־עֲבָדָ֥יו וְאֶת־שָׂרָ֖יו וְאֶת־כׇּל־עַמּֽוֹ ׃ 20 וְאֵת֙ כׇּל־הָעֶ֔רֶב וְאֵ֕ת כׇּל־מַלְכֵ֖י אֶ֣רֶץ הָע֑וּץ וְאֵ֗ת כׇּל־מַלְכֵ֞י אֶ֤רֶץ פְּלִשְׁתִּים֙ וְאֶת־אַשְׁקְל֣וֹן וְאֶת־עַזָּ֔ה וְאֶת־עֶקְר֖וֹן וְאֵ֥ת שְׁאֵרִ֥ית אַשְׁדּֽוֹד ׃ 21 אֶת־אֱד֥וֹם וְאֶת־מוֹאָ֖ב וְאֶת־בְּנֵ֥י עַמּֽוֹן ׃ 22 וְאֵת֙ כׇּל־מַלְכֵי־צֹ֔ר וְאֵ֖ת כׇּל־מַלְכֵ֣י צִיד֑וֹן וְאֵת֙ מַלְכֵ֣י הָאִ֔י אֲשֶׁ֖ר בְּעֵ֥בֶר הַיָּֽם ׃ 23 וְאֶת־דְּדָ֤ן וְאֶת־תֵּימָא֙ וְאֶת־בּ֔וּז וְאֵ֖ת כׇּל־קְצוּצֵ֥י פֵאָֽה ׃ 24 וְאֵ֖ת כׇּל־מַלְכֵ֣י עֲרָ֑ב וְאֵת֙ כׇּל־מַלְכֵ֣י הָעֶ֔רֶב הַשֹּׁכְנִ֖ים בַּמִּדְבָּֽר ׃ 25 וְאֵ֣ת ׀ כׇּל־מַלְכֵ֣י זִמְרִ֗י וְאֵת֙ כׇּל־מַלְכֵ֣י עֵילָ֔ם וְאֵ֖ת כׇּל־מַלְכֵ֥י מָדָֽי ׃ 26 וְאֵ֣ת ׀ כׇּל־מַלְכֵ֣י הַצָּפ֗וֹן הַקְּרֹבִ֤ים וְהָֽרְחֹקִים֙ אִ֣ישׁ אֶל־אָחִ֔יו וְאֵת֙ כׇּל־הַמַּמְלְכ֣וֹת הָאָ֔רֶץ אֲשֶׁ֖ר עַל־פְּנֵ֣י הָאֲדָמָ֑ה וּמֶ֥לֶךְ שֵׁשַׁ֖ךְ יִשְׁתֶּ֥ה אַחֲרֵיהֶֽם ׃

27 וְאָמַרְתָּ֣ אֲלֵיהֶ֡ם ס כֹּֽה־אָמַר֩ יְהֹוָ֨ה צְבָא֜וֹת אֱלֹהֵ֣י יִשְׂרָאֵ֗ל שְׁת֤וּ וְשִׁכְרוּ֙ וּקְי֔וּ וְנִפְל֖וּ וְלֹ֣א תָק֑וּמוּ מִפְּנֵ֣י הַחֶ֔רֶב אֲשֶׁ֥ר אָנֹכִ֖י שֹׁלֵ֥חַ בֵּינֵיכֶֽם ׃ 28 וְהָיָ֗ה כִּ֧י יְמָאֲנ֛וּ לָקַֽחַת־הַכּ֥וֹס מִיָּדְךָ֖ לִשְׁתּ֑וֹת וְאָמַרְתָּ֣ אֲלֵיהֶ֗ם כֹּ֥ה אָמַ֛ר יְהֹוָ֥ה צְבָא֖וֹת שָׁת֥וֹ תִשְׁתּֽוּ ׃ 29 כִּי֩ הִנֵּ֨ה בָעִ֜יר אֲשֶׁ֧ר נִקְרָא־שְׁמִ֣י עָלֶ֗יהָ אָֽנֹכִי֙ מֵחֵ֣ל לְהָרַ֔ע וְאַתֶּ֖ם הִנָּקֵ֣ה תִנָּק֑וּ לֹ֣א תִנָּק֔וּ כִּ֣י חֶ֗רֶב אֲנִ֤י קֹרֵא֙ עַל־כׇּל־יֹשְׁבֵ֣י הָאָ֔רֶץ נְאֻ֖ם יְהֹוָ֥ה צְבָאֽוֹת ׃

30 וְאַתָּה֙ תִּנָּבֵ֣א אֲלֵיהֶ֔ם אֵ֥ת כׇּל־הַדְּבָרִ֖ים הָאֵ֑לֶּה וְאָמַרְתָּ֣ אֲלֵיהֶ֔ם

יְהֹוָ֞ה מִמָּר֣וֹם יִשְׁאָ֗ג
וּמִמְּע֤וֹן קׇדְשׁוֹ֙ יִתֵּ֣ן קוֹל֔וֹ
שָׁאֹ֥ג יִשְׁאַ֖ג עַל־נָוֵ֑הוּ

He utters shouts like the grape-treaders,
Against all the dwellers on earth.
31Tumult has reached the ends of the earth,
For the LORD has a case against the nations,
He contends with all flesh.
He delivers the wicked to the sword
     —declares the LORD.
32Thus said the LORD of Hosts:
Disaster goes forth
From nation to nation;
A great storm is unleashed
From the remotest parts of earth.

33In that day, the earth shall be strewn with
the slain of the LORD from one end to the other.
They shall not be mourned, or gathered and
buried; they shall become dung upon the face
of the earth.

34Howl, you shepherds, and yell,
Strew [dust] on yourselves, you lords of the
    flock!
For the day of your slaughter draws near.
d-I will break you in pieces,-d
And you shall fall like a precious vessel.
35Flight shall fail the shepherds,
And escape, the lords of the flock.
36Hark, the outcry of the shepherds,
And the howls of the lords of the flock!
For the LORD is ravaging their pasture.
37The peaceful meadows shall be wiped out
By the fierce wrath of the LORD.
38Like a lion, He has gone forth from His lair;
The land has become a desolation,
Because of the oppressived wrath,
Because of His fierce anger.

26 At the beginning of the reign of King
Jehoiakim son of Josiah of Judah, this word
came from the LORD:

הֵידָד֙ כְּדֹרְכִ֣ים יַֽעֲנֶ֔ה
אֶ֥ל כָּל־יֹשְׁבֵ֖י הָאָֽרֶץ׃
31 בָּ֤א שָׁאוֹן֙ עַד־קְצֵ֣ה הָאָ֔רֶץ
כִּ֣י רִ֤יב לַֽיהוָה֙ בַּגּוֹיִ֔ם
נִשְׁפָּ֥ט ה֖וּא לְכָל־בָּשָׂ֑ר
הָרְשָׁעִ֛ים נְתָנָ֥ם לַחֶ֖רֶב
נְאֻם־יְהוָֽה׃ ס
32 כֹּ֤ה אָמַר֙ יְהוָ֣ה צְבָא֔וֹת
הִנֵּ֥ה רָעָ֛ה יֹצֵ֖את מִגּ֣וֹי אֶל־גּ֑וֹי
וְסַ֣עַר גָּד֔וֹל יֵע֖וֹר
מִיַּרְכְּתֵי־אָֽרֶץ׃
33 וְהָי֞וּ חַֽלְלֵ֤י יְהוָה֙ בַּיּ֣וֹם הַה֔וּא מִקְצֵ֥ה
הָאָ֖רֶץ וְעַד־קְצֵ֣ה הָאָ֑רֶץ לֹ֣א יִסָּפְד֗וּ וְלֹ֤א
יֵאָֽסְפוּ֙ וְלֹ֣א יִקָּבֵ֔רוּ לְדֹ֛מֶן עַל־פְּנֵ֥י הָֽאֲדָמָ֖ה
יִֽהְיֽוּ׃
34 הֵילִ֤ילוּ הָֽרֹעִים֙ וְזַֽעֲק֔וּ
וְהִֽתְפַּלְּשׁוּ֙ אַדִּירֵ֣י הַצֹּ֔אן
כִּֽי־מָלְא֥וּ יְמֵיכֶ֖ם לִטְב֑וֹחַ
וּתְפוֹצ֣וֹתִיכֶ֔ם
וּנְפַלְתֶּ֖ם כִּכְלִ֥י חֶמְדָּֽה׃
35 וְאָבַ֥ד מָנ֖וֹס מִן־הָֽרֹעִ֑ים
וּפְלֵיטָ֖ה מֵֽאַדִּירֵ֥י הַצֹּֽאן׃
36 ק֚וֹל צַֽעֲקַ֣ת הָֽרֹעִ֔ים
וְיִֽלְלַ֖ת אַדִּירֵ֣י הַצֹּ֑אן
כִּֽי־שֹׁדֵ֥ד יְהוָ֖ה אֶת־מַרְעִיתָֽם׃
37 וְנָדַ֖מּוּ נְא֣וֹת הַשָּׁל֑וֹם
מִפְּנֵ֖י חֲר֥וֹן אַף־יְהוָֽה׃
38 עָזַ֥ב כַּכְּפִ֖יר סֻכּ֑וֹ
כִּֽי־הָֽיְתָ֤ה אַרְצָם֙ לְשַׁמָּ֔ה
מִפְּנֵי֙ חֲר֣וֹן הַיּוֹנָ֔ה
וּמִפְּנֵ֖י חֲר֥וֹן אַפּֽוֹ׃ פ

כו בְּרֵאשִׁ֗ית מַמְלְכ֛וּת יְהֽוֹיָקִ֥ים בֶּן־
יֹֽאשִׁיָּ֖הוּ מֶ֣לֶךְ יְהוּדָ֑ה הָיָה֙ הַדָּבָ֣ר הַזֶּ֔ה
מֵאֵ֥ת יְהוָ֖ה לֵאמֹֽר׃

2"Thus said the LORD: Stand in the court of the House of the LORD, and speak to [the men of] all the towns of Judah, who are coming to worship in the House of the LORD, all the words which I command you to speak to them. Do not omit anything. 3Perhaps they will listen and turn back, each from his evil way, that I may renounce the punishment I am planning to bring upon them for their wicked acts.

4"Say to them: Thus said the LORD: If you do not obey Me, abiding by the Teaching that I have set before you, 5heeding the words of My servants the prophets whom I have been sending to you persistently—but you have not heeded—6then I will make this House like Shiloh, and I will make this city a curse[a] for all the nations of earth."

7The priests and prophets and all the people heard Jeremiah speaking these words in the House of the LORD. 8And when Jeremiah finished speaking all that the LORD had commanded him to speak to all the people, the priests and the prophets and all the people seized him, shouting, "You shall die! 9How dare you prophesy in the name of the LORD that this House shall become like Shiloh and this city be made desolate, without inhabitants?" And all the people crowded about Jeremiah in the House of the LORD.

10When the officials of Judah heard about this, they went up from the king's palace to the House of the LORD and held a session at the entrance of the New Gate of [b-]the House of[-b] the LORD. 11The priests and prophets said to the officials and to all the people, "This man deserves the death penalty, for he has prophesied against this city, as you yourselves have heard."

12Jeremiah said to the officials and to all the people, "It was the LORD who sent me to prophesy against this House and this city all the words

2 כֹּה ׀ אָמַ֣ר יְהוָ֗ה עֲמֹד֮ בַּחֲצַר֮ בֵּית־יְהוָה֒ וְדִבַּרְתָּ֞ עַל־כָּל־עָרֵ֤י יְהוּדָה֙ הַבָּאִ֔ים לְהִֽשְׁתַּחֲוֺ֖ת בֵּית־יְהוָ֑ה אֵ֣ת כָּל־הַדְּבָרִ֗ים אֲשֶׁ֤ר צִוִּיתִ֙יךָ֙ לְדַבֵּ֣ר אֲלֵיהֶ֔ם אַל־תִּגְרַ֖ע דָּבָֽר׃ 3 אוּלַ֣י יִשְׁמְע֔וּ וְיָשֻׁ֕בוּ אִ֖ישׁ מִדַּרְכּ֣וֹ הָרָעָ֑ה וְנִחַמְתִּ֣י אֶל־הָרָעָ֗ה אֲשֶׁ֨ר אָנֹכִ֤י חֹשֵׁב֙ לַעֲשׂ֣וֹת לָהֶ֔ם מִפְּנֵ֖י רֹ֥עַ מַֽעַלְלֵיהֶֽם׃ 4 וְאָמַרְתָּ֣ אֲלֵיהֶ֗ם כֹּ֚ה אָמַ֣ר יְהוָ֔ה אִם־לֹ֤א תִשְׁמְעוּ֙ אֵלַ֔י לָלֶ֙כֶת֙ בְּתֽוֹרָתִ֔י אֲשֶׁ֥ר נָתַ֖תִּי לִפְנֵיכֶֽם׃ 5 לִשְׁמֹ֗עַ עַל־דִּבְרֵ֤י עֲבָדַי֙ הַנְּבִאִ֔ים אֲשֶׁ֥ר אָנֹכִ֖י שֹׁלֵ֣חַ אֲלֵיכֶ֑ם וְהַשְׁכֵּ֥ם וְשָׁלֹ֖חַ וְלֹ֥א שְׁמַעְתֶּֽם׃ 6 וְנָתַתִּ֛י אֶת־הַבַּ֥יִת הַזֶּ֖ה כְּשִׁלֹ֑ה וְאֶת־הָעִ֤יר הזאתה [הַזֹּאת֙] אֶתֵּ֣ן לִקְלָלָ֔ה לְכֹ֖ל גּוֹיֵ֥י הָאָֽרֶץ׃ ס

7 וַֽיִּשְׁמְע֤וּ הַכֹּהֲנִים֙ וְהַנְּבִאִ֔ים וְכָל־הָעָ֑ם אֶֽת־יִרְמְיָ֔הוּ מְדַבֵּ֛ר אֶת־הַדְּבָרִ֥ים הָאֵ֖לֶּה בְּבֵ֥ית יְהוָֽה׃ 8 וַיְהִ֣י ׀ כְּכַלּ֣וֹת יִרְמְיָ֗הוּ לְדַבֵּר֙ אֵ֣ת כָּל־אֲשֶׁר־צִוָּ֣ה יְהוָ֔ה לְדַבֵּ֖ר אֶל־כָּל־הָעָ֑ם וַיִּתְפְּשׂ֨וּ אֹת֜וֹ הַכֹּהֲנִ֧ים וְהַנְּבִאִ֛ים וְכָל־הָעָ֥ם לֵאמֹ֖ר מ֥וֹת תָּמֽוּת׃ 9 מַדּ֜וּעַ נִבֵּ֣יתָ* בְשֵׁם־יְהוָה֮ לֵאמֹר֒ כְּשִׁלוֹ֙ יִהְיֶ֣ה הַבַּ֣יִת הַזֶּ֔ה וְהָעִ֥יר הַזֹּ֛את תֶּחֱרַ֖ב מֵאֵ֣ין יוֹשֵׁ֑ב וַיִּקָּהֵ֧ל כָּל־הָעָ֛ם אֶֽל־יִרְמְיָ֖הוּ בְּבֵ֥ית יְהוָֽה׃

10 וַֽיִּשְׁמְע֣וּ ׀ שָׂרֵ֣י יְהוּדָ֗ה אֵ֚ת הַדְּבָרִ֣ים הָאֵ֔לֶּה וַיַּעֲל֥וּ מִבֵּית־הַמֶּ֖לֶךְ בֵּ֣ית יְהוָ֑ה וַיֵּ֣שְׁב֔וּ בְּפֶ֛תַח שַֽׁעַר־יְהוָ֖ה* הֶחָדָֽשׁ׃ ס 11 וַיֹּ֨אמְר֜וּ הַכֹּהֲנִ֤ים וְהַנְּבִאִים֙ אֶל־הַשָּׂרִ֔ים וְאֶל־כָּל־הָעָ֖ם לֵאמֹ֑ר מִשְׁפַּט־מָ֙וֶת֙ לָאִ֣ישׁ הַזֶּ֔ה כִּ֣י נִבָּ֔א אֶל־הָעִ֖יר הַזֹּ֑את כַּאֲשֶׁ֥ר שְׁמַעְתֶּ֖ם בְּאָזְנֵיכֶֽם׃ 12 וַיֹּ֣אמֶר יִרְמְיָ֗הוּ אֶל־כָּל־הַשָּׂרִים֙ וְאֶל־כָּל־הָעָ֣ם לֵאמֹ֑ר יְהוָ֣ה שְׁלָחַ֗נִי לְהִנָּבֵ֞א אֶל־הַבַּ֤יִת הַזֶּה֙ וְאֶל־הָעִ֣יר הַזֹּ֔את אֵ֖ת

a Cf. note at 24.9.
b-b So many mss. and ancient versions; other mss. and the editions omit these words.

1075

you heard. ¹³Therefore mend your ways and your acts, and heed the LORD your God, that the LORD may renounce the punishment He has decreed for you. ¹⁴As for me, I am in your hands: do to me what seems good and right to you. ¹⁵But know that if you put me to death, you and this city and its inhabitants will be guilty of shedding the blood of an innocent man. For in truth the LORD has sent me to you, to speak all these words to you."

¹⁶Then the officials and all the people said to the priests and prophets, "This man does not deserve the death penalty, for he spoke to us in the name of the LORD our God."

¹⁷And some of the elders of the land arose and said to the entire assemblage of the people, ¹⁸"Micah the Morashtite, who prophesied in the days of King Hezekiah of Judah, said to all the people of Judah: 'Thus said the LORD of Hosts:

Zion shall be plowed as a field,
Jerusalem shall become heaps of ruins
And the Temple Mount a shrine in the woods.'ᶜ

¹⁹"Did King Hezekiah of Judah, and all Judah, put him to death? Did he not rather fear the LORD and implore the LORD, so that the LORD renounced the punishment He had decreed against them? We are about to do great injury to ourselves!"

²⁰There was also a man prophesying in the name of the LORD, Uriah son of Shemaiah from Kiriath-jearim, who prophesied against this city and this land the same things as Jeremiah. ²¹King Jehoiakim and all his warriors and all the officials heard about his address, and the king wanted to put him to death. Uriah heard of this and fled in fear, and came to Egypt. ²²But King Jehoiakim sent men to Egypt, Elnathan son of

c Cf. Mic. 3.12.

כָּל־הַדְּבָרִים אֲשֶׁר שְׁמַעְתֶּם: 13 וְעַתָּה הֵיטִיבוּ דַרְכֵיכֶם וּמַעַלְלֵיכֶם וְשִׁמְעוּ בְּקוֹל יְהוָה אֱלֹהֵיכֶם וְיִנָּחֵם יְהוָה אֶל־הָרָעָה אֲשֶׁר דִּבֶּר עֲלֵיכֶם: 14 וַאֲנִי הִנְנִי בְיֶדְכֶם עֲשׂוּ־לִי כַּטּוֹב וְכַיָּשָׁר בְּעֵינֵיכֶם: 15 אַךְ ׀ יָדֹעַ תֵּדְעוּ כִּי אִם־מְמִתִים אַתֶּם אֹתִי כִּי־דָם נָקִי אַתֶּם נֹתְנִים עֲלֵיכֶם וְאֶל־הָעִיר הַזֹּאת וְאֶל־יֹשְׁבֶיהָ כִּי בֶאֱמֶת שְׁלָחַנִי יְהוָה עֲלֵיכֶם לְדַבֵּר בְּאָזְנֵיכֶם אֵת כָּל־הַדְּבָרִים הָאֵלֶּה: ס

16 וַיֹּאמְרוּ הַשָּׂרִים וְכָל־הָעָם אֶל־הַכֹּהֲנִים וְאֶל־הַנְּבִיאִים אֵין־לָאִישׁ הַזֶּה מִשְׁפַּט־מָוֶת כִּי בְּשֵׁם יְהוָה אֱלֹהֵינוּ דִּבֶּר אֵלֵינוּ: 17 וַיָּקֻמוּ אֲנָשִׁים מִזִּקְנֵי הָאָרֶץ וַיֹּאמְרוּ אֶל־כָּל־קְהַל הָעָם לֵאמֹר: 18 מִיכָה המוֹרַשְׁתִּי הָיָה נִבָּא בִּימֵי חִזְקִיָּהוּ מֶלֶךְ־יְהוּדָה וַיֹּאמֶר אֶל־כָּל־עַם יְהוּדָה לֵאמֹר כֹּה־אָמַר ׀ יְהוָה צְבָאוֹת

צִיּוֹן שָׂדֶה תֵחָרֵשׁ
וִירוּשָׁלַיִם עִיִּים תִּהְיֶה
וְהַר הַבַּיִת לְבָמוֹת יָעַר:

19 הֶהָמֵת הֱמִתֻהוּ חִזְקִיָּהוּ מֶלֶךְ־יְהוּדָה וְכָל־יְהוּדָה הֲלֹא יָרֵא אֶת־יְהוָה וַיְחַל אֶת־פְּנֵי יְהוָה וַיִּנָּחֶם יְהוָה אֶל־הָרָעָה אֲשֶׁר־דִּבֶּר עֲלֵיהֶם וַאֲנַחְנוּ עֹשִׂים רָעָה גְדוֹלָה עַל־נַפְשׁוֹתֵינוּ:

20 וְגַם־אִישׁ הָיָה מִתְנַבֵּא בְּשֵׁם יְהוָה אוּרִיָּהוּ בֶּן־שְׁמַעְיָהוּ מִקִּרְיַת הַיְּעָרִים וַיִּנָּבֵא עַל־הָעִיר הַזֹּאת וְעַל־הָאָרֶץ הַזֹּאת כְּכֹל דִּבְרֵי יִרְמְיָהוּ: 21 וַיִּשְׁמַע הַמֶּלֶךְ־יְהוֹיָקִים וְכָל־גִּבּוֹרָיו וְכָל־הַשָּׂרִים אֶת־דְּבָרָיו וַיְבַקֵּשׁ הַמֶּלֶךְ הֲמִיתוֹ וַיִּשְׁמַע אוּרִיָּהוּ וַיִּרָא וַיִּבְרַח וַיָּבֹא מִצְרָיִם: 22 וַיִּשְׁלַח הַמֶּלֶךְ יְהוֹיָקִים אֲנָשִׁים מִצְרָיִם אֵת אֶלְנָתָן בֶּן־עַכְבּוֹר וַאֲנָשִׁים אִתּוֹ אֶל־

Achbor and men with him to Egypt. ²³They took Uriah out of Egypt and brought him to King Jehoiakim, who had him put to the sword and his body thrown into the burial place of the common people. ²⁴However, Ahikam son of Shaphan protected Jeremiah, so that he was not handed over to the people for execution.

27

At the beginning of the reign of King Jehoiakim[a] son of Josiah of Judah, this word came to Jeremiah from the Lord:

²Thus said the Lord to me: Make for yourself thongs and bars of a yoke, and put them on your neck. ³[b]And send them[b] to the king of Edom, the king of Moab, the king of the Ammonites, the king of Tyre, and the king of Sidon, by envoys who have come to King Zedekiah of Judah in Jerusalem; ⁴and give them this charge to their masters: Thus said the Lord of Hosts, the God of Israel: Say this to your masters:

⁵"It is I who made the earth, and the men and beasts who are on the earth, by My great might and My outstretched arm; and I give it to whomever I deem proper. ⁶I herewith deliver all these lands to My servant, King Nebuchadnezzar of Babylon; I even give him the wild beasts to serve him. ⁷All nations shall serve him, his son and his grandson—until the turn of his own land comes, when many nations and great kings shall subjugate him. ⁸The nation or kingdom that does not serve him—King Nebuchadnezzar of Babylon—and does not put its neck under the yoke of the king of Babylon, that nation I will visit—declares the Lord—with sword, famine, and pestilence, until I have destroyed it by his hands. ⁹As for you, give no heed to your prophets, augurs, dreamers,[c] diviners, and sorcerers,

מִצְרָיִם: 23 וַיּוֹצִיאוּ אֶת־אוּרִיָּהוּ מִמִּצְרַיִם וַיְבִאֻהוּ אֶל־הַמֶּלֶךְ יְהוֹיָקִים וַיַּכֵּהוּ בֶּחָרֶב וַיַּשְׁלֵךְ אֶת־נִבְלָתוֹ אֶל־קִבְרֵי בְּנֵי הָעָם: 24 אַךְ יַד אֲחִיקָם בֶּן־שָׁפָן הָיְתָה אֶת־יִרְמְיָהוּ לְבִלְתִּי תֵּת־אֹתוֹ בְיַד־הָעָם לַהֲמִיתוֹ: פ

כז בְּרֵאשִׁית מַמְלֶכֶת יְהוֹיָקִם בֶּן־יֹאושִׁיָּהוּ מֶלֶךְ יְהוּדָה הָיָה הַדָּבָר הַזֶּה אֶל־יִרְמְיָה מֵאֵת יְהוָה לֵאמֹר:

2 כֹּה־אָמַר יְהוָה אֵלַי עֲשֵׂה לְךָ מוֹסֵרוֹת וּמֹטוֹת וּנְתַתָּם עַל־צַוָּארֶךָ: 3 וְשִׁלַּחְתָּם אֶל־מֶלֶךְ אֱדוֹם וְאֶל־מֶלֶךְ מוֹאָב וְאֶל־מֶלֶךְ בְּנֵי עַמּוֹן וְאֶל־מֶלֶךְ צֹר וְאֶל־מֶלֶךְ צִידוֹן בְּיַד מַלְאָכִים הַבָּאִים יְרוּשָׁלַם אֶל־צִדְקִיָּהוּ מֶלֶךְ יְהוּדָה: 4 וְצִוִּיתָ אֹתָם אֶל־אֲדֹנֵיהֶם לֵאמֹר כֹּה־אָמַר יְהוָה צְבָאוֹת אֱלֹהֵי יִשְׂרָאֵל כֹּה תֹאמְרוּ אֶל־אֲדֹנֵיכֶם: 5 אָנֹכִי עָשִׂיתִי אֶת־הָאָרֶץ אֶת־הָאָדָם וְאֶת־הַבְּהֵמָה אֲשֶׁר עַל־פְּנֵי הָאָרֶץ בְּכֹחִי הַגָּדוֹל וּבִזְרוֹעִי הַנְּטוּיָה וּנְתַתִּיהָ לַאֲשֶׁר יָשַׁר בְּעֵינָי: 6 וְעַתָּה אָנֹכִי נָתַתִּי אֶת־כָּל־הָאֲרָצוֹת הָאֵלֶּה בְּיַד נְבוּכַדְנֶאצַּר מֶלֶךְ־בָּבֶל עַבְדִּי וְגַם אֶת־חַיַּת הַשָּׂדֶה נָתַתִּי לוֹ לְעָבְדוֹ: 7 וְעָבְדוּ אֹתוֹ כָּל־הַגּוֹיִם וְאֶת־בְּנוֹ וְאֶת־בֶּן־בְּנוֹ עַד בֹּא־עֵת אַרְצוֹ גַּם־הוּא וְעָבְדוּ בוֹ גּוֹיִם רַבִּים וּמְלָכִים גְּדֹלִים: 8 וְהָיָה הַגּוֹי וְהַמַּמְלָכָה אֲשֶׁר לֹא־יַעַבְדוּ אֹתוֹ אֶת־נְבוּכַדְנֶאצַּר מֶלֶךְ־בָּבֶל וְאֵת אֲשֶׁר לֹא־יִתֵּן אֶת־צַוָּארוֹ בְּעֹל מֶלֶךְ בָּבֶל בַּחֶרֶב וּבָרָעָב וּבַדֶּבֶר אֶפְקֹד עַל־הַגּוֹי הַהוּא נְאֻם־יְהוָה עַד־תֻּמִּי אֹתָם בְּיָדוֹ: 9 וְאַתֶּם אַל־תִּשְׁמְעוּ אֶל־נְבִיאֵיכֶם וְאֶל־קֹסְמֵיכֶם וְאֶל חֲלֹמֹתֵיכֶם וְאֶל־עֹנְנֵיכֶם

---

who say to you, 'Do not serve the king of Babylon.' [10]For they prophesy falsely to you—with the result that you shall be banished from your land; I will drive you out and you shall perish. [11]But the nation that puts its neck under the yoke of the king of Babylon, and serves him, will be left by Me on its own soil—declares the LORD—to till it and dwell on it."

[12]I also spoke to King Zedekiah of Judah in just the same way: "Put your necks under the yoke of the king of Babylon; serve him and his people, and live! [13]Otherwise you will die together with your people, by sword, famine, and pestilence, as the LORD has decreed against any nation that does not serve the king of Babylon. [14]Give no heed to the words of the prophets who say to you, 'Do not serve the king of Babylon,' for they prophesy falsely to you. [15]I have not sent them—declares the LORD—and they prophesy falsely in My name, with the result that I will drive you out and you shall perish, together with the prophets who prophesy to you."

[16]And to the priests and to all that people I said: "Thus said the LORD: Give no heed to the words of the prophets who prophesy to you, 'The vessels of the House of the LORD shall shortly be brought back from Babylon,' for they prophesy falsely to you. [17]Give them no heed. Serve the king of Babylon, and live! Otherwise this city shall become a ruin. [18]If they are really prophets and the word of the LORD is with them, let them intercede with the LORD of Hosts not to let the vessels remaining in the House of the LORD, in the royal palace of Judah, and in Jerusalem, go to Babylon!

[19]"For thus said the LORD of Hosts concerning the columns, the tank,[d] the stands, and the rest of the vessels remaining in this city, [20]which King Nebuchadnezzar of Babylon did not take

d   Lit. "sea"; cf. 1 Kings 7.23 ff.

וְאֶל־כַּשְׂפֵיכֶם אֲשֶׁר־הֵם אֹמְרִים אֲלֵיכֶם לֵאמֹר לֹא תַעַבְדוּ אֶת־מֶלֶךְ בָּבֶל: 10 כִּי שֶׁקֶר הֵם נִבְּאִים לָכֶם לְמַעַן הַרְחִיק אֶתְכֶם מֵעַל אַדְמַתְכֶם וְהִדַּחְתִּי אֶתְכֶם וַאֲבַדְתֶּם: 11 וְהַגּוֹי אֲשֶׁר יָבִיא אֶת־צַוָּארוֹ בְּעֹל מֶלֶךְ־בָּבֶל וַעֲבָדוֹ וְהִנַּחְתִּיו עַל־אַדְמָתוֹ נְאֻם־יְהוָה וַעֲבָדָהּ וְיָשַׁב בָּהּ:

12 וְאֶל־צִדְקִיָּה מֶלֶךְ־יְהוּדָה דִּבַּרְתִּי כְּכָל־הַדְּבָרִים הָאֵלֶּה לֵאמֹר הָבִיאוּ אֶת־צַוְּארֵיכֶם בְּעֹל מֶלֶךְ־בָּבֶל וְעִבְדוּ אֹתוֹ וְעַמּוֹ וִחְיוּ: 13 לָמָּה תָמוּתוּ אַתָּה וְעַמֶּךָ בַּחֶרֶב בָּרָעָב וּבַדָּבֶר כַּאֲשֶׁר דִּבֶּר יְהוָה אֶל־הַגּוֹי אֲשֶׁר לֹא־יַעֲבֹד אֶת־מֶלֶךְ בָּבֶל: 14 וְאַל־תִּשְׁמְעוּ אֶל־דִּבְרֵי הַנְּבִאִים הָאֹמְרִים אֲלֵיכֶם לֵאמֹר לֹא תַעַבְדוּ אֶת־מֶלֶךְ בָּבֶל כִּי שֶׁקֶר הֵם נִבְּאִים לָכֶם: 15 כִּי לֹא שְׁלַחְתִּים נְאֻם־יְהוָה וְהֵם נִבְּאִים בִּשְׁמִי לַשָּׁקֶר לְמַעַן הַדִּיחִי אֶתְכֶם וַאֲבַדְתֶּם אַתֶּם וְהַנְּבִאִים הַנִּבְּאִים לָכֶם:

16 וְאֶל־הַכֹּהֲנִים וְאֶל־כָּל־הָעָם הַזֶּה דִּבַּרְתִּי לֵאמֹר כֹּה אָמַר יְהוָה אַל־תִּשְׁמְעוּ אֶל־דִּבְרֵי נְבִיאֵיכֶם הַנִּבְּאִים לָכֶם לֵאמֹר הִנֵּה כְלֵי בֵית־יְהוָה מוּשָׁבִים מִבָּבֶלָה עַתָּה מְהֵרָה כִּי שֶׁקֶר הֵמָּה נִבְּאִים לָכֶם: 17 אַל־תִּשְׁמְעוּ אֲלֵיהֶם עִבְדוּ אֶת־מֶלֶךְ־בָּבֶל וִחְיוּ לָמָּה תִהְיֶה הָעִיר הַזֹּאת חָרְבָּה: 18 וְאִם־נְבִאִים הֵם וְאִם־יֵשׁ דְּבַר־יְהוָה אִתָּם יִפְגְּעוּ־נָא בַּיהוָה צְבָאוֹת לְבִלְתִּי־בֹאוּ הַכֵּלִים ׀ הַנּוֹתָרִים בְּבֵית־יְהוָה וּבֵית מֶלֶךְ יְהוּדָה וּבִירוּשָׁלִָם בָּבֶלָה: פ

19 כִּי כֹה אָמַר יְהוָה צְבָאוֹת אֶל־הָעַמֻּדִים וְעַל־הַיָּם וְעַל־הַמְּכֹנוֹת וְעַל יֶתֶר הַכֵּלִים הַנּוֹתָרִים בָּעִיר הַזֹּאת: 20 אֲשֶׁר לֹא־

when he exiled King Jeconiah son of Jehoiakim of Judah, from Jerusalem to Babylon, with all the nobles of Judah and Jerusalem; ²¹for thus said the Lord of Hosts, the God of Israel, concerning the vessels remaining in the House of the Lord, in the royal palace of Judah, and in Jerusalem: ²²They shall be brought to Babylon, and there they shall remain, until I take note of them—declares the Lord of Hosts—and bring them up and restore them to this place."

28 That year, early in the reign of King Zedekiah of Judah, in the fifth month of the fourth year, the prophet Hananiah son of Azzur, who was from Gibeon, spoke to me in the House of the Lord, in the presence of the priests and all the people. He said: ²"Thus said the Lord of Hosts, the God of Israel: I hereby break the yoke of the king of Babylon. ³In two years, I will restore to this place all the vessels of the House of the Lord which King Nebuchadnezzar of Babylon took from this place and brought to Babylon. ⁴And I will bring back to this place King Jeconiah son of Jehoiakim of Judah, and all the Judean exiles who went to Babylon—declares the Lord. Yes, I will break the yoke of the king of Babylon."

⁵Then the prophet Jeremiah answered the prophet Hananiah in the presence of the priests and of all the people who were standing in the House of the Lord. ⁶The prophet Jeremiah said: "Amen! May the Lord do so! May the Lord fulfill what you have prophesied and bring back from Babylon to this place the vessels of the House of the Lord and all the exiles! ⁷But just listen to this word which I address to you and to all the people: ⁸The prophets who lived before you and me from ancient times prophesied war, disaster, and pestilence against many lands and

לְקַחַם נְבוּכַדְנֶאצַּר מֶלֶךְ בָּבֶל בַּגְלוֹתוֹ אֶת־יְכָנְיָה* בֶּן־יְהוֹיָקִים מֶלֶךְ־יְהוּדָה מִירוּשָׁלַם בָּבֶלָה וְאֵת כָּל־חֹרֵי יְהוּדָה וִירוּשָׁלָם: ס ²¹ כִּי כֹה אָמַר יְהוָה צְבָאוֹת אֱלֹהֵי יִשְׂרָאֵל עַל־הַכֵּלִים הַנּוֹתָרִים בֵּית יְהוָה וּבֵית מֶלֶךְ־יְהוּדָה וִירוּשָׁלָם: ²² בָּבֶלָה יוּבָאוּ וְשָׁמָּה יִהְיוּ עַד יוֹם פָּקְדִי אֹתָם נְאֻם־יְהוָה וְהַעֲלִיתִים וַהֲשִׁיבֹתִים אֶל־הַמָּקוֹם הַזֶּה: פ

כח וַיְהִי ׀ בַּשָּׁנָה הַהִיא בְּרֵאשִׁית מַמְלֶכֶת צִדְקִיָּה מֶלֶךְ־יְהוּדָה בשנת בַּשָּׁנָה הָרְבִיעִית בַּחֹדֶשׁ הַחֲמִישִׁי אָמַר אֵלַי חֲנַנְיָה בֶן־עַזּוּר הַנָּבִיא אֲשֶׁר מִגִּבְעוֹן בְּבֵית יְהוָה לְעֵינֵי הַכֹּהֲנִים וְכָל־הָעָם לֵאמֹר: ² כֹּה־אָמַר יְהוָה צְבָאוֹת אֱלֹהֵי יִשְׂרָאֵל לֵאמֹר שָׁבַרְתִּי אֶת־עֹל מֶלֶךְ בָּבֶל: ³ בְּעוֹד ׀ שְׁנָתַיִם יָמִים אֲנִי מֵשִׁיב אֶל־הַמָּקוֹם הַזֶּה אֶת־כָּל־כְּלֵי בֵּית יְהוָה אֲשֶׁר לָקַח נְבוּכַדְנֶאצַּר מֶלֶךְ־בָּבֶל מִן־הַמָּקוֹם הַזֶּה וַיְבִיאֵם בָּבֶל: ⁴ וְאֶת־יְכָנְיָה בֶן־יְהוֹיָקִים מֶלֶךְ־יְהוּדָה וְאֶת־כָּל־גָּלוּת יְהוּדָה הַבָּאִים בָּבֶלָה אֲנִי מֵשִׁיב אֶל־הַמָּקוֹם הַזֶּה נְאֻם־יְהוָה כִּי אֶשְׁבֹּר אֶת־עֹל מֶלֶךְ בָּבֶל:

⁵ וַיֹּאמֶר יִרְמְיָה הַנָּבִיא אֶל־חֲנַנְיָה הַנָּבִיא לְעֵינֵי הַכֹּהֲנִים וּלְעֵינֵי כָל־הָעָם הָעֹמְדִים בְּבֵית יְהוָה: ⁶ וַיֹּאמֶר יִרְמְיָה הַנָּבִיא אָמֵן כֵּן יַעֲשֶׂה יְהוָה יָקֵם יְהוָה אֶת־דְּבָרֶיךָ אֲשֶׁר נִבֵּאתָ לְהָשִׁיב כְּלֵי בֵית־יְהוָה וְכָל־הַגּוֹלָה מִבָּבֶל אֶל־הַמָּקוֹם הַזֶּה: ⁷ אַךְ־שְׁמַע־נָא הַדָּבָר הַזֶּה אֲשֶׁר אָנֹכִי דֹּבֵר בְּאָזְנֶיךָ וּבְאָזְנֵי כָּל־הָעָם: ⁸ הַנְּבִיאִים אֲשֶׁר הָיוּ לְפָנַי וּלְפָנֶיךָ מִן־הָעוֹלָם וַיִּנָּבְאוּ אֶל־אֲרָצוֹת רַבּוֹת וְעַל־מַמְלָכוֹת גְּדֹלוֹת

great kingdoms. 9So if a prophet prophesies good fortune, then only when the word of the prophet comes true can it be known that the LORD really sent him."

10But the prophet Hananiah removed the bar from the neck of the prophet Jeremiah, and broke it; 11and Hananiah said in the presence of all the people, "Thus said the LORD: So will I break the yoke of King Nebuchadnezzar of Babylon from off the necks of all the nations, in two years." And the prophet Jeremiah went on his way.

12After the prophet Hananiah had broken the bar from off the neck of the prophet Jeremiah, the word of the LORD came to Jeremiah: 13"Go say to Hananiah: Thus said the LORD: You broke bars of wood, but a-you shall-a make bars of iron instead. 14For thus said the LORD of Hosts, the God of Israel: I have put an iron yoke upon the necks of all those nations, that they may serve King Nebuchadnezzar of Babylon—and serve him they shall! I have even given the wild beasts to him."

15And the prophet Jeremiah said to the prophet Hananiah, "Listen, Hananiah! The LORD did not send you, and you have given this people lying assurances. 16Assuredly, thus said the LORD: I am going to banish you from off the earth. This year you shall die, for you have urged disloyalty to the LORD."

17And the prophet Hananiah died that year, in the seventh month.

29
This is the text of the letter which the prophet Jeremiah sent from Jerusalem to the priests, the prophets, the rest of the elders of the exile community, and to all the people whom Nebuchadnezzar had exiled from Jerusalem to Babylon—2after King Jeconiah, the queen mother, the eunuchs, the officials of Judah and

לַמִּלְחָמָ֖ה וּלְרָעָ֣ה וּלְדָ֑בֶר: 9 הַנָּבִ֗יא אֲשֶׁ֤ר יִנָּבֵא֙ לְשָׁל֔וֹם בְּבֹא֙ דְּבַ֣ר הַנָּבִ֔יא יִוָּדַע֙ הַנָּבִ֔יא אֲשֶׁר־שְׁלָח֖וֹ יְהֹוָ֥ה בֶּאֱמֶֽת: 10 וַיִּקַּ֞ח חֲנַנְיָ֣ה הַנָּבִ֗יא אֶת־הַמּוֹטָ֔ה מֵעַ֕ל צַוַּ֖אר יִרְמְיָ֣ה הַנָּבִ֑יא וַֽיִּשְׁבְּרֵֽהוּ: 11 *וַיֹּ֣אמֶר חֲנַנְיָ֣ה לְעֵינֵ֣י כׇל־הָעָם֮ לֵאמֹר֒ כֹּה֮ אָמַ֣ר יְהֹוָה֒ כָּ֣כָה אֶשְׁבֹּ֞ר אֶת־עֹ֣ל ׀ נְבֻֽכַדְנֶאצַּ֣ר מֶֽלֶךְ־בָּבֶ֗ל בְּע֤וֹד שְׁנָתַ֙יִם֙ יָמִ֔ים מֵעַ֕ל־צַוַּ֖אר כׇּל־הַגּוֹיִ֑ם וַיֵּ֛לֶךְ יִרְמְיָ֥ה הַנָּבִ֖יא לְדַרְכּֽוֹ: פ

12 וַיְהִ֥י דְבַר־יְהֹוָ֖ה אֶֽל־יִרְמְיָ֑ה אַחֲרֵ֞י שְׁב֣וֹר חֲנַנְיָ֣ה הַנָּבִ֗יא אֶת־הַמּוֹטָה֙ מֵעַ֕ל צַוַּ֕אר יִרְמְיָ֥ה הַנָּבִ֖יא לֵאמֹֽר: 13 הָל֞וֹךְ וְאָמַרְתָּ֣ אֶל־חֲנַנְיָה֮ לֵאמֹר֒ כֹּ֚ה אָמַ֣ר יְהֹוָ֔ה מוֹטֹ֥ת עֵ֖ץ שָׁבָ֑רְתָּ וְעָשִׂ֥יתָ תַחְתֵּיהֶ֖ן מֹט֥וֹת בַּרְזֶֽל: 14 כִּ֣י כֹֽה־אָמַר֩ יְהֹוָ֨ה צְבָא֜וֹת אֱלֹהֵ֣י יִשְׂרָאֵ֗ל עֹ֣ל בַּרְזֶ֡ל נָתַ֜תִּי עַל־צַוַּ֣אר ׀ כׇּל־הַגּוֹיִ֣ם הָאֵ֗לֶּה לַעֲבֹ֛ד אֶת־נְבֻכַדְנֶאצַּ֥ר מֶֽלֶךְ־בָּבֶ֖ל וַעֲבָדֻ֑הוּ וְגַ֛ם אֶת־חַיַּ֥ת הַשָּׂדֶ֖ה נָתַ֥תִּי לֽוֹ: 15 וַיֹּ֨אמֶר יִרְמְיָ֧ה הַנָּבִ֛יא אֶל־חֲנַנְיָ֥ה הַנָּבִ֖יא שְׁמַֽע־נָ֣א חֲנַנְיָ֑ה לֹא־שְׁלָחֲךָ֣ יְהֹוָ֔ה וְאַתָּ֗ה הִבְטַ֛חְתָּ אֶת־הָעָ֥ם הַזֶּ֖ה עַל־שָֽׁקֶר: 16 לָכֵ֗ן כֹּ֚ה אָמַ֣ר יְהֹוָ֔ה הִנְנִי֙ מְשַׁלֵּֽחֲךָ֙ מֵעַ֣ל פְּנֵ֣י הָאֲדָמָ֔ה הַשָּׁנָ֖ה אַתָּ֣ה מֵ֑ת כִּֽי־סָרָ֥ה דִבַּ֖רְתָּ אֶל־יְהֹוָֽה: 17 וַיָּ֛מׇת חֲנַנְיָ֥ה הַנָּבִ֖יא בַּשָּׁנָ֣ה הַהִ֑יא בַּחֹ֖דֶשׁ הַשְּׁבִיעִֽי: פ

כט וְאֵ֙לֶּה֙ דִּבְרֵ֣י הַסֵּ֔פֶר אֲשֶׁ֥ר שָׁלַ֖ח יִרְמְיָ֣ה הַנָּבִ֑יא מִירוּשָׁלָ֗͏ִם אֶל־יֶ֜תֶר זִקְנֵ֣י הַגּוֹלָ֗ה וְאֶל־הַכֹּהֲנִ֤ים וְאֶל־הַנְּבִיאִים֙ וְאֶל־כׇּל־הָעָ֔ם אֲשֶׁ֨ר הֶגְלָ֧ה נְבֽוּכַדְנֶאצַּ֛ר מִירוּשָׁלַ֖͏ִם בָּבֶֽלָה: 2 אַחֲרֵ֣י צֵ֣את יְכׇנְיָֽה־הַמֶּ֩לֶךְ֩ וְהַגְּבִירָ֨ה וְהַסָּרִיסִ֜ים שָׂרֵ֧י יְהוּדָ֛ה

Jerusalem, and the craftsmen and smiths had left Jerusalem. ³[The letter was sent] through Elasah son of Shaphan and Gemariah son of Hilkiah, whom King Zedekiah of Judah had dispatched to Babylon, to King Nebuchadnezzar of Babylon.

⁴Thus said the LORD of Hosts, the God of Israel, to the whole community which I exiled from Jerusalem to Babylon: ⁵Build houses and live in them, plant gardens and eat their fruit. ⁶Take wives and beget sons and daughters; and take wives for your sons, and give your daughters to husbands, that they may bear sons and daughters. Multiply there, do not decrease. ⁷And seek the welfare of the city to which I have exiled you and pray to the LORD in its behalf; for in its prosperity you shall prosper.

⁸For thus said the LORD of Hosts, the God of Israel: Let not the prophets and diviners in your midst deceive you, and pay no heed to the dreams they^a dream. ⁹For they prophesy to you in My name falsely; I did not send them—declares the LORD.

¹⁰For thus said the LORD: When Babylon's seventy years are over, I will take note of you, and I will fulfill to you My promise of favor—to bring you back to this place. ¹¹For I am mindful of the plans I have made concerning you—declares the LORD—plans for your welfare, not for disaster, to give you a hopeful future. ¹²When you call Me, and come and pray to Me, I will give heed to you. ¹³You will search for Me and find Me, if only you seek Me wholeheartedly. ¹⁴I will be at hand for you—declares the LORD—and I will restore your fortunes. And I will gather you from all the nations and from all the places to which I have banished you—declares the LORD—and I will bring you back to the place from which I have exiled you.

a   Heb. "you."

1081

וִירוּשָׁלַ֖͏ִם וְהֶחָרָ֣שׁ וְהַמַּסְגֵּ֑ר מִירוּשָׁלָֽ͏ִם: ³ בְּיַד֩ אֶלְעָשָׂ֨ה בֶן־שָׁפָ֜ן וּגְמַרְיָ֣ה בֶן־חִלְקִיָּ֗ה אֲשֶׁ֨ר שָׁלַ֜ח צִדְקִיָּ֣ה מֶֽלֶךְ־יְהוּדָ֗ה אֶל־ נְבֽוּכַדְנֶאצַּ֛ר מֶ֥לֶךְ בָּבֶ֖ל בָּבֶ֣לָה לֵאמֹֽר: ס

⁴ כֹּ֣ה אָמַ֞ר יְהוָ֤ה צְבָאוֹת֙ אֱלֹהֵ֣י יִשְׂרָאֵ֔ל לְכָל־הַגּוֹלָ֕ה אֲשֶׁר־הִגְלֵ֖יתִי מִירוּשָׁלַ֥͏ִם בָּבֶֽלָה: ⁵ בְּנ֥וּ בָתִּ֖ים וְשֵׁ֑בוּ וְנִטְע֣וּ גַנּ֔וֹת וְאִכְל֖וּ אֶת־פִּרְיָֽן: ⁶ קְח֣וּ נָשִׁים֮ וְהוֹלִ֣ידוּ֒ בָּנִ֣ים וּבָנ֗וֹת וּקְח֤וּ לִבְנֵיכֶם֙ נָשִׁ֔ים וְאֶת־ בְּנֽוֹתֵיכֶם֙ תְּנ֣וּ לַֽאֲנָשִׁ֔ים וְתֵלַ֖דְנָה בָּנִ֣ים וּבָנ֑וֹת וּרְבוּ־שָׁ֖ם וְאַל־תִּמְעָֽטוּ: ⁷ וְדִרְשׁ֞וּ אֶת־שְׁל֣וֹם הָעִ֗יר אֲשֶׁ֨ר הִגְלֵ֤יתִי אֶתְכֶם֙ שָׁ֔מָּה וְהִתְפַּֽלְל֥וּ בַֽעֲדָ֖הּ אֶל־יְהוָ֑ה כִּ֣י בִשְׁלוֹמָ֔הּ יִהְיֶ֥ה לָכֶ֖ם שָׁלֽוֹם: פ ⁸ כִּי֩ כֹ֨ה אָמַ֜ר יְהוָ֤ה צְבָאוֹת֙ אֱלֹהֵ֣י יִשְׂרָאֵ֔ל אַל־יַשִּׁ֧יאוּ לָכֶ֛ם נְבִֽיאֵיכֶ֥ם אֲשֶׁר־בְּקִרְבְּכֶ֖ם וְקֹֽסְמֵיכֶ֑ם וְאַל־תִּשְׁמְעוּ֙ אֶל־חֲלֹ֣מֹֽתֵיכֶ֔ם אֲשֶׁ֥ר אַתֶּ֖ם מַחְלְמִֽים: ⁹ כִּ֣י בְשֶׁ֔קֶר הֵ֛ם נִבְּאִ֥ים לָכֶ֖ם בִּשְׁמִ֑י לֹ֥א שְׁלַחְתִּ֖ים נְאֻם־ יְהוָֽה: ס

¹⁰ כִּי־כֹה֙ אָמַ֣ר יְהוָ֔ה כִּ֠י לְפִ֞י מְלֹ֧את לְבָבֶ֛ל שִׁבְעִ֥ים שָׁנָ֖ה אֶפְקֹ֣ד אֶתְכֶ֑ם וַהֲקִֽמֹתִ֤י עֲלֵיכֶם֙ אֶת־דְּבָרִ֣י הַטּ֔וֹב לְהָשִׁ֥יב אֶתְכֶ֖ם אֶל־הַמָּק֥וֹם הַזֶּֽה: ¹¹ כִּ֣י אָנֹכִ֗י יָדַ֜עְתִּי אֶת־ הַמַּחֲשָׁבֹ֗ת אֲשֶׁ֧ר אָנֹכִ֛י חֹשֵׁ֥ב עֲלֵיכֶ֖ם נְאֻם־ יְהוָ֑ה מַחְשְׁב֤וֹת שָׁלוֹם֙ וְלֹ֣א לְרָעָ֔ה לָתֵ֥ת לָכֶ֖ם אַחֲרִ֥ית וְתִקְוָֽה: ¹² וּקְרָאתֶ֤ם אֹתִי֙ וַֽהֲלַכְתֶּ֔ם וְהִתְפַּלַּלְתֶּ֖ם אֵלָ֑י וְשָׁמַעְתִּ֖י אֲלֵיכֶֽם: ¹³ וּבִקַּשְׁתֶּ֥ם אֹתִ֖י וּמְצָאתֶ֑ם כִּ֥י תִדְרְשֻׁ֖נִי בְּכָל־לְבַבְכֶֽם: ¹⁴ וְנִמְצֵ֨אתִי לָכֶם֮ נְאֻם־יְהוָה֒ וְשַׁבְתִּ֣י אֶת־שְׁבִ֣יתְכֶם וְקִבַּצְתִּ֣י אֶתְכֶ֗ם מִֽכָּל־הַגּוֹיִם֙ וּמִכָּל־ הַמְּקוֹמוֹת֙ אֲשֶׁ֨ר הִדַּ֧חְתִּי אֶתְכֶ֛ם שָׁ֖ם נְאֻם־ יְהוָ֑ה וַהֲשִׁבֹתִ֣י אֶתְכֶ֔ם אֶל־הַ֨מָּק֔וֹם אֲשֶׁר־ הִגְלֵ֥יתִי אֶתְכֶ֖ם מִשָּֽׁם:

¹⁵But you say, "The LORD has raised up prophets for us in Babylon."ᵇ

¹⁶Thus said the LORD concerning the king who sits on the throne of David, and concerning all the people who dwell in this city, your brothers who did not go out with you into exile—¹⁷thus said the LORD of Hosts: I am going to let loose sword, famine, and pestilence against them and I will treat them as loathsome figs, so bad that they cannot be eaten.ᶜ ¹⁸I will pursue them with the sword, with famine, and with pestilence; and I will make them a horror to all the kingdoms of the earth, a curse and an object of horror and hissingᵈ and scorn among all the nations to which I shall banish them, ¹⁹ because they did not heed My words—declares the LORD—when I persistently sent to them My servants, the prophets, and theyᵈ did not heed—declares the LORD.

²⁰But you, the whole exile community which I banished from Jerusalem to Babylon, hear the word of the LORD! ²¹Thus said the LORD of Hosts, the God of Israel, concerning Ahab son of Kolaiah and Zedekiah son of Maaseiah, who prophesy falsely to you in My name: I am going to deliver them into the hands of King Nebuchadrezzar of Babylon, and he shall put them to death before your eyes. ²²And the whole community of Judah in Babylonia shall use a curse derived from their fate: "May God make you like Zedekiah and Ahab, whom the king of Babylon consigned to the flames!"—²³because they did vile things in Israel, committing adultery with the wives of their fellows and speaking in My name false words which I had not commanded them. I am He who knows and bears witness—declares the LORD.

²⁴Concerning Shemaiah the Nehelamite youᵉ shall say: ²⁵Thus said the LORD of Hosts, the God

---

ᵇ This verse is continued in vv. 20 ff.
ᶜ Cf. 24.1 ff.
ᵈ Cf. note at 18.16.
ᵉ I.e., Jeremiah.

¹⁵ כִּ֣י אֲמַרְתֶּ֔ם הֵקִ֨ים לָ֥נוּ יְהֹוָ֖ה נְבִאִ֑ים בָּבֶֽלָה׃ ס
¹⁶ כִּי־כֹ֣ה ׀ אָמַ֣ר יְהֹוָ֗ה אֶל־הַמֶּ֙לֶךְ֙ הַיּוֹשֵׁב֙ אֶל־כִּסֵּ֣א דָוִ֔ד וְאֶל־כׇּל־הָעָ֔ם הַיּוֹשֵׁ֖ב בָּעִ֣יר הַזֹּ֑את אֲחֵיכֶ֕ם אֲשֶׁ֛ר לֹא־יָצְא֥וּ אִתְּכֶ֖ם בַּגּוֹלָֽה׃ ¹⁷ כֹּ֤ה אָמַר֙ יְהֹוָ֣ה צְבָא֔וֹת הִנְנִ֗י מְשַׁלֵּ֤חַ בָּם֙ אֶת־הַחֶ֙רֶב֙ אֶת־הָ֣רָעָ֔ב וְאֶת־הַדָּ֑בֶר וְנָתַתִּ֣י אוֹתָ֗ם כַּתְּאֵנִים֙ הַשֹּׁ֣עָרִ֔ים אֲשֶׁ֥ר לֹא־תֵאָכַ֖לְנָה מֵרֹֽעַ׃ ¹⁸ וְרָ֣דַפְתִּ֗י אַֽחֲרֵיהֶם֙ בַּחֶ֙רֶב֙ בָּרָעָ֣ב וּבַדָּ֔בֶר וּנְתַתִּ֣ים לזועה לְזַעֲוָ֗ה לְכֹ֣ל ׀ מַמְלְכ֣וֹת הָאָ֔רֶץ לְאָלָ֤ה וּלְשַׁמָּה֙ וְלִשְׁרֵקָ֣ה וּלְחֶרְפָּ֔ה בְּכׇל־הַגּוֹיִ֖ם אֲשֶׁר־הִדַּחְתִּ֥ים שָֽׁם׃ ¹⁹ תַּ֣חַת אֲשֶֽׁר־לֹא־שָׁמְע֣וּ אֶל־דְּבָרַ֗י נְאֻם־יְהֹוָ֑ה אֲשֶׁר֩ שָׁלַ֨חְתִּי אֲלֵיהֶ֜ם אֶת־עֲבָדַ֤י הַנְּבִאִים֙ הַשְׁכֵּ֣ם וְשָׁלֹ֔חַ וְלֹ֥א שְׁמַעְתֶּ֖ם נְאֻם־יְהֹוָֽה׃
²⁰ וְאַתֶּ֖ם שִׁמְע֣וּ דְבַר־יְהֹוָ֑ה כׇּל־הַ֨גּוֹלָ֔ה אֲשֶׁר־שִׁלַּ֥חְתִּי מִירוּשָׁלַ֖͏ִם בָּבֶֽלָה׃ ס ²¹ כֹּה־אָמַר֩ יְהֹוָ֨ה צְבָא֜וֹת אֱלֹהֵ֣י יִשְׂרָאֵ֗ל אֶל־אַחְאָ֤ב בֶּן־קֽוֹלָיָה֙ וְאֶל־צִדְקִיָּ֣הוּ בֶן־מַ֣עֲשֵׂיָ֔ה הַֽנִּבְּאִ֥ים לָכֶ֛ם בִּשְׁמִ֖י שָׁ֑קֶר הִנְנִ֣י ׀ נֹתֵ֣ן אֹתָ֗ם בְּיַד֙ נְבֽוּכַדְרֶאצַּ֣ר מֶֽלֶךְ־בָּבֶ֔ל וְהִכָּ֖ם לְעֵינֵיכֶֽם׃ ²² וְלֻקַּ֤ח מֵהֶם֙ קְלָלָ֔ה לְכֹל֙ גָּל֣וּת יְהוּדָ֔ה אֲשֶׁ֥ר בְּבָבֶ֖ל לֵאמֹ֑ר יְשִֽׂמְךָ֤ יְהֹוָה֙ כְּצִדְקִיָּ֣הוּ וּכְאֶחָ֔ב אֲשֶׁר־קָלָ֥ם מֶֽלֶךְ־בָּבֶ֖ל בָּאֵֽשׁ׃ ²³ יַ֡עַן אֲשֶׁר֩ עָשׂ֨וּ נְבָלָ֜ה בְּיִשְׂרָאֵ֗ל וַיְנַֽאֲפוּ֙ אֶת־נְשֵׁ֣י רֵֽעֵיהֶ֔ם וַיְדַבְּר֤וּ דָבָר֙ בִּשְׁמִ֣י שֶׁ֔קֶר אֲשֶׁ֖ר ל֣וֹא צִוִּיתִ֑ם וְאָנֹכִ֛י הוֹיֵ֥דֵֽעַ וָעֵ֖ד נְאֻם־יְהֹוָֽה׃ ס
²⁴ וְאֶל־שְׁמַעְיָ֥הוּ הַנֶּחֱלָמִ֖י תֹּאמַ֥ר לֵאמֹֽר׃ ²⁵ כֹּֽה־אָמַ֞ר יְהֹוָ֧ה צְבָא֛וֹת אֱלֹהֵ֥י יִשְׂרָאֵ֖ל

of Israel: Because you sent letters in your own name to all the people in Jerusalem, to Zephaniah son of Maaseiah and to the rest of the priests, as follows, ²⁶"The LORD appointed you priest in place of the priest Jehoiada,ᶠ to exercise authority-ᶠ in the House of the LORD over every madman who wants to play the prophet, to put him into the stocksᵍ and into the pillory.ᵍ ²⁷Now why have you not rebuked Jeremiah the Anathothite, who plays the prophet among you? ²⁸For he has actually sent a message to us in Babylon to this effect: It will be a long time. Build houses and live in them, plant gardens and enjoy their fruit."—

²⁹When the priest Zephaniah read this letter in the hearing of the prophet Jeremiah, ³⁰the word of the LORD came to Jeremiah: ³¹Send a message to the entire exile community: "Thus said the LORD concerning Shemaiah the Nehelamite: Because Shemaiah prophesied to you, though I did not send him, and made you false promises, ³²assuredly, thus said the LORD: I am going to punish Shemaiah the Nehelamite and his offspring. There shall be no man of his line dwelling among this people or seeing the good things I am going to do for My people— declares the LORD—for he has urged disloyalty toward the LORD."

30 The word which came to Jeremiah from the LORD: ²Thus said the LORD, the God of Israel: Write down in a scroll all the words that I have spoken to you. ³For days are coming— declares the LORD—when I will restore the fortunes of My people Israel and Judah, said the LORD; and I will bring them back to the land that I gave their fathers, and they shall possess it. ⁴And these are the words that the LORD spoke concerning Israel and Judah:

לֵאמֹר יַעַן אֲשֶׁר אַתָּה שָׁלַחְתָּ בְשִׁמְכָה* סְפָרִים אֶל־כָּל־הָעָם אֲשֶׁר בִּירוּשָׁלַ͏ִם וְאֶל־צְפַנְיָה בֶן־מַעֲשֵׂיָה הַכֹּהֵן וְאֶל כָּל־הַכֹּהֲנִים לֵאמֹר: 26 יְהֹוָה נְתָנְךָ כֹהֵן תַּחַת יְהוֹיָדָע הַכֹּהֵן לִהְיוֹת פְּקִדִים בֵּית יְהֹוָה לְכָל־אִישׁ מְשֻׁגָּע וּמִתְנַבֵּא וְנָתַתָּה אֹתוֹ אֶל־הַמַּהְפֶּכֶת וְאֶל־הַצִּינֹק: 27 וְעַתָּה לָמָּה לֹא גָעַרְתָּ בְּיִרְמְיָהוּ הָעֲנְתֹתִי הַמִּתְנַבֵּא לָכֶם: 28 כִּי עַל־כֵּן שָׁלַח אֵלֵינוּ בָּבֶל לֵאמֹר אֲרֻכָּה הִיא בְּנוּ בָתִּים וְשֵׁבוּ וְנִטְעוּ גַנּוֹת וְאִכְלוּ אֶת־פְּרִיהֶן:

29 וַיִּקְרָא צְפַנְיָה הַכֹּהֵן אֶת־הַסֵּפֶר הַזֶּה בְּאָזְנֵי יִרְמְיָהוּ הַנָּבִיא: פ 30 וַיְהִי דְּבַר־ יְהֹוָה אֶל־יִרְמְיָהוּ לֵאמֹר: 31 שְׁלַח עַל־ כָּל־הַגּוֹלָה לֵאמֹר כֹּה אָמַר יְהֹוָה אֶל־ שְׁמַעְיָה הַנֶּחֱלָמִי יַעַן אֲשֶׁר נִבָּא לָכֶם שְׁמַעְיָה וַאֲנִי לֹא שְׁלַחְתִּיו וַיַּבְטַח אֶתְכֶם עַל־שָׁקֶר: 32 לָכֵן כֹּה־אָמַר יְהֹוָה הִנְנִי פֹקֵד עַל־שְׁמַעְיָה הַנֶּחֱלָמִי וְעַל־זַרְעוֹ לֹא־ יִהְיֶה לוֹ אִישׁ ׀ יוֹשֵׁב ׀ בְּתוֹךְ־הָעָם הַזֶּה וְלֹא־יִרְאֶה בַטּוֹב אֲשֶׁר־אֲנִי עֹשֶׂה־לְעַמִּי נְאֻם־יְהֹוָה כִּי־סָרָה דִבֶּר עַל־יְהֹוָה: ס

ל הַדָּבָר אֲשֶׁר הָיָה אֶל־יִרְמְיָהוּ מֵאֵת יְהֹוָה לֵאמֹר: 2 כֹּה־אָמַר יְהֹוָה אֱלֹהֵי יִשְׂרָאֵל לֵאמֹר כְּתָב־לְךָ אֵת כָּל־הַדְּבָרִים אֲשֶׁר־דִּבַּרְתִּי אֵלֶיךָ אֶל־סֵפֶר: 3 כִּי הִנֵּה יָמִים בָּאִים נְאֻם־יְהֹוָה וְשַׁבְתִּי אֶת־ שְׁבוּת עַמִּי יִשְׂרָאֵל וִיהוּדָה אָמַר יְהֹוָה וַהֲשִׁבֹתִים אֶל־הָאָרֶץ אֲשֶׁר־נָתַתִּי לַאֲבוֹתָם וִירֵשׁוּהָ: פ 4 וְאֵלֶּה הַדְּבָרִים אֲשֶׁר דִּבֶּר יְהֹוָה אֶל־יִשְׂרָאֵל וְאֶל־יְהוּדָה:

ᶠ⁻ᶠ Lit. "that there might be officials."
ᵍ Meaning of Heb. uncertain.

5Thus said the LORD:

We have heard cries of panic,

Terror without relief.

6Ask and see:

Surely males do not bear young!

Why then do I see every man

With his hands on his loins

Like a woman in labor?

Why have all faces turned pale?

7Ah, that day is awesome;

There is none like it!

It is a time of trouble for Jacob,

But he shall be delivered from it.

8In that day—declares the LORD of Hosts—I will break the yoke from off your neck and I will rip off your bonds. Strangers shall no longer make slaves of them; 9instead, they shall serve the LORD their God and David, the king whom I will raise up for them.

10But you,

Have no fear, My servant Jacob

—declares the LORD—

Be not dismayed, O Israel!

I will deliver you from far away,

Your folk from their land of captivity.

And Jacob shall again have calm

And quiet with none to trouble him;

11For I am with you to deliver you

—declares the LORD.

I will make an end of all the nations

Among which I have dispersed you;

But I will not make an end of you!

I will not leave you unpunished,

But will chastise you in measure.

12For thus said the LORD:

Your injury is incurable,

5 כִּי־כֹה֙ אָמַ֣ר יְהֹוָ֔ה

ק֥וֹל חֲרָדָ֖ה שָׁמָ֑עְנוּ

פַּ֖חַד וְאֵ֥ין שָׁלֽוֹם׃

6 שַׁאֲלוּ־נָ֣א וּרְא֔וּ

אִם־יֹלֵ֖ד זָכָ֑ר

מַדּוּעַ֩ רָאִ֨יתִי כׇל־גֶּ֜בֶר

יָדָ֤יו עַל־חֲלָצָיו֙

כַּיּֽוֹלֵדָ֔ה

וְנֶהֶפְכ֥וּ כׇל־פָּנִ֖ים לְיֵרָקֽוֹן׃

7 ה֗וֹי כִּ֥י גָד֛וֹל הַיּ֥וֹם הַה֖וּא

מֵאַ֣יִן כָּמֹ֑הוּ

וְעֵֽת־צָרָ֥ה הִיא֙ לְיַֽעֲקֹ֔ב

וּמִמֶּ֖נָּה יִוָּשֵֽׁעַ׃

8 וְהָיָה֩ בַיּ֨וֹם הַה֜וּא נְאֻ֣ם ׀ יְהֹוָ֣ה צְבָא֗וֹת

אֶשְׁבֹּ֤ר עֻלּוֹ֙ מֵעַ֣ל צַוָּארֶ֔ךָ וּמוֹסְרוֹתֶ֖יךָ

אֲנַתֵּ֑ק וְלֹא־יַעַבְדוּ־ב֥וֹ ע֖וֹד זָרִֽים׃ 9 וְעָ֣בְד֔וּ

אֵ֖ת יְהֹוָ֣ה אֱלֹהֵיהֶ֑ם וְאֵת֙ דָּוִ֣ד מַלְכָּ֔ם אֲשֶׁ֥ר

אָקִ֖ים לָהֶֽם׃ ס

10 וְאַתָּ֣ה

אַל־תִּירָ֤א עַבְדִּי֙ יַֽעֲקֹ֔ב

נְאֻם־יְהֹוָ֔ה

וְאַל־תֵּחַ֖ת יִשְׂרָאֵ֑ל

כִּ֠י הִנְנִ֤י מוֹשִֽׁיעֲךָ֙ מֵֽרָח֔וֹק

וְאֶֽת־זַרְעֲךָ֖ מֵאֶ֣רֶץ שִׁבְיָ֑ם

וְשָׁ֧ב יַעֲקֹ֛ב וְשָׁקַ֥ט

וְשַׁאֲנַ֖ן וְאֵ֥ין מַחֲרִֽיד׃

11 כִּֽי־אִתְּךָ֥ אֲנִ֛י

נְאֻם־יְהֹוָ֖ה לְהֽוֹשִׁיעֶ֑ךָ

כִּי֩ אֶעֱשֶׂ֨ה כָלָ֜ה בְּכׇל־הַגּוֹיִ֣ם ׀

אֲשֶׁ֧ר הֲפִצוֹתִ֣יךָ שָּׁ֗ם

אַ֤ךְ אֹֽתְךָ֙ לֹֽא־אֶעֱשֶׂ֣ה כָלָ֔ה

וְיִסַּרְתִּ֨יךָ֙ לַמִּשְׁפָּ֔ט

וְנַקֵּ֖ה לֹ֥א אֲנַקֶּֽךָּ׃ פ

12 כִּ֣י כֹ֥ה אָמַ֖ר יְהֹוָ֑ה

אָנ֣וּשׁ לְשִׁבְרֵ֔ךְ

Your wound severe;

13a-No one pleads for the healing of your sickness,-a

There is no remedy, no recovery for you.

14All your lovers have forgotten you,

They do not seek you out;

For I have struck you as an enemy strikes,

With cruel chastisement,

Because your iniquity was so great

And your sins so many.

15Why cry out over your injury,

That your wound is incurable?

I did these things to you

Because your iniquity was so great

And your sins so many.

16Assuredly,

All who wanted to devour you shall be devoured,

And every one of your foes shall go into captivity;

Those who despoiled you shall be despoiled,

And all who pillaged you I will give up to pillage.

17But I will bring healing to you

And cure you of your wounds

        —declares the LORD.

Though they called you "Outcast,

That Zion whom no one seeks out,"

18Thus said the LORD:

I will restore the fortunes of Jacob's tents

And have compassion upon his dwellings.

The city shall be rebuilt on its mound,b

And the fortress in its proper place.

19From them shall issue thanksgiving

And the sound of dancers.

I will multiply them,

And they shall not be few;

I will make them honored,

נַחְלָ֖ה מַכָּתֵֽךְ׃

13 אֵֽין־דָּ֥ן דִּינֵ֖ךְ לְמָז֑וֹר

רְפֻא֥וֹת תְּעָלָ֖ה אֵ֥ין לָֽךְ׃

14 כׇּל־מְאַהֲבַ֣יִךְ שְׁכֵח֔וּךְ

אוֹתָ֖ךְ לֹ֣א יִדְרֹ֑שׁוּ

כִּי֩ מַכַּ֨ת אוֹיֵ֤ב הִכִּיתִיךְ֙

מוּסַ֣ר אַכְזָרִ֔י

עַ֖ל רֹ֣ב עֲוֺנֵ֑ךְ

עָצְמ֖וּ חַטֹּאתָֽיִךְ׃

15 מַה־תִּזְעַק֙ עַל־שִׁבְרֵ֔ךְ

אָנ֖וּשׁ מַכְאֹבֵ֑ךְ

עַ֣ל ׀ רֹ֣ב עֲוֺנֵ֗ךְ

עָֽצְמוּ֙ חַטֹּאתַ֔יִךְ

עָשִׂ֥יתִי אֵ֖לֶּה לָֽךְ׃

16 לָכֵ֞ן

כׇּל־אֹכְלַ֙יִךְ֙ יֵאָכֵ֔לוּ

וְכׇל־צָרַ֥יִךְ כֻּלָּ֖ם בַּשְּׁבִ֣י יֵלֵ֑כוּ

וְהָי֤וּ שֹׁאסַ֙יִךְ֙* לִמְשִׁסָּ֔ה

וְכׇל־בֹּזְזַ֖יִךְ אֶתֵּ֥ן לָבַֽז׃

17 כִּי֩ אַעֲלֶ֨ה אֲרֻכָ֤ה לָךְ֙

וּמִמַּכּוֹתַ֥יִךְ אֶרְפָּאֵ֖ךְ

נְאֻם־יְהֹוָ֑ה

כִּ֤י נִדָּחָה֙ קָ֣רְאוּ לָ֔ךְ

צִיּ֣וֹן הִ֔יא דֹּרֵ֖שׁ אֵ֥ין לָֽהּ׃ ס

18 כֹּ֣ה ׀ אָמַ֣ר יְהֹוָ֗ה

הִנְנִי־שָׁב֙ שְׁבוּת֙ אׇהֳלֵ֣י יַֽעֲק֔וֹב*

וּמִשְׁכְּנֹתָ֖יו אֲרַחֵ֑ם

וְנִבְנְתָ֥ה עִיר֙ עַל־תִּלָּ֔הּ

וְאַרְמ֖וֹן עַל־מִשְׁפָּט֥וֹ יֵשֵֽׁב׃

19 וְיָצָ֥א מֵהֶ֛ם תּוֹדָ֖ה

וְק֣וֹל מְשַׂחֲקִ֑ים

וְהִרְבִּתִים֙

וְלֹ֣א יִמְעָ֔טוּ

וְהִכְבַּדְתִּ֖ים

v. 16.   יתיר א'
v. 18.   מלא ו'

a-a   Meaning of Heb. uncertain.
b   I.e., on the mound of ruins left after its previous destruction.

And they shall not be humbled.

20His children shall be as of old,

And his community shall be established by
My grace;

And I will deal with all his oppressors.

21His chieftain shall be one of his own,

His ruler shall come from his midst;

I will bring him near, that he may approach
Me

—declares the LORD—

For who would otherwise dare approach Me?

22You shall be My people,

And I will be your God.

23Lo, the storm of the LORD goes forth in fury,

A raging tempest;

It shall whirl down upon the head of the
wicked.

24The anger of the LORD shall not turn back

Till it has fulfilled and completed His purposes.

In the days to come

You shall perceive it.

[31]1cAt that time—declares the LORD—I
will be God to all the clans of Israel, and they
shall be My people.

31 2Thus said the LORD:

The people escaped from the sword,

Found favor in the wilderness;

When Israel was marching homeward

3The LORD revealed Himself to mea of old.

Eternal love I conceived for you then;

Therefore I continue My grace to you.

4I will build you firmly again,

O Maiden Israel!

Again you shall take up your timbrels

וְלֹא יִצְעָרוּ׃

20 וְהָיוּ בָנָיו כְּקֶדֶם
וַעֲדָתוֹ לְפָנַי תִּכּוֹן
וּפָקַדְתִּי עַל כָּל־לֹחֲצָיו׃

21 וְהָיָה אַדִּירוֹ מִמֶּנּוּ
וּמֹשְׁלוֹ מִקִּרְבּוֹ יֵצֵא
וְהִקְרַבְתִּיו וְנִגַּשׁ אֵלָי
כִּי מִי הוּא־זֶה עָרַב אֶת־לִבּוֹ לָגֶשֶׁת
אֵלַי
נְאֻם־יְהֹוָה׃

22 וִהְיִיתֶם לִי לְעָם
וְאָנֹכִי אֶהְיֶה לָכֶם לֵאלֹהִים׃ ס

23 הִנֵּה ׀ סַעֲרַת יְהֹוָה חֵמָה יָצְאָה
סַעַר מִתְגּוֹרֵר
עַל רֹאשׁ רְשָׁעִים יָחוּל׃

24 לֹא יָשׁוּב חֲרוֹן אַף־יְהֹוָה
עַד־עֲשֹׂתוֹ וְעַד־הֲקִימוֹ מְזִמּוֹת לִבּוֹ
בְּאַחֲרִית הַיָּמִים
תִּתְבּוֹנְנוּ בָהּ׃

1 בָּעֵת הַהִיא נְאֻם־יְהֹוָה אֶהְיֶה לֵאלֹהִים
לְכֹל מִשְׁפְּחוֹת יִשְׂרָאֵל וְהֵמָּה יִהְיוּ־לִי
לְעָם׃ ס

לא

2 כֹּה אָמַר יְהֹוָה
מָצָא חֵן בַּמִּדְבָּר
עַם שְׂרִידֵי חָרֶב
הָלוֹךְ לְהַרְגִּיעוֹ יִשְׂרָאֵל׃

3 מֵרָחוֹק יְהֹוָה נִרְאָה לִי
וְאַהֲבַת עוֹלָם אֲהַבְתִּיךְ
עַל־כֵּן מְשַׁכְתִּיךְ חָסֶד׃

4 עוֹד אֶבְנֵךְ וְנִבְנֵית
בְּתוּלַת יִשְׂרָאֵל
עוֹד תַּעְדִּי תֻפַּיִךְ

---

c   *In some editions this verse is 30.25.*

a   *Emendation yields "him."*

And go forth to the rhythm of the dancers.
⁵Again you shall plant vineyards
On the hills of Samaria;
Men shall plant and live to enjoy them.
⁶For the day is coming when watchmen
Shall proclaim on the heights of Ephraim:
Come, let us go up to Zion,
To the Lord our God!

⁷For thus said the Lord:
Cry out in joy for Jacob,
Shout at the crossroads[b] of the nations!
Sing aloud in praise, and say:
c-Save, O Lord, Your people,-c
The remnant of Israel.
⁸I will bring them in from the northland,
Gather them from the ends of the earth—
The blind and the lame among them,
Those with child and those in labor—
In a vast throng they shall return here.
⁹They shall come with weeping,
And with compassion[d] will I guide them.
I will lead them to streams of water,
By a level road where they will not stumble.
For I am ever a Father to Israel,
Ephraim is My first-born.

¹⁰Hear the word of the Lord, O nations,
And tell it in the isles afar.
Say:
He who scattered Israel will gather them,
And will guard them as a shepherd his flock.
¹¹For the Lord will ransom Jacob,
Redeem him from one too strong for him.
¹²They shall come and shout on the heights
    of Zion,
Radiant over the bounty of the Lord—
Over new grain and wine and oil,

וְיָצְאָ֖ה בִּמְחֹ֥ול מְשַׂחֲקִֽים׃
5 ע֚וֹד תִּטְּעִ֣י כְרָמִ֔ים
בְּהָרֵ֖י שֹׁמְרֹ֑ון
נָטְע֥וּ נֹטְעִ֖ים וְחִלֵּֽלוּ׃
6 כִּ֣י יֶשׁ־יֹ֔ום
קָרְא֥וּ נֹצְרִ֖ים בְּהַ֣ר אֶפְרָ֑יִם
ק֚וּמוּ וְנַעֲלֶ֣ה צִיֹּ֔ון
אֶל־יְהוָ֖ה אֱלֹהֵֽינוּ׃ פ

7 כִּי־כֹ֣ה ׀ אָמַ֣ר יְהוָ֗ה
רָנּ֤וּ לְיַֽעֲקֹב֙ שִׂמְחָ֔ה
וְצַהֲל֖וּ בְּרֹ֣אשׁ הַגֹּויִ֑ם
הַשְׁמִ֤יעוּ הַֽלְלוּ֙ וְאִמְר֔וּ
הֹושַׁ֤ע יְהוָה֙ אֶֽת־עַמְּךָ֔
אֵ֖ת שְׁאֵרִ֥ית יִשְׂרָאֵֽל׃
8 הִנְנִי֩ מֵבִ֨יא אֹותָ֜ם מֵאֶ֣רֶץ צָפֹ֗ון
וְקִבַּצְתִּים֮ מִיַּרְכְּתֵי־אָרֶץ֒
בָּ֚ם עִוֵּ֣ר וּפִסֵּ֔חַ
הָרָ֥ה וְיֹלֶ֖דֶת יַחְדָּ֑ו
קָהָ֥ל גָּדֹ֖ול יָשׁ֥וּבוּ הֵֽנָּה׃
9 בִּבְכִ֣י יָבֹ֗אוּ
וּֽבְתַחֲנוּנִים֮ אֹֽובִילֵם֒
אֹֽולִיכֵם֙ אֶל־נַ֣חֲלֵי מַ֔יִם
בְּדֶ֣רֶךְ יָשָׁ֔ר לֹ֥א יִכָּשְׁל֖וּ בָּ֑הּ
כִּֽי־הָיִ֤יתִי לְיִשְׂרָאֵל֙ לְאָ֔ב
וְאֶפְרַ֖יִם בְּכֹ֥רִי הֽוּא׃ ס

10 שִׁמְע֤וּ דְבַר־יְהוָה֙ גֹּויִ֔ם
וְהַגִּ֥ידוּ בָאִיִּ֖ים מִמֶּרְחָ֑ק
וְאִמְר֗וּ
מְזָרֵ֤ה יִשְׂרָאֵל֙ יְקַבְּצֶ֔נּוּ
וּשְׁמָרֹ֖ו כְּרֹעֶ֥ה עֶדְרֹֽו׃
11 כִּֽי־פָדָ֥ה יְהוָ֖ה אֶֽת־יַעֲקֹ֑ב
וּגְאָלֹ֕ו מִיַּ֖ד חָזָ֥ק מִמֶּֽנּוּ׃
12 וּבָ֨אוּ֙ וְרִנְּנ֣וּ בִמְרֹום־צִיֹּ֔ון
וְנָהֲר֖וּ אֶל־ט֣וּב יְהוָ֑ה
עַל־דָּגָן֙ וְעַל־תִּירֹ֣שׁ וְעַל־יִצְהָ֔ר

---

b   Lit. "head."
c-c Emendation yields "The Lord has saved His people."
d   For this meaning, cf. Zech. 12.10.

And over sheep and cattle.
They shall fare like a watered garden,
They shall never languish again.
¹³Then shall maidens dance gaily,
Young men and old alike.
I will turn their mourning to joy,
I will comfort them and cheer them in their
    grief.
¹⁴I will give the priests their fill of fatness,
And My people shall enjoy My full bounty
                    —declares the Lord.

¹⁵Thus said the Lord:
A cry is heard ᵉ-in Ramah-ᵉ—
Wailing, bitter weeping—
Rachel weeping for her children.
She refuses to be comforted
For her children, who are gone.
¹⁶Thus said the Lord:
Restrain your voice from weeping,
Your eyes from shedding tears;
For there is a reward for your labor
                    —declares the Lord:
They shall return from the enemy's land.
¹⁷And there is hope for your future
                    —declares the Lord:
Your children shall return to their country.

¹⁸I can hear Ephraim lamenting:
You have chastised me, and I am chastised
Like a calf that has not been broken.
Receive me back, let me return,
For You, O Lord, are my God.
¹⁹Now that I have turned back, I am filled with
    remorse;
Now that I am made aware, I strike my thigh.ᶠ
I am ashamed and humiliated,
For I bear the disgrace of my youth.
²⁰Truly, Ephraim is a dear son to Me,
A child that is dandled!

וְעַל־בְּנֵי־צֹאן וּבָקָר
וְהָיְתָה נַפְשָׁם כְּגַן רָוֶה
וְלֹא־יוֹסִיפוּ לְדַאֲבָה עוֹד׃
¹³אָז תִּשְׂמַח בְּתוּלָה בְּמָחוֹל
וּבַחֻרִים וּזְקֵנִים יַחְדָּו
וְהָפַכְתִּי אֶבְלָם לְשָׂשׂוֹן
וְנִחַמְתִּים וְשִׂמַּחְתִּים מִיגוֹנָם׃
¹⁴וְרִוֵּיתִי נֶפֶשׁ הַכֹּהֲנִים דָּשֶׁן
וְעַמִּי אֶת־טוּבִי יִשְׂבָּעוּ
נְאֻם־יְהֹוָה׃ ס
¹⁵כֹּה ׀ אָמַר יְהֹוָה
קוֹל בְּרָמָה נִשְׁמָע
נְהִי בְּכִי תַמְרוּרִים
רָחֵל מְבַכָּה עַל־בָּנֶיהָ
מֵאֲנָה לְהִנָּחֵם
עַל־בָּנֶיהָ כִּי אֵינֶנּוּ׃ ס
¹⁶כֹּה ׀ אָמַר יְהֹוָה
מִנְעִי קוֹלֵךְ מִבֶּכִי
וְעֵינַיִךְ מִדִּמְעָה
כִּי יֵשׁ שָׂכָר לִפְעֻלָּתֵךְ
נְאֻם־יְהֹוָה
וְשָׁבוּ מֵאֶרֶץ אוֹיֵב׃
¹⁷וְיֵשׁ־תִּקְוָה לְאַחֲרִיתֵךְ
נְאֻם־יְהֹוָה
וְשָׁבוּ בָנִים לִגְבוּלָם׃ ס
¹⁸שָׁמוֹעַ שָׁמַעְתִּי אֶפְרַיִם מִתְנוֹדֵד
יִסַּרְתַּנִי וָאִוָּסֵר
כְּעֵגֶל לֹא לֻמָּד
הֲשִׁיבֵנִי וְאָשׁוּבָה
כִּי אַתָּה יְהֹוָה אֱלֹהָי׃
¹⁹כִּי־אַחֲרֵי שׁוּבִי נִחַמְתִּי
וְאַחֲרֵי הִוָּדְעִי סָפַקְתִּי עַל־יָרֵךְ
בֹּשְׁתִּי וְגַם־נִכְלַמְתִּי
כִּי נָשָׂאתִי חֶרְפַּת נְעוּרָי׃
²⁰הֲבֵן יַקִּיר לִי אֶפְרַיִם
אִם יֶלֶד שַׁעֲשֻׁעִים

ᵉ⁻ᵉ Or "on a height."
ᶠ I.e., as a gesture of self-reproach.

Whenever I have turned*g* against him,
My thoughts would dwell on him still.
That is why My heart yearns for him;
I will receive him back in love
          —declares the LORD.
21Erect markers,
Set up signposts;*h*
Keep in mind the highway,
The road that you traveled.
Return, Maiden Israel!
Return to these towns of yours!
22How long will you waver,
O rebellious daughter?
(For the LORD has created something new on
  earth:
A woman courts*h* a man.)

23Thus said the LORD of Hosts, the God of Israel: They shall again say this in the land of Judah
and in its towns, when I restore their fortunes:
"The LORD bless you,
Abode of righteousness,
O holy mountain!"
24Judah and all its towns alike shall be inhabited by the farmers and *i*-such as move about-*i*
with the flocks. 25For I will give the thirsty abundant drink, and satisfy all who languish.

26At this I awoke and looked about, and my
sleep*j* had been pleasant to me.

27See, a time is coming—declares the LORD—
when I will sow the House of Israel and the
House of Judah with seed of men and seed of
cattle; 28and just as I was watchful over them
to uproot and to pull down, to overthrow and
to destroy and to bring disaster, so I will be
watchful over them to build and to plant—
declares the LORD. 29In those days, they shall no

כִּֽי־מִדֵּ֤י דַבְּרִי֙ בּ֔וֹ
זָכֹ֥ר אֶזְכְּרֶ֖נּוּ ע֑וֹד
עַל־כֵּ֗ן הָמ֤וּ מֵעַי֙ ל֔וֹ
רַחֵ֥ם אֲֽרַחֲמֶ֖נּוּ
נְאֻם־יְהוָֽה׃ ס
21 הַצִּ֧יבִי לָ֣ךְ צִיֻּנִ֗ים
שִׂ֤מִי לָךְ֙ תַּמְרוּרִ֔ים
שִׁ֣תִי לִבֵּ֔ךְ לַֽמְסִלָּ֖ה
דֶּ֣רֶךְ הלכתי הָלָ֑כְתְּ
שׁ֚וּבִי בְּתוּלַ֣ת יִשְׂרָאֵ֔ל
שֻׁ֖בִי אֶל־עָרַ֥יִךְ אֵֽלֶּה׃
22 עַד־מָתַי֙ תִּתְחַמָּקִ֔ין
הַבַּ֖ת הַשּֽׁוֹבֵבָ֑ה
כִּֽי־בָרָ֨א יְהוָ֤ה חֲדָשָׁה֙ בָּאָ֔רֶץ
נְקֵבָ֖ה תְּס֥וֹבֵֽב גָּֽבֶר׃ ס

23 כֹּֽה־אָמַ֞ר יְהוָ֤ה צְבָאוֹת֙ אֱלֹהֵ֣י יִשְׂרָאֵ֔ל
ע֣וֹד יֹאמְר֞וּ אֶת־הַדָּבָ֣ר הַזֶּ֗ה בְּאֶ֤רֶץ יְהוּדָה֙
וּבְעָרָ֔יו בְּשׁוּבִ֖י אֶת־שְׁבוּתָ֑ם
יְבָרֶכְךָ֧ יְהוָ֛ה
נְוֵה־צֶ֖דֶק
הַ֥ר הַקֹּֽדֶשׁ׃
24 וְיָ֥שְׁבוּ בָ֛הּ יְהוּדָ֖ה וְכָל־עָרָ֣יו יַחְדָּ֑ו
אִכָּרִ֕ים וְנָסְע֖וּ בַּעֵֽדֶר׃ 25 כִּ֤י הִרְוֵ֙יתִי֙ נֶ֣פֶשׁ
עֲיֵפָ֔ה וְכָל־נֶ֥פֶשׁ דָּאֲבָ֖ה מִלֵּֽאתִי׃

26 עַל־זֹ֖את הֱקִיצֹ֣תִי וָֽאֶרְאֶ֑ה וּשְׁנָתִ֖י עָ֥רְבָה
לִּֽי׃ ס

27 הִנֵּ֛ה יָמִ֥ים בָּאִ֖ים נְאֻם־יְהוָ֑ה וְזָ֣רַעְתִּ֗י
אֶת־בֵּ֤ית יִשְׂרָאֵל֙ וְאֶת־בֵּ֣ית יְהוּדָ֔ה זֶ֥רַע
אָדָ֖ם וְזֶ֥רַע בְּהֵמָֽה׃ 28 וְהָיָ֞ה כַּאֲשֶׁ֧ר שָׁקַ֣דְתִּי
עֲלֵיהֶ֗ם לִנְת֧וֹשׁ וְלִנְת֛וֹץ וְלַהֲרֹ֥ס וּלְהַאֲבִ֖יד
וּלְהָרֵ֑עַ כֵּ֣ן אֶשְׁקֹ֧ד עֲלֵיהֶ֛ם לִבְנ֥וֹת
וְלִנְט֖וֹעַ נְאֻם־יְהוָֽה׃ 29 בַּיָּמִ֣ים הָהֵ֔ם לֹא־

---

g Lit. "spoken."
h Meaning of Heb. uncertain.
i-i Lit. "they shall travel."
j I.e., the vision in the preceding verses.

longer say, "Parents have eaten sour grapes and children's teeth are blunted."[k] [30]But every one shall die for his own sins: whosoever eats sour grapes, his teeth shall be blunted.

[31]See, a time is coming—declares the LORD—when I will make a new covenant with the House of Israel and the House of Judah. [32]It will not be like the covenant I made with their fathers, when I took them by the hand to lead them out of the land of Egypt, a covenant which they broke, though I espoused[l] them—declares the LORD. [33]But such is the covenant I will make with the House of Israel after these days—declares the LORD: I will put My Teaching into their inmost being and inscribe it upon their hearts. Then I will be their God, and they shall be My people. [34]No longer will they need to teach one another and say to one another, "Heed the LORD"; for all of them, from the least of them to the greatest, shall heed Me—declares the LORD.

For I will forgive their iniquities,
And remember their sins no more.

[35]Thus said the LORD,
Who established the sun for light by day,
The laws of moon and stars for light by night,
Who stirs up the sea into roaring waves,
Whose name is LORD of Hosts:
[36]If these laws should ever be annulled by Me
——declares the LORD—
Only then would the offspring of Israel cease
To be a nation before Me for all time.

[37]Thus said the LORD: If the heavens above could be measured, and the foundations of the earth below could be fathomed, only then would I reject all the offspring of Israel for all that they have done—declares the LORD.

---

k Others "set on edge."
l Meaning of Heb. uncertain; compare 3.14.

יֹאמְרוּ עוֹד אָבוֹת אָכְלוּ בֹסֶר וְשִׁנֵּי
בָנִים תִּקְהֶינָה: 30 כִּי אִם־אִישׁ בַּעֲוֹנוֹ
יָמוּת כָּל־הָאָדָם הָאֹכֵל הַבֹּסֶר תִּקְהֶינָה
שִׁנָּיו: ס

31 הִנֵּה יָמִים בָּאִים נְאֻם־יְהֹוָה וְכָרַתִּי
אֶת־בֵּית יִשְׂרָאֵל וְאֶת־בֵּית יְהוּדָה בְּרִית
חֲדָשָׁה: 32 לֹא כַבְּרִית אֲשֶׁר כָּרַתִּי אֶת־
אֲבוֹתָם בְּיוֹם הֶחֱזִיקִי בְיָדָם לְהוֹצִיאָם
מֵאֶרֶץ מִצְרָיִם אֲשֶׁר־הֵמָּה הֵפֵרוּ אֶת־
בְּרִיתִי וְאָנֹכִי בָּעַלְתִּי בָם נְאֻם־יְהֹוָה: 33 כִּי
זֹאת הַבְּרִית אֲשֶׁר אֶכְרֹת אֶת־בֵּית יִשְׂרָאֵל
אַחֲרֵי הַיָּמִים הָהֵם נְאֻם־יְהֹוָה נָתַתִּי
אֶת־תּוֹרָתִי בְּקִרְבָּם וְעַל־לִבָּם אֶכְתֲּבֶנָּה
וְהָיִיתִי לָהֶם לֵאלֹהִים וְהֵמָּה יִהְיוּ־לִי
לְעָם: 34 וְלֹא יְלַמְּדוּ עוֹד אִישׁ אֶת־רֵעֵהוּ
וְאִישׁ אֶת־אָחִיו לֵאמֹר דְּעוּ אֶת־יְהֹוָה
כִּי־כוּלָּם יֵדְעוּ אוֹתִי לְמִקְּטַנָּם וְעַד־גְּדוֹלָם
נְאֻם־יְהֹוָה

כִּי אֶסְלַח לַעֲוֹנָם
וּלְחַטָּאתָם לֹא אֶזְכָּר־עוֹד: ס

35 כֹּה ׀ אָמַר יְהֹוָה
נֹתֵן שֶׁמֶשׁ לְאוֹר יוֹמָם
חֻקֹּת יָרֵחַ וְכוֹכָבִים לְאוֹר לָיְלָה
רֹגַע הַיָּם וַיֶּהֱמוּ גַלָּיו
יְהֹוָה צְבָאוֹת שְׁמוֹ:
36 אִם־יָמֻשׁוּ הַחֻקִּים הָאֵלֶּה מִלְּפָנַי
נְאֻם־יְהֹוָה
גַּם זֶרַע יִשְׂרָאֵל יִשְׁבְּתוּ
מִהְיוֹת גּוֹי לְפָנַי כָּל־הַיָּמִים: ס

37 כֹּה ׀ אָמַר יְהֹוָה אִם־יִמַּדּוּ שָׁמַיִם
מִלְמַעְלָה וְיֵחָקְרוּ מוֹסְדֵי־אֶרֶץ לְמָטָּה
גַּם־אֲנִי אֶמְאַס בְּכָל־זֶרַע יִשְׂרָאֵל עַל־כָּל־
אֲשֶׁר עָשׂוּ נְאֻם־יְהֹוָה: ס

38See, a time is coming—declares the LORD— when the city shall be rebuilt for the LORD from the Tower of Hananel to the Corner Gate; 39and the measuring line shall go straight out to the Gareb Hill, and then turn toward Goah. 40And the entire Valley of the Corpses and Ashes, and all the fields as far as the Wadi Kidron, and the corner of the Horse Gate on the east, shall be holy to the LORD. They shall never again be uprooted or overthrown.

32 The word which came to Jeremiah from the LORD in the tenth year of King Zedekiah of Judah, which was the eighteenth year of Nebuchadrezzar. 2At that time the army of the king of Babylon was besieging Jerusalem, and the prophet Jeremiah was confined in the prison compound attached to the palace of the king of Judah. 3For King Zedekiah of Judah had confined him, saying, "How dare you prophesy: 'Thus said the LORD: I am delivering this city into the hands of the king of Babylon, and he shall capture it. 4And King Zedekiah of Judah shall not escape from the Chaldeans; he shall be delivered into the hands of the king of Babylon, a-and he shall speak to him face to face and see him in person.-a 5And Zedekiah shall be brought to Babylon, there to remain until I take note of him—declares the LORD. When you wage war against the Chaldeans, you shall not be successful.'"

6Jeremiah said: The word of the LORD came to me: 7Hanamel, the son of your uncle Shallum, will come to you and say, "Buy my land in Anathoth, b-for you are next in succession to redeem it by purchase."-b 8And just as the LORD had said, my cousin Hanamel came to me in the prison compound and said to me, "Please

---

38 הִנֵּה יָמִים [בָּאִים*] נְאֻם־יְהֹוָה וְנִבְנְתָה הָעִיר לַיהֹוָה מִמִּגְדַּל חֲנַנְאֵל שַׁעַר הַפִּנָּה׃ 39 וְיָצָא עוֹד קוה קָו הַמִּדָּה נֶגְדּוֹ עַל גִּבְעַת גָּרֵב וְנָסַב גֹּעָתָה׃ 40 וְכׇל־הָעֵמֶק הַפְּגָרִים וְהַדֶּשֶׁן וְכׇל־הַשְּׁרֵמוֹת הַשְּׁדֵמוֹת עַד־נַחַל קִדְרוֹן עַד־פִּנַּת שַׁעַר הַסּוּסִים מִזְרָחָה קֹדֶשׁ לַיהֹוָה לֹא־יִנָּתֵשׁ וְלֹא־יֵהָרֵס עוֹד לְעוֹלָם׃ ס

לב הַדָּבָר אֲשֶׁר־הָיָה אֶל־יִרְמְיָהוּ מֵאֵת יְהֹוָה בשנת בַּשָּׁנָה הָעֲשִׂרִית לְצִדְקִיָּהוּ מֶלֶךְ יְהוּדָה הִיא הַשָּׁנָה שְׁמֹנֶה־עֶשְׂרֵה שָׁנָה לִנְבוּכַדְרֶאצַּר׃ 2 וְאָז חֵיל מֶלֶךְ בָּבֶל צָרִים עַל־יְרוּשָׁלָ͏ִם וְיִרְמְיָהוּ הַנָּבִיא הָיָה כָלוּא בַּחֲצַר הַמַּטָּרָה אֲשֶׁר בֵּית־מֶלֶךְ יְהוּדָה׃ 3 אֲשֶׁר כְּלָאוֹ צִדְקִיָּהוּ מֶלֶךְ־יְהוּדָה לֵאמֹר מַדּוּעַ אַתָּה נִבָּא לֵאמֹר כֹּה אָמַר יְהֹוָה הִנְנִי נֹתֵן אֶת־הָעִיר הַזֹּאת בְּיַד מֶלֶךְ־בָּבֶל וּלְכָדָהּ׃ 4 וְצִדְקִיָּהוּ מֶלֶךְ יְהוּדָה לֹא יִמָּלֵט מִיַּד הַכַּשְׂדִּים כִּי הִנָּתֹן יִנָּתֵן בְּיַד מֶלֶךְ־בָּבֶל וְדִבֶּר־פִּיו עִם־פִּיו וְעֵינָיו אֶת־עֵינָו תִּרְאֶינָה׃ 5 וּבָבֶל יוֹלִךְ אֶת־צִדְקִיָּהוּ וְשָׁם יִהְיֶה עַד־פׇּקְדִי אֹתוֹ נְאֻם־יְהֹוָה כִּי תִלָּחֲמוּ אֶת־הַכַּשְׂדִּים לֹא תַצְלִיחוּ׃ פ

6 וַיֹּאמֶר יִרְמְיָהוּ הָיָה דְּבַר־יְהֹוָה אֵלַי לֵאמֹר׃ 7 הִנֵּה חֲנַמְאֵל בֶּן־שַׁלֻּם דֹּדְךָ בָּא אֵלֶיךָ לֵאמֹר קְנֵה לְךָ אֶת־שָׂדִי אֲשֶׁר בַּעֲנָתוֹת כִּי לְךָ מִשְׁפַּט הַגְּאֻלָּה לִקְנוֹת׃ 8 וַיָּבֹא אֵלַי חֲנַמְאֵל בֶּן־דֹּדִי כִּדְבַר יְהֹוָה אֶל־חֲצַר הַמַּטָּרָה וַיֹּאמֶר אֵלַי קְנֵה נָא

v. 38. קריא ולא כתיב

---

a-a   Lit. "and his mouth shall speak with his mouth, and his eyes shall see his eyes."

b-b   Lit. "for yours is the procedure of redemption by purchase."

buy my land in Anathoth, in the territory of Benjamin; for the right of succession is yours, and you have the duty of redemption. Buy it." Then I knew that it was indeed the word of the LORD.

⁹So I bought the land in Anathoth from my cousin Hanamel. I weighed out the money to him, seventeen shekels of silver. ¹⁰I wrote a deed, sealed it, and had it witnessed; and I weighed out the silver on a balance. ¹¹I took the deed of purchase, the sealed text and the open one c-according to rule and law,-c ¹²and gave the deed to Baruch son of Neriah son of Mahseiah in the presence of my kinsman Hanamel, of the witnesses d-who were named-d in the deed, and all the Judeans who were sitting in the prison compound. ¹³In their presence I charged Baruch as follows: ¹⁴Thus said the LORD of Hosts, the God of Israel: "Take these documents, this deed of purchase, the sealed text and the open one, and put them into an earthen jar, so that they may last a long time." ¹⁵For thus said the LORD of Hosts, the God of Israel: "Houses, fields, and vineyards shall again be purchased in this land."

¹⁶But after I had given the deed to Baruch son of Neriah, I prayed to the LORD: ¹⁷"Ah, Lord GOD! You made heaven and earth with Your great might and outstretched arm. Nothing is too wondrous for You! ¹⁸You show kindness to the thousandth generation, but visit the guilt of the fathers upon their children after them. O great and mighty God whose name is LORD of Hosts, ¹⁹wondrous in purpose and mighty in deed, whose eyes observe all the ways of men, so as to repay every man according to his ways, and with the proper fruit of his deeds! ²⁰You displayed signs and marvels in the land of Egypt

אֶת־שָׂדִי אֲשֶׁר־בַּעֲנָתוֹת אֲשֶׁר ׀ בְּאֶרֶץ בִּנְיָמִין כִּי־לְךָ מִשְׁפַּט הַיְרֻשָּׁה וּלְךָ הַגְּאֻלָּה קְנֵה־לָךְ וָאֵדַע כִּי דְבַר־יְהוָה הוּא: ⁹וָאֶקְנֶה אֶת־הַשָּׂדֶה מֵאֵת חֲנַמְאֵל בֶּן־דֹּדִי אֲשֶׁר בַּעֲנָתוֹת וָאֶשְׁקֲלָה־לּוֹ אֶת־הַכֶּסֶף שִׁבְעָה שְׁקָלִים וַעֲשָׂרָה הַכָּסֶף: ¹⁰וָאֶכְתֹּב בַּסֵּפֶר וָאֶחְתֹּם וָאָעֵד עֵדִים וָאֶשְׁקֹל הַכֶּסֶף בְּמֹאזְנָיִם: ¹¹וָאֶקַּח אֶת־סֵפֶר הַמִּקְנָה אֶת־הֶחָתוּם הַמִּצְוָה וְהַחֻקִּים וְאֶת־הַגָּלוּי: ¹²וָאֶתֵּן אֶת־הַסֵּפֶר הַמִּקְנָה אֶל־בָּרוּךְ בֶּן־נֵרִיָּה בֶּן־מַחְסֵיָה לְעֵינֵי חֲנַמְאֵל דֹּדִי וּלְעֵינֵי הָעֵדִים הַכֹּתְבִים* בְּסֵפֶר הַמִּקְנָה לְעֵינֵי כָּל־הַיְּהוּדִים הַיֹּשְׁבִים בַּחֲצַר הַמַּטָּרָה: ¹³וָאֲצַוֶּה אֶת־בָּרוּךְ לְעֵינֵיהֶם לֵאמֹר: ¹⁴כֹּה־אָמַר יְהוָה צְבָאוֹת אֱלֹהֵי יִשְׂרָאֵל לָקוֹחַ אֶת־הַסְּפָרִים הָאֵלֶּה אֵת סֵפֶר הַמִּקְנָה הַזֶּה וְאֵת הֶחָתוּם וְאֵת סֵפֶר הַגָּלוּי הַזֶּה וּנְתַתָּם בִּכְלִי־חָרֶשׂ לְמַעַן יַעַמְדוּ יָמִים רַבִּים: ס ¹⁵כִּי כֹה אָמַר יְהוָה צְבָאוֹת אֱלֹהֵי יִשְׂרָאֵל עוֹד יִקָּנוּ בָתִּים וְשָׂדוֹת וּכְרָמִים בָּאָרֶץ הַזֹּאת: פ

¹⁶וָאֶתְפַּלֵּל אֶל־יְהוָה אַחֲרֵי תִתִּי אֶת־סֵפֶר הַמִּקְנָה אֶל־בָּרוּךְ בֶּן־נֵרִיָּה לֵאמֹר: ¹⁷אֲהָהּ אֲדֹנָי יְהוִה הִנֵּה ׀ אַתָּה עָשִׂיתָ אֶת־הַשָּׁמַיִם וְאֶת־הָאָרֶץ בְּכֹחֲךָ הַגָּדוֹל וּבִזְרֹעֲךָ הַנְּטוּיָה לֹא־יִפָּלֵא מִמְּךָ כָּל־דָּבָר: ¹⁸עֹשֶׂה חֶסֶד לַאֲלָפִים וּמְשַׁלֵּם עֲוֹן אָבוֹת אֶל־חֵיק בְּנֵיהֶם אַחֲרֵיהֶם הָאֵל הַגָּדוֹל הַגִּבּוֹר יְהוָה צְבָאוֹת שְׁמוֹ: ¹⁹גְּדֹל הָעֵצָה וְרַב הָעֲלִילִיָּה אֲשֶׁר־עֵינֶיךָ פְקֻחוֹת עַל־כָּל־דַּרְכֵי בְּנֵי אָדָם לָתֵת לְאִישׁ כִּדְרָכָיו וְכִפְרִי מַעֲלָלָיו: ²⁰אֲשֶׁר־שַׂמְתָּ אֹתוֹת

v. 12. בנוסח אחר "הכתובים"

---

c-c   *Force of Heb. uncertain.*
d-d   *With many mss. and ancient versions; so ancient Near Eastern practice. Other mss. and the editions read "who wrote" (i.e., signed their names).*

e-with lasting effect,-e and won renown in Israel and among mankind to this very day. 21You freed Your people Israel from the land of Egypt with signs and marvels, with a strong hand and an outstretched arm, and with great terror. 22You gave them this land that You had sworn to their fathers to give them, a land flowing with milk and honey, 23and they came and took possession of it. But they did not listen to You or follow Your Teaching; they did nothing of what You commanded them to do. Therefore you have caused all this misfortune to befall them. 24Here are the siegemounds, raised against the city to storm it; and the city, because of sword and famine and pestilence, is at the mercy of the Chaldeans who are attacking it. What You threatened has come to pass—as You see. 25Yet You, Lord GOD, said to me: Buy the land for money and call in witnesses—when the city is at the mercy of the Chaldeans!"

26Then the word of the LORD came to Jeremiah:

27"Behold I am the LORD, the God of all flesh. Is anything too wondrous for Me? 28Assuredly, thus said the LORD: I am delivering this city into the hands of the Chaldeans and of King Nebuchadrezzar of Babylon, and he shall capture it. 29And the Chaldeans who have been attacking this city shall come and set this city on fire and burn it down—with the houses on whose roofs they made offerings to Baal and poured out libations to other gods, so as to vex Me. 30For the people of Israel and Judah have done nothing but evil in My sight since their youth; the people of Israel have done nothing but vex Me by their conduct—declares the LORD. 31This city has aroused My anger and My wrath from the day it was built until this day; so that it must be removed from My sight 32because of all the wick-

 וּמֹֽפְתִים֙ בְּאֶ֣רֶץ־מִצְרַ֔יִם עַד־הַיּ֖וֹם הַזֶּ֑ה וּבְיִשְׂרָאֵ֖ל וּבָֽאָדָ֑ם וַתַּֽעֲשֶׂה־לְּךָ֥ שֵׁ֖ם כַּיּ֥וֹם הַזֶּֽה׃ 21 וַתֹּצֵ֤א אֶת־עַמְּךָ֙ אֶת־יִשְׂרָאֵ֔ל מֵאֶ֖רֶץ מִצְרָ֑יִם בְּאֹת֣וֹת וּבְמֽוֹפְתִ֗ים וּבְיָ֤ד חֲזָקָה֙ וּבְאֶזְר֣וֹעַ נְטוּיָ֔ה וּבְמוֹרָ֖א גָּדֽוֹל׃ 22 וַתִּתֵּ֤ן לָהֶם֙ אֶת־הָאָ֣רֶץ הַזֹּ֔את אֲשֶׁר־ נִשְׁבַּ֥עְתָּ לַֽאֲבוֹתָ֖ם לָתֵ֣ת לָהֶ֑ם אֶ֛רֶץ זָבַ֥ת חָלָ֖ב וּדְבָֽשׁ׃ 23 וַיָּבֹ֜אוּ וַיִּֽרְשׁ֣וּ אֹתָ֗הּ וְלֹֽא־ שָׁמְע֣וּ בְקוֹלֶ֗ךָ וּבְתֹֽרֹתְךָ֘ וּבְתוֹרָֽתְךָ֣ לֹ֣א־ הָלָ֔כוּ אֵ֣ת כָּל־אֲשֶׁ֥ר צִוִּ֛יתָה לָהֶ֖ם לַֽעֲשׂ֑וֹת לֹ֣א עָשׂ֔וּ וַתַּקְרֵ֣א אֹתָ֔ם אֵ֥ת כָּל־הָֽרָעָ֖ה הַזֹּֽאת׃ 24 הִנֵּ֣ה הַסֹּֽלְל֗וֹת בָּ֣אוּ הָעִיר֮ לְלָכְדָהּ֒ וְהָעִ֣יר נִתְּנָ֗ה בְּיַ֤ד הַכַּשְׂדִּים֙ הַנִּלְחָמִ֣ים עָלֶ֔יהָ מִפְּנֵ֛י הַחֶ֥רֶב וְהָֽרָעָ֖ב וְהַדָּ֑בֶר וַֽאֲשֶׁ֥ר דִּבַּ֛רְתָּ הָיָ֖ה וְהִנְּךָ֥ רֹאֶֽה׃ 25 וְאַתָּ֞ה אָמַ֤רְתָּ אֵלַי֙ אֲדֹנָ֣י יְהֹוִ֔ה קְנֵֽה־לְךָ֧ הַשָּׂדֶ֛ה בַּכֶּ֖סֶף וְהָעֵ֣ד עֵדִ֑ים וְהָעִ֖יר נִתְּנָ֥ה בְּיַ֥ד הַכַּשְׂדִּֽים׃

26 וַֽיְהִי֙ דְּבַר־יְהֹוָ֔ה אֶֽל־יִרְמְיָ֖הוּ לֵאמֹֽר׃ 27 הִנֵּה֙ אֲנִ֣י יְהֹוָ֔ה אֱלֹהֵ֖י כָּל־בָּשָׂ֑ר הֲמִמֶּ֥נִּי יִפָּלֵ֖א כָּל־דָּבָֽר׃ 28 לָכֵ֕ן כֹּ֖ה אָמַ֣ר יְהֹוָ֑ה הִנְנִ֣י נֹתֵן֩ אֶת־הָעִ֨יר הַזֹּ֜את בְּיַ֣ד הַכַּשְׂדִּ֗ים וּבְיַ֛ד נְבֽוּכַדְרֶאצַּ֥ר מֶֽלֶךְ־בָּבֶ֖ל וּלְכָדָֽהּ׃ 29 וּבָ֣אוּ הַכַּשְׂדִּ֗ים הַנִּלְחָמִים֙ עַל־הָעִ֣יר הַזֹּ֔את וְהִצִּ֜יתוּ אֶת־הָעִ֥יר הַזֹּ֛את בָּאֵ֖שׁ וּשְׂרָפ֑וּהָ וְאֵ֣ת הַבָּתִּ֡ים אֲשֶׁר֩ קִטְּר֨וּ עַל־ גַּגּֽוֹתֵיהֶ֜ם לַבַּ֗עַל וְהִסִּ֤כוּ נְסָכִים֙ לֵאלֹהִ֣ים אֲחֵרִ֔ים לְמַ֖עַן הַכְעִסֵ֑נִי׃ 30 כִּֽי־הָי֣וּ בְנֵֽי־ יִשְׂרָאֵ֗ל וּבְנֵ֤י יְהוּדָה֙ אַ֣ךְ עֹשִׂ֥ים הָרַ֛ע בְּעֵינַ֖י מִנְּעֻֽרֹֽתֵיהֶ֑ם כִּ֣י בְנֵֽי־יִשְׂרָאֵ֗ל אַ֤ךְ מַכְעִסִ֣ים אֹתִ֔י בְּמַֽעֲשֵׂ֥ה יְדֵיהֶ֖ם נְאֻם־יְהֹוָֽה׃ 31 כִּ֣י עַל־אַפִּ֞י וְעַל־חֲמָתִ֗י הָ֤יְתָה לִּי֙ הָעִ֣יר הַזֹּ֔את לְמִן־הַיּוֹם֙ אֲשֶׁ֣ר בָּנ֣וּ אוֹתָ֔הּ וְעַ֖ד הַיּ֣וֹם הַזֶּ֑ה לַֽהֲסִירָ֖הּ מֵעַ֥ל פָּנָֽי׃ 32 עַל֩

edness of the people of Israel and Judah who have so acted as to vex Me—they, their kings, their officials, their priests and prophets, and the men of Judah and the inhabitants of Jerusalem. [33]They turned their backs to Me, not their faces; though I have taught them persistently, they do not give heed or accept rebuke. [34]They placed their abominations in the House which bears My name and defiled it; [35]and they built the shrines of Baal which are in the Valley of Ben-hinnom, where they offered up their sons and daughters to Molech—when I had never commanded, or even thought [of commanding], that they should do such an abominable thing, and so bring guilt on Judah.

[36]But now, assuredly, thus said the LORD, the God of Israel, concerning this city of which you say, "It is being delivered into the hands of the king of Babylon through the sword, through famine, and through pestilence": [37]See, I will gather them from all the lands to which I have banished them in My anger and wrath, and in great rage; and I will bring them back to this place and let them dwell secure. [38]They shall be My people, and I will be their God. [39]I will give them a single heart and a single nature to revere Me for all time, and it shall be well with them and their children after them. [40]And I will make an everlasting covenant with them that I will not turn away from them and that I will treat them graciously; and I will put into their hearts reverence for Me, so that they do not turn away from Me. [41]I will delight in treating them graciously, and I will plant them in this land faithfully, with all My heart and soul.

[42]For thus said the LORD: As I have brought this terrible disaster upon this people, so I am going to bring upon them the vast good fortune which I have promised for them. [43]And fields

כָּל־רָעַ֞ת בְּנֵֽי־יִשְׂרָאֵ֣ל וּבְנֵ֣י יְהוּדָ֗ה אֲשֶׁ֤ר עָשׂוּ֙ לְהַכְעִסֵ֔נִי הֵ֤מָּה מַלְכֵיהֶם֙ שָׂרֵיהֶ֔ם כֹּהֲנֵיהֶ֖ם וּנְבִֽיאֵיהֶ֑ם וְאִ֣ישׁ יְהוּדָ֔ה וְיֹשְׁבֵ֖י יְרוּשָׁלָֽ͏ִם׃ [33] וַיִּפְנ֥וּ אֵלַ֛י עֹ֖רֶף וְלֹ֣א פָנִ֑ים וְלַמֵּ֤ד אֹתָם֙ הַשְׁכֵּ֣ם וְלַמֵּ֔ד וְאֵינָ֥ם שֹׁמְעִ֖ים לָקַ֥חַת מוּסָֽר׃ [34] וַיָּשִׂ֣ימוּ שִׁקּֽוּצֵיהֶ֗ם בַּבַּ֛יִת אֲשֶׁר־נִקְרָֽא־שְׁמִ֥י עָלָ֖יו לְטַמְּאֽוֹ׃ [35] וַיִּבְנוּ֩ אֶת־בָּמ֨וֹת הַבַּ֜עַל אֲשֶׁ֣ר ׀ בְּגֵ֣יא בֶן־הִנֹּ֗ם לְ֠הַעֲבִ֠יר אֶת־בְּנֵיהֶ֤ם וְאֶת־בְּנֽוֹתֵיהֶם֙ לַמֹּ֔לֶךְ אֲשֶׁ֣ר לֹֽא־צִוִּיתִ֗ים וְלֹ֤א עָֽלְתָה֙ עַל־לִבִּ֔י לַעֲשׂ֖וֹת הַתּוֹעֵבָ֣ה הַזֹּ֑את לְמַ֖עַן הַחֲטִ֥י אֶת־יְהוּדָֽה׃ ס

[36] וְעַתָּ֕ה לָכֵ֛ן כֹּֽה־אָמַ֥ר יְהֹוָ֖ה אֱלֹהֵ֣י יִשְׂרָאֵ֑ל אֶל־הָעִ֣יר הַזֹּ֗את אֲשֶׁ֣ר ׀ אַתֶּ֣ם אֹמְרִ֗ים נִתְּנָה֙ בְּיַ֣ד מֶֽלֶךְ־בָּבֶ֔ל בַּחֶ֖רֶב וּבָרָעָ֥ב וּבַדָּֽבֶר׃ [37] הִנְנִ֣י מְקַבְּצָ֗ם מִכָּל־הָ֣אֲרָצ֔וֹת אֲשֶׁ֨ר הִדַּחְתִּ֥ים שָׁ֛ם בְּאַפִּ֥י וּבַחֲמָתִ֖י וּבְקֶ֣צֶף גָּד֑וֹל וַהֲשִֽׁבֹתִים֙ אֶל־הַמָּק֣וֹם הַזֶּ֔ה וְהֹשַׁבְתִּ֖ים לָבֶֽטַח׃ [38] וְהָ֥יוּ לִ֖י לְעָ֑ם וַאֲנִ֕י אֶהְיֶ֥ה לָהֶ֖ם לֵאלֹהִֽים׃ [39] וְנָתַתִּ֨י לָהֶ֜ם לֵ֤ב אֶחָד֙ וְדֶ֣רֶךְ אֶחָ֔ד לְיִרְאָ֥ה אוֹתִ֖י כָּל־הַיָּמִ֑ים לְט֣וֹב לָהֶ֔ם וְלִבְנֵיהֶ֖ם אַחֲרֵיהֶֽם׃ [40] וְכָרַתִּ֤י לָהֶם֙ בְּרִ֣ית עוֹלָ֔ם אֲשֶׁ֤ר לֹֽא־אָשׁוּב֙ מֵאַ֣חֲרֵיהֶ֔ם לְהֵיטִיבִ֖י אוֹתָ֑ם וְאֶת־יִרְאָתִי֙ אֶתֵּ֣ן בִּלְבָבָ֔ם לְבִלְתִּ֖י ס֥וּר מֵעָלָֽי׃ [41] וְשַׂשְׂתִּ֥י עֲלֵיהֶ֖ם לְהֵטִ֣יב אוֹתָ֑ם וּנְטַעְתִּ֞ים בָּאָ֤רֶץ הַזֹּאת֙ בֶּאֱמֶ֔ת בְּכָל־לִבִּ֖י וּבְכָל־נַפְשִֽׁי׃ ס

[42] כִּי־כֹה֙ אָמַ֣ר יְהֹוָ֔ה כַּאֲשֶׁ֤ר הֵבֵ֙אתִי֙ אֶל־הָעָ֣ם הַזֶּ֔ה אֵ֛ת כָּל־הָרָעָ֥ה הַגְּדוֹלָ֖ה הַזֹּ֑את כֵּ֣ן אָנֹכִ֞י מֵבִ֤יא עֲלֵיהֶם֙ אֶת־כָּל־הַטּוֹבָ֔ה אֲשֶׁ֥ר אָנֹכִ֖י דֹּבֵ֥ר עֲלֵיהֶֽם׃ [43] וְנִקְנָ֥ה הַשָּׂדֶ֖ה

shall again be purchased in this land of which you say, "It is a desolation, without man or beast; it is delivered into the hands of the Chaldeans."

⁴⁴Fields shall be purchased, and deeds written and sealed, and witnesses called in the land of Benjamin and in the environs of Jerusalem, and in the towns of Judah; the towns of the hill country, the towns of the Shephelah, and the towns of the Negeb. For I will restore their fortunes— declares the LORD.

33 The word of the LORD came to Jeremiah a second time, while he was still confined in the prison compound, as follows:

²Thus said the LORD who is planning it,
The LORD who is shaping it to bring it about,
Whose name is LORD:
³Call to Me, and I will answer you,
And I will tell you wondrous things,
Secrets you have not known.

⁴For thus said the LORD, the God of Israel, concerning the houses of this city and the palaces of the kings of Judah that were torn down ᵃ-for [defense] against the siegemounds and against the sword, ⁵and were filled by those who went to fight the Chaldeans,-ᵃ—with the corpses of the men whom I struck down in My anger and rage, hiding My face from this city because of all their wickedness: ⁶I am going to bring her relief and healing. I will heal them and reveal to them abundanceᵃ of true favor. ⁷And I will restore the fortunes of Judah and Israel, and I will rebuild them as of old. ⁸And I will purge them of all the sins which they committed against Me, and I will pardon all the sins which they committed against Me, by which they re-

בָּאָרֶץ הַזֹּאת אֲשֶׁר ׀ אַתֶּם אֹמְרִים שְׁמָמָה הִיא מֵאֵין אָדָם וּבְהֵמָה נִתְּנָה בְּיַד הַכַּשְׂדִּים: ⁴⁴ שָׂדוֹת בַּכֶּסֶף יִקְנוּ וְכָתוֹב בַּסֵּפֶר ׀ וְחָתוֹם וְהָעֵד עֵדִים בְּאֶרֶץ בִּנְיָמִן וּבִסְבִיבֵי יְרוּשָׁלִַם וּבְעָרֵי יְהוּדָה וּבְעָרֵי הָהָר וּבְעָרֵי הַשְּׁפֵלָה וּבְעָרֵי הַנֶּגֶב כִּי־אָשִׁיב אֶת־שְׁבוּתָם נְאֻם־יְהוָה: פ

לג וַיְהִי דְבַר־יְהוָה אֶל־יִרְמְיָהוּ שֵׁנִית וְהוּא עוֹדֶנּוּ עָצוּר בַּחֲצַר הַמַּטָּרָה לֵאמֹר:

² כֹּה־אָמַר יְהוָה עֹשָׂה יְהוָה יוֹצֵר אוֹתָהּ לַהֲכִינָהּ יְהוָה שְׁמוֹ: ³ קְרָא אֵלַי וְאֶעֱנֶךָּ וְאַגִּידָה לְּךָ גְּדֹלוֹת וּבְצֻרוֹת לֹא יְדַעְתָּם: ס

⁴ כִּי כֹה אָמַר יְהוָה אֱלֹהֵי יִשְׂרָאֵל עַל־בָּתֵּי הָעִיר הַזֹּאת וְעַל־בָּתֵּי מַלְכֵי יְהוּדָה הַנְּתֻצִים אֶל־הַסֹּלְלוֹת וְאֶל־הֶחָרֶב: ⁵ בָּאִים לְהִלָּחֵם אֶת־הַכַּשְׂדִּים וּלְמַלְאָם אֶת־פִּגְרֵי הָאָדָם אֲשֶׁר־הִכֵּיתִי בְאַפִּי וּבַחֲמָתִי וַאֲשֶׁר הִסְתַּרְתִּי פָנַי מֵהָעִיר הַזֹּאת עַל כָּל־רָעָתָם: ⁶ הִנְנִי מַעֲלֶה־לָּהּ אֲרֻכָה וּמַרְפֵּא וּרְפָאתִים וְגִלֵּיתִי לָהֶם עֲתֶרֶת שָׁלוֹם וֶאֱמֶת: ⁷ וַהֲשִׁבֹתִי אֶת־שְׁבוּת יְהוּדָה וְאֵת שְׁבוּת יִשְׂרָאֵל וּבְנִתִים כְּבָרִאשֹׁנָה: ⁸ וְטִהַרְתִּים מִכָּל־עֲוֹנָם אֲשֶׁר חָטְאוּ־לִי וְסָלַחְתִּי לְכוֹל לְכָל־עֲוֹנוֹתֵיהֶם

ᵃ⁻ᵃ Meaning of Heb. uncertain.

belled against Me. [9]And she shall gain through Me renown, joy, fame, and glory above all the nations on earth, when they hear of all the good fortune I provide for them.[b] They will thrill and quiver because of all the good fortune and all the prosperity that I provide for her.

[10]Thus said the LORD: Again there shall be heard in this place, which you say is ruined, without man or beast—in the towns of Judah and the streets of Jerusalem that are desolate, without man, without inhabitants, without beast—[11]the sound of mirth and gladness, the voice of bridegroom and bride, the voice of those who cry, "Give thanks to the LORD of Hosts, for the LORD is good, for His kindness is everlasting!" as they bring thanksgiving offerings to the House of the LORD. For I will restore the fortunes of the land as of old—said the LORD.

[12]Thus said the LORD of Hosts: In this ruined place, without man and beast, and in all its towns, there shall again be a pasture for shepherds, where they can rest their flocks. [13]In the towns of the hill country, in the towns of the Shephelah, and in the towns of the Negeb, in the land of Benjamin and in the environs of Jerusalem and in the towns of Judah, sheep shall pass again under the hands of one who counts them—said the LORD. [14]See, days are coming—declares the LORD—when I will fulfill the promise that I made concerning the House of Israel and the House of Judah. [15]In those days and at that time, I will raise up a true branch of David's line, and he shall do what is just and right in the land. [16]In those days Judah shall be delivered and Israel shall dwell secure. And this is what she shall be called: "The LORD is our Vindicator." [17]For thus said the LORD: There shall never be an end to men of David's line who sit upon the throne of the House of Israel. [18]Nor shall

9 וְהָיְתָה לִּי פְּשָׁעוּ בִי וַאֲשֶׁר חָטְאוּ־לִי וַאֲשֶׁר לְשֵׁם שָׂשׂוֹן לִתְהִלָּה וּלְתִפְאֶרֶת לְכֹל גּוֹיֵי הָאָרֶץ אֲשֶׁר יִשְׁמְעוּ אֶת־כָּל־הַטּוֹבָה אֲשֶׁר אָנֹכִי עֹשֶׂה אֹתָם וּפָחֲדוּ וְרָגְזוּ עַל כָּל־הַטּוֹבָה וְעַל כָּל־הַשָּׁלוֹם אֲשֶׁר אָנֹכִי עֹשֶׂה לָּהּ׃ ס

10 כֹּה ׀ אָמַר יְהוָֹה עוֹד יִשָּׁמַע בַּמָּקוֹם־הַזֶּה אֲשֶׁר אַתֶּם אֹמְרִים חָרֵב הוּא מֵאֵין אָדָם וּמֵאֵין בְּהֵמָה בְּעָרֵי יְהוּדָה וּבְחֻצוֹת יְרוּשָׁלִַם הַנְשַׁמּוֹת מֵאֵין אָדָם וּמֵאֵין יוֹשֵׁב וּמֵאֵין בְּהֵמָה׃ 11 קוֹל שָׂשׂוֹן וְקוֹל שִׂמְחָה קוֹל חָתָן וְקוֹל כַּלָּה קוֹל אֹמְרִים הוֹדוּ אֶת־יְהוָֹה צְבָאוֹת כִּי־טוֹב יְהוָֹה כִּי־לְעוֹלָם חַסְדּוֹ מְבִאִים תּוֹדָה בֵּית יְהוָֹה כִּי־אָשִׁיב אֶת־שְׁבוּת־הָאָרֶץ כְּבָרִאשֹׁנָה אָמַר יְהוָֹה׃ ס

12 כֹּה־אָמַר יְהוָֹה צְבָאוֹת עוֹד יִהְיֶה ׀ בַּמָּקוֹם הַזֶּה הֶחָרֵב מֵאֵין־אָדָם וְעַד־בְּהֵמָה וּבְכָל־עָרָיו נְוֵה רֹעִים מַרְבִּצִים צֹאן׃ 13 בְּעָרֵי הָהָר בְּעָרֵי הַשְּׁפֵלָה וּבְעָרֵי הַנֶּגֶב וּבְאֶרֶץ בִּנְיָמִן וּבִסְבִיבֵי יְרוּשָׁלִַם וּבְעָרֵי יְהוּדָה עֹד תַּעֲבֹרְנָה הַצֹּאן עַל־יְדֵי מוֹנֶה אָמַר יְהוָֹה׃ ס 14 הִנֵּה יָמִים בָּאִים נְאֻם־יְהוָֹה וַהֲקִמֹתִי אֶת־הַדָּבָר הַטּוֹב אֲשֶׁר דִּבַּרְתִּי אֶל־בֵּית יִשְׂרָאֵל וְעַל־בֵּית יְהוּדָה׃ 15 בַּיָּמִים הָהֵם וּבָעֵת הַהִיא אַצְמִיחַ לְדָוִד צֶמַח צְדָקָה וְעָשָׂה מִשְׁפָּט וּצְדָקָה בָּאָרֶץ׃ 16 בַּיָּמִים הָהֵם תִּוָּשַׁע יְהוּדָה וִירוּשָׁלִַם תִּשְׁכּוֹן לָבֶטַח וְזֶה אֲשֶׁר־יִקְרָא־לָהּ יְהוָֹה ׀ צִדְקֵנוּ׃ ס 17 כִּי־כֹה אָמַר יְהוָֹה לֹא־יִכָּרֵת לְדָוִד אִישׁ

there ever be an end to the line of the levitical priests before Me, of those who present burnt offerings and turn the meal offering to smoke and perform sacrifices.

19The word of the LORD came to Jeremiah: 20Thus said the LORD: If you could break My covenant with the day and My covenant with the night, so that day and night should not come at their proper time, 21only then could My covenant with My servant David be broken—so that he would not have a descendant reigning upon his throne—or with My ministrants, the levitical priests. 22Like the host of heaven which cannot be counted, and the sand of the sea which cannot be measured, so will I multiply the offspring of My servant David, and of the Levites who minister to Me.

23The word of the LORD came to Jeremiah: 24You see what this people said: "The two families which the LORD chose have now been rejected by Him." Thus they despise My people, a-and regard them as no longer a nation.-a 25Thus said the LORD: As surely as I have established My covenant with day and night—the laws of heaven and earth——26so I will never reject the offspring of Jacob and My servant David; I will never fail to take from his offspring rulers for the descendants of Abraham, Isaac, and Jacob. Indeed, I will restore their fortunes and take them back in love.

34 The word which came to Jeremiah from the LORD, when King Nebuchadrezzar of Babylon and all his army, and all the kingdoms of the earth and all the peoples under his sway, were waging war against Jerusalem and all its towns:

2Thus said the LORD, the God of Israel: Go

יֹשֵׁב עַל־כִּסֵּא בֵית־יִשְׂרָאֵל: 18 וְלַכֹּהֲנִים הַלְוִיִּם לֹא־יִכָּרֵת אִישׁ מִלְּפָנָי מַעֲלֶה עוֹלָה וּמַקְטִיר מִנְחָה וְעֹשֶׂה־זֶּבַח כָּל־ הַיָּמִים: ס

19 וַיְהִי דְּבַר־יְהֹוָה אֶל־יִרְמְיָהוּ לֵאמוֹר*: 20 כֹּה אָמַר יְהֹוָה אִם־תָּפֵרוּ אֶת־בְּרִיתִי הַיּוֹם וְאֶת־בְּרִיתִי הַלָּיְלָה וּלְבִלְתִּי הֱיוֹת יוֹמָם־וָלַיְלָה בְּעִתָּם: 21 גַּם־בְּרִיתִי תֻפַר אֶת־דָּוִד עַבְדִּי מִהְיוֹת־לוֹ בֵן מֹלֵךְ עַל־ כִּסְאוֹ וְאֶת־הַלְוִיִּם הַכֹּהֲנִים מְשָׁרְתָי: 22 אֲשֶׁר לֹא־יִסָּפֵר צְבָא הַשָּׁמַיִם וְלֹא יִמַּד חוֹל הַיָּם כֵּן אַרְבֶּה אֶת־זֶרַע דָּוִד עַבְדִּי וְאֶת־הַלְוִיִּם מְשָׁרְתֵי אֹתִי: ס

23 וַיְהִי דְּבַר־יְהֹוָה אֶל־יִרְמְיָהוּ לֵאמֹר: 24 הֲלוֹא רָאִיתָ מָה־הָעָם הַזֶּה דִּבְּרוּ לֵאמֹר שְׁתֵּי הַמִּשְׁפָּחוֹת אֲשֶׁר בָּחַר יְהֹוָה בָּהֶם וַיִּמְאָסֵם וְאֶת־עַמִּי יִנְאָצוּן מִהְיוֹת עוֹד גּוֹי לִפְנֵיהֶם: ס 25 כֹּה אָמַר יְהֹוָה אִם־לֹא בְרִיתִי יוֹמָם וָלָיְלָה חֻקּוֹת שָׁמַיִם וָאָרֶץ לֹא־שָׂמְתִּי: 26 גַּם־זֶרַע יַעֲקוֹב וְדָוִד עַבְדִּי אֶמְאַס מִקַּחַת מִזַּרְעוֹ מֹשְׁלִים אֶל־ זֶרַע אַבְרָהָם יִשְׂחָק וְיַעֲקֹב כִּי־אָשׁוּב אֶת־שְׁבוּתָם וְרִחַמְתִּים: ס

לד הַדָּבָר אֲשֶׁר־הָיָה אֶל־יִרְמְיָהוּ מֵאֵת יְהֹוָה וּנְבוּכַדְרֶאצַּר מֶלֶךְ־בָּבֶל | וְכָל־חֵילוֹ וְכָל־מַמְלְכוֹת אֶרֶץ מֶמְשֶׁלֶת יָדוֹ וְכָל־הָעַמִּים נִלְחָמִים עַל־יְרוּשָׁלַ͏ִם וְעַל־כָּל־עָרֶיהָ לֵאמֹר: 2 כֹּה־אָמַר יְהֹוָה אֱלֹהֵי יִשְׂרָאֵל הָלֹךְ

speak to King Zedekiah of Judah, and say to him: "Thus said the LORD: I am going to deliver this city into the hands of the king of Babylon, and he will destroy it by fire. ³And you will not escape from him; you will be captured and handed over to him. ᵃ-And you will see the king of Babylon face to face and speak to him in person;-ᵃ and you will be brought to Babylon. ⁴But hear the word of the LORD, O King Zedekiah of Judah! Thus said the LORD concerning you: You will not die by the sword. ⁵You will die a peaceful death; and as incenseᵇ was burned for your ancestors, the earlier kings who preceded you, so they will burn incenseᵇ for you, and they will lament for you 'Ah, lord!' For I Myself have made the promise—declares the LORD."

⁶The prophet Jeremiah spoke all these words to King Zedekiah of Judah in Jerusalem, ⁷when the army of the king of Babylon was waging war against Jerusalem and against the remaining towns of Judah—against Lachish and Azekah, for they were the only fortified towns of Judah that were left.

⁸The word which came to Jeremiah from the LORD after King Zedekiah had made a covenant with all the people in Jerusalem to proclaim a releaseᶜ among them—⁹that everyone should set free his Hebrew slaves, both male and female, and that no one should keep his fellow Judean enslaved.

¹⁰Everyone, officials and people, who had entered into the covenant agreed to set their male and female slaves free and not keep them enslaved any longer; they complied and let them go. ¹¹But afterward they turned about and brought back the men and women they had set free, and forced them into slavery again. ¹²Then it was that the word of the LORD came to Jeremiah from the LORD:

וְאָמַרְתָּ֙ אֶל־צִדְקִיָּ֣הוּ מֶֽלֶךְ־יְהוּדָ֔ה וְאָמַרְתָּ֖
אֵלָ֑יו כֹּ֚ה אָמַ֣ר יְהוָ֔ה הִנְנִ֨י נֹתֵ֜ן אֶת־הָעִ֤יר
הַזֹּאת֙ בְּיַ֣ד מֶֽלֶךְ־בָּבֶ֔ל וּשְׂרָפָ֖הּ בָּאֵֽשׁ׃ ³ וְאַתָּ֗ה לֹ֤א תִמָּלֵט֙ מִיָּד֔וֹ כִּ֚י תָּפֹ֣שׂ תִּתָּפֵ֔שׂ
וּבְיָד֖וֹ תִּנָּתֵ֑ן וְ֠עֵינֶ֠יךָ אֶת־עֵינֵ֨י מֶֽלֶךְ־בָּבֶ֜ל
תִּרְאֶ֗ינָה וּפִ֛יהוּ אֶת־פִּ֥יךָ יְדַבֵּ֖ר וּבָבֶ֥ל
תָּבֽוֹא׃ ⁴ אַ֚ךְ שְׁמַ֣ע דְּבַר־יְהוָ֔ה צִדְקִיָּ֖הוּ
מֶ֣לֶךְ יְהוּדָ֑ה כֹּֽה־אָמַ֤ר יְהוָה֙ עָלֶ֔יךָ
לֹ֥א תָמ֖וּת בֶּחָֽרֶב׃ ⁵ בְּשָׁל֣וֹם תָּמ֗וּת
וּֽכְמִשְׂרְפ֣וֹת אֲ֠בוֹתֶ֠יךָ הַמְּלָכִ֨ים הָרִֽאשֹׁנִ֜ים
אֲשֶׁר־הָי֣וּ לְפָנֶ֗יךָ כֵּ֣ן יִשְׂרְפוּ־לָ֔ךְ וְה֥וֹי אָד֖וֹן
יִסְפְּדוּ־לָ֑ךְ כִּֽי־דָבָ֥ר אֲנִֽי־דִבַּ֖רְתִּי נְאֻם־
יְהוָֽה׃ ס
⁶ וַיְדַבֵּר֙ יִרְמְיָ֣הוּ הַנָּבִ֔יא אֶל־צִדְקִיָּ֖הוּ מֶ֣לֶךְ
יְהוּדָ֑ה אֵ֛ת כָּל־הַדְּבָרִ֥ים הָאֵ֖לֶּה
בִּירוּשָׁלָֽ͏ִם׃ ⁷ וְחֵ֣יל מֶֽלֶךְ־בָּבֶ֗ל נִלְחָמִים֙
עַל־יְר֣וּשָׁלַ֔͏ִם וְעַ֛ל כָּל־עָרֵ֥י יְהוּדָ֖ה
הַנּֽוֹתָר֑וֹת אֶל־לָכִ֣ישׁ וְאֶל־עֲזֵקָ֔ה כִּ֣י הֵ֗נָּה
נִשְׁאֲר֛וּ בְּעָרֵ֥י יְהוּדָ֖ה עָרֵ֥י מִבְצָֽר׃ פ

⁸ הַדָּבָ֞ר אֲשֶׁר־הָיָ֧ה אֶֽל־יִרְמְיָ֛הוּ מֵאֵ֥ת
יְהוָ֖ה אַֽחֲרֵ֑י כְּרֹ֨ת הַמֶּ֤לֶךְ צִדְקִיָּ֨הוּ֙ בְּרִית֙
אֶת־כָּל־הָעָ֣ם אֲשֶׁ֣ר בִּירֽוּשָׁלַ֔͏ִם לִקְרֹ֥א לָהֶ֖ם
דְּרֽוֹר׃ ⁹ לְ֠שַׁלַּ֠ח אִ֣ישׁ אֶת־עַבְדּ֞וֹ וְאִ֣ישׁ
אֶת־שִׁפְחָת֗וֹ הָעִבְרִ֤י וְהָֽעִבְרִיָּה֙ חָפְשִׁ֔ים
לְבִלְתִּ֧י עֲבָד־בָּ֛ם בִּֽיהוּדִ֥י אָחִ֖יהוּ אִֽישׁ׃
¹⁰ וַיִּשְׁמְעוּ֩ כָל־הַשָּׂרִ֨ים וְכָל־הָעָ֜ם אֲשֶׁר־
בָּ֣אוּ בַבְּרִ֗ית לְשַׁלַּ֞ח אִ֣ישׁ אֶת־עַבְדּ֞וֹ וְאִ֣ישׁ
אֶת־שִׁפְחָת֛וֹ חָפְשִׁ֖ים לְבִלְתִּ֥י עֲבָד־בָּ֑ם
ע֖וֹד וַֽיִּשְׁמְע֥וּ וַֽיְשַׁלֵּֽחוּ׃ ¹¹ וַיָּשׁ֙וּבוּ֙ אַֽחֲרֵי־
כֵ֔ן וַיָּשִׁ֗בוּ אֶת־הָֽעֲבָדִים֙ וְאֶת־הַשְּׁפָח֔וֹת
אֲשֶׁ֥ר שִׁלְּח֖וּ חָפְשִׁ֑ים וַֽיִּכְבְּשׁ֔וּם
לַֽעֲבָדִ֖ים וְלִשְׁפָחֽוֹת׃ ס ¹² וַֽיְהִ֤י דְבַר־
יְהוָה֙ אֶֽל־יִרְמְיָ֔הוּ מֵאֵ֥ת יְהוָ֖ה לֵאמֹֽר׃

13Thus said the Lord, the God of Israel: I made a covenant with your fathers when I brought them out of the land of Egypt, the house of bondage, saying: 14"In the seventh year[d] each of you must let go any fellow Hebrew [e]who may be sold[-e] to you; when he has served you six years, you must set him free." But your fathers would not obey Me or give ear. 15Lately you turned about and did what is proper in My sight, and each of you proclaimed a release to his countrymen; and you made a covenant accordingly before Me in the House which bears My name. 16But now you have turned back and have profaned My name; each of you has brought back the men and women whom you had given their freedom, and forced them to be your slaves again.

17Assuredly, thus said the Lord: You would not obey Me and proclaim a release, each to his kinsman and countryman. Lo! I proclaim your release—declares the Lord—to the sword, to pestilence, and to famine; and I will make you a horror to all the kingdoms of the earth. 18I will make the men who violated My covenant, who did not fulfill the terms of the covenant which they made before Me, [like] the calf which they cut in two so as to pass between the halves:[f] 19The officers of Judah and Jerusalem, the officials, the priests, and all the people of the land who passed between the halves of the calf 20shall be handed over to their enemies, to those who seek to kill them. Their carcasses shall become food for the birds of the sky and the beasts of the earth. 21I will hand over King Zedekiah of Judah and his officers to their enemies, who seek to kill them—to the army of the king of Babylon which has withdrawn from you. 22I hereby give the command—declares the Lord—by which I will bring them back against

---

13 כֹּה־אָמַ֞ר יְהוָ֣ה אֱלֹהֵ֣י יִשְׂרָאֵ֗ל אָנֹכִ֞י כָּרַ֤תִּי בְרִית֙ אֶת־אֲב֣וֹתֵיכֶ֔ם בְּי֨וֹם הוֹצִאִ֤י אוֹתָם֙ מֵאֶ֣רֶץ מִצְרַ֔יִם מִבֵּ֥ית עֲבָדִ֖ים לֵאמֹֽר׃ 14 מִקֵּ֣ץ שֶׁ֣בַע שָׁנִ֡ים תְּֽשַׁלְּח֡וּ אִישׁ֩ אֶת־אָחִ֨יו הָעִבְרִ֜י אֲשֶֽׁר־יִמָּכֵ֣ר לְךָ֗ וַעֲבָֽדְךָ֙ שֵׁ֣שׁ שָׁנִ֔ים וְשִׁלַּחְתּ֥וֹ חָפְשִׁ֖י מֵֽעִמָּ֑ךְ וְלֹֽא־שָׁמְע֤וּ אֲבֽוֹתֵיכֶם֙ אֵלַ֔י וְלֹ֥א הִטּ֖וּ אֶת־אָזְנָֽם׃ 15 וַתָּשֻׁ֨בוּ אַתֶּ֜ם הַיּ֗וֹם וַתַּעֲשׂ֤וּ אֶת־הַיָּשָׁר֙ בְּעֵינַ֔י לִקְרֹ֥א דְר֖וֹר אִ֣ישׁ לְרֵעֵ֑הוּ וַתִּכְרְת֤וּ בְרִית֙ לְפָנַ֔י בַּבַּ֕יִת אֲשֶׁר־נִקְרָ֥א שְׁמִ֖י עָלָֽיו׃ 16 וַתָּשֻׁ֙בוּ֙ וַתְּחַלְּל֣וּ אֶת־שְׁמִ֔י וַתָּשִׁ֗בוּ אִ֤ישׁ אֶת־עַבְדּוֹ֙ וְאִ֣ישׁ אֶת־שִׁפְחָת֔וֹ אֲשֶׁר־שִׁלַּחְתֶּ֥ם חָפְשִׁ֖ים לְנַפְשָׁ֑ם וַתִּכְבְּשׁ֣וּ אֹתָ֔ם לִֽהְי֣וֹת לָכֶ֔ם לַעֲבָדִ֖ים וְלִשְׁפָחֽוֹת׃ ס

17 לָכֵן֮ כֹּה־אָמַ֣ר יְהוָה֒ אַתֶּם֙ לֹֽא־שְׁמַעְתֶּ֣ם אֵלַ֔י לִקְרֹ֣א דְר֔וֹר אִ֥ישׁ לְאָחִ֖יו וְאִ֣ישׁ לְרֵעֵ֑הוּ הִנְנִ֣י קֹרֵא֩ לָכֶ֨ם דְּר֜וֹר נְאֻם־יְהוָ֗ה אֶל־הַחֶ֙רֶב֙ אֶל־הַדֶּ֣בֶר וְאֶל־הָרָעָ֔ב וְנָתַתִּ֤י אֶתְכֶם֙ לִזְוָעָה לְכֹ֖ל מַמְלְכ֥וֹת הָאָֽרֶץ׃ 18 וְנָתַתִּ֣י אֶת־הָאֲנָשִׁ֗ים הָעֹֽבְרִים֙ אֶת־בְּרִתִ֔י אֲשֶׁ֤ר לֹֽא־הֵקִ֙ימוּ֙ אֶת־דִּבְרֵ֣י הַבְּרִ֔ית אֲשֶׁ֥ר כָּרְת֖וּ לְפָנָ֑י הָעֵ֙גֶל֙ אֲשֶׁ֣ר כָּרְת֣וּ לִשְׁנַ֔יִם וַיַּעַבְר֖וּ בֵּ֥ין בְּתָרָֽיו׃ 19 שָׂרֵ֨י יְהוּדָ֜ה וְשָׂרֵ֣י יְרוּשָׁלִַ֗ם הַסָּֽרִסִים֙ וְהַכֹּ֣הֲנִ֔ים וְכֹ֖ל עַ֣ם הָאָ֑רֶץ הָעֹ֣בְרִ֔ים בֵּ֖ין בִּתְרֵ֥י הָעֵֽגֶל׃ 20 וְנָתַתִּ֤י אוֹתָם֙ בְּיַ֣ד אֹֽיְבֵיהֶ֔ם וּבְיַ֖ד מְבַקְשֵׁ֣י נַפְשָׁ֑ם וְהָיְתָ֤ה נִבְלָתָם֙ לְמַֽאֲכָ֔ל לְע֥וֹף הַשָּׁמַ֖יִם וּלְבֶהֱמַ֥ת הָאָֽרֶץ׃ 21 וְאֶת־צִדְקִיָּ֨הוּ מֶֽלֶךְ־יְהוּדָ֜ה וְאֶת־שָׂרָ֗יו אֶתֵּן֙ בְּיַ֣ד אֹֽיְבֵיהֶ֔ם וּבְיַ֖ד מְבַקְשֵׁ֣י נַפְשָׁ֑ם וּבְיַ֗ד חֵ֚יל מֶ֣לֶךְ בָּבֶ֔ל הָעֹלִ֖ים מֵעֲלֵיכֶֽם׃ 22 הִנְנִ֨י מְצַוֶּ֜ה נְאֻם־יְהוָ֗ה וַהֲשִׁבֹתִים֙ אֶל־הָעִ֣יר הַזֹּ֔את

---

d   I.e., of servitude. Lit. "After a period of seven years"; cf. Deut. 14.28 and 15.1.

e-e   Or "who sells himself."

f   Cf. Gen. 15.9–10, 17–21.

this city. They shall attack it and capture it, and burn it down. I will make the towns of Judah a desolation, without inhabitant.

35

The word which came to Jeremiah from the LORD in the days of King Jehoiakim son of Josiah of Judah:

2Go to the house of the Rechabites and speak to them, and bring them to the House of the LORD, to one of the chambers, and give them wine to drink.

3So I took Jaazaniah son of Jeremiah son of Habazziniah, and his brothers, all his sons, and the whole household of the Rechabites; 4and I brought them to the House of the LORD, to the chamber of the sons of Hanan son of Igdaliah, the man of God, which is next to the chamber of the officials and above the chamber of Maaseiah son of Shallum, the guardian of the threshold. 5I set bowls full of wine and cups before the men of the house of the Rechabites, and said to them, "Have some wine."

6They replied, "We will not drink wine, for our ancestor, Jonadab son of Rechab, commanded us: 'You shall never drink wine, either you or your children. 7Nor shall you build houses or sow fields*a* or plant vineyards, nor shall you own such things; but you shall live in tents all your days, so that you may live long upon the land where you sojourn.' 8And we have obeyed our ancestor Jonadab son of Rechab in all that he commanded us: we never drink wine, neither we nor our wives nor our sons and daughters. 9Nor do we build houses to live in, and we do not own vineyards or fields for sowing; 10but we live in tents. We have obeyed and done all that our ancestor Jonadab commanded us. 11But when King Nebuchadrezzar of Babylon invaded the country, we said, 'Come, let us

a Lit. "seed."

וְנִלְחֲמ֣וּ עָלֶ֔יהָ וּלְכָד֖וּהָ וּשְׂרָפֻ֣הָ בָאֵ֑שׁ
וְאֶת־עָרֵ֧י יְהוּדָ֛ה אֶתֵּ֥ן שְׁמָמָ֖ה מֵאֵ֥ין
יֹשֵֽׁב: פ

לה הַדָּבָ֞ר אֲשֶׁר־הָיָ֤ה אֶֽל־יִרְמְיָ֙הוּ֙
מֵאֵ֣ת יְהוָ֔ה בִּימֵ֛י יְהוֹיָקִ֥ים בֶּן־יֹאשִׁיָּ֖הוּ
מֶ֥לֶךְ יְהוּדָ֖ה לֵאמֹֽר: 2 הָלוֹךְ֙ אֶל־בֵּ֣ית הָרֵכָבִ֔ים וְדִבַּרְתָּ֖ אוֹתָ֑ם
וַהֲבִאוֹתָם֙ בֵּ֣ית יְהוָ֔ה אֶל־אַחַ֖ת הַלְּשָׁכ֑וֹת
וְהִשְׁקִיתָ֥ אוֹתָ֖ם יָֽיִן: 3 וָאֶקַּ֞ח אֶת־יַאֲזַנְיָ֤ה בֶן־יִרְמְיָ֙הוּ֙ בֶּן־
חֲבַצִּנְיָ֔ה וְאֶת־אֶחָ֖יו וְאֶת־כָּל־בָּנָ֑יו וְאֵ֖ת
כָּל־בֵּ֥ית הָרֵכָבִֽים: 4 וָאָבִ֣א אֹתָם֮ בֵּ֣ית
יְהוָה֒ אֶל־לִשְׁכַּ֗ת בְּנֵ֛י חָנָ֥ן בֶּן־יִגְדַּלְיָ֖הוּ
אִ֣ישׁ הָאֱלֹהִ֑ים אֲשֶׁר־אֵ֙צֶל֙ לִשְׁכַּ֣ת הַשָּׂרִ֔ים
אֲשֶׁ֣ר מִמַּ֗עַל לְלִשְׁכַּ֛ת מַעֲשֵׂיָ֥הוּ בֶן־שַׁלֻּ֖ם
שֹׁמֵ֥ר הַסַּֽף: 5 וָאֶתֵּ֞ן לִפְנֵ֣י | בְּנֵ֣י בֵית־
הָרֵכָבִ֗ים גְּבִעִ֛ים מְלֵאִ֥ים יַ֖יִן וְכֹס֑וֹת וָאֹמַ֥ר
אֲלֵיהֶ֖ם שְׁתוּ־יָֽיִן: 6 וַיֹּאמְר֖וּ לֹ֣א נִשְׁתֶּה־יָּ֑יִן כִּ֣י יוֹנָדָ֣ב בֶּן־רֵכָ֣ב
אָבִ֡ינוּ צִוָּ֣ה עָלֵינוּ֩ לֵאמֹ֨ר לֹ֤א תִשְׁתּוּ־יַ֙יִן֙
אַתֶּ֣ם וּבְנֵיכֶ֔ם עַד־עוֹלָֽם: 7 וּבַ֣יִת לֹֽא־תִבְנ֗וּ
וְזֶ֤רַע לֹֽא־תִזְרָ֙עוּ֙ וְכֶ֣רֶם לֹֽא־תִטָּ֔עוּ וְלֹ֣א
יִהְיֶ֖ה לָכֶ֑ם כִּ֠י בָּאֳהָלִ֤ים תֵּשְׁבוּ֙ כָּל־יְמֵיכֶ֔ם
לְמַ֙עַן֙ תִּֽחְי֣וּ יָמִ֣ים רַבִּ֔ים עַל־פְּנֵ֣י הָֽאֲדָמָ֔ה
אֲשֶׁ֥ר אַתֶּ֖ם גָּרִ֥ים שָֽׁם: 8 וַנִּשְׁמַ֗ע בְּק֞וֹל
יְהוֹנָדָ֤ב בֶּן־רֵכָב֙ אָבִ֔ינוּ לְכֹ֖ל אֲשֶׁ֣ר צִוָּ֑נוּ
לְבִלְתִּ֤י שְׁתֽוֹת־יַ֙יִן֙ כָּל־יָמֵ֔ינוּ אֲנַ֖חְנוּ נָשֵׁ֑ינוּ
בָּנֵ֖ינוּ וּבְנֹתֵֽינוּ: 9 וּלְבִלְתִּ֛י בְּנ֥וֹת בָּתִּ֖ים
לְשִׁבְתֵּ֑נוּ וְכֶ֧רֶם וְשָׂדֶ֛ה וָזֶ֖רַע לֹ֥א יִֽהְיֶה־לָּֽנוּ:
10 וַנֵּ֖שֶׁב בָּאֳהָלִ֑ים וַנִּשְׁמַ֣ע וַנַּ֔עַשׂ כְּכֹ֥ל
אֲשֶׁר־צִוָּ֖נוּ יוֹנָדָ֥ב אָבִֽינוּ: 11 וַיְהִ֗י בַּעֲל֨וֹת
נְבוּכַדְרֶאצַּ֥ר מֶֽלֶךְ־בָּבֶל֮ אֶל־הָאָרֶץ֒ וַנֹּ֗אמֶר

1100

go into Jerusalem because of the army of the Chaldeans and the army of Aram.' And so we are living in Jerusalem."

12Then the word of the LORD came to Jeremiah:

13Thus said the LORD of Hosts, the God of Israel: Go say to the men of Judah and the inhabitants of Jerusalem: "You can learn a lesson [here] about obeying My commands—declares the LORD. 14The commands of Jonadab son of Rechab have been fulfilled: he charged his children not to drink wine, and to this day they have not drunk, in obedience to the charge of their ancestor. But I spoke to you persistently, and you did not listen to Me. 15I persistently sent you all My servants, the prophets, to say: 'Turn back, every one of you, from your wicked ways and mend your deeds; do not follow other gods or serve them. Then you may remain on the land that I gave to you and your fathers.' But you did not give ear or listen to Me. 16The family of Jonadab son of Rechab have indeed fulfilled the charge which their ancestor gave them; but this people has not listened to Me. 17Assuredly, thus said the LORD, the God of Hosts, the God of Israel: I am going to bring upon Judah and upon all the inhabitants of Jerusalem all the disaster with which I have threatened them; for I spoke to them, but they would not listen; I called to them, but they would not respond."

18And to the family of the Rechabites Jeremiah said: "Thus said the LORD of Hosts, the God of Israel: Because you have obeyed the charge of your ancestor Jonadab and kept all his commandments, and done all that he enjoined upon you, 19assuredly, thus said the LORD of Hosts, the God of Israel: There shall never cease to be a man of the line of Jonadab son of Rechab standing before Me."

בֹּאוּ וְנָבוֹא יְרוּשָׁלַ͏ִם מִפְּנֵי חֵיל הַכַּשְׂדִּים וּמִפְּנֵי חֵיל אֲרָם וַנֵּשֶׁב בִּירוּשָׁלָ͏ִם: פ 12 וַיְהִי דְּבַר־יְהֹוָה אֶל־יִרְמְיָהוּ לֵאמֹר: 13 כֹּה־אָמַר יְהֹוָה צְבָאוֹת אֱלֹהֵי יִשְׂרָאֵל הָלֹךְ וְאָמַרְתָּ לְאִישׁ יְהוּדָה וּלְיוֹשְׁבֵי יְרוּשָׁלָ͏ִם הֲלוֹא תִקְחוּ מוּסָר לִשְׁמֹעַ אֶל־דְּבָרַי נְאֻם־יְהֹוָה: 14 הוּקַם אֶת־דִּבְרֵי יְהוֹנָדָב בֶּן־רֵכָב אֲשֶׁר־צִוָּה אֶת־בָּנָיו לְבִלְתִּי שְׁתוֹת־יַיִן וְלֹא שָׁתוּ עַד־הַיּוֹם הַזֶּה כִּי שָׁמְעוּ אֵת מִצְוַת אֲבִיהֶם וְאָנֹכִי דִּבַּרְתִּי אֲלֵיכֶם הַשְׁכֵּם וְדַבֵּר וְלֹא שְׁמַעְתֶּם אֵלָי: 15 וָאֶשְׁלַח אֲלֵיכֶם אֶת־כׇּל־עֲבָדַי הַנְּבִאִים | הַשְׁכֵּים וְשָׁלֹחַ | לֵאמֹר שֻׁבוּ־נָא אִישׁ מִדַּרְכּוֹ הָרָעָה וְהֵיטִיבוּ מַעַלְלֵיכֶם וְאַל־תֵּלְכוּ אַחֲרֵי אֱלֹהִים אֲחֵרִים לְעׇבְדָם וּשְׁבוּ אֶל־הָאֲדָמָה אֲשֶׁר־נָתַתִּי לָכֶם וְלַאֲבֹתֵיכֶם וְלֹא הִטִּיתֶם אֶת־אׇזְנְכֶם וְלֹא שְׁמַעְתֶּם אֵלָי: 16 כִּי הֵקִימוּ בְּנֵי יְהוֹנָדָב בֶּן־רֵכָב אֶת־מִצְוַת אֲבִיהֶם אֲשֶׁר צִוָּם וְהָעָם הַזֶּה לֹא שָׁמְעוּ אֵלָי: ס 17 לָכֵן כֹּה־אָמַר יְהֹוָה אֱלֹהֵי צְבָאוֹת אֱלֹהֵי יִשְׂרָאֵל הִנְנִי מֵבִיא אֶל־יְהוּדָה וְאֶל כׇּל־יוֹשְׁבֵי יְרוּשָׁלַ͏ִם אֵת כׇּל־הָרָעָה אֲשֶׁר דִּבַּרְתִּי עֲלֵיהֶם יַעַן דִּבַּרְתִּי אֲלֵיהֶם וְלֹא שָׁמֵעוּ וָאֶקְרָא לָהֶם וְלֹא עָנוּ: 18 וּלְבֵית הָרֵכָבִים אָמַר יִרְמְיָהוּ כֹּה־אָמַר יְהֹוָה צְבָאוֹת אֱלֹהֵי יִשְׂרָאֵל יַעַן אֲשֶׁר שְׁמַעְתֶּם עַל־מִצְוַת יְהוֹנָדָב אֲבִיכֶם וַתִּשְׁמְרוּ אֶת־כׇּל־מִצְוֺתָיו וַתַּעֲשׂוּ כְּכֹל אֲשֶׁר־צִוָּה אֶתְכֶם: ס 19 לָכֵן כֹּה אָמַר יְהֹוָה צְבָאוֹת אֱלֹהֵי יִשְׂרָאֵל לֹא־יִכָּרֵת אִישׁ לְיוֹנָדָב בֶּן־רֵכָב עֹמֵד לְפָנַי כׇּל־הַיָּמִים: פ

36 In the fourth year of King Jehoiakim son of Josiah of Judah, this word came to Jeremiah from the LORD:

²Get a scroll and write upon it all the words that I have spoken to you—concerning Israel and Judah and all the nations—from the time I first spoke to you in the days of Josiah to this day. ³Perhaps when the House of Judah hear of all the disasters I intend to bring upon them, they will turn back from their wicked ways, and I will pardon their iniquity and their sin. ⁴So Jeremiah called Baruch son of Neriah; and Baruch wrote down in the scroll, at Jeremiah's dictation, all the words which the LORD had spoken to him.

⁵Jeremiah instructed Baruch, "I am in hiding; I cannot go to the House of the LORD. ⁶But you go and read aloud the words of the LORD from the scroll which you wrote at my dictation, to all the people in the House of the LORD on a fast day; thus you will also be reading them to all the Judeans who come in from the towns. ⁷Perhaps their entreaty will be accepted by the LORD, if they turn back from their wicked ways. For great is the anger and wrath with which the LORD has threatened this people."

⁸Baruch son of Neriah did just as the prophet Jeremiah had instructed him, about reading the words of the LORD from the scroll in the House of the LORD. ⁹In the ninth month of the fifth year of King Jehoiakim son of Josiah of Judah, all the people in Jerusalem and all the people coming from Judah proclaimed a fast before the LORD in Jerusalem. ¹⁰It was then that Baruch—in the chamber of Gemariah son of Shaphan the scribe, in the upper court, near the new gateway of the House of the LORD—read the words of Jeremiah from the scroll to all the people in the House of the LORD.

לו
וַיְהִי֙ בַּשָּׁנָ֣ה הָרְבִיעִ֔ת לִיהֽוֹיָקִ֛ים
בֶּן־יֹאשִׁיָּ֖הוּ מֶ֣לֶךְ יְהוּדָ֑ה הָיָ֞ה הַדָּבָ֤ר הַזֶּה֙
אֶֽל־יִרְמְיָ֔הוּ מֵאֵ֥ת יְהוָ֖ה לֵאמֹֽר׃ ² קַח־לְךָ֮ מְגִלַּת־סֵפֶר֒ וְכָתַבְתָּ֣ אֵלֶ֗יהָ אֵ֣ת
כָּל־הַדְּבָרִ֞ים אֲשֶׁר־דִּבַּ֧רְתִּי אֵלֶ֛יךָ עַל־
יִשְׂרָאֵ֧ל וְעַל־יְהוּדָ֛ה וְעַל־כָּל־הַגּוֹיִ֖ם מִיּ֥וֹם
דִּבַּ֤רְתִּי אֵלֶ֙יךָ֙ מִימֵ֣י יֹאשִׁיָּ֔הוּ וְעַ֖ד הַיּ֥וֹם
הַזֶּֽה׃ ³ אוּלַ֣י יִשְׁמְע֗וּ בֵּ֣ית יְהוּדָ֔ה אֵ֚ת
כָּל־הָ֣רָעָ֔ה אֲשֶׁ֛ר אָנֹכִ֥י חֹשֵׁ֖ב לַעֲשׂ֣וֹת לָהֶ֑ם
לְמַ֣עַן יָשׁ֗וּבוּ אִ֚ישׁ מִדַּרְכּ֣וֹ הָרָעָ֔ה וְסָלַחְתִּ֥י
לַעֲוֺנָ֖ם וּלְחַטָּאתָֽם׃ ס ⁴ וַיִּקְרָ֣א יִרְמְיָ֗הוּ
אֶת־בָּר֣וּךְ בֶּן־נֵֽרִיָּ֑ה וַיִּכְתֹּ֨ב בָּר֜וּךְ מִפִּ֣י
יִרְמְיָ֗הוּ אֵ֣ת כָּל־דִּבְרֵ֧י יְהוָ֛ה אֲשֶׁר־דִּבֶּ֥ר
אֵלָ֖יו עַל־מְגִלַּת־סֵֽפֶר׃ ⁵ וַיְצַוֶּ֣ה יִרְמְיָ֔הוּ אֶת־בָּר֖וּךְ לֵאמֹ֑ר אֲנִ֣י
עָצ֔וּר לֹ֣א אוּכַ֔ל לָב֖וֹא בֵּ֥ית יְהוָֽה׃ ⁶ וּבָאתָ֣
אַתָּ֡ה וְקָרָ֣אתָ בַמְּגִלָּ֣ה אֲשֶׁר־כָּתַבְתָּֽ־מִפִּי֩
אֶת־דִּבְרֵ֨י יְהוָ֤ה בְּאָזְנֵ֣י הָעָם֙ בֵּ֣ית יְהוָ֔ה
בְּי֣וֹם צ֑וֹם וְגַ֗ם בְּאָזְנֵ֛י כָל־יְהוּדָ֖ה הַבָּאִ֣ים
מֵעָרֵיהֶ֖ם תִּקְרָאֵֽם׃ ⁷ אוּלַ֞י תִּפֹּ֤ל תְּחִנָּתָם֙
לִפְנֵ֣י יְהוָ֔ה וְיָשֻׁ֕בוּ אִ֖ישׁ מִדַּרְכּ֣וֹ הָרָעָ֑ה
כִּֽי־גָד֤וֹל הָאַף֙ וְהַ֣חֵמָ֔ה אֲשֶׁר־דִּבֶּ֥ר יְהוָ֖ה
אֶל־הָעָ֥ם הַזֶּֽה׃ ⁸ וַיַּ֗עַשׂ בָּרוּךְ֙ בֶּן־נֵ֣רִיָּ֔ה כְּכֹ֥ל אֲשֶׁר־צִוָּ֖הוּ
יִרְמְיָ֣הוּ הַנָּבִ֑יא לִקְרֹ֥א בַסֵּ֛פֶר דִּבְרֵ֥י יְהוָ֖ה
בֵּ֥ית יְהוָֽה׃ ס ⁹ וַיְהִ֣י בַשָּׁנָ֣ה הַחֲמִשִׁ֗ית
לִֽיהוֹיָקִ֤ים בֶּן־יֹאשִׁיָּ֙הוּ֙ מֶ֣לֶךְ יְהוּדָ֔ה בַּחֹ֖דֶשׁ
הַתְּשִׁעִ֑י קָרְא֨וּ צ֜וֹם לִפְנֵ֤י יְהוָה֙ כָּל־הָעָ֣ם
בִּירֽוּשָׁלִַ֔ם וְכָל־הָעָ֗ם הַבָּאִ֛ים מֵעָרֵ֥י יְהוּדָ֖ה
בִּירֽוּשָׁלָֽ͏ִם׃ ¹⁰ וַיִּקְרָ֨א בָר֜וּךְ בַּסֵּ֗פֶר אֶת־
דִּבְרֵ֣י יִרְמְיָ֮הוּ֮ בֵּ֣ית יְהוָה֒ בְּלִשְׁכַּ֗ת גְּמַרְיָ֨הוּ
בֶן־שָׁפָ֣ן הַסֹּפֵר֮ בֶּחָצֵ֣ר הָעֶלְיוֹן֒ פֶּ֜תַח שַׁ֤עַר
בֵּית־יְהוָה֙ הֶֽחָדָ֔שׁ בְּאָזְנֵ֖י כָּל־הָעָֽם׃

¹¹Micaiah son of Gemariah son of Shaphan heard all the words of the Lᴏʀᴅ [read] from the scroll, ¹²and he went down to the king's palace, to the chamber of the scribe. There he found all the officials in session: Elishama the scribe, Delaiah son of Shemaiah, Elnathan son of Achbor, Gemariah son of Shaphan, Zedekiah son of Hananiah, and all the other officials. ¹³And Micaiah told them all that he had heard as Baruch read from the scroll in the hearing of the people.

¹⁴Then all the officials sent Jehudi son of Nethaniah son of Shelemiah son of Cushi to say to Baruch, "Take that scroll from which you read to the people, and come along!" And Baruch took the scroll and came to them.

¹⁵They said, ᵃ-"Sit down and read it-ᵃ to us." And Baruch read it to them. ¹⁶When they heard all these words, they turned to each other in fear; and they said to Baruch, "We must report all this to the king."

¹⁷And they questioned Baruch further, "Tell us how you wrote down all these words ᵇ-that he spoke."-ᵇ ¹⁸He answered them, "He himself recited all those words to me, and I would write them down in the scroll in ink."

¹⁹The officials said to Baruch, "Go into hiding, you and Jeremiah. Let no man know where you are!" ²⁰And they went to the king in the court, after leaving the scroll in the chamber of the scribe Elishama. And they reported all these matters to the king.

²¹The king sent Jehudi to get the scroll and he fetched it from the chamber of the scribe Elishama. Jehudi read it to the king and to all the officials who were in attendance on the king. ²²Since it was the ninth month, the king was sitting in the winter house, with a fire burning in the brazier before him. ²³And every time Jehudi

---

a-a   Change of vocalization yields "Read it again"; cf. Targum and
       Septuagint.
b-b   Force of Heb. uncertain.

11 וַיִּשְׁמַ֞ע מִכָ֣יְהוּ בֶן־גְּמַרְיָ֤הוּ בֶן־שָׁפָן֙ אֶת־
כָּל־דִּבְרֵ֥י יְהוָ֖ה מֵעַ֥ל הַסֵּֽפֶר׃ 12 וַיֵּ֣רֶד בֵּית־
הַמֶּ֗לֶךְ עַל־לִשְׁכַּ֣ת הַסֹּפֵר֒ וְהִ֨נֵּה־שָׁ֜ם כָּל־
הַשָּׂרִ֣ים יֽוֹשְׁבִ֗ים אֱלִישָׁמָ֣ע הַסֹּפֵ֡ר וּדְלָיָ֣הוּ
בֶן־שְׁמַעְיָ֡הוּ וְאֶלְנָתָ֣ן בֶּן־עַכְבּוֹר֩ וּגְמַרְיָ֨הוּ
בֶן־שָׁפָ֜ן וְצִדְקִיָּ֣הוּ בֶן־חֲנַנְיָ֗הוּ וְכָל־
הַשָּׂרִֽים׃ 13 וַיַּגֵּ֤ד לָהֶם֙ מִכָ֔יְהוּ אֵ֥ת כָּל־
הַדְּבָרִ֖ים אֲשֶׁ֣ר שָׁמֵ֑עַ בִּקְרֹ֥א בָר֛וּךְ בַּסֵּ֖פֶר
בְּאָזְנֵ֥י הָעָֽם׃

14 וַיִּשְׁלְח֨וּ כָל־הַשָּׂרִ֜ים אֶל־בָּר֗וּךְ אֶת־
יְהוּדִ֡י בֶּן־נְתַנְיָ֠הוּ בֶּן־שֶׁלֶמְיָ֣הוּ בֶן־כּוּשִׁי֮
לֵאמֹר֒ הַמְּגִלָּ֗ה אֲשֶׁ֨ר קָרָ֤אתָ בָּהּ֙ בְּאָזְנֵ֣י
הָעָ֔ם קָחֶ֥נָּה בְיָדְךָ֖ וָלֵ֑ךְ וַיִּקַּ֞ח בָּר֤וּךְ בֶּן־
נֵרִיָּ֨הוּ֙ אֶת־הַמְּגִלָּ֣ה בְּיָד֔וֹ וַיָּבֹ֖א אֲלֵיהֶֽם׃
15 וַיֹּאמְר֣וּ אֵלָ֔יו שֵׁ֣ב נָ֔א וּקְרָאֶ֖נָּה בְּאָזְנֵ֑ינוּ
וַיִּקְרָ֥א בָר֖וּךְ בְּאָזְנֵיהֶֽם׃ 16 וַיְהִ֗י כְּשָׁמְעָם֙
אֶת־כָּל־הַדְּבָרִ֔ים פָּחֲד֖וּ אִ֣ישׁ אֶל־רֵעֵ֑הוּ
וַיֹּֽאמְרוּ֙ אֶל־בָּר֔וּךְ הַגֵּ֤יד נַגִּיד֙ לַמֶּ֔לֶךְ אֵ֥ת
כָּל־הַדְּבָרִ֖ים הָאֵֽלֶּה׃

17 וְאֶת־בָּר֔וּךְ שָׁאֲל֖וּ לֵאמֹ֑ר הַגֶּד־נָ֣א לָ֔נוּ
אֵ֗יךְ כָּתַ֛בְתָּ אֶת־כָּל־הַדְּבָרִ֥ים הָאֵ֖לֶּה
מִפִּֽיו׃ 18 וַיֹּ֤אמֶר לָהֶם֙ בָּר֔וּךְ מִפִּיו֙ יִקְרָ֣א
אֵלַ֔י אֵ֥ת כָּל־הַדְּבָרִ֖ים הָאֵ֑לֶּה וַאֲנִ֛י כֹּתֵ֥ב
עַל־הַסֵּ֖פֶר בַּדְּיֽוֹ׃ פ

19 וַיֹּאמְר֤וּ הַשָּׂרִים֙ אֶל־בָּר֔וּךְ לֵ֥ךְ הִסָּתֵ֖ר
אַתָּ֣ה וְיִרְמְיָ֑הוּ וְאִ֥ישׁ אַל־יֵדַ֖ע אֵיפֹ֥ה
אַתֶּֽם׃ 20 וַיָּבֹ֣אוּ אֶל־הַמֶּלֶךְ֮ חָצֵרָה֒ וְאֶת־
הַמְּגִלָּ֣ה הִפְקִ֔דוּ בְּלִשְׁכַּ֖ת אֱלִישָׁמָ֣ע הַסֹּפֵ֑ר
וַיַּגִּ֙ידוּ֙ בְּאָזְנֵ֣י הַמֶּ֔לֶךְ אֵ֖ת כָּל־הַדְּבָרִֽים׃
21 וַיִּשְׁלַ֨ח הַמֶּ֜לֶךְ אֶת־יְהוּדִ֗י לָקַ֙חַת֙ אֶת־
הַמְּגִלָּ֔ה וַיִּקָּחֶ֕הָ מִלִּשְׁכַּ֖ת אֱלִישָׁמָ֣ע הַסֹּפֵ֑ר
וַיִּקְרָאֶ֣הָ יְהוּדִ֗י בְּאָזְנֵ֣י הַמֶּ֔לֶךְ וּבְאָזְנֵי֙ כָּל־
הַשָּׂרִ֔ים הָעֹמְדִ֖ים מֵעַ֣ל הַמֶּֽלֶךְ׃ 22 וְהַמֶּ֗לֶךְ
יוֹשֵׁב֙ בֵּ֣ית הַחֹ֔רֶף בַּחֹ֖דֶשׁ הַתְּשִׁיעִ֑י וְאֶת־
הָאָ֖ח לְפָנָ֥יו מְבֹעָֽרֶת׃ 23 וַיְהִ֣י ׀ כִּקְר֣וֹא

read three or four columns, [the king] would cut it up with a scribe's knife and throw it into the fire in the brazier, until the entire scroll was consumed by the fire in the brazier. ²⁴Yet the king and all his courtiers who heard all these words showed no fear and did not tear their garments; ²⁵moreover, Elnathan, Delaiah, and Gemariah begged the king not to burn the scroll, but he would not listen to them.

²⁶The king ordered Jerahmeel, the king's son, and Seraiah son of Azriel, and Shelemiah son of Abdeel to arrest the scribe Baruch and the prophet Jeremiah. But the Lord hid them.

²⁷The word of the Lord came to Jeremiah after the king had burned the scroll containing the words that Baruch had written at Jeremiah's dictation: ²⁸Get yourself another scroll, and write upon it the same words that were in the first scroll that was burned by King Jehoiakim of Judah. ²⁹And concerning King Jehoiakim of Judah you shall say: Thus said the Lord: You burned that scroll, saying, "How dare you write in it that the king of Babylon will come and destroy this land and cause man and beast to cease from it?" ³⁰Assuredly, thus said the Lord concerning King Jehoiakim of Judah: He shall not have any of his line sitting on the throne of David; and his own corpse shall be left exposed to the heat by day and the cold by night. ³¹And I will punish him and his offspring and his courtiers for their iniquity; I will bring on them and on the inhabitants of Jerusalem and on all the men of Judah all the disasters of which I have warned them—but they would not listen.

³²So Jeremiah got another scroll and gave it to the scribe Baruch son of Neriah. And at Jeremiah's dictation, he wrote in it the whole text

יְהוּדִי שָׁלֹשׁ דְּלָתוֹת וְאַרְבָּעָה יִקְרָעֶהָ בְּתַעַר הַסֹּפֵר וְהַשְׁלֵךְ אֶל־הָאֵשׁ אֲשֶׁר אֶל־הָאָח עַד־תֹּם כָּל־הַמְּגִלָּה עַל־הָאֵשׁ אֲשֶׁר עַל־הָאָח: 24 וְלֹא פָחֲדוּ וְלֹא קָרְעוּ אֶת־בִּגְדֵיהֶם הַמֶּלֶךְ וְכָל־עֲבָדָיו הַשֹּׁמְעִים אֵת כָּל־הַדְּבָרִים הָאֵלֶּה: 25 וְגַם אֶלְנָתָן וּדְלָיָהוּ וּגְמַרְיָהוּ הִפְגִּעוּ בַמֶּלֶךְ לְבִלְתִּי שְׂרֹף אֶת־הַמְּגִלָּה וְלֹא שָׁמַע אֲלֵיהֶם: 26 וַיְצַוֶּה הַמֶּלֶךְ אֶת־יְרַחְמְאֵל בֶּן־הַמֶּלֶךְ וְאֶת־שְׂרָיָהוּ בֶן־עַזְרִיאֵל וְאֶת־שֶׁלֶמְיָהוּ בֶּן־עַבְדְּאֵל לָקַחַת אֶת־בָּרוּךְ הַסֹּפֵר וְאֵת יִרְמְיָהוּ הַנָּבִיא וַיַּסְתִּרֵם יְהֹוָה: ס

27 וַיְהִי דְבַר־יְהֹוָה אֶל־יִרְמְיָהוּ אַחֲרֵי | שְׂרֹף הַמֶּלֶךְ אֶת־הַמְּגִלָּה וְאֶת־הַדְּבָרִים אֲשֶׁר כָּתַב בָּרוּךְ מִפִּי יִרְמְיָהוּ לֵאמֹר: 28 שׁוּב קַח־לְךָ מְגִלָּה אַחֶרֶת וּכְתֹב עָלֶיהָ אֵת כָּל־הַדְּבָרִים הָרִאשֹׁנִים אֲשֶׁר הָיוּ עַל־הַמְּגִלָּה הָרִאשֹׁנָה אֲשֶׁר שָׂרַף יְהוֹיָקִים מֶלֶךְ־יְהוּדָה: 29 וְעַל־יְהוֹיָקִים מֶלֶךְ־ יְהוּדָה תֹאמַר כֹּה אָמַר יְהֹוָה אַתָּה שָׂרַפְתָּ אֶת־הַמְּגִלָּה הַזֹּאת לֵאמֹר מַדּוּעַ כָּתַבְתָּ עָלֶיהָ לֵאמֹר בֹּא־יָבוֹא מֶלֶךְ־בָּבֶל וְהִשְׁחִית אֶת־הָאָרֶץ הַזֹּאת וְהִשְׁבִּית מִמֶּנָּה אָדָם וּבְהֵמָה: ס 30 לָכֵן כֹּה־ אָמַר יְהֹוָה עַל־יְהוֹיָקִים מֶלֶךְ יְהוּדָה לֹא־יִהְיֶה־לּוֹ יוֹשֵׁב עַל־כִּסֵּא דָוִד וְנִבְלָתוֹ תִּהְיֶה מֻשְׁלֶכֶת לַחֹרֶב בַּיּוֹם וְלַקֶּרַח בַּלָּיְלָה: 31 וּפָקַדְתִּי עָלָיו וְעַל־זַרְעוֹ וְעַל־ עֲבָדָיו אֶת־עֲוֹנָם וְהֵבֵאתִי עֲלֵיהֶם וְעַל־ יֹשְׁבֵי יְרוּשָׁלַם וְאֶל־אִישׁ יְהוּדָה אֵת כָּל־הָרָעָה אֲשֶׁר־דִּבַּרְתִּי אֲלֵיהֶם וְלֹא שָׁמֵעוּ: ס

32 וְיִרְמְיָהוּ לָקַח | מְגִלָּה אַחֶרֶת וַיִּתְּנָהּ אֶל־בָּרוּךְ בֶּן־נֵרִיָּהוּ הַסֹּפֵר וַיִּכְתֹּב עָלֶיהָ מִפִּי יִרְמְיָהוּ אֵת כָּל־דִּבְרֵי הַסֵּפֶר אֲשֶׁר

of the scroll that King Jehoiakim of Judah had burned; and more of the like was added.

37 Zedekiah son of Josiah became king instead of Coniah son of Jehoiakim, for King Nebuchadrezzar of Babylon set him up as king over the land of Judah. [2]Neither he nor his courtiers nor the people of the land gave heed to the words which the LORD spoke through the prophet Jeremiah.

[3]Yet King Zedekiah sent Jehucal son of Shelemiah and Zephaniah son of the priest Maaseiah to the prophet Jeremiah, to say, "Please pray on our behalf to the LORD our God." [4](Jeremiah could still go in and out among the people, for they had not yet put him in prison. [5]The army of Pharaoh had set out from Egypt; and when the Chaldeans who were besieging Jerusalem heard the report, they raised the siege of Jerusalem.)

[6]Then the word of the LORD came to the prophet Jeremiah: [7]Thus said the LORD, the God of Israel: Thus shall you say to the king of Judah who sent you to Me to inquire of Me: "The army of Pharaoh, which set out to help you, will return to its own land, to Egypt. [8]And the Chaldeans will come back and attack this city and they will capture it and destroy it by fire."

[9]Thus said the LORD: Do not delude yourselves into thinking, "The Chaldeans will go away from us." They will not. [10]Even if you defeated the whole army of the Chaldeans that are fighting against you, and only wounded men were left lying in their tents, they would get up and burn this city down!

[11]When the army of the Chaldeans raised the siege of Jerusalem on account of the army of

שָׂרַף יְהוֹיָקִים מֶלֶךְ־יְהוּדָה בָּאֵשׁ וְעוֹד
נוֹסַף עֲלֵיהֶם דְּבָרִים רַבִּים כָּהֵמָּה: ס

לז וַיִּמְלָךְ־מֶלֶךְ צִדְקִיָּהוּ בֶּן־יֹאשִׁיָּהוּ
תַּחַת כָּנְיָהוּ בֶּן־יְהוֹיָקִים אֲשֶׁר הִמְלִיךְ
נְבוּכַדְרֶאצַּר מֶלֶךְ־בָּבֶל בְּאֶרֶץ יְהוּדָה:
[2] וְלֹא שָׁמַע הוּא וַעֲבָדָיו וְעַם הָאָרֶץ
אֶל־דִּבְרֵי יְהוָה אֲשֶׁר דִּבֶּר בְּיַד יִרְמְיָהוּ
הַנָּבִיא:

[3] וַיִּשְׁלַח הַמֶּלֶךְ צִדְקִיָּהוּ אֶת־יְהוּכַל בֶּן־
שֶׁלֶמְיָה וְאֶת־צְפַנְיָהוּ בֶן־מַעֲשֵׂיָה הַכֹּהֵן
אֶל־יִרְמְיָהוּ הַנָּבִיא לֵאמֹר הִתְפַּלֶּל־
נָא בַעֲדֵנוּ אֶל־יְהוָה אֱלֹהֵינוּ: [4] וְיִרְמְיָהוּ
בָּא וְיֹצֵא בְּתוֹךְ הָעָם וְלֹא־נָתְנוּ אֹתוֹ
בֵּית הַכְּלִיא: [5] וְחֵיל פַּרְעֹה
יָצָא מִמִּצְרָיִם וַיִּשְׁמְעוּ הַכַּשְׂדִּים הַצָּרִים
עַל־יְרוּשָׁלִַם אֶת־שִׁמְעָם וַיֵּעָלוּ מֵעַל
יְרוּשָׁלִָם: פ

[6] וַיְהִי דְּבַר־יְהוָה אֶל־יִרְמְיָהוּ הַנָּבִיא
לֵאמֹר: [7] כֹּה־אָמַר יְהוָה אֱלֹהֵי יִשְׂרָאֵל
כֹּה תֹאמְרוּ אֶל־מֶלֶךְ יְהוּדָה הַשֹּׁלֵחַ
אֶתְכֶם אֵלַי לְדָרְשֵׁנִי הִנֵּה ׀ חֵיל פַּרְעֹה
הַיֹּצֵא לָכֶם לְעֶזְרָה שָׁב לְאַרְצוֹ מִצְרָיִם:
[8] וְשָׁבוּ הַכַּשְׂדִּים וְנִלְחֲמוּ עַל־הָעִיר הַזֹּאת
וּלְכָדֻהָ וּשְׂרָפֻהָ בָאֵשׁ: ס
[9] כֹּה ׀ אָמַר יְהוָה אַל־תַּשִּׁאוּ נַפְשֹׁתֵיכֶם
לֵאמֹר הָלֹךְ יֵלְכוּ מֵעָלֵינוּ הַכַּשְׂדִּים כִּי־לֹא
יֵלֵכוּ: [10] כִּי אִם־הִכִּיתֶם כָּל־חֵיל כַּשְׂדִּים
הַנִּלְחָמִים אִתְּכֶם וְנִשְׁאֲרוּ בָם אֲנָשִׁים
מְדֻקָּרִים אִישׁ בְּאָהֳלוֹ יָקוּמוּ וְשָׂרְפוּ אֶת־
הָעִיר הַזֹּאת בָּאֵשׁ:

[11] וְהָיָה בְּהֵעָלוֹת חֵיל הַכַּשְׂדִּים מֵעַל
יְרוּשָׁלִָם מִפְּנֵי חֵיל פַּרְעֹה: ס [12] וַיֵּצֵא

Pharaoh, 12Jeremiah was going to leave Jerusalem and go to the territory of Benjamin *a-to share in some property there-a* among the people. 13When he got to the Benjamin Gate, there was a guard officer there named Irijah son of Shelemiah son of Hananiah; and he arrested the prophet Jeremiah, saying, "You are defecting to the Chaldeans!" 14Jeremiah answered, "That's a lie! I'm not defecting to the Chaldeans!" But Irijah would not listen to him; he arrested Jeremiah and brought him to the officials. 15The officials were furious with Jeremiah; they beat him and put him into prison, in the house of the scribe Jonathan—for it had been made into a jail. 16Thus Jeremiah came to the *a-pit and the cells,-a* and Jeremiah remained there a long time.

17Then King Zedekiah sent for him, and the king questioned him secretly in his palace. He asked, "Is there any word from the LORD?" "There is!" Jeremiah answered, and he continued, "You will be delivered into the hands of the king of Babylon." 18And Jeremiah said to King Zedekiah, "What wrong have I done to you, to your courtiers, and to this people, that you have put me in jail? 19And where are those prophets of yours who prophesied to you that the king of Babylon would never move against you and against this land? 20Now, please hear me, O lord king, and grant my plea: Don't send me back to the house of the scribe Jonathan *b-to die there."-b*

21So King Zedekiah gave instructions to lodge Jeremiah in the prison compound and to supply him daily with a loaf of bread from the Bakers' Street—until all the bread in the city was gone. Jeremiah remained in the prison compound.

38 Shephatiah son of Mattan, Gedaliah son of Pashhur, Jucal son of Shelemiah, and

יִרְמְיָהוּ מִירוּשָׁלַ֫ם לָלֶ֫כֶת אֶ֫רֶץ בִּנְיָמִ֫ן לַחֲלֹ֫ק מִשָּׁ֫ם בְּת֫וֹךְ הָעָֽם: 13 וַֽיְהִי־ה֫וּא בְּשַׁ֫עַר בִּנְיָמִן֙ וְשָׁ֫ם בַּ֫עַל פְּקִדֻ֫ת וּשְׁמ֫וֹ יִרְאִיָּ֗ה בֶּן־שֶֽׁלֶמְיָ֖ה בֶּן־חֲנַנְיָ֑ה וַיִּתְפֹּ֤שׂ אֶֽת־יִרְמְיָ֙הוּ֙ הַנָּבִ֔יא לֵאמֹ֕ר אֶל־הַכַּשְׂדִּ֖ים אַתָּ֥ה נֹפֵֽל: 14 וַיֹּ֤אמֶר יִרְמְיָ֙הוּ֙ שֶׁ֔קֶר אֵינֶ֫נִּי נֹפֵל֙ עַל־הַכַּשְׂדִּ֔ים וְלֹ֥א שָׁמַ֖ע אֵלָ֑יו וַיִּתְפֹּ֤שׂ יִרְאִיָּה֙ בְּיִרְמְיָ֔הוּ וַיְבִאֵ֖הוּ אֶל־הַשָּׂרִֽים: 15 וַיִּקְצְפ֥וּ הַשָּׂרִ֖ים עַֽל־יִרְמְיָ֑הוּ וְהִכּ֣וּ אֹת֗וֹ וְנָתְנ֤וּ אוֹתוֹ֙ בֵּ֣ית הָאֵס֔וּר בֵּ֖ית יְהוֹנָתָ֣ן הַסֹּפֵ֑ר כִּֽי־אֹת֥וֹ עָשׂ֖וּ לְבֵ֥ית הַכֶּֽלֶא: 16 כִּ֣י בָ֤א יִרְמְיָ֙הוּ֙ אֶל־בֵּ֣ית הַבּ֔וֹר וְאֶל־הַֽחֲנֻי֑וֹת וַיֵּֽשֶׁב־שָׁ֥ם יִרְמְיָ֖הוּ יָמִ֥ים רַבִּֽים: פ

17 וַיִּשְׁלַח֩ הַמֶּ֙לֶךְ צִדְקִיָּ֜הוּ וַיִּקָּחֵ֗הוּ וַיִּשְׁאָלֵ֙הוּ הַמֶּ֤לֶךְ בְּבֵיתוֹ֙ בַּסֵּ֔תֶר וַיֹּ֕אמֶר הֲיֵ֥שׁ דָּבָ֖ר מֵאֵ֣ת יְהוָ֑ה וַיֹּ֤אמֶר יִרְמְיָ֙הוּ֙ יֵ֔שׁ וַיֹּ֕אמֶר בְּיַ֥ד מֶֽלֶךְ־בָּבֶ֖ל תִּנָּתֵֽן: ס 18 וַיֹּ֣אמֶר יִרְמְיָ֔הוּ אֶל־הַמֶּ֖לֶךְ צִדְקִיָּ֑הוּ מֶ֣ה חָטָ֤אתִי לְךָ֙ וְלַֽעֲבָדֶ֔יךָ וְלָעָ֖ם הַזֶּ֑ה כִּֽי־נְתַתֶּ֥ם אוֹתִ֖י אֶל־בֵּ֥ית הַכֶּֽלֶא: 19 וְאַיּוֹ֙ נְבִ֣יאֵיכֶ֔ם אֲשֶׁר־נִבְּא֥וּ לָכֶ֖ם לֵאמֹ֑ר לֹֽא־יָבֹ֤א מֶֽלֶךְ־בָּבֶל֙ עֲלֵיכֶ֔ם וְעַ֖ל הָאָ֥רֶץ הַזֹּֽאת: 20 וְעַתָּ֕ה שְֽׁמַֽע־נָ֖א אֲדֹנִ֣י הַמֶּ֑לֶךְ תִּפָּל־נָ֤א תְחִנָּתִי֙ לְפָנֶ֔יךָ וְאַל־תְּשִׁבֵ֗נִי בֵּ֚ית יְהוֹנָתָ֣ן הַסֹּפֵ֔ר וְלֹ֥א אָמ֖וּת שָֽׁם: 21 וַיְצַוֶּ֞ה הַמֶּ֣לֶךְ צִדְקִיָּ֗הוּ וַיַּפְקִ֙דוּ֙ אֶֽת־יִרְמְיָ֙הוּ֙ בַּחֲצַ֣ר הַמַּטָּרָ֔ה וְנָתֹן֩ ל֙וֹ כִכַּר־לֶ֜חֶם לַיּ֗וֹם מִחוּץ֙ הָֽאֹפִ֔ים עַד־תֹּ֥ם כָּל־הַלֶּ֖חֶם מִן־הָעִ֑יר וַיֵּ֣שֶׁב יִרְמְיָ֔הוּ בַּחֲצַ֖ר הַמַּטָּרָֽה:

לח

וַיִּשְׁמַ֞ע שְׁפַטְיָ֣ה בֶן־מַתָּ֗ן וּגְדַלְיָ֙הוּ֙ בֶּן־פַּשְׁח֔וּר וְיוּכַל֙ בֶּן־שֶֽׁלֶמְיָ֔הוּ

---

a-a Meaning of Heb. uncertain.
b-b Lit. "and let me not die there."

1106

Pashhur son of Malchiah heard what Jeremiah was saying to all the people: ²"Thus said the LORD: Whoever remains in this city shall die by the sword, by famine, and by pestilence; but whoever surrenders to the Chaldeans shall live; ᵃ-he shall at least gain his life-ᵃ and shall live. ³Thus said the LORD: This city shall be delivered into the hands of the king of Babylon's army, and he shall capture it."

⁴Then the officials said to the king, "Let that man be put to death, for he disheartensᵇ the soldiers, and all the people who are left in this city, by speaking such things to them. That man is not seeking the welfare of this people, but their harm!" ⁵King Zedekiah replied, "He is in your hands; the king cannot oppose you in anything!"

⁶So they took Jeremiah and put him down in the pit of Malchiah, the king's son, which was in the prison compound; they let Jeremiah down by ropes. There was no water in the pit, only mud, and Jeremiah sank into the mud.

⁷Ebed-melech the Cushite, a eunuch who was in the king's palace, heard that they had put Jeremiah in the pit. The king was then sitting at the Benjamin Gate; ⁸so Ebed-melech left the king's palace, and spoke to the king: ⁹"O lord king, those men have acted wickedly in all they did to the prophet Jeremiah; they have put him down in the pit, to die there of hunger." For there was no more bread in the city.

¹⁰Then the king instructed Ebed-melech the Cushite, "Take with you thirtyᶜ men from here, and pull the prophet Jeremiah up from the pit before he dies." ¹¹So Ebed-melech took the men with him, and went to the king's palace, to ᵈ-a place below-ᵈ the treasury. There they got worn cloths and rags, which they let down to Jeremiah in the pit by ropes. ¹²And Ebed-melech the

---

a-a Lit. "he shall have his life as booty"; cf. 21.9.
b Lit. "weakens the hands of."
c One ms. reads "three."
d-d Emendation yields "the wardrobe of."

וּפַשְׁח֤וּר בֶּן־מַלְכִּיָּה֙ אֶת־הַדְּבָרִ֔ים אֲשֶׁ֥ר יִרְמְיָ֖הוּ מְדַבֵּ֣ר אֶל־כָּל־הָעָ֑ם לֵאמֹֽר׃ ס

2 כֹּ֣ה ׀ אָמַ֣ר יְהוָ֗ה הַיֹּשֵׁב֙ בָּעִ֣יר הַזֹּ֔את יָמ֕וּת בַּחֶ֖רֶב בָּרָעָ֣ב וּבַדָּ֑בֶר וְהַיֹּצֵ֤א אֶל־הַכַּשְׂדִּים֙ יִחְיֶ֣ה וְחָיָ֔ה וְהָֽיְתָה־לּ֥וֹ נַפְשׁ֛וֹ לְשָׁלָ֖ל וָחָֽי׃ ס

3 כֹּ֖ה אָמַ֣ר יְהוָ֑ה הִנָּתֹ֨ן תִּנָּתֵ֜ן הָעִ֣יר הַזֹּ֗את בְּיַ֛ד חֵ֥יל מֶֽלֶךְ־בָּבֶ֖ל וּלְכָדָֽהּ׃

4 וַיֹּאמְר֨וּ הַשָּׂרִ֜ים אֶל־הַמֶּ֗לֶךְ י֣וּמַת נָא֮ אֶת־הָאִ֣ישׁ הַזֶּה֒ כִּֽי־עַל־כֵּ֡ן הֽוּא־מְרַפֵּ֡א אֶת־יְדֵי֩ אַנְשֵׁ֨י הַמִּלְחָמָ֜ה הַֽנִּשְׁאָרִ֣ים ׀ בָּעִ֣יר הַזֹּ֗את וְאֵת֙ יְדֵ֣י כָל־הָעָ֔ם לְדַבֵּ֣ר אֲלֵיהֶ֔ם כַּדְּבָרִ֖ים הָאֵ֑לֶּה כִּ֣י ׀ הָאִ֣ישׁ הַזֶּ֗ה אֵינֶ֨נּוּ דֹרֵ֧שׁ לְשָׁל֛וֹם לָעָ֥ם הַזֶּ֖ה כִּ֥י אִם־לְרָעָֽה׃

5 וַיֹּ֙אמֶר֙ הַמֶּ֣לֶךְ צִדְקִיָּ֔הוּ הִנֵּה־ה֖וּא בְּיֶדְכֶ֑ם כִּֽי־אֵ֣ין הַמֶּ֔לֶךְ יוּכַ֥ל אֶתְכֶ֖ם דָּבָֽר׃

6 וַיִּקְח֣וּ אֶֽת־יִרְמְיָ֗הוּ וַיַּשְׁלִ֨כוּ אֹת֜וֹ אֶל־הַבּ֣וֹר ׀ מַלְכִּיָּ֣הוּ בֶן־הַמֶּ֗לֶךְ אֲשֶׁר֙ בַּחֲצַ֣ר הַמַּטָּרָ֔ה וַיְשַׁלְּח֥וּ אֶֽת־יִרְמְיָ֖הוּ בַּחֲבָלִ֑ים וּבַבּ֤וֹר אֵֽין־מַ֙יִם֙ כִּ֣י אִם־טִ֔יט וַיִּטְבַּ֥ע יִרְמְיָ֖הוּ בַּטִּֽיט׃ ס

7 וַיִּשְׁמַ֡ע עֶֽבֶד־מֶ֨לֶךְ הַכּוּשִׁ֜י אִ֣ישׁ סָרִ֗יס וְהוּא֙ בְּבֵ֣ית הַמֶּ֔לֶךְ כִּֽי־נָתְנ֥וּ אֶֽת־יִרְמְיָ֖הוּ אֶל־הַבּ֑וֹר וְהַמֶּ֥לֶךְ יוֹשֵׁ֖ב בְּשַׁ֥עַר בִּנְיָמִֽן׃

8 וַיֵּצֵ֥א עֶֽבֶד־מֶ֖לֶךְ מִבֵּ֣ית הַמֶּ֑לֶךְ וַיְדַבֵּ֥ר אֶל־הַמֶּ֖לֶךְ לֵאמֹֽר׃

9 אֲדֹנִ֣י הַמֶּ֗לֶךְ הֵרֵ֜עוּ הָאֲנָשִׁ֤ים הָאֵ֙לֶּה֙ אֵ֣ת כָּל־אֲשֶׁ֤ר עָשׂוּ֙ לְיִרְמְיָ֣הוּ הַנָּבִ֔יא אֵ֥ת אֲשֶׁר־הִשְׁלִ֖יכוּ אֶל־הַבּ֑וֹר וַיָּ֤מָת תַּחְתָּיו֙ מִפְּנֵ֣י הָרָעָ֔ב כִּ֣י אֵ֥ין הַלֶּ֛חֶם ע֖וֹד בָּעִֽיר׃

10 וַיְצַוֶּ֣ה הַמֶּ֔לֶךְ אֵ֛ת עֶֽבֶד־מֶ֥לֶךְ הַכּוּשִׁ֖י לֵאמֹ֑ר קַ֣ח בְּיָדְךָ֤ מִזֶּה֙ שְׁלֹשִׁ֣ים אֲנָשִׁ֔ים וְֽהַעֲלִ֜יתָ אֶֽת־יִרְמְיָ֧הוּ הַנָּבִ֛יא מִן־הַבּ֖וֹר בְּטֶ֥רֶם יָמֽוּת׃

11 וַיִּקַּ֣ח ׀ עֶֽבֶד־מֶ֨לֶךְ אֶת־הָאֲנָשִׁ֜ים בְּיָד֗וֹ וַיָּבֹ֤א בֵית־הַמֶּ֙לֶךְ֙ אֶל־תַּ֣חַת הָאוֹצָ֔ר וַיִּקַּ֤ח מִשָּׁם֙ בְּלוֹיֵ֣ הַסְּחָב֔וֹת וּבְלוֹיֵ֖ מְלָחִ֑ים וַיְשַׁלְּחֵ֧ם אֶֽל־יִרְמְיָ֛הוּ אֶל־

Cushite called to Jeremiah, "Put the worn cloths and rags under your armpits, inside the ropes." Jeremiah did so, [13]and they pulled Jeremiah up by the ropes and got him out of the pit. And Jeremiah remained in the prison compound.

[14]King Zedekiah sent for the prophet Jeremiah, and had him brought to him at the third entrance of the House of the LORD. And the king said to Jeremiah, "I want to ask you something; don't conceal anything from me."

[15]Jeremiah answered the king, "If I tell you, you'll surely kill me; and if I give you advice, you won't listen to me."

[16]Thereupon King Zedekiah secretly promised Jeremiah on oath: "As the LORD lives who has *e*-given us this life,-*e* I will not put you to death or leave you in the hands of those men who seek your life."

[17]Then Jeremiah said to Zedekiah, "Thus said the LORD, the God of Hosts, the God of Israel: If you surrender to the officers of the king of Babylon, your life will be spared and this city will not be burned down. You and your household will live. [18]But if you do not surrender to the officers of the king of Babylon, this city will be delivered into the hands of the Chaldeans, who will burn it down; and you will not escape from them."

[19]King Zedekiah said to Jeremiah, "I am worried about the Judeans who have defected to the Chaldeans; that they [the Chaldeans] might hand me over to them to abuse me."

[20]"They will not hand you over," Jeremiah replied. "Listen to the voice of the LORD, to what I tell you, that it may go well with you and your life be spared. [21]For this is what the LORD has

e-e Meaning of Heb. uncertain.

הַבּוֹר בַּחֲבָלִים: 12 וַיֹּאמֶר עֶבֶד־מֶלֶךְ הַכּוּשִׁי אֶל־יִרְמְיָהוּ שִׂים נָא בְּלוֹאֵי הַסְּחָבוֹת וְהַמְּלָחִים תַּחַת אַצִּלוֹת יָדֶיךָ מִתַּחַת לַחֲבָלִים וַיַּעַשׂ יִרְמְיָהוּ כֵּן: 13 וַיִּמְשְׁכוּ אֶת־יִרְמְיָהוּ בַּחֲבָלִים וַיַּעֲלוּ אֹתוֹ מִן־הַבּוֹר וַיֵּשֶׁב יִרְמְיָהוּ בַּחֲצַר הַמַּטָּרָה: ס

14 וַיִּשְׁלַח הַמֶּלֶךְ צִדְקִיָּהוּ וַיִּקַּח אֶת־יִרְמְיָהוּ הַנָּבִיא אֵלָיו אֶל־מָבוֹא הַשְּׁלִישִׁי אֲשֶׁר בְּבֵית יְהוָה וַיֹּאמֶר הַמֶּלֶךְ אֶל־יִרְמְיָהוּ שֹׁאֵל אֲנִי אֹתְךָ דָּבָר אַל־תְּכַחֵד מִמֶּנִּי דָּבָר: 15 וַיֹּאמֶר יִרְמְיָהוּ אֶל־צִדְקִיָּהוּ כִּי אַגִּיד לְךָ הֲלוֹא הָמֵת תְּמִיתֵנִי וְכִי אִיעָצְךָ לֹא תִשְׁמַע אֵלָי: 16 וַיִּשָּׁבַע הַמֶּלֶךְ צִדְקִיָּהוּ אֶל־יִרְמְיָהוּ בַּסֵּתֶר לֵאמֹר חַי־יְהוָה אֵת* אֲשֶׁר עָשָׂה־לָנוּ אֶת־הַנֶּפֶשׁ הַזֹּאת אִם־אֲמִיתֶךָ וְאִם־אֶתֶּנְךָ בְּיַד הָאֲנָשִׁים הָאֵלֶּה אֲשֶׁר מְבַקְשִׁים אֶת־נַפְשֶׁךָ: ס 17 וַיֹּאמֶר יִרְמְיָהוּ אֶל־צִדְקִיָּהוּ כֹּה־אָמַר יְהוָה אֱלֹהֵי צְבָאוֹת אֱלֹהֵי יִשְׂרָאֵל אִם־יָצֹא תֵצֵא אֶל־שָׂרֵי מֶלֶךְ־בָּבֶל וְחָיְתָה נַפְשֶׁךָ וְהָעִיר הַזֹּאת לֹא תִשָּׂרֵף בָּאֵשׁ וְחָיִתָה אַתָּה וּבֵיתֶךָ: 18 וְאִם לֹא־תֵצֵא אֶל־שָׂרֵי מֶלֶךְ בָּבֶל וְנִתְּנָה הָעִיר הַזֹּאת בְּיַד הַכַּשְׂדִּים וּשְׂרָפוּהָ בָּאֵשׁ וְאַתָּה לֹא־תִמָּלֵט מִיָּדָם: ס 19 וַיֹּאמֶר הַמֶּלֶךְ צִדְקִיָּהוּ אֶל־יִרְמְיָהוּ אֲנִי דֹאֵג אֶת־הַיְּהוּדִים אֲשֶׁר נָפְלוּ אֶל־הַכַּשְׂדִּים פֶּן־יִתְּנוּ אֹתִי בְּיָדָם וְהִתְעַלְּלוּ־בִי: פ 20 וַיֹּאמֶר יִרְמְיָהוּ לֹא יִתֵּנוּ שְׁמַע־נָא בְּקוֹל יְהוָה לַאֲשֶׁר אֲנִי דֹּבֵר אֵלֶיךָ וְיִיטַב לְךָ וּתְחִי נַפְשֶׁךָ: 21 וְאִם־מָאֵן אַתָּה לָצֵאת

shown me if you refuse to surrender: [22]All the women who are left in the palace of the king of Judah shall be brought out to the officers of the king of Babylon; and they shall say:

The men who were your friends
Have seduced you and vanquished you.
Now that your feet are sunk in the mire,
They have turned their backs [on you].

[23]They will bring out all your wives and children to the Chaldeans, and you yourself will not escape from them. You will be captured by the king of Babylon, and *f*-this city shall be burned down."-*f*

[24]Zedekiah said to Jeremiah, "Don't let anyone know about this conversation, *g*-or you will die.-*g* [25]If the officials should hear that I have spoken with you, and they should come and say to you, 'Tell us what you said to the king; hide nothing from us, *h*-or we'll kill you.-*h* And what did the king say to you?' [26]say to them, 'I was presenting my petition to the king not to send me back to the house of Jonathan to die there.'"

[27]All the officials did come to Jeremiah to question him; and he replied to them just as the king had instructed him. So they stopped questioning him, for the conversation had not been overheard. [28]Jeremiah remained in the prison compound until the day Jerusalem was captured.

When Jerusalem was captured...*i*

39

In the ninth year of King Zedekiah of Judah, in the tenth month, King Nebuchadrezzar of Babylon moved against Jerusalem with his whole army, and they laid siege to it. [2]And in the eleventh year of Zedekiah, on the ninth

זֶה הַדָּבָר אֲשֶׁר הִרְאַנִי יְהֹוָה: [22] וְהִנֵּה כָל־הַנָּשִׁים אֲשֶׁר נִשְׁאֲרוּ בְּבֵית מֶלֶךְ־יְהוּדָה מוּצָאוֹת אֶל־שָׂרֵי מֶלֶךְ בָּבֶל וְהֵנָּה אֹמְרֹות

הִסִּיתוּךָ וְיָכְלוּ לְךָ
אַנְשֵׁי שְׁלֹמֶךָ
הָטְבְּעוּ בַבֹּץ רַגְלֶךָ
נָסֹגוּ אָחֽוֹר׃

[23] וְאֶת־כָּל־נָשֶׁיךָ וְאֶת־בָּנֶיךָ מוֹצִאִים אֶל־הַכַּשְׂדִּים וְאַתָּה לֹא־תִמָּלֵט מִיָּדָם כִּי בְיַד מֶלֶךְ־בָּבֶל תִּתָּפֵשׂ וְאֶת־הָעִיר הַזֹּאת תִּשְׂרֹף* בָּאֵשׁ׃ פ

[24] וַיֹּאמֶר צִדְקִיָּהוּ אֶל־יִרְמְיָהוּ אִישׁ אַל־יֵדַע בַּדְּבָרִים־הָאֵלֶּה וְלֹא תָמֽוּת׃ [25] וְכִי־יִשְׁמְעוּ הַשָּׂרִים כִּי־דִבַּרְתִּי אִתָּךְ וּבָאוּ אֵלֶיךָ וְאָמְרוּ אֵלֶיךָ הַגִּידָה־נָּא לָנוּ מַה־דִּבַּרְתָּ אֶל־הַמֶּלֶךְ אַל־תְּכַחֵד מִמֶּנּוּ וְלֹא נְמִיתֶךָ וּמַה־דִּבֶּר אֵלֶיךָ הַמֶּלֶךְ׃ [26] וְאָמַרְתָּ אֲלֵיהֶם מַפִּיל־אֲנִי תְחִנָּתִי לִפְנֵי הַמֶּלֶךְ לְבִלְתִּי הֲשִׁיבֵנִי בֵּית יְהוֹנָתָן לָמוּת שָׁם׃ פ

[27] וַיָּבֹאוּ כָל־הַשָּׂרִים אֶל־יִרְמְיָהוּ וַיִּשְׁאֲלוּ אֹתוֹ וַיַּגֵּד לָהֶם כְּכָל־הַדְּבָרִים הָאֵלֶּה אֲשֶׁר צִוָּה הַמֶּלֶךְ וַיַּחֲרִשׁוּ מִמֶּנּוּ כִּי לֹא־נִשְׁמַע הַדָּבָֽר׃ פ [28] וַיֵּשֶׁב יִרְמְיָהוּ בַּחֲצַר הַמַּטָּרָה עַד־יוֹם אֲשֶׁר־נִלְכְּדָה יְרוּשָׁלִָם ס

וְהָיָה כַּאֲשֶׁר נִלְכְּדָה יְרוּשָׁלִָֽם׃ פ

לט בַּשָּׁנָה הַתְּשִׁעִית לְצִדְקִיָּהוּ מֶלֶךְ־יְהוּדָה בַּחֹדֶשׁ הָעֲשִׂירִי בָּא נְבוּכַדְרֶאצַּר מֶלֶךְ־בָּבֶל וְכָל־חֵילוֹ אֶל־יְרוּשָׁלִַם וַיָּצֻרוּ עָלֶיהָ׃ ס [2] בְּעַשְׁתֵּי־עֶשְׂרֵה שָׁנָה לְצִדְקִיָּהוּ בַּחֹדֶשׁ הָרְבִיעִי

---

f-f So Targum and Septuagint and some mss. Most mss. and the editions read "you will burn down this city by fire."
g-g Lit. "that you may not die."
h-h Lit. "that we may not kill you."
i This clause would read well before 39.3.

v. 23. בנוסח אחר "תִּשְׂרֵף" כלומר שני תנועות

day of the fourth month, the [walls of] the city were breached. ³All the officers of the king of Babylon entered, and took up quarters at the middle gate—Nergal-sarezer, Samgar-nebo, Sarsechim the Rab-saris,ᵃ Nergal-sarezer the Rab-mag,ᵃ and all the rest of the officers of the king of Babylon.

⁴When King Zedekiah of Judah saw them, he and all the soldiers fled. They left the city at night, by way of the king's garden, through the gate between the double walls; and he set out toward the Arabah.ᵇ ⁵But the Chaldean troops pursued them, and they overtook Zedekiah in the steppes of Jericho. They captured him and brought him before King Nebuchadrezzar of Babylon at Riblah in the region of Hamath; and he put him on trial. ⁶The king of Babylon had Zedekiah's children slaughtered at Riblah before his eyes; the king of Babylon had all the nobles of Judah slaughtered. ⁷Then the eyes of Zedekiah were put out and he was chained in bronze fetters, that he might be brought to Babylon.

⁸The Chaldeans burned down the king's palace and the housesᶜ of the people by fire, and they tore down the walls of Jerusalem. ⁹The remnant of the people that was left in the city, and the defectors who had gone over to him—the remnant of the people that was left—were exiled by Nebuzaradan, the chief of the guards, to Babylon. ¹⁰But some of the poorest people who owned nothing were left in the land of Judah by Nebuzaradan, the chief of the guards, and he gave them vineyards and fields at that time.

¹¹King Nebuchadrezzar of Babylon had given orders to Nebuzaradan, the chief of the guards, concerning Jeremiah: ¹²"Take him and look after him; do him no harm, but grant whatever he asks of you." ¹³So Nebuzaradan, the chief of

---

בְּתִשְׁעָה לַחֹדֶשׁ הֻבְקְעָה הָעִיר: 3 וַיָּבֹאוּ כֹּל שָׂרֵי מֶלֶךְ־בָּבֶל וַיֵּשְׁבוּ בְּשַׁעַר הַתָּוֶךְ נֵרְגַל שַׂר־אֶצֶר* סַמְגַּר־נְבוּ שַׂר־סְכִים רַב־סָרִיס נֵרְגַל שַׂר־אֶצֶר* רַב־מָג וְכָל־שְׁאֵרִית שָׂרֵי מֶלֶךְ בָּבֶל:

4 וַיְהִי כַּאֲשֶׁר רָאָם צִדְקִיָּהוּ מֶלֶךְ־יְהוּדָה וְכֹל ׀ אַנְשֵׁי הַמִּלְחָמָה וַיִּבְרְחוּ וַיֵּצְאוּ לַיְלָה מִן־הָעִיר דֶּרֶךְ גַּן הַמֶּלֶךְ בְּשַׁעַר בֵּין הַחֹמֹתָיִם וַיֵּצֵא דֶּרֶךְ הָעֲרָבָה: 5 וַיִּרְדְּפוּ חֵיל־כַּשְׂדִּים אַחֲרֵיהֶם וַיַּשִּׂגוּ אֶת־צִדְקִיָּהוּ בְּעַרְבוֹת יְרֵחוֹ וַיִּקְחוּ אֹתוֹ וַיַּעֲלֻהוּ אֶל־נְבוּכַדְרֶאצַּר מֶלֶךְ־בָּבֶל רִבְלָתָה בְּאֶרֶץ חֲמָת וַיְדַבֵּר אִתּוֹ מִשְׁפָּטִים: 6 וַיִּשְׁחַט מֶלֶךְ בָּבֶל אֶת־בְּנֵי צִדְקִיָּהוּ בְּרִבְלָה לְעֵינָיו וְאֵת כָּל־חֹרֵי יְהוּדָה שָׁחַט מֶלֶךְ בָּבֶל: 7 וְאֶת־עֵינֵי צִדְקִיָּהוּ עִוֵּר וַיַּאַסְרֵהוּ בַּנְחֻשְׁתַּיִם לָבִיא* אֹתוֹ בָּבֶלָה:

8 וְאֶת־בֵּית הַמֶּלֶךְ וְאֶת־בֵּית הָעָם שָׂרְפוּ הַכַּשְׂדִּים בָּאֵשׁ וְאֶת־חֹמוֹת יְרוּשָׁלַ͏ִם נָתָצוּ: 9 וְאֵת יֶתֶר הָעָם הַנִּשְׁאָרִים בָּעִיר וְאֶת־הַנֹּפְלִים אֲשֶׁר נָפְלוּ עָלָיו וְאֵת יֶתֶר הָעָם הַנִּשְׁאָרִים הֶגְלָה נְבוּזַר־אֲדָן רַב־טַבָּחִים בָּבֶל: 10 וּמִן־הָעָם הַדַּלִּים אֲשֶׁר אֵין־לָהֶם מְאוּמָה הִשְׁאִיר נְבוּזַרְאֲדָן רַב־טַבָּחִים בְּאֶרֶץ יְהוּדָה וַיִּתֵּן לָהֶם כְּרָמִים וִיגֵבִים בַּיּוֹם הַהוּא:

11 וַיְצַו נְבוּכַדְרֶאצַּר מֶלֶךְ־בָּבֶל עַל־יִרְמְיָהוּ בְּיַד נְבוּזַרְאֲדָן רַב־טַבָּחִים לֵאמֹר: 12 קָחֶנּוּ וְעֵינֶיךָ שִׂים עָלָיו וְאַל־תַּעַשׂ לוֹ מְאוּמָה רָּע* כִּי אם* כַּאֲשֶׁר יְדַבֵּר אֵלֶיךָ כֵּן עֲשֵׂה עִמּוֹ: 13 וַיִּשְׁלַח נְבוּזַרְאֲדָן רַב־טַבָּחִים וּנְבוּשַׁזְבָּן* רַב־סָרִיס וְנֵרְגַל שַׂר־אֶצֶר* רַב־

ᵃ   Titles of officers.
ᵇ   Hoping to escape across the Jordan.
ᶜ   Taking Heb. singular as collective, with Kimhi.

the guards, and Nebushazban the Rab-saris, and Nergal-sarezer the Rab-mag, and all the commanders of the king of Babylon sent [14]and had Jeremiah brought from the prison compound. They committed him to the care of Gedaliah son of Ahikam son of Shaphan, *d*-that he might be left at liberty in a house.-*d* So he dwelt among the people.

[15]The word of the Lord had come to Jeremiah while he was still confined in the prison compound: [16]Go and say to Ebed-melech the Ethiopian: "Thus said the Lord of Hosts, the God of Israel: I am going to fulfill My words concerning this city—for disaster, not for good— and they shall come true on that day in your presence. [17]But I will save you on that day—declares the Lord; you shall not be delivered into the hands of the men you dread. [18]I will rescue you, and you shall not fall by the sword. *e*-You shall escape with your life,-*e* because you trusted Me—declares the Lord."

40

The word that came to Jeremiah from the Lord, after Nebuzaradan, the chief of the guards, set him free at Ramah, to which he had taken him, chained in fetters, among those from Jerusalem and Judah who were being exiled to Babylon.

[2]The chief of the guards took charge of Jeremiah, and he said to him, "The Lord your God threatened this place with this disaster; [3]and now the Lord has brought it about. He has acted as He threatened, because you sinned against the Lord and did not obey Him. That is why this has happened to you. [4]Now, I release you this day from the fetters which were on your hands. If you would like to go with me to Babylon, come, and I will look after you. And if you

מָג וְכֹל רַבֵּי מֶלֶךְ־בָּבֶל: 14 וַיִּשְׁלְחוּ וַיִּקְחוּ אֶת־יִרְמְיָהוּ מֵחֲצַר הַמַּטָּרָה וַיִּתְּנוּ אֹתוֹ אֶל־גְּדַלְיָהוּ בֶּן־אֲחִיקָם בֶּן־שָׁפָן לְהוֹצִאֵהוּ אֶל־הַבָּיִת וַיֵּשֶׁב בְּתוֹךְ הָעָם: ס

15 וְאֶל־יִרְמְיָהוּ הָיָה דְבַר־יְהוָה בִּהְיֹתוֹ עָצוּר בַּחֲצַר הַמַּטָּרָה לֵאמֹר: 16 הָלוֹךְ וְאָמַרְתָּ לְעֶבֶד־מֶלֶךְ הַכּוּשִׁי לֵאמֹר כֹּה־ אָמַר יְהוָה צְבָאוֹת אֱלֹהֵי יִשְׂרָאֵל הִנְנִי מֵבִי אֶת־דְּבָרַי אֶל־הָעִיר הַזֹּאת לְרָעָה וְלֹא לְטוֹבָה וְהָיוּ לְפָנֶיךָ בַּיּוֹם הַהוּא: 17 וְהִצַּלְתִּיךָ בַיּוֹם־הַהוּא נְאֻם־ יְהוָה וְלֹא תִנָּתֵן בְּיַד הָאֲנָשִׁים אֲשֶׁר־אַתָּה יָגוֹר מִפְּנֵיהֶם: 18 כִּי מַלֵּט אֲמַלֶּטְךָ וּבַחֶרֶב לֹא תִפֹּל וְהָיְתָה לְךָ נַפְשְׁךָ לְשָׁלָל כִּי־ בָטַחְתָּ בִּי נְאֻם־יְהוָה: ס

מ הַדָּבָר אֲשֶׁר־הָיָה אֶל־יִרְמְיָהוּ מֵאֵת יְהוָה אַחַר ׀ שַׁלַּח אֹתוֹ נְבוּזַרְאֲדָן רַב־ טַבָּחִים מִן־הָרָמָה בְּקַחְתּוֹ אֹתוֹ וְהוּא־ אָסוּר בָּאזִקִּים* בְּתוֹךְ כָּל־גָּלוּת יְרוּשָׁלַ͏ִם וִיהוּדָה הַמֻּגְלִים בָּבֶלָה: 2 וַיִּקַּח רַב־טַבָּחִים לְיִרְמְיָהוּ וַיֹּאמֶר אֵלָיו יְהוָה אֱלֹהֶיךָ דִּבֶּר אֶת־הָרָעָה הַזֹּאת אֶל־הַמָּקוֹם הַזֶּה: 3 וַיָּבֵא וַיַּעַשׂ יְהוָה כַּאֲשֶׁר דִּבֵּר כִּי־חֲטָאתֶם לַיהוָה וְלֹא־ שְׁמַעְתֶּם בְּקוֹלוֹ וְהָיָה לָכֶם דבר הַדָּבָר הַזֶּה: 4 וְעַתָּה הִנֵּה פִתַּחְתִּיךָ הַיּוֹם מִן־ הָאזִקִּים* אֲשֶׁר עַל־יָדֶךָ אִם־טוֹב בְּעֵינֶיךָ לָבוֹא אִתִּי בָבֶל בֹּא וְאָשִׂים אֶת־עֵינִי עָלֶיךָ וְאִם־רַע בְּעֵינֶיךָ לָבוֹא־אִתִּי בָבֶל

---

d-d   Meaning of Heb. uncertain.
e-e   See note at 38.2.

don't want to come with me to Babylon, you
need not. See, the whole land is before you:
go wherever seems good and right to you."—
5ᵃ-But [Jeremiah] still did not turn back. -ᵃ—"Or
go to Gedaliah son of Ahikam son of Shaphan,
whom the king of Babylon has put in charge of
the towns of Judah, and stay with him among
the people, or go wherever you want to go."

The chief of the guards gave him an allowance
of food, and dismissed him. 6So Jeremiah came
to Gedaliah son of Ahikam at Mizpah, and
stayed with him among the people who were
left in the land.

7The officers of the troops in the open country, and their men with them, heard that the
king of Babylon had put Gedaliah son of
Ahikam in charge of the region, and that he
had put in his charge the men, women, and
children—of the poorest in the land—those
who had not been exiled to Babylon. 8So they
with their men came to Gedaliah at Mizpah—
Ishmael son of Nethaniah; Johanan and Jonathan the sons of Kareah; Seraiah son of Tanhumeth; the sons of Ephai the Netophathite;
and Jezaniah son of the Maacathite. 9Gedaliah
son of Ahikam son of Shaphan reassuredᵇ them
and their men, saying, "Do not be afraid to serve
the Chaldeans. Stay in the land and serve the
king of Babylon, and it will go well with you.
10I am going to stay in Mizpah to attend upon
the Chaldeans who will come to us. But you may
gather wine and figsᶜ and oil and put them in
your own vessels, and settle in the towns you
have occupied."

11Likewise, all the Judeans who were in Moab,
Ammon, and Edom, or who were in other lands,
heard that the king of Babylon had let a remnant
stay in Judah, and that he had put Gedaliah son

חֲדַל רְאֵה כָּל־הָאָ֫רֶץ לְפָנֶ֫יךָ אֶל־ט֫וֹב
וְאֶל־הַיָּשָׁ֥ר בְּעֵינֶ֫יךָ לָלֶ֫כֶת שָׁ֫מָּה לֵֽךְ:
5 וְעוֹדֶ֫נּוּ לֹֽא־יָשׁ֫וּב וְשֻׁ֫בָה אֶל־גְּדַלְיָ֫ה בֶן־
אֲחִיקָ֣ם בֶּן־שָׁפָ֗ן אֲשֶׁ֩ר הִפְקִ֨יד מֶֽלֶךְ־בָּבֶ֜ל
בְּעָרֵ֣י יְהוּדָ֗ה וְשֵׁ֤ב אִתּוֹ֙ בְּת֣וֹךְ הָעָ֔ם א֚וֹ
אֶל־כָּל־הַיָּשָׁ֖ר בְּעֵינֶ֑יךָ לָלֶ֑כֶת לֵ֑ךְ

וַיִּתֶּן־ל֧וֹ רַב־טַבָּחִ֛ים אֲרֻחָ֥ה וּמַשְׂאֵ֖ת
וַֽיְשַׁלְּחֵֽהוּ: 6 וַיָּבֹ֧א יִרְמְיָ֛הוּ אֶל־גְּדַלְיָ֥ה בֶן־
אֲחִיקָ֖ם הַמִּצְפָּ֑תָה וַיֵּ֤שֶׁב אִתּוֹ֙ בְּת֣וֹךְ הָעָ֔ם
הַנִּשְׁאָרִ֖ים בָּאָֽרֶץ: ס

7 וַיִּשְׁמְעוּ֩ כָל־שָׂרֵ֨י הַחֲיָלִ֜ים אֲשֶׁ֣ר בַּשָּׂדֶ֗ה
הֵ֚מָּה וְאַנְשֵׁיהֶ֔ם כִּֽי־הִפְקִ֥יד מֶֽלֶךְ־בָּבֶ֖ל
אֶת־גְּדַלְיָ֣הוּ בֶן־אֲחִיקָ֑ם בָּאָ֗רֶץ וְכִ֣י ׀
הִפְקִ֣יד אִתּ֗וֹ אֲנָשִׁ֤ים וְנָשִׁים֙ וָטָ֔ף וּמִדַּלַּ֣ת
הָאָ֔רֶץ מֵאֲשֶׁ֖ר לֹֽא־הָגְל֥וּ בָּבֶֽלָה: 8 וַיָּבֹ֣אוּ
אֶל־גְּדַלְיָה֮ הַמִּצְפָּתָה֒ וְיִשְׁמָעֵ֣אל בֶּן־
נְתַנְיָ֡הוּ וְיֽוֹחָנָ֣ן וְיוֹנָתָ֣ן בְּנֵֽי־קָ֠רֵחַ וּשְׂרָיָ֨ה
בֶן־תַּנְחֻ֜מֶת וּבְנֵ֣י ׀ עֵיפַ֣י הַנְּטֹפָתִ֗י
וִֽיזַנְיָ֙הוּ֙ בֶּן־הַמַּֽעֲכָתִ֔י הֵ֖מָּה וְאַנְשֵׁיהֶֽם:
9 וַיִּשָּׁבַ֨ע לָהֶ֜ם גְּדַלְיָ֨הוּ בֶן־אֲחִיקָ֤ם בֶּן־שָׁפָן֙
וּלְאַנְשֵׁיהֶ֣ם לֵאמֹ֔ר אַל־תִּֽירְא֖וּ מֵעֲב֣וֹד
הַכַּשְׂדִּ֑ים שְׁב֣וּ בָאָ֗רֶץ וְעִבְד֛וּ אֶת־מֶ֥לֶךְ־
בָּבֶ֖ל וְיִיטַ֥ב לָכֶֽם: 10 וַאֲנִ֗י הִנְנִ֤י יֹשֵׁב֙
בַּמִּצְפָּ֔ה לַֽעֲמֹד֙ לִפְנֵ֣י הַכַּשְׂדִּ֔ים אֲשֶׁ֥ר יָבֹ֖אוּ
אֵלֵ֑ינוּ וְאַתֶּ֡ם אִסְפוּ֩ יַ֨יִן וָקַ֜יִץ וְשֶׁ֗מֶן וְשִׂ֙מוּ֙
בִּכְלֵיכֶ֔ם וּשְׁב֖וּ בְּעָרֵיכֶ֥ם אֲשֶׁר־תְּפַשְׂתֶּֽם:
11 וְגַ֣ם כָּֽל־הַיְּהוּדִ֡ים אֲשֶׁר־בְּמוֹאָ֣ב ׀ וּבִבְנֵֽי־
עַמּ֨וֹן וּבֶאֱד֜וֹם וַאֲשֶׁ֣ר בְּכָל־הָֽאֲרָצ֗וֹת
שָֽׁמְעוּ֙ כִּֽי־נָתַ֤ן מֶֽלֶךְ־בָּבֶל֙ שְׁאֵרִ֣ית לִֽיהוּדָ֔ה
וְכִי֙ הִפְקִ֣יד עֲלֵיהֶ֔ם אֶת־גְּדַלְיָ֖הוּ בֶּן־

---

a-a Meaning of Heb. uncertain.
b Lit. "swore to."
c Lit. "summer fruit."

of Ahikam son of Shaphan in charge of them. [12]All these Judeans returned from all the places to which they had scattered. They came to the land of Judah, to Gedaliah at Mizpah, and they gathered large quantities of wine and figs.[c]

[13]Johanan son of Kareah, and all the officers of the troops in the open country, came to Gedaliah at Mizpah [14]and said to him, "Do you know that King Baalis of Ammon has sent Ishmael son of Nethaniah to kill you?" But Gedaliah son of Ahikam would not believe them. [15]Johanan son of Kareah also said secretly to Gedaliah at Mizpah, "Let me go and strike down Ishmael son of Nethaniah before anyone knows about it; otherwise he will kill you, and all the Judeans who have gathered about you will be dispersed, and the remnant of Judah will perish!"

[16]But Gedaliah son of Ahikam answered Johanan son of Kareah, "Do not do such a thing: what you are saying about Ishmael is not true!"

41

In the seventh month, Ishmael son of Nethaniah son of Elishama, who was of royal descent and one of the king's commanders, came with ten men to Gedaliah son of Ahikam at Mizpah; and they ate together there at Mizpah. [2]Then Ishmael son of Nethaniah and the ten men who were with him arose and struck down Gedaliah son of Ahikam son of Shaphan with the sword and killed him, because the king of Babylon had put him in charge of the land. [3]Ishmael also killed all the Judeans who were with him—with Gedaliah in Mizpah—and the Chaldean soldiers who were stationed there.

[4]The second day after Gedaliah was killed, when no one yet knew about it, [5]eighty men came from Shechem, Shiloh, and Samaria, their beards shaved, their garments torn, and their bodies gashed, carrying meal offerings and

אֲחִיקָ֖ם בֶּן־שָׁפָֽן׃ 12 וַיָּשֻׁ֣בוּ כָל־הַיְּהוּדִ֗ים מִכָּל־הַמְּקֹמוֹת֙ אֲשֶׁ֣ר נִדְּחוּ־שָׁ֔ם וַיָּבֹ֧אוּ אֶֽרֶץ־יְהוּדָ֛ה אֶל־גְּדַלְיָ֖הוּ הַמִּצְפָּ֑תָה וַיַּאַסְפ֛וּ יַ֥יִן וָקַ֖יִץ הַרְבֵּ֥ה מְאֹֽד׃ פ 13 וְיֽוֹחָנָ֣ן בֶּן־קָרֵ֗חַ וְכָל־שָׂרֵ֧י הַחֲיָלִ֛ים אֲשֶׁ֥ר בַּשָּׂדֶ֖ה בָּ֣אוּ אֶל־גְּדַלְיָ֑הוּ הַמִּצְפָּֽתָה׃ 14 וַיֹּאמְר֣וּ אֵלָ֗יו הֲיָדֹ֤עַ תֵּדַע֙ כִּ֞י בַּעֲלִ֣יס ׀ מֶ֣לֶךְ בְּנֵֽי־עַמּ֗וֹן שָׁלַח֙ אֶת־יִשְׁמָעֵ֣אל בֶּן־נְתַנְיָ֔ה לְהַכֹּתְךָ֖ נָ֑פֶשׁ וְלֹא־הֶאֱמִ֣ין לָהֶ֔ם גְּדַלְיָ֖הוּ בֶּן־אֲחִיקָֽם׃ 15 וְיֽוֹחָנָ֣ן בֶּן־קָרֵ֗חַ אָמַ֣ר אֶל־גְּדַלְיָהוּ֮ בַסֵּ֣תֶר בַּמִּצְפָּה֮ לֵאמֹר֒ אֵ֤לְכָה נָּא֙ וְאַכֶּה֙ אֶת־יִשְׁמָעֵ֣אל בֶּן־נְתַנְיָ֔ה וְאִ֖ישׁ לֹ֣א יֵדָ֑ע לָ֧מָּה יַכֶּ֣כָּה נֶּ֗פֶשׁ וְנָפֹ֙צוּ֙ כָּל־יְהוּדָ֔ה הַנִּקְבָּצִ֣ים אֵלֶ֔יךָ וְאָבְדָ֖ה שְׁאֵרִ֥ית יְהוּדָֽה׃ 16 וַיֹּ֨אמֶר גְּדַלְיָ֤הוּ בֶן־אֲחִיקָם֙ אֶל־יֽוֹחָנָ֣ן בֶּן־קָרֵ֔חַ אַל־תַּ֖עַשׂ אֶת־הַדָּבָ֣ר הַזֶּ֑ה כִּי־שֶׁ֛קֶר אַתָּ֥ה דֹבֵ֖ר אֶל־יִשְׁמָעֵֽאל׃ ס

מא וַיְהִ֣י ׀ בַּחֹ֣דֶשׁ הַשְּׁבִיעִ֗י בָּ֣א יִשְׁמָעֵ֣אל בֶּן־נְתַנְיָ֣ה בֶן־אֱלִישָׁמָ֣ע מִזֶּ֣רַע הַמְּלוּכָ֡ה וְרַבֵּ֣י הַמֶּ֠לֶךְ וַעֲשָׂרָ֨ה אֲנָשִׁ֤ים אִתּוֹ֙ אֶל־גְּדַלְיָ֣הוּ בֶן־אֲחִיקָ֔ם הַמִּצְפָּ֑תָה וַיֹּ֨אכְלוּ שָׁ֥ם לֶ֛חֶם יַחְדָּ֖ו בַּמִּצְפָּֽה׃ 2 וַיָּ֣קָם יִשְׁמָעֵ֣אל בֶּן־נְתַנְיָ֗ה וַעֲשֶׂ֨רֶת הָאֲנָשִׁ֣ים ׀ אֲשֶׁר־הָי֣וּ אִתּ֗וֹ וַיַּכּ֛וּ אֶת־גְּדַלְיָ֥הוּ בֶן־אֲחִיקָ֖ם בֶּן־שָׁפָ֑ן בַּחֶ֛רֶב וַיָּ֣מֶת אֹת֔וֹ אֲשֶׁר־הִפְקִ֥יד מֶֽלֶךְ־בָּבֶ֖ל בָּאָֽרֶץ׃ 3 וְאֵ֣ת כָּל־הַיְּהוּדִ֗ים אֲשֶׁר־הָי֤וּ אִתּוֹ֙ אֶת־גְּדַלְיָ֔הוּ בַּמִּצְפָּ֔ה וְאֶת־הַכַּשְׂדִּ֖ים אֲשֶׁ֣ר נִמְצְאוּ־שָׁ֑ם אֵ֚ת אַנְשֵׁ֣י הַמִּלְחָמָ֔ה הִכָּ֖ה יִשְׁמָעֵֽאל׃ 4 וַיְהִ֗י בַּיּ֤וֹם הַשֵּׁנִי֙ לְהָמִ֣ית אֶת־גְּדַלְיָ֔הוּ וְאִ֖ישׁ לֹ֥א יָדָֽע׃ 5 וַיָּבֹ֣אוּ אֲ֠נָשִׁים מִשְּׁכֶ֞ם מִשִּׁל֤וֹ וּמִשֹּֽׁמְרוֹן֙ שְׁמֹנִ֣ים אִ֔ישׁ מְגֻלְּחֵ֤י זָקָן֙ וּקְרֻעֵ֣י בְגָדִ֔ים וּמִתְגֹּֽדְדִ֑ים וּמִנְחָ֤ה וּלְבוֹנָה֙

frankincense to present at the House of the LORD. [6]Ishmael son of Nethaniah went out from Mizpah to meet them, weeping as he walked. As he met them, he said to them, "Come to Gedaliah son of Ahikam." [7]When they came inside the town, Ishmael son of Nethaniah and the men who were with him slaughtered them [and threw their bodies] into a cistern.

[8]But there were ten men among them who said to Ishmael, "Don't kill us! We have stores hidden in a field—wheat, barley, oil, and honey." So he stopped, and did not kill them along with their fellows.—[9]The cistern into which Ishmael threw all the corpses of the men he had killed [a]-in the affair of Gedaliah was the one that-[a] King Asa had constructed on account of King Baasha of Israel. That was the one which Ishmael son of Nethaniah filled with corpses.— [10]Ishmael carried off all the rest of the people who were in Mizpah, including the daughters of the king—all the people left in Mizpah, over whom Nebuzaradan, the chief of the guards, had appointed Gedaliah son of Ahikam. Ishmael son of Nethaniah carried them off, and set out to cross over to the Ammonites.

[11]Johanan son of Kareah, and all the army officers with him, heard of all the crimes committed by Ishmael son of Nethaniah. [12]They took all their men and went to fight against Ishmael son of Nethaniah; and they encountered him by the great pool in Gibeon. [13]When all the people held by Ishmael saw Johanan son of Kareah and all the army officers with him, they were glad; [14]all the people whom Ishmael had carried off from Mizpah turned back and went over to Johanan son of Kareah. [15]But Ishmael son of Nethaniah escaped from Johanan with eight men, and went to the Ammonites.

[16]Johanan son of Kareah and all the army officers with him took all the rest of the people

a-a Septuagint reads "was a large cistern, which…"

בְּיָדָ֑ם לְהָבִ֖יא בֵּ֥ית יְהֹוָֽה׃ [6] וַיֵּצֵ֞א יִשְׁמָעֵ֣אל בֶּן־נְתַנְיָ֗ה לִקְרָאתָם֙ מִן־הַמִּצְפָּ֔ה הֹלֵ֥ךְ הָלֹ֖ךְ וּבֹכֶ֑ה וַיְהִי֙ כִּפְגֹ֣שׁ אֹתָ֔ם וַיֹּ֣אמֶר אֲלֵיהֶ֔ם בֹּ֖אוּ אֶל־גְּדַלְיָ֥הוּ בֶן־אֲחִיקָֽם׃ ס [7] וַיְהִ֕י כְּבוֹאָ֖ם אֶל־תּ֣וֹךְ הָעִ֑יר וַיִּשְׁחָטֵ֞ם יִשְׁמָעֵ֤אל בֶּן־נְתַנְיָה֙ אֶל־תּ֣וֹךְ הַבּ֔וֹר ה֖וּא וְהָאֲנָשִׁ֥ים אֲשֶׁר־אִתּֽוֹ׃ [8] וַעֲשָׂרָ֣ה אֲנָשִׁ֗ים נִמְצְאוּ־בָם֮ וַיֹּֽאמְר֣וּ אֶל־יִשְׁמָעֵאל֒ אַל־תְּמִתֵ֔נוּ כִּֽי־יֶשׁ־לָ֤נוּ מַטְמֹנִים֙ בַּשָּׂדֶ֔ה חִטִּ֥ים וּשְׂעֹרִ֖ים וְשֶׁ֣מֶן וּדְבָ֑שׁ וַיֶּחְדַּ֕ל וְלֹ֥א הֱמִיתָ֖ם בְּת֥וֹךְ אֲחֵיהֶֽם׃ [9] וְהַבּ֗וֹר אֲשֶׁר֩ הִשְׁלִ֨יךְ שָׁ֜ם יִשְׁמָעֵ֗אל אֵ֣ת ׀ כָּל־פִּגְרֵ֣י הָאֲנָשִׁ֗ים אֲשֶׁ֤ר הִכָּה֙ בְּיַד־גְּדַלְיָ֔הוּ ה֗וּא אֲשֶׁ֨ר עָשָׂ֜ה הַמֶּ֤לֶךְ אָסָא֙ מִפְּנֵ֣י בַּעְשָׁ֣א מֶֽלֶךְ־יִשְׂרָאֵ֔ל אֹת֣וֹ מִלֵּ֛א יִשְׁמָעֵ֥אל בֶּן־נְתַנְיָ֖הוּ חֲלָלִֽים׃ [10] וַיִּ֣שְׁבְּ ׀ יִשְׁמָעֵ֡אל אֶת־כָּל־שְׁאֵרִית֩ הָעָ֨ם אֲשֶׁ֤ר בַּמִּצְפָּה֙ אֶת־בְּנ֣וֹת הַמֶּ֔לֶךְ וְאֶת־כָּל־הָעָם֙ הַנִּשְׁאָרִ֣ים בַּמִּצְפָּ֔ה אֲשֶׁ֣ר הִפְקִ֗יד נְבֽוּזַרְאֲדָ֛ן רַב־טַבָּחִ֖ים אֶת־גְּדַלְיָ֣הוּ בֶּן־אֲחִיקָ֑ם וַיִּשְׁבֵּם֙ יִשְׁמָעֵ֣אל בֶּן־נְתַנְיָ֔ה וַיֵּ֕לֶךְ לַעֲבֹ֖ר אֶל־בְּנֵ֥י עַמּֽוֹן׃ ס [11] וַיִּשְׁמַ֞ע יוֹחָנָ֣ן בֶּן־קָרֵ֗חַ וְכָל־שָׂרֵ֤י הַחֲיָלִים֙ אֲשֶׁ֣ר אִתּ֔וֹ אֵ֤ת כָּל־הָֽרָעָה֙ אֲשֶׁ֣ר עָשָׂ֔ה יִשְׁמָעֵ֖אל בֶּן־נְתַנְיָֽה׃ [12] וַיִּקְחוּ֙ אֶת־כָּל־הָ֣אֲנָשִׁ֔ים וַיֵּ֣לְכ֔וּ לְהִלָּחֵ֖ם עִם־יִשְׁמָעֵ֣אל בֶּן־נְתַנְיָ֑ה וַיִּמְצְא֣וּ אֹת֔וֹ אֶל־מַ֥יִם רַבִּ֖ים אֲשֶׁ֥ר בְּגִבְעֽוֹן׃ [13] וַיְהִ֗י כִּרְא֤וֹת כָּל־הָעָם֙ אֲשֶׁ֣ר אֶת־יִשְׁמָעֵ֔אל אֶת־יֽוֹחָנָ֣ן בֶּן־קָרֵ֔חַ וְאֵ֛ת כָּל־שָׂרֵ֥י הַחֲיָלִ֖ים אֲשֶׁ֣ר אִתּ֑וֹ וַיִּשְׂמָֽחוּ׃ [14] וַיָּסֹ֨בּוּ֙ כָּל־הָעָ֔ם אֲשֶׁר־שָׁבָ֥ה יִשְׁמָעֵ֖אל מִן־הַמִּצְפָּ֑ה וַיָּשֻׁ֙בוּ֙ וַיֵּ֣לְכ֔וּ אֶל־יֽוֹחָנָ֖ן בֶּן־קָרֵֽחַ׃ [15] וְיִשְׁמָעֵ֣אל בֶּן־נְתַנְיָ֗ה נִמְלַט֙ בִּשְׁמֹנָ֣ה אֲנָשִׁ֔ים מִפְּנֵ֖י יֽוֹחָנָ֑ן וַיֵּ֖לֶךְ אֶל־בְּנֵ֥י עַמּֽוֹן׃ ס [16] וַיִּקַּח֩ יֽוֹחָנָ֨ן בֶּן־קָרֵ֜חַ וְכָל־שָׂרֵ֧י הַחֲיָלִ֣ים אֲשֶׁר־אִתּ֗וֹ אֵ֧ת כָּל־שְׁאֵרִ֣ית הָעָ֗ם אֲשֶׁ֣ר

whom *b*-he had rescued from Ishmael son of Nethaniah-*b* from Mizpah after he had murdered Gedaliah son of Ahikam—the men, soldiers, women, children, and eunuchs whom [Johanan] had brought back from Gibeon. 17They set out, and they stopped at Geruth*c* Chimham, near Bethlehem, on their way to go to Egypt 18because of the Chaldeans. For they were afraid of them, because Ishmael son of Nethaniah had killed Gedaliah son of Ahikam, whom the king of Babylon had put in charge of the land.

הֵשִׁיב מֵאֵת יִשְׁמָעֵאל בֶּן־נְתַנְיָה מִן־הַמִּצְפָּה אַחַר הִכָּה אֶת־גְּדַלְיָהוּ בֶּן־אֲחִיקָם גִּבֹּרִים אַנְשֵׁי הַמִּלְחָמָה וְנָשִׁים וְטַף וְסָרִסִים אֲשֶׁר הֵשִׁיב מִגִּבְעוֹן: 17 וַיֵּלְכוּ וַיֵּשְׁבוּ בְּגֵרוּת כמוהם כִּמְהָם אֲשֶׁר־אֵצֶל בֵּית לָחֶם לָלֶכֶת לָבוֹא מִצְרָיִם: 18 מִפְּנֵי הַכַּשְׂדִּים כִּי יָרְאוּ מִפְּנֵיהֶם כִּי־הִכָּה יִשְׁמָעֵאל בֶּן־נְתַנְיָה אֶת־גְּדַלְיָהוּ בֶּן־אֲחִיקָם אֲשֶׁר־הִפְקִיד מֶלֶךְ־בָּבֶל בָּאָרֶץ: ס

42

Then all the army officers, with Johanan son of Kareah, Jezaniah son of Hoshaiah, and all the rest of the people, great and small, approached 2the prophet Jeremiah and said, "Grant our plea, and pray for us to the LORD your God, for all this remnant! For we remain but a few out of many, as you can see. 3Let the LORD your God tell us where we should go and what we should do."

4The prophet Jeremiah answered them, "Agreed: I will pray to the LORD your God as you request, and I will tell you whatever response the LORD gives for you. I will withhold nothing from you."

5Thereupon they said to Jeremiah, "Let the LORD be a true and faithful witness against us! We swear that we will do exactly as the LORD your God instructs us through you—6Whether it is pleasant or unpleasant, we will obey the LORD our God to whom we send you, in order that it may go well with us when we obey the LORD our God."

7After ten days, the word of the LORD came to Jeremiah. 8He called Johanan son of Kareah and all the army officers, and the rest of the peo-

מב וַיִּגְּשׁוּ כָּל־שָׂרֵי הַחֲיָלִים וְיוֹחָנָן בֶּן־קָרֵחַ וִיזַנְיָה בֶּן־הוֹשַׁעְיָה וְכָל־הָעָם מִקָּטֹן וְעַד־גָּדוֹל: 2 וַיֹּאמְרוּ אֶל־יִרְמְיָהוּ הַנָּבִיא תִּפָּל־נָא תְחִנָּתֵנוּ לְפָנֶיךָ וְהִתְפַּלֵּל בַּעֲדֵנוּ אֶל־יְהוָה אֱלֹהֶיךָ בְּעַד כָּל־הַשְּׁאֵרִית הַזֹּאת כִּי־נִשְׁאַרְנוּ מְעַט מֵהַרְבֵּה כַּאֲשֶׁר עֵינֶיךָ רֹאוֹת אֹתָנוּ: 3 וְיַגֶּד־לָנוּ יְהוָה אֱלֹהֶיךָ אֶת־הַדֶּרֶךְ אֲשֶׁר נֵלֶךְ־בָּהּ וְאֶת־הַדָּבָר אֲשֶׁר נַעֲשֶׂה: 4 וַיֹּאמֶר אֲלֵיהֶם יִרְמְיָהוּ הַנָּבִיא שָׁמַעְתִּי הִנְנִי מִתְפַּלֵּל אֶל־יְהוָה אֱלֹהֵיכֶם כְּדִבְרֵיכֶם וְהָיָה כָּל־הַדָּבָר אֲשֶׁר־יַעֲנֶה יְהוָה אֶתְכֶם אַגִּיד לָכֶם לֹא־אֶמְנַע מִכֶּם דָּבָר: 5 וְהֵמָּה אָמְרוּ אֶל־יִרְמְיָהוּ יְהִי יְהוָה בָּנוּ לְעֵד אֱמֶת וְנֶאֱמָן אִם־לֹא כְּכָל־הַדָּבָר אֲשֶׁר יִשְׁלָחֲךָ יְהוָה אֱלֹהֶיךָ אֵלֵינוּ כֵּן נַעֲשֶׂה: 6 אִם־טוֹב וְאִם־רָע בְּקוֹל ׀ יְהוָה אֱלֹהֵינוּ אֲשֶׁר אנו אֲנַחְנוּ שֹׁלְחִים אֹתְךָ אֵלָיו נִשְׁמָע לְמַעַן אֲשֶׁר יִיטַב־לָנוּ כִּי נִשְׁמַע בְּקוֹל יְהוָה אֱלֹהֵינוּ: ס

7 וַיְהִי מִקֵּץ עֲשֶׂרֶת יָמִים וַיְהִי דְבַר־יְהוָה אֶל־יִרְמְיָהוּ: 8 וַיִּקְרָא אֶל־יוֹחָנָן בֶּן־קָרֵחַ

---

b-b Emendation yields "Ishmael son of Nethaniah had carried off."
c Aquila reads "the sheepfolds of."

ple, great and small, 9and said to them, "Thus said the LORD, the God of Israel, to whom you sent me to present your supplication before Him: 10If you remain in this land, I will build you and not overthrow, I will plant you and not uproot; for I regret the punishment I have brought upon you. 11Do not be afraid of the king of Babylon, whom you fear; do not be afraid of him—declares the LORD—for I am with you to save you and to rescue you from his hands. 12I will dispose him to be merciful to you: he shall show you mercy and a-bring you back to-a your own land.

13"But if you say, 'We will not stay in this land'—thus disobeying the LORD your God— 14if you say, 'No! We will go to the land of Egypt, so that we may not see war or hear the sound of the horn, and so that we may not hunger for bread; there we will stay,' 15then hear the word of the LORD, O remnant of Judah! Thus said the LORD of Hosts, the God of Israel: If you turn your faces toward Egypt, and you go and sojourn there, 16the sword that you fear shall overtake you there, in the land of Egypt, and the famine you worry over shall follow at your heels in Egypt too; and there you shall die. 17All the men who turn their faces toward Egypt, in order to sojourn there, shall die by the sword, by famine, and by pestilence. They shall have no surviving remnant of the disaster that I will bring upon them. 18For thus said the LORD of Hosts, the God of Israel: As My anger and wrath were poured out upon the inhabitants of Jerusalem, so will My wrath be poured out on you if you go to Egypt. You shall become b-an execration of woe, a curse-b and a mockery; and you shall never again see this place. 19The LORD has spoken against you, O remnant of Judah! Do not go to Egypt! Know well, then—for I warn you

a-a   *Change of vocalization yields "let you dwell in."*
b-b   *I.e., a standard by which men execrate and curse; cf. note at 24.9.*

וְאֶל כָּל־שָׂרֵי הַחֲיָלִים אֲשֶׁר אִתּוֹ וּלְכָל־הָעָם לְמִקָּטֹן וְעַד־גָּדוֹל: 9 וַיֹּאמֶר אֲלֵיהֶם כֹּה־אָמַר יְהוָה אֱלֹהֵי יִשְׂרָאֵל אֲשֶׁר שְׁלַחְתֶּם אֹתִי אֵלָיו לְהַפִּיל תְּחִנַּתְכֶם לְפָנָיו: 10 אִם־שׁוֹב תֵּשְׁבוּ בָּאָרֶץ הַזֹּאת וּבָנִיתִי אֶתְכֶם וְלֹא אֶהֱרֹס וְנָטַעְתִּי אֶתְכֶם וְלֹא אֶתּוֹשׁ כִּי נִחַמְתִּי אֶל־הָרָעָה אֲשֶׁר עָשִׂיתִי לָכֶם: 11 אַל־תִּירְאוּ מִפְּנֵי מֶלֶךְ בָּבֶל אֲשֶׁר־אַתֶּם יְרֵאִים מִפָּנָיו אַל־תִּירְאוּ מִמֶּנּוּ נְאֻם־יְהוָה כִּי־אִתְּכֶם אָנִי לְהוֹשִׁיעַ אֶתְכֶם וּלְהַצִּיל אֶתְכֶם מִיָּדוֹ: 12 וְאֶתֵּן לָכֶם רַחֲמִים וְרִחַם אֶתְכֶם וְהֵשִׁיב אֶתְכֶם אֶל־אַדְמַתְכֶם:

13 וְאִם־אֹמְרִים אַתֶּם לֹא נֵשֵׁב בָּאָרֶץ הַזֹּאת לְבִלְתִּי שְׁמֹעַ בְּקוֹל יְהוָה אֱלֹהֵיכֶם: 14 לֵאמֹר לֹא כִּי אֶרֶץ מִצְרַיִם נָבוֹא אֲשֶׁר לֹא־נִרְאֶה מִלְחָמָה וְקוֹל שׁוֹפָר לֹא נִשְׁמָע וְלַלֶּחֶם לֹא־נִרְעָב וְשָׁם נֵשֵׁב: 15 וְעַתָּה לָכֵן שִׁמְעוּ דְבַר־יְהוָה שְׁאֵרִית יְהוּדָה כֹּה־אָמַר יְהוָה צְבָאוֹת אֱלֹהֵי יִשְׂרָאֵל אִם־אַתֶּם שׂוֹם תְּשִׂמוּן פְּנֵיכֶם לָבֹא מִצְרַיִם וּבָאתֶם לָגוּר שָׁם: 16 וְהָיְתָה הַחֶרֶב אֲשֶׁר אַתֶּם יְרֵאִים מִמֶּנָּה שָׁם תַּשִּׂיג אֶתְכֶם בְּאֶרֶץ מִצְרָיִם וְהָרָעָב אֲשֶׁר־אַתֶּם ׀ דֹּאֲגִים מִמֶּנּוּ שָׁם יִדְבַּק אַחֲרֵיכֶם מִצְרַיִם וְשָׁם תָּמֻתוּ: 17 וְיִהְיוּ כָל־הָאֲנָשִׁים אֲשֶׁר־שָׂמוּ אֶת־פְּנֵיהֶם לָבוֹא מִצְרַיִם לָגוּר שָׁם יָמוּתוּ בַּחֶרֶב בָּרָעָב וּבַדָּבֶר וְלֹא־יִהְיֶה לָהֶם שָׂרִיד וּפָלִיט מִפְּנֵי הָרָעָה אֲשֶׁר אֲנִי מֵבִיא עֲלֵיהֶם: ס 18 כִּי כֹה אָמַר יְהוָה צְבָאוֹת אֱלֹהֵי יִשְׂרָאֵל כַּאֲשֶׁר נִתַּךְ אַפִּי וַחֲמָתִי עַל־יֹשְׁבֵי יְרוּשָׁלִַם כֵּן תִּתַּךְ חֲמָתִי עֲלֵיכֶם בְּבֹאֲכֶם מִצְרָיִם וִהְיִיתֶם לְאָלָה וּלְשַׁמָּה וְלִקְלָלָה וּלְחֶרְפָּה וְלֹא־תִרְאוּ עוֹד אֶת־הַמָּקוֹם הַזֶּה: 19 דִּבֶּר יְהוָה עֲלֵיכֶם

this day ²⁰that you were deceitful at heart when you sent me to the Lord your God, saying, 'Pray for us to the Lord our God; and whatever the Lord our God may say, just tell us and we will do it.' ²¹I told you today, and you have not obeyed the Lord your God in respect to all that He sent me to tell you—²²know well, then, that you shall die by the sword, by famine, and by pestilence in the place where you want to go and sojourn."

43 When Jeremiah had finished speaking all these words to all the people—all the words of the Lord their God, with which the Lord their God had sent him to them—²Azariah son of Hoshaiah and Johanan son of Kareah and all the arrogant men said to Jeremiah, "You are lying! The Lord our God did not send you to say, 'Don't go to Egypt and sojourn there'! ³It is Baruch son of Neriah who is inciting you against us, so that we will be delivered into the hands of the Chaldeans to be killed or to be exiled to Babylon!"

⁴So Johanan son of Kareah and all the army officers and the rest of the people did not obey the Lord's command to remain in the land of Judah. ⁵Instead, Johanan son of Kareah and all the army officers took the entire remnant of Judah—those who had returned from all the countries to which they had been scattered and had sojourned in the land of Judah, ⁶men, women, and children; and the daughters of the king and all the people whom Nebuzaradan the chief of the guards had left with Gedaliah son of Ahikam son of Shaphan, as well as the prophet Jeremiah and Baruch son of Neriah—⁷and they went to Egypt. They did not obey the Lord.

שְׁאֵרִית יְהוּדָה אַל־תָּבֹאוּ אֶל־מִצְרַיִם יָדֹעַ תֵּדְעוּ כִּי־הַעִידֹתִי בָכֶם הַיּֽוֹם׃ 20 כִּי הִתְעֵתֶם בְּנַפְשֽׁוֹתֵיכֶם כִּי־אַתֶּם שְׁלַחְתֶּם אֹתִי אֶל־יְהוָה אֱלֹֽהֵיכֶם לֵאמֹר הִתְפַּלֵּל בַּעֲדֵנוּ אֶל־יְהוָה אֱלֹהֵינוּ וּכְכֹל אֲשֶׁר יֹאמַר יְהוָה אֱלֹהֵינוּ כֵּן הַגֶּד־לָנוּ וְעָשִֽׂינוּ׃ 21 וָאַגִּד לָכֶם הַיּוֹם וְלֹא שְׁמַעְתֶּם בְּקוֹל יְהוָה אֱלֹֽהֵיכֶם וּלְכֹל אֲשֶׁר־שְׁלָחַנִי אֲלֵיכֶֽם׃ 22 וְעַתָּה יָדֹעַ תֵּדְעוּ כִּי בַּחֶרֶב בָּרָעָב וּבַדֶּבֶר תָּמוּתוּ בַּמָּקוֹם אֲשֶׁר חֲפַצְתֶּם לָבוֹא לָגוּר שָֽׁם׃ ס

מג וַיְהִי כְּכַלּוֹת יִרְמְיָהוּ לְדַבֵּר אֶל־כָּל־הָעָם אֶת־כָּל־דִּבְרֵי יְהוָה אֱלֹהֵיהֶם אֲשֶׁר שְׁלָחוֹ יְהוָה אֱלֹהֵיהֶם אֲלֵיהֶם אֵת כָּל־הַדְּבָרִים הָאֵֽלֶּה׃ ס 2 וַיֹּאמֶר עֲזַרְיָה בֶן־הוֹשַֽׁעְיָה וְיוֹחָנָן בֶּן־קָרֵחַ וְכָל־הָאֲנָשִׁים הַזֵּדִים אֹמְרִים אֶל־יִרְמְיָהוּ שֶׁקֶר אַתָּה מְדַבֵּר לֹא שְׁלָחֲךָ יְהוָה אֱלֹהֵינוּ לֵאמֹר לֹא־תָבֹאוּ מִצְרַיִם לָגוּר שָֽׁם׃ 3 כִּי בָּרוּךְ בֶּן־נֵרִיָּה מַסִּית אֹתְךָ בָּנוּ לְמַעַן תֵּת אֹתָנוּ בְיַד־הַכַּשְׂדִּים לְהָמִית אֹתָנוּ וּלְהַגְלוֹת אֹתָנוּ בָּבֶֽל׃ 4 וְלֹא־שָׁמַע יוֹחָנָן בֶּן־קָרֵחַ וְכָל־שָׂרֵי הַחֲיָלִים וְכָל־הָעָם בְּקוֹל יְהוָה לָשֶׁבֶת בְּאֶרֶץ יְהוּדָֽה׃ 5 וַיִּקַּח יוֹחָנָן בֶּן־קָרֵחַ וְכָל־שָׂרֵי הַחֲיָלִים אֵת כָּל־שְׁאֵרִית יְהוּדָה אֲשֶׁר־שָׁבוּ מִכָּל־הַגּוֹיִם אֲשֶׁר נִדְּחוּ־שָׁם לָגוּר בְּאֶרֶץ יְהוּדָֽה׃ 6 אֶת־הַגְּבָרִים וְאֶת־הַנָּשִׁים וְאֶת־הַטַּף וְאֶת־בְּנוֹת הַמֶּלֶךְ וְאֵת כָּל־הַנֶּפֶשׁ אֲשֶׁר הִנִּיחַ נְבוּזַרְאֲדָן רַב־טַבָּחִים אֶת־גְּדַלְיָהוּ בֶּן־אֲחִיקָם בֶּן־שָׁפָן וְאֵת יִרְמְיָהוּ הַנָּבִיא וְאֶת־בָּרוּךְ בֶּן־נֵרִיָּֽהוּ׃ 7 וַיָּבֹאוּ אֶרֶץ מִצְרַיִם כִּי לֹא שָׁמְעוּ בְּקוֹל יְהוָה

They arrived at Tahpanhes, [8]and the word of the LORD came to Jeremiah in Tahpanhes: [9]Get yourself large stones, and embed them in mortar in the brick structure at the entrance to Pharaoh's palace in Tahpanhes, with some Judeans looking on. [10]And say to them: "Thus said the LORD of Hosts, the God of Israel: I am sending for My servant King Nebuchadrezzar of Babylon, and I[a] will set his throne over these stones which I have embedded. He will spread out his pavilion[b] over them. [11]He will come and attack the land of Egypt, delivering

Those destined for the plague, to the plague,
Those destined for captivity, to captivity,
And those destined for the sword, to the sword.

[12]And I[a] will set fire to the temples of the gods of Egypt; he will burn them down and carry them[c] off. He shall wrap himself up in the land of Egypt, as a shepherd wraps himself up in his garment. And he shall depart from there in safety. [13]He shall smash the obelisks of the Temple of the Sun which is in the land of Egypt, and he shall burn down the temples of the gods of Egypt.

44

The word which came to Jeremiah for all the Judeans living in the land of Egypt, living in Migdol, Tahpanhes, and Noph, and in the land of Pathros:

[2]Thus said the LORD of Hosts, the God of Israel: You have seen all the disaster that I brought on Jerusalem and on all the towns of Judah. They are a ruin today, and no one inhabits them, [3]on account of the wicked things they did to vex Me, going to make offerings in worship of other gods which they had not known—neither they nor you nor your fathers. [4]Yet I persistently sent

---

a   *Septuagint reads "he."*
b   *Meaning of Heb. uncertain.*
c   *I.e., the gods.*

8 וַיְהִ֥י דְבַר־ ס ‏וַיָּבֹ֖אוּ עַד־תַּחְפַּנְחֵֽס׃
יְהוָה֙ אֶֽל־יִרְמְיָ֔הוּ בְּתַחְפַּנְחֵ֖ס לֵאמֹֽר׃
9 קַ֣ח בְּיָדְךָ֞ אֲבָנִ֣ים גְּדֹל֗וֹת וּטְמַנְתָּ֤ם
בַּמֶּ֙לֶט֙ בַּמַּלְבֵּ֔ן אֲשֶׁ֖ר בְּפֶ֣תַח בֵּית־
פַּרְעֹ֖ה בְּתַחְפַּנְחֵ֑ס לְעֵינֵ֖י אֲנָשִׁ֥ים יְהוּדִֽים׃
10 וְאָמַרְתָּ֣ אֲלֵיהֶ֡ם כֹּֽה־אָמַר֩ יְהוָ֨ה צְבָא֜וֹת
אֱלֹהֵ֣י יִשְׂרָאֵ֗ל הִנְנִ֤י שֹׁלֵ֙חַ֙ וְלָקַחְתִּ֜י אֶת־
נְבוּכַדְרֶאצַּ֤ר מֶֽלֶךְ־בָּבֶל֙ עַבְדִּ֔י וְשַׂמְתִּ֣י
כִסְא֔וֹ מִמַּ֖עַל לָאֲבָנִ֣ים הָאֵ֑לֶּה אֲשֶׁ֣ר טָמָ֑נְתִּי
וְנָטָ֥ה אֶת־שפרורו שַׁפְרִיר֖וֹ עֲלֵיהֶֽם׃
11 ובאה וּבָ֕א וְהִכָּ֖ה אֶת־אֶ֥רֶץ מִצְרָ֑יִם
אֲשֶׁ֧ר לַמָּ֣וֶת לַמָּ֗וֶת
וַאֲשֶׁ֥ר לַשְּׁבִ֖י לַשֶּׁ֑בִי
וַאֲשֶׁ֥ר לַחֶ֖רֶב לֶחָֽרֶב׃
12 וְהִצַּ֣תִּי אֵ֗שׁ בְּבָתֵּ֛י אֱלֹהֵ֥י מִצְרַ֖יִם וּשְׂרָפָ֑ם
וְשָׁבָ֗ם וְעָטָה֙ אֶת־אֶ֣רֶץ מִצְרַ֔יִם כַּאֲשֶׁר־
יַעְטֶ֤ה הָֽרֹעֶה֙ אֶת־בִּגְד֔וֹ וְיָצָ֥א מִשָּׁ֖ם
בְּשָׁל֑וֹם׃ 13 וְשִׁבַּ֗ר אֶת־מַצְּבוֹת֙ בֵּ֣ית שֶׁ֔מֶשׁ
אֲשֶׁ֖ר בְּאֶ֣רֶץ מִצְרָ֑יִם וְאֶת־בָּתֵּ֥י אֱלֹהֵֽי־
מִצְרַ֖יִם יִשְׂרֹ֥ף בָּאֵֽשׁ׃ ס

מד

הַדָּבָר֙ אֲשֶׁ֣ר הָיָ֣ה אֶֽל־יִרְמְיָ֔הוּ
אֶ֚ל כָּל־הַיְּהוּדִ֔ים הַיֹּשְׁבִ֖ים בְּאֶ֣רֶץ מִצְרָ֑יִם
הַיֹּשְׁבִ֤ים בְּמִגְדֹּל֙ וּבְתַחְפַּנְחֵ֣ס וּבְנֹ֔ף וּבְאֶ֣רֶץ
פַּתְר֖וֹס לֵאמֹֽר׃ ס
2 כֹּֽה־אָמַ֞ר יְהוָ֤ה צְבָאוֹת֙ אֱלֹהֵ֣י יִשְׂרָאֵ֔ל
אַתֶּ֣ם רְאִיתֶ֗ם אֵ֤ת כָּל־הָֽרָעָה֙ אֲשֶׁ֣ר
הֵבֵ֙אתִי֙ עַל־יְר֣וּשָׁלִַ֔ם וְעַ֖ל כָּל־עָרֵ֣י יְהוּדָ֑ה
וְהִנָּ֤ם חָרְבָּה֙ הַיּ֣וֹם הַזֶּ֔ה וְאֵ֥ין בָּהֶ֖ם יוֹשֵֽׁב׃
3 מִפְּנֵ֣י רָעָתָ֗ם אֲשֶׁ֤ר עָשׂוּ֙ לְהַכְעִסֵ֔נִי לָלֶ֙כֶת֙
לְקַטֵּ֗ר לַעֲבֹד֙ לֵאלֹהִ֣ים אֲחֵרִ֔ים אֲשֶׁר֙ לֹ֣א
יְדָע֔וּם הֵ֖מָּה אַתֶּ֣ם וַאֲבֹתֵיכֶֽם׃ 4 וָאֶשְׁלַ֣ח

to you all My servants the prophets, to say, "I beg you not to do this abominable thing which I hate." [5]But they would not listen or give ear, to turn back from their wickedness and not make offerings to other gods; [6]so My fierce anger was poured out, and it blazed against the towns of Judah and the streets of Jerusalem. And they became a desolate ruin, as they still are today.

[7]And now, thus said the Lord, the God of Hosts, the God of Israel: Why are you doing such great harm to yourselves, so that every man and woman, child and infant of yours shall be cut off from the midst of Judah, and no remnant shall be left of you? [8]For you vex me by your deeds, making offering to other gods in the land of Egypt where you have come to sojourn, so that you shall be cut off and become a curse[a] and a mockery among all the nations of earth. [9]Have you forgotten the wicked acts of your forefathers, of the kings of Judah and their[b] wives, and your own wicked acts and those of your wives, which were committed in the land of Judah and in the streets of Jerusalem? [10]No one has shown contrition to this day, and no one has shown reverence. You[c] have not followed the Teaching and the laws that I set before you and before your fathers.

[11]Assuredly, thus said the Lord of Hosts, the God of Israel: I am going to set My face against you for punishment, to cut off all of Judah. [12]I will take the remnant of Judah who turned their faces toward the land of Egypt, to go and sojourn there, and they shall be utterly consumed in the land of Egypt. They shall fall by the sword, they shall be consumed by famine; great and small alike shall die by the sword and by famine, and they shall become an execration[a] and a desolation, a curse[a] and a mockery. [13]I will punish

---

a   *See note at 24.9; 42.18.*
b   *Heb. "his."*
c   *Heb. "They."*

אֲלֵיכֶ֗ם אֶת־כָּל־עֲבָדַ֛י הַנְּבִיאִ֖ים הַשְׁכֵּ֣ים וְשָׁלֹ֣חַ לֵאמֹ֑ר אַל־נָ֣א תַעֲשׂ֗וּ אֵ֧ת דְּבַר־ הַתֹּעֵבָ֛ה הַזֹּ֖את אֲשֶׁ֥ר שָׂנֵֽאתִי׃ 5 וְלֹ֤א שָׁמְעוּ֙ וְלֹא־הִטּ֣וּ אֶת־אָזְנָ֔ם לָשׁ֖וּב מֵרָ֣עָתָ֑ם לְבִלְתִּ֥י קַטֵּ֖ר לֵאלֹהִ֥ים אֲחֵרִֽים׃ 6 וַתִּתַּ֤ךְ חֲמָתִי֙ וְאַפִּ֔י וַתִּבְעַר֙ בְּעָרֵ֣י יְהוּדָ֔ה וּבְחֻצ֖וֹת יְרֽוּשָׁלִָ֑ם וַתִּהְיֶ֛ינָה לְחָרְבָּ֥ה לִשְׁמָמָ֖ה כַּיּ֥וֹם הַזֶּֽה׃ ס

7 וְעַתָּ֡ה כֹּֽה־אָמַ֣ר יְהוָה֩ אֱלֹהֵ֨י צְבָא֜וֹת אֱלֹהֵ֣י יִשְׂרָאֵ֗ל לָמָה֩ אַתֶּ֨ם עֹשִׂ֜ים רָעָ֣ה גְדוֹלָה֮ אֶל־נַפְשֹׁתֵכֶם֒ לְהַכְרִ֣ית לָכֶ֗ם אִישׁ־ וְאִשָּׁ֛ה עוֹלֵ֥ל וְיוֹנֵ֖ק מִתּ֣וֹךְ יְהוּדָ֑ה לְבִלְתִּ֛י הוֹתִ֥יר לָכֶ֖ם שְׁאֵרִֽית׃ 8 לְהַכְעִסֵ֙נִי֙ בְּמַעֲשֵׂ֣י יְדֵיכֶ֔ם לְקַטֵּ֞ר לֵאלֹהִ֤ים אֲחֵרִים֙ בְּאֶ֣רֶץ מִצְרַ֔יִם אֲשֶׁר־אַתֶּ֥ם בָּאִ֖ים לָג֣וּר שָׁ֑ם לְמַ֙עַן֙ הַכְרִ֣ית לָכֶ֔ם וּלְמַ֤עַן הֱיֽוֹתְכֶם֙ לִקְלָלָ֣ה וּלְחֶרְפָּ֔ה בְּכֹ֖ל גּוֹיֵ֥י הָאָֽרֶץ׃ 9 הַֽשְׁכַחְתֶּם֙ אֶת־רָע֣וֹת אֲבוֹתֵיכֶ֔ם וְאֶת־רָע֣וֹת ׀ מַלְכֵ֣י יְהוּדָ֗ה וְאֵת֙ רָע֣וֹת נָשָׁ֔יו וְאֵת֙ רָעֹ֣תְכֶ֔ם וְאֵ֖ת רָעֹ֣ת נְשֵׁיכֶ֑ם אֲשֶׁ֤ר עָשׂוּ֙ בְּאֶ֣רֶץ יְהוּדָ֔ה וּבְחֻצ֖וֹת יְרֽוּשָׁלִָֽם׃ 10 לֹ֣א דֻכְּא֔וּ עַ֖ד הַיּ֣וֹם הַזֶּ֑ה וְלֹ֤א יָֽרְאוּ֙ וְלֹֽא־הָלְכ֣וּ בְתֽוֹרָתִ֗י וּבְחֻקֹּתַ֛י אֲשֶׁר־נָתַ֥תִּי לִפְנֵיכֶ֖ם וְלִפְנֵ֥י אֲבוֹתֵיכֶֽם׃ ס

11 לָכֵ֗ן כֹּֽה־אָמַ֞ר יְהוָ֤ה צְבָאוֹת֙ אֱלֹהֵ֣י יִשְׂרָאֵ֔ל הִנְנִ֨י שָׂ֥ם פָּנַ֛י בָּכֶ֖ם לְרָעָ֑ה וּלְהַכְרִ֖ית אֶת־כָּל־יְהוּדָֽה׃ 12 וְלָקַחְתִּ֞י אֶת־שְׁאֵרִ֣ית יְהוּדָ֗ה אֲשֶׁר־שָׂ֨מוּ פְנֵיהֶ֜ם לָב֣וֹא אֶֽרֶץ־מִצְרַיִם֮ לָג֣וּר שָׁם֒ וְתַ֙מּוּ֙ כֹ֔ל בְּאֶ֣רֶץ מִצְרַ֔יִם יִפֹּ֕לוּ בַּחֶ֥רֶב בָּֽרָעָ֖ב יִתַּ֑מּוּ מִקָּטֹן֙ וְעַד־גָּד֔וֹל בַּחֶ֥רֶב וּבָרָעָ֖ב יָמֻ֑תוּ וְהָיוּ֙ לְאָלָ֣ה לְשַׁמָּ֔ה וְלִקְלָלָ֖ה וּלְחֶרְפָּֽה׃ 13 וּפָֽקַדְתִּ֗י עַ֤ל הַיּֽוֹשְׁבִים֙ בְּאֶ֣רֶץ מִצְרַ֔יִם כַּאֲשֶׁ֥ר פָּקַ֖דְתִּי עַל־יְרֽוּשָׁלִָ֑ם בַּחֶ֥רֶב בָּרָעָ֖ב

those who live in the land of Egypt as I punished Jerusalem, with the sword, with famine, and with pestilence. [14]Of the remnant of Judah who came to sojourn here in the land of Egypt, no survivor or fugitive shall be left to return to the land of Judah. Though they all long to return and dwell there, none shall return except [a few] survivors.

[15]Thereupon they answered Jeremiah—all the men who knew that their wives made offerings to other gods; all the women present, a large gathering; and all the people who lived in Pathros in the land of Egypt: [16]"We will not listen to you in the matter about which you spoke to us in the name of the LORD. [17]On the contrary, we will do *d*-everything that we have vowed-*d*—to make offerings to the Queen of Heaven and to pour libations to her, as we used to do,*e* we and our fathers, our kings and our officials, in the towns of Judah and the streets of Jerusalem. For then we had plenty to eat, we were well-off, and suffered no misfortune. [18]But ever since we stopped making offerings to the Queen of Heaven and pouring libations to her, we have lacked everything, and we have been consumed by the sword and by famine. [19]And when we make offerings to the Queen of Heaven and pour libations to her, is it without our husbands' approval that we have made cakes *f*-in her likeness-*f* and poured libations to her?"

[20]Jeremiah replied to all the people, men and women—all the people who argued with him. He said, [21]"Indeed, the offerings you presented in the towns of Judah and the streets of Jerusalem—you, your fathers, your kings, your officials, and the people of the land—were remembered by the LORD and brought to mind! [22]When the LORD could no longer bear your evil practices and the abominations you committed,

וּבַדֶּ֔בֶר: 14 וְלֹ֨א יִהְיֶ֜ה פָּלִ֤יט וְשָׂרִיד֙ לִשְׁאֵרִ֣ית יְהוּדָ֔ה הַבָּאִ֥ים לָגֽוּר־שָׁ֖ם בְּאֶ֣רֶץ מִצְרָ֑יִם וְלָשׁ֣וּב ׀ אֶ֣רֶץ יְהוּדָ֗ה אֲשֶׁר־הֵ֜מָּה מְנַשְּׂאִ֤ים אֶת־נַפְשָׁם֙ לָשׁוּב֙ לָשֶׁ֣בֶת שָׁ֔ם כִּ֥י לֹֽא־יָשׁ֖וּבוּ כִּ֥י אִם־פְּלֵטִֽים: ס

15 וַיַּעֲנ֣וּ אֶֽת־יִרְמְיָ֗הוּ כָּל־הָאֲנָשִׁ֤ים הַיֹּדְעִים֙ כִּֽי־מְקַטְּר֤וֹת נְשֵׁיהֶם֙ לֵאלֹהִ֣ים אֲחֵרִ֔ים וְכָל־הַנָּשִׁ֥ים הָעֹמְד֖וֹת קָהָ֣ל גָּד֑וֹל וְכָל־הָעָ֛ם הַיֹּשְׁבִ֥ים בְּאֶֽרֶץ־מִצְרַ֖יִם בְּפַתְר֥וֹס לֵאמֹֽר: 16 הַדָּבָ֛ר אֲשֶׁר־דִּבַּ֥רְתָּ אֵלֵ֖ינוּ בְּשֵׁ֣ם יְהֹוָ֑ה אֵינֶ֥נּוּ שֹׁמְעִ֖ים אֵלֶֽיךָ: 17 כִּ֣י עָשֹׂ֣ה נַעֲשֶׂ֗ה אֶת־כָּל־הַדָּבָ֣ר ׀ אֲשֶׁר־יָצָ֣א מִפִּ֡ינוּ לְקַטֵּ֣ר לִמְלֶ֣כֶת הַשָּׁמַ֡יִם וְהַסֵּֽיךְ־לָ֣הּ נְסָכִים֩ כַּאֲשֶׁ֨ר עָשִׂ֜ינוּ אֲנַ֣חְנוּ וַאֲבֹתֵ֡ינוּ מְלָכֵ֣ינוּ וְשָׂרֵ֣ינוּ בְּעָרֵ֣י יְהוּדָ֗ה וּבְחֻצ֣וֹת יְרֽוּשָׁלִָ֔ם וַנִּֽשְׂבַּֽע־לֶ֖חֶם וַנִּֽהְיֶ֣ה טוֹבִ֑ים וְרָעָ֖ה לֹ֥א רָאִֽינוּ: 18 וּמִן־אָ֡ז חָדַ֡לְנוּ לְקַטֵּ֞ר לִמְלֶ֣כֶת הַשָּׁמַ֗יִם וְהַסֵּֽךְ־לָ֛הּ נְסָכִ֖ים חָסַ֣רְנוּ כֹ֑ל וּבַחֶ֥רֶב וּבָרָעָ֖ב תָּֽמְנוּ: 19 וְכִֽי־אֲנַ֤חְנוּ מְקַטְּרִים֙ לִמְלֶ֣כֶת הַשָּׁמַ֔יִם וּלְהַסֵּ֥ךְ לָ֖הּ נְסָכִ֑ים הֲמִבַּלְעֲדֵ֣י אֲנָשֵׁ֗ינוּ עָשִׂ֤ינוּ לָהּ֙ כַּוָּנִ֣ים לְהַֽעֲצִבָ֔הּ וְהַסֵּ֥ךְ לָ֖הּ נְסָכִֽים: פ

20 וַיֹּ֤אמֶר יִרְמְיָ֙הוּ֙ אֶל־כָּל־הָעָ֔ם עַל־הַגְּבָרִ֤ים וְעַל־הַנָּשִׁים֙ וְעַל־כָּל־הָעָ֔ם הָעֹנִ֥ים אֹת֖וֹ דָּבָ֥ר לֵאמֹֽר: 21 הֲל֣וֹא אֶת־הַקִּטֵּ֗ר אֲשֶׁ֨ר קִטַּרְתֶּ֜ם בְּעָרֵ֤י יְהוּדָה֙ וּבְחֻצ֣וֹת יְרוּשָׁלִַ֔ם אַתֶּ֖ם וַאֲבֽוֹתֵיכֶ֑ם מַלְכֵיכֶ֤ם וְשָׂרֵיכֶם֙ וְעַ֣ם הָאָ֔רֶץ אֹתָ֖ם זָכַ֣ר יְהֹוָ֔ה וַתַּעֲלֶ֖ה עַל־לִבּֽוֹ: 22 וְלֹֽא־יוּכַל֩ יְהֹוָ֨ה ע֜וֹד לָשֵׂ֗את מִפְּנֵי֙ רֹ֣עַ מַעַלְלֵיכֶ֔ם מִפְּנֵ֥י הַתּוֹעֵבֹ֖ת אֲשֶׁ֣ר עֲשִׂיתֶ֑ם וַתְּהִ֣י אַרְצְכֶ֗ם לְחָרְבָּ֧ה וּלְשַׁמָּ֛ה וְלִקְלָלָ֖ה מֵאֵ֥ין יוֹשֵֽׁב

d-d Lit. "everything that has gone forth from our mouth."
e Cf. 7.18.
f-f Meaning of Heb. uncertain.

your land became a desolate ruin and a curse,[a] without inhabitant, as is still the case. [23]Because you burned incense and sinned against the LORD and did not obey the LORD, and because you did not follow His Teaching, His laws, and His exhortations, therefore this disaster has befallen you, as is still the case."

[24]Jeremiah further said to all the people and to all the women: "Hear the word of the LORD, all Judeans in the land of Egypt! [25]Thus said the LORD of Hosts, the God of Israel: You and your wives have [g]-confirmed by deed what you spoke in words:[g] 'We will fulfill the vows which we made, to burn incense to the Queen of Heaven and to pour libations to her.' So fulfill your vows; perform your vows!

[26]"Yet hear the word of the LORD, all Judeans who dwell in the land of Egypt! Lo, I swear by My great name—said the LORD—that none of the men of Judah in all the land of Egypt shall ever again invoke My name, saying, 'As the Lord GOD lives!' [27]I will be watchful over them to their hurt, not to their benefit; all the men of Judah in the land of Egypt shall be consumed by sword and by famine, until they cease to be. [28]Only the few who survive the sword shall return from the land of Egypt to the land of Judah. All the remnant of Judah who came to the land of Egypt to sojourn there shall learn whose word will be fulfilled—Mine or theirs!

[29]"And this shall be the sign to you—declares the LORD—that I am going to deal with you in this place, so that you may know that My threats of punishment against you will be fulfilled: [30]Thus said the LORD: I will deliver Pharaoh Hophra, king of Egypt, into the hands of his enemies, those who seek his life, just as I delivered King Zedekiah of Judah into the hands of King Nebuchadrezzar of Babylon, his enemy who sought his life."

כְּהַיּ֣וֹם הַזֶּ֑ה: 23 מִפְּנֵי֩ אֲשֶׁ֨ר קִטַּרְתֶּ֜ם וַאֲשֶׁ֧ר חֲטָאתֶ֣ם לַֽיהוָ֗ה וְלֹ֤א שְׁמַעְתֶּם֙ בְּק֣וֹל יְהוָ֔ה וּבְתֹֽרָת֧וֹ וּבְחֻקֹּתָ֛יו וּבְעֵדְוֺתָ֖יו לֹ֣א הֲלַכְתֶּ֑ם עַל־כֵּ֞ן קָרָ֥את אֶתְכֶ֛ם הָרָעָ֥ה הַזֹּ֖את כַּיּ֥וֹם הַזֶּֽה: ס

24 וַיֹּ֣אמֶר יִרְמְיָ֗הוּ אֶל־כָּל־הָעָ֖ם וְאֶל־כָּל־הַנָּשִׁ֑ים שִׁמְעוּ֙ דְּבַר־יְהוָ֔ה כָּל־יְהוּדָ֕ה אֲשֶׁ֖ר בְּאֶ֥רֶץ מִצְרָֽיִם: ס 25 כֹּֽה־אָמַ֣ר יְהוָֽה־צְבָאוֹת֩ אֱלֹהֵ֨י יִשְׂרָאֵ֜ל לֵאמֹ֗ר אַתֶּ֤ם וּנְשֵׁיכֶם֙ וַתְּדַבֵּ֣רְנָה בְּפִיכֶ֔ם וּבִידֵיכֶ֖ם מִלֵּאתֶ֣ם ׀ לֵאמֹ֗ר עָשֹׂ֤ה נַעֲשֶׂה֙ אֶת־נְדָרֵ֔ינוּ אֲשֶׁ֣ר נָדַ֔רְנוּ לְקַטֵּר֙ לִמְלֶ֣כֶת הַשָּׁמַ֔יִם וּלְהַסֵּ֥ךְ לָ֖הּ נְסָכִ֑ים הָקֵ֨ים תָּקִ֜ימְנָה אֶת־נִדְרֵיכֶ֗ם וְעָשֹׂ֥ה תַעֲשֶׂ֖ינָה אֶת־נִדְרֵיכֶֽם: פ

26 לָכֵן֙ שִׁמְע֣וּ דְבַר־יְהוָ֔ה כָּל־יְהוּדָ֕ה הַיֹּשְׁבִ֖ים בְּאֶ֣רֶץ מִצְרָ֑יִם הִנְנִ֨י נִשְׁבַּ֜עְתִּי בִּשְׁמִ֤י הַגָּדוֹל֙ אָמַ֣ר יְהוָ֔ה אִם־יִהְיֶה֩ ע֨וֹד שְׁמִ֜י נִקְרָ֣א ׀ בְּפִ֣י ׀ כָּל־אִ֣ישׁ יְהוּדָ֗ה אֹמֵ֧ר חַי־אֲדֹנָ֣י יְהוִ֗ה בְּכָל־אֶ֥רֶץ מִצְרָֽיִם: 27 הִנְנִ֨י שֹׁקֵ֧ד עֲלֵיהֶ֛ם לְרָעָ֖ה וְלֹ֣א לְטוֹבָ֑ה וְתַ֨מּוּ כָל־אִ֤ישׁ יְהוּדָה֙ אֲשֶׁ֣ר בְּאֶֽרֶץ־מִצְרַ֔יִם בַּחֶ֥רֶב וּבָרָעָ֖ב עַד־כְּלוֹתָֽם: 28 וּפְלִיטֵ֣י חֶ֡רֶב יְשֻׁבוּן֩ מִן־אֶ֨רֶץ מִצְרַ֜יִם אֶ֧רֶץ יְהוּדָ֛ה מְתֵ֥י מִסְפָּ֖ר וְיָֽדְע֞וּ כָּל־שְׁאֵרִ֣ית יְהוּדָ֗ה הַבָּאִ֤ים לְאֶֽרֶץ־מִצְרַ֙יִם֙ לָג֣וּר שָׁ֔ם דְּבַר־מִ֥י יָק֖וּם מִמֶּ֥נִּי וּמֵהֶֽם:

29 וְזֹאת־לָכֶ֤ם הָאוֹת֙ נְאֻם־יְהוָ֔ה כִּֽי־פֹקֵ֥ד אֲנִ֛י עֲלֵיכֶ֖ם בַּמָּק֣וֹם הַזֶּ֑ה לְמַ֨עַן֙ תֵּֽדְע֔וּ כִּי֩ ק֨וֹם יָק֧וּמוּ דְבָרַ֛י עֲלֵיכֶ֖ם לְרָעָֽה: ס 30 כֹּ֣ה ׀ אָמַ֣ר יְהוָ֗ה הִנְנִ֣י נֹתֵ֞ן אֶת־פַּרְעֹ֨ה חָפְרַ֤ע מֶֽלֶךְ־מִצְרַ֙יִם֙ בְּיַ֣ד אֹֽיְבָ֔יו וּבְיַ֖ד מְבַקְשֵׁ֣י נַפְשׁ֑וֹ כַּאֲשֶׁ֨ר נָתַ֜תִּי אֶת־צִדְקִיָּ֣הוּ מֶֽלֶךְ־יְהוּדָ֗ה בְּיַ֛ד נְבֽוּכַדְרֶאצַּ֥ר מֶֽלֶךְ־בָּבֶ֖ל אֹיְב֑וֹ וּמְבַקֵּ֖שׁ נַפְשֽׁוֹ: ס

---

g-g   Lit. "spoken with your mouth and fulfilled by your hands."

45

The word which the prophet Jeremiah spoke to Baruch son of Neriah, when he was writing these words in a scroll at Jeremiah's dictation, in the fourth year of King Jehoiakim son of Josiah of Judah:

2Thus said the LORD, the God of Israel, concerning you, Baruch: 3You say, "Woe is me! The LORD has added grief to my pain. I am worn out with groaning, and I have found no rest." 4Thus shall you speak to him: "Thus said the LORD: I am going to overthrow what I have built, and uproot what I have planted—*a*-this applies to the whole land.-*a* 5And do you expect great things for yourself? Don't expect them. For I am going to bring disaster upon all flesh—declares the LORD—but I will *b*-at least grant you your life-*b* in all the places where you may go."

46

The word of the LORD to the prophet Jeremiah concerning the nations.

2Concerning Egypt, about the army of Pharaoh Neco, king of Egypt, which was at the river Euphrates near Carchemish, and which was defeated by King Nebuchadrezzar of Babylon, in the fourth year of King Jehoiakim son of Josiah of Judah.

3Get ready buckler and shield,
And move forward to battle!
4Harness the horses;
Mount, you horsemen!
Fall in line, helmets on!
Burnish the lances,
Don your armor!
5Why do I see them dismayed,
Yielding ground?

a-a   *Meaning of Heb. uncertain.*
b-b   *Cf. note at 21.9.*

מה הַדָּבָר אֲשֶׁר דִּבֶּר יִרְמְיָהוּ הַנָּבִיא אֶל־בָּרוּךְ בֶּן־נֵרִיָּה בְּכָתְבוֹ אֶת־הַדְּבָרִים הָאֵלֶּה עַל־סֵפֶר מִפִּי יִרְמְיָהוּ בַּשָּׁנָה הָרְבִעִית לִיהוֹיָקִים בֶּן־יֹאשִׁיָּהוּ מֶלֶךְ יְהוּדָה לֵאמֹר: ס

2כֹּה־אָמַר יְהוָה אֱלֹהֵי יִשְׂרָאֵל עָלֶיךָ בָּרוּךְ: 3אָמַרְתָּ אוֹי־נָא לִי כִּי־יָסַף יְהוָה יָגוֹן עַל־מַכְאֹבִי יָגַעְתִּי בְּאַנְחָתִי וּמְנוּחָה לֹא מָצָאתִי: ס 4כֹּה ׀ תֹּאמַר אֵלָיו כֹּה אָמַר יְהוָה הִנֵּה אֲשֶׁר־בָּנִיתִי אֲנִי הֹרֵס וְאֵת אֲשֶׁר־נָטַעְתִּי אֲנִי נֹתֵשׁ וְאֶת־כָּל־הָאָרֶץ הִיא: 5וְאַתָּה תְּבַקֶּשׁ־לְךָ גְדֹלוֹת אַל־תְּבַקֵּשׁ כִּי הִנְנִי מֵבִיא רָעָה עַל־כָּל־בָּשָׂר נְאֻם־יְהוָה וְנָתַתִּי לְךָ אֶת־נַפְשְׁךָ לְשָׁלָל עַל כָּל־הַמְּקֹמוֹת אֲשֶׁר תֵּלֶךְ־שָׁם: ס

מו אֲשֶׁר הָיָה דְבַר־יְהוָה אֶל־יִרְמְיָהוּ הַנָּבִיא עַל־הַגּוֹיִם: 2לְמִצְרַיִם עַל־חֵיל פַּרְעֹה נְכוֹ מֶלֶךְ מִצְרַיִם אֲשֶׁר־הָיָה עַל־נְהַר־פְּרָת בְּכַרְכְּמִשׁ אֲשֶׁר הִכָּה נְבוּכַדְרֶאצַּר מֶלֶךְ בָּבֶל בִּשְׁנַת הָרְבִיעִית לִיהוֹיָקִים בֶּן־יֹאשִׁיָּהוּ מֶלֶךְ יְהוּדָה:

3עִרְכוּ מָגֵן וְצִנָּה
וּגְשׁוּ לַמִּלְחָמָה:
4אִסְרוּ הַסּוּסִים
וַעֲלוּ הַפָּרָשִׁים
וְהִתְיַצְּבוּ בְּכוֹבָעִים
מִרְקוּ הָרְמָחִים
לִבְשׁוּ הַסִּרְיֹנֹת:
5מַדּוּעַ רָאִיתִי הֵמָּה חַתִּים
נְסֹגִים אָחוֹר

Their fighters are crushed,
They flee in haste
And do not turn back—
Terror all around!

    —declares the LORD.

6a-The swift cannot get away,
The warrior cannot escape.-a
In the north, by the river Euphrates,
They stagger and fall.

7Who is this that rises like the Nile,
Like streams whose waters surge?
8It is Egypt that rises like the Nile,
Like streams whose waters surge,
That said, "I will rise,
I will cover the earth,
I will wipe out towns
And those who dwell in them.
9Advance, O horses,
Dash madly, O chariots!
Let the warriors go forth,
Cush and Put, that grasp the shield,
And the Ludim who grasp and draw the bow!"

10But that day shall be for the Lord GOD of Hosts a day when He exacts retribution from His foes. The sword shall devour; it shall be sated and drunk with their blood. For the Lord GOD of Hosts is preparing a sacrifice in the northland, by the river Euphrates.

11Go up to Gilead and get balm,
Fair Maiden Egypt.
In vain do you seek many remedies,
There is no healing for you.
12Nations have heard your shame;
The earth resounds with your screams.
For warrior stumbles against warrior;
The two fall down together.

וְגִבּוֹרֵיהֶם יֻכַּתּוּ
וּמָנוֹס נָסוּ
וְלֹא הִפְנוּ
מָגוֹר מִסָּבֵיב
נְאֻם־יְהֹוָה:
6 אַל־יָנוּס הַקַּל
וְאַל־יִמָּלֵט הַגִּבּוֹר
צָפוֹנָה עַל־יַד נְהַר־פְּרָת
כָּשְׁלוּ וְנָפָלוּ:

7 מִי־זֶה כַּיְאֹר יַעֲלֶה
כַּנְּהָרוֹת יִתְגָּעֲשׁוּ מֵימָיו:
8 מִצְרַיִם כַּיְאֹר יַעֲלֶה
וְכַנְּהָרוֹת יִתְגָּעֲשׁוּ מָיִם
וַיֹּאמֶר אַעֲלֶה
אֲכַסֶּה־אֶרֶץ
אֹבִידָה עִיר
וְיֹשְׁבֵי בָהּ:
9 עֲלוּ הַסּוּסִים
וְהִתְהֹלְלוּ הָרֶכֶב
וְיֵצְאוּ הַגִּבּוֹרִים
כּוּשׁ וּפוּט תֹּפְשֵׂי מָגֵן
וְלוּדִים תֹּפְשֵׂי דֹּרְכֵי קָשֶׁת:

10 וְהַיּוֹם הַהוּא לַאדֹנָי יְהֹוִה צְבָאוֹת יוֹם נְקָמָה לְהִנָּקֵם מִצָּרָיו וְאָכְלָה חֶרֶב וְשָׂבְעָה וְרָוְתָה מִדָּמָם כִּי זֶבַח לַאדֹנָי יְהֹוִה צְבָאוֹת בְּאֶרֶץ צָפוֹן אֶל־נְהַר־פְּרָת:
11 עֲלִי גִלְעָד וּקְחִי צֳרִי
בְּתוּלַת בַּת־מִצְרָיִם
לַשָּׁוְא הִרְבֵּיתי הִרְבֵּית רְפֻאוֹת
תְּעָלָה אֵין לָךְ:
12 שָׁמְעוּ גוֹיִם קְלוֹנֵךְ
וְצִוְחָתֵךְ מָלְאָה הָאָרֶץ
כִּי־גִבּוֹר בְּגִבּוֹר כָּשָׁלוּ
יַחְדָּו נָפְלוּ שְׁנֵיהֶם: פ

---

a-a Lit. "Let not the swift get away, / Let not the warrior escape."

13The word which the LORD spoke to the prophet Jeremiah about the coming of King Nebuchadrezzar of Babylon to attack the land of Egypt:

14Declare in Egypt, proclaim in Migdol,
Proclaim in Noph and Tahpanhes!
Say: Take your posts and stand ready,
For the sword has devoured all around you!
15Why are your stalwarts swept away?
They did not stand firm,
For the LORD thrust them down;
16He made many stumble,
They fell over one another.

They said:
"Up! let us return to our people,
To the land of our birth,
Because of the deadlyᵇ sword."
17There they called Pharaoh king of Egypt:
ᵇ-"Braggart who let the hour go by."-ᵇ

18As I live—declares the King,
Whose name is LORD of Hosts—
ᵇ-As surely as Tabor is among the mountains
And Carmel is by the sea,
So shall this come to pass.-ᵇ
19Equip yourself for exile,
Fair Egypt, you who dwell secure!
For Noph shall become a waste,
Desolate, without inhabitants.
20Egypt is a handsome heifer—
A gadflyᶜ from the north ᵈ-is coming, coming!-ᵈ
21The mercenaries, too, in her midst
Are like stall-fed calves;
They too shall turn tail,
Flee as one, and make no stand.

13 הַדָּבָר֙ אֲשֶׁ֣ר דִּבֶּ֣ר יְהֹוָ֔ה אֶֽל־יִרְמְיָ֖הוּ הַנָּבִ֑יא לָב֗וֹא נְבֽוּכַדְרֶאצַּר֙ מֶ֣לֶךְ בָּבֶ֔ל לְהַכּ֖וֹת אֶת־אֶ֥רֶץ מִצְרָֽיִם׃

14 הַגִּ֤ידוּ בְמִצְרַ֙יִם֙ וְהַשְׁמִ֣יעוּ בְמִגְדּ֔וֹל וְהַשְׁמִ֥יעוּ בְנֹ֖ף וּבְתַחְפַּנְחֵ֑ס אִמְר֗וּ הִתְיַצֵּב֙ וְהָכֵ֣ן לָ֔ךְ כִּֽי־אָכְלָ֥ה חֶ֖רֶב סְבִיבֶֽיךָ׃
15 מַדּ֖וּעַ נִסְחַ֣ף אַבִּירֶ֑יךָ לֹ֣א עָמַ֔ד כִּ֥י יְהֹוָ֖ה הֲדָפֽוֹ׃
16 הִרְבָּ֖ה כּוֹשֵׁ֑ל גַּם־נָפַ֞ל אִ֣ישׁ אֶל־רֵעֵ֗הוּ
וַיֹּֽאמְרוּ֙
ק֣וּמָה ׀ וְנָשֻׁ֣בָה אֶל־עַמֵּ֗נוּ וְאֶל־אֶ֙רֶץ֙ מֽוֹלַדְתֵּ֔נוּ מִפְּנֵ֖י חֶ֥רֶב הַיּוֹנָֽה׃
17 קָרְא֖וּ שָׁ֑ם פַּרְעֹ֤ה מֶֽלֶךְ־מִצְרַ֙יִם֙ שָׁא֔וֹן הֶעֱבִ֖יר הַמּוֹעֵֽד׃
18 חַי־אָ֙נִי֙ נְאֻם־הַמֶּ֔לֶךְ יְהֹוָ֥ה צְבָא֖וֹת שְׁמ֑וֹ כִּ֚י כְּתָב֣וֹר בֶּהָרִ֔ים וּכְכַרְמֶ֖ל בַּיָּ֥ם יָבֽוֹא׃
19 כְּלֵ֤י גוֹלָה֙ עֲשִׂ֣י לָ֔ךְ יוֹשֶׁ֖בֶת בַּת־מִצְרָ֑יִם כִּֽי־נֹף֙ לְשַׁמָּ֣ה תִֽהְיֶ֔ה וְנִצְּתָ֖ה מֵאֵ֥ין יוֹשֵֽׁב׃ ס
20 עֶגְלָ֥ה יְפֵֽה־פִיָּ֖ה מִצְרָ֑יִם קֶ֥רֶץ מִצָּפ֖וֹן בָּ֥א בָֽא׃
21 גַּם־שְׂכִרֶ֤יהָ בְקִרְבָּהּ֙ כְּעֶגְלֵ֣י מַרְבֵּ֔ק כִּֽי־גַם־הֵ֧מָּה הִפְנ֛וּ נָ֥סוּ יַחְדָּ֖יו לֹ֣א עָמָ֑דוּ

ᵇ Meaning of Heb. uncertain.
ᶜ Or "butcher"; meaning of Heb. uncertain.
ᵈ-ᵈ Many mss. read "will come upon her."

Their day of disaster is upon them,
The hour of their doom.
²²ᵇ-She shall rustle away like a snake-ᵇ
As they come marching in force;
They shall come against her with axes,
Like hewers of wood.
²³They shall cut down her forest
      —declares the LORD—
Though it cannot be measured;
For they are more numerous than locusts,
And cannot be counted.
²⁴Fair Egypt shall be shamed,
Handed over to the people of the north.

²⁵The LORD of Hosts, the God of Israel, has said: I will inflict punishment on Amonᵉ of No and on Pharaoh—on Egypt, her gods, and her kings—on Pharaoh and all who rely on him. ²⁶I will deliver them into the hands of those who seek to kill them, into the hands of King Nebuchadrezzar of Babylon and into the hands of his subjects. But afterward she shall be inhabited again as in former days, declares the LORD.

²⁷But you,
Have no fear, My servant Jacob,
Be not dismayed, O Israel!
I will deliver you from far away,
Your folk from their land of captivity;
And Jacob again shall have calm
And quiet, with none to trouble him.
²⁸But you, have no fear,
My servant Jacob
      —declares the LORD—
For I am with you.
I will make an end of all the nations
Among which I have banished you,
But I will not make an end of you!
I will not leave you unpunished,
But I will chastise you in measure.

כִּי יוֹם אֵידָם בָּא עֲלֵיהֶם
עֵת פְּקֻדָּתָם:
22 קוֹלָהּ כַּנָּחָשׁ יֵלֵךְ
כִּי־בְחַיִל יֵלֵכוּ
וּבְקַרְדֻּמּוֹת בָּאוּ לָהּ
כְּחֹטְבֵי עֵצִים:
23 כָּרְתוּ יַעְרָהּ
נְאֻם־יְהֹוָה
כִּי לֹא יֵחָקֵר
כִּי רַבּוּ מֵאַרְבֶּה
וְאֵין לָהֶם מִסְפָּר:
24 הֹבִישָׁה בַּת־מִצְרָיִם
נִתְּנָה בְּיַד עַם־צָפוֹן:

25 אָמַר יְהֹוָה צְבָאוֹת אֱלֹהֵי יִשְׂרָאֵל הִנְנִי
פוֹקֵד אֶל־אָמוֹן מִנֹּא וְעַל־פַּרְעֹה וְעַל־
מִצְרַיִם וְעַל־אֱלֹהֶיהָ וְעַל־מְלָכֶיהָ וְעַל־
פַּרְעֹה וְעַל הַבֹּטְחִים בּוֹ: 26 וּנְתַתִּים בְּיַד
מְבַקְשֵׁי נַפְשָׁם וּבְיַד נְבוּכַדְרֶאצַּר מֶלֶךְ־
בָּבֶל וּבְיַד־עֲבָדָיו וְאַחֲרֵי־כֵן תִּשְׁכֹּן כִּימֵי־
קֶדֶם נְאֻם־יְהֹוָה: ס

27 וְאַתָּה
אַל־תִּירָא עַבְדִּי יַעֲקֹב
וְאַל־תֵּחַת יִשְׂרָאֵל
כִּי הִנְנִי מוֹשִׁעֲךָ מֵרָחוֹק
וְאֶת־זַרְעֲךָ מֵאֶרֶץ שִׁבְיָם
וְשָׁב יַעֲקוֹב* וְשָׁקַט
וְשַׁאֲנַן וְאֵין מַחֲרִיד: ס
28 אַתָּה אַל־תִּירָא
עַבְדִּי יַעֲקֹב
נְאֻם־יְהֹוָה
כִּי אִתְּךָ אָנִי
כִּי אֶעֱשֶׂה כָלָה בְּכָל־הַגּוֹיִם ׀
אֲשֶׁר הִדַּחְתִּיךָ שָׁמָּה
וְאֹתְךָ לֹא־אֶעֱשֶׂה כָלָה
וְיִסַּרְתִּיךָ לַמִּשְׁפָּט
וְנַקֵּה לֹא אֲנַקֶּךָּ: ס

ᵉ   *Tutelary deity of the city No (Thebes); cf. Nah. 3.8.*

47 The word of the LORD that came to the prophet Jeremiah concerning the Philistines, before Pharaoh conquered Gaza.

²Thus said the LORD:
See, waters are rising from the north,
They shall become a raging torrent,
They shall flood the land and its creatures,
The towns and their inhabitants.
Men shall cry out,
All the inhabitants of the land shall howl,
³At the clatter of the stamping hoofs of his
    stallions,
At the noise of his chariots,
The rumbling of their wheels,
Fathers shall not look to their children
Out of ᵃ-sheer helplessness-ᵃ
⁴Because of the day that is coming
For ravaging all the Philistines,
For cutting off every last ally
Of Tyre and Sidon.
For the LORD will ravage the Philistines,
The remnant from the island of Caphtor.
⁵Baldnessᵇ has come upon Gaza,
Ashkelon is destroyed.
O remnant of ᶜ-their valley,-ᶜ
How long will you ᵇ-gash yourself?-ᵇ

⁶"O sword of the LORD,
When will you be quiet at last?
Withdraw into your sheath,
Rest and be still!"

⁷How can itᵈ be quiet
When the LORD has given it orders
Against Ashkelon and the seacoast,
Given it assignment there?

a-a   Lit. "weakness of hands."
b   Shaving the head and gashing the body were expressions of
    mourning; cf. Deut. 14.1.
c-c   Septuagint reads "the Anakites"; cf. Josh. 11.22.
d   Heb. "you."

מז אֲשֶׁר הָיָה דְבַר־יְהֹוָה אֶל־יִרְמְיָהוּ
הַנָּבִיא אֶל־פְּלִשְׁתִּים בְּטֶרֶם יַכֶּה פַרְעֹה
אֶת־עַזָּה: ס

2 כֹּה ׀ אָמַר יְהֹוָה
הִנֵּה־מַיִם עֹלִים מִצָּפוֹן
וְהָיוּ לְנַחַל שׁוֹטֵף
וְיִשְׁטְפוּ אֶרֶץ וּמְלוֹאָהּ
עִיר וְיֹשְׁבֵי בָהּ
וְזָעֲקוּ הָאָדָם
וְהֵילִל כֹּל יוֹשֵׁב הָאָרֶץ:
3 מִקּוֹל שַׁעֲטַת פַּרְסוֹת אַבִּירָיו
מֵרַעַשׁ לְרִכְבּוֹ
הֲמוֹן גַּלְגִּלָּיו
לֹא־הִפְנוּ אָבוֹת אֶל־בָּנִים
מֵרִפְיוֹן יָדָיִם:
4 עַל־הַיּוֹם הַבָּא
לִשְׁדוֹד אֶת־כׇּל־פְּלִשְׁתִּים
לְהַכְרִית לְצֹר וּלְצִידוֹן
כֹּל שָׂרִיד עֹזֵר
כִּי־שֹׁדֵד יְהֹוָה אֶת־פְּלִשְׁתִּים
שְׁאֵרִית אִי כַפְתּוֹר:
5 בָּאָה קׇרְחָה אֶל־עַזָּה
נִדְמְתָה אַשְׁקְלוֹן
שְׁאֵרִית עִמְקָם
עַד־מָתַי תִּתְגּוֹדָדִי: ס
6 הוֹי חֶרֶב לַיהֹוָה
עַד־אָנָה לֹא תִשְׁקֹטִי
הֵאָסְפִי אַל־תַּעְרֵךְ
הֵרָגְעִי וָדֹמִּי:
7 אֵיךְ תִּשְׁקֹטִי
וַיהֹוָה צִוָּה־לָהּ
אֶל־אַשְׁקְלוֹן וְאֶל־חוֹף הַיָּם
שָׁם יְעָדָהּ: ס

48 Concerning Moab.ᵃ

מח לְמוֹאָב

Thus said the Lord of Hosts, the God of Israel:

Alas, that Nebo should be ravaged,
Kiriathaim captured and shamed,
ᵇ-The stronghold-ᵇ shamed and dismayed!
²Moab's glory is no more;
In Heshbon they have plannedᶜ evil against
her:
"Come, let us make an end of her as a nation!"
You too, O Madmen, shall be silenced;ᵈ
The sword is following you.
³Hark! an outcry from Horonaim,
Destruction and utter ruin!

⁴Moab is broken;
ᵉ-Her young ones cry aloud;-ᵉ
⁵They climb to Luhith
Weeping continually;
On the descent to Horonaim
A distressing cry of anguish is heard:
⁶Flee, save your lives!
ᶠ-And be like Aroer in the desert.-ᶠ

⁷Surely, because of your trust
In your wealth and in your treasures,
You too shall be captured.
And Chemosh shall go forth to exile,
Together with his priests and attendants.
⁸The ravager shall come to every town;
No town shall escape.
The valley shall be devastated
And the tableland laid waste
—because the Lord has spoken.
⁹Give ᶠwings to Moab,

כֹּה־אָמַ֞ר יְהֹוָ֤ה צְבָאוֹת֙ אֱלֹהֵ֣י יִשְׂרָאֵ֔ל
ה֤וֹי אֶל־נְבוֹ֙ כִּ֣י שֻׁדָּ֔דָה
הֹבִ֥ישָׁה נִלְכְּדָ֖ה קִרְיָתָ֑יִם
הֹבִ֥ישָׁה הַמִּשְׂגָּ֖ב וָחָֽתָּה׃
² אֵ֣ין עוֹד֙ תְּהִלַּ֣ת מוֹאָ֔ב
בְּחֶשְׁבּ֗וֹן חָשְׁב֤וּ עָלֶ֙יהָ֙ רָעָ֔ה
לְכ֥וּ וְנַכְרִיתֶ֖נָּה מִגּ֑וֹי
גַּם־מַדְמֵ֣ן תִּדֹּ֔מִּי
אַחֲרַ֖יִךְ תֵּ֥לֶךְ חָֽרֶב׃
³ ק֥וֹל צְעָקָ֖ה מֵחֹרוֹנָ֑יִם
שֹׁ֖ד וָשֶׁ֥בֶר גָּדֽוֹל׃

⁴ נִשְׁבְּרָ֖ה מוֹאָ֑ב
הִשְׁמִ֥יעוּ זְּעָקָ֖ה צְעוֹרֶ֥יהָ צְעִירֶֽיהָ׃
⁵ כִּ֣י מַעֲלֵ֣ה הַלֻּחִית֙
בִּבְכִ֔י יַעֲלֶה־בֶּ֑כִי
כִּ֚י בְּמוֹרַ֣ד חוֹרֹנַ֔יִם
צָרֵ֥י צַעֲקַת־שֶׁ֖בֶר שָׁמֵֽעוּ׃
⁶ נֻ֖סוּ מַלְּט֣וּ נַפְשְׁכֶ֑ם
וְתִֽהְיֶ֕ינָה כַּעֲרוֹעֵ֖ר בַּמִּדְבָּֽר׃

⁷ כִּ֠י יַ֚עַן בִּטְחֵ֣ךְ
בְּמַעֲשַׂ֙יִךְ֙ וּבְא֣וֹצְרוֹתַ֔יִךְ
גַּם־אַ֖תְּ תִּלָּכֵ֑דִי
וְיָצָ֤א כְמוֹשׁ֙ בַּגּוֹלָ֔ה
כֹּהֲנָ֥יו וְשָׂרָ֖יו יַחַ֥ד יַחְדָּֽיו׃
⁸ וְיָבֹ֨א שֹׁדֵ֜ד אֶל־כָּל־עִ֗יר
וְעִיר֙ לֹ֣א תִמָּלֵ֔ט
וְאָבַ֥ד הָעֵ֖מֶק
וְנִשְׁמַ֣ד הַמִּישֹׁ֑ר
אֲשֶׁ֖ר אָמַ֥ר יְהֹוָֽה׃
⁹ תְּנוּ־צִ֖יץ לְמוֹאָב֙

ᵃ   *A number of parallels to this chapter occur in Isa. 15–16.*
ᵇ⁻ᵇ   *Or "Misgab."*
ᶜ   *Heb.* ḥashebu, *play on Heshbon.*
ᵈ   *Heb.* tiddommi, *play on Madmen, the name of a town.*
ᵉ⁻ᵉ   *Emendation yields "They cry aloud as far as Zoar"; cf. Isa. 15.5.*
ᶠ⁻ᶠ   *Meaning of Heb. uncertain.*

For she must go hence.-ƒ
Her towns shall become desolate,
With no one living in them.

¹⁰Cursed be he who is slack in doing the
LORD's work! Cursed be he who withholds his
sword from blood!

¹¹Moab has been secure from his youth on—
He is settled on his lees
And has not been poured from vessel to
 vessel—
He has never gone into exile.
Therefore his fine flavor has remained
And his bouquet is unspoiled.

¹²But days are coming—declares the LORD—
when I will send men against him to tip him
over; they shall empty his vessels and smash his
jars. ¹³And Moab shall be shamed because of
Chemosh, as the House of Israel were shamed
because of Bethel, on whom they relied.

¹⁴How can you say: We are warriors,
Valiant men for war?
¹⁵Moab is ravaged,
His towns have been entered,
His choice young men
Have gone down to the slaughter
                    —declares the King whose
                name is LORD of Hosts.
¹⁶The doom of Moab is coming close,
His downfall is approaching swiftly.
¹⁷Condole with him, all who live near him,
All you who know him by name!
Say: "Alas, the strong rod is broken,
The lordly staff!"

¹⁸Descend from glory
And sit in thirst,ƒ

כִּי נָצֹא תֵּצֵא
וְעָרֶיהָ לְשַׁמָּה תִהְיֶינָה
מֵאֵין יוֹשֵׁב בָּהֵן:

10 אָר֗וּר עֹשֶׂה מְלֶאכֶת יְהֹוָה רְמִיָּה וְאָר֗וּר
מֹנֵעַ חַרְבּוֹ מִדָּם:

11 שַׁאֲנַן מוֹאָב מִנְּעוּרָיו
וְשֹׁקֵט הוּא אֶל־שְׁמָרָיו
וְלֹא־הוּרַק מִכְּלִי אֶל־כֶּלִי
וּבַגּוֹלָה לֹא הָלָךְ
עַל־כֵּן עָמַד טַעְמוֹ בּוֹ
וְרֵיחוֹ לֹא נָמָר: ס

12 לָכֵן הִנֵּה־יָמִים בָּאִים נְאֻם־יְהֹוָה
וְשִׁלַּחְתִּי־לוֹ צֹעִים וְצֵעֻהוּ וְכֵלָיו יָרִיקוּ
וְנִבְלֵיהֶם יְנַפֵּצוּ: 13 וּבֹשׁ מוֹאָב מִכְּמוֹשׁ
כַּאֲשֶׁר־בֹּשׁוּ בֵּית יִשְׂרָאֵל מִבֵּית אֵל
מִבְטֶחָם:

14 אֵיךְ תֹּאמְרוּ גִּבּוֹרִים אֲנָחְנוּ
וְאַנְשֵׁי־חַיִל לַמִּלְחָמָה:
15 שֻׁדַּד מוֹאָב
וְעָרֶיהָ עָלָה
וּמִבְחַר בַּחוּרָיו יָרְדוּ לַטָּבַח
נְאֻם־הַמֶּלֶךְ יְהֹוָה צְבָאוֹת שְׁמוֹ:
16 קָרוֹב אֵיד־מוֹאָב לָבוֹא
וְרָעָתוֹ מִהֲרָה מְאֹד:
17 נֻדוּ לוֹ כָּל־סְבִיבָיו
וְכֹל יֹדְעֵי שְׁמוֹ
אִמְרוּ אֵיכָה נִשְׁבַּר מַטֵּה־עֹז
מַקֵּל תִּפְאָרָה:

18 רְדִי מִכָּבוֹד
ישבי וּשְׁבִי בַצָּמָא

O inhabitant of Fair Dibon;

For the ravager of Moab has entered your
　　town,

He has destroyed your fortresses.

19Stand by the road and look out,

O inhabitant of Aroer.

Ask of him who is fleeing

And of her who is escaping:

Say, "What has happened?"

20Moab is shamed and dismayed;

Howl and cry aloud!

Tell at the Arnon

That Moab is ravaged!

21Judgment has come upon the tableland—
upon Holon, Jahzah, and Mephaath; 22upon
Dibon, Nebo, and Beth-diblathaim; 23upon
Kiriathaim, Beth-gamul, and Beth-meon;
24upon Kerioth and Bozrah—upon all the
towns of the land of Moab, far and near.

25The might of Moab has been cut down,

His strength is broken

　　　　　　　　—declares the Lord.

26Get him drunk

For he vaunted himself against the Lord.

Moab shall vomit till he is drained,

And he too shall be a laughingstock.

27Wasn't Israel a laughingstock to you?

Was he ever caught among thieves,

That you should g-shake your head-g

Whenever you speak of him?

28Desert the cities

And dwell in the crags,

O inhabitants of Moab!

Be like a dove that nests

In the sides of a pit.

g-g　I.e., in mockery.

יֹשֶׁבֶת בַּת־דִּיבוֹן

כִּי־שֹׁדֵד מוֹאָב עָלָה בָךְ

שִׁחֵת מִבְצָרָיִךְ:

19 אֶל־דֶּרֶךְ עִמְדִי וְצַפִּי

יוֹשֶׁבֶת עֲרוֹעֵר

שַׁאֲלִי־נָס

וְנִמְלָטָה

אִמְרִי מַה־נֶּהְיָתָה:

20 הֹבִישׁ מוֹאָב כִּי־חַתָּה

הֵילִילִי וזעקי | וּזְעָקוּ

הַגִּידוּ בְאַרְנוֹן

כִּי שֻׁדַּד מוֹאָב:

21 וּמִשְׁפָּט בָּא אֶל־אֶרֶץ הַמִּישֹׁר אֶל־חֹלוֹן
וְאֶל־יַהְצָה וְעַל־מופעת מֵיפָעַת: 22 וְעַל־
דִּיבוֹן וְעַל־נְבוֹ וְעַל־בֵּית דִּבְלָתָיִם: 23 וְעַל
קִרְיָתַיִם וְעַל־בֵּית גָּמוּל וְעַל־בֵּית מְעוֹן:
24 וְעַל־קְרִיּוֹת וְעַל־בָּצְרָה וְעַל כָּל־עָרֵי
אֶרֶץ מוֹאָב הָרְחֹקוֹת וְהַקְּרֹבוֹת:

25 נִגְדְּעָה קֶרֶן מוֹאָב

וּזְרֹעוֹ נִשְׁבָּרָה

נְאֻם יְהוָה:

26 הַשְׁכִּירֻהוּ

כִּי עַל־יְהוָה הִגְדִּיל

וְסָפַק מוֹאָב בְּקִיאוֹ

וְהָיָה לִשְׂחֹק גַּם־הוּא:

27 וְאִם | לוֹא הַשְּׂחֹק הָיָה לְךָ יִשְׂרָאֵל

אִם־בְּגַנָּבִים נמצאה נִמְצָא

כִּי־מִדֵּי דְבָרֶיךָ בּוֹ

תִּתְנוֹדָד:

28 עִזְבוּ עָרִים

וְשִׁכְנוּ בַּסֶּלַע

יֹשְׁבֵי מוֹאָב

וִהְיוּ כְיוֹנָה תְּקַנֵּן

בְּעֶבְרֵי פִי־פָחַת:

29We have heard of Moab's pride—
Most haughty is he—
Of his arrogance and pride,
His haughtiness and self-exaltation.
30I know his insolence—declares the LORD—
the wickedness that is in him,*h* the wickedness
i-he has-*i* committed.
31Therefore I will howl for Moab,
I will cry out for all Moab,
I*j* will moan for the men of Kir-heres.
32With greater weeping than for Jazer
I weep for you, O vine of Sibmah,
Whose tendrils crossed the sea,
Reached to the sea,*f* to Jazer.
A ravager has come down
Upon your fig and grape harvests.
33Rejoicing and gladness
Are gone from the farm land,
From the country of Moab;
I have put an end to wine in the presses,
No one treads [the grapes] with shouting—
*f*The shout is a shout no more.*f*
34There is an outcry from Heshbon to Elealeh,
They raise their voices as far as Jahaz,
From Zoar to Horonaim and Eglath-
　　shelishiah.
The waters of Nimrim
Shall also become desolation.
35And I will make an end in Moab
　　　　　　—declares the LORD—
Of those who offer at a shrine
And burn incense to their god.
36Therefore,
My heart moans for Moab like a flute;
Like a flute my heart moans
For the men of Kir-heres—
*f*Therefore,
The gains they have made shall vanish-*f*—
37For every head is bald

29 שָׁמַעְנוּ גְאוֹן־מוֹאָב
גֵּאֶה מְאֹד
גׇּבְהוֹ וּגְאוֹנוֹ
וְגַאֲוָתוֹ וְרֻם לִבּֽוֹ׃
30 אֲנִי יָדַעְתִּי נְאֻם־יְהֹוָה עֶבְרָתוֹ וְלֹא־כֵן
בַּדָּיו לֹא־כֵן עָשֽׂוּ׃
31 עַל־כֵּן עַל־מוֹאָב אֲיֵלִיל
וּלְמוֹאָב כֻּלֹּה אֶזְעָק
אֶל־אַנְשֵׁי קִיר־חֶרֶשׂ יֶהְגֶּֽה׃
32 מִבְּכִי יַעְזֵר
אֶבְכֶּה־לָּךְ הַגֶּפֶן שִׂבְמָה
נְטִישֹׁתַיִךְ עָבְרוּ יָם
עַד יָם יַעְזֵר נָגָעוּ
עַל־קֵיצֵךְ וְעַל־בְּצִירֵךְ
שֹׁדֵד נָפָֽל׃
33 וְנֶאֶסְפָה שִׂמְחָה וָגִיל
מִכַּרְמֶל
וּמֵאֶרֶץ מוֹאָב
וְיַיִן מִיקָבִים הִשְׁבַּתִּי
לֹא־יִדְרֹךְ הֵידָד
הֵידָד לֹא הֵידָֽד׃
34 מִזַּעֲקַת חֶשְׁבּוֹן עַד־אֶלְעָלֵה
עַד־יַהַץ נָתְנוּ קוֹלָם
מִצֹּעַר עַד־חֹרֹנַיִם עֶגְלַת שְׁלִשִׁיָּה
כִּי גַּם־מֵי נִמְרִים
לִמְשַׁמּוֹת יִהְיֽוּ׃
35 וְהִשְׁבַּתִּי לְמוֹאָב
נְאֻם־יְהֹוָה
מַעֲלֶה בָמָה
וּמַקְטִיר לֵאלֹהָֽיו׃
36 עַל־כֵּן
לִבִּי לְמוֹאָב כַּחֲלִלִים יֶהֱמֶה
וְלִבִּי אֶל־אַנְשֵׁי קִיר־חֶרֶשׂ
כַּחֲלִילִים יֶהֱמֶה
עַל־כֵּן
יִתְרַת עָשָׂה אָבָֽדוּ׃
37 כִּי כׇל־רֹאשׁ קׇרְחָה

---

h Cf. note at Isa. 16.6.
i-i Heb. "they have."
j Heb. "He."

1130

And every beard is shorn;
On all hands there are gashes,
And on the loins sackcloth.
³⁸On all the roofs of Moab,
And in its squares
There is naught but lamentation;
For I have broken Moab
Like a vessel no one wants
         —declares the LORD.
³⁹How he is dismayed! Wail!
How Moab has turned his back in shame!
Moab shall be a laughingstock
And a shock to all those near him.

⁴⁰For thus said the LORD:
See, he soars like an eagle
And spreads out his wings against Moab!
⁴¹Kerioth shall be captured
And the strongholds shall be seized.
In that day, the heart of Moab's warriors
Shall be like the heart of a woman in travail.
⁴²And Moab shall be destroyed as a people,
For he vaunted himself against the LORD.
⁴³^k-Terror, and pit, and trap-^k
Upon you who dwell in Moab!
         —declares the LORD.
⁴⁴He who flees from the terror
Shall fall into the pit;
And he who climbs out of the pit
Shall be caught in the trap.
For I will bring upon Moab
The year of their doom
         —declares the LORD.

⁴⁵In the shelter of Heshbon
Fugitives halt exhausted;
For fire went forth from Heshbon,

k-k See note at Isa. 24.17.

וְכָל־זָקָן גְּרֻעָה
עַל כָּל־יָדַיִם גְּדֻדֹת
וְעַל־מָתְנַיִם שָׂק:
38 עַל כָּל־גַּגּוֹת מוֹאָב
וּבִרְחֹבֹתֶיהָ
כֻּלֹּה מִסְפֵּד
כִּי־שָׁבַרְתִּי אֶת־מוֹאָב
כִּכְלִי אֵין־חֵפֶץ בּוֹ
נְאֻם־יְהוָה:
39 אֵיךְ חַתָּה הֵילִילוּ
אֵיךְ הִפְנָה־עֹרֶף מוֹאָב בּוֹשׁ
וְהָיָה מוֹאָב לִשְׂחֹק
וְלִמְחִתָּה לְכָל־סְבִיבָיו: ס

40 כִּי־כֹה אָמַר יְהוָה
הִנֵּה כַנֶּשֶׁר יִדְאֶה
וּפָרַשׂ כְּנָפָיו אֶל־מוֹאָב:
41 נִלְכְּדָה הַקְּרִיּוֹת
וְהַמְּצָדוֹת נִתְפָּשָׂה
וְהָיָה לֵב גִּבּוֹרֵי מוֹאָב בַּיּוֹם הַהוּא
כְּלֵב אִשָּׁה מְצֵרָה:
42 וְנִשְׁמַד מוֹאָב מֵעָם
כִּי עַל־יְהוָה הִגְדִּיל:
43 פַּחַד וָפַחַת וָפָח
עָלֶיךָ יוֹשֵׁב מוֹאָב
נְאֻם־יְהוָה:
44 הַנִּיס הַנָּס מִפְּנֵי הַפַּחַד
יִפֹּל אֶל־הַפַּחַת
וְהָעֹלֶה מִן־הַפַּחַת
יִלָּכֵד בַּפָּח
כִּי־אָבִיא אֵלֶיהָ אֶל־מוֹאָב
שְׁנַת פְּקֻדָּתָם
נְאֻם־יְהוָה:

45 בְּצֵל חֶשְׁבּוֹן
עָמְדוּ מִכֹּחַ נָסִים
כִּי־אֵשׁ יָצָא* מֵחֶשְׁבּוֹן

v. 45. סבירין ומטעין "יצאה"

Flame from the midst*l* of Sihon,
Consuming the brow of Moab,
The pate of the people of Shaon.*m*
⁴⁶Woe to you, O Moab!
The people of Chemosh are undone,
For your sons are carried off into captivity,
Your daughters into exile.
⁴⁷But I will restore the fortunes of Moab in
the days to come—declares the LORD.

Thus far is the judgment on Moab.

וְלֶהָבָה מִבֵּין סִיחוֹן
וַתֹּאכַל פְּאַת מוֹאָב
וְקָדְקֹד בְּנֵי שָׁאוֹן:
46 אוֹי־לְךָ מוֹאָב
אָבַד עַם־כְּמוֹשׁ
כִּי־לֻקְּחוּ בָנֶיךָ בַּשֶּׁבִי
וּבְנֹתֶיךָ בַּשִּׁבְיָה:
47 וְשַׁבְתִּי שְׁבוּת־מוֹאָב בְּאַחֲרִית הַיָּמִים
נְאֻם־יְהוָה

עַד־הֵנָּה מִשְׁפַּט מוֹאָב: ס

49 Concerning the Ammonites.

מט לִבְנֵי עַמּוֹן

Thus said the LORD:
Has Israel no sons,
Has he no heir?
Then why has Milcom*a* dispossessed Gad,
And why have his people settled in Gad's*b*
    towns?
²Assuredly, days are coming
          —declares the LORD—
When I will sound the alarm of war
Against Rabbah of the Ammonites;
It shall become a desolate mound,
And its villages shall be set on fire.
And Israel shall dispossess
Those who dispossessed him
          —said the LORD.
³Howl, O Heshbon, for Ai is ravaged!
Cry out, O daughters of Rabbah!
Gird on sackcloth, lament,
c-And run to and fro in the sheepfolds.-*c*
For Milcom shall go into exile,
Together with his priests and attendants.

כֹּה אָמַר יְהוָה
הֲבָנִים אֵין לְיִשְׂרָאֵל
אִם־יוֹרֵשׁ אֵין לוֹ
מַדּוּעַ יָרַשׁ מַלְכָּם אֶת־גָּד
וְעַמּוֹ בְּעָרָיו יָשָׁב:
2 לָכֵן הִנֵּה יָמִים בָּאִים
נְאֻם־יְהוָה
וְהִשְׁמַעְתִּי אֶל־רַבַּת בְּנֵי־עַמּוֹן
תְּרוּעַת מִלְחָמָה
וְהָיְתָה לְתֵל שְׁמָמָה
וּבְנֹתֶיהָ בָּאֵשׁ תִּצַּתְנָה
וְיָרַשׁ יִשְׂרָאֵל
אֶת־יֹרְשָׁיו
אָמַר יְהוָה:
3 הֵילִילִי חֶשְׁבּוֹן כִּי שֻׁדְּדָה־עַי
צְעַקְנָה בְּנוֹת רַבָּה
חֲגֹרְנָה שַׂקִּים סְפֹדְנָה
וְהִתְשׁוֹטַטְנָה בַּגְּדֵרוֹת
כִּי מַלְכָּם בַּגּוֹלָה יֵלֵךְ
כֹּהֲנָיו וְשָׂרָיו יַחְדָּיו:

---

l   *Emendation yields "house."*
m   *Or "tumult."*

a   *The name of the Ammonite deity; vocalized Malcam here and*
     in v. 3.
b   *Heb. "his."*
c-c *Meaning of Heb. uncertain.*

^{4d-}Why do you glory in strength,
Your strength is drained,^{-d}
O rebellious daughter,
You who relied on your treasures,
[Who said:] Who dares attack me?
⁵I am bringing terror upon you
    —declares the Lord G<small>OD</small> of Hosts—
From all those around you.
Every one of you shall be driven ^{e-}in every
    direction,^{-e}
And none shall gather in the fugitives.
⁶But afterward I will restore the fortunes of
the Ammonites—declares the L<small>ORD</small>.

⁷Concerning Edom.

Thus said the L<small>ORD</small> of Hosts:
Is there no more wisdom in Teman?
Has counsel vanished from the prudent?
Has their wisdom gone stale?
⁸Flee, turn away, sit down low,
O inhabitants of Dedan,
For I am bringing Esau's doom upon him,
The time when I deal with him.
^{9f-}If vintagers were to come upon you,
Would they leave no gleanings?
Even thieves in the night
Would destroy only for their needs!^{-f}
¹⁰But it is I who have bared Esau,
Have exposed his place of concealment;
He cannot hide.
His offspring is ravaged,
His kin and his neighbors—
^{g-}He is no more.^{-g}
¹¹"Leave your orphans with me,
I will rear them;
Let your widows rely on me!"

מַה־תִּתְהַלְלִי בָּעֲמָקִים 4
זָב עִמְקֵךְ
הַבַּת הַשּׁוֹבֵבָה
הַבֹּטְחָה בְּאֹצְרֹתֶיהָ
מִי יָבוֹא אֵלָי:
הִנְנִי מֵבִיא עָלַיִךְ פַּחַד 5
נְאֻם־אֲדֹנָי יְהוִה צְבָאוֹת
מִכָּל־סְבִיבָיִךְ
וְנִדַּחְתֶּם אִישׁ לְפָנָיו
וְאֵין מְקַבֵּץ לַנֹּדֵד:
וְאַחֲרֵי־כֵן אָשִׁיב אֶת־שְׁבוּת בְּנֵי־עַמּוֹן 6
נְאֻם־יְהוָה: ס

לֶאֱדוֹם 7

כֹּה אָמַר יְהוָה צְבָאוֹת
הַאֵין עוֹד חָכְמָה בְּתֵימָן
אָבְדָה עֵצָה מִבָּנִים
נִסְרְחָה חָכְמָתָם:
נֻסוּ הָפְנוּ הֶעְמִיקוּ לָשֶׁבֶת 8
יֹשְׁבֵי דְּדָן
כִּי אֵיד עֵשָׂו הֵבֵאתִי עָלָיו
עֵת פְּקַדְתִּיו:
אִם־בֹּצְרִים בָּאוּ לָךְ 9
לֹא יַשְׁאִרוּ עוֹלֵלוֹת
אִם־גַּנָּבִים בַּלַּיְלָה
הִשְׁחִיתוּ דַיָּם:
כִּי־אֲנִי חָשַׂפְתִּי אֶת־עֵשָׂו 10
גִּלֵּיתִי אֶת־מִסְתָּרָיו
וְנֶחְבָּה לֹא יוּכָל
שֻׁדַּד זַרְעוֹ
וְאֶחָיו וּשְׁכֵנָיו
וְאֵינֶנּוּ:
עָזְבָה יְתֹמֶיךָ 11
אֲנִי אֲחַיֶּה
וְאַלְמְנֹתֶיךָ עָלַי תִּבְטָחוּ: ס

---

^{d-d}   *Meaning of Heb. uncertain; for "strength" cf. Akkadian*
     emuqu.
^{e-e}   *Lit. "each man straight ahead."*
^{f-f}   *Obad. 1.5 reads: "If thieves were to come to you, / Marauders*
     by night, / They would steal no more than they needed. / If
     vintagers came to you, / They would surely leave some
     gleanings."

  ^{g-g}   *Some Septuagint mss. read "And there is none to say."*

12For thus said the Lord: If they who rightly should not drink of the cup must drink it, are you the one to go unpunished? You shall not go unpunished: you will have to drink! 13For by Myself I swear—declares the Lord—Bozrah shall become a desolation, a mockery, a ruin, and a curse;h and all its towns shall be ruins for all time.

14I have received tidings from the Lord,
And an envoy is sent out among the nations:
Assemble, and move against her,
And rise up for war!
15For I will make you least among nations,
Most despised among men.
16c-Your horrible nature,-c
Your arrogant heart has seduced you,
You who dwell in clefts of the rock,
Who occupy the height of the hill!
Should you nest as high as the eagle,
From there I will pull you down
               —declares the Lord.

17And Edom shall be a cause of appallment; whoever passes by will be appalled and will hissi at all its wounds. 18It shall be like the overthrow of Sodom and Gomorrah and their neighbors— said the Lord: no man shall live there, no human shall sojourn there. 19It shall be as when a lion comes up out of the jungle of the Jordan against a secure pasture: in a moment j-I can harry him out of it and appoint over it anyone I choose.-j Then who is like Me? Who can summon Me? Who is the shepherd that can stand up against Me? 20Hear, then, the plan which the Lord has devised against Edom, and what He has purposed against the inhabitants of Teman:

---

12 כִּי־כֹה ׀ אָמַר יְהֹוָה הִנֵּה אֲשֶׁר־אֵין מִשְׁפָּטָם לִשְׁתּוֹת הַכּוֹס שָׁתוֹ יִשְׁתּוּ וְאַתָּה הוּא נָקֹה תִּנָּקֶה לֹא תִנָּקֶה כִּי שָׁתֹה תִשְׁתֶּה: 13 כִּי בִי נִשְׁבַּעְתִּי נְאֻם־יְהֹוָה כִּי־לְשַׁמָּה לְחֶרְפָּה לְחֹרֶב וְלִקְלָלָה תִּהְיֶה בָצְרָה וְכׇל־עָרֶיהָ תִהְיֶינָה לְחׇרְבוֹת עוֹלָם:

14 שְׁמוּעָה שָׁמַעְתִּי מֵאֵת יְהֹוָה
וְצִיר בַּגּוֹיִם שָׁלוּחַ
הִתְקַבְּצוּ וּבֹאוּ עָלֶיהָ
וְקוּמוּ לַמִּלְחָמָה:
15 כִּי־הִנֵּה קָטֹן נְתַתִּיךָ בַּגּוֹיִם
בָּזוּי בָּאָדָם:
16 תִּפְלַצְתְּךָ
הִשִּׁיא אֹתָךְ זְדוֹן לִבֶּךָ
שֹׁכְנִי בְּחַגְוֵי הַסֶּלַע
תֹּפְשִׂי מְרוֹם גִּבְעָה
כִּי־תַגְבִּיהַ כַּנֶּשֶׁר קִנֶּךָ
מִשָּׁם אוֹרִידְךָ
נְאֻם־יְהֹוָה:

17 וְהָיְתָה אֱדוֹם לְשַׁמָּה כֹּל עֹבֵר עָלֶיהָ יִשֹּׁם וְיִשְׁרֹק עַל־כׇּל־מַכּוֹתֶהָ: 18 כְּמַהְפֵּכַת סְדֹם וַעֲמֹרָה וּשְׁכֵנֶיהָ אָמַר יְהֹוָה לֹא־יֵשֵׁב שָׁם אִישׁ וְלֹא־יָגוּר בָּהּ בֶּן־אָדָם: 19 הִנֵּה כְּאַרְיֵה יַעֲלֶה מִגְּאוֹן הַיַּרְדֵּן אֶל־נְוֵה אֵיתָן כִּי־אַרְגִּיעָה אֲרִיצֶנּוּ מֵעָלֶיהָ וּמִי בָחוּר אֵלֶיהָ אֶפְקֹד כִּי מִי כָמוֹנִי וּמִי יוֹעִדֶנִּי וּמִי־זֶה רֹעֶה אֲשֶׁר יַעֲמֹד לְפָנָי: ס 20 לָכֵן שִׁמְעוּ עֲצַת־יְהֹוָה אֲשֶׁר יָעַץ אֶל־אֱדוֹם וּמַחְשְׁבוֹתָיו אֲשֶׁר חָשַׁב אֶל־יֹשְׁבֵי תֵימָן

---

h   Cf. note at 24.9 and 42.18.
i   Cf. note at 18.16.
j-j Emendation yields "he can harry them [i.e., the sheep] out of it; and what champion could one place in charge of them?"

Surely the shepherd boys
Shall drag them away;
Surely the pasture shall be
Aghast because of them.
21At the sound of their downfall
The earth shall shake;
The sound of screaming
Shall be heard at the Sea of Reeds.
22See, like an eagle he flies up,
He soars and spreads his wings against
　　　Bozrah;
And the heart of Edom's warriors in that day
Shall be like the heart of a woman in travail.

23Concerning Damascus.

Hamath and Arpad are shamed,
For they have heard bad news.
They shake with anxiety,
Like[k] the sea which cannot rest.
24Damascus has grown weak,
She has turned around to flee;
Trembling has seized her,
Pain and anguish have taken hold of her,
Like a woman in childbirth.
25l-How has the glorious city not been
　　　deserted,-l
The citadel of my joy!
26Assuredly, her young men shall lie fallen in
　　　her squares.
And all her warriors shall be stilled in that day
　　　　　　—declares the LORD of Hosts.
27I will set fire to the wall of Damascus,
And it shall consume the fortresses of Ben-
　　　hadad.

28Concerning Kedar and the kingdoms of
　　　Hazor, which King Nebuchadrezzar of
　　　Babylon conquered.

אִם־לֹא יִסְחָב֖וּם
צְעִירֵ֣י הַצֹּ֑אן
אִם־לֹ֥א יַשִּׁ֛ים
עֲלֵיהֶ֖ם נְוֵהֶֽם׃
21מִקּ֣וֹל נִפְלָ֗ם
רָעֲשָׁ֣ה הָאָ֑רֶץ
צְעָקָ֕ה
בְּיַם־ס֖וּף נִשְׁמַ֥ע קוֹלָֽהּ׃
22הִנֵּ֤ה כַנֶּ֙שֶׁר֙ יַעֲלֶ֣ה
וְיִדְאֶ֔ה וְיִפְרֹ֥שׂ כְּנָפָ֖יו עַל־בָּצְרָ֑ה
וְֽהָיָ֞ה לֵ֣ב גִּבּוֹרֵ֤י אֱדוֹם֙ בַּיּ֣וֹם הַה֔וּא
כְּלֵ֖ב אִשָּׁ֥ה מְצֵרָֽה׃ ס

23לְדַמֶּ֗שֶׂק

בּ֣וֹשָֽׁה חֲמָ֤ת וְאַרְפָּד֙
כִּֽי־שְׁמֻעָ֥ה רָעָ֛ה שָׁמְע֖וּ
נָמֹ֑גוּ
בַּיָּ֣ם* דְּאָגָ֔ה הַשְׁקֵ֖ט לֹ֥א יוּכָֽל׃
24רָפְתָ֥ה דַמֶּ֖שֶׂק
הִפְנְתָ֣ה לָנ֑וּס
וְרֶ֣טֶט ׀ הֶחֱזִ֔יקָה
צָרָ֧ה וַחֲבָלִ֛ים אֲחָזַ֖תָּה
כַּיּוֹלֵדָֽה׃
25אֵ֥יךְ לֹֽא־עֻזְּבָ֖ה עִ֣יר תְּהִלָּ֑ת
קִרְיַ֖ת מְשׂוֹשִֽׂי׃
26לָכֵ֛ן יִפְּל֥וּ בַחוּרֶ֖יהָ בִּרְחֹבֹתֶ֑יהָ
וְכׇל־אַנְשֵׁ֨י הַמִּלְחָמָ֤ה יִדַּ֙מּוּ֙ בַּיּ֣וֹם הַה֔וּא
נְאֻ֖ם יְהֹוָ֥ה צְבָאֽוֹת׃
27וְהִצַּ֥תִּי אֵ֖שׁ בְּחוֹמַ֣ת דַּמָּ֑שֶׂק
וְאָכְלָ֖ה אַרְמְנ֥וֹת בֶּן־הֲדָֽד׃ ס

28לְקֵדָ֣ר ׀ וּֽלְמַמְלְכ֣וֹת חָצ֗וֹר אֲשֶׁ֤ר
הִכָּה֙ נְבֽוּכַדְרֶאצַּ֣ר מֶֽלֶךְ־
בָּבֶ֔ל

k　So a few mss. Most mss. and editions read "In."
l-l　Emendation yields "How has the glorious city been deserted";
　　　so Vulgate.

Thus said the LORD:

Arise, march against Kedar,
And ravage the Kedemites!

29They will take away their tents and their
  flocks,

Their tent cloths and all their gear;
They shall carry off their camels,
And shall proclaim against them:
Terror all around!

30Flee, wander far,
Sit down low, O inhabitants of Hazor
                            —says the LORD.

For King Nebuchadrezzar of Babylon
Has devised a plan against you
And formed a purpose against you:

31Rise up, attack a tranquil nation
That dwells secure
                            —says the LORD—

That has no barred gates,
That dwells alone.

32Their camels shall become booty,
And their abundant flocks a spoil;
And I will scatter to every quarter
Those who have their hair clipped;
And from every direction I will bring
Disaster upon them
                            —says the LORD.

33Hazor shall become a lair of jackals,
A desolation for all time.
No man shall live there,
No human shall sojourn there.

34The word of the LORD that came to the
prophet Jeremiah concerning Elam, at the beginning of the reign of King Zedekiah of Judah:

35Thus said the LORD of Hosts: I am going
to break the bow of Elam, the mainstay of their
strength. 36And I shall bring four winds against
Elam from the four quarters of heaven, and
scatter them to all those winds. There shall not

כֹּה אָמַר יְהֹוָה
קוּמוּ עֲלוּ אֶל־קֵדָר
וְשָׁדְדוּ אֶת־בְּנֵי־קֶדֶם:
29 אׇהֳלֵיהֶם וְצֹאנָם יִקָּחוּ
יְרִיעוֹתֵיהֶם וְכׇל־כְּלֵיהֶם
וּגְמַלֵּיהֶם יִשְׂאוּ לָהֶם
וְקָרְאוּ עֲלֵיהֶם
מָגוֹר מִסָּבִיב:
30 נֻסוּ נֻּדוּ מְאֹד
הֶעְמִיקוּ לָשֶׁבֶת יֹשְׁבֵי חָצוֹר
נְאֻם־יְהֹוָה
כִּי־יָעַץ עֲלֵיכֶם
נְבוּכַדְרֶאצַּר מֶלֶךְ־בָּבֶל עֵצָה
וְחָשַׁב עליהם עֲלֵיכֶם מַחֲשָׁבָה:
31 קוּמוּ עֲלוּ אֶל־גּוֹי שְׁלֵיו
יוֹשֵׁב לָבֶטַח
נְאֻם־יְהֹוָה
לֹא־דְלָתַיִם וְלֹא־בְרִיחַ לוֹ
בָּדָד יִשְׁכֹּנוּ:
32 וְהָיוּ גְמַלֵּיהֶם לָבַז
וַהֲמוֹן מִקְנֵיהֶם לְשָׁלָל
וְזֵרִתִים לְכׇל־רוּחַ
קְצוּצֵי פֵאָה
וּמִכׇּל־עֲבָרָיו אָבִיא
אֶת־אֵידָם
נְאֻם־יְהֹוָה:
33 וְהָיְתָה חָצוֹר לִמְעוֹן תַּנִּים
שְׁמָמָה עַד־עוֹלָם
לֹא־יֵשֵׁב שָׁם אִישׁ
וְלֹא־יָגוּר בָּהּ בֶּן־אָדָם: ס
34 אֲשֶׁר הָיָה דְבַר־יְהֹוָה אֶל־יִרְמְיָהוּ
הַנָּבִיא אֶל־עֵילָם בְּרֵאשִׁית מַלְכוּת
צִדְקִיָּה מֶלֶךְ־יְהוּדָה לֵאמֹר:
35 כֹּה אָמַר יְהֹוָה צְבָאוֹת הִנְנִי שֹׁבֵר אֶת־
קֶשֶׁת עֵילָם רֵאשִׁית גְּבוּרָתָם: 36 וְהֵבֵאתִי
אֶל־עֵילָם אַרְבַּע רוּחוֹת מֵאַרְבַּע קְצוֹת

be a nation to which the fugitives from Elam do not come. [37]And I will break Elam before their enemies, before those who seek their lives; and I will bring disaster upon them, My flaming wrath—declares the LORD. And I will dispatch the sword after them until I have consumed them.

[38]And I will set My throne in Elam,
And wipe out from there king and officials
—says the LORD.

[39]But in the days to come I will restore the fortunes of Elam—declares the LORD.

50

The word which the LORD spoke concerning Babylon, the land of the Chaldeans, through the prophet Jeremiah:

[2]Declare among the nations, and proclaim;
Raise a standard, proclaim;
Hide nothing! Say:
Babylon is captured,
Bel[a] is shamed,
Merodach[a] is dismayed.
Her idols are shamed,
Her fetishes dismayed.

[3]For a nation from the north has attacked her,
It will make her land a desolation.
No one shall dwell in it,
Both man and beast shall wander away.

[4]In those days and at that time—declares the LORD—the people of Israel together with the people of Judah shall come, and they shall weep as they go to seek the LORD their God. [5]They shall inquire for Zion; in that direction their faces shall turn; [b]they shall come-[b] and attach themselves to the LORD by a covenant for all

הַשָּׁמַיִם וְזֵרִתִים לְכֹל הָרֻחוֹת הָאֵלֶּה וְלֹא־יִהְיֶה הַגּוֹי אֲשֶׁר לֹא־יָבוֹא שָׁם נִדְחֵי עוֹלָם עֵילָם: [37] וְהַחְתַּתִּי אֶת־עֵילָם לִפְנֵי אֹיְבֵיהֶם וְלִפְנֵי ׀ מְבַקְשֵׁי נַפְשָׁם וְהֵבֵאתִי עֲלֵיהֶם ׀ רָעָה אֶת־חֲרוֹן אַפִּי נְאֻם־יְהֹוָה וְשִׁלַּחְתִּי אַחֲרֵיהֶם אֶת־הַחֶרֶב עַד כַּלּוֹתִי אוֹתָם:

[38] וְשַׂמְתִּי כִסְאִי בְּעֵילָם
וְהַאֲבַדְתִּי מִשָּׁם מֶלֶךְ וְשָׂרִים
נְאֻם־יְהֹוָה:

[39] וְהָיָה ׀ בְּאַחֲרִית הַיָּמִים אָשִׁיב אֶת־שְׁבִית שְׁבוּת עֵילָם נְאֻם־יְהֹוָה: ס

נ הַדָּבָר אֲשֶׁר דִּבֶּר יְהֹוָה אֶל־בָּבֶל אֶל־אֶרֶץ כַּשְׂדִּים בְּיַד יִרְמְיָהוּ הַנָּבִיא:

[2] הַגִּידוּ בַגּוֹיִם וְהַשְׁמִיעוּ
וּשְׂאוּ־נֵס הַשְׁמִיעוּ
אַל־תְּכַחֵדוּ אִמְרוּ
נִלְכְּדָה בָבֶל
הֹבִישׁ בֵּל
חַת מְרֹדָךְ
הֹבִישׁוּ עֲצַבֶּיהָ
חַתּוּ גִּלּוּלֶיהָ:

[3] כִּי עָלָה עָלֶיהָ גּוֹי מִצָּפוֹן
הוּא־יָשִׁית אֶת־אַרְצָהּ לְשַׁמָּה
וְלֹא־יִהְיֶה יוֹשֵׁב בָּהּ
מֵאָדָם וְעַד־בְּהֵמָה נָדוּ הָלָכוּ:

[4] בַּיָּמִים הָהֵמָּה וּבָעֵת הַהִיא נְאֻם־יְהֹוָה יָבֹאוּ בְנֵי־יִשְׂרָאֵל הֵמָּה וּבְנֵי־יְהוּדָה יַחְדָּו הָלוֹךְ וּבָכוֹ יֵלֵכוּ וְאֶת־יְהֹוָה אֱלֹהֵיהֶם יְבַקֵּשׁוּ: [5] צִיּוֹן יִשְׁאָלוּ דֶּרֶךְ הֵנָּה פְנֵיהֶם בֹּאוּ וְנִלְווּ אֶל־יְהֹוָה בְּרִית עוֹלָם לֹא תִשָּׁכֵחַ: ס [6] צֹאן אֹבְדוֹת הָיָה עַמִּי

---

a   *Names of the city god of Babylon.*
b-b   *Heb. "come ye."*

time, which shall never be forgotten. ⁶My people were lost sheep: their shepherds led them astray, they drove them out to the mountains, they roamed from mount to hill, they forgot their own resting place. ⁷All who encountered them devoured them; and their foes said, "We shall not be held guilty, because they have sinned against the Lord, the true Pasture, the Hope of their fathers—the Lord."

⁸Flee from Babylon,
Leave the land of the Chaldeans,
And be like he-goats that lead the flock!
⁹For see, I am rousing and leading
An assemblage of great nations against Babylon
From the lands of the north.
They shall draw up their lines against her,
There she shall be captured.
Their arrows are like those of ᶜ-a skilled warrior-ᶜ
Who does not turn back without hitting the mark.
¹⁰Chaldea shall be despoiled,
All her spoilers shall be sated
                              —declares the Lord.
¹¹For you rejoiced, you exulted,
You who plundered My possession;
You stamped like a heifer treading grain,
You neighed like steeds.
¹²So your mother will be utterly shamed,
She who bore you will be disgraced.
Behold the end of the nations—
Wilderness, desert, and steppe!
¹³Because of the Lord's wrath she shall not
     be inhabited;
She shall be utterly desolate.
Whoever passes by Babylon will be appalled
And will hiss at all her wounds.

רֹעֵיהֶם הִתְעוּם הָרִים שׁוֹבֵבִים שְׁוֹבְבוּם
מֵהַר אֶל־גִּבְעָה הָלָכוּ שָׁכְחוּ רִבְצָם:
7 כָּל־מוֹצְאֵיהֶם אֲכָלוּם וְצָרֵיהֶם אָמְרוּ
לֹא נֶאְשָׁם תַּחַת אֲשֶׁר חָטְאוּ לַיהֹוָה
נְוֵה־צֶדֶק וּמִקְוֵה אֲבוֹתֵיהֶם יְהֹוָה: ס

8 נֻדוּ מִתּוֹךְ בָּבֶל
וּמֵאֶרֶץ כַּשְׂדִּים יצאו צֵאוּ
וִהְיוּ כְּעַתּוּדִים לִפְנֵי־צֹאן:
9 כִּי הִנֵּה אָנֹכִי מֵעִיר וּמַעֲלֶה
עַל־בָּבֶל קְהַל־גּוֹיִם גְּדֹלִים
מֵאֶרֶץ צָפוֹן
וְעָרְכוּ לָהּ
מִשָּׁם תִּלָּכֵד
חִצָּיו כְּגִבּוֹר מַשְׁכִּיל
לֹא יָשׁוּב רֵיקָם:
10 וְהָיְתָה כַשְׂדִּים לְשָׁלָל
כָּל־שֹׁלְלֶיהָ יִשְׂבָּעוּ
נְאֻם־יְהֹוָה:
11 כִּי תשמחי תִשְׂמְחוּ כִּי תעלזי תַעַלְזוּ
שֹׁסֵי נַחֲלָתִי
כִּי תפושי תָפוּשׁוּ כְּעֶגְלָה דָשָׁה
ותצהלי וְתִצְהֲלוּ כָּאַבִּרִים:
12 בּוֹשָׁה אִמְּכֶם מְאֹד
חָפְרָה יוֹלַדְתְּכֶם
הִנֵּה אַחֲרִית גּוֹיִם
מִדְבָּר צִיָּה וַעֲרָבָה:
13 מִקֶּצֶף יְהֹוָה לֹא תֵשֵׁב
וְהָיְתָה שְׁמָמָה כֻּלָּהּ
כֹּל עֹבֵר עַל־בָּבֶל יִשֹּׁם
וְיִשְׁרֹק עַל־כָּל־מַכּוֹתֶיהָ:

ᶜ⁻ᶜ So many mss., editions, and versions; other mss. and editions
     read "a warrior who bereaves."

14Range yourselves roundabout Babylon,
All you who draw the bow;
Shoot at her, don't spare arrows,
For she has sinned against the LORD.
15Raise a shout against her all about!
d-She has surrendered;-d
Her bastions have fallen,
Her walls are thrown down—
This is the LORD's vengeance.
Take vengeance on her,
Do to her as she has done!
16Make an end in Babylon of sowers,
And of wielders of the sickle at harvest time.
Because of the deadlye sword,
Each man shall turn back to his people,
They shall flee every one to his land.

17Israel are scattered sheep, harried by lions.
First the king of Assyria devoured them, and
in the end King Nebuchadrezzar of Babylon
crunched their bones. 18Assuredly, thus said the
LORD of Hosts, the God of Israel: I will deal with
the king of Babylon and his land as I dealt with
the king of Assyria. 19And I will lead Israel back
to his pasture, and he shall graze in Carmel and
Bashan, and eat his fill in the hill country of
Ephraim and in Gilead.

20In those days and at that time
    —declares the LORD—
The iniquity of Israel shall be sought,
And there shall be none;
The sins of Judah,
And none shall be found;
For I will pardon those I allow to survive.

21Advance against her—e-the land of Mera-
    thaim-e—
And against the inhabitants of Pekod;

עֶרְכ֧וּ עַל־בָּבֶ֛ל ׀ סָבִיב֩ 14
כָּל־דֹּ֣רְכֵי קֶ֗שֶׁת
יְד֤וּ אֵלֶ֙יהָ֙ אַל־תַּחְמְל֣וּ אֶל־חֵ֔ץ
כִּ֥י לַיהֹוָ֖ה חָטָֽאָה׃
הָרִ֥יעוּ עָלֶ֛יהָ סָבִ֖יב 15
נָתְנָ֣ה יָדָ֔הּ
נָֽפְלוּ֙ אשְׁיוֹתֶ֔יהָ
נֶהֶרְס֖וּ חֽוֹמוֹתֶ֑יהָ
כִּי֩ נִקְמַ֨ת יְהֹוָ֥ה הִיא֙
הִנָּ֣קְמוּ בָ֔הּ
כַּאֲשֶׁ֥ר עָשְׂתָ֖ה עֲשׂוּ־לָֽהּ׃
כִּרְת֤וּ זוֹרֵ֙עַ֙ מִבָּבֶ֔ל 16
וְתֹפֵ֥שׂ מַגָּ֖ל בְּעֵ֣ת קָצִ֑יר
מִפְּנֵי֙ חֶ֣רֶב הַיּוֹנָ֔ה
אִ֥ישׁ אֶל־עַמּ֖וֹ יִפְנ֔וּ
וְאִ֥ישׁ לְאַרְצ֖וֹ יָנֻֽסוּ׃ ס

שֶׂ֧ה פְזוּרָ֛ה יִשְׂרָאֵ֖ל אֲרָי֣וֹת הִדִּ֑יחוּ 17
הָרִאשׁ֤וֹן אֲכָלוֹ֙ מֶ֣לֶךְ אַשּׁ֔וּר וְזֶ֤ה הָאַחֲרוֹן֙
עִצְּמ֔וֹ נְבוּכַדְרֶאצַּ֖ר מֶ֥לֶךְ בָּבֶֽל׃ ס לָכֵ֗ן 18
כֹּֽה־אָמַ֞ר יְהֹוָ֤ה צְבָאוֹת֙ אֱלֹהֵ֣י יִשְׂרָאֵ֔ל
הִנְנִ֥י פֹקֵ֛ד אֶל־מֶ֥לֶךְ בָּבֶ֖ל וְאֶל־אַרְצ֑וֹ כַּאֲשֶׁ֥ר
פָּקַ֖דְתִּי אֶל־מֶ֥לֶךְ אַשּֽׁוּר׃ וְשֹׁבַבְתִּ֣י אֶת־ 19
יִשְׂרָאֵל֮ אֶל־נָוֵהוּ֒ וְרָעָ֤ה הַכַּרְמֶל֙ וְהַבָּשָׁ֔ן
וּבְהַ֥ר אֶפְרַ֛יִם וְהַגִּלְעָ֖ד תִּשְׂבַּ֥ע נַפְשֽׁוֹ׃

בַּיָּמִ֣ים הָהֵם֩ וּבָעֵ֨ת הַהִ֜יא 20
נְאֻם־יְהֹוָ֗ה
יְבֻקַּ֞שׁ אֶת־עֲוֺ֤ן יִשְׂרָאֵל֙
וְאֵינֶ֔נּוּ
וְאֶת־חַטֹּ֣את יְהוּדָ֔ה
וְלֹ֖א תִמָּצֶ֑אינָה
כִּ֥י אֶסְלַ֖ח לַאֲשֶׁ֥ר אַשְׁאִֽיר׃

עַל־הָאָ֤רֶץ מְרָתַ֙יִם֙ עֲלֵ֣ה עָלֶ֔יהָ 21
וְאֶל־יוֹשְׁבֵ֖י פְּק֑וֹד

d-d   Lit. "She has given her hand"; meaning of Heb. uncertain.
e   Meaning of Heb. uncertain.

1139

Ruin and destroy after them to the last
    —says the LORD—
Do just as I have commanded you.
²²Hark! War in the land
And vast destruction!
²³How the hammer of the whole earth
Has been hacked and shattered!
How Babylon has become
An appallment among the nations!
²⁴I set a snare for you, O Babylon,
And you were trapped unawares;
You were found and caught,
Because you challenged the LORD.
²⁵The LORD has opened His armory
And brought out the weapons of His wrath;
For that is the task
Of my Lord GOD of Hosts
In the land of the Chaldeans.
²⁶Come against her ^{e-}from every quarter;^{-e}
Break open her granaries,
^{e-}Pile her up like heaps of grain,^{-e}
And destroy her, let her have no remnant!
^{27f-}Destroy all^{-f} her bulls,
Let them go down to slaughter.
Alas for them, their day is come,
The hour of their doom!
²⁸Hark! fugitives are escaping
From the land of Babylon,
To tell in Zion of the vengeance of the LORD
    our God,
Vengeance for His Temple.

²⁹Summon archers against Babylon,
All who draw the bow!
Encamp against her roundabout,
Let none of her people escape.
Pay her back for her actions,

חָרֹב וְהַחֲרֵם אַחֲרֵיהֶם
נְאֻם־יְהוָה
וַעֲשֵׂה כְּכֹל אֲשֶׁר צִוִּיתִךָ: ס
²² קוֹל מִלְחָמָה בָּאָרֶץ
וְשֶׁבֶר גָּדוֹל:
²³ אֵיךְ נִגְדַּע וַיִּשָּׁבֵר
פַּטִּישׁ כָּל־הָאָרֶץ
אֵיךְ הָיְתָה לְשַׁמָּה
בָּבֶל בַּגּוֹיִם:
²⁴ יָקֹשְׁתִּי לָךְ וְגַם־נִלְכַּדְתְּ בָּבֶל
וְאַתְּ לֹא יָדָעַתְּ
נִמְצֵאת וְגַם־נִתְפָּשְׂתְּ
כִּי בַיהוָה הִתְגָּרִית:
²⁵ פָּתַח יְהוָה אֶת־אוֹצָרוֹ
וַיּוֹצֵא אֶת־כְּלֵי זַעְמוֹ
כִּי־מְלָאכָה הִיא
לַאדֹנָי יְהוִה צְבָאוֹת
בְּאֶרֶץ כַּשְׂדִּים:
²⁶ בֹּאוּ־לָהּ מִקֵּץ
פִּתְחוּ מַאֲבֻסֶיהָ
סָלּוּהָ כְמוֹ־עֲרֵמִים
וְהַחֲרִימוּהָ אַל־תְּהִי־לָהּ שְׁאֵרִית:
²⁷ חִרְבוּ כָּל־פָּרֶיהָ
יֵרְדוּ לַטָּבַח
הוֹי עֲלֵיהֶם כִּי־בָא יוֹמָם
עֵת פְּקֻדָּתָם: ס
²⁸ קוֹל נָסִים וּפְלֵטִים
מֵאֶרֶץ בָּבֶל
לְהַגִּיד בְּצִיּוֹן אֶת־נִקְמַת יְהוָה אֱלֹהֵינוּ
נִקְמַת הֵיכָלוֹ:

²⁹ הַשְׁמִיעוּ אֶל־בָּבֶל ׀ רַבִּים
כָּל־דֹּרְכֵי קֶשֶׁת
חֲנוּ עָלֶיהָ סָבִיב
אַל־יְהִי־[לָהּ*] פְּלֵטָה
שַׁלְּמוּ־לָהּ כְּפָעֳלָהּ

_{f-f} *Emendation yields "A sword against"; cf. vv. 35 ff.*

Do to her just what she has done;
For she has acted insolently against the LORD,
The Holy One of Israel.
30Assuredly, her young men shall fall in her
    squares,
And all her warriors shall perish in that day
                    —declares the LORD.
31I am going to deal with you, O Insolence
            —declares the Lord GOD of Hosts—
For your day is come, the time when I doom
    you:
32Insolence shall stumble and fall,
With none to raise her up.
I will set her cities on fire,
And it shall consume everything around her.

33Thus said the LORD of Hosts:
The people of Israel are oppressed,
And so too the people of Judah;
All their captors held them,
They refused to let them go.
34Their Redeemer is mighty,
His name is LORD of Hosts.
He will champion their cause—
So as to give rest to the earth,
And unrest to the inhabitants of Babylon.

35A sword against the Chaldeans
                —declares the LORD—
And against the inhabitants of Babylon,
Against its officials and its wise men!
36A sword against the diviners, that they be
    made fools of!
A sword against the warriors, that they be dis-
    mayed!
37A sword against its horses and chariots,
And against all the motley crowd in its midst,
That they become like women!
A sword against its treasuries, that they be
    pillaged!

כְּכֹל אֲשֶׁר עָשְׂתָה עֲשׂוּ־לָהּ
כִּי אֶל־יְהֹוָה זָדָה
אֶל־קְדוֹשׁ יִשְׂרָאֵל:
30 לָכֵן יִפְּלוּ בַחוּרֶיהָ בִּרְחֹבֹתֶיהָ
וְכׇל־אַנְשֵׁי מִלְחַמְתָּהּ יִדַּמּוּ בַּיּוֹם הַהוּא
נְאֻם־יְהֹוָה: ס
31 הִנְנִי אֵלֶיךָ זָדוֹן
נְאֻם־אֲדֹנָי יְהֹוִה צְבָאוֹת
כִּי בָּא יוֹמְךָ
עֵת פְּקַדְתִּיךָ:
32 וְכָשַׁל זָדוֹן וְנָפַל
וְאֵין לוֹ מֵקִים
וְהִצַּתִּי אֵשׁ בְּעָרָיו
וְאָכְלָה כׇּל־סְבִיבֹתָיו: ס

33 כֹּה אָמַר יְהֹוָה צְבָאוֹת
עֲשׁוּקִים בְּנֵי־יִשְׂרָאֵל
וּבְנֵי־יְהוּדָה יַחְדָּו
וְכׇל־שֹׁבֵיהֶם הֶחֱזִיקוּ בָם
מֵאֲנוּ שַׁלְּחָם:
34 גֹּאֲלָם ׀ חָזָק
יְהֹוָה צְבָאוֹת שְׁמוֹ
רִיב יָרִיב אֶת־רִיבָם
לְמַעַן הִרְגִּיעַ אֶת־הָאָרֶץ
וְהִרְגִּיז לְיֹשְׁבֵי בָבֶל:

35 חֶרֶב עַל־כַּשְׂדִּים
נְאֻם־יְהֹוָה
וְאֶל־יֹשְׁבֵי בָבֶל
וְאֶל־שָׂרֶיהָ וְאֶל־חֲכָמֶיהָ:
36 חֶרֶב אֶל־הַבַּדִּים וְנֹאָלוּ
חֶרֶב אֶל־גִּבּוֹרֶיהָ וָחָתּוּ:
37 חֶרֶב אֶל־סוּסָיו וְאֶל־רִכְבּוֹ
וְאֶל־כׇּל־הָעֶרֶב אֲשֶׁר בְּתוֹכָהּ
וְהָיוּ לְנָשִׁים
חֶרֶב אֶל־אוֹצְרֹתֶיהָ וּבֻזָּזוּ:

38A drought*g* against its waters, that they be
  dried up!
For it is a land of idols;
They are besotted by their *e*-dread images.-*e*
39Assuredly,
e-Wildcats and hyenas-*e* shall dwell [there],
And ostriches shall dwell there;
It shall never be settled again,
Nor inhabited throughout the ages.

40It shall be as when God overthrew Sodom
and Gomorrah and their neighbors—declares
the LORD; no man shall live there, no human
shall sojourn there.

41Lo, a people comes from the northland;
A great nation and many kings are roused
From the remotest parts of the earth.
42They grasp the bow and javelin,
They are cruel, they show no mercy;
The sound of them is like the roaring sea.
They ride upon horses,
Accoutered like a man for battle,
Against you, O Fair Babylon!
43The king of Babylon has heard the report
  of them,
And his hands are weakened;
Anguish seizes him,
Pangs like a woman in childbirth.

44It shall be as when a lion comes out of the
jungle of the Jordan against a secure pasture:
in a moment *h*-I can harry them out of it and
appoint over it anyone I choose.-*h* Then who is
like Me? Who can summon Me? Who is the
shepherd that can stand up against Me? 45Hear,
then, the plan that the LORD has devised against
Babylon, and has purposed against the land of
Chaldea:

38 חֶ֧רֶב אֶל־מֵימֶ֛יהָ וְיָבֵ֑שׁוּ
כִּ֣י אֶ֤רֶץ פְּסִלִים֙ הִ֔יא
וּבָאֵימִ֖ים יִתְהֹלָֽלוּ:
39 לָכֵ֗ן
יֵשְׁב֤וּ צִיִּים֙ אֶת־אִיִּ֔ים
וְיָ֥שְׁבוּ בָ֖הּ בְּנ֣וֹת יַֽעֲנָ֑ה
וְלֹא־תֵשֵׁ֥ב עוֹד֙ לָנֶ֔צַח
וְלֹ֥א תִשְׁכּ֖וֹן עַד־דּ֥וֹר וָדֽוֹר:

40 כְּמַהְפֵּכַ֣ת אֱלֹהִ֗ים אֶת־סְדֹ֤ם וְאֶת־
עֲמֹרָה֙ וְאֶת־שְׁכֵנֶ֔יהָ נְאֻם־יְהוָ֑ה לֹֽא־יֵשֵׁ֥ב
שָׁם֙ אִ֔ישׁ וְלֹֽא־יָג֥וּר בָּ֖הּ בֶּן־אָדָֽם:

41 הִנֵּ֛ה עַ֥ם בָּ֖א מִצָּפ֑וֹן
וְג֤וֹי גָּדוֹל֙ וּמְלָכִ֣ים רַבִּ֔ים יֵעֹ֖רוּ
מִיַּרְכְּתֵי־אָֽרֶץ:
42 קֶ֣שֶׁת וְכִידֹן֮ יַחֲזִ֒יקוּ֒
אַכְזָרִ֥י הֵ֙מָּה֙ וְלֹ֣א יְרַחֵ֔מוּ
קוֹלָם֙ כַּיָּ֣ם יֶהֱמֶ֔ה
וְעַל־סוּסִ֖ים יִרְכָּ֑בוּ
עָר֗וּךְ כְּאִישׁ֙ לַמִּלְחָמָ֔ה
עָלַ֖יִךְ בַּת־בָּבֶֽל:
43 שָׁמַ֧ע מֶֽלֶךְ־בָּבֶ֛ל אֶת־שִׁמְעָ֖ם
וְרָפ֣וּ יָדָ֑יו
צָרָה֙ הֶחֱזִיקַ֔תְהוּ
חִ֖יל כַּיּוֹלֵדָֽה:

44 הִ֠נֵּה כְּאַרְיֵ֞ה יַעֲלֶ֨ה מִגְּא֣וֹן הַיַּרְדֵּן֮ אֶל־
נְוֵ֣ה אֵיתָן֒ כִּֽי־אַרְגִּ֤עָה אֲרִיצֵם֙
מֵֽעָלֶ֔יהָ וּמִ֥י בָח֖וּר אֵלֶ֣יהָ אֶפְקֹ֑ד כִּ֣י מִ֤י
כָמ֙וֹנִי֙ וּמִ֣י יֹעִידֶ֔נִּי וּמִֽי־זֶ֣ה רֹעֶ֔ה אֲשֶׁ֥ר יַעֲמֹ֖ד
לְפָנָֽי: 45 לָכֵ֞ן שִׁמְע֣וּ עֲצַת־יְהוָ֗ה אֲשֶׁ֤ר יָעַץ֙
אֶל־בָּבֶ֔ל וּמַ֨חְשְׁבוֹתָ֔יו אֲשֶׁ֥ר חָשַׁ֖ב אֶל־אֶ֣רֶץ
כַּשְׂדִּ֑ים

---

g Horeb, play on ḥereb, "sword" in preceding verses.
h-h See note at 49.19.

Surely the shepherd boys
Shall drag them away;
Surely the pasture shall be
Aghast because of them.
46At the sound of Babylon's capture
The earth quakes,
And an outcry is heard among the nations.

אִם־לֹא יִסְחָב֖וּם
צְעִירֵ֣י הַצֹּ֑אן
אִם־לֹ֥א יַשִּׁ֛ים
עֲלֵיהֶ֖ם נָוֶֽה׃
46מִקּוֹל֙ נִתְפְּשָׂ֣ה בָבֶ֔ל
נִרְעֲשָׁ֖ה הָאָ֑רֶץ
וּזְעָקָ֖ה בַּגּוֹיִ֥ם נִשְׁמָֽע׃ ס

51 Thus said the LORD:

נא כֹּ֚ה אָמַ֣ר יְהֹוָ֔ה

See, I am rousing a destructive wind
Against Babylon and the inhabitants of Leb-
kamai.ᵃ
2I will send strangersᵇ against Babylon, and
they shall winnow her.
And they shall strip her land bare;
They shall beset her on all sides
On the day of disaster.
3Letᶜ the archer draw his bow,
And let him stand ready in his coat of mail!
Show no pity to her young men,
Wipe out all her host!
4Let them fall slain in the land of Chaldea,
Pierced through in her streets.

הִנְנִ֤י מֵעִיר֙ עַל־בָּבֶ֔ל
וְאֶל־יֹשְׁבֵ֖י לֵ֥ב קָמָ֑י ר֖וּחַ מַשְׁחִֽית׃
2וְשִׁלַּחְתִּ֨י לְבָבֶ֤ל ׀ זָרִים֙
וְזֵר֔וּהָ
וִיבֹקְק֖וּ אֶת־אַרְצָ֑הּ
כִּֽי־הָי֧וּ עָלֶ֛יהָ מִסָּבִ֖יב
בְּי֥וֹם רָעָֽה׃
3אֶֽל־יִדְרֹ֤ךְ יִדְרֹךְ֙ הַדֹּרֵ֣ךְ* קַשְׁתּ֔וֹ
וְאֶל־יִתְעַ֖ל בְּסִרְיֹנ֑וֹ
וְאַל־תַּחְמְלוּ֙ אֶל־בַּחֻרֶ֔יהָ
הַחֲרִ֖ימוּ כָּל־צְבָאָֽהּ׃
4וְנָפְל֥וּ חֲלָלִ֖ים בְּאֶ֣רֶץ כַּשְׂדִּ֑ים
וּמְדֻקָּרִ֖ים בְּחוּצוֹתֶֽיהָ׃

5For Israel and Judah were not bereftᵈ
Of their God the LORD of Hosts,
But their land was filled with guilt
Before the Holy One of Israel.

5כִּ֠י לֹֽא־אַלְמָ֨ן יִשְׂרָאֵ֤ל וִֽיהוּדָה֙
מֵאֱלֹהָ֔יו מֵיְהֹוָ֖ה צְבָא֑וֹת
כִּ֤י אַרְצָם֙ מָלְאָ֣ה אָשָׁ֔ם
מִקְּד֖וֹשׁ יִשְׂרָאֵֽל׃

6Flee from the midst of Babylon
And save your lives, each of you!
Do not perish for her iniquity;
For this is a time of vengeance for the LORD,
He will deal retribution to her.

6נֻ֤סוּ ׀ מִתּ֣וֹךְ בָּבֶ֔ל
וּמַלְּט֖וּ אִ֣ישׁ נַפְשׁ֑וֹ
אַל־תִּדַּ֖מּוּ בַּעֲוֺנָ֑הּ
כִּי֩ עֵ֨ת נְקָמָ֥ה הִיא֙ לַֽיהֹוָ֔ה
גְּמ֕וּל ה֖וּא מְשַׁלֵּ֥ם לָֽהּ׃

ᵃ A cipher for Kasdim, "Chaldea."
ᵇ Change of vocalization yields "winnowers."
ᶜ Some Heb. mss. and ancient versions read "Let not" here and
   in next line.
ᵈ Lit. "widowed."

7Babylon was a golden cup in the LORD's
   hand,
It made the whole earth drunk;
The nations drank of her wine—
That is why the nations are mad.
8Suddenly Babylon has fallen and is shattered;
Howl over her!
Get balm for her wounds:
Perhaps she can be healed.
9We tried to cure Babylon
But she was incurable.
Let us leave her and go,
Each to his own land;
For her punishment reaches to heaven,
It is as high as the sky.
10The LORD has proclaimed our vindication;
Come, let us recount in Zion
The deeds of the LORD our God.

11Polish the arrows,
Fill the quivers!
The LORD has roused the spirit of the kings
   of Media,
For His plan against Babylon is to destroy her.
This is the vengeance of the LORD,
Vengeance for His Temple.

12Raise a standard against the walls of Bab-
   ylon!
Set up a blockade; station watchmen;
Prepare those in ambush.
For the LORD has both planned and per-
   formed
What He decreed against the inhabitants of
   Babylon.

13O you who dwell by great waters,
With vast storehouses,
Your time is come, e-the hour of your end.-e
14The LORD of Hosts has sworn by Himself:

7 כּוֹס־זָהָב בָּבֶל בְּיַד־יְהֹוָה
מְשַׁכֶּרֶת כָּל־הָאָרֶץ
מִיֵּינָהּ שָׁתוּ גוֹיִם
עַל־כֵּן יִתְהֹלְלוּ גוֹיִם׃
8 פִּתְאֹם נָפְלָה בָבֶל וַתִּשָּׁבֵר
הֵילִילוּ עָלֶיהָ
קְחוּ צֳרִי לְמַכְאוֹבָהּ
אוּלַי תֵּרָפֵא׃
9 רִפְּאנוּ רִפִּינוּ אֶת־בָּבֶל
וְלֹא נִרְפָּתָה*
עִזְבוּהָ וְנֵלֵךְ
אִישׁ לְאַרְצוֹ
כִּי־נָגַע אֶל־הַשָּׁמַיִם מִשְׁפָּטָהּ
וְנִשָּׂא עַד־שְׁחָקִים׃
10 הוֹצִיא יְהֹוָה אֶת־צִדְקֹתֵינוּ
בֹּאוּ וּנְסַפְּרָה בְצִיּוֹן
אֶת־מַעֲשֵׂה יְהֹוָה אֱלֹהֵינוּ׃

11 הָבֵרוּ הַחִצִּים
מִלְאוּ הַשְּׁלָטִים
הֵעִיר יְהֹוָה אֶת־רוּחַ מַלְכֵי מָדַי
כִּי־עַל־בָּבֶל מְזִמָּתוֹ לְהַשְׁחִיתָהּ
כִּי־נִקְמַת יְהֹוָה הִיא
נִקְמַת הֵיכָלוֹ׃

12 אֶל־חוֹמֹת בָּבֶל שְׂאוּ־נֵס
הַחֲזִיקוּ הַמִּשְׁמָר הָקִימוּ שֹׁמְרִים
הָכִינוּ הָאֹרְבִים
כִּי גַם־זָמַם יְהֹוָה גַּם־עָשָׂה
אֵת אֲשֶׁר־דִּבֶּר אֶל־יֹשְׁבֵי בָבֶל׃

13 שֹׁכַנְתְּי עַל־מַיִם רַבִּים
רַבַּת אוֹצָרֹת
בָּא קִצֵּךְ אַמַּת בִּצְעֵךְ׃
14 נִשְׁבַּע יְהֹוָה צְבָאוֹת בְּנַפְשׁוֹ

e-e Meaning of Heb. uncertain.

I will fill you with men like a locust swarm,
They will raise a shout against you.

15He made the earth by His might,
Established the world by His wisdom,
And by His understanding stretched out the
   skies.
16*f*-When He makes His voice heard,*-f*
There is a rumbling of waters in the skies;
He makes vapors rise from the end of the
   earth,
He makes lightning for the rain,
And brings forth wind from His treasuries.
17Every man is proved dull, without knowl-
   edge;
Every goldsmith is put to shame because of
   the idol,
For his molten image is a deceit—
There is no breath in them.
18They are delusion, a work of mockery;
In their hour of doom, they shall perish.
19Not like these in the Portion of Jacob,
For it is He who formed all things;
And [Israel is] His very own tribe.
LORD of Hosts is His name.

20You are My war club, [My] weapons of
   battle;
With you I clubbed nations,
With you I destroyed kingdoms;
21With you I clubbed horse and rider,
With you I clubbed chariot and driver,
22With you I clubbed man and woman,
With you I clubbed graybeard and boy,
With you I clubbed youth and maiden;
23With you I clubbed shepherd and flock,
With you I clubbed plowman and team,
With you I clubbed governors and prefects.
24But I will requite Babylon and all the in-
   habitants of Chaldea

כִּי אִם־מִלֵּאתִיךְ אָדָם כַּיֶּלֶק
וְעָנוּ עָלַיִךְ הֵידָד׃ ס

15 עֹשֵׂה אֶרֶץ בְּכֹחוֹ
מֵכִין תֵּבֵל בְּחׇכְמָתוֹ
וּבִתְבוּנָתוֹ נָטָה שָׁמָיִם׃
16 לְקוֹל תִּתּוֹ
הֲמוֹן מַיִם בַּשָּׁמַיִם
וַיַּעַל נְשִׂאִים מִקְצֵה־אָרֶץ
בְּרָקִים לַמָּטָר עָשָׂה
וַיּוֹצֵא רוּחַ מֵאֹצְרֹתָיו׃
17 נִבְעַר כׇּל־אָדָם מִדַּעַת
הֹבִישׁ כׇּל־צֹרֵף מִפָּסֶל
כִּי שֶׁקֶר נִסְכּוֹ
וְלֹא־רוּחַ בָּם׃
18 הֶבֶל הֵמָּה מַעֲשֵׂה תַּעְתֻּעִים
בְּעֵת פְּקֻדָּתָם יֹאבֵדוּ׃
19 לֹא־כְאֵלֶּה חֵלֶק יַעֲקֹב*
כִּי־יוֹצֵר הַכֹּל הוּא
וְשֵׁבֶט נַחֲלָתוֹ
יְהֹוָה צְבָאוֹת שְׁמוֹ׃ ס

20 מַפֵּץ־אַתָּה לִי כְּלֵי מִלְחָמָה
וְנִפַּצְתִּי בְךָ גּוֹיִם
וְהִשְׁחַתִּי בְךָ מַמְלָכוֹת׃
21 וְנִפַּצְתִּי בְךָ סוּס וְרֹכְבוֹ
וְנִפַּצְתִּי בְךָ רֶכֶב וְרֹכְבוֹ׃
22 וְנִפַּצְתִּי בְךָ אִישׁ וְאִשָּׁה
וְנִפַּצְתִּי בְךָ זָקֵן וָנָעַר
וְנִפַּצְתִּי בְךָ בָּחוּר וּבְתוּלָה׃
23 וְנִפַּצְתִּי בְךָ רֹעֶה וְעֶדְרוֹ
וְנִפַּצְתִּי בְךָ אִכָּר וְצִמְדּוֹ
וְנִפַּצְתִּי בְךָ פַּחוֹת וּסְגָנִים׃
24 וְשִׁלַּמְתִּי לְבָבֶל וּלְכֹל ׀ יוֹשְׁבֵי כַשְׂדִּים

v. 19. מלא ו׳

f-f Lit. "At the sound of His making."

For all the wicked things they did to Zion before your eyes

       —declares the LORD.

25See, I will deal with you, O mountain of the
destroyer

       —declares the LORD—

Destroyer of the whole earth!
I will stretch out My hand against you
And roll you down from the crags,
And make you a burnt-out mountain.
26They shall never take from you
A cornerstone or foundation stone;
You shall be a desolation for all time

       —declares the LORD.

27Raise a standard on earth,
Sound a horn among the nations,
Appoint nations against her,
Assemble kingdoms against her—
Ararat, Minni, and Ashkenaz—
Designate a marshal against her,
Bring up horses like swarming[e] locusts!
28Appoint nations for war against her—
The kings of Media,
Her governors and all her prefects,
And all the lands they rule!

29Then the earth quakes and writhes,
For the LORD's purpose is fulfilled against
   Babylon,
To make the land of Babylon
A waste without inhabitant.
30The warriors of Babylon stop fighting,
They sit in the strongholds,
Their might is dried up,
They become women.
Her dwellings are set afire,
Her bars are broken.
31Runner dashes to meet runner,
Messenger to meet messenger,

אֵת כָּל־רָעָתָם אֲשֶׁר־עָשׂוּ בְצִיּוֹן
לְעֵינֵיכֶם
נְאֻם יְהֹוָה: ס
25 הִנְנִי אֵלֶיךָ הַר הַמַּשְׁחִית
נְאֻם־יְהֹוָה
הַמַּשְׁחִית אֶת־כָּל־הָאָרֶץ
וְנָטִיתִי אֶת־יָדִי עָלֶיךָ
וְגִלְגַּלְתִּיךָ מִן־הַסְּלָעִים
וּנְתַתִּיךָ לְהַר שְׂרֵפָה:
26 וְלֹא־יִקְחוּ מִמְּךָ
אֶבֶן לְפִנָּה וְאֶבֶן לְמוֹסָדוֹת
כִּי־שִׁמְמוֹת עוֹלָם תִּהְיֶה
נְאֻם־יְהֹוָה:
27 שְׂאוּ־נֵס בָּאָרֶץ
תִּקְעוּ שׁוֹפָר בַּגּוֹיִם
קַדְּשׁוּ עָלֶיהָ גּוֹיִם
הַשְׁמִיעוּ עָלֶיהָ מַמְלָכוֹת
אֲרָרַט מִנִּי וְאַשְׁכְּנָז
פִּקְדוּ עָלֶיהָ טִפְסָר
הַעֲלוּ־סוּס כְּיֶלֶק סָמָר:
28 קַדְּשׁוּ עָלֶיהָ גוֹיִם
אֶת־מַלְכֵי מָדַי
אֶת־פַּחוֹתֶיהָ וְאֶת־כָּל־סְגָנֶיהָ
וְאֵת כָּל־אֶרֶץ מֶמְשַׁלְתּוֹ:

29 וַתִּרְעַשׁ הָאָרֶץ וַתָּחֹל
כִּי קָמָה עַל־בָּבֶל מַחְשְׁבוֹת יְהֹוָה
לָשׂוּם אֶת־אֶרֶץ בָּבֶל
לְשַׁמָּה מֵאֵין יוֹשֵׁב:
30 חָדְלוּ גִבּוֹרֵי בָבֶל לְהִלָּחֵם
יָשְׁבוּ בַּמְּצָדוֹת
נָשְׁתָה גְבוּרָתָם
הָיוּ לְנָשִׁים
הִצִּיתוּ מִשְׁכְּנֹתֶיהָ
נִשְׁבְּרוּ בְרִיחֶיהָ:
31 רָץ לִקְרַאת־רָץ יָרוּץ
וּמַגִּיד לִקְרַאת מַגִּיד

To report to the king of Babylon
That his city is captured, from end to end.

לְהַגִּיד לְמֶלֶךְ בָּבֶל
כִּי־נִלְכְּדָה עִירוֹ מִקָּצֶה:

³²The fords are captured,
And the swamp thickets[e] are consumed in
   fire;
And the fighting men are in panic.

³² וְהַמַּעְבָּרוֹת נִתְפָּשׂוּ
וְאֶת־הָאֲגַמִּים שָׂרְפוּ בָאֵשׁ
וְאַנְשֵׁי הַמִּלְחָמָה נִבְהָלוּ: ס

³³For thus said the Lord of Hosts, the God
   of Israel:
Fair Babylon is like a threshing floor
Ready to be trodden;
In a little while her harvesttime will come.

³³ כִּי כֹה אָמַר יְהוָה צְבָאוֹת אֱלֹהֵי
יִשְׂרָאֵל
בַּת־בָּבֶל כְּגֹרֶן
עֵת הִדְרִיכָהּ
עוֹד מְעַט וּבָאָה עֵת־הַקָּצִיר לָהּ:

³⁴"Nebuchadrezzar king of Babylon
Devoured me and discomfited me;
He swallowed me like a dragon,
He filled his belly with my dainties,
And set me down like an empty dish;
Then he [e-]rinsed me out.[-e]
³⁵Let the violence done me and my kindred
Be upon Babylon,"
Says the inhabitant of Zion;
"And let my blood be upon the inhabitants
   of Chaldea,"
Says Jerusalem.

³⁴ אֲכָלַנוּ אֲכָלָנִי הֲמָמַנִי הֲמָמַנִי
נְבוּכַדְרֶאצַּר מֶלֶךְ בָּבֶל
הִצִּיגַנוּ הִצִּיגַנִי כְּלִי רִיק
בְּלָעַנוּ בְּלָעַנִי כַּתַּנִּין
מִלָּא כְרֵשׂוֹ מֵעֲדָנָי
הֱדִיחָנוּ הֱדִיחָנִי:
³⁵ חֲמָסִי וּשְׁאֵרִי
עַל־בָּבֶל
תֹּאמַר יֹשֶׁבֶת צִיּוֹן
וְדָמִי אֶל־יֹשְׁבֵי כַשְׂדִּים
תֹּאמַר יְרוּשָׁלָ͏ִם: ס

³⁶Assuredly, thus said the Lord:
I am going to uphold your cause
And take vengeance for you;
I will dry up her sea
And make her fountain run dry.
³⁷Babylon shall become rubble,
A den for jackals,
An object of horror and hissing,[g]
Without inhabitant.
³⁸Like lions, they roar together,
They growl like lion cubs.
³⁹[h-]When they are heated, I will set out their
   drink

³⁶ לָכֵן כֹּה אָמַר יְהוָה
הִנְנִי־רָב אֶת־רִיבֵךְ
וְנִקַּמְתִּי אֶת־נִקְמָתֵךְ
וְהַחֲרַבְתִּי אֶת־יַמָּהּ
וְהֹבַשְׁתִּי אֶת־מְקוֹרָהּ:
³⁷ וְהָיְתָה בָבֶל | לְגַלִּים |
מְעוֹן־תַּנִּים
שַׁמָּה וּשְׁרֵקָה
מֵאֵין יוֹשֵׁב:
³⁸ יַחְדָּו כַּכְּפִרִים יִשְׁאָגוּ
נָעֲרוּ כְּגוֹרֵי אֲרָיוֹת:
³⁹ בְּחֻמָּם אָשִׁית אֶת־מִשְׁתֵּיהֶם

---

g   See note at 18.16.
h-h   Emendation yields "With poison [so Syriac] will I set out their
      drink / And get them drunk till they fall unconscious" (so
      ancient versions).

And get them drunk, that they may become

hilarious-*h*

And then sleep an endless sleep,

Never to awake

               —declares the LORD.

40I will bring them down like lambs for

slaughter,

Like rams and he-goats.

41How has Sheshach*i* been captured,

The praise of the whole earth been taken!

How has Babylon become

A horror to the nations!

42The sea has risen over Babylon,

She is covered by its roaring waves.

43Her towns are a desolation,

A land of desert and steppe,

A land no man lives in

And no human passes through.

44And I will deal with Bel in Babylon,

And make him disgorge what he has swal-

lowed,

And nations shall no more gaze on him with

joy.

Even the wall of Babylon shall fall.

45Depart from there, O My people,

Save your lives, each of you,

From the furious anger of the LORD.

46Do not be downhearted or afraid

At the rumors heard in the land:

A rumor will come one year,

And another rumor the next year

Of violence in the land,

And of ruler against ruler.

47Assuredly, days are coming,

When I will deal with Babylon's images;

Her whole land shall be shamed,

And all her slain shall fall in her midst.

48Heavens and earth and all that is in them

Shall shout over Babylon;

וְהִשְׁכַּרְתִּים לְמַעַן יַעֲלֹזוּ

וְיָשְׁנוּ שְׁנַת־עוֹלָם

וְלֹא יָקִיצוּ

נְאֻם יְהוָה:

40 אוֹרִידֵם כְּכָרִים לִטְבוֹחַ

כְּאֵילִים עִם־עַתּוּדִים:

41 אֵיךְ נִלְכְּדָה שֵׁשַׁךְ

וַתִּתָּפֵשׂ תְּהִלַּת כָּל־הָאָרֶץ

אֵיךְ הָיְתָה לְשַׁמָּה

בָּבֶל בַּגּוֹיִם:

42 עָלָה עַל־בָּבֶל הַיָּם

בַּהֲמוֹן גַּלָּיו נִכְסָתָה:

43 הָיוּ עָרֶיהָ לְשַׁמָּה

אֶרֶץ צִיָּה וַעֲרָבָה

אֶרֶץ לֹא־יֵשֵׁב בָּהֵן כָּל־אִישׁ

וְלֹא־יַעֲבֹר בָּהֵן בֶּן־אָדָם:

44 וּפָקַדְתִּי עַל־בֵּל בְּבָבֶל

וְהֹצֵאתִי אֶת־בִּלְעוֹ מִפִּיו

וְלֹא־יִנְהֲרוּ אֵלָיו עוֹד גּוֹיִם

גַּם־חוֹמַת בָּבֶל נָפָלָה:

45 צְאוּ מִתּוֹכָהּ עַמִּי

וּמַלְּטוּ אִישׁ אֶת־נַפְשׁוֹ

מֵחֲרוֹן אַף־יְהוָה:

46 וּפֶן־יֵרַךְ לְבַבְכֶם וְתִירְאוּ

בַּשְּׁמוּעָה הַנִּשְׁמַעַת בָּאָרֶץ

וּבָא בַשָּׁנָה הַשְּׁמוּעָה

וְאַחֲרָיו בַּשָּׁנָה הַשְּׁמוּעָה

וְחָמָס בָּאָרֶץ

וּמֹשֵׁל עַל־מֹשֵׁל:

47 לָכֵן הִנֵּה יָמִים בָּאִים

וּפָקַדְתִּי עַל־פְּסִילֵי בָבֶל

וְכָל־אַרְצָהּ תֵּבוֹשׁ

וְכָל־חֲלָלֶיהָ יִפְּלוּ בְתוֹכָהּ:

48 וְרִנְּנוּ עַל־בָּבֶל

שָׁמַיִם וָאָרֶץ וְכֹל אֲשֶׁר בָּהֶם

---

i   See note at 25.26.

For the ravagers shall come upon her from
the north

          —declares the LORD.

⁴⁹Yes, Babylon is to fall
[For] the slain of Israel,
As the slain of all the earth
Have fallen through Babylon.

⁵⁰You fugitives from the sword,
Go, don't delay!
Remember the LORD from afar,
And call Jerusalem to mind.
⁵¹"We were shamed, we heard taunts;
Humiliation covered our faces,
When aliens entered
The sacred areas of the LORD's House."
⁵²Assuredly, days are coming

          —declares the LORD—

When I will deal with her images,
And throughout her land the dying shall
groan.
⁵³Though Babylon should climb to the skies,
Though she fortify her strongholds up to
heaven,
The ravagers would come against her from
Me

          —declares the LORD.

⁵⁴Hark! an outcry from Babylon,
Great destruction from the land of the Chal-
deans.
⁵⁵For the LORD is ravaging Babylon;
He will put an end to her great din,
Whose roar is like waves of mighty waters,
Whose tumultuous noise resounds.
⁵⁶For a ravager is coming upon Babylon,
Her warriors shall be captured, their bows
shall be snapped.
For the LORD is a God of requital,
He deals retribution.
⁵⁷I will make her officials and wise men drunk,

כִּי מִצָּפוֹן יָבוֹא*־לָהּ הַשּׁוֹדְדִים
נְאֻם־יְהוָה:
גַּם־בָּבֶל לִנְפֹּל 49
חַלְלֵי יִשְׂרָאֵל
גַּם־לְבָבֶל נָפְלוּ
חַלְלֵי כָל־הָאָרֶץ:

פְּלֵטִים מֵחֶרֶב 50
הִלְכוּ אַל־תַּעֲמֹדוּ
זִכְרוּ מֵרָחוֹק אֶת־יְהוָה
וִירוּשָׁלַ‍ִם תַּעֲלֶה עַל־לְבַבְכֶם:
בֹּשְׁנוּ כִּי־שָׁמַעְנוּ חֶרְפָּה 51
כִּסְּתָה כְלִמָּה פָּנֵינוּ
כִּי בָּאוּ זָרִים
עַל־מִקְדְּשֵׁי בֵּית יְהוָה: ס
לָכֵן הִנֵּה־יָמִים בָּאִים 52
נְאֻם־יְהוָה
וּפָקַדְתִּי עַל־פְּסִילֶיהָ
וּבְכָל־אַרְצָהּ יֶאֱנֹק חָלָל:
כִּי־תַעֲלֶה בָבֶל הַשָּׁמַיִם 53
וְכִי תְבַצֵּר מְרוֹם עֻזָּהּ
מֵאִתִּי יָבֹאוּ שֹׁדְדִים לָהּ
נְאֻם־יְהוָה: ס
קוֹל זְעָקָה מִבָּבֶל 54
וְשֶׁבֶר גָּדוֹל מֵאֶרֶץ כַּשְׂדִּים:
כִּי־שֹׁדֵד יְהוָה אֶת־בָּבֶל 55
וְאִבַּד מִמֶּנָּה קוֹל גָּדוֹל
וְהָמוּ גַלֵּיהֶם כְּמַיִם רַבִּים
נִתַּן שְׁאוֹן קוֹלָם:
כִּי בָא עָלֶיהָ עַל־בָּבֶל שׁוֹדֵד 56
וְנִלְכְּדוּ גִּבּוֹרֶיהָ חִתְּתָה קַשְּׁתוֹתָם
כִּי אֵל גְּמֻלוֹת יְהוָה
שַׁלֵּם יְשַׁלֵּם:
וְהִשְׁכַּרְתִּי שָׂרֶיהָ וַחֲכָמֶיהָ 57

סְבִירִין וּמַטְעִין לְשׁוֹן רַבִּים   v. 48.

Her governors and prefects and warriors;
And they shall sleep an endless sleep,
Never to awaken

     —declares the King whose
     name is LORD of Hosts.
⁵⁸Thus said the LORD of Hosts:
Babylon's broad wall shall be knocked down,
And her high gates set afire.
Peoples shall labor for naught,
And nations have wearied themselves for fire.

⁵⁹The instructions that the prophet Jeremiah gave to Seraiah son of Neriah son of Mahseiah, when the latter went with[j] King Zedekiah of Judah to Babylonia, in the fourth year of [Zedekiah's] reign. Seraiah was quartermaster.[e] ⁶⁰Jeremiah wrote down in one scroll all the disaster that would come upon Babylon, all these things that are written concerning Babylon. ⁶¹And Jeremiah said to Seraiah, "When you get to Babylon, see that you read out all these words. ⁶²And say, 'O LORD, You Yourself have declared concerning this place that it shall be cut off, without inhabitant, man or beast; that it shall be a desolation for all time.' ⁶³And when you finish reading this scroll, tie a stone to it and hurl it into the Euphrates. ⁶⁴And say, 'Thus shall Babylon sink and never rise again, because of the disaster that I will bring upon it. And [nations] shall have wearied themselves [for fire].'"[k]

Thus far the words of Jeremiah.

52 ^aZedekiah was twenty-one years old when he became king, and he reigned in Jerusalem for eleven years. His mother's name was Hamutal, daughter of Jeremiah of Libnah. ²He did what was displeasing to the LORD, just as

פַּחוֹתֶיהָ וּסְגָנֶיהָ וְגִבּוֹרֶיהָ
וְיָשְׁנוּ שְׁנַת־עוֹלָם
וְלֹא יָקִיצוּ
נְאֻם־הַמֶּלֶךְ יְהוָה צְבָאוֹת שְׁמוֹ: ס
58 כֹּה־אָמַר יְהוָה צְבָאוֹת
חֹמוֹת בָּבֶל הָרְחָבָה עַרְעֵר תִּתְעַרְעָר
וּשְׁעָרֶיהָ הַגְּבֹהִים בָּאֵשׁ יִצַּתּוּ
וְיִגְעוּ עַמִּים בְּדֵי־רִיק
וּלְאֻמִּים בְּדֵי־אֵשׁ וְיָעֵפוּ: ס

59 הַדָּבָר אֲשֶׁר־צִוָּה | יִרְמְיָהוּ הַנָּבִיא אֶת־שְׂרָיָה בֶן־נֵרִיָּה בֶּן־מַחְסֵיָה בְּלֶכְתּוֹ אֶת־צִדְקִיָּהוּ מֶלֶךְ־יְהוּדָה בָּבֶל בִּשְׁנַת הָרְבִעִית לְמָלְכוֹ וּשְׂרָיָה שַׂר מְנוּחָה: 60 וַיִּכְתֹּב יִרְמְיָהוּ אֵת כָּל־הָרָעָה אֲשֶׁר־תָּבוֹא אֶל־בָּבֶל אֶל־סֵפֶר אֶחָד אֵת כָּל־הַדְּבָרִים הָאֵלֶּה הַכְּתֻבִים אֶל־בָּבֶל: 61 וַיֹּאמֶר יִרְמְיָהוּ אֶל־שְׂרָיָה כְּבֹאֲךָ בָבֶל וְרָאִיתָ וְקָרָאתָ אֵת כָּל־הַדְּבָרִים הָאֵלֶּה: 62 וְאָמַרְתָּ יְהוָה אַתָּה דִבַּרְתָּ אֶל־הַמָּקוֹם הַזֶּה לְהַכְרִיתוֹ לְבִלְתִּי הֱיוֹת־בּוֹ יוֹשֵׁב לְמֵאָדָם וְעַד־בְּהֵמָה כִּי־שִׁמְמוֹת עוֹלָם תִּהְיֶה: 63 וְהָיָה כְּכַלֹּתְךָ לִקְרֹא אֶת־הַסֵּפֶר הַזֶּה תִּקְשֹׁר עָלָיו אֶבֶן וְהִשְׁלַכְתּוֹ אֶל־תּוֹךְ פְּרָת: 64 וְאָמַרְתָּ כָּכָה תִּשְׁקַע בָּבֶל וְלֹא־תָקוּם מִפְּנֵי הָרָעָה אֲשֶׁר אָנֹכִי מֵבִיא עָלֶיהָ וְיָעֵפוּ

עַד־הֵנָּה דִּבְרֵי יִרְמְיָהוּ: ס

נב בֶּן־עֶשְׂרִים וְאַחַת שָׁנָה צִדְקִיָּהוּ בְמָלְכוֹ וְאַחַת עֶשְׂרֵה שָׁנָה מָלַךְ בִּירוּשָׁלִָם וְשֵׁם אִמּוֹ חֲמִיטַל בַּת־יִרְמְיָהוּ מִלִּבְנָה: 2 וַיַּעַשׂ הָרַע בְּעֵינֵי יְהוָה כְּכֹל

j   *Emendation yields "at the instance of."*

k   *Cf. v. 58, last line.*

a   *For this chapter cf. chap. 39 above and 2 Kings 24–25.*

Jehoiakim had done. ³Indeed, Jerusalem and Judah *b-were a cause of anger for the LORD, so that-b* He cast them out of His presence.

Zedekiah rebelled against the king of Babylon. ⁴And in the ninth year of his*c* reign, on the tenth day of the tenth month, King Nebuchadrezzar moved against Jerusalem with his whole army. They besieged it and built towers against it all around. ⁵The city continued in a state of siege until the eleventh year of King Zedekiah. ⁶By the ninth day of the fourth month, the famine had become acute in the city; there was no food left for the common people.

⁷Then [the wall of] the city was breached. All the soldiers fled; they left the city by night through the gate between the double walls, which is near the king's garden—the Chaldeans were all around the city—and they set out for the Arabah.*d* ⁸But the Chaldean troops pursued the king, and they overtook Zedekiah in the steppes of Jericho, as his entire force left him and scattered. ⁹They captured the king and brought him before the king of Babylon at Riblah, in the region of Hamath; and he put him on trial. ¹⁰The king of Babylon had Zedekiah's sons slaughtered before his eyes; he also had all the officials of Judah slaughtered at Riblah. ¹¹Then the eyes of Zedekiah were put out, and he was chained in bronze fetters. The king of Babylon brought him to Babylon and put him in prison, [where he remained] to the day of his death.

¹²On the tenth day of the fifth month—that was the nineteenth year of King Nebuchadrezzar, the king of Babylon—Nebuzaradan, the chief of the guards, came *e-to represent-e* the king of Babylon in Jerusalem. ¹³He burned the House of the LORD, the king's palace, and all

---

³ כִּי ׀ עַל־אַף יְהֹוָה הָיְתָה בִּירוּשָׁלַ֙͏ִם וִיהוּדָ֔ה עַד־הִשְׁלִיכֽוֹ אוֹתָ֖ם מֵעַ֥ל פָּנָ֑יו ⁴ וַיְהִ֣י בַשָּׁנָ֣ה וַיִּמְרֹ֥ד צִדְקִיָּ֖הוּ בְּמֶ֥לֶךְ בָּבֶֽל׃ הַתְּשִׁעִ֜ית לְמׇלְכ֗וֹ בַּחֹ֚דֶשׁ הָעֲשִׂירִי֙ בֶּֽעָשׂ֣וֹר לַחֹ֔דֶשׁ בָּ֠א נְבוּכַדְרֶאצַּ֨ר מֶֽלֶךְ־בָּבֶ֥ל ה֛וּא וְכׇל־חֵיל֖וֹ עַל־יְרוּשָׁלַ֑͏ִם וַיַּחֲנ֣וּ עָלֶ֔יהָ וַיִּבְנ֥וּ עָלֶ֛יהָ דָּיֵ֖ק סָבִֽיב׃ ⁵ וַתָּבֹ֥א הָעִ֖יר בַּמָּצ֑וֹר עַ֚ד עַשְׁתֵּ֣י עֶשְׂרֵ֣ה שָׁנָ֔ה לַמֶּ֖לֶךְ צִדְקִיָּֽהוּ׃ ⁶ בַּחֹ֣דֶשׁ הָרְבִיעִי֮ בְּתִשְׁעָ֣ה לַחֹ֒דֶשׁ֒ וַיֶּחֱזַ֨ק הָרָעָ֣ב בָּעִ֔יר וְלֹא־הָ֥יָה לֶ֖חֶם לְעַ֥ם הָאָֽרֶץ׃ ⁷ וַתִּבָּקַ֣ע הָעִ֗יר וְכׇל־אַנְשֵׁ֤י הַמִּלְחָמָה֙ יִבְרְח֜וּ וַיֵּצְא֥וּ מֵהָעִ֣יר לַ֗יְלָה דֶּ֜רֶךְ שַׁ֚עַר בֵּין־הַחֹמֹתַ֙יִם֙ אֲשֶׁר֙ עַל־גַּ֣ן הַמֶּ֔לֶךְ וְכַשְׂדִּ֥ים עַל־הָעִ֖יר סָבִ֑יב וַיֵּלְכ֖וּ דֶּ֥רֶךְ הָעֲרָבָֽה׃ ⁸ וַיִּרְדְּפ֤וּ חֵיל־כַּשְׂדִּים֙ אַחֲרֵ֣י הַמֶּ֔לֶךְ וַיַּשִּׂ֥יגוּ אֶת־צִדְקִיָּ֖הוּ בְּעַֽרְבֹ֣ת יְרֵח֑וֹ וְכׇל־חֵיל֔וֹ נָפֹ֖צוּ מֵעָלָֽיו׃ ⁹ וַיִּתְפְּשׂוּ֙ אֶת־הַמֶּ֔לֶךְ וַיַּעֲל֨וּ אֹת֜וֹ אֶל־מֶ֧לֶךְ בָּבֶ֛ל רִבְלָ֖תָה בְּאֶ֣רֶץ חֲמָ֑ת וַיְדַבֵּ֥ר אִתּ֖וֹ מִשְׁפָּטִֽים׃ ¹⁰ וַיִּשְׁחַ֧ט מֶֽלֶךְ־בָּבֶ֛ל אֶת־בְּנֵ֥י צִדְקִיָּ֖הוּ לְעֵינָ֑יו וְגַ֛ם אֶת־כׇּל־שָׂרֵ֥י יְהוּדָ֖ה שָׁחַ֥ט בְּרִבְלָֽתָה׃ ¹¹ וְאֶת־עֵינֵ֥י צִדְקִיָּ֖הוּ עִוֵּ֑ר וַיַּאַסְרֵ֣הוּ בַֽנְחֻשְׁתַּ֗יִם וַיְבִאֵ֤הוּ מֶֽלֶךְ־בָּבֶל֙ בָּבֶ֔לָה וַיִּתְּנֵ֥הוּ בבית־[בֵֽית־]הַפְּקֻדֹּ֖ת עַד־י֥וֹם מוֹתֽוֹ׃

¹² וּבַחֹ֤דֶשׁ הַחֲמִישִׁי֙ בֶּעָשׂ֣וֹר לַחֹ֔דֶשׁ הִ֗יא שְׁנַ֚ת תְּשַֽׁע־עֶשְׂרֵה֙ שָׁנָ֔ה לַמֶּ֖לֶךְ נְבוּכַדְרֶאצַּ֣ר מֶֽלֶךְ־בָּבֶ֑ל בָּ֗א נְבֽוּזַרְאֲדָ֞ן רַב־טַבָּחִ֗ים עָמַ֛ד לִפְנֵ֥י מֶֽלֶךְ־בָּבֶ֖ל בִּירוּשָׁלָֽ͏ִם׃ ¹³ וַיִּשְׂרֹ֥ף אֶת־בֵּית־יְהֹוָ֖ה וְאֶת־בֵּ֣ית הַמֶּ֑לֶךְ

---

b-b Meaning of Heb. uncertain.
c I.e., Zedekiah's.
d See note at 39.4.
e-e Lit. "he stood before."

the houses of Jerusalem; he burned down the house of *b*-every notable person.-*b* 14The entire Chaldean force that was with the chief of the guards tore down all the walls of Jerusalem on every side. 15The remnant of the people left in the city, the defectors who had gone over to the king of Babylon, and what remained of the craftsmen*f* were taken into exile by Nebuzaradan, the chief of the guards. But some of the poorest elements of the population—16some of the poorest in the land—were left by Nebuzaradan, the chief of the guards, to be vine-dressers and field hands.

17The Chaldeans broke up the bronze columns of the House of the LORD, the stands, and the bronze tank that was in the House of the LORD; and they carried all the bronze away to Babylon. 18They also took the pails, scrapers, snuffers, sprinkling bowls, ladles, and all the other bronze vessels used in the service. 19The chief of the guards took whatever was of gold and whatever was of silver: basins, fire pans, sprinkling bowls, pails, lampstands, ladles, and jars. 20The two columns, the one tank and the twelve bronze oxen which supported it, and the stands, which King Solomon had provided for the House of the LORD—all these objects contained bronze beyond weighing. 21As for the columns, each was eighteen cubits high and twelve cubits in circumference; it was hollow, and [the metal] was four fingers thick. 22It had a bronze capital above it; the height of each capital was five cubits, and there was a meshwork [decorated] with pomegranates about the capital, all made of bronze; and so for the second column, also with pomegranates. 23There were ninety-six pomegranates *b*-facing outward;-*b* all the pomegranates around the meshwork amounted to one hundred.

24The chief of the guards also took Seraiah the

---

f Apparently after the deportation of 2 Kings 24.14; meaning of Heb. uncertain.

וְאֵת כָּל־בָּתֵּי יְרוּשָׁלַ֫ם וְאֶת־כָּל־בֵּית הַגָּדוֹל שָׂרַף בָּאֵשׁ: 14 וְאֶת־כָּל־חֹמ֣וֹת יְרוּשָׁלַ֫ם סָבִיב נָתְצוּ כָּל־חֵיל כַּשְׂדִּ֫ים אֲשֶׁר אֶת־רַב־טַבָּחִים: 15 וּמִדַּלּוֹת הָעָם וְאֶת־יֶ֫תֶר הָעָם ׀ הַנִּשְׁאָרִים בָּעִיר וְאֶת־הַנֹּֽפְלִים אֲשֶׁר נָפְלוּ אֶל־מֶ֫לֶךְ בָּבֶל וְאֵת יֶ֫תֶר הָאָמ֑וֹן הֶגְלָה נְבוּזַרְאֲדָן רַב־טַבָּחִים: 16 וּמִדַּלּוֹת הָאָ֫רֶץ הִשְׁאִיר נְבוּזַרְאֲדָן רַב־טַבָּחִים לְכֹרְמִים וּלְיֹגְבִים: 17 וְאֶת־עַמּוּדֵי הַנְּחֹ֫שֶׁת אֲשֶׁר לְבֵית־יְהוָה וְאֶת־הַמְּכֹנוֹת וְאֶת־יָם הַנְּחֹ֫שֶׁת אֲשֶׁר בְּבֵית־יְהוָה שִׁבְּרוּ כַשְׂדִּים וַיִּשְׂאוּ אֶת־כָּל־נְחֻשְׁתָּם בָּבֶֽלָה: 18 וְאֶת־הַסִּירוֹת וְאֶת־הַיָּעִים וְאֶת־הַֽמְזַמְּרוֹת וְאֶת־הַמִּזְרָקֹת וְאֶת־הַכַּפּוֹת וְאֵת כָּל־כְּלֵי הַנְּחֹ֫שֶׁת אֲשֶׁר־יְשָׁרְתוּ בָהֶם לָקָֽחוּ: 19 וְאֶת־הַסִּפִּים וְאֶת־הַמַּחְתּוֹת וְאֶת־הַמִּזְרָקוֹת וְאֶת־הַסִּירוֹת וְאֶת־הַמְּנֹרוֹת וְאֶת־הַכַּפּוֹת וְאֶת־הַמְּנַקִיּוֹת אֲשֶׁר זָהָב זָהָב וַאֲשֶׁר־כֶּ֫סֶף כָּ֫סֶף לָקַח רַב־טַבָּחִים: 20 הָעַמּוּדִים ׀ שְׁנַ֫יִם הַיָּם אֶחָד וְהַבָּקָר שְׁנֵים־עָשָׂר נְחֹ֫שֶׁת אֲשֶׁר־תַּ֫חַת הַמְּכֹנוֹת אֲשֶׁר עָשָׂה הַמֶּ֫לֶךְ שְׁלֹמֹה לְבֵית יְהוָה לֹא־הָיָה מִשְׁקָל לִנְחֻשְׁתָּם כָּל־הַכֵּלִים הָאֵֽלֶּה: 21 וְהָעַמּוּדִים שְׁמֹנֶה עֶשְׂרֵה אַמָּה קוֹמָה קוֹמַת הָעַמֻּד הָאֶחָד וְחוּט שְׁתֵּים־עֶשְׂרֵה אַמָּה יְסֻבֶּנּוּ וְעָבְיוֹ אַרְבַּע אַצְבָּעוֹת נָבוּב: 22 וְכֹתֶ֫רֶת עָלָיו נְחֹ֫שֶׁת וְקוֹמַת הַכֹּתֶ֫רֶת הָאַחַת חָמֵשׁ אַמּוֹת וּשְׂבָכָה וְרִמּוֹנִים עַל־הַכּוֹתֶ֫רֶת סָבִיב הַכֹּל נְחֹ֫שֶׁת וְכָאֵ֫לֶּה לָעַמּוּד הַשֵּׁנִי וְרִמּוֹנִים: 23 וַיִּהְיוּ הָרִמֹּנִים תִּשְׁעִים וְשִׁשָּׁה ר֑וּחָה כָּל־הָרִמּוֹנִים מֵאָה עַל־הַשְּׂבָכָה סָבִיב: 24 וַיִּקַּח רַב־טַבָּחִים אֶת־שְׂרָיָה כֹּהֵן הָרֹאשׁ וְאֶת־צְפַנְיָה כֹּהֵן הַמִּשְׁנֶה וְאֶת־שְׁלֹ֫שֶׁת שֹׁמְרֵי הַסַּֽף: 25 וּמִן־הָעִיר לָקַח

chief priest and Zephaniah, the deputy priest, and the three guardians of the threshold. ²⁵And from the city he took a eunuch who was in command of the soldiers; seven royal privy councilors, who were present in the city; the scribe of the army commander, who was in charge of mustering the people of the land; and sixty of the common people who were inside the city. ²⁶Nebuzaradan, the chief of the guards, took them and brought them to the king of Babylon at Riblah. ²⁷The king of Babylon had them struck down and put to death at Riblah, in the region of Hamath.

Thus Judah was exiled from its land. ²⁸This is the number of those whom Nebuchadrezzar exiled in the seventh year: 3,023 Judeans. ²⁹In the eighteenth year of Nebuchadrezzar, 832 persons [were exiled] from Jerusalem. ³⁰And in the twenty-third year of Nebuchadrezzar, Nebuzaradan, the chief of the guards, exiled 745 Judeans. The total amounted to 4,600 persons.

³¹In the thirty-seventh year of the exile of King Jehoiachin of Judah, on the twenty-fifth day of the twelfth month, King Evil-merodach of Babylon, in the year he became king, ᵍ-took note of-ᵍ King Jehoiachin of Judah and released him from prison. ³²He spoke kindly to him, and gave him a throne above those of other kings who were with him in Babylon. ³³He removed his prison garments and [Jehoiachin] ate regularly in his presence the rest of his life. ³⁴A regular allotment of food was given him by order of the king of Babylon, an allotment for each day, to the day of his death—all the days of his life.

סָרִיס אֶחָד אֲשֶׁר־הָיָה פָקִיד ׀ עַל־אַנְשֵׁי הַמִּלְחָמָה וְשִׁבְעָה אֲנָשִׁים מֵרֹאֵי פְנֵי־הַמֶּלֶךְ אֲשֶׁר נִמְצְאוּ בָעִיר וְאֵת סֹפֵר שַׂר הַצָּבָא הַמַּצְבִּא אֶת־עַם הָאָרֶץ וְשִׁשִּׁים אִישׁ מֵעַם הָאָרֶץ הַנִּמְצְאִים בְּתוֹךְ הָעִיר: ²⁶ וַיִּקַּח אוֹתָם נְבוּזַרְאֲדָן רַב־טַבָּחִים וַיֹּלֶךְ אוֹתָם אֶל־מֶלֶךְ בָּבֶל רִבְלָתָה: ²⁷ וַיַּכֶּה אוֹתָם מֶלֶךְ בָּבֶל וַיְמִתֵם בְּרִבְלָה בְּאֶרֶץ חֲמָת

וַיִּגֶל יְהוּדָה מֵעַל אַדְמָתוֹ: ²⁸ זֶה הָעָם אֲשֶׁר הֶגְלָה נְבוּכַדְרֶאצַּר בִּשְׁנַת־שֶׁבַע יְהוּדִים שְׁלֹשֶׁת אֲלָפִים וְעֶשְׂרִים וּשְׁלֹשָׁה: ²⁹ בִּשְׁנַת שְׁמוֹנֶה עֶשְׂרֵה לִנְבוּכַדְרֶאצַּר מִירוּשָׁלִַם נֶפֶשׁ שְׁמֹנֶה מֵאוֹת שְׁלֹשִׁים וּשְׁנָיִם: ³⁰ בִּשְׁנַת שָׁלֹשׁ וְעֶשְׂרִים לִנְבוּכַדְרֶאצַּר הֶגְלָה נְבוּזַרְאֲדָן רַב־טַבָּחִים יְהוּדִים נֶפֶשׁ שְׁבַע מֵאוֹת אַרְבָּעִים וַחֲמִשָּׁה כָּל־נֶפֶשׁ אַרְבַּעַת אֲלָפִים וְשֵׁשׁ מֵאוֹת: פ

³¹ וַיְהִי בִשְׁלֹשִׁים וָשֶׁבַע שָׁנָה לְגָלוּת יְהוֹיָכִן מֶלֶךְ־יְהוּדָה בִּשְׁנֵים עָשָׂר חֹדֶשׁ בְּעֶשְׂרִים וַחֲמִשָּׁה לַחֹדֶשׁ נָשָׂא אֱוִיל מְרֹדַךְ מֶלֶךְ בָּבֶל בִּשְׁנַת מַלְכֻתוֹ אֶת־רֹאשׁ יְהוֹיָכִין מֶלֶךְ־יְהוּדָה וַיֹּצֵא אוֹתוֹ מִבֵּית הַכְּלִיא הַכְּלוּא: ³² וַיְדַבֵּר אִתּוֹ טֹבוֹת וַיִּתֵּן אֶת־כִּסְאוֹ מִמַּעַל לְכִסֵּא מלכים הַמְּלָכִים אֲשֶׁר אִתּוֹ בְּבָבֶל: ³³ וְשִׁנָּה אֵת בִּגְדֵי כִלְאוֹ וְאָכַל לֶחֶם לְפָנָיו תָּמִיד כָּל־יְמֵי חַיָּו*: ³⁴ וַאֲרֻחָתוֹ אֲרֻחַת תָּמִיד נִתְּנָה־לּוֹ מֵאֵת מֶלֶךְ־בָּבֶל דְּבַר־יוֹם בְּיוֹמוֹ עַד־יוֹם מוֹתוֹ כֹּל יְמֵי חַיָּיו*:

תם ונשלם תהילה לאל בורא עולם

EZEKIEL

1 In the thirtieth year,[a] on the fifth day of the fourth month, when I was in the community of exiles by the Chebar Canal, the heavens opened and I saw visions of God. [2]On the fifth day of the month—it was the fifth year of the exile of King Jehoiachin—[3]the word of the LORD came to the priest Ezekiel son of Buzi, by the Chebar Canal, in the land of the Chaldeans. And the hand of the LORD came upon him there.

[4]I looked, and lo, a stormy wind came sweeping out of the north—a huge cloud and flashing fire, surrounded by a radiance; and in the center of it, in the center of the fire, a gleam as of amber. [5]In the center of it were also the figures of four creatures. And this was their appearance:

They had the figures of human beings. [6]However, each had four faces, and each of them had four wings; [7]the legs of each were [fused into] a single rigid leg, and the feet of each were like a single calf's hoof;[b] and their sparkle[c] was like the luster of burnished bronze. [8]They had human hands below their wings. The four of them had their faces and their wings on their four sides. [9]Each one's wings touched those of the other. They did not turn when they moved; each could move in the direction of any of its faces.

[10]Each of them had a human face [at the front]; each of the four had the face of a lion on the right; each of the four had the face of an ox on the left; and each of the four had the face of an eagle [at the back]. [11]Such were their

א וַיְהִי ׀ בִּשְׁלֹשִׁים שָׁנָה בָּרְבִיעִי בַּחֲמִשָּׁה לַחֹדֶשׁ וַאֲנִי בְתוֹךְ־הַגּוֹלָה עַל־נְהַר־כְּבָר נִפְתְּחוּ הַשָּׁמַיִם וָאֶרְאֶה מַרְאוֹת אֱלֹהִים: 2 בַּחֲמִשָּׁה לַחֹדֶשׁ הִיא הַשָּׁנָה הַחֲמִישִׁית לְגָלוּת הַמֶּלֶךְ יוֹיָכִין: 3 הָיֹה הָיָה דְבַר־יְהֹוָה אֶל־יְחֶזְקֵאל בֶּן־בּוּזִי הַכֹּהֵן בְּאֶרֶץ כַּשְׂדִּים עַל־נְהַר־כְּבָר וַתְּהִי עָלָיו שָׁם יַד־יְהֹוָה:

4 וָאֵרֶא וְהִנֵּה רוּחַ סְעָרָה בָּאָה מִן־הַצָּפוֹן עָנָן גָּדוֹל וְאֵשׁ מִתְלַקַּחַת וְנֹגַהּ לוֹ סָבִיב וּמִתּוֹכָהּ כְּעֵין הַחַשְׁמַל מִתּוֹךְ הָאֵשׁ: 5 וּמִתּוֹכָהּ דְּמוּת אַרְבַּע חַיּוֹת וְזֶה מַרְאֵיהֶן

דְּמוּת אָדָם לָהֵנָּה: 6 וְאַרְבָּעָה פָנִים לְאֶחָת וְאַרְבַּע כְּנָפַיִם לְאַחַת לָהֶם: 7 וְרַגְלֵיהֶם רֶגֶל יְשָׁרָה וְכַף רַגְלֵיהֶם כְּכַף רֶגֶל עֵגֶל וְנֹצְצִים כְּעֵין נְחֹשֶׁת קָלָל: 8 וְיָדוֹ אָדָם מִתַּחַת כַּנְפֵיהֶם עַל אַרְבַּעַת רִבְעֵיהֶם וּפְנֵיהֶם וְכַנְפֵיהֶם לְאַרְבַּעְתָּם: 9 חֹבְרֹת אִשָּׁה אֶל־אֲחוֹתָהּ כַּנְפֵיהֶם לֹא־יִסַּבּוּ בְלֶכְתָּן אִישׁ אֶל־עֵבֶר פָּנָיו יֵלֵכוּ: 10 וּדְמוּת פְּנֵיהֶם פְּנֵי אָדָם וּפְנֵי אַרְיֵה אֶל־הַיָּמִין לְאַרְבַּעְתָּם וּפְנֵי־שׁוֹר מֵהַשְּׂמֹאול* לְאַרְבַּעְתָּן וּפְנֵי־נֶשֶׁר לְאַרְבַּעְתָּן: 11 וּפְנֵיהֶם וְכַנְפֵיהֶם פְּרֻדוֹת מִלְמָעְלָה

---

a We do not know the 30th of what.
b I.e., cleft in front.
c Or "plumage."

1155

faces. As for their wings, they were separated: above, each had two touching those of the others, while the other two covered its body. [12]And each could move in the direction of any of its faces; they went wherever the spirit impelled them to go, without turning when they moved.

[13]Such then was the appearance of the creatures. With them was something that looked like burning coals of fire. This fire, suggestive of torches, kept moving about among the creatures; the fire had a radiance, and lightning issued from the fire. [14]d-Dashing to and fro [among] the creatures was something that looked like flares.-d

[15]As I gazed on the creatures, I saw one wheel on the ground next to each of the four-faced creatures. [16]As for the appearance and structure of the wheels, they gleamed like beryl. All four had the same form; the appearance and structure of each was as of two wheels cutting through each other. [17]And when they moved, each could move in the direction of any of its four quarters; they did not veer when they moved. [18]Their rims were tall and frightening, for the rims of all four were covered all over with eyes. [19]And when the creatures moved forward, the wheels moved at their sides; and when the creatures were borne above the earth, the wheels were borne too. [20]Wherever the spirit impelled them to go, they went—wherever the spirit impelled them—and the wheels were borne alongside them; for the spirit of the creatures was in the wheels. [21]When those moved, these moved; and when those stood still, these stood still; and when those were borne above the earth, the wheels were borne alongside them—for the spirit of the creatures was in the wheels.

[22]Above the heads of the creatures was a form: an expanse, with an awe-inspiring gleam as of crystal, was spread out above their heads. [23]Under the expanse, each had one pair of wings ex-

לְאִישׁ שְׁתַּיִם חֹבְרוֹת אִישׁ וּשְׁתַּיִם מְכַסּוֹת אֵת גְּוִיֹתֵיהֶנָה: 12 וְאִישׁ אֶל־עֵבֶר פָּנָיו יֵלֵכוּ אֶל אֲשֶׁר יִהְיֶה־שָּׁמָּה הָרוּחַ לָלֶכֶת יֵלֵכוּ לֹא יִסַּבּוּ בְּלֶכְתָּן: 13 וּדְמוּת הַחַיּוֹת מַרְאֵיהֶם כְּגַחֲלֵי־אֵשׁ בֹּעֲרוֹת כְּמַרְאֵה הַלַּפִּדִים הִיא מִתְהַלֶּכֶת בֵּין הַחַיּוֹת וְנֹגַהּ לָאֵשׁ וּמִן־הָאֵשׁ יוֹצֵא בָרָק: 14 וְהַחַיּוֹת רָצוֹא וָשׁוֹב כְּמַרְאֵה הַבָּזָק: 15 וָאֵרֶא הַחַיּוֹת וְהִנֵּה אוֹפַן אֶחָד בָּאָרֶץ אֵצֶל הַחַיּוֹת לְאַרְבַּעַת פָּנָיו: 16 מַרְאֵה הָאוֹפַנִּים וּמַעֲשֵׂיהֶם כְּעֵין תַּרְשִׁישׁ וּדְמוּת אֶחָד לְאַרְבַּעְתָּן וּמַרְאֵיהֶם וּמַעֲשֵׂיהֶם כַּאֲשֶׁר יִהְיֶה הָאוֹפַן בְּתוֹךְ הָאוֹפָן: 17 עַל־ אַרְבַּעַת רִבְעֵיהֶן בְּלֶכְתָּם יֵלֵכוּ לֹא יִסַּבּוּ בְּלֶכְתָּן: 18 וְגַבֵּיהֶן וְגֹבַהּ לָהֶם וְיִרְאָה לָהֶם וְגַבֹּתָם מְלֵאֹת עֵינַיִם סָבִיב לְאַרְבַּעְתָּן: 19 וּבְלֶכֶת הַחַיּוֹת יֵלֵכוּ הָאוֹפַנִּים אֶצְלָם וּבְהִנָּשֵׂא הַחַיּוֹת מֵעַל הָאָרֶץ יִנָּשְׂאוּ הָאוֹפַנִּים: 20 עַל אֲשֶׁר יִהְיֶה־שָּׁם הָרוּחַ לָלֶכֶת יֵלֵכוּ שָׁמָּה הָרוּחַ לָלֶכֶת וְהָאוֹפַנִּים יִנָּשְׂאוּ לְעֻמָּתָם כִּי רוּחַ הַחַיָּה בָּאוֹפַנִּים: 21 בְּלֶכְתָּם יֵלֵכוּ וּבְעָמְדָם יַעֲמֹדוּ וּבְהִנָּשְׂאָם מֵעַל הָאָרֶץ יִנָּשְׂאוּ הָאוֹפַנִּים לְעֻמָּתָם כִּי רוּחַ הַחַיָּה בָּאוֹפַנִּים: 22 וּדְמוּת עַל־רָאשֵׁי הַחַיָּה רָקִיעַ כְּעֵין הַקֶּרַח הַנּוֹרָא נָטוּי עַל־רָאשֵׁיהֶם מִלְמָעְלָה: 23 וְתַחַת הָרָקִיעַ כַּנְפֵיהֶם יְשָׁרוֹת אִשָּׁה אֶל־אֲחוֹתָהּ לְאִישׁ שְׁתַּיִם

---

d-d   *Meaning of Heb. uncertain.*

tended toward those of the others; and each had another pair covering its body. 24When they moved, I could hear the sound of their wings like the sound of mighty waters, like the sound of Shaddai,*e* a tumult like the din of an army. When they stood still, they would let their wings droop. 25*d*-From above the expanse over their heads came a sound.-*d* When they stood still, they would let their wings droop.

26Above the expanse over their heads was the semblance of a throne, in appearance like sapphire; and on top, upon this semblance of a throne, there was the semblance of a human form. 27From what appeared as his loins up, I saw a gleam as of amber—-*d*what looked like a fire encased in a frame;-*d* and from what appeared as his loins down, I saw what looked like fire. There was a radiance all about him. 28Like the appearance of the bow which shines in the clouds on a day of rain, such was the appearance of the surrounding radiance. That was the appearance of the semblance of the Presence of the LORD. When I beheld it, I flung myself down on my face. And I heard the voice of someone speaking.

2 And He said to me, "O mortal, stand up on your feet that I may speak to you." 2As He spoke to me, a spirit entered into me and set me upon my feet; and I heard what was being spoken to me. 3He said to me, "O mortal, I am sending you to the people of Israel, that nation of rebels, who have rebelled against Me.—They as well as their fathers have defied Me to this very day; 4for the sons are brazen of face and stubborn of heart. I send you to them, and you shall say to them: 'Thus said the Lord GOD'—5whether they listen or not, for they are a rebellious breed—that they may know that there was a prophet among them.

מְכַסּוֹת֙ לָהֵ֔נָּה וּלְאִ֕ישׁ שְׁתַּ֥יִם מְכַסּ֖וֹת לָהֵ֑נָּה אֵ֖ת גְּוִיֹּתֵיהֶֽם׃ 24 וָאֶשְׁמַ֣ע אֶת־ק֣וֹל כַּנְפֵיהֶ֡ם כְּקוֹל֩ מַ֨יִם רַבִּ֤ים כְּקוֹל־שַׁדַּי֙ בְּלֶכְתָּ֔ם ק֥וֹל הֲמֻלָּ֖ה כְּק֣וֹל מַחֲנֶ֑ה בְּעָמְדָ֖ם תְּרַפֶּ֥ינָה כַנְפֵיהֶֽן׃ 25 וַֽיְהִי־ק֕וֹל מֵעַ֣ל לָרָקִ֔יעַ אֲשֶׁ֖ר עַל־רֹאשָׁ֑ם בְּעָמְדָ֖ם תְּרַפֶּ֥ינָה כַנְפֵיהֶֽן׃

26 וּמִמַּ֗עַל לָרָקִ֙יעַ֙ אֲשֶׁ֣ר עַל־רֹאשָׁ֔ם כְּמַרְאֵ֥ה אֶֽבֶן־סַפִּ֛יר דְּמ֣וּת כִּסֵּ֑א וְעַל֙ דְּמ֣וּת הַכִּסֵּ֔א דְּמ֞וּת כְּמַרְאֵ֥ה אָדָ֛ם עָלָ֖יו מִלְמָֽעְלָה׃ 27 וָאֵ֣רֶא ׀ כְּעֵ֣ין חַשְׁמַ֗ל כְּמַרְאֵה־אֵ֤שׁ בֵּֽית־לָהּ֙ סָבִ֔יב מִמַּרְאֵ֥ה מָתְנָ֖יו וּלְמָ֑עְלָה וּמִמַּרְאֵ֤ה מָתְנָיו֙ וּלְמַ֔טָּה רָאִ֙יתִי֙ כְּמַרְאֵה־אֵ֔שׁ וְנֹ֥גַֽהּ ל֖וֹ סָבִֽיב׃ 28 כְּמַרְאֵ֣ה הַקֶּ֡שֶׁת אֲשֶׁר֩ יִֽהְיֶ֨ה בֶעָנָ֜ן בְּי֣וֹם הַגֶּ֗שֶׁם כֵּ֣ן מַרְאֵ֤ה הַנֹּ֙גַהּ֙ סָבִ֔יב ה֕וּא מַרְאֵ֖ה דְּמ֣וּת כְּבוֹד־יְהֹוָ֑ה וָֽאֶרְאֶה֙ וָאֶפֹּ֣ל עַל־פָּנַ֔י וָאֶשְׁמַ֖ע ק֥וֹל מְדַבֵּֽר׃ ס

ב וַיֹּ֖אמֶר אֵלָ֑י בֶּן־אָדָם֙ עֲמֹ֣ד עַל־רַגְלֶ֔יךָ וַאֲדַבֵּ֖ר אֹתָֽךְ׃ 2 וַתָּ֧בֹא בִ֣י ר֗וּחַ כַּֽאֲשֶׁר֙ דִּבֶּ֣ר אֵלַ֔י וַתַּעֲמִדֵ֖נִי עַל־רַגְלָ֑י וָאֶשְׁמַ֕ע אֵ֖ת מִדַּבֵּ֥ר אֵלָֽי׃ פ 3 וַיֹּ֣אמֶר אֵלַ֗י בֶּן־אָדָם֙ שׁוֹלֵ֨חַ אֲנִ֤י אֽוֹתְךָ֙ אֶל־בְּנֵ֣י יִשְׂרָאֵ֔ל אֶל־גּוֹיִ֥ם הַמּוֹרְדִ֖ים אֲשֶׁ֣ר מָרְדוּ־בִ֑י הֵ֤מָּה וַאֲבוֹתָם֙ פָּ֣שְׁעוּ בִ֔י עַ֖ד עֶ֥צֶם הַיּ֥וֹם הַזֶּֽה׃ 4 וְהַבָּנִ֗ים קְשֵׁ֤י פָנִים֙ וְחִזְקֵי־לֵ֔ב אֲנִ֛י שׁוֹלֵ֥חַ אֽוֹתְךָ֖ אֲלֵיהֶ֑ם וְאָמַרְתָּ֣ אֲלֵיהֶ֔ם כֹּ֥ה אָמַ֖ר אֲדֹנָ֥י יֱהֹוִֽה׃ 5 וְהֵ֙מָּה֙ אִם־יִשְׁמְע֣וּ וְאִם־יֶחְדָּ֔לוּ כִּ֛י בֵּ֥ית מְרִ֖י הֵ֑מָּה וְיָ֣דְע֔וּ כִּ֥י נָבִ֖יא הָיָ֥ה בְתוֹכָֽם׃ פ

---

e   Traditionally "the Almighty"; see Gen. 17.1.

6"And you, mortal, do not fear them and do not fear their words, though thistles and thorns *press against*[a] you, and you sit upon scorpions. Do not be afraid of their words and do not be dismayed by them, though they are a rebellious breed; 7but speak My words to them, whether they listen or not, for they are rebellious.

8"And you, mortal, heed what I say to you: Do not be rebellious like that rebellious breed. Open your mouth and eat what I am giving you." 9As I looked, there was a hand stretched out to me, holding a written scroll. 10He unrolled it before me, and it was inscribed on both the front and the back; on it were written lamentations, dirges, and woes.

3 He said to me, "Mortal, eat what is offered you; eat this scroll, and go speak to the House of Israel." 2So I opened my mouth, and He gave me this scroll to eat, 3as He said to me, "Mortal, feed your stomach and fill your belly with this scroll that I give you." I ate it, and it tasted as sweet as honey to me.

4Then He said to me, "Mortal, go to the House of Israel and repeat My very words to them. 5For you are sent, not to a people of unintelligible speech and difficult language, but to the House of Israel—6not to the many peoples of unintelligible speech and difficult language, whose talk you cannot understand. If I sent you to them, they would listen to you. 7But the House of Israel will refuse to listen to you, for they refuse to listen to Me; for the whole House of Israel are brazen of forehead and stubborn of heart. 8But I will make your face as hard as theirs, and your forehead as brazen as theirs. 9I will make your forehead like adamant, harder than flint. Do not fear them, and do not be dis-

6 וְאַתָּה בֶן־אָדָם אַל־תִּירָא מֵהֶם וּמִדִּבְרֵיהֶם אַל־תִּירָא כִּי סָרָבִים וְסַלּוֹנִים אוֹתָךְ וְאֶל־עַקְרַבִּים אַתָּה יוֹשֵׁב מִדִּבְרֵיהֶם אַל־תִּירָא וּמִפְּנֵיהֶם אַל־תֵּחָת כִּי בֵּית מְרִי הֵמָּה: 7 וְדִבַּרְתָּ אֶת־דְּבָרַי אֲלֵיהֶם אִם־יִשְׁמְעוּ וְאִם־יֶחְדָּלוּ כִּי מְרִי הֵמָּה: פ

8 וְאַתָּה בֶן־אָדָם שְׁמַע אֵת אֲשֶׁר־אֲנִי מְדַבֵּר אֵלֶיךָ אַל־תְּהִי־מֶרִי כְּבֵית הַמֶּרִי פְּצֵה פִיךָ וֶאֱכֹל אֵת אֲשֶׁר־אֲנִי נֹתֵן אֵלֶיךָ: 9 וָאֶרְאֶה וְהִנֵּה־יָד שְׁלוּחָה אֵלָי וְהִנֵּה־בוֹ מְגִלַּת־סֵפֶר: 10 וַיִּפְרֹשׂ אוֹתָהּ לְפָנַי וְהִיא כְתוּבָה פָּנִים וְאָחוֹר וְכָתוּב אֵלֶיהָ קִנִים וָהֶגֶה וָהִי: ס

ג 1 וַיֹּאמֶר אֵלַי בֶּן־אָדָם אֵת אֲשֶׁר־תִּמְצָא אֱכוֹל אֱכוֹל אֶת־הַמְּגִלָּה הַזֹּאת וְלֵךְ דַּבֵּר אֶל־בֵּית יִשְׂרָאֵל: 2 וָאֶפְתַּח אֶת־פִּי וַיַּאֲכִלֵנִי אֵת הַמְּגִלָּה הַזֹּאת: 3 וַיֹּאמֶר אֵלַי בֶּן־אָדָם בִּטְנְךָ תַאֲכֵל וּמֵעֶיךָ תְמַלֵּא אֵת הַמְּגִלָּה הַזֹּאת אֲשֶׁר אֲנִי נֹתֵן אֵלֶיךָ וָאֹכְלָה וַתְּהִי בְּפִי כִּדְבַשׁ לְמָתוֹק: פ

4 וַיֹּאמֶר אֵלַי בֶּן־אָדָם לֶךְ־בֹּא אֶל־בֵּית יִשְׂרָאֵל וְדִבַּרְתָּ בִדְבָרַי אֲלֵיהֶם: 5 כִּי לֹא אֶל־עַם עִמְקֵי שָׂפָה וְכִבְדֵי לָשׁוֹן אַתָּה שָׁלוּחַ אֶל־בֵּית יִשְׂרָאֵל: 6 לֹא אֶל־עַמִּים רַבִּים עִמְקֵי שָׂפָה וְכִבְדֵי לָשׁוֹן אֲשֶׁר לֹא־תִשְׁמַע דִּבְרֵיהֶם אִם־לֹא אֲלֵיהֶם שְׁלַחְתִּיךָ הֵמָּה יִשְׁמְעוּ אֵלֶיךָ: 7 וּבֵית יִשְׂרָאֵל לֹא יֹאבוּ לִשְׁמֹעַ אֵלֶיךָ כִּי־אֵינָם אֹבִים לִשְׁמֹעַ אֵלָי כִּי כָּל־בֵּית יִשְׂרָאֵל חִזְקֵי־מֵצַח וּקְשֵׁי־לֵב הֵמָּה: 8 הִנֵּה נָתַתִּי אֶת־פָּנֶיךָ חֲזָקִים לְעֻמַּת פְּנֵיהֶם וְאֶת־מִצְחֲךָ חָזָק לְעֻמַּת מִצְחָם: 9 כְּשָׁמִיר חָזָק

---

a-a Lit. "are with."

mayed by them, though they are a rebellious breed."

¹⁰Then He said to me: "Mortal, listen with your ears and receive into your mind all the words that I speak to you. ¹¹Go to your people, the exile community, and speak to them. Say to them: Thus says the Lord God—whether they listen or not." ¹²Then a spirit carried me away, and behind me I heard a great roaring sound: ᵃ-"Blessed is the Presence of the Lord, in His place,"-ᵃ ¹³with the sound of the wings of the creatures beating against one another, and the sound of the wheels beside them—a great roaring sound. ¹⁴A spirit seized me and carried me away. I went in bitterness, in the fury of my spirit, while the hand of the Lord was strong upon me. ¹⁵And I came to the exile community that dwelt in Tel Abib by the Chebar Canal, and I remained where they dwelt. And for seven days I sat there stunned among them.

¹⁶After those seven days, the word of the Lord came to me: ¹⁷"O mortal, I appoint you watchman for the House of Israel; and when you hear a word from My mouth, you must warn them for Me. ¹⁸If I say to a wicked man, 'You shall die,' and you do not warn him—you do not speak to warn the wicked man of his wicked course in order to save his life—he, the wicked man, shall die for his iniquity, but I will require a reckoning for his blood from you. ¹⁹But if you do warn the wicked man, and he does not turn back from his wickedness and his wicked course, he shall die for his iniquity, but you will have saved your own life. ²⁰Again, if a righteous man abandons his righteousness and does wrong, when I put a stumbling block before him, he shall die. He shall die for his sins; the righteous deeds that he did shall not be remembered; but because you did not warn him, I will require a reckoning for his blood from you. ²¹If,

---

מִצָּר נָתַתִּי מִצְחֲךָ לֹא־תִירָא אוֹתָם וְלֹא־תֵחַת מִפְּנֵיהֶם כִּי בֵּית־מְרִי הֵמָּה: פ
¹⁰ וַיֹּאמֶר אֵלָי בֶּן־אָדָם אֶת־כָּל־דְּבָרַי אֲשֶׁר אֲדַבֵּר אֵלֶיךָ קַח בִּלְבָבְךָ וּבְאָזְנֶיךָ שְׁמָע: ¹¹ וְלֵךְ בֹּא אֶל־הַגּוֹלָה אֶל־בְּנֵי עַמֶּךָ וְדִבַּרְתָּ אֲלֵיהֶם וְאָמַרְתָּ אֲלֵיהֶם כֹּה אָמַר אֲדֹנָי יְהֹוִה אִם־יִשְׁמְעוּ וְאִם־יֶחְדָּלוּ: ¹² וַתִּשָּׂאֵנִי רוּחַ וָאֶשְׁמַע אַחֲרַי קוֹל רַעַשׁ גָּדוֹל בָּרוּךְ כְּבוֹד־יְהֹוָה מִמְּקוֹמוֹ: ¹³ וְקוֹל | כַּנְפֵי הַחַיּוֹת מַשִּׁיקוֹת אִשָּׁה אֶל־אֲחוֹתָהּ וְקוֹל הָאוֹפַנִּים לְעֻמָּתָם וְקוֹל רַעַשׁ גָּדוֹל: ¹⁴ וְרוּחַ נְשָׂאַתְנִי וַתִּקָּחֵנִי וָאֵלֵךְ מַר בַּחֲמַת רוּחִי וְיַד־יְהֹוָה עָלַי חָזָקָה: ¹⁵ וָאָבוֹא אֶל־הַגּוֹלָה תֵּל אָבִיב הַיֹּשְׁבִים אֶל־נְהַר־כְּבָר וָאֵשֵׁר הֵמָּה יוֹשְׁבִים שָׁם וָאֵשֵׁב שָׁם שִׁבְעַת יָמִים מַשְׁמִים בְּתוֹכָם: ¹⁶ וַיְהִי מִקְצֵה שִׁבְעַת יָמִים ס וַיְהִי דְבַר־יְהֹוָה אֵלַי לֵאמֹר: ¹⁷ בֶּן־אָדָם צֹפֶה נְתַתִּיךָ לְבֵית יִשְׂרָאֵל וְשָׁמַעְתָּ מִפִּי דָּבָר וְהִזְהַרְתָּ אוֹתָם מִמֶּנִּי: ¹⁸ בְּאָמְרִי לָרָשָׁע מוֹת תָּמוּת וְלֹא הִזְהַרְתּוֹ וְלֹא דִבַּרְתָּ לְהַזְהִיר רָשָׁע מִדַּרְכּוֹ הָרְשָׁעָה לְחַיֹּתוֹ הוּא רָשָׁע בַּעֲוֹנוֹ יָמוּת וְדָמוֹ מִיָּדְךָ אֲבַקֵּשׁ: ¹⁹ וְאַתָּה כִּי־הִזְהַרְתָּ רָשָׁע וְלֹא־שָׁב מֵרִשְׁעוֹ וּמִדַּרְכּוֹ הָרְשָׁעָה הוּא בַּעֲוֹנוֹ יָמוּת וְאַתָּה אֶת־נַפְשְׁךָ הִצַּלְתָּ: ס ²⁰ וּבְשׁוּב צַדִּיק מִצִּדְקוֹ וְעָשָׂה עָוֶל וְנָתַתִּי מִכְשׁוֹל לְפָנָיו הוּא יָמוּת כִּי לֹא הִזְהַרְתּוֹ בְּחַטָּאתוֹ יָמוּת וְלֹא תִזָּכַרְןָ צִדְקֹתָו אֲשֶׁר עָשָׂה וְדָמוֹ מִיָּדְךָ אֲבַקֵּשׁ: ²¹ וְאַתָּה כִּי

ᵃ⁻ᵃ   *Emendation yields* "as the Presence of the Lord rose from where it stood."

however, you warn the righteous man not to sin, and he, the righteous, does not sin, he shall live because he took warning, and you will have saved your own life."

²²Then the hand of the LORD came upon me there, and He said to me, "Arise, go out to the valley, and there I will speak with you." ²³I arose and went out to the valley, and there stood the Presence of the LORD, like the Presence that I had seen at the Chebar Canal; and I flung myself down on my face. ²⁴And a spirit entered into me and set me upon my feet. And He spoke to me, and said to me: "Go, shut yourself up in your house. ²⁵As for you, O mortal, cords have been placed upon you, and you have been bound with them, and you shall not go out among them.ᵇ ²⁶And I will make your tongue cleave to your palate, and you shall be dumb; you shall not be a reprover to them, for they are a rebellious breed. ²⁷But when I speak with you, I will open your mouth, and you shall say to them, 'Thus says the Lord GOD!' He who listens will listen, and he who does not will not—for they are a rebellious breed."

4 "And you, O mortal, take a brick and put it in front of you, and incise on it a city, Jerusalem. ²Set up a siege against it, and build towers against it, and cast a mound against it; pitch camps against it, and bring up battering rams roundabout it. ³Then take an iron plate and place it as an iron wall between yourself and the city, and set your face against it. ᵃThus it shall be under siege, you shall besiege it. This shall be an omen for the House of Israel.

⁴"Then lie on your left side, and let it bear the punishment of the House of Israel;ᵇ for as

הֻזְהַרְתּוֹ צַדִּיק לְבִלְתִּי חֲטֹא צַדִּיק וְהוּא לֹא־חָטָא חָיוֹ יִחְיֶה כִּי נִזְהָר וְאַתָּה אֶת־נַפְשְׁךָ הִצַּלְתָּ׃ ס

²² וַתְּהִי עָלַי שָׁם יַד־יְהוָה וַיֹּאמֶר אֵלַי קוּם צֵא אֶל־הַבִּקְעָה וְשָׁם אֲדַבֵּר אוֹתָךְ׃ ²³ וָאָקוּם וָאֵצֵא אֶל־הַבִּקְעָה וְהִנֵּה־שָׁם כְּבוֹד־יְהוָה עֹמֵד כַּכָּבוֹד אֲשֶׁר רָאִיתִי עַל־נְהַר־כְּבָר וָאֶפֹּל עַל־פָּנָי׃ ²⁴ וַתָּבֹא־בִי רוּחַ וַתַּעֲמִדֵנִי עַל־רַגְלָי וַיְדַבֵּר אֹתִי וַיֹּאמֶר אֵלַי בֹּא הִסָּגֵר בְּתוֹךְ בֵּיתֶךָ׃ ²⁵ וְאַתָּה בֶן־אָדָם הִנֵּה נָתְנוּ עָלֶיךָ עֲבוֹתִים וַאֲסָרוּךָ בָּהֶם וְלֹא תֵצֵא בְּתוֹכָם׃ ²⁶ וּלְשׁוֹנְךָ אַדְבִּיק אֶל־חִכֶּךָ וְנֶאֱלַמְתָּ וְלֹא־תִהְיֶה לָהֶם לְאִישׁ מוֹכִיחַ כִּי בֵּית מְרִי הֵמָּה׃ ²⁷ וּבְדַבְּרִי אוֹתְךָ אֶפְתַּח אֶת־פִּיךָ וְאָמַרְתָּ אֲלֵיהֶם כֹּה אָמַר אֲדֹנָי יְהוִה הַשֹּׁמֵעַ ׀ יִשְׁמָע וְהֶחָדֵל ׀ יֶחְדָּל כִּי בֵּית מְרִי הֵמָּה׃ ס

ד וְאַתָּה בֶן־אָדָם קַח־לְךָ לְבֵנָה וְנָתַתָּה אוֹתָהּ לְפָנֶיךָ וְחַקּוֹתָ עָלֶיהָ עִיר אֶת־יְרוּשָׁלָ͏ִם׃ ² וְנָתַתָּה עָלֶיהָ מָצוֹר וּבָנִיתָ עָלֶיהָ דָּיֵק וְשָׁפַכְתָּ עָלֶיהָ סֹלְלָה וְנָתַתָּה עָלֶיהָ מַחֲנוֹת וְשִׂים־עָלֶיהָ כָּרִים סָבִיב׃ ³ וְאַתָּה קַח־לְךָ מַחֲבַת בַּרְזֶל וְנָתַתָּה אוֹתָהּ קִיר בַּרְזֶל בֵּינְךָ וּבֵין הָעִיר וַהֲכִינֹתָה אֶת־פָּנֶיךָ אֵלֶיהָ וְהָיְתָה בַמָּצוֹר וְצַרְתָּ עָלֶיהָ אוֹת הִיא לְבֵית יִשְׂרָאֵל׃ ס

⁴ וְאַתָּה שְׁכַב עַל־צִדְּךָ הַשְּׂמָאלִי וְשַׂמְתָּ

ᵇ   *I.e., the people.*

ᵃ   *I.e., in hostility.*

ᵇ   *Since left and right also denote north and south (e.g., 16.46), the left side represents Israel, the northern kingdom, and the right side Judah, the southern kingdom.*

many days as you lie on it you shall bear their punishment. [5]For I impose upon you three hundred and ninety days, corresponding to the number of the years of their punishment; and so you shall bear the punishment for the House of Israel. [6]When you have completed these, you shall lie another forty days on your right side, and bear the punishment of the House of Judah.[b] I impose on you one day for each year.

[7]"Then, with bared arm, set your face toward besieged Jerusalem and prophesy against it. [8]Now I put cords upon you, so that you cannot turn from side to side until you complete your days of siege.

[9]"Further, take wheat, barley, beans, lentils, millet, and emmer. Put them into one vessel and bake them into bread. Eat it as many days as you lie on your side: three hundred and ninety. [10]The food that you eat shall be by weight, twenty shekels a day; this you shall eat in the space of a day. [11]And you shall drink water by measure; drink a sixth of a *hin* in the space of a day.

[12]"Eat it as a barley[c] cake; you shall bake it on human excrement before their eyes. [13]So," said the Lord, "shall the people of Israel eat their bread, unclean, among the nations to which I will banish them." [14]Then I said, "Ah, Lord GOD, my person was never defiled; nor have I eaten anything that died of itself or was torn by beasts from my youth until now, nor has foul flesh entered my mouth." [15]He answered me, "See, I allow you cow's dung instead of human excrement; prepare your bread on that."

[16d]And He said to me, "O mortal, I am going to break the staff of bread in Jerusalem, and they shall eat bread by weight, in anxiety, and drink water by measure, in horror, [17]so that, lacking bread and water, they shall stare at each other,

---

c   *Meaning of Heb. uncertain.*
d   *Resuming the thought of v. 11.*

אֶת־עֲוֺ֥ן בֵּֽית־יִשְׂרָאֵ֖ל עָלָ֑יו מִסְפַּ֣ר הַיָּמִ֗ים
אֲשֶׁ֤ר תִּשְׁכַּב֙ עָלָ֔יו תִּשָּׂ֖א אֶת־עֲוֺנָֽם׃ 5 וַאֲנִ֗י
נָתַ֤תִּי לְךָ֙ אֶת־שְׁנֵ֣י עֲוֺנָ֔ם לְמִסְפַּ֣ר יָמִ֔ים
שְׁלֹשׁ־מֵא֥וֹת וְתִשְׁעִ֖ים י֑וֹם וְנָשָׂ֖אתָ עֲוֺ֥ן
בֵּֽית־יִשְׂרָאֵֽל׃ 6 וְכִלִּיתָ֣ אֶת־אֵ֔לֶּה וְשָׁכַבְתָּ֞
עַל־צִדְּךָ֤ הַיְמָנִי֙ שֵׁנִ֔ית וְנָשָׂ֖אתָ
אֶת־עֲוֺ֣ן בֵּֽית־יְהוּדָ֑ה אַרְבָּעִ֣ים י֔וֹם
י֥וֹם לַשָּׁנָ֛ה י֥וֹם לַשָּׁנָ֖ה נְתַתִּ֥יו לָֽךְ׃
7 וְאֶל־מְצ֤וֹר יְרוּשָׁלִַ֙ם֙ תָּכִ֣ין פָּנֶ֔יךָ וּֽזְרֹעֲךָ֖
חֲשׂוּפָ֑ה וְנִבֵּ֖אתָ עָלֶֽיהָ׃ 8 וְהִנֵּ֛ה נָתַ֥תִּי עָלֶ֖יךָ
עֲבוֹתִ֑ים וְלֹֽא־תֵהָפֵ֤ךְ מִֽצִּדְּךָ֙ אֶל־צִדְּךָ֔ עַד־
כַּלּוֹתְךָ֖ יְמֵ֥י מְצוּרֶֽךָ׃
9 וְאַתָּ֣ה קַח־לְךָ֡ חִטִּ֡ין וּ֠שְׂעֹרִים וּפ֨וֹל
וַעֲדָשִׁ֜ים וְדֹ֣חַן וְכֻסְּמִ֗ים וְנָתַתָּ֤ה אוֹתָם֙
בִּכְלִ֣י אֶחָ֔ד וְעָשִׂ֧יתָ אוֹתָ֛ם לְךָ֖ לְלָ֑חֶם
מִסְפַּ֤ר הַיָּמִים֙ אֲשֶׁר־אַתָּ֣ה ׀ שׁוֹכֵ֣ב עַל־
צִדְּךָ֗ שְׁלֹשׁ־מֵא֧וֹת וְתִשְׁעִ֛ים י֖וֹם תֹּאכֲלֶֽנּוּ׃
10 וּמַאֲכָֽלְךָ֙ אֲשֶׁ֣ר תֹּֽאכֲלֶ֔נּוּ בְּמִשְׁק֕וֹל
עֶשְׂרִ֥ים שֶׁ֖קֶל לַיּ֑וֹם מֵעֵ֥ת עַד־עֵ֖ת תֹּאכֲלֶֽנּוּ׃
11 וּמַ֕יִם בִּמְשׂוּרָ֥ה תִשְׁתֶּ֖ה שִׁשִּׁ֣ית הַהִ֑ין
מֵעֵ֥ת עַד־עֵ֖ת תִּשְׁתֶּֽה׃
12 וְעֻגַ֥ת שְׂעֹרִ֖ים תֹּֽאכֲלֶ֑נָּה וְהִ֗יא בְּגֶֽלְלֵי֙
צֵאַ֣ת הָֽאָדָ֔ם תְּעֻגֶ֖נָה לְעֵינֵיהֶֽם׃ ס
13 וַיֹּ֣אמֶר יְהֹוָ֔ה כָּ֣כָה יֹאכְל֧וּ בְנֵֽי־יִשְׂרָאֵ֛ל
אֶת־לַחְמָ֥ם טָמֵ֖א בַּגּוֹיִ֑ם אֲשֶׁ֥ר אַדִּיחֵ֖ם
שָֽׁם׃ 14 וָאֹמַ֗ר אֲהָ֙הּ֙ אֲדֹנָ֣י יֱהֹוִ֔ה הִנֵּ֥ה נַפְשִׁ֖י
לֹ֣א מְטֻמָּאָ֑ה וּנְבֵלָ֨ה וּטְרֵפָ֤ה לֹֽא־אָכַ֙לְתִּי֙
מִנְּעוּרַ֣י וְעַד־עַ֔תָּה וְלֹא־בָ֥א בְּפִ֖י בְּשַׂ֥ר
פִּגּֽוּל׃ ס 15 וַיֹּ֣אמֶר אֵלַ֗י רְאֵה֙ נָתַ֣תִּי לְךָ֔
אֶת־צְפוּעֵ֣י הַבָּקָ֔ר תַּ֖חַת גֶּלְלֵ֣י
הָאָדָ֑ם וְעָשִׂ֥יתָ אֶת־לַחְמְךָ֖ עֲלֵיהֶֽם׃ ס
16 וַיֹּ֣אמֶר אֵלַ֗י בֶּן־אָדָם֙ הִנְנִ֣י שֹׁבֵ֤ר מַטֵּה־
לֶ֙חֶם֙ בִּיר֣וּשָׁלִַ֔ם וְאָכְלוּ־לֶ֥חֶם בְּמִשְׁקָ֖ל
וּבִדְאָגָ֑ה וּמַ֕יִם בִּמְשׂוּרָ֥ה וּבְשִׁמָּמ֖וֹן יִשְׁתּֽוּ׃
17 לְמַ֥עַן יַחְסְר֖וּ לֶ֣חֶם וָמָ֑יִם וְנָשַׁ֙מּוּ֙ אִ֣ישׁ

5

heartsick over their iniquity. ¹And you, O
mortal, take a sharp knife; use it as a bar-
ber's razor and pass it over your head and beard.
Then take scales and divide the hair.ᵃ ²When
the days of siege are completed, destroy a third
part in fire in the city, take a third and strike
it with the sword all around ᵇ-the city,-ᵇ and scatter a third to the wind and unsheatheᶜ a sword
after them.

³"Take also a few [hairs] from there and tie
them up in your skirts. ⁴And take some more
of them and cast them into the fire, and burn
them in the fire. From this a fire shall go out
upon the whole House of Israel."

⁵Thus said the Lord GOD: I set this Jerusalem
in the midst of nations, with countries round
about her. ⁶But she rebelled against My rules
and My laws, acting more wickedly than the nations and the countries round about her; sheᵈ
rejected My rules and disobeyed My laws. ⁷Assuredly, thus said the Lord GOD: Because you
have outdone the nations that are round about
you—you have not obeyed My laws or followed
My rules, nor have you observed the rules of
the nations round about you—⁸assuredly, thus
said the Lord GOD: I, in turn, am going to deal
with you, and I will execute judgments in your
midst in the sight of the nations. ⁹On account
of all your abominations, I will do among you
what I have never done, and the like of which
I will never do again.

¹⁰Assuredly, parents shall eat their children
in your midst, and children shall eat their
parents. I will execute judgments against you,
and I will scatter all your survivors in every
direction.

¹¹Assuredly, as I live—said the Lord GOD—
because you defiled My Sanctuary with all your

וְאָחִ֔יו וְנָמַ֖קּוּ בַּעֲוֺנָֽם׃ פ ¹וְאַתָּ֣ה
בֶן־אָדָ֗ם קַח־לְךָ֣ ׀ חֶ֤רֶב חַדָּה֙ תַּ֣עַר
הַגַּלָּבִים֙ תִּקָּחֶ֣נָּה לָּ֔ךְ וְהַעֲבַרְתָּ֥
עַל־רֹאשְׁךָ֖ וְעַל־זְקָנֶ֑ךָ וְלָקַחְתָּ֥ לְךָ֛ מֹאזְנֵ֥י מִשְׁקָ֖ל
וְחִלַּקְתָּֽם׃ ²שְׁלִשִׁ֗ית בָּא֤וּר תַּבְעִיר֙ בְּת֣וֹךְ
הָעִ֔יר כִּמְלֹ֖את יְמֵ֣י הַמָּצ֑וֹר וְלָקַחְתָּ֣
אֶת־הַשְּׁלִשִׁ֗ית תַּכֶּ֤ה בַחֶ֙רֶב֙ סְבִיבוֹתֶ֔יהָ
וְהַשְּׁלִשִׁ֗ית תִּזְרֶ֣ה לָר֔וּחַ וְחֶ֖רֶב אָרִ֥יק
אַחֲרֵיהֶֽם׃ ³וְלָקַחְתָּ֥ מִשָּׁ֖ם מְעַ֣ט בְּמִסְפָּ֑ר וְצַרְתָּ֥ אוֹתָ֖ם
בִּכְנָפֶֽיךָ׃ ⁴וּמֵהֶם֙ ע֣וֹד תִּקָּ֔ח וְהִשְׁלַכְתָּ֤
אוֹתָם֙ אֶל־תּ֣וֹךְ הָאֵ֔שׁ וְשָׂרַפְתָּ֥ אֹתָ֖ם בָּאֵ֑שׁ
מִמֶּ֣נּוּ תֵצֵא־אֵ֔שׁ אֶל־כָּל־בֵּ֥ית יִשְׂרָאֵֽל׃ פ

⁵כֹּ֤ה אָמַר֙ אֲדֹנָ֣י יְהֹוִ֔ה זֹ֚את יְר֣וּשָׁלַ֔͏ִם בְּת֥וֹךְ
הַגּוֹיִ֖ם שַׂמְתִּ֑יהָ וּסְבִיבוֹתֶ֖יהָ אֲרָצֽוֹת׃
⁶וַתֶּ֨מֶר אֶת־מִשְׁפָּטַ֤י לְרִשְׁעָה֙ מִן־הַגּוֹיִ֔ם
וְאֶת־חֻקּוֹתַ֕י מִן־הָ֣אֲרָצ֔וֹת אֲשֶׁ֖ר סְבִיבוֹתֶ֑יהָ
כִּ֤י בְמִשְׁפָּטַי֙ מָאָ֔סוּ וְחֻקּוֹתַ֖י לֹא־הָלְכ֥וּ
בָהֶֽם׃ ס ⁷לָכֵ֞ן כֹּה־אָמַ֣ר ׀ אֲדֹנָ֣י יְהֹוִ֗ה
יַ֤עַן הֲמָנְכֶם֙ מִן־הַגּוֹיִם֙ אֲשֶׁ֣ר סְבִיבֽוֹתֵיכֶ֔ם
בְּחֻקּוֹתַי֙ לֹ֣א הֲלַכְתֶּ֔ם וְאֶת־מִשְׁפָּטַ֖י
לֹ֣א עֲשִׂיתֶ֑ם וּֽכְמִשְׁפְּטֵ֞י הַגּוֹיִ֗ם אֲשֶׁ֤ר
סְבִיבֽוֹתֵיכֶם֙ לֹ֣א עֲשִׂיתֶֽם׃ ס ⁸לָכֵ֗ן כֹּ֤ה
אָמַר֙ אֲדֹנָ֣י יְהֹוִ֔ה הִנְנִ֥י עָלַ֖יִךְ גַּם־אָ֑נִי
וְעָשִׂ֧יתִי בְתוֹכֵ֛ךְ מִשְׁפָּטִ֖ים לְעֵינֵ֥י הַגּוֹיִֽם׃
⁹וְעָשִׂ֣יתִי בָ֗ךְ אֵ֚ת אֲשֶׁ֣ר לֹֽא־עָשִׂ֔יתִי וְאֵ֛ת
אֲשֶֽׁר־לֹֽא־אֶעֱשֶׂ֥ה כָמֹ֖הוּ ע֑וֹד יַ֖עַן כָּל־
תּוֹעֲבֹתָֽיִךְ׃ ס
¹⁰לָכֵ֗ן אָב֞וֹת יֹאכְל֤וּ בָנִים֙ בְּתוֹכֵ֔ךְ וּבָנִ֖ים
יֹאכְל֣וּ אֲבוֹתָ֑ם וְעָשִׂ֤יתִי בָךְ֙ שְׁפָטִ֔ים וְזֵרִיתִ֥י
אֶת־כָּל־שְׁאֵרִיתֵ֖ךְ לְכָל־רֽוּחַ׃ פ
¹¹לָכֵ֣ן חַי־אָ֗נִי נְאֻם֙ אֲדֹנָ֣י יְהֹוִ֔ה אִם־לֹ֗א
יַ֜עַן אֶת־מִקְדָּשִׁ֤י טִמֵּאת֙ בְּכָל־שִׁקּוּצַ֙יִךְ֙

---

a   Lit. "them."
b-b Heb. "it."
c   Cf. v. 12; lit. "I will unsheathe."
d   Heb. "they."

detestable things and all your abominations, I
in turn will shear [you] away*e* and show no pity.
I in turn will show no compassion: ¹²One-third
of you shall die of pestilence or perish in your
midst by famine, one-third shall fall by the
sword around you, and I will scatter one-third
in every direction and will unsheathe the sword
after them. ¹³I will vent all My anger and satisfy
My fury upon them; and when I vent all My fury
upon them, they shall know that I the Lord have
spoken in My passion. ¹⁴I will make you a ruin
and a mockery among the nations roundabout
you, in the sight of every passerby. ¹⁵And when
I execute judgment upon you in anger and rage
and furious chastisement, you*f* shall be a mockery and a derision, a warning and a horror, to
the nations roundabout you: I the Lord have
spoken. ¹⁶When I loose the deadly arrows of
famine against those doomed to destruction,
when I loose them against you to destroy you,
I will heap more famine upon you and break
your staff of bread. ¹⁷I will let loose against you
famine and wild beasts and they shall bereave
you; pestilence and bloodshed shall sweep
through you, and I will bring the sword upon
you. I the Lord have spoken.

6 The word of the Lord came to me: ²O mortal, turn your face toward the mountains of Israel and prophesy to them ³and say: O mountains of Israel, hear the word of the Lord God.
Thus said the Lord God to the mountains and
the hills, to the streams and the valleys: See, I
will bring a sword against you and destroy your
shrines. ⁴Your altars shall be wrecked and your
incense stands smashed, and I will hurl down
your slain in front of your fetishes. ⁵I will cast
the corpses of the people of Israel in front of

וּבְכָל־תּוֹעֲבֹתַיִךְ וְגַם־אֲנִי אֶגְרַע וְלֹא־
תָחוֹס עֵינִי וְגַם־אֲנִי לֹא אֶחְמוֹל׃
¹² שְׁלִשָׁתֵיךְ* בַּדֶּבֶר יָמוּתוּ וּבָרָעָב יִכְלוּ
בְתוֹכֵךְ וְהַשְּׁלִשִׁית בַּחֶרֶב יִפְּלוּ סְבִיבוֹתָיִךְ
וְהַשְּׁלִישִׁית לְכָל־רוּחַ אֱזָרֶה וְחֶרֶב אָרִיק
אַחֲרֵיהֶם׃ ¹³ וְכָלָה אַפִּי וַהֲנִחוֹתִי חֲמָתִי
בָּם וְהִנֶּחָמְתִּי וְיָדְעוּ כִּי־אֲנִי יְהוָה דִּבַּרְתִּי
בְּקִנְאָתִי בְּכַלּוֹתִי חֲמָתִי בָּם׃ ¹⁴ וְנָתַתִּי
לְחָרְבָּה וּלְחֶרְפָּה בַּגּוֹיִם אֲשֶׁר סְבִיבוֹתָיִךְ
לְעֵינֵי כָּל־עוֹבֵר׃ ¹⁵ וְהָיְתָה חֶרְפָּה וּגְדוּפָה
מוּסָר וּמְשַׁמָּה לַגּוֹיִם אֲשֶׁר סְבִיבוֹתָיִךְ
בַּעֲשׂוֹתִי בָךְ שְׁפָטִים בְּאַף וּבְחֵמָה
וּבְתֹכְחוֹת חֵמָה אֲנִי יְהוָה דִּבַּרְתִּי׃
¹⁶ בְּשַׁלְּחִי אֶת־חִצֵּי הָרָעָב הָרָעִים בָּהֶם
אֲשֶׁר הָיוּ לְמַשְׁחִית אֲשֶׁר־אֲשַׁלַּח אוֹתָם
לְשַׁחֶתְכֶם וְרָעָב אֹסֵף עֲלֵיכֶם וְשָׁבַרְתִּי
לָכֶם מַטֵּה־לָחֶם׃ ¹⁷ וְשִׁלַּחְתִּי עֲלֵיכֶם רָעָב
וְחַיָּה רָעָה וְשִׁכְּלֻךְ וְדֶבֶר וָדָם יַעֲבָר־בָּךְ
וְחֶרֶב אָבִיא עָלַיִךְ אֲנִי יְהוָה דִּבַּרְתִּי׃ פ

^ו וַיְהִי דְבַר־יְהוָה אֵלַי לֵאמֹר׃ ² בֶּן־אָדָם
שִׂים פָּנֶיךָ אֶל־הָרֵי יִשְׂרָאֵל וְהִנָּבֵא
אֲלֵיהֶם׃ ³ וְאָמַרְתָּ הָרֵי יִשְׂרָאֵל שִׁמְעוּ
דְּבַר־אֲדֹנָי יְהוָה כֹּה־אָמַר אֲדֹנָי יְהוָה
לֶהָרִים וְלַגְּבָעוֹת לָאֲפִיקִים וְלַגֵּאָיֹת
וְלַגֵּאָיוֹת הִנְנִי אֲנִי מֵבִיא עֲלֵיכֶם חֶרֶב
וְאִבַּדְתִּי בָּמוֹתֵיכֶם׃ ⁴ וְנָשַׁמּוּ מִזְבְּחוֹתֵיכֶם
וְנִשְׁבְּרוּ חַמָּנֵיכֶם וְהִפַּלְתִּי חַלְלֵיכֶם לִפְנֵי
גִּלּוּלֵיכֶם׃ ⁵ וְנָתַתִּי אֶת־פִּגְרֵי בְּנֵי יִשְׂרָאֵל
לִפְנֵי גִּלּוּלֵיהֶם וְזֵרִיתִי אֶת־עַצְמוֹתֵיכֶם

v. 12. חסר י׳ וחסר י׳ ומלא י׳

---

*e   Cf. Isa. 15.2 and Jer. 48.37; here an allusion to the symbolism
      in v. 1.*
f   Heb. "she."

their fetishes, and scatter your bones around your altars 6in all your settlements. The towns shall be laid waste and the shrines shall be devastated. Thus your altars shall be laid waste and a-bear their punishment;-a your fetishes shall be smashed and annihilated, your incense stands cut down, and your handiwork wiped out; 7and the slain shall fall in your midst. Then you shall know that I am the LORD. 8Yet I will leave a remnant, in that some of you shall escape the sword among the nations and be scattered through the lands. 9And those of you that escape will remember Me among the nations where they have been taken captive, b-how I was brokenhearted through-b their faithless hearts which turned away from Me, and through their eyes which lusted after their fetishes. And they shall loathe themselves for all the evil they committed and for all their abominable deeds. 10Then they shall realize it was not without cause that I the LORD resolved to bring this evil upon them.

11Thus said the Lord GOD: Strike your hands together and stamp your feet and cry: Aha! over all the vile abominations of the House of Israel who shall fall by the sword, by famine, and by pestilence. 12He who is far away shall die of pestilence, and he who is near shall fall by the sword, and he who survives and is protected shall die of famine. Thus I will spend My fury upon them. 13And you shall know that I am the LORD, when your slain lie among the fetishes round about their altars, on every high hill, on all the mountaintops, under every green tree, and under every leafy oak—wherever they presented pleasing odors to all their fetishes.

14I will stretch out My hand against them, and lay the land waste and desolate in all their settlements, from the wilderness as far as Diblah;c then they shall know that I am the LORD.

סְבִיב֥וֹת מִזְבְּחוֹתֵיכֶ֖ם׃ 6 בְּכֹל֙ מוֹשְׁבֽוֹתֵיכֶ֔ם הֶעָרִ֣ים תֶּחֱרַ֔בְנָה וְהַבָּמ֖וֹת תִּישָׁ֑מְנָה לְמַ֩עַן֩ יֶחֶרְב֨וּ וְיֶאְשְׁמ֜וּ מִזְבְּחֽוֹתֵיכֶ֗ם וְנִשְׁבְּר֤וּ וְנִשְׁבְּתוּ֙ גִּלּ֣וּלֵיכֶ֔ם וְנִגְדְּעוּ֙ חַמָּ֣נֵיכֶ֔ם וְנִמְח֖וּ מַעֲשֵׂיכֶֽם׃ 7 וְנָפַ֥ל חָלָ֖ל בְּתֽוֹכְכֶ֑ם וִֽידַעְתֶּ֖ם כִּֽי־אֲנִ֥י יְהֹוָֽה׃ 8 וְהוֹתַרְתִּ֗י בִּהְי֥וֹת לָכֶ֛ם פְּלִ֥יטֵי חֶ֖רֶב בַּגּוֹיִ֑ם בְּהִזָּרֽוֹתֵיכֶ֖ם בָּאֲרָצֽוֹת׃ 9 וְזָכְר֣וּ פְלִֽיטֵיכֶ֗ם אוֹתִי֙ בַּגּוֹיִם֙ אֲשֶׁ֣ר נִשְׁבּוּ־ שָׁ֔ם אֲשֶׁ֣ר נִשְׁבַּ֗רְתִּי אֶת־לִבָּ֤ם הַזּוֹנֶה֙ אֲשֶׁר־ סָ֣ר מֵֽעָלַ֔י וְאֵת֙ עֵ֣ינֵיהֶ֔ם הַזֹּנ֖וֹת אַחֲרֵ֣י גִלּֽוּלֵיהֶ֑ם וְנָקֹ֙טוּ֙ בִּפְנֵיהֶ֔ם אֶל־הָֽרָעוֹת֙ אֲשֶׁ֣ר עָשׂ֔וּ לְכֹ֖ל תּוֹעֲבֹֽתֵיהֶֽם׃ 10 וְיָדְע֖וּ כִּֽי־אֲנִ֣י יְהֹוָ֑ה לֹ֤א אֶל־חִנָּם֙ דִּבַּ֔רְתִּי לַעֲשׂ֥וֹת לָהֶ֖ם הָרָעָ֥ה הַזֹּֽאת׃ פ

11 כֹּֽה־אָמַ֞ר אֲדֹנָ֣י יְהֹוִ֗ה הַכֵּ֤ה בְכַפְּךָ֙ וּרְקַ֣ע בְּרַגְלְךָ֔ וֶֽאֱמָר־אָ֕ח אֶ֥ל כָּל־תּוֹעֲב֖וֹת רָע֣וֹת בֵּ֣ית יִשְׂרָאֵ֑ל אֲשֶׁ֗ר בַּחֶ֛רֶב בָּרָעָ֥ב וּבַדֶּ֖בֶר יִפֹּֽלוּ׃ 12 הָרָח֞וֹק בַּדֶּ֣בֶר יָמ֗וּת וְהַקָּרוֹב֙ בַּחֶ֣רֶב יִפּ֔וֹל וְהַנִּשְׁאָר֙ וְהַנָּצ֔וּר בָּרָעָ֣ב יָמ֑וּת וְכִלֵּיתִ֥י חֲמָתִ֖י בָּֽם׃ 13 וִֽידַעְתֶּם֙ כִּֽי־אֲנִ֣י יְהֹוָ֔ה בִּֽהְי֣וֹת חַלְלֵיהֶ֗ם בְּתוֹךְ֙ גִּלּ֣וּלֵיהֶ֔ם סְבִיב֖וֹת מִזְבְּחֽוֹתֵיהֶ֑ם אֶל֩ כָּל־גִּבְעָ֨ה רָמָ֜ה בְּכֹ֣ל ׀ רָאשֵׁ֣י הֶהָרִ֗ים וְתַ֨חַת כָּל־עֵ֤ץ רַֽעֲנָן֙ וְתַ֙חַת֙ כָּל־אֵלָ֣ה עֲבֻתָּ֔ה מְק֗וֹם אֲשֶׁ֤ר נָֽתְנוּ־שָׁם֙ רֵ֣יחַ נִיחֹ֔חַ לְכֹ֖ל גִּלּֽוּלֵיהֶֽם׃ 14 וְנָטִ֤יתִי אֶת־יָדִי֙ עֲלֵיהֶ֔ם וְנָתַתִּ֣י אֶת־ הָאָ֗רֶץ שְׁמָמָ֤ה וּמְשַׁמָּה֙ מִמִּדְבַּ֣ר דִּבְלָ֔תָה בְּכֹ֖ל מוֹשְׁבֽוֹתֵיהֶ֑ם וְיָדְע֖וּ כִּֽי־אֲנִ֥י יְהֹוָֽה׃ פ

---

a-a   Targum and other ancient versions read "shall be devastated."
b-b   Emendation yields "how I broke."
c   A few Heb. mss. read "Riblah"; cf. 2 Kings 23.33; 25.6 ff.

7 The word of the Lord came to me: ²You, O mortal, [say:] Thus said the Lord God to the land of Israel: Doom! Doom is coming upon the four corners of the land. ³Now doom is upon you! I will let loose My anger against you and judge you according to your ways; I will requite you for all your abominations. ⁴I will show you no pity and no compassion; but I will requite you for your ways and for the abominations in your midst. And you shall know that I am the Lord.

⁵Thus said the Lord God: *ᵃ-A singular disaster; a disaster-ᵃ* is coming. ⁶Doom is coming! The hour of doom is coming! It stirs against you; there it comes! ⁷*ᵇ-The cycle has come around for you, O inhabitants of the land; the time has come; the day is near. There is panic on the mountains, not joy.-ᵇ* ⁸Very soon I will pour out My wrath upon you and spend My anger on you; I will judge you according to your ways, and I will requite you for all your abominations. ⁹I will show you no pity and no compassion; but I will requite you for your ways, and for the abominations in your midst. And you shall know it was I the Lord who punished.

¹⁰Here is the day! See, the *ᵇ-*cycle has come round; it has appeared. The rod has blossomed; arrogance has budded, ¹¹lawlessness has grown into a rod of wickedness. Nothing comes of them, nor of their abundance, nor of their wealth; nor is there preeminence among them.*-ᵇ* ¹²The time has come, the day has arrived. Let not the buyer rejoice nor the seller mourn—for divine wrath shall overtake all her multitude. ¹³For the seller shall not return to what he sold so long as they remain among the living. For the vision concerns all her multitude, it shall not be revoked. And because of his guilt, no man shall hold fast to his life.

ז

² וַיְהִ֥י דְבַר־יְהֹוָ֖ה אֵלַ֥י לֵאמֹֽר׃ וְאַתָּ֣ה בֶן־אָדָ֗ם כֹּה־אָמַ֞ר אֲדֹנָ֤י יְהֹוִה֙ לְאַדְמַ֣ת יִשְׂרָאֵ֔ל קֵ֖ץ בָּ֣א הַקֵּ֑ץ עַל־אַרְבַּ֖עת כַּנְפ֥וֹת הָאָֽרֶץ׃ ³ עַתָּה֙ הַקֵּ֣ץ עָלַ֔יִךְ וְשִׁלַּחְתִּ֤י אַפִּי֙ בָּ֔ךְ וּשְׁפַטְתִּ֖יךְ כִּדְרָכָ֑יִךְ וְנָתַתִּ֣י עָלַ֔יִךְ אֵ֖ת כׇּל־תּוֹעֲבֹתָֽיִךְ׃ ⁴ וְלֹא־תָח֤וֹס עֵינִי֙ עָלַ֔יִךְ וְלֹ֖א אֶחְמ֑וֹל כִּ֣י דְרָכַ֜יִךְ עָלַ֣יִךְ אֶתֵּ֗ן וְתוֹעֲבוֹתַ֙יִךְ֙ בְּתוֹכֵ֣ךְ תִּֽהְיֶ֔יןָ וִידַעְתֶּ֖ם כִּֽי־אֲנִ֥י יְהֹוָֽה׃ פ

⁵ כֹּ֥ה אָמַ֖ר אֲדֹנָ֣י יְהֹוִ֑ה רָעָ֛ה אַחַ֥ת רָעָ֖ה הִנֵּ֥ה בָאָֽה׃ ⁶ קֵ֣ץ בָּ֔א בָּ֥א הַקֵּ֖ץ הֵקִ֣יץ אֵלָ֑יִךְ הִנֵּ֖ה בָּאָֽה׃ ⁷ בָּ֧אָה הַצְּפִירָ֛ה אֵלֶ֖יךָ יוֹשֵׁ֣ב הָאָ֑רֶץ בָּ֣א הָעֵ֗ת קָר֛וֹב הַיּ֥וֹם מְהוּמָ֖ה וְלֹא־הֵ֥ד הָרִֽים׃ ⁸ עַתָּ֣ה מִקָּר֗וֹב אֶשְׁפּ֤וֹךְ חֲמָתִי֙ עָלַ֔יִךְ וְכִלֵּיתִ֤י אַפִּי֙ בָּ֔ךְ וּשְׁפַטְתִּ֖יךְ כִּדְרָכָ֑יִךְ וְנָתַתִּ֣י עָלַ֔יִךְ אֵ֖ת כׇּל־תּוֹעֲבוֹתָֽיִךְ׃ ⁹ וְלֹא־תָח֥וֹס עֵינִ֖י וְלֹ֣א אֶחְמ֑וֹל כִּדְרָכַ֜יִךְ עָלַ֣יִךְ אֶתֵּ֗ן וְתוֹעֲבוֹתַ֙יִךְ֙ בְּתוֹכֵ֣ךְ תִּֽהְיֶ֔יןָ וִידַעְתֶּ֕ם כִּ֛י אֲנִ֥י יְהֹוָ֖ה מַכֶּֽה׃

¹⁰ הִנֵּ֥ה הַיּ֖וֹם הִנֵּ֣ה בָאָ֑ה יָֽצְאָה֙ הַצְּפִרָ֔ה צָ֚ץ הַמַּטֶּ֔ה פָּרַ֖ח הַזָּדֽוֹן׃ ¹¹ הֶחָמָ֣ס ׀ קָ֠ם לְמַטֵּה־רֶ֔שַׁע לֹא־מֵהֶ֥ם וְלֹ֛א מֵהֲמוֹנָ֖ם וְלֹ֣א מֶהֱמֵהֶ֑ם וְלֹא־נֹ֖הַּ בָּהֶֽם׃ ¹² בָּ֤א הָעֵת֙ הִגִּ֣יעַ הַיּ֔וֹם הַקּוֹנֶה֙ אַל־יִשְׂמָ֔ח וְהַמּוֹכֵ֖ר אַל־יִתְאַבָּ֑ל כִּ֥י חָר֖וֹן אֶל־כׇּל־הֲמוֹנָֽהּ׃ ¹³ כִּ֣י הַמּוֹכֵ֗ר אֶל־הַמִּמְכָּר֙ לֹ֣א יָשׁ֔וּב וְע֥וֹד בַּחַיִּ֖ים חַיָּתָ֑ם כִּֽי־חָז֤וֹן אֶל־כׇּל־הֲמוֹנָהּ֙ לֹ֣א יָשׁ֔וּב וְאִ֧ישׁ בַּעֲוֺנ֛וֹ חַיָּת֖וֹ לֹ֥א יִתְחַזָּֽקוּ׃

14They have sounded the horn, and all is prepared; but no one goes to battle, for My wrath is directed against all her multitude. 15The sword is outside and pestilence and famine are inside; he who is in the open shall die by the sword, he who is in the town shall be devoured by famine and pestilence. 16And if any survive, they shall take to the mountains; they shall be c-like doves of the valley, moaning together-c— every one for his iniquity. 17All hands shall grow weak, and all knees shall turn to water. 18They shall gird on sackcloth, and horror shall cover them; every face shall betray shame, and every head shall be made bald.

19They shall throw their silver into the streets, and their gold shall be treated as something unclean. Their silver and gold shall not avail to save them in the day of the LORD's wrath—to satisfy their hunger or to fill their stomachs. Because they made them stumble into guilt—20for out of their beautiful adornments, in which they took pride, they made their images and their detestable abominations—therefore I will make themd an unclean thing to them. 21I will give them as spoil to strangers, and as plunder to the wicked of the earth; and they shall defile them. 22I will turn My face from them, and My treasures shall be defiled; ruffians shall invade it and defile it.

23b-Forge the chain,-b for the land is full of bloody crimes, and the city is full of lawlessness. 24I will bring in the worst of the nations to take possession of their houses; so shall I turn to naught the pride of the powerful, and their sanctuaries shall be defiled.

25Horrorb comes, and they shall seek safety, but there shall be none. 26Calamity shall follow calamity, and rumor follow rumor. Then they shall seek vision from the prophet in vain; instruction shall perish from the priest, and coun-

14 תָּקְע֤וּ בַתָּק֙וֹעַ֙ וְהָכִ֣ין הַכֹּ֔ל וְאֵ֥ין הֹלֵ֖ךְ לַמִּלְחָמָ֑ה כִּ֥י חֲרוֹנִ֖י אֶל־כָּל־הֲמוֹנָֽהּ׃ 15 הַחֶ֣רֶב בַּח֔וּץ וְהַדֶּ֥בֶר וְהָרָעָ֖ב מִבָּ֑יִת אֲשֶׁ֤ר בַּשָּׂדֶה֙ בַּחֶ֣רֶב יָמ֔וּת וַאֲשֶׁ֣ר בָּעִ֔יר רָעָ֥ב וָדֶ֖בֶר יֹאכְלֶֽנּוּ׃ 16 וּפָֽלְטוּ֙ פְּלִ֣יטֵיהֶ֔ם וְהָי֣וּ אֶל־הֶהָרִ֗ים כְּיוֹנֵ֧י הַגֵּאָי֛וֹת כֻּלָּ֖ם הֹמ֑וֹת אִ֖ישׁ בַּעֲוֺנֽוֹ׃ 17 כָּל־הַיָּדַ֖יִם תִּרְפֶּ֑ינָה וְכָל־בִּרְכַּ֖יִם תֵּלַ֥כְנָה מָּֽיִם׃ 18 וְחָגְר֣וּ שַׂקִּ֔ים וְכִסְּתָ֥ה אוֹתָ֖ם פַּלָּצ֑וּת וְאֶ֤ל כָּל־פָּנִים֙ בּוּשָׁ֔ה וּבְכָל־רָאשֵׁיהֶ֖ם קָרְחָֽה׃ 19 כַּסְפָּ֞ם בַּחוּצ֣וֹת יַשְׁלִ֗יכוּ וּזְהָבָם֮ לְנִדָּ֣ה יִֽהְיֶה֒ כַּסְפָּ֧ם וּזְהָבָ֛ם לֹֽא־יוּכַ֥ל לְהַצִּילָ֖ם בְּי֣וֹם עֶבְרַ֣ת יְהֹוָ֑ה נַפְשָׁם֙ לֹ֣א יְשַׂבֵּ֔עוּ וּמֵעֵיהֶ֖ם לֹ֣א יְמַלֵּ֑אוּ כִּֽי־מִכְשׁ֥וֹל עֲוֺנָ֖ם הָיָֽה׃ 20 וּצְבִ֤י עֶדְיוֹ֙ לְגָא֣וֹן שָׂמָ֔הוּ וְצַלְמֵ֧י תוֹעֲבֹתָ֛ם שִׁקּוּצֵיהֶ֖ם עָ֣שׂוּ ב֑וֹ עַל־כֵּ֛ן נְתַתִּ֥יו לָהֶ֖ם לְנִדָּֽה׃ 21 וּנְתַתִּ֤יו בְּיַד־הַזָּרִים֙ לָבַ֔ז וּלְרִשְׁעֵ֥י הָאָ֖רֶץ לְשָׁלָ֑ל וְחִלְּלֽוּהוּ׃ 22 וַהֲסִבּוֹתִ֤י פָנַי֙ מֵהֶ֔ם וְחִלְּל֖וּ אֶת־צְפוּנִ֑י וּבָאוּ־בָ֥הּ פָּרִיצִ֖ים וְחִלְּלֽוּהָ׃ פ 23 עֲשֵׂ֖ה הָֽרַתּ֑וֹק כִּ֣י הָאָ֗רֶץ מָֽלְאָה֙ מִשְׁפַּ֣ט דָּמִ֔ים וְהָעִ֖יר מָלְאָ֥ה חָמָֽס׃ 24 וְהֵֽבֵאתִי֙ רָעֵ֣י גוֹיִ֔ם וְיָרְשׁ֖וּ אֶת־בָּֽתֵּיהֶ֑ם וְהִשְׁבַּתִּי֙ גְּא֣וֹן עַזִּ֔ים וְנִחֲל֖וּ מְקַֽדְשֵׁיהֶֽם׃ 25 קְפָ֣דָה־בָ֑א* וּבִקְשׁ֥וּ שָׁל֖וֹם וָאָֽיִן׃ 26 הֹוָ֤ה עַל־הֹוָה֙ תָּב֔וֹא וּשְׁמֻעָ֖ה אֶל־שְׁמוּעָ֣ה תִֽהְיֶ֑ה וּבִקְשׁ֤וּ חָזוֹן֙ מִנָּבִ֔יא וְתוֹרָ֖ה תֹּאבַ֥ד

c-c Emendation yields "like moaning doves. All of them shall perish."
d I.e., their adornments.

sel from the elders. ²⁷The king shall mourn, the prince shall clothe himself with desolation, and the hands of the people of the land shall tremble. I will treat them in accordance with their own ways and judge them according to their deserts. And they shall know that I am the LORD.

8 In the sixth year, on the fifth day of the sixth month, I was sitting at home, and the elders of Judah were sitting before me, and there the hand of the Lord GOD fell upon me. ²As I looked, there was a figure that had the appearance of fire:*a* from what appeared as his loins down, [he was] fire; and from his loins up, his appearance was resplendent and had the color of amber. ³He stretched out the form of a hand, and took me by the hair of my head. A spirit lifted me up between heaven and earth and brought me in visions of God to Jerusalem, to the entrance of the Penimith*b* Gate that faces north; that was the site of the infuriating image that provokes fury. ⁴And the Presence of the God of Israel appeared there, like the vision that I had seen in the valley.*c*

⁵And He said to me, "O mortal, turn your eyes northward." I turned my eyes northward, and there, *d*-north of the gate of the altar, was-*d* that infuriating image on the approach.*b* ⁶And He said to me, "Mortal, do you see what they are doing, the terrible abominations that the House of Israel is practicing here, *e*-to drive Me far-*e* from My Sanctuary? You shall yet see even greater abominations!"

⁷Then He brought me to the entrance of the court;*f* and I looked, and there was a hole in the wall. ⁸He said to me, "Mortal, break through the wall"; so I broke through the wall and found

---

מִכֹּהֵן וְעֵצָה מִזְּקֵנִים׃ 27 הַמֶּלֶךְ יִתְאַבָּל וְנָשִׂיא יִלְבַּשׁ שְׁמָמָה וִידֵי עַם־הָאָרֶץ תִּבָּהַלְנָה מִדַּרְכָּם אֶעֱשֶׂה אוֹתָם וּבְמִשְׁפְּטֵיהֶם אֶשְׁפְּטֵם וְיָדְעוּ כִּי־אֲנִי יְהוָה׃ פ

ח וַיְהִי ׀ בַּשָּׁנָה הַשִּׁשִּׁית בַּשִּׁשִּׁי בַּחֲמִשָּׁה לַחֹדֶשׁ אֲנִי יוֹשֵׁב בְּבֵיתִי וְזִקְנֵי יְהוּדָה יוֹשְׁבִים לְפָנָי וַתִּפֹּל עָלַי שָׁם יַד אֲדֹנָי יְהוִה׃ 2 וָאֶרְאֶה וְהִנֵּה דְּמוּת כְּמַרְאֵה־אֵשׁ מִמַּרְאֵה מָתְנָיו וּלְמַטָּה אֵשׁ וּמִמָּתְנָיו וּלְמַעְלָה כְּמַרְאֵה־זֹהַר כְּעֵין הַחַשְׁמַלָה׃ 3 וַיִּשְׁלַח תַּבְנִית יָד וַיִּקָּחֵנִי בְּצִיצִת רֹאשִׁי וַתִּשָּׂא אֹתִי רוּחַ ׀ בֵּין־ הָאָרֶץ וּבֵין הַשָּׁמַיִם וַתָּבֵא אֹתִי יְרוּשָׁלְַמָה בְּמַרְאוֹת אֱלֹהִים אֶל־פֶּתַח שַׁעַר הַפְּנִימִית הַפּוֹנֶה צָפוֹנָה אֲשֶׁר־שָׁם מוֹשַׁב סֵמֶל הַקִּנְאָה הַמַּקְנֶה׃ 4 וְהִנֵּה־שָׁם כְּבוֹד אֱלֹהֵי יִשְׂרָאֵל כַּמַּרְאֶה אֲשֶׁר רָאִיתִי בַּבִּקְעָה׃

5 וַיֹּאמֶר אֵלַי בֶּן־אָדָם שָׂא־נָא עֵינֶיךָ דֶּרֶךְ צָפוֹנָה וָאֶשָּׂא עֵינַי דֶּרֶךְ צָפוֹנָה וְהִנֵּה מִצָּפוֹן לְשַׁעַר הַמִּזְבֵּחַ סֵמֶל הַקִּנְאָה הַזֶּה בַּבִּאָה׃ 6 וַיֹּאמֶר אֵלַי בֶּן־אָדָם הֲרֹאֶה אַתָּה מהם מָה הֵם עֹשִׂים תּוֹעֵבוֹת גְּדֹלוֹת אֲשֶׁר בֵּית־יִשְׂרָאֵל ׀ עֹשִׂים פֹּה לְרָחֳקָה מֵעַל מִקְדָּשִׁי וְעוֹד תָּשׁוּב תִּרְאֶה תּוֹעֵבוֹת גְּדֹלוֹת׃ ס 7 וַיָּבֵא אֹתִי אֶל־פֶּתַח הֶחָצֵר וָאֶרְאֶה וְהִנֵּה חֹר־אֶחָד בַּקִּיר׃ 8 וַיֹּאמֶר אֵלַי בֶּן־ אָדָם חֲתָר־נָא בַקִּיר וָאֶחְתֹּר בַּקִּיר וְהִנֵּה

---

a   *Septuagint "a man."*
b   *Meaning of Heb. uncertain.*
c   *See chap. 1 and 3.22–23.*
d-d *Meaning of Heb. uncertain; emendation yields "north of the gate was the altar of."*
e-e *Or "at a distance."*
f   *I.e., the outer court of the Temple.*

an entrance. 9And He said to me, "Enter and see the vile abominations that they are practicing here." 10I entered and looked, and there all detestable forms of creeping things and beasts and all the fetishes of the House of Israel were depicted over the entire wall. 11Before them stood seventy men, elders of the House of Israel, with Jaazaniah son of Shaphan standing in their midst. Everyone had a censer in his hand, and a thick cloud of incense smoke ascended. 12Again He spoke to me, "O mortal, have you seen what the elders of the House of Israel are doing in the darkness, everyone in his image-covered chamber? For they say, 'The LORD does not see us; the LORD has abandoned the country.'" 13And He said to me, "You shall see even more terrible abominations which they practice."

14Next He brought me to the entrance of the north *g*-gate of the House of the LORD;-*g* and there sat the women bewailing Tammuz.*h* 15He said to me, "Have you seen, O mortal? You shall see even more terrible abominations than these."

16Then He brought me into the inner court of the House of the LORD, and there, at the entrance to the Temple of the LORD, between the portico and the altar, were about twenty-five men, their backs to the Temple of the LORD and their faces to the east; they were bowing low to the sun in the east. 17And He said to me, "Do you see, O mortal? Is it not enough for the House of Judah to practice the abominations that they have committed here, that they must fill the country with lawlessness and provoke Me still further and *i*-thrust the branch to their nostrils?-*i* 18I in turn will act with fury, I will show no pity or compassion; though they cry aloud to Me, I will not listen to them."

---

g-g *I.e., the gate of the inner court.*
h   *A Babylonian god.*
i-i *Apparently meaning "goad Me to fury"; "their" is a euphemism for "My."*

פֶּתַח אֶחָֽד׃ 9 וַיֹּ֣אמֶר אֵלַ֔י בֹּ֣א וּרְאֵ֔ה אֶת־הַתּוֹעֵב֥וֹת הָרָע֖וֹת אֲשֶׁ֣ר הֵ֣ם עֹשִׂ֣ים פֹּֽה׃ 10 וָֽאָבוֹא֮ וָֽאֶרְאֶה֒ וְהִנֵּ֨ה כׇל־תַּבְנִ֜ית רֶ֤מֶשׂ וּבְהֵמָה֙ שֶׁ֔קֶץ וְכׇל־גִּלּוּלֵ֖י בֵּ֣ית יִשְׂרָאֵ֑ל מְחֻקֶּ֥ה עַל־הַקִּ֖יר סָבִ֥יב ׀ סָבִֽיב׃ 11 וְשִׁבְעִ֣ים אִ֣ישׁ מִזִּקְנֵ֣י בֵֽית־יִשְׂרָאֵ֗ל וְיַֽאֲזַנְיָ֨הוּ בֶן־שָׁפָ֜ן עֹמֵ֣ד בְּתוֹכָם֮ עֹמְדִ֣ים לִפְנֵיהֶם֒ וְאִ֗ישׁ מִקְטַרְתּ֤וֹ בְיָדוֹ֙ וַעֲתַ֥ר עֲנַֽן־הַקְּטֹ֖רֶת עֹלֶֽה׃ 12 וַיֹּ֣אמֶר אֵלַי֮ הֲרָאִ֣יתָ בֶן־אָדָם֒ אֲשֶׁ֨ר זִקְנֵ֣י בֵֽית־יִשְׂרָאֵל֮ עֹשִׂ֣ים בַּחֹ֒שֶׁךְ֒ אִ֚ישׁ בְּחַדְרֵ֣י מַשְׂכִּית֔וֹ כִּ֣י אֹמְרִ֔ים אֵ֤ין יְהֹוָה֙ רֹאֶ֣ה אֹתָ֔נוּ עָזַ֥ב יְהֹוָ֖ה אֶת־הָאָֽרֶץ׃ 13 וַיֹּ֖אמֶר אֵלָ֑י ע֣וֹד תָּשׁ֣וּב תִּרְאֶ֔ה תּוֹעֵב֥וֹת גְּדֹל֖וֹת אֲשֶׁר־הֵ֥מָּה עֹשִֽׂים׃ 14 וַיָּבֵ֣א אֹתִ֗י אֶל־פֶּ֙תַח֙ שַׁ֣עַר בֵּית־יְהֹוָ֔ה אֲשֶׁ֖ר אֶל־הַצָּפ֑וֹנָה וְהִנֵּה־שָׁם֙ הַנָּשִׁ֣ים יֹשְׁב֔וֹת מְבַכּ֖וֹת אֶת־הַתַּמּֽוּז׃ ס 15 וַיֹּ֥אמֶר אֵלַ֖י הֲרָאִ֣יתָ בֶן־אָדָ֑ם ע֣וֹד תָּשׁ֥וּב תִּרְאֶ֛ה תּוֹעֵב֥וֹת גְּדֹל֖וֹת מֵאֵֽלֶּה׃ 16 וַיָּבֵ֣א אֹתִ֗י אֶל־חֲצַ֣ר בֵּית־יְהֹוָה֮ הַפְּנִימִית֒ וְהִנֵּה־פֶ֜תַח הֵיכַ֣ל יְהֹוָ֗ה בֵּ֤ין הָֽאוּלָם֙ וּבֵ֣ין הַמִּזְבֵּ֔חַ כְּעֶשְׂרִ֥ים וַחֲמִשָּׁ֖ה אִ֑ישׁ אֲחֹרֵיהֶ֞ם אֶל־הֵיכַ֤ל יְהֹוָה֙ וּפְנֵיהֶ֣ם קֵ֔דְמָה וְהֵ֛מָּה מִשְׁתַּחֲוִיתֶ֥ם קֵ֖דְמָה לַשָּֽׁמֶשׁ׃ 17 וַיֹּ֣אמֶר אֵלַי֮ הֲרָאִ֣יתָ בֶן־אָדָם֒ הֲנָקֵל֙ לְבֵ֣ית יְהוּדָ֔ה מֵעֲשׂ֕וֹת אֶת־הַתּוֹעֵב֖וֹת אֲשֶׁ֣ר עָֽשׂוּ־פֹ֑ה כִּי־מָלְא֨וּ אֶת־הָאָ֜רֶץ חָמָ֗ס וַיָּשֻׁ֙בוּ֙ לְהַכְעִיסֵ֔נִי וְהִנָּ֛ם שֹׁלְחִ֥ים אֶת־הַזְּמוֹרָ֖ה אֶל־אַפָּֽם׃ 18 וְגַם־אֲנִי֙ אֶעֱשֶׂ֣ה בְחֵמָ֔ה לֹֽא־תָח֥וֹס עֵינִ֖י וְלֹ֣א אֶחְמֹ֑ל וְקָרְא֤וּ בְאׇזְנַי֙ ק֣וֹל גָּד֔וֹל וְלֹ֥א אֶשְׁמַ֖ע אוֹתָֽם׃

9 Then He called loudly in my hearing, saying, "Approach, you men in charge of the city, each bearing his weapons of destruction!" [2]And six men entered by way of the upper gate that faces north, each with his club in his hand; and among them was another, clothed in linen, with a writing case at his waist. They came forward and stopped at the bronze altar. [3]Now the Presence of the God of Israel had moved from the cherub on which it had rested to the platform[a] of the House. He called to the man clothed in linen with the writing case at his waist; [4]and the LORD said to him, "Pass through the city, through Jerusalem, and put a mark on the foreheads of the men who moan and groan because of all the abominations that are committed in it." [5]To the others He said in my hearing, "Follow him through the city and strike; show no pity or compassion. [6]Kill off graybeard, youth and maiden, women and children; but do not touch any person who bears the mark. Begin here at My Sanctuary." So they began with the elders who were in front of the House. [7]And He said to them, "Defile the House and fill the courts with the slain. Then go forth." So they went forth and began to kill in the city. [8]When they were out killing, and I remained alone, I flung myself on my face and cried out, "Ah, Lord GOD! Are you going to annihilate all that is left of Israel, pouring out Your fury upon Jerusalem?" [9]He answered me, "The iniquity of the Houses of Judah and Israel is very very great, the land is full of crime and the city is full of corruption. For they say, 'The LORD has forsaken the land, and the LORD does not see.' [10]I, in turn, will show no pity or compassion; I will give them their deserts." [11]And then the man clothed in linen with the writing case at his waist brought back word, saying, "I have done as You commanded me."

ט וַיִּקְרָ֣א בְאָזְנַ֗י ק֤וֹל גָּדוֹל֙ לֵאמֹ֔ר קָרְב֖וּ פְּקֻדּ֣וֹת הָעִ֑יר וְאִ֛ישׁ כְּלִ֥י מַשְׁחֵת֖וֹ בְּיָדֽוֹ׃ [2]וְהִנֵּ֣ה שִׁשָּׁ֣ה אֲנָשִׁ֡ים בָּאִ֣ים ׀ מִדֶּרֶךְ־שַׁ֩עַר֩ הָעֶלְי֨וֹן אֲשֶׁ֤ר ׀ מׇפְנֶ֣ה צָפ֔וֹנָה וְאִ֨ישׁ כְּלִ֤י מַפָּצוֹ֙ בְּיָד֔וֹ וְאִישׁ־אֶחָ֤ד בְּתוֹכָם֙ לָבֻ֣שׁ בַּדִּ֔ים וְקֶ֥סֶת הַסֹּפֵ֖ר בְּמׇתְנָ֑יו וַיָּבֹ֙אוּ֙ וַיַּ֣עַמְד֔וּ אֵ֖צֶל מִזְבַּ֥ח הַנְּחֹֽשֶׁת׃ [3]וּכְב֣וֹד ׀ אֱלֹהֵ֣י יִשְׂרָאֵ֗ל נַעֲלָה֙ מֵעַ֤ל הַכְּרוּב֙ אֲשֶׁ֣ר הָיָ֣ה עָלָ֔יו אֶ֖ל מִפְתַּ֣ן הַבָּ֑יִת וַיִּקְרָ֗א אֶל־הָאִישׁ֙ הַלָּבֻ֣שׁ הַבַּדִּ֔ים אֲשֶׁ֛ר קֶ֥סֶת הַסֹּפֵ֖ר בְּמׇתְנָֽיו׃ [4]וַיֹּ֤אמֶר יְהֹוָה֙ אֵלָ֔ו עֲבֹר֙ בְּת֣וֹךְ הָעִ֔יר בְּת֖וֹךְ יְרוּשָׁלָ֑͏ִם וְהִתְוִ֨יתָ תָּ֜ו עַל־מִצְח֣וֹת הָאֲנָשִׁ֗ים הַנֶּֽאֱנָחִים֙ וְהַנֶּ֣אֱנָקִ֔ים עַ֚ל כׇּל־הַתּ֣וֹעֵב֔וֹת הַֽנַּעֲשׂ֖וֹת בְּתוֹכָֽהּ׃ [5]וּלְאֵ֜לֶּה אָמַ֤ר בְּאׇזְנַי֙ עִבְר֤וּ בָעִיר֙ אַחֲרָ֔יו וְהַכּ֖וּ עַל־[תָּחֹ֥ס] אַל־תָּחֹ֥ס עיניכם [עֵינְכֶ֖ם] וְאַל־תַּחְמֹֽלוּ׃ [6]זָקֵ֡ן בָּח֣וּר וּבְתוּלָה֩ וְטַ֨ף וְנָשִׁ֜ים תַּהַרְג֣וּ לְמַשְׁחִ֗ית וְעַֽל־כׇּל־אִ֨ישׁ אֲשֶׁר־עָלָ֤יו הַתָּו֙ אַל־תִּגַּ֔שׁוּ וּמִמִּקְדָּשִׁ֖י תָּחֵ֑לּוּ וַיָּחֵ֙לּוּ֙ בָּאֲנָשִׁ֣ים הַזְּקֵנִ֔ים אֲשֶׁ֖ר לִפְנֵ֥י הַבָּֽיִת׃ [7]וַיֹּ֨אמֶר אֲלֵיהֶ֜ם טַמְּא֣וּ אֶת־הַבַּ֗יִת וּמַלְא֧וּ אֶת־הַחֲצֵר֛וֹת חֲלָלִ֖ים צֵ֑אוּ וְיָצְא֖וּ וְהִכּ֥וּ בָעִֽיר׃ [8]וַֽיְהִי֙ כְּהַכּוֹתָ֔ם וְנֵֽאשֲׁאַ֣ר* אָ֔נִי וָאֶפְּלָ֥ה עַל־פָּנַ֖י וָאֶזְעַ֑ק וָאֹמַ֗ר אֲהָהּ֙ אֲדֹנָ֣י יֱהֹוִ֔ה הֲמַשְׁחִ֣ית אַתָּ֗ה אֵ֚ת כׇּל־שְׁאֵרִ֣ית יִשְׂרָאֵ֔ל בְּשׇׁפְכְּךָ֥ אֶת־חֲמָתְךָ֖ עַל־יְרוּשָׁלָֽ͏ִם׃ [9]וַיֹּ֣אמֶר אֵלַ֗י עֲוֺ֨ן בֵּֽית־יִשְׂרָאֵ֤ל וִֽיהוּדָה֙ גָּדוֹל֙ בִּמְאֹ֣ד מְאֹ֔ד וַתִּמָּלֵ֤א הָאָ֙רֶץ֙ דָּמִ֔ים וְהָעִ֖יר מָלְאָ֣ה מֻטֶּ֑ה כִּ֣י אָמְר֗וּ עָזַ֤ב יְהֹוָה֙ אֶת־הָאָ֔רֶץ וְאֵ֥ין יְהֹוָ֖ה רֹאֶֽה׃ [10]וְגַ֙ם־אֲנִ֔י לֹא־תָח֥וֹס עֵינִ֖י וְלֹ֣א אֶחְמֹ֑ל דַּרְכָּ֖ם בְּרֹאשָׁ֥ם נָתָֽתִּי׃ [11]וְהִנֵּ֞ה הָאִ֣ישׁ ׀ לְבֻ֣שׁ הַבַּדִּ֗ים אֲשֶׁ֤ר הַקֶּ֙סֶת֙ בְּמׇתְנָ֔יו מֵשִׁ֥יב דָּבָ֖ר לֵאמֹ֑ר עָשִׂ֕יתִי כאשר [כְּכֹ֖ל] אֲשֶׁ֥ר צִוִּיתָֽנִי׃ ס

---

a   *The raised platform on which the Temple stood; cf. 47.1.*

10

I looked, and on the expanse over the heads of the cherubs, there was something like a sapphire stone; an appearance resembling a throne could be seen over them. ²He spoke to the man clothed in linen and said, "Step inside the wheelwork, under the cherubs, and fill your hands with glowing coals from among the cherubs, and scatter them over the city." And he went in as I looked on. ³Now the cherubs were standing on the south side of the House when the man entered, and the cloud filled the inner court. ⁴But when the Presence of the LORD moved from the cherubs to the platform^a of the House, the House was filled with the cloud, and the court was filled with the radiance of the Presence of the LORD. ⁵The sound of the cherubs' wings could be heard as far as the outer court, like the voice of El Shaddai^b when He speaks.

⁶When He commanded the man dressed in linen: "Take fire from among the cherubs within the wheelwork," he went in and stood beside a wheel. ⁷And a cherub stretched out his hand among the cherubs to the fire that was among the cherubs; he took some and put it into the hands of him who was clothed in linen, who took it and went out. ⁸The cherubs appeared to have the form of a man's hand under their wings.

⁹I could see that there were four wheels beside the cherubs, one wheel beside each of the cherubs; as for the appearance of the wheels, they gleamed like the beryl stone. ¹⁰In appearance, the four had the same form, as if there were two wheels cutting through each other. ¹¹And when they moved, each could move in the direction of any of its four quarters; they did not veer as they moved. The [cherubs] moved in the direction in which one of the heads faced, without turning as they moved. ¹²Their entire bodies—

---

a   See note at 47.1.
b   See note at Gen. 17.1.

ל

וָאֶרְאֶ֗ה וְהִנֵּ֤ה אֶל־הָרָקִ֙יעַ֙ אֲשֶׁר֙ עַל־רֹ֣אשׁ הַכְּרֻבִ֔ים כְּאֶ֣בֶן סַפִּ֔יר כְּמַרְאֵ֖ה דְּמ֣וּת כִּסֵּ֑א נִרְאָ֖ה עֲלֵיהֶֽם׃ ²וַיֹּ֜אמֶר אֶל־הָאִ֣ישׁ ׀ לְבֻ֣שׁ הַבַּדִּ֗ים וַיֹּ֡אמֶר בֹּא֩ אֶל־בֵּינ֨וֹת לַגַּלְגַּ֜ל אֶל־תַּ֣חַת לַכְּר֗וּב וּמַלֵּ֨א חָפְנֶ֤יךָ גַֽחֲלֵי־אֵשׁ֙ מִבֵּינ֣וֹת לַכְּרֻבִ֔ים וּזְרֹ֖ק עַל־הָעִ֑יר וַיָּבֹ֖א לְעֵינָֽי׃ ³וְהַכְּרֻבִ֗ים עֹֽמְדִ֛ים מִימִ֥ין לַבַּ֖יִת בְּבֹא֣וֹ הָאִ֑ישׁ וְהֶעָנָ֣ן מָלֵ֔א אֶת־הֶחָצֵ֖ר הַפְּנִימִֽית׃ ⁴וַיָּ֤רׇם כְּבוֹד־יְהֹוָה֙ מֵעַ֣ל הַכְּר֔וּב עַ֖ל מִפְתַּ֣ן הַבָּ֑יִת וַיִּמָּלֵ֤א הַבַּ֙יִת֙ אֶת־הֶ֣עָנָ֔ן וְהֶֽחָצֵר֙ מָֽלְאָ֔ה אֶת־נֹ֖גַהּ כְּב֥וֹד יְהֹוָֽה׃ ⁵וְק֙וֹל֙ כַּנְפֵ֣י הַכְּרוּבִ֔ים נִשְׁמַ֖ע עַד־הֶחָצֵ֣ר הַחִיצֹנָ֑ה כְּק֥וֹל אֵל־שַׁדַּ֖י בְּדַבְּרֽוֹ׃ ⁶וַיְהִ֗י בְּצַוֺּתוֹ֙ אֶת־הָאִ֤ישׁ לְבֻשׁ־הַבַּדִּים֙ לֵאמֹ֔ר קַ֥ח אֵשׁ֙ מִבֵּינ֣וֹת לַגַּלְגַּ֔ל מִבֵּינ֖וֹת לַכְּרוּבִ֑ים וַיָּבֹא֙ וַֽיַּעֲמֹ֔ד אֵ֖צֶל הָאוֹפָֽן׃ ⁷וַיִּשְׁלַח֩ הַכְּר֨וּב אֶת־יָד֜וֹ מִבֵּינ֣וֹת לַכְּרוּבִ֗ים אֶל־הָאֵשׁ֙ אֲשֶׁר֙ בֵּינ֣וֹת הַכְּרֻבִ֔ים וַיִּשָּׂא֙ וַיִּתֵּ֔ן אֶל־חׇפְנֵ֖י לְבֻ֣שׁ הַבַּדִּ֑ים וַיִּקַּ֖ח וַיֵּצֵֽא׃ ⁸וַיֵּרָ֛א לַכְּרֻבִ֖ים תַּבְנִ֣ית יַד־אָדָ֑ם תַּ֖חַת כַּנְפֵיהֶֽם׃ ⁹וָאֶרְאֶ֗ה וְהִנֵּ֨ה אַרְבָּעָ֤ה אֽוֹפַנִּים֙ אֵ֣צֶל הַכְּרוּבִ֔ים אוֹפַ֣ן אֶחָ֗ד אֵ֚צֶל הַכְּר֣וּב אֶחָ֔ד וְאוֹפַ֣ן אֶחָ֔ד אֵ֖צֶל הַכְּר֣וּב אֶחָ֑ד וּמַרְאֵה֙ הָא֣וֹפַנִּ֔ים כְּעֵ֖ין אֶ֥בֶן תַּרְשִֽׁישׁ׃ ¹⁰וּמַ֨רְאֵיהֶ֔ם דְּמ֥וּת אֶחָ֖ד לְאַרְבַּעְתָּ֑ם כַּאֲשֶׁ֛ר יִהְיֶ֥ה הָאוֹפַ֖ן בְּת֥וֹךְ הָאוֹפָֽן׃ ¹¹בְּלֶכְתָּ֗ם אֶל־אַרְבַּ֤עַת רִבְעֵיהֶם֙ יֵלֵ֔כוּ לֹ֥א יִסַּ֖בּוּ בְּלֶכְתָּ֑ם כִּ֣י הַמָּק֞וֹם אֲשֶׁר־יִפְנֶ֤ה הָרֹאשׁ֙ אַחֲרָ֣יו יֵלֵ֔כוּ לֹ֥א יִסַּ֖בּוּ

---

backs, hands, and wings—and the wheels, the wheels of the four of them, were covered all over with eyes. [13]It was these wheels that I had heard called "the wheelwork."[c] [14]Each one had four faces: One was a cherub's face, the second a human face, the third a lion's face, and the fourth an eagle's face.

[15]The cherubs ascended; those were the creatures that I had seen by the Chebar Canal. [16]Whenever the cherubs went, the wheels went beside them; and when the cherubs lifted their wings to ascend from the earth, the wheels did not roll away from their side. [17]When those stood still, these stood still; and when those ascended, these ascended with them, for the spirit of the creature was in them.

[18]Then the Presence of the Lord left the platform[a] of the House and stopped above the cherubs. [19]And I saw the cherubs lift their wings and rise from the earth, with the wheels beside them as they departed; and they[d] stopped at the entrance of the eastern gate of the House of the Lord, with the Presence of the God of Israel above them. [20]They were the same creatures that I had seen below the God of Israel at the Chebar Canal; so now I knew that they were cherubs.[e] [21]Each one had four faces and each had four wings, with the form of human hands under the wings. [22]As for the form of their faces, they were the very faces that I had seen by the Chebar Canal—their appearance and [f]their features[f]—and each could move in the direction of any of its faces.

11

Then a spirit lifted me up and brought me to the east gate of the House of the Lord, which faces eastward; and there, at the entrance of the gate, were twenty-five men, among whom

---

c   See v. 2.
d   Lit. "it."
e   Because they had been called "cherubs" (cf. v. 2).
f-f Lit. "themselves."

בְּלֶכְתָּם: 12 וְכָל־בְּשָׂרָם וְגַבֵּהֶם וִידֵיהֶם וְכַנְפֵיהֶם וְהָאוֹפַנִּים מְלֵאִים עֵינַיִם סָבִיב לְאַרְבַּעְתָּם אוֹפַנֵּיהֶם: 13 לָאוֹפַנִּים* לָהֶם קוֹרָא הַגַּלְגַּל בְּאָזְנָי: 14 וְאַרְבָּעָה פָנִים לְאֶחָד פְּנֵי הָאֶחָד פְּנֵי הַכְּרוּב וּפְנֵי הַשֵּׁנִי פְּנֵי אָדָם וְהַשְּׁלִישִׁי פְּנֵי אַרְיֵה וְהָרְבִיעִי פְּנֵי־נָשֶׁר:

15 וַיֵּרֹמּוּ הַכְּרוּבִים הִיא הַחַיָּה אֲשֶׁר רָאִיתִי בִּנְהַר־כְּבָר: 16 וּבְלֶכֶת הַכְּרוּבִים יֵלְכוּ הָאוֹפַנִּים אֶצְלָם וּבִשְׂאֵת הַכְּרוּבִים אֶת־כַּנְפֵיהֶם לָרוּם מֵעַל הָאָרֶץ לֹא־יִסַּבּוּ הָאוֹפַנִּים גַּם־הֵם מֵאֶצְלָם: 17 בְּעָמְדָם יַעֲמֹדוּ וּבְרוֹמָם יֵרוֹמּוּ אוֹתָם כִּי רוּחַ הַחַיָּה בָּהֶם:

18 וַיֵּצֵא כְּבוֹד יְהוָה מֵעַל מִפְתַּן הַבָּיִת וַיַּעֲמֹד עַל־הַכְּרוּבִים: 19 וַיִּשְׂאוּ הַכְּרוּבִים אֶת־כַּנְפֵיהֶם וַיֵּרוֹמּוּ מִן־הָאָרֶץ לְעֵינַי בְּצֵאתָם וְהָאוֹפַנִּים לְעֻמָּתָם וַיַּעֲמֹד פֶּתַח שַׁעַר בֵּית־יְהוָה הַקַּדְמוֹנִי וּכְבוֹד אֱלֹהֵי־יִשְׂרָאֵל עֲלֵיהֶם מִלְמָעְלָה: 20 הִיא הַחַיָּה אֲשֶׁר רָאִיתִי תַּחַת אֱלֹהֵי־יִשְׂרָאֵל בִּנְהַר־כְּבָר וָאֵדַע כִּי כְרוּבִים הֵמָּה: 21 אַרְבָּעָה אַרְבָּעָה פָנִים לְאֶחָד וְאַרְבַּע כְּנָפַיִם לְאֶחָד וּדְמוּת יְדֵי אָדָם תַּחַת כַּנְפֵיהֶם: 22 וּדְמוּת פְּנֵיהֶם הֵמָּה הַפָּנִים אֲשֶׁר רָאִיתִי עַל־נְהַר־כְּבָר מַרְאֵיהֶם וְאוֹתָם אִישׁ אֶל־עֵבֶר פָּנָיו יֵלֵכוּ:

יא 11 וַתִּשָּׂא אֹתִי רוּחַ וַתָּבֵא אֹתִי אֶל־שַׁעַר בֵּית־יְהוָה הַקַּדְמוֹנִי הַפּוֹנֶה קָדִימָה וְהִנֵּה בְּפֶתַח הַשַּׁעַר עֶשְׂרִים וַחֲמִשָּׁה אִישׁ וָאֶרְאֶה בְתוֹכָם אֶת־יַאֲזַנְיָה

I saw Jaazaniah son of Azzur and Pelatiah son of Benaiah, leaders of the people. [2][The Lord] said to me, "O mortal, these are the men who plan iniquity and plot wickedness in this city, [3]who say: 'There is no need now to build houses; this [city] is the pot, and we are the meat.'[a] [4]I adjure you, prophesy against them; prophesy, O mortal!"

[5]Thereupon the spirit of the Lord fell upon me, and He said to me, "Speak: Thus said the Lord: Such are your thoughts, O House of Israel; I know what comes into your mind. [6]Many have you slain in this city; you have filled its streets with corpses. [7]Assuredly, thus says the Lord God: The corpses that you have piled up in it are the meat for which it is the pot; but you shall be taken out of it. [8]You feared the sword, and the sword I will bring upon you—declares the Lord God. [9]I will take you out of it and deliver you into the hands of strangers, and I will execute judgments upon you. [10]You shall fall by the sword; I will punish you at the border of Israel. And you shall know that I am the Lord. [11]This [city] shall not be a pot for you, nor you the meat in it; I will punish you at the border of Israel. [12]Then you shall know that I am the Lord, whose laws you did not follow and whose rules you did not obey, acting instead according to the rules of the nations around you."

[13]Now, as I prophesied, Pelatiah son of Benaiah dropped dead. I threw myself upon my face and cried out aloud, "Ah, Lord God! You are wiping out the remnant of Israel!"

[14]Then the word of the Lord came to me: [15]"O mortal, [I will save] your brothers, your brothers, the men of your kindred,[b] all of that very House of Israel to whom the inhabitants of Jerusalem say, 'Keep far from the Lord; the land has been given as a heritage to us.' [16]Say

בֶּן־עַזֻּר וְאֶת־פְּלַטְיָהוּ בֶן־בְּנָיָהוּ שָׂרֵי הָעָם: פ 2 וַיֹּאמֶר אֵלַי בֶּן־אָדָם אֵלֶּה הָאֲנָשִׁים הַחֹשְׁבִים אָוֶן וְהַיֹּעֲצִים עֲצַת־רָע בָּעִיר הַזֹּאת: 3 הָאֹמְרִים לֹא בְקָרוֹב בְּנוֹת בָּתִּים הִיא הַסִּיר וַאֲנַחְנוּ הַבָּשָׂר: 4 לָכֵן הִנָּבֵא עֲלֵיהֶם הִנָּבֵא בֶּן־אָדָם: 5 וַתִּפֹּל עָלַי רוּחַ יְהֹוָה וַיֹּאמֶר אֵלַי אֱמֹר כֹּה־אָמַר יְהֹוָה כֵּן אֲמַרְתֶּם בֵּית יִשְׂרָאֵל וּמַעֲלוֹת רוּחֲכֶם אֲנִי יְדַעְתִּיהָ: 6 הִרְבֵּיתֶם חַלְלֵיכֶם בָּעִיר הַזֹּאת וּמִלֵּאתֶם חוּצֹתֶיהָ חָלָל: פ 7 לָכֵן כֹּה־אָמַר אֲדֹנָי יֱהֹוִה חַלְלֵיכֶם אֲשֶׁר שַׂמְתֶּם בְּתוֹכָהּ הֵמָּה הַבָּשָׂר וְהִיא הַסִּיר וְאֶתְכֶם הוֹצִיא מִתּוֹכָהּ: 8 חֶרֶב יְרֵאתֶם וְחֶרֶב אָבִיא עֲלֵיכֶם נְאֻם אֲדֹנָי יֱהֹוִה: 9 וְהוֹצֵאתִי אֶתְכֶם מִתּוֹכָהּ וְנָתַתִּי אֶתְכֶם בְּיַד־זָרִים וְעָשִׂיתִי בָכֶם שְׁפָטִים: 10 בַּחֶרֶב תִּפֹּלוּ עַל־גְּבוּל יִשְׂרָאֵל אֶשְׁפּוֹט אֶתְכֶם וִידַעְתֶּם כִּי־אֲנִי יְהֹוָה: 11 הִיא לֹא־תִהְיֶה לָכֶם לְסִיר וְאַתֶּם תִּהְיוּ בְתוֹכָהּ לְבָשָׂר אֶל־גְּבוּל יִשְׂרָאֵל אֶשְׁפֹּט אֶתְכֶם: 12 וִידַעְתֶּם כִּי־אֲנִי יְהֹוָה אֲשֶׁר בְּחֻקַּי לֹא הֲלַכְתֶּם וּמִשְׁפָּטַי לֹא עֲשִׂיתֶם וּכְמִשְׁפְּטֵי הַגּוֹיִם אֲשֶׁר סְבִיבוֹתֵיכֶם עֲשִׂיתֶם: 13 וַיְהִי כְּהִנָּבְאִי וּפְלַטְיָהוּ בֶן־בְּנָיָה מֵת וָאֶפֹּל עַל־פָּנַי וָאֶזְעַק קוֹל־גָּדוֹל וָאֹמַר אֲהָהּ אֲדֹנָי יֱהֹוִה כָּלָה אַתָּה עֹשֶׂה אֵת שְׁאֵרִית יִשְׂרָאֵל: פ 14 וַיְהִי דְבַר־יְהֹוָה אֵלַי לֵאמֹר: 15 בֶּן־אָדָם אַחֶיךָ אַחֶיךָ אַנְשֵׁי גְאֻלָּתֶךָ וְכָל־בֵּית יִשְׂרָאֵל כֻּלֹּה אֲשֶׁר אָמְרוּ לָהֶם יֹשְׁבֵי יְרוּשָׁלַ͏ִם רַחֲקוּ מֵעַל יְהֹוָה לָנוּ הִיא נִתְּנָה הָאָרֶץ לְמוֹרָשָׁה: ס 16 לָכֵן אֱמֹר כֹּה

---

then: Thus said the Lord GOD: I have indeed removed them far among the nations and have
scattered them among the countries, and I have
become to them a diminished sanctity in the
countries whither they have gone. [17]Yet say:
Thus said the Lord GOD: I will gather you[b] from
the peoples and assemble you out of the countries where you have been scattered, and I will
give you the Land of Israel. [18]And they shall return there, and do away with all its detestable
things and all its abominations. [19]I will give
them one heart and put a new spirit in them;[c]
I will remove the heart of stone from their bodies and give them a heart of flesh, [20]that they
may follow My laws and faithfully observe My
rules. Then they shall be My people and I will
be their God. [21]But as for them whose heart is
set upon their detestable things and their abominations, I will repay them for their conduct—
declares the Lord GOD."

[22]Then the cherubs, with the wheels beside
them, lifted their wings, while the Presence of
the God of Israel rested above them. [23]The Presence of the LORD ascended from the midst of
the city and stood on the hill east of the city.
[24]A spirit carried me away and brought me in
a vision by the spirit of God to the exile community in Chaldea. Then the vision that I had
seen left me, [25]and I told the exiles all the things
that the LORD had shown me.

12

The word of the LORD came to me: [2]O
mortal, you dwell among the rebellious breed.
They have eyes to see but see not, ears to hear
but hear not; for they are a rebellious breed.
[3]Therefore, mortal, get yourself gear for exile,
and go into exile by day before their eyes. Go
into exile from your home to another place be-

אָמַר אֲדֹנָי יְהֹוִה כִּי הִרְחַקְתִּים בַּגּוֹיִם וְכִי
הֲפִיצוֹתִים בָּאֲרָצוֹת וָאֱהִי לָהֶם לְמִקְדָּשׁ
מְעַט בָּאֲרָצוֹת אֲשֶׁר־בָּאוּ שָׁם: ס
17 לָכֵן אֱמֹר כֹּה־אָמַר אֲדֹנָי יְהֹוִה וְקִבַּצְתִּי
אֶתְכֶם מִן־הָעַמִּים וְאָסַפְתִּי אֶתְכֶם מִן־
הָאֲרָצוֹת אֲשֶׁר נְפֹצוֹתֶם בָּהֶם וְנָתַתִּי
לָכֶם אֶת־אַדְמַת יִשְׂרָאֵל: 18 וּבָאוּ־
שָׁמָּה* וְהֵסִירוּ אֶת־כָּל־שִׁקּוּצֶיהָ וְאֶת־
כָּל־תּוֹעֲבוֹתֶיהָ מִמֶּנָּה: 19 וְנָתַתִּי לָהֶם לֵב
אֶחָד וְרוּחַ חֲדָשָׁה אֶתֵּן בְּקִרְבְּכֶם וַהֲסִרֹתִי
לֵב הָאֶבֶן מִבְּשָׂרָם וְנָתַתִּי לָהֶם לֵב
בָּשָׂר: 20 לְמַעַן בְּחֻקֹּתַי יֵלֵכוּ וְאֶת־מִשְׁפָּטַי
יִשְׁמְרוּ וְעָשׂוּ אֹתָם וְהָיוּ־לִי לְעָם וַאֲנִי
אֶהְיֶה לָהֶם לֵאלֹהִים: 21 וְאֶל־לֵב
שִׁקּוּצֵיהֶם וְתוֹעֲבוֹתֵיהֶם לִבָּם הֹלֵךְ דַּרְכָּם
בְּרֹאשָׁם נָתַתִּי נְאֻם אֲדֹנָי יְהֹוִה:

22 וַיִּשְׂאוּ הַכְּרוּבִים אֶת־כַּנְפֵיהֶם
וְהָאוֹפַנִּים לְעֻמָּתָם וּכְבוֹד אֱלֹהֵי־יִשְׂרָאֵל
עֲלֵיהֶם מִלְמָעְלָה: 23 וַיַּעַל כְּבוֹד יְהֹוָה
מֵעַל תּוֹךְ הָעִיר וַיַּעֲמֹד עַל־הָהָר אֲשֶׁר
מִקֶּדֶם לָעִיר: 24 וְרוּחַ נְשָׂאַתְנִי וַתְּבִיאֵנִי
כַשְׂדִּימָה אֶל־הַגּוֹלָה בַּמַּרְאֶה בְּרוּחַ
אֱלֹהִים וַיַּעַל מֵעָלַי הַמַּרְאֶה אֲשֶׁר רָאִיתִי:
25 וָאֲדַבֵּר אֶל־הַגּוֹלָה אֵת כָּל־דִּבְרֵי יְהֹוָה
אֲשֶׁר הֶרְאָנִי: פ

יב וַיְהִי דְבַר־יְהֹוָה אֵלַי לֵאמֹר: 2 בֶּן־
אָדָם בְּתוֹךְ בֵּית־הַמֶּרִי אַתָּה יֹשֵׁב אֲשֶׁר
עֵינַיִם לָהֶם לִרְאוֹת וְלֹא רָאוּ אָזְנַיִם לָהֶם
לִשְׁמֹעַ וְלֹא שָׁמֵעוּ כִּי בֵּית מְרִי הֵם:
3 וְאַתָּה בֶן־אָדָם עֲשֵׂה לְךָ כְּלֵי גוֹלָה וּגְלֵה
יוֹמָם לְעֵינֵיהֶם וְגָלִיתָ מִמְּקוֹמְךָ אֶל־מָקוֹם

---

c Heb. "you."

שני טעמים v. 18.

1173

fore their very eyes; perhaps they will take note, even though they are a rebellious breed. ⁴Carry out your gear as gear for exile by day before their very eyes; and go out again in the evening before their eyes, as one who goes out into exile. ⁵Before their eyes, break through the wall and carry [the gear] out through it; ⁶before their eyes, carry it on your shoulder. Take it out in the dark, and cover your face that you may not see the land; for I make you a portent to the House of Israel.

⁷I did just as I was ordered: I took out my gear by day as gear for exile, and in the evening I broke through the wall ᵃ-with my own hands.-ᵃ In the darkness I carried [the gear] out on my shoulder, carrying it before their eyes.

⁸In the morning, the word of the Lᴏʀᴅ came to me: ⁹O mortal, did not the House of Israel, that rebellious breed, ask you, "What are you doing?" ¹⁰Say to them: "Thus said the Lord Gᴏᴅ: This pronouncement concerns the prince in Jerusalem and all the House of Israel who are in it." ¹¹Say: "I am a portent for you: As I have done, so shall it be done to them; they shall go into exile, into captivity. ¹²And the prince among them shall carry his gear on his shoulder as he goes out in the dark. Heᵇ shall break through the wall in order to carry [his gear] out through it; he shall cover his face, because he himself shall not see the land with his eyes." ¹³I will spread My net over him, and he shall be caught in My snare. I will bring him to Babylon, the land of the Chaldeans, but he shall not see it;ᶜ and there he shall die. ¹⁴And all those around him, his helpers and all his troops, I will scatter in every direction; and I will unsheathe the sword after them. ¹⁵Then, when I have scattered them among the nations and dispersed them through the countries, they shall know that I am the Lᴏʀᴅ. ¹⁶But I will spare a few of them from

אַחַר֙ לְעֵ֣ינֵיהֶ֔ם אוּלַ֣י יִרְא֔וּ כִּ֛י בֵּ֥ית מְרִ֖י הֵֽמָּה׃ ⁴ וְהוֹצֵאתָ֙ כֵלֶ֜יךָ כִּכְלֵ֥י גוֹלָ֛ה יוֹמָ֖ם לְעֵֽינֵיהֶ֑ם וְאַתָּ֗ה תֵּצֵ֤א בָעֶ֨רֶב֙ לְעֵ֣ינֵיהֶ֔ם כְּמוֹצָאֵ֖י גּוֹלָֽה׃ ⁵ לְעֵינֵיהֶ֖ם חֲתׇר־לְךָ֣ בַקִּ֑יר וְהוֹצֵאתָ֖ בּֽוֹ׃ ⁶ לְעֵינֵיהֶ֞ם עַל־כָּתֵ֣ף תִּשָּׂ֗א בָּעֲלָטָ֤ה תוֹצִיא֙ פָּנֶ֣יךָ תְכַסֶּ֔ה וְלֹ֥א תִרְאֶ֖ה אֶת־הָאָ֑רֶץ כִּֽי־מוֹפֵ֥ת נְתַתִּ֖יךָ לְבֵ֥ית יִשְׂרָאֵֽל׃

⁷ וָאַ֣עַשׂ כֵּן֮ כַּאֲשֶׁ֣ר צֻוֵּ֒יתִי֒ כֵּלַ֞י הוֹצֵ֤אתִי כִּכְלֵ֤י גוֹלָה֙ יוֹמָ֔ם וּבָעֶ֛רֶב חָתַֽרְתִּי־לִ֥י בַקִּ֖יר בְּיָ֑ד בָּעֲלָטָ֥ה הוֹצֵ֛אתִי עַל־כָּתֵ֥ף נָשָׂ֖אתִי לְעֵינֵיהֶֽם׃ פ

⁸ וַיְהִ֧י דְבַר־יְהֹוָ֛ה אֵלַ֖י בַּבֹּ֥קֶר לֵאמֹֽר׃ ⁹ בֶּן־ אָדָ֕ם הֲלֹ֨א אָמְר֤וּ אֵלֶ֨יךָ֙ בֵּ֣ית יִשְׂרָאֵ֔ל בֵּ֖ית הַמֶּ֑רִי מָ֥ה אַתָּ֖ה עֹשֶֽׂה׃ ¹⁰ אֱמֹ֣ר אֲלֵיהֶ֔ם כֹּ֥ה אָמַ֖ר אֲדֹנָ֣י יֱהֹוִ֑ה הַנָּשִׂ֞יא הַמַּשָּׂ֤א הַזֶּה֙ בִּיר֣וּשָׁלַ֔͏ִם וְכׇל־בֵּ֥ית יִשְׂרָאֵ֖ל אֲשֶׁר־הֵ֥מָּה בְתוֹכָֽם׃ ¹¹ אֱמֹ֖ר אֲנִ֣י מֽוֹפֶתְכֶ֑ם כַּאֲשֶׁ֤ר עָשִׂ֨יתִי֙ כֵּ֣ן יֵעָשֶׂ֣ה לָהֶ֔ם בַּגּוֹלָ֥ה בַשְּׁבִ֖י יֵלֵֽכוּ׃ ¹² וְהַנָּשִׂ֣יא אֲשֶׁר־בְּתוֹכָ֗ם אֶל־כָּתֵ֤ף יִשָּׂא֙ בָּעֲלָטָ֣ה וְיֵצֵ֔א בַּקִּ֥יר יַחְתְּר֖וּ לְה֣וֹצִיא ב֑וֹ פָּנָ֣יו יְכַסֶּ֔ה יַ֗עַן אֲשֶׁ֨ר לֹא־יִרְאֶ֥ה לַעַ֛יִן ה֖וּא אֶת־הָאָֽרֶץ׃ ¹³ וּפָרַשְׂתִּ֤י אֶת־רִשְׁתִּי֙ עָלָ֔יו וְנִתְפַּ֖שׂ בִּמְצֽוּדָתִ֑י וְהֵבֵאתִ֨י אֹת֤וֹ בָבֶ֨לָה֙ אֶ֣רֶץ כַּשְׂדִּ֔ים וְאוֹתָ֥הּ לֹֽא־יִרְאֶ֖ה וְשָׁ֥ם יָמֽוּת׃ ¹⁴ וְכֹל֩ אֲשֶׁ֨ר סְבִֽיבֹתָ֜יו עֶזְרֹ֤ה עֶזְרֹה֙ וְכׇל־אֲגַפָּ֔יו אֱזָרֶ֖ה לְכׇל־ר֑וּחַ וְחֶ֖רֶב אָרִ֥יק אַחֲרֵיהֶֽם׃ ¹⁵ וְיָדְע֖וּ כִּֽי־אֲנִ֣י יְהֹוָ֑ה בַּהֲפִיצִ֤י אוֹתָם֙ בַּגּוֹיִ֔ם וְזֵרִיתִ֥י אוֹתָ֖ם בָּאֲרָצֽוֹת׃ ¹⁶ וְהוֹתַרְתִּ֤י מֵהֶם֙ אַנְשֵׁ֣י מִסְפָּ֔ר

---

the sword, from famine, and from pestilence, that they may recount all their abominable deeds among the nations to which they come; and they shall know that I am the Lord!

17The word of the Lord came to me: 18O mortal, eat your bread in trembling and drink your water in fear and anxiety. 19And say to the people of the land: Thus said the Lord God concerning the inhabitants of Jerusalem in the land of Israel: They shall eat their bread in anxiety and drink their water in desolation, because their land will be desolate of its multitudes on account of the lawlessness of all its inhabitants. 20The inhabited towns shall be laid waste and the land shall become a desolation; then you shall know that I am the Lord.

21The word of the Lord came to me: 22O mortal, what is this proverb that you have in the land of Israel, that you say, "The days grow many and every vision comes to naught?" 23Assuredly, say to them, Thus said the Lord God: I will put an end to this proverb; it shall not be used in Israel any more. Speak rather to them: The days draw near, and the fulfillment of every vision. 24For there shall no longer be any false vision or soothing divination in the House of Israel. 25But whenever I the Lord speak what I speak, that word shall be fulfilled without any delay; in your days, O rebellious breed, I will fulfill every word I speak—declares the Lord God.

26The word of the Lord came to me: 27See, O mortal, the House of Israel says, "The vision that he sees is far ahead, and he prophesies for the distant future." 28Assuredly, say to them: Thus said the Lord God: There shall be no more delay; whenever I speak a word, that word shall be fulfilled—declares the Lord God.

מֵחֶ֣רֶב מֵרָעָ֣ב וּמִדָּ֑בֶר לְמַ֣עַן יְסַפְּר֗וּ אֶת־
כָּל־תּוֹעֲבֽוֹתֵיהֶ֖ם בַּגּוֹיִ֣ם אֲשֶׁר־בָּ֣אוּ שָׁ֑ם
וְיָדְע֖וּ כִּֽי־אֲנִ֥י יְהֹוָֽה׃ פ

17 וַיְהִ֥י דְבַר־יְהֹוָ֖ה אֵלַ֥י לֵאמֹֽר׃ 18 בֶּן־אָדָ֗ם
לַחְמְךָ֙ בְּרַ֣עַשׁ תֹּאכֵ֔ל וּמֵימֶ֕יךָ בְּרׇגְזָ֥ה
וּבִדְאָגָ֖ה תִּשְׁתֶּֽה׃ 19 וְאָמַרְתָּ֣ אֶל־עַם־
הָאָ֗רֶץ כֹּֽה־אָמַ֞ר אֲדֹנָ֣י יְהֹוִה֮ לְיוֹשְׁבֵ֣י
יְרוּשָׁלַ֙͏ִם֙ אֶל־אַדְמַ֣ת יִשְׂרָאֵ֔ל לַחְמָ֞ם
בִּדְאָגָ֣ה יֹאכֵ֗לוּ וּמֵֽימֵיהֶם֙ בְּשִׁמָּמ֣וֹן יִשְׁתּ֔וּ
לְמַ֙עַן֙ תֵּשַׁ֣ם אַרְצָ֔הּ מִמְּלֹאָ֔הּ מֵחֲמַ֖ס כׇּל־
הַיֹּשְׁבִ֥ים בָּֽהּ׃ 20 וְהֶעָרִ֤ים הַנּֽוֹשָׁבוֹת֙
תֶּחֱרַ֔בְנָה וְהָאָ֖רֶץ שְׁמָמָ֣ה תִֽהְיֶ֑ה וִידַעְתֶּ֖ם
כִּֽי־אֲנִ֥י יְהֹוָֽה׃ פ

21 וַיְהִ֥י דְבַר־יְהֹוָ֖ה אֵלַ֥י לֵאמֹֽר׃ 22 בֶּן־אָדָ֗ם
מָֽה־הַמָּשָׁ֤ל הַזֶּה֙ לָכֶ֔ם עַל־אַדְמַ֥ת יִשְׂרָאֵ֖ל
לֵאמֹ֑ר יַֽאַרְכוּ֙ הַיָּמִ֔ים וְאָבַ֖ד כׇּל־חָזֽוֹן׃
23 לָכֵ֞ן אֱמֹ֣ר אֲלֵיהֶ֗ם כֹּֽה־אָמַר֮ אֲדֹנָ֣י יְהֹוִה֒
הִשְׁבַּ֙תִּי֙ אֶת־הַמָּשָׁ֣ל הַזֶּ֔ה וְלֹֽא־יִמְשְׁל֥וּ
אֹת֛וֹ ע֖וֹד בְּיִשְׂרָאֵ֑ל כִּ֚י אִם־דַּבֵּ֣ר אֲלֵיהֶ֔ם
קָֽרְבוּ֙ הַיָּמִ֔ים וּדְבַ֖ר כׇּל־חָזֽוֹן׃ 24 כִּ֣י לֹ֥א
יִֽהְיֶ֛ה ע֖וֹד כׇּל־חֲז֣וֹן שָׁ֑וְא וּמִקְסַ֣ם חָלָ֔ק
בְּת֖וֹךְ בֵּ֥ית יִשְׂרָאֵֽל׃ 25 כִּ֣י ׀ אֲנִ֣י יְהֹוָ֗ה
אֲדַבֵּר֙ אֵת֩ אֲשֶׁ֨ר אֲדַבֵּ֤ר דָּבָר֙ וְיֵ֣עָשֶׂ֔ה לֹ֥א
תִמָּשֵׁ֖ךְ ע֑וֹד כִּ֣י בִֽימֵיכֶ֞ם בֵּ֣ית הַמֶּ֗רִי אֲדַבֵּ֤ר
דָּבָר֙ וַֽעֲשִׂיתִ֔יו נְאֻ֖ם אֲדֹנָ֥י יְהֹוִֽה׃ פ

26 וַיְהִ֥י דְבַר־יְהֹוָ֖ה אֵלַ֥י לֵאמֹֽר׃ 27 בֶּן־אָדָ֗ם
הִנֵּ֤ה בֵֽית־יִשְׂרָאֵל֙ אֹֽמְרִ֔ים הֶחָז֛וֹן אֲשֶׁר־
ה֥וּא חֹזֶ֖ה לְיָמִ֣ים רַבִּ֑ים וּלְעִתִּ֥ים רְחוֹק֖וֹת
ה֥וּא נִבָּֽא׃ 28 לָכֵ֞ן אֱמֹ֣ר אֲלֵיהֶ֗ם כֹּ֤ה אָמַר֙
אֲדֹנָ֣י יְהֹוִ֔ה לֹא־תִמָּשֵׁ֥ךְ ע֖וֹד כׇּל־דְּבָרָ֑י
אֲשֶׁ֨ר אֲדַבֵּ֤ר דָּבָר֙ וְיֵ֣עָשֶׂ֔ה נְאֻ֖ם אֲדֹנָ֥י
יְהֹוִֽה׃ ס

13

The word of the Lord came to me: 2O mortal, prophesy against the prophets of Israel who prophesy; say to those who prophesy out of their own imagination: Hear the word of the Lord! 3Thus said the Lord God: Woe to the degenerate prophets, who follow their own fancy, without having had a vision! 4Your prophets, O Israel, have been like jackals among ruins. 5You did not enter the breaches and repair the walls for the House of Israel, that they might stand up in battle in the day of the Lord. 6They prophesied falsehood and lying divination; they said, "Declares the Lord," when the Lord did not send them, and then they waited for their word to be fulfilled. 7It was false visions you prophesied and lying divination you uttered, saying, "Declares the Lord," when I had not spoken.

8Assuredly, thus said the Lord God: Because you speak falsehood and prophesy lies, assuredly, I will deal with you—declares the Lord God. 9My hand will be against the prophets who prophesy falsehood and utter lying divination. They shall not remain in the assembly of My people, they shall not be inscribed in the lists of the House of Israel, and they shall not come back to the land of Israel. Thus shall you know that I am the Lord God.

10Inasmuch as they have misled My people, saying, "It is well," when nothing is well, daubing with plaster the flimsy wall which a-the people-a were building, 11say to those daubers of plaster: It shall collapse; a driving rain shall descend—and you, O great hailstones, shall fall—and a hurricane wind shall rend it. 12Then, when the wall collapses, you will be asked, "What became of the plaster you daubed on?"

13Assuredly, thus said the Lord God: In My fury I will let loose hurricane winds; in My anger

a-a Heb. "it."

רג

2 וַיְהִי דְבַר־יְהֹוָה אֵלַי לֵאמֹר: בֶּן־
אָדָם הִנָּבֵא אֶל־נְבִיאֵי יִשְׂרָאֵל הַנִּבָּאִים
וְאָמַרְתָּ לִנְבִיאֵי מִלִּבָּם שִׁמְעוּ דְּבַר־יְהֹוָה:
3 כֹּה אָמַר אֲדֹנָי יֱהֹוִה הוֹי עַל־הַנְּבִיאִים
הַנְּבָלִים אֲשֶׁר הֹלְכִים אַחַר רוּחָם וּלְבִלְתִּי
רָאוּ: 4 כְּשֻׁעָלִים בׇּחֳרָבוֹת נְבִיאֶיךָ יִשְׂרָאֵל
הָיוּ: 5 לֹא עֲלִיתֶם בַּפְּרָצוֹת וַתִּגְדְּרוּ גָדֵר
עַל־בֵּית יִשְׂרָאֵל לַעֲמֹד בַּמִּלְחָמָה בְּיוֹם
יְהֹוָה: 6 חָזוּ שָׁוְא וְקֶסֶם כָּזָב הָאֹמְרִים
נְאֻם־יְהֹוָה וַיהֹוָה לֹא שְׁלָחָם וְיִחֲלוּ לְקַיֵּם
דָּבָר: 7 הֲלוֹא מַחֲזֵה־שָׁוְא חֲזִיתֶם וּמִקְסַם
כָּזָב אֲמַרְתֶּם וְאֹמְרִים נְאֻם־יְהֹוָה וַאֲנִי
לֹא דִבַּרְתִּי: ס

8 לָכֵן כֹּה אָמַר אֲדֹנָי יֱהֹוִה יַעַן דַּבֶּרְכֶם
שָׁוְא וַחֲזִיתֶם כָּזָב לָכֵן הִנְנִי אֲלֵיכֶם נְאֻם
אֲדֹנָי יֱהֹוִה: 9 וְהָיְתָה יָדִי אֶל־הַנְּבִיאִים
הַחֹזִים שָׁוְא וְהַקֹּסְמִים כָּזָב בְּסוֹד עַמִּי
לֹא־יִהְיוּ וּבִכְתָב בֵּית־יִשְׂרָאֵל לֹא יִכָּתֵבוּ
וְאֶל־אַדְמַת יִשְׂרָאֵל לֹא יָבֹאוּ וִידַעְתֶּם כִּי
אֲנִי אֲדֹנָי יֱהֹוִה:

10 יַעַן וּבְיַעַן הִטְעוּ אֶת־עַמִּי לֵאמֹר שָׁלוֹם
וְאֵין שָׁלוֹם וְהוּא בֹּנֶה חַיִץ וְהִנָּם טָחִים
אֹתוֹ תָּפֵל: 11 אֱמֹר אֶל־טָחֵי תָפֵל וְיִפֹּל
הָיָה ׀ גֶּשֶׁם שׁוֹטֵף וְאַתֵּנָה אַבְנֵי אֶלְגָּבִישׁ
תִּפֹּלְנָה וְרוּחַ סְעָרוֹת תְּבַקֵּעַ: 12 וְהִנֵּה נָפַל
הַקִּיר הֲלוֹא יֵאָמֵר אֲלֵיכֶם אַיֵּה הַטִּיחַ
אֲשֶׁר טַחְתֶּם: ס

13 לָכֵן כֹּה אָמַר אֲדֹנָי יֱהֹוִה וּבִקַּעְתִּי
רוּחַ־סְעָרוֹת בַּחֲמָתִי וְגֶשֶׁם שֹׁטֵף בְּאַפִּי

a driving rain shall descend, and great hailstones in destructive fury. [14]I will throw down the wall that you daubed with plaster, and I will raze it to the ground so that its foundation is exposed; and when it falls, you shall perish in its midst; then you shall know that I am the LORD. [15]And when I have spent My fury upon the wall and upon those who daubed it with plaster, I will say to you: Gone is the wall and gone are its daubers, [16]the prophets of Israel who prophesy about Jerusalem and see a vision of well-being for her when there is no well-being—declares the Lord GOD.

[17]And you, O mortal, set your face against the women of your people, who prophesy out of their own imagination. Prophesy against them [18]and say: Thus said the Lord GOD: Woe to those who sew pads[b] on all arm-joints and make bonnets[b] for the head of every person, in order to entrap! Can you hunt down lives among My people, while you preserve your own lives? [19]You have profaned [c]My name[c] among My people in return for handfuls of barley and morsels of bread; you have announced the death of persons who will not die and the survival of persons who will not live—lying to My people, who listen to your lies.

[20]Assuredly, thus said the Lord GOD: I am going to deal with your pads,[b] [d]by which[d] you hunt down lives like birds, and I will tear them from your arms and free the persons whose lives you hunt down like birds. [21]I will tear off your bonnets[b] and rescue My people from your hands, and they shall no longer be prey in your hands; then you shall know that I am the LORD. [22]Because you saddened the heart of the innocent with lies, when I would not inflict suffering on him, and encouraged the wicked not to repent of his evil ways and so gain life—

---

b　Meaning of Heb. uncertain.
c-c　Heb. "Me."
d-d　Heb. "where."

יִהְיֶה וְאַבְנֵי אֶלְגָּבִישׁ בְּחֵמָה לְכָלָה׃
14 וְהָרַסְתִּי אֶת־הַקִּיר אֲשֶׁר־טַחְתֶּם תָּפֵל וְהִגַּעְתִּיהוּ אֶל־הָאָרֶץ וְנִגְלָה יְסֹדוֹ וְנָפְלָה וּכְלִיתֶם בְּתוֹכָהּ וִידַעְתֶּם כִּי־אֲנִי יְהוָה׃
15 וְכִלֵּיתִי אֶת־חֲמָתִי בַּקִּיר וּבַטָּחִים אֹתוֹ תָּפֵל וְאֹמַר לָכֶם אֵין הַקִּיר וְאֵין הַטָּחִים אֹתוֹ׃ 16 נְבִיאֵי יִשְׂרָאֵל הַנִּבְּאִים אֶל־יְרוּשָׁלַ͏ִם וְהַחֹזִים לָהּ חֲזוֹן שָׁלֹם וְאֵין שָׁלֹם נְאֻם אֲדֹנָי יְהוִה׃ פ
17 וְאַתָּה בֶן־אָדָם שִׂים פָּנֶיךָ אֶל־בְּנוֹת עַמְּךָ הַמִּתְנַבְּאוֹת מִלִּבְּהֶן וְהִנָּבֵא עֲלֵיהֶן׃
18 וְאָמַרְתָּ כֹּה־אָמַר ׀ אֲדֹנָי יְהוִה הוֹי לִמְתַפְּרוֹת כְּסָתוֹת עַל ׀ כָּל־אַצִּילֵי יָדַי וְעֹשׂוֹת הַמִּסְפָּחוֹת עַל־רֹאשׁ כָּל־קוֹמָה לְצוֹדֵד נְפָשׁוֹת הַנְּפָשׁוֹת תְּצוֹדֵדְנָה לְעַמִּי וּנְפָשׁוֹת לָכֶנָה תְחַיֶּינָה׃ 19 וַתְּחַלֶּלְנָה אֹתִי אֶל־עַמִּי בְּשַׁעֲלֵי שְׂעֹרִים וּבִפְתוֹתֵי לֶחֶם לְהָמִית נְפָשׁוֹת אֲשֶׁר לֹא־תְמוּתֶנָה וּלְחַיּוֹת נְפָשׁוֹת אֲשֶׁר לֹא־תִחְיֶינָה בְּכַזֶּבְכֶם לְעַמִּי שֹׁמְעֵי כָזָב׃ ס
20 לָכֵן כֹּה־אָמַר ׀ אֲדֹנָי יְהוִה הִנְנִי אֶל־כִּסְּתוֹתֵיכֶנָה אֲשֶׁר אַתֵּנָה מְצֹדְדוֹת שָׁם אֶת־הַנְּפָשׁוֹת לְפֹרְחוֹת וְקָרַעְתִּי אֹתָם מֵעַל זְרוֹעֹתֵיכֶם וְשִׁלַּחְתִּי אֶת־הַנְּפָשׁוֹת אֲשֶׁר אַתֶּם מְצֹדְדוֹת אֶת־נְפָשִׁים לְפֹרְחֹת׃
21 וְקָרַעְתִּי אֶת־מִסְפְּחֹתֵיכֶם וְהִצַּלְתִּי אֶת־עַמִּי מִיֶּדְכֶן וְלֹא־יִהְיוּ עוֹד בְּיֶדְכֶן לִמְצוּדָה וִידַעְתֶּן כִּי־אֲנִי יְהוָה׃ 22 יַעַן הַכְאוֹת לֵב־צַדִּיק שֶׁקֶר וַאֲנִי לֹא הִכְאַבְתִּיו וּלְחַזֵּק יְדֵי רָשָׁע לְבִלְתִּי־שׁוּב מִדַּרְכּוֹ הָרָע

²³assuredly, you shall no longer prophesy lies or practice divination! I will save My people from your hands, and you shall know that I am the LORD.

14 Certain elders of Israel came to me and sat down before me. ²And the word of the LORD came to me: ³O mortal, these men have turned their thoughts upon their fetishes and set their minds upon the sin through which they stumbled: Shall I respond to their inquiry? ⁴Now speak to them and tell them: Thus said the Lord GOD: If anyone of the House of Israel turns his thoughts upon his fetishes and sets his mind upon the sin through which he stumbled, and yet comes to the prophet, I the LORD will respond to him ᵃ-as he comes with-ᵃ his multitude of fetishes. ⁵Thus I will hold the House of Israel to account for their thoughts, because they have all been estranged from Me through their fetishes.

⁶Now say to the House of Israel: Thus said the Lord GOD: Repent, and turn back from your fetishes and turn your minds away from all your abominations. ⁷For if any man of the House of Israel, or of the strangers who dwell in Israel, breaks away from Me and turns his thoughts upon his fetishes and sets his mind upon the sins through which he stumbled, and then goes to the prophet to inquire of Me through him, I the LORD will respond to him directly. ⁸I will set My face against that man and make him a sign and a byword, and I will cut him off from the midst of My people. Then you shall know that I am the LORD.

⁹And if a prophet is seduced and does speak a word [to such a man], it was I the LORD who seduced that prophet; I will stretch out My hand against him and destroy him from among My

לְהַחֲיֹתֽוֹ׃ 23 לָכֵ֣ן שָׁ֤וְא לֹ֣א תֶחֱזֶ֙ינָה֙ וְקֶ֣סֶם לֹא־תִקְסַ֣מְנָה ע֑וֹד וְהִצַּלְתִּ֤י אֶת־עַמִּי֙ מִיֶּדְכֶ֔ן וִידַעְתֶּ֖ן כִּֽי־אֲנִ֥י יְהוָֽה׃

יד וַיָּב֤וֹא* אֵלַי֙ אֲנָשִׁים֙ מִזִּקְנֵ֣י יִשְׂרָאֵ֔ל וַיֵּשְׁב֖וּ לְפָנָֽי׃ פ 2 וַיְהִ֥י דְבַר־יְהוָ֖ה אֵלַ֥י לֵאמֹֽר׃ 3 בֶּן־אָדָ֗ם הָאֲנָשִׁ֤ים הָאֵ֙לֶּה֙ הֶעֱל֤וּ גִלּֽוּלֵיהֶם֙ עַל־לִבָּ֔ם וּמִכְשׁ֧וֹל עֲוֺנָ֛ם נָתְנ֖וּ נֹ֣כַח פְּנֵיהֶ֑ם הַאִדָּרֹ֥שׁ אִדָּרֵ֖שׁ לָהֶֽם׃ ס 4 לָכֵ֣ן דַּבֵּר־א֠וֹתָ֠ם וְאָמַרְתָּ֨ אֲלֵיהֶ֜ם כֹּֽה־אָמַ֣ר ׀ אֲדֹנָ֣י יְהֹוִ֗ה אִ֣ישׁ אִ֣ישׁ מִבֵּ֣ית יִשְׂרָאֵ֡ל אֲשֶׁר֩ יַעֲלֶ֨ה אֶת־גִּלּוּלָ֜יו אֶל־לִבּ֗וֹ וּמִכְשׁ֤וֹל עֲוֺנוֹ֙ יָשִׂים֙ נֹ֣כַח פָּנָ֔יו וּבָ֖א אֶל־הַנָּבִ֑יא אֲנִ֣י יְהוָ֗ה נַעֲנֵ֧יתִי ל֦וֹ בה בָ֖א בְּרֹ֥ב גִּלּוּלָֽיו׃ 5 לְמַ֛עַן תְּפֹ֥שׂ אֶת־בֵּֽית־יִשְׂרָאֵ֖ל בְּלִבָּ֑ם אֲשֶׁ֤ר נָזֹ֙רוּ֙ מֵֽעָלַ֔י בְּגִלּֽוּלֵיהֶ֖ם כֻּלָּֽם׃ ס 6 לָכֵ֞ן אֱמֹ֣ר ׀ אֶל־בֵּ֣ית יִשְׂרָאֵ֗ל כֹּ֤ה אָמַר֙ אֲדֹנָ֣י יְהֹוִ֔ה שׁ֣וּבוּ וְהָשִׁ֔יבוּ מֵעַ֖ל גִּלּ֣וּלֵיכֶ֑ם וּמֵעַ֥ל כׇּל־תּוֹעֲבֹתֵיכֶ֖ם הָשִׁ֥יבוּ פְנֵיכֶֽם׃ 7 כִּי֩ אִ֨ישׁ אִ֜ישׁ מִבֵּ֣ית יִשְׂרָאֵ֗ל וּמֵהַגֵּר֮ אֲשֶׁר־יָג֣וּר בְּיִשְׂרָאֵל֒ וְיִנָּזֵ֣ר מֵֽאַחֲרַ֗י וְיַ֤עַל גִּלּוּלָיו֙ אֶל־לִבּ֔וֹ וּמִכְשׁ֣וֹל עֲוֺנ֔וֹ יָשִׂ֖ים נֹ֣כַח פָּנָ֑יו וּבָ֤א אֶל־הַנָּבִיא֙ לִדְרׇשׁ־ל֣וֹ בִ֔י אֲנִ֣י יְהוָ֔ה נַעֲנֶה־לּ֖וֹ בִּֽי׃ 8 וְנָתַתִּ֨י פָנַ֜י בָּאִ֣ישׁ הַה֗וּא וַהֲשִׂמֹתִ֙יהוּ֙ לְא֣וֹת וְלִמְשָׁלִ֔ים וְהִכְרַתִּ֖יו מִתּ֣וֹךְ עַמִּ֑י וִידַעְתֶּ֖ם כִּֽי־אֲנִ֥י יְהוָֽה׃ ס 9 וְהַנָּבִ֣יא כִֽי־יְפֻתֶּה֮ וְדִבֶּ֣ר דָּבָר֒ אֲנִ֤י יְהוָה֙ פִּתֵּ֙יתִי֙ אֵ֣ת הַנָּבִ֣יא הַה֔וּא וְנָטִ֤יתִי אֶת־יָדִי֙ עָלָ֔יו וְהִ֨שְׁמַדְתִּ֔יו מִתּ֖וֹךְ עַמִּ֥י יִשְׂרָאֵֽל׃

---

a-a Emendation yields "directly, because of"; cf. v. 7.   סבירין ומטעין לשון רבים   v. 1.

people Israel. ¹⁰Thus they shall bear their punishment: The punishment of the inquirer and the punishment of the prophet shall be the same, ¹¹so that the House of Israel may never again stray from Me and defile itself with all its transgressions. Then they shall be My people and I will be their God—declares the Lord God.

¹²The word of the Lord came to me: ¹³O mortal, if a land were to sin against Me and commit a trespass, and I stretched out My hand against it and broke its staff of bread, and sent famine against it and cut off man and beast from it, ¹⁴even if these three men—Noah, Daniel, and Job—should be in it, they would by their righteousness save only themselves—declares the Lord God. ¹⁵Or, if I were to send wild beasts to roam the land and they depopulated it, and it became a desolation with none passing through it because of the beasts, ¹⁶as I live—declares the Lord God—those three men in it would save neither sons nor daughters; they alone would be saved, but the land would become a desolation. ¹⁷Or, if I were to bring the sword upon that land and say, "Let a sword sweep through the land so that I may cut off from it man and beast," ¹⁸if those three men should be in it, as I live—declares the Lord God—they would save neither sons nor daughters, but they alone would be saved. ¹⁹Or, if I let loose a pestilence against that land, and poured out My fury upon it in blood, cutting off from it man and beast, ²⁰should Noah, Daniel, and Job be in it, as I live—declares the Lord God—they would save neither son nor daughter; they would save themselves alone by their righteousness.

²¹Assuredly, thus said the Lord God: How much less [should any escape] now that I have let loose against Jerusalem all four of My terrible punishments—the sword, famine, wild beasts,

¹⁰ וְנָשְׂא֖וּ עֲוֺנָ֑ם כַּעֲוֺן֙ הַדֹּרֵ֔שׁ כַּעֲוֺ֖ן הַנָּבִ֥יא יִהְיֶֽה׃ ¹¹ לְ֠מַעַן לֹֽא־יִתְע֨וּ ע֤וֹד בֵּֽית־יִשְׂרָאֵל֙ מֵאַֽחֲרַ֔י וְלֹֽא־יִטַּמְּא֥וּ ע֖וֹד בְּכָל־פִּשְׁעֵיהֶ֑ם וְהָ֤יוּ לִי֙ לְעָ֔ם וַֽאֲנִי֙ אֶהְיֶ֣ה לָהֶ֣ם לֵֽאלֹהִ֔ים נְאֻ֖ם אֲדֹנָ֥י יְהֹוִֽה׃ ס

¹² וַיְהִ֥י דְבַר־יְהֹוָ֖ה אֵלַ֥י לֵאמֹֽר׃ ¹³ בֶּן־אָדָ֗ם אֶ֚רֶץ כִּ֣י תֶֽחֱטָא־לִ֔י לִמְעׇל־מַ֔עַל וְנָטִ֤יתִי יָדִי֙ עָלֶ֔יהָ וְשָׁבַ֥רְתִּי לָ֖הּ מַטֵּה־לָ֑חֶם וְהִשְׁלַחְתִּי־בָ֣הּ רָעָ֔ב וְהִכְרַתִּ֥י מִמֶּ֖נָּה אָדָ֥ם וּבְהֵמָֽה׃ ¹⁴ וְ֠הָיוּ שְׁלֹ֨שֶׁת הָאֲנָשִׁ֤ים הָאֵ֙לֶּה֙ בְּתוֹכָ֔הּ נֹ֛חַ דָּנִיֵּ֥אל וְאִיּ֖וֹב הֵ֑מָּה בְּצִדְקָתָ֞ם יְנַצְּל֣וּ נַפְשָׁ֗ם נְאֻ֖ם אֲדֹנָ֥י יְהֹוִֽה׃ ¹⁵ לֽוּ־חַיָּ֥ה רָעָ֛ה אַעֲבִ֥יר בָּאָ֖רֶץ וְשִׁכְּלָ֑תָּה וְהָיְתָ֤ה שְׁמָמָה֙ מִבְּלִ֣י עוֹבֵ֔ר מִפְּנֵ֖י הַחַיָּֽה׃ ¹⁶ שְׁלֹ֨שֶׁת הָאֲנָשִׁ֣ים הָאֵ֘לֶּה֮ בְּתוֹכָהּ֒ חַי־אָ֗נִי נְאֻם֙ אֲדֹנָ֣י יְהֹוִ֔ה אִם־בָּנִ֥ים וְאִם־בָּנ֖וֹת יַצִּ֑ילוּ הֵ֤מָּה לְבַדָּם֙ יִנָּצֵ֔לוּ וְהָאָ֖רֶץ תִּֽהְיֶ֥ה שְׁמָמָֽה׃ ¹⁷ א֛וֹ חֶ֥רֶב אָבִ֖יא עַל־הָאָ֣רֶץ הַהִ֑יא וְאָמַרְתִּ֗י חֶ֚רֶב תַּֽעֲבֹ֣ר בָּאָ֔רֶץ וְהִכְרַתִּ֥י מִמֶּ֖נָּה אָדָ֥ם וּבְהֵמָֽה׃ ¹⁸ וּשְׁלֹ֨שֶׁת הָאֲנָשִׁ֣ים הָאֵ֘לֶּה֮ בְּתוֹכָהּ֒ חַי־אָ֙נִי֙ נְאֻם֙ אֲדֹנָ֣י יְהֹוִ֔ה לֹ֥א יַצִּ֖ילוּ בָּנִ֣ים וּבָנ֑וֹת כִּ֛י הֵ֥ם לְבַדָּ֖ם יִנָּצֵֽלוּ׃ ¹⁹ א֛וֹ דֶּ֥בֶר אֲשַׁלַּ֖ח אֶל־הָאָ֣רֶץ הַהִ֑יא וְשָׁפַכְתִּ֨י חֲמָתִ֤י עָלֶ֙יהָ֙ בְּדָ֔ם לְהַכְרִ֥ית מִמֶּ֖נָּה אָדָ֥ם וּבְהֵמָֽה׃ ²⁰ וְ֠נֹחַ דָּנִיֵּ֥אל וְאִיּוֹב֮ בְּתוֹכָהּ֒ חַי־אָ֙נִי֙ נְאֻם֙ אֲדֹנָ֣י יְהֹוִ֔ה אִם־בֵּ֥ן אִם־בַּ֖ת יַצִּ֑ילוּ הֵ֥מָּה בְצִדְקָתָ֖ם יַצִּ֥ילוּ נַפְשָֽׁם׃ פ

²¹ כִּי֩ כֹ֨ה אָמַ֜ר אֲדֹנָ֣י יְהֹוִ֗ה אַ֣ף כִּֽי־אַרְבַּ֣עַת שְׁפָטַ֣י ׀ הָרָעִ֡ים חֶ֠רֶב וְרָעָ֞ב וְחַיָּ֤ה רָעָה֙ וָדֶ֔בֶר שִׁלַּ֖חְתִּי אֶל־יְרֽוּשָׁלָ֑͏ִם לְהַכְרִ֥ית

and pestilence—to cut off man and beast from it! ²²Yet there are survivors left of it, *b-sons and daughters who are being brought out.-b* They are coming out to you; and when you see their ways and their deeds, you will be consoled for the disaster that I brought on Jerusalem, for all that I brought on it. ²³You will be consoled through them, when you see their ways and their deeds and realize that not without cause did I do all that I did in it—declares the Lord GOD.

15 The word of the LORD came to me: ²O mortal, how is the wood of the grapevine better than the wood of any branch to be found among the trees of the forest? ³Can wood be taken from it for use in any work? Can one take a peg from it to hang any vessel on? ⁴Now suppose it was thrown into the fire as fuel and the fire consumed its two ends and its middle was charred—is it good for any use? ⁵Even when it was whole it could not be used for anything; how much less when fire has consumed it and it is charred! Can it still be used for anything?

⁶Assuredly, thus said the Lord GOD: Like the wood of the grapevine among the trees of the forest, which I have designated to be fuel for fire, so will I treat the inhabitants of Jerusalem. ⁷I will set My face against them; they escaped from fire, but fire shall consume them. When I set my face against them, you shall know that I am the LORD. ⁸I will make the land a desolation, because they committed trespass—declares the Lord GOD.

16 The word of the LORD came to me: ²O mortal, proclaim Jerusalem's abominations to her, ³and say: Thus said the Lord GOD to Jeru-

מִמֶּנָּה אָדָם וּבְהֵמָה׃ 22 וְהִנֵּה נוֹתְרָה־בָּהּ פְּלֵטָה הַמּוּצָאִים בָּנִים וּבָנוֹת הִנָּם יוֹצְאִים אֲלֵיכֶם וּרְאִיתֶם אֶת־דַּרְכָּם וְאֶת־עֲלִילוֹתָם וְנִחַמְתֶּם עַל־הָרָעָה אֲשֶׁר הֵבֵאתִי עַל־יְרוּשָׁלַםִ אֵת כָּל־אֲשֶׁר הֵבֵאתִי עָלֶיהָ׃ 23 וְנִחֲמוּ אֶתְכֶם כִּי־תִרְאוּ אֶת־דַּרְכָּם וְאֶת־עֲלִילוֹתָם וִידַעְתֶּם כִּי לֹא חִנָּם עָשִׂיתִי אֵת כָּל־אֲשֶׁר־עָשִׂיתִי בָהּ נְאֻם אֲדֹנָי יְהוִֹה׃ פ

טו וַיְהִי דְבַר־יְהוָה אֵלַי לֵאמֹר׃ 2 בֶּן־ אָדָם מַה־יִּהְיֶה עֵץ־הַגֶּפֶן מִכָּל־עֵץ הַזְּמוֹרָה אֲשֶׁר הָיָה בַּעֲצֵי הַיָּעַר׃ 3 הֲיֻקַּח מִמֶּנּוּ עֵץ לַעֲשׂוֹת לִמְלָאכָה אִם־יִקְחוּ מִמֶּנּוּ יָתֵד לִתְלוֹת עָלָיו כָּל־כֶּלִי׃ 4 הִנֵּה לָאֵשׁ נִתַּן לְאָכְלָה אֵת שְׁנֵי קְצוֹתָיו אָכְלָה הָאֵשׁ וְתוֹכוֹ נָחָר הֲיִצְלַח לִמְלָאכָה׃ 5 הִנֵּה בִּהְיוֹתוֹ תָמִים לֹא יֵעָשֶׂה לִמְלָאכָה אַף כִּי־אֵשׁ אֲכָלַתְהוּ וַיֵּחָר וְנַעֲשָׂה עוֹד לִמְלָאכָה׃ ס

6 לָכֵן כֹּה אָמַר אֲדֹנָי יְהוִֹה כַּאֲשֶׁר עֵץ־ הַגֶּפֶן בְּעֵץ הַיַּעַר אֲשֶׁר־נְתַתִּיו לָאֵשׁ לְאָכְלָה כֵּן נָתַתִּי אֶת־יֹשְׁבֵי יְרוּשָׁלָםִ׃ 7 וְנָתַתִּי אֶת־פָּנַי בָּהֶם מֵהָאֵשׁ יָצָאוּ וְהָאֵשׁ תֹּאכְלֵם וִידַעְתֶּם כִּי־אֲנִי יְהוָה בְּשׂוּמִי אֶת־פָּנַי בָּהֶם׃ 8 וְנָתַתִּי אֶת־הָאָרֶץ שְׁמָמָה יַעַן מָעֲלוּ מַעַל נְאֻם אֲדֹנָי יְהוִֹה׃ פ

טז וַיְהִי דְבַר־יְהוָה אֵלַי לֵאמֹר׃ 2 בֶּן־ אָדָם הוֹדַע אֶת־יְרוּשָׁלַםִ אֶת־תּוֹעֲבֹתֶיהָ׃ 3 וְאָמַרְתָּ כֹּה־אָמַר אֲדֹנָי יְהוִֹה לִירוּשָׁלַםִ

---

b-b Several ancient versions read "who are bringing out sons and daughters."

salem: By origin and birth you are from the land of the Canaanites—your father was an Amorite and your mother a Hittite. [4]As for your birth, when you were born your navel cord was not cut, and you were not bathed in water to *a-smooth you;-a* you were not rubbed with salt, nor were you swaddled. [5]No one pitied you enough to do any one of these things for you out of compassion for you; on the day you were born, you were left lying, rejected, in the open field. [6]When I passed by you and saw you wallowing in your blood, I said to you: "Live in spite of your blood." *b-Yea, I said to you: "Live in spite of your blood."-b* [7]I let you grow like the plants of the field; and you continued to grow up until you attained *a-to womanhood,-a* until your breasts became firm and your hair sprouted.

You were still naked and bare [8]when I passed by you [again] and saw that your time for love had arrived. *c-So I spread My robe over you-c* and covered your nakedness, and I entered into a covenant with you by oath—declares the Lord God; thus you became Mine. [9]I bathed you in water, and washed the blood off you, and anointed you with oil. [10]I clothed you with embroidered garments, and gave you sandals of *a-dolphin leather-a* to wear, and wound fine linen about your head, and dressed you in silks. [11]I decked you out in finery and put bracelets on your arms and a chain around your neck. [12]I put a ring in your nose, and earrings in your ears, and a splendid crown on your head. [13]You adorned yourself with gold and silver, and your apparel was of fine linen, silk, and embroidery. Your food was choice flour, honey, and oil. You grew more and more beautiful, and became fit for royalty. [14]Your beauty won you fame among the nations, for it was perfected through the splendor which I set upon you—declares the Lord God.

מְכֹרֹתַ֙יִךְ֙ וּמֹלְדֹתַ֔יִךְ מֵאֶ֖רֶץ הַֽכְּנַעֲנִ֑י אָבִ֣יךְ הָאֱמֹרִ֔י וְאִמֵּ֖ךְ חִתִּֽית׃ 4 וּמוֹלְדוֹתַ֗יִךְ בְּי֨וֹם הוּלֶּ֤דֶת אֹתָךְ֙ לֹֽא־כׇרַּ֣ת שׇׁרֵּ֔ךְ* וּבְמַ֥יִם לֹֽא־רֻחַ֖צְתְּ לְמִשְׁעִ֑י וְהׇמְלֵ֙חַ֙ לֹ֣א הֻמְלַ֔חַתְּ וְהׇחְתֵּ֖ל לֹ֥א חֻתָּֽלְתְּ׃ 5 לֹא־חָ֣סָה עָלַ֣יִךְ עַ֗יִן לַעֲשׂ֥וֹת לָ֛ךְ אַחַ֥ת מֵאֵ֖לֶּה לְחֻמְלָ֣ה עָלָ֑יִךְ וַֽתֻּשְׁלְכִ֞י אֶל־פְּנֵ֤י הַשָּׂדֶה֙ בְּגֹ֣עַל נַפְשֵׁ֔ךְ בְּי֖וֹם הֻלֶּ֥דֶת אֹתָֽךְ׃ 6 וָאֶעֱבֹ֤ר עָלַ֙יִךְ֙ וָאֶרְאֵ֔ךְ מִתְבּוֹסֶ֖סֶת בְּדָמָ֑יִךְ וָאֹ֤מַר לָךְ֙ בְּדָמַ֣יִךְ חֲיִ֔י וָאֹ֥מַר לָ֖ךְ בְּדָמַ֥יִךְ חֲיִֽי׃ 7 רְבָבָ֗ה כְּצֶ֤מַח הַשָּׂדֶה֙ נְתַתִּ֔יךְ וַתִּרְבִּי֙ וַֽתִּגְדְּלִ֔י וַתָּבֹ֖אִי בַּעֲדִ֣י עֲדָיִ֑ים שָׁדַ֤יִם נָכֹ֙נוּ֙ וּשְׂעָרֵ֣ךְ צִמֵּ֔חַ וְאַ֖תְּ עֵרֹ֥ם וְעֶרְיָֽה׃ 8 וָאֶעֱבֹ֨ר עָלַ֜יִךְ וָאֶרְאֵ֗ךְ וְהִנֵּ֤ה עִתֵּךְ֙ עֵ֣ת דֹּדִ֔ים וָאֶפְרֹ֤שׂ כְּנָפִי֙ עָלַ֔יִךְ וָאֲכַסֶּ֖ה עֶרְוָתֵ֑ךְ וָאֶשָּׁ֣בַֽע לָ֠ךְ וָאָב֙וֹא בִבְרִ֤ית אֹתָךְ֙ נְאֻ֣ם אֲדֹנָ֣י יֱהֹוִ֔ה וַתִּ֖הְיִי לִֽי׃ 9 וָאֶרְחָצֵ֣ךְ בַּמַּ֔יִם וָאֶשְׁטֹ֥ף דָּמַ֖יִךְ מֵֽעָלָ֑יִךְ וָאֲסֻכֵ֖ךְ בַּשָּֽׁמֶן׃ 10 וָאַלְבִּישֵׁ֣ךְ רִקְמָ֗ה וָאֶנְעֲלֵ֖ךְ תָּ֑חַשׁ וָאֶחְבְּשֵׁ֣ךְ בַּשֵּׁ֔שׁ וַאֲכַסֵּ֖ךְ מֶֽשִׁי׃ 11 וָאֶעְדֵּ֖ךְ עֶ֑דִי וָאֶתְּנָ֤ה צְמִידִים֙ עַל־יָדַ֔יִךְ וְרָבִ֖יד עַל־גְּרוֹנֵֽךְ׃ 12 וָאֶתֵּ֥ן נֶ֙זֶם֙ עַל־אַפֵּ֔ךְ וַעֲגִילִ֖ים עַל־אׇזְנָ֑יִךְ וַעֲטֶ֥רֶת תִּפְאֶ֖רֶת בְּרֹאשֵֽׁךְ׃ 13 וַתַּעְדִּ֞י זָהָ֣ב וָכֶ֗סֶף וּמַלְבּוּשֵׁךְ֙ שֵׁ֤ש וָמֶ֙שִׁי֙ וְרִקְמָ֔ה סֹ֧לֶת וּדְבַ֛שׁ וָשֶׁ֖מֶן אכלתי (אָכָ֑לְתְּ) וַתִּ֣יפִי בִּמְאֹ֣ד מְאֹ֔ד וַֽתִּצְלְחִ֖י לִמְלוּכָֽה׃ 14 וַיֵּ֙צֵא לָ֥ךְ שֵׁ֛ם בַּגּוֹיִ֖ם בְּיׇפְיֵ֑ךְ כִּ֣י ׀ כָּלִ֣יל ה֗וּא בַּהֲדָרִי֙ אֲשֶׁר־שַׂ֣מְתִּי עָלַ֔יִךְ נְאֻ֖ם אֲדֹנָ֥י יֱהֹוִֽה׃

---

a-a   Meaning of Heb. uncertain.

b-b   This sentence is missing from some ancient versions and a few Heb. mss.

c-c   An act symbolizing espousal; cf. note at Deut. 23.1, Ruth 3.9.

ר' דגושה פעמיים   v. 4.

¹⁵But confident in your beauty and fame, you played the harlot: you lavished your favors on every passerby; *a*-they were his.-*a* ¹⁶You even took some of your cloths and made yourself *a*-tapestried platforms-*a* and fornicated on them—*d*-not in the future; not in time to come.-*d* ¹⁷You took your beautiful things, made of the gold and silver that I had given you, and you made yourself phallic images and fornicated with them. ¹⁸You took your embroidered cloths to cover them; and you set My oil and My incense before them. ¹⁹The food that I had given you—the choice flour, the oil, and the honey, which I had provided for you to eat—you set it before them for a pleasing odor.*e* And so it went—declares the Lord GOD. ²⁰You even took the sons and daughters that you bore to Me and sacrificed them to those [images] as food—as if your harlotries were not enough, ²¹you slaughtered My children and presented them as offerings to them! ²²In all your abominations and harlotries, you did not remember the days of your youth, when you were naked and bare, and lay wallowing in your blood.

²³After all your wickedness (woe, woe to you!)—declares the Lord GOD—²⁴you built yourself an eminence and made yourself a mound in every square. ²⁵You built your mound at every crossroad; and you sullied your beauty and spread your legs to every passerby, and you multiplied your harlotries. ²⁶You played the whore with your neighbors, the lustful*f* Egyptians—you multiplied your harlotries to anger Me. ²⁷Now, I will stretch out My arm against you and withhold your maintenance; and I will surrender you to the will of your enemies, the Philistine women, who are shocked by your lewd behavior.

²⁸In your insatiable lust you also played the whore with the Assyrians; you played the whore

15 וַתִּבְטְחִי בְיָפְיֵךְ וַתִּזְנִי עַל־שְׁמֵךְ וַתִּשְׁפְּכִי אֶת־תַּזְנוּתַיִךְ עַל־כָּל־עוֹבֵר לוֹ־
יֶהִי: 16 וַתִּקְחִי מִבְּגָדַיִךְ וַתַּעֲשִׂי־לָךְ בָּמוֹת טְלֻאוֹת וַתִּזְנִי עֲלֵיהֶם לֹא בָאוֹת וְלֹא יִהְיֶה: 17 וַתִּקְחִי כְּלֵי תִפְאַרְתֵּךְ מִזְּהָבִי וּמִכַּסְפִּי אֲשֶׁר נָתַתִּי לָךְ וַתַּעֲשִׂי־לָךְ צַלְמֵי זָכָר וַתִּזְנִי־בָם: 18 וַתִּקְחִי אֶת־בִּגְדֵי רִקְמָתֵךְ וַתְּכַסִּים וְשַׁמְנִי וּקְטָרְתִּי נתתי נָתַתְּ לִפְנֵיהֶם: 19 וְלַחְמִי אֲשֶׁר־נָתַתִּי לָךְ סֹלֶת וָשֶׁמֶן וּדְבַשׁ הֶאֱכַלְתִּיךְ וּנְתַתִּיהוּ לִפְנֵיהֶם לְרֵיחַ נִיחֹחַ וַיֶּהִי נְאֻם אֲדֹנָי יְהֹוִה: 20 וַתִּקְחִי אֶת־בָּנַיִךְ וְאֶת־בְּנוֹתַיִךְ אֲשֶׁר יָלַדְתְּ לִי וַתִּזְבָּחִים לָהֶם לֶאֱכוֹל הַמְעַט מתזנתך מִתַּזְנוּתָיִךְ: 21 וַתִּשְׁחֲטִי אֶת־בָּנָי וַתִּתְּנִים בְּהַעֲבִיר אוֹתָם לָהֶם: 22 וְאֵת כָּל־תּוֹעֲבֹתַיִךְ וְתַזְנֻתַיִךְ לֹא זָכַרְתִּ אֶת־יְמֵי נְעוּרָיִךְ בִּהְיוֹתֵךְ עֵרֹם וְעֶרְיָה מִתְבּוֹסֶסֶת בְּדָמֵךְ הָיִית: 23 וַיְהִי אַחֲרֵי כָּל־רָעָתֵךְ אוֹי אוֹי לָךְ נְאֻם אֲדֹנָי יְהֹוִה: 24 וַתִּבְנִי־לָךְ גֶּב וַתַּעֲשִׂי־לָךְ רָמָה בְּכָל־רְחוֹב: 25 אֶל־כָּל־רֹאשׁ דֶּרֶךְ בָּנִית רָמָתֵךְ וַתְּתַעֲבִי אֶת־יָפְיֵךְ וַתְּפַשְּׂקִי אֶת־רַגְלַיִךְ לְכָל־עוֹבֵר וַתַּרְבִּי אֶת־תזנתך תַּזְנוּתָיִךְ: 26 וַתִּזְנִי אֶל־בְּנֵי־מִצְרַיִם שְׁכֵנַיִךְ גִּדְלֵי בָשָׂר וַתַּרְבִּי אֶת־תַּזְנֻתֵךְ לְהַכְעִיסֵנִי: 27 וְהִנֵּה נָטִיתִי יָדִי עָלַיִךְ וָאֶגְרַע חֻקֵּךְ וָאֶתְּנֵךְ בְּנֶפֶשׁ שֹׂנְאוֹתַיִךְ בְּנוֹת פְּלִשְׁתִּים הַנִּכְלָמוֹת מִדַּרְכֵּךְ זִמָּה: 28 וַתִּזְנִי אֶל־בְּנֵי אַשּׁוּר מִבִּלְתִּי שָׂבְעָתֵךְ וַתִּזְנִים וְגַם לֹא שָׂבָעַתְּ: 29 וַתַּרְבִּי אֶת־

---

d-d See note at Exod. 25.4.
e I.e., as a sacrifice; cf. Lev. 2.2.
f Lit. "big of phallus"; cf. 23.20.

with them, but were still unsated. ²⁹You multiplied your harlotries with Chaldea, that land of traders; yet even with this you were not satisfied.

³⁰g‑How sick was your heart‑g—declares the Lord GOD—when you did all those things, the acts of a self-willed whore, ³¹building your eminence at every crossroad and setting your mound in every square! Yet you were not like a prostitute, for you spurned fees; ³²[you were like] the adulterous wife who welcomes strangers instead of her husband. ³³Gifts are made to all prostitutes, but you made gifts to all your lovers, and bribed them to come to you from every quarter for your harlotries. ³⁴You were the opposite of other women: you solicited instead of being solicited; you paid fees instead of being paid fees. Thus you were just the opposite!

³⁵Now, O harlot, hear the word of the LORD. ³⁶Thus said the Lord GOD: Because of your brazen effrontery, offering your nakedness to your lovers for harlotry—h‑just like the blood of your children, which you gave to all your abominable fetishes:‑h—³⁷I will assuredly assemble all the lovers to whom you gave your favors, along with everybody you accepted and everybody you rejected. I will assemble them against you from every quarter, and I will expose your nakedness to them, and they shall see all your nakedness. ³⁸I will inflict upon you the punishment of women who commit adultery and murder, and I will direct bloody and impassioned fury against you. ³⁹I will deliver you into their hands, and they shall tear down your eminence and level your mounds; and they shall strip you of your clothing and take away your dazzling jewels, leaving you naked and bare. ⁴⁰Then they shall assemble a mob against you to pelt you with stones and pierce you with their swords.

תַּזְנוּתֵ֛ךְ אֶל־אֶ֥רֶץ כְּנַ֖עַן כַּשְׂדִּ֑ימָה וְגַם־בְּזֹ֖את לֹ֥א שָׂבָֽעַתְּ׃
³⁰ מָ֤ה אֲמֻלָה֙ לִבָּתֵ֔ךְ נְאֻ֖ם אֲדֹנָ֣י יְהֹוִ֑ה בַּעֲשׂוֹתֵךְ֙ אֶת־כׇּל־אֵ֔לֶּה מַעֲשֵׂ֖ה אִשָּֽׁה־זוֹנָ֥ה שַׁלָּֽטֶת׃ ³¹ בִּבְנוֹתַ֣יִךְ גַּבֵּ֗ךְ בְּרֹאשׁ֙ כׇּל־דֶּ֔רֶךְ וְרָמָתֵ֥ךְ עָשִׂ֖ית בְּכׇל־רְח֑וֹב וְלֹא־הָיִ֥ית כַּזּוֹנָ֖ה לְקַלֵּ֥ס אֶתְנָֽן׃ ³² הָאִשָּׁ֖ה הַמְּנָאָ֑פֶת תַּ֣חַת אִישָׁ֔הּ תִּקַּ֖ח אֶת־זָרִֽים׃ ³³ לְכׇל־זֹנ֖וֹת יִתְּנוּ־נֵ֑דֶה וְאַ֨תְּ נָתַ֤תְּ אֶת־נְדָנַ֙יִךְ֙ לְכׇל־מְאַֽהֲבַ֔יִךְ וַתִּשְׁחֳדִ֣י אוֹתָ֔ם לָב֥וֹא אֵלַ֛יִךְ מִסָּבִ֖יב בְּתַזְנוּתָֽיִךְ׃ ³⁴ וַיְהִי־בָ֨ךְ הֵ֤פֶךְ מִן־הַנָּשִׁים֙ בְּתַזְנוּתַ֔יִךְ וְאַחֲרַ֖יִךְ לֹ֣א זוּנָּ֑ה וּבְתִתֵּ֣ךְ אֶתְנָ֗ן וְאֶתְנַ֛ן לֹ֥א נִתַּן־לָ֖ךְ וַתְּהִ֥י לְהֶֽפֶךְ׃ ³⁵ לָכֵ֣ן זוֹנָ֔ה שִׁמְעִ֖י דְּבַר־יְהֹוָֽה׃ פ ³⁶ כֹּֽה־אָמַ֞ר אֲדֹנָ֣י יְהֹוִ֗ה יַ֣עַן הִשָּׁפֵ֤ךְ נְחֻשְׁתֵּךְ֙ וַתִּגָּלֶ֣ה עֶרְוָתֵ֔ךְ בְּתַזְנוּתַ֖יִךְ עַל־מְאַהֲבָ֑יִךְ וְעַל֙ כׇּל־גִּלּוּלֵ֣י תוֹעֲבוֹתַ֔יִךְ וְכִדְמֵ֣י בָנַ֔יִךְ אֲשֶׁ֥ר נָתַ֖תְּ לָהֶֽם׃ ³⁷ לָכֵ֣ן הִנְנִ֣י מְקַבֵּ֣ץ אֶת־כׇּל־מְאַֽהֲבַ֗יִךְ אֲשֶׁ֤ר עָרַ֙בְתְּ֙ עֲלֵיהֶ֔ם וְאֵת֙ כׇּל־אֲשֶׁ֣ר אָהַ֔בְתְּ עַ֖ל כׇּל־אֲשֶׁ֣ר שָׂנֵ֑את וְקִבַּצְתִּ֨י אֹתָ֤ם עָלַ֙יִךְ֙ מִסָּבִ֔יב וְגִלֵּיתִ֤י עֶרְוָתֵךְ֙ אֲלֵהֶ֔ם וְרָא֖וּ אֶת־כׇּל־עֶרְוָתֵֽךְ׃ ³⁸ וּשְׁפַטְתִּיךְ֙ מִשְׁפְּטֵ֣י נֹאֲפ֔וֹת וְשֹׁפְכֹ֖ת דָּ֑ם וּנְתַתִּ֕יךְ דַּ֥ם חֵמָ֖ה וְקִנְאָֽה׃ ³⁹ וְנָתַתִּ֨י אוֹתָ֜ךְ בְּיָדָ֗ם וְהָרְס֤וּ גַבֵּךְ֙ וְנִתְּצ֣וּ רָמֹתַ֔יִךְ וְהִפְשִׁ֤יטוּ אוֹתָךְ֙ בְּגָדַ֔יִךְ וְלָקְח֖וּ כְּלֵ֣י תִפְאַרְתֵּ֑ךְ וְהִנִּיח֖וּךְ עֵירֹ֥ם וְעֶרְיָֽה׃ ⁴⁰ וְהֶעֱל֤וּ עָלַ֙יִךְ֙ קָהָ֔ל וְרָגְמ֥וּ אוֹתָ֖ךְ בָּאָ֑בֶן וּבִתְּק֖וּךְ

---

g‑g   *Change of vocalization yields* "How furious I was with you"; *lit.* "How I was filled with your fury" (libbat, *as in Akkadian and Old Aramaic*).

h‑h   *Construction of Heb. uncertain.*

⁴¹They shall put your houses to the flames and execute punishment upon you in the sight of many women; thus I will put a stop to your harlotry, and you shall pay no more fees. ⁴²When I have satisfied My fury upon you and My rage has departed from you, then I will be tranquil; I will be angry no more.

⁴³Because you did not remember the days of your youth, but infuriated Me with all those things, I ʰ-will pay you back for your conduct-ʰ—declares the Lord GOD.

Have you not committed depravity on top of all your other abominations? ⁴⁴Why, everyone who uses proverbs applies to you the proverb "Like mother, like daughter." ⁴⁵You are the daughter of your mother, who rejected her husband and children. And you are the sister of your sisters, who rejected their husbands and children; for you are daughters of a Hittite mother and an Amorite father. ⁴⁶Your elder sister was Samaria, who lived with her daughters to the north of you; your younger sister was Sodom, who lived with her daughters to the south of you. ⁴⁷Did you not walk in their ways and practice their abominations? Why, you were almostᵃ more corrupt than they in all your ways. ⁴⁸As I live—declares the Lord GOD—your sister Sodom and her daughters did not do what you and your daughters did. ⁴⁹Only this was the sin of your sister Sodom: arrogance! She and her daughters had plenty of bread and untroubled tranquillity; yet she did not support the poor and the needy. ⁵⁰In their haughtiness, they committed abomination before Me; and so I removed them, as you saw.ⁱ ⁵¹Nor did Samaria commit even half your sins. You committed more abominations than they, and by all the abominations that you committed you made your sisters look righteous. ⁵²Truly, you must bear the disgrace of serving as your sisters' ad-

בְּחֵרְבוֹתָם : ⁴¹ וְשָׂרְפוּ בָתַּיִךְ בָּאֵשׁ וְעָשׂוּ־
בָךְ שְׁפָטִים לְעֵינֵי נָשִׁים רַבּוֹת וְהִשְׁבַּתִּיךְ
מִזּוֹנָה וְגַם־אֶתְנַן לֹא תִתְּנִי־עוֹד :
⁴² וַהֲנִחֹתִי חֲמָתִי בָּךְ וְסָרָה קִנְאָתִי מִמֵּךְ
וְשָׁקַטְתִּי וְלֹא אֶכְעַס עוֹד :
⁴³ יַעַן אֲשֶׁר לֹא־זָכַרְתְּ אֶת־יְמֵי
נְעוּרַיִךְ וַתִּרְגְּזִי־לִי בְּכָל־אֵלֶּה וְגַם־אֲנִי הֵא
דַרְכֵּךְ | בְּרֹאשׁ נָתַתִּי נְאֻם אֲדֹנָי יְהוִֹה
וְלֹא עָשִׂית אֶת־הַזִּמָּה עַל כָּל־
תּוֹעֲבֹתָיִךְ : ⁴⁴ הִנֵּה כָּל־הַמֹּשֵׁל עָלַיִךְ
יִמְשֹׁל לֵאמֹר כְּאִמָּה בִּתָּה : ⁴⁵ בַּת־אִמֵּךְ
אַתְּ גֹּעֶלֶת אִישָׁהּ וּבָנֶיהָ וַאֲחוֹת אֲחוֹתֵךְ
אַתְּ אֲשֶׁר גָּעֲלוּ אַנְשֵׁיהֶן וּבְנֵיהֶן אִמְּכֶן
חִתִּית וַאֲבִיכֶן אֱמֹרִי : ⁴⁶ וַאֲחוֹתֵךְ הַגְּדוֹלָה
שֹׁמְרוֹן הִיא וּבְנוֹתֶיהָ הַיּוֹשֶׁבֶת עַל־
שְׂמֹאולֵךְ* וַאֲחוֹתֵךְ הַקְּטַנָּה מִמֵּךְ
הַיּוֹשֶׁבֶת מִימִינֵךְ סְדֹם וּבְנוֹתֶיהָ : ⁴⁷ וְלֹא
בְדַרְכֵיהֶן הָלַכְתְּ וּבְתוֹעֲבוֹתֵיהֶן עָשִׂיתי
עָשִׂית כִּמְעַט קָט וַתַּשְׁחִתִי מֵהֵן בְּכָל־
דְּרָכָיִךְ : ⁴⁸ חַי־אָנִי נְאֻם אֲדֹנָי יְהוִֹה אִם־
עָשְׂתָה סְדֹם אֲחוֹתֵךְ הִיא וּבְנוֹתֶיהָ כַּאֲשֶׁר
עָשִׂית אַתְּ וּבְנוֹתָיִךְ : ⁴⁹ הִנֵּה־זֶה הָיָה עֲוֹן
סְדֹם אֲחוֹתֵךְ גָּאוֹן שִׂבְעַת־לֶחֶם וְשַׁלְוַת
הַשְׁקֵט הָיָה לָהּ וְלִבְנוֹתֶיהָ וְיַד־עָנִי וְאֶבְיוֹן
לֹא הֶחֱזִיקָה : ⁵⁰ וַתִּגְבְּהֶינָה וַתַּעֲשֶׂינָה
תוֹעֵבָה לְפָנָי וָאָסִיר אֶתְהֶן כַּאֲשֶׁר
רָאִיתִי : ס ⁵¹ וְשֹׁמְרוֹן כַּחֲצִי חַטֹּאתַיִךְ
לֹא חָטָאָה וַתַּרְבִּי אֶת־תּוֹעֲבוֹתַיִךְ מֵהֵנָּה
וַתְּצַדְּקִי אֶת־אֲחוֹתֵךְ אֲחוֹתָיִךְ בְּכָל־
תּוֹעֲבוֹתַיִךְ אֲשֶׁר עָשִׂית : ⁵² גַּם־
אַתְּ | שְׂאִי כְלִמָּתֵךְ אֲשֶׁר פִּלַּלְתְּ לַאֲחוֹתֵךְ

ⁱ Construed as second-person feminine; cf. qere, vv. 47 and 51; and see above vv. 13, 18, 22, 31, 43.

מלא ו׳   v. 46.

vocate: Since you have sinned more abominably than they, they appear righteous in comparison. So be ashamed and bear your disgrace, because you have made your sisters look righteous.

⁵³I will restore their fortunes—the fortunes of Sodom and her daughters and the fortunes of Samaria and her daughters—and your fortunes along with theirs. ⁵⁴Thus you shall bear your disgrace and feel your disgrace for behaving in such a way that they could take comfort. ⁵⁵Then your sister Sodom and her daughters shall return to their former state, and Samaria and her daughters shall return to their former state, and you and your daughters shall return to your former state. ⁵⁶Was not your sister Sodom a byword in your mouth in the days of your pride, ⁵⁷before your own wickedness was exposed? So must you now bear the mockery of the daughters of Aram *j* and all her neighbors, the daughters of Philistia who jeer at you on every side. ⁵⁸You yourself must bear your depravity and your abominations—declares the LORD.

⁵⁹Truly, thus said the Lord GOD: I will deal with you as you have dealt, for you have spurned the pact and violated the covenant. ⁶⁰Nevertheless, I will remember the covenant I made with you in the days of your youth, and I will establish it with you as an everlasting covenant. ⁶¹You shall remember your ways and feel ashamed, when you receive your older sisters and your younger sisters, and I give them to you as daughters, though they are not of your covenant. ⁶²I will establish My covenant with you, and you shall know that I am the LORD. ⁶³Thus you shall remember and feel shame, and you shall be too abashed to open your mouth again, when I have forgiven you for all that you did—declares the Lord GOD.

---

j Many Heb. mss. and editions read "Edom."

בְּחַטֹּאתַ֙יִךְ֙ אֲשֶׁר־הִתְעַ֔בְתְּ מֵהֵ֖ן תִּצְדַּ֑קְנָה מִמֵּ֑ךְ וְגַם־אַ֣תְּ בּ֗וֹשִׁי וּשְׂאִ֤י כְלִמָּתֵךְ֙ בְּצַדֶּקְתֵּ֖ךְ אַחְיוֹתֵֽךְ׃ ⁵³ וְשַׁבְתִּי֙ אֶת־שְׁבִ֣יתְהֶ֔ן אֶת־שְׁב֣וּת סְדֹם֙ וּבְנוֹתֶ֔יהָ וְאֶת־שְׁב֖וּת שֹׁמְר֣וֹן וּבְנוֹתֶ֑יהָ ושבית וּשְׁב֥וּת שְׁבִיתַ֖יִךְ בְּתוֹכֵֽהְנָה׃ ⁵⁴ לְמַ֙עַן֙ תִּשְׂאִ֣י כְלִמָּתֵ֔ךְ וְנִכְלַ֕מְתְּ מִכֹּ֖ל אֲשֶׁ֣ר עָשִׂ֑ית בְּנַחֲמֵ֖ךְ אֹתָֽן׃ ⁵⁵ וַאֲחוֹתַ֗יִךְ סְדֹ֤ם וּבְנוֹתֶ֙יהָ֙ תָּשֹׁ֣בְןָ לְקַדְמָתָ֔ן וְשֹֽׁמְרוֹן֙ וּבְנוֹתֶ֔יהָ תָּשֹׁ֖בְןָ לְקַדְמָתָ֑ן וְאַ֙תְּ֙ וּבְנוֹתַ֔יִךְ תְּשֻׁבֶ֖יןָ לְקַדְמַתְכֶֽן׃ ⁵⁶ וְל֤וֹא הָֽיְתָה֙ סְדֹ֣ם אֲחוֹתֵ֔ךְ לִשְׁמוּעָ֖ה בְּפִ֑יךְ בְּי֖וֹם גְּאוֹנָֽיִךְ׃ ⁵⁷ בְּטֶ֩רֶם֩ תִּגָּלֶ֨ה רָעָתֵ֜ךְ כְּמ֣וֹ עֵ֗ת חֶרְפַּת֙ בְּנוֹת־אֲרָ֔ם וְכָל־סְבִיבוֹתֶ֖יהָ בְּנ֣וֹת פְּלִשְׁתִּ֑ים הַשָּׁאט֥וֹת* אוֹתָ֖ךְ מִסָּבִֽיב׃ ⁵⁸ אֶת־זִמָּתֵ֥ךְ וְאֶת־תּוֹעֲבוֹתַ֖יִךְ אַ֣תְּ נְשָׂאתִ֑ים נְאֻ֖ם יְהוָֽה׃ ס

⁵⁹ כִּ֣י כֹ֤ה אָמַר֙ אֲדֹנָ֣י יְהוִ֔ה ועשית וְעָשִׂ֥ית אוֹתָ֖ךְ כַּאֲשֶׁ֣ר עָשִׂ֑ית אֲשֶׁר־בָּזִ֥ית אָלָ֖ה לְהָפֵ֥ר בְּרִֽית׃ ⁶⁰ וְזָכַרְתִּ֨י אֲנִ֧י אֶת־בְּרִיתִ֛י אוֹתָ֖ךְ בִּימֵ֣י נְעוּרָ֑יִךְ וַהֲקִמוֹתִ֥י לָ֖ךְ בְּרִ֥ית עוֹלָֽם׃ ⁶¹ וְזָכַ֣רְתְּ אֶת־דְּרָכַ֗יִךְ וְנִכְלַ֙מְתְּ֙ בְּקַחְתֵּ֞ךְ אֶת־אֲחוֹתַ֙יִךְ֙ הַגְּדֹל֣וֹת מִמֵּ֔ךְ אֶל־הַקְּטַנּ֖וֹת מִמֵּ֑ךְ וְנָתַתִּ֨י אֶתְהֶ֥ן לָ֛ךְ לְבָנ֖וֹת וְלֹ֥א מִבְּרִיתֵֽךְ׃ ⁶² וַהֲקִימוֹתִ֥י אֲנִ֛י אֶת־בְּרִיתִ֖י אִתָּ֑ךְ וְיָדַ֖עַתְּ כִּֽי־אֲנִ֥י יְהוָֽה׃ ⁶³ לְמַ֙עַן֙ תִּזְכְּרִ֣י וָבֹ֔שְׁתְּ וְלֹ֨א יִֽהְיֶה־לָּ֥ךְ עוֹד֙ פִּתְח֣וֹן פֶּ֔ה מִפְּנֵ֖י כְּלִמָּתֵ֑ךְ בְּכַפְּרִי־לָךְ֙ לְכָל־אֲשֶׁ֣ר עָשִׂ֔ית נְאֻ֖ם אֲדֹנָ֥י יְהוִֽה׃ ס

---

17 The word of the LORD came to me: 2O mortal, propound a riddle and relate an allegory to the House of Israel. 3Say: Thus said the Lord GOD: The great eagle with the great wings and the long pinions, *a*-with the full plumage and the brilliant colors,-*a* came to the Lebanon range and seized the top of the cedar. 4He plucked off its topmost bough and carried it off to the land of traders*b* and set it in a city of merchants. 5He then took some of the seed of the land*c* and planted it in a fertile field; *d*-he planted and set it like a willow-*d* beside abundant waters. 6It grew and became a spreading vine of low stature; it became a vine, produced branches, and sent out boughs. [He had intended] that its twigs should turn to him, and that its roots should stay under him.

7But there was another great eagle with great wings and full plumage; and this vine now bent its roots in his direction and sent out its twigs toward him, that he might water it more than the bed where it was planted—8though it was planted in rich soil beside abundant water—so that it might grow branches and produce boughs and be a noble vine.

9Say: Thus said the Lord GOD: Will it thrive? Will he*e* not tear out its roots and rip off its crown, so that its entire foliage withers? It shall wither, despite any strong arm or mighty army [that may come] to remove it from its roots. 10And suppose it is transplanted, will it thrive? When the east wind strikes it, it shall wither— wither upon the bed where it is growing.

11Then the word of the LORD came to me: 12Say to the rebellious breed: Do you not know what these things mean? Say: The king of Bab-

---

יז וַיְהִ֥י דְבַר־יְהֹוָ֖ה אֵלַ֥י לֵאמֹֽר: 2 בֶּן־
אָדָ֕ם ח֥וּד חִידָ֖ה וּמְשֹׁ֣ל מָשָׁ֑ל אֶל־בֵּ֖ית
יִשְׂרָאֵֽל: 3 וְאָמַרְתָּ֞ כֹּה־אָמַ֣ר ׀ אֲדֹנָ֣י יְהֹוִ֗ה
הַנֶּ֤שֶׁר הַגָּדוֹל֙ גְּד֤וֹל הַכְּנָפַ֙יִם֙ אֶ֣רֶךְ הָאֵ֔בֶר
מָלֵא֙ הַנּוֹצָ֔ה אֲשֶׁר־ל֖וֹ הָרִקְמָ֑ה בָּ֣א אֶל־
הַלְּבָנ֔וֹן וַיִּקַּ֖ח אֶת־צַמֶּ֥רֶת הָאָֽרֶז: 4 אֵ֣ת
רֹ֤אשׁ יְנִיקוֹתָיו֙ קָטָ֔ף וַיְבִיאֵ֖הוּ אֶל־אֶ֣רֶץ
כְּנַ֑עַן בְּעִ֥יר רֹכְלִ֖ים שָׂמֽוֹ: 5 וַיִּקַּח֙ מִזֶּ֣רַע
הָאָ֔רֶץ וַיִּתְּנֵ֖הוּ בִּשְׂדֵה־זָ֑רַע קָ֚ח עַל־מַ֣יִם
רַבִּ֔ים צַפְצָפָ֖ה שָׂמֽוֹ: 6 וַיִּצְמַ֡ח וַיְהִי֩ לְגֶ֨פֶן
סֹרַ֜חַת שִׁפְלַ֣ת קוֹמָ֗ה לִפְנ֤וֹת דָּֽלִיּוֹתָיו֙ אֵלָ֔יו
וְשָֽׁרָשָׁ֖יו תַּחְתָּ֣יו יִֽהְי֑וּ וַתְּהִ֣י לְגֶ֔פֶן וַתַּ֣עַשׂ
בַּדִּ֔ים וַתְּשַׁלַּ֖ח פֹּארֽוֹת:
7 וַיְהִ֤י נֶֽשֶׁר־אֶחָד֙ גָּד֔וֹל גְּד֥וֹל כְּנָפַ֖יִם וְרַב־
נוֹצָ֑ה וְהִנֵּה֩ הַגֶּ֨פֶן הַזֹּ֜את כָּפְנָ֧ה שׇׁרָשֶׁ֣יהָ
עָלָ֗יו וְדָֽלִיּוֹתָיו֙ שִׁלְחָה־ל֔וֹ* לְהַשְׁק֣וֹת
אוֹתָ֔הּ מֵעֲרֻג֖וֹת מַטָּעָֽהּ: 8 אֶל־שָׂדֶ֥ה ט֛וֹב
אֶל־מַ֥יִם רַבִּ֖ים הִ֣יא שְׁתוּלָ֑ה לַעֲשׂ֤וֹת עָנָף֙
וְלָשֵׂ֣את פֶּ֔רִי לִהְי֖וֹת לְגֶ֥פֶן אַדָּֽרֶת: ס
9 אֱמֹ֗ר כֹּ֥ה אָמַ֖ר אֲדֹנָ֣י יְהֹוִ֑ה תִּצְלָ֔ח הֲל֣וֹא
אֶת־שָׁרָשֶׁ֣יהָ יְנַתֵּ֗ק וְאֶת־פִּרְיָ֤הּ ׀ יְקוֹסֵ֣ס
וְיָבֵ֗שׁ כׇּל־טַרְפֵּ֤י צִמְחָהּ֙ תִּיבָ֔שׁ וְלֹֽא־
בִזְרֹ֤עַ גְּדוֹלָה֙ וּבְעַם־רָ֔ב לְמַשְׂא֥וֹת אוֹתָ֖הּ
מִשׇּׁרָשֶֽׁיהָ: 10 וְהִנֵּ֥ה שְׁתוּלָ֖ה הֲתִצְלָ֑ח
הֲלֹא֩ כְגַ֨עַת בָּ֜הּ ר֤וּחַ הַקָּדִים֙ תִּיבַ֣שׁ יָבֹ֔שׁ
עַל־עֲרֻגֹ֥ת צִמְחָ֖הּ תִּיבָֽשׁ: פ
11 וַיְהִ֥י דְבַר־יְהֹוָ֖ה אֵלַ֥י לֵאמֹֽר: 12 אֱמׇר־נָא֙
לְבֵ֣ית הַמֶּ֔רִי הֲלֹ֥א יְדַעְתֶּ֖ם מָה־אֵ֑לֶּה אֱמֹ֗ר

---

a-a *This description suggests the golden eagle; the vulture, called by the same word in Heb. (*nesher*) has a bald head (Mic. 1.16) and dark feathers.*

b *Cf. 16.29.*

c *Emendation yields "cedar."*

d-d *Meaning of Heb. uncertain.*

e *I.e., the first eagle.*

ל' רפה   v. 7.

ylon came to Jerusalem, and carried away its king and its officers and brought them back with him to Babylon. [13]He took one of the seed royal and made a covenant with him and imposed an oath on him, and he carried away the nobles of the land—[14]so that it might be a humble kingdom and not exalt itself, but keep his covenant and so endure.

[15]But [that prince] rebelled against him and sent his envoys to Egypt to get horses and a large army. Will he succeed? Will he who does such things escape? Shall he break a covenant and escape? [16]As I live—declares the Lord GOD—in the very homeland of the king who made him king, whose oath he flouted and whose covenant he broke—right there, in Babylon, he shall die. [17]Pharaoh will not fight at his side with a great army and with numerous troops in the war, when mounds are thrown up and siege towers erected to destroy many lives. [18]He flouted a pact and broke a covenant; he gave his promise and did all these things—he shall not escape. [19]Assuredly, thus said the Lord GOD: As I live, I will pay him back for flouting My pact and breaking My covenant. [20]I will spread My net over him and he shall be caught in My snare; I will carry him to Babylon and enter with him into judgment there for the trespass which he committed against Me. [21]And all the fugitives[f] of all his battalions shall fall by the sword, and those who remain shall scatter in every direction; then you will know that I the LORD have spoken.

[22]Thus said the Lord GOD: Then I in turn will take and set [in the ground a slip] from the lofty top of the cedar; I will pluck a tender twig from the tip of its crown, and I will plant it on a tall, towering mountain. [23]I will plant it in Israel's lofty highlands, and it shall bring forth boughs and produce branches[g] and grow into a noble

---

f   Many mss. read "picked men."
g   Others "fruit."

הִנֵּה־בָ֤א מֶֽלֶךְ־בָּבֶל֙ יְר֣וּשָׁלִַ֔ם וַיִּקַּ֣ח אֶת־
מַלְכָּהּ֙ וְאֶת־שָׂרֶ֔יהָ וַיָּבֵ֥א אוֹתָ֛ם אֵלָ֖יו
בָּבֶֽלָה׃ 13 וַיִּקַּח֙ מִזֶּ֣רַע הַמְּלוּכָ֔ה וַיִּכְרֹ֥ת
אִתּ֖וֹ בְּרִ֑ית וַיָּבֵ֤א אֹתוֹ֙ בְּאָלָ֔ה וְאֶת־אֵילֵ֥י
הָאָ֖רֶץ לָקָֽח׃ 14 לִֽהְיוֹת֙ מַמְלָכָ֣ה שְׁפָלָ֔ה
לְבִלְתִּ֖י הִתְנַשֵּׂ֑א לִשְׁמֹ֥ר אֶת־בְּרִית֖וֹ
לְעָמְדָֽהּ׃

15 וַיִּמְרָד־בּ֗וֹ לִשְׁלֹ֤חַ מַלְאָכָיו֙ מִצְרַ֔יִם
לָתֶת־ל֥וֹ סוּסִ֖ים וְעַם־רָ֑ב הֲיִצְלָ֤ח הֲיִמָּלֵט֙
הָעֹשֵׂ֣ה אֵ֔לֶּה וְהֵפֵ֥ר בְּרִ֖ית וְנִמְלָֽט׃ 16 חַי־
אָ֗נִי נְאֻם֮ אֲדֹנָ֣י יְהוִה֒ אִם־לֹ֗א בִּמְקוֹם֙
הַמֶּ֙לֶךְ֙ הַמַּמְלִ֣יךְ אֹת֔וֹ אֲשֶׁ֤ר בָּזָה֙ אֶת־אָ֣לָת֔וֹ
וַאֲשֶׁ֥ר הֵפֵ֖ר אֶת־בְּרִית֑וֹ אִתּ֥וֹ בְתֽוֹךְ־בָּבֶ֖ל
יָמֽוּת׃ 17 וְלֹא֩ בְחַ֨יִל גָּד֜וֹל וּבְקָהָ֣ל רָ֗ב
יַעֲשֶׂ֨ה אוֹת֤וֹ פַרְעֹה֙ בַּמִּלְחָמָ֔ה בִּשְׁפֹּ֥ךְ
סֹלְלָ֖ה וּבִבְנ֣וֹת דָּיֵ֑ק לְהַכְרִ֖ית נְפָשׁ֥וֹת
רַבּֽוֹת׃ 18 וּבָזָ֥ה אָלָ֖ה לְהָפֵ֣ר בְּרִ֑ית וְהִנֵּ֨ה
נָתַ֥ן יָד֛וֹ וְכָל־אֵ֥לֶּה עָשָׂ֖ה לֹ֥א יִמָּלֵֽט׃ ס
19 לָכֵ֞ן כֹּה־אָמַ֨ר אֲדֹנָ֣י יְהוִה֮ חַי־אָנִי֒ אִם־
לֹ֗א אָֽלָתִי֙ אֲשֶׁ֣ר בָּזָ֔ה וּבְרִיתִ֖י אֲשֶׁ֣ר הֵפִ֑יר
וּנְתַתִּ֖יו בְּרֹאשֽׁוֹ׃ 20 וּפָרַשְׂתִּ֤י עָלָיו֙ רִשְׁתִּ֔י
וְנִתְפַּ֖שׂ בִּמְצֽוּדָתִ֑י וַהֲבִיאוֹתִ֤יהוּ בָבֶ֙לָה֙
וְנִשְׁפַּטְתִּ֤י אִתּוֹ֙ שָׁ֔ם מַעֲל֖וֹ אֲשֶׁ֥ר מָֽעַל־בִּֽי׃
21 וְאֵ֨ת כָּל־מִבְרָחָ֤ו בְּכָל־אֲגַפָּיו֙
בַּחֶ֣רֶב יִפֹּ֔לוּ וְהַנִּשְׁאָרִ֖ים לְכָל־ר֣וּחַ יִפָּרֵ֑שׂוּ
וִֽידַעְתֶּ֕ם כִּ֛י אֲנִ֥י יְהוָ֖ה דִּבַּֽרְתִּי׃ ס
22 כֹּ֤ה אָמַר֙ אֲדֹנָ֣י יְהוִ֔ה וְלָקַ֣חְתִּי אָ֗נִי
מִצַּמֶּ֤רֶת הָאֶ֙רֶז֙ הָרָמָ֔ה וְנָתָ֑תִּי מֵרֹ֧אשׁ
יֹֽנְקוֹתָ֛יו רַ֥ךְ אֶקְטֹ֖ף וְשָׁתַ֣לְתִּי אָ֑נִי עַ֥ל
הַר־גָּבֹ֖הַ וְתָלֽוּל׃ 23 בְּהַ֤ר מְרֽוֹם יִשְׂרָאֵל֙
אֶשְׁתֳּלֶ֔נּוּ וְנָשָׂ֥א עָנָ֖ף וְעָ֣שָׂה פֶ֑רִי וְהָיָ֖ה
לְאֶ֣רֶז אַדִּ֑יר וְשָׁכְנ֣וּ תַחְתָּ֗יו כֹּ֚ל צִפּ֣וֹר

cedar. Every bird of every feather shall take shelter under it, shelter in the shade of its boughs. 24Then shall all the trees of the field know that it is I the LORD who have abased the lofty tree and exalted the lowly tree, who have dried up the green tree and made the withered tree bud. I the LORD have spoken, and I will act.

18

The word of the LORD came to me: 2What do you mean by quoting this proverb upon the soil of Israel, "Parents eat sour grapes and their children's teeth are blunted"?a 3As I live— declares the Lord GOD—this proverb shall no longer be current among you in Israel. 4Consider, all lives are Mine; the life of the parent and the life of the child are both Mine. The person who sins, only he shall die.

5Thus, if a man is righteous and does what is just and right: 6If he has not eaten on the mountainsb or raised his eyes to the fetishes of the House of Israel; if he has not defiled another man's wife or approached a menstruous woman; 7if he has not wronged anyone; if he has returned the debtor's pledge to him and has taken nothing by robbery; if he has given bread to the hungry and clothed the naked; 8if he has not lent at advance interest or exacted accrued interest;c if he has abstained from wrongdoing and executed true justice between man and man; 9if he has followed My laws and kept My rules and acted honestly—he is righteous. Such a man shall live—declares the Lord GOD.

10Suppose, now, that he has begotten a son who is a ruffian, a shedder of blood, who d-does any of these things,-d 11whereas he himself did none of these things. That is, [the son] has eaten on the mountains,b has defiled another man's

כָּל־כָּנָף בְּצֵל דָּלִיּוֹתָיו תִּשְׁכֹּנָּה: 24 וְיָדְעוּ כָּל־עֲצֵי הַשָּׂדֶה כִּי אֲנִי יְהוָה הִשְׁפַּלְתִּי | עֵץ גָּבֹהַ הִגְבַּהְתִּי עֵץ שָׁפָל הוֹבַשְׁתִּי עֵץ לָח וְהִפְרַחְתִּי עֵץ יָבֵשׁ אֲנִי יְהוָה דִּבַּרְתִּי וְעָשִׂיתִי: פ

יח וַיְהִי דְבַר־יְהוָה אֵלַי לֵאמֹר: 2 מַה־לָּכֶם אַתֶּם מֹשְׁלִים אֶת־הַמָּשָׁל הַזֶּה עַל־אַדְמַת יִשְׂרָאֵל לֵאמֹר אָבוֹת יֹאכְלוּ בֹסֶר וְשִׁנֵּי הַבָּנִים תִּקְהֶינָה: 3 חַי־אָנִי נְאֻם אֲדֹנָי יְהוִה אִם־יִהְיֶה לָכֶם עוֹד מְשֹׁל הַמָּשָׁל הַזֶּה בְּיִשְׂרָאֵל: 4 הֵן כָּל־הַנְּפָשׁוֹת לִי הֵנָּה כְּנֶפֶשׁ הָאָב וּכְנֶפֶשׁ הַבֵּן לִי־הֵנָּה הַנֶּפֶשׁ הַחֹטֵאת הִיא תָמוּת: ס 5 וְאִישׁ כִּי־יִהְיֶה צַדִּיק וְעָשָׂה מִשְׁפָּט וּצְדָקָה: 6 אֶל־הֶהָרִים לֹא אָכָל וְעֵינָיו לֹא נָשָׂא אֶל־גִּלּוּלֵי בֵּית יִשְׂרָאֵל וְאֶת־אֵשֶׁת רֵעֵהוּ לֹא טִמֵּא וְאֶל־אִשָּׁה נִדָּה לֹא יִקְרָב: 7 וְאִישׁ לֹא יוֹנֶה חֲבֹלָתוֹ חוֹב יָשִׁיב גְּזֵלָה לֹא יִגְזֹל לַחְמוֹ לְרָעֵב יִתֵּן וְעֵירֹם יְכַסֶּה־בָּגֶד: 8 בַּנֶּשֶׁךְ לֹא־יִתֵּן וְתַרְבִּית לֹא יִקָּח מֵעָוֶל יָשִׁיב יָדוֹ מִשְׁפַּט אֱמֶת יַעֲשֶׂה בֵּין אִישׁ לְאִישׁ: 9 בְּחֻקּוֹתַי יְהַלֵּךְ וּמִשְׁפָּטַי שָׁמַר לַעֲשׂוֹת אֱמֶת צַדִּיק הוּא חָיֹה יִחְיֶה נְאֻם אֲדֹנָי יְהוִה: 10 וְהוֹלִיד בֵּן־פָּרִיץ שֹׁפֵךְ דָּם וְעָשָׂה אָח מֵאַחַד מֵאֵלֶּה: 11 וְהוּא אֶת־כָּל־אֵלֶּה לֹא עָשָׂה כִּי גַם אֶל־הֶהָרִים אָכָל וְאֶת־אֵשֶׁת

---

a   Others "set on edge."
b   I.e., in idolatry. Emendation yields "with the blood"; cf. 33.25; Lev. 17.10–11, 19.26.
c   I.e., interest deducted in advance or interest added at the time of repayment; cf. Lev. 25.36.
d-d   Meaning of Heb. uncertain.

wife, [12]has wronged the poor and the needy, has taken by robbery, has not returned a pledge, has raised his eyes to the fetishes, has committed abomination, [13]has lent at advance interest, or exacted accrued interest—shall he live? He shall not live! If he has committed any of these abominations, he shall die; he has forfeited his life.

[14]Now suppose that he, in turn, has begotten a son who has seen all the sins that his father committed, but has taken heed and has not imitated them: [15]He has not eaten on the mountains[b] or raised his eyes to the fetishes of the House of Israel; he has not defiled another man's wife; [16]he has not wronged anyone; he has not seized a pledge or taken anything by robbery; he has given his bread to the hungry and clothed the naked; [17]he has [e-]refrained from oppressing the poor;[-e] he has not exacted advance or accrued interest; he has obeyed My rules and followed My laws—he shall not die for the iniquity of his father, but shall live. [18]To be sure, his father, because he practiced fraud, robbed his brother, and acted wickedly among his kin, did die for his iniquity; [19]and now you ask, "Why has not the son shared the burden of his father's guilt?" But the son has done what is right and just, and has carefully kept all My laws: he shall live!

[20]The person who sins, he alone shall die. A child shall not share the burden of a parent's guilt, nor shall a parent share the burden of a child's guilt; the righteousness of the righteous shall be accounted to him alone, and the wickedness of the wicked shall be accounted to him alone.

[21]Moreover, if the wicked one repents of all the sins that he committed and keeps all My laws and does what is just and right, he shall live; he shall not die. [22]None of the transgressions he committed shall be remembered against him;

רֵעֵהוּ טִמֵּא׃ 12 עָנִי וְאֶבְיוֹן הוֹנָה גְּזֵלוֹת גָּזָל חֲבֹל לֹא יָשִׁיב וְאֶל־הַגִּלּוּלִים נָשָׂא עֵינָיו תּוֹעֵבָה עָשָׂה׃ 13 בַּנֶּשֶׁךְ נָתַן וְתַרְבִּית לָקַח וָחָי לֹא יִחְיֶה אֵת כָּל־הַתּוֹעֵבוֹת הָאֵלֶּה עָשָׂה מוֹת יוּמָת דָּמָיו בּוֹ יִהְיֶה׃ 14 וְהִנֵּה הוֹלִיד בֵּן וַיַּרְא אֶת־כָּל־חַטֹּאת אָבִיו אֲשֶׁר עָשָׂה וַיִּרְאֶה וְלֹא יַעֲשֶׂה כָּהֵן׃ 15 עַל־הֶהָרִים לֹא אָכָל וְעֵינָיו לֹא נָשָׂא אֶל־גִּלּוּלֵי בֵּית יִשְׂרָאֵל אֶת־אֵשֶׁת רֵעֵהוּ לֹא טִמֵּא׃ 16 וְאִישׁ לֹא הוֹנָה חֲבֹל לֹא חָבָל וּגְזֵלָה לֹא גָזָל לַחְמוֹ לְרָעֵב נָתָן וְעֵרוֹם כִּסָּה־בָגֶד׃ 17 מֵעָנִי הֵשִׁיב יָדוֹ נֶשֶׁךְ וְתַרְבִּית לֹא לָקָח מִשְׁפָּטַי עָשָׂה בְּחֻקּוֹתַי הָלָךְ הוּא לֹא יָמוּת בַּעֲוֹן אָבִיו חָיֹה יִחְיֶה׃ 18 אָבִיו כִּי־עָשַׁק עֹשֶׁק גָּזַל גֵּזֶל אָח וַאֲשֶׁר לֹא־טוֹב עָשָׂה בְּתוֹךְ עַמָּיו וְהִנֵּה־מֵת בַּעֲוֹנוֹ׃ 19 וַאֲמַרְתֶּם מַדּוּעַ לֹא־נָשָׂא הַבֵּן בַּעֲוֹן הָאָב וְהַבֵּן מִשְׁפָּט וּצְדָקָה עָשָׂה אֵת כָּל־חֻקּוֹתַי שָׁמַר וַיַּעֲשֶׂה אֹתָם חָיֹה יִחְיֶה׃ 20 הַנֶּפֶשׁ הַחֹטֵאת הִיא תָמוּת בֵּן לֹא־יִשָּׂא בַּעֲוֹן הָאָב וְאָב לֹא יִשָּׂא בַּעֲוֹן הַבֵּן צִדְקַת הַצַּדִּיק עָלָיו תִּהְיֶה וְרִשְׁעַת רָשָׁע עָלָיו תִּהְיֶה׃ ס 21 וְהָרָשָׁע כִּי יָשׁוּב מִכָּל־חַטֹּאתוֹ אֲשֶׁר עָשָׂה וְשָׁמַר אֶת־כָּל־חֻקּוֹתַי וְעָשָׂה מִשְׁפָּט וּצְדָקָה חָיֹה יִחְיֶה לֹא יָמוּת׃ 22 כָּל־פְּשָׁעָיו אֲשֶׁר עָשָׂה לֹא יִזָּכְרוּ לוֹ

---

e-e   Lit. "turned his hand back from the poor." Emendation yields "abstained from wrongdoing"; cf. v. 8.

because of the righteousness he has practiced, he shall live. [23]Is it my desire that a wicked person shall die?—says the Lord God. It is rather that he shall turn back from his ways and live.

[24]So, too, if a righteous person turns away from his righteousness and does wrong, practicing the very abominations that the wicked person practiced, shall he live? None of the righteous deeds that he did shall be remembered; because of the treachery he has practiced and the sins he has committed—because of these, he shall die.

[25]Yet you say, "The way of the Lord is unfair." Listen, O House of Israel: Is My way unfair? It is your ways that are unfair! [26]When a righteous person turns away from his righteousness and does wrong, he shall die for it; he shall die for the wrong he has done. [27]And if a wicked person turns back from the wickedness that he practiced and does what is just and right, such a person shall save his life. [28]Because he took heed and turned back from all the transgressions that he committed, he shall live; he shall not die.

[29]Yet the House of Israel say, "The way of the Lord is unfair." Are My ways unfair, O House of Israel? It is your ways that are unfair! [30]Be assured, O House of Israel, I will judge each one of you according to his ways—declares the Lord God. Repent and turn back from your transgressions; let them not be a stumbling block of guilt for you. [31]Cast away all the transgressions by which you have offended, and get yourselves a new heart and a new spirit, that you may not die, O House of Israel. [32]For it is not My desire that anyone shall die—declares the Lord God. Repent, therefore, and live!

19 And you are to intone a dirge over the princes of Israel, [2]and say:

בְּצִדְקָתוֹ אֲשֶׁר־עָשָׂה יִחְיֶה: [23] הֶחָפֹץ אֶחְפֹּץ מוֹת רָשָׁע נְאֻם אֲדֹנָי יְהוִה הֲלוֹא בְּשׁוּבוֹ מִדְּרָכָיו וְחָיָה: ס

[24] וּבְשׁוּב צַדִּיק מִצִּדְקָתוֹ וְעָשָׂה עָוֶל כְּכֹל הַתּוֹעֵבוֹת אֲשֶׁר־עָשָׂה הָרָשָׁע יַעֲשֶׂה וָחָי כָּל־צִדְקֹתָו אֲשֶׁר־עָשָׂה לֹא תִזָּכַרְנָה בְּמַעֲלוֹ אֲשֶׁר־מָעַל וּבְחַטָּאתוֹ אֲשֶׁר־חָטָא בָּם יָמוּת:

[25] וַאֲמַרְתֶּם לֹא יִתָּכֵן דֶּרֶךְ אֲדֹנָי שִׁמְעוּ־נָא בֵּית יִשְׂרָאֵל הֲדַרְכִּי לֹא יִתָּכֵן הֲלֹא דַרְכֵיכֶם לֹא יִתָּכֵנוּ: [26] בְּשׁוּב־צַדִּיק מִצִּדְקָתוֹ וְעָשָׂה עָוֶל וּמֵת עֲלֵיהֶם בְּעַוְלוֹ אֲשֶׁר־עָשָׂה יָמוּת: ס [27] וּבְשׁוּב רָשָׁע מֵרִשְׁעָתוֹ אֲשֶׁר עָשָׂה וַיַּעַשׂ מִשְׁפָּט וּצְדָקָה הוּא אֶת־נַפְשׁוֹ יְחַיֶּה: [28] וַיִּרְאֶה וַישׁוֹב [וַיָּשָׁב] מִכָּל־פְּשָׁעָיו אֲשֶׁר עָשָׂה חָיוֹ יִחְיֶה לֹא יָמוּת:

[29] וְאָמְרוּ בֵּית יִשְׂרָאֵל לֹא יִתָּכֵן דֶּרֶךְ אֲדֹנָי הַדְּרָכַי לֹא יִתָּכֵנוּ בֵּית יִשְׂרָאֵל הֲלֹא דַרְכֵיכֶם לֹא יִתָּכֵן: [30] לָכֵן אִישׁ כִּדְרָכָיו אֶשְׁפֹּט אֶתְכֶם בֵּית יִשְׂרָאֵל נְאֻם אֲדֹנָי יְהוִה שׁוּבוּ וְהָשִׁיבוּ מִכָּל־פִּשְׁעֵיכֶם וְלֹא־יִהְיֶה לָכֶם לְמִכְשׁוֹל עָוֹן: [31] הַשְׁלִיכוּ מֵעֲלֵיכֶם אֶת־כָּל־פִּשְׁעֵיכֶם אֲשֶׁר פְּשַׁעְתֶּם בָּם וַעֲשׂוּ לָכֶם לֵב חָדָשׁ וְרוּחַ חֲדָשָׁה וְלָמָּה תָמֻתוּ בֵּית יִשְׂרָאֵל: [32] כִּי לֹא אֶחְפֹּץ בְּמוֹת הַמֵּת נְאֻם אֲדֹנָי יְהוִה וְהָשִׁיבוּ וִחְיוּ: פ

יט וְאַתָּה שָׂא קִינָה אֶל־נְשִׂיאֵי יִשְׂרָאֵל: [2] וְאָמַרְתָּ

What a lioness was your mother
Among the lions!
Crouching among the great beasts,
She reared her cubs.
3She raised up one of her cubs,
He became a great beast;
He learned to hunt prey—
He devoured men.
4Nations heeded [the call] against him;
He was caught in their snare.
They dragged him off with hooks
To the land of Egypt.
5When she saw herself frustrated,
Her hope defeated,
She took another of her cubs
And set him up as a great beast.
6He stalked among the lions,
He was a great beast;
He learned to hunt prey—
He devoured men.
7He a-ravished their widows,-a
Laid waste their cities;
The land and all in it were appalled
At the sound of his roaring.
8Nations from the countries roundabout
Arrayed themselves against him.
They spread their net over him,
He was caught in their snare.
9With hooks he was put in a cage,
They carried him off to the king of Babylon
And confined him in a fortress,
So that never again should his roar be heard
On the hills of Israel.

10Your mother was like a vine b-in your
   blood,-b
Planted beside streams,

a-a *Emendation yields "ravaged their castles."*
b-b *Meaning of Heb. uncertain; emendation yields "in a vineyard."*

מָה אִמְּךָ לְבִיָּא
בֵּין אֲרָיוֹת
רָבְצָה בְּתוֹךְ כְּפִרִים
רִבְּתָה גוּרֶיהָ׃
3וַתַּעַל אֶחָד מִגֻּרֶיהָ
כְּפִיר הָיָה
וַיִּלְמַד לִטְרָף־טֶרֶף
אָדָם אָכָל׃
4וַיִּשְׁמְעוּ אֵלָיו גּוֹיִם
בְּשַׁחְתָּם נִתְפָּשׂ
וַיְבִאֻהוּ בַחַחִים
אֶל־אֶרֶץ מִצְרָיִם׃
5וַתֵּרֶא כִּי נוֹחֲלָה
אָבְדָה תִּקְוָתָהּ
וַתִּקַּח אֶחָד מִגֻּרֶיהָ
כְּפִיר שָׂמָתְהוּ׃
6וַיִּתְהַלֵּךְ בְּתוֹךְ־אֲרָיוֹת
כְּפִיר הָיָה
וַיִּלְמַד לִטְרָף־טֶרֶף
אָדָם אָכָל׃
7וַיֵּדַע אַלְמְנוֹתָיו
וְעָרֵיהֶם הֶחֱרִיב
וַתֵּשַׁם אֶרֶץ וּמְלֹאָהּ
מִקּוֹל שַׁאֲגָתוֹ׃
8וַיִּתְּנוּ עָלָיו גּוֹיִם
סָבִיב מִמְּדִינוֹת
וַיִּפְרְשׂוּ עָלָיו רִשְׁתָּם
בְּשַׁחְתָּם נִתְפָּשׂ׃
9וַיִּתְּנֻהוּ בַסּוּגַר בַּחַחִים
וַיְבִאֻהוּ אֶל־מֶלֶךְ בָּבֶל
יְבִאֻהוּ בַּמְּצֹדוֹת
לְמַעַן לֹא־יִשָּׁמַע קוֹלוֹ עוֹד
אֶל־הָרֵי יִשְׂרָאֵל׃ פ

10אִמְּךָ כַגֶּפֶן בְּדָמְךָ
עַל־מַיִם שְׁתוּלָה

With luxuriant boughs and branches
Thanks to abundant waters.
11And she had a mighty rod^c

פְּרִיָּה֙ וַעֲנֵפָ֣ה הָיְתָ֔ה
מִמַּ֖יִם רַבִּֽים׃
11 וַיִּֽהְיוּ־לָ֞הּ מַטּ֣וֹת עֹ֗ז

Fit for a ruler's scepter.^c
It towered highest ^damong the leafy trees,^{-d}
It was conspicuous by its height,
By the abundance of its boughs.

אֶל־שִׁבְטֵי֙ מֹֽשְׁלִ֔ים
וַתִּגְבַּ֤הּ קֽוֹמָתוֹ֙ עַל־בֵּ֣ין עֲבֹתִ֔ים
וַיֵּרָ֥א בְגׇבְה֖וֹ
בְּרֹ֥ב דָּלִיֹּתָֽיו׃

12But plucked up in a fury,
She was hurled to the ground.
The east wind withered her branches,
They broke apart and dried up;
And her mighty rod was consumed by fire.

12 וַתֻּתַּ֤שׁ בְּחֵמָה֙
לָאָ֣רֶץ הֻשְׁלָ֔כָה
וְר֥וּחַ הַקָּדִ֖ים הוֹבִ֣ישׁ פִּרְיָ֑הּ
הִתְפָּֽרְק֥וּ וְיָבֵ֖שׁוּ
מַטֵּ֥ה עֻזָּ֖הּ אֵ֥שׁ אֲכָלָֽתְהוּ׃

13Now she is planted in the desert,
In ground that is arid and parched.
14Fire has issued from her twig-laden branch
And has consumed her boughs,
She is left without a mighty rod,
A scepter to rule with.

13 וְעַתָּ֖ה שְׁתוּלָ֣ה בַמִּדְבָּ֑ר
בְּאֶ֖רֶץ צִיָּ֥ה וְצָמָֽא׃
14 וַתֵּצֵ֨א אֵ֜שׁ מִמַּטֵּ֤ה בַדֶּ֙יהָ֙
פִּרְיָ֣הּ אָכָ֔לָה
וְלֹא־הָ֥יָה בָ֛הּ מַטֵּה־עֹ֖ז
שֵׁ֣בֶט לִמְשׁ֑וֹל

This is a dirge, and it has become a [familiar] dirge.

קִינָ֥ה הִ֖יא וַתְּהִ֥י לְקִינָֽה׃ פ

20 In the seventh year, on the tenth day of the fifth month, certain elders of Israel came to inquire of the LORD, and sat down before me. 2And the word of the LORD came to me:

3O mortal, speak to the elders of Israel and say to them: Thus said the Lord GOD: Have you come to inquire of Me? As I live, I will not respond to your inquiry—declares the Lord GOD. 4a-Arraign, arraign them, O mortal!-a Declare to them the abhorrent deeds of their fathers. 5Say to them: Thus said the Lord GOD:

On the day that I chose Israel, I b-gave My oath-b to the stock of the House of Jacob; when I made Myself known to them in the land of

כ וַיְהִ֣י ׀ בַּשָּׁנָ֣ה הַשְּׁבִיעִ֗ית בַּֽחֲמִשִׁ֞י
בֶּעָשׂ֤וֹר לַחֹ֙דֶשׁ֙ בָּ֣אוּ אֲנָשִׁ֔ים מִזִּקְנֵ֖י יִשְׂרָאֵ֑ל
לִדְרֹ֣שׁ אֶת־יְהֹוָ֔ה וַיֵּשְׁב֖וּ לְפָנָֽי׃ ס 2 וַיְהִ֥י
דְבַר־יְהֹוָ֖ה אֵלַ֥י לֵאמֹֽר׃
3 בֶּן־אָדָ֗ם דַּבֵּ֞ר אֶת־זִקְנֵ֤י יִשְׂרָאֵל֙ וְאָמַרְתָּ֣
אֲלֵהֶ֔ם כֹּ֤ה אָמַר֙ אֲדֹנָ֣י יֱהֹוִ֔ה הֲלִדְרֹ֥שׁ אֹתִ֖י
אַתֶּ֣ם בָּאִ֑ים חַי־אָ֙נִי֙ אִם־אִדָּרֵ֣שׁ לָכֶ֔ם נְאֻ֖ם
אֲדֹנָ֥י יֱהֹוִֽה׃
4 הֲתִשְׁפֹּ֥ט אֹתָ֖ם הֲתִשְׁפּ֣וֹט בֶּן־אָדָ֑ם אֶת־
תּוֹעֲבֹ֥ת אֲבוֹתָ֖ם הוֹדִיעֵֽם׃ 5 וְאָמַרְתָּ֣
אֲלֵיהֶ֗ם כֹּֽה־אָמַר֮ אֲדֹנָ֣י יְהֹוִה֒
בְּיוֹם֙ בׇּחֳרִ֣י בְיִשְׂרָאֵ֔ל וָאֶשָּׂ֣א יָדִ֗י לְזֶ֙רַע֙
בֵּ֣ית יַֽעֲקֹ֔ב וָאִוָּדַ֥ע לָהֶ֖ם בְּאֶ֣רֶץ מִצְרַ֑יִם

Egypt, I gave my oath to them. When I said, "I the LORD am your God," ⁶that same day I swore to them to take them out of the land of Egypt into a land flowing with milk and honey, a land which I had sought out for them, the fairest of all lands.

⁷I also said to them: Cast away, every one of you, the detestable things ᶜ-that you are drawn to,-ᶜ and do not defile yourselves with the fetishes of Egypt—I the LORD am your God. ⁸But they defied Me and refused to listen to Me. They did not cast away the detestable things they were drawn to, nor did they give up the fetishes of Egypt. Then I resolved to pour out My fury upon them, to vent all My anger upon them there, in the land of Egypt. ⁹But I acted for the sake of My name, that it might not be profaned in the sight of the nations among whom they were. For it was before their eyes that I had made Myself known to Israelᵈ to bring them out of the land of Egypt.

¹⁰I brought them out of the land of Egypt and I led them into the wilderness. ¹¹I gave them My laws and taught them My rules, by the pursuit of which a man shall live. ¹²Moreover, I gave them My sabbaths to serve as a sign between Me and them, that they might know that it is I the LORD who sanctify them. ¹³But the House of Israel rebelled against Me in the wilderness; they did not follow My laws and they rejected My rules—by the pursuit of which a man shall live—and they grossly desecrated My sabbaths. Then I thought to pour out My fury upon them in the wilderness and to make an end of them; ¹⁴but I acted for the sake of My name, that it might not be profaned in the sight of the nations before whose eyes I had led them out. ¹⁵However, I sworeᵇ to them in the wilderness that I would not bring them into the land flowing with milk and honey, the fairest of all lands, which

---

c-c Lit. "of his eyes."
d Lit. "them."

וָאֶשָּׂ֨א יָדִ֤י לָהֶם֙ לֵאמֹ֔ר אֲנִ֖י יְהוָ֣ה אֱלֹהֵיכֶֽם׃ 6 בַּיּ֣וֹם הַה֗וּא נָשָׂ֤אתִי יָדִי֙ לָהֶ֔ם לְהֽוֹצִיאָ֖ם מֵאֶ֣רֶץ מִצְרָ֑יִם אֶל־אֶ֜רֶץ אֲשֶׁר־תַּ֣רְתִּי לָהֶ֗ם זָבַ֤ת חָלָב֙ וּדְבַ֔שׁ צְבִ֥י הִ֖יא לְכָל־הָאֲרָצֽוֹת׃ 7 וָאֹמַ֣ר אֲלֵהֶ֗ם אִ֣ישׁ שִׁקּוּצֵ֤י עֵינָיו֙ הַשְׁלִ֔יכוּ וּבְגִלּוּלֵ֥י מִצְרַ֖יִם אַל־תִּטַּמָּ֑אוּ אֲנִ֖י יְהוָ֥ה אֱלֹהֵיכֶֽם׃ 8 וַיַּמְרוּ־בִ֗י וְלֹ֤א אָבוּ֙ לִשְׁמֹ֣עַ אֵלַ֔י אִ֣ישׁ אֶת־שִׁקּוּצֵ֤י עֵֽינֵיהֶם֙ לֹ֣א הִשְׁלִ֔יכוּ וְאֶת־גִּלּוּלֵ֥י מִצְרַ֖יִם לֹ֣א עָזָ֑בוּ וָאֹמַ֞ר לִשְׁפֹּ֧ךְ חֲמָתִ֣י עֲלֵיהֶ֗ם לְכַלּ֤וֹת אַפִּי֙ בָּהֶ֔ם בְּת֖וֹךְ אֶ֥רֶץ מִצְרָֽיִם׃ 9 וָאַ֙עַשׂ֙ לְמַ֣עַן שְׁמִ֔י לְבִלְתִּ֥י הֵחֵ֖ל לְעֵינֵ֣י הַגּוֹיִ֑ם אֲשֶׁר־הֵ֣מָּה בְתוֹכָ֔ם אֲשֶׁ֨ר נוֹדַ֤עְתִּי אֲלֵיהֶם֙ לְעֵ֣ינֵיהֶ֔ם לְהוֹצִיאָ֖ם מֵאֶ֥רֶץ מִצְרָֽיִם׃ 10 וָאֽוֹצִיאֵ֖ם מֵאֶ֣רֶץ מִצְרָ֑יִם וָאֲבִאֵ֖ם אֶל־הַמִּדְבָּֽר׃ 11 וָאֶתֵּ֤ן לָהֶם֙ אֶת־חֻקּוֹתַ֔י וְאֶת־מִשְׁפָּטַ֖י הוֹדַ֣עְתִּי אוֹתָ֑ם אֲשֶׁ֨ר יַעֲשֶׂ֥ה אוֹתָ֛ם הָאָדָ֖ם וָחַ֥י בָּהֶֽם׃ 12 וְגַ֤ם אֶת־שַׁבְּתוֹתַי֙ נָתַ֣תִּי לָהֶ֔ם לִהְי֣וֹת לְא֔וֹת בֵּינִ֖י וּבֵֽינֵיהֶ֑ם לָדַ֕עַת כִּ֛י אֲנִ֥י יְהוָ֖ה מְקַדְּשָֽׁם׃ 13 וַיַּמְרוּ־בִ֣י בֵֽית־יִשְׂרָאֵ֣ל בַּמִּדְבָּ֗ר בְּחֻקּוֹתַ֤י לֹא־הָלָ֙כוּ֙ וְאֶת־מִשְׁפָּטַ֣י מָאָ֔סוּ אֲשֶׁ֨ר יַעֲשֶׂ֥ה אֹתָ֛ם הָאָדָ֖ם וָחַ֣י בָּהֶ֑ם וְאֶת־שַׁבְּתֹתַ֖י חִלְּל֣וּ מְאֹ֑ד וָאֹמַ֞ר לִשְׁפֹּ֧ךְ חֲמָתִ֛י עֲלֵיהֶ֖ם בַּמִּדְבָּ֖ר לְכַלּוֹתָֽם׃ 14 וָאֶעֱשֶׂ֖ה לְמַ֣עַן שְׁמִ֑י לְבִלְתִּ֤י הֵחֵל֙ לְעֵינֵ֣י הַגּוֹיִ֔ם אֲשֶׁ֥ר הוֹצֵאתִ֖ים לְעֵינֵיהֶֽם׃ 15 וְגַם־אֲנִ֗י נָשָׂ֧אתִי יָדִ֛י לָהֶ֖ם בַּמִּדְבָּ֑ר לְבִלְתִּי֙ הָבִ֣יא אוֹתָ֔ם אֶל־הָאָ֙רֶץ֙ אֲשֶׁר־נָתַ֔תִּי זָבַ֥ת חָלָ֖ב

I had assigned [to them], [16]for they had rejected My rules, disobeyed My laws, and desecrated My sabbaths; their hearts followed after their fetishes. [17]But I had pity on them and did not destroy them; I did not make an end of them in the wilderness.

[18]I warned their children in the wilderness: Do not follow the practices of your fathers, do not keep their ways, and do not defile yourselves with their fetishes. [19]I the LORD am your God: Follow My laws and be careful to observe My rules. [20]And hallow My sabbaths, that they may be a sign between Me and you, that you may know that I the LORD am your God.

[21]But the children rebelled against Me: they did not follow My laws and did not faithfully observe My rules, by the pursuit of which man shall live; they profaned My sabbaths. Then I resolved to pour out My fury upon them, to vent all My anger upon them, in the wilderness. [22]But I held back My hand and acted for the sake of My name, that it might not be profaned in the sight of the nations before whose eyes I had led them out. [23]However, I swore[b] to them in the wilderness that I would scatter them among the nations and disperse them through the lands, [24]because they did not obey My rules, but rejected My laws, profaned My sabbaths, and looked with longing to the fetishes of their fathers. [25]Moreover, I gave them laws that were not good and rules by which they could not live: [26]When they set aside every first issue of the womb, I defiled them by their very gifts[e]—that I might render them desolate,[f] that they might know that I am the LORD.

[27]Now, O mortal, speak to the House of Israel and say to them: Thus said the Lord GOD: By this too your fathers affronted Me and committed trespass against Me: [28]When I brought them to the land that I had sworn[b] to give them,

e   See v. 31.
f   Emendation yields "guilty."

וּדְבַ֥שׁ צְבִ֛י הִ֖יא לְכָל־הָאֲרָצֽוֹת׃ 16 יַ֜עַן בְּמִשְׁפָּטַ֣י מָאָ֗סוּ וְאֶת־חֻקּוֹתַי֙ לֹא־הָלְכ֣וּ בָהֶ֔ם וְאֶת־שַׁבְּתוֹתַ֖י חִלֵּ֑לוּ כִּ֛י אַחֲרֵ֥י גִלּוּלֵיהֶ֖ם לִבָּ֥ם הֹלֵֽךְ׃ 17 וַתָּ֧חָס עֵינִ֛י עֲלֵיהֶ֖ם מִֽשַּׁחֲתָ֑ם וְלֹא־עָשִׂ֧יתִי אוֹתָ֛ם כָּלָ֖ה בַּמִּדְבָּֽר׃

18 וָאֹמַ֤ר אֶל־בְּנֵיהֶם֙ בַּמִּדְבָּ֔ר בְּחוּקֵּ֤י אֲבֽוֹתֵיכֶם֙ אַל־תֵּלֵ֔כוּ וְאֶת־מִשְׁפְּטֵיהֶ֖ם אַל־תִּשְׁמֹ֑רוּ וּבְגִלּֽוּלֵיהֶ֖ם אַל־תִּטַּמָּֽאוּ׃ 19 אֲנִ֖י יְהֹוָ֣ה אֱלֹֽהֵיכֶ֑ם בְּחֻקּוֹתַ֣י לֵ֔כוּ וְאֶת־מִשְׁפָּטַ֥י שִׁמְר֖וּ וַעֲשׂ֥וּ אוֹתָֽם׃ 20 וְאֶת־שַׁבְּתוֹתַ֖י קַדֵּ֑שׁוּ וְהָי֤וּ לְאוֹת֙ בֵּינִ֣י וּבֵֽינֵיכֶ֔ם לָדַ֕עַת כִּ֛י אֲנִ֥י יְהֹוָ֖ה אֱלֹהֵיכֶֽם׃

21 וַיַּמְרוּ־בִ֣י הַבָּנִ֗ים בְּחֻקּוֹתַ֣י לֹא־הָלָ֡כוּ וְאֶת־מִשְׁפָּטַ֣י לֹא־שָׁמְרוּ֩ לַעֲשׂ֨וֹת אוֹתָ֜ם אֲשֶׁר֩ יַעֲשֶׂ֨ה אוֹתָ֤ם הָֽאָדָם֙ וָחַ֣י בָּהֶ֔ם אֶת־שַׁבְּתוֹתַ֖י חִלֵּ֑לוּ וָאֹמַ֞ר לִשְׁפֹּ֧ךְ חֲמָתִ֣י עֲלֵיהֶ֗ם לְכַלּ֥וֹת אַפִּ֛י בָּ֖ם בַּמִּדְבָּֽר׃ 22 וַהֲשִׁבֹ֙תִי֙ אֶת־יָדִ֔י וָאַ֖עַשׂ לְמַ֣עַן שְׁמִ֑י לְבִלְתִּ֤י הֵחֵל֙ לְעֵינֵ֣י הַגּוֹיִ֔ם אֲשֶׁר־הוֹצֵ֥אתִי אוֹתָ֖ם לְעֵינֵיהֶֽם׃ 23 גַּם־אֲנִ֗י נָשָׂ֧אתִי אֶת־יָדִ֛י לָהֶ֖ם בַּמִּדְבָּ֑ר לְהָפִ֤יץ אֹתָם֙ בַּגּוֹיִ֔ם וּלְזָר֥וֹת אוֹתָ֖ם בָּאֲרָצֽוֹת׃ 24 יַ֜עַן מִשְׁפָּטַ֣י לֹא־עָשׂ֗וּ וְחֻקּוֹתַ֤י מָאָ֙סוּ֙ וְאֶת־שַׁבְּתוֹתַ֣י חִלֵּ֔לוּ וְאַֽחֲרֵי֙ גִּלּוּלֵ֣י אֲבוֹתָ֔ם הָי֖וּ עֵינֵיהֶֽם׃ 25 וְגַם־אֲנִי֙ נָתַ֣תִּי לָהֶ֔ם חֻקִּ֖ים לֹ֣א טוֹבִ֑ים וּמִ֨שְׁפָּטִ֔ים לֹ֥א יִֽחְי֖וּ בָּהֶֽם׃ 26 וָאֲטַמֵּ֤א אוֹתָם֙ בְּמַתְּנוֹתָ֔ם בְּהַעֲבִ֖יר כָּל־פֶּ֣טֶר רָ֑חַם לְמַ֣עַן אֲשִׁמֵּ֔ם לְמַ֙עַן֙ אֲשֶׁ֣ר יֵֽדְע֔וּ אֲשֶׁ֖ר אֲנִ֥י יְהֹוָֽה׃ ס

27 לָכֵ֞ן דַּבֵּ֨ר אֶל־בֵּ֤ית יִשְׂרָאֵל֙ בֶּן־אָדָ֔ם וְאָמַרְתָּ֣ אֲלֵיהֶ֔ם כֹּ֥ה אָמַ֖ר אֲדֹנָ֣י יְהֹוִ֑ה ע֗וֹד זֹ֚את גִּדְּפ֤וּ אוֹתִי֙ אֲב֣וֹתֵיכֶ֔ם בְּמַעֲלָ֥ם בִּ֖י מָֽעַל׃ 28 וָאֲבִיאֵם֙ אֶל־הָאָ֔רֶץ אֲשֶׁ֤ר נָשָׂ֙אתִי֙

and they saw any high hill or any leafy tree, they slaughtered their sacrifices there and presented their offensive offerings there; there they produced their pleasing odors and poured out their libations. 29Then I said to them, "What is this shrine which you visit?" (Therefore such [a shrine] is called bamah^g to this day.)

30Now say to the House of Israel: Thus said the Lord God: If you defile yourselves as your fathers did and go astray after their detestable things, 31and if to this very day you defile yourselves in the presentation of your gifts by making your children pass through the fire to all your fetishes, shall I respond to your inquiry, O House of Israel? As I live—declares the Lord God—I will not respond to you. 32And what you have in mind shall never come to pass—when you say, "We will be like the nations, like the families of the lands, worshiping wood and stone." 33As I live—declares the Lord God—I will reign over you with a strong hand, and with an outstretched arm, and with overflowing fury. 34With a strong hand and an outstretched arm and overflowing fury I will bring you out from the peoples and gather you from the lands where you are scattered, 35and I will bring you into the wilderness of the peoples; and there I will enter into judgment with you face to face. 36As I entered into judgment with your fathers in the wilderness of the land of Egypt, so will I enter into judgment with you—declares the Lord God. 37I will make you pass under the shepherd's staff,^h and I will bring you into the bondⁱ of the covenant. 38I will remove from you those who rebel and transgress against Me; I will take them out of the countries where they sojourn, but they shall not enter the land of Israel. Then you shall know that I am the Lord.

אֶת־יָדִי לָתֵת אוֹתָהּ לָהֶם וַיִּרְאוּ כָל־גִּבְעָה רָמָה וְכָל־עֵץ עָבֹת וַיִּזְבְּחוּ־שָׁם אֶת־זִבְחֵיהֶם וַיִּתְּנוּ־שָׁם כַּעַס קָרְבָּנָם וַיָּשִׂימוּ שָׁם רֵיחַ נִיחוֹחֵיהֶם וַיַּסִּיכוּ שָׁם אֶת־נִסְכֵּיהֶם׃ 29 וָאֹמַר אֲלֵהֶם מָה הַבָּמָה אֲשֶׁר־אַתֶּם הַבָּאִים שָׁם וַיִּקָּרֵא שְׁמָהּ בָּמָה עַד הַיּוֹם הַזֶּה׃

30 לָכֵן אֱמֹר ׀ אֶל־בֵּית יִשְׂרָאֵל כֹּה אָמַר אֲדֹנָי יְהוִֹה הַבְּדֶרֶךְ אֲבוֹתֵיכֶם אַתֶּם נִטְמְאִים וְאַחֲרֵי שִׁקּוּצֵיהֶם אַתֶּם זֹנִים׃ 31 וּבִשְׂאֵת מַתְּנֹתֵיכֶם בְּהַעֲבִיר בְּנֵיכֶם בָּאֵשׁ אַתֶּם נִטְמְאִים לְכָל־גִּלּוּלֵיכֶם עַד־הַיּוֹם וַאֲנִי אִדָּרֵשׁ לָכֶם בֵּית יִשְׂרָאֵל חַי־אָנִי נְאֻם ׀ אֲדֹנָי יְהוִֹה אִם־אִדָּרֵשׁ לָכֶם׃ 32 וְהָעֹלָה עַל־רוּחֲכֶם הָיוֹ לֹא תִהְיֶה אֲשֶׁר ׀ אַתֶּם אֹמְרִים נִהְיֶה כַגּוֹיִם כְּמִשְׁפְּחוֹת הָאֲרָצוֹת לְשָׁרֵת עֵץ וָאָבֶן׃ 33 חַי־אָנִי נְאֻם אֲדֹנָי יְהוִֹה אִם־לֹא בְּיָד חֲזָקָה וּבִזְרוֹעַ נְטוּיָה וּבְחֵמָה שְׁפוּכָה אֶמְלוֹךְ עֲלֵיכֶם׃ 34 וְהוֹצֵאתִי אֶתְכֶם מִן־הָעַמִּים וְקִבַּצְתִּי אֶתְכֶם מִן־הָאֲרָצוֹת אֲשֶׁר נְפוֹצֹתֶם בָּם בְּיָד חֲזָקָה וּבִזְרוֹעַ נְטוּיָה וּבְחֵמָה שְׁפוּכָה׃ 35 וְהֵבֵאתִי אֶתְכֶם אֶל־מִדְבַּר הָעַמִּים וְנִשְׁפַּטְתִּי אִתְּכֶם שָׁם פָּנִים אֶל־פָּנִים׃ 36 כַּאֲשֶׁר נִשְׁפַּטְתִּי אֶת־אֲבוֹתֵיכֶם בְּמִדְבַּר אֶרֶץ מִצְרָיִם כֵּן אִשָּׁפֵט אִתְּכֶם נְאֻם אֲדֹנָי יְהוִֹה׃ 37 וְהַעֲבַרְתִּי אֶתְכֶם תַּחַת הַשָּׁבֶט וְהֵבֵאתִי אֶתְכֶם בְּמָסֹרֶת* הַבְּרִית׃ 38 וּבָרוֹתִי מִכֶּם הַמֹּרְדִים וְהַפּוֹשְׁעִים בִּי מֵאֶרֶץ מְגוּרֵיהֶם אוֹצִיא אוֹתָם וְאֶל־אַדְמַת יִשְׂרָאֵל לֹא יָבוֹא* וִידַעְתֶּם כִּי־אֲנִי יְהוָֹה׃

g   As if from ba "visit" and mah "what."
h   I.e., to be counted; see Lev. 27.32.
i   Meaning of Heb. uncertain.

³⁹As for you, O House of Israel, thus said the Lord GOD: Go, every one of you, and worship his fetishes and continue,ⁱ if you will not obey Me; but do not profane My holy name any more with your idolatrous gifts. ⁴⁰For only on My holy mountain, on the lofty mount of Israel— declares the Lord GOD—there, in the land, the entire House of Israel, all of it, must worship Me. There I will accept them, and there I will take note of your contributions and the choicest offerings of all your sacred things. ⁴¹When I bring you out from the peoples and gather you from the lands in which you are scattered, I will accept you as a pleasing odor; and I will be sanctified through you in the sight of the nations. ⁴²Then, when I have brought you to the land of Israel, to the country that I swordᵇ to give to your fathers, you shall know that I am the LORD. ⁴³There you will recall your ways and all the acts by which you defiled yourselves; and you will loathe yourselves for all the evils that you committed. ⁴⁴Then, O House of Israel, you shall know that I am the LORD, when I deal with you for My name's sake—not in accordance with your evil ways and corrupt acts—declares the Lord GOD.

21 The word of the LORD came to me: ²O mortal, set your face toward Teman,ᵃ and proclaim to Darom,ᵃ and prophesy against the brushland of the Negeb.ᵃ ³Say to the brushland of the Negeb: Hear the word of the LORD. Thus said the Lord GOD: I am going to kindle a fire in you, which shall devour every tree of yours, both green and withered. Its leaping flame shall not go out, and every face from south to north shall be scorched by it. ⁴Then all flesh shall recognize that I the LORD have kindled it; it shall

---

39 וְאַתֶּם בֵּית־יִשְׂרָאֵל כֹּה־אָמַר ׀ אֲדֹנָי
יֱהֹוִה אִישׁ גִּלּוּלָיו לְכוּ עֲבֹדוּ וְאַחַר אִם־
אֵינְכֶם שֹׁמְעִים אֵלָי וְאֶת־שֵׁם קָדְשִׁי לֹא
תְחַלְּלוּ־עוֹד בְּמַתְּנוֹתֵיכֶם וּבְגִלּוּלֵיכֶם:
40 כִּי בְהַר־קָדְשִׁי בְּהַר ׀ מְרוֹם יִשְׂרָאֵל
נְאֻם אֲדֹנָי יֱהֹוִה שָׁם יַעַבְדֻנִי כָּל־בֵּית
יִשְׂרָאֵל כֻּלֹּה בָּאָרֶץ שָׁם אֶרְצֵם וְשָׁם
אֶדְרוֹשׁ אֶת־תְּרוּמֹֽתֵיכֶם וְאֶת־רֵאשִׁית
מַשְׂאֽוֹתֵיכֶם בְּכָל־קָדְשֵׁיכֶם: 41 בְּרֵיחַ
נִיחֹחַ אֶרְצֶה אֶתְכֶם בְּהוֹצִיאִי אֶתְכֶם
מִן־הָעַמִּים וְקִבַּצְתִּי אֶתְכֶם מִן־הָאֲרָצוֹת
אֲשֶׁר נְפֹצֹתֶם בָּם וְנִקְדַּשְׁתִּי בָכֶם לְעֵינֵי
הַגּוֹיִם: 42 וִידַעְתֶּם כִּי־אֲנִי יֱהֹוִה בַּהֲבִיאִי
אֶתְכֶם אֶל־אַדְמַת יִשְׂרָאֵל אֶל־הָאָרֶץ
אֲשֶׁר נָשָׂאתִי אֶת־יָדִי לָתֵת אוֹתָהּ
לַאֲבֽוֹתֵיכֶם: 43 וּזְכַרְתֶּם־שָׁם אֶת־דַּרְכֵיכֶם
וְאֵת כָּל־עֲלִילֽוֹתֵיכֶם אֲשֶׁר נִטְמֵאתֶם
בָּם וּנְקֹטֹתֶם בִּפְנֵיכֶם בְּכָל־רָעוֹתֵיכֶם
אֲשֶׁר עֲשִׂיתֶם: 44 וִידַעְתֶּם כִּי־אֲנִי יֱהֹוָה
בַּעֲשׂוֹתִי אִתְּכֶם לְמַעַן שְׁמִי לֹא כְדַרְכֵיכֶם
הָרָעִים וְכַעֲלִילֽוֹתֵיכֶם הַנִּשְׁחָתוֹת בֵּית
יִשְׂרָאֵל נְאֻם אֲדֹנָי יֱהֹוִה: פ

כא וַיְהִי דְבַר־יְהֹוָה אֵלַי לֵאמֹר:
2 בֶּן־אָדָם שִׂים פָּנֶיךָ דֶּרֶךְ תֵּימָנָה וְהַטֵּף
אֶל־דָּרוֹם וְהִנָּבֵא אֶל־יַעַר הַשָּׂדֶה נֶגֶב:
3 וְאָמַרְתָּ לְיַעַר הַנֶּגֶב שְׁמַע דְּבַר־יְהֹוָה
כֹּה־אָמַר אֲדֹנָי יֱהֹוִה הִנְנִי מַצִּית־בְּךָ ׀ אֵשׁ
וְאָכְלָה בְךָ כָל־עֵץ־לַח וְכָל־עֵץ יָבֵשׁ
לֹא־תִכְבֶּה לַהֶבֶת שַׁלְהֶבֶת וְנִצְרְבוּ־בָהּ
כָּל־פָּנִים מִנֶּגֶב צָפוֹנָה: 4 וְרָאוּ כָּל־בָּשָׂר
כִּי אֲנִי יְהֹוָה בִּעַרְתִּיהָ לֹא תִכְבֶּה: 5 וָאֹמַר

ᵃ Teman, Darom, Negeb are three terms for "the south." The allusion is to Jerusalem (v. 7), which was always approached from Babylon by way of the north.

1196

not go out. 5And I said, "Ah, Lord God! They say of me: He is just a riddlemonger."

6Then the word of the Lord came to me: 7O mortal, set your face toward Jerusalem and proclaim against her sanctuaries and prophesy against the land of Israel. 8Say to the land of Israel: Thus said the Lord: I am going to deal with you! I will draw My sword from its sheath, and I will wipe out from you both the righteous and the wicked. 9In order to wipe out from you both the righteous and the wicked, My sword shall assuredly be unsheathed against all flesh from south to north; 10and all flesh shall know that I the Lord have drawn My sword from its sheath, not to be sheathed again.

11And you, O mortal, sigh; with tottering limbs and bitter grief, sigh before their eyes. 12And when they ask you, "Why do you sigh?" answer, "Because of the tidings that have come." Every heart shall sink and all hands hang nerveless; every spirit shall grow faint and all knees turn to water because of the tidings that have come. It is approaching, it shall come to pass— declares the Lord God.

13The word of the Lord came to me: 14O mortal, prophesy and say: Thus said the Lord God: A sword! A sword has been whetted and polished. 15It has been whetted to wreak slaughter; b-[therefore] it has been ground to a brilliant polish.-b c-How can we rejoice? My son, it scorns-c the rod and every stick. 16It has been given to be polished and then grasped in the hand; for this has the sword been whetted, for this polished—to be put into the hand of a slayer. 17Cry and wail, O mortal, for this shall befall My people, this shall befall all the chieftains of Israel: they shall be cast before the sword together with My people; oh, strike the thigh [in grief]. 18c-Consider: How shall it fail to hap-

אֲהָהּ אֲדֹנָי יְהוִֹה הֵמָּה אֹמְרִים לִי הֲלֹא
מְמַשֵּׁל מְשָׁלִים הוּא: פ

6 וַיְהִי דְבַר־יְהוָה אֵלַי לֵאמֹר: 7 בֶּן־אָדָם
שִׂים פָּנֶיךָ אֶל־יְרוּשָׁלִַם וְהַטֵּף אֶל־
מִקְדָּשִׁים וְהִנָּבֵא אֶל־אַדְמַת יִשְׂרָאֵל:
8 וְאָמַרְתָּ לְאַדְמַת יִשְׂרָאֵל כֹּה אָמַר יְהוָה
הִנְנִי אֵלַיִךְ וְהוֹצֵאתִי חַרְבִּי מִתַּעְרָהּ
וְהִכְרַתִּי מִמֵּךְ צַדִּיק וְרָשָׁע: 9 יַעַן אֲשֶׁר־
הִכְרַתִּי מִמֵּךְ צַדִּיק וְרָשָׁע לָכֵן תֵּצֵא חַרְבִּי
מִתַּעְרָהּ אֶל־כָּל־בָּשָׂר מִנֶּגֶב צָפוֹן: 10 וְיָדְעוּ
כָל־בָּשָׂר כִּי אֲנִי יְהוָה הוֹצֵאתִי חַרְבִּי
מִתַּעְרָהּ לֹא תָשׁוּב עוֹד: ס

11 וְאַתָּה בֶן־אָדָם הֵאָנַח בְּשִׁבְרוֹן מָתְנַיִם
וּבִמְרִירוּת תֵּאָנַח לְעֵינֵיהֶם: 12 וְהָיָה כִּי־
יֹאמְרוּ אֵלֶיךָ עַל־מָה אַתָּה נֶאֱנָח וְאָמַרְתָּ
אֶל־שְׁמוּעָה כִי־בָאָה וְנָמֵס כָּל־לֵב וְרָפוּ
כָל־יָדַיִם וְכִהֲתָה כָל־רוּחַ וְכָל־בִּרְכַּיִם
תֵּלַכְנָה מַּיִם הִנֵּה בָאָה וְנִהְיָתָה נְאֻם
אֲדֹנָי יְהוִֹה: פ

13 וַיְהִי דְבַר־יְהוָה אֵלַי לֵאמֹר: 14 בֶּן־אָדָם
הִנָּבֵא וְאָמַרְתָּ כֹּה אָמַר אֲדֹנָי אֱמֹר חֶרֶב
חֶרֶב הוּחַדָּה וְגַם־מְרוּטָה: 15 לְמַעַן טְבֹחַ
טֶבַח הוּחַדָּה לְמַעַן־הֱיֵה־לָהּ בָּרָק מֹרָטָּה
אוֹ נָשִׂישׂ שֵׁבֶט בְּנִי מֹאֶסֶת כָּל־עֵץ: 16 וַיִּתֵּן
אֹתָהּ לְמָרְטָה לִתְפֹּשׂ בַּכָּף הִיא־הוּחַדָּה
חֶרֶב וְהִיא מֹרָטָּה לָתֵת אוֹתָהּ בְּיַד־הוֹרֵג:
17 זְעַק וְהֵילֵל בֶּן־אָדָם כִּי־הִיא הָיְתָה
בְעַמִּי הִיא בְּכָל־נְשִׂיאֵי יִשְׂרָאֵל מְגוּרֵי
אֶל־חֶרֶב הָיוּ אֶת־עַמִּי לָכֵן סְפֹק אֶל־יָרֵךְ:

---

b-b   Lit. "it has been polished in order that it may have lightning."
c-c   Meaning of Heb. uncertain.

pen, seeing that it even scorns the rod?-*c*—says the Lord God.

¹⁹Further, O mortal, prophesy, striking hand against hand. Let the sword strike a second time and yet a third time; it is a sword for massacre, a sword for great carnage, that presses*c* upon them. ²⁰Thus hearts shall lose courage and many shall fall. At all their gates I have appointed slaughter*c* by the sword. Ah! it is made to flash brilliantly, it is honed*c* for slaughter. ²¹Be united,*d* go to the right, turn left; whither are you bound? ²²I, too, will strike hand against hand and will satisfy My fury upon you; I the Lord have spoken.

²³The word of the Lord came to me: ²⁴And you, O mortal, choose two roads on which the sword of the king of Babylon may advance, both issuing from the same country; and select a spot, select it where roads branch off to [two] cities. ²⁵Choose a way for the sword to advance on Rabbah of the Ammonites or on fortified Jerusalem in Judah. ²⁶For the king of Babylon has stood at the fork of the road, where two roads branch off, to perform divination: He has shaken arrows, consulted teraphim, and inspected the liver.*e* ²⁷In his right hand came up the omen against Jerusalem—to set battering rams, to proclaim murder, to raise battle shouts, to set battering rams against the gates, to cast up mounds, to erect towers.

²⁸*f* In their eyes, the oaths they had sworn to them were like empty divination; but this shall serve to recall their guilt, for which they shall be taken to task. ²⁹Assuredly, thus said the Lord God: For causing your guilt to be recalled, your transgressions to be uncovered, and your sins to be revealed—all your misdeeds—because you have brought yourselves to [My] mind, you shall be taken to task.

18 כִּי בֹחַן וּמָה אִם־גַּם־שֵׁבֶט מֹאֶסֶת לֹא
יִהְיֶה נְאֻם אֲדֹנָי יְהוִה: פ
19 וְאַתָּה בֶן־אָדָם הִנָּבֵא וְהַךְ כַּף אֶל־כַּף
וְתִכָּפֵל חֶרֶב שְׁלִישִׁתָה חֶרֶב חֲלָלִים הִיא
חֶרֶב חָלָל הַגָּדוֹל הַחֹדֶרֶת לָהֶם: 20 לְמַעַן ׀
לָמוּג לֵב וְהַרְבֵּה הַמִּכְשֹׁלִים עַל כָּל־
שַׁעֲרֵיהֶם נָתַתִּי אִבְחַת־חָרֶב אָח עֲשׂוּיָה
לְבָרָק מְעֻטָּה לְטָבַח: 21 הִתְאַחֲדִי הֵימִנִי
הָשִׂימִי הַשְׂמִילִי* אָנָה פָּנַיִךְ מֻעָדוֹת:
22 וְגַם־אֲנִי אַכֶּה כַפִּי אֶל־כַּפִּי וַהֲנִחֹתִי
חֲמָתִי אֲנִי יְהוִה דִּבַּרְתִּי: פ
23 וַיְהִי דְבַר־יְהוָה אֵלַי לֵאמֹר: 24 וְאַתָּה
בֶן־אָדָם שִׂים־לְךָ ׀ שְׁנַיִם דְּרָכִים לָבוֹא
חֶרֶב מֶלֶךְ־בָּבֶל מֵאֶרֶץ אֶחָד יֵצְאוּ שְׁנֵיהֶם
וְיָד בָּרֵא בְּרֹאשׁ דֶּרֶךְ־עִיר בָּרֵא: 25 דֶּרֶךְ
תָּשִׂים לָבוֹא חֶרֶב אֵת רַבַּת בְּנֵי־עַמּוֹן
וְאֶת־יְהוּדָה בִירוּשָׁלִַם בְּצוּרָה: 26 כִּי־
עָמַד מֶלֶךְ־בָּבֶל אֶל־אֵם הַדֶּרֶךְ בְּרֹאשׁ שְׁנֵי
הַדְּרָכִים לִקְסָם־קָסֶם קִלְקַל בַּחִצִּים שָׁאַל
בַּתְּרָפִים רָאָה בַּכָּבֵד: 27 בִּימִינוֹ הָיָה ׀
הַקֶּסֶם יְרוּשָׁלִַם לָשׂוּם כָּרִים לִפְתֹּחַ פֶּה
בְּרֶצַח לְהָרִים קוֹל בִּתְרוּעָה לָשׂוּם כָּרִים
עַל־שְׁעָרִים לִשְׁפֹּךְ סֹלְלָה לִבְנוֹת דָּיֵק:
28 וְהָיָה לָהֶם כקסום כִּקְסָם־שָׁוְא בְּעֵינֵיהֶם
שְׁבֻעֵי שְׁבֻעוֹת לָהֶם וְהוּא־מַזְכִּיר עָוֹן
לְהִתָּפֵשׂ: פ 29 לָכֵן כֹּה־אָמַר אֲדֹנָי
יְהוִה יַעַן הַזְכַּרְכֶם עֲוֹנְכֶם בְּהִגָּלוֹת
פִּשְׁעֵיכֶם לְהֵרָאוֹת חַטֹּאותֵיכֶם* בְּכֹל
עֲלִילוֹתֵיכֶם יַעַן הִזָּכֶרְכֶם בַּכַּף
תִּתָּפֵשׂוּ: פ

---

d   *Meaning of Heb. uncertain; Targum reads "Be whetted." Cf. vv.*
    14–16.
e   *I.e., of a sacrificed animal.*
f   *The inhabitants of Jerusalem disregarded their oaths to the Bab-*
    ylonians; cf. 17.13 ff.

חסר א׳   v. 21.
מלא ו׳   v. 29.

1198

30And to you, O dishonored wicked prince of Israel, whose day has come—the time set for your punishment—31thus said the Lord GOD: Remove the turban and lift off the crown! This shall not remain as it is; exalt the low and abase the high. 32Ruin, an utter ruin I will make it. c-It shall be no more-c until he comes to whom it rightfully belongs; and I will give it to him.

33Further, O mortal, prophesy and say: Thus said the Lord GOD concerning the Ammonites and their blasphemies: Proclaim: O sword! O sword unsheathed for slaughter, polished to the utmost, to a flashing brilliance! 34Because they have prophesied falsely about you and have divined deceitfully concerning you, you shall be wielded over the necks of the dishonored wicked ones, for their day has come, the time c-set for their punishment.-c

35g-Return it to its sheath!-g In the place where you were created, in the land of your origin, I will judge you. 36I will pour out My indignation upon you, I will blow upon you with the fire of My wrath; and I will deliver you into the hands of barbarians, craftsmen of destruction. 37You shall be fuel for the fire, your blood shall sink into the earth, you shall not be remembered, for I the LORD have spoken.

22 The word of the LORD came to me: 2Further, O mortal, a-arraign, arraign-a the city of bloodshed; declare to her all her abhorrent deeds! 3Say: Thus said the Lord GOD: O city in whose midst blood is shed, so that your hour is approaching; within which fetishes are made, so that you have become unclean! 4You stand guilty of the blood you have shed, defiled by the

30 וְאַתָּה חָלָל רָשָׁע נְשִׂיא יִשְׂרָאֵל אֲשֶׁר־בָּא יוֹמוֹ בְּעֵת עֲוֺן קֵץ: ס 31 כֹּה אָמַר אֲדֹנָי יְהֹוִה הָסִיר הַמִּצְנֶפֶת וְהָרִים הָעֲטָרָה זֹאת לֹא־זֹאת הַשָּׁפָלָה הַגְבֵּהַ וְהַגָּבֹהַ הַשְׁפִּיל: 32 עַוָּה עַוָּה עַוָּה אֲשִׂימֶנָּה גַּם־זֹאת לֹא הָיָה עַד־בֹּא אֲשֶׁר־לוֹ הַמִּשְׁפָּט וּנְתַתִּיו: פ

33 וְאַתָּה בֶן־אָדָם הִנָּבֵא וְאָמַרְתָּ כֹּה אָמַר אֲדֹנָי יְהֹוִה אֶל־בְּנֵי עַמּוֹן וְאֶל־חֶרְפָּתָם וְאָמַרְתָּ חֶרֶב חֶרֶב פְּתוּחָה לְטֶבַח מְרוּטָה לְהָכִיל לְמַעַן בָּרָק: 34 בַּחֲזוֹת לָךְ שָׁוְא בִּקְסָם־לָךְ כָּזָב לָתֵת אוֹתָךְ אֶל־צַוְּארֵי חַלְלֵי רְשָׁעִים אֲשֶׁר־בָּא יוֹמָם בְּעֵת עֲוֺן קֵץ:

35 הָשַׁב אֶל־תַּעְרָהּ בִּמְקוֹם אֲשֶׁר־נִבְרֵאת בְּאֶרֶץ מְכֻרוֹתַיִךְ אֶשְׁפֹּט אֹתָךְ: 36 וְשָׁפַכְתִּי עָלַיִךְ זַעְמִי בְּאֵשׁ עֶבְרָתִי אָפִיחַ עָלָיִךְ וּנְתַתִּיךְ בְּיַד אֲנָשִׁים בֹּעֲרִים חָרָשֵׁי מַשְׁחִית: 37 לָאֵשׁ תִּהְיֶה לְאָכְלָה דָּמֵךְ יִהְיֶה בְּתוֹךְ הָאָרֶץ לֹא תִזָּכֵרִי כִּי אֲנִי יְהֹוָה דִּבַּרְתִּי: פ

כב וַיְהִי דְבַר־יְהֹוָה אֵלַי לֵאמֹר: 2 וְאַתָּה בֶן־אָדָם הֲתִשְׁפֹּט הֲתִשְׁפֹּט אֶת־עִיר הַדָּמִים וְהוֹדַעְתָּהּ אֵת כָּל־תּוֹעֲבוֹתֶיהָ: 3 וְאָמַרְתָּ כֹּה אָמַר אֲדֹנָי יְהֹוִה עִיר שֹׁפֶכֶת דָּם בְּתוֹכָהּ לָבוֹא עִתָּהּ וְעָשְׂתָה גִלּוּלִים עָלֶיהָ לְטָמְאָה: 4 בְּדָמֵךְ אֲשֶׁר־שָׁפַכְתְּ אָשַׁמְתְּ וּבְגִלּוּלַיִךְ אֲשֶׁר־

---

g-g   *Emendation yields "Return to your scabbard!" In this and the following verses, the prophet describes the future punishment of Babylon, still symbolized by the sword.*

a-a   *Lit. "will you arraign, arraign."*

fetishes you have made. You have brought on your day; b-you have reached your year.-b Therefore I will make you the mockery of the nations and the scorn of all the lands. 5Both the near and the far shall scorn you, O besmirched of name, O laden with iniquity!

6Every one of the princes of Israel in your midst used his strength for the shedding of blood. 7Fathers and mothers have been humiliated within you; strangers have been cheated in your midst; orphans and widows have been wronged within you. 8You have despised My holy things and profaned My sabbaths.

9Basec men in your midst were intent on shedding blood; in you they have eaten d-upon the mountains;-d and they have practiced depravity in your midst. 10In you they have uncovered their fathers' nakedness;e in you they have ravished women during their impurity. 11They have committed abhorrent acts with other men's wives; in their depravity they have defiled their own daughters-in-law; in you they have ravished their own sisters, daughters of their fathers. 12They have taken bribes within you to shed blood. You have taken advance and accrued interest;f you have defrauded your countrymen to your profit. You have forgotten Me—declares the Lord GOD.

13Lo, I will strike My hands over the ill-gotten gains that you have amassed, and over the bloodshed that has been committed in your midst. 14Will your courage endure, will your hands remain firm in the days when I deal with you? I the LORD have spoken and I will act. 15I will scatter you among the nations and disperse you through the lands; I will consume the uncleanness out of you. 16You shall be dishonored

עָשִׂית֙ טָמֵ֔את וַתַּקְרִ֣יבִי יָמַ֔יִךְ וַתָּב֖וֹא
עַד־שְׁנוֹתָ֑יִךְ עַל־כֵּ֗ן נְתַתִּ֤יךְ חֶרְפָּה֙ לַגּוֹיִ֔ם
וְקַלָּסָ֖ה לְכָל־הָאֲרָצֽוֹת׃ 5 הַקְּרֹב֣וֹת
וְהָרְחֹק֤וֹת מִמֵּךְ֙ יִתְקַלְּסוּ־בָ֔ךְ טְמֵאַ֣ת הַשֵּׁ֔ם
רַבַּ֖ת הַמְּהוּמָֽה׃
6 הִנֵּה֙ נְשִׂיאֵ֣י יִשְׂרָאֵ֔ל אִ֛ישׁ לִזְרֹע֖וֹ הָ֣יוּ בָ֑ךְ
לְמַ֖עַן שְׁפָךְ־דָּֽם׃ 7 אָ֤ב וָאֵם֙ הֵקַ֣לּוּ בָ֔ךְ
לַגֵּ֛ר עָשׂ֥וּ בַעֹ֖שֶׁק בְּתוֹכֵ֑ךְ יָת֤וֹם וְאַלְמָנָה֙
ה֣וֹנוּ בָֽךְ׃ 8 קָדָשַׁ֖י בָּזִ֑ית וְאֶת־שַׁבְּתֹתַ֖י
חִלָּֽלְתְּ׃
9 אַנְשֵׁ֥י רָכִ֛יל הָ֥יוּ בָ֖ךְ לְמַ֣עַן שְׁפָךְ־דָּ֑ם
וְאֶל־הֶֽהָרִים֙ אָ֣כְלוּ בָ֔ךְ זִמָּ֖ה עָשׂ֥וּ בְתוֹכֵֽךְ׃
10 עֶרְוַת־אָ֖ב גִּלָּה־בָ֑ךְ טְמֵאַ֥ת הַנִּדָּ֖ה עִנּוּ־
בָֽךְ׃ 11 וְאִ֣ישׁ ׀ אֶת־אֵ֣שֶׁת רֵעֵ֗הוּ עָשָׂה֙
תּֽוֹעֵבָ֔ה וְאִ֗ישׁ אֶת־כַּלָּת֛וֹ טִמֵּ֖א בְּזִמָּ֑ה
וְאִ֛ישׁ אֶת־אֲחֹת֥וֹ בַת־אָבִ֖יו עִנָּה־בָֽךְ׃
12 שֹׁ֣חַד לָֽקְחוּ־בָ֔ךְ לְמַ֖עַן שְׁפָךְ־דָּ֑ם נֶ֧שֶׁךְ
וְתַרְבִּ֣ית לָקַ֗חַתְּ וַתְּבַצְּעִ֤י רֵעַ֙יִךְ֙ בַּעֹ֔שֶׁק
וְאֹתִ֥י שָׁכַ֖חַתְּ נְאֻ֥ם אֲדֹנָ֥י יְהֹוִֽה׃
13 וְהִנֵּה֙ הִכֵּ֣יתִי כַפִּ֔י אֶל־בִּצְעֵ֖ךְ אֲשֶׁ֣ר
עָשִׂ֑ית וְעַ֨ל־דָּמֵ֔ךְ אֲשֶׁ֥ר הָי֖וּ בְּתוֹכֵֽךְ׃
14 הֲיַעֲמֹ֤ד לִבֵּךְ֙ אִם־תֶּחֱזַ֣קְנָה יָדַ֔יִךְ לַיָּמִ֕ים
אֲשֶׁ֥ר אֲנִ֖י עֹשֶׂ֣ה אוֹתָ֑ךְ אֲנִ֧י יְהֹוָ֛ה דִּבַּ֖רְתִּי
וְעָשִֽׂיתִי׃ 15 וַהֲפִיצוֹתִ֤י אוֹתָךְ֙ בַּגּוֹיִ֔ם
וְזֵרִיתִ֖יךְ בָּאֲרָצ֑וֹת וַהֲתִמֹּתִ֥י טֻמְאָתֵ֖ךְ

---

b-b   Some Babylonian mss. and ancient versions read "the time of your years has come."

c   Meaning of Heb. uncertain.

d-d   I.e., in idolatry. Emendation yields "with the blood"; cf. Lev. 19.26.

e   I.e., have cohabited with a former wife of the father; cf. Lev. 18.7–8.

f   Cf. note at 18.8.

in the sight of nations, and you shall know that I am the LORD.

17The word of the LORD came to me: 18O mortal, the House of Israel has become dross to Me; they are all copper, tin, iron, and lead. c-But in a crucible, the dross shall turn into silver.-c 19Assuredly, thus said the Lord GOD: Because you have all become dross, I will gather you into Jerusalem. 20As silver, copper, iron, lead, and tin are gathered into a crucible to blow the fire upon them, so as to melt them, so will I gather you in My fierce anger and cast you [into the fire] and melt you. 21I will gather you and I will blow upon you the fire of My fury, and you shall be melted in it. 22As silver is melted in a crucible, so shall you be melted in it. And you shall know that I the LORD have poured out My fury upon you.

23The word of the LORD came to me: 24O mortal, say to her: You are an uncleansed land, c-not to be washed with rain-c on the day of indignation. 25g-Her gang of prophets-g are like roaring lions in her midst, rending prey. They devour human beings; they seize treasure and wealth; they have widowed many women in her midst. 26Her priests have violated My Teaching: they have profaned what is sacred to Me, they have not distinguished between the sacred and the profane, they have not taught the difference between the unclean and the clean, and they have closed their eyes to My sabbaths. I am profaned in their midst. 27Her officials are like wolves rending prey in her midst; they shed blood and destroy lives to win ill-gotten gain. 28Her prophets, too, daub the wall for them with plaster:h They prophesy falsely and divine deceitfully for them; they say, "Thus said the Lord GOD," when the LORD has not spoken. 29And

---

g-g Septuagint reads "Whose chieftains."
h   Cf. 13.10 ff.

מִמֵּךְ ׃ 16 וְנִחַלְתְּ בָּ֖ךְ לְעֵינֵ֣י גוֹיִ֑ם וְיָדַ֖עַתְּ כִּֽי־אֲנִ֥י יְהוָֽה ׃ פ

17 וַיְהִ֥י דְבַר־יְהוָ֖ה אֵלַ֥י לֵאמֹֽר ׃ 18 בֶּן־אָדָ֗ם הָֽיוּ־לִ֤י בֵֽית־יִשְׂרָאֵל֙ לְסוּג לְסִיג כֻּלָּ֗ם נְחֹ֨שֶׁת וּבְדִ֤יל וּבַרְזֶל֙ וְעוֹפֶ֔רֶת בְּת֖וֹךְ כּ֑וּר סִגִ֥ים כֶּ֖סֶף הָיֽוּ ׃ ס 19 לָכֵ֗ן כֹּ֤ה אָמַר֙ אֲדֹנָ֣י יְהוִ֔ה יַ֛עַן הֱי֥וֹת כֻּלְּכֶ֖ם לְסִגִ֑ים לָכֵ֗ן הִנְנִ֤י קֹבֵ֤ץ אֶתְכֶם֙ אֶל־תּ֣וֹךְ יְרוּשָׁלִָ֑ם ׃ 20 קְבֻ֣צַת כֶּ֡סֶף וּנְחֹשֶׁת֩ וּבַרְזֶ֨ל וְעוֹפֶ֤רֶת וּבְדִיל֙ אֶל־תּ֣וֹךְ כּ֔וּר לָפַֽחַת־עָלָ֥יו אֵ֖שׁ לְהַנְתִּ֑יךְ כֵּ֤ן אֶקְבֹּץ֙ בְּאַפִּ֣י וּבַחֲמָתִ֔י וְהִנַּחְתִּ֖י וְהִתַּכְתִּ֥י אֶתְכֶֽם ׃ 21 וְכִנַּסְתִּ֣י אֶתְכֶ֔ם וְנָפַחְתִּ֥י עֲלֵיכֶ֖ם בְּאֵ֣שׁ עֶבְרָתִ֑י וְנִתַּכְתֶּ֖ם בְּתוֹכָֽהּ ׃ 22 כְּהִתּ֤וּךְ כֶּ֙סֶף֙ בְּת֣וֹךְ כּ֔וּר כֵּ֖ן תֻּתְּכ֣וּ בְתוֹכָ֑הּ וִֽידַעְתֶּ֕ם כִּֽי־אֲנִ֣י יְהוָ֔ה שָׁפַ֥כְתִּי חֲמָתִ֖י עֲלֵיכֶֽם ׃ פ

23 וַיְהִ֥י דְבַר־יְהוָ֖ה אֵלַ֥י לֵאמֹֽר ׃ 24 בֶּן־אָדָ֗ם אֱמָר־לָ֕הּ אַ֣תְּ אֶ֗רֶץ לֹ֤א מְטֹהָרָה֙ הִ֔יא לֹ֥א גֻשְׁמָ֖הּ בְּי֥וֹם זָֽעַם ׃ 25 קֶ֤שֶׁר נְבִיאֶ֙יהָ֙ בְּתוֹכָ֔הּ כַּֽאֲרִ֥י שׁוֹאֵ֖ג טֹ֣רֵֽף טָ֑רֶף נֶ֣פֶשׁ אָכָ֗לוּ חֹ֤סֶן וִיקָר֙ יִקָּ֔חוּ אַלְמְנוֹתֶ֖יהָ הִרְבּ֥וּ בְתוֹכָֽהּ ׃ 26 כֹּהֲנֶ֜יהָ חָמְס֣וּ תוֹרָתִ֗י וַיְחַלְּלוּ֙ קָדָשַׁ֔י בֵּֽין־קֹ֤דֶשׁ לְחֹל֙ לֹ֣א הִבְדִּ֔ילוּ וּבֵֽין־הַטָּמֵ֥א לְטָה֖וֹר לֹ֣א הוֹדִ֑יעוּ וּמִשַּׁבְּתוֹתַי֙ הֶעְלִ֣ימוּ עֵֽינֵיהֶ֔ם וָאֵחַ֖ל בְּתוֹכָֽם ׃ 27 שָׂרֶ֣יהָ בְקִרְבָּ֗הּ כִּזְאֵבִים֙ טֹ֣רְפֵי טָ֔רֶף לִשְׁפָּךְ־דָּם֙ לְאַבֵּ֣ד נְפָשׁ֔וֹת לְמַ֖עַן בְּצֹ֥עַ בָּֽצַע ׃ 28 וּנְבִיאֶ֗יהָ טָח֤וּ לָהֶם֙ תָּפֵ֔ל חֹזִ֣ים שָׁ֔וְא וְקֹסְמִ֥ים לָהֶ֖ם כָּזָ֑ב אֹֽמְרִ֗ים כֹּ֤ה אָמַר֙ אֲדֹנָ֣י יְהוִ֔ה וַֽיהוָ֖ה לֹ֥א

the people of the land have practiced fraud and committed robbery; they have wronged the poor and needy, have defrauded the stranger without redress. ³⁰And I sought a man among them to repair the wall or to stand in the breach before Me in behalf of this land, that I might not destroy it; but I found none. ³¹I have therefore poured out My indignation upon them; I will consume them with the fire of My fury. I will repay them for their conduct—declares the Lord GOD.

23

The word of the LORD came to me: ²O mortal, once there were two women, daughters of one mother. ³They played the whore in Egypt; they played the whore while still young. There their breasts were squeezed, and there their virgin nipples were handled. ⁴Their names were: the elder one, Oholah;^a and her sister, Oholibah.^b They became Mine, and they bore sons and daughters. As for their names, Oholah is Samaria, and Oholibah is Jerusalem.

⁵Oholah whored while she was Mine, and she lusted after her lovers, after the Assyrians, warriors^c ⁶clothed in blue, governors and prefects, horsemen mounted on steeds—all of them handsome young fellows. ⁷She bestowed her favors upon them—upon all the pick of the Assyrians—and defiled herself with all their fetishes after which she lusted. ⁸She did not give up the whoring she had begun with the Egyptians; for they had lain with her in her youth, and they had handled her virgin nipples and had poured out their lust upon her. ⁹Therefore I delivered her into the hands of her lovers, into the hands of the Assyrians after whom she lusted. ¹⁰They exposed her nakedness; they seized her sons and daughters, and she herself was put to the sword. And because of the punishment

---

a   I.e., "Tent."
b   I.e., "My Tent Is in Her."
c   Meaning of Heb. uncertain.

דָּבֵּר: 29 עַם הָאָרֶץ עָשְׁקוּ עֹשֶׁק וְגָזְלוּ גָּזֵל וְעָנִי וְאֶבְיוֹן הוֹנוּ וְאֶת־הַגֵּר עָשְׁקוּ בְּלֹא מִשְׁפָּט: 30 וָאֲבַקֵּשׁ מֵהֶם אִישׁ גֹּדֵר־גָּדֵר וְעֹמֵד בַּפֶּרֶץ לְפָנַי בְּעַד הָאָרֶץ לְבִלְתִּי שַׁחֲתָהּ וְלֹא מָצָאתִי: 31 וָאֶשְׁפֹּךְ עֲלֵיהֶם זַעְמִי בְּאֵשׁ עֶבְרָתִי כִּלִּיתִים דַּרְכָּם בְּרֹאשָׁם נָתַתִּי נְאֻם אֲדֹנָי יְהוִה: פ

כג וַיְהִי דְבַר־יְהוָה אֵלַי לֵאמֹר: 2 בֶּן־אָדָם שְׁתַּיִם נָשִׁים בְּנוֹת אֵם־אַחַת הָיוּ: 3 וַתִּזְנֶינָה בְמִצְרַיִם בִּנְעוּרֵיהֶן זָנוּ שָׁמָּה מֹעֲכוּ שְׁדֵיהֶן וְשָׁם עִשּׂוּ דַּדֵּי בְּתוּלֵיהֶן: 4 וּשְׁמוֹתָן אָהֳלָה הַגְּדוֹלָה וְאָהֳלִיבָה אֲחוֹתָהּ וַתִּהְיֶינָה לִי וַתֵּלַדְנָה בָּנִים וּבָנוֹת וּשְׁמוֹתָן שֹׁמְרוֹן אָהֳלָה וִירוּשָׁלַ͏ִם אָהֳלִיבָה: 5 וַתִּזֶן אָהֳלָה תַּחְתָּי וַתַּעְגַּב עַל־מְאַהֲבֶיהָ אֶל־אַשּׁוּר קְרוֹבִים: 6 לְבֻשֵׁי תְכֵלֶת פַּחוֹת וּסְגָנִים בַּחוּרֵי חֶמֶד כֻּלָּם פָּרָשִׁים רֹכְבֵי סוּסִים: 7 וַתִּתֵּן תַּזְנוּתֶיהָ עֲלֵיהֶם מִבְחַר בְּנֵי־אַשּׁוּר כֻּלָּם וּבְכֹל אֲשֶׁר־עָגְבָה בְּכָל־גִּלּוּלֵיהֶם נִטְמָאָה: 8 וְאֶת־תַּזְנוּתֶיהָ מִמִּצְרַיִם לֹא עָזָבָה כִּי אוֹתָהּ שָׁכְבוּ בִנְעוּרֶיהָ וְהֵמָּה עִשּׂוּ דַּדֵּי בְתוּלֶיהָ וַיִּשְׁפְּכוּ תַזְנוּתָם עָלֶיהָ: 9 לָכֵן נְתַתִּיהָ בְּיַד־מְאַהֲבֶיהָ בְּיַד בְּנֵי אַשּׁוּר אֲשֶׁר עָגְבָה עֲלֵיהֶם: 10 הֵמָּה גִּלּוּ עֶרְוָתָהּ בָּנֶיהָ

inflicted upon her, she became a byword among women.

¹¹Her sister Oholibah saw this; yet her lusting was more depraved than her sister's, and her whoring more debased. ¹²She lusted after the Assyrians, governors and prefects, warriorsᶜ gorgeously clad, horsemen mounted on steeds—all of them handsome young fellows. ¹³And I saw how she had defiled herself. Both of them followed the same course, ¹⁴but she carried her harlotries further. For she saw men sculptured upon the walls, figures of Chaldeans drawn in vermilion, ¹⁵girded with belts round their waists, and with flowing turbans on their heads, all of them looking like officers—a picture of Babylonians whose native land was Chaldea. ¹⁶At the very sight of them she lusted after them, and she sent messengers for them to Chaldea. ¹⁷So the Babylonians came to her for lovemaking and defiled her with their whoring; and she defiled herself with them until she turned from them in disgust. ¹⁸She flaunted her harlotries and exposed her nakedness, and I turned from her in disgust, as I had turned disgusted from her sister. ¹⁹But she whored still more, remembering how in her youth she had played the whore in the land of Egypt; ²⁰she lusted for concubinage with them, whose members were like those of asses and whose organsᶜ were like those of stallions. ²¹Thus you reverted to the wantonness of your youth, rememberingᵈ your youthful breasts, when the men of Egypt handled your nipples.

²²Assuredly, Oholibah, thus said the Lord GOD: I am going to rouse against you the lovers from whom you turned in disgust, and I will bring them upon you from all around—²³the Babylonians and all the Chaldeans, [the people of] Pekod, Shoa, and Koa, and all the Assyrians with them, all of them handsome young fellows,

---

d Lit. "for the sake of."

וּבְנוֹתֶיהָ לָקָחוּ וְאוֹתָהּ בַּחֶרֶב הָרָגוּ וַתְּהִי־
שֵׁם לַנָּשִׁים וּשְׁפוּטִים עָשׂוּ בָהּ׃ ס ¹¹ וַתֵּרֶא
אֲחוֹתָהּ אָהֳלִיבָה וַתַּשְׁחֵת עַגְבָתָהּ מִמֶּנָּה
וְאֶת־תַּזְנוּתֶיהָ מִזְּנוּנֵי אֲחוֹתָהּ׃ ¹² אֶל־בְּנֵי
אַשּׁוּר עָגָבָה פַּחוֹת וּסְגָנִים קְרֹבִים לְבֻשֵׁי
מִכְלוֹל פָּרָשִׁים רֹכְבֵי סוּסִים בַּחוּרֵי חֶמֶד
כֻּלָּם׃ ¹³ וָאֵרֶא כִּי נִטְמָאָה דֶּרֶךְ אֶחָד
לִשְׁתֵּיהֶן׃ ¹⁴ וַתּוֹסֶף אֶל־תַּזְנוּתֶיהָ וַתֵּרֶא
אַנְשֵׁי מְחֻקֶּה עַל־הַקִּיר צַלְמֵי כשדיים כַשְׂדִּים
חֲקֻקִים בַּשָּׁשַׁר׃ ¹⁵ חֲגוֹרֵי אֵזוֹר בְּמָתְנֵיהֶם
סְרוּחֵי טְבוּלִים בְּרָאשֵׁיהֶם מַרְאֵה שָׁלִשִׁים
כֻּלָּם דְּמוּת בְּנֵי־בָבֶל כַּשְׂדִּים אֶרֶץ
מוֹלַדְתָּם׃ ¹⁶ ותעגב וַתַּעְגְּבָה עֲלֵיהֶם לְמַרְאֵה
עֵינֶיהָ וַתִּשְׁלַח מַלְאָכִים אֲלֵיהֶם כַּשְׂדִּימָה׃
¹⁷ וַיָּבֹאוּ אֵלֶיהָ בְנֵי־בָבֶל לְמִשְׁכַּב דֹּדִים
וַיְטַמְּאוּ אוֹתָהּ בְּתַזְנוּתָם וַתִּטְמָא־בָם
וַתֵּקַע נַפְשָׁהּ מֵהֶם׃ ¹⁸ וַתְּגַל תַּזְנוּתֶיהָ
וַתְּגַל אֶת־עֶרְוָתָהּ וַתֵּקַע נַפְשִׁי מֵעָלֶיהָ
כַּאֲשֶׁר נָקְעָה נַפְשִׁי מֵעַל אֲחוֹתָהּ׃ ¹⁹
וַתַּרְבֶּה אֶת־תַּזְנוּתֶיהָ לִזְכֹּר אֶת־יְמֵי
נְעוּרֶיהָ אֲשֶׁר זָנְתָה בְּאֶרֶץ מִצְרָיִם׃ ²⁰
וַתַּעְגְּבָה עַל פִּלַגְשֵׁיהֶם אֲשֶׁר בְּשַׂר־
חֲמוֹרִים בְּשָׂרָם וְזִרְמַת סוּסִים זִרְמָתָם׃
²¹ וַתִּפְקְדִי אֵת זִמַּת נְעוּרָיִךְ בַּעְשׂוֹת
מִמִּצְרַיִם דַּדַּיִךְ לְמַעַן שְׁדֵי נְעוּרָיִךְ׃ ס
²² לָכֵן אָהֳלִיבָה כֹּה־אָמַר אֲדֹנָי יְהוִה הִנְנִי
מֵעִיר אֶת־מְאַהֲבַיִךְ עָלַיִךְ אֵת אֲשֶׁר־נָקְעָה
נַפְשֵׁךְ מֵהֶם וַהֲבֵאתִים עָלַיִךְ מִסָּבִיב׃
²³ בְּנֵי בָבֶל וְכָל־כַּשְׂדִּים פְּקוֹד וְשׁוֹעַ וְקוֹעַ
כָּל־בְּנֵי אַשּׁוּר אוֹתָם בַּחוּרֵי חֶמֶד פַּחוֹת
וּסְגָנִים כֻּלָּם שָׁלִשִׁים וּקְרוּאִים רֹכְבֵי

governors and prefects, officers and warriors,[c] all of them riding on horseback. [24]They shall attack you with fleets[c] of wheeled chariots and a host of troops; they shall set themselves against you on all sides with bucklers, shields, and helmets. And I will entrust your punishment to them, and they shall inflict their punishments on you. [25]I will direct My passion against you, and they shall deal with you in fury: they shall cut off your nose and ears. The last of you shall fall by the sword; they[e] shall take away your sons and daughters, and your remnant shall be devoured by fire. [26]They shall strip you of your clothing and take away your dazzling jewels. [27]I will put an end to your wantonness and to your whoring in the land of Egypt, and you shall not long for them or remember Egypt any more.

[28]For thus said the Lord GOD: I am going to deliver you into the hands of those you hate, into the hands of those from whom you turned in disgust. [29]They shall treat you with hate, and they shall take away all you have toiled for, and leave you naked and bare; your naked whoredom, wantonness, and harlotry will be exposed. [30]These things shall be done to you for your harlotries with the nations, for defiling yourself with their fetishes. [31]You walked in your sister's path; therefore I will put her cup into your hand.

[32]Thus said the Lord GOD:

You shall drink of your sister's cup,
So deep and wide;
It shall cause derision and scorn,
It holds so much.
[33]You shall be filled with drunkenness and
   woe.
The cup of desolation and horror,
The cup of your sister Samaria—
[34]You shall drink it and drain it,
[c]-And gnaw its shards;[-c]
And you shall tear your breasts.

---

e   *I.e., the former lovers, vv. 22 ff.*

סוּסִ֖ים כֻּלָּֽם׃ 24 וּבָ֣אוּ עָלַ֡יִךְ הֹ֩צֶן֩ רֶ֨כֶב
וְגַלְגַּ֜ל וּבִקְהַ֣ל עַמִּ֗ים צִנָּ֤ה וּמָגֵן֙ וְקוֹבַ֔ע
יָשִׂ֤ימוּ עָלַ֙יִךְ֙ סָבִ֔יב וְנָתַתִּ֤י לִפְנֵיהֶם֙ מִשְׁפָּ֔ט
וּשְׁפָט֖וּךְ בְּמִשְׁפְּטֵיהֶֽם׃ 25 וְנָתַתִּ֤י קִנְאָתִי֙
בָּ֔ךְ וְעָשׂ֤וּ אוֹתָךְ֙ בְּחֵמָ֔ה אַפֵּ֤ךְ וְאָזְנַ֙יִךְ֙ יָסִ֔ירוּ
וְאַחֲרִיתֵ֖ךְ בַּחֶ֣רֶב תִּפּ֑וֹל הֵ֗מָּה בָּנַ֤יִךְ
וּבְנוֹתַ֙יִךְ֙ יִקָּ֔חוּ וְאַחֲרִיתֵ֖ךְ תֵּאָכֵ֥ל בָּאֵֽשׁ׃
26 וְהִפְשִׁיט֖וּךְ אֶת־בְּגָדָ֑יִךְ וְלָקְח֖וּ כְּלֵ֥י
תִפְאַרְתֵּֽךְ׃ 27 וְהִשְׁבַּתִּ֤י זִמָּתֵךְ֙ מִמֵּ֔ךְ וְאֶת־
זְנוּתֵ֖ךְ מֵאֶ֣רֶץ מִצְרָ֑יִם וְלֹֽא־תִשְׂאִ֤י עֵינַ֙יִךְ֙
אֲלֵיהֶ֔ם וּמִצְרַ֖יִם לֹ֥א תִזְכְּרִי־עֽוֹד׃ ס
28 כִּ֣י כֹ֤ה אָמַר֙ אֲדֹנָ֣י יְהֹוִ֔ה הִנְנִ֤י נֹֽתְנָךְ֙ בְּיַ֔ד
אֲשֶׁ֣ר שָׂנֵ֑את בְּיַ֖ד אֲשֶׁר־נָקְעָ֥ה נַפְשֵׁ֖ךְ מֵהֶֽם׃
29 וְעָשׂ֨וּ אוֹתָ֜ךְ בְּשִׂנְאָ֗ה וְלָקְחוּ֙ כָּל־יְגִיעֵ֔ךְ
וַעֲזָב֖וּךְ עֵירֹ֣ם וְעֶרְיָ֑ה וְנִגְלָה֙ עֶרְוַ֣ת זְנוּנַ֔יִךְ
וְזִמָּתֵ֖ךְ וְתַזְנוּתָֽיִךְ׃ 30 עָשֹׂ֥ה אֵ֖לֶּה לָ֑ךְ
בִּזְנוֹתֵךְ֙ אַחֲרֵ֣י גוֹיִ֔ם עַ֥ל אֲשֶׁר־נִטְמֵ֖את
בְּגִלּוּלֵיהֶֽם׃ 31 בְּדֶ֥רֶךְ אֲחוֹתֵ֖ךְ הָלָ֑כְתְּ
וְנָתַתִּ֥י כוֹסָ֖הּ בְּיָדֵֽךְ׃ ס
32 כֹּ֤ה אָמַר֙ אֲדֹנָ֣י יְהֹוִ֔ה

כּ֣וֹס אֲחוֹתֵ֤ךְ תִּשְׁתִּי֙
הָעֲמֻקָּ֣ה וְהָרְחָבָ֔ה
תִּהְיֶ֥ה לִצְחֹ֖ק וּלְלַ֑עַג
מִרְבָּ֖ה לְהָכִֽיל׃
33 שִׁכָּר֥וֹן וְיָג֖וֹן תִּמָּלֵ֑אִי
כּ֚וֹס שַׁמָּ֣ה וּשְׁמָמָ֔ה
כּ֖וֹס אֲחוֹתֵ֥ךְ שֹׁמְרֽוֹן׃
34 וְשָׁתִ֨ית אוֹתָ֜הּ וּמָצִ֗ית
וְאֶת־חֲרָשֶׂ֛יהָ תְּגָרֵ֖מִי
וְשָׁדַ֣יִךְ תְּנַתֵּ֑קִי

For I have spoken—declares the Lord GOD.

³⁵Assuredly, thus said the Lord GOD: Because you have forgotten Me and cast Me behind your back, you in turn must suffer for your wanton whoring.

³⁶Then the LORD said to me: O mortal, arraign*f* Oholah and Oholibah, and charge them with their abominations. ³⁷For they have committed adultery, and blood is on their hands; truly they have committed adultery with their fetishes, and have even offered to them as food the children they bore to Me. ³⁸At the same time they also did this to Me: they defiled My Sanctuary and profaned My sabbaths. ³⁹On the very day that they slaughtered their children to their fetishes, they entered My Sanctuary to desecrate it. That is what they did in My House.

⁴⁰Moreover, they sent for men to come from afar, [men] to whom a messenger was sent; and they came. For them, [Oholibah,] you bathed, painted your eyes, and donned your finery; ⁴¹and you sat on a grand couch with a set table in front of it—and it was My incense and My oil you laid upon it. ⁴²And the noise of a carefree multitude was there, *c*-of numerous men brought drunk from the desert;-*c* and they put bracelets on their arms and splendid crowns upon their heads. ⁴³Then I said, *c*-"To destruction with adultery! Look, they are still going on with those same fornications of hers."-*c* ⁴⁴And they would go to her as one goes to a prostitute; that is how they went to Oholah and Oholibah, wanton women. ⁴⁵But righteous men shall punish them with the punishments for adultery and for bloodshed, for they are adulteresses and have blood on their hands.

⁴⁶For thus said the Lord GOD: Summon an assembly against them, and make them an object of horror and plunder. ⁴⁷Let the assembly pelt them with stones and cut them down with

כִּי אֲנִי דִבַּרְתִּי נְאֻם אֲדֹנָי יְהֹוִה: ס
35 לָכֵן כֹּה אָמַר אֲדֹנָי יְהֹוִה יַעַן שָׁכַחַתְּ
אוֹתִי וַתַּשְׁלִיכִי אוֹתִי אַחֲרֵי גַוֵּךְ וְגַם־אַתְּ
שְׂאִי זִמָּתֵךְ וְאֶת־תַּזְנוּתָיִךְ: ס
36 וַיֹּאמֶר יְהֹוָה אֵלַי בֶּן־אָדָם הֲתִשְׁפּוֹט
אֶת־אָהֳלָה וְאֶת־אָהֳלִיבָה וְהַגֵּד לָהֶן אֵת
תּוֹעֲבוֹתֵיהֶן: 37 כִּי נִאֵפוּ וְדָם בִּידֵיהֶן
וְאֶת־גִּלּוּלֵיהֶן נִאֵפוּ וְגַם אֶת־בְּנֵיהֶן אֲשֶׁר
יָלְדוּ־לִי הֶעֱבִירוּ לָהֶם לְאָכְלָה: 38 עוֹד
זֹאת עָשׂוּ לִי טִמְּאוּ אֶת־מִקְדָּשִׁי בַּיּוֹם
הַהוּא וְאֶת־שַׁבְּתוֹתַי חִלֵּלוּ: 39 וּבְשַׁחֲטָם
אֶת־בְּנֵיהֶם לְגִלּוּלֵיהֶם וַיָּבֹאוּ אֶל־מִקְדָּשִׁי
בַּיּוֹם הַהוּא לְחַלְּלוֹ וְהִנֵּה־כֹה עָשׂוּ בְּתוֹךְ
בֵּיתִי:
40 וְאַף כִּי תִשְׁלַחְנָה לַאֲנָשִׁים בָּאִים
מִמֶּרְחָק אֲשֶׁר מַלְאָךְ שָׁלוּחַ אֲלֵיהֶם וְהִנֵּה־
בָאוּ לַאֲשֶׁר רָחַצְתְּ כָּחַלְתְּ עֵינַיִךְ וְעָדִית
עֶדִי: 41 וְיָשַׁבְתְּ עַל־מִטָּה כְבוּדָּה וְשֻׁלְחָן
עָרוּךְ לְפָנֶיהָ וּקְטָרְתִּי וְשַׁמְנִי שַׂמְתְּ עָלֶיהָ:
42 וְקוֹל הָמוֹן שָׁלֵו בָהּ* וְאֶל־אֲנָשִׁים מֵרֹב
אָדָם מוּבָאִים סוֹבָאִים מִמִּדְבָּר
וַיִּתְּנוּ צְמִידִים אֶל־יְדֵיהֶן וַעֲטֶרֶת תִּפְאֶרֶת
עַל־רָאשֵׁיהֶן: 43 וָאֹמַר לַבָּלָה נִאוּפִים עת
עַתָּה יזנה יִזְנוּ תַזְנוּתֶהָ וָהִיא: 44 וַיָּבוֹא*
אֵלֶיהָ כְּבוֹא אֶל־אִשָּׁה זוֹנָה כֵּן בָּאוּ
אֶל־אָהֳלָה וְאֶל־אָהֳלִיבָה אִשֹּׁת הַזִּמָּה:
45 וַאֲנָשִׁים צַדִּיקִם הֵמָּה יִשְׁפְּטוּ אוֹתְהֶם
מִשְׁפַּט נֹאֲפוֹת וּמִשְׁפַּט שֹׁפְכוֹת דָּם כִּי
נֹאֲפֹת הֵנָּה וְדָם בִּידֵיהֶן: ס
46 כִּי כֹּה אָמַר אֲדֹנָי יְהֹוִה הַעֲלֵה עֲלֵיהֶם
קָהָל וְנָתֹן אֶתְהֶן לְזַעֲוָה וְלָבַז: 47 וְרָגְמוּ
עֲלֵיהֶן אֶבֶן קָהָל וּבָרֵא אוֹתְהֶן בְּחַרְבוֹתָם

---

f Lit. "will you arraign"; cf. 22.2.

their swords; let them kill their sons and daughters, and burn down their homes. ⁴⁸I will put an end to wantonness in the land; and all the women shall take warning not to imitate your wantonness. ⁴⁹They shall punish you for your wantonness, and you shall suffer the penalty for your sinful idolatry. And you shall know that I am the Lord GOD.

בְּנֵיהֶם וּבְנוֹתֵיהֶם יַהֲרֹגוּ וּבָתֵּיהֶן בָּאֵשׁ
יִשְׂרֹפוּ: 48 וְהִשְׁבַּתִּי זִמָּה מִן־הָאָרֶץ וְנִוַּסְּרוּ
כָּל־הַנָּשִׁים וְלֹא תַעֲשֶׂינָה כְּזִמַּתְכֶנָה:
49 וְנָתְנוּ זִמַּתְכֶנָה עֲלֵיכֶן וַחֲטָאֵי גִלּוּלֵיכֶן
תִּשֶּׂאינָה* וִידַעְתֶּם כִּי אֲנִי אֲדֹנָי יְהוִה: פ

24

In the ninth year, on the tenth day of the tenth month, the word of the LORD came to me: ²O mortal, record this date, this exact day; for this very day the king of Babylon has laid siege to Jerusalem. ³Further, speak in an allegory to the rebellious breed and say to them: Thus said the Lord GOD:

כד וַיְהִי דְבַר־יְהוָה אֵלַי בַּשָּׁנָה
הַתְּשִׁיעִית בַּחֹדֶשׁ הָעֲשִׂירִי בֶּעָשׂוֹר לַחֹדֶשׁ
לֵאמֹר: 2 בֶּן־אָדָם כְּתָב־לְךָ אֶת־שֵׁם
הַיּוֹם אֶת־עֶצֶם הַיּוֹם הַזֶּה סָמַךְ מֶלֶךְ־בָּבֶל
אֶל־יְרוּשָׁלִַם בְּעֶצֶם הַיּוֹם הַזֶּה: 3 וּמְשֹׁל
אֶל־בֵּית־הַמֶּרִי מָשָׁל וְאָמַרְתָּ אֲלֵיהֶם כֹּה
אָמַר אֲדֹנָי יְהוִה

Put the caldron [on the fire], put it on,
And then pour water into it.
⁴Collect in it the pieces [of meat].
Every choice piece, thigh and shoulder;
Fill it with the best cutsª—
⁵Take the best of the flock.
Also pile the cutsᵇ under it;
Get it boiling briskly,
And cook the cuts in it.
⁶Assuredly, thus said the Lord GOD:
Woe to the city of blood—
A caldron whose scumᶜ is in it,
Whose scum has not been cleaned out!
Empty it piece by piece;
ᵈ-No lot has fallen upon it.-ᵈ
⁷For the blood she shed is still in her;
She set it upon a bare rock;
She did not pour it out on the ground
To cover it with earth.

שְׁפֹת הַסִּיר שְׁפֹת
וְגַם־יְצֹק בּוֹ מָיִם:
4 אֱסֹף נְתָחֶיהָ אֵלֶיהָ
כָּל־נֵתַח טוֹב יָרֵךְ וְכָתֵף
מִבְחַר עֲצָמִים מַלֵּא:
5 מִבְחַר הַצֹּאן לָקוֹחַ
וְגַם דּוּר הָעֲצָמִים תַּחְתֶּיהָ
רַתַּח רְתָחֶיהָ
גַּם־בָּשְׁלוּ עֲצָמֶיהָ בְּתוֹכָהּ: ס
6 לָכֵן כֹּה־אָמַר ׀ אֲדֹנָי יְהוִה
אוֹי עִיר הַדָּמִים
סִיר אֲשֶׁר חֶלְאָתָה* בָהּ
וְחֶלְאָתָהּ לֹא יָצְאָה מִמֶּנָּה
לִנְתָחֶיהָ לִנְתָחֶיהָ הוֹצִיאָהּ
לֹא־נָפַל עָלֶיהָ גּוֹרָל:
7 כִּי דָמָהּ בְּתוֹכָהּ הָיָה
עַל־צְחִיחַ סֶלַע שָׂמָתְהוּ
לֹא שְׁפָכַתְהוּ עַל־הָאָרֶץ
לְכַסּוֹת עָלָיו עָפָר:

---

a   Lit. "limbs."
b   Emendation yields "wood"; cf. v. 10.
c   Or "rust."
d-d   Meaning of Heb. uncertain.

8She‍e set her blood upon the bare rock,
So that it was not covered,
So that it may stir up [My] fury
To take vengeance.
9Assuredly, thus said the Lord GOD:
Woe to the city of blood!
I in turn will make a great blaze.
10Pile on the logs,
Kindle the fire,
Cook the meat through
And f-stew it completely,-f
And let the bones be charred.
11Let it stand empty on the coals,
Until it becomes so hot
That the copper glows.
Then its uncleanness shall melt away in it,
And its rust be consumed.
12d-It has frustrated all effort,
Its thick scum will not leave it—
Into the fire with its scum!-d
13For your vile impurity—because I sought to cleanse you of your impurity, but you would not be cleansed—you shall never be clean again until I have satisfied My fury upon you. 14I the LORD have spoken: It shall come to pass and I will do it. I will not refrain or spare or relent. You shall be punished according to your ways and your deeds—declares the Lord GOD.

15The word of the LORD came to me: 16O mortal, I am about to take away the delight of your eyes from you through pestilence; but you shall not lament or weep or let your tears flow. 17Moan softly; observe no mourning for the dead: Put on your turban and put your sandals on your feet; do not cover over your upper lip, and do not eat the bread of comforters."g

18In the evening my wife died, and in the morning I did as I had been commanded. And when I spoke to the people that morning, 19the

---

8לְהַעֲל֤וֹת חֵמָה֙ לִנְקֹ֣ם נָקָ֔ם
נָתַ֧תִּי אֶת־דָּמָ֛הּ עַל־צְחִ֥יחַ סָ֖לַע
לְבִלְתִּ֥י הִכָּסֽוֹת: פ
9לָכֵ֗ן כֹּ֤ה אָמַר֙ אֲדֹנָ֣י יְהוִ֔ה
א֖וֹי עִ֣יר הַדָּמִ֑ים
גַּם־אֲנִ֖י אַגְדִּ֥יל הַמְּדוּרָֽה:
10הַרְבֵּ֣ה הָעֵצִ֗ים
הַדְלֵ֣ק הָאֵ֔שׁ
הָתֵ֖ם הַבָּשָׂ֑ר
וְהַרְקַח֙ הַמֶּרְקָחָ֔ה
וְהָעֲצָמ֖וֹת יֵחָֽרוּ:
11וְהַעֲמִידֶ֥הָ עַל־גֶּחָלֶ֖יהָ רֵקָ֑ה
לְמַ֨עַן תֵּחַ֜ם וְחָ֣רָה נְחֻשְׁתָּ֗הּ
וְנִתְּכָ֤ה בְתוֹכָהּ֙ טֻמְאָתָ֔הּ
תִּתֻּ֖ם חֶלְאָתָֽהּ:
12תְּאֻנִ֖ים הֶלְאָ֑ת
וְלֹֽא־תֵצֵ֤א מִמֶּ֙נָּה֙ רַבַּ֣ת חֶלְאָתָ֔הּ
בְּאֵ֖שׁ חֶלְאָתָֽהּ:
13בְּטֻמְאָתֵ֖ךְ זִמָּ֑ה יַ֧עַן טִֽהַרְתִּ֛יךְ וְלֹ֥א טָהַ֖רְתְּ
מִטֻּמְאָתֵ֗ךְ לֹ֤א תִטְהֲרִי־עוֹד֙ עַד־הֲנִיחִ֤י
אֶת־חֲמָתִ֖י בָּֽךְ: 14אֲנִ֧י יְהוָ֣ה דִּבַּ֗רְתִּי בָּאָ֤ה
וְעָשִׂ֙יתִי֙ לֹֽא־אֶפְרַ֤ע וְלֹא־אָח֙וּס֙ וְלֹ֣א
אֶנָּחֵ֔ם כִּדְרָכַ֥יִךְ וְכַעֲלִילוֹתַ֖יִךְ שְׁפָט֑וּךְ נְאֻ֖ם
אֲדֹנָ֥י יְהוִֽה: פ

15וַיְהִ֥י דְבַר־יְהוָ֖ה אֵלַ֥י לֵאמֹֽר: 16בֶּן־אָדָ֗ם
הִנְנִ֨י לֹקֵ֤חַ מִמְּךָ֙ אֶת־מַחְמַ֣ד עֵינֶ֔יךָ בְּמַגֵּפָ֑ה
וְלֹ֤א תִסְפֹּד֙ וְלֹ֣א תִבְכֶּ֔ה וְל֥וֹא תָב֖וֹא
דִּמְעָתֶֽךָ: 17הֵאָנֵ֣ק ׀ דֹּ֗ם מֵתִים֙ אֵ֣בֶל
לֹֽא־תַעֲשֶׂ֔ה פְּאֵֽרְךָ֙ חֲב֣וֹשׁ עָלֶ֔יךָ וּנְעָלֶ֖יךָ
תָּשִׂ֣ים בְּרַגְלֶ֔יךָ וְלֹ֤א תַעְטֶה֙ עַל־שָׂפָ֔ם
וְלֶ֥חֶם אֲנָשִׁ֖ים לֹ֥א תֹאכֵֽל:
18וָאֲדַבֵּ֤ר אֶל־הָעָם֙ בַּבֹּ֔קֶר וַתָּ֥מָת אִשְׁתִּ֖י
בָּעָ֑רֶב וָאַ֥עַשׂ בַּבֹּ֖קֶר כַּאֲשֶׁ֥ר צֻוֵּֽיתִי:

---

people asked me, "Will you not tell us what these things portend for us, that you are acting so?" ²⁰I answered them, "The word of the Lord has come to me: ²¹Tell the House of Israel: Thus said the Lord God: 'I am going to desecrate My Sanctuary, your pride and glory, the delight of your eyes and the desire of your heart; and the sons and daughters you have left behind shall fall by the sword. ²⁴^hAnd Ezekiel shall become a portent for you: you shall do just as he has done, when it happens; and you shall know that I am the Lord God.' ²²Accordingly, you shall do as I have done: you shall not cover over your upper lips or eat the bread of comforters;^g ²³and your turbans shall remain on your heads, and your sandals upon your feet. You shall not lament or weep, but you shall be heartsick because of your iniquities and shall moan to one another."^h

²⁵You, O mortal, take note: On the day that I take their stronghold from them, their pride and joy, the delight of their eyes and the longing of their hearts—their sons and daughters—²⁶on that day a fugitive will come to you, to let you hear it with your own ears. ²⁷On that day your mouth shall be opened to the fugitive, and you shall speak and no longer be dumb. So you shall be a portent for them, and they shall know that I am the Lord.

25

The word of the Lord came to me: ²O mortal, set your face toward the Ammonites and prophesy against them. ³Say to the Ammonites: Hear the word of the Lord God! Thus said the Lord God: Because you cried "Aha!" over My Sanctuary when it was desecrated, and over the land of Israel when it was laid waste, and over the House of Judah when it went into exile—⁴assuredly, I will deliver you to the

---

19 וַיֹּאמְר֣וּ אֵלַ֔י הָעָ֔ם הֲלֹֽא־תַגִּ֥יד לָ֖נוּ מָה־ אֵ֥לֶּה לָּ֖נוּ כִּ֥י אַתָּ֖ה עֹשֶֽׂה: 20 וָאֹמַ֖ר אֲלֵיהֶ֑ם דְּבַר־יְהֹוָ֔ה הָיָ֥ה אֵלַ֖י לֵאמֹֽר: 21 אֱמֹ֣ר ׀ לְבֵ֣ית יִשְׂרָאֵ֗ל כֹּֽה־אָמַר֮ אֲדֹנָ֣י יְהֹוִה֒ הִנְנִ֨י מְחַלֵּ֤ל אֶת־מִקְדָּשִׁי֙ גְּא֣וֹן עֻזְּכֶ֔ם מַחְמַ֥ד עֵינֵיכֶ֖ם וּמַחְמַ֣ל נַפְשְׁכֶ֑ם וּבְנֵיכֶ֧ם וּבְנֽוֹתֵיכֶ֛ם אֲשֶׁ֥ר עֲזַבְתֶּ֖ם בַּחֶ֥רֶב יִפֹּֽלוּ: 22 וַעֲשִׂיתֶ֖ם כַּאֲשֶׁ֣ר עָשִׂ֑יתִי עַל־שָׂפָם֙ לֹ֣א תַעְט֔וּ וְלֶ֥חֶם אֲנָשִׁ֖ים לֹ֥א תֹאכֵֽלוּ: 23 וּפְאֵרֵכֶ֣ם עַל־רָאשֵׁיכֶ֗ם וְנַֽעֲלֵיכֶם֙ בְּרַגְלֵיכֶ֔ם לֹ֥א תִסְפְּד֖וּ וְלֹ֣א תִבְכּ֑וּ וּנְמַקֹּתֶם֙ בַּעֲוֺנֹ֣תֵיכֶ֔ם וּנְהַמְתֶּ֖ם אִ֥ישׁ אֶל־אָחִֽיו: 24 וְהָיָ֨ה יְחֶזְקֵ֤אל לָכֶם֙ לְמוֹפֵ֔ת כְּכֹ֥ל אֲשֶׁר־ עָשָׂ֖ה תַּעֲשׂ֑וּ בְּבֹאָ֕הּ וִידַעְתֶּ֕ם כִּ֥י אֲנִ֖י אֲדֹנָ֥י יְהֹוִֽה: ס

25 וְאַתָּ֣ה בֶן־אָדָ֗ם הֲל֣וֹא בְּי֨וֹם קַחְתִּ֤י מֵהֶם֙ אֶת־מָ֣עוּזָּ֔ם מְשׂ֖וֹשׂ תִּפְאַרְתָּ֑ם אֶת־ מַחְמַ֤ד עֵֽינֵיהֶם֙ וְאֶת־מַשָּׂ֣א נַפְשָׁ֔ם בְּנֵיהֶ֖ם וּבְנֽוֹתֵיהֶֽם: 26 בַּיּ֣וֹם הַה֔וּא יָב֥וֹא הַפָּלִ֖יט אֵלֶ֑יךָ לְהַשְׁמָע֖וּת אָזְנָֽיִם: 27 בַּיּ֣וֹם הַה֗וּא יִפָּ֤תַח פִּ֨יךָ֙ אֶת־הַפָּלִ֔יט וּתְדַבֵּ֖ר וְלֹ֣א תֵֽאָלֵ֣ם ע֑וֹד וְהָיִ֤יתָ לָהֶם֙ לְמוֹפֵ֔ת וְיָדְע֖וּ כִּֽי־אֲנִ֥י יְהֹוָֽה: ס

כה וַיְהִ֥י דְבַר־יְהֹוָ֖ה אֵלַ֥י לֵאמֹֽר: 2 בֶּן־אָדָ֕ם שִׂ֥ים פָּנֶ֖יךָ אֶל־בְּנֵ֣י עַמּ֑וֹן וְהִנָּבֵ֖א עֲלֵיהֶֽם: 3 וְאָמַרְתָּ֙ לִבְנֵ֣י עַמּ֔וֹן שִׁמְע֖וּ דְּבַר־ אֲדֹנָ֣י יְהֹוִ֑ה כֹּֽה־אָמַ֞ר אֲדֹנָ֣י יְהֹוִ֗ה יַ֠עַן אׇמְרֵ֨ךְ הֶאָ֜ח אֶל־מִקְדָּשִׁ֣י כִֽי־נִחָ֗ל וְאֶל־ אַדְמַ֤ת יִשְׂרָאֵל֙ כִּ֣י נָשַׁ֔מָּה וְאֶל־בֵּ֣ית יְהוּדָ֔ה כִּ֥י הָלְכ֖וּ בַּגּוֹלָֽה: 4 לָכֵ֡ן הִנְנִי֩ נֹתְנָ֨ךְ לִבְנֵי־

Kedemites as a possession. They shall set up their encampments among you and pitch their dwellings in your midst; they shall eat your produce and they shall drink your milk. ⁵I will make Rabbah a pasture for camels and Ammon a place for sheep to lie down. And you shall know that I am the LORD.

⁶For thus said the Lord GOD: Because you clapped your hands and stamped your feet and rejoiced over the land of Israel with such utter scorn—⁷assuredly, I will stretch out My hand against you and give you as booty to the nations; I will cut you off from among the peoples and wipe you out from among the countries and destroy you. And you shall know that I am the LORD.

⁸Thus said the Lord GOD: Because Moab ᵃ-and Seir-ᵃ said, "See, the House of Judah is like all other nations"—⁹assuredly, I will lay bare the flank of Moab, all its towns to the last one—Beth-jeshimoth, Baal-meon, and Kiriathaim, the glory of the country. ¹⁰I will deliver it, together with Ammon, to the Kedemites as their possession. Thus Ammon shall not be remembered among the nations, ¹¹and I will mete out punishments to Moab. And they shall know that I am the LORD.

¹²Thus said the Lord GOD: Because Edom acted vengefully against the House of Judah and incurred guilt by wreaking revenge upon it—¹³assuredly, thus said the Lord GOD: I will stretch out My hand against Edom and cut off from it man and beast, and I will lay it in ruins; from Tema to Dedan they shall fall by the sword. ¹⁴I will wreak My vengeance on Edom through My people Israel, and they shall take action against Edom in accordance with My blazing anger; and they shall know My vengeance—declares the Lord GOD.

קֶ֛דֶם לְמֽוֹרָשָׁ֖ה וְיָשְׁב֣וּ טִירֽוֹתֵיהֶ֣ם בָּ֑ךְ וְנָ֤תְנוּ בָךְ֙ מִשְׁכְּנֵיהֶ֔ם הֵ֚מָּה יֹאכְל֣וּ פִרְיֵ֔ךְ וְהֵ֖מָּה יִשְׁתּ֥וּ חֲלָבֵֽךְ׃ ⁵וְנָתַתִּ֤י אֶת־רַבָּה֙ לִנְוֵ֣ה גְמַלִּ֔ים וְאֶת־בְּנֵ֥י עַמּ֖וֹן לְמִרְבַּץ־צֹ֑אן וִֽידַעְתֶּ֖ם כִּֽי־אֲנִ֥י יְהוָֽה׃ ס

⁶כִּ֣י כֹ֤ה אָמַר֙ אֲדֹנָ֣י יְהוִ֔ה יַ֚עַן מַחְאֲךָ֣ יָ֔ד וְרַקְעֲךָ֖ בְּרָ֑גֶל וַתִּשְׂמַ֤ח בְּכָל־שָֽׁאטְךָ֙* בְּנֶ֔פֶשׁ אֶל־אַדְמַ֖ת יִשְׂרָאֵֽל׃ ⁷לָכֵ֗ן הִנְנִ֤י נָטִ֨יתִי֙ אֶת־יָדִ֣י עָלֶ֔יךָ וּנְתַתִּ֥יךָ לְבַ֖ז לַגּוֹיִ֑ם וְהִכְרַתִּ֨יךָ֙ מִן־הָ֣עַמִּ֔ים וְהַאֲבַדְתִּ֖יךָ מִן־הָאֲרָצ֑וֹת אַשְׁמִ֣ידְךָ֔ וְיָדַעְתָּ֖ כִּֽי־אֲנִ֥י יְהוָֽה׃ ס

⁸כֹּ֤ה אָמַר֙ אֲדֹנָ֣י יְהוִ֔ה יַ֗עַן אֲמֹ֤ר מוֹאָב֙ וְשֵׂעִ֔יר הִנֵּ֥ה כְּכָל־הַגּוֹיִ֖ם בֵּ֥ית יְהוּדָֽה׃ ⁹לָכֵן֙ הִנְנִ֣י פֹתֵ֔חַ אֶת־כֶּ֥תֶף מוֹאָ֖ב מֵהֶעָרִ֑ים מֵֽעָרָ֣יו מִקָּצֵ֗הוּ צְבִ֤י אֶ֨רֶץ֙ בֵּ֣ית הַיְשִׁימֹ֔ת בַּ֥עַל מְע֖וֹן וְקִרְיָתָֽיְמָה׃ ¹⁰לִבְנֵי־קֶ֜דֶם עַל־בְּנֵ֤י עַמּוֹן֙ וּנְתַתִּ֣יהָ לְמֽוֹרָשָׁ֔ה לְמַ֛עַן לֹֽא־תִזָּכֵ֥ר בְּנֵֽי־עַמּ֖וֹן בַּגּוֹיִֽם׃ ¹¹וּבְמוֹאָ֖ב אֶעֱשֶׂ֣ה שְׁפָטִ֑ים וְיָדְע֖וּ כִּֽי־אֲנִ֥י יְהוָֽה׃ ס

¹²כֹּ֤ה אָמַר֙ אֲדֹנָ֣י יְהוִ֔ה יַ֣עַן עֲשׂ֥וֹת אֱד֛וֹם בִּנְקֹ֥ם נָקָ֖ם לְבֵ֣ית יְהוּדָ֑ה וַיֶּאְשְׁמ֥וּ אָשׁ֖וֹם וְנִקְּמ֥וּ בָהֶֽם׃ ¹³לָכֵ֗ן כֹּ֤ה אָמַר֙ אֲדֹנָ֣י יְהוִ֔ה וְנָטִ֤תִי יָדִי֙ עַל־אֱד֔וֹם וְהִכְרַתִּ֥י מִמֶּ֖נָּה אָדָ֣ם וּבְהֵמָ֑ה וּנְתַתִּ֤יהָ חָרְבָּה֙ מִתֵּימָ֔ן וּדְדָ֖נֶה בַּחֶ֥רֶב יִפֹּֽלוּ׃ ¹⁴וְנָתַתִּ֨י אֶת־נִקְמָתִ֜י בֶּאֱד֗וֹם בְּיַד֙ עַמִּ֣י יִשְׂרָאֵ֔ל וְעָשׂ֣וּ בֶאֱד֔וֹם כְּאַפִּ֖י וְכַחֲמָתִ֑י וְיָדְע֖וּ אֶת־נִקְמָתִ֔י נְאֻ֖ם אֲדֹנָ֥י יְהוִֽה׃ פ

---

a-a Lacking in some Septuagint mss.   יתיר א׳   *v.* 6.

15Thus said the Lord God: Because the Philistines, in their ancient hatred, acted vengefully, and with utter scorn sought revenge and destruction—16assuredly, thus said the Lord God: I will stretch out My hand against the Philistines and cut off the Cherethites and wipe out the last survivors of the seacoast. 17I will wreak frightful vengeance upon them by furious punishment; and when I inflict My vengeance upon them, they shall know that I am the Lord.

26

In the eleventh year, on the first of the month,a the word of the Lord came to me: 2O mortal, because Tyre gloated over Jerusalem, "Aha! The gatewayb of the peoples is broken, it has become mine; I shall be filled, now that it is laid in ruins"—3assuredly, thus said the Lord God:

I am going to deal with you, O Tyre!
I will hurl many nations against you,
As the sea hurls its waves.
4They shall destroy the walls of Tyre
And demolish her towers;
And I will scrape her soil off her
And leave her a naked rock.
5She shall be in the heart of the sea
A place for dryingc nets;
For I have spoken it
    —declares the Lord God.
She shall become spoil for the nations,
6And her daughter-towns in the country
Shall be put to the sword.
And they shall know that I am the Lord.

7For thus said the Lord God: I will bring from the north, against Tyre, King Nebuchadrezzar of Babylon, a king of kings, with horses, chariots, and horsemen—a great mass of troops.

---

a   *The month is not indicated.*
b   *Targum reads "trafficker"; cf. 27.3.*
c   *Lit. "spreading out."*

15 כֹּה אָמַר אֲדֹנָי יְהֹוִה יַעַן עֲשׂוֹת פְּלִשְׁתִּים בִּנְקָמָה וַיִּנָּקְמוּ נָקָם בִּשְׁאָט בְּנֶפֶשׁ לְמַשְׁחִית אֵיבַת עוֹלָם: 16 לָכֵן כֹּה אָמַר אֲדֹנָי יְהֹוִה הִנְנִי נוֹטֶה יָדִי עַל־פְּלִשְׁתִּים וְהִכְרַתִּי אֶת־כְּרֵתִים וְהַאֲבַדְתִּי אֶת־שְׁאֵרִית חוֹף הַיָּם: 17 וְעָשִׂיתִי בָם נְקָמוֹת גְּדֹלוֹת בְּתוֹכְחוֹת חֵמָה וְיָדְעוּ כִּי־אֲנִי יְהֹוָה בְּתִתִּי אֶת־נִקְמָתִי בָּם: ס

כו 1 *וַיְהִי בְּעַשְׁתֵּי־עֶשְׂרֵה שָׁנָה בְּאֶחָד לַחֹדֶשׁ הָיָה דְבַר־יְהֹוָה אֵלַי לֵאמֹר: 2 בֶּן־אָדָם יַעַן אֲשֶׁר־אָמְרָה צֹּר עַל־יְרוּשָׁלַ͏ִם הֶאָח נִשְׁבְּרָה דַּלְתוֹת הָעַמִּים נָסֵבָּה אֵלָי אִמָּלְאָה הׇחֳרָבָה: 3 לָכֵן כֹּה אָמַר אֲדֹנָי יְהֹוִה

הִנְנִי עָלַיִךְ צֹר
וְהַעֲלֵיתִי עָלַיִךְ גּוֹיִם רַבִּים
כְּהַעֲלוֹת הַיָּם לְגַלָּיו:
4 וְשִׁחֲתוּ חֹמוֹת צֹר
וְהָרְסוּ מִגְדָּלֶיהָ
וְסִחֵיתִי עֲפָרָהּ מִמֶּנָּה
וְנָתַתִּי אוֹתָהּ לִצְחִיחַ סָלַע:
5 מִשְׁטַח חֲרָמִים תִּהְיֶה
בְּתוֹךְ הַיָּם
כִּי אֲנִי דִבַּרְתִּי
נְאֻם אֲדֹנָי יְהֹוִה
וְהָיְתָה לְבַז לַגּוֹיִם:
6 וּבְנוֹתֶיהָ אֲשֶׁר בַּשָּׂדֶה
בַּחֶרֶב תֵּהָרַגְנָה
וְיָדְעוּ כִּי־אֲנִי יְהֹוָה: פ

7 כִּי כֹה אָמַר אֲדֹנָי יְהֹוִה הִנְנִי מֵבִיא אֶל־צֹר נְבוּכַדְרֶאצַּר מֶלֶךְ־בָּבֶל מִצָּפוֹן מֶלֶךְ מְלָכִים בְּסוּס וּבְרֶכֶב וּבְפָרָשִׁים וְקָהָל וְעַם־רָב:

⁸Your daughter-towns in the country
He shall put to the sword;
He shall erect towers against you,
And cast up mounds against you,
And raise [a wall of] bucklers against you.
⁹He shall turn the force of his battering rams
Against your walls
And smash your towers with his axes.^d
¹⁰From the cloud raised by his horses
Dust shall cover you;
From the clatter of horsemen
And wheels and chariots,
Your walls shall shake—
When he enters your gates
As men enter a breached city.
¹¹With the hoofs of his steeds
He shall trample all your streets.
He shall put your people to the sword,
And your mighty pillars shall crash to the
   ground.
¹²They shall plunder your wealth
And loot your merchandise.
They shall raze your walls
And tear down your splendid houses,
And they shall cast into the water
Your stones and timber and soil.
¹³I will put an end to the murmur of your
   songs,
And the sound of your lyres shall be heard
   no more.
¹⁴I will make you a naked rock,
You shall be a place for drying^e nets;
You shall never be rebuilt.
For I have spoken

          —declares the Lord GOD.

¹⁵Thus said the Lord GOD to Tyre: The coast-
lands shall quake at the sound of your downfall,
when the wounded groan, when slaughter is rife
within you. ¹⁶All the rulers of the sea shall descend from their thrones; they shall remove

---

^d Lit. "swords."

בְּנוֹתַ֥יִךְ בַּשָּׂדֶ֖ה 8
בַּחֶ֣רֶב יַהֲרֹ֑ג
וְנָתַ֨ן עָלַ֜יִךְ דָּיֵ֗ק
וְשָׁפַ֤ךְ עָלַ֙יִךְ֙ סֹֽלְלָ֔ה
וְהֵקִ֥ים עָלַ֖יִךְ צִנָּֽה׃
וּמְחִ֣י קָֽבֳלּ֔וֹ יִתֵּ֖ן 9
בְּחֹֽמוֹתָ֑יִךְ
וּמִ֨גְדְּלֹתַ֔יִךְ יִתֹּ֖ץ בְּחַרְבוֹתָֽיו׃
מִשִּׁפְעַ֥ת סוּסָ֖יו 10
יְכַסֵּ֣ךְ אֲבָקָ֑ם
מִקּוֹל֩ פָּרַ֨שׁ
וְגַלְגַּ֜ל וָרֶ֗כֶב
תִּרְעַ֙שְׁנָה֙ חֽוֹמוֹתַ֔יִךְ
בְּבֹאוֹ֙ בִּשְׁעָרַ֔יִךְ
כִּמְבוֹאֵ֖י עִ֥יר מְבֻקָּעָֽה׃
בְּפַרְס֣וֹת סוּסָ֔יו 11
יִרְמֹ֖ס אֶת־כָּל־חֽוּצוֹתָ֑יִךְ
עַמֵּךְ֙ בַּחֶ֣רֶב יַהֲרֹ֔ג
וּמַצְּב֥וֹת עֻזֵּ֖ךְ לָאָ֥רֶץ תֵּרֵֽד׃
וְשָׁלְל֣וּ חֵילֵ֗ךְ וּבָֽזְז֣וּ רְכֻלָּתֵ֔ךְ 12
וְהָֽרְסוּ֙ חֽוֹמוֹתַ֔יִךְ
וּבָתֵּ֥י חֶמְדָּתֵ֖ךְ יִתֹּ֑צוּ
וַאֲבָנַ֤יִךְ וְעֵצַ֙יִךְ֙ וַֽעֲפָרֵ֔ךְ
בְּת֥וֹךְ מַ֖יִם יָשִֽׂימוּ׃
וְהִשְׁבַּתִּ֖י הֲמ֣וֹן שִׁירָ֑יִךְ 13
וְק֣וֹל כִּנּוֹרַ֔יִךְ לֹ֥א יִשָּׁמַ֖ע עֽוֹד׃
וּנְתַתִּ֗יךְ לִצְחִ֣יחַ סֶ֔לַע 14
מִשְׁטַ֥ח חֲרָמִ֖ים תִּֽהְיֶ֑ה
לֹ֤א תִבָּנֶה֙ ע֔וֹד
כִּ֛י אֲנִ֥י יְהוָ֖ה דִּבַּ֑רְתִּי
נְאֻ֖ם אֲדֹנָ֥י יְהוִֽה׃ ס

כֹּ֥ה אָמַ֛ר אֲדֹנָ֥י יְהוִ֖ה לְצ֑וֹר הֲלֹ֣א ׀ מִקּ֣וֹל 15
מַפַּלְתֵּ֗ךְ בֶּאֱנֹ֤ק חָלָל֙ בֵּהָ֤רֵֽג הֶ֙רֶג֙ בְּתוֹכֵ֔ךְ
יִרְעֲשׁ֖וּ הָֽאִיִּֽים׃ וְֽיָרְד֞וּ מֵעַ֣ל כִּסְאוֹתָ֗ם 16
כֹּ֚ל נְשִׂיאֵ֣י הַיָּ֔ם וְהֵסִ֙ירוּ֙ אֶת־מְעִ֣ילֵיהֶ֔ם

their robes and strip off their embroidered garments. They shall clothe themselves with trembling, and shall sit on the ground; they shall
tremble every moment, and they shall be aghast
at you. [17]And they shall intone a dirge over you,
and they shall say to you:

How you have perished, *e*-you who were
    peopled-*e* from the seas,
O renowned city!
Mighty on the sea were she and her inhabi-
    tants,
Who cast their terror on all *f*-its inhabitants.-*f*
[18]Now shall the coastlands tremble
On the day of your downfall,
And the coastlands by the sea
Be terrified at your end.

[19]For thus said the Lord GOD: When I make
you a ruined city, like cities empty of inhabitants; when I bring the deep over you, and its
mighty waters cover you, [20]then I will bring you
down, with those who go down to the Pit, to
the people of old. I will install you in the netherworld, with those that go down to the Pit, like
the ruins of old, so that you shall not be inhabited and shall not radiate*g* splendor in the land
of the living. [21]I will make you a horror, and
you shall cease to be; you shall be sought, but
shall never be found again—declares the Lord
GOD.

27 The word of the LORD came to me:
[2]Now you, O mortal, intone a dirge over Tyre.
[3]Say to Tyre:

O you who dwell at the gateway of the sea,
Who trade with the peoples on many coast-
    lands:
Thus said the Lord GOD:

וְאֶת־בִּגְדֵי רִקְמָתָם יִפְשֹׁטוּ חֲרָדֹות |
יִלְבָּשׁוּ עַל־הָאָרֶץ יֵשֵׁבוּ וְחָרְדוּ לִרְגָעִים
וְשָׁמְמוּ עָלָיִךְ: 17 וְנָשְׂאוּ עָלַיִךְ קִינָה
וְאָמְרוּ לָךְ

אֵיךְ אָבַדְתְּ נוֹשֶׁבֶת מִיַּמִּים
הָעִיר הַהֻלָּלָה
אֲשֶׁר הָיְתָה חֲזָקָה בַיָּם הִיא וְיֹשְׁבֶיהָ
אֲשֶׁר־נָתְנוּ חִתִּיתָם לְכָל־יוֹשְׁבֶיהָ:
18 עַתָּה יֶחְרְדוּ הָאִיִּן
יֹום מַפַּלְתֵּךְ
וְנִבְהֲלוּ הָאִיִּים אֲשֶׁר־בַּיָּם
מִצֵּאתֵךְ:

19 כִּי כֹה אָמַר אֲדֹנָי יְהוִה בְּתִתִּי אֹתָךְ
עִיר נֶחֱרֶבֶת כֶּעָרִים אֲשֶׁר לֹא־נוֹשָׁבוּ
בְּהַעֲלֹות עָלַיִךְ אֶת־תְּהֹום וְכִסּוּךְ הַמַּיִם
הָרַבִּים: 20 וְהֹורַדְתִּיךְ אֶת־יֹורְדֵי בֹור אֶל־
עַם עֹולָם וְהֹושַׁבְתִּיךְ בְּאֶרֶץ תַּחְתִּיֹּות
כָּחֳרָבֹות מֵעֹולָם אֶת־יֹורְדֵי בֹור לְמַעַן
לֹא תֵשֵׁבִי וְנָתַתִּי צְבִי בְּאֶרֶץ חַיִּים:
21 בַּלָּהֹות אֶתְּנֵךְ וְאֵינֵךְ וּתְבֻקְשִׁי וְלֹא־
תִמָּצְאִי עֹוד לְעֹולָם נְאֻם אֲדֹנָי יְהוִה: ס

כז וַיְהִי דְבַר־יְהוָה אֵלַי לֵאמֹר:
2 וְאַתָּה בֶן־אָדָם שָׂא עַל־צֹר קִינָה:
3 וְאָמַרְתָּ לְצֹור

הַיֹּשֶׁבֶתֿ עַל־מְבֹואֹת יָם
רֹכֶלֶת הָעַמִּים אֶל־אִיִּים רַבִּים
כֹּה אָמַר אֲדֹנָי יְהוִה

---

e-e   Septuagint reads "vanished."
f-f   I.e., of the sea. Emendation yields "the dry land."
g   Understanding nathatti as second-person singular feminine; cf.
     16.50 and note. But meaning of Heb. uncertain.

^aO Tyre, you boasted,
I am perfect in beauty.^{-a}
⁴Your frontiers were on the high seas,
Your builders perfected your beauty.
⁵From cypress trees of Senir
They fashioned your planks;
They took a cedar from Lebanon
To make a mast for you.
⁶From oak trees of Bashan
They made your oars;
Of boxwood from the isles of Kittim,
Inlaid with ivory,
They made your decks.
⁷Embroidered linen from Egypt
Was the cloth
That served you for sails;
Of blue and purple from the coasts of Elishah
Were your awnings.
⁸The inhabitants of Sidon and Arvad
Were your rowers;
^bYour skilled men, O Tyre,^{-b} were within you,
They were your pilots.
⁹Gebal's elders and craftsmen were within you,
Making your repairs.

All the ships of the sea, with their crews,
Were ^cin your harbor^{-c}
To traffic in your wares.
¹⁰Men of Paras, Lud, and Put
Were in your army,
Your fighting men;
They hung shields and helmets in your midst,
They lent splendor to you.
¹¹Men of Arvad and Helech
Manned your walls all around,
And men of Gammad were stationed in your towers;

צֹר אַתְּ אָמַרְתְּ
אֲנִי כְּלִילַת יֹפִי:
4 בְּלֵב יַמִּים גְּבוּלָיִךְ
בֹּנַיִךְ כָּלְלוּ יָפְיֵךְ:
5 בְּרוֹשִׁים מִשְּׂנִיר
בָּנוּ לָךְ אֵת כָּל־לֻחֹתָיִם
אֶרֶז מִלְּבָנוֹן לָקָחוּ
לַעֲשׂוֹת תֹּרֶן עָלָיִךְ:
6 אַלּוֹנִים מִבָּשָׁן
עָשׂוּ מִשּׁוֹטָיִךְ
קַרְשֵׁךְ עָשׂוּ־שֵׁן בַּת־אֲשֻׁרִים
מֵאִיֵּי כִּתִּיִּם:
7 שֵׁשׁ־בְּרִקְמָה מִמִּצְרַיִם
הָיָה מִפְרָשֵׂךְ
לִהְיוֹת לָךְ לְנֵס
תְּכֵלֶת וְאַרְגָּמָן מֵאִיֵּי אֱלִישָׁה
הָיָה מְכַסֵּךְ:
8 יֹשְׁבֵי צִידוֹן וְאַרְוַד
הָיוּ שָׁטִים לָךְ
חֲכָמַיִךְ צוֹר הָיוּ בָךְ
הֵמָּה חֹבְלָיִךְ:
9 זִקְנֵי גְבַל וַחֲכָמֶיהָ הָיוּ בָךְ
מַחֲזִיקֵי בִּדְקֵךְ
כָּל־אֳנִיּוֹת הַיָּם
וּמַלָּחֵיהֶם הָיוּ בָךְ
לַעֲרֹב מַעֲרָבֵךְ:
10 פָּרַס וְלוּד וּפוּט
הָיוּ בְחֵילֵךְ
אַנְשֵׁי מִלְחַמְתֵּךְ
מָגֵן וְכוֹבַע תִּלּוּ־בָךְ
הֵמָּה נָתְנוּ הֲדָרֵךְ:
11 בְּנֵי אַרְוַד וְחֵילֵךְ
עַל־חוֹמוֹתַיִךְ סָבִיב
וְגַמָּדִים בְּמִגְדְּלוֹתַיִךְ הָיוּ

---

a-a   *Emendation yields: "O Tyre, you are a ship / Perfect in beauty."*
b-b   *Emendation yields "The skilled men of Zemar"; cf. Gen. 10.18.*
c-c   *Lit. "in you."*

They hung their quivers all about your walls;
They perfected your beauty.

¹²Tarshish traded with you because of your wealth of all kinds of goods; they bartered silver, iron, tin, and lead for your wares. ¹³Javan, Tubal, and Meshech—they were your merchants; they trafficked with you in human beings and copper utensils. ¹⁴From Beth-togarmah they bartered horses, horsemen, and mules for your wares. ¹⁵The people of Dedan were your merchants; many coastlands traded under your rule and rendered you tribute in ivory tusks and ebony. ¹⁶Aram traded with you because of your wealth of merchandise, dealing with you in turquoise, purple stuff, embroidery, fine linen, coral, and agate.ᵈ ¹⁷Judah and the land of Israel were your merchants; they trafficked with you in wheat of ᵉ-Minnith and Pannag,-ᵉ honey, oil, and balm. ¹⁸Because of your wealth of merchandise, because of your great wealth, Damascus traded with you in Helbon wine and white wool. ¹⁹ᶠ-Vedan and Javan from Uzal traded for your wares; they trafficked with you in polished iron, cassia, and calamus. ²⁰Dedan was your merchant in saddlecloths for riding.-ᶠ ²¹Arabia and all Kedar's chiefs were traders under your rule; they traded with you in lambs, rams, and goats. ²²The merchants of Sheba and Raamah were your merchants; they bartered for your wares all the finest spices, all kinds of precious stones, and gold. ²³Haran, Canneh, and Eden, the merchants of Sheba, Assyria, and Chilmad traded with you. ²⁴ᶠThese were your merchants in choice fabrics, embroidered cloaks of blue, and many-colored carpets tied up with cords and preserved with cedar—among your wares.-ᶠ ²⁵The ships of Tarshish were in the service of your trade.

ᵍSo you were full and richly laden

שִׁלְטֵיהֶם֙ תִּלּ֣וּ עַל־חוֹמוֹתַ֙יִךְ֙ סָבִ֔יב הֵ֖מָּה כָּלְל֥וּ יָפְיֵֽךְ׃

¹² תַּרְשִׁ֥ישׁ סֹחַרְתֵּ֖ךְ מֵרֹ֣ב כָּל־ה֑וֹן בְּכֶ֤סֶף בַּרְזֶ֙ל בְּדִ֣יל וְעוֹפֶ֔רֶת נָתְנ֖וּ עִזְבוֹנָֽיִךְ׃ ¹³ יָוָ֤ן תֻּבַל֙ וָמֶ֔שֶׁךְ הֵ֖מָּה רֹֽכְלָ֑יִךְ בְּנֶ֤פֶשׁ אָדָם֙ וּכְלֵ֣י נְחֹ֔שֶׁת נָתְנ֖וּ מַעֲרָבֵֽךְ׃ ¹⁴ מִבֵּ֖ית תּוֹגַרְמָ֑ה סוּסִ֤ים וּפָֽרָשִׁים֙ וּפְרָדִ֔ים נָתְנ֖וּ עִזְבוֹנָֽיִךְ׃ ¹⁵ בְּנֵ֤י דְדָן֙ רֹֽכְלַ֔יִךְ אִיִּ֥ים רַבִּ֖ים סְחֹרַ֣ת יָדֵ֑ךְ קַרְנ֥וֹת שֵׁן֙ והובנים וְהׇבְנִ֔ים הֵשִׁ֖יבוּ אֶשְׁכָּרֵֽךְ׃ ¹⁶ אֲרָ֥ם סֹחַרְתֵּ֖ךְ מֵרֹ֣ב מַעֲשָׂ֑יִךְ בְּ֠נֹ֠פֶךְ אַרְגָּמָ֨ן וְרִקְמָ֤ה וּבוּץ֙ וְרָאמֹ֣ת וְכַדְכֹּ֔ד נָתְנ֖וּ בְּעִזְבוֹנָֽיִךְ׃ ¹⁷ יְהוּדָה֙ וְאֶ֣רֶץ יִשְׂרָאֵ֔ל הֵ֖מָּה רֹֽכְלָ֑יִךְ בְּחִטֵּ֣י מִנִּ֗ית וּפַנַּ֤ג וּדְבַשׁ֙ וָשֶׁ֣מֶן וָצֹ֔רִי נָתְנ֖וּ מַעֲרָבֵֽךְ׃ ¹⁸ דַּמֶּ֧שֶׂק סֹחַרְתֵּ֛ךְ בְּרֹ֥ב מַעֲשַׂ֖יִךְ מֵרֹ֣ב כָּל־ה֑וֹן בְּיֵ֥ין חֶלְבּ֖וֹן וְצֶ֥מֶר צָֽחַר׃ ¹⁹ וְדָ֤ן וְיָוָן֙ מְאוּזָּ֔ל בְּעִזְבוֹנַ֖יִךְ נָתָ֑נּוּ בַּרְזֶ֤ל עָשׁוֹת֙ קִדָּ֣ה וְקָנֶ֔ה בְּמַעֲרָבֵ֖ךְ הָיָֽה׃ ²⁰ דְּדָן֙ רֹֽכַלְתֵּ֔ךְ בְבִגְדֵי־חֹ֖פֶשׁ לְרִכְבָּֽה׃ ²¹ עֲרַ֤ב וְכָל־נְשִׂיאֵ֣י קֵדָ֔ר הֵ֖מָּה סֹחֲרֵ֣י יָדֵ֑ךְ בְּכָרִ֤ים וְאֵילִים֙ וְעַתּוּדִ֔ים בָּ֖ם סֹחֲרָֽיִךְ׃ ²² רֹכְלֵ֤י שְׁבָא֙ וְרַעְמָ֔ה הֵ֖מָּה רֹֽכְלָ֑יִךְ בְּרֹ֨אשׁ כָּל־בֹּ֜שֶׂם וּבְכָל־אֶ֤בֶן יְקָרָה֙ וְזָהָ֔ב נָתְנ֖וּ עִזְבוֹנָֽיִךְ׃ ²³ חָרָ֤ן וְכַנֵּה֙ וָעֶ֔דֶן רֹכְלֵ֖י שְׁבָ֑א אַשּׁ֖וּר כִּלְמַ֥ד רֹכַלְתֵּֽךְ׃ ²⁴ הֵ֤מָּה רֹֽכְלַ֙יִךְ֙ בְּמַכְלֻלִ֔ים בִּגְלוֹמֵי֙ תְּכֵ֣לֶת וְרִקְמָ֔ה וּבְגִנְזֵ֖י בְּרֹמִ֑ים בַּחֲבָלִ֧ים חֲבֻשִׁ֛ים וַאֲרֻזִ֖ים בְּמַרְכֻלְתֵּֽךְ׃ ²⁵ אֳנִיּ֣וֹת תַּרְשִׁ֔ישׁ שָׁרוֹתַ֖יִךְ מַעֲרָבֵ֑ךְ

וַתִּמָּלְאִ֧י וַתִּכְבְּדִ֛י מְאֹ֖ד

ᵈ   The exact identity of these stones is uncertain.
ᵉ-ᵉ   Meaning of Heb. uncertain; cf. "Minnith," Judg. 11.33.
ᶠ-ᶠ   Meaning of Heb. uncertain.
ᵍ   Resuming the description of Tyre as a ship, as in vv. 3b–9a.

On the high seas.

²⁶Your oarsmen brought you out
Into the mighty waters;
The tempest wrecked you
On the high seas.
²⁷Your wealth, your wares, your merchandise,
Your sailors and your pilots,
The men who made your repairs,
Those who carried on your traffic,
And all the fighting men within you—
All the multitude within you—
Shall go down into the depths of the sea
On the day of your downfall.
²⁸At the outcry of your pilots
The billows shall heave;
²⁹And all the oarsmen and mariners,
All the pilots of the sea,
Shall come down from their ships
And stand on the ground.
³⁰They shall raise their voices over you
And cry out bitterly;
They shall cast dust on their heads
And strew ashes on themselves.
³¹On your account, they shall make
Bald patches on their heads,
And shall gird themselves with sackcloth.
They shall weep over you, brokenhearted,
With bitter lamenting;
³²They shall intone a dirge over you as they wail,
And lament for you thus:

Who was like Tyre when she was silenced
In the midst of the sea?
³³When your wares were unloaded from the seas,
You satisfied many peoples;
With your great wealth and merchandise
You enriched the kings of the earth.

בְּלֵב יַמִּֽים׃

26 בְּמַ֤יִם רַבִּים֙ הֱבִיא֔וּךְ
הַשָּׁטִ֖ים אֹתָ֑ךְ
ר֚וּחַ הַקָּדִ֔ים שְׁבָרֵ֖ךְ
בְּלֵ֥ב יַמִּֽים׃

27 הוֹנֵ֤ךְ וְעִזְבוֹנַ֙יִךְ֙
מַעֲרָבֵ֔ךְ מַלָּחַ֖יִךְ וְחֹבְלָ֑יִךְ
מַחֲזִיקֵ֣י בִדְקֵ֗ךְ
וְעֹֽרְבֵ֣י מַעֲרָבֵ֔ךְ
וְכׇל־אַנְשֵׁ֤י מִלְחַמְתֵּךְ֙ אֲשֶׁר־בָּ֔ךְ
וּבְכׇל־קְהָלֵ֖ךְ אֲשֶׁ֣ר בְּתוֹכֵ֑ךְ
יִפְּלוּ֙ בְּלֵ֣ב יַמִּ֔ים
בְּי֖וֹם מַפַּלְתֵּֽךְ׃

28 לְק֖וֹל זַעֲקַ֣ת חֹבְלָ֑יִךְ
יִרְעֲשׁ֖וּ מִגְרֹשֽׁוֹת׃

29 וְֽיָרְד֞וּ מֵאֳנִיּֽוֹתֵיהֶ֗ם
כֹּ֚ל תֹּפְשֵׂ֣י מָשׁ֔וֹט
מַלָּחִ֕ים כֹּ֖ל חֹבְלֵ֣י הַיָּ֑ם
אֶל־הָאָ֖רֶץ יַעֲמֹֽדוּ׃

30 וְהִשְׁמִ֤יעוּ עָלַ֙יִךְ֙ בְּקוֹלָ֔ם
וְיִזְעֲק֖וּ מָרָ֑ה
וְיַעֲל֤וּ עָֽפָר֙ עַל־רָ֣אשֵׁיהֶ֔ם
בָּאֵ֖פֶר יִתְפַּלָּֽשׁוּ׃

31 וְהִקְרִ֤יחוּ אֵלַ֙יִךְ֙ קׇרְחָ֔ה
וְחָגְר֖וּ שַׂקִּ֑ים
וּבָכ֥וּ אֵלַ֛יִךְ בְּמַר־נֶ֖פֶשׁ
מִסְפֵּ֥ד מָֽר׃

32 וְנָשְׂא֨וּ אֵלַ֤יִךְ בְּנִיהֶם֙ קִינָ֔ה
וְקוֹנְנ֖וּ עָלָ֑יִךְ

מִ֣י כְצ֔וֹר כְּדֻמָ֖ה
בְּת֥וֹךְ הַיָּֽם׃

33 בְּצֵ֤את עִזְבוֹנַ֙יִךְ֙ מִיַּמִּ֔ים
הִשְׂבַּ֖עַתְּ עַמִּ֣ים רַבִּ֑ים
בְּרֹ֤ב הוֹנַ֙יִךְ֙ וּמַעֲרָבַ֔יִךְ
הֶעֱשַׁ֖רְתְּ מַלְכֵי־אָֽרֶץ׃

³⁴But when you were wrecked on the seas,
In the deep waters sank your merchandise
And all the crew aboard you.
³⁵All the inhabitants of the coastlands
Are appalled over you;
Their kings are aghast,
Their faces contorted.ᶠ
³⁶The merchants among the peoples hissedʰ
  at you;
You have become a horror,
And have ceased to be forever.

28

The word of the LORD came to me: ²O
mortal, say to the prince of Tyre: Thus said the
Lord GOD:

Because you have been so haughty and have
said, "I am a god; I sit enthroned like a god in
the heart of the seas," whereas you are not a god
but a man, though you deemed your mind equal
to a god'sᵃ—

³Yes, you are wiser than Daniel;
In no hidden matter can anyone
Compare to you.
⁴By your shrewd understanding
You have gained riches,
And have amassed gold and silver
In your treasuries.
⁵By your great shrewdness in trade
You have increased your wealth,
And you have grown haughty
Because of your wealth.
⁶Assuredly, thus said the Lord GOD: Because
you have deemed your mind equal to a god's,
⁷I swear I will bring against you
Strangers, the most ruthless of nations.
They shall unsheathe their swords
Against your prized shrewdness,
And they shall strike downᵇ your splendor.

---

h   *I.e., to ward off the calamity from the viewer; cf. Jer. 18.16, 49.17;*
    Job 27.23; Lam. 2.15.

a   *This sentence is continued in v. 6; vv. 3–5 are parenthetical.*
b   *Meaning of Heb. uncertain.*

³⁴ עֵת נִשְׁבֶּ֫רֶת מִיַּמִּ֔ים
בְּמַֽעֲמַקֵּי־מָ֑יִם
מַֽעֲרָבֵ֧ךְ וְכָל־קְהָלֵ֛ךְ בְּתוֹכֵ֖ךְ נָפָֽלוּ׃
³⁵ כֹּ֚ל יֹֽשְׁבֵ֣י הָֽאִיִּ֔ים
שָֽׁמְמ֖וּ עָלָ֑יִךְ
וּמַלְכֵיהֶם֙ שָֽׂעֲר֣וּ שַׂ֔עַר
רָֽעֲמ֖וּ פָּנִֽים׃
³⁶ סֹֽחֲרִים֙ בָּֽעַמִּ֔ים שָֽׁרְק֖וּ עָלָ֑יִךְ
בַּלָּה֣וֹת הָיִ֔ית
וְאֵינֵ֖ךְ עַד־עוֹלָֽם׃ ס

כח

וַיְהִ֥י דְבַר־יְהֹוָ֖ה אֵלַ֥י לֵאמֹֽר׃
² בֶּן־אָדָ֡ם אֱמֹר֩ לִנְגִ֨יד צֹ֜ר כֹּֽה־אָמַ֣ר ׀ אֲדֹנָ֣י
יֱהֹוִ֗ה
יַ֣עַן גָּבַ֤הּ לִבְּךָ֙ וַתֹּ֔אמֶר אֵ֣ל אָ֗נִי מוֹשַׁ֧ב
אֱלֹהִ֛ים יָשַׁ֖בְתִּי בְּלֵ֣ב יַמִּ֑ים וְאַתָּ֤ה אָדָם֙
וְלֹא־אֵ֔ל וַתִּתֵּ֥ן לִבְּךָ֖ כְּלֵ֥ב אֱלֹהִֽים׃
³ הִנֵּ֥ה חָכָ֛ם אַתָּ֖ה מדנאל מִדָּֽנִיֵּ֑אל
כָּל־סָת֖וּם
לֹ֥א עֲמָמֽוּךָ׃
⁴ בְּחׇכְמָֽתְךָ֙ וּבִתְבֽוּנָ֣תְךָ֔
עָשִׂ֥יתָ לְּךָ֖ חָ֑יִל
וַתַּ֛עַשׂ זָהָ֥ב וָכֶ֖סֶף
בְּאֽוֹצְרוֹתֶֽיךָ׃
⁵ בְּרֹ֧ב חׇכְמָֽתְךָ֛ בִּרְכֻלָּֽתְךָ֖
הִרְבִּ֣יתָ חֵילֶ֑ךָ
וַיִּגְבַּ֥הּ לְבָבְךָ֖
בְּחֵילֶֽךָ׃ ס
⁶ לָכֵ֕ן כֹּ֥ה אָמַ֖ר אֲדֹנָ֣י יֱהֹוִ֑ה יַ֛עַן תִּתְּךָ֥
אֶת־לְבָבְךָ֖ כְּלֵ֥ב אֱלֹהִֽים׃
⁷ לָכֵ֗ן הִנְנִ֨י מֵבִ֤יא עָלֶ֙יךָ֙
זָרִ֔ים עָֽרִיצֵ֖י גּוֹיִ֑ם
וְהֵרִ֤יקוּ חַרְבוֹתָם֙
עַל־יְפִ֣י חׇכְמָתֶ֔ךָ
וְחִלְּל֖וּ יִפְעָתֶֽךָ׃

8They shall bring you down to the Pit;
In the heart of the sea you shall die
The death of the slain.
9Will you still say, "I am a god"
Before your slayers,
When you are proved a man, not a god,
At the hands of those who strike you down?
10By the hands of strangers you shall die
The death of the uncircumcised;c
For I have spoken
         —declares the Lord GOD.

11The word of the LORD came to me: 12O mortal, intone a dirge over the king of Tyre and say to him: Thus said the Lord GOD:
You were the seal of perfection,
Full of wisdom and flawless in beauty.
13You were in Eden, the garden of God;
Every precious stone was your adornment:
Carnelian, chrysolite, and amethyst;
Beryl, lapis lazuli, and jasper;
Sapphire, turquoise, and emerald;
And gold d-beautifully wrought for you,
Mined for you, prepared the day you were
  created.-d
14b-I created you as a cherub
With outstretched shielding wings;-b
And you resided on God's holy mountain;
You walked among stones of fire.
15You were blameless in your ways,
From the day you were created
Until wrongdoing was found in you.
16By your far-flung commerce
You were filled with lawlessness
And you sinned.
So I have struck you down
From the mountain of God,
And I have destroyed you, O shielding
  cherub,

---

c *According to popular belief, those who die uncircumcised and those left unburied are relegated to the lower level of the netherworld; cf. 31.18; 32.19 ff.*
d-d *Meaning of Heb. uncertain. On the stones, see note at Exod. 28.17.*

8 לְשַׁ֤חַת יֽוֹרִד֙וּךָ
וָמַ֛תָּה מְמוֹתֵ֥י חָלָ֖ל
בְּלֵ֥ב יַמִּֽים׃
9 הֶאָמֹ֤ר תֹּאמַר֙ אֱלֹהִ֣ים אָ֔נִי
לִפְנֵ֖י הֹֽרְגֶ֑ךָ
וְאַתָּ֥ה אָדָ֛ם וְלֹא־אֵ֖ל
בְּיַ֥ד מְחַלְלֶֽיךָ׃
10 מוֹתֵ֧י עֲרֵלִ֛ים
תָּמ֖וּת בְּיַד־זָרִ֑ים
כִּ֚י אֲנִ֣י דִבַּ֔רְתִּי
נְאֻ֖ם אֲדֹנָ֥י יְהֹוִֽה׃ ס

11 וַיְהִ֥י דְבַר־יְהֹוָ֖ה אֵלַ֥י לֵאמֹֽר׃ 12 בֶּן־אָדָ֗ם
שָׂ֤א קִינָה֙ עַל־מֶ֣לֶךְ צ֔וֹר וְאָמַרְתָּ֣ לּ֔וֹ כֹּ֤ה
אָמַר֙ אֲדֹנָ֣י יְהֹוִ֔ה
אַתָּה֙ חוֹתֵ֣ם תׇּכְנִ֔ית
מָלֵ֥א חׇכְמָ֖ה וּכְלִ֥יל יֹֽפִי׃
13 בְּעֵ֨דֶן גַּן־אֱלֹהִ֜ים הָיִ֗יתָ
כׇּל־אֶ֨בֶן יְקָרָ֤ה מְסֻכָתֶ֙ךָ֙
אֹ֤דֶם פִּטְדָה֙ וְיָ֣הֲלֹ֔ם
תַּרְשִׁ֥ישׁ שֹׁ֖הַם וְיָ֣שְׁפֵ֑ה
סַפִּ֣יר נֹ֔פֶךְ וּבָרְקַ֖ת
וְזָהָ֑ב מְלֶ֨אכֶת תֻּפֶּ֤יךָ
וּנְקָבֶ֙יךָ֙ בָּ֔ךְ בְּי֥וֹם הִבָּרַאֲךָ֖ כּוֹנָֽנוּ׃
14 אַתְּ־כְּר֔וּב
מִמְשַׁ֖ח הַסּוֹכֵ֑ךְ
וּנְתַתִּ֗יךָ בְּהַ֨ר קֹ֤דֶשׁ אֱלֹהִים֙ הָיִ֔יתָ
בְּת֥וֹךְ אַבְנֵי־אֵ֖שׁ הִתְהַלָּֽכְתָּ׃
15 תָּמִ֤ים אַתָּה֙ בִּדְרָכֶ֔יךָ
מִיּ֖וֹם הִבָּֽרְאָ֑ךְ
עַד־נִמְצָ֥א עַוְלָ֖תָה בָּֽךְ׃
16 בְּרֹ֣ב רְכֻלָּתְךָ֗
מָלֽוּ* תוֹכְךָ֤ חָמָס֙
וַֽתֶּחֱטָ֔א
וָאֶחַלֶּלְךָ֗
מֵהַ֣ר אֱלֹהִ֔ים
וָֽאַבֶּדְךָ֛ כְּר֥וּב הַסֹּכֵ֖ךְ

From among the stones of fire.
¹⁷You grew haughty because of your beauty,
You debased your wisdom for the sake of your
    splendor;
I have cast you to the ground,
I have made you an object for kings to stare
    at.
¹⁸By the greatness of your guilt,
Through the dishonesty of your trading,
You desecrated your sanctuaries.
So I made a fire issue from you,
And it has devoured you;
I have reduced you to ashes on the ground,
In the sight of all who behold you.
¹⁹All who knew you among the peoples
Are appalled at your doom.
You have become a horror
And have ceased to be, forever.

²⁰The word of the LORD came to me: ²¹O mortal, set your face toward Sidon and prophesy against her. ²²Say: Thus said the Lord GOD:
I am going to deal with you, O Sidon.
I will gain glory in your midst;
And they shall know that I am the LORD,
When I wreak punishment upon her
And show Myself holy through her.
²³I will let pestilence loose against her
And bloodshed into her streets.
And the slain shall fall in her midst
When the sword comes upon her from all
    sides.
And they shall know that I am the LORD.
²⁴Then shall the House of Israel no longer be afflicted with prickling briers and lacerating thorns from all the neighbors who despise them; and they shall know that I am the Lord GOD.
²⁵Thus said the Lord GOD: When I have gathered the House of Israel from the peoples among which they have been dispersed, and have shown Myself holy through them in the sight

מִתּוֹךְ אַבְנֵי־אֵשׁ:
17 גָּבַהּ לִבְּךָ בְּיָפְיֶךָ
שִׁחַתָּ חָכְמָתְךָ עַל־יִפְעָתֶךָ
עַל־אֶרֶץ הִשְׁלַכְתִּיךָ
לִפְנֵי מְלָכִים נְתַתִּיךָ לְרַאֲוָה בָךְ:
18 מֵרֹב עֲוֺנֶיךָ
בְּעֶוֶל רְכֻלָּתְךָ
חִלַּלְתָּ מִקְדָּשֶׁיךָ
וָאוֹצִא־אֵשׁ מִתּוֹכְךָ
הִיא אֲכָלַתְךָ
וָאֶתֶּנְךָ לְאֵפֶר עַל־הָאָרֶץ
לְעֵינֵי כָּל־רֹאֶיךָ:
19 כָּל־יוֹדְעֶיךָ בָּעַמִּים
שָׁמְמוּ עָלֶיךָ
בַּלָּהוֹת הָיִיתָ
וְאֵינְךָ עַד־עוֹלָם: פ

20 וַיְהִי דְבַר־יְהֹוָה אֵלַי לֵאמֹר: 21 בֶּן־אָדָם
שִׂים פָּנֶיךָ אֶל־צִידוֹן וְהִנָּבֵא עָלֶיהָ:
22 וְאָמַרְתָּ כֹּה אָמַר אֲדֹנָי יְהֹוִה
הִנְנִי עָלַיִךְ צִידוֹן
וְנִכְבַּדְתִּי בְּתוֹכֵךְ
וְיָדְעוּ כִּי־אֲנִי יְהֹוָה
בַּעֲשׂוֹתִי בָהּ שְׁפָטִים
וְנִקְדַּשְׁתִּי בָהּ:
23 וְשִׁלַּחְתִּי־בָהּ דֶּבֶר
וָדָם בְּחוּצוֹתֶיהָ
וְנִפְלַל חָלָל בְּתוֹכָהּ
בְּחֶרֶב עָלֶיהָ מִסָּבִיב
וְיָדְעוּ כִּי־אֲנִי יְהֹוָה:
24 וְלֹא־יִהְיֶה עוֹד לְבֵית יִשְׂרָאֵל סִלּוֹן
מַמְאִיר וְקוֹץ מַכְאִב מִכֹּל סְבִיבֹתָם
הַשָּׁאטִים* אוֹתָם וְיָדְעוּ כִּי אֲנִי אֲדֹנָי
יְהֹוִה: ס
25 כֹּה־אָמַר אֲדֹנָי יְהֹוִה בְּקַבְּצִי | אֶת־
בֵּית יִשְׂרָאֵל מִן־הָעַמִּים אֲשֶׁר נָפֹצוּ בָם

of the nations, they shall settle on their own soil, which I gave to My servant Jacob, ²⁶and they shall dwell on it in security. They shall build houses and plant vineyards, and shall dwell on it in security, when I have meted out punishment to all those about them who despise them. And they shall know that I the Lord am their God.

29 In the tenth year, on the twelfth day of the tenth month, the word of the Lord came to me: ²O mortal, turn your face against Pharaoh king of Egypt, and prophesy against him and against all Egypt. ³Speak these words:

Thus said the Lord God:

I am going to deal with you, O Pharaoh king
    of Egypt,
Mighty monster, sprawling in your[a] chan-
    nels,
Who said,
My Nile is my own;
I made it for myself.
⁴I will put hooks in your jaws,
And make the fish of your channels
Cling to your scales;
I will haul you up from your channels,
With all the fish of your channels
Clinging to your scales.
⁵And I will fling you into the desert,
With all the fish of your channels.
You shall be left lying in the open,
Ungathered and unburied:
I have given you as food
To the beasts of the earth
And the birds of the sky.
⁶Then all the inhabitants of Egypt shall know
That I am the Lord.
Because you[b] were a staff of reed
To the House of Israel:

---

a Lit. "its."
b Lit. "they."

וְנִקְדַּשְׁתִּי בָם לְעֵינֵי הַגּוֹיִם וְיָשְׁבוּ עַל־
אַדְמָתָם אֲשֶׁר נָתַתִּי לְעַבְדִּי לְיַעֲקֹב: ²⁶וְיָשְׁבוּ עָלֶיהָ לָבֶטַח וּבָנוּ בָתִּים וְנָטְעוּ
כְרָמִים וְיָשְׁבוּ לָבֶטַח בַּעֲשׂוֹתִי שְׁפָטִים
בְּכֹל הַשָּׁאטִים* אֹתָם מִסְּבִיבוֹתָם וְיָדְעוּ
כִּי אֲנִי יְהֹוָה אֱלֹהֵיהֶם: ס

כט בַּשָּׁנָה הָעֲשִׂירִית בָּעֲשִׂרִי בִּשְׁנֵים
עָשָׂר לַחֹדֶשׁ הָיָה דְבַר־יְהֹוָה אֵלַי לֵאמֹר:
²בֶּן־אָדָם שִׂים פָּנֶיךָ עַל־פַּרְעֹה מֶלֶךְ
מִצְרָיִם וְהִנָּבֵא עָלָיו וְעַל־מִצְרַיִם כֻּלָּהּ:
³דַּבֵּר וְאָמַרְתָּ

כֹּה־אָמַר | אֲדֹנָי יְהֹוִה
הִנְנִי עָלֶיךָ פַּרְעֹה מֶלֶךְ־מִצְרַיִם
הַתַּנִּים הַגָּדוֹל הָרֹבֵץ בְּתוֹךְ יְאֹרָיו
אֲשֶׁר אָמַר
לִי יְאֹרִי
וַאֲנִי עֲשִׂיתִנִי:
⁴וְנָתַתִּי חַחִיים בִּלְחָיֶיךָ
וְהִדְבַּקְתִּי דְגַת־יְאֹרֶיךָ
בְּקַשְׂקְשֹׂתֶיךָ
וְהַעֲלִיתִיךָ מִתּוֹךְ יְאֹרֶיךָ
וְאֵת כָּל־דְּגַת יְאֹרֶיךָ
בְּקַשְׂקְשֹׂתֶיךָ תִּדְבָּק:
⁵וּנְטַשְׁתִּיךָ הַמִּדְבָּרָה
אוֹתְךָ וְאֵת כָּל־דְּגַת יְאֹרֶיךָ
עַל־פְּנֵי הַשָּׂדֶה תִּפּוֹל
לֹא תֵאָסֵף וְלֹא תִקָּבֵץ
לְחַיַּת הָאָרֶץ
וּלְעוֹף הַשָּׁמַיִם
נְתַתִּיךָ לְאָכְלָה:
⁶וְיָדְעוּ כָּל־יֹשְׁבֵי מִצְרַיִם
כִּי אֲנִי יְהֹוָה
יַעַן הֱיוֹתָם מִשְׁעֶנֶת קָנֶה

7When they grasped you with the hand, you
  would splinter,
And wound all their shoulders,c
And when they leaned on you, you would
  break,
And make all their loins unsteady.d

8Assuredly, thus said the Lord GOD: Lo, I will
bring a sword against you, and will cut off man
and beast from you, 9so that the land of Egypt
shall fall into desolation and ruin. And they shall
know that I am the LORD—because he boasted,
"The Nile is mine, and I made it." 10Assuredly,
I am going to deal with you and your channels,
and I will reduce the land of Egypt to utter ruin
and desolation, e-from Migdol to Syene, all the
way to the border of Nubia.-e 11No foot of man
shall traverse it, and no foot of beast shall traverse it; and it shall remain uninhabited for forty
years. 12For forty years I will make the land of
Egypt the most desolate of desolate lands, and
its cities shall be the most desolate of ruined
cities. And I will scatter the Egyptians among
the nations and disperse them throughout the
countries.

13Further, thus said the Lord GOD: After a period of forty years I will gather the Egyptians
from the peoples among whom they were dispersed. 14I will restore the fortunes of the Egyptians and bring them back to the land of their
origin, the land of Pathros,f and there they shall
be a lowly kingdom. 15It shall be the lowliest of
all the kingdoms, and shall not lord it over the
nations again. I will reduce the Egyptians,g so
that they shall have no dominion over the nations. 16Never again shall they be the trust of
the House of Israel, recalling its guilt in having
turned to them. And they shall know that I am
the Lord GOD.

לְבֵית יִשְׂרָאֵל:
7 בְּתׇפְשָׂם בְּךָ בכפך תֵּרוֹץ
וּבָקַעְתָּ לָהֶם כָּל־כָּתֵף
וּבְהִשָּׁעֲנָם עָלֶיךָ תִּשָּׁבֵר
וְהַעֲמַדְתָּ לָהֶם כָּל־מׇתְנָיִם: ס
8 לָכֵן כֹּה אָמַר אֲדֹנָי יֱהֹוִה הִנְנִי מֵבִיא
עָלַיִךְ חָרֶב וְהִכְרַתִּי מִמֵּךְ אָדָם וּבְהֵמָה:
9 וְהָיְתָה אֶרֶץ־מִצְרַיִם לִשְׁמָמָה וְחׇרְבָּה
וְיָדְעוּ כִּי־אֲנִי יְהֹוָה יַעַן אָמַר יְאֹר לִי וַאֲנִי
עָשִׂיתִי: 10 לָכֵן הִנְנִי אֵלֶיךָ וְאֶל־יְאֹרֶיךָ
וְנָתַתִּי אֶת־אֶרֶץ מִצְרַיִם לְחׇרְבוֹת חֹרֶב
שְׁמָמָה מִמִּגְדֹּל סְוֵנֵה וְעַד־גְּבוּל כּוּשׁ:
11 לֹא תַעֲבָר־בָּהּ רֶגֶל אָדָם וְרֶגֶל בְּהֵמָה
לֹא תַעֲבָר־בָּהּ וְלֹא תֵשֵׁב אַרְבָּעִים שָׁנָה:
12 וְנָתַתִּי אֶת־אֶרֶץ מִצְרַיִם שְׁמָמָה בְּתוֹךְ ׀
אֲרָצוֹת נְשַׁמּוֹת וְעָרֶיהָ בְּתוֹךְ עָרִים
מׇחֳרָבוֹת תִּהְיֶיןָ שְׁמָמָה אַרְבָּעִים שָׁנָה
וַהֲפִצֹתִי אֶת־מִצְרַיִם בַּגּוֹיִם וְזֵרִיתִים
בָּאֲרָצוֹת: פ
13 כִּי כֹּה אָמַר אֲדֹנָי יֱהֹוִה מִקֵּץ אַרְבָּעִים
שָׁנָה אֲקַבֵּץ אֶת־מִצְרַיִם מִן־הָעַמִּים
אֲשֶׁר־נָפֹצוּ שָׁמָּה: 14 וְשַׁבְתִּי אֶת־שְׁבוּת
מִצְרַיִם וַהֲשִׁבֹתִי אֹתָם אֶרֶץ פַּתְרוֹס עַל־
אֶרֶץ מְכוּרָתָם וְהָיוּ שָׁם מַמְלָכָה שְׁפָלָה:
15 מִן־הַמַּמְלָכוֹת תִּהְיֶה שְׁפָלָה וְלֹא־
תִתְנַשֵּׂא עוֹד עַל־הַגּוֹיִם וְהִמְעַטְתִּים
לְבִלְתִּי רְדוֹת בַּגּוֹיִם: 16 וְלֹא יִהְיֶה־עוֹד
לְבֵית יִשְׂרָאֵל לְמִבְטָח מַזְכִּיר עָוֺן בִּפְנוֹתָם
אַחֲרֵיהֶם וְיָדְעוּ כִּי אֲנִי אֲדֹנָי יְהֹוִה: פ

c   Septuagint and Syriac read "palms"; cf. 2 Kings 18.21; Isa. 36.6.
d   Taking ʿamad as a byform of maʿad; cf. Syriac translation.
e-e I.e., the length of Egypt, from north to south. Syene is modern
     Aswan.
f   I.e., southern Egypt.
g   Heb. "them."

17In the twenty-seventh year, on the first day of the first month, the word of the LORD came to me: 18O mortal, King Nebuchadrezzar of Babylon has made his army expend vast labor on Tyre; every head is rubbed bald and every shoulder scraped. But he and his army have had no return for the labor he expended on Tyre. 19Assuredly, thus said the Lord GOD: I will give the land of Egypt to Nebuchadrezzar, king of Babylon. He shall carry off her wealth and take her spoil and seize her booty; and she shall be the recompense of his army. 20As the wage for which he labored, for what they did for Me, I give him the land of Egypt—declares the Lord GOD.

21On that day I will *h*-endow the House of Israel with strength, and you shall be vindicated-*h* among them. And they shall know that I am the LORD.

30 The word of the LORD came to me: 2O mortal, prophesy and say: Thus said the Lord GOD:

Wail, alas for the day!
3For a day is near;
A day of the LORD is near.
It will be a day of cloud,
An hour of [invading] nations.
4A sword shall pierce Egypt,
And Nubia shall be seized with trembling,
When men fall slain in Egypt
And her wealth is seized
And her foundations are overthrown.
5Nubia, Put, and Lud, and all *a*-the mixed populations,-*a* and Cub, and the inhabitants of the allied countries shall fall by the sword with them.

---

17 וַיְהִ֗י בְּעֶשְׂרִ֤ים וָשֶׁ֙בַע֙ שָׁנָ֣ה בָּֽרִאשׁ֔וֹן בְּאֶחָ֣ד לַחֹ֔דֶשׁ הָיָ֥ה דְבַר־יְהֹוָ֖ה אֵלַ֥י לֵאמֹֽר: 18 בֶּן־אָדָ֗ם נְבוּכַדְרֶאצַּ֣ר מֶֽלֶךְ־בָּ֠בֶל הֶעֱבִ֨יד אֶת־חֵיל֜וֹ עֲבֹדָ֤ה גְדֹלָה֙ אֶל־צֹ֔ר כָּל־רֹ֣אשׁ מֻקְרָ֔ח וְכָל־כָּתֵ֖ף מְרוּטָ֑ה וְ֠שָׂכָ֠ר לֹא־הָ֨יָה ל֤וֹ וּלְחֵילוֹ֙ מִצֹּ֔ר עַל־הָעֲבֹדָ֖ה אֲשֶׁר־עָבַ֥ד עָלֶֽיהָ: ס 19 לָכֵ֗ן כֹּ֤ה אָמַר֙ אֲדֹנָ֣י יֱהֹוִ֔ה הִנְנִ֥י נֹתֵ֛ן לִנְבוּכַדְרֶאצַּ֥ר מֶֽלֶךְ־בָּבֶ֖ל אֶת־אֶ֣רֶץ מִצְרָ֑יִם וְנָשָׂ֨א הֲמֹנָ֜הּ וְשָׁלַ֤ל שְׁלָלָהּ֙ וּבָזַ֣ז בִּזָּ֔הּ וְהָיְתָ֥ה שָׂכָ֖ר לְחֵילֽוֹ: 20 פְּעֻלָּתוֹ֙ אֲשֶׁר־עָ֣בַד בָּ֔הּ נָתַ֥תִּי ל֖וֹ אֶת־אֶ֣רֶץ מִצְרָ֑יִם אֲשֶׁר֙ עָ֣שׂוּ לִ֔י נְאֻ֖ם אֲדֹנָ֥י יֱהֹוִֽה: ס

21 בַּיּ֣וֹם הַה֗וּא אַצְמִ֤יחַ קֶ֙רֶן֙ לְבֵ֣ית יִשְׂרָאֵ֔ל וּלְךָ֛ אֶתֵּ֥ן פִּתְח֥וֹן־פֶּ֖ה בְּתוֹכָ֑ם וְיָדְע֖וּ כִּי־אֲנִ֥י יְהֹוָֽה: פ

ל 1 וַיְהִ֥י דְבַר־יְהֹוָ֖ה אֵלַ֥י לֵאמֹֽר: 2 בֶּן־אָדָ֕ם הִנָּבֵא֙ וְאָ֣מַרְתָּ֔ כֹּ֥ה אָמַ֖ר אֲדֹנָ֣י יֱהֹוִ֑ה

הֵילִ֖ילוּ הָ֥הּ לַיּֽוֹם:
3 כִּֽי־קָר֥וֹב י֖וֹם
וְקָר֥וֹב י֖וֹם לַֽיהֹוָ֑ה
י֣וֹם עָנָ֔ן
עֵ֥ת גּוֹיִ֖ם יִֽהְיֶֽה:
4 וּבָ֤אָה חֶ֙רֶב֙ בְּמִצְרַ֔יִם
וְהָיְתָ֤ה חַלְחָלָה֙ בְּכ֔וּשׁ
בִּנְפֹ֥ל חָלָ֖ל בְּמִצְרָ֑יִם
וְלָקְח֣וּ הֲמוֹנָ֔הּ
וְנֶהֶרְס֖וּ יְסֹֽדוֹתֶֽיהָ:
5 כּ֣וּשׁ וּפ֤וּט וְלוּד֙ וְכָל־הָעֶ֔רֶב וְכ֖וּב וּבְנֵ֣י אֶ֣רֶץ הַבְּרִ֑ית אִתָּ֖ם בַּחֶ֥רֶב יִפֹּֽלוּ: פ

---

h-h Lit. "cause a horn to sprout for the House of Israel, and I will grant you opening of the mouth."

a-a Meaning of Heb. uncertain.

6Thus said the LORD:
Those who support Egypt shall fall,
And her proud strength shall sink;
There they shall fall by the sword,
From Migdol to Syene
             —declares the Lord GOD.

7They shall be the most desolate of desolate lands, and her cities shall be the most ruined of cities, 8when I set fire to Egypt and all who help her are broken. Thus they shall know that I am the LORD.

9On that day, messengers shall set out at My bidding to strike terror into confident Nubia. And they shall be seized with trembling on Egypt's day [of doom]—for it is at hand.

10Thus said the Lord GOD: I will put an end to the wealth of Egypt through King Nebuchadrezzar of Babylon. 11He, together with his troops, the most ruthless of the nations, shall be brought to ravage the land. And they shall unsheathe the sword against Egypt and fill the land with the slain.

12I will turn the channels into dry ground, and I will deliver the land into the hands of evil men. I will lay waste the land and everything in it by the hands of strangers. I the LORD have spoken.

13Thus said the Lord GOD: I will destroy the fetishes and make an end of the idols in Noph; and no longer shall there be a prince in the land of Egypt; and I will strike the land of Egypt with fear. 14I will lay Pathros waste, I will set fire to Zoan, and I will execute judgment on No. 15I will pour out my anger upon Sin, the stronghold of Egypt, and I will destroy the wealth of No. 16I will set fire to Egypt; Sin shall writhe in anguish and No shall be torn apart; a-and Noph [shall face] adversaries in broad daylight.-a 17The young men of Avenb and Pi-beseth shall fall by the sword, and those [towns] shall go into

b   Elsewhere called "On"; cf. Gen. 41.45, 50; 46.20.

6 כֹּה אָמַר יְהֹוָה
וְנָֽפְלוּ סֹמְכֵי מִצְרַיִם
וְיָרַד גְּאוֹן עֻזָּהּ
מִמִּגְדֹּל סְוֵנֵה
בַּחֶרֶב יִפְּלוּ־בָהּ
נְאֻם אֲדֹנָי יְהֹוִה:

7 וְנָשַׁמּוּ בְּתוֹךְ אֲרָצוֹת נְשַׁמּוֹת וְעָרָיו
בְּתוֹךְ־עָרִים נַחֲרָבוֹת תִּהְיֶינָה: 8 וְיָדְעוּ
כִּי־אֲנִי יְהֹוָה בְּתִתִּי־אֵשׁ בְּמִצְרַיִם וְנִשְׁבְּרוּ
כָּל־עֹזְרֶיהָ:

9 בַּיּוֹם הַהוּא יֵצְאוּ מַלְאָכִים מִלְּפָנַי בַּצִּים
לְהַחֲרִיד אֶת־כּוּשׁ בֶּטַח וְהָיְתָה חַלְחָלָה
בָהֶם בְּיוֹם מִצְרַיִם כִּי הִנֵּה בָּאָה: ס

10 כֹּה אָמַר אֲדֹנָי יְהֹוִה וְהִשְׁבַּתִּי אֶת־הֲמוֹן
מִצְרַיִם בְּיַד נְבוּכַדְרֶאצַּר מֶלֶךְ־בָּבֶל:
11 הוּא וְעַמּוֹ אִתּוֹ עָרִיצֵי גוֹיִם מוּבָאִים
לְשַׁחֵת הָאָרֶץ וְהֵרִיקוּ חַרְבוֹתָם עַל־
מִצְרַיִם וּמָלְאוּ אֶת־הָאָרֶץ חָלָל:
12 וְנָתַתִּי יְאֹרִים חָרָבָה וּמָכַרְתִּי אֶת־
הָאָרֶץ בְּיַד־רָעִים וַהֲשִׁמֹּתִי אֶרֶץ וּמְלֹאָהּ
בְּיַד־זָרִים אֲנִי יְהֹוָה דִּבַּרְתִּי: ס

13 כֹּה־אָמַר אֲדֹנָי יְהֹוִה וְהַאֲבַדְתִּי גִלּוּלִים
וְהִשְׁבַּתִּי אֱלִילִים מִנֹּף וְנָשִׂיא מֵאֶרֶץ־
מִצְרַיִם לֹא יִהְיֶה־עוֹד וְנָתַתִּי יִרְאָה בְּאֶרֶץ
מִצְרָיִם: 14 וַהֲשִׁמֹּתִי אֶת־פַּתְרוֹס וְנָתַתִּי
אֵשׁ בְּצֹעַן וְעָשִׂיתִי שְׁפָטִים בְּנֹא:
15 וְשָׁפַכְתִּי חֲמָתִי עַל־סִין מָעוֹז מִצְרָיִם
וְהִכְרַתִּי אֶת־הֲמוֹן נֹא: 16 וְנָתַתִּי אֵשׁ
בְּמִצְרַיִם חוּל תָּחִיל סִין וְנֹא תִּהְיֶה
לְהִבָּקֵעַ וְנֹף צָרֵי יוֹמָם: 17 בַּחוּרֵי אָוֶן
וּפִי־בֶסֶת בַּחֶרֶב יִפֹּלוּ וְהֵנָּה בַּשְּׁבִי

captivity. [18]In Tehaphnehes[c] daylight shall be withheld,[d] when I break there the power of Egypt, and there her proud strength comes to an end. [The city] itself shall be covered with cloud, and its daughter towns shall go into captivity.

[19]Thus I will execute judgment on Egypt;
And they shall know that I am the Lord.

[20]In the eleventh year, on the seventh day of the first month, the word of the Lord came to me: [21]O mortal, I have broken the arm of Pharaoh king of Egypt; it has not been bound up to be healed nor firmly bandaged to make it strong enough to grasp the sword. [22]Assuredly, thus said the Lord God: I am going to deal with Pharaoh king of Egypt. I will break his arms, both the sound one and the injured, and make the sword drop from his hand. [23]I will scatter the Egyptians among the nations and disperse them throughout the countries. [24]I will strengthen the arms of the king of Babylon and put My sword in his hand; and I will break the arms of Pharaoh, and he shall groan before him with the groans of one struck down. [25]I will make firm the arms of the king of Babylon, but the arms of Pharaoh shall fail. And they shall know that I am the Lord, when I put My sword into the hand of the king of Babylon, and he lifts it against the land of Egypt. [26]I will scatter the Egyptians among the nations and disperse them throughout the countries. Thus they shall know that I am the Lord.

31

In the eleventh year, on the first day of the third month, the word of the Lord came to me: [2]O mortal, say to Pharaoh king of Egypt and his hordes:

---

c   *Elsewhere vocalized "Tahpanhes"; e.g., Jer. 2.16; 44.1.*
d   *Some Heb. mss. and editions read "darkened."*

תֵלַכְנָה: 18 וּבִתְחַפְנְחֵס חָשַׂךְ הַיּוֹם בְּשִׁבְרִי־שָׁם אֶת־מֹטוֹת מִצְרַיִם וְנִשְׁבַּת־בָּהּ גְּאוֹן עֻזָּהּ הִיא עָנָן יְכַסֶּנָּה וּבְנוֹתֶיהָ בַּשְּׁבִי תֵלַכְנָה:
19 וְעָשִׂיתִי שְׁפָטִים בְּמִצְרָיִם וְיָדְעוּ כִּי־אֲנִי יְהוָה: פ

20 וַיְהִי בְּאַחַת עֶשְׂרֵה שָׁנָה בָּרִאשׁוֹן בְּשִׁבְעָה לַחֹדֶשׁ הָיָה דְבַר־יְהוָה אֵלַי לֵאמֹר: 21 בֶּן־אָדָם אֶת־זְרוֹעַ פַּרְעֹה מֶלֶךְ־מִצְרַיִם שָׁבָרְתִּי וְהִנֵּה לֹא־חֻבְּשָׁה לָתֵת רְפֻאוֹת לָשׂוּם חִתּוּל לְחָבְשָׁהּ לְחָזְקָהּ לִתְפֹּשׂ בֶּחָרֶב: ס 22 לָכֵן כֹּה־אָמַר | אֲדֹנָי יְהוִה הִנְנִי אֶל־פַּרְעֹה מֶלֶךְ־מִצְרַיִם וְשָׁבַרְתִּי אֶת־זְרֹעֹתָיו אֶת־הַחֲזָקָה וְאֶת־הַנִּשְׁבָּרֶת וְהִפַּלְתִּי אֶת־הַחֶרֶב מִיָּדוֹ: 23 וַהֲפִצוֹתִי אֶת־מִצְרַיִם בַּגּוֹיִם וְזֵרִיתִם בָּאֲרָצוֹת: 24 וְחִזַּקְתִּי אֶת־זְרֹעוֹת מֶלֶךְ בָּבֶל וְנָתַתִּי אֶת־חַרְבִּי בְּיָדוֹ וְשָׁבַרְתִּי אֶת־זְרֹעוֹת פַּרְעֹה וְנָאַק נַאֲקוֹת חָלָל לְפָנָיו: 25 וְהַחֲזַקְתִּי אֶת־זְרֹעוֹת מֶלֶךְ בָּבֶל וּזְרֹעוֹת פַּרְעֹה תִּפֹּלְנָה וְיָדְעוּ כִּי־אֲנִי יְהוָה בְּתִתִּי חַרְבִּי בְּיַד מֶלֶךְ־בָּבֶל וְנָטָה אוֹתָהּ אֶל־אֶרֶץ מִצְרָיִם: 26 וַהֲפִצוֹתִי אֶת־מִצְרַיִם בַּגּוֹיִם וְזֵרִיתִי אוֹתָם בָּאֲרָצוֹת וְיָדְעוּ כִּי־אֲנִי יְהוָה: ס

לא
וַיְהִי בְּאַחַת עֶשְׂרֵה שָׁנָה בַּשְּׁלִישִׁי בְּאֶחָד לַחֹדֶשׁ הָיָה דְבַר־יְהוָה אֵלַי לֵאמֹר: 2 בֶּן־אָדָם אֱמֹר אֶל־פַּרְעֹה מֶלֶךְ־מִצְרַיִם וְאֶל־הֲמוֹנוֹ

Who was comparable to you in greatness?

³Assyria was a cedar in Lebanon

With beautiful branches and ᵃ-shady thickets,-ᵃ

Of lofty stature,

With its top among ᵇ-leafy trees.-ᵇ

⁴Waters nourished it,

The deep made it grow tall,

Washing with its streams

The place where it was planted,

Making its channels well up

ᶜ-To all-ᶜ the trees of the field.

⁵Therefore it exceeded in stature

All the trees of the field;

Its branches multiplied and its boughs grew long

Because of the abundant water

That welled up for it.

⁶In its branches nested

All the birds of the sky;

All the beasts of the field

Bore their young under its boughs,

And in its shadow lived

All the great nations.

⁷It was beautiful in its height,

In the length of its branches,

Because its stock stood

By abundant waters.

⁸Cedars in the garden of God

Could not compare with it;

Cypresses could not match its boughs,

And plane trees could not vie with its branches;

No tree in the garden of God

Was its peer in beauty.

⁹I made it beautiful

In the profusion of its branches;

And all the trees of Eden envied it

In the garden of God.

אֶל־מִי דָמִיתָ בְּגֹדֶל׃

3 הִנֵּה אַשּׁוּר אֶרֶז בַּלְּבָנוֹן

יְפֵה עָנָף וְחֹרֶשׁ מֵצַל

וּגְבַהּ קוֹמָה

וּבֵין עֲבֹתִים הָיְתָה צַמַּרְתּוֹ׃

4 מַיִם גִּדְּלוּהוּ

תְּהוֹם רֹמְמָתְהוּ

אֶת־נַהֲרֹתֶיהָ

הֹלֵךְ סְבִיבוֹת מַטָּעָהּ

וְאֶת־תְּעָלֹתֶיהָ שִׁלְחָה*

אֶל כָּל־עֲצֵי הַשָּׂדֶה׃

5 עַל־כֵּן גָּבְהָא* קֹמָתוֹ

מִכֹּל עֲצֵי הַשָּׂדֶה

וַתִּרְבֶּינָה סַרְעַפֹּתָיו וַתֶּאֱרַכְנָה פֹארֹתֹו
פֹארֹתָיו

מִמַּיִם רַבִּים

בְּשַׁלְּחוֹ׃

6 בִּסְעַפֹּתָיו קִנְנוּ

כָּל־עוֹף הַשָּׁמַיִם

וְתַחַת פֹּארֹתָיו יָלְדוּ

כֹּל חַיַּת הַשָּׂדֶה

וּבְצִלּוֹ יֵשְׁבוּ

כֹּל גּוֹיִם רַבִּים׃

7 וַיְּיִף בְּגָדְלוֹ

בְּאֹרֶךְ דָּלִיּוֹתָיו

כִּי־הָיָה שָׁרְשׁוֹ

אֶל־מַיִם רַבִּים׃

8 אֲרָזִים לֹא־עֲמָמֻהוּ בְּגַן־אֱלֹהִים

בְּרוֹשִׁים לֹא דָמוּ אֶל־סְעַפֹּתָיו

וְעַרְמֹנִים לֹא־הָיוּ כְּפֹארֹתָיו

כָּל־עֵץ בְּגַן־אֱלֹהִים

לֹא־דָמָה אֵלָיו בְּיָפְיוֹ׃

9 יָפֶה עֲשִׂיתִיו

בְּרֹב דָּלִיּוֹתָיו

וַיְקַנְאֻהוּ כָּל־עֲצֵי־עֵדֶן

אֲשֶׁר בְּגַן הָאֱלֹהִים׃ ס

ᵃ-ᵃ   *Meaning of Heb. uncertain.*

ᵇ-ᵇ   *Septuagint reads "clouds."*

ᶜ-ᶜ   *Meaning of Heb. uncertain; emendation yields "more than for all."*

10Assuredly, thus said the Lord GOD: Because it[d] towered high in stature, and thrust its top up among the [b]-leafy trees,-[b] and it was arrogant in its height, 11I delivered it into the hands of the mightiest of nations. They treated it as befitted its wickedness. I banished it. 12Strangers, the most ruthless of nations, cut it down and abandoned it; its branches fell on the mountains and in every valley; its boughs were splintered in every watercourse of the earth; and all the peoples of the earth departed from its shade and abandoned it. 13Upon its fallen trunk all the birds of the sky nest, and all the beasts of the field lodge among its boughs—14so that no trees by water should exalt themselves in stature or set their tops among the [b]-leafy trees,-[b] and that no well-watered tree may reach up to them in height. For they are all consigned to death, to the lowest part of the netherworld,[e] together with human beings who descend into the Pit.

15Thus said the Lord GOD: On the day it went down to Sheol, I closed[f] the deep over it and covered it; I held back its streams, and the great waters were checked. I made Lebanon mourn deeply for it, and all the trees of the field languished on its account. 16I made nations quake at the crash of its fall, when I cast it down to Sheol with those who descend into the Pit; and all the trees of Eden, the choicest and best of Lebanon, all that were well watered, were consoled in the lowest part of the netherworld. 17They also descended with it into Sheol, to those slain by the sword, together with its supporters,[g] they who had lived under its shadow among the nations.

18[Now you know] who is comparable to you in glory and greatness among the trees of Eden. And you too shall be brought down with the

10 לָכֵ֞ן כֹּ֤ה אָמַר֙ אֲדֹנָ֣י יְהֹוִ֔ה יַ֕עַן אֲשֶׁ֥ר גָּבַ֖הְתָּ בְּקוֹמָ֑ה וַיִּתֵּ֤ן צַמַּרְתּוֹ֙ אֶל־בֵּ֣ין עֲבוֹתִ֔ים וְרָ֥ם לְבָב֖וֹ בְּגׇבְה֑וֹ: 11 וְאֶ֨תְּנֵ֔הוּ בְּיַ֖ד אֵ֣יל גּוֹיִ֑ם עָשׂ֤וֹ יַעֲשֶׂה֙ ל֔וֹ כְּרִשְׁע֖וֹ גֵּרַשְׁתִּֽהוּ: 12 וַיִּכְרְתֻ֣הוּ זָרִ֗ים עָרִיצֵ֣י גוֹיִם֮ וַֽיִּטְּשֻׁ֒הוּ֒ אֶל־הֶהָרִ֣ים וּבְכׇל־גֵּ֣אָי֗וֹת נָֽפְל֤וּ דָֽלִיּוֹתָיו֙ וַתִּשָּׁבַ֣רְנָה פֹֽארֹתָ֔יו בְּכֹ֖ל אֲפִיקֵ֣י הָאָ֑רֶץ וַיֵּרְד֧וּ מִצִּלּ֛וֹ כׇּל־עַמֵּ֥י הָאָ֖רֶץ וַֽיִּטְּשֻֽׁהוּ: 13 עַל־מַפַּלְתּ֖וֹ יִשְׁכְּנ֣וּ כׇּל־ע֣וֹף הַשָּׁמָ֑יִם וְאֶל־פֹּֽארֹתָ֖יו הָי֖וּ כֹּ֥ל חַיַּ֥ת הַשָּׂדֶֽה: 14 לְמַ֡עַן אֲשֶׁר֩ לֹא־יִגְבְּה֨וּ בְקוֹמָתָ֜ם כׇּל־עֲצֵי־מַ֗יִם וְלֹא־יִתְּנ֤וּ אֶת־צַמַּרְתָּם֙ אֶל־בֵּ֣ין עֲבֹתִ֔ים וְלֹא־יַעַמְד֧וּ אֵלֵיהֶ֛ם בְּגׇבְהָ֖ם כׇּל־שֹׁ֣תֵי מָ֑יִם כִּֽי־כֻלָּ֞ם נִתְּנ֤וּ לַמָּ֙וֶת֙ אֶל־אֶ֣רֶץ תַּחְתִּ֔ית בְּת֖וֹךְ בְּנֵ֣י אָדָ֑ם אֶל־י֖וֹרְדֵ֥י בֽוֹר: ס

15 כֹּה־אָמַ֞ר אֲדֹנָ֣י יְהֹוִ֗ה בְּי֨וֹם רִדְתּ֤וֹ שְׁא֙וֹלָה֙ הֶאֱבַ֣לְתִּי כִּסֵּ֧תִי עָלָ֛יו אֶת־תְּה֖וֹם וָֽאֶמְנַ֣ע נַהֲרוֹתֶ֗יהָ וַיִּכָּֽלְא֖וּ מַ֣יִם רַבִּ֑ים וָאַקְדִּ֤ר עָלָיו֙ לְבָנ֔וֹן וְכׇל־עֲצֵ֥י הַשָּׂדֶ֖ה עָלָ֥יו עֻלְפֶּֽה: 16 מִקּ֤וֹל מַפַּלְתּוֹ֙ הִרְעַ֣שְׁתִּי גוֹיִ֔ם בְּהוֹרִדִ֥י אֹת֛וֹ שְׁא֖וֹלָה אֶת־י֣וֹרְדֵי ב֑וֹר וַיִּנָּ֨חֲמ֜וּ בְּאֶ֤רֶץ תַּחְתִּית֙ כׇּל־עֲצֵי־עֵ֔דֶן מִבְחַ֥ר וְטוֹב־לְבָנ֖וֹן כׇּל־שֹׁ֥תֵי מָֽיִם: 17 גַּם־הֵ֗ם אִתּ֛וֹ יָרְד֥וּ שְׁא֖וֹלָה אֶל־חַלְלֵי־חָ֑רֶב וּזְרֹע֛וֹ יָשְׁב֥וּ בְצִלּ֖וֹ בְּת֥וֹךְ גּוֹיִֽם: 18 אֶל־מִ֨י דָמִ֤יתָ כָּ֙כָה֙ בְּכָב֣וֹד וּבְגֹ֔דֶל בַּעֲצֵי־עֵ֑דֶן וְהוֹרַדְתָּ֙ אֶת־עֲצֵי־עֵ֜דֶן אֶל־אֶ֣רֶץ

---

d   Heb. "you."
e   To which popular belief relegated those who died uncircumcised or by the sword; cf. v. 18.
f   Cf. Aramaic 'abulla, "gate."
g   Heb. "arm."

trees of Eden to the lowest part of the nether-world; you shall lie among the uncircumcised and those slain by the sword. Such shall be [the fate of] Pharaoh and all his hordes—declares the Lord GOD.

32

In the twelfth year, on the first day of the twelfth month, the word of the LORD came to me: ²O mortal, intone a dirge over Pharaoh king of Egypt. Say to him:

ᵃ-O great beast among the nations,-ᵃ you are
    doomed!
You are like the dragon in the seas,
Thrusting through theirᵇ streams,
Stirring up the water with your feet
And muddying their streams!
³Thus said the Lord GOD:
I will cast My net over you
In an assembly of many peoples,
And you shall be hauled up in My toils.
⁴And I will fling you to the ground,
Hurl you upon the open field.
I will cause all the birds of the sky
To settle upon you.
I will cause the beasts of all the earth
To batten on you.
⁵I will cast your carcass upon the hills
And fill the valleys with your ᵃ-rotting flesh.-ᵃ
⁶I will drench the earth
With your oozing blood upon the hills,
And the watercourses shall be filled with your
    [gore].
⁷When you are snuffed out,
I will cover the sky
And darken its stars;
I will cover the sun with clouds
And the moon shall not give its light.
⁸All the lights that shine in the sky

---

a-a   Meaning of Heb. uncertain.
b   Heb. "your."

תַּחְתִּית בְּתוֹךְ עֲרֵלִים תִּשְׁכַּב אֶת־חַלְלֵי־
חֶרֶב הוּא פַרְעֹה וְכָל־הֲמוֹנֹה נְאֻם
אֲדֹנָי יְהוִה: ס

לב וַיְהִי בִּשְׁתֵּי עֶשְׂרֵה שָׁנָה בִּשְׁנֵי־
עָשָׂר חֹדֶשׁ בְּאֶחָד לַחֹדֶשׁ הָיָה דְבַר־יְהוָה
אֵלַי לֵאמֹר: ² בֶּן־אָדָם שָׂא קִינָה עַל־
פַּרְעֹה מֶלֶךְ־מִצְרַיִם וְאָמַרְתָּ אֵלָיו
כְּפִיר גּוֹיִם נִדְמֵיתָ
וְאַתָּה כַּתַּנִּים בַּיַּמִּים
וַתָּגַח בְּנַהֲרוֹתֶיךָ
וַתִּדְלַח־מַיִם בְּרַגְלֶיךָ
וַתִּרְפֹּס נַהֲרוֹתָם:
³ כֹּה אָמַר אֲדֹנָי יְהוִה
וּפָרַשְׂתִּי עָלֶיךָ אֶת־רִשְׁתִּי
בִּקְהַל עַמִּים רַבִּים
וְהֶעֱלוּךָ בְּחֶרְמִי:
⁴ וּנְטַשְׁתִּיךָ בָאָרֶץ
עַל־פְּנֵי הַשָּׂדֶה אֲטִילֶךָ
וְהִשְׁכַּנְתִּי עָלֶיךָ
כָּל־עוֹף הַשָּׁמַיִם
וְהִשְׂבַּעְתִּי מִמְּךָ
חַיַּת כָּל־הָאָרֶץ:
⁵ וְנָתַתִּי אֶת־בְּשָׂרְךָ עַל־הֶהָרִים
וּמִלֵּאתִי הַגֵּאָיוֹת רָמוּתֶךָ:
⁶ וְהִשְׁקֵיתִי אֶרֶץ צָפָתְךָ
מִדָּמְךָ אֶל־הֶהָרִים
וַאֲפִקִים יִמָּלְאוּן מִמֶּךָּ:
⁷ וְכִסֵּיתִי בְכַבּוֹתְךָ שָׁמַיִם
וְהִקְדַּרְתִּי אֶת־כֹּכְבֵיהֶם
שֶׁמֶשׁ בֶּעָנָן אֲכַסֶּנּוּ
וְיָרֵחַ לֹא־יָאִיר אוֹרוֹ:
⁸ כָּל־מְאוֹרֵי אוֹר בַּשָּׁמַיִם

I will darken above you;
And I will bring darkness upon your land
    —declares the Lord GOD.
⁹I will vex the hearts of many peoples
When I bring your ᶜ-shattered remnants-ᶜ
    among the nations,
To countries which you never knew.
¹⁰I will strike many peoples with horror over
    your fate;
And their kings shall be aghast over you,
When I brandish My sword before them.
They shall tremble continually,
Each man for his own life,
On the day of your downfall.
¹¹For thus said the Lord GOD:
The sword of the king of Babylon shall come
    upon you.
¹²I will cause your multitude to fall
By the swords of warriors,
All the most ruthless among the nations.
They shall ravage the splendor of Egypt,
And all her masses shall be wiped out.
¹³I will make all her cattle vanish from beside
    abundant waters;
The feet of man shall not muddy them any
    more,
Nor shall the hoofs of cattle muddy them.
¹⁴Then I will let their waters settle,
And make their rivers flow like oil
    —declares the Lord GOD:
¹⁵When I lay the land of Egypt waste,
When the land is emptied of [the life] that
    filled it,
When I strike down all its inhabitants.
And they shall know that I am the LORD.
¹⁶This is a dirge, and it shall be intoned;
The women of the nations shall intone it,
They shall intone it over Egypt and all her
    multitude
    —declares the Lord GOD.

אַקְדִּ֤יר עָלֶ֙יךָ֙
וְנָתַ֤תִּי חֹ֙שֶׁךְ֙ עַל־אַרְצֶ֔ךָ
נְאֻ֖ם אֲדֹנָ֥י יְהוִֽה׃
9 וְ֠הִכְעַסְתִּ֠י לֵ֣ב עַמִּ֤ים רַבִּים֙
בַּהֲבִיאִ֤י שִׁבְרְךָ֙ בַּגּוֹיִ֔ם
עַל־אֲרָצ֖וֹת אֲשֶׁ֥ר לֹֽא־יְדַעְתָּֽם׃
10 וַהֲשִׁמּוֹתִ֤י עָלֶ֙יךָ֙ עַמִּ֣ים רַבִּ֔ים
וּמַלְכֵיהֶ֞ם יִשְׂעֲר֤וּ עָלֶ֙יךָ֙ שַׂ֔עַר
בְּעוֹפְפִ֥י חַרְבִּ֖י עַל־פְּנֵיהֶ֑ם
וְחָרְד֤וּ לִרְגָעִים֙
אִ֣ישׁ לְנַפְשׁ֔וֹ
בְּי֖וֹם מַפַּלְתֶּֽךָ׃ ס
11 כִּ֛י כֹּ֥ה אָמַ֖ר אֲדֹנָ֣י יְהוִ֑ה
חֶ֥רֶב מֶֽלֶךְ־בָּבֶ֖ל תְּבוֹאֶֽךָ׃
12 בְּחַרְב֣וֹת גִּבּוֹרִים֮
אַפִּ֣יל הֲמוֹנֶ֒ךָ֒
עָרִיצֵ֥י גוֹיִ֖ם כֻּלָּ֑ם
וְשָֽׁדְדוּ֙ אֶת־גְּא֣וֹן מִצְרַ֔יִם
וְנִשְׁמַ֖ד כָּל־הֲמוֹנָֽהּ׃
13 וְהַ֣אֲבַדְתִּ֗י אֶת־כָּל־בְּהֶמְתָּ֔הּ מֵעַ֖ל מַ֣יִם
רַבִּ֑ים
וְלֹ֙א תִדְלָחֵ֜ם רֶֽגֶל־אָדָ֣ם ע֗וֹד
וּפַרְס֥וֹת בְּהֵמָ֖ה לֹ֥א תִדְלָחֵֽם׃
14 אָ֚ז אַשְׁקִ֣יעַ מֵֽימֵיהֶ֔ם
וְנַהֲרוֹתָ֖ם כַּשֶּׁ֣מֶן אוֹלִ֑יךְ
נְאֻ֖ם אֲדֹנָ֥י יְהוִֽה׃
15 בְּתִתִּי֩ אֶת־אֶ֨רֶץ מִצְרַ֜יִם שְׁמָמָ֗ה
וּנְשַׁמָּ֤ה אֶ֙רֶץ֙ מִמְּלֹאָ֔הּ
בְּהַכּוֹתִ֖י אֶת־כָּל־י֣וֹשְׁבֵי בָ֑הּ
וְיָדְע֖וּ כִּֽי־אֲנִ֥י יְהוִֽה׃
16 קִינָ֥ה הִיא֙ וְק֣וֹנְנ֔וּהָ
בְּנ֥וֹת הַגּוֹיִ֖ם תְּקוֹנֵ֣נָּה אוֹתָ֑הּ
עַל־מִצְרַ֙יִם֙ וְעַל־כָּל־הֲמוֹנָ֔הּ תְּקוֹנֵ֣נָּה
אוֹתָ֑הּ
נְאֻ֖ם אֲדֹנָ֥י יְהוִֽה׃ פ

---

c-c   Septuagint reads "captives."

17In the twelfth year, on the fifteenth day of the month,*d* the word of the LORD came to me: 18*e*O mortal, wail [the dirge]—along with the women of the mighty nations—over the masses of Egypt, accompanying their descent to the lowest part of the netherworld, among those who have gone down into the Pit. 19*f*-Whom do you surpass in beauty? Down with you, and be laid to rest with the uncircumcised! 20They shall lie amid those slain by the sword,-*f* *e*[amid those slain by] the sword [Egypt] has been dragged and left with all her masses.

21From the depths of Sheol the mightiest of warriors speak to him and his allies; the uncircumcised, the slain by the sword, have gone down and lie [there]. 22Assyria is there with all her company, their graves round about, all of them slain, fallen by the sword. 23Their graves set in the farthest recesses of the Pit, all her company are round about her tomb, all of them slain, fallen by the sword—they who struck terror in the land of the living. 24There too is Elam and all her masses round about her tomb, all of them slain, fallen by the sword—they who descended uncircumcised to the lowest part of the netherworld, who struck terror in the land of the living—now they bear their shame with those who have gone down to the Pit. 25They made a bed for her among the slain, with all her masses; their graves are round about her. They are all uncircumcised, slain by the sword. Though their terror was once spread over the land of the living, they bear their shame with those who have gone into the Pit; they are placed among the slain. 26Meshech and Tubal and all their masses are there; their graves are round about. They are all uncircumcised, pierced through by the sword—they who once struck terror in the land of the living. 27And they do not lie with the fallen uncircumcised warriors,

17 וַיְהִי בִּשְׁתֵּי עֶשְׂרֵה שָׁנָה בַּחֲמִשָּׁה עָשָׂר לַחֹדֶשׁ הָיָה דְבַר־יְהוָה אֵלַי לֵאמֹר׃ 18 בֶּן־אָדָם נְהֵה עַל־הֲמוֹן מִצְרַיִם וְהוֹרִדֵהוּ אוֹתָהּ וּבְנוֹת גּוֹיִם אַדִּרִם אֶל־אֶרֶץ תַּחְתִּיּוֹת אֶת־יוֹרְדֵי בוֹר׃ 19 מִמִּי נָעָמְתָּ רְדָה וְהָשְׁכְּבָה אֶת־עֲרֵלִים׃ 20 בְּתוֹךְ חַלְלֵי־חֶרֶב יִפֹּלוּ חֶרֶב נִתָּנָה מָשְׁכוּ אוֹתָהּ וְכָל־הֲמוֹנֶיהָ׃

21 יְדַבְּרוּ־לוֹ אֵלֵי גִבּוֹרִים מִתּוֹךְ שְׁאוֹל אֶת־עֹזְרָיו יָרְדוּ שָׁכְבוּ הָעֲרֵלִים חַלְלֵי־חָרֶב׃ 22 שָׁם אַשּׁוּר וְכָל־קְהָלָהּ סְבִיבוֹתָיו קִבְרֹתָיו כֻּלָּם חֲלָלִים הַנֹּפְלִים בֶּחָרֶב׃ 23 אֲשֶׁר נִתְּנוּ קִבְרֹתֶיהָ בְּיַרְכְּתֵי־בוֹר וַיְהִי קְהָלָהּ סְבִיבוֹת קְבֻרָתָהּ כֻּלָּם חֲלָלִים נֹפְלִים בַּחֶרֶב אֲשֶׁר־נָתְנוּ חִתִּית בְּאֶרֶץ חַיִּים׃ 24 שָׁם עֵילָם וְכָל־הֲמוֹנָהּ סְבִיבוֹת קְבֻרָתָהּ כֻּלָּם חֲלָלִים הַנֹּפְלִים בַּחֶרֶב אֲשֶׁר־יָרְדוּ עֲרֵלִים ׀ אֶל־אֶרֶץ תַּחְתִּיּוֹת אֲשֶׁר נָתְנוּ חִתִּיתָם בְּאֶרֶץ חַיִּים וַיִּשְׂאוּ כְלִמָּתָם אֶת־יוֹרְדֵי בוֹר׃ 25 בְּתוֹךְ חֲלָלִים נָתְנוּ מִשְׁכָּב לָהּ בְּכָל־הֲמוֹנָהּ סְבִיבוֹתָיו קִבְרֹתֶהָ כֻּלָּם עֲרֵלִים חַלְלֵי־חֶרֶב כִּי־נִתַּן חִתִּיתָם בְּאֶרֶץ חַיִּים וַיִּשְׂאוּ כְלִמָּתָם אֶת־יוֹרְדֵי בוֹר בְּתוֹךְ חֲלָלִים נִתָּן׃ 26 שָׁם מֶשֶׁךְ תֻּבַל וְכָל־הֲמוֹנָהּ סְבִיבוֹתָיו קִבְרוֹתֶיהָ כֻּלָּם עֲרֵלִים מְחֻלְלֵי חֶרֶב כִּי־נָתְנוּ חִתִּיתָם בְּאֶרֶץ חַיִּים׃ 27 וְלֹא יִשְׁכְּבוּ אֶת־גִּבּוֹרִים נֹפְלִים מֵעֲרֵלִים אֲשֶׁר

---

d Presumably the twelfth month; cf. v. 1.
e Construction of these verses uncertain.
f-f Cf. 31.18 ff. and note e on 31.14.

who went down to Sheol with their battle gear, who put their swords beneath their heads and their iniquities*g* upon their bones—for the terror of the warriors was upon the land of the living. [28]And you too shall be shattered amid the uncircumcised, and lie among those slain by the sword. [29]Edom is there, her kings and all her chieftains, who, for all their might, are laid among those who are slain by the sword; they too lie with the uncircumcised and with those who have gone down to the Pit. [30]All the princes of the north and all the Sidonians are there, who went down in disgrace with the slain, in spite of the terror that their might inspired; and they lie, uncircumcised, with those who are slain by the sword, and bear their shame with those who have gone down to the Pit.

[31]These Pharaoh shall see, and he shall be consoled for all his masses, those of Pharaoh's men slain by the sword and all his army— declares the Lord GOD. [32]*h*-I strike terror into the land of the living; Pharaoh-*h* and all his masses are laid among the uncircumcised, along with those who were slain by the sword—said the Lord GOD.

33

The word of the LORD came to me: [2]O mortal, speak to your fellow countrymen and say to them: When I bring the sword against a country, the citizens of that country take one of their number and appoint him their watchman. [3]Suppose he sees the sword advancing against the country, and he blows the horn and warns the people. [4]If anybody hears the sound of the horn but ignores the warning, and the sword comes and dispatches him, his blood shall be on his own head. [5]Since he heard the sound of the horn but ignored the warning, his bloodguilt shall be upon himself; had he taken

---

g   *Emendation yields "shields."*
h-h   *Emendation yields "because he struck terror in the land of the living, Pharaoh."*

יָרְדוּ־שָׁא֜וּל בִּכְלֵי־מִלְחַמְתָּם֒ וַיִּתְּנ֣וּ אֶת־חַרְבוֹתָם֙ תַּ֣חַת רָאשֵׁיהֶ֔ם וַתְּהִ֤י עֲוֺנֹתָם֙ עַל־עַצְמוֹתָ֔ם כִּֽי־חִתִּ֥ית גִּבּוֹרִ֖ים בְּאֶ֥רֶץ חַיִּֽים׃ [28] וְאַתָּ֗ה בְּת֧וֹךְ עֲרֵלִ֛ים תִּשָּׁבַ֥ר וְתִשְׁכַּ֖ב אֶת־חַלְלֵי־חָֽרֶב׃ [29] שָׁ֣מָּה אֱד֤וֹם מְלָכֶ֙יהָ֙ וְכׇל־נְשִׂיאֶ֔יהָ אֲשֶׁר־נִתְּנ֥וּ בִגְבוּרָתָ֖ם אֶת־חַלְלֵי־חָ֑רֶב הֵ֛מָּה אֶת־עֲרֵלִ֥ים יִשְׁכָּ֖בוּ וְאֶת־יֹ֥רְדֵי בֽוֹר׃ [30] שָׁ֣מָּה נְסִיכֵ֥י צָפ֛וֹן כֻּלָּ֖ם וְכׇל־צִֽדֹנִ֑י אֲשֶׁר־יָרְד֣וּ אֶת־חֲלָלִ֗ים בְּחִתִּיתָ֥ם מִגְּבֽוּרָתָם֙ בּוֹשִׁ֔ים וַיִּשְׁכְּב֤וּ עֲרֵלִים֙ אֶת־חַלְלֵי־חֶ֔רֶב וַיִּשְׂא֥וּ כְלִמָּתָ֖ם אֶת־י֥וֹרְדֵי בֽוֹר׃

[31] אוֹתָ֨ם יִרְאֶ֤ה פַרְעֹה֙ וְנִחַ֣ם עַל־כׇּל־הֲמוֹנ֔וֹ חַלְלֵי־חֶ֙רֶב֙ פַּרְעֹ֣ה וְכׇל־חֵיל֔וֹ נְאֻ֖ם אֲדֹנָ֥י יְהֹוִֽה׃ [32] כִּֽי־נָתַ֥תִּי אֶת־חִתִּיתִ֖י בְּאֶ֣רֶץ חַיִּ֑ים וְהֻשְׁכַּב֩ בְּת֨וֹךְ עֲרֵלִ֜ים אֶת־חַלְלֵי־חֶ֗רֶב פַּרְעֹה֙ וְכׇל־הֲמוֹנ֔וֹ נְאֻ֖ם אֲדֹנָ֥י יְהֹוִֽה׃ פ

לג

וַיְהִ֥י דְבַר־יְהֹוָ֖ה אֵלַ֥י לֵאמֹֽר׃ [2] בֶּן־אָדָ֗ם דַּבֵּ֤ר אֶל־בְּנֵֽי־עַמְּךָ֙ וְאָמַרְתָּ֣ אֲלֵיהֶ֔ם אֶ֕רֶץ כִּֽי־אָבִ֥יא עָלֶ֖יהָ חָ֑רֶב וְלָקְח֣וּ עַם־הָאָ֗רֶץ אִ֤ישׁ אֶחָד֙ מִקְצֵיהֶ֔ם וְנָתְנ֥וּ אֹת֛וֹ לָהֶ֖ם לְצֹפֶֽה׃ [3] וְרָאָ֥ה אֶת־הַחֶ֖רֶב בָּאָ֣ה עַל־הָאָ֑רֶץ וְתָקַ֥ע בַּשּׁוֹפָ֖ר וְהִזְהִ֥יר אֶת־הָעָֽם׃ [4] וְשָׁמַ֨ע הַשֹּׁמֵ֜עַ אֶת־ק֣וֹל הַשּׁוֹפָ֗ר וְלֹ֣א נִזְהָ֔ר וַתָּ֥בוֹא חֶ֖רֶב וַתִּקָּחֵ֑הוּ דָּמ֥וֹ בְרֹאשׁ֖וֹ יִהְיֶֽה׃ [5] אֵת֩ ק֨וֹל הַשּׁוֹפָ֤ר שָׁמַע֙ וְלֹ֣א נִזְהָ֔ר דָּמ֖וֹ בּ֣וֹ יִהְיֶ֑ה וְה֖וּא נִזְהָ֥ר

the warning, he would have saved his life. ⁶But if the watchman sees the sword advancing and does not blow the horn, so that the people are not warned, and the sword comes and destroys one of them, that person was destroyed for his own sins; however, I will demand a reckoning for his blood from the watchman.

⁷Now, O mortal, I have appointed you a watchman for the House of Israel; and whenever you hear a message from My mouth, you must transmit My warning to them. ⁸When I say to the wicked, "Wicked man, you shall die," but you have not spoken to warn the wicked man against his way, he, that wicked man, shall die for his sins, but I will demand a reckoning for his blood from you. ⁹But if you have warned the wicked man to turn back from his way, and he has not turned from his way, he shall die for his own sins, but you will have saved your life.

¹⁰Now, O mortal, say to the House of Israel: This is what you have been saying: "Our transgressions and our sins weigh heavily upon us; we are sick at heart about them. How can we survive?" ¹¹Say to them: As I live—declares the Lord God—it is not My desire that the wicked shall die, but that the wicked turn from his [evil] ways and live. Turn back, turn back from your evil ways, that you may not die, O House of Israel!

¹²Now, O mortal, say to your fellow countrymen: The righteousness of the righteous shall not save him when he transgresses, nor shall the wickedness of the wicked cause him to stumble when he turns back from his wickedness. The righteous shall not survive through ᵃ-his righteousness-ᵃ when he sins. ¹³When I say of the righteous "He shall surely live," and, relying on his righteousness, he commits iniquity, none of his righteous deeds shall be remembered; but for the iniquity that he has committed he shall die. ¹⁴So, too, when I say to the wicked, "You

נַפְשׁ֥וֹ מִלֵּֽט׃ ⁶וְֽהַצֹּפֶ֡ה כִּֽי־יִרְאֶ֣ה אֶת־ הַחֶ֩רֶב֩ בָּאָ֨ה וְלֹֽא־תָקַ֜ע בַּשּׁוֹפָ֗ר וְהָעָ֣ם לֹֽא־נִזְהָ֗ר וַתָּב֥וֹא חֶ֙רֶב֙ וַתִּקַּ֣ח מֵהֶ֣ם נָ֔פֶשׁ ה֥וּא בַּעֲוֺנ֖וֹ נִלְקָ֑ח וְדָמ֥וֹ מִיַּֽד־הַצֹּפֶ֖ה אֶדְרֹֽשׁ׃ ס

⁷וְאַתָּ֣ה בֶן־אָדָ֔ם צֹפֶ֥ה נְתַתִּ֖יךָ לְבֵ֣ית יִשְׂרָאֵ֑ל וְשָׁמַעְתָּ֤ מִפִּי֙ דָּבָ֔ר וְהִזְהַרְתָּ֥ אֹתָ֖ם מִמֶּֽנִּי׃ ⁸בְּאׇמְרִ֣י לָרָשָׁ֗ע רָשָׁע֙ מ֣וֹת תָּמ֔וּת וְלֹ֣א דִבַּ֔רְתָּ לְהַזְהִ֥יר רָשָׁ֖ע מִדַּרְכּ֑וֹ ה֤וּא רָשָׁע֙ בַּעֲוֺנ֣וֹ יָמ֔וּת וְדָמ֖וֹ מִיָּדְךָ֥ אֲבַקֵּֽשׁ׃ ⁹וְ֠אַתָּ֠ה כִּֽי־הִזְהַ֨רְתָּ רָשָׁ֤ע מִדַּרְכּוֹ֙ לָשׁ֣וּב מִמֶּ֔נָּה וְלֹא־שָׁ֖ב מִדַּרְכּ֑וֹ ה֚וּא בַּעֲוֺנ֣וֹ יָמ֔וּת וְאַתָּ֖ה נַפְשְׁךָ֥ הִצַּֽלְתָּ׃ ס

¹⁰וְאַתָּ֣ה בֶן־אָדָ֗ם אֱמֹר֙ אֶל־בֵּ֣ית יִשְׂרָאֵ֔ל כֵּ֤ן אֲמַרְתֶּם֙ לֵאמֹ֔ר כִּֽי־פְשָׁעֵ֥ינוּ וְחַטֹּאתֵ֖ינוּ עָלֵ֑ינוּ וּבָ֛ם אֲנַ֥חְנוּ נְמַקִּ֖ים וְאֵ֥יךְ נִֽחְיֶֽה׃ ¹¹אֱמֹ֨ר אֲלֵיהֶ֜ם חַי־אָ֣נִי ׀ נְאֻ֣ם ׀ אֲדֹנָ֣י יֱהֹוִ֗ה אִם־אֶחְפֹּץ֙ בְּמ֣וֹת הָרָשָׁ֔ע כִּ֣י אִם־בְּשׁ֥וּב רָשָׁ֛ע מִדַּרְכּ֖וֹ וְחָיָ֑ה שׁ֣וּבוּ שׁ֗וּבוּ מִדַּרְכֵיכֶ֤ם הָֽרָעִים֙ וְלָ֣מָּה תָמ֔וּתוּ בֵּ֖ית יִשְׂרָאֵֽל׃ פ

¹²וְאַתָּ֣ה בֶן־אָדָ֗ם אֱמֹ֤ר אֶל־בְּנֵֽי־עַמְּךָ֙ צִדְקַ֣ת הַצַּדִּ֗יק לֹ֤א תַצִּילֶ֙נּוּ֙ בְּי֣וֹם פִּשְׁע֔וֹ וְרִשְׁעַ֤ת הָֽרָשָׁע֙ לֹֽא־יִכָּ֣שֶׁל בָּ֔הּ בְּי֖וֹם שׁוּב֣וֹ מֵֽרִשְׁע֑וֹ וְצַדִּ֗יק לֹ֥א יוּכַ֛ל לִֽחְי֥וֹת בָּ֖הּ בְּי֥וֹם חֲטֹאתֽוֹ׃ ¹³בְּאׇמְרִ֤י לַצַּדִּיק֙ חָיֹ֣ה יִֽחְיֶ֔ה וְהֽוּא־בָטַ֥ח עַל־צִדְקָת֖וֹ וְעָ֣שָׂה עָ֑וֶל כׇּל־ צִדְקֹתָו֙ לֹ֣א תִזָּכַ֔רְנָה וּבְעַוְל֥וֹ אֲשֶׁר־ עָשָׂ֖ה בּ֣וֹ יָמֽוּת׃ ¹⁴וּבְאׇמְרִ֥י לָֽרָשָׁ֖ע מ֥וֹת

shall die," and he turns back from his sinfulness and does what is just and right—15if the wicked man restores a pledge, makes good what he has taken by robbery, follows the laws of life,[b] and does not commit iniquity—he shall live, he shall not die. 16None of the sins that he committed shall be remembered against him; since he does what is just and right, he shall live.

17Your fellow countrymen say, "The way of the Lord is unfair." But it is their way that is unfair! 18When a righteous man turns away from his righteous deeds and commits iniquity, he shall die [c-for it.-c] 19And when a wicked man turns back from his wickedness and does what is just and right, it is he who shall live by virtue of these things. 20And will you say, "The way of the Lord is unfair"? I will judge each one of you according to his ways, O House of Israel!

21In the twelfth year of our exile, on the fifth day of the tenth month, a fugitive came to me from Jerusalem and reported, "The city has fallen." 22Now the hand of the Lord had come upon me the evening before the fugitive arrived, and He opened my mouth before he came to me in the morning; thus my mouth was opened and I was no longer speechless.

23The word of the Lord came to me: 24O mortal, those who live in these ruins in the land of Israel argue, "Abraham was but one man, yet he was granted possession of the land. We are many; surely, the land has been given as a possession to us." 25Therefore say to them: Thus said the Lord God: You eat with the blood, you raise your eyes to your fetishes, and you shed blood—yet you expect to possess the land! 26You have relied on your sword, you have committed abominations, you have all defiled other men's wives—yet you expect to possess the land!

---

b Cf. Lev. 18.5.
c-c Or "in spite of them," i.e., his righteous deeds.

תָּמוּת וְשָׁב מֵחַטָּאתוֹ וְעָשָׂה מִשְׁפָּט וּצְדָקָה: 15 חֲבֹל יָשִׁיב רָשָׁע גְּזֵלָה יְשַׁלֵּם בְּחֻקּוֹת הַחַיִּים הָלַךְ לְבִלְתִּי עֲשׂוֹת עָוֶל חָיוֹ יִחְיֶה לֹא יָמוּת: 16 כָּל־חַטֹּאתָו אֲשֶׁר חָטָא לֹא תִזָּכַרְנָה לוֹ מִשְׁפָּט וּצְדָקָה עָשָׂה חָיוֹ יִחְיֶה: 17 וְאָמְרוּ בְּנֵי עַמְּךָ לֹא יִתָּכֵן דֶּרֶךְ אֲדֹנָי וְהֵמָּה דַּרְכָּם לֹא־יִתָּכֵן: 18 בְּשׁוּב־צַדִּיק מִצִּדְקָתוֹ וְעָשָׂה עָוֶל וּמֵת בָּהֶם: 19 וּבְשׁוּב רָשָׁע מֵרִשְׁעָתוֹ וְעָשָׂה מִשְׁפָּט וּצְדָקָה עֲלֵיהֶם הוּא יִחְיֶה: 20 וַאֲמַרְתֶּם לֹא יִתָּכֵן דֶּרֶךְ אֲדֹנָי אִישׁ כִּדְרָכָיו אֶשְׁפּוֹט אֶתְכֶם בֵּית יִשְׂרָאֵל: פ

21 וַיְהִי בִּשְׁתֵּי עֶשְׂרֵה שָׁנָה בָּעֲשִׂרִי בַּחֲמִשָּׁה לַחֹדֶשׁ לְגָלוּתֵנוּ בָּא־אֵלַי הַפָּלִיט מִירוּשָׁלַ͏ִם לֵאמֹר הֻכְּתָה הָעִיר: 22 וְיַד־יְהוָה הָיְתָה אֵלַי בָּעֶרֶב לִפְנֵי בּוֹא הַפָּלִיט וַיִּפְתַּח אֶת־פִּי עַד־בּוֹא אֵלַי בַּבֹּקֶר וַיִּפָּתַח פִּי וְלֹא נֶאֱלַמְתִּי עוֹד: פ

23 וַיְהִי דְבַר־יְהוָה אֵלַי לֵאמֹר: 24 בֶּן־אָדָם יֹשְׁבֵי הֶחֳרָבוֹת הָאֵלֶּה עַל־אַדְמַת יִשְׂרָאֵל אֹמְרִים לֵאמֹר אֶחָד הָיָה אַבְרָהָם וַיִּירַשׁ אֶת־הָאָרֶץ וַאֲנַחְנוּ רַבִּים לָנוּ נִתְּנָה הָאָרֶץ לְמוֹרָשָׁה: ס 25 לָכֵן אֱמֹר אֲלֵיהֶם כֹּה־אָמַר ׀ אֲדֹנָי ׀ יְהוִֹה עַל־הַדָּם ׀ תֹּאכֵלוּ וְעֵינֵכֶם תִּשְׂאוּ אֶל־גִּלּוּלֵיכֶם וְדָם תִּשְׁפֹּכוּ וְהָאָרֶץ תִּירָשׁוּ: 26 עֲמַדְתֶּם עַל־חַרְבְּכֶם עֲשִׂיתֶן תּוֹעֵבָה וְאִישׁ אֶת־אֵשֶׁת רֵעֵהוּ טִמֵּאתֶם וְהָאָרֶץ תִּירָשׁוּ: ס

27Thus shall you speak to them: Thus said the Lord GOD: As I live, those who are in the ruins shall fall by the sword, and those who are in the open I have allotted as food to the beasts, and those who are in the strongholds and caves shall die by pestilence. 28I will make the land a desolate waste, and her proud glory shall cease; and the mountains of Israel shall be desolate, with none passing through. 29And they shall know that I am the LORD, when I make the land a desolate waste on account of all the abominations which they have committed.

30Note well, O mortal: your fellow countrymen who converse about you by the walls and in the doorways of their houses and say to each other and propose to one another, "Come and hear what word has issued from the LORD." 31They will come to you *d*-in crowds and sit before you in throngs-*d* and will hear your words, but they will not obey them. For *e*-they produce nothing but lust with their mouths;-*e* and their hearts pursue nothing but gain. 32To them you are just a singer of bawdy songs, who has a sweet voice and plays skillfully; they hear your words, but will not obey them. 33But when it*f* comes—and come it will—they shall know that a prophet has been among them.

34

The word of the LORD came to me: 2O mortal, prophesy against the shepherds*a* of Israel. Prophesy, and say to them:

To the shepherds: Thus said the Lord GOD: Ah, you shepherds of Israel, who have been tending yourselves! Is it not the flock that the shepherds ought to tend? 3You partake of the fat,*b* you clothe yourselves with the wool, and

27 כֹּה־תֹאמַ֣ר אֲלֵהֶ֗ם כֹּֽה־אָמַר֮ אֲדֹנָ֣י יְהֹוִה֒ חַי־אָ֗נִי אִם־לֹ֞א אֲשֶׁ֤ר בֶּֽחֳרָבוֹת֙ בַּחֶ֣רֶב יִפֹּ֔לוּ וַֽאֲשֶׁר֙ עַל־פְּנֵ֣י הַשָּׂדֶ֔ה לַחַיָּ֥ה נְתַתִּ֖יו לְאׇכְל֑וֹ וַֽאֲשֶׁ֛ר בַּמְּצָד֥וֹת וּבַמְּעָר֖וֹת בַּדֶּ֥בֶר יָמֽוּתוּ׃ 28 וְנָתַתִּ֤י אֶת־הָאָ֙רֶץ֙ שְׁמָמָ֣ה וּמְשַׁמָּ֔ה וְנִשְׁבַּ֖ת גְּא֣וֹן עֻזָּ֑הּ וְשָֽׁמְמ֛וּ הָרֵ֥י יִשְׂרָאֵ֖ל מֵאֵ֥ין עוֹבֵֽר׃ 29 וְיָדְע֖וּ כִּֽי־אֲנִ֣י יְהֹוָ֑ה בְּתִתִּ֤י אֶת־הָאָ֙רֶץ֙ שְׁמָמָ֣ה וּמְשַׁמָּ֔ה עַ֥ל כׇּל־תּֽוֹעֲבֹתָ֖ם אֲשֶׁ֥ר עָשֽׂוּ׃ ס

30 וְאַתָּ֣ה בֶן־אָדָ֗ם בְּנֵ֤י עַמְּךָ֙ הַנִּדְבָּרִ֣ים בְּךָ֔ אֵ֣צֶל הַקִּיר֔וֹת וּבְפִתְחֵ֖י הַבָּתִּ֑ים וְדִבֶּר־חַ֣ד אֶת־אַחַ֗ד אִ֤ישׁ אֶת־אָחִיו֙ לֵאמֹ֔ר בֹּֽאוּ־נָ֣א וְשִׁמְע֔וּ מָ֣ה הַדָּבָ֔ר הַיּוֹצֵ֖א מֵאֵ֥ת יְהֹוָֽה׃ 31 וְיָב֣וֹאוּ אֵ֠לֶ֠יךָ כִּמְבוֹא־עָ֞ם וְיֵשְׁב֣וּ לְפָנֶ֗יךָ עַמִּי֙ וְשָֽׁמְעוּ֙ אֶת־דְּבָרֶ֔יךָ וְאוֹתָ֖ם לֹ֣א יַֽעֲשׂ֑וּ כִּֽי־עֲגָבִ֤ים בְּפִיהֶם֙ הֵ֣מָּה עֹשִׂ֔ים אַֽחֲרֵ֥י בִצְעָ֖ם לִבָּ֥ם הֹלֵֽךְ׃ 32 וְהִנְּךָ֤ לָהֶם֙ כְּשִׁ֣יר עֲגָבִ֔ים יְפֵ֥ה ק֖וֹל וּמֵטִ֣ב נַגֵּ֑ן וְשָֽׁמְעוּ֙ אֶת־דְּבָרֶ֔יךָ וְעֹשִׂ֥ים אֵינָ֖ם אוֹתָֽם׃ 33 וּבְבֹאָ֥הּ הִנֵּ֣ה בָאָ֑ה וְיָ֣דְע֔וּ כִּ֥י נָבִ֖יא הָיָ֥ה בְתוֹכָֽם׃ ס

לד

1 וַיְהִ֥י דְבַר־יְהֹוָ֖ה אֵלַ֥י לֵאמֹֽר׃ 2 בֶּן־אָדָ֕ם הִנָּבֵ֖א עַל־רוֹעֵ֣י יִשְׂרָאֵ֑ל הִנָּבֵ֣א וְאָֽמַרְתָּ֩ אֲלֵיהֶ֨ם לָֽרֹעִ֜ים כֹּ֥ה אָמַ֣ר ׀ אֲדֹנָ֣י יְהֹוִ֗ה ה֣וֹי רֹעֵֽי־יִשְׂרָאֵל֙ אֲשֶׁ֤ר הָיוּ֙ רֹעִ֣ים אוֹתָ֔ם הֲל֣וֹא הַצֹּ֔אן יִרְע֖וּ הָרֹעִֽים׃ 3 אֶת־הַחֵ֤לֶב תֹּאכֵ֙לוּ֙ וְאֶת־הַצֶּ֣מֶר תִּלְבָּ֔שׁוּ הַבְּרִיאָ֣ה

---

d-d Meaning of Heb. uncertain. Lit. "as a people come, and sit before you as My people."
e-e Meaning of Heb. uncertain.
f I.e., the punishment predicted.

a I.e., rulers.
b Septuagint and Vulgate, reading the Hebrew consonants with different vowels, translate "milk."

you slaughter the fatlings; but you do not tend the flock. ⁴You have not sustained the weak, healed the sick, or bandaged the injured; you have not brought back the strayed, or looked for the lost; but you have driven them with harsh rigor, ⁵and they have been scattered for want of anyone to tend them; scattered, they have become prey for every wild beast. ⁶My sheep stray through all the mountains and over every lofty hill; My flock is scattered all over the face of the earth, with none to take thought of them and none to seek them. ⁷Hear then, O shepherds, the word of the Lord! ⁸As I live—declares the Lord God: Because My flock has been a spoil—My flock has been a prey for all the wild beasts, for want of anyone to tend them since My shepherds have not taken thought of My flock, for the shepherds tended themselves instead of tending the flock—⁹hear indeed, O shepherds, the word of the Lord: ¹⁰Thus said the Lord God: I am going to deal with the shepherds! I will demand a reckoning of them for My flock, and I will dismiss them from tending the flock. The shepherds shall not tend themselves any more; for I will rescue My flock from their mouths, and it shall not be their prey. ¹¹For thus said the Lord God: Here am I! I am going to take thought for My flock and I will seek them out. ¹²As a shepherd seeks out his flock when some [animals] in his flock have gotten separated, so I will seek out My flock, I will rescue them from all the places to which they were scattered on a day of cloud and gloom. ¹³I will take them out from the peoples and gather them from the countries, and I will bring them to their own land, and will pasture them on the mountains of Israel, by the watercourses and in all the settled portions of the land. ¹⁴I will feed them in good grazing land, and the lofty hills of Israel shall be their pasture. There, in the hills of Israel, they shall lie down in a good pasture and shall

תִּזְבְּחוּ הַצֹּאן לֹא תִרְעוּ: 4 אֶת־הַנַּחְלוֹת לֹא חִזַּקְתֶּם וְאֶת־הַחוֹלָה לֹא־רִפֵּאתֶם וְלַנִּשְׁבֶּרֶת לֹא חֲבַשְׁתֶּם וְאֶת־הַנִּדַּחַת לֹא הֲשֵׁבֹתֶם וְאֶת־הָאֹבֶדֶת לֹא בִקַּשְׁתֶּם וּבְחָזְקָה רְדִיתֶם אֹתָם וּבְפָרֶךְ: 5 וַתְּפוּצֶינָה מִבְּלִי רֹעֶה וַתִּהְיֶינָה לְאָכְלָה לְכָל־חַיַּת הַשָּׂדֶה וַתְּפוּצֶינָה: 6 יִשְׁגּוּ צֹאנִי בְּכָל־הֶהָרִים וְעַל כָּל־גִּבְעָה רָמָה וְעַל כָּל־פְּנֵי הָאָרֶץ נָפֹצוּ צֹאנִי וְאֵין דּוֹרֵשׁ וְאֵין מְבַקֵּשׁ: 7 לָכֵן רֹעִים שִׁמְעוּ אֶת־דְּבַר יְהֹוָה: 8 חַי־אָנִי נְאֻם | אֲדֹנָי יֱהֹוִה אִם־לֹא יַעַן הֱיוֹת־צֹאנִי | לָבַז וַתִּהְיֶינָה צֹאנִי לְאָכְלָה לְכָל־חַיַּת הַשָּׂדֶה מֵאֵין רֹעֶה וְלֹא־דָרְשׁוּ רֹעַי אֶת־צֹאנִי וַיִּרְעוּ הָרֹעִים אוֹתָם וְאֶת־צֹאנִי לֹא רָעוּ: ס 9 לָכֵן הָרֹעִים שִׁמְעוּ דְּבַר־יְהֹוָה: 10 כֹּה־אָמַר אֲדֹנָי יֱהֹוִה הִנְנִי אֶל־הָרֹעִים וְדָרַשְׁתִּי אֶת־צֹאנִי מִיָּדָם וְהִשְׁבַּתִּים מֵרְעוֹת צֹאן וְלֹא־יִרְעוּ עוֹד הָרֹעִים אוֹתָם וְהִצַּלְתִּי צֹאנִי מִפִּיהֶם וְלֹא־תִהְיֶין לָהֶם לְאָכְלָה: ס 11 כִּי כֹּה אָמַר אֲדֹנָי יֱהֹוִה הִנְנִי־אָנִי וְדָרַשְׁתִּי אֶת־צֹאנִי וּבִקַּרְתִּים: 12 כְּבַקָּרַת רֹעֶה עֶדְרוֹ בְּיוֹם־הֱיוֹתוֹ בְתוֹךְ־צֹאנוֹ נִפְרָשׁוֹת כֵּן אֲבַקֵּר אֶת־צֹאנִי וְהִצַּלְתִּי אֶתְהֶם מִכָּל־הַמְּקוֹמֹת אֲשֶׁר נָפֹצוּ שָׁם בְּיוֹם עָנָן וַעֲרָפֶל: 13 וְהוֹצֵאתִים מִן־הָעַמִּים וְקִבַּצְתִּים מִן־הָאֲרָצוֹת וַהֲבִיאֹתִים אֶל־אַדְמָתָם וּרְעִיתִים אֶל־הָרֵי יִשְׂרָאֵל בָּאֲפִיקִים וּבְכֹל מוֹשְׁבֵי הָאָרֶץ: 14 בְּמִרְעֶה־טּוֹב אֶרְעֶה אֹתָם וּבְהָרֵי מְרוֹם־יִשְׂרָאֵל יִהְיֶה נְוֵהֶם שָׁם תִּרְבַּצְנָה בְּנָוֶה טּוֹב וּמִרְעֶה שָׁמֵן תִּרְעֶינָה

feed on rich grazing land. ¹⁵I Myself will graze My flock, and I Myself will let them lie down—declares the Lord God. ¹⁶I will look for the lost, and I will bring back the strayed; I will bandage the injured, and I will sustain the weak; and the fat and healthy ones I will destroy.ᶜ I will tend them rightly.

¹⁷And as for you, My flock, thus said the Lord God: I am going to judge between one animal and another.

To the rams and the bucks: ¹⁸Is it not enough for you to graze on choice grazing ground, but you must also trample with your feet what is left from your grazing? And is it not enough for you to drink ᵈ-clear water,-ᵈ but you must also muddy with your feet what is left? ¹⁹And must My flock graze on what your feet have trampled and drink what your feet have muddied? ²⁰Assuredly, thus said the Lord God to them: Here am I, I am going to decide between the stout animals and the lean. ²¹Because you pushed with flank and shoulder against the feeble ones and butted them with your horns until you scattered them abroad, ²²I will rescue My flock and they shall no longer be a spoil. I will decide between one animal and another.

²³Then I will appoint a single shepherd over them to tend them—My servant David. He shall tend them, he shall be a shepherd to them. ²⁴I the Lord will be their God, and My servant David shall be a ruler among them—I the Lord have spoken. ²⁵And I will grant them a covenant of friendship. I will banish vicious beasts from their land, and they shall live secure in the wasteland, they shall even sleep in the woodland. ²⁶I will make ᵉ-these and the environs of My hill-ᵉ a blessing: I will send down the rain in its season, rains that bring blessing. ²⁷The trees of the field shall yield their fruit and the land shall yield its

---

אֶל־הָרֵי יִשְׂרָאֵל׃ 15 אֲנִי אֶרְעֶה צֹאנִי וַאֲנִי אַרְבִּיצֵם נְאֻם אֲדֹנָי יְהוִֹה׃ 16 אֶת־הָאֹבֶדֶת אֲבַקֵּשׁ וְאֶת־הַנִּדַּחַת אָשִׁיב וְלַנִּשְׁבֶּרֶת אֶחֱבֹשׁ וְאֶת־הַחוֹלָה אֲחַזֵּק וְאֶת־הַשְּׁמֵנָה וְאֶת־הַחֲזָקָה אַשְׁמִיד אֶרְעֶנָּה בְמִשְׁפָּט׃ 17 וְאַתֵּנָה צֹאנִי כֹּה אָמַר אֲדֹנָי יְהוִֹה הִנְנִי שֹׁפֵט בֵּין־שֶׂה לָשֶׂה לָאֵילִים וְלָעַתּוּדִים׃ 18 הַמְעַט מִכֶּם הַמִּרְעֶה הַטּוֹב תִּרְעוּ וְיֶתֶר מִרְעֵיכֶם תִּרְמְסוּ בְּרַגְלֵיכֶם וּמִשְׁקַע־מַיִם תִּשְׁתּוּ וְאֵת הַנּוֹתָרִים בְּרַגְלֵיכֶם תִּרְפֹּשׂוּן׃ 19 וְצֹאנִי מִרְמַס רַגְלֵיכֶם תִּרְעֶינָה וּמִרְפַּשׂ רַגְלֵיכֶם תִּשְׁתֶּינָה׃ ס 20 לָכֵן כֹּה אָמַר אֲדֹנָי יְהוִֹה אֲלֵיהֶם הִנְנִי־אָנִי וְשָׁפַטְתִּי בֵּין־שֶׂה בִרְיָה וּבֵין שֶׂה רָזֶה׃ 21 יַעַן בְּצַד וּבְכָתֵף תֶּהְדֹּפוּ וּבְקַרְנֵיכֶם תְּנַגְּחוּ כָּל־הַנַּחְלוֹת עַד אֲשֶׁר הֲפִיצוֹתֶם אוֹתָנָה אֶל־הַחוּצָה׃ 22 וְהוֹשַׁעְתִּי לְצֹאנִי וְלֹא־תִהְיֶינָה עוֹד לָבַז וְשָׁפַטְתִּי בֵּין שֶׂה לָשֶׂה׃ 23 וַהֲקִמֹתִי עֲלֵיהֶם רֹעֶה אֶחָד וְרָעָה אֶתְהֶן אֵת עַבְדִּי דָוִיד הוּא יִרְעֶה אֹתָם וְהוּא־יִהְיֶה לָהֶן לְרֹעֶה׃ 24 וַאֲנִי יְהוָה אֶהְיֶה לָהֶם לֵאלֹהִים וְעַבְדִּי דָוִד נָשִׂיא בְתוֹכָם אֲנִי יְהוָה דִּבַּרְתִּי׃ 25 וְכָרַתִּי לָהֶם בְּרִית שָׁלוֹם וְהִשְׁבַּתִּי חַיָּה־רָעָה מִן־הָאָרֶץ וְיָשְׁבוּ בַמִּדְבָּר לָבֶטַח וְיָשְׁנוּ בַּיְּעָרִים׃ 26 וְנָתַתִּי אוֹתָם וּסְבִיבוֹת גִּבְעָתִי בְּרָכָה וְהוֹרַדְתִּי הַגֶּשֶׁם בְּעִתּוֹ גִּשְׁמֵי בְרָכָה יִהְיוּ׃ 27 וְנָתַן עֵץ הַשָּׂדֶה אֶת־פִּרְיוֹ וְהָאָרֶץ

---

c   Several ancient versions read "guard."
d-d Lit. "water that has settled."
e-e Meaning of Heb. uncertain.

produce. [My people] shall continue secure on its own soil. They shall know that I am the LORD when I break the bars of their yoke and rescue them from those who enslave them. [28] They shall no longer be a spoil for the nations, and the beasts of the earth shall not devour them; they shall dwell secure and untroubled. [29] I shall establish for them *e-a planting of renown;-e* they shall no more be carried off by famine, and they shall not have to bear again the taunts of the nations.*f* [30] They shall know that I the LORD their God am with them and they, the House of Israel, are My people—declares the Lord GOD.

[31] For you, My flock, flock that I tend, are men; and I am your God—declares the Lord GOD.

35 The word of the LORD came to me: [2] O mortal, set your face against Mount Seir and prophesy against it. [3] Say to it: Thus said the Lord GOD: I am going to deal with you, Mount Seir: I will stretch out My hand against you and make you an utter waste. [4] I will turn your towns into ruins, and you shall be a desolation; then you shall know that I am the LORD. [5] Because you harbored an ancient hatred and handed the people of Israel over to the sword in their time of calamity, the time set for their punishment— [6] assuredly, as I live, declares the Lord GOD, *a-I will doom you with blood; blood shall pursue you; I swear that, for your bloodthirsty hatred, blood shall pursue you.-a* [7] I will make Mount Seir an utter waste, and I will keep all passersby away from it. [8] I will cover its mountains with the slain; men slain by the sword shall lie on your hills, in your valleys, and in all your watercourses. [9] I will make you a desolation for all time; your towns shall never be inhabited. And you shall know that I am the LORD.

תִּתֵּן יְבוּלָהּ וְהָיוּ עַל־אַדְמָתָם לָבֶטַח
וְיָדְעוּ כִּי־אֲנִי יְהֹוָה בְּשִׁבְרִי אֶת־מֹטוֹת
עֻלָּם וְהִצַּלְתִּים מִיַּד הָעֹבְדִים בָּהֶם:
28 וְלֹא־יִהְיוּ עוֹד בַּז לַגּוֹיִם וְחַיַּת הָאָרֶץ
לֹא תֹאכְלֵם וְיָשְׁבוּ לָבֶטַח וְאֵין מַחֲרִיד:
29 וַהֲקִמֹתִי לָהֶם מַטָּע לְשֵׁם וְלֹא־יִהְיוּ
עוֹד אֲסֻפֵי רָעָב בָּאָרֶץ וְלֹא־יִשְׂאוּ עוֹד
כְּלִמַּת הַגּוֹיִם: 30 וְיָדְעוּ כִּי אֲנִי יְהֹוָה
אֱלֹהֵיהֶם אִתָּם וְהֵמָּה עַמִּי בֵּית יִשְׂרָאֵל
נְאֻם אֲדֹנָי יְהֹוִה:
31 וְאַתֵּן צֹאנִי צֹאן מַרְעִיתִי אָדָם אַתֶּם
אֲנִי אֱלֹהֵיכֶם נְאֻם אֲדֹנָי יְהֹוִה: פ

לה וַיְהִי דְבַר־יְהֹוָה אֵלַי לֵאמֹר:
2 בֶּן־אָדָם שִׂים פָּנֶיךָ עַל־הַר שֵׂעִיר וְהִנָּבֵא
עָלָיו: 3 וְאָמַרְתָּ לּוֹ כֹּה אָמַר אֲדֹנָי יְהֹוִה
הִנְנִי אֵלֶיךָ הַר־שֵׂעִיר וְנָטִיתִי יָדִי עָלֶיךָ
וּנְתַתִּיךָ שְׁמָמָה וּמְשַׁמָּה: 4 עָרֶיךָ חָרְבָּה
אָשִׂים וְאַתָּה שְׁמָמָה תִהְיֶה וְיָדַעְתָּ כִּי־
אֲנִי יְהֹוָה: 5 יַעַן הֱיוֹת לְךָ אֵיבַת עוֹלָם
וַתַּגֵּר אֶת־בְּנֵי־יִשְׂרָאֵל עַל־יְדֵי־חָרֶב בְּעֵת
אֵידָם בְּעֵת עֲוֹן קֵץ: 6 לָכֵן חַי־אָנִי נְאֻם
אֲדֹנָי יְהֹוִה כִּי־לְדָם אֶעֶשְׂךָ וְדָם יִרְדְּפֶךָ
אִם־לֹא דָם שָׂנֵאתָ וְדָם יִרְדְּפֶךָ: 7 וְנָתַתִּי
אֶת־הַר שֵׂעִיר לְשִׁמְמָה וּשְׁמָמָה וְהִכְרַתִּי
מִמֶּנּוּ עֹבֵר וָשָׁב: 8 וּמִלֵּאתִי אֶת־הָרָיו
חֲלָלָיו גִּבְעוֹתֶיךָ וְגֵאוֹתֶיךָ וְכָל־אֲפִיקֶיךָ
חַלְלֵי־חֶרֶב יִפְּלוּ בָהֶם: 9 שִׁמְמוֹת עוֹלָם
אֶתֶּנְךָ וְעָרֶיךָ לֹא תישבנה [תֵשַׁבְנָה] וִידַעְתֶּם
כִּי־אֲנִי יְהֹוָה:

---

f   *Cf. 36.30.*

a-a   *Meaning of Heb. uncertain.*

10Because you thought "The two nations and the two lands shall be mine and we shall possess them"—b-although the Lord was there-b—11assuredly, as I live, declares the Lord God, I will act with the same anger and passion that you acted with in your hatred of them. And I will make Myself known through them when I judge you. 12You shall know that I the Lord have heard all the taunts you uttered against the hills of Israel: "They have been laid waste; they have been given to us as prey." 13And you spoke arrogantly against Me and c-multiplied your words-c against Me: I have heard it.

14Thus said the Lord God: When the whole earth rejoices, I will make you a desolation. 15As you rejoiced when the heritage of the House of Israel was laid waste, so will I treat you: the hill country of Seir and the whole of Edom, all of it, shall be laid waste. And they shall know that I am the Lord.

36 And you, O mortal, prophesy to the mountains of Israel and say: O mountains of Israel, hear the word of the Lord:

2Thus said the Lord God: Because the enemy gloated over you, "Aha! Those ancient heights have become our possession!" 3therefore prophesy, and say: Thus said the Lord God: Just because a-they eagerly lusted to see you become a possession of the other nations round about, so that you have become the butt of gossip in every language and of the jibes from every people-a—4truly, you mountains of Israel, hear the word of the Lord God: Thus said the Lord God to the mountains and the hills, to the watercourses and the valleys, and to the desolate wastes and deserted cities which have become

10 יַ֣עַן אֲמָרְךָ֗ אֶת־שְׁנֵ֤י הַגּוֹיִם֙ וְאֶת־שְׁתֵּ֣י הָאֲרָצ֔וֹת לִ֥י תִֽהְיֶ֖ינָה וִֽירַשְׁנ֑וּהָ וַֽיהוָ֖ה שָׁ֥ם הָיָֽה: 11 לָכֵ֣ן חַי־אָ֗נִי נְאֻם֮ אֲדֹנָ֣י יְהוִה֒ וְעָשִׂ֙יתִי֙ כְּאַפְּךָ֣ וּכְקִנְאָֽתְךָ֔ אֲשֶׁ֣ר עָשִׂ֗יתָה מִשִּׂנְאָתֶ֙יךָ֙ בָּ֔ם וְנוֹדַ֥עְתִּי בָ֖ם כַּֽאֲשֶׁ֥ר אֶשְׁפְּטֶֽךָ׃ 12 וְֽיָדַעְתָּ֮ כִּֽי־אֲנִ֣י יְהוָה֒ שָׁמַ֣עְתִּי ׀ אֶת־כָּל־נָֽאָצוֹתֶ֗יךָ אֲשֶׁ֥ר אָמַ֛רְתָּ עַל־הָרֵ֥י יִשְׂרָאֵ֖ל לֵאמֹ֑ר ׀ שׁמֵ֣מה שָׁמֵ֔מוּ לָ֥נוּ נִתְּנ֖וּ לְאָכְלָֽה: 13 וַתַּגְדִּ֤ילוּ עָלַי֙ בְּפִיכֶ֔ם וְהַעְתַּרְתֶּ֥ם עָלַ֖י דִּבְרֵיכֶ֑ם אֲנִ֖י שָׁמָֽעְתִּי: ס

14 כֹּ֤ה אָמַר֙ אֲדֹנָ֣י יְהוִ֔ה כִּשְׂמֹ֙חַ֙ כָּל־הָאָ֔רֶץ שְׁמָמָ֖ה אֶֽעֱשֶׂה־לָּֽךְ: 15 כְּשִׂמְחָ֙תְךָ֜ לְנַחֲלַ֧ת בֵּֽית־יִשְׂרָאֵ֛ל עַ֥ל אֲשֶׁר־שָׁמֵ֖מָה כֵּ֣ן אֶֽעֱשֶׂה־לָּ֑ךְ שְׁמָמָ֙ה תִֽהְיֶ֜ה הַר־שֵׂעִ֛יר וְכָל־אֱד֥וֹם כֻּלָּ֖הּ וְיָֽדְע֖וּ כִּֽי־אֲנִ֥י יְהוָֽה: פ

לו 1 וְאַתָּ֣ה בֶן־אָדָ֔ם הִנָּבֵ֖א אֶל־הָרֵ֣י יִשְׂרָאֵ֑ל וְאָ֣מַרְתָּ֔ הָרֵי֙ יִשְׂרָאֵ֔ל שִׁמְע֖וּ דְּבַר־יְהוָֽה:

2 כֹּ֤ה אָמַר֙ אֲדֹנָ֣י יְהוִ֔ה יַ֣עַן אָמַ֧ר הָאוֹיֵ֛ב עֲלֵיכֶ֖ם הֶאָ֑ח וּבָמ֣וֹת עוֹלָ֔ם לְמֽוֹרָשָׁ֖ה הָ֥יְתָה לָּֽנוּ: 3 לָכֵן֙ הִנָּבֵ֣א וְאָֽמַרְתָּ֔ כֹּ֥ה אָמַ֖ר אֲדֹנָ֣י יְהוִ֑ה יַ֣עַן בְּיַ֙עַן֙ שַׁמּ֤וֹת וְשָׁאֹף֙ אֶתְכֶ֣ם מִסָּבִ֔יב לִֽהְיֽוֹתְכֶ֣ם מֽוֹרָשָׁ֔ה לִשְׁאֵרִ֖ית הַגּוֹיִ֑ם וַתֵּֽעֲל֛וּ עַל־שְׂפַ֥ת לָשׁ֖וֹן וְדִבַּת־עָֽם: 4 לָכֵן֙ הָרֵ֣י יִשְׂרָאֵ֔ל שִׁמְע֖וּ דְּבַר־אֲדֹנָ֣י יְהוִ֑ה כֹּֽה־אָמַ֣ר אֲדֹנָ֣י יְהוִ֗ה לֶֽהָרִ֤ים וְלַגְּבָעוֹת֙ לָאֲפִיקִ֣ים וְלַגֵּאָי֔וֹת וְלֶחֳרָב֥וֹת הַשֹּֽׁמְמ֛וֹת

---

b-b   *Meaning of Heb. uncertain; emendation yields "and the Lord heard it."*

c-c   *Emendation yields "and spoke arrogantly."*

a-a   *Meaning of Heb. uncertain.*

a prey and a laughingstock to the other nations round about:

⁵Assuredly, thus said the Lord God: I have indeed spoken in My blazing wrath against the other nations and against all of Edom which, ᵃ-with wholehearted glee and with contempt, have made My land a possession for themselves for pasture and for prey.-ᵃ ⁶Yes, prophesy about the land of Israel, and say to the mountains and the hills, to the watercourses and to the valleys, Thus said the Lord God: Behold, I declare in My blazing wrath: Because you have suffered the taunting of the nations, ⁷thus said the Lord God: I hereby swear that the nations which surround you shall, in their turn, suffer disgrace. ⁸But you, O mountains of Israel, shall yield your produce and bear your fruit for My people Israel, for their return is near. ⁹For I will care for you: I will turn to you, and you shall be tilled and sown. ¹⁰I will settle a large population on you, the whole House of Israel; the towns shall be resettled, and the ruined sites rebuilt. ¹¹I will multiply men and beasts upon you, and they shall increase and be fertile, and I will resettle you as you were formerly, and will make you more prosperous than you were at first. And you shall know that I am the Lord. ¹²I will lead men—My people Israel—to you, and they shall possess you. You shall be their heritage, and you shall not again cause them to be bereaved.

¹³Thus said the Lord God: Because they say to you, "You are [a land] that devours men, you have been a bereaver of your nations,"ᵇ ¹⁴assuredly, you shall devour men no more, you shall never again bereave your nations— declares the Lord God. ¹⁵No more will I allow the jibes of the nations to be heard against you, no longer shall you suffer the taunting of the peoples; and never again shall you cause your nations to stumbleᶜ—declares the Lord God.

וְלֶעָרִ֗ים הַנֶּעֱזָבוֹת֙ אֲשֶׁ֣ר הָי֔וּ לְבַ֥ז וּלְלַ֖עַג לִשְׁאֵרִ֥ית הַגּוֹיִ֖ם אֲשֶׁ֣ר מִסָּבִ֑יב: ס ⁵לָכֵ֗ן כֹּֽה־אָמַר֮ אֲדֹנָ֣י יְהוִה֒ אִם־לֹ֠א בְּאֵ֨שׁ קִנְאָתִ֥י דִבַּ֛רְתִּי עַל־שְׁאֵרִ֥ית הַגּוֹיִ֖ם וְעַל־ אֱד֣וֹם כֻּלָּ֑א* אֲשֶׁ֣ר נָתְנֽוּ־אֶת־אַרְצִ֣י ׀ לָהֶ֣ם לְמ֣וֹרָשָׁ֗ה בְּשִׂמְחַ֤ת כָּל־לֵבָב֙ בִּשְׁאָ֣ט נֶ֔פֶשׁ לְמַ֥עַן מִגְרָשָׁ֖הּ לָבַֽז: ⁶לָכֵ֕ן הִנָּבֵ֖א עַל־ אַדְמַ֣ת יִשְׂרָאֵ֑ל וְאָמַרְתָּ֡ לֶהָרִ֣ים וְלַגְּבָעוֹת֩ לָאֲפִיקִ֨ים וְלַגֵּאָי֜וֹת כֹּֽה־אָמַ֣ר ׀ אֲדֹנָ֣י יְהוִ֗ה הִנְנִ֨י בְקִנְאָתִ֤י וּבַחֲמָתִי֙ דִּבַּ֔רְתִּי יַ֛עַן כְּלִמַּ֥ת גּוֹיִ֖ם נְשָׂאתֶֽם: ⁷לָכֵ֗ן כֹּ֤ה אָמַר֙ אֲדֹנָ֣י יְהוִ֔ה אֲנִ֖י נָשָׂ֣אתִי אֶת־יָדִ֑י אִם־לֹ֤א הַגּוֹיִם֙ אֲשֶׁ֣ר לָכֶ֣ם מִסָּבִ֔יב הֵ֖מָּה כְּלִמָּתָ֥ם יִשָּֽׂאוּ: ⁸וְאַתֶּ֞ם הָרֵ֤י יִשְׂרָאֵל֙ עַנְפְּכֶ֣ם תִּתֵּ֔נוּ וּפֶרְיְכֶ֥ם תִּשְׂא֖וּ לְעַמִּ֣י יִשְׂרָאֵ֑ל כִּ֥י קֵרְב֖וּ לָבֽוֹא: ⁹כִּ֖י הִנְנִ֣י אֲלֵיכֶ֑ם וּפָנִ֣יתִי אֲלֵיכֶ֔ם וְנֶעֱבַדְתֶּ֖ם וְנִזְרַעְתֶּֽם: ¹⁰וְהִרְבֵּיתִ֤י עֲלֵיכֶם֙ אָדָ֔ם כָּל־בֵּ֥ית יִשְׂרָאֵ֖ל כֻּלֹּ֑ה וְנֹֽשְׁבוּ֙ הֶֽעָרִ֔ים וְהֶחֳרָב֖וֹת תִּבָּנֶֽינָה: ¹¹וְהִרְבֵּיתִ֧י עֲלֵיכֶ֛ם אָדָ֥ם וּבְהֵמָ֖ה וְרָב֣וּ וּפָר֑וּ וְהוֹשַׁבְתִּ֨י אֶתְכֶ֜ם כְּקַדְמֽוֹתֵיכֶ֗ם וְהֵטִֽבֹתִי֙ מֵרִאשֹׁ֣תֵיכֶ֔ם וִֽידַעְתֶּ֖ם כִּֽי־אֲנִ֥י יְהוָֽה: ¹²וְהוֹלַכְתִּי֩ עֲלֵיכֶ֨ם אָדָ֜ם אֶת־עַמִּ֤י יִשְׂרָאֵל֙ וִֽירֵשׁ֔וּךָ וְהָיִ֥יתָ לָהֶ֖ם לְנַחֲלָ֑ה וְלֹא־תוֹסִ֥ף ע֖וֹד לְשַׁכְּלָֽם: ס

¹³כֹּ֤ה אָמַר֙ אֲדֹנָ֣י יְהוִ֔ה יַ֚עַן אֹמְרִ֣ים לָכֶ֔ם אֹכֶ֥לֶת אָדָ֖ם אתי (אָ֑תְּ) וּמְשַׁכֶּ֥לֶת גּוֹיַ֖יִךְ הָיִֽית: ¹⁴לָכֵ֗ן אָדָם֙ לֹא־תֹ֣אכְלִי ע֔וֹד וגוייך (וְגוֹיַ֖יִךְ) לֹ֣א תכשלי (תְשַׁכְּלִי)־ע֑וֹד נְאֻ֖ם אֲדֹנָ֥י יְהוִֽה: ¹⁵וְלֹא־אַשְׁמִ֨יעַ אֵלַ֤יִךְ עוֹד֙ כְּלִמַּ֣ת הַגּוֹיִ֔ם וְחֶרְפַּ֥ת עַמִּ֖ים לֹ֣א תִשְׂאִי־ע֑וֹד וגויך (וְגוֹיַ֛יִךְ) לֹא־תַכְשִׁ֥לִי ע֖וֹד נְאֻ֖ם אֲדֹנָ֥י יְהוִֽה: ס

---

b   I.e., Israel and Judah; cf. 37.15–22.
c   Many mss. read "be bereaved"; cf. vv. 13–14.

v. 5. א' במקום ה' *

16The word of the Lord came to me: 17O mortal, when the House of Israel dwelt on their own soil, they defiled it with their ways and their deeds; their ways were in My sight like the uncleanness of a menstruous woman. 18So I poured out My wrath on them for the blood which they shed upon their land, and for the fetishes with which they defiled it. 19I scattered them among the nations, and they were dispersed through the countries: I punished them in accordance with their ways and their deeds. 20But when they came *d*-to those nations,-*d* they caused My holy name to be profaned,*e* in that it was said of them, "These are the people of the Lord, yet they had to leave His land." 21Therefore I am concerned for My holy name, which the House of Israel have caused to be profaned among the nations to which they have come.

22Say to the House of Israel: Thus said the Lord God: Not for your sake will I act, O House of Israel, but for My holy name, which you have caused to be profaned among the nations to which you have come. 23I will sanctify My great name which has been profaned among the nations—among whom you have caused it to be profaned. And the nations shall know that I am the Lord—declares the Lord God—when I manifest My holiness before their eyes through you. 24I will take you from among the nations and gather you from all the countries, and I will bring you back to your own land. 25I will sprinkle clean water upon you, and you shall be clean: I will cleanse you from all your uncleanness and from all your fetishes. 26And I will give you a new heart and put a new spirit into you: I will remove the heart of stone from your body and give you a heart of flesh; 27and I will put My spirit into you. Thus I will cause you to follow My laws and faithfully to observe My rules. 28Then you shall dwell in the land which I gave to your

16 וַיְהִ֥י דְבַר־יְהֹוָ֖ה אֵלַ֥י לֵאמֹֽר׃ 17 בֶּן־אָדָ֗ם בֵּ֤ית יִשְׂרָאֵל֙ יֹשְׁבִ֣ים עַל־אַדְמָתָ֔ם וַיְטַמְּא֣וּ אוֹתָ֔הּ בְּדַרְכָּ֖ם וּבַעֲלִ֣ילוֹתָ֑ם כְּטֻמְאַת֙ הַנִּדָּ֔ה הָיְתָ֥ה דַרְכָּ֖ם לְפָנָֽי׃ 18 וָאֶשְׁפֹּ֤ךְ חֲמָתִי֙ עֲלֵיהֶ֔ם עַל־הַדָּ֖ם אֲשֶׁר־שָׁפְכ֣וּ עַל־הָאָ֑רֶץ וּבְגִלּוּלֵיהֶ֖ם טִמְּאֽוּהָ׃ 19 וָאָפִ֤יץ אֹתָם֙ בַּגּוֹיִ֔ם וַיִּזָּר֖וּ בָּאֲרָצ֑וֹת כְּדַרְכָּ֥ם וְכַעֲלִ֣ילוֹתָ֖ם שְׁפַטְתִּֽים׃ 20 וַיָּבוֹא֙* אֶל־הַגּוֹיִם֙ אֲשֶׁר־בָּ֣אוּ שָׁ֔ם וַיְחַלְּל֖וּ אֶת־שֵׁ֣ם קׇדְשִׁ֑י בֶּאֱמֹ֤ר לָהֶם֙ עַם־יְהֹוָ֣ה אֵ֔לֶּה וּמֵאַרְצ֖וֹ יָצָֽאוּ׃ 21 וָאֶחְמֹ֖ל עַל־שֵׁ֣ם קׇדְשִׁ֑י אֲשֶׁ֤ר חִלְּל֙וּהוּ֙ בֵּ֣ית יִשְׂרָאֵ֔ל בַּגּוֹיִ֖ם אֲשֶׁר־בָּ֥אוּ שָֽׁמָּה׃ ס

22 לָכֵ֞ן אֱמֹ֣ר לְבֵֽית־יִשְׂרָאֵ֗ל כֹּ֤ה אָמַר֙ אֲדֹנָ֣י יֱהֹוִ֔ה לֹ֧א לְמַעַנְכֶ֛ם אֲנִ֥י עֹשֶׂ֖ה בֵּ֣ית יִשְׂרָאֵ֑ל כִּ֣י אִם־לְשֵׁם־קׇדְשִׁ֗י אֲשֶׁ֤ר חִלַּלְתֶּם֙ בַּגּוֹיִ֔ם אֲשֶׁר־בָּ֥אתֶם שָֽׁם׃ 23 וְקִדַּשְׁתִּ֞י אֶת־שְׁמִ֣י הַגָּד֗וֹל הַֽמְחֻלָּל֙ בַּגּוֹיִ֔ם אֲשֶׁ֥ר חִלַּלְתֶּ֖ם בְּתוֹכָ֑ם וְיָדְע֣וּ הַגּוֹיִ֗ם כִּֽי־אֲנִ֣י יְהֹוָה֙ נְאֻם֙ אֲדֹנָ֣י יֱהֹוִ֔ה בְּהִקָּדְשִׁ֥י בָכֶ֖ם לְעֵינֵיהֶֽם׃ 24 וְלָקַחְתִּ֤י אֶתְכֶם֙ מִן־הַגּוֹיִ֔ם וְקִבַּצְתִּ֥י אֶתְכֶ֖ם מִכׇּל־הָאֲרָצ֑וֹת וְהֵבֵאתִ֥י אֶתְכֶ֖ם אֶל־אַדְמַתְכֶֽם׃ 25 וְזָרַקְתִּ֧י עֲלֵיכֶ֛ם מַ֥יִם טְהוֹרִ֖ים וּטְהַרְתֶּ֑ם מִכֹּ֧ל טֻמְאוֹתֵיכֶ֛ם וּמִכׇּל־גִּלּ֣וּלֵיכֶ֖ם אֲטַהֵ֥ר אֶתְכֶֽם׃ 26 וְנָתַתִּ֤י לָכֶם֙ לֵ֣ב חָדָ֔שׁ וְר֥וּחַ חֲדָשָׁ֖ה אֶתֵּ֣ן בְּקִרְבְּכֶ֑ם וַהֲסִרֹתִ֞י אֶת־לֵ֤ב הָאֶ֙בֶן֙ מִבְּשַׂרְכֶ֔ם וְנָתַתִּ֥י לָכֶ֖ם לֵ֥ב בָּשָֽׂר׃ 27 וְאֶת־רוּחִ֖י אֶתֵּ֣ן בְּקִרְבְּכֶ֑ם וְעָשִׂ֗יתִי אֵ֤ת אֲשֶׁר־בְּחֻקַּי֙ תֵּלֵ֔כוּ וּמִשְׁפָּטַ֥י תִּשְׁמְר֖וּ וַעֲשִׂיתֶֽם׃ 28 וִישַׁבְתֶּ֣ם

---

d-d Lit. "the nations they came to."
e I.e., the exile of Israel was taken by the nations to be evidence of the Lord's weakness.

fathers, and you shall be My people and I will be your God.

²⁹And when I have delivered you from all your uncleanness, I will summon the grain and make it abundant, and I will not bring famine upon you. ³⁰I will make the fruit of your trees and the crops of your fields abundant, so that you shall never again be humiliated before the nations because of famine. ³¹Then you shall recall your evil ways and your base conduct, and you shall loathe yourselves for your iniquities and your abhorrent practices. ³²Not for your sake will I act—declares the Lord GOD—take good note! Be ashamed and humiliated because of your ways, O House of Israel!

³³Thus said the Lord GOD: When I have cleansed you of all your iniquities, I will people your settlements, and the ruined places shall be rebuilt; ³⁴and the desolate land, after lying waste in the sight of every passerby, shall again be tilled. ³⁵And men shall say, "That land, once desolate, has become like the garden of Eden; and the cities, once ruined, desolate, and ravaged, are now populated and fortified." ³⁶And the nations that are left around you shall know that I the LORD have rebuilt the ravaged places and replanted the desolate land. I the LORD have spoken and will act.

³⁷Thus said the Lord GOD: Moreover, in this I will respond to the House of Israel and act for their sake: I will multiply their people like sheep. ³⁸As Jerusalem is filled with sacrificial sheep during her festivals, so shall the ruined cities be filled with flocks of people. And they shall know that I am the LORD.

37

The hand of the LORD came upon me. He took me out by the spirit of the LORD and set me down in the valley. It was full of bones.

בָּאָ֗רֶץ אֲשֶׁ֤ר נָתַ֙תִּי֙ לַאֲבֹ֣תֵיכֶ֔ם וִהְיִ֤יתֶם לִי֙ לְעָ֔ם וְאָ֣נֹכִ֔י אֶהְיֶ֥ה לָכֶ֖ם לֵאלֹהִֽים׃ 29 וְהוֹשַׁעְתִּ֣י אֶתְכֶ֔ם מִכֹּ֖ל טֻמְאֽוֹתֵיכֶ֑ם וְקָרָ֤אתִי אֶל־הַדָּגָן֙ וְהִרְבֵּיתִ֣י אֹת֔וֹ וְלֹא־ אֶתֵּ֥ן עֲלֵיכֶ֖ם רָעָֽב׃ 30 וְהִרְבֵּיתִי֙ אֶת־פְּרִ֣י הָעֵ֔ץ וּתְנוּבַ֖ת הַשָּׂדֶ֑ה לְמַ֗עַן אֲשֶׁ֨ר לֹ֤א תִקְח֥וּ ע֛וֹד חֶרְפַּ֥ת רָעָ֖ב בַּגּוֹיִֽם׃ 31 וּזְכַרְתֶּם֙ אֶת־דַּרְכֵיכֶ֣ם הָרָעִ֔ים וּמַעַלְלֵיכֶ֖ם אֲשֶׁ֣ר לֹא־טוֹבִ֑ים וּנְקֹֽטֹתֶם֙ בִּפְנֵיכֶ֔ם עַ֚ל עֲוֺנֹ֣תֵיכֶ֔ם וְעַ֖ל תּוֹעֲבֽוֹתֵיכֶֽם׃ 32 לֹ֧א לְמַעַנְכֶ֣ם אֲנִֽי־ עֹשֶׂה֙ נְאֻם֙ אֲדֹנָ֣י יְהֹוִ֔ה יִוָּדַ֖ע לָכֶ֑ם בּ֧וֹשׁוּ וְהִכָּלְמ֛וּ מִדַּרְכֵיכֶ֖ם בֵּ֥ית יִשְׂרָאֵֽל׃ ס 33 כֹּ֤ה אָמַר֙ אֲדֹנָ֣י יְהֹוִ֔ה בְּיוֹם֙ טַהֲרִ֣י אֶתְכֶ֔ם מִכֹּ֖ל עֲוֺנֽוֹתֵיכֶ֑ם וְהֽוֹשַׁבְתִּי֙ אֶת־הֶ֣עָרִ֔ים וְנִבְנ֖וּ הֶחֳרָבֽוֹת׃ 34 וְהָאָ֥רֶץ הַנְּשַׁמָּ֖ה תֵּֽעָבֵ֑ד תַּ֣חַת אֲשֶׁ֣ר הָיְתָ֣ה שְׁמָמָ֔ה לְעֵינֵ֖י כׇּל־ עוֹבֵֽר׃ 35 וְאָמְר֗וּ הָאָ֤רֶץ הַלֵּ֙זוּ֙ הַנְּשַׁמָּ֔ה הָיְתָ֖ה כְּגַן־עֵ֑דֶן וְהֶעָרִ֧ים הֶחֳרֵב֛וֹת וְהַֽנְשַׁמּ֥וֹת וְהַנֶּהֱרָס֖וֹת בְּצוּר֥וֹת יָשָֽׁבוּ׃ 36 וְיָדְע֣וּ הַגּוֹיִ֗ם אֲשֶׁ֣ר יִֽשָּׁאֲרוּ֮ סְבִיבֽוֹתֵיכֶם֒ כִּ֣י ׀ אֲנִ֣י יְהֹוָ֗ה בָּנִ֙יתִי֙ הַנֶּ֣הֱרָס֔וֹת נָטַ֖עְתִּי הַנְּשַׁמָּ֑ה אֲנִ֥י יְהֹוָ֖ה דִּבַּ֥רְתִּי וְעָשִֽׂיתִי׃ ס 37 כֹּ֤ה אָמַר֙ אֲדֹנָ֣י יְהֹוִ֔ה ע֗וֹד זֹ֛את אִדָּרֵ֥שׁ לְבֵֽית־יִשְׂרָאֵ֖ל לַעֲשׂ֣וֹת לָהֶ֑ם אַרְבֶּ֥ה אֹתָ֛ם כַּצֹּ֖אן אָדָֽם׃ 38 כְּצֹ֣אן קׇֽדָשִׁ֗ים כְּצֹ֤אן יְרוּשָׁלַ֙͏ִם֙ בְּמ֣וֹעֲדֶ֔יהָ כֵּ֤ן תִּהְיֶ֙ינָה֙ הֶעָרִ֣ים הֶחֳרֵב֔וֹת מְלֵא֖וֹת צֹ֣אן אָדָ֑ם וְיָדְע֖וּ כִּֽי־אֲנִ֥י יְהֹוָֽה׃ ס

לז

הָיְתָ֣ה עָלַי֮ יַד־יְהֹוָה֒ וַיּוֹצִאֵ֤נִי בְר֙וּחַ֙ יְהֹוָ֔ה וַיְנִיחֵ֖נִי בְּת֣וֹךְ הַבִּקְעָ֑ה וְהִ֖יא מְלֵאָ֥ה עֲצָמֽוֹת׃ 2 וְהֶעֱבִירַ֥נִי עֲלֵיהֶ֖ם סָבִ֣יב ׀ סָבִ֑יב

²He led me all around them; there were very many of them spread over the valley, and they were very dry. ³He said to me, "O mortal, can these bones live again?" I replied, "O Lord GOD, only You know." ⁴And He said to me, "Prophesy over these bones and say to them: O dry bones, hear the word of the LORD! ⁵Thus said the Lord GOD to these bones: I will cause breath to enter you and you shall live again. ⁶I will lay sinews upon you, and cover you with flesh, and form skin over you. And I will put breath into you, and you shall live again. And you shall know that I am the LORD!"

⁷I prophesied as I had been commanded. And while I was prophesying, suddenly there was a sound of rattling, and the bones came together, bone to matching bone. ⁸I looked, and there were sinews on them, and flesh had grown, and skin had formed over them; but there was no breath in them. ⁹Then He said to me, "Prophesy to the breath, prophesy, O mortal! Say to the breath: Thus said the Lord GOD: Come, O breath, from the four winds, and breathe into these slain, that they may live again." ¹⁰I prophesied as He commanded me. The breath entered them, and they came to life and stood up on their feet, a vast multitude.

¹¹And He said to me, "O mortal, these bones are the whole House of Israel. They say, 'Our bones are dried up, our hope is gone; we are doomed.' ¹²Prophesy, therefore, and say to them: Thus said the Lord GOD: I am going to open your graves and lift you out of the graves, O My people, and bring you to the land of Israel. ¹³You shall know, O My people, that I am the LORD, when I have opened your graves and lifted you out of your graves. ¹⁴I will put My breath into you and you shall live again, and I will set you upon your own soil. Then you shall know that I the LORD have spoken and have acted"—declares the LORD.

וְהֶעֱבִירַנִי עֲלֵיהֶם סָבִיב ׀ סָבִיב וְהִנֵּה רַבּוֹת מְאֹד עַל־פְּנֵי הַבִּקְעָה וְהִנֵּה יְבֵשׁוֹת מְאֹד: ³וַיֹּאמֶר אֵלַי בֶּן־אָדָם הֲתִחְיֶינָה הָעֲצָמוֹת הָאֵלֶּה וָאֹמַר אֲדֹנָי יְהֹוִה אַתָּה יָדָעְתָּ: ⁴וַיֹּאמֶר אֵלַי הִנָּבֵא עַל־הָעֲצָמוֹת הָאֵלֶּה וְאָמַרְתָּ אֲלֵיהֶם הָעֲצָמוֹת הַיְבֵשׁוֹת שִׁמְעוּ דְּבַר־יְהֹוָה: ⁵כֹּה אָמַר אֲדֹנָי יְהֹוִה לָעֲצָמוֹת הָאֵלֶּה הִנֵּה אֲנִי מֵבִיא בָכֶם רוּחַ וִחְיִיתֶם: ⁶וְנָתַתִּי עֲלֵיכֶם גִּדִים וְהַעֲלֵתִי עֲלֵיכֶם בָּשָׂר וְקָרַמְתִּי עֲלֵיכֶם עוֹר וְנָתַתִּי בָכֶם רוּחַ וִחְיִיתֶם וִידַעְתֶּם כִּי־אֲנִי יְהֹוָה: ⁷וְנִבֵּאתִי כַּאֲשֶׁר צֻוֵּיתִי וַיְהִי־קוֹל כְּהִנָּבְאִי וְהִנֵּה־רַעַשׁ וַתִּקְרְבוּ עֲצָמוֹת עֶצֶם אֶל־עַצְמוֹ: ⁸וְרָאִיתִי וְהִנֵּה־עֲלֵיהֶם גִּדִים וּבָשָׂר עָלָה וַיִּקְרַם עֲלֵיהֶם עוֹר מִלְמָעְלָה וְרוּחַ אֵין בָּהֶם: ⁹וַיֹּאמֶר אֵלַי הִנָּבֵא אֶל־הָרוּחַ הִנָּבֵא בֶן־אָדָם וְאָמַרְתָּ אֶל־הָרוּחַ כֹּה־אָמַר ׀ אֲדֹנָי יְהֹוִה מֵאַרְבַּע רוּחוֹת בֹּאִי הָרוּחַ וּפְחִי בַּהֲרוּגִים הָאֵלֶּה וְיִחְיוּ: ¹⁰וְהִנַּבֵּאתִי כַּאֲשֶׁר צִוָּנִי וַתָּבוֹא בָהֶם הָרוּחַ וַיִּחְיוּ וַיַּעַמְדוּ עַל־רַגְלֵיהֶם חַיִל גָּדוֹל מְאֹד־מְאֹד: ס
¹¹וַיֹּאמֶר אֵלַי בֶּן־אָדָם הָעֲצָמוֹת הָאֵלֶּה כָּל־בֵּית יִשְׂרָאֵל הֵמָּה הִנֵּה אֹמְרִים יָבְשׁוּ עַצְמוֹתֵינוּ וְאָבְדָה תִקְוָתֵנוּ נִגְזַרְנוּ לָנוּ: ¹²לָכֵן הִנָּבֵא וְאָמַרְתָּ אֲלֵיהֶם כֹּה־אָמַר אֲדֹנָי יְהֹוִה הִנֵּה אֲנִי פֹתֵחַ אֶת־קִבְרוֹתֵיכֶם וְהַעֲלֵיתִי אֶתְכֶם מִקִּבְרוֹתֵיכֶם עַמִּי וְהֵבֵאתִי אֶתְכֶם אֶל־אַדְמַת יִשְׂרָאֵל: ס ¹³וִידַעְתֶּם כִּי־אֲנִי יְהֹוָה בְּפִתְחִי אֶת־קִבְרוֹתֵיכֶם וּבְהַעֲלוֹתִי אֶתְכֶם מִקִּבְרוֹתֵיכֶם עַמִּי: ¹⁴וְנָתַתִּי רוּחִי בָכֶם וִחְיִיתֶם וְהִנַּחְתִּי אֶתְכֶם עַל־אַדְמַתְכֶם וִידַעְתֶּם כִּי־אֲנִי יְהֹוָה דִּבַּרְתִּי וְעָשִׂיתִי נְאֻם־יְהֹוָה: פ

¹⁵The word of the LORD came to me: ¹⁶And you, O mortal, take a stick and write on it, "Of Judah and the Israelites associated with him"; and take another stick and write on it, "Of Joseph—the stick of Ephraim—and all the House of Israel associated with him." ¹⁷Bring them close to each other, so that they become one stick, joined together in your hand. ¹⁸And when any of your people ask you, "Won't you tell us what these actions of yours mean?" ¹⁹answer them, "Thus said the Lord GOD: I am going to take the stick of Joseph—which is in the hand of Ephraim—and of the tribes of Israel associated with him, and I will place the stick of Judah ^a-upon it-^a and make them into one stick; they shall be joined in My hand." ²⁰You shall hold up before their eyes the sticks which you have inscribed, ²¹and you shall declare to them: Thus said the Lord GOD: I am going to take the Israelite people from among the nations they have gone to, and gather them from every quarter, and bring them to their own land. ²²I will make them a single nation in the land, on the hills of Israel, and one king shall be king of them all. Never again shall they be two nations, and never again shall they be divided into two kingdoms. ²³Nor shall they ever again defile themselves by their fetishes and their abhorrent things, and by their other transgressions. I will save them in all their settlements where they sinned, and I will cleanse them. Then they shall be My people, and I will be their God.

²⁴My servant David shall be king over them; there shall be one shepherd for all of them. They shall follow My rules and faithfully obey My laws. ²⁵Thus they shall remain in the land which I gave to My servant Jacob and in which your fathers dwelt; they and their children and their children's children shall dwell there forever, with My servant David as their prince for all

¹⁵ וַיְהִ֥י דְבַר־יְהֹוָ֖ה אֵלַ֥י לֵאמֹֽר׃ ¹⁶ וְאַתָּ֣ה בֶן־אָדָ֗ם קַח־לְךָ֙ עֵ֣ץ אֶחָ֔ד וּכְתֹ֤ב עָלָיו֙ לִֽיהוּדָ֔ה וְלִבְנֵ֥י יִשְׂרָאֵ֖ל חֲבֵרָ֑ו וּלְקַח֙ עֵ֣ץ אֶחָ֔ד וּכְת֣וֹב עָלָ֗יו לְיוֹסֵף֙ עֵ֣ץ אֶפְרַ֔יִם וְכׇל־בֵּ֥ית יִשְׂרָאֵ֖ל חֲבֵרָֽו׃ ¹⁷ וְקָרַ֨ב אֹתָ֜ם אֶחָ֧ד אֶל־אֶחָ֛ד לְךָ֖ לְעֵ֣ץ אֶחָ֑ד וְהָי֥וּ לַאֲחָדִ֖ים בְּיָדֶֽךָ׃ ¹⁸ וְכַֽאֲשֶׁר֙ יֹאמְר֣וּ אֵלֶ֔יךָ בְּנֵ֥י עַמְּךָ֖ לֵאמֹ֑ר הֲלֽוֹא־תַגִּ֥יד לָ֖נוּ מָה־אֵ֥לֶּה לָּֽךְ׃ ¹⁹ דַּבֵּ֣ר אֲלֵהֶ֗ם כֹּֽה־אָמַר֮ אֲדֹנָ֣י יְהֹוִה֒ הִנֵּה֩ אֲנִ֨י לֹקֵ֜חַ אֶת־עֵ֤ץ יוֹסֵף֙ אֲשֶׁ֣ר בְּיַד־אֶפְרַ֔יִם וְשִׁבְטֵ֥י יִשְׂרָאֵ֖ל חֲבֵרָ֑ו וְנָתַתִּי֩ אוֹתָ֨ם עָלָ֜יו אֶת־עֵ֣ץ יְהוּדָ֗ה וַֽעֲשִׂיתִם֙ לְעֵ֣ץ אֶחָ֔ד וְהָי֥וּ אֶחָ֖ד בְּיָדִֽי׃ ²⁰ וְהָי֨וּ הָעֵצִ֜ים אֲ‍ֽשֶׁר־תִּכְתֹּ֧ב עֲלֵיהֶ֛ם בְּיָדְךָ֖ לְעֵינֵיהֶֽם׃ ²¹ וְדַבֵּ֣ר אֲלֵיהֶ֗ם כֹּֽה־אָמַר֮ אֲדֹנָ֣י יְהֹוִה֒ הִנֵּ֨ה אֲנִ֤י לֹקֵ֙חַ֙ אֶת־בְּנֵ֣י יִשְׂרָאֵ֔ל מִבֵּ֥ין הַגּוֹיִ֖ם אֲשֶׁ֣ר הָֽלְכוּ־שָׁ֑ם וְקִבַּצְתִּ֤י אֹתָם֙ מִסָּבִ֔יב וְהֵבֵאתִ֥י אוֹתָ֖ם אֶל־אַדְמָתָֽם׃ ²² וְעָשִׂ֣יתִי אֹ֠תָ֠ם לְג֨וֹי אֶחָ֤ד בָּאָ֙רֶץ֙ בְּהָרֵ֣י יִשְׂרָאֵ֔ל וּמֶ֧לֶךְ אֶחָ֛ד יִהְיֶ֥ה לְכֻלָּ֖ם לְמֶ֑לֶךְ וְלֹ֤א ^{יהיה} יִֽהְיוּ־עוֹד֙ לִשְׁנֵ֣י גוֹיִ֔ם וְלֹ֨א יֵחָ֧צוּ ע֛וֹד לִשְׁתֵּ֥י מַמְלָכ֖וֹת עֽוֹד׃ ²³ וְלֹ֧א יִֽטַמְּא֣וּ ע֗וֹד בְּגִלּֽוּלֵיהֶם֙ וּבְשִׁקּ֣וּצֵיהֶ֔ם וּבְכֹ֖ל פִּשְׁעֵיהֶ֑ם וְהוֹשַׁעְתִּ֣י אֹתָ֗ם מִכֹּ֤ל מוֹשְׁבֹֽתֵיהֶם֙ אֲשֶׁ֣ר חָטְא֣וּ בָהֶ֔ם וְטִהַרְתִּ֥י אוֹתָ֖ם וְהָֽיוּ־לִ֣י לְעָ֑ם וַאֲנִ֕י אֶהְיֶ֥ה לָהֶ֖ם לֵֽאלֹהִֽים׃ ²⁴ וְעַבְדִּ֤י דָוִד֙ מֶ֣לֶךְ עֲלֵיהֶ֔ם וְרוֹעֶ֥ה אֶחָ֖ד יִהְיֶ֣ה לְכֻלָּ֑ם וּבְמִשְׁפָּטַ֣י יֵלֵ֔כוּ וְחֻקֹּתַ֥י יִשְׁמְר֖וּ וְעָשׂ֥וּ אוֹתָֽם׃ ²⁵ וְיָשְׁב֣וּ עַל־הָאָ֗רֶץ אֲשֶׁ֤ר נָתַ֙תִּי֙ לְעַבְדִּ֣י לְיַֽעֲקֹ֔ב אֲשֶׁ֥ר יָֽשְׁבוּ־בָ֖הּ אֲבֽוֹתֵיכֶ֑ם וְיָשְׁב֣וּ עָלֶ֡יהָ הֵ֠מָּה וּבְנֵיהֶ֞ם וּבְנֵ֤י בְנֵיהֶם֙ עַד־עוֹלָ֔ם וְדָוִ֣ד עַבְדִּ֔י נָשִׂ֥יא לָהֶ֖ם

---

a-a Meaning of Heb. uncertain.

time. ²⁶I will make a covenant of friendship with them—it shall be an everlasting covenant with them—I will establishᵃ them and multiply them, and I will place My Sanctuary among them forever. ²⁷My Presenceᵇ shall rest over them; I will be their God and they shall be My people. ²⁸And when My Sanctuary abides among them forever, the nations shall know that I the LORD do sanctify Israel.

38 The word of the LORD came to me: ²O mortal, turn your face toward Gog of the land of Magog, the chief prince of Meshech and Tubal. Prophesy against him ³and say: Thus said the Lord GOD: Lo, I am coming to deal with you, O Gog, chief prince of Meshech and Tubal! ⁴I will turn you around and put hooks in your jaws, and lead you out with all your army, horses, and horsemen, all of them clothed in splendor, a vast assembly, all of them with bucklers and shields, wielding swords. ⁵Among them shall be Persia, Nubia, and Put, everyone with shield and helmet; ⁶Gomer and all its cohorts, Beth-togarmah [in] the remotest parts of the north and all its cohorts—the many peoples with you.ᵃ ⁷Be ready, prepare yourselves, you and all the battalions mustered about you, and hold yourself in reserve for them.ᵇ ⁸After a long time you shall be summoned; in the distant future you shall march against the land [of a people] restored from the sword, gathered from the midst of many peoples—against the mountains of Israel, which have long lain desolate—[a people] liberated from the nations, and now all dwelling secure. ⁹You shall advance, coming like a storm; you shall be like a cloud covering the earth, you and all your cohorts, and the many peoples with you.

לְעוֹלָֽם: 26 וְכָרַתִּ֤י לָהֶם֙ בְּרִ֣ית שָׁל֔וֹם בְּרִ֤ית עוֹלָם֙ יִהְיֶ֣ה אוֹתָ֔ם וּנְתַתִּים֙ וְהִרְבֵּיתִ֣י אוֹתָ֔ם וְנָתַתִּ֥י אֶת־מִקְדָּשִׁ֖י בְּתוֹכָ֑ם לְעוֹלָֽם: 27 וְהָיָ֤ה מִשְׁכָּנִי֙ עֲלֵיהֶ֔ם וְהָיִ֥יתִי לָהֶ֖ם לֵֽאלֹהִ֑ים וְהֵ֖מָּה יִֽהְיוּ־לִ֥י לְעָֽם: 28 וְיָֽדְעוּ֙ הַגּוֹיִ֔ם כִּ֚י אֲנִ֣י יְהוָ֔ה מְקַדֵּ֖שׁ אֶת־יִשְׂרָאֵ֑ל בִּֽהְי֧וֹת מִקְדָּשִׁ֛י בְּתוֹכָ֖ם לְעוֹלָֽם: ס

לח וַיְהִ֥י דְבַר־יְהוָ֖ה אֵלַ֥י לֵאמֹֽר: 2 בֶּן־אָדָ֗ם שִׂ֤ים פָּנֶ֨יךָ֙ אֶל־גּוֹג֙ אֶ֣רֶץ הַמָּג֔וֹג נְשִׂ֕יא רֹ֖אשׁ מֶ֣שֶׁךְ וְתֻבָ֑ל וְהִנָּבֵ֖א עָלָֽיו: 3 וְאָ֣מַרְתָּ֔ כֹּ֥ה אָמַ֖ר אֲדֹנָ֣י יְהוִ֑ה הִנְנִ֤י אֵלֶ֨יךָ֙ גּ֔וֹג נְשִׂ֕יא רֹ֖אשׁ מֶ֥שֶׁךְ וְתֻבָֽל: 4 וְשׁ֣וֹבַבְתִּ֔יךָ וְנָתַתִּ֤י חַחִים֙ בִּלְחָיֶ֔יךָ וְהוֹצֵאתִ֤י אוֹתְךָ֙ וְאֶת־כָּל־חֵילֶ֔ךָ סוּסִ֖ים וּפָרָשִׁ֑ים לְבֻשֵׁ֤י מִכְלוֹל֙ כֻּלָּ֔ם קָהָ֥ל רָ֖ב צִנָּ֣ה וּמָגֵ֑ן תֹּפְשֵׂ֥י חֲרָב֖וֹת כֻּלָּֽם: 5 פָּרַ֛ס כּ֥וּשׁ וּפ֖וּט אִתָּ֑ם כֻּלָּ֖ם מָגֵ֥ן וְכוֹבָֽע: 6 גֹּ֚מֶר וְכָל־אֲגַפֶּ֔יהָ בֵּ֖ית תּוֹגַרְמָ֑ה יַרְכְּתֵ֥י צָפ֖וֹן וְאֶת־כָּל־אֲגַפָּ֑יו עַמִּ֥ים רַבִּ֖ים אִתָּֽךְ: 7 הִכֹּ֣ן וְהָכֵ֤ן לְךָ֙ אַתָּ֔ה וְכָל־קְהָלֶ֖ךָ הַנִּקְהָלִ֣ים עָלֶ֑יךָ וְהָיִ֥יתָ לָהֶ֖ם לְמִשְׁמָֽר: 8 מִיָּמִ֣ים רַבִּים֮ תִּפָּקֵד֒ בְּאַחֲרִ֣ית הַשָּׁנִ֗ים תָּב֣וֹא ׀ אֶל־אֶ֣רֶץ ׀ מְשׁוֹבֶ֣בֶת מֵחֶ֔רֶב מְקֻבֶּ֤צֶת מֵֽעַמִּים֙ רַבִּ֔ים עַ֖ל הָרֵ֣י יִשְׂרָאֵ֔ל אֲשֶׁר־הָי֥וּ לְחָרְבָּ֖ה תָּמִ֑יד וְהִ֨יא מֵעַמִּ֣ים הוּצָ֔אָה וְיָשְׁב֥וּ לָבֶ֖טַח כֻּלָּֽם: 9 וְעָלִ֨יתָ֙ כַּשֹּׁאָ֣ה תָב֔וֹא כֶּֽעָנָ֛ן לְכַסּ֥וֹת הָאָ֖רֶץ תִּֽהְיֶ֑ה אַתָּה֙ וְכָל־אֲגַפֶּ֔יךָ וְעַמִּ֥ים רַבִּ֖ים אוֹתָֽךְ: ס

---

b   Lit. "dwelling place."

a   I.e., with Gog.
b   Septuagint reads "Me."

10Thus said the Lord God: On that day, a thought will occur to you, and you will conceive a wicked design. 11You will say, "I will invade a land of open towns, I will fall upon a tranquil people living secure, all of them living in unwalled towns and lacking bars and gates, 12in order to take spoil and seize plunder"—to turn your hand against repopulated wastes, and against a people gathered from among nations, acquiring livestock and possessions, living at the center of the earth. 13Sheba and Dedan, and the merchants and all the magnates of Tarshish will say to you, "Have you come to take spoil? Is it to seize plunder that you assembled your hordes—to carry off silver and gold, to make off with livestock and goods, to gather an immense booty?"

14Therefore prophesy, O mortal, and say to Gog: Thus said the Lord God: Surely, on that day, when My people Israel are living secure, you will c-take note,-c 15and you will come from your home in the farthest north, you and many peoples with you—all of them mounted on horses, a vast horde, a mighty army—16and you will advance upon My people Israel, like a cloud covering the earth. This shall happen on that distant day: I will bring you to My land, that the nations may know Me when, before their eyes, I manifest My holiness through you, O Gog!

17Thus said the Lord God: Why, you are the one I spoke of in ancient days through My servants, the prophets of Israel, who prophesied for years in those days that I would bring you against them!

18On that day, when Gog sets foot on the soil of Israel—declares the Lord God—My raging anger shall flare up. 19For I have decreed in My indignation and in My blazing wrath: On that day, a terrible earthquake shall befall the land

---

c-c Septuagint reads "rouse yourself."

10 כֹּה אָמַר אֲדֹנָי יְהוִה וְהָיָה ׀ בַּיּוֹם הַהוּא יַעֲלוּ דְבָרִים עַל־לְבָבֶךָ וְחָשַׁבְתָּ מַחֲשֶׁבֶת רָעָה: 11 וְאָמַרְתָּ אֶעֱלֶה עַל־אֶרֶץ פְּרָזוֹת אָבוֹא הַשֹּׁקְטִים יֹשְׁבֵי לָבֶטַח כֻּלָּם יֹשְׁבִים בְּאֵין חוֹמָה וּבְרִיחַ וּדְלָתַיִם אֵין לָהֶם: 12 לִשְׁלֹל שָׁלָל וְלָבֹז בַּז לְהָשִׁיב יָדְךָ עַל־חֳרָבוֹת נוֹשָׁבֹת וְאֶל־עַם מְאֻסָּף מִגּוֹיִם עֹשֶׂה מִקְנֶה וְקִנְיָן יֹשְׁבֵי עַל־טַבּוּר הָאָרֶץ: 13 שְׁבָא וּדְדָן וְסֹחֲרֵי תַרְשִׁישׁ וְכָל־כְּפִרֶיהָ יֹאמְרוּ לְךָ הֲלִשְׁלֹל שָׁלָל אַתָּה בָא הֲלָבֹז בַּז הִקְהַלְתָּ קְהָלֶךָ לָשֵׂאת ׀ כֶּסֶף וְזָהָב לָקַחַת מִקְנֶה וְקִנְיָן לִשְׁלֹל שָׁלָל גָּדוֹל: ס 14 לָכֵן הִנָּבֵא בֶן־אָדָם וְאָמַרְתָּ לְגוֹג כֹּה אָמַר אֲדֹנָי יְהוִה הֲלוֹא ׀ בַּיּוֹם הַהוּא בְּשֶׁבֶת עַמִּי יִשְׂרָאֵל לָבֶטַח תֵּדָע: 15 וּבָאתָ מִמְּקוֹמְךָ מִיַּרְכְּתֵי צָפוֹן אַתָּה וְעַמִּים רַבִּים אִתָּךְ רֹכְבֵי סוּסִים כֻּלָּם קָהָל גָּדוֹל וְחַיִל רָב: 16 וְעָלִיתָ עַל־עַמִּי יִשְׂרָאֵל כֶּעָנָן לְכַסּוֹת הָאָרֶץ בְּאַחֲרִית הַיָּמִים תִּהְיֶה וַהֲבִאוֹתִיךָ עַל־אַרְצִי לְמַעַן דַּעַת הַגּוֹיִם אֹתִי בְּהִקָּדְשִׁי בְךָ לְעֵינֵיהֶם גּוֹג: ס 17 כֹּה־אָמַר אֲדֹנָי יְהוִה הַאַתָּה־הוּא אֲשֶׁר־דִּבַּרְתִּי בְּיָמִים קַדְמוֹנִים בְּיַד עֲבָדַי נְבִיאֵי יִשְׂרָאֵל הַנִּבְּאִים בַּיָּמִים הָהֵם שָׁנִים לְהָבִיא אֹתְךָ עֲלֵיהֶם: ס 18 וְהָיָה ׀ בַּיּוֹם הַהוּא בְּיוֹם בּוֹא גוֹג עַל־אַדְמַת יִשְׂרָאֵל נְאֻם אֲדֹנָי יְהוִה תַּעֲלֶה חֲמָתִי בְּאַפִּי: 19 וּבְקִנְאָתִי בְאֵשׁ־עֶבְרָתִי דִבַּרְתִּי אִם־לֹא ׀ בַּיּוֹם הַהוּא

of Israel. ²⁰The fish of the sea, the birds of the sky, the beasts of the field, all creeping things that move on the ground, and every human being on earth shall quake before Me. Mountains shall be overthrown, cliffs shall topple, and every wall shall crumble to the ground. ²¹*-I will then summon the sword against him throughout My mountains-*^d—declares the Lord GOD—and every man's sword shall be turned against his brother. ²²I will punish him with pestilence and with bloodshed; and I will pour torrential rain, hailstones, and sulfurous fire upon him and his hordes and the many peoples with him. ²³Thus will I manifest My greatness and My holiness, and make Myself known in the sight of many nations. And they shall know that I am the LORD.

39

And you, O mortal, prophesy against Gog and say: Thus said the Lord GOD: I am going to deal with you, O Gog, chief prince of Meshech and Tubal! ²I will turn you around and *-drive you on,-^a and I will take you from the far north and lead you toward the mountains of Israel. ³I will strike your bow from your left hand and I will loosen the arrows from your right hand. ⁴You shall fall on the mountains of Israel, you and all your battalions and the peoples who are with you; and I will give you as food to carrion birds of every sort and to the beasts of the field, ⁵as you lie in the open field. For I have spoken—declares the Lord GOD. ⁶And I will send a fire against Magog and against those who dwell secure in the coastlands. And they shall know that I am the LORD. ⁷I will make My holy name known among My people Israel, and never again will I let My holy name be profaned. And the nations shall know that I the LORD

יִהְיֶה֩ רַ֨עַשׁ גָּד֔וֹל עַ֖ל אַדְמַ֥ת יִשְׂרָאֵֽל׃
²⁰ וְרָעֲשׁ֣וּ מִפָּנַ֡י דְּגֵ֣י הַיָּם֩ וְע֨וֹף הַשָּׁמַ֜יִם וְחַיַּ֣ת הַשָּׂדֶ֗ה וְכׇל־הָרֶ֙מֶשׂ֙ הָרֹמֵ֣שׂ עַל־הָ֣אֲדָמָ֔ה וְכֹל֙ הָֽאָדָ֔ם אֲשֶׁ֖ר עַל־פְּנֵ֣י הָאֲדָמָ֑ה וְנֶהֶרְס֣וּ הֶהָרִ֗ים וְנָֽפְלוּ֙ הַמַּדְרֵג֔וֹת וְכׇל־חוֹמָ֖ה לָאָ֥רֶץ תִּפּֽוֹל׃
²¹ וְקָרָ֨אתִי עָלָ֤יו לְכׇל־הָרַי֙ חֶ֔רֶב נְאֻ֖ם אֲדֹנָ֣י יֱהֹוִ֑ה חֶ֥רֶב אִ֖ישׁ בְּאָחִ֥יו תִּֽהְיֶֽה׃
²² וְנִשְׁפַּטְתִּ֥י אִתּ֖וֹ בְּדֶ֣בֶר וּבְדָ֑ם וְגֶ֣שֶׁם שׁוֹטֵף֩ וְאַבְנֵ֨י אֶלְגָּבִ֜ישׁ אֵ֣שׁ וְגׇפְרִ֗ית אַמְטִ֤יר עָלָיו֙ וְעַל־אֲגַפָּ֔יו וְעַל־עַמִּ֥ים רַבִּ֖ים אֲשֶׁ֥ר אִתּֽוֹ׃
²³ וְהִתְגַּדִּלְתִּי֙ וְהִ֨תְקַדִּשְׁתִּ֔י וְנ֣וֹדַעְתִּ֔י לְעֵינֵ֖י גּוֹיִ֣ם רַבִּ֑ים וְיָדְע֖וּ כִּֽי־אֲנִ֥י יְהֹוָֽה׃ ס

לט

וְאַתָּ֤ה בֶן־אָדָם֙ הִנָּבֵ֣א עַל־גּ֔וֹג וְאָ֣מַרְתָּ֔ כֹּ֥ה אָמַ֖ר אֲדֹנָ֣י יֱהֹוִ֑ה הִנְנִ֤י אֵלֶ֙יךָ֙ גּ֔וֹג נְשִׂ֕יא רֹ֖אשׁ מֶ֥שֶׁךְ וְתֻבָֽל׃
² וְשֹׁבַבְתִּ֙יךָ֙ וְשִׁשֵּׁאתִ֔יךָ* וְהַעֲלִיתִ֖יךָ מִיַּרְכְּתֵ֣י צָפ֑וֹן וַהֲבִאוֹתִ֖ךָ עַל־הָרֵ֥י יִשְׂרָאֵֽל׃
³ וְהִכֵּיתִ֥י קַשְׁתְּךָ֖ מִיַּ֣ד שְׂמֹאולֶ֑ךָ* וְחִצֶּ֕יךָ מִיַּ֥ד יְמִינְךָ֖ אַפִּֽיל׃
⁴ עַל־הָרֵ֨י יִשְׂרָאֵ֜ל תִּפּ֗וֹל אַתָּה֙ וְכׇל־אֲגַפֶּ֔יךָ וְעַמִּ֖ים אֲשֶׁ֣ר אִתָּ֑ךְ לְעֵ֨יט צִפּ֧וֹר כׇּל־כָּנָ֛ף וְחַיַּ֥ת הַשָּׂדֶ֖ה נְתַתִּ֥יךָ לְאׇכְלָֽה׃
⁵ עַל־פְּנֵ֥י הַשָּׂדֶ֖ה תִּפּ֑וֹל כִּ֚י אֲנִ֣י דִבַּ֔רְתִּי נְאֻ֖ם אֲדֹנָ֥י יֱהֹוִֽה׃
⁶ וְשִׁלַּחְתִּי־אֵ֣שׁ בְּמָג֔וֹג וּבְיֹשְׁבֵ֥י הָאִיִּ֖ים לָבֶ֑טַח וְיָדְע֖וּ כִּֽי־אֲנִ֥י יְהֹוָֽה׃
⁷ וְאֶת־שֵׁ֨ם קׇדְשִׁ֜י אוֹדִ֗יעַ בְּת֙וֹךְ֙ עַמִּ֣י יִשְׂרָאֵ֔ל וְלֹֽא־אַחֵ֥ל אֶת־שֵׁם־קׇדְשִׁ֖י ע֑וֹד וְיָדְע֤וּ הַגּוֹיִם֙ כִּֽי־אֲנִ֣י יְהֹוָ֔ה קָד֖וֹשׁ

---

d-d   *Meaning of Heb. uncertain.*

a-a   *Meaning of Heb. uncertain.*

           א׳ נחה   *v.* 2.
           מלא ו׳   *v.* 3.

am holy in Israel. ⁸Ah! it has come, it has happened—declares the Lord GOD: this is that day that I decreed.

⁹Then the inhabitants of the cities of Israel will go out and make fires and feed them with the weapons—shields and bucklers, bows and arrows, clubs and spears; they shall use them as fuel for seven years. ¹⁰They will not gather firewood in the fields or cut any in the forests, but will use the weapons as fuel for their fires. They will despoil those who despoiled them and plunder those who plundered them—declares the Lord GOD.

¹¹On that day I will assign to Gog a burial site there in Israel—the Valley of the Travelers, east of the Sea. It shall block the path of travelers, for there Gog and all his multitude will be buried. It shall be called the Valley of Gog's Multitude. ¹²The House of Israel shall spend seven months burying them, in order to cleanse the land; ¹³all the people of the land shall bury them. ᵃ-The day I manifest My glory shall bring renown to them-ᵃ—declares the Lord GOD. ¹⁴And they shall appoint men to serve permanently, to traverse the land and bury any invaders who remain above ground, in order to cleanse it. The search shall go on for a period of seven months. ¹⁵As those who traverse the country make their rounds, any one of them who sees a human bone shall erect a marker beside it, until the buriers have interred them in the Valley of Gog's Multitude. ¹⁶ᵃ-There shall also be a city named Multitude.-ᵃ And thus the land shall be cleansed.

¹⁷And you, O mortal, say to every winged bird and to all the wild beasts: Thus said the Lord GOD: Assemble, come and gather from all around for the sacrificial feast that I am preparing for you—a great sacrificial feast—upon

בְּיִשְׂרָאֵל: ⁸ הִנֵּה בָאָה וְנִהְיָ֫תָה נְאֻם אֲדֹנָ֣י יְהוִ֑ה ה֣וּא הַיּ֔וֹם אֲשֶׁ֖ר דִּבַּֽרְתִּי:

⁹ וְֽיָצְא֞וּ יֹשְׁבֵ֣י ׀ עָרֵ֣י יִשְׂרָאֵ֗ל וּבִעֲר֡וּ וְ֠הִשִּׂ֠יקוּ בְּנֶ֨שֶׁק וּמָגֵ֤ן וְצִנָּה֙ בְּקֶ֣שֶׁת וּבְחִצִּ֔ים וּבְמַקֵּ֥ל יָ֖ד וּבְרֹ֑מַח וּבִעֲר֥וּ בָהֶ֛ם אֵ֖שׁ שֶׁ֥בַע שָׁנִֽים: ¹⁰ וְלֹֽא־יִשְׂא֨וּ עֵצִ֜ים מִן־הַשָּׂדֶ֗ה וְלֹ֤א יַחְטְבוּ֙ מִן־הַיְּעָרִ֔ים כִּ֥י בַנֶּ֖שֶׁק יְבַעֲרוּ־אֵ֑שׁ וְשָׁלְל֣וּ אֶת־שֹׁלְלֵיהֶ֗ם וּבָֽזְזוּ֙ אֶת־בֹּ֣זְזֵיהֶ֔ם נְאֻ֖ם אֲדֹנָ֥י יְהוִֽה: ס

¹¹ וְהָיָ֣ה בַיּ֣וֹם הַה֡וּא אֶתֵּ֣ן לְגוֹג֩ ׀ מְקֽוֹם־שָׁ֨ם קֶ֜בֶר בְּיִשְׂרָאֵ֗ל גֵּ֤י הָעֹֽבְרִים֙ קִדְמַ֣ת הַיָּ֔ם וְחֹסֶ֥מֶת הִ֖יא אֶת־הָעֹֽבְרִ֑ים וְקָ֣בְרוּ שָׁ֗ם אֶת־גּוֹג֙ וְאֶת־כָּל־הֲמוֹנ֔וֹ וְקָ֣רְא֔וּ גֵּ֖יא הֲמ֥וֹן גּֽוֹג: ¹² וּקְבָרוּם֙ בֵּ֣ית יִשְׂרָאֵ֔ל לְמַ֖עַן טַהֵ֣ר אֶת־הָאָ֑רֶץ שִׁבְעָ֥ה חֳדָשִֽׁים: ¹³ וְקָֽבְרוּ֙ כָּל־עַ֣ם הָאָ֔רֶץ וְהָיָ֥ה לָהֶ֖ם לְשֵׁ֑ם י֗וֹם הִכָּ֣בְדִ֔י נְאֻ֖ם אֲדֹנָ֥י יְהוִֽה: ¹⁴ וְאַנְשֵׁ֨י תָמִ֤יד יַבְדִּ֨ילוּ֙ עֹבְרִ֣ים בָּאָ֔רֶץ מְקַבְּרִ֣ים אֶת־הָעֹבְרִ֗ים אֶת־הַנּוֹתָרִ֛ים עַל־פְּנֵ֥י הָאָ֖רֶץ לְטַֽהֲרָ֑הּ מִקְצֵ֥ה שִׁבְעָֽה־חֳדָשִׁ֖ים יַחְקֹֽרוּ: ¹⁵ וְעָֽבְר֤וּ הָעֹֽבְרִים֙ בָּאָ֔רֶץ וְרָאָה֙ עֶ֣צֶם אָדָ֔ם וּבָנָ֥ה אֶצְל֖וֹ צִיּ֑וּן עַ֣ד קָבְר֤וּ אֹתוֹ֙ הַֽמְקַבְּרִ֔ים אֶל־גֵּ֖יא הֲמ֥וֹן גּֽוֹג: ¹⁶ וְגַ֥ם שֶׁם־עִ֖יר הֲמוֹנָ֑ה וְטִהֲר֖וּ הָאָֽרֶץ: ס

¹⁷ וְאַתָּ֨ה בֶן־אָדָ֜ם כֹּֽה־אָמַ֣ר ׀ אֲדֹנָ֣י יְהוִ֗ה אֱמֹר֩ לְצִפּ֨וֹר כָּל־כָּנָ֜ף וּלְכֹ֣ל ׀ חַיַּ֣ת הַשָּׂדֶ֗ה הִקָּֽבְצ֤וּ וָבֹ֨אוּ֙ הֵאָסְפ֣וּ מִסָּבִ֔יב עַל־זִבְחִ֗י אֲשֶׁ֨ר אֲנִ֜י זֹבֵ֤חַ לָכֶם֙ זֶ֣בַח גָּד֔וֹל עַ֖ל הָרֵ֥י

the mountains of Israel, and eat flesh and drink blood. [18]You shall eat the flesh of warriors and drink the blood of the princes of the earth: rams, lambs, he-goats, and bulls—fatlings of Bashan all of them. [19]You shall eat fat to satiety and drink your fill of blood from the sacrificial feast that I have prepared for you. [20]And you shall sate yourselves at My table with horses, charioteers,[b] warriors, and all fighting men—declares the Lord GOD. [21]Thus will I manifest My glory among the nations, and all the nations shall see the judgment that I executed and the power that I wielded against them.

[22]From that time on, the House of Israel shall know that I the LORD am their God. [23]And the nations shall know that the House of Israel were exiled only for their iniquity, because they trespassed against Me, so that I hid My face from them and delivered them into the hands of their adversaries, and they all fell by the sword. [24]When I hid My face from them, I dealt with them according to their uncleanness and their transgressions.

[25]Assuredly, thus said the Lord GOD: I will now restore the fortunes of Jacob and take the whole House of Israel back in love; and I will be zealous for My holy name. [26]They will bear[c] their shame and all their trespasses that they committed against Me, when they dwell in their land secure and untroubled, [27]when I have brought them back from among the peoples and gathered them out of the lands of their enemies and have manifested My holiness through them in the sight of many nations. [28]They shall know that I the Lord am their GOD when, having exiled them among the nations, I gather them back into their land and leave none of them behind. [29]I will never again hide My face from them, for I will pour out My spirit upon the House of Israel—declares the Lord GOD.

יִשְׂרָאֵל וַאֲכַלְתֶּם בָּשָׂר וּשְׁתִיתֶם דָּם:
18 בְּשַׂר גִּבּוֹרִים תֹּאכֵלוּ וְדַם־נְשִׂיאֵי
הָאָרֶץ תִּשְׁתּוּ אֵילִים כָּרִים וְעַתּוּדִים
פָּרִים מְרִיאֵי בָשָׁן כֻּלָּם: 19 וַאֲכַלְתֶּם־חֵלֶב
לְשָׂבְעָה וּשְׁתִיתֶם דָּם לְשִׁכָּרוֹן מִזִּבְחִי
אֲשֶׁר־זָבַחְתִּי לָכֶם: 20 וּשְׂבַעְתֶּם עַל־
שֻׁלְחָנִי סוּס וָרֶכֶב גִּבּוֹר וְכָל־אִישׁ מִלְחָמָה
נְאֻם אֲדֹנָי יְהוִה: 21 וְנָתַתִּי אֶת־כְּבוֹדִי
בַּגּוֹיִם וְרָאוּ כָל־הַגּוֹיִם אֶת־מִשְׁפָּטִי אֲשֶׁר
עָשִׂיתִי וְאֶת־יָדִי אֲשֶׁר־שַׂמְתִּי בָהֶם:
22 וְיָדְעוּ בֵּית יִשְׂרָאֵל כִּי אֲנִי יְהוָה
אֱלֹהֵיהֶם מִן־הַיּוֹם הַהוּא וָהָלְאָה:
23 וְיָדְעוּ הַגּוֹיִם כִּי בַעֲוֹנָם גָּלוּ בֵית־יִשְׂרָאֵל
עַל אֲשֶׁר מָעֲלוּ־בִי וָאַסְתִּר פָּנַי מֵהֶם
וָאֶתְּנֵם בְּיַד צָרֵיהֶם וַיִּפְּלוּ בַחֶרֶב כֻּלָּם:
24 כְּטֻמְאָתָם וּכְפִשְׁעֵיהֶם עָשִׂיתִי אֹתָם
וָאַסְתִּר פָּנַי מֵהֶם: ס
25 לָכֵן כֹּה אָמַר אֲדֹנָי יְהוִה עַתָּה אָשִׁיב
אֶת־שְׁבִות יַעֲקֹב וְרִחַמְתִּי כָּל־בֵּית
יִשְׂרָאֵל וְקִנֵּאתִי לְשֵׁם קָדְשִׁי: 26 וְנָשׂוּ*
אֶת־כְּלִמָּתָם וְאֶת־כָּל־מַעֲלָם אֲשֶׁר מָעֲלוּ־
בִי בְּשִׁבְתָּם עַל־אַדְמָתָם לָבֶטַח וְאֵין
מַחֲרִיד: 27 בְּשׁוֹבְבִי אוֹתָם מִן־הָעַמִּים
וְקִבַּצְתִּי אֹתָם מֵאַרְצוֹת אֹיְבֵיהֶם
וְנִקְדַּשְׁתִּי בָם לְעֵינֵי הַגּוֹיִם רַבִּים: 28 וְיָדְעוּ
כִּי אֲנִי יְהוָה אֱלֹהֵיהֶם בְּהַגְלוֹתִי אֹתָם
אֶל־הַגּוֹיִם וְכִנַּסְתִּים עַל־אַדְמָתָם וְלֹא־
אוֹתִיר עוֹד מֵהֶם שָׁם: 29 וְלֹא־אַסְתִּיר
עוֹד פָּנַי מֵהֶם אֲשֶׁר שָׁפַכְתִּי אֶת־רוּחִי
עַל־בֵּית יִשְׂרָאֵל נְאֻם אֲדֹנָי יְהוִה: פ

---

b   Lit. "chariots"; Septuagint reads "riders."
c   Change of diacritical point yields "forget."

40 In the twenty-fifth year of our exile,[a] the fourteenth year after the city had fallen, at the beginning of the year, the tenth day of the month—on that very day—the hand of the LORD came upon me, and He brought me there. [2]He brought me, in visions of God, to the Land of Israel, and He set me down on a very high mountain[b] on which there seemed to be the outline of a city [c]-on the south.-[c] [3]He brought me over to it, and there, standing at the gate, was a man who shone like copper. In his hand were a cord of linen and a measuring rod. [4]The man spoke to me: "Mortal, look closely and listen attentively and note well everything I am going to show you—for you have been brought here in order to be shown—and report everything you see to the House of Israel."

[5]Along the outside of the Temple [area] ran a wall on every side. The rod that the man held was six cubits long, plus one handbreadth for each cubit; and when he applied it to that structure, it measured one rod deep[d] and one rod high.

[6]He went up to the gate that faced eastward and mounted its steps. He measured the threshold of the gate; it was one rod deep[d]—[e]-the one threshold was one rod deep.-[e] [7]Each recess was one rod wide and one rod deep, with [a partition of] 5 cubits between recesses; and the threshold of the gate, at the inner vestibule of the gate, was one rod deep. [8][e]-For when he measured it at the inner vestibule of the gate, it was one rod [deep].-[e] [9]Next he measured the vestibule of the gate, and it measured 8 cubits and its supports

---

מ בְּעֶשְׂרִ֣ים וְחָמֵ֣שׁ שָׁנָ֣ה לְגָל֠וּתֵנוּ בְּרֹ֨אשׁ הַשָּׁנָ֜ה בֶּעָשׂ֣וֹר לַחֹ֗דֶשׁ בְּאַרְבַּ֤ע עֶשְׂרֵה֙ שָׁנָ֔ה אַחַ֕ר אֲשֶׁ֥ר הֻכְּתָ֖ה הָעִ֑יר בְּעֶ֣צֶם ׀ הַיּ֣וֹם הַזֶּ֗ה הָיְתָ֤ה עָלַי֙ יַד־יְהֹוָ֔ה וַיָּבֵ֥א אֹתִ֖י שָֽׁמָּה׃ [2]בְּמַרְא֣וֹת אֱלֹהִ֔ים הֱבִיאַ֖נִי אֶל־אֶ֣רֶץ יִשְׂרָאֵ֑ל וַיְנִיחֵ֗נִי אֶל־הַ֤ר גָּבֹ֙הַּ֙ מְאֹ֔ד וְעָלָ֥יו כְּמִבְנֵה־עִ֖יר מִנֶּֽגֶב׃ [3]וַיָּבֵ֨יא אוֹתִ֜י שָׁ֗מָּה וְהִנֵּה־אִישׁ֙ מַרְאֵ֙הוּ֙ כְּמַרְאֵ֣ה נְחֹ֔שֶׁת וּפְתִיל־פִּשְׁתִּ֥ים בְּיָד֖וֹ וּקְנֵ֣ה הַמִּדָּ֑ה וְה֥וּא עֹמֵ֖ד בַּשָּֽׁעַר׃ [4]וַיְדַבֵּ֨ר אֵלַ֜י הָאִ֗ישׁ בֶּן־אָדָ֡ם רְאֵ֣ה בְעֵינֶ֩יךָ֩ וּבְאׇזְנֶ֨יךָ שְּׁמָ֜ע וְשִׂ֣ים לִבְּךָ֗ לְכֹ֤ל אֲשֶׁר־אֲנִי֙ מַרְאֶ֣ה אוֹתָ֔ךְ כִּ֛י לְמַ֥עַן הַרְאוֹתְכָ֖ה* הֻבָ֣אתָה הֵ֑נָּה הַגֵּ֛ד אֶת־כׇּל־אֲשֶׁר־אַתָּ֥ה רֹאֶ֖ה לְבֵ֥ית יִשְׂרָאֵֽל׃

[5]וְהִנֵּ֥ה חוֹמָ֛ה מִח֥וּץ לַבַּ֖יִת סָבִ֣יב ׀ סָבִ֑יב וּבְיַ֨ד הָאִ֜ישׁ קְנֵ֤ה הַמִּדָּה֙ שֵׁשׁ־אַמּ֣וֹת בָּֽאַמָּ֣ה וָטֹ֔פַח וַיָּ֜מׇד אֶת־רֹ֤חַב הַבִּנְיָן֙ קָנֶ֣ה אֶחָ֔ד וְקוֹמָ֖ה קָנֶ֥ה אֶחָֽד׃ [6]וַיָּב֗וֹא אֶל־שַׁ֙עַר֙ אֲשֶׁ֤ר פָּנָיו֙ דֶּ֣רֶךְ הַקָּדִ֔ימָה וַיַּ֖עַל *במעלותו* בְּמַֽעֲלוֹתָ֑יו וַיָּ֣מׇד ׀ אֶת־סַ֣ף הַשַּׁ֗עַר קָנֶ֤ה אֶחָד֙ רֹ֔חַב וְאֵ֗ת סַ֤ף אֶחָד֙ קָנֶ֥ה אֶחָ֖ד רֹֽחַב׃ [7]וְהַתָּ֗א קָנֶ֨ה אֶחָ֥ד אֹ֙רֶךְ֙ וְקָנֶ֤ה אֶחָד֙ רֹ֔חַב וּבֵ֥ין הַתָּאִ֖ים חָמֵ֣שׁ אַמּ֑וֹת וְסַ֣ף הַ֠שַּׁעַר מֵאֵ֨צֶל אוּלָ֥ם הַשַּׁ֛עַר מֵהַבַּ֖יִת קָנֶ֥ה אֶחָֽד׃ [8]וַיָּ֛מׇד אֶת־אֻלָ֥ם הַשַּׁ֖עַר מֵהַבַּ֑יִת קָנֶ֥ה אֶחָֽד׃ [9]וַיָּ֜מׇד אֶת־אֻלָ֤ם הַשַּׁ֙עַר֙ שְׁמֹנֶ֣ה אַמּ֔וֹת *ואילו* וְאֵילָ֖יו שְׁתַּ֣יִם אַמּ֑וֹת וְאֻלָ֥ם

v. 4. יתיר ה'

---

a   I.e., the exile of King Jehoiachin; see 1.2.
b   Cf. Isa. 2.1; Mic. 4.1.
c-c   Septuagint reads "in the distance."
d   In this description, the Hebrew word which ordinarily corresponds to English "width" sometimes designates a measurement from an opening or outer surface inward, and so corresponds to the English "depth"; and the word which ordinarily corresponds to English "length" designates the distance from side to side of a vestibule or a passage, and so corresponds to the English "width."
e-e   Meaning of Heb. uncertain.

2 cubits; the vestibule of the gate was at its inner end. [10]fOn either side of this eastern gate there were three recesses, all three of the same size; of identical sizes were also the supportsg on either side. [11]He measured the opening of the gate and found it 10 cubits wide, while the gate itself measured 13 cubits across.h [12]At the fronts of the recesses on either side were e-barriers of one cubit;-e the recesses on either side were 6 cubits [deep]. [13]Their openings faced each other directly across the gate passage, so that when he measured from reare of recess to reare of recess he obtained a width of 25 cubits.i [14]e-He made the vestiblej—60 cubits—and the gate next to the support on every side of the court.-e [15]And [the distance] from the front of the outere gate to the front of the inner vestibule of the gate was 50 cubits. [16]The recesses—and their supports—had windows e-with frames-e on the interior of the gate complex on both sides, and the interiors of the vestibules also had windows on both sides; and the supports were adorned with palms.

[17]He took me into the outer court. There were chambers there, and there was a pavement laid out all around the court. There were 30 chambers on the pavement. [18]The pavements flanked the gates; the depth of the lowerk pavements paralleled that of the gates. [19]Then he measured the width of l-the lowerk court, from in front of the inner gate to in front of the outer gate-l—100 cubits.

e-After the east [gate], the north [gate].-e [20]Next he measured the gate of the outer court that faced north: its length and its width, [21]its

הַשַּׁעַר מֵהַבָּיִת: 10 וְתָאֵי הַשַּׁעַר דֶּרֶךְ הַקָּדִים שְׁלֹשָׁה מִפֹּה וּשְׁלֹשָׁה מִפֹּה מִדָּה אַחַת לִשְׁלָשְׁתָּם וּמִדָּה אַחַת לָאֵילִם מִפֹּה וּמִפּוֹ: 11 וַיָּמָד אֶת־רֹחַב פֶּתַח־הַשַּׁעַר עֶשֶׂר אַמּוֹת אֹרֶךְ הַשַּׁעַר שְׁלוֹשׁ עֶשְׂרֵה אַמּוֹת: 12 וּגְבוּל לִפְנֵי הַתָּאוֹת אַמָּה אֶחָת וְאַמָּה־אַחַת גְּבוּל מִפֹּה וְהַתָּא שֵׁשׁ־אַמּוֹת מִפֹּה וְשֵׁשׁ אַמּוֹת מִפּוֹ: 13 וַיָּמָד אֶת־הַשַּׁעַר מִגַּג הַתָּא לְגַגּוֹ רֹחַב עֶשְׂרִים וְחָמֵשׁ אַמּוֹת פֶּתַח נֶגֶד פָּתַח: 14 וַיַּעַשׂ אֶת־ אֵילִים שִׁשִּׁים אַמָּה וְאֶל־אֵיל הֶחָצֵר הַשַּׁעַר סָבִיב | סָבִיב: 15 וְעַל פְּנֵי הַשַּׁעַר הָאִיתוֹן עַל־לִפְנֵי אֻלָם הַשַּׁעַר הַפְּנִימִי חֲמִשִּׁים אַמָּה: 16 וְחַלֹּנוֹת אֲטֻמוֹת אֶל־הַתָּאִים וְאֶל אֵלֵיהֵמָה לִפְנִימָה לַשַּׁעַר סָבִיב | סָבִיב וְכֵן לָאֵלַמּוֹת וְחַלּוֹנוֹת סָבִיב | סָבִיב לִפְנִימָה וְאֶל־אַיִל תִּמֹרִים:

17 וַיְבִיאֵנִי אֶל־הֶחָצֵר הַחִיצוֹנָה וְהִנֵּה לְשָׁכוֹת וְרִצְפָה עָשׂוּי לֶחָצֵר סָבִיב | סָבִיב שְׁלֹשִׁים לְשָׁכוֹת אֶל־הָרִצְפָה: 18 וְהָרִצְפָה אֶל־כֶּתֶף הַשְּׁעָרִים לְעֻמַּת אֹרֶךְ הַשְּׁעָרִים הָרִצְפָה הַתַּחְתּוֹנָה: 19 וַיָּמָד רֹחַב מִלִּפְנֵי הַשַּׁעַר הַתַּחְתּוֹנָה לִפְנֵי הֶחָצֵר הַפְּנִימִי מִחוּץ מֵאָה אַמָּה הַקָּדִים וְהַצָּפוֹן: 20 וְהַשַּׁעַר אֲשֶׁר פָּנָיו דֶּרֶךְ הַצָּפוֹן לֶחָצֵר הַחִיצוֹנָה מָדַד אָרְכּוֹ וְרָחְבּוֹ: 21 וְתָאָו וְתָאָיו שְׁלוֹשָׁה מִפּוֹ

---

f   This verse would read well before v. 7.
g   In connection with recesses, the "supports" are partitions.
h   The opening was perhaps narrowed by a stone on each side for receiving the hinge of a door-leaf.
i   Since each of the recesses was 6 cubits deep (v. 7a) and the passage in the middle was 13 cubits wide (v. 11).
j   Elim here is the same as elam in vv. 16, 21, 22, etc.
k   The outer court and its gates were 8 steps lower than the inner ones: v. 34.
l-l   In this rendering, the adjectives "lower" and "inner" are construed, not with the nouns they stand next to in the Hebrew, but with those with which they agree in gender.

three recesses on either side and its supports, as also its vestibule. It measured, like the first gate, 50 cubits in length and 25 cubits in width. ²²Its windows and [those of] its vestibule, as also its palm trees, corresponded to those of the gate that faced east. [From the outside] one had to climb 7 steps to reach it, and its vestibule was ^m-ahead of them.-^m ²³Like the east gate, the north gate faced a gate leading into the inner forecourt; and when he measured the distance from gate to gate, it was 100 cubits.

²⁴Then he took me to the south side. There was also a gate on the south side, and he got the same measurements as before for its supports and its vestibule. ²⁵Both it and its vestibule had windows like the aforementioned ones. It was 50 cubits long and 25 cubits wide. ²⁶Its staircase consisted of 7 steps; its vestibule was ^m-ahead of them,-^m and its supports were decorated on both sides with palm trees. ²⁷The inner court likewise had a gate facing south; and on the south side, too, he measured a distance of 100 cubits from the [outer] gate to the [inner] gate.

²⁸He now took me into the inner forecourt through its south gate. When he measured this south gate, it had the same measurements as the foregoing. ²⁹Its recesses, its supports, and its vestibule had the same measurements. Both it and its vestibule had windows on both sides; it was 50 cubits long and 25 cubits wide—³⁰ⁿ-vestibules on both sides, 25 cubits long, 5 cubits wide.-ⁿ ³¹Its vestibule, however, gave on the outer court.^o Its supports were adorned on either side with palms, and its staircase consisted of 8 steps.

³²Then he took me to the eastern side of the inner forecourt; and when he measured the gate there, he got the same measurements: ³³its re-

וּשְׁלֹשָׁ֣ה מִפֹּ֣ו וָאֵילָ֣ו וְ֜אֵילָ֗ו וְאֵלַמֹּ֣ו וְאֵלַמָּ֡יו הָיָ֣ה כְּמִדַּ֣ת הַשַּׁ֣עַר הָרִאשֹׁ֗ון חֲמִשִּׁ֤ים אַמָּה֙ אָרְכֹּ֔ו וְרֹ֕חַב חָמֵ֥שׁ וְעֶשְׂרִ֖ים בָּאַמָּֽה: ²² וְחַלֹּונָ֤ו וְאֵלַמֹּו֙ וְאֵלַמָּ֔יו וְתִ֣מֹרָ֔יו כְּמִדַּ֣ת הַשַּׁ֔עַר אֲשֶׁ֥ר פָּנָ֖יו דֶּ֣רֶךְ הַקָּדִ֑ים וּבְמַעֲלֹ֤ות שֶׁ֙בַע֙ יַֽעֲלוּ־בֹ֔ו וְאֵֽילַמָּ֖יו לִפְנֵיהֶֽם: ²³ וְשַׁ֙עַר֙ לֶחָצֵ֣ר הַפְּנִימִ֔י נֶ֚גֶד הַשַּׁ֔עַר לַצָּפֹ֖ון וְלַקָּדִ֑ים וַיָּ֧מָד מִשַּׁ֛עַר אֶל־שַׁ֖עַר מֵאָ֥ה אַמָּֽה:

²⁴ וַיֹּֽולִכֵ֙נִי֙ דֶּ֣רֶךְ הַדָּרֹ֔ום וְהִנֵּה־שַׁ֖עַר דֶּ֣רֶךְ הַדָּרֹ֑ום וּמָדַ֤ד אֵילֹו֙ וְאֵ֣ילַמָּ֔יו כַּמִּדֹּ֖ות הָאֵֽלֶּה: ²⁵ וְחַלֹּונִ֣ים לֹ֣ו וּלְאֵֽילַמָּ֣יו סָבִ֣יב ׀ סָבִ֗יב כְּהַֽחַלֹּנֹ֣ות הָאֵ֑לֶּה חֲמִשִּׁ֤ים אַמָּה֙ אֹ֔רֶךְ וְרֹ֕חַב חָמֵ֥שׁ וְעֶשְׂרִ֖ים אַמָּֽה: ²⁶ וּמַעֲלֹ֤ות שִׁבְעָה֙ עֹלֹותָ֔ו וְאֵֽלַמֹּ֖ו לִפְנֵיהֶ֑ם וְתִמֹרִ֣ים לֹ֗ו אֶחָ֥ד מִפֹּ֛ו וְאֶחָ֥ד מִפֹּ֖ו אֶל־אֵילָֽו: ²⁷ וְשַׁ֙עַר֙ לֶחָצֵ֣ר הַפְּנִימִ֔י דֶּ֖רֶךְ הַדָּרֹ֑ום וַיָּ֧מָד מִשַּׁ֛עַר אֶל־הַשַּׁ֖עַר דֶּ֣רֶךְ הַדָּרֹ֖ום מֵאָ֥ה אַמֹּֽות: ²⁸ וַיְבִיאֵ֙נִי֙ אֶל־חָצֵ֣ר הַפְּנִימִ֔י בְּשַׁ֖עַר הַדָּרֹ֑ום וַיָּ֙מָד֙ אֶת־הַשַּׁ֣עַר הַדָּרֹ֔ום כַּמִּדֹּ֖ות הָאֵֽלֶּה: ²⁹ וְתָאָ֞ו וְאֵילָ֤ו וְאֵֽילַמָּו֙ כַּמִּדֹּ֣ות הָאֵ֔לֶּה וְחַלֹּונֹ֥ות לֹ֛ו וּלְאֵילַמָּ֖יו סָבִ֣יב ׀ סָבִ֑יב חֲמִשִּׁ֤ים אַמָּה֙ אֹ֔רֶךְ וְרֹ֕חַב עֶשְׂרִ֥ים וְחָמֵ֖שׁ אַמֹּֽות: ³⁰ וְאֵֽלַמֹּ֖ות סָבִ֣יב ׀ סָבִ֑יב אֹ֗רֶךְ חָמֵ֤שׁ וְעֶשְׂרִים֙ אַמָּ֔ה וְרֹ֖חַב חָמֵ֥שׁ אַמֹּֽות: ³¹ וְאֵֽלַמֹּ֗ו אֶל־חָצֵר֙ הַחִ֣צֹונָ֔ה וְתִמֹרִ֖ים אֶל־אֵילָ֑ו וּמַעֲלֹ֥ות שְׁמֹונֶ֖ה מַעֲלָֽו: ³² וַיְבִיאֵ֛נִי אֶל־הֶֽחָצֵ֥ר הַפְּנִימִ֖י דֶּ֣רֶךְ הַקָּדִ֑ים וַיָּ֣מָד אֶת־הַשַּׁ֔עַר כַּמִּדֹּ֖ות הָאֵֽלֶּה: ³³ וְתָאָ֞ו

m-m   Septuagint reads "at its inner end."
n-n   Connection unclear; wanting in some Heb. mss. and versions.
o   I.e., in the inner gates the vestibules were situated at their entrances, and so they were true vestibules, in contrast to the "inner vestibules" of the outer gates.

cesses, supports, and vestibule had the above measurements. Both it and its vestibule had windows on both sides; it was 50 cubits long and 25 cubits wide, 34and its vestibule gave on the outer court. Its supports were decorated on both sides with palm trees, and its staircase consisted of 8 steps.

35Then he took me to the north gate, and found its measurements to be identical, 36with the same recesses, supports, vestibule, windows on both sides, and a length of 50 cubits and a width of 25 cubits. 37Its supports*p* gave on the outer court; its supports were decorated on both sides with palm trees; and its staircase consisted of eight steps.

38A chamber opened into the gate;*q* there the burnt offering would be washed. 39And inside the vestibule of the gate, there were two tables on each side, at which the burnt offering, the sin offering, and the guilt offering were to be slaughtered; 40while outside—*r*-as one goes up toward-*r* the opening of the north gate—there were two tables on one side, and there were two tables on the other side of the gate's vestibule. 41Thus there were four tables on either flank of the gate—eight tables in all—at which [the sacrifices] were to be slaughtered. 42As for the four tables for the burnt offering*s*—they were of hewn stone, one and a half cubits long, one and a half cubits wide, and one cubit high—*t*-on them were laid out the instruments with which burnt offerings and sacrifices were slaughtered.-*t* 43Shelves,*e* one handbreadth wide, were attached all around the inside; and the sacrificial flesh was [laid] on the tables.

44There were *u*-chambers for singers-*u* in the inner forecourt: [one] beside the north gate fac-

---

p   Septuagint reads "vestibules"; cf. vv. 31, 34.

q   Heb. "gates"; the reference is apparently to the north gate; cf. v. 40 and Lev. 1.11; 4.24; 7.2.

r-r   Emendation yields "the vestibule at."

s   See v. 39.

t-t   This clause would read well after v. 43.

u-u Septuagint reads "two chambers."

וְתָאָ֞יו ואלו וְאֵלָ֣יו ואלמו וְאֵלַמָּ֗יו כַּמִּדּ֣וֹת הָאֵ֔לֶּה וְחַלּוֹנ֥וֹת ל֛וֹ ולאלמו וּלְאֵלַמָּ֖יו סָבִ֑יב ׀ סָבֵ֣יב אֹ֔רֶךְ חֲמִשִּׁ֣ים אַמָּ֔ה וְרֹ֕חַב חָמֵ֥שׁ וְעֶשְׂרִ֖ים אַמָּֽה׃ 34 ואלמו וְאֵלַמָּ֗יו לֶחָצֵר֙ הַחִ֣יצוֹנָ֔ה וְתִמֹרִ֥ים אֶל־אֵלָ֖יו אֵלָ֑יו מִפּ֣וֹ וּמִפּ֑וֹ וּשְׁמֹנֶ֥ה מַעֲל֖וֹת מעלו מַעֲלָֽו׃

35 וַיְבִיאֵ֖נִי אֶל־שַׁ֣עַר הַצָּפ֑וֹן וּמָדַ֖ד כַּמִּדּ֥וֹת הָאֵֽלֶּה׃ 36 תאו תָּאָ֤יו אלו אֵלָ֙יו וְאֵלַמָּ֔יו וְחַלּוֹנ֥וֹת ל֛וֹ סָבִ֖יב ׀ סָבֵ֑יב אֹ֗רֶךְ חֲמִשִּׁ֣ים אַמָּ֔ה וְרֹ֕חַב חָמֵ֥שׁ וְעֶשְׂרִ֖ים אַמָּֽה׃ 37 ואילו וְאֵילָ֗יו לֶחָצֵר֙ הַחִ֣יצוֹנָ֔ה וְתִמֹרִ֥ים אֶל־אֵילָ֛יו אֵילָ֖יו מִפּ֣וֹ וּמִפּ֑וֹ וּשְׁמֹנֶ֥ה מַעֲל֖וֹת מעלו מַעֲלָֽו׃

38 וְלִשְׁכָּ֣ה וּפִתְחָ֔הּ בְּאֵילִ֖ים הַשְּׁעָרִ֑ים שָׁ֖ם יָדִ֥יחוּ אֶת־הָעֹלָֽה׃ 39 וּבְאֻלָ֣ם הַשַּׁ֗עַר שְׁנַ֤יִם שֻׁלְחָנוֹת֙ מִפּ֔וֹ וּשְׁנַ֥יִם שֻׁלְחָנ֖וֹת מִפֹּ֑ה לִשְׁח֤וֹט אֲלֵיהֶם֙ הָעוֹלָ֔ה וְהַחַטָּ֖את וְהָאָשָֽׁם׃ 40 וְאֶל־הַכָּתֵ֣ף מִח֗וּצָה לָעוֹלֶה֙ לְפֶ֙תַח֙ הַשַּׁ֣עַר הַצָּפ֔וֹנָה שְׁנַ֖יִם שֻׁלְחָנ֑וֹת וְאֶל־הַכָּתֵ֣ף הָאַחֶ֗רֶת אֲשֶׁר֙ לְאֻלָ֣ם הַשַּׁ֔עַר שְׁנַ֖יִם שֻׁלְחָנֽוֹת׃ 41 אַרְבָּעָ֣ה שֻׁלְחָנ֣וֹת מִפֹּ֗ה וְאַרְבָּעָ֤ה שֻׁלְחָנוֹת֙ מִפֹּ֔ה לְכֶ֖תֶף הַשָּׁ֑עַר שְׁמוֹנָ֣ה שֻׁלְחָנ֔וֹת אֲלֵיהֶ֖ם יִשְׁחָֽטוּ׃ 42 וְאַרְבָּעָה֩ שֻׁלְחָנ֨וֹת לָעוֹלָ֜ה אַבְנֵ֣י גָזִ֗ית אֹ֡רֶךְ אַמָּ֨ה אַחַ֤ת וָחֵ֙צִי֙ וְרֹ֨חַב אַמָּ֤ה אַחַת֙ וָחֵ֔צִי וְגֹ֖בַהּ אַמָּ֣ה אֶחָ֑ת אֲלֵיהֶ֗ם וְיַנִּ֤יחוּ אֶת־הַכֵּלִים֙ אֲשֶׁ֨ר יִשְׁחֲט֧וּ אֶת־הָעוֹלָ֛ה בָּ֖ם וְהַזָּֽבַח׃ 43 וְהַֽשְׁפַתַּ֗יִם טֹ֣פַח אֶחָ֞ד מוּכָנִ֥ים בַּבַּ֖יִת סָבִ֣יב ׀ סָבֵ֑יב וְאֶל־הַשֻּׁלְחָנ֖וֹת בְּשַׂ֥ר הַקָּרְבָּֽן׃ 44 וּמִחוּצָה֩ לַשַּׁ֨עַר הַפְּנִימִ֜י לִֽשְׁכ֣וֹת שָׁרִ֗ים בֶּחָצֵ֤ר הַפְּנִימִי֙ אֲשֶׁ֣ר אֶל־כֶּ֔תֶף שַׁ֖עַר הַצָּפ֑וֹן

ing south, and one beside the east[v] gate facing north. 45[The man] explained to me: "The chamber that faces south is for the priests who perform the duties of the Temple; 46and the chamber that faces north is for the priests who perform the duties of the altar—they are the descendants of Zadok, who alone of the descendants of Levi may approach the Lord to minister to Him."

47He then measured the forecourt: 100 cubits long and 100 cubits broad—foursquare. In front of the Temple stood the altar. 48He took me into the portico of the Temple and measured it. The jambs[w] of the portico were 5 cubits deep on either side. The width of the gate-opening was x-[14 cubits, and the flanking wall of the gate was]-x 3 cubits on either side. 49The portico was 20 cubits wide[y] and 11[z] cubits deep, and aa-it was by steps that it was reached.-aa There were columns by the jambs on either side.

41 He then led me into the great hall. He measured the jambs, 6 cubits on either side; such was the depth[a] of each jamb.[b] 2The entrance was 10 cubits wide, and the flanking walls of the entrance were each 5 cubits wide. Next he measured the depth [of the hall], 40 cubits, and the width, 20 cubits. 3And then he entered the inner room. He measured each jamb of the entrance, 2 cubits [deep]; the entrance itself, 6 cubits across; and the width of c-[the flanking wall on either side of]-c the entrance, 7 cubits. 4Then he measured the depth, 20 cubits; and

וּפְנֵיהֶם דֶּרֶךְ הַדָּרוֹם אֶחָד אֶל־כֶּתֶף שַׁעַר הַקָּדִים פְּנֵי דֶּרֶךְ הַצָּפֹן: 45 וַיְדַבֵּר אֵלָי זֶה הַלִּשְׁכָּה אֲשֶׁר פָּנֶיהָ דֶּרֶךְ הַדָּרוֹם לַכֹּהֲנִים שֹׁמְרֵי מִשְׁמֶרֶת הַבָּיִת: 46 וְהַלִּשְׁכָּה אֲשֶׁר פָּנֶיהָ דֶּרֶךְ הַצָּפוֹן לַכֹּהֲנִים שֹׁמְרֵי מִשְׁמֶרֶת הַמִּזְבֵּחַ הֵמָּה בְנֵי־צָדוֹק הַקְּרֵבִים מִבְּנֵי־לֵוִי אֶל־יְהוָה לְשָׁרְתוֹ:

47 וַיָּמָד אֶת־הֶחָצֵר אֹרֶךְ ׀ מֵאָה אַמָּה וְרֹחַב מֵאָה אַמָּה מְרֻבָּעַת וְהַמִּזְבֵּחַ לִפְנֵי הַבָּיִת: 48 וַיְבִאֵנִי אֶל־אֻלָם הַבַּיִת וַיָּמָד אֵל אֻלָם חָמֵשׁ אַמּוֹת מִפֹּה וְחָמֵשׁ אַמּוֹת מִפֹּה וְרֹחַב הַשַּׁעַר שָׁלֹשׁ אַמּוֹת מִפּוֹ וְשָׁלֹשׁ אַמּוֹת מִפֹּה: 49 אֹרֶךְ הָאֻלָם עֶשְׂרִים אַמָּה וְרֹחַב עַשְׁתֵּי עֶשְׂרֵה אַמָּה וּבַמַּעֲלוֹת אֲשֶׁר יַעֲלוּ אֵלָיו וְעַמֻּדִים אֶל־הָאֵילִים אֶחָד מִפֹּה וְאֶחָד מִפֹּה:

מא וַיְבִיאֵנִי אֶל־הַהֵיכָל וַיָּמָד אֶת־הָאֵילִים שֵׁשׁ־אַמּוֹת רֹחַב־מִפּוֹ וְשֵׁשׁ־אַמּוֹת־רֹחַב מִפּוֹ רֹחַב הָאֹהֶל: 2 וְרֹחַב הַפֶּתַח עֶשֶׂר אַמּוֹת וְכִתְפוֹת הַפֶּתַח חָמֵשׁ אַמּוֹת מִפּוֹ וְחָמֵשׁ אַמּוֹת מִפּוֹ וַיָּמָד אָרְכּוֹ אַרְבָּעִים אַמָּה וְרֹחַב עֶשְׂרִים אַמָּה: 3 וּבָא לִפְנִימָה וַיָּמָד אֵיל־הַפֶּתַח שְׁתַּיִם אַמּוֹת וְהַפֶּתַח שֵׁשׁ אַמּוֹת וְרֹחַב הַפֶּתַח שֶׁבַע אַמּוֹת: 4 וַיָּמָד אֶת־אָרְכּוֹ עֶשְׂרִים אַמָּה

---

v   Septuagint reads "south."
w   I.e., the edges of the flanking walls.
x-x   Preserved in the Septuagint.
y   See note on v. 5.
z   Septuagint reads "12"; see note j on 41.13.
aa-aa Septuagint reads "it was reached by ten steps."

a   See note on 40.5.
b   This sense is demanded by the context; usually, ohel means "tent."
c-c   Preserved in the Septuagint.

the width at the inner end of the great hall was also 20 cubits. And he said to me, "This is the Holy of Holies."

⁵Then he measured the wall of the Temple. [It was] 6 cubits [thick] on every side of the Temple, and the side-chamber measured 4 cubits [across].*d* ⁶The side chambers were arranged one above the other, in 33 sections.*e* All around, there were projections in the Temple wall to serve the side chambers as supports, so that [their] supports should not be the Temple wall itself. ⁷The *f*-winding passage-*f* of the side chambers widened from story to story; *g*-and since the structure was furnished all over with winding passages from story to story, the structure itself became wider from story to story.-*g* It was by this means that one ascended from the bottom story to the top one by way of the middle one.

⁸I observed that the Temple was surrounded by a raised pavement—the foundations of the side chambers; its elevation was a rod's length, or 6 cubits. ⁹The outer wall of the side chamber was 5 cubits thick, and that which served as a walk between the Temple's side chambers ¹⁰and the chamber complexes*h* was 20 cubits wide all around the Temple. ¹¹Of entrances to the side chambers giving on the walk, there was one entrance on the north side and one entrance on the south side; and the space*i* of the walk was 5 cubits thick all around. ¹²And the structure that fronted on the vacant space at the [Temple's] western end was 70 cubits deep;*a* the walls of the structure were 5 cubits thick on every side; and it was 90 cubits wide.*a*

¹³He measured the [total] depth of the Tem-

---

d   *I.e., on the ground level; cf. v. 7.*

e   *Lit. "times." Emendation yields "in three sections of three tiers each," i.e., one section next to each of the two side walls of the Temple and one next to its rear wall; cf. v. 7.*

f-f   *So Targum; cf. Mishnah Tamid 1.1.*

g-g   *Exact meaning of Heb. uncertain, but for the general sense cf. 1 Kings 6.6a, 8b.*

h   *See 42.1 ff.*

i   *Emendation yields "parapet."*

וְרֹ֣חַב עֶשְׂרִ֤ים אַמָּה֙ אֶל־פְּנֵ֣י הַהֵיכָ֔ל וַיֹּ֣אמֶר אֵלַ֔י זֶ֖ה קֹ֥דֶשׁ הַקֳּדָשִֽׁים׃

⁵ וַיָּ֣מָד קִֽיר־הַבַּ֗יִת שֵׁ֣שׁ אַמּ֑וֹת וְרֹ֣חַב הַצֵּלָ֡ע אַרְבַּ֣ע אַמּ֛וֹת סָבִ֥יב ׀ סָבִ֖יב לַבַּ֥יִת סָבִֽיב׃ ⁶ וְהַצְּלָעוֹת֩ צֵלָ֨ע אֶל־צֵלָ֜ע שָׁל֧וֹשׁ וּשְׁלֹשִׁ֣ים פְּעָמִ֗ים וּ֠בָאוֹת בַּקִּ֤יר אֲשֶׁר־לַבַּ֨יִת֙ לַצְּלָע֤וֹת סָבִ֣יב ׀ סָבִ֔יב לִהְי֖וֹת אֲחוּזִ֑ים וְלֹֽא־יִהְי֥וּ אֲחוּזִ֖ים בְּקִ֥יר הַבָּֽיִת׃ ⁷ וְֽרָחֲבָ֡ה וְֽנָסְבָה֩ לְמַ֨עְלָה לְמַ֜עְלָה לַצְּלָע֗וֹת כִּ֣י מֽוּסַב־הַ֠בַּיִת לְמַ֨עְלָה לְמַ֜עְלָה סָבִ֤יב ׀ סָבִיב֙ לַבַּ֔יִת עַל־כֵּ֥ן רֹֽחַב־לַבַּ֖יִת לְמָ֑עְלָה וְכֵ֧ן הַתַּחְתּוֹנָ֛ה יַעֲלֶ֥ה עַל־הָעֶלְיוֹנָ֖ה לַתִּיכוֹנָֽה׃

⁸ וְרָאִ֧יתִי לַבַּ֛יִת גֹּ֖בַהּ סָבִ֣יב ׀ סָבִ֑יב מִוּסְדוֹת֩ מוּסְד֨וֹת הַצְּלָע֜וֹת מְל֣וֹ הַקָּנֶ֗ה שֵׁ֛שׁ אַמּ֖וֹת אַצִּֽילָה׃ ⁹ רֹ֣חַב הַקִּ֧יר אֲֽשֶׁר־לַצֵּלָ֛ע אֶל־הַח֖וּץ חָמֵ֣שׁ אַמּ֑וֹת וַאֲשֶׁ֣ר מֻנָּ֔ח בֵּ֥ית צְלָע֖וֹת אֲשֶׁ֥ר לַבָּֽיִת׃ ¹⁰ וּבֵ֨ין הַלְּשָׁכ֜וֹת רֹ֣חַב עֶשְׂרִ֥ים אַמָּ֛ה סָבִ֥יב לַבַּ֖יִת סָבִ֥יב ׀ סָבִֽיב׃ ¹¹ וּפֶ֤תַח הַצֵּלָע֙ לַמֻּנָּ֔ח פֶּ֥תַח אֶחָד֙ דֶּ֣רֶךְ הַצָּפ֔וֹן וּפֶ֥תַח אֶחָ֖ד לַדָּר֑וֹם וְרֹ֨חַב֙ מְק֣וֹם הַמֻּנָּ֔ח חָמֵ֥שׁ אַמּ֖וֹת סָבִ֥יב ׀ סָבִֽיב׃ ¹² וְהַבִּנְיָ֡ן אֲשֶׁר֩ אֶל־פְּנֵ֨י הַגִּזְרָ֜ה פְּאַ֣ת דֶּֽרֶךְ־הַיָּ֗ם רֹ֚חַב שִׁבְעִ֣ים אַמָּ֔ה וְקִ֧יר הַבִּנְיָ֛ן חָֽמֵשׁ־אַמּ֥וֹת רֹ֖חַב סָבִ֣יב ׀ סָבִ֑יב וְאָרְכּ֖וֹ תִּשְׁעִ֥ים אַמָּֽה׃

¹³ וּמָדַ֣ד אֶת־הַבַּ֗יִת אֹ֚רֶךְ מֵאָ֣ה אַמָּ֔ה

ple, 100 cubits;[j] and the depth of the vacant space and of the structure, with its walls, also came to 100 cubits.[k] [14] The front side of the Temple, like the vacant space on the east, was 100 cubits wide.[l] [15] He also measured the width[a] of the structure facing the vacant space in the rear, inclusive of its ledges,[m] 100 cubits.

Both the great hall inside and the portico next to the court—[16n] the thresholds-[n]—and the windows [o] with frames-[o] and the ledges[p] at the threshold, all over the three parts of each, were completely overlaid[o] with wood. There was wainscoting from the floor to the windows, including the window [frame]s [17] and extending above the openings, [q] both in the inner Temple and outside.-[q] And all over the wall, [q] both in the inner one and in the outer,-[q] ran a pattern.[o] [18] It consisted of cherubs and palm trees, with a palm tree between every two cherubs. Each cherub had two faces: [19] a human face turned toward the palm tree on one side and a lion's face turned toward the palm tree on the other side. This was repeated all over the Temple; [20] the cherubs and the palm trees were carved on[r] the wall from the floor to above the openings.

As regards the great hall, [21] the great hall had four doorposts; and before the Shrine was something resembling [22] a wooden altar 3 cubits high and 2 cubits long and having inner cor-

וְהַגִּזְרָה וְהַבִּנְיָ֔ה וְקִירוֹתֶ֖יהָ אֹ֥רֶךְ מֵאָ֣ה אַמָּֽה׃ [14] וְרֹ֙חַב֙ פְּנֵ֣י הַבַּ֔יִת וְהַגִּזְרָ֖ה לַקָּדִ֑ים מֵאָ֥ה אַמָּֽה׃ [15] וּמָדַ֞ד אֹֽרֶךְ־הַבִּנְיָ֗ן אֶל־פְּנֵ֤י הַגִּזְרָה֙ אֲשֶׁ֣ר עַל־אַחֲרֶ֔יהָ ואתוקיהא וְאַתִּיקֶ֖יהָֽ* מִפּ֣וֹ וּמִפּ֑וֹ מֵאָ֣ה אַמָּ֑ה וְהַהֵיכָל֙ הַפְּנִימִ֔י וְאֻֽלַמֵּ֖י הֶחָצֵֽר׃ [16] הַסִּפִּ֡ים וְהַחַלּוֹנִ֣ים הָאֲטֻמ֣וֹת וְהָאַתִּיקִ֣ים ׀ סָבִ֣יב לִשְׁלׇשְׁתָּ֗ם נֶ֧גֶד הַסַּ֛ף שְׂחִ֥יף עֵ֖ץ סָבִ֣יב ׀ סָבִ֑יב וְהָאָ֙רֶץ֙ עַד־הַֽחַלֹּנ֔וֹת וְהַֽחַלֹּנ֖וֹת מְכֻסּֽוֹת׃ [17] עַל־מֵעַ֣ל הַפֶּ֗תַח וְעַד־הַבַּ֙יִת֙ הַפְּנִימִ֣י וְלַח֔וּץ וְאֶל־כׇּל־הַקִּ֥יר סָבִ֖יב ׀ סָבִ֑יב בַּפְּנִימִ֖י וּבַחִיצ֥וֹן מִדּֽוֹת׃ [18] וְעָשׂ֥וּי כְּרוּבִ֖ים וְתִמֹרִ֑ים וְתִֽמֹרָה֙ בֵּין־כְּר֣וּב לִכְר֔וּב וּשְׁנַ֥יִם פָּנִ֖ים לַכְּרֽוּב׃ [19] וּפְנֵ֤י אָדָם֙ אֶל־הַתִּֽמֹרָה֙ מִפּ֔וֹ וּפְנֵי־כְפִ֥יר אֶל־הַתִּֽמֹרָ֖ה מִפּ֑וֹ עָשׂ֥וּי אֶל־כׇּל־הַבַּ֖יִת סָבִ֥יב ׀ סָבִֽיב׃ [20] מֵהָאָ֙רֶץ֙ עַד־מֵעַ֣ל הַפֶּ֔תַח הַכְּרוּבִ֥ים וְהַתִּמֹרִ֖ים עֲשׂוּיִ֑ם וְקִ֥יר הַֽהֵיכָֽל*׃ [21] הַֽהֵיכָ֕ל מְזוּזַ֖ת רְבֻעָ֑ה וּפְנֵ֣י הַקֹּ֔דֶשׁ הַמַּרְאֶ֖ה כַּמַּרְאֶֽה׃ [22] הַמִּזְבֵּ֡חַ עֵ֣ץ שָׁל֣וֹשׁ אַמּוֹת֩ גָּבֹ֨הַּ וְאׇרְכּ֜וֹ שְׁתַּֽיִם־

v. 15. יתיר א'
v. 20. ניקוד על ה' ה' י' כ' ל'

---

j   Comprising the 5 cubits of 40.48, the 12 of 40.49 (see note there), the 6 of 41.1, the 40 of 41.2, the 2 of 41.3, the 20 of 41.4, the 6 of 41.5a, the 4 of 41.5b, and the 5 of 41.9.

k   The structure was 70 cubits deep and its front and rear walls each 5 cubits thick (v. 12). The remaining 20 cubits are accounted for by the vacant space; cf. 42.1–2.

l   To the inside width of 20 cubits (40.49; 41.2–4) must be added on each side: one Temple wall of 6 cubits equals 12; one side-chamber wall of 5 cubits equals 10; one side chamber's inner depth of 4 cubits equals 8; a walk's width of 20 cubits (40.9–10) equals 40; and a parapet's thickness of 5 cubits (v. 11) equals 10; totaling 100 cubits.

m   Emendation yields "walls"; cf. v. 12.

n-n   Septuagint reads "were paneled."

o-o   Meaning of Heb. uncertain.

p   Here perhaps designating the door frames, since it is these that (as required by the continuation of the verse) are situated at the threshold and consist of three parts (a lintel and two doorposts).

q-q   Meaning perhaps the great hall and the vestibule; cf. v. 5.

r   Heb. "and."

ners;⁵ and its length*t* and its walls were of wood. And he said to me, "This is the table*u* that stands before the LORD." ²³The great hall had a double door, and the Shrine likewise had ²⁴a double door, and each door had two *o*-swinging leaves:-*o* two for the one door and two *o*-such leaves-*o* for the other. ²⁵Cherubs and palm trees were carved on these—on the doors of the hall—just as they were carved on the walls; and there was a lattice*o* of wood outside in front of the portico. ²⁶And there were windows *o*-with frames-*o* and palm trees on the flanking walls of the portico on either side [of the entrance] *o*-and [on] the Temple's side chambers and [on] the lattices.-*o*

42

He took me out, by way of the northern gate, into the outer court, and he led me [westward] up to a *a*-complex of chambers-*a* that ran parallel to the northern ends of the vacant space and the structure. ²The width*b* of its façade—*c*-its north side, the one from which it was entered-*c*—was 100 cubits, and its depth*b* was 50 cubits. ³At right angles to the 20 cubits*d* of the inner court and to the pavement of the outer court,*e* the complex rose ledge by ledge*f* in three tiers. ⁴There was an areaway, 10 cubits wide and *g*-a road of one cubit,-*g* running along the inner-court side of the chamber complex, but its entrances were on its north side. ⁵Here its upper chambers were cut back, because ledges took away from them as construction proceeded backward from the bottom ones and

אַמּוֹת וּמִקְצֹעוֹתָיו לוֹ וְאָרְכּוֹ וְקִירֹתָיו עֵץ
וַיְדַבֵּר אֵלַי זֶה הַשֻּׁלְחָן אֲשֶׁר לִפְנֵי
יְהוָה: 23 וּשְׁתַּיִם דְּלָתוֹת לַהֵיכָל וְלַקֹּדֶשׁ:
24 וּשְׁתַּיִם דְּלָתוֹת לַדְּלָתוֹת שְׁתַּיִם
מוּסַבּוֹת דְּלָתוֹת שְׁתַּיִם לְדֶלֶת אֶחָת
וּשְׁתֵּי דְלָתוֹת לָאַחֶרֶת: 25 וַעֲשׂוּיָה אֲלֵיהֶן
אֶל־דַּלְתוֹת הַהֵיכָל כְּרוּבִים וְתִמֹרִים
כַּאֲשֶׁר עֲשׂוּיִם לַקִּירוֹת וְעָב עֵץ אֶל־פְּנֵי
הָאוּלָם מֵהַחוּץ: 26 וְחַלּוֹנִים אֲטֻמוֹת
וְתִמֹרִים מִפּוֹ וּמִפּוֹ אֶל־כִּתְפוֹת הָאוּלָם
וְצַלְעוֹת הַבַּיִת וְהָעֻבִּים:

מב וַיּוֹצִאֵנִי אֶל־הֶחָצֵר הַחִיצוֹנָה
הַדֶּרֶךְ דֶּרֶךְ הַצָּפוֹן וַיְבִאֵנִי אֶל־הַלִּשְׁכָּה
אֲשֶׁר נֶגֶד הַגִּזְרָה וַאֲשֶׁר־נֶגֶד הַבִּנְיָן אֶל־
הַצָּפוֹן: 2 אֶל־פְּנֵי־אֹרֶךְ אַמּוֹת הַמֵּאָה
פֶּתַח הַצָּפוֹן וְהָרֹחַב חֲמִשִּׁים אַמּוֹת: 3 נֶגֶד
הָעֶשְׂרִים אֲשֶׁר לֶחָצֵר הַפְּנִימִי וְנֶגֶד רִצְפָה
אֲשֶׁר לֶחָצֵר הַחִיצוֹנָה אַתִּיק אֶל־פְּנֵי־
אַתִּיק בַּשְּׁלִשִׁים: 4 וְלִפְנֵי הַלְּשָׁכוֹת מַהֲלַךְ
עֶשֶׂר אַמּוֹת רֹחַב אֶל־הַפְּנִימִית דֶּרֶךְ אַמָּה
אֶחָת וּפִתְחֵיהֶם לַצָּפוֹן: 5 וְהַלְּשָׁכוֹת
הָעֶלְיוֹנֹת קְצֻרוֹת כִּי־יוֹכְלוּ* אַתִּיקִים

---

s   *Apparently meaning that it had a rim around the top, like the table of Exod. 25.25; see the final note on the present verse.*
t   *Septuagint reads "base."*
u   *Serving to hold the bread of display; cf. Exod. 25.30; 40.22–23; 1 Kings 7.48.*

a-a *Heb. simply "chambers," and so elsewhere.*
b   *See note d at 40.6.*
c-c *Lit. "the north entrance"; but cf. v. 4.*
d   *I.e., the vacant space; cf. 41.13 with note k.*
e   *Cf. 40.17.*
f   *Because this part of the inner court was considerably higher than the outer; 40.28–31 and 41.8, 9b–10.*
g-g *Septuagint and Syriac read "and 100 cubits long"; cf. vv. 2–3.*

then from the middle ones. [6]For they were arranged in three tiers, and they had no columns like those of the chambers in the courts.[h] That is why the rise proceeded by stages: from the ground, from the bottom ones, and from the middle ones. [7]In the outer court, a wall 50 cubits long ran parallel to the chamber complex up to the chambers in the outer court;[h] [8]for the chambers in the outer court were themselves 50 cubits deep, thus completing 100 cubits alongside the edifice.[i] [9]Thus, at the foot of that complex of chambers ran a passage [j]—[k]of a width set by the wall in the outer court-[k]—which one entered from the east in order to gain access to them from the outer court.

[10]There was another chamber complex to the east[l] of the vacant space and the structure, [11]likewise with a passage in front—just like the complex on the north side, with which this one agreed in width[b] and depth[b] and in the exact layout of its exits and entrances. [12]Accordingly, the entrances to the chamber complex on the south side were approached from the east by the entrance at the head of [m]the corresponding passage along the matching wall.-[m]

[13]And he said to me, "The northern chambers and the southern chambers by the vacant space are the consecrated chambers in which the priests who have access to the Lord shall eat the most holy offerings. There they shall deposit the most holy offerings—the meal offerings, the sin offerings, and the guilt offerings, for the place is consecrated. [14]When the priests enter, they shall not proceed from the consecrated place to the outer court without first leaving here the vestments in which they minister; for the [vestments] are consecrated. Before proceeding to

---

h   See vv. 8–9 referring to chambers along the west wall.
i   Apparently meaning the chamber complex of v. 1.
j   So kethib; qere "thing giving access."
k-k Brought up from v. 10 for clarity.
l   Septuagint reads "south"; cf. v. 13.
m-m Exact meaning of Heb. uncertain; the phrase apparently
        refers to vv. 7–8.

מֵהֵנָּה מֵהַתַּחְתֹּנ֛וֹת וּמֵהַתִּֽכֹנ֖וֹת בִּנְיָֽן׃ [6] כִּ֣י מְשֻׁלָּשׁוֹת֮ הֵ֒נָּה֒ וְאֵ֤ין לָהֶן֙ עַמּוּדִ֔ים כְּעַמּוּדֵ֖י הַחֲצֵר֑וֹת עַל־כֵּ֣ן נֶֽאֱצַ֗ל מֵהַתַּחְתּוֹנ֛וֹת וּמֵהַתִּֽיכֹנ֖וֹת מֵהָאָֽרֶץ׃ [7] וְגָדֵ֤ר אֲשֶׁר־לַחוּץ֙ לְעֻמַּ֣ת הַלְּשָׁכ֔וֹת דֶּ֛רֶךְ הֶחָצֵ֥ר הַחִֽצוֹנָ֖ה אֶל־פְּנֵ֣י הַלְּשָׁכ֑וֹת אׇרְכּ֖וֹ חֲמִשִּׁ֥ים אַמָּֽה׃ [8] כִּֽי־אֹ֣רֶךְ הַלְּשָׁכ֗וֹת אֲשֶׁ֛ר לֶחָצֵ֥ר הַחִֽצוֹנָ֖ה חֲמִשִּׁ֣ים אַמָּ֑ה וְהִנֵּ֛ה עַל־פְּנֵ֥י הַהֵיכָ֖ל מֵאָ֥ה אַמָּֽה׃ [9] וּמִתַּ֖חַת הַלְּשָׁכ֣וֹת הָאֵ֑לֶּה הַמֵּבִיא֙ מֵהַקָּדִ֔ים בְּבֹא֣וֹ לָהֵ֔נָּה מֵהֶחָצֵ֖ר הַחִצֹנָֽה׃ [10] בְּרֹ֣חַב ׀ גֶּ֣דֶר הֶחָצֵ֗ר דֶּ֧רֶךְ הַקָּדִ֛ים אֶל־פְּנֵ֥י הַגִּזְרָ֖ה וְאֶל־פְּנֵ֣י הַבִּנְיָ֑ן לְשָׁכֽוֹת׃ [11] וְדֶ֨רֶךְ֙ לִפְנֵיהֶ֔ם כְּמַרְאֵ֣ה הַלְּשָׁכ֗וֹת אֲשֶׁר֙ דֶּ֣רֶךְ הַצָּפ֔וֹן כְּאׇרְכָּ֖ן כֵּ֣ן רׇחְבָּ֑ן וְכֹל֙ מוֹצָ֣אֵיהֶ֔ן וּכְמִשְׁפְּטֵיהֶ֖ן וּכְפִתְחֵיהֶֽן׃ [12] וּכְפִתְחֵ֣י הַלְּשָׁכ֗וֹת אֲשֶׁר֙ דֶּ֣רֶךְ הַדָּר֔וֹם פֶּ֖תַח בְּרֹ֣אשׁ דָּ֑רֶךְ דֶּ֗רֶךְ בִּפְנֵי֙ הַגְּדֶ֣רֶת הֲגִינָ֔ה דֶּ֥רֶךְ הַקָּדִ֖ים בְּבוֹאָֽן׃ [13] וַיֹּ֣אמֶר אֵלַ֗י לִֽשְׁכ֤וֹת הַצָּפוֹן֙ לִֽשְׁכ֣וֹת הַדָּר֔וֹם אֲשֶׁר֙ אֶל־פְּנֵ֣י הַגִּזְרָ֔ה הֵ֣נָּה ׀ לִֽשְׁכ֣וֹת הַקֹּ֗דֶשׁ אֲשֶׁ֣ר יֹאכְלוּ־שָׁ֤ם הַכֹּהֲנִים֙ אֲשֶׁר־קְרוֹבִ֣ים לַֽיהֹוָ֔ה קׇדְשֵׁ֖י הַקֳּדָשִׁ֑ים שָׁ֞ם יַנִּ֣יחוּ ׀ קׇדְשֵׁ֣י הַקֳּדָשִׁ֗ים וְהַמִּנְחָה֙ וְהַחַטָּ֣את וְהָֽאָשָׁ֔ם כִּ֥י הַמָּק֖וֹם קָדֹֽשׁ׃ [14] בְּבֹאָ֣ם הַכֹּהֲנִ֗ים וְלֹא־יֵצְא֤וּ מֵהַקֹּ֙דֶשׁ֙ אֶל־הֶחָצֵ֣ר הַחִֽיצוֹנָ֔ה וְשָׁ֞ם יַנִּ֣יחוּ בִגְדֵיהֶ֗ם אֲשֶׁר־

1255

the area open to the people,[n] they shall put on other garments."

[15]When he had finished the measurements of the inner Temple [area], he led me out by way of the gate which faces east, and he measured off the entire area. [16]He measured the east side with the measuring rod, 500 [cubits]—in rods, by the measuring rod. He turned [17][and] measured the north side: 500 [cubits]—in rods, by the measuring rod. He turned [18][and] measured the south side: 500 [cubits]—in rods, by the measuring rod. [19]Then he turned to the west side [and] measured it: 500 cubits—in rods, by the measuring rod. [20]Thus he measured it on the four sides; it had a wall completely surrounding it, 500 [cubits] long [o]-on each side,-[o] to separate the consecrated from the unconsecrated.

43

Then he led me to a gate, the gate that faced east. [2]And there, coming from the east with a roar like the roar of mighty waters, was the Presence of the God of Israel, and the earth was lit up by His Presence. [3]The vision was like the vision I had seen when I[a] came to destroy the city, the very same vision that I had seen by the Chebar Canal. Forthwith, I fell on my face.

[4]The Presence of the LORD entered the Temple by the gate that faced eastward. [5]A spirit carried me into the inner court, and lo, the Presence of the LORD filled the Temple; [6]and I heard speech addressed to me from the Temple, though [the] man[b] was standing beside me. [7]It said to me:

O mortal, this is the place of My throne and the place for the soles of My feet, where I will dwell in the midst of the people Israel forever. The House of Israel and their kings must not

יִשְׁרְתוּ בָהֵן כִּי־קֹדֶשׁ הֵנָּה יִלְבְּשׁוּ וְלָבְשׁוּ
בְּגָדִים אֲחֵרִים וְקָרְבוּ אֶל־אֲשֶׁר לָעָם:
15 וְכִלָּה אֶת־מִדּוֹת הַבַּיִת הַפְּנִימִי
וְהוֹצִיאַנִי דֶּרֶךְ הַשַּׁעַר אֲשֶׁר פָּנָיו דֶּרֶךְ
הַקָּדִים וּמְדָדוֹ סָבִיב ׀ סָבִיב: 16 מָדַד רוּחַ
הַקָּדִים בִּקְנֵה הַמִּדָּה חֲמֵשׁ־אֵמוֹת מֵאוֹת
קָנִים בִּקְנֵה הַמִּדָּה סָבִיב: 17 מָדַד רוּחַ
הַצָּפוֹן חֲמֵשׁ־מֵאוֹת קָנִים בִּקְנֵה הַמִּדָּה
סָבִיב: 18 אֵת רוּחַ הַדָּרוֹם מָדַד חֲמֵשׁ־
מֵאוֹת קָנִים בִּקְנֵה הַמִּדָּה: 19 סָבַב אֶל־
רוּחַ הַיָּם מָדַד חֲמֵשׁ־מֵאוֹת קָנִים בִּקְנֵה
הַמִּדָּה: 20 לְאַרְבַּע רוּחוֹת מְדָדוֹ חוֹמָה לוֹ
סָבִיב ׀ סָבִיב אֹרֶךְ חֲמֵשׁ מֵאוֹת וְרֹחַב
חֲמֵשׁ מֵאוֹת לְהַבְדִּיל בֵּין הַקֹּדֶשׁ לְחֹל:

מג וַיּוֹלִכֵנִי אֶל־הַשַּׁעַר שַׁעַר אֲשֶׁר
פֹּנֶה דֶּרֶךְ הַקָּדִים: 2 וְהִנֵּה כְּבוֹד אֱלֹהֵי
יִשְׂרָאֵל בָּא מִדֶּרֶךְ הַקָּדִים וְקוֹלוֹ כְּקוֹל
מַיִם רַבִּים וְהָאָרֶץ הֵאִירָה מִכְּבֹדוֹ:
3 וּכְמַרְאֵה הַמַּרְאֶה אֲשֶׁר רָאִיתִי כַּמַּרְאֶה
אֲשֶׁר־רָאִיתִי בְּבֹאִי לְשַׁחֵת אֶת־הָעִיר
וּמַרְאוֹת כַּמַּרְאֶה אֲשֶׁר רָאִיתִי אֶל־נְהַר־
כְּבָר וָאֶפֹּל אֶל־פָּנָי:
4 וּכְבוֹד יְהוָה בָּא אֶל־הַבָּיִת דֶּרֶךְ שַׁעַר
אֲשֶׁר פָּנָיו דֶּרֶךְ הַקָּדִים: 5 וַתִּשָּׂאֵנִי רוּחַ
וַתְּבִיאֵנִי אֶל־הֶחָצֵר הַפְּנִימִי וְהִנֵּה מָלֵא
כְבוֹד־יְהוָה הַבָּיִת: 6 וָאֶשְׁמַע מִדַּבֵּר אֵלַי
מֵהַבָּיִת וְאִישׁ הָיָה עֹמֵד אֶצְלִי: 7 וַיֹּאמֶר
אֵלַי
בֶּן־אָדָם אֶת־מְקוֹם כִּסְאִי וְאֶת־מְקוֹם
כַּפּוֹת רַגְלַי אֲשֶׁר אֶשְׁכָּן־שָׁם בְּתוֹךְ בְּנֵי־
יִשְׂרָאֵל לְעוֹלָם וְלֹא יְטַמְּאוּ עוֹד בֵּית־

---

n   Cf. 44.19 and note d.
o-o   Lit. "and 500 wide."

a   Six mss. and two ancient versions read "He."
b   I.e., the guide of 40.3 ff.

again defile My holy name by their apostasy and by the corpses of their kings c-at their death.-c 8When they placed their threshold next to My threshold and their doorposts next to My doorposts with only a wall between Me and them,d they would defile My holy name by the abominations that they committed, and I consumed them in My anger. 9Therefore, let them put their apostasy and the corpses of their kings far from Me, and I will dwell among them forever.

10[Now] you, O mortal, describe the Temple to the House of Israel,e and let them measure its design. But let them be ashamed of their iniquities: 11When they are ashamed of all they have done, make known to them the plan of the Temple and its layout, its exits and entrances—its entire plan, and all the laws and instructions pertaining to its entire plan. Write it down before their eyes, that they may faithfully follow its entire plan and all its laws. 12Such are the instructions for the Temple on top of the mountain: the entire area of its enclosure shall be most holy. Thus far the instructions for the Temple.

13fAnd these are the dimensions of the altar, in cubits where each is a cubit and a handbreadth. The trenchg shall be a cubit deep and a cubit wide, with a rim one span high around its edge. And the heighth shall be as follows: 14From the trench in the ground to the lower ledge, which shall be a cubit wide: 2 cubits; from the i-lower ledge to the upper-i ledge, which shall likewise be a cubit wide: 4 cubits; 15and the height of the altar hearth shall be 4 cubits, with 4 horns projecting upward from the hearth:

יִשְׂרָאֵל שֵׁם קָדְשִׁי הֵמָּה וּמַלְכֵיהֶם בִּזְנוּתָם וּבְפִגְרֵי מַלְכֵיהֶם בָּמוֹתָם*: 8 בְּתִתָּם סִפָּם אֶת־סִפִּי וּמְזוּזָתָם אֵצֶל מְזוּזָתִי וְהַקִּיר בֵּינִי וּבֵינֵיהֶם וְטִמְּאוּ | אֶת־שֵׁם קָדְשִׁי בְּתוֹעֲבוֹתָם אֲשֶׁר עָשׂוּ וָאֲכַל אֹתָם בְּאַפִּי: 9 עַתָּה יְרַחֲקוּ אֶת־זְנוּתָם וּפִגְרֵי מַלְכֵיהֶם מִמֶּנִּי וְשָׁכַנְתִּי בְתוֹכָם לְעוֹלָם: ס

10 אַתָּה בֶן־אָדָם הַגֵּד אֶת־בֵּית־יִשְׂרָאֵל אֶת־הַבַּיִת וְיִכָּלְמוּ מֵעֲוֹנוֹתֵיהֶם וּמָדְדוּ אֶת־תָּכְנִית: 11 וְאִם־נִכְלְמוּ מִכֹּל אֲשֶׁר־עָשׂוּ צוּרַת הַבַּיִת וּתְכוּנָתוֹ וּמוֹצָאָיו וּמוֹבָאָיו וְכָל־צוּרֹתָו צוּרֹתָיו וְאֵת כָּל־חֻקֹּתָיו וְכָל־צוּרֹתי צוּרֹתָיו וְכָל־תּוֹרֹתו תּוֹרֹתָיו הוֹדַע אוֹתָם וּכְתֹב לְעֵינֵיהֶם וְיִשְׁמְרוּ אֶת־כָּל־צוּרָתוֹ וְאֶת־כָּל־חֻקֹּתָיו וְעָשׂוּ אוֹתָם: 12 זֹאת תּוֹרַת הַבָּיִת עַל־רֹאשׁ הָהָר כָּל־גְּבֻלוֹ סָבִיב | סָבִיב קֹדֶשׁ קָדָשִׁים הִנֵּה־זֹאת תּוֹרַת הַבָּיִת:

13 וְאֵלֶּה מִדּוֹת הַמִּזְבֵּחַ בָּאַמּוֹת אַמָּה אַמָּה וָטֹפַח וְחֵיק הָאַמָּה וְאַמָּה־רֹחַב וּגְבוּלָהּ אֶל־שְׂפָתָהּ סָבִיב זֶרֶת הָאֶחָד וְזֶה גַּב הַמִּזְבֵּחַ: 14 וּמֵחֵיק הָאָרֶץ עַד־הָעֲזָרָה הַתַּחְתּוֹנָה שְׁתַּיִם אַמּוֹת וְרֹחַב אַמָּה אֶחָת וּמֵהָעֲזָרָה הַקְּטַנָּה עַד־הָעֲזָרָה הַגְּדוֹלָה אַרְבַּע אַמּוֹת וְרֹחַב הָאַמָּה: 15 וְהַהַרְאֵל אַרְבַּע אַמּוֹת וּמֵהָאֲרִאֵיל וּמֵהָאֲרִיאֵל וּלְמַעְלָה הַקְּרָנוֹת אַרְבַּע:

v. 7. בנסח אחר ״בָּמוֹתָם״ כלומר שני תנועה

c-c So with a number of Heb. mss. The usual vocalization yields "their shrines."
d The south wall of the First Temple enclosure was also the north wall of the royal enclosure; the two communicated by the Gate of the Guard (2 Kings 11.19). Thus Temple and palace could be regarded as a single dwelling ("tent") in the sense of Num. 19.14, and the death of a king in the palace would defile the Temple. Hence the zoning provisions of 45.2 ff.
e In accordance with the three preceding chapters; cf. 40.4.
f Some of the terms and details in vv. 13–17 are obscure.
g Lit. "bosom."
h Lit. "bulge."
i-i Lit. "lesser ledge to the greater."

4 cubits. [16]Now the hearth shall be 12 cubits long and 12 broad, square, with 4 equal sides. [17]Hence, the [upper] base[j] shall be 14 cubits broad, with 4 equal sides. The surrounding rim shall be half a cubit [high],[k] and the surrounding trench shall measure one cubit. And the ramp[l] shall face east.

[18]Then he[b] said to me: O mortal, thus said the Lord GOD: These are the directions for the altar on the day it is erected, so that burnt offerings may be offered up on it and blood dashed against it. [19]You shall give to the levitical priests who are of the stock of Zadok, and so eligible to minister to Me—declares the Lord GOD—a young bull of the herd for a sin offering. [20]You shall take some of its blood and apply it to [m]the four horns [of the altar],[-m] to the four corners of the base, and to the surrounding rim; thus you shall purge it and perform purification upon it. [21]Then you shall take the bull of sin offering and burn it in the [n]designated area[-n] of the Temple, outside the Sanctuary.

[22]On the following day, you shall offer a goat without blemish as a sin offering; and the altar shall be purged [with it] just as it was purged with the bull. [23]When you have completed the ritual of purging, you shall offer a bull of the herd without blemish and a ram of the flock without blemish. [24]Offer them to the LORD; let the priests throw salt on them and offer them up as a burnt offering to the LORD. [25]Every day, for seven days, you shall present a goat of sin offering, as well as a bull of the herd and a ram of the flock; you[o] shall present unblemished ones. [26]Seven days they shall purge the altar and cleanse it; [p]thus shall it be consecrated.[-p]

16 וְהָאֲרִאֵיל שְׁתֵּים עֶשְׂרֵה אֹרֶךְ בִּשְׁתֵּים עֶשְׂרֵה רֹחַב רָב֫וּעַ אֶל אַרְבַּעַת רְבָעָיו: 17 וְהָעֲזָרָ֡ה אַרְבַּ֣ע עֶשְׂרֵה֩ אֹ֨רֶךְ בְּאַרְבַּ֤ע עֶשְׂרֵה֙ רֹ֔חַב אֶ֖ל אַרְבַּ֣עַת רְבָעֶ֑יהָ וְהַגְּבוּל֩ סָבִ֨יב אוֹתָ֜הּ חֲצִ֣י הָאַמָּ֗ה וְהַֽחֵ֨יק־לָ֥הּ אַמָּ֛ה סָבִ֖יב וּמַֽעֲלֹתֵ֑הוּ פְּנ֥וֹת קָדִֽים: 18 וַיֹּ֣אמֶר אֵלַ֗י בֶּן־אָדָם֙ כֹּ֤ה אָמַר֙ אֲדֹנָ֣י יְהֹוִ֔ה אֵ֚לֶּה חֻקּ֣וֹת הַמִּזְבֵּ֔חַ בְּי֖וֹם הֵעָשׂוֹת֑וֹ לְהַעֲל֤וֹת עָלָיו֙ עוֹלָ֔ה וְלִזְרֹ֥ק עָלָ֖יו דָּֽם: 19 וְנָתַתָּ֡ה אֶל־הַכֹּהֲנִ֣ים הַלְוִיִּם֩ אֲשֶׁ֨ר הֵ֜ם מִזֶּ֤רַע צָדוֹק֙ הַקְּרֹבִ֣ים אֵלַ֔י נְאֻ֖ם אֲדֹנָ֣י יְהֹוִ֑ה לְשָׁ֣רְתֵ֑נִי פַּ֥ר בֶּן־בָּקָ֖ר לְחַטָּֽאת: 20 וְלָקַחְתָּ֣ מִדָּמ֗וֹ וְנָ֨תַתָּ֜ה עַל־אַרְבַּ֤ע קַרְנֹתָיו֙ וְאֶל־אַרְבַּע֙ פִּנּ֣וֹת הָעֲזָרָ֔ה וְאֶל־הַגְּב֖וּל סָבִ֑יב וְחִטֵּאתָ֥ אוֹת֖וֹ וְכִפַּרְתָּֽהוּ: 21 וְלָ֣קַחְתָּ֔ אֵ֖ת הַפָּ֣ר הַֽחַטָּ֑את וּשְׂרָפוֹ֙ בְּמִפְקַ֣ד הַבַּ֔יִת מִח֖וּץ לַמִּקְדָּֽשׁ: 22 וּבַיּוֹם֙ הַשֵּׁנִ֔י תַּקְרִ֛יב שְׂעִיר־עִזִּ֥ים תָּמִ֖ים לְחַטָּ֑את וְחִטְּאוּ֙ אֶת־הַמִּזְבֵּ֔חַ כַּאֲשֶׁ֥ר חִטְּא֖וּ בַּפָּֽר: 23 בְּכַלּוֹתְךָ֖ מֵֽחַטֵּ֑א תַּקְרִיב֙ פַּ֣ר בֶּן־בָּקָ֣ר תָּמִ֔ים וְאַ֥יִל מִן־הַצֹּ֖אן תָּמִֽים: 24 וְהִקְרַבְתָּ֖ם לִפְנֵ֣י יְהֹוָ֑ה וְהִשְׁלִ֤יכוּ הַכֹּֽהֲנִים֙ עֲלֵיהֶ֣ם מֶ֔לַח וְהֶעֱל֥וּ אוֹתָ֛ם עֹלָ֖ה לַֽיהֹוָֽה: 25 שִׁבְעַ֣ת יָמִ֗ים תַּֽעֲשֶׂ֤ה שְׂעִיר־חַטָּאת֙ לַיּ֔וֹם וּפַ֧ר בֶּן־בָּקָ֛ר וְאַ֥יִל מִן־הַצֹּ֖אן תְּמִימִ֥ים יַעֲשֽׂוּ: 26 שִׁבְעַ֣ת יָמִ֔ים יְכַפְּרוּ֙ אֶת־הַמִּזְבֵּ֔חַ וְטִֽהֲר֖וּ אֹת֑וֹ וּמִלְא֖וּ יָדָֽיו:

---

j Heb. 'azarah, which in v. 14 means "ledge." The altar consists of 3 blocks, each smaller than the one below it.
k Half a cubit is identical with the one span of v. 13.
l Leading up to the altar; cf. Exod. 20.23.
m-m Heb. "its four horns."
n-n Meaning of Heb. uncertain. Emendation yields "burning place"; cf. Lev. 6.2; Isa. 33.14; Ps. 102.4 (for the word), and Lev. 4.12; 6.4 (for the place).
o Heb. "they."
p-p Lit. "they shall fill its hands"; cf. note at Exod. 28.41.

27And when these days are over, then from the eighth day onward the priests shall offer your burnt offerings and your offerings of well-being on the altar; and I will extend My favor to you—declares the Lord God.

44 Then he led me back to the outer gate of the Sanctuary that faced eastward; it was shut. 2And the Lord said to me: This gate is to be kept shut and is not to be opened! No one shall enter by it because the Lord, the God of Israel, has entered by it; therefore it shall remain shut. 3Only the prince may sit in it and eat bread before the Lord, since he is a prince; he shall enter by way of *a-the vestibule of the gate,-a* and shall depart by the same way.

4Then he led me, by way of the north gate, to the front of the Temple. I looked, and lo! the Presence of the Lord filled the Temple of the Lord; and I fell upon my face. 5Then the Lord said to me: O mortal, mark well, look closely and listen carefully to everything that I tell you regarding all the laws of the Temple of the Lord and all the instructions regarding it. Note well who may enter the Temple and all who must be excluded from the Sanctuary. 6And say to the rebellious House of Israel: Thus said the Lord God: Too long, O House of Israel, have you committed all your abominations, 7admitting aliens, uncircumcised of spirit and uncircumcised of flesh, to be in My Sanctuary and profane My very Temple, when you offer up My food—the fat and the blood. You*b* have broken My covenant with all your abominations. 8You have not discharged the duties concerning My sacred offerings, but have appointed them to discharge the duties of My Sanctuary for you.

9Thus said the Lord God: Let no alien, uncircumcised in spirit and flesh, enter My

27 וְכִלּוּ אֶת־הַיָּמִים ס וְהָיָה בַיּוֹם הַשְּׁמִינִי וָהָלְאָה יַעֲשׂוּ הַכֹּהֲנִים עַל־הַמִּזְבֵּחַ אֶת־עוֹלוֹתֵיכֶם וְאֶת־שַׁלְמֵיכֶם וְרָצִאתִי* אֶתְכֶם נְאֻם אֲדֹנָי יְהֹוִה: ס

מד וַיָּשֶׁב אֹתִי דֶּרֶךְ שַׁעַר הַמִּקְדָּשׁ הַחִיצוֹן הַפֹּנֶה קָדִים וְהוּא סָגוּר: 2 וַיֹּאמֶר אֵלַי יְהֹוָה הַשַּׁעַר הַזֶּה סָגוּר יִהְיֶה לֹא יִפָּתֵחַ וְאִישׁ לֹא־יָבֹא בוֹ כִּי יְהֹוָה אֱלֹהֵי־יִשְׂרָאֵל בָּא בוֹ וְהָיָה סָגוּר: 3 אֶת־הַנָּשִׂיא נָשִׂיא הוּא יֵשֶׁב־בּוֹ לֶאֱכוֹל לֶחֶם לִפְנֵי יְהֹוָה מִדֶּרֶךְ אֻלָם הַשַּׁעַר יָבוֹא וּמִדַּרְכּוֹ יֵצֵא:

4 וַיְבִיאֵנִי דֶּרֶךְ־שַׁעַר הַצָּפוֹן אֶל־פְּנֵי הַבַּיִת וָאֵרֶא וְהִנֵּה מָלֵא כְבוֹד־יְהֹוָה אֶת־בֵּית יְהֹוָה וָאֶפֹּל אֶל־פָּנָי: 5 וַיֹּאמֶר אֵלַי יְהֹוָה בֶּן־אָדָם שִׂים לִבְּךָ וּרְאֵה בְעֵינֶיךָ וּבְאָזְנֶיךָ שְׁמָע אֵת כָּל־אֲשֶׁר אֲנִי מְדַבֵּר אֹתָךְ לְכָל־חֻקּוֹת בֵּית־יְהֹוָה וּלְכָל־תּוֹרֹתָו תּוֹרֹתָיו וְשַׂמְתָּ לִבְּךָ לִמְבוֹא הַבַּיִת בְּכֹל מוֹצָאֵי הַמִּקְדָּשׁ: 6 וְאָמַרְתָּ אֶל־מֶרִי אֶל־בֵּית יִשְׂרָאֵל כֹּה אָמַר אֲדֹנָי יְהֹוִה רַב־לָכֶם מִכָּל־תּוֹעֲבוֹתֵיכֶם בֵּית יִשְׂרָאֵל: 7 בַּהֲבִיאֲכֶם בְּנֵי־נֵכָר עַרְלֵי־לֵב וְעַרְלֵי בָשָׂר לִהְיוֹת בְּמִקְדָּשִׁי לְחַלְּלוֹ אֶת־בֵּיתִי בְּהַקְרִיבְכֶם אֶת־לַחְמִי חֵלֶב וָדָם וַיָּפֵרוּ אֶת־בְּרִיתִי אֶל כָּל־תּוֹעֲבוֹתֵיכֶם: 8 וְלֹא שְׁמַרְתֶּם מִשְׁמֶרֶת קָדָשָׁי וַתְּשִׂימוּן לְשֹׁמְרֵי מִשְׁמַרְתִּי בְּמִקְדָּשִׁי לָכֶם:

9 כֹּה־אָמַר אֲדֹנָי יְהֹוִה כָּל־בֶּן־נֵכָר עֶרֶל לֵב וְעֶרֶל בָּשָׂר לֹא יָבוֹא אֶל־מִקְדָּשִׁי

---

a-a   *This does not contradict v. 2 because the vestibule is at the inner end of the gate; cf. 40.9.*
b   *Heb. "They."*

יְ' בִּמְקוֹם א' v. 27.

Sanctuary—no alien whatsoever among the people of Israel. [10]But the Levites who forsook Me when Israel went astray—straying from Me to follow their fetishes—shall suffer their punishment: [11]They shall be servitors in My Sanctuary, appointed over the Temple gates, and performing the chores of My Temple; they shall slaughter the burnt offerings and the sacrifices for the people. They shall attend on them and serve them. [12]Because they served the House of Israel in the presence of their fetishes and made them stumble into guilt, therefore—declares the Lord GOD—I have sworn concerning them that they shall suffer their punishment: [13]They shall not approach Me to serve Me as priests, to come near any of My sacred offerings, the most holy things. They shall bear their shame for the abominations that they committed. [14]I will make them watchmen of the Temple, to perform all its chores, everything that needs to be done in it.

[15c]-But the levitical priests descended from Zadok,-[c] who maintained the service of My Sanctuary when the people of Israel went astray from Me—they shall approach Me to minister to Me; they shall stand before Me to offer Me fat and blood—declares the Lord GOD. [16]They alone may enter My Sanctuary and they alone shall approach My table to minister to Me; and they shall keep My charge. [17]And when they enter the gates of the inner court, they shall wear linen vestments: they shall have nothing woolen upon them when they minister inside the gates of the inner court. [18]They shall have linen turbans on their heads and linen breeches on their loins; they shall not gird themselves with anything that causes sweat. [19]When they go out to the outer court—the outer court where the people are—they shall remove the vestments in

---

c-c By contrast with the Levite-priests whose demotion has just been announced.

לְכָל־בֶּן־נֵכָר אֲשֶׁר בְּתוֹךְ בְּנֵי יִשְׂרָאֵל: [10] כִּי אִם־הַלְוִיִּם אֲשֶׁר רָחֲקוּ מֵעָלַי בִּתְעוֹת יִשְׂרָאֵל אֲשֶׁר תָּעוּ מֵעָלַי אַחֲרֵי גִּלּוּלֵיהֶם וְנָשְׂאוּ עֲוֺנָם: [11] וְהָיוּ בְמִקְדָּשִׁי מְשָׁרְתִים פְּקֻדּוֹת אֶל־שַׁעֲרֵי הַבַּיִת וּמְשָׁרְתִים אֶת־הַבָּיִת הֵמָּה יִשְׁחֲטוּ אֶת־הָעֹלָה וְאֶת־הַזֶּבַח לָעָם וְהֵמָּה יַעַמְדוּ לִפְנֵיהֶם לְשָׁרְתָם: [12] יַעַן אֲשֶׁר יְשָׁרְתוּ אוֹתָם לִפְנֵי גִלּוּלֵיהֶם וְהָיוּ לְבֵית־יִשְׂרָאֵל לְמִכְשׁוֹל עָוֺן עַל־כֵּן נָשָׂאתִי יָדִי עֲלֵיהֶם נְאֻם אֲדֹנָי יְהֹוִה וְנָשְׂאוּ עֲוֺנָם: [13] וְלֹא־ יִגְּשׁוּ אֵלַי לְכַהֵן לִי וְלָגֶשֶׁת עַל־כָּל־קָדָשַׁי אֶל־קָדְשֵׁי הַקֳּדָשִׁים וְנָשְׂאוּ כְּלִמָּתָם וְתוֹעֲבוֹתָם אֲשֶׁר עָשׂוּ: [14] וְנָתַתִּי אוֹתָם שֹׁמְרֵי מִשְׁמֶרֶת הַבָּיִת לְכֹל עֲבֹדָתוֹ וּלְכֹל אֲשֶׁר יֵעָשֶׂה בּוֹ: פ

[15] וְהַכֹּהֲנִים הַלְוִיִּם בְּנֵי צָדוֹק אֲשֶׁר שָׁמְרוּ אֶת־מִשְׁמֶרֶת מִקְדָּשִׁי בִּתְעוֹת בְּנֵי־יִשְׂרָאֵל מֵעָלַי הֵמָּה יִקְרְבוּ אֵלַי לְשָׁרְתֵנִי וְעָמְדוּ לְפָנַי לְהַקְרִיב לִי חֵלֶב וָדָם נְאֻם אֲדֹנָי יְהֹוִה: [16] הֵמָּה יָבֹאוּ אֶל־מִקְדָּשִׁי וְהֵמָּה יִקְרְבוּ אֶל־שֻׁלְחָנִי לְשָׁרְתֵנִי וְשָׁמְרוּ אֶת־מִשְׁמַרְתִּי: [17] וְהָיָה בְּבוֹאָם אֶל־שַׁעֲרֵי הֶחָצֵר הַפְּנִימִית בִּגְדֵי פִשְׁתִּים יִלְבָּשׁוּ וְלֹא־יַעֲלֶה עֲלֵיהֶם צֶמֶר בְּשָׁרְתָם בְּשַׁעֲרֵי הֶחָצֵר הַפְּנִימִית וָבָיְתָה: [18] פַּאֲרֵי פִשְׁתִּים יִהְיוּ עַל־רֹאשָׁם וּמִכְנְסֵי פִשְׁתִּים יִהְיוּ עַל־מָתְנֵיהֶם לֹא יַחְגְּרוּ בַּיָּזַע: [19] וּבְצֵאתָם אֶל־הֶחָצֵר הַחִיצוֹנָה אֶל־הֶחָצֵר הַחִיצוֹנָה אֶל־הָעָם יִפְשְׁטוּ אֶת־בִּגְדֵיהֶם אֲשֶׁר־הֵמָּה מְשָׁרְתִם בָּם וְהִנִּיחוּ אוֹתָם בְּלִשְׁכֹת

which they minister and shall deposit them in the sacred chambers;[d] they shall put on other garments, lest they make the people consecrated[e] by [contact with] their vestments. 20They shall neither shave their heads nor let their hair go untrimmed; they shall keep their hair trimmed. 21No priest shall drink wine when he enters into the inner court. 22They shall not marry widows[f] or divorced women; they may marry only virgins of the stock of the House of Israel, or widows who are widows of priests.

23They shall declare to My people what is sacred and what is profane, and inform them what is clean and what is unclean. 24In lawsuits, too, it is they who shall act as judges; they shall decide them in accordance with My rules. They shall preserve My teachings and My laws regarding all My fixed occasions; and they shall maintain the sanctity of My sabbaths.

25[A priest] shall not defile himself by entering [a house] where there is a dead person. He shall defile himself only for father or mother, son or daughter, brother or unmarried sister. 26After he has become clean, seven days shall be counted off for him; 27and on the day that he reenters the inner court of the Sanctuary to minister in the Sanctuary, he shall present his sin offering—declares the Lord God.

28This shall be their portion, for I am their portion; and no holding shall be given them in Israel, for I am their holding. 29The meal offerings, sin offerings, and guilt offerings shall be consumed by them. Everything proscribed[g] in Israel shall be theirs. 30All the choice first fruits of every kind, and all the gifts of every kind—of all your contributions—shall go to the priests. You shall further give the first of the yield of your baking[h] to the priest, that a blessing may rest upon your home.

הַקֹּדֶשׁ וְלָבְשׁוּ בְּגָדִים אֲחֵרִים וְלֹא־יְקַדְּשׁוּ אֶת־הָעָם בְּבִגְדֵיהֶם: 20 וְרֹאשָׁם לֹא יְגַלֵּחוּ וּפֶרַע לֹא יְשַׁלֵּחוּ כָּסוֹם יִכְסְמוּ אֶת־רָאשֵׁיהֶם: 21 וְיַיִן לֹא־יִשְׁתּוּ כָּל־כֹּהֵן בְּבוֹאָם אֶל־הֶחָצֵר הַפְּנִימִית: 22 וְאַלְמָנָה וּגְרוּשָׁה לֹא־יִקְחוּ לָהֶם לְנָשִׁים כִּי אִם־בְּתוּלֹת מִזֶּרַע בֵּית יִשְׂרָאֵל וְהָאַלְמָנָה אֲשֶׁר תִּהְיֶה אַלְמָנָה מִכֹּהֵן יִקָּחוּ: 23 וְאֶת־עַמִּי יוֹרוּ בֵּין קֹדֶשׁ לְחֹל וּבֵין־טָמֵא לְטָהוֹר יוֹדִעֻם: 24 וְעַל־רִיב הֵמָּה יַעַמְדוּ לשפט לְמִשְׁפָּט בְּמִשְׁפָּטַי ושפטהו יִשְׁפְּטֻהוּ וְאֶת־תּוֹרֹתַי וְאֶת־חֻקֹּתַי בְּכָל־מוֹעֲדַי יִשְׁמֹרוּ וְאֶת־שַׁבְּתוֹתַי יְקַדֵּשׁוּ: 25 וְאֶל־מֵת אָדָם לֹא יָבוֹא לְטָמְאָה כִּי אִם־לְאָב וּלְאֵם וּלְבֵן וּלְבַת לְאָח וּלְאָחוֹת אֲשֶׁר־לֹא־הָיְתָה לְאִישׁ יִטַּמָּאוּ: 26 וְאַחֲרֵי טָהֳרָתוֹ שִׁבְעַת יָמִים יִסְפְּרוּ־לוֹ: 27 וּבְיוֹם בֹּאוֹ אֶל־הַקֹּדֶשׁ אֶל־הֶחָצֵר הַפְּנִימִית לְשָׁרֵת בַּקֹּדֶשׁ יַקְרִיב חַטָּאתוֹ נְאֻם אֲדֹנָי יֱהֹוִה: 28 וְהָיְתָה לָהֶם לְנַחֲלָה אֲנִי נַחֲלָתָם וַאֲחֻזָּה לֹא־תִתְּנוּ לָהֶם בְּיִשְׂרָאֵל אֲנִי אֲחֻזָּתָם: 29 הַמִּנְחָה וְהַחַטָּאת וְהָאָשָׁם הֵמָּה יֹאכְלוּם וְכָל־חֵרֶם בְּיִשְׂרָאֵל לָהֶם יִהְיֶה: 30 וְרֵאשִׁית כָּל־בִּכּוּרֵי כֹל וְכָל־תְּרוּמַת כֹּל מִכֹּל תְּרוּמוֹתֵיכֶם לַכֹּהֲנִים יִהְיֶה וְרֵאשִׁית עֲרִסוֹתֵיכֶם תִּתְּנוּ לַכֹּהֵן לְהָנִיחַ בְּרָכָה אֶל־בֵּיתֶךָ:

---

d   Cf. 42.13–14.
e   Thereby rendering the people unfit for ordinary activity.
f   I.e., of laymen.
g   See Lev. 27.28.
h   See Num. 15.20–21.

³¹Priests shall not eat anything, whether bird or animal, that died or was torn by beasts.

45 When you allot the land as an inheritance, you shall set aside from the land, as a gift sacred to the Lᴏʀᴅ, an areaᵃ 25,000 [cubits] long and 10,000ᵇ wide: this shall be holy through its entire extent. ²Of this, a square measuring a full 500 by 500 shall be reserved for the Sanctuary,ᶜ and 50 cubits for an open space all around it. ³Of the aforesaid area, you shall measure off, as most holy and destined to include the Sanctuary, [a space] 25,000 long by 10,000 wide; ⁴it is a sacred portion of the land; it shall provide space for houses for the priests, the ministrants of the Sanctuary who are qualified to minister to the Lᴏʀᴅ, as well as holy ground for the Sanctuary. ⁵Another [space], 25,000 long by 10,000 wide, shall be the property of the Levites, the servants of the Temple—ᵈtwenty chambers.ᵈ ⁶Alongside the sacred reserve, you shall set aside [a space] 25,000 long by 5,000 wide, as the property of the city; it shall belong to the whole House of Israel. ⁷And to the prince shall belong, on both sides of the sacred reserve and the property of the city and alongside the sacred reserve and the property of the city, on the west extending westward and on the east extending eastward, a portionᵈ corresponding to one of the [tribal] portions that extend from the western border to the eastern border ⁸of the land.ᵉ That shall be his property in Israel; and My princes shall no more defraud My people, but shall leave the rest of the land to the several tribes of the House of Israel.

⁹Thus said the Lord Gᴏᴅ: Enough, princes of Israel! Make an end of lawlessness and rapine, and do what is right and just! Put a stop to your

---

a   Lit. "length."
b   Septuagint reads 20,000; cf. vv. 3–5.
c   Cf. 42.15 ff.
d-d   Septuagint reads "for towns to dwell in."
e   Cf. for all the foregoing 48.1 ff.

מה וּבְהַפִּילְכֶם אֶת־הָאָרֶץ בְּנַחֲלָה
תָּרִימוּ תְרוּמָה לַיהוָה ׀ קֹדֶשׁ מִן־הָאָרֶץ
אֹרֶךְ חֲמִשָּׁה וְעֶשְׂרִים אֶלֶף אֹרֶךְ וְרֹחַב
עֲשָׂרָה אֶלֶף קֹדֶשׁ־הוּא בְכָל־גְּבוּלָהּ
סָבִיב: ²יִהְיֶה מִזֶּה אֶל־הַקֹּדֶשׁ חָמֵשׁ
מֵאוֹת בַּחֲמֵשׁ מֵאוֹת מְרֻבָּע סָבִיב
וַחֲמִשִּׁים אַמָּה מִגְרָשׁ לוֹ סָבִיב: ³וּמִן־
הַמִּדָּה הַזֹּאת תָּמוֹד אֹרֶךְ חמש חֲמִשָּׁה
וְעֶשְׂרִים אֶלֶף וְרֹחַב עֲשֶׂרֶת אֲלָפִים וּבוֹ־
יִהְיֶה הַמִּקְדָּשׁ קֹדֶשׁ קָדָשִׁים: ⁴קֹדֶשׁ מִן־
הָאָרֶץ הוּא לַכֹּהֲנִים מְשָׁרְתֵי הַמִּקְדָּשׁ
יִהְיֶה הַקְּרֵבִים לְשָׁרֵת אֶת־יְהוָה וְהָיָה
לָהֶם מָקוֹם לְבָתִּים וּמִקְדָּשׁ לַמִּקְדָּשׁ:
⁵וַחֲמִשָּׁה וְעֶשְׂרִים אֶלֶף אֹרֶךְ וַעֲשֶׂרֶת
אֲלָפִים רֹחַב יהיה וְהָיָה לַלְוִיִּם מְשָׁרְתֵי
הַבַּיִת לָהֶם לַאֲחֻזָּה עֶשְׂרִים לְשָׁכֹת:
⁶וַאֲחֻזַּת הָעִיר תִּתְּנוּ חֲמֵשֶׁת אֲלָפִים
רֹחַב וְאֹרֶךְ חֲמִשָּׁה וְעֶשְׂרִים אֶלֶף
לְעֻמַּת תְּרוּמַת הַקֹּדֶשׁ לְכָל־בֵּית יִשְׂרָאֵל
יִהְיֶה: ⁷וְלַנָּשִׂיא מִזֶּה וּמִזֶּה לִתְרוּמַת
הַקֹּדֶשׁ וְלַאֲחֻזַּת הָעִיר אֶל־פְּנֵי תְרוּמַת־
הַקֹּדֶשׁ וְאֶל־פְּנֵי אֲחֻזַּת הָעִיר מִפְּאַת־יָם
יָמָּה וּמִפְּאַת־קֵדְמָה קָדִימָה וְאֹרֶךְ
לְעֻמּוֹת אַחַד הַחֲלָקִים מִגְּבוּל יָם אֶל־
גְּבוּל קָדִימָה: ⁸לָאָרֶץ יִהְיֶה־לּוֹ
לַאֲחֻזָּה בְּיִשְׂרָאֵל וְלֹא־יוֹנוּ עוֹד נְשִׂיאַי
אֶת־עַמִּי וְהָאָרֶץ יִתְּנוּ לְבֵית־יִשְׂרָאֵל
לְשִׁבְטֵיהֶם: ס
⁹כֹּה־אָמַר אֲדֹנָי יְהוִֹה רַב־לָכֶם נְשִׂיאֵי
יִשְׂרָאֵל חָמָס וָשֹׁד הָסִירוּ וּמִשְׁפָּט וּצְדָקָה
עֲשׂוּ הָרִימוּ גְרֻשֹׁתֵיכֶם מֵעַל עַמִּי נְאֻם

evictions of My people—declares the Lord GOD. ¹⁰Have honest balances, an honest *ephah*, and an honest *bath*.*f* ¹¹The *ephah* and the *bath* shall comprise the same volume, the *bath* a tenth of a *homer* and the *ephah* a tenth of a *homer*; their capacity shall be gauged by the *homer*. ¹²And the shekel shall weigh 20 *gerahs*. *g*-20 shekels, 25 shekels [and] 10 plus 5 shekels shall count with you as a *mina*.-*g*

¹³This is the contribution you shall make: One-sixth of an *ephah* from every *homer* of wheat and one-sixth of an *ephah* from every *homer* of barley, ¹⁴while the due from the oil—*h*-the oil being measured by the *bath*-*h*—shall be one-tenth of a *bath* from every *kor*.—As 10 *bath*s make a *homer*, so 10 *bath*s make a *homer*.*i*—¹⁵And [the due] from the flock shall be one animal from every 200. [All these shall be contributed] from Israel's products*h* for meal offerings, burnt offerings, and offerings of well-being, to make expiation for them—declares the Lord GOD. ¹⁶In this contribution, the entire population must join with the prince in Israel.

¹⁷But the burnt offerings, the meal offerings, and the libations on festivals, new moons, sabbaths—all fixed occasions—of the House of Israel shall be the obligation of the prince; he shall provide the sin offerings, the meal offerings, the burnt offerings, and the offerings of well-being, to make expiation for the House of Israel.

¹⁸Thus said the Lord GOD: On the first day of the first month, you shall take a bull of the herd without blemish, and you shall cleanse the Sanctuary. ¹⁹The priest shall take some of the blood of the sin offering and apply it to the doorposts of the Temple, to the four corners of the

אֲדֹנָ֥י יְהֹוִֽה׃ 10 מֹ֥אזְנֵי־צֶ֛דֶק וְאֵֽיפַת־צֶ֖דֶק וּבַת־צֶ֑דֶק יְהִ֖י לָכֶֽם׃ 11 הָאֵיפָ֣ה וְהַבַּ֗ת תֹּ֤כֶן אֶחָד֙ יִֽהְיֶ֔ה לָשֵׂ֕את מַעְשַׂ֥ר הַחֹ֖מֶר הַבָּ֑ת וַעֲשִׂירִ֤ת הַחֹ֙מֶר֙ הָֽאֵיפָ֔ה אֶל־הַחֹ֖מֶר יִהְיֶ֥ה מַתְכֻּנְתּֽוֹ׃ 12 וְהַשֶּׁ֖קֶל עֶשְׂרִ֣ים גֵּרָ֑ה עֶשְׂרִ֨ים שְׁקָלִ֜ים חֲמִשָּׁ֧ה וְעֶשְׂרִ֣ים שְׁקָלִ֗ים עֲשָׂרָ֤ה וַחֲמִשָּׁה֙ שֶׁ֔קֶל הַמָּנֶ֖ה יִֽהְיֶ֥ה לָכֶֽם׃ 13 זֹ֥את הַתְּרוּמָ֖ה אֲשֶׁ֣ר תָּרִ֑ימוּ שִׁשִּׁ֤ית הָֽאֵיפָה֙ מֵחֹ֣מֶר הַֽחִטִּ֔ים וְשִׁשִּׁיתֶ֣ם הָֽאֵיפָ֔ה מֵחֹ֖מֶר הַשְּׂעֹרִֽים׃ 14 וְחֹ֣ק הַשֶּׁ֗מֶן הַבַּ֣ת הַשֶּׁ֔מֶן מַעְשַׂ֥ר הַבַּ֖ת מִן־הַכֹּ֑ר עֲשֶׂ֤רֶת הַבַּתִּים֙ חֹ֔מֶר כִּֽי־עֲשֶׂ֥רֶת הַבַּתִּ֖ים חֹֽמֶר׃ 15 וְשֶׂה־אַחַ֨ת מִן־הַצֹּ֤אן מִן־הַמָּאתַ֙יִם֙ מִמַּשְׁקֵ֣ה יִשְׂרָאֵ֔ל לְמִנְחָ֖ה וּלְעוֹלָ֣ה וְלִשְׁלָמִ֑ים לְכַפֵּ֥ר עֲלֵיהֶ֖ם נְאֻ֥ם אֲדֹנָ֥י יְהֹוִֽה׃ 16 כֹּ֚ל הָעָ֣ם הָאָ֔רֶץ יִהְי֖וּ אֶל־הַתְּרוּמָ֣ה הַזֹּ֑את לַנָּשִׂ֖יא בְּיִשְׂרָאֵֽל׃ 17 וְעַֽל־הַנָּשִׂ֣יא יִהְיֶ֗ה הָעוֹל֣וֹת וְהַמִּנְחָה֮ וְהַנֵּ֒סֶךְ֒ בַּֽחַגִּ֤ים וּבֶֽחֳדָשִׁים֙ וּבַשַּׁבָּת֔וֹת בְּכׇֽל־מוֹעֲדֵ֖י בֵּ֣ית יִשְׂרָאֵ֑ל הֽוּא־יַעֲשֶׂ֞ה אֶת־הַחַטָּ֣את וְאֶת־הַמִּנְחָ֗ה וְאֶת־הָֽעוֹלָה֙ וְאֶת־הַשְּׁלָמִ֔ים לְכַפֵּ֖ר בְּעַ֥ד בֵּֽית־יִשְׂרָאֵֽל׃ ס 18 כֹּֽה־אָמַר֮ אֲדֹנָ֣י יְהֹוִה֒ בָּֽרִאשׁוֹן֙ בְּאֶחָ֣ד לַחֹ֔דֶשׁ תִּקַּ֥ח פַּר־בֶּן־בָּקָ֖ר תָּמִ֑ים וְחִטֵּאתָ֖ אֶת־הַמִּקְדָּֽשׁ׃ 19 וְלָקַ֨ח הַכֹּהֵ֜ן מִדַּ֣ם הַחַטָּ֗את וְנָתַן֙ אֶל־מְזוּזַ֣ת הַבַּ֔יִת וְאֶל־אַרְבַּ֛ע פִּנּ֥וֹת הָעֲזָרָ֖ה לַמִּזְבֵּ֑חַ וְעַ֨ל־מְזוּזַ֔ת

---

f The *ephah* is used for dry measure and the *bath* for liquid measure.

g-g The Mesopotamian *mina* of 60 shekels; but meaning of Heb. uncertain.

h-h Meaning of Heb. uncertain.

i The Vulgate reads "kor"; *homer* and *kor* are synonyms.

ledge[h] of the altar, and to the doorposts of the gate of the inner court. [20]You shall do the same [j]on the seventh day of the month[j] to purge the Temple from uncleanness caused by unwitting or ignorant persons.

[21]On the fourteenth day of the first month you shall have the passover sacrifice; and during a festival of seven days unleavened bread shall be eaten. [22]On that day, the prince shall provide a bull of sin offering on behalf of himself and of the entire population; [23]and during the seven days of the festival, he shall provide daily—for seven days—seven bulls and seven rams, without blemish, for a burnt offering to the LORD, and one goat daily for a sin offering. [24]He shall provide a meal offering of an *ephah*[k] for each bull and an *ephah* for each ram, with a *hin* of oil to every *ephah*. [25]So, too, during the festival of the seventh month, for seven days from the fifteenth day on, he shall provide the same sin offerings, burnt offerings, meal offerings, and oil.

46 Thus said the Lord GOD: The gate of the inner court which faces east shall be closed on the six working days; it shall be opened on the sabbath day and it shall be opened on the day of the new moon. [2]The prince shall enter by way of the vestibule outside the gate, and shall attend at the gatepost while the priests sacrifice his burnt offering and his offering of well-being; he shall then bow low at the threshold of the gate and depart. The gate, however, shall not be closed until evening. [3]The common people[a] shall worship before the LORD on sabbaths and new moons at the entrance of the same gate.

[4]The burnt offering which the prince presents to the LORD on the sabbath day shall consist of

---

j-j   *Septuagint reads "in the seventh month."*
k   *Of choice flour.*

a   *I.e., those other than the priests, the Levites, and the prince; lit. "the people of the land."*

שַׁ֥עַר הֶחָצֵ֖ר הַפְּנִימִ֑ית: 20 וְכֵ֤ן תַּעֲשֶׂה֙ בְּשִׁבְעָ֣ה בַחֹ֔דֶשׁ מֵאִ֥ישׁ שֹׁגֶ֖ה וּמִפֶּ֑תִי וְכִפַּרְתֶּ֖ם אֶת־הַבָּֽיִת:

21 בָּ֠רִאשׁוֹן בְּאַרְבָּעָ֨ה עָשָׂ֥ר יוֹם֙ לַחֹ֔דֶשׁ יִהְיֶ֥ה לָכֶ֖ם הַפָּ֑סַח חָ֕ג שְׁבֻע֣וֹת יָמִ֔ים מַצּ֖וֹת יֵאָכֵֽל: 22 וְעָשָׂ֣ה הַנָּשִׂ֗יא בַּיּ֥וֹם הַה֛וּא בַּעֲד֖וֹ וּבְעַ֣ד כָּל־עַ֣ם הָאָ֑רֶץ פַּ֖ר חַטָּֽאת: 23 וְשִׁבְעַ֨ת יְמֵֽי־הֶחָ֜ג יַעֲשֶׂ֧ה עוֹלָ֣ה לַֽיהֹוָ֗ה שִׁבְעַ֣ת פָּ֠רִים וְשִׁבְעַ֨ת אֵילִ֤ים תְּמִימִם֙ לַיּ֔וֹם שִׁבְעַ֖ת הַיָּמִ֑ים וְחַטָּ֕את שְׂעִ֥יר עִזִּ֖ים לַיּֽוֹם: 24 וּמִנְחָ֗ה אֵיפָ֤ה לַפָּר֙ וְאֵיפָ֣ה לָאַ֔יִל יַעֲשֶׂ֑ה וְשֶׁ֕מֶן הִ֖ין לָאֵיפָֽה: 25 בַּשְּׁבִיעִ֡י בַּחֲמִשָּׁה֩ עָשָׂ֨ר י֤וֹם לַחֹ֙דֶשׁ֙ בֶּחָ֔ג יַעֲשֶׂ֥ה כָאֵ֖לֶּה שִׁבְעַ֣ת הַיָּמִ֑ים כַּֽחַטָּאת֙ כָּֽעֹלָ֔ה וְכַמִּנְחָ֖ה וְכַשָּֽׁמֶן: ס

מו כֹּה־אָמַר֮ אֲדֹנָ֣י יְהֹוִה֒ שַׁ֜עַר הֶחָצֵ֤ר הַפְּנִימִית֙ הַפֹּנֶ֣ה קָדִ֔ים יִהְיֶ֣ה סָג֔וּר שֵׁ֖שֶׁת יְמֵ֣י הַֽמַּעֲשֶׂ֑ה וּבְי֧וֹם הַשַּׁבָּ֛ת יִפָּתֵ֖חַ וּבְי֥וֹם הַחֹ֖דֶשׁ יִפָּתֵֽחַ: 2 וּבָ֣א הַנָּשִׂ֡יא דֶּרֶךְ֩ אוּלָ֨ם הַשַּׁ֜עַר מִח֗וּץ וְעָמַד֙ עַל־מְזוּזַ֣ת הַשַּׁ֔עַר וְעָשׂ֣וּ הַכֹּהֲנִ֗ים אֶת־עֽוֹלָתוֹ֙ וְאֶת־שְׁלָמָ֔יו וְהִֽשְׁתַּחֲוָ֛ה עַל־מִפְתַּ֥ן הַשַּׁ֖עַר וְיָצָ֑א וְהַשַּׁ֥עַר לֹֽא־יִסָּגֵ֖ר עַד־הָעָֽרֶב: 3 וְהִשְׁתַּחֲו֣וּ עַם־הָאָ֗רֶץ פֶּ֜תַח הַשַּׁ֤עַר הַהוּא֙ בַּשַּׁבָּת֣וֹת וּבֶֽחֳדָשִׁ֔ים לִפְנֵ֖י יְהֹוָֽה: 4 וְהָ֣עֹלָ֔ה אֲשֶׁר־יַקְרִ֥ב הַנָּשִׂ֖יא לַֽיהֹוָ֑ה בְּי֣וֹם הַשַּׁבָּ֗ת שִׁשָּׁ֧ה כְבָשִׂ֛ים תְּמִימִ֖ם וְאַ֥יִל

six lambs without blemish and one ram without blemish—[5]with a meal offering of an *ephah* for the ram, a meal offering of as much as he wishes for the lambs, and a *hin* of oil with every *ephah*. [6]And on the day of the new moon, it shall consist of a bull of the herd without blemish, and six lambs and a ram—they shall be without blemish. [7]And he shall provide a meal offering of an *ephah* for the bull, an *ephah* for the ram, and as much as he can afford for the lambs, with a *hin* of oil to every *ephah*.

[8]When the prince enters, he shall come in by way of the vestibule of the gate, and he shall go out the same way.

[9]But on the fixed occasions, when the common people come before the LORD, whoever enters by the north gate to bow low shall leave by the south gate; and whoever enters by the south gate shall leave by the north gate. They shall not go back through the gate by which they came in, but shall go out *b-*by the opposite one.*-b* [10]And as for the prince, he shall enter with them when they enter and leave when they leave.

[11]On festivals and fixed occasions, the meal offering shall be an *ephah* for each bull, an *ephah* for each ram, and as much as he wishes for the lambs, with a *hin* of oil for every *ephah*.

[12]The gate that faces east shall also be opened for the prince whenever he offers a freewill offering—be it burnt offering or offering of well-being—freely offered to the LORD, so that he may offer his burnt offering or his offering of well-being just as he does on the sabbath day. Then he shall leave, and the gate shall be closed after he leaves.

[13]Each day you shall offer a lamb of the first year without blemish, as a daily burnt offering to the LORD; you shall offer one every morning. [14]And every morning regularly you shall offer a meal offering with it: a sixth of an *ephah*, with

תָּמִֽים: 5 וּמִנְחָה אֵיפָ֣ה לָאַ֗יִל וְלַכְּבָשִׂים֙ מִנְחָה֙ מַתַּ֣ת יָד֔וֹ וְשֶׁ֖מֶן הִ֥ין לָאֵיפָֽה: 6 וּבְי֣וֹם הַחֹ֗דֶשׁ פַּ֧ר בֶּן־בָּקָ֛ר תְּמִימִ֖ם וְשֵׁ֣שֶׁת כְּבָשִׂ֑ם וָאַ֖יִל תְּמִימִ֥ם יִהְיֽוּ: 7 וְאֵיפָ֣ה לַפָּ֡ר וְאֵיפָ֣ה לָאַ֩יִל֩ יַעֲשֶׂ֨ה מִנְחָ֜ה וְלַכְּבָשִׂ֗ים כַּאֲשֶׁ֛ר תַּשִּׂ֥יג יָד֖וֹ וְשֶׁ֥מֶן הִ֥ין לָאֵיפָֽה: 8 וּבְב֖וֹא הַנָּשִׂ֑יא דֶּ֣רֶךְ אוּלָ֤ם הַשַּׁ֙עַר֙ יָב֔וֹא וּבְדַרְכּ֖וֹ יֵצֵֽא: 9 וּבְב֨וֹא עַם־הָאָ֜רֶץ לִפְנֵ֣י יְהוָה֮ בַּמּֽוֹעֲדִים֒ הַבָּ֡א דֶּֽרֶךְ־שַׁ֨עַר צָפ֜וֹן לְהִֽשְׁתַּחֲוֺ֗ת יֵצֵא֙ דֶּֽרֶךְ־שַׁ֣עַר נֶ֔גֶב וְהַבָּא֙ דֶּֽרֶךְ־שַׁ֣עַר נֶ֔גֶב יֵצֵ֖א דֶּֽרֶךְ־שַׁ֣עַר צָפ֑וֹנָה לֹ֣א יָשׁ֗וּב דֶּ֤רֶךְ הַשַּׁ֙עַר֙ אֲשֶׁר־בָּ֣א ב֔וֹ כִּ֥י נִכְח֖וֹ *יצאו* יֵצֵֽא: 10 וְהַנָּשִׂ֖יא בְּתוֹכָ֑ם בְּבוֹאָם֙ יָב֔וֹא וּבְצֵאתָ֖ם יֵצֵֽאוּ: 11 וּבַחַגִּ֣ים וּבַמּֽוֹעֲדִ֗ים תִּהְיֶ֤ה הַמִּנְחָה֙ אֵיפָ֤ה לַפָּר֙ וְאֵיפָ֣ה לָאַ֔יִל וְלַכְּבָשִׂ֖ים מַתַּ֣ת יָד֑וֹ וְשֶׁ֖מֶן הִ֥ין לָאֵיפָֽה: ס 12 וְכִֽי־יַעֲשֶׂה֩ הַנָּשִׂ֨יא נְדָבָ֜ה עוֹלָ֣ה אֽוֹ־שְׁלָמִים֮ נְדָבָ֣ה לַֽיהוָה֒ וּפָ֣תַֽח ל֗וֹ אֶת־הַשַּׁ֙עַר֙ הַפֹּנֶ֣ה קָדִ֔ים וְעָשָׂ֤ה אֶת־עֹֽלָתוֹ֙ וְאֶת־שְׁלָמָ֔יו כַּאֲשֶׁ֥ר יַעֲשֶׂ֖ה בְּי֣וֹם הַשַּׁבָּ֑ת וְיָצָ֗א וְסָגַ֤ר אֶת־הַשַּׁ֙עַר֙ אַחֲרֵ֣י צֵאתֽוֹ: 13 וְכֶ֨בֶשׂ בֶּן־שְׁנָת֜וֹ תָּמִ֗ים תַּעֲשֶׂ֥ה עוֹלָ֛ה לַיּ֖וֹם לַֽיהוָ֑ה בַּבֹּ֥קֶר בַּבֹּ֖קֶר תַּעֲשֶׂ֥ה אֹתֽוֹ: 14 וּמִנְחָה֩ תַעֲשֶׂ֨ה עָלָ֤יו בַּבֹּ֙קֶר֙ בַּבֹּ֔קֶר שִׁשִּׁ֣ית הָאֵיפָ֗ה וְשֶׁ֜מֶן שְׁלִישִׁ֤ית הַהִין֙ לָרֹ֣ס

---

b-b   Lit. "straight before him."

a third of a *hin* of oil to moisten the choice flour, as a meal offering to the LORD—a law for all time. [15]The lamb, the meal offering, and oil shall be presented every morning as a regular burnt offering.

[16]Thus said the Lord GOD: If the prince makes a gift to any of his sons, it shall become the latter's inheritance; it shall pass on to his sons; it is their holding by inheritance. [17]But if he makes a gift from his inheritance to any of his subjects, it shall only belong to the latter until the year of release.[c] Then it shall revert to the prince; his inheritance must by all means pass on to his sons.

[18]But the prince shall not take property away from any of the people and rob them of their holdings. Only out of his own holdings shall he endow his sons, in order that My people may not be dispossessed of their holdings.

[19]Then he led me into the passage at the side of the gate to the sacred chambers of the priests, which face north, and there, at the rear of it, in the west, I saw a space. [20]He said to me, "This is the place where the priests shall boil the guilt offerings and the sin offerings, and where they shall bake the meal offerings, so as not to take them into the outer court and [d-]make the people consecrated."[-d] [21]Then he led me into the outer court and led me past the four corners of the court; and in each corner of the court there was an enclosure. [22]These unroofed[e] enclosures, [each] 40 [cubits] long and 30 wide, were in the four corners of the court; the four corner enclosures had the same measurements. [23][On the inside,] running round the four of them, there was a row of masonry, equipped with hearths under the rows all around. [24]He said to me, "These are the kitchens where the Temple servitors shall boil the sacrifices of the people."

אֶת־הַסֹּלֶת מִנְחָה לַיהֹוָה חֻקּוֹת עוֹלָם
תָּמִיד: [15] וְעָשׂוּ יַעֲשׂוּ אֶת־הַכֶּבֶשׂ וְאֶת־
הַמִּנְחָה וְאֶת־הַשֶּׁמֶן בַּבֹּקֶר בַּבֹּקֶר עוֹלַת
תָּמִיד: פ

[16] כֹּה־אָמַר אֲדֹנָי יֱהֹוִה כִּי־יִתֵּן הַנָּשִׂיא
מַתָּנָה לְאִישׁ מִבָּנָיו נַחֲלָתוֹ הִיא לְבָנָיו
תִּהְיֶה אֲחֻזָּתָם הִיא בְּנַחֲלָה: [17] וְכִי־יִתֵּן
מַתָּנָה מִנַּחֲלָתוֹ לְאַחַד מֵעֲבָדָיו וְהָיְתָה
לּוֹ עַד־שְׁנַת הַדְּרוֹר וְשָׁבַת לַנָּשִׂיא אַךְ
נַחֲלָתוֹ בָּנָיו לָהֶם תִּהְיֶה:
[18] וְלֹא־יִקַּח הַנָּשִׂיא מִנַּחֲלַת הָעָם
לְהוֹנֹתָם מֵאֲחֻזָּתָם מֵאֲחֻזָּתוֹ יַנְחִל אֶת־
בָּנָיו לְמַעַן אֲשֶׁר לֹא־יָפֻצוּ עַמִּי אִישׁ
מֵאֲחֻזָּתוֹ:
[19] וַיְבִיאֵנִי בַמָּבוֹא אֲשֶׁר עַל־כֶּתֶף הַשַּׁעַר
אֶל־הַלִּשְׁכוֹת הַקֹּדֶשׁ אֶל־הַכֹּהֲנִים הַפֹּנוֹת
צָפוֹנָה וְהִנֵּה־שָׁם מָקוֹם בַּיַּרְכָתִם
בַּיַּרְכָתַיִם יָמָּה: ס [20] וַיֹּאמֶר אֵלַי זֶה
הַמָּקוֹם אֲשֶׁר יְבַשְּׁלוּ־שָׁם הַכֹּהֲנִים אֶת־
הָאָשָׁם וְאֶת־הַחַטָּאת אֲשֶׁר יֹאפוּ אֶת־
הַמִּנְחָה לְבִלְתִּי הוֹצִיא אֶל־הֶחָצֵר
הַחִיצוֹנָה לְקַדֵּשׁ אֶת־הָעָם: [21] וַיּוֹצִיאֵנִי
אֶל־הֶחָצֵר הַחִיצֹנָה וַיַּעֲבִירֵנִי אֶל־אַרְבַּעַת
מִקְצוֹעֵי הֶחָצֵר וְהִנֵּה חָצֵר בְּמִקְצֹעַ
הֶחָצֵר חָצֵר בְּמִקְצֹעַ הֶחָצֵר: [22] בְּאַרְבַּעַת
מִקְצֹעוֹת הֶחָצֵר חֲצֵרוֹת קְטֻרוֹת אַרְבָּעִים
אֹרֶךְ וּשְׁלֹשִׁים רֹחַב מִדָּה אַחַת
לְאַרְבַּעְתָּם מְהֻקְצָעוֹת*: [23] וְטוּר סָבִיב
בָּהֶם סָבִיב לְאַרְבַּעְתָּם וּמְבַשְּׁלוֹת עָשׂוּי
מִתַּחַת הַטִּירוֹת סָבִיב: [24] וַיֹּאמֶר אֵלַי
אֵלֶּה בֵּית הַמְבַשְּׁלִים אֲשֶׁר יְבַשְּׁלוּ־שָׁם
מְשָׁרְתֵי הַבַּיִת אֶת־זֶבַח הָעָם:

---

c   Cf. Lev. 25.10.
d-d   See note e at 44.19.
e   So Mishnah Middoth 2.5; emendation yields "small."

47 He led me back to the entrance of the Temple, and I found that water was issuing from below the platform*a* of the Temple—eastward, since the Temple faced east—but the water was running out at the *b*-south of the altar,-*b* under the south wall of the Temple. [2]Then he led me out by way of the northern gate and led me around to the outside of the outer gate that faces in the direction of the east;*c* and I found that water was gushing from [under] the south wall. [3]As the man went on eastward with a measuring line in his hand, he measured off a thousand cubits and led me across the water; the water was ankle deep. [4]Then he measured off another thousand and led me across the water; the water was knee deep. He measured off a further thousand and led me across the water; the water was up to the waist. [5]When he measured yet another thousand, it was a stream I could not cross; for the water had swollen into a stream that could not be crossed except by swimming. [6]"Do you see, O mortal?" he said to me; and he led me back to the bank of the stream.

[7]As I came back, I saw trees in great profusion on both banks of the stream. [8]"This water," he told me, "runs out to the eastern region, and flows into the Arabah; and when it comes into the sea, into *d*-the sea of foul waters,-*d* the water will become wholesome. [9]Every living creature that swarms will be able to live wherever this stream goes; the fish will be very abundant once these waters have reached there. It will be wholesome, and everything will live wherever this stream goes. [10]Fishermen shall stand beside it all the way from En-gedi to En-eglaim; it shall be a place for drying nets; and the fish will be

מז וַיְשִׁבֵנִי אֶל־פֶּתַח הַבַּיִת וְהִנֵּה־מַיִם יֹצְאִים מִתַּחַת מִפְתַּן הַבַּיִת קָדִימָה כִּי־פְנֵי הַבַּיִת קָדִים וְהַמַּיִם יֹרְדִים מִתַּחַת מִכֶּתֶף הַבַּיִת הַיְמָנִית מִנֶּגֶב לַמִּזְבֵּחַ: [2] וַיּוֹצִאֵנִי דֶּרֶךְ־שַׁעַר צָפוֹנָה וַיְסִבֵּנִי דֶּרֶךְ חוּץ אֶל־שַׁעַר הַחוּץ דֶּרֶךְ הַפּוֹנֶה קָדִים וְהִנֵּה־מַיִם מְפַכִּים מִן־הַכָּתֵף הַיְמָנִית: [3] בְּצֵאת־הָאִישׁ קָדִים וְקָו בְּיָדוֹ וַיָּמָד אֶלֶף בָּאַמָּה וַיַּעֲבִרֵנִי בַמַּיִם מֵי אָפְסָיִם: [4] וַיָּמָד אֶלֶף וַיַּעֲבִרֵנִי בַמַּיִם מַיִם בִּרְכָּיִם וַיָּמָד אֶלֶף וַיַּעֲבִרֵנִי מֵי מָתְנָיִם: [5] וַיָּמָד אֶלֶף נַחַל אֲשֶׁר לֹא־אוּכַל לַעֲבֹר כִּי־גָאוּ הַמַּיִם מֵי שָׂחוּ נַחַל אֲשֶׁר לֹא־יֵעָבֵר: [6] וַיֹּאמֶר אֵלַי הֲרָאִיתָ בֶן־אָדָם וַיּוֹלִכֵנִי וַיְשִׁבֵנִי שְׂפַת הַנָּחַל: [7] בְּשׁוּבֵנִי וְהִנֵּה אֶל־שְׂפַת הַנַּחַל עֵץ רַב מְאֹד מִזֶּה וּמִזֶּה: [8] וַיֹּאמֶר אֵלַי הַמַּיִם הָאֵלֶּה יוֹצְאִים אֶל־הַגְּלִילָה הַקַּדְמוֹנָה וְיָרְדוּ עַל־הָעֲרָבָה וּבָאוּ הַיָּמָּה אֶל־הַיָּמָּה הַמּוּצָאִים וְנִרְפְּאוּ* הַמָּיִם: [9] וְהָיָה כָל־נֶפֶשׁ חַיָּה ׀ אֲשֶׁר־יִשְׁרֹץ אֶל כָּל־אֲשֶׁר יָבוֹא שָׁם נַחֲלַיִם יִחְיֶה וְהָיָה הַדָּגָה רַבָּה מְאֹד כִּי בָאוּ שָׁמָּה הַמַּיִם הָאֵלֶּה וְיֵרָפְאוּ וָחָי כֹּל אֲשֶׁר־יָבוֹא שָׁמָּה הַנָּחַל: [10] וְהָיָה יעמדו עָמְדוּ עָלָיו דַּוָּגִים מֵעֵין גֶּדִי וְעַד־עֵין עֶגְלַיִם מִשְׁטוֹחַ לַחֲרָמִים יִהְיוּ לְמִינָה*

---

a See note at 9.3.
b-b Connection unclear. Emendation yields "southeast."
c The end of the verse explains why he could not have made the detour by way of the south gate. For the reasons why he could not have proceeded to his present position directly by way of the east gate, see 43.1–2; 44.1–2.
d-d I.e., the Dead Sea.

חסר א' v. 8.
ה' רפה v. 10.

of various kinds [and] most plentiful, like the fish of the Great Sea. [11]But its swamps and marshes shall not become wholesome; they will serve to [supply] salt. [12]All kinds of trees for food will grow up on both banks of the stream. Their leaves will not wither nor their fruit fail; they will yield new fruit every month, because the water for them flows from the Temple. Their fruit will serve for food and their leaves for healing."

[13]Thus said the Lord GOD: These shall be the boundaries of the land that you shall allot to the twelve tribes of Israel. Joseph shall receive two portions, [14]and you shall share the rest equally. As I swore to give it to your fathers, so shall this land fall to you as your heritage. [15]These are the boundaries of the land:

As the northern limit: From the Great Sea by way of Hethlon, Lebo-e-hamath,-e Zedad, [16]Berathah, Sibraim—which lies between the border of Damascus and the border of Hamath—[down to] Hazer-hatticon, which is on the border of Hauran. [17]Thus the boundary shall run from the Sea to f-Hazar-enon,-f to the north of the territory of Damascus, with the territory of Hamath to the north of it. That shall be the northern limit.

[18]As the eastern limit: A line between Hauran and Damascus, and between Gilead and the land of Israel: with the Jordan as a boundary, you shall measure down to the d-Eastern Sea.-d That shall be the eastern limit.

[19]The southern limit shall run: A line from Tamar to the waters of Meriboth-kadesh, along the Wadi [of Egypt and] the Great Sea. That is the southern limit.

[20]And as the western limit: The Great Sea shall be the boundary up to a point opposite Lebo-hamath. That shall be the western limit.

תִּהְיֶה דְגָתָם כְּדְגַת הַיָּם הַגָּדוֹל רַבָּה מְאֹד: 11 בצאתו בְּצֵאתָיו וּגְבָאָיו וְלֹא יֵרָפְאוּ לְמֶלַח נִתָּנוּ: 12 וְעַל־הַנַּחַל יַעֲלֶה עַל־שְׂפָתוֹ מִזֶּה | וּמִזֶּה | כָּל־עֵץ־מַאֲכָל לֹא־יִבּוֹל עָלֵהוּ וְלֹא־יִתֹּם פִּרְיוֹ לָחֳדָשָׁיו יְבַכֵּר כִּי מֵימָיו מִן־הַמִּקְדָּשׁ הֵמָּה יוֹצְאִים וְהָיָה פִרְיוֹ לְמַאֲכָל וְעָלֵהוּ לִתְרוּפָה: ס

13 כֹּה אָמַר אֲדֹנָי יְהֹוִה גֵּה גְּבוּל אֲשֶׁר תִּתְנַחֲלוּ אֶת־הָאָרֶץ לִשְׁנֵי עָשָׂר שִׁבְטֵי יִשְׂרָאֵל יוֹסֵף חֲבָלִים: 14 וּנְחַלְתֶּם אוֹתָהּ אִישׁ כְּאָחִיו אֲשֶׁר נָשָׂאתִי אֶת־יָדִי לְתִתָּהּ לַאֲבֹתֵיכֶם וְנָפְלָה הָאָרֶץ הַזֹּאת לָכֶם בְּנַחֲלָה: 15 וְזֶה גְּבוּל הָאָרֶץ לִפְאַת צָפוֹנָה מִן־הַיָּם הַגָּדוֹל הַדֶּרֶךְ חֶתְלֹן לְבוֹא צְדָדָה: 16 חֲמָת | בֵּרוֹתָה סִבְרַיִם אֲשֶׁר בֵּין־גְּבוּל דַּמֶּשֶׂק וּבֵין גְּבוּל חֲמָת חָצֵר הַתִּיכוֹן אֲשֶׁר אֶל־גְּבוּל חַוְרָן: 17 וְהָיָה גְבוּל מִן־הַיָּם חֲצַר עֵינוֹן גְּבוּל דַּמֶּשֶׂק וְצָפוֹן | צָפוֹנָה וּגְבוּל חֲמָת וְאֵת פְּאַת צָפוֹן: 18 וּפְאַת קָדִים מִבֵּין חַוְרָן וּמִבֵּין־דַּמֶּשֶׂק וּמִבֵּין הַגִּלְעָד וּמִבֵּין אֶרֶץ יִשְׂרָאֵל הַיַּרְדֵּן מִגְּבוּל עַל־הַיָּם הַקַּדְמוֹנִי תָּמֹדּוּ וְאֵת פְּאַת קָדִימָה: 19 וּפְאַת נֶגֶב תֵּימָנָה מִתָּמָר עַד־מֵי מְרִיבוֹת קָדֵשׁ נַחֲלָה אֶל־הַיָּם הַגָּדוֹל וְאֵת פְּאַת־תֵּימָנָה נֶגְבָּה: 20 וּפְאַת־יָם הַיָּם הַגָּדוֹל מִגְּבוּל עַד־נֹכַח לְבוֹא חֲמָת זֹאת פְּאַת־יָם:

---

e-e *Brought up from v. 16 for clarity.*
f-f *Apparently identical with Hazer-hatticon in v. 16.*

²¹This land you shall divide for yourselves among the tribes of Israel. ²²You shall allot it as a heritage for yourselves and for the strangers who reside among you, who have begotten children among you. You shall treat them as Israelite citizens; they shall receive allotments along with you among the tribes of Israel. ²³You shall give the stranger an allotment within the tribe where he resides—declares the Lord GOD.

48

These are the names of the tribes:

At the northern end, along the Hethlon road, [from] Lebo-hamath to Hazar-enan—which is the border of Damascus, with Hamath to the north—from the eastern border to the Sea: Dan—one [tribe].

²Adjoining the territory of Dan, from the eastern border to the western border: Asher—one.

³Adjoining the territory of Asher, from the eastern border to the western border: Naphtali—one.

⁴Adjoining the territory of Naphtali, from the eastern border to the western border: Manasseh—one.

⁵Adjoining the territory of Manasseh, from the eastern border to the western border: Ephraim—one.

⁶Adjoining the territory of Ephraim, from the eastern border to the western border: Reuben—one.

⁷Adjoining the territory of Reuben, from the eastern border to the western border: Judah—one.

⁸Adjoining the territory of Judah, from the eastern border to the western border, shall be the reserve that you set aside: 25,000 [cubits] in breadth and in length equal to one of the portions from the eastern border to the western

וְחִלַּקְתֶּ֞ם אֶת־הָאָ֤רֶץ הַזֹּאת֙ לָכֶ֔ם ²¹
לְשִׁבְטֵ֖י יִשְׂרָאֵֽל׃ ²² וְהָיָ֗ה תַּפִּ֣לוּ אוֹתָהּ֮
בְּנַחֲלָה֒ לָכֶ֗ם וּלְהַגֵּרִ֛ים הַגָּרִ֥ים בְּתוֹכְכֶ֖ם
אֲשֶׁר־הוֹלִ֣דוּ בָנִ֣ים בְּתוֹכְכֶ֑ם וְהָי֣וּ לָכֶ֗ם
כְּאֶזְרָח֙ בִּבְנֵ֣י יִשְׂרָאֵ֔ל אִתְּכֶם֙ יִפְּל֣וּ בְנַחֲלָ֔ה
בְּת֖וֹךְ שִׁבְטֵ֣י יִשְׂרָאֵֽל׃ ²³ וְהָיָ֣ה בַשֵּׁ֔בֶט
אֲשֶׁר־גָּ֥ר הַגֵּ֖ר אִתּ֑וֹ שָׁ֚ם תִּתְּנ֣וּ נַחֲלָת֔וֹ נְאֻ֖ם
אֲדֹנָ֥י יְהֹוִֽה׃ ס

מח

וְאֵ֖לֶּה שְׁמ֣וֹת הַשְּׁבָטִ֑ים
מִקְצֵ֣ה צָפ֡וֹנָה אֶל־יַ֣ד דֶּֽרֶךְ־חֶתְלֹ֣ן ׀ לְבוֹא־
חֲמָ֗ת חֲצַ֤ר עֵינָן֙ גְּב֣וּל דַּמֶּ֣שֶׂק צָפ֔וֹנָה
אֶל־יַ֣ד חֲמָ֑ת וְהָיוּ־ל֧וֹ פְאַת־קָדִ֛ים הַיָּ֖ם דָּ֥ן
אֶחָֽד׃
² וְעַ֣ל ׀ גְּב֣וּל דָּ֗ן מִפְּאַ֥ת קָדִ֖ים עַד־פְּאַת־
יָ֑מָּה אָשֵׁ֖ר אֶחָֽד׃
³ וְעַ֣ל ׀ גְּב֣וּל אָשֵׁ֗ר מִפְּאַ֤ת קָדִ֙ימָה֙ וְעַד־
פְּאַת־יָ֔מָּה נַפְתָּלִ֖י אֶחָֽד׃
⁴ וְעַ֣ל ׀ גְּב֣וּל נַפְתָּלִ֗י מִפְּאַ֤ת קָדִ֙מָה֙ עַד־
פְּאַת־יָ֔מָּה מְנַשֶּׁ֖ה אֶחָֽד׃
⁵ וְעַ֣ל ׀ גְּב֣וּל מְנַשֶּׁ֗ה מִפְּאַ֤ת קָדִ֙מָה֙ עַד־
פְּאַת־יָ֔מָּה אֶפְרַ֖יִם אֶחָֽד׃
⁶ וְעַ֣ל ׀ גְּב֣וּל אֶפְרַ֗יִם מִפְּאַ֤ת קָדִים֙ וְעַד־
פְּאַת־יָ֔מָּה רְאוּבֵ֖ן אֶחָֽד׃
⁷ וְעַ֣ל ׀ גְּב֣וּל רְאוּבֵ֗ן מִפְּאַ֤ת קָדִים֙ עַד־
פְּאַת־יָ֔מָּה יְהוּדָ֖ה אֶחָֽד׃
⁸ וְעַל֙ גְּב֣וּל יְהוּדָ֔ה מִפְּאַ֥ת קָדִ֖ים עַד־
פְּאַת־יָ֑מָּה תִּהְיֶ֣ה הַתְּרוּמָ֡ה אֲשֶׁר־תָּרִ֩ימוּ֩
חֲמִשָּׁ֨ה וְעֶשְׂרִ֥ים אֶ֙לֶף֙ רֹ֔חַב וְאֹ֕רֶךְ כְּאַחַ֤ד
הַחֲלָקִים֙ מִפְּאַ֣ת קָדִ֔ימָה עַד־פְּאַת־יָ֔מָּה

border; the Sanctuary shall be in the middle of it. 9The reserve that you set aside for the LORD shall be 25,000 long and 10,000*a* wide. 10It shall be apportioned to the following: The sacred reserve for the priests shall measure 25,000 [cubits] on the north, *b*-10,000 on the west, 10,000 on the east, and 25,000 on the south,-*b* with the LORD's Sanctuary in the middle of it. 11This consecrated area shall be for the priests of the line of Zadok, who kept My charge and did not go astray, as the Levites did when the people of Israel went astray. 12It shall be a special reserve for them out of the [total] reserve from the land, most holy, adjoining the territory of the Levites. 13Alongside the territory of the priests, the Levites shall have [an area] 25,000 long by 10,000 wide; the total length shall be 25,000 and the breadth 10,000.*c* 14None of it—the choicest of the land—may be sold, exchanged, or transferred; it is sacred to the LORD.

15The remaining 5,000 in breadth by 25,000 shall be for common use—serving the city for dwellings and pasture. The city itself shall be in the middle of it; 16and these shall be its measurements: On the north side 4,500 cubits, on the south side 4,500, on the east side 4,500, and on the west side 4,500. 17The pasture shall extend 250 cubits to the north of the city, 250 to the south, 250 to the east, and 250 to the west. 18As for the remaining 10,000 to the east and 10,000 to the west, adjoining the long side*d* of the sacred reserve, the produce of these areas adjoining the sacred reserve shall serve as food for the workers in the city; 19the workers in the city from all the tribes of Israel shall cultivate it. 20The entire reserve, 25,000 square, you shall set aside as the sacred reserve plus the city prop-

---

a   *Emendation yields "25,000"; cf. 45.3–6.*
b-b   *Lit. "10,000 in breadth on the west; 10,000 in breadth on the east; and 25,000 in length on the south."*
c   *Septuagint reads "20,000"; cf. note a.*
d   *I.e., the south side.*

וְהָיָה הַמִּקְדָּשׁ בְּתוֹכוֹ: 9 הַתְּרוּמָה אֲשֶׁר תָּרִימוּ לַיהוָה אֹרֶךְ חֲמִשָּׁה וְעֶשְׂרִים אֶלֶף וְרֹחַב עֲשֶׂרֶת אֲלָפִים: 10 וּלְאֵלֶּה* תִּהְיֶה תְרוּמַת־הַקֹּדֶשׁ לַכֹּהֲנִים צָפוֹנָה חֲמִשָּׁה וְעֶשְׂרִים אֶלֶף וְיָמָּה רֹחַב עֲשֶׂרֶת אֲלָפִים וְקָדִימָה רֹחַב עֲשֶׂרֶת אֲלָפִים וְנֶגְבָּה אֹרֶךְ חֲמִשָּׁה וְעֶשְׂרִים אָלֶף וְהָיָה מִקְדַּשׁ־יְהוָה בְּתוֹכוֹ: 11 לַכֹּהֲנִים הַמְקֻדָּשׁ מִבְּנֵי צָדוֹק אֲשֶׁר שָׁמְרוּ מִשְׁמַרְתִּי אֲשֶׁר לֹא־תָעוּ בִּתְעוֹת בְּנֵי יִשְׂרָאֵל כַּאֲשֶׁר תָּעוּ הַלְוִיִּם: ס 12 וְהָיְתָה לָהֶם תְּרוּמִיָּה מִתְּרוּמַת הָאָרֶץ קֹדֶשׁ קָדָשִׁים אֶל־גְּבוּל הַלְוִיִּם: 13 וְהַלְוִיִּם לְעֻמַּת גְּבוּל הַכֹּהֲנִים חֲמִשָּׁה וְעֶשְׂרִים אֶלֶף אֹרֶךְ וְרֹחַב עֲשֶׂרֶת אֲלָפִים כָּל־אֹרֶךְ חֲמִשָּׁה וְעֶשְׂרִים אֶלֶף וְרֹחַב עֲשֶׂרֶת אֲלָפִים: 14 וְלֹא־יִמְכְּרוּ מִמֶּנּוּ וְלֹא יָמֵר וְלֹא יעבור יַעֲבִיר רֵאשִׁית הָאָרֶץ כִּי־קֹדֶשׁ לַיהוָה:

15 וַחֲמֵשֶׁת אֲלָפִים הַנּוֹתָר בָּרֹחַב עַל־פְּנֵי חֲמִשָּׁה וְעֶשְׂרִים אֶלֶף חֹל־הוּא לָעִיר לְמוֹשָׁב וּלְמִגְרָשׁ וְהָיְתָה הָעִיר בְּתוֹכֹה בְּתוֹכוֹ: 16 וְאֵלֶּה מִדּוֹתֶיהָ פְּאַת צָפוֹן חֲמֵשׁ מֵאוֹת וְאַרְבַּעַת אֲלָפִים וּפְאַת־נֶגֶב חֲמֵשׁ חמש* מֵאוֹת וְאַרְבַּעַת אֲלָפִים וּמִפְּאַת קָדִים חֲמֵשׁ מֵאוֹת וְאַרְבַּעַת אֲלָפִים וּפְאַת־יָמָּה חֲמֵשׁ מֵאוֹת וְאַרְבַּעַת אֲלָפִים: 17 וְהָיָה מִגְרָשׁ לָעִיר צָפוֹנָה חֲמִשִּׁים וּמָאתַיִם וְנֶגְבָּה חֲמִשִּׁים וּמָאתַיִם וְקָדִימָה חֲמִשִּׁים וּמָאתַיִם וְיָמָּה חֲמִשִּׁים וּמָאתָיִם: 18 וְהַנּוֹתָר בָּאֹרֶךְ לְעֻמַּת | תְּרוּמַת הַקֹּדֶשׁ עֲשֶׂרֶת אֲלָפִים קָדִימָה וַעֲשֶׂרֶת אֲלָפִים יָמָּה וְהָיָה לְעֻמַּת תְּרוּמַת הַקֹּדֶשׁ וְהָיְתָה תְבוּאָתֹה תְבוּאָתוֹ לְלֶחֶם לְעֹבְדֵי הָעִיר: 19 וְהָעֹבֵד הָעִיר

שני טעמים   v. 10.
כתיב ולא קריא   v. 16.

erty. ²¹What remains on either side of the sacred
reserve and the city property shall belong to the
prince. The prince shall own [the land] from
the border of the 25,000 ^e-of the reserve-^e up to
the eastern boundary, and from the border of
the 25,000 on the west up to the western boundary, corresponding to the [tribal] portions. The
sacred reserve, with the Temple Sanctuary in the
middle of it ²²and the property of the Levites
and the city property as well, shall be in the middle of the [area belonging] to the prince; [the
rest of the land] between the territory of Judah
and the territory of Benjamin shall belong to the
prince.

²³As for the remaining tribes:^f From the east-
ern border to the western border: Benjamin—
one.

²⁴Adjoining the territory of Benjamin, from
the eastern border to the western border:
Simeon—one.

²⁵Adjoining the territory of Simeon, from
the eastern border to the western border:
Issachar—one.

²⁶Adjoining the territory of Issachar, from
the eastern border to the western border:
Zebulun—one.

²⁷Adjoining the territory of Zebulun, from
the eastern border to the western border: Gad—
one.

²⁸The other border of Gad shall be the south-
ern boundary. This boundary shall run from
Tamar to the waters of Meribath-kadesh, to the
Wadi [of Egypt], and to the Great Sea.

²⁹That is the land which you shall allot as a
heritage to the tribes of Israel, and those are their
portions—declares the Lord God.

³⁰And these are the exits from the city: On its
northern side, measuring 4,500 cubits, ³¹the
gates of the city shall be—three gates on the
north—named for the tribes of Israel: the Reu-

20 כָּל־יַעֲבֹד֜וּהוּ מִכֹּ֖ל שִׁבְטֵ֥י יִשְׂרָאֵ֑ל׃
הַתְּרוּמָ֡ה חֲמִשָּׁ֣ה וְעֶשְׂרִים֩ אֶ֨לֶף בַּחֲמִשָּׁ֧ה
וְעֶשְׂרִ֛ים אֶ֖לֶף רְבִיעִ֑ית תָּרִ֙ימוּ֙ אֶת־
תְּרוּמַ֣ת הַקֹּ֔דֶשׁ אֶל־אֲחֻזַּ֖ת הָעִֽיר׃
21 וְהַנּוֹתָ֣ר לַנָּשִׂ֣יא מִזֶּ֣ה ׀ וּמִזֶּ֣ה ׀ לִתְרֽוּמַת־
הַקֹּ֣דֶשׁ וְלַאֲחֻזַּ֣ת הָעִ֗יר אֶל־פְּנֵ֞י חֲמִשָּׁ֣ה
וְעֶשְׂרִ֣ים אֶ֗לֶף ׀ תְּרוּמָה֮ עַד־גְּב֣וּל קָדִ֣ימָה
וְיָ֣מָּה עַל־פְּנֵ֠י חֲמִשָּׁ֨ה וְעֶשְׂרִ֥ים אֶ֙לֶף֙ עַל־
גְּב֣וּל יָ֔מָּה לְעֻמַּ֥ת חֲלָקִ֖ים לַנָּשִׂ֑יא וְהָיְתָ֞ה
תְּרוּמַ֤ת הַקֹּ֙דֶשׁ֙ וּמִקְדַּ֣שׁ הַבַּ֔יִת בְּתוֹכֹֽה
22 וּמֵאֲחֻזַּ֣ת הַלְוִיִּ֗ם וּמֵאֲחֻזַּ֣ת הָעִ֔יר
בְּת֗וֹךְ אֲשֶׁ֤ר לַנָּשִׂיא֙ יִֽהְיֶ֔ה בֵּ֣ין ׀ גְּב֣וּל יְהוּדָ֗ה
וּבֵ֛ין גְּב֥וּל בִּנְיָמִ֖ן לַנָּשִׂ֥יא יִהְיֶֽה׃
23 וְיֶ֖תֶר הַשְּׁבָטִ֑ים מִפְּאַ֥ת קָדִ֛ימָה עַד־
פְּאַת־יָ֖מָּה בִּנְיָמִ֥ן אֶחָֽד׃
24 וְעַ֣ל ׀ גְּב֣וּל בִּנְיָמִ֗ן מִפְּאַ֥ת קָדִ֛ימָה
עַד־פְּאַת־יָ֖מָּה שִׁמְע֥וֹן אֶחָֽד׃
25 וְעַ֣ל ׀ גְּב֣וּל שִׁמְע֗וֹן מִפְּאַ֥ת קָדִ֛ימָה
עַד־פְּאַת־יָ֖מָּה יִשָּׂשכָ֥ר אֶחָֽד׃
26 וְעַ֣ל ׀ גְּב֣וּל יִשָּׂשכָ֗ר מִפְּאַ֥ת קָדִ֛ימָה
עַד־פְּאַת־יָ֖מָּה זְבוּלֻ֥ן אֶחָֽד׃
27 וְעַ֣ל ׀ גְּב֣וּל זְבוּלֻ֗ן מִפְּאַ֥ת קָדְמָ֖ה עַד־
פְּאַת־יָ֖מָּה גָּ֥ד אֶחָֽד׃
28 וְעַל֙ גְּב֣וּל גָּ֔ד אֶל־פְּאַ֖ת נֶ֣גֶב תֵּימָ֑נָה וְהָיָ֣ה
גְב֞וּל מִתָּמָ֗ר מֵ֚י מְרִיבַ֣ת קָדֵ֔שׁ נַחֲלָ֖ה
עַל־הַיָּ֥ם הַגָּדֽוֹל׃
29 זֹ֣את הָאָ֗רֶץ אֲשֶׁר־תַּפִּ֤ילוּ מִֽנַּחֲלָה֙
לְשִׁבְטֵ֣י יִשְׂרָאֵ֔ל וְאֵ֖לֶּה מַחְלְקוֹתָ֑ם נְאֻ֖ם
אֲדֹנָ֥י יְהֹוִֽה׃ פ
30 וְאֵ֗לֶּה תּוֹצְאֹ֤ת הָעִיר֙ מִפְּאַ֣ת צָפ֔וֹן חֲמֵ֥שׁ
מֵא֖וֹת וְאַרְבַּ֥עַת אֲלָפִ֖ים מִדָּֽה׃ 31 וְשַׁעֲרֵ֣י
הָעִ֗יר עַל־שְׁמוֹת֙ שִׁבְטֵ֣י יִשְׂרָאֵ֔ל שְׁעָרִ֥ים

---

^{e-e} *Emendation yields "on the east."*
^f *The tribes not provided for in vv. 1–7, and lying south of the sacred*
  gift.

ben Gate: one; the Judah Gate: one; the Levi Gate: one. ³²On the eastern side, [measuring] 4,500 cubits—there shall be three gates: the Joseph Gate: one; the Benjamin Gate: one; and the Dan Gate: one. ³³On the southern side, measuring 4,500 cubits, there shall be three gates: the Simeon Gate: one; the Issachar Gate: one; and the Zebulun Gate: one. ³⁴And on the western side, [measuring] 4,500 cubits—there shall be three gates: the Gad Gate: one; the Asher Gate: one; the Naphtali Gate: one.

³⁵Its circumference [shall be] 18,000 [cubits]; and the name of the city from that day on shall be "The Lᴏʀᴅ Is There."

שְׁלוֹשָׁה צָפוֹנָה שַׁעַר רְאוּבֵן אֶחָד שַׁעַר
יְהוּדָה אֶחָד שַׁעַר לֵוִי אֶחָד: 32 וְאֶל־פְּאַת
קָדִימָה חֲמֵשׁ מֵאוֹת וְאַרְבַּעַת אֲלָפִים
וּשְׁעָרִים שְׁלֹשָׁה וְשַׁעַר יוֹסֵף אֶחָד שַׁעַר
בִּנְיָמִן אֶחָד שַׁעַר דָּן אֶחָד: 33 וּפְאַת־נֶגְבָּה
חֲמֵשׁ מֵאוֹת וְאַרְבַּעַת אֲלָפִים מִדָּה
וּשְׁעָרִים שְׁלֹשָׁה שַׁעַר שִׁמְעוֹן אֶחָד שַׁעַר
יִשָּׂשכָר אֶחָד שַׁעַר זְבוּלֻן אֶחָד: 34 פְּאַת־
יָמָּה חֲמֵשׁ מֵאוֹת וְאַרְבַּעַת אֲלָפִים
שַׁעֲרֵיהֶם שְׁלֹשָׁה שַׁעַר גָּד אֶחָד שַׁעַר
אָשֵׁר אֶחָד שַׁעַר נַפְתָּלִי אֶחָד:
35 סָבִיב שְׁמֹנָה עָשָׂר אָלֶף וְשֵׁם־הָעִיר
מִיּוֹם יְהוָה | שָׁמָּה:*

תם ונשלם תהילה לאל בורא עולם

HOSEA

1 The word of the LORD that came to Hosea son of Beeri, in the reigns of Kings Uzziah, Jotham, Ahaz, and Hezekiah of Judah, and in the reign of King Jeroboam son of Joash of Israel.

²When the LORD first spoke to Hosea, the LORD said to Hosea, "Go, get yourself *a*-a wife of whoredom and children of whoredom; for the land will stray*b* from following the LORD."-*a* ³So he went and married Gomer daughter of Diblaim. She conceived and bore him a son, ⁴and the LORD instructed him, "Name him Jezreel; for, I will soon punish the House of Jehu*c* for the *d*-bloody deeds at Jezreel-*d* and put an end to the monarchy of the House of Israel. ⁵In that day, I will break the bow of Israel in the Valley of Jezreel."

⁶She conceived again and bore a daughter; and He said to him, "Name her Lo-ruhamah;*e* for I will no longer accept the House of Israel*f*-or pardon them.-*f* (⁷But I will accept the House of Judah. And I will give them victory through the LORD their God; I will not give them victory with bow and sword and battle, by horses and riders.)"

⁸After weaning Lo-ruhamah, she conceived and bore a son. ⁹Then He said, "Name him Lo-ammi;*g* for you*h* are not My people, and *i*-I will not be your [God]."-*i*

---

a-a   Force of Heb. uncertain.
b   Lit. "whore away."
c   Emendation yields "Israel"; cf. next note.
d-d   See 1 Kings 21.1–24; 2 Kings 9.21–35. Emendation yields "the Baal days"; cf. 2.15.
e   I.e., "Not-accepted"; cf. 2.3, 6, and 25.
f-f   Meaning of Heb. uncertain; emendation yields "but will disown them"; cf. 9.15 and elsewhere.
g   I.e., "Not-My-People."
h   I.e., you and your fellow countrymen.
i-i   Cf. 2.25.

הוֹשֵׁעַ

א דְּבַר־יְהוָה ׀ אֲשֶׁר הָיָה אֶל־הוֹשֵׁעַ בֶּן־בְּאֵרִי בִּימֵי עֻזִּיָּה יוֹתָם אָחָז יְחִזְקִיָּה מַלְכֵי יְהוּדָה וּבִימֵי יָרָבְעָם בֶּן־יוֹאָשׁ מֶלֶךְ יִשְׂרָאֵל:

2 תְּחִלַּת דִּבֶּר־יְהוָה בְּהוֹשֵׁעַ ס וַיֹּאמֶר יְהוָה אֶל־הוֹשֵׁעַ לֵךְ קַח־לְךָ אֵשֶׁת זְנוּנִים וְיַלְדֵי זְנוּנִים כִּי־זָנֹה תִזְנֶה הָאָרֶץ מֵאַחֲרֵי יְהוָה: 3 וַיֵּלֶךְ וַיִּקַּח אֶת־גֹּמֶר בַּת־דִּבְלָיִם וַתַּהַר וַתֵּלֶד־לוֹ בֵּן: 4 וַיֹּאמֶר יְהוָה אֵלָיו קְרָא שְׁמוֹ יִזְרְעֶאל כִּי־עוֹד מְעַט וּפָקַדְתִּי אֶת־דְּמֵי יִזְרְעֶאל עַל־בֵּית יֵהוּא וְהִשְׁבַּתִּי מַמְלְכוּת בֵּית יִשְׂרָאֵל: 5 וְהָיָה בַּיּוֹם הַהוּא וְשָׁבַרְתִּי אֶת־קֶשֶׁת יִשְׂרָאֵל בְּעֵמֶק יִזְרְעֶאל:

6 וַתַּהַר עוֹד וַתֵּלֶד בַּת וַיֹּאמֶר לוֹ קְרָא שְׁמָהּ לֹא רֻחָמָה כִּי לֹא אוֹסִיף עוֹד אֲרַחֵם אֶת־בֵּית יִשְׂרָאֵל כִּי־נָשֹׂא אֶשָּׂא לָהֶם: 7 וְאֶת־בֵּית יְהוּדָה אֲרַחֵם וְהוֹשַׁעְתִּים בַּיהוָה אֱלֹהֵיהֶם וְלֹא אוֹשִׁיעֵם בְּקֶשֶׁת וּבְחֶרֶב וּבְמִלְחָמָה בְּסוּסִים וּבְפָרָשִׁים: 8 וַתִּגְמֹל אֶת־לֹא רֻחָמָה וַתַּהַר וַתֵּלֶד בֵּן: 9 וַיֹּאמֶר קְרָא שְׁמוֹ לֹא עַמִּי כִּי אַתֶּם לֹא עַמִּי וְאָנֹכִי לֹא־אֶהְיֶה לָכֶם: ס

2 ^aThe number of the people of Israel shall be like that of the sands of the sea, which cannot be measured or counted; and instead of being told, "You are Not-My-People,"^b they shall be called Children-of-the-Living-God. ²The people of Judah and the people of Israel shall assemble together and appoint one head over them; and they shall rise from the ground^c—for marvelous shall be ^d-the day of Jezreel!-^d

³Oh, call^e your brothers "My People,"
And your sisters "Lovingly Accepted!"

⁴Rebuke^e your mother, rebuke her—
For she is not My wife
And I am not her husband—
And let her put away her harlotry from her
    face
And her adultery from between her breasts.
⁵Else will I strip her naked
And leave her as on the day she was born:
And I will make her like a wilderness,
Render her like desert land,
And let her die of thirst.
⁶I will also disown her children;
For they are now a harlot's brood,
⁷In that their mother has played the harlot,
She that conceived them has acted shamelessly—
Because she thought,
"I will go after my lovers,
Who supply my bread and my water,
My wool and my linen,
My oil and my drink."

¹ וְהָיָ֞ה מִסְפַּ֤ר בְּנֵֽי־יִשְׂרָאֵל֙ כְּח֣וֹל הַיָּ֔ם
אֲשֶׁ֥ר לֹֽא־יִמַּ֖ד וְלֹ֣א יִסָּפֵ֑ר וְֽהָיָ֞ה בִּמְק֣וֹם
אֲשֶׁר־יֵאָמֵ֤ר לָהֶם֙ לֹֽא־עַמִּ֣י אַתֶּ֔ם יֵאָמֵ֥ר
לָהֶ֖ם בְּנֵ֥י אֵל־חָֽי: ² וְ֠נִקְבְּצוּ בְּנֵֽי־יְהוּדָ֨ה
וּבְנֵֽי־יִשְׂרָאֵ֜ל יַחְדָּ֗ו וְשָׂמ֤וּ לָהֶם֙ רֹ֣אשׁ אֶחָ֔ד
וְעָל֖וּ מִן־הָאָ֑רֶץ כִּ֥י גָד֖וֹל י֥וֹם יִזְרְעֶֽאל:
³ אִמְר֥וּ לַאֲחֵיכֶ֖ם עַמִּ֑י
וְלַאֲחֽוֹתֵיכֶ֖ם רֻחָֽמָה:

⁴ רִ֤יבוּ בְאִמְּכֶם֙ רִ֔יבוּ
כִּֽי־הִיא֙ לֹ֣א אִשְׁתִּ֔י
וְאָנֹכִ֖י לֹ֣א אִישָׁ֑הּ
וְתָסֵ֤ר זְנוּנֶ֙יהָ֙ מִפָּנֶ֔יה
וְנַאֲפוּפֶ֖יהָ מִבֵּ֥ין שָׁדֶֽיהָ:
⁵ פֶּן־אַפְשִׁיטֶ֣נָּה עֲרֻמָּ֔ה
וְהִ֨צַּגְתִּ֔יהָ כְּי֖וֹם הִוָּֽלְדָ֑הּ
וְשַׂמְתִּ֣יהָ כַמִּדְבָּ֔ר
וְשַׁתִּ֙הָ֙ כְּאֶ֣רֶץ צִיָּ֔ה
וַהֲמִתִּ֖יהָ בַּצָּמָֽא:
⁶ וְאֶת־בָּנֶ֖יהָ לֹ֣א אֲרַחֵ֑ם
כִּֽי־בְנֵ֥י זְנוּנִ֖ים הֵֽמָּה:
⁷ כִּ֤י זָֽנְתָה֙ אִמָּ֔ם
הֹבִ֖ישָׁה הֽוֹרָתָ֑ם
כִּ֣י אָמְרָ֗ה
אֵלְכָ֞ה אַחֲרֵ֣י מְאַהֲבַ֗י
נֹתְנֵ֤י לַחְמִי֙ וּמֵימַ֔י
צַמְרִ֣י וּפִשְׁתִּ֔י
שַׁמְנִ֖י וְשִׁקּוּיָֽי:

⁸ לָכֵ֛ן
הִנְנִי־שָׂ֥ךְ אֶת־דַּרְכֵּ֖ךְ בַּסִּירִ֑ים

<table>
<tr><td>

8Assuredly,
I will hedge up her*f* roads with thorns
And raise walls against her,
And she shall not find her paths.
9Pursue her lovers as she will,
She shall not overtake them;
And seek them as she may,
She shall never find them.
Then she will say,
"I will go and return
To my first husband,
For then I fared better than now."
10And she did not consider this:
It was I who bestowed on her
The new grain and wine and oil;
I who lavished silver on her
And gold—which they used for Baal.
11Assuredly,
I will take back My new grain in its time
And My new wine in its season,
And I will snatch away My wool and My linen
That serve to cover her nakedness.
12Now will I uncover her shame
In the very sight of her lovers,
And none shall save her from Me.
13And I will end all her rejoicing:
Her festivals, new moons, and sabbaths—
All her festive seasons.
14I will lay waste her vines and her fig trees,
Which she thinks are a fee
She received from her lovers;
I will turn them into brushwood,
And beasts of the field shall devour them.
15Thus will I punish her
For the days of the Baalim,
On which she brought them offerings;
When, decked with earrings and jewels,
She would go after her lovers,
Forgetting Me
       —declares the LORD.

</td><td>

וְגָדַרְתִּי אֶת־גְּדֵרָה
וּנְתִיבוֹתֶיהָ לֹא תִמְצָא:
9 וְרִדְּפָה אֶת־מְאַהֲבֶיהָ
וְלֹא־תַשִּׂיג אֹתָם
וּבִקְשָׁתַם
וְלֹא תִמְצָא
וְאָמְרָה
אֵלְכָה וְאָשׁוּבָה
אֶל־אִישִׁי הָרִאשׁוֹן
כִּי טוֹב לִי אָז מֵעָתָּה:
10 וְהִיא לֹא יָדְעָה
כִּי אָנֹכִי נָתַתִּי לָהּ
הַדָּגָן וְהַתִּירוֹשׁ וְהַיִּצְהָר
וְכֶסֶף הִרְבֵּיתִי לָהּ
וְזָהָב עָשׂוּ לַבָּעַל:
11 לָכֵן
אָשׁוּב וְלָקַחְתִּי דְגָנִי בְּעִתּוֹ
וְתִירוֹשִׁי בְּמוֹעֲדוֹ
וְהִצַּלְתִּי צַמְרִי וּפִשְׁתִּי
לְכַסּוֹת אֶת־עֶרְוָתָהּ:
12 וְעַתָּה אֲגַלֶּה אֶת־נַבְלֻתָהּ
לְעֵינֵי מְאַהֲבֶיהָ
וְאִישׁ לֹא־יַצִּילֶנָּה מִיָּדִי:
13 וְהִשְׁבַּתִּי כָּל־מְשׂוֹשָׂהּ
חַגָּהּ חָדְשָׁהּ וְשַׁבַּתָּהּ
וְכֹל מוֹעֲדָהּ:
14 וַהֲשִׁמֹּתִי גַּפְנָהּ וּתְאֵנָתָהּ
אֲשֶׁר אָמְרָה אֶתְנָה הֵמָּה לִי
אֲשֶׁר נָתְנוּ־לִי מְאַהֲבָי
וְשַׂמְתִּים לְיַעַר
וַאֲכָלָתַם חַיַּת הַשָּׂדֶה:
15 וּפָקַדְתִּי עָלֶיהָ
אֶת־יְמֵי הַבְּעָלִים
אֲשֶׁר תַּקְטִיר לָהֶם
וַתַּעַד נִזְמָהּ וְחֶלְיָתָהּ
וַתֵּלֶךְ אַחֲרֵי מְאַהֲבֶיהָ
וְאֹתִי שָׁכְחָה
נְאֻם־יְהֹוָה: פ

</td></tr>
</table>

---

f Heb. "your." Vv. 8–9 would read well after v. 15.

16Assuredly,

I will speak coaxingly to her

And lead her through the wildernessg

And speak to her tenderly.

17I will give her her vineyards from there,

And the Valley of Achorh as a i-plowland of
hope.-i

There she shall respond as in the days of her
youth,

When she came up from the land of Egypt.

18And in that day

—declares the LORD—

You will call [Me] Ishi,j

And no more will you call Me Baali.j

19For I will remove the names of the Baalim
from her mouth,

And they shall nevermore be mentioned by
name.

20In that day, I will make a covenant for them
with the beasts of the field, the birds of the air,
and the creeping things of the ground; I will also
banishk bow, sword, and war from the land.
Thus I will let them lie down in safety.

21And I will espouse you forever:

I will espouse you l-with righteousness and
justice,

And with goodness and mercy,

22And I will espouse you with faithfulness;-l

Then you shall be devoted to the LORD.

23In that day,

I will respond

—declares the LORD—

I will respond to the sky,

16 לָכֵן

הִנֵּה אָנֹכִי מְפַתֶּיהָ

וְהֹלַכְתִּיהָ הַמִּדְבָּר

וְדִבַּרְתִּי עַל־לִבָּהּ:

17 וְנָתַתִּי לָהּ אֶת־כְּרָמֶיהָ מִשָּׁם

וְאֶת־עֵמֶק עָכוֹר לְפֶתַח תִּקְוָה

וְעָנְתָה שָּׁמָּה כִּימֵי נְעוּרֶיהָ

וּכְיוֹם עֲלֹתָהּ מֵאֶרֶץ־מִצְרָיִם: ס

18 וְהָיָה בַיּוֹם־הַהוּא

נְאֻם־יְהֹוָה

תִּקְרְאִי אִישִׁי

וְלֹא־תִקְרְאִי־לִי עוֹד בַּעְלִי:

19 וַהֲסִרֹתִי אֶת־שְׁמוֹת הַבְּעָלִים מִפִּיהָ

וְלֹא־יִזָּכְרוּ עוֹד בִּשְׁמָם:

20 וְכָרַתִּי לָהֶם בְּרִית בַּיּוֹם הַהוּא עִם־חַיַּת
הַשָּׂדֶה וְעִם־עוֹף הַשָּׁמַיִם וְרֶמֶשׂ הָאֲדָמָה
וְקֶשֶׁת וְחֶרֶב וּמִלְחָמָה אֶשְׁבּוֹר מִן־הָאָרֶץ
וְהִשְׁכַּבְתִּים לָבֶטַח:

21 וְאֵרַשְׂתִּיךְ לִי לְעוֹלָם

וְאֵרַשְׂתִּיךְ לִי בְּצֶדֶק וּבְמִשְׁפָּט

וּבְחֶסֶד וּבְרַחֲמִים:

22 וְאֵרַשְׂתִּיךְ לִי בֶּאֱמוּנָה

וְיָדַעַתְּ אֶת־יְהֹוָה: ס

23 וְהָיָה | בַּיּוֹם הַהוּא

אֶעֱנֶה

נְאֻם־יְהֹוָה

אֶעֱנֶה אֶת־הַשָּׁמַיִם

---

g I.e., her ravaged land (see vv. 5, 10–11, 14); so Ibn Ezra.

h A desolate region; cf. Isa. 65.10; see further Josh. 7.25–26.

i-i Connecting pethah with pittah "to plow" (see Isa. 28.24).
Meaning of Heb. uncertain; others "door of hope."

j Both Ishi and Baali mean "my husband," but the latter also means
"my Baal."

k Lit. "break."

l-l As the bride-price which the bridegroom will pay, He will confer
these qualities on her, so that she will never offend again.

And it shall respond to the earth;

24And the earth shall respond
With new grain and wine and oil,
And they shall respond to Jezreel.*m*

25I will sow her in the land as My own;
And take Lo-ruhamah back in favor;
And I will say to Lo-ammi, "You are My peo-
ple,"
And he will respond, "[You are] my God."

3 The LORD said to me further, "Go, *a*-be-
friend a woman who, while befriended by a
companion, consorts with others, just as the
LORD befriends the Israelites,-*a* but they turn
b-to other gods and love the cups of the grape."-*b*

2Then I hired her for fifteen [shekels of] silver,
a *ḥomer* of barley, and *c*-a *lethech* of barley;-*c*
3and I stipulated with her, *d*-"In return,-*d* you are
to go a long time without either fornicating or
marrying; even I [shall not cohabit] with you."

4For the Israelites shall go a long time without
king and without officials, without sacrifice*e*
and without cult pillars, and without ephod and
teraphim. 5Afterward, the Israelites will turn
back and will seek the LORD their God and David
their king—and they will thrill over the LORD
and over His bounty in the days to come.

4 Hear the word of the LORD,
O people of Israel!
For the LORD has a case
Against the inhabitants of this land,
Because there is no honesty and no goodness

וְהֵם יַעֲנוּ אֶת־הָאָרֶץ:

24 וְהָאָרֶץ תַּעֲנֶה
אֶת־הַדָּגָן וְאֶת־הַתִּירוֹשׁ וְאֶת־הַיִּצְהָר
וְהֵם יַעֲנוּ אֶת־יִזְרְעֶאל:

25 וּזְרַעְתִּיהָ לִּי בָּאָרֶץ
וְרִחַמְתִּי אֶת־לֹא רֻחָמָה
וְאָמַרְתִּי לְלֹא־עַמִּי עַמִּי־אַתָּה
וְהוּא יֹאמַר אֱלֹהָי: פ

ג וַיֹּאמֶר יְהוָה אֵלַי עוֹד לֵךְ אֱהַב־אִשָּׁה
אֲהֻבַת רֵעַ וּמְנָאָפֶת כְּאַהֲבַת יְהוָה אֶת־
בְּנֵי יִשְׂרָאֵל וְהֵם פֹּנִים אֶל־אֱלֹהִים אֲחֵרִים
וְאֹהֲבֵי אֲשִׁישֵׁי עֲנָבִים:
2 וָאֶכְּרֶהָ לִּי בַּחֲמִשָּׁה עָשָׂר כָּסֶף וְחֹמֶר
שְׂעֹרִים וְלֵתֶךְ שְׂעֹרִים: 3 וָאֹמַר אֵלֶיהָ
יָמִים רַבִּים תֵּשְׁבִי לִי לֹא תִזְנִי וְלֹא תִהְיִי
לְאִישׁ וְגַם־אֲנִי אֵלָיִךְ:
4 כִּי | יָמִים רַבִּים יֵשְׁבוּ בְּנֵי יִשְׂרָאֵל אֵין
מֶלֶךְ וְאֵין שָׂר וְאֵין זֶבַח וְאֵין מַצֵּבָה
וְאֵין אֵפוֹד וּתְרָפִים: 5 אַחַר יָשֻׁבוּ בְּנֵי
יִשְׂרָאֵל וּבִקְשׁוּ אֶת־יְהוָה אֱלֹהֵיהֶם וְאֵת
דָּוִד מַלְכָּם וּפָחֲדוּ אֶל־יְהוָה וְאֶל־טוּבוֹ
בְּאַחֲרִית הַיָּמִים: פ

ד שִׁמְעוּ דְבַר־יְהוָה
בְּנֵי יִשְׂרָאֵל
כִּי רִיב לַיהוָה
עִם־יוֹשְׁבֵי הָאָרֶץ
כִּי אֵין־אֱמֶת וְאֵין־חֶסֶד

---

m   I.e., "God sows." The names of Hosea's children (1.3–8) are
      applied here to Israel.

a-a   For "befriend," see Deut. 10.19. For God's befriending Israel,
      see Hos. 2.10.

b-b   Meaning of Heb. uncertain; emendation yields "'to other gods.'
      And so I befriended a woman of lust."

c-c   Septuagint reads "a jar of wine."

d-d   Lit. "for me."

e   Emendation yields "altar."

And no obedience to God in the land.

²[False] swearing, dishonesty, and murder,

And theft and adultery are rife;

Crime follows upon crime!

³For that, the earth is withered:

Everything that dwells on it languishes—

Beasts of the field and birds of the sky—

Even the fish of the sea perish.

⁴"Let no man rebuke, let no man protest!"

ᵃ⁻For this your people has a grievance against
[you],

O priest!⁻ᵃ

⁵So you shall stumble by day,

And by night ᵇ⁻a prophet⁻ᵇ shall stumble as
well,

And I will destroy your kindred.ᶜ

⁶My people is destroyed because of [your]
disobedience!

Because you have rejected obedience,

I reject you as My priest;

Because you have spurned the teaching of
your God,

I, in turn, will spurn your children.

⁷The more they increased, the more they
sinned against Me:

I will change their dignity to dishonor.

⁸They feed on My people's sin offerings,

And so they desire its iniquity.

⁹Therefore, the people shall fare like the
priests:

I will punish it for its conduct,

I will requite it for its deeds.

¹⁰Truly, they shall eat, but not be sated;

They shall swill,ᵈ but not be satisfied,

Because they have forsaken the LORD

To practiceᵉ ¹¹lechery.

וְאֵין־דַּעַת אֱלֹהִים בָּאָרֶץ:

2 אָלֹה וְכַחֵשׁ וְרָצֹחַ

וְגָנֹב וְנָאֹף פָּרָצוּ

וְדָמִים בְּדָמִים נָגָעוּ:

3 עַל־כֵּן ׀ תֶּאֱבַל הָאָרֶץ

וְאֻמְלַל כָּל־יוֹשֵׁב בָּהּ

בְּחַיַּת הַשָּׂדֶה וּבְעוֹף הַשָּׁמָיִם

וְגַם־דְּגֵי הַיָּם יֵאָסֵפוּ:

4 אַךְ אִישׁ אַל־יָרֵב וְאַל־יוֹכַח אִישׁ

וְעַמְּךָ כִּמְרִיבֵי

כֹהֵן:

5 וְכָשַׁלְתָּ הַיּוֹם

וְכָשַׁל גַּם־נָבִיא עִמְּךָ לָיְלָה

וְדָמִיתִי אִמֶּךָ:

6 נִדְמוּ עַמִּי מִבְּלִי הַדָּעַת

כִּי־אַתָּה הַדַּעַת מָאַסְתָּ

וְאֶמְאָסְאךָ* מִכַּהֵן לִי

וַתִּשְׁכַּח תּוֹרַת אֱלֹהֶיךָ

אֶשְׁכַּח בָּנֶיךָ גַּם־אָנִי:

7 כְּרֻבָּם כֵּן חָטְאוּ־לִי

כְּבוֹדָם בְּקָלוֹן אָמִיר:

8 חַטַּאת עַמִּי יֹאכֵלוּ

וְאֶל־עֲוֹנָם יִשְׂאוּ נַפְשׁוֹ*:

9 וְהָיָה כָעָם כַּכֹּהֵן

וּפָקַדְתִּי עָלָיו דְּרָכָיו

וּמַעֲלָלָיו אָשִׁיב לוֹ:

10 וְאָכְלוּ וְלֹא יִשְׂבָּעוּ

הִזְנוּ וְלֹא יִפְרֹצוּ

כִּי־אֶת־יְהוָה עָזְבוּ

לִשְׁמֹר: 11 זְנוּת

---

a-a   For failing to reprove; but meaning of Heb. uncertain.

b-b   Emendation yields "your children"; cf. v. 6 end.

c   Lit. "mother."

d   For this meaning of hiznah cf. v. 18.

e   Cf. 12.7.

v. 6.   יתיר א'

v. 8.   סבירין ומטעין "נפשם"

Wine*f* and new wine destroy

The mind of [12]My people:

It consults its stick,*g*

Its rod*g* directs it!

A lecherous impulse has made them go wrong,

And they have strayed*h* from submission to their God.

[13]They sacrifice on the mountaintops

And offer on the hills,

Under oaks, poplars, and terebinths

Whose shade is so pleasant.

That is why their*i* daughters fornicate

And their daughters-in-law commit adultery!

[14]I will not punish their daughters for fornicating

Nor their daughters-in-law for committing adultery;

For they themselves*j*-turn aside-*j* with whores

And sacrifice with prostitutes,

And a people that is without sense*k* must stumble.

[15]If you are a lecher, Israel—

Let not Judah incur guilt—

Do not come to Gilgal,*l*

Do not make pilgrimages to Beth-aven,*m*

And do not swear by the LORD!*n*

[16]Ah, Israel has balked

Like a stubborn cow;

Therefore,

The LORD will graze him

וְיַיִן וְתִירוֹשׁ יִקַּח־

לֵב: 12 עַמִּי

בְּעֵצוֹ יִשְׁאָל

וּמַקְלוֹ יַגִּיד לוֹ

כִּי רוּחַ זְנוּנִים הִתְעָה

וַיִּזְנוּ מִתַּחַת אֱלֹהֵיהֶם:

13 עַל־רָאשֵׁי הֶהָרִים יְזַבֵּחוּ

וְעַל־הַגְּבָעוֹת יְקַטֵּרוּ

תַּחַת אַלּוֹן וְלִבְנֶה וְאֵלָה

כִּי טוֹב צִלָּהּ

עַל־כֵּן תִּזְנֶינָה בְּנוֹתֵיכֶם

וְכַלּוֹתֵיכֶם תְּנָאַפְנָה:

14 לֹא־אֶפְקוֹד עַל־בְּנוֹתֵיכֶם כִּי תִזְנֶינָה

וְעַל־כַּלּוֹתֵיכֶם כִּי תְנָאַפְנָה

כִּי־הֵם עִם־הַזֹּנוֹת יְפָרֵדוּ

וְעִם־הַקְּדֵשׁוֹת יְזַבֵּחוּ

וְעָם לֹא־יָבִין יִלָּבֵט:

15 אִם־זֹנֶה אַתָּה יִשְׂרָאֵל

אַל־יֶאְשַׁם יְהוּדָה

וְאַל־תָּבֹאוּ הַגִּלְגָּל

וְאַל־תַּעֲלוּ בֵּית אָוֶן

וְאַל־תִּשָּׁבְעוּ חַי־יְהוָה:

16 כִּי כְּפָרָה סֹרֵרָה

סָרַר יִשְׂרָאֵל

עַתָּה יִרְעֵם יְהוָה

---

f   Emendation yields "New grain"; cf. 7.14; 9.1–2.

g   I.e., its phallus, meaning "its lust."

h   See note b at 1.2.

i   Heb. "your," here and through v. 14.

j-j   Meaning of Heb. uncertain.

k   Cf. vv. 11–12.

l   One who participates in the debaucheries of the open-air shrines is not fit to visit a temple building.

m   Lit. "House of Delusion," substituted for Bethel (cf. Amos 4.4).

n   I.e., you are not fit to profess His religion; see Jer. 12.16.

On the range, like a sheep.ᵒ

¹⁷ᵖEphraim is addicted to images—

Let him be.

¹⁸They drink to excess—

Their liquor turns against them.

They "love" beyond measure—

Disgrace is the "gift"

¹⁹Which the wind q-is bringing;-q

They shall garner shame from their sacrifices.

כְּכֶ֖בֶשׂ בַּמֶּרְחָֽב׃
¹⁷ חֲב֧וּר עֲצַבִּ֛ים אֶפְרָ֖יִם
הַֽנַּֽח־לֽוֹ׃
¹⁸ סָ֖ר סָבְאָ֑ם
הַזְנֵ֣ה הִזְנ֔וּ
אָהֲב֥וּ הֵב֖וּ
קָל֥וֹן מָגִנֶּֽיהָ׃
¹⁹ צָרַ֥ר ר֛וּחַ אוֹתָ֖הּ בִּכְנָפֶ֑יהָ
וְיֵבֹ֖שׁוּ מִזִּבְחוֹתָֽם׃ ס

5 Hear this, O priests,

Attend, O Houseᵃ of Israel,

And give ear, O royal house;

For right conduct is your responsibility!

But you have been a snare to Mizpah

And a net spread out over Tabor;

²ᵇ-For when trappers dug deep pitfalls,

I was the only reprover of them all.-ᵇ

³Yes, I have watched Ephraim,

Israel has not escaped my notice:

Behold, you have fornicated, O Ephraim;

Israel has defiled himself!

⁴Their habits do not let them

Turn back to their God;

Because of the lecherous impulse within

    them,

They pay no heed to the LORD.

⁵ᶜIsrael's pride shall be humbled before his

    very eyes,

As Israel and Ephraim fall because of their sin

(And Judah falls with them).

⁶Then they will go with their sheep and cattle

To seek the LORD, but they will not find

    Him.-ᶜ

ה שִׁמְעוּ־זֹאת֙ הַכֹּ֣הֲנִ֔ים
וְהַקְשִׁ֣יבוּ ׀ בֵּ֣ית יִשְׂרָאֵ֗ל
וּבֵ֤ית הַמֶּ֙לֶךְ֙ הַאֲזִ֔ינוּ
כִּ֥י לָכֶ֖ם הַמִּשְׁפָּ֑ט
כִּֽי־פַח֙ הֱיִיתֶ֣ם לְמִצְפָּ֔ה
וְרֶ֖שֶׁת פְּרוּשָׂ֥ה עַל־תָּבֽוֹר׃
² וְשַׁחֲטָ֥ה שֵׂטִ֖ים הֶעְמִ֑יקוּ
וַאֲנִ֖י מוּסָ֥ר לְכֻלָּֽם׃
³ אֲנִי֙ יָדַ֣עְתִּי אֶפְרַ֔יִם
וְיִשְׂרָאֵ֖ל לֹֽא־נִכְחַ֣ד מִמֶּ֑נִּי
כִּ֤י עַתָּה֙ הִזְנֵ֣יתָ אֶפְרַ֔יִם
נִטְמָ֖א יִשְׂרָאֵֽל׃
⁴ לֹ֤א יִתְּנוּ֙ מַ֣עַלְלֵיהֶ֔ם
לָשׁ֖וּב אֶל־אֱלֹֽהֵיהֶ֑ם
כִּ֣י ר֤וּחַ זְנוּנִים֙ בְּקִרְבָּ֔ם
וְאֶת־יְהוָ֖ה לֹ֥א יָדָֽעוּ׃
⁵ וְעָנָ֥ה גְאֽוֹן־יִשְׂרָאֵ֖ל בְּפָנָ֑יו
וְיִשְׂרָאֵ֣ל וְאֶפְרַ֗יִם יִכָּֽשְׁלוּ֙ בַּעֲוֺנָ֔ם
כָּשַׁ֥ל גַּם־יְהוּדָ֖ה עִמָּֽם׃
⁶ בְּצֹאנָ֣ם וּבִבְקָרָ֔ם יֵלְכ֖וּ
לְבַקֵּ֣שׁ אֶת־יְהוָ֑ה וְלֹ֖א יִמְצָ֑אוּ

---

o   *Instead of giving them fodder in return for their work; cf. Isa.*
    30.23–24.

p   *Meaning of vv. 17–19 uncertain in part.*

q-q   *Lit. "has bound up in the corners of its garment"; see note at*
    Mal. 3.20.

a   *Emendation yields "prophets."*

b-b   *Meaning of Heb. uncertain.*

c-c   *This passage would read well after 5.15; cf. 5.6 with 6.6.*

b-He has cast them off:-*b*

7[Because] they have broken faith with the
LORD,
Because *d*-they have-*d* begotten
Alien children.
Therefore, *b*-the new moon
Shall devour their portion.-*b*

חָלַק מֵהֶם:

7 בַּיהוָה בָּגָדוּ
כִּי־בָנִים זָרִים
יָלָדוּ
עַתָּה יֹאכְלֵם חֹדֶשׁ
אֶת־חֶלְקֵיהֶם: ס

8Sound a ram's horn in Gibeah,
A trumpet in Ramah;
Give the alarm in Beth-aven;*e*
f-After you,-*f* Benjamin!
9Ephraim is stricken with horror
On a day of chastisement.

8 תִּקְעוּ שׁוֹפָר בַּגִּבְעָה
חֲצֹצְרָה בָּרָמָה
הָרִיעוּ בֵּית אָוֶן
אַחֲרֶיךָ בִּנְיָמִין:
9 אֶפְרַיִם לְשַׁמָּה תִהְיֶה
בְּיוֹם תּוֹכֵחָה

Against the tribes*g* of Israel
I proclaim certainties:
10The officers of Judah have acted
Like shifters of field boundaries;
On them I will pour out
My wrath like water.
11Ephraim is defrauded,
Robbed of redress,
Because he has witlessly
Gone after futility.*h*
12For it is I who am like rot to Ephraim,
Like decay to the House of Judah;*i*
13Yet when Ephraim became aware of his
sickness,
Judah*i* of his sores,
Ephraim repaired to Assyria—
He sent envoys to a patron*j* king!
He will never be able to cure you,
Will not heal you of your sores.
14No, I will be like a lion to Ephraim,

בְּשִׁבְטֵי יִשְׂרָאֵל
הוֹדַעְתִּי נֶאֱמָנָה:
10 הָיוּ שָׂרֵי יְהוּדָה
כְּמַסִּיגֵי גְּבוּל
עֲלֵיהֶם אֶשְׁפּוֹךְ
כַּמַּיִם עֶבְרָתִי:
11 עָשׁוּק אֶפְרַיִם
רְצוּץ מִשְׁפָּט
כִּי הוֹאִיל
הָלַךְ אַחֲרֵי־צָו:
12 וַאֲנִי כָעָשׁ לְאֶפְרַיִם
וְכָרָקָב לְבֵית יְהוּדָה:
13 וַיַּרְא אֶפְרַיִם אֶת־חָלְיוֹ
וִיהוּדָה אֶת־מְזֹרוֹ
וַיֵּלֶךְ אֶפְרַיִם אֶל־אַשּׁוּר
וַיִּשְׁלַח אֶל־מֶלֶךְ יָרֵב
וְהוּא לֹא יוּכַל לִרְפֹּא לָכֶם
וְלֹא־יִגְהֶה מִכֶּם מָזוֹר:
14 כִּי אָנֹכִי כַשַּׁחַל לְאֶפְרַיִם

---

d-d   Emendation yields "He has."
e   The three towns named, in the territory of Benjamin, are now
      being wrested from Israel by Judah; see v. 10.
f-f   Emendation yields "Stir up."
g   I.e., the kingdoms of Judah and Israel (Ephraim).
h   Cf. Targum and Septuagint; but meaning of Heb. uncertain.
i   Emendation yields "Israel."
j   Compare the verb ryb in the sense of "to champion, uphold the
      cause of," in Isa. 1.17; 3.13; 19.20 end; 51.22.

Like a great beast to the House of Judah;[i]
I, I will attack and stride away,
Carrying the prey that no one can rescue;
[15]And I will return to My abode—
Till they realize their guilt.
In their distress, they will seek Me
And beg for My favor.

וְכַכְּפִיר לְבֵית יְהוּדָה
אֲנִי אֲנִי אֶטְרֹף וְאֵלֵךְ
אֶשָּׂא וְאֵין מַצִּיל׃
15 אֵלֵךְ אָשׁוּבָה אֶל־מְקוֹמִי
עַד אֲשֶׁר־יֶאְשְׁמוּ
וּבִקְשׁוּ פָנַי בַּצַּר לָהֶם
יְשַׁחֲרֻנְנִי׃

6 [a]"Come, let us turn back to the LORD:
He attacked, and He can heal us;
He wounded, and He can bind us up.
[2]In two days He will make us whole again;
On the third day He will raise us up,
And we shall be whole by His favor.
[3]Let us pursue obedience to the LORD,
And we shall become obedient.
His appearance is as sure as daybreak,
And He will come to us like rain,
Like latter rain that refreshes[b] the earth."

ו לְכוּ וְנָשׁוּבָה אֶל־יְהֹוָה
כִּי הוּא טָרָף וְיִרְפָּאֵנוּ
יַךְ וְיַחְבְּשֵׁנוּ׃
2 יְחַיֵּנוּ מִיֹּמָיִם
בַּיּוֹם הַשְּׁלִישִׁי יְקִמֵנוּ
וְנִחְיֶה לְפָנָיו׃
3 וְנֵדְעָה
נִרְדְּפָה לָדַעַת אֶת־יְהֹוָה
כְּשַׁחַר נָכוֹן מוֹצָאוֹ
וְיָבוֹא כַגֶּשֶׁם לָנוּ
כְּמַלְקוֹשׁ יוֹרֶה אָרֶץ׃

[4]What can I do for you, Ephraim,
What can I do for you, Judah,[c]
When your goodness is like morning clouds,
Like dew so early gone?
[5]That is why I have hewn down [d]-the
    prophets,-[d]
Have slain them with the words of My mouth:
[e]-And the day that dawned [brought on] your
    punishment.-[e]
[6]For I desire goodness, not sacrifice;
Obedience to God, rather than burnt
    offerings.
[7][f]But they, to a man, have transgressed the
    Covenant.
This is where they have been false to Me:

4 מָה אֶעֱשֶׂה־לְּךָ אֶפְרַיִם
מָה אֶעֱשֶׂה־לְּךָ יְהוּדָה
וְחַסְדְּכֶם כַּעֲנַן־בֹּקֶר
וְכַטַּל מַשְׁכִּים הֹלֵךְ׃
5 עַל־כֵּן חָצַבְתִּי בַּנְּבִיאִים
הֲרַגְתִּים בְּאִמְרֵי־פִי
וּמִשְׁפָּטֶיךָ אוֹר יֵצֵא׃
6 כִּי חֶסֶד חָפַצְתִּי וְלֹא־זָבַח
וְדַעַת אֱלֹהִים מֵעֹלוֹת׃
7 וְהֵמָּה כְּאָדָם עָבְרוּ בְרִית
שָׁם בָּגְדוּ בִי׃

---

a   As anticipated at the end of chapter 5, Israel seeks the LORD's
    favor; His answer begins with v. 4.
b   Taking yoreh as equivalent of yarweh.
c   Emendation yields "Israel"; cf. "Ephraim...Israel" in v. 10.
d-d Emendation yields "your children"; cf. 9.13.
e-e Cf. v. 3; but meaning of Heb. uncertain.
f   Meaning of vv. 7–11 unclear in part.

⁸Gilead is a city of evildoers,
Tracked up with blood.
⁹The gang of priests is
Like the ambuscade of bandits
Who murder on the road to Shechem,
For they have encouraged*g* depravity.
¹⁰In *h-*the House of Israel*-h* I have seen
A horrible thing;
Ephraim has fornicated there,
Israel has defiled himself.
¹¹*i-*(Even Judah has reaped a harvest of you!)*-i*

7 When I would restore My people's fortunes,
¹When I would heal Israel,
The guilt of Ephraim reveals itself
And the wickedness of Samaria.
For they have acted treacherously,
With thieves breaking in
And bands raiding outside.
²And they do not consider
That I remembered all their wickedness.
Why, their misdeeds have been all around
   them,*a*
They have been ever before Me.

³*b*In malice they make a king merry,
And officials in treachery.
⁴They *c-*commit adultery,*-c* all of them,
Like an oven fired by a baker,
Who desists from stoking only
From the kneading of the dough to its leav-
   ening.
⁵The day they made our king sick
[And] officials with the poison of wine,
*d-*He gave his hand to traitors.*-d*

---

8 גִּלְעָ֕ד קִרְיַ֖ת פֹּ֣עֲלֵי אָ֑וֶן
עֲקֻבָּ֖ה מִדָּֽם׃
9 וּכְחַכֵּ֨י אִ֜ישׁ גְּדוּדִ֗ים
חֶ֚בֶר כֹּ֣הֲנִ֔ים
דֶּ֖רֶךְ יְרַצְּחוּ־שֶׁ֑כְמָה
כִּ֥י זִמָּ֖ה עָשֽׂוּ׃
10 בְּבֵית֙ יִשְׂרָאֵ֔ל רָאִ֖יתִי
שַׁעֲרֽוּרִיָּ֑ה
שָׁ֚ם זְנ֣וּת לְאֶפְרַ֔יִם
נִטְמָ֖א יִשְׂרָאֵֽל׃
11 גַּם־יְהוּדָ֕ה שָׁ֥ת קָצִ֖יר לָ֑ךְ

בְּשׁוּבִ֖י שְׁב֥וּת עַמִּֽי׃ פ
ז 1 כְּרׇפְאִ֣י לְיִשְׂרָאֵ֗ל
וְנִגְלָ֞ה עֲוֺ֤ן אֶפְרַ֙יִם֙
וְרָע֣וֹת שֹֽׁמְר֔וֹן
כִּ֖י פָעֲל֣וּ שָׁ֑קֶר
וְגַנָּ֣ב יָב֔וֹא
פָּשַׁ֥ט גְּד֖וּד בַּחֽוּץ׃
2 וּבַל־יֹֽאמְרוּ֙ לִלְבָבָ֔ם
כׇּל־רָעָתָ֖ם זָכָ֑רְתִּי
עַתָּה֙ סְבָב֣וּם מַֽעַלְלֵיהֶ֔ם
נֶ֥גֶד פָּנַ֖י הָיֽוּ׃
3 בְּרָעָתָ֖ם יְשַׂמְּחוּ־מֶ֑לֶךְ
וּבְכַחֲשֵׁיהֶ֖ם שָׂרִֽים׃
4 כֻּלָּם֙ מְנָ֣אֲפִ֔ים
כְּמ֣וֹ תַנּ֔וּר בֹּעֵ֖רָה מֵֽאֹפֶ֑ה
יִשְׁבּ֣וֹת מֵעִ֔יר
מִלּ֥וּשׁ בָּצֵ֖ק עַד־חֻמְצָתֽוֹ׃
5 י֣וֹם מַלְכֵּ֔נוּ הֶחֱל֥וּ
שָׂרִ֖ים חֲמַ֣ת מִיָּ֑יִן
מָשַׁ֥ךְ יָד֖וֹ אֶת־לֹֽצְצִֽים׃

---

g   *Heb. "done"; cf. 5.1–3.*
h-h   *Emendation yields "Beth-shean."*
i-i   *Cf. 5.9–10; but meaning of clause uncertain.*

a   *Emendation yields "Me."*
b   *Vv. 3–6 would read well in the order 4, 6, 3, 5.*
c-c   *Emendation yields "rage."*
d-d   *I.e., he trusted traitors; but meaning of verse uncertain.*

6e-For they approach their ambush
With their hearts like an oven:-e
Through the night
Their bakerᶜ has slept;
In the morning, it flares up
Like a blazing fire.
⁷They all get heated like an oven
And devour their rulers—
None of them calls to Me.
All their kings have fallen [by their hand].

8e-Ephraim is among the peoples;
He is rotting away.
Ephraim is like a cake—
Incapable of turning.-e
⁹Strangers have consumed his strength,
But he has taken no notice;
Also, moldᶠ is scattered over him,
But he has taken no notice.
¹⁰Though Israel's pride has been humbled
Before his very eyes,
They have not turned back
To their God the Lᴏʀᴅ;
They have not sought Him
In spite of everything.
¹¹Instead, Ephraim has acted
Like a silly dove with no mind:
They have appealed to Egypt!
They have gone to Assyria!
¹²When they go, I will spread
My net over them,
I will bring them down
Like birds of the sky;
e-I will chastise them
When I hear their bargaining.-e
¹³Woe to them
For straying from Me;

6 כִּי־קֵרְב֖וּ
כַתַּנּ֥וּר לִבָּ֖ם בְּאָרְבָּ֑ם
כָּל־הַלַּ֗יְלָה
יָשֵׁן֙ אֹֽפֵהֶ֔ם
בֹּ֕קֶר ה֥וּא בֹעֵ֖ר
כְּאֵ֥שׁ לֶהָבָֽה׃
7 כֻּלָּ֤ם יֵחַ֙מּוּ֙ כַּתַּנּ֔וּר
וְאָכְל֖וּ אֶת־שֹֽׁפְטֵיהֶ֑ם
כָּל־מַלְכֵיהֶ֣ם נָפָ֔לוּ
אֵין־קֹרֵ֥א בָהֶ֖ם אֵלָֽי׃

8 אֶפְרַ֕יִם בָּעַמִּ֖ים
ה֣וּא יִתְבּוֹלָ֑ל
אֶפְרַ֕יִם הָיָ֥ה עֻגָ֖ה
בְּלִ֥י הֲפוּכָֽה׃
9 אָכְל֤וּ זָרִים֙ כֹּח֔וֹ
וְה֖וּא לֹ֣א יָדָ֑ע
גַּם־שֵׂיבָה֙ זָ֣רְקָה בּ֔וֹ
וְה֖וּא לֹ֥א יָדָֽע׃
10 וְעָנָ֥ה גְאֽוֹן־יִשְׂרָאֵ֖ל
בְּפָנָ֑יו
וְלֹא־שָׁ֙בוּ֙
אֶל־יְהוָ֣ה אֱלֹֽהֵיהֶ֔ם
וְלֹ֥א בִקְשֻׁ֖הוּ
בְּכָל־זֹֽאת׃
11 וַיְהִ֣י אֶפְרַ֔יִם
כְּיוֹנָ֥ה פוֹתָ֖ה אֵ֣ין לֵ֑ב
מִצְרַ֥יִם קָרָ֖אוּ
אַשּׁ֥וּר הָלָֽכוּ׃
12 כַּאֲשֶׁ֣ר יֵלֵ֔כוּ אֶפְר֤וֹשׂ
עֲלֵיהֶם֙ רִשְׁתִּ֔י
כְּע֥וֹף הַשָּׁמַ֖יִם
אֽוֹרִידֵ֑ם
אַיְסִרֵ֕ם
כְּשֵׁ֖מַע לַעֲדָתָֽם׃ ס
13 א֥וֹי לָהֶם֙
כִּי־נָדְד֣וּ מִמֶּ֔נִּי

---

e-e   Meaning of Heb. uncertain.
f   Like Akkadian shību; others "gray hairs."

Destruction to them
For rebelling against Me!
For I was their Redeemer;
Yet they have plotted treason against Me.

שֹׁד לָהֶם
כִּי־פָשְׁעוּ בִי
וְאָנֹכִי אֶפְדֵּם
וְהֵמָּה דִּבְּרוּ עָלַי כְּזָבִים׃

14gBut they did not cry out to Me sincerely
As they h-lay wailing.-h
They debauchi over new grain and new wine,
They are faithlessj to Me.

14 וְלֹא־זָעֲקוּ אֵלַי בְּלִבָּם
כִּי יְיֵלִילוּ עַל־מִשְׁכְּבוֹתָם
עַל־דָּגָן וְתִירוֹשׁ יִתְגּוֹרָרוּ
יָסוּרוּ בִי׃

15I braced, I strengthened their arms,
And they plot evil against Me!
16They come back;
They have been of no use,e
Like a slack bow.
Their officers shall fall by the sword,
Because of the stammeringk of their tongues.
Such shall be [the results of] their jabberingl
In the land of Egypt.

15 וַאֲנִי יִסַּרְתִּי חִזַּקְתִּי זְרוֹעֹתָם
וְאֵלַי יְחַשְּׁבוּ־רָע׃
16 יָשׁוּבוּ ׀
לֹא עָל הָיוּ
כְּקֶשֶׁת רְמִיָּה
יִפְּלוּ בַחֶרֶב שָׂרֵיהֶם
מִזַּעַם לְשׁוֹנָם
זוֹ לַעְגָּם
בְּאֶרֶץ מִצְרָיִם׃

8 [Put] a ram's horn to your mouth—
a-Like an eagle-a over the House of b-the
 Lord;-b
Because they have transgressed My covenant
And been faithless to My teaching.
2Israel cries out to Me,
"O my God, we are devoted to You."c

ח אֶל־חִכְּךָ שֹׁפָר
כַּנֶּשֶׁר עַל־בֵּית יְהוָה
יַעַן עָבְרוּ בְרִיתִי
וְעַל־תּוֹרָתִי פָּשָׁעוּ׃
2 לִי יִזְעָקוּ
אֱלֹהַי יְדַעֲנוּךָ יִשְׂרָאֵל׃

3Israel rejects what is good;
d-An enemy shall pursue him.-d
4They have made kings,
But not with My sanction;

3 זָנַח יִשְׂרָאֵל טוֹב
אוֹיֵב יִרְדְּפוֹ׃
4 הֵם הִמְלִיכוּ
וְלֹא מִמֶּנִּי

g   This verse would read well after 8.2.
h-h   I.e., in penitence; cf. Isa. 58.5.
i   Cf. Aramaic gar/yegur "to commit adultery"; for the thought,
    cf. 4.11.
j   Taking yasuru as equivalent to yasoru, from sarar; cf. 9.15 end.
k   Cf. Arabic zaghūm and zughmūm "a stammerer."
l   I.e., the negotiations conducted in the Egyptian language.

a-a   Meaning of Heb. uncertain.
b-b   Emendation yields "Israel."
c   See note g at 7.14.
d-d   Emendation yields "They pursue delusion."

They have made officers,
But not of My choice.
Of their silver and gold
They have made themselves images,
To their own undoing.
⁵*ᵉ-He rejects-ᵉ* your calf, Samaria!
I am furious with them!
Will they never be capable of *ᶠ*-purity?
⁶For it was Israel's doing;-*ᶠ*
It was only made by a joiner,
It is not a god.
No, the calf of Samaria shall be
Reduced to splinters!

⁷They sow wind,
And they shall reap whirlwind—
Standing stalks devoid of ears
And yielding no flour.
If they do yield any,
Strangers shall devour it.
⁸Israel is bewildered;*ᵍ*
They have now become among the nations
Like an unwanted vessel,
⁹[Like] a lonely wild ass.
For they have gone up to Assyria,
ʰ-Ephraim has-*ʰ* courted friendship.
¹⁰And while they are courting among the nations,
ⁱ-There I will hold them fast;-*ⁱ*
ᵃ-And they shall begin to diminish in number
From the burden of king [and] officers.-*ᵃ*

¹¹For Ephraim has multiplied altars—for guilt;
His altars have redounded to his guilt:
¹²The many teachings I wrote for him
Have been treated as something alien.

הֵשִׂירוּ
וְלֹא יָדָעְתִּי
כַּסְפָּם וּזְהָבָם
עָשׂוּ לָהֶם עֲצַבִּים
לְמַעַן יִכָּרֵת׃
⁵ זָנַח עֶגְלֵךְ שֹׁמְרוֹן
חָרָה אַפִּי בָּם
עַד־מָתַי לֹא יוּכְלוּ נִקָּיֹן׃
⁶ כִּי מִיִּשְׂרָאֵל
וְהוּא חָרָשׁ עָשָׂהוּ
וְלֹא אֱלֹהִים הוּא
כִּי־שְׁבָבִים יִהְיֶה
עֵגֶל שֹׁמְרוֹן׃

⁷ כִּי רוּחַ יִזְרָעוּ
וְסוּפָתָה יִקְצֹרוּ
קָמָה אֵין־לוֹ צֶמַח
בְּלִי יַעֲשֶׂה־קֶּמַח
אוּלַי יַעֲשֶׂה
זָרִים יִבְלָעֻהוּ׃
⁸ נִבְלַע יִשְׂרָאֵל
עַתָּה הָיוּ בַגּוֹיִם
כִּכְלִי אֵין־חֵפֶץ בּוֹ׃
⁹ כִּי־הֵמָּה עָלוּ אַשּׁוּר
פֶּרֶא בּוֹדֵד לוֹ
אֶפְרַיִם הִתְנוּ אֲהָבִים׃
¹⁰ גַּם כִּי־יִתְנוּ בַגּוֹיִם
עַתָּה אֲקַבְּצֵם
וַיָּחֵלּוּ מְּעָט
מִמַּשָּׂא מֶלֶךְ שָׂרִים׃

¹¹ כִּי־הִרְבָּה אֶפְרַיִם מִזְבְּחֹת לַחֲטֹא
הָיוּ־לוֹ מִזְבְּחוֹת לַחֲטֹא׃
¹² אכתוב אֶכְתָּב־לוֹ רבו רֻבֵּי תּוֹרָתִי
כְּמוֹ־זָר נֶחְשָׁבוּ׃

ᵉ-ᵉ   *Emendation yields "I reject."*
ᶠ-ᶠ   *Emendation yields "understanding, / That House of Israel?"*
ᵍ   *A play on words: The Heb. root* bala', *which means "bewildered" here (cf. Isa. 28.7), means "devour" in the preceding verse.*
ʰ-ʰ   *Emendation yields "In Egypt they have."*
ⁱ-ⁱ   *Cf. 9.6; but meaning of Heb. uncertain.*

13 a-When they present sacrifices to Me,-a
It is but flesh for them to eat:
The LORD has not accepted them.
Behold, He remembers their iniquity,
He will punish their sins:
Back to Egypt with them!
14 Israel has ignored his Maker
And built temples
(And Judah has fortified many cities).
So I will set fire to his cities,
And it shall consume their fortresses.

9 Rejoice not, O Israel,
As other peoples exult;
For you have strayed
Away from your God:
a-You have loved a harlot's fee
By every threshing floor of new grain.
2 Threshing floor and winepress
Shall not join them,
And the new wine shall betray her.-a
3 They shall not be able to remain
In the land of the LORD.
But Ephraim shall return to Egypt
And shall eat unclean food in Assyria.b
4 It shall be for them like the food of mourners,
All who partake of which are defiled.
They will offer no libations of wine to the
  LORD,
And no sacrifices of theirs will be pleasing to
  Him;
But their food will be only for their hunger,
It shall not come into the House of the LORD.
5 What will you do about feast days,
About the festivals of the LORD?
6 Behold, they have gone c-from destruction-c

זִבְחֵי הַבְהָבַי יִזְבְּחוּ 13
בָשָׂר וַיֹּאכֵלוּ
יְהֹוָה לֹא רָצָם
עַתָּה יִזְכֹּר עֲוֺנָם
וְיִפְקֹד חַטֹּאותָם
הֵמָּה מִצְרַיִם יָשׁוּבוּ:
וַיִּשְׁכַּח יִשְׂרָאֵל אֶת־עֹשֵׂהוּ 14
וַיִּבֶן הֵיכָלוֹת
וִיהוּדָה הִרְבָּה עָרִים בְּצֻרוֹת
וְשִׁלַּחְתִּי־אֵשׁ בְּעָרָיו
וְאָכְלָה אַרְמְנֹתֶיהָ: ס

אַל־תִּשְׂמַח יִשְׂרָאֵל | **ט**
אֶל־גִּיל כָּעַמִּים
כִּי זָנִיתָ
מֵעַל אֱלֹהֶיךָ
אָהַבְתָּ אֶתְנָן
עַל כָּל־גָּרְנוֹת דָּגָן:
גֹּרֶן וָיֶקֶב 2
לֹא יִרְעֵם
וְתִירוֹשׁ יְכַחֶשׁ בָּהּ*:
לֹא יֵשְׁבוּ 3
בְּאֶרֶץ יְהֹוָה
וְשָׁב אֶפְרַיִם מִצְרַיִם
וּבְאַשּׁוּר טָמֵא יֹאכֵלוּ:
לֹא־יִסְּכוּ לַיהֹוָה | יַיִן 4
וְלֹא יֶעֶרְבוּ־לוֹ זִבְחֵיהֶם
כְּלֶחֶם אוֹנִים לָהֶם
כָּל־אֹכְלָיו יִטַּמָּאוּ
כִּי־לַחְמָם לְנַפְשָׁם
לֹא יָבוֹא בֵּית יְהֹוָה:
מַה־תַּעֲשׂוּ לְיוֹם מוֹעֵד 5
וּלְיוֹם חַג־יְהֹוָה:
כִּי־הִנֵּה הָלְכוּ מִשֹּׁד 6

---

a-a *Emendation and rearrangement yield: "You have loved
    fornication / By every threshing floor and press; / The new grain
    shall not join them, / And the new wine shall fail them."*
b   *The lands of the heathen and the food there are unclean; cf. Ezek.
    4.13; Amos 7.17.*
c-c *Emendation yields "to Assyria."*

[With] the silver they treasure.

Egypt shall *d*-hold them fast,-*d*

Moph*e* shall receive them in burial.

Weeds are their heirs;

Prickly shrubs occupy their [old] homes.

⁷The days of punishment have come

For your heavy guilt;

The days of requital have come—

Let Israel know it!

The prophet was distraught,

The inspired man driven mad

By constant harassment.

⁸Ephraim watches for *f*-my God.

As for the prophet,-*f*

Fowlers' snares are on all his paths,

Harassment in the House of his God.

⁹They have been as grievously corrupt

As in the days of Gibeah;*g*

He will remember their iniquity,

He will punish their sins.

¹⁰I found Israel [as pleasing]

As grapes in the wilderness;

Your fathers seemed to Me

h-Like the first fig to ripen on a fig tree.-*h*

But when they came to Baal-peor,

They turned aside to shamefulness;*i*

j-Then they became as detested

As they had been loved.-*j*

¹¹From birth, from the womb, from conception

Ephraim's glory shall be

Like birds that fly away.*k*

¹²Even if they rear their infants,

מִצְרַ֣יִם תְּקַבְּצֵ֔ם

מֹ֖ף תְּקַבְּרֵ֑ם

מַחְמַ֣ד לְכַסְפָּ֗ם

קִמּ֣וֹשׂ יִֽירָשֵׁ֔ם

ח֖וֹחַ בְּאׇהֳלֵיהֶֽם׃

⁷ בָּ֣אוּ ׀ יְמֵ֣י הַפְּקֻדָּ֗ה

בָּ֙אוּ֙ יְמֵ֣י הַשִׁלֻּ֔ם

יֵדְע֖וּ יִשְׂרָאֵ֑ל

אֱוִ֣יל הַנָּבִ֗יא

מְשֻׁגָּע֙ אִ֣ישׁ הָר֔וּחַ

עַ֚ל רֹ֣ב עֲוֺנְךָ֔

וְרַבָּ֖ה מַשְׂטֵמָֽה׃

⁸ צֹפֶ֥ה אֶפְרַ֖יִם עִם־אֱלֹהָ֑י

נָבִ֗יא

פַּ֤ח יָקוֹשׁ֙ עַל־כׇּל־דְּרָכָ֔יו

מַשְׂטֵמָ֖ה בְּבֵ֥ית אֱלֹהָֽיו׃

⁹ הֶעְמִֽיקוּ־שִׁחֵ֖תוּ

כִּימֵ֣י הַגִּבְעָ֑ה

יִזְכּ֣וֹר עֲוֺנָ֔ם

יִפְק֖וֹד חַטֹּאותָ֑ם*׃ ס

¹⁰ כַּעֲנָבִ֣ים בַּמִּדְבָּ֗ר

מָצָ֙אתִי֙ יִשְׂרָאֵ֔ל

כְּבִכּוּרָ֤ה בִתְאֵנָה֙ בְּרֵ֣אשִׁיתָ֔הּ

רָאִ֖יתִי אֲבֽוֹתֵיכֶ֑ם

הֵ֙מָּה֙ בָּ֣אוּ בַֽעַל־פְּע֔וֹר

וַיִּנָּֽזְרוּ֙ לַבֹּ֔שֶׁת

וַיִּהְי֥וּ שִׁקּוּצִ֖ים

כְּאׇהֳבָֽם׃

¹¹ אֶפְרַ֕יִם

כָּע֖וֹף יִתְעוֹפֵ֣ף כְּבוֹדָ֑ם

מִלֵּדָ֥ה וּמִבֶּ֖טֶן וּמֵהֵרָיֽוֹן׃

¹² כִּ֤י אִם־יְגַדְּלוּ֙ אֶת־בְּנֵיהֶ֔ם

---

d-d   Cf. 8.10.

e   *Believed to be Memphis, elsewhere called Noph.*

f-f   *Emendation yields "the prophet of my God."*

g   *See Judg. 19–20.*

h-h   *Emendation yields "like a ripe fig in a waterless waste"; cf.*

    13.5.

i   *Cf. Num. 25.1–3.*

j-j   *Meaning of Heb. uncertain.*

k   *V. 16 would read well after v. 11.*

I will bereave them of men.
l-Woe to them indeed
When I turn away from them!-*l*
13*j*-It shall go with Ephraim
As I have seen it go with Tyre,
Which was planted in a meadow;-*j*
Ephraim too must bring out
His children to slayers.
14Give them, O Lord—give them what?
Give them a womb that miscarries,
And shriveled breasts!
15All their misfortune [began] at Gilgal,
For there I disowned them.*m*
For their evil deeds
I will drive them out of My House.
I will accept them no more;
n-All their officials are-*n* disloyal.

16*k*Ephraim*o* is stricken,
Their stock is withered;
They can produce no fruit.
Even if they do bear children,
I will slay their cherished offspring.

17My God rejects them
Because they have not obeyed Him,
And they shall go wandering
Among the nations.

10 Israel is a ravaged vine
And its fruit is like it.
When his fruit was plentiful,
He made altars aplenty;
When his land was bountiful,
Cult pillars abounded.

וְשִׁכַּלְתִּים מֵאָדָם
כִּי־גַם־א֣וֹי לָהֶ֔ם
בְּשׂוּרִ֖י מֵהֶֽם׃
13 אֶפְרַ֕יִם
כַּאֲשֶׁר־רָאִ֥יתִי לְצ֖וֹר
שְׁתוּלָ֣ה בְנָוֶ֑ה
וְאֶפְרַ֖יִם לְהוֹצִ֥יא
אֶל־הֹרֵ֖ג בָּנָֽיו׃
14 תֵּן־לָהֶ֥ם יְהוָ֖ה מַה־תִּתֵּ֑ן
תֵּן־לָהֶם֙ רֶ֣חֶם מַשְׁכִּ֔יל
וְשָׁדַ֖יִם צֹמְקִֽים׃
15 כָּל־רָעָתָ֣ם בַּגִּלְגָּ֗ל
כִּי־שָׁ֖ם שְׂנֵאתִ֑ים
עַ֚ל רֹ֣עַ מַֽעַלְלֵיהֶ֔ם
מִבֵּיתִ֖י אֲגָרְשֵׁ֑ם
לֹ֤א אוֹסֵף֙ אַהֲבָתָ֔ם
כָּל־שָׂרֵיהֶ֖ם סֹרְרִֽים׃
16 הֻכָּ֣ה אֶפְרַ֔יִם
שָׁרְשָׁ֥ם יָבֵ֖שׁ
פְּרִ֣י בלי־ בַֽל־יַעֲשׂ֑וּן
גַּ֚ם כִּ֣י יֵֽלֵד֔וּן
וְהֵמַתִּ֖י מַחֲמַדֵּ֥י בִטְנָֽם׃ ס
17 יִמְאָסֵ֣ם אֱלֹהַ֔י
כִּ֛י לֹ֥א שָׁמְע֖וּ ל֑וֹ
וְיִהְי֥וּ נֹדְדִ֖ים
בַּגּוֹיִֽם׃ ס

גֶּ֤פֶן בּוֹקֵק֙ יִשְׂרָאֵ֔ל
פְּרִ֖י יְשַׁוֶּה־לּ֑וֹ
כְּרֹ֣ב לְפִרְי֗וֹ
הִרְבָּה֙ לַֽמִּזְבְּח֔וֹת
כְּט֣וֹב לְאַרְצ֔וֹ
הֵיטִ֖יבוּ מַצֵּבֽוֹת׃

---

l-l   Emendation yields: "Even if they wean their babes, / They shall
       be dismayed because of them."
m   The specific allusion is uncertain.
n-n   Emendation yields "They are all."
o   Targum reads "Their crown," i.e., of a tree.

²Now that his boughs^a are broken up,
He feels his guilt;
He himself pulls apart his altars,
Smashes his pillars.

³Truly, now they say,
"We have no king;
For, since we do not fear the LORD,
What can a king do to us?"
⁴So they conclude agreements and make cov-
enants
With false oaths,
And justice ^b-degenerates into poison weeds,
Breaking out-^b on the furrows of the fields.

⁵The inhabitants of Samaria fear
For the calf of Beth-aven;^c
Indeed, its people and priestlings,
^d-Whose joy it once was,-^d
Mourn over it for the glory
That is departed from it.
⁶It too shall be brought to Assyria
As tribute to a patron^e king;
Ephraim shall be chagrined,
Israel shall be dismayed
Because of his plans.^f
⁷Samaria's monarchy^g is vanishing
Like foam upon water,
⁸Ruined shall be the shrines of [Beth-]aven,^c
That sin of Israel.
Thorns and thistles
Shall grow on their altars.
They shall call to the mountains, "Bury us!"
To the hills, "Fall on us!"

⁹You have sinned more, O Israel,
Than in the days of Gibeah.^h

חָלַק לִבָּם ²
עַתָּה יֶאְשָׁמוּ
הוּא יַעֲרֹף מִזְבְּחוֹתָם
יְשֹׁדֵד מַצֵּבוֹתָם:

כִּי עַתָּה יֹאמְרוּ ³
אֵין מֶלֶךְ לָנוּ
כִּי לֹא יָרֵאנוּ אֶת־יְהֹוָה
וְהַמֶּלֶךְ מַה־יַּעֲשֶׂה־לָּנוּ:
דִּבְּרוּ דְבָרִים ⁴
אָלוֹת שָׁוְא כָּרֹת בְּרִית
וּפָרַח כָּרֹאשׁ מִשְׁפָּט
עַל תַּלְמֵי שָׂדָי:

לְעֶגְלוֹת בֵּית אָוֶן ⁵
יָגוּרוּ שְׁכַן שֹׁמְרוֹן
כִּי־אָבַל עָלָיו
עַמּוֹ וּכְמָרָיו
עָלָיו יָגִילוּ עַל־כְּבוֹדוֹ
כִּי־גָלָה מִמֶּנּוּ:
גַּם־אוֹתוֹ לְאַשּׁוּר יוּבָל ⁶
מִנְחָה לְמֶלֶךְ יָרֵב
בָּשְׁנָה אֶפְרַיִם יִקָּח
וְיֵבוֹשׁ יִשְׂרָאֵל
מֵעֲצָתוֹ:
נִדְמֶה שֹׁמְרוֹן מַלְכָּהּ ⁷
כְּקֶצֶף עַל־פְּנֵי־מָיִם:
וְנִשְׁמְדוּ בָּמוֹת אָוֶן ⁸
חַטַּאת יִשְׂרָאֵל
קוֹץ וְדַרְדַּר
יַעֲלֶה עַל־מִזְבְּחוֹתָם
וְאָמְרוּ לֶהָרִים כַּסּוּנוּ
וְלַגְּבָעוֹת נִפְלוּ עָלֵינוּ: ס

מִימֵי הַגִּבְעָה ⁹
חָטָאתָ יִשְׂרָאֵל

---

^a   *Cf. 2 Sam. 18.14, where the word is rendered "thick growth."*
^{b-b} *Cf. Amos 6.12; lit. "breaks out like poison weeds."*
^c   *See note m at 4.15.*
^{d-d} *Meaning of Heb. uncertain.*
^e   *See note j at 5.13.*
^f   *Emendation yields "image," referring to the calf.*
^g   *The Heb. verb agrees with this word, not with "Samaria."*
^h   *See note at 9.9.*

d-There they stand [as] at Gibeah!

Shall they not be overtaken

By a war upon scoundrels

¹⁰As peoples gather against them?-*d*

When I chose [them], I broke them in,

Harnessing them for two furrows.

¹¹Ephraim became a trained heifer,

But preferred to thresh;

I *i*-placed a yoke

Upon her sleek neck.-*i*

I will make Ephraim *j*-do advance plowing;-*j*

Judah*k* shall do [main] plowing!

Jacob shall do final plowing!

¹²"Sow righteousness for yourselves;

Reap *l*-the fruits of-*l* goodness;

Break for yourselves betimes fresh ground

Of seeking the Lord,

So that you may obtain *m*-a teacher-*m* of right-

   eousness."

¹³You have plowed wickedness,

You have reaped iniquity—

[And] you shall eat the fruits of treachery—

Because you relied on your way,*n*

On your host of warriors.

¹⁴But the din of war shall arise in your own

   people,

And all your fortresses shall be ravaged

As Beth-arbel was ravaged by Shalman*o*

On a day of battle,

When mothers and babes were dashed to

   death together.

¹⁵This *p*-is what Bethel has done to you-*p*

For your horrible wickedness:

שָׁם עָמְדוּ

לֹא־תַשִּׂיגֵם בַּגִּבְעָה

מִלְחָמָה עַל־בְּנֵי עַלְוָה:

¹⁰ בְּאַוָּתִי וְאֶסֳּרֵם

וְאֻסְּפוּ עֲלֵיהֶם עַמִּים

בְּאָסְרָם לִשְׁתֵּי עֵינֹתָם עוֹנֹתָם:

¹¹ וְאֶפְרַיִם עֶגְלָה מְלֻמָּדָה

אֹהַבְתִּי לָדוּשׁ

וַאֲנִי עָבַרְתִּי

עַל־טוּב צַוָּארָהּ

אַרְכִּיב אֶפְרַיִם

יַחֲרוֹשׁ יְהוּדָה

יְשַׂדֶּד־לוֹ יַעֲקֹב:

¹² זִרְעוּ לָכֶם לִצְדָקָה

קִצְרוּ לְפִי־חֶסֶד

נִירוּ לָכֶם נִיר

וְעֵת לִדְרוֹשׁ אֶת־יְהֹוָה

עַד־יָבוֹא וְיֹרֶה צֶדֶק לָכֶם:

¹³ חֲרַשְׁתֶּם־רֶשַׁע

עַוְלָתָה קְצַרְתֶּם

אֲכַלְתֶּם פְּרִי־כָחַשׁ

כִּי־בָטַחְתָּ בְדַרְכְּךָ

בְּרֹב גִּבּוֹרֶיךָ:

¹⁴ וְקָאם* שָׁאוֹן בְּעַמֶּךָ

וְכָל־מִבְצָרֶיךָ יוּשַּׁד

כְּשֹׁד שַׁלְמַן בֵּית אַרְבֵאל

בְּיוֹם מִלְחָמָה

אֵם עַל־בָּנִים רֻטָּשָׁה:

¹⁵ כָּכָה עָשָׂה לָכֶם בֵּית־אֵל

מִפְּנֵי רָעַת רָעַתְכֶם

---

i-i   Lit. "passed over the comeliness of its neck."

j-j   Taking rkb in the sense of the Arabic krb.

k   Emendation yields "Israel."

l-l   Lit. "according to."

m-m Meaning of Heb. uncertain; Septuagint reads "the fruits."

n   Septuagint reads "chariots."

o   Perhaps identical with the Shallum of 2 Kings 15.10 ff.; cf. the

      atrocities of Shallum's rival, ibid., v. 16.

p-p   Emendation yields "will I do to you, O House of Israel."

q-At dawn-*q* shall Israel's monarchy
Utterly perish.

בַּשַּׁ֕חַר
נִדְמֹ֥ה נִדְמָ֖ה מֶ֣לֶךְ יִשְׂרָאֵֽל׃

11
I fell in love with Israel
When he was still a child;
And I have called [him] My son
Ever since Egypt.

²*a*Thus were they called,
But they went their own way;
They sacrifice to Baalim*b*
And offer to carved images.

³I have pampered Ephraim,
Taking them in My*c* arms;
But they have ignored
My healing care.

⁴I drew them with human ties,
With cords of love;
But I seemed to them as one
Who imposed a yoke on their jaws,
Though I was offering them food.

⁵No!
They return to the land of Egypt,
And Assyria is their king.
Because they refuse to repent,

⁶A sword shall descend upon their towns*d*
And consume their limbs
And devour *e*-[them] because of their designs.-*e*

⁷*f*-For My people persists
In its defection from Me;
When it is summoned upward,
It does not rise at all.-*f*

⁸How can I give you up, O Ephraim?
How surrender you, O Israel?

יא כִּ֛י נַ֥עַר יִשְׂרָאֵ֖ל
וָאֹֽהֲבֵ֑הוּ
וּמִמִּצְרַ֖יִם
קָרָ֥אתִי לִבְנִֽי׃
² קָרְא֖וּ לָהֶ֑ם
כֵּ֖ן הָלְכ֣וּ מִפְּנֵיהֶ֑ם
לַבְּעָלִים֙ יְזַבֵּ֔חוּ
וְלַפְּסִלִ֖ים יְקַטֵּרֽוּן׃
³ וְאָנֹכִ֤י תִרְגַּ֙לְתִּי֙ לְאֶפְרַ֔יִם
קָחָ֖ם עַל־זְרֽוֹעֹתָ֑יו
וְלֹ֥א יָדְע֖וּ
כִּ֥י רְפָאתִֽים׃
⁴ בְּחַבְלֵ֨י אָדָ֤ם אֶמְשְׁכֵם֙
בַּעֲבֹת֣וֹת אַהֲבָ֔ה
וָאֶהְיֶ֥ה לָהֶ֛ם
כִּמְרִ֥ימֵי עֹ֖ל עַ֣ל לְחֵיהֶ֑ם
וְאַ֥ט אֵלָ֖יו אוֹכִֽיל׃
⁵ לֹ֤א
יָשׁוּב֙ אֶל־אֶ֣רֶץ מִצְרַ֔יִם
וְאַשּׁ֖וּר ה֣וּא מַלְכּ֑וֹ
כִּ֥י מֵאֲנ֖וּ לָשֽׁוּב׃
⁶ וְחָלָ֥ה חֶ֙רֶב֙ בְּעָרָ֔יו
וְכִלְּתָ֥ה בַדָּ֖יו
וְאָכָ֑לָה מִֽמֹּעֲצֽוֹתֵיהֶֽם׃
⁷ וְעַמִּ֥י תְלוּאִ֖ים
לִמְשֽׁוּבָתִ֑י
וְאֶל־עַל֙ יִקְרָאֻ֔הוּ
יַ֖חַד לֹ֥א יְרוֹמֵֽם׃

⁸ אֵ֣יךְ אֶתֶּנְךָ֣ אֶפְרַ֗יִם
אֲמַגֶּנְךָ֣ יִשְׂרָאֵ֔ל

---

q-q   Meaning, perhaps, "swiftly as the dawn"; cf. v. 7 above, "like
        foam upon water."

a   Meaning of parts of vv. 2–7 uncertain.
b   Emendation yields "calves"; cf. 8.4–6; 13.2.
c   Heb. "his."
d   Emendation yields "bodies," lit. "skins"; cf. Job. 18.13.
e-e Emendation yields "their bones."
f-f Meaning of Heb. uncertain.

How can I make you like Admah,
Render you like Zeboiim?g
I have had a change of heart,
All My tenderness is stirred.
9I will not act on My wrath,
Will not turn to destroy Ephraim.
For I am God, not man,
f-The Holy One in your midst:
I will not come in fury.-f

10The LORD will roar like a lion,
And they shall march behind Him;
When He roars, His children shall come
Fluttering out of the west.
11They shall flutter from Egypt like sparrows,
From the land of Assyria like doves;
And I will settle them in their homes
                              —declares the LORD.

אֵ֤יךְ אֶתֶּנְךָ֙ כְאַדְמָ֔ה
אֲשִֽׂימְךָ֙ כִּצְבֹאיִ֔ם*
נֶהְפַּ֤ךְ עָלַי֙ לִבִּ֔י
יַ֖חַד נִכְמְר֥וּ נִחוּמָֽי׃
9לֹ֤א אֶֽעֱשֶׂה֙ חֲר֣וֹן אַפִּ֔י
לֹ֥א אָשׁ֖וּב לְשַׁחֵ֣ת אֶפְרָ֑יִם
כִּ֣י אֵ֤ל אָֽנֹכִי֙ וְלֹא־אִ֔ישׁ
בְּקִרְבְּךָ֖ קָד֑וֹשׁ
וְלֹ֥א אָב֖וֹא בְּעִֽיר׃
10 אַחֲרֵ֧י יְהוָ֛ה יֵלְכ֖וּ
כְּאַרְיֵ֣ה יִשְׁאָ֑ג
כִּֽי־ה֣וּא יִשְׁאַ֗ג
וְיֶחֶרְד֥וּ בָנִ֖ים מִיָּֽם׃
11 יֶחֶרְד֤וּ כְצִפּוֹר֙ מִמִּצְרַ֔יִם
וּכְיוֹנָ֖ה מֵאֶ֣רֶץ אַשּׁ֑וּר
וְהוֹשַׁבְתִּ֥ים עַל־בָּתֵּיהֶ֖ם
נְאֻם־יְהוָֽה׃ ס

12 Ephraim surrounds Me with deceit,
The House of Israel with guile.a
b-(But Judah stands firm with God
And is faithful to the Holy One.)-b
2Ephraim tends the wind
And pursues the gale;
He is forever adding
Illusion to calamity.c
Now they make a covenant with Assyria,
Now oil is carried to Egypt.d

יב סְבָבֻ֤נִי בְכַ֨חַשׁ֙ אֶפְרַ֔יִם
וּבְמִרְמָ֖ה בֵּ֣ית יִשְׂרָאֵ֑ל
וִֽיהוּדָ֗ה עֹ֥ד רָ֛ד עִם־אֵ֖ל
וְעִם־קְדוֹשִׁ֥ים נֶאֱמָֽן׃
2 אֶפְרַ֜יִם רֹעֶ֥ה ר֨וּחַ֙
וְרֹדֵ֣ף קָדִ֔ים
כָּל־הַיּ֕וֹם
כָּזָ֥ב וָשֹׁ֖ד יַרְבֶּ֑ה
וּבְרִית֙ עִם־אַשּׁ֣וּר יִכְרֹ֔תוּ
וְשֶׁ֖מֶן לְמִצְרַ֥יִם יוּבָֽל׃

3The LORD once indicted Judah,e
And punished Jacob for his conduct,

3 וְרִ֥יב לַֽיהוָ֖ה עִם־יְהוּדָ֑ה
וְלִפְקֹ֤ד עַֽל־יַעֲקֹב֙ כִּדְרָכָ֔יו

---

g   *Admah and Zeboiim were destroyed with neighboring Sodom
    and Gomorrah; cf. Gen. 10.19; 14.2, 8; Deut. 29.22.*

a   *I.e., the deceit and guile they practice on each other (below vv.
    8–9) is constantly noted by the LORD.*
b-b   *Meaning of Heb. uncertain.*
c   *Septuagint reads "futility."*
d   *I.e., they foolishly depend on alliances instead of on the LORD;
    cf. 5.13; 7.10–11.*
e   *Presumably the patriarch Judah. Emendation would yield "Is-
    rael"; cf. next note.*

יתיר א׳   v. 8.

Requited him for his deeds.
4In the womb he tried to supplant his brother;
Grown to manhood, he strove with a divine
  being,*f*
5He strove with an angel and prevailed—
The other had to weep and implore him.
At Bethel [Jacob] would meet him,
There to commune with him.*g*
6Yet the LORD, the God of Hosts,
Must be invoked as "LORD."*h*
7You must return to your God!
Practice goodness and justice,
And constantly trust in your God.

8A trader who uses false balances,
Who loves to overreach,
9Ephraim thinks,
"Ah, I have become rich;
I have gotten power!
*b-*All my gains do not amount
To an offense which is real guilt."-*b*
10I the LORD have been your God
Ever since the land of Egypt.
I will let you dwell in your tents*i* again
As in the days of old,*j*
11When I spoke to the prophets;
For I granted many visions,
*b-*And spoke parables through the prophets.
12As for Gilead, it is worthless;
And to no purpose-*b* have they
Been sacrificing oxen in Gilgal:
The altars of these are also
Like stone heaps upon a plowed field.*k*

13Then Jacob had to flee*l* to the land of Aram;
There Israel served for a wife,

כְּמַעֲלָלָיו יָשִׁיב לֽוֹ:
4 בַּבֶּטֶן עָקַב אֶת־אָחִיו
וּבְאוֹנוֹ שָׂרָה אֶת־אֱלֹהִֽים:
5 וַיָּשַׂר אֶל־מַלְאָךְ וַיֻּכָל
בָּכָה וַיִּתְחַנֶּן־לוֹ
בֵּֽית־אֵל יִמְצָאֶנּוּ
וְשָׁם יְדַבֵּר עִמָּֽנוּ:
6 וַֽיהֹוָה אֱלֹהֵי הַצְּבָאוֹת
יְהֹוָה זִכְרֽוֹ:
7 וְאַתָּה בֵּאלֹהֶיךָ תָשׁוּב
חֶסֶד וּמִשְׁפָּט שְׁמֹר
וְקַוֵּה אֶל־אֱלֹהֶיךָ תָּמִֽיד:

8 כְּנַעַן בְּיָדוֹ מֹאזְנֵי מִרְמָה
לַעֲשֹׁק אָהֵֽב:
9 וַיֹּאמֶר* אֶפְרַיִם
אַךְ עָשַׁרְתִּי
מָצָאתִי אוֹן לִי
כָּל־יְגִיעַי לֹא יִמְצְאוּ־לִי
עָוֹן אֲשֶׁר־חֵֽטְא:
10 וְאָנֹכִי יְהֹוָה אֱלֹהֶיךָ
מֵאֶרֶץ מִצְרָיִם
עֹד אוֹשִֽׁיבְךָ בָאֳהָלִים
כִּימֵי מוֹעֵֽד:
11 וְדִבַּרְתִּי עַל־הַנְּבִיאִים
וְאָנֹכִי חָזוֹן הִרְבֵּיתִי
וּבְיַד הַנְּבִיאִים אֲדַמֶּֽה:
12 אִם־גִּלְעָד אָוֶן
אַךְ־שָׁוְא הָיוּ
בַּגִּלְגָּל שְׁוָרִים זִבֵּחוּ
גַּם מִזְבְּחוֹתָם
כְּגַלִּים עַל תַּלְמֵי שָׂדָֽי:

13 וַיִּבְרַח יַעֲקֹב שְׂדֵה אֲרָם
וַיַּעֲבֹד יִשְׂרָאֵל בְּאִשָּׁה

---

f   Cf. Gen. 25.26 and 32.29.
g   Heb. "us."
h   I.e., one should not invoke any of the angelic hosts.
i   I.e., securely; see 2 Kings 13.5.
j   Lit. "fixed season."
k   I.e., the cults of Gilead and Gilgal are as worthless as that of Bethel.
l   This is the punishment mentioned in 12.3.

v. 9.   סבירין וּמטעין לשון רבים

For a wife he had to guard [sheep].
14But when the LORD
Brought Israel up from Egypt,
It was through a prophet;[m]
Through a prophet[m] they were guarded.
15[n]Ephraim gave bitter offense,
And his Lord cast his crimes upon him
And requited him for his mockery.

וּבְאִשָּׁה שָׁמָֽר:
14 וּבְנָבִ֗יא
הֶעֱלָ֧ה יְהֹוָ֛ה
אֶת־יִשְׂרָאֵ֖ל מִמִּצְרָ֑יִם
וּבְנָבִ֖יא נִשְׁמָֽר:
15 הִכְעִ֥יס אֶפְרַ֖יִם תַּמְרוּרִ֑ים
וְדָמָיו֙ עָלָ֣יו יִטּ֔וֹשׁ
וְחֶ֨רְפָּת֔וֹ יָשִׁ֥יב ל֖וֹ אֲדֹנָֽיו:

13 When Ephraim spoke piety,
He was exalted in Israel;
But he incurred guilt through Baal,[a]
And so he died.
2And now they go on sinning;
They have made them molten images,
Idols, by their skill, from their silver,
Wholly the work of craftsmen.
[b]-Yet for these they appoint men to sacrifice;-[b]
They are wont to kiss calves!
3Assuredly,
They shall be like morning clouds,
Like dew so early gone;
Like chaff whirled away from the threshing
   floor.
And like smoke from a lattice.
4Only I the LORD have been your God
Ever since the land of Egypt;
You have never known a [true] God but Me,
You have never had a helper other than Me.
5I looked after you in the desert,
In a thirsty land.
6When they grazed, they were sated;
When they were sated, they grew haughty;
And so they forgot Me.
7So I am become like a lion to them,
Like a leopard I lurk on the way;

יג כְּדַבֵּ֤ר אֶפְרַ֙יִם֙ רְתֵ֔ת
נָשָׂ֥א ה֖וּא בְּיִשְׂרָאֵ֑ל
וַיֶּאְשַׁ֥ם בַּבַּ֖עַל
וַיָּמֹֽת:
2 וְעַתָּ֣ה ׀ יוֹסִ֣פוּ לַחֲטֹ֗א
וַיַּעְשׂ֣וּ לָהֶם֩ מַסֵּכָ֨ה
מִכַּסְפָּ֜ם כִּתְבוּנָ֤ם עֲצַבִּים֙
מַעֲשֵׂ֥ה חָרָשִׁ֖ים כֻּלֹּ֑ה
לָהֶם֙ הֵ֣ם אֹמְרִ֔ים זֹבְחֵ֣י אָדָ֔ם
עֲגָלִ֖ים יִשָּׁקֽוּן:
3 לָכֵ֗ן
יִֽהְיוּ֙ כַּעֲנַן־בֹּ֔קֶר
וְכַטַּ֖ל מַשְׁכִּ֣ים הֹלֵ֑ךְ
כְּמֹץ֙ יְסֹעֵ֣ר מִגֹּ֔רֶן
וּכְעָשָׁ֖ן מֵאֲרֻבָּֽה:
4 וְאָנֹכִ֛י יְהֹוָ֥ה אֱלֹהֶ֖יךָ
מֵאֶ֣רֶץ מִצְרָ֑יִם
וֵאלֹהִ֤ים זֽוּלָתִי֙ לֹ֣א תֵדָ֔ע
וּמוֹשִׁ֥יעַ אַ֖יִן בִּלְתִּֽי:
5 אֲנִ֥י יְדַעְתִּ֖יךָ בַּמִּדְבָּ֑ר
בְּאֶ֖רֶץ תַּלְאֻבֽוֹת:
6 כְּמַרְעִיתָם֙ וַיִּשְׂבָּ֔עוּ
שָׂבְע֖וּ וַיָּ֣רָם לִבָּ֑ם
עַל־כֵּ֖ן שְׁכֵחֽוּנִי:
7 וָאֱהִ֥י לָהֶ֖ם כְּמוֹ־שָׁ֑חַל
כְּנָמֵ֖ר עַל־דֶּ֥רֶךְ אָשֽׁוּר:

---

m   *I.e., not through an angel.*
n   *Meaning of 12.15–13.1 uncertain.*

a   *I.e., Baal-peor; cf. 9.10.*
b-b   *Meaning of Heb. uncertain.*

⁸Like a bear robbed of her young I attack them
And rip open the casing of their hearts;
ᶜ-I will devour them there like a lion,-ᶜ
The beasts of the field shall mangle them.

⁹ᵇ-You are undone, O Israel!
You had no help but Me.-ᵇ
¹⁰Where now is your king?
Let him save you!
Where are the chieftains in all your towns
Whom you demanded:
"Give me a king and officers"?
¹¹I give you kings in my ire,
And take them away in My wrath.

¹²Ephraim's guilt is bound up,
His sin is stored away.ᵈ
¹³Pangs of childbirth assail him,
ᵇ-And the babe is not wise—
For this is no time to survive
At the birthstool of babes.-ᵇ

¹⁴ᵉFrom Sheol itself I will save them,
Redeem them from very Death.
Where, O Death, are your plagues?
Your pestilence where, O Sheol?
ᶠ-Revenge shall be far from My thoughts.-ᶠ
¹⁵For though he flourish among reeds,
A blast, a wind of the LORD,
Shall come blowing up from the wilderness;
His fountain shall be parched,
His spring dried up.
That [wind] shall plunder treasures,
Every lovely object.

14 Samaria must bear her guilt,
For she has defied her God.

⁸ אֶפְגְּשֵׁם כְּדֹב שַׁכּוּל
וְאֶקְרַע סְגוֹר לִבָּם
וְאֹכְלֵם שָׁם כְּלָבִיא
חַיַּת הַשָּׂדֶה תְּבַקְּעֵם:

⁹ שִׁחֶתְךָ יִשְׂרָאֵל
כִּי־בִי בְעֶזְרֶךָ:
¹⁰ אֱהִי מַלְכְּךָ אֵפוֹא
וְיוֹשִׁיעֲךָ
בְּכָל־עָרֶיךָ וְשֹׁפְטֶיךָ
אֲשֶׁר אָמַרְתָּ
תְּנָה־לִּי מֶלֶךְ וְשָׂרִים:
¹¹ אֶתֶּן־לְךָ מֶלֶךְ בְּאַפִּי
וְאֶקַּח בְּעֶבְרָתִי: ס

¹² צָרוּר עֲוֹן אֶפְרָיִם
צְפוּנָה חַטָּאתוֹ:
¹³ חֶבְלֵי יוֹלֵדָה יָבֹאוּ לוֹ
הוּא־בֵן לֹא חָכָם
כִּי־עֵת לֹא־יַעֲמֹד
בְּמִשְׁבַּר בָּנִים:

¹⁴ מִיַּד שְׁאוֹל אֶפְדֵּם
מִמָּוֶת אֶגְאָלֵם
אֱהִי דְבָרֶיךָ מָוֶת
אֱהִי קָטָבְךָ שְׁאוֹל
נֹחַם יִסָּתֵר מֵעֵינָי:
¹⁵ כִּי הוּא בֵּן אַחִים יַפְרִיא
יָבוֹא קָדִים רוּחַ יְהוָה
מִמִּדְבָּר
עֹלֶה וְיֵבוֹשׁ מְקוֹרוֹ
וְיֶחֱרַב מַעְיָנוֹ
הוּא יִשְׁסֶה אוֹצַר
כָּל־כְּלִי חֶמְדָּה:

יד תֶּאְשַׁם שֹׁמְרוֹן
כִּי מָרְתָה בֵּאלֹהֶיהָ

ᶜ-ᶜ *Emendation yields "There dogs shall devour them"; cf. Septuagint.*
ᵈ *I.e., for future retribution.*
ᵉ *This verse would read well before 14.5.*
ᶠ-ᶠ *Lit. "Satisfaction (for this meaning of nḥm see Deut. 32.36; Isa. 1.24) shall be hidden from My eyes."*

They shall fall by the sword,
Their infants shall be dashed to death,
And their women with child ripped open.

²Return, O Israel, to the Lord your God,
For you have fallen because of your sin.
³Take words with you
And return to the Lord.
Say to Him:
a-"Forgive all guilt
And accept what is good;
Instead of bulls we will pay
[The offering of] our lips.-*a*
⁴Assyria shall not save us,
No more will we ride on steeds;*b*
Nor ever again will we call
Our handiwork our god,
Since in You alone orphans find pity!"
⁵I will heal their affliction,*c*
Generously will I take them back in love;
For My anger has turned away from them.*d*
⁶I will be to Israel like dew;
He shall blossom like the lily,
He shall strike root like a *e*-Lebanon tree.-*e*
⁷His boughs shall spread out far,
His beauty shall be like the olive tree's,
His fragrance like that of Lebanon.
⁸They who sit in his shade shall be revived:
They shall bring to life new grain,
They shall blossom like the vine;
His scent shall be like the wine of Lebanon.*f*
⁹Ephraim [shall say]:
"What more have I to do with idols?
When I respond and look to Him,
I become like a verdant cypress."
a-Your fruit is provided by Me.-*a*

בַּחֶרֶב יִפֹּלוּ
עֹלְלֵיהֶם יְרֻטָּשׁוּ
וְהָרִיּוֹתָיו יְבֻקָּעוּ: פ

²שׁוּבָה יִשְׂרָאֵל עַד יְהֹוָה אֱלֹהֶיךָ
כִּי כָשַׁלְתָּ בַּעֲוֹנֶךָ:
³קְחוּ עִמָּכֶם דְּבָרִים
וְשׁוּבוּ אֶל־יְהֹוָה
אִמְרוּ אֵלָיו
כָּל־תִּשָּׂא עָוֹן
וְקַח־טוֹב
וּנְשַׁלְמָה פָרִים
שְׂפָתֵינוּ:
⁴אַשּׁוּר ׀ לֹא יוֹשִׁיעֵנוּ
עַל־סוּס לֹא נִרְכָּב
וְלֹא־נֹאמַר עוֹד
אֱלֹהֵינוּ לְמַעֲשֵׂה יָדֵינוּ
אֲשֶׁר־בְּךָ יְרֻחַם יָתוֹם:
⁵אֶרְפָּא מְשׁוּבָתָם
אֹהֲבֵם נְדָבָה
כִּי שָׁב אַפִּי מִמֶּנּוּ:
⁶אֶהְיֶה כַטַּל לְיִשְׂרָאֵל
יִפְרַח כַּשּׁוֹשַׁנָּה
וְיַךְ שָׁרָשָׁיו כַּלְּבָנוֹן:
⁷יֵלְכוּ יֹנְקוֹתָיו
וִיהִי כַזַּיִת הוֹדוֹ
וְרֵיחַ לוֹ כַּלְּבָנוֹן:
⁸יָשֻׁבוּ יֹשְׁבֵי בְצִלּוֹ
יְחַיּוּ דָגָן
וְיִפְרְחוּ כַגָּפֶן
זִכְרוֹ כְּיֵין לְבָנוֹן: ס
⁹אֶפְרַיִם
מַה־לִּי עוֹד לָעֲצַבִּים
אֲנִי עָנִיתִי וַאֲשׁוּרֶנּוּ
אֲנִי כִּבְרוֹשׁ רַעֲנָן
מִמֶּנִּי פֶּרְיְךָ נִמְצָא:

---

a-a   Meaning of Heb. uncertain.
b   I.e., we will no longer depend on an alliance with Egypt; cf.
     2 Kings 18.24 (Isa. 36.9); Isa. 30.16.
c   For this meaning of *meshubah* see Jer. 2.19; 3.22.
d   Heb. "him."
e-e   Emendation yields "poplar."
f   Emendation yields "Helbon"; cf. Ezek. 27.18.

10He who is wise will consider these words,
He who is prudent will take note of them.
For the paths of the LORD are smooth;
The righteous can walk on them,
While sinners stumble on them.

10 מִי חָכָם֙ וְיָ֣בֵֽן אֵ֔לֶּה
נָב֖וֹן וְיֵֽדָעֵ֑ם
כִּֽי־יְשָׁרִ֞ים דַּרְכֵ֣י יְהוָ֗ה
וְצַדִּקִים֙ יֵ֣לְכוּ בָ֔ם
וּפֹשְׁעִ֖ים יִכָּ֥שְׁלוּ בָֽם׃

JOEL

1 The word of the LORD that came to Joel son
of Pethuel.

2Listen to this, O elders,
Give ear, all inhabitants of the land.
Has the like of this happened in your days
Or in the days of your fathers?
3Tell your children about it,
And let your children tell theirs,
And their children the next generation!
4What the cutter*a* has left, the locust has de-
    voured;
What the locust has left, the grub has de-
    voured;
And what the grub has left, the hopper has
    devoured.
5Wake up, you drunkards, and weep,
Wail, all you swillers of wine—
For the new wine that is *b-*denied you!-*b*
6For a nation has invaded my land,
Vast beyond counting,
With teeth like the teeth of a lion,
With the fangs of a lion's breed.
7They have laid my vines waste
And splintered my fig trees:
They have stripped off their bark and thrown
    [it] away;
Their runners have turned white.

8Lament—like a maiden girt with sackcloth
For the husband of her youth!

---

a   The Heb. terms translated "cutter, locust, grub, and hopper" are
     of uncertain meaning; they probably designate stages in the
     development of the locust.
b-b   Lit. "cut off from your mouth."

א דְּבַר־יְהוָה֙ אֲשֶׁ֣ר הָיָ֔ה אֶל־יוֹאֵ֖ל בֶּן־
פְּתוּאֵֽל׃

2 שִׁמְעוּ־זֹאת֙ הַזְּקֵנִ֔ים
וְהַֽאֲזִ֔ינוּ כֹּ֖ל יוֹשְׁבֵ֣י הָאָ֑רֶץ
הֶהָ֤יְתָה זֹּאת֙ בִּֽימֵיכֶ֔ם
וְאִ֖ם בִּימֵ֥י אֲבֹֽתֵיכֶֽם׃
3 עָלֶ֖יהָ לִבְנֵיכֶ֣ם סַפֵּ֑רוּ
וּבְנֵיכֶם֙ לִבְנֵיהֶ֔ם
וּבְנֵיהֶ֖ם לְד֥וֹר אַחֵֽר׃
4 יֶ֤תֶר הַגָּזָם֙ אָכַ֣ל הָֽאַרְבֶּ֔ה
וְיֶ֥תֶר הָֽאַרְבֶּ֖ה אָכַ֣ל הַיָּ֑לֶק
וְיֶ֥תֶר הַיֶּ֖לֶק אָכַ֥ל הֶחָסִֽיל׃
5 הָקִ֤יצוּ שִׁכּוֹרִים֙ וּבְכ֔וּ
וְהֵילִ֖לוּ כָּל־שֹׁ֣תֵי יָ֑יִן
עַל־עָסִ֕יס כִּ֥י נִכְרַ֖ת מִפִּיכֶֽם׃
6 כִּֽי־גוֹי֙ עָלָ֣ה עַל־אַרְצִ֔י
עָצ֖וּם וְאֵ֣ין מִסְפָּ֑ר
שִׁנָּיו֙ שִׁנֵּ֣י אַרְיֵ֔ה
וּֽמְתַלְּע֥וֹת לָבִ֖יא לֽוֹ׃
7 שָׂ֤ם גַּפְנִי֙ לְשַׁמָּ֔ה
וּתְאֵנָתִ֖י לִקְצָפָ֑ה
חָשֹׂ֤ף חֲשָׂפָהּ֙ וְהִשְׁלִ֔יךְ
הִלְבִּ֖ינוּ שָׂרִיגֶֽיהָ׃

8 אֱלִ֕י כִּבְתוּלָ֥ה חֲגֻֽרַת־שַׂ֖ק
עַל־בַּ֥עַל נְעוּרֶֽיהָ׃

9Offering and libation have ceased
From the House of the LORD;
The priests must mourn
Who minister to the LORD.
10The country is ravaged,
The ground must mourn;
For the new grain is ravaged,
The new wine is dried up,
The new oil has failed.
11Farmers are dismayed
And vine dressers wail
Over wheat and barley;
For the crops of the field are lost.
12The vine has dried up,
The fig tree withers,
Pomegranate, palm, and apple—
All the trees of the field are sear.
And joy has dried up
Among men.

13Gird yourselves and lament, O priests,
Wail, O ministers of the altar;
Come, spend the night in sackcloth,
O ministers of my God.
For offering and libation are withheld
From the House of your God.
14Solemnize a fast,
Proclaim an assembly;
Gather the elders—all the inhabitants of the
    land—
In the House of the LORD your God,
And cry out to the LORD.

15Alas for the day!
For the day of the LORD is near;
It shall come like havoc from Shaddai.c
16For food is cut off
Before our very eyes,

---

c Traditionally "the Almighty"; see Gen. 17.1.

9 הָכְרַ֨ת מִנְחָ֤ה וָנֶ֙סֶךְ֙
מִבֵּ֣ית יְהוָ֔ה
אָֽבְלוּ֙ הַכֹּ֣הֲנִ֔ים
מְשָׁרְתֵ֖י יְהוָֽה:
10 שֻׁדַּ֣ד שָׂדֶ֔ה
אָבְלָ֖ה אֲדָמָ֑ה
כִּ֚י שֻׁדַּ֣ד דָּגָ֔ן
הוֹבִ֥ישׁ תִּיר֖וֹשׁ
אֻמְלַ֥ל יִצְהָֽר:
11 הֹבִ֣ישׁוּ אִכָּרִ֗ים
הֵילִ֙ילוּ֙ כֹּֽרְמִ֔ים
עַל־חִטָּ֖ה וְעַל־שְׂעֹרָ֑ה
כִּ֥י אָבַ֖ד קְצִ֥יר שָׂדֶֽה:
12 הַגֶּ֣פֶן הוֹבִ֔ישָׁה
וְהַתְּאֵנָ֖ה אֻמְלָ֑לָה
רִמּ֞וֹן גַּם־תָּמָ֣ר וְתַפּ֗וּחַ
כָּל־עֲצֵ֤י הַשָּׂדֶה֙ יָבֵ֔שׁוּ
כִּֽי־הֹבִ֥ישׁ שָׂשׂ֖וֹן
מִן־בְּנֵ֥י אָדָֽם: ס

13 חִגְר֨וּ וְסִפְד֜וּ הַכֹּֽהֲנִ֗ים
הֵילִ֙ילוּ֙ מְשָׁרְתֵ֣י מִזְבֵּ֔חַ
בֹּ֚אוּ לִ֣ינוּ בַשַּׂקִּ֔ים
מְשָׁרְתֵ֖י אֱלֹהָ֑י
כִּ֥י נִמְנַ֛ע מִבֵּ֥ית אֱלֹֽהֵיכֶ֖ם
מִנְחָ֥ה וָנָֽסֶךְ:
14 קַדְּשׁוּ־צוֹם֙
קִרְא֣וּ עֲצָרָ֔ה
אִסְפ֣וּ זְקֵנִ֗ים כֹּ֚ל יֹשְׁבֵ֣י הָאָ֔רֶץ
בֵּ֖ית יְהוָ֣ה אֱלֹהֵיכֶ֑ם
וְזַעֲק֖וּ אֶל־יְהוָֽה:

15 אֲהָ֖הּ לַיּ֑וֹם
כִּ֤י קָרוֹב֙ י֣וֹם יְהוָ֔ה
וּכְשֹׁ֖ד מִשַּׁדַּ֥י יָבֽוֹא:
16 הֲל֛וֹא נֶ֥גֶד עֵינֵ֖ינוּ
אֹ֣כֶל נִכְרָ֑ת

And joy and gladness
From the House of our God.
17d-The seeds have shriveled
Under their clods.-d
The granaries are desolate,
Barns are in ruins,
For the new grain has failed.
18How the beasts groan!
The herds of cattle are bewildered
Because they have no pasture,
And the flocks of sheep are dazed.d

19To You, O LORD, I call.
For firee has consumed
The pastures in the wilderness,
And flamee has devoured
All the trees of the countryside.
20The very beasts of the field
Cry out to You;
For the watercourses are dried up,
And fire has consumed
The pastures in the wilderness.

מִבֵּית אֱלֹהֵינוּ
שִׂמְחָה וָגִיל:
17 עָבְשׁוּ פְרֻדוֹת
תַּחַת מֶגְרְפֹתֵיהֶם
נָשַׁמּוּ אֹצָרוֹת
נֶהֶרְסוּ מַמְּגֻרוֹת
כִּי הֹבִישׁ דָּגָן:
18 מַה־נֶּאֶנְחָה בְהֵמָה
נָבֹכוּ עֶדְרֵי בָקָר
כִּי אֵין מִרְעֶה לָהֶם
גַּם־עֶדְרֵי הַצֹּאן נֶאְשָׁמוּ:

19 אֵלֶיךָ יְהֹוָה אֶקְרָא
כִּי אֵשׁ אָכְלָה
נְאוֹת מִדְבָּר
וְלֶהָבָה לִהֲטָה
כָּל־עֲצֵי הַשָּׂדֶה:
20 גַּם־בַּהֲמוֹת שָׂדֶה
תַּעֲרוֹג אֵלֶיךָ
כִּי יָבְשׁוּ אֲפִיקֵי מָיִם
וְאֵשׁ אָכְלָה
נְאוֹת הַמִּדְבָּר: פ

2 Blow a horn in Zion,
Sound an alarm on My holy mount!
Let all dwellers on earth tremble,
For the day of the LORD has come!
It is close—
2A day of darkness and gloom,
A day of densest cloud
Spread like soot over the hills.
A vast, enormous horde—
Nothing like it has ever happened,
And it shall never happen again
Through the years and ages.

ב תִּקְעוּ שׁוֹפָר בְּצִיּוֹן
וְהָרִיעוּ בְּהַר קָדְשִׁי
יִרְגְּזוּ כֹּל יֹשְׁבֵי הָאָרֶץ
כִּי־בָא יוֹם־יְהֹוָה
כִּי קָרוֹב:
2 יוֹם חֹשֶׁךְ וַאֲפֵלָה
יוֹם עָנָן וַעֲרָפֶל
כְּשַׁחַר פָּרֻשׂ עַל־הֶהָרִים
עַם רַב וְעָצוּם
כָּמֹהוּ לֹא נִהְיָה מִן־הָעוֹלָם
וְאַחֲרָיו לֹא יוֹסֵף
עַד־שְׁנֵי דּוֹר וָדוֹר:

d-d Meaning of Heb. uncertain.
e I.e., scorching heat.

3Their vanguard is a consuming fire,
Their rear guard a devouring flame.
Before them the land was like the Garden of
  Eden,
Behind them, a desolate waste:
Nothing has escaped them.
4They have the appearance of horses,
They gallop just like steeds.
5With a clatter as of chariots
They bound on the hilltops,
With a noise like a blazing fire
Consuming straw;
Like an enormous horde
Arrayed for battle.
6Peoples tremble before them,
All faces a-turn ashen.-a
7They rush like warriors,
They scale a wall like fighters.
And each keeps to his own track.
Their paths never cross;b
8No one jostles another,
Each keeps to his own course.
b-And should they fall through a loophole,
They do not get hurt.-b
9They rush up the wall,
They dash about in the city;
They climb into the houses,
They enter like thieves
By way of the windows.
10Before them earth trembles,
Heaven shakes,
Sun and moon are darkened,
And stars withdraw their brightness.
11And the Lord roars aloud
At the head of His army;
For vast indeed is His host,
Numberless are those that do His bidding.
For great is the day of the Lord,

לְפָנָיו אָכְלָה אֵשׁ 3
וְאַחֲרָיו תְּלַהֵט לֶהָבָה
כְּגַן־עֵדֶן הָאָרֶץ לְפָנָיו
וְאַחֲרָיו מִדְבַּר שְׁמָמָה
וְגַם־פְּלֵיטָה לֹא־הָיְתָה לּוֹ׃
כְּמַרְאֵה סוּסִים מַרְאֵהוּ 4
וּכְפָרָשִׁים כֵּן יְרוּצוּן׃
כְּקוֹל מַרְכָּבוֹת 5
עַל־רָאשֵׁי הֶהָרִים יְרַקֵּדוּן
כְּקוֹל לַהַב אֵשׁ
אֹכְלָה קָשׁ
כְּעַם עָצוּם
עֲרוּךְ מִלְחָמָה׃
מִפָּנָיו יָחִילוּ עַמִּים 6
כָּל־פָּנִים קִבְּצוּ פָארוּר׃
כְּגִבּוֹרִים יְרֻצוּן 7
כְּאַנְשֵׁי מִלְחָמָה יַעֲלוּ חוֹמָה
וְאִישׁ בִּדְרָכָיו יֵלֵכוּן
וְלֹא יְעַבְּטוּן אֹרְחוֹתָם׃
וְאִישׁ אָחִיו לֹא יִדְחָקוּן 8
גֶּבֶר בִּמְסִלָּתוֹ יֵלֵכוּן
וּבְעַד הַשֶּׁלַח יִפֹּלוּ
לֹא יִבְצָעוּ׃
בָּעִיר יָשֹׁקּוּ 9
בַּחוֹמָה יְרֻצוּן
בַּבָּתִּים יַעֲלוּ
בְּעַד הַחַלּוֹנִים
יָבֹאוּ כַּגַּנָּב׃
לְפָנָיו רָגְזָה אֶרֶץ 10
רָעֲשׁוּ שָׁמָיִם
שֶׁמֶשׁ וְיָרֵחַ קָדָרוּ
וְכוֹכָבִים אָסְפוּ נָגְהָם׃
וַיהוָה נָתַן קוֹלוֹ 11
לִפְנֵי חֵילוֹ
כִּי רַב מְאֹד מַחֲנֵהוּ
כִּי עָצוּם עֹשֵׂה דְבָרוֹ
כִּי־גָדוֹל יוֹם־יְהוָה

---

a-a Meaning of Heb. uncertain; cf. Nah. 2.11.
b   Meaning of Heb. uncertain.

Most terrible—who can endure it?

12"Yet even now"—says the LORD—
"Turn back to Me with all your hearts,
And with fasting, weeping, and lamenting."

13Rend your hearts
Rather than your garments,
And turn back to the LORD your God.
For He is gracious and compassionate,
Slow to anger, abounding in kindness,
And renouncing punishment.

14Who knows but He may turn and relent,
And leave a blessing behind
For meal offering and drink offering
To the LORD your God?c

15Blow a horn in Zion,
Solemnize a fast,
Proclaim an assembly!

16Gather the people,
Bid the congregation purify themselves.d
Bring together the old,
Gather the babes
And the sucklings at the breast;
Let the bridegroom come out of his chamber,
The bride from her canopied couch.

17Between the portico and the altar,
Let the priests, the LORD's ministers, weep
And say:
"Oh, spare Your people, LORD!
Let not Your possession become a mockery,
To be taunted by nations!
Let not the peoples say,
'Where is their God?'"

18Then the LORD was roused
On behalf of His land
And had compassion

וְנוֹרָא מְאֹד וּמִי יְכִילֶֽנּוּ׃
12 וְגַם־עַתָּה נְאֻם־יְהֹוָה
שֻׁבוּ עָדַי בְּכָל־לְבַבְכֶם
וּבְצוֹם וּבִבְכִי וּבְמִסְפֵּֽד׃
13 וְקִרְעוּ לְבַבְכֶם
וְאַל־בִּגְדֵיכֶם
וְשׁוּבוּ אֶל־יְהֹוָה אֱלֹֽהֵיכֶם
כִּֽי־חַנּוּן וְרַחוּם הוּא
אֶרֶךְ אַפַּיִם וְרַב־חֶסֶד
וְנִחָם עַל־הָרָעָֽה׃
14 מִי יוֹדֵעַ יָשׁוּב וְנִחָם
וְהִשְׁאִיר אַחֲרָיו בְּרָכָה
מִנְחָה וָנֶסֶךְ
לַיהֹוָה אֱלֹהֵיכֶֽם׃ פ

15 תִּקְעוּ שׁוֹפָר בְּצִיּוֹן
קַדְּשׁוּ־צוֹם
קִרְאוּ עֲצָרָֽה׃
16 אִסְפוּ־עָם
קַדְּשׁוּ קָהָל
קִבְצוּ זְקֵנִים
אִסְפוּ עוֹלָלִים
וְיֹנְקֵי שָׁדָיִם
יֵצֵא חָתָן מֵחֶדְרוֹ
וְכַלָּה מֵחֻפָּתָֽהּ׃
17 בֵּין הָאוּלָם וְלַמִּזְבֵּחַ
יִבְכּוּ הַכֹּהֲנִים מְשָׁרְתֵי יְהֹוָה
וְיֹאמְרוּ
חוּסָה יְהֹוָה עַל־עַמֶּךָ
וְאַל־תִּתֵּן נַחֲלָתְךָ לְחֶרְפָּה
לִמְשָׁל־בָּם גּוֹיִם
לָמָּה יֹאמְרוּ בָעַמִּים
אַיֵּה אֱלֹהֵיהֶֽם׃

18 וַיְקַנֵּא יְהֹוָה
לְאַרְצוֹ
וַיַּחְמֹל

---

c When the locusts depart, there will again be yield enough for
   offerings; see 1.9.
d Cf. Exod. 19.10; Zeph. 1.7.

Upon His people.

19In response to His people
The LORD declared:
"I will grant you the new grain,
The new wine, and the new oil,
And you shall have them in abundance.
Nevermore will I let you be
A mockery among the nations.
20I will drive the northerner[e] far from you,
I will thrust it into a parched and desolate
    land—
Its van to the Eastern Sea[f]
And its rear to the Western Sea;[g]
And the stench of it shall go up,
And the foul smell rise."
For [the LORD] shall work great deeds.

21Fear not, O soil, rejoice and be glad;
For the LORD has wrought great deeds.
22Fear not, O beasts of the field,
For the pastures in the wilderness
Are clothed with grass.
The trees have borne their fruit;
Fig tree and vine
Have yielded their strength.
23O children of Zion, be glad,
Rejoice in the LORD your God.
For He has given you the early rain in [His]
    kindness,
Now He makes the rain fall [as] formerly—
The early rain and the late—
24And threshing floors shall be piled with
    grain,
And vats shall overflow with new wine and
    oil.

25"I will repay you [h]-for the years-[h]
Consumed by swarms and hoppers,

עַל־עַמּֽוֹ׃

19 וַיַּ֖עַן יְהֹוָ֑ה
וַיֹּ֣אמֶר לְעַמּ֗וֹ
הִנְנִ֨י שֹׁלֵ֤חַ לָכֶם֙ אֶת־הַדָּגָ֔ן
וְהַתִּיר֖וֹשׁ וְהַיִּצְהָ֑ר
וּשְׂבַעְתֶּ֖ם אֹת֑וֹ
וְלֹא־אֶתֵּ֨ן אֶתְכֶ֥ם ע֛וֹד
חֶרְפָּ֖ה בַּגּוֹיִֽם׃

20 וְאֶת־הַצְּפוֹנִ֞י אַרְחִ֣יק מֵֽעֲלֵיכֶ֗ם
וְהִדַּחְתִּיו֮ אֶל־אֶ֣רֶץ צִיָּ֣ה וּשְׁמָמָה֒
אֶת־פָּנָ֗יו אֶל־הַיָּם֙ הַקַּדְמֹנִ֔י
וְסֹפ֖וֹ אֶל־הַיָּ֣ם הָאַֽחֲר֑וֹן
וְעָלָ֣ה בׇאְשׁ֗וֹ
וְתַ֙עַל֙ צַֽחֲנָת֔וֹ
כִּ֥י הִגְדִּ֖יל לַעֲשֽׂוֹת׃

21 אַל־תִּֽירְאִ֖י אֲדָמָ֑ה גִּ֣ילִי וּשְׂמָ֔חִי
כִּֽי־הִגְדִּ֥יל יְהֹוָ֖ה לַעֲשֽׂוֹת׃
22 אַל־תִּֽירְאוּ֙ בַּֽהֲמ֣וֹת שָׂדַ֔י
כִּ֥י דָשְׁא֖וּ נְא֣וֹת מִדְבָּ֑ר
כִּֽי־עֵץ֙ נָשָׂ֣א פִרְי֔וֹ
תְּאֵנָ֥ה וָגֶ֖פֶן
נָתְנ֥וּ חֵילָֽם׃
23 וּבְנֵ֣י צִיּ֗וֹן גִּ֤ילוּ
וְשִׂמְחוּ֙ בַּֽיהֹוָ֣ה אֱלֹֽהֵיכֶ֔ם
כִּֽי־נָתַ֥ן לָכֶ֛ם אֶת־הַמּוֹרֶ֖ה לִצְדָקָ֑ה
וַיּ֣וֹרֶד לָכֶ֗ם גֶּ֛שֶׁם
מוֹרֶ֥ה וּמַלְק֖וֹשׁ בָּרִאשֽׁוֹן׃
24 וּמָלְא֥וּ הַגֳּרָנ֖וֹת בָּ֑ר
וְהֵשִׁ֥יקוּ הַיְקָבִ֖ים תִּיר֥וֹשׁ וְיִצְהָֽר׃

25 וְשִׁלַּמְתִּ֤י לָכֶם֙ אֶת־הַשָּׁנִ֔ים
אֲשֶׁר֙ אָכַ֣ל הָֽאַרְבֶּ֔ה הַיֶּ֖לֶק

---

e   I.e., the locusts. Emendation yields "My multitude"; cf. "nation"
    (1.6), "horde," "army," and "host" (2.2, 5, 11, and 25).
f   The Dead Sea.
g   The Mediterranean Sea.
h-h   Emendation yields "double what was."

By grubs and locusts,
The great army I let loose against you.
26And you shall eat your fill
And praise the name of the LORD your God
Who dealt so wondrously with you—
My people shall be shamed no more.
27And you shall know
That I am in the midst of Israel:
That I the LORD am your God
And there is no other.
And My people shall be shamed no more."

וְהֶחָסִיל וְהַגָּזָם
חֵילִי הַגָּדוֹל אֲשֶׁר שִׁלַּחְתִּי בָּכֶם:
26 וַאֲכַלְתֶּם אָכוֹל וְשָׂבוֹעַ
וְהִלַּלְתֶּם אֶת־שֵׁם יְהוָה אֱלֹהֵיכֶם
אֲשֶׁר־עָשָׂה עִמָּכֶם לְהַפְלִיא
וְלֹא־יֵבֹשׁוּ עַמִּי לְעוֹלָם:
27 וִידַעְתֶּם
כִּי בְקֶרֶב יִשְׂרָאֵל אָנִי
וַאֲנִי יְהוָה אֱלֹהֵיכֶם
וְאֵין עוֹד
וְלֹא־יֵבֹשׁוּ עַמִּי לְעוֹלָם: ס

3 After that,
I will pour out My spirit on all flesh;
Your sons and daughters shall prophesy;
Your old men shall dream dreams,
And your young men shall see visions.
2I will even pour out My spirit
Upon male and female slaves in those days.

ג וְהָיָה אַחֲרֵי־כֵן
אֶשְׁפּוֹךְ אֶת־רוּחִי עַל־כָּל־בָּשָׂר
וְנִבְּאוּ בְּנֵיכֶם וּבְנוֹתֵיכֶם
זִקְנֵיכֶם חֲלֹמוֹת יַחֲלֹמוּן
בַּחוּרֵיכֶם חֶזְיֹנוֹת יִרְאוּ:
2 וְגַם עַל־הָעֲבָדִים וְעַל־הַשְּׁפָחוֹת
בַּיָּמִים הָהֵמָּה
אֶשְׁפּוֹךְ אֶת־רוּחִי:

3a-Before the great and terrible day of the
LORD comes,-a
I will set portents in the sky and on earth:
Blood and fire and pillars of smoke;
4The sun shall turn into darkness
And the moon into blood.
5But everyone who invokes the name of the
LORD shall escape; for there shall be a remnant
on Mount Zion and in Jerusalem, as the LORD
promised. b-Anyone who invokes the LORD will
be among the survivors.-b

3 וְנָתַתִּי מוֹפְתִים בַּשָּׁמַיִם וּבָאָרֶץ
דָּם וָאֵשׁ וְתִימֲרוֹת עָשָׁן:
4 הַשֶּׁמֶשׁ יֵהָפֵךְ לְחֹשֶׁךְ
וְהַיָּרֵחַ לְדָם
לִפְנֵי בּוֹא יוֹם יְהוָה הַגָּדוֹל וְהַנּוֹרָא:
5 וְהָיָה כֹּל אֲשֶׁר־יִקְרָא בְּשֵׁם יְהוָה יִמָּלֵט
כִּי בְּהַר־צִיּוֹן וּבִירוּשָׁלַ͏ִם תִּהְיֶה פְלֵיטָה
כַּאֲשֶׁר אָמַר יְהוָה וּבַשְּׂרִידִים אֲשֶׁר יְהוָה
קֹרֵא:

4 For lo! in those days
And in that time,
When I restore the fortunes
Of Judah and Jerusalem,

ד כִּי הִנֵּה בַּיָּמִים הָהֵמָּה
וּבָעֵת הַהִיא
אֲשֶׁר אָשׁוּב אָשִׁיב אֶת־שְׁבוּת
יְהוּדָה וִירוּשָׁלָ͏ִם:

---

a-a   *Brought up from v. 4 for clarity.*
b-b   *Meaning of Heb. uncertain.*

²I will gather all the nations
And bring them down to the Valley of Jeho-
 shaphat.ᵃ
There I will contend with them
Over My very own people, Israel,
Which they scattered among the nations.
For they divided My land among themselves
³And cast lots over My people;
And they bartered a boy for a whore,
And sold a girl for wine, which they drank.

⁴What is this you are doing to Me, O Tyre,
Sidon, and all the districts of Philistia? Are you
requiting Me for something I have done, or are
you doing something for My benefit? Quick as
a flash, I will pay you back; ⁵for you have taken
My gold and My silver, and have carried off My
precious treasures to your palaces; ⁶and you
have sold the people of Judah and the people
of Jerusalem to the Ionians, so that you have
removed them far away from their homeland.
⁷Behold, I will rouse them to leave the place you
have sold them to, and I will pay you back: ⁸I
will deliver your sons and daughters into the
hands of the people of Judah, and they will sell
them into captivity to a distant nation—for the
LORD has spoken.

⁹Proclaim this among the nations:
Prepare for battle!
Arouse the warriors,
Let all the fighters come and draw near!
¹⁰Beat your plowsharesᵇ into swords,
And your pruning hooks into spears.
Let even the weakling say, "I am strong."
¹¹ᶜ-Rouse yourselves-ᶜ and come,
All you nations;
Come together
From roundabout.

² וְקִבַּצְתִּי אֶת־כָּל־הַגּוֹיִם
וְהוֹרַדְתִּים אֶל־עֵמֶק יְהוֹשָׁפָט
וְנִשְׁפַּטְתִּי עִמָּם שָׁם
עַל־עַמִּי וְנַחֲלָתִי יִשְׂרָאֵל
אֲשֶׁר פִּזְּרוּ בַגּוֹיִם
וְאֶת־אַרְצִי חִלֵּקוּ:
³ וְאֶל־עַמִּי יַדּוּ גוֹרָל
וַיִּתְּנוּ הַיֶּלֶד בַּזּוֹנָה
וְהַיַּלְדָּה מָכְרוּ בַיַּיִן וַיִּשְׁתּוּ:

⁴ וְגַם מָה־אַתֶּם לִי צֹר וְצִידוֹן וְכֹל גְּלִילוֹת
פְּלָשֶׁת הַגְּמוּל אַתֶּם מְשַׁלְּמִים עָלָי וְאִם־
גֹּמְלִים אַתֶּם עָלַי קַל מְהֵרָה אָשִׁיב
גְּמֻלְכֶם בְּרֹאשְׁכֶם: ⁵ אֲשֶׁר־כַּסְפִּי וּזְהָבִי
לְקַחְתֶּם וּמַחֲמַדַּי הַטֹּבִים הֲבֵאתֶם
לְהֵיכְלֵיכֶם: ⁶ וּבְנֵי יְהוּדָה וּבְנֵי יְרוּשָׁלַ͏ִם
מְכַרְתֶּם לִבְנֵי הַיְּוָנִים לְמַעַן הַרְחִיקָם
מֵעַל גְּבוּלָם: ⁷ הִנְנִי מְעִירָם מִן־הַמָּקוֹם
אֲשֶׁר־מְכַרְתֶּם אֹתָם שָׁמָּה וַהֲשִׁבֹתִי
גְמֻלְכֶם בְּרֹאשְׁכֶם: ⁸ וּמָכַרְתִּי אֶת־בְּנֵיכֶם
וְאֶת־בְּנוֹתֵיכֶם בְּיַד בְּנֵי יְהוּדָה וּמְכָרוּם
לִשְׁבָאִים אֶל־גּוֹי רָחוֹק כִּי יְהוָה דִּבֵּר: ס

⁹ קִרְאוּ־זֹאת בַּגּוֹיִם
קַדְּשׁוּ מִלְחָמָה
הָעִירוּ הַגִּבּוֹרִים
יִגְּשׁוּ יַעֲלוּ כֹּל אַנְשֵׁי הַמִּלְחָמָה:
¹⁰ כֹּתּוּ אִתֵּיכֶם לַחֲרָבוֹת
וּמַזְמְרֹתֵיכֶם לִרְמָחִים
הַחַלָּשׁ יֹאמַר גִּבּוֹר אָנִי:
¹¹ עוּשׁוּ וָבֹאוּ
כָל־הַגּוֹיִם
מִסָּבִיב
וְנִקְבָּצוּ

ᵃ Here understood as "The LORD contends"; contrast v. 12.
ᵇ See note at Isa. 2.4.
ᶜ-ᶜ Meaning of Heb. uncertain.

There *c*-bring down-*c*
Your warriors, O LORD!

12Let the nations rouse themselves and march
  up
To the Valley of Jehoshaphat;*d*
For there I will sit in judgment
Over all the nations roundabout.

13Swing the sickle,
For the crop is ripe;
Come and tread,
For the winepress is full,
The vats are overflowing!
For great is their wickedness.

14Multitudes upon multitudes
In the Valley of Decision!
For the day of the LORD is at hand
In the Valley of Decision.

15Sun and moon are darkened,
And stars withdraw their brightness.

16And the LORD will roar from Zion,
And shout aloud from Jerusalem,
So that heaven and earth tremble.
But the LORD will be a shelter to His people,
A refuge to the children of Israel.

17And you shall know that I the LORD your
  God
Dwell in Zion, My holy mount.
And Jerusalem shall be holy;
Nevermore shall strangers pass through it.

18And in that day,
The mountains shall drip with wine,
The hills shall flow with milk,
And all the watercourses of Judah shall flow
  with water;
A spring shall issue from the House of the
  LORD
And shall water the Wadi of the Acacias.

19Egypt shall be a desolation,

שָׁמָּה הַנְחַת
יְהוָה גִּבּוֹרֶיךָ:
12 יֵעוֹרוּ וְיַעֲלוּ הַגּוֹיִם
אֶל־עֵמֶק יְהוֹשָׁפָט
כִּי שָׁם אֵשֵׁב לִשְׁפֹּט
אֶת־כָּל־הַגּוֹיִם מִסָּבִיב:
13 שִׁלְחוּ מַגָּל
כִּי בָשַׁל קָצִיר
בֹּאוּ רְדוּ
כִּי־מָלְאָה גַּת
הֵשִׁיקוּ הַיְקָבִים
כִּי רַבָּה רָעָתָם:

14 הֲמוֹנִים הֲמוֹנִים
בְּעֵמֶק הֶחָרוּץ
כִּי קָרוֹב יוֹם יְהוָה
בְּעֵמֶק הֶחָרוּץ:
15 שֶׁמֶשׁ וְיָרֵחַ קָדָרוּ
וְכוֹכָבִים אָסְפוּ נָגְהָם:
16 וַיהוָה מִצִּיּוֹן יִשְׁאָג
וּמִירוּשָׁלַ͏ִם יִתֵּן קוֹלוֹ
וְרָעֲשׁוּ שָׁמַיִם וָאָרֶץ
וַיהוָה מַחֲסֶה לְעַמּוֹ
וּמָעוֹז לִבְנֵי יִשְׂרָאֵל:
17 וִידַעְתֶּם כִּי אֲנִי יְהוָה אֱלֹהֵיכֶם
שֹׁכֵן בְּצִיּוֹן הַר־קָדְשִׁי
וְהָיְתָה יְרוּשָׁלַ͏ִם קֹדֶשׁ
וְזָרִים לֹא־יַעַבְרוּ־בָהּ עוֹד: ס
18 וְהָיָה בַיּוֹם הַהוּא
יִטְּפוּ הֶהָרִים עָסִיס
וְהַגְּבָעוֹת תֵּלַכְנָה חָלָב
וְכָל־אֲפִיקֵי יְהוּדָה יֵלְכוּ מָיִם
וּמַעְיָן מִבֵּית יְהוָה יֵצֵא
וְהִשְׁקָה אֶת־נַחַל הַשִּׁטִּים:
19 מִצְרַיִם לִשְׁמָמָה תִהְיֶה

d Here understood as "The LORD judges"; contrast v. 2.

And Edom a desolate waste,
Because of the outrage to the people of Judah,
In whose land they shed the blood of the in-
nocent.
20But Judah shall be inhabited forever,
And Jerusalem throughout the ages.
21Thus e-I will treat as innocent their blood
Which I have not treated as innocent;-e
And the Lord shall dwell in Zion.

וֶאֱדֹום לְמִדְבַּר שְׁמָמָה תִהְיֶה
מֵחֲמַס בְּנֵי יְהוּדָה
אֲשֶׁר־שָׁפְכוּ דָם־נָקִיא* בְּאַרְצָם׃
20 וִיהוּדָה לְעֹולָם תֵּשֵׁב
וִירוּשָׁלַ͏ִם לְדֹור וָדֹור׃
21 וְנִקֵּיתִי דָמָם
לֹא־נִקֵּיתִי
וַיהוָה שֹׁכֵן בְּצִיֹּון׃

---

e-e   *Emendation yields "their unavenged blood shall be avenged."*

AMOS

1 The words of Amos, a sheepbreeder from Tekoa, who prophesied concerning Israel in the reigns of Kings Uzziah of Judah and Jeroboam son of Joash of Israel, two years before the earthquake.[a]

²He proclaimed:

The LORD roars from Zion,
Shouts aloud from Jerusalem;
And the pastures of the shepherds shall languish,
And the summit of Carmel shall wither.

³Thus said the LORD:
For three transgressions of Damascus,
For four, I will not revoke it:[b]
Because they threshed Gilead
With threshing boards of iron.
⁴I will send down[c] fire upon the palace of Hazael,
And it shall devour the fortresses of Ben-hadad.[d]
⁵I will break the gate bars of Damascus,
And wipe out the inhabitants from the Vale of Aven
And the sceptered ruler of Beth-eden;
And the people of Aram shall be exiled to Kir
—said the LORD.

⁶Thus said the LORD:
For three transgressions of Gaza,
For four, I will not revoke it:

א ¹דִּבְרֵי עָמוֹס אֲשֶׁר־הָיָה בַנֹּקְדִים מִתְּקוֹעַ אֲשֶׁר חָזָה עַל־יִשְׂרָאֵל בִּימֵי | עֻזִּיָּה מֶלֶךְ־יְהוּדָה וּבִימֵי יָרָבְעָם בֶּן־יוֹאָשׁ מֶלֶךְ יִשְׂרָאֵל שְׁנָתַיִם לִפְנֵי הָרָעַשׁ:

²וַיֹּאמַר |
יְהוָה מִצִּיּוֹן יִשְׁאָג
וּמִירוּשָׁלַ͏ִם יִתֵּן קוֹלוֹ
וְאָבְלוּ נְאוֹת הָרֹעִים
וְיָבֵשׁ רֹאשׁ הַכַּרְמֶל: פ

³כֹּה אָמַר יְהוָה
עַל־שְׁלֹשָׁה פִּשְׁעֵי דַמֶּשֶׂק
וְעַל־אַרְבָּעָה לֹא אֲשִׁיבֶנּוּ
עַל־דּוּשָׁם
בַּחֲרֻצוֹת הַבַּרְזֶל אֶת־הַגִּלְעָד:
⁴וְשִׁלַּחְתִּי אֵשׁ בְּבֵית חֲזָאֵל
וְאָכְלָה אַרְמְנוֹת בֶּן־הֲדָד:
⁵וְשָׁבַרְתִּי בְּרִיחַ דַּמֶּשֶׂק
וְהִכְרַתִּי יוֹשֵׁב מִבִּקְעַת־אָוֶן
וְתוֹמֵךְ שֵׁבֶט מִבֵּית עֶדֶן
וְגָלוּ עַם־אֲרָם קִירָה
אָמַר יְהוָה: פ

⁶כֹּה אָמַר יְהוָה
עַל־שְׁלֹשָׁה פִּשְׁעֵי עַזָּה
וְעַל־אַרְבָּעָה לֹא אֲשִׁיבֶנּוּ

---

a See Zech. 14.5.
b I.e., the decree of punishment.
c Cf. Lam. 1.13.
d Cf. 2 Kings 13.22–25.

Because they exiled^e an entire population,
Which they delivered to Edom.^f
⁷I will send down fire upon the wall of Gaza,
And it shall devour its fortresses;
⁸And I will wipe out the inhabitants of Ash-
    dod
And the sceptered ruler of Ashkelon;
And I will turn My hand against Ekron,
And the Philistines shall perish to the last man
         —said the Lord God.

⁹Thus said the Lord:
For three transgressions of Tyre,
For four, I will not revoke it:
Because they handed over
An entire population to Edom,^g
Ignoring the covenant of brotherhood.^h
¹⁰I will send down fire upon the wall of Tyre,
And it shall devour its fortresses.

¹¹Thus said the Lord:
For three transgressions of Edom,
For four, I will not revoke it:
Because he pursued his brother with the
    sword
And repressed all pity,
Because his anger raged unceasing
And his fury stormedⁱ unchecked.
¹²I will send down fire upon Teman,
And it shall devour the fortresses of Bozrah.

¹³Thus said the Lord:
For three transgressions of the Ammonites,
For four, I will not revoke it:
Because they ripped open the pregnant
    women of Gilead
In order to enlarge their own territory.

עַל־הַגְלוֹתָם גָּלוּת שְׁלֵמָה
לְהַסְגִּיר לֶאֱדוֹם:
7 וְשִׁלַּחְתִּי אֵשׁ בְּחוֹמַת עַזָּה
וְאָכְלָה אַרְמְנֹתֶיהָ:
8 וְהִכְרַתִּי יוֹשֵׁב מֵאַשְׁדּוֹד
וְתוֹמֵךְ שֵׁבֶט מֵאַשְׁקְלוֹן
וַהֲשִׁיבוֹתִי יָדִי עַל־עֶקְרוֹן
וְאָבְדוּ שְׁאֵרִית פְּלִשְׁתִּים
אָמַר אֲדֹנָי יְהוִה: פ

9 כֹּה אָמַר יְהוָה
עַל־שְׁלֹשָׁה פִּשְׁעֵי־צֹר
וְעַל־אַרְבָּעָה לֹא אֲשִׁיבֶנּוּ
עַל־הַסְגִּירָם
גָּלוּת שְׁלֵמָה לֶאֱדוֹם
וְלֹא זָכְרוּ בְּרִית אַחִים:
10 וְשִׁלַּחְתִּי אֵשׁ בְּחוֹמַת צֹר
וְאָכְלָה אַרְמְנֹתֶיהָ: פ

11 כֹּה אָמַר יְהוָה
עַל־שְׁלֹשָׁה פִּשְׁעֵי אֱדוֹם
וְעַל־אַרְבָּעָה לֹא אֲשִׁיבֶנּוּ
עַל־רָדְפוֹ בַחֶרֶב אָחִיו
וְשִׁחֵת רַחֲמָיו
וַיִּטְרֹף לָעַד אַפּוֹ
וְעֶבְרָתוֹ שְׁמָרָה נֶצַח:
12 וְשִׁלַּחְתִּי אֵשׁ בְּתֵימָן
וְאָכְלָה אַרְמְנוֹת בָּצְרָה: פ

13 כֹּה אָמַר יְהוָה
עַל־שְׁלֹשָׁה פִּשְׁעֵי בְנֵי־עַמּוֹן
וְעַל־אַרְבָּעָה לֹא אֲשִׁיבֶנּוּ
עַל־בִּקְעָם הָרוֹת הַגִּלְעָד
לְמַעַן הַרְחִיב אֶת־גְּבוּלָם:

---

^e *I.e., they cooperated in the annexation of Israelite territory; cf.*
    Jer. 13.19 with note.
^f *Emendation yields "Aram"; cf. Isa. 9.11.*
^g *Emendation yields "Aram."*
^h *Cf. 1 Kings 5.26; 9.12–13.*
ⁱ *Cf. Akkadian* shamaru *and Jer. 3.5.*

¹⁴I will set fire to the wall of Rabbah,
And it shall devour its fortresses,
Amid shouting on a day of battle,
On a day of violent tempest.
¹⁵Their king and his officers shall go
Into exile together
      —said the LORD.

2 Thus said the LORD:
For three transgressions of Moab,
For four, I will not revoke it:
Because he burned the bones
Of the king of Edom to lime.
²I will send down fire upon Moab,
And it shall devour the fortresses of Kerioth.
And Moab shall die in tumult,
Amid shouting and the blare of horns;
³I will wipe out the ruler from within her
And slay all her officials along with him
      —said the LORD.

⁴Thus said the LORD:
For three transgressions of Judah,
For four, I will not revoke it:
Because they have spurned the Teaching of
   the LORD
And have not observed His laws;
They are beguiled by the delusions
After which their fathers walked.
⁵I will send down fire upon Judah,
And it shall devour the fortresses of Jeru-
   salem.

⁶Thus said the LORD:
For three transgressions of Israel,
For four, I will not revoke it:
Because they have sold for silver
Those whose cause was just,
And the needy for a pair of sandals.

14 וְהִצַּתִּי אֵשׁ בְּחוֹמַת רַבָּה
וְאָכְלָה אַרְמְנוֹתֶיהָ
בִּתְרוּעָה בְּיוֹם מִלְחָמָה
בְּסַעַר בְּיוֹם סוּפָה:
15 וְהָלַךְ מַלְכָּם בַּגּוֹלָה
הוּא וְשָׂרָיו יַחְדָּו
אָמַר יְהֹוָה: פ

ב 1 כֹּה אָמַר יְהֹוָה
עַל־שְׁלֹשָׁה פִּשְׁעֵי מוֹאָב
וְעַל־אַרְבָּעָה לֹא אֲשִׁיבֶנּוּ
עַל־שָׂרְפוֹ עַצְמוֹת
מֶלֶךְ־אֱדוֹם לַשִּׂיד:
2 וְשִׁלַּחְתִּי־אֵשׁ בְּמוֹאָב
וְאָכְלָה אַרְמְנוֹת הַקְּרִיּוֹת
וּמֵת בְּשָׁאוֹן מוֹאָב
בִּתְרוּעָה בְּקוֹל שׁוֹפָר:
3 וְהִכְרַתִּי שׁוֹפֵט מִקִּרְבָּהּ
וְכָל־שָׂרֶיהָ אֶהֱרוֹג עִמּוֹ
אָמַר יְהֹוָה: פ

4 כֹּה אָמַר יְהֹוָה
עַל־שְׁלֹשָׁה פִּשְׁעֵי יְהוּדָה
וְעַל־אַרְבָּעָה לֹא אֲשִׁיבֶנּוּ
עַל־מָאֳסָם אֶת־תּוֹרַת יְהֹוָה
וְחֻקָּיו לֹא שָׁמָרוּ
וַיַּתְעוּם כִּזְבֵיהֶם
אֲשֶׁר־הָלְכוּ אֲבוֹתָם אַחֲרֵיהֶם:
5 וְשִׁלַּחְתִּי אֵשׁ בִּיהוּדָה
וְאָכְלָה אַרְמְנוֹת יְרוּשָׁלָ͏ִם: פ

6 כֹּה אָמַר יְהֹוָה
עַל־שְׁלֹשָׁה פִּשְׁעֵי יִשְׂרָאֵל
וְעַל־אַרְבָּעָה לֹא אֲשִׁיבֶנּוּ
עַל־מִכְרָם בַּכֶּסֶף
צַדִּיק
וְאֶבְיוֹן בַּעֲבוּר נַעֲלָיִם:

7[Ah,] you ᵃ-who trample the heads of the poor
Into the dust of the ground,
And make the humble walk a twisted course!-ᵃ
Father and son go to the same girl,
And thereby profane My holy name.
8They recline by every altar
On garments taken in pledge,
And drink in the House of their God
Wine bought with fines they imposed.
9Yet I
Destroyed the Amorite before them,
Whose stature was like the cedar's
And who was stout as the oak,
Destroying his boughs above
And his trunk below!
10And I
Brought you up from the land of Egypt
And led you through the wilderness forty years,
To possess the land of the Amorite!
11And I raised up prophets from among your sons
And nazirites from among your young men.
Is that not so, O people of Israel?
——says the Lord.
12But you made the nazirites drink wine
And ordered the prophets not to prophesy.
13ᵇ-Ah, I will slow your movements
As a wagon is slowed
When it is full of cut grain.-ᵇ
14Flight shall fail the swift,
The strong shall find no strength,
And the warrior shall not save his life.
15The bowman shall not hold his ground,
And the fleet-footed shall not escape,

7 הַשֹּׁאֲפִ֤ים עַל־עֲפַר־אֶ֙רֶץ֙
בְּרֹ֣אשׁ דַּלִּ֔ים
וְדֶ֥רֶךְ עֲנָוִ֖ים יַטּ֑וּ
וְאִ֣ישׁ וְאָבִ֗יו יֵֽלְכוּ֙ אֶל־הַֽנַּעֲרָ֔ה
לְמַ֥עַן חַלֵּ֖ל אֶת־שֵׁ֥ם קׇדְשִֽׁי׃
8 וְעַל־בְּגָדִ֣ים חֲבֻלִ֔ים
יַטּ֖וּ אֵ֣צֶל כׇּל־מִזְבֵּ֑חַ
וְיֵ֤ין עֲנוּשִׁים֙
יִשְׁתּ֔וּ בֵּ֖ית אֱלֹהֵיהֶֽם׃
9 וְאָ֨נֹכִ֜י
הִשְׁמַ֤דְתִּי אֶת־הָֽאֱמֹרִי֙ מִפְּנֵיהֶ֔ם
אֲשֶׁ֨ר כְּגֹ֤בַהּ אֲרָזִים֙ גׇּבְה֔וֹ
וְחָסֹ֥ן ה֖וּא כָּֽאַלּוֹנִ֑ים
וָֽאַשְׁמִ֤יד פִּרְיוֹ֙ מִמַּ֔עַל
וְשׇׁרָשָׁ֖יו מִתָּֽחַת׃
10 וְאָנֹכִ֛י
הֶעֱלֵ֥יתִי אֶתְכֶ֖ם מֵאֶ֣רֶץ מִצְרָ֑יִם
וָאוֹלֵ֨ךְ אֶתְכֶ֤ם בַּמִּדְבָּר֙ אַרְבָּעִ֣ים שָׁנָ֔ה
לָרֶ֖שֶׁת אֶת־אֶ֥רֶץ הָאֱמֹרִֽי׃
11 וָאָקִ֤ים מִבְּנֵיכֶם֙ לִנְבִיאִ֔ים
וּמִבַּחוּרֵיכֶ֖ם לִנְזִרִ֑ים
הַאַ֥ף אֵֽין־זֹ֛את בְּנֵ֥י יִשְׂרָאֵ֖ל
נְאֻם־יְהֹוָֽה׃
12 וַתַּשְׁק֥וּ אֶת־הַנְּזִרִ֖ים יָ֑יִן
וְעַל־הַנְּבִיאִים֙ צִוִּיתֶ֣ם לֵאמֹ֔ר לֹ֖א תִּנָּבְאֽוּ׃
13 הִנֵּ֛ה אָנֹכִ֥י מֵעִ֖יק תַּחְתֵּיכֶ֑ם
כַּאֲשֶׁ֤ר תָּעִיק֙ הָעֲגָלָ֔ה
הַֽמְלֵאָ֥ה לָ֖הּ עָמִֽיר׃
14 וְאָבַ֤ד מָנוֹס֙ מִקָּ֔ל
וְחָזָ֖ק לֹא־יְאַמֵּ֣ץ כֹּח֑וֹ
וְגִבּ֖וֹר לֹא־יְמַלֵּ֥ט נַפְשֽׁוֹ׃
15 וְתֹפֵ֤שׂ הַקֶּ֙שֶׁת֙ לֹ֣א יַעֲמֹ֔ד
וְקַ֥ל בְּרַגְלָ֖יו לֹ֣א יְמַלֵּ֑ט

ᵃ-ᵃ Understanding sho'afim as equivalent to shafim. Emendation yields: "Who crush on the ground / The heads of the poor, / And push off the road / The humble of the land"; cf. Job 24.4.
ᵇ-ᵇ Meaning of verse uncertain; alternatively: "I will slow your movements / As a threshing sledge (cf. Isa. 28.27–28) is slowed / When clogged by cut grain."

Nor the horseman save his life.

16Even the most stouthearted warrior

Shall run away unarmed^c that day

—declares the Lord.

3 Hear this word, O people of Israel,

That the Lord has spoken concerning you,

Concerning the whole family that I brought

    up from the land of Egypt:

2You alone have I singled out

Of all the families of the earth—

That is why I will call you to account

For all your iniquities.

3Can two walk together

Without having met?

4Does a lion roar in the forest

When he has no prey?

Does a great beast let out a cry from its den

Without having made a capture?

5Does a bird drop on the ground—in a trap—

With no snare there?

Does a trap spring up from the ground

Unless it has caught something?

6When a ram's horn is sounded in a town,

Do the people not take alarm?

Can misfortune come to a town

If the Lord has not caused it?

7Indeed, my Lord God does nothing

Without having revealed His purpose

To His servants the prophets.

8A lion has roared,

Who can but fear?

My Lord God has spoken,

Who can but prophesy?

9Proclaim in the fortresses of Ashdod^a

And in the fortresses of the land of Egypt!

---

c *Lit. "naked."*

a *Septuagint reads "Assyria."*

וְרֹכֵ֣ב הַסּ֔וּס לֹ֥א יְמַלֵּ֖ט נַפְשֽׁוֹ׃

16 וְאַמִּ֥יץ לִבּ֖וֹ בַּגִּבּוֹרִ֑ים

עָר֛וֹם יָנ֥וּס בַּיּוֹם־הַה֖וּא

נְאֻם־יְהֹוָֽה׃ פ

ג שִׁמְע֞וּ אֶת־הַדָּבָ֣ר הַזֶּ֗ה

אֲשֶׁ֨ר דִּבֶּ֧ר יְהֹוָ֛ה עֲלֵיכֶ֖ם בְּנֵ֣י יִשְׂרָאֵ֑ל

עַ֚ל כׇּל־הַמִּשְׁפָּחָ֔ה אֲשֶׁ֥ר הֶעֱלֵ֖יתִי מֵאֶ֥רֶץ

מִצְרַ֖יִם לֵאמֹֽר׃

2 רַ֚ק אֶתְכֶ֣ם יָדַ֔עְתִּי

מִכֹּ֖ל מִשְׁפְּח֣וֹת הָאֲדָמָ֑ה

עַל־כֵּן֙ אֶפְקֹ֣ד עֲלֵיכֶ֔ם

אֵ֖ת כׇּל־עֲוֺנֹֽתֵיכֶֽם׃

3 הֲיֵֽלְכ֥וּ שְׁנַ֖יִם יַחְדָּ֑ו

בִּלְתִּ֖י אִם־נוֹעָֽדוּ׃

4 הֲיִשְׁאַ֤ג אַרְיֵה֙ בַּיַּ֔עַר

וְטֶ֖רֶף אֵ֣ין ל֑וֹ

הֲיִתֵּ֨ן כְּפִ֤יר קוֹלוֹ֙ מִמְּעֹ֣נָת֔וֹ

בִּלְתִּ֖י אִם־לָכָֽד׃

5 הֲתִפֹּ֤ל צִפּוֹר֙ עַל־פַּ֣ח הָאָ֔רֶץ

וּמוֹקֵ֖שׁ אֵ֣ין לָ֑הּ

הֲיַֽעֲלֶה־פַּח֙ מִן־הָ֣אֲדָמָ֔ה

וְלָכ֖וֹד לֹ֥א יִלְכּֽוֹד׃

6 אִם־יִתָּקַ֤ע שׁוֹפָר֙ בְּעִ֔יר

וְעָ֖ם לֹ֣א יֶחֱרָ֑דוּ

אִם־תִּהְיֶ֤ה רָעָה֙ בְּעִ֔יר

וַיהֹוָ֖ה לֹ֥א עָשָֽׂה׃

7 כִּ֣י לֹ֧א יַעֲשֶׂ֛ה אֲדֹנָ֥י יֱהֹוִ֖ה דָּבָ֑ר

כִּ֚י אִם־גָּלָ֣ה סוֹד֔וֹ

אֶל־עֲבָדָ֖יו הַנְּבִיאִֽים׃

8 אַרְיֵ֥ה שָׁאָ֖ג

מִ֣י לֹ֣א יִירָ֑א

אֲדֹנָ֤י יֱהֹוִה֙ דִּבֶּ֔ר

מִ֖י לֹ֥א יִנָּבֵֽא׃

9 הַשְׁמִ֙יעוּ֙ עַל־אַרְמְנ֣וֹת בְּאַשְׁדּ֔וֹד

וְעַֽל־אַרְמְנ֖וֹת בְּאֶ֣רֶץ מִצְרָ֑יִם

Say:
Gather on the hill[b] of Samaria
And witness the great outrages within her
And the oppression in her midst.
[10]They are incapable of doing right
     —declares the LORD;
They store up lawlessness and rapine
In their fortresses.
[11]Assuredly,
Thus said my Lord GOD:
An enemy, all about the land!
He shall strip you of your splendor,
And your fortresses shall be plundered.
[12]Thus said the LORD:
As a shepherd rescues from the lion's jaws
Two shank bones or the tip of an ear,
So shall the Israelites escape
Who dwell in Samaria—
With the leg[c] of a bed or the head[c] of a couch.

[13]Hear [this], and warn the House of Jacob
  —says my Lord GOD, the God of Hosts—
[14]That when I punish Israel for its transgres-
  sions,
I will wreak judgment on the altar[d] of Bethel,
And the horns of the altar shall be cut off
And shall fall to the ground.
[15]I will wreck the winter palace
Together with the summer palace;
The ivory palaces shall be demolished,
And the great houses shall be destroyed
     —declares the LORD.

4 Hear this word, you cows of Bashan
On the hill of Samaria—
Who defraud the poor,
Who rob the needy;

וְאָמְרוּ
הֵאָסְפוּ עַל־הָרֵי שֹׁמְרֹון
וּרְאוּ מְהוּמֹת רַבֹּות בְּתֹוכָהּ
וַעֲשׁוּקִים בְּקִרְבָּהּ׃
10 וְלֹא־יָדְעוּ עֲשֹׂות־נְכֹחָה
נְאֻם־יְהוָה
הָאֹוצְרִים חָמָס וָשֹׁד
בְּאַרְמְנֹותֵיהֶם׃ פ
11 לָכֵן
כֹּה אָמַר אֲדֹנָי יְהוִה
צַר וּסְבִיב הָאָרֶץ
וְהֹורִד מִמֵּךְ עֻזֵּךְ
וְנָבֹזּוּ אַרְמְנֹותָיִךְ׃
12 כֹּה אָמַר יְהוָה
כַּאֲשֶׁר יַצִּיל הָרֹעֶה מִפִּי הָאֲרִי
שְׁתֵּי כְרָעַיִם אֹו בְדַל־אֹזֶן
כֵּן יִנָּצְלוּ בְּנֵי יִשְׂרָאֵל
הַיֹּשְׁבִים בְּשֹׁמְרֹון
בִּפְאַת מִטָּה וּבִדְמֶשֶׁק עָרֶשׂ׃

13 שִׁמְעוּ וְהָעִידוּ בְּבֵית יַעֲקֹב
נְאֻם־אֲדֹנָי יְהוִה אֱלֹהֵי הַצְּבָאֹות׃
14 כִּי בְּיֹום פָּקְדִי פִשְׁעֵי־יִשְׂרָאֵל עָלָיו
וּפָקַדְתִּי עַל־מִזְבְּחֹות בֵּית־אֵל
וְנִגְדְּעוּ קַרְנֹות הַמִּזְבֵּחַ
וְנָפְלוּ לָאָרֶץ׃
15 וְהִכֵּיתִי בֵית־הַחֹרֶף
עַל־בֵּית הַקָּיִץ
וְאָבְדוּ בָּתֵּי הַשֵּׁן
וְסָפוּ בָּתִּים רַבִּים
נְאֻם־יְהוָה׃ ס

ד שִׁמְעוּ הַדָּבָר הַזֶּה פָּרֹות הַבָּשָׁן
אֲשֶׁר בְּהַר שֹׁמְרֹון
הָעֹשְׁקֹות דַּלִּים
הָרֹצְצֹות אֶבְיֹונִים

---

b *Heb. plural; but cf. 4.1; 6.1.*
c *Meaning of Heb. uncertain.*
d *Heb. plural, but cf. "altar" in next line.*

Who say to your[a] husbands,
"Bring, and let's carouse!"

²My Lord GOD swears by His holiness:
Behold, days are coming upon you
[b-]When you will be carried off in baskets,
And, to the last one, in fish baskets,
³And taken out [of the city]—
Each one through a breach straight ahead—
And flung on the refuse heap[-b]
          —declares the LORD.

⁴Come to Bethel and transgress;
To Gilgal, and transgress even more:
Present your sacrifices the next morning
And your tithes on the third day;
⁵And burn a thank offering of leavened
  bread;[c]
And proclaim freewill offerings loudly.
For you love that sort of thing, O Israelites
          —declares my Lord GOD.

⁶I, on My part, have given you
Cleanness of teeth in all your towns,
And lack of food in all your settlements.
Yet you did not turn back to Me
          —declares the LORD.

⁷I therefore withheld the rain from you
Three months before harvesttime:
I would make it rain on one town
And not on another;
One field would be rained upon
While another on which it did not rain
Would wither.
⁸So two or three towns would wander
To a single town to drink water,
But their thirst would not be slaked.
Yet you did not turn back to Me
          —declares the LORD.

⁹I scourged you with blight and mildew;
Repeatedly[b] your gardens and vineyards,

הָאֹמְרֹת לַאֲדֹנֵיהֶם
הָבִיאָה וְנִשְׁתֶּה:
² נִשְׁבַּע אֲדֹנָי יְהוִה בְּקָדְשׁוֹ
כִּי הִנֵּה יָמִים בָּאִים עֲלֵיכֶם
וְנִשָּׂא אֶתְכֶם בְּצִנּוֹת
וְאַחֲרִיתְכֶן בְּסִירוֹת דּוּגָה:
³ וּפְרָצִים תֵּצֶאנָה
אִשָּׁה נֶגְדָּהּ
וְהִשְׁלַכְתֶּנָה הַהַרְמוֹנָה
נְאֻם־יְהוָה:
⁴ בֹּאוּ בֵית־אֵל וּפִשְׁעוּ
הַגִּלְגָּל הַרְבּוּ לִפְשֹׁעַ
וְהָבִיאוּ לַבֹּקֶר זִבְחֵיכֶם
לִשְׁלֹשֶׁת יָמִים מַעְשְׂרֹתֵיכֶם:
⁵ וְקַטֵּר מֵחָמֵץ תּוֹדָה
וְקִרְאוּ נְדָבוֹת הַשְׁמִיעוּ
כִּי כֵן אֲהַבְתֶּם בְּנֵי יִשְׂרָאֵל
נְאֻם אֲדֹנָי יְהוִה:
⁶ וְגַם־אֲנִי נָתַתִּי לָכֶם
נִקְיוֹן שִׁנַּיִם בְּכָל־עָרֵיכֶם
וְחֹסֶר לֶחֶם בְּכֹל מְקוֹמֹתֵיכֶם
וְלֹא־שַׁבְתֶּם עָדַי
נְאֻם־יְהוָה:
⁷ וְגַם אָנֹכִי מָנַעְתִּי מִכֶּם אֶת־הַגֶּשֶׁם
בְּעוֹד שְׁלֹשָׁה חֳדָשִׁים לַקָּצִיר
וְהִמְטַרְתִּי עַל־עִיר אֶחָת
וְעַל־עִיר אַחַת לֹא אַמְטִיר
חֶלְקָה אַחַת תִּמָּטֵר
וְחֶלְקָה אֲשֶׁר־לֹא־תַמְטִיר עָלֶיהָ
תִּיבָשׁ:
⁸ וְנָעוּ שְׁתַּיִם שָׁלֹשׁ עָרִים
אֶל־עִיר אַחַת לִשְׁתּוֹת מַיִם
וְלֹא יִשְׂבָּעוּ
וְלֹא־שַׁבְתֶּם עָדַי
נְאֻם־יְהוָה:
⁹ הִכֵּיתִי אֶתְכֶם בַּשִּׁדָּפוֹן וּבַיֵּרָקוֹן
הַרְבּוֹת גַּנּוֹתֵיכֶם וְכַרְמֵיכֶם

---

a   Heb. "their."
b-b Meaning of Heb. uncertain.
c   Cf. Lev. 7.12–14; where, however, the bread is not to be burned.

Your fig trees and olive trees
Were devoured by locusts.
Yet you did not turn back to Me
    —declares the LORD.

10 I sent against you pestilence
In the manner of Egypt;^d
I slew your young men with the sword,
Together with your captured horses,
And I made the stench of your armies
Rise in your very nostrils.
Yet you did not turn back to Me
    —declares the LORD.

11 I have wrought destruction among you
As when God destroyed Sodom and Gomor-
    rah;
You have become like a brand plucked from
    burning.
Yet you have not turned back to Me
    —declares the LORD.

12 Assuredly,
e-Because I am doing that to you,-e
Even so will I act toward you, O Israel—
Prepare to meet your God, O Israel!

13 Behold,
He who formed the mountains,
And created the wind,
And has told man what His wish^b is,
Who turns blackness^f into daybreak,
And treads upon the high places of the
    earth—
His name is the LORD, the God of Hosts.

5 Hear this word which I intone
As a dirge over you, O House of Israel:
2 Fallen, not to rise again,

וּתְאֵנֵיכֶ֣ם וְזֵיתֵיכֶ֗ם
יֹאכַ֖ל הַגָּזָ֑ם
וְלֹֽא־שַׁבְתֶּ֥ם עָדַ֖י
נְאֻם־יְהוָֽה: ס

10 שִׁלַּ֨חְתִּי בָכֶ֥ם דֶּ֙בֶר֙
בְּדֶ֣רֶךְ מִצְרַ֔יִם
הָרַ֤גְתִּי בַחֶ֙רֶב֙ בַּח֣וּרֵיכֶ֔ם
עִ֖ם שְׁבִ֣י סֽוּסֵיכֶ֑ם
וָאַעֲלֶ֞ה בְּאֹ֤שׁ מַחֲנֵיכֶם֙
וּֽבְאַפְּכֶ֔ם
וְלֹֽא־שַׁבְתֶּ֥ם עָדַ֖י
נְאֻם־יְהוָֽה:

11 הָפַ֣כְתִּי בָכֶ֗ם
כְּמַהְפֵּכַ֤ת אֱלֹהִים֙ אֶת־סְדֹ֣ם וְאֶת־
עֲמֹרָ֔ה
וַתִּהְי֕וּ כְּא֖וּד מֻצָּ֣ל מִשְּׂרֵפָ֑ה
וְלֹֽא־שַׁבְתֶּ֥ם עָדַ֖י
נְאֻם־יְהוָֽה: ס

12 לָכֵ֕ן
כֹּ֥ה אֶֽעֱשֶׂה־לְּךָ֖ יִשְׂרָאֵ֑ל
עֵ֚קֶב כִּֽי־זֹ֣את אֶֽעֱשֶׂה־לָּ֔ךְ
הִכּ֥וֹן לִקְרַאת־אֱלֹהֶ֖יךָ יִשְׂרָאֵֽל:

13 כִּ֡י הִנֵּה֩
יוֹצֵ֨ר הָרִ֜ים
וּבֹרֵ֣א ר֗וּחַ
וּמַגִּ֤יד לְאָדָם֙ מַה־שֵּׂח֔וֹ
עֹשֵׂ֥ה שַׁ֙חַר֙ עֵיפָ֔ה
וְדֹרֵ֖ךְ עַל־בָּ֣מֳתֵי אָ֑רֶץ
יְהוָ֥ה אֱלֹהֵֽי־צְבָא֖וֹת שְׁמֽוֹ: ס

ה שִׁמְע֞וּ אֶת־הַדָּבָ֣ר הַזֶּ֗ה אֲשֶׁ֨ר אָנֹכִ֜י
נֹשֵׂ֧א
עֲלֵיכֶ֛ם קִינָ֖ה בֵּ֥ית יִשְׂרָאֵֽל:
2 נָפְלָה֙ לֹֽא־תוֹסִ֣יף ק֔וּם

---

d   *Alluding to the plagues at the time of the Exodus.*
e-e   *Emendation yields "Because you are acting thus toward Me."*
f   *Cf. Joel 2.2. Emendation yields "darkness"; cf. 5.8.*

Is Maiden Israel;
Abandoned on her soil
With none to lift her up.
³For thus said my Lord GOD
About the House of Israel:
The town that marches out a thousand strong
Shall have a hundred left,
And the one that marches out a hundred strong
Shall have but ten left.
⁴Thus said the LORD
To the House of Israel:
Seek Me, and you will live.
⁵Do not seek Bethel,
Nor go to Gilgal,
Nor cross over^a to Beer-sheba;
For Gilgal shall go into exile,
And Bethel shall become a delusion.
⁶Seek the LORD, and you will live,
^{b-}Else He will rush like fire upon-^b the House of Joseph
And consume Bethel^c with none to quench it.

⁷[Ah,] you who turn justice into wormwood
And hurl righteousness to the ground!
[Seek the LORD,]
⁸Who made the Pleiades and Orion,
Who turns deep darkness into dawn
And darkens day into night,
Who summons the waters of the sea
And pours them out upon the earth—
His name is the LORD!
⁹^{b-}It is He who hurls destruction upon strongholds,
So that ruin comes upon fortresses!^{-b}

¹⁰They hate the arbiter in the gate,
And detest him whose plea is just.

בְּתוּלַת יִשְׂרָאֵל
נִטְּשָׁה עַל־אַדְמָתָהּ
אֵין מְקִימָהּ:
³ כִּי כֹה אָמַר אֲדֹנָי יְהֹוִה
הָעִיר הַיֹּצֵאת אֶלֶף
תַּשְׁאִיר מֵאָה
וְהַיּוֹצֵאת מֵאָה
תַּשְׁאִיר עֲשָׂרָה
לְבֵית יִשְׂרָאֵל: ס
⁴ כִּי כֹה אָמַר יְהֹוָה
לְבֵית יִשְׂרָאֵל
דִּרְשׁוּנִי וִחְיוּ:
⁵ וְאַל־תִּדְרְשׁוּ בֵּית־אֵל
וְהַגִּלְגָּל לֹא תָבֹאוּ
וּבְאֵר שֶׁבַע לֹא תַעֲבֹרוּ
כִּי הַגִּלְגָּל גָּלֹה יִגְלֶה
וּבֵית־אֵל יִהְיֶה לְאָוֶן:
⁶ דִּרְשׁוּ אֶת־יְהֹוָה וִחְיוּ
פֶּן־יִצְלַח כָּאֵשׁ בֵּית יוֹסֵף
וְאָכְלָה וְאֵין־מְכַבֶּה לְבֵית־אֵל:

⁷ הַהֹפְכִים לְלַעֲנָה מִשְׁפָּט
וּצְדָקָה לָאָרֶץ הִנִּיחוּ:
⁸ עֹשֵׂה כִימָה וּכְסִיל
וְהֹפֵךְ לַבֹּקֶר צַלְמָוֶת
וְיוֹם לַיְלָה הֶחְשִׁיךְ
הַקּוֹרֵא לְמֵי־הַיָּם
וַיִּשְׁפְּכֵם עַל־פְּנֵי הָאָרֶץ
יְהֹוָה שְׁמוֹ: ס
⁹ הַמַּבְלִיג שֹׁד עַל־עָז
וְשֹׁד עַל־מִבְצָר יָבוֹא:

¹⁰ שָׂנְאוּ בַשַּׁעַר מוֹכִיחַ
וְדֹבֵר תָּמִים יְתָעֵבוּ:

_a   *I.e., into Judah; cf. 1 Kings 19.3.*
_{b-b}   *Meaning of Heb. uncertain.*
_c   *Septuagint reads "the House of Israel."*

11Assuredly,

Because you *b*-impose a tax-*b* on the poor
And exact from him a levy of grain,
You have built houses of hewn stone,
But you shall not live in them;
You have planted delightful vineyards,
But shall not drink their wine.
12For I have noted how many are your crimes,
And how countless your sins—
You enemies of the righteous,
You takers of bribes,
You who subvert in the gate
The cause of the needy!

13Assuredly,

At such a time the prudent man keeps silent,
For it is an evil time.

14Seek good and not evil,
That you may live,
And that the LORD, the God of Hosts,
May truly be with you,
As you think.
15Hate evil and love good,
And establish justice in the gate;
Perhaps the LORD, the God of Hosts,
Will be gracious to the remnant of Joseph.

16Assuredly,
Thus said the LORD,
My Lord, the God of Hosts:
In every square there shall be lamenting,
In every street cries of "Ah, woe!"
And the farm hand shall be
Called to mourn,
And those skilled in wailing
To lament;

11 לָכֵן
יַ֫עַן בּוֹשַׁסְכֶ֣ם עַל־דָּ֗ל
וּמַשְׂאַת־בַּר֙ תִּקְח֣וּ מִמֶּ֔נּוּ
בָּתֵּ֥י גָזִ֛ית בְּנִיתֶ֖ם
וְלֹא־תֵ֣שְׁבוּ בָ֑ם
כַּרְמֵי־חֶ֣מֶד נְטַעְתֶּ֔ם
וְלֹ֥א תִשְׁתּ֖וּ אֶת־יֵינָֽם׃
12 כִּ֤י יָדַ֙עְתִּי֙ רַבִּ֣ים פִּשְׁעֵיכֶ֔ם
וַעֲצֻמִ֖ים חַטֹּֽאתֵיכֶ֑ם
צֹרְרֵ֤י צַדִּיק֙
לֹ֣קְחֵי כֹ֔פֶר
וְאֶבְיוֹנִ֖ים
בַּשַּׁ֥עַר הִטּֽוּ׃
13 לָכֵ֗ן
הַמַּשְׂכִּ֛יל בָּעֵ֥ת הַהִ֖יא יִדֹּ֑ם
כִּ֛י עֵ֥ת רָעָ֖ה הִֽיא׃
14 דִּרְשׁוּ־ט֥וֹב וְאַל־רָ֖ע
לְמַ֣עַן תִּֽחְי֑וּ
וִיהִי־כֵ֞ן
יְהוָ֧ה אֱלֹהֵֽי־צְבָא֛וֹת אִתְּכֶ֖ם
כַּאֲשֶׁ֥ר אֲמַרְתֶּֽם׃
15 שִׂנְאוּ־רָע֙ וְאֶ֣הֱבוּ ט֔וֹב
וְהַצִּ֥יגוּ בַשַּׁ֖עַר מִשְׁפָּ֑ט
אוּלַ֗י יֶֽחֱנַ֛ן יְהוָ֥ה אֱלֹהֵֽי־צְבָא֖וֹת
שְׁאֵרִ֥ית יוֹסֵֽף׃ ס
16 לָכֵ֡ן
כֹּֽה־אָמַ֣ר יְהוָה֩
אֱלֹהֵ֨י צְבָא֜וֹת אֲדֹנָ֗י
בְּכָל־רְחֹב֣וֹת מִסְפֵּ֔ד
וּבְכָל־חוּצ֖וֹת יֹאמְר֣וּ הוֹ־ה֑וֹ
וְקָרְא֥וּ אִכָּ֛ר
אֶל־אֵ֖בֶל
וּמִסְפֵּ֑ד
אֶל־י֥וֹדְעֵי נֶֽהִי׃

¹⁷For there shall be lamenting
In every vineyard, too,
When I pass through your midst
           —said the Lord.

¹⁸Ah, you who wish
For the day of the Lord!
Why should you want
The day of the Lord?
It shall be darkness, not light!—
¹⁹As if a man should run from a lion
And be attacked by a bear;
Or if he got indoors,
Should lean his hand on the wall
And be bitten by a snake!
²⁰Surely the day of the Lord shall be
Not light, but darkness,
Blackest night without a glimmer.

²¹I loathe, I spurn your festivals,
I am not appeased by your solemn assemblies.
²²If you offer Me burnt offerings—or your
   meal offerings—
I will not accept them;
I will pay no heed
To your gifts of fatlings.
²³Spare Me the sound of your hymns,
And let Me not hear the music of your lutes.
²⁴But let justice well up like water,
Righteousness like an unfailing stream.
²⁵Did you offer sacrifice and oblation to Me
Those forty years in the wilderness,
O House of Israel?

^{26d}And you shall carry off your "king"—
Sikkuth^e and Kiyyun,^e
The images you have made for yourselves
Of your astral deity—

---

d   Vv. 26–27 would read well after 6.14.
*e   Two Akkadian names applied to Saturn, here deliberately
    pointed with the vowels of Heb. shiqquṣ, "detestable thing."*

17 וּבְכָל־כְּרָמִים
מִסְפֵּד
כִּי־אֶעֱבֹר בְּקִרְבְּךָ
אָמַר יְהֹוָה: ס

18 הוֹי הַמִּתְאַוִּים
אֶת־יוֹם יְהֹוָה
לָמָּה־זֶּה לָכֶם
יוֹם יְהֹוָה
הוּא־חֹשֶׁךְ וְלֹא־אוֹר:
19 כַּאֲשֶׁר יָנוּס אִישׁ מִפְּנֵי* הָאֲרִי
וּפְגָעוֹ הַדֹּב
וּבָא הַבַּיִת
וְסָמַךְ יָדוֹ עַל־הַקִּיר
וּנְשָׁכוֹ הַנָּחָשׁ:
20 הֲלֹא־חֹשֶׁךְ יוֹם יְהֹוָה
וְלֹא־אוֹר
וְאָפֵל וְלֹא־נֹגַהּ לוֹ:

21 שָׂנֵאתִי מָאַסְתִּי חַגֵּיכֶם
וְלֹא אָרִיחַ בְּעַצְּרֹתֵיכֶם:
22 כִּי אִם־תַּעֲלוּ־לִי עֹלוֹת וּמִנְחֹתֵיכֶם
לֹא אֶרְצֶה
וְשֶׁלֶם מְרִיאֵיכֶם
לֹא אַבִּיט:
23 הָסֵר מֵעָלַי הֲמוֹן שִׁרֶיךָ
וְזִמְרַת נְבָלֶיךָ לֹא אֶשְׁמָע:
24 וְיִגַּל כַּמַּיִם מִשְׁפָּט
וּצְדָקָה כְּנַחַל אֵיתָן:
25 הַזְּבָחִים וּמִנְחָה הִגַּשְׁתֶּם־לִי
בַּמִּדְבָּר אַרְבָּעִים שָׁנָה
בֵּית יִשְׂרָאֵל:

26 וּנְשָׂאתֶם
אֵת סִכּוּת מַלְכְּכֶם וְאֵת כִּיּוּן
צַלְמֵיכֶם כּוֹכַב אֱלֹהֵיכֶם
אֲשֶׁר עֲשִׂיתֶם לָכֶם:

v. 19. סבירין ומטעין "מפי"

27As I drive you into exile beyond Damascus
—Said the Lord, whose
name is God of Hosts.*f*

27 וְהִגְלֵיתִ֥י אֶתְכֶ֖ם מֵהָ֣לְאָה לְדַמָּ֑שֶׂק
אָמַ֧ר יְהֹוָ֛ה אֱלֹהֵֽי־צְבָא֖וֹת שְׁמֽוֹ׃ פ

6 Ah, you who are at ease in Zion*a*
And confident on the hill of Samaria,
You notables of the leading nation
On whom the House of Israel *b*-pin their
    hopes:-*b*
2Cross over to Calneh and see,
Go from there to Great Hamath,
And go down to Gath of the Philistines:
Are [you] better than those kingdoms,
c-Or is their territory larger than yours?-*c*
3*d*-Yet you ward off [the thought of] a day of
    woe
And convene a session of lawlessness.-*d*
4They lie on ivory beds,
Lolling on their couches,
Feasting on lambs from the flock
And on calves from the stalls.
5*d*-They hum snatches of song
To the tune of the lute—
They account themselves musicians-*d* like
    David.
6They drink [straight] from the wine bowls
And anoint themselves with the choicest
    oils—
But they are not concerned about the ruin of
    Joseph.
7Assuredly, right soon
They shall head the column of exiles;
They shall loll no more at festive meals.

ו 1 ה֤וֹי הַשַּׁאֲנַנִּים֙ בְּצִיּ֔וֹן
וְהַבֹּטְחִ֖ים בְּהַ֣ר שֹׁמְר֑וֹן
נְקֻבֵי֙ רֵאשִׁ֣ית הַגּוֹיִ֔ם
וּבָ֥אוּ לָהֶ֖ם בֵּ֥ית יִשְׂרָאֵֽל׃
2 עִבְר֤וּ כַֽלְנֵה֙ וּרְא֔וּ
וּלְכ֥וּ מִשָּׁ֖ם חֲמַ֣ת רַבָּ֑ה
וּרְד֖וּ גַת־פְּלִשְׁתִּ֑ים
הֲטוֹבִים֙ מִן־הַמַּמְלָכ֣וֹת הָאֵ֔לֶּה
אִם־רַ֥ב גְּבוּלָ֖ם מִגְּבֻלְכֶֽם׃
3 הַֽמְנַדִּ֖ים לְי֣וֹם רָ֑ע
וַתַּגִּישׁ֖וּן שֶׁ֥בֶת חָמָֽס׃
4 הַשֹּֽׁכְבִים֙ עַל־מִטּ֣וֹת שֵׁ֔ן
וּסְרֻחִ֖ים עַל־עַרְשׂוֹתָ֑ם
וְאֹכְלִ֤ים כָּרִים֙ מִצֹּ֔אן
וַעֲגָלִ֖ים מִתּ֥וֹךְ מַרְבֵּֽק׃
5 הַפֹּֽרְטִ֖ים עַל־פִּ֣י הַנָּ֑בֶל
כְּדָוִ֕יד
חָשְׁב֥וּ לָהֶ֖ם כְּלֵי־שִֽׁיר׃
6 הַשֹּׁתִ֤ים בְּמִזְרְקֵי֙ יַ֔יִן
וְרֵאשִׁ֥ית שְׁמָנִ֖ים יִמְשָׁ֑חוּ
וְלֹ֥א נֶחְל֖וּ עַל־שֵׁ֥בֶר יוֹסֵֽף׃
7 לָכֵ֥ן עַתָּ֛ה
יִגְל֖וּ בְּרֹ֣אשׁ גֹּלִ֑ים
וְסָ֖ר מִרְזַ֥ח סְרוּחִֽים׃ פ

---

f   I.e., who is Lord of all the astral bodies.

a   Emendation yields "Joseph," cf. v. 6, and 5.6, 15, where "Joseph"
       denotes the northern kingdom.
b-b Taking ba' l- as synonymous with ba' 'ad; see Isa. 45.24 and
       note i-i.
c-c Emendation yields "Or is your territory larger than theirs?"
d-d Meaning of Heb. uncertain.

⁸My Lord GOD swears by Himself:
I loathe ᵉ-the Pride of Jacob,-ᵉ
And I detest his fortresses.
I will declare forfeit city and inhabitants alike
—declares the LORD, the God of Hosts.

⁹If ten people are left in one house, they shall
die. ¹⁰ᵈ-And if someone's kinsman—who is to
burn incense for him—comes to carry the remains out of a house,-ᵈ and he calls to the one
at the rear of the house, "Are there any alive besides you?" he will answer, "No, none." And he
will say, "Hush!"—so that no one may utter the
name of the LORD.

¹¹For the LORD will command,
And the great house shall be smashed to bits,
And the little house to splinters.

¹²Can horses gallop on a rock?
ᶠ-Can it be plowed with oxen?-ᶠ
Yet you have turned justice into poison weed
And the fruit of righteousness to wormwood.
¹³[Ah,] those who are so happy about
    Lo-dabar,ᵍ
Who exult, "By our might
We have captured Karnaim"!ᵍ
¹⁴But I, O House of Israel,
Will raise up a nation against you
—declares the LORD, the God of Hosts—
Who will harass you from Lebo-Hamath
To the Wadi Arabah.

7 This is what my Lord GOD showed me: He
was creating [a plague of] locusts at the time
when the late-sown crops were beginning to
sprout—ᵃ-the late-sown crops after the king's

⁸נִשְׁבַּ֛ע אֲדֹנָ֥י יְהוִ֖ה בְּנַפְשׁ֑וֹ
נְאֻם־יְהוָה֙ אֱלֹהֵ֣י צְבָא֔וֹת
מְתָאֵ֤ב אָֽנֹכִי֙ אֶת־גְּא֣וֹן יַעֲקֹ֔ב
וְאַרְמְנֹתָ֖יו שָׂנֵ֑אתִי
וְהִסְגַּרְתִּ֖י עִ֥יר וּמְלֹאָֽהּ׃
⁹וְהָיָ֗ה אִם־יִוָּ֨תְר֜וּ עֲשָׂרָ֧ה אֲנָשִׁ֛ים בְּבַ֥יִת
אֶחָ֖ד וָמֵֽתוּ׃ ¹⁰וּנְשָׂא֞וֹ דּוֹד֣וֹ וּמְסָרְפ֗וֹ
לְהוֹצִ֣יא עֲצָמִים֮ מִן־הַבַּיִת֒ וְאָמַ֞ר לַאֲשֶׁ֨ר
בְּיַרְכְּתֵ֤י הַבַּ֙יִת֙ הַע֣וֹד עִמָּ֔ךְ וְאָמַ֖ר אָ֑פֶס
וְאָמַ֣ר הָ֔ס כִּ֛י לֹ֥א לְהַזְכִּ֖יר בְּשֵׁ֥ם יְהוָֽה׃
¹¹כִּֽי־הִנֵּ֤ה יְהוָה֙ מְצַוֶּ֔ה
וְהִכָּ֛ה הַבַּ֥יִת הַגָּד֖וֹל רְסִיסִ֑ים
וְהַבַּ֥יִת הַקָּטֹ֖ן בְּקִעִֽים׃

¹²הַיְרֻצ֤וּן בַּסֶּ֙לַע֙ סוּסִ֔ים
אִֽם־יַחֲר֖וֹשׁ בַּבְּקָרִ֑ים
כִּֽי־הֲפַכְתֶּ֤ם לְרֹאשׁ֙ מִשְׁפָּ֔ט
וּפְרִ֥י צְדָקָ֖ה לְלַעֲנָֽה׃
¹³הַשְּׂמֵחִ֖ים לְלֹ֣א דָבָ֑ר
הָאֹ֣מְרִ֔ים הֲל֣וֹא בְחָזְקֵ֔נוּ
לָקַ֥חְנוּ לָ֖נוּ קַרְנָֽיִם׃
¹⁴כִּ֡י הִנְנִי֩ מֵקִ֨ים עֲלֵיכֶ֜ם בֵּ֣ית יִשְׂרָאֵ֗ל
נְאֻם־יְהוָ֖ה אֱלֹהֵ֣י הַצְּבָא֑וֹת
גּ֔וֹי
וְלָחֲצ֣וּ אֶתְכֶ֔ם מִלְּב֥וֹא חֲמָ֖ת
עַד־נַ֥חַל הָעֲרָבָֽה׃ ס

ז כֹּ֤ה הִרְאַ֙נִי֙ אֲדֹנָ֣י יְהוִ֔ה וְהִנֵּה֙ יוֹצֵ֣ר גֹּבַ֔י
בִּתְחִלַּ֖ת עֲל֣וֹת הַלָּ֑קֶשׁ וְהִנֵּה־לֶ֖קֶשׁ אַחַ֥ר

---

e-e   *A poetic designation of the northern kingdom.*
f-f   *Meaning of Heb. uncertain; emendation yields "Can one plow
the sea with oxen?"*
g   *Two towns east of the Jordan recovered for Israel by Jeroboam
II (see 2 Kings 14.25). For Lo-dabar, cf. 2 Sam. 9.4, 5; 17.27;
for Karnaim, cf. Gen. 14.5.*

a-a   *Meaning of Heb. uncertain. The king's reaping of fodder
apparently occurred near the end of the rainy season, and
whatever the locust destroyed after that could not be replaced
for another year.*

reaping.-ᵃ ²When it had finished devouring the herbage in the land, I said, "O Lord GOD, pray forgive. How will Jacob survive? He is so small."
³The LORD relented concerning this. "It shall not come to pass," said the LORD.

⁴This is what the Lord GOD showed me: Lo, my Lord GOD was summoning ᵇ-to contend by-ᵇ fire which consumed the Great Deep and was consuming the fields. ⁵I said, "Oh, Lord GOD, refrain! How will Jacob survive? He is so small."
⁶The LORD relented concerning this. "That shall not come to pass, either," said my Lord GOD.

⁷This is what He showed me: He was standing on a wall ᶜ-checked with a plumb line-ᶜ and He was holding a plumb line.ᵈ ⁸And the LORD asked me, "What do you see, Amos?" "A plumb line,"ᵈ I replied. And my Lord declared, "I am going to apply a plumb lineᵈ to My people Israel; I will pardon them no more. ⁹The shrines of Isaac shall be laid waste, and the sanctuaries of Israel reduced to ruins; and I will turn upon the House of Jeroboam with the sword."

¹⁰Amaziah, the priest of Bethel, sent this message to King Jeroboam of Israel: "Amos is conspiring against you within the House of Israel. The country cannot endure the things he is saying. ¹¹For Amos has said, 'Jeroboam shall die by the sword, and Israel shall be exiled from its soil.'"

¹²Amaziah also said to Amos, "Seer, off with you to the land of Judah! ᵉ-Earn your living-ᵉ there, and do your prophesying there. ¹³But don't ever prophesy again at Bethel; for it is a king's sanctuary and a royal palace." ¹⁴Amos answered Amaziah: "I am not a prophet,ᶠ and I am not a prophet's disciple. I am a cattle breederᵍ and a tender of sycamore figs. ¹⁵But

---

b-b *Emendation yields "flaming."*
c-c *Or "destined for the pickax"; meaning of Heb. uncertain.*
d *Or "pickax"; meaning of Heb. uncertain.*
e-e *Lit. "eat bread."*
f *I.e., by profession.*
g *Meaning of Heb. uncertain; emendation yields "sheep breeder"; cf. the next verse and 1.1.*

גִּזֵּי הַמֶּלֶךְ: ²וְהָיָה אִם־כִּלָּה לֶאֱכוֹל אֶת־
עֵשֶׂב הָאָרֶץ וָאֹמַר אֲדֹנָי יְהוִה סְלַח־נָא
מִי יָקוּם יַעֲקֹב כִּי קָטֹן הוּא: ³נִחַם יְהוָה
עַל־זֹאת לֹא תִהְיֶה אָמַר יְהוָה:
⁴כֹּה הִרְאַנִי אֲדֹנָי יְהוִה וְהִנֵּה קֹרֵא לָרִב
בָּאֵשׁ אֲדֹנָי יְהוִה וַתֹּאכַל אֶת־תְּהוֹם רַבָּה
וְאָכְלָה אֶת־הַחֵלֶק: ⁵וָאֹמַר אֲדֹנָי יְהוִה
חֲדַל־נָא מִי יָקוּם יַעֲקֹב כִּי קָטֹן הוּא:
⁶נִחַם יְהוָה עַל־זֹאת גַּם־הִיא לֹא תִהְיֶה
אָמַר אֲדֹנָי יְהוִה: ס
⁷כֹּה הִרְאַנִי וְהִנֵּה אֲדֹנָי נִצָּב עַל־חוֹמַת
אֲנָךְ וּבְיָדוֹ אֲנָךְ: ⁸וַיֹּאמֶר יְהוָה אֵלַי
מָה־אַתָּה רֹאֶה עָמוֹס וָאֹמַר אֲנָךְ וַיֹּאמֶר
אֲדֹנָי הִנְנִי שָׂם אֲנָךְ בְּקֶרֶב עַמִּי יִשְׂרָאֵל
לֹא־אוֹסִיף עוֹד עֲבוֹר לוֹ: ⁹וְנָשַׁמּוּ בָּמוֹת
יִשְׂחָק וּמִקְדְּשֵׁי יִשְׂרָאֵל יֶחֱרָבוּ וְקַמְתִּי
עַל־בֵּית יָרָבְעָם בֶּחָרֶב: פ

¹⁰וַיִּשְׁלַח אֲמַצְיָה כֹּהֵן בֵּית־אֵל אֶל־
יָרָבְעָם מֶלֶךְ־יִשְׂרָאֵל לֵאמֹר קָשַׁר עָלֶיךָ
עָמוֹס בְּקֶרֶב בֵּית יִשְׂרָאֵל לֹא־תוּכַל
הָאָרֶץ לְהָכִיל אֶת־כָּל־דְּבָרָיו: ¹¹כִּי־כֹה
אָמַר עָמוֹס בַּחֶרֶב יָמוּת יָרָבְעָם וְיִשְׂרָאֵל
גָּלֹה יִגְלֶה מֵעַל אַדְמָתוֹ: ס
¹²וַיֹּאמֶר אֲמַצְיָה אֶל־עָמוֹס חֹזֶה לֵךְ
בְּרַח־לְךָ אֶל־אֶרֶץ יְהוּדָה וֶאֱכָל־שָׁם לֶחֶם
וְשָׁם תִּנָּבֵא: ¹³וּבֵית־אֵל לֹא־תוֹסִיף עוֹד
לְהִנָּבֵא כִּי מִקְדַּשׁ־מֶלֶךְ הוּא וּבֵית
מַמְלָכָה הוּא: ס ¹⁴וַיַּעַן עָמוֹס וַיֹּאמֶר
אֶל־אֲמַצְיָה לֹא־נָבִיא אָנֹכִי וְלֹא בֶן־נָבִיא
אָנֹכִי כִּי־בוֹקֵר אָנֹכִי וּבוֹלֵס שִׁקְמִים:

the LORD took me away from following the flock, and the LORD said to me, 'Go, prophesy to My people Israel.' [16]And so, hear the word of the LORD. You say I must not prophesy about the House of Israel or preach about the House of Isaac; [17]but this, I swear, is what the LORD said: Your wife shall ^h-play the harlot^-h in the town, your sons and daughters shall fall by the sword, and your land shall be divided up with a measuring line. And you yourself shall die on unclean soil;^i for Israel shall be exiled from its soil."

8 This is what my Lord GOD showed me: There was a basket of figs.^a [2]He said, "What do you see, Amos?" "A basket of figs," I replied. And the LORD said to me: "The ^b-hour of doom-^b has come for My people Israel; I will not pardon them again. [3]And the singing women of the palace shall howl on that day—declares my Lord GOD:

So many corpses
Left lying everywhere!
Hush!"

[4]Listen to this, you ^c-who devour the needy, annihilating the poor of the land,-^c [5]saying, "If only the new moon were over, so that we could sell grain; the sabbath, so that we could offer wheat for sale, ^d-using an *ephah* that is too small, and a shekel that is too big,-^d tilting a dishonest scale, [6]and selling grain refuse as grain! We will buy the poor for silver, the needy for a pair of sandals." [7]The LORD swears by^e the Pride of Jacob: "I will never forget any of their doings."

---

15 וַיִּקָּחֵ֤נִי יְהוָה֙ מֵאַחֲרֵ֣י הַצֹּ֔אן וַיֹּ֥אמֶר אֵלַ֖י יְהוָ֑ה לֵ֥ךְ הִנָּבֵ֖א אֶל־עַמִּ֥י יִשְׂרָאֵֽל׃ 16 וְעַתָּ֖ה שְׁמַ֣ע דְּבַר־יְהוָ֑ה אַתָּ֣ה אֹמֵ֗ר לֹ֤א תִנָּבֵא֙ עַל־יִשְׂרָאֵ֔ל וְלֹ֥א תַטִּ֖יף עַל־בֵּ֥ית יִשְׂחָֽק׃ 17 לָכֵ֞ן כֹּה־אָמַ֣ר יְהוָ֗ה אִשְׁתְּךָ֞ בָּעִ֣יר תִּזְנֶ֗ה וּבָנֶ֤יךָ וּבְנֹתֶ֙יךָ֙ בַּחֶ֣רֶב יִפֹּ֔לוּ וְאַדְמָתְךָ֖ בַּחֶ֣בֶל תְּחֻלָּ֑ק וְאַתָּ֗ה עַל־אֲדָמָ֤ה טְמֵאָה֙ תָּמ֔וּת וְיִ֨שְׂרָאֵ֔ל גָּלֹ֥ה יִגְלֶ֖ה מֵעַ֥ל אַדְמָתֽוֹ׃ ס

ח **8** כֹּ֥ה הִרְאַ֖נִי אֲדֹנָ֣י יְהוִ֑ה וְהִנֵּ֖ה כְּל֥וּב קָֽיִץ׃ 2 וַיֹּ֗אמֶר מָֽה־אַתָּ֤ה רֹאֶה֙ עָמ֔וֹס וָאֹמַ֖ר כְּל֣וּב קָ֑יִץ וַיֹּ֨אמֶר יְהוָ֜ה אֵלַ֗י בָּ֤א הַקֵּץ֙ אֶל־עַמִּ֣י יִשְׂרָאֵ֔ל לֹא־אוֹסִ֥יף ע֖וֹד עֲב֥וֹר לֽוֹ׃ 3 וְהֵילִ֜ילוּ שִׁיר֤וֹת הֵיכָל֙ בַּיּ֣וֹם הַה֔וּא נְאֻ֖ם אֲדֹנָ֣י יְהוִ֑ה רַ֣ב הַפֶּ֔גֶר בְּכָל־מָק֖וֹם הִשְׁלִ֥יךְ הָֽס׃ פ

4 שִׁמְעוּ־זֹ֕את הַשֹּׁאֲפִ֖ים אֶבְי֑וֹן וְלַשְׁבִּ֖ית עֲנִוֵּי־אָֽרֶץ׃ 5 לֵאמֹ֗ר מָתַ֞י יַעֲבֹ֤ר הַחֹ֙דֶשׁ֙ וְנַשְׁבִּ֣ירָה שֶּׁ֔בֶר וְהַשַּׁבָּ֖ת וְנִפְתְּחָה־בָּ֑ר לְהַקְטִ֤ין אֵיפָה֙ וּלְהַגְדִּ֣יל שֶׁ֔קֶל וּלְעַוֵּ֖ת מֹאזְנֵ֥י מִרְמָֽה׃ 6 לִקְנ֤וֹת בַּכֶּ֙סֶף֙ דַּלִּ֔ים וְאֶבְי֖וֹן בַּעֲב֣וּר נַעֲלָ֑יִם וּמַפַּ֥ל בַּ֖ר נַשְׁבִּֽיר׃ 7 נִשְׁבַּ֥ע יְהוָ֖ה בִּגְא֣וֹן יַעֲקֹ֑ב אִם־אֶשְׁכַּ֥ח לָנֶ֖צַח כָּל־מַעֲשֵׂיהֶֽם׃

---

h-h   Emendation yields "be ravished"; cf. Lam. 5.11.
i   Cf. Hos. 9.3 and note.

a   Heb. *qayiṣ*, lit. "summer fruit."
b-b   Heb. *qeṣ*.
c-c   Emendation yields "who on every new moon devour the needy, and on every sabbath the humble of the land"; cf. v. 5.
d-d   Giving short measures of grain, but using oversize weights for the silver received in payment.
e   Or "concerning"; cf. 6.8 with note.

8Shall not the earth shake for this
And all that dwell on it mourn?
Shall it not all rise like the Nile
And surge and subside like the Nile of Egypt?
9And in that day
     —declares my Lord GOD—
I will make the sun set at noon,
I will darken the earth on a sunny day.
10I will turn your festivals into mourning
And all your songs into dirges;
I will put sackcloth on all loins
And tonsures on every head.
I will make it*f* mourn as for an only child,
All*g* of it as on a bitter day.

11A time is coming—declares my Lord
GOD—when I will send a famine upon the land:
not a hunger for bread or a thirst for water, but
for hearing the words of the LORD. 12Men shall
wander from *h*-sea to sea-*h* and from north to
east to seek the word of the LORD, but they shall
not find it.

13In that day, the beautiful maidens and the
young men shall faint with thirst—
14Those who swear by the guilt of Samaria,
Saying, "As your god lives, Dan,"*i*
And "As the way to Beer-sheba lives"*j*—
They shall fall to rise no more.

9 I saw my LORD standing by the altar, and
He said: *a*-Strike the capitals so that the thresholds quake, and make an end of the first of them
all.-*a* And I will slay the last of them with the

8 הֲעַ֤ל זֹאת֙ לֹֽא־תִרְגַּ֣ז הָאָ֔רֶץ
וְאָבַ֖ל כָּל־יוֹשֵׁ֣ב בָּ֑הּ
וְעָלְתָ֤ה כָאֹר֙ כֻּלָּ֔הּ
וְנִגְרְשָׁ֛ה ונשקה וְנִשְׁקְעָ֖ה כִּיא֥וֹר
מִצְרָֽיִם: ס
9 וְהָיָ֣ה ׀ בַּיּ֣וֹם הַה֗וּא
נְאֻם֙ אֲדֹנָ֣י יְהֹוִ֔ה
וְהֵבֵאתִ֥י הַשֶּׁ֖מֶשׁ בַּֽצָּהֳרָ֑יִם
וְהַחֲשַׁכְתִּ֥י לָאָ֛רֶץ בְּי֥וֹם אֽוֹר:
10 וְהָפַכְתִּ֨י חַגֵּיכֶ֜ם לְאֵ֗בֶל
וְכָל־שִֽׁירֵיכֶם֙ לְקִינָ֔ה
וְהַעֲלֵיתִ֤י עַל־כָּל־מָתְנַ֨יִם֙ שָׂ֔ק
וְעַל־כָּל־רֹ֖אשׁ קָרְחָ֑ה
וְשַׂמְתִּ֨יהָ֙ כְּאֵ֣בֶל יָחִ֔יד
וְאַחֲרִיתָ֖הּ כְּי֥וֹם מָֽר:

11 הִנֵּ֣ה ׀ יָמִ֣ים בָּאִ֗ים נְאֻם֙ אֲדֹנָ֣י יְהֹוִ֔ה
וְהִשְׁלַחְתִּ֥י רָעָ֖ב בָּאָ֑רֶץ לֹֽא־רָעָ֤ב לַלֶּ֨חֶם֙
וְלֹֽא־צָמָ֣א לַמַּ֔יִם כִּ֣י אִם־לִשְׁמֹ֔עַ אֵ֖ת דִּבְרֵ֥י
יְהֹוָֽה: 12 וְנָעוּ֙ מִיָּ֣ם עַד־יָ֔ם וּמִצָּפ֖וֹן וְעַד־
מִזְרָ֑ח יְשֽׁוֹטְט֛וּ לְבַקֵּ֥שׁ אֶת־דְּבַר־יְהֹוָ֖ה וְלֹ֥א
יִמְצָֽאוּ:

13 בַּיּ֨וֹם הַה֜וּא תִּ֠תְעַלַּ֠פְנָה הַבְּתוּלֹ֧ת
הַיָּפ֛וֹת וְהַבַּחוּרִ֖ים בַּצָּמָֽא: 14 הַנִּשְׁבָּעִים֙ בְּאַשְׁמַ֣ת שֹׁמְר֔וֹן
וְאָמְר֗וּ חֵ֤י אֱלֹהֶ֨יךָ֙ דָּ֔ן
וְחֵ֖י דֶּ֣רֶךְ בְּאֵֽר־שָׁ֑בַע
וְנָפְל֖וּ וְלֹא־יָק֥וּמוּ עֽוֹד: ס

ט רָאִ֨יתִי אֶת־אֲדֹנָ֜י נִצָּ֣ב עַל־הַמִּזְבֵּ֗חַ
וַיֹּאמֶר֩ הַ֨ךְ הַכַּפְתּ֜וֹר וְיִרְעֲשׁ֣וּ הַסִּפִּ֗ים
וּבְצַעַ֣ם בְּרֹ֣אשׁ כֻּלָּ֔ם וְאַחֲרִיתָ֖ם בַּחֶ֣רֶב

---

f *I.e., the earth; cf. vv. 8 and 9d.*
g *Lit. "the end."*
h-h *Emendation yields "south to west."*
i *See 1 Kings 12.28–29.*
j *See 5.5 with note.*

a-a *Meaning of Heb. uncertain.*

sword; not one of them shall escape, and not one of them shall survive.

²If they burrow down to Sheol,
From there My hand shall take them;
And if they ascend to heaven,
From there I will bring them down.
³If they hide on the top of Carmel,
There I will search them out and seize them;
And if they conceal themselves from My sight
At the bottom of the sea,
There I will command
The serpent to bite them.
⁴And if they go into captivity
Before their enemies,
There I will command
The sword to slay them.
I will fix My eye on them for evil
And not for good.

⁵It is my Lord the GOD of Hosts
At whose touch the earth trembles
And all who dwell on it mourn,
And all of it swells like the Nile
And subsides like the Nile of Egypt;
⁶Who built His chambers in heaven
And founded His vault on the earth,
Who summons the waters of the sea
And pours them over the land—
His name is the LORD.

⁷To Me, O Israelites, you are
Just like the Ethiopians
——declares the LORD.
True, I brought Israel up
From the land of Egypt,
But also the Philistines from Caphtor
And the Arameans from Kir.

אֶהֱרֹג לֹא־יָנוּס לָהֶם נָס וְלֹא־יִמָּלֵט לָהֶם
פָּלִיט:
2 אִם־יַחְתְּרוּ בִשְׁאוֹל
מִשָּׁם יָדִי תִקָּחֵם
וְאִם־יַעֲלוּ הַשָּׁמַיִם
מִשָּׁם אוֹרִידֵם:
3 וְאִם־יֵחָבְאוּ בְּרֹאשׁ הַכַּרְמֶל
מִשָּׁם אֲחַפֵּשׂ וּלְקַחְתִּים
וְאִם־יִסָּתְרוּ מִנֶּגֶד עֵינַי
בְּקַרְקַע הַיָּם
מִשָּׁם אֲצַוֶּה
אֶת־הַנָּחָשׁ וּנְשָׁכָם:
4 וְאִם־יֵלְכוּ בַשְּׁבִי
לִפְנֵי אֹיְבֵיהֶם
מִשָּׁם אֲצַוֶּה
אֶת־הַחֶרֶב וַהֲרָגָתַם
וְשַׂמְתִּי עֵינִי עֲלֵיהֶם לְרָעָה
וְלֹא לְטוֹבָה:

5 וַאדֹנָי יְהוִֹה הַצְּבָאוֹת
הַנּוֹגֵעַ בָּאָרֶץ וַתָּמוֹג
וְאָבְלוּ כָּל־יוֹשְׁבֵי בָהּ
וְעָלְתָה כַיְאֹר כֻּלָּהּ
וְשָׁקְעָה כִּיאֹר מִצְרָיִם:
6 הַבּוֹנֶה בַשָּׁמַיִם מַעֲלוֹתָו מַעֲלוֹתָיו
וַאֲגֻדָּתוֹ עַל־אֶרֶץ יְסָדָהּ
הַקֹּרֵא לְמֵי־הַיָּם
וַיִּשְׁפְּכֵם עַל־פְּנֵי הָאָרֶץ
יְהוָה שְׁמוֹ:

7 הֲלוֹא כִבְנֵי כֻשִׁיִּים
אַתֶּם לִי בְּנֵי יִשְׂרָאֵל
נְאֻם־יְהוָה
הֲלוֹא אֶת־יִשְׂרָאֵל הֶעֱלֵיתִי
מֵאֶרֶץ מִצְרַיִם
וּפְלִשְׁתִּיִּים מִכַּפְתּוֹר
וַאֲרָם מִקִּיר:

8Behold, the Lord GOD has His eye
Upon the sinful kingdom:
I will wipe it off
The face of the earth!

But, I will not wholly wipe out
The House of Jacob
　　　　　　　—declares the LORD.
9For I will give the order
And shake the House of Israel—
Through all the nations—
As one shakes [sand] in a sieve,b
And not a pebble falls to the ground.
10All the sinners of My people
Shall perish by the sword,
Who boast,
"Never shall the evil
Overtake us or come near us."

11In that day,
I will set up again the fallen booth of David:
I will mend its breaches and set up its ruins
　　anew.
I will build it firm as in the days of old,
12c-So that they shall possess the rest of Edom
And all the nations once attached to My
　　name-c
　　　　　　　—declares the LORD who
　　　　　　　will bring this to pass.
13A time is coming
　　　　　　　—declares the LORD—
When the plowman shall meet the reaper,d
And the treader of grapes
Him who holds the [bag of] seed;
When the mountains shall drip wine
And all the hills shall wave [with grain].

---

b　A coarse sieve used for cleansing grain of straw and stones, or
　　sand of pebbles and shells.
c-c　I.e., the House of David shall reestablish its authority over the
　　nations that were ruled by David.
d　Cf. Lev. 26.5.

8 הִנֵּה עֵינֵי ׀ אֲדֹנָי יְהֹוִה
בַּמַּמְלָכָה הַחַטָּאָה
וְהִשְׁמַדְתִּי אֹתָהּ
מֵעַל פְּנֵי הָאֲדָמָה

אֶפֶס כִּי לֹא הַשְׁמֵיד אַשְׁמִיד
אֶת־בֵּית יַעֲקֹב
נְאֻם־יְהֹוָה׃
9 כִּי־הִנֵּה אָנֹכִי מְצַוֶּה
וַהֲנִעוֹתִי בְכָל־הַגּוֹיִם
אֶת־בֵּית יִשְׂרָאֵל
כַּאֲשֶׁר יִנּוֹעַ בַּכְּבָרָה
וְלֹא־יִפּוֹל צְרוֹר אָרֶץ׃
10 בַּחֶרֶב יָמוּתוּ
כֹּל חַטָּאֵי עַמִּי
הָאֹמְרִים
לֹא־תַגִּישׁ
וְתַקְדִּים בַּעֲדֵינוּ הָרָעָה׃

11 בַּיּוֹם הַהוּא
אָקִים אֶת־סֻכַּת דָּוִיד הַנֹּפֶלֶת
וְגָדַרְתִּי אֶת־פִּרְצֵיהֶן וַהֲרִסֹתָיו אָקִים
וּבְנִיתִיהָ כִּימֵי עוֹלָם׃
12 לְמַעַן יִירְשׁוּ אֶת־שְׁאֵרִית אֱדוֹם
וְכָל־הַגּוֹיִם אֲשֶׁר־נִקְרָא שְׁמִי עֲלֵיהֶם
נְאֻם־יְהֹוָה עֹשֶׂה זֹּאת׃ פ
13 הִנֵּה יָמִים בָּאִים
נְאֻם־יְהֹוָה
וְנִגַּשׁ חוֹרֵשׁ בַּקֹּצֵר
וְדֹרֵךְ עֲנָבִים
בְּמֹשֵׁךְ הַזָּרַע
וְהִטִּיפוּ הֶהָרִים עָסִיס
וְכָל־הַגְּבָעוֹת תִּתְמוֹגַגְנָה׃

14I will restore My people Israel.
They shall rebuild ruined cities and inhabit
　　them;
They shall plant vineyards and drink their
　　wine;
They shall till gardens and eat their fruits.
15And I will plant them upon their soil,
Nevermore to be uprooted
From the soil I have given them
　　　　　　　—said the LORD your God.

14 וְשַׁבְתִּי֙ אֶת־שְׁב֣וּת עַמִּ֣י יִשְׂרָאֵ֔ל
וּבָנ֞וּ עָרִ֤ים נְשַׁמּוֹת֙ וְיָשָׁ֔בוּ
וְנָטְע֣וּ כְרָמִ֔ים וְשָׁת֖וּ אֶת־יֵינָ֑ם
וְעָשׂ֣וּ גַנּ֔וֹת וְאָכְל֖וּ אֶת־פְּרִיהֶֽם׃
15 וּנְטַעְתִּ֖ים עַל־אַדְמָתָ֑ם
וְלֹ֨א יִנָּתְשׁ֜וּ ע֗וֹד
מֵעַ֤ל אַדְמָתָם֙ אֲשֶׁ֣ר נָתַ֣תִּי לָהֶ֔ם
אָמַ֖ר יְהוָ֥ה אֱלֹהֶֽיךָ׃

OBADIAH

1 The prophecy of Obadiah.

We have received tidings from the LORD,
And an envoy has been sent out among the
    nations:
"Up! Let us rise up against her for battle."

Thus said my Lord GOD concerning Edom:
²I will make you least among nations,
You shall be most despised.
³Your arrogant heart has seduced you,
You who dwell in clefts of the rock,
In your lofty abode.
You think in your heart,
"Who can pull me down to earth?"
⁴Should you nest as high as the eagle,
Should your eyrie be lodged 'mong the stars,
Even from there I will pull you down
               —declares the LORD.

⁵If thieves were to come to you,
Marauders by night,
They would steal no more than they needed.
If vintagers came to you,
They would surely leave some gleanings.
How utterly you are destroyed!
⁶How thoroughly rifled is Esau,
How ransacked his hoards!
⁷All your allies turned you back
At the frontier;
Your own confederates
Have duped and overcome you;

חֲז֖וֹן עֹבַדְיָ֑ה **א**

כֹּה־אָמַר֩ אֲדֹנָ֨י יְהֹוִ֜ה לֶאֱד֗וֹם
שְׁמוּעָ֤ה שָׁמַ֙עְנוּ֙ מֵאֵ֣ת יְהֹוָ֔ה
וְצִיר֙ בַּגּוֹיִ֣ם שֻׁלָּ֔ח
ק֛וּמוּ וְנָק֥וּמָה עָלֶ֖יהָ לַמִּלְחָמָֽה׃
הִנֵּ֥ה קָטֹ֛ן נְתַתִּ֖יךָ בַּגּוֹיִ֑ם ²
בָּז֥וּי אַתָּ֖ה מְאֹֽד׃
זְד֤וֹן לִבְּךָ֙ הִשִּׁיאֶ֔ךָ ³
שֹׁכְנִ֥י בְחַגְוֵי־סֶ֖לַע
מְר֣וֹם שִׁבְתּ֑וֹ
אֹמֵ֣ר בְּלִבּ֔וֹ
מִ֥י יוֹרִדֵ֖נִי אָֽרֶץ׃
אִם־תַּגְבִּ֣יהַּ כַּנֶּ֔שֶׁר ⁴
וְאִם־בֵּ֥ין כּֽוֹכָבִ֖ים שִׂ֣ים קִנֶּ֑ךָ
מִשָּׁ֥ם אוֹרִֽידְךָ֖
נְאֻם־יְהֹוָֽה׃

אִם־גַּנָּבִ֤ים בָּאֽוּ־לְךָ֙ ⁵
אִם־שׁ֣וֹדְדֵי לַ֔יְלָה
אֵ֣יךְ נִדְמֵ֔יתָה
הֲל֥וֹא יִגְנְב֖וּ דַּיָּ֑ם
אִם־בֹּֽצְרִים֙ בָּ֣אוּ לָ֔ךְ
הֲל֖וֹא יַשְׁאִ֥ירוּ עֹלֵלֽוֹת׃
אֵ֚יךְ נֶחְפְּשׂ֣וּ עֵשָׂ֔ו ⁶
נִבְע֖וּ מַצְפֻּנָֽיו׃
עַד־הַגְּב֣וּל ⁷
שִׁלְּח֗וּךָ כֹּ֚ל אַנְשֵׁ֣י בְרִיתֶ֔ךָ
הִשִּׁיא֛וּךָ יָכְל֥וּ לְךָ֖
אַנְשֵׁ֣י שְׁלֹמֶ֑ךָ

[Those who ate] your bread
Have planted snares under you.

He is bereft of understanding.
8In that day

—declares the LORD—

I will make the wise vanish from Edom,
Understanding from Esau's mount.
9Your warriors shall lose heart, O Teman,
And not a man on Esau's mount
Shall survive the slaughter.

10For the outrage to your brother Jacob,
Disgrace shall engulf you,
And you shall perish forever.
11On that day when you stood aloof,
When aliens carried off his goods,
When foreigners entered his gates
And cast lots for Jerusalem,
You were as one of them.

12a-How could you-a gaze with glee
On your brother that day,
On his day of calamity!
How could you gloat
Over the people of Judah
On that day of ruin!
How could you loudly jeer
On a day of anguish!
13How could you enter the gate of My people
On its day of disaster,
Gaze in glee with the others
On its misfortune
On its day of disaster,
And lay hands on its wealth
On its day of disaster!
14How could you stand at the passes*b*

---

a-a Lit. "Do not," and so through v. 14.
b   Meaning of Heb. uncertain.

לְחַמְךָ
יָשִׂימוּ מָזוֹר תַּחְתֶּיךָ
אֵין תְּבוּנָה בּוֹ:
8הֲלוֹא בַּיּוֹם הַהוּא
נְאֻם־יְהוָה
וְהַאֲבַדְתִּי חֲכָמִים מֵאֱדוֹם
וּתְבוּנָה מֵהַר עֵשָׂו:
9וְחַתּוּ גִבּוֹרֶיךָ תֵּימָן
לְמַעַן יִכָּרֶת־אִישׁ מֵהַר עֵשָׂו
מִקָּטֶל:
10מֵחֲמַס אָחִיךָ יַעֲקֹב
תְּכַסְּךָ בוּשָׁה
וְנִכְרַתָּ לְעוֹלָם:
11בְּיוֹם עֲמָדְךָ מִנֶּגֶד
בְּיוֹם שְׁבוֹת זָרִים חֵילוֹ
וְנָכְרִים בָּאוּ שְׁעָרָו
וְעַל־יְרוּשָׁלִַם יַדּוּ גוֹרָל
גַּם־אַתָּה כְּאַחַד מֵהֶם:
12וְאַל־תֵּרֶא
בְיוֹם־אָחִיךָ
בְּיוֹם נָכְרוֹ
וְאַל־תִּשְׂמַח
לִבְנֵי־יְהוּדָה
בְּיוֹם אָבְדָם
וְאַל־תַּגְדֵּל פִּיךָ
בְּיוֹם צָרָה:
13אַל־תָּבוֹא בְשַׁעַר־עַמִּי
בְּיוֹם אֵידָם
אַל־תֵּרֶא גַם־אַתָּה
בְּרָעָתוֹ
בְּיוֹם אֵידוֹ
וְאַל־תִּשְׁלַחְנָה בְחֵילוֹ
בְּיוֹם אֵידוֹ:
14וְאַל־תַּעֲמֹד עַל־הַפֶּרֶק

To cut down its fugitives!
How could you betray those who fled
On that day of anguish!
15As you did, so shall it be done to you;
Your conduct shall be requited.

לְהַכְרִית אֶת־פְּלִיטָיו
וְאַל־תַּסְגֵּר שְׂרִידָיו
בְּיוֹם צָרָה:
15 כִּי־קָרוֹב יוֹם־יְהוָה
עַל־כָּל־הַגּוֹיִם
כַּאֲשֶׁר עָשִׂיתָ יֵעָשֶׂה לָּךְ
גְּמֻלְךָ יָשׁוּב בְּרֹאשֶׁךָ:

Yea, against all nations
The day of the LORD is at hand.
16That same cup that youc drank on My Holy
Mount
Shall all nations drink evermore,d
Drink till their speech grows thick,
And they become as though they had never
been.
17But on Zion's mount a remnant shall sur-
vive,
And it shall be holy.e
The House of Jacob shall dispossess
Those who dispossessed them.
18The House of Jacob shall be fire,
And the House of Joseph flame,
And the House of Esau shall be straw;
They shall burn it and devour it,
And no survivor shall be left of the House of
Esau
      —for the LORD has spoken.

16 כִּי כַּאֲשֶׁר שְׁתִיתֶם עַל־הַר קָדְשִׁי
יִשְׁתּוּ כָל־הַגּוֹיִם תָּמִיד
וְשָׁתוּ וְלָעוּ
וְהָיוּ כְּלוֹא הָיוּ:
17 וּבְהַר צִיּוֹן תִּהְיֶה פְלֵיטָה
וְהָיָה קֹדֶשׁ
וְיָרְשׁוּ בֵּית יַעֲקֹב
אֵת מוֹרָשֵׁיהֶם:
18 וְהָיָה בֵית־יַעֲקֹב אֵשׁ
וּבֵית יוֹסֵף לֶהָבָה
וּבֵית עֵשָׂו לְקַשׁ
וְדָלְקוּ בָהֶם וַאֲכָלוּם
וְלֹא־יִהְיֶה שָׂרִיד לְבֵית עֵשָׂו
כִּי יְהוָה דִּבֵּר:

19fThus they shall possess the Negeb and
Mount Esau as well, the Shephelah and Philistia.
They shall possess the Ephraimite country and
the district of Samaria,g and Benjaminh along
with Gilead. 20And that exiled force of Israelites
[shall possess] what belongs to the Phoenicians
as far as Zarephath,i while the Jerusalemite exile

19 וְיָרְשׁוּ הַנֶּגֶב אֶת־הַר עֵשָׂו וְהַשְּׁפֵלָה
אֶת־פְּלִשְׁתִּים וְיָרְשׁוּ אֶת־שְׂדֵה אֶפְרַיִם
וְאֵת שְׂדֵה שֹׁמְרוֹן וּבִנְיָמִן אֶת־הַגִּלְעָד:
20 וְגָלֻת הַחֵל־הַזֶּה לִבְנֵי יִשְׂרָאֵל אֲשֶׁר־

---

c   I.e., the Israelites.
d   Emendation yields "at My hand," cf. Isa. 51.17; Jer. 25.15; Ps.
      75.9.
e   I.e., inviolate; cf. Jer. 2.3.
f   Meaning of parts of vv. 19–21 uncertain.
g   After the exile of the northern tribes, the city and district of
      Samaria were occupied mainly by non-Israelites.
h   Emendation yields "the land of the Ammonites."
i   A town in southern Phoenicia; see 1 Kings 17.9.

community of Sepharad*j* shall possess the towns of the Negeb. [21] For *k-*liberators shall march up*-k* on Mount Zion to wreak judgment on Mount Esau; and dominion shall be the LORD's.

כְּנַעֲנִים֙ עַד־צָ֣רְפַ֔ת וְגָלֻ֥ת יְרוּשָׁלַ֖͏ִם אֲשֶׁ֣ר בִּסְפָרַ֑ד יִֽרְשׁ֕וּ אֵ֖ת עָרֵ֥י הַנֶּֽגֶב: [21] וְעָל֣וּ מֽוֹשִׁעִים֙ בְּהַ֣ר צִיּ֔וֹן לִשְׁפֹּ֖ט אֶת־הַ֣ר עֵשָׂ֑ו וְהָיְתָ֥ה לַֽיהֹוָ֖ה הַמְּלוּכָֽה:

j Probably Asia Minor, called Saparda in Persian cuneiform inscriptions.

k-k Several ancient versions read, "they [the exiles from Jerusalem named in the preceding verse] shall march up victorious."

1332

JONAH

יוֹנָה

1 The word of the LORD came to Jonah[a] son of Amittai: ²Go at once to Nineveh, that great city, and proclaim judgment upon it; for their wickedness has come before Me.

³Jonah, however, started out to flee to Tarshish from the LORD's service. He went down to Joppa and found a ship going to Tarshish. He paid the fare and went aboard to sail with the others to Tarshish, away from the service of the LORD.

⁴But the LORD cast a mighty wind upon the sea, and such a great tempest came upon the sea that the ship was in danger of breaking up. ⁵In their fright, the sailors cried out, each to his own god; and they flung the ship's cargo overboard to make it lighter for them. Jonah, meanwhile, had gone down into the hold of the vessel where he lay down and fell asleep. ⁶The captain went over to him and cried out, "How can you be sleeping so soundly! Up, call upon your god! Perhaps the god will be kind to us and we will not perish."

⁷The men said to one another, "Let us cast lots and find out on whose account this misfortune has come upon us." They cast lots and the lot fell on Jonah. ⁸They said to him, "Tell us, you who have brought this misfortune upon us, what is your business? Where have you come from? What is your country, and of what people are you?" ⁹"I am a Hebrew," he replied. "I worship the LORD, the God of Heaven, who made both sea and land." ¹⁰The men were greatly terrified, and they asked him, "What have you

א וַיְהִי דְּבַר־יְהֹוָה אֶל־יוֹנָה בֶן־אֲמִתַּי
לֵאמֹר: 2 קוּם לֵךְ אֶל־נִינְוֵה הָעִיר הַגְּדוֹלָה
וּקְרָא עָלֶיהָ כִּי־עָלְתָה רָעָתָם לְפָנָי:
3 וַיָּקָם יוֹנָה לִבְרֹחַ תַּרְשִׁישָׁה מִלִּפְנֵי יְהֹוָה
וַיֵּרֶד יָפוֹ וַיִּמְצָא אָנִיָּה ׀ בָּאָה תַרְשִׁישׁ
וַיִּתֵּן שְׂכָרָהּ וַיֵּרֶד בָּהּ לָבוֹא עִמָּהֶם
תַּרְשִׁישָׁה מִלִּפְנֵי יְהֹוָה:
4 וַיהֹוָה הֵטִיל רוּחַ־גְּדוֹלָה אֶל־הַיָּם וַיְהִי
סַעַר־גָּדוֹל בַּיָּם וְהָאֳנִיָּה חִשְּׁבָה לְהִשָּׁבֵר:
5 וַיִּירְאוּ הַמַּלָּחִים וַיִּזְעֲקוּ אִישׁ אֶל־אֱלֹהָיו
וַיָּטִלוּ אֶת־הַכֵּלִים אֲשֶׁר בָּאֳנִיָּה אֶל־הַיָּם
לְהָקֵל מֵעֲלֵיהֶם וְיוֹנָה יָרַד אֶל־יַרְכְּתֵי
הַסְּפִינָה וַיִּשְׁכַּב וַיֵּרָדַם: 6 וַיִּקְרַב אֵלָיו רַב
הַחֹבֵל וַיֹּאמֶר לוֹ מַה־לְּךָ נִרְדָּם קוּם קְרָא
אֶל־אֱלֹהֶיךָ אוּלַי יִתְעַשֵּׁת הָאֱלֹהִים לָנוּ
וְלֹא נֹאבֵד:
7 וַיֹּאמְרוּ אִישׁ אֶל־רֵעֵהוּ לְכוּ וְנַפִּילָה
גוֹרָלוֹת וְנֵדְעָה בְּשֶׁלְּמִי הָרָעָה הַזֹּאת לָנוּ
וַיַּפִּלוּ גּוֹרָלוֹת וַיִּפֹּל הַגּוֹרָל עַל־יוֹנָה:
8 וַיֹּאמְרוּ אֵלָיו הַגִּידָה־נָּא לָנוּ בַּאֲשֶׁר
לְמִי־הָרָעָה הַזֹּאת לָנוּ מַה־מְּלַאכְתְּךָ
וּמֵאַיִן תָּבוֹא מָה אַרְצֶךָ וְאֵי־מִזֶּה עַם
אָתָּה: 9 וַיֹּאמֶר אֲלֵיהֶם עִבְרִי אָנֹכִי וְאֶת־
יְהֹוָה אֱלֹהֵי הַשָּׁמַיִם אֲנִי יָרֵא אֲשֶׁר
עָשָׂה אֶת־הַיָּם וְאֶת־הַיַּבָּשָׁה: 10 וַיִּירְאוּ
הָאֲנָשִׁים יִרְאָה גְדוֹלָה וַיֹּאמְרוּ אֵלָיו

---

a *Mentioned in 2 Kings 14.25.*

done?" And when the men learned that he was fleeing from the service of the LORD—for so he told them—11they said to him, "What must we do to you to make the sea calm around us?" For the sea was growing more and more stormy. 12He answered, "Heave me overboard, and the sea will calm down for you; for I know that this terrible storm came upon you on my account." 13Nevertheless, the men rowed hard to regain the shore, but they could not, for the sea was growing more and more stormy about them. 14Then they cried out to the LORD: "Oh, please, LORD, do not let us perish on account of this man's life. Do not hold us guilty of killing an innocent person! For You, O LORD, by Your will, have brought this about." 15And they heaved Jonah overboard, and the sea stopped raging.

16The men feared the LORD greatly; they offered a sacrifice to the LORD and they made vows.

מַה־זֹּאת עָשִׂיתָ כִּי־יָדְעוּ הָאֲנָשִׁים כִּי־
מִלִּפְנֵי יְהוָה הוּא בֹרֵחַ כִּי הִגִּיד לָהֶם:
11 וַיֹּאמְרוּ אֵלָיו מַה־נַּעֲשֶׂה לָּךְ וְיִשְׁתֹּק
הַיָּם מֵעָלֵינוּ כִּי הַיָּם הוֹלֵךְ וְסֹעֵר:
12 וַיֹּאמֶר אֲלֵיהֶם שָׂאוּנִי וַהֲטִילֻנִי אֶל־הַיָּם
וְיִשְׁתֹּק הַיָּם מֵעֲלֵיכֶם כִּי יוֹדֵעַ אָנִי כִּי
בְשֶׁלִּי הַסַּעַר הַגָּדוֹל הַזֶּה עֲלֵיכֶם:
13 וַיַּחְתְּרוּ הָאֲנָשִׁים לְהָשִׁיב אֶל־הַיַּבָּשָׁה
וְלֹא יָכֹלוּ כִּי הַיָּם הוֹלֵךְ וְסֹעֵר עֲלֵיהֶם:
14 וַיִּקְרְאוּ אֶל־יְהוָה וַיֹּאמְרוּ אָנָּה יְהוָה
אַל־נָא נֹאבְדָה בְּנֶפֶשׁ הָאִישׁ הַזֶּה וְאַל־
תִּתֵּן עָלֵינוּ דָּם נָקִיא* כִּי־אַתָּה יְהוָה
כַּאֲשֶׁר חָפַצְתָּ עָשִׂיתָ: 15 וַיִּשְׂאוּ אֶת־יוֹנָה
וַיְטִלֻהוּ אֶל־הַיָּם וַיַּעֲמֹד הַיָּם מִזַּעְפּוֹ:
16 וַיִּירְאוּ הָאֲנָשִׁים יִרְאָה גְדוֹלָה אֶת־
יְהוָה וַיִּזְבְּחוּ־זֶבַח לַיהוָה וַיִּדְּרוּ נְדָרִים:

2 The LORD provided a huge fish to swallow Jonah; and Jonah remained in the fish's belly three days and three nights. 2Jonah prayed to the LORD his God from the belly of the fish. 3He said:

ב וַיְמַן יְהוָה דָּג גָּדוֹל לִבְלֹעַ אֶת־יוֹנָה
וַיְהִי יוֹנָה בִּמְעֵי הַדָּג שְׁלֹשָׁה יָמִים
וּשְׁלֹשָׁה לֵילוֹת: 2 וַיִּתְפַּלֵּל יוֹנָה אֶל־יְהוָה
אֱלֹהָיו מִמְּעֵי הַדָּגָה: 3 וַיֹּאמֶר

In my trouble I called to the LORD,
And He answered me;
From the belly of Sheol I cried out,
And You heard my voice.
4You cast me into the depths,
Into the heart of the sea,
The floods engulfed me;
All Your breakers and billows
Swept over me.
5I thought I was driven away
Out of Your sight:

קָרָאתִי מִצָּרָה לִי אֶל־יְהוָה
וַיַּעֲנֵנִי
מִבֶּטֶן שְׁאוֹל שִׁוַּעְתִּי
שָׁמַעְתָּ קוֹלִי:
4 וַתַּשְׁלִיכֵנִי מְצוּלָה
בִּלְבַב יַמִּים
וְנָהָר יְסֹבְבֵנִי
כָּל־מִשְׁבָּרֶיךָ וְגַלֶּיךָ
עָלַי עָבָרוּ:
5 וַאֲנִי אָמַרְתִּי נִגְרַשְׁתִּי
מִנֶּגֶד עֵינֶיךָ

Would I ever gaze again
Upon Your holy Temple?
⁶The waters closed in over me,
The deep engulfed me.
Weeds twined around my head.
⁷I sank to the base of the mountains;
The bars of the earth closed upon me forever.
Yet You brought my life up from the pit,
O LORD my God!
⁸When my life was ebbing away,
I called the LORD to mind;
And my prayer came before You,
Into Your holy Temple.
⁹They who cling to empty folly
Forsake their own welfare,ᵃ
¹⁰But I, with loud thanksgiving,
Will sacrifice to You;
What I have vowed I will perform.
Deliverance is the LORD's!

¹¹The LORD commanded the fish, and it spewed Jonah out upon dry land.

אַךְ אוֹסִיף לְהַבִּיט
אֶל־הֵיכַל קָדְשֶׁךָ׃
6 אֲפָפ֣וּנִי מַ֙יִם֙ עַד־נֶ֔פֶשׁ
תְּה֖וֹם יְסֹבְבֵ֑נִי
ס֖וּף חָב֥וּשׁ לְרֹאשִֽׁי׃
7 לְקִצְבֵ֤י הָרִים֙ יָרַ֔דְתִּי
הָאָ֛רֶץ בְּרִחֶ֥יהָ בַעֲדִ֖י לְעוֹלָ֑ם
וַתַּ֧עַל מִשַּׁ֛חַת חַיַּ֖י
יְהוָ֥ה אֱלֹהָֽי׃
8 בְּהִתְעַטֵּ֤ף עָלַי֙ נַפְשִׁ֔י
אֶת־יְהוָ֖ה זָכָ֑רְתִּי
וַתָּב֤וֹא אֵלֶ֙יךָ֙ תְּפִלָּתִ֔י
אֶל־הֵיכַ֖ל קָדְשֶֽׁךָ׃
9 מְשַׁמְּרִ֖ים הַבְלֵי־שָׁ֑וְא
חַסְדָּ֖ם יַעֲזֹֽבוּ׃
10 וַאֲנִ֗י בְּק֤וֹל תּוֹדָה֙
אֶזְבְּחָה־לָּ֔ךְ
אֲשֶׁ֥ר נָדַ֖רְתִּי אֲשַׁלֵּ֑מָה
יְשׁוּעָ֖תָה לַֽיהוָֽה׃ ס

11 וַיֹּ֥אמֶר יְהוָ֖ה לַדָּ֑ג וַיָּקֵ֥א אֶת־יוֹנָ֖ה אֶל־
הַיַּבָּשָֽׁה׃ פ

3 The word of the LORD came to Jonah a second time: ²"Go at once to Nineveh, that great city, and proclaim to it what I tell you." ³Jonah went at once to Nineveh in accordance with the LORD's command.

Nineveh was ᵃ-an enormously large city-ᵃ a three days' walk across. ⁴Jonah started out and made his way into the city the distance of one day's walk, and proclaimed: "Forty days more, and Nineveh shall be overthrown!"

⁵The people of Nineveh believed God. They proclaimed a fast, and great and small alike put on sackcloth. ⁶When the news reached the king

ג וַיְהִ֧י דְבַר־יְהוָ֛ה אֶל־יוֹנָ֖ה שֵׁנִ֥ית
לֵאמֹֽר׃ 2 ק֛וּם לֵ֥ךְ אֶל־נִֽינְוֵ֖ה הָעִ֣יר הַגְּדוֹלָ֑ה
וּקְרָ֤א אֵלֶ֙יהָ֙ אֶת־הַקְּרִיאָ֔ה אֲשֶׁ֥ר אָנֹכִ֖י דֹּבֵ֥ר
אֵלֶֽיךָ׃ 3 וַיָּ֣קָם יוֹנָ֗ה וַיֵּ֛לֶךְ אֶל־נִֽינְוֵ֖ה כִּדְבַ֣ר
יְהוָ֑ה
וְנִֽינְוֵ֗ה הָיְתָ֤ה עִיר־גְּדוֹלָה֙ לֵֽאלֹהִ֔ים מַהֲלַ֖ךְ
שְׁלֹ֥שֶׁת יָמִֽים׃ 4 וַיָּ֤חֶל יוֹנָה֙ לָב֣וֹא בָעִ֔יר
מַהֲלַ֖ךְ י֣וֹם אֶחָ֑ד וַיִּקְרָא֙ וַיֹּאמַ֔ר ע֚וֹד
אַרְבָּעִ֣ים י֔וֹם וְנִֽינְוֵ֖ה נֶהְפָּֽכֶת׃
5 וַֽיַּאֲמִ֛ינוּ אַנְשֵׁ֥י נִֽינְוֵ֖ה בֵּֽאלֹהִ֑ים וַיִּקְרְאוּ־
צוֹם֙ וַיִּלְבְּשׁ֣וּ שַׂקִּ֔ים מִגְּדוֹלָ֖ם וְעַד־קְטַנָּֽם׃

ᵃ Meaning of Heb. uncertain.

ᵃ⁻ᵃ Lit. "a large city of God."

of Nineveh, he rose from his throne, took off his robe, put on sackcloth, and sat in ashes. 7And he had the word cried through Nineveh: "By decree of the king and his nobles: No man or beast—of flock or herd—shall taste anything! They shall not graze, and they shall not drink water! 8They shall be covered with sackcloth—man and beast—and shall cry mightily to God. Let everyone turn back from his evil ways and from the injustice of which he is guilty. 9Who knows but that God may turn and relent? He may turn back from His wrath, so that we do not perish."

10God saw what they did, how they were turning back from their evil ways. And God renounced the punishment He had planned to bring upon them, and did not carry it out.

4 This displeased Jonah greatly, and he was grieved. 2He prayed to the LORD, saying, "O LORD! Isn't this just what I said when I was still in my own country? That is why I fled beforehand to Tarshish. For I know that You are a compassionate and gracious God, slow to anger, abounding in kindness, renouncing punishment. 3Please, LORD, take my life, for I would rather die than live." 4The LORD replied, "Are you that deeply grieved?"

5Now Jonah had left the city and found a place east of the city. He made a booth there and sat under it in the shade, until he should see what happened to the city. 6The LORD God provided a ricinus plant,a which grew up over Jonah, to provide shade for his head and save him from discomfort. Jonah was very happy about the plant. 7But the next day at dawn God provided a worm, which attacked the plant so that it withered. 8And when the sun rose, God provided a sultryb east wind; the sun beat down on Jonah's

---

6 וַיִּגַּע הַדָּבָר אֶל־מֶלֶךְ נִינְוֵה וַיָּקָם מִכִּסְאוֹ וַיַּעֲבֵר אַדַּרְתּוֹ מֵעָלָיו וַיְכַס שַׂק וַיֵּשֶׁב עַל־הָאֵפֶר׃ 7 וַיַּזְעֵק וַיֹּאמֶר בְּנִינְוֵה מִטַּעַם הַמֶּלֶךְ וּגְדֹלָיו לֵאמֹר הָאָדָם וְהַבְּהֵמָה הַבָּקָר וְהַצֹּאן אַל־יִטְעֲמוּ מְאוּמָה אַל־יִרְעוּ וּמַיִם אַל־יִשְׁתּוּ׃ 8 וְיִתְכַּסּוּ שַׂקִּים הָאָדָם וְהַבְּהֵמָה וְיִקְרְאוּ אֶל־אֱלֹהִים בְּחָזְקָה וְיָשֻׁבוּ אִישׁ מִדַּרְכּוֹ הָרָעָה וּמִן־הֶחָמָס אֲשֶׁר בְּכַפֵּיהֶם׃ 9 מִי־יוֹדֵעַ יָשׁוּב וְנִחַם הָאֱלֹהִים וְשָׁב מֵחֲרוֹן אַפּוֹ וְלֹא נֹאבֵד׃

10 וַיַּרְא הָאֱלֹהִים אֶת־מַעֲשֵׂיהֶם כִּי־שָׁבוּ מִדַּרְכָּם הָרָעָה וַיִּנָּחֶם הָאֱלֹהִים עַל־הָרָעָה אֲשֶׁר־דִּבֶּר לַעֲשׂוֹת־לָהֶם וְלֹא עָשָׂה׃

ד וַיֵּרַע אֶל־יוֹנָה רָעָה גְדוֹלָה וַיִּחַר לוֹ׃ 2 וַיִּתְפַּלֵּל אֶל־יְהֹוָה וַיֹּאמַר אָנָּה יְהֹוָה הֲלוֹא־זֶה דְבָרִי עַד־הֱיוֹתִי עַל־אַדְמָתִי עַל־כֵּן קִדַּמְתִּי לִבְרֹחַ תַּרְשִׁישָׁה כִּי יָדַעְתִּי כִּי אַתָּה אֵל־חַנּוּן וְרַחוּם אֶרֶךְ אַפַּיִם וְרַב־חֶסֶד וְנִחָם עַל־הָרָעָה׃ 3 וְעַתָּה יְהֹוָה קַח־נָא אֶת־נַפְשִׁי מִמֶּנִּי כִּי טוֹב מוֹתִי מֵחַיָּי׃ ס 4 וַיֹּאמֶר יְהֹוָה הַהֵיטֵב חָרָה לָךְ׃

5 וַיֵּצֵא יוֹנָה מִן־הָעִיר וַיֵּשֶׁב מִקֶּדֶם לָעִיר וַיַּעַשׂ לוֹ שָׁם סֻכָּה וַיֵּשֶׁב תַּחְתֶּיהָ בַּצֵּל עַד אֲשֶׁר יִרְאֶה מַה־יִּהְיֶה בָּעִיר׃ 6 וַיְמַן יְהֹוָה־אֱלֹהִים קִיקָיוֹן וַיַּעַל ׀ מֵעַל לְיוֹנָה לִהְיוֹת צֵל עַל־רֹאשׁוֹ לְהַצִּיל לוֹ מֵרָעָתוֹ וַיִּשְׂמַח יוֹנָה עַל־הַקִּיקָיוֹן שִׂמְחָה גְדוֹלָה׃ 7 וַיְמַן הָאֱלֹהִים תּוֹלַעַת בַּעֲלוֹת הַשַּׁחַר לַמׇּחֳרָת וַתַּךְ אֶת־הַקִּיקָיוֹן וַיִּיבָשׁ׃ 8 וַיְהִי ׀ כִּזְרֹחַ הַשֶּׁמֶשׁ וַיְמַן אֱלֹהִים רוּחַ קָדִים

---

head, and he became faint. He begged for death, saying, "I would rather die than live." ⁹Then God said to Jonah, "Are you so deeply grieved about the plant?" "Yes," he replied, "so deeply that I want to die."

¹⁰Then the Lord said: "You cared about the plant, which you did not work for and which you did not grow, which appeared overnight and perished overnight. ¹¹And should not I care about Nineveh, that great city, in which there are more than a hundred and twenty thousand persons who do not yet know their right hand from their left, and many beasts as well!"ᶜ

חֲרִישִׁית וַתַּךְ הַשֶּׁמֶשׁ עַל־רֹאשׁ יוֹנָה
וַיִּתְעַלָּף וַיִּשְׁאַל אֶת־נַפְשׁוֹ לָמוּת וַיֹּאמֶר
טוֹב מוֹתִי מֵחַיָּי: ⁹ וַיֹּאמֶר אֱלֹהִים אֶל־
יוֹנָה הַהֵיטֵב חָרָה־לְךָ עַל־הַקִּיקָיוֹן וַיֹּאמֶר
הֵיטֵב חָרָה־לִי עַד־מָוֶת:
¹⁰ וַיֹּאמֶר יְהֹוָה אַתָּה חַסְתָּ עַל־הַקִּיקָיוֹן
אֲשֶׁר לֹא־עָמַלְתָּ בּוֹ וְלֹא גִדַּלְתּוֹ שֶׁבִּן־
לַיְלָה הָיָה וּבִן־לַיְלָה אָבָד: ¹¹ וַאֲנִי לֹא
אָחוּס עַל־נִינְוֵה הָעִיר הַגְּדוֹלָה אֲשֶׁר
יֶשׁ־בָּהּ הַרְבֵּה מִשְׁתֵּים־עֶשְׂרֵה רִבּוֹ אָדָם
אֲשֶׁר לֹא־יָדַע בֵּין־יְמִינוֹ לִשְׂמֹאלוֹ וּבְהֵמָה
רַבָּה:

ᶜ   *Infants and beasts are not held responsible for their actions.*

MICAH

1 The word of the Lord that came to Micah the Morashtite, who prophesied concerning Samaria and Jerusalem in the reigns of Kings Jotham, Ahaz, and Hezekiah of Judah.

2Listen, all you peoples,
Give heed, O earth, and all it holds;
And let my Lord God be your accuser—
My Lord from His holy abode.
3For lo! the Lord
Is coming forth from His dwelling-place,
He will come down and stride
Upon the heights of the earth.
4The mountains shall melt under Him
And the valleys burst open—
Like wax before fire,
Like water cascading down a slope.

5All this is for the transgression of Jacob,
And for the sins of the House of Israel.
What is the transgression of Jacob
But Samaria,
And what the shrines*a* of Judah
But Jerusalem?
6So I will turn Samaria
Into a ruin in open country,
Into ground for planting vineyards;
For I will tumble her stones into the valley
And lay her foundations bare.
7All her sculptured images shall be smashed,
And all her harlot's wealth be burned,

---

a Emendation yields "sins."

א דְּבַר־יְהֹוָה ׀ אֲשֶׁר הָיָה אֶל־מִיכָה
הַמֹּרַשְׁתִּי בִּימֵי יוֹתָם אָחָז יְחִזְקִיָּה מַלְכֵי
יְהוּדָה אֲשֶׁר־חָזָה עַל־שֹׁמְרוֹן וִירוּשָׁלָֽ͏ִם:

2 שִׁמְעוּ עַמִּים כֻּלָּם
הַקְשִׁיבִי אֶרֶץ וּמְלֹאָהּ
וִיהִי אֲדֹנָי יֱהֹוִה בָּכֶם לְעֵד
אֲדֹנָי מֵהֵיכַל קׇדְשֽׁוֹ:
3 כִּי־הִנֵּה יְהֹוָה
יֹצֵא מִמְּקוֹמוֹ
וְיָרַד וְדָרַךְ
עַל־במותי בָּמֳתֵי אָֽרֶץ:
4 וְנָמַסּוּ הֶהָרִים תַּחְתָּיו
וְהָעֲמָקִים יִתְבַּקָּעוּ
כַּדּוֹנַג מִפְּנֵי הָאֵשׁ
כְּמַיִם מֻגָּרִים בְּמוֹרָֽד:

5 בְּפֶשַׁע יַעֲקֹב כׇּל־זֹאת
וּבְחַטֹּאות* בֵּית יִשְׂרָאֵל
מִי־פֶשַׁע יַעֲקֹב
הֲלוֹא שֹׁמְרוֹן
וּמִי בָּמוֹת יְהוּדָה
הֲלוֹא יְרוּשָׁלָֽ͏ִם:
6 וְשַׂמְתִּי שֹׁמְרוֹן
לְעִי הַשָּׂדֶה
לְמַטָּעֵי כָרֶם
וְהִגַּרְתִּי לַגַּי אֲבָנֶיהָ
וִיסֹדֶיהָ אֲגַלֶּֽה:
7 וְכׇל־פְּסִילֶיהָ יֻכַּתּוּ
וְכׇל־אֶתְנַנֶּיהָ יִשָּׂרְפוּ בָאֵשׁ

מלא ו׳ v. 5.

And I will make a waste heap of all her idols,
For they were amassed from fees for harlotry,
And they shall become harlots' fees again.

⁸Because of this I will lament and wail;
I will go stripped and naked!
I will lament as sadly as the jackals,
As mournfully as the ostriches.
⁹For her^b wound is incurable,
It has reached Judah,
It has spread to the gate of my people,
To Jerusalem.

¹⁰^cTell it not in Gath,
Refrain from weeping;^d
In Beth-leaphrah,
Strew dust^e over your [head].
¹¹Pass on, inhabitants of Shaphir!
Did not the inhabitants of Zaanan
Have to go forth naked in shame?
There is lamentation in Beth-ezel—
It will withdraw its support from you.
¹²Though the inhabitants of Maroth
Hoped for good,
Yet disaster from the LORD descended
Upon the gate of Jerusalem.
¹³Hitch the steeds to the chariot,
Inhabitant of Lachish!
It is the beginning
Of Fair Zion's guilt;
Israel's transgressions
Can be traced to you!
¹⁴Truly, you must give a farewell gift
To Moresheth-gath.
^fThe houses of Achzib are-^f
To the kings of Israel

וְכָל־עֲצַבֶּיהָ יֻכַּתּוּ אָשִׂים שְׁמָמָה
כִּי מֵאֶתְנַן זוֹנָה קִבָּצָה
וְעַד־אֶתְנַן זוֹנָה יָשׁוּבוּ:

8 עַל־זֹאת אֶסְפְּדָה וְאֵילִילָה
אֵילְכָה שׁילַל שׁוֹלָל וְעָרוֹם
אֶעֱשֶׂה מִסְפֵּד כַּתַּנִּים
וְאֵבֶל כִּבְנוֹת יַעֲנָה:
9 כִּי אֲנוּשָׁה מַכּוֹתֶיהָ
כִּי־בָאָה עַד־יְהוּדָה
נָגַע עַד־שַׁעַר עַמִּי
עַד־יְרוּשָׁלָ͏ִם:

10 בְּגַת אַל־תַּגִּידוּ
בָּכוֹ אַל־תִּבְכּוּ
בְּבֵית לְעַפְרָה
עָפָר הִתְפַּלָּשְׁתִּי הִתְפַּלָּשִׁי:
11 עִבְרִי לָכֶם יוֹשֶׁבֶת שָׁפִיר
עֶרְיָה־בֹשֶׁת
לֹא יָצְאָה יוֹשֶׁבֶת צַאֲנָן
מִסְפַּד בֵּית הָאֵצֶל
יִקַּח מִכֶּם עֶמְדָּתוֹ:
12 כִּי־חָלָה לְטוֹב
יוֹשֶׁבֶת מָרוֹת
כִּי־יָרַד רָע מֵאֵת יְהֹוָה
לְשַׁעַר יְרוּשָׁלָ͏ִם:
13 רְתֹם הַמֶּרְכָּבָה לָרֶכֶשׁ
יוֹשֶׁבֶת לָכִישׁ
רֵאשִׁית
חַטָּאת הִיא לְבַת־צִיּוֹן
כִּי־בָךְ נִמְצְאוּ
פִּשְׁעֵי יִשְׂרָאֵל:
14 לָכֵן תִּתְּנִי שִׁלּוּחִים
עַל מוֹרֶשֶׁת גַּת
בָּתֵּי אַכְזִיב
לְאַכְזָב

---

^b   *I.e., the nation's.*
^c   *Meaning of much of vv. 10–13 uncertain. They may refer to the transfer of part of western Judah to Philistine rule by Sennacherib of Assyria in the year 701 B.C.E.*
^d   *So that enemies may not gloat; cf. 2 Sam. 1.20.*
^e   *Heb. 'aphar, a play on Beth-leaphrah; vv. 10–15 contain several similar puns.*
^{f-f} *Emendation yields "Fair Achzib is."*

Like a spring that fails.

15A dispossessor will I bring to you
Who dwell in Mareshah;
At Adullam the glory
Of Israel shall set.

16gShear off your hair and make yourself bald
For the children you once delighted in;
Make yourself as bald as a vulture,
For they have been banished from you.

2 Ah, those who plan iniquity
And design evil on their beds;
When morning dawns, they do it,
For they have the power.

2They covet fields, and seize them;
Houses, and take them away.
They defraud men of their homes,
And people of their land.

3Assuredly, thus said the LORD: I am planning such a misfortune against this clan that you will not be able to free your necks from it. You will not be able to walk erect; it will be such a time of disaster.

4In that day,
One shall recite a poem about you,
And utter a bitter lament,
And shall say:
a-"My people's portion changes hands;
How it slips away from me!
Our field is allotted to a rebel.b
We are utterly ravaged."-a

5Truly, none of you
Shall cast a lot cordc
In the assembly of the LORD!

6"Stop preaching!" they preach.
"That's no way to preach;

לְמַלְכֵי יִשְׂרָאֵל׃

15 עֹד הַיֹּרֵשׁ אָבִי* לָךְ
יוֹשֶׁבֶת מָרֵשָׁה
עַד־עֲדֻלָּם יָבוֹא
כְּבוֹד יִשְׂרָאֵל׃

16 קָרְחִי וָגֹזִּי
עַל־בְּנֵי תַּעֲנוּגָיִךְ
הַרְחִבִי קָרְחָתֵךְ כַּנֶּשֶׁר
כִּי גָלוּ מִמֵּךְ׃ ס

ב הוֹי חֹשְׁבֵי־אָוֶן
וּפֹעֲלֵי רָע עַל־מִשְׁכְּבוֹתָם
בְּאוֹר הַבֹּקֶר יַעֲשׂוּהָ
כִּי יֶשׁ־לְאֵל יָדָם׃

2 וְחָמְדוּ שָׂדוֹת וְגָזָלוּ
וּבָתִּים וְנָשָׂאוּ
וְעָשְׁקוּ גֶּבֶר וּבֵיתוֹ
וְאִישׁ וְנַחֲלָתוֹ׃ פ

3 לָכֵן כֹּה אָמַר יְהֹוָה הִנְנִי חֹשֵׁב עַל־הַמִּשְׁפָּחָה הַזֹּאת רָעָה אֲשֶׁר לֹא־תָמִישׁוּ מִשָּׁם צַוְּארֹתֵיכֶם וְלֹא תֵלְכוּ רוֹמָה כִּי עֵת רָעָה הִיא׃

4 בַּיּוֹם הַהוּא
יִשָּׂא עֲלֵיכֶם מָשָׁל
וְנָהָה נְהִי נִהְיָה
אָמַר
שָׁדוֹד נְשַׁדֻּנוּ
חֵלֶק עַמִּי יָמִיר
אֵיךְ יָמִישׁ לִי
לְשׁוֹבֵב שָׂדֵינוּ יְחַלֵּק׃

5 לָכֵן לֹא־יִהְיֶה לְךָ
מַשְׁלִיךְ חֶבֶל בְּגוֹרָל
בִּקְהַל יְהֹוָה׃

6 אַל־תַּטִּפוּ יַטִּיפוּן
לֹא־יַטִּפוּ לָאֵלֶּה

---

g   A common rite of mourning; cf. Jer. 7.29.

a-a   Meaning of Heb. uncertain.
b   Emendation yields "ravager."
c   On a piece of land, thus acquiring title to it; cf. Josh. 18.6 and
      Ps. 16.6.

חסר א׳   v. 15.

a-Shame shall not overtake [us].

⁷Is the House of Jacob condemned?-*a*

Is the LORD's patience short?

Is such His practice?"

To be sure, My words are friendly

To those who walk in rectitude;

⁸But *d*-an enemy arises against-*d* My people.

You strip the mantle *e*-with the cloak-*e*

Off such as pass unsuspecting,

a-Who are turned away from war.-*a*

⁹You drive the women of My people away

From their pleasant homes;

You deprive their infants

Of My glory forever.

¹⁰Up and depart!

This is no resting place

a-Because of [your] defilement.

Terrible destruction shall befall.-*a*

¹¹If a man were to go about uttering

Windy, baseless falsehoods:

"I'll preach to you in favor of wine and
    liquor"—

He would be a preacher [acceptable] to that
    people.

¹²*f*I will assemble Jacob, all of you;

I will bring together the remnant of Israel;

I will make them all like sheep *g*-of Bozrah,-*g*

Like a flock inside its pen*a*—

They will be noisy with people.

¹³One who makes a breach

Goes before them;

They enlarge it to a gate

And leave by it.

לֹא יִסַּג כְּלִמּוֹת:

⁷ הֶאָמוּר בֵּית־יַעֲקֹב

הֲקָצַר רוּחַ יְהֹוָה

אִם־אֵלֶּה מַעֲלָלָיו

הֲלוֹא דְבָרַי יֵיטִיבוּ

עִם הַיָּשָׁר הוֹלֵךְ:

⁸ וְאֶתְמוּל עַמִּי לְאוֹיֵב יְקוֹמֵם

מִמּוּל שַׂלְמָה אֶדֶר תַּפְשִׁטוּן

מֵעֹבְרִים בֶּטַח

שׁוּבֵי מִלְחָמָה:

⁹ נְשֵׁי עַמִּי תְּגָרְשׁוּן

מִבֵּית תַּעֲנֻגֶיהָ

מֵעַל עֹלָלֶיהָ

תִּקְחוּ הֲדָרִי לְעוֹלָם:

¹⁰ קוּמוּ וּלְכוּ

כִּי לֹא־זֹאת הַמְּנוּחָה

בַּעֲבוּר טָמְאָה

תְּחַבֵּל וְחֶבֶל נִמְרָץ:

¹¹ לוּ־אִישׁ הֹלֵךְ

רוּחַ וָשֶׁקֶר כִּזֵּב

אַטִּף לְךָ לַיַּיִן וְלַשֵּׁכָר

וְהָיָה מַטִּיף הָעָם הַזֶּה:

¹² אָסֹף אֶאֱסֹף יַעֲקֹב כֻּלָּךְ

קַבֵּץ אֲקַבֵּץ שְׁאֵרִית יִשְׂרָאֵל

יַחַד אֲשִׂימֶנּוּ כְּצֹאן בָּצְרָה

כְּעֵדֶר בְּתוֹךְ הַדָּבְרוֹ

תְּהִימֶנָה מֵאָדָם:

¹³ עָלָה הַפֹּרֵץ

לִפְנֵיהֶם

פָּרְצוּ וַיַּעֲבֹרוּ שַׁעַר

וַיֵּצְאוּ בוֹ

---

d-d Meaning of Heb. uncertain; emendation yields "you arise as
    enemies against."

e-e Meaning of Heb. uncertain; emendation yields "off peaceful
    folk."

f Vv. 12–13 may be an example of such "acceptable" preaching.

g-g Emendation yields "in a fold [Arabic sīrah]."

Their king marches before them,
The LORD at their head.

וַיַּעֲבֹ֤ר מַלְכָּם֙ לִפְנֵיהֶ֔ם
וַיהֹוָ֖ה בְּרֹאשָֽׁם׃ פ

3

3 I said:

Listen, you rulers of Jacob,
You chiefs of the House of Israel!
For you ought to know what is right,
2*a*But you hate good and love evil.
3You have devoured My people's flesh;
You have flayed the skin off them,
And their flesh off their bones.
b-And after tearing their skins off them,
And their flesh off their bones,-*b*
And breaking their bones to bits,
You have cut it up *c*-as into-*c* a pot,
Like meat in a caldron.
4Someday they shall cry out to the LORD,
But He will not answer them;
At that time He will hide His face from them,
In accordance with the wrongs they have done.

ג וָאֹמַ֕ר
שִׁמְעוּ־נָא֙ רָאשֵׁ֣י יַעֲקֹ֔ב
וּקְצִינֵ֖י בֵּ֣ית יִשְׂרָאֵ֑ל
הֲל֣וֹא לָכֶ֔ם לָדַ֖עַת אֶת־הַמִּשְׁפָּֽט׃
2 שֹׂ֥נְאֵי ט֖וֹב וְאֹ֣הֲבֵי רעה רָ֑ע
גֹּזְלֵ֤י עוֹרָם֙ מֵֽעֲלֵיהֶ֔ם
וּשְׁאֵרָ֖ם מֵעַ֥ל עַצְמוֹתָֽם׃
3 וַאֲשֶׁ֣ר אָכְלוּ֮ שְׁאֵ֣ר עַמִּי֒
וְעוֹרָם֙ מֵעֲלֵיהֶ֣ם הִפְשִׁ֔יטוּ
וְאֶת־עַצְמֹֽתֵיהֶ֖ם פִּצֵּ֑חוּ
וּפָרְשׂוּ֙ כַּאֲשֶׁ֣ר בַּסִּ֔יר
וּכְבָשָׂ֖ר בְּת֥וֹךְ קַלָּֽחַת׃
4 אָ֚ז יִזְעֲק֣וּ אֶל־יְהֹוָ֔ה
וְלֹ֥א יַעֲנֶ֖ה אוֹתָ֑ם
וְיַסְתֵּ֨ר פָּנָ֤יו מֵהֶם֙ בָּעֵ֣ת הַהִ֔יא
כַּאֲשֶׁ֥ר הֵרֵ֖עוּ מַעַלְלֵיהֶֽם׃ פ

5Thus said the LORD to the prophets
Who lead My people astray,
Who cry "Peace!"
When they have something to chew,
But launch a war on him
Who fails to fill their mouths:
6Assuredly,
It shall be night for you
So that you cannot prophesy,
And it shall be dark for you
So that you cannot divine;
The sun shall set on the prophets,
And the day shall be darkened for them.
7The seers shall be shamed
And the diviners confounded;

5 כֹּ֚ה אָמַ֣ר יְהֹוָ֔ה עַל־הַנְּבִיאִ֖ים
הַמַּתְעִ֣ים אֶת־עַמִּ֑י
הַנֹּשְׁכִ֤ים בְּשִׁנֵּיהֶם֙
וְקָרְא֣וּ שָׁל֔וֹם
וַאֲשֶׁר֙ לֹא־יִתֵּ֣ן עַל־פִּיהֶ֔ם
וְקִדְּשׁ֥וּ עָלָ֖יו מִלְחָמָֽה׃
6 לָכֵ֞ן
לַ֤יְלָה לָכֶם֙
מֵֽחָז֔וֹן
וְחָשְׁכָ֥ה לָכֶ֖ם
מִקְּסֹ֑ם
וּבָ֤אָה הַשֶּׁ֙מֶשׁ֙ עַל־הַנְּבִיאִ֔ים
וְקָדַ֥ר עֲלֵיהֶ֖ם הַיּֽוֹם׃
7 וּבֹ֣שׁוּ הַחֹזִ֗ים
וְחָֽפְרוּ֙ הַקֹּֽסְמִ֔ים

---

a   Syntax of vv. 2–3 uncertain.
b-b   Brought down from v. 2 for clarity.
c-c   Meaning of Heb. uncertain; Septuagint and Syriac read "like flesh in."

They shall cover their upper lips,[d]
Because no response comes from God.
8But I,
I am filled with strength by the spirit of the
   Lord,
And with judgment and courage,
To declare to Jacob his transgressions
And to Israel his sin.

9Hear this, you rulers of the House of Jacob,
You chiefs of the House of Israel,
Who detest justice
And make crooked all that is straight,
10Who build Zion with crime,
Jerusalem with iniquity!
11Her rulers judge for gifts,
Her priests give rulings for a fee,
And her prophets divine for pay;
Yet they rely upon the Lord, saying,
"The Lord is in our midst;
No calamity shall overtake us."
12Assuredly, because of you
Zion shall be plowed as a field,
And Jerusalem shall become heaps of ruins,
And the Temple Mount
A shrine in the woods.

4 aIn the days to come,
The Mount of the Lord's House shall stand
Firm above the mountains;
And it shall tower above the hills.
The peoples shall gaze on it with joy,
2And the many nations shall go and shall say:
"Come,
Let us go up to the Mount of the Lord,
To the House of the God of Jacob;
That He may instruct us in His ways,

וְעָטוּ עַל־שָׂפָם כֻּלָּם
כִּי אֵין מַעֲנֵה אֱלֹהִים:
8 וְאוּלָם אָנֹכִי
מָלֵאתִי כֹחַ אֶת־רוּחַ יְהוָה
וּמִשְׁפָּט וּגְבוּרָה
לְהַגִּיד לְיַעֲקֹב פִּשְׁעוֹ
וּלְיִשְׂרָאֵל חַטָּאתוֹ: ס

9 שִׁמְעוּ־נָא זֹאת רָאשֵׁי בֵּית יַעֲקֹב
וּקְצִינֵי בֵּית יִשְׂרָאֵל
הַמְתַעֲבִים מִשְׁפָּט
וְאֵת כָּל־הַיְשָׁרָה יְעַקֵּשׁוּ:
10 בֹּנֶה צִיּוֹן בְּדָמִים
וִירוּשָׁלַםִ בְּעַוְלָה:
11 רָאשֶׁיהָ ׀ בְּשֹׁחַד יִשְׁפֹּטוּ
וְכֹהֲנֶיהָ בִּמְחִיר יוֹרוּ
וּנְבִיאֶיהָ בְּכֶסֶף יִקְסֹמוּ
וְעַל־יְהוָה יִשָּׁעֵנוּ לֵאמֹר
הֲלוֹא יְהוָה בְּקִרְבֵּנוּ
לֹא־תָבוֹא עָלֵינוּ רָעָה:
12 ⁎ לָכֵן בִּגְלַלְכֶם
צִיּוֹן שָׂדֶה תֵחָרֵשׁ
וִירוּשָׁלַםִ עִיִּין תִּהְיֶה
וְהַר הַבַּיִת
לְבָמוֹת יָעַר: פ

ד וְהָיָה ׀ בְּאַחֲרִית הַיָּמִים
יִהְיֶה הַר בֵּית־יְהוָה נָכוֹן
בְּרֹאשׁ הֶהָרִים
וְנִשָּׂא הוּא מִגְּבָעוֹת
וְנָהֲרוּ עָלָיו עַמִּים:
2 וְהָלְכוּ גּוֹיִם רַבִּים וְאָמְרוּ
לְכוּ ׀
וְנַעֲלֶה אֶל־הַר־יְהוָה
וְאֶל־בֵּית אֱלֹהֵי יַעֲקֹב
וְיוֹרֵנוּ מִדְּרָכָיו

---

d   As a sign of mourning; cf. Ezek. 24.17, 22; Lev. 13.45.
a   For vv. 1–3 cf. Isa. 2.2–4.

חצי הספר בפסוקים   v. 12.

And that we may walk in His paths."
For instruction shall come forth[b] from Zion,
The word of the LORD from Jerusalem.
[3]Thus He will judge among the many peoples,
And arbitrate for the multitude of nations,
However distant;
And they shall beat their swords into plow-
   shares[c]
And their spears into pruning hooks.
Nation shall not take up
Sword against nation;
They shall never again know[d] war;
[4]But every man shall sit
Under his grapevine or fig tree
With no one to disturb him.
For it was the LORD of Hosts who spoke.
[5]Though all the peoples walk
Each in the names of its gods,
We will walk
In the name of the LORD our God
Forever and ever.

[6]In that day

    —declares the LORD—

I will assemble the lame [sheep]
And will gather the outcast
And those I have treated harshly;
[7]And I will turn the lame into a remnant
And the expelled[e] into a populous nation.
And the LORD will reign over them on Mount
   Zion
Now and for evermore.

[8]And you, O Migdal-eder,[f]
[g]-Outpost of Fair Zion,
It shall come to you:-[g]

וְנֵלְכָ֖ה בְּאֹרְחֹתָ֑יו
כִּ֤י מִצִּיּוֹן֙ תֵּ֣צֵא תוֹרָ֔ה
וּדְבַר־יְהוָ֖ה מִירוּשָׁלָֽםִ׃
³וְשָׁפַ֗ט בֵּ֚ין עַמִּ֣ים רַבִּ֔ים
וְהוֹכִ֛יחַ לְגוֹיִ֥ם עֲצֻמִ֖ים
עַד־רָח֑וֹק
וְכִתְּת֨וּ חַרְבֹתֵיהֶ֜ם לְאִתִּ֗ים
וַחֲנִיתֹֽתֵיהֶם֙ לְמַזְמֵר֔וֹת
לֹא־יִשְׂא֞וּ גּ֤וֹי
אֶל־גּוֹי֙ חֶ֔רֶב
וְלֹא־יִלְמְד֥וּן ע֖וֹד מִלְחָמָֽה׃
⁴וְיָשְׁב֗וּ אִ֣ישׁ
תַּ֧חַת גַּפְנ֛וֹ וְתַ֥חַת תְּאֵנָת֖וֹ
וְאֵ֣ין מַחֲרִ֑יד
כִּי־פִ֛י יְהוָ֥ה צְבָא֖וֹת דִּבֵּֽר׃
⁵כִּ֚י כָּל־הָ֣עַמִּ֔ים יֵלְכ֕וּ
אִ֖ישׁ בְּשֵׁ֣ם אֱלֹהָ֑יו
וַאֲנַ֗חְנוּ נֵלֵ֛ךְ
בְּשֵׁם־יְהוָ֥ה אֱלֹהֵ֖ינוּ
לְעוֹלָ֥ם וָעֶֽד׃ פ

⁶בַּיּ֨וֹם הַה֤וּא
נְאֻם־יְהוָ֔ה
אֹֽסְפָה֙ הַצֹּ֣לֵעָ֔ה
וְהַנִּדָּחָ֖ה אֲקַבֵּ֑צָה
וַאֲשֶׁ֖ר הֲרֵעֹֽתִי׃
⁷וְשַׂמְתִּ֤י אֶת־הַצֹּֽלֵעָה֙ לִשְׁאֵרִ֔ית
וְהַנַּהֲלָאָ֖ה לְג֣וֹי עָצ֑וּם
וּמָלַ֨ךְ יְהוָ֤ה עֲלֵיהֶם֙ בְּהַ֣ר צִיּ֔וֹן
מֵעַתָּ֖ה וְעַד־עוֹלָֽם׃ פ

⁸וְאַתָּ֣ה מִגְדַּל־עֵ֗דֶר
עֹ֛פֶל בַּת־צִיּ֖וֹן
עָדֶ֣יךָ תֵּאתֶ֑ה

---

b   *I.e., oracles will be obtainable.*
c   *More exactly, the iron points with which wooden plows were*
    tipped.
d   *Cf. Judg. 3.2.*
e   *Meaning of Heb. uncertain; emendation yields "weaklings"; cf.*
    Ezek. 34.4.
f   *Apparently near Bethlehem; see Gen. 35.19–21.*
g-g   *Meaning of Heb. uncertain.*

The former monarchy shall return—
The kingship of *h*-Fair Jerusalem.-*h*

9Now why do you utter such cries?
Is there no king in you,
Have your advisors perished,
That you have been seized by writhing
Like a woman in travail?
10Writhe and scream,*g* Fair Zion,
Like a woman in travail!
For now you must leave the city
And dwell in the country—
And you will reach Babylon.
There you shall be saved,
There the LORD will redeem you
From the hands of your foes.
11Indeed, many nations
Have assembled against you
Who think, "Let our eye
g-Obscenely gaze-*g* on Zion."
12But they do not know
The design of the LORD,
They do not divine His intent:
He has gathered them
Like cut grain to the threshing floor.
13Up and thresh, Fair Zion!
For I will give you horns of iron
And provide you with hoofs of bronze,
And you will crush the many peoples.
You*i* will devote their riches to the LORD,
Their wealth to the Lord of all the earth.

14Now you gash yourself *g*-in grief.-*g*
They have laid siege to us;
They strike the ruler of Israel
On the cheek with a staff.

וּבָאָ֞ה הַמֶּמְשָׁלָ֣ה הָרִֽאשֹׁנָ֗ה
מַמְלֶ֖כֶת לְבַת־יְרֽוּשָׁלָֽ͏ִם׃

9עַתָּ֕ה לָ֥מָּה תָרִ֖יעִי רֵ֑עַ
הֲמֶ֣לֶךְ אֵֽין־בָּ֗ךְ
אִֽם־יוֹעֲצֵךְ֙ אָבָ֔ד
כִּֽי־הֶחֱזִיקֵ֥ךְ חִ֖יל
כַּיּוֹלֵדָֽה׃
10ח֧וּלִי וָגֹ֛חִי בַּת־צִיּ֖וֹן
כַּיּֽוֹלֵדָ֑ה
כִּֽי־עַתָּה֩ תֵצְאִ֨י מִקִּרְיָ֜ה
וְשָׁכַ֣נְתְּ בַּשָּׂדֶ֗ה
וּבָ֖את עַד־בָּבֶ֑ל
שָׁ֣ם תִּנָּצֵ֔לִי
שָׁ֚ם יִגְאָלֵ֣ךְ יְהֹוָ֔ה
מִכַּ֖ף אֹיְבָֽיִךְ׃
11וְעַתָּ֛ה נֶֽאֶסְפ֥וּ עָלַ֖יִךְ
גּוֹיִ֣ם רַבִּ֑ים
הָאֹמְרִ֣ים תֶּחֱנָ֔ף
וְתַ֥חַז בְּצִיּ֖וֹן עֵינֵֽינוּ׃
12וְהֵ֗מָּה לֹ֤א יָֽדְעוּ֙
מַחְשְׁב֣וֹת יְהֹוָ֔ה
וְלֹ֥א הֵבִ֖ינוּ עֲצָת֑וֹ
כִּ֥י קִבְּצָ֖ם
כֶּעָמִ֥יר גֹּֽרְנָה׃
13ק֧וּמִי וָד֣וֹשִׁי בַת־צִיּ֗וֹן
כִּֽי־קַרְנֵ֞ךְ אָשִׂ֤ים בַּרְזֶל֙
וּפַרְסֹתַ֙יִךְ֙ אָשִׂ֣ים נְחוּשָׁ֔ה
וַהֲדִקּ֖וֹת עַמִּ֣ים רַבִּ֑ים
וְהַחֲרַמְתִּ֤י לַֽיהֹוָה֙ בִּצְעָ֔ם
וְחֵילָ֖ם לַאֲד֥וֹן כׇּל־הָאָֽרֶץ׃

14עַתָּה֙ תִּתְגֹּֽדְדִ֣י בַת־גְּד֔וּד
מָצ֖וֹר שָׂ֣ם עָלֵ֑ינוּ
בַּשֵּׁ֙בֶט֙ יַכּ֣וּ עַֽל־הַלְּחִ֔י
אֵ֖ת שֹׁפֵ֥ט יִשְׂרָאֵֽל׃ ס

---

h-h   Emendation yields "the House of Israel"; *cf.* 5.1–2.
i   Heb. -*ti serves here as the ending of the second-person singular
    feminine; cf. Judg. 5.7 and note; Jer. 2.20; etc.*

5 And you, O Bethlehem of Ephrath,[a]
  Least among the clans of Judah,
From you one shall come forth
  To rule Israel for Me—
One whose origin is from of old,
  From ancient times.
[2b]Truly, He will leave them [helpless]
  Until she who is to bear has borne;[c]
Then the rest of his countrymen
  Shall return to the children of Israel.[-b]
[3]He shall stand and shepherd
  By the might of the LORD,
By the power of the name
  Of the LORD his God,
And they shall dwell [secure].
  For lo, he shall wax great
To the ends of the earth;
[4]And that shall afford safety.
  Should Assyria invade our land
And tread upon our fortresses,[d]
  We will set up over it[e] seven shepherds,
Eight princes of men,
[5]Who will shepherd Assyria's land with
    swords,
The land of Nimrod [f]in its gates.[-f]
  Thus he will deliver [us]
From Assyria, should it invade our land,
  And should it trample our country.

[6]The remnant of Jacob shall be,
  In the midst of the many peoples,
Like dew from the LORD,
  Like droplets on grass—
Which do not look to any man
  Nor place their hope in mortals.

ה וְאַתָּ֞ה בֵּֽית־לֶ֣חֶם אֶפְרָ֗תָה

צָעִיר֙ לִֽהְיוֹת֙ בְּאַלְפֵ֣י יְהוּדָ֔ה

מִמְּךָ֙ לִ֣י יֵצֵ֔א

לִֽהְי֥וֹת מוֹשֵׁ֖ל בְּיִשְׂרָאֵ֑ל

וּמוֹצָאֹתָ֥יו מִקֶּ֖דֶם

מִימֵ֥י עוֹלָֽם׃

2 לָכֵ֣ן יִתְּנֵ֔ם

עַד־עֵ֥ת יוֹלֵדָ֖ה יָלָ֑דָה

וְיֶ֣תֶר אֶחָ֔יו

יְשׁוּב֖וּן עַל־בְּנֵ֥י יִשְׂרָאֵֽל׃

3 וְעָמַ֣ד וְרָעָ֔ה

בְּעֹ֣ז יְהוָ֔ה

בִּגְא֕וֹן שֵׁ֖ם

יְהוָ֣ה אֱלֹהָ֑יו

וְיָשָׁ֕בוּ

כִּֽי־עַתָּ֥ה יִגְדַּ֖ל

עַד־אַפְסֵי־אָֽרֶץ׃

4 וְהָיָ֥ה זֶ֖ה שָׁל֑וֹם

אַשּׁ֣וּר ׀ כִּֽי־יָב֣וֹא בְאַרְצֵ֗נוּ

וְכִ֣י יִדְרֹךְ֮ בְּאַרְמְנֹתֵינוּ֒

וַהֲקֵמֹ֤נוּ עָלָיו֙ שִׁבְעָ֣ה רֹעִ֔ים

וּשְׁמֹנָ֖ה נְסִיכֵ֥י אָדָֽם׃

5 וְרָע֞וּ אֶת־אֶ֤רֶץ אַשּׁוּר֙ בַּחֶ֔רֶב

וְאֶת־אֶ֥רֶץ נִמְרֹ֖ד בִּפְתָחֶ֑יהָ

וְהִצִּ֣יל

מֵֽאַשּׁ֔וּר כִּֽי־יָב֣וֹא בְאַרְצֵ֔נוּ

וְכִ֥י יִדְרֹ֖ךְ בִּגְבוּלֵֽנוּ׃ ס

6 וְהָיָ֣ה ׀ שְׁאֵרִ֣ית יַעֲקֹ֗ב

בְּקֶ֙רֶב֙ עַמִּ֣ים רַבִּ֔ים

כְּטַל֙ מֵאֵ֣ת יְהוָ֔ה

כִּרְבִיבִ֖ים עֲלֵי־עֵ֑שֶׂב

אֲשֶׁ֤ר לֹֽא־יְקַוֶּה֙ לְאִ֔ישׁ

וְלֹ֥א יְיַחֵ֖ל לִבְנֵ֥י אָדָֽם׃

---

a   *The clan to which the Bethlehemites belonged; see 1 Sam. 17.12;*
     Ruth 1.2; 4.11.
b-b *Meaning of Heb. uncertain.*
c   *I.e., a ruler, shepherd (v. 3), to deliver Israel from the Assyrians*
     (vv. 4–5).
d   *Septuagint and Syriac read "soil"; cf. v. 5.*
e   *I.e., Assyria.*
f-f *Emendation yields "with drawn blades"; cf. Ps. 37.14; 55.22.*

7The remnant of Jacob
Shall be among the nations,
In the midst of the many peoples,
Like a lion among beasts of the wild,
Like a fierce lion among flocks of sheep,
Which tramples wherever it goes
And rends, with none to deliver.
8Your hand shall prevail over your foes,
And all your enemies shall be cut down!
9In that day

         —declares the Lord—

I will destroy the horses in your midst
And wreck your chariots.
10I will destroy the cities of your land
And demolish all your fortresses.
11I will destroy the sorcery you practice,
And you shall have no more soothsayers.
12I will destroy your idols
And the sacred pillars in your midst;
And no more shall you bow down
To the work of your hands.
13I will tear down the sacred posts in your
    midst
And destroy your cities.g
14In anger and wrath
Will I wreak retribution
On the nationsh that have not obeyed.

6 Hear what the Lord is saying:
Come, present [My] case before the moun-
    tains,
And let the hills hear you pleading.

2Hear, you mountains, the case of the Lord—
a-You firm-a foundations of the earth!
For the Lord has a case against His people,
He has a suit against Israel.

---

g Emendation yields "idols."
h Emendation yields "arrogant."

a-a Emendation yields "Give ear, you."

וְהָיָ֣ה ׀ שְׁאֵרִ֣ית יַעֲקֹ֗ב 7
בַּגּוֹיִ֔ם
בְּקֶ֖רֶב עַמִּ֣ים רַבִּ֑ים
כְּאַרְיֵה֙ בְּבַהֲמ֣וֹת יַ֔עַר
כִּכְפִ֖יר בְּעֶדְרֵי־צֹ֑אן
אֲשֶׁ֧ר אִם־עָבַ֛ר וְרָמַ֥ס
וְטָרַ֖ף וְאֵ֥ין מַצִּֽיל׃
תָּרֹ֥ם יָדְךָ֖ עַל־צָרֶ֑יךָ 8
וְכָל־אֹיְבֶ֖יךָ יִכָּרֵֽתוּ׃ פ
וְהָיָ֣ה בַיּוֹם־הַה֗וּא 9
נְאֻם־יְהֹוָ֔ה
וְהִכְרַתִּ֥י סוּסֶ֖יךָ מִקִּרְבֶּ֑ךָ
וְהַאֲבַדְתִּ֖י מַרְכְּבֹתֶֽיךָ׃
וְהִכְרַתִּ֖י עָרֵ֣י* אַרְצֶ֑ךָ 10
וְהָרַסְתִּ֖י כָּל־מִבְצָרֶֽיךָ׃
וְהִכְרַתִּ֥י כְשָׁפִ֖ים מִיָּדֶ֑ךָ 11
וּמְע֣וֹנְנִ֔ים לֹ֥א יִֽהְיוּ־לָֽךְ׃
וְהִכְרַתִּ֧י פְסִילֶ֛יךָ 12
וּמַצֵּבוֹתֶ֖יךָ מִקִּרְבֶּ֑ךָ
וְלֹֽא־תִשְׁתַּחֲוֶ֥ה ע֖וֹד
לְמַעֲשֵׂ֥ה יָדֶֽיךָ׃
וְנָתַשְׁתִּ֥י אֲשֵׁירֶ֖יךָ מִקִּרְבֶּ֑ךָ 13
וְהִשְׁמַדְתִּ֖י עָרֶֽיךָ*׃
וְעָשִׂ֥יתִי בְּאַ֖ף 14
וּבְחֵמָ֣ה נָקָ֑ם
אֶת־הַגּוֹיִ֖ם אֲשֶׁ֥ר לֹ֥א שָׁמֵֽעוּ׃ ס

שִׁמְעוּ־נָ֕א אֵ֥ת אֲשֶׁר־יְהֹוָ֖ה אֹמֵ֑ר ו
ק֚וּם רִ֣יב אֶת־הֶהָרִ֔ים
וְתִשְׁמַ֖עְנָה הַגְּבָע֥וֹת קוֹלֶֽךָ׃

שִׁמְע֤וּ הָרִים֙ אֶת־רִ֣יב יְהֹוָ֔ה 2
וְהָאֵתָנִ֖ים מֹ֣סְדֵי אָ֑רֶץ
כִּ֣י רִ֤יב לַֽיהֹוָה֙ עִם־עַמּ֔וֹ
וְעִם־יִשְׂרָאֵ֖ל יִתְוַכָּֽח׃

---

v. 10. לשון שנאה
v. 13. לשון שנאה

3"My people!
What wrong have I done you?
What hardship have I caused you?
Testify against Me.
4In fact,
I brought you up from the land of Egypt,
I redeemed you from the house of bondage,
And I sent before you
Moses, Aaron, and Miriam.

5"My people,
Remember what Balak king of Moab
Plotted against you,
And how Balaam son of Beor
Responded to him.
[Recall your passage]
From Shittim to Gilgal[b]—
And you will recognize
The gracious acts of the Lord."

6With what shall I approach the Lord,
Do homage to God on high?
Shall I approach Him with burnt offerings,
With calves a year old?
7Would the Lord be pleased with thousands
of rams,
With myriads of streams of oil?
Shall I give my first-born for my transgres-
sion,
The fruit of my body for my sins?

8"He has told you, O man, what is good,
And what the Lord requires of you:
Only to do justice
And to love goodness,
And [c]-to walk modestly with your God;-[c]
9[d]-Then will your name achieve wisdom."-[d]

Hark! The Lord
Summons the city:

3 עַמִּי
מֶה־עָשִׂיתִי לְךָ
וּמָה הֶלְאֵתִיךָ
עֲנֵה בִי:
4 כִּי
הֶעֱלִתִיךָ מֵאֶרֶץ מִצְרַיִם
וּמִבֵּית עֲבָדִים פְּדִיתִיךָ
וָאֶשְׁלַח לְפָנֶיךָ
אֶת־מֹשֶׁה אַהֲרֹן וּמִרְיָם:

5 עַמִּי
זְכָר־נָא מַה־יָּעַץ
בָּלָק מֶלֶךְ מוֹאָב
וּמֶה־עָנָה אֹתוֹ
בִּלְעָם בֶּן־בְּעוֹר
מִן־הַשִּׁטִּים
עַד־הַגִּלְגָּל
לְמַעַן דַּעַת
צִדְקוֹת יְהוָה:

6 בַּמָּה אֲקַדֵּם יְהוָה
אִכַּף לֵאלֹהֵי מָרוֹם
הַאֲקַדְּמֶנּוּ בְעוֹלוֹת
בַּעֲגָלִים בְּנֵי שָׁנָה:
7 הֲיִרְצֶה יְהוָה בְּאַלְפֵי אֵילִים
בְּרִבְבוֹת נַחֲלֵי־שָׁמֶן
הַאֶתֵּן בְּכוֹרִי פִּשְׁעִי
פְּרִי בִטְנִי חַטַּאת נַפְשִׁי:

8 הִגִּיד לְךָ אָדָם מַה־טּוֹב
וּמָה־יְהוָה דּוֹרֵשׁ מִמְּךָ
כִּי אִם־עֲשׂוֹת מִשְׁפָּט
וְאַהֲבַת חֶסֶד
וְהַצְנֵעַ לֶכֶת עִם־אֱלֹהֶיךָ: פ
9 קוֹל יְהוָה
לָעִיר יִקְרָא
וְתוּשִׁיָּה יִרְאֶה שְׁמֶךָ

---

b   *I.e., the crossing of the Jordan; see Josh. 3.1, 14–4.19.*
c-c   *Or "It is prudent to serve your God."*
d-d   *Emendation yields "And it is worthwhile to revere His name."*

*e-*Hear, O scepter;

For who can direct her [10]but you?-*e*

Will I overlook,*f* in the wicked man's house,

The granaries of wickedness

And the accursed short *ephah*?*g*

[11]Shall he*h* be acquitted despite wicked balances

And a bag of fraudulent weights?—

[12]*i*Whose rich men are full of lawlessness,

And whose inhabitants speak treachery,

With tongues of deceit in their mouths.

[13]I, in turn, have beaten you sore,

Have stunned [you] for your sins:

[14]You have been eating without getting your fill,

*e-*And there is a gnawing at your vitals;

You have been conceiving without bearing young,-*e*

And what you bore I would deliver to the sword.

[15]You have been sowing, but have nothing to reap;

You have trod olives, but have no oil for rubbing,

And grapes*j* but have no wine to drink.

[16]Yet *k-*you have kept-*k* the laws of Omri,

And all the practices of the House of Ahab,

And have followed what they devised.

Therefore I will make you an object of horror

And *l-*her inhabitants-*l* an object of hissing;*m*

And you shall bear the mockery of peoples.*n*

שִׁמְע֖וּ מַטֶּ֥ה

10 וּמִ֣י יְעָדָ֑הּ ע֚וֹד

הַאִשׁ֙* בֵּ֣ית רָשָׁ֔ע

אֹצְר֖וֹת רֶ֑שַׁע

וְאֵיפַ֥ת רָז֖וֹן זְעוּמָֽה׃

11 הַאֶזְכֶּ֖ה בְּמֹ֣אזְנֵי רֶ֑שַׁע

וּבְכִ֖יס אַבְנֵ֥י מִרְמָֽה׃

12 אֲשֶׁ֤ר עֲשִׁירֶ֙יהָ֙ מָלְא֣וּ חָמָ֔ס

וְיֹשְׁבֶ֖יהָ דִּבְּרוּ־שָׁ֑קֶר

וּלְשׁוֹנָ֖ם רְמִיָּ֥ה בְּפִיהֶֽם׃

13 וְגַם־אֲנִ֥י הֶחֱלֵ֖יתִי הַכּוֹתֶ֑ךָ

הַשְׁמֵ֖ם עַל־חַטֹּאתֶֽךָ׃

14 אַתָּ֤ה תֹאכַל֙ וְלֹ֣א תִשְׂבָּ֔ע

וְיֶשְׁחֲךָ֖ בְּקִרְבֶּ֑ךָ

וְתַסֵּג֙ וְלֹ֣א תַפְלִ֔יט

וַאֲשֶׁ֥ר תְּפַלֵּ֖ט לַחֶ֥רֶב אֶתֵּֽן׃

15 אַתָּ֥ה תִזְרַ֖ע וְלֹ֣א תִקְצ֑וֹר

אַתָּ֤ה תִדְרֹךְ־זַ֙יִת֙ וְלֹא־תָס֣וּךְ שֶׁ֔מֶן

וְתִיר֖וֹשׁ וְלֹ֥א תִשְׁתֶּה־יָּֽיִן׃

16 וְיִשְׁתַּמֵּ֞ר חֻקּ֣וֹת עָמְרִ֗י

וְכֹל֙ מַעֲשֵׂ֣ה בֵית־אַחְאָ֔ב

וַתֵּלְכ֖וּ בְּמֹעֲצוֹתָ֑ם

לְמַ֩עַן֩ תִּתִּ֨י אֹתְךָ֜ לְשַׁמָּ֗ה

וְיֹשְׁבֶ֙יהָ֙ לִשְׁרֵקָ֔ה

וְחֶרְפַּ֥ת עַמִּ֖י תִּשָּֽׂאוּ׃ פ

---

e-e   *Meaning of Heb. uncertain.*

f   *Taking ish as from* nashah *"to forget"; cf. Deut. 32.18.*

g   *Cf. Amos 8.4–5.*

h   *Heb. "I"; change of vocalization yields "Will I acquit him."*

i   *This verse would read well after "city" in v. 9.*

j   *Lit. "new wine."*

k-k *Heb. "is kept."*

l-l   *I.e., those of the city of v. 9, apparently Samaria.*

m   *See note at Jer. 18.16.*

n   *Heb. "My people."*

7

7 Woe is me!*a*

I am become like leavings of a fig harvest,
Like gleanings when the vintage is over,
There is not a cluster to eat,
Not a ripe fig I could desire.
²The pious are vanished from the land,
None upright are left among men;
All lie in wait to commit crimes,
One traps the other in his net.
³*b*-They are eager to do evil:
The magistrate makes demands,
And the judge [judges] for a fee;
The rich man makes his crooked plea,
And they grant it.-*b*
⁴The best of them is like a prickly shrub;
The [most] upright, worse than a barrier of
   thorns.
b-On the day you waited for,-*b* your doom has
   come—
Now their confusion shall come to pass.
⁵Trust no friend,
Rely on no intimate;
Be guarded in speech
With her who lies in your bosom.
⁶For son spurns father,
Daughter rises up against mother,
Daughter-in-law against mother-in-law—
A man's own household
Are his enemies.
⁷Yet I will look to the LORD,
I will wait for the God who saves me,
My God will hear me.

⁸Do not rejoice over me,
O my enemy!*c*
Though I have fallen, I rise again;
Though I sit in darkness, the LORD is my light.

אֱלָלַי לִ֔י ז ١

כִּ֣י הָיִ֗יתִי כְּאׇסְפֵּי־קַ֔יִץ

כְּעֹלְלֹ֖ת בָּצִ֑יר

אֵין־אֶשְׁכּ֣וֹל לֶאֱכ֔וֹל

בִּכּוּרָ֖ה אִוְּתָ֥ה נַפְשִֽׁי׃

אָבַ֤ד חָסִיד֙ מִן־הָאָ֔רֶץ ٢

וְיָשָׁ֥ר בָּאָדָ֖ם אָ֑יִן

כֻּלָּם֙ לְדָמִ֣ים יֶאֱרֹ֔בוּ

אִ֥ישׁ אֶת־אָחִ֖יהוּ יָצ֥וּדוּ חֵֽרֶם׃

עַל־הָרַ֤ע כַּפַּ֙יִם֙ לְהֵיטִ֔יב ٣

הַשַּׂ֣ר שֹׁאֵ֗ל

וְהַשֹּׁפֵ֣ט בַּשִּׁלּ֔וּם

וְהַגָּד֗וֹל דֹּבֵ֛ר הַוַּ֥ת נַפְשׁ֖וֹ ה֑וּא

וַֽיְעַבְּתֽוּהָ׃

טוֹבָ֣ם כְּחֵ֔דֶק ٤

יָשָׁ֖ר מִמְּסוּכָ֑ה

י֤וֹם מְצַפֶּ֙יךָ֙ פְּקֻדָּתְךָ֣ בָ֔אָה

עַתָּ֥ה תִהְיֶ֖ה מְבוּכָתָֽם׃

אַל־תַּאֲמִ֣ינוּ בְרֵ֔עַ ٥

אַֽל־תִּבְטְח֖וּ בְּאַלּ֑וּף

מִשֹּׁכֶ֣בֶת חֵיקֶ֔ךָ

שְׁמֹ֖ר פִּתְחֵי־פִֽיךָ׃

כִּֽי־בֵן֙ מְנַבֵּ֣ל אָ֔ב ٦

בַּ֖ת קָמָ֣ה בְאִמָּ֑הּ

כַּלָּ֖ה בַּחֲמֹתָ֑הּ

אֹיְבֵ֥י אִ֖ישׁ

אַנְשֵׁ֥י בֵיתֽוֹ׃

וַאֲנִי֙ בַּיהֹוָ֣ה אֲצַפֶּ֔ה ٧

אוֹחִ֖ילָה לֵאלֹהֵ֣י יִשְׁעִ֑י

יִשְׁמָעֵ֖נִי אֱלֹהָֽי׃

אַֽל־תִּשְׂמְחִ֤י ٨

אֹיַ֙בְתִּי֙ לִ֔י

כִּ֣י נָפַ֖לְתִּי קָ֑מְתִּי

כִּֽי־אֵשֵׁ֣ב בַּחֹ֔שֶׁךְ יְהֹוָ֖ה א֥וֹר לִֽי׃ ס

---

a   *The speaker is feminine (cf. 'elohayikh, v. 10), probably Samaria
     personified; cf. note l-l at 6.16.*
b-b *Meaning of Heb. uncertain.*
c   *Heb. feminine, apparently referring to Damascus.*

⁹I must bear the anger of the Lord,
Since I have sinned against Him,
Until He champions my cause
And upholds my claim.
He will let me out into the light;
I will enjoy vindication by Him.
¹⁰When my enemyᶜ sees it,
She shall be covered with shame,
She who taunts me with "Where is He,
The Lord your God?"
My eyes shall behold her [downfall];
Lo, she shall be for trampling
Like mud in the streets.
¹¹A day for mending your wallsᵈ—
That is a far-off day.
¹²This is rather a day when to you
[Tramplers] will come streaming
From Assyria and the towns of Egypt—
From [every land from] Egypt to the Euphra-
    tes,
From sea to sea and from mountain to moun-
    tain—
¹³And yourᵉ land shall become a desolation—
Because of those who dwell in it—
As the fruit of their misdeeds.

¹⁴Oh, shepherd Your people with Your staff,
Your very own flock.
May they who dwell isolated
ᶠIn a woodland surrounded by farmland-ᶠ
Grazeᵍ Bashan and Gilead
As in olden days.
¹⁵ʰ-I will show him-ʰ wondrous deeds
As in the days when You sallied forth from
    the land of Egypt.
¹⁶Let nations behold and be ashamed

⁹ זַעַף יְהֹוָה אֶשָּׂא
כִּי חָטָאתִי לֹו
עַד אֲשֶׁר יָרִיב רִיבִי
וְעָשָׂה מִשְׁפָּטִי
יֹוצִיאֵנִי לָאֹור
אֶרְאֶה בְּצִדְקָתֹו:
¹⁰ וְתֵרֶא אֹיַבְתִּי
וּתְכַסֶּהָ בוּשָׁה
הָאֹמְרָה אֵלַי אַיֹּו
יְהֹוָה אֱלֹהָיִךְ
עֵינַי תִּרְאֶינָה* בָּהּ
עַתָּה תִּהְיֶה לְמִרְמָס
כְּטִיט חוּצֹות:
¹¹ יֹום לִבְנֹות גְּדֵרָיִךְ
יֹום הַהוּא יִרְחַק־חֹק:
¹² יֹום הוּא וְעָדֶיךָ
יָבֹוא
לְמִנִּי אַשּׁוּר וְעָרֵי מָצֹור
וּלְמִנִּי מָצֹור וְעַד־נָהָר
וְיָם מִיָּם וְהַר הָהָר:
¹³ וְהָיְתָה הָאָרֶץ לִשְׁמָמָה
עַל־יֹשְׁבֶיהָ
מִפְּרִי מַעַלְלֵיהֶם: ס

¹⁴ רְעֵה עַמְּךָ בְשִׁבְטֶךָ
צֹאן נַחֲלָתֶךָ
שֹׁכְנִי לְבָדָד
יַעַר בְּתֹוךְ כַּרְמֶל
יִרְעוּ בָשָׁן וְגִלְעָד
כִּימֵי עֹולָם:
¹⁵ כִּימֵי צֵאתְךָ מֵאֶרֶץ מִצְרָיִם
אַרְאֶנּוּ נִפְלָאֹות:
¹⁶ יִרְאוּ גֹויִם וְיֵבֹשׁוּ

ᵈ To keep out tramplers (end of preceding verse); cf. Isa. 5.5;
   Ps. 80.13–14.
ᵉ Heb. "the."
ᶠ-ᶠ I.e., the land west of the Jordan, which is represented as far less
   fertile than adjacent regions.
ᵍ Emendation yields "possess."
ʰ-ʰ Emendation yields "Show us."

Despite all their might;

Let them put hand to mouth;

Let their ears be deafened!

¹⁷Let them lick dust like snakes,

Like crawling things on the ground!

ᵇ-Let them come trembling out of their
    strongholds-*ᵇ*

To the Lᴏʀᴅ our God;

Let them fear and dread You!

¹⁸Who is a God like You,

Forgiving iniquity

And remitting transgression;

Who has not maintained His wrath forever

Against the remnant of His own people,

Because He loves graciousness!

¹⁹He will take us back in love;

He will cover up our iniquities,

You will hurl all our*ⁱ* sins

Into the depths of the sea.

²⁰You will keep faith with Jacob,

Loyalty to Abraham,

As You promised on oath to our fathers

In days gone by.

מִכֹּל גְּבוּרָתֶֽם

יָשִׂימוּ יָד֙ עַל־פֶּ֔ה

אָזְנֵיהֶ֖ם תֶּחֱרַֽשְׁנָה׃

17 יְלַחֲכ֤וּ עָפָר֙ כַּנָּחָ֔שׁ

כְּזֹחֲלֵ֣י אֶ֔רֶץ

יִרְגְּז֖וּ מִמִּסְגְּרֹֽתֵיהֶ֑ם

אֶל־יְהֹוָ֤ה אֱלֹהֵ֙ינוּ֙

יִפְחָ֔דוּ וְיִֽרְא֖וּ מִמֶּֽךָּ׃

18 מִי־אֵ֣ל כָּמ֗וֹךָ

נֹשֵׂ֤א עָוֺן֙

וְעֹבֵ֣ר עַל־פֶּ֔שַׁע

לִשְׁאֵרִ֖ית נַחֲלָת֑וֹ

לֹא־הֶחֱזִ֤יק לָעַד֙ אַפּ֔וֹ

כִּֽי־חָפֵ֥ץ חֶ֖סֶד הֽוּא׃

19 יָשׁ֣וּב יְרַחֲמֵ֔נוּ

יִכְבֹּ֖שׁ עֲוֺנֹתֵ֑ינוּ

וְתַשְׁלִ֛יךְ בִּמְצֻל֥וֹת יָ֖ם

כָּל־חַטֹּאותָֽם׃*

20 תִּתֵּ֤ן אֱמֶת֙ לְיַעֲקֹ֔ב

חֶ֖סֶד לְאַבְרָהָ֑ם

אֲשֶׁר־נִשְׁבַּ֥עְתָּ לַאֲבֹתֵ֖ינוּ

מִ֥ימֵי קֶֽדֶם׃

ⁱ   Heb. *"their."*   מלא ו'   *v. 19.*

NAHUM

1

A pronouncement on Nineveh: The Book of the Prophecy of Nahum the Elkoshite.

2The LORD is a passionate, avenging God;
The LORD is vengeful and fierce in wrath.
The LORD takes vengeance on His enemies,
He rages against His foes.
3The LORD is slow to anger and of great for-
    bearance,
But the LORD does not remit all punishment.
He travels in whirlwind and storm,
And clouds are the dust on His feet.
4He rebukes the sea and dries it up,
And He makes all rivers fail;
Bashan and Carmel languish,
And the blossomsa of Lebanon wither.
5The mountains quake because of Him,
And the hills melt.
The earth heavesb before Him,
The world and all that dwell therein.
6Who can stand before His wrath?
Who can resist His fury?
His anger pours out like fire,
And rocks are shattered because of Him.
7The LORD is good to [those who hope in
    Him],
A haven on a day of distress;
He is mindful of those who seek refuge in
    Him.
8And with a sweeping flood
He makes an end of c-her place,-c

---

a   Lit. "bud."
b   Meaning of Heb. uncertain.
c-c Meaning of Heb. uncertain; emendation yields "those who
    oppose Him."

נַחוּם

א מַשָּׂא נִינְוֵה סֵפֶר חֲזוֹן נַחוּם
הָאֶלְקֹשִׁי:

2 אֵל קַנּוֹא וְנֹקֵם יְהֹוָה
נֹקֵם יְהֹוָה וּבַעַל חֵמָה
נֹקֵם יְהֹוָה לְצָרָיו
וְנוֹטֵר הוּא לְאֹיְבָיו:
3 יְהֹוָה אֶרֶךְ אַפַּיִם וגדול וּגְדָל־כֹּחַ
וְנַקֵּה לֹא יְנַקֶּה
יְהֹוָה בְּסוּפָה וּבִשְׂעָרָה דַּרְכּוֹ
וְעָנָן אֲבַק רַגְלָיו:
4 גּוֹעֵר בַּיָּם וַיַּבְּשֵׁהוּ
וְכָל־הַנְּהָרוֹת הֶחֱרִיב
אֻמְלַל בָּשָׁן וְכַרְמֶל
וּפֶרַח לְבָנוֹן אֻמְלָל:
5 הָרִים רָעֲשׁוּ מִמֶּנּוּ
וְהַגְּבָעוֹת הִתְמֹגָגוּ
וַתִּשָּׂא הָאָרֶץ מִפָּנָיו
וְתֵבֵל וְכָל־יֹשְׁבֵי בָהּ:
6 לִפְנֵי זַעְמוֹ מִי יַעֲמוֹד
וּמִי יָקוּם בַּחֲרוֹן אַפּוֹ
חֲמָתוֹ נִתְּכָה כָאֵשׁ
וְהַצֻּרִים נִתְּצוּ מִמֶּנּוּ:
7 טוֹב יְהֹוָה
לְמָעוֹז בְּיוֹם צָרָה
וְיֹדֵעַ חֹסֵי בוֹ:
8 וּבְשֶׁטֶף עֹבֵר
כָּלָה יַעֲשֶׂה מְקוֹמָהּ

And chases His enemies into darkness.
⁹Why will you plot against the Lord?
He wreaks utter destruction;
No adversary*d* opposes Him twice!
¹⁰*b*-For like men besotted with drink,
They are burned up like tangled thorns,
Like straw that is thoroughly dried.-*b*

¹¹*e*The base plotter
Who designed evil against the Lord
Has left you.
¹²Thus said the Lord:
b-"Even as they*f* were full and many,
Even so are they over and gone;
As surely as I afflicted you,
I will afflict you no more."-*b*
¹³And now
I will break off his yoke bar from you
And burst your cords apart.
¹⁴The Lord has commanded concerning
   him:*g*
b-No posterity shall continue your name.-*b*
I will do away with
The carved and graven images
In the temples of your gods;
I will make your grave
b-Accord with your worthlessness.-*b*

וְאֹיְבָ֖יו יְרַדֶּף־חֹֽשֶׁךְ׃
9 מַה־תְּחַשְּׁבוּן֙ אֶל־יְהֹוָ֔ה
כָּלָ֖ה ה֣וּא עֹשֶׂ֑ה
לֹֽא־תָק֥וּם פַּעֲמַ֖יִם צָרָֽה׃
10 כִּ֚י עַד־סִירִ֣ים סְבֻכִ֔ים
וּכְסׇבְאָ֖ם סְבוּאִ֑ים
אֻ֨כְּל֔וּ כְּקַ֥שׁ יָבֵ֖שׁ מָלֵֽא׃

11 מִמֵּ֖ךְ יָצָ֑א
חֹשֵׁ֥ב עַל־יְהֹוָ֖ה רָעָ֑ה
יֹעֵ֖ץ בְּלִיָּֽעַל׃ ס
12 כֹּ֣ה ׀ אָמַ֣ר יְהֹוָ֗ה
אִם־שְׁלֵמִים֙ וְכֵ֣ן רַבִּ֔ים
וְכֵ֥ן נָגֹ֖זּוּ וְעָבָ֑ר
וְעִנִּתִ֕ךְ
לֹ֥א אֲעַנֵּ֖ךְ עֽוֹד׃
13 וְעַתָּ֕ה
אֶשְׁבֹּ֥ר מֹטֵ֖הוּ מֵעָלָ֑יִךְ
וּמוֹסְרֹתַ֖יִךְ אֲנַתֵּֽק׃
14 וְצִוָּ֤ה עָלֶ֙יךָ֙ יְהֹוָ֔ה
לֹֽא־יִזָּרַ֥ע מִשִּׁמְךָ֖ ע֑וֹד
מִבֵּ֣ית אֱלֹהֶ֗יךָ
אַכְרִ֛ית
פֶּ֥סֶל וּמַסֵּכָ֖ה
אָשִׂ֣ים קִבְרֶ֑ךָ
כִּ֥י קַלּֽוֹתָ׃ פ

2 Behold on the hills
The footsteps of a herald
Announcing good fortune!
"Celebrate your festivals, O Judah,
Fulfill your vows.
Never again shall scoundrels invade you,
They have totally vanished."

ב הִנֵּ֨ה עַל־הֶהָרִ֜ים
רַגְלֵ֤י מְבַשֵּׂר֙
מַשְׁמִ֣יעַ שָׁל֔וֹם
חׇגִּ֧י יְהוּדָ֛ה חַגַּ֖יִךְ
שַׁלְּמִ֣י נְדָרָ֑יִךְ
כִּי֩ לֹ֨א יוֹסִ֥יף ע֛וֹד לַעֲבׇר־בָּ֥ךְ
בְּלִיַּ֖עַל
כֻּלֹּ֥ה נִכְרָֽת׃

---

d Cf. Ugaritic ṣrt.
e Vv. 11–14 would read well after 2.1.
f I.e., the days of your affliction.
g Heb. "you."

2^aA shatterer has come up against you.
Man the guard posts,
Watch the road;
Steady your loins,
Brace all your strength!

³For the LORD has restored ^b-the Pride^c of Jacob
As well as the Pride^c of Israel,-^b
Though marauders have laid them waste
And ravaged their branches.

⁴His warriors' shields are painted red,
And the soldiers are clothed in crimson;
The chariots are like flaming torches,^d
On the day they are made ready.
^e-The [arrows of] cypress wood are poisoned,-^e
⁵The chariots dash about frenzied in the fields,
They rush through the meadows.
They appear like torches,
They race like streaks of lightning.
⁶^f-He commands his burly men;
They stumble as they advance,
They hasten up to her wall,
Where ^g-wheeled shelters-^g are set up.-^f
⁷^h-The floodgates are opened,
And the palace is deluged.-^h
⁸ⁱ-And Huzzab is exiled and carried away,-ⁱ
While her handmaidens ^j-escort [her]-^j
As with the voices of doves,

עָלָה מֵפִיץ עַל־פָּנַיִךְ
נָצוֹר מְצֻרָה
צַפֵּה־דֶּרֶךְ
חַזֵּק מָתְנַיִם
אַמֵּץ כֹּחַ מְאֹד: 2

כִּי שָׁב יְהוָה אֶת־גְּאוֹן יַעֲקֹב
כִּגְאוֹן יִשְׂרָאֵל
כִּי בְקָקוּם בֹּקְקִים
וּזְמֹרֵיהֶם שִׁחֵתוּ: 3

מָגֵן גִּבֹּרֵיהוּ מְאָדָּם
אַנְשֵׁי־חַיִל מְתֻלָּעִים
בְּאֵשׁ־פְּלָדוֹת הָרֶכֶב
בְּיוֹם הֲכִינוֹ
וְהַבְּרֹשִׁים הָרְעָלוּ: 4
בַּחוּצוֹת יִתְהוֹלְלוּ הָרֶכֶב
יִשְׁתַּקְשְׁקוּן בָּרְחֹבוֹת
מַרְאֵיהֶן כַּלַּפִּידִם
כַּבְּרָקִים יְרוֹצֵצוּ: 5
יִזְכֹּר אַדִּירָיו
יִכָּשְׁלוּ בהלכותם בַּהֲלִיכָתָם
יְמַהֲרוּ חוֹמָתָהּ
וְהֻכַן הַסֹּכֵךְ: 6
שַׁעֲרֵי הַנְּהָרוֹת נִפְתָּחוּ
וְהַהֵיכָל נָמוֹג: 7
וְהֻצַּב גֻּלְּתָה הֹעֲלָתָה
וְאַמְהֹתֶיהָ מְנַהֲגוֹת
כְּקוֹל יוֹנִים 8

---

a   This verse would read well after v. 3.
b-b "Jacob" refers to the northern kingdom (cf. Amos 6.8; 8.7); Israel refers to the southern kingdom, regarded as the remnant of Israel after the fall of the northern kingdom (cf. Mic. 1.13–15).
c   Emendation yields "vine."
d   Understanding peladoth as equivalent to lappidoth.
e-e Meaning of Heb. uncertain. Emendation yields "The horsemen charge"; cf. 3.3.
f-f   Meaning of Heb. uncertain.
g-g To protect the crews that swung the battering rams.
h-h I.e., the walls are breached and the palace is overrun.
i-i   Meaning of Heb. uncertain. Emendation yields "And its mistress is led out and exiled."
j-j   Emendation yields "moan."

Beating their breasts.

9Nineveh has been like a [placid] pool of
    water
f-From earliest times;-f
Now they flee.
"Stop! Stop!"—
But none can turn them back.
10"Plunder silver! Plunder gold!"
There is no limit to the treasure;
It is a hoard of all precious objects.

11Desolation, devastation, and destruction!
Spirits sink,
Knees buckle,
All loins tremble,
All faces k-turn ashen.-k
12What has become of that lions' den,
That pasture*l* of great beasts,
Where lion and lion's breed walked,
And lion's cub—with none to disturb them?
13[Where is] the lion that tore victims for his
    cubs
And strangled for his lionesses,
And filled his lairs with prey
And his dens with mangled flesh?
14I am going to deal with you
         —declares the Lord of Hosts:
I will burn down m-her chariots in smoke,-m
And the sword shall devour your great beasts;
I will stamp out your killings from the earth,
And the sound of your messengers*n*
Shall be heard no more.

3 Ah, city of crime,
Utterly treacherous,
Full of violence,
Where killing never stops!

מִתֹּפְפֹ֖ת עַל־לִבְבֵהֶֽן׃

9וְנִֽינְוֵ֥ה כִבְרֵכַת־מַ֖יִם

מִ֣ימֵי הִ֑יא

וְהֵ֣מָּה נָסִ֔ים

עִמְד֥וּ עֲמֹ֖דוּ

וְאֵ֥ין מַפְנֶֽה׃

10בֹּ֥זּוּ כֶ֖סֶף בֹּ֣זּוּ זָהָ֑ב

וְאֵ֥ין קֵ֙צֶה֙ לַתְּכוּנָ֔ה

כָּבֹ֕ד מִכֹּ֖ל כְּלִ֥י חֶמְדָּֽה׃

11בּוּקָ֥ה וּמְבוּקָ֖ה וּמְבֻלָּקָ֑ה

וְלֵ֣ב נָמֵ֗ס

וּפִ֣ק בִּרְכַּ֔יִם

וְחַלְחָלָה֙ בְּכָל־מָתְנַ֔יִם

וּפְנֵ֥י כֻלָּ֖ם קִבְּצ֥וּ פָארֽוּר׃

12אַיֵּה֙ מְע֣וֹן אֲרָי֔וֹת

וּמִרְעֶ֥ה ה֖וּא לַכְּפִרִ֑ים

אֲשֶׁ֣ר הָלַךְ֩ אַרְיֵ֨ה לָבִ֥יא שָׁ֛ם

גּ֥וּר אַרְיֵ֖ה וְאֵ֥ין מַחֲרִֽיד׃

13אַרְיֵ֤ה טֹרֵף֙ בְּדֵ֣י גֹֽרוֹתָ֔יו

וּמְחַנֵּ֖ק לְלִבְאֹתָ֑יו

וַיְמַלֵּא־טֶ֣רֶף חֹרָ֔יו

וּמְעֹֽנֹתָ֖יו טְרֵפָֽה׃

14הִנְנִ֣י אֵלַ֗יִךְ

נְאֻם֙ יְהֹוָ֣ה צְבָא֔וֹת

וְהִבְעַרְתִּ֤י בֶֽעָשָׁן֙ רִכְבָּ֔הּ

וּכְפִירַ֖יִךְ תֹּ֣אכַל חָ֑רֶב

וְהִכְרַתִּ֤י מֵאֶ֙רֶץ֙ טַרְפֵּ֔ךְ

וְלֹֽא־יִשָּׁמַ֥ע עוֹד֖

ק֥וֹל מַלְאָכֵֽכֵה׃ ס

ג ה֖וֹי עִ֣יר דָּמִ֑ים

כֻּלָּ֣הּ כַּ֔חַשׁ

פֶּ֖רֶק מְלֵאָ֑ה

לֹ֥א יָמִ֖ישׁ טָֽרֶף׃

---

k-k *Meaning of Heb. uncertain; cf. note at Joel 2.6.*
l   *Emendation yields "cave."*
m-m *Emendation yields "your thicket in fire."*
n   *Emendation yields "devouring."*

2Crack of whip

קוֹל שׁוֹט 2

And rattle of wheel,

וְקוֹל רַעַשׁ אוֹפָן

Galloping steed

וְסוּס דֹּהֵר

And bounding chariot!

וּמֶרְכָּבָה מְרַקֵּדָה:

3Charging horsemen,

פָּרָשׁ מַעֲלֶה 3

Flashing swords,

וְלַהַב חֶרֶב

And glittering spears!

וּבְרַק חֲנִית

Hosts of slain

וְרֹב חָלָל

And heaps of corpses,

וְכֹבֶד פָּגֶר

Dead bodies without number—

וְאֵין קֵצֶה לַגְּוִיָּה

They stumble over bodies.

יכשלו וְכָשְׁלוּ בִּגְוִיָּתָם:

4Because of the countless harlotries of the
    harlot,

מֵרֹב זְנוּנֵי זוֹנָה 4

The winsome mistress of sorcery,

טוֹבַת חֵן בַּעֲלַת כְּשָׁפִים

Who ensnared*a* nations with her harlotries

הַמֹּכֶרֶת גּוֹיִם בִּזְנוּנֶיהָ

And peoples with her sorcery,

וּמִשְׁפָּחוֹת בִּכְשָׁפֶיהָ:

5I am going to deal with you

הִנְנִי אֵלַיִךְ 5

     —declares the Lord of Hosts.

נְאֻם יְהוָה צְבָאוֹת

I will lift up your skirts over your face

וְגִלֵּיתִי שׁוּלַיִךְ עַל־פָּנָיִךְ

And display your nakedness to the nations

וְהַרְאֵיתִי גוֹיִם מַעְרֵךְ

And your shame to kingdoms.

וּמַמְלָכוֹת קְלוֹנֵךְ:

6I will throw loathsome things over you

וְהִשְׁלַכְתִּי עָלַיִךְ שִׁקֻּצִים 6

And disfigure you

וְנִבַּלְתִּיךְ

And make a spectacle of you.

וְשַׂמְתִּיךְ כְּרֹאִי:

7All who see you will recoil from you

וְהָיָה כָל־רֹאַיִךְ יִדּוֹד מִמֵּךְ 7

And will say,

וְאָמַר

"Nineveh has been ravaged!"

שָׁדְּדָה נִינְוֵה

Who will console her?

מִי יָנוּד לָהּ

Where shall I look for

מֵאַיִן אֲבַקֵּשׁ

Anyone to comfort you?

מְנַחֲמִים לָךְ:

8Were you any better than No-amon,*b*

הֲתֵיטְבִי מִנֹּא אָמוֹן 8

Which sat by the Nile,

הַיֹּשְׁבָה בַּיְאֹרִים

Surrounded by water—

מַיִם סָבִיב לָהּ

Its rampart a river,*c*

אֲשֶׁר־חֵיל יָם

Its wall *d*-consisting of sea?-*d*

מִיָּם חוֹמָתָהּ:

9Populous Nubia

כּוּשׁ עָצְמָה 9

And teeming Egypt,

וּמִצְרַיִם וְאֵין קֵצֶה

Put and the Libyans—

פּוּט וְלוּבִים

---

a   *Meaning of Heb. uncertain.*

b   *Amon was the tutelary deity of No (Thebes; cf. Jer. 46.25), which
    the Assyrians had sacked in 663 B.C.E.*

c   *Heb. "sea."*

d-d   *Change of vocalization yields "water."*

They were her^e helpers.

¹⁰Yet even she was exiled,
She went into captivity.
Her babes, too, were dashed in pieces
At every street corner.
Lots were cast for her honored men,
And all her nobles were bound in chains.

¹¹You too shall be drunk
And utterly overcome;^a
You too shall seek
A refuge from the enemy.

¹²All your forts are fig trees
With^f ripe fruit;
If shaken they will fall
Into the mouths of devourers.

¹³Truly, the troops within you are women;
The gates of your land have opened them-
   selves
To your enemies;
Fire has consumed your gate bars.

¹⁴Draw water for the siege,
Strengthen your forts;
Tread the clay,
Trample the mud,
Grasp the brick mold!

¹⁵There fire will devour you,
The sword will put an end to you;
It will devour you like the grub.
^{a-}Multiply like grubs,
Multiply like locusts!^{-a}

¹⁶You had more traders
Than the sky has stars—
The grubs cast their skins and fly away.

¹⁷Your guards were like locusts,
Your marshals like piles of hoppers
Which settle on the stone fences

הָיוּ בְעֶזְרָתֵךְ:

10 גַּם־הִיא לַגֹּלָה
הָלְכָה בַשֶּׁבִי
גַּם עֹלָלֶיהָ יְרֻטְּשׁוּ
בְּרֹאשׁ כָּל־חוּצוֹת
וְעַל־נִכְבַּדֶּיהָ יַדּוּ גוֹרָל
וְכָל־גְּדוֹלֶיהָ רֻתְּקוּ בַזִּקִּים:

11 גַּם־אַתְּ תִּשְׁכְּרִי
תְּהִי נַעֲלָמָה
גַּם־אַתְּ תְּבַקְשִׁי
מָעוֹז מֵאוֹיֵב:

12 כָּל־מִבְצָרַיִךְ תְּאֵנִים
עִם־בִּכּוּרִים
אִם־יִנּוֹעוּ וְנָפְלוּ
עַל־פִּי אוֹכֵל:

13 הִנֵּה עַמֵּךְ נָשִׁים בְּקִרְבֵּךְ
לְאֹיְבַיִךְ
פָּתוֹחַ נִפְתְּחוּ שַׁעֲרֵי אַרְצֵךְ
אָכְלָה אֵשׁ בְּרִיחָיִךְ:

14 מֵי מָצוֹר שַׁאֲבִי־לָךְ
חַזְּקִי מִבְצָרָיִךְ
בֹּאִי בַטִּיט
וְרִמְסִי בַחֹמֶר
הַחֲזִיקִי מַלְבֵּן:

15 שָׁם תֹּאכְלֵךְ אֵשׁ
תַּכְרִיתֵךְ חֶרֶב
תֹּאכְלֵךְ כַּיָּלֶק
הִתְכַּבֵּד כַּיֶּלֶק
הִתְכַּבְּדִי כָּאַרְבֶּה:

16 הִרְבֵּית רֹכְלַיִךְ
מִכּוֹכְבֵי הַשָּׁמָיִם
יֶלֶק פָּשַׁט וַיָּעֹף:

17 מִנְּזָרַיִךְ כָּאַרְבֶּה
וְטַפְסְרַיִךְ כְּגוֹב גֹּבָי
הַחוֹנִים בַּגְּדֵרוֹת

---

^e Heb. "your."
^f Emendation yields "Your troops are"; cf. next verse.

On a chilly day;
When the sun comes out, they fly away,
And where they are nobody knows.
¹⁸Your shepherds are slumbering,
O king of Assyria;
Your sheepmasters are ᵍ-lying inert;-ᵍ
Your people are scattered*a* over the hills,
And there is none to gather them.
¹⁹There is no healing*h* for your injury;
Your wound is grievous.
All who hear the news about you
Clap their hands over you.
For who has not suffered
From your constant malice?

בְּיוֹם קָרָה
שֶׁמֶשׁ זָרְחָה֙ וְנוֹדַ֔ד
וְלֹא־נוֹדַ֥ע מְקוֹמ֖וֹ אַיָּ֑ם׃
18 נָמ֣וּ רֹעֶ֗יךָ
מֶ֣לֶךְ אַשּׁ֔וּר
יִשְׁכְּנ֖וּ אַדִּירֶ֑יךָ
נָפֹ֧שׁוּ עַמְּךָ֛ עַל־הֶהָרִ֖ים
וְאֵ֥ין מְקַבֵּֽץ׃
19 אֵין־כֵּהָ֣ה לְשִׁבְרֶ֗ךָ
נַחְלָ֖ה מַכָּתֶ֑ךָ
כֹּ֣ל ׀ שֹׁמְעֵ֣י שִׁמְעֲךָ֗
תָּקְע֥וּ כַף֙ עָלֶ֔יךָ
כִּ֗י עַל־מִ֛י לֹֽא־עָבְרָ֥ה
רָעָתְךָ֖ תָּמִֽיד׃

---

g-g   *Lit. "dwelling"; emendation yields "asleep."*
h   *Heb.* kehah, *a variant of* gehah; *see Prov. 17.22.*

HABAKKUK

1 The pronouncement made by the prophet Habakkuk.

²How long, O Lord, shall I cry out
And You not listen,
Shall I shout to You, "Violence!"
And You not save?
³Why do You make me see iniquity
ᵃ-[Why] do You look-ᵃ upon wrong?—
Raiding and violence are before me,
Strife continues and contention ᵇ-goes on.-ᵇ
⁴That is why decision fails
And justice never emerges;
For the villain hedges in the just man—
Therefore judgment emerges deformed.

⁵"Look among the nations,
Observe well and be utterly astounded;
For a work is being wrought in your days
Which you would not believe if it were told.
⁶For lo, I am raising up the Chaldeans,
That fierce, impetuous nation,
Who cross the earth's wide spaces
To seize homes not their own.
⁷They are terrible, dreadful;
ᶜ-They make their own laws and rules.-ᶜ
⁸Their horses are swifter than leopards,
Fleeter than wolves of the steppe.ᵈ
Their steeds gallop—ᵉ-their steeds-ᵉ
Come flying from afar.

a-a Targum and Syriac "So that I look."
b-b Meaning of Heb. uncertain.
c-c Lit. "Their law and majesty proceed from themselves."
d Understanding 'ereb as synonymous with 'arabah; cf. Jer. 5.6.
e-e The Qumran Habakkuk commentary (hereafter 1QpHab) reads "and spread [wings]."

א הַמַּשָּׂא֙ אֲשֶׁ֣ר חָזָ֔ה חֲבַקּ֖וּק הַנָּבִֽיא׃

2 עַד־אָ֧נָה יְהֹוָ֛ה שִׁוַּ֖עְתִּי
וְלֹ֣א תִשְׁמָ֑ע
אֶזְעַ֥ק אֵלֶ֛יךָ חָמָ֖ס
וְלֹ֥א תוֹשִֽׁיעַ׃
3 לָ֣מָּה תַרְאֵ֤נִי אָ֨וֶן֙
וְעָמָ֣ל תַּבִּ֔יט
וְשֹׁ֥ד וְחָמָ֖ס לְנֶגְדִּ֑י
וַיְהִ֧י רִ֦יב וּמָד֖וֹן יִשָּֽׂא׃
4 עַל־כֵּן֙ תָּפ֣וּג תּוֹרָ֔ה
וְלֹא־יֵצֵ֥א לָנֶ֖צַח מִשְׁפָּ֑ט
כִּ֤י רָשָׁע֙ מַכְתִּ֣יר אֶת־הַצַּדִּ֔יק
עַל־כֵּ֛ן יֵצֵ֥א מִשְׁפָּ֖ט מְעֻקָּֽל׃

5 רְא֤וּ בַגּוֹיִם֙
וְֽהַבִּ֔יטוּ וְהִֽתַּמְּה֖וּ תְּמָ֑הוּ
כִּי־פֹ֨עַל֙ פֹּעֵ֣ל בִּֽימֵיכֶ֔ם
לֹ֥א תַאֲמִ֖ינוּ כִּ֥י יְסֻפָּֽר׃
6 כִּֽי־הִנְנִ֤י מֵקִים֙ אֶת־הַכַּשְׂדִּ֔ים
הַגּ֖וֹי הַמַּ֣ר וְהַנִּמְהָ֑ר
הַֽהוֹלֵךְ֙ לְמֶרְחֲבֵי־אֶ֔רֶץ
לָרֶ֥שֶׁת מִשְׁכָּנ֖וֹת לֹא־לֽוֹ׃
7 אָיֹ֥ם וְנוֹרָ֖א ה֑וּא
מִמֶּ֕נּוּ מִשְׁפָּט֥וֹ וּשְׂאֵת֖וֹ יֵצֵֽא׃
8 וְקַלּ֨וּ מִנְּמֵרִ֜ים סוּסָ֗יו
וְחַדּוּ֙ מִזְּאֵ֣בֵי עֶ֔רֶב
וּפָ֖שׁוּ פָּרָשָׁ֑יו וּפָרָשָׁ֣יו
מֵרָח֣וֹק יָבֹ֔אוּ יָעֻ֖פוּ

Like vultures rushing toward food,
⁹They all come, bent on rapine.
The thrust[b] of their van is forward,
And they amass captives like sand.
¹⁰Kings they hold in derision,
And princes are a joke to them;
They laugh at every fortress,
They pile up earth and capture it.
¹¹[b-]Then they pass on like the wind,
They transgress and incur guilt,
For they ascribe their might to their god."[-b]

¹²You, O LORD, are from everlasting;
My holy God, You[f] never die.
O LORD, You have made them a subject of
    contention;
O Rock, You have made them a cause for
    complaint.
¹³You whose eyes are too pure to look upon
    evil,
Who cannot countenance wrongdoing,
Why do You countenance treachery,
And stand by idle
While the one in the wrong devours
The one in the right?
¹⁴You have made mankind like the fish of the
    sea,
Like creeping things [g-]that have no ruler.[-g]
¹⁵He has fished them all up with a line,
Pulled them up in his trawl,
And gathered them in his net.
That is why he rejoices and is glad.
¹⁶That is why he sacrifices to his trawl
And makes offerings to his net;
For through them his portion[h] is rich
And his nourishment fat.
¹⁷Shall he then keep [i-]emptying his trawl,[-i]
And slaying nations without pity?

כְּנֶשֶׁר חָשׁ לֶאֱכֽוֹל:
9 כֻּלֹּה לְחָמָס יָבוֹא
מְגַמַּת פְּנֵיהֶם קָדִימָה
וַיֶּאֱסֹף כַּחוֹל שֶֽׁבִי:
10 וְהוּא בַּמְּלָכִים יִתְקַלָּס
וְרֹזְנִים מִשְׂחָק לוֹ
הוּא לְכָל־מִבְצָר יִשְׂחָק
וַיִּצְבֹּר עָפָר וַיִּלְכְּדָֽהּ:
11 אָז חָלַף רוּחַ
וַֽיַּעֲבֹר וְאָשֵׁם
זוּ כֹחוֹ לֵאלֹהֽוֹ:
12 הֲלוֹא אַתָּה מִקֶּדֶם יְהוָה
אֱלֹהַי קְדֹשִׁי לֹא נָמוּת
יְהוָה לְמִשְׁפָּט שַׂמְתּוֹ
וְצוּר לְהוֹכִיחַ יְסַדְתּֽוֹ:
13 טְהוֹר עֵינַיִם מֵרְאוֹת רָע
וְהַבִּיט אֶל־עָמָל לֹא תוּכָל
לָמָּה תַבִּיט בּוֹגְדִים
תַּחֲרִישׁ
בְּבַלַּע רָשָׁע
צַדִּיק מִמֶּֽנּוּ:
14 וַתַּעֲשֶׂה אָדָם כִּדְגֵי הַיָּם
כְּרֶמֶשׂ לֹא־מֹשֵׁל בּֽוֹ:
15 כֻּלֹּה בְּחַכָּה הֵעֲלָה
יְגֹרֵהוּ בְחֶרְמוֹ
וְיַאַסְפֵהוּ בְּמִכְמַרְתּוֹ
עַל־כֵּן יִשְׂמַח וְיָגִֽיל:
16 עַל־כֵּן יְזַבֵּחַ לְחֶרְמוֹ
וִיקַטֵּר לְמִכְמַרְתּוֹ
כִּי בָהֵמָּה שָׁמֵן חֶלְקוֹ
וּמַאֲכָלוֹ בְּרִאָֽה:
17 הַעַל כֵּן יָרִיק חֶרְמוֹ
וְתָמִיד לַהֲרֹג גּוֹיִם לֹא יַחְמֽוֹל: ס

---

f   Heb. "we," a change made by a pious scribe.
g-g   1QpHab "[for him] to rule over"; cf. Gen. 1.28; Ps. 8.7–9.
h   Emendation yields "bread"; cf. Gen. 49.20.
i-i   1QpHab "drawing his sword."

2 I will stand on my watch,
Take up my station at the[a] post,
And wait to see what He will say to me,
What He[b] will reply to my complaint.

2The LORD answered me and said:
Write the prophecy down,
Inscribe it clearly on tablets,
So that it can be read easily.
3For [c]there is yet a prophecy[c] for a set term,
A truthful witness for a time that will come.
Even if it tarries, wait for it still;
For it will surely come, without delay:
4[d]Lo, his spirit within him is puffed up, not
    upright,
But[d] the righteous man is rewarded with life
For his fidelity.
5How much less then shall the defiant[e] go un-
    punished,
The treacherous, arrogant man
Who has made his maw as wide as Sheol,
Who is as insatiable as Death,
Who has harvested all the nations
And gathered in all the peoples!
6Surely all these shall pronounce a satire
    against him,
A pointed epigram concerning him.
They shall say:
Ah, you who pile up what is not yours—
How much longer?—
And make ever heavier your load of indebted-
    ness!
7Right suddenly will your creditors[f] arise,

ב עַל־מִשְׁמַרְתִּי אֶעֱמֹדָה
וְאֶתְיַצְּבָה עַל־מָצֽוֹר
וַאֲצַפֶּה לִרְאוֹת מַה־יְדַבֶּר־בִּי
וּמָה אָשִׁיב עַל־תּוֹכַחְתִּֽי׃

2 וַיַּעֲנֵנִי יְהוָה וַיֹּאמֶר
כְּתוֹב חָזוֹן
וּבָאֵר עַל־הַלֻּחוֹת
לְמַעַן יָרוּץ קוֹרֵא בֽוֹ׃

3 כִּי עוֹד חָזוֹן לַמּוֹעֵד
וְיָפֵחַ לַקֵּץ וְלֹא יְכַזֵּב
אִם־יִתְמַהְמָהּ חַכֵּה־לוֹ
כִּי־בֹא יָבֹא לֹא יְאַחֵֽר׃

4 הִנֵּה עֻפְּלָה לֹא־יָשְׁרָה נַפְשׁוֹ בּוֹ
וְצַדִּיק בֶּאֱמוּנָתוֹ יִחְיֶֽה׃

5 וְאַף כִּי־הַיַּיִן בּוֹגֵד
גֶּבֶר יָהִיר וְלֹא יִנְוֶה
אֲשֶׁר הִרְחִיב כִּשְׁאוֹל נַפְשׁוֹ
וְהוּא כַמָּוֶת וְלֹא יִשְׂבָּע
וַיֶּאֱסֹף אֵלָיו כָּל־הַגּוֹיִם
וַיִּקְבֹּץ אֵלָיו כָּל־הָעַמִּֽים׃

6 הֲלוֹא־אֵלֶּה כֻלָּם עָלָיו מָשָׁל יִשָּׂאוּ
וּמְלִיצָה חִידוֹת לוֹ
וְיֹאמַר
הוֹי הַמַּרְבֶּה לֹּא־לוֹ
עַד־מָתַי
וּמַכְבִּיד עָלָיו עַבְטִֽיט׃

7 הֲלוֹא פֶתַע יָקוּמוּ נֹשְׁכֶיךָ

---

a   1QpHab reads "my."
b   Taking 'ashib as equivalent to yashib.
c-c Emendation yields "the prophecy is a witness."
d-d Meaning of Heb. uncertain. Emendation yields "Lo, there is
    a reward for the upright— / the life breath within him— /
    And..."
e   Connecting hyyn (1 QpHab hwn) with the root hwn, Deut. 1.41;
    for the thought cf. Prov. 11.31. Meaning of rest of line uncertain.
f   Lit. "usurers."

And those who remind^g you will awake,
And you will be despoiled by them.
⁸Because you plundered many nations,
All surviving peoples shall plunder you—
For crimes against men and wrongs against
    lands,
Against cities and all their inhabitants.

וְיִקְצוּ מְזַעְזְעֶיךָ
וְהָיִיתָ לִמְשִׁסּוֹת לָמוֹ:
8 כִּי אַתָּה שַׁלּוֹתָ גּוֹיִם רַבִּים
יְשָׁלּוּךָ כָּל־יֶתֶר עַמִּים
מִדְּמֵי אָדָם וַחֲמַס־אֶרֶץ
קִרְיָה וְכָל־יֹשְׁבֵי בָהּ: פ

⁹Ah, you who have acquired gains
To the detriment of your own house,
^{h-}Who have destroyed many peoples^{-h}
In order to set your nest on high
To escape disaster!
¹⁰You have plotted shame for your own
    house,
And guilt for yourself;
¹¹For a stone shall cry out from the wall,
And a rafter shall answer it from the wood-
    work.

9 הוֹי בֹּצֵעַ בֶּצַע
רָע לְבֵיתוֹ
לָשׂוּם בַּמָּרוֹם קִנּוֹ
לְהִנָּצֵל
מִכַּף־רָע:
10 יָעַצְתָּ בֹּשֶׁת לְבֵיתֶךָ
קְצוֹת־עַמִּים רַבִּים וְחוֹטֵא נַפְשֶׁךָ:
11 כִּי־אֶבֶן מִקִּיר תִּזְעָק
וְכָפִיס מֵעֵץ יַעֲנֶנָּה: פ

¹²Ah, you who have built a town with crime,
And established a city with infamy,
¹³So that peoples have had to toil for the fire,ⁱ
And nations to weary themselves for naught!
^jBehold, it is from the LORD of Hosts:
^{14k-}For the earth shall be filled
With awe for the glory of the LORD
As water covers the sea.^{-k}

12 הוֹי בֹּנֶה עִיר בְּדָמִים
וְכוֹנֵן קִרְיָה בְּעַוְלָה:
13 הֲלוֹא הִנֵּה מֵאֵת יְהוָה צְבָאוֹת
וְיִיגְעוּ עַמִּים בְּדֵי־אֵשׁ
וּלְאֻמִּים בְּדֵי־רִיק יִעָפוּ:
14 כִּי תִּמָּלֵא הָאָרֶץ
לָדַעַת אֶת־כְּבוֹד יְהוָה
כַּמַּיִם יְכַסּוּ עַל־יָם: ס

¹⁵Ah, you who make others drink to intoxi-
    cation
^{l-}As you pour out^{-l} your wrath,
In order to gaze upon their nakedness!^m
¹⁶You shall be sated with shame
Rather than glory:

15 הוֹי מַשְׁקֵה רֵעֵהוּ
מְסַפֵּחַ חֲמָתְךָ וְאַף שַׁכֵּר
לְמַעַן הַבִּיט עַל־מְעוֹרֵיהֶם:
16 שָׂבַעְתָּ קָלוֹן
מִכָּבוֹד

---

g   Lit. "shake"; the same verb means "to call to mind" in Samaritan
     Aramaic.
h-h   Brought up from v. 10 for clarity.
i   I.e., without profit.
j   Connection with the next four lines uncertain; they might read
     better after v. 20.
k-k   Cf. Isa. 11.9.
l-l   Meaning of Heb. uncertain. Emendation yields "from the bowl
     of."
m   Cf. Gen. 9.21–22.

Drink in your turn and stagger!ⁿ
The cup in the right hand of the Lord
Shall come around to you,
And ^{o-}disgrace to^{-o} your glory.
^{17p-}For the lawlessness against Lebanon shall
   cover you,
The destruction of beasts shall overwhelm
   you^{-p}—
For crimes against men and wrongs against
   lands,
Against cities and all their inhabitants.
^{18q}What has the carved image availed,
That he who fashioned it has carved it
For an image and a false oracle—
That he who fashioned his product has
   trusted in it,
Making dumb idols?
¹⁹Ah, you who say, "Wake up" to wood,
"Awaken," to inert stone!
Can that give an oracle?
Why, it is encased in gold and silver,
But there is no breath inside it.
²⁰But the Lord in His holy Abode—
Be silent before Him all the earth!

3 A prayer of the prophet Habakkuk. In the
mode of *Shigionoth.*^a

²O Lord! I have learned of Your renown;
I am awed, O Lord, by Your deeds.
Renew them in these years,
Oh, make them known in these years!
Though angry, may You remember compas-
   sion.

³God is coming from Teman,
The Holy One from Mount Paran.   *Selah.*^b

שָׁתֵה גַם־אַתָּה וְהֵעָרֵל
תִּסּוֹב עָלֶיךָ
כּוֹס יְמִין יְהֹוָה
וְקִיקָלוֹן עַל־כְּבוֹדֶךָ:
17 כִּי חֲמַס לְבָנוֹן יְכַסֶּךָ
וְשֹׁד בְּהֵמוֹת יְחִיתַן
מִדְּמֵי אָדָם וַחֲמַס־אֶרֶץ
קִרְיָה וְכָל־יֹשְׁבֵי בָהּ: ס
18 מָה־הוֹעִיל פֶּסֶל
כִּי פְסָלוֹ יֹצְרוֹ
מַסֵּכָה וּמוֹרֶה שָּׁקֶר
כִּי בָטַח יֹצֵר יִצְרוֹ עָלָיו
לַעֲשׂוֹת אֱלִילִים אִלְּמִים: ס
19 הוֹי אֹמֵר לָעֵץ הָקִיצָה
עוּרִי לְאֶבֶן דּוּמָם
הוּא יוֹרֶה
הִנֵּה־הוּא תָּפוּשׂ זָהָב וָכֶסֶף
וְכָל־רוּחַ אֵין בְּקִרְבּוֹ:
20 וַיהֹוָה בְּהֵיכַל קָדְשׁוֹ
הַס מִפָּנָיו כָּל־הָאָרֶץ: פ

ג תְּפִלָּה לַחֲבַקּוּק הַנָּבִיא עַל שִׁגְיֹנוֹת:

2 יְהֹוָה שָׁמַעְתִּי שִׁמְעֲךָ
יָרֵאתִי יְהֹוָה פָּעָלְךָ
בְּקֶרֶב שָׁנִים חַיֵּיהוּ
בְּקֶרֶב שָׁנִים תּוֹדִיעַ
בְּרֹגֶז רַחֵם תִּזְכּוֹר:

3 אֱלוֹהַ מִתֵּימָן יָבוֹא
וְקָדוֹשׁ מֵהַר־פָּארָן סֶלָה

---

n   *Emendation yields "uncover yourself"; cf. Lam. 4.21.*
o-o *Or "vomit of disgrace upon."*
p-p *Meaning of Heb. uncertain.*
q   *This verse would read well after v. 19.*

a   *Meaning uncertain; perhaps "psalms of supplication"; cf. Ps. 7.1.*
b   *A musical direction of uncertain meaning.*

His majesty covers the skies,
His splendor fills the earth:
4c-It is a brilliant light
Which gives off rays on every side—
And therein His glory is enveloped.-c
5Pestilence marches before Him,
And plague comes forth at His heels.
6When He stands, He makes the earth shake;d
When He glances, He makes nations tremble.
The age-old mountains are shattered,
The primeval hills sink low.
c-His are the ancient routes:
7As a scene of havoc I behold-c
The tents of Cushan;
Shaken are the pavilions
Of the land of Midian!

8Are You wroth, O LORD, with Neharim?
Is Your anger against Neharim,
Your rage against Yame—
That You are driving Your steeds,
Your victorious chariot?
9All bared and ready is Your bow.
c-Sworn are the rods of the word.-c   Selah.
You make the earth burst into streams,
10The mountains rock at the sight of You,
A torrent of rain comes down;
Loud roars the deep,
c-The sky returns the echo.-c
11Sun [and] moon stand still on high
As Your arrows fly in brightness,
Your flashing spear in brilliance.
12You tread the earth in rage,
You trample nations in fury.
13You have come forth to deliver Your people,
To deliver Your anointed.f

כִּסָּה שָׁמַיִם הוֹדוֹ
וּתְהִלָּתוֹ מָלְאָה הָאָרֶץ:
4 וְנֹגַהּ כָּאוֹר תִּהְיֶה
קַרְנַיִם מִיָּדוֹ לוֹ
וְשָׁם חֶבְיוֹן עֻזֹּה:
5 לְפָנָיו יֵלֶךְ דָּבֶר
וְיֵצֵא רֶשֶׁף לְרַגְלָיו:
6 עָמַד ׀ וַיְמֹדֶד אֶרֶץ
רָאָה וַיַּתֵּר גּוֹיִם
וַיִּתְפֹּצְצוּ הַרְרֵי־עַד
שַׁחוּ גִּבְעוֹת עוֹלָם
הֲלִיכוֹת עוֹלָם לוֹ:
7 תַּחַת אָוֶן רָאִיתִי
אָהֳלֵי כוּשָׁן
יִרְגְּזוּן יְרִיעוֹת
אֶרֶץ מִדְיָן: ס

8 הֲבִנְהָרִים חָרָה יְהוָה
אִם בַּנְּהָרִים אַפֶּךָ
אִם־בַּיָּם עֶבְרָתֶךָ
כִּי תִרְכַּב עַל־סוּסֶיךָ
מַרְכְּבֹתֶיךָ יְשׁוּעָה:
9 עֶרְיָה תֵעוֹר קַשְׁתֶּךָ
שְׁבֻעוֹת מַטּוֹת אֹמֶר   סֶלָה
נְהָרוֹת תְּבַקַּע־אָרֶץ:
10 רָאוּךָ יָחִילוּ הָרִים
זֶרֶם מַיִם עָבָר
נָתַן תְּהוֹם קוֹלוֹ
רוֹם יָדֵיהוּ נָשָׂא:
11 שֶׁמֶשׁ יָרֵחַ עָמַד זְבֻלָה
לְאוֹר חִצֶּיךָ יְהַלֵּכוּ
לְנֹגַהּ בְּרַק חֲנִיתֶךָ:
12 בְּזַעַם תִּצְעַד־אָרֶץ
בְּאַף תָּדוּשׁ גּוֹיִם:
13 יָצָאתָ לְיֵשַׁע עַמֶּךָ
לְיֵשַׁע אֶת־מְשִׁיחֶךָ

---

c-c   *Meaning of Heb. uncertain.*
d   *Cf. Targum and Septuagint.*
e   *Neharim (lit. "Floods") and Yam (lit. "Sea") were marine
monsters vanquished by the LORD in hoary antiquity. On Yam
see Ps. 74.13; Job 7.12. A being called both Yam and Nahar figures
in early Canaanite literature.*
f   *I.e., the king of Judah.*

g-You will smash the roof of the villain's house,

Raze it from foundation to top. *Selah.*

14You will crack [his] skull with Your[h] bludgeon;

Blown away shall be his warriors,

Whose delight is to crush me suddenly,

To devour a poor man in an ambush.-g

15iYou will make Your steeds tread the sea,

Stirring the mighty waters.

16I heard and my bowels quaked,

My lips quivered at the sound;

Rot entered into my bone,

I trembled where I stood.

Yet I wait calmly for the day of distress,

For a people to come to attack us.

17Though the fig tree does not bud

And no yield is on the vine,

Though the olive crop has failed

And the fields produce no grain,

Though sheep have vanished from the fold

And no cattle are in the pen,-i

18Yet will I rejoice in the LORD,

Exult in the God who delivers me.

19My Lord GOD is my strength:

He makes my feet like the deer's

And lets me stride upon the heights.

c-For the leader; with instrumental music.-c

מְחַצְתָּ רֹּאשׁ* מִבֵּית רָשָׁע
עָרוֹת יְסוֹד עַד־צַוָּאר סֶלָה: פ
14 נָקַבְתָּ בְמַטָּיו רֹאשׁ
פְּרָזָו יִסְעֲרוּ
לַהֲפִיצֵנִי עֲלִיצֻתָם
כְּמוֹ־לֶאֱכֹל עָנִי בַּמִּסְתָּר:
15 דָּרַכְתָּ בַיָּם סוּסֶיךָ
חֹמֶר מַיִם רַבִּים:
16 שָׁמַעְתִּי | וַתִּרְגַּז בִּטְנִי
לְקוֹל צָלֲלוּ שְׂפָתַי
יָבוֹא רָקָב בַּעֲצָמַי
וְתַחְתַּי אֶרְגָּז
אֲשֶׁר אָנוּחַ לְיוֹם צָרָה
לַעֲלוֹת לְעַם יְגוּדֶנּוּ:
17 כִּי־תְאֵנָה לֹא־תִפְרָח
וְאֵין יְבוּל בַּגְּפָנִים
כִּחֵשׁ מַעֲשֵׂה־זַיִת
וּשְׁדֵמוֹת לֹא־עָשָׂה אֹכֶל
גָּזַר מִמִּכְלָה צֹאן
וְאֵין בָּקָר בָּרְפָתִים:
18 וַאֲנִי בַּיהוָה אֶעְלוֹזָה
אָגִילָה בֵּאלֹהֵי יִשְׁעִי:
19 יְהוִה אֲדֹנָי חֵילִי
וַיָּשֶׂם רַגְלַי כָּאַיָּלוֹת
וְעַל בָּמוֹתַי יַדְרִכֵנִי:

לַמְנַצֵּחַ בִּנְגִינוֹתָי:

---

g-g *Emendation yields: You will strike the heads of men of evil, / Smash the pates of Your adversaries. Selah. / You will crack their skulls with Your bludgeon; / Dispersed, blown like chaff shall be they / Who lie in wait to swallow the innocent, / To devour the poor in an ambush.*

h   Heb. "His."

i-i *Or:* 15You will make Your steeds tread the sea, / Stirring the mighty waters, / 16That I may have rest on a day of distress, / When a people come up to attack us. / But this report made my bowels quake, / These tidings made my lips quiver; / Rot entered into my bone, / I trembled where I stood: 17That the fig tree does not bud, / And no yield is on the vine; / The olive crop has failed, / And the fields produce no grain; / The sheep have vanished from the fold, / And no cattle are in the pen.

ZEPHANIAH

1 The word of the Lord that came to Zephaniah son of Cushi son of Gedaliah son of Amariah son of Hezekiah, during the reign of King Josiah son of Amon of Judah.

²I will sweep everything away
From the face of the earth
    —declares the Lord.
³I will sweep away man and beast;
I will sweep away the birds of the sky
And the fish of the sea.
^{a-}I will make the wicked stumble,^{-a}
And I will destroy mankind
From the face of the earth
    —declares the Lord.

⁴I will stretch out My arm against Judah
And against all who dwell in Jerusalem;
And I will wipe out from this place
Every vestige of Baal,
And the name of the priestlings^b along with
 the priests;
⁵And those who bow down on the roofs
To the host of heaven;
And those who bow down and swear to the
 Lord
But also swear by Malcam;^c
⁶And those who have forsaken the Lord,
And those who have not sought the Lord
And have not turned to Him.

אֶל־צְפַנְיָ֣ה הָיָה֙ אֲשֶׁ֤ר ׀ דְּבַר־יְהוָ֞ה א
בֶּן־חִזְקִיָּ֑ה בֶּן־אֲמַרְיָ֖ה גְּדַלְיָ֥ה בֶן־כּוּשִׁ֣י
יְהוּדָֽה׃ מֶ֥לֶךְ אָמ֖וֹן בֶּן־ יֹאשִׁיָּ֥הוּ בִּימֵ֛י

כֹּ֔ל אָסֵ֣ף אָסֹ֥ף 2
הָֽאֲדָמָ֑ה פְּנֵ֣י מֵעַ֖ל
נְאֻם־יְהוָֽה׃
וּבְהֵמָ֔ה אָדָ֣ם אָסֵ֤ף 3
הַשָּׁמַ֙יִם֙ עוֹף־ אָסֵ֤ף
הַיָּ֔ם וּדְגֵ֣י
אֶת־הָרְשָׁעִ֑ים וְהַמַּכְשֵׁל֖וֹת
אֶת־הָ֣אָדָ֔ם וְהִכְרַתִּ֣י
הָֽאֲדָמָ֑ה פְּנֵ֣י מֵעַ֖ל
נְאֻם־יְהוָֽה׃

עַל־יְהוּדָ֔ה יָדִי֙ * וְנָטִ֤יתִי 4
יְרוּשָׁלָ֑͏ִם יֽוֹשְׁבֵ֣י כָּל־ וְעַ֖ל
הַזֶּ֔ה הַמָּק֣וֹם מִן־ וְהִכְרַתִּ֞י
הַבַּ֔עַל אֶת־שְׁאָ֣ר
עִם־הַכֹּהֲנִֽים׃ הַכְּמָרִ֖ים אֶת־שֵׁ֥ם
עַל־הַגַּגּ֔וֹת הַמִּֽשְׁתַּחֲוִים֙ וְאֶת־ 5
הַשָּׁמָ֑יִם לִצְבָ֣א
לַֽיהוָ֔ה הַנִּשְׁבָּעִ֣ים הַמִּֽשְׁתַּחֲוִים֙ וְאֶת־
בְּמַלְכָּֽם׃ וְהַנִּשְׁבָּעִ֖ים
יְהוָ֑ה מֵאַחֲרֵ֖י הַנְּסוֹגִ֖ים וְאֶת־ 6
אֶת־יְהוָ֖ה לֹֽא־בִקְשׁ֥וּ וַאֲשֶׁ֛ר
דְרָשֻֽׁהוּ׃ וְלֹ֥א

v. 4. חסר "את"

---

a-a *Meaning of Heb. uncertain.*
b   *Heb.* kemarim, *a term used only of priests of heathen gods.*
c   *Apparently identical with "Milcom the abomination of the Ammonites"; cf.* 1 Kings 11.5.

7Be silent before my Lord GOD,

For the day of the LORD is approaching;

For the LORD has prepared a d-sacrificial feast,-d

Has bidden His guests purify themselves.

8And on the day of the LORD's sacrifice

I will punish the officials

And the king's sons,e

f-And all who don a foreign vestment.

9I will also punish on that day

Everyone who steps over the threshold,-f

Who fill their master'sg palace

With lawlessness and fraud.

10In that day there shall be

—declares the LORD—

A loud outcry from the Fish Gate,

And howling from the Mishneh,h

And a sound of great anguish from the hills.

11The dwellers of the Machteshi howl;

For all the tradesmen have perished,

All who weigh silver are wiped out.

12At that time,

I will search Jerusalem with lamps;

And I will punish the men

Who rest untroubled on their lees,

Who say to themselves,

"The LORD will do nothing, good or bad."

13Their wealth shall be plundered

And their homes laid waste.

They shall build houses and not dwell in them,

Plant vineyards and not drink their wine.

14The great day of the LORD is approaching,

Approaching most swiftly.

7 הַס מִפְּנֵי אֲדֹנָי יְהֹוִה

כִּי קָרוֹב יוֹם יְהֹוָה

כִּי־הֵכִין יְהֹוָה זֶבַח

הִקְדִּישׁ קְרֻאָיו:

8 וְהָיָה בְּיוֹם זֶבַח יְהֹוָה

וּפָקַדְתִּי עַל־הַשָּׂרִים

וְעַל־בְּנֵי הַמֶּלֶךְ

וְעַל כָּל־הַלֹּבְשִׁים מַלְבּוּשׁ נָכְרִי:

9 וּפָקַדְתִּי עַל כָּל־הַדּוֹלֵג עַל־הַמִּפְתָּן

בַּיּוֹם הַהוּא

הַמְמַלְאִים בֵּית אֲדֹנֵיהֶם

חָמָס וּמִרְמָה: ס

10 וְהָיָה בַיּוֹם הַהוּא

נְאֻם־יְהֹוָה

קוֹל צְעָקָה מִשַּׁעַר הַדָּגִים

וִילָלָה מִן־הַמִּשְׁנֶה

וְשֶׁבֶר גָּדוֹל מֵהַגְּבָעוֹת:

11 הֵילִילוּ יֹשְׁבֵי הַמַּכְתֵּשׁ

כִּי נִדְמָה כָּל־עַם כְּנַעַן

נִכְרְתוּ כָּל־נְטִילֵי כָסֶף:

12 וְהָיָה בָּעֵת הַהִיא

אֲחַפֵּשׂ אֶת־יְרוּשָׁלַ͏ִם בַּנֵּרוֹת

וּפָקַדְתִּי עַל־הָאֲנָשִׁים

הַקֹּפְאִים עַל־שִׁמְרֵיהֶם

הָאֹמְרִים בִּלְבָבָם

לֹא־יֵיטִיב יְהֹוָה וְלֹא יָרֵעַ:

13 וְהָיָה חֵילָם לִמְשִׁסָּה

וּבָתֵּיהֶם לִשְׁמָמָה

וּבָנוּ בָתִּים וְלֹא יֵשֵׁבוּ

וְנָטְעוּ כְרָמִים וְלֹא יִשְׁתּוּ אֶת־יֵינָם:

14 קָרוֹב יוֹם־יְהֹוָה הַגָּדוֹל

קָרוֹב וּמַהֵר מְאֹד

---

d-d I.e., a slaughter of sinners.

e Apparently brothers of King Amon, who exercised influence during the minority of King Josiah (2 Kings 22.1).

f-f Apparently references to two customs of heathen worship; cf.
2 Kings 10.22 and 1 Sam. 5.5.

g I.e., King Josiah's.

h A quarter of Jerusalem; cf. 2 Kings 22.14.

i Another quarter of Jerusalem.

j-Hark, the day of the LORD!	קוֹל יוֹם יְהֹוָה
It is bitter:	מַר
There a warrior shrieks!-*j*	צֹרֵחַ שָׁם גִּבּוֹר׃
15That day shall be a day of wrath,	15 יוֹם עֶבְרָה הַיּוֹם הַהוּא
A day of trouble and distress,	יוֹם צָרָה וּמְצוּקָה
A day of calamity and desolation,	יוֹם שֹׁאָה וּמְשׁוֹאָה
A day of darkness and deep gloom,	יוֹם חֹשֶׁךְ וַאֲפֵלָה
A day of densest clouds,	יוֹם עָנָן וַעֲרָפֶל׃
16A day of horn blasts and alarms—	16 יוֹם שׁוֹפָר וּתְרוּעָה
Against the fortified towns	עַל הֶעָרִים הַבְּצֻרוֹת
And the lofty corner towers.	וְעַל הַפִּנּוֹת הַגְּבֹהוֹת׃
17I will bring distress on the people,	17 וַהֲצֵרֹתִי לָאָדָם
And they shall walk like blind men,	וְהָלְכוּ כַּעִוְרִים
Because they sinned against the LORD;	כִּי לַיהֹוָה חָטָאוּ
Their blood shall be spilled like dust,	וְשֻׁפַּךְ דָּמָם כֶּעָפָר
And their fat*k* like dung.	וּלְחֻמָם כַּגְּלָלִים׃
18Moreover, their silver and gold	18 גַּם־כַּסְפָּם גַּם־זְהָבָם
Shall not avail to save them.	לֹא־יוּכַל לְהַצִּילָם
On the day of the LORD's wrath,	בְּיוֹם עֶבְרַת יְהֹוָה
In the fire of His passion,	וּבְאֵשׁ קִנְאָתוֹ
The whole land shall be consumed;	תֵּאָכֵל כָּל־הָאָרֶץ
For He will make a terrible end	כִּי־כָלָה אַךְ־נִבְהָלָה יַעֲשֶׂה
Of all who dwell in the land.	אֵת כָּל־יֹשְׁבֵי הָאָרֶץ׃ ס

2 Gather together, gather,	ב הִתְקוֹשְׁשׁוּ וָקוֹשּׁוּ
a-O nation without shame,	הַגּוֹי לֹא נִכְסָף׃
2Before the day the decree is born—	2 בְּטֶרֶם לֶדֶת חֹק
The day flies by like chaff-*a*—	כְּמֹץ עָבַר יוֹם
Before the fierce anger	בְּטֶרֶם לֹא־יָבוֹא עֲלֵיכֶם
Of the LORD overtakes you,	חֲרוֹן אַף־יְהֹוָה
Before the day of anger	בְּטֶרֶם לֹא־יָבוֹא עֲלֵיכֶם
Of the LORD overtakes you.	יוֹם אַף־יְהֹוָה׃
3Seek the LORD,	3 בַּקְּשׁוּ אֶת־יְהֹוָה
All you humble of the land	כָּל־עַנְוֵי הָאָרֶץ
Who have fulfilled His law;	אֲשֶׁר מִשְׁפָּטוֹ פָּעָלוּ

j-j   *Emendation yields: "The day of the LORD is faster than a runner, / Fleeter than a warrior"; cf. Ps. 19.6.*
k   *Or "marrow"; meaning of Heb. uncertain.*

a-a   *Meaning of Heb. uncertain. Emendation yields: "O straw [Aramaic gel] not gathered in, / Before you are driven like flying chaff"; cf. Ps. 35.5.*

Seek righteousness,
Seek humility.
Perhaps you will find shelter
On the day of the LORD's anger.

4Indeed, Gaza shall be deserted
And Ashkelon desolate;
Ashdod's people shall be expelled in broad
    daylight,
And Ekron shall be uprooted.
5Ah, nation of Cherethites
Who inhabit the seacoast!
There is a word of the LORD against you,
O Canaan,b land of the Philistines:
I will lay you waste
Without inhabitants.

6The seacoast Cherothc shall become
An abode for shepherds and folds for flocks,
7And shall be a portion for the remnant of the
    House of Judah;
On these [pastures] they shall graze [their
    flocks],
They shall d-lie down-d at eventide
In the houses of Ashkelon.
For the LORD their God will take note of them
And restore their fortunes.

8I have heard the insults of Moab
And the jeers of the Ammonites,
Who have insulted My people
And gloated over their country.
9Assuredly, as I live
        —declares the LORD of Hosts,
            the God of Israel—
Moab shall become like Sodom
And the Ammonites like Gomorrah:

בַּקְּשׁוּ־צֶ֫דֶק
בַּקְּשׁ֣וּ עֲנָוָ֔ה
אוּלַי֙ תִּסָּ֣תְר֔וּ
בְּי֖וֹם אַף־יְהֹוָֽה׃

4 כִּ֤י עַזָּה֙ עֲזוּבָ֣ה תִֽהְיֶ֔ה
וְאַשְׁקְל֖וֹן לִשְׁמָמָ֑ה
אַשְׁדּוֹד֙ בַּֽצׇּהֳרַ֣יִם יְגָ֣רְשׁ֔וּהָ
וְעֶקְר֖וֹן תֵּעָקֵֽר׃ ס
5 ה֗וֹי יֹֽשְׁבֵ֛י חֶ֥בֶל הַיָּ֖ם
גּ֣וֹי כְּרֵתִ֑ים
דְּבַר־יְהֹוָ֣ה עֲלֵיכֶ֗ם
כְּנַ֙עַן֙ אֶ֣רֶץ פְּלִשְׁתִּ֔ים
וְהַֽאֲבַדְתִּ֖יךְ
מֵאֵ֥ין יוֹשֵֽׁב׃

6 וְֽהָיְתָ֞ה חֶ֤בֶל הַיָּם֙
נְוֺ֣ת כְּרֹ֣ת רֹעִ֔ים וְגִדְר֖וֹת צֹֽאן׃
7 וְהָ֣יָה חֶ֗בֶל לִשְׁאֵרִ֛ית בֵּ֥ית יְהוּדָ֖ה
עֲלֵיהֶ֣ם יִרְע֑וּן
בְּבָתֵּ֣י אַשְׁקְל֗וֹן
בָּעֶ֙רֶב֙ יִרְבָּצ֔וּן
כִּ֧י יִפְקְדֵ֛ם יְהֹוָ֥ה אֱלֹֽהֵיהֶ֖ם
וְשָׁ֥ב שבותם שְׁבִיתָֽם׃

8 שָׁמַ֙עְתִּי֙ חֶרְפַּ֣ת מוֹאָ֔ב
וְגִדּוּפֵ֖י בְּנֵ֣י עַמּ֑וֹן
אֲשֶׁ֤ר חֵֽרְפוּ֙ אֶת־עַמִּ֔י
וַיַּגְדִּ֖ילוּ עַל־גְּבוּלָֽם׃
9 לָכֵ֣ן חַי־אָ֡נִי
נְאֻם֩ יְהֹוָ֨ה צְבָא֜וֹת אֱלֹהֵ֣י יִשְׂרָאֵ֗ל
כִּֽי־מוֹאָ֞ב כִּסְדֹ֣ם תִּֽהְיֶ֗ה
וּבְנֵ֤י עַמּוֹן֙ כַּֽעֲמֹרָ֔ה

---

b   Or "Phoenicia," of which Philistia is regarded as an extension
southward.
c   Meaning of Heb. uncertain.
d-d   Change of vocalization yields "rest [them]"; cf. Song of Songs
    1.7.

Clumps*c* of weeds and patches*c* of salt,
And desolation evermore.
The remnant of My people shall plunder
   them,
The remainder of My nation shall possess
   them.
10That is what they'll get for their haughti-
   ness,
For insulting and jeering
At the people of the Lord of Hosts.
11The Lord will show Himself terrible against
   them,
Causing all the gods on earth to shrivel;*c*
And all the coastlands of the nations
Shall bow down to Him—
Every man in his own home.

12You Cushites too—
e-They shall be slain by My sword.-*e*
13And He will stretch out His arm against the
   north
And destroy Assyria;
He will make Nineveh a desolation,
Arid as the desert.
14In it flocks shall lie down,
Every *c*-species of beast,
While jackdaws and owls roost on its capitals,
The great owl hoots in the window,
And the raven [croaks] on the threshold.
For he has stripped its cedarwork bare.-*c*

15Is this the gay city
That dwelt secure,
That thought in her heart,
"I am, and there is none but me"?
Alas, she is become a waste,
A lair of wild beasts!
Everyone who passes by her
Hisses and gestures with his hand.*f*

מִמְשַׁק חָרוּל וּמִכְרֵה-מֶלַח
וּשְׁמָמָה עַד-עוֹלָם
שְׁאֵרִית עַמִּי יְבָזּוּם
וְיֶתֶר גּוֹיִ יִנְחָלוּם:
10 זֹאת לָהֶם תַּחַת גְּאוֹנָם
כִּי חֵרְפוּ וַיַּגְדִּלוּ
עַל-עַם יְהֹוָה צְבָאוֹת:
11 נוֹרָא יְהֹוָה עֲלֵיהֶם
כִּי רָזָה אֵת כָּל-אֱלֹהֵי הָאָרֶץ
וְיִשְׁתַּחֲווּ-לוֹ
אִישׁ מִמְּקוֹמוֹ
כֹּל אִיֵּי הַגּוֹיִם:

12 גַּם-אַתֶּם כּוּשִׁים
חַלְלֵי חַרְבִּי הֵמָּה:
13 וְיֵט * יָדוֹ עַל-צָפוֹן
וִיאַבֵּד אֶת-אַשּׁוּר
וְיָשֵׂם אֶת-נִינְוֵה לִשְׁמָמָה
צִיָּה כַּמִּדְבָּר:
14 וְרָבְצוּ בְתוֹכָהּ עֲדָרִים
כָּל-חַיְתוֹ-גוֹי
גַּם-קָאַת גַּם-קִפֹּד בְּכַפְתֹּרֶיהָ יָלִינוּ
קוֹל יְשׁוֹרֵר בַּחַלּוֹן
חֹרֶב בַּסַּף
כִּי אַרְזָה* עֵרָה:

15 זֹאת* הָעִיר הָעַלִּיזָה
הַיּוֹשֶׁבֶת לָבֶטַח
הָאֹמְרָה בִּלְבָבָהּ
אֲנִי וְאַפְסִי עוֹד
אֵיךְ ׀ הָיְתָה לְשַׁמָּה
מַרְבֵּץ לַחַיָּה
כֹּל עוֹבֵר עָלֶיהָ
יִשְׁרֹק יָנִיעַ יָדוֹ: ס

v. 13. חסר "את"
v. 14. ה' רפה
v. 15. שני טעמים

e-e   Emendation yields "shall be slain by the sword of the Lord."
f   To ward off a like fate from himself; cf. Jer. 18.16 and note.

3 Ah, sullied, polluted,
Overbearing[a] city!
[2]She has been disobedient,
Has learned no lesson;
She has not trusted in the LORD,
Has not drawn near to her God.
[3]The officials within her
Are roaring lions;
Her judges are wolves [b]-of the steppe,
They leave no bone until morning.-[b]
[4]Her prophets are reckless,
Faithless fellows;
Her priests profane what is holy,
They give perverse rulings.
[5]But the LORD in her midst is righteous,
He does no wrong;
He issues judgment every morning,
As unfailing as the light.

The wrongdoer knows no shame!
[6]I wiped out nations:
Their corner towers are desolate;
I turned their thoroughfares into ruins,
With none passing by;
Their towns lie waste without people,
Without inhabitants.
[7]And I thought that she[c] would fear Me,
Would learn a lesson,
And that the punishment I brought on them[d]
Would not be [e]-lost on her.-[e]
Instead, all the more eagerly
They have practiced corruption in all their
   deeds.

ג הֹ֥וי מֹראָ֖ה וְנִגְאָלָ֑ה
הָעִ֖יר הַיּוֹנָֽה:
2 לֹ֤א שָֽׁמְעָה֙ בְּק֔וֹל
לֹ֥א לָקְחָ֖ה מוּסָ֑ר
בַּֽיהוָה֙ לֹ֣א בָטָ֔חָה
אֶל־אֱלֹהֶ֖יהָ לֹ֥א קָרֵֽבָה:
3 שָׂרֶ֣יהָ בְקִרְבָּ֔הּ
אֲרָי֖וֹת שֹֽׁאֲגִ֑ים
שֹׁפְטֶ֙יהָ֙ זְאֵ֣בֵי עֶ֔רֶב
לֹ֥א גָרְמ֖וּ לַבֹּֽקֶר:
4 נְבִיאֶ֙יהָ֙ פֹּֽחֲזִ֔ים
אַנְשֵׁ֖י בֹּֽגְד֑וֹת
כֹּהֲנֶ֙יהָ֙ חִלְּלוּ־קֹ֔דֶשׁ
חָמְס֖וּ תּוֹרָֽה:
5 יְהוָ֤ה צַדִּיק֙ בְּקִרְבָּ֔הּ
לֹ֥א יַעֲשֶׂ֖ה עַוְלָ֑ה
בַּבֹּ֤קֶר בַּבֹּ֙קֶר֙ מִשְׁפָּט֣וֹ יִתֵּ֔ן
לָאוֹר֙ לֹ֣א נֶעְדָּ֔ר
וְלֹֽא־יוֹדֵ֥עַ עַוָּ֖ל בֹּֽשֶׁת:
6 הִכְרַ֣תִּי גוֹיִ֗ם
נָשַׁ֙מּוּ֙ פִּנּוֹתָ֔ם
הֶחֱרַ֖בְתִּי חֽוּצוֹתָ֑ם
מִבְּלִ֖י עוֹבֵ֑ר
נִצְדּ֤וּ עָרֵיהֶם֙ מִבְּלִי־אִ֔ישׁ
מֵאֵ֖ין יוֹשֵֽׁב:
7 אָמַ֜רְתִּי אַךְ־תִּירְאִ֤י אוֹתִי֙
תִּקְחִ֣י מוּסָ֔ר
וְלֹֽא־יִכָּרֵ֣ת מְעוֹנָ֔הּ
כֹּ֥ל אֲשֶׁר־פָּקַ֖דְתִּי עָלֶ֑יהָ
אָכֵן֙ הִשְׁכִּ֣ימוּ
הִשְׁחִ֖יתוּ כֹּ֥ל עֲלִילוֹתָֽם:

---

a   *Meaning of Heb. uncertain. Emendation yields "harlot"; cf. Isa.*
    1.21.
b-b *Meaning of Heb. uncertain.*
c   *Heb. "you."*
d   *Heb. "her."*
e-e *Lit. "cut off [from] her vision."*

8But wait for Me—says the LORD—
For the day when I arise as an accuser;*f*
When I decide to gather nations,
To bring kingdoms together,
To pour out My indignation on them,
All My blazing anger.
Indeed, by the fire of My passion
All the earth shall be consumed.
9For then I will make the peoples pure of
    speech,
So that they all invoke the LORD by name
And serve Him with one accord.*g*
10From beyond the rivers of Cush, My
    suppliants*b*
Shall bring offerings to Me in Fair Puzai.*h*
11In that day,
You will no longer be shamed for all the deeds
By which you have defied Me.
For then I will remove
The proud and exultant within you,
And you will be haughty no more
On My sacred mount.*i*
12But I will leave within you
A poor, humble folk,
And they shall find refuge
In the name of the LORD.
13The remnant of Israel
Shall do no wrong
And speak no falsehood;
A deceitful tongue
Shall not be in their mouths.
Only such as these shall graze and lie down,
With none to trouble them.

14Shout for joy, Fair Zion,
Cry aloud, O Israel!

8 לָכֵן חַכּוּ־לִ֤י נְאֻם־יְהוָ֔ה
לְי֖וֹם קוּמִ֣י לְעַ֑ד
כִּ֣י מִשְׁפָּטִי֩ לֶאֱסֹ֨ף גּוֹיִ֜ם
לְקָבְצִ֣י מַמְלָכ֗וֹת
לִשְׁפֹּ֤ךְ עֲלֵיהֶם֙
זַעְמִ֔י כֹּ֖ל חֲר֣וֹן אַפִּ֑י
כִּ֚י בְּאֵ֣שׁ קִנְאָתִ֔י
תֵּאָכֵ֖ל כָּל־הָאָֽרֶץ׃
9 כִּֽי־אָ֛ז אֶהְפֹּ֥ךְ אֶל־עַמִּ֖ים שָׂפָ֣ה בְרוּרָ֑ה
לִקְרֹ֤א כֻלָּם֙ בְּשֵׁ֣ם יְהוָ֔ה
לְעָבְד֖וֹ שְׁכֶ֥ם אֶחָֽד׃
10 מֵעֵ֖בֶר לְנַהֲרֵי־כ֑וּשׁ עֲתָרַי֙
בַּת־פּוּצַ֔י יוֹבִל֖וּן מִנְחָתִֽי׃
11 בַּיּ֣וֹם הַה֗וּא
לֹ֤א תֵב֙וֹשִׁי֙ מִכֹּ֣ל עֲלִילֹתַ֔יִךְ
אֲשֶׁ֥ר פָּשַׁ֖עַתְּ בִּ֑י
כִּי־אָ֣ז ׀ אָסִ֣יר
מִקִּרְבֵּ֗ךְ עַלִּיזֵי֙ גַּאֲוָתֵ֔ךְ
וְלֹֽא־תוֹסִ֧פִי לְגָבְהָ֛ה ע֖וֹד
בְּהַ֥ר קָדְשִֽׁי׃
12 וְהִשְׁאַרְתִּ֣י בְקִרְבֵּ֔ךְ
עַ֥ם עָנִ֖י וָדָ֑ל
וְחָס֖וּ
בְּשֵׁ֥ם יְהוָֽה׃
13 שְׁאֵרִ֨ית יִשְׂרָאֵ֜ל
לֹֽא־יַעֲשׂ֤וּ עַוְלָה֙
וְלֹא־יְדַבְּר֣וּ כָזָ֔ב
וְלֹֽא־יִמָּצֵ֥א בְּפִיהֶ֖ם
לְשׁ֣וֹן תַּרְמִ֑ית
כִּי־הֵ֛מָּה יִרְע֥וּ וְרָבְצ֖וּ
וְאֵ֥ין מַחֲרִֽיד׃ ס
14 רָנִּי֙ בַּת־צִיּ֔וֹן
הָרִ֖יעוּ יִשְׂרָאֵ֑ל

---

f *Understanding* 'ad *as equivalent to* 'ed, *with Septuagint and
    Syriac.*
g *Lit.* "back," *i.e., like beasts of burden.*
h *Emendation yields* "Zion." *For the thought, cf. Isa. 18.1, 7.*
i *I.e., in My holy land; cf. Isa. 11.9; 57.13; 65.25.*

Rejoice and be glad with all your heart,

Fair Jerusalem!

¹⁵The LORD has annulled the judgment
   against you,

He has swept away your foes.

Israel's Sovereign the LORD is within you;

You need fear misfortune no more.

¹⁶In that day,

This shall be said to Jerusalem:

Have no fear, O Zion;

Let not your hands droop!

¹⁷Your God the LORD is in your midst,

A warrior who brings triumph.

He will rejoice over you and be glad,

He will shout over you with jubilation.

He will ʲ-soothe with His love

¹⁸Those long disconsolate.-ʲ

I will take away from you ᵇ-the woe

Over which you endured mockery.-ᵇ

¹⁹At that time I will make [an end]

Of all who afflicted you.

And I will rescue the lame [sheep]

And gather the strayed;

And I will exchange their disgrace

For fame and renown in all the earth.

²⁰At that time I will gather you,

And at [that] time I will bring you [home];

For I will make you renowned and famous

Among all the peoples on earth,

When I restore your fortunes

Before theirᵏ very eyes

         —said the LORD.

שִׂמְחִי וְעָלְזִי֙ בְּכָל־לֵ֔ב

בַּ֖ת יְרוּשָׁלָֽ͏ִם׃

15 הֵסִ֤יר יְהֹוָה֙ מִשְׁפָּטַ֔יִךְ

פִּנָּ֖ה אֹיְבֵ֑ךְ

מֶ֣לֶךְ יִשְׂרָאֵ֤ל ׀ יְהֹוָה֙ בְּקִרְבֵּ֔ךְ

לֹא־תִֽירְאִ֥י רָ֖ע עֽוֹד׃

16 בַּיּ֣וֹם הַה֔וּא

יֵאָמֵ֥ר לִירוּשָׁלַ֖͏ִם

אַל־תִּירָ֑אִי צִיּ֕וֹן

אַל־יִרְפּ֖וּ יָדָֽיִךְ׃

17 יְהֹוָ֧ה אֱלֹהַ֛יִךְ בְּקִרְבֵּ֖ךְ

גִּבּ֣וֹר יוֹשִׁ֑יעַ

יָשִׂ֤ישׂ עָלַ֙יִךְ֙ בְּשִׂמְחָ֔ה

יַחֲרִ֖ישׁ בְּאַהֲבָת֑וֹ

יָגִ֥יל עָלַ֖יִךְ בְּרִנָּֽה׃

18 נוּגֵ֥י מִמּוֹעֵ֖ד

אָסַ֑פְתִּי מִמֵּ֖ךְ הָי֑וּ

מַשְׂאֵ֥ת עָלֶ֖יהָ חֶרְפָּֽה׃

19 הִנְנִ֥י עֹשֶׂ֛ה אֶת־כָּל־מְעַנַּ֖יִךְ

בָּעֵ֣ת הַהִ֑יא

וְהוֹשַׁעְתִּי֙ אֶת־הַצֹּ֣לֵעָ֔ה

וְהַנִּדָּחָה֙ אֲקַבֵּ֔ץ

וְשַׂמְתִּים֙ לִתְהִלָּ֣ה וּלְשֵׁ֔ם

בְּכָל־הָאָ֖רֶץ בָּשְׁתָּֽם׃

20 בָּעֵ֤ת הַהִיא֙ אָבִ֣יא אֶתְכֶ֔ם

וּבָעֵ֖ת קַבְּצִ֣י אֶתְכֶ֑ם

כִּֽי־אֶתֵּ֨ן אֶתְכֶ֜ם לְשֵׁ֣ם וְלִתְהִלָּ֗ה

בְּכֹל֙ עַמֵּ֣י הָאָ֔רֶץ

בְּשׁוּבִ֧י אֶת־שְׁבוּתֵיכֶ֛ם

לְעֵינֵיכֶ֖ם

אָמַ֥ר יְהֹוָֽה׃

ʲ-ʲ   *Meaning of Heb. uncertain. Emendation yields "renew His love*
    / As in the days of old."

ᵏ   *Heb. "your."*

HAGGAI

1 In the second year of King Darius, on the first day of the sixth month, this word of the LORD came through the prophet Haggai to Zerubbabel son of Shealtiel, the governor of Judah, and to Joshua son of Jehozadak, the high priest:

2Thus said the LORD of Hosts: These people say, a-"The time has not yet come-a for rebuilding the House of the LORD."

3And the word of the LORD through the prophet Haggai continued:

4Is it a time for you to dwell in your paneled houses, while this House is lying in ruins? 5Now thus said the LORD of Hosts: Consider how you have been faring! 6You have sowed much and brought in little; you eat without being satisfied; you drink without getting your fill; you clothe yourselves, but no one gets warm; and he who earns anything earns it for a leaky purse.

7bThus said the LORD of Hosts: Consider how you have fared: 8Go up to the hills and get timber, and rebuild the House; then I will look on it with favor and I will c-be glorified-c—said the LORD.

9You have been expecting much and getting little; and when you brought it home, I would blow on it!d Because of what?—says the LORD of Hosts. Because of My House which lies in ruins, while you all hurry to your own houses! 10That is why the skies above you have withheld [their] moisture and the earth has withheld its yield, 11and I have summoned fierce heat upon

א בִּשְׁנַ֣ת שְׁתַּ֔יִם לְדָרְיָ֖וֶשׁ הַמֶּ֑לֶךְ בַּחֹ֨דֶשׁ הַשִּׁשִּׁ֜י בְּי֤וֹם אֶחָד֙ לַחֹ֔דֶשׁ הָיָ֣ה דְבַר־יְהֹוָ֗ה בְּיַד־חַגַּ֣י הַנָּבִ֔יא אֶל־זְרֻבָּבֶ֤ל בֶּן־שְׁאַלְתִּיאֵל֙ פַּחַ֣ת יְהוּדָ֔ה וְאֶל־יְהוֹשֻׁ֧עַ בֶּן־יְהוֹצָדָ֛ק הַכֹּהֵ֥ן הַגָּד֖וֹל לֵאמֹֽר׃

2 כֹּ֥ה אָמַ֛ר יְהֹוָ֥ה צְבָא֖וֹת לֵאמֹ֑ר הָעָ֤ם הַזֶּה֙ אָמְר֔וּ לֹ֥א עֶת־בֹּ֖א עֶת־בֵּ֥ית יְהֹוָ֖ה לְהִבָּנֽוֹת׃ פ

3 וַיְהִי֙ דְּבַר־יְהֹוָ֔ה בְּיַד־חַגַּ֥י הַנָּבִ֖יא לֵאמֹֽר׃ 4 הַעֵ֣ת לָכֶ֗ם אַתֶּ֛ם לָשֶׁ֥בֶת בְּבָתֵּיכֶ֖ם סְפוּנִ֑ים וְהַבַּ֥יִת הַזֶּ֖ה חָרֵֽב׃ 5 וְעַתָּ֕ה כֹּ֥ה אָמַ֖ר יְהֹוָ֣ה צְבָא֑וֹת שִׂ֥ימוּ לְבַבְכֶ֖ם עַל־דַּרְכֵיכֶֽם׃ 6 זְרַעְתֶּ֨ם הַרְבֵּ֜ה וְהָבֵ֣א מְעָ֗ט אָכ֤וֹל וְאֵין־לְשׇׂבְעָה֙ שָׁת֣וֹ וְאֵין־לְשׇׁכְרָ֔ה לָב֖וֹשׁ וְאֵין־לְחֹ֣ם ל֑וֹ וְהַ֨מִּשְׂתַּכֵּ֔ר מִשְׂתַּכֵּ֖ר אֶל־צְר֥וֹר נָקֽוּב׃ פ

7 כֹּ֥ה אָמַ֖ר יְהֹוָ֣ה צְבָא֑וֹת שִׂ֥ימוּ לְבַבְכֶ֖ם עַל־דַּרְכֵיכֶֽם׃ 8 עֲל֤וּ הָהָר֙ וַהֲבֵאתֶ֣ם עֵ֔ץ וּבְנ֖וּ הַבָּ֑יִת וְאֶרְצֶה־בּ֥וֹ וְאֶכָּבְדָ֖ה אָמַ֥ר יְהֹוָֽה׃ 9 פָּנֹ֤ה אֶל־הַרְבֵּה֙ וְהִנֵּ֣ה לִמְעָ֔ט וַהֲבֵאתֶ֥ם הַבַּ֖יִת וְנָפַ֣חְתִּי ב֑וֹ יַ֣עַן מֶ֗ה נְאֻם֙ יְהֹוָ֣ה צְבָא֔וֹת יַ֗עַן בֵּיתִי֙ אֲשֶׁר־ה֣וּא חָרֵ֔ב וְאַתֶּ֥ם רָצִ֖ים אִ֥ישׁ לְבֵיתֽוֹ׃ 10 עַל־כֵּ֗ן עֲלֵיכֶם֙ כָּלְא֣וּ שָׁמַ֖יִם מִטָּ֑ל וְהָאָ֖רֶץ כָּלְאָ֥ה יְבוּלָֽהּ׃ 11 וָאֶקְרָ֨א חֹ֜רֶב עַל־הָאָ֣רֶץ וְעַל־הֶהָרִ֗ים

---

a-a Lit. "It is not time for the coming of the time."
b Vv. 7–8 would read well after v. 11.
c-c Emendation yields "glorify it"; see 2.7–9.
d Meaning, perhaps, cast a curse on.

the land—upon the hills, upon the new grain and wine and oil, upon all that the ground produces, upon man and beast, and upon all the fruits of labor.

¹²Zerubbabel son of Shealtiel and the high priest Joshua son of Jehozadak and all the rest of the people gave heed to the summons of the LORD their God and to the words of the prophet Haggai, when the LORD their God sent him; the people feared the LORD. ¹³And Haggai, the LORD's messenger, fulfilling the LORD's mission, spoke to the people, "I am with you—declares the LORD."

¹⁴Then the LORD roused the spirit of Zerubbabel son of Shealtiel, the governor of Judah, and the spirit of the high priest Joshua son of Jehozadak, and the spirit of all the rest of the people: They came and set to work on the House of the LORD of Hosts, their God, ¹⁵on the twenty-fourth day of the sixth month. In the second
2 year of King Darius, ¹on the twenty-first day of the seventh month, the word of the LORD came through the prophet Haggai:

²Speak to Zerubbabel son of Shealtiel, the governor of Judah, and to the high priest Joshua son of Jehozadak, and to the rest of the people: ³Who is there left among you who saw this House in its former splendor? How does it look to you now? It must seem like nothing to you. ⁴But be strong, O Zerubbabel—says the LORD—be strong, O high priest Joshua son of Jehozadak; be strong, all you people of the land—says the LORD—and act! For I am with you—says the LORD of Hosts. ⁵So I promised you when you came out of Egypt, and My spirit is still in your midst. Fear not!

⁶For thus said the LORD of Hosts: In just a little while longer I will shake the heavens and

וְעַל־הַדָּגָן וְעַל־הַתִּירוֹשׁ וְעַל־הַיִּצְהָר וְעַל אֲשֶׁר תּוֹצִיא הָאֲדָמָה וְעַל־הָאָדָם וְעַל־ הַבְּהֵמָה וְעַל כָּל־יְגִיעַ כַּפָּיִם: ס

¹² וַיִּשְׁמַע זְרֻבָּבֶל ׀ בֶּן־שַׁלְתִּיאֵל וִיהוֹשֻׁעַ בֶּן־יְהוֹצָדָק הַכֹּהֵן הַגָּדוֹל וְכֹל ׀ שְׁאֵרִית הָעָם בְּקוֹל יְהוָה אֱלֹהֵיהֶם וְעַל־דִּבְרֵי חַגַּי הַנָּבִיא כַּאֲשֶׁר שְׁלָחוֹ יְהוָה אֱלֹהֵיהֶם וַיִּירְאוּ הָעָם מִפְּנֵי יְהוָה: ¹³ וַיֹּאמֶר חַגַּי מַלְאַךְ יְהוָה בְּמַלְאֲכוּת יְהוָה לָעָם לֵאמֹר אֲנִי אִתְּכֶם נְאֻם־יְהוָה:

¹⁴ וַיָּעַר יְהוָה אֶת־רוּחַ זְרֻבָּבֶל ׀ בֶּן־ שַׁלְתִּיאֵל* פַּחַת יְהוּדָה וְאֶת־רוּחַ יְהוֹשֻׁעַ בֶּן־יְהוֹצָדָק הַכֹּהֵן הַגָּדוֹל וְאֶת־רוּחַ כֹּל שְׁאֵרִית הָעָם וַיָּבֹאוּ וַיַּעֲשׂוּ מְלָאכָה בְּבֵית־יְהוָה צְבָאוֹת אֱלֹהֵיהֶם: פ ¹⁵ בְּיוֹם עֶשְׂרִים וְאַרְבָּעָה לַחֹדֶשׁ בַּשִּׁשִּׁי בִּשְׁנַת שְׁתַּיִם לְדָרְיָוֶשׁ הַמֶּלֶךְ: ¹ בַּשְּׁבִיעִי בְּעֶשְׂרִים וְאֶחָד לַחֹדֶשׁ הָיָה דְּבַר־ ב יְהוָה בְּיַד־חַגַּי הַנָּבִיא לֵאמֹר: ² אֱמָר־נָא אֶל־זְרֻבָּבֶל בֶּן־שַׁלְתִּיאֵל* פַּחַת יְהוּדָה וְאֶל־יְהוֹשֻׁעַ בֶּן־יְהוֹצָדָק הַכֹּהֵן הַגָּדוֹל וְאֶל־שְׁאֵרִית הָעָם לֵאמֹר: ³ מִי בָכֶם הַנִּשְׁאָר אֲשֶׁר רָאָה אֶת־הַבַּיִת הַזֶּה בִּכְבוֹדוֹ הָרִאשׁוֹן וּמָה אַתֶּם רֹאִים אֹתוֹ עַתָּה הֲלוֹא כָמֹהוּ כְּאַיִן בְּעֵינֵיכֶם: ⁴ וְעַתָּה חֲזַק זְרֻבָּבֶל ׀ נְאֻם־יְהוָה וַחֲזַק יְהוֹשֻׁעַ בֶּן־יְהוֹצָדָק הַכֹּהֵן הַגָּדוֹל וַחֲזַק כָּל־עַם הָאָרֶץ נְאֻם־יְהוָה וַעֲשׂוּ כִּי־אֲנִי אִתְּכֶם נְאֻם יְהוָה צְבָאוֹת: ⁵ אֶת־הַדָּבָר אֲשֶׁר־ כָּרַתִּי אִתְּכֶם בְּצֵאתְכֶם מִמִּצְרַיִם וְרוּחִי עֹמֶדֶת בְּתוֹכְכֶם אַל־תִּירָאוּ: ס

⁶ כִּי כֹה אָמַר יְהוָה צְבָאוֹת עוֹד אַחַת מְעַט הִיא וַאֲנִי מַרְעִישׁ אֶת־הַשָּׁמַיִם

v. 14. חסר א'

v. 2. חסר א'

the earth, the sea and the dry land; 7I will shake all the nations. And the precious things of all the nations shall come [here], and I will fill this House with glory, said the LORD of Hosts. 8Silver is Mine and gold is Mine—says the LORD of Hosts. 9The glory of this latter House shall be greater than that of the former one, said the LORD of Hosts; and in this place I will grant prosperity—declares the LORD of Hosts.

10On the twenty-fourth day of the ninth [month], in the second year of Darius, the word of the LORD came to the prophet Haggai:

11Thus said the LORD of Hosts: Seek a ruling from the priests, as follows: 12If a man is carrying sacrificial flesh in a fold of his garment, and with that fold touches bread, stew, wine, oil, or any other food, will the latter become holy? In reply, the priests said, "No." 13Haggai went on, "If someone defiled by a corpse touches any of these, will it be defiled?" And the priests responded, "Yes."

14Thereupon Haggai said: That is how this people and that is how this nation looks to Me—declares the LORD—and so, too, the work of their hands: Whatever they offer there is defiled. 15And now take thought, from this day backward:a As long as no stone had been laid on another in the House of the LORD, 16if one came to a heap of twenty measures,b it would yield only ten; and if one came to a wine vat to skim off fifty measures, the press would yield only twenty. 17I struck you—all the works of your hands—with blight and mildew and hail, but cyou did not return-c to Me—declares the LORD. 18Take note, from this day forward— from the twenty-fourth day of the ninth month, from the day when the foundation was laid for the LORD's Temple—take note 19while the seed is still in the granary, and the vine, fig tree,

וְאֶת־הָאָֽרֶץ וְאֶת־הַיָּ֖ם וְאֶת־הֶחָרָבָֽה׃
7 וְהִרְעַשְׁתִּי֙ אֶת־כָּל־הַגּוֹיִ֔ם וּבָ֖אוּ חֶמְדַּ֣ת כָּל־הַגּוֹיִ֑ם וּמִלֵּאתִ֞י אֶת־הַבַּ֤יִת הַזֶּה֙ כָּב֔וֹד אָמַ֖ר יְהֹוָ֥ה צְבָאֽוֹת׃ 8 לִ֥י הַכֶּ֖סֶף וְלִ֣י הַזָּהָ֑ב נְאֻ֖ם יְהֹוָ֥ה צְבָאֽוֹת׃ 9 גָּד֣וֹל יִֽהְיֶ֡ה כְּבוֹד֩ הַבַּ֨יִת הַזֶּ֤ה הָאַחֲרוֹן֙ מִן־הָ֣רִאשׁ֔וֹן אָמַ֖ר יְהֹוָ֣ה צְבָא֑וֹת וּבַמָּק֤וֹם הַזֶּה֙ אֶתֵּ֣ן שָׁל֔וֹם נְאֻ֖ם יְהֹוָ֥ה צְבָאֽוֹת׃ פ

10 בְּעֶשְׂרִ֤ים וְאַרְבָּעָה֙ לַתְּשִׁיעִ֔י בִּשְׁנַ֥ת שְׁתַּ֖יִם לְדָרְיָ֑וֶשׁ הָיָה֙ דְּבַר־יְהֹוָ֔ה אֶל־חַגַּ֥י הַנָּבִ֖יא לֵאמֹֽר׃ 11 כֹּ֥ה אָמַ֖ר יְהֹוָ֣ה צְבָא֑וֹת שְׁאַל־נָ֧א אֶת־הַכֹּהֲנִ֛ים תּוֹרָ֖ה לֵאמֹֽר׃ 12 הֵ֣ן ׀ יִשָּׂא־אִ֣ישׁ בְּשַׂר־קֹ֗דֶשׁ בִּכְנַ֣ף בִּגְד֒וֹ וְנָגַ֣ע בִּ֠כְנָפ֠וֹ אֶל־הַלֶּ֨חֶם וְאֶל־הַנָּזִ֜יד וְאֶל־הַיַּ֣יִן וְאֶל־שֶׁ֗מֶן וְאֶל־כָּל־מַאֲכָ֛ל הֲיִקְדָּ֑שׁ וַיַּעֲנ֧וּ הַכֹּהֲנִ֛ים וַיֹּאמְר֖וּ לֹֽא׃ 13 וַיֹּ֣אמֶר חַגַּ֔י אִם־יִגַּ֧ע טְמֵא־נֶ֛פֶשׁ בְּכָל־אֵ֖לֶּה הֲיִטְמָ֑א וַיַּעֲנ֧וּ הַכֹּהֲנִ֛ים וַיֹּאמְר֖וּ יִטְמָֽא׃ 14 וַיַּ֨עַן חַגַּ֜י וַיֹּ֗אמֶר כֵּ֣ן הָֽעָם־הַזֶּ֩ה וְכֵן־הַגּ֨וֹי הַזֶּ֤ה לְפָנַי֙ נְאֻם־יְהֹוָ֔ה וְכֵ֖ן כָּל־מַעֲשֵׂ֣ה יְדֵיהֶ֑ם וַאֲשֶׁ֥ר יַקְרִ֛יבוּ שָׁ֖ם טָמֵ֥א הֽוּא׃ 15 וְעַתָּה֙ שִֽׂימוּ־נָ֣א לְבַבְכֶ֔ם מִן־הַיּ֥וֹם הַזֶּ֖ה וָמָ֑עְלָה מִטֶּ֧רֶם שֽׂוּם־אֶ֛בֶן אֶל־אֶ֖בֶן בְּהֵיכַ֥ל יְהֹוָֽה׃ 16 מִֽהְיוֹתָ֥ם בָּ֣א אֶל־עֲרֵמַ֣ת עֶשְׂרִ֗ים וְהָיְתָ֖ה עֲשָׂרָ֑ה בָּ֣א אֶל־הַיֶּ֗קֶב לַחְשֹׂף֙ חֲמִשִּׁ֣ים פּוּרָ֔ה וְהָיְתָ֖ה עֶשְׂרִֽים׃ 17 הִכֵּ֨יתִי אֶתְכֶ֜ם בַּשִּׁדָּפ֤וֹן וּבַיֵּֽרָקוֹן֙ וּבַבָּרָ֔ד אֵ֖ת כָּל־מַעֲשֵׂ֣ה יְדֵיכֶ֑ם וְאֵין־אֶתְכֶ֥ם אֵלַ֖י נְאֻם־יְהֹוָֽה׃ 18 שִֽׂימוּ־נָ֣א לְבַבְכֶ֔ם מִן־הַיּ֥וֹם הַזֶּ֖ה וָמָ֑עְלָה מִיּוֹם֩ עֶשְׂרִ֨ים וְאַרְבָּעָ֜ה לַתְּשִׁיעִ֗י לְמִן־הַיּ֛וֹם אֲשֶׁר־יֻסַּ֥ד הֵֽיכַל־יְהֹוָ֖ה שִׂ֥ימוּ לְבַבְכֶֽם׃ 19 הַע֤וֹד הַזֶּ֨רַע֙ בַּמְּגוּרָ֔ה וְעַד־

---

a   Or "forward."
b   I.e., of grain.
c-c   Lit. "there was not with you to Me"; cf. Amos 4.9.

1381

pomegranate, and olive tree have not yet borne fruit. For from this day on I will send blessings.

²⁰And the word of the LORD came to Haggai a second time on the twenty-fourth day of the month: ²¹Speak to Zerubbabel the governor of Judah: I am going to shake the heavens and the earth. ²²And I will overturn the thrones of kingdoms and destroy the might of the kingdoms of the nations. I will overturn chariots and their drivers. Horses and their riders shall fall, each by the sword of his fellow. ²³On that day—declares the LORD of Hosts—I will take you, O My servant Zerubbabel son of Shealtiel—declares the LORD—and make you as a signet;*d* for I have chosen you—declares the LORD of Hosts.

הַגֶּפֶן וְהַתְּאֵנָה וְהָרִמּוֹן וְעֵץ הַזַּיִת לֹא
נָשָׂא מִן־הַיּוֹם הַזֶּה אֲבָרֵךְ: ס
²⁰ וַיְהִי דְבַר־יְהוָה ׀ שֵׁנִית אֶל־חַגַּי
בְּעֶשְׂרִים וְאַרְבָּעָה לַחֹדֶשׁ לֵאמֹר: ²¹ אֱמֹר
אֶל־זְרֻבָּבֶל פַּחַת־יְהוּדָה לֵאמֹר אֲנִי
מַרְעִישׁ אֶת־הַשָּׁמַיִם וְאֶת־הָאָרֶץ:
²² וְהָפַכְתִּי כִּסֵּא מַמְלָכוֹת וְהִשְׁמַדְתִּי חֹזֶק
מַמְלְכוֹת הַגּוֹיִם וְהָפַכְתִּי מֶרְכָּבָה וְרֹכְבֶיהָ
וְיָרְדוּ סוּסִים וְרֹכְבֵיהֶם אִישׁ בְּחֶרֶב אָחִיו:
²³ בַּיּוֹם הַהוּא נְאֻם־יְהוָה צְבָאוֹת אֶקָּחֲךָ
זְרֻבָּבֶל בֶּן־שְׁאַלְתִּיאֵל עַבְדִּי נְאֻם־יְהוָה
וְשַׂמְתִּיךָ כַּחוֹתָם כִּי־בְךָ בָחַרְתִּי נְאֻם
יְהוָה צְבָאוֹת:

---

d *I.e., bring you close to Me; contrast Jer. 22.24–30.*

ZECHARIAH

1 In the eighth month of the second year of Darius, this word of the LORD came to the prophet Zechariah son of Berechiah son of Iddo:[a] 2The LORD was very angry with your fathers. 3Say to them further:

Thus said the LORD of Hosts: Turn back to me—says the LORD of Hosts—and I will turn back to you—said the LORD of Hosts. 4Do not be like your fathers! For when the earlier prophets called to them, "Thus said the LORD of Hosts: Come, turn back from your evil ways and your evil deeds, they did not obey or give heed to Me—declares the LORD. 5Where are your fathers now? And did the prophets live forever? 6But the warnings and the decrees with which I charged My servants the prophets overtook your fathers—did they not?—and in the end they had to admit, 'The LORD has dealt with us according to our ways and our deeds, just as He purposed.'"

7On the twenty-fourth day of the eleventh month of the second year of Darius—the month of Shebat—this word of the LORD came to the prophet Zechariah son of Berechiah son of Iddo:

8In the night, I had a vision. I saw a man, mounted on a bay horse, standing b-among the myrtles-b in the Deep, and behind him were bay,c sorrel,d and white horses. 9I asked, "What

אבַּחֹ֙דֶשׁ֙ הַשְּׁמִינִ֔י בִּשְׁנַ֥ת שְׁתַּ֖יִם
לְדָרְיָ֑וֶשׁ הָיָ֣ה דְבַר־יְהֹוָ֗ה אֶל־זְכַרְיָה֙ בֶּן־
בֶּרֶכְיָ֧ה בֶּן־עִדּ֛וֹ הַנָּבִ֖יא לֵאמֹֽר: 2קָצַ֧ף
יְהֹוָ֛ה עַל־אֲבֽוֹתֵיכֶ֖ם קָֽצֶף: 3וְאָמַרְתָּ֣
אֲלֵהֶ֗ם

כֹּ֤ה אָמַר֙ יְהֹוָ֣ה צְבָא֔וֹת שׁ֣וּבוּ אֵלַ֔י נְאֻ֖ם
יְהֹוָ֣ה צְבָא֑וֹת וְאָשׁ֣וּב אֲלֵיכֶ֔ם אָמַ֖ר יְהֹוָ֥ה
צְבָאֽוֹת: 4אַל־תִּֽהְי֣וּ כַאֲבֹֽתֵיכֶ֡ם אֲשֶׁ֣ר
קָרְא֣וּ־אֲלֵיהֶם֩ הַנְּבִיאִ֨ים הָרִֽאשֹׁנִ֜ים לֵאמֹ֗ר
כֹּ֣ה אָמַר֮ יְהֹוָ֣ה צְבָאוֹת֒ שׁ֣וּבוּ נָ֣א
מִדַּרְכֵיכֶ֤ם הָֽרָעִים֙ ומעליליכם וּמַֽעַלְלֵיכֶ֣ם
הָֽרָעִ֔ים וְלֹ֥א שָֽׁמְע֛וּ וְלֹא־הִקְשִׁ֥יבוּ
אֵלַ֖י נְאֻם־יְהֹוָֽה: 5אֲבֽוֹתֵיכֶ֖ם אַיֵּה־הֵ֑ם
וְהַ֨נְּבִאִ֔ים הַלְעוֹלָ֖ם יִֽחְיֽוּ: 6אַ֣ךְ ׀ דְּבָרַ֣י
וְחֻקַּ֗י אֲשֶׁ֤ר צִוִּ֙יתִי֙ אֶת־עֲבָדַ֣י הַנְּבִיאִ֔ים
הֲל֥וֹא הִשִּׂ֖יגוּ אֲבֹֽתֵיכֶ֑ם וַיָּשׁ֣וּבוּ וַיֹּֽאמְר֗וּ
כַּאֲשֶׁ֨ר זָמַ֜ם יְהֹוָ֤ה צְבָאוֹת֙ לַעֲשׂ֣וֹת לָ֔נוּ
כִּדְרָכֵ֙ינוּ֙ וּכְמַ֣עֲלָלֵ֔ינוּ כֵּ֖ן עָשָׂ֥ה אִתָּֽנוּ: ס

7בְּיוֹם֩ עֶשְׂרִ֨ים וְאַרְבָּעָ֜ה לְעַשְׁתֵּֽי־עָשָׂ֥ר
חֹ֙דֶשׁ֙ הוּא־חֹ֣דֶשׁ שְׁבָ֔ט בִּשְׁנַ֥ת שְׁתַּ֖יִם
לְדָרְיָ֑וֶשׁ הָיָ֣ה דְבַר־יְהֹוָ֗ה אֶל־זְכַרְיָה֙ בֶּן־
בֶּרֶכְיָ֧הוּ בֶּן־עִדּ֛וֹא הַנָּבִ֖יא לֵאמֹֽר:
8רָאִ֣יתִי ׀ הַלַּ֗יְלָה וְהִנֵּה־אִישׁ֙ רֹכֵב֙ עַל־
ס֣וּס אָדֹ֔ם וְה֣וּא עֹמֵ֔ד בֵּ֥ין הַהֲדַסִּ֖ים אֲשֶׁ֣ר
בַּמְּצֻלָ֑ה וְאַֽחֲרָ֗יו סוּסִ֛ים אֲדֻמִּ֥ים שְׂרֻקִּ֖ים

---

a A clause like "Say to the people" is here understood; cf. 7.5.
b-b Septuagint reads "between the mountains"; cf. 6.1. In 6.1 ff. four teams of horses leave the LORD's abode to roam the four quarters of the earth; in 1.8 ff. they are about to reenter His abode after such a reconnaissance.
c Septuagint adds "dappled"; cf. 6.3.
d Meaning of Heb. uncertain. Emendation yields "black"; cf. 6.2.

are those, my lord?" And the angel who talked with me answered, "I will let you know what they are." [10]Then the man who was standing [b-]among the myrtles[-b] spoke up and said, "These were sent out by the LORD to roam the earth."

[11]And in fact, they reported to the angel of the LORD who was standing [b-]among the myrtles,[-b] "We have roamed the earth, and have found all the earth dwelling in tranquility."[e] [12]Thereupon the angel of the LORD exclaimed, "O LORD of Hosts! How long will You withhold pardon from Jerusalem and the towns of Judah, which You placed under a curse seventy years ago?"

[13]The LORD replied with kind, comforting words to the angel who talked with me.

[14]Then the angel who talked with me said to me: "Proclaim! Thus said the LORD of Hosts: I am very jealous for Jerusalem—for Zion—[15]and I am very angry with those nations that are at ease; for I was only angry a little, but they overdid the punishment. [16]Assuredly, thus said the LORD: I graciously return to Jerusalem. My House shall be built in her—declares the LORD of Hosts—the measuring line is being applied to Jerusalem. [17]Proclaim further: Thus said the LORD of Hosts: My towns shall yet overflow with bounty. For the LORD will again comfort Zion; He will choose Jerusalem again."

2 I looked up, and I saw four horns.[a] [2]I asked the angel who talked with me, "What are those?" "Those," he replied, "are the horns that tossed Judah, Israel, and Jerusalem."[a] [3]Then the LORD showed me four smiths. [4]"What are they coming to do?" I asked. He replied: "Those are the

---

ולבנים: 9 וָאֹמַ֕ר מָה־אֵ֖לֶּה אֲדֹנִ֑י וַיֹּ֣אמֶר אֵלַ֗י הַמַּלְאָךְ֙ הַדֹּבֵ֣ר בִּ֔י אֲנִ֥י אַרְאֶ֖ךָּ מָה־הֵ֥מָּה אֵֽלֶּה: 10 וַיַּ֗עַן הָאִ֛ישׁ הָעֹמֵ֥ד בֵּין־הַהֲדַסִּ֖ים וַיֹּאמַ֑ר אֵ֚לֶּה אֲשֶׁ֣ר שָׁלַ֣ח יְהוָ֔ה לְהִתְהַלֵּ֖ךְ בָּאָֽרֶץ:

11 וַֽיַּעֲנ֞וּ אֶת־מַלְאַ֣ךְ יְהוָ֗ה הָֽעֹמֵד֙ בֵּ֣ין הַהֲדַסִּ֔ים וַיֹּאמְר֖וּ הִתְהַלַּ֣כְנוּ בָאָ֑רֶץ וְהִנֵּ֥ה כָל־הָאָ֖רֶץ יֹשֶׁ֥בֶת וְשֹׁקָֽטֶת: 12 וַיַּ֣עַן מַלְאַךְ־יְהוָה֮ וַיֹּאמַר֒ יְהוָ֣ה צְבָא֔וֹת עַד־מָתַ֗י אַתָּה֙ לֹֽא־תְרַחֵ֣ם אֶת־יְרוּשָׁלִַ֔ם וְאֵ֖ת עָרֵ֣י יְהוּדָ֑ה אֲשֶׁ֣ר זָעַ֔מְתָּה זֶ֖ה שִׁבְעִ֥ים שָׁנָֽה:

13 וַיַּ֣עַן יְהוָ֗ה אֶת־הַמַּלְאָ֛ךְ הַדֹּבֵ֥ר בִּ֖י דְּבָרִ֣ים טוֹבִ֑ים דְּבָרִ֖ים נִחֻמִֽים: 14 וַיֹּ֣אמֶר אֵלַ֗י הַמַּלְאָךְ֙ הַדֹּבֵ֣ר בִּ֔י קְרָ֣א לֵאמֹ֔ר כֹּ֥ה אָמַ֖ר יְהוָ֣ה צְבָא֑וֹת קִנֵּ֧אתִי לִירוּשָׁלִַ֛ם וּלְצִיּ֖וֹן קִנְאָ֥ה גְדוֹלָֽה: 15 וְקֶ֤צֶף גָּדוֹל֙ אֲנִ֣י קֹצֵ֔ף עַל־הַגּוֹיִ֖ם הַשַּֽׁאֲנַנִּ֑ים אֲשֶׁ֤ר אֲנִי֙ קָצַ֣פְתִּי מְּעָ֔ט וְהֵ֖מָּה עָזְר֥וּ לְרָעָֽה: 16 לָכֵ֞ן כֹּֽה־אָמַ֣ר יְהוָ֗ה שַׁ֤בְתִּי לִירֽוּשָׁלִַ֙ם֙ בְּֽרַחֲמִ֔ים בֵּיתִי֙ יִבָּ֣נֶה בָּ֔הּ נְאֻ֖ם יְהוָ֣ה צְבָא֑וֹת וקוה וְקָ֥ו יִנָּטֶ֖ה עַל־יְרֽוּשָׁלָֽיִם: 17 ע֣וֹד | קְרָ֣א לֵאמֹ֗ר כֹּ֤ה אָמַר֙ יְהוָ֣ה צְבָא֔וֹת ע֛וֹד תְּפוּצֶ֥ינָה עָרַ֖י מִטּ֑וֹב וְנִחַ֨ם יְהוָ֥ה עוֹד֙ אֶת־צִיּ֔וֹן וּבָחַ֥ר ע֖וֹד בִּירֽוּשָׁלִָֽם: ס

ב וָאֶשָּׂ֥א אֶת־עֵינַ֖י וָאֵ֑רֶא וְהִנֵּ֖ה אַרְבַּ֥ע קְרָנֽוֹת: 2 וָאֹמַ֗ר אֶל־הַמַּלְאָ֛ךְ הַדֹּבֵ֥ר בִּ֖י מָה־אֵ֑לֶּה וַיֹּ֣אמֶר אֵלַ֔י אֵ֤לֶּה הַקְּרָנוֹת֙ אֲשֶׁ֣ר זֵר֣וּ אֶת־יְהוּדָ֔ה אֶת־יִשְׂרָאֵ֖ל וִירֽוּשָׁלִָֽם: ס 3 וַיַּרְאֵ֣נִי יְהוָ֔ה אַרְבָּעָ֖ה חָרָשִֽׁים: 4 וָאֹמַ֕ר

---

e   *Upheavals at the start of Darius' reign had encouraged hopes of an early restoration of the Davidic dynasty (cf. Hag. 2.21 ff.). Now these hopes were dashed.*

a   *The four horns correspond to the four winds of v. 10.*

horns that tossed Judah, so that no man could raise his head; and these men have come *b*-to throw them into a panic,-*b* to *c*-hew down-*c* the horns of the nations that raise a horn against the land of Judah, to toss it."

⁵I looked up, and I saw a man holding a measuring line. ⁶"Where are you going?" I asked. "To measure Jerusalem," he replied, "to see how long and wide it is to be." ⁷But the angel who talked with me came forward, and another angel came forward to meet him. ⁸The former said to him, "Run to that young man and tell him:

"Jerusalem shall be peopled as a city without walls, so many shall be the men and cattle it contains. ⁹And I Myself—declares the LORD—will be a wall of fire all around it, and I will be a glory inside it.

¹⁰"Away, away! Flee from the land of the north—says the LORD—though I swept you [there] like the four winds of heaven—declares the LORD."

¹¹Away, escape, O Zion, you who dwell in Fair Babylon! ¹²For thus said the LORD of Hosts— He *d*-who sent me after glory-*d*—concerning the nations that have taken you as spoil: "Whoever touches you touches the pupil of *e*-his own-*e* eye. ¹³For I will lift My hand against them, and they shall be spoil for those they enslaved."— Then you shall know that I was sent by the LORD of Hosts.

¹⁴Shout for joy, Fair Zion! For lo, I come; and I will dwell in your midst—declares the LORD. ¹⁵In that day many nations will attach themselves to the LORD and become His*f* people, and He*g* will dwell in your midst. Then you will know that I was sent to you by the LORD of Hosts.

מָה אֵלֶּה בָאִים לַעֲשׂוֹת וַיֹּאמֶר לֵאמֹר
אֵלֶּה הַקְּרָנוֹת אֲשֶׁר־זֵרוּ אֶת־יְהוּדָה כְּפִי־
אִישׁ לֹא־נָשָׂא רֹאשׁוֹ וַיָּבֹאוּ אֵלֶּה לְהַחֲרִיד
אֹתָם לְיַדּוֹת אֶת־קַרְנוֹת הַגּוֹיִם הַנֹּשְׂאִים
קֶרֶן אֶל־אֶרֶץ יְהוּדָה לְזָרוֹתָהּ׃ ס
5 וָאֶשָּׂא עֵינַי וָאֵרֶא וְהִנֵּה־אִישׁ וּבְיָדוֹ חֶבֶל
מִדָּה׃ 6 וָאֹמַר אָנָה אַתָּה הֹלֵךְ וַיֹּאמֶר אֵלַי
לָמֹד אֶת־יְרוּשָׁלִַם לִרְאוֹת כַּמָּה־רָחְבָּהּ
וְכַמָּה אָרְכָּהּ׃ 7 וְהִנֵּה הַמַּלְאָךְ הַדֹּבֵר
בִּי יֹצֵא וּמַלְאָךְ אַחֵר יֹצֵא לִקְרָאתוֹ׃
8 וַיֹּאמֶר אֵלוֹ אֵלָיו רֻץ דַּבֵּר אֶל־הַנַּעַר הַלָּז
לֵאמֹר
פְּרָזוֹת תֵּשֵׁב יְרוּשָׁלִַם מֵרֹב אָדָם וּבְהֵמָה
בְּתוֹכָהּ׃ 9 וַאֲנִי אֶהְיֶה־לָּהּ נְאֻם־יְהוָה
חוֹמַת אֵשׁ סָבִיב וּלְכָבוֹד אֶהְיֶה
בְתוֹכָהּ׃ פ
10 הוֹי הוֹי וְנֻסוּ מֵאֶרֶץ צָפוֹן נְאֻם־יְהוָה
כִּי כְּאַרְבַּע רוּחוֹת הַשָּׁמַיִם פֵּרַשְׂתִּי אֶתְכֶם
נְאֻם־יְהוָה׃
11 הוֹי צִיּוֹן הִמָּלְטִי יוֹשֶׁבֶת בַּת־בָּבֶל׃ ס
12 כִּי כֹה אָמַר יְהוָה צְבָאוֹת אַחַר כָּבוֹד
שְׁלָחַנִי אֶל־הַגּוֹיִם הַשֹּׁלְלִים אֶתְכֶם כִּי
הַנֹּגֵעַ בָּכֶם נֹגֵעַ בְּבָבַת עֵינוֹ׃ 13 כִּי הִנְנִי
מֵנִיף אֶת־יָדִי עֲלֵיהֶם וְהָיוּ שָׁלָל
לְעַבְדֵיהֶם וִידַעְתֶּם כִּי־יְהוָה צְבָאוֹת
שְׁלָחָנִי׃ ס

14 רָנִּי וְשִׂמְחִי בַּת־צִיּוֹן כִּי הִנְנִי־בָא
וְשָׁכַנְתִּי בְתוֹכֵךְ נְאֻם־יְהוָה׃ 15 וְנִלְווּ גוֹיִם
רַבִּים אֶל־יְהוָה בַּיּוֹם הַהוּא וְהָיוּ לִי לְעָם
וְשָׁכַנְתִּי בְתוֹכֵךְ וְיָדַעַתְּ כִּי־יְהוָה צְבָאוֹת
שְׁלָחַנִי אֵלָיִךְ׃

---

b-b Meaning of Heb. uncertain; emendation yields "to sharpen ax heads."
c-c Meaning of Heb. uncertain.
d-d Emendation yields "whose Presence sent me."
e-e According to ancient Jewish tradition, a scribal change for "My."
f Heb. "My."
g Heb. "I."

16The Lord will h-take Judah to Himself as His portion-h in the Holy Land, and He will choose Jerusalem once more.

17Be silent, all flesh, before the Lord! For He is roused from His holy habitation.

3 He further showed me Joshua, the high priest, standing before the angel of the Lord, and the Accusera standing at his right to accuse him. 2But [the angel of] the Lord said to the Accuser, "The Lord rebuke you, O Accuser; may the Lord who has chosen Jerusalem rebuke you! For this is a brand plucked from the fire."b 3Now Joshua was clothed in filthy garments when he stood before the angel. 4The latter spoke up and said to his attendants, "Take the filthy garments off him!" And he said to him, "See, I have removed your guilt from you, and you shall be clothed in [priestly] robes." 5Then hec gave the order, "Let a pured diadem be placed on his head." And they placed the pure diadem on his head and clothed him in [priestly] garments,e as the angel of the Lord stood by.

6And the angel of the Lord charged Joshua as follows: 7"Thus said the Lord of Hosts: If you walk in My paths and keep My charge, you in turn will rule My House and guard My courts, and I will permit you to move about among these attendants. 8Hearken well, O High Priest Joshua, you and your fellow priests sitting before you! For those men are a sign that I am going to bring My servant the Branch.f 9For mark well this stone which I place before Joshua, a

16 וְנָחַל יְהוָה אֶת־יְהוּדָה חֶלְקוֹ עַל אַדְמַת הַקֹּדֶשׁ וּבָחַר עוֹד בִּירוּשָׁלָ͏ִם׃

17 הַס כָּל־בָּשָׂר מִפְּנֵי יְהוָה כִּי נֵעוֹר מִמְּעוֹן קָדְשׁוֹ׃ ס

ג וַיַּרְאֵנִי אֶת־יְהוֹשֻׁעַ הַכֹּהֵן הַגָּדוֹל עֹמֵד לִפְנֵי מַלְאַךְ יְהוָה וְהַשָּׂטָן עֹמֵד עַל־יְמִינוֹ לְשִׂטְנוֹ׃ 2 וַיֹּאמֶר יְהוָה אֶל־הַשָּׂטָן יִגְעַר יְהוָה בְּךָ הַשָּׂטָן וְיִגְעַר יְהוָה בְּךָ הַבֹּחֵר בִּירוּשָׁלָ͏ִם הֲלוֹא זֶה אוּד מֻצָּל מֵאֵשׁ׃ 3 וִיהוֹשֻׁעַ הָיָה לָבֻשׁ בְּגָדִים צוֹאִים וְעֹמֵד לִפְנֵי הַמַּלְאָךְ׃ 4 וַיַּעַן וַיֹּאמֶר אֶל־הָעֹמְדִים לְפָנָיו לֵאמֹר הָסִירוּ הַבְּגָדִים הַצֹּאִים מֵעָלָיו וַיֹּאמֶר אֵלָיו רְאֵה הֶעֱבַרְתִּי מֵעָלֶיךָ עֲוֺנֶךָ וְהַלְבֵּשׁ אֹתְךָ מַחֲלָצוֹת׃ 5 וָאֹמַר יָשִׂימוּ צָנִיף טָהוֹר עַל־רֹאשׁוֹ וַיָּשִׂימוּ הַצָּנִיף הַטָּהוֹר עַל־רֹאשׁוֹ וַיַּלְבִּשֻׁהוּ בְּגָדִים וּמַלְאַךְ יְהוָה עֹמֵד׃ 6 וַיָּעַד מַלְאַךְ יְהוָה בִּיהוֹשֻׁעַ לֵאמֹר׃ 7 כֹּה־אָמַר יְהוָה צְבָאוֹת אִם־בִּדְרָכַי תֵּלֵךְ וְאִם אֶת־מִשְׁמַרְתִּי תִשְׁמֹר וְגַם־אַתָּה תָּדִין אֶת־בֵּיתִי וְגַם תִּשְׁמֹר אֶת־חֲצֵרָי וְנָתַתִּי לְךָ מַהְלְכִים בֵּין הָעֹמְדִים הָאֵלֶּה׃ 8 שְׁמַע־נָא יְהוֹשֻׁעַ ׀ הַכֹּהֵן הַגָּדוֹל אַתָּה וְרֵעֶיךָ הַיֹּשְׁבִים לְפָנֶיךָ כִּי־אַנְשֵׁי מוֹפֵת הֵמָּה כִּי־הִנְנִי מֵבִיא אֶת־עַבְדִּי צֶמַח׃ 9 כִּי ׀ הִנֵּה הָאֶבֶן אֲשֶׁר נָתַתִּי לִפְנֵי יְהוֹשֻׁעַ

---

h-h   *Emendation yields "allot to Judah its portion"; cf. Num. 34.17.*

a   *Others "Satan."*
b   *Joshua's father (Hag. 1.1; 1 Chron. 5.40–41) was exiled and his grandfather executed (2 Kings 25.18–21) by the Babylonians, but Joshua returned.*
c   *Heb. "I."*
d   *I.e., ritually pure.*
e   *Joshua has now been rendered fit to associate with the heavenly beings (v. 7); cf. Isa. 6.6–8.*
f   *I.e., the future king of David's line. See 6.12; Jer. 23.5–6; 33.15–16; cf. Isa. 11.1.*

single stone with seven eyes.*g* I will execute its engraving—declares the LORD of Hosts—and I will remove that country's guilt in a single day. ¹⁰In that day—declares the LORD of Hosts—you will be inviting each other to the shade of vines and fig trees."

4 The angel who talked with me came back and woke me as a man is wakened from sleep. ²He said to me, "What do you see?" And I answered, "I see a lampstand all of gold, with a bowl above it. The lamps on it are seven in number, and the *a*-lamps above it have-*a* seven pipes; ³and by it are two olive trees, one on the right of the bowl and one on its left." ⁴I, in turn, asked the angel who talked with me, "What do those things mean, my lord?" ⁵"Do you not know what those things mean?" asked the angel who talked with me; and I said, "No, my lord." ⁶Then he explained to me as follows:*b*

"This is the word of the LORD to Zerubbabel:*c* Not by might, nor by power, but by My spirit*d*—said the LORD of Hosts. ⁷Whoever you are, O great mountain in the path of Zerubbabel, turn into level ground! For he shall produce that excellent stone; it shall be greeted with shouts of 'Beautiful! Beautiful!'"

⁸And the word of the LORD came to me: ⁹"Zerubbabel's hands have founded this House and Zerubbabel's hands shall complete it. Then you shall know that it was the LORD of Hosts who sent me to you. ¹⁰Does anyone scorn a day of small beginnings? When they see *e*-the stone of distinction-*e* in the hand of Zerubbabel, they shall rejoice.

עַל־אֶבֶן אַחַת שִׁבְעָה עֵינָיִם הִנְנִי מְפַתֵּחַ פִּתֻּחָהּ נְאֻם יְהוָה צְבָאוֹת וּמַשְׁתִּי אֶת־עֲוֹן הָאָרֶץ־הַהִיא בְּיוֹם אֶחָד׃ 10 בַּיּוֹם הַהוּא נְאֻם יְהוָה צְבָאוֹת תִּקְרְאוּ אִישׁ לְרֵעֵהוּ אֶל־תַּחַת גֶּפֶן וְאֶל־תַּחַת תְּאֵנָה׃

ד וַיָּשָׁב הַמַּלְאָךְ הַדֹּבֵר בִּי וַיְעִירֵנִי כְּאִישׁ אֲשֶׁר־יֵעוֹר מִשְּׁנָתוֹ׃ 2 וַיֹּאמֶר אֵלַי מָה אַתָּה רֹאֶה ויאמר וָאֹמַר רָאִיתִי ׀ וְהִנֵּה מְנוֹרַת זָהָב כֻּלָּהּ וְגֻלָּהּ עַל־רֹאשָׁהּ וְשִׁבְעָה נֵרֹתֶיהָ עָלֶיהָ שִׁבְעָה וְשִׁבְעָה מוּצָקוֹת לַנֵּרוֹת אֲשֶׁר עַל־רֹאשָׁהּ׃ 3 וּשְׁנַיִם זֵיתִים עָלֶיהָ אֶחָד מִימִין הַגֻּלָּה וְאֶחָד עַל־שְׂמֹאלָהּ׃ 4 וָאַעַן וָאֹמַר אֶל־הַמַּלְאָךְ הַדֹּבֵר בִּי לֵאמֹר מָה־אֵלֶּה אֲדֹנִי׃ 5 וַיַּעַן הַמַּלְאָךְ הַדֹּבֵר בִּי וַיֹּאמֶר אֵלַי הֲלוֹא יָדַעְתָּ מָה־הֵמָּה אֵלֶּה וָאֹמַר לֹא אֲדֹנִי׃ 6 וַיַּעַן וַיֹּאמֶר אֵלַי לֵאמֹר

זֶה דְּבַר־יְהוָה אֶל־זְרֻבָּבֶל לֵאמֹר לֹא בְחַיִל וְלֹא בְכֹחַ כִּי אִם־בְּרוּחִי אָמַר יְהוָה צְבָאוֹת׃ 7 מִי־אַתָּה הַר־הַגָּדוֹל לִפְנֵי זְרֻבָּבֶל לְמִישֹׁר וְהוֹצִיא אֶת־הָאֶבֶן הָרֹאשָׁה תְּשֻׁאוֹת חֵן חֵן לָהּ׃ פ 8 וַיְהִי דְבַר־יְהוָה אֵלַי לֵאמֹר׃ 9 יְדֵי זְרֻבָּבֶל יִסְּדוּ הַבַּיִת הַזֶּה וְיָדָיו תְּבַצַּעְנָה וְיָדַעְתָּ כִּי־יְהוָה צְבָאוֹת שְׁלָחַנִי אֲלֵיכֶם׃ 10 כִּי מִי בַז לְיוֹם קְטַנּוֹת וְשָׂמְחוּ וְרָאוּ אֶת־הָאֶבֶן הַבְּדִיל בְּיַד זְרֻבָּבֶל

---

g Meaning of Heb. uncertain. The stone apparently symbolizes the God-given power of the future Davidic ruler; see below 4.6–7.

a-a Emendation yields "bowl above it has."
b The explanation is given in the last sentence of v. 10.
c A grandson of King Jehoiachin (1 Chron. 3.17–19) and the secular head of the repatriated community (Hag. 1.1; etc.).
d I.e., Zerubbabel will succeed by means of spiritual gifts conferred upon him by the LORD; cf. Isa. 11.2. ff.
e-e Meaning of Heb. uncertain; others "plummet."

"Those seven are the eyes of the Lord, ranging over the whole earth."

¹¹"And what," I asked him, "are those two olive trees, one on the right and one on the left of the lampstand?" ¹²And I further asked him, "What are the two tops*f* of the olive trees that feed their gold*g* through those two golden tubes?"*h* ¹³He asked me, "Don't you know what they are?" And I replied, "No, my lord." ¹⁴Then he explained, "They are the two *i*-anointed dignitaries-*i* who attend the Lord of all the earth."

5 I looked up again, and I saw a flying scroll. ²"What do you see?" he asked. And I replied, "A flying scroll, twenty cubits long and ten cubits wide." ³"That," he explained to me, "is the curse which goes out over the whole land. *a*-For everyone who has stolen, as is forbidden on one side [of the scroll], has gone unpunished; and everyone who has sworn [falsely], as is forbidden on the other side of it, has gone unpunished.-*a* ⁴[But] I have sent it forth—declares the Lord of Hosts—and [the curse] shall enter the house of the thief and the house of the one who swears falsely by My name, and it shall lodge inside their houses and shall consume them to the last timber and stone."

⁵Then the angel who talked with me came forward and said, "Now look up and note this other object that is approaching." ⁶I asked, "What is it?" And he said, "This tub*b* that is approaching—this," said he, "is their eye*c* in all the land." ⁷And behold, a disk of lead was lifted, revealing a woman seated inside the tub. ⁸"That," he said,

---

שִׁבְעָה־אֵלֶּה עֵינֵי יְהוָה הֵמָּה מְשׁוֹטְטִים בְּכָל־הָאָרֶץ: ¹¹ וָאַעַן וָאֹמַר אֵלָיו מַה־שְּׁנֵי הַזֵּיתִים הָאֵלֶּה עַל־יְמִין הַמְּנוֹרָה וְעַל־שְׂמֹאולָה*: ¹² וָאַעַן שֵׁנִית וָאֹמַר אֵלָיו מַה־שְׁתֵּי שִׁבֲּלֵי הַזֵּיתִים אֲשֶׁר בְּיַד שְׁנֵי צַנְתְּרוֹת הַזָּהָב הַמְרִיקִים מֵעֲלֵיהֶם הַזָּהָב: ¹³ וַיֹּאמֶר אֵלַי לֵאמֹר הֲלוֹא יָדַעְתָּ מָה־אֵלֶּה וָאֹמַר לֹא אֲדֹנִי: ¹⁴ וַיֹּאמֶר אֵלֶּה שְׁנֵי בְנֵי־הַיִּצְהָר הָעֹמְדִים עַל־אֲדוֹן כָּל־הָאָרֶץ:

ה וָאָשׁוּב וָאֶשָּׂא עֵינַי וָאֶרְאֶה וְהִנֵּה מְגִלָּה עָפָה: ² וַיֹּאמֶר אֵלַי מָה אַתָּה רֹאֶה וָאֹמַר אֲנִי רֹאֶה מְגִלָּה עָפָה אָרְכָּהּ עֶשְׂרִים בָּאַמָּה וְרָחְבָּהּ עֶשֶׂר בָּאַמָּה: ³ וַיֹּאמֶר אֵלַי זֹאת הָאָלָה הַיּוֹצֵאת עַל־פְּנֵי כָל־הָאָרֶץ כִּי כָל־הַגֹּנֵב מִזֶּה כָּמוֹהָ נִקָּה וְכָל־הַנִּשְׁבָּע מִזֶּה כָּמוֹהָ נִקָּה: ⁴ הוֹצֵאתִיהָ נְאֻם יְהוָה צְבָאוֹת וּבָאָה אֶל־בֵּית הַגַּנָּב וְאֶל־בֵּית הַנִּשְׁבָּע בִּשְׁמִי לַשָּׁקֶר וְלָנֶה בְּתוֹךְ בֵּיתוֹ וְכִלַּתּוּ וְאֶת־עֵצָיו וְאֶת־אֲבָנָיו: ⁵ וַיֵּצֵא הַמַּלְאָךְ הַדֹּבֵר בִּי וַיֹּאמֶר אֵלַי שָׂא נָא עֵינֶיךָ וּרְאֵה מָה הַיּוֹצֵאת הַזֹּאת: ⁶ וָאֹמַר מַה־הִיא וַיֹּאמֶר זֹאת הָאֵיפָה הַיּוֹצֵאת וַיֹּאמֶר זֹאת עֵינָם בְּכָל־הָאָרֶץ: ⁷ וְהִנֵּה כִּכַּר עֹפֶרֶת נִשֵּׂאת וְזֹאת אִשָּׁה אַחַת יוֹשֶׁבֶת בְּתוֹךְ הָאֵיפָה: ⁸ וַיֹּאמֶר זֹאת

v. 11. מלא ו׳

---

f Meaning of Heb. uncertain; literally "ears" (as of grain).
g Emendation yields "oil"; cf. v. 14.
h Or "funnels"; through them the oil runs from the olive trees into the bowl of vv. 2 and 3.
i-i I.e., the high priest and the king (cf. 3.8–9 with note); lit. "sons of oil."

a-a Meaning of Heb. uncertain.
b Heb. ephah, a measure of capacity.
c Septuagint and Syriac read "guilt."

"is Wickedness"; and, thrusting her down into the tub, he pressed the leaden weight into its mouth.

⁹I looked up again and saw two women come soaring with the wind in their wings—they had wings like those of a stork—and carry off the tub between earth and sky. ¹⁰"Where are they taking the tub?" I asked the angel who talked with me. ¹¹And he answered, "To build a shrine for it in the land of Shinar;ᵈ [a stand] shall be erected for it, and it shall be set down there upon the stand."

6 I looked up again, and I saw: Four chariots were coming out from between the two mountains; the mountains were of copper. ²The horses of the first chariot were bay, the horses of the second chariot were black; ³the horses of the third chariot were white, and the horses of the fourth chariot were spotted—dappled. ⁴And I spoke up and asked the angel who talked with me: "What are those, my lord?" ⁵In reply, the angel said to me, "Those are the four winds of heaven coming out after presenting themselves to the Lord of all the earth. ⁶The one with the black horses is going out to the region of the north; the white ones ᵃ-have gone out-ᵃ to ᵇ-what is to the west of them;-ᵇ the spotted ones ᵃ-have gone out-ᵃ to the region of the south; ⁷and ᶜ-the dappled ones have gone out…"-ᶜ They were ready to start out and range the earth, and he gave them the order, "Start out and range the earth!" And they ranged the earth. ⁸Then he alerted me, and said to me, "Take good note! Those that went out to the region of the north

ד ‏הָרִשְׁעָה וַיַּשְׁלֵךְ אֹתָהּ אֶל־תּוֹךְ הָאֵיפָה וַיַּשְׁלֵךְ אֶת־אֶבֶן הָעֹפֶרֶת אֶל־פִּיהָ: ס ‎⁹ וָאֶשָּׂא עֵינַי וָאֵרֶא וְהִנֵּה שְׁתַּיִם נָשִׁים יוֹצְאוֹת וְרוּחַ בְּכַנְפֵיהֶם וְלָהֵנָּה כְנָפַיִם כְּכַנְפֵי הַחֲסִידָה וַתִּשֶּׂאנָה אֶת־הָאֵיפָה בֵּין הָאָרֶץ וּבֵין הַשָּׁמָיִם: ‎¹⁰ וָאֹמַר אֶל־הַמַּלְאָךְ הַדֹּבֵר בִּי אָנָה הֵמָּה מוֹלִכוֹת אֶת־הָאֵיפָה: ‎¹¹ וַיֹּאמֶר אֵלַי לִבְנוֹת־לָהּ* בַיִת בְּאֶרֶץ שִׁנְעָר וְהוּכַן וְהֻנִּיחָה שָּׁם עַל־מְכֻנָתָהּ: ס

ו וָאָשֻׁב וָאֶשָּׂא עֵינַי וָאֶרְאֶה וְהִנֵּה אַרְבַּע מַרְכָּבוֹת יֹצְאוֹת מִבֵּין שְׁנֵי הֶהָרִים וְהֶהָרִים הָרֵי נְחֹשֶׁת: ‎² בַּמֶּרְכָּבָה הָרִאשֹׁנָה סוּסִים אֲדֻמִּים וּבַמֶּרְכָּבָה הַשֵּׁנִית סוּסִים שְׁחֹרִים: ‎³ וּבַמֶּרְכָּבָה הַשְּׁלִשִׁית סוּסִים לְבָנִים וּבַמֶּרְכָּבָה הָרְבִעִית סוּסִים בְּרֻדִּים אֲמֻצִּים: ‎⁴ וָאַעַן וָאֹמַר אֶל־הַמַּלְאָךְ הַדֹּבֵר בִּי מָה־אֵלֶּה אֲדֹנִי: ‎⁵ וַיַּעַן הַמַּלְאָךְ וַיֹּאמֶר אֵלַי אֵלֶּה אַרְבַּע רֻחוֹת הַשָּׁמַיִם יוֹצְאוֹת מֵהִתְיַצֵּב עַל־אֲדוֹן כָּל־הָאָרֶץ: ‎⁶ אֲשֶׁר־בָּהּ הַסּוּסִים הַשְּׁחֹרִים יֹצְאִים אֶל־אֶרֶץ צָפוֹן וְהַלְּבָנִים יָצְאוּ אֶל־אַחֲרֵיהֶם וְהַבְּרֻדִּים יָצְאוּ אֶל־אֶרֶץ הַתֵּימָן: ‎⁷ וְהָאֲמֻצִּים יָצְאוּ וַיְבַקְשׁוּ לָלֶכֶת לְהִתְהַלֵּךְ בָּאָרֶץ וַיֹּאמֶר* לְכוּ הִתְהַלְּכוּ בָאָרֶץ וַתִּתְהַלַּכְנָה בָּאָרֶץ: ‎⁸ וַיַּזְעֵק אֹתִי וַיְדַבֵּר אֵלַי לֵאמֹר רְאֵה

ד I.e., Babylonia; cf. Gen. 10.10; 11.2, 9.

a-a Change of vocalization yields "will go out."
b-b Cf. ʾaḥor, "west," Isa. 9.11. Emendation yields "the region of the west."
c-c Emendation yields "the bay ones will go out to the region of the east."

have *d-done my pleasure-d* in the region of the north."*e*

⁹The word of the LORD came to me: ¹⁰Receive from*f* the exiled community—from Heldai, Tobijah, and Jedaiah, who have come from Babylon—and you, in turn, proceed the same day to the house of Josiah son of Zephaniah. ¹¹Take silver and gold and make crowns. Place [one] on the head of High Priest Joshua son of Jehozadak, ¹²and say to him, "Thus said the LORD of Hosts: Behold, a man called the Branch*g* shall branch out from the place where he is, and he shall build the Temple of the LORD. ¹³He shall build the Temple of the LORD and shall assume majesty, and he shall sit on his throne and rule. And there shall also be a priest *h*-seated on his throne,-*h* and harmonious understanding shall prevail between them."

¹⁴The crowns shall remain in the Temple of the LORD as a memorial to Helem,*i* Tobijah, Jedaiah, and Hen*j* son of Zephaniah. ¹⁵Men from far away shall come and take part in the building of the Temple of the LORD, and you shall know that I have been sent to you by the LORD of Hosts—if only you will obey the LORD your God!

7 In the fourth year of King Darius, on the fourth day of the ninth month, Kislev, the word of the LORD came to Zechariah—²when Bethel-sharezer *a*-and Regem-melech and his men sent-*a* to entreat the favor of the LORD, ³[and] to address this inquiry to the priests of the House of the LORD and to the prophets: "Shall

הַיּוֹצְאִים אֶל־אֶרֶץ צָפוֹן הֵנִיחוּ אֶת־רוּחִי בְּאֶרֶץ צָפוֹן: ס

⁹ וַיְהִי דְבַר־יְהוָה אֵלַי לֵאמֹר: ¹⁰ לָקוֹחַ מֵאֵת הַגּוֹלָה מֵחֶלְדַּי וּמֵאֵת טוֹבִיָּה וּמֵאֵת יְדַעְיָה וּבָאתָ אַתָּה בַּיּוֹם הַהוּא וּבָאתָ בֵּית יֹאשִׁיָּה בֶן־צְפַנְיָה אֲשֶׁר־בָּאוּ מִבָּבֶל: ¹¹ וְלָקַחְתָּ כֶסֶף־וְזָהָב וְעָשִׂיתָ עֲטָרוֹת וְשַׂמְתָּ בְּרֹאשׁ יְהוֹשֻׁעַ בֶּן־יְהוֹצָדָק הַכֹּהֵן הַגָּדוֹל: ¹² וְאָמַרְתָּ אֵלָיו לֵאמֹר כֹּה אָמַר יְהוָה צְבָאוֹת לֵאמֹר הִנֵּה־אִישׁ צֶמַח שְׁמוֹ וּמִתַּחְתָּיו יִצְמָח וּבָנָה אֶת־הֵיכַל יְהוָה: ¹³ וְהוּא יִבְנֶה אֶת־הֵיכַל יְהוָה וְהוּא־יִשָּׂא הוֹד וְיָשַׁב וּמָשַׁל עַל־כִּסְאוֹ וְהָיָה כֹהֵן עַל־כִּסְאוֹ וַעֲצַת שָׁלוֹם תִּהְיֶה בֵּין שְׁנֵיהֶם: ¹⁴ וְהָעֲטָרֹת תִּהְיֶה לְחֵלֶם וּלְטוֹבִיָּה וְלִידַעְיָה וּלְחֵן בֶּן־צְפַנְיָה לְזִכָּרוֹן בְּהֵיכַל יְהוָה: ¹⁵ וּרְחוֹקִים | יָבֹאוּ וּבָנוּ בְּהֵיכַל יְהוָה וִידַעְתֶּם כִּי־יְהוָה צְבָאוֹת שְׁלָחַנִי אֲלֵיכֶם וְהָיָה אִם־שָׁמוֹעַ תִּשְׁמְעוּן בְּקוֹל יְהוָה אֱלֹהֵיכֶם: ס

ז ¹ וַיְהִי בִּשְׁנַת אַרְבַּע לְדָרְיָוֶשׁ הַמֶּלֶךְ הָיָה דְבַר־יְהוָה אֶל־זְכַרְיָה בְּאַרְבָּעָה לַחֹדֶשׁ הַתְּשִׁעִי בְּכִסְלֵו: ² וַיִּשְׁלַח בֵּית־אֵל שַׂר־אֶצֶר* וְרֶגֶם מֶלֶךְ וַאֲנָשָׁיו לְחַלּוֹת אֶת־פְּנֵי יְהוָה: ³ לֵאמֹר אֶל־הַכֹּהֲנִים אֲשֶׁר לְבֵית־יְהוָה צְבָאוֹת וְאֶל־הַנְּבִיאִים לֵאמֹר

---

d-d   Cf. postbiblical naḥath ruaḥ, "gratification." Emendation yields, "done the LORD's pleasure."

e   I.e., Babylonia, whose communication with Judah was via North Mesopotamia and Syria; cf. 2.10–11.

f   Emendation yields "the gift of."

g   See note at 3.8.

h-h   Septuagint reads "on his right side."

i   The Syriac version reads "Heldai"; cf. v. 10.

j   In v. 10, "Josiah."

a-a   Emendation yields "sent Regem-melech and his men."

v. 2. כן למדינחאי, ובנוסח אחר "שראצר", כלומר בסימן ימנית

I weep and practice abstinence in the fifth month,[b] as I have been doing all these years?"

⁴Thereupon the word of the Lord of Hosts came to me: ⁵Say to all the people of the land and to the priests: When you fasted and lamented in the fifth and seventh months all these seventy years, did you fast for my benefit? ⁶And when you eat and drink, who but you does the eating, and who but you does the drinking? ⁷Look, this is the message that the Lord proclaimed through the earlier prophets, when Jerusalem and the towns about her were peopled and tranquil, when the Negeb and the Shephelah were peopled.

⁸And the word of the Lord to Zechariah continued: ⁹Thus said the Lord of Hosts: Execute true justice; deal loyally and compassionately with one another. ¹⁰Do not defraud the widow, the orphan, the stranger, and the poor; and do not plot evil against one another.—¹¹But they refused to pay heed. They presented a balky back and turned a deaf ear. ¹²They hardened their hearts like adamant against heeding the instruction and admonition that the Lord of Hosts sent to them by His spirit through the earlier prophets; and a terrible wrath issued from the Lord of Hosts. ¹³Even as He called and they would not listen, "So," said the Lord of Hosts, "let them call and I will not listen." ¹⁴I dispersed them among all those nations which they had not known, and the land was left behind them desolate, without any who came and went. They caused a delightful land to be turned into a desolation.

8

The word of the Lord of Hosts came [to me]:

²Thus said the Lord of Hosts: I am very jealous for Zion, I am fiercely jealous for her. ³Thus

b   Because of the destruction of the Temple and Jerusalem; cf. 2 Kings 25.8 ff.

1391

הָאֶבְכֶּה֙ בַּחֹ֣דֶשׁ הַֽחֲמִשִׁ֔י הִנָּזֵ֖ר כַּאֲשֶׁ֣ר עָשִׂ֔יתִי זֶ֖ה כַּמֶּ֥ה שָׁנִֽים׃ פ ⁴וַיְהִ֛י דְּבַר־יְהוָ֥ה צְבָא֖וֹת אֵלַ֥י לֵאמֹֽר׃ ⁵אֱמֹר֙ אֶל־כָּל־עַ֣ם הָאָ֔רֶץ וְאֶל־הַכֹּהֲנִ֖ים לֵאמֹ֑ר כִּֽי־צַמְתֶּ֨ם וְסָפ֜וֹד בַּחֲמִישִׁ֣י וּבַשְּׁבִיעִ֗י וְזֶה֙ שִׁבְעִ֣ים שָׁנָ֔ה הֲצ֥וֹם צַמְתֻּ֖נִי אָֽנִי׃ ⁶וְכִ֥י תֹאכְל֖וּ וְכִ֣י תִשְׁתּ֑וּ הֲל֤וֹא אַתֶּם֙ הָאֹ֣כְלִ֔ים וְאַתֶּ֖ם הַשֹּׁתִֽים׃ ⁷הֲל֣וֹא אֶת־הַדְּבָרִ֗ים אֲשֶׁ֨ר קָרָ֤א יְהוָה֙ בְּיַד֙ הַנְּבִיאִ֣ים הָרִֽאשֹׁנִ֔ים בִּֽהְי֤וֹת יְרוּשָׁלִַ֙ם֙ יֹשֶׁ֣בֶת וּשְׁלֵוָ֔ה וְעָרֶ֖יהָ סְבִיבֹתֶ֑יהָ וְהַנֶּ֥גֶב וְהַשְּׁפֵלָ֖ה יֹשֵֽׁב׃ פ

⁸וַיְהִי֙ דְּבַר־יְהוָ֔ה אֶל־זְכַרְיָ֖ה לֵאמֹֽר׃ ⁹כֹּ֥ה אָמַ֛ר יְהוָ֥ה צְבָא֖וֹת לֵאמֹ֑ר מִשְׁפַּ֤ט אֱמֶת֙ שְׁפֹ֔טוּ וְחֶ֣סֶד וְרַֽחֲמִ֔ים עֲשׂ֖וּ אִ֥ישׁ אֶת־אָחִֽיו׃ ¹⁰וְאַלְמָנָ֧ה וְיָת֛וֹם גֵּ֥ר וְעָנִ֖י אַֽל־תַּֽעֲשֹׁ֑קוּ וְרָעַת֙ אִ֣ישׁ אָחִ֔יו אַֽל־תַּחְשְׁב֖וּ בִּלְבַבְכֶֽם׃ ¹¹וַיְמָאֲנ֣וּ לְהַקְשִׁ֔יב וַיִּתְּנ֥וּ כָתֵ֖ף סֹרָ֑רֶת וְאָזְנֵיהֶ֖ם הִכְבִּ֥ידוּ מִשְּׁמֽוֹעַ׃ ¹²וְלִבָּ֞ם שָׂ֣מוּ שָׁמִ֗יר מִ֠שְּׁמ֠וֹעַ אֶת־הַתּוֹרָ֤ה וְאֶת־הַדְּבָרִים֙ אֲשֶׁ֨ר שָׁלַ֜ח יְהוָ֤ה צְבָאוֹת֙ בְּרוּח֔וֹ בְּיַ֖ד הַנְּבִיאִ֣ים הָרִֽאשֹׁנִ֑ים וַֽיְהִי֙ קֶ֣צֶף גָּד֔וֹל מֵאֵ֖ת יְהוָ֥ה צְבָאֽוֹת׃ ¹³וַיְהִ֥י כַֽאֲשֶׁר־קָרָ֛א וְלֹ֥א שָׁמֵ֖עוּ כֵּ֣ן יִקְרְא֛וּ וְלֹ֥א אֶשְׁמָ֖ע אָמַ֖ר יְהוָ֥ה צְבָאֽוֹת׃ ¹⁴וְאֵ֣סָעֲרֵ֗ם עַ֤ל כָּל־הַגּוֹיִם֙ אֲשֶׁ֣ר לֹֽא־יְדָע֔וּם וְהָאָ֙רֶץ֙ נָשַׁ֣מָּה אַֽחֲרֵיהֶ֔ם מֵעֹבֵ֖ר וּמִשָּׁ֑ב וַיָּשִׂ֥ימוּ אֶֽרֶץ־חֶמְדָּ֖ה לְשַׁמָּֽה׃ פ

ח ¹וַיְהִ֛י דְּבַר־יְהוָ֥ה צְבָא֖וֹת לֵאמֹֽר׃ ²כֹּ֤ה אָמַר֙ יְהוָ֣ה צְבָא֔וֹת קִנֵּ֥אתִי לְצִיּ֖וֹן קִנְאָ֣ה גְדוֹלָ֑ה וְחֵמָ֥ה גְדוֹלָ֖ה קִנֵּ֥אתִי לָֽהּ׃

said the LORD: I have returned to Zion, and I will dwell in Jerusalem. Jerusalem will be called the City of Faithfulness, and the mount of the LORD of Hosts the Holy Mount.

⁴Thus said the LORD of Hosts: There shall yet be old men and women in the squares of Jerusalem, each with staff in hand because of their great age. ⁵And the squares of the city shall be crowded with boys and girls playing in the squares. ⁶Thus said the LORD of Hosts: Though it will seem impossible to the remnant of this people in those days, shall it also be impossible to Me?—declares the LORD of Hosts. ⁷Thus said the LORD of Hosts: I will rescue My people from the lands of the east and from the lands of the west, ⁸and I will bring them home to dwell in Jerusalem. They shall be My people, and I will be their God—in truth and sincerity.

⁹Thus said the LORD of Hosts: Take courage, you who now hear these words which the prophets spoke when the foundations were laid for the rebuilding of the Temple, the House of the LORD of Hosts.

¹⁰ᵃFor before that time, the earnings of men were nil, and profits from beasts were nothing. It was not safe to go about one's business on account of enemies; and I set all men against one another. ¹¹But now I will not treat the remnant of this people as before—declares the LORD of Hosts—¹²but what it sows shall prosper: The vine shall produce its fruit, the ground shall produce its yield, and the skies shall provide their moisture. I will bestow all these things upon the remnant of this people. ¹³And just as you were a curseᵇ among the nations, O House of Judah and House of Israel, so, when I vindicate you, you shall become a blessing.ᵇ Have no fear; take courage!

¹⁴For thus said the LORD of Hosts: Just as I planned to afflict you and did not relent when

---

a   Cf. Hag. 1.6.
b   I.e., a standard by which men curse or bless; cf. Gen. 12.2 and note.

---

3 כֹּה אָמַר יְהוָה שַׁבְתִּי אֶל־צִיּוֹן וְשָׁכַנְתִּי בְּתוֹךְ יְרוּשָׁלָ͏ִם וְנִקְרְאָה יְרוּשָׁלַ͏ִם עִיר־הָאֱמֶת וְהַר־יְהוָה צְבָאוֹת הַר הַקֹּדֶשׁ: ס

4 כֹּה אָמַר יְהוָה צְבָאוֹת עֹד יֵשְׁבוּ זְקֵנִים וּזְקֵנוֹת בִּרְחֹבוֹת יְרוּשָׁלָ͏ִם וְאִישׁ מִשְׁעַנְתּוֹ בְּיָדוֹ מֵרֹב יָמִים: 5 וּרְחֹבוֹת הָעִיר יִמָּלְאוּ יְלָדִים וִילָדוֹת מְשַׂחֲקִים בִּרְחֹבֹתֶיהָ: ס

6 כֹּה אָמַר יְהוָה צְבָאוֹת כִּי יִפָּלֵא בְּעֵינֵי שְׁאֵרִית הָעָם הַזֶּה בַּיָּמִים הָהֵם גַּם־בְּעֵינַי יִפָּלֵא נְאֻם יְהוָה צְבָאוֹת: פ 7 כֹּה אָמַר יְהוָה צְבָאוֹת הִנְנִי מוֹשִׁיעַ אֶת־עַמִּי מֵאֶרֶץ מִזְרָח וּמֵאֶרֶץ מְבוֹא הַשָּׁמֶשׁ: 8 וְהֵבֵאתִי אֹתָם וְשָׁכְנוּ בְּתוֹךְ יְרוּשָׁלָ͏ִם וְהָיוּ־לִי לְעָם וַאֲנִי אֶהְיֶה לָהֶם לֵאלֹהִים בֶּאֱמֶת וּבִצְדָקָה: ס

9 כֹּה־אָמַר יְהוָה צְבָאוֹת תֶּחֱזַקְנָה יְדֵיכֶם הַשֹּׁמְעִים בַּיָּמִים הָאֵלֶּה אֵת הַדְּבָרִים הָאֵלֶּה מִפִּי הַנְּבִיאִים אֲשֶׁר בְּיוֹם יֻסַּד בֵּית־יְהוָה צְבָאוֹת הַהֵיכָל לְהִבָּנוֹת: 10 כִּי לִפְנֵי הַיָּמִים הָהֵם שְׂכַר הָאָדָם לֹא נִהְיָה וּשְׂכַר הַבְּהֵמָה אֵינֶנָּה וְלַיּוֹצֵא וְלַבָּא אֵין־שָׁלוֹם מִן־הַצָּר וַאֲשַׁלַּח אֶת־כָּל־הָאָדָם אִישׁ בְּרֵעֵהוּ: 11 וְעַתָּה לֹא כַיָּמִים הָרִאשֹׁנִים אֲנִי לִשְׁאֵרִית הָעָם הַזֶּה נְאֻם יְהוָה צְבָאוֹת: 12 כִּי־זֶרַע הַשָּׁלוֹם הַגֶּפֶן תִּתֵּן פִּרְיָהּ וְהָאָרֶץ תִּתֵּן אֶת־יְבוּלָהּ וְהַשָּׁמַיִם יִתְּנוּ טַלָּם וְהִנְחַלְתִּי אֶת־שְׁאֵרִית הָעָם הַזֶּה אֶת־כָּל־אֵלֶּה: 13 וְהָיָה כַּאֲשֶׁר הֱיִיתֶם קְלָלָה בַּגּוֹיִם בֵּית יְהוּדָה וּבֵית יִשְׂרָאֵל כֵּן אוֹשִׁיעַ אֶתְכֶם וִהְיִיתֶם בְּרָכָה אַל־תִּירָאוּ תֶּחֱזַקְנָה יְדֵיכֶם: ס

14 כִּי כֹה אָמַר יְהוָה צְבָאוֹת כַּאֲשֶׁר זָמַמְתִּי לְהָרַע לָכֶם בְּהַקְצִיף אֲבֹתֵיכֶם אֹתִי אָמַר יְהוָה צְבָאוֹת וְלֹא נִחָמְתִּי:

your fathers provoked Me to anger—said the LORD of Hosts—¹⁵so, at this time, I have turned and planned to do good to Jerusalem and to the House of Judah. Have no fear! ¹⁶These are the things you are to do: Speak the truth to one another, render true and perfect justice in your gates. ¹⁷And do not contrive evil against one another, and do not love perjury, because all those are things that I hate—declares the LORD.

¹⁸And the word of the LORD of Hosts came to me, saying, ¹⁹Thus said the LORD of Hosts: The fast of the fourth month, the fast of the fifth month, the fast of the seventh month, and the fast of the tenth month^c shall become occasions for joy and gladness, happy festivals for the House of Judah; but you must love honesty and integrity.

²⁰Thus said the LORD of Hosts: Peoples and the inhabitants of many cities shall yet come—²¹the inhabitants of one shall go to the other and say, "Let us go and entreat the favor of the LORD, let us seek the LORD of Hosts; I will go, too." ²²The many peoples and the multitude of nations shall come to seek the LORD of Hosts in Jerusalem and to entreat the favor of the LORD. ²³Thus said the LORD of Hosts: In those days, ten men from nations of every tongue will take hold—they will take hold of every Jew by a corner of his cloak and say, "Let us go with you, for we have heard that God is with you."

9
A pronouncement: The word of the LORD.

He will reside in the land of Hadrach and
    Damascus;
For all men's eyes will turn to the LORD—
Like all the tribes of Israel—
²Including Hamath, which borders on it,^a

---

c *Commemorating, respectively, the events of 2 Kings 25.3 ff. (Jer. 52.6 ff.); 2 Kings 25.8 ff. (Jer. 52.12 ff.); 2 Kings 25.25 ff. (Jer. 41); 2 Kings 25.1 ff. (Jer. 52.4).*

a *I.e., on the land of Hadrach and Damascus.*

15 כֵּן שַׁבְתִּי זָמַמְתִּי בַּיָּמִים הָאֵלֶּה לְהֵיטִיב אֶת־יְרוּשָׁלַ͏ִם וְאֶת־בֵּית יְהוּדָה אַל־תִּירָאוּ: 16 אֵלֶּה הַדְּבָרִים אֲשֶׁר תַּעֲשׂוּ דַּבְּרוּ אֱמֶת אִישׁ אֶת־רֵעֵהוּ אֱמֶת וּמִשְׁפַּט שָׁלוֹם שִׁפְטוּ בְּשַׁעֲרֵיכֶם: 17 וְאִישׁ ׀ אֶת־רָעַת רֵעֵהוּ אַל־תַּחְשְׁבוּ בִּלְבַבְכֶם וּשְׁבֻעַת שֶׁקֶר אַל־תֶּאֱהָבוּ כִּי אֶת־כָּל־אֵלֶּה אֲשֶׁר שָׂנֵאתִי נְאֻם־יְהֹוָה: ס

18 וַיְהִי דְּבַר־יְהֹוָה צְבָאוֹת אֵלַי לֵאמֹר: 19 כֹּה־אָמַר יְהֹוָה צְבָאוֹת צוֹם הָרְבִיעִי וְצוֹם הַחֲמִישִׁי וְצוֹם הַשְּׁבִיעִי וְצוֹם הָעֲשִׂירִי יִהְיֶה לְבֵית־יְהוּדָה לְשָׂשׂוֹן וּלְשִׂמְחָה וּלְמֹעֲדִים טוֹבִים וְהָאֱמֶת וְהַשָּׁלוֹם אֱהָבוּ: פ

20 כֹּה אָמַר יְהֹוָה צְבָאוֹת עֹד אֲשֶׁר יָבֹאוּ עַמִּים וְיֹשְׁבֵי עָרִים רַבּוֹת: 21 וְהָלְכוּ יֹשְׁבֵי אַחַת אֶל־אַחַת לֵאמֹר נֵלְכָה הָלוֹךְ לְחַלּוֹת אֶת־פְּנֵי יְהֹוָה וּלְבַקֵּשׁ אֶת־יְהֹוָה צְבָאוֹת אֵלְכָה גַּם־אָנִי: 22 וּבָאוּ עַמִּים רַבִּים וְגוֹיִם עֲצוּמִים לְבַקֵּשׁ אֶת־יְהֹוָה צְבָאוֹת בִּירוּשָׁלָ͏ִם וּלְחַלּוֹת אֶת־פְּנֵי יְהֹוָה: ס 23 כֹּה אָמַר יְהֹוָה צְבָאוֹת בַּיָּמִים הָהֵמָּה אֲשֶׁר יַחֲזִיקוּ עֲשָׂרָה אֲנָשִׁים מִכֹּל לְשֹׁנוֹת הַגּוֹיִם וְהֶחֱזִיקוּ בִּכְנַף אִישׁ יְהוּדִי לֵאמֹר נֵלְכָה עִמָּכֶם כִּי שָׁמַעְנוּ אֱלֹהִים עִמָּכֶם: ס

ט מַשָּׂא דְבַר־יְהֹוָה

בְּאֶרֶץ חַדְרָךְ וְדַמֶּשֶׂק מְנֻחָתוֹ
כִּי לַיהֹוָה עֵין אָדָם
וְכֹל שִׁבְטֵי יִשְׂרָאֵל:
2 וְגַם־חֲמָת תִּגְבָּל־בָּהּ

And Tyre and Sidon, though they are very
  wise.

³Tyre has built herself a fortress;
She has amassed silver like dust,
And gold like the mud in the streets.

⁴But my Lord will impoverish her;
He will defeat her forces at sea,
And she herself shall be consumed by fire.

⁵Ashkelon shall see it and be frightened,
Gaza shall tremble violently,
And Ekron, at the collapse of her hopes.
Kingship shall vanish from Gaza,
Ashkelon shall be without inhabitants,

⁶And b-a mongrel people-b shall settle in Ashdod.
I will uproot the grandeur of Philistia.

⁷But I will clean out the blood from its mouth,
And the detestable things from between its
  teeth.
Its survivors, too, shall belong to our God:
They shall become like a clan in Judah,
And Ekron shall be like the Jebusites.

⁸And I will encamp in My House c-against
  armies,-c
Against any that come and go,
And no oppressor shall ever overrun them
  again;
For I have now taken note d-with My own
  eyes.-d

⁹Rejoice greatly, Fair Zion;
Raise a shout, Fair Jerusalem!
Lo, your king is coming to you.
He is victorious, triumphant,
Yet humble, riding on an ass,
On a donkey foaled by a she-ass.

צֹ֤ר וְצִידוֹן֙ כִּ֣י חָכְמָ֣ה מְאֹֽד׃
3 וַתִּ֥בֶן צֹ֖ר מָצ֣וֹר לָ֑הּ
וַתִּצְבָּר־כֶּ֙סֶף֙ כֶּֽעָפָ֔ר
וְחָר֖וּץ כְּטִ֥יט חוּצֽוֹת׃
4 הִנֵּ֤ה אֲדֹנָי֙ יֽוֹרִשֶׁ֔נָּה
וְהִכָּ֥ה בַיָּ֖ם חֵילָ֑הּ
וְהִ֖יא בָּאֵ֥שׁ תֵּאָכֵֽל׃

5 תֵּרֶ֨א אַשְׁקְל֜וֹן וְתִירָ֗א
וְעַזָּה֙ וְתָחִ֣יל מְאֹ֔ד
וְעֶקְר֖וֹן כִּֽי־הֹבִ֣ישׁ מֶבָּטָ֑הּ
וְאָ֤בַד מֶ֙לֶךְ֙ מֵֽעַזָּ֔ה
וְאַשְׁקְל֖וֹן לֹ֥א תֵשֵֽׁב׃
6 וְיָשַׁ֥ב מַמְזֵ֖ר בְּאַשְׁדּ֑וֹד
וְהִכְרַתִּ֖י גְּא֥וֹן פְּלִשְׁתִּֽים׃

7 וַהֲסִרֹתִ֤י דָמָיו֙ מִפִּ֔יו
וְשִׁקֻּצָיו֙ מִבֵּ֣ין שִׁנָּ֔יו
וְנִשְׁאַ֥ר גַּם־ה֖וּא לֵֽאלֹהֵ֑ינוּ
וְהָיָה֙ כְּאַלֻּ֣ף בִּֽיהוּדָ֔ה
וְעֶקְר֖וֹן כִּיבוּסִֽי׃

8 וְחָנִ֨יתִי לְבֵיתִ֤י מִצָּבָה֙
מֵעֹבֵ֣ר וּמִשָּׁ֔ב
וְלֹֽא־יַעֲבֹ֧ר עֲלֵיהֶ֛ם ע֖וֹד נֹגֵ֑שׂ
כִּ֥י עַתָּ֖ה רָאִ֥יתִי בְעֵינָֽי׃ ס

9 גִּ֣ילִי מְאֹד֮ בַּת־צִיּוֹן֒
הָרִ֙יעִי֙ בַּ֣ת יְרֽוּשָׁלַ֔͏ִם
הִנֵּ֤ה מַלְכֵּךְ֙ יָ֣בוֹא לָ֔ךְ
צַדִּ֥יק וְנוֹשָׁ֖ע ה֑וּא
עָנִי֙ וְרֹכֵ֣ב עַל־חֲמ֔וֹר
וְעַל־עַ֖יִר בֶּן־אֲתֹנֽוֹת׃

---

b-b   Heb. mamzer; cf. note at Deut. 23.3.
c-c   Change of vocalization yields "as a garrison."
d-d   Emendation yields "of their suffering"; cf. 1 Sam. 1.11.

¹⁰Heᵉ shall banish chariots from Ephraim
And horses from Jerusalem;
The warrior's bow shall be banished.
He shall call on the nations to surrender,ᶠ
And his rule shall extend from sea to sea
And from ocean to land's end.

¹¹ᵍYou, for your part, have releasedʰ
Your prisoners from the dry pit,ⁱ
For the sake of the blood of your covenant,
¹²[Saying], "Return to Bizzaron,ʲ
You prisoners of hope."
In return [I] announce this day:
I will repay you double.
¹³For I have drawn Judah taut,
And applied [My hand] to Ephraim as to a
   bow,
And I will arouse your sons, O Zion,
Against your sons, O Javan,
And make you like a warrior's sword.

¹⁴And the LORD will manifest Himself to
   them,ᵏ
And His arrows shall flash like lightning;
My Lord GOD shall sound the ram's horn
And advance in a stormy tempest.ˡ
¹⁵The LORD of Hosts will protect them:
ᵐ[His] slingstones shall devour and conquer;
They shall ⁿ-drink, shall rage as with-ⁿ wine,
And be filled [with it] like a dashing bowl,
Like the corners of an altar.
¹⁶The LORD their God shall prosper them
On that day;

10 וְהִכְרַתִּי־רֶ֫כֶב מֵֽאֶפְרַ֗יִם
וְסוּס֙ מִיר֣וּשָׁלַ֔͏ִם
וְנִכְרְתָה֙ קֶ֣שֶׁת מִלְחָמָ֔ה
וְדִבֶּ֥ר שָׁל֖וֹם לַגּוֹיִ֑ם
וּמָשְׁלוֹ֙ מִיָּ֣ם עַד־יָ֔ם
וּמִנָּהָ֖ר עַד־אַפְסֵי־אָֽרֶץ׃

11 גַּם־אַ֕תְּ
בְּדַם־בְּרִיתֵ֖ךְ
שִׁלַּ֤חְתִּי אֲסִירַ֙יִךְ֙ מִבּ֔וֹר אֵ֥ין מַ֖יִם בּֽוֹ׃
12 שׁ֚וּבוּ לְבִצָּר֔וֹן
אֲסִירֵ֖י הַתִּקְוָ֑ה
גַּם־הַיּ֛וֹם מַגִּ֥יד
מִשְׁנֶ֖ה אָשִׁ֥יב לָֽךְ׃
13 כִּֽי־דָרַ֨כְתִּי לִ֤י יְהוּדָה֙
קֶ֚שֶׁת מִלֵּ֣אתִי אֶפְרַ֔יִם
וְעוֹרַרְתִּ֤י בָנַ֙יִךְ֙ צִיּ֔וֹן
עַל־בָּנַ֖יִךְ יָוָ֑ן
וְשַׂמְתִּ֖יךְ כְּחֶ֥רֶב גִּבּֽוֹר׃

14 וַֽיהוָה֙ עֲלֵיהֶ֣ם יֵֽרָאֶ֔ה
וְיָצָ֥א כַבָּרָ֖ק חִצּ֑וֹ
וַֽאדֹנָ֤י יְהוִֹה֙ בַּשּׁוֹפָ֣ר יִתְקָ֔ע
וְהָלַ֖ךְ בְּסַעֲר֥וֹת תֵּימָֽן׃
15 יְהוָ֣ה צְבָאוֹת֮ יָגֵ֣ן עֲלֵיהֶם֒
וְאָכְל֗וּ וְכָבְשׁוּ֙ אַבְנֵי־קֶ֔לַע
וְשָׁת֥וּ הָמ֖וּ כְּמוֹ־יָ֑יִן
וּמָֽלְאוּ֙ כַּמִּזְרָ֔ק
כְּזָוִיּ֖וֹת מִזְבֵּֽחַ׃
16 וְֽהוֹשִׁיעָ֞ם יְהוָ֧ה אֱלֹהֵיהֶ֛ם
בַּיּ֥וֹם הַה֖וּא

---

e   Heb. "I."
f   Cf. Deut. 20.10–12 and note.
g   Exact meaning and connection of vv. 11–12 uncertain.
h   Taking shillaḥti as a second-person singular feminine form, with
     Septuagint; cf. Judg. 5.7 with note.
i   I.e., a pit that serves as a dungeon rather than a cistern (both
     are called bor in Heb.).
j   Perhaps a nickname ("fortress") for Samaria (Heb. Shomeron).
k   I.e., Judah.
l   Lit. "tempests of wind"; for teman in the sense of wind, cf. Job
     9.9; 39.26.
m   The meaning of much of the rest of the chapter is uncertain.
n-n Some Septuagint mss. read "drink blood like."

[He shall pasture] His people like sheep.
[They shall be] like crown jewels glittering on
    His soil.
17How lovely, how beautiful they shall be,
Producing young men like new grain,
Young women like new wine!

כְּצֹאן עַמּוֹ
כִּי אַבְנֵי־נֵזֶר מִתְנוֹסְסוֹת עַל־אַדְמָתוֹ:
17 כִּי מַה־טּוּבוֹ וּמַה־יָּפְיוֹ
דָּגָן בַּחוּרִים
וְתִירוֹשׁ יְנוֹבֵב בְּתֻלוֹת:

10 Ask the LORD for rain
In the *a*-season of late rain.-*a*
It is the LORD who causes storms;*b*
And He will provide rainstorms *c*-for them,
Grass in the fields for everyone.-*c*

ל
שַׁאֲלוּ מֵיהוָה מָטָר
בְּעֵת מַלְקוֹשׁ
יְהוָה עֹשֶׂה חֲזִיזִים
וּמְטַר־גֶּשֶׁם יִתֵּן לָהֶם
לְאִישׁ עֵשֶׂב בַּשָּׂדֶה:

2For the teraphim*d* spoke delusion,
The augurs predicted falsely;
And dreamers speak lies
And console with illusions.
That is why My people have strayed*b* like a
    flock,
They suffer*b* for lack of a shepherd.
3My anger is roused against the shepherds,
And I will punish the he-goats.*e*

2 כִּי הַתְּרָפִים דִּבְּרוּ־אָוֶן
וְהַקּוֹסְמִים חָזוּ שֶׁקֶר
וַחֲלֹמוֹת הַשָּׁוְא יְדַבֵּרוּ
הֶבֶל יְנַחֵמוּן
עַל־כֵּן נָסְעוּ כְמוֹ־צֹאן
יַעֲנוּ כִּי־אֵין רֹעֶה: פ
3 עַל־הָרֹעִים חָרָה אַפִּי
וְעַל־הָעַתּוּדִים אֶפְקוֹד

For the LORD of Hosts has taken thought
In behalf of His flock, the House of Judah;
He will make them like majestic chargers in
    battle.
4From them shall come *f*-cornerstones,
From them tent pegs,-*f*
From them bows of combat,
And every captain shall also arise from them.
5And together they shall be like warriors in
    battle,
Tramping in the dirt of the streets;

כִּי־פָקַד יְהוָה צְבָאוֹת
אֶת־עֶדְרוֹ אֶת־בֵּית יְהוּדָה
וְשָׂם אוֹתָם כְּסוּס הוֹדוֹ בַּמִּלְחָמָה:
4 מִמֶּנּוּ פִנָּה
מִמֶּנּוּ יָתֵד
מִמֶּנּוּ קֶשֶׁת מִלְחָמָה
מִמֶּנּוּ יֵצֵא כָל־נוֹגֵשׂ יַחְדָּו:
5 וְהָיוּ כְגִבֹּרִים
בּוֹסִים בְּטִיט חוּצוֹת בַּמִּלְחָמָה

a-a   Septuagint reads "in its season / The early rain and the late."
       Cf. Deut. 11.14.
b   Meaning of Heb. uncertain.
c-c   Emendation yields "[producing] food for men, / Grass in the
       fields for cattle." Cf. Deut. 11.14–15.
d   Idols consulted for oracles; cf. 1 Sam. 15.23; Ezek. 21.26.
e   I.e., oppressive leaders; cf. Ezek. 34.17 ff.
f-f   Emendation yields "shields and bucklers."

They shall fight, for the LORD shall be with
   them,

And they shall put horsemen to shame.

⁶I will give victory to the House of Judah,

And triumph to the House of Joseph.

I will restore them, for I have pardoned them,

And they shall be as though I had never disowned them;

For I the LORD am their God,

And I will answer their prayers.

⁷ᵍ-Ephraim shall be like a warrior,

And they-ᵍ shall exult as with wine;

Their children shall see it and rejoice,

They shall exult in the LORD.

⁸I will whistle to them and gather them,

For I will redeem them;

They shall increase ᵇ-and continue increasing.-ᵇ

⁹For though I sowed them among the nations,

In the distant places they shall remember Me,

They shall escape with their children and shall
   return.

¹⁰I will bring them back from the land of
   Egypt

And gather them from Assyria;

And I will bring them to the lands of Gilead
   and Lebanon,

And even they shall not suffice for them.

¹¹ᵇ-A hemmed-in force shall pass over the sea

And shall stir up waves in the sea;-ᵇ

And all the deeps of the Nile shall dry up.

Down shall come the pride of Assyria,

And the scepter of Egypt shall pass away.

¹²But I will make themʰ mighty through the
   LORD,

And they shall ⁱ-march proudly-ⁱ in His name
   —declares the LORD.

וְנִלְחֲמוּ כִּי יְהֹוָה עִמָּם
וְהֹבִישׁוּ רֹכְבֵי סוּסִים:
6 וְגִבַּרְתִּי ׀ אֶת־בֵּית יְהוּדָה
וְאֶת־בֵּית יוֹסֵף אוֹשִׁיעַ
וְהוֹשְׁבוֹתִים כִּי רִחַמְתִּים
וְהָיוּ כַּאֲשֶׁר לֹא־זְנַחְתִּים
כִּי אֲנִי יְהֹוָה אֱלֹהֵיהֶם
וְאֶעֱנֵם:
7 וְהָיוּ כְגִבּוֹר אֶפְרַיִם
וְשָׂמַח לִבָּם כְּמוֹ־יָיִן
וּבְנֵיהֶם יִרְאוּ וְשָׂמֵחוּ
יָגֵל לִבָּם בַּיהֹוָה:
8 אֶשְׁרְקָה לָהֶם וַאֲקַבְּצֵם
כִּי פְדִיתִים
וְרָבוּ כְּמוֹ רָבוּ:
9 וְאֶזְרָעֵם בָּעַמִּים
וּבַמֶּרְחַקִּים יִזְכְּרוּנִי
וְחָיוּ אֶת־בְּנֵיהֶם וָשָׁבוּ:
10 וַהֲשִׁיבוֹתִים מֵאֶרֶץ מִצְרַיִם
וּמֵאַשּׁוּר אֲקַבְּצֵם
וְאֶל־אֶרֶץ גִּלְעָד וּלְבָנוֹן אֲבִיאֵם
וְלֹא יִמָּצֵא לָהֶם:
11 וְעָבַר בַּיָּם צָרָה
וְהִכָּה בַיָּם גַּלִּים
וְהֹבִישׁוּ כֹּל מְצוּלוֹת יְאֹר
וְהוּרַד גְּאוֹן אַשּׁוּר
וְשֵׁבֶט מִצְרַיִם יָסוּר:
12 וְגִבַּרְתִּים בַּיהֹוָה
וּבִשְׁמוֹ יִתְהַלָּכוּ
נְאֻם יְהֹוָה: ס

---

g-g   *Emendation yields "And when Ephraim is victorious, /
    They…"*

h   *I.e., Judah and Ephraim.*

i-i   *Meaning of Heb. uncertain. Emendation yields "have glory";
    cf. Isa. 45.25.*

11 Throw open your gates, O Lebanon,
And let fire consume your cedars!
²Howl, cypresses, for cedars have fallen!
How the mighty are ravaged!
Howl, you oaks of Bashan,
For the stately forest is laid low!
³Hark, the wailing of the shepherds,
For their *a-rich pastures-a* are ravaged;
Hark, the roaring of the great beasts,
For the jungle of the Jordan is ravaged.

⁴Thus said my God the Lord: Tend the sheep meant for slaughter, ⁵whose buyers will slaughter them with impunity, whose seller will say, "Praised be the Lord! I'll get rich," and whose shepherd will not pity them. ⁶For I will pity the inhabitants of the land no more—declares the Lord—but I will place every man at the mercy of every other man and at the mercy of his king; they shall break the country to bits, and I will not rescue it from their hands.

⁷So I tended the sheep meant for slaughter, *b-for those poor men of the sheep.-b* I got two staffs, one of which I named Favor and the other Unity, and I proceeded to tend the sheep. ⁸But I lost *c-the three shepherds-c* in one month; then my patience with them was at an end, and they in turn were disgusted with me. ⁹So I declared, "I am not going to tend you; let the one that is to die die and the one that is to get lost get lost; and let the rest devour each other's flesh!"

¹⁰Taking my staff Favor, I cleft it in two, so as to annul the covenant I had made with all the peoples;*d* ¹¹and when it was annulled that day, *e-the same poor men of the sheep-e* who watched*f* me realized that it was a message from

יא א פְּתַח לְבָנוֹן דְּלָתֶיךָ
וְתֹאכַל אֵשׁ בַּאֲרָזֶיךָ:
2 הֵילֵל בְּרוֹשׁ כִּי־נָפַל אֶרֶז
אֲשֶׁר אַדִּרִים שֻׁדָּדוּ
הֵילִילוּ אַלּוֹנֵי בָשָׁן
כִּי יָרַד יַעַר הבצור הַבָּצִיר:
3 קוֹל יִלְלַת הָרֹעִים
כִּי שֻׁדְּדָה אַדַּרְתָּם
קוֹל שַׁאֲגַת כְּפִירִים
כִּי שֻׁדַּד גְּאוֹן הַיַּרְדֵּן: ס

4 כֹּה אָמַר יְהוָה אֱלֹהָי רְעֵה אֶת־צֹאן
הַהֲרֵגָה: 5 אֲשֶׁר קֹנֵיהֶן יַהֲרֻגֵן וְלֹא יֶאְשָׁמוּ
וּמֹכְרֵיהֶן יֹאמַר בָּרוּךְ יְהוָה וַאעשׁר*
וְרֹעֵיהֶם לֹא יַחְמוֹל עֲלֵיהֶן: 6 כִּי לֹא
אֶחְמוֹל עוֹד עַל־יֹשְׁבֵי הָאָרֶץ נְאֻם־יְהוָה
וְהִנֵּה אָנֹכִי מַמְצִיא אֶת־הָאָדָם אִישׁ
בְּיַד־רֵעֵהוּ וּבְיַד מַלְכּוֹ וְכִתְּתוּ אֶת־הָאָרֶץ
וְלֹא אַצִּיל מִיָּדָם:

7 וָאֶרְעֶה אֶת־צֹאן הַהֲרֵגָה לָכֵן עֲנִיֵּי הַצֹּאן
וָאֶקַּח־לִי שְׁנֵי מַקְלוֹת לְאַחַד קָרָאתִי
נֹעַם וּלְאַחַד קָרָאתִי חֹבְלִים וָאֶרְעֶה
אֶת־הַצֹּאן: 8 וָאַכְחִד אֶת־שְׁלֹשֶׁת הָרֹעִים
בְּיֶרַח אֶחָד וַתִּקְצַר נַפְשִׁי בָּהֶם וְגַם־
נַפְשָׁם בָּחֲלָה בִי: 9 וָאֹמַר לֹא אֶרְעֶה
אֶתְכֶם הַמֵּתָה תָמוּת וְהַנִּכְחֶדֶת תִּכָּחֵד
וְהַנִּשְׁאָרוֹת תֹּאכַלְנָה אִשָּׁה אֶת־בְּשַׂר
רְעוּתָהּ:

10 וָאֶקַּח אֶת־מַקְלִי אֶת־נֹעַם וָאֶגְדַּע אֹתוֹ
לְהָפִיר אֶת־בְּרִיתִי אֲשֶׁר כָּרַתִּי אֶת־כָּל־
הָעַמִּים: 11 וַתֻּפַר בַּיּוֹם הַהוּא וַיֵּדְעוּ כֵן
עֲנִיֵּי הַצֹּאן הַשֹּׁמְרִים אֹתִי כִּי דְבַר־יְהוָה

---

a-a   *Meaning of Heb. uncertain.*
b-b   *Emendation yields "for the sheep dealers"; cf. the word rendered "trader" in 14.21.*
c-c   *Emendation yields "a third of the flock."*
d   *Perhaps alluding to the prediction of 14.1–3.*
e-e   *Emendation yields "the sheep dealers."*
f   *Emendation yields "hired."*

the Lord. ¹²Then I said to them, "If you are satisfied, pay me my wages; if not, don't." So they weighed out my wages, thirty shekels of silver—¹³ᵃ-the noble sum that I was worth in their estimation.-ᵃ The Lord said to me, "Deposit it in the treasury."ᵃ And I took the thirty shekels and deposited it in the treasury in the House of the Lord. ¹⁴Then I cleft in two my second staff, Unity, in order to annul the brotherhood between Judah and Israel.ᵍ

¹⁵The Lord said to me further: Get yourself the gear of a foolish shepherd. ¹⁶For I am going to raise up in the land a shepherd who will neither miss the lost [sheep], nor seek the strayed,ᵃ nor heal the injured, nor sustain the frail,ᵃ but will feast on the flesh of the fat ones and ᵃ-tear off their hoofs.-ᵃ

¹⁷Oh, the worthless shepherd
Who abandons the flock!
Let a sword descend upon his arm
And upon his right eye!
His arm shall shrivel up;
His right eye shall go blind.

12

A pronouncement: The word of the Lord concerning Israel.

The utterance of the Lord,
Who stretched out the skies
And made firm the earth,
And created man's breath within him:

²Behold, I will make Jerusalem a bowl of reeling for the peoples all around. Judah shall be caught up in the siege upon Jerusalem, ³when all the nations of the earth gather against her. In that day, I will make Jerusalem a stone for all the peoples to lift; all who lift it shall injure themselves. ⁴In that day—declares the Lord—I

הוּא: 12 וָאֹמַ֣ר אֲלֵיהֶ֗ם אִם־ט֧וֹב בְּעֵֽינֵיכֶ֛ם הָב֥וּ שְׂכָרִ֖י וְאִם־לֹ֣א ׀ חֲדָ֑לוּ וַיִּשְׁקְל֥וּ אֶת־שְׂכָרִ֖י שְׁלֹשִׁ֥ים כָּֽסֶף: 13 וַיֹּ֨אמֶר יְהֹוָ֜ה אֵלַ֗י הַשְׁלִיכֵ֨הוּ֙ אֶל־הַיּוֹצֵ֔ר אֶ֣דֶר הַיְקָ֔ר אֲשֶׁ֥ר יָקַ֖רְתִּי מֵֽעֲלֵיהֶ֑ם וָֽאֶקְחָ֞ה שְׁלֹשִׁ֣ים הַכֶּ֗סֶף וָֽאַשְׁלִ֥יךְ אֹת֛וֹ בֵּ֥ית יְהֹוָ֖ה אֶל־ הַיּוֹצֵֽר: 14 וָֽאֶגְדַּע֙ אֶת־מַקְלִ֣י הַשֵּׁנִ֔י אֵ֖ת הַחֹ֣בְלִ֑ים לְהָפֵר֙ אֶת־הָ֣אַֽחֲוָ֔ה בֵּ֥ין יְהוּדָ֖ה וּבֵ֥ין יִשְׂרָאֵֽל: ס

15 וַיֹּ֨אמֶר יְהֹוָ֜ה אֵלַ֗י ע֚וֹד קַח־לְךָ֔ כְּלִ֖י רֹעֶ֥ה אֱוִלִֽי: 16 כִּ֣י הִנֵּֽה־אָנֹכִי֩ מֵקִ֨ים רֹעֶ֜ה בָּאָ֗רֶץ הַנִּכְחָד֤וֹת לֹֽא־יִפְקֹד֙ הַנַּ֣עַר לֹֽא־יְבַקֵּ֔שׁ וְהַנִּשְׁבֶּ֖רֶת לֹ֣א יְרַפֵּ֑א הַנִּצָּבָה֙ לֹ֣א יְכַלְכֵּ֔ל וּבְשַׂ֤ר הַבְּרִיאָה֙ יֹאכַ֔ל וּפַרְסֵיהֶ֖ן יְפָרֵֽק: ס

17 ה֣וֹי רֹעִ֤י הָֽאֱלִיל֙
עֹזְבִ֣י הַצֹּ֔אן
חֶ֥רֶב עַל־זְרוֹע֖וֹ
וְעַל־עֵ֣ין יְמִינ֑וֹ
זְרֹעוֹ֙ יָב֣וֹשׁ תִּיבָ֔שׁ
וְעֵ֥ין יְמִינ֖וֹ כָּהֹ֥ה תִכְהֶֽה: ס

יב

מַשָּׂ֥א דְבַר־יְהֹוָ֖ה עַל־יִשְׂרָאֵ֑ל

נְאֻם־יְהֹוָ֗ה
נֹטֶ֤ה שָׁמַ֙יִם֙
וְיֹסֵ֣ד אָ֔רֶץ
וְיֹצֵ֥ר רֽוּחַ־אָדָ֖ם בְּקִרְבּֽוֹ: פ

2 הִנֵּ֣ה אָ֠נֹכִ֠י שָׂ֣ם אֶת־יְרֽוּשָׁלַ֗͏ִם סַף־רַ֛עַל לְכׇל־הָֽעַמִּ֖ים סָבִ֑יב וְגַ֧ם עַל־יְהוּדָ֛ה יִֽהְיֶ֥ה בַמָּצ֖וֹר עַל־יְרֽוּשָׁלָֽ͏ִם: 3 וְהָיָ֣ה בַיּֽוֹם־הַה֗וּא אָשִׂ֨ים אֶת־יְרֽוּשָׁלַ֜͏ִם אֶ֤בֶן מַֽעֲמָסָה֙ לְכׇל־הָ֣עַמִּ֔ים כׇּל־עֹמְסֶ֖יהָ שָׂר֣וֹט יִשָּׂרֵ֑טוּ וְנֶֽאֶסְפ֣וּ עָלֶ֔יהָ כֹּ֖ל גּוֹיֵ֥י הָאָֽרֶץ: 4 בַּיּ֨וֹם הַה֜וּא

ᵍ Two mss. of the Septuagint have "Jerusalem"; cf. 12.2–3; 14.14.

will strike every horse with panic and its rider with madness. But I will *a*-watch over the House of Judah while I strike every horse of-*a* the peoples with blindness. 5And the clans of Judah will say to themselves, *b*-"The dwellers of Jerusalem are a task set for us by-*b* their God, the LORD of Hosts." 6In that day, I will make the clans of Judah like a flaming brazier among sticks and like a flaming torch among sheaves. They shall devour all the besieging peoples right and left; and Jerusalem shall continue on its site, in Jerusalem.*c*

7The LORD will give victory to the tents of Judah first, so that the glory of the House of David and the glory of the inhabitants of Jerusalem may not be too great for Judah. 8In that day, the LORD will shield the inhabitants of Jerusalem; and the feeblest of them shall be in that day like David, and the House of David like a divine being—like an angel of the LORD—at their head.

9In that day I will *d*-all but annihilate-*d* all the nations that came up against Jerusalem. 10But I will fill the House of David and the inhabitants of Jerusalem with a spirit of pity and compassion; and they shall lament*e* to Me about those who are slain, wailing over them as over a favorite son and showing bitter grief as over a first-born. 11In that day, the wailing in Jerusalem shall be as great as the wailing at Hadadrimmon in the plain of Megiddon.*f* 12The land shall wail, each family by itself: The family of the House of David by themselves, and their womenfolk by themselves; the family of the House of Nathan by themselves, and their womenfolk by themselves; 13the family of the

נְאֻם־יְהֹוָה אַכֶּה כָל־סוּס בַּתִּמָּהוֹן וְרֹכְבוֹ
בַּשִּׁגָּעוֹן וְעַל־בֵּית יְהוּדָה אֶפְקַח אֶת־עֵינַי
וְכֹל סוּס הָעַמִּים אַכֶּה בַּעִוָּרוֹן: 5 וְאָמְרוּ
אַלֻּפֵי יְהוּדָה בְּלִבָּם אַמְצָה לִי יֹשְׁבֵי
יְרוּשָׁלַ͏ִם בַּיהֹוָה צְבָאוֹת אֱלֹהֵיהֶם: 6 בַּיּוֹם
הַהוּא אָשִׂים אֶת־אַלֻּפֵי יְהוּדָה כְּכִיּוֹר
אֵשׁ בְּעֵצִים וּכְלַפִּיד אֵשׁ בְּעָמִיר וְאָכְלוּ
עַל־יָמִין וְעַל־שְׂמֹאול* אֶת־כָּל־הָעַמִּים
סָבִיב וְיָשְׁבָה יְרוּשָׁלַ͏ִם עוֹד תַּחְתֶּיהָ
בִּירוּשָׁלָ͏ִם: פ

7 וְהוֹשִׁיעַ יְהֹוָה אֶת־אָהֳלֵי יְהוּדָה
בָּרִאשֹׁנָה לְמַעַן לֹא־תִגְדַּל תִּפְאֶרֶת בֵּית־
דָּוִיד וְתִפְאֶרֶת יֹשֵׁב יְרוּשָׁלַ͏ִם עַל־יְהוּדָה:
8 בַּיּוֹם הַהוּא יָגֵן יְהֹוָה בְּעַד יוֹשֵׁב יְרוּשָׁלַ͏ִם
וְהָיָה הַנִּכְשָׁל בָּהֶם בַּיּוֹם הַהוּא כְּדָוִיד
וּבֵית דָּוִיד כֵּאלֹהִים כְּמַלְאַךְ יְהֹוָה
לִפְנֵיהֶם:

9 וְהָיָה בַּיּוֹם הַהוּא אֲבַקֵּשׁ לְהַשְׁמִיד
אֶת־כָּל־הַגּוֹיִם הַבָּאִים עַל־יְרוּשָׁלָ͏ִם:
10 וְשָׁפַכְתִּי עַל־בֵּית דָּוִיד וְעַל יוֹשֵׁב
יְרוּשָׁלַ͏ִם רוּחַ חֵן וְתַחֲנוּנִים וְהִבִּיטוּ אֵלַי
אֵת אֲשֶׁר־דָּקָרוּ וְסָפְדוּ עָלָיו כְּמִסְפֵּד עַל־
הַיָּחִיד וְהָמֵר עָלָיו כְּהָמֵר עַל־הַבְּכוֹר:
11 בַּיּוֹם הַהוּא יִגְדַּל הַמִּסְפֵּד בִּירוּשָׁלַ͏ִם
כְּמִסְפַּד הֲדַד־רִמּוֹן בְּבִקְעַת מְגִדּוֹן:
12 וְסָפְדָה הָאָרֶץ מִשְׁפָּחוֹת מִשְׁפָּחוֹת לְבָד
מִשְׁפַּחַת בֵּית־דָּוִיד לְבָד וּנְשֵׁיהֶם לְבָד
מִשְׁפַּחַת בֵּית־נָתָן לְבָד וּנְשֵׁיהֶם לְבָד:

---

a-a   Emendation yields "open the eyes of Judah while I strike all."
b-b   Emendation yields "We will save the dwellers of Jerusalem with the help of."
c   Emendation yields "safety."
d-d   For the idiom cf. Gen. 43.30; it is also attested in postbiblical Hebrew.
e   Meaning of Heb. uncertain.
f   Usually "Megiddo."

House of Levi by themselves, and their womenfolk by themselves; the family of the Shimeites
by themselves, and their womenfolk by themselves; [14]and all the other families, every family
by itself, with their womenfolk by themselves.[g]

13 In that day a fountain shall be open to
the House of David and the inhabitants of Jerusalem for purging and cleansing.

[2]In that day, too—declares the LORD of
Hosts—I will erase the very names of the idols
from the land; they shall not be uttered any
more. And I will also make the "prophets" and
the [a]unclean spirit[a] vanish from the land. [3]If
anyone "prophesies" thereafter, his own father
and mother, who brought him into the world,
will say to him, "You shall die, for you have lied
in the name of the LORD"; and his own father
and mother, who brought him into the world,
will put him to death when he "prophesies." [4]In
that day, every "prophet" will be ashamed of the
"visions" [he had] when he "prophesied." In order to deceive, he[b] will not wear a hairy mantle,[c]
[5]and he will declare, "I am not a 'prophet'; [d]I
am a tiller of the soil;[d] you see, [e]I was plied with
the red stuff[e] from my youth on." [6]And if he
is asked, "What are those[f] sores on your back?"[f]
he will reply, "From being beaten in the homes
of my friends."[g]

[7][h]O sword!
Rouse yourself against My shepherd,

---

g   *In this way, apparently, they will prevail upon the LORD to spare
the remnant of the besieging nations; cf. v. 10.*

a-a   *To which abnormal human behavior was attributed.*
b   *Heb. "They."*
c   *In imitation of Elijah; cf. 2 Kings 1.8.*
d-d   *I.e., I was addicted to wine like Noah, the tiller of the soil (cf.
Gen. 9.20–21), hence my hallucinations and ravings; cf. Prov.
23.33.*
e-e   *Connecting 'adam with 'adom "red" (cf. Prov. 23.31); but
meaning of Heb. uncertain.*
f-f   *Lit. "sores between your arms"; cf. 2 Kings 9.24. Sores are
sometimes symptoms of hysteria.*
g   *Presumably for making drunken scenes; cf. Prov. 23.35.*
h   *Vv. 7–9 would read well after 11.17.*

1401

---

13 מִשְׁפַּ֧חַת בֵּית־לֵוִ֛י לְבָ֖ד וּנְשֵׁיהֶ֣ם לְבָ֑ד
מִשְׁפַּ֣חַת הַשִּׁמְעִ֔י לְבָ֖ד וּנְשֵׁיהֶ֥ם לְבָֽד׃
14 כֹּ֗ל הַמִּשְׁפָּחוֹת֙ הַנִּשְׁאָר֔וֹת מִשְׁפָּחֹ֥ת
מִשְׁפָּחֹ֖ת לְבָ֑ד וּנְשֵׁיהֶ֖ם לְבָֽד׃ ס

יג בַּיּ֣וֹם הַה֗וּא יִֽהְיֶה֙ מָק֣וֹר נִפְתָּ֔ח
לְבֵ֥ית דָּוִ֖יד וּלְיֹשְׁבֵ֣י יְרוּשָׁלָ֑͏ִם לְחַטַּ֖את
וּלְנִדָּֽה׃

2 וְהָיָה֩ בַיּ֨וֹם הַה֜וּא נְאֻ֣ם ׀ יְהוָ֣ה צְבָא֗וֹת
אַכְרִ֞ית אֶת־שְׁמ֤וֹת הָֽעֲצַבִּים֙ מִן־הָאָ֔רֶץ
וְלֹ֥א יִזָּכְר֖וּ ע֑וֹד וְגַ֧ם אֶת־הַנְּבִיאִ֛ים וְאֶת־
ר֥וּחַ הַטֻּמְאָ֖ה אַעֲבִ֥יר מִן־הָאָֽרֶץ׃ 3 וְהָיָ֗ה
כִּֽי־יִנָּבֵ֣א אִישׁ֮ עוֹד֒ וְאָמְר֣וּ אֵלָ֗יו אָבִ֤יו
וְאִמּוֹ֙ יֹֽלְדָ֔יו לֹ֣א תִֽחְיֶ֔ה כִּ֛י שֶׁ֥קֶר דִּבַּ֖רְתָּ
בְּשֵׁ֣ם יְהוָ֑ה וּדְקָרֻ֜הוּ אָבִ֧יהוּ וְאִמּ֛וֹ יֹלְדָ֖יו
בְּהִנָּֽבְאֽוֹ׃ 4 וְהָיָ֣ה ׀ בַּיּ֣וֹם הַה֗וּא יֵבֹ֛שׁוּ
הַנְּבִיאִ֛ים אִ֥ישׁ מֵחֶזְיֹנ֖וֹ בְּהִנָּֽבְא֑וֹ וְלֹ֧א
יִלְבְּשׁ֛וּ אַדֶּ֥רֶת שֵׂעָ֖ר לְמַ֥עַן כַּחֵֽשׁ׃ 5 וְאָמַ֕ר
לֹ֥א נָבִ֖יא אָנֹ֑כִי אִישׁ־עֹבֵ֤ד אֲדָמָה֙ אָנֹ֔כִי
כִּ֥י אָדָ֖ם הִקְנַ֥נִי מִנְּעוּרָֽי׃ 6 וְאָמַ֣ר אֵלָ֔יו מָ֧ה
הַמַּכּ֛וֹת הָאֵ֖לֶּה בֵּ֣ין יָדֶ֑יךָ וְאָמַ֕ר אֲשֶׁ֥ר
הֻכֵּ֖יתִי בֵּ֥ית מְאַהֲבָֽי׃ ס

7 חֶ֗רֶב
ע֤וּרִי עַל־רֹעִי֙

The man i-in charge of My flock-i
      —says the LORD of Hosts.
Strike down the shepherd
And let the flock scatter;
And I will also turn My hand
Against all the shepherd boys.
⁸Throughout the land
      —declares the LORD—
Two-thirds shall perish, shall die,
And one-third of it shall survive.
⁹That third I will put into the fire,
And I will smelt them as one smelts silver
And test them as one tests gold.
They will invoke Me by name,
And I will respond to them.
I will declare, "You are My people,"
And they will declare,
"The LORD is our God!"

וְעַל־גֶּבֶר עֲמִיתִי
נְאֻם יְהֹוָה צְבָאֹות
הַךְ אֶת־הָרֹעֶה
וּתְפוּצֶיןָ הַצֹּאן
וַהֲשִׁבֹתִי יָדִי
עַל־הַצֹּעֲרִים:
⁸וְהָיָה בְכָל־הָאָרֶץ
נְאֻם־יְהֹוָה
פִּי־שְׁנַיִם בָּהּ יִכָּרְתוּ יִגְוָעוּ
וְהַשְּׁלִשִׁית יִוָּתֶר בָּהּ:
⁹וְהֵבֵאתִי אֶת־הַשְּׁלִשִׁית בָּאֵשׁ
וּצְרַפְתִּים כִּצְרֹף אֶת־הַכֶּסֶף
וּבְחַנְתִּים כִּבְחֹן אֶת־הַזָּהָב
הוּא | יִקְרָא בִשְׁמִי
וַאֲנִי אֶעֱנֶה אֹתֹו
אָמַרְתִּי עַמִּי הוּא
וְהוּא יֹאמַר
יְהֹוָה אֱלֹהָי: ס

14 Lo, a day of the LORD is coming when yourᵃ spoil shall be divided in your very midst! ²For I will gather all the nations to Jerusalem for war: The city shall be captured, the houses plundered, and the women violated; and a part of the city shall go into exile. But the rest of the population shall not be uprooted from the city.

³Then the LORD will come forth and make war on those nations as He is wont to make war on a day of battle. ⁴On that day, He will set His feet on the Mount of Olives, near Jerusalem on the east; and the Mount of Olives shall split across from east to west, and one part of the Mount shall shift to the north and the other to the south, a huge gorge. ⁵ᵇAnd the Valley in the Hills shall be stopped up, for the Valley of the Hills

יד הִנֵּה יֹום־בָּא לַיהֹוָה וְחֻלַּק שְׁלָלֵךְ
בְּקִרְבֵּךְ: ²וְאָסַפְתִּי אֶת־כָּל־הַגֹּויִם | אֶל־
יְרוּשָׁלַם לַמִּלְחָמָה וְנִלְכְּדָה הָעִיר וְנָשַׁסּוּ
הַבָּתִּים וְהַנָּשִׁים תשגלנה תִּשָּׁכַבְנָה וְיָצָא
חֲצִי הָעִיר בַּגֹּולָה וְיֶתֶר הָעָם לֹא יִכָּרֵת
מִן־הָעִיר:
³וְיָצָא יְהֹוָה וְנִלְחַם בַּגֹּויִם הָהֵם כְּיֹום
הִלָּחֲמֹו בְּיֹום קְרָב: ⁴וְעָמְדוּ רַגְלָיו בַּיֹּום־
הַהוּא עַל־הַר הַזֵּתִים אֲשֶׁר עַל־פְּנֵי
יְרוּשָׁלַם מִקֶּדֶם וְנִבְקַע הַר הַזֵּיתִים מֵחֶצְיֹו
מִזְרָחָה וָיָמָּה גֵּיא גְדֹולָה מְאֹד וּמָשׁ חֲצִי
הָהָר צָפֹונָה וְחֶצְיֹו־נֶגְבָּה: ⁵וְנַסְתֶּם גֵּיא־
הָרַי כִּי־יַגִּיעַ גֵּי־הָרִים אֶל־אָצַל וְנַסְתֶּם

---

i-i   *Meaning of Heb. uncertain.*

a   *Jerusalem is addressed.*

b   *Vocalizing [we] nistam with Targum, Septuagint, and an old Heb. ms. Other mss. and printed editions read, "You [pl.] shall flee [to] the Valley in the Hills, for the Valley of the Hills shall reach up to Azal. You shall flee as you fled because of the earthquake…"*

1402

shall reach only to Azal; it shall be stopped up as it was stopped up as a result of the earthquake in the days of King Uzziah of Judah.—And the LORD my God, with all the holy beings, will come to you.

6cIn that day, there shall be neither sunlight nor cold moonlight, 7but there shall be a continuous day—only the LORD knows when—of neither day nor night, and there shall be light at eventide.

8In that day, fresh water shall flow from Jerusalem, part of it to the Eastern Sea*d* and part to the Western Sea,*e* throughout the summer and winter.

9And the LORD shall be king over all the earth; in that day there shall be one LORD with one name.*f*

10Then the whole country shall become like the Arabah,*g* *h*-from Geba to Rimmon south of Jerusalem.-*h* The latter, however, shall perch high up where it is, and *i*-shall be inhabited-*i* from the Gate of Benjamin to the site of the Old Gate, down to the Corner Gate, and from the Tower of Hananel to the king's winepresses. 11Never again shall destruction be decreed, and Jerusalem shall dwell secure.

12As for those peoples that warred against Jerusalem, the LORD will smite them with this plague: Their flesh shall rot away while they stand on their feet; their eyes shall rot away in their sockets; and their tongues shall rot away in their mouths.

13In that day, a great panic from the LORD shall fall upon them, and everyone shall snatch at the hand of another, and everyone shall raise his hand against everyone else's hand. 14Judah shall join the fighting in Jerusalem, and the

כַּאֲשֶׁר נַסְתֶּם מִפְּנֵי הָרַעַשׁ בִּימֵי עֻזִּיָּה מֶלֶךְ־יְהוּדָה וּבָא יְהוָה אֱלֹהַי כָּל־קְדֹשִׁים עִמָּךְ׃

6 וְהָיָה בַּיּוֹם הַהוּא לֹא־יִהְיֶה אוֹר יְקָרוֹת יקפאון וְקִפָּאוֹן׃ 7 וְהָיָה יוֹם־אֶחָד הוּא יִוָּדַע לַיהוָה לֹא־יוֹם וְלֹא־לָיְלָה וְהָיָה לְעֵת־עֶרֶב יִהְיֶה־אוֹר׃

8 וְהָיָה ׀ בַּיּוֹם הַהוּא יֵצְאוּ מַיִם־חַיִּים מִירוּשָׁלַ͏ִם חֶצְיָם אֶל־הַיָּם הַקַּדְמוֹנִי וְחֶצְיָם אֶל־הַיָּם הָאַחֲרוֹן בַּקַּיִץ וּבָחֹרֶף יִהְיֶה׃

9 וְהָיָה יְהוָה לְמֶלֶךְ עַל־כָּל־הָאָרֶץ בַּיּוֹם הַהוּא יִהְיֶה יְהוָה אֶחָד וּשְׁמוֹ אֶחָד׃

10 יִסּוֹב כָּל־הָאָרֶץ כָּעֲרָבָה מִגֶּבַע לְרִמּוֹן נֶגֶב יְרוּשָׁלָ͏ִם וְרָאֲמָה וְיָשְׁבָה תַחְתֶּיהָ לְמִשַּׁעַר בִּנְיָמִן עַד־מְקוֹם שַׁעַר הָרִאשׁוֹן עַד־שַׁעַר הַפִּנִּים וּמִגְדַּל חֲנַנְאֵל עַד יִקְבֵי הַמֶּלֶךְ׃ 11 וְיָשְׁבוּ בָהּ וְחֵרֶם לֹא יִהְיֶה־עוֹד וְיָשְׁבָה יְרוּשָׁלַ͏ִם לָבֶטַח׃

12 וְזֹאת ׀ תִּהְיֶה הַמַּגֵּפָה אֲשֶׁר יִגֹּף יְהוָה אֶת־כָּל־הָעַמִּים אֲשֶׁר צָבְאוּ עַל־יְרוּשָׁלָ͏ִם הָמֵק ׀ בְּשָׂרוֹ וְהוּא עֹמֵד עַל־רַגְלָיו וְעֵינָיו תִּמַּקְנָה בְחֹרֵיהֶן וּלְשׁוֹנוֹ תִּמַּק בְּפִיהֶם׃

13 וְהָיָה בַּיּוֹם הַהוּא תִּהְיֶה מְהוּמַת־יְהוָה רַבָּה בָּהֶם וְהֶחֱזִיקוּ אִישׁ יַד רֵעֵהוּ וְעָלְתָה יָדוֹ עַל־יַד רֵעֵהוּ׃ 14 וְגַם־יְהוּדָה תִּלָּחֵם

---

c   *Meaning of verse uncertain; cf. Job 21.26.*
d   *I.e., the Dead Sea; cf. Joel 2.20.*
e   *I.e., the Mediterranean Sea; cf. Joel 2.20.*
f   *I.e., the LORD alone shall be worshiped and shall be invoked by His true name.*
g   *I.e., shall be depressed like the Jordan Valley.*
h-h *I.e., from the northern border of the Kingdom of Judah (1 Kings 15.22; 2 Kings 23.8) to the southern border (Josh. 15.32; 19.7).*
i-i *Brought up from v. 11 for clarity.*

wealth of all the nations roundabout—vast quantities of gold, silver, and clothing—shall be gathered in.

[15]The same plague shall strike the horses, the mules, the camels, and the asses; the plague shall affect all the animals in those camps.

[16]All who survive of all those nations that came up against Jerusalem shall make a pilgrimage year by year to bow low to the King Lord of Hosts and to observe the Feast of Booths. [17]Any of the earth's communities that does not make the pilgrimage to Jerusalem to bow low to the King Lord of Hosts shall receive no rain. [18]However, if the community of Egypt does not make this pilgrimage, it shall not be visited by the same affliction with which the Lord will strike the other nations that do not come up to observe the Feast of Booths.*j* [19]Such shall be the punishment of Egypt and of all other nations that do not come up to observe the Feast of Booths.

[20]In that day, even the bells on the horses shall be inscribed "Holy to the Lord." The metal pots in the House of the Lord shall be like the basins before the altar; [21]indeed, every metal pot in Jerusalem and in Judah shall be holy to the Lord of Hosts. And all those who sacrifice shall come and take of these to boil [their sacrificial meat] in; in that day there shall be no more traders*k* in the House of the Lord of Hosts.

בִּירוּשָׁלָ֑͏ִם וְאָסַף֩ חֵ֨יל כָּל־הַגּוֹיִ֜ם סָבִ֗יב זָהָ֧ב וָכֶ֛סֶף וּבְגָדִ֖ים לָרֹ֥ב מְאֹֽד: [15]וְכֵ֨ן תִּֽהְיֶ֜ה מַגֵּפַ֣ת הַסּ֗וּס הַפֶּ֨רֶד֙ הַגָּמָ֣ל וְהַֽחֲמ֔וֹר וְכָל־הַ֨בְּהֵמָ֔ה אֲשֶׁ֥ר יִֽהְיֶ֖ה בַּֽמַּֽחֲנ֣וֹת הָהֵ֑מָּה כַּמַּגֵּפָ֖ה הַזֹּֽאת: [16]וְהָיָ֗ה כָּל־הַנּוֹתָר֙ מִכָּל־הַגּוֹיִ֔ם הַבָּאִ֖ים עַל־יְרֽוּשָׁלָ֑͏ִם וְעָל֞וּ מִדֵּ֧י שָׁנָ֣ה בְשָׁנָ֗ה לְהִֽשְׁתַּֽחֲוֺת֙ לְמֶ֨לֶךְ֙ יְהֹוָ֣ה צְבָא֔וֹת וְלָחֹ֖ג אֶת־חַ֥ג הַסֻּכּֽוֹת: [17]וְ֠הָיָ֠ה אֲשֶׁ֨ר לֹֽא־יַֽעֲלֶ֜ה מֵאֵ֨ת מִשְׁפְּח֤וֹת הָאָ֨רֶץ֙ אֶל־יְר֣וּשָׁלַ֔͏ִם לְהִֽשְׁתַּֽחֲוֺ֔ת לְמֶ֖לֶךְ יְהֹוָ֣ה צְבָא֑וֹת וְלֹ֥א עֲלֵיהֶ֖ם יִֽהְיֶ֥ה הַגָּֽשֶׁם: [18]וְאִם־מִשְׁפַּ֨חַת מִצְרַ֧יִם לֹֽא־תַֽעֲלֶ֛ה וְלֹ֥א בָ֨אָה֙ וְלֹ֣א עֲלֵיהֶ֔ם תִּֽהְיֶ֣ה הַמַּגֵּפָ֗ה אֲשֶׁ֨ר יִגֹּ֤ף יְהֹוָה֙ אֶת־הַגּוֹיִ֔ם אֲשֶׁר֙ לֹ֣א יַֽעֲל֔וּ לָחֹ֖ג אֶת־חַ֥ג הַסֻּכּֽוֹת: [19]זֹ֥את תִּֽהְיֶ֖ה חַטַּ֣את מִצְרָ֑יִם וְחַטַּאת֙ כָּל־הַגּוֹיִ֔ם אֲשֶׁר֙ לֹ֣א יַֽעֲל֔וּ לָחֹ֖ג אֶת־חַ֥ג הַסֻּכּֽוֹת: [20]בַּיּ֣וֹם הַה֗וּא יִֽהְיֶה֙ עַל־מְצִלּ֣וֹת הַסּ֔וּס קֹ֖דֶשׁ לַֽיהֹוָ֑ה וְהָיָ֤ה הַסִּירוֹת֙ בְּבֵ֣ית יְהֹוָ֔ה כַּמִּזְרָקִ֖ים לִפְנֵ֥י הַמִּזְבֵּֽחַ: [21]וְ֠הָיָ֠ה כָּל־סִ֨יר בִּירֽוּשָׁלַ֜͏ִם וּבִֽיהוּדָ֗ה קֹ֚דֶשׁ לַֽיהֹוָ֣ה צְבָא֔וֹת וּבָ֨אוּ֙ כָּל־הַזֹּ֣בְחִ֔ים וְלָֽקְח֥וּ מֵהֶ֖ם וּבִשְּׁל֣וּ בָהֶ֑ם וְלֹֽא־יִהְיֶ֨ה כְנַֽעֲנִ֥י ע֛וֹד בְּבֵית־יְהֹוָ֥ה צְבָא֖וֹת בַּיּ֥וֹם הַהֽוּא:

---

j Because Egypt is not dependent on rain, it will suffer some other punishment, presumably that described in v. 12.

k To sell ritually pure vessels.

MALACHI

1 A pronouncement: The word of the Lord to Israel through Malachi.

2I have shown you love, said the Lord. But you ask, "How have You shown us love?" After all—declares the Lord—Esau is Jacob's brother; yet I have accepted Jacob 3and have rejected Esau. I have made his hills a desolation, his territory *a-a home for beasts-a* of the desert. 4If Edom thinks, "Though crushed, we can build the ruins again," thus said the Lord of Hosts: They may build, but I will tear down. And so they shall be known as the region of wickedness, the people damned forever of the Lord. 5Your eyes shall behold it, and you shall declare, "Great is the Lord beyond the borders of Israel!"

6A son should honor his father, and a slave*b* his master. Now if I am a father, where is the honor due Me? And if I am a master, where is the reverence due Me?—said the Lord of Hosts to you, O priests who scorn My name. But you ask, "How have we scorned Your name?" 7You offer defiled food on My altar. But you ask, "How have we defiled You?"*c* By saying, "The table of the Lord can be treated with scorn." 8When you present a blind animal for sacrifice—it doesn't matter! When you present a lame or sick one—it doesn't matter! Just offer it to your governor: Will he accept you? Will he show you favor?—said the Lord of Hosts. 9And now implore the favor of God! Will He

א מַשָּׂא דְבַר־יְהֹוָה אֶל־יִשְׂרָאֵל בְּיַד
מַלְאָכִי:

2 אָהַבְתִּי אֶתְכֶם אָמַר יְהֹוָה וַאֲמַרְתֶּם
בַּמָּה אֲהַבְתָּנוּ הֲלוֹא־אָח עֵשָׂו לְיַעֲקֹב
נְאֻם־יְהֹוָה וָאֹהַב אֶת־יַעֲקֹב: 3 וְאֶת־עֵשָׂו
שָׂנֵאתִי וָאָשִׂים אֶת־הָרָיו שְׁמָמָה וְאֶת־
נַחֲלָתוֹ לְתַנּוֹת מִדְבָּר: 4 כִּי־תֹאמַר אֱדוֹם
רֻשַּׁשְׁנוּ וְנָשׁוּב וְנִבְנֶה חֳרָבוֹת כֹּה אָמַר
יְהֹוָה צְבָאוֹת הֵמָּה יִבְנוּ וַאֲנִי אֶהֱרוֹס
וְקָרְאוּ לָהֶם גְּבוּל רִשְׁעָה וְהָעָם אֲשֶׁר־זָעַם
יְהֹוָה עַד־עוֹלָם: 5 וְעֵינֵיכֶם תִּרְאֶינָה
וְאַתֶּם תֹּאמְרוּ יִגְדַּל יְהֹוָה מֵעַל לִגְבוּל
יִשְׂרָאֵל:

6 בֵּן יְכַבֵּד אָב וְעֶבֶד אֲדֹנָיו וְאִם־אָב אָנִי
אַיֵּה כְבוֹדִי וְאִם־אֲדוֹנִים אָנִי אַיֵּה מוֹרָאִי
אָמַר | יְהֹוָה צְבָאוֹת לָכֶם הַכֹּהֲנִים
בּוֹזֵי שְׁמִי וַאֲמַרְתֶּם בַּמֶּה בָזִינוּ אֶת־
שְׁמֶךָ: 7 מַגִּישִׁים עַל־מִזְבְּחִי לֶחֶם מְגֹאָל
וַאֲמַרְתֶּם בַּמֶּה גֵאַלְנוּךָ בֶּאֱמָרְכֶם שֻׁלְחַן
יְהֹוָה נִבְזֶה הוּא: 8 וְכִי־תַגִּשׁוּן עִוֵּר לִזְבֹּחַ
אֵין רָע וְכִי תַגִּישׁוּ פִּסֵּחַ וְחֹלֶה אֵין רָע
הַקְרִיבֵהוּ נָא לְפֶחָתֶךָ הֲיִרְצְךָ אוֹ הֲיִשָּׂא
פָנֶיךָ אָמַר יְהֹוָה צְבָאוֹת: 9 וְעַתָּה חַלּוּ־נָא

---

a-a Meaning of Heb. uncertain.
b Septuagint and Targum add "should reverence"; cf. next part of verse.
c Septuagint "it."

be gracious to us? This is what you have done—will He accept any of you?

The Lord of Hosts has said: [10]If only you would lock My doors, and not kindle fire on My altar to no purpose! I take no pleasure in you—said the Lord of Hosts—and I will accept no offering from you. [11]For from where the sun rises to where it sets, My name is honored among the nations, and everywhere incense and pure oblation are offered to My name; for My name is honored among the nations—said the Lord of Hosts. [12]But you profane it when you say, "The table of the Lord is defiled and the meat,[a] the food, can be treated with scorn." [13]You say, "Oh, what a bother!" And so you degrade[a] it—said the Lord of Hosts—and you bring the stolen, the lame, and the sick; and you offer such as an oblation. Will I accept it from you?—said the Lord.

[14]A curse on the cheat who has an [unblemished] male in his flock, but for his vow sacrifices a blemished animal to the Lord! For I am a great King—said the Lord of Hosts—and My name is revered among the nations.

2 And now, O priests, this charge is for you: [2]Unless you obey and unless you lay it to heart, and do honor to My name—said the Lord of Hosts—I will send a curse and turn your blessings into curses. (Indeed, I have turned them into curses, because you do not lay it to heart.) [3]I will [a]-put your seed under a ban,-[a] and I will strew dung upon your faces, the dung of your festal sacrifices, and you shall be carried out to its [heap].

[4]Know, then, that I have sent this charge to you that My covenant with Levi may endure—said the Lord of Hosts. [5]I had with him a covenant of life and well-being, which I gave to

פָּנֶי־אֵל וִיחׇנֵּנוּ מִיֶּדְכֶם הָיְתָה זֹּאת הֲיִשָּׂא מִכֶּם פָּנִים

אָמַר יְהֹוָה צְבָאֽוֹת: [10] מִי גַם־בָּכֶם וְיִסְגֹּר דְּלָתַיִם וְלֹא־תָאִירוּ מִזְבְּחִי חִנָּם אֵין־לִי חֵפֶץ בָּכֶם אָמַר יְהֹוָה צְבָאוֹת וּמִנְחָה לֹא־אֶרְצֶה מִיֶּדְכֶם: [11] כִּי מִמִּזְרַח־שֶׁמֶשׁ וְעַד־מְבוֹאוֹ גָּדוֹל שְׁמִי בַּגּוֹיִם וּבְכׇל־מָקוֹם מֻקְטָר מֻגָּשׁ לִשְׁמִי וּמִנְחָה טְהוֹרָה כִּי־ גָדוֹל שְׁמִי בַּגּוֹיִם אָמַר יְהֹוָה צְבָאֽוֹת: [12] וְאַתֶּם מְחַלְּלִים אוֹתוֹ בֶּאֱמׇרְכֶם שֻׁלְחַן אֲדֹנָי מְגֹאָל הוּא וְנִיבוֹ נִבְזֶה אׇכְלֽוֹ: [13] וַאֲמַרְתֶּם הִנֵּה מַתְּלָאָה וְהִפַּחְתֶּם אוֹתוֹ אָמַר יְהֹוָה צְבָאוֹת וַהֲבֵאתֶם גָּזוּל וְאֶת־ הַפִּסֵּחַ וְאֶת־הַחוֹלֶה וַהֲבֵאתֶם אֶת־ הַמִּנְחָה הַאֶרְצֶה אוֹתָהּ מִיֶּדְכֶם אָמַר יְהֹוָה: ס

[14] וְאָרוּר נוֹכֵל וְיֵשׁ בְּעֶדְרוֹ זָכָר וְנֹדֵר וְזֹבֵחַ מׇשְׁחָת לַאדֹנָי כִּי מֶלֶךְ גָּדוֹל אָנִי אָמַר יְהֹוָה צְבָאוֹת וּשְׁמִי נוֹרָא בַגּוֹיִֽם:

ב וְעַתָּה אֲלֵיכֶם הַמִּצְוָה הַזֹּאת הַכֹּהֲנִים: [2] אִם־לֹא תִשְׁמְעוּ וְאִם־לֹא תָשִׂימוּ עַל־לֵב לָתֵת כָּבוֹד לִשְׁמִי אָמַר יְהֹוָה צְבָאוֹת וְשִׁלַּחְתִּי בָכֶם אֶת־הַמְּאֵרָה וְאָרוֹתִי אֶת־בִּרְכוֹתֵיכֶם וְגַם אָרוֹתִיהָ כִּי אֵינְכֶם שָׂמִים עַל־לֵב: [3] הִנְנִי גֹעֵר לָכֶם אֶת־הַזֶּרַע וְזֵרִיתִי פֶרֶשׁ עַל־פְּנֵיכֶם פֶּרֶשׁ חַגֵּיכֶם וְנָשָׂא אֶתְכֶם אֵלָיו:

[4] וִידַעְתֶּם כִּי שִׁלַּחְתִּי אֲלֵיכֶם אֵת הַמִּצְוָה הַזֹּאת לִהְיוֹת בְּרִיתִי אֶת־לֵוִי אָמַר יְהֹוָה צְבָאוֹת: [5] בְּרִיתִי | הָיְתָה אִתּוֹ הַחַיִּים

a-a   *Meaning of Heb. uncertain.*

him, and of reverence, which he showed Me.
For he stood in awe of My name.
6bProper rulings were in his mouth,
And nothing perverse was on his lips;
He served Me with complete loyalty
And held the many back from iniquity.
7c-For the lips of a priest guard knowledge,
And men seek rulings from his mouth;-c
For he is a messenger of the LORD of Hosts.
8But you have turned away from that course:
You have made the many stumble through your
rulings;d you have corrupted the covenant of
the Levites—said the LORD of Hosts. 9And I, in
turn, have made you despicable and vile in the
eyes of all the people, because you disregard My
ways and show partiality in your rulings.

10Have we not all one Father? Did not one
God create us? Why do we break faith with one
another, profaning the covenant of our ancestors? 11Judah has broken faith; abhorrent things
have been done in Israel and in Jerusalem. For
Judah has profaned what is holy to the LORD—
what He desires—and espoused daughters of
alien gods. 12May the LORD leave to him who
does this a-no descendants-a dwelling in the tents
of Jacob and presenting offerings to the LORD
of Hosts. 13And this you do e-as well:-e You cover
the altar of the LORD with tears, weeping, and
moaning, so that He refuses to regard the oblation any more and to accept f-what you offer.-f
14But you ask, "Because of what?" Because the
LORD is a witness between you and the wife of
your youth with whom you have broken faith,
though she is your partner and covenanted
spouse. 15Did not the One make [all,] a-so that
all remaining life-breath is His? And what does

וְהַשָּׁלוֹם וָאֶתְּנֶם־לוֹ מוֹרָא וַיִּירָאֵנִי וּמִפְּנֵי
שְׁמִי נִחַת הוּא:
6 תּוֹרַת אֱמֶת הָיְתָה בְּפִיהוּ
וְעַוְלָה לֹא־נִמְצָא בִשְׂפָתָיו
בְּשָׁלוֹם וּבְמִישׁוֹר הָלַךְ אִתִּי
וְרַבִּים הֵשִׁיב מֵעָוֺן:
7 כִּי־שִׂפְתֵי כֹהֵן יִשְׁמְרוּ־דַעַת
וְתוֹרָה יְבַקְשׁוּ מִפִּיהוּ
כִּי מַלְאַךְ יְהוָה־צְבָאוֹת הוּא:
8 וְאַתֶּם סַרְתֶּם מִן־הַדֶּרֶךְ הִכְשַׁלְתֶּם
רַבִּים בַּתּוֹרָה שִׁחַתֶּם בְּרִית הַלֵּוִי אָמַר
יְהוָה צְבָאוֹת: 9 וְגַם־אֲנִי נָתַתִּי אֶתְכֶם
נִבְזִים וּשְׁפָלִים לְכָל־הָעָם כְּפִי אֲשֶׁר
אֵינְכֶם שֹׁמְרִים אֶת־דְּרָכַי וְנֹשְׂאִים פָּנִים
בַּתּוֹרָה: פ

10 הֲלוֹא אָב אֶחָד לְכֻלָּנוּ הֲלוֹא אֵל אֶחָד
בְּרָאָנוּ מַדּוּעַ נִבְגַּד אִישׁ בְּאָחִיו לְחַלֵּל
בְּרִית אֲבֹתֵינוּ: 11 בָּגְדָה יְהוּדָה וְתוֹעֵבָה
נֶעֶשְׂתָה בְיִשְׂרָאֵל וּבִירוּשָׁלָ͏ִם כִּי ׀ חִלֵּל
יְהוּדָה קֹדֶשׁ יְהוָה אֲשֶׁר אָהֵב וּבָעַל
בַּת־אֵל נֵכָר: 12 יַכְרֵת יְהוָה לָאִישׁ אֲשֶׁר
יַעֲשֶׂנָּה עֵר וְעֹנֶה מֵאׇהֳלֵי יַעֲקֹב וּמַגִּישׁ
מִנְחָה לַיהוָה צְבָאוֹת: פ 13 וְזֹאת
שֵׁנִית תַּעֲשׂוּ כַּסּוֹת דִּמְעָה אֶת־מִזְבַּח
יְהוָה בְּכִי וַאֲנָקָה מֵאֵין עוֹד פְּנוֹת
אֶל־הַמִּנְחָה וְלָקַחַת רָצוֹן מִיֶּדְכֶם:
14 וַאֲמַרְתֶּם עַל־מָה עַל כִּי־יְהוָה הֵעִיד
בֵּינְךָ וּבֵין ׀ אֵשֶׁת נְעוּרֶיךָ אֲשֶׁר אַתָּה
בָּגַדְתָּה בָּהּ וְהִיא חֲבֶרְתְּךָ וְאֵשֶׁת בְּרִיתֶךָ:
15 וְלֹא־אֶחָד עָשָׂה וּשְׁאָר רוּחַ לוֹ וּמָה

---

b   See Hag. 2.10–13; cf. Lev. 10.8–11, Deut. 33.8, 10.
c-c Or: For the lips of a priest are observed; / Knowledge and ruling
     are sought from his mouth.
d   By ruling falsely that an act was licit or an object ritually pure.
e-e Lit. "a second time"; Septuagint reads "which I detest"; cf.
     v. 16.
f-f Lit. "from your hand."

that One seek but godly folk? So be careful of your life-breath,-*a* and let no one break faith with the wife of his youth. [16]For I detest divorce—said the Lord, the God of Israel—*a*-and covering oneself with lawlessness as with a garment-*a*—said the Lord of Hosts. So be careful of your life-breath and do not act treacherously.

[17]You have wearied the Lord with your talk. But you ask, "By what have we wearied [Him]?" By saying, "All who do evil are good in the sight of the Lord, and in them He delights," or else, "Where is the God of justice?"

3 Behold, I am sending My messenger to clear the way before Me, and the Lord whom you seek shall come to His Temple suddenly. As for the angel of the covenant*a* that you desire, he is already coming. [2]But who can endure the day of his coming, and who can hold out when he appears? For he is like a smelter's fire and like fuller's lye. [3]He shall act*b* like a smelter and purger of silver; and he shall purify the descendants of Levi and refine them like gold and silver, so that they shall present offerings in righteousness. [4]Then the offerings of Judah and Jerusalem shall be pleasing to the Lord as in the days of yore and in the years of old. [5]But [first] I will step forward to contend against you, and I will act as a relentless accuser against those who have no fear of Me: Who practice sorcery, who commit adultery, who swear falsely, who cheat laborers of their hire, and who subvert [the cause of] the widow, orphan, and stranger, said the Lord of Hosts.

[6c]For I am the Lord—I have not changed; and you are the children of Jacob—you have not

הָאֶחָד מְבַקֵּשׁ זֶרַע אֱלֹהִים וְנִשְׁמַרְתֶּם בְּרוּחֲכֶם וּבְאֵשֶׁת נְעוּרֶיךָ אַל־יִבְגֹּד: 16 כִּי־שָׂנֵא שַׁלַּח אָמַר יְהוָה אֱלֹהֵי יִשְׂרָאֵל וְכִסָּה חָמָס עַל־לְבוּשׁוֹ אָמַר יְהוָה צְבָאוֹת וְנִשְׁמַרְתֶּם בְּרוּחֲכֶם וְלֹא תִבְגֹּדוּ: ס

17 הוֹגַעְתֶּם יְהוָה בְּדִבְרֵיכֶם וַאֲמַרְתֶּם בַּמָּה הוֹגָעְנוּ בֶּאֱמָרְכֶם כָּל־עֹשֵׂה רָע טוֹב בְּעֵינֵי יְהוָה וּבָהֶם הוּא חָפֵץ אוֹ אַיֵּה אֱלֹהֵי הַמִּשְׁפָּט:

ג הִנְנִי שֹׁלֵחַ מַלְאָכִי וּפִנָּה־דֶרֶךְ לְפָנָי וּפִתְאֹם יָבוֹא אֶל־הֵיכָלוֹ הָאָדוֹן | אֲשֶׁר־אַתֶּם מְבַקְשִׁים וּמַלְאַךְ הַבְּרִית אֲשֶׁר־אַתֶּם חֲפֵצִים הִנֵּה־בָא אָמַר יְהוָה צְבָאוֹת: 2 וּמִי מְכַלְכֵּל אֶת־יוֹם בּוֹאוֹ וּמִי הָעֹמֵד בְּהֵרָאוֹתוֹ כִּי־הוּא כְּאֵשׁ מְצָרֵף וּכְבֹרִית מְכַבְּסִים: 3 וְיָשַׁב מְצָרֵף וּמְטַהֵר כֶּסֶף וְטִהַר אֶת־בְּנֵי־לֵוִי וְזִקַּק אֹתָם כַּזָּהָב וְכַכָּסֶף וְהָיוּ לַיהוָה מַגִּישֵׁי מִנְחָה בִּצְדָקָה: 4 וְעָרְבָה לַיהוָה מִנְחַת יְהוּדָה וִירוּשָׁלָ͏ִם כִּימֵי עוֹלָם וּכְשָׁנִים קַדְמֹנִיּוֹת: 5 וְקָרַבְתִּי אֲלֵיכֶם לַמִּשְׁפָּט וְהָיִיתִי | עֵד מְמַהֵר בַּמְכַשְּׁפִים וּבַמְנָאֲפִים וּבַנִּשְׁבָּעִים לַשֶּׁקֶר וּבְעֹשְׁקֵי שְׂכַר־שָׂכִיר אַלְמָנָה וְיָתוֹם וּמַטֵּי־גֵר* וְלֹא יְרֵאוּנִי אָמַר יְהוָה צְבָאוֹת:

6 כִּי אֲנִי יְהוָה לֹא שָׁנִיתִי וְאַתֶּם בְּנֵי־יַעֲקֹב לֹא כְלִיתֶם: 7 לְמִימֵי אֲבֹתֵיכֶם סַרְתֶּם

v. 5. ' י' במקום ה

---

a   Apparently the messenger of the previous sentence is regarded as Israel's tutelary angel.
b   Lit. "sit."
c   Vv. 6–12 resume the thought of 1.2–5.

ceased to be. [7]From the very days of your fathers you have turned away from My laws and have not observed them. Turn back to Me, and I will turn back to you—said the LORD of Hosts. But you ask, "How shall we turn back?" [8]Ought man to defraud[d] God? Yet you are defrauding Me. And you ask, "How have we been defrauding You?" In tithe and contribution.[e] [9]You are suffering under a curse, yet you go on defrauding Me—the whole nation of you. [10]Bring the full tithe into the storehouse,[f] and let there be food in My House, and thus put Me to the test—said the LORD of Hosts. I will surely open the floodgates of the sky for you and pour down blessings on you; [11]and I will banish the locusts[g] from you, so that they will not destroy the yield of your soil; and your vines in the field shall no longer miscarry—said the LORD of Hosts. [12]And all the nations shall account you happy, for you shall be the most desired of lands—said the LORD of Hosts.

[13]You have spoken hard words against Me—said the LORD. But you ask, "What have we been saying among ourselves against You?" [14]You have said, "It is useless to serve God. What have we gained by keeping His charge and walking in abject awe of the LORD of Hosts? [15]And so, we account the arrogant happy: they have indeed done evil and endured; they have indeed dared God and escaped." [16]In this vein have those who revere the LORD been talking to one another. The LORD has heard and noted it, and a scroll of remembrance has been written at His behest concerning those who revere the LORD and esteem His name. [17]And on the day that I am preparing, said the LORD of Hosts, they shall be My treasured possession; I will be tender toward them as a man is tender toward a son who

מְחָקִי וְלֹא שְׁמַרְתֶּם שׁוּבוּ אֵלַי וְאָשׁוּבָה אֲלֵיכֶם אָמַר יְהֹוָה צְבָאוֹת וַאֲמַרְתֶּם בַּמֶּה נָשׁוּב: [8] הֲיִקְבַּע אָדָם אֱלֹהִים כִּי אַתֶּם קֹבְעִים אֹתִי וַאֲמַרְתֶּם בַּמֶּה קְבַעֲנוּךָ הַמַּעֲשֵׂר וְהַתְּרוּמָה: [9] בַּמְּאֵרָה אַתֶּם נֵאָרִים וְאֹתִי אַתֶּם קֹבְעִים הַגּוֹי כֻּלּוֹ: [10] הָבִיאוּ אֶת־כָּל־הַמַּעֲשֵׂר אֶל־בֵּית הָאוֹצָר וִיהִי טֶרֶף בְּבֵיתִי וּבְחָנוּנִי נָא בָּזֹאת אָמַר יְהֹוָה צְבָאוֹת אִם־לֹא אֶפְתַּח לָכֶם אֵת אֲרֻבּוֹת הַשָּׁמַיִם וַהֲרִיקֹתִי לָכֶם בְּרָכָה עַד־בְּלִי־דָי: [11] וְגָעַרְתִּי לָכֶם בָּאֹכֵל וְלֹא־יַשְׁחִת לָכֶם אֶת־פְּרִי הָאֲדָמָה וְלֹא־תְשַׁכֵּל לָכֶם הַגֶּפֶן בַּשָּׂדֶה אָמַר יְהֹוָה צְבָאוֹת: [12] וְאִשְּׁרוּ אֶתְכֶם כָּל־הַגּוֹיִם כִּי־תִהְיוּ אַתֶּם אֶרֶץ חֵפֶץ אָמַר יְהֹוָה צְבָאוֹת: ס

[13] חָזְקוּ עָלַי דִּבְרֵיכֶם אָמַר יְהֹוָה וַאֲמַרְתֶּם מַה־נִּדְבַּרְנוּ עָלֶיךָ: [14] אֲמַרְתֶּם שָׁוְא עֲבֹד אֱלֹהִים וּמַה־בֶּצַע כִּי שָׁמַרְנוּ מִשְׁמַרְתּוֹ וְכִי הָלַכְנוּ קְדֹרַנִּית מִפְּנֵי יְהֹוָה צְבָאוֹת: [15] וְעַתָּה אֲנַחְנוּ מְאַשְּׁרִים זֵדִים גַּם־נִבְנוּ עֹשֵׂי רִשְׁעָה גַּם בָּחֲנוּ אֱלֹהִים וַיִּמָּלֵטוּ: [16] אָז נִדְבְּרוּ יִרְאֵי יְהֹוָה אִישׁ אֶת־רֵעֵהוּ וַיַּקְשֵׁב יְהֹוָה וַיִּשְׁמָע וַיִּכָּתֵב סֵפֶר זִכָּרוֹן לְפָנָיו לְיִרְאֵי יְהֹוָה וּלְחֹשְׁבֵי שְׁמוֹ: [17] וְהָיוּ לִי אָמַר יְהֹוָה צְבָאוֹת לַיּוֹם אֲשֶׁר אֲנִי עֹשֶׂה סְגֻלָּה וְחָמַלְתִּי עֲלֵיהֶם כַּאֲשֶׁר יַחְמֹל אִישׁ עַל־בְּנוֹ הָעֹבֵד אֹתוֹ:

---

d   Heb. qaba', a play on the name of Jacob (v. 6); cf. Gen. 27.36.
e   I.e., the contributions to the priests from the new grain, oil, and
     wine; see Num. 18.12.
f   I.e., the public storehouse; see Neh. 13.10–13.
g   Lit. "devourer."

ministers to him. [18]And you shall come to see the difference between the righteous and the wicked, between him who has served God and him who has not served Him.

[19]For lo! That day is at hand, burning like an oven. All the arrogant and all the doers of evil shall be straw, and the day that is coming—said the Lord of Hosts—shall burn them to ashes and leave of them neither stock nor boughs. [20]But for you who revere My name a sun of victory shall rise [h]-to bring healing.-[h] You shall go forth and stamp like stall-fed calves, [21]and you shall trample the wicked to a pulp, for they shall be dust beneath your feet on the day that I am preparing—said the Lord of Hosts.

[22]Be mindful of the Teaching of My servant Moses, whom I charged at Horeb with laws and rules for all Israel.

[23]Lo, I will send the prophet Elijah to you before the coming of the awesome, fearful day of the Lord. [24]He shall reconcile parents with children and children with their parents, so that, when I come, I do not strike the whole land with utter destruction.

Lo, I will send the prophet Elijah to you before the coming of the awesome, fearful day of the Lord.

18 וּשַׁבְתֶּם וּרְאִיתֶם בֵּין צַדִּיק לְרָשָׁע בֵּין עֹבֵד אֱלֹהִים לַאֲשֶׁר לֹא עֲבָדוֹ: ס 19 כִּי־הִנֵּה הַיּוֹם בָּא בֹּעֵר כַּתַּנּוּר וְהָיוּ כָל־זֵדִים וְכָל־עֹשֵׂה רִשְׁעָה קַשׁ וְלִהַט אֹתָם הַיּוֹם הַבָּא אָמַר יְהוָה צְבָאוֹת אֲשֶׁר לֹא־יַעֲזֹב לָהֶם שֹׁרֶשׁ וְעָנָף: 20 וְזָרְחָה לָכֶם יִרְאֵי שְׁמִי שֶׁמֶשׁ צְדָקָה וּמַרְפֵּא בִּכְנָפֶיהָ וִיצָאתֶם וּפִשְׁתֶּם כְּעֶגְלֵי מַרְבֵּק: 21 וְעַסּוֹתֶם רְשָׁעִים כִּי־יִהְיוּ אֵפֶר תַּחַת כַּפּוֹת רַגְלֵיכֶם בַּיּוֹם אֲשֶׁר אֲנִי עֹשֶׂה אָמַר יְהוָה צְבָאוֹת: פ

22 זִכְרוּ תּוֹרַת מֹשֶׁה עַבְדִּי אֲשֶׁר צִוִּיתִי אוֹתוֹ בְחֹרֵב עַל־כָּל־יִשְׂרָאֵל חֻקִּים וּמִשְׁפָּטִים:

23 הִנֵּה אָנֹכִי שֹׁלֵחַ לָכֶם אֵת אֵלִיָּה הַנָּבִיא לִפְנֵי בּוֹא יוֹם יְהוָה הַגָּדוֹל וְהַנּוֹרָא: 24 וְהֵשִׁיב לֵב־אָבוֹת עַל־בָּנִים וְלֵב בָּנִים עַל־אֲבוֹתָם פֶּן־אָבוֹא וְהִכֵּיתִי אֶת־הָאָרֶץ חֵרֶם: * *

[הִנֵּה אָנֹכִי שֹׁלֵחַ לָכֶם אֵת אֵלִיָּה הַנָּבִיא לִפְנֵי בּוֹא יוֹם יְהוָה הַגָּדוֹל וְהַנּוֹרָא:*]

תם ונשלם תהילה לאל בורא עולם

[h-h] Lit. "with healing in the folds of its garments"; others "with healing in its wings."

v. 24. סכום הפסוקים של ספר 1,050 וחציו מיכה 3.12
v. 24. סכום הפסוקים של נביאים 9,285
end. במסורת הקריאה נשנה הפסוק לפני האחרון

KETHUVIM THE WRITINGS

PSALMS	תהילים
PROVERBS	משלי
JOB	איוב
THE SONG OF SONGS	שיר השירים
RUTH	רות
LAMENTATIONS	איכה
ECCLESIASTES	קהלת
ESTHER	אסתר
DANIEL	דניאל
EZRA	עזרא
NEHEMIAH	נחמיה
1 CHRONICLES	דברי הימים א
2 CHRONICLES	דברי הימים ב

PSALMS

תהלים

1 Happy is the man who has not followed the
counsel of the wicked,
or taken the path of sinners,
or joined the company of the insolent;
²rather, the teaching of the Lord is his delight,
and he studies[a] that teaching day and night.
³He is like a tree planted beside streams of water,
which yields its fruit in season,
whose foliage never fades,
and whatever [b]-it produces thrives.-[b]

⁴Not so the wicked;
rather, they are like chaff that wind blows away.
⁵Therefore the wicked will not survive judgment,
nor will sinners, in the assembly of the righteous.
⁶For the Lord cherishes the way of the righteous,
but the way of the wicked is doomed.

2 Why do nations assemble,
and peoples plot[a] vain things;
²kings of the earth take their stand,
and regents intrigue together
against the Lord and against His anointed?
³"Let us break the cords of their yoke,
shake off their ropes from us!"

א *אַשְׁרֵי־הָאִישׁ אֲשֶׁר ׀ לֹא הָלַךְ֙
בַּעֲצַ֪ת רְשָׁעִ֫ים
וּבְדֶ֣רֶךְ חַ֭טָּאִים לֹ֣א עָמָ֑ד
וּבְמוֹשַׁ֥ב לֵ֝צִ֗ים לֹ֣א יָשָֽׁב׃
2 כִּ֤י אִ֥ם בְּתוֹרַ֥ת יְהֹוָ֗ה חֶ֫פְצ֥וֹ
וּֽבְתוֹרָת֥וֹ יֶהְגֶּ֗ה יוֹמָ֥ם וָלָֽיְלָה׃
3 וְֽהָיָ֗ה כְּעֵץ֮ שָׁת֢וּל עַֽל־פַּלְגֵ֫י מָ֥יִם
אֲשֶׁ֤ר פִּרְי֨וֹ ׀ יִתֵּ֬ן בְּעִתּ֗וֹ
וְעָלֵ֥הוּ לֹֽא־יִבּ֑וֹל
וְכֹ֖ל אֲשֶׁר־יַעֲשֶׂ֣ה יַצְלִֽיחַ׃

4 לֹא־כֵ֥ן הָרְשָׁעִ֑ים
כִּ֥י אִם־כַּ֝מֹּ֗ץ אֲֽשֶׁר־תִּדְּפֶ֥נּוּ רֽוּחַ׃
5 עַל־כֵּ֤ן ׀ לֹא־יָקֻ֣מוּ רְ֭שָׁעִים
בַּמִּשְׁפָּ֑ט
וְ֝חַטָּאִ֗ים בַּעֲדַ֥ת צַדִּיקִֽים׃
6 כִּֽי־יוֹדֵ֣עַ יְ֭הֹוָה דֶּ֣רֶךְ צַדִּיקִ֑ים
וְדֶ֖רֶךְ רְשָׁעִ֣ים תֹּאבֵֽד׃

ב לָ֭מָּה רָגְשׁ֣וּ גוֹיִ֑ם
וּ֝לְאֻמִּ֗ים יֶהְגּוּ־רִֽיק׃
2 יִ֥תְיַצְּב֨וּ ׀ מַלְכֵי־אֶ֗רֶץ
וְרוֹזְנִ֥ים נֽוֹסְדוּ־יָ֑חַד
עַל־יְ֝הֹוָה וְעַל־מְשִׁיחֽוֹ׃
3 נְֽ֭נַתְּקָה אֶת־מֽוֹסְרוֹתֵ֑ימוֹ
וְנַשְׁלִ֖יכָה מִמֶּ֣נּוּ עֲבֹתֵֽימוֹ׃

---

a   Or "recites"; lit. "utters."
b-b   Or "he does prospers."

a   Lit. "utter."

v. 1.   בכתב היד שלנו כל פרק בספר בצורת שירה

⁴He who is enthroned in heaven laughs;

the Lord mocks at them.

⁵Then He speaks to them in anger,

terrifying them in His rage,

⁶"But I have installed My king

on Zion, My holy mountain!"

⁷Let me tell of the decree:

the Lord said to me,

^b"You are My son,

I have fathered you this day.-^b

⁸Ask it of Me,

and I will make the nations your domain;

your estate, the limits of the earth.

⁹You can smash them with an iron mace,

shatter them like potter's ware."

¹⁰So now, O kings, be prudent;

accept discipline, you rulers of the earth!

¹¹Serve the Lord in awe;

^ctremble with fright,-^c

^{12d}pay homage in good faith,-^d

lest He be angered, and your way be doomed

in the mere flash of His anger.

Happy are all who take refuge in Him.

4 יוֹשֵׁב בַּשָּׁמַיִם יִשְׂחָק

אֲדֹנָי יִלְעַג־לָמוֹ:

5 אָז יְדַבֵּר אֵלֵימוֹ בְאַפּוֹ

וּבַחֲרוֹנוֹ יְבַהֲלֵמוֹ:

6 וַאֲנִי נָסַכְתִּי מַלְכִּי

עַל־צִיּוֹן הַר־קָדְשִׁי:

7 אֲסַפְּרָה אֶל חֹק

יְהֹוָה אָמַר אֵלַי

בְּנִי אַתָּה

אֲנִי הַיּוֹם יְלִדְתִּיךָ:

8 שְׁאַל מִמֶּנִּי

וְאֶתְּנָה גוֹיִם נַחֲלָתֶךָ

וַאֲחֻזָּתְךָ אַפְסֵי־אָרֶץ:

9 תְּרֹעֵם בְּשֵׁבֶט בַּרְזֶל

כִּכְלִי יוֹצֵר תְּנַפְּצֵם:

10 וְעַתָּה מְלָכִים הַשְׂכִּילוּ

הִוָּסְרוּ שֹׁפְטֵי אָרֶץ:

11 עִבְדוּ אֶת־יְהֹוָה בְּיִרְאָה

וְגִילוּ בִּרְעָדָה:

12 נַשְּׁקוּ־בַר

פֶּן־יֶאֱנַף | וְתֹאבְדוּ דֶרֶךְ

כִּי־יִבְעַר כִּמְעַט אַפּוֹ

אַשְׁרֵי כָּל־חוֹסֵי בוֹ:

3 A psalm of David when he fled from his son Absalom.

ג מִזְמוֹר לְדָוִד בְּבָרְחוֹ מִפְּנֵי | אַבְשָׁלוֹם בְּנוֹ:

²O Lord, my foes are so many!

Many are those who attack me;

³many say of me,

"There is no deliverance for him through

God." *Selah.*^a

⁴But You, O Lord, are a shield about me,

my glory, He who holds my head high.

2 יְהֹוָה מָה־רַבּוּ צָרָי

רַבִּים קָמִים עָלָי:

3 רַבִּים אֹמְרִים לְנַפְשִׁי

אֵין יְשׁוּעָתָה לּוֹ בֵאלֹהִים   סֶלָה:

4 וְאַתָּה יְהֹוָה מָגֵן בַּעֲדִי

כְּבוֹדִי וּמֵרִים רֹאשִׁי:

---

b-b   Compare 2 Sam. 7.14, and Ps. 89.27 ff.

c-c   Meaning of Heb. uncertain; others "rejoice with trembling."

d-d   Meaning of Heb. uncertain.

a   A liturgical direction of uncertain meaning.

⁵I cry aloud to the LORD,

and He answers me from His holy mountain.

Selah.

⁶I lie down and sleep and wake again,

for the LORD sustains me.

⁷I have no fear of the myriad forces

arrayed against me on every side.

⁸Rise, O LORD!

Deliver me, O my God!

For You slap all my enemies in the face;*b*

You break the teeth of the wicked.

⁹Deliverance is the LORD's;

Your blessing be upon Your people!   *Selah.*

4 *ᵃ-*For the leader; with instrumental music.*-ᵃ* A psalm of David.

²Answer me when I call,

O God, my vindicator!

You freed me from distress;

have mercy on me and hear my prayer.

³You men, how long will my glory be mocked,

will you love illusions,

have recourse to frauds?   *Selah.*

⁴Know that the LORD singles out the faithful for Himself;

the LORD hears when I call to Him.

⁵So tremble, and sin no more;

ponder it on your bed, and sigh.*b*

⁶Offer sacrifices in righteousness

and trust in the LORD.

⁷Many say, "O for good days!"

*c-*Bestow Your favor on us,*-c* O LORD.

⁸You put joy into my heart

---

⁵ קוֹלִי אֶל־יְהוָה אֶקְרָא

וַיַּעֲנֵנִי מֵהַר קָדְשׁוֹ   סֶלָה:

⁶ אֲנִי שָׁכַבְתִּי וָאִישָׁנָה הֱקִיצוֹתִי

כִּי יְהוָה יִסְמְכֵנִי:

⁷ לֹא־אִירָא מֵרִבְבוֹת עָם

אֲשֶׁר סָבִיב שָׁתוּ עָלָי:

⁸ קוּמָה יְהוָה |

הוֹשִׁיעֵנִי אֱלֹהַי

כִּי־הִכִּיתָ אֶת־כָּל־אֹיְבַי לֶחִי

שִׁנֵּי רְשָׁעִים שִׁבַּרְתָּ:

⁹ לַיהוָה הַיְשׁוּעָה

עַל־עַמְּךָ בִרְכָתֶךָ   סֶלָה:

ד לַמְנַצֵּחַ בִּנְגִינוֹת מִזְמוֹר לְדָוִד:

² בְּקָרְאִי עֲנֵנִי |

אֱלֹהֵי צִדְקִי

בַּצָּר הִרְחַבְתָּ לִּי

חָנֵּנִי וּשְׁמַע תְּפִלָּתִי:

³ בְּנֵי אִישׁ עַד־מֶה כְבוֹדִי לִכְלִמָּה

תֶּאֱהָבוּן רִיק

תְּבַקְשׁוּ כָזָב   סֶלָה:

⁴ וּדְעוּ כִּי־הִפְלָה יְהוָה חָסִיד לוֹ

יְהוָה יִשְׁמַע בְּקָרְאִי אֵלָיו:

⁵ רִגְזוּ וְאַל־תֶּחֱטָאוּ

אִמְרוּ בִלְבַבְכֶם עַל־מִשְׁכַּבְכֶם

וְדֹמּוּ סֶלָה:

⁶ זִבְחוּ זִבְחֵי־צֶדֶק

וּבִטְחוּ אֶל־יְהוָה:

⁷ רַבִּים אֹמְרִים מִי־יַרְאֵנוּ טוֹב

נְסָה־עָלֵינוּ אוֹר פָּנֶיךָ יְהוָה:

⁸ נָתַתָּה שִׂמְחָה בְלִבִּי

מֵעֵת דְּגָנָם וְתִירוֹשָׁם רָבּוּ:

---

b Lit. "cheek."

a-a Meaning of Heb. uncertain.

b Others "be still."

c-c Lit. "Lift up the light of Your countenance upon us"; cf. Num. 6.25 f.

when their grain and wine show increase.

9Safe and sound, I lie down and sleep,

  d-for You alone, O LORD, keep me secure.-d

בְּשָׁלֹום יַחְדָּו֮ אֶשְׁכְּבָ֪ה וְאִ֫ישָׁ֥ן 9

כִּֽי־אַתָּ֣ה יְהֹוָ֣ה לְבָדָ֑ד לָבֶ֥טַח

תּֽוֹשִׁיבֵֽנִי׃

5
a-For the leader; on *neḥiloth*.-a A psalm of David.

2Give ear to my speech, O LORD;

  consider my utterance.

3Heed the sound of my cry,

  my king and God,

  for I pray to You.

4Hear my voice, O LORD, at daybreak;

  at daybreak I plead before You, and wait.

5For You are not a God who desires wickedness;

  evil cannot abide with You;

  6wanton men cannot endure in Your sight.

You detest all evildoers;

  7You doom those who speak lies;

  murderous, deceitful men the LORD abhors.

8But I, through Your abundant love, enter Your house;

  I bow down in awe at Your holy temple.

9O LORD, b-lead me along Your righteous [path]-b

  because of my watchful foes;

  make Your way straight before me.

10For there is no sincerity on their lips;c

  their heart is [filled with] malice;

  their throat is an open grave;

  their tongue slippery.

11Condemn them, O God;

  let them fall by their own devices;

  cast them out for their many crimes,

  for they defy You.

12But let all who take refuge in You rejoice,

ה לַמְנַצֵּ֥חַ אֶל־הַנְּחִילֹות֮ מִזְמֹ֪ור
לְדָוִֽד׃

אֲמָרַ֖י הַאֲזִ֥ינָה ׀ יְהֹוָ֗ה 2
בִּ֣ינָה הֲגִֽיגִי׃

הַקְשִׁ֤יבָה ׀ לְקֹ֬ול שַׁוְעִ֗י 3
מַלְכִּ֥י וֵֽאלֹהָ֑י
כִּֽי־אֵלֶ֥יךָ אֶתְפַּלָּֽל׃

יְֽהֹוָ֗ה בֹּ֭קֶר תִּשְׁמַ֣ע קֹולִ֑י 4
בֹּ֥קֶר אֶעֱרׇךְ־לְ֝ךָ֗ וַאֲצַפֶּֽה׃

כִּ֤י ׀ לֹ֤א אֵֽל־חָפֵ֘ץ רֶ֥שַׁע ׀ אָ֑תָּה 5
לֹ֖א יְגֻרְךָ֣ רָֽע׃

לֹֽא־יִתְיַצְּב֣וּ הֹֽולְלִים֮ לְנֶ֪גֶד עֵינֶ֥יךָ 6
שָׂ֝נֵ֗אתָ כׇּל־פֹּ֥עֲלֵי אָֽוֶן׃

תְּאַבֵּד֮ דֹּבְרֵ֪י כָ֫זָ֥ב 7
אִישׁ־דָּמִ֥ים וּמִרְמָ֗ה יְתָ֘עֵ֥ב ׀ יְהֹוָֽה׃

וַאֲנִ֗י בְּרֹ֣ב חַ֭סְדְּךָ אָבֹ֣וא בֵיתֶ֑ךָ 8
אֶשְׁתַּחֲוֶ֥ה אֶל־הֵֽיכַל־קׇ֝דְשְׁךָ֗
בְּיִרְאָתֶֽךָ׃

יְהֹוָ֤ה ׀ נְחֵ֬נִי בְצִדְקָתֶ֗ךָ 9
לְמַ֥עַן שֹׁורְרָ֑י
הושר (הַיְשַׁ֖ר) לְפָנַ֣י דַּרְכֶּֽךָ׃

כִּ֤י אֵ֪ין בְּפִ֡יהוּ נְכֹונָה֮ 10
קִרְבָּ֪ם הַ֫וֹּ֥ות
קֶבֶר־פָּת֥וּחַ גְּרֹונָ֑ם
לְ֝שֹׁונָ֗ם יַחֲלִיקֽוּן׃

הַאֲשִׁימֵ֨ם ׀ אֱֽלֹהִ֗ים 11
יִפְּלוּ֮ מִֽמֹּעֲצֹ֪ותֵ֫יהֶ֥ם
בְּרֹ֣ב פִּ֭שְׁעֵיהֶם הַדִּיחֵ֑מֹו
כִּי־מָ֥רוּ בָֽךְ׃

וְיִשְׂמְח֥וּ כׇל־חֹ֪וסֵי בָ֡ךְ 12

---

d-d   *Or "for You, O LORD, keep me alone and secure."*

a-a   *Meaning of Heb. uncertain.*

b-b   *Or "as You are righteous, lead me."*

c   *Lit. "mouth."*

ever jubilant as You shelter them;
   and let those who love Your name exult in You.
13For You surely bless the righteous man, O LORD,
   encompassing him with favor like a shield.

לְעוֹלָם יְרַנֵּנוּ וְתָסֵךְ עָלֵימוֹ
וְיַעְלְצוּ בְךָ אֹהֲבֵי שְׁמֶךָ׃
13 כִּי־אַתָּה תְּבָרֵךְ צַדִּיק יְהֹוָה
כַּצִּנָּה רָצוֹן תַּעְטְרֶנּוּ׃

6

a-For the leader; with instrumental music on the *sheminith.-a* A psalm of David.

לַמְנַצֵּחַ בִּנְגִינוֹת עַל־הַשְּׁמִינִית
מִזְמוֹר לְדָוִד׃

2O LORD, do not punish me in anger,
   do not chastise me in fury.
3Have mercy on me, O LORD, for I languish;
   heal me, O LORD, for my bones shake with terror.
4My whole being is stricken with terror,
   while You, LORD—O, how long!
5O LORD, turn! Rescue me!
Deliver me as befits Your faithfulness.
6For there is no praise of You among the dead;
   in Sheol, who can acclaim You?

2 יְהֹוָה אַל־בְּאַפְּךָ תוֹכִיחֵנִי
וְאַל־בַּחֲמָתְךָ תְיַסְּרֵנִי׃
3 חָנֵּנִי יְהֹוָה כִּי אֻמְלַל אָנִי
רְפָאֵנִי יְהֹוָה כִּי נִבְהֲלוּ עֲצָמָי׃
4 וְנַפְשִׁי נִבְהֲלָה מְאֹד
ואת וְאַתָּה יְהֹוָה עַד־מָתָי׃
5 שׁוּבָה יְהֹוָה חַלְּצָה נַפְשִׁי
הוֹשִׁיעֵנִי לְמַעַן חַסְדֶּךָ׃
6 כִּי אֵין בַּמָּוֶת זִכְרֶךָ
בִּשְׁאוֹל מִי יוֹדֶה־לָּךְ׃

7I am weary with groaning;
   every night I drench my bed,
   I melt my couch in tears.
8My eyes are wasted by vexation,
   worn out because of all my foes.
9Away from me, all you evildoers,
   for the LORD heeds the sound of my weeping.
10The LORD heeds my plea,
   the LORD accepts my prayer.
11All my enemies will be frustrated and stricken with terror;
   they will turn back in an instant, frustrated.

7 יָגַעְתִּי ׀ בְּאַנְחָתִי
אַשְׂחֶה בְכָל־לַיְלָה מִטָּתִי
בְּדִמְעָתִי עַרְשִׂי אַמְסֶה׃
8 עָשְׁשָׁה מִכַּעַס עֵינִי
עָתְקָה בְּכָל־צוֹרְרָי׃
9 סוּרוּ מִמֶּנִּי כָּל־פֹּעֲלֵי אָוֶן
כִּי־שָׁמַע יְהֹוָה קוֹל בִּכְיִי׃
10 שָׁמַע יְהֹוָה תְּחִנָּתִי
יְהֹוָה תְּפִלָּתִי יִקָּח׃
11 יֵבֹשׁוּ ׀ וְיִבָּהֲלוּ מְאֹד כָּל־אֹיְבָי
יָשֻׁבוּ יֵבֹשׁוּ רָגַע׃

7

a-*Shiggaion* of David,-a which he sang to the LORD, concerning Cush, a Benjaminite.

שִׁגָּיוֹן לְדָוִד אֲשֶׁר־שָׁר לַיהֹוָה עַל־
דִּבְרֵי־כוּשׁ בֶּן־יְמִינִי׃

a-a *Meaning of Heb. uncertain.*
a-a *Meaning of Heb. uncertain.*

²O Lord, my God, in You I seek refuge;
   deliver me from all my pursuers and save me,
  ³lest, like a lion, they tear me apart,
   rending in pieces, and no one save me.
⁴O Lord, my God, if I have done such things,
   if my hands bear the guilt of wrongdoing,
  ⁵if I have dealt evil to my ally—
  ^bI who rescued my foe without reward-^b—
  ⁶then let the enemy pursue and overtake me;
   let him trample my life to the ground,
   and lay my body in the dust.   *Selah.*

⁷Rise, O Lord, in Your anger;
   assert Yourself ^cagainst the fury of my foes;-^c
   bestir Yourself on my behalf;
   You have ordained judgment.
^{8a}Let the assembly of peoples gather about You,
   with You enthroned above, on high.-^a
⁹The Lord judges the peoples;
   vindicate me, O Lord,
   for the righteousness and blamelessness that
    are mine.
¹⁰Let the evil of the wicked come to an end,
   but establish the righteous;
   he who probes the mind and conscience^d is
    God the righteous.
^{11e}I look to God to shield me;-^e
   the deliverer of the upright.
¹²God vindicates the righteous;
   God ^fpronounces doom-^f each day.
^{13g}If one does not turn back, but whets his sword,
   bends his bow and aims it,
  ¹⁴then against himself he readies deadly weap-
    ons,
   and makes his arrows sharp.-^g

2 יְהוָה אֱלֹהַי בְּךָ חָסִיתִי
הוֹשִׁיעֵנִי מִכָּל־רֹדְפַי וְהַצִּילֵנִי:
3 פֶּן־יִטְרֹף כְּאַרְיֵה נַפְשִׁי
פֹּרֵק וְאֵין מַצִּיל:
4 יְהוָה אֱלֹהַי אִם־עָשִׂיתִי זֹאת
אִם־יֶשׁ־עָוֶל בְּכַפָּי:
5 אִם־גָּמַלְתִּי שׁוֹלְמִי רָע
וָאֲחַלְּצָה צוֹרְרִי רֵיקָם:
6 יִרַדֹּף אוֹיֵב ׀ נַפְשִׁי וְיַשֵּׂג
וְיִרְמֹס לָאָרֶץ חַיָּי
וּכְבוֹדִי ׀ לֶעָפָר יַשְׁכֵּן סֶלָה:

7 קוּמָה יְהוָה ׀ בְּאַפֶּךָ
הִנָּשֵׂא בְּעַבְרוֹת צוֹרְרָי
וְעוּרָה אֵלַי מִשְׁפָּט צִוִּיתָ:
8 וַעֲדַת לְאֻמִּים תְּסוֹבְבֶךָּ
וְעָלֶיהָ לַמָּרוֹם שׁוּבָה:
9 יְהוָה יָדִין עַמִּים
שָׁפְטֵנִי יְהוָה
כְּצִדְקִי וּכְתֻמִּי עָלָי:
10 יִגְמָר־נָא רַע ׀ רְשָׁעִים
וּתְכוֹנֵן צַדִּיק
וּבֹחֵן לִבּוֹת וּכְלָיוֹת אֱלֹהִים צַדִּיק:
11 מָגִנִּי עַל־אֱלֹהִים
מוֹשִׁיעַ יִשְׁרֵי־לֵב:
12 אֱלֹהִים שׁוֹפֵט צַדִּיק
וְאֵל זֹעֵם בְּכָל־יוֹם:
13 אִם־לֹא יָשׁוּב חַרְבּוֹ יִלְטוֹשׁ
קַשְׁתּוֹ דָרַךְ וַיְכוֹנְנֶהָ:
14 וְלוֹ הֵכִין כְּלֵי־מָוֶת
חִצָּיו לְדֹלְקִים יִפְעָל:

---

b-b   *Meaning of Heb. uncertain; others "or stripped my foe clean."*
c-c   *Or "in Your fury against my foes."*
d   *Lit. "kidneys."*
e-e   *Cf. Ibn Ezra and Kimhi; lit. "My Shield is upon God."*
f-f   *Others "has indignation."*
g-g   *Meaning of vv. 13–14 uncertain; an alternate rendering, with God*
    as the main subject, is: ¹³*If one does not turn back, He whets His sword,*
    / bends His bow and aims it; / ¹⁴*deadly weapons He prepares for him,*
    / and makes His arrows sharp.

15See, he hatches evil, conceives mischief,
   and gives birth to fraud.
16He has dug a pit and deepened it,
   and will fall into the trap he made.
17His mischief will recoil upon his own head;
   his lawlessness will come down upon his skull.
18I will praise the LORD for His righteousness,
   and sing a hymn to the name of the LORD Most
   High.

הִנֵּה יְחַבֶּל־אָוֶן וְהָרָה עָמָל 15
וְיָלַד שָׁקֶר׃
בּוֹר כָּרָה וַיַּחְפְּרֵהוּ 16
וַיִּפֹּל בְּשַׁחַת יִפְעָל׃
יָשׁוּב עֲמָלוֹ בְרֹאשׁוֹ 17
וְעַל קָדְקֳדוֹ חֲמָסוֹ יֵרֵד׃
אוֹדֶה יְהוָה כְּצִדְקוֹ 18
וַאֲזַמְּרָה שֵׁם־יְהוָה עֶלְיוֹן׃

8 *a*-For the leader; on the *gittith.-a* A psalm of
David.

2O LORD, our Lord,
   How majestic is Your name throughout the
    earth,
   b-You who have covered the heavens with
    Your splendor!-*b*
3*a*-From the mouths of infants and sucklings
   You have founded strength on account of Your
    foes,
   to put an end to enemy and avenger.-*a*
4When I behold Your heavens, the work of Your
    fingers,
   the moon and stars that You set in place,
5what is man that You have been mindful of
    him,
   mortal man that You have taken note of him,
6that You have made him little less than divine,*c*
   and adorned him with glory and majesty;
7You have made him master over Your handi-
    work,
   laying the world at his feet,
8sheep and oxen, all of them,
   and wild beasts, too;
9the birds of the heavens, the fish of the sea,
   whatever travels the paths of the seas.

ח לַמְנַצֵּחַ עַל־הַגִּתִּית מִזְמוֹר לְדָוִד׃

יְהוָה אֲדֹנֵינוּ 2
מָה־אַדִּיר שִׁמְךָ בְּכָל־הָאָרֶץ
אֲשֶׁר תְּנָה הוֹדְךָ עַל־הַשָּׁמָיִם׃
מִפִּי עוֹלְלִים ׀ וְיֹנְקִים 3
יִסַּדְתָּ עֹז לְמַעַן צוֹרְרֶיךָ
לְהַשְׁבִּית אוֹיֵב וּמִתְנַקֵּם׃
כִּי־אֶרְאֶה שָׁמֶיךָ מַעֲשֵׂי 4
אֶצְבְּעֹתֶיךָ
יָרֵחַ וְכוֹכָבִים אֲשֶׁר כּוֹנָנְתָּה׃
מָה־אֱנוֹשׁ כִּי־תִזְכְּרֶנּוּ 5
וּבֶן־אָדָם כִּי תִפְקְדֶנּוּ׃
וַתְּחַסְּרֵהוּ מְּעַט מֵאֱלֹהִים 6
וְכָבוֹד וְהָדָר תְּעַטְּרֵהוּ׃
תַּמְשִׁילֵהוּ בְּמַעֲשֵׂי יָדֶיךָ 7
כֹּל שַׁתָּה תַחַת־רַגְלָיו׃
צֹנֶה וַאֲלָפִים כֻּלָּם 8
וְגַם בַּהֲמוֹת שָׂדָי׃
צִפּוֹר שָׁמַיִם וּדְגֵי הַיָּם 9
עֹבֵר אָרְחוֹת יַמִּים׃

---

a-a   *Meaning of Heb. uncertain.*
b-b   *Meaning of Heb. uncertain; or "You whose splendor is celebrated*
     all over the heavens!"
c   *Or "the angels."*

10O LORD, our Lord, how majestic is Your name
throughout the earth!

10 יְהוָה אֲדֹנֵינוּ מָה־אַדִּיר שִׁמְךָ
בְּכָל־הָאָרֶץ׃

ט 9 *a*-For the leader; '*almuth labben.-a* A psalm of
David.

ט לַמְנַצֵּחַ עַלְמוּת לַבֵּן מִזְמוֹר לְדָוִד׃

2I will praise You, LORD, with all my heart;
I will tell all Your wonders.

3I will rejoice and exult in You,
singing a hymn to Your name, O Most High.

אוֹדֶה יְהוָה בְּכָל־לִבִּי 2
אֲסַפְּרָה כָּל־נִפְלְאוֹתֶיךָ׃
אֶשְׂמְחָה וְאֶעֶלְצָה בָךְ 3
אֲזַמְּרָה שִׁמְךָ עֶלְיוֹן׃

4When my enemies retreat,
they stumble to their doom at Your presence.

5For You uphold my right and claim,
enthroned as righteous judge.

6You blast the nations;
You destroy the wicked;
You blot out their name forever.

7*b*-The enemy is no more—
ruins everlasting;
You have torn down their cities;
their very names are lost.-*b*

8But the LORD abides forever;
He has set up His throne for judgment;

9it is He who judges the world with righteousness,
rules the peoples with equity.

10The LORD is a haven for the oppressed,
a haven in times of trouble.

11Those who know Your name trust You,
for You do not abandon those who turn to You,
O LORD.

12Sing a hymn to the LORD, *c*-who reigns in Zion;-*c*
declare His deeds among the peoples.

13*d*-For He does not ignore the cry of the afflicted;
He who requites bloodshed is mindful of
them.-*d*

בְּשׁוּב־אוֹיְבַי אָחוֹר 4
יִכָּשְׁלוּ וְיֹאבְדוּ מִפָּנֶיךָ׃
כִּי־עָשִׂיתָ מִשְׁפָּטִי וְדִינִי 5
יָשַׁבְתָּ לְכִסֵּא שׁוֹפֵט צֶדֶק׃
גָּעַרְתָּ גוֹיִם 6
אִבַּדְתָּ רָשָׁע
שְׁמָם מָחִיתָ לְעוֹלָם וָעֶד׃
הָאוֹיֵב ׀ תַּמּוּ 7
חֳרָבוֹת לָנֶצַח
וְעָרִים* נָתַשְׁתָּ
אָבַד זִכְרָם הֵמָּה׃
וַיהוָה לְעוֹלָם יֵשֵׁב 8
כּוֹנֵן לַמִּשְׁפָּט כִּסְאוֹ׃
וְהוּא יִשְׁפֹּט־תֵּבֵל בְּצֶדֶק 9
יָדִין לְאֻמִּים בְּמֵישָׁרִים׃
וִיהִי יְהוָה מִשְׂגָּב לַדָּךְ 10
מִשְׂגָּב לְעִתּוֹת בַּצָּרָה׃
וְיִבְטְחוּ בְךָ יוֹדְעֵי שְׁמֶךָ 11
כִּי לֹא־עָזַבְתָּ דֹרְשֶׁיךָ יְהוָה׃
זַמְּרוּ לַיהוָה יֹשֵׁב צִיּוֹן 12
הַגִּידוּ בָעַמִּים עֲלִילוֹתָיו׃
כִּי־דֹרֵשׁ דָּמִים אוֹתָם זָכָר 13
לֹא־שָׁכַח צַעֲקַת עניים עֲנָוִים׃

---

a-a Meaning of Heb. uncertain; some mss. and ancient versions, '*al muth labben,* as though "over the death of the son."

b-b Meaning of Heb. uncertain.

c-c Or "O You who dwell in Zion."

d-d Order of Hebrew clauses inverted for clarity.

v. 7. לשון שנאה

14Have mercy on me, O Lord;

see my affliction at the hands of my foes,

You who lift me from the gates of death,

15so that in the gates of *e*-Fair Zion-*e*

I might tell all Your praise,

I might exult in Your deliverance.

16The nations sink in the pit they have made;

their own foot is caught in the net they have

hidden.

17The Lord has made Himself known:

He works judgment;

the wicked man is snared by his own devices.

Higgaion.[b]   *Selah.*

18Let the wicked be[f] in Sheol,

all the nations who ignore God!

19Not always shall the needy be ignored,

nor the hope of the afflicted forever lost.

20Rise, O Lord!

Let not men have power;

let the nations be judged in Your presence.

21[b]-Strike fear into them,-[b] O Lord;

let the nations know they are only men.   *Selah.*

14 חָנְנֵ֬נִי יְהֹוָ֗ה

רְאֵ֣ה עָ֭נְיִי מִשֹּׂנְאָ֑י

מְ֝רוֹמְמִ֗י מִשַּׁ֥עֲרֵי מָֽוֶת׃

15 לְמַ֥עַן אֲסַפְּרָ֗ה כׇּֽל־תְּהִלָּ֫תֶ֥יךָ

בְּשַֽׁעֲרֵ֥י בַת־צִיּ֑וֹן

אָ֝גִ֗ילָה בִּישׁוּעָתֶֽךָ׃

16 טָבְע֣וּ ג֭וֹיִם בְּשַׁ֣חַת עָשׂ֑וּ

בְּרֶֽשֶׁת־ז֥וּ טָמָ֗נוּ נִלְכְּדָ֥ה רַגְלָֽם׃

17 נ֤וֹדַ֨ע ׀ יְהֹוָה֮

מִשְׁפָּ֢ט עָ֫שָׂ֥ה

בְּפֹ֣עַל כַּ֭פָּיו נוֹקֵ֣שׁ רָשָׁ֑ע הִגָּי֥וֹן

סֶֽלָה׃

18 יָשׁ֣וּבוּ רְשָׁעִ֣ים לִשְׁא֑וֹלָה

כׇּל־גּ֝וֹיִ֗ם שְׁכֵחֵ֥י אֱלֹהִֽים׃

19 כִּ֤י לֹ֣א לָ֭נֶצַח יִשָּׁכַ֣ח אֶבְי֑וֹן

תִּקְוַ֥ת עֲנָוִ֗ים עֲנִיִּ֗ים תֹּאבַ֥ד לָעַֽד׃

20 קוּמָ֣ה יְ֭הֹוָה

אַל־יָעֹ֣ז אֱנ֑וֹשׁ

יִשָּׁפְט֥וּ ג֝וֹיִ֗ם עַל־פָּנֶֽיךָ׃

21 שִׁ֘יתָ֤ה יְהֹוָ֨ה ׀ מוֹרָ֗ה לָ֫הֶ֥ם

יֵדְע֥וּ גוֹיִ֑ם אֱנ֖וֹשׁ הֵ֣מָּה סֶּֽלָה׃

10

Why, O Lord, do You stand aloof,

heedless in times of trouble?

2The wicked in his arrogance hounds the lowly—

a-may they be caught in the schemes they

devise! -*a*

3[b]-The wicked crows about his unbridled lusts;

the grasping man reviles and scorns the Lord.

4The wicked, arrogant as he is,

in all his scheming [thinks],-[b]

"He does not call to account;

c-God does not care."-*c*

5His ways prosper at all times;

Your judgments are far beyond him;

י   לָמָ֣ה יְ֭הֹוָה תַּעֲמֹ֣ד בְּרָח֑וֹק

תַּ֝עְלִ֗ים לְעִתּ֥וֹת בַּצָּרָֽה׃

2 בְּגַאֲוַ֣ת רָ֭שָׁע יִדְלַ֣ק עָנִ֑י

יִתָּפְשׂ֓וּ ׀ בִּמְזִמּ֖וֹת ז֣וּ חָשָֽׁבוּ׃

3 כִּֽי־הִלֵּ֣ל רָ֭שָׁע עַל־תַּאֲוַ֣ת נַפְשׁ֑וֹ

וּבֹצֵ֥עַ בֵּ֝רֵ֗ךְ נִ֘אֵ֥ץ ׀ יְהֹוָֽה׃

4 רָשָׁ֗ע כְּגֹ֣בַהּ אַ֭פּוֹ

בַּל־יִדְרֹ֑שׁ

אֵ֥ין אֱ֝לֹהִ֗ים

כׇּל־מְזִמּוֹתָֽיו׃

5 יָ֘חִ֤ילוּ דְרָכָ֨ו ׀ בְּכׇל־עֵ֗ת

מָר֣וֹם מִ֭שְׁפָּטֶיךָ מִנֶּגְדּ֑וֹ

---

e-e   Lit. *"the Daughter of Zion."*

f   Others *"return to."*

a-a   Or *"they (i.e., the lowly) are caught by the schemes they devised."*

b-b   Meaning of Heb. uncertain.

c-c   Lit. *"There is no God."*

he snorts at all his foes.

6He thinks, "I shall not be shaken,
   through all time never be in trouble."

7His mouth is full of oaths, deceit, and fraud;
   mischief and evil are under his tongue.

8He lurks in outlying places;
   from a covert he slays the innocent;
   his eyes spy out the hapless.

9He waits in a covert like a lion in his lair;
   waits to seize the lowly;
   he seizes the lowly as he pulls his net shut;

10he stoops, he crouches,
   b-and the hapless fall prey to his might.-b

11He thinks, "God is not mindful,
   He hides His face, He never looks."

12Rise, O LORD!

d-Strike at him,-d O God!

Do not forget the lowly.

13Why should the wicked man scorn God,
   thinking You do not call to account?

14You do look!

You take note of mischief and vexation!

b-To requite is in Your power.-b

To You the hapless can entrust himself;
   You have ever been the orphan's help.

15O break the power of the wicked and evil man,
   so that when You e-look for-e his wickedness
   You will find it no more.

16The LORD is king for ever and ever;
   the nations will perish from His land.

17You will listen to the entreaty of the lowly,
   O LORD,
   You will make their hearts firm;
   You will incline Your ear

18to champion the orphan and the downtrodden,
   b-that men who are of the earth tyrannize no
   more.-b

כָּל־צוֹרְרָ֗יו יָפִ֥יחַ בָּהֶֽם׃

6 אָמַ֣ר בְּ֭לִבּוֹ בַּל־אֶמּ֑וֹט
לְדֹ֥ר וָ֝דֹ֗ר אֲשֶׁ֣ר לֹֽא־בְרָֽע׃

7 אָלָ֤ה ׀ פִּ֣יהוּ מָ֭לֵא וּמִרְמ֣וֹת וָתֹ֑ךְ
תַּ֥חַת לְ֝שׁוֹנ֗וֹ עָמָ֥ל וָאָֽוֶן׃

8 יֵשֵׁ֤ב ׀ בְּמַאְרַ֬ב חֲצֵרִ֗ים
בַּֽמִּסְתָּ֭רִים יַהֲרֹ֣ג נָקִ֑י
עֵ֝ינָ֗יו לְֽחֵלְכָ֥ה יִצְפֹּֽנוּ׃

9 יֶאֱרֹ֬ב בַּמִּסְתָּ֨ר ׀ כְּאַרְיֵ֬ה בְסֻכֹּ֗ה
יֶ֭אֱרֹב לַחֲט֣וֹף עָנִ֑י
יַחְטֹ֥ף עָ֝נִ֗י בְּמָשְׁכ֥וֹ בְרִשְׁתּֽוֹ׃

10 ודכה יִדְכֶּ֣ה יָשֹׁ֑חַ
וְנָפַ֥ל בַּ֝עֲצוּמָ֗יו חלכאים חֵ֣יל כָּאִֽים׃

11 אָמַ֣ר בְּ֭לִבּוֹ שָׁ֣כַֽח אֵ֑ל
הִסְתִּ֥יר פָּ֝נָ֗יו בַּל־רָאָ֥ה לָנֶֽצַח׃

12 קוּמָ֤ה יְהֹוָ֗ה
אֵ֭ל נְשָׂ֣א יָדֶ֑ךָ
אַל־תִּשְׁכַּ֥ח עֲנָוִֽים׃

13 עַל־מֶ֤ה ׀ נִאֵ֖ץ רָשָׁ֥ע ׀ אֱלֹהִ֑ים
אָמַ֥ר בְּ֝לִבּ֗וֹ לֹ֣א תִדְרֹֽשׁ׃

14 רָאִ֡תָה כִּֽי־אַתָּ֨ה ׀
עָמָ֖ל וָכַ֣עַס ׀ תַּבִּיט֮
לָתֵ֢ת בְּיָ֫דֶ֥ךָ עָלֶ֗יךָ יַעֲזֹ֥ב חֵלֶ֑כָה
יָ֝ת֗וֹם אַתָּ֤ה ׀ הָיִ֥יתָ עוֹזֵֽר׃

15 שְׁ֭בֹר זְר֣וֹעַ רָשָׁ֑ע וָ֝רָ֗ע
תִּֽדְרוֹשׁ־רִשְׁע֥וֹ
בַל־תִּמְצָֽא׃

16 יְהֹוָ֣ה מֶ֭לֶךְ עוֹלָ֣ם וָעֶ֑ד
אָבְד֥וּ ג֝וֹיִ֗ם מֵֽאַרְצֽוֹ׃

17 תַּאֲוַ֬ת עֲנָוִ֣ים שָׁמַ֣עְתָּ יְהֹוָ֑ה
תָּכִ֥ין לִ֝בָּ֗ם
תַּקְשִׁ֥יב אָזְנֶֽךָ׃

18 לִשְׁפֹּ֥ט יָת֗וֹם וָ֫דָ֥ךְ
בַּל־יוֹסִ֥יף ע֑וֹד לַעֲרֹ֥ץ אֱ֝נ֗וֹשׁ מִן־
הָאָֽרֶץ׃

---

d-d   Lit. "Lift Your hand."
e-e   A play on darash, which in vv. 4 and 13 means "to call to account."

11 For the leader. Of David.

יא לַמְנַצֵּחַ לְדָוִד

בַּיהוָה ׀ חָסִיתִי

In the Lord I take refuge;
how can you say to me,
"Take to ᵃthe hills like a bird!-ᵃ

אֵיךְ תֹּאמְרוּ לְנַפְשִׁי
נוּדוּ הַרְכֶם צִפּוֹר:

2For see, the wicked bend the bow,
they set their arrow on the string
to shoot from the shadows at the upright.

2 כִּי הִנֵּה הָרְשָׁעִים יִדְרְכוּן קֶשֶׁת
כּוֹנְנוּ חִצָּם עַל־יֶתֶר
לִירוֹת בְּמוֹ־אֹפֶל לְיִשְׁרֵי־לֵב:

3ᵇ-When the foundations are destroyed,
what can the righteous man do?"-ᵇ

3 כִּי הַשָּׁתוֹת יֵהָרֵסוּן
צַדִּיק מַה־פָּעָל:

4The Lord is in His holy palace;
the Lord—His throne is in heaven;
His eyes behold, His gaze searches mankind.

4 יְהוָה ׀ בְּהֵיכַל קָדְשׁוֹ
יְהוָה בַּשָּׁמַיִם כִּסְאוֹ
עֵינָיו יֶחֱזוּ עַפְעַפָּיו יִבְחֲנוּ בְּנֵי אָדָם:

5The Lord seeks out the righteous man,
but loathes the wicked one who loves injustice.

5 יְהוָה צַדִּיק יִבְחָן
וְרָשָׁע וְאֹהֵב חָמָס שָׂנְאָה נַפְשׁוֹ:

6He will rain down upon the wicked blazing coals
and sulfur;
a scorching wind shall be ᶜtheir lot.-ᶜ

6 יַמְטֵר עַל־רְשָׁעִים פַּחִים אֵשׁ וְגָפְרִית
וְרוּחַ זִלְעָפוֹת מְנָת כּוֹסָם:

7For the Lord is righteous;
He loves righteous deeds;
the upright shall behold His face.

7 כִּי־צַדִּיק יְהוָה
צְדָקוֹת אָהֵב
יָשָׁר יֶחֱזוּ פָנֵימוֹ:

12 For the leader; on the *sheminith*. A psalm of David.

יב לַמְנַצֵּחַ עַל־הַשְּׁמִינִית מִזְמוֹר לְדָוִד:

2Help, O Lord!
For the faithful are no more;
the loyal have vanished from among men.

2 הוֹשִׁיעָה יְהוָה
כִּי־גָמַר חָסִיד
כִּי־פַסּוּ אֱמוּנִים מִבְּנֵי אָדָם:

3Men speak lies to one another;
their speech is smooth;
they talk with duplicity.

3 שָׁוְא ׀ יְדַבְּרוּ אִישׁ אֶת־רֵעֵהוּ
שְׂפַת חֲלָקוֹת
בְּלֵב וָלֵב יְדַבֵּרוּ:

4May the Lord cut off all flattering lips,
every tongue that speaks arrogance.

4 יַכְרֵת יְהוָה כָּל־שִׂפְתֵי חֲלָקוֹת
לָשׁוֹן מְדַבֶּרֶת גְּדֹלוֹת:

---

a-a *Meaning of Heb. uncertain; lit.* "your hill, bird!"
b-b *Or* "For the foundations are destroyed; what has the Righteous One done?" *Or* "If the foundations are destroyed, what has the righteous man accomplished?"
c-c *Lit.* "the portion of their cup."

5They say, "By our tongues we shall prevail;
   with lips such as ours, who can be our master?"

6"Because of the groans of the plundered poor
    and needy,
   I will now act," says the LORD.
   a-"I will give help," He affirms to him.-a
7The words of the LORD are pure words,
   silver purged in an earthen crucible,
   refined sevenfold.
8You, O LORD, will keep them,
   guarding each a-from this age-a evermore.
9On every side the wicked roam
   a-when baseness is exalted among men.-a

5 אֲשֶׁר אָמְר�֮וּ ׀ לִלְשֹׁנֵ֣נוּ נַגְבִּ֑יר
שְׂפָתֵ֥ינוּ אִתָּ֑נוּ מִ֖י אָד֣וֹן לָֽנוּ׃

6 מִשֹּׁ֥ד עֲנִיִּים֮ מֵאַנְקַ֢ת אֶבְי֫וֹנִ֥ים
עַתָּ֣ה אָ֭קוּם יֹאמַ֣ר* יְהוָ֑ה
אָשִׁ֥ית בְּ֝יֵ֗שַׁע יָפִ֥יחַֽ לֽוֹ׃

7 אִמֲר֣וֹת יְהוָה֮ אֲמָר֢וֹת טְהֹ֫ר֥וֹת
כֶּ֣סֶף צָ֭רוּף בַּעֲלִ֣יל לָאָ֑רֶץ
מְ֝זֻקָּ֗ק שִׁבְעָתָֽיִם׃

8 אַתָּֽה־יְהוָ֥ה תִּשְׁמְרֵ֑ם
תִּצְּרֶ֓נּוּ ׀ מִן־הַדּ֖וֹר ז֣וּ לְעוֹלָֽם׃

9 סָבִ֗יב רְשָׁעִ֥ים יִתְהַלָּכ֑וּן
כְּרֻ֥ם זֻ֝לּ֗וּת לִבְנֵ֥י אָדָֽם׃

13 For the leader. A psalm of David.

2How long, O LORD; will You ignore me forever?
How long will You hide Your face from me?
3How long will I have cares on my mind,
   grief in my heart all day?
How long will my enemy have the upper hand?
4Look at me, answer me, O LORD, my God!
Restore the luster to my eyes,
   lest I sleep the sleep of death;
5lest my enemy say, "I have overcome him,"
   my foes exult when I totter.
6But I trust in Your faithfulness,
   my heart will exult in Your deliverance.
I will sing to the LORD,
   for He has been good to me.

יג לַמְנַצֵּ֗חַ מִזְמ֥וֹר לְדָוִֽד׃

2 עַד־אָ֣נָה יְ֭הוָה תִּשְׁכָּחֵ֣נִי נֶ֑צַח
עַד־אָ֓נָה ׀ תַּסְתִּ֖יר אֶת־פָּנֶ֣יךָ מִמֶּֽנִּי׃

3 עַד־אָ֣נָה אָשִׁ֪ית עֵצ֡וֹת בְּנַפְשִׁ֡י
יָג֣וֹן בִּלְבָבִ֣י יוֹמָ֑ם
עַד־אָ֓נָה ׀ יָר֖וּם אֹיְבִ֣י עָלָֽי׃

4 הַבִּ֣יטָֽה עֲ֭נֵנִי יְהוָ֣ה אֱלֹהָ֑י
הָאִ֥ירָה עֵ֝ינַ֗י
פֶּן־אִישַׁ֥ן הַמָּֽוֶת׃

5 פֶּן־יֹאמַ֣ר אֹיְבִ֣י יְכָלְתִּ֑יו
צָרַ֥י יָ֝גִ֗ילוּ כִּ֣י אֶמּֽוֹט׃

6 וַאֲנִ֤י ׀ בְּחַסְדְּךָ֣ בָטַחְתִּי֮
יָ֤גֵ֥ל לִ֭בִּי בִּ֥ישׁוּעָתֶ֑ךָ
אָשִׁ֥ירָה לַיהוָ֑ה
כִּ֖י גָמַ֣ל עָלָֽי׃

14 a-For the leader. Of David.

The benighted man thinks,
   b-"God does not care."-b

יד לַמְנַצֵּ֗חַ לְדָוִֽד

אָמַ�.֤ר נָבָ֣ל בְּלִבּ֑וֹ
אֵ֣ין אֱלֹהִ֑ים

---

a-a   *Meaning of Heb. uncertain.*
a   *Cf. Ps. 53.*
b-b   *Lit. "There is no God"; cf. Ps. 10.4.*

v. 6. סְבִירִין וּמַטְעִין "אֹמֵר"

Man's deeds are corrupt and loathsome;
    no one does good.

²The LORD looks down from heaven on mankind
    to find a man of understanding,
    a man mindful of God.

³All have turned bad,
    altogether foul;
    there is none who does good,
    not even one.

⁴Are they so witless, all those evildoers,
    who devour my people as they devour food,
    and do not invoke the LORD?

⁵There they will be seized with fright,
    for God is present in the circle of the righteous.

⁶You may set at naught the counsel of the lowly,
    but the LORD is his refuge.

⁷O that the deliverance of Israel might come from
    Zion!
When the LORD restores the fortunes of His
    people,
    Jacob will exult, Israel will rejoice.

הִשְׁחִיתוּ הִתְעִיבוּ עֲלִילָה
אֵין עֹשֵׂה־טוֹב:
2 יְהוָה מִשָּׁמַיִם הִשְׁקִיף עַל־בְּנֵי־
אָדָם
לִרְאוֹת הֲיֵשׁ מַשְׂכִּיל
דֹּרֵשׁ אֶת־אֱלֹהִים:
3 הַכֹּל סָר
יַחְדָּו נֶאֱלָחוּ
אֵין עֹשֵׂה־טוֹב
אֵין גַּם־אֶחָד:
4 הֲלֹא יָדְעוּ כָּל־פֹּעֲלֵי אָוֶן
אֹכְלֵי עַמִּי אָכְלוּ לֶחֶם
יְהוָה לֹא קָרָאוּ:
5 שָׁם ׀ פָּחֲדוּ פָחַד
כִּי־אֱלֹהִים בְּדוֹר צַדִּיק:
6 עֲצַת־עָנִי תָבִישׁוּ
כִּי יְהוָה מַחְסֵהוּ:
7 מִי יִתֵּן מִצִּיּוֹן יְשׁוּעַת יִשְׂרָאֵל
בְּשׁוּב יְהוָה שְׁבוּת עַמּוֹ
יָגֵל יַעֲקֹב יִשְׂמַח יִשְׂרָאֵל:

15 A psalm of David.

LORD, who may sojourn in Your tent,
    who may dwell on Your holy mountain?

²He who lives without blame,
    who does what is right,
    and in his heart acknowledges the truth;

³ᵃ-whose tongue is not given to evil;-ᵃ
who has never done harm to his fellow,
or borne reproach for [his acts toward] his
    neighbor;

⁴for whom a contemptible man is abhorrent,
    but who honors those who fear the LORD;
who stands by his oath even to his hurt;

⁵who has never lent money at interest,

טו מִזְמוֹר לְדָוִד

יְהוָה מִי־יָגוּר בְּאָהֳלֶךָ
מִי־יִשְׁכֹּן בְּהַר קָדְשֶׁךָ:
2 הוֹלֵךְ תָּמִים
וּפֹעֵל צֶדֶק
וְדֹבֵר אֱמֶת בִּלְבָבוֹ:
3 לֹא־רָגַל ׀ עַל־לְשֹׁנוֹ
לֹא־עָשָׂה לְרֵעֵהוּ רָעָה
וְחֶרְפָּה לֹא־נָשָׂא עַל־קְרֹבוֹ:
4 נִבְזֶה ׀ בְּעֵינָיו נִמְאָס
וְאֶת־יִרְאֵי יְהוָה יְכַבֵּד
נִשְׁבַּע לְהָרַע וְלֹא יָמִר:
5 כַּסְפּוֹ ׀ לֹא־נָתַן בְּנֶשֶׁךְ

a-a   *Meaning of Heb. uncertain; or "who has no slander upon his tongue."*

or accepted a bribe against the innocent.   וְשֹׁ֥חַד עַל־נָקִ֗י לֹ֥א לָ֫קָ֥ח
The man who acts thus shall never be shaken.   עֹֽשֵׂה־אֵ֑לֶּה לֹ֖א יִמּ֣וֹט לְעוֹלָֽם׃

16 A *michtam*[a] of David.

טז מִכְתָּ֥ם לְדָוִ֑ד

Protect me, O God, for I seek refuge in You.   שָׁמְרֵ֥נִי אֵ֑ל כִּֽי־חָסִ֥יתִי בָֽךְ׃
[2]I say to the LORD,   2 אָמַ֣רְתְּ לַֽיהוָה
     "You are my Lord, [b]my benefactor;   אֲדֹנָ֥י אָ֑תָּה ט֜וֹבָתִ֗י
     there is none above You."[-b]   בַּל־עָלֶֽיךָ׃
[3c]As to the holy and mighty ones that are in the   3 לִ֭קְדוֹשִׁים אֲשֶׁר־בָּאָ֣רֶץ הֵ֑מָּה
     land,   וְ֜אַדִּירֵ֗י כָּל־חֶפְצִי־בָֽם׃
     my whole desire concerning them is that
[4]those who espouse another [god]   4 יִרְבּ֥וּ עַצְּבוֹתָם֮
     may have many sorrows![-c]   אַחֵ֪ר מָ֫הָ֥רוּ
I will have no part of their bloody libations;   בַּל־אַסִּ֣יךְ נִסְכֵּיהֶ֣ם מִדָּ֑ם
     their names will not pass my lips.   וּֽבַל־אֶשָּׂ֥א אֶת־שְׁ֜מוֹתָ֗ם עַל־שְׂפָתָֽי׃
[5]The LORD is my allotted share and portion;[d]   5 יְֽהוָ֗ה מְנָת־חֶלְקִ֥י וְכוֹסִ֑י
     You control my fate.   אַ֜תָּ֗ה תּוֹמִ֥יךְ גּוֹרָלִֽי׃
[6]Delightful country has fallen to my lot;   6 חֲבָלִ֥ים נָֽפְלוּ־לִ֥י בַּנְּעִמִ֑ים
     lovely indeed is my estate.   אַף־נַ֜חֲלָ֗ת שָֽׁפְרָ֥ה עָלָֽי׃
[7]I bless the LORD who has guided me;   7 אֲבָרֵ֗ךְ אֶת־יְ֖הוָה אֲשֶׁ֣ר יְעָצָ֑נִי
     my conscience[e] admonishes me at night.   אַף־לֵ֜יל֗וֹת יִסְּר֥וּנִי כִלְיוֹתָֽי׃
[8]I am ever mindful of the LORD's presence;   8 שִׁוִּ֬יתִי יְהוָ֣ה לְנֶגְדִּ֣י תָמִ֑יד
     He is at my right hand; I shall never be shaken.   כִּ֥י מִֽ֜ימִינִ֗י בַּל־אֶמּֽוֹט׃
[9]So my heart rejoices,   9 לָכֵ֤ן ׀ שָׂמַ֣ח לִ֭בִּי
     my whole being exults,   וַיָּ֣גֶל כְּבוֹדִ֑י
     and my body rests secure.   אַף־בְּ֜שָׂרִ֗י יִשְׁכֹּ֥ן לָבֶֽטַח׃
[10]For You will not abandon me to Sheol,   10 כִּ֤י ׀ לֹא־תַעֲזֹ֣ב נַפְשִׁ֣י לִשְׁא֑וֹל
     or let Your faithful one see the Pit.   לֹֽא־תִתֵּ֥ן חֲ֜סִידְךָ֗ לִרְא֥וֹת שָֽׁחַת׃
[11]You will teach me the path of life.   11 תּֽוֹדִיעֵנִי֮ אֹ֤רַח חַ֫יִּ֥ים
In Your presence is perfect joy;   שֹׂ֣בַע שְׂ֖מָחוֹת אֶת־פָּנֶ֑יךָ
     delights are ever in Your right hand.   נְעִמ֖וֹת בִּימִֽינְךָ֣ נֶֽצַח׃

---

a   *Meaning of Heb. uncertain.*
b-b *Others "I have no good but in You."*
c-c *Meaning of Heb. uncertain; "holy and mighty ones" taken as epithets*
    for divine beings; cf. qedoshim in Ps. 89.6, 8, and 'addirim in 1 Sam.
    4.8.
d   *Lit. "cup."*
e   *Lit. "kidneys."*

17 A prayer of David.

יז תְּפִלָּה לְדָוִד

Hear, O LORD, what is just;
>heed my cry, give ear to my prayer,
>>uttered without guile.

שִׁמְעָה יְהֹוָה ׀ צֶדֶק
הַקְשִׁיבָה רִנָּתִי הַאֲזִינָה תְפִלָּתִי
בְּלֹא שִׂפְתֵי מִרְמָה׃

2My vindication will come from You;
>Your eyes will behold what is right.

2מִלְּפָנֶיךָ מִשְׁפָּטִי יֵצֵא
עֵינֶיךָ תֶּחֱזֶינָה מֵישָׁרִים׃

3You have visited me at night, probed my mind,
>You have tested me and found nothing amiss;
>>a-I determined that my mouth should not
>>transgress.

3בָּחַנְתָּ לִבִּי ׀ פָּקַדְתָּ לַּיְלָה
צְרַפְתַּנִי בַל־תִּמְצָא
זַמֹּתִי בַּל־יַעֲבָר־פִּי׃

4As for man's dealings,
>in accord with the command of Your lips,-a
>I have kept in view the fate[b] of the lawless.

4לִפְעֻלּוֹת אָדָם
בִּדְבַר שְׂפָתֶיךָ
אֲנִי שָׁמַרְתִּי אָרְחוֹת פָּרִיץ׃

5My feet have held to Your paths;
>my legs have not given way.

5תָּמֹךְ אֲשֻׁרַי בְּמַעְגְּלוֹתֶיךָ
בַּל־נָמוֹטּוּ פְעָמָי׃

6I call on You;
>You will answer me, God;
>turn Your ear to me,
>hear what I say.

6אֲנִי־קְרָאתִיךָ
כִי־תַעֲנֵנִי אֵל
הַט־אָזְנְךָ לִי
שְׁמַע אִמְרָתִי׃

7Display Your faithfulness in wondrous deeds,
>You who deliver with Your right hand
>those who seek refuge from assailants.

7הַפְלֵה חֲסָדֶיךָ
מוֹשִׁיעַ חוֹסִים
מִמִּתְקוֹמְמִים בִּימִינֶךָ׃

8Guard me like the apple of Your eye;
>hide me in the shadow of Your wings
9from the wicked who despoil me,
>c-my mortal enemies who-c encircle me.

8שָׁמְרֵנִי כְּאִישׁוֹן בַּת־עָיִן
בְּצֵל כְּנָפֶיךָ תַּסְתִּירֵנִי׃
9מִפְּנֵי רְשָׁעִים זוּ שַׁדּוּנִי
אֹיְבַי בְּנֶפֶשׁ יַקִּיפוּ עָלָי׃

10a-Their hearts are closed to pity;-a
>they mouth arrogance;
11now they hem in our feet on every side;
>they set their eyes roaming over the land.

10חֶלְבָּמוֹ סָגְרוּ
פִּימוֹ דִּבְּרוּ בְגֵאוּת׃
11אַשֻּׁרֵינוּ עַתָּה סבבוני סְבָבוּנוּ
עֵינֵיהֶם יָשִׁיתוּ לִנְטוֹת בָּאָרֶץ׃

12He is like a lion eager for prey,
>a king of beasts lying in wait.

12דִּמְיֹנוֹ כְּאַרְיֵה יִכְסוֹף לִטְרוֹף
וְכִכְפִיר יֹשֵׁב בְּמִסְתָּרִים׃

13Rise, O LORD! Go forth to meet him.
Bring him down;

13קוּמָה יְהֹוָה קַדְּמָה פָנָיו
הַכְרִיעֵהוּ

---

a-a   Meaning of Heb. uncertain.
b   Cf. Prov. 1.19; lit. "paths."
c-c   Or "from my enemies who avidly."

rescue me from the wicked with Your sword,

14a-from men, O Lord, with Your hand,

from men whose share in life is fleeting.

But as to Your treasured ones,

fill their bellies.-a

Their sons too shall be satisfied,

and have something to leave over for their young.

15Then I, justified, will behold Your face;

awake, I am filled with the vision of You.

פַּלְּטָה נַפְשִׁי מֵרָשָׁע חַרְבֶּךָ׃

14 מִמְתִים יָדְךָ ׀ יְהֹוָה

מִמְתִים מֵחֶלֶד חֶלְקָם בַּחַיִּים

וּצְפוּנְךָ תְּמַלֵּא בִטְנָם

יִשְׂבְּעוּ בָנִים

וְהִנִּיחוּ יִתְרָם לְעוֹלְלֵיהֶם׃

15 אֲנִי בְּצֶדֶק אֶחֱזֶה פָנֶיךָ

אֶשְׂבְּעָה בְהָקִיץ תְּמוּנָתֶךָ׃

18

a-For the leader. Of David, the servant of the Lord, who addressed the words of this song to the Lord after the Lord had saved him from the hands of all his enemies and from the clutches of Saul.

2He said:

b-I adore you, O Lord, my strength,-b

3O Lord, my crag, my fortress, my rescuer,

my God, my rock in whom I seek refuge,

my shield, my c-mighty champion,-c my haven.

4d-All praise! I called on the Lord-d

and was delivered from my enemies.

5Ropese of Death encompassed me;

torrents of Belialf terrified me;

6ropes of Sheol encircled me;

snares of Death confronted me.

7In my distress I called on the Lord,

cried out to my God;

in His temple He heard my voice;

my cry to Him reached His ears.

8Then the earth rocked and quaked;

the foundations of the mountains shook,

rocked by His indignation;

9smoke went up from His nostrils,

from His mouth came devouring fire;

live coals blazed forth from Him.

יח לַמְנַצֵּחַ ׀ לְעֶבֶד יְהֹוָה לְדָוִד

אֲשֶׁר דִּבֶּר ׀ לַיהֹוָה אֶת־דִּבְרֵי הַשִּׁירָה

הַזֹּאת בְּיוֹם הִצִּיל־יְהֹוָה אוֹתוֹ מִכַּף

כָּל־אֹיְבָיו וּמִיַּד שָׁאוּל׃

2 וַיֹּאמַר

אֶרְחָמְךָ יְהֹוָה חִזְקִי׃

3 יְהֹוָה ׀ סַלְעִי וּמְצוּדָתִי וּמְפַלְטִי

אֵלִי צוּרִי אֶחֱסֶה־בּוֹ

מָגִנִּי וְקֶרֶן־יִשְׁעִי מִשְׂגַּבִּי׃

4 מְהֻלָּל אֶקְרָא יְהֹוָה

וּמִן־אֹיְבַי אִוָּשֵׁעַ׃

5 אֲפָפוּנִי חֶבְלֵי־מָוֶת

וְנַחֲלֵי בְלִיַּעַל יְבַעֲתוּנִי׃

6 חֶבְלֵי שְׁאוֹל סְבָבוּנִי

קִדְּמוּנִי מוֹקְשֵׁי מָוֶת׃

7 בַּצַּר־לִי ׀ אֶקְרָא יְהֹוָה

וְאֶל־אֱלֹהַי אֲשַׁוֵּעַ

יִשְׁמַע מֵהֵיכָלוֹ קוֹלִי

וְשַׁוְעָתִי לְפָנָיו ׀ תָּבוֹא בְאָזְנָיו׃

8 וַתִּגְעַשׁ וַתִּרְעַשׁ ׀ הָאָרֶץ

וּמוֹסְדֵי הָרִים יִרְגָּזוּ

וַיִּתְגָּעֲשׁוּ כִּי־חָרָה לוֹ׃

9 עָלָה עָשָׁן ׀ בְּאַפּוֹ

וְאֵשׁ־מִפִּיו תֹּאכֵל

גֶּחָלִים בָּעֲרוּ מִמֶּנּוּ׃

---

a   This poem occurs again at 2 Sam. 22, with a number of variations, some of which are cited in the following notes.

b-b   Not in 2 Sam. 22.2.

c-c   Lit. "horn of rescue."

d-d   Construction of Heb. uncertain.

e   2 Sam. 22.5, "breakers."

f   I.e., the netherworld, like "Death" and "Sheol."

10He bent the sky and came down,

thick cloud beneath His feet.

11He mounted a cherub and flew,

gliding on the wings of the wind.

12He made darkness His screen;

dark thunderheads, dense clouds of the sky

were His pavilion round about Him.

13Out of the brilliance before Him,

hail and fiery coals g-pierced His clouds.-g

14Then the LORD thundered from heaven,

the Most High gave forth His voice—

h-hail and fiery coals.-h

15He let fly His shafts and scattered them;

He discharged lightning and routed them.

16The ocean bed was exposed;

the foundations of the world were laid bare

by Your mighty roaring, O LORD,

at the blast of the breath of Your nostrils.

17He reached down from on high, He took me;

He drew me out of the mighty waters;

18He saved me from my fierce enemy,

from foes too strong for me.

19They confronted me on the day of my calamity,

but the LORD was my support.

20He brought me out to freedom;

He rescued me because He was pleased with me.

21The LORD rewarded me according to my merit;

He requited the cleanness of my hands;

22for I have kept to the ways of the LORD,

and have not been guilty before my God;

23for I am mindful of all His rules;

I have not disregarded His laws.

24I have been blameless toward Him,

and have guarded myself against sinning;

25and the LORD has requited me according to

my merit,

the cleanness of my hands in His sight.

10 וַיֵּט שָׁמַיִם וַיֵּרַד

וַעֲרָפֶל תַּחַת רַגְלָיו:

11 וַיִּרְכַּב עַל־כְּרוּב וַיָּעֹף

וַיֵּדֶא עַל־כַּנְפֵי־רוּחַ:

12 יָשֶׁת חֹשֶׁךְ ׀ סִתְרוֹ

סְבִיבוֹתָיו סֻכָּתוֹ

חֶשְׁכַת־מַיִם עָבֵי שְׁחָקִים:

13 מִנֹּגַהּ נֶגְדּוֹ עָבָיו עָבְרוּ

בָּרָד וְגַחֲלֵי־אֵשׁ:

14 וַיַּרְעֵם בַּשָּׁמַיִם ׀ יְהֹוָה

וְעֶלְיוֹן יִתֵּן קֹלוֹ

בָּרָד וְגַחֲלֵי־אֵשׁ:

15 וַיִּשְׁלַח חִצָּיו וַיְפִיצֵם

וּבְרָקִים רָב וַיְהֻמֵּם:

16 וַיֵּרָאוּ ׀ אֲפִיקֵי מַיִם

וַיִּגָּלוּ מוֹסְדוֹת תֵּבֵל

מִגַּעֲרָתְךָ יְהֹוָה

מִנִּשְׁמַת רוּחַ אַפֶּךָ:

17 יִשְׁלַח מִמָּרוֹם יִקָּחֵנִי

יַמְשֵׁנִי מִמַּיִם רַבִּים:

18 יַצִּילֵנִי מֵאֹיְבִי עָז

וּמִשֹּׂנְאַי כִּי־אָמְצוּ מִמֶּנִּי:

19 יְקַדְּמוּנִי בְיוֹם־אֵידִי

וַיְהִי־יְהֹוָה לְמִשְׁעָן לִי:

20 וַיּוֹצִיאֵנִי לַמֶּרְחָב

יְחַלְּצֵנִי כִּי חָפֵץ בִּי:

21 יִגְמְלֵנִי יְהֹוָה כְּצִדְקִי

כְּבֹר יָדַי יָשִׁיב לִי:

22 כִּי־שָׁמַרְתִּי דַּרְכֵי יְהֹוָה

וְלֹא־רָשַׁעְתִּי מֵאֱלֹהָי:

23 כִּי כָל־מִשְׁפָּטָיו לְנֶגְדִּי

וְחֻקֹּתָיו לֹא־אָסִיר מֶנִּי:

24 וָאֱהִי תָמִים עִמּוֹ

וָאֶשְׁתַּמֵּר מֵעֲוֹנִי:

25 וַיָּשֶׁב־יְהֹוָה לִי כְצִדְקִי

כְּבֹר יָדַי לְנֶגֶד עֵינָיו:

g-g   2 Sam. 22.13, "blazed."
h-h   Not in 2 Sam. 22.14.

1429

26With the loyal, You deal loyally;

  with the blameless man, blamelessly.

27With the pure, You act purely,

  and with the perverse, You are wily.

28It is You who deliver lowly folk,

  but haughty eyes You humble.

29It is You who light my lamp;

  the Lord, my God, lights up my darkness.

30With You, I can rush a barrier;[i]

  with my God I can scale a wall;

31the way of God is perfect;

  the word of the Lord is pure;

  He is a shield to all who seek refuge in Him.

32Truly, who is a god except the Lord,

  who is a rock but our God?—

33the God who girded me with might,

  who made my way perfect;

34who made my legs like a deer's,

  and let me stand firm on the[j] heights;

35who trained my hands for battle;

  my arms can bend a bow of bronze.

36You have given me the shield of Your protection;

  Your right hand has sustained me,

  Your care[k] has made me great.

37You have let me stride on freely;

  my feet have not slipped.

38I pursued my enemies and overtook them;

  I did not turn back till I destroyed them.

39I struck them down,

  and they could rise no more;

  they lay fallen at my feet.

40You have girded me with strength for battle,

  brought my adversaries low before me,

41made my enemies turn tail before me;

  I wiped out my foes.

42They cried out, but there was none to deliver;

  [cried] to the Lord, but He did not answer them.

---

i *Cf. note to 2 Sam. 22.30; or "troop."*

j *Taking bamothai as a poetic form of bamoth; cf. Hab. 3.19; others "my."*

k *Meaning of Heb. uncertain; others "condescension."*

26 עִם־חָסִיד תִּתְחַסָּד

עִם־גְּבַר תָּמִים תִּתַּמָּם:

27 עִם־נָבָר תִּתְבָּרָר

וְעִם־עִקֵּשׁ תִּתְפַּתָּל:

28 כִּי־אַתָּה עַם־עָנִי תוֹשִׁיעַ

וְעֵינַיִם רָמוֹת תַּשְׁפִּיל:

29 כִּי־אַתָּה תָּאִיר נֵרִי

יְהוָה אֱלֹהַי יַגִּיהַּ חָשְׁכִּי:

30 כִּי־בְךָ אָרֻץ גְּדוּד

וּבֵאלֹהַי אֲדַלֶּג־שׁוּר:

31 הָאֵל תָּמִים דַּרְכּוֹ

אִמְרַת־יְהוָה צְרוּפָה

מָגֵן הוּא לְכֹל ׀ הַחֹסִים בּוֹ:

32 כִּי מִי אֱלוֹהַּ מִבַּלְעֲדֵי יְהוָה

וּמִי צוּר זוּלָתִי אֱלֹהֵינוּ:

33 הָאֵל הַמְאַזְּרֵנִי חָיִל

וַיִּתֵּן תָּמִים דַּרְכִּי:

34 מְשַׁוֶּה רַגְלַי כָּאַיָּלוֹת

וְעַל בָּמֹתַי יַעֲמִידֵנִי:

35 מְלַמֵּד יָדַי לַמִּלְחָמָה

וְנִחֲתָה קֶשֶׁת־נְחוּשָׁה זְרוֹעֹתָי:

36 וַתִּתֶּן־לִי מָגֵן יִשְׁעֶךָ

וִימִינְךָ תִסְעָדֵנִי

וְעַנְוַתְךָ תַרְבֵּנִי:

37 תַּרְחִיב צַעֲדִי תַחְתָּי

וְלֹא מָעֲדוּ קַרְסֻלָּי:

38 אֶרְדּוֹף אוֹיְבַי וְאַשִּׂיגֵם

וְלֹא־אָשׁוּב עַד־כַּלּוֹתָם:

39 אֶמְחָצֵם

וְלֹא־יֻכְלוּ קוּם

יִפְּלוּ תַּחַת רַגְלָי:

40 וַתְּאַזְּרֵנִי חַיִל לַמִּלְחָמָה

תַּכְרִיעַ קָמַי תַּחְתָּי:

41 וְאֹיְבַי נָתַתָּה לִּי עֹרֶף

וּמְשַׂנְאַי אַצְמִיתֵם:

42 יְשַׁוְּעוּ וְאֵין־מוֹשִׁיעַ

עַל־יְהוָה וְלֹא עָנָם:

43I ground them fine as windswept dust;
  I trod them flat as dirt of the streets.

44You have rescued me from the strife of people;
  You have set me at the head of nations;
  peoples I knew not must serve me.

45At the mere report of me they are submissive;
  foreign peoples cower before me;
46foreign peoples lose courage,
  l-and come trembling out of their strongholds.-l

47The LORD lives! Blessed is my rock!
Exalted be God, my deliverer,
  48the God who has vindicated me
and made peoples subject to me,
  49who rescued me from my enemies,
  who raised me clear of my adversaries,
  saved me from lawless men.
50For this I sing Your praise among the nations,
  LORD,
  and hymn Your name:
51m-He accords great victories-m to His king,
  keeps faith with His anointed,
  with David and his offspring forever.

מג וְאֶשְׁחָקֵם כְּעָפָר עַל־פְּנֵי־רֻוּחַ
כְּטִיט חוּצוֹת אֲרִיקֵם:
מד תְּפַלְּטֵנִי מֵרִיבֵי עָם
תְּשִׂימֵנִי לְרֹאשׁ גּוֹיִם
עַם לֹא־יָדַעְתִּי יַעַבְדוּנִי:
מה לְשֵׁמַע אֹזֶן יִשָּׁמְעוּ לִי
בְּנֵי־נֵכָר יְכַחֲשׁוּ־לִי:
מו בְּנֵי־נֵכָר יִבֹּלוּ
וְיַחְרְגוּ מִמִּסְגְּרוֹתֵיהֶם:
מז חַי־יְהוָה וּבָרוּךְ צוּרִי
וְיָרוּם אֱלוֹהֵי* יִשְׁעִי:
מח הָאֵל הַנּוֹתֵן נְקָמוֹת לִי
וַיַּדְבֵּר עַמִּים תַּחְתָּי:
מט מְפַלְּטִי מֵאֹיְבָי
אַף מִן־קָמַי תְּרוֹמְמֵנִי
מֵאִישׁ חָמָס תַּצִּילֵנִי:
נ עַל־כֵּן ׀ אוֹדְךָ בַגּוֹיִם ׀ יְהוָה
וּלְשִׁמְךָ אֲזַמֵּרָה:
נא מַגְדִּל מַגְדִּיל יְשׁוּעוֹת מַלְכּוֹ
וְעֹשֶׂה חֶסֶד ׀ לִמְשִׁיחוֹ
לְדָוִד וּלְזַרְעוֹ עַד־עוֹלָם:

19 For the leader. A psalm of David.

יט לַמְנַצֵּחַ מִזְמוֹר לְדָוִד:

2The heavens declare the glory of God,
  the sky proclaims His handiwork.
3Day to day makes utterance,
  night to night speaks out.
4There is no utterance,
  there are no words,
  a-whose sound goes unheard.-a
5Their voiceb carries throughout the earth,
  their words to the end of the world.
He placed in themc a tent for the sun,

ב הַשָּׁמַיִם מְסַפְּרִים כְּבוֹד־אֵל
וּמַעֲשֵׂה יָדָיו מַגִּיד הָרָקִיעַ:
ג יוֹם לְיוֹם יַבִּיעַ אֹמֶר
וְלַיְלָה לְּלַיְלָה יְחַוֶּה־דָּעַת:
ד אֵין־אֹמֶר
וְאֵין דְּבָרִים
בְּלִי נִשְׁמָע קוֹלָם:
ה בְּכָל־הָאָרֶץ ׀ יָצָא קַוָּם
וּבִקְצֵה תֵבֵל מִלֵּיהֶם
לַשֶּׁמֶשׁ שָׂם־אֹהֶל בָּהֶם:

---

l-l   Meaning of Heb. uncertain.
m-m   2 Sam. 22.51, "Tower of victory."

a-a   With Septuagint, Symmachus, and Vulgate; or "their sound is not
        heard."
b   Cf. Septuagint, Symmachus, and Vulgate; Arabic qawwah, "to shout."
c   Viz., the heavens.

מלא ו׳   v. 47.

6who is like a groom coming forth from the
    chamber,
    like a hero, eager to run his course.
7His rising-place is at one end of heaven,
    and his circuit reaches the other;
    nothing escapes his heat.

8The teaching of the LORD is perfect,
    renewing life;
    the decrees of the LORD are enduring,
    making the simple wise;
9The precepts of the LORD are just,
    rejoicing the heart;
    the instruction of the LORD is lucid,
    making the eyes light up.
10The fear of the LORD is pure,
    abiding forever;
    the judgments of the LORD are true,
    righteous altogether,
11more desirable than gold,
    than much fine gold;
    sweeter than honey,
    than drippings of the comb.
12Your servant pays them heed;
    in obeying them there is much reward.
13Who can be aware of errors?
    Clear me of unperceived guilt,
14and from d-willful sins-d keep Your servant;
    let them not dominate me;
    then shall I be blameless
    and clear of grave offense.
15May the words of my mouth
    and the prayer of my hearte
    be acceptable to You,
    O LORD, my rock and my redeemer.

6 וְהוּא כְּחָתָן יֹצֵא מֵחֻפָּתוֹ
יָשִׂישׂ כְּגִבּוֹר לָרוּץ אֹרַח:
7 מִקְצֵה הַשָּׁמַיִם ׀ מוֹצָאוֹ
וּתְקוּפָתוֹ עַל־קְצוֹתָם
וְאֵין נִסְתָּר מֵחַמָּתוֹ:

8 תּוֹרַת יְהוָה תְּמִימָה
מְשִׁיבַת נָפֶשׁ
עֵדוּת יְהוָה נֶאֱמָנָה
מַחְכִּימַת פֶּתִי:
9 פִּקּוּדֵי יְהוָה יְשָׁרִים
מְשַׂמְּחֵי־לֵב
מִצְוַת יְהוָה בָּרָה
מְאִירַת עֵינָיִם:
10 יִרְאַת יְהוָה ׀ טְהוֹרָה
עוֹמֶדֶת לָעַד
מִשְׁפְּטֵי־יְהוָה אֱמֶת
צָדְקוּ יַחְדָּו:
11 הַנֶּחֱמָדִים מִזָּהָב
וּמִפַּז רָב
וּמְתוּקִים מִדְּבַשׁ
וְנֹפֶת צוּפִים:
12 גַּם־עַבְדְּךָ נִזְהָר בָּהֶם
בְּשָׁמְרָם עֵקֶב רָב:
13 שְׁגִיאוֹת מִי־יָבִין
מִנִּסְתָּרוֹת נַקֵּנִי:
14 גַּם מִזֵּדִים ׀ חֲשֹׂךְ עַבְדֶּךָ
אַל־יִמְשְׁלוּ־בִי
אָז אֵיתָם
וְנִקֵּיתִי מִפֶּשַׁע רָב:
15 יִהְיוּ לְרָצוֹן ׀
אִמְרֵי־פִי
וְהֶגְיוֹן לִבִּי לְפָנֶיךָ
יְהוָה צוּרִי וְגֹאֲלִי:

---

d-d Or "arrogant men"; cf. Ps. 119.51.
e For leb as a source of speech, see note to Eccl. 5.1.

20 For the leader. A psalm of David.

כ   לַמְנַצֵּחַ מִזְמוֹר לְדָוִד:

2May the LORD answer you in time of trouble,
   the name of Jacob's God keep you safe.

²יַעַנְךָ יְהוָה בְּיוֹם צָרָה
   יְשַׂגֶּבְךָ שֵׁם ׀ אֱלֹהֵי יַעֲקֹב:

3May He send you help from the sanctuary,
   and sustain you from Zion.

³יִשְׁלַח־עֶזְרְךָ מִקֹּדֶשׁ
   וּמִצִּיּוֹן יִסְעָדֶךָּ:

4May He receive the tokens[a] of all your meal
   offerings,
   and approve[b] your burnt offerings.   *Selah.*

⁴יִזְכֹּר כָּל־מִנְחֹתֶךָ
   וְעוֹלָתְךָ יְדַשְּׁנֶה   סֶלָה:

5May He grant you your desire,
   and fulfill your every plan.

⁵יִתֶּן־לְךָ כִלְבָבֶךָ
   וְכָל־עֲצָתְךָ יְמַלֵּא:

6May we shout for joy in your victory,
   arrayed by standards in the name of our God.
May the LORD fulfill your every wish.

⁶נְרַנְּנָה ׀ בִּישׁוּעָתֶךָ
   וּבְשֵׁם־אֱלֹהֵינוּ נִדְגֹּל
יְמַלֵּא יְהוָה כָּל־מִשְׁאֲלוֹתֶיךָ:

7Now I know that the LORD will give victory to
   His anointed,
   will answer him from His heavenly sanctuary
   with the mighty victories of His right arm.

⁷עַתָּה יָדַעְתִּי כִּי הוֹשִׁיעַ ׀ יְהוָה
   מְשִׁיחוֹ
יַעֲנֵהוּ מִשְּׁמֵי קָדְשׁוֹ
   בִּגְבֻרוֹת יֵשַׁע יְמִינוֹ:

8They [call] on chariots, they [call] on horses,
   but we call on the name of the LORD our God.

⁸אֵלֶּה בָרֶכֶב וְאֵלֶּה בַסּוּסִים
   וַאֲנַחְנוּ ׀ בְּשֵׁם־יְהוָה אֱלֹהֵינוּ
נַזְכִּיר:

9They collapse and lie fallen,
   but we rally and gather strength.

⁹הֵמָּה כָּרְעוּ וְנָפָלוּ
   וַאֲנַחְנוּ קַּמְנוּ וַנִּתְעוֹדָד:

10cO LORD, grant victory!
May the King answer us when we call.-c

¹⁰יְהוָה הוֹשִׁיעָה
   הַמֶּלֶךְ יַעֲנֵנוּ בְיוֹם־קָרְאֵנוּ:

21 For the leader. A psalm of David.

כא   לַמְנַצֵּחַ מִזְמוֹר לְדָוִד:

2O LORD, the king rejoices in Your strength;
   how greatly he exults in Your victory!

²יְהוָה בְּעָזְּךָ יִשְׂמַח־מֶלֶךְ
   וּבִישׁוּעָתְךָ מַה־יָּגֶיל* מְאֹד:

3You have granted him the desire of his heart,
   have not denied the request of his lips.   *Selah.*

³תַּאֲוַת לִבּוֹ נָתַתָּה לּוֹ
   וַאֲרֶשֶׁת שְׂפָתָיו בַּל־מָנַעְתָּ   סֶלָה:

4You have proffered him blessings of good things,
   have set upon his head a crown of fine gold.

⁴כִּי־תְקַדְּמֶנּוּ בִּרְכוֹת טוֹב
   תָּשִׁית לְרֹאשׁוֹ עֲטֶרֶת פָּז:

---

a   Reference to azkara, "token portion" of meal offering; Lev. 2.2, 9, 16,
   etc.
b   Meaning of Heb. uncertain.
c-c   Or in the light of v. 7, "O LORD, grant victory to the king; may He
   answer us when we call."

v. 2. יָתֵיר י׳

⁵He asked You for life; You granted it;
    a long life, everlasting.

⁶Great is his glory through Your victory;
    You have endowed him with splendor and
      majesty.

⁷You have made him blessed forever,
    gladdened him with the joy of Your presence.

⁸For the king trusts in the Lᴏʀᴅ;
    Through the faithfulness of the Most High
    he will not be shaken.

⁹Your hand is equal to all Your enemies;
    Your right hand overpowers Your foes.

¹⁰You set them ablaze like a furnace
    ᵃ-when You show Your presence.-ᵃ
The Lᴏʀᴅ in anger destroys them;
    fire consumes them.

¹¹You wipe their offspring from the earth,
    their issue from among men.

¹²For they schemed against You;
    they laid plans,
    but could not succeed.

¹³ᵇ-For You make them turn back-ᵇ
    by Your bows aimed at their face.

¹⁴Be exalted, O Lᴏʀᴅ, through Your strength;
    we will sing and chant the praises of Your
      mighty deeds.

22   For the leader; on ᵃ-ayyeleth ha-shaḥar.-ᵃ
A psalm of David.

²My God, my God,
    why have You abandoned me;
    why so far from delivering me
    and from my anguished roaring?

³My God,
    I cry by day—You answer not;
    by night, and have no respite.

---

5 חַיִּים ׀ שָׁאַל מִמְּךָ נָתַתָּה לּוֹ
אֹרֶךְ יָמִים עוֹלָם וָעֶד:

6 גָּדוֹל כְּבוֹדוֹ בִּישׁוּעָתֶךָ
הוֹד וְהָדָר תְּשַׁוֶּה עָלָיו:

7 כִּי־תְשִׁיתֵהוּ בְרָכוֹת לָעַד
תְּחַדֵּהוּ בְשִׂמְחָה אֶת־פָּנֶיךָ:

8 כִּי־הַמֶּלֶךְ בֹּטֵחַ בַּיהוָה
וּבְחֶסֶד עֶלְיוֹן
בַּל־יִמּוֹט:

9 תִּמְצָא יָדְךָ לְכָל־אֹיְבֶיךָ
יְמִינְךָ תִּמְצָא שֹׂנְאֶיךָ:

10 תְּשִׁיתֵמוֹ ׀ כְּתַנּוּר אֵשׁ
לְעֵת פָּנֶיךָ
יְהוָה בְּאַפּוֹ יְבַלְּעֵם
וְתֹאכְלֵם אֵשׁ:

11 פִּרְיָמוֹ מֵאֶרֶץ תְּאַבֵּד
וְזַרְעָם מִבְּנֵי אָדָם:

12 כִּי־נָטוּ עָלֶיךָ רָעָה
חָשְׁבוּ מְזִמָּה
בַּל־יוּכָלוּ:

13 כִּי תְּשִׁיתֵמוֹ שֶׁכֶם
בְּמֵיתָרֶיךָ תְּכוֹנֵן עַל־פְּנֵיהֶם:

14 רוּמָה יְהוָה בְּעֻזֶּךָ
נָשִׁירָה וּנְזַמְּרָה גְּבוּרָתֶךָ:

כב לַמְנַצֵּחַ עַל־אַיֶּלֶת הַשַּׁחַר
מִזְמוֹר לְדָוִד:

2 אֵלִי אֵלִי
לָמָה עֲזַבְתָּנִי
רָחוֹק מִישׁוּעָתִי
דִּבְרֵי שַׁאֲגָתִי:

3 אֱלֹהַי
אֶקְרָא יוֹמָם וְלֹא תַעֲנֶה
וְלַיְלָה וְלֹא־דוּמִיָּה לִי:

---

a-a   Or "at the time of Your anger."
b-b   Meaning of Heb. uncertain.

a-a   Meaning of Heb. uncertain.

4b-But You are the Holy One,
   enthroned,
   the Praise of Israel.-b

5In You our fathers trusted;
   they trusted, and You rescued them.

6To You they cried out
   and they escaped;
   in You they trusted
   and were not disappointed.

7But I am a worm, less than human;
   scorned by men, despised by people.

8All who see me mock me;
   c-they curl their lips,-c
   they shake their heads.

9"Let him commit himself to the LORD;
   let Him rescue him,
   let Him save him,
   for He is pleased with him."

10You a-drew me-a from the womb,
   made me secure at my mother's breast.

11I became Your charge at birth;
   from my mother's womb You have been my
      God.

12Do not be far from me,
   for trouble is near,
   and there is none to help.

13Many bulls surround me,
   mighty ones of Bashan encircle me.

14They open their mouths at me
   like tearing, roaring lions.

15d-My life ebbs away:-d
   all my bones are disjointed;
   my heart is like wax,
   melting within me;

16my vigor dries up like a shard;
   my tongue cleaves to my palate;
   You commit me to the dust of death.

4 וְאַתָּה קָדוֹשׁ
יוֹשֵׁב
תְּהִלּוֹת יִשְׂרָאֵל:
5 בְּךָ בָּטְחוּ אֲבֹתֵינוּ
בָּטְחוּ וַתְּפַלְּטֵמוֹ:
6 אֵלֶיךָ זָעֲקוּ
וְנִמְלָטוּ
בְּךָ בָטְחוּ
וְלֹא־בוֹשׁוּ:

7 וְאָנֹכִי תוֹלַעַת וְלֹא־אִישׁ
חֶרְפַּת אָדָם וּבְזוּי עָם:
8 כָּל־רֹאַי יַלְעִגוּ לִי
יַפְטִירוּ בְשָׂפָה
יָנִיעוּ רֹאשׁ:
9 גֹּל אֶל־יְהוָה
יְפַלְּטֵהוּ
יַצִּילֵהוּ
כִּי חָפֵץ בּוֹ:
10 כִּי־אַתָּה גֹחִי מִבָּטֶן
מַבְטִיחִי עַל־שְׁדֵי אִמִּי:
11 עָלֶיךָ הָשְׁלַכְתִּי מֵרָחֶם
מִבֶּטֶן אִמִּי אֵלִי אָתָּה:
12 אַל־תִּרְחַק מִמֶּנִּי
כִּי־צָרָה קְרוֹבָה
כִּי־אֵין עוֹזֵר:
13 סְבָבוּנִי פָּרִים רַבִּים
אַבִּירֵי בָשָׁן כִּתְּרוּנִי:
14 פָּצוּ עָלַי פִּיהֶם
אַרְיֵה טֹרֵף וְשֹׁאֵג:
15 כַּמַּיִם נִשְׁפַּכְתִּי
וְהִתְפָּרְדוּ כָּל־עַצְמוֹתָי
הָיָה לִבִּי כַּדּוֹנָג
נָמֵס בְּתוֹךְ מֵעָי:
16 יָבֵשׁ כַּחֶרֶשׂ ׀ כֹּחִי
וּלְשׁוֹנִי מֻדְבָּק מַלְקוֹחָי
וְלַעֲפַר־מָוֶת תִּשְׁפְּתֵנִי:

b-b   Or "But You are holy, enthroned upon the praises of Israel."
c-c   Lit. "they open wide with a lip."
d-d   Lit. "I am poured out like water."

17Dogs surround me;

  a pack of evil ones closes in on me,

  e-like lions [they maul] my hands and feet.-e

18I take the count of all my bones

  while they look on and gloat.

19They divide my clothes among themselves,

  casting lots for my garments.

20But You, O Lord, be not far off;

  my strength, hasten to my aid.

21Save my life from the sword,

  my precious lifef from the clutches of a dog.

22Deliver me from a lion's mouth;

  from the horns of wild oxen rescueg me.

23Then will I proclaim Your fame to my brethren,

  praise You in the congregation.

24You who fear the Lord, praise Him!

All you offspring of Jacob, honor Him!

Be in dread of Him, all you offspring of Israel!

25For He did not scorn, He did not spurn

  the pleah of the lowly;

  He did not hide His face from him;

  when he cried out to Him, He listened.

26i-Because of You I offer praise-i in the great con-

    gregation;

  I pay my vows in the presence of His wor-

    shipers.

27Let the lowly eat and be satisfied;

  let all who seek the Lord praise Him.

Always be of good cheer!

28Let all the ends of the earth pay heed and turn

    to the Lord,

  and the peoples of all nations prostrate them-

    selves before You;

29for kingship is the Lord's

  and He rules the nations.

17 כִּי סְבָבוּנִי כְּלָבִים
עֲדַת מְרֵעִים הִקִּיפוּנִי
כָּאֲרִי יָדַי וְרַגְלָי:
18 אֲסַפֵּר כָּל־עַצְמוֹתָי
הֵמָּה יַבִּיטוּ יִרְאוּ־בִי:
19 יְחַלְּקוּ בְגָדַי לָהֶם
וְעַל־לְבוּשִׁי יַפִּילוּ גוֹרָל:

20 וְאַתָּה יְהוָה אַל־תִּרְחָק
אֱיָלוּתִי לְעֶזְרָתִי חוּשָׁה:
21 הַצִּילָה מֵחֶרֶב נַפְשִׁי
מִיַּד־כֶּלֶב יְחִידָתִי:
22 הוֹשִׁיעֵנִי מִפִּי אַרְיֵה
וּמִקַּרְנֵי רֵמִים עֲנִיתָנִי:
23 אֲסַפְּרָה שִׁמְךָ לְאֶחָי
בְּתוֹךְ קָהָל אֲהַלְלֶךָּ:

24 יִרְאֵי יְהוָה | הַלְלוּהוּ
כָּל־זֶרַע יַעֲקֹב כַּבְּדוּהוּ
וְגוּרוּ מִמֶּנּוּ כָּל־זֶרַע יִשְׂרָאֵל:
25 כִּי לֹא־בָזָה וְלֹא שִׁקַּץ
עֱנוּת עָנִי
וְלֹא־הִסְתִּיר פָּנָיו מִמֶּנּוּ
וּבְשַׁוְּעוֹ אֵלָיו שָׁמֵעַ:
26 מֵאִתְּךָ תְהִלָּתִי בְּקָהָל רָב
נְדָרַי אֲשַׁלֵּם נֶגֶד יְרֵאָיו:
27 יֹאכְלוּ עֲנָוִים | וְיִשְׂבָּעוּ
יְהַלְלוּ יְהוָה דֹּרְשָׁיו
יְחִי לְבַבְכֶם לָעַד:
28 יִזְכְּרוּ | וְיָשֻׁבוּ אֶל־יְהוָה כָּל־
אַפְסֵי־אָרֶץ
וְיִשְׁתַּחֲווּ לְפָנֶיךָ כָּל־מִשְׁפְּחוֹת
גּוֹיִם:
29 כִּי לַיהוָה הַמְּלוּכָה
וּמֹשֵׁל בַּגּוֹיִם:

---

e-e   With Rashi; cf. Isa. 38.13.

f   Lit. "only one."

g   Lit. "answer."

h   Or "plight."

i-i   Lit. "From You is my praise."

30j-All those in full vigor shall eat and prostrate
   themselves;
  all those at death's door, whose spirits flag,
  shall bend the knee before Him.-j
31Offspring shall serve Him;
  the Lord's fame shall be proclaimed to the
   generation 32to come;
  they shall tell of His beneficence to people
   yet to be born,
  for He has acted.

אָכְלוּ וַיִּשְׁתַּחֲווּ ׀ כָּל־דִּשְׁנֵי־אֶ֫רֶץ 30
לְפָנָיו יִכְרְעוּ
כָּל־יוֹרְדֵי עָפָר וְנַפְשׁוֹ לֹא חִיָּה׃
זֶרַע יַעַבְדֶ֑נּוּ 31
יְסֻפַּר לַאדֹנָ֥י לַדּוֹר׃ יָבֹאוּ 32
וְיַגִּידוּ צִדְקָתוֹ לְעַ֣ם נוֹלָד
כִּי עָשָׂה׃

23 A psalm of David.

The Lord is my shepherd;
  I lack nothing.
2He makes me lie down in green pastures;
  He leads me to a-water in places of repose;-a
  3He renews my life;
  He guides me in right paths
  as befits His name.
4Though I walk through b-a valley of deepest
   darkness,-b
  I fear no harm, for You are with me;
  Your rod and Your staff—they comfort me.

5You spread a table for me in full view of my
   enemies;
  You anoint my head with oil;
  my drink is abundant.
6Only goodness and steadfast love shall pursue me
  all the days of my life,
  and I shall dwell in the house of the Lord
  for many long years.

כג מִזְמוֹר לְדָוִד

יְהֹוָה רֹ֫עִי
לֹא אֶחְסָר׃
בִּנְאוֹת דֶּשֶׁא יַרְבִּיצֵנִי 2
עַל־מֵי מְנֻחוֹת יְנַהֲלֵנִי׃
נַפְשִׁי יְשׁוֹבֵב 3
יַנְחֵנִי בְמַעְגְּלֵי־צֶדֶק
לְמַעַן שְׁמוֹ׃
גַּם כִּי־אֵלֵךְ בְּגֵיא צַלְמָ֫וֶת 4
לֹא־אִירָא רָע כִּי־אַתָּה עִמָּדִי
שִׁבְטְךָ וּמִשְׁעַנְתֶּ֗ךָ הֵמָּה יְנַחֲמֻנִי׃

תַּעֲרֹךְ לְפָנַ֨י ׀ שֻׁלְחָן נֶגֶד צֹרְרָ֫י 5
דִּשַּׁנְתָּ בַשֶּׁמֶן רֹאשִׁי
כּוֹסִי רְוָיָה׃
אַךְ ׀ טוֹב וָחֶסֶד יִרְדְּפוּנִי 6
כָּל־יְמֵי חַיָּי
וְשַׁבְתִּי בְּבֵית־יְהֹוָה
לְאֹרֶךְ יָמִים׃

j-j   *Meaning of Heb. uncertain; others "All the fat ones of the earth shall*
     eat and worship; / All they that go down to the dust shall kneel before
     Him, / Even he that cannot keep his soul alive."

a-a   *Others "still waters."*
b-b   *Others "the valley of the shadow of death."*

24 Of David. A psalm.

The earth is the LORD's and all that it holds,
   the world and its inhabitants.
²For He founded it upon the ocean,
   set it on the nether-streams.

³Who may ascend the mountain of the LORD?
Who may stand in His holy place?—
⁴He who has clean hands and a pure heart,
   who has not taken a false oath by My[a] life
   or sworn deceitfully.
⁵He shall carry away a blessing from the LORD,
   a just reward from God, his deliverer.
⁶Such is the circle[b] of those who turn to Him,
   Jacob, who seek Your presence.   *Selah.*

⁷O gates, lift up your heads!
Up high, you everlasting doors,
   so the King of glory may come in!
⁸Who is the King of glory?—
   the LORD, mighty and valiant,
   the LORD, valiant in battle.
⁹O gates, lift up your heads!
Lift them up, you everlasting doors,
   so the King of glory may come in!
¹⁰Who is the King of glory?—
   the LORD of hosts,
   He is the King of glory!   *Selah.*

25 Of David.

א O LORD, I set my hope on You;
ב ²my God, in You I trust;
   may I not be disappointed,
   may my enemies not exult over me.

כד לְדָוִ֗ד מִזְמ֥וֹר
לַֽ֭יהוָה הָאָ֣רֶץ וּמְלוֹאָ֑הּ
תֵּ֝בֵ֗ל וְיֹ֣שְׁבֵי בָֽהּ׃
2 כִּי־ה֭וּא עַל־יַמִּ֣ים יְסָדָ֑הּ
וְעַל־נְ֝הָר֗וֹת יְכוֹנְנֶֽהָ׃

3 מִֽי־יַעֲלֶ֥ה בְהַר־יְהוָ֑ה
וּמִי־יָ֝ק֗וּם בִּמְק֥וֹם קָדְשֽׁוֹ׃
4 נְקִ֥י כַפַּ֗יִם וּֽבַר־לֵ֫בָ֥ב
אֲשֶׁ֤ר ׀ לֹא־נָשָׂ֣א לַשָּׁ֣וְא נַפְשִׁ֑י
וְלֹ֖א נִשְׁבַּ֣ע לְמִרְמָֽה׃
5 יִשָּׂ֣א בְ֭רָכָה מֵאֵ֣ת יְהוָ֑ה
וּ֝צְדָקָ֗ה מֵאֱלֹהֵ֥י יִשְׁעֽוֹ׃
6 זֶ֣ה דּ֭וֹר דֹּרְשָׁ֑יו
מְבַקְשֵׁ֖י פָנֶ֣יךָ יַעֲקֹ֣ב סֶֽלָה׃

7 שְׂא֤וּ שְׁעָרִ֨ים ׀ רָֽאשֵׁיכֶ֗ם
וְֽ֭הִנָּשְׂאוּ פִּתְחֵ֣י עוֹלָ֑ם
וְ֝יָב֗וֹא מֶ֣לֶךְ הַכָּבֽוֹד׃
8 מִ֥י זֶה֮ מֶ֤לֶךְ הַכָּ֫ב֥וֹד
יְ֭הוָה עִזּ֣וּז וְגִבּ֑וֹר
יְ֝הוָ֗ה גִּבּ֥וֹר מִלְחָמָֽה׃
9 שְׂא֤וּ שְׁעָרִ֨ים ׀ רָֽאשֵׁיכֶ֗ם
וּ֭שְׂאוּ פִּתְחֵ֣י עוֹלָ֑ם
וְ֝יָבֹא מֶ֣לֶךְ הַכָּבֽוֹד׃
10 מִ֤י ה֣וּא זֶה֮ מֶ֤לֶךְ הַכָּ֫ב֥וֹד
יְהוָ֥ה צְבָא֑וֹת
ה֤וּא מֶ֖לֶךְ הַכָּב֣וֹד סֶֽלָה׃

כה לְדָוִ֡ד
אֵלֶ֥יךָ יְ֝הוָ֗ה נַפְשִׁ֥י אֶשָּֽׂא׃
2 אֱֽלֹהַ֗י בְּךָ֣ בָ֭טַחְתִּי
אַל־אֵב֑וֹשָׁה
אַל־יַֽעַלְצ֖וּ אֹיְבַ֣י לִֽי׃

---

a *Ancient versions and some mss. read "His."*
b *Lit. "generation."*

3 גַּם כָּל־קֹוֶיךָ לֹא יֵבֹשׁוּ
יֵבֹשׁוּ הַבּוֹגְדִים רֵיקָם:
4 דְּרָכֶיךָ יְהֹוָה הוֹדִיעֵנִי
אֹרְחוֹתֶיךָ לַמְּדֵנִי:
5 הַדְרִיכֵנִי בַאֲמִתֶּךָ ׀ וְלַמְּדֵנִי
כִּי־אַתָּה אֱלֹהֵי יִשְׁעִי
אוֹתְךָ קִוִּיתִי כָּל־הַיּוֹם:
6 זְכֹר־רַחֲמֶיךָ יְהֹוָה
וַחֲסָדֶיךָ
כִּי מֵעוֹלָם הֵמָּה:
7 חַטֹּאות* נְעוּרַי ׀ וּפְשָׁעַי אַל־
תִּזְכֹּר
כְּחַסְדְּךָ זְכָר־לִי־אַתָּה
לְמַעַן טוּבְךָ יְהֹוָה:
8 טוֹב־וְיָשָׁר יְהֹוָה
עַל־כֵּן יוֹרֶה חַטָּאִים בַּדָּרֶךְ:
9 יַדְרֵךְ עֲנָוִים בַּמִּשְׁפָּט
וִילַמֵּד עֲנָוִים דַּרְכּוֹ:
10 כָּל־אָרְחוֹת יְהֹוָה חֶסֶד וֶאֱמֶת
לְנֹצְרֵי בְרִיתוֹ וְעֵדֹתָיו:
11 לְמַעַן־שִׁמְךָ יְהֹוָה
וְסָלַחְתָּ לַעֲוֹנִי כִּי רַב־הוּא:
12 מִי־זֶה הָאִישׁ יְרֵא יְהֹוָה
יוֹרֶנּוּ בְּדֶרֶךְ יִבְחָר:
13 נַפְשׁוֹ בְּטוֹב תָּלִין
וְזַרְעוֹ יִירַשׁ אָרֶץ:
14 סוֹד יְהֹוָה לִירֵאָיו
וּבְרִיתוֹ לְהוֹדִיעָם:
15 עֵינַי תָּמִיד אֶל־יְהֹוָה
כִּי הוּא־יוֹצִיא מֵרֶשֶׁת רַגְלָי:
16 פְּנֵה־אֵלַי וְחָנֵּנִי
כִּי־יָחִיד וְעָנִי אָנִי:
17 צָרוֹת לְבָבִי הִרְחִיבוּ
מִמְּצוּקוֹתַי הוֹצִיאֵנִי:
18 רְאֵה עָנְיִי וַעֲמָלִי
וְשָׂא לְכָל־חַטֹּאותָי*:

3 ³O let none who look to You be disappointed;
   let the faithless be disappointed, empty-
     handed.

ד ⁴Let me know Your paths, O LORD;
   teach me Your ways;

הו ⁵guide me in Your true way and teach me,
   for You are God, my deliverer;
   it is You I look to at all times.

ז ⁶O LORD, be mindful of Your compassion
   and Your faithfulness;
   they are old as time.

ח ⁷Be not mindful of my youthful sins and trans-
    gressions;
   in keeping with Your faithfulness consider
    what is in my favor,
   as befits Your goodness, O LORD.

ט ⁸Good and upright is the LORD;
   therefore He shows sinners the way.

י ⁹He guides the lowly in the right path,
   and teaches the lowly His way.

כ ¹⁰All the LORD's paths are steadfast love
   for those who keep the decrees of His covenant.

ל ¹¹As befits Your name, O LORD,
   pardon my iniquity though it be great.

מ ¹²Whoever fears the LORD,
   he shall be shown what path to choose.

נ ¹³He shall live a happy life,
   and his children shall inherit the land.

ס ¹⁴The counsel[a] of the LORD is for those who fear
    Him;
   to them He makes known His covenant.

ע ¹⁵My eyes are ever toward the LORD,
   for He will loose my feet from the net.

פ ¹⁶Turn to me, have mercy on me,
   for I am alone and afflicted.

צ ¹⁷b-My deep distress-b increases;
   deliver me from my straits.

ר ¹⁸Look at my affliction and suffering,
   and forgive all my sins.

v. 7. מלא ו'
v. 18. מלא ו'

a Or "secret."
b-b Lit. "The distress of my heart."

¹⁹See how numerous my enemies are,
   and how unjustly they hate me!

ש ²⁰Protect me and save me;
   let me not be disappointed,
   for I have sought refuge in You.

ת ²¹May integrity and uprightness watch over me,
   for I look to You.
     ²²O God, redeem Israel
   from all its distress.

19 רְאֵה־אוֹיְבַי כִּי־רָבּוּ
וְשִׂנְאַת חָמָס שְׂנֵאוּנִי:
20 שָׁמְרָה נַפְשִׁי וְהַצִּילֵנִי
אַל־אֵבוֹשׁ
כִּי־חָסִיתִי בָךְ:
21 תֹּם־וָיֹשֶׁר יִצְּרוּנִי
כִּי קִוִּיתִיךָ:
22 פְּדֵה אֱלֹהִים אֶת־יִשְׂרָאֵל
מִכֹּל צָרוֹתָיו:

26 Of David.

Vindicate me, O LORD,
   for I have walked without blame;
   I have trusted in the LORD;
   I have not faltered.
²Probe me, O LORD, and try me,
   test my ^{a-}heart and mind;^{-a}
    ^{3b-}for my eyes are on Your steadfast love;
   I have set my course by it.^{-b}
⁴I do not consort with scoundrels,
   or mix with hypocrites;
⁵I detest the company of evil men,
   and do not consort with the wicked;
⁶I wash my hands in innocence,
   and walk around Your altar, O LORD,
⁷raising my voice in thanksgiving,
   and telling all Your wonders.
⁸O LORD, I love Your temple abode,
   the dwelling-place of Your glory.
⁹Do not sweep me away with sinners,
   or [snuff out] my life with murderers,
    ¹⁰who have schemes at their fingertips,
   and hands full of bribes.
¹¹But I walk without blame;
   redeem me, have mercy on me!

כו לְדָוִד |

שָׁפְטֵנִי יְהוָה
כִּי־אֲנִי בְּתֻמִּי הָלַכְתִּי
וּבַיהוָה בָּטַחְתִּי
לֹא אֶמְעָד:
2 בְּחָנֵנִי יְהוָה וְנַסֵּנִי
צָרְפָה כִלְיוֹתַי וְלִבִּי:
3 כִּי־חַסְדְּךָ לְנֶגֶד עֵינָי
וְהִתְהַלַּכְתִּי בַּאֲמִתֶּךָ:
4 לֹא־יָשַׁבְתִּי עִם־מְתֵי־שָׁוְא
וְעִם נַעֲלָמִים לֹא אָבוֹא:
5 שָׂנֵאתִי קְהַל מְרֵעִים
וְעִם־רְשָׁעִים לֹא אֵשֵׁב:
6 אֶרְחַץ בְּנִקָּיוֹן כַּפָּי
וַאֲסֹבְבָה אֶת־מִזְבַּחֲךָ יְהוָה:
7 לַשְׁמִעַ* בְּקוֹל תּוֹדָה
וּלְסַפֵּר כָּל־נִפְלְאוֹתֶיךָ:
8 יְהוָה אָהַבְתִּי מְעוֹן בֵּיתֶךָ
וּמְקוֹם מִשְׁכַּן כְּבוֹדֶךָ:
9 אַל־תֶּאֱסֹף עִם־חַטָּאִים נַפְשִׁי
וְעִם־אַנְשֵׁי דָמִים חַיָּי:
10 אֲשֶׁר־בִּידֵיהֶם זִמָּה
וִימִינָם מָלְאָה שֹּׁחַד:
11 וַאֲנִי בְּתֻמִּי אֵלֵךְ
פְּדֵנִי וְחָנֵּנִי:

---

^{a-a} Lit. "kidneys and heart."
^{b-b} Or "I am aware of Your faithfulness, and always walk in Your true
   [path]."

¹²My feet are on level ground.
In assemblies I will bless the LORD.

¹²רַגְלִי עָמְדָה בְמִישׁוֹר
בְּמַקְהֵלִים אֲבָרֵךְ יְהוָה:

27 Of David.

כז לְדָוִד

The LORD is my light and my help;
    whom should I fear?
The LORD is the stronghold of my life,
    whom should I dread?
²When evil men assail me
    ^ato devour my flesh^{-a}—
it is they, my foes and my enemies,
    who stumble and fall.
³Should an army besiege me,
    my heart would have no fear;
should war beset me,
    still would I be confident.

יְהוָה ׀ אוֹרִי וְיִשְׁעִי
מִמִּי אִירָא
יְהוָה מָעוֹז־חַיַּי
מִמִּי אֶפְחָד:
²בִּקְרֹב עָלַי ׀ מְרֵעִים
לֶאֱכֹל אֶת־בְּשָׂרִי
צָרַי וְאֹיְבַי לִי
הֵמָּה כָשְׁלוּ וְנָפָלוּ:
³אִם־תַּחֲנֶה עָלַי ׀ מַחֲנֶה
לֹא־יִירָא לִבִּי
אִם־תָּקוּם עָלַי מִלְחָמָה
בְּזֹאת אֲנִי בוֹטֵחַ:

⁴One thing I ask of the LORD,
    only that do I seek:
to live in the house of the LORD
    all the days of my life,
to gaze upon the beauty of the LORD,
    ^bto frequent^{-b} His temple.
⁵He will shelter me in His pavilion
    on an evil day,
grant me the protection of His tent,
    raise me high upon a rock.
⁶Now is my head high
    over my enemies roundabout;
I sacrifice in His tent with shouts of joy,
    singing and chanting a hymn to the LORD.

⁴אַחַת ׀ שָׁאַלְתִּי מֵאֵת־יְהוָה
אוֹתָהּ אֲבַקֵּשׁ
שִׁבְתִּי בְּבֵית־יְהוָה
כָּל־יְמֵי חַיַּי
לַחֲזוֹת בְּנֹעַם־יְהוָה
וּלְבַקֵּר בְּהֵיכָלוֹ:
⁵כִּי יִצְפְּנֵנִי ׀ בְּסֻכֹּה
בְּיוֹם רָעָה
יַסְתִּרֵנִי בְּסֵתֶר אָהֳלוֹ
בְּצוּר יְרוֹמְמֵנִי:
⁶וְעַתָּה יָרוּם רֹאשִׁי
עַל אֹיְבַי סְבִיבוֹתַי
וְאֶזְבְּחָה בְאָהֳלוֹ זִבְחֵי תְרוּעָה
אָשִׁירָה וַאֲזַמְּרָה לַיהוָה:

⁷Hear, O LORD, when I cry aloud;
    have mercy on me, answer me.
^{8b}In Your behalf^{-b} my heart says:
    "Seek My face!"

⁷שְׁמַע־יְהוָה קוֹלִי אֶקְרָא
וְחָנֵּנִי וַעֲנֵנִי:
⁸לְךָ ׀ אָמַר לִבִּי
בַּקְּשׁוּ פָנָי

---

^{a-a} Or "to slander me"; cf. Dan. 3.8; 6.25.
^{b-b} Meaning of Heb. uncertain.

O Lᴏʀᴅ, I seek Your face.

9Do not hide Your face from me;
   do not thrust aside Your servant in anger;
   You have ever been my help.

Do not forsake me, do not abandon me,
   O God, my deliverer.

10Though my father and mother abandon me,
   the Lᴏʀᴅ will take me in.

11Show me Your way, O Lᴏʀᴅ,
   and lead me on a level path
   because of my watchful foes.

12Do not subject me to the will of my foes,
   for false witnesses and unjust accusers
   have appeared against me.

13Had I not the assurance
   that I would enjoy the goodness of the Lᴏʀᴅ
   in the land of the living…

14Look to the Lᴏʀᴅ;
   be strong and of good courage!
   O look to the Lᴏʀᴅ!

28 Of David.

O Lᴏʀᴅ, I call to You;
   my rock, do not disregard me,
   for if You hold aloof from me,
   I shall be like those gone down into the Pit.

2Listen to my plea for mercy
   when I cry out to You,
   when I lift my hands
   toward Your inner sanctuary.

3Do not ᵃ-count me-ᵃ with the wicked and evildoers
   who profess goodwill toward their fellows
   while malice is in their heart.

4Pay them according to their deeds,
   their malicious acts;

אֶת־פָּנֶיךָ יְהוָה אֲבַקֵּשׁ:
9 אַל־תַּסְתֵּר פָּנֶיךָ ׀ מִמֶּנִּי
אַל־תַּט־בְּאַף עַבְדֶּךָ עֶזְרָתִי הָיִיתָ
אַל־תִּטְּשֵׁנִי וְאַל־תַּעַזְבֵנִי
אֱלֹהֵי יִשְׁעִי:
10 כִּי־אָבִי וְאִמִּי עֲזָבוּנִי
וַיהוָה יַאַסְפֵנִי:
11 הוֹרֵנִי יְהוָה דַּרְכֶּךָ
וּנְחֵנִי בְּאֹרַח מִישׁוֹר
לְמַעַן שׁוֹרְרָי:
12 אַל־תִּתְּנֵנִי בְּנֶפֶשׁ צָרָי
כִּי קָמוּ־בִי
עֵדֵי־שֶׁקֶר וִיפֵחַ חָמָס:
13 לוּלֵא* הֶאֱמַנְתִּי
לִרְאוֹת בְּטוּב־יְהוָה
בְּאֶרֶץ חַיִּים:

14 קַוֵּה אֶל־יְהוָה
חֲזַק וְיַאֲמֵץ לִבֶּךָ
וְקַוֵּה אֶל־יְהוָה:

כח לְדָוִד

אֵלֶיךָ יְהוָה ׀ אֶקְרָא
צוּרִי אַל־תֶּחֱרַשׁ מִמֶּנִּי
פֶּן־תֶּחֱשֶׁה מִמֶּנִּי
וְנִמְשַׁלְתִּי עִם־יוֹרְדֵי בוֹר:
2 שְׁמַע קוֹל תַּחֲנוּנַי
בְּשַׁוְּעִי אֵלֶיךָ
בְּנָשְׂאִי יָדַי
אֶל־דְּבִיר קָדְשֶׁךָ:
3 אַל־תִּמְשְׁכֵנִי עִם־רְשָׁעִים וְעִם־
פֹּעֲלֵי אָוֶן
דֹּבְרֵי שָׁלוֹם עִם־רֵעֵיהֶם
וְרָעָה בִּלְבָבָם:
4 תֶּן־לָהֶם כְּפָעֳלָם
וּכְרֹעַ מַעַלְלֵיהֶם

---

a-a Or "drag me off"; Meaning of Heb. uncertain.

נקוד על ל' ל' א' וגם מלמטה   .v. 13

according to their handiwork pay them,
    give them their deserts.

כְּמַעֲשֵׂה יְדֵיהֶם תֵּן לָהֶם
הָשֵׁב גְּמוּלָם לָהֶם:

5For they do not consider the LORD's deeds,
    the work of His hands.

5 כִּי לֹא יָבִינוּ אֶל־פְּעֻלֹּת יְהֹוָה
וְאֶל־מַעֲשֵׂה יָדָיו

May He tear them down,
    never to rebuild them!

יֶהֶרְסֵם
וְלֹא יִבְנֵם:

6Blessed is the LORD,
    for He listens to my plea for mercy.

6 בָּרוּךְ יְהֹוָה
כִּי־שָׁמַע קוֹל תַּחֲנוּנָי:

7The LORD is my strength and my shield;
    my heart trusts in Him.

7 יְהֹוָה | עֻזִּי וּמָגִנִּי
בּוֹ בָטַח לִבִּי

I was helped,b and my heart exulted,
    so I will glorify Him with my song.

וְנֶעֱזָרְתִּי וַיַּעֲלֹז לִבִּי
וּמִשִּׁירִי אֲהוֹדֶנּוּ:

8The LORD is c-their strength;-c
    He is a stronghold for the deliverance of His
    anointed.

8 יְהֹוָה עֹז־לָמוֹ
וּמָעוֹז יְשׁוּעוֹת מְשִׁיחוֹ הוּא:

9Deliver and bless Your very own people;
    tend them and sustain them forever.

9 הוֹשִׁיעָה | אֶת־עַמֶּךָ וּבָרֵךְ אֶת־
נַחֲלָתֶךָ
וּרְעֵם וְנַשְּׂאֵם עַד־הָעוֹלָם:

29 A psalm of David.

כט מִזְמוֹר לְדָוִד

Ascribe to the LORD, O divine beings,
    ascribe to the LORD glory and strength.

הָבוּ לַיהֹוָה בְּנֵי אֵלִים
הָבוּ לַיהֹוָה כָּבוֹד וָעֹז:

2Ascribe to the LORD the glory of His name;
    bow down to the LORD, majestic in holiness.

2 הָבוּ לַיהֹוָה כְּבוֹד שְׁמוֹ
הִשְׁתַּחֲווּ לַיהֹוָה בְּהַדְרַת־קֹדֶשׁ:

3The voice of the LORD is over the waters;
    the God of glory thunders,
    the LORD, over the mighty waters.

3 קוֹל יְהֹוָה עַל־הַמָּיִם
אֵל־הַכָּבוֹד הִרְעִים
יְהֹוָה עַל־מַיִם רַבִּים:

4The voice of the LORD is power;
    the voice of the LORD is majesty;

4 קוֹל־יְהֹוָה בַּכֹּחַ
קוֹל יְהֹוָה בֶּהָדָר:

5the voice of the LORD breaks cedars;
    the LORD shatters the cedars of Lebanon.

5 קוֹל יְהֹוָה שֹׁבֵר אֲרָזִים
וַיְשַׁבֵּר יְהֹוָה אֶת־אַרְזֵי הַלְּבָנוֹן:

6a-He makes Lebanon skip like a calf,-a
    Sirion, like a young wild ox.

6 וַיַּרְקִידֵם כְּמוֹ־עֵגֶל
לְבָנוֹן וְשִׂרְיֹן כְּמוֹ בֶן־רְאֵמִים:

7The voice of the LORD kindles flames of fire;

7 קוֹל־יְהֹוָה חֹצֵב לַהֲבוֹת אֵשׁ:

8the voice of the LORD convulses the wilderness;
    the LORD convulses the wilderness of Kadesh;

8 קוֹל יְהֹוָה יָחִיל מִדְבָּר
יָחִיל יְהֹוָה מִדְבַּר קָדֵשׁ:

---

b   Or "strengthened."

c-c Septuagint, Saadia, and others render, and some mss. read, 'oz
      le'ammo, "the strength of His people."

a-a Lit. "He makes them skip like a calf, Lebanon and Sirion, etc."

⁹the voice of the Lord causes hinds to calve,
  ^b-and strips forests bare;-^b
    while in His temple all say "Glory!"
¹⁰The Lord sat enthroned at the Flood;
  the Lord sits enthroned, king forever.

¹¹May the Lord grant strength to His people;
  may the Lord bestow on His people wellbeing.

9 קוֹל יְהֹוָה ׀ יְחוֹלֵל אַיָּלוֹת
וַיֶּחֱשֹׂף יְעָרוֹת
וּבְהֵיכָלוֹ כֻּלּוֹ אֹמֵר כָּבוֹד:
10 יְהֹוָה לַמַּבּוּל יָשָׁב
וַיֵּשֶׁב יְהֹוָה מֶלֶךְ לְעוֹלָם:

11 יְהֹוָה עֹז לְעַמּוֹ יִתֵּן
יְהֹוָה ׀ יְבָרֵךְ אֶת־עַמּוֹ בַשָּׁלוֹם:

30

A psalm of David. A song for the dedication of the House.^a

ל מִזְמוֹר שִׁיר־חֲנֻכַּת הַבַּיִת לְדָוִד:

²I extol You, O Lord,
  for You have lifted me up,
    and not let my enemies rejoice over me.
³O Lord, my God,
  I cried out to You,
    and You healed me.
⁴O Lord, You brought me up from Sheol,
  preserved me from going down into the Pit.

2 אֲרוֹמִמְךָ יְהֹוָה
כִּי דִלִּיתָנִי
וְלֹא־שִׂמַּחְתָּ אֹיְבַי לִי:
3 יְהֹוָה אֱלֹהָי
שִׁוַּעְתִּי אֵלֶיךָ
וַתִּרְפָּאֵנִי:
4 יְהֹוָה הֶעֱלִיתָ מִן־שְׁאוֹל נַפְשִׁי
חִיִּיתַנִי מיורדי מִיָּרְדִי־בוֹר:

⁵O you faithful of the Lord, sing to Him,
  and praise His holy name.
⁶For He is angry but a moment,
  and when He is pleased there is life.
  ^b-One may lie down weeping at nightfall;-^b
    but at dawn there are shouts of joy.

5 זַמְּרוּ לַיהֹוָה חֲסִידָיו
וְהוֹדוּ לְזֵכֶר קָדְשׁוֹ:
6 כִּי רֶגַע ׀ בְּאַפּוֹ
חַיִּים בִּרְצוֹנוֹ
בָּעֶרֶב יָלִין בֶּכִי
וְלַבֹּקֶר רִנָּה:

⁷When I was untroubled,
  I thought, "I shall never be shaken,"
⁸for You, O Lord, when You were pleased,
  made [me]^c firm as a mighty mountain.
When You hid Your face,
  I was terrified.
⁹I called to You, O Lord;
  to my Lord I made appeal,

7 וַאֲנִי אָמַרְתִּי בְשַׁלְוִי
בַּל־אֶמּוֹט לְעוֹלָם:
8 יְהֹוָה בִּרְצוֹנְךָ
הֶעֱמַדְתָּה לְהַרְרִי עֹז
הִסְתַּרְתָּ פָנֶיךָ
הָיִיתִי נִבְהָל:
9 אֵלֶיךָ יְהֹוָה אֶקְרָא
וְאֶל־אֲדֹנָי אֶתְחַנָּן:

---

^{b-b} Or "brings ewes to early birth."

^a I.e., the Temple.
^{b-b} Or "Weeping may linger for the night."
^c Following Saadia, R. Isaiah of Trani; cf. Ibn Ezra.

10"What is to be gained from my death,^d
from my descent into the Pit?
Can dust praise You?
Can it declare Your faithfulness?

11Hear, O Lᴏʀᴅ, and have mercy on me;
O Lᴏʀᴅ, be my help!"

12You turned my lament into dancing,
you undid my sackcloth and girded me with
   joy,
13that [my] whole being might sing hymns to
   You endlessly;
O Lᴏʀᴅ my God, I will praise You forever.

10 מַה־בֶּ֥צַע בְּדָמִי֮
בְּרִדְתִּ֢י אֶל־שָׁ֥חַת
הֲיוֹדְךָ֥ עָפָ֑ר
הֲיַגִּ֥יד אֲמִתֶּֽךָ׃
11 שְׁמַע־יְהֹוָ֥ה וְחָנֵּ֑נִי
יְהֹוָ֗ה הֱיֵה־עֹזֵ֥ר לִֽי׃
12 הָפַ֣כְתָּ מִסְפְּדִי֮ לְמָח֢וֹל לִ֥י
פִּתַּ֥חְתָּ שַׂקִּ֑י וַֽתְּאַזְּרֵ֥נִי שִׂמְחָֽה׃
13 לְמַ֤עַן ׀ יְזַמֶּרְךָ֣ כָ֭בוֹד וְלֹ֣א יִדֹּ֑ם
יְהֹוָ֥ה אֱ֝לֹהַ֗י לְעוֹלָ֥ם אוֹדֶֽךָּ׃

31 For the leader. A psalm of David.

לא לַמְנַצֵּ֗חַ מִזְמ֥וֹר לְדָוִֽד׃

2I seek refuge in You, O Lᴏʀᴅ;
may I never be disappointed;
as You are righteous, rescue me.
3Incline Your ear to me;
be quick to save me;
be a rock, a stronghold for me,
a citadel, for my deliverance.
4For You are my rock and my fortress;
You lead me and guide me as befits Your name.
5You free me from the net laid for me,
for You are my stronghold.
6Into Your hand I entrust my spirit;
You redeem me, O Lᴏʀᴅ, faithful God.
7I detest those who rely on empty folly,
but I trust in the Lᴏʀᴅ.
8Let me exult and rejoice in Your faithfulness
when You notice my affliction,
are mindful of my deep distress,
9and do not hand me over to my enemy,
but ^a-grant me relief.-^a

2 בְּךָ֣ יְהֹוָ֣ה חָ֭סִיתִי
אַל־אֵב֣וֹשָׁה לְעוֹלָ֑ם
בְּצִדְקָתְךָ֥ פַלְּטֵֽנִי׃
3 הַטֵּ֤ה אֵלַ֨י ׀ אׇזְנְךָ֮
מְהֵרָ֢ה הַצִּ֫ילֵ֥נִי
הֱיֵ֤ה לִ֨י ׀ לְֽצוּר־מָ֭עוֹז
לְבֵ֥ית מְצוּד֗וֹת לְהוֹשִׁיעֵֽנִי׃
4 כִּֽי־סַלְעִ֣י וּמְצוּדָתִ֣י אָ֑תָּה
וּלְמַ֥עַן שִׁ֝מְךָ֗ תַּֽנְחֵ֥נִי וּֽתְנַהֲלֵֽנִי׃
5 תּֽוֹצִיאֵ֗נִי מֵרֶ֣שֶׁת ז֭וּ טָ֣מְנוּ לִ֑י
כִּֽי־אַ֝תָּ֗ה מָעוּזִּֽי׃
6 בְּיָדְךָ֮ אַפְקִ֢יד ר֫וּחִ֥י
פָּדִ֖יתָה אוֹתִ֥י יְהֹוָ֗ה אֵ֣ל אֱמֶֽת׃
7 שָׂנֵ֗אתִי הַשֹּׁמְרִ֥ים הַבְלֵי־שָׁ֑וְא
וַ֝אֲנִ֗י אֶל־יְהֹוָ֥ה בָּטָֽחְתִּי׃
8 אָגִ֥ילָה וְאֶשְׂמְחָ֗ה בְּחַ֫סְדֶּ֥ךָ
אֲשֶׁ֣ר רָ֭אִיתָ אֶת־עׇנְיִ֑י
יָ֝דַ֗עְתָּ בְּצָר֥וֹת נַפְשִֽׁי׃
9 וְלֹ֣א הִ֭סְגַּרְתַּנִי בְּיַד־אוֹיֵ֑ב
הֶעֱמַ֖דְתָּ בַמֶּרְחָ֣ב רַגְלָֽי׃

d   Lit. "blood."

a-a   Lit. "make my feet stand in a broad place."

10Have mercy on me, O Lord,
   for I am in distress;
   my eyes are wasted by vexation,
   b-my substance and body too.-*b*
11My life is spent in sorrow,
   my years in groaning;
   my strength fails because of my iniquity,
   my limbs waste away.
12Because of all my foes
   I am the particular butt of my neighbors,
   a horror to my friends;
   those who see me on the street avoid me.
13I am put out of mind like the dead;
   I am like an object given up for lost.
14I hear the whisperings of many,
   intrigue*c* on every side,
   as they scheme together against me,
   plotting to take my life.

15But I trust in You, O Lord;
   I say, "You are my God!"
16My fate is in Your hand;
   save me from the hand of my enemies and pursuers.
17Show favor to Your servant;
   as You are faithful, deliver me.
18O Lord, let me not be disappointed when I call You;
   let the wicked be disappointed;
   let them be silenced in Sheol;
19let lying lips be stilled
   that speak haughtily against the righteous
   with arrogance and contempt.
20How abundant is the good
   that You have in store for those who fear You,
   that You do in the full view of men
   for those who take refuge in You.
21You grant them the protection of Your presence
   b-against scheming men;-*b*

10 חָנֵּנִי יְהֹוָה
כִּי צַר־לִי
עָשְׁשָׁה בְכַעַס עֵינִי
נַפְשִׁי וּבִטְנִי:
11 כִּי כָלוּ בְיָגוֹן חַיַּי
וּשְׁנוֹתַי בַּאֲנָחָה
כָּשַׁל בַּעֲוֺנִי כֹחִי
וַעֲצָמַי עָשֵׁשׁוּ:
12 מִכָּל־צֹרְרַי
הָיִיתִי חֶרְפָּה וְלִשְׁכֵנַי ׀ מְאֹד
וּפַחַד לִמְיֻדָּעָי
רֹאַי בַּחוּץ נָדְדוּ מִמֶּנִּי:
13 נִשְׁכַּחְתִּי כְּמֵת מִלֵּב
הָיִיתִי כִּכְלִי אֹבֵד:
14 כִּי שָׁמַעְתִּי ׀ דִּבַּת רַבִּים
מָגוֹר מִסָּבִיב
בְּהִוָּסְדָם יַחַד עָלַי
לָקַחַת נַפְשִׁי זָמָמוּ:
15 וַאֲנִי ׀ עָלֶיךָ בָטַחְתִּי יְהֹוָה
אָמַרְתִּי אֱלֹהַי אָתָּה:
16 בְּיָדְךָ עִתֹּתָי
הַצִּילֵנִי מִיַּד־אוֹיְבַי וּמֵרֹדְפָי:
17 הָאִירָה פָנֶיךָ עַל־עַבְדֶּךָ
הוֹשִׁיעֵנִי בְחַסְדֶּךָ:
18 יְהֹוָה אַל־אֵבוֹשָׁה כִּי קְרָאתִיךָ
יֵבֹשׁוּ רְשָׁעִים
יִדְּמוּ לִשְׁאוֹל:
19 תֵּאָלַמְנָה שִׂפְתֵי שָׁקֶר
הַדֹּבְרוֹת עַל־צַדִּיק עָתָק
בְּגַאֲוָה וָבוּז:
20 מָה רַב־טוּבְךָ
אֲשֶׁר־צָפַנְתָּ לִּירֵאֶיךָ
פָּעַלְתָּ לַחֹסִים בָּךְ
נֶגֶד בְּנֵי אָדָם:
21 תַּסְתִּירֵם ׀ בְּסֵתֶר פָּנֶיךָ
מֵרֻכְסֵי אִישׁ

You shelter them in Your pavilion
   from contentious tongues.

²²Blessed is the Lord,
   for He has been wondrously faithful to me,
   a veritable bastion.

²³Alarmed, I had thought,
   "I am thrust out of Your sight";
   yet You listened to my plea for mercy
   when I cried out to You.

²⁴So love the Lord, all you faithful;
   the Lord guards the loyal,
   and more than requites
   him who acts arrogantly.

²⁵Be strong and of good courage,
   all you who wait for the Lord.

תִּצְפְּנֵם בְּסֻכָּה
מֵרִיב לְשֹׁנוֹת:
²² בָּרוּךְ יְהוָה
כִּי הִפְלִיא חַסְדּוֹ לִי
בְּעִיר מָצוֹר:
²³ וַאֲנִי ׀ אָמַרְתִּי בְחָפְזִי
נִגְרַזְתִּי מִנֶּגֶד עֵינֶיךָ
אָכֵן שָׁמַעְתָּ קוֹל תַּחֲנוּנַי
בְּשַׁוְּעִי אֵלֶיךָ:
²⁴ אֶהֱבוּ אֶת־יְהוָה כָּל־חֲסִידָיו
אֱמוּנִים נֹצֵר יְהוָה
וּמְשַׁלֵּם עַל־יֶתֶר
עֹשֵׂה גַאֲוָה:
²⁵ חִזְקוּ וְיַאֲמֵץ לְבַבְכֶם
כָּל־הַמְיַחֲלִים לַיהוָה:

32

Of David. ᵃ-A *maskil.*-ᵃ

לב לְדָוִד מַשְׂכִּיל

Happy is he whose transgression is forgiven,
   whose sin is covered over.

²Happy the man whom the Lord does not hold
   guilty,
   and in whose spirit there is no deceit.

אַשְׁרֵי נְשׂוּי־פֶּשַׁע
כְּסוּי חֲטָאָה:
² אַשְׁרֵי אָדָם לֹא יַחְשֹׁב יְהוָה לוֹ
עָוֺן
וְאֵין בְּרוּחוֹ רְמִיָּה:

³As long as I said nothing,
   my limbs wasted away
   from my anguished roaring all day long.

⁴For night and day
   Your hand lay heavy on me;
   my vigor waned
   as in the summer drought.   *Selah.*

⁵Then I acknowledged my sin to You;
   I did not cover up my guilt;
   I resolved, "I will confess my transgressions to
     the Lord,"
   and You forgave the guilt of my sin.   *Selah.*

⁶Therefore let every faithful man pray to You

³ כִּי־הֶחֱרַשְׁתִּי
בָּלוּ עֲצָמָי
בְּשַׁאֲגָתִי כָּל־הַיּוֹם:
⁴ כִּי ׀ יוֹמָם וָלַיְלָה
תִּכְבַּד עָלַי יָדֶךָ
נֶהְפַּךְ לְשַׁדִּי
בְּחַרְבֹנֵי קַיִץ סֶלָה:
⁵ חַטָּאתִי אוֹדִיעֲךָ
וַעֲוֺנִי לֹא־כִסִּיתִי
אָמַרְתִּי אוֹדֶה עֲלֵי פְשָׁעַי לַיהוָה
וְאַתָּה נָשָׂאתָ עֲוֺן חַטָּאתִי סֶלָה:
⁶ עַל־זֹאת יִתְפַּלֵּל כָּל־חָסִיד ׀ אֵלֶיךָ

ᵃ-ᵃ *Meaning of Heb. uncertain.*

b-upon discovering [his sin],-*b*
that the rushing mighty waters
not overtake him.

7You are my shelter;
You preserve me from distress;
You surround me with the joyous shouts of
deliverance.   *Selah.*

8Let me enlighten you
and show you which way to go;
let me offer counsel; my eye is on you.

9Be not like a senseless horse or mule
    a-whose movement must be curbed by bit and
        bridle;-*a*
    c-far be it from you!-*c*

10Many are the torments of the wicked,
but he who trusts in the Lord
shall be surrounded with favor.

11Rejoice in the Lord and exult, O you righteous;
shout for joy, all upright men!

לְעֵת מְצֹא רַק
לְשֵׁטֶף מַיִם רַבִּים
אֵלָיו לֹא יַגִּיעוּ:

7 אַתָּה ׀ סֵתֶר לִי
מִצַּר תִּצְּרֵנִי
רָנֵּי פַלֵּט תְּסוֹבְבֵנִי   סֶלָה:

8 אַשְׂכִּילְךָ ׀
וְאוֹרְךָ בְּדֶרֶךְ־זוּ תֵלֵךְ
אִיעֲצָה עָלֶיךָ עֵינִי:

9 אַל־תִּהְיוּ ׀ כְּסוּס כְּפֶרֶד אֵין הָבִין
בְּמֶתֶג־וָרֶסֶן עֶדְיוֹ לִבְלוֹם
בַּל קְרֹב אֵלֶיךָ:

10 רַבִּים מַכְאוֹבִים לָרָשָׁע
וְהַבּוֹטֵחַ בַּיהֹוָה
חֶסֶד יְסוֹבְבֶנּוּ:

11 שִׂמְחוּ בַיהֹוָה וְגִילוּ צַדִּיקִים
וְהַרְנִינוּ כָּל־יִשְׁרֵי־לֵב:

33 Sing forth, O you righteous, to the Lord;
it is fit that the upright acclaim Him.

2Praise the Lord with the lyre;
with the ten-stringed harp sing to Him;

3sing Him a new song;
play sweetly with shouts of joy.

4For the word of the Lord is right;
His every deed is faithful.

5He loves what is right and just;
the earth is full of the Lord's faithful care.

6By the word of the Lord the heavens were made,
by the breath of His mouth, all their host.

7He heaps up the ocean waters like a mound,
stores the deep in vaults.

8Let all the earth fear the Lord;
let all the inhabitants of the world dread Him.

לג רַנְּנוּ צַדִּיקִים בַּיהֹוָה
לַיְשָׁרִים נָאוָה תְהִלָּה:

2 הוֹדוּ לַיהֹוָה בְּכִנּוֹר
בְּנֵבֶל עָשׂוֹר זַמְּרוּ־לוֹ:

3 שִׁירוּ־לוֹ שִׁיר חָדָשׁ
הֵיטִיבוּ נַגֵּן בִּתְרוּעָה:

4 כִּי־יָשָׁר דְּבַר־יְהֹוָה
וְכָל־מַעֲשֵׂהוּ בֶּאֱמוּנָה:

5 אֹהֵב צְדָקָה וּמִשְׁפָּט
חֶסֶד יְהֹוָה מָלְאָה הָאָרֶץ:

6 בִּדְבַר יְהֹוָה שָׁמַיִם נַעֲשׂוּ
וּבְרוּחַ פִּיו כָּל־צְבָאָם:

7 כֹּנֵס כַּנֵּד מֵי הַיָּם
נֹתֵן בְּאֹצָרוֹת תְּהוֹמוֹת:

8 יִירְאוּ מֵיְהֹוָה כָּל־הָאָרֶץ
מִמֶּנּוּ יָגוּרוּ כָּל־יֹשְׁבֵי תֵבֵל:

---

b-b Meaning of Heb. uncertain; others "in a time when You may be
        found."

c-c Meaning of Heb. uncertain; for this rendering *cf.* Ibn Ezra.

1448

9For He spoke, and it was;
  He commanded, and it endured.
10The Lord frustrates the plans of nations,
  brings to naught the designs of peoples.
11What the Lord plans endures forever,
  what He designs, for ages on end.

12Happy the nation whose God is the Lord,
  the people He has chosen to be His own.
13The Lord looks down from heaven;
  He sees all mankind.
14From His dwelling-place He gazes
  on all the inhabitants of the earth—
15He who fashions the hearts of them all,
  who discerns all their doings.

16Kings are not delivered by a large force;
  warriors are not saved by great strength;
17horses are a false hope for deliverance;
  for all their great power they provide no escape.
18Truly the eye of the Lord is on those who fear
    Him,
  who wait for His faithful care
19to save them from death,
  to sustain them in famine.
20We set our hope on the Lord,
  He is our help and shield;
21in Him our hearts rejoice,
  for in His holy name we trust.
22May we enjoy, O Lord, Your faithful care,
  as we have put our hope in You.

34 Of David, a-when he feigned madness in the presence of Abimelech, who turned him out, and he left.-a

א 2I bless the Lord at all times;
  praise of Him is ever in my mouth.

---

9 כִּי הוּא אָמַר וַיֶּהִי
הוּא־צִוָּה וַיַּעֲמֹד׃
10 יְהֹוָה הֵפִיר עֲצַת־גּוֹיִם
הֵנִיא מַחְשְׁבוֹת עַמִּים׃
11 עֲצַת יְהֹוָה לְעוֹלָם תַּעֲמֹד
מַחְשְׁבוֹת לִבּוֹ לְדֹר וָדֹר׃

12 אַשְׁרֵי הַגּוֹי אֲשֶׁר־יְהֹוָה אֱלֹהָיו
הָעָם ׀ בָּחַר לְנַחֲלָה לוֹ׃
13 מִשָּׁמַיִם הִבִּיט יְהֹוָה
רָאָה אֶת־כָּל־בְּנֵי הָאָדָם׃
14 מִמְּכוֹן־שִׁבְתּוֹ הִשְׁגִּיחַ
אֶל כָּל־יֹשְׁבֵי הָאָרֶץ׃
15 הַיֹּצֵר יַחַד לִבָּם
הַמֵּבִין אֶל־כָּל־מַעֲשֵׂיהֶם׃

16 אֵין־הַמֶּלֶךְ נוֹשָׁע בְּרָב־חָיִל
גִּבּוֹר לֹא־יִנָּצֵל בְּרָב־כֹּחַ׃
17 שֶׁקֶר הַסּוּס לִתְשׁוּעָה
וּבְרֹב חֵילוֹ לֹא יְמַלֵּט׃
18 הִנֵּה עֵין יְהֹוָה אֶל־יְרֵאָיו
לַמְיַחֲלִים לְחַסְדּוֹ׃
19 לְהַצִּיל מִמָּוֶת נַפְשָׁם
וּלְחַיּוֹתָם בָּרָעָב׃
20 נַפְשֵׁנוּ חִכְּתָה לַיהֹוָה
עֶזְרֵנוּ וּמָגִנֵּנוּ הוּא׃
21 כִּי־בוֹ יִשְׂמַח לִבֵּנוּ
כִּי בְשֵׁם קָדְשׁוֹ בָטָחְנוּ׃
22 יְהִי־חַסְדְּךָ יְהֹוָה עָלֵינוּ
כַּאֲשֶׁר יִחַלְנוּ לָךְ׃

לד לְדָוִד בְּשַׁנּוֹתוֹ אֶת־טַעְמוֹ לִפְנֵי
אֲבִימֶלֶךְ וַיְגָרֲשֵׁהוּ וַיֵּלַךְ׃

2 אֲבָרֲכָה אֶת־יְהֹוָה בְּכָל־עֵת
תָּמִיד תְּהִלָּתוֹ בְּפִי׃

ב 3I glory in the LORD;

    let the lowly hear it and rejoice.

ג 4Exalt the LORD with me;

    let us extol His name together.

ד 5I turned to the LORD, and He answered me;

    He saved me from all my terrors.

ה 6Men look to Him and are radiant;

ו   let their faces not be downcast.

ז 7Here was a lowly man who called,

    and the LORD listened,

    and delivered him from all his troubles.

ח 8The angel of the LORD camps around those who

      fear Him

    and rescues them.

ט 9Taste and see how good the LORD is;

    happy the man who takes refuge in Him!

י 10Fear the LORD,* you His consecrated ones,

    for those who fear Him lack nothing.

כ 11Lions have been reduced to starvation,

    but those who turn to the LORD shall not lack

      any good.

ל 12Come, my sons, listen to me;

    I will teach you what it is to fear the LORD.

מ 13Who is the man who is eager for life,

    who desires years of good fortune?

נ 14Guard your tongue from evil,

    your lips from deceitful speech.

ס 15Shun evil and do good,

    seek amity[b] and pursue it.

ע 16The eyes of the LORD are on the righteous,

    His ears attentive to their cry.

פ 17The face of the LORD is set against evildoers,

    to erase their names from the earth.

צ 18They[c] cry out, and the LORD hears,

    and saves them from all their troubles.

ק 19The LORD is close to the brokenhearted;

    those crushed in spirit He delivers.

ר 20Though the misfortunes of the righteous be

    many,

3 בַּיהוָה תִּתְהַלֵּל נַפְשִׁי

יִשְׁמְעוּ עֲנָוִים וְיִשְׂמָחוּ:

4 גַּדְּלוּ לַיהוָה אִתִּי

וּנְרוֹמְמָה שְׁמוֹ יַחְדָּו:

5 דָּרַשְׁתִּי אֶת־יְהוָה וְעָנָנִי

וּמִכָּל־מְגוּרוֹתַי הִצִּילָנִי:

6 הִבִּיטוּ אֵלָיו וְנָהָרוּ

וּפְנֵיהֶם אַל־יֶחְפָּרוּ:

7 זֶה עָנִי קָרָא

וַיהוָה שָׁמֵעַ

וּמִכָּל־צָרוֹתָיו הוֹשִׁיעוֹ:

8 חֹנֶה מַלְאַךְ־יְהוָה סָבִיב לִירֵאָיו

וַיְחַלְּצֵם:

9 טַעֲמוּ וּרְאוּ כִּי־טוֹב יְהוָה

אַשְׁרֵי הַגֶּבֶר יֶחֱסֶה־בּוֹ:

10 יְראוּ* אֶת־יְהוָה קְדֹשָׁיו

כִּי־אֵין מַחְסוֹר לִירֵאָיו:

11 כְּפִירִים רָשׁוּ וְרָעֵבוּ

וְדֹרְשֵׁי יְהוָה לֹא־יַחְסְרוּ כָל־טוֹב:

12 לְכוּ־בָנִים שִׁמְעוּ־לִי

יִרְאַת יְהוָה אֲלַמֶּדְכֶם:

13 מִי־הָאִישׁ הֶחָפֵץ חַיִּים

אֹהֵב יָמִים לִרְאוֹת טוֹב:

14 נְצֹר לְשׁוֹנְךָ מֵרָע

וּשְׂפָתֶיךָ מִדַּבֵּר מִרְמָה:

15 סוּר מֵרָע וַעֲשֵׂה־טוֹב

בַּקֵּשׁ שָׁלוֹם וְרָדְפֵהוּ:

16 עֵינֵי יְהוָה אֶל־צַדִּיקִים

וְאָזְנָיו אֶל־שַׁוְעָתָם:

17 פְּנֵי יְהוָה בְּעֹשֵׂי רָע

לְהַכְרִית מֵאֶרֶץ זִכְרָם:

18 צָעֲקוּ וַיהוָה שָׁמֵעַ

וּמִכָּל־צָרוֹתָם הִצִּילָם:

19 קָרוֹב יְהוָה לְנִשְׁבְּרֵי־לֵב

וְאֶת־דַּכְּאֵי־רוּחַ יוֹשִׁיעַ:

20 רַבּוֹת רָעוֹת צַדִּיק

---

b   Or "integrity."

c   Viz., the righteous of v. 16.

the LORD will save him from them all,

ש 21Keeping all his bones intact,
not one of them being broken.

ת 22One misfortune is the deathblow of the wicked;
the foes of the righteous shall be ruined.

23The LORD redeems the life of His servants;
all who take refuge in Him shall not be ruined.

35 Of David.

O LORD, strive with my adversaries,
give battle to my foes,
2take up shield and buckler,
and come to my defense;
3ready the spear and javelin
against my pursuers;
tell me, "I am your deliverance."

4Let those who seek my life
be frustrated and put to shame;
let those who plan to harm me
fall back in disgrace.

5Let them be as chaff in the wind,
the LORD's angel driving them on.

6Let their path be dark and slippery,
with the LORD's angel in pursuit.

7For without cause they hid a net to trap me;
without cause they dug a pit[a] for me.

8Let disaster overtake them unawares;
let the net they hid catch them;
let them fall into it when disaster [strikes].

9Then shall I exult in the LORD,
rejoice in His deliverance.

10All my bones shall say,
"LORD, who is like You?
You save the poor from one stronger than he,
the poor and needy from his despoiler."

וּמִכֻּלָּם יַצִּילֶנּוּ יְהוָה׃

21 שֹׁמֵר כָּל־עַצְמוֹתָיו
אַחַת מֵהֵנָּה לֹא נִשְׁבָּרָה׃

22 תְּמוֹתֵת רָשָׁע רָעָה
וְשֹׂנְאֵי צַדִּיק יֶאְשָׁמוּ׃

23 פּוֹדֶה יְהוָה נֶפֶשׁ עֲבָדָיו
וְלֹא יֶאְשְׁמוּ כָּל־הַחֹסִים בּוֹ׃

לה לְדָוִד ׀

רִיבָה יְהוָה אֶת־יְרִיבַי
לְחַם אֶת־לֹחֲמָי׃

2 הַחֲזֵק מָגֵן וְצִנָּה
וְקוּמָה בְּעֶזְרָתִי׃

3 וְהָרֵק חֲנִית וּסְגֹר
לִקְרַאת רֹדְפָי
אֱמֹר לְנַפְשִׁי יְשֻׁעָתֵךְ אָנִי׃

4 יֵבֹשׁוּ וְיִכָּלְמוּ
מְבַקְשֵׁי נַפְשִׁי
יִסֹּגוּ אָחוֹר וְיַחְפְּרוּ
חֹשְׁבֵי רָעָתִי׃

5 יִהְיוּ כְּמֹץ לִפְנֵי־רוּחַ
וּמַלְאַךְ יְהוָה דּוֹחֶה׃

6 יְהִי־דַרְכָּם חֹשֶׁךְ וַחֲלַקְלַקּוֹת
וּמַלְאַךְ יְהוָה רֹדְפָם׃

7 כִּי־חִנָּם טָמְנוּ־לִי שַׁחַת רִשְׁתָּם
חִנָּם חָפְרוּ לְנַפְשִׁי׃

8 תְּבוֹאֵהוּ שׁוֹאָה לֹא־יֵדָע
וְרִשְׁתּוֹ אֲשֶׁר־טָמַן תִּלְכְּדוֹ
בְּשׁוֹאָה יִפָּל־בָּהּ׃

9 וְנַפְשִׁי תָּגִיל בַּיהוָה
תָּשִׂישׂ בִּישׁוּעָתוֹ׃

10 כָּל עַצְמוֹתַי ׀ תֹּאמַרְנָה
יְהוָה מִי כָמוֹךָ
מַצִּיל עָנִי מֵחָזָק מִמֶּנּוּ
וְעָנִי וְאֶבְיוֹן מִגֹּזְלוֹ׃

---

a Transferred from first clause for clarity.

11Malicious witnesses appear
who question me about things I do not know.

12They repay me evil for good,
[seeking] my bereavement.

13Yet, when they were ill,
my dress was sackcloth,
I kept a fast—
b-may what I prayed for happen to me!-b

14I walked about as though it were my friend or
my brother;
I was bowed with gloom, like one mourning
for his mother.

15But when I stumble, they gleefully gather;
wretches gather against me,
I know not why;
c-they tear at me without end.

16With impious, mocking grimace-c
they gnash their teeth at me.

17O Lord, how long will You look on?
Rescue me c-from their attacks,-c
my precious life, from the lions,

18that I may praise You in a great congregation,
acclaim You in a mighty throng.

19Let not my treacherous enemies rejoice over me,
or those who hate me without reason wink
their eyes.

20For they do not offer amity,
but devise fraudulent schemes against harm-
less folk.

21They open wide their mouths at me,
saying, "Aha, aha, we have seen it!"

22You have seen it, O Lord;
do not hold aloof!
O Lord, be not far from me!

23Wake, rouse Yourself for my cause,
for my claim, O my God and my Lord!

11 יָק֣וּמוּן עֵדֵ֣י חָמָ֑ס
אֲשֶׁ֥ר לֹא־יָ֝דַ֗עְתִּי יִשְׁאָלֽוּנִי׃

12 יְשַׁלְּמ֣וּנִי רָ֭עָה תַּ֣חַת טוֹבָ֑ה
שְׁכ֥וֹל לְנַפְשִֽׁי׃

13 וַאֲנִ֤י ׀ בַּחֲלוֹתָ֡ם
לְב֬וּשִׁי שָׂ֗ק
עִנֵּ֣יתִי בַצּ֣וֹם נַפְשִׁ֑י
וּ֝תְפִלָּתִ֗י עַל־חֵיקִ֥י תָשֽׁוּב׃

14 כְּרֵֽעַ־כְּאָ֣ח לִ֭י הִתְהַלָּ֑כְתִּי
כַּאֲבֶל־אֵ֝֗ם קֹדֵ֥ר שַׁחֽוֹתִי׃

15 וּבְצַלְעִי֮ שָׂמְח֪וּ וְֽנֶ֫אֱסָ֥פוּ
נֶאֶסְפ֬וּ עָלַ֣י נֵ֭כִים
וְלֹ֣א יָדַ֑עְתִּי
קָרְע֥וּ וְלֹא־דָֽמּוּ׃

16 בְּ֭חַנְפֵי לַעֲגֵ֣י מָע֑וֹג
חָרֹ֖ק עָלַ֣י שִׁנֵּֽימוֹ׃

17 אֲדֹנָי֮ כַּמָּ֪ה תִּ֫רְאֶ֥ה
הָשִׁ֣יבָה נַ֭פְשִׁי מִשֹּׁאֵיהֶ֑ם
מִ֝כְּפִירִ֗ים יְחִידָתִֽי׃

18 א֭וֹדְךָ בְּקָהָ֣ל רָ֑ב
בְּעַ֖ם עָצ֣וּם אֲהַלְלֶֽךָּ׃

19 אַֽל־יִשְׂמְחוּ־לִ֣י אֹיְבַ֣י שֶׁ֑קֶר
שֹׂנְאַ֥י חִ֝נָּ֗ם יִקְרְצוּ־עָֽיִן׃

20 כִּ֤י לֹ֥א שָׁל֗וֹם יְדַ֫בֵּ֥רוּ וְעַ֥ל רִגְעֵי־
אֶ֑רֶץ
דִּבְרֵ֥י מִ֝רְמ֗וֹת יַחֲשֹׁבֽוּן׃

21 וַיַּרְחִ֥יבוּ עָלַ֗י פִּ֫יהֶ֥ם
אָ֭מְרוּ הֶאָ֣ח ׀ הֶאָ֑ח רָאֲתָ֥ה עֵינֵֽינוּ׃

22 רָאִ֣יתָה יְ֭הוָה אַֽל־תֶּחֱרַ֑שׁ
אֲ֝דֹנָ֗י אַל־תִּרְחַ֥ק מִמֶּֽנִּי׃

23 הָעִ֣ירָה וְ֭הָקִיצָה לְמִשְׁפָּטִ֑י
אֱלֹהַ֖י וַֽאדֹנָ֣י לְרִיבִֽי׃

b-b Meaning of Heb. uncertain; lit. "my prayer returns upon my bosom."
c-c Meaning of Heb. uncertain.

24Take up my cause, O LORD my God, as You are
beneficent,
  and let them not rejoice over me.
25Let them not think,
  "Aha, just what we wished!"
Let them not say,
  "We have destroyed him!"
26May those who rejoice at my misfortune
  be frustrated and utterly disgraced;
  may those who vaunt themselves over me
  be clad in frustration and shame.
27May those who desire my vindication
  sing forth joyously;
  may they always say,
  "Extolled be the LORD
  who desires the well-being of His servant,"
28while my tongue shall recite Your beneficent
  acts,
  Your praises all day long.

שָׁפְטֵנִי כְצִדְקְךָ יְהֹוָה אֱלֹהָי 24
וְאַל־יִשְׂמְחוּ־לִי:
אַל־יֹאמְרוּ בְלִבָּם 25
הֶאָח נַפְשֵׁנוּ
אַל־יֹאמְרוּ
בִּלַּעֲנוּהוּ:
יֵבֹשׁוּ וְיַחְפְּרוּ ׀ 26
יַחְדָּו שְׂמֵחֵי רָעָתִי
יִלְבְּשׁוּ־בֹשֶׁת וּכְלִמָּה
הַמַּגְדִּילִים עָלָי:
יָרֹנּוּ וְיִשְׂמְחוּ 27
חֲפֵצֵי צִדְקִי
וְיֹאמְרוּ תָמִיד
יִגְדַּל יְהֹוָה
הֶחָפֵץ שְׁלוֹם עַבְדּוֹ:
וּלְשׁוֹנִי תֶּהְגֶּה צִדְקֶךָ 28
כָּל־הַיּוֹם תְּהִלָּתֶךָ:

36 For the leader. Of the servant of the LORD,
of David.

לַמְנַצֵּחַ ׀ לְעֶבֶד־יְהֹוָה לְדָוִד: **לו**

2a-I know-a what Transgression says to the wicked;
  he has no sense of the dread of God,
  3b-because its speech is seductive to him
  till his iniquity be found out and he be hated.-b
4His words are evil and deceitful;
  he will not consider doing good.
5In bed he plots mischief;
  he is set on a path of no good,
  he does not reject evil.

נְאֻם־פֶּשַׁע לָרָשָׁע בְּקֶרֶב לִבִּי 2
אֵין־פַּחַד אֱלֹהִים לְנֶגֶד עֵינָיו:
כִּי־הֶחֱלִיק אֵלָיו בְּעֵינָיו 3
לִמְצֹא עֲוֺנוֹ לִשְׂנֹא:
דִּבְרֵי־פִיו אָוֶן וּמִרְמָה 4
חָדַל לְהַשְׂכִּיל לְהֵיטִיב:
אָוֶן ׀ יַחְשֹׁב עַל־מִשְׁכָּבוֹ 5
יִתְיַצֵּב עַל־דֶּרֶךְ לֹא־טוֹב
רָע לֹא יִמְאָס:

6O LORD, Your faithfulness reaches to heaven;
  Your steadfastness to the sky;
  7Your beneficence is like the high mountains;
  Your justice like the great deep;
  man and beast You deliver, O LORD.

יְהֹוָה בְּהַשָּׁמַיִם חַסְדֶּךָ 6
אֱמוּנָתְךָ עַד־שְׁחָקִים:
צִדְקָתְךָ ׀ כְּהַרְרֵי־אֵל 7
מִשְׁפָּטֶךָ תְּהוֹם רַבָּה
אָדָם־וּבְהֵמָה תוֹשִׁיעַ יְהֹוָה:

---

a-a Lit. "In my heart is."
b-b Meaning of Heb. uncertain.

8How precious is Your faithful care, O God!   8 מַה־יָּקָ֥ר חַסְדְּךָ֗ אֱלֹ֫הִ֥ים
Mankind shelters in the shadow of Your wings.   וּבְנֵ֥י אָדָ֑ם בְּצֵ֥ל כְּ֝נָפֶ֗יךָ יֶחֱסָי֥וּן :
9They feast on the rich fare of Your house;   9 יִ֭רְוְיֻן מִדֶּ֣שֶׁן בֵּיתֶ֑ךָ
   You let them drink at Your refreshing stream.   וְנַ֖חַל עֲדָנֶ֣יךָ תַשְׁקֵֽם :
10With You is the fountain of life;   10 כִּֽי־עִ֭מְּךָ מְק֣וֹר חַיִּ֑ים
   by Your light do we see light.   בְּ֝אוֹרְךָ֗ נִרְאֶה־אֽוֹר :
11Bestow Your faithful care on those devoted to   11 מְשֹׁ֣ךְ חַ֭סְדְּךָ לְיֹדְעֶ֑יךָ
     You,   וְ֝צִדְקָֽתְךָ֗ לְיִשְׁרֵי־לֵֽב :
   and Your beneficence on upright men.   12 אַל־תְּ֭בוֹאֵנִי רֶ֣גֶל גַּאֲוָ֑ה
12Let not the foot of the arrogant tread on me,   וְיַד־רְ֝שָׁעִ֗ים אַל־תְּנִדֵֽנִי :
   or the hand of the wicked drive me away.   13 שָׁ֣ם נָ֭פְלוּ פֹּ֣עֲלֵי אָ֑וֶן
13There lie the evildoers, fallen,   דֹּ֝ח֗וּ וְלֹא־יָ֥כְלוּ קֽוּם :
   thrust down, unable to rise.

37 Of David.   לְדָוִ֨ד **לז**

א Do not be vexed by evil men;   אַל־תִּתְחַ֥ר בַּמְּרֵעִ֑ים
   do not be incensed by wrongdoers;   אַל־תְּ֝קַנֵּ֗א בְּעֹשֵׂ֥י עַוְלָֽה :
2for they soon wither like grass,   2 כִּ֣י כֶ֭חָצִיר מְהֵרָ֣ה יִמָּ֑לוּ
   like verdure fade away.   וּכְיֶ֥רֶק דֶּ֝֗שֶׁא יִבּוֹלֽוּן :
ב 3Trust in the LORD and do good,   3 בְּטַ֣ח בַּ֭יהוָה וַעֲשֵׂה־ט֑וֹב
   abide in the land and remain loyal.   שְׁכָן־אֶ֝֗רֶץ וּרְעֵ֥ה אֱמוּנָֽה :
4Seek the favor of the LORD,   4 וְהִתְעַנַּ֥ג עַל־יְהוָ֑ה
   and He will grant you the desires of your heart.   וְיִֽתֶּן־לְ֝ךָ֗ מִשְׁאֲלֹ֥ת לִבֶּֽךָ :
ג 5Leave all[a] to the LORD;   5 גּ֣וֹל עַל־יְהוָ֣ה דַּרְכֶּ֑ךָ
   trust in Him; He will do it.   וּבְטַ֥ח עָ֝לָ֗יו וְה֣וּא יַעֲשֶֽׂה :
6He will cause your vindication to shine forth like   6 וְהוֹצִ֣יא כָא֣וֹר צִדְקֶ֑ךָ
     the light,   וּ֝מִשְׁפָּטֶ֗ךָ כַּֽצָּהֳרָֽיִם :
   the justice of your case, like the noonday sun.   7 דּ֤וֹם לַיהוָה֮ וְהִתְח֪וֹלֵ֫ל ל֥וֹ
ד 7Be patient and wait for the LORD,   אַל־תִּ֭תְחַר בְּמַצְלִ֣יחַ דַּרְכּ֑וֹ
   do not be vexed by the prospering man   בְּ֝אִ֗ישׁ עֹשֶׂ֥ה מְזִמּֽוֹת :
   who carries out his schemes.

ה 8Give up anger, abandon fury,   8 הֶ֣רֶף מֵ֭אַף וַעֲזֹ֣ב חֵמָ֑ה
   do not be vexed;   אַל־תִּ֝תְחַ֗ר
   it can only do harm.   אַךְ־לְהָרֵֽעַ :
9For evil men will be cut off,   9 כִּֽי־מְ֭רֵעִים יִכָּרֵת֑וּן
   but those who look to the LORD—   וְקֹוֵ֥י יְ֝הוָ֗ה

a Lit. "your way."

they shall inherit the land.

ו 10A little longer and there will be no wicked man;
you will look at where he was—
he will be gone.

11But the lowly shall inherit the land,
and delight in abundant well-being.

ז 12The wicked man schemes against the righteous,
and gnashes his teeth at him.

13The Lord laughs at him,
for He knows that his day will come.

ח 14The wicked draw their swords, bend their bows,
to bring down the lowly and needy,
to slaughter b-upright men.-b

15Their swords shall pierce their own hearts,
and their bows shall be broken.

ט 16Better the little that the righteous man has
than the great abundance of the wicked.

17For the arms of the wicked shall be broken,
but the Lord is the support of the righteous.

י 18The Lord is concerned for the needsᶜ of the
blameless;
their portion lasts forever;

19they shall not come to grief in bad times;
in famine, they shall eat their fill.

כ 20But the wicked shall perish,
and the enemies of the Lord shall be consumed,
like meadow grassᵈ consumed in smoke.

ל 21The wicked man borrows and does not repay;
the righteous is generous and keeps giving.

22Those blessed by Him shall inherit the land,
but those cursed by Him shall be cut off.

מ 23The steps of a man are made firm by the Lord,
when He delights in his way.

24Though he stumbles, he does not fall down,
for the Lord gives him support.

נ 25I have been young and am now old,
but I have never seen a righteous man abandoned,

הֵ֫מָּה יִ֥ירְשׁוּ־אָֽרֶץ׃

ו 10 וְע֣וֹד מְ֭עַט וְאֵ֣ין רָשָׁ֑ע
וְהִתְבּוֹנַ֖נְתָּ עַל־מְקוֹמ֣וֹ
וְאֵינֶֽנּוּ׃

11 וַעֲנָוִ֥ים יִֽירְשׁוּ־אָ֑רֶץ
וְ֝הִֽתְעַנְּג֗וּ עַל־רֹ֥ב שָׁלֽוֹם׃

12 זֹמֵ֣ם רָ֭שָׁע לַצַּדִּ֑יק
וְחֹרֵ֖ק עָלָ֣יו שִׁנָּֽיו׃

13 אֲדֹנָ֥י יִשְׂחַק־ל֑וֹ
כִּֽי־רָ֝אָ֗ה כִּֽי־יָבֹ֥א יוֹמֽוֹ׃

14 חֶ֤רֶב ׀ פָּֽתְח֣וּ רְשָׁעִים֮ וְדָרְכ֪וּ
קַשְׁ֫תָּ֥ם
לְ֭הַפִּיל עָנִ֣י וְאֶבְי֑וֹן
לִ֝טְב֗וֹחַ יִשְׁרֵי־דָֽרֶךְ׃

15 חַ֭רְבָּם תָּב֣וֹא בְלִבָּ֑ם
וְ֝קַשְּׁתוֹתָ֗ם תִּשָּׁבַֽרְנָה׃

16 טֽוֹב־מְ֭עַט לַצַּדִּ֑יק
מֵ֝הֲמ֗וֹן רְשָׁעִ֥ים רַבִּֽים׃

17 כִּ֤י זְרוֹע֣וֹת רְ֭שָׁעִים תִּשָּׁבַ֑רְנָה
וְסוֹמֵ֖ךְ צַדִּיקִ֣ים יְהֹוָֽה׃

18 יוֹדֵ֣עַ יְ֭הֹוָה יְמֵ֣י תְמִימִ֑ם
וְ֝נַחֲלָתָ֗ם לְעוֹלָ֥ם תִּהְיֶֽה׃

19 לֹֽא־יֵ֭בֹשׁוּ בְּעֵ֣ת רָעָ֑ה
וּבִימֵ֖י רְעָב֣וֹן יִשְׂבָּֽעוּ׃

20 כִּ֤י רְשָׁעִ֨ים ׀ יֹאבֵ֗דוּ
וְאֹיְבֵ֣י יְ֭הֹוָה כִּיקַ֣ר כָּרִ֑ים
כָּל֖וּ בֶעָשָׁ֣ן כָּֽלוּ׃

21 לֹוֶ֣ה רָ֭שָׁע וְלֹ֣א יְשַׁלֵּ֑ם
וְצַדִּ֗יק חוֹנֵ֥ן וְנוֹתֵֽן׃

22 כִּ֣י מְ֭בֹרָכָיו יִ֣ירְשׁוּ אָ֑רֶץ
וּ֝מְקֻלָּלָ֗יו יִכָּרֵֽתוּ׃

23 מֵ֭יְהֹוָה מִֽצְעֲדֵי־גֶ֥בֶר כּוֹנָ֑נוּ
וְדַרְכּ֥וֹ יֶחְפָּֽץ׃

24 כִּֽי־יִפֹּ֥ל לֹֽא־יוּטָ֑ל
כִּֽי־יְ֝הֹוָ֗ה סוֹמֵ֥ךְ יָדֽוֹ׃

25 נַ֤עַר ׀ הָיִ֗יתִי גַּם־זָ֫קַ֥נְתִּי
וְֽלֹא־רָ֭אִיתִי צַדִּ֣יק נֶעֱזָ֑ב

---

b-b Lit. "those whose way is upright."
c Lit. "days."
d Meaning of Heb. uncertain.

or his children seeking bread.

26He is always generous, and lends,
    and his children are held blessed.

ס 27Shun evil and do good,
    and you shall abide forever.

28For the Lord loves what is right,
    He does not abandon His faithful ones.
They are preserved forever,
    while the children of the wicked will be cut off.

29The righteous shall inherit the land,
    and abide forever in it.

פ 30The mouth of the righteous utters wisdom,
    and his tongue speaks what is right.

31The teaching of his God is in his heart;
    his feet do not slip.

צ 32The wicked watches for the righteous,
    seeking to put him to death;

33the Lord will not abandon him to his power;
He will not let him be condemned in judgment.

ק 34Look to the Lord and keep to His way,
    and He will raise you high that you may inherit
        the land;
    when the wicked are cut off, you shall see it.

ר 35I saw a wicked man, powerful,
    well-rooted like a robust native tree.

36Suddenly he vanished and was gone;
    I sought him, but he was not to be found.

ש 37Mark the blameless, note the upright,
    for there is a future for the man of integrity.

38But transgressors shall be utterly destroyed,
    the future of the wicked shall be cut off.

ת 39The deliverance of the righteous comes from
        the Lord,
    their stronghold in time of trouble.

40The Lord helps them and rescues them,
    rescues them from the wicked and delivers
        them,
    for they seek refuge in Him.

וְזַרְעוֹ מְבַקֶּשׁ־לָחֶם:

26 כָּל־הַיּוֹם חוֹנֵן וּמַלְוֶה
וְזַרְעוֹ לִבְרָכָה:

27 סוּר מֵרָע וַעֲשֵׂה־טוֹב
וּשְׁכֹן לְעוֹלָם:

28 כִּי יְהֹוָה ׀ אֹהֵב מִשְׁפָּט
וְלֹא־יַעֲזֹב אֶת־חֲסִידָיו
לְעוֹלָם נִשְׁמָרוּ
וְזֶרַע רְשָׁעִים נִכְרָת:

29 צַדִּיקִים יִירְשׁוּ־אָרֶץ
וְיִשְׁכְּנוּ לָעַד עָלֶיהָ:

30 פִּי־צַדִּיק יֶהְגֶּה חָכְמָה
וּלְשׁוֹנוֹ תְּדַבֵּר מִשְׁפָּט:

31 תּוֹרַת אֱלֹהָיו בְּלִבּוֹ
לֹא תִמְעַד אֲשֻׁרָיו:

32 צוֹפֶה רָשָׁע לַצַּדִּיק
וּמְבַקֵּשׁ לַהֲמִיתוֹ:

33 יְהֹוָה לֹא־יַעַזְבֶנּוּ בְיָדוֹ
וְלֹא יַרְשִׁיעֶנּוּ בְּהִשָּׁפְטוֹ:

34 קַוֵּה אֶל־יְהֹוָה ׀ וּשְׁמֹר דַּרְכּוֹ
וִירוֹמִמְךָ לָרֶשֶׁת אָרֶץ
בְּהִכָּרֵת רְשָׁעִים תִּרְאֶה:

35 רָאִיתִי רָשָׁע עָרִיץ
וּמִתְעָרֶה כְּאֶזְרָח רַעֲנָן:

36 וַיַּעֲבֹר וְהִנֵּה אֵינֶנּוּ
וָאֲבַקְשֵׁהוּ וְלֹא נִמְצָא:

37 שְׁמָר־תָּם וּרְאֵה יָשָׁר
כִּי־אַחֲרִית לְאִישׁ שָׁלוֹם:

38 וּפֹשְׁעִים נִשְׁמְדוּ יַחְדָּו
אַחֲרִית רְשָׁעִים נִכְרָתָה:

39 וּתְשׁוּעַת צַדִּיקִים מֵיְהֹוָה
מָעוּזָּם בְּעֵת צָרָה:

40 וַיַּעְזְרֵם יְהֹוָה וַיְפַלְּטֵם
יְפַלְּטֵם מֵרְשָׁעִים וְיוֹשִׁיעֵם
כִּי־חָסוּ בוֹ:

38

38 A psalm of David. *Lehazkir.ᵃ*

לח מִזְמ֥וֹר לְדָוִ֗ד לְהַזְכִּֽיר׃

²O Lord, do not punish me in wrath;
  do not chastise me in fury.

²יְֽהֹוָ֗ה אַל־בְּקֶצְפְּךָ֥ תוֹכִיחֵ֑נִי
  וּֽבַחֲמָתְךָ֥ תְיַסְּרֵֽנִי׃

³For Your arrows have struck me;
  Your blows have fallen upon me.

³כִּֽי־חִ֭צֶּיךָ נִ֣חֲתוּ בִ֑י
  וַתִּנְחַ֖ת עָלַ֣י יָדֶֽךָ׃

⁴There is no soundness in my flesh because of
    Your rage,
  no wholeness in my bones because of my sin.

⁴אֵין־מְתֹ֣ם בִּ֭בְשָׂרִי מִפְּנֵ֣י זַעְמֶ֑ךָ
  אֵין־שָׁל֥וֹם בַּ֝עֲצָמַ֗י מִפְּנֵ֥י חַטָּאתִֽי׃

⁵For my iniquities have ᵇ-overwhelmed me;-ᵇ
  they are like a heavy burden, more than I can
    bear.

⁵כִּ֣י עֲ֭וֹנֹתַי עָבְר֣וּ רֹאשִׁ֑י
  כְּמַשָּׂ֥א כָ֝בֵ֗ד יִכְבְּד֥וּ מִמֶּֽנִּי׃

⁶My wounds stink and fester
  because of my folly.

⁶הִבְאִ֣ישׁוּ נָ֭מַקּוּ חַבּוּרֹתָ֑י
  מִ֝פְּנֵ֗י אִוַּלְתִּֽי׃

⁷I am all bent and bowed;
  I walk about in gloom all day long.

⁷נַעֲוֵ֣יתִי שַׁחֹ֣תִי עַד־מְאֹ֑ד
  כָּל־הַ֝יּ֗וֹם קֹדֵ֥ר הִלָּֽכְתִּי׃

⁸For my sinews are full of fever;
  there is no soundness in my flesh.

⁸כִּֽי־כְ֭סָלַי מָלְא֣וּ נִקְלֶ֑ה
  וְאֵ֥ין מְ֝תֹ֗ם בִּבְשָׂרִֽי׃

⁹I am all benumbed and crushed;
  I roar because of the turmoil in my mind.

⁹נְפוּג֣וֹתִי וְנִדְכֵּ֣יתִי עַד־מְאֹ֑ד
  שָׁ֝אַ֗גְתִּי מִֽנַּהֲמַ֥ת לִבִּֽי׃

¹⁰O Lord, You are aware of all my entreaties;
  my groaning is not hidden from You.

¹⁰אֲֽדֹנָ֗י נֶגְדְּךָ֥ כָל־תַּאֲוָתִ֑י
  וְ֝אַנְחָתִ֗י מִמְּךָ֥ לֹא־נִסְתָּֽרָה׃

¹¹My mind reels;
  my strength fails me;
  my eyes too have lost their luster.

¹¹לִבִּ֣י סְ֭חַרְחַר
  עֲזָבַ֣נִי כֹחִ֑י
  וְאוֹר־עֵינַ֥י גַּם־הֵ֝֗ם אֵ֣ין אִתִּֽי׃

¹²My friends and companions stand back from
    my affliction;
  my kinsmen stand far off.

¹²אֹֽהֲבַ֤י ׀ וְרֵעַ֗י מִנֶּ֣גֶד נִגְעִ֣י יַעֲמֹ֑דוּ
  וּ֝קְרוֹבַ֗י מֵרָחֹ֥ק עָמָֽדוּ׃

¹³Those who seek my life lay traps;
  those who wish me harm speak malice;
  they utter deceit all the time.

¹³וַיְנַקְשׁ֤וּ ׀ מְבַקְשֵׁ֬י נַפְשִׁ֗י
  וְדֹרְשֵׁ֣י רָ֭עָתִי דִּבְּר֣וּ הַוּ֑וֹת
  וּ֝מִרְמֹ֗ות כָּל־הַיּ֥וֹם יֶהְגּֽוּ׃

¹⁴But I am like a deaf man, unhearing,
  like a dumb man who cannot speak up;

¹⁴וַאֲנִ֣י כְ֭חֵרֵשׁ לֹ֣א אֶשְׁמָ֑ע
  וּ֝כְאִלֵּ֗ם לֹ֣א יִפְתַּח־פִּֽיו׃

¹⁵I am like one who does not hear,
  who has no retort on his lips.

¹⁵וָאֱהִ֗י כְּ֭אִישׁ אֲשֶׁ֣ר לֹא־שֹׁמֵ֑עַ
  וְאֵ֥ין בְּ֝פִ֗יו תּוֹכָחֽוֹת׃

¹⁶But I wait for You, O Lord;
  You will answer, O Lord, my God.

¹⁶כִּֽי־לְךָ֣ יְהֹוָ֣ה הוֹחָ֑לְתִּי
  אַתָּ֥ה תַ֝עֲנֶ֗ה אֲדֹנָ֥י אֱלֹהָֽי׃

ᵃ Meaning of Heb. uncertain.
ᵇ⁻ᵇ Lit. "passed over my head."

17For I fear they will rejoice over me;

    when my foot gives way they will vaunt them-

      selves against me.

18For I am on the verge of collapse;

    my pain is always with me.

19I acknowledge my iniquity;

    I am fearful over my sin;

    20for my mortal enemies are numerous;

    my treacherous foes are many.

21Those who repay evil for good

    harass me for pursuing good.

22Do not abandon me, O LORD;

    my God, be not far from me;

    23hasten to my aid,

    O Lord, my deliverance.

39 For the leader; for *Jeduthun.*
A psalm of David.

2I resolved I would watch my step

    lest I offend by my speech;

    I would keep my mouth muzzled

    while the wicked man was in my presence.

3I was dumb, silent;

    I was very*a* still

    while my pain was intense.

4My mind was in a rage,

    my thoughts were all aflame;

    I spoke out:

    5Tell me, O LORD, what my term is,

    what is the measure of my days;

    I would know how fleeting my life is.

6You have made my life just handbreadths long;

    its span is as nothing in Your sight;

    b-no man endures any longer than a breath.-*b*

    Selah.

17 כִּי־אָמַרְתִּי פֶּן־יִשְׂמְחוּ־לִי

בְּמוֹט רַגְלִי עָלַי הִגְדִּילוּ׃

18 כִּי־אֲנִי לְצֶלַע נָכוֹן

וּמַכְאוֹבִי נֶגְדִּי תָמִיד׃

19 כִּי־עֲוֹנִי אַגִּיד

אֶדְאַג מֵחַטָּאתִי׃

20 וְאֹיְבַי חַיִּים עָצֵמוּ

וְרַבּוּ שֹׂנְאַי שָׁקֶר׃

21 וּמְשַׁלְּמֵי רָעָה תַּחַת טוֹבָה

יִשְׂטְנוּנִי תַּחַת רדופי רָדְפִי־טוֹב׃

22 אַל־תַּעַזְבֵנִי יְהֹוָה

אֱלֹהַי אַל־תִּרְחַק מִמֶּנִּי׃

23 חוּשָׁה לְעֶזְרָתִי

אֲדֹנָי תְּשׁוּעָתִי׃

לט
לַמְנַצֵּחַ לידיתון לִידוּתוּן

מִזְמוֹר לְדָוִד׃

2 אָמַרְתִּי אֶשְׁמְרָה דְרָכַי

מֵחֲטוֹא בִלְשׁוֹנִי

אֶשְׁמְרָה לְפִי מַחְסוֹם

בְּעֹד רָשָׁע לְנֶגְדִּי׃

3 נֶאֱלַמְתִּי דוּמִיָּה

הֶחֱשֵׁיתִי מִטּוֹב

וּכְאֵבִי נֶעְכָּר׃

4 חַם־לִבִּי ׀ בְּקִרְבִּי

בַּהֲגִיגִי תִבְעַר־אֵשׁ

דִּבַּרְתִּי בִּלְשׁוֹנִי׃

5 הוֹדִיעֵנִי יְהֹוָה ׀ קִצִּי

וּמִדַּת יָמַי מַה־הִיא

אֵדְעָה מֶה־חָדֵל אָנִי׃

6 הִנֵּה טְפָחוֹת ׀ נָתַתָּה יָמַי

וְחֶלְדִּי כְאַיִן נֶגְדֶּךָ

אַךְ כָּל־הֶבֶל כָּל־אָדָם נִצָּב סֶלָה׃

---

a   Cf. use of ṭwb in Hos. 10.1; Jonah 4.4.

b-b   Meaning of Heb. uncertain.

7Man walks about as a mere shadow;

   mere futility is his hustle and bustle,

   amassing and not knowing who will gather in.

8What, then, can I count on, O Lord?

In You my hope lies.

9Deliver me from all my transgressions;

   make me not the butt of the benighted.

10I am dumb, I do not speak up,

   for it is Your doing.

11Take away Your plague from me;

   I perish from Your blows.

12You chastise a man in punishment for his sin,

   consuming like a moth what he treasures.

No man is more than a breath.   *Selah.*

13Hear my prayer, O Lord;

   give ear to my cry;

   do not disregard my tears;

   for like all my forebears

   I am an alien, resident with You.

14Look away from me, *b-*that I may recover,*-b*

   before I pass away and am gone.

40 For the leader. A psalm of David.

2I put my hope in the Lord;

   He inclined toward me,

   and heeded my cry.

3He lifted me out of the miry pit,

   the slimy clay,

   and set my feet on a rock,

   steadied my legs.

4He put a new song into my mouth,

   a hymn to our God.

May many see it and stand in awe,

   and trust in the Lord.

5Happy is the man who makes the Lord his trust,

7 אַךְ־בְּצֶ֤לֶם ׀ יִֽתְהַלֶּךְ־אִ֗ישׁ

אַךְ־הֶ֥בֶל יֶהֱמָי֑וּן

יִ֝צְבֹּ֗ר וְֽלֹא־יֵדַ֥ע מִי־אֹסְפָֽם׃

8 וְעַתָּ֣ה מַה־קִּוִּ֣יתִי אֲדֹנָ֑י

תּ֝וֹחַלְתִּ֗י לְךָ֣ הִֽיא׃

9 מִכָּל־פְּשָׁעַ֥י הַצִּילֵ֑נִי

חֶרְפַּ֥ת נָ֝בָ֗ל אַל־תְּשִׂימֵֽנִי׃

10 נֶ֭אֱלַמְתִּי לֹ֣א אֶפְתַּח־פִּ֑י

כִּ֖י אַתָּ֣ה עָשִֽׂיתָ׃

11 הָסֵ֣ר מֵעָלַ֣י נִגְעֶ֑ךָ

מִתִּגְרַ֥ת יָ֝דְךָ֗ אֲנִ֣י כָלִֽיתִי׃

12 בְּֽתוֹכָ֘ח֤וֹת עַל־עָוֺ֨ן ׀ יִסַּ֬רְתָּ אִ֗ישׁ

וַתֶּ֣מֶס כָּעָ֣שׁ חֲמוּד֑וֹ

אַ֤ךְ הֶ֖בֶל כָּל־אָדָ֣ם סֶֽלָה׃

13 שִֽׁמְעָ֥ה־תְפִלָּתִ֨י ׀ יְהֹוָ֡ה

וְשַׁוְעָתִ֨י ׀ הַאֲזִ֗ינָה

אֶֽל־דִּמְעָתִ֗י אַֽל־תֶּ֫חֱרַ֥שׁ

כִּ֤י גֵ֣ר אָנֹכִ֣י עִמָּ֑ךְ

תּ֝וֹשָׁ֗ב כְּכָל־אֲבוֹתָֽי׃

14 הָשַׁ֣ע מִמֶּ֣נִּי וְאַבְלִ֑יגָה

בְּטֶ֖רֶם אֵלֵ֣ךְ וְאֵינֶֽנִּי׃

מ לַמְנַצֵּ֗חַ לְדָוִ֥ד מִזְמֽוֹר׃

2 קַוֺּ֣ה קִוִּ֣יתִי יְהֹוָ֑ה

וַיֵּ֥ט אֵ֝לַ֗י

וַיִּשְׁמַ֥ע שַׁוְעָתִֽי׃

3 וַיַּעֲלֵ֤נִי ׀ מִבּ֥וֹר שָׁא֗וֹן

מִטִּ֗יט הַיָּ֫וֵ֥ן

וַיָּ֖קֶם עַל־סֶ֥לַע רַגְלַ֗י

כּוֹנֵ֥ן אֲשֻׁרָֽי׃

4 וַיִּתֵּ֬ן בְּפִ֨י ׀ שִׁ֥יר חָדָשׁ֮

תְּהִלָּ֢ה לֵֽאלֹ֫הֵ֥ינוּ

יִרְא֣וּ רַבִּ֣ים וְיִירָ֑אוּ

וְ֝יִבְטְח֗וּ בַּיהֹוָֽה׃

who turns not to the arrogant or to followers
of falsehood.

6a-You, O LORD my God, have done many things;
the wonders You have devised for us
cannot be set out before You;-a
I would rehearse the tale of them,
but they are more than can be told.

7b-You gave me to understand that-b
You do not desire sacrifice and meal offering;
You do not ask for burnt offering and sin
offering.

8Then I said,
b-"See, I will bring a scroll recounting what befell me."-b

9To do what pleases You, my God, is my desire;
Your teaching is in my inmost parts.

10I proclaimed [Your] righteousness in a great
congregation;
see, I did not withhold my words;
O LORD, You must know it.

11I did not keep Your beneficence to myself;
I declared Your faithful deliverance;
I did not fail to speak of Your steadfast love in
a great congregation.

12O LORD, You will not withhold from me Your
compassion;
Your steadfast love will protect me always.

13For misfortunes without number envelop me;
my iniquities have caught up with me;
I cannot see;
they are more than the hairs of my head;
c-I am at my wits' end.-c

14dO favor me, LORD, and save me;
O LORD, hasten to my aid.

15Let those who seek to destroy my life
be frustrated and disgraced;

5 אַשְׁרֵי הַגֶּבֶר אֲשֶׁר־שָׂם יְהֹוָה
מִבְטַחוֹ
וְלֹא־פָנָה אֶל־רְהָבִים וְשָׂטֵי כָזָב:
6 רַבּוֹת עָשִׂיתָ ׀ אַתָּה ׀ יְהֹוָה אֱלֹהַי
נִפְלְאֹתֶיךָ וּמַחְשְׁבֹתֶיךָ אֵלֵינוּ
אֵין ׀ עֲרֹךְ אֵלֶיךָ
אַגִּידָה וַאֲדַבֵּרָה
עָצְמוּ מִסַּפֵּר:
7 זֶבַח וּמִנְחָה ׀ לֹא־חָפַצְתָּ
אָזְנַיִם כָּרִיתָ לִּי
עוֹלָה וַחֲטָאָה לֹא שָׁאָלְתָּ:
8 אָז אָמַרְתִּי
הִנֵּה־בָאתִי בִּמְגִלַּת־סֵפֶר כָּתוּב
עָלָי:
9 לַעֲשׂוֹת־רְצוֹנְךָ אֱלֹהַי חָפָצְתִּי
וְתוֹרָתְךָ בְּתוֹךְ מֵעָי:
10 בִּשַּׂרְתִּי צֶדֶק ׀ בְּקָהָל רָב
הִנֵּה שְׂפָתַי לֹא אֶכְלָא
יְהֹוָה אַתָּה יָדָעְתָּ:
11 צִדְקָתְךָ לֹא־כִסִּיתִי ׀ בְּתוֹךְ לִבִּי
אֱמוּנָתְךָ וּתְשׁוּעָתְךָ אָמַרְתִּי
לֹא־כִחַדְתִּי חַסְדְּךָ וַאֲמִתְּךָ לְקָהָל
רָב:
12 אַתָּה יְהֹוָה לֹא־תִכְלָא רַחֲמֶיךָ
מִמֶּנִּי
חַסְדְּךָ וַאֲמִתְּךָ תָּמִיד יִצְּרוּנִי:
13 כִּי אָפְפוּ־עָלַי ׀ רָעוֹת עַד־אֵין
מִסְפָּר
הִשִּׂיגוּנִי עֲוֺנֹתַי
וְלֹא־יָכֹלְתִּי לִרְאוֹת
עָצְמוּ מִשַּׂעֲרוֹת רֹאשִׁי
וְלִבִּי עֲזָבָנִי:
14 רְצֵה יְהֹוָה לְהַצִּילֵנִי
יְהֹוָה לְעֶזְרָתִי חוּשָׁה:
15 יֵבֹשׁוּ וְיַחְפְּרוּ ׀
יַחַד מְבַקְשֵׁי נַפְשִׁי לִסְפּוֹתָהּ

---

a-a   Or "You, O LORD my God, have done many things— / the wonders
You have devised for us; / none can equal You."
b-b   Meaning of Heb. uncertain.
c-c   Or "my courage fails me."
d   With vv. 14–18, cf. Ps. 70.

let those who wish me harm
fall back in shame.

16Let those who say "Aha! Aha!" over me
be desolate because of their frustration.

17But let all who seek You be glad and rejoice
in You;
let those who are eager for Your deliverance
always say, "Extolled be the LORD!"

18But I am poor and needy;
may the Lord devise [deliverance] for me.
You are my help and my rescuer;
my God, do not delay.

יִסֹּגוּ אָחוֹר וְיִכָּלְמוּ
חֲפֵצֵי רָעָתִי:

16 יָשֹׁמּוּ עַל־עֵקֶב בָּשְׁתָּם
הָאֹמְרִים לִי הֶאָח ׀ הֶאָח:

17 יָשִׂישׂוּ וְיִשְׂמְחוּ ׀ בְּךָ כָּל־
מְבַקְשֶׁיךָ
יֹאמְרוּ תָמִיד יִגְדַּל יְהֹוָה אֹהֲבֵי
תְּשׁוּעָתֶךָ:

18 וַאֲנִי ׀ עָנִי וְאֶבְיוֹן
אֲדֹנָי יַחֲשָׁב לִי
עֶזְרָתִי וּמְפַלְטִי אַתָּה
אֱלֹהַי אַל־תְּאַחַר:

41

For the leader. A psalm of David.

מא לַמְנַצֵּחַ מִזְמוֹר לְדָוִד:

2Happy is he who is thoughtful of the wretched;
in bad times may the LORD keep him from
harm.

3May the LORD guard him and preserve him;
and may he be thought happy in the land.
Do not subject him to the will of his enemies.

4The LORD will sustain him on his sickbed;
a-You shall wholly transform his bed of
suffering.-a

5I said, "O LORD, have mercy on me,
heal me, for I have sinned against You."

6My enemies speak evilly of me,
"When will he die and his name perish?"

7If one comes to visit, he speaks falsely;
his mind stores up evil thoughts;
once outside, he speaks them.

8All my enemies whisper together against me,
imagining the worst for me.

9"Something baneful has settled in him;
he'll not rise from his bed again."

10My ally in whom I trusted,
even he who shares my bread,

2 אַשְׁרֵי מַשְׂכִּיל אֶל־דָּל
בְּיוֹם רָעָה יְמַלְּטֵהוּ יְהֹוָה:

3 יְהֹוָה ׀ יִשְׁמְרֵהוּ וִיחַיֵּהוּ
יְאֻשַּׁר וְאֶשֶׁר בָּאָרֶץ
וְאַל־תִּתְּנֵהוּ בְּנֶפֶשׁ אֹיְבָיו:

4 יְהֹוָה יִסְעָדֶנּוּ עַל־עֶרֶשׂ דְּוָי
כָּל־מִשְׁכָּבוֹ הָפַכְתָּ בְחָלְיוֹ:

5 אֲנִי־אָמַרְתִּי יְהֹוָה חָנֵּנִי
רְפָאָה נַפְשִׁי כִּי־חָטָאתִי לָךְ:

6 אוֹיְבַי יֹאמְרוּ רַע לִי
מָתַי יָמוּת וְאָבַד שְׁמוֹ:

7 וְאִם־בָּא לִרְאוֹת ׀ שָׁוְא יְדַבֵּר
לִבּוֹ יִקְבָּץ־אָוֶן לוֹ
יֵצֵא לַחוּץ יְדַבֵּר:

8 יַחַד עָלַי יִתְלַחֲשׁוּ כָּל־שֹׂנְאָי
עָלַי ׀ יַחְשְׁבוּ רָעָה לִי:

9 דְּבַר־בְּלִיַּעַל יָצוּק בּוֹ
וַאֲשֶׁר שָׁכַב לֹא־יוֹסִיף לָקוּם:

10 גַּם־אִישׁ שְׁלוֹמִי ׀ אֲשֶׁר־בָּטַחְתִּי
בוֹ
אוֹכֵל לַחְמִי

a-a Meaning of Heb. uncertain.

^a-has been utterly false to me.-^a

¹¹But You, O Lord, have mercy on me;

   let me rise again and repay them.

¹²Then shall I know that You are pleased with me:

   when my enemy cannot shout in triumph over

   me.

¹³You will support me because of my integrity,

   and let me abide in Your presence forever.

¹⁴Blessed is the Lord, God of Israel,

   from eternity to eternity.

   Amen and Amen.

הִגְדִּיל עָלַי עָקֵב:

11 וְאַתָּה יְהוָה חָנֵּנִי וַהֲקִימֵנִי

וַאֲשַׁלְּמָה לָהֶם:

12 בְּזֹאת יָדַעְתִּי כִּי־חָפַצְתָּ בִּי

כִּי לֹא־יָרִיעַ אֹיְבִי עָלָי:

13 וַאֲנִי בְּתֻמִּי תָּמַכְתָּ בִּי

וַתַּצִּיבֵנִי לְפָנֶיךָ לְעוֹלָם:

14 בָּרוּךְ יְהוָה | אֱלֹהֵי יִשְׂרָאֵל

מֵהָעוֹלָם וְעַד הָעוֹלָם

אָמֵן | וְאָמֵן:

BOOK TWO   ספר שני

42 For the leader. A *maskil* of the Korahites.   מב לַמְנַצֵּחַ מַשְׂכִּיל לִבְנֵי־קֹרַח:

²Like a hind crying for water,^a

   my soul cries for You, O God;

³my soul thirsts for God, the living God;

   O when will I come to appear before God!

⁴My tears have been my food day and night;

   I am ever taunted with, "Where is your God?"

⁵When I think of this, I pour out my soul:

   how I ^b-walked with the crowd, moved with

      them,-^b

   the festive throng, to the House of God

   with joyous shouts of praise.

⁶Why so downcast, my soul,

   why disquieted within me?

Have hope in God;

   I will yet praise Him

   ^c-for His saving presence.-^c

2 כְּאַיָּל תַּעֲרֹג עַל־אֲפִיקֵי־מָיִם

כֵּן נַפְשִׁי תַעֲרֹג אֵלֶיךָ אֱלֹהִים:

3 צָמְאָה נַפְשִׁי | לֵאלֹהִים לְאֵל חָי

מָתַי אָבוֹא

וְאֵרָאֶה פְּנֵי אֱלֹהִים:

4 הָיְתָה־לִּי דִמְעָתִי לֶחֶם יוֹמָם

וָלָיְלָה

בֶּאֱמֹר אֵלַי כָּל־הַיּוֹם אַיֵּה אֱלֹהֶיךָ:

5 אֵלֶּה אֶזְכְּרָה | וְאֶשְׁפְּכָה עָלַי |

נַפְשִׁי

כִּי אֶעֱבֹר | בַּסָּךְ

אֶדַּדֵּם עַד־בֵּית אֱלֹהִים

בְּקוֹל־רִנָּה וְתוֹדָה הָמוֹן חוֹגֵג:

6 מַה־תִּשְׁתּוֹחֲחִי | נַפְשִׁי

וַתֶּהֱמִי עָלָי

הוֹחִילִי לֵאלֹהִים

כִּי־עוֹד אוֹדֶנּוּ

יְשׁוּעוֹת פָּנָיו:

---

a   Lit. "watercourses."

b-b   Meaning of Heb. uncertain.

c-c   Several ancient versions and Heb. mss. connect the first word in

      v. 7 with the end of 6, reading yeshu'ot panai we'Elohai, "my

      ever-present help, my God," as in vv. 12 and Ps. 43.5.

7O my God, my soul is downcast;

  therefore I think of You

  in this land of Jordan and Hermon,

  in Mount Mizar,

  8where deep calls to deep

  in the roar of ᵇ-Your cataracts;-ᵇ

  all Your breakers and billows have swept over

    me.

9By day may the LORD vouchsafe His faithful care,

  so that at night a song to Him may be with me,

  a prayer to the God of my life.

10I say to God, my rock,

  "Why have You forgotten me,

  why must I walk in gloom,

  oppressed by my enemy?"

11ᵇ-Crushing my bones,-ᵇ

  my foes revile me,

  taunting me always with, "Where is your God?"

12Why so downcast, my soul,

  why disquieted within me?

Have hope in God;

  I will yet praise Him,

  my ever-present help, my God.

43 ᵃVindicate me, O God,

  champion my cause

  against faithless people;

  rescue me from the treacherous, dishonest

    man.

2For You are my God, my stronghold;

  why have You rejected me?

Why must I walk in gloom,

  oppressed by the enemy?

3Send forth Your light and Your truth;

  they will lead me;

  they will bring me to Your holy mountain,

  to Your dwelling-place,

7 אֱלֹהַי עָלַי נַפְשִׁי תִשְׁתּוֹחָח

עַל־כֵּן אֶזְכָּרְךָ

מֵאֶרֶץ יַרְדֵּן וְחֶרְמוֹנִים

מֵהַר מִצְעָר:

8 תְּהוֹם־אֶל־תְּהוֹם קוֹרֵא

לְקוֹל צִנּוֹרֶיךָ

כָּל־מִשְׁבָּרֶיךָ וְגַלֶּיךָ עָלַי עָבָרוּ:

9 יוֹמָם ׀ יְצַוֶּה יְהוָה ׀ חַסְדּוֹ

וּבַלַּיְלָה שִׁירֹה עִמִּי

תְּפִלָּה לְאֵל חַיָּי:

10 אוֹמְרָה ׀ לְאֵל סַלְעִי

לָמָה שְׁכַחְתָּנִי

לָמָה־קֹדֵר אֵלֵךְ

בְּלַחַץ אוֹיֵב:

11 בְּרֶצַח ׀ בְּעַצְמוֹתַי

חֵרְפוּנִי צוֹרְרָי

בְּאָמְרָם אֵלַי כָּל־הַיּוֹם אַיֵּה

אֱלֹהֶיךָ:

12 מַה־תִּשְׁתּוֹחֲחִי ׀ נַפְשִׁי

וּמַה־תֶּהֱמִי עָלָי

הוֹחִילִי לֵאלֹהִים

כִּי־עוֹד אוֹדֶנּוּ

יְשׁוּעֹת פָּנַי וֵאלֹהָי:

מג שָׁפְטֵנִי אֱלֹהִים ׀

וְרִיבָה רִיבִי

מִגּוֹי לֹא־חָסִיד

מֵאִישׁ־מִרְמָה וְעַוְלָה תְפַלְּטֵנִי:

2 כִּי־אַתָּה ׀ אֱלֹהֵי מָעוּזִּי

לָמָה זְנַחְתָּנִי

לָמָה־קֹדֵר אֶתְהַלֵּךְ

בְּלַחַץ אוֹיֵב:

3 שְׁלַח־אוֹרְךָ וַאֲמִתְּךָ

הֵמָּה יַנְחוּנִי

יְבִיאוּנִי אֶל־הַר־קָדְשְׁךָ

וְאֶל־מִשְׁכְּנוֹתֶיךָ:

a   A continuation of Ps. 42.

4that I may come to the altar of God,
God, my delight, my joy;
that I may praise You with the lyre,
O God, my God.

5Why so downcast, my soul,
why disquieted within me?
Have hope in God;
I will yet praise Him,
my ever-present help, my God.

וְאָב֤וֹאָה ׀ אֶל־מִזְבַּ֬ח אֱלֹהִ֗ים
אֶל־אֵל֮ שִׂמְחַ֪ת גִּ֫ילִ֥י
וְאוֹדְךָ֥ בְכִנּ֑וֹר
אֱלֹהִ֥ים אֱלֹהָֽי׃

מַה־תִּשְׁתּ֬וֹחֲחִ֨י ׀ נַפְשִׁי֮
וּֽמַה־תֶּהֱמִ֪י עָ֫לָ֥י
הוֹחִ֣ילִי לֵֽ֭אלֹהִים
כִּי־ע֣וֹד אוֹדֶ֑נּוּ
יְשׁוּעֹ֥ת פָּ֝נַ֗י וֵֽאלֹהָֽי׃

44 For the leader. Of the Korahites. A *maskil.*

לַמְנַצֵּ֬חַ לִבְנֵי־קֹ֬רַח מַשְׂכִּֽיל׃   **מד**

2We have heard, O God,
our fathers have told us
the deeds You performed in their time,
in days of old.

3With Your hand You planted them,
displacing nations;
You brought misfortune on peoples,
and drove them out.

4It was not by their sword that they took the land,
their arm did not give them victory,
but Your right hand, Your arm, and Your
goodwill,
for You favored them.

5You are my king, O God;
decree victories for Jacob!

6Through You we gore our foes;
by Your name we trample our adversaries;

7I do not trust in my bow;
it is not my sword that gives me victory;

8You give us victory over our foes;
You thwart those who hate us.

9In God we glory at all times,
and praise Your name unceasingly. *Selah.*

10Yet You have rejected and disgraced us;
You do not go with our armies.

אֱלֹהִ֤ים ׀ בְּאָזְנֵ֬ינוּ שָׁמַ֗עְנוּ
אֲבוֹתֵ֥ינוּ סִפְּרוּ־לָ֑נוּ
פֹּ֥עַל פָּעַ֥לְתָּ בִֽימֵיהֶ֗ם
בִּ֣ימֵי קֶֽדֶם׃

אַתָּ֤ה ׀ יָדְךָ֮ גּוֹיִ֪ם ה֫וֹרַ֥שְׁתָּ
וַתִּטָּעֵ֑ם
תָּרַ֥ע לְ֝אֻמִּ֗ים
וַֽתְּשַׁלְּחֵֽם׃

כִּ֤י לֹ֪א בְחַרְבָּ֡ם יָ֥רְשׁוּ אָ֗רֶץ
וּזְרוֹעָם֮ לֹא־הוֹשִׁ֪יעָ֫ה לָּ֥מוֹ
כִּֽי־יְמִֽינְךָ֣ וּ֭זְרוֹעֲךָ וְא֥וֹר פָּנֶ֗יךָ
כִּ֣י רְצִיתָֽם׃

אַתָּה־ה֣וּא מַלְכִּ֣י אֱלֹהִ֑ים
צַ֝וֵּ֗ה יְשׁוּע֥וֹת יַעֲקֹֽב׃

בְּ֭ךָ צָרֵ֣ינוּ נְנַגֵּ֑חַ
בְּ֝שִׁמְךָ֗ נָב֥וּס קָמֵֽינוּ׃

כִּ֤י לֹ֣א בְקַשְׁתִּ֣י אֶבְטָ֑ח
וְ֝חַרְבִּ֗י לֹ֣א תוֹשִׁיעֵֽנִי׃

כִּ֣י ה֭וֹשַׁעְתָּנוּ מִצָּרֵ֑ינוּ
וּמְשַׂנְאֵ֥ינוּ הֱבִישֽׁוֹת׃

בֵּֽ֭אלֹהִים הִלַּ֣לְנוּ כָל־הַיּ֑וֹם
וְשִׁמְךָ֓ ׀ לְעוֹלָ֖ם נוֹדֶ֣ה סֶֽלָה׃

אַף־זָ֭נַחְתָּ וַתַּכְלִימֵ֑נוּ
וְלֹא־תֵ֝צֵ֗א בְּצִבְאוֹתֵֽינוּ׃

11You make us retreat before our foe;
our enemies plunder us at will.

12You let them devour us like sheep;
You disperse us among the nations.

13You sell Your people for no fortune,
You set no high price on them.

14You make us the butt of our neighbors,
the scorn and derision of those around us.

15You make us a byword among the nations,
a laughingstock[a] among the peoples.

16I am always aware of my disgrace;
I am wholly covered with shame

17at the sound of taunting revilers,
in the presence of the vengeful foe.

18All this has come upon us,
yet we have not forgotten You,
or been false to Your covenant.

19Our hearts have not gone astray,
nor have our feet swerved from Your path,

20though You cast us, crushed, to where the
[b]-sea monster-[b] is,
and covered us over with deepest darkness.

21If we forgot the name of our God
and spread forth our hands to a foreign god,

22God would surely search it out,
for He knows the secrets of the heart.

23It is for Your sake that we are slain all day long,
that we are regarded as sheep to be slaughtered.

24Rouse Yourself; why do You sleep, O Lord?
Awaken, do not reject us forever!

25Why do You hide Your face,
ignoring our affliction and distress?

26We lie prostrate in the dust;
our body clings to the ground.

27Arise and help us,
redeem us, as befits Your faithfulness.

11 תְּשִׁיבֵנוּ אָחוֹר מִנִּי־צָר
וּמְשַׂנְאֵינוּ שָׁסוּ לָמוֹ:
12 תִּתְּנֵנוּ כְּצֹאן מַאֲכָל
וּבַגּוֹיִם זֵרִיתָנוּ:
13 תִּמְכֹּר־עַמְּךָ בְלֹא־הוֹן
וְלֹא־רִבִּיתָ בִּמְחִירֵיהֶם:
14 תְּשִׂימֵנוּ חֶרְפָּה לִשְׁכֵנֵינוּ
לַעַג וָקֶלֶס לִסְבִיבוֹתֵינוּ:
15 תְּשִׂימֵנוּ מָשָׁל בַּגּוֹיִם
מְנוֹד־רֹאשׁ בַּל־אֻמִּים*:
16 כָּל־הַיּוֹם כְּלִמָּתִי נֶגְדִּי
וּבֹשֶׁת פָּנַי כִּסָּתְנִי:
17 מִקּוֹל מְחָרֵף וּמְגַדֵּף
מִפְּנֵי אוֹיֵב וּמִתְנַקֵּם:
18 כָּל־זֹאת בָּאַתְנוּ
וְלֹא שְׁכַחֲנוּךָ
וְלֹא־שִׁקַּרְנוּ בִּבְרִיתֶךָ:
19 לֹא־נָסוֹג אָחוֹר לִבֵּנוּ
וַתֵּט אֲשֻׁרֵינוּ מִנִּי אָרְחֶךָ:
20 כִּי דִכִּיתָנוּ בִּמְקוֹם תַּנִּים
וַתְּכַס עָלֵינוּ בְצַלְמָוֶת:
21 אִם־שָׁכַחְנוּ שֵׁם אֱלֹהֵינוּ
וַנִּפְרֹשׂ כַּפֵּינוּ לְאֵל זָר:
22 הֲלֹא אֱלֹהִים יַחֲקָר־זֹאת
כִּי־הוּא יֹדֵעַ תַּעֲלֻמוֹת לֵב:
23 כִּי־עָלֶיךָ הֹרַגְנוּ כָל־הַיּוֹם
נֶחְשַׁבְנוּ כְּצֹאן טִבְחָה:
24 עוּרָה ׀ לָמָּה תִישַׁן ׀ אֲדֹנָי
הָקִיצָה אַל־תִּזְנַח לָנֶצַח:
25 לָמָּה־פָנֶיךָ תַסְתִּיר
תִּשְׁכַּח עָנְיֵנוּ וְלַחֲצֵנוּ:
26 כִּי שָׁחָה לֶעָפָר נַפְשֵׁנוּ
דָּבְקָה לָאָרֶץ בִּטְנֵנוּ:
27 קוּמָה עֶזְרָתָה לָּנוּ
וּפְדֵנוּ לְמַעַן חַסְדֶּךָ:

a Lit. "a wagging of the head."
b-b Heb. tannim = tannin, as in Ezek. 29.3 and 32.2.

בנוסח אחר "בלאמים" v. 15.

45

For the leader; *a*-on *shoshannim.*-*a* Of the
Korahites. A *maskil.* A love song.

מה לַמְנַצֵּחַ עַל־שֹׁשַׁנִּים לִבְנֵי־
קֹרַח מַשְׂכִּיל שִׁיר יְדִידֹת:

2My heart is astir with gracious words;

    I speak my poem to a king;

    my tongue is the pen of an expert scribe.

3You are fairer than all men;

    your speech is endowed with grace;

    rightly has God given you an eternal blessing.

4Gird your sword upon your thigh, O hero,

    in your splendor and glory;

    5*a*-in your glory, win success;

    ride on in the cause of truth and meekness and

      right;

    and let your right hand lead you to awesome

      deeds.-*a*

6Your arrows, sharpened,

    b-[pierce] the breast of the king's enemies;

    peoples fall at your feet.-*b*

7Your *c*-divine throne-*c* is everlasting;

    your royal scepter is a scepter of equity.

8You love righteousness and hate wickedness;

    rightly has God, your God, chosen to anoint

      you

    with oil of gladness over all your peers.

9All your robes [are fragrant] with

    myrrh and aloes and cassia;

    from ivoried palaces

    lutes entertain you.

10Royal princesses are your favorites;

    the consort stands at your right hand,

    decked in gold of Ophir.

11Take heed, lass, and note,

    incline your ear:

    forget your people and your father's house,

    12and let the king be aroused by your beauty;

רָחַשׁ לִבִּי ׀ דָּבָר טוֹב 2
אֹמֵר אָנִי מַעֲשַׂי לְמֶלֶךְ
לְשׁוֹנִי עֵט ׀ סוֹפֵר מָהִיר:

יָפְיָפִיתָ מִבְּנֵי אָדָם 3
הוּצַק חֵן בְּשִׂפְתוֹתֶיךָ
עַל־כֵּן בֵּרַכְךָ אֱלֹהִים לְעוֹלָם:
חֲגוֹר־חַרְבְּךָ עַל־יָרֵךְ גִּבּוֹר 4
הוֹדְךָ וַהֲדָרֶךָ:
וַהֲדָרְךָ ׀ צְלַח 5
רְכַב עַל־דְּבַר־אֱמֶת וְעַנְוָה־צֶדֶק
וְתוֹרְךָ נוֹרָאוֹת יְמִינֶךָ:
חִצֶּיךָ שְׁנוּנִים 6
עַמִּים תַּחְתֶּיךָ יִפְּלוּ
בְּלֵב אוֹיְבֵי הַמֶּלֶךְ:
כִּסְאֲךָ אֱלֹהִים עוֹלָם וָעֶד 7
שֵׁבֶט מִישֹׁר שֵׁבֶט מַלְכוּתֶךָ:
אָהַבְתָּ צֶּדֶק וַתִּשְׂנָא רֶשַׁע 8
עַל־כֵּן ׀ מְשָׁחֲךָ אֱלֹהִים אֱלֹהֶיךָ
שֶׁמֶן שָׂשׂוֹן מֵחֲבֵרֶיךָ:
מֹר־וַאֲהָלוֹת קְצִיעוֹת 9
כָּל־בִּגְדֹתֶיךָ
מִן־הֵיכְלֵי שֵׁן
מִנִּי שִׂמְּחוּךָ:
בְּנוֹת מְלָכִים בְּיִקְּרוֹתֶיךָ* 10
נִצְּבָה שֵׁגַל לִימִינְךָ
בְּכֶתֶם אוֹפִיר:
שִׁמְעִי־בַת וּרְאִי 11
וְהַטִּי אָזְנֵךְ
וְשִׁכְחִי עַמֵּךְ וּבֵית אָבִיךְ:
וְיִתְאָו הַמֶּלֶךְ יָפְיֵךְ 12

---

a-a   *Meaning of Heb. uncertain.*
b-b   *Order of Heb. clauses inverted for clarity.*
c-c   *Cf. 1 Chron. 29.23.*

since he is your lord, bow to him.

13O Tyrian lass,

the wealthiest people will court your favor with gifts,

14a-goods of all sorts.

The royal princess,

her dress embroidered with golden mountings,

15is led inside to the king;-a

maidens in her train, her companions,

are presented to you.

16They are led in with joy and gladness;

they enter the palace of the king.

17Your sons will succeed your ancestors;

you will appoint them princes throughout the land.

18I commemorate your fame for all generations,

so peoples will praise you forever and ever.

46 For the leader. Of the Korahites;

a-on *alamoth*.-a A song.

2God is our refuge and stronghold,

a help in trouble, very near.

3Therefore we are not afraid

though the earth reels,

though mountains topple into the sea—

4its waters rage and foam;

in its swell mountains quake. *Selah.*

5There is a river whose streams gladden God's city,

the holy dwelling-place of the Most High.

6God is in its midst, it will not be toppled;

by daybreak God will come to its aid.

7Nations rage, kingdoms topple;

at the sound of His thunder the earth dissolves.

כִּי־הוּא אֲדֹנַיִךְ וְהִשְׁתַּחֲוִי־לוֹ:

13 וּבַת־צֹר ׀

בְּמִנְחָה פָּנַיִךְ יְחַלּוּ עֲשִׁירֵי עָם:

14 כָּל־כְּבוּדָּה

בַת־מֶלֶךְ פְּנִימָה

מִמִּשְׁבְּצוֹת זָהָב לְבוּשָׁהּ:

15 לִרְקָמוֹת תּוּבַל לַמֶּלֶךְ

בְּתוּלוֹת אַחֲרֶיהָ רֵעוֹתֶיהָ

מוּבָאוֹת לָךְ:

16 תּוּבַלְנָה בִּשְׂמָחֹת וָגִיל

תְּבֹאֶינָה בְּהֵיכַל מֶלֶךְ:

17 תַּחַת אֲבֹתֶיךָ יִהְיוּ בָנֶיךָ

תְּשִׁיתֵמוֹ לְשָׂרִים בְּכָל־הָאָרֶץ:

18 אַזְכִּירָה שִׁמְךָ בְּכָל־דֹּר וָדֹר

עַל־כֵּן עַמִּים יְהוֹדֻךָ לְעֹלָם וָעֶד:

מו לַמְנַצֵּחַ לִבְנֵי־קֹרַח

עַל־עֲלָמוֹת שִׁיר:

2 אֱלֹהִים לָנוּ מַחֲסֶה וָעֹז

עֶזְרָה בְצָרוֹת נִמְצָא מְאֹד:

3 עַל־כֵּן לֹא־נִירָא

בְּהָמִיר אָרֶץ

וּבְמוֹט הָרִים בְּלֵב יַמִּים:

4 יֶהֱמוּ יֶחְמְרוּ מֵימָיו

יִרְעֲשׁוּ־הָרִים בְּגַאֲוָתוֹ סֶלָה:

5 נָהָר פְּלָגָיו יְשַׂמְּחוּ עִיר־אֱלֹהִים

קְדֹשׁ מִשְׁכְּנֵי עֶלְיוֹן:

6 אֱלֹהִים בְּקִרְבָּהּ בַּל־תִּמּוֹט

יַעְזְרֶהָ אֱלֹהִים לִפְנוֹת בֹּקֶר:

7 הָמוּ גוֹיִם מָטוּ מַמְלָכוֹת

נָתַן בְּקוֹלוֹ תָּמוּג אָרֶץ:

---

a-a   *Meaning of Heb. uncertain.*

8The Lord of hosts is with us;
    the God of Jacob is our haven.   *Selah.*

9Come and see what the Lord has done,
    how He has wrought desolation on the earth.
10He puts a stop to wars throughout the earth,
    breaking the bow, snapping the spear,
    consigning wagons to the flames.
11"Desist! Realize that I am God!
    I dominate the nations;
    I dominate the earth."
12The Lord of hosts is with us;
    the God of Jacob is our haven.   *Selah.*

8 יְהֹוָה צְבָא֣וֹת עִמָּ֑נוּ
מִשְׂגָּֽב־לָ֝֗נוּ אֱלֹהֵ֣י יַעֲקֹ֣ב סֶֽלָה׃

9 לְכֽוּ־חֲ֭זוּ מִפְעֲל֣וֹת יְהֹוָ֑ה
אֲשֶׁר־שָׂ֖ם שַׁמּ֣וֹת בָּאָֽרֶץ׃
10 מַשְׁבִּ֥ית מִלְחָמוֹת֮ עַד־קְצֵ֢ה
הָ֫אָ֥רֶץ
קֶ֣שֶׁת יְ֭שַׁבֵּר וְקִצֵּ֣ץ חֲנִ֑ית
עֲ֝גָל֗וֹת יִשְׂרֹ֥ף בָּאֵֽשׁ׃
11 הַרְפּ֣וּ וּ֭דְעוּ כִּֽי־אָנֹכִ֣י אֱלֹהִ֑ים
אָר֥וּם בַּ֝גּוֹיִ֗ם
אָר֥וּם בָּאָֽרֶץ׃
12 יְהֹוָ֣ה צְבָא֣וֹת עִמָּ֑נוּ
מִשְׂגָּֽב־לָ֝֗נוּ אֱלֹהֵ֣י יַעֲקֹ֣ב סֶֽלָה׃

47 For the leader. Of the Korahites. A psalm.

מז לַמְנַצֵּ֓חַ ׀ לִבְנֵי־קֹ֬רַח מִזְמֽוֹר׃

2All you peoples, clap your hands,
    raise a joyous shout for God.
3For the Lord Most High is awesome,
    great king over all the earth;
4He subjects peoples to us,
    sets nations at our feet.
5He chose our heritage for us,
    the pride of Jacob whom He loved.   *Selah.*

6God ascends midst acclamation;
    the Lord, to the blasts of the horn.
7Sing, O sing to God;
    sing, O sing to our king;
8for God is king over all the earth;
    sing a hymn.[a]
9God reigns over the nations;
    God is seated on His holy throne.
10The great of the peoples are gathered together,
    the retinue of Abraham's God;

2 כׇּל־הָ֭עַמִּים תִּקְעוּ־כָ֑ף
הָרִ֥יעוּ לֵ֝אלֹהִ֗ים בְּק֣וֹל רִנָּֽה׃
3 כִּֽי־יְהֹוָ֣ה עֶלְי֣וֹן נוֹרָ֑א
מֶ֥לֶךְ גָּ֝ד֗וֹל עַל־כׇּל־הָאָֽרֶץ׃
4 יַדְבֵּ֣ר עַמִּ֣ים תַּחְתֵּ֑ינוּ
וּ֝לְאֻמִּ֗ים תַּ֣חַת רַגְלֵֽינוּ׃
5 יִבְחַר־לָ֥נוּ אֶת־נַחֲלָתֵ֑נוּ
אֶ֥ת* גְּא֣וֹן יַעֲקֹ֣ב אֲשֶׁר־אָהֵ֣ב
סֶֽלָה׃

6 עָלָ֣ה אֱ֭לֹהִים בִּתְרוּעָ֑ה
יְ֝הֹוָ֗ה בְּק֣וֹל שׁוֹפָֽר׃
7 זַמְּר֣וּ אֱלֹהִ֣ים זַמֵּ֑רוּ
זַמְּר֖וּ לְמַלְכֵּ֣נוּ זַמֵּֽרוּ׃
8 כִּ֤י מֶ֖לֶךְ כׇּל־הָאָ֥רֶץ אֱלֹהִ֑ים
זַמְּר֥וּ מַשְׂכִּֽיל׃
9 מָלַ֣ךְ אֱ֭לֹהִים עַל־גּוֹיִ֑ם
אֱ֝לֹהִ֗ים יָשַׁ֤ב ׀ עַל־כִּסֵּ֬א קׇדְשֽׁוֹ׃
10 נְדִ֘יבֵ֤י עַמִּ֨ים ׀ נֶאֱסָ֗פוּ
עַם֮ אֱלֹהֵ֢י אַבְרָ֫הָ֥ם

---

a   Heb. *maskil, a musical term of uncertain meaning.*

for the guardians of the earth belong to God;
He is greatly exalted.

כִּי לֵאלֹהִים מָגִנֵּי־אֶרֶץ
מְאֹד נַעֲלָה:

48 A song. A psalm of the Korahites.

מח שִׁיר מִזְמוֹר לִבְנֵי־קֹרַח:

2The LORD is great and much acclaimed
in the city of our God,
His holy mountain—
3fair-crested, joy of all the earth,
Mount Zion, summit of Zaphon,ᵃ
city of the great king.
4Through its citadels, God has made Himself
known as a haven.
5See, the kings joined forces;
they advanced together.
6At the mere sight of it they were stunned,
they were terrified, they panicked;
7they were seized there with a trembling,
like a woman in the throes of labor,
8as the Tarshish fleet was wrecked
in an easterly gale.ᵇ
9The likes of what we heard we have now witnessed
in the city of the LORD of hosts,
in the city of our God—
may God preserve it forever!   Selah.

2 גָּדוֹל יְהֹוָה וּמְהֻלָּל מְאֹד
בְּעִיר אֱלֹהֵינוּ
הַר־קָדְשׁוֹ:
3 יְפֵה נוֹף מְשׂוֹשׂ כָּל־הָאָרֶץ
הַר־צִיּוֹן יַרְכְּתֵי צָפוֹן
קִרְיַת מֶלֶךְ רָב:
4 אֱלֹהִים בְּאַרְמְנוֹתֶיהָ נוֹדַע
לְמִשְׂגָּב:
5 כִּי־הִנֵּה הַמְּלָכִים נוֹעֲדוּ
עָבְרוּ יַחְדָּו:
6 הֵמָּה רָאוּ כֵּן תָּמָהוּ
נִבְהֲלוּ נֶחְפָּזוּ:
7 רְעָדָה אֲחָזָתַם שָׁם
חִיל כַּיּוֹלֵדָה:
8 בְּרוּחַ קָדִים
תְּשַׁבֵּר אֳנִיּוֹת תַּרְשִׁישׁ:
9 כַּאֲשֶׁר שָׁמַעְנוּ ׀ כֵּן רָאִינוּ
בְּעִיר־יְהֹוָה צְבָאוֹת
בְּעִיר אֱלֹהֵינוּ
אֱלֹהִים יְכוֹנְנֶהָ עַד־עוֹלָם סֶלָה:

10In Your temple, God,
we meditate upon Your faithful care.
11The praise of You, God, like Your name,
reaches to the ends of the earth;
Your right hand is filled with beneficence.
12Let Mount Zion rejoice!
Let the townsᶜ of Judah exult,
because of Your judgments.

10 דִּמִּינוּ אֱלֹהִים חַסְדֶּךָ
בְּקֶרֶב הֵיכָלֶךָ:
11 כְּשִׁמְךָ אֱלֹהִים כֵּן תְּהִלָּתְךָ
עַל־קַצְוֵי־אֶרֶץ
צֶדֶק מָלְאָה יְמִינֶךָ:
12 יִשְׂמַח ׀ הַר־צִיּוֹן
תָּגֵלְנָה בְּנוֹת יְהוּדָה
לְמַעַן מִשְׁפָּטֶיךָ:

13Walk around Zion,
circle it;

13 סֹבּוּ צִיּוֹן
וְהַקִּיפוּהָ

a   A term for the divine abode.
b   See 1 Kings 22.49.
c   Or "women."

count its towers,
14take note of its ramparts;
^dgo through-^d its citadels,
that you may recount it to a future age.
15For God—He is our God forever;
He will lead us ^devermore.^{-d}

סִפְרוּ מִגְדָּלֶיהָ׃
14 שִׁיתוּ לִבְּכֶם ׀ לְחֵילָה
פַּסְּגוּ אַרְמְנוֹתֶיהָ
לְמַעַן תְּסַפְּרוּ לְדוֹר אַחֲרוֹן׃
15 כִּי זֶה ׀ אֱלֹהִים אֱלֹהֵינוּ עוֹלָם וָעֶד
הוּא יְנַהֲגֵנוּ עַל־מוּת׃

49　For the leader. Of the Korahites. A psalm.　מט לַמְנַצֵּחַ ׀ לִבְנֵי־קֹרַח מִזְמוֹר׃

2Hear this, all you peoples;
give ear, all inhabitants of the world,
3men of all estates,
rich and poor alike.
4My mouth utters wisdom,
my speech^a is full of insight.
5I will turn my attention to a theme,
set forth my lesson to the music of a lyre.

6In time of trouble, why should I fear
the encompassing evil of those who would supplant me—
7men who trust in their riches,
who glory in their great wealth?
8b-Ah, it-b cannot redeem a man,
or pay his ransom to God;
9the price of life is too high;
and so one ceases to be, forever.
10Shall he live eternally,
and never see the grave?
11For one sees that the wise die,
that the foolish and ignorant both perish,
leaving their wealth to others.
12Their grave^c is their eternal home,
the dwelling-place for all generations
of those once famous on earth.

2 שִׁמְעוּ־זֹאת כָּל־הָעַמִּים
הַאֲזִינוּ כָּל־יֹשְׁבֵי חָלֶד׃
3 גַּם־בְּנֵי אָדָם גַּם־בְּנֵי־אִישׁ
יַחַד עָשִׁיר וְאֶבְיוֹן׃
4 פִּי יְדַבֵּר חָכְמוֹת
וְהָגוּת לִבִּי תְבוּנוֹת׃
5 אַטֶּה לְמָשָׁל אָזְנִי
אֶפְתַּח בְּכִנּוֹר חִידָתִי׃
6 לָמָּה אִירָא בִּימֵי רָע
עֲוֺן עֲקֵבַי יְסוּבֵּנִי׃
7 הַבֹּטְחִים עַל־חֵילָם
וּבְרֹב עָשְׁרָם יִתְהַלָּלוּ׃
8 אָח לֹא־פָדֹה יִפְדֶּה אִישׁ
לֹא־יִתֵּן לֵאלֹהִים כָּפְרוֹ׃
9 וְיֵקַר פִּדְיוֹן נַפְשָׁם
וְחָדַל לְעוֹלָם׃
10 וִיחִי־עוֹד לָנֶצַח
לֹא יִרְאֶה הַשָּׁחַת׃
11 כִּי יִרְאֶה ׀ חֲכָמִים יָמוּתוּ
יַחַד כְּסִיל וָבַעַר יֹאבֵדוּ
וְעָזְבוּ לַאֲחֵרִים חֵילָם׃
12 קִרְבָּם בָּתֵּימוֹ ׀ לְעוֹלָם
מִשְׁכְּנֹתָם לְדֹר וָדֹר
קָרְאוּ בִשְׁמוֹתָם עֲלֵי אֲדָמוֹת׃

d-d　Meaning of Heb. uncertain.
a　Lit. "utterance of my heart"; on leb, cf. Ps. 19.15.
b-b　Or "A brother."
c　Taken with ancient versions and medieval commentators as the equivalent of qibram.

¹³Man does not abide in honor;
   he is like the beasts that perish.

¹⁴Such is the fate of those who are self-confident,
   ^d-the end of those pleased with their own talk.-^d
   Selah.

¹⁵Sheeplike they head for Sheol,
   with Death as their shepherd.
The upright shall rule over them at daybreak,
   ^d-and their form shall waste away in Sheol
   till its nobility be gone.-^d
¹⁶But God will redeem my life from the clutches
   of Sheol,
   for He will take me.   *Selah.*

¹⁷Do not be afraid when a man becomes rich,
   when his household goods increase;
   ¹⁸for when he dies he can take none of it along;
   his goods cannot follow him down.
¹⁹Though he congratulates himself in his lifetime
   —^d-"They must admit that you did well by
     yourself"-^d—
   ²⁰yet he must join the company of his ancestors,
   who will never see daylight again.
²¹Man does not understand honor;
   he is like the beasts that perish.

50 A psalm of Asaph.

^a-God, the LORD God-^a spoke
   and summoned the world from east to west.
²From Zion, perfect in beauty,
   God appeared
   ³—let our God come and not fail to act!
Devouring fire preceded Him;
   it stormed around Him fiercely.

---

^{d-d} *Meaning of Heb. uncertain.*
^{a-a} *Heb. 'El 'Elohim YHWH.*

13 וְאָדָ֣ם בִּ֭יקָר בַּל־יָלִ֑ין
נִמְשַׁ֖ל כַּבְּהֵמ֣וֹת נִדְמֽוּ׃

14 זֶ֣ה דַ֭רְכָּם כֵּ֣סֶל לָ֑מוֹ
וְאַחֲרֵיהֶ֓ם ׀ בְּפִיהֶ֖ם יִרְצ֣וּ סֶֽלָה׃

15 כַּצֹּ֤אן ׀ לִשְׁא֣וֹל שַׁתּוּ֘
מָ֤וֶת יִ֫רְעֵ֥ם
וַיִּרְדּ֘וּ בָ֤ם יְשָׁרִ֨ים ׀ לַבֹּ֗קֶר
וְצוּרָם לְבַלּ֣וֹת שְׁא֑וֹל
מִזְּבֻ֥ל לֽוֹ׃

16 אַךְ־אֱלֹהִ֗ים יִפְדֶּ֣ה נַ֭פְשִׁי מִיַּד־
שְׁא֑וֹל
כִּ֖י יִקָּחֵ֣נִי סֶֽלָה׃

17 אַל־תִּ֭ירָא כִּֽי־יַעֲשִׁ֣ר אִ֑ישׁ
כִּֽי־יִ֝רְבֶּ֗ה כְּב֣וֹד בֵּיתֽוֹ׃

18 כִּ֤י לֹ֣א בְ֭מוֹתוֹ יִקַּ֣ח הַכֹּ֑ל
לֹא־יֵרֵ֖ד אַחֲרָ֣יו כְּבוֹדֽוֹ׃

19 כִּֽי־נַ֭פְשׁוֹ בְּחַיָּ֣יו יְבָרֵ֑ךְ
וְ֝יוֹדֻ֗ךָ כִּֽי־תֵיטִ֥יב לָֽךְ׃

20 תָּ֭בוֹא עַד־דּ֣וֹר אֲבוֹתָ֑יו
עַד־נֵ֝֗צַח לֹ֣א יִרְאוּ־אֽוֹר׃

21 אָדָ֣ם בִּ֭יקָר וְלֹ֣א יָבִ֑ין
נִמְשַׁ֖ל כַּבְּהֵמ֣וֹת נִדְמֽוּ׃

נ מִזְמ֗וֹר לְאָ֫סָ֥ף

אֵ֤ל ׀ אֱֽלֹהִ֡ים יְֽהוָ֗ה דִּבֶּ֥ר
וַיִּקְרָא־אָ֑רֶץ מִמִּזְרַח־שֶׁ֝֗מֶשׁ עַד־
מְבֹאֽוֹ׃

2 מִצִּיּ֥וֹן מִכְלַל־יֹ֗פִי
אֱלֹהִ֥ים הוֹפִֽיעַ׃

3 יָבֹ֤א אֱלֹהֵ֗ינוּ וְֽאַל־יֶ֫חֱרַ֥שׁ
אֵשׁ־לְפָנָ֥יו תֹּאכֵ֑ל
וּ֝סְבִיבָ֗יו נִשְׂעֲרָ֥ה מְאֹֽד׃

4He summoned the heavens above,
  and the earth, for the trial of His people.
5"Bring in My devotees,
  who made a covenant with Me over sacrifice!"
6Then the heavens proclaimed His righteousness,
  for He is a God who judges.   *Selah.*

7"Pay heed, My people, and I will speak,
  O Israel, and I will arraign you.
I am God, your God.
8I censure you not for your sacrifices,
  and your burnt offerings, made to Me daily;
9I claim no bull from your estate,
  no he-goats from your pens.
10For Mine is every animal of the forest,
  the beasts on b-a thousand mountains.-b
11I know every bird of the mountains,
  the creatures of the field are subject to Me.
12Were I hungry, I would not tell you,
  for Mine is the world and all it holds.
13Do I eat the flesh of bulls,
  or drink the blood of he-goats?
14Sacrifice a thank offering to God,
  and pay your vows to the Most High.
15Call upon Me in time of trouble;
  I will rescue you, and you shall honor Me."

16And to the wicked, God said:
  "Who are you to recite My laws,
  and mouth the terms of My covenant,
17seeing that you spurn My discipline,
  and brush My words aside?
18When you see a thief, you fall in with him,
  and throw in your lot with adulterers;
19you devote your mouth to evil,
  and yoke your tongue to deceit;
20you are busy maligning your brother,
  defaming the son of your mother.

b-b *Meaning of Heb. uncertain.*

יִקְרָא אֶל־הַשָּׁמַיִם מֵעָל 4
וְאֶל־הָאָרֶץ לָדִין עַמּוֹ:
אִסְפוּ־לִי חֲסִידָי 5
כֹּרְתֵי בְרִיתִי עֲלֵי־זָבַח:
וַיַּגִּידוּ שָׁמַיִם צִדְקוֹ 6
כִּי־אֱלֹהִים שֹׁפֵט הוּא סֶלָה:

שִׁמְעָה עַמִּי וַאֲדַבֵּרָה 7
יִשְׂרָאֵל וְאָעִידָה בָּךְ
אֱלֹהִים אֱלֹהֶיךָ אָנֹכִי:
לֹא עַל־זְבָחֶיךָ אוֹכִיחֶךָ 8
וְעוֹלֹתֶיךָ לְנֶגְדִּי תָמִיד:
לֹא־אֶקַּח מִבֵּיתְךָ פָר 9
מִמִּכְלְאֹתֶיךָ עַתּוּדִים:
כִּי־לִי כָל־חַיְתוֹ־יָעַר 10
בְּהֵמוֹת בְּהַרְרֵי־אָלֶף:
יָדַעְתִּי כָּל־עוֹף הָרִים 11
וְזִיז שָׂדַי עִמָּדִי:
אִם־אֶרְעַב לֹא־אֹמַר לָךְ 12
כִּי־לִי תֵבֵל וּמְלֹאָהּ:
הַאוֹכַל בְּשַׂר אַבִּירִים 13
וְדַם עַתּוּדִים אֶשְׁתֶּה:
זְבַח לֵאלֹהִים תּוֹדָה 14
וְשַׁלֵּם לְעֶלְיוֹן נְדָרֶיךָ:
וּקְרָאֵנִי בְּיוֹם צָרָה 15
אֲחַלֶּצְךָ וּתְכַבְּדֵנִי:

וְלָרָשָׁע אָמַר אֱלֹהִים 16
מַה־לְּךָ לְסַפֵּר חֻקָּי
וַתִּשָּׂא בְרִיתִי עֲלֵי־פִיךָ:
וְאַתָּה שָׂנֵאתָ מוּסָר 17
וַתַּשְׁלֵךְ דְּבָרַי אַחֲרֶיךָ:
אִם־רָאִיתָ גַנָּב וַתִּרֶץ עִמּוֹ 18
וְעִם מְנָאֲפִים חֶלְקֶךָ:
פִּיךָ שָׁלַחְתָּ בְרָעָה 19
וּלְשׁוֹנְךָ תַּצְמִיד מִרְמָה:
תֵּשֵׁב בְּאָחִיךָ תְדַבֵּר 20
בְּבֶן־אִמְּךָ תִּתֶּן־דֹּפִי:

²¹If I failed to act when you did these things,
   you would fancy that I was like you;
   so I censure you and confront you with charges.
²²Mark this, you who are unmindful of God,
   lest I tear you apart and no one save you.

²³He who sacrifices a thank offering honors Me,
   ^b-and to him who improves his way-^b
   I will show the salvation of God."

21 אֵלֶּה עָשִׂיתָ ׀ וְהֶחֱרַשְׁתִּי
דִּמִּיתָ הֱיוֹת־אֶהְיֶה כָמוֹךָ
אוֹכִיחֲךָ וְאֶעֶרְכָה לְעֵינֶיךָ׃
22 בִּינוּ־נָא זֹאת שֹׁכְחֵי אֱלוֹהַּ
פֶּן־אֶטְרֹף וְאֵין מַצִּיל׃

23 זֹבֵחַ תּוֹדָה יְכַבְּדָנְנִי
וְשָׂם דֶּרֶךְ
אַרְאֶנּוּ בְּיֵשַׁע אֱלֹהִים׃

51 For the leader. A psalm of David, ²when Nathan the prophet came to him after he had come to Bathsheba.^a

נא לַמְנַצֵּחַ מִזְמוֹר לְדָוִד׃ 2 בְּבוֹא־
אֵלָיו נָתָן הַנָּבִיא כַּאֲשֶׁר־בָּא אֶל־בַּת־
שָׁבַע׃

³Have mercy upon me, O God,
   as befits Your faithfulness;
   in keeping with Your abundant compassion,
   blot out my transgressions.
⁴Wash me thoroughly of my iniquity,
   and purify me of my sin;
⁵for I recognize my transgressions,
   and am ever conscious of my sin.
⁶Against You alone have I sinned,
   and done what is evil in Your sight;
   so You are just in Your sentence,
   and right in Your judgment.
⁷Indeed I was born with iniquity;
   with sin my mother conceived me.
⁸^b-Indeed You desire truth about that which is hidden;
   teach me wisdom about secret things.-^b

3 חָנֵּנִי אֱלֹהִים
כְּחַסְדֶּךָ
כְּרֹב רַחֲמֶיךָ
מְחֵה פְשָׁעָי׃
4 הֶרֶב כַּבְּסֵנִי מֵעֲוֺנִי
וּמֵחַטָּאתִי טַהֲרֵנִי׃
5 כִּי־פְשָׁעַי אֲנִי אֵדָע
וְחַטָּאתִי נֶגְדִּי תָמִיד׃
6 לְךָ לְבַדְּךָ ׀ חָטָאתִי
וְהָרַע בְּעֵינֶיךָ עָשִׂיתִי
לְמַעַן תִּצְדַּק בְּדָבְרֶךָ
תִּזְכֶּה בְשָׁפְטֶךָ׃
7 הֵן־בְּעָווֹן חוֹלָלְתִּי
וּבְחֵטְא יֶחֱמַתְנִי אִמִּי׃
8 הֵן־אֱמֶת חָפַצְתָּ בַטֻּחוֹת
וּבְסָתֻם חָכְמָה תוֹדִיעֵנִי׃

⁹Purge me with hyssop till I am pure;
   wash me till I am whiter than snow.
¹⁰Let me hear tidings of joy and gladness;
   let the bones You have crushed exult.
¹¹Hide Your face from my sins;
   blot out all my iniquities.

9 תְּחַטְּאֵנִי בְאֵזוֹב וְאֶטְהָר
תְּכַבְּסֵנִי וּמִשֶּׁלֶג אַלְבִּין׃
10 תַּשְׁמִיעֵנִי שָׂשׂוֹן וְשִׂמְחָה
תָּגֵלְנָה עֲצָמוֹת דִּכִּיתָ׃
11 הַסְתֵּר פָּנֶיךָ מֵחֲטָאָי
וְכָל־עֲוֺנֹתַי מְחֵה׃

a   Cf. 2 Sam. 12.
b-b Meaning of Heb. uncertain.

¹²Fashion a pure heart for me, O God;
   create in me a steadfast spirit.
¹³Do not cast me out of Your presence,
   or take Your holy spirit away from me.
¹⁴Let me again rejoice in Your help;
   let a vigorous spirit sustain me.
¹⁵I will teach transgressors Your ways,
   that sinners may return to You.

¹⁶Save me from bloodguilt,
   O God, God, my deliverer,
   that I may sing forth Your beneficence.
¹⁷O Lord, open my lips,
   and let my mouth declare Your praise.
¹⁸You do not want me to bring sacrifices;
   You do not desire burnt offerings;
¹⁹True sacrifice to God is a contrite spirit;
   God, You will not despise
   a contrite and crushed heart.

²⁰May it please You to make Zion prosper;
   rebuild the walls of Jerusalem.
²¹Then You will want sacrifices offered in righteousness,
   burnt and whole offerings;
   then bulls will be offered on Your altar.

52 For the leader. A *maskil* of David, ²when
Doeg the Edomite came and informed Saul, telling
him, "David came to Ahimelech's house."ᵃ

³Why do you boast of your evil, brave fellow?
   God's faithfulness ᵇ-never ceases.-ᵇ
⁴Your tongue devises mischief,
   like a sharpened razor that works treacherously.
⁵You prefer evil to good,
   the lie, to speaking truthfully. *Selah.*

12 לֵב טָהוֹר בְּרָא־לִי אֱלֹהִים
וְרוּחַ נָכוֹן חַדֵּשׁ בְּקִרְבִּי:
13 אַל־תַּשְׁלִיכֵנִי מִלְּפָנֶיךָ
וְרוּחַ קָדְשְׁךָ אַל־תִּקַּח מִמֶּנִּי:
14 הָשִׁיבָה לִּי שְׂשׂוֹן יִשְׁעֶךָ
וְרוּחַ נְדִיבָה תִסְמְכֵנִי:
15 אֲלַמְּדָה פֹשְׁעִים דְּרָכֶיךָ
וְחַטָּאִים אֵלֶיךָ יָשׁוּבוּ:

16 הַצִּילֵנִי מִדָּמִים |
אֱלֹהִים אֱלֹהֵי תְּשׁוּעָתִי
תְּרַנֵּן לְשׁוֹנִי צִדְקָתֶךָ:
17 אֲדֹנָי שְׂפָתַי תִּפְתָּח
וּפִי יַגִּיד תְּהִלָּתֶךָ:
18 כִּי | לֹא־תַחְפֹּץ זֶבַח וְאֶתֵּנָה
עוֹלָה לֹא תִרְצֶה:
19 זִבְחֵי אֱלֹהִים רוּחַ נִשְׁבָּרָה
לֵב־נִשְׁבָּר וְנִדְכֶּה
אֱלֹהִים לֹא תִבְזֶה:

20 הֵיטִיבָה בִרְצוֹנְךָ אֶת־צִיּוֹן
תִּבְנֶה חוֹמוֹת יְרוּשָׁלִָם:
21 אָז תַּחְפֹּץ זִבְחֵי־צֶדֶק
עוֹלָה וְכָלִיל
אָז יַעֲלוּ עַל־מִזְבַּחֲךָ פָרִים:

נב לַמְנַצֵּחַ מַשְׂכִּיל לְדָוִד: 2 בְּבוֹא |
דּוֹאֵג הָאֲדֹמִי וַיַּגֵּד לְשָׁאוּל וַיֹּאמֶר לוֹ
בָּא דָוִד אֶל־בֵּית אֲחִימֶלֶךְ:

3 מַה־תִּתְהַלֵּל בְּרָעָה הַגִּבּוֹר
חֶסֶד אֵל כָּל־הַיּוֹם:
4 הַוּוֹת תַּחְשֹׁב לְשׁוֹנֶךָ
כְּתַעַר מְלֻטָּשׁ עֹשֵׂה רְמִיָּה:
5 אָהַבְתָּ רָּע* מִטּוֹב
שֶׁקֶר | מִדַּבֵּר צֶדֶק סֶלָה:

ר' דגושה   v. 5.

ᵃ Cf. 1 Sam. 22.9 ff.
ᵇ⁻ᵇ Lit. "is all the day."

⁶You love all pernicious words,
  treacherous speech.
⁷So God will tear you down for good,
  will break you and pluck you from your tent,
  and root you out of the land of the living.
    Selah.
⁸The righteous, seeing it, will be awestruck;
  they will jibe at him, saying,
⁹"Here was a fellow who did not make God his
      refuge,
  but trusted in his great wealth,
  relied upon his mischief."

¹⁰But I am like a thriving olive tree in God's house;
  I trust in the faithfulness of God forever and
      ever.
¹¹I praise You forever, for You have acted;
  c-I declare that Your name is good-c
  in the presence of Your faithful ones.

53

ᵃFor the leader; on *mahalath.*ᵇ
A *maskil* of David.

²The benighted man thinks,
  c-"God does not care."-c
Man's wrongdoing is corrupt and loathsome;
  no one does good.
³God looks down from heaven on mankind
  to find a man of understanding,
  a man mindful of God.
⁴Everyone is dross,
  altogether foul;
  there is none who does good,
  not even one.
⁵Are they so witless, those evildoers,
  who devour my people as they devour food,
  and do not invoke God?

אָהַבְתָּ כָל־דִּבְרֵי־בָלַע
לְשׁוֹן מִרְמָה:
גַּם־אֵל יִתָּצְךָ לָנֶצַח
יַחְתְּךָ וְיִסָּחֲךָ מֵאֹהֶל
וְשֵׁרֶשְׁךָ מֵאֶרֶץ חַיִּים סֶלָה:
וְיִרְאוּ צַדִּיקִים וְיִירָאוּ וְעָלָיו
יִשְׂחָקוּ:
הִנֵּה הַגֶּבֶר לֹא יָשִׂים אֱלֹהִים
מָעוּזּוֹ
וַיִּבְטַח בְּרֹב עָשְׁרוֹ
יָעֹז בְּהַוָּתוֹ:

וַאֲנִי ׀ כְּזַיִת רַעֲנָן בְּבֵית אֱלֹהִים
בָּטַחְתִּי בְחֶסֶד־אֱלֹהִים עוֹלָם וָעֶד:
אוֹדְךָ לְעוֹלָם כִּי עָשִׂיתָ
וַאֲקַוֶּה שִׁמְךָ כִי־טוֹב
נֶגֶד חֲסִידֶיךָ:

נג לַמְנַצֵּחַ עַל־מָחֲלַת
מַשְׂכִּיל לְדָוִד:

אָמַר נָבָל בְּלִבּוֹ
אֵין אֱלֹהִים
הִשְׁחִיתוּ וְהִתְעִיבוּ עָוֶל
אֵין עֹשֵׂה־טוֹב:
אֱלֹהִים מִשָּׁמַיִם הִשְׁקִיף עַל־בְּנֵי
אָדָם
לִרְאוֹת הֲיֵשׁ מַשְׂכִּיל
דֹּרֵשׁ אֶת־אֱלֹהִים:
כֻּלּוֹ סָג
יַחְדָּו נֶאֱלָחוּ
אֵין עֹשֵׂה־טוֹב
אֵין גַּם־אֶחָד:
הֲלֹא יָדְעוּ פֹּעֲלֵי אָוֶן
אֹכְלֵי עַמִּי אָכְלוּ לֶחֶם

---

c-c   *Meaning of Heb. uncertain; others "I will wait for Your name for it
  is good."*

a   *Cf. Ps. 14.*
b   *Meaning of Heb. unknown.*
c-c   *Lit. "There is no God"; cf. Ps. 10.4.*

⁶There they will be seized with fright
  —ᵈ-never was there such a fright—
  for God has scattered the bones of your be-
    siegers;
  you have put them to shame,-ᵈ
  for God has rejected them.

⁷O that the deliverance of Israel might come from
    Zion!
  When God restores the fortunes of His people,
    Jacob will exult, Israel will rejoice.

אֱלֹהִים לֹא קְרָאוּ:
6 שָׁם | פָּחֲדוּ־פַחַד
לֹא־הָיָה פָחַד
כִּי־אֱלֹהִים פִּזַּר עַצְמוֹת חֹנָךְ
הֱבִשֹׁתָה
כִּי־אֱלֹהִים מְאָסָם:

7 מִי יִתֵּן מִצִּיּוֹן יְשֻׁעוֹת יִשְׂרָאֵל
בְּשׁוּב אֱלֹהִים שְׁבוּת עַמּוֹ
יָגֵל יַעֲקֹב יִשְׂמַח יִשְׂרָאֵל:

54 For the leader; with instrumental music. A
maskil of David, ²when the Ziphites came and told
Saul, "Know, David is in hiding among us."ᵃ

נד לַמְנַצֵּחַ בִּנְגִינֹת מַשְׂכִּיל לְדָוִד:
2 בְּבוֹא הַזִּיפִים וַיֹּאמְרוּ לְשָׁאוּל הֲלֹא
דָוִד מִסְתַּתֵּר עִמָּנוּ:

³O God, deliver me by Your name;
  by Your power vindicate me.
⁴O God, hear my prayer;
  give ear to the words of my mouth.
⁵For strangers have risen against me,
  and ruthless men seek my life;
  they are unmindful of God.   *Selah.*

⁶See, God is my helper;
  the Lord is my support.
⁷He will repay the evil of my watchful foes;
  by Your faithfulness, destroy them!
⁸Then I will offer You a freewill sacrifice;
  I will praise Your name, Lᴏʀᴅ, for it is good,
⁹for it has saved me from my foes,
  and let me gaze triumphant upon my enemies.

3 אֱלֹהִים בְּשִׁמְךָ הוֹשִׁיעֵנִי
וּבִגְבוּרָתְךָ תְדִינֵנִי:
4 אֱלֹהִים שְׁמַע תְּפִלָּתִי
הַאֲזִינָה לְאִמְרֵי־פִי:
5 כִּי זָרִים | קָמוּ עָלַי
וְעָרִיצִים בִּקְשׁוּ נַפְשִׁי
לֹא שָׂמוּ אֱלֹהִים לְנֶגְדָּם   סֶלָה:

6 הִנֵּה אֱלֹהִים עֹזֵר לִי
אֲדֹנָי בְּסֹמְכֵי נַפְשִׁי:
7 יָשִׁיב הָרַע לְשֹׁרְרָי
בַּאֲמִתְּךָ הַצְמִיתֵם:
8 בִּנְדָבָה אֶזְבְּחָה־לָּךְ
אוֹדֶה שִּׁמְךָ יְהוָה כִּי־טוֹב:
9 כִּי מִכָּל־צָרָה הִצִּילָנִי
וּבְאֹיְבַי רָאֲתָה עֵינִי:

d-d   *Meaning of Heb. uncertain.*
a   *Cf. 1 Sam. 23.19.*

55

55 For the leader; with instrumental music.
A *maskil* of David.

²Give ear, O God, to my prayer;
  do not ignore my plea;
  ³pay heed to me and answer me.
I am tossed about, complaining and moaning
  ⁴at the clamor of the enemy,
  because of the oppression of the wicked;
  for they bring evil upon me
  and furiously harass me.
⁵My heart is convulsed within me;
  terrors of death assail me.
⁶Fear and trembling invade me;
  I am clothed with horror.
⁷I said,
  "O that I had the wings of a dove!
  I would fly away and find rest;
  ⁸surely, I would flee far off;
  I would lodge in the wilderness;   *selah*
  ⁹I would soon find me a refuge
  from the sweeping wind,
  from the tempest."

¹⁰O Lord, confound their speech, confuse it!
For I see lawlessness and strife in the city;
  ¹¹day and night they make their rounds on its
    walls;
  evil and mischief are inside it.
¹²Malice is within it;
  fraud and deceit never leave its square.

¹³It is not an enemy who reviles me
  —I could bear that;
  it is not my foe who vaunts himself against me
  —I could hide from him;
  ¹⁴but it is you, my equal,

נה לַמְנַצֵּחַ בִּנְגִינֹת מַשְׂכִּיל לְדָוִד׃

2 הַאֲזִינָה אֱלֹהִים תְּפִלָּתִי
וְאַל־תִּתְעַלַּם מִתְּחִנָּתִי׃
3 הַקְשִׁיבָה לִּי וַעֲנֵנִי
אָרִיד בְּשִׂיחִי וְאָהִימָה׃
4 מִקּוֹל אוֹיֵב
מִפְּנֵי עָקַת רָשָׁע
כִּי־יָמִיטוּ עָלַי אָוֶן
וּבְאַף יִשְׂטְמוּנִי׃
5 לִבִּי יָחִיל בְּקִרְבִּי
וְאֵימוֹת מָוֶת נָפְלוּ עָלָי׃
6 יִרְאָה וָרַעַד יָבֹא בִי
וַתְּכַסֵּנִי פַּלָּצוּת׃
7 וָאֹמַר
מִי־יִתֶּן־לִי אֵבֶר כַּיּוֹנָה
אָעוּפָה וְאֶשְׁכֹּנָה׃
8 הִנֵּה אַרְחִיק נְדֹד
אָלִין בַּמִּדְבָּר   סֶלָה׃
9 אָחִישָׁה מִפְלָט לִי
מֵרוּחַ סֹעָה
מִסָּעַר׃

10 בַּלַּע אֲדֹנָי פַּלַּג לְשׁוֹנָם
כִּי־רָאִיתִי חָמָס וְרִיב בָּעִיר׃
11 יוֹמָם וָלַיְלָה יְסוֹבְבֻהָ עַל־
חוֹמֹתֶיהָ
וְאָוֶן וְעָמָל בְּקִרְבָּהּ׃
12 הַוּוֹת בְּקִרְבָּהּ
וְלֹא־יָמִישׁ מֵרְחֹבָהּ תֹּךְ וּמִרְמָה׃

13 כִּי לֹא־אוֹיֵב יְחָרְפֵנִי
וְאֶשָּׂא
לֹא־מְשַׂנְאִי עָלַי הִגְדִּיל
וְאֶסָּתֵר מִמֶּנּוּ׃
14 וְאַתָּה אֱנוֹשׁ כְּעֶרְכִּי

my companion, my friend;

15sweet was our fellowship;

we walked together in God's house.

16Let Him incite death against them;

may they go down alive into Sheol!

For where they dwell,

there evil is.

17As for me, I call to God;

the LORD will deliver me.

18Evening, morning, and noon,

I complain and moan,

and He hears my voice.

19He redeems me unharmed

from the battle against me;

a-it is as though many are on my side.-a

20God who has reigned from the first,

who will have no successor,

hears and humbles those who have no fear of

God. *Selah.*

21Heb harmed his ally,

he broke his pact;

22his talk was smoother than butter,

yet his mind was on war;

his words were more soothing than oil,

yet they were drawn swords.

23Cast your burden on the LORD and He will sus-

tain you;

He will never let the righteous man collapse.

24For You, O God, will bring them down to the

nethermost Pit—

those murderous, treacherous men;

they shall not live out half their days;

but I trust in You.

אַלּוּפִי וּמְיֻדָּעִי:

15 אֲשֶׁר יַחְדָּו נַמְתִּיק סוֹד

בְּבֵית אֱלֹהִים נְהַלֵּךְ בְּרָגֶשׁ:

16 יַשִּׁימָוֶת עָלֵימוֹ

יֵרְדוּ שְׁאוֹל חַיִּים

כִּי־רָעוֹת בִּמְגוּרָם

בְּקִרְבָּם:

17 אֲנִי אֶל־אֱלֹהִים אֶקְרָא

וַיהוָה יוֹשִׁיעֵנִי:

18 עֶרֶב וָבֹקֶר וְצָהֳרַיִם

אָשִׂיחָה וְאֶהֱמֶה

וַיִּשְׁמַע קוֹלִי:

19 פָּדָה בְשָׁלוֹם נַפְשִׁי

מִקְּרָב־לִי

כִּי־בְרַבִּים הָיוּ עִמָּדִי:

20 יִשְׁמַע ׀ אֵל ׀ וְיַעֲנֵם

וְיֹשֵׁב קֶדֶם סֶלָה

אֲשֶׁר אֵין חֲלִיפוֹת לָמוֹ

וְלֹא יָרְאוּ אֱלֹהִים:

21 שָׁלַח יָדָיו בִּשְׁלֹמָיו חִלֵּל בְּרִיתוֹ:

22 חָלְקוּ ׀ מַחְמָאֹת פִּיו

וּקְרָב־לִבּוֹ

רַכּוּ דְבָרָיו מִשֶּׁמֶן

וְהֵמָּה פְתִחוֹת:

23 הַשְׁלֵךְ עַל־יְהוָה ׀ יְהָבְךָ וְהוּא

יְכַלְכְּלֶךָ

לֹא־יִתֵּן לְעוֹלָם מוֹט לַצַּדִּיק:

24 וְאַתָּה אֱלֹהִים ׀ תּוֹרִדֵם ׀ לִבְאֵר

שַׁחַת

אַנְשֵׁי דָמִים וּמִרְמָה

לֹא־יֶחֱצוּ יְמֵיהֶם

וַאֲנִי אֶבְטַח־בָּךְ:

---

a-a   *Meaning of Heb. uncertain.*

b   *I.e., the friend of v. 14.*

56

For the leader; *a*-on *yonath elem reḥokim.*-*a*
Of David. A *michtam*; when the Philistines seized
him in Gath.

נו לַמְנַצֵּחַ ׀ עַל־יוֹנַת אֵלֶם רְחֹקִים
לְדָוִד מִכְתָּם בֶּאֱחֹז אֹתוֹ פְלִשְׁתִּים
בְּגַת:

2Have mercy on me, O God,
    for men persecute me;
        all day long my adversary oppresses me.
3My watchful foes persecute me all day long;
    many are my adversaries, O Exalted One.
4When I am afraid, I trust in You,
    5in God, whose word I praise,
    in God I trust;
    I am not afraid;
        what can mortals*b* do to me?
6All day long *a*-they cause me grief in my affairs,-*a*
    they plan only evil against me.
7They plot, they lie in ambush;
    they watch my every move, hoping for my
        death.
8Cast them out for their evil;
    subdue peoples in Your anger, O God.

9*a*-You keep count of my wanderings;
    put my tears into Your flask,
    into Your record.-*a*
10Then my enemies will retreat when I call on You;
    this I know, that God is for me.
11In God, whose word I praise,
    in the LORD, whose word I praise,
    12in God I trust;
    I am not afraid;
        what can man do to me?
13I must pay my vows to You, O God;
    I will render thank offerings to You.
14For You have saved me from death,

2 חָנֵּנִי אֱלֹהִים
כִּי־שְׁאָפַנִי אֱנוֹשׁ
כָּל־הַיּוֹם לֹחֵם יִלְחָצֵנִי:
3 שָׁאֲפוּ שׁוֹרְרַי כָּל־הַיּוֹם
כִּי־רַבִּים לֹחֲמִים לִי מָרוֹם:
4 יוֹם אִירָא אֲנִי אֵלֶיךָ אֶבְטָח:
5 בֵּאלֹהִים אֲהַלֵּל דְּבָרוֹ
בֵּאלֹהִים בָּטַחְתִּי
לֹא אִירָא
מַה־יַּעֲשֶׂה בָשָׂר לִי:
6 כָּל־הַיּוֹם דְּבָרַי יְעַצֵּבוּ
עָלַי כָּל־מַחְשְׁבֹתָם לָרָע:
7 יָגוּרוּ ׀ יצפינו יִצְפּוֹנוּ
הֵמָּה עֲקֵבַי יִשְׁמֹרוּ כַּאֲשֶׁר קִוּוּ
נַפְשִׁי:
8 עַל־אָוֶן פַּלֶּט־לָמוֹ
בְּאַף עַמִּים ׀ הוֹרֵד אֱלֹהִים:
9 נֹדִי סָפַרְתָּה אָתָּה
שִׂימָה דִמְעָתִי בְנֹאדֶךָ
הֲלֹא בְּסִפְרָתֶךָ:
10 אָז יָשׁוּבוּ אוֹיְבַי אָחוֹר בְּיוֹם
אֶקְרָא
זֶה־יָדַעְתִּי כִּי־אֱלֹהִים לִי:
11 בֵּאלֹהִים אֲהַלֵּל דָּבָר
בַּיהוָה אֲהַלֵּל דָּבָר:
12 בֵּאלֹהִים בָּטַחְתִּי
לֹא אִירָא
מַה־יַּעֲשֶׂה אָדָם לִי:
13 עָלַי אֱלֹהִים נְדָרֶיךָ
אֲשַׁלֵּם תּוֹדֹת לָךְ:
14 כִּי הִצַּלְתָּ נַפְשִׁי מִמָּוֶת

---

a-a   *Meaning of Heb. uncertain.*
b   *Lit. "flesh."*

my foot from stumbling,
that I may walk before God in the light of life.

הֲלֹא רַגְלַי מִדֶּ֑חִי
לְהִֽתְהַלֵּ֗ךְ לִפְנֵ֥י אֱלֹהִ֑ים בְּא֗וֹר
הַֽחַיִּֽים׃

57

For the leader; *a-al tashḥeth.-a* Of David. A *michtam*; when he fled from Saul into a cave.

נז לַמְנַצֵּ֣חַ אַל־תַּ֭שְׁחֵת לְדָוִ֣ד מִכְתָּ֑ם
בְּבָרְח֥וֹ מִפְּנֵי־שָׁא֗וּל בַּמְּעָרָֽה׃

²Have mercy on me, O God, have mercy on me,
  for I seek refuge in You,
  I seek refuge in the shadow of Your wings,
  until danger passes.
³I call to God Most High,
  to God who is good to me.
⁴He will reach down from heaven and deliver me:
  God will send down His steadfast love;
  my persecutor reviles.   *Selah.*

²חָנֵּ֣נִי אֱלֹהִים֮ ׀ חָ֫נֵּ֥נִי
כִּ֥י בְךָ֮ חָסָ֪יָה נַ֫פְשִׁ֥י וּבְצֵֽל־כְּנָפֶ֥יךָ
אֶחְסֶ֑ה
עַ֝֗ד יַעֲבֹ֥ר הַוּֽוֹת׃
³אֶ֭קְרָא לֵֽאלֹהִ֣ים עֶלְי֑וֹן
לָ֝אֵ֗ל גֹּמֵ֥ר עָלָֽי׃
⁴יִשְׁלַ֤ח מִשָּׁמַ֨יִם ׀ וְֽיוֹשִׁיעֵ֗נִי
חֵרֵ֣ף שֹׁאֲפִ֣י סֶ֑לָה
יִשְׁלַ֥ח אֱ֝לֹהִ֗ים חַסְדּ֥וֹ וַאֲמִתּֽוֹ׃

⁵As for me, I lie down among man-eating lions
  whose teeth are spears and arrows,
  whose tongue is a sharp sword.
⁶Exalt Yourself over the heavens, O God,
  let Your glory be over all the earth!
⁷They prepared a net for my feet *b-to ensnare me;-b*
  they dug a pit for me,
  but they fell into it.   *Selah.*

⁵נַפְשִׁ֤י ׀ בְּת֥וֹךְ לְבָאִם֮ אֶשְׁכְּבָ֪ה
לֹ֫הֲטִ֥ים בְּֽנֵי־אָדָ֗ם
שִׁ֭נֵּיהֶם חֲנִ֣ית וְחִצִּ֑ים
וּ֝לְשׁוֹנָ֗ם חֶ֣רֶב חַדָּֽה׃
⁶ר֣וּמָה עַל־הַשָּׁמַ֣יִם אֱלֹהִ֑ים
עַ֖ל כָּל־הָאָ֣רֶץ כְּבוֹדֶֽךָ׃
⁷רֶ֤שֶׁת ׀ הֵכִ֣ינוּ לִפְעָמַי֮ כָּפַ֪ף נַ֫פְשִׁ֥י
כָּר֣וּ לְפָנַ֣י שִׁיחָ֑ה
נָפְל֖וּ בְתוֹכָ֣הּ סֶֽלָה׃

⁸cMy heart is firm, O God;
  my heart is firm;
  I will sing, I will chant a hymn.
⁹Awake, O my soul!
  Awake, O harp and lyre!
  I will wake the dawn.
¹⁰I will praise You among the peoples, O Lord;
  I will sing a hymn to You among the nations;
¹¹for Your faithfulness is as high as heaven;
  Your steadfastness reaches to the sky.

⁸נָכ֣וֹן לִבִּ֣י אֱלֹהִ֑ים
נָכ֣וֹן לִבִּ֑י
אָ֝שִׁ֗ירָה וַאֲזַמֵּֽרָה׃
⁹ע֤וּרָה כְבוֹדִ֗י
ע֭וּרָֽה הַנֵּ֥בֶל וְכִנּ֗וֹר
אָעִ֥ירָה שָּֽׁחַר׃
¹⁰אוֹדְךָ֖ בָעַמִּ֥ים ׀ אֲדֹנָ֑י
אֲ֝זַמֶּרְךָ֗ בַּל־אֻמִּֽים*׃
¹¹כִּֽי־גָדֹ֣ל עַד־שָׁמַ֣יִם חַסְדֶּ֑ךָ
וְֽעַד־שְׁחָקִ֥ים אֲמִתֶּֽךָ׃

---

a-a   *Meaning of Heb. uncertain.*
b-b   *Cf. Mishnaic Heb.* kefifah, *a wicker basket used in fishing.*
c   *With vv. 8–12, cf. Ps. 108.2–6.*

¹²Exalt Yourself over the heavens, O God,
let Your glory be over all the earth!

רוּמָה עַל־שָׁמַיִם אֱלֹהִים 12
עַל כָּל־הָאָרֶץ כְּבוֹדֶךָ:

58 For the leader; *al tashḥeth.* Of David.
A *michtam.*

נח לַמְנַצֵּחַ אַל־תַּשְׁחֵת לְדָוִד
מִכְתָּם:

²^a-O mighty ones,^{-a} do you really decree what is
just?
Do you judge mankind with equity?
³In your minds you devise wrongdoing in the
land;
^a-with your hands you deal out lawlessness.^{-a}
⁴The wicked are defiant from birth;
the liars go astray from the womb.
⁵Their venom is like that of a snake,
a deaf viper that stops its ears
⁶so as not to hear the voice of charmers
or the expert mutterer of spells.

הַאֻמְנָם אֵלֶם צֶדֶק תְּדַבֵּרוּן 2
מֵישָׁרִים תִּשְׁפְּטוּ בְּנֵי אָדָם:
אַף־בְּלֵב עוֹלֹת תִּפְעָלוּן בָּאָרֶץ 3
חֲמַס יְדֵיכֶם תְּפַלֵּסוּן:
זֹרוּ רְשָׁעִים מֵרָחֶם 4
תָּעוּ מִבֶּטֶן דֹּבְרֵי כָזָב:
חֲמַת־לָמוֹ כִּדְמוּת חֲמַת־נָחָשׁ 5
כְּמוֹ־פֶתֶן חֵרֵשׁ יַאְטֵם אָזְנוֹ:
אֲשֶׁר לֹא־יִשְׁמַע לְקוֹל מְלַחֲשִׁים 6
חוֹבֵר חֲבָרִים מְחֻכָּם:

⁷O God, smash their teeth in their mouth;
shatter the fangs of lions, O L<small>ORD</small>;
⁸let them melt, let them vanish like water;
let Him aim His arrows that they be cut down;
⁹^a-like a snail that melts away as it moves;^{-a}
like a woman's stillbirth, may they never see
the sun!
¹⁰Before ^a-the thorns grow into a bramble,
may He whirl them away alive in fury.^{-a}

אֱלֹהִים הֲרָס־שִׁנֵּימוֹ בְּפִימוֹ 7
מַלְתְּעוֹת כְּפִירִים נְתֹץ | יְהוָה:
יִמָּאֲסוּ כְמוֹ־מַיִם יִתְהַלְּכוּ־לָמוֹ 8
יִדְרֹךְ חִצָּו כְּמוֹ יִתְמֹלָלוּ:
כְּמוֹ שַׁבְּלוּל תֶּמֶס יַהֲלֹךְ 9
נֵפֶל אֵשֶׁת בַּל־חָזוּ שָׁמֶשׁ:
בְּטֶרֶם יָבִינוּ סִּירֹתֵיכֶם אָטָד 10
כְּמוֹ־חַי כְּמוֹ־חָרוֹן יִשְׂעָרֶנּוּ:

¹¹The righteous man will rejoice when he sees re-
venge;
he will bathe his feet in the blood of the wicked.
¹²Men will say,
"There is, then, a reward for the righteous;
there is, indeed, divine justice on earth."

יִשְׂמַח צַדִּיק כִּי־חָזָה נָקָם 11
פְּעָמָיו יִרְחַץ בְּדַם הָרָשָׁע:
וְיֹאמַר אָדָם 12
אַךְ־פְּרִי לַצַּדִּיק
אַךְ יֵשׁ־אֱלֹהִים שֹׁפְטִים בָּאָרֶץ:

---

^{a-a} *Meaning of Heb. uncertain.*

59

נט

For the leader; *al tashḥeth*. Of David. A *michtam*; when Saul sent men to watch his house in order to put him to death.[a]

לַמְנַצֵּחַ אַל־תַּשְׁחֵת לְדָוִד
מִכְתָּם בִּשְׁלֹחַ שָׁאוּל וַיִּשְׁמְרוּ אֶת־
הַבַּיִת לַהֲמִיתוֹ:

2 Save me from my enemies, O my God;
  secure me against my assailants.
3 Save me from evildoers;
  deliver me from murderers.
4 For see, they lie in wait for me;
  fierce men plot against me
  for no offense of mine,
  for no transgression, O Lord;
5 for no guilt of mine
  do they rush to array themselves against me.
Look, rouse Yourself on my behalf!
6 You, O Lord God of hosts,
  God of Israel,
  bestir Yourself to bring all nations to account;
  have no mercy on any treacherous villain.
    Selah.

2 הַצִּילֵנִי מֵאֹיְבַי ׀ אֱלֹהָי
מִמִּתְקוֹמְמַי תְּשַׂגְּבֵנִי:
3 הַצִּילֵנִי מִפֹּעֲלֵי אָוֶן
וּמֵאַנְשֵׁי דָמִים הוֹשִׁיעֵנִי:
4 כִּי הִנֵּה אָרְבוּ לְנַפְשִׁי
יָגוּרוּ עָלַי עַזִּים
לֹא־פִשְׁעִי
וְלֹא־חַטָּאתִי יְהוָה:
5 בְּלִי־עָוֹן
יְרֻצוּן וְיִכּוֹנָנוּ
עוּרָה לִקְרָאתִי וּרְאֵה:
6 וְאַתָּה יְהוָה־אֱלֹהִים ׀ צְבָאוֹת
אֱלֹהֵי יִשְׂרָאֵל
הָקִיצָה לִפְקֹד כָּל־הַגּוֹיִם
אַל־תָּחֹן כָּל־בֹּגְדֵי אָוֶן   סֶלָה:

7 They come each evening growling like dogs,
  roaming the city.
8 They rave with their mouths,
  b-sharp words-*b* are on their lips;
  [they think,] "Who hears?"
9 But You, O Lord, laugh at them;
  You mock all the nations.

7 יָשׁוּבוּ לָעֶרֶב יֶהֱמוּ כַכָּלֶב
וִיסוֹבְבוּ עִיר:
8 הִנֵּה ׀ יַבִּיעוּן בְּפִיהֶם
חֲרָבוֹת בְּשִׂפְתוֹתֵיהֶם
כִּי־מִי שֹׁמֵעַ:
9 וְאַתָּה יְהוָה תִּשְׂחַק־לָמוֹ
תִּלְעַג לְכָל־גּוֹיִם:

10 O my[c] strength, I wait for You;
  for God is my haven.
11 My faithful God will come to aid me;
  God will let me gloat over my watchful foes.
12 Do not kill them lest my people be unmindful;
  with Your power make wanderers of them;
  bring them low, O our shield, the Lord,
13 because of their sinful mouths,

10 עֻזּוֹ אֵלֶיךָ אֶשְׁמֹרָה
כִּי־אֱלֹהִים מִשְׂגַּבִּי:
11 אֱלֹהֵי חַסְדּוֹ חַסְדִּי יְקַדְּמֵנִי
אֱלֹהִים יַרְאֵנִי בְשֹׁרְרָי:
12 אַל־תַּהַרְגֵם ׀ פֶּן־יִשְׁכְּחוּ עַמִּי
הֲנִיעֵמוֹ בְחֵילְךָ
וְהוֹרִידֵמוֹ מָגִנֵּנוּ אֲדֹנָי:
13 חַטַּאת־פִּימוֹ

---

a   Cf. 1 Sam. 19.11.
b-b   Lit. "swords."
c   With several mss.; cf. v. 18; lit. "His."

the words on their lips.   דְּבַר־שְׂפָתֵימוֹ

Let them be trapped by their pride,   וְיִלָּכְדוּ בִגְאוֹנָם

  and by the imprecations and lies they utter.   וּמֵאָלָה וּמִכַּחַשׁ יְסַפֵּרוּ׃

14In Your fury put an end to them;   14 כַּלֵּה בְחֵמָה

  put an end to them that they be no more;   כַּלֵּה וְאֵינֵמוֹ

  that it may be known to the ends of the earth   וְיֵדְעוּ כִּי־אֱלֹהִים מֹשֵׁל בְּיַעֲקֹב

  that God does rule over Jacob.   *Selah.*   לְאַפְסֵי הָאָרֶץ סֶלָה׃

15They come each evening growling like dogs,   15 וְיָשׁוּבוּ לָעֶרֶב יֶהֱמוּ כַכָּלֶב

  roaming the city.   וִיסוֹבְבוּ עִיר׃

16They wander in search of food;   16 הֵמָּה יְנִיעוּן יְנִיעוּן לֶאֱכֹל

  and whine if they are not satisfied.   אִם־לֹא יִשְׂבְּעוּ וַיָּלִינוּ׃

17But I will sing of Your strength,   17 וַאֲנִי אָשִׁיר עֻזֶּךָ

  extol each morning Your faithfulness;   וַאֲרַנֵּן לַבֹּקֶר חַסְדֶּךָ

  for You have been my haven,   כִּי־הָיִיתָ מִשְׂגָּב לִי

  a refuge in time of trouble.   וּמָנוֹס בְּיוֹם צַר־לִי׃

18O my strength, to You I sing hymns;   18 עֻזִּי אֵלֶיךָ אֲזַמֵּרָה

  for God is my haven, my faithful God.   כִּי־אֱלֹהִים מִשְׂגַּבִּי אֱלֹהֵי חַסְדִּי׃

60 For the leader; on *a-shushan eduth.-a* A *michtam* of David (to be taught), 2when he fought with Aram-Naharaim and Aram-Zobah, and Joab returned and defeated Edom—[an army] of twelve thousand men—in the Valley of Salt.b

ס לַמְנַצֵּחַ עַל־שׁוּשַׁן עֵדוּת מִכְתָּם לְדָוִד לְלַמֵּד׃ 2 בְּהַצּוֹתוֹ אֶת אֲרַם נַהֲרַיִם וְאֶת־אֲרַם צוֹבָה וַיָּשָׁב יוֹאָב וַיַּךְ אֶת־אֱדוֹם בְּגֵיא־מֶלַח שְׁנֵים עָשָׂר אָלֶף׃

3O God, You have rejected us,

  You have made a breach in us;

  You have been angry;

    restore us!

4You have made the land quake;

  You have torn it open.

Mend its fissures,

  for it is collapsing.

5You have made Your people suffer hardship;

  c-You have given us wine that makes us reel.-c

3 אֱלֹהִים זְנַחְתָּנוּ

פְרַצְתָּנוּ

אָנַפְתָּ

תְּשׁוֹבֵב לָנוּ׃

4 הִרְעַשְׁתָּה אֶרֶץ

פְּצַמְתָּהּ

רְפָה שְׁבָרֶיהָ

כִי־מָטָה׃

5 הִרְאִיתָה עַמְּךָ קָשָׁה

הִשְׁקִיתָנוּ יַיִן תַּרְעֵלָה׃

---

a-a   *Meaning of Heb. uncertain.*
b   *Cf. 2 Sam. 8; 1 Chron. 18.*
c-c   *Or "You have sated Your people with a bitter draft."*

סגול בלי מקף   v. 2.

6a-Give those who fear You because of Your truth
   a banner for rallying.-a   *Selah*.

7dThat those whom You love might be rescued,
   deliver with Your right hand and answer me.

8God promised e-in His sanctuary-e
   that I would exultingly divide up Shechem,
   and measure the Valley of Sukkoth;
9Gilead and Manasseh would be mine,
   Ephraim my chief stronghold,
   Judah my scepter;
10Moab would be my washbasin;
   on Edom I would cast my shoe;
   acclaim me, O Philistia!

11Would that I were brought to the bastion!
   Would that I were led to Edom!

12But You have rejected us, O God;
   God, You do not march with our armies.
13Grant us Your aid against the foe,
   for the help of man is worthless.
14With God we shall triumph;
   He will trample our foes.

61 For the leader; with instrumental music. Of
David.

2Hear my cry, O God,
   heed my prayer.
3From the end of the earth I call to You;
   when my heart is faint,
   You lead me to a rock that is high above me.
4For You have been my refuge,
   a tower of strength against the enemy.
5O that I might dwell in Your tent forever,
   take refuge under Your protecting wings.
   Selah.

---

6 נָתַתָּה לִּירֵאֶיךָ נֵּס לְהִתְנוֹסֵס
מִפְּנֵי קֹשֶׁט סֶלָה:
7 לְמַעַן יֵחָלְצוּן יְדִידֶיךָ
הוֹשִׁיעָה יְמִינְךָ וַעֲנֵנִי:

8 אֱלֹהִים | דִּבֶּר בְּקָדְשׁוֹ
אֶעְלֹזָה אֲחַלְּקָה שְׁכֶם
וְעֵמֶק סֻכּוֹת אֲמַדֵּד:
9 לִי גִלְעָד | וְלִי מְנַשֶּׁה
וְאֶפְרַיִם מָעוֹז רֹאשִׁי
יְהוּדָה מְחֹקְקִי:
10 מוֹאָב | סִיר רַחְצִי
עַל־אֱדוֹם אַשְׁלִיךְ נַעֲלִי
עָלַי פְּלֶשֶׁת הִתְרֹעָעִי:

11 מִי יֹבִלֵנִי עִיר מָצוֹר
מִי נָחַנִי עַד־אֱדוֹם:

12 הֲלֹא־אַתָּה אֱלֹהִים זְנַחְתָּנוּ
וְלֹא־תֵצֵא אֱלֹהִים בְּצִבְאוֹתֵינוּ:
13 הָבָה־לָּנוּ עֶזְרָת מִצָּר
וְשָׁוְא תְּשׁוּעַת אָדָם:
14 בֵּאלֹהִים נַעֲשֶׂה־חָיִל
וְהוּא יָבוּס צָרֵינוּ:

סא לַמְנַצֵּחַ | עַל־נְגִינַת לְדָוִד:

2 שִׁמְעָה אֱלֹהִים רִנָּתִי
הַקְשִׁיבָה תְּפִלָּתִי:
3 מִקְצֵה הָאָרֶץ | אֵלֶיךָ אֶקְרָא
בַּעֲטֹף לִבִּי
בְּצוּר־יָרוּם מִמֶּנִּי תַנְחֵנִי:
4 כִּי־הָיִיתָ מַחְסֶה לִי
מִגְדַּל־עֹז מִפְּנֵי אוֹיֵב:
5 אָגוּרָה בְאָהָלְךָ עוֹלָמִים
אֶחֱסֶה בְסֵתֶר כְּנָפֶיךָ   סֶלָה:

---

d   Cf. Ps. 108.7–14.
e-e   Or "by His holiness."

6O God, You have heard my vows;
    grant the request*a* of those who fear Your name.
7Add days to the days of the king;
    may his years extend through generations;
8may he dwell in God's presence forever;
    appoint*b* steadfast love to guard him.
9So I will sing hymns to Your name forever,
    as I fulfill my vows day after day.

6 כִּי־אַתָּה אֱלֹהִים שָׁמַעְתָּ לִנְדָרָי
נָתַתָּ יְרֻשַּׁת יִרְאֵי שְׁמֶךָ:
7 יָמִים עַל־יְמֵי־מֶלֶךְ תּוֹסִיף
שְׁנוֹתָיו כְּמוֹ־דֹר וָדֹר:
8 יֵשֵׁב עוֹלָם לִפְנֵי אֱלֹהִים
חֶסֶד וֶאֱמֶת מַן יִנְצְרֻהוּ:
9 כֵּן אֲזַמְּרָה שִׁמְךָ לָעַד
לְשַׁלְּמִי נְדָרַי יוֹם ׀ יוֹם:

62 For the leader; on *Jeduthun*. A psalm of David.

2Truly my soul waits quietly for God;
    my deliverance comes from Him.
3Truly He is my rock and deliverance,
    my haven; I shall never be shaken.
4How long will all of you attack*a* a man,
    to crush*a* him, as though he were
    a leaning wall, a tottering fence?
5They lay plans to topple him from his rank;
    they delight in falsehood;
    they bless with their mouths,
    while inwardly they curse.   *Selah.*

סב לַמְנַצֵּחַ עַל־יְדוּתוּן מִזְמוֹר לְדָוִד:
2 אַךְ אֶל־אֱלֹהִים דּוּמִיָּה נַפְשִׁי
מִמֶּנּוּ יְשׁוּעָתִי:
3 אַךְ־הוּא צוּרִי וִישׁוּעָתִי
מִשְׂגַּבִּי לֹא־אֶמּוֹט רַבָּה:
4 עַד־אָנָה ׀ תְּהוֹתְתוּ עַל־אִישׁ
תְּרָצְּחוּ כֻלְּכֶם
כְּקִיר נָטוּי גָּדֵר הַדְּחוּיָה:
5 אַךְ מִשְּׂאֵתוֹ ׀ יָעֲצוּ לְהַדִּיחַ
יִרְצוּ כָזָב
בְּפִיו יְבָרֵכוּ
וּבְקִרְבָּם יְקַלְלוּ־סֶלָה:

6Truly, wait quietly for God, O my soul,
    for my hope comes from Him.
7He is my rock and deliverance,
    my haven; I shall not be shaken.
8I rely on God, my deliverance and glory,
    my rock of strength;
    in God is my refuge.
9Trust in Him at all times, O people;
    pour out your hearts before Him;
    God is our refuge.   *Selah.*

6 אַךְ לֵאלֹהִים דּוֹמִּי נַפְשִׁי
כִּי־מִמֶּנּוּ תִּקְוָתִי:
7 אַךְ־הוּא צוּרִי וִישׁוּעָתִי
מִשְׂגַּבִּי לֹא אֶמּוֹט:
8 עַל־אֱלֹהִים יִשְׁעִי וּכְבוֹדִי
צוּר־עֻזִּי
מַחְסִי בֵּאלֹהִים:
9 בִּטְחוּ בוֹ בְכָל־עֵת ׀ עָם
שִׁפְכוּ־לְפָנָיו לְבַבְכֶם
אֱלֹהִים מַחֲסֶה־לָּנוּ סֶלָה:

10Men are mere breath;
    mortals, illusion;

10 אַךְ ׀ הֶבֶל בְּנֵי־אָדָם
כָּזָב בְּנֵי אִישׁ

---

a Taking the noun *yršt* as an alternate form of *'ršt*; cf. Ps. 21.3.
b Meaning of Heb. uncertain.

a Meaning of Heb. uncertain.

placed on a scale all together,
   they weigh even less than a breath.
¹¹Do not trust in violence,
   or put false hopes in robbery;
   if force bears fruit pay it no mind.
¹²One thing God has spoken;
   two things have I heard:
   that might belongs to God,
   ¹³and faithfulness is Yours, O Lord,
   to reward each man according to his deeds.

בְּמֹאזְנַיִם לַעֲלוֹת
הֵמָּה מֵהֶבֶל יָחַד׃
11 אַל־תִּבְטְחוּ בְעֹשֶׁק
וּבְגָזֵל אַל־תֶּהְבָּלוּ
חַיִל ׀ כִּי־יָנוּב אַל־תָּשִׁיתוּ לֵב׃
12 אַחַת ׀ דִּבֶּר אֱלֹהִים
שְׁתַּיִם־זוּ שָׁמָעְתִּי
כִּי עֹז לֵאלֹהִים׃
13 וּלְךָ־אֲדֹנָי חָסֶד
כִּי־אַתָּה תְשַׁלֵּם לְאִישׁ כְּמַעֲשֵׂהוּ׃

63 A psalm of David, when he was in the Wilderness of Judah.

סג מִזְמוֹר לְדָוִד בִּהְיוֹתוֹ בְּמִדְבַּר
יְהוּדָה׃

²God, You are my God;
   I search for You,
   my soul thirsts for You,
   my body yearns for You,
   as a parched and thirsty land that has no water.
³I shall behold You in the sanctuary,
   and see Your might and glory,
⁴Truly Your faithfulness is better than life;
   my lips declare Your praise.
⁵I bless You all my life;
   I lift up my hands, invoking Your name.
⁶I am sated as with a ^arich feast,^{-a}
   I sing praises with joyful lips
⁷when I call You to mind upon my bed,
   when I think of You in the watches of the night;
⁸for You are my help,
   and in the shadow of Your wings
   I shout for joy.
⁹My soul is attached to You;
   Your right hand supports me.

¹⁰May those who seek to destroy my life
   enter the depths of the earth.

2 אֱלֹהִים ׀ אֵלִי אַתָּה
אֲשַׁחֲרֶךָּ
צָמְאָה לְךָ ׀ נַפְשִׁי
כָּמַהּ לְךָ בְשָׂרִי
בְּאֶרֶץ־צִיָּה וְעָיֵף בְּלִי־מָיִם׃
3 כֵּן בַּקֹּדֶשׁ חֲזִיתִיךָ
לִרְאוֹת עֻזְּךָ וּכְבוֹדֶךָ׃
4 כִּי־טוֹב חַסְדְּךָ מֵחַיִּים
שְׂפָתַי יְשַׁבְּחוּנְךָ׃
5 כֵּן אֲבָרֶכְךָ בְחַיָּי
בְּשִׁמְךָ אֶשָּׂא כַפָּי׃
6 כְּמוֹ חֵלֶב וָדֶשֶׁן תִּשְׂבַּע נַפְשִׁי
וְשִׂפְתֵי רְנָנוֹת יְהַלֶּל־פִּי׃
7 אִם־זְכַרְתִּיךָ עַל־יְצוּעָי
בְּאַשְׁמֻרוֹת אֶהְגֶּה־בָּךְ׃
8 כִּי־הָיִיתָ עֶזְרָתָה לִּי
וּבְצֵל כְּנָפֶיךָ
אֲרַנֵּן׃
9 דָּבְקָה נַפְשִׁי אַחֲרֶיךָ
בִּי תָּמְכָה יְמִינֶךָ׃

10 וְהֵמָּה לְשׁוֹאָה יְבַקְשׁוּ נַפְשִׁי
יָבֹאוּ בְּתַחְתִּיּוֹת הָאָרֶץ׃

---

^{a-a} Lit. "suet and fat."

11May they be gutted by the sword;
   may they be prey to jackals.
12But the king shall rejoice in God;
   all who swear by Him shall exult,
   when the mouth of liars is stopped.

11 יַגִּירֻהוּ עַל־יְדֵי־חָרֶב
מְנָת שֻׁעָלִים יִהְיוּ:
12 וְהַמֶּלֶךְ יִשְׂמַח בֵּאלֹהִים
יִתְהַלֵּל כָּל־הַנִּשְׁבָּע בּוֹ
כִּי יִסָּכֵר פִּי דוֹבְרֵי־שָׁקֶר:

64 For the leader. A psalm of David.

סד לַמְנַצֵּחַ מִזְמוֹר לְדָוִד:

2Hear my voice, O God, when I plead;
   guard my life from the enemy's terror.
3Hide me from a band of evil men,
   from a crowd of evildoers,
   4who whet their tongues like swords;
   they aim their arrows—cruel words—
   5to shoot from hiding at the blameless man;
   they shoot him suddenly and without fear.
6a-They arm themselves with an evil word;
   when they speak, it is to conceal traps;-a
   they think, "Who will see them?"
7bLet the wrongdoings c-they have concealed,-c
   each one inside him, his secret thoughts,
   be wholly exposed.
8God shall shoot them with arrows;
   they shall be struck down suddenly.
9Their tongue shall be their downfall;
   all who see them shall recoil in horror;
   10all men shall stand in awe;
   they shall proclaim the work of God
   and His deed which they perceived.
11The righteous shall rejoice in the LORD,
   and take refuge in Him;
   all the upright shall exult.

2 שְׁמַע־אֱלֹהִים קוֹלִי בְשִׂיחִי
מִפַּחַד אוֹיֵב תִּצֹּר חַיָּי:
3 תַּסְתִּירֵנִי מִסּוֹד מְרֵעִים
מֵרִגְשַׁת פֹּעֲלֵי אָוֶן:
4 אֲשֶׁר שָׁנְנוּ כַחֶרֶב לְשׁוֹנָם
דָּרְכוּ חִצָּם דָּבָר מָר:
5 לִירוֹת בַּמִּסְתָּרִים תָּם
פִּתְאֹם יֹרֻהוּ וְלֹא יִירָאוּ:
6 יְחַזְּקוּ־לָמוֹ ׀ דָּבָר רָע
יְסַפְּרוּ לִטְמוֹן מוֹקְשִׁים
אָמְרוּ מִי יִרְאֶה־לָּמוֹ:
7 יַחְפְּשׂוּ־עוֹלֹת
תַּמְנוּ* חֵפֶשׂ מְחֻפָּשׂ
וְקֶרֶב אִישׁ וְלֵב עָמֹק:
8 וַיֹּרֵם אֱלֹהִים חֵץ פִּתְאוֹם
הָיוּ מַכּוֹתָם:
9 וַיַּכְשִׁילוּהוּ עָלֵימוֹ לְשׁוֹנָם
יִתְנֹדֲדוּ כָּל־רֹאֵה בָם:
10 וַיִּירְאוּ כָּל־אָדָם
וַיַּגִּידוּ פֹּעַל אֱלֹהִים
וּמַעֲשֵׂהוּ הִשְׂכִּילוּ:
11 יִשְׂמַח צַדִּיק בַּיהוָה
וְחָסָה בוֹ
וְיִתְהַלֲלוּ כָּל־יִשְׁרֵי־לֵב:

a-a Meaning of Heb. uncertain.
b Meaning of verse uncertain.
c-c Reading ṭamnu with some mss. (cf. Minḥat Shai) and Rashi; most printed editions tamnu, traditionally rendered "they have accomplished."

v. 7. בנוסח אחר "טמנו"

65
For the leader. A psalm of David. A song.

סה לַמְנַצֵּחַ מִזְמוֹר לְדָוִד שִׁיר:

[2]Praise befits You in Zion, O God;
  vows are paid to You;
  [3]all mankind[a] comes to You,
  You who hear prayer.
[4]When all manner of sins overwhelm me,
  it is You who forgive our iniquities.
[5]Happy is the man You choose and bring near
  to dwell in Your courts;
  may we be sated with the blessings of Your
    house,
  Your holy temple.

[6]Answer us with victory through awesome deeds,
  O God, our deliverer,
  in whom all the ends of the earth
  and the distant seas
  put their trust;
[7]who by His power fixed the mountains firmly,
  who is girded with might,
[8]who stills the raging seas,
  the raging waves,
  and tumultuous peoples.
[9]Those who live at the ends of the earth are awed
    by Your signs;
  You make the lands of sunrise and sunset shout
    for joy.
[10]You take care of the earth and irrigate it;
  You enrich it greatly,
  with the channel of God full of water;
  You provide grain for men;
  for so do You prepare it.
[11]Saturating its furrows,
  leveling its ridges,
  You soften it with showers,
  You bless its growth.
[12]You crown the year with Your bounty;

לְךָ דֻמִיָּה תְהִלָּה אֱלֹהִים בְּצִיּוֹן
וּלְךָ יְשֻׁלַּם־נֶדֶר:
שֹׁמֵעַ תְּפִלָּה
עָדֶיךָ כָּל־בָּשָׂר יָבֹאוּ:
דִּבְרֵי עֲוֺנֹת גָּבְרוּ מֶנִּי
פְּשָׁעֵינוּ אַתָּה תְכַפְּרֵם:
אַשְׁרֵי ׀ תִּבְחַר וּתְקָרֵב
יִשְׁכֹּן חֲצֵרֶיךָ
נִשְׂבְּעָה בְּטוּב בֵּיתֶךָ
קְדֹשׁ הֵיכָלֶךָ:

נוֹרָאוֹת ׀ בְּצֶדֶק תַּעֲנֵנוּ
אֱלֹהֵי יִשְׁעֵנוּ
מִבְטָח
כָּל־קַצְוֵי־אֶרֶץ
וְיָם רְחֹקִים:
מֵכִין הָרִים בְּכֹחוֹ
נֶאְזָר בִּגְבוּרָה:
מַשְׁבִּיחַ ׀ שְׁאוֹן יַמִּים
שְׁאוֹן גַּלֵּיהֶם
וַהֲמוֹן לְאֻמִּים:
וַיִּירְאוּ ׀ יֹשְׁבֵי קְצָוֺת מֵאוֹתֹתֶיךָ
מוֹצָאֵי־בֹקֶר וָעֶרֶב תַּרְנִין:
פָּקַדְתָּ הָאָרֶץ ׀ וַתְּשֹׁקְקֶהָ
רַבַּת תַּעְשְׁרֶנָּה
פֶּלֶג אֱלֹהִים מָלֵא מָיִם
תָּכִין דְּגָנָם
כִּי־כֵן תְּכִינֶהָ:
תְּלָמֶיהָ רַוֵּה
נַחֵת גְּדוּדֶיהָ
בִּרְבִיבִים תְּמֹגְגֶנָּה
צִמְחָהּ תְּבָרֵךְ:
עִטַּרְתָּ שְׁנַת טוֹבָתֶךָ

---

a   Lit. "flesh."

fatness is distilled in Your paths; וּמַעְגָּלֶיךָ יִרְעֲפוּן דָּשֶׁן:

13the pasturelands distill it; 13 יִרְעֲפוּ נְאוֹת מִדְבָּר

the hills are girded with joy. וְגִיל גְּבָעוֹת תַּחְגֹּרְנָה:

14The meadows are clothed with flocks, 14 לָבְשׁוּ כָרִים | הַצֹּאן

the valleys mantled with grain; וַעֲמָקִים יַעַטְפוּ־בָר

they raise a shout, they break into song. יִתְרוֹעֲעוּ אַף־יָשִׁירוּ:

66 For the leader. A song. A psalm. סו לַמְנַצֵּחַ שִׁיר מִזְמוֹר

Raise a shout for God, all the earth; הָרִיעוּ לֵאלֹהִים כָּל־הָאָרֶץ:

2sing the glory of His name, 2 זַמְּרוּ כְבוֹד־שְׁמוֹ

make glorious His praise. שִׂימוּ כָבוֹד תְּהִלָּתוֹ:

3Say to God, 3 אִמְרוּ לֵאלֹהִים

"How awesome are Your deeds, מַה־נּוֹרָא מַעֲשֶׂיךָ

Your enemies cower before Your great בְּרֹב עֻזְּךָ יְכַחֲשׁוּ לְךָ אֹיְבֶיךָ:

strength;

4all the earth bows to You, 4 כָּל־הָאָרֶץ | יִשְׁתַּחֲווּ לְךָ

and sings hymns to You; וִיזַמְּרוּ־לָךְ

all sing hymns to Your name."   *Selah.* יְזַמְּרוּ שִׁמְךָ   סֶלָה:

5Come and see the works of God, 5 לְכוּ וּרְאוּ מִפְעֲלוֹת אֱלֹהִים

who is held in awe by men for His acts. נוֹרָא עֲלִילָה עַל־בְּנֵי אָדָם:

6He turned the sea into dry land; 6 הָפַךְ יָם | לְיַבָּשָׁה

they crossed the river on foot; בַּנָּהָר יַעַבְרוּ בְרָגֶל

we therefore rejoice in Him. שָׁם נִשְׂמְחָה־בּוֹ:

7He rules forever in His might; 7 מֹשֵׁל בִּגְבוּרָתוֹ | עוֹלָם

His eyes scan the nations; עֵינָיו בַּגּוֹיִם תִּצְפֶּינָה

let the rebellious not assert themselves.   *Selah.* הַסּוֹרְרִים | אַל־יָרִימוּ יָרוּמוּ לָמוֹ

סֶלָה:

8O peoples, bless our God, 8 בָּרְכוּ עַמִּים | אֱלֹהֵינוּ

celebrate His praises; וְהַשְׁמִיעוּ קוֹל תְּהִלָּתוֹ:

9who has granted us life, 9 הַשָּׂם נַפְשֵׁנוּ בַּחַיִּים

and has not let our feet slip. וְלֹא־נָתַן לַמּוֹט רַגְלֵנוּ:

10You have tried us, O God, 10 כִּי־בְחַנְתָּנוּ אֱלֹהִים

refining us, as one refines silver. צְרַפְתָּנוּ כִּצְרָף־כָּסֶף:

11You have caught us in a net, 11 הֲבֵאתָנוּ בַמְּצוּדָה

a-caught us in trammels.-*a*

שַׂמְתָּ מוּעָקָה בְמָתְנֵינוּ:

12You have let men ride over us;

12 הִרְכַּבְתָּ אֱנוֹשׁ לְרֹאשֵׁנוּ

  we have endured fire and water,

בָּאנוּ־בָאֵשׁ וּבַמַּיִם

  and You have brought us through to prosperity.

וַתּוֹצִיאֵנוּ לָרְוָיָה:

13I enter Your house with burnt offerings,

13 אָבוֹא בֵיתְךָ בְעוֹלוֹת

  I pay my vows to You,

אֲשַׁלֵּם לְךָ נְדָרָי:

  14[vows] that my lips pronounced,

14 אֲשֶׁר־פָּצוּ שְׂפָתָי

  that my mouth uttered in my distress.

וְדִבֶּר־פִּי בַּצַּר־לִי:

15I offer up fatlings to You,

15 עֹלוֹת מֵחִים אַעֲלֶה־לָּךְ

  with the odor of burning rams;

עִם־קְטֹרֶת אֵילִים

  I sacrifice bulls and he-goats.   *Selah.*

אֶעֱשֶׂה בָקָר עִם־עַתּוּדִים   סֶלָה:

16Come and hear, all God-fearing men,

16 לְכוּ־שִׁמְעוּ וַאֲסַפְּרָה כָּל־יִרְאֵי

  as I tell what He did for me.

אֱלֹהִים

17I called aloud to Him,

אֲשֶׁר עָשָׂה לְנַפְשִׁי:

  glorification on my tongue.

17 אֵלָיו פִּי־קָרָאתִי

18Had I an evil thought in my mind,

וְרוֹמַם תַּחַת לְשׁוֹנִי:

  the Lord would not have listened.

18 אָוֶן אִם־רָאִיתִי בְלִבִּי

19But God did listen;

לֹא יִשְׁמַע ׀ אֲדֹנָי:

  He paid heed to my prayer.

19 אָכֵן שָׁמַע אֱלֹהִים

20Blessed is God who has not turned away my prayer,

הִקְשִׁיב בְּקוֹל תְּפִלָּתִי:

  or His faithful care from me.

20 בָּרוּךְ אֱלֹהִים

אֲשֶׁר לֹא־הֵסִיר תְּפִלָּתִי וְחַסְדּוֹ

מֵאִתִּי:

67 For the leader; with instrumental music. A psalm. A song.

סז לַמְנַצֵּחַ בִּנְגִינֹת מִזְמוֹר שִׁיר:

אֱלֹהִים יְחָנֵּנוּ וִיבָרְכֵנוּ

2May God be gracious to us and bless us;

יָאֵר פָּנָיו אִתָּנוּ   סֶלָה:

  may He show us favor,   *selah*

3 לָדַעַת בָּאָרֶץ דַּרְכֶּךָ

  3that Your way be known on earth,

בְּכָל־גּוֹיִם יְשׁוּעָתֶךָ:

  Your deliverance among all nations.

4 יוֹדוּךָ עַמִּים ׀ אֱלֹהִים

4Peoples will praise You, O God;

יוֹדוּךָ עַמִּים כֻּלָּם:

  all peoples will praise You.

5 יִשְׂמְחוּ וִירַנְּנוּ לְאֻמִּים

5Nations will exult and shout for joy,

a-a   Lit. *"put a trammel on our loins."*

for You rule the peoples with equity,

You guide the nations of the earth.   *Selah.*

כִּי־תִשְׁפֹּט עַמִּים מִישֹׁור

וּלְאֻמִּים ׀ בָּאָרֶץ תַּנְחֵם סֶלָה:

6The peoples will praise You, O God;

all peoples will praise You.

‏6 יוֹדוּךָ עַמִּים ׀ אֱלֹהִים

יוֹדוּךָ עַמִּים כֻּלָּם:

7May the earth yield its produce;

may God, our God, bless us.

‏7 אֶרֶץ נָתְנָה יְבוּלָהּ

יְבָרְכֵנוּ אֱלֹהִים אֱלֹהֵינוּ:

8May God bless us,

and be revered to the ends of the earth.

‏8 יְבָרְכֵנוּ אֱלֹהִים

וְיִירְאוּ אֹתוֹ כָּל־אַפְסֵי־אָרֶץ:

68 *a*For the leader. Of David. A psalm. A song.

סח לַמְנַצֵּחַ לְדָוִד מִזְמוֹר שִׁיר:

2God will arise,

His enemies shall be scattered,

His foes shall flee before Him.

‏2 יָקוּם אֱלֹהִים

יָפוּצוּ אוֹיְבָיו

וְיָנוּסוּ מְשַׂנְאָיו מִפָּנָיו:

3Disperse them as smoke is dispersed;

as wax melts at fire,

so the wicked shall perish before God.

‏3 כְּהִנְדֹּף עָשָׁן תִּנְדֹּף

כְּהִמֵּס דּוֹנַג מִפְּנֵי־אֵשׁ

יֹאבְדוּ רְשָׁעִים מִפְּנֵי אֱלֹהִים:

4But the righteous shall rejoice;

they shall exult in the presence of God;

they shall be exceedingly joyful.

‏4 וְצַדִּיקִים יִשְׂמְחוּ

יַעַלְצוּ לִפְנֵי אֱלֹהִים

וְיָשִׂישׂוּ בְשִׂמְחָה:

5Sing to God, chant hymns to His name;

extol Him who rides the clouds;

the Lord is His name.

Exult in His presence—

‏5 שִׁירוּ ׀ לֵאלֹהִים זַמְּרוּ שְׁמוֹ

סֹלּוּ לָרֹכֵב בָּעֲרָבוֹת

בְּיָהּ שְׁמוֹ

וְעִלְזוּ לְפָנָיו:

6the father of orphans, the champion of

widows,

God, in His holy habitation.

‏6 אֲבִי יְתוֹמִים וְדַיַּן אַלְמָנוֹת

אֱלֹהִים בִּמְעוֹן קָדְשׁוֹ:

7God restores the lonely to their homes,

sets free the imprisoned, safe and sound,

while the rebellious must live in a parched land.

‏7 אֱלֹהִים ׀ מוֹשִׁיב יְחִידִים ׀ בַּיְתָה

מוֹצִיא אֲסִירִים בַּכּוֹשָׁרוֹת

אַךְ סוֹרְרִים שָׁכְנוּ צְחִיחָה:

8O God, when You went at the head of Your army,

when You marched through the desert,

selah

‏8 אֱלֹהִים בְּצֵאתְךָ לִפְנֵי עַמֶּךָ

בְּצַעְדְּךָ בִישִׁימוֹן סֶלָה:

9the earth trembled, the sky rained because of

God,

‏9 אֶרֶץ רָעָשָׁה ׀ אַף־שָׁמַיִם נָטְפוּ

מִפְּנֵי אֱלֹהִים

---

a   *The coherence of this psalm and the meaning of many of its passages are uncertain.*

yon Sinai, because of God, the God of Israel.

¹⁰You released a bountiful rain, O God;
  when Your own land languished, You sustained
    it.

¹¹Your tribe dwells there;
  O God, in Your goodness You provide for the
    needy.

¹²The Lord gives a command;
  the women who bring the news are a great host:

¹³"The kings and their armies are in headlong
    flight;
  housewives are sharing in the spoils;

¹⁴even for those of you who lie among the
    sheepfolds
  there are wings of a dove sheathed in silver,
  its pinions in fine gold."

¹⁵When Shaddai scattered the kings,
  it seemed like a snowstorm in Zalmon.

¹⁶O majestic mountain, Mount Bashan;
  O jagged mountain, Mount Bashan;

¹⁷why so hostile, O jagged mountains,
  toward the mountain God desired as His
    dwelling?
The LORD shall abide there forever.

¹⁸God's chariots are myriads upon myriads,
    thousands upon thousands;
  the Lord is among them as in Sinai in holiness.

¹⁹You went up to the heights, having taken cap-
    tives,
  having received tribute of men,
  even of those who rebel
  against the LORD God's abiding there.

²⁰Blessed is the Lord.
Day by day He supports us,
  God, our deliverance. *Selah.*

זֶה סִינַי מִפְּנֵי אֱלֹהִים אֱלֹהֵי
יִשְׂרָאֵל:

10 גֶּשֶׁם נְדָבוֹת תָּנִיף אֱלֹהִים
נַחֲלָתְךָ וְנִלְאָה אַתָּה כוֹנַנְתָּהּ:

11 חַיָּתְךָ יָשְׁבוּ־בָהּ
תָּכִין בְּטוֹבָתְךָ לֶעָנִי אֱלֹהִים:

12 אֲדֹנָי יִתֶּן־אֹמֶר
הַמְבַשְּׂרוֹת צָבָא רָב:

13 מַלְכֵי צְבָאוֹת יִדֹּדוּן יִדֹּדוּן
וּנְוַת בַּיִת תְּחַלֵּק שָׁלָל:

14 אִם־תִּשְׁכְּבוּן בֵּין שְׁפַתָּיִם
כַּנְפֵי יוֹנָה נֶחְפָּה בַכֶּסֶף
וְאֶבְרוֹתֶיהָ בִּירַקְרַק חָרוּץ:

15 בְּפָרֵשׂ שַׁדַּי מְלָכִים בָּהּ תַּשְׁלֵג
בְּצַלְמוֹן:

16 הַר־אֱלֹהִים הַר־בָּשָׁן
הַר גַּבְנֻנִּים הַר־בָּשָׁן:

17 לָמָּה ׀ תְּרַצְּדוּן הָרִים גַּבְנֻנִּים
הָהָר חָמַד אֱלֹהִים לְשִׁבְתּוֹ
אַף־יְהוָה יִשְׁכֹּן לָנֶצַח:

18 רֶכֶב אֱלֹהִים רִבֹּתַיִם
אַלְפֵי שִׁנְאָן
אֲדֹנָי בָם סִינַי בַּקֹּדֶשׁ:

19 עָלִיתָ לַמָּרוֹם ׀ שָׁבִיתָ שֶּׁבִי
לָקַחְתָּ מַתָּנוֹת בָּאָדָם
וְאַף סוֹרְרִים
לִשְׁכֹּן ׀ יָהּ אֱלֹהִים:

20 בָּרוּךְ אֲדֹנָי
יוֹם ׀ יוֹם יַעֲמָס־לָנוּ
הָאֵל יְשׁוּעָתֵנוּ סֶלָה:

²¹God is for us a God of deliverance;
   Goᴅ the Lord provides an escape from death.
²²God will smash the heads of His enemies,
   the hairy crown of him who walks about in his
     guilt.
²³The Lord said, "I will retrieve from Bashan,
   I will retrieve from the depths of the sea;
    ²⁴that your feet may wade through blood;
   that the tongue of your dogs may have its por-
     tion of your enemies."

²⁵Men see Your processions, O God,
   the processions of my God, my king,
     into the sanctuary.
²⁶First come singers, then musicians,
   amidst maidens playing timbrels.
²⁷In assemblies bless God,
   the Lᴏʀᴅ, O you who are from the fountain of
     Israel.
²⁸There is little Benjamin who rules them,
   the princes of Judah who command them,
     the princes of Zebulun and Naphtali.

²⁹Your God has ordained strength for you,
   the strength, O God,
     which You displayed for us
       ³⁰from Your temple above Jerusalem.
The kings bring You tribute.
³¹Blast the beast of the marsh,
   the herd of bulls among the peoples, the calves,
   till they come cringing with pieces of silver.
Scatter the peoples who delight in wars!
³²Tribute-bearers shall come from Egypt;
   Cush shall hasten its gifts to God.

³³O kingdoms of the earth,
   sing to God;
   chant hymns to the Lord,   *selah*

21 הָאֵל ׀ לָנוּ אֵל לְמוֹשָׁעוֹת
וְלֵיהוִֹה אֲדֹנָי לַמָּוֶת תּוֹצָאוֹת:
22 אַךְ־אֱלֹהִים יִמְחַץ רֹאשׁ אֹיְבָיו
קׇדְקֹד שֵׂעָר
מִתְהַלֵּךְ בַּאֲשָׁמָיו:
23 אָמַר אֲדֹנָי מִבָּשָׁן אָשִׁיב
אָשִׁיב מִמְּצֻלוֹת יָם:
24 לְמַעַן ׀ תִּמְחַץ רַגְלְךָ בְּדָם
לְשׁוֹן כְּלָבֶיךָ מֵאֹיְבִים מִנֵּהוּ:

25 רָאוּ הֲלִיכוֹתֶיךָ אֱלֹהִים
הֲלִיכוֹת אֵלִי מַלְכִּי
בַקֹּדֶשׁ:
26 קִדְּמוּ שָׁרִים אַחַר נֹגְנִים
בְּתוֹךְ עֲלָמוֹת תּוֹפֵפוֹת:
27 בְּמַקְהֵלוֹת בָּרְכוּ אֱלֹהִים
יְהוָֹה מִמְּקוֹר יִשְׂרָאֵל:
28 שָׁם בִּנְיָמִן ׀ צָעִיר רֹדֵם
שָׂרֵי יְהוּדָה רִגְמָתָם
שָׂרֵי זְבֻלוּן שָׂרֵי נַפְתָּלִי:

29 צִוָּה אֱלֹהֶיךָ עֻזֶּךָ
עוּזָּה אֱלֹהִים
זוּ פָּעַלְתָּ לָּנוּ:
30 מֵהֵיכָלֶךָ עַל־יְרוּשָׁלָ͏ִם
לְךָ יוֹבִילוּ מְלָכִים שָׁי:
31 גְּעַר חַיַּת קָנֶה
עֲדַת אַבִּירִים ׀ בְּעֶגְלֵי עַמִּים
מִתְרַפֵּס בְּרַצֵּי־כָסֶף
בִּזַּר עַמִּים קְרָבוֹת יֶחְפָּצוּ:
32 יֶאֱתָיוּ חַשְׁמַנִּים מִנִּי מִצְרָיִם
כּוּשׁ תָּרִיץ יָדָיו לֵאלֹהִים:

33 מַמְלְכוֹת הָאָרֶץ
שִׁירוּ לֵאלֹהִים
זַמְּרוּ אֲדֹנָי סֶלָה:

34to Him who rides the ancient highest heavens,
who thunders forth with His mighty voice.

35Ascribe might to God,
whose majesty is over Israel,
whose might is in the skies.

36You are awesome, O God, in Your holy places;
it is the God of Israel who gives might and
power to the people.
Blessed is God.

34 לָרֹכֵב בִּשְׁמֵי שְׁמֵי־קֶדֶם
הֵן יִתֵּן בְּקוֹלוֹ קוֹל עֹז׃

35 תְּנוּ עֹז לֵאלֹהִים
עַל־יִשְׂרָאֵל גַּאֲוָתוֹ
וְעֻזּוֹ בַּשְּׁחָקִים׃

36 נוֹרָא אֱלֹהִים מִמִּקְדָּשֶׁיךָ
אֵל יִשְׂרָאֵל הוּא נֹתֵן ׀ עֹז
וְתַעֲצֻמוֹת לָעָם
בָּרוּךְ אֱלֹהִים׃

69 For the leader. On *shoshannim*.[a] Of David.

סט לַמְנַצֵּחַ עַל־שׁוֹשַׁנִּים לְדָוִד׃

2Deliver me, O God,
for the waters have reached my neck;

3I am sinking into the slimy deep
and find no foothold;
I have come into the watery depths;
the flood sweeps me away.

4I am weary with calling;
my throat is dry;
my eyes fail
while I wait for God.

5More numerous than the hairs of my head
are those who hate me without reason;
many are those who would destroy me,
my treacherous enemies.
Must I restore what I have not stolen?

6God, You know my folly;
my guilty deeds are not hidden from You.

7Let those who look to You,
O Lord, GOD of hosts,
not be disappointed on my account;
let those who seek You,
O God of Israel,
not be shamed because of me.

8It is for Your sake that I have been reviled,
that shame covers my face;

2 הוֹשִׁיעֵנִי אֱלֹהִים
כִּי בָאוּ מַיִם עַד־נָפֶשׁ׃

3 טָבַעְתִּי ׀ בִּיוֵן מְצוּלָה
וְאֵין מָעֳמָד
בָּאתִי בְמַעֲמַקֵּי־מַיִם
וְשִׁבֹּלֶת שְׁטָפָתְנִי׃

4 יָגַעְתִּי בְקָרְאִי
נִחַר גְּרוֹנִי
כָּלוּ עֵינַי
מְיַחֵל לֵאלֹהָי׃

5 רַבּוּ ׀ מִשַּׂעֲרוֹת רֹאשִׁי
שֹׂנְאַי חִנָּם
עָצְמוּ מַצְמִיתַי
אֹיְבַי שֶׁקֶר
אֲשֶׁר לֹא־גָזַלְתִּי אָז אָשִׁיב׃

6 אֱלֹהִים אַתָּה יָדַעְתָּ לְאִוַּלְתִּי
וְאַשְׁמוֹתַי מִמְּךָ לֹא־נִכְחָדוּ׃

7 אַל־יֵבֹשׁוּ בִי ׀
קֹוֶיךָ
אֲדֹנָי יְהוִה צְבָאוֹת
אַל־יִכָּלְמוּ בִי
מְבַקְשֶׁיךָ
אֱלֹהֵי יִשְׂרָאֵל׃

8 כִּי־עָלֶיךָ נָשָׂאתִי חֶרְפָּה
כִּסְּתָה כְלִמָּה פָנָי׃

a   Meaning of Heb. uncertain.

9I am a stranger to my brothers,
an alien to my kin.

10My zeal for Your house has been my undoing;
the reproaches of those who revile You have
fallen upon me.

11When I wept and fasted,
I was reviled for it.

12I made sackcloth my garment;
I became a byword among them.

13Those who sit in the gate talk about me;
I am the taunt of drunkards.

14As for me, may my prayer come to You, O LORD,
at a favorable moment;
O God, in Your abundant faithfulness,
answer me with Your sure deliverance.

15Rescue me from the mire;
let me not sink;
let me be rescued from my enemies,
and from the watery depths.

16Let the floodwaters not sweep me away;
let the deep not swallow me;
let the mouth of the Pit not close over me.

17Answer me, O LORD,
according to Your great steadfastness;
in accordance with Your abundant mercy
turn to me;
18do not hide Your face from Your servant,
for I am in distress;
answer me quickly.

19Come near to me and redeem me;
free me from my enemies.

20You know my reproach,
my shame, my disgrace;
You are aware of all my foes.

21Reproach breaks my heart,
I am in despair;*a*

9 מָזוֹר הָיִיתִי לְאֶחָי
וְנָכְרִי לִבְנֵי אִמִּי:

10 כִּי־קִנְאַת בֵּיתְךָ אֲכָלָתְנִי
וְחֶרְפּוֹת חוֹרְפֶיךָ נָפְלוּ עָלָי:

11 וָאֶבְכֶּה בַצּוֹם נַפְשִׁי
וַתְּהִי לַחֲרָפוֹת לִי:

12 וָאֶתְּנָה לְבוּשִׁי שָׂק
וָאֱהִי לָהֶם לְמָשָׁל:

13 יָשִׂיחוּ בִי יֹשְׁבֵי שָׁעַר
וּנְגִינוֹת שׁוֹתֵי שֵׁכָר:

14 וַאֲנִי תְפִלָּתִי־לְךָ ׀ יְהֹוָה
עֵת רָצוֹן
אֱלֹהִים בְּרָב־חַסְדֶּךָ
עֲנֵנִי בֶּאֱמֶת יִשְׁעֶךָ:

15 הַצִּילֵנִי מִטִּיט
וְאַל־אֶטְבָּעָה
אִנָּצְלָה מִשֹּׂנְאַי
וּמִמַּעֲמַקֵּי־מָיִם:

16 אַל־תִּשְׁטְפֵנִי ׀ שִׁבֹּלֶת מַיִם
וְאַל־תִּבְלָעֵנִי מְצוּלָה
וְאַל־תֶּאְטַר־עָלַי בְּאֵר פִּיהָ:

17 עֲנֵנִי יְהֹוָה
כִּי־טוֹב חַסְדֶּךָ
כְּרֹב רַחֲמֶיךָ
פְּנֵה אֵלָי:

18 וְאַל־תַּסְתֵּר פָּנֶיךָ מֵעַבְדֶּךָ
כִּי־צַר־לִי
מַהֵר עֲנֵנִי:

19 קָרְבָה אֶל־נַפְשִׁי גְאָלָהּ
לְמַעַן אֹיְבַי פְּדֵנִי:

20 אַתָּה יָדַעְתָּ חֶרְפָּתִי
וּבָשְׁתִּי וּכְלִמָּתִי
נֶגְדְּךָ כָּל־צוֹרְרָי:

21 חֶרְפָּה ׀ שָׁבְרָה לִבִּי
וָאָנוּשָׁה

I hope for consolation, but there is none,
for comforters, but find none.

²²They give me gall for food,
vinegar to quench my thirst.

²³May their table be a trap for them,
a snare for their allies.

²⁴May their eyes grow dim so that they cannot
see;
may their loins collapse continually.

²⁵Pour out Your wrath on them;
may Your blazing anger overtake them;

²⁶may their encampments be desolate;
may their tents stand empty.

²⁷For they persecute those You have struck;
they talk about the pain of those You have
felled.

²⁸Add that to their guilt;
let them have no share of Your beneficence;

²⁹may they be erased from the book of life,
and not be inscribed with the righteous.

³⁰But I am lowly and in pain;
Your help, O God, keeps me safe.

³¹I will extol God's name with song,
and exalt Him with praise.

³²That will please the LORD more than oxen,
than bulls with horns and hooves.

³³The lowly will see and rejoice;
you who are mindful of God, take heart!

³⁴For the LORD listens to the needy,
and does not spurn His captives.

³⁵Heaven and earth shall extol Him,
the seas, and all that moves in them.

³⁶For God will deliver Zion
and rebuild the cities of Judah;
they shall live there and inherit it;

³⁷the offspring of His servants shall possess it;
those who cherish His name shall dwell there.

וָאֲקַוֶּה לָנוּד וָאַיִן
וְלַמְנַחֲמִים וְלֹא מָצָאתִי:

22 וַיִּתְּנוּ בְּבָרוּתִי רֹאשׁ
וְלִצְמָאִי יַשְׁקוּנִי חֹמֶץ:

23 יְהִי־שֻׁלְחָנָם לִפְנֵיהֶם לְפָח
וְלִשְׁלוֹמִים לְמוֹקֵשׁ:

24 תֶּחְשַׁכְנָה עֵינֵיהֶם מֵרְאוֹת
וּמָתְנֵיהֶם תָּמִיד הַמְעַד:

25 שְׁפָךְ־עֲלֵיהֶם זַעְמֶךָ
וַחֲרוֹן אַפְּךָ יַשִּׂיגֵם:

26 תְּהִי־טִירָתָם נְשַׁמָּה
בְּאָהֳלֵיהֶם אַל־יְהִי יֹשֵׁב:

27 כִּי־אַתָּה אֲשֶׁר־הִכִּיתָ רָדָפוּ
וְאֶל־מַכְאוֹב חֲלָלֶיךָ יְסַפֵּרוּ:

28 תְּנָה־עָוֹן עַל־עֲוֹנָם
וְאַל־יָבֹאוּ בְּצִדְקָתֶךָ:

29 יִמָּחוּ מִסֵּפֶר חַיִּים
וְעִם צַדִּיקִים אַל־יִכָּתֵבוּ:

30 וַאֲנִי עָנִי וְכוֹאֵב
יְשׁוּעָתְךָ אֱלֹהִים תְּשַׂגְּבֵנִי:

31 אֲהַלְלָה שֵׁם־אֱלֹהִים בְּשִׁיר
וַאֲגַדְּלֶנּוּ בְתוֹדָה:

32 וְתִיטַב לַיהוָה מִשּׁוֹר פָּר מַקְרִן
מַפְרִיס:

33 רָאוּ עֲנָוִים יִשְׂמָחוּ
דֹּרְשֵׁי אֱלֹהִים וִיחִי לְבַבְכֶם:

34 כִּי־שֹׁמֵעַ אֶל־אֶבְיוֹנִים יְהוָה
וְאֶת־אֲסִירָיו לֹא בָזָה:

35 יְהַלְלוּהוּ שָׁמַיִם וָאָרֶץ
יַמִּים וְכָל־רֹמֵשׂ בָּם:

36 כִּי אֱלֹהִים ׀ יוֹשִׁיעַ צִיּוֹן
וְיִבְנֶה עָרֵי יְהוּדָה
וְיָשְׁבוּ שָׁם וִירֵשׁוּהָ:

37 וְזֶרַע עֲבָדָיו יִנְחָלוּהָ
וְאֹהֲבֵי שְׁמוֹ יִשְׁכְּנוּ־בָהּ:

70

ע

For the leader. Of David. *Lehazkir.*ᵃ

לַמְנַצֵּחַ לְדָוִד לְהַזְכִּיר:

²ᵇHasten, O God, to save me;
O Lord, to aid me!
³Let those who seek my life
be frustrated and disgraced;
let those who wish me harm,
fall back in shame.
⁴Let those who say, "Aha! Aha!"
turn back because of their frustration.

⁵But let all who seek You be glad and rejoice in
You;
let those who are eager for Your deliverance al-
ways say,
"Extolled be God!"
⁶But I am poor and needy;
O God, hasten to me!
You are my help and my rescuer;
O Lord, do not delay.

² אֱלֹהִים לְהַצִּילֵנִי
יְהֹוָה לְעֶזְרָתִי חֽוּשָׁה:
³ יֵבֹשׁוּ וְיַחְפְּרוּ
מְבַקְשֵׁי נַפְשִׁי
יִסֹּגוּ אָחוֹר וְיִכָּלְמוּ
חֲפֵצֵי רָעָתִי:
⁴ יָשׁוּבוּ עַל־עֵקֶב בָּשְׁתָּם
הָאֹמְרִים הֶאָח ׀ הֶאָֽח:

⁵ יָשִׂישׂוּ וְיִשְׂמְחוּ ׀ בְּךָ כָּל־מְבַקְשֶׁיךָ
וְיֹאמְרוּ תָמִיד יִגְדַּל אֱלֹהִים
אֹהֲבֵי יְשׁוּעָתֶֽךָ:
⁶ וַאֲנִי ׀ עָנִי וְאֶבְיוֹן
אֱלֹהִים חֽוּשָׁה־לִּי
עֶזְרִי וּמְפַלְטִי אַתָּה
יְהֹוָה אַל־תְּאַחַֽר:

71

עא

I seek refuge in You, O Lord;
may I never be disappointed.
²As You are beneficent, save me and rescue me;
incline Your ear to me and deliver me.
³Be a sheltering rock for me to which I may always
repair;
decree my deliverance,
for You are my rock and my fortress.
⁴My God, rescue me from the hand of the wicked,
from the grasp of the unjust and the lawless.
⁵For You are my hope,
O Lord God,
my trust from my youth.
⁶While yet unborn, I depended on You;
in the womb of my mother, You were my
support;ᵃ

בְּךָ־יְהֹוָה חָסִיתִי
אַל־אֵבוֹשָׁה לְעוֹלָֽם:
² בְּצִדְקָתְךָ תַּצִּילֵנִי וּתְפַלְּטֵנִי
הַטֵּה־אֵלַי אָזְנְךָ וְהוֹשִׁיעֵֽנִי:
³ הֱיֵה לִי ׀ לְצוּר מָעוֹן לָבוֹא תָּמִיד
צִוִּיתָ לְהוֹשִׁיעֵנִי
כִּי־סַלְעִי וּמְצוּדָתִי אָֽתָּה:
⁴ אֱלֹהַי פַּלְּטֵנִי מִיַּד רָשָׁע
מִכַּף מְעַוֵּל וְחוֹמֵֽץ:
⁵ כִּי־אַתָּה תִקְוָתִי
אֲדֹנָי יְהֹוִה
מִבְטַחִי מִנְּעוּרָֽי:
⁶ עָלֶיךָ ׀ נִסְמַכְתִּי מִבֶּטֶן
מִמְּעֵי אִמִּי אַתָּה גוֹזִי

---

a   *Meaning of Heb. uncertain.*
b   *Cf. Ps. 40.14–18.*

   a   *Meaning of Heb. uncertain.*

I sing Your praises always.

⁷I have become an example for many,
  since You are my mighty refuge.

⁸My mouth is full of praise to You,
  glorifying You all day long.

⁹Do not cast me off in old age;
  when my strength fails, do not forsake me!

¹⁰For my enemies talk against me;
  those who wait for me are of one mind,

¹¹saying, "God has forsaken him;
  chase him and catch him,
  for no one will save him!"

¹²O God, be not far from me;
  my God, hasten to my aid!

¹³Let my accusers perish in frustration;
  let those who seek my ruin be clothed in re-
    proach and disgrace!

¹⁴As for me, I will hope always,
  and add to the many praises of You.

¹⁵My mouth tells of Your beneficence,
  of Your deliverance all day long,
  though I know not how to tell it.

¹⁶I come with praise of Your mighty acts, O Lord
  GOD;
  I celebrate Your beneficence, Yours alone.

¹⁷You have let me experience it, God, from my
  youth;
  until now I have proclaimed Your wondrous
    deeds,

¹⁸and even in hoary old age do not forsake me,
  God,
  until I proclaim Your strength to the next gen-
    eration,
  Your mighty acts, to all who are to come,

¹⁹Your beneficence, high as the heavens, O
  God,
  You who have done great things;
  O God, who is Your peer!

בְּךָ תְהִלָּתִי תָמִיד:

⁷ כְּמוֹפֵת הָיִיתִי לְרַבִּים
וְאַתָּה מַחֲסִי־עֹז:

⁸ יִמָּלֵא פִי תְּהִלָּתֶךָ
כָּל־הַיּוֹם תִּפְאַרְתֶּךָ:

⁹ אַל־תַּשְׁלִיכֵנִי לְעֵת זִקְנָה
כִּכְלוֹת כֹּחִי אַל־תַּעַזְבֵנִי:

¹⁰ כִּי־אָמְרוּ אוֹיְבַי לִי
וְשֹׁמְרֵי נַפְשִׁי נוֹעֲצוּ יַחְדָּו:

¹¹ לֵאמֹר אֱלֹהִים עֲזָבוֹ
רִדְפוּ וְתִפְשׂוּהוּ
כִּי־אֵין מַצִּיל:

¹² אֱלֹהִים אַל־תִּרְחַק מִמֶּנִּי
אֱלֹהַי לְעֶזְרָתִי חישה חוּשָׁה:

¹³ יֵבֹשׁוּ יִכְלוּ שֹׂטְנֵי נַפְשִׁי
יַעֲטוּ חֶרְפָּה וּכְלִמָּה מְבַקְשֵׁי
רָעָתִי:

¹⁴ וַאֲנִי תָּמִיד אֲיַחֵל
וְהוֹסַפְתִּי עַל־כָּל־תְּהִלָּתֶךָ:

¹⁵ פִּי ׀ יְסַפֵּר צִדְקָתֶךָ
כָּל־הַיּוֹם תְּשׁוּעָתֶךָ
כִּי לֹא יָדַעְתִּי סְפֹרוֹת:

¹⁶ אָבוֹא בִּגְבֻרוֹת אֲדֹנָי יְהֹוִה
אַזְכִּיר צִדְקָתְךָ לְבַדֶּךָ:

¹⁷ אֱלֹהִים לִמַּדְתַּנִי מִנְּעוּרָי
וְעַד־הֵנָּה אַגִּיד נִפְלְאוֹתֶיךָ:

¹⁸ וְגַם עַד־זִקְנָה ׀ וְשֵׂיבָה אֱלֹהִים
אַל־תַּעַזְבֵנִי
עַד־אַגִּיד זְרוֹעֲךָ לְדוֹר
לְכָל־יָבוֹא גְּבוּרָתֶךָ:

¹⁹ וְצִדְקָתְךָ אֱלֹהִים עַד־מָרוֹם
אֲשֶׁר־עָשִׂיתָ גְדֹלוֹת
אֱלֹהִים מִי כָמוֹךָ:

20You who have made me undergo many troubles
and misfortunes
   will revive me again,
     and raise me up from the depths of the earth.
21You will grant me much greatness,
   You will turn and comfort me.
22Then I will acclaim You to the music of the lyre
   for Your faithfulness, O my God;
   I will sing a hymn to You with a harp,
    O Holy One of Israel.
23My lips shall be jubilant, as I sing a hymn to
You,
   my whole being, which You have redeemed.
24All day long my tongue shall recite Your beneficent acts,
   how those who sought my ruin were frustrated
    and disgraced.

20 אֲשֶׁר הִרְאִיתַנוּ הִרְאִיתַ֣נִי ׀ צָר֥וֹת
רַבּ֗וֹת וְרָע֥וֹת
תָּשׁ֥וּב תחיינו תְּחַיֵּ֑ינִי
וּֽמִתְּהֹמ֥וֹת הָ֝אָ֗רֶץ תָּשׁ֥וּב תַּעֲלֵֽנִי׃
21 תֶּ֤רֶב ׀ גְּדֻלָּתִ֗י וְתִסֹּ֥ב תְּֽנַחֲמֵֽנִי׃
22 גַּם־אֲנִ֤י ׀ אוֹדְךָ֣ בִכְלִי־נֶבֶל֮
אֲמִתְּךָ֢ אֱלֹ֫הָ֥י
אֲזַמְּרָ֣ה לְךָ֣ בְכִנּ֑וֹר
קְ֝ד֗וֹשׁ יִשְׂרָאֵֽל׃
23 תְּרַנֵּ֣נָּה שְׂ֭פָתַי כִּ֣י אֲזַמְּרָה־לָּ֑ךְ
וְ֝נַפְשִׁ֗י אֲשֶׁ֣ר פָּדִֽיתָ׃
24 גַּם־לְשׁוֹנִ֗י כָּל־הַ֭יּוֹם תֶּהְגֶּ֣ה
צִדְקָתֶ֑ךָ
כִּי־בֹ֥שׁוּ כִֽי־חָ֝פְר֗וּ מְבַקְשֵׁ֥י רָעָתִֽי׃

72 Of Solomon.

O God, endow the king with Your judgments,
   the king's son with Your righteousness;
2that he may judge Your people rightly,
   Your lowly ones, justly.
3Let the mountains produce well-being for the
people,
   the hills, the reward of justice.
4Let him champion the lowly among the people,
   deliver the needy folk,
   and crush those who wrong them.
5Let them fear You as long as the sun shines,
   while the moon lasts, generations on end.
6Let him be like rain that falls on a mown field,
   like a downpour of rain on the ground,
7that the righteous may flourish in his time,
   and well-being abound, till the moon is no
more.
8Let him rule from sea to sea,
   from the river to the ends of the earth.

עב לִשְׁלֹמֹ֨ה ׀
אֱלֹהִ֗ים מִ֭שְׁפָּטֶיךָ לְמֶ֣לֶךְ תֵּ֑ן
וְצִדְקָתְךָ֥ לְבֶן־מֶֽלֶךְ׃
2 יָדִ֣ין עַמְּךָ֣ בְצֶ֑דֶק
וַעֲנִיֶּ֥יךָ בְמִשְׁפָּֽט׃
3 יִשְׂא֤וּ הָרִ֓ים שָׁ֖לוֹם לָעָ֑ם
וּ֝גְבָע֗וֹת בִּצְדָקָֽה׃
4 יִשְׁפֹּ֤ט ׀ עֲ‍ֽנִיֵּי־עָ֗ם
י֭וֹשִׁיעַ לִבְנֵ֣י אֶבְי֑וֹן
וִֽידַכֵּ֣א עוֹשֵֽׁק׃
5 יִֽירָא֥וּךָ עִם־שָׁ֑מֶשׁ
וְלִפְנֵ֥י יָ֝רֵ֗חַ דּ֣וֹר דּוֹרִֽים׃
6 יֵ֭רֵד כְּמָטָ֣ר עַל־גֵּ֑ז
כִּ֝רְבִיבִ֗ים זַרְזִ֥יף אָֽרֶץ׃
7 יִֽפְרַח־בְּיָמָ֥יו צַדִּ֑יק
וְרֹ֥ב שָׁ֝ל֗וֹם עַד־בְּלִ֥י יָרֵֽחַ׃
8 וְ֭יֵרְדְּ מִיָּ֣ם עַד־יָ֑ם
וּ֝מִנָּהָ֗ר עַד־אַפְסֵי־אָֽרֶץ׃

9Let desert-dwellers kneel before him,
and his enemies lick the dust.

9לְפָנָיו יִכְרְעוּ צִיִּים
וְאֹיְבָיו עָפָר יְלַחֵכוּ:

10Let kings of Tarshish and the islands pay tribute,
kings of Sheba and Seba offer gifts.

10מַלְכֵי תַרְשִׁישׁ וְאִיִּים מִנְחָה
יָשִׁיבוּ
מַלְכֵי שְׁבָא וּסְבָא אֶשְׁכָּר יַקְרִיבוּ:

11Let all kings bow to him,
and all nations serve him.

11וְיִשְׁתַּחֲווּ־לוֹ כָל־מְלָכִים
כָּל־גּוֹיִם יַעַבְדוּהוּ:

12For he saves the needy who cry out,
the lowly who have no helper.

12כִּי־יַצִּיל אֶבְיוֹן מְשַׁוֵּעַ
וְעָנִי וְאֵין־עֹזֵר לוֹ:

13He cares about the poor and the needy;
He brings the needy deliverance.

13יָחֹס עַל־דַּל וְאֶבְיוֹן
וְנַפְשׁוֹת אֶבְיוֹנִים יוֹשִׁיעַ:

14He redeems them from fraud and lawlessness;
a-the shedding of their blood weighs heavily
upon him.-a

14מִתּוֹךְ וּמֵחָמָס יִגְאַל נַפְשָׁם
וְיֵיקַר דָּמָם בְּעֵינָיו:

15So let him live, and receive gold of Sheba;
let prayers for him be said always,
blessings on him invoked at all times.

15וִיחִי וְיִתֶּן־לוֹ מִזְּהַב שְׁבָא
וְיִתְפַּלֵּל בַּעֲדוֹ תָמִיד
כָּל־הַיּוֹם יְבָרֲכֶנְהוּ:

16b-Let abundant grain be in the land, to the tops
of the mountains;
let his crops thrive like the forest of Lebanon;
and let men sprout up in towns like country
grass.

16יְהִי פִסַּת־בַּר | בָּאָרֶץ בְּרֹאשׁ
הָרִים
יִרְעַשׁ כַּלְּבָנוֹן פִּרְיוֹ
וְיָצִיצוּ מֵעִיר כְּעֵשֶׂב הָאָרֶץ:

17May his name be eternal;
while the sun lasts, may his name endure;-b
let men invoke his blessedness upon themselves;
let all nations count him happy.

17יְהִי שְׁמוֹ לְעוֹלָם
לִפְנֵי־שֶׁמֶשׁ יִנּוֹן שְׁמוֹ
וְיִתְבָּרְכוּ בוֹ
כָּל־גּוֹיִם יְאַשְּׁרוּהוּ:

18Blessed is the LORD God, God of Israel,
who alone does wondrous things;

18בָּרוּךְ | יְהוָה אֱלֹהִים אֱלֹהֵי
יִשְׂרָאֵל
עֹשֵׂה נִפְלָאוֹת לְבַדּוֹ:

19Blessed is His glorious name forever;
His glory fills the whole world.
Amen and Amen.

19וּבָרוּךְ | שֵׁם כְּבוֹדוֹ לְעוֹלָם
וְיִמָּלֵא כְבוֹדוֹ אֶת־כֹּל הָאָרֶץ
אָמֵן | וְאָמֵן:

20End of the prayers of David son of Jesse.

20כָּלּוּ תְפִלּוֹת דָּוִד בֶּן־יִשָׁי:

a-a Or "their life is precious in his sight."
b-b Meaning of some Heb. phrases in these verses uncertain.

73 A psalm of Asaph.

עג מִזְמוֹר לְאָסָף

God is truly good to Israel,
 to those whose heart is pure.
²As for me, my feet had almost strayed,
 my steps were nearly led off course,
³for I envied the wanton;
 I saw the wicked at ease.
⁴Death has no pangs for them;
 their body is healthy.
⁵They have no part in the travail of men;
 they are not afflicted like the rest of mankind.
⁶So pride adorns their necks,
 lawlessness enwraps them as a mantle.
⁷ᵃ-Fat shuts out their eyes;
 their fancies are extravagant.-ᵃ
⁸They scoff and plan evil;
 from their eminence they plan wrongdoing.
⁹They set their mouths against heaven,
 and their tongues range over the earth.
¹⁰ᵃ-So they pound His people again and again,
 until they are drained of their very last tear.-ᵃ
¹¹Then they say, "How could God know?
 Is there knowledge with the Most High?"
¹²Such are the wicked;
 ever tranquil, they amass wealth.

¹³It was for nothing that I kept my heart pure
 and washed my hands in innocence,
 ¹⁴seeing that I have been constantly afflicted,
 that each morning brings new punishments.
¹⁵Had I decided to say these things,
 I should have been false to the circle of Your
 disciples.
¹⁶So I applied myself to understand this,
 but it seemed a hopeless task

אַךְ טוֹב לְיִשְׂרָאֵל אֱלֹהִים
 לְבָרֵי לֵבָב:
² וַאֲנִי כִּמְעַט נָטוּי נָטָיוּ רַגְלָי
 כְּאַיִן שֻׁפְּכָה שֻׁפְּכוּ אֲשֻׁרָי:
³ כִּי־קִנֵּאתִי בַּהוֹלְלִים
 שְׁלוֹם רְשָׁעִים אֶרְאֶה:
⁴ כִּי אֵין חַרְצֻבּוֹת לְמוֹתָם וּבָרִיא
 אוּלָם:
⁵ בַּעֲמַל אֱנוֹשׁ אֵינֵמוֹ
 וְעִם־אָדָם לֹא יְנֻגָּעוּ:
⁶ לָכֵן עֲנָקַתְמוֹ גַאֲוָה
 יַעֲטָף־שִׁית חָמָס לָמוֹ:
⁷ יָצָא מֵחֵלֶב עֵינֵמוֹ
 עָבְרוּ מַשְׂכִּיּוֹת לֵבָב:
⁸ יָמִיקוּ | וִידַבְּרוּ בְרָע עֹשֶׁק
 מִמָּרוֹם יְדַבֵּרוּ:
⁹ שַׁתּוּ בַשָּׁמַיִם פִּיהֶם
 וּלְשׁוֹנָם תִּהֲלַךְ בָּאָרֶץ:
¹⁰ לָכֵן | יָשִׁיב יָשׁוּב עַמּוֹ הֲלֹם
 וּמֵי מָלֵא יִמָּצוּ לָמוֹ:
¹¹ וְאָמְרוּ אֵיכָה יָדַע־אֵל
 וְיֵשׁ דֵּעָה בְעֶלְיוֹן:
¹² הִנֵּה־אֵלֶּה רְשָׁעִים
 וְשַׁלְוֵי עוֹלָם הִשְׂגּוּ־חָיִל:

¹³ אַךְ־רִיק זִכִּיתִי לְבָבִי
 וָאֶרְחַץ בְּנִקָּיוֹן כַּפָּי:
¹⁴ וָאֱהִי נָגוּעַ כָּל־הַיּוֹם
 וְתוֹכַחְתִּי לַבְּקָרִים:
¹⁵ אִם־אָמַרְתִּי אֲסַפְּרָה כְמוֹ
 הִנֵּה דוֹר בָּנֶיךָ בָגָדְתִּי:
¹⁶ וָאֲחַשְּׁבָה לָדַעַת זֹאת
 עָמָל היא הוּא בְעֵינָי:

ᵃ⁻ᵃ *Meaning of Heb. uncertain.*

17till I entered God's sanctuary
and reflected on their fate.

18You surround them with flattery;
You make them fall through blandishments.
19How suddenly are they ruined,
wholly swept away by terrors.
20a-When You are aroused You despise their
image,
as one does a dream after waking, O Lord.-a

21My mind was stripped of its reason,
b-my feelings were numbed.-b
22I was a dolt, without knowledge;
I was brutish toward You.

23Yet I was always with You,
You held my right hand;
24You guided me by Your counsel
c-and led me toward honor.-c
25Whom else have I in heaven?
And having You, I want no one on earth.
26My body and mind fail;
but God is the stayd of my mind, my portion
forever.
27Those who keep far from You perish;
You annihilate all who are untrue to You.
28As for me, nearness to God is good;
I have made the Lord GOD my refuge,
that I may recount all Your works.

74 A *maskil* of Asaph.

Why, O God, do You forever reject us,
do You fume in anger at the flock that You tend?
2Remember the community You made Yours
long ago,

עד 17 עַד־אָב֭וֹא אֶל־מִקְדְּשֵׁי־אֵ֑ל
אָ֝בִ֗ינָה לְאַחֲרִיתָֽם׃
18 אַ֣ךְ בַּ֭חֲלָקוֹת תָּשִׁ֣ית לָ֑מוֹ
הִ֝פַּלְתָּ֗ם לְמַשּׁוּאֽוֹת׃
19 אֵ֤יךְ הָי֣וּ לְשַׁמָּ֣ה כְרָ֑גַע
סָ֥פוּ תַ֝֗מּוּ מִן־בַּלָּהֽוֹת׃
20 כַּחֲל֥וֹם מֵהָקִ֑יץ
אֲ֝דֹנָ֗י בָּעִ֤יר ׀ צַלְמָ֬ם תִּבְזֶֽה׃
21 כִּ֭י יִתְחַמֵּ֣ץ לְבָבִ֑י
וְ֝כִלְיוֹתַ֗י אֶשְׁתּוֹנָֽן׃
22 וַאֲנִי־בַ֭עַר וְלֹ֣א אֵדָ֑ע
בְּ֝הֵמ֗וֹת הָיִ֥יתִי עִמָּֽךְ׃
23 וַאֲנִ֣י תָמִ֣יד עִמָּ֑ךְ
אָ֝חַ֗זְתָּ בְּיַד־יְמִינִֽי׃
24 בַּעֲצָתְךָ֥ תַנְחֵ֑נִי
וְ֝אַחַ֗ר כָּב֥וֹד תִּקָּחֵֽנִי׃
25 מִי־לִ֥י בַשָּׁמָ֑יִם
וְ֝עִמְּךָ֗ לֹא־חָפַ֥צְתִּי בָאָֽרֶץ׃
26 כָּלָ֥ה שְׁאֵרִ֗י וּלְבָ֫בִ֥י
צוּר־לְבָבִ֥י וְחֶלְקִ֑י אֱלֹהִ֣ים לְעוֹלָֽם׃
27 כִּֽי־הִנֵּ֣ה רְחֵקֶ֣יךָ יֹאבֵ֑דוּ
הִ֝צְמַ֗תָּה כָּל־זוֹנֶ֥ה מִמֶּֽךָּ׃
28 וַאֲנִ֤י ׀ קִֽרֲבַ֥ת אֱלֹהִ֗ים לִ֫י־ט֥וֹב
שַׁתִּ֤י ׀ בַּאדֹנָ֣י יְהֹוִ֣ה מַחְסִ֑י
לְ֝סַפֵּ֗ר כָּל־מַלְאֲכוֹתֶֽיךָ׃

עד מַשְׂכִּ֗יל לְאָ֫סָ֥ף
לָמָ֣ה אֱ֭לֹהִים זָנַ֣חְתָּ לָנֶ֑צַח
יֶעְשַׁ֥ן אַ֝פְּךָ֗ בְּצֹ֣אן מַרְעִיתֶֽךָ׃
2 זְכֹ֤ר עֲדָתְךָ֨ ׀ קָנִ֣יתָ קֶּ֗דֶם

b-b   Lit. "I was pierced through in my kidneys."
c-c   Meaning of Heb. uncertain; others "And afterward receive me with
     glory."
d   Lit. "rock."

Your very own tribe that You redeemed,
Mount Zion, where You dwell.

3 *a*-Bestir Yourself-*a* because of the *b*-perpetual tumult,-*b*
all the outrages of the enemy in the sanctuary.

4 Your foes roar inside Your meeting-place;
they take their signs for true signs.

5 *b*-It is like men wielding axes
against a gnarled tree;

6 with hatchet and pike
they hacked away at its carved work.-*b*

7 They made Your sanctuary go up in flames;
they brought low in dishonor the dwelling-place of Your presence.

8 They resolved, "Let us destroy them altogether!"
They burned all God's tabernacles in the land.

9 No signs appear for us;
there is no longer any prophet;
no one among us knows for how long.

10 Till when, O God, will the foe blaspheme,
will the enemy forever revile Your name?

11 Why do You hold back Your hand, Your right hand?
b-Draw it out of Your bosom!-*b*

12 O God, my King from of old,
who brings deliverance throughout the land;

13 it was You who drove back the sea with Your might,
who smashed the heads of the monsters in the waters;

14 it was You who crushed the heads of Leviathan,
who left him as food for *c*-the denizens of the desert;-*c*

15 it was You who released springs and torrents,
who made mighty rivers run dry;

16 the day is Yours, the night also;

גָּאַלְתָּ שֵׁבֶט נַחֲלָתֶךָ
הַר־צִיּוֹן זֶה ׀ שָׁכַנְתָּ בּוֹ׃

3 הָרִימָה פְעָמֶיךָ לְמַשֻּׁאוֹת נֶצַח
כָּל־הֵרַע אוֹיֵב בַּקֹּדֶשׁ׃

4 שָׁאֲגוּ צֹרְרֶיךָ בְּקֶרֶב מוֹעֲדֶךָ
שָׂמוּ אוֹתֹתָם אֹתוֹת׃

5 יִוָּדַע כְּמֵבִיא לְמָעְלָה
בִּסְבָךְ־עֵץ קַרְדֻּמּוֹת׃

6 וְעַתָּה פִּתּוּחֶיהָ יָּחַד
בְּכַשִּׁיל וְכֵילַפֹּת יַהֲלֹמוּן׃

7 שִׁלְחוּ* בָאֵשׁ מִקְדָּשֶׁךָ
לָאָרֶץ חִלְּלוּ מִשְׁכַּן־שְׁמֶךָ׃

8 אָמְרוּ בְלִבָּם נִינָם יָחַד
שָׂרְפוּ כָל־מוֹעֲדֵי־אֵל בָּאָרֶץ׃

9 אוֹתֹתֵינוּ לֹא רָאִינוּ
אֵין־עוֹד נָבִיא
וְלֹא־אִתָּנוּ יֹדֵעַ עַד־מָה׃

10 עַד־מָתַי אֱלֹהִים יְחָרֶף צָר
יְנָאֵץ אוֹיֵב שִׁמְךָ לָנֶצַח׃

11 לָמָּה תָשִׁיב יָדְךָ וִימִינֶךָ
מִקֶּרֶב חוקר חֵיקְךָ כַלֵּה׃

12 וֵאלֹהִים מַלְכִּי מִקֶּדֶם
פֹּעֵל יְשׁוּעוֹת בְּקֶרֶב הָאָרֶץ׃

13 אַתָּה פוֹרַרְתָּ בְעָזְּךָ יָם
שִׁבַּרְתָּ רָאשֵׁי תַנִּינִים עַל־הַמָּיִם׃

14 אַתָּה רִצַּצְתָּ רָאשֵׁי לִוְיָתָן
תִּתְּנֶנּוּ מַאֲכָל לְעָם לְצִיִּים׃

15 אַתָּה בָקַעְתָּ מַעְיָן וָנָחַל
אַתָּה הוֹבַשְׁתָּ נַהֲרוֹת אֵיתָן׃

16 לְךָ יוֹם אַף־לְךָ לָיְלָה

---

a-a   Lit. "Lift up Your feet."
b-b   Meaning of Heb. uncertain.
c-c   Or "seafaring men"; meaning of Heb. uncertain.

v. 7. ל' רפה

it was You who set in place the orb of the sun;

17You fixed all the boundaries of the earth;

   summer and winter—You made them.

אַתָּה הֲכִינוֹתָ מָאוֹר וָשָׁמֶשׁ:

17 אַתָּה הִצַּבְתָּ כָּל־גְּבוּלוֹת אָרֶץ

קַיִץ וָחֹרֶף אַתָּה יְצַרְתָּם:

18Be mindful of how the enemy blasphemes the

   LORD,

   how base people revile Your name.

19Do not deliver Your dove to the wild beast;

   do not ignore forever the band of Your lowly

   ones.

20Look to the covenant!

For the dark places of the land are full of the

   haunts of lawlessness.

21Let not the downtrodden turn away disap-

   pointed;

   let the poor and needy praise Your name.

22Rise, O God, champion Your cause;

   be mindful that You are blasphemed by base

   men all day long.

23Do not ignore the shouts of Your foes,

   the din of Your adversaries that ascends all

   the time.

18 זְכָר־זֹאת אוֹיֵב חֵרֵף ׀ יְהוָה

וְעַם נָבָל נִאֲצוּ שְׁמֶךָ:

19 אַל־תִּתֵּן לְחַיַּת נֶפֶשׁ תּוֹרֶךָ

חַיַּת עֲנִיֶּיךָ אַל־תִּשְׁכַּח לָנֶצַח:

20 הַבֵּט לַבְּרִית

כִּי מָלְאוּ מַחֲשַׁכֵּי־אֶרֶץ נְאוֹת

חָמָס:

21 אַל־יָשֹׁב דַּךְ נִכְלָם

עָנִי וְאֶבְיוֹן יְהַלְלוּ שְׁמֶךָ:

22 קוּמָה אֱלֹהִים רִיבָה רִיבֶךָ

זְכֹר חֶרְפָּתְךָ מִנִּי־נָבָל כָּל־הַיּוֹם:

23 אַל־תִּשְׁכַּח קוֹל צֹרְרֶיךָ

שְׁאוֹן קָמֶיךָ עֹלֶה תָמִיד:

75 For the leader; *al tashḥeth.*

A psalm of Asaph, a song.

עד לַמְנַצֵּחַ אַל־תַּשְׁחֵת

מִזְמוֹר לְאָסָף שִׁיר:

2We praise You, O God;

   we praise You;

   Your presence is near;

   men tell of Your wondrous deeds.

2 הוֹדִינוּ לְּךָ ׀ אֱלֹהִים

הוֹדִינוּ

וְקָרוֹב שְׁמֶךָ

סִפְּרוּ נִפְלְאוֹתֶיךָ:

3"At the time I choose,

   I will give judgment equitably.

4Earth and all its inhabitants dissolve;

   it is I who keep its pillars firm.   *Selah.*

5To wanton men I say, 'Do not be wanton!'

   to the wicked, 'Do not lift up your horns!'"

3 כִּי אֶקַּח מוֹעֵד

אֲנִי מֵישָׁרִים אֶשְׁפֹּט:

4 נְמֹגִים אֶרֶץ וְכָל־יֹשְׁבֶיהָ

אָנֹכִי תִכַּנְתִּי עַמּוּדֶיהָ   סֶלָה:

5 אָמַרְתִּי לַהוֹלְלִים אַל־תָּהֹלּוּ

וְלָרְשָׁעִים אַל־תָּרִימוּ קָרֶן:

6Do not lift your horns up high
  a-in vainglorious bluster.-*a*
7For what lifts a man comes not from the east
  or the west or the wilderness;*b*
8for God it is who gives judgment;
  He brings down one man, He lifts up another.
9There is a cup in the LORD's hand
  with foaming wine fully mixed;
  from this He pours;
  all the wicked of the earth drink,
  draining it to the very dregs.
10As for me, I will declare forever,
  I will sing a hymn to the God of Jacob.

11"All the horns of the wicked I will cut;
  but the horns of the righteous shall be lifted
  up."

76

For the leader; with instrumental music.
A psalm of Asaph, a song.

2God has made Himself known in Judah,
  His name is great in Israel;
3Salem became His abode;
  Zion, His den.
4There He broke the fiery arrows of the bow,
  the shield and the sword of war.   *Selah.*

5You were resplendent,
  glorious, on the mountains of prey.
6The stout-hearted were despoiled;
  they were in a stupor;
  the bravest of men could not lift a hand.
7At Your blast, O God of Jacob,
  horse and chariot lay stunned.
8O You! You are awesome!
Who can withstand You
  when You are enraged?

6 אַל־תָּרִימוּ לַמָּרוֹם קַרְנְכֶם
תְּדַבְּרוּ בְצַוָּאר עָתָק:
7 כִּי לֹא מִמּוֹצָא וּמִמַּעֲרָב
וְלֹא מִמִּדְבַּר הָרִים:
8 כִּי־אֱלֹהִים שֹׁפֵט
זֶה יַשְׁפִּיל וְזֶה יָרִים:
9 כִּי כוֹס בְּיַד־יְהֹוָה
וְיַיִן חָמַר ׀ מָלֵא מֶסֶךְ
וַיַּגֵּר מִזֶּה
אַךְ־שְׁמָרֶיהָ יִמְצוּ יִשְׁתּוּ
כֹּל רִשְׁעֵי־אָרֶץ:
10 וַאֲנִי אַגִּיד לְעֹלָם
אֲזַמְּרָה לֵאלֹהֵי יַעֲקֹב:

11 וְכָל־קַרְנֵי רְשָׁעִים אֲגַדֵּעַ
תְּרוֹמַמְנָה קַרְנוֹת צַדִּיק:

עו לַמְנַצֵּחַ בִּנְגִינֹת
מִזְמוֹר לְאָסָף שִׁיר:

2 נוֹדָע בִּיהוּדָה אֱלֹהִים
בְּיִשְׂרָאֵל גָּדוֹל שְׁמוֹ:
3 וַיְהִי בְשָׁלֵם סֻכּוֹ
וּמְעוֹנָתוֹ בְצִיּוֹן:
4 שָׁמָּה שִׁבַּר רִשְׁפֵי־קָשֶׁת
מָגֵן וְחֶרֶב וּמִלְחָמָה   סֶלָה:

5 נָאוֹר אַתָּה
אַדִּיר מֵהַרְרֵי־טָרֶף:
6 אֶשְׁתּוֹלְלוּ ׀ אַבִּירֵי לֵב
נָמוּ שְׁנָתָם
וְלֹא־מָצְאוּ כָל־אַנְשֵׁי־חַיִל יְדֵיהֶם:
7 מִגַּעֲרָתְךָ אֱלֹהֵי יַעֲקֹב
נִרְדָּם וְרֶכֶב וָסוּס:
8 אַתָּה ׀ נוֹרָא אַתָּה
וּמִי־יַעֲמֹד לְפָנֶיךָ
מֵאָז אַפֶּךָ:

---

a-a   Lit. "with arrogant neck you speak."
b   Reading *midbār* with many mss.

9In heaven You pronounced sentence;
   the earth was numbed with fright
10as God rose to execute judgment,
   to deliver all the lowly of the earth.   *Selah.*

⁹ מִשָּׁמַיִם הִשְׁמַעְתָּ דִּין
אֶרֶץ יָרְאָה וְשָׁקָטָה:
10 בְּקוּם־לַמִּשְׁפָּט אֱלֹהִים
לְהוֹשִׁיעַ כָּל־עַנְוֵי־אֶרֶץ   סֶלָה:

11ᵃ-The fiercest of men shall acknowledge You,
   when You gird on the last bit of fury.-ᵃ
12Make vows and pay them to the Lᴏʀᴅ your God;
   ᵃ-all who are around Him shall bring tribute to
      the Awesome One.-ᵃ
13He curbs the spirit of princes,
   inspires awe in the kings of the earth.

11 כִּי־חֲמַת אָדָם תּוֹדֶךָּ
שְׁאֵרִית חֵמֹת תַּחְגֹּר:
12 נִדְרוּ וְשַׁלְּמוּ לַיהוָה אֱלֹהֵיכֶם
כָּל־סְבִיבָיו יוֹבִילוּ שַׁי לַמּוֹרָא:
13 יִבְצֹר רוּחַ נְגִידִים
נוֹרָא לְמַלְכֵי־אָרֶץ:

77

For the leader; on *Jeduthun.*
Of Asaph. A psalm.

עז לַמְנַצֵּחַ עַל־יְדִיתוּן יְדוּתוּן
לְאָסָף מִזְמוֹר:

2I cry aloud to God;
   I cry to God that He may give ear to me.
3In my time of distress I turn to the Lord,
   ᵃ-with my hand [uplifted];
   [my eyes] flow all night without respite;-ᵃ
   I will not be comforted.
4I call God to mind, I moan,
   I complain, my spirit fails.   *Selah.*

2 קוֹלִי אֶל־אֱלֹהִים וְאֶצְעָקָה
קוֹלִי אֶל־אֱלֹהִים וְהַאֲזִין אֵלָי:
3 בְּיוֹם צָרָתִי אֲדֹנָי דָּרָשְׁתִּי
יָדִי |
לַיְלָה נִגְּרָה וְלֹא תָפוּג
מֵאֲנָה הִנָּחֵם נַפְשִׁי:
4 אֶזְכְּרָה אֱלֹהִים וְאֶהֱמָיָה
אָשִׂיחָה | וְתִתְעַטֵּף רוּחִי   סֶלָה:

5You have held my eyelids open;
   I am overwrought, I cannot speak.
6My thoughts turn to days of old,
   to years long past.
7I recall at night their jibes at me;
   I commune with myself;
   my spirit inquires,
8"Will the Lord reject forever
   and never again show favor?
9Has His faithfulness disappeared forever?
Will His promise be unfulfilled for all time?
10Has God forgotten how to pity?
Has He in anger stifled His compassion?" *Selah.*

5 אָחַזְתָּ שְׁמֻרוֹת עֵינָי
נִפְעַמְתִּי וְלֹא אֲדַבֵּר:
6 חִשַּׁבְתִּי יָמִים מִקֶּדֶם
שְׁנוֹת עוֹלָמִים:
7 אֶזְכְּרָה נְגִינָתִי בַּלָּיְלָה
עִם־לְבָבִי אָשִׂיחָה
וַיְחַפֵּשׂ רוּחִי:
8 הַלְעוֹלָמִים יִזְנַח | אֲדֹנָי
וְלֹא־יֹסִיף לִרְצוֹת עוֹד:
9 הֶאָפֵס לָנֶצַח חַסְדּוֹ
גָּמַר אֹמֶר לְדֹר וָדֹר:
10 הֲשָׁכַח חַנּוֹת אֵל
אִם־קָפַץ בְּאַף רַחֲמָיו   סֶלָה:

a-a   *Meaning of Heb. uncertain.*
a-a   *Meaning of Heb. uncertain.*

1506

11And I said, *a*-"It is my fault
　　that the right hand of the Most High has
　　　changed."-*a*

12I recall the deeds of the LORD;
　　yes, I recall Your wonders of old;
　　　13I recount all Your works;
　　　　I speak of Your acts.

14O God, Your ways are holiness;
　　what god is as great as God?

15You are the God who works wonders;
　　You have manifested Your strength among the
　　　peoples.

16By Your arm You redeemed Your people,
　　the children of Jacob and Joseph.　　*Selah.*

17The waters saw You, O God,
　　the waters saw You and were convulsed;
　　the very deep quaked as well.

18Clouds streamed water;
　　the heavens rumbled;
　　Your arrows flew about;
　　　19Your thunder rumbled like wheels;
　　lightning lit up the world;
　　the earth quaked and trembled.

20Your way was through the sea,
　　Your path, through the mighty waters;
　　Your tracks could not be seen.

21You led Your people like a flock
　　in the care of Moses and Aaron.

78 A *maskil* of Asaph.

Give ear, my people, to my teaching,
　　turn your ear to what I say.
2I will expound a theme,
　　hold forth on the lessons of the past,
　　　3things we have heard and known,
　　　that our fathers have told us.

וָאֹמַר חַלּוֹתִי הִיא 11
שְׁנוֹת יְמִין עֶלְיוֹן:

אֶזְכִּיר אַזְכּוֹר מַעֲלָלֵי־יָהּ 12
כִּי־אֶזְכְּרָה מִקֶּדֶם פִּלְאֶךָ:
וְהָגִיתִי בְכָל־פָּעֳלֶךָ 13
וּבַעֲלִילוֹתֶיךָ אָשִׂיחָה:
אֱלֹהִים בַּקֹּדֶשׁ דַּרְכֶּךָ 14
מִי־אֵל גָּדוֹל כֵּאלֹהִים:
אַתָּה הָאֵל עֹשֵׂה פֶלֶא 15
הוֹדַעְתָּ בָעַמִּים עֻזֶּךָ:
גָּאַלְתָּ בִּזְרוֹעַ עַמֶּךָ 16
בְּנֵי־יַעֲקֹב וְיוֹסֵף　סֶלָה:
רָאוּךָ מַּיִם ׀ אֱלֹהִים 17
רָאוּךָ מַּיִם יָחִילוּ
אַף יִרְגְּזוּ תְהֹמוֹת:
זֹרְמוּ מַיִם ׀ עָבוֹת 18
קוֹל נָתְנוּ שְׁחָקִים
אַף־חֲצָצֶיךָ יִתְהַלָּכוּ:
קוֹל רַעַמְךָ ׀ בַּגַּלְגַּל 19
הֵאִירוּ בְרָקִים תֵּבֵל
רָגְזָה וַתִּרְעַשׁ הָאָרֶץ:
בַּיָּם דַּרְכֶּךָ 20
ושבילוך וּשְׁבִילְךָ בְּמַיִם רַבִּים
וְעִקְּבוֹתֶיךָ לֹא נֹדָעוּ:
נָחִיתָ כַצֹּאן עַמֶּךָ 21
בְּיַד־מֹשֶׁה וְאַהֲרֹן:

עח מַשְׂכִּיל לְאָסָף

הַאֲזִינָה עַמִּי תּוֹרָתִי
הַטּוּ אָזְנְכֶם לְאִמְרֵי־פִי:
אֶפְתְּחָה בְמָשָׁל פִּי 2
אַבִּיעָה חִידוֹת מִנִּי־קֶדֶם:
אֲשֶׁר שָׁמַעְנוּ וַנֵּדָעֵם 3
וַאֲבוֹתֵינוּ סִפְּרוּ־לָנוּ:

4We will not withhold them from their children,
  telling the coming generation
  the praises of the LORD and His might,
  and the wonders He performed.

5He established a decree in Jacob,
  ordained a teaching in Israel,
  charging our fathers
  to make them known to their children,
6that a future generation might know
  —children yet to be born—
  and in turn tell their children
7that they might put their confidence in God,
  and not forget God's great deeds,
  but observe His commandments,
8and not be like their fathers,
  a wayward and defiant generation,
  a generation whose heart was inconstant,
  whose spirit was not true to God.

9Like the Ephraimite bowmen
  who played false in the day of battle,
10they did not keep God's covenant,
  they refused to follow His instruction;
11they forgot His deeds
  and the wonders that He showed them.
12He performed marvels in the sight of their
    fathers,
  in the land of Egypt, the plain of Zoan.
13He split the sea and took them through it;
  He made the waters stand like a wall.
14He led them with a cloud by day,
  and throughout the night by the light of fire.
15He split rocks in the wilderness
  and gave them drink as if from the great deep.
16He brought forth streams from a rock
  and made them flow down like a river.

17But they went on sinning against Him,
  defying the Most High in the parched land.

4 לֹא נְכַחֵד ׀ מִבְּנֵיהֶם
לְדוֹר אַחֲרוֹן מְסַפְּרִים
תְּהִלּוֹת יְהוָה וֶעֱזוּזוֹ
וְנִפְלְאֹתָיו אֲשֶׁר עָשָׂה:
5 וַיָּקֶם עֵדוּת ׀ בְּיַעֲקֹב
וְתוֹרָה שָׂם בְּיִשְׂרָאֵל
אֲשֶׁר צִוָּה אֶת־אֲבוֹתֵינוּ
לְהוֹדִיעָם לִבְנֵיהֶם:
6 לְמַעַן יֵדְעוּ ׀ דּוֹר אַחֲרוֹן
בָּנִים יִוָּלֵדוּ
יָקֻמוּ וִיסַפְּרוּ לִבְנֵיהֶם:
7 וְיָשִׂימוּ בֵאלֹהִים כִּסְלָם
וְלֹא יִשְׁכְּחוּ מַעַלְלֵי־אֵל
וּמִצְוֹתָיו יִנְצֹרוּ:
8 וְלֹא יִהְיוּ ׀ כַּאֲבוֹתָם
דּוֹר סוֹרֵר וּמֹרֶה
דּוֹר לֹא־הֵכִין לִבּוֹ
וְלֹא־נֶאֶמְנָה אֶת־אֵל רוּחוֹ:
9 בְּנֵי־אֶפְרַיִם נוֹשְׁקֵי רוֹמֵי־קָשֶׁת
הָפְכוּ בְּיוֹם קְרָב:
10 לֹא שָׁמְרוּ בְּרִית אֱלֹהִים
וּבְתוֹרָתוֹ מֵאֲנוּ לָלֶכֶת:
11 וַיִּשְׁכְּחוּ עֲלִילוֹתָיו
וְנִפְלְאוֹתָיו אֲשֶׁר הֶרְאָם:
12 נֶגֶד אֲבוֹתָם עָשָׂה פֶלֶא
בְּאֶרֶץ מִצְרַיִם שְׂדֵה־צֹעַן:
13 בָּקַע יָם וַיַּעֲבִירֵם
וַיַּצֶּב־מַיִם כְּמוֹ־נֵד:
14 וַיַּנְחֵם בֶּעָנָן יוֹמָם
וְכָל־הַלַּיְלָה בְּאוֹר אֵשׁ:
15 יְבַקַּע צֻרִים בַּמִּדְבָּר
וַיַּשְׁקְ כִּתְהֹמוֹת רַבָּה:
16 וַיּוֹצִא נוֹזְלִים מִסָּלַע
וַיּוֹרֶד כַּנְּהָרוֹת מָיִם:
17 וַיּוֹסִיפוּ עוֹד לַחֲטֹא־לוֹ
לַמְרוֹת עֶלְיוֹן בַּצִּיָּה:

18To test God was in their mind
  when they demanded food for themselves.
19They spoke against God, saying,
  "Can God spread a feast in the wilderness?
20True, He struck the rock and waters flowed,
  streams gushed forth;
  but can He provide bread?
Can He supply His people with meat?"
21The Lord heard and He raged;
  fire broke out against Jacob,
  anger flared up at Israel,
22because they did not put their trust in God,
  did not rely on His deliverance.
23So He commanded the skies above,
  He opened the doors of heaven
24and rained manna upon them for food,
  giving them heavenly grain.
25Each man ate a hero's meal;
  He sent them provision in plenty.
26He set the east wind moving in heaven,
  and drove the south wind by His might.
27He rained meat on them like dust,
  winged birds like the sands of the sea,
28making them come down inside His camp,
  around His dwelling-place.
29They ate till they were sated;
  He gave them what they craved.
30They had not yet wearied of what they craved,
  the food was still in their mouths
31when God's anger flared up at them.
He slew their sturdiest,
  struck down the youth of Israel.
32Nonetheless, they went on sinning
  and had no faith in His wonders.
33He made their days end in futility,
  their years in sudden death.
34When He struck[a] them, they turned to Him
  and sought God once again.

---

a Lit. "killed."

18 וַיְנַסּוּ־אֵל בִּלְבָבָם
לִשְׁאָל־אֹכֶל לְנַפְשָׁם׃
19 וַיְדַבְּרוּ בֵּאלֹהִים אָמְרוּ
הֲיוּכַל אֵל לַעֲרֹךְ שֻׁלְחָן בַּמִּדְבָּר׃
20 הֵן הִכָּה־צוּר ׀ וַיָּזוּבוּ מַיִם
וּנְחָלִים יִשְׁטֹפוּ
הֲגַם־לֶחֶם יוּכַל תֵּת
אִם־יָכִין שְׁאֵר לְעַמּוֹ׃
21 לָכֵן ׀ שָׁמַע יְהֹוָה וַיִּתְעַבָּר
וְאֵשׁ נִשְּׂקָה בְיַעֲקֹב
וְגַם־אַף עָלָה בְיִשְׂרָאֵל׃
22 כִּי לֹא הֶאֱמִינוּ בֵּאלֹהִים
וְלֹא בָטְחוּ בִּישׁוּעָתוֹ׃
23 וַיְצַו שְׁחָקִים מִמָּעַל
וְדַלְתֵי שָׁמַיִם פָּתָח׃
24 וַיַּמְטֵר עֲלֵיהֶם מָן לֶאֱכֹל
וּדְגַן־שָׁמַיִם נָתַן לָמוֹ׃
25 לֶחֶם אַבִּירִים אָכַל אִישׁ
צֵידָה שָׁלַח לָהֶם לָשֹׂבַע׃
26 יַסַּע קָדִים בַּשָּׁמָיִם
וַיְנַהֵג בְּעֻזּוֹ תֵימָן׃
27 וַיַּמְטֵר עֲלֵיהֶם כֶּעָפָר שְׁאֵר
וּכְחוֹל יַמִּים עוֹף כָּנָף׃
28 וַיַּפֵּל בְּקֶרֶב מַחֲנֵהוּ
סָבִיב לְמִשְׁכְּנֹתָיו׃
29 וַיֹּאכְלוּ וַיִּשְׂבְּעוּ מְאֹד
וְתַאֲוָתָם יָבִא לָהֶם׃
30 לֹא־זָרוּ מִתַּאֲוָתָם
עוֹד אָכְלָם בְּפִיהֶם׃
31 וְאַף אֱלֹהִים ׀ עָלָה בָהֶם
וַיַּהֲרֹג בְּמִשְׁמַנֵּיהֶם
וּבַחוּרֵי יִשְׂרָאֵל הִכְרִיעַ׃
32 בְּכָל־זֹאת חָטְאוּ־עוֹד
וְלֹא־הֶאֱמִינוּ בְּנִפְלְאוֹתָיו׃
33 וַיְכַל־בַּהֶבֶל יְמֵיהֶם
וּשְׁנוֹתָם בַּבֶּהָלָה׃
34 אִם־הֲרָגָם וּדְרָשׁוּהוּ
וְשָׁבוּ וְשִׁחֲרוּ־אֵל׃

35They remembered that God was their rock,
  God Most High, their Redeemer.
36Yet they deceived Him with their speech,
  lied to Him with their words;
37their hearts were inconstant toward Him;
  they were untrue to His covenant.
38But He, being merciful, forgave iniquity
  and would not destroy;
  He restrained His wrath time and again
  and did not give full vent to His fury;
39for He remembered that they were but flesh,
  a passing breath that does not return.

40How often did they defy Him in the wilderness,
  did they grieve Him in the wasteland!
41Again and again they tested God,
  vexed[b] the Holy One of Israel.
42They did not remember His strength,
  or the day He redeemed them from the foe;
43how He displayed His signs in Egypt,
  His wonders in the plain of Zoan.
44He turned their rivers into blood;
  He made their waters undrinkable.
45He inflicted upon them swarms of insects to
    devour them,
  frogs to destroy them.
46He gave their crops over to grubs,
  their produce to locusts.
47He killed their vines with hail,
  their sycamores [c-with frost.-c]
48He gave their beasts over to hail,
  their cattle to lightning bolts.
49He inflicted His burning anger upon them,
  wrath, indignation, trouble,
  a band of deadly messengers.
50He cleared a path for His anger;
  He did not stop short of slaying them,
  but gave them over to pestilence.

35 וַיִּזְכְּרוּ כִּי־אֱלֹהִים צוּרָם
  וְאֵל עֶלְיוֹן גֹּאֲלָם:
36 *וַיְפַתּוּהוּ בְּפִיהֶם
  וּבִלְשׁוֹנָם יְכַזְּבוּ־לֽוֹ:
37 וְלִבָּם לֹא־נָכוֹן עִמּוֹ
  וְלֹא נֶאֶמְנוּ בִּבְרִיתֽוֹ:
38 וְהוּא רַחוּם | יְכַפֵּר עָוֺן
  וְלֹא־יַשְׁחִית
  וְהִרְבָּה לְהָשִׁיב אַפּוֹ
  וְלֹא־יָעִיר כָּל־חֲמָתֽוֹ:
39 וַיִּזְכֹּר כִּי־בָשָׂר הֵמָּה
  רוּחַ הוֹלֵךְ וְלֹא יָשֽׁוּב:
40 כַּמָּה יַמְרוּהוּ בַמִּדְבָּר
  יַעֲצִיבוּהוּ בִּישִׁימֽוֹן:
41 וַיָּשׁוּבוּ וַיְנַסּוּ אֵל
  וּקְדוֹשׁ יִשְׂרָאֵל הִתְווּ:
42 לֹא־זָכְרוּ אֶת־יָדוֹ
  יוֹם אֲשֶׁר־פָּדָם מִנִּי־צָֽר:
43 אֲשֶׁר־שָׂם בְּמִצְרַיִם אֹתוֹתָיו
  וּמוֹפְתָיו בִּשְׂדֵה־צֹֽעַן:
44 וַיַּהֲפֹךְ לְדָם יְאֹרֵיהֶם
  וְנֹזְלֵיהֶם בַּל־יִשְׁתָּיֽוּן:
45 יְשַׁלַּח בָּהֶם עָרֹב וַיֹּאכְלֵם
  וּצְפַרְדֵּעַ וַתַּשְׁחִיתֵֽם:
46 וַיִּתֵּן לֶחָסִיל יְבוּלָם
  וִיגִיעָם לָאַרְבֶּֽה:
47 יַהֲרֹג בַּבָּרָד גַּפְנָם
  וְשִׁקְמוֹתָם בַּחֲנָמַֽל:
48 וַיַּסְגֵּר לַבָּרָד בְּעִירָם
  וּמִקְנֵיהֶם לָרְשָׁפִֽים:
49 יְשַׁלַּח־בָּם | חֲרוֹן אַפּוֹ
  עֶבְרָה וָזַעַם וְצָרָה
  מִשְׁלַחַת מַלְאֲכֵי רָעִֽים:
50 יְפַלֵּס נָתִיב לְאַפּוֹ
  לֹא־חָשַׂךְ מִמָּוֶת נַפְשָׁם
  וְחַיָּתָם לַדֶּבֶר הִסְגִּֽיר:

⁵¹He struck every first-born in Egypt,
    the first fruits of their vigor in the tents of Ham.

⁵²He set His people moving like sheep,
    drove them like a flock in the wilderness.

⁵³He led them in safety; they were unafraid;
    as for their enemies, the sea covered them.

⁵⁴He brought them to His holy realm,ᵈ
    the mountain His right hand had acquired.

⁵⁵He expelled nations before them,
    ᵉ-settled the tribes of Israel in their tents,
    allotting them their portion by the line.-ᵉ

⁵⁶Yet they defiantly tested God Most High,
    and did not observe His decrees.

⁵⁷They fell away, disloyal like their fathers;
    they played false like a treacherous bow.

⁵⁸They vexed Him with their high places;
    they incensed Him with their idols.

⁵⁹God heard it and was enraged;
    He utterly rejected Israel.

⁶⁰He forsook the tabernacle of Shiloh,
    the tent He had set among men.

⁶¹He let His mightᶠ go into captivity,
    His glory into the hands of the foe.

⁶²He gave His people over to the sword;
    He was enraged at His very own.

⁶³Fire consumed their young men,
    and their maidens ᵍ-remained unwed.-ᵍ

⁶⁴Their priests fell by the sword,
    and their widows could not weep.

⁶⁵The Lord awoke as from sleep,
    like a warrior ᶜ-shaking off-ᶜ wine.

⁶⁶He beat back His foes,
    dealing them lasting disgrace.

⁶⁷He rejected the clan of Joseph;
    He did not choose the tribe of Ephraim.

---

51 וַיַּ֣ךְ כָּל־בְּכ֣וֹר בְּמִצְרָ֑יִם
רֵאשִׁ֥ית א֝וֹנִ֗ים בְּאָהֳלֵי־חָֽם׃

52 וַיַּסַּ֣ע כַּצֹּ֣אן עַמּ֑וֹ
וַֽיְנַהֲגֵ֥ם כַּ֝עֵ֗דֶר בַּמִּדְבָּֽר׃

53 וַיַּנְחֵ֣ם לָ֭בֶטַח וְלֹ֣א פָחָ֑דוּ
וְאֶת־א֝וֹיְבֵיהֶ֗ם כִּסָּ֥ה הַיָּֽם׃

54 וַ֭יְבִיאֵם אֶל־גְּב֣וּל קָדְשׁ֑וֹ
הַר־זֶ֝֗ה קָנְתָ֥ה יְמִינֽוֹ׃

55 וַיְגָ֤רֶשׁ מִפְּנֵיהֶ֨ם ׀ גּוֹיִ֗ם
וַֽ֭יַּפִּילֵם בְּחֶ֣בֶל נַחֲלָ֑ה
וַיַּשְׁכֵּ֥ן בְּ֝אָהֳלֵיהֶ֗ם שִׁבְטֵ֥י יִשְׂרָאֵֽל׃

56 וַיְנַסּ֣וּ וַ֭יַּמְר֤וּ אֶת־אֱלֹהִ֣ים עֶלְי֑וֹן
וְ֝עֵדוֹתָ֗יו לֹ֣א שָׁמָֽרוּ׃

57 וַיִּסֹּ֣גוּ וַֽ֭יִּבְגְּדוּ כַּאֲבוֹתָ֑ם
נֶ֝הְפְּכ֗וּ כְּקֶ֣שֶׁת רְמִיָּֽה׃

58 וַיַּכְעִיס֥וּהוּ בְּבָמוֹתָ֑ם
וּ֝בִפְסִילֵיהֶ֗ם יַקְנִיאֽוּהוּ׃

59 שָׁמַ֣ע אֱ֭לֹהִים וַֽיִּתְעַבָּ֑ר
וַיִּמְאַ֥ס מְ֝אֹ֗ד בְּיִשְׂרָאֵֽל׃

60 וַ֭יִּטֹּשׁ מִשְׁכַּ֣ן שִׁל֑וֹ
אֹ֝֗הֶל שִׁכֵּ֥ן בָּאָדָֽם׃

61 וַיִּתֵּ֣ן לַשְּׁבִ֣י עֻזּ֑וֹ
וְֽתִפְאַרְתּ֥וֹ בְיַד־צָֽר׃

62 וַיַּסְגֵּ֣ר לַחֶ֣רֶב עַמּ֑וֹ
וּ֝בְנַחֲלָת֗וֹ הִתְעַבָּֽר׃

63 בַּחוּרָ֥יו אָכְלָה־אֵ֑שׁ
וּ֝בְתוּלֹתָ֗יו לֹ֣א הוּלָּֽלוּ׃

64 כֹּ֭הֲנָיו בַּחֶ֣רֶב נָפָ֑לוּ
וְ֝אַלְמְנֹתָ֗יו לֹ֣א תִבְכֶּֽינָה׃

65 וַיִּקַ֖ץ* כְּיָשֵׁ֥ן ׀ אֲדֹנָ֑י
כְּ֝גִבּ֗וֹר מִתְרוֹנֵ֥ן מִיָּֽיִן׃

66 וַיַּךְ־צָרָ֥יו אָח֑וֹר
חֶרְפַּ֥ת ע֝וֹלָ֗ם נָ֣תַן לָֽמוֹ׃

67 וַ֭יִּמְאַס בְּאֹ֣הֶל יוֹסֵ֑ף
וּֽבְשֵׁ֥בֶט אֶ֝פְרַ֗יִם לֹ֣א בָחָֽר׃

---

d Or "hill" with Septuagint and Saadia.
e-e Inverted for clarity.
f I.e., the Ark; cf. Ps. 132.8.
g-g Lit. "had no nuptial song."

חסר י' בשורש v. 65.

68He did choose the tribe of Judah,
  Mount Zion, which He loved.
69He built His Sanctuary like the heavens,
  like the earth that He established forever.
70He chose David, His servant,
  and took him from the sheepfolds.
71He brought him from minding the nursing ewes
  to tend His people Jacob, Israel, His very own.
72He tended them with blameless heart;
  with skillful hands he led them.

68 וַיִּבְחַר אֶת־שֵׁבֶט יְהוּדָה
אֶת־הַר צִיּוֹן אֲשֶׁר אָהֵב:
69 וַיִּבֶן כְּמוֹ־רָמִים מִקְדָּשׁוֹ
כְּאֶרֶץ יְסָדָהּ לְעוֹלָם:
70 וַיִּבְחַר בְּדָוִד עַבְדּוֹ
וַיִּקָּחֵהוּ מִמִּכְלְאֹת צֹאן:
71 מֵאַחַר עָלוֹת הֱבִיאוֹ
לִרְעוֹת בְּיַעֲקֹב עַמּוֹ וּבְיִשְׂרָאֵל
נַחֲלָתוֹ:
72 וַיִּרְעֵם כְּתֹם לְבָבוֹ
וּבִתְבוּנוֹת כַּפָּיו יַנְחֵם:

79 A psalm of Asaph.

עט מִזְמוֹר לְאָסָף

O God, heathens have entered Your domain,
  defiled Your holy temple,
  and turned Jerusalem into ruins.
2They have left Your servants' corpses
  as food for the fowl of heaven,
  and the flesh of Your faithful for the wild beasts.
3Their blood was shed like water around Jerusalem,
  with none to bury them.
4We have become the butt of our neighbors,
  the scorn and derision of those around us.

5How long, O LORD, will You be angry forever,
  will Your indignation blaze like fire?
6Pour out Your fury on the nations that do not
  know You,
  upon the kingdoms that do not invoke Your
  name,
    7for they have devoured Jacob
  and desolated his home.
8Do not hold our former iniquities against us;
  let Your compassion come swiftly toward us,
  for we have sunk very low.

אֱלֹהִים בָּאוּ גוֹיִם ׀ בְּנַחֲלָתֶךָ
טִמְּאוּ אֶת־הֵיכַל קָדְשֶׁךָ
שָׂמוּ אֶת־יְרוּשָׁלַ͏ִם לְעִיִּים:
2 נָתְנוּ אֶת־נִבְלַת עֲבָדֶיךָ
מַאֲכָל לְעוֹף הַשָּׁמָיִם
בְּשַׂר חֲסִידֶיךָ לְחַיְתוֹ־אָרֶץ:
3 שָׁפְכוּ דָמָם ׀ כַּמַּיִם סְבִיבוֹת
יְרוּשָׁלָ͏ִם
וְאֵין קוֹבֵר:
4 הָיִינוּ חֶרְפָּה לִשְׁכֵנֵינוּ
לַעַג וָקֶלֶס לִסְבִיבוֹתֵינוּ:
5 עַד־מָה יְהוָה תֶּאֱנַף לָנֶצַח
תִּבְעַר כְּמוֹ־אֵשׁ קִנְאָתֶךָ:
6 שְׁפֹךְ חֲמָתְךָ אֶל־הַגּוֹיִם אֲשֶׁר לֹא־
יְדָעוּךָ
וְעַל מַמְלָכוֹת אֲשֶׁר בְּשִׁמְךָ לֹא
קָרָאוּ:
7 כִּי אָכַל אֶת־יַעֲקֹב
וְאֶת־נָוֵהוּ הֵשַׁמּוּ:
8 אַל־תִּזְכָּר־לָנוּ עֲוֹנֹת רִאשֹׁנִים
מַהֵר יְקַדְּמוּנוּ רַחֲמֶיךָ
כִּי דַלּוֹנוּ מְאֹד:

9Help us, O God, our deliverer,
   for the sake of the glory of Your name.
Save us and forgive our sin,
   for the sake of Your name.
10Let the nations not say, "Where is their God?"
Before our eyes let it be known among the nations
   that You avenge the spilled blood of Your servants.
11Let the groans of the prisoners reach You;
   reprieve those condemned to death,
   as befits Your great strength.
12Pay back our neighbors sevenfold
   for the abuse they have flung at You, O Lord.
13Then we, Your people,
   the flock You shepherd,
   shall glorify You forever;
   for all time we shall tell Your praises.

9 עָזְרֵנוּ ׀ אֱלֹהֵי יִשְׁעֵנוּ
עַל־דְּבַר כְּבוֹד־שְׁמֶךָ
וְהַצִּילֵנוּ וְכַפֵּר עַל־חַטֹּאתֵינוּ
לְמַעַן שְׁמֶךָ׃
10 לָמָּה ׀ יֹאמְרוּ הַגּוֹיִם אַיֵּה
אֱלֹהֵיהֶם
יִוָּדַע בַּגֹּיִים לְעֵינֵינוּ
נִקְמַת דַּם־עֲבָדֶיךָ הַשָּׁפוּךְ׃
11 תָּבוֹא לְפָנֶיךָ אֶנְקַת אָסִיר
כְּגֹדֶל זְרוֹעֲךָ
הוֹתֵר בְּנֵי תְמוּתָה׃
12 וְהָשֵׁב לִשְׁכֵנֵינוּ שִׁבְעָתַיִם אֶל־
חֵיקָם
חֶרְפָּתָם אֲשֶׁר חֵרְפוּךָ אֲדֹנָי׃
13 וַאֲנַחְנוּ עַמְּךָ ׀
וְצֹאן מַרְעִיתֶךָ
נוֹדֶה לְּךָ לְעוֹלָם
לְדֹר וָדֹר נְסַפֵּר תְּהִלָּתֶךָ׃

80
For the leader; on *shoshannim, eduth.*
Of Asaph. A psalm.

פ לַמְנַצֵּחַ אֶל־שֹׁשַׁנִּים עֵדוּת
לְאָסָף מִזְמוֹר׃

2Give ear, O shepherd of Israel
   who leads Joseph like a flock!
Appear, You who are enthroned on the cherubim,
   3at the head of Ephraim, Benjamin, and Manasseh!
Rouse Your might and come to our help!
4Restore us, O God;
   show Your favor that we may be delivered.

2 רֹעֵה יִשְׂרָאֵל ׀ הַאֲזִינָה
נֹהֵג כַּצֹּאן יוֹסֵף
יֹשֵׁב הַכְּרוּבִים הוֹפִיעָה׃
3 לִפְנֵי* אֶפְרַיִם ׀ וּבִנְיָמִן וּמְנַשֶּׁה
עוֹרְרָה אֶת־גְּבוּרָתֶךָ וּלְכָה
לִישֻׁעָתָה לָּנוּ׃
4 אֱלֹהִים הֲשִׁיבֵנוּ
וְהָאֵר פָּנֶיךָ וְנִוָּשֵׁעָה׃

5O Lord, God of hosts,
   how long will You be wrathful
   toward the prayers of Your people?
6You have fed them tears as their daily bread,
   made them drink great measures of tears.
7You set us at strife with our neighbors;

5 יְהוָה אֱלֹהִים צְבָאוֹת
עַד־מָתַי עָשַׁנְתָּ
בִּתְפִלַּת עַמֶּךָ׃
6 הֶאֱכַלְתָּם לֶחֶם דִּמְעָה
וַתַּשְׁקֵמוֹ בִּדְמָעוֹת שָׁלִישׁ׃
7 תְּשִׂימֵנוּ מָדוֹן לִשְׁכֵנֵינוּ

v. 3. סבירין ומטעין "לבני"

our enemies mock us at will.

8O God of hosts, restore us;

   show Your favor that we may be delivered.

9You plucked up a vine from Egypt;

   You expelled nations and planted it.

10You cleared a place for it;

   it took deep root and filled the land.

11The mountains were covered by its shade,

   mighty cedars by its boughs.

12Its branches reached the sea,

   its shoots, the river.

13Why did You breach its wall

   so that every passerby plucks its fruit,

14wild boars gnaw at it,

   and creatures of the field feed on it?

15O God of hosts, turn again,

   look down from heaven and see;

   take note of that vine,

16the stock planted by Your right hand,

   the stem^a you have taken as Your own.

17For it is burned by fire and cut down,

   perishing before Your angry blast.

18Grant Your help^b to the man at Your right hand,

   the one You have taken as Your own.

19We will not turn away from You;

   preserve our life that we may invoke Your

   name.

20O Lord, God of hosts, restore us;

   show Your favor that we may be delivered.

וְאֹיְבֵ֫ינוּ יִלְעֲגוּ־לָֽמוֹ׃

8 אֱלֹהִ֣ים צְבָא֣וֹת הֲשִׁיבֵ֑נוּ

וְהָאֵ֥ר פָּ֝נֶ֗יךָ וְנִוָּשֵֽׁעָה׃

9 גֶּ֭פֶן מִמִּצְרַ֣יִם תַּסִּ֑יעַ

תְּגָרֵ֥שׁ גּ֝וֹיִ֗ם וַתִּטָּעֶֽהָ׃

10 פִּנִּ֥יתָ לְפָנֶ֑יהָ

וַתַּשְׁרֵ֥שׁ שָׁ֝רָשֶׁ֗יהָ וַתְּמַלֵּא־אָֽרֶץ׃

11 כָּסּ֣וּ הָרִ֣ים צִלָּ֑הּ

וַעֲנָפֶ֗יהָ אַֽרְזֵי־אֵֽל׃

12 תְּשַׁלַּ֣ח קְצִירֶ֣הָ עַד־יָ֑ם

וְאֶל־נָ֝הָ֗ר יֽוֹנְקוֹתֶֽיהָ׃

13 לָ֭מָּה פָּרַ֣צְתָּ גְדֵרֶ֑יהָ

וְ֝אָר֗וּהָ כָּל־עֹ֥בְרֵי דָֽרֶךְ׃

14 יְכַרְסְמֶ֣נָּֽה חֲזִ֣יר מִיָּ֑עַר*

וְזִ֖יז שָׂדַ֣י יִרְעֶֽנָּה׃

15 אֱלֹהִ֣ים צְבָאוֹת֮ שֽׁוּב־נָ֥א

הַבֵּ֥ט מִשָּׁמַ֖יִם וּרְאֵ֑ה

וּפְקֹ֥ד גֶּ֣פֶן זֹֽאת׃

16 וְ֭כַנָּה אֲשֶׁר־נָטְעָ֣ה יְמִינֶ֑ךָ

וְעַל־בֵּ֝֗ן אִמַּ֥צְתָּה לָּֽךְ׃

17 שְׂרֻפָ֣ה בָאֵ֣שׁ כְּסוּחָ֑ה

מִגַּעֲרַ֖ת פָּנֶ֣יךָ יֹאבֵֽדוּ׃

18 תְּֽהִי־יָ֭דְךָ עַל־אִ֣ישׁ יְמִינֶ֑ךָ

עַל־בֶּן־אָ֝דָ֗ם אִמַּ֥צְתָּ לָּֽךְ׃

19 וְלֹא־נָס֥וֹג מִמֶּ֑ךָּ

תְּ֝חַיֵּ֗נוּ וּבְשִׁמְךָ֥ נִקְרָֽא׃

20 יְהֹוָ֤ה אֱלֹהִ֣ים צְבָא֣וֹת הֲשִׁיבֵ֑נוּ

הָאֵ֥ר פָּ֝נֶ֗יךָ וְנִוָּשֵֽׁעָה׃

81 For the leader; on the *gittith*. Of Asaph.

2Sing joyously to God, our strength;

   raise a shout for the God of Jacob.

3Take up the song,

פא לַמְנַצֵּ֬חַ ׀ עַֽל־הַגִּתִּ֬ית לְאָסָֽף׃

2 הַ֭רְנִ֣ינוּ לֵאלֹהִ֣ים עוּזֵּ֑נוּ

הָ֝רִ֗יעוּ לֵאלֹהֵ֥י יַעֲקֹֽב׃

3 שְׂאֽוּ־זִ֭מְרָה

a Lit. "son."
b Lit. "hand."

ע׳ תלויה   v. 14.

sound the timbrel,
  the melodious lyre and harp.

⁴Blow the horn on the new moon,
  on the full moon for our feast day.

⁵For it is a law for Israel,
  a ruling of the God of Jacob;

⁶He imposed it as a decree upon Joseph
  when ᵃ-he went forth from-ᵃ the land of Egypt;
  I heard a language that I knew not.

⁷I relieved his shoulder of the burden,
  his hands were freed from the basket.

⁸In distress you called and I rescued you;
  I answered you from the ᵇ-secret place of
    thunder-ᵇ
  I tested you at the waters of Meribah.   *Selah.*

⁹Hear, My people, and I will admonish you;
  Israel, if you would but listen to Me!

¹⁰You shall have no foreign god,
  you shall not bow to an alien god.

¹¹I the Lord am your God
  who brought you out of the land of Egypt;
  open your mouth wide and I will fill it.

¹²But My people would not listen to Me,
  Israel would not obey Me.

¹³So I let them go after their willful heart
  that they might follow their own devices.

¹⁴If only My people would listen to Me,
  if Israel would follow My paths,

¹⁵then would I subdue their enemies at once,
  strike their foes again and again.

¹⁶Those who hate the Lord shall cower before
    Him;
  their doom shall be eternal.

¹⁷He fed themᶜ the finest wheat;
  I sated you with honey from the rock.

וּתְנוּ־תֹף

כִּנּוֹר נָעִים עִם־נָבֶל:

4 תִּקְעוּ בַחֹדֶשׁ שׁוֹפָר

בַּכֵּסֶה לְיוֹם חַגֵּנוּ:

5 כִּי חֹק לְיִשְׂרָאֵל הוּא

מִשְׁפָּט לֵאלֹהֵי יַעֲקֹב:

6 עֵדוּת ׀ בִּיהוֹסֵף שָׂמוֹ

בְּצֵאתוֹ עַל־אֶרֶץ מִצְרָיִם

שְׂפַת לֹא־יָדַעְתִּי אֶשְׁמָע:

7 הֲסִירוֹתִי מִסֵּבֶל שִׁכְמוֹ

כַּפָּיו מִדּוּד תַּעֲבֹרְנָה:

8 בַּצָּרָה קָרָאתָ וָאֲחַלְּצֶךָּ

אֶעֶנְךָ בְּסֵתֶר רַעַם

אֶבְחָנְךָ עַל־מֵי מְרִיבָה סֶלָה:

9 שְׁמַע עַמִּי וְאָעִידָה בָּךְ

יִשְׂרָאֵל אִם־תִּשְׁמַע־לִי:

10 לֹא־יִהְיֶה בְךָ אֵל זָר

וְלֹא תִשְׁתַּחֲוֶה לְאֵל נֵכָר:

11 אָנֹכִי ׀ יְהוָה אֱלֹהֶיךָ

הַמַּעַלְךָ מֵאֶרֶץ מִצְרָיִם

הַרְחֶב־פִּיךָ וַאֲמַלְאֵהוּ:

12 וְלֹא־שָׁמַע עַמִּי לְקוֹלִי

וְיִשְׂרָאֵל לֹא־אָבָה לִי:

13 וָאֲשַׁלְּחֵהוּ בִּשְׁרִירוּת לִבָּם

יֵלְכוּ בְּמוֹעֲצוֹתֵיהֶם:

14 לוּ עַמִּי שֹׁמֵעַ לִי

יִשְׂרָאֵל בִּדְרָכַי יְהַלֵּכוּ:

15 כִּמְעַט אוֹיְבֵיהֶם אַכְנִיעַ

וְעַל צָרֵיהֶם אָשִׁיב יָדִי:

16 מְשַׂנְאֵי יְהוָה יְכַחֲשׁוּ־לוֹ

וִיהִי עִתָּם לְעוֹלָם:

17 וַיַּאֲכִילֵהוּ מֵחֵלֶב חִטָּה

וּמִצּוּר דְּבַשׁ אַשְׂבִּיעֶךָ:

---

a-a   Or "He went forth against."
b-b   Meaning of Heb. uncertain.
c   Lit. "him," i.e., Israel.

82 A psalm of Asaph.

God stands in the divine assembly;
   among the divine beings He pronounces judg-
      ment.
2How long will you judge perversely,
   showing favor to the wicked?   *Selah.*
3Judge the wretched and the orphan,
   vindicate the lowly and the poor,
4rescue the wretched and the needy;
   save them from the hand of the wicked.

5They neither know nor understand,
   they go about in darkness;
   all the foundations of the earth totter.
6I had taken you for divine beings,
   sons of the Most High, all of you;
7but you shall die as men do,
   fall like any prince.

8Arise, O God, judge the earth,
   for all the nations are Your possession.

83 A song, a psalm of Asaph.

2O God, do not be silent;
   do not hold aloof;
   do not be quiet, O God!
3For Your enemies rage,
   Your foes *a*-assert themselves.-*a*
4They plot craftily against Your people,
   take counsel against Your treasured ones.
5They say, "Let us wipe them out as a nation;
   Israel's name will be mentioned no more."
6Unanimous in their counsel
   they have made an alliance against You—
7the clans of Edom and the Ishmaelites,

פב מִזְמוֹר לְאָסָף

אֱלֹהִים נִצָּב בַּעֲדַת־אֵל
בְּקֶרֶב אֱלֹהִים יִשְׁפֹּט:
2 עַד־מָתַי תִּשְׁפְּטוּ־עָוֶל
וּפְנֵי רְשָׁעִים תִּשְׂאוּ־סֶלָה:
3 שִׁפְטוּ־דַל וְיָתוֹם
עָנִי וָרָשׁ הַצְדִּיקוּ:
4 פַּלְּטוּ־דַל וְאֶבְיוֹן
מִיַּד רְשָׁעִים הַצִּילוּ:

5 לֹא יָדְעוּ ׀ וְלֹא יָבִינוּ
בַּחֲשֵׁכָה יִתְהַלָּכוּ
יִמּוֹטוּ כָּל־מוֹסְדֵי אָרֶץ:
6 אֲנִי־אָמַרְתִּי אֱלֹהִים אַתֶּם
וּבְנֵי עֶלְיוֹן כֻּלְּכֶם:
7 אָכֵן כְּאָדָם תְּמוּתוּן
וּכְאַחַד הַשָּׂרִים תִּפֹּלוּ:

8 קוּמָה אֱלֹהִים שָׁפְטָה הָאָרֶץ
כִּי־אַתָּה תִנְחַל בְּכָל־הַגּוֹיִם:

פג שִׁיר מִזְמוֹר לְאָסָף:

2 אֱלֹהִים אַל־דֳּמִי־לָךְ
אַל־תֶּחֱרַשׁ
וְאַל־תִּשְׁקֹט אֵל:
3 כִּי־הִנֵּה אוֹיְבֶיךָ יֶהֱמָיוּן
וּמְשַׂנְאֶיךָ נָשְׂאוּ רֹאשׁ:
4 עַל־עַמְּךָ יַעֲרִימוּ סוֹד
וְיִתְיָעֲצוּ עַל־צְפוּנֶיךָ:
5 אָמְרוּ לְכוּ וְנַכְחִידֵם מִגּוֹי
וְלֹא־יִזָּכֵר שֵׁם־יִשְׂרָאֵל עוֹד:
6 כִּי נוֹעֲצוּ לֵב יַחְדָּו
עָלֶיךָ בְּרִית יִכְרֹתוּ:
7 אָהֳלֵי אֱדוֹם וְיִשְׁמְעֵאלִים

---

a-a   Lit. "lift up the head."

Moab and the Hagrites,
⁸Gebal, Ammon, and Amalek,
Philistia with the inhabitants of Tyre;
⁹Assyria too joins forces with them;
they give support to the sons of Lot.   *Selah.*

מוֹאָב וְהַגְרִים׃
8 גְּבָל וְעַמּוֹן וַעֲמָלֵק
פְּלֶשֶׁת עִם־יֹשְׁבֵי צוֹר׃
9 גַּם־אַשּׁוּר נִלְוָה עִמָּם
הָיוּ זְרוֹעַ לִבְנֵי־לוֹט   סֶלָה׃

¹⁰Deal with them as You did with Midian,
with Sisera, with Jabin,
at the brook Kishon—
¹¹who were destroyed at En-dor,
who became dung for the field.
¹²Treat their great men like Oreb and Zeeb,
all their princes like Zebah and Zalmunna,
¹³who said, "Let us take the meadows of God
as our possession."
¹⁴O my God, make them like thistledown,
like stubble driven by the wind.
¹⁵As a fire burns a forest,
as flames scorch the hills,
¹⁶pursue them with Your tempest,
terrify them with Your storm.
¹⁷Cover[b] their faces with shame
so that they seek Your name, O Lᴏʀᴅ.
¹⁸May they be frustrated and terrified,
disgraced and doomed forever.
¹⁹May they know
that Your name, Yours alone, is the Lᴏʀᴅ,
supreme over all the earth.

10 עֲשֵׂה־לָהֶם כְּמִדְיָן
כְּסִיסְרָא כְיָבִין
בְּנַחַל קִישׁוֹן׃
11 נִשְׁמְדוּ בְעֵין־דֹּאר
הָיוּ דֹּמֶן לָאֲדָמָה׃
12 שִׁיתֵמוֹ נְדִיבֵמוֹ כְּעֹרֵב וְכִזְאֵב
וּכְזֶבַח וּכְצַלְמֻנָּע כָּל־נְסִיכֵמוֹ׃
13 אֲשֶׁר אָמְרוּ נִירֲשָׁה לָּנוּ
אֵת נְאוֹת אֱלֹהִים׃
14 אֱלֹהַי שִׁיתֵמוֹ כַגַּלְגַּל
כְּקַשׁ לִפְנֵי־רוּחַ׃
15 כְּאֵשׁ תִּבְעַר־יָעַר
וּכְלֶהָבָה תְּלַהֵט הָרִים׃
16 כֵּן תִּרְדְּפֵם בְּסַעֲרֶךָ
וּבְסוּפָתְךָ תְבַהֲלֵם׃
17 מַלֵּא פְנֵיהֶם קָלוֹן
וִיבַקְשׁוּ שִׁמְךָ יְהוָה׃
18 יֵבֹשׁוּ וְיִבָּהֲלוּ עֲדֵי־עַד וְיַחְפְּרוּ
וְיֹאבֵדוּ׃
19 וְיֵדְעוּ
כִּי־אַתָּה שִׁמְךָ יְהוָה לְבַדֶּךָ
עֶלְיוֹן עַל־כָּל־הָאָרֶץ׃

84 For the leader; on the *gittith.*
Of the Korahites. A psalm.

פד לַמְנַצֵּחַ עַל־הַגִּתִּית
לִבְנֵי־קֹרַח מִזְמוֹר׃

²How lovely is Your dwelling-place,
O Lᴏʀᴅ of hosts.
³I long, I yearn for the courts of the Lᴏʀᴅ;
my body and soul shout for joy to the living
God.

2 מַה־יְּדִידוֹת מִשְׁכְּנוֹתֶיךָ
יְהוָה צְבָאוֹת׃
3 נִכְסְפָה וְגַם־כָּלְתָה ׀ נַפְשִׁי
לְחַצְרוֹת יְהוָה
לִבִּי וּבְשָׂרִי יְרַנְּנוּ אֶל אֵל־חָי׃

---

b   Lit. "Fill."

4Even the sparrow has found a home,
  and the swallow a nest for herself
  in which to set her young,
  near Your altar, O LORD of hosts,
  my king and my God.
5Happy are those who dwell in Your house;
  they forever praise You.   *Selah.*

6Happy is the man who finds refuge in You,
  whose mind is on the [pilgrim] highways.
7They pass through the Valley of Baca,
  a-regarding it as a place of springs,
  as if the early rain had covered it with blessing.-*a*
8They go from *b*-rampart to rampart,-*b*
  appearing before God in Zion.
9O LORD, God of hosts,
  hear my prayer;
  give ear, O God of Jacob.   *Selah.*
10O God, behold our shield,
  look upon the face of Your anointed.

11Better one day in Your courts than a thousand
    [anywhere else];
  I would rather stand at the threshold of God's
    house
  than dwell in the tents of the wicked.
12For the LORD God is sun*c* and shield;
  the LORD bestows grace and glory;
  He does not withhold His bounty from those
    who live without blame.
13O LORD of hosts,
  happy is the man who trusts in You.

85 For the leader. Of the Korahites. A psalm.

2O LORD, You *a*-will favor-*a* Your land,
  restore*b* Jacob's fortune;

---

a-a   Meaning of Heb. uncertain.
b-b   Others "strength to strength."
c   Or "bulwark," with Targum; cf. Isa. 54.12.

a-a   Or "have favored."
b   Or "have restored."

4 גַּם־צִפּוֹר ׀ מָצְאָה בַיִת
וּדְרוֹר ׀ קֵן לָהּ
אֲשֶׁר־שָׁתָה אֶפְרֹחֶיהָ
אֶת־מִזְבְּחוֹתֶיךָ יְהוָה צְבָאוֹת
מַלְכִּי וֵאלֹהָי:
5 אַשְׁרֵי יוֹשְׁבֵי בֵיתֶךָ
עוֹד יְהַלְלוּךָ סֶּלָה:

6 אַשְׁרֵי אָדָם עוֹז־לוֹ בָךְ
מְסִלּוֹת בִּלְבָבָם:
7 עֹבְרֵי ׀ בְּעֵמֶק הַבָּכָא
מַעְיָן יְשִׁיתוּהוּ
גַּם־בְּרָכוֹת יַעְטֶה מוֹרֶה:
8 יֵלְכוּ מֵחַיִל אֶל־חָיִל
יֵרָאֶה אֶל־אֱלֹהִים בְּצִיּוֹן:
9 יְהוָה אֱלֹהִים צְבָאוֹת
שִׁמְעָה תְפִלָּתִי
הַאֲזִינָה אֱלֹהֵי יַעֲקֹב סֶלָה:
10 מָגִנֵּנוּ רְאֵה אֱלֹהִים
וְהַבֵּט פְּנֵי מְשִׁיחֶךָ:

11 כִּי טוֹב־יוֹם בַּחֲצֵרֶיךָ מֵאָלֶף
בָּחַרְתִּי הִסְתּוֹפֵף בְּבֵית אֱלֹהַי
מִדּוּר בְּאָהֳלֵי־רֶשַׁע:
12 כִּי שֶׁמֶשׁ ׀ וּמָגֵן יְהוָה אֱלֹהִים
חֵן וְכָבוֹד יִתֵּן יְהוָה
לֹא יִמְנַע־טוֹב לַהֹלְכִים בְּתָמִים:
13 יְהוָה צְבָאוֹת
אַשְׁרֵי אָדָם בֹּטֵחַ בָּךְ:

פה לַמְנַצֵּחַ ׀ לִבְנֵי־קֹרַח מִזְמוֹר:

2 רָצִיתָ יְהוָה אַרְצֶךָ
שַׁבְתָּ שְׁבוּת יַעֲקֹב:

³נָשָׂאתָ עֲוֺן עַמֶּךָ

כִּסִּיתָ כָל־חַטָּאתָם סֶלָה׃

⁴אָסַפְתָּ כָל־עֶבְרָתֶךָ

הֱשִׁיבוֹתָ מֵחֲרוֹן אַפֶּךָ׃

⁵שׁוּבֵנוּ אֱלֹהֵי יִשְׁעֵנוּ

וְהָפֵר כַּעַסְךָ עִמָּנוּ׃

⁶הַלְעוֹלָם תֶּאֱנַף־בָּנוּ

תִּמְשֹׁךְ אַפְּךָ לְדֹר וָדֹר׃

⁷הֲלֹא־אַתָּה תָּשׁוּב תְּחַיֵּנוּ

וְעַמְּךָ יִשְׂמְחוּ־בָךְ׃

⁸הַרְאֵנוּ יְהוָה חַסְדֶּךָ

וְיֶשְׁעֲךָ תִּתֶּן־לָנוּ׃

⁹אֶשְׁמְעָה מַה־יְדַבֵּר הָאֵל ׀ יְהוָה

כִּי ׀ יְדַבֵּר שָׁלוֹם אֶל־עַמּוֹ וְאֶל־

חֲסִידָיו

וְאַל־יָשׁוּבוּ לְכִסְלָה׃

¹⁰אַךְ ׀ קָרוֹב לִירֵאָיו יִשְׁעוֹ

לִשְׁכֹּן כָּבוֹד בְּאַרְצֵנוּ׃

¹¹חֶסֶד־וֶאֱמֶת נִפְגָּשׁוּ

צֶדֶק וְשָׁלוֹם נָשָׁקוּ׃

¹²אֱמֶת מֵאֶרֶץ תִּצְמָח

וְצֶדֶק מִשָּׁמַיִם נִשְׁקָף׃

¹³גַּם־יְהוָה יִתֵּן הַטּוֹב

וְאַרְצֵנוּ תִּתֵּן יְבוּלָהּ׃

¹⁴צֶדֶק לְפָנָיו יְהַלֵּךְ

וְיָשֵׂם לְדֶרֶךְ פְּעָמָיו׃

פו תְּפִלָּה לְדָוִד

הַטֵּה־יְהוָה אָזְנְךָ

עֲנֵנִי

כִּי־עָנִי וְאֶבְיוֹן אָנִי׃

²שָׁמְרָה נַפְשִׁי כִּי־חָסִיד אָנִי

הוֹשַׁע עַבְדְּךָ אַתָּה אֱלֹהַי

הַבּוֹטֵחַ אֵלֶיךָ׃

³You c-will forgive-c Your people's iniquity,
   pardon^d all their sins; *selah*
⁴You e-will withdraw-e all Your anger,
   turn^f away from Your rage.
⁵Turn again, O God, our helper,
   revoke Your displeasure with us.
⁶Will You be angry with us forever,
   prolong Your wrath for all generations?
⁷Surely You will revive us again,
   so that Your people may rejoice in You.
⁸Show us, O LORD, Your faithfulness;
   grant us Your deliverance.

⁹Let me hear what God, the LORD, will speak;
   He will promise well-being to His people, His
      faithful ones;
   may they not turn to folly.
¹⁰His help is very near those who fear Him,
   to make His glory dwell in our land.
¹¹Faithfulness and truth meet;
   justice and well-being kiss.
¹²Truth springs up from the earth;
   justice looks down from heaven.
¹³The LORD also bestows His bounty;
   our land yields its produce.
¹⁴Justice goes before Him
   as He sets out on His way.

86 A prayer of David.

Incline Your ear, O LORD,
   answer me,
      for I am poor and needy.
²Preserve my life, for I am steadfast;
   O You, my God,
      deliver Your servant who trusts in You.

---

c-c Or "have forgiven."
d Or "have pardoned."
e-e Or "have withdrawn."
f Or "have turned."

³Have mercy on me, O Lord,
  for I call to You all day long;
⁴bring joy to Your servant's life,
  for on You, Lord, I set my hope.
⁵For You, Lord, are good and forgiving,
  abounding in steadfast love to all who call on
  You.
⁶Give ear, O LORD, to my prayer;
  heed my plea for mercy.
⁷In my time of trouble I call You,
  for You will answer me.

⁸There is none like You among the gods, O Lord,
  and there are no deeds like Yours.
⁹All the nations You have made
  will come to bow down before You, O Lord,
  and they will pay honor to Your name.
¹⁰For You are great and perform wonders;
  You alone are God.
¹¹Teach me Your way, O LORD;
  I will walk in Your truth;
  let my heart be undivided in reverence for Your
  name.
¹²I will praise You, O Lord, my God, with all my
  heart
  and pay honor to Your name forever.
¹³For Your steadfast love toward me is great;
  You have saved me from the depths of Sheol.

¹⁴O God, arrogant men have risen against me;
  a band of ruthless men seek my life;
  they are not mindful of You.
¹⁵But You, O Lord, are a God
  compassionate and merciful,
  slow to anger, abounding in steadfast love and
  faithfulness.
¹⁶Turn to me and have mercy on me;
  grant Your strength to Your servant
  and deliver the son of Your maidservant.
¹⁷Show me a sign of Your favor,

3 חָנֵּנִי אֲדֹנָי
כִּי אֵלֶיךָ אֶקְרָא כָּל־הַיּוֹם:
4 שַׂמֵּחַ נֶפֶשׁ עַבְדֶּךָ
כִּי אֵלֶיךָ אֲדֹנָי נַפְשִׁי אֶשָּׂא:
5 כִּי־אַתָּה אֲדֹנָי טוֹב וְסַלָּח
וְרַב־חֶסֶד לְכָל־קֹרְאֶיךָ:
6 הַאֲזִינָה יְהוָה תְּפִלָּתִי
וְהַקְשִׁיבָה בְּקוֹל תַּחֲנוּנוֹתָי:
7 בְּיוֹם צָרָתִי אֶקְרָאֶךָּ
כִּי תַעֲנֵנִי:

8 אֵין־כָּמוֹךָ בָאֱלֹהִים ׀ אֲדֹנָי
וְאֵין כְּמַעֲשֶׂיךָ:
9 כָּל־גּוֹיִם ׀ אֲשֶׁר עָשִׂיתָ
יָבוֹאוּ ׀ וְיִשְׁתַּחֲווּ לְפָנֶיךָ אֲדֹנָי
וִיכַבְּדוּ לִשְׁמֶךָ:
10 כִּי־גָדוֹל אַתָּה וְעֹשֵׂה נִפְלָאוֹת
אַתָּה אֱלֹהִים לְבַדֶּךָ:
11 הוֹרֵנִי יְהוָה ׀ דַּרְכֶּךָ
אֲהַלֵּךְ בַּאֲמִתֶּךָ
יַחֵד לְבָבִי לְיִרְאָה שְׁמֶךָ:
12 אוֹדְךָ ׀ אֲדֹנָי אֱלֹהַי בְּכָל־לְבָבִי
וַאֲכַבְּדָה שִׁמְךָ לְעוֹלָם:
13 כִּי־חַסְדְּךָ גָּדוֹל עָלָי
וְהִצַּלְתָּ נַפְשִׁי מִשְּׁאוֹל תַּחְתִּיָּה:

14 אֱלֹהִים ׀ זֵדִים קָמוּ־עָלַי
וַעֲדַת עָרִיצִים בִּקְשׁוּ נַפְשִׁי
וְלֹא שָׂמוּךָ לְנֶגְדָּם:
15 וְאַתָּה אֲדֹנָי
אֵל־רַחוּם וְחַנּוּן
אֶרֶךְ אַפַּיִם וְרַב־חֶסֶד וֶאֱמֶת:
16 פְּנֵה אֵלַי וְחָנֵּנִי
תְּנָה־עֻזְּךָ לְעַבְדֶּךָ
וְהוֹשִׁיעָה לְבֶן־אֲמָתֶךָ:
17 עֲשֵׂה־עִמִּי אוֹת לְטוֹבָה

that my enemies may see and be frustrated
because You, O LORD, have given me aid and
comfort.

וְיִרְאוּ שֹׂנְאַי וְיֵבֹשׁוּ
כִּי־אַתָּה יְהֹוָה עֲזַרְתַּנִי וְנִחַמְתָּנִי׃

87 ^{a1-2}Of the Korahites. A psalm. A song.

פז לִבְנֵי־קֹרַח מִזְמוֹר שִׁיר

^bThe LORD loves the gates of Zion,
  His foundation on the holy mountains,^{-b}
  more than all the dwellings of Jacob.
³Glorious things are spoken of you,
  O city of God.   *Selah.*
⁴I mention Rahab^cand Babylon among those who
    acknowledge Me;
  Philistia, and Tyre, and Cush—each was born
    there.
⁵Indeed, it shall be said of Zion,
  "Every man was born there."
^d-He, the Most High, will preserve it.^{-d}
⁶The LORD will inscribe in the register of peoples
  that each was born there.   *Selah.*
⁷Singers and dancers alike [will say]:
  "All my roots^e are in You."

יְסוּדָתוֹ בְּהַרְרֵי־קֹדֶשׁ׃
² אֹהֵב יְהֹוָה שַׁעֲרֵי צִיּוֹן
מִכֹּל מִשְׁכְּנוֹת יַעֲקֹב׃
³ נִכְבָּדוֹת מְדֻבָּר בָּךְ
עִיר הָאֱלֹהִים סֶלָה׃
⁴ אַזְכִּיר ׀ רַהַב וּבָבֶל לְיֹדְעָי
הִנֵּה פְלֶשֶׁת וְצוֹר עִם־כּוּשׁ זֶה
יֻלַּד־שָׁם׃
⁵ וּלְצִיּוֹן ׀ יֵאָמַר
אִישׁ וְאִישׁ יֻלַּד־בָּהּ
וְהוּא יְכוֹנְנֶהָ עֶלְיוֹן׃
⁶ יְהֹוָה יִסְפֹּר בִּכְתוֹב עַמִּים
זֶה יֻלַּד־שָׁם סֶלָה׃
⁷ וְשָׁרִים כְּחֹלְלִים
כָּל־מַעְיָנַי בָּךְ׃

88 A song. A psalm of the Korahites. For the
leader; ^a-on *maḥalath leannoth.*^{-a} A *maskil* of Heman
the Ezrahite.

פח שִׁיר מִזְמוֹר לִבְנֵי קֹרַח
לַמְנַצֵּחַ עַל־מָחֲלַת לְעַנּוֹת מַשְׂכִּיל
לְהֵימָן הָאֶזְרָחִי׃

²O LORD, God of my deliverance,
  ^b-when I cry out in the night^{-b} before You,
³let my prayer reach You;
  incline Your ear to my cry.
⁴For I am sated with misfortune;
  I am at the brink of Sheol.

² יְהֹוָה אֱלֹהֵי יְשׁוּעָתִי
יוֹם־צָעַקְתִּי בַלַּיְלָה נֶגְדֶּךָ׃
³ תָּבוֹא לְפָנֶיךָ תְּפִלָּתִי
הַטֵּה־אָזְנְךָ לְרִנָּתִי׃
⁴ כִּי־שָׂבְעָה בְרָעוֹת נַפְשִׁי
וְחַיַּי לִשְׁאוֹל הִגִּיעוּ׃

---

^a   *The meaning of many passages in this psalm is uncertain.*
^{b-b}   *Order of lines inverted for clarity.*
^c   *A primeval monster; here, a poetic term for Egypt; cf. Isa. 30.7.*
^{d-d}   *Or "He will preserve it supreme."*
^e   *Lit. "sources."*

^{a-a}   *Meaning of Heb. uncertain.*
^{b-b}   *Or "by day I cry out [and] by night."*

⁵I am numbered with those who go down to the
   Pit;
   I am a helpless man
⁶abandonedᶜ among the dead,
   like bodies lying in the grave
of whom You are mindful no more,
   and who are cut off from Your care.
⁷You have put me at the bottom of the Pit,
   in the darkest places, in the depths.
⁸Your fury lies heavy upon me;
   You afflict me with all Your breakers.   *Selah.*
⁹You make my companions shun me;
   You make me abhorrent to them;
   I am shut in and do not go out.
¹⁰My eyes pine away from affliction;
   I call to You, O LORD, each day;
   I stretch out my hands to You.

¹¹Do You work wonders for the dead?
   Do the shades rise to praise You?   *Selah.*
¹²Is Your faithful care recounted in the grave,
   Your constancy in the place of perdition?
¹³Are Your wonders made known in the netherworld,ᵈ
   Your beneficent deeds in the land of oblivion?

¹⁴As for me, I cry out to You, O LORD;
   each morning my prayer greets You.
¹⁵Why, O LORD, do You reject me,
   do You hide Your face from me?
¹⁶From my youth I have been afflicted
   and near death;
   I suffer Your terrors ᵉ-wherever I turn.-ᵉ
¹⁷Your fury overwhelms me;
   Your terrors destroy me.
¹⁸They swirl about me like water all day long;
   they encircle me on every side.
¹⁹You have put friend and neighbor far from me
   and my companions out of my sight.ᶠ

נֶחְשַׁבְתִּי עִם־יוֹרְדֵי בוֹר 5
הָיִיתִי כְּגֶבֶר אֵין־אֱיָל:
בַּמֵּתִים חָפְשִׁי 6
כְּמוֹ חֲלָלִים ׀ שֹׁכְבֵי קֶבֶר
אֲשֶׁר לֹא זְכַרְתָּם עוֹד
וְהֵמָּה מִיָּדְךָ נִגְזָרוּ:
שַׁתַּנִי בְּבוֹר תַּחְתִּיּוֹת 7
בְּמַחֲשַׁכִּים בִּמְצֹלוֹת:
עָלַי סָמְכָה חֲמָתֶךָ 8
וְכָל־מִשְׁבָּרֶיךָ עִנִּיתָ סֶּלָה:
הִרְחַקְתָּ מְיֻדָּעַי מִמֶּנִּי 9
שַׁתַּנִי תוֹעֵבוֹת לָמוֹ
כָּלֻא וְלֹא אֵצֵא:
עֵינִי דָאֲבָה מִנִּי עֹנִי 10
קְרָאתִיךָ יְהוָה בְּכָל־יוֹם
שִׁטַּחְתִּי אֵלֶיךָ כַפָּי:

הֲלַמֵּתִים תַּעֲשֶׂה־פֶּלֶא 11
אִם־רְפָאִים יָקוּמוּ ׀ יוֹדוּךָ סֶּלָה:
הַיְסֻפַּר בַּקֶּבֶר חַסְדֶּךָ 12
אֱמוּנָתְךָ בָּאֲבַדּוֹן:
הֲיִוָּדַע בַּחֹשֶׁךְ פִּלְאֶךָ 13
וְצִדְקָתְךָ בְּאֶרֶץ נְשִׁיָּה:

וַאֲנִי ׀ אֵלֶיךָ יְהוָה שִׁוַּעְתִּי 14
וּבַבֹּקֶר תְּפִלָּתִי תְקַדְּמֶךָּ:
לָמָה יְהוָה תִּזְנַח נַפְשִׁי 15
תַּסְתִּיר פָּנֶיךָ מִמֶּנִּי:
עָנִי אֲנִי 16
וְגֹוֵעַ מִנֹּעַר
נָשָׂאתִי אֵמֶיךָ אָפוּנָה:
עָלַי עָבְרוּ חֲרוֹנֶיךָ 17
בִּעוּתֶיךָ צִמְּתוּתֻנִי:
סַבּוּנִי כַמַּיִם כָּל־הַיּוֹם 18
הִקִּיפוּ עָלַי יָחַד:
הִרְחַקְתָּ מִמֶּנִּי אֹהֵב וָרֵעַ 19
מְיֻדָּעַי מַחְשָׁךְ:

---

c   *Lit. "released."*
d   *Lit. "darkness."*
e-e   *Following Saadia; meaning of Heb. uncertain.*
f   *Lit. "into darkness."*

89

A *maskil* of Ethan the Ezrahite.

²I will sing of the Lord's steadfast love forever;
to all generations I will proclaim Your faithfulness with my mouth.
³I declare, "Your steadfast love is confirmed forever;
there in the heavens You establish Your faithfulness."

⁴"I have made a covenant with My chosen one;
I have sworn to My servant David:
⁵I will establish your offspring forever,
I will confirm your throne for all generations."
Selah.

⁶Your wonders, O Lord, are praised by the heavens,
Your faithfulness, too, in the assembly of holy beings.
⁷For who in the skies can equal the Lord,
can compare with the Lord among the divine beings,
⁸a God greatly dreaded in the council of holy beings,
held in awe by all around Him?
⁹O Lord, God of hosts,
who is mighty like You, O Lord?
Your faithfulness surrounds You;
¹⁰You rule the swelling of the sea;
when its waves surge, You still them.
¹¹You crushed Rahab; he was like a corpse;
with Your powerful arm You scattered Your enemies.
¹²The heaven is Yours,
the earth too;
the world and all it holds—
You established them.

פט מַשְׂכִּיל לְאֵיתָן הָאֶזְרָחִי:

² חַסְדֵי יְהוָה עוֹלָם אָשִׁירָה
לְדֹר וָדֹר ׀ אוֹדִיעַ אֱמוּנָתְךָ בְּפִי:
³ כִּי־אָמַרְתִּי עוֹלָם חֶסֶד יִבָּנֶה
שָׁמַיִם ׀ תָּכִן אֱמוּנָתְךָ בָהֶם:

⁴ כָּרַתִּי בְרִית לִבְחִירִי
נִשְׁבַּעְתִּי לְדָוִד עַבְדִּי:
⁵ עַד־עוֹלָם אָכִין זַרְעֶךָ
וּבָנִיתִי לְדֹר־וָדוֹר כִּסְאֲךָ   סֶלָה:

⁶ וְיוֹדוּ שָׁמַיִם פִּלְאֲךָ יְהוָה
אַף־אֱמוּנָתְךָ בִּקְהַל קְדֹשִׁים:
⁷ כִּי מִי בַשַּׁחַק יַעֲרֹךְ לַיהוָה
יִדְמֶה לַיהוָה בִּבְנֵי אֵלִים:
⁸ אֵל נַעֲרָץ בְּסוֹד־קְדֹשִׁים רַבָּה
וְנוֹרָא עַל־כָּל־סְבִיבָיו:
⁹ יְהוָה ׀ אֱלֹהֵי צְבָאוֹת
מִי־כָמוֹךָ חֲסִין ׀ יָהּ
וֶאֱמוּנָתְךָ סְבִיבוֹתֶיךָ:
¹⁰ אַתָּה מוֹשֵׁל בְּגֵאוּת הַיָּם
בְּשׂוֹא גַלָּיו אַתָּה תְשַׁבְּחֵם:
¹¹ אַתָּה דִכִּאתָ כֶחָלָל רָהַב
בִּזְרוֹעַ עֻזְּךָ פִּזַּרְתָּ אוֹיְבֶיךָ:
¹² לְךָ שָׁמַיִם
אַף־לְךָ אָרֶץ
תֵּבֵל וּמְלֹאָהּ
אַתָּה יְסַדְתָּם:

13North and south—
　You created them;
　Tabor and Hermon sing forth Your name.
14Yours is an arm endowed with might;
　Your hand is strong;
　Your right hand, exalted.
15Righteousness and justice are the base of Your
　　throne;
　steadfast love and faithfulness stand before
　　You.

16Happy is the people who know the joyful shout;
　O LORD, they walk in the light of Your presence.
17They rejoice in Your name all day long;
　they are exalted through Your righteousness.
18For You are their strength in which they glory;
　our horn is exalted through Your favor.
19Truly our shield is of the LORD,
　our king, of the Holy One of Israel.

20Then[a] You spoke to Your faithful ones in a
　　vision
　and said, "I have conferred power upon a
　　warrior;
　I have exalted one chosen out of the people.
21I have found David, My servant;
　anointed him with My sacred oil.
22My hand shall be constantly with him,
　and My arm shall strengthen him.
23No enemy shall [b]-oppress him,-[b]
　no vile man afflict him.
24I will crush his adversaries before him;
　I will strike down those who hate him.
25My faithfulness and steadfast love shall be with
　　him;
　his horn shall be exalted through My name.
26I will set his hand upon the sea,
　his right hand upon the rivers.
27He shall say to Me,

13 צָפֹון וְיָמִין
אַתָּה בְרָאתָם
תָּבֹור וְחֶרְמֹון בְּשִׁמְךָ יְרַנֵּנוּ׃
14 לְךָ זְרֹועַ עִם־גְּבוּרָה
תָּעֹז יָדְךָ
תָּרוּם יְמִינֶךָ׃
15 צֶדֶק וּמִשְׁפָּט מְכֹון כִּסְאֶךָ
חֶסֶד וֶאֱמֶת יְקַדְּמוּ פָנֶיךָ׃
16 אַשְׁרֵי הָעָם יֹדְעֵי תְרוּעָה
יְהֹוָה בְּאֹור־פָּנֶיךָ יְהַלֵּכוּן׃
17 בְּשִׁמְךָ יְגִילוּן כָּל־הַיֹּום
וּבְצִדְקָתְךָ יָרוּמוּ׃
18 כִּי־תִפְאֶרֶת עֻזָּמֹו אָתָּה
וּבִרְצֹנְךָ תָּרים תָּרוּם קַרְנֵנוּ׃
19 כִּי לַיהוָה מָגִנֵּנוּ
וְלִקְדֹושׁ יִשְׂרָאֵל מַלְכֵּנוּ׃
20 אָז דִּבַּרְתָּ־בְחָזֹון לַחֲסִידֶיךָ
וַתֹּאמֶר שִׁוִּיתִי עֵזֶר עַל־גִּבֹּור
הֲרִימֹותִי בָחוּר מֵעָם׃
21 מָצָאתִי דָּוִד עַבְדִּי
בְּשֶׁמֶן קָדְשִׁי מְשַׁחְתִּיו׃
22 אֲשֶׁר יָדִי תִּכֹּון עִמֹּו
אַף־זְרֹועִי תְאַמְּצֶנּוּ׃
23 לֹא־יַשִּׁא אֹויֵב בֹּו
וּבֶן־עַוְלָה לֹא יְעַנֶּנּוּ׃
24 וְכַתֹּותִי מִפָּנָיו צָרָיו
וּמְשַׂנְאָיו אֶגֹּוף׃
25 וֶאֱמוּנָתִי וְחַסְדִּי עִמֹּו
וּבִשְׁמִי תָּרוּם קַרְנֹו׃
26 וְשַׂמְתִּי בַיָּם יָדֹו
וּבַנְּהָרֹות יְמִינֹו׃
27 הוּא יִקְרָאֵנִי

---

a　Referring to vv. 4–5; cf. 2 Sam. 7.1–17.
b-b　Meaning of Heb. uncertain.

'You are my father, my God, the rock of my
    deliverance.'

28I will appoint him first-born,
    highest of the kings of the earth.

29I will maintain My steadfast love for him always;
    My covenant with him shall endure.

30I will establish his line forever,
    his throne, as long as the heavens last.

31If his sons forsake My Teaching
    and do not live by My rules;
32if they violate My laws,
    and do not observe My commands,
33I will punish their transgression with the rod,
    their iniquity with plagues.

34But I will not take away My steadfast love from
    him;
    I will not betray My faithfulness.

35I will not violate My covenant,
    or change what I have uttered.

36I have sworn by My holiness, once and for all;
    I will not be false to David.

37His line shall continue forever,
    his throne, as the sun before Me,
38as the moon, established forever,
    an enduring witness in the sky."   *Selah.*

39Yet You have rejected, spurned,
    and become enraged at Your anointed.

40You have repudiated the covenant with Your
    servant;
    You have dragged his dignity in the dust.

41You have breached all his defenses,
    shattered his strongholds.

42All who pass by plunder him;
    he has become the butt of his neighbors.

43You have exalted the right hand of his adver-
    saries,
    and made all his enemies rejoice.

44You have turned back the blade of his sword,

אָבִי אָתָּה אֵלִי וְצוּר יְשׁוּעָתִי:
28 אַף־אָנִי בְּכוֹר אֶתְּנֵהוּ
עֶלְיוֹן לְמַלְכֵי־אָרֶץ:
29 לְעוֹלָם אשמור אֶשְׁמָר־לוֹ חַסְדִּי
וּבְרִיתִי נֶאֱמֶנֶת לוֹ:
30 וְשַׂמְתִּי לָעַד זַרְעוֹ
וְכִסְאוֹ כִּימֵי שָׁמָיִם:
31 אִם־יַעַזְבוּ בָנָיו תּוֹרָתִי
וּבְמִשְׁפָּטַי לֹא יֵלֵכוּן:
32 אִם־חֻקֹּתַי יְחַלֵּלוּ
וּמִצְוֹתַי לֹא יִשְׁמֹרוּ:
33 וּפָקַדְתִּי בְשֵׁבֶט פִּשְׁעָם
וּבִנְגָעִים עֲוֺנָם:
34 וְחַסְדִּי לֹא־אָפִיר מֵעִמּוֹ
וְלֹא־אֲשַׁקֵּר בֶּאֱמוּנָתִי:
35 לֹא־אֲחַלֵּל בְּרִיתִי
וּמוֹצָא שְׂפָתַי לֹא אֲשַׁנֶּה:
36 אַחַת נִשְׁבַּעְתִּי בְקָדְשִׁי
אִם־לְדָוִד אֲכַזֵּב:
37 זַרְעוֹ לְעוֹלָם יִהְיֶה
וְכִסְאוֹ כַשֶּׁמֶשׁ נֶגְדִּי:
38 כְּיָרֵחַ יִכּוֹן עוֹלָם
וְעֵד בַּשַּׁחַק נֶאֱמָן   סֶלָה:
39 וְאַתָּה זָנַחְתָּ וַתִּמְאָס
הִתְעַבַּרְתָּ עִם־מְשִׁיחֶךָ:
40 נֵאַרְתָּה בְּרִית עַבְדֶּךָ
חִלַּלְתָּ לָאָרֶץ נִזְרוֹ:
41 פָּרַצְתָּ כָל־גְּדֵרֹתָיו
שַׂמְתָּ מִבְצָרָיו מְחִתָּה:
42 שַׁסֻּהוּ כָּל־עֹבְרֵי דָרֶךְ
הָיָה חֶרְפָּה לִשְׁכֵנָיו:
43 הֲרִימוֹתָ יְמִין צָרָיו
הִשְׂמַחְתָּ כָּל־אוֹיְבָיו:
44 אַף־תָּשִׁיב צוּר חַרְבּוֹ

and have not sustained him in battle.

וְלֹא הֲקֵימֹתוֹ בַּמִּלְחָמָה:

⁴⁵You have brought *b*-his splendor-*b* to an end

and have hurled his throne to the ground.

⁴⁵ הִשְׁבַּתָּ מִטְּהָרוֹ

וְכִסְאוֹ לָאָרֶץ מִגַּרְתָּה:

⁴⁶You have cut short the days of his youth;

You have covered him with shame.   *Selah.*

⁴⁶ הִקְצַרְתָּ יְמֵי עֲלוּמָיו

הֶעֱטִיתָ עָלָיו בּוּשָׁה   סֶלָה:

⁴⁷How long, O LORD; will You forever hide Your

face,

will Your fury blaze like fire?

⁴⁷ עַד־מָה יְהוָה תִּסָּתֵר לָנֶצַח

תִּבְעַר כְּמוֹ־אֵשׁ חֲמָתֶךָ:

⁴⁸O remember *b*-how short my life is;-*b*

why should You have created every man in

vain?

⁴⁸ זְכָר־אֲנִי מֶה־חָלֶד

עַל־מַה־שָּׁוְא בָּרָאתָ כָל־בְּנֵי־אָדָם:

⁴⁹What man can live and not see death,

can save himself from the clutches of Sheol?

Selah.

⁴⁹ מִי גֶבֶר יִחְיֶה וְלֹא יִרְאֶה־מָּוֶת

יְמַלֵּט נַפְשׁוֹ מִיַּד־שְׁאוֹל   סֶלָה:

⁵⁰O Lord, where is Your steadfast love of old

which You swore to David in Your faithfulness?

⁵⁰ אַיֵּה | חֲסָדֶיךָ הָרִאשֹׁנִים | אֲדֹנָי

נִשְׁבַּעְתָּ לְדָוִד בֶּאֱמוּנָתֶךָ:

⁵¹Remember, O Lord, the abuse flung at Your ser-

vants

b-that I have borne in my bosom [from] many

peoples,-*b*

⁵¹ זְכֹר אֲדֹנָי חֶרְפַּת עֲבָדֶיךָ

שְׂאֵתִי בְחֵיקִי כָּל־רַבִּים עַמִּים:

⁵²how Your enemies, O LORD, have flung abuse,

abuse at Your anointed at every step.

⁵² אֲשֶׁר חֵרְפוּ אוֹיְבֶיךָ | יְהוָה

אֲשֶׁר חֵרְפוּ עִקְּבוֹת מְשִׁיחֶךָ:

⁵³Blessed is the LORD forever;

Amen and Amen.

⁵³ בָּרוּךְ יְהוָה לְעוֹלָם

אָמֵן | וְאָמֵן:

BOOK FOUR

ספר רביעי

90 A prayer of Moses, the man of God.

צ תְּפִלָּה לְמֹשֶׁה אִישׁ־הָאֱלֹהִים

O Lord, You have been our refuge in every gen-

eration.

אֲדֹנָי מָעוֹן אַתָּה הָיִיתָ לָּנוּ בְּדֹר

וָדֹר:

²Before the mountains came into being,

before You brought forth the earth and the

world,

from eternity to eternity You are God.

² בְּטֶרֶם | הָרִים יֻלָּדוּ

וַתְּחוֹלֵל אֶרֶץ וְתֵבֵל

וּמֵעוֹלָם עַד־עוֹלָם אַתָּה אֵל:

³You return man to dust;ᵃ

  You decreed, "Return you mortals!"

³ תָּשֵׁב אֱנוֹשׁ עַד־דַּכָּא

וַתֹּאמֶר שׁוּבוּ בְנֵי־אָדָם:

⁴ᵇFor in Your sight a thousand years

  are like yesterday that has passed,

  like a watch of the night.

⁴ כִּי אֶלֶף שָׁנִים בְּעֵינֶיךָ

כְּיוֹם אֶתְמוֹל כִּי יַעֲבֹר

וְאַשְׁמוּרָה בַלָּיְלָה:

⁵You engulf men in sleep;⁻ᵇ

  at daybreak they are like grass that renews itself;

⁵ זְרַמְתָּם שֵׁנָה יִהְיוּ

בַּבֹּקֶר כֶּחָצִיר יַחֲלֹף:

⁶at daybreak it flourishes anew;

  by dusk it withers and dries up.

⁶ בַּבֹּקֶר יָצִיץ וְחָלָף

לָעֶרֶב יְמוֹלֵל וְיָבֵשׁ:

⁷So we are consumed by Your anger,

  terror-struck by Your fury.

⁷ כִּי־כָלִינוּ בְאַפֶּךָ

וּבַחֲמָתְךָ נִבְהָלְנוּ:

⁸You have set our iniquities before You,

  our hidden sins in the light of Your face.

⁸ שַׁתָּ עֲוֺנֹתֵינוּ לְנֶגְדֶּךָ

עֲלֻמֵנוּ לִמְאוֹר פָּנֶיךָ:

⁹All our days pass away in Your wrath;

  we spend our years like a sigh.

⁹ כִּי כָל־יָמֵינוּ פָּנוּ בְעֶבְרָתֶךָ

כִּלִּינוּ שָׁנֵינוּ כְמוֹ־הֶגֶה:

¹⁰The span of our life is seventy years,

  or, given the strength, eighty years;

  but the ᵇ-best of them-ᵇ are trouble and sorrow.

They pass by speedily, and we ᶜ-are in darkness.⁻ᶜ

¹⁰ יְמֵי־שְׁנוֹתֵינוּ בָהֶם שִׁבְעִים שָׁנָה

וְאִם בִּגְבוּרֹת שְׁמוֹנִים שָׁנָה

וְרָהְבָּם עָמָל וָאָוֶן

כִּי־גָז חִישׁ וַנָּעֻפָה:

¹¹Who can know Your furious anger?

Your wrath matches the fear of You.

¹¹ מִי־יוֹדֵעַ עֹז אַפֶּךָ

וּכְיִרְאָתְךָ עֶבְרָתֶךָ:

¹²Teach us to count our days rightly,

  that we may obtain a wise heart.

¹² לִמְנוֹת יָמֵינוּ כֵּן הוֹדַע

וְנָבִא לְבַב חָכְמָה:

¹³Turn, O Lᴏʀᴅ!

How long?

Show mercy to Your servants.

¹³ שׁוּבָה יְהוָה

עַד־מָתָי

וְהִנָּחֵם עַל־עֲבָדֶיךָ:

¹⁴Satisfy us at daybreak with Your steadfast love

  that we may sing for joy all our days.

¹⁴ שַׂבְּעֵנוּ בַבֹּקֶר חַסְדֶּךָ

וּנְרַנְּנָה וְנִשְׂמְחָה בְּכָל־יָמֵינוּ:

¹⁵Give us joy for as long as You have afflicted us,

  for the years we have suffered misfortune.

¹⁵ שַׂמְּחֵנוּ כִּימוֹת עִנִּיתָנוּ

שְׁנוֹת רָאִינוּ רָעָה:

¹⁶Let Your deeds be seen by Your servants,

  Your glory by their children.

¹⁶ יֵרָאֶה אֶל־עֲבָדֶיךָ פָעֳלֶךָ

וַהֲדָרְךָ עַל־בְּנֵיהֶם:

¹⁷May the favor of the Lord, our God, be

  upon us;

  let the work of our hands prosper,

  O prosper the work of our hands!

¹⁷ וִיהִי נֹעַם אֲדֹנָי אֱלֹהֵינוּ עָלֵינוּ

וּמַעֲשֵׂה יָדֵינוּ כּוֹנְנָה עָלֵינוּ

וּמַעֲשֵׂה יָדֵינוּ כּוֹנְנֵהוּ:

ᵃ Or "contrition."

ᵇ⁻ᵇ Meaning of Heb. uncertain.

ᶜ⁻ᶜ Or "fly away."

91

O you who dwell in the shelter of the Most High

and abide in the protection of Shaddai—
²I say of the LORD, my refuge and stronghold,
my God in whom I trust,
³that He will save you from the fowler's trap,
from the destructive plague.
⁴He will cover you with His pinions;
you will find refuge under His wings;
His fidelity is an encircling shield.
⁵You need not fear the terror by night,
or the arrow that flies by day,
⁶the plague that stalks in the darkness,
or the scourge that ravages at noon.
⁷A thousand may fall at your left side,
ten thousand at your right,
but it shall not reach you.
⁸You will see it with your eyes,
you will witness the punishment of the wicked.
⁹Because you took the LORD—my refuge,
the Most High—as your haven,
¹⁰no harm will befall you,
no disease touch your tent.
¹¹For He will order His angels
to guard you wherever you go.
¹²They will carry you in their hands
lest you hurt your foot on a stone.
¹³You will tread on cubs and vipers;
you will trample lions and asps.

¹⁴"Because he is devoted to Me I will deliver him;
I will keep him safe, for he knows My name.
¹⁵When he calls on Me, I will answer him;
I will be with him in distress;
I will rescue him and make him honored;
¹⁶I will let him live to a ripe old age,
and show him My salvation."

צא יֹשֵׁב בְּסֵתֶר עֶלְיֹון
בְּצֵל שַׁדַּי יִתְלֹונָן׃
2 אֹמַר לַיהוָה מַחְסִי וּמְצוּדָתִי
אֱלֹהַי אֶבְטַח־בֹּו׃
3 כִּי הוּא יַצִּילְךָ מִפַּח יָקוּשׁ
מִדֶּבֶר הַוֹּות׃
4 בְּאֶבְרָתֹו ׀ יָסֶךְ לָךְ
וְתַחַת־כְּנָפָיו תֶּחְסֶה
צִנָּה וְסֹחֵרָה אֲמִתֹּו׃
5 לֹא־תִירָא מִפַּחַד לָיְלָה
מֵחֵץ יָעוּף יֹומָם׃
6 מִדֶּבֶר בָּאֹפֶל יַהֲלֹךְ
מִקֶּטֶב יָשׁוּד צָהֳרָיִם׃
7 יִפֹּל מִצִּדְּךָ ׀ אֶלֶף
וּרְבָבָה מִימִינֶךָ
אֵלֶיךָ לֹא יִגָּשׁ׃
8 רַק בְּעֵינֶיךָ תַבִּיט
וְשִׁלֻּמַת רְשָׁעִים תִּרְאֶה׃
9 כִּי־אַתָּה יְהוָה מַחְסִי
עֶלְיֹון שַׂמְתָּ מְעֹונֶךָ׃
10 לֹא־תְאֻנֶּה אֵלֶיךָ רָעָה
וְנֶגַע לֹא־יִקְרַב בְּאָהֳלֶךָ׃
11 כִּי מַלְאָכָיו יְצַוֶּה־לָּךְ
לִשְׁמָרְךָ בְּכָל־דְּרָכֶיךָ׃
12 עַל־כַּפַּיִם יִשָּׂאוּנְךָ
פֶּן־תִּגֹּף בָּאֶבֶן רַגְלֶךָ׃
13 עַל־שַׁחַל וָפֶתֶן תִּדְרֹךְ
תִּרְמֹס כְּפִיר וְתַנִּין׃

14 כִּי בִי חָשַׁק וַאֲפַלְּטֵהוּ
אֲשַׂגְּבֵהוּ כִּי־יָדַע שְׁמִי׃
15 יִקְרָאֵנִי ׀ וְאֶעֱנֵהוּ
עִמֹּו־אָנֹכִי בְצָרָה
אֲחַלְּצֵהוּ וַאֲכַבְּדֵהוּ׃
16 אֹרֶךְ יָמִים אַשְׂבִּיעֵהוּ
וְאַרְאֵהוּ בִּישׁוּעָתִי׃

92 A psalm. A song; for the sabbath day.

צב מִזְמוֹר שִׁיר לְיוֹם הַשַּׁבָּת:

2It is good to praise the LORD,
   to sing hymns to Your name, O Most High,
3To proclaim Your steadfast love at daybreak,
   Your faithfulness each night
4With a ten-stringed harp,
   with voice and lyre together.
5You have gladdened me by Your deeds, O LORD;
   I shout for joy at Your handiwork.
6How great are Your works, O LORD,
   how very subtle[a] Your designs!
7A brutish man cannot know,
   a fool cannot understand this:
8though the wicked sprout like grass,
   though all evildoers blossom,
   it is only that they may be destroyed forever.

9But You are exalted, O LORD, for all time.

10Surely, Your enemies, O LORD,
   surely, Your enemies perish;
   all evildoers are scattered.
11You raise my horn high like that of a wild ox;
   I am soaked in freshening oil.
12I shall see the defeat of my watchful foes,
   hear of the downfall of the wicked who beset
   me.
13The righteous bloom like a date-palm;
   they thrive like a cedar in Lebanon;
14planted in the house of the LORD,
   they flourish in the courts of our God.
15In old age they still produce fruit;
   they are full of sap and freshness,
16attesting that the LORD is upright,
   my rock, in whom there is no wrong.

2 טוֹב לְהֹדוֹת לַיהוָה
וּלְזַמֵּר לְשִׁמְךָ עֶלְיוֹן:
3 לְהַגִּיד בַּבֹּקֶר חַסְדֶּךָ
וֶאֱמוּנָתְךָ בַּלֵּילוֹת:
4 עֲלֵי־עָשׂוֹר וַעֲלֵי־נָבֶל
עֲלֵי הִגָּיוֹן בְּכִנּוֹר:
5 כִּי שִׂמַּחְתַּנִי יְהוָה בְּפָעֳלֶךָ
בְּמַעֲשֵׂי יָדֶיךָ אֲרַנֵּן:
6 מַה־גָּדְלוּ מַעֲשֶׂיךָ יְהוָה
מְאֹד עָמְקוּ מַחְשְׁבֹתֶיךָ:
7 אִישׁ־בַּעַר לֹא יֵדָע
וּכְסִיל לֹא־יָבִין אֶת־זֹאת:
8 בִּפְרֹחַ רְשָׁעִים כְּמוֹ עֵשֶׂב
וַיָּצִיצוּ כָּל־פֹּעֲלֵי אָוֶן
לְהִשָּׁמְדָם עֲדֵי־עַד:

9 וְאַתָּה מָרוֹם לְעֹלָם יְהוָה:

10 כִּי הִנֵּה אֹיְבֶיךָ ׀ יְהוָה
כִּי־הִנֵּה אֹיְבֶיךָ יֹאבֵדוּ
יִתְפָּרְדוּ כָּל־פֹּעֲלֵי אָוֶן:
11 וַתָּרֶם כִּרְאֵים קַרְנִי
בַּלֹּתִי בְּשֶׁמֶן רַעֲנָן:
12 וַתַּבֵּט עֵינִי בְּשׁוּרָי
בַּקָּמִים עָלַי מְרֵעִים תִּשְׁמַעְנָה
אָזְנָי:
13 צַדִּיק כַּתָּמָר יִפְרָח
כְּאֶרֶז בַּלְּבָנוֹן יִשְׂגֶּה:
14 שְׁתוּלִים בְּבֵית יְהוָה
בְּחַצְרוֹת אֱלֹהֵינוּ יַפְרִיחוּ:
15 עוֹד יְנוּבוּן בְּשֵׂיבָה
דְּשֵׁנִים וְרַעֲנַנִּים יִהְיוּ:
16 לְהַגִּיד כִּי־יָשָׁר יְהוָה
צוּרִי וְלֹא־עַלְתָה בּוֹ:

a   Or "profound."

93

The LORD is king,
   He is robed in grandeur;
   the LORD is robed,
   He is girded with strength.
The world stands firm;
   it cannot be shaken.
²Your throne stands firm from of old;
   from eternity You have existed.
³The ocean sounds, O LORD,
   the ocean sounds its thunder,
   the ocean sounds its pounding.
⁴Above the thunder of the mighty waters,
   more majestic than the breakers of the sea
   is the LORD, majestic on high.
⁵Your decrees are indeed enduring;
   holiness befits Your house,
   O LORD, for all times.

צג יְהוָ֣ה מָלָךְ֮
גֵּא֪וּת לָ֫בֵ֥שׁ
לָבֵ֣שׁ יְהוָה֮
עֹ֣ז הִתְאַזָּ֥ר
אַף־תִּכּ֥וֹן תֵּבֵ֗ל
בַּל־תִּמּֽוֹט׃
²נָכ֣וֹן כִּסְאֲךָ֣ מֵאָ֑ז
מֵעוֹלָ֣ם אָֽתָּה׃
³נָשְׂא֣וּ נְהָר֨וֹת ׀ יְהֹוָ֗ה
נָשְׂא֣וּ נְהָר֣וֹת קוֹלָ֑ם
יִשְׂא֖וּ נְהָר֣וֹת דׇּכְיָֽם׃
⁴מִקֹּל֨וֹת ׀ מַ֤יִם רַבִּ֗ים
אַדִּירִ֣ים מִשְׁבְּרֵי־יָ֑ם
אַדִּ֖יר בַּמָּר֣וֹם יְהוָֽה׃
⁵עֵֽדֹתֶ֨יךָ ׀ נֶֽאֶמְנ֬וּ מְאֹ֗ד
לְבֵיתְךָ֥ נַאֲוָה־קֹ֑דֶשׁ
יְ֝הוָ֗ה לְאֹ֣רֶךְ יָמִֽים׃

94

God of retribution, LORD,
   God of retribution, appear!
²Rise up, judge of the earth,
   give the arrogant their deserts!
³How long shall the wicked, O LORD,
   how long shall the wicked exult,
⁴shall they utter insolent speech,
   shall all evildoers vaunt themselves?
⁵They crush Your people, O LORD,
   they afflict Your very own;
⁶they kill the widow and the stranger;
   they murder the fatherless,
⁷thinking, "The LORD does not see it,
   the God of Jacob does not pay heed."

⁸Take heed, you most brutish people;
   fools, when will you get wisdom?
⁹Shall He who implants the ear not hear,

צד אֵל־נְקָמ֥וֹת יְהוָ֑ה
אֵ֖ל נְקָמ֣וֹת הוֹפִֽיעַ׃
²הִ֭נָּשֵׂא שֹׁפֵ֣ט הָאָ֑רֶץ
הָשֵׁ֥ב גְּ֝מ֗וּל עַל־גֵּאִֽים׃
³עַד־מָתַ֖י רְשָׁעִ֥ים ׀ יְהֹוָ֑ה
עַד־מָ֝תַ֗י רְשָׁעִ֥ים יַעֲלֹֽזוּ׃
⁴יַבִּ֣יעוּ יְדַבְּר֣וּ עָתָ֑ק
יִ֝תְאַמְּר֗וּ כׇּל־פֹּ֥עֲלֵי אָֽוֶן׃
⁵עַמְּךָ֣ יְהוָ֣ה יְדַכְּא֑וּ
וְֽנַחֲלָתְךָ֥ יְעַנּֽוּ׃
⁶אַ֭לְמָנָה וְגֵ֣ר יַהֲרֹ֑גוּ
וִ֖יתוֹמִ֣ים יְרַצֵּֽחוּ׃
⁷וַ֭יֹּ֣אמְרוּ לֹ֣א יִרְאֶה־יָּ֑הּ
וְלֹא־יָ֝בִ֗ין אֱלֹהֵ֥י יַעֲקֹֽב׃
⁸בִּ֭ינוּ בֹּעֲרִ֣ים בָּעָ֑ם
וּ֝כְסִילִ֗ים מָתַ֥י תַּשְׂכִּֽילוּ׃
⁹הֲנֹ֣טַֽע אֹ֭זֶן הֲלֹ֣א יִשְׁמָ֑ע

He who forms the eye not see?

10Shall He who disciplines nations not punish,

    He who instructs men in knowledge?

11The Lord knows the designs of men to be futile.

אִם־יֹצֵ֣ר עַ֭יִן הֲלֹ֣א יַבִּֽיט׃

10 הֲיֹסֵ֣ר גּ֭וֹיִם הֲלֹ֣א יוֹכִ֑יחַ

הַֽמְלַמֵּ֖ד אָדָ֣ם דָּֽעַת׃

11 יְהֹוָ֗ה יֹ֭דֵעַ מַחְשְׁב֣וֹת אָדָ֑ם

כִּי־הֵ֥מָּה הָֽבֶל׃

12Happy is the man whom You discipline, O

    Lord,

    the man You instruct in Your teaching,

13to give him tranquillity in times of misfor-

    tune,

    until a pit be dug for the wicked.

14For the Lord will not forsake His people;

    He will not abandon His very own.

15Judgment shall again accord with justice

    and all the upright shall rally to it.

12 אַשְׁרֵ֤י ׀ הַגֶּ֣בֶר אֲשֶׁר־תְּיַסְּרֶ֣נּוּ יָּ֑הּ

וּֽמִתּוֹרָתְךָ֥ תְלַמְּדֶֽנּוּ׃

13 לְהַשְׁקִ֣יט ל֭וֹ מִ֣ימֵי רָ֑ע

עַ֤ד יִכָּרֶ֖ה לָרָשָׁ֣ע שָֽׁחַת׃

14 כִּ֤י ׀ לֹא־יִטֹּ֣שׁ יְהֹוָ֣ה עַמּ֑וֹ

וְ֝נַחֲלָת֗וֹ לֹ֣א יַעֲזֹֽב׃

15 כִּֽי־עַד־צֶ֭דֶק יָשׁ֣וּב מִשְׁפָּ֑ט

וְ֝אַחֲרָ֗יו כׇּל־יִשְׁרֵי־לֵֽב׃

16Who will take my part against evil men?

    Who will stand up for me against wrongdoers?

17Were not the Lord my help,

    I should soon dwell in silence.

18When I think my foot has given way,

    Your faithfulness, O Lord, supports me.

19When I am filled with cares,

    Your assurance soothes my soul.

16 מִֽי־יָק֣וּם לִ֭י עִם־מְרֵעִ֑ים

מִֽי־יִתְיַצֵּ֥ב לִ֝֗י עִם־פֹּ֣עֲלֵי אָֽוֶן׃

17 לוּלֵ֣י יְ֭הֹוָה עֶזְרָ֣תָה לִּ֑י

כִּמְעַ֓ט ׀ שָֽׁכְנָ֖ה דוּמָ֣ה נַפְשִֽׁי׃

18 אִם־אָ֭מַרְתִּי מָ֣טָה רַגְלִ֑י

חַסְדְּךָ֥ יְ֝הֹוָ֗ה יִסְעָדֵֽנִי׃

19 בְּרֹ֣ב שַׂרְעַפַּ֣י בְּקִרְבִּ֑י

תַּ֝נְחוּמֶ֗יךָ יְֽשַׁעַשְׁע֥וּ נַפְשִֽׁי׃

20Shall the seat of injustice be Your partner,

    that frames mischief by statute?

21They band together to do away with the right-

    eous;

    they condemn the innocent to death.

22But the Lord is my haven;

    my God is my sheltering rock.

23He will make their evil recoil upon them,

    annihilate them through their own wickedness;

    the Lord our God will annihilate them.

20 הַֽיְחׇבְרְךָ֮ כִּסֵּ֢א הַ֫וּ֥וֹת

יֹצֵ֖ר עָמָ֣ל עֲלֵי־חֹֽק׃

21 יָ֭גוֹדּוּ עַל־נֶ֣פֶשׁ צַדִּ֑יק

וְדָ֖ם נָקִ֣י יַרְשִֽׁיעוּ׃

22 וַיְהִ֬י יְהֹוָ֣ה לִ֣י לְמִשְׂגָּ֑ב

וֵ֝אלֹהַ֗י לְצ֣וּר מַחְסִֽי׃

23 וַיָּ֤שֶׁב עֲלֵיהֶ֨ם ׀ אֶת־אוֹנָ֗ם

וּבְרָעָתָ֥ם יַצְמִיתֵ֑ם

יַ֝צְמִיתֵ֗ם יְהֹוָ֥ה אֱלֹהֵֽינוּ׃

95 Come, let us sing joyously to the Lord,

    raise a shout for our rock and deliverer;

2let us come into His presence with praise;

צה לְ֭כוּ נְרַנְּנָ֣ה לַיהֹוָ֑ה

נָ֝רִ֗יעָה לְצ֣וּר יִשְׁעֵֽנוּ׃

2 נְקַדְּמָ֣ה פָנָ֣יו בְּתוֹדָ֑ה

let us raise a shout for Him in song!

³For the LORD is a great God,

the great king of all divine beings.

⁴In His hand are the depths of the earth;

the peaks of the mountains are His.

⁵His is the sea, He made it;

and the land, which His hands fashioned.

⁶Come, let us bow down and kneel,

bend the knee before the LORD our maker,

⁷for He is our God,

and we are the people He tends, the flock in

His care.

O, if you would but heed His charge this day:

⁸Do not be stubborn as at Meribah,

as on the day of Massah, in the wilderness,

⁹when your fathers put Me to the test,

tried Me, though they had seen My deeds.

¹⁰Forty years I was provoked by that generation;

I thought, "They are a senseless people;

they would not know My ways."

¹¹Concerning them I swore in anger,

"They shall never come to My resting-place!"

בְּזִמְרוֹת נָרִיעַ לוֹ:

3 כִּי אֵל גָּדוֹל יְהוָה

וּמֶלֶךְ גָּדוֹל עַל־כָּל־אֱלֹהִים:

4 אֲשֶׁר בְּיָדוֹ מֶחְקְרֵי־אָרֶץ

וְתוֹעֲפוֹת הָרִים לוֹ:

5 אֲשֶׁר־לוֹ הַיָּם וְהוּא עָשָׂהוּ

וְיַבֶּשֶׁת יָדָיו יָצָרוּ:

6 בֹּאוּ נִשְׁתַּחֲוֶה וְנִכְרָעָה

נִבְרְכָה לִפְנֵי־יְהוָה עֹשֵׂנוּ:

7 כִּי הוּא אֱלֹהֵינוּ

וַאֲנַחְנוּ עַם מַרְעִיתוֹ וְצֹאן יָדוֹ

הַיּוֹם אִם־בְּקֹלוֹ תִשְׁמָעוּ:

8 אַל־תַּקְשׁוּ לְבַבְכֶם כִּמְרִיבָה

כְּיוֹם מַסָּה בַּמִּדְבָּר:

9 אֲשֶׁר נִסּוּנִי אֲבוֹתֵיכֶם

בְּחָנוּנִי גַּם־רָאוּ פָעֳלִי:

10 אַרְבָּעִים שָׁנָה ׀ אָקוּט בְּדוֹר

וָאֹמַר עַם תֹּעֵי לֵבָב הֵם

וְהֵם לֹא־יָדְעוּ דְרָכָי:

11 אֲשֶׁר־נִשְׁבַּעְתִּי בְאַפִּי

אִם־יְבֹאוּן אֶל־מְנוּחָתִי:

96

ᵃSing to the LORD a new song,

sing to the LORD, all the earth.

²Sing to the LORD, bless His name,

proclaim His victory day after day.

³Tell of His glory among the nations,

His wondrous deeds, among all peoples.

⁴For the LORD is great and much acclaimed,

He is held in awe by all divine beings.

⁵All the gods of the peoples are mere idols,

but the LORD made the heavens.

⁶Glory and majesty are before Him;

strength and splendor are in His temple.

צו שִׁירוּ לַיהוָה שִׁיר חָדָשׁ

שִׁירוּ לַיהוָה כָּל־הָאָרֶץ:

2 שִׁירוּ לַיהוָה בָּרְכוּ שְׁמוֹ

בַּשְּׂרוּ מִיּוֹם־לְיוֹם יְשׁוּעָתוֹ:

3 סַפְּרוּ בַגּוֹיִם כְּבוֹדוֹ

בְּכָל־הָעַמִּים נִפְלְאוֹתָיו:

4 כִּי גָדוֹל יְהוָה וּמְהֻלָּל מְאֹד

נוֹרָא הוּא עַל־כָּל־אֱלֹהִים:

5 כִּי ׀ כָּל־אֱלֹהֵי הָעַמִּים אֱלִילִים

וַיהוָה שָׁמַיִם עָשָׂה:

6 הוֹד־וְהָדָר לְפָנָיו

עֹז וְתִפְאֶרֶת בְּמִקְדָּשׁוֹ:

a   Cf. 1 Chron. 16.23–33.

7Ascribe to the Lᴏʀᴅ, O families of the peoples,
  ascribe to the Lᴏʀᴅ glory and strength.

8Ascribe to the Lᴏʀᴅ the glory of His name,
  bring tribute and enter His courts.

9Bow down to the Lᴏʀᴅ majestic in holiness;
  tremble in His presence, all the earth!

10Declare among the nations, "The Lᴏʀᴅ is king!"
  the world stands firm; it cannot be shaken;
  He judges the peoples with equity.

11Let the heavens rejoice and the earth exult;
  let the sea and all within it thunder,

12the fields and everything in them exult;
  then shall all the trees of the forest shout for
    joy

13at the presence of the Lᴏʀᴅ, for He is coming,
  for He is coming to rule the earth;
  He will rule the world justly,
  and its peoples in faithfulness.

הָבוּ לַיהוָה מִשְׁפְּחוֹת עַמִּים
הָבוּ לַיהוָה כָּבוֹד וָעֹז:
8 הָבוּ לַיהוָה כְּבוֹד שְׁמוֹ
שְׂאוּ־מִנְחָה וּבֹאוּ לְחַצְרוֹתָיו:
9 הִשְׁתַּחֲווּ לַיהוָה בְּהַדְרַת־קֹדֶשׁ
חִילוּ מִפָּנָיו כָּל־הָאָרֶץ:
10 אִמְרוּ בַגּוֹיִם | יְהוָה מָלָךְ
אַף־תִּכּוֹן תֵּבֵל בַּל־תִּמּוֹט
יָדִין עַמִּים בְּמֵישָׁרִים:
11 יִשְׂמְחוּ הַשָּׁמַיִם וְתָגֵל הָאָרֶץ
יִרְעַם הַיָּם וּמְלֹאוֹ:
12 יַעֲלֹז שָׂדַי וְכָל־אֲשֶׁר־בּוֹ
אָז יְרַנְּנוּ כָּל־עֲצֵי־יָעַר:
13 לִפְנֵי יְהוָה | כִּי בָא
כִּי בָא לִשְׁפֹּט הָאָרֶץ
יִשְׁפֹּט־תֵּבֵל בְּצֶדֶק
וְעַמִּים בֶּאֱמוּנָתוֹ:

97 The Lᴏʀᴅ is king!

Let the earth exult,
  the many islands rejoice!

2Dense clouds are around Him,
  righteousness and justice are the base of His
    throne.

3Fire is His vanguard,
  burning His foes on every side.

4His lightnings light up the world;
  the earth is convulsed at the sight;

5mountains melt like wax at the Lᴏʀᴅ's pres-
    ence,
  at the presence of the Lord of all the earth.

6The heavens proclaim His righteousness
  and all peoples see His glory.

7All who worship images,
  who vaunt their idols,
    are dismayed;
  all divine beings bow down to Him.

צז יְהוָה מָלָךְ
תָּגֵל הָאָרֶץ
יִשְׂמְחוּ אִיִּים רַבִּים:
2 עָנָן וַעֲרָפֶל סְבִיבָיו
צֶדֶק וּמִשְׁפָּט מְכוֹן כִּסְאוֹ:
3 אֵשׁ לְפָנָיו תֵּלֵךְ
וּתְלַהֵט סָבִיב צָרָיו:
4 הֵאִירוּ בְרָקָיו תֵּבֵל
רָאֲתָה וַתָּחֵל הָאָרֶץ:
5 הָרִים כַּדּוֹנַג נָמַסּוּ מִלִּפְנֵי יְהוָה
מִלִּפְנֵי אֲדוֹן כָּל־הָאָרֶץ:
6 הִגִּידוּ הַשָּׁמַיִם צִדְקוֹ
וְרָאוּ כָל־הָעַמִּים כְּבוֹדוֹ:
7 יֵבֹשׁוּ |
כָּל־עֹבְדֵי פֶסֶל
הַמִּתְהַלְלִים בָּאֱלִילִים
הִשְׁתַּחֲווּ־לוֹ כָּל־אֱלֹהִים:

8Zion, hearing it, rejoices,
   the towns[a] of Judah exult,
      because of Your judgments, O Lord.
9For You, Lord, are supreme over all the earth;
   You are exalted high above all divine beings.

10O you who love the Lord, hate evil!
He guards the lives of His loyal ones,
   saving them from the hand of the wicked.
11Light is sown for the righteous,
   radiance[b] for the upright.
12O you righteous, rejoice in the Lord
   and acclaim His holy name!

צ שָׁמְעָ֤ה וַתִּשְׂמַ֨ח ׀ צִיּ֗וֹן
וַ֭תָּגֵלְנָה בְּנ֣וֹת יְהוּדָ֑ה
לְמַ֖עַן מִשְׁפָּטֶ֣יךָ יְהוָֽה׃
9 כִּֽי־אַתָּ֬ה יְהוָ֗ה עֶלְי֥וֹן עַל־כָּל־
הָאָ֑רֶץ
מְאֹ֥ד נַ֝עֲלֵ֗יתָ עַל־כָּל־אֱלֹהִֽים׃

10 אֹהֲבֵ֥י יְהוָ֗ה שִׂנְא֫וּ רָ֥ע
שֹׁ֭מֵר נַפְשׁ֣וֹת חֲסִידָ֑יו
מִיַּ֥ד רְ֝שָׁעִ֗ים יַצִּילֵֽם׃
11 א֣וֹר זָרֻ֣עַ לַצַּדִּ֑יק
וּֽלְיִשְׁרֵי־לֵ֥ב שִׂמְחָֽה׃
12 שִׂמְח֣וּ צַ֭דִּיקִים בַּֽיהוָ֑ה
וְ֝הוֹד֗וּ לְזֵ֣כֶר קָדְשֽׁוֹ׃

98 A psalm.

צח מִזְמ֡וֹר

Sing to the Lord a new song,
   for He has worked wonders;
   His right hand, His holy arm,
      has won Him victory.
2The Lord has manifested His victory,
   has displayed His triumph in the sight of the
      nations.
3He was mindful of His steadfast love and faith-
      fulness toward the house of Israel;
   all the ends of the earth beheld the victory of
      our God.
4Raise a shout to the Lord, all the earth,
   break into joyous songs of praise!
5Sing praise to the Lord with the lyre,
   with the lyre and melodious song.
6With trumpets and the blast of the horn
   raise a shout before the Lord, the King.
7Let the sea and all within it thunder,
   the world and its inhabitants;
8let the rivers clap their hands,

שִׁ֣ירוּ לַֽיהוָ֨ה ׀ שִׁ֣יר חָדָ֗שׁ
כִּֽי־נִפְלָא֥וֹת עָשָׂ֑ה
הוֹשִֽׁיעָה־לּ֥וֹ
יְ֝מִינ֗וֹ וּזְר֥וֹעַ קָדְשֽׁוֹ׃
2 הוֹדִ֣יעַ יְ֭הוָה יְשׁוּעָת֑וֹ
לְעֵינֵ֥י הַ֝גּוֹיִ֗ם גִּלָּ֥ה צִדְקָתֽוֹ׃
3 זָ֘כַ֤ר חַסְדּ֨וֹ ׀ וֶֽאֱמֽוּנָתוֹ֮
לְבֵ֪ית יִשְׂרָ֫אֵ֥ל
רָא֥וּ כָל־אַפְסֵי־אָ֑רֶץ אֵ֝֗ת יְשׁוּעַ֥ת
אֱלֹהֵֽינוּ׃
4 הָרִ֥יעוּ לַֽ֭יהוָה כָּל־הָאָ֑רֶץ
פִּצְח֖וּ וְרַנְּנ֣וּ וְזַמֵּֽרוּ׃
5 זַמְּר֣וּ לַֽיהוָ֣ה בְּכִנּ֑וֹר
בְּ֝כִנּ֗וֹר וְק֣וֹל זִמְרָֽה׃
6 בַּ֭חֲצֹ֣צְרוֹת וְק֣וֹל שׁוֹפָ֑ר
הָ֝רִ֗יעוּ לִפְנֵ֤י ׀ הַמֶּ֬לֶךְ יְהוָֽה׃
7 יִרְעַ֣ם הַ֭יָּם וּמְלֹא֑וֹ
תֵּ֝בֵ֗ל וְיֹ֣שְׁבֵי בָֽהּ׃
8 נְהָר֥וֹת יִמְחֲאוּ־כָ֑ף

---

a   Or "women."
b   Others "joy."

the mountains sing joyously together
9at the presence of the Lord,
for He is coming to rule the earth;
He will rule the world justly,
and its peoples with equity.

צט יְהֹוָה מָלָךְ יִרְגְּזוּ עַמִּים
יֹשֵׁב כְּרוּבִים תָּנוּט הָאָרֶץ:
2יְהֹוָה בְּצִיּוֹן גָּדוֹל
וְרָם הוּא עַל־כָּל־הָעַמִּים:
3יוֹדוּ שִׁמְךָ גָּדוֹל וְנוֹרָא
קָדוֹשׁ הוּא:

99 a-The Lord, enthroned on cherubim, is
king,
peoples tremble, the earth quakes.-a
2The Lord is great in Zion,
and exalted above all peoples.
3They praise Your name as great and awesome;
He is holy!

4b-Mighty king-b who loves justice,
it was You who established equity,
You who worked righteous judgment in Jacob.
5Exalt the Lord our God
and bow down to His footstool;
He is holy!

4וְעֹז מֶלֶךְ מִשְׁפָּט אָהֵב
אַתָּה כּוֹנַנְתָּ מֵישָׁרִים
מִשְׁפָּט וּצְדָקָה בְּיַעֲקֹב | אַתָּה
עָשִׂיתָ:
5רוֹמְמוּ יְהֹוָה אֱלֹהֵינוּ
וְהִשְׁתַּחֲווּ לַהֲדֹם רַגְלָיו
קָדוֹשׁ הוּא:

6Moses and Aaron among His priests,
Samuel, among those who call on His name—
when they called to the Lord,
He answered them.
7He spoke to them in a pillar of cloud;
they obeyed His decrees,
the law He gave them.
8O Lord our God, You answered them;
You were a forgiving God for them,
but You exacted retribution for their misdeeds.

6מֹשֶׁה וְאַהֲרֹן | בְּכֹהֲנָיו
וּשְׁמוּאֵל בְּקֹרְאֵי שְׁמוֹ
קֹרִאים* אֶל־יְהֹוָה
וְהוּא יַעֲנֵם:
7בְּעַמּוּד עָנָן יְדַבֵּר אֲלֵיהֶם
שָׁמְרוּ עֵדֹתָיו
וְחֹק נָתַן־לָמוֹ:
8יְהֹוָה אֱלֹהֵינוּ אַתָּה עֲנִיתָם
אֵל נֹשֵׂא הָיִיתָ לָהֶם
וְנֹקֵם עַל־עֲלִילוֹתָם:

9Exalt the Lord our God,
and bow toward His holy hill,
for the Lord our God is holy.

9רוֹמְמוּ יְהֹוָה אֱלֹהֵינוּ
וְהִשְׁתַּחֲווּ לְהַר קָדְשׁוֹ
כִּי־קָדוֹשׁ יְהֹוָה אֱלֹהֵינוּ:

a-a   *Clauses transposed for clarity.*
b-b   *Meaning of Heb. uncertain.*

100 A psalm *a*-for praise.-*a*

Raise a shout for the Lord, all the earth;
  [2]worship the Lord in gladness;
  come into His presence with shouts of joy.
[3]Acknowledge that the Lord is God;
  He made us and *b*-we are His,-*b*
  His people, the flock He tends.
[4]Enter His gates with praise,
  His courts with acclamation.
Praise Him!
Bless His name!
[5]For the Lord is good;
  His steadfast love is eternal;
  His faithfulness is for all generations.

ק מִזְמוֹר לְתוֹדָה

הָרִיעוּ לַיהֹוָה כָּל־הָאָרֶץ:
[2] עִבְדוּ אֶת־יְהֹוָה בְּשִׂמְחָה
בֹּאוּ לְפָנָיו בִּרְנָנָה:
[3] דְּעוּ כִּי־יְהֹוָה הוּא אֱלֹהִים
הוּא־עָשָׂנוּ וְלֹא וְלוֹ אֲנַחְנוּ
עַמּוֹ וְצֹאן מַרְעִיתוֹ:
[4] בֹּאוּ שְׁעָרָיו | בְּתוֹדָה
חֲצֵרֹתָיו בִּתְהִלָּה
הוֹדוּ־לוֹ
בָּרְכוּ שְׁמוֹ:
[5] כִּי־טוֹב יְהֹוָה
לְעוֹלָם חַסְדּוֹ
וְעַד־דֹּר וָדֹר אֱמוּנָתוֹ:

101 Of David. A psalm.

I will sing of faithfulness and justice;
  I will chant a hymn to You, O Lord.
[2]I will study the way of the blameless;
  when shall I attain it?
I will live without blame within my house.
[3]I will not set before my eyes anything base;
  I hate crooked dealing;
  I will have none of it.
[4]Perverse thoughts will be far from me;
  I will know nothing of evil.
[5]He who slanders his friend in secret I will destroy;
  I cannot endure the haughty and proud man.
[6]My eyes are on the trusty men of the land,
  to have them at my side.
He who follows the way of the blameless

קא לְדָוִד מִזְמוֹר

חֶסֶד־וּמִשְׁפָּט אָשִׁירָה
לְךָ יְהֹוָה אֲזַמֵּרָה:
[2] אַשְׂכִּילָה | בְּדֶרֶךְ תָּמִים
מָתַי תָּבוֹא אֵלָי
אֶתְהַלֵּךְ בְּתָם־לְבָבִי בְּקֶרֶב בֵּיתִי:
[3] לֹא־אָשִׁית | לְנֶגֶד עֵינַי דְּבַר־
בְּלִיָּעַל
עֲשֹׂה־סֵטִים שָׂנֵאתִי
לֹא יִדְבַּק בִּי:
[4] לֵבָב עִקֵּשׁ יָסוּר מִמֶּנִּי
רָע לֹא אֵדָע:
[5] מְלָשְׁנִי בַסֵּתֶר | רֵעֵהוּ
אוֹתוֹ אַצְמִית
גְּבַהּ־עֵינַיִם וּרְחַב לֵבָב אֹתוֹ לֹא
אוּכָל:
[6] עֵינַי | בְּנֶאֶמְנֵי־אֶרֶץ
לָשֶׁבֶת עִמָּדִי
הֹלֵךְ בְּדֶרֶךְ תָּמִים

---

a-a Traditionally "for the thanksgiving offering."
b-b So qere; kethib *and some ancient versions* "not we ourselves."

shall be in my service.

7He who deals deceitfully
  shall not live in my house;
  he who speaks untruth
  shall not stand before my eyes.

8Each morning I will destroy
  all the wicked of the land,
  to rid the city of the Lord
  of all evildoers.

הוּא יְשָׁרְתֵנִי:

7 לֹא־יֵשֵׁב ׀ בְּקֶרֶב בֵּיתִי
עֹשֵׂה רְמִיָּה
דֹּבֵר שְׁקָרִים
לֹא־יִכּוֹן לְנֶגֶד עֵינָי:

8 לַבְּקָרִים אַצְמִית
כָּל־רִשְׁעֵי־אָרֶץ
לְהַכְרִית מֵעִיר־יְהֹוָה
כָּל־פֹּעֲלֵי אָוֶן:

102 A prayer of the lowly man when he is faint and pours forth his plea before the Lord.

קב תְּפִלָּה לְעָנִי כִי־יַעֲטֹף וְלִפְנֵי
יְהֹוָה יִשְׁפֹּךְ שִׂיחוֹ:

2O Lord, hear my prayer;
  let my cry come before You.

3Do not hide Your face from me
  in my time of trouble;
  turn Your ear to me;
  when I cry, answer me speedily.

4For my days have vanished like smoke
  and my bones are charred like a hearth.

5My body is stricken and withered like grass;
  a-too wasted-a to eat my food;

6on account of my vehement groaning
  my bones b-show through my skin.-b

7I am like a great owl in the wilderness,
  an owl among the ruins.

8I lie awake; I am like
  a lone bird upon a roof.

9All day long my enemies revile me;
  my deriders use my name to curse.

10For I have eaten ashes like bread
  and mixed my drink with tears,
  11because of Your wrath and Your fury;
  for You have cast me far away.

12My days are like a lengthening shadow;
  I wither like grass.

2 יְהֹוָה שִׁמְעָה תְפִלָּתִי
וְשַׁוְעָתִי אֵלֶיךָ תָבוֹא:

3 אַל־תַּסְתֵּר פָּנֶיךָ ׀ מִמֶּנִּי
בְּיוֹם צַר לִי
הַטֵּה־אֵלַי אָזְנֶךָ
בְּיוֹם אֶקְרָא מַהֵר עֲנֵנִי:

4 כִּי־כָלוּ בְעָשָׁן יָמָי
וְעַצְמוֹתַי כְּמוֹקֵד נִחָרוּ:

5 הוּכָּה־כָעֵשֶׂב וַיִּבַשׁ לִבִּי
כִּי־שָׁכַחְתִּי מֵאֲכֹל לַחְמִי:

6 מִקּוֹל אַנְחָתִי
דָּבְקָה עַצְמִי לִבְשָׂרִי:

7 דָּמִיתִי לִקְאַת מִדְבָּר
הָיִיתִי כְּכוֹס חֳרָבוֹת:

8 שָׁקַדְתִּי וָאֶהְיֶה
כְּצִפּוֹר בּוֹדֵד עַל־גָּג:

9 כָּל־הַיּוֹם חֵרְפוּנִי אוֹיְבָי
מְהוֹלָלַי בִּי נִשְׁבָּעוּ:

10 כִּי־אֵפֶר כַּלֶּחֶם אָכָלְתִּי
וְשִׁקֻּוַי בִּבְכִי מָסָכְתִּי:

11 מִפְּנֵי־זַעַמְךָ וְקִצְפֶּךָ
כִּי נְשָׂאתַנִי וַתַּשְׁלִיכֵנִי:

12 יָמַי כְּצֵל נָטוּי
וַאֲנִי כָּעֵשֶׂב אִיבָשׁ:

a-a Others "I forget."
b-b Lit. "cling to my flesh."

13But You, O Lᴏʀᴅ, are enthroned forever;

Your fame endures throughout the ages.

14You will surely arise and take pity on Zion,

for it is time to be gracious to her;

the appointed time has come.

15Your servants take delight in its stones,

and cherish its dust.

16The nations will fear the name of the Lᴏʀᴅ,

all the kings of the earth, Your glory.

17For the Lᴏʀᴅ has built Zion;

He has appeared in all His glory.

18He has turned to the prayer ᶜ-of the destitute-ᶜ

and has not spurned their prayer.

19May this be written down for a coming generation,

that people yet to be created may praise the Lᴏʀᴅ.

20For He looks down from His holy height;

the Lᴏʀᴅ beholds the earth from heaven

21to hear the groans of the prisoner,

to release those condemned to death;

22that the fame of the Lᴏʀᴅ may be recounted in Zion,

His praises in Jerusalem,

23when the nations gather together,

the kingdoms, to serve the Lᴏʀᴅ.

24He drained my strength in mid-course,

He shortened my days.

25I say, "O my God, do not take me away

in the midst of my days,

You whose years go on for generations on end.

26Of old You established the earth;

the heavens are the work of Your hands.

27They shall perish, but You shall endure;

they shall all wear out like a garment;

You change them like clothing and they pass away.

28But You are the same, and Your years never end.

---

c-c *Meaning of Heb. uncertain.*

29May the children of Your servants dwell securely
and their offspring endure in Your presence."

29 בְּנֵי־עֲבָדֶיךָ יִשְׁכּוֹנוּ
וְזַרְעָם לְפָנֶיךָ יִכּוֹן:

103 Of David.

קג לְדָוִד |

Bless the LORD, O my soul,
    all my being, His holy name.

בָּרֲכִי נַפְשִׁי אֶת־יְהֹוָה
וְכָל־קְרָבַי אֶת־שֵׁם קָדְשׁוֹ:

2Bless the LORD, O my soul
    and do not forget all His bounties.

2 בָּרֲכִי נַפְשִׁי אֶת־יְהֹוָה
וְאַל־תִּשְׁכְּחִי כָּל־גְּמוּלָיו:

3He forgives all your sins,
    heals all your diseases.

3 הַסֹּלֵחַ לְכָל־עֲוֺנֵכִי
הָרֹפֵא לְכָל־תַּחֲלֻאָיְכִי:

4He redeems your life from the Pit,
    surrounds you with steadfast love and mercy.

4 הַגּוֹאֵל מִשַּׁחַת חַיָּיְכִי
הַמְעַטְּרֵכִי חֶסֶד וְרַחֲמִים:

5He satisfies you with good things in ^athe prime
    of life,-^a
    so that your youth is renewed like the eagle's.

5 הַמַּשְׂבִּיעַ בַּטּוֹב עֶדְיֵךְ
תִּתְחַדֵּשׁ כַּנֶּשֶׁר נְעוּרָיְכִי:

6The LORD executes righteous acts
    and judgments for all who are wronged.

6 עֹשֵׂה צְדָקוֹת יְהֹוָה
וּמִשְׁפָּטִים לְכָל־עֲשׁוּקִים:

7He made known His ways to Moses,
    His deeds to the children of Israel.

7 יוֹדִיעַ דְּרָכָיו לְמֹשֶׁה
לִבְנֵי יִשְׂרָאֵל עֲלִילוֹתָיו:

8The LORD is compassionate and gracious,
    slow to anger, abounding in steadfast love.

8 רַחוּם וְחַנּוּן יְהֹוָה
אֶרֶךְ אַפַּיִם וְרַב־חָסֶד:

9He will not contend forever,
    or nurse His anger for all time.

9 לֹא־לָנֶצַח יָרִיב
וְלֹא לְעוֹלָם יִטּוֹר:

10He has not dealt with us according to our sins,
    nor has He requited us according to our
    iniquities.

10 לֹא כַחֲטָאֵינוּ עָשָׂה לָנוּ
וְלֹא כַעֲוֺנֹתֵינוּ גָּמַל עָלֵינוּ:

11For as the heavens are high above the earth,
    so great is His steadfast love toward those who
    fear Him.

11 כִּי כִגְבֹהַּ שָׁמַיִם עַל־הָאָרֶץ
גָּבַר חַסְדּוֹ עַל־יְרֵאָיו:

12As east is far from west,
    so far has He removed our sins from us.

12 כִּרְחֹק מִזְרָח מִמַּעֲרָב
הִרְחִיק מִמֶּנּוּ אֶת־פְּשָׁעֵינוּ:

13As a father has compassion for his children,
    so the LORD has compassion for those who fear
    Him.

13 כְּרַחֵם אָב עַל־בָּנִים
רִחַם יְהֹוָה עַל־יְרֵאָיו:

14For He knows how we are formed;
    He is mindful that we are dust.

14 כִּי־הוּא יָדַע יִצְרֵנוּ
זָכוּר כִּי־עָפָר אֲנָחְנוּ:

a-a   Meaning of Heb. uncertain.

15Man, his days are like those of grass;

he blooms like a flower of the field;

16a wind passes by and it is no more,

its own place no longer knows it.

17But the LORD's steadfast love is for all eternity

toward those who fear Him,

and His beneficence is for the children's chil-

dren

18of those who keep His covenant

and remember to observe His precepts.

19The LORD has established His throne in heaven,

and His sovereign rule is over all.

20Bless the LORD, O His angels,

mighty creatures who do His bidding,

ever obedient to His bidding;

21bless the LORD, all His hosts,

His servants who do His will;

22bless the LORD, all His works,

through the length and breadth of His realm;

bless the LORD, O my soul.

104 Bless the LORD, O my soul;

O LORD, my God, You are very great;

You are clothed in glory and majesty,

2wrapped in a robe of light;

You spread the heavens like a tent cloth.

3He sets the rafters of His lofts in the waters,

makes the clouds His chariot,

moves on the wings of the wind.

4He makes the winds His messengers,

fiery flames His servants.

5He established the earth on its foundations,

so that it shall never totter.

6You made the deep cover it as a garment;

the waters stood above the mountains.

7They fled at Your blast,

rushed away at the sound of Your thunder,

15 אֱנוֹשׁ כֶּחָצִיר יָמָיו

כְּצִיץ הַשָּׂדֶה כֵּן יָצִיץ:

16 כִּי רוּחַ עָבְרָה־בּוֹ וְאֵינֶנּוּ

וְלֹא־יַכִּירֶנּוּ עוֹד מְקוֹמוֹ:

17 וְחֶסֶד יְהוָה ׀ מֵעוֹלָם וְעַד־עוֹלָם

עַל־יְרֵאָיו

וְצִדְקָתוֹ לִבְנֵי בָנִים:

18 לְשֹׁמְרֵי בְרִיתוֹ

וּלְזֹכְרֵי פִקֻּדָיו לַעֲשׂוֹתָם:

19 יְהוָה בַּשָּׁמַיִם הֵכִין כִּסְאוֹ

וּמַלְכוּתוֹ בַּכֹּל מָשָׁלָה:

20 בָּרֲכוּ יְהוָה מַלְאָכָיו

גִּבֹּרֵי כֹחַ עֹשֵׂי דְבָרוֹ

לִשְׁמֹעַ בְּקוֹל דְּבָרוֹ:

21 בָּרֲכוּ יְהוָה כָּל־צְבָאָיו

מְשָׁרְתָיו עֹשֵׂי רְצוֹנוֹ:

22 בָּרֲכוּ יְהוָה ׀ כָּל־מַעֲשָׂיו

בְּכָל־מְקֹמוֹת מֶמְשַׁלְתּוֹ

בָּרֲכִי נַפְשִׁי אֶת־יְהוָה:

קד בָּרֲכִי נַפְשִׁי אֶת־יְהוָה

יְהוָה אֱלֹהַי גָּדַלְתָּ מְּאֹד

הוֹד וְהָדָר לָבָשְׁתָּ:

2 עֹטֶה־אוֹר כַּשַּׂלְמָה

נוֹטֶה שָׁמַיִם כַּיְרִיעָה:

3 הַמְקָרֶה בַמַּיִם עֲלִיּוֹתָיו

הַשָּׂם־עָבִים רְכוּבוֹ

הַמְהַלֵּךְ עַל־כַּנְפֵי־רוּחַ:

4 עֹשֶׂה מַלְאָכָיו רוּחוֹת

מְשָׁרְתָיו אֵשׁ לֹהֵט:

5 יָסַד־אֶרֶץ עַל־מְכוֹנֶיהָ

בַּל־תִּמּוֹט עוֹלָם וָעֶד:

6 תְּהוֹם כַּלְּבוּשׁ כִּסִּיתוֹ

עַל־הָרִים יַעַמְדוּ־מָיִם:

7 מִן־גַּעֲרָתְךָ יְנוּסוּן

מִן־קוֹל רַעַמְךָ יֵחָפֵזוּן:

8—mountains rising, valleys sinking—
  to the place You established for them.
9You set bounds they must not pass
  so that they never again cover the earth.

10You make springs gush forth in torrents;
  they make their way between the hills,
11giving drink to all the wild beasts;
  the wild asses slake their thirst.
12The birds of the sky dwell beside them
  and sing among the foliage.
13You water the mountains from Your[a] lofts;
  the earth is sated from the fruit of Your work.
14You make the grass grow for the cattle,
  and herbage for man's labor
  that he may get food out of the earth—
15wine that cheers the hearts of men
  [b]-oil that makes the face shine,-[b]
  and bread that sustains man's life.
16The trees of the LORD drink their fill,
  the cedars of Lebanon, His own planting,
17where birds make their nests;
  the stork has her home in the junipers.
18The high mountains are for wild goats;
  the crags are a refuge for rock-badgers.

19He made the moon to mark the seasons;
  the sun knows when to set.
20You bring on darkness and it is night,
  when all the beasts of the forests stir.
21The lions roar for prey,
  seeking their food from God.
22When the sun rises, they come home
  and couch in their dens.
23Man then goes out to his work,
  to his labor until the evening.

a   Lit. "His."
b-b   Lit. "to make the face shine from oil."

יַעֲל֣וּ הָ֭רִים יֵרְד֣וּ בְקָע֑וֹת 8
אֶל־מְק֥וֹם זֶ֝֗ה ׀ יָסַ֥דְתָּ לָהֶֽם׃
גְּֽבוּל־שַׂ֭מְתָּ בַּל־יַֽעֲבֹר֑וּן 9
בַּל־יְ֝שׁוּב֗וּן לְכַסּ֥וֹת הָאָֽרֶץ׃

הַֽמְשַׁלֵּ֣חַ מַ֭עְיָנִים בַּנְּחָלִ֑ים 10
בֵּ֥ין הָ֝רִ֗ים יְהַלֵּכֽוּן׃
יַ֭שְׁקוּ כָּל־חַיְת֣וֹ שָׂדָ֑י 11
יִשְׁבְּר֖וּ פְרָאִ֣ים צְמָאָֽם׃
עֲ֭לֵיהֶם עוֹף־הַשָּׁמַ֣יִם יִשְׁכּ֑וֹן 12
מִבֵּ֥ין עֳ֝פָאיִם* יִתְּנוּ־קֽוֹל׃
מַשְׁקֶ֣ה הָ֭רִים מֵעֲלִיּוֹתָ֑יו 13
מִפְּרִ֥י מַ֝עֲשֶׂ֗יךָ תִּשְׂבַּ֥ע הָאָֽרֶץ׃
מַצְמִ֤יחַ חָצִ֨יר ׀ לַבְּהֵמָ֗ה 14
וְ֭עֵשֶׂב לַעֲבֹדַ֣ת הָאָדָ֑ם
לְה֥וֹצִיא לֶ֝֗חֶם מִן־הָאָֽרֶץ׃
וְיַ֤יִן ׀ יְשַׂמַּ֬ח לְֽבַב־אֱנ֗וֹשׁ 15
לְהַצְהִ֣יל פָּנִ֣ים מִשָּׁ֑מֶן
וְ֝לֶ֗חֶם לְֽבַב־אֱנ֥וֹשׁ יִסְעָֽד׃
יִ֭שְׂבְּעוּ עֲצֵ֣י יְהוָ֑ה 16
אַֽרְזֵ֥י לְ֝בָנ֗וֹן אֲשֶׁ֣ר נָטָֽע׃
אֲשֶׁר־שָׁ֭ם צִפֳּרִ֣ים יְקַנֵּ֑נוּ 17
חֲ֝סִידָ֗ה בְּרוֹשִׁ֥ים בֵּיתָֽהּ׃
הָרִ֣ים הַ֭גְּבֹהִים לַיְּעֵלִ֑ים 18
סְ֝לָעִ֗ים מַחְסֶ֥ה לַֽשְׁפַנִּֽים׃

עָשָׂ֣ה יָ֭רֵחַ לְמוֹעֲדִ֑ים 19
שֶׁ֝֗מֶשׁ יָדַ֥ע מְבוֹאֽוֹ׃
תָּֽשֶׁת־חֹ֭שֶׁךְ וִ֣יהִי לָ֑יְלָה 20
בּֽוֹ־תִ֝רְמֹ֗שׂ כָּל־חַיְתוֹ־יָֽעַר׃
הַ֭כְּפִירִים שֹׁאֲגִ֣ים לַטָּ֑רֶף 21
וּלְבַקֵּ֖שׁ מֵאֵ֣ל אָכְלָֽם׃
תִּזְרַ֣ח הַ֭שֶּׁמֶשׁ יֵאָסֵפ֑וּן 22
וְאֶל־מְ֝עֽוֹנֹתָ֗ם יִרְבָּצֽוּן׃
יֵצֵ֣א אָדָ֣ם לְפָעֳל֑וֹ 23
וְֽלַעֲבֹ֖דָת֣וֹ עֲדֵי־עָֽרֶב׃

א׳ נחה   v. 12.

24How many are the things You have made, O
   LORD;
   You have made them all with wisdom;
   the earth is full of Your creations.
25There is the sea, vast and wide,
   with its creatures beyond number,
   living things, small and great.
26There go the ships,
   and Leviathan that You formed to sport with.
27All of them look to You
   to give them their food when it is due.
28Give it to them, they gather it up;
   open Your hand, they are well satisfied;
29hide Your face, they are terrified;
   take away their breath, they perish
   and turn again into dust;
30send back Your breath, they are created,
   and You renew the face of the earth.

31May the glory of the LORD endure forever;
   may the LORD rejoice in His works!
32He looks at the earth and it trembles;
   He touches the mountains and they smoke.
33I will sing to the LORD as long as I live;
   all my life I will chant hymns to my God.
34May my prayer be pleasing to Him;
   I will rejoice in the LORD.
35May sinners disappear from the earth,
   and the wicked be no more.
Bless the LORD, O my soul.
   Hallelujah.

105 Praise the LORD;
   call on His name;
   proclaim His deeds among the peoples.
2Sing praises to Him;
   speak of all His wondrous acts.

24 מָה־רַבּ֬וּ מַעֲשֶׂ֨יךָ ׀ יְהֹוָ֗ה
כֻּ֭לָּם בְּחָכְמָ֣ה עָשִׂ֑יתָ
מָלְאָ֥ה הָ֝אָ֗רֶץ קִנְיָנֶֽךָ׃
25 זֶ֤ה ׀ הַיָּ֥ם גָּדוֹל֮ וּרְחַ֢ב יָ֫דָ֥יִם
שָֽׁם־רֶ֭מֶשׂ וְאֵ֣ין מִסְפָּ֑ר
חַיּ֥וֹת קְ֝טַנּ֗וֹת עִם־גְּדֹלֽוֹת׃
26 שָׁ֭ם אֳנִיּ֣וֹת יְהַלֵּכ֑וּן
לִ֝וְיָתָ֗ן זֶֽה־יָצַ֥רְתָּ לְשַֽׂחֶק־בּֽוֹ׃
27 כֻּ֭לָּם אֵלֶ֣יךָ יְשַׂבֵּר֑וּן
לָתֵ֖ת אׇכְלָ֣ם בְּעִתּֽוֹ׃
28 תִּתֵּ֣ן לָ֭הֶם יִלְקֹט֑וּן
תִּפְתַּ֥ח יָֽ֝דְךָ֗ יִשְׂבְּע֥וּן טֽוֹב׃
29 תַּסְתִּ֥יר פָּנֶיךָ֮ יִֽבָּהֵ֫ל֥וּן
תֹּסֵ֣ף ר֭וּחָם יִגְוָע֑וּן
וְֽאֶל־עֲפָרָ֥ם יְשׁוּבֽוּן׃
30 תְּשַׁלַּ֣ח ר֭וּחֲךָ יִבָּרֵא֑וּן
וּ֝תְחַדֵּ֗שׁ פְּנֵ֣י אֲדָמָֽה׃

31 יְהִ֤י כְב֣וֹד יְהֹוָ֣ה לְעוֹלָ֑ם
יִשְׂמַ֖ח יְהֹוָ֣ה בְּמַעֲשָֽׂיו׃
32 הַמַּבִּ֣יט לָ֭אָרֶץ וַתִּרְעָ֑ד
יִגַּ֖ע בֶּהָרִ֣ים וְֽיֶעֱשָֽׁנוּ׃
33 אָשִׁ֣ירָה לַיהֹוָ֣ה בְּחַיָּ֑י
אֲזַמְּרָ֖ה לֵאלֹהַ֣י בְּעוֹדִֽי׃
34 יֶעֱרַ֣ב עָלָ֣יו שִׂיחִ֑י
אָ֝נֹכִ֗י אֶשְׂמַ֥ח בַּיהֹוָֽה׃
35 יִתַּ֤מּוּ חַטָּאִ֨ים ׀ מִן־הָאָ֡רֶץ
וּרְשָׁעִ֤ים ׀ ע֤וֹד אֵינָ֗ם
בָּרְכִ֣י נַ֭פְשִׁי אֶת־יְהֹוָ֗ה
הַֽלְלוּ־יָֽהּ׃

קה הוֹד֣וּ לַ֭יהֹוָה
קִרְא֣וּ בִשְׁמ֑וֹ
הוֹדִ֥יעוּ בָ֝עַמִּ֗ים עֲלִילוֹתָֽיו׃
2 שִֽׁירוּ־ל֭וֹ זַמְּרוּ־ל֑וֹ
שִׂ֝֗יחוּ בְּכׇל־נִפְלְאוֹתָֽיו׃

3Exult in His holy name;
   let all who seek the LORD rejoice.
4Turn to the LORD, to His might;[a]
   seek His presence constantly.
5Remember the wonders He has done,
   His portents and the judgments He has pro-
     nounced,
6O offspring of Abraham, His servant,
   O descendants of Jacob, His chosen ones.

7He is the LORD our God;
   His judgments are throughout the earth.
8He is ever mindful of His covenant,
   the promise He gave for a thousand genera-
     tions,
9that He made with Abraham,
   swore to Isaac,
10and confirmed in a decree for Jacob,
   for Israel, as an eternal covenant,
11saying, "To you I will give the land of Canaan
   as your allotted heritage."

12They were then few in number,
   a mere handful, sojourning there,
13wandering from nation to nation,
   from one kingdom to another.
14He allowed no one to oppress them;
   He reproved kings on their account,
15"Do not touch My anointed ones;
   do not harm My prophets."

16He called down a famine on the land,
   destroyed every staff of bread.
17He sent ahead of them a man,
   Joseph, sold into slavery.
18His feet were subjected to fetters;
   an iron collar was put on his neck.
19Until his prediction came true
   the decree of the LORD purged him.

---

a I.e., the Ark; cf. Ps. 78.61; 132.8.

1543

3 הִתְהַלְלוּ בְּשֵׁם קָדְשׁוֹ
יִשְׂמַח לֵב ׀ מְבַקְשֵׁי יְהוָה:
4 דִּרְשׁוּ יְהוָה וְעֻזּוֹ
בַּקְּשׁוּ פָנָיו תָּמִיד:
5 זִכְרוּ נִפְלְאוֹתָיו אֲשֶׁר־עָשָׂה
מֹפְתָיו וּמִשְׁפְּטֵי־פִיו:
6 זֶרַע אַבְרָהָם עַבְדּוֹ
בְּנֵי יַעֲקֹב בְּחִירָיו:

7 הוּא יְהוָה אֱלֹהֵינוּ
בְּכָל־הָאָרֶץ מִשְׁפָּטָיו:
8 זָכַר לְעוֹלָם בְּרִיתוֹ
דָּבָר צִוָּה לְאֶלֶף דּוֹר:
9 אֲשֶׁר כָּרַת אֶת־אַבְרָהָם
וּשְׁבוּעָתוֹ לְיִשְׂחָק:
10 וַיַּעֲמִידֶהָ לְיַעֲקֹב לְחֹק
לְיִשְׂרָאֵל בְּרִית עוֹלָם:
11 לֵאמֹר לְךָ אֶתֵּן אֶת־אֶרֶץ־כְּנָעַן
חֶבֶל נַחֲלַתְכֶם:

12 בִּהְיוֹתָם מְתֵי מִסְפָּר
כִּמְעַט וְגָרִים בָּהּ:
13 וַיִּתְהַלְּכוּ מִגּוֹי אֶל־גּוֹי
מִמַּמְלָכָה אֶל־עַם אַחֵר:
14 לֹא־הִנִּיחַ אָדָם לְעָשְׁקָם
וַיּוֹכַח עֲלֵיהֶם מְלָכִים:
15 אַל־תִּגְּעוּ בִמְשִׁיחָי
וְלִנְבִיאַי אַל־תָּרֵעוּ:

16 וַיִּקְרָא רָעָב עַל־הָאָרֶץ
כָּל־מַטֵּה־לֶחֶם שָׁבָר:
17 שָׁלַח לִפְנֵיהֶם אִישׁ
לְעֶבֶד נִמְכַּר יוֹסֵף:
18 עִנּוּ בַכֶּבֶל רַגְלָיו
בַּרְזֶל בָּאָה נַפְשׁוֹ:
19 עַד־עֵת בֹּא־דְבָרוֹ
אִמְרַת יְהוָה צְרָפָתְהוּ:

20The king sent to have him freed;
   the ruler of nations released him.

21He made him the lord of his household,
   empowered him over all his possessions,

22to discipline his princes at will,
   to teach his elders wisdom.

23Then Israel came to Egypt;
   Jacob sojourned in the land of Ham.

24He made His people very fruitful,
   more numerous than their foes.

25b-He changed their heart-b to hate His people,
   to plot against His servants.

26He sent His servant Moses,
   and Aaron, whom He had chosen.

27They performed His signs among them,
   His wonders, against the land of Ham.

28He sent darkness; it was very dark;
   c-did they not defy His word?-c

29He turned their waters into blood
   and killed their fish.

30Their land teemed with frogs,
   even the rooms of their king.

31Swarms of insects came at His command,
   lice, throughout their country.

32He gave them hail for rain,
   and flaming fire in their land.

33He struck their vines and fig trees,
   broke down the trees of their country.

34Locusts came at His command,
   grasshoppers without number.

35They devoured every green thing in the land;
   they consumed the produce of the soil.

36He struck down every first-born in the land,
   the first fruit of their vigor.

37He led Israeld out with silver and gold;
   none among their tribes faltered.

20 שָׁלַח מֶלֶךְ וַיַתִּירֵהוּ
מֹשֵׁל עַמִּים וַיְפַתְּחֵהוּ:
21 שָׂמוֹ אָדוֹן לְבֵיתוֹ
וּמֹשֵׁל בְּכָל־קִנְיָנוֹ:
22 לֶאְסֹר שָׂרָיו בְּנַפְשׁוֹ
וּזְקֵנָיו יְחַכֵּם:
23 וַיָּבֹא יִשְׂרָאֵל מִצְרָיִם
וְיַעֲקֹב גָּר בְּאֶרֶץ־חָם:
24 וַיֶּפֶר אֶת־עַמּוֹ מְאֹד
וַיַּעֲצִמֵהוּ מִצָּרָיו:
25 הָפַךְ לִבָּם לִשְׂנֹא עַמּוֹ
לְהִתְנַכֵּל בַּעֲבָדָיו:
26 שָׁלַח מֹשֶׁה עַבְדּוֹ
אַהֲרֹן אֲשֶׁר בָּחַר־בּוֹ:
27 שָׂמוּ־בָם דִּבְרֵי אֹתוֹתָיו
וּמֹפְתִים בְּאֶרֶץ חָם:
28 שָׁלַח חֹשֶׁךְ וַיַּחְשִׁךְ
וְלֹא־מָרוּ אֶת־דברוו דְּבָרוֹ:
29 הָפַךְ אֶת־מֵימֵיהֶם לְדָם
וַיָּמֶת אֶת־דְּגָתָם:
30 שָׁרַץ אַרְצָם צְפַרְדְּעִים
בְּחַדְרֵי מַלְכֵיהֶם:
31 אָמַר וַיָּבֹא עָרֹב
כִּנִּים בְּכָל־גְּבוּלָם:
32 נָתַן גִּשְׁמֵיהֶם בָּרָד
אֵשׁ לֶהָבוֹת בְּאַרְצָם:
33 וַיַּךְ גַּפְנָם וּתְאֵנָתָם
וַיְשַׁבֵּר עֵץ גְּבוּלָם:
34 אָמַר וַיָּבֹא אַרְבֶּה
וְיֶלֶק וְאֵין מִסְפָּר:
35 וַיֹּאכַל כָּל־עֵשֶׂב בְּאַרְצָם
וַיֹּאכַל פְּרִי אַדְמָתָם:
36 וַיַּךְ כָּל־בְּכוֹר בְּאַרְצָם
רֵאשִׁית לְכָל־אוֹנָם:
37 וַיּוֹצִיאֵם בְּכֶסֶף וְזָהָב
וְאֵין בִּשְׁבָטָיו כּוֹשֵׁל:

b-b   Or "Their heart changed."
c-c   Meaning of Heb. uncertain.
d   Lit. "them."

³⁸Egypt rejoiced when they left,
   for dread of Israel^d had fallen upon them.

³⁹He spread a cloud for a cover,
   and fire to light up the night.
⁴⁰They asked and He brought them quail,
   and satisfied them with food from heaven.
⁴¹He opened a rock so that water gushed forth;
   it flowed as a stream in the parched land.
⁴²Mindful of His sacred promise
   to His servant Abraham,
⁴³He led His people out in gladness,
   His chosen ones with joyous song.
⁴⁴He gave them the lands of nations;
   they inherited the wealth of peoples,
⁴⁵that they might keep His laws
   and observe His teachings.
   Hallelujah.

106 Hallelujah.

Praise the LORD for He is good;
   His steadfast love is eternal.
²Who can tell the mighty acts of the LORD,
   proclaim all His praises?

³Happy are those who act justly,
   who do right at all times.
⁴Be mindful of me, O LORD, when You favor Your
   people;
   take note of me when You deliver them,
⁵that I may enjoy the prosperity of Your chosen
   ones,
   share the joy of Your nation,
   glory in Your very own people.

⁶We have sinned like our forefathers;
   we have gone astray, done evil.

שָׂמַח מִצְרַיִם בְּצֵאתָם 38
כִּי־נָפַל פַּחְדָּם עֲלֵיהֶם:

פָּרַשׂ עָנָן לְמָסָךְ 39
וְאֵשׁ לְהָאִיר לָיְלָה:
שָׁאַל וַיָּבֵא שְׂלָו 40
וְלֶחֶם שָׁמַיִם יַשְׂבִּיעֵם:
פָּתַח צוּר וַיָּזוּבוּ מָיִם 41
הָלְכוּ בַּצִּיּוֹת נָהָר:
כִּי־זָכַר אֶת־דְּבַר קָדְשׁוֹ 42
אֶת־אַבְרָהָם עַבְדּוֹ:
וַיּוֹצִא עַמּוֹ בְשָׂשׂוֹן 43
בְּרִנָּה אֶת־בְּחִירָיו:
וַיִּתֵּן לָהֶם אַרְצוֹת גּוֹיִם 44
וַעֲמַל לְאֻמִּים יִירָשׁוּ:
בַּעֲבוּר ׀ יִשְׁמְרוּ חֻקָּיו 45
וְתוֹרֹתָיו יִנְצֹרוּ
הַלְלוּ־יָהּ:

קו הַלְלוּיָהּ ׀

הוֹדוּ לַיהוָה כִּי־טוֹב
כִּי לְעוֹלָם חַסְדּוֹ:
מִי יְמַלֵּל גְּבוּרוֹת יְהוָה 2
יַשְׁמִיעַ כָּל־תְּהִלָּתוֹ:

אַשְׁרֵי שֹׁמְרֵי מִשְׁפָּט 3
עֹשֵׂה צְדָקָה בְכָל־עֵת:
זָכְרֵנִי יְהוָה בִּרְצוֹן עַמֶּךָ 4
פָּקְדֵנִי בִּישׁוּעָתֶךָ:
לִרְאוֹת ׀ בְּטוֹבַת בְּחִירֶיךָ 5
לִשְׂמֹחַ בְּשִׂמְחַת גּוֹיֶךָ
לְהִתְהַלֵּל עִם־נַחֲלָתֶךָ:

חָטָאנוּ עִם־אֲבוֹתֵינוּ 6
הֶעֱוִינוּ הִרְשָׁעְנוּ:

7Our forefathers in Egypt did not perceive Your
   wonders;
   they did not remember Your abundant love,
   but rebelled at the sea, at the Sea of Reeds.

8Yet He saved them, as befits His name,
   to make known His might.

9He sent His blast against the Sea of Reeds;
   it became dry;
   He led them through the deep as through a wilderness.

10He delivered them from the foe,
   redeemed them from the enemy.

11Water covered their adversaries;
   not one of them was left.

12Then they believed His promise,
   and sang His praises.

13But they soon forgot His deeds;
   they would not wait to learn His plan.

14They were seized with craving in the wilderness,
   and put God to the test in the wasteland.

15He gave them what they asked for,
   then made them waste away.

16There was envy of Moses in the camp,
   and of Aaron, the holy one of the LORD.

17The earth opened up and swallowed Dathan,
   closed over the party of Abiram.

18A fire blazed among their party,
   a flame that consumed the wicked.

19They made a calf at Horeb
   and bowed down to a molten image.

20They exchanged their glory
   for the image of a bull that feeds on grass.

21They forgot God who saved them,
   who performed great deeds in Egypt,

22wondrous deeds in the land of Ham,
   awesome deeds at the Sea of Reeds.

23He would have destroyed them
   had not Moses His chosen one

אֲבוֹתֵינוּ בְמִצְרַיִם ׀ לֹא־הִשְׂכִּילוּ 7
נִפְלְאוֹתֶיךָ
לֹא זָכְרוּ אֶת־רֹב חֲסָדֶיךָ
וַיַּמְרוּ עַל־יָם בְּיַם־סוּף:
וַיּוֹשִׁיעֵם לְמַעַן שְׁמוֹ 8
לְהוֹדִיעַ אֶת־גְּבוּרָתוֹ:
וַיִּגְעַר בְּיַם־סוּף 9
וַיֶּחֱרָב
וַיּוֹלִיכֵם בַּתְּהֹמוֹת כַּמִּדְבָּר:
וַיּוֹשִׁיעֵם מִיַּד שׂוֹנֵא 10
וַיִּגְאָלֵם מִיַּד אוֹיֵב:
וַיְכַסּוּ־מַיִם צָרֵיהֶם 11
אֶחָד מֵהֶם לֹא נוֹתָר:
וַיַּאֲמִינוּ בִדְבָרָיו 12
יָשִׁירוּ תְּהִלָּתוֹ:
מִהֲרוּ שָׁכְחוּ מַעֲשָׂיו 13
לֹא־חִכּוּ לַעֲצָתוֹ:
וַיִּתְאַוּוּ תַאֲוָה בַּמִּדְבָּר 14
וַיְנַסּוּ־אֵל בִּישִׁימוֹן:
וַיִּתֵּן לָהֶם שֶׁאֱלָתָם 15
וַיְשַׁלַּח רָזוֹן בְּנַפְשָׁם:
וַיְקַנְאוּ לְמֹשֶׁה בַּמַּחֲנֶה 16
לְאַהֲרֹן קְדוֹשׁ יְהוָה:
תִּפְתַּח־אֶרֶץ וַתִּבְלַע דָּתָן 17
וַתְּכַס עַל־עֲדַת אֲבִירָם:
וַתִּבְעַר־אֵשׁ בַּעֲדָתָם 18
לֶהָבָה תְּלַהֵט רְשָׁעִים:
יַעֲשׂוּ־עֵגֶל בְּחֹרֵב 19
וַיִּשְׁתַּחֲווּ לְמַסֵּכָה:
וַיָּמִירוּ אֶת־כְּבוֹדָם 20
בְּתַבְנִית שׁוֹר אֹכֵל עֵשֶׂב:
שָׁכְחוּ אֵל מוֹשִׁיעָם 21
עֹשֶׂה גְדֹלוֹת בְּמִצְרָיִם:
נִפְלָאוֹת בְּאֶרֶץ חָם 22
נוֹרָאוֹת עַל־יַם־סוּף:
וַיֹּאמֶר לְהַשְׁמִידָם 23
לוּלֵי מֹשֶׁה בְחִירוֹ

confronted Him in the breach
to avert His destructive wrath.
24They rejected the desirable land,
and put no faith in His promise.
25They grumbled in their tents
and disobeyed the LORD.
26So He raised His hand in oath
to make them fall in the wilderness,
27to disperse*a* their offspring among the nations
and scatter them through the lands.
28They attached themselves to Baal Peor,
ate sacrifices offered to the dead.
29They provoked anger by their deeds,
and a plague broke out among them.
30Phinehas stepped forth and intervened,
and the plague ceased.
31It was reckoned to his merit
for all generations, to eternity.
32They provoked wrath at the waters of Meribah
and Moses suffered on their account,
33because they rebelled against Him
and he spoke rashly.

34They did not destroy the nations
as the LORD had commanded them,
35but mingled with the nations
and learned their ways.
36They worshiped their idols,
which became a snare for them.
37Their own sons and daughters
they sacrificed to demons.
38They shed innocent blood,
the blood of their sons and daughters,
whom they sacrificed to the idols of Canaan;
so the land was polluted with bloodguilt.
39Thus they became defiled by their acts,
debauched through their deeds.

a   *Cf. Targum, Kimhi.*

עָמַד בַּפֶּרֶץ לְפָנָיו
לְהָשִׁיב חֲמָתוֹ מֵהַשְׁחִית:
24 וַיִּמְאֲסוּ בְּאֶרֶץ חֶמְדָּה
לֹא־הֶאֱמִינוּ לִדְבָרוֹ:
25 וַיֵּרָגְנוּ בְאָהֳלֵיהֶם
לֹא שָׁמְעוּ בְּקוֹל יְהֹוָה:
26 וַיִּשָּׂא יָדוֹ לָהֶם
לְהַפִּיל אוֹתָם בַּמִּדְבָּר:
27 וּלְהַפִּיל זַרְעָם בַּגּוֹיִם
וּלְזָרוֹתָם בָּאֲרָצוֹת:
28 וַיִּצָּמְדוּ לְבַעַל פְּעוֹר
וַיֹּאכְלוּ זִבְחֵי מֵתִים:
29 וַיַּכְעִיסוּ בְּמַעַלְלֵיהֶם
וַתִּפְרָץ־בָּם מַגֵּפָה:
30 וַיַּעֲמֹד פִּינְחָס וַיְפַלֵּל
וַתֵּעָצַר הַמַּגֵּפָה:
31 וַתֵּחָשֶׁב לוֹ לִצְדָקָה
לְדֹר וָדֹר עַד־עוֹלָם:
32 וַיַּקְצִיפוּ עַל־מֵי מְרִיבָה
וַיֵּרַע לְמֹשֶׁה בַּעֲבוּרָם:
33 כִּי־הִמְרוּ אֶת־רוּחוֹ
וַיְבַטֵּא בִּשְׂפָתָיו:

34 לֹא־הִשְׁמִידוּ אֶת־הָעַמִּים
אֲשֶׁר אָמַר יְהֹוָה לָהֶם:
35 וַיִּתְעָרְבוּ בַגּוֹיִם
וַיִּלְמְדוּ מַעֲשֵׂיהֶם:
36 וַיַּעַבְדוּ אֶת־עֲצַבֵּיהֶם
וַיִּהְיוּ לָהֶם לְמוֹקֵשׁ:
37 וַיִּזְבְּחוּ אֶת־בְּנֵיהֶם
וְאֶת־בְּנוֹתֵיהֶם לַשֵּׁדִים:
38 וַיִּשְׁפְּכוּ דָם נָקִי
דַּם־בְּנֵיהֶם וּבְנוֹתֵיהֶם
אֲשֶׁר זִבְּחוּ לַעֲצַבֵּי כְנַעַן
וַתֶּחֱנַף הָאָרֶץ בַּדָּמִים:
39 וַיִּטְמְאוּ בְמַעֲשֵׂיהֶם
וַיִּזְנוּ בְּמַעַלְלֵיהֶם:

40The LORD was angry with His people
   and He abhorred His inheritance.
41He handed them over to the nations;
   their foes ruled them.
42Their enemies oppressed them
   and they were subject to their power.
43He saved them time and again,
   but they were deliberately rebellious,
   and so they were brought low by their iniquity.
44When He saw that they were in distress,
   when He heard their cry,
45He was mindful of His covenant
   and in His great faithfulness relented.
46He made all their captors kindly disposed toward them.

47Deliver us, O LORD our God,
   and gather us from among the nations,
   to acclaim Your holy name,
   to glory in Your praise.

48Blessed is the LORD, God of Israel,
From eternity to eternity.
Let all the people say, "Amen."
   Hallelujah.

BOOK FIVE

107
  "Praise the LORD, for He is good;
   His steadfast love is eternal!"
2Thus let the redeemed of the LORD say,
   those He redeemed from adversity,
   3whom He gathered in from the lands,
   from east and west,
   from the north and from the sea.

40 וַיִּחַר־אַ֣ף יְהֹוָ֣ה בְּעַמּ֑וֹ
וַיְתָעֵ֥ב אֶת־נַחֲלָתֽוֹ׃
41 וַיִּתְּנֵ֥ם בְּיַד־גּוֹיִ֑ם
וַֽיִּמְשְׁל֥וּ בָ֝הֶ֗ם שֹׂנְאֵיהֶֽם׃
42 וַיִּלְחָצ֥וּם אוֹיְבֵיהֶ֑ם
וַ֝יִּכָּנְע֗וּ תַּ֣חַת יָדָֽם׃
43 פְּעָמִ֥ים רַבּ֗וֹת יַ֫צִּילֵ֥ם
וְ֭הֵמָּה יַמְר֣וּ בַעֲצָתָ֑ם
וַ֝יָּמֹ֗כּוּ בַּעֲוֺנָֽם׃
44 וַ֭יַּרְא בַּצַּ֣ר לָהֶ֑ם
בְּ֝שׇׁמְע֗וֹ אֶת־רִנָּתָֽם׃
45 וַיִּזְכֹּ֣ר לָהֶ֣ם בְּרִית֑וֹ
וַ֝יִּנָּחֵ֗ם כְּרֹ֣ב חֲסָדָֽו׃
46 וַיִּתֵּ֣ן אוֹתָ֣ם לְרַחֲמִ֑ים לִ֝פְנֵ֗י כׇּל־
שׁוֹבֵיהֶֽם׃

47 הוֹשִׁיעֵ֨נוּ ׀ יְהֹוָ֣ה אֱלֹהֵינוּ֮
וְקַבְּצֵנוּ֮ מִֽן־הַגּ֫וֹיִ֥ם
לְ֭הֹדוֹת לְשֵׁ֣ם קׇדְשֶׁ֑ךָ
לְ֝הִשְׁתַּבֵּ֗חַ בִּתְהִלָּתֶֽךָ׃

48 בָּ֤רוּךְ־יְהֹוָ֨ה אֱלֹהֵ֪י יִשְׂרָאֵ֡ל
מִן־הָ֨עוֹלָ֤ם ׀ וְעַ֬ד הָעוֹלָ֗ם
וְאָמַ֖ר כׇּל־הָעָ֥ם אָמֵ֗ן
הַֽלְלוּ־יָֽהּ׃

ספר חמישי

קז הֹד֣וּ לַיהֹוָ֣ה כִּי־ט֑וֹב
כִּ֖י לְעוֹלָ֣ם חַסְדּֽוֹ׃
2 יֹ֭אמְרוּ גְּאוּלֵ֣י יְהֹוָ֑ה
אֲשֶׁ֥ר גְּ֝אָלָ֗ם מִיַּד־צָֽר׃
3 וּֽמֵאֲרָצ֗וֹת קִ֫בְּצָ֥ם
מִמִּזְרָ֥ח וּמִֽמַּעֲרָ֑ב
מִצָּפ֥וֹן וּמִיָּֽם׃

4Some lost their way in the wilderness,
  in the wasteland;
  they found no settled place.

5Hungry and thirsty,
  their spirit failed.

6In their adversity they cried to the LORD,
  and He rescued them from their troubles.

7He showed them a direct way
  to reach a settled place.

8Let them praise the LORD for His steadfast love,
  His wondrous deeds for mankind;

9for He has satisfied the thirsty,
  filled the hungry with all good things.

10Some lived in deepest darkness,
  bound in cruel irons,

11because they defied the word of God,
  spurned the counsel of the Most High.

12He humbled their hearts through suffering;
  they stumbled with no one to help.

13In their adversity they cried to the LORD,
  and He rescued them from their troubles.

14He brought them out of deepest darkness,
  broke their bonds asunder.

15Let them praise the LORD for His steadfast love,
  His wondrous deeds for mankind,

16For He shattered gates of bronze,
  He broke their iron bars.

17There were fools who suffered for their sinful
  way,
  and for their iniquities.

18All food was loathsome to them;
  they reached the gates of death.

19In their adversity they cried to the LORD
  and He saved them from their troubles.

20He gave an order and healed them;
  He delivered them from the pits.ᵃ

4 תָּעוּ בַמִּדְבָּר
בִּישִׁימוֹן דָּרֶךְ
עִיר מוֹשָׁב לֹא מָצָאוּ:
5 רְעֵבִים גַּם־צְמֵאִים
נַפְשָׁם בָּהֶם תִּתְעַטָּף:
6 וַיִּצְעֲקוּ אֶל־יְהוָה בַּצַּר לָהֶם
מִמְּצוּקוֹתֵיהֶם יַצִּילֵם:
7 וַיַּדְרִיכֵם בְּדֶרֶךְ יְשָׁרָה
לָלֶכֶת אֶל־עִיר מוֹשָׁב:
8 יוֹדוּ לַיהוָה חַסְדּוֹ
וְנִפְלְאוֹתָיו לִבְנֵי אָדָם:
9 כִּי־הִשְׂבִּיעַ נֶפֶשׁ שֹׁקֵקָה
וְנֶפֶשׁ רְעֵבָה מִלֵּא־טוֹב:
10 יֹשְׁבֵי חֹשֶׁךְ וְצַלְמָוֶת
אֲסִירֵי עֳנִי וּבַרְזֶל:
11 כִּי־הִמְרוּ אִמְרֵי־אֵל
וַעֲצַת עֶלְיוֹן נָאָצוּ:
12 וַיַּכְנַע בֶּעָמָל לִבָּם
כָּשְׁלוּ וְאֵין עֹזֵר:
13 וַיִּזְעֲקוּ אֶל־יְהוָה בַּצַּר לָהֶם
מִמְּצֻקוֹתֵיהֶם יוֹשִׁיעֵם:
14 יוֹצִיאֵם מֵחֹשֶׁךְ וְצַלְמָוֶת
וּמוֹסְרוֹתֵיהֶם יְנַתֵּק:
15 יוֹדוּ לַיהוָה חַסְדּוֹ
וְנִפְלְאוֹתָיו לִבְנֵי אָדָם:
16 כִּי־שִׁבַּר דַּלְתוֹת נְחֹשֶׁת
וּבְרִיחֵי בַרְזֶל גִּדֵּעַ:
17 אֱוִלִים מִדֶּרֶךְ פִּשְׁעָם
וּמֵעֲוֺנֹתֵיהֶם יִתְעַנּוּ:
18 כָּל־אֹכֶל תְּתַעֵב נַפְשָׁם
וַיַּגִּיעוּ עַד־שַׁעֲרֵי מָוֶת:
19 וַיִּזְעֲקוּ אֶל־יְהוָה בַּצַּר לָהֶם
מִמְּצֻקוֹתֵיהֶם יוֹשִׁיעֵם:
20 יִשְׁלַח דְּבָרוֹ וְיִרְפָּאֵם
וִימַלֵּט מִשְּׁחִיתוֹתָם:

---

a Viz., of death.

1549

21Let them praise the LORD for His steadfast love,
His wondrous deeds for mankind.
22Let them offer thanksgiving sacrifices,
and tell His deeds in joyful song.

23Others go down to the sea in ships,
ply their trade in the mighty waters;
24they have seen the works of the LORD
and His wonders in the deep.
25By His word He raised a storm wind
that made the waves surge.
26Mounting up to the heaven,
plunging down to the depths,
disgorging in their misery,
27they reeled and staggered like a drunken man,
all their skill to no avail.
28In their adversity they cried to the LORD,
and He saved them from their troubles.
29He reduced the storm to a whisper;
the waves were stilled.
30They rejoiced when all was quiet,
and He brought them to the port they desired.
31Let them praise the LORD for His steadfast love,
His wondrous deeds for mankind.
32Let them exalt Him in the congregation of the
people,
acclaim Him in the assembly of the elders.

33He turns the rivers into a wilderness,
springs of water into thirsty land,
34fruitful land into a salt marsh,
because of the wickedness of its inhabitants.
35He turns the wilderness into pools,
parched land into springs of water.
36There He settles the hungry;
they build a place to settle in.
37They sow fields and plant vineyards
that yield a fruitful harvest.

נ*21 יוֹד֣וּ לַיהֹוָ֣ה חַסְדּ֑וֹ
וְנִ֝פְלְאוֹתָ֗יו לִבְנֵ֣י אָדָֽם׃
נ*22 וְיִזְבְּח֖וּ זִבְחֵ֣י תוֹדָ֑ה
וִֽיסַפְּר֖וּ מַעֲשָׂ֣יו בְּרִנָּֽה׃

נ*23 יוֹרְדֵ֣י הַ֭יָּם בׇּאֳנִיּ֑וֹת
עֹשֵׂ֥י מְ֝לָאכָ֗ה בְּמַ֣יִם רַבִּֽים׃
נ*24 הֵ֣מָּה רָ֭אוּ מַעֲשֵׂ֣י יְהֹוָ֑ה
וְ֝נִפְלְאוֹתָ֗יו בִּמְצוּלָֽה׃
נ*25 וַיֹּ֗אמֶר וַֽ֭יַּעֲמֵד ר֣וּחַ סְעָרָ֑ה
וַתְּרוֹמֵ֥ם גַּלָּֽיו׃
נ*26 יַעֲל֣וּ שָׁ֭מַיִם
יֵרְד֣וּ תְהוֹמ֑וֹת
נַ֝פְשָׁ֗ם בְּרָעָ֥ה תִתְמוֹגָֽג׃
27 יָח֣וֹגּוּ וְ֭יָנוּעוּ כַּשִּׁכּ֑וֹר
וְכׇל־חׇ֝כְמָתָ֗ם תִּתְבַּלָּֽע׃
28 וַיִּצְעֲק֣וּ אֶל־יְ֭הֹוָה בַּצַּ֣ר לָהֶ֑ם
וּֽ֝מִמְּצ֥וּקֹתֵיהֶ֗ם יוֹצִיאֵֽם׃
29 יָקֵ֣ם סְ֭עָרָה לִדְמָמָ֑ה
וַ֝יֶּחֱשׁ֗וּ גַּלֵּיהֶֽם׃
30 וַיִּשְׂמְח֥וּ כִֽי־יִשְׁתֹּ֑קוּ
וַ֝יַּנְחֵ֗ם אֶל־מְח֥וֹז חֶפְצָֽם׃
31 יוֹד֣וּ לַיהֹוָ֣ה חַסְדּ֑וֹ
וְ֝נִפְלְאוֹתָ֗יו לִבְנֵ֣י אָדָֽם׃
32 וִֽ֭ירֹמְמוּהוּ בִּקְהַל־עָ֑ם
וּבְמוֹשַׁ֖ב זְקֵנִ֣ים יְהַלְלֽוּהוּ׃

33 יָשֵׂ֣ם נְהָר֣וֹת לְמִדְבָּ֑ר
וּמֹצָ֥אֵי מַ֝֗יִם לְצִמָּאֽוֹן׃
34 אֶ֣רֶץ פְּ֭רִי לִמְלֵחָ֑ה
מֵ֝רָעַ֗ת יֹ֣שְׁבֵי בָֽהּ׃
35 יָשֵׂ֣ם מִ֭דְבָּר לַאֲגַם־מַ֑יִם
וְאֶ֥רֶץ צִ֝יָּ֗ה לְמֹצָ֥אֵי מָֽיִם׃
36 וַיּ֣וֹשֶׁב שָׁ֣ם רְעֵבִ֑ים
וַ֝יְכוֹנְנ֗וּ עִ֣יר מוֹשָֽׁב׃
37 וַיִּזְרְע֣וּ שָׂ֭דוֹת וַיִּטְּע֣וּ כְרָמִ֑ים
וַ֝יַּעֲשׂ֗וּ פְּרִ֣י תְבוּאָֽה׃

v. 21–26.   סימנית מנוזרת, וגם נקרא נ' הפוכה

38He blesses them and they increase greatly;
and He does not let their cattle decrease,
  39after they had been few and crushed
by oppression, misery, and sorrow.
40He pours contempt on great men
and makes them lose their way in trackless
deserts;
  41but the needy He secures from suffering,
and increases their families like flocks.

42The upright see it and rejoice;
the mouth of all wrongdoers is stopped.
43The wise man will take note of these things;
he will consider the steadfast love of the LORD.

108   A song. A psalm of David.

2*a*My heart is firm, O God;
I will sing and chant a hymn with all my soul.
3Awake, O harp and lyre!
I will wake the dawn.
4I will praise You among the peoples, O LORD,
sing a hymn to You among the nations;
5for Your faithfulness is higher than the
heavens;
Your steadfastness reaches to the sky.
6Exalt Yourself over the heavens, O God;
let Your glory be over all the earth!
7*b*That those whom You love may be rescued,
deliver with Your right hand and answer me.

8God promised *c*-in His sanctuary-*c*
that I would exultingly divide up Shechem,
and measure the Valley of Sukkoth;
9Gilead and Manasseh would be mine,
Ephraim my chief stronghold,
Judah my scepter;
10Moab would be my washbasin;

קח שִׁיר מִזְמוֹר לְדָוִד:

2 נָכוֹן לִבִּי אֱלֹהִים
אָשִׁירָה וַאֲזַמְּרָה אַף־כְּבוֹדִי:
3 עוּרָה הַנֵּבֶל וְכִנּוֹר
אָעִירָה שָּׁחַר:
4 אוֹדְךָ בָעַמִּים ׀ יְהוָה
וַאֲזַמֶּרְךָ בַּל־אֻמִּים*:
5 כִּי־גָדוֹל מֵעַל־שָׁמַיִם חַסְדֶּךָ
וְעַד־שְׁחָקִים אֲמִתֶּךָ:
6 רוּמָה עַל־שָׁמַיִם אֱלֹהִים
וְעַל כָּל־הָאָרֶץ כְּבוֹדֶךָ:
7 לְמַעַן יֵחָלְצוּן יְדִידֶיךָ
הוֹשִׁיעָה יְמִינְךָ וַעֲנֵנִי:

8 אֱלֹהִים ׀ דִּבֶּר בְּקָדְשׁוֹ
אֶעְלֹזָה אֲחַלְּקָה שְׁכֶם
וְעֵמֶק סֻכּוֹת אֲמַדֵּד:
9 לִי גִלְעָד ׀ לִי מְנַשֶּׁה
וְאֶפְרַיִם מָעוֹז רֹאשִׁי
יְהוּדָה מְחֹקְקִי:
10 מוֹאָב ׀ סִיר רַחְצִי

38 וַיְבָרְכֵם וַיִּרְבּוּ מְאֹד
וּבְהֶמְתָּם לֹא יַמְעִיט:
39 וַיִּמְעֲטוּ וַיָּשֹׁחוּ
מֵעֹצֶר רָעָה וְיָגוֹן:
40 שֹׁפֵךְ בּוּז עַל־נְדִיבִים
וַיַּתְעֵם בְּתֹהוּ לֹא־דָרֶךְ:
41 וַיְשַׂגֵּב אֶבְיוֹן מֵעוֹנִי
וַיָּשֶׂם כַּצֹּאן מִשְׁפָּחוֹת:
42 יִרְאוּ יְשָׁרִים וְיִשְׂמָחוּ
וְכָל־עַוְלָה קָפְצָה פִּיהָ:
43 מִי־חָכָם וְיִשְׁמָר־אֵלֶּה
וְיִתְבּוֹנְנוּ חַסְדֵי יְהוָה:

---

a   With vv. 2–6, cf. Ps. 57.8–12.
b   With vv. 7–14, cf. Ps. 60.7–14.
c-c   Or "by His holiness."

v. 40. סימנית מנוזרת, וגם נקרא נ' הפוכה
v. 4. בנוסח אחר "בלאמים"

on Edom I would cast my shoe;

I would raise a shout over Philistia.

11Would that I were brought to the bastion!

Would that I were led to Edom!

12But You have rejected us, O God;

God, You do not march with our armies.

13Grant us Your aid against the foe,

for the help of man is worthless.

14With God we shall triumph;

He will trample our foes.

עַל־אֱדוֹם אַשְׁלִיךְ נַעֲלִי

עֲלֵי־פְלֶשֶׁת אֶתְרוֹעָע׃

11 מִי יֹבִלֵנִי עִיר מִבְצָר

מִי נָחַנִי עַד־אֱדוֹם׃

12 הֲלֹא־אֱלֹהִים זְנַחְתָּנוּ

וְלֹא־תֵצֵא אֱלֹהִים בְּצִבְאֹתֵינוּ׃

13 הָבָה־לָּנוּ עֶזְרָת מִצָּר

וְשָׁוְא תְּשׁוּעַת אָדָם׃

14 בֵּאלֹהִים נַעֲשֶׂה־חָיִל

וְהוּא יָבוּס צָרֵינוּ׃

109 For the leader. Of David. A psalm.

קט לַמְנַצֵּחַ לְדָוִד מִזְמוֹר

O God of my praise,

do not keep aloof,

2for the wicked and the deceitful

open their mouth against me;

they speak to me with lying tongue.

3They encircle me with words of hate;

they attack me without cause.

4They answer my love with accusation

a-and I must stand judgment.-a

5They repay me with evil for good,

with hatred for my love.

6Appoint a wicked man over him;

may an accuser stand at his right side;

7may he be tried and convicted;

may he be judged and found guilty.

8May his days be few;

may another take over b-his position.-b

9May his children be orphans,

his wife a widow.

10May his children wander from their hovels,

begging in search of [bread].

אֱלֹהֵי תְהִלָּתִי

אַל־תֶּחֱרַשׁ׃

2 כִּי פִי רָשָׁע וּפִי־מִרְמָה

עָלַי פָּתָחוּ

דִּבְּרוּ אִתִּי לְשׁוֹן שָׁקֶר׃

3 וְדִבְרֵי שִׂנְאָה סְבָבוּנִי

וַיִּלָּחֲמוּנִי חִנָּם׃

4 תַּחַת־אַהֲבָתִי יִשְׂטְנוּנִי

וַאֲנִי תְפִלָּה׃

5 וַיָּשִׂימוּ עָלַי רָעָה תַּחַת טוֹבָה

וְשִׂנְאָה תַּחַת אַהֲבָתִי׃

6 הַפְקֵד עָלָיו רָשָׁע

וְשָׂטָן יַעֲמֹד עַל־יְמִינוֹ׃

7 בְּהִשָּׁפְטוֹ יֵצֵא רָשָׁע

וּתְפִלָּתוֹ תִּהְיֶה לַחֲטָאָה׃

8 יִהְיוּ־יָמָיו מְעַטִּים

פְּקֻדָּתוֹ יִקַּח אַחֵר׃

9 יִהְיוּ־בָנָיו יְתוֹמִים

וְאִשְׁתּוֹ אַלְמָנָה׃

10 וְנוֹעַ יָנוּעוּ בָנָיו וְשִׁאֵלוּ

וְדָרְשׁוּ מֵחָרְבוֹתֵיהֶם׃

---

a-a   Or "but I am all prayer"; meaning of Heb. uncertain, but see v. 7.

b-b   Meaning of Heb. uncertain.

11May his creditor seize all his possessions;

may strangers plunder his wealth.

12May no one show him mercy;

may none pity his orphans;

13may his posterity be cut off;

may their names be blotted out in the next generation.

14May God be ever mindful of his father's iniquity,

and may the sin of his mother not be blotted out.

15May the LORD be aware of them always

and cause their names to be cut off from the earth,

16because he was not minded to act kindly,

and hounded to death the poor and needy man,

one crushed in spirit.

17He loved to curse—may a curse come upon him!

He would not bless—may blessing be far from him!

18May he be clothed in a curse like a garment,

may it enter his body like water,

his bones like oil.

19Let it be like the cloak he wraps around him,

like the belt he always wears.

20May the LORD thus repay my accusers,

all those who speak evil against me.

21Now You, O GOD, my Lord,

act on my behalf as befits Your name.

Good and faithful as You are, save me.

22For I am poor and needy,

and my heart is pierced within me.

23I fade away like a lengthening shadow;

I am shaken off like locusts.

24My knees give way from fasting;

my flesh is lean, has lost its fat.

25I am the object of their scorn;

---

11 יְנַקֵּשׁ נוֹשֶׁה לְכָל־אֲשֶׁר־ל֑וֹ
וְיָבֹ֖זּוּ זָרִ֣ים יְגִיעֽוֹ׃

12 אַל־יְהִי־ל֭וֹ מֹשֵׁ֣ךְ חָ֑סֶד
וְֽאַל־יְהִ֥י ח֝וֹנֵ֗ן לִיתוֹמָֽיו׃

13 יְהִֽי־אַחֲרִית֥וֹ לְהַכְרִ֑ית
בְּד֥וֹר אַ֝חֵ֗ר יִמַּ֥ח שְׁמָֽם׃

14 יִזָּכֵ֤ר ׀ עֲוֺ֣ן אֲ֭בֹתָיו אֶל־יְהֹוָ֑ה
וְחַטַּ֥את אִ֝מּ֗וֹ אַל־תִּמָּֽח׃

15 יִהְי֣וּ נֶֽגֶד־יְהֹוָ֣ה תָּמִ֑יד
וְיַכְרֵ֖ת מֵאֶ֣רֶץ זִכְרָֽם׃

16 יַ֗עַן אֲשֶׁ֤ר ׀ לֹ֥א זָכַר֮ עֲשׂ֢וֹת חָ֥סֶד
וַיִּרְדֹּ֡ף אִישׁ־עָנִ֣י וְ֭אֶבְיוֹן
וְנִכְאֵ֨ה לֵבָ֬ב לְמוֹתֵֽת׃

17 וַיֶּאֱהַ֣ב קְ֭לָלָה וַתְּבוֹאֵ֑הוּ
וְֽלֹא־חָפֵ֥ץ בִּ֝בְרָכָ֗ה וַתִּרְחַ֥ק מִמֶּֽנּוּ׃

18 וַיִּלְבַּ֥שׁ קְלָלָ֗ה כְּמַ֫דּ֥וֹ
וַתָּבֹ֣א כַמַּ֣יִם בְּקִרְבּ֑וֹ
וְ֝כַשֶּׁ֗מֶן בְּעַצְמוֹתָֽיו׃

19 תְּהִי־ל֭וֹ כְּבֶ֣גֶד יַעְטֶ֑ה
וּ֝לְמֵ֗זַח תָּמִ֥יד יַחְגְּרֶֽהָ׃

20 זֹ֤את פְּעֻלַּ֣ת שֹׂ֭טְנַי מֵאֵ֣ת יְהֹוָ֑ה
וְהַדֹּבְרִ֥ים רָ֝֗ע עַל־נַפְשִֽׁי׃

21 וְאַתָּ֤ה ׀ יְהֹוִ֣ה אֲדֹנָי֮
עֲשֵֽׂה־אִ֭תִּי לְמַ֣עַן שְׁמֶ֑ךָ
כִּי־ט֥וֹב חַ֝סְדְּךָ֗ הַצִּילֵֽנִי׃

22 כִּֽי־עָנִ֣י וְאֶבְי֣וֹן אָנֹ֑כִי
וְ֝לִבִּ֗י חָלַ֥ל בְּקִרְבִּֽי׃

23 כְּצֵל־כִּנְטוֹת֥וֹ נֶהֱלָ֑כְתִּי
נִ֝נְעַ֗רְתִּי כָּֽאַרְבֶּֽה׃

24 בִּ֭רְכַּי כָּשְׁל֣וּ מִצּ֑וֹם
וּ֝בְשָׂרִ֗י כָּחַ֥שׁ מִשָּֽׁמֶן׃

25 וַאֲנִ֤י ׀ הָיִ֣יתִי חֶרְפָּ֣ה לָהֶ֑ם

when they see me, they shake their head.

וְרָאוּנִי יְנִיעוּן רֹאשָֽׁם:

26Help me, O LORD, my God;

26 עׇזְרֵנִי יְהֹוָה אֱלֹהָי

save me in accord with Your faithfulness,

הֽוֹשִׁיעֵנִי כְחַסְדֶּֽךָ:

27that men may know that it is Your hand,

27 וְֽיֵדְעוּ כִּי־יָדְךָ זֹּאת

that You, O LORD, have done it.

אַתָּה יְהֹוָה עֲשִׂיתָֽהּ:

28Let them curse, but You bless;

28 יְקַֽלְלוּ־הֵמָּה וְאַתָּה תְבָרֵךְ

let them rise up, but come to grief,

קָמוּ ׀ וַיֵּבֹשׁוּ

while Your servant rejoices.

וְֽעַבְדְּךָ יִשְׂמָֽח:

29My accusers shall be clothed in shame,

29 יִלְבְּשׁוּ שׂוֹטְנַי כְּלִמָּה

wrapped in their disgrace as in a robe.

וְיַעֲטוּ כַמְעִיל בׇּשְׁתָּֽם:

30My mouth shall sing much praise to the LORD;

30 אוֹדֶה יְהֹוָה מְאֹד בְּפִי

I will acclaim Him in the midst of a throng,

וּבְתוֹךְ רַבִּים אֲהַלְלֶֽנּוּ:

31because He stands at the right hand of the needy,

31 כִּֽי־יַעֲמֹד לִימִין אֶבְיוֹן

to save him from those who would condemn him.

לְהוֹשִׁיעַ מִשֹּׁפְטֵי נַפְשֽׁוֹ*:

110 Of David. A psalm.

קי לְדָוִד מִזְמוֹר

The LORD said to my lord,

נְאֻם יְהֹוָה ׀ לַֽאדֹנִי

"Sit at My right hand

שֵׁב לִֽימִינִי

while I make your enemies your footstool."

עַד־אָשִׁית אֹיְבֶיךָ הֲדֹם לְרַגְלֶֽיךָ:

2The LORD will stretch forth from Zion your mighty scepter;

2 מַטֵּֽה־עֻזְּךָ יִשְׁלַח יְהֹוָה מִצִּיּוֹן

hold sway over your enemies!

רְדֵה בְּקֶרֶב אֹיְבֶֽיךָ:

3a-Your people come forward willingly on your day of battle.

3 עַמְּךָ נְדָבֹת בְּיוֹם חֵילֶךָ

In majestic holiness, from the womb,

בְּהַדְרֵי־קֹדֶשׁ מֵרֶחֶם

from the dawn, yours was the dew of youth.-a

מִשְׁחָר לְךָ טַל יַלְדֻתֶֽיךָ:

4The LORD has sworn and will not relent,

4 נִשְׁבַּע יְהֹוָה ׀ וְלֹא יִנָּחֵם אַתָּה־

"You are a priest forever, b-a rightful king by My decree."-b

כֹהֵן לְעוֹלָם עַל־דִּבְרָתִי מַלְכִּי־צֶֽדֶק:

5The Lord is at your right hand.

5 אֲדֹנָי עַל־יְמִֽינְךָ

He crushes kings in the day of His anger.

מָחַץ בְּיוֹם־אַפּוֹ מְלָכִֽים:

v. 31. סבירין ומטעין "נפשם"

a-a　Meaning of Heb. uncertain.
b-b　Or "after the manner of Melchizedek."

⁶He works judgment upon the nations,

    heaping up bodies,

    crushing heads far and wide.

⁷He drinks from the stream on his way;

    therefore he holds his head high.

ידין בגוים   ⁶

מלא גויות

מחץ ראש על־ארץ רבה:

מנחל בדרך ישתה   ⁷

על־כן ירים ראש:

111 Hallelujah.

א   I praise the LORD with all my heart

ב   in the assembled congregation of the upright.

ג   ²The works of the LORD are great,

ד   ^awithin reach of all who desire them.^{-a}

ה   ³His deeds are splendid and glorious;

ו   His beneficence is everlasting;

ז   ⁴He has won renown for His wonders.

ח   The LORD is gracious and compassionate;

ט   ⁵He gives food to those who fear Him;

י   He is ever mindful of His covenant.

כ   ⁶He revealed to His people His powerful works,

ל   in giving them the heritage of nations.

מ   ⁷His handiwork is truth and justice;

נ   all His precepts are enduring,

ס   ⁸well-founded for all eternity,

ע   wrought of truth and equity.

פ   ⁹He sent redemption to His people;

צ   He ordained His covenant for all time;

ק   His name is holy and awesome.

ר   ¹⁰The beginning^b of wisdom is the fear of the LORD;

ש   all who practice it gain sound understanding.

ת   Praise of Him is everlasting.

קיא   הללו יה |

אודה יהוה בכל־לבב

בסוד ישרים ועדה:

גדלים מעשי יהוה   ²

דרושים לכל־חפציהם:

הוד־והדר פעלו   ³

וצדקתו עמדת לעד:

זכר עשה לנפלאתיו   ⁴

חנון ורחום יהוה:

טרף נתן ליראיו   ⁵

יזכר לעולם בריתו:

כח מעשיו הגיד לעמו   ⁶

לתת להם נחלת גוים:

מעשי ידיו אמת ומשפט   ⁷

נאמנים כל־פקודיו:

סמוכים לעד לעולם   ⁸

עשוים באמת וישר:

פדות | שלח לעמו   ⁹

צוה־לעולם בריתו

קדוש ונורא שמו:

ראשית חכמה | יראת יהוה   ¹⁰

שכל טוב לכל־עשיהם

תהלתו עמדת לעד:

112 Hallelujah.

א   Happy is the man who fears the LORD,

ב   who is ardently devoted to His commandments.

ג   ²His descendants will be mighty in the land,

קיב   הללו יה |

אשרי־איש ירא את־יהוה

במצותיו חפץ מאד:

גבור בארץ יהיה זרעו   ²

---

a-a   *Meaning of Heb. uncertain.*

b   *Or "chief part."*

ד   a blessed generation of upright men.   דּוֹר יְשָׁרִים יְבֹרָךְ׃

ה   ³Wealth and riches are in his house,   3 הוֹן־וָעֹשֶׁר בְּבֵיתוֹ

ו   and his beneficence lasts forever.   וְצִדְקָתוֹ עֹמֶדֶת לָעַד׃

ז   ⁴ᵃA light shines⁻ᵃ for the upright in the darkness;   4 זָרַח בַּחֹשֶׁךְ אוֹר לַיְשָׁרִים

ח   he is gracious, compassionate, and beneficent.   חַנּוּן וְרַחוּם וְצַדִּיק׃

ט   ⁵All goes well with the man who lends generously,   5 טוֹב־אִישׁ חוֹנֵן וּמַלְוֶה

י   who conducts his affairs with equity.   יְכַלְכֵּל דְּבָרָיו בְּמִשְׁפָּט׃

כ   ⁶He shall never be shaken;   6 כִּי־לְעוֹלָם לֹא־יִמּוֹט

ל   the beneficent man will be remembered for-   לְזֵכֶר עוֹלָם יִהְיֶה צַדִּיק׃
     ever.

מ   ⁷He is not afraid of evil tidings;   7 מִשְּׁמוּעָה רָעָה לֹא יִירָא

נ   his heart is firm, he trusts in the Lord.   נָכוֹן לִבּוֹ בָּטֻחַ בַּיהוָה׃

ס   ⁸His heart is resolute, he is unafraid;   8 סָמוּךְ לִבּוֹ לֹא יִירָא

ע   in the end he will see the fall of his foes.   עַד אֲשֶׁר־יִרְאֶה בְצָרָיו׃

פ   ⁹He gives freely to the poor;   9 פִּזַּר ׀ נָתַן לָאֶבְיוֹנִים

צ   his beneficence lasts forever;   צִדְקָתוֹ עֹמֶדֶת לָעַד

ק   his horn is exalted in honor.   קַרְנוֹ תָּרוּם בְּכָבוֹד׃

ר   ¹⁰The wicked man shall see it and be vexed;   10 רָשָׁע יִרְאֶה ׀ וְכָעָס

ש   he shall gnash his teeth; his courage shall fail.   שִׁנָּיו יַחֲרֹק וְנָמָס

ת   The desire of the wicked shall come to nothing.   תַּאֲוַת רְשָׁעִים תֹּאבֵד׃

113 Hallelujah.   קיג הַלְלוּ יָהּ ׀

O servants of the Lord, give praise;   הַלְלוּ עַבְדֵי יְהוָה

praise the name of the Lord.   הַלְלוּ אֶת־שֵׁם יְהוָה׃

²Let the name of the Lord be blessed   2 יְהִי שֵׁם יְהוָה מְבֹרָךְ

now and forever.   מֵעַתָּה וְעַד־עוֹלָם׃

³From east to west   3 מִמִּזְרַח־שֶׁמֶשׁ עַד־מְבוֹאוֹ

the name of the Lord is praised.   מְהֻלָּל שֵׁם יְהוָה׃

⁴The Lord is exalted above all nations;   4 רָם עַל־כָּל־גּוֹיִם ׀ יְהוָה

His glory is above the heavens.   עַל הַשָּׁמַיִם כְּבוֹדוֹ׃

⁵Who is like the Lord our God,   5 מִי כַּיהוָה אֱלֹהֵינוּ

who, enthroned on high,   הַמַּגְבִּיהִי לָשָׁבֶת׃

⁶sees what is below,   6 הַמַּשְׁפִּילִי לִרְאוֹת

in heaven and on earth?   בַּשָּׁמַיִם וּבָאָרֶץ׃

⁷He raises the poor from the dust,   7 מְקִימִי מֵעָפָר דָּל

lifts up the needy from the refuse heap   מֵאַשְׁפֹּת יָרִים אֶבְיוֹן׃

⁸to set them with the great,   8 לְהוֹשִׁיבִי עִם־נְדִיבִים

with the great men of His people.

a-a Or "He shines as a light."

9He sets the childless woman among her household
as a happy mother of children.
Hallelujah.

עִם נְדִיבֵי עַמּוֹ:
9 מוֹשִׁיבִי | עֲקֶרֶת הַבַּיִת
אֵם־הַבָּנִים שְׂמֵחָה
הַלְלוּ־יָהּ:

114 When Israel went forth from Egypt,
the house of Jacob from a people of strange
speech,
2Judah became His a-holy one,-a
Israel, His dominion.
3The sea saw them and fled,
Jordan ran backward,
4mountains skipped like rams,
hills like sheep.
5What alarmed you, O sea, that you fled,
Jordan, that you ran backward,
6mountains, that you skipped like rams,
hills, like sheep?
7Tremble, O earth, at the presence of the Lord,
at the presence of the God of Jacob,
8who turned the rock into a pool of water,
the flinty rock into a fountain.

קיד בְּצֵאת יִשְׂרָאֵל מִמִּצְרָיִם
בֵּית יַעֲקֹב מֵעַם לֹעֵז:
2 הָיְתָה יְהוּדָה לְקָדְשׁוֹ
יִשְׂרָאֵל מַמְשְׁלוֹתָיו:
3 הַיָּם רָאָה וַיָּנֹס
הַיַּרְדֵּן יִסֹּב לְאָחוֹר:
4 הֶהָרִים רָקְדוּ כְאֵילִים
גְּבָעוֹת כִּבְנֵי־צֹאן:
5 מַה־לְּךָ הַיָּם כִּי תָנוּס
הַיַּרְדֵּן תִּסֹּב לְאָחוֹר:
6 הֶהָרִים תִּרְקְדוּ כְאֵילִים
גְּבָעוֹת כִּבְנֵי־צֹאן:
7 מִלִּפְנֵי אָדוֹן חוּלִי אָרֶץ
מִלִּפְנֵי אֱלוֹהַּ יַעֲקֹב:
8 הַהֹפְכִי הַצּוּר אֲגַם־מָיִם
חַלָּמִישׁ לְמַעְיְנוֹ־מָיִם:

115 Not to us, O LORD, not to us
but to Your name bring glory
for the sake of Your love and Your faithfulness.
2Let the nations not say,
"Where, now, is their God?"
3when our God is in heaven
and all that He wills He accomplishes.
4aTheir idols are silver and gold,
the work of men's hands.
5They have mouths, but cannot speak,
eyes, but cannot see;
6they have ears, but cannot hear,
noses, but cannot smell;

קטו *לֹא לָנוּ יְהוָה לֹא לָנוּ
כִּי־לְשִׁמְךָ תֵּן כָּבוֹד
עַל־חַסְדְּךָ עַל־אֲמִתֶּךָ:
2 לָמָּה יֹאמְרוּ הַגּוֹיִם
אַיֵּה־נָא אֱלֹהֵיהֶם:
3 וֵאלֹהֵינוּ בַשָּׁמָיִם
כֹּל אֲשֶׁר־חָפֵץ עָשָׂה:
4 עֲצַבֵּיהֶם כֶּסֶף וְזָהָב
מַעֲשֵׂה יְדֵי אָדָם:
5 פֶּה־לָהֶם וְלֹא יְדַבֵּרוּ
עֵינַיִם לָהֶם וְלֹא יִרְאוּ:
6 אָזְנַיִם לָהֶם וְלֹא יִשְׁמָעוּ
אַף לָהֶם וְלֹא יְרִיחוּן:

a-a   Or "sanctuary."
a   With vv. 4–11, cf. Ps. 135.15–20.

v. 1. המשך של שירה הקודמת בכתב היד שלנו,
ולפי זה, אין בו סכום הפרקים של ספר 150
149 אלא

7they have hands, but cannot touch,
    feet, but cannot walk;
    they can make no sound in their throats.
8Those who fashion them,
    all who trust in them,
    shall become like them.
9O Israel, trust in the Lord!
He is their help and shield.
10O house of Aaron, trust in the Lord!
He is their help and shield.
11O you who fear the Lord, trust in the Lord!
He is their help and shield.

12The Lord is mindful of us.
He will bless us;
    He will bless the house of Israel;
    He will bless the house of Aaron;
13He will bless those who fear the Lord,
    small and great alike.

14May the Lord increase your numbers,
    yours and your children's also.
15May you be blessed by the Lord,
    Maker of heaven and earth.
16The heavens belong to the Lord,
    but the earth He gave over to man.
17The dead cannot praise the Lord,
    nor any who go down into silence.
18But we will bless the Lord
    now and forever.
    Hallelujah.

116 a-I love the Lord
    for He hears-a my voice, my pleas;
2for He turns His ear to me
    whenever I call.

7 יְדֵיהֶ֤ם ׀ וְלֹ֬א יְמִישׁ֗וּן
רַ֭גְלֵיהֶם וְלֹ֣א יְהַלֵּ֑כוּ
לֹֽא־יֶ֝הְגּ֗וּ בִּגְרוֹנָֽם׃
8 כְּ֭מוֹהֶם יִהְי֣וּ
עֹשֵׂיהֶ֑ם
כֹּ֖ל אֲשֶׁר־בֹּטֵ֣חַ בָּהֶֽם׃
9 יִ֭שְׂרָאֵל בְּטַ֣ח בַּֽיהֹוָ֑ה
עֶזְרָ֖ם וּמָגִנָּ֣ם הֽוּא׃
10 בֵּ֣ית אַ֭הֲרֹן בִּטְח֣וּ בַֽיהֹוָ֑ה
עֶזְרָ֖ם וּמָגִנָּ֣ם הֽוּא׃
11 יִרְאֵ֣י יְ֭הֹוָה בִּטְח֣וּ בַֽיהֹוָ֑ה
עֶזְרָ֖ם וּמָגִנָּ֣ם הֽוּא׃
12 יְהֹוָה֮ זְכָרָ֢נוּ
יְבָ֫רֵ֥ךְ
יְ֭בָרֵךְ אֶת־בֵּ֣ית יִשְׂרָאֵ֑ל
יְ֝בָרֵ֗ךְ אֶת־בֵּ֥ית אַהֲרֹֽן׃
13 יְ֭בָרֵךְ יִרְאֵ֣י יְהֹוָ֑ה
הַ֝קְּטַנִּ֗ים עִם־הַגְּדֹלִֽים׃
14 יֹסֵ֣ף יְהֹוָ֣ה עֲלֵיכֶ֑ם
עֲ֝לֵיכֶ֗ם וְעַל־בְּנֵיכֶֽם׃
15 בְּרוּכִ֣ים אַ֭תֶּם לַֽיהֹוָ֑ה
עֹ֝שֵׂ֗ה שָׁמַ֥יִם וָאָֽרֶץ׃
16 הַשָּׁמַ֣יִם שָׁ֭מַיִם לַֽיהֹוָ֑ה
וְ֝הָאָ֗רֶץ נָתַ֥ן לִבְנֵי־אָדָֽם׃
17 לֹ֣א הַ֭מֵּתִים יְהַֽלְלוּ־יָ֑הּ
וְ֝לֹ֗א כׇּל־יֹרְדֵ֥י דוּמָֽה׃
18 וַאֲנַ֤חְנוּ ׀ נְבָ֘רֵ֤ךְ יָ֗הּ
מֵֽעַתָּ֥ה וְעַד־עוֹלָ֗ם
הַֽלְלוּ־יָֽהּ׃

קטז אָ֭הַבְתִּי כִּֽי־יִשְׁמַ֥ע ׀ יְהֹוָ֑ה
אֶת־ק֝וֹלִ֗י תַּחֲנוּנָֽי׃
2 כִּֽי־הִטָּ֣ה אׇזְנ֣וֹ לִ֑י
וּבְיָמַ֥י אֶקְרָֽא׃

a-a   Heb. transposed for clarity; others "I would love that the Lord hear,"
    etc.

³The bonds of death encompassed me;
   the torments of Sheol overtook me.
I came upon trouble and sorrow
   ⁴and I invoked the name of the Lᴏʀᴅ,
   "O Lᴏʀᴅ, save my life!"

⁵The Lᴏʀᴅ is gracious and beneficent;
   our God is compassionate.
⁶The Lᴏʀᴅ protects the simple;
   I was brought low and He saved me.
⁷Be at rest, once again, O my soul,
   for the Lᴏʀᴅ has been good to you.
⁸You*ᵇ* have delivered me from death,
   my eyes from tears,
   my feet from stumbling.
⁹I shall walk before the Lᴏʀᴅ
   in the lands of the living.
¹⁰*c*-I trust [in the Lᴏʀᴅ];
   out of great suffering I spoke-*c*
¹¹and said rashly,
   "All men are false."

¹²How can I repay the Lᴏʀᴅ
   for all His bounties to me?
¹³I raise the cup of deliverance
   and invoke the name of the Lᴏʀᴅ.
¹⁴I will pay my vows to the Lᴏʀᴅ
   in the presence of all His people.
¹⁵The death of His faithful ones
   is grievous in the Lᴏʀᴅ's sight.

¹⁶O Lᴏʀᴅ,
   I am Your servant,
   Your servant, the son of Your maidservant;
   You have undone the cords that bound me.
¹⁷I will sacrifice a thank offering to You
   and invoke the name of the Lᴏʀᴅ.

ᵇ *I.e., God.*
c-c *Meaning of Heb. uncertain.*

³ אֲפָפ֤וּנִי ׀ חֶבְלֵי־מָ֗וֶת
וּמְצָרֵ֣י שְׁא֣וֹל מְצָא֑וּנִי
צָרָ֖ה וְיָג֣וֹן אֶמְצָֽא׃
⁴ וּבְשֵֽׁם־יְהוָ֥ה אֶקְרָ֑א
אָנָּ֥ה יְ֝הוָ֗ה מַלְּטָ֥ה נַפְשִֽׁי׃

⁵ חַנּ֣וּן יְהֹוָ֣ה וְצַדִּ֑יק
וֵ֖אלֹהֵ֣ינוּ מְרַחֵֽם׃
⁶ שֹׁמֵ֣ר פְּתָאיִם֮* יְהֹ֫וָ֥ה
דַּלֹּ֗תִי וְלִ֣י יְהוֹשִֽׁיעַ׃
⁷ שׁוּבִ֣י נַ֭פְשִׁי לִמְנוּחָ֑יְכִי
כִּֽי־יְ֝הוָ֗ה גָּמַ֥ל עָלָֽיְכִי׃
⁸ כִּ֤י חִלַּ֪צְתָּ נַפְשִׁ֡י מִמָּ֗וֶת
אֶת־עֵינִ֥י מִן־דִּמְעָ֑ה
אֶת־רַגְלִ֥י מִדֶּֽחִי׃
⁹ אֶ֭תְהַלֵּךְ לִפְנֵ֣י יְהוָ֑ה
בְּ֝אַרְצ֗וֹת הַֽחַיִּֽים׃
¹⁰ הֶ֭אֱמַנְתִּי כִּ֣י אֲדַבֵּ֑ר
אֲ֝נִ֗י עָנִ֥יתִי מְאֹֽד׃
¹¹ אֲנִ֗י אָמַ֥רְתִּי בְחׇפְזִ֑י
כׇּל־הָאָדָ֥ם כֹּזֵֽב׃

¹² מָֽה־אָשִׁ֥יב לַיהוָ֑ה
כׇּֽל־תַּגְמוּל֥וֹהִי עָלָֽי׃
¹³ כּוֹס־יְשׁוּע֥וֹת אֶשָּׂ֑א
וּבְשֵׁ֖ם יְהוָ֣ה אֶקְרָֽא׃
¹⁴ נְ֭דָרַי לַיהוָ֣ה אֲשַׁלֵּ֑ם
נֶגְדָה־נָּ֗א לְכׇל־עַמּֽוֹ׃
¹⁵ יָ֭קָר בְּעֵינֵ֣י יְהוָ֑ה
הַ֝מָּ֗וְתָה לַחֲסִידָֽיו׃
¹⁶ אָֽנָּ֣ה יְהֹוָה֮
כִּֽי־אֲנִ֢י עַ֫בְדֶּ֥ךָ
אֲ‍ֽנִי־עַ֭בְדְּךָ בֶּן־אֲמָתֶ֑ךָ
פִּ֝תַּ֗חְתָּ לְמוֹסֵרָֽי׃
¹⁷ לְֽךָ־אֶ֭זְבַּח זֶ֣בַח תּוֹדָ֑ה
וּבְשֵׁ֖ם יְהוָ֣ה אֶקְרָֽא׃

¹⁸I will pay my vows to the Lord
in the presence of all His people,
¹⁹in the courts of the house of the Lord,
in the midst of^d Jerusalem.
Hallelujah.

¹⁸נְדָרַי לַיהֹוָה אֲשַׁלֵּם
נֶגְדָה־נָּא לְכָל־עַמּוֹ׃
¹⁹בְּחַצְרוֹת ׀ בֵּית יְהֹוָה
בְּתוֹכֵכִי יְרוּשָׁלָ͏ִם
הַלְלוּ־יָהּ׃

117 Praise the Lord, all you nations;
extol Him, all you peoples,
²for great is His steadfast love toward us;
the faithfulness of the Lord endures forever.
Hallelujah.

קיז הַלְלוּ אֶת־יְהֹוָה כָּל־גּוֹיִם
שַׁבְּחוּהוּ כָּל־הָאֻמִּים׃
²כִּי גָבַר עָלֵינוּ ׀ חַסְדּוֹ
וֶאֱמֶת־יְהֹוָה לְעוֹלָם
הַלְלוּ־יָהּ׃

118 Praise the Lord, for He is good,
His steadfast love is eternal.
²Let Israel declare,
"His steadfast love is eternal."
³Let the house of Aaron declare,
"His steadfast love is eternal."
⁴Let those who fear the Lord declare,
"His steadfast love is eternal."

קיח הוֹדוּ לַיהֹוָה כִּי־טוֹב
²כִּי לְעוֹלָם חַסְדּוֹ׃
יֹאמַר־נָא יִשְׂרָאֵל
כִּי לְעוֹלָם חַסְדּוֹ׃
³יֹאמְרוּ־נָא בֵית־אַהֲרֹן
כִּי לְעוֹלָם חַסְדּוֹ׃
⁴יֹאמְרוּ־נָא יִרְאֵי יְהֹוָה
כִּי לְעוֹלָם חַסְדּוֹ׃

⁵In distress I called on the Lord;
the Lord answered me and brought me relief.
⁶The Lord is on my side,
I have no fear;
what can man do to me?
⁷With the Lord on my side as my helper,
I will see the downfall of my foes.

⁵מִן־הַמֵּצַר קָרָאתִי יָּהּ
עָנָנִי בַמֶּרְחָב יָהּ׃
⁶יְהֹוָה לִי
לֹא אִירָא
מַה־יַּעֲשֶׂה לִי אָדָם׃
⁷יְהֹוָה לִי בְּעֹזְרָי
וַאֲנִי אֶרְאֶה בְשֹׂנְאָי׃

⁸It is better to take refuge in the Lord
than to trust in mortals;
⁹it is better to take refuge in the Lord
than to trust in the great.

⁸טוֹב לַחֲסוֹת בַּיהֹוָה
מִבְּטֹחַ בָּאָדָם׃
⁹טוֹב לַחֲסוֹת בַּיהֹוָה
מִבְּטֹחַ בִּנְדִיבִים׃

¹⁰All nations have beset me;
by the name of the Lord I will surely ^acut them
down.^{-a}

¹⁰כָּל־גּוֹיִם סְבָבוּנִי
בְּשֵׁם יְהֹוָה כִּי אֲמִילַם׃

---

d   Others "of you."

a-a   Meaning of 'amilam *in this and the following two verses uncertain.*

11They beset me, they surround me;
  by the name of the Lord I will surely cut them
    down.

12They have beset me like bees;
  they shall be extinguished like burning thorns;
  by the name of the Lord I will surely cut them
    down.

13You*b* pressed me hard,
  I nearly fell;
  but the Lord helped me.

14The Lord is my strength and might;*c*
  He has become my deliverance.

15The tents of the victorious*d* resound with joyous
    shouts of deliverance,
  "The right hand of the Lord is triumphant!

16The right hand of the Lord is exalted!
The right hand of the Lord is triumphant!"

17I shall not die but live
  and proclaim the works of the Lord.

18The Lord punished me severely,
  but did not hand me over to death.

19Open the gates of victory*e* for me
  that I may enter them and praise the Lord.

20This is the gateway to the Lord—
  the victorious*d* shall enter through it.

21I praise You, for You have answered me,
  and have become my deliverance.

22The stone that the builders rejected
  has become the chief cornerstone.

23This is the Lord's doing;
  it is marvelous in our sight.

24This is the day that the Lord has made—
  let us exult and rejoice on it.

---

11 סַבּ֥וּנִי גַם־סְבָב֑וּנִי
בְּשֵׁ֥ם יְ֝הֹוָ֗ה כִּ֣י אֲמִילַֽם׃
12 סַבּ֤וּנִי כִדְבוֹרִ֗ים
דֹּ֭עֲכוּ כְּאֵ֣שׁ קוֹצִ֑ים
בְּשֵׁ֥ם יְ֝הֹוָ֗ה כִּ֣י אֲמִילַֽם׃
13 דַּחֹ֣ה דְחִיתַ֣נִי
לִנְפֹּ֑ל
וַיהֹוָ֥ה עֲזָרָֽנִי׃
14 עׇזִּ֣י וְזִמְרָ֣ת יָ֑הּ
וַֽיְהִי־לִ֝֗י לִֽישׁוּעָֽה׃
15 ק֤וֹל ׀ רִנָּ֬ה וִישׁוּעָ֗ה בְּאׇהֳלֵ֥י
צַדִּיקִ֑ים
יְמִ֥ין יְ֝הֹוָ֗ה עֹ֣שָׂה חָֽיִל׃
16 יְמִ֣ין יְ֭הֹוָה רוֹמֵמָ֑ה
יְמִ֥ין יְ֝הֹוָ֗ה עֹ֣שָׂה חָֽיִל׃
17 לֹֽא־אָמ֥וּת כִּי־אֶחְיֶ֑ה
וַ֝אֲסַפֵּ֗ר מַֽעֲשֵׂ֥י יָֽהּ׃
18 יַסֹּ֣ר יִסְּרַ֣נִּי יָּ֑הּ
וְ֝לַמָּ֗וֶת לֹ֣א נְתָנָֽנִי׃
19 פִּתְחוּ־לִ֥י שַׁעֲרֵי־צֶ֑דֶק
אָבֹא־בָ֝֗ם אוֹדֶ֥ה יָֽהּ׃
20 זֶה־הַשַּׁ֥עַר לַיהֹוָ֑ה
צַ֝דִּיקִ֗ים יָבֹ֥אוּ בֽוֹ׃
21 א֭וֹדְךָ כִּ֣י עֲנִיתָ֑נִי
וַתְּהִי־לִ֝֗י לִישׁוּעָֽה׃
22 אֶ֭בֶן מָאֲס֣וּ הַבּוֹנִ֑ים
הָ֝יְתָ֗ה לְרֹ֣אשׁ פִּנָּֽה׃
23 מֵאֵ֣ת יְ֭הֹוָה הָ֣יְתָה זֹּ֑את
הִ֖יא נִפְלָ֣את בְּעֵינֵֽינוּ׃
24 זֶה־הַ֭יּוֹם עָשָׂ֣ה יְהֹוָ֑ה
נָגִ֖ילָה וְנִשְׂמְחָ֣ה בֽוֹ׃

---

b   I.e., the enemy.
c   Others "song."
d   Or "righteous."
e   Or "righteousness."

25O Lord, deliver us!
O Lord, let us prosper!

26May he who enters be blessed in the name of
the Lord;
we bless you from the House of the Lord.
27The Lord is God;
He has given us light;
f-bind the festal offering to the horns of the altar
with cords.-f
28You are my God and I will praise You;
You are my God and I will extol You.
29Praise the Lord for He is good,
His steadfast love is eternal.

25 אָנָּא יְהֹוָה הוֹשִׁיעָה נָּא
אָנָּא יְהֹוָה הַצְלִיחָה נָּא׃
26 בָּרוּךְ הַבָּא בְּשֵׁם יְהֹוָה
בֵּרַכְנוּכֶם מִבֵּית יְהֹוָה׃
27 אֵל ׀ יְהֹוָה
וַיָּאֶר לָנוּ
אִסְרוּ־חַג בַּעֲבֹתִים עַד־קַרְנוֹת
הַמִּזְבֵּחַ׃
28 אֵלִי אַתָּה וְאוֹדֶךָּ
אֱלֹהַי אֲרוֹמְמֶךָּ׃
29 הוֹדוּ לַיהֹוָה כִּי־טוֹב
כִּי לְעוֹלָם חַסְדּוֹ׃

119 א Happy are those whose way is
blameless,
who follow the teaching of the Lord.
2Happy are those who observe His decrees,
who turn to Him wholeheartedly.
3They have done no wrong,
but have followed His ways.
4You have commanded that Your precepts
be kept diligently.
5Would that my ways were firm
in keeping Your laws;
6then I would not be ashamed
when I regard all Your commandments.
7I will praise You with a sincere heart
as I learn Your just rules.
8I will keep Your laws;
do not utterly forsake me.

ב 9How can a young man keep his way pure?—
by holding to Your word.
10I have turned to You with all my heart;
do not let me stray from Your commandments.
11In my heart I treasure Your promise;

קיט אַשְׁרֵי תְמִימֵי־דָרֶךְ
הַהֹלְכִים בְּתוֹרַת יְהֹוָה׃
2 אַשְׁרֵי נֹצְרֵי עֵדֹתָיו
בְּכָל־לֵב יִדְרְשׁוּהוּ׃
3 אַף לֹא־פָעֲלוּ עַוְלָה
בִּדְרָכָיו הָלָכוּ׃
4 אַתָּה צִוִּיתָה פִקֻּדֶיךָ
לִשְׁמֹר מְאֹד׃
5 אַחֲלַי יִכֹּנוּ דְרָכָי
לִשְׁמֹר חֻקֶּיךָ׃
6 אָז לֹא־אֵבוֹשׁ
בְּהַבִּיטִי אֶל־כָּל־מִצְוֹתֶיךָ׃
7 אוֹדְךָ בְּיֹשֶׁר לֵבָב
בְּלָמְדִי מִשְׁפְּטֵי צִדְקֶךָ׃
8 אֶת־חֻקֶּיךָ אֶשְׁמֹר
אַל־תַּעַזְבֵנִי עַד־מְאֹד׃
9 בַּמֶּה יְזַכֶּה־נַּעַר אֶת־אָרְחוֹ
לִשְׁמֹר כִּדְבָרֶךָ׃
10 בְּכָל־לִבִּי דְרַשְׁתִּיךָ
אַל־תַּשְׁגֵּנִי מִמִּצְוֹתֶיךָ׃
11 בְּלִבִּי צָפַנְתִּי אִמְרָתֶךָ

f-f Meaning of Heb. uncertain.

therefore I do not sin against You.

12Blessed are You, O Lord;

train me in Your laws.

13With my lips I rehearse

all the rules You proclaimed.

14I rejoice over the way of Your decrees

as over all riches.

15I study Your precepts;

I regard Your ways;

16I take delight in Your laws;

I will not neglect Your word.

17Deal kindly with Your servant,

that I may live to keep Your word.

18Open my eyes, that I may perceive

the wonders of Your teaching.

19I am only a sojourner in the land;

do not hide Your commandments from me.

20My soul is consumed with longing

for Your rules at all times.

21You blast the accursed insolent ones

who stray from Your commandments.

22Take away from me taunt and abuse,

because I observe Your decrees.

23Though princes meet and speak against me,

Your servant studies Your laws.

24For Your decrees are my delight,

my intimate companions.

25My soul clings to the dust;

revive me in accordance with Your word.

26I have declared my way, and You have answered

me;

train me in Your laws.

27Make me understand the way of Your precepts,

that I may study Your wondrous acts.

28I am racked with grief;

sustain me in accordance with Your word.

לְמַעַן לֹא אֶחֱטָא־לָךְ:

12 בָּרוּךְ אַתָּה יְהֹוָה

לַמְּדֵנִי חֻקֶּיךָ:

13 בִּשְׂפָתַי סִפַּרְתִּי

כֹּל מִשְׁפְּטֵי־פִיךָ:

14 בְּדֶרֶךְ עֵדְוֺתֶיךָ שַׂשְׂתִּי

כְּעַל כָּל־הוֹן:

15 בְּפִקֻּדֶיךָ אָשִׂיחָה

וְאַבִּיטָה אֹרְחֹתֶיךָ:

16 בְּחֻקֹּתֶיךָ אֶשְׁתַּעֲשָׁע

לֹא אֶשְׁכַּח דְּבָרֶךָ:

17 גְּמֹל עַל־עַבְדְּךָ

אֶחְיֶה וְאֶשְׁמְרָה דְבָרֶךָ:

18 גַּל־עֵינַי וְאַבִּיטָה

נִפְלָאוֹת מִתּוֹרָתֶךָ:

19 גֵּר אָנֹכִי בָאָרֶץ

אַל־תַּסְתֵּר מִמֶּנִּי מִצְוֺתֶיךָ:

20 גָּרְסָה נַפְשִׁי לְתַאֲבָה

אֶל־מִשְׁפָּטֶיךָ בְכָל־עֵת:

21 גָּעַרְתָּ זֵדִים אֲרוּרִים

הַשֹּׁגִים מִמִּצְוֺתֶיךָ:

22 גַּל מֵעָלַי חֶרְפָּה וָבוּז

כִּי עֵדֹתֶיךָ נָצָרְתִּי:

23 גַּם יָשְׁבוּ שָׂרִים בִּי נִדְבָּרוּ

עַבְדְּךָ יָשִׂיחַ בְּחֻקֶּיךָ:

24 גַּם־עֵדֹתֶיךָ שַׁעֲשֻׁעָי

אַנְשֵׁי עֲצָתִי:

25 דָּבְקָה לֶעָפָר נַפְשִׁי

חַיֵּנִי כִּדְבָרֶךָ:

26 דְּרָכַי סִפַּרְתִּי וַתַּעֲנֵנִי

לַמְּדֵנִי חֻקֶּיךָ:

27 דֶּרֶךְ־פִּקּוּדֶיךָ הֲבִינֵנִי

וְאָשִׂיחָה בְּנִפְלְאוֹתֶיךָ:

28 דָּלְפָה נַפְשִׁי מִתּוּגָה

קַיְּמֵנִי כִּדְבָרֶךָ:

29Remove all false ways from me;
  favor me with Your teaching.
30I have chosen the way of faithfulness;
  I have set Your rules before me.
31I cling to Your decrees;
  O LORD, do not put me to shame.
32I eagerly pursue Your commandments,
  for You broaden my understanding.

ה 33Teach me, O LORD, the way of Your laws;
  I will observe them *a*-to the utmost.-*a*
34Give me understanding, that I may observe
    Your teaching
  and keep it wholeheartedly.
35Lead me in the path of Your commandments,
  for that is my concern.
36Turn my heart to Your decrees
  and not to love of gain.
37Avert my eyes from seeing falsehood;
  by Your ways preserve me.
38Fulfill Your promise to Your servant,
  which is for those who worship You.
39Remove the taunt that I dread,
  for Your rules are good.
40See, I have longed for Your precepts;
  by Your righteousness preserve me.

ו 41May Your steadfast love reach me, O LORD,
  Your deliverance, as You have promised.
42I shall have an answer for those who taunt me,
  for I have put my trust in Your word.
43Do not utterly take the truth away from my
    mouth,
  for I have put my hope in Your rules.
44I will always obey Your teaching,
  forever and ever.
45I will walk about at ease,
  for I have turned to Your precepts.

29 דֶּרֶךְ־שֶׁקֶר הָסֵר מִמֶּנִּי
וְתוֹרָתְךָ חָנֵּנִי:
30 דֶּרֶךְ־אֱמוּנָה בָחָרְתִּי
מִשְׁפָּטֶיךָ שִׁוִּיתִי:
31 דָּבַקְתִּי בְעֵדְוֺתֶיךָ
יְהֹוָה אַל־תְּבִישֵׁנִי:
32 דֶּרֶךְ־מִצְוֺתֶיךָ אָרוּץ
כִּי תַרְחִיב לִבִּי:
33 הוֹרֵנִי יְהֹוָה דֶּרֶךְ חֻקֶּיךָ
וְאֶצְּרֶנָּה עֵקֶב:
34 הֲבִינֵנִי וְאֶצְּרָה תוֹרָתֶךָ
וְאֶשְׁמְרֶנָּה בְכָל־לֵב:
35 הַדְרִיכֵנִי בִּנְתִיב מִצְוֺתֶיךָ
כִּי־בוֹ חָפָצְתִּי:
36 הַט־לִבִּי אֶל־עֵדְוֺתֶיךָ
וְאַל אֶל־בָּצַע:
37 הַעֲבֵר עֵינַי מֵרְאוֹת שָׁוְא
בִּדְרָכֶךָ חַיֵּנִי:
38 הָקֵם לְעַבְדְּךָ אִמְרָתֶךָ
אֲשֶׁר לְיִרְאָתֶךָ:
39 הַעֲבֵר חֶרְפָּתִי אֲשֶׁר יָגֹרְתִּי
כִּי מִשְׁפָּטֶיךָ טוֹבִים:
40 הִנֵּה תָּאַבְתִּי לְפִקֻּדֶיךָ
בְּצִדְקָתְךָ חַיֵּנִי:
41 וִיבֹאֻנִי חֲסָדֶךָ יְהֹוָה
תְּשׁוּעָתְךָ כְּאִמְרָתֶךָ:
42 וְאֶעֱנֶה חֹרְפִי דָבָר
כִּי־בָטַחְתִּי בִּדְבָרֶךָ:
43 וְאַל־תַּצֵּל מִפִּי דְבַר־אֱמֶת עַד־
מְאֹד
כִּי לְמִשְׁפָּטֶךָ יִחָלְתִּי:
44 וְאֶשְׁמְרָה תוֹרָתְךָ תָמִיד
לְעוֹלָם וָעֶד:
45 וְאֶתְהַלְּכָה בָרְחָבָה
כִּי פִקֻּדֶיךָ דָרָשְׁתִּי:

a-a Meaning of Heb. uncertain.

46I will speak of Your decrees,
   and not be ashamed in the presence of kings.
47I will delight in Your commandments,
   which I love.
48I reach out for Your commandments, which I
   love;
   I study Your laws.

49Remember Your word to Your servant
   through which You have given me hope.
50This is my comfort in my affliction,
   that Your promise has preserved me.
51Though the arrogant have cruelly mocked me,
   I have not swerved from Your teaching.
52I remember Your rules of old, O LORD,
   and find comfort in them.
53I am seized with rage
   because of the wicked who forsake Your teaching.
54Your laws are b-a source of strength to me-b
   wherever I may dwell.
55I remember Your name at night, O LORD,
   and obey Your teaching.
56This has been my lot,
   for I have observed Your precepts.

57The LORD is my portion;
   I have resolved to keep Your words.
58I have implored You with all my heart;
   have mercy on me, in accordance with Your
   promise.
59I have considered my ways,
   and have turned back to Your decrees.
60I have hurried and not delayed
   to keep Your commandments.
61Though the bonds of the wicked are coiled
   round me,
   I have not neglected Your teaching.
62I arise at midnight to praise You
   for Your just rules.

46 וַאֲדַבְּרָה בְעֵדֹתֶיךָ
נֶגֶד מְלָכִים וְלֹא אֵבוֹשׁ:
47 וְאֶשְׁתַּעֲשַׁע בְּמִצְוֺתֶיךָ
אֲשֶׁר אָהָבְתִּי:
48 וְאֶשָּׂא־כַפַּי אֶל־מִצְוֺתֶיךָ אֲשֶׁר
אָהָבְתִּי
וְאָשִׂיחָה בְחֻקֶּיךָ:

49 זְכֹר־דָּבָר לְעַבְדֶּךָ
עַל אֲשֶׁר יִחַלְתָּנִי:
50 זֹאת נֶחָמָתִי בְעָנְיִי
כִּי אִמְרָתְךָ חִיָּתְנִי:
51 זֵדִים הֱלִיצֻנִי עַד־מְאֹד
מִתּוֹרָתְךָ לֹא נָטִיתִי:
52 זָכַרְתִּי מִשְׁפָּטֶיךָ מֵעוֹלָם ׀ יְהֹוָה
וָאֶתְנֶחָם:
53 זַלְעָפָה אֲחָזַתְנִי מֵרְשָׁעִים
עֹזְבֵי תּוֹרָתֶךָ:
54 זְמִרוֹת הָיוּ־לִי חֻקֶּיךָ
בְּבֵית מְגוּרָי:
55 זָכַרְתִּי בַלַּיְלָה שִׁמְךָ יְהֹוָה
וָאֶשְׁמְרָה תּוֹרָתֶךָ:
56 זֹאת הָיְתָה־לִּי
כִּי פִקֻּדֶיךָ נָצָרְתִּי:

57 חֶלְקִי יְהֹוָה
אָמַרְתִּי לִשְׁמֹר דְּבָרֶיךָ:
58 חִלִּיתִי פָנֶיךָ בְכָל־לֵב
חָנֵּנִי כְּאִמְרָתֶךָ:
59 חִשַּׁבְתִּי דְרָכָי
וָאָשִׁיבָה רַגְלַי אֶל־עֵדֹתֶיךָ:
60 חַשְׁתִּי וְלֹא הִתְמַהְמָהְתִּי
לִשְׁמֹר מִצְוֺתֶיךָ:
61 חֶבְלֵי רְשָׁעִים עִוְּדֻנִי
תּוֹרָתְךָ לֹא שָׁכָחְתִּי:
62 חֲצוֹת־לַיְלָה אָקוּם לְהוֹדוֹת לָךְ
עַל מִשְׁפְּטֵי צִדְקֶךָ:

ז

ח

---

b-b Or "songs for me."

63I am a companion to all who fear You,
    to those who keep Your precepts.
64Your steadfast love, O LORD, fills the earth;
    teach me Your laws.

ט 65You have treated Your servant well,
    according to Your word, O LORD.
66Teach me good sense and knowledge,
    for I have put my trust in Your command-
    ments.
67Before I was humbled I went astray,
    but now I keep Your word.
68You are good and beneficent;
    teach me Your laws.
69Though the arrogant have accused me falsely,
    I observe Your precepts wholeheartedly.
70Their minds are thick like fat;
    as for me, Your teaching is my delight.
71It was good for me that I was humbled,
    so that I might learn Your laws.
72I prefer the teaching You proclaimed
    to thousands of gold and silver pieces.

י 73Your hands made me and fashioned me;
    give me understanding that I may learn Your
    commandments.
74Those who fear You will see me and rejoice,
    for I have put my hope in Your word.
75I know, O LORD, that Your rulings are just;
    rightly have You humbled me.
76May Your steadfast love comfort me
    in accordance with Your promise to Your serv-
    ant.
77May Your mercy reach me, that I might live,
    for Your teaching is my delight.
78Let the insolent be dismayed, for they have
    wronged me without cause;
    I will study Your precepts.
79May those who fear You,
    those who know Your decrees,

63 חָבֵר אָנִי לְכָל־אֲשֶׁר יְרֵאוּךָ
וּלְשֹׁמְרֵי פִּקּוּדֶיךָ:
64 חַסְדְּךָ יְהֹוָה מָלְאָה הָאָרֶץ
חֻקֶּיךָ לַמְּדֵנִי:

65 טוֹב עָשִׂיתָ עִם־עַבְדְּךָ
יְהֹוָה כִּדְבָרֶךָ:
66 טוּב טַעַם וָדַעַת לַמְּדֵנִי
כִּי בְמִצְוֺתֶיךָ הֶאֱמָנְתִּי:
67 טֶרֶם אֶעֱנֶה אֲנִי שֹׁגֵג
וְעַתָּה אִמְרָתְךָ שָׁמָרְתִּי:
68 טוֹב־אַתָּה וּמֵטִיב
לַמְּדֵנִי חֻקֶּיךָ:
69 טָפְלוּ עָלַי שֶׁקֶר זֵדִים
אֲנִי בְּכָל־לֵב ׀ אֶצֹּר פִּקּוּדֶיךָ:
70 טָפַשׁ כַּחֵלֶב לִבָּם
אֲנִי תּוֹרָתְךָ שִׁעֲשָׁעְתִּי:
71 טוֹב־לִי כִי־עֻנֵּיתִי
לְמַעַן אֶלְמַד חֻקֶּיךָ:
72 טוֹב־לִי תוֹרַת־פִּיךָ
מֵאַלְפֵי זָהָב וָכָסֶף:

73 יָדֶיךָ עָשׂוּנִי וַיְכוֹנְנוּנִי
הֲבִינֵנִי וְאֶלְמְדָה מִצְוֺתֶיךָ:
74 יְרֵאֶיךָ יִרְאוּנִי וְיִשְׂמָחוּ
כִּי לִדְבָרְךָ יִחָלְתִּי:
75 יָדַעְתִּי יְהֹוָה כִּי־צֶדֶק מִשְׁפָּטֶיךָ
וֶאֱמוּנָה עִנִּיתָנִי:
76 יְהִי־נָא חַסְדְּךָ לְנַחֲמֵנִי
כְּאִמְרָתְךָ לְעַבְדֶּךָ:
77 יְבֹאוּנִי רַחֲמֶיךָ וְאֶחְיֶה
כִּי־תוֹרָתְךָ שַׁעֲשֻׁעָי:
78 יֵבֹשׁוּ זֵדִים כִּי־שֶׁקֶר עִוְּתוּנִי
אֲנִי אָשִׂיחַ בְּפִקּוּדֶיךָ:
79 יָשׁוּבוּ לִי
יְרֵאֶיךָ

turn again to me.

80May I wholeheartedly follow Your laws
    so that I do not come to grief.

כ 81I long for Your deliverance;
    I hope for Your word.

82My eyes pine away for Your promise;
    I say, "When will You comfort me?"

83Though I have become like a water-skin dried
    in smoke,
    I have not neglected Your laws.

84How long has Your servant to live?
    when will You bring my persecutors to judg-
    ment?

85The insolent have dug pits for me,
    flouting Your teaching.

86All Your commandments are enduring;
    I am persecuted without cause; help me!

87Though they almost wiped me off the earth,
    I did not abandon Your precepts.

88As befits Your steadfast love, preserve me,
    so that I may keep the decree You proclaimed.

ל 89The Lord exists forever;
    Your word stands firm in heaven.

90Your faithfulness is for all generations;
    You have established the earth, and it stands.

91They stand this day to [carry out] Your rulings,
    for all are Your servants.

92Were not Your teaching my delight
    I would have perished in my affliction.

93I will never neglect Your precepts,
    for You have preserved my life through them.

94I am Yours; save me!
    For I have turned to Your precepts.

95The·wicked hope to destroy me,
    but I ponder Your decrees.

96I have seen that all things have their limit,
    but Your commandment is broad beyond
    measure.

וִידְעוּ וְיֹדְעֵי עֵדֹתֶיךָ:

80 יְהִי־לִבִּי תָמִים בְּחֻקֶּיךָ
לְמַעַן לֹא אֵבוֹשׁ:

81 כָּלְתָה לִתְשׁוּעָתְךָ נַפְשִׁי
לִדְבָרְךָ יִחָלְתִּי:

82 כָּלוּ עֵינַי לְאִמְרָתֶךָ
לֵאמֹר מָתַי תְּנַחֲמֵנִי:

83 כִּי־הָיִיתִי כְּנֹאד בְּקִיטוֹר
חֻקֶּיךָ לֹא שָׁכָחְתִּי:

84 כַּמָּה יְמֵי־עַבְדֶּךָ
מָתַי תַּעֲשֶׂה בְרֹדְפַי מִשְׁפָּט:

85 כָּרוּ־לִי זֵדִים שִׁיחוֹת
אֲשֶׁר לֹא כְתוֹרָתֶךָ:

86 כָּל־מִצְוֹתֶיךָ אֱמוּנָה
שֶׁקֶר רְדָפוּנִי עָזְרֵנִי:

87 כִּמְעַט כִּלּוּנִי בָאָרֶץ
וַאֲנִי לֹא־עָזַבְתִּי פִקֻּדֶיךָ:

88 כְּחַסְדְּךָ חַיֵּנִי
וְאֶשְׁמְרָה עֵדוּת פִּיךָ:

89 לְעוֹלָם יְהוָה
דְּבָרְךָ נִצָּב בַּשָּׁמָיִם:

90 לְדֹר וָדֹר אֱמוּנָתֶךָ
כּוֹנַנְתָּ אֶרֶץ וַתַּעֲמֹד:

91 לְמִשְׁפָּטֶיךָ עָמְדוּ הַיּוֹם
כִּי הַכֹּל עֲבָדֶיךָ:

92 לוּלֵי תוֹרָתְךָ שַׁעֲשֻׁעָי
אָז אָבַדְתִּי בְעָנְיִי:

93 לְעוֹלָם לֹא־אֶשְׁכַּח פִּקּוּדֶיךָ
כִּי בָם חִיִּיתָנִי:

94 לְךָ־אֲנִי הוֹשִׁיעֵנִי
כִּי פִקּוּדֶיךָ דָרָשְׁתִּי:

95 לִי קִוּוּ רְשָׁעִים לְאַבְּדֵנִי
עֵדֹתֶיךָ אֶתְבּוֹנָן:

96 לְכָל־תִּכְלָה רָאִיתִי קֵץ
רְחָבָה מִצְוָתְךָ מְאֹד:

מ 97O how I love Your teaching!
It is my study all day long.

98Your commandments make me wiser than my
enemies;
they always stand by me.

99I have gained more insight than all my teachers,
for Your decrees are my study.

100I have gained more understanding than my
elders,
for I observe Your precepts.

101I have avoided every evil way
so that I may keep Your word.

102I have not departed from Your rules,
for You have instructed me.

103How pleasing is Your word to my palate,
sweeter than honey.

104I ponder Your precepts;
therefore I hate every false way.

נ 105Your word is a lamp to my feet,
a light for my path.

106I have firmly sworn
to keep Your just rules.

107I am very much afflicted;
O LORD, preserve me in accordance with Your
word.

108Accept, O LORD, my freewill offerings;
teach me Your rules.

109Though my life is always in danger,
I do not neglect Your teaching.

110Though the wicked have set a trap for me,
I have not strayed from Your precepts.

111Your decrees are my eternal heritage;
they are my heart's delight.

112I am resolved to follow Your laws
a-to the utmost-a forever.

ס 113I hate men of divided heart,
but I love Your teaching.

97 מָה־אָהַבְתִּי תוֹרָתֶךָ
כָּל־הַיּוֹם הִיא שִׂיחָתִי:

98 מֵאֹיְבַי תְּחַכְּמֵנִי מִצְוֺתֶךָ
כִּי לְעוֹלָם הִיא־לִי:

99 מִכָּל־מְלַמְּדַי הִשְׂכַּלְתִּי
כִּי עֵדְוֺתֶיךָ שִׂיחָה לִי:

100 מִזְּקֵנִים אֶתְבּוֹנָן
כִּי פִקּוּדֶיךָ נָצָרְתִּי:

101 מִכָּל־אֹרַח רָע כָּלִאתִי רַגְלָי
לְמַעַן אֶשְׁמֹר דְּבָרֶךָ:

102 מִמִּשְׁפָּטֶיךָ לֹא־סָרְתִּי
כִּי־אַתָּה הוֹרֵתָנִי:

103 מַה־נִּמְלְצוּ לְחִכִּי אִמְרָתֶךָ
מִדְּבַשׁ לְפִי:

104 מִפִּקּוּדֶיךָ אֶתְבּוֹנָן
עַל־כֵּן שָׂנֵאתִי ׀ כָּל־אֹרַח שָׁקֶר:

105 נֵר־לְרַגְלִי דְבָרֶךָ
וְאוֹר לִנְתִיבָתִי:

106 נִשְׁבַּעְתִּי וָאֲקַיֵּמָה
לִשְׁמֹר מִשְׁפְּטֵי צִדְקֶךָ:

107 נַעֲנֵיתִי עַד־מְאֹד
יְהֹוָה חַיֵּנִי כִדְבָרֶךָ:

108 נִדְבוֹת פִּי רְצֵה־נָא יְהֹוָה
וּמִשְׁפָּטֶיךָ לַמְּדֵנִי:

109 נַפְשִׁי בְכַפִּי תָמִיד
וְתוֹרָתְךָ לֹא שָׁכָחְתִּי:

110 נָתְנוּ רְשָׁעִים פַּח לִי
וּמִפִּקּוּדֶיךָ לֹא תָעִיתִי:

111 נָחַלְתִּי עֵדְוֺתֶיךָ לְעוֹלָם
כִּי־שְׂשׂוֹן לִבִּי הֵמָּה:

112 נָטִיתִי לִבִּי לַעֲשׂוֹת חֻקֶּיךָ
לְעוֹלָם עֵקֶב:

113 סֵעֲפִים שָׂנֵאתִי
וְתוֹרָתְךָ אָהָבְתִּי:

114You are my protection and my shield;
  I hope for Your word.

115Keep away from me, you evildoers,
  that I may observe the commandments of my
    God.

116Support me as You promised, so that I may live;
  do not thwart my expectation.

117Sustain me that I may be saved,
  and I will always muse upon Your laws.

118You reject all who stray from Your laws,
  for they are false and deceitful.

119You do away with the wicked as if they were
    dross;
  rightly do I love Your decrees.

120My flesh creeps from fear of You;
  I am in awe of Your rulings.

ע 121I have done what is just and right;
  do not abandon me to those who would wrong
    me.

122Guarantee Your servant's well-being;
  do not let the arrogant wrong me.

123My eyes pine away for Your deliverance,
  for Your promise of victory.

124Deal with Your servant as befits Your steadfast
    love;
  teach me Your laws.

125I am Your servant;
  give me understanding,
  that I might know Your decrees.

126It is a time to act for the LORD,
  for they have violated Your teaching.

127Rightly do I love Your commandments
  more than gold, even fine gold.

128Truly c-by all [Your] precepts I walk straight;-c
  I hate every false way.

פ 129Your decrees are wondrous;
  rightly do I observe them.

114 סִתְרִי וּמָגִנִּי אָתָּה
לִדְבָרְךָ יִחָלְתִּי:

115 סוּרוּ־מִמֶּנִּי מְרֵעִים
וְאֶצְּרָה מִצְוֹת אֱלֹהָי:

116 סָמְכֵנִי כְאִמְרָתְךָ וְאֶחְיֶה
וְאַל־תְּבִישֵׁנִי מִשִּׂבְרִי:

117 סְעָדֵנִי וְאִוָּשֵׁעָה
וְאֶשְׁעָה בְחֻקֶּיךָ תָמִיד:

118 סָלִיתָ כָּל־שׁוֹגִים מֵחֻקֶּיךָ
כִּי־שֶׁקֶר תַּרְמִיתָם:

119 סִגִים הִשְׁבַּתָּ כָל־רִשְׁעֵי־אָרֶץ
לָכֵן אָהַבְתִּי עֵדֹתֶיךָ:

120 סָמַר מִפַּחְדְּךָ בְשָׂרִי
וּמִמִּשְׁפָּטֶיךָ יָרֵאתִי:

121 עָשִׂיתִי מִשְׁפָּט וָצֶדֶק
בַּל־תַּנִּיחֵנִי לְעֹשְׁקָי:

122 עֲרֹב עַבְדְּךָ לְטוֹב
אַל־יַעַשְׁקֻנִי זֵדִים:

123 עֵינַי כָּלוּ לִישׁוּעָתֶךָ
וּלְאִמְרַת צִדְקֶךָ:

124 עֲשֵׂה עִם־עַבְדְּךָ כְחַסְדֶּךָ
וְחֻקֶּיךָ לַמְּדֵנִי:

125 עַבְדְּךָ־אָנִי הֲבִינֵנִי
וְאֵדְעָה עֵדֹתֶיךָ:

126 עֵת לַעֲשׂוֹת לַיהוָה
הֵפֵרוּ תּוֹרָתֶךָ:

127 עַל־כֵּן אָהַבְתִּי מִצְוֹתֶיךָ
מִזָּהָב וּמִפָּז:

128 עַל־כֵּן ׀ כָּל־פִּקּוּדֵי כֹל יִשָּׁרְתִּי
כָּל־אֹרַח שֶׁקֶר שָׂנֵאתִי:

129 פְּלָאוֹת עֵדְוֹתֶיךָ
עַל־כֵּן נְצָרָתַם נַפְשִׁי:

c-c Or "I declare all [Your] precepts to be just."

130*d*-The words You inscribed give-*d* light,
  and grant understanding to the simple.

131I open my mouth wide, I pant,
  longing for Your commandments.

132Turn to me and be gracious to me,
  as is Your rule with those who love Your name.

133Make my feet firm through Your promise;
  do not let iniquity dominate me.

134Redeem me from being wronged by man,
  that I may keep Your precepts.

135Show favor to Your servant,
  and teach me Your laws.

136My eyes shed streams of water
  because men do not obey Your teaching.

ᴢ 137You are righteous, O Lᴏʀᴅ;
  Your rulings are just.

138You have ordained righteous decrees;
  they are firmly enduring.

139I am consumed with rage
  over my foes' neglect of Your words.

140Your word is exceedingly pure,
  and Your servant loves it.

141Though I am belittled and despised,
  I have not neglected Your precepts.

142Your righteousness is eternal;
  Your teaching is true.

143Though anguish and distress come upon me,
  Your commandments are my delight.

144Your righteous decrees are eternal;
  give me understanding, that I might live.

ᴋ 145I call with all my heart;
  answer me, O Lᴏʀᴅ,
  that I may observe Your laws.

146I call upon You; save me,

d-d With Targum; or *"The exposition of Your words gives"; meaning
    of Heb. uncertain.*

130 פֶּתַח דְּבָרֶיךָ יָאִיר
מֵבִין פְּתָיִים:

131 פִּי־פָעַרְתִּי וָאֶשְׁאָפָה
כִּי לְמִצְוֺתֶיךָ יָאָבְתִּי:

132 פְּנֵה־אֵלַי וְחָנֵּנִי
כְּמִשְׁפָּט לְאֹהֲבֵי שְׁמֶךָ:

133 פְּעָמַי הָכֵן בְּאִמְרָתֶךָ
וְאַל־תַּשְׁלֶט־בִּי כָל־אָוֶן:

134 פְּדֵנִי מֵעֹשֶׁק אָדָם
וְאֶשְׁמְרָה פִּקּוּדֶיךָ:

135 פָּנֶיךָ הָאֵר בְּעַבְדֶּךָ
וְלַמְּדֵנִי אֶת־חֻקֶּיךָ:

136 פַּלְגֵי־מַיִם יָרְדוּ עֵינָי
עַל לֹא־שָׁמְרוּ תוֹרָתֶךָ:

137 צַדִּיק אַתָּה יְהֹוָה
וְיָשָׁר מִשְׁפָּטֶיךָ:

138 צִוִּיתָ צֶדֶק עֵדֹתֶיךָ
וֶאֱמוּנָה מְאֹד:

139 צִמְּתַתְנִי קִנְאָתִי
כִּי־שָׁכְחוּ דְבָרֶיךָ צָרָי:

140 צְרוּפָה אִמְרָתְךָ מְאֹד
וְעַבְדְּךָ אֲהֵבָהּ:

141 צָעִיר אָנֹכִי וְנִבְזֶה
פִּקֻּדֶיךָ לֹא שָׁכָחְתִּי:

142 צִדְקָתְךָ צֶדֶק לְעוֹלָם
וְתוֹרָתְךָ אֱמֶת:

143 צַר־וּמָצוֹק מְצָאוּנִי
מִצְוֺתֶיךָ שַׁעֲשֻׁעָי:

144 צֶדֶק עֵדְוֺתֶיךָ לְעוֹלָם
הֲבִינֵנִי וְאֶחְיֶה:

145 קָרָאתִי בְכָל־לֵב
עֲנֵנִי יְהֹוָה
חֻקֶּיךָ אֶצֹּרָה:

146 קְרָאתִיךָ הוֹשִׁיעֵנִי

that I may keep Your decrees.

147I rise before dawn and cry for help;
    I hope for Your word.

148My eyes greet each watch of the night,
    as I meditate on Your promise.

149Hear my voice as befits Your steadfast love;
    O LORD, preserve me, as is Your rule.

150Those who pursue intrigue draw near;
    they are far from Your teaching.

151You, O LORD, are near,
    and all Your commandments are true.

152I know from Your decrees of old
    that You have established them forever.

ר 153See my affliction and rescue me,
    for I have not neglected Your teaching.

154Champion my cause and redeem me;
    preserve me according to Your promise.

155Deliverance is far from the wicked,
    for they have not turned to Your laws.

156Your mercies are great, O LORD;
    as is Your rule, preserve me.

157Many are my persecutors and foes;
    I have not swerved from Your decrees.

158I have seen traitors and loathed*e* them,
    because they did not keep Your word in mind.

159See that I have loved Your precepts;
    O LORD, preserve me, as befits Your steadfast
    love.

160Truth is the essence of Your word;
    Your just rules are eternal.

ש 161Princes have persecuted me without reason;
    my heart thrills at Your word.

162I rejoice over Your promise
    as one who obtains great spoil.

163I hate and abhor falsehood;
    I love Your teaching.

---

e Or "have contended with."

וְאֶשְׁמְרָ֖ה עֵדֹתֶֽיךָ׃

147 קִדַּ֣מְתִּי בַ֭נֶּשֶׁף וָאֲשַׁוֵּ֑עָה
לדבריך לִדְבָרְךָ֥ יִחָֽלְתִּי׃

148 קִדְּמ֣וּ עֵ֭ינַי אַשְׁמֻר֑וֹת
לָ֝שִׂ֗יחַ בְּאִמְרָתֶֽךָ׃

149 ק֭וֹלִי שִׁמְעָ֣ה כְחַסְדֶּ֑ךָ
יְ֝הֹוָ֗ה כְּֽמִשְׁפָּטֶ֥ךָ חַיֵּֽנִי׃

150 קָ֭רְבוּ רֹדְפֵ֣י זִמָּ֑ה
מִתּוֹרָֽתְךָ֥ רָחָֽקוּ׃

151 קָר֣וֹב אַתָּ֣ה יְהֹוָ֑ה
וְֽכָל־מִצְוֺתֶ֥יךָ אֱמֶֽת׃

152 קֶ֣דֶם יָ֭דַעְתִּי מֵעֵדֹתֶ֑יךָ
כִּ֖י לְעוֹלָ֣ם יְסַדְתָּֽם׃

153 רְאֵֽה־עׇנְיִ֥י וְחַלְּצֵ֑נִי
כִּי־תֽוֹרָתְךָ֗ לֹ֣א שָׁכָֽחְתִּי׃

154 רִיבָ֣ה רִ֭יבִי וּגְאָלֵ֑נִי
לְאִמְרָתְךָ֥ חַיֵּֽנִי׃

155 רָח֣וֹק מֵרְשָׁעִ֣ים יְשׁוּעָ֑ה
כִּֽי־חֻקֶּ֥יךָ לֹ֣א דָרָֽשׁוּ׃

156 רַחֲמֶ֖יךָ רַבִּ֥ים ׀ יְהֹוָ֑ה
כְּֽמִשְׁפָּטֶ֥יךָ חַיֵּֽנִי׃

157 רַ֭בִּים רֹדְפַ֣י וְצָרָ֑י
מֵ֝עֵדְוֺתֶ֗יךָ לֹ֣א נָטִֽיתִי׃

158 רָאִ֣יתִי בֹ֭גְדִים וָאֶתְקוֹטָ֑טָה
אֲשֶׁ֥ר אִ֝מְרָתְךָ֗ לֹ֣א שָׁמָֽרוּ׃

159 רְ֭אֵה כִּֽי־פִקּוּדֶ֣יךָ אָהָ֑בְתִּי
יְ֝הֹוָ֗ה כְּֽחַסְדְּךָ֥ חַיֵּֽנִי׃

160 רֹאשׁ־דְּבָרְךָ֥ אֱמֶ֑ת
וּ֝לְעוֹלָ֗ם כָּל־מִשְׁפַּ֥ט צִדְקֶֽךָ׃

161 שָׂ֭רִים רְדָפ֣וּנִי חִנָּ֑ם
ומדבריך וּ֝מִדְּבָרְךָ֗ פָּחַ֥ד לִבִּֽי׃

162 שָׂ֣שׂ אָ֭נֹכִי עַל־אִמְרָתֶ֑ךָ
כְּ֝מוֹצֵ֗א שָׁלָ֥ל רָֽב׃

163 שֶׁ֣קֶר שָׂ֭נֵאתִי וַאֲתַעֵ֑בָה
תּוֹרָתְךָ֥ אָהָֽבְתִּי׃

164I praise You seven times each day
for Your just rules.

165Those who love Your teaching enjoy well-
being;
they encounter no adversity.

166I hope for Your deliverance, O Lord;
I observe Your commandments.

167I obey Your decrees
and love them greatly.

168I obey Your precepts and decrees;
all my ways are before You.

ת 169May my plea reach You, O Lord;
grant me understanding according to Your
word.

170May my petition come before You;
save me in accordance with Your promise.

171My lips shall pour forth praise,
for You teach me Your laws.

172My tongue shall declare Your promise,
for all Your commandments are just.

173Lend Your hand to help me,
for I have chosen Your precepts.

174I have longed for Your deliverance, O Lord;
Your teaching is my delight.

175Let me live, that I may praise You;
may Your rules be my help;

176I have strayed like a lost sheep;
search for Your servant,
for I have not neglected Your commandments.

164 שֶׁבַע בַּיּוֹם הִלַּלְתִּיךָ
עַל מִשְׁפְּטֵי צִדְקֶךָ:
165 שָׁלוֹם רָב לְאֹהֲבֵי תוֹרָתֶךָ
וְאֵין־לָמוֹ מִכְשׁוֹל:
166 שִׂבַּרְתִּי לִישׁוּעָתְךָ יְהוָה
וּמִצְוֺתֶיךָ עָשִׂיתִי:
167 שָׁמְרָה נַפְשִׁי עֵדֹתֶיךָ
וָאֹהֲבֵם מְאֹד:
168 שָׁמַרְתִּי פִקּוּדֶיךָ וְעֵדֹתֶיךָ
כִּי כָל־דְּרָכַי נֶגְדֶּךָ:
169 תִּקְרַב רִנָּתִי לְפָנֶיךָ יְהוָה
כִּדְבָרְךָ הֲבִינֵנִי:
170 תָּבוֹא תְּחִנָּתִי לְפָנֶיךָ
כְּאִמְרָתְךָ הַצִּילֵנִי:
171 תַּבַּעְנָה שְׂפָתַי תְּהִלָּה
כִּי תְלַמְּדֵנִי חֻקֶּיךָ:
172 תַּעַן לְשׁוֹנִי אִמְרָתֶךָ
כִּי כָל־מִצְוֺתֶיךָ צֶּדֶק:
173 תְּהִי־יָדְךָ לְעָזְרֵנִי
כִּי פִקּוּדֶיךָ בָחָרְתִּי:
174 תָּאַבְתִּי לִישׁוּעָתְךָ יְהוָה
וְתוֹרָתְךָ שַׁעֲשֻׁעָי:
175 תְּחִי־נַפְשִׁי וּתְהַלְלֶךָּ
וּמִשְׁפָּטֶךָ יַעְזְרֻנִי:
176 תָּעִיתִי כְּשֶׂה אֹבֵד
בַּקֵּשׁ עַבְדֶּךָ
כִּי מִצְוֺתֶיךָ לֹא שָׁכָחְתִּי:

120 A song of ascents.a

In my distress I called to the Lord
and He answered me.

2O Lord, save me from treacherous lips,
from a deceitful tongue!

3What can you profit,

קכ שִׁיר הַמַּעֲלוֹת

אֶל־יְהוָה בַּצָּרָתָה לִּי
קָרָאתִי וַיַּעֲנֵנִי:
2 יְהוָה הַצִּילָה נַפְשִׁי מִשְּׂפַת־שֶׁקֶר
מִלָּשׁוֹן רְמִיָּה:
3 מַה־יִּתֵּן לְךָ

a A term of uncertain meaning.

what can you gain,
  O deceitful tongue?
4A warrior's sharp arrows,
  with hot coals of broom-wood.

5Woe is me, that I live with Meshech,
  that I dwell among the clans of Kedar.
6Too long have I dwelt with those who hate peace.
7I am all peace;
  but when I speak,
  they are for war.

וּמַה־יֹּסִיף לָךְ
לָשׁוֹן רְמִיָּה׃
4 חִצֵּי גִבּוֹר שְׁנוּנִים
עִם גַּחֲלֵי רְתָמִים׃

5 אוֹיָה־לִי כִּי־גַרְתִּי מֶשֶׁךְ
שָׁכַנְתִּי עִם־אָהֳלֵי קֵדָר׃
6 רַבַּת שָׁכְנָה־לָּהּ נַפְשִׁי עִם שׂוֹנֵא
שָׁלוֹם׃
7 אֲנִי־שָׁלוֹם
וְכִי אֲדַבֵּר
הֵמָּה לַמִּלְחָמָה׃

121 A song for ascents.

כקא שִׁיר לַמַּעֲלוֹת

I turn my eyes to the mountains;
  from where will my help come?
2My help comes from the LORD,
  maker of heaven and earth.
3He will not let your foot give way;
  your guardian will not slumber;
4See, the guardian of Israel
  neither slumbers nor sleeps!
5The LORD is your guardian,
  the LORD is your protection
  at your right hand.
6By day the sun will not strike you,
  nor the moon by night.
7The LORD will guard you from all harm;
  He will guard your life.
8The LORD will guard your going and coming
  now and forever.

אֶשָּׂא עֵינַי אֶל־הֶהָרִים
מֵאַיִן יָבֹא עֶזְרִי׃
2 עֶזְרִי מֵעִם יְהוָה
עֹשֵׂה שָׁמַיִם וָאָרֶץ׃
3 אַל־יִתֵּן לַמּוֹט רַגְלֶךָ
אַל־יָנוּם שֹׁמְרֶךָ׃
4 הִנֵּה לֹא־יָנוּם וְלֹא יִישָׁן
שׁוֹמֵר יִשְׂרָאֵל׃
5 יְהוָה שֹׁמְרֶךָ
יְהוָה צִלְּךָ
עַל־יַד יְמִינֶךָ׃
6 יוֹמָם הַשֶּׁמֶשׁ לֹא־יַכֶּכָּה
וְיָרֵחַ בַּלָּיְלָה׃
7 יְהוָה יִשְׁמָרְךָ מִכָּל־רָע
יִשְׁמֹר אֶת־נַפְשֶׁךָ׃
8 יְהוָה יִשְׁמָר־צֵאתְךָ וּבוֹאֶךָ
מֵעַתָּה וְעַד־עוֹלָם׃

122

122 A song of ascents. Of David.

קכב שִׁיר הַמַּעֲלוֹת לְדָוִד

שָׂמַחְתִּי בְּאֹמְרִים לִי
בֵּית יְהוָה נֵלֵךְ:

I rejoiced when they said to me,
"We are going to the House of the LORD."

²Our feet stood inside your gates, O Jerusalem,

³Jerusalem built up, a city knit together,

⁴to which tribes would make pilgrimage,
the tribes of the LORD,
—as was enjoined upon Israel—
to praise the name of the LORD.

⁵There the thrones of judgment stood,
thrones of the house of David.

⁶Pray for the well-being of Jerusalem;
"May those who love you be at peace.

⁷May there be well-being within your ramparts,
peace in your citadels."

⁸For the sake of my kin and friends,
I pray for your well-being;

⁹for the sake of the house of the LORD our God,
I seek your good.

² עֹמְדוֹת הָיוּ רַגְלֵינוּ בִּשְׁעָרָיִךְ
יְרוּשָׁלָ͏ִם:

³ יְרוּשָׁלַ͏ִם הַבְּנוּיָה כְּעִיר שֶׁחֻבְּרָה-
לָּהּ יַחְדָּו:

⁴ שֶׁשָּׁם עָלוּ שְׁבָטִים
שִׁבְטֵי-יָהּ
עֵדוּת לְיִשְׂרָאֵל
לְהֹדוֹת לְשֵׁם יְהוָה:

⁵ כִּי שָׁמָּה | יָשְׁבוּ כִסְאוֹת לְמִשְׁפָּט
כִּסְאוֹת לְבֵית דָּוִיד:

⁶ שַׁאֲלוּ שְׁלוֹם יְרוּשָׁלָ͏ִם
יִשְׁלָיוּ אֹהֲבָיִךְ:

⁷ יְהִי-שָׁלוֹם בְּחֵילֵךְ
שַׁלְוָה בְּאַרְמְנוֹתָיִךְ:

⁸ לְמַעַן אַחַי וְרֵעָי
אֲדַבְּרָה-נָּא שָׁלוֹם בָּךְ:

⁹ לְמַעַן בֵּית-יְהוָה אֱלֹהֵינוּ
אֲבַקְשָׁה טוֹב לָךְ:

123

123 A song of ascents.

קכג שִׁיר הַמַּעֲלוֹת

To You, enthroned in heaven,
I turn my eyes.

²As the eyes of slaves follow their master's hand,
as the eyes of a slave-girl follow the hand of her
mistress,
so our eyes are toward the LORD our God,
awaiting His favor.

³Show us favor, O LORD,
show us favor!
We have had more than enough of contempt.

אֵלֶיךָ נָשָׂאתִי אֶת-עֵינַי
הַיֹּשְׁבִי בַּשָּׁמָיִם:

² הִנֵּה כְעֵינֵי עֲבָדִים אֶל-יַד
אֲדוֹנֵיהֶם
כְּעֵינֵי שִׁפְחָה אֶל-יַד גְּבִרְתָּהּ
כֵּן עֵינֵינוּ אֶל-יְהוָה אֱלֹהֵינוּ
עַד שֶׁיְּחָנֵּנוּ:

³ חָנֵּנוּ יְהוָה
חָנֵּנוּ
כִּי-רַב שָׂבַעְנוּ בוּז:

4Long enough have we endured
the scorn of the complacent,
the contempt of the haughty.

4 רַבַּת֙ שָֽׂבְעָה־לָּ֣הּ נַפְשֵׁ֑נוּ
הַלַּ֥עַג הַשַּׁאֲנַנִּ֑ים
הַבּ֑וּז לִגְאֵ֥יֹונִֽם לִגְאֵ֥י יֹונִֽים׃

124   A song of ascents. Of David.

קכד   שִׁ֥יר הַֽמַּעֲלֹ֗ות לְדָ֫וִ֥ד

Were it not for the LORD, who was on our side,
let Israel now declare,
2were it not for the LORD, who was on our side
when men assailed us,
3they would have swallowed us alive
in their burning rage against us;
4the waters would have carried us off,
the torrent would have swept over us;
5over us would have swept
the seething waters.
6Blessed is the LORD, who did not let us
be ripped apart by their teeth.
7We are like a bird escaped from the fowler's trap;
the trap broke and we escaped.
8Our help is the name of the LORD,
maker of heaven and earth.

לוּלֵ֣י יְ֭הוָה שֶׁהָ֣יָה לָ֑נוּ
יֹֽאמַר־נָ֝א יִשְׂרָאֵֽל׃
2 לוּלֵ֣י יְ֭הוָה שֶׁהָ֣יָה לָ֑נוּ
בְּק֖וּם עָלֵ֣ינוּ אָדָֽם׃
3 אֲ֭זַי חַיִּ֣ים בְּלָע֑וּנוּ
בַּחֲרֹ֖ות אַפָּ֣ם בָּֽנוּ׃
4 אֲ֭זַי הַמַּ֣יִם שְׁטָפ֑וּנוּ
נַ֝֗חְלָה עָבַ֥ר עַל־נַפְשֵֽׁנוּ׃
5 אֲ֭זַי עָבַ֣ר עַל־נַפְשֵׁ֑נוּ
הַ֝מַּ֗יִם הַזֵּידֹונִֽים׃
6 בָּר֥וּךְ יְהוָ֑ה שֶׁלֹּ֥א נְתָנָ֥נוּ
טֶ֝֗רֶף לְשִׁנֵּיהֶֽם׃
7 נַפְשֵׁ֗נוּ כְּצִפֹּ֥ור נִמְלְטָה֮ מִפַּ֪ח
יֹ֫וקְשִׁ֥ים
הַפַּ֥ח נִשְׁבָּ֗ר וַאֲנַ֥חְנוּ נִמְלָֽטְנוּ׃
8 עֶ֭זְרֵנוּ בְּשֵׁ֣ם יְהוָ֑ה
עֹ֝שֵׂ֗ה שָׁמַ֥יִם וָאָֽרֶץ׃

125   A song of ascents.

קכה   שִׁ֗יר הַֽמַּ֫עֲלֹ֥ות

Those who trust in the LORD
are like Mount Zion
that cannot be moved,
enduring forever.
2Jerusalem, hills enfold it,
and the LORD enfolds His people
now and forever.
3a-The scepter of the wicked shall never rest
upon the land allotted to the righteous,

הַבֹּטְחִ֥ים בַּיהוָ֑ה
כְּֽהַר־צִיֹּ֥ון
לֹא־יִ֝מֹּ֗וט
לְעֹולָ֥ם יֵשֵֽׁב׃
2 יְֽרוּשָׁלִַ֗ם הָרִים֮ סָבִ֪יב לָ֥הּ
וַ֭יהוָה סָבִ֣יב לְעַמֹּ֑ו
מֵ֝עַתָּ֗ה וְעַד־עֹולָֽם׃
3 כִּ֤י לֹ֪א יָנ֡וּחַ שֵׁ֤בֶט הָרֶ֗שַׁע
עַ֥ל גֹּורַ֪ל הַֽצַּ֫דִּיקִ֥ים

---

a-a   *Meaning of Heb. uncertain.*

that the righteous not set their hand to
   wrongdoing.-*a*

4Do good, O LORD, to the good,
   to the upright in heart.

5*a*-But those who in their crookedness act
   corruptly,-*a*
   let the LORD make them go the way of evildoers.
May it be well with Israel!

לְמַעַן לֹא־יִשְׁלְחוּ הַצַּדִּיקִים
בְּעַוְלָתָה יְדֵיהֶם׃
4 הֵיטִיבָה יְהֹוָה לַטּוֹבִים
וְלִישָׁרִים בְּלִבּוֹתָם׃
5 וְהַמַּטִּים עֲקַלְקַלּוֹתָם
יוֹלִיכֵם יְהֹוָה אֶת־פֹּעֲלֵי הָאָוֶן
שָׁלוֹם עַל־יִשְׂרָאֵל׃

126 A song of ascents.

קכו שִׁיר הַמַּעֲלוֹת

When the LORD restores the fortunes of Zion
   —*a*-we see it as in a dream-*a*—
2our mouths shall be filled with laughter,
   our tongues, with songs of joy.
Then shall they say among the nations,
   "The LORD has done great things for them!"
3The LORD will do great things for us
   and we shall rejoice.

בְּשׁוּב יְהֹוָה אֶת־שִׁיבַת צִיּוֹן
הָיִינוּ כְּחֹלְמִים׃
2 אָז יִמָּלֵא שְׂחוֹק פִּינוּ
וּלְשׁוֹנֵנוּ רִנָּה
אָז יֹאמְרוּ בַגּוֹיִם
הִגְדִּיל יְהֹוָה לַעֲשׂוֹת עִם־אֵלֶּה׃
3 הִגְדִּיל יְהֹוָה לַעֲשׂוֹת עִמָּנוּ
הָיִינוּ שְׂמֵחִים׃

4Restore our fortunes, O LORD,
   like watercourses in the Negeb.
5They who sow in tears
   shall reap with songs of joy.
6Though he goes along weeping,
   carrying the seed-bag,
   he shall come back with songs of joy,
   carrying his sheaves.

4 שׁוּבָה יְהֹוָה אֶת־שְׁבוּתֵנוּ
כַּאֲפִיקִים בַּנֶּגֶב׃
5 הַזֹּרְעִים בְּדִמְעָה
בְּרִנָּה יִקְצֹרוּ׃
6 הָלוֹךְ יֵלֵךְ ׀ וּבָכֹה
נֹשֵׂא מֶשֶׁךְ־הַזָּרַע
בֹּא־יָבוֹא בְרִנָּה
נֹשֵׂא אֲלֻמֹּתָיו׃

127 A song of ascents. Of Solomon.

קכז שִׁיר הַמַּעֲלוֹת לִשְׁלֹמֹה

Unless the LORD builds the house,
   its builders labor in vain on it;
   unless the LORD watches over the city,
   the watchman keeps vigil in vain.
2In vain do you rise early
   and stay up late,

אִם־יְהֹוָה ׀ לֹא־יִבְנֶה בַיִת
שָׁוְא ׀ עָמְלוּ בוֹנָיו בּוֹ
אִם־יְהֹוָה לֹא־יִשְׁמָר־עִיר
שָׁוְא ׀ שָׁקַד שׁוֹמֵר׃
2 שָׁוְא לָכֶם ׀ מַשְׁכִּימֵי קוּם
מְאַחֲרֵי־שֶׁבֶת

---

a-a Lit. "we are veritable dreamers."

you who toil for the bread you eat;
  a-He provides as much for His loved ones while
    they sleep.-*a*

אֹכְלֵי לֶחֶם הָעֲצָבִים
כֵּן יִתֵּן לִידִידוֹ שֵׁנָא*:

3Sons are the provision*b* of the Lord;
  the fruit of the womb, His reward.
4Like arrows in the hand of a warrior
  are sons born to a man in his youth.
5Happy is the man who fills his quiver with them;
  they shall not be put to shame
  when they contend with the enemy in the gate.

3הִנֵּה נַחֲלַת יְהֹוָה בָּנִים
שָׂכָר פְּרִי הַבָּטֶן:
4כְּחִצִּים בְּיַד־גִּבּוֹר
כֵּן בְּנֵי הַנְּעוּרִים:
5אַשְׁרֵי הַגֶּבֶר אֲשֶׁר מִלֵּא אֶת־
אַשְׁפָּתוֹ מֵהֶם
לֹא־יֵבֹשׁוּ
כִּי־יְדַבְּרוּ אֶת־אוֹיְבִים בַּשָּׁעַר:

128 A song of ascents.

שִׁיר הַמַּעֲלוֹת קכח

Happy are all who fear the Lord,
  who follow His ways.
2You shall enjoy the fruit of your labors;
  you shall be happy and you shall prosper.
3Your wife shall be like a fruitful vine within your
    house;
  your sons, like olive saplings around your table.
4So shall the man who fears the Lord be blessed.

5May the Lord bless you from Zion;
  may you share the prosperity of Jerusalem
  all the days of your life,
    6and live to see your children's children.
May all be well with Israel!

אַשְׁרֵי כָּל־יְרֵא יְהֹוָה
הַהֹלֵךְ בִּדְרָכָיו:
2יְגִיעַ כַּפֶּיךָ כִּי תֹאכֵל
אַשְׁרֶיךָ וְטוֹב לָךְ:
3אֶשְׁתְּךָ ׀ כְּגֶפֶן פֹּרִיָּה בְּיַרְכְּתֵי
בֵיתֶךָ
בָּנֶיךָ כִּשְׁתִלֵי זֵיתִים סָבִיב
לְשֻׁלְחָנֶךָ:
4הִנֵּה כִי־כֵן יְבֹרַךְ גָּבֶר יְרֵא יְהֹוָה:
5יְבָרֶכְךָ יְהֹוָה מִצִּיּוֹן
וּרְאֵה בְּטוּב יְרוּשָׁלָ͏ִם
כֹּל יְמֵי חַיֶּיךָ:
6וּרְאֵה־בָנִים לְבָנֶיךָ*
שָׁלוֹם עַל־יִשְׂרָאֵל:

129 A song of ascents.

שִׁיר הַמַּעֲלוֹת קכט

Since my youth they have often assailed me,
  let Israel now declare,
    2since my youth they have often assailed me,
  but they have never overcome me.

רַבַּת צְרָרוּנִי מִנְּעוּרַי
יֹאמַר־נָא יִשְׂרָאֵל:
2רַבַּת צְרָרוּנִי מִנְּעוּרָי
גַּם לֹא־יָכְלוּ לִי:

---

a-a Meaning of Heb. uncertain.
b   Lit. "heritage."

א' במקום ה'   *v. 2.*

³Plowmen plowed across my back;
   they made long furrows.
⁴The Lord, the righteous one,
   has snapped the cords of the wicked.

⁵Let all who hate Zion
   fall back in disgrace.
⁶Let them be like grass on roofs
   that fades before it can be pulled up,
⁷that affords no handful for the reaper,
   no armful for the gatherer of sheaves,
⁸no exchange with passersby:
   "The blessing of the Lord be upon you."
"We bless you by the name of the Lord."

³עַל־גַּבִּי חָרְשׁוּ חֹרְשִׁים
הֶאֱרִיכוּ למענותם לְמַעֲנִיתָם:
⁴יְהֹוָה צַדִּיק
קִצֵּץ עֲבוֹת רְשָׁעִים:

⁵יֵבֹשׁוּ וְיִסֹּגוּ אָחוֹר
כֹּל שֹׂנְאֵי צִיּוֹן:
⁶יִהְיוּ כַּחֲצִיר גַּגּוֹת
שֶׁקַּדְמַת שָׁלַף יָבֵשׁ:
⁷שֶׁלֹּא מִלֵּא כַפּוֹ קוֹצֵר
וְחִצְנוֹ מְעַמֵּר:
⁸וְלֹא אָמְרוּ ׀ הָעֹבְרִים
בִּרְכַּת־יְהֹוָה אֲלֵיכֶם
בֵּרַכְנוּ אֶתְכֶם בְּשֵׁם יְהֹוָה:

130 A song of ascents.

קל שִׁיר הַמַּעֲלוֹת

Out of the depths I call You, O Lord.
²O Lord, listen to my cry;
   let Your ears be attentive
   to my plea for mercy.
³If You keep account of sins, O Lord,
   Lord, who will survive?
⁴Yours is the power to forgive
   so that You may be held in awe.

⁵I look to the Lord;
   I look to Him;
   I await His word.
⁶I am more eager for the Lord
   than watchmen for the morning,
   watchmen for the morning.

⁷O Israel, wait for the Lord;
   for with the Lord is steadfast love
   and great power to redeem.
⁸It is He who will redeem Israel from all their
   iniquities.

מִמַּעֲמַקִּים קְרָאתִיךָ יְהֹוָה:
²אֲדֹנָי שִׁמְעָה בְקוֹלִי
תִּהְיֶינָה אָזְנֶיךָ קַשֻּׁבוֹת
לְקוֹל תַּחֲנוּנָי:
³אִם־עֲוֹנוֹת תִּשְׁמָר־יָהּ
אֲדֹנָי מִי יַעֲמֹד:
⁴כִּי־עִמְּךָ הַסְּלִיחָה
לְמַעַן תִּוָּרֵא:

⁵קִוִּיתִי יְהֹוָה
קִוְּתָה נַפְשִׁי
וְלִדְבָרוֹ הוֹחָלְתִּי:
⁶נַפְשִׁי לַאדֹנָי
מִשֹּׁמְרִים לַבֹּקֶר
שֹׁמְרִים לַבֹּקֶר:

⁷יַחֵל יִשְׂרָאֵל אֶל־יְהֹוָה
כִּי־עִם־יְהֹוָה הַחֶסֶד
וְהַרְבֵּה עִמּוֹ פְדוּת:
⁸וְהוּא יִפְדֶּה אֶת־יִשְׂרָאֵל מִכֹּל
עֲוֹנֹתָיו:

131 A song of ascents. Of David.

קלא שִׁיר הַמַּעֲלוֹת לְדָוִד

O LORD, my heart is not proud
    nor my look haughty;
I do not aspire to great things
    or to what is beyond me;
²ᵃ-but I have taught myself to be contented
    like a weaned child with its mother;
    like a weaned child am I in my mind.⁻ᵃ
³O Israel, wait for the LORD
    now and forever.

יְהֹוָה ׀ לֹא־גָבַהּ לִבִּי
וְלֹא־רָמוּ עֵינַי
וְלֹא־הִלַּכְתִּי ׀ בִּגְדֹלוֹת
וּבְנִפְלָאוֹת מִמֶּנִּי:
2 אִם־לֹא שִׁוִּיתִי ׀ וְדוֹמַמְתִּי נַפְשִׁי
כְּגָמֻל עֲלֵי אִמּוֹ
כַּגָּמֻל עָלַי נַפְשִׁי:
3 יַחֵל יִשְׂרָאֵל אֶל־יְהֹוָה
מֵעַתָּה וְעַד־עוֹלָם:

132 A song of ascents.

קלב שִׁיר הַמַּעֲלוֹת

O LORD, remember in David's favor
    his extreme self-denial,
²how he swore to the LORD,
    vowed to the Mighty One of Jacob,
³"I will not enter my house,
    nor will I mount my bed,
⁴I will not give sleep to my eyes,
    or slumber to my eyelidsᵃ
⁵until I find a place for the LORD,
    an abode for the Mighty One of Jacob."

זְכוֹר־יְהֹוָה לְדָוִד
אֵת כָּל־עֻנּוֹתוֹ:
2 אֲשֶׁר נִשְׁבַּע לַיהֹוָה
נָדַר לַאֲבִיר יַעֲקֹב:
3 אִם־אָבֹא בְּאֹהֶל בֵּיתִי
אִם־אֶעֱלֶה עַל־עֶרֶשׂ יְצוּעָי:
4 אִם־אֶתֵּן שְׁנַת לְעֵינָי
לְעַפְעַפַּי תְּנוּמָה:
5 עַד־אֶמְצָא מָקוֹם לַיהֹוָה
מִשְׁכָּנוֹת לַאֲבִיר יַעֲקֹב:

⁶We heard it was in Ephrath;
    we came upon it in the region of Jaar.ᵇ
⁷Let us enter His abode,
    bow at His footstool.
⁸Advance, O LORD, to Your resting-place,
    You and Your mighty Ark!
⁹Your priests are clothed in triumph;
    Your loyal ones sing for joy.
¹⁰For the sake of Your servant David
    do not reject Your anointed one.
¹¹The LORD swore to David

6 הִנֵּה־שְׁמַעֲנוּהָ בְאֶפְרָתָה
מְצָאנוּהָ בִּשְׂדֵי־יָעַר:
7 נָבוֹאָה לְמִשְׁכְּנוֹתָיו
נִשְׁתַּחֲוֶה לַהֲדֹם רַגְלָיו:
8 קוּמָה יְהֹוָה לִמְנוּחָתֶךָ
אַתָּה וַאֲרוֹן עֻזֶּךָ:
9 כֹּהֲנֶיךָ יִלְבְּשׁוּ־צֶדֶק
וַחֲסִידֶיךָ יְרַנֵּנוּ:
10 בַּעֲבוּר דָּוִד עַבְדֶּךָ
אַל־תָּשֵׁב פְּנֵי מְשִׁיחֶךָ:
11 נִשְׁבַּע־יְהֹוָה ׀ לְדָוִד

---

a-a   *Meaning of Heb. uncertain.*

a   *Lit. "eyes."*
b   *Cf. 1 Sam. 7.1–2; 1 Chron. 13.5–6.*

a firm oath that He will not renounce,
"One of your own issue I will set upon your
throne.

אֱמֶת לֹא־יָשׁוּב מִמֶּנָּה
מִפְּרִי בִטְנְךָ אָשִׁית לְכִסֵּא־לָךְ:

12If your sons keep My covenant
and My decrees that I teach them,
then their sons also,
to the end of time,
shall sit upon your throne."

12 אִם־יִשְׁמְרוּ בָנֶיךָ | בְּרִיתִי
וְעֵדֹתִי זוֹ אֲלַמְּדֵם
גַּם־בְּנֵיהֶם
עֲדֵי־עַד
יֵשְׁבוּ לְכִסֵּא־לָךְ:

13For the LORD has chosen Zion;
He has desired it for His seat.

13 כִּי־בָחַר יְהֹוָה בְּצִיּוֹן
אִוָּהּ לְמוֹשָׁב לוֹ:

14"This is my resting-place for all time;
here I will dwell, for I desire it.

14 זֹאת־מְנוּחָתִי עֲדֵי־עַד
פֹּה־אֵשֵׁב כִּי אִוִּתִיהָ:

15I will amply bless its store of food,
give its needy their fill of bread.

15 צֵידָהּ בָּרֵךְ אֲבָרֵךְ
אֶבְיוֹנֶיהָ אַשְׂבִּיעַ לָחֶם:

16I will clothe its priests in victory,
its loyal ones shall sing for joy.

16 וְכֹהֲנֶיהָ אַלְבִּישׁ יֶשַׁע
וַחֲסִידֶיהָ רַנֵּן יְרַנֵּנוּ:

17There I will make a horn sprout for David;
I have prepared a lamp for My anointed one.

17 שָׁם אַצְמִיחַ קֶרֶן לְדָוִד
עָרַכְתִּי נֵר לִמְשִׁיחִי:

18I will clothe his enemies in disgrace,
while on him his crown shall sparkle."

18 אוֹיְבָיו אַלְבִּישׁ בֹּשֶׁת
וְעָלָיו יָצִיץ נִזְרוֹ:

133 A song of ascents. Of David.

קלג שִׁיר הַמַּעֲלוֹת לְדָוִד

How good and how pleasant it is
that brothers dwell together.

הִנֵּה מַה־טּוֹב וּמַה־נָּעִים
שֶׁבֶת אַחִים גַּם־יָחַד:

2It is like fine oil on the head
running down onto the beard,
the beard of Aaron,
that comes down over the collar of his robe;
3like the dew of Hermon
that falls upon the mountains of Zion.
There the LORD ordained blessing,
everlasting life.

2 כַּשֶּׁמֶן הַטּוֹב | עַל־הָרֹאשׁ
יֹרֵד עַל־הַזָּקָן
זְקַן־אַהֲרֹן
שֶׁיֹּרֵד עַל־פִּי מִדּוֹתָיו:
3 כְּטַל־חֶרְמוֹן
שֶׁיֹּרֵד עַל־הַרְרֵי צִיּוֹן
כִּי שָׁם | צִוָּה יְהֹוָה אֶת־הַבְּרָכָה
חַיִּים עַד־הָעוֹלָם:

134 A song of ascents.

קלד שִׁיר הַמַּעֲלוֹת

Now bless the LORD,
all you servants of the LORD

הִנֵּה | בָּרְכוּ אֶת־יְהֹוָה
כָּל־עַבְדֵי יְהֹוָה

who stand nightly
in the house of the LORD.
²Lift your hands toward the sanctuary
and bless the LORD.
³May the LORD,
maker of heaven and earth,
bless you from Zion.

הָעֹמְדִים בְּבֵית־יְהֹוָה
בַּלֵּילוֹת:
² שְׂאוּ־יְדֵכֶם קֹדֶשׁ
וּבָרְכוּ אֶת־יְהֹוָה:
³ יְבָרֶכְךָ יְהֹוָה
מִצִּיּוֹן
עֹשֵׂה שָׁמַיִם וָאָרֶץ:

135 Hallelujah.

Praise the name of the LORD;
give praise, you servants of the LORD
²who stand in the house of the LORD,
in the courts of the house of our God.
³Praise the LORD, for the LORD is good;
sing hymns to His name, for it is pleasant.
⁴For the LORD has chosen Jacob for Himself,
Israel, as His treasured possession.

⁵For I know that the LORD is great,
that our Lord is greater than all gods.
⁶Whatever the LORD desires He does
in heaven and earth,
in the seas and all the depths.
⁷He makes clouds rise from the end of the earth;
He makes lightning for the rain;
He releases the wind from His vaults.
⁸He struck down the first-born of Egypt,
man and beast alike;
⁹He sent signs and portents against[a] Egypt,
against Pharaoh and all his servants;
¹⁰He struck down many nations
and slew numerous kings—
¹¹Sihon, king of the Amorites,
Og, king of Bashan,
and all the royalty of Canaan—

קלה הַלְלוּ יָהּ |

הַלְלוּ אֶת־שֵׁם יְהֹוָה
הַלְלוּ עַבְדֵי יְהֹוָה:
² שֶׁעֹמְדִים בְּבֵית יְהֹוָה
בְּחַצְרוֹת בֵּית אֱלֹהֵינוּ:
³ הַלְלוּ־יָהּ כִּי־טוֹב יְהֹוָה
זַמְּרוּ לִשְׁמוֹ כִּי נָעִים:
⁴ כִּי־יַעֲקֹב בָּחַר לוֹ יָהּ
יִשְׂרָאֵל לִסְגֻלָּתוֹ:

⁵ כִּי אֲנִי יָדַעְתִּי כִּי־גָדוֹל יְהֹוָה
וַאֲדֹנֵינוּ מִכָּל־אֱלֹהִים:
⁶ כֹּל אֲשֶׁר־חָפֵץ יְהֹוָה עָשָׂה
בַּשָּׁמַיִם וּבָאָרֶץ
בַּיַּמִּים וְכָל־תְּהוֹמוֹת:
⁷ מַעֲלֶה נְשִׂאִים מִקְצֵה הָאָרֶץ
בְּרָקִים לַמָּטָר עָשָׂה
מוֹצֵא־רוּחַ מֵאוֹצְרוֹתָיו:
⁸ שֶׁהִכָּה בְּכוֹרֵי מִצְרָיִם
מֵאָדָם עַד־בְּהֵמָה:
⁹ שָׁלַח | אֹתוֹת וּמֹפְתִים בְּתוֹכֵכִי
מִצְרָיִם
בְּפַרְעֹה וּבְכָל־עֲבָדָיו:
¹⁰ שֶׁהִכָּה גּוֹיִם רַבִּים
וְהָרַג מְלָכִים עֲצוּמִים:
¹¹ לְסִיחוֹן | מֶלֶךְ הָאֱמֹרִי
וּלְעוֹג מֶלֶךְ הַבָּשָׁן
וּלְכֹל מַמְלְכוֹת כְּנָעַן:

a   Others "against you."

1581

¹²and gave their lands as a heritage,
as a heritage to His people Israel.

12 וְנָתַן אַרְצָם נַחֲלָה
נַחֲלָה לְיִשְׂרָאֵל עַמּֽוֹ:

¹³O Lord, Your name endures forever,
Your fame, O Lord, through all generations;
¹⁴for the Lord will champion His people,
and obtain satisfaction for His servants.

13 יְהוָה שִׁמְךָ לְעוֹלָם
יְהוָה זִכְרְךָ לְדֹר־וָדֹֽר:
14 כִּֽי־יָדִין יְהוָה עַמּוֹ
וְעַל־עֲבָדָיו יִתְנֶחָֽם:

^{15b}The idols of the nations are silver and gold,
the work of men's hands.
¹⁶They have mouths, but cannot speak;
they have eyes, but cannot see;
¹⁷they have ears, but cannot hear,
nor is there breath in their mouths.
¹⁸Those who fashion them,
all who trust in them,
shall become like them.

15 עֲצַבֵּי הַגּוֹיִם כֶּסֶף וְזָהָב
מַעֲשֵׂה יְדֵי אָדָֽם:
16 פֶּֽה־לָהֶם וְלֹא יְדַבֵּרוּ
עֵינַיִם לָהֶם וְלֹא יִרְאֽוּ:
17 אָזְנַיִם לָהֶם וְלֹא יַאֲזִינוּ
אַף אֵין־יֶשׁ־רוּחַ בְּפִיהֶֽם:
18 כְּמוֹהֶם יִהְיוּ
עֹשֵׂיהֶם
כֹּל אֲשֶׁר־בֹּטֵחַ בָּהֶֽם:

¹⁹O house of Israel, bless the Lord;
O house of Aaron, bless the Lord;
²⁰O house of Levi, bless the Lord;
you who fear the Lord, bless the Lord.
²¹Blessed is the Lord from Zion,
He who dwells in Jerusalem.
Hallelujah.

19 בֵּית יִשְׂרָאֵל בָּרֲכוּ אֶת־יְהוָה
בֵּית אַהֲרֹן בָּרֲכוּ אֶת־יְהוָה:
20 בֵּית הַלֵּוִי בָּרֲכוּ אֶת־יְהוָה
יִרְאֵי יְהוָה בָּרֲכוּ אֶת־יְהוָה:
21 בָּרוּךְ יְהוָה ׀ מִצִּיּוֹן
שֹׁכֵן יְרוּשָׁלִָם
הַֽלְלוּ־יָֽהּ:

136 Praise the Lord; for He is good,
His steadfast love is eternal.
²Praise the God of gods,
His steadfast love is eternal.
³Praise the Lord of lords,
His steadfast love is eternal;
⁴Who alone works great marvels,
His steadfast love is eternal;
⁵Who made the heavens with wisdom,
His steadfast love is eternal;

קלו הוֹדוּ לַיהוָה כִּי־טוֹב
כִּי לְעוֹלָם חַסְדּֽוֹ:
2 הוֹדוּ לֵאלֹהֵי הָאֱלֹהִים
כִּי לְעוֹלָם חַסְדּֽוֹ:
3 הוֹדוּ לַאֲדֹנֵי הָאֲדֹנִים
כִּי לְעוֹלָם חַסְדּֽוֹ:
4 לְעֹשֵׂה נִפְלָאוֹת גְּדֹלוֹת לְבַדּוֹ
כִּי לְעוֹלָם חַסְדּֽוֹ:
5 לְעֹשֵׂה הַשָּׁמַיִם בִּתְבוּנָה
כִּי לְעוֹלָם חַסְדּֽוֹ:

---

^b *With vv. 15–20, cf. Ps. 115.4–11.*

6Who spread the earth over the water,
  His steadfast love is eternal;

7Who made the great lights,
  His steadfast love is eternal;

8the sun to dominate the day,
  His steadfast love is eternal;

9the moon and the stars to dominate the night,
  His steadfast love is eternal;

10Who struck Egypt through their first-born,
  His steadfast love is eternal;

11and brought Israel out of their midst,
  His steadfast love is eternal;

12with a strong hand and outstretched arm,
  His steadfast love is eternal;

13Who split apart the Sea of Reeds,
  His steadfast love is eternal;

14and made Israel pass through it,
  His steadfast love is eternal;

15Who hurled Pharaoh and his army into the Sea
  of Reeds,
  His steadfast love is eternal;

16Who led His people through the wilderness,
  His steadfast love is eternal;

17Who struck down great kings,
  His steadfast love is eternal;

18and slew mighty kings—
  His steadfast love is eternal;

19Sihon, king of the Amorites,
  His steadfast love is eternal;

20Og, king of Bashan—
  His steadfast love is eternal;

21and gave their land as a heritage,
  His steadfast love is eternal;

22a heritage to His servant Israel,
  His steadfast love is eternal;

23Who took note of us in our degradation,
  His steadfast love is eternal;

6 לְרֹקַע הָאָרֶץ עַל־הַמָּיִם
כִּי לְעוֹלָם חַסְדּוֹ:

7 לְעֹשֵׂה אוֹרִים גְּדֹלִים
כִּי לְעוֹלָם חַסְדּוֹ:

8 אֶת־הַשֶּׁמֶשׁ לְמֶמְשֶׁלֶת בַּיּוֹם
כִּי לְעוֹלָם חַסְדּוֹ:

9 אֶת־הַיָּרֵחַ וְכוֹכָבִים לְמֶמְשְׁלוֹת
בַּלָּיְלָה
כִּי לְעוֹלָם חַסְדּוֹ:

10 לְמַכֵּה מִצְרַיִם בִּבְכוֹרֵיהֶם
כִּי לְעוֹלָם חַסְדּוֹ:

11 וַיּוֹצֵא יִשְׂרָאֵל מִתּוֹכָם
כִּי לְעוֹלָם חַסְדּוֹ:

12 בְּיָד חֲזָקָה וּבִזְרוֹעַ נְטוּיָה
כִּי לְעוֹלָם חַסְדּוֹ:

13 לְגֹזֵר יַם־סוּף לִגְזָרִים
כִּי לְעוֹלָם חַסְדּוֹ:

14 וְהֶעֱבִיר יִשְׂרָאֵל בְּתוֹכוֹ
כִּי לְעוֹלָם חַסְדּוֹ:

15 וְנִעֵר פַּרְעֹה וְחֵילוֹ בְיַם־סוּף
כִּי לְעוֹלָם חַסְדּוֹ:

16 לְמוֹלִיךְ עַמּוֹ בַּמִּדְבָּר
כִּי לְעוֹלָם חַסְדּוֹ:

17 לְמַכֵּה מְלָכִים גְּדֹלִים
כִּי לְעוֹלָם חַסְדּוֹ:

18 וַיַּהֲרֹג מְלָכִים אַדִּירִים
כִּי לְעוֹלָם חַסְדּוֹ:

19 לְסִיחוֹן מֶלֶךְ הָאֱמֹרִי
כִּי לְעוֹלָם חַסְדּוֹ:

20 וּלְעוֹג מֶלֶךְ הַבָּשָׁן
כִּי לְעוֹלָם חַסְדּוֹ:

21 וְנָתַן אַרְצָם לְנַחֲלָה
כִּי לְעוֹלָם חַסְדּוֹ:

22 נַחֲלָה לְיִשְׂרָאֵל עַבְדּוֹ
כִּי לְעוֹלָם חַסְדּוֹ:

23 שֶׁבְּשִׁפְלֵנוּ זָכַר לָנוּ
כִּי לְעוֹלָם חַסְדּוֹ:

24and rescued us from our enemies,
His steadfast love is eternal;

25Who gives food to all flesh,
His steadfast love is eternal.

26Praise the God of heaven,
His steadfast love is eternal.

24 וַיִּפְרְקֵנוּ מִצָּרֵינוּ
כִּי לְעוֹלָם חַסְדּוֹ:

25 נֹתֵן לֶחֶם לְכָל־בָּשָׂר
כִּי לְעוֹלָם חַסְדּוֹ:

26 הוֹדוּ לְאֵל הַשָּׁמָיִם
כִּי לְעוֹלָם חַסְדּוֹ:

137 By the rivers of Babylon,
there we sat,
sat and wept,
as we thought of Zion.

2There on the poplars
we hung up our lyres,

3for our captors asked us there for songs,
our tormentors,*a* for amusement,
"Sing us one of the songs of Zion."

4How can we sing a song of the LORD
on alien soil?

5If I forget you, O Jerusalem,
let my right hand wither;*b*

6let my tongue stick to my palate
if I cease to think of you,
if I do not keep Jerusalem in memory
even at my happiest hour.

7Remember, O LORD, against the Edomites
the day of Jerusalem's fall;
how they cried, "Strip her, strip her
to her very foundations!"

8Fair Babylon, you predator,*c*
a blessing on him who repays you in kind
what you have inflicted on us;

9a blessing on him who seizes your babies
and dashes them against the rocks!

קלז עַל נַהֲרוֹת ׀ בָּבֶל
שָׁם יָשַׁבְנוּ
גַּם־בָּכִינוּ
בְּזָכְרֵנוּ אֶת־צִיּוֹן:

2 עַל־עֲרָבִים בְּתוֹכָהּ
תָּלִינוּ כִּנֹּרוֹתֵינוּ:

3 כִּי שָׁם שְׁאֵלוּנוּ שׁוֹבֵינוּ דִּבְרֵי־שִׁיר
וְתוֹלָלֵינוּ שִׂמְחָה
שִׁירוּ לָנוּ מִשִּׁיר צִיּוֹן:

4 אֵיךְ נָשִׁיר אֶת־שִׁיר־יְהֹוָה
עַל אַדְמַת נֵכָר:

5 אִם־אֶשְׁכָּחֵךְ יְרוּשָׁלָ͏ִם
תִּשְׁכַּח יְמִינִי:

6 תִּדְבַּק־לְשׁוֹנִי ׀ לְחִכִּי
אִם־לֹא אֶזְכְּרֵכִי
אִם־לֹא אַעֲלֶה אֶת־יְרוּשָׁלַ͏ִם
עַל רֹאשׁ שִׂמְחָתִי:

7 זְכֹר יְהֹוָה ׀ לִבְנֵי אֱדוֹם
אֵת יוֹם יְרוּשָׁלָ͏ִם
הָאֹמְרִים עָרוּ ׀ עָרוּ
עַד הַיְסוֹד בָּהּ:

8 בַּת־בָּבֶל הַשְּׁדוּדָה
אַשְׁרֵי שֶׁיְשַׁלֶּם־לָךְ
אֶת־גְּמוּלֵךְ שֶׁגָּמַלְתְּ לָנוּ:

9 אַשְׁרֵי ׀ שֶׁיֹּאחֵז וְנִפֵּץ אֶת־עֹלָלַיִךְ
אֶל־הַסָּלַע:

---

a   *Meaning of Heb. uncertain.*
b   *Others "forget its cunning."*
c   *With Targum; others "who are to be destroyed."*

138 Of David.

קלח | לְדָוִ֨ד ׀

I praise You with all my heart,
   sing a hymn to You before the divine beings;
²I bow toward Your holy temple
   and praise Your name for Your steadfast love
     and faithfulness,
   because You have exalted ᵃ-Your name, Your
     word, above all.-ᵃ
³When I called, You answered me,
   ᵃ-You inspired me with courage.-ᵃ
⁴All the kings of the earth shall praise You,
   O Lᴏʀᴅ,
   for they have heard the words You spoke.
⁵They shall sing of the ways of the Lᴏʀᴅ,
   "Great is the majesty of the Lᴏʀᴅ!"
⁶High though the Lᴏʀᴅ is, He sees the lowly;
   lofty, He perceives from afar.
⁷Though I walk among enemies,
   You preserve me in the face of my foes;
   You extend Your hand;
   with Your right hand You deliver me.
⁸The Lᴏʀᴅ will settle accounts for me.
O Lᴏʀᴅ, Your steadfast love is eternal;
   do not forsake the work of Your hands.

אֽוֹדְךָ֥ בְכָל־לִבִּ֑י
נֶ֖גֶד אֱלֹהִ֣ים אֲזַמְּרֶֽךָּ׃
²אֶשְׁתַּחֲוֶ֨ה אֶל־הֵיכַ֪ל קָדְשְׁךָ֡
וְא֘וֹדֶ֤ה אֶת־שְׁמֶ֗ךָ עַל־חַסְדְּךָ֥ וְעַל־
אֲמִתֶּ֑ךָ
כִּֽי־הִגְדַּ֥לְתָּ עַל־כָּל־שִׁמְךָ֗ אִמְרָתֶֽךָ׃
³בְּי֣וֹם קָ֭רָֽאתִי וַֽתַּעֲנֵ֑נִי
תַּרְהִבֵ֖נִי בְנַפְשִׁ֣י עֹֽז׃
⁴יוֹד֣וּךָ יְ֭הֹוָה כָּל־מַלְכֵי־אָ֑רֶץ
כִּ֥י שָׁ֝מְע֗וּ אִמְרֵי־פִֽיךָ׃
⁵וְ֭יָשִׁירוּ בְּדַרְכֵ֣י יְהֹוָ֑ה
כִּ֥י גָ֝ד֗וֹל כְּב֣וֹד יְהֹוָֽה׃
⁶כִּי־רָ֣ם יְ֭הֹוָה וְשָׁפָ֣ל יִרְאֶ֑ה
וְ֝גָבֹ֗הַּ מִמֶּרְחָ֥ק יְיֵדָֽע׃
⁷אִם־אֵלֵ֤ךְ ׀ בְּקֶ֥רֶב צָרָ֗ה
תְּחַ֫יֵּ֥נִי עַ֤ל אַ֣ף אֹ֭יְבַי
תִּשְׁלַ֣ח יָדֶ֑ךָ
וְת֖וֹשִׁיעֵ֣נִי יְמִינֶֽךָ׃
⁸יְהֹוָה֮ יִגְמֹ֢ר בַּֽעֲ֫דִ֥י
יְ֭הֹוָה חַסְדְּךָ֣ לְעוֹלָ֑ם
מַעֲשֵׂ֖י יָדֶ֣יךָ אַל־תֶּֽרֶף׃

139 For the leader. Of David. A psalm.

קלט לַמְנַצֵּ֗חַ לְדָוִ֥ד מִזְמ֑וֹר

O Lᴏʀᴅ, You have examined me and know me.
²When I sit down or stand up You know it;
   You discern my thoughts from afar.
³ᵃ-You observe-ᵃ my walking and reclining,
   and are familiar with all my ways.
⁴There is not a word on my tongue
   but that You, O Lᴏʀᴅ, know it well.
⁵You hedge me before and behind;
   You lay Your hand upon me.

יְהֹוָ֥ה חֲ֝קַרְתַּ֗נִי וַתֵּדָֽע׃
²אַתָּ֣ה יָ֭דַעְתָּ שִׁבְתִּ֣י וְקוּמִ֑י
בַּ֥נְתָּה לְ֝רֵעִ֗י מֵרָחֽוֹק׃
³אָרְחִ֣י וְרִבְעִ֣י זֵרִ֑יתָ
וְֽכָל־דְּרָכַ֥י הִסְכַּֽנְתָּה׃
⁴כִּ֤י אֵ֣ין מִ֭לָּה בִּלְשׁוֹנִ֑י
הֵ֥ן יְ֝הֹוָ֗ה יָדַ֥עְתָּ כֻלָּֽהּ׃
⁵אָח֣וֹר וָקֶ֣דֶם צַרְתָּ֑נִי
וַתָּ֖שֶׁת עָלַ֣י כַּפֶּֽכָה*׃

ᵃ⁻ᵃ   *Meaning of Heb. uncertain.*
ᵃ⁻ᵃ   *Meaning of Heb. uncertain.*

יתיר ה'   *v. 5.*

⁶It is beyond my knowledge;

it is a mystery; I cannot fathom it.

⁷Where can I escape from Your spirit?

Where can I flee from Your presence?

⁸If I ascend to heaven, You are there;

if I descend to Sheol, You are there too.

⁹If I take wing with the dawn

to come to rest on the western horizon,

¹⁰even there Your hand will be guiding me,

Your right hand will be holding me fast.

¹¹If I say, "Surely darkness ᵇ-will conceal me,

night will provide me with cover,"-ᵇ

¹²darkness is not dark for You;

night is as light as day;

darkness and light are the same.

¹³It was You who created my conscience;ᶜ

You fashioned me in my mother's womb.

¹⁴I praise You,

for I am awesomely, wondrously made;

Your work is wonderful;

I know it very well.

¹⁵My frame was not concealed from You

when I was shaped in a hidden place,

knit together in the recesses of the earth.

¹⁶Your eyes saw my unformed limbs;

they were all recorded in Your book;

in due time they were formed,

ᵃ-to the very last one of them.-ᵃ

¹⁷How weighty Your thoughts seem to me,

O God,

how great their number!

¹⁸I count them—they exceed the grains of sand;

I end—but am still with You.

¹⁹O God, if You would only slay the wicked—

you murderers, away from me!—

²⁰ᵃ-who invoke You for intrigue,

Your enemies who swear by You falsely.-ᵃ

ᵇ⁻ᵇ   Cf. Rashi, Ibn Ezra; meaning of Heb. uncertain.

ᶜ   Lit. "kidneys."

---

⁶ פְּלִיאָה דַעַת מִמֶּנִּי

נִשְׂגְּבָה לֹא־אוּכַל לָהּ׃

⁷ אָנָה אֵלֵךְ מֵרוּחֶךָ

וְאָנָה מִפָּנֶיךָ אֶבְרָח׃

⁸ אִם־אֶסַּק שָׁמַיִם שָׁם אָתָּה

וְאַצִּיעָה שְּׁאוֹל הִנֶּךָּ׃

⁹ אֶשָּׂא כַנְפֵי־שָׁחַר

אֶשְׁכְּנָה בְּאַחֲרִית יָם׃

¹⁰ גַּם־שָׁם יָדְךָ תַנְחֵנִי

וְתֹאחֲזֵנִי יְמִינֶךָ׃

¹¹ וָאֹמַר אַךְ־חֹשֶׁךְ יְשׁוּפֵנִי

וְלַיְלָה אוֹר בַּעֲדֵנִי׃

¹² גַּם־חֹשֶׁךְ לֹא־יַחְשִׁיךְ מִמֶּךָ

וְלַיְלָה כַּיּוֹם יָאִיר

כַּחֲשֵׁיכָה כָּאוֹרָה׃

¹³ כִּי־אַתָּה קָנִיתָ כִלְיֹתָי

תְּסֻכֵּנִי בְּבֶטֶן אִמִּי׃

¹⁴ אוֹדְךָ

עַל כִּי נוֹרָאוֹת נִפְלֵיתִי

נִפְלָאִים מַעֲשֶׂיךָ

וְנַפְשִׁי יֹדַעַת מְאֹד׃

¹⁵ לֹא־נִכְחַד עָצְמִי מִמֶּךָּ

אֲשֶׁר־עֻשֵּׂיתִי בַסֵּתֶר

רֻקַּמְתִּי בְּתַחְתִּיּוֹת אָרֶץ׃

¹⁶ גָּלְמִי ׀ רָאוּ עֵינֶיךָ

וְעַל־סִפְרְךָ כֻּלָּם יִכָּתֵבוּ

יָמִים יֻצָּרוּ

ולא וְלוֹ אֶחָד בָּהֶם׃

¹⁷ וְלִי מַה־יָּקְרוּ רֵעֶיךָ אֵל

מֶה עָצְמוּ רָאשֵׁיהֶם׃

¹⁸ אֶסְפְּרֵם מֵחוֹל יִרְבּוּן

הֱקִיצֹתִי וְעוֹדִי עִמָּךְ׃

¹⁹ אִם־תִּקְטֹל אֱלוֹהַּ ׀ רָשָׁע

וְאַנְשֵׁי דָמִים סוּרוּ מֶנִּי׃

²⁰ אֲשֶׁר יֹאמְרֻךָ לִמְזִמָּה

נָשֻׂא לַשָּׁוְא עָרֶיךָ׃*

---

v. 20. לשון שנאה

²¹O Lᴏʀᴅ, You know I hate those who hate You,
   and loathe Your adversaries.
²²I feel a perfect hatred toward them;
   I count them my enemies.

²³Examine me, O God, and know my mind;
   probe me and know my thoughts.
²⁴See if I have vexatious ways,
   and guide me in ways everlasting.

21 הֲלֽוֹא־מְשַׂנְאֶ֖יךָ יְהֹוָ֥ה ׀ אֶשְׂנָ֑א
וּ֝בִתְקוֹמְמֶ֗יךָ אֶתְקוֹטָֽט׃
22 תַּכְלִ֣ית שִׂנְאָ֣ה שְׂנֵאתִ֑ים
לְ֝אוֹיְבִ֗ים הָ֣יוּ לִֽי׃

23 חׇקְרֵ֣נִי אֵ֭ל וְדַ֣ע לְבָבִ֑י
בְּ֝חָנֵ֗נִי וְדַ֣ע שַׂרְעַפָּֽי׃
24 וּרְאֵ֗ה אִם־דֶּֽרֶךְ־עֹ֥צֶב בִּ֑י
וּ֝נְחֵ֗נִי בְּדֶ֣רֶךְ עוֹלָֽם׃

140 For the leader. A psalm of David.

קמ לַמְנַצֵּ֗חַ מִזְמ֥וֹר לְדָוִֽד׃

²Rescue me, O Lᴏʀᴅ, from evil men;
   save me from the lawless,
³whose minds are full of evil schemes,
   who plot war every day.
⁴They sharpen their tongues like serpents;
   spiders' poison is on their lips.   *Selah.*

⁵O Lᴏʀᴅ, keep me out of the clutches of the
     wicked;
   save me from lawless men
   who scheme to ᵃ-make me fall.-ᵃ
⁶Arrogant men laid traps with ropes for me;
   they spread out a net along the way;
   they set snares for me.   *Selah.*

⁷I said to the Lᴏʀᴅ: You are my God;
   give ear, O Lᴏʀᴅ, to my pleas for mercy.
⁸O Gᴏᴅ, my Lord, the strength of my deliverance,
   You protected my head on the day of battle.ᵇ
⁹O Lᴏʀᴅ, do not grant the desires of the wicked;
   do not let their plan succeed,
   ᶜ-else they be exalted.   *Selah.*

¹⁰May the heads of those who beset me
   be covered with the mischief of their lips.-ᶜ

2 חַלְּצֵ֣נִי יְ֭הֹוָה מֵאָדָ֣ם רָ֑ע
מֵאִ֖ישׁ חֲמָסִ֣ים תִּנְצְרֵֽנִי׃
3 אֲשֶׁ֤ר חָשְׁב֣וּ רָע֣וֹת בְּלֵ֑ב
כׇּל־י֝֗וֹם יָג֥וּרוּ מִלְחָמֽוֹת׃
4 שָׁנְנ֣וּ לְשׁוֹנָם֮ כְּֽמוֹ־נָ֫חָ֥שׁ חֲמַ֥ת
עַכְשׁ֑וּב
תַּ֖חַת שְׂפָתֵ֣ימוֹ סֶֽלָה׃

5 שׇׁמְרֵ֤נִי יְהֹוָ֨ה ׀ מִ֘ידֵ֤י רָשָׁ֗ע
מֵאִ֣ישׁ חֲמָסִ֣ים תִּנְצְרֵ֑נִי
אֲשֶׁ֥ר חָ֝שְׁב֗וּ לִדְח֥וֹת פְּעָמָֽי׃
6 טָֽמְנֽוּ־גֵאִ֨ים ׀ פַּ֡ח לִ֗י וַחֲבָלִ֗ים
פָּ֣רְשׂוּ רֶ֭שֶׁת לְיַד־מַעְגָּ֑ל
מֹקְשִׁ֖ים שָֽׁתוּ־לִ֣י סֶֽלָה׃

7 אָמַ֣רְתִּי לַ֭יהֹוָה אֵ֣לִי אָ֑תָּה
הַאֲזִ֥ינָה יְ֝הֹוָ֗ה ק֣וֹל תַּחֲנוּנָֽי׃
8 יֱהֹוִ֣ה אֲ֭דֹנָי עֹ֣ז יְשׁוּעָתִ֑י
סַכֹּ֥תָה לְ֝רֹאשִׁ֗י בְּי֣וֹם נָֽשֶׁק׃
9 אַל־תִּתֵּ֣ן יְהֹוָה֮ מַאֲוַיֵּ֢י רָ֫שָׁ֥ע
זְמָמ֥וֹ אַל־תָּפֵ֗ק
יָר֥וּמוּ סֶֽלָה׃

10 רֹ֤אשׁ מְסִבָּ֑י
עֲמַ֖ל שְׂפָתֵ֣ימוֹ יְכַסּֽוֹמוֹ (יְכַסֵּֽימוֹ)׃

ᵃ⁻ᵃ Lit. *"push my feet."*
ᵇ   Lit. *"arms."*
ᶜ⁻ᶜ *Meaning of Heb. uncertain.*

¹¹may coals of fire drop down upon them,
   and they be cast into pits, never to rise again.

¹²Let slanderers have no place in the land;
   let the evil of the lawless man drive him into
   corrals.

¹³I know that the LORD will champion
   the cause of the poor, the right of the needy.

¹⁴Righteous men shall surely praise Your name;
   the upright shall dwell in Your presence.

11 יַמִּיטוּ יִמּוֹטוּ עֲלֵיהֶם גֶּחָלִים בָּאֵשׁ
יַפִּלֵם
בְּמַהֲמֹרוֹת בַּל־יָקוּמוּ׃

12 אִישׁ לָשׁוֹן בַּל־יִכּוֹן בָּאָרֶץ אִישׁ־
חָמָס רָע
יְצוּדֶנּוּ לְמַדְחֵפֹת׃

13 יָדַעְתִּ כִּי־יַעֲשֶׂה יְהֹוָה דִּין
עָנִי
מִשְׁפַּט אֶבְיֹנִים׃

14 אַךְ צַדִּיקִים יוֹדוּ לִשְׁמֶךָ
יֵשְׁבוּ יְשָׁרִים אֶת־פָּנֶיךָ׃

141   A psalm of David.

I call You, O LORD, hasten to me;
   give ear to my cry when I call You.

²Take my prayer as an offering of incense,
   my upraised hands as an evening sacrifice.

³O LORD, set a guard over my mouth,
   a watch at the door of my lips;

⁴let my mind not turn to an evil thing,
   to practice deeds of wickedness
   with men who are evildoers;
   let me not feast on their dainties.

^{5a}Let the righteous man strike me in loyalty,
   let him reprove me;
   let my head not refuse such choice oil.
My prayers are still against their^b evil deeds.

⁶May their judges slip on the rock,
   but let my words be heard, for they are sweet.

⁷As when the earth is cleft and broken up
   our bones are scattered at the mouth of Sheol.

⁸My eyes are fixed upon You, O GOD my Lord;
   I seek refuge in You, do not put me in jeopardy.

⁹Keep me from the trap laid for me,
   and from the snares of evildoers.

קמא מִזְמוֹר לְדָוִד

יְהֹוָה קְרָאתִיךָ חוּשָׁה לִּי
הַאֲזִינָה קוֹלִי בְּקָרְאִי־לָךְ׃

2 תִּכּוֹן תְּפִלָּתִי קְטֹרֶת לְפָנֶיךָ
מַשְׂאַת כַּפַּי מִנְחַת־עָרֶב׃

3 שִׁיתָה יְהֹוָה שָׁמְרָה לְפִי
נִצְּרָה עַל־דַּל שְׂפָתָי׃

4 אַל־תַּט־לִבִּי לְדָבָר ׀ רָע
לְהִתְעוֹלֵל עֲלִלוֹת ׀ בְּרֶשַׁע
אֶת־אִישִׁים פֹּעֲלֵי־אָוֶן
וּבַל־אֶלְחַם בְּמַנְעַמֵּיהֶם׃

5 יֶהֶלְמֵנִי־צַדִּיק ׀ חֶסֶד
וְיוֹכִיחֵנִי
שֶׁמֶן רֹאשׁ אַל־יָנִי רֹאשִׁי
כִּי־עוֹד וּתְפִלָּתִי בְּרָעוֹתֵיהֶם׃

6 נִשְׁמְטוּ בִידֵי־סֶלַע שֹׁפְטֵיהֶם
וְשָׁמְעוּ אֲמָרַי כִּי נָעֵמוּ׃

7 כְּמוֹ פֹלֵחַ וּבֹקֵעַ בָּאָרֶץ
נִפְזְרוּ עַצְמֵינוּ לְפִי שְׁאוֹל׃

8 כִּי אֵלֶיךָ ׀ יְהֹוָה אֲדֹנָי עֵינָי
בְּכָה* חָסִיתִי אַל־תְּעַר נַפְשִׁי׃

9 שָׁמְרֵנִי מִידֵי פַח יָקְשׁוּ לִי
וּמֹקְשׁוֹת פֹּעֲלֵי אָוֶן׃

---

a   Meaning of vv. 5–7 uncertain.
b   I.e., the evildoers of v. 4.

יתיר ה'   v. 8.

¹⁰Let the wicked fall into their nets
while I alone come through.

142 A *maskil* of David,
while he was in the cave.^a A prayer.

²I cry aloud to the LORD;
I appeal to the LORD loudly for mercy.
³I pour out my complaint before Him;
I lay my trouble before Him
⁴when my spirit fails within me.
You know my course;
they have laid a trap in the path I walk.
⁵Look at my right and see—
I have no friend;
there is nowhere I can flee,
no one cares about me.
⁶So I cry to You, O LORD;
I say, "You are my refuge,
all I have in the land of the living."
⁷Listen to my cry, for I have been brought very
low;
save me from my pursuers,
for they are too strong for me.
⁸Free me from prison,
that I may praise Your name.
The righteous ^b-shall glory in me-^b
for Your gracious dealings with me.

143 A psalm of David.

O LORD, hear my prayer;
give ear to my plea, as You are faithful;
answer me, as You are beneficent.
²Do not enter into judgment with Your servant,
for before You no creature is in the right.

קמב ¹⁰ יִפְּל֥וּ בְמַכְמֹרָ֖יו רְשָׁעִ֑ים
יַ֥חַד אָ֝נֹכִ֗י עַֽד־אֶעֱבֽוֹר׃

קמב מַשְׂכִּ֥יל לְדָוִ֑ד
בִּהְיוֹת֖וֹ בַמְּעָרָ֣ה תְפִלָּֽה׃

² קוֹלִ֣י אֶל־יְהֹוָ֣ה אֶזְעָ֑ק
קוֹלִ֥י אֶל־יְ֝הֹוָ֗ה אֶתְחַנָּֽן׃
³ אֶשְׁפֹּ֣ךְ לְפָנָ֣יו שִׂיחִ֑י
צָ֝רָתִ֗י לְפָנָ֥יו אַגִּֽיד׃
⁴ בְּהִתְעַטֵּ֬ף עָלַ֨י ׀ רוּחִ֗י
וְאַתָּה֮ יָדַ֢עְתָּ נְֽתִיבָ֫תִ֥י
בְּאֹֽרַח־ז֥וּ אֲהַלֵּ֑ךְ טָמְנ֖וּ פַ֣ח לִֽי׃
⁵ הַבֵּ֤יט יָמִ֨ין ׀ וּרְאֵה֮
וְאֵֽין־לִ֪י מַ֫כִּ֥יר
אָבַ֣ד מָנ֣וֹס מִמֶּ֑נִּי
אֵ֖ין דּוֹרֵ֣שׁ לְנַפְשִֽׁי׃
⁶ זָעַ֥קְתִּי אֵלֶ֗יךָ יְהֹ֫וָ֥ה
אָ֭מַרְתִּי אַתָּ֣ה מַחְסִ֑י
חֶ֝לְקִ֗י בְּאֶ֣רֶץ הַֽחַיִּֽים׃
⁷ הַקְשִׁ֤יבָה ׀ אֶֽל־רִנָּתִי֮ כִּֽי־דַלּ֪וֹתִ֫י
מְאֹ֥ד
הַצִּילֵ֥נִי מֵרֹדְפַ֑י
כִּ֖י אָמְצ֣וּ מִמֶּֽנִּי׃
⁸ ה֘וֹצִ֤יאָה מִמַּסְגֵּ֨ר ׀ נַפְשִׁי֮
לְהוֹד֪וֹת אֶת־שְׁ֫מֶ֥ךָ
בִּ֭י יַכְתִּ֣רוּ צַדִּיקִ֑ים
כִּ֖י תִגְמֹ֣ל עָלָֽי׃

קמג מִזְמ֥וֹר לְדָוִ֑ד
יְהֹוָ֤ה ׀ שְׁמַ֬ע תְּפִלָּתִ֗י
הַאֲזִ֥ינָה אֶל־תַּחֲנוּנַ֑י
בֶּאֱמֻנָתְךָ֥ עֲ֝נֵ֗נִי בְּצִדְקָתֶֽךָ׃
² וְאַל־תָּב֣וֹא בְ֭מִשְׁפָּט אֶת־עַבְדֶּ֑ךָ
כִּ֤י לֹֽא־יִצְדַּ֖ק לְפָנֶ֣יךָ כָל־חָֽי׃

---

^a *Cf. 1 Sam. 24.3–4.*
^{b-b} *Meaning of Heb. uncertain.*

³My foe hounded me;
  he crushed me to the ground;
  he made me dwell in darkness
    like those long dead.
⁴My spirit failed within me;
  my mind was numbed with horror.
⁵Then I thought of the days of old;
  I rehearsed all Your deeds,
  recounted the work of Your hands.
⁶I stretched out my hands to You,
  longing for You like thirsty earth.   *Selah.*

⁷Answer me quickly, O LORD;
  my spirit can endure no more.
Do not hide Your face from me,
  or I shall become like those who descend into
    the Pit.
⁸Let me learn of Your faithfulness by daybreak,
  for in You I trust;
  let me know the road I must take,
  for on You I have set my hope.
⁹Save me from my foes, O LORD;
  ᵃ-to You I look for cover.-ᵃ
¹⁰Teach me to do Your will,
  for You are my God.
Let Your gracious spirit lead me
  on level ground.
¹¹For the sake of Your name, O LORD, preserve
  me;
  as You are beneficent, free me from distress.
¹²As You are faithful, put an end to my foes;
  destroy all my mortal enemies,
  for I am Your servant.

144 Of David.

Blessed is the LORD, my rock,
  who trains my hands for battle,
  my fingers for warfare;

³ כִּי רָדַף אוֹיֵב ׀ נַפְשִׁי
דִּכָּא לָאָרֶץ חַיָּתִי
הוֹשִׁיבַנִי בְמַחֲשַׁכִּים
כְּמֵתֵי עוֹלָם:
⁴ וַתִּתְעַטֵּף עָלַי רוּחִי
בְּתוֹכִי יִשְׁתּוֹמֵם לִבִּי:
⁵ זָכַרְתִּי יָמִים ׀ מִקֶּדֶם
הָגִיתִי בְכָל־פָּעֳלֶךָ
בְּמַעֲשֵׂה יָדֶיךָ אֲשׂוֹחֵחַ:
⁶ פֵּרַשְׂתִּי יָדַי אֵלֶיךָ
נַפְשִׁי ׀ כְּאֶרֶץ־עֲיֵפָה לְךָ   סֶלָה:

⁷ מַהֵר עֲנֵנִי ׀ יְהֹוָה
כָּלְתָה רוּחִי
אַל־תַּסְתֵּר פָּנֶיךָ מִמֶּנִּי
וְנִמְשַׁלְתִּי עִם־יֹרְדֵי בוֹר:
⁸ הַשְׁמִיעֵנִי בַבֹּקֶר ׀ חַסְדֶּךָ
כִּי־בְךָ בָטָחְתִּי
הוֹדִיעֵנִי דֶּרֶךְ־זוּ אֵלֵךְ
כִּי־אֵלֶיךָ נָשָׂאתִי נַפְשִׁי:
⁹ הַצִּילֵנִי מֵאֹיְבַי ׀ יְהֹוָה
אֵלֶיךָ כִסִּתִי:
¹⁰ לַמְּדֵנִי ׀ לַעֲשׂוֹת רְצוֹנֶךָ
כִּי־אַתָּה אֱלוֹהָי
רוּחֲךָ טוֹבָה תַּנְחֵנִי
בְּאֶרֶץ מִישׁוֹר:
¹¹ לְמַעַן־שִׁמְךָ יְהֹוָה תְּחַיֵּנִי
בְּצִדְקָתְךָ ׀ תּוֹצִיא מִצָּרָה נַפְשִׁי:
¹² וּבְחַסְדְּךָ תַּצְמִית אֹיְבָי
וְהַאֲבַדְתָּ כָּל־צֹרְרֵי נַפְשִׁי
כִּי אֲנִי עַבְדֶּךָ:

קמד לְדָוִד ׀

בָּרוּךְ יְהֹוָה ׀ צוּרִי
הַמְלַמֵּד יָדַי לַקְרָב
אֶצְבְּעוֹתַי לַמִּלְחָמָה:

---

a-a   Meaning of Heb. uncertain.

2my faithful one, my fortress,
my haven and my deliverer,
my shield, in whom I take shelter,
who makes peoples*a* subject to me.

3O LORD, what is man that You should care about
him,
mortal man, that You should think of him?
4Man is like a breath;
his days are like a passing shadow.
5O LORD, bend Your sky and come down;
touch the mountains and they will smoke.
6Make lightning flash and scatter them;
shoot Your arrows and rout them.
7Reach Your hand down from on high;
rescue me, save me from the mighty waters,
from the hands of foreigners,
8whose mouths speak lies,
and whose oaths*b* are false.

9O God, I will sing You a new song,
sing a hymn to You with a ten-stringed harp,
10to You who give victory to kings,
who rescue His servant David from the deadly
sword.
11Rescue me, save me from the hands of
foreigners,
whose mouths speak lies,
and whose oaths*b* are false.

12*c*For our sons are like saplings,
well-tended in their youth;
our daughters are like cornerstones
trimmed to give shape to a palace.
13Our storehouses are full,
supplying produce of all kinds;
our flocks number thousands,
even myriads, in our fields;
14our cattle are well cared for.

2 חַסְדִּי וּמְצוּדָתִי
מִשְׂגַּבִּי וּמְפַלְטִי
לִי מָגִנִּי וּבוֹ חָסִיתִי
הָרוֹדֵד עַמִּי* תַחְתָּי:

3 יְהֹוָה מָה־אָדָם וַתֵּדָעֵהוּ
בֶּן־אֱנוֹשׁ וַתְּחַשְּׁבֵהוּ:
4 אָדָם לַהֶבֶל דָּמָה
יָמָיו כְּצֵל עוֹבֵר:
5 יְהֹוָה הַט־שָׁמֶיךָ וְתֵרֵד
גַּע בֶּהָרִים וְיֶעֱשָׁנוּ:
6 בְּרוֹק בָּרָק וּתְפִיצֵם
שְׁלַח חִצֶּיךָ וּתְהֻמֵּם:
7 שְׁלַח יָדֶיךָ מִמָּרוֹם
פְּצֵנִי וְהַצִּילֵנִי מִמַּיִם רַבִּים
מִיַּד בְּנֵי נֵכָר:
8 אֲשֶׁר פִּיהֶם דִּבֶּר־שָׁוְא
וִימִינָם יְמִין שָׁקֶר:

9 אֱלֹהִים שִׁיר חָדָשׁ אָשִׁירָה לָּךְ
בְּנֵבֶל עָשׂוֹר אֲזַמְּרָה־לָּךְ:
10 הַנּוֹתֵן תְּשׁוּעָה לַמְּלָכִים
הַפּוֹצֶה אֶת־דָּוִד עַבְדּוֹ מֵחֶרֶב
רָעָה:
11 פְּצֵנִי וְהַצִּילֵנִי מִיַּד בְּנֵי־נֵכָר
אֲשֶׁר פִּיהֶם דִּבֶּר־שָׁוְא
וִימִינָם יְמִין שָׁקֶר:

12 אֲשֶׁר בָּנֵינוּ ׀ כִּנְטִעִים
מְגֻדָּלִים בִּנְעוּרֵיהֶם
בְּנוֹתֵינוּ כְזָוִיֹּת
מְחֻטָּבוֹת תַּבְנִית הֵיכָל:
13 מְזָוֵינוּ מְלֵאִים
מְפִיקִים מִזַּן אֶל־זַן
צֹאונֵנוּ מַאֲלִיפוֹת
מְרֻבָּבוֹת בְּחוּצוֹתֵינוּ:
14 אַלּוּפֵינוּ מְסֻבָּלִים

---

a So Targum, Saadia; others "my people."
b With Rashi; lit. "right hand."
c The meaning of several phrases in vv. 12–14 is uncertain.

v. 2. סבירין ומטעין "עמים"

There is no breaching and no sortie,
   and no wailing in our streets.

אֵין־פֶּרֶץ וְאֵין יוֹצֵאת
וְאֵין צְוָחָה בִּרְחֹבֹתֵינוּ׃

15Happy the people who have it so;
   happy the people whose God is the Lord.

15 אַשְׁרֵי הָעָם שֶׁכָּכָה לּוֹ
אַשְׁרֵי הָעָם שֶׁיהוה אֱלֹהָיו׃

145 A song of praise. Of David.

קמה תְּהִלָּה לְדָוִד

א I will extol You, my God and king,
   and bless Your name forever and ever.

אֲרוֹמִמְךָ אֱלוֹהַי הַמֶּלֶךְ
וַאֲבָרְכָה שִׁמְךָ לְעוֹלָם וָעֶד׃

ב 2Every day will I bless You
   and praise Your name forever and ever.

2 בְּכָל־יוֹם אֲבָרְכֶךָּ
וַאֲהַלְלָה שִׁמְךָ לְעוֹלָם וָעֶד׃

ג 3Great is the Lord and much acclaimed;
   His greatness cannot be fathomed.

3 גָּדוֹל יהוה וּמְהֻלָּל מְאֹד
וְלִגְדֻלָּתוֹ אֵין חֵקֶר׃

ד 4One generation shall laud Your works to another
   and declare Your mighty acts.

4 דּוֹר לְדוֹר יְשַׁבַּח מַעֲשֶׂיךָ
וּגְבוּרֹתֶיךָ יַגִּידוּ׃

ה 5The glorious majesty of Your splendor
   a-and Your wondrous acts-a will I recite.

5 הֲדַר כְּבוֹד הוֹדֶךָ
וְדִבְרֵי נִפְלְאוֹתֶיךָ אָשִׂיחָה׃

ו 6Men shall talk of the might of Your awesome deeds,
   and I will recount Your greatness.

6 וֶעֱזוּז נוֹרְאֹתֶיךָ יֹאמֵרוּ
וּגְדוּלָּתִיךָ וּגְדוּלָּתְךָ אֲסַפְּרֶנָּה׃

ז 7They shall celebrate Your abundant goodness,
   and sing joyously of Your beneficence.

7 זֵכֶר רַב־טוּבְךָ יַבִּיעוּ
וְצִדְקָתְךָ יְרַנֵּנוּ׃

ח 8The Lord is gracious and compassionate,
   slow to anger and abounding in kindness.

8 חַנּוּן וְרַחוּם יהוה
אֶרֶךְ אַפַּיִם וּגְדָל־חָסֶד׃

ט 9The Lord is good to all,
   and His mercy is upon all His works.

9 טוֹב־יהוה לַכֹּל
וְרַחֲמָיו עַל־כָּל־מַעֲשָׂיו׃

י 10All Your works shall praise You, O Lord,
   and Your faithful ones shall bless You.

10 יוֹדוּךָ יהוה כָּל־מַעֲשֶׂיךָ
וַחֲסִידֶיךָ יְבָרְכוּכָה*׃

כ 11They shall talk of the majesty of Your kingship,
   and speak of Your might,

11 כְּבוֹד מַלְכוּתְךָ יֹאמֵרוּ
וּגְבוּרָתְךָ יְדַבֵּרוּ׃

ל 12to make His mighty acts known among men
   and the majestic glory of His kingship.

12 לְהוֹדִיעַ ׀ לִבְנֵי הָאָדָם גְּבוּרֹתָיו
וּכְבוֹד הֲדַר מַלְכוּתוֹ׃

מ 13Your kingship is an eternal kingship;
   Your dominion is for all generations.

13 מַלְכוּתְךָ מַלְכוּת כָּל־עֹלָמִים
וּמֶמְשַׁלְתְּךָ בְּכָל־דּוֹר וָדוֹר׃

ס 14The Lord supports all who stumble,
   and makes all who are bent stand straight.

14 סוֹמֵךְ יהוה לְכָל־הַנֹּפְלִים
וְזוֹקֵף לְכָל־הַכְּפוּפִים׃

---

a-a *A Qumran Pss. scroll reads: "they will speak of, and Your wonders."*

v. 10. יתיר ה׳

ע 15The eyes of all look to You expectantly,
and You give them their food when it is due.

פ 16You give it openhandedly,
feeding every creature to its heart's content.

צ 17The LORD is beneficent in all His ways
and faithful in all His works.

ק 18The LORD is near to all who call Him,
to all who call Him with sincerity.

ר 19He fulfills the wishes of those who fear Him;
He hears their cry and delivers them.

ש 20The LORD watches over all who love Him,
but all the wicked He will destroy.

ת 21My mouth shall utter the praise of the LORD,
and all creatures*b* shall bless His holy name forever and ever.

146 Hallelujah.

Praise the LORD, O my soul!

2I will praise the LORD all my life,
sing hymns to my God while I exist.

3Put not your trust in the great,
in mortal man who cannot save.

4His breath departs;
he returns to the dust;
on that day his plans come to nothing.

5Happy is he who has the God of Jacob for his
help,
whose hope is in the LORD his God,

6maker of heaven and earth,
the sea and all that is in them;
who keeps faith forever;

7who secures justice for those who are wronged,
gives food to the hungry.
The LORD sets prisoners free;

15 עֵינֵי־כֹל אֵלֶיךָ יְשַׂבֵּרוּ
וְאַתָּה נוֹתֵן־לָהֶם אֶת־אָכְלָם
בְּעִתּוֹ:

16 פּוֹתֵחַ אֶת־יָדֶךָ
וּמַשְׂבִּיעַ לְכָל־חַי רָצוֹן:

17 צַדִּיק יְהֹוָה בְּכָל־דְּרָכָיו
וְחָסִיד בְּכָל־מַעֲשָׂיו:

18 קָרוֹב יְהֹוָה לְכָל־קֹרְאָיו
לְכֹל אֲשֶׁר יִקְרָאֻהוּ בֶאֱמֶת:

19 רְצוֹן־יְרֵאָיו יַעֲשֶׂה
וְאֶת־שַׁוְעָתָם יִשְׁמַע וְיוֹשִׁיעֵם:

20 שׁוֹמֵר יְהֹוָה אֶת־כָּל־אֹהֲבָיו
וְאֵת כָּל־הָרְשָׁעִים יַשְׁמִיד:

21 תְּהִלַּת יְהֹוָה יְדַבֶּר־פִּי
וִיבָרֵךְ כָּל־בָּשָׂר שֵׁם קָדְשׁוֹ לְעוֹלָם
וָעֶד:

קמו הַלְלוּ־יָהּ
הַלְלִי נַפְשִׁי אֶת־יְהֹוָה:

2 אֲהַלְלָה יְהֹוָה בְּחַיָּי
אֲזַמְּרָה לֵאלֹהַי בְּעוֹדִי:

3 אַל־תִּבְטְחוּ בִנְדִיבִים
בְּבֶן־אָדָם | שֶׁאֵין לוֹ תְשׁוּעָה:

4 תֵּצֵא רוּחוֹ
יָשֻׁב לְאַדְמָתוֹ
בַּיּוֹם הַהוּא אָבְדוּ עֶשְׁתֹּנֹתָיו:

5 אַשְׁרֵי שֶׁאֵל יַעֲקֹב בְּעֶזְרוֹ
שִׂבְרוֹ עַל־יְהֹוָה אֱלֹהָיו:

6 עֹשֶׂה | שָׁמַיִם וָאָרֶץ
אֶת־הַיָּם וְאֶת־כָּל־אֲשֶׁר־בָּם
הַשֹּׁמֵר אֱמֶת לְעוֹלָם:

7 עֹשֶׂה מִשְׁפָּט | לָעֲשׁוּקִים
נֹתֵן לֶחֶם לָרְעֵבִים
יְהֹוָה מַתִּיר אֲסוּרִים:

---

b   Lit. *"flesh."*

8The Lord restores sight to the blind;
  the Lord makes those who are bent stand
    straight;
  the Lord loves the righteous;
9The Lord watches over the stranger;
  He gives courage to the orphan and widow,
  but makes the path of the wicked tortuous.

10The Lord shall reign forever,
  your God, O Zion, for all generations.
  Hallelujah.

147 Hallelujah.

It is good to chant hymns to our God;
  it is pleasant to sing glorious praise.

2The Lord rebuilds Jerusalem;
  He gathers in the exiles of Israel.
3He heals their broken hearts,
  and binds up their wounds.
4He reckoned the number of the stars;
  to each He gave its name.
5Great is our Lord and full of power;
  His wisdom is beyond reckoning.
6The Lord gives courage to the lowly,
  and brings the wicked down to the dust.

7Sing to the Lord a song of praise,
  chant a hymn with a lyre to our God,
8who covers the heavens with clouds,
  provides rain for the earth,
  makes mountains put forth grass;
9who gives the beasts their food,
  to the raven's brood what they cry for.
10He does not prize the strength of horses,
  nor value the fleetness[a] of men;

a Lit. "thighs."

---

8 יְהֹוָה ׀ פֹּקֵחַ עִוְרִים
יְהֹוָה זֹקֵף כְּפוּפִים
יְהֹוָה אֹהֵב צַדִּיקִים:
9 יְהֹוָה ׀ שֹׁמֵר אֶת־גֵּרִים
יָתוֹם וְאַלְמָנָה יְעוֹדֵד
וְדֶרֶךְ רְשָׁעִים יְעַוֵּת:

10 יִמְלֹךְ יְהֹוָה ׀ לְעוֹלָם
אֱלֹהַיִךְ צִיּוֹן לְדֹר וָדֹר
הַלְלוּ־יָהּ:

קמז הַלְלוּ יָהּ ׀

כִּי־טוֹב זַמְּרָה אֱלֹהֵינוּ
כִּי־נָעִים נָאוָה תְהִלָּה:

2 בּוֹנֵה יְרוּשָׁלַ͏ִם יְהֹוָה
נִדְחֵי יִשְׂרָאֵל יְכַנֵּס:
3 הָרֹפֵא לִשְׁבוּרֵי לֵב
וּמְחַבֵּשׁ לְעַצְּבוֹתָם:
4 מוֹנֶה מִסְפָּר לַכּוֹכָבִים
לְכֻלָּם שֵׁמוֹת יִקְרָא:
5 גָּדוֹל אֲדוֹנֵינוּ וְרַב־כֹּחַ
לִתְבוּנָתוֹ אֵין מִסְפָּר:
6 מְעוֹדֵד עֲנָוִים יְהֹוָה
מַשְׁפִּיל רְשָׁעִים עֲדֵי־אָרֶץ:

7 עֱנוּ לַיהֹוָה בְּתוֹדָה
זַמְּרוּ לֵאלֹהֵינוּ בְכִנּוֹר:
8 הַמְכַסֶּה שָׁמַיִם ׀ בְּעָבִים
הַמֵּכִין לָאָרֶץ מָטָר
הַמַּצְמִיחַ הָרִים חָצִיר:
9 נוֹתֵן לִבְהֵמָה לַחְמָהּ
לִבְנֵי עֹרֵב אֲשֶׁר יִקְרָאוּ:
10 לֹא בִגְבוּרַת הַסּוּס יֶחְפָּץ
לֹא־בְשׁוֹקֵי הָאִישׁ יִרְצֶה:

¹¹but the LORD values those who fear Him,
those who depend on His faithful care.

¹²O Jerusalem, glorify the LORD;
praise your God, O Zion!
¹³For He made the bars of your gates strong,
and blessed your children within you.
¹⁴He endows your realm with well-being,
and satisfies you with choice wheat.

¹⁵He sends forth His word to the earth;
His command runs swiftly.
¹⁶He lays down snow like fleece,
scatters frost like ashes.
¹⁷He tosses down hail like crumbs—
who can endure His icy cold?
¹⁸He issues a command—it melts them;
He breathes—the waters flow.
¹⁹He issued His commands to Jacob,
His statutes and rules to Israel.
²⁰He did not do so for any other nation;
of such rules they know nothing.
Hallelujah.

148 Hallelujah.

Praise the LORD from the heavens;
praise Him on high.
²Praise Him, all His angels,
praise Him, all His hosts.
³Praise Him, sun and moon,
praise Him, all bright stars.
⁴Praise Him, highest heavens,
and you waters that are above the heavens.
⁵Let them praise the name of the LORD,
for it was He who commanded that they be
created.
⁶He made them endure forever,

11 רוֹצֶה יְהֹוָה אֶת־יְרֵאָיו
אֶת־הַמְיַחֲלִים לְחַסְדּוֹ:

12 שַׁבְּחִי יְרוּשָׁלַ͏ִם אֶת־יְהֹוָה
הַלְלִי אֱלֹהַיִךְ צִיּוֹן:
13 כִּי־חִזַּק בְּרִיחֵי שְׁעָרָיִךְ
בֵּרַךְ בָּנַיִךְ בְּקִרְבֵּךְ:
14 הַשָּׂם־גְּבוּלֵךְ שָׁלוֹם
חֵלֶב חִטִּים יַשְׂבִּיעֵךְ:

15 הַשֹּׁלֵחַ אִמְרָתוֹ אָרֶץ
עַד־מְהֵרָה יָרוּץ דְּבָרוֹ:
16 הַנֹּתֵן שֶׁלֶג כַּצָּמֶר
כְּפוֹר כָּאֵפֶר יְפַזֵּר:
17 מַשְׁלִיךְ קַרְחוֹ כְפִתִּים
לִפְנֵי קָרָתוֹ מִי יַעֲמֹד:
18 יִשְׁלַח דְּבָרוֹ וְיַמְסֵם
יַשֵּׁב רוּחוֹ יִזְּלוּ־מָיִם:
19 מַגִּיד דְּבָרָו לְיַעֲקֹב
חֻקָּיו וּמִשְׁפָּטָיו לְיִשְׂרָאֵל:
20 לֹא עָשָׂה כֵן ׀ לְכָל־גּוֹי
וּמִשְׁפָּטִים בַּל־יְדָעוּם
הַלְלוּ־יָהּ:

קמח הַלְלוּ יָהּ ׀

הַלְלוּ אֶת־יְהֹוָה מִן־הַשָּׁמַיִם
הַלְלוּהוּ בַּמְּרוֹמִים:
2 הַלְלוּהוּ כָל־מַלְאָכָיו
הַלְלוּהוּ כָּל־צְבָאָו:
3 הַלְלוּהוּ שֶׁמֶשׁ וְיָרֵחַ
הַלְלוּהוּ כָּל־כּוֹכְבֵי אוֹר:
4 הַלְלוּהוּ שְׁמֵי הַשָּׁמָיִם
וְהַמַּיִם אֲשֶׁר ׀ מֵעַל הַשָּׁמָיִם:
5 יְהַלְלוּ אֶת־שֵׁם יְהֹוָה
כִּי הוּא צִוָּה וְנִבְרָאוּ:
6 וַיַּעֲמִידֵם לָעַד לְעוֹלָם

establishing an order that shall never change.

7Praise the LORD, O you who are on earth,
all sea monsters and ocean depths,
8fire and hail, snow and smoke,
storm wind that executes His command,
9all mountains and hills,
all fruit trees and cedars,
10all wild and tamed beasts,
creeping things and winged birds,
11all kings and peoples of the earth,
all princes of the earth and its judges,
12youths and maidens alike,
old and young together.
13Let them praise the name of the LORD,
for His name, His alone, is sublime;
His splendor covers heaven and earth.
14He has exalted the horn of His people
for the glory of all His faithful ones,
Israel, the people close to Him.
Hallelujah.

149 Hallelujah.
Sing to the LORD a new song,
His praises in the congregation of the faithful.
2Let Israel rejoice in its maker;
let the children of Zion exult in their king.
3Let them praise His name in dance;
with timbrel and lyre let them chant His praises.
4For the LORD delights in His people;
He adorns the lowly with victory.
5Let the faithful exult in glory;
let them shout for joy upon their couches,
6with paeans to God in their throats
and two-edged swords in their hands,
7to impose retribution upon the nations,
punishment upon the peoples,

חָק־נָתַן וְלֹא יַעֲבוֹר׃
7 הַלְלוּ אֶת־יְהוָה מִן־הָאָרֶץ
תַּנִּינִים וְכָל־תְּהֹמוֹת׃
8 אֵשׁ וּבָרָד שֶׁלֶג וְקִיטוֹר
רוּחַ סְעָרָה עֹשָׂה דְבָרוֹ׃
9 הֶהָרִים וְכָל־גְּבָעוֹת
עֵץ פְּרִי וְכָל־אֲרָזִים׃
10 הַחַיָּה וְכָל־בְּהֵמָה
רֶמֶשׂ וְצִפּוֹר כָּנָף׃
11 מַלְכֵי־אֶרֶץ וְכָל־לְאֻמִּים
שָׂרִים וְכָל־שֹׁפְטֵי אָרֶץ׃
12 בַּחוּרִים וְגַם־בְּתוּלוֹת
זְקֵנִים עִם־נְעָרִים׃
13 יְהַלְלוּ ׀ אֶת־שֵׁם יְהוָה
כִּי־נִשְׂגָּב שְׁמוֹ לְבַדּוֹ
הוֹדוֹ עַל־אֶרֶץ וְשָׁמָיִם׃
14 וַיָּרֶם קֶרֶן ׀ לְעַמּוֹ
תְּהִלָּה לְכָל־חֲסִידָיו
לִבְנֵי יִשְׂרָאֵל עַם־קְרֹבוֹ
הַלְלוּ־יָהּ׃

קמט הַלְלוּ יָהּ ׀
שִׁירוּ לַיהוָה שִׁיר חָדָשׁ
תְּהִלָּתוֹ בִּקְהַל חֲסִידִים׃
2 יִשְׂמַח יִשְׂרָאֵל בְּעֹשָׂיו
בְּנֵי־צִיּוֹן יָגִילוּ בְמַלְכָּם׃
3 יְהַלְלוּ שְׁמוֹ בְמָחוֹל
בְּתֹף וְכִנּוֹר יְזַמְּרוּ־לוֹ׃
4 כִּי־רוֹצֶה יְהוָה בְּעַמּוֹ
יְפָאֵר עֲנָוִים בִּישׁוּעָה׃
5 יַעְלְזוּ חֲסִידִים בְּכָבוֹד
יְרַנְּנוּ עַל־מִשְׁכְּבוֹתָם׃
6 רוֹמְמוֹת אֵל בִּגְרוֹנָם
וְחֶרֶב פִּיפִיּוֹת בְּיָדָם׃
7 לַעֲשׂוֹת נְקָמָה בַּגּוֹיִם
תּוֹכֵחֹת בַּל־אֻמִּים׃*

v. 7. בנוסח אחר "בלאמים"

⁸binding their kings with shackles,
   their nobles with chains of iron,
   ⁹executing the doom decreed against them.
This is the glory of all His faithful.
   Hallelujah.

⁸ לֶאְסֹר מַלְכֵיהֶם בְּזִקִּים
וְנִכְבְּדֵיהֶם בְּכַבְלֵי בַרְזֶל׃
⁹ לַעֲשׂוֹת בָּהֶם ׀ מִשְׁפָּט כָּתוּב
הָדָר הוּא לְכָל־חֲסִידָיו
הַלְלוּ־יָהּ׃

150 Hallelujah.

Praise God in His sanctuary;
   praise Him in the sky, His stronghold.
²Praise Him for His mighty acts;
   praise Him forᵃ His exceeding greatness.
³Praise Him with blasts of the horn;
   praise Him with harp and lyre.
⁴Praise Him with timbrel and dance;
   praise Him with lute and pipe.
⁵Praise Him with resounding cymbals;
   praise Him with loud-clashing cymbals.
⁶Let all that breathes praise the Lord.
   Hallelujah.

קנ הַלְלוּ יָהּ ׀
הַלְלוּ־אֵל בְּקָדְשׁוֹ
הַלְלוּהוּ בִּרְקִיעַ עֻזּוֹ׃
² הַלְלוּהוּ בִגְבוּרֹתָיו
הַלְלוּהוּ כְּרֹב גֻּדְלוֹ׃
³ הַלְלוּהוּ בְּתֵקַע שׁוֹפָר
הַלְלוּהוּ בְּנֵבֶל וְכִנּוֹר׃
⁴ הַלְלוּהוּ בְתֹף וּמָחוֹל
הַלְלוּהוּ בְּמִנִּים וְעוּגָב׃
⁵ הַלְלוּהוּ בְצִלְצְלֵי־שָׁמַע
הַלְלוּהוּ בְּצִלְצְלֵי תְרוּעָה׃
⁶ כֹּל הַנְּשָׁמָה תְּהַלֵּל יָהּ
הַלְלוּ־יָהּ׃*

תם ונשלם תהילה לאל בורא עולם

ᵃ   Or "as befits."

PROVERBS

1 The proverbs of Solomon son of David, king of Israel:

²For learning wisdom and discipline;
For understanding words of discernment;
³For acquiring the discipline for success,
Righteousness, justice, and equity;
⁴For endowing the simple with shrewdness,
The young with knowledge and foresight.
⁵—The wise man, hearing them, will gain more
wisdom;
The discerning man will learn to be adroit;
⁶For understanding proverb and epigram,
The words of the wise and their riddles.

⁷The fear of the Lᴏʀᴅ is the beginning[a] of knowledge;
Fools despise wisdom and discipline.

⁸My son, heed the discipline of your father,
And do not forsake the instruction of your
mother;
⁹For they are a graceful wreath upon your head,
A necklace about your throat.

¹⁰My son, if sinners entice you, do not yield;
¹¹If they say, "Come with us,
Let us set an ambush to shed blood,
Let us lie in wait for the innocent
(Without cause!)
¹²Like Sheol, let us swallow them alive;
Whole, like those who go down into the Pit.

מִשְׁלֵי

א *מִשְׁלֵי שְׁלֹמֹה בֶן־דָּוִד מֶלֶךְ
יִשְׂרָאֵל:
² לָדַעַת חָכְמָה וּמוּסָר
לְהָבִין אִמְרֵי בִינָה:
³ לָקַחַת מוּסַר הַשְׂכֵּל
צֶדֶק וּמִשְׁפָּט וּמֵישָׁרִים:
⁴ לָתֵת לִפְתָאיִם* עָרְמָה
לְנַעַר דַּעַת וּמְזִמָּה:
⁵ יִשְׁמַע חָכָם וְיוֹסֶף לֶקַח
וְנָבוֹן תַּחְבֻּלוֹת יִקְנֶה:
⁶ לְהָבִין מָשָׁל וּמְלִיצָה
דִּבְרֵי חֲכָמִים וְחִידֹתָם:

⁷ יִרְאַת יְהוָה רֵאשִׁית דָּעַת
חָכְמָה וּמוּסָר אֱוִילִים בָּזוּ: פ

⁸ שְׁמַע בְּנִי מוּסַר אָבִיךָ
וְאַל־תִּטֹּשׁ תּוֹרַת אִמֶּךָ:
⁹ כִּי | לִוְיַת חֵן הֵם לְרֹאשֶׁךָ
וַעֲנָקִים לְגַרְגְּרֹתֶיךָ:

¹⁰ בְּנִי אִם־יְפַתּוּךָ חַטָּאִים אַל־
תֹּבֵא:
¹¹ אִם־יֹאמְרוּ לְכָה אִתָּנוּ
נֶאֶרְבָה לְדָם
נִצְפְּנָה לְנָקִי
חִנָּם:
¹² נִבְלָעֵם כִּשְׁאוֹל חַיִּים
וּתְמִימִים כְּיוֹרְדֵי בוֹר:

---

a   Or "best part."

v. 1. בכתב היד שלנו, כל הספר בצורת שירה
v. 4. יתיר א'

¹³We shall obtain every precious treasure;
We shall fill our homes with loot.
¹⁴Throw in your lot with us;
We shall all have a common purse."
¹⁵My son, do not set out with them;
Keep your feet from their path.
¹⁶For their feet run to evil;
They hurry to shed blood.
¹⁷In the eyes of every winged creature
The outspread net means nothing.
¹⁸But they lie in ambush for their own blood;
They lie in wait for their own lives.
¹⁹Such is the fate of all who pursue unjust gain;
It takes the life of its possessor.

²⁰Wisdom^b cries aloud in the streets,
Raises her voice in the squares.
²¹At the head of the busy streets she calls;
At the entrance of the gates, in the city, she speaks
    out:
²²"How long will you simple ones love simplicity,
You scoffers be eager to scoff,
You dullards hate knowledge?
²³You are indifferent to my rebuke;
I will now speak my mind to you,
And let you know my thoughts.
²⁴Since you refused me when I called,
And paid no heed when I extended my hand,
²⁵You spurned all my advice,
And would not hear my rebuke,
²⁶I will laugh at your calamity,
And mock when terror comes upon you,
²⁷When terror comes like a disaster,
And calamity arrives like a whirlwind,
When trouble and distress come upon you.
²⁸Then they shall call me but I will not answer;
They shall seek me but not find me.

b   *In Proverbs, wisdom is personified as a woman.*

13 כָּל־הוֹן יָקָר נִמְצָא
נְמַלֵּא בָתֵּינוּ שָׁלָל:
14 גּוֹרָלְךָ תַּפִּיל בְּתוֹכֵנוּ
כִּיס אֶחָד יִהְיֶה לְכֻלָּנוּ:
15 בְּנִי אַל־תֵּלֵךְ בְּדֶרֶךְ אִתָּם
מְנַע רַגְלְךָ מִנְּתִיבָתָם:
16 כִּי רַגְלֵיהֶם לָרַע יָרוּצוּ
וִימַהֲרוּ לִשְׁפָּךְ־דָּם:
17 כִּי־חִנָּם מְזֹרָה הָרָשֶׁת
בְּעֵינֵי כָל־בַּעַל כָּנָף:
18 וְהֵם לְדָמָם יֶאֱרֹבוּ*
יִצְפְּנוּ לְנַפְשֹׁתָם:
19 כֵּן אָרְחוֹת כָּל־בֹּצֵעַ בָּצַע
אֶת־נֶפֶשׁ בְּעָלָיו יִקָּח: פ

20 חָכְמוֹת בַּחוּץ תָּרֹנָּה
בָּרְחֹבוֹת תִּתֵּן קוֹלָהּ:
21 בְּרֹאשׁ הֹמִיּוֹת תִּקְרָא
בְּפִתְחֵי שְׁעָרִים בָּעִיר אֲמָרֶיהָ
תֹאמֵר:
22 עַד־מָתַי ׀ פְּתָיִם תְּאֵהֲבוּ פֶתִי
וְלֵצִים לָצוֹן חָמְדוּ לָהֶם
וּכְסִילִים יִשְׂנְאוּ־דָעַת:
23 תָּשׁוּבוּ לְתוֹכַחְתִּי
הִנֵּה אַבִּיעָה לָכֶם רוּחִי
אוֹדִיעָה דְבָרַי אֶתְכֶם:
24 יַעַן קָרָאתִי וַתְּמָאֵנוּ
נָטִיתִי* יָדִי וְאֵין מַקְשִׁיב:
25 וַתִּפְרְעוּ כָל־עֲצָתִי
וְתוֹכַחְתִּי לֹא אֲבִיתֶם:
26 גַּם־אֲנִי בְּאֵידְכֶם אֶשְׂחָק
אֶלְעַג בְּבֹא פַחְדְּכֶם:
27 בְּבֹא כשׁאוה כְשׁוֹאָה ׀ פַּחְדְּכֶם
וְאֵידְכֶם כְּסוּפָה יֶאֱתֶה
בְּבֹא עֲלֵיכֶם צָרָה וְצוּקָה:
28 אָז יִקְרָאֻנְנִי וְלֹא אֶעֱנֶה
יְשַׁחֲרֻנְנִי וְלֹא יִמְצָאֻנְנִי:

29Because they hated knowledge,
And did not choose fear of the Lord;
30They refused my advice,
And disdained all my rebukes,
31They shall eat the fruit of their ways,
And have their fill of their own counsels.
32The tranquillity of the simple will kill them,
And the complacency of dullards will destroy
   them.
33But he who listens to me will dwell in safety,
Untroubled by the terror of misfortune."

29 תַּחַת כִּי־שָׂנְאוּ דָעַת
וְיִרְאַת יְהֹוָה לֹא בָחָרוּ:
30 לֹא־אָבוּ לַעֲצָתִי
נָאֲצוּ כָּל־תּוֹכַחְתִּי:
31 וְיֹאכְלוּ מִפְּרִי דַרְכָּם
וּמִמֹּעֲצֹתֵיהֶם יִשְׂבָּעוּ:
32 כִּי מְשׁוּבַת פְּתָיִם תַּהַרְגֵם
וְשַׁלְוַת כְּסִילִים תְּאַבְּדֵם:
33 וְשֹׁמֵעַ לִי יִשְׁכָּן־בֶּטַח
וְשַׁאֲנַן מִפַּחַד רָעָה: פ

2 My son, if you accept my words
And treasure up my commandments;
2If you make your ear attentive to wisdom
And your mind open to discernment;
3If you call to understanding
And cry aloud to discernment,
4If you seek it as you do silver
And search for it as for treasures,
5Then you will understand the fear of the Lord
And attain knowledge of God.
6For the Lord grants wisdom;
Knowledge and discernment are by His decree.
7He reserves ability for the upright
And is a shield for those who live blamelessly,
8Guarding the paths of justice,
Protecting the way of those loyal to Him.
9You will then understand what is right, just,
And equitable—every good course.
10For wisdom will enter your mind
And knowledge will delight you.
11Foresight will protect you,
And discernment will guard you.
12It will save you from the way of evil men,
From men who speak duplicity,
13Who leave the paths of rectitude

ב בְּנִי אִם־תִּקַּח אֲמָרָי
וּמִצְוֹתַי תִּצְפֹּן אִתָּךְ:
2 לְהַקְשִׁיב לַחָכְמָה אָזְנֶךָ
תַּטֶּה לִבְּךָ לַתְּבוּנָה:
3 כִּי אִם לַבִּינָה תִקְרָא
לַתְּבוּנָה תִּתֵּן קוֹלֶךָ:
4 אִם־תְּבַקְשֶׁנָּה כַכָּסֶף
וְכַמַּטְמוֹנִים תַּחְפְּשֶׂנָּה:
5 אָז תָּבִין יִרְאַת יְהֹוָה
וְדַעַת אֱלֹהִים תִּמְצָא:
6 כִּי־יְהֹוָה יִתֵּן חָכְמָה
מִפִּיו דַּעַת וּתְבוּנָה:
7 וְצָפַן יִצְפֹּן לַיְשָׁרִים תּוּשִׁיָּה
מָגֵן לְהֹלְכֵי תֹם:
8 לִנְצֹר אָרְחוֹת מִשְׁפָּט
וְדֶרֶךְ חֲסִידָו יִשְׁמֹר:
9 אָז תָּבִין צֶדֶק וּמִשְׁפָּט
וּמֵישָׁרִים כָּל־מַעְגַּל־טוֹב:
10 כִּי־תָבוֹא חָכְמָה בְלִבֶּךָ
וְדַעַת לְנַפְשְׁךָ יִנְעָם:
11 מְזִמָּה תִּשְׁמֹר עָלֶיךָ
תְּבוּנָה תִנְצְרֶכָּה*:
12 לְהַצִּילְךָ מִדֶּרֶךְ רָע
מֵאִישׁ מְדַבֵּר תַּהְפֻּכוֹת:
13 הַעֹזְבִים אָרְחוֹת יֹשֶׁר

v. 11. יתיר ה׳

To follow the ways of darkness,
14Who rejoice in doing evil
And exult in the duplicity of evil men,
15Men whose paths are crooked
And who are devious in their course.
16It will save you from the forbidden^a woman,
From the alien woman whose talk is smooth,
17Who forsakes the companion of her youth
And disregards the covenant of her God.
18Her house sinks down to Death,
And her course leads to the shades.
19All who go to her cannot return
And find again the paths of life.

20So follow the way of the good
And keep to the paths of the just.
21For the upright will inhabit the earth,
The blameless will remain in it.
22While the wicked will vanish from the land
And the treacherous will be rooted out of it.

לָלֶכֶת בְּדַרְכֵי־חֹשֶׁךְ:
14 הַשְּׂמֵחִים לַעֲשׂוֹת רָע
יָגִילוּ בְּתַהְפֻּכוֹת רָע:
15 אֲשֶׁר אָרְחֹתֵיהֶם עִקְּשִׁים
וּנְלוֹזִים בְּמַעְגְּלוֹתָם:
16 לְהַצִּילְךָ מֵאִשָּׁה זָרָה
מִנָּכְרִיָּה אֲמָרֶיהָ הֶחֱלִיקָה:
17 הַעֹזֶבֶת אַלּוּף נְעוּרֶיהָ
וְאֶת־בְּרִית אֱלֹהֶיהָ שָׁכֵחָה:
18 כִּי שָׁחָה אֶל־מָוֶת בֵּיתָהּ
וְאֶל־רְפָאִים מַעְגְּלֹתֶיהָ:
19 כָּל־בָּאֶיהָ לֹא יְשׁוּבוּן
וְלֹא־יַשִּׂיגוּ אָרְחוֹת חַיִּים:

20 לְמַעַן תֵּלֵךְ בְּדֶרֶךְ טוֹבִים
וְאָרְחוֹת צַדִּיקִים תִּשְׁמֹר:
21 כִּי־יְשָׁרִים יִשְׁכְּנוּ־אָרֶץ
וּתְמִימִים יִוָּתְרוּ בָהּ:
22 וּרְשָׁעִים מֵאֶרֶץ יִכָּרֵתוּ
וּבוֹגְדִים יִסְּחוּ מִמֶּנָּה: פ

3 My son, do not forget my teaching,
But let your mind retain my commandments;
2For they will bestow on you length of days,
Years of life and well-being.
3Let fidelity and steadfastness not leave you;
Bind them about your throat,
Write them on the tablet of your mind,
4And you will find favor and approbation
In the eyes of God and man.
5Trust in the LORD with all your heart,
And do not rely on your own understanding.
6In all your ways acknowledge Him,
And He will make your paths smooth.
7Do not be wise in your own eyes;
Fear the LORD and shun evil.

ג בְּנִי תּוֹרָתִי אַל־תִּשְׁכָּח
וּמִצְוֹתַי יִצֹּר לִבֶּךָ:
2 כִּי אֹרֶךְ יָמִים וּשְׁנוֹת חַיִּים
וְשָׁלוֹם יוֹסִיפוּ לָךְ:
3 חֶסֶד וֶאֱמֶת אַל־יַעַזְבֻךָ
קָשְׁרֵם עַל־גַּרְגְּרוֹתֶיךָ
כָּתְבֵם עַל־לוּחַ לִבֶּךָ:
4 וּמְצָא־חֵן וְשֵׂכֶל־טוֹב
בְּעֵינֵי אֱלֹהִים וְאָדָם: פ
5 בְּטַח אֶל־יְהוָה בְּכָל־לִבֶּךָ
וְאֶל־בִּינָתְךָ אַל־תִּשָּׁעֵן:
6 בְּכָל־דְּרָכֶיךָ דָעֵהוּ
וְהוּא יְיַשֵּׁר אֹרְחֹתֶיךָ:
7 אַל־תְּהִי חָכָם בְּעֵינֶיךָ
יְרָא אֶת־יְהוָה וְסוּר מֵרָע:

a Lit. "strange."

⁸It will be a cure for your body,^a
A tonic for your bones.
⁹Honor the LORD with your wealth,
With the best of all your income,
¹⁰And your barns will be filled with grain,
Your vats will burst with new wine.
¹¹Do not reject the discipline of the LORD,
  my son;
Do not abhor His rebuke.
¹²For whom the LORD loves, He rebukes,
As a father the son whom he favors.

¹³Happy is the man who finds wisdom,
The man who attains understanding.
¹⁴Her value in trade is better than silver,
Her yield, greater than gold.
¹⁵She is more precious than rubies;
All of your goods cannot equal her.
¹⁶In her right hand is length of days,
In her left, riches and honor.
¹⁷Her ways are pleasant ways,
And all her paths, peaceful.
¹⁸She is a tree of life to those who grasp her,
And whoever holds on to her is happy.

¹⁹The LORD founded the earth by wisdom;
He established the heavens by understanding;
²⁰By His knowledge the depths burst apart,
And the skies distilled dew.
²¹My son, do not lose sight of them;
Hold on to resourcefulness and foresight.
²²They will give life to your spirit
And grace to your throat.
²³Then you will go your way safely
And not injure your feet.
²⁴When you lie down you will be unafraid;
You will lie down and your sleep will be sweet.

---

a   Lit. "navel."

רְפָאוּת תְּהִי לְשָׁרֶּךָ* ⁸
וְשִׁקּוּי לְעַצְמוֹתֶיךָ:
כַּבֵּד אֶת־יְהֹוָה מֵהוֹנֶךָ ⁹
וּמֵרֵאשִׁית כָּל־תְּבוּאָתֶךָ:
וְיִמָּלְאוּ אֲסָמֶיךָ שָׂבָע ¹⁰
וְתִירוֹשׁ יְקָבֶיךָ יִפְרֹצוּ: פ
מוּסַר יְהֹוָה בְּנִי אַל־תִּמְאָס ¹¹
וְאַל־תָּקֹץ בְּתוֹכַחְתּוֹ:
כִּי אֶת* אֲשֶׁר יֶאֱהַב יְהֹוָה יוֹכִיחַ ¹²
וּכְאָב אֶת־בֵּן יִרְצֶה:

אַשְׁרֵי אָדָם מָצָא חָכְמָה ¹³
וְאָדָם יָפִיק תְּבוּנָה:
כִּי טוֹב סַחְרָהּ מִסְּחַר־כָּסֶף ¹⁴
וּמֵחָרוּץ תְּבוּאָתָהּ:
יְקָרָה הִיא מִפְּנִיִּים ¹⁵
וְכָל־חֲפָצֶיךָ לֹא יִשְׁווּ־בָהּ:
אֹרֶךְ יָמִים בִּימִינָהּ ¹⁶
בִּשְׂמֹאולָהּ* עֹשֶׁר וְכָבוֹד:
דְּרָכֶיהָ דַרְכֵי־נֹעַם ¹⁷
וְכָל־נְתִיבוֹתֶיהָ שָׁלוֹם:
עֵץ־חַיִּים הִיא לַמַּחֲזִיקִים בָּהּ ¹⁸
וְתֹמְכֶיהָ מְאֻשָּׁר: פ

יְהֹוָה בְּחָכְמָה יָסַד־אָרֶץ ¹⁹
כּוֹנֵן שָׁמַיִם בִּתְבוּנָה:
בְּדַעְתּוֹ תְּהוֹמוֹת נִבְקָעוּ ²⁰
וּשְׁחָקִים יִרְעֲפוּ־טָל:
בְּנִי אַל־יָלֻזוּ מֵעֵינֶיךָ ²¹
נְצֹר תֻּשִׁיָּה וּמְזִמָּה:
וְיִהְיוּ חַיִּים לְנַפְשֶׁךָ ²²
וְחֵן לְגַרְגְּרֹתֶיךָ:
אָז תֵּלֵךְ לָבֶטַח דַּרְכֶּךָ ²³
וְרַגְלְךָ לֹא תִגּוֹף:
אִם־תִּשְׁכַּב לֹא־תִפְחָד ²⁴
וְשָׁכַבְתָּ וְעָרְבָה שְׁנָתֶךָ:

ר' דגושה   v. 8.
סגול בלי מקף   v. 12.
מלא ו'   v. 16.

1603

25You will not fear sudden terror
Or the disaster that comes upon the wicked,
26For the LORD will be your trust;
He will keep your feet from being caught.

27Do not withhold good from one who
　deserves it
When you have the power to do it [for him].
28Do not say to your fellow, "Come back again;
I'll give it to you tomorrow," when you have it
　with you.
29Do not devise harm against your fellow
Who lives trustfully with you.
30Do not quarrel with a man for no cause,
When he has done you no harm.
31Do not envy a lawless man,
Or choose any of his ways;
32For the devious man is an abomination to the
　LORD,
But He is intimate with the straightforward.
33The curse of the LORD is on the house of the
　wicked,
But He blesses the abode of the righteous.
34At scoffers He scoffs,
But to the lowly He shows grace.
35The wise shall obtain honor,
But dullards get disgrace as their portion.

4 Sons, heed the discipline of a father;
Listen and learn discernment,
2For I give you good instruction;
Do not forsake my teaching.

3Once I was a son to my father,
The tender darling of my mother.
4He instructed me and said to me,
"Let your mind hold on to my words;
Keep my commandments and you will live.

25 אַל־תִּירָא מִפַּחַד פִּתְאֹם
וּמִשֹּׁאַת רְשָׁעִים כִּי תָבֹא:
26 כִּי־יְהֹוָה יִהְיֶה בְכִסְלֶךָ
וְשָׁמַר רַגְלְךָ מִלָּכֶד:
27 אַל־תִּמְנַע־טוֹב מִבְּעָלָיו
בִּהְיוֹת לְאֵל יָדְךָ לַעֲשׂוֹת:
28 אַל־תֹּאמַר לְרֵעֲךָ לֵךְ וָשׁוּב
וּמָחָר אֶתֵּן וְיֵשׁ אִתָּךְ:
29 אַל־תַּחֲרֹשׁ עַל־רֵעֲךָ רָעָה
וְהוּא־יוֹשֵׁב לָבֶטַח אִתָּךְ:
30 אַל־תָּרוֹב עִם־אָדָם חִנָּם
אִם־לֹא גְמָלְךָ רָעָה:
31 אַל־תְּקַנֵּא בְּאִישׁ חָמָס
וְאַל־תִּבְחַר בְּכָל־דְּרָכָיו:
32 כִּי תוֹעֲבַת יְהֹוָה נָלוֹז
וְאֶת־יְשָׁרִים סוֹדוֹ:
33 מְאֵרַת יְהֹוָה בְּבֵית רָשָׁע
וּנְוֵה צַדִּיקִים יְבָרֵךְ:
34 אִם־לַלֵּצִים הוּא־יָלִיץ
ולַעֲנִיִּים וְלַעֲנָוִים יִתֶּן־חֵן:
35 כָּבוֹד חֲכָמִים יִנְחָלוּ
וּכְסִילִים מֵרִים קָלוֹן: פ

ד שִׁמְעוּ בָנִים מוּסַר אָב
וְהַקְשִׁיבוּ לָדַעַת בִּינָה:
2 כִּי לֶקַח טוֹב נָתַתִּי לָכֶם
תּוֹרָתִי אַל־תַּעֲזֹבוּ:
3 כִּי־בֵן הָיִיתִי לְאָבִי
רַךְ וְיָחִיד לִפְנֵי* אִמִּי:
4 וַיֹּרֵנִי וַיֹּאמֶר לִי
יִתְמָךְ־דְּבָרַי לִבֶּךָ
שְׁמֹר מִצְוֺתַי וֶחְיֵה:

v. 3. סבירין ומטעין "לבני"

1604

⁵Acquire wisdom, acquire discernment;
Do not forget and do not swerve from my words.
⁶Do not forsake her and she will guard you;
Love her and she will protect you.
⁷The beginning^a of wisdom is—acquire wisdom;
With all your acquisitions, acquire discernment.
⁸Hug her to you and she will exalt you;
She will bring you honor if you embrace her.
⁹She will adorn your head with a graceful wreath;
Crown you with a glorious diadem."

¹⁰My son, heed and take in my words,
And you will have many years of life.
¹¹I instruct you in the way of wisdom;
I guide you in straight courses.
¹²You will walk without breaking stride;
When you run, you will not stumble.
¹³Hold fast to discipline; do not let go;
Keep it; it is your life.
¹⁴Do not enter on the path of the wicked;
Do not walk on the way of evil men.
¹⁵Avoid it; do not pass through it;
Turn away from it; pass it by.
¹⁶For they cannot sleep unless they have done evil;
Unless they make someone fall they are robbed
   of sleep.
¹⁷They eat the bread of wickedness
And drink the wine of lawlessness.
¹⁸The path of the righteous is like radiant sunlight,
Ever brightening until noon.
¹⁹The way of the wicked is all darkness;
They do not know what will make them stumble.

²⁰My son, listen to my speech;
Incline your ear to my words.
²¹Do not lose sight of them;
Keep them in your mind.

---

a   Or "best part."

5 קְנֵה חָכְמָה קְנֵה בִינָה
אַל־תִּשְׁכַּח וְאַל־תֵּט מֵאִמְרֵי־פִי:
6 אַל־תַּעַזְבֶהָ וְתִשְׁמְרֶךָּ
אֱהָבֶהָ וְתִצְּרֶךָּ:
7 רֵאשִׁית חָכְמָה קְנֵה חָכְמָה
וּבְכָל־קִנְיָנְךָ קְנֵה בִינָה:
8 סַלְסְלֶהָ וּתְרוֹמְמֶךָּ
תְּכַבֵּדְךָ כִּי תְחַבְּקֶנָּה:
9 תִּתֵּן לְרֹאשְׁךָ לִוְיַת־חֵן
עֲטֶרֶת תִּפְאֶרֶת תְּמַגְּנֶךָּ:

10 שְׁמַע בְּנִי וְקַח אֲמָרָי
וְיִרְבּוּ לְךָ שְׁנוֹת חַיִּים:
11 בְּדֶרֶךְ חָכְמָה הֹרֵתִיךָ
הִדְרַכְתִּיךָ בְּמַעְגְּלֵי־יֹשֶׁר:
12 בְּלֶכְתְּךָ לֹא־יֵצַר צַעֲדֶךָ
וְאִם־תָּרוּץ לֹא תִכָּשֵׁל:
13 הַחֲזֵק בַּמּוּסָר אַל־תֶּרֶף
נִצְּרֶהָ כִּי־הִיא חַיֶּיךָ:
14 בְּאֹרַח רְשָׁעִים אַל־תָּבֹא
וְאַל־תְּאַשֵּׁר בְּדֶרֶךְ רָעִים:
15 פְּרָעֵהוּ אַל־תַּעֲבָר־בּוֹ
שְׂטֵה מֵעָלָיו וַעֲבוֹר:
16 כִּי לֹא יִשְׁנוּ אִם־לֹא יָרֵעוּ
וְנִגְזְלָה שְׁנָתָם אִם־לֹא יכשולו
יַכְשִׁילוּ:
17 כִּי לָחֲמוּ לֶחֶם רֶשַׁע
וְיֵין חֲמָסִים יִשְׁתּוּ:
18 וְאֹרַח צַדִּיקִים כְּאוֹר נֹגַהּ
הוֹלֵךְ וָאוֹר עַד־נְכוֹן הַיּוֹם:
19 דֶּרֶךְ רְשָׁעִים כָּאֲפֵלָה
לֹא יָדְעוּ בַּמֶּה יִכָּשֵׁלוּ: פ

20 בְּנִי לִדְבָרַי הַקְשִׁיבָה
לַאֲמָרַי הַט־אָזְנֶךָ:
21 אַל־יַלִּיזוּ מֵעֵינֶיךָ
שָׁמְרֵם בְּתוֹךְ לְבָבֶךָ:

22They are life to him who finds them,
Healing for his whole body.
23More than all that you guard, guard your mind,
For it is the source of life.
24Put crooked speech away from you;
Keep devious talk far from you.
25Let your eyes look forward,
Your gaze be straight ahead.
26Survey the course you take,
And all your ways will prosper.
27Do not swerve to the right or the left;
Keep your feet from evil.

5 My son, listen to my wisdom;
Incline your ear to my insight,
2That you may have foresight,
While your lips hold fast to knowledge.
3For the lips of a forbidden[a] woman drip honey;
Her mouth is smoother than oil;
4But in the end she is as bitter as wormwood,
Sharp as a two-edged sword.
5Her feet go down to Death;
Her steps take hold of Sheol.
6She does not chart a path of life;
Her course meanders for lack of knowledge.
7So now, sons, pay heed to me,
And do not swerve from the words of my mouth.
8Keep yourself far away from her;
Do not come near the doorway of her house
9Lest you give up your vigor to others,
Your years to a ruthless one;
10Lest strangers eat their fill of your strength,
And your toil be for the house of another;
11And in the end you roar,
When your flesh and body are consumed,
12And say,
"O how I hated discipline,

22 כִּי־חַיִּים הֵם לְמֹצְאֵיהֶם
וּלְכָל־בְּשָׂרוֹ מַרְפֵּא׃
23 מִכָּל־מִשְׁמָר נְצֹר לִבֶּךָ
כִּי־מִמֶּנּוּ תּוֹצְאוֹת חַיִּים׃
24 הָסֵר מִמְּךָ עִקְּשׁוּת פֶּה
וּלְזוּת שְׂפָתַיִם הַרְחֵק מִמֶּךָּ׃
25 עֵינֶיךָ לְנֹכַח יַבִּיטוּ
וְעַפְעַפֶּיךָ יַיְשִׁרוּ נֶגְדֶּךָ׃
26 פַּלֵּס מַעְגַּל רַגְלֶךָ
וְכָל־דְּרָכֶיךָ יִכֹּנוּ׃
27 אַל־תֵּט־יָמִין וּשְׂמֹאול*
הָסֵר רַגְלְךָ מֵרָע׃

ה בְּנִי לְחָכְמָתִי הַקְשִׁיבָה
לִתְבוּנָתִי הַט־אָזְנֶךָ׃
2 לִשְׁמֹר מְזִמּוֹת
וְדַעַת שְׂפָתֶיךָ יִנְצֹרוּ׃
3 כִּי נֹפֶת תִּטֹּפְנָה שִׂפְתֵי זָרָה
וְחָלָק מִשֶּׁמֶן חִכָּהּ׃
4 וְאַחֲרִיתָהּ מָרָה כַלַּעֲנָה
חַדָּה כְּחֶרֶב פִּיּוֹת׃
5 רַגְלֶיהָ יֹרְדוֹת מָוֶת
שְׁאוֹל צְעָדֶיהָ יִתְמֹכוּ׃
6 אֹרַח חַיִּים פֶּן־תְּפַלֵּס
נָעוּ מַעְגְּלֹתֶיהָ לֹא תֵדָע׃ פ
7 וְעַתָּה בָנִים שִׁמְעוּ־לִי
וְאַל־תָּסוּרוּ מֵאִמְרֵי־פִי׃
8 הַרְחֵק מֵעָלֶיהָ דַרְכֶּךָ
וְאַל־תִּקְרַב אֶל־פֶּתַח בֵּיתָהּ׃
9 פֶּן־תִּתֵּן לַאֲחֵרִים הוֹדֶךָ
וּשְׁנֹתֶיךָ לְאַכְזָרִי׃
10 פֶּן־יִשְׂבְּעוּ זָרִים כֹּחֶךָ
וַעֲצָבֶיךָ בְּבֵית נָכְרִי׃
11 וְנָהַמְתָּ בְאַחֲרִיתֶךָ
בִּכְלוֹת בְּשָׂרְךָ וּשְׁאֵרֶךָ׃
12 וְאָמַרְתָּ אֵיךְ שָׂנֵאתִי מוּסָר
וְתוֹכַחַת נָאַץ לִבִּי׃

a Lit. "strange."

And heartily spurned rebuke.

¹³I did not pay heed to my teachers,
Or incline my ear to my instructors.

¹⁴Soon I was in dire trouble
Amidst the assembled congregation."

¹⁵Drink water from your own cistern,
Running water from your own well.

¹⁶Your springs will gush forth
In streams in the public squares.

¹⁷They will be yours alone,
Others having no part with you.

¹⁸Let your fountain be blessed;
Find joy in the wife of your youth—

¹⁹A loving doe, a graceful mountain goat.
Let her breasts satisfy you at all times;
Be infatuated with love of her always.

²⁰Why be infatuated, my son, with a forbidden*
woman?
Why clasp the bosom of an alien woman?

²¹For a man's ways are before the eyes of God;
He surveys his entire course.

²²The wicked man will be trapped in his iniquities;
He will be caught up in the ropes of his sin.

²³He will die for lack of discipline,
Infatuated by his great folly.

6 My son, if you have stood surety for your fellow,
Given your hand for another,*

²You have been trapped by the words of your
mouth,
Snared by the words of your mouth.

³Do this, then, my son, to extricate yourself,
For you have come into the power of your fellow:
Go grovel—and badger your fellow;

⁴Give your eyes no sleep,
Your pupils no slumber.

⁵Save yourself like a deer out of the hand [of a
hunter],
Like a bird out of the hand of a fowler.

---

¹³ וְלֹא־שָׁמַעְתִּי בְּקוֹל מוֹרָי
וְלִמְלַמְּדַי לֹא־הִטֵּיתִי אָזְנִי:
¹⁴ כִּמְעַט הָיִיתִי בְכָל־רָע
בְּתוֹךְ קָהָל וְעֵדָה:
¹⁵ שְׁתֵה־מַיִם מִבּוֹרֶךָ
וְנֹזְלִים מִתּוֹךְ בְּאֵרֶךָ:
¹⁶ יָפוּצוּ מַעְיְנֹתֶיךָ חוּצָה
בָּרְחֹבוֹת פַּלְגֵי־מָיִם:
¹⁷ יִהְיוּ־לְךָ לְבַדֶּךָ
וְאֵין לְזָרִים אִתָּךְ:
¹⁸ יְהִי־מְקוֹרְךָ בָרוּךְ
וּשְׂמַח מֵאֵשֶׁת נְעוּרֶךָ:
¹⁹ אַיֶּלֶת אֲהָבִים וְיַעֲלַת־חֵן
דַּדֶּיהָ יְרַוֻּךָ בְכָל־עֵת
בְּאַהֲבָתָהּ תִּשְׁגֶּה תָמִיד:
²⁰ וְלָמָּה תִשְׁגֶּה בְנִי בְזָרָה
וּתְחַבֵּק חֵק נָכְרִיָּה:
²¹ כִּי נֹכַח ׀ עֵינֵי יְהוָה דַּרְכֵי־אִישׁ
וְכָל־מַעְגְּלֹתָיו מְפַלֵּס:
²² עֲווֹנוֹתָיו יִלְכְּדֻנוֹ אֶת־הָרָשָׁע
וּבְחַבְלֵי חַטָּאתוֹ יִתָּמֵךְ:
²³ הוּא יָמוּת בְּאֵין מוּסָר
וּבְרֹב אִוַּלְתּוֹ יִשְׁגֶּה: פ

ר ¹ בְּנִי אִם־עָרַבְתָּ לְרֵעֶךָ
תָּקַעְתָּ לַזָּר כַּפֶּיךָ:
² נוֹקַשְׁתָּ בְאִמְרֵי־פִיךָ
נִלְכַּדְתָּ בְּאִמְרֵי־פִיךָ:
³ עֲשֵׂה זֹאת אֵפוֹא ׀ בְּנִי וְהִנָּצֵל
כִּי בָאתָ בְכַף־רֵעֶךָ
לֵךְ הִתְרַפֵּס וּרְהַב רֵעֶיךָ:
⁴ אַל־תִּתֵּן שֵׁנָה לְעֵינֶיךָ
וּתְנוּמָה לְעַפְעַפֶּיךָ:
⁵ הִנָּצֵל כִּצְבִי מִיָּד
וּכְצִפּוֹר מִיַּד יָקוּשׁ: פ

---

a   Or "a stranger."

6Lazybones, go to the ant;
Study its ways and learn.

7Without leaders, officers, or rulers,

8It lays up its stores during the summer,
Gathers in its food at the harvest.

9How long will you lie there, lazybones;
When will you wake from your sleep?

10A bit more sleep, a bit more slumber,
A bit more hugging yourself in bed,

11And poverty will come *b*-calling upon you,-*b*
And want, like a man with a shield.

12A scoundrel, an evil man
Lives by crooked speech,

13Winking his eyes,
Shuffling his feet,
Pointing his finger.

14Duplicity is in his heart;
He plots evil all the time;
He incites quarrels.

15Therefore calamity will come upon him without warning;
Suddenly he will be broken beyond repair.

16Six things the Lord hates;
Seven are an abomination to Him:

17A haughty bearing,
A lying tongue,
Hands that shed innocent blood,

18A mind that hatches evil plots,
Feet quick to run to evil,

19A false witness testifying lies,
And one who incites brothers to quarrel.

20My son, keep your father's commandment;
Do not forsake your mother's teaching.

21Tie them over your heart always;
Bind them around your throat.

6 לֵךְ־אֶל־נְמָלָה עָצֵל
רְאֵה דְרָכֶיהָ וַחֲכָם:

7 אֲשֶׁר אֵין־לָהּ קָצִין שֹׁטֵר וּמֹשֵׁל:

8 תָּכִין בַּקַּיִץ לַחְמָהּ
אָגְרָה בַקָּצִיר מַאֲכָלָהּ:

9 עַד־מָתַי עָצֵל ׀ תִּשְׁכָּב
מָתַי תָּקוּם מִשְּׁנָתֶךָ:

10 מְעַט שֵׁנוֹת מְעַט תְּנוּמוֹת
מְעַט ׀ חִבֻּק יָדַיִם לִשְׁכָּב:

11 וּבָא־כִמְהַלֵּךְ רֵאשֶׁךָ*
וּמַחְסֹרְךָ כְּאִישׁ מָגֵן: פ

12 אָדָם בְּלִיַּעַל אִישׁ אָוֶן
הוֹלֵךְ עִקְּשׁוּת פֶּה:

13 קֹרֵץ בְּעֵינוֹ בְּרַגְלָו
מֹלֵל בְּרַגְלָו בְּאֶצְבְּעֹתָיו:

14 תַּהְפֻּכוֹת ׀ בְּלִבּוֹ
חֹרֵשׁ רָע בְּכָל־עֵת
מִדְיָנִים יְשַׁלֵּחַ:

15 עַל־כֵּן פִּתְאֹם יָבוֹא אֵידוֹ
פֶּתַע יִשָּׁבֵר וְאֵין מַרְפֵּא: פ

16 שֶׁשׁ־הֵנָּה שָׂנֵא יְהוָה
וְשֶׁבַע תּוֹעֲבוֹת תּוֹעֲבַת נַפְשׁוֹ:

17 עֵינַיִם רָמוֹת
לְשׁוֹן שָׁקֶר
וְיָדַיִם שֹׁפְכוֹת דָּם־נָקִי:

18 לֵב חֹרֵשׁ מַחְשְׁבוֹת אָוֶן
רַגְלַיִם מְמַהֲרוֹת לָרוּץ לָרָעָה:

19 יָפִיחַ כְּזָבִים עֵד שָׁקֶר
וּמְשַׁלֵּחַ מְדָנִים בֵּין אַחִים: פ

20 נְצֹר בְּנִי מִצְוַת אָבִיךָ
וְאַל־תִּטֹּשׁ תּוֹרַת אִמֶּךָ:

21 קָשְׁרֵם עַל־לִבְּךָ תָמִיד
עָנְדֵם עַל־גַּרְגְּרֹתֶךָ:

---

b-b Meaning of Heb. uncertain.

22When you walk it will lead you;
When you lie down it will watch over you;
And when you are awake it will talk with you.
23For the commandment is a lamp,
The teaching is a light,
And the way to life is the rebuke that disciplines.
24It will keep you from an evil woman,
From the smooth tongue of a forbidden[c] woman.
25Do not lust for her beauty
Or let her captivate you with her eyes.
26The last loaf of bread will go for a harlot;
A married woman will snare a person of honor.
27Can a man rake embers into his bosom
Without burning his clothes?
28Can a man walk on live coals
Without scorching his feet?
29It is the same with one who sleeps with his fel-
low's wife;
None who touches her will go unpunished.
30A thief is not held in contempt
For stealing to appease his hunger;
31Yet if caught he must pay sevenfold;
He must give up all he owns.
32He who commits adultery is devoid of sense;
Only one who would destroy himself does such
a thing.
33He will meet with disease and disgrace;
His reproach will never be expunged.
34The fury of the husband will be passionate;
He will show no pity on his day of vengeance.
35He will not have regard for any ransom;
He will refuse your bribe, however great.

7 My son, heed my words;
And store up my commandments with you.
2Keep my commandments and live,
My teaching, as the apple of your eye.

22 בְּהִתְהַלֶּכְךָ ׀ תַּנְחֶה אֹתָךְ
בְּשָׁכְבְּךָ תִּשְׁמֹר עָלֶיךָ
וַהֲקִיצֹ֫וֹתָ הִיא תְשִׂיחֶךָ:
23 כִּי נֵר מִצְוָה וְתוֹרָה אוֹר
וְדֶרֶךְ חַיִּים תּוֹכְחוֹת מוּסָר:
24 לִשְׁמָרְךָ מֵאֵשֶׁת רָע
מֵחֶלְקַת לָשׁוֹן נָכְרִיָּה:
25 אַל־תַּחְמֹד יָפְיָהּ בִּלְבָבֶךָ
וְאַל־תִּקָּחֲךָ בְּעַפְעַפֶּיהָ:
26 כִּי בְעַד־אִשָּׁה זוֹנָה עַד־כִּכַּר
לָחֶם
וְאֵשֶׁת אִישׁ
נֶפֶשׁ יְקָרָה תָצוּד: פ
27 הֲיַחְתֶּה אִישׁ אֵשׁ בְּחֵיקוֹ
וּבְגָדָיו לֹא תִשָּׂרַפְנָה:
28 אִם־יְהַלֵּךְ אִישׁ עַל־הַגֶּחָלִים
וְרַגְלָיו לֹא תִכָּוֶינָה:
29 כֵּן הַבָּא אֶל־אֵשֶׁת רֵעֵהוּ
לֹא יִנָּקֶה כָּל־הַנֹּגֵעַ בָּהּ:
30 לֹא־יָבוּזוּ לַגַּנָּב כִּי יִגְנוֹב
לְמַלֵּא נַפְשׁוֹ כִּי יִרְעָב:
31 וְנִמְצָא יְשַׁלֵּם שִׁבְעָתָיִם
אֶת־כָּל־הוֹן בֵּיתוֹ יִתֵּן:
32 נֹאֵף אִשָּׁה חֲסַר־לֵב
מַשְׁחִית נַפְשׁוֹ הוּא יַעֲשֶׂנָּה:
33 נֶגַע־וְקָלוֹן יִמְצָא
וְחֶרְפָּתוֹ לֹא תִמָּחֶה:
34 כִּי־קִנְאָה חֲמַת־גָּבֶר
וְלֹא־יַחְמוֹל בְּיוֹם נָקָם:
35 לֹא־יִשָּׂא פְּנֵי כָל־כֹּפֶר
וְלֹא־יֹאבֶה כִּי תַרְבֶּה־שֹׁחַד: פ

ז
בְּנִי שְׁמֹר אֲמָרָי
וּמִצְוֹתַי תִּצְפֹּן אִתָּךְ:
2 שְׁמֹר מִצְוֹתַי וֶחְיֵה
וְתוֹרָתִי כְּאִישׁוֹן עֵינֶיךָ:

c   Lit. "alien."

3Bind them on your fingers;
Write them on the tablet of your mind.
4Say to Wisdom, "You are my sister,"
And call Understanding a kinswoman.
5She will guard you from a forbidden*a* woman;
From an alien woman whose talk is smooth.

6From the window of my house,
Through my lattice, I looked out
7And saw among the simple,
Noticed among the youths,
A lad devoid of sense.
8He was crossing the street near her corner,
Walking toward her house
9In the dusk of evening,
In the dark hours of night.
10A woman comes toward him
b-Dressed like a harlot, with set purpose.-*b*
11She is bustling and restive;
She is never at home.
12Now in the street, now in the square,
She lurks at every corner.
13She lays hold of him and kisses him;
Brazenly she says to him,
14"I had to make a sacrifice of well-being;
Today I fulfilled my vows.
15Therefore I have come out to you,
Seeking you, and have found you.
16I have decked my couch with covers
Of dyed Egyptian linen;
17I have sprinkled my bed
With myrrh, aloes, and cinnamon.
18Let us drink our fill of love till morning;
Let us delight in amorous embrace.
19For the man of the house is away;
He is off on a distant journey.
20He took his bag of money with him
And will return only at mid-month."

a Lit. "strange."
b-b Meaning of Heb. uncertain.

³ קִשְׁרֵ֥ם עַל־אֶצְבְּעֹתֶ֑יךָ
כָּ֝תְבֵ֗ם עַל־ל֥וּחַ לִבֶּֽךָ׃
⁴ אֱמֹ֣ר לַֽ֭חָכְמָה אֲחֹ֣תִי אָ֑תְּ
וּ֝מֹדָ֗ע לַבִּינָ֥ה תִקְרָֽא׃
⁵ לִ֭שְׁמָרְךָ מֵאִשָּׁ֣ה זָרָ֑ה
מִ֝נָּכְרִיָּ֗ה אֲמָרֶ֥יהָ הֶחֱלִֽיקָה׃

⁶ כִּ֭י בְּחַלּ֣וֹן בֵּיתִ֑י
בְּעַ֖ד אֶשְׁנַבִּ֣י נִשְׁקָֽפְתִּי׃
⁷ וָאֵ֤רֶא בַפְּתָאיִם֙*
אָבִ֤ינָה בַבָּנִ֔ים
נַ֖עַר חֲסַר־לֵֽב׃
⁸ עֹבֵ֣ר בַּ֭שּׁוּק אֵ֣צֶל פִּנָּ֑הּ
וְדֶ֖רֶךְ בֵּיתָ֣הּ יִצְעָֽד׃
⁹ בְּנֶֽשֶׁף־בְּעֶ֥רֶב י֑וֹם
בְּאִישׁ֥וֹן לַ֝֗יְלָה וַאֲפֵלָֽה׃
¹⁰ וְהִנֵּ֣ה אִ֭שָּׁה לִקְרָאת֑וֹ
שִׁ֥ית ז֝וֹנָ֗ה וּנְצֻ֥רַת לֵֽב׃
¹¹ הֹמִיָּ֣ה הִ֭יא וְסֹרָ֑רֶת
בְּ֝בֵיתָ֗הּ לֹא־יִשְׁכְּנ֥וּ רַגְלֶֽיהָ׃
¹² פַּ֤עַם ׀ בַּח֗וּץ פַּ֥עַם בָּרְחֹב֑וֹת
וְאֵ֖צֶל כָּל־פִּנָּ֣ה תֶאֱרֹֽב׃
¹³ וְהֶחֱזִ֣יקָה בּ֭וֹ וְנָ֣שְׁקָה־לּ֑וֹ
הֵעֵ֥זָה פָ֝נֶ֗יהָ וַתֹּ֣אמַר לֽוֹ׃
¹⁴ זִבְחֵ֣י שְׁלָמִ֣ים עָלָ֑י
הַ֝יּ֗וֹם שִׁלַּ֥מְתִּי נְדָרָֽי׃
¹⁵ עַל־כֵּ֭ן יָצָ֣אתִי לִקְרָאתֶ֑ךָ
לְשַׁחֵ֥ר פָּ֝נֶ֗יךָ וָאֶמְצָאֶֽךָּ׃
¹⁶ מַ֭רְבַדִּים רָבַ֣דְתִּי עַרְשִׂ֑י
חֲ֝טֻב֗וֹת אֵט֥וּן מִצְרָֽיִם׃
¹⁷ נַ֥פְתִּי מִשְׁכָּבִ֑י
מֹ֥ר אֲ֝הָלִ֗ים וְקִנָּמֽוֹן׃
¹⁸ לְכָ֤ה נִרְוֶ֣ה דֹ֭דִים עַד־הַבֹּ֑קֶר
נִ֝תְעַלְּסָ֗ה בָּאֳהָבִֽים׃
¹⁹ כִּ֤י אֵ֣ין הָאִ֣ישׁ בְּבֵית֑וֹ
הָ֝לַ֗ךְ בְּדֶ֣רֶךְ מֵרָחֽוֹק׃
²⁰ צְֽרוֹר־הַ֭כֶּסֶף לָקַ֣ח בְּיָד֑וֹ
לְי֥וֹם הַ֝כֵּ֗סֶא יָבֹ֥א בֵיתֽוֹ׃

²¹She sways him with her eloquence,
Turns him aside with her smooth talk.
²²Thoughtlessly he follows her,
Like an ox going to the slaughter,
^{b-}Like a fool to the stocks for punishment^{-b}—
²³Until the arrow pierces his liver.
He is like a bird rushing into a trap,
Not knowing his life is at stake.
²⁴Now, sons, listen to me;
Pay attention to my words;
²⁵Let your mind not wander down her ways;
Do not stray onto her paths.
²⁶For many are those she has struck dead,
And numerous are her victims.
²⁷Her house is a highway to Sheol
Leading down to Death's inner chambers.

21 הִטַּתּוּ בְּרֹב לִקְחָהּ
בְּחֵלֶק שְׂפָתֶיהָ תַּדִּיחֶנּוּ׃
22 הֹולֵךְ אַחֲרֶיהָ פִּתְאֹם
כְּשֹׁור אֶל־טֶבַח יָבֹוא
וּכְעֶכֶס אֶל־מוּסַר אֱוִיל׃
23 עַד יְפַלַּח חֵץ כְּבֵדֹו
כְּמַהֵר צִפֹּור אֶל־פָּח
וְלֹא־יָדַע כִּי־בְנַפְשֹׁו הוּא׃ פ
24 וְעַתָּה בָנִים שִׁמְעוּ־לִי
וְהַקְשִׁיבוּ לְאִמְרֵי־פִי׃
25 אַל־יֵשְׂטְ אֶל־דְּרָכֶיהָ לִבֶּךָ
אַל־תֵּתַע בִּנְתִיבֹותֶיהָ׃
26 כִּי־רַבִּים חֲלָלִים הִפִּילָה
וַעֲצֻמִים כָּל־הֲרֻגֶיהָ׃
27 דַּרְכֵי שְׁאֹול בֵּיתָהּ
יֹרְדֹות אֶל־חַדְרֵי־מָוֶת׃ פ

8 It is Wisdom calling,
Understanding raising her voice.
²She takes her stand at the topmost heights,
By the wayside, at the crossroads,
³Near the gates at the city entrance;
At the entryways, she shouts,
⁴"O men, I call to you;
My cry is to all mankind.
⁵O simple ones, learn shrewdness;
O dullards, instruct your minds.
⁶Listen, for I speak noble things;
Uprightness comes from my lips.
⁷My mouth utters truth;
Wickedness is abhorrent to my lips.
⁸All my words are just,
None of them perverse or crooked;
⁹All are straightforward to the intelligent man,
And right to those who have attained knowledge.

ח הֲלֹא־חָכְמָה תִקְרָא
וּתְבוּנָה תִּתֵּן קֹולָהּ׃
2 בְּרֹאשׁ־מְרֹומִים עֲלֵי־דָרֶךְ
בֵּית נְתִיבֹות נִצָּבָה׃
3 לְיַד־שְׁעָרִים לְפִי־קָרֶת
מְבֹוא פְתָחִים תָּרֹנָּה׃
4 אֲלֵיכֶם אִישִׁים אֶקְרָא
וְקֹולִי אֶל־בְּנֵי אָדָם׃
5 הָבִינוּ פְתָאיִם* עָרְמָה
וּכְסִילִים הָבִינוּ לֵב׃
6 שִׁמְעוּ כִּי־נְגִידִים אֲדַבֵּר
וּמִפְתַּח שְׂפָתַי מֵישָׁרִים׃
7 כִּי־אֱמֶת יֶהְגֶּה חִכִּי
וְתֹועֲבַת שְׂפָתַי רֶשַׁע׃
8 בְּצֶדֶק כָּל־אִמְרֵי־פִי
אֵין בָּהֶם נִפְתָּל וְעִקֵּשׁ׃
9 כֻּלָּם נְכֹחִים לַמֵּבִין
וִישָׁרִים לְמֹצְאֵי דָעַת׃

¹⁰Accept my discipline rather than silver,
Knowledge rather than choice gold.
¹¹For wisdom is better than rubies;
No goods can equal her.

¹²"I, Wisdom, live with Prudence;
I attain knowledge and foresight.
¹³To fear the LORD is to hate evil;
I hate pride, arrogance, the evil way,
And duplicity in speech.
¹⁴Mine are counsel and resourcefulness;
I am understanding; courage is mine.
¹⁵Through me kings reign
And rulers decree just laws;
¹⁶Through me princes rule,
Great men and all the ^a-righteous judges.-^a
¹⁷Those who love me I love,
And those who seek me will find me.
¹⁸Riches and honor belong to me,
Enduring wealth and success.
¹⁹My fruit is better than gold, fine gold,
And my produce better than choice silver.
²⁰I walk on the way of righteousness,
On the paths of justice.
²¹I endow those who love me with substance;
I will fill their treasuries.

²²"The LORD created me at the beginning of His
course
As the first of His works of old.
²³In the distant past I was fashioned,
At the beginning, at the origin of earth.
²⁴There was still no deep when I was brought
forth,
No springs rich in water;
²⁵Before [the foundation of] the mountains were
sunk,
Before the hills I was born.
²⁶He had not yet made earth and fields,

10 קְחֽוּ־מוּסָרִ֥י וְאַל־כֶּ֑סֶף
וְ֝דַ֗עַת מֵחָר֥וּץ נִבְחָֽר׃
11 כִּֽי־טוֹבָ֣ה חָ֭כְמָה מִפְּנִינִ֑ים
וְכָל־חֲ֝פָצִ֗ים לֹ֣א יִֽשְׁווּ־בָֽהּ׃
12 אֲֽנִי־חָ֭כְמָה שָׁכַ֣נְתִּי עָרְמָ֑ה
וְדַ֖עַת מְזִמּ֣וֹת אֶמְצָֽא׃
13 יִֽרְאַ֫ת יְהֹוָ֗ה שְֽׂנֹ֫את רָ֥ע
גֵּאָ֣ה וְגָא֣וֹן ׀ וְדֶ֣רֶךְ רָ֑ע
וּפִ֖י תַהְפֻּכ֣וֹת שָׂנֵֽאתִי׃
14 לִֽי־עֵ֭צָה וְתוּשִׁיָּ֑ה
אֲנִ֥י בִ֝ינָ֗ה לִ֣י גְבוּרָֽה׃
15 בִּ֭י מְלָכִ֣ים יִמְלֹ֑כוּ
וְ֝רוֹזְנִ֗ים יְחֹ֣קְקוּ צֶֽדֶק׃
16 בִּ֭י שָׂרִ֣ים יָשֹׂ֑רוּ
וּ֝נְדִיבִ֗ים כָּל־שֹׁ֥פְטֵי צֶֽדֶק׃*
17 אֲ֭נִי *אֹהֲבֶ֣יהָ* אֵהָ֑ב
וּ֝מְשַׁחֲרַ֗י יִמְצָאֻֽנְנִי׃
18 עֹֽשֶׁר־וְכָב֥וֹד אִתִּ֑י
ה֥וֹן עָ֝תֵ֗ק וּצְדָקָֽה׃
19 ט֣וֹב פִּ֭רְיִי מֵחָר֣וּץ וּמִפָּ֑ז
וּ֝תְבוּאָתִ֗י מִכֶּ֥סֶף נִבְחָֽר׃
20 בְּאֹֽרַח־צְדָקָ֥ה אֲהַלֵּ֑ךְ
בְּ֝ת֗וֹךְ נְתִיב֥וֹת מִשְׁפָּֽט׃
21 לְהַנְחִ֖יל אֹהֲבַ֥י ׀ יֵ֑שׁ
וְאֹצְרֹֽתֵיהֶ֣ם אֲמַלֵּֽא׃ פ
22 יְֽהֹוָ֗ה קָ֭נָנִי רֵאשִׁ֣ית דַּרְכּ֑וֹ
קֶ֖דֶם מִפְעָלָ֣יו מֵאָֽז׃
23 מֵ֭עוֹלָם נִסַּ֥כְתִּי מֵרֹ֗אשׁ מִקַּדְמֵי־אָֽרֶץ׃
24 בְּאֵין־תְּהֹמ֥וֹת חוֹלָ֑לְתִּי
בְּאֵ֥ין מַ֝עְיָנ֗וֹת נִכְבַּדֵּי־מָֽיִם׃
25 בְּטֶ֣רֶם הָרִ֣ים הׇטְבָּ֑עוּ
לִפְנֵ֖י גְבָע֣וֹת חוֹלָֽלְתִּי׃
26 עַד־לֹ֣א עָ֭שָׂה אֶ֣רֶץ וְחוּצ֑וֹת

_{v. 16.} בנוסח אחר "שפטי ארץ"

---

^{a-a} *According to some Heb. mss. and printed editions, "judges of the earth."*

Or the world's first clumps of clay.
27I was there when He set the heavens into place;
When He fixed the horizon upon the deep;
28When He made the heavens above firm,
And the fountains of the deep gushed forth;
29When He assigned the sea its limits,
So that its waters never transgress His command;
When He fixed the foundations of the earth,
30I was with Him as a confidant,
A source of delight every day,
Rejoicing before Him at all times,
31Rejoicing in His inhabited world,
Finding delight with mankind.
32Now, sons, listen to me;
Happy are they who keep my ways.
33Heed discipline and become wise;
Do not spurn it.
34Happy is the man who listens to me,
Coming early to my gates each day,
Waiting outside my doors.
35For he who finds me finds life
And obtains favor from the LORD.
36But he who misses me destroys himself;
All who hate me love death."

וְרֹאשׁ עַפְרוֹת תֵּבֵל:
27 בַּהֲכִינוֹ שָׁמַיִם שָׁם אָנִי
בְּחוּקוֹ חוּג עַל־פְּנֵי תְהוֹם:
28 בְּאַמְּצוֹ שְׁחָקִים מִמָּעַל
בַּעֲזוֹז עִינוֹת תְּהוֹם:
29 בְּשׂוּמוֹ לַיָּם ׀ חֻקּוֹ
וּמַיִם לֹא יַעַבְרוּ־פִיו
בְּחוּקוֹ מוֹסְדֵי אָרֶץ:
30 וָאֶהְיֶה אֶצְלוֹ אָמוֹן
וָאֶהְיֶה שַׁעֲשֻׁעִים יוֹם ׀ יוֹם
מְשַׂחֶקֶת לְפָנָיו בְּכָל־עֵת:
31 מְשַׂחֶקֶת בְּתֵבֵל אַרְצוֹ
וְשַׁעֲשֻׁעַי אֶת־בְּנֵי אָדָם: פ
32 וְעַתָּה בָנִים שִׁמְעוּ־לִי
וְאַשְׁרֵי דְּרָכַי יִשְׁמֹרוּ:
33 שִׁמְעוּ מוּסָר וַחֲכָמוּ
וְאַל־תִּפְרָעוּ:
34 אַשְׁרֵי אָדָם שֹׁמֵעַ לִי
לִשְׁקֹד עַל־דַּלְתֹתַי יוֹם ׀ יוֹם
לִשְׁמֹר מְזוּזֹת פְּתָחָי:
35 כִּי מֹצְאִי מצאי מָצָא חַיִּים
וַיָּפֶק רָצוֹן מֵיהֹוָה:
36 וְחֹטְאִי חֹמֵס נַפְשׁוֹ
כָּל־מְשַׂנְאַי אָהֲבוּ מָוֶת: פ

9 Wisdom has built her house,
She has hewn her seven pillars.
2She has prepared the feast,
Mixed the wine,
And also set the table.
3She has sent out her maids to announce
On the heights of the town,
4"Let the simple enter here";
To those devoid of sense she says,
5"Come, eat my food
And drink the wine that I have mixed;
6Give up simpleness and live,
Walk in the way of understanding."

ט חָכְמוֹת בָּנְתָה בֵיתָהּ
חָצְבָה עַמּוּדֶיהָ שִׁבְעָה:
2 טָבְחָה טִבְחָהּ מָסְכָה יֵינָהּ
אַף עָרְכָה שֻׁלְחָנָהּ:
3 שָׁלְחָה נַעֲרֹתֶיהָ תִקְרָא
עַל־גַּפֵּי מְרֹמֵי קָרֶת:
4 מִי־פֶתִי יָסֻר הֵנָּה
חֲסַר־לֵב אָמְרָה לּוֹ:
5 לְכוּ לַחֲמוּ בְלַחֲמִי
וּשְׁתוּ בְּיַיִן מָסָכְתִּי:
6 עִזְבוּ פְתָאיִם* וִחְיוּ
וְאִשְׁרוּ בְּדֶרֶךְ בִּינָה:

v. 6. יתיר א'

7To correct a scoffer,

a-Or rebuke a wicked man for his blemish,

Is to call down abuse on oneself.-*a*

8Do not rebuke a scoffer, for he will hate you;

Reprove a wise man, and he will love you.

9Instruct a wise man, and he will grow wiser;

Teach a righteous man, and he will gain in
learning.

10The beginning of wisdom is fear of the LORD,

And knowledge of the Holy One is understanding.

11For through me your days will increase,

And years be added to your life.

12If you are wise, you are wise for yourself;

If you are a scoffer, you bear it alone.

13The stupid woman bustles about;

She is simple and knows nothing.

14She sits in the doorway of her house,

Or on a chair at the heights of the town,

15Calling to all the wayfarers

Who go about their own affairs,

16"Let the simple enter here";

And to those devoid of sense she says,

17"Stolen waters are sweet,

And bread eaten furtively is tasty."

18He does not know that the shades are there,

That her guests are in the depths of Sheol.

10 The proverbs of Solomon:

A wise son brings joy to his father;

A dull son is his mother's sorrow.

2Ill-gotten wealth is of no avail,

But righteousness saves from death.

3The LORD will not let the righteous go hungry,

But He denies the wicked what they crave.

4Negligent hands cause poverty,

But diligent hands enrich.

7 יֹסֵר ׀ לֵץ

לֹקֵחַ לוֹ קָלוֹן

וּמוֹכִיחַ לְרָשָׁע מוּמוֹ:

8 אַל־תּוֹכַח לֵץ פֶּן־יִשְׂנָאֶךָּ

הוֹכַח לְחָכָם וְיֶאֱהָבֶךָּ:

9 תֵּן לְחָכָם וְיֶחְכַּם־עוֹד

הוֹדַע לְצַדִּיק וְיוֹסֶף לֶקַח: פ

10 תְּחִלַּת חָכְמָה יִרְאַת יְהֹוָה

וְדַעַת קְדֹשִׁים בִּינָה:

11 כִּי־בִי יִרְבּוּ יָמֶיךָ

וְיוֹסִיפוּ לְּךָ שְׁנוֹת חַיִּים:

12 אִם־חָכַמְתָּ חָכַמְתָּ לָּךְ

וְלַצְתָּ לְבַדְּךָ תִשָּׂא:

13 אֵשֶׁת כְּסִילוּת הֹמִיָּה

פְּתַיּוּת וּבַל־יָדְעָה מָּה:

14 וְיָשְׁבָה לְפֶתַח בֵּיתָהּ

עַל־כִּסֵּא מְרֹמֵי קָרֶת:

15 לִקְרֹא לְעֹבְרֵי־דָרֶךְ

הַמְיַשְּׁרִים אֹרְחוֹתָם:

16 מִי־פֶתִי יָסֻר הֵנָּה

וַחֲסַר־לֵב וְאָמְרָה לּוֹ:

17 מַיִם־גְּנוּבִים יִמְתָּקוּ

וְלֶחֶם סְתָרִים יִנְעָם:

18 וְלֹא־יָדַע כִּי־רְפָאִים שָׁם

בְּעִמְקֵי שְׁאוֹל קְרֻאֶיהָ: פ

ל מִשְׁלֵי שְׁלֹמֹה ס

בֵּן חָכָם יְשַׂמַּח־אָב

וּבֵן כְּסִיל תּוּגַת אִמּוֹ:

2 לֹא־יוֹעִילוּ אוֹצְרוֹת רֶשַׁע

וּצְדָקָה תַּצִּיל מִמָּוֶת:

3 לֹא־יַרְעִיב יְהֹוָה נֶפֶשׁ צַדִּיק

וְהַוַּת רְשָׁעִים יֶהְדֹּף:

4 רָאשׁ* עֹשֶׂה כַף־רְמִיָּה

וְיַד חָרוּצִים תַּעֲשִׁיר:

---

a-a   Clauses transposed for clarity.

יתיר א' v. 4.

⁵He who lays in stores during the summer is a capable son,

But he who sleeps during the harvest is an incompetent.

⁶Blessings light upon the head of the righteous,

But lawlessness covers the mouth of the wicked.

⁷The name of the righteous is invoked in blessing,

But the fame of the wicked rots.

⁸He whose heart is wise accepts commands,

But he whose speech is foolish comes to grief.

⁹He who lives blamelessly lives safely,

But he who walks a crooked path will be found out.

¹⁰He who winks his eye causes sorrow;

He whose speech is foolish comes to grief.

¹¹The mouth of the righteous is a fountain of life,

But lawlessness covers the mouth of the wicked.

¹²Hatred stirs up strife,

But love covers up all faults.

¹³Wisdom is to be found on the lips of the intelligent,

But a rod is ready for the back of the senseless.

¹⁴The wise store up knowledge;

The mouth of the fool is an imminent ruin.

¹⁵The wealth of a rich man is his fortress;

The poverty of the poor is his ruin.

¹⁶The labor of the righteous man makes for life;

The produce of the wicked man makes for want.

¹⁷He who follows discipline shows the way to life,

But he who ignores reproof leads astray.

¹⁸He who conceals hatred has lying lips,

While he who speaks forth slander is a dullard.

¹⁹Where there is much talking, there is no lack of transgressing,

But he who curbs his tongueᵃ shows sense.

²⁰The tongue of a righteous man is choice silver,

But the mind of the wicked is of little worth.

²¹The lips of the righteous sustain many,

But fools die for lack of sense.

ᵃ Lit. "lips."

אֹגֵר בַּקַּיִץ בֵּן מַשְׂכִּיל ⁵

נִרְדָּם בַּקָּצִיר בֵּן מֵבִישׁ׃

בְּרָכוֹת לְרֹאשׁ צַדִּיק ⁶

וּפִי רְשָׁעִים יְכַסֶּה חָמָס׃

זֵכֶר צַדִּיק לִבְרָכָה ⁷

וְשֵׁם רְשָׁעִים יִרְקָב׃

חֲכַם־לֵב יִקַּח מִצְוֺת ⁸

וֶאֱוִיל שְׂפָתַיִם יִלָּבֵט׃

הוֹלֵךְ בַּתֹּם יֵלֶךְ בֶּטַח ⁹

וּמְעַקֵּשׁ דְּרָכָיו יִוָּדֵעַ׃

קֹרֵץ עַיִן יִתֵּן עַצָּבֶת ¹⁰

וֶאֱוִיל שְׂפָתַיִם יִלָּבֵט׃

מְקוֹר חַיִּים פִּי צַדִּיק ¹¹

וּפִי רְשָׁעִים יְכַסֶּה חָמָס׃

שִׂנְאָה תְּעוֹרֵר מְדָנִים ¹²

וְעַל כָּל־פְּשָׁעִים תְּכַסֶּה אַהֲבָה׃

בְּשִׂפְתֵי נָבוֹן תִּמָּצֵא חָכְמָה ¹³

וְשֵׁבֶט לְגֵו חֲסַר־לֵב׃

חֲכָמִים יִצְפְּנוּ־דָעַת ¹⁴

וּפִי־אֱוִיל מְחִתָּה קְרֹבָה׃

הוֹן עָשִׁיר קִרְיַת עֻזּוֹ ¹⁵

מְחִתַּת דַּלִּים רֵישָׁם׃

פְּעֻלַּת צַדִּיק לְחַיִּים ¹⁶

תְּבוּאַת רָשָׁע לְחַטָּאת׃

אֹרַח לְחַיִּים שׁוֹמֵר מוּסָר ¹⁷

וְעוֹזֵב תּוֹכַחַת מַתְעֶה׃

מְכַסֶּה שִׂנְאָה שִׂפְתֵי־שָׁקֶר ¹⁸

וּמוֹצִא דִבָּה הוּא כְסִיל׃

בְּרֹב דְּבָרִים לֹא יֶחְדַּל־פָּשַׁע ¹⁹

וְחֹשֵׂךְ שְׂפָתָיו מַשְׂכִּיל׃

כֶּסֶף נִבְחָר לְשׁוֹן צַדִּיק ²⁰

לֵב רְשָׁעִים כִּמְעָט׃

שִׂפְתֵי צַדִּיק יִרְעוּ רַבִּים ²¹

וֶאֱוִילִים בַּחֲסַר־לֵב יָמוּתוּ׃

22It is the blessing of the LORD that enriches,
And no toil can increase it.

23As mischief is sport for the dullard,
So is wisdom for the man of understanding.

24What the wicked man plots overtakes him;
What the righteous desire is granted.

25When the storm passes the wicked man is gone,
But the righteous is an everlasting foundation.

26Like vinegar to the teeth,
Like smoke to the eyes,
Is a lazy man to those who send him on a mission.

27The fear of the LORD prolongs life,
While the years of the wicked will be shortened.

28The righteous can look forward to joy,
But the hope of the wicked is doomed.

29The way of the LORD is a stronghold for the
    blameless,
But a ruin for evildoers.

30The righteous will never be shaken;
The wicked will not inhabit the earth.

31The mouth of the righteous produces wisdom,
But the treacherous tongue shall be cut off.

32The lips of the righteous know what is pleasing;
The mouth of the wicked [knows] duplicity.

11 False scales are an abomination to the LORD;
An honest[a] weight pleases Him.

2When arrogance appears, disgrace follows,
But wisdom is with those who are unassuming.

3The integrity of the upright guides them;
The deviousness of the treacherous leads them to
    ruin.

4Wealth is of no avail on the day of wrath,
But righteousness saves from death.

5The righteousness of the blameless man smooths
    his way,
But the wicked man is felled by his wickedness.

6The righteousness of the upright saves them,

22 בִּרְכַּת יְהוָה הִיא תַעֲשִׁיר
וְלֹא־יוֹסִף עֶצֶב עִמָּהּ׃

23 כִּשְׂחוֹק לִכְסִיל עֲשׂוֹת זִמָּה
וְחָכְמָה לְאִישׁ תְּבוּנָה׃

24 מְגוֹרַת רָשָׁע הִיא תְבוֹאֶנּוּ
וְתַאֲוַת צַדִּיקִים יִתֵּן׃

25 כַּעֲבוֹר סוּפָה וְאֵין רָשָׁע
וְצַדִּיק יְסוֹד עוֹלָם׃

26 כַּחֹמֶץ ׀ לַשִּׁנַּיִם
וְכֶעָשָׁן לָעֵינָיִם
כֵּן הֶעָצֵל לְשֹׁלְחָיו׃

27 יִרְאַת יְהוָה תּוֹסִיף יָמִים
וּשְׁנוֹת רְשָׁעִים תִּקְצֹרְנָה׃

28 תּוֹחֶלֶת צַדִּיקִים שִׂמְחָה
וְתִקְוַת רְשָׁעִים תֹּאבֵד׃

29 מָעוֹז לַתֹּם דֶּרֶךְ יְהוָה
וּמְחִתָּה לְפֹעֲלֵי אָוֶן׃

30 צַדִּיק לְעוֹלָם בַּל־יִמּוֹט
וּרְשָׁעִים לֹא יִשְׁכְּנוּ־אָרֶץ׃

31 פִּי־צַדִּיק יָנוּב חָכְמָה
וּלְשׁוֹן תַּהְפֻּכוֹת תִּכָּרֵת׃

32 שִׂפְתֵי צַדִּיק יֵדְעוּן רָצוֹן
וּפִי רְשָׁעִים תַּהְפֻּכוֹת׃

יא מֹאזְנֵי מִרְמָה תּוֹעֲבַת יְהוָה
וְאֶבֶן שְׁלֵמָה רְצוֹנוֹ׃

2 בָּא־זָדוֹן וַיָּבֹא קָלוֹן
וְאֶת־צְנוּעִים חָכְמָה׃

3 תֻּמַּת יְשָׁרִים תַּנְחֵם
וְסֶלֶף בּוֹגְדִים וְשָׁדֵּם יְשָׁדֵּם׃

4 לֹא־יוֹעִיל הוֹן בְּיוֹם עֶבְרָה
וּצְדָקָה תַּצִּיל מִמָּוֶת׃

5 צִדְקַת תָּמִים תְּיַשֵּׁר דַּרְכּוֹ
וּבְרִשְׁעָתוֹ יִפֹּל רָשָׁע׃

6 צִדְקַת יְשָׁרִים תַּצִּילֵם

---

a   Lit. "whole."

But the treacherous are trapped by their malice.

7At death the hopes of a wicked man are doomed,
And the ambition of evil men comes to nothing.

8The righteous man is rescued from trouble
And the wicked man takes his place.

9The impious man destroys his neighbor through
    speech,
But through their knowledge the righteous are
    rescued.

10When the righteous prosper the city exults;
When the wicked perish there are shouts of joy.

11A city is built up by the blessing of the upright,
But it is torn down by the speech of the wicked.

12He who speaks contemptuously of his fellow-
    man is devoid of sense;
A prudent man keeps his peace.

13A base fellow gives away secrets,
But a trustworthy soul keeps a confidence.

14For want of strategy an army falls,
But victory comes with much planning.

15Harm awaits him who stands surety for
    another;[b]
He who spurns pledging shall be secure.

16A graceful woman obtains honor;
Ruthless men obtain wealth.

17A kindly man benefits himself;
A cruel man makes trouble for himself.

18The wicked man earns illusory wages,
But he who sows righteousness has a true reward.

19Righteousness is a prop of life,
But to pursue evil leads to death.

20Men of crooked mind are an abomination to
    the LORD,
But those whose way is blameless please Him.

21Assuredly,[c] the evil man will not escape,
But the offspring of the righteous will be safe.

22Like a gold ring in the snout of a pig
Is a beautiful woman bereft of sense.

23What the righteous desire can only be good;

וּבְהַוַּת בֹּגְדִים יִלָּכֵדוּ:

7 בְּמוֹת אָדָם רָשָׁע תֹּאבַד תִּקְוָה
וְתוֹחֶלֶת אוֹנִים אָבָדָה:

8 צַדִּיק מִצָּרָה נֶחֱלָץ
וַיָּבֹא רָשָׁע תַּחְתָּיו:

9 בְּפֶה חָנֵף יַשְׁחִת רֵעֵהוּ
וּבְדַעַת צַדִּיקִים יֵחָלֵצוּ:

10 בְּטוּב צַדִּיקִים תַּעֲלֹץ קִרְיָה
וּבַאֲבֹד רְשָׁעִים רִנָּה:

11 בְּבִרְכַּת יְשָׁרִים תָּרוּם קָרֶת
וּבְפִי רְשָׁעִים תֵּהָרֵס:

12 בָּז־לְרֵעֵהוּ חֲסַר־לֵב
וְאִישׁ תְּבוּנוֹת יַחֲרִישׁ:

13 הוֹלֵךְ רָכִיל מְגַלֶּה־סּוֹד
וְנֶאֱמַן־רוּחַ מְכַסֶּה דָבָר:

14 בְּאֵין תַּחְבֻּלוֹת יִפָּל־עָם
וּתְשׁוּעָה בְּרֹב יוֹעֵץ:

15 רַע־יֵרוֹעַ כִּי־עָרַב זָר
וְשֹׂנֵא תֹקְעִים בּוֹטֵחַ:

16 אֵשֶׁת־חֵן תִּתְמֹךְ כָּבוֹד
וְעָרִיצִים יִתְמְכוּ־עֹשֶׁר:

17 גֹּמֵל נַפְשׁוֹ אִישׁ חָסֶד
וְעֹכֵר שְׁאֵרוֹ אַכְזָרִי:

18 רָשָׁע עֹשֶׂה פְעֻלַּת־שָׁקֶר
וְזֹרֵעַ צְדָקָה שֶׂכֶר אֱמֶת:

19 כֵּן־צְדָקָה לְחַיִּים
וּמְרַדֵּף רָעָה לְמוֹתוֹ:

20 תּוֹעֲבַת יְהוָה עִקְּשֵׁי־לֵב
וּרְצוֹנוֹ תְּמִימֵי דָרֶךְ:

21 יָד לְיָד לֹא־יִנָּקֶה רָּע*
וְזֶרַע צַדִּיקִים נִמְלָט:

22 נֶזֶם זָהָב בְּאַף חֲזִיר
אִשָּׁה יָפָה וְסָרַת טָעַם:

23 תַּאֲוַת צַדִּיקִים אַךְ־טוֹב

v. 21. ר׳ דגושה

b   Or "a stranger."
c   Lit. "Hand to hand"; meaning of Heb. uncertain.

What the wicked hope for [stirs] wrath.

24One man gives generously and ends with more;

Another stints on doing the right thing and incurs
a loss.

25A generous person enjoys prosperity;

He who satisfies others shall himself be sated.

26He who withholds grain earns the curses of the
people,

But blessings are on the head of the one who dis-
penses it.

27He who earnestly seeks what is good pursues
what is pleasing;

He who is bent on evil, upon him it shall come.

28He who trusts in his wealth shall fall,

But the righteous shall flourish like foliage.

29He who makes trouble for his household shall
inherit the wind;

A fool is a slave to the wise-hearted.

30The fruit of the righteous is a tree of life;

A wise man captivates people.

31If the righteous on earth get their deserts,

How much more the wicked man and the sinner.

תִּקְוַת רְשָׁעִים עֶבְרָה׃

24 יֵשׁ מְפַזֵּר וְנוֹסָף עוֹד

וְחוֹשֵׂךְ מִיֹּשֶׁר אַךְ־לְמַחְסוֹר׃

25 נֶפֶשׁ־בְּרָכָה תְדֻשָּׁן

וּמַרְוֶה גַּם־הוּא יוֹרֶא*׃

26 מֹנֵעַ בָּר יִקְּבֻהוּ לְאוֹם

וּבְרָכָה לְרֹאשׁ מַשְׁבִּיר׃

27 שֹׁחֵר טוֹב יְבַקֵּשׁ רָצוֹן

וְדֹרֵשׁ רָעָה תְבוֹאֶנּוּ׃

28 בּוֹטֵחַ בְּעָשְׁרוֹ הוּא יִפֹּל

וְכֶעָלֶה צַדִּיקִים יִפְרָחוּ׃

29 עוֹכֵר בֵּיתוֹ יִנְחַל־רוּחַ

וְעֶבֶד אֱוִיל לַחֲכַם־לֵב׃

30 פְּרִי־צַדִּיק עֵץ חַיִּים

וְלֹקֵחַ נְפָשׁוֹת חָכָם׃

31 הֵן צַדִּיק בָּאָרֶץ יְשֻׁלָּם

אַף כִּי־רָשָׁע וְחוֹטֵא׃

12

He who loves discipline loves knowledge;

He who spurns reproof is a brutish man.

2A good man earns the favor of the LORD,

A man of intrigues, His condemnation.

3A man cannot be established in wickedness,

But the root of the righteous will not be shaken
loose.

4A capable wife is a crown for her husband,

But an incompetent one is like rot in his bones.

5The purposes of the righteous are justice,

The schemes of the wicked are deceit.

6The words of the wicked are a deadly ambush,

But the speech of the upright saves them.

7Overturn the wicked and they are gone,

But the house of the righteous will endure.

יב אֹהֵב מוּסָר אֹהֵב דָּעַת

וְשֹׂנֵא תוֹכַחַת בָּעַר׃

2 טוֹב יָפִיק רָצוֹן מֵיהוָה

וְאִישׁ מְזִמּוֹת יַרְשִׁיעַ׃

3 לֹא־יִכּוֹן אָדָם בְּרֶשַׁע

וְשֹׁרֶשׁ צַדִּיקִים בַּל־יִמּוֹט׃

4 אֵשֶׁת־חַיִל עֲטֶרֶת בַּעְלָהּ

וּכְרָקָב בְּעַצְמוֹתָיו מְבִישָׁה׃

5 מַחְשְׁבוֹת צַדִּיקִים מִשְׁפָּט

תַּחְבֻּלוֹת רְשָׁעִים מִרְמָה׃

6 דִּבְרֵי רְשָׁעִים אֱרָב־דָּם

וּפִי יְשָׁרִים יַצִּילֵם׃

7 הָפוֹךְ רְשָׁעִים וְאֵינָם

וּבֵית צַדִּיקִים יַעֲמֹד׃

א' במקום ה'   v. 25.

8A man is commended according to his intelligence;
A twisted mind is held up to contempt.

9Better to be lightly esteemed and have a servant
Than to put on airs and have no food.

10A righteous man knows the needs of his beast,
But the compassion of the wicked is cruelty.

11He who tills his land shall have food in plenty,
But he who pursues vanities is devoid of sense.

12a-The wicked covet the catch of evil men;
The root of the righteous yields [fruit].-a

13Sinful speech is a trap for the evil man,
But the righteous escapes from trouble.

14A man gets his fill of good from the fruit of his
speech;
One is repaid in kind for one's deeds.

15The way of a fool is right in his own eyes;
But the wise man accepts advice.

16A fool's vexation is known at once,
But a clever man conceals his humiliation.

17He who testifies faithfully tells the truth,
But a false witness, deceit.

18There is blunt talk like sword-thrusts,
But the speech of the wise is healing.

19Truthful speech abides forever,
A lying tongue for but a moment.

20Deceit is in the minds of those who plot evil;
For those who plan good there is joy.

21No harm befalls the righteous,
But the wicked have their fill of misfortune.

22Lying speech is an abomination to the LORD,
But those who act faithfully please Him.

23A clever man conceals what he knows,
But the mind of a dullard cries out folly.

24The hand of the diligent wields authority;
The negligent are held in subjection.

25If there is anxiety in a man's mind let him
quash it,
And turn it into joy with a good word.

8 לְפִי־שִׂכְלוֹ יְהֻלַּל־אִישׁ
וְנַעֲוֵה־לֵב יִהְיֶה לָבוּז:
9 טוֹב נִקְלֶה וְעֶבֶד לוֹ
מִמְּתַכַּבֵּד וַחֲסַר־לָחֶם:
10 יוֹדֵעַ צַדִּיק נֶפֶשׁ בְּהֶמְתּוֹ
וְרַחֲמֵי רְשָׁעִים אַכְזָרִי:
11 עֹבֵד אַדְמָתוֹ יִשְׂבַּע־לָחֶם
וּמְרַדֵּף רֵיקִים חֲסַר־לֵב:
12 חָמַד רָשָׁע מְצוֹד רָעִים
וְשֹׁרֶשׁ צַדִּיקִים יִתֵּן:
13 בְּפֶשַׁע שְׂפָתַיִם מוֹקֵשׁ רָע
וַיֵּצֵא מִצָּרָה צַדִּיק:
14 מִפְּרִי פִי־אִישׁ יִשְׂבַּע־טוֹב
וּגְמוּל יְדֵי־אָדָם ישוב יָשִׁיב לוֹ:
15 דֶּרֶךְ אֱוִיל יָשָׁר בְּעֵינָיו
וְשֹׁמֵעַ לְעֵצָה חָכָם:
16 אֱוִיל בַּיּוֹם יִוָּדַע כַּעְסוֹ
וְכֹסֶה קָלוֹן עָרוּם:
17 יָפִיחַ אֱמוּנָה יַגִּיד צֶדֶק
וְעֵד שְׁקָרִים מִרְמָה:
18 יֵשׁ בּוֹטֶה כְּמַדְקְרוֹת חָרֶב
וּלְשׁוֹן חֲכָמִים מַרְפֵּא:
19 שְׂפַת־אֱמֶת תִּכּוֹן לָעַד
וְעַד־אַרְגִּיעָה לְשׁוֹן שָׁקֶר:
20 מִרְמָה בְּלֶב־חֹרְשֵׁי רָע
וּלְיֹעֲצֵי שָׁלוֹם שִׂמְחָה:
21 לֹא־יְאֻנֶּה לַצַּדִּיק כָּל־אָוֶן
וּרְשָׁעִים מָלְאוּ רָע:
22 תּוֹעֲבַת יְהוָה שִׂפְתֵי־שָׁקֶר
וְעֹשֵׂי אֱמוּנָה רְצוֹנוֹ:
23 אָדָם עָרוּם כֹּסֶה דָּעַת
וְלֵב כְּסִילִים יִקְרָא אִוֶּלֶת:
24 יַד־חָרוּצִים תִּמְשׁוֹל
וּרְמִיָּה תִּהְיֶה לָמַס:
25 דְּאָגָה בְלֶב־אִישׁ יַשְׁחֶנָּה
וְדָבָר טוֹב יְשַׂמְּחֶנָּה:

a-a   *Meaning of Heb. uncertain.*

²⁶A righteous man ᵃ-gives his friend direction,-ᵃ
But the way of the wicked leads astray.

²⁷A negligent man never has game to roast;
ᵃ-A diligent man has precious wealth.-ᵃ

²⁸The road of righteousness leads to life;
By way of its path there is no death.

26	יַ֭תֵּר מֵרֵעֵ֣הוּ צַדִּ֑יק וְדֶ֖רֶךְ רְשָׁעִ֣ים תַּתְעֵֽם׃
27	לֹא־יַחֲרֹ֣ךְ רְמִיָּ֣ה צֵידֹ֑ו וְהֹון־אָדָ֖ם יָקָ֣ר חָרֽוּץ׃
28	בְּאֹֽרַח־צְדָקָ֥ה חַיִּ֑ים וְדֶ֖רֶךְ נְתִיבָ֣ה אַל*־מָֽוֶת׃

13 ‎ רג

A wise son—it is through the discipline of his father;
A scoffer—he never heard reproof.

²A man enjoys good from the fruit of his speech;
But out of the throat of the treacherous comes lawlessness.

³He who guards his tongueᵃ preserves his life;
He who opens wide his lips, it is his ruin.

⁴A lazy man craves, but has nothing;
The diligent shall feast on rich fare.

⁵A righteous man hates lies;
The wicked man is vile and disgraceful.

⁶Righteousness protects him whose way is blameless;
Wickedness subverts the sinner.

⁷One man pretends to be rich and has nothing;
Another professes to be poor and has much wealth.

⁸Riches are ransom for a man's life,
The poor never heard a reproof.

⁹The light of the righteous is radiant;
The lamp of the wicked is extinguished.

¹⁰ᵇ-Arrogance yields nothing but strife;-ᵇ
Wisdom belongs to those who seek advice.

¹¹Wealth may dwindle to less than nothing,
But he who gathers little by little increases it.

¹²Hope deferred sickens the heart,
But desire realized is a tree of life.

¹³He who disdains a precept will be injured thereby;
He who respects a command will be rewarded.

	בֵּ֣ן חָ֭כָם מ֣וּסַר אָ֑ב וְ֝לֵ֗ץ לֹא־שָׁמַ֥ע גְּעָרָֽה׃
2	מִפְּרִ֣י פִי־אִ֭ישׁ יֹ֣אכַל ט֑וֹב וְנֶ֖פֶשׁ בֹּגְדִ֣ים חָמָֽס׃
3	נֹצֵ֣ר פִּ֭יו שֹׁמֵ֣ר נַפְשֹׁ֑ו פֹּשֵׂ֥ק שְׂ֝פָתָ֗יו מְחִתָּה־לֹֽו׃
4	מִתְאַוָּ֣ה וָ֭אַיִן נַפְשֹׁ֣ו עָצֵ֑ל וְנֶ֖פֶשׁ חָרֻצִ֣ים תְּדֻשָּֽׁן׃
5	דְּבַר־שֶׁ֭קֶר יִשְׂנָ֣א צַדִּ֑יק וְ֝רָשָׁ֗ע יַבְאִ֥ישׁ וְיַחְפִּֽיר׃
6	צְ֭דָקָה תִּצֹּ֣ר תָּם־דָּ֑רֶךְ וְ֝רִשְׁעָ֗ה תְּסַלֵּ֥ף חַטָּֽאת׃
7	יֵ֣שׁ מִ֭תְעַשֵּׁר וְאֵ֣ין כֹּ֑ל מִ֝תְרוֹשֵׁ֗שׁ וְהֹ֣ון רָֽב׃
8	כֹּ֣פֶר נֶֽפֶשׁ־אִ֣ישׁ עָשְׁרֹ֑ו וְ֝רָ֗שׁ לֹא־שָׁמַ֥ע גְּעָרָֽה׃
9	אֹֽור־צַדִּיקִ֥ים יִשְׂמָ֑ח וְנֵ֖ר רְשָׁעִ֣ים יִדְעָֽךְ׃
10	רַק־בְּ֭זָדֹון יִתֵּ֣ן מַצָּ֑ה וְאֶת־נֹ֖ועָצִ֣ים חָכְמָֽה׃
11	הֹ֭ון מֵהֶ֣בֶל יִמְעָ֑ט וְקֹבֵ֖ץ עַל־יָ֣ד יַרְבֶּֽה׃
12	תֹּוחֶ֣לֶת מְ֭מֻשָּׁכָה מַחֲלָה־לֵ֑ב וְעֵ֥ץ חַ֝יִּ֗ים תַּאֲוָ֥ה בָאָֽה׃
13	בָּ֣ז לְ֭דָבָר יֵחָ֣בֶל לֹ֑ו וִירֵ֥א מִ֝צְוָ֗ה ה֣וּא יְשֻׁלָּֽם׃

ᵃ Lit. "mouth."
ᵇ⁻ᵇ Meaning of Heb. uncertain.

סבירין ומטעין "אַל", כלומר שנוי תנועה   v. 28.

14The instruction of a wise man is a fountain of
  life,
Enabling one to avoid deadly snares.
15Good sense wins favor;
The way of treacherous men is unchanging.c
16Every clever man acts knowledgeably,
But a dullard exposes his stupidity.
17Harm befalls a wicked messenger;
A faithful courier brings healing.
18Poverty and humiliation are for him who spurns
  discipline;
But he who takes reproof to heart gets honor.
19Desire realized is sweet to the soul;
To turn away from evil is abhorrent to the stupid.
20He who keeps company with the wise becomes
  wise,
But he who consorts with dullards comes to grief.
21Misfortune pursues sinners,
But the righteous are well rewarded.
22A good man has what to bequeath to his grandchildren,
For the wealth of sinners is stored up for the righteous.
23The tillage of the poor yields much food;
But substance is swept away for lack of moder-
  ation.
24He who spares the rod hates his son,
But he who loves him disciplines him early.
25The righteous man eats to his heart's content,
But the belly of the wicked is empty.

14 The wisest of women builds her house,
But folly tears it down with its own hands.
2He who maintains his integrity fears the Lord;
A man of devious ways scorns Him.
3In the mouth of a fool is a rod of haughtiness,
But the lips of the wise protect them.
4If there are no oxen the crib is clean,

14 תּוֹרַת חָכָם מְקוֹר חַיִּים
לָסוּר מִמֹּקְשֵׁי מָוֶת:
15 שֵׂכֶל־טוֹב יִתֶּן־חֵן
וְדֶרֶךְ בֹּגְדִים אֵיתָן:
16 כָּל־עָרוּם יַעֲשֶׂה בְדָעַת
וּכְסִיל יִפְרֹשׂ אִוֶּלֶת:
17 מַלְאָךְ רָשָׁע יִפֹּל בְּרָע
וְצִיר אֱמוּנִים מַרְפֵּא:
18 רֵישׁ וְקָלוֹן פּוֹרֵעַ מוּסָר
וְשׁוֹמֵר תּוֹכַחַת יְכֻבָּד:
19 תַּאֲוָה נִהְיָה תֶּעֱרַב לְנָפֶשׁ
וְתוֹעֲבַת כְּסִילִים סוּר מֵרָע:
20 הֹלֵךְ אֶת־חֲכָמִים וחכם
יֶחְכָּם
וְרֹעֶה כְסִילִים יֵרוֹעַ:
21 חַטָּאִים תְּרַדֵּף רָעָה
וְאֶת־צַדִּיקִים יְשַׁלֶּם־טוֹב:
22 טוֹב יַנְחִיל בְּנֵי־בָנִים
וְצָפוּן לַצַּדִּיק חֵיל חוֹטֵא:
23 רָב־אֹכֶל נִיר רָאשִׁים*
וְיֵשׁ נִסְפֶּה בְּלֹא מִשְׁפָּט:
24 חוֹשֵׂךְ שִׁבְטוֹ שׂוֹנֵא בְנוֹ
וְאֹהֲבוֹ שִׁחֲרוֹ מוּסָר:
25 צַדִּיק אֹכֵל לְשֹׂבַע נַפְשׁוֹ
וּבֶטֶן רְשָׁעִים תֶּחְסָר: פ

יד חַכְמוֹת נָשִׁים בָּנְתָה בֵיתָהּ
וְאִוֶּלֶת בְּיָדֶיהָ תֶהֶרְסֶנּוּ:
2 הוֹלֵךְ בְּיָשְׁרוֹ יְרֵא יְהוָה
וּנְלוֹז דְּרָכָיו בּוֹזֵהוּ:
3 בְּפִי־אֱוִיל חֹטֶר גַּאֲוָה
וְשִׂפְתֵי חֲכָמִים תִּשְׁמוּרֵם:
4 בְּאֵין אֲלָפִים אֵבוּס בָּר

---

c Or "harsh."   יתיר א' v. 23.

But a rich harvest comes through the strength of
the ox.

5An honest witness will not lie;
A false witness testifies lies.

6A scoffer seeks wisdom in vain,
But knowledge comes easily to the intelligent
man.

7Keep your distance from a dullard,
For you will not learn wise speech.

8It is the wisdom of a clever man to understand
his course;
But the stupidity of the dullard is delusion.

9Reparations mediate between fools,
Between the upright, good will.

10The heart alone knows its bitterness,
And no outsider can share in its joy.

11The house of the wicked will be demolished,
But the tent of the upright will flourish.

12A road may seem right to a man,
But in the end it is a road to death.

13The heart may ache even in laughter,
And joy may end in grief.

14An unprincipled man reaps the fruits of his
ways;
a-A good man, of his deeds.-*a*

15A simple person believes anything;
A clever man ponders his course.

16A wise man is diffident and shuns evil,
But a dullard rushes in confidently.

17An impatient man commits folly;
A man of intrigues will be hated.

18Folly is the lot of the simple,
But clever men *b*-glory in knowledge.-*b*

19Evil men are brought low before the good,
So are the wicked at the gates of the righteous.

20A pauper is despised even by his peers,
But a rich man has many friends.

21He who despises his fellow is wrong;
He who shows pity for the lowly is happy.

וְרָב־תְּבוּאוֹת בְּכֹחַ שׁוֹר׃

5 עֵד אֱמוּנִים לֹא יְכַזֵּב
וְיָפִיחַ כְּזָבִים עֵד שָׁקֶר׃

6 בִּקֶּשׁ־לֵץ חָכְמָה וָאָיִן
וְדַעַת לְנָבוֹן נָקָל׃

7 לֵךְ מִנֶּגֶד לְאִישׁ כְּסִיל
וּבַל־יָדַעְתָּ שִׂפְתֵי־דָעַת׃

8 חָכְמַת עָרוּם הָבִין דַּרְכּוֹ
וְאִוֶּלֶת כְּסִילִים מִרְמָה׃

9 אֱוִלִים יָלִיץ אָשָׁם
וּבֵין יְשָׁרִים רָצוֹן׃

10 לֵב יוֹדֵעַ מָרַּת* נַפְשׁוֹ
וּבְשִׂמְחָתוֹ לֹא־יִתְעָרַב זָר׃

11 בֵּית רְשָׁעִים יִשָּׁמֵד
וְאֹהֶל יְשָׁרִים יַפְרִיחַ׃

12 יֵשׁ דֶּרֶךְ יָשָׁר לִפְנֵי־אִישׁ
וְאַחֲרִיתָהּ דַּרְכֵי־מָוֶת׃

13 גַּם־בִּשְׂחוֹק יִכְאַב־לֵב
וְאַחֲרִיתָהּ שִׂמְחָה תוּגָה׃

14 מִדְּרָכָיו יִשְׂבַּע סוּג לֵב
וּמֵעָלָיו אִישׁ טוֹב׃

15 פֶּתִי יַאֲמִין לְכָל־דָּבָר
וְעָרוּם יָבִין לַאֲשֻׁרוֹ׃

16 חָכָם יָרֵא וְסָר מֵרָע
וּכְסִיל מִתְעַבֵּר וּבוֹטֵחַ׃

17 קְצַר־אַפַּיִם יַעֲשֶׂה אִוֶּלֶת
וְאִישׁ מְזִמּוֹת יִשָּׂנֵא׃

18 נָחֲלוּ פְתָאיִם* אִוֶּלֶת
וַעֲרוּמִים יַכְתִּרוּ דָעַת׃

19 שַׁחוּ רָעִים לִפְנֵי טוֹבִים
וּרְשָׁעִים עַל־שַׁעֲרֵי צַדִּיק׃

20 גַּם־לְרֵעֵהוּ יִשָּׂנֵא רָשׁ
וְאֹהֲבֵי עָשִׁיר רַבִּים׃

21 בָּז־לְרֵעֵהוּ חוֹטֵא
וּמְחוֹנֵן עֲנִיִּים עֲנָוִים אַשְׁרָיו׃

v. 10. ר׳ דגושה
v. 18. יתיר א׳

---

a-a   Taking '*al* as from '*ll*; cf. Hos. 12.3.
b-b   Meaning of Heb. uncertain.

22Surely those who plan evil go astray,
While those who plan good earn steadfast love.

22 הֲלוֹא־יִתְעוּ חֹרְשֵׁי רָע
וְחֶסֶד וֶאֱמֶת חֹרְשֵׁי טוֹב׃

23From all toil there is some gain,
But idle chatter is pure loss.

23 בְּכָל־עֶצֶב יִהְיֶה מוֹתָר
וּדְבַר־שְׂפָתַיִם אַךְ־לְמַחְסוֹר׃

24The ornament of the wise is their wealth;
The stupidity of dullards is stupidity.

24 עֲטֶרֶת חֲכָמִים עָשְׁרָם
אִוֶּלֶת כְּסִילִים אִוֶּלֶת׃

25A truthful witness saves lives;
He who testifies lies [spreads] deceit.

25 מַצִּיל נְפָשׁוֹת עֵד אֱמֶת
וְיָפִחַ כְּזָבִים מִרְמָה׃

26Fear of the LORD is a stronghold,
A refuge for a man's children.

26 בְּיִרְאַת יְהוָה מִבְטַח־עֹז
וּלְבָנָיו יִהְיֶה מַחְסֶה׃

27Fear of the LORD is a fountain of life,
Enabling one to avoid deadly snares.

27 יִרְאַת יְהוָה מְקוֹר חַיִּים
לָסוּר מִמֹּקְשֵׁי מָוֶת׃

28A numerous people is the glory of a king;
Without a nation a ruler is ruined.

28 בְּרָב־עָם הַדְרַת־מֶלֶךְ
וּבְאֶפֶס לְאֹם מְחִתַּת רָזוֹן׃

29Patience results in much understanding;
Impatience gets folly as its portion.

29 אֶרֶךְ אַפַּיִם רַב־תְּבוּנָה
וּקְצַר־רוּחַ מֵרִים אִוֶּלֶת׃

30A calm disposition gives bodily health;
Passion is rot to the bones.

30 חַיֵּי בְשָׂרִים לֵב מַרְפֵּא
וּרְקַב עֲצָמוֹת קִנְאָה׃

31He who withholds what is due to the poor
   affronts his Maker;
He who shows pity for the needy honors Him.

31 עֹשֵׁק־דָּל חֵרֵף עֹשֵׂהוּ
וּמְכַבְּדוֹ חֹנֵן אֶבְיוֹן׃

32The wicked man is felled by his own evil;
The righteous man finds security in his death.

32 בְּרָעָתוֹ יִדָּחֶה רָשָׁע
וְחֹסֶה בְמוֹתוֹ צַדִּיק׃

33Wisdom rests quietly in the mind of a prudent
   man,
But among dullards it makes itself known.

33 בְּלֵב נָבוֹן תָּנוּחַ חָכְמָה
וּבְקֶרֶב כְּסִילִים תִּוָּדֵעַ׃

34Righteousness exalts a nation;
Sin is a reproach to any people.

34 צְדָקָה תְרוֹמֵם־גּוֹי
וְחֶסֶד לְאֻמִּים חַטָּאת׃

35The king favors a capable servant;
He rages at an incompetent one.

35 רְצוֹן־מֶלֶךְ לְעֶבֶד מַשְׂכִּיל
וְעֶבְרָתוֹ תִּהְיֶה מֵבִישׁ׃

15

A gentle response allays wrath;
A harsh word provokes anger.

טו מַעֲנֶה־רַּךְ* יָשִׁיב חֵמָה
וּדְבַר־עֶצֶב יַעֲלֶה־אָף׃

2The tongue of the wise produces much knowledge,
But the mouth of dullards pours out folly.

2 לְשׁוֹן חֲכָמִים תֵּיטִיב דָּעַת
וּפִי כְסִילִים יַבִּיעַ אִוֶּלֶת׃

3The eyes of the LORD are everywhere,
Observing the bad and the good.

3 בְּכָל־מָקוֹם עֵינֵי יְהוָה
צֹפוֹת רָעִים וְטוֹבִים׃

ר׳ דגושה   v. 1.

⁴A healing tongue is a tree of life,
But a devious one makes for a broken spirit.

⁵A fool spurns the discipline of his father,
But one who heeds reproof becomes clever.

⁶In the house of the righteous there is much
   treasure,
But in the harvest of the wicked there is trouble.

⁷The lips of the wise disseminate knowledge;
Not so the minds of dullards.

⁸The sacrifice of the wicked is an abomination to
   the Lord,
But the prayer of the upright pleases Him.

⁹The way of the wicked is an abomination to the
   Lord,
But He loves him who pursues righteousness.

¹⁰Discipline seems bad to him who forsakes the
   way;
He who spurns reproof will die.

¹¹Sheol and Abaddon lie exposed to the Lord,
How much more the minds of men!

¹²The scoffer dislikes being reproved;
He will not resort to the wise.

¹³A joyful heart makes a cheerful face;
A sad heart makes a despondent mood.

¹⁴The mind of a prudent man seeks knowledge;
The mouth of the dullard pursues folly.

¹⁵All the days of a poor man are wretched,
But contentment is a feast without end.

¹⁶Better a little with fear of the Lord
Than great wealth with confusion.

¹⁷Better a meal of vegetables where there is love
Than a fattened ox where there is hate.

¹⁸A hot-tempered man provokes a quarrel;
A patient man calms strife.

¹⁹The way of a lazy man is like a hedge of thorns,
But the path of the upright is paved.

²⁰A wise son makes his father happy;
A fool of a man humiliates his mother.

²¹Folly is joy to one devoid of sense;

4 מַרְפֵּא לָשׁוֹן עֵץ חַיִּים
וְסֶלֶף בָּהּ שֶׁבֶר בְּרוּחַ:

5 אֱוִיל יִנְאַץ מוּסַר אָבִיו
וְשֹׁמֵר תּוֹכַחַת יַעְרִם:

6 בֵּית צַדִּיק חֹסֶן רָב
וּבִתְבוּאַת רָשָׁע נֶעְכָּרֶת:

7 שִׂפְתֵי חֲכָמִים יְזָרוּ דָעַת
וְלֵב כְּסִילִים לֹא־כֵן:

8 זֶבַח רְשָׁעִים תּוֹעֲבַת יְהוָה
וּתְפִלַּת יְשָׁרִים רְצוֹנוֹ:

9 תּוֹעֲבַת יְהוָה דֶּרֶךְ רָשָׁע
וּמְרַדֵּף צְדָקָה יֶאֱהָב:

10 מוּסָר רָע לְעֹזֵב אֹרַח
שׂוֹנֵא תוֹכַחַת יָמוּת:

11 שְׁאוֹל וַאֲבַדּוֹן נֶגֶד יְהוָה
אַף כִּי־לִבּוֹת בְּנֵי־אָדָם:

12 לֹא יֶאֱהַב־לֵץ הוֹכֵחַ לוֹ
אֶל־חֲכָמִים לֹא יֵלֵךְ:

13 לֵב שָׂמֵחַ יֵיטִב פָּנִים
וּבְעַצְּבַת־לֵב רוּחַ נְכֵאָה:

14 לֵב נָבוֹן יְבַקֶּשׁ־דָּעַת
וּפְנֵי כְסִילִים יִרְעֶה אִוֶּלֶת:

15 כָּל־יְמֵי עָנִי רָעִים
וְטוֹב־לֵב מִשְׁתֶּה תָמִיד:

16 טוֹב־מְעַט בְּיִרְאַת יְהוָה
מֵאוֹצָר רָב וּמְהוּמָה בוֹ:

17 טוֹב אֲרֻחַת יָרָק וְאַהֲבָה־שָׁם
מִשּׁוֹר אָבוּס וְשִׂנְאָה־בוֹ:

18 אִישׁ חֵמָה יְגָרֶה מָדוֹן
וְאֶרֶךְ אַפַּיִם יַשְׁקִיט רִיב:

19 דֶּרֶךְ עָצֵל כִּמְשֻׂכַת חָדֶק
וְאֹרַח יְשָׁרִים סְלֻלָה:

20 בֵּן חָכָם יְשַׂמַּח־אָב
וּכְסִיל אָדָם בּוֹזֶה אִמּוֹ:

21 אִוֶּלֶת שִׂמְחָה לַחֲסַר־לֵב

A prudent man walks a straight path.

²²Plans are foiled for want of counsel,

But they succeed through many advisers.

²³A ready response is a joy to a man,

And how good is a word rightly timed!

²⁴For an intelligent man the path of life leads up-

ward,

In order to avoid Sheol below.

²⁵The Lord will tear down the house of the proud,

But He will establish the homestead of the widow.

²⁶Evil thoughts are an abomination to the Lord,

But pleasant words are pure.

²⁷He who pursues ill-gotten gain makes trouble

for his household;

He who spurns gifts will live long.

²⁸The heart[a] of the righteous man rehearses his

answer,

But the mouth of the wicked blurts out evil things.

²⁹The Lord is far from the wicked,

But He hears the prayer of the righteous.

³⁰What brightens the eye gladdens the heart;

Good news puts fat on the bones.

³¹He whose ear heeds the discipline of life

Lodges among the wise.

³²He who spurns discipline hates himself;

He who heeds reproof gains understanding.

³³The fear of the Lord is the discipline of wisdom;

Humility precedes honor.

16 A man may arrange his thoughts,

But what he says depends on the Lord.

²All the ways of a man seem right to him,

But the Lord probes motives.

³Entrust your affairs to the Lord,

And your plans will succeed.

⁴The Lord made everything for a purpose,

Even the wicked for an evil day.

⁵Every haughty person is an abomination to the

Lord;

וְאִ֥ישׁ תְּבוּנָ֗ה יְיַשֶּׁר־לָֽכֶת׃

²² הָפֵ֣ר מַ֭חֲשָׁבוֹת בְּאֵ֣ין ס֑וֹד

וּבְרֹ֖ב יוֹעֲצִ֣ים תָּקֽוּם׃

²³ שִׂמְחָ֣ה לָ֭אִישׁ בְּמַעֲנֵה־פִ֑יו

וְדָבָ֖ר בְּעִתּ֣וֹ מַה־טּֽוֹב׃

²⁴ אֹ֣רַח חַ֭יִּים לְמַ֣עְלָה לְמַשְׂכִּ֑יל

לְמַ֥עַן ס֝֗וּר מִשְּׁא֥וֹל מָֽטָּה׃

²⁵ בֵּ֣ית גֵּ֭אִים יִסַּ֥ח ׀ יְהֹוָ֑ה

וְ֝יַצֵּ֗ב גְּב֣וּל אַלְמָנָֽה׃

²⁶ תּוֹעֲבַ֣ת יְ֭הֹוָה מַחְשְׁב֣וֹת רָ֑ע

וּ֝טְהֹרִ֗ים אִמְרֵי־נֹֽעַם׃

²⁷ עֹכֵ֣ר בֵּ֭יתוֹ בּוֹצֵ֣עַ בָּ֑צַע

וְשׂוֹנֵ֖א מַתָּנֹ֣ת יִחְיֶֽה׃

²⁸ לֵ֣ב צַ֭דִּיק יֶהְגֶּ֣ה לַעֲנ֑וֹת

וּפִ֥י רְ֝שָׁעִ֗ים יַבִּ֥יעַ רָעֽוֹת׃

²⁹ רָח֣וֹק יְ֭הֹוָה מֵרְשָׁעִ֑ים

וּתְפִלַּ֖ת צַדִּיקִ֣ים יִשְׁמָֽע׃

³⁰ מְאֽוֹר־עֵ֭ינַיִם יְשַׂמַּֽח־לֵ֑ב

שְׁמוּעָ֥ה ט֝וֹבָ֗ה תְּדַשֶּׁן־עָֽצֶם׃

³¹ אֹ֗זֶן שֹׁ֭מַעַת תּוֹכַ֣חַת חַיִּ֑ים

בְּקֶ֖רֶב חֲכָמִ֣ים תָּלִֽין׃

³² פּוֹרֵ֣עַ מ֭וּסָר מוֹאֵ֣ס נַפְשׁ֑וֹ

וְשׁוֹמֵ֥עַ תּ֝וֹכַ֗חַת ק֣וֹנֶה לֵּֽב׃

³³ יִרְאַ֣ת יְ֭הֹוָה מוּסַ֣ר חׇכְמָ֑ה

וְלִפְנֵ֖י כָב֣וֹד עֲנָוָֽה׃

טז לְאָדָ֥ם מַעַרְכֵי־לֵ֑ב

וּ֝מֵֽיְהֹוָ֗ה מַעֲנֵ֥ה לָשֽׁוֹן׃

² כׇּֽל־דַּרְכֵי־אִ֭ישׁ זַ֣ךְ בְּעֵינָ֑יו

וְתֹכֵ֖ן רוּח֣וֹת יְהֹוָֽה׃

³ גֹּ֣ל אֶל־יְהֹוָ֣ה מַעֲשֶׂ֑יךָ

וְ֝יִכֹּ֗נוּ מַחְשְׁבֹתֶֽיךָ׃

⁴ כֹּ֤ל פָּעַ֣ל יְ֭הֹוָה לַֽמַּעֲנֵ֑הוּ

וְגַם־רָ֝שָׁ֗ע לְי֣וֹם רָעָֽה׃

⁵ תּוֹעֲבַ֣ת יְ֭הֹוָה כׇּל־גְּבַהּ־לֵ֑ב

---

a For *leb* as a source of speech, see note to Eccl. 5.1.

Assuredly,[a] he will not go unpunished.

6Iniquity is expiated by loyalty and faithfulness,
And evil is avoided through fear of the LORD.

7When the LORD is pleased with a man's conduct,
He may turn even his enemies into allies.

8Better a little with righteousness
Than a large income with injustice.

9A man may plot out his course,
But it is the LORD who directs his steps.

10There is magic on the lips of the king;
He cannot err in judgment.

11Honest scales and balances are the LORD's;
All the weights in the bag are His work.

12Wicked deeds are an abomination to kings,
For the throne is established by righteousness.

13Truthful speech wins the favor of kings;
They love those who speak honestly.

14The king's wrath is a messenger of death,
But a wise man can appease it.

15The king's smile means life;
His favor is like a rain cloud in spring.

16How much better to acquire wisdom than gold;
To acquire understanding is preferable to silver.

17The highway of the upright avoids evil;
He who would preserve his life watches his way.

18Pride goes before ruin,
Arrogance, before failure.

19Better to be humble and among the lowly
Than to share spoils with the proud.

20He who is adept in a matter will attain success;
Happy is he who trusts in the LORD.

21The wise-hearted is called discerning;
One whose speech is pleasing gains wisdom.

22Good sense is a fountain of life to those who
    have it,
And folly is the punishment of fools.

---

a   Lit. "Hand to hand"; meaning of Heb. uncertain.

יָ֣ד לְ֭יָד לֹ֣א יִנָּקֶ֑ה׃

6 בְּחֶ֣סֶד וֶ֭אֱמֶת יְכֻפַּ֣ר עָוֺ֑ן
וּבְיִרְאַ֥ת יְ֝הֹוָ֗ה ס֣וּר מֵרָֽע׃

7 בִּרְצ֣וֹת יְ֭הֹוָה דַּרְכֵי־אִ֑ישׁ
גַּם־א֝וֹיְבָ֗יו יַשְׁלִ֥ם אִתּֽוֹ׃

8 טוֹב־מְ֭עַט בִּצְדָקָ֑ה
מֵרֹ֥ב תְּ֝בוּא֗וֹת בְּלֹ֣א מִשְׁפָּֽט׃

9 לֵ֣ב אָ֭דָם יְחַשֵּׁ֣ב דַּרְכּ֑וֹ
וַ֝יהֹוָ֗ה יָכִ֥ין צַעֲדֽוֹ׃

10 קֶ֤סֶם ׀ עַֽל־שִׂפְתֵי־מֶ֑לֶךְ
בְּ֝מִשְׁפָּ֗ט לֹ֣א יִמְעַל־פִּֽיו׃

11 פֶּ֤לֶס ׀ וּמֹאזְנֵ֣י מִ֭שְׁפָּט לַֽיהֹוָ֑ה
מַ֝עֲשֵׂ֗הוּ כׇּל־אַבְנֵי־כִֽיס׃

12 תּוֹעֲבַ֣ת מְ֭לָכִים עֲשׂ֣וֹת רֶ֑שַׁע
כִּ֥י בִ֝צְדָקָ֗ה יִכּ֥וֹן כִּסֵּֽא׃

13 רְצ֣וֹן מְ֭לָכִים שִׂפְתֵי־צֶ֑דֶק
וְדֹבֵ֖ר יְשָׁרִ֣ים יֶֽאֱהָֽב׃

14 חֲמַת־מֶ֥לֶךְ מַלְאֲכֵי־מָ֑וֶת
וְאִ֖ישׁ חָכָ֣ם יְכַפְּרֶֽנָּה׃

15 בְּאוֹר־פְּנֵי־מֶ֥לֶךְ חַיִּ֑ים
וּ֝רְצוֹנ֗וֹ כְּעָ֣ב מַלְקֽוֹשׁ׃

16 קְנֹֽה־חׇכְמָ֗ה מַה־טּ֥וֹב מֵחָר֑וּץ
וּקְנ֥וֹת בִּ֝ינָ֗ה נִבְחָ֥ר מִכָּֽסֶף׃

17 מְסִלַּ֣ת יְ֭שָׁרִים ס֣וּר מֵרָ֑ע
שֹׁמֵ֥ר נַ֝פְשׁ֗וֹ נֹצֵ֥ר דַּרְכּֽוֹ׃

18 * לִפְנֵי־שֶׁ֥בֶר גָּא֑וֹן
וְלִפְנֵ֥י כִ֝שָּׁל֗וֹן גֹּ֣בַהּ רֽוּחַ׃

19 ט֣וֹב שְׁפַל־ר֭וּחַ אֶת־עֲנָוִ֑ים
מֵֽחַלֵּ֥ק שָׁ֝לָ֗ל אֶת־גֵּאִֽים׃

20 מַשְׂכִּ֣יל עַל־דָּ֭בָר יִמְצָא־ט֑וֹב
וּבוֹטֵ֖חַ בַּיהֹוָ֣ה אַשְׁרָֽיו׃

21 לַחֲכַם־לֵ֭ב יִקָּרֵ֣א נָב֑וֹן
וּמֶ֥תֶק שְׂ֝פָתַ֗יִם יֹסִ֥יף לֶֽקַח׃

22 מְק֣וֹר חַ֭יִּים שֵׂ֣כֶל בְּעָלָ֑יו
וּמוּסַ֖ר אֱוִלִ֣ים אִוֶּֽלֶת׃

23The mind of the wise man makes his speech
   effective
And increases the wisdom on his lips.

24Pleasant words are like a honeycomb,
Sweet to the palate and a cure for the body.

25A road may seem right to a man,
But in the end it is a road to death.

26The appetite of a laborer labors for him,
Because his hunger[b] [c-]forces him on.[-c]

27A scoundrel plots[c] evil;
What is on his lips is like a scorching fire.

28A shifty man stirs up strife,
And a querulous one alienates his friend.

29A lawless man misleads his friend,
Making him take the wrong way.

30He closes his eyes while meditating deception;
He purses his lips while deciding upon evil.

31Gray hair is a crown of glory;
It is attained by the way of righteousness.

32Better to be forbearing than mighty,
To have self-control than to conquer a city.

33Lots are cast into the lap;
The decision depends on the LORD.

17

Better a dry crust with peace
Than a house full of feasting with strife.

2A capable servant will dominate an incompetent
   son
And share the inheritance with the brothers.

3For silver—the crucible;
For gold—the furnace,
And the LORD tests the mind.

4An evildoer listens to mischievous talk;
A liar gives ear to malicious words.

5He who mocks the poor affronts his Maker;

23 לֵ֣ב חָ֭כָם יַשְׂכִּ֣יל פִּ֑יהוּ
וְעַל־שְׂ֝פָתָ֗יו יֹסִ֥יף לֶֽקַח׃

24 צוּף־דְּ֭בַשׁ אִמְרֵי־נֹ֑עַם
מָת֥וֹק לַ֝נֶּ֗פֶשׁ וּמַרְפֵּ֥א לָעָֽצֶם׃

25 יֵ֤שׁ דֶּ֣רֶךְ יָ֭שָׁר לִפְנֵי־אִ֑ישׁ
וְ֝אַחֲרִיתָ֗הּ דַּרְכֵי־מָֽוֶת׃

26 נֶ֣פֶשׁ עָ֭מֵל עָ֣מְלָה לּ֑וֹ
כִּֽי־אָכַ֖ף עָלָ֣יו פִּֽיהוּ׃

27 אִ֣ישׁ בְּ֭לִיַּעַל כֹּרֶ֣ה רָעָ֑ה
וְעַל־שְׂ֝פָתָ֗יו כְּאֵ֣שׁ צָרָֽבֶת׃

28 אִ֣ישׁ תַּ֭הְפֻּכוֹת יְשַׁלַּ֣ח מָד֑וֹן
וְ֝נִרְגָּ֗ן* מַפְרִ֥יד אַלּֽוּף׃

29 אִ֣ישׁ חָ֭מָס יְפַתֶּ֣ה רֵעֵ֑הוּ
וְ֝הוֹלִיכ֗וֹ בְּדֶ֣רֶךְ לֹא־טֽוֹב׃

30 עֹצֶ֣ה עֵ֭ינָיו לַחְשֹׁ֣ב תַּהְפֻּכ֑וֹת
קֹרֵ֥ץ שְׂ֝פָתָ֗יו כִּלָּ֥ה רָעָֽה׃

31 עֲטֶ֣רֶת תִּפְאֶ֣רֶת שֵׂיבָ֑ה
בְּדֶ֥רֶךְ צְ֝דָקָ֗ה תִּמָּצֵֽא׃

32 ט֤וֹב אֶ֣רֶךְ אַ֭פַּיִם מִגִּבּ֑וֹר
וּמֹשֵׁ֥ל בְּ֝רוּח֗וֹ מִלֹּכֵ֥ד עִֽיר׃

33 בַּ֭חֵיק יוּטַ֣ל אֶת־הַגּוֹרָ֑ל
וּ֝מֵיְהֹוָ֗ה כׇּל־מִשְׁפָּטֽוֹ׃

יז ט֤וֹב פַּ֣ת חֲ֭רֵבָה וְשַׁלְוָה־בָ֑הּ
מִ֝בַּ֗יִת מָלֵ֥א זִבְחֵי־רִֽיב׃

2 עֶֽבֶד־מַשְׂכִּ֗יל יִ֭מְשֹׁל בְּבֵ֣ן מֵבִ֑ישׁ
וּבְת֥וֹךְ אַ֝חִ֗ים יַחֲלֹ֥ק נַחֲלָֽה׃

3 מַצְרֵ֣ף לַכֶּסֶף֮
וְכ֢וּר לַזָּ֫הָ֥ב
וּבֹחֵ֖ן לִבּ֣וֹת יְהֹוָֽה׃

4 מֵ֭רַע מַקְשִׁ֣יב עַל־שְׂפַת־אָ֑וֶן
שֶׁ֥קֶר מֵ֝זִ֗ין עַל־לְשׁ֥וֹן הַוֺּֽת׃

5 לֹעֵ֣ג לָ֭רָשׁ חֵרֵ֣ף עֹשֵׂ֑הוּ

b   Lit. "mouth."
c-c   Meaning of Heb. uncertain.

He who rejoices over another's misfortune will
not go unpunished.

שָׂמֵחַ לְאֵיד לֹא יִנָּקֶה:

6Grandchildren are the crown of their elders,
And the glory of children is their parents.

6 עֲטֶרֶת זְקֵנִים בְּנֵי בָנִים
וְתִפְאֶרֶת בָּנִים אֲבוֹתָם:

7Lofty words are not fitting for a villain;
Much less lying words for a great man.

7 לֹא־נָאוָה לְנָבָל שְׂפַת־יֶתֶר
אַף כִּי־לְנָדִיב שְׂפַת־שָׁקֶר:

8A bribe seems like a charm to him who uses it;
He succeeds at every turn.

8 אֶבֶן־חֵן הַשֹּׁחַד בְּעֵינֵי בְעָלָיו
אֶל־כָּל־אֲשֶׁר יִפְנֶה יַשְׂכִּיל:

9He who seeks love overlooks faults,
But he who harps on a matter alienates his friend.

9 מְכַסֶּה־פֶּשַׁע מְבַקֵּשׁ אַהֲבָה
וְשֹׁנֶה בְדָבָר מַפְרִיד אַלּוּף:

10A rebuke works on an intelligent man
More than one hundred blows on a fool.

10 תֵּחַת גְּעָרָה בְמֵבִין
מֵהַכּוֹת כְּסִיל מֵאָה:

11An evil man seeks only to rebel;
A ruthless messenger will be sent against him.

11 אַךְ־מְרִי יְבַקֶּשׁ־רָע
וּמַלְאָךְ אַכְזָרִי יְשֻׁלַּח־בּוֹ:

12Sooner meet a bereaved she-bear
Than a fool with his nonsense.

12 פָּגוֹשׁ דֹּב שַׁכּוּל בְּאִישׁ
וְאַל־כְּסִיל בְּאִוַּלְתּוֹ:

13Evil will never depart from the house
Of him who repays good with evil.

13 מֵשִׁיב רָעָה תַּחַת טוֹבָה
לֹא־תָמוּשׁ רָעָה מִבֵּיתוֹ:

14To start a quarrel is to open a sluice;
Before a dispute a-flares up,-a drop it.

14 פּוֹטֵר מַיִם רֵאשִׁית מָדוֹן
וְלִפְנֵי הִתְגַּלַּע הָרִיב נְטוֹשׁ:

15To acquit the guilty and convict the innocent—
Both are an abomination to the LORD.

15 מַצְדִּיק רָשָׁע וּמַרְשִׁיעַ צַדִּיק
תּוֹעֲבַת יְהוָה גַּם־שְׁנֵיהֶם:

16What good is money in the hand of a fool
To purchase wisdom, when he has no mind?

16 לָמָּה־זֶּה מְחִיר בְּיַד־כְּסִיל
לִקְנוֹת חָכְמָה וְלֶב־אָיִן:

17A friend is devoted at all times;
A brother is born to share adversity.

17 בְּכָל־עֵת אֹהֵב הָרֵעַ
וְאָח לְצָרָה יִוָּלֵד:

18Devoid of sense is he who gives his hand
To stand surety for his fellow.

18 אָדָם חֲסַר־לֵב תּוֹקֵעַ כָּף
עֹרֵב עֲרֻבָּה לִפְנֵי רֵעֵהוּ:

19He who loves transgression loves strife;
He who builds a high threshold invites broken
bones.

19 אֹהֵב פֶּשַׁע אֹהֵב מַצָּה
מַגְבִּיהַּ פִּתְחוֹ מְבַקֶּשׁ־שָׁבֶר:

20Man of crooked mind comes to no good,
And he who speaks duplicity falls into trouble.

20 עִקֶּשׁ־לֵב לֹא יִמְצָא־טוֹב
וְנֶהְפָּךְ בִּלְשׁוֹנוֹ יִפּוֹל בְּרָעָה:

21One begets a dullard to one's own grief;
The father of a villain has no joy.

21 יֹלֵד כְּסִיל לְתוּגָה לוֹ
וְלֹא־יִשְׂמַח אֲבִי נָבָל:

22A joyful heart makes for b-good health;-b
Despondency dries up the bones.

22 לֵב שָׂמֵחַ יֵיטִב גֵּהָה
וְרוּחַ נְכֵאָה תְּיַבֶּשׁ־גָּרֶם:

23The wicked man draws a bribe out of his bosom
To pervert the course of justice.

23 שֹׁחַד מֵחֵיק רָשָׁע יִקָּח
לְהַטּוֹת אָרְחוֹת מִשְׁפָּט:

---

a-a   Meaning of Heb. uncertain.
b-b   Or "a cheerful face"; meaning of Heb. uncertain.

24Wisdom lies before the intelligent man;
The eyes of the dullard range to the ends of the
earth.

25A stupid son is vexation for his father
And a heartache for the woman who bore him.

26To punish the innocent is surely not right,
Or to flog the great for their uprightness.

27A knowledgeable man is sparing with his words;
A man of understanding is reticent.

28Even a fool, if he keeps silent, is deemed wise;
Intelligent, if he seals his lips.

18 *a*-He who isolates himself pursues his desires;
He disdains all competence.-*a*

2The fool does not desire understanding,
But only to air his thoughts.

3Comes the wicked man comes derision,
And with the rogue, contempt.

4The words a man speaks are deep waters,
A flowing stream, a fountain of wisdom.

5It is not right to be partial to the guilty
And subvert the innocent in judgment.

6The words of a fool lead to strife;
His speech invites blows.

7The fool's speech is his ruin;
His words are a trap for him.

8The words of a querulous man are bruising;*a*
They penetrate one's inmost parts.

9One who is slack in his work
Is a brother to a vandal.

10The name of the LORD is a tower of strength
To which the righteous man runs and is safe.

11The wealth of a rich man is his fortress;
a-In his fancy-*a* it is a protective wall.

12Before ruin a man's heart is proud;
Humility goes before honor.

13To answer a man before hearing him out

a-a Meaning of Heb. uncertain.

24 אֶת־פְּנֵי מֵבִין חָכְמָה
וְעֵינֵי כְסִיל בִּקְצֵה־אָרֶץ׃
25 כַּעַס לְאָבִיו בֵּן כְּסִיל
וּמֶמֶר לְיוֹלַדְתּוֹ׃
26 גַּם עֲנוֹשׁ לַצַּדִּיק לֹא־טוֹב
לְהַכּוֹת נְדִיבִים עַל־יֹשֶׁר׃
27 חוֹשֵׂךְ אֲמָרָיו יוֹדֵעַ דָּעַת
וקר יְקַר־רוּחַ אִישׁ תְּבוּנָה׃
28 גַּם אֱוִיל מַחֲרִישׁ חָכָם יֵחָשֵׁב
אֹטֵם שְׂפָתָיו נָבוֹן׃

יח לְתַאֲוָה יְבַקֵּשׁ נִפְרָד
בְּכָל־תּוּשִׁיָּה יִתְגַּלָּע׃
2 לֹא־יַחְפֹּץ כְּסִיל בִּתְבוּנָה
כִּי אִם־בְּהִתְגַּלּוֹת לִבּוֹ׃
3 בְּבוֹא־רָשָׁע בָּא גַם־בּוּז
וְעִם־קָלוֹן חֶרְפָּה׃
4 מַיִם עֲמֻקִּים דִּבְרֵי פִי־אִישׁ
נַחַל נֹבֵעַ מְקוֹר חָכְמָה׃
5 שְׂאֵת פְּנֵי־רָשָׁע לֹא־טוֹב
לְהַטּוֹת צַדִּיק בַּמִּשְׁפָּט׃
6 שִׂפְתֵי כְסִיל יָבֹאוּ בְרִיב
וּפִיו לְמַהֲלֻמוֹת יִקְרָא׃
7 פִּי־כְסִיל מְחִתָּה־לוֹ
וּשְׂפָתָיו מוֹקֵשׁ נַפְשׁוֹ׃
8 דִּבְרֵי נִרְגָּן כְּמִתְלַהֲמִים
וְהֵם יָרְדוּ חַדְרֵי־בָטֶן׃
9 גַּם מִתְרַפֶּה בִמְלַאכְתּוֹ
אָח הוּא לְבַעַל מַשְׁחִית׃
10 מִגְדַּל־עֹז שֵׁם יְהוָה
בּוֹ־יָרוּץ צַדִּיק וְנִשְׂגָּב׃
11 הוֹן עָשִׁיר קִרְיַת עֻזּוֹ
וּכְחוֹמָה נִשְׂגָּבָה בְּמַשְׂכִּיתוֹ׃
12 לִפְנֵי־שֶׁבֶר יִגְבַּהּ לֵב־אִישׁ
וְלִפְנֵי כָבוֹד עֲנָוָה׃
13 מֵשִׁיב דָּבָר בְּטֶרֶם יִשְׁמָע

Is foolish and disgraceful.

14A man's spirit can sustain him through illness;
But low spirits—who can bear them?

15The mind of an intelligent man acquires knowledge;
The ears of the wise seek out knowledge.

16A man's gift eases his way
And gives him access to the great.

17The first to plead his case seems right
Till the other party examines him.

18The lot puts an end to strife
And separates those locked in dispute.

19A brother offended is more formidable than a
stronghold;
Such strife is like the bars of a fortress.

20A man's belly is filled by the fruit of his mouth;
He will be filled by the produce of his lips.

21Death and life are in the power of the tongue;
Those who love it will eat its fruit.

22He who finds a wife has found happiness
And has won the favor of the LORD.

23The poor man speaks beseechingly;
The rich man's answer is harsh.

24There are companions to keep one company,
And there is a friend more devoted than a brother.

19 Better a poor man who lives blamelessly
Than one who speaks perversely and is a dullard.

2A person without knowledge is surely not good;
He who moves hurriedly blunders.

3A man's folly subverts his way,
And his heart rages against the LORD.

4Wealth makes many friends,
But a poor man loses his last friend.

5A false witness will not go unpunished;
He who testifies lies will not escape.

6Many court the favor of a great man,
And all are the friends of a dispenser of gifts.

אִוֶּלֶת הִיא־לֹו וּכְלִמָּה:

14 רֽוּחַ־אִישׁ יְכַלְכֵּל מַחֲלֵהוּ
וְרוּחַ נְכֵאָה מִי יִשָּׂאֶנָּה:

15 לֵב נָבֹון יִקְנֶה־דָּעַת
וְאֹזֶן חֲכָמִים תְּבַקֶּשׁ־דָּעַת:

16 מַתָּן אָדָם יַרְחִיב לֹו
וְלִפְנֵי גְדֹלִים יַנְחֶנּוּ:

17 צַדִּיק הָרִאשֹׁון בְּרִיבֹו
יבא ובָֽא־רֵעֵהוּ וַחֲקָרֹו:

18 מִדְיָנִים יַשְׁבִּית הַגֹּורָל
וּבֵין עֲצוּמִים יַפְרִיד:

19 אָח נִפְשָׁע מִקִּרְיַת־עֹז
ומדונים וּמִדְיָנִים כִּבְרִיחַ אַרְמֹון:

20 מִפְּרִי פִי־אִישׁ תִּשְׂבַּע בִּטְנֹו
תְּבוּאַת שְׂפָתָיו יִשְׂבָּע:

21 מָוֶת וְחַיִּים בְּיַד־לָשֹׁון
וְאֹהֲבֶיהָ יֹאכַל פִּרְיָהּ:

22 מָצָא אִשָּׁה מָצָא טֹוב
וַיָּפֶק רָצֹון מֵיְהוָֽה:

23 תַּחֲנוּנִים יְדַבֶּר־רָשׁ
וְעָשִׁיר יַעֲנֶה עַזֹּות:

24 אִישׁ* רֵעִים לְהִתְרֹעֵעַ
וְיֵשׁ אֹהֵב דָּבֵק מֵאָח:

יט טֹוב־רָשׁ הֹולֵךְ בְּתֻמֹּו
מֵעִקֵּשׁ שְׂפָתָיו וְהוּא כְסִיל:

2 גַּם בְּלֹא־דַעַת נֶפֶשׁ לֹא־טֹוב
וְאָץ בְּרַגְלַיִם חֹוטֵא:

3 אִוֶּלֶת אָדָם תְּסַלֵּף דַּרְכֹּו
וְעַל־יְהוָה יִזְעַף לִבֹּו:

4 הֹון יֹסִיף רֵעִים רַבִּים
וְדָל מֵרֵעֵהוּ יִפָּרֵד:

5 עֵד שְׁקָרִים לֹא יִנָּקֶה
וְיָפִיחַ כְּזָבִים לֹא יִמָּלֵט:

6 רַבִּים יְחַלּוּ פְנֵי־נָדִיב
וְכָל־הָרֵעַ לְאִישׁ מַתָּן:

⁷All the brothers of a poor man despise him;

How much more is he shunned by his friends!

^{a-}He who pursues words—they are of no avail.^{-a}

⁸He who acquires wisdom is his own best friend;

He preserves understanding and attains happiness.

⁹A false witness will not go unpunished;

He who testifies falsely is doomed.

¹⁰Luxury is not fitting for a dullard,

Much less that a servant rule over princes.

¹¹A man shows intelligence by his forebearance;

It is his glory when he overlooks an offense.

¹²The rage of a king is like the roar of a lion;

His favor is like dew upon the grass.

¹³A stupid son is a calamity to his father;

The nagging of a wife is like the endless dripping of water.

¹⁴Property and riches are bequeathed by fathers,

But an efficient wife comes from the Lord.

¹⁵Laziness induces sleep,

And a negligent person will go hungry.

¹⁶He who has regard for his life pays regard to commandments;

He who is heedless of his ways will die.

¹⁷He who is generous to the poor makes a loan to the Lord;

He will repay him his due.

¹⁸Discipline your son while there is still hope,

And^b do not ^{c-}set your heart on his destruction.^{-c}

¹⁹A hot-tempered man incurs punishment;

^{a-}If you try to save him you will only make it worse.^{-a}

²⁰Listen to advice and accept discipline

In order that you may be wise in the end.

²¹Many designs are in a man's mind,

But it is the Lord's plan that is accomplished.

^{22a-}Greed is a reproach to a man;^{-a}

Better be poor than a liar.

²³He who fears the Lord earns life;

7 כָּל אֲחֵי־רָשׁ ׀ שְׂנֵאֻהוּ
אַף כִּי מְרֵעֵהוּ רָחֲקוּ מִמֶּנּוּ
מְרַדֵּף אֲמָרִים לא לו־הֵמָּה:
8 קֹנֶה־לֵּב אֹהֵב נַפְשׁוֹ
שֹׁמֵר תְּבוּנָה לִמְצֹא־טוֹב:
9 עֵד שְׁקָרִים לֹא יִנָּקֶה
וְיָפִיחַ כְּזָבִים יֹאבֵד: פ
10 לֹא־נָאוֶה לִכְסִיל תַּעֲנוּג
אַף כִּי־לְעֶבֶד ׀ מְשֹׁל בְּשָׂרִים:
11 שֵׂכֶל אָדָם הֶאֱרִיךְ אַפּוֹ
וְתִפְאַרְתּוֹ עֲבֹר עַל־פָּשַׁע:
12 נַהַם כַּכְּפִיר זַעַף מֶלֶךְ
וּכְטַל עַל־עֵשֶׂב רְצוֹנוֹ:
13 הַוֹּת לְאָבִיו בֵּן כְּסִיל
וְדֶלֶף טֹרֵד מִדְיְנֵי אִשָּׁה:
14 בַּיִת וָהוֹן נַחֲלַת אָבוֹת
וּמֵיְהֹוָה אִשָּׁה מַשְׂכָּלֶת:
15 עַצְלָה תַּפִּיל תַּרְדֵּמָה
וְנֶפֶשׁ רְמִיָּה תִרְעָב:
16 שֹׁמֵר מִצְוָה שֹׁמֵר נַפְשׁוֹ
בּוֹזֵה דְרָכָיו יומת יָמוּת:
17 מַלְוֵה יְהֹוָה חוֹנֵן דָּל
וּגְמֻלוֹ יְשַׁלֶּם־לוֹ:
18 יַסֵּר בִּנְךָ כִּי־יֵשׁ תִּקְוָה
וְאֶל־הֲמִיתוֹ אַל־תִּשָּׂא נַפְשֶׁךָ:
19 גְּרָל גְּדָל־חֵמָה נֹשֵׂא עֹנֶשׁ
כִּי אִם־תַּצִּיל וְעוֹד תּוֹסִף:
20 שְׁמַע עֵצָה וְקַבֵּל מוּסָר
לְמַעַן תֶּחְכַּם בְּאַחֲרִיתֶךָ:
21 רַבּוֹת מַחֲשָׁבוֹת בְּלֶב־אִישׁ
וַעֲצַת יְהֹוָה הִיא תָקוּם:
22 תַּאֲוַת אָדָם חַסְדּוֹ
וְטוֹב־רָשׁ מֵאִישׁ כָּזָב:
23 יִרְאַת יְהֹוָה לְחַיִּים

a-He shall abide in contentment,-*a*
Free from misfortune.

וְשָׂבֵעַ יָלִין
בַּל־יִפָּקֶד רָע:

24The lazy man buries his hand in the bowl;
He will not even bring it to his mouth.

24 טָמַן עָצֵל יָדוֹ בַּצַּלָּחַת
גַּם־אֶל־פִּיהוּ לֹא יְשִׁיבֶנָּה:

25Beat the scoffer and the simple will become
   clever;
Reprove an intelligent man and he gains knowledge.

25 לֵץ תַּכֶּה וּפֶתִי יַעְרִם
וְהוֹכִיחַ לְנָבוֹן יָבִין דָּעַת:

26A son who causes shame and disgrace
Plunders his father, puts his mother to flight.

26 מְשַׁדֶּד־אָב יַבְרִיחַ אֵם
בֵּן מֵבִישׁ וּמַחְפִּיר:

27My son, cease to stray from words of knowledge
And receive discipline.

27 חֲדַל־בְּנִי לִשְׁמֹעַ מוּסָר
לִשְׁגוֹת מֵאִמְרֵי־דָעַת:

28A malicious witness scoffs at justice,
And the speech of the wicked conceals mischief.

28 עֵד בְּלִיַּעַל יָלִיץ מִשְׁפָּט
וּפִי רְשָׁעִים יְבַלַּע־אָוֶן:

29Punishments are in store for scoffers
And blows for the backs of dullards.

29 נָכוֹנוּ לַלֵּצִים שְׁפָטִים
וּמַהֲלֻמוֹת לְגֵו כְּסִילִים:

20 Wine is a scoffer, strong drink a roisterer;
He who is muddled by them will not grow wise.

כ לֵץ הַיַּיִן הֹמֶה שֵׁכָר
וְכָל־שֹׁגֶה בּוֹ לֹא יֶחְכָּם:

2The terror of a king is like the roar of a lion;
He who provokes his anger risks his life.

2 נַהַם כַּכְּפִיר אֵימַת מֶלֶךְ
מִתְעַבְּרוֹ חוֹטֵא נַפְשׁוֹ:

3It is honorable for a man to desist from strife,
But every fool *a*-becomes embroiled.-*a*

3 כָּבוֹד לָאִישׁ שֶׁבֶת מֵרִיב
וְכָל־אֱוִיל יִתְגַּלָּע:

4In winter the lazy man does not plow;
At harvesttime he seeks, and finds nothing.

4 מֵחֹרֶף עָצֵל לֹא־יַחֲרֹשׁ
ישאל וְשָׁאַל בַּקָּצִיר וָאָיִן:

5The designs in a man's mind are deep waters,
But a man of understanding can draw them out.

5 מַיִם עֲמֻקִּים עֵצָה בְלֶב־אִישׁ
וְאִישׁ תְּבוּנָה יִדְלֶנָּה:

6He calls many a man his loyal friend,
But who can find a faithful man?

6 רָב־אָדָם יִקְרָא אִישׁ חַסְדּוֹ
וְאִישׁ אֱמוּנִים מִי יִמְצָא:

7The righteous man lives blamelessly;
Happy are his children who come after him.

7 מִתְהַלֵּךְ בְּתֻמּוֹ צַדִּיק
אַשְׁרֵי בָנָיו אַחֲרָיו:

8The king seated on the throne of judgment
Can winnow out all evil by his glance.

8 מֶלֶךְ יוֹשֵׁב עַל־כִּסֵּא־דִין
מְזָרֶה בְעֵינָיו כָּל־רָע:

9Who can say, "I have cleansed my heart,
I am purged of my sin"?

9 מִי־יֹאמַר זִכִּיתִי לִבִּי
טָהַרְתִּי מֵחַטָּאתִי:

10False weights and false measures,
Both are an abomination to the LORD.

10 אֶבֶן וָאֶבֶן אֵיפָה וְאֵיפָה
תּוֹעֲבַת יְהוָה גַּם־שְׁנֵיהֶם:

a-a *Meaning of Heb. uncertain.*

11A child may be dissembling in his behavior
Even though his actions are blameless and proper.

12The ear that hears, the eye that sees—
The LORD made them both.

13Do not love sleep lest you be impoverished;
Keep your eyes open and you will have plenty of
    food.

14"Bad, bad," says the buyer,
But having moved off, he congratulates himself.

15Gold is plentiful, jewels abundant,
But wise speech is a precious object.

16Seize his garment, for he stood surety for
    another;b
Take it as a pledge, [for he stood surety] for an
    unfamiliar woman.

17Bread gained by fraud may be tasty to a man,
But later his mouth will be filled with gravel.

18Plans laid in council will succeed;
Wage war with stratagems.

19He who gives away secrets is a base fellow;
Do not take up with a garrulous man.

20One who reviles his father or mother,
Light will fail him when darkness comes.

21An estate acquired in haste at the outset
Will not be blessed in the end.

22Do not say, "I will requite evil";
Put your hope in the LORD and He will deliver
    you.

23False weights are an abomination to the LORD;
Dishonest scales are not right.

24A man's steps are decided by the LORD;
What does a man know about his own way?

25It is a snare for a man a-to pledge a sacred gift
    rashly-a
And to give thought to his vows only after they
    have been made.

26A wise king winnows out the wicked,
And turns the wheel upon them.

27The lifebreath of man is the lamp of the LORD

11 גַּם בְּמַעֲלָלָיו יִתְנַכֶּר־נָעַר
אִם־זַךְ וְאִם־יָשָׁר פָּעֳלוֹ:
12 אֹזֶן שֹׁמַעַת וְעַיִן רֹאָה
יְהֹוָה עָשָׂה גַּם־שְׁנֵיהֶם:
13 אַל־תֶּאֱהַב שֵׁנָה פֶּן־תִּוָּרֵשׁ
פְּקַח עֵינֶיךָ שְׂבַע־לָחֶם:
14 רַע רַע יֹאמַר הַקּוֹנֶה
וְאֹזֵל לוֹ אָז יִתְהַלָּל:
15 יֵשׁ זָהָב וְרָב־פְּנִינִים
וּכְלִי יְקָר שִׂפְתֵי־דָעַת:
16 לְקַח־בִּגְדוֹ כִּי־עָרַב זָר
וּבְעַד נׇכְרִיָּה חַבְלֵהוּ:
17 עָרֵב לָאִישׁ לֶחֶם שָׁקֶר
וְאַחַר יִמָּלֵא־פִיהוּ חָצָץ:
18 מַחֲשָׁבוֹת בְּעֵצָה תִכּוֹן
וּבְתַחְבֻּלוֹת עֲשֵׂה מִלְחָמָה:
19 גּוֹלֶה־סּוֹד הוֹלֵךְ רָכִיל
וּלְפֹתֶה שְׂפָתָיו לֹא תִתְעָרָב:
20 מְקַלֵּל אָבִיו וְאִמּוֹ
יִדְעַךְ נֵרוֹ בֶּאֱשׁוּן חֹשֶׁךְ:
21 נַחֲלָה מְבֹחֶלֶת בָּרִאשֹׁנָה
וְאַחֲרִיתָהּ לֹא תְבֹרָךְ:
22 אַל־תֹּאמַר אֲשַׁלְּמָה־רָע
קַוֵּה לַיהֹוָה וְיֹשַׁע לָךְ:
23 תּוֹעֲבַת יְהֹוָה אֶבֶן וָאָבֶן
וּמֹאזְנֵי מִרְמָה לֹא־טוֹב:
24 מֵיְהֹוָה מִצְעֲדֵי־גָבֶר
וְאָדָם מַה־יָּבִין דַּרְכּוֹ:
25 מוֹקֵשׁ אָדָם יָלַע קֹדֶשׁ
וְאַחַר נְדָרִים לְבַקֵּר:
26 מְזָרֶה רְשָׁעִים מֶלֶךְ חָכָם
וַיָּשֶׁב עֲלֵיהֶם אוֹפָן:
27 נֵר יְהֹוָה נִשְׁמַת אָדָם

---

b Or "a stranger."

Revealing all his inmost parts.

28Faithfulness and loyalty protect the king;

He maintains his throne by faithfulness.

29The glory of youths is their strength;

The majesty of old men is their gray hair.

30Bruises and wounds are repayment[a] for evil,

Striking at one's inmost parts.

חֹפֵשׂ כָּל־חַדְרֵי־בָטֶן:

28 חֶסֶד וֶאֱמֶת יִצְּרוּ־מֶלֶךְ

וְסָעַד בַּחֶסֶד כִּסְאוֹ:

29 תִּפְאֶרֶת בַּחוּרִים כֹּחָם

וַהֲדַר זְקֵנִים שֵׂיבָה:

30 חַבֻּרוֹת פֶּצַע תמריק תַּמְרוּק בְּרָע

וּמַכּוֹת חַדְרֵי־בָטֶן:

21 Like channeled water is the mind of the king
in the LORD's hand;

He directs it to whatever He wishes.

2All the ways of a man seem right to him,

But the LORD probes the mind.

3To do what is right and just

Is more desired by the LORD than sacrifice.

4Haughty looks, a proud heart—

The tillage of the wicked is sinful.

5The plans of the diligent make only for gain;

All rash haste makes only for loss.

6Treasures acquired by a lying tongue

a-Are like driven vapor, heading for extinction.-a

7The violence of the wicked sweeps them away,

For they refuse to act justly.

8The way of a man may be tortuous and strange,

Though his actions are blameless and proper.

9Dwelling in the corner of a roof is better

Than a contentious wife in a a-spacious house.-a

10The desire of the wicked is set upon evil;

His fellowman finds no favor in his eyes.

11When a scoffer is punished, the simple man is
edified;

When a wise man is taught, he gains insight.

12The Righteous One observes the house of the
wicked man;

He subverts the wicked to their ruin.

13Who stops his ears at the cry of the wretched,

He too will call and not be answered.

14A gift in secret subdues anger,

כא פַּלְגֵי־מַיִם לֶב־מֶלֶךְ בְּיַד־
יְהוָה

עַל־כָּל־אֲשֶׁר יַחְפֹּץ יַטֶּנּוּ:

2 כָּל־דֶּרֶךְ־אִישׁ יָשָׁר בְּעֵינָיו

וְתֹכֵן לִבּוֹת יְהוָה:

3 עֲשֹׂה צְדָקָה וּמִשְׁפָּט

נִבְחָר לַיהוָה מִזָּבַח:

4 רוּם־עֵינַיִם וּרְחַב־לֵב

נֵר רְשָׁעִים חַטָּאת:

5 מַחְשְׁבוֹת חָרוּץ אַךְ־לְמוֹתָר

וְכָל־אָץ אַךְ־לְמַחְסוֹר:

6 פֹּעַל אוֹצָרוֹת בִּלְשׁוֹן שָׁקֶר

הֶבֶל נִדָּף מְבַקְשֵׁי־מָוֶת:

7 שֹׁד־רְשָׁעִים יְגוֹרֵם

כִּי מֵאֲנוּ לַעֲשׂוֹת מִשְׁפָּט:

8 הֲפַכְפַּךְ דֶּרֶךְ אִישׁ וָזָר

וְזַךְ יָשָׁר פָּעֳלוֹ:

9 טוֹב לָשֶׁבֶת עַל־פִּנַּת־גָּג

מֵאֵשֶׁת מִדְיָנִים וּבֵית חָבֶר:

10 נֶפֶשׁ רָשָׁע אִוְּתָה־רָע

לֹא־יֻחַן בְּעֵינָיו רֵעֵהוּ:

11 בַּעְנָשׁ־לֵץ יֶחְכַּם־פֶּתִי

וּבְהַשְׂכִּיל לְחָכָם יִקַּח־דָּעַת:

12 מַשְׂכִּיל צַדִּיק לְבֵית רָשָׁע

מְסַלֵּף רְשָׁעִים לָרָע:

13 אֹטֵם אָזְנוֹ מִזַּעֲקַת־דָּל

גַּם־הוּא יִקְרָא וְלֹא יֵעָנֶה:

14 מַתָּן בַּסֵּתֶר יִכְפֶּה־אָף

---

a-a   Meaning of Heb. uncertain.

A present in private, fierce rage.

15Justice done is a joy to the righteous,
To evildoers, ruination.

16A man who strays from the path of prudence
Will rest in the company of ghosts.

17He who loves pleasure comes to want;
He who loves wine and oil does not grow rich.

18The wicked are the ransom of the righteous;
The traitor comes in place of the upright.

19It is better to live in the desert
Than with a contentious, vexatious wife.

20Precious treasure and oil are in the house of the
wise man,
And a fool of a man will run through them.

21He who strives to do good and kind deeds
Attains life, success, and honor.

22One wise man prevailed over a city of warriors
And brought down its mighty stronghold.

23He who guards his mouth and tongue
Guards himself from trouble.

24The proud, insolent man, scoffer is his name,
Acts in a frenzy of insolence.

25The craving of a lazy man kills him,
For his hands refuse to work.

26All day long he is seized with craving
While the righteous man gives without stint.

27The sacrifice of the wicked man is an abomination,
The more so as he offers it in depravity.

28A false witness is doomed,
But one who really heard will testify with success.

29The wicked man is brazen-faced;
The upright man discerns his course.

30No wisdom, no prudence, and no counsel
Can prevail against the LORD.

31The horse is readied for the day of battle,
But victory comes from the LORD.

וְשֹׁ֣חַד בַּחֵ֑ק חֵמָ֥ה עַזָּֽה׃

15 שִׂמְחָ֣ה לַ֭צַּדִּיק עֲשׂ֣וֹת מִשְׁפָּ֑ט
וּ֝מְחִתָּ֗ה לְפֹ֣עֲלֵי אָֽוֶן׃

16 אָדָ֗ם תּ֭וֹעֶה מִדֶּ֣רֶךְ הַשְׂכֵּ֑ל
בִּקְהַ֖ל רְפָאִ֣ים יָנֽוּחַ׃

17 אִ֣ישׁ מַ֭חְסוֹר אֹהֵ֣ב שִׂמְחָ֑ה
אֹהֵ֖ב יַ֥יִן־וָ֝שֶׁ֗מֶן לֹ֣א יַעֲשִֽׁיר׃

18 כֹּ֣פֶר לַצַּדִּ֣יק רָשָׁ֑ע
וְתַ֖חַת יְשָׁרִ֣ים בּוֹגֵֽד׃

19 ט֗וֹב שֶׁ֥בֶת בְּאֶֽרֶץ־מִדְבָּ֑ר
מֵאֵ֖שֶׁת מִדְיָנִ֣ים וָכָֽעַס׃

20 אוֹצָ֤ר ׀ נֶחְמָ֣ד וָ֭שֶׁמֶן בִּנְוֵ֣ה חָכָ֑ם
וּכְסִ֖יל אָדָ֣ם יְבַלְּעֶֽנּוּ׃

21 רֹ֭דֵף צְדָקָ֣ה וָחָ֑סֶד
יִמְצָ֥א חַ֝֗יִּים צְדָקָ֥ה וְכָבֽוֹד׃

22 עִ֣יר גִּ֭בֹּרִים עָלָ֣ה חָכָ֑ם
וַ֝יֹּ֗רֶד עֹ֣ז מִבְטֶחָֽה׃

23 שֹׁמֵ֣ר פִּ֭יו וּלְשׁוֹנ֑וֹ
שֹׁמֵ֖ר מִצָּר֣וֹת נַפְשֽׁוֹ׃

24 זֵ֣ד יָ֭הִיר לֵ֣ץ שְׁמ֑וֹ
ע֝וֹשֶׂ֗ה בְּעֶבְרַ֥ת זָדֽוֹן׃

25 תַּאֲוַ֣ת עָצֵ֣ל תְּמִיתֶ֑נּוּ
כִּֽי־מֵאֲנ֖וּ יָדָ֣יו לַעֲשֽׂוֹת׃

26 כָּל־הַ֭יּוֹם הִתְאַוָּ֣ה תַאֲוָ֑ה
וְצַדִּ֥יק יִ֝תֵּ֗ן וְלֹ֣א יַחְשֹֽׂךְ׃

27 זֶ֣בַח רְ֭שָׁעִים תּוֹעֵבָ֑ה
אַ֝֗ף כִּֽי־בְזִמָּ֥ה יְבִיאֶֽנּוּ׃

28 עֵד־כְּזָבִ֥ים יֹאבֵ֑ד
וְאִ֥ישׁ שׁוֹמֵ֗עַ לָנֶ֥צַח יְדַבֵּֽר׃

29 הֵעֵ֬ז אִ֣ישׁ רָשָׁ֣ע בְּפָנָ֑יו
וְ֝יָשָׁ֗ר ה֤וּא ׀ יָכִ֬ין דרכיו יָבִ֥ין דַּרְכּֽוֹ׃

30 אֵ֣ין חָ֭כְמָה וְאֵ֣ין תְּבוּנָ֑ה
וְאֵ֥ין עֵ֝צָ֗ה לְנֶ֣גֶד יְהוָֽה׃ פ

31 ס֗וּס מ֭וּכָן לְי֣וֹם מִלְחָמָ֑ה
וְ֝לַֽיהוָ֗ה הַתְּשׁוּעָֽה׃

כב

22 Repute is preferable to great wealth,
Grace is better than silver and gold.
²Rich man and poor man meet;
The LORD made them both.
³The shrewd man saw trouble and took cover;
The simple kept going and paid the penalty.
⁴The effect of humility is fear of the LORD,
Wealth, honor, and life.
⁵Thorns and snares are in the path of the crooked;
He who values his life will keep far from them.
⁶Train a lad in the way he ought to go;
He will not swerve from it even in old age.
⁷The rich rule the poor,
And the borrower is a slave to the lender.
⁸He who sows injustice shall reap misfortune;
His rod of wrath shall fail.
⁹The generous man is blessed,
For he gives of his bread to the poor.
¹⁰Expel the scoffer and contention departs,
Quarrel and contumely cease.
¹¹A pure-hearted friend,
His speech is gracious;
He has the king for his companion.
¹²The eyes of the LORD watch the wise man;
He subverts the words of the treacherous.
¹³The lazy man says, "There's a lion in the street;
I shall be killed ᵃ-if I step outside."-ᵃ
¹⁴The mouth of a forbiddenᵇ woman is a deep pit;
He who is doomed by the LORD falls into it.
¹⁵If folly settles in the heart of a lad,
The rod of discipline will remove it.
¹⁶To profit by withholding what is due to the poor
Is like making gifts to the rich—pure loss.

¹⁷Incline your ear and listen to the words of the
    sages;
Pay attention to my wisdom.
¹⁸It is good that you store them inside you,

נִבְחָר שֵׁם מֵעֹשֶׁר רָב
מִכֶּסֶף וּמִזָּהָב חֵן טוֹב:
2 עָשִׁיר וָרָשׁ נִפְגָּשׁוּ
עֹשֵׂה כֻלָּם יְהוָה:
3 עָרוּם ׀ רָאָה רָעָה ויסתר וְנִסְתָּר
וּפְתָיִים עָבְרוּ וְנֶעֱנָשׁוּ:
4 עֵקֶב עֲנָוָה יִרְאַת יְהוָה
עֹשֶׁר וְכָבוֹד וְחַיִּים:
5 צִנִּים פַּחִים בְּדֶרֶךְ עִקֵּשׁ
שׁוֹמֵר נַפְשׁוֹ יִרְחַק מֵהֶם:
6 חֲנֹךְ לַנַּעַר עַל־פִּי דַרְכּוֹ
גַּם כִּי־יַזְקִין לֹא־יָסוּר מִמֶּנָּה:
7 עָשִׁיר בְּרָשִׁים יִמְשׁוֹל
וְעֶבֶד לֹוֶה לְאִישׁ מַלְוֶה:
8 זוֹרֵעַ עַוְלָה יקצור יִקְצָר־אָוֶן
וְשֵׁבֶט עֶבְרָתוֹ יִכְלֶה:
9 טוֹב־עַיִן הוּא יְבֹרָךְ
כִּי־נָתַן מִלַּחְמוֹ לַדָּל:
10 גָּרֵשׁ לֵץ וְיֵצֵא מָדוֹן
וְיִשְׁבֹּת דִּין וְקָלוֹן:
11 אֹהֵב טהור טְהָר־לֵב
חֵן שְׂפָתָיו רֵעֵהוּ מֶלֶךְ:
12 עֵינֵי יְהוָה נָצְרוּ דָעַת
וַיְסַלֵּף דִּבְרֵי בֹגֵד:
13 אָמַר עָצֵל אֲרִי בַחוּץ
בְּתוֹךְ רְחֹבוֹת אֵרָצֵחַ:
14 שׁוּחָה עֲמֻקָּה פִּי זָרוֹת
זְעוּם יְהוָה יפול יִפָּל־שָׁם:
15 אִוֶּלֶת קְשׁוּרָה בְלֶב־נָעַר
שֵׁבֶט מוּסָר יַרְחִיקֶנָּה מִמֶּנּוּ:
16 עֹשֵׁק דָּל לְהַרְבּוֹת לוֹ
נֹתֵן לְעָשִׁיר אַךְ־לְמַחְסוֹר:
17 הַט אָזְנְךָ וּשְׁמַע דִּבְרֵי חֲכָמִים
וְלִבְּךָ תָּשִׁית לְדַעְתִּי:
18 כִּי־נָעִים כִּי־תִשְׁמְרֵם בְּבִטְנֶךָ

---

a-a Lit. "in the square."
b   Lit. "strange."

And that all of them be constantly on your lips,

יִכֹּנוּ יַחְדָּו עַל־שְׂפָתֶיךָ׃

19That you may put your trust in the LORD.

19 לִהְיוֹת בַּיהוָה מִבְטַחֶךָ

I let you know today—yes, you—

הוֹדַעְתִּיךָ הַיּוֹם אַף־אָתָּה׃

20Indeed, I wrote down for you c-a threefold lore,-c

20 הֲלֹא כָתַבְתִּי לְךָ שלשום

Wise counsel,

שָׁלִישִׁים

21To let you know truly reliable words,

בְּמוֹעֵצֹת וָדָעַת׃

That you may give a faithful reply to him who sent
  you.

21 לְהוֹדִיעֲךָ קֹשְׁטְ אִמְרֵי אֱמֶת

לְהָשִׁיב אֲמָרִים אֱמֶת לְשֹׁלְחֶיךָ׃ פ

22Do not rob the wretched because he is wretched;

22 אַל־תִּגְזָל־דָּל כִּי דַל־הוּא

Do not crush the poor man in the gate;

וְאַל־תְּדַכֵּא עָנִי בַשָּׁעַר׃

23For the LORD will take up their cause

23 כִּי־יְהוָה יָרִיב רִיבָם

And despoil those who despoil them of life.

וְקָבַע אֶת־קֹבְעֵיהֶם נָפֶשׁ׃

24Do not associate with an irascible man,

24 אַל־תִּתְרַע אֶת־בַּעַל אָף

Or go about with one who is hot-tempered,

וְאֶת־אִישׁ חֵמוֹת לֹא תָבוֹא׃

25Lest you learn his ways

25 פֶּן־תֶּאֱלַף אֹרְחֹתָו אֹרְחֹתֶיךָ

And find yourself ensnared.

וְלָקַחְתָּ מוֹקֵשׁ לְנַפְשֶׁךָ׃

26Do not be one of those who give their hand,

26 אַל־תְּהִי בְתֹקְעֵי־כָף

Who stand surety for debts,

בַּעֹרְבִים מַשָּׁאוֹת׃

27Lest your bed be taken from under you

27 אִם־אֵין־לְךָ לְשַׁלֵּם

When you have no money to pay.

לָמָּה יִקַּח מִשְׁכָּבְךָ מִתַּחְתֶּיךָ׃

28Do not remove the ancient boundary stone

28 אַל־תַּסֵּג גְּבוּל עוֹלָם

That your ancestors set up.

אֲשֶׁר עָשׂוּ אֲבוֹתֶיךָ׃

29See a man skilled at his work—

29 חָזִיתָ אִישׁ ׀ מָהִיר בִּמְלַאכְתּוֹ

He shall attend upon kings;

לִפְנֵי־מְלָכִים יִתְיַצָּב

He shall not attend upon c-obscure men.-c

בַּל־יִתְיַצֵּב לִפְנֵי חֲשֻׁכִּים׃ פ

23 When you sit down to dine with a ruler,

כג כִּי־תֵשֵׁב לִלְחוֹם אֶת־מוֹשֵׁל

Consider well who is before you.

בִּין תָּבִין אֶת־אֲשֶׁר לְפָנֶיךָ׃

2Thrust a knife into your gullet

2 וְשַׂמְתָּ שַׂכִּין בְּלֹעֶךָ

If you have a large appetite.

אִם־בַּעַל נֶפֶשׁ אָתָּה׃

3Do not crave for his dainties,

3 אַל־תִּתְאָו לְמַטְעַמּוֹתָיו

For they are counterfeit food.

וְהוּא לֶחֶם כְּזָבִים׃

4Do not toil to gain wealth;

4 אַל־תִּיגַע לְהַעֲשִׁיר

Have the sense to desist.

מִבִּינָתְךָ חֲדָל׃

5You see it, then it is gone;

5 התעוף הֲתָעִיף עֵינֶיךָ בּוֹ וְאֵינֶנּוּ

c-c   Meaning of Heb. uncertain.

It grows wings and flies away,
Like an eagle, heavenward.

כִּי עָשֹׂה יַעֲשֶׂה־לּוֹ כְנָפַיִם
כְּנֶשֶׁר ועיף יָעוּף הַשָּׁמָיִם: פ

6Do not eat of a stingy man's food;
Do not crave for his dainties;
7He is like one keeping accounts;
"Eat and drink," he says to you,
But he does not really mean it.
8The morsel you eat you will vomit;
You will waste your courteous words.

6 אַל־תִּלְחַם אֶת־לֶחֶם רַע עָיִן
וְאַל־תתאו תִּתְאָיו לְמַטְעַמֹּתָיו:
7 כִּי | כְּמוֹ־שָׁעַר בְּנַפְשׁוֹ
כֶּן־הוּא אֱכֹל וּשְׁתֵה יֹאמַר לָךְ
וְלִבּוֹ בַּל־עִמָּךְ:
8 פִּתְּךָ־אָכַלְתָּ תְקִיאֶנָּה
וְשִׁחַתָּ דְּבָרֶיךָ הַנְּעִימִים:

9Do not speak to a dullard,
For he will disdain your sensible words.
10Do not remove ancient boundary stones;
Do not encroach upon the field of orphans,
11For they have a mighty Kinsman,
And He will surely take up their cause with you.

9 בְּאָזְנֵי כְסִיל אַל־תְּדַבֵּר
כִּי־יָבוּז לְשֵׂכֶל מִלֶּיךָ:
10 אַל־תַּסֵּג גְּבוּל עוֹלָם
וּבִשְׂדֵי יְתוֹמִים אַל־תָּבֹא:
11 כִּי־גֹאֲלָם חָזָק
הוּא־יָרִיב אֶת־רִיבָם אִתָּךְ:

12Apply your mind to discipline
And your ears to wise sayings.
13Do not withhold discipline from a child;
If you beat him with a rod he will not die.
14Beat him with a rod
And you will save him from the grave.

12 הָבִיאָה לַמּוּסָר לִבֶּךָ
וְאָזְנְךָ לְאִמְרֵי־דָעַת:
13 אַל־תִּמְנַע מִנַּעַר מוּסָר
כִּי־תַכֶּנּוּ בַשֵּׁבֶט לֹא יָמוּת:
14 אַתָּה בַּשֵּׁבֶט תַּכֶּנּוּ
וְנַפְשׁוֹ מִשְּׁאוֹל תַּצִּיל:

15My son, if your mind gets wisdom,
My mind, too, will be gladdened.
16I shall rejoice with all my heart[a]
When your lips speak right things.
17Do not envy sinners in your heart,
But only God-fearing men, at all times,
18For then you will have a future,
And your hope will never fail.

15 בְּנִי אִם־חָכַם לִבֶּךָ
יִשְׂמַח לִבִּי גַם־אָנִי:
16 וְתַעְלֹזְנָה כִלְיוֹתָי
בְּדַבֵּר שְׂפָתֶיךָ מֵישָׁרִים:
17 אַל־יְקַנֵּא לִבְּךָ בַּחַטָּאִים
כִּי אִם־בְּיִרְאַת־יְהֹוָה כָּל־הַיּוֹם:
18 כִּי אִם־יֵשׁ אַחֲרִית
וְתִקְוָתְךָ לֹא תִכָּרֵת:

19Listen, my son, and get wisdom;
Lead your mind in a [proper] path.
20Do not be of those who guzzle wine,
Or glut themselves on meat;

19 שְׁמַע־אַתָּה בְנִי וַחֲכָם
וְאַשֵּׁר בַּדֶּרֶךְ לִבֶּךָ:
20 אַל־תְּהִי בְסֹבְאֵי־יַיִן
בְּזֹלֲלֵי בָשָׂר לָמוֹ:

a Lit. "kidneys."

21For guzzlers and gluttons will be impoverished,
And drowsing will clothe you in tatters.

כא כִּי־סֹבֵא וְזוֹלֵל יִוָּרֵשׁ
וּקְרָעִים תַּלְבִּישׁ נוּמָה׃

22Listen to your father who begot you;
Do not disdain your mother when she is old.

כב שְׁמַע לְאָבִיךָ זֶה יְלָדֶךָ
וְאַל־תָּבוּז כִּי־זָקְנָה אִמֶּךָ׃

23Buy truth and never sell it,
And wisdom, discipline, and understanding.

כג אֱמֶת קְנֵה וְאַל־תִּמְכֹּר
חָכְמָה וּמוּסָר וּבִינָה׃

24The father of a righteous man will exult;
He who begets a wise son will rejoice in him.

כד גּוֹל יָגוּל גִּיל יָגִיל אֲבִי צַדִּיק
יוֹלֵד וְיוֹלֵד חָכָם וְיִשְׂמַח יִשְׂמַח־בּוֹ׃

25Your father and mother will rejoice;
She who bore you will exult.

כה יִשְׂמַח־אָבִיךָ וְאִמֶּךָ
וְתָגֵל יוֹלַדְתֶּךָ׃

26Give your mind to me, my son;
Let your eyes watch my ways.

כו תְּנָה־בְנִי לִבְּךָ לִי
וְעֵינֶיךָ דְּרָכַי תרצנה תִּצֹּרְנָה׃

27A harlot is a deep pit;
A forbidden[b] woman is a narrow well.

כז כִּי־שׁוּחָה עֲמֻקָּה זוֹנָה
וּבְאֵר צָרָה נָכְרִיָּה׃

28She too lies in wait as if for prey,
And destroys the unfaithful among men.

כח אַף־הִיא כְּחֶתֶף תֶּאֱרֹב
וּבוֹגְדִים בְּאָדָם תּוֹסִף׃

29Who cries, "Woe!" who, "Alas!";
Who has quarrels, who complaints;
Who has wounds without cause;
Who has bleary eyes?

כט לְמִי אוֹי לְמִי אֲבוֹי
לְמִי מִדוֹנִים מִדְיָנִים ׀ לְמִי שִׂיחַ
לְמִי פְּצָעִים חִנָּם
לְמִי חַכְלִלוּת עֵינָיִם׃

30Those whom wine keeps till the small hours,
Those who gather to drain the cups.

ל לַמְאַחֲרִים עַל־הַיָּיִן
לַבָּאִים לַחְקֹר מִמְסָךְ׃

31Do not ogle that red wine
As it lends its color to the cup,
As it flows on smoothly;

לא אַל־תֵּרֶא יַיִן כִּי יִתְאַדָּם
כִּי־יִתֵּן בכיס בַּכּוֹס עֵינוֹ
יִתְהַלֵּךְ בְּמֵישָׁרִים׃

32In the end, it bites like a snake;
It spits like a basilisk.

לב אַחֲרִיתוֹ כְּנָחָשׁ יִשָּׁךְ
וּכְצִפְעֹנִי יַפְרִשׁ׃

33Your eyes will see strange sights;
Your heart[c] will speak distorted things.

לג עֵינֶיךָ יִרְאוּ זָרוֹת
וְלִבְּךָ יְדַבֵּר תַּהְפֻּכוֹת׃

34You will be like one lying in bed on high seas,
Like one lying [d-]on top of the rigging.[-d]

לד וְהָיִיתָ כְּשֹׁכֵב בְּלֶב־יָם
וּכְשֹׁכֵב בְּרֹאשׁ חִבֵּל׃

35"They struck me, but I felt no hurt;
They beat me, but I was unaware;
As often as I wake,
I go after it again."

לה הִכּוּנִי בַל־חָלִיתִי
הֲלָמוּנִי בַּל־יָדָעְתִּי
מָתַי אָקִיץ
אוֹסִיף אֲבַקְשֶׁנּוּ עוֹד׃

---

b   Lit. "alien."
c   See note to 15.28.
d-d   Meaning of Heb. uncertain.

24

Do not envy evil men;
Do not desire to be with them;
²For their hearts^a talk violence,
And their lips speak mischief.

³A house is built by wisdom,
And is established by understanding;
⁴By knowledge are its rooms filled
With all precious and beautiful things.

⁵A wise man is strength;
A knowledgeable man exerts power;
⁶For by stratagems you wage war,
And victory comes with much planning.

⁷Wisdom is too lofty for a fool;
He does not open his mouth in the gate.
⁸He who lays plans to do harm
Is called by men a schemer.
⁹The schemes of folly are sin,
And a scoffer is an abomination to men.

¹⁰If you showed yourself slack in time of trouble,
Wanting in power,
¹¹If you refrained from rescuing those taken off
　to death,
Those condemned to slaughter—
¹²If you say, "We knew nothing of it,"
Surely He who fathoms hearts will discern [the
　truth],
He who watches over your life will know it,
And He will pay each man as he deserves.
¹³My son, eat honey, for it is good;
Let its sweet drops be on your palate.
¹⁴Know: such is wisdom for your soul;
If you attain it, there is a future;
Your hope will not be cut off.

כד אַל־תְּקַנֵּא בְּאַנְשֵׁי רָעָה
וְאַל־תתאו [תִּתְאָו] לִהְיוֹת אִתָּם:
² כִּי־שֹׁד יֶהְגֶּה לִבָּם
וְעָמָל שִׂפְתֵיהֶם תְּדַבֵּרְנָה:

³ בְּחָכְמָה יִבָּנֶה בָּיִת
וּבִתְבוּנָה יִתְכּוֹנָן:
⁴ וּבְדַעַת חֲדָרִים יִמָּלְאוּ
כָּל־הוֹן יָקָר וְנָעִים:

⁵ גֶּבֶר־חָכָם בַּעוֹז
וְאִישׁ־דַּעַת מְאַמֶּץ־כֹּחַ:
⁶ כִּי בְתַחְבֻּלוֹת תַּעֲשֶׂה־לְּךָ
מִלְחָמָה
וּתְשׁוּעָה בְּרֹב יוֹעֵץ:

⁷ רָאמוֹת לֶאֱוִיל חָכְמוֹת
בַּשַּׁעַר לֹא יִפְתַּח־פִּיהוּ:
⁸ מְחַשֵּׁב לְהָרֵעַ
לוֹ בַּעַל־מְזִמּוֹת יִקְרָאוּ:
⁹ זִמַּת אִוֶּלֶת חַטָּאת
וְתוֹעֲבַת לְאָדָם לֵץ:

¹⁰ הִתְרַפִּיתָ בְּיוֹם צָרָה צַר
כֹּחָכָה*:
¹¹ הַצֵּל לְקֻחִים לַמָּוֶת
וּמָטִים לַהֶרֶג אִם־תַּחְשׂוֹךְ:
¹² כִּי־תֹאמַר הֵן לֹא־יָדַעְנוּ זֶה
הֲלֹא־תֹכֵן לִבּוֹת ׀ הוּא־יָבִין
וְנֹצֵר נַפְשְׁךָ הוּא יֵדָע
וְהֵשִׁיב לְאָדָם כְּפָעֳלוֹ:
¹³ אֱכָל־בְּנִי דְבַשׁ כִּי־טוֹב
וְנֹפֶת מָתוֹק עַל־חִכֶּךָ:
¹⁴ כֵּן ׀ דְּעֶה חָכְמָה לְנַפְשֶׁךָ
אִם־מָצָאתָ וְיֵשׁ אַחֲרִית
וְתִקְוָתְךָ לֹא תִכָּרֵת: פ

v. 10. יתיר ה'

1640

15Wicked man! Do not lurk by the home of the
righteous man;
Do no violence to his dwelling.
16Seven times the righteous man falls and gets up,
While the wicked are tripped by one misfortune.

17If your enemy falls, do not exult;
If he trips, let your heart not rejoice,
18Lest the LORD see it and be displeased,
And avert His wrath from him.

19Do not be vexed by evildoers;
Do not be incensed by the wicked;
20For there is no future for the evil man;
The lamp of the wicked goes out.

21Fear the LORD, my son, and the king,
And do not mix with dissenters,
22For disaster comes from them suddenly;
The doom both decree who can foreknow?

23These also are by the sages:

It is not right to be partial in judgment.
24He who says to the guilty, "You are innocent,"
Shall be cursed by peoples,
Damned by nations;
25But it shall go well with them who decide justly;
Blessings of good things will light upon them.

26Giving a straightforward reply
Is like giving a kiss.
27Put your external affairs in order,
Get ready what you have in the field,
Then build yourself a home.
28Do not be a witness against your fellow without
good cause;
Would you mislead with your speech?

אַל־תֶּאֱרֹב רָשָׁע לִנְוֵה צַדִּיק 15
אַל־תְּשַׁדֵּד רִבְצוֹ:
כִּי שֶׁבַע ׀ יִפּוֹל צַדִּיק וָקָם 16
וּרְשָׁעִים יִכָּשְׁלוּ בְרָעָה:

בִּנְפֹל אוֹיִבְךָ אַל־תִּשְׂמָח 17
וּבִכָּשְׁלוֹ אַל־יָגֵל לִבֶּךָ:
פֶּן־יִרְאֶה יְהֹוָה וְרַע בְּעֵינָיו 18
וְהֵשִׁיב מֵעָלָיו אַפּוֹ:

אַל־תִּתְחַר בַּמְּרֵעִים 19
אַל־תְּקַנֵּא בָּרְשָׁעִים:
כִּי ׀ לֹא־תִהְיֶה אַחֲרִית לָרָע 20
נֵר רְשָׁעִים יִדְעָךְ:

יְרָא־אֶת־יְהֹוָה בְּנִי וָמֶלֶךְ 21
עִם־שׁוֹנִים אַל־תִּתְעָרָב:
כִּי־פִתְאֹם יָקוּם אֵידָם 22
וּפִיד שְׁנֵיהֶם מִי יוֹדֵעַ: ס

גַּם־אֵלֶּה לַחֲכָמִים 23

הַכֵּר־פָּנִים בְּמִשְׁפָּט בַּל־טוֹב:
אֹמֵר ׀ לְרָשָׁע צַדִּיק אָתָּה 24
יִקְּבֻהוּ עַמִּים
יִזְעָמוּהוּ לְאֻמִּים:
וְלַמּוֹכִיחִים יִנְעָם 25
וַעֲלֵיהֶם תָּבוֹא בִרְכַּת־טוֹב:

שְׂפָתַיִם יִשָּׁק 26
מֵשִׁיב דְּבָרִים נְכֹחִים:
הָכֵן בַּחוּץ ׀ מְלַאכְתֶּךָ וְעַתְּדָהּ 27
בַּשָּׂדֶה לָךְ
אַחַר וּבָנִיתָ בֵיתֶךָ: פ
אַל־תְּהִי עֵד־חִנָּם בְּרֵעֶךָ 28
וַהֲפִתִּיתָ בִּשְׂפָתֶיךָ:

29Do not say, "I will do to him what he did to me;
I will pay the man what he deserves."

29 אַל־תֹּאמַר כַּאֲשֶׁר עָשָׂה־לִי כֵּן
אֶעֱשֶׂה־לֹּו
אָשִׁיב לָאִישׁ כְּפָעֳלֹו:

30I passed by the field of a lazy man,
By the vineyard of a man lacking sense.

30 עַל־שְׂדֵה אִישׁ־עָצֵל עָבַרְתִּי
וְעַל־כֶּרֶם אָדָם חֲסַר־לֵב:

31It was all overgrown with thorns;
Its surface was covered with chickweed,
And its stone fence lay in ruins.

31 וְהִנֵּה עָלָה כֻלֹּו ׀ קִמְּשֹׂנִים
כָּסּוּ פָנָיו חֲרֻלִּים
וְגֶדֶר אֲבָנָיו נֶהֱרָסָה:

32I observed and took it to heart;
I saw it and learned a lesson.

32 וָאֶחֱזֶה אָנֹכִי אָשִׁית לִבִּי
רָאִיתִי לָקַחְתִּי מוּסָר:

33A bit more sleep, a bit more slumber,
A bit more hugging yourself in bed,

33 מְעַט שֵׁנֹות מְעַט תְּנוּמֹות
מְעַט ׀ חִבֻּק יָדַיִם לִשְׁכָּב:

34And poverty will come b-calling upon you,-b
And want, like a man with a shield.

34 וּבָא־מִתְהַלֵּךְ רֵישֶׁךָ
וּמַחְסֹרֶיךָ כְּאִישׁ מָגֵן: פ

25 These too are proverbs of Solomon, which the men of King Hezekiah of Judah copied:

כה גַּם־אֵלֶּה מִשְׁלֵי שְׁלֹמֹה אֲשֶׁר
הֶעְתִּיקוּ אַנְשֵׁי ׀ חִזְקִיָּה מֶלֶךְ־יְהוּדָה:

2It is the glory of God to conceal a matter,
And the glory of a king to plumb a matter.

2 כְּבֹד אֱלֹהִים הַסְתֵּר דָּבָר
וּכְבֹד מְלָכִים חֲקֹר דָּבָר:

3Like the heavens in their height, like the earth
   in its depth,
Is the mind of kings—unfathomable.

3 שָׁמַיִם לָרוּם וָאָרֶץ לָעֹמֶק
וְלֵב מְלָכִים אֵין חֵקֶר:

4The dross having been separated from the silver,
A vessel emerged for the smith.

4 הָגֹו סִיגִים מִכָּסֶף
וַיֵּצֵא לַצֹּרֵף כֶּלִי:

5Remove the wicked from the king's presence,
And his throne will be established in justice.

5 הָגֹו רָשָׁע לִפְנֵי־מֶלֶךְ
וְיִכֹּון בַּצֶּדֶק כִּסְאֹו:

6Do not exalt yourself in the king's presence;
Do not stand in the place of nobles.

6 אַל־תִּתְהַדַּר לִפְנֵי־מֶלֶךְ
וּבִמְקֹום גְּדֹלִים אַל־תַּעֲמֹד:

7For it is better to be told, "Step up here,"
Than to be degraded in the presence of the great.

7 כִּי טֹוב אֲמָר־לְךָ עֲלֵה הֵנָּה
מֵהַשְׁפִּילְךָ לִפְנֵי נָדִיב

Do not let what your eyes have seen

אֲשֶׁר רָאוּ עֵינֶיךָ:

8Be vented rashly in a quarrel;
Thinka of what it will effect in the end,

8 אַל־תֵּצֵא לָרִב מַהֵר
פֶּן מַה־תַּעֲשֶׂה בְּאַחֲרִיתָהּ

---

b-b   *Meaning of Heb. uncertain.*

a   *Lit. "Lest."*

When your fellow puts you to shame.

9Defend your right against your fellow,
But do not give away the secrets of another,

10Lest he who hears it reproach you,
And your bad repute never end.

11Like golden apples in silver showpieces*b*
Is a phrase well turned.

12Like a ring of gold, a golden ornament,
Is a wise man's reproof in a receptive ear.

13Like the coldness of snow at harvesttime
Is a trusty messenger to those who send him;
He lifts his master's spirits.

14Like clouds, wind—but no rain—
Is one who boasts of gifts not given.

15Through forbearance a ruler may be won over;
A gentle tongue can break bones.

16If you find honey, eat only what you need,
Lest, surfeiting yourself, you throw it up.

17Visit your neighbor sparingly,
Lest he have his surfeit of you and loathe you.

18Like a club, a sword, a sharpened arrow,
Is a man who testifies falsely against his fellow.

19Like a loose tooth and an unsteady leg,
Is a treacherous support in time of trouble.

20Disrobing on a chilly day,
Like vinegar on natron,
Is one who sings songs to a sorrowful soul.

21If your enemy is hungry, give him bread to eat;
If he is thirsty, give him water to drink.

22You will be heaping live coals on his head,
And the LORD will reward you.

23A north wind produces rain,
And whispered words, a glowering face.

24Dwelling in the corner of a roof is better

b *Meaning of Heb. uncertain.*

בְּהַכְלִים אֹתְךָ רֵעֶךָ׃

9 רִיבְךָ רִיב אֶת־רֵעֶךָ
וְסוֹד אַחֵר אַל־תְּגָל׃

10 פֶּן־יְחַסֶּדְךָ שֹׁמֵעַ
וְדִבָּתְךָ לֹא תָשׁוּב׃

11 תַּפּוּחֵי זָהָב בְּמַשְׂכִּיּוֹת כָּסֶף
דָּבָר דָּבֻר עַל־אָפְנָיו׃

12 נֶזֶם זָהָב וַחֲלִי־כָתֶם
מוֹכִיחַ חָכָם עַל־אֹזֶן שֹׁמָעַת׃

13 כְּצִנַּת־שֶׁלֶג ׀ בְּיוֹם קָצִיר צִיר
נֶאֱמָן לְשֹׁלְחָיו
וְנֶפֶשׁ אֲדֹנָיו יָשִׁיב׃ פ

14 נְשִׂיאִים* וְרוּחַ וְגֶשֶׁם אָיִן
אִישׁ מִתְהַלֵּל בְּמַתַּת־שָׁקֶר׃

15 בְּאֹרֶךְ אַפַּיִם יְפֻתֶּה קָצִין
וְלָשׁוֹן רַכָּה תִּשְׁבָּר־גָּרֶם׃

16 דְּבַשׁ מָצָאתָ אֱכֹל דַּיֶּךָּ
פֶּן־תִּשְׂבָּעֶנּוּ וַהֲקֵאתוֹ׃

17 הֹקַר רַגְלְךָ מִבֵּית רֵעֶךָ
פֶּן־יִשְׂבָּעֲךָ וּשְׂנֵאֶךָ׃

18 מֵפִיץ וְחֶרֶב וְחֵץ שָׁנוּן
אִישׁ עֹנֶה בְרֵעֵהוּ עֵד שָׁקֶר׃

19 שֵׁן רֹעָה וְרֶגֶל מוּעָדֶת
מִבְטָח בּוֹגֵד בְּיוֹם צָרָה׃

20 מַעֲדֶה בֶּגֶד ׀ בְּיוֹם קָרָה
חֹמֶץ עַל־נָתֶר
וְשָׁר בַּשִּׁרִים עַל לֶב־רָע׃ פ

21 אִם־רָעֵב שֹׂנַאֲךָ הַאֲכִלֵהוּ לָחֶם
וְאִם־צָמֵא הַשְׁקֵהוּ מָיִם׃

22 כִּי גֶחָלִים אַתָּה חֹתֶה עַל־רֹאשׁוֹ
וַיהוָה יְשַׁלֶּם־לָךְ׃

23 רוּחַ צָפוֹן תְּחוֹלֵל גָּשֶׁם
וּפָנִים נִזְעָמִים לְשׁוֹן סָתֶר׃

24 טוֹב שֶׁבֶת עַל־פִּנַּת־גָּג

Than a contentious woman in *b*-a spacious
 house.-*b*

מֵאֵשֶׁת מדונים מִדְיָנִים 'וּבֵית חָבֶר:

25Like cold water to a parched throat
Is good news from a distant land.

25 מַיִם קָרִים עַל־נֶפֶשׁ עֲיֵפָה
וּשְׁמוּעָה טוֹבָה מֵאֶרֶץ מֶרְחָק:

26Like a muddied spring, a ruined fountain,
Is a righteous man fallen before a wicked one.

26 מַעְיָן נִרְפָּשׂ וּמָקוֹר מָשְׁחָת
צַדִּיק מָט לִפְנֵי־רָשָׁע:

27It is not good to eat much honey,
b-Nor is it honorable to search for honor.-*b*

27 אָכֹל דְּבַשׁ הַרְבּוֹת לֹא־טוֹב
וְחֵקֶר כְּבֹדָם כָּבוֹד:

28Like an open city without walls
Is a man whose temper is uncurbed.

28 עִיר פְּרוּצָה אֵין חוֹמָה
אִישׁ אֲשֶׁר אֵין מַעְצָר לְרוּחוֹ:

26 Like snow in summer and rain at harvest-
 time,
So honor is not fitting for a dullard.

כו

כַּשֶּׁלֶג ׀ בַּקַּיִץ וְכַמָּטָר בַּקָּצִיר
כֵּן לֹא־נָאוֶה לִכְסִיל כָּבוֹד:

2As a sparrow must flit and a swallow fly,
So a gratuitous curse must backfire.*a*

2 כַּצִּפּוֹר לָנוּד כַּדְּרוֹר לָעוּף
כֵּן קִלְלַת חִנָּם לֹא תָבֹא:

3A whip for a horse and a bridle for a donkey,
And a rod for the back of dullards.

3 שׁוֹט לַסּוּס מֶתֶג לַחֲמוֹר
וְשֵׁבֶט לְגֵו כְּסִילִים:

4Do not answer a dullard in accord with his folly,
Else you will become like him.

4 אַל־תַּעַן כְּסִיל כְּאִוַּלְתּוֹ
פֶּן־תִּשְׁוֶה־לּוֹ גַם־אָתָּה:

5Answer a dullard in accord with his folly,
Else he will think himself wise.

5 עֲנֵה כְסִיל כְּאִוַּלְתּוֹ
פֶּן־יִהְיֶה חָכָם בְּעֵינָיו:

6He who sends a message by a dullard
Will wear out legs and *b*-must put up with-*b* lawlessness.

6 מְקַצֶּה רַגְלַיִם חָמָס שֹׁתֶה
שֹׁלֵחַ דְּבָרִים בְּיַד־כְּסִיל:

7As legs hang limp on a cripple,
So is a proverb in the mouth of dullards.

7 דַּלְיוּ שֹׁקַיִם מִפִּסֵּחַ
וּמָשָׁל בְּפִי כְסִילִים:

8Like a pebble in a sling,
So is paying honor to a dullard.

8 כִּצְרוֹר אֶבֶן בְּמַרְגֵּמָה
כֵּן־נוֹתֵן לִכְסִיל כָּבוֹד:

9As a thorn comes to the hand of a drunkard,
So a proverb to the mouth of a dullard.

9 חוֹחַ עָלָה בְיַד־שִׁכּוֹר
וּמָשָׁל בְּפִי כְסִילִים:

10*c*-A master can produce anything,-*c*
But he who hires a dullard is as one who hires
 transients.*c*

10 רַב מְחוֹלֵל־כֹּל
וְשֹׂכֵר כְּסִיל וְשֹׂכֵר עֹבְרִים:

11As a dog returns to his vomit,
So a dullard repeats his folly.

11 כְּכֶלֶב שָׁב עַל־קֵאוֹ
כְּסִיל שׁוֹנֶה בְאִוַּלְתּוֹ:

12If you see a man who thinks himself wise,
There is more hope for a dullard than for him.

12 רָאִיתָ אִישׁ חָכָם בְּעֵינָיו
תִּקְוָה לִכְסִיל מִמֶּנּוּ:

---

a   Kethib, "fail."
b-b Lit. "drink."
c-c Meaning of Heb. uncertain.

¹³A lazy man says,
"There's a cub on the road, a lion in the squares."

¹⁴The door turns on its hinge,
And the lazy man on his bed.

¹⁵The lazy man buries his hand in the bowl;
He will not even bring it to his mouth.

¹⁶The lazy man thinks himself wiser
Than seven men who give good advice.

¹⁷A passerby who gets embroiled in someone
else's quarrel
Is like one who seizes a dog by its ears.

¹⁸Like a madman⁻ᶜ scattering deadly firebrands,
arrows,

¹⁹Is one who cheats his fellow and says, "I was only
joking."

²⁰For lack of wood a fire goes out,
And without a querulous man contention is
stilled.

²¹Charcoal for embers and wood for a fire
And a contentious man for kindling strife.

²²The words of a querulous man are bruising;ᶜ
They penetrate one's inmost parts.

²³Base silver laid over earthenware
Are ardent lips with an evil mind.

²⁴An enemy dissembles with his speech,
Inwardly he harbors deceit.

²⁵Though he be fair-spoken do not trust him,
For seven abominations are in his mind.

²⁶His hatred may be concealed by dissimulation,
But his evil will be exposed to public view.

²⁷He who digs a pit will fall in it,
And whoever rolls a stone, it will roll back on him.

²⁸A lying tongue hates ᶜ⁻those crushed by it;⁻ᶜ
Smooth speech throws one down.

אָמַר עָצֵל שַׁחַל בַּדָּרֶךְ 13
אֲרִי בֵּין הָרְחֹבוֹת:
הַדֶּלֶת תִּסּוֹב עַל־צִירָהּ 14
וְעָצֵל עַל־מִטָּתוֹ:
טָמַן עָצֵל יָדוֹ בַּצַּלָּחַת 15
נִלְאָה לַהֲשִׁיבָהּ אֶל־פִּיו:
חָכָם עָצֵל בְּעֵינָיו 16
מִשִּׁבְעָה מְשִׁיבֵי טָעַם:

מַחֲזִיק בְּאָזְנֵי־כָלֶב 17
עֹבֵר מִתְעַבֵּר עַל־רִיב לֹא־לוֹ:
כְּמִתְלַהְלֵהַּ הַיֹּרֶה זִקִּים חִצִּים 18
וָמָוֶת:
כֵּן־אִישׁ רִמָּה אֶת־רֵעֵהוּ 19
וְאָמַר הֲלֹא־מְשַׂחֵק אָנִי:

בְּאֶפֶס עֵצִים תִּכְבֶּה־אֵשׁ 20
וּבְאֵין נִרְגָּן יִשְׁתֹּק מָדוֹן:
פֶּחָם לְגֶחָלִים וְעֵצִים לְאֵשׁ 21
וְאִישׁ מדונים מִדְיָנִים לְחַרְחַר־
רִיב: פ
דִּבְרֵי נִרְגָּן כְּמִתְלַהֲמִים 22
וְהֵם יָרְדוּ חַדְרֵי־בָטֶן:

כֶּסֶף סִיגִים מְצֻפֶּה עַל־חָרֶשׂ 23
שְׂפָתַיִם דֹּלְקִים וְלֶב־רָע:
בשפתו בִּשְׂפָתָיו יִנָּכֵר שׂוֹנֵא 24
וּבְקִרְבּוֹ יָשִׁית מִרְמָה:
כִּי־יְחַנֵּן קוֹלוֹ אַל־תַּאֲמֶן־בּוֹ 25
כִּי שֶׁבַע תּוֹעֵבוֹת בְּלִבּוֹ:
תִּכַּסֶּה שִׂנְאָה בְּמַשָּׁאוֹן 26
תִּגָּלֶה רָעָתוֹ בְקָהָל:

כֹּרֶה־שַּׁחַת בָּהּ יִפֹּל 27
וְגֹלֵל אֶבֶן אֵלָיו תָּשׁוּב:
לְשׁוֹן־שֶׁקֶר יִשְׂנָא דַכָּיו 28
וּפֶה חָלָק יַעֲשֶׂה מִדְחֶה:

27

Do not boast of tomorrow,

For you do not know what the day will bring.

2Let the mouth of another praise you, not yours,

The lips of a stranger, not your own.

3A stone has weight, sand is heavy,

But a fool's vexation outweighs them both.

4There is the cruelty of fury, the overflowing of anger,

But who can withstand jealousy?

5Open reproof is better than concealed love.

6Wounds by a loved one are long lasting;

The kisses of an enemy are profuse.

7A sated person disdains honey,

But to a hungry man anything bitter seems sweet.

8Like a sparrow wandering from its nest

Is a man who wanders from his home.

9Oil and incense gladden the heart,

And the sweetness of a friend is better than one's own counsel.

10Do not desert your friend and your father's friend;

Do not enter your brother's house in your time of misfortune;

A close neighbor is better than a distant brother.

11Get wisdom, my son, and gladden my heart,

That I may have what to answer those who taunt me.

12The shrewd man saw trouble and took cover;

The simple kept going and paid the penalty.

13Seize his garment, for he stood surety for another;[a]

Take it as a pledge, [for he stood surety] for an unfamiliar woman.

14He who greets his fellow loudly early in the morning

Shall have it reckoned to him as a curse.

15An endless dripping on a rainy day

And a contentious wife are alike;

כז אַל־תִּתְהַלֵּל בְּיוֹם מָחָר

כִּי לֹא־תֵדַע מַה־יֵּלֶד יוֹם׃

2 יְהַלֶּלְךָ זָר וְלֹא־פִיךָ

נָכְרִי וְאַל־שְׂפָתֶיךָ׃

3 כֹּבֶד־אֶבֶן וְנֵטֶל הַחוֹל

וְכַעַס אֱוִיל כָּבֵד מִשְּׁנֵיהֶם׃

4 אַכְזְרִיּוּת חֵמָה וְשֶׁטֶף אָף

וּמִי יַעֲמֹד לִפְנֵי קִנְאָה׃

5 טוֹבָה תּוֹכַחַת מְגֻלָּה

מֵאַהֲבָה מְסֻתָּרֶת׃

6 נֶאֱמָנִים פִּצְעֵי אוֹהֵב

וְנַעְתָּרוֹת נְשִׁיקוֹת שׂוֹנֵא׃

7 נֶפֶשׁ שְׂבֵעָה תָּבוּס נֹפֶת

וְנֶפֶשׁ רְעֵבָה כָּל־מַר מָתוֹק׃

8 כְּצִפּוֹר נוֹדֶדֶת מִן־קִנָּהּ

כֵּן־אִישׁ נוֹדֵד מִמְּקוֹמוֹ׃

9 שֶׁמֶן וּקְטֹרֶת יְשַׂמַּח־לֵב

וּמֶתֶק רֵעֵהוּ מֵעֲצַת־נָפֶשׁ׃

10 רֵעֲךָ ורעה וְרֵעַ אָבִיךָ אַל־תַּעֲזֹב

וּבֵית אָחִיךָ אַל־תָּבוֹא בְּיוֹם אֵידֶךָ

טוֹב שָׁכֵן קָרוֹב מֵאָח רָחוֹק׃

11 חֲכַם בְּנִי וְשַׂמַּח לִבִּי

וְאָשִׁיבָה חֹרְפִי דָבָר׃

12 עָרוּם רָאָה רָעָה נִסְתָּר

פְּתָאיִם* עָבְרוּ נֶעֱנָשׁוּ׃

13 קַח־בִּגְדוֹ כִּי־עָרַב זָר

וּבְעַד נָכְרִיָּה חַבְלֵהוּ׃

14 מְבָרֵךְ רֵעֵהוּ ׀ בְּקוֹל גָּדוֹל בַּבֹּקֶר הַשְׁכֵּים

קְלָלָה תֵּחָשֶׁב לוֹ׃

15 דֶּלֶף טוֹרֵד בְּיוֹם סַגְרִיר

וְאֵשֶׁת מדונים מִדְיָנִים נִשְׁתָּוָה׃

---

a Or "a stranger."

¹⁶As soon repress her as repress the wind,
Or declare one's right hand to be oil.
¹⁷As iron sharpens iron
So a man sharpens the wit^b of his friend.
¹⁸He who tends a fig tree will enjoy its fruit,
And he who cares for his master will be honored.
¹⁹As face answers to face in water,
So does one man's heart to another.
²⁰Sheol and Abaddon cannot be satisfied,
Nor can the eyes of man be satisfied.
²¹For silver—the crucible, for gold—the furnace,
And a man is tested by his praise.
²²Even if you pound the fool in a mortar
With a pestle along with grain,
His folly will not leave him.

²³Mind well the looks of your flock;
Pay attention to your herds;
²⁴For property does not last forever,
Or a crown for all generations.
²⁵Grass vanishes, new grass appears,
And the herbage of the hills is gathered in.
²⁶The lambs will provide you with clothing,
The he-goats, the price of a field.
²⁷The goats' milk will suffice for your food,
The food of your household,
And the maintenance of your maids.

28 The wicked flee though no one gives chase,
But the righteous are as confident as a lion.
²When there is rebellion in the land, many are its
rulers;
^a-But with a man who has understanding and
knowledge, stability will last.-^a
³A poor man who withholds what is due to the
wretched

צָפְנֶיהָ צָפַן־רוּחַ 16
וְשֶׁמֶן יְמִינוֹ יִקְרָא:
בַּרְזֶל בְּבַרְזֶל יָחַד 17
וְאִישׁ יַחַד פְּנֵי־רֵעֵהוּ:
נֹצֵר תְּאֵנָה יֹאכַל פִּרְיָהּ 18
וְשֹׁמֵר אֲדֹנָיו יְכֻבָּד:
כַּמַּיִם הַפָּנִים לַפָּנִים 19
כֵּן לֵב־הָאָדָם לָאָדָם:
שְׁאוֹל ואבדה וַאֲבַדּוֹ לֹא תִשְׂבַּעְנָה 20
וְעֵינֵי הָאָדָם לֹא תִשְׂבַּעְנָה:
מַצְרֵף לַכֶּסֶף וְכוּר לַזָּהָב 21
וְאִישׁ לְפִי מַהֲלָלוֹ:
אִם תִּכְתּוֹשׁ־אֶת־הָאֱוִיל ׀ בַּמַּכְתֵּשׁ 22
בְּתוֹךְ הָרִיפוֹת בַּעֱלִי
לֹא־תָסוּר מֵעָלָיו אִוַּלְתּוֹ: פ
יָדֹעַ תֵּדַע פְּנֵי צֹאנֶךָ 23
שִׁית לִבְּךָ לַעֲדָרִים:
כִּי לֹא לְעוֹלָם חֹסֶן 24
וְאִם־נֵזֶר לְדוֹר דּוֹר וָדוֹר:
גָּלָה חָצִיר וְנִרְאָה־דֶשֶׁא 25
וְנֶאֶסְפוּ עִשְּׂבוֹת הָרִים:
כְּבָשִׂים לִלְבוּשֶׁךָ 26
וּמְחִיר שָׂדֶה עַתּוּדִים:
וְדֵי ׀ חֲלֵב עִזִּים לְלַחְמְךָ 27
לְלֶחֶם בֵּיתֶךָ
וְחַיִּים לְנַעֲרוֹתֶיךָ:

כח נָסוּ וְאֵין־רֹדֵף רָשָׁע
וְצַדִּיקִים כִּכְפִיר יִבְטָח:
בְּפֶשַׁע אֶרֶץ רַבִּים שָׂרֶיהָ 2
וּבְאָדָם מֵבִין יֹדֵעַ כֵּן יַאֲרִיךְ:
גֶּבֶר רָשׁ וְעֹשֵׁק דַּלִּים 3

---

b   Lit. "face."

a-a   Meaning of Heb. uncertain.

Is like a destructive rain that leaves no food.

4Those who forsake instruction praise the wicked,

But those who heed instruction fight them.

5Evil men cannot discern judgment,

But those who seek the LORD discern all things.

6Better is a poor man who lives blamelessly

Than a rich man whose ways are crooked.

7An intelligent son heeds instruction,

But he who keeps company with gluttons disgraces his father.

8He who increases his wealth by loans at discount or interest

Amasses it for one who is generous to the poor.

9He who turns a deaf ear to instruction—

His prayer is an abomination.

10He who misleads the upright into an evil course

Will fall into his own pit,

But the blameless will prosper.

11A rich man is clever in his own eyes,

But a perceptive poor man can see through him.

12When the righteous exult there is great glory,

But when the wicked rise up men make themselves scarce.

13He who covers up his faults will not succeed;

He who confesses and gives them up will find mercy.

14Happy is the man who is anxious always,

But he who hardens his heart falls into misfortune.

15A roaring lion and a prowling bear

Is a wicked man ruling a helpless people.

16A prince who lacks understanding is very oppressive;

He who spurns ill-gotten gains will live long.

17A man oppressed by bloodguilt will flee to a pit;

Let none give him support.

18He who lives blamelessly will be delivered,

But he who is crooked in his ways will fall all at once.

מָטָר סֹחֵף וְאֵין לָחֶם:

4 עֹזְבֵי תוֹרָה יְהַלְלוּ רָשָׁע

וְשֹׁמְרֵי תוֹרָה יִתְגָּרוּ בָם: פ

5 אַנְשֵׁי־רָע לֹא־יָבִינוּ מִשְׁפָּט

וּמְבַקְשֵׁי יְהֹוָה יָבִינוּ כֹל:

6 טוֹב־רָשׁ הוֹלֵךְ בְּתֻמּוֹ

מֵעִקֵּשׁ דְּרָכַיִם וְהוּא עָשִׁיר:

7 נוֹצֵר תּוֹרָה בֵּן מֵבִין

וְרֹעֶה זוֹלְלִים יַכְלִים אָבִיו:

8 מַרְבֶּה הוֹנוֹ בְּנֶשֶׁךְ ובתרבית וְתַרְבִּית

לְחוֹנֵן דַּלִּים יִקְבְּצֶנּוּ:

9 מֵסִיר אָזְנוֹ מִשְּׁמֹעַ תּוֹרָה

גַּם־תְּפִלָּתוֹ תּוֹעֵבָה:

10 מַשְׁגֶּה יְשָׁרִים ׀ בְּדֶרֶךְ רָע

בִּשְׁחוּתוֹ הוּא־יִפּוֹל

וּתְמִימִים יִנְחֲלוּ־טוֹב:

11 חָכָם בְּעֵינָיו אִישׁ עָשִׁיר

וְדַל מֵבִין יַחְקְרֶנּוּ:

12 בַּעֲלֹץ צַדִּיקִים רַבָּה תִפְאָרֶת

וּבְקוּם רְשָׁעִים יְחֻפַּשׂ אָדָם:

13 מְכַסֶּה פְשָׁעָיו לֹא יַצְלִיחַ

וּמוֹדֶה וְעֹזֵב יְרֻחָם:

14 אַשְׁרֵי אָדָם מְפַחֵד תָּמִיד

וּמַקְשֶׁה לִבּוֹ יִפּוֹל בְּרָעָה:

15 אֲרִי־נֹהֵם וְדֹב שׁוֹקֵק

מֹשֵׁל רָשָׁע עַל עַם־דָּל:

16 נָגִיד חֲסַר תְּבוּנוֹת וְרַב מַעֲשַׁקּוֹת

שֹׂנְאֵי שֶׁנֶא בֶצַע יַאֲרִיךְ יָמִים: פ

17 אָדָם עָשֻׁק בְּדַם־נָפֶשׁ

עַד־בּוֹר יָנוּס אַל־יִתְמְכוּ־בוֹ:

18 הוֹלֵךְ תָּמִים יִוָּשֵׁעַ

וְנֶעְקַשׁ דְּרָכַיִם יִפּוֹל בְּאֶחָת:

¹⁹He who tills his land will have food in plenty,
But he who pursues vanities will have poverty in
   plenty.
²⁰A dependable man will receive many blessings,
But one in a hurry to get rich will not go un-
   punished.
²¹To be partial is not right;
A man may do wrong for a piece of bread.
²²A miserly man runs after wealth;
He does not realize that loss will overtake it.
²³He who reproves a man will in the end
Find more favor than he who flatters him.
²⁴He who robs his father and mother and says,
   "It is no offense,"
Is a companion to vandals.
²⁵A greedy man provokes quarrels,
But he who trusts the Lord shall enjoy prosperity.
²⁶He who trusts his own instinct is a dullard,
But he who lives by wisdom shall escape.
²⁷He who gives to the poor will not be in want,
But he who shuts his eyes will be roundly cursed.
²⁸When the wicked rise up, men go into hiding,
But when they perish the righteous increase.

29

One oft reproved may become stiffnecked,
But he will be suddenly broken beyond repair.
²When the righteous become great the people re-
   joice,
But when the wicked dominate the people groan.
³A man who loves wisdom brings joy to his father,
But he who keeps company with harlots will lose
   his wealth.
⁴By justice a king sustains the land,
But a fraudulent man tears it down.
⁵A man who flatters his fellow
Spreads a net for his feet.
⁶An evil man's offenses are a trap for himself,
But the righteous sing out joyously.

עֹבֵד אַדְמָתוֹ יִשְׂבַּֽע־לָחֶם 19
וּמְרַדֵּף רֵקִים יִֽשְׂבַּע־רִֽישׁ׃
אִישׁ אֱמוּנוֹת רַב־בְּרָכוֹת 20
וְאָץ לְהַעֲשִׁיר לֹא יִנָּקֶֽה׃
הַכֵּר־פָּנִים לֹא־טוֹב 21
וְעַל־פַּת־לֶחֶם יִפְשַׁע־גָּֽבֶר׃
נִֽבְהָל לַהוֹן אִישׁ רַע עָיִן 22
וְלֹֽא־יֵדַע כִּי־חֶסֶר יְבֹאֶֽנּוּ׃
מוֹכִיחַ אָדָם אַחֲרַי חֵן יִמְצָא 23
מִֽמַּחֲלִיק לָשֽׁוֹן׃
גּוֹזֵל ׀ אָבִיו וְאִמּוֹ וְאֹמֵר אֵֽין־ 24
פָּשַׁע
חָבֵר הוּא לְאִישׁ מַשְׁחִֽית׃
רְחַב־נֶפֶשׁ יְגָרֶה מָדוֹן 25
וּבוֹטֵחַ עַל־יְהוָה יְדֻשָּֽׁן׃
בּוֹטֵחַ בְּלִבּוֹ הוּא כְסִיל 26
וְהוֹלֵךְ בְּחָכְמָה הוּא יִמָּלֵֽט׃
נוֹתֵן לָרָשׁ אֵין מַחְסוֹר 27
וּמַעְלִים עֵינָיו רַב־מְאֵרֽוֹת׃
בְּקוּם רְשָׁעִים יִסָּתֵר אָדָם 28
וּבְאָבְדָם יִרְבּוּ צַדִּיקִֽים׃

כט אִישׁ תּֽוֹכָחוֹת מַקְשֶׁה־עֹרֶף
פֶּתַע יִשָּׁבֵר וְאֵין מַרְפֵּֽא׃
בִּרְבוֹת צַדִּיקִים יִשְׂמַח הָעָם 2
וּבִמְשֹׁל רָשָׁע יֵאָנַֽח עָֽם׃
אִישׁ־אֹהֵב חָכְמָה יְשַׂמַּח אָבִיו 3
וְרֹעֶה זוֹנוֹת יְאַבֶּד־הֽוֹן׃
מֶלֶךְ בְּמִשְׁפָּט יַעֲמִיד אָרֶץ 4
וְאִישׁ תְּרוּמוֹת יֶהֶרְסֶֽנָּה׃
גֶּבֶר מַחֲלִיק עַל־רֵעֵהוּ 5
רֶשֶׁת פּוֹרֵשׂ עַל־פְּעָמָֽיו׃
בְּפֶשַׁע אִישׁ רָע מוֹקֵשׁ 6
וְצַדִּיק יָרוּן וְשָׂמֵֽחַ׃

7A righteous man is concerned with the cause of
   the wretched;
A wicked man cannot understand such concern.

8Scoffers inflame a city,
But the wise allay anger.

9When a wise man enters into litigation with a
   fool
There is ranting and ridicule, but no satisfaction.

10Bloodthirsty men detest the blameless,
But the upright seek them out.

11A dullard vents all his rage,
But a wise man calms it down.

12A ruler who listens to lies,
All his ministers will be wicked.

13A poor man and a fraudulent man meet;
The LORD gives luster to the eyes of both.

14A king who judges the wretched honestly,
His throne will be established forever.

15Rod and reproof produce wisdom,
But a lad out of control is a disgrace to his mother.

16When the wicked increase, offenses increase,
But the righteous will see their downfall.

17Discipline your son and he will give you peace;
He will gratify you with dainties.

18For lack of vision a people lose restraint,
But happy is he who heeds instruction.

19A slave cannot be disciplined by words;
Though he may comprehend, he does not respond.

20If you see a man hasty in speech,
There is more hope for a fool than for him.

21A slave pampered from youth
a-Will come to a bad end.-a

22An angry man provokes a quarrel;
A hot-tempered man commits many offenses.

23A man's pride will humiliate him,
But a humble man will obtain honor.

24He who shares with a thief is his own enemy;
He hears the imprecation and does not tell.b

7 יֹדֵעַ צַדִּיק דִּין דַּלִּים
רָשָׁע לֹא־יָבִין דָּעַת׃
8 אַנְשֵׁי לָצוֹן יָפִיחוּ קִרְיָה
וַחֲכָמִים יָשִׁיבוּ אָף׃
9 אִישׁ־חָכָם נִשְׁפָּט אֶת־אִישׁ אֱוִיל
וְרָגַז וְשָׂחַק וְאֵין נָחַת׃
10 אַנְשֵׁי דָמִים יִשְׂנְאוּ־תָם
וִישָׁרִים יְבַקְשׁוּ נַפְשׁוֹ׃
11 כָּל־רוּחוֹ יוֹצִיא כְסִיל
וְחָכָם בְּאָחוֹר יְשַׁבְּחֶנָּה׃
12 מֹשֵׁל מַקְשִׁיב עַל־דְּבַר־שָׁקֶר
כָּל־מְשָׁרְתָיו רְשָׁעִים׃
13 רָשׁ וְאִישׁ תְּכָכִים נִפְגָּשׁוּ
מֵאִיר־עֵינֵי שְׁנֵיהֶם יְהוָה׃
14 מֶלֶךְ שׁוֹפֵט בֶּאֱמֶת דַּלִּים
כִּסְאוֹ לָעַד יִכּוֹן׃
15 שֵׁבֶט וְתוֹכַחַת יִתֵּן חָכְמָה
וְנַעַר מְשֻׁלָּח מֵבִישׁ אִמּוֹ׃
16 בִּרְבוֹת רְשָׁעִים יִרְבֶּה־פָּשַׁע
וְצַדִּיקִים בְּמַפַּלְתָּם יִרְאוּ׃
17 יַסֵּר בִּנְךָ וִינִיחֶךָ
וְיִתֵּן מַעֲדַנִּים לְנַפְשֶׁךָ׃ פ
18 בְּאֵין חָזוֹן יִפָּרַע עָם
וְשֹׁמֵר תּוֹרָה אַשְׁרֵהוּ׃
19 בִּדְבָרִים לֹא־יִוָּסֶר עָבֶד
כִּי־יָבִין וְאֵין מַעֲנֶה׃
20 חָזִיתָ אִישׁ אָץ בִּדְבָרָיו
תִּקְוָה לִכְסִיל מִמֶּנּוּ׃
21 מְפַנֵּק מִנֹּעַר עַבְדּוֹ
וְאַחֲרִיתוֹ יִהְיֶה מָנוֹן׃
22 אִישׁ־אַף יְגָרֶה מָדוֹן
וּבַעַל חֵמָה רַב־פָּשַׁע׃
23 גַּאֲוַת אָדָם תַּשְׁפִּילֶנּוּ
וּשְׁפַל־רוּחַ יִתְמֹךְ כָּבוֹד׃
24 חוֹלֵק עִם־גַּנָּב שׂוֹנֵא נַפְשׁוֹ
אָלָה יִשְׁמַע וְלֹא יַגִּיד׃

---

a-a   Meaning of Heb. uncertain.
b   Cf. Lev. 5.1.

²⁵A man's fears become a trap for him,

But he who trusts in the LORD shall be safeguarded.

²⁶Many seek audience with a ruler,

But it is from the LORD that a man gets justice.

²⁷The unjust man is an abomination to the right-
eous,

And he whose way is straight is an abomination
to the wicked.

30
The words of Agur son of Jakeh, [man of]
Massa; The speech of the man to Ithiel, to Ithiel and
Ucal:

²I am brutish, less than a man;

I lack common sense.

³I have not learned wisdom,

Nor do I possess knowledge of the Holy One.

⁴Who has ascended heaven and come down?

Who has gathered up the wind in the hollow of
his hand?

Who has wrapped the waters in his garment?

Who has established all the extremities of the
earth?

What is his name or his son's name, if you
know it?

⁵Every word of God is pure,

A shield to those who take refuge in Him.

⁶Do not add to His words,

Lest He indict you and you be proved a liar.

⁷Two things I ask of you; do not deny them to
me before I die:

⁸Keep lies and false words far from me;

Give me neither poverty nor riches,

But provide me with my daily bread,

⁹Lest, being sated, I renounce, saying,

25 חֶרְדַּת אָדָם יִתֵּן מוֹקֵשׁ

וּבוֹטֵחַ בַּיהוָה יְשֻׂגָּב:

26 רַבִּים מְבַקְשִׁים פְּנֵי־מוֹשֵׁל

וּמֵיהוָה מִשְׁפַּט־אִישׁ:

27 תּוֹעֲבַת צַדִּיקִים אִישׁ עָוֶל

וְתוֹעֲבַת רָשָׁע יְשַׁר־דָּרֶךְ: פ

ל

דִּבְרֵי ׀ אָגוּר בִּן־יָקֶה הַמַּשָּׂא נְאֻם
הַגֶּבֶר לְאִיתִיאֵל לְאִיתִיאֵל וְאֻכָל:

2 כִּי בַעַר אָנֹכִי מֵאִישׁ

וְלֹא־בִינַת אָדָם לִי:

3 וְלֹא־לָמַדְתִּי חָכְמָה

וְדַעַת קְדֹשִׁים אֵדָע:

4 מִי עָלָה־שָׁמַיִם ׀ וַיֵּרַד

מִי אָסַף־רוּחַ ׀ בְּחָפְנָיו

מִי צָרַר־מַיִם ׀ בַּשִּׂמְלָה

מִי הֵקִים כָּל־אַפְסֵי־אָרֶץ

מַה־שְּׁמוֹ וּמַה־שֶּׁם־בְּנוֹ כִּי תֵדָע:

5 כָּל־אִמְרַת אֱלוֹהַּ צְרוּפָה

מָגֵן הוּא לַחֹסִים בּוֹ:

6 אַל־תּוֹסְףְּ עַל־דְּבָרָיו

פֶּן־יוֹכִיחַ בְּךָ וְנִכְזָבְתָּ: פ

7 שְׁתַּיִם שָׁאַלְתִּי מֵאִתָּךְ

אַל־תִּמְנַע מִמֶּנִּי בְּטֶרֶם אָמוּת:

8 שָׁוְא ׀ וּדְבַר־כָּזָב הַרְחֵק מִמֶּנִּי

רֵאשׁ* וָעֹשֶׁר אַל־תִּתֶּן־לִי

הַטְרִיפֵנִי לֶחֶם חֻקִּי:

9 פֶּן אֶשְׂבַּע ׀ וְכִחַשְׁתִּי וְאָמַרְתִּי

v. 8. א׳ במקום ר׳

"Who is the LORD?"
Or, being impoverished, I take to theft
And profane[a] the name of my God.
10 Do not inform on a slave to his master,
Lest he curse you and you incur guilt.

11 There is a breed of men that brings a curse on
its fathers
And brings no blessing to its mothers,
12 A breed that thinks itself pure,
Though it is not washed of its filth;
13 A breed so haughty of bearing, so supercilious;
14 A breed whose teeth are swords,
Whose jaws are knives,
Ready to devour the poor of the land,
The needy among men.

15 The leech has two daughters, "Give!" and
"Give!"
Three things are insatiable;
Four never say, "Enough!":
16 Sheol, a barren womb,
Earth that cannot get enough water,
And fire which never says, "Enough!"

17 The eye that mocks a father
And disdains the homage due a mother—
The ravens of the brook will gouge it out,
Young eagles will devour it.

18 Three things are beyond me;
Four I cannot fathom:
19 How an eagle makes its way over the sky;
How a snake makes its way over a rock;
How a ship makes its way through the high seas;
How a man has his way with a maiden.
20 Such is the way of an adulteress:
She eats, wipes her mouth,
And says, "I have done no wrong."

מִי יְהוָה
וּפֶן־אִוָּרֵשׁ וְגָנַבְתִּי
וְתָפַשְׂתִּי שֵׁם אֱלֹהָי: פ
10 אַל־תַּלְשֵׁן עֶבֶד אֶל־אֲדֹנָו
פֶּן־יְקַלֶּלְךָ וְאָשָׁמְתָּ:

11 דּוֹר אָבִיו יְקַלֵּל
וְאֶת־אִמּוֹ לֹא יְבָרֵךְ:
12 דּוֹר טָהוֹר בְּעֵינָיו
וּמִצֹּאָתוֹ לֹא רֻחָץ:
13 דּוֹר מָה־רָמוּ עֵינָיו
וְעַפְעַפָּיו יִנָּשֵׂאוּ:
14 דּוֹר ׀ חֲרָבוֹת שִׁנָּיו
וּמַאֲכָלוֹת מְתַלְּעֹתָיו
לֶאֱכֹל עֲנִיִּים מֵאֶרֶץ
וְאֶבְיוֹנִים מֵאָדָם: פ

15 לַעֲלוּקָה ׀ שְׁתֵּי בָנוֹת הַב ׀ הַב
שָׁלוֹשׁ הֵנָּה לֹא תִשְׂבַּעְנָה
אַרְבַּע לֹא־אָמְרוּ הוֹן:
16 שְׁאוֹל וְעֹצֶר רָחַם אֶרֶץ לֹא־
שָׂבְעָה מַּיִם
וְאֵשׁ לֹא־אָמְרָה הוֹן:

17 עַיִן ׀ תִּלְעַג לְאָב
וְתָבוּז לִיקֲּהַת־אֵם
יִקְּרוּהָ עֹרְבֵי־נַחַל
וְיֹאכְלוּהָ בְנֵי־נָשֶׁר: פ

18 שְׁלֹשָׁה הֵמָּה נִפְלְאוּ מִמֶּנִּי
וְארבע וְאַרְבָּעָה לֹא יְדַעְתִּים:
19 דֶּרֶךְ הַנֶּשֶׁר ׀ בַּשָּׁמַיִם
דֶּרֶךְ נָחָשׁ עֲלֵי צוּר
דֶּרֶךְ־אֳנִיָּה בְלֶב־יָם
וְדֶרֶךְ גֶּבֶר בְּעַלְמָה:
20 כֵּן ׀ דֶּרֶךְ אִשָּׁה מְנָאָפֶת
אָכְלָה וּמָחֲתָה פִיהָ
וְאָמְרָה לֹא־פָעַלְתִּי אָוֶן: פ

a Meaning of Heb. uncertain.

21The earth shudders at three things,
At four which it cannot bear:
22A slave who becomes king;
A scoundrel sated with food;
23A loathsome woman who gets married;
A slave-girl who supplants her mistress.

24Four are among the tiniest on earth,
Yet they are the wisest of the wise:
25Ants are a folk without power,
Yet they prepare food for themselves in summer;
26The badger is a folk without strength,
Yet it makes its home in the rock;
27The locusts have no king,
Yet they all march forth in formation;
28You can catch the lizard[b] in your hand,
Yet it is found in royal palaces.

29There are three that are stately of stride,
Four that carry themselves well:
30The lion is mightiest among the beasts,
And recoils before none;
31a-The greyhound, the he-goat,
The king whom none dares resist.-a

32If you have been scandalously arrogant,
If you have been a schemer,
Then clap your hand to your mouth.
33As milk under pressure produces butter,
And a nose under pressure produces blood,
So patience under pressure produces strife.

31 The words of Lemuel, king of Massa, with which his mother admonished him:

2No, my son!
No, O son of my womb!
No, O son of my vows!

21 תַּחַת שָׁלוֹשׁ רָגְזָה אֶרֶץ
וְתַחַת אַרְבַּע לֹא־תוּכַל שְׂאֵת:
22 תַּחַת־עֶבֶד כִּי יִמְלוֹךְ
וְנָבָל כִּי יִשְׂבַּע־לָחֶם:
23 תַּחַת שְׂנוּאָה כִּי תִבָּעֵל
וְשִׁפְחָה כִּי־תִירַשׁ גְּבִרְתָּהּ: פ

24 אַרְבָּעָה הֵם קְטַנֵּי־אָרֶץ
וְהֵמָּה חֲכָמִים מְחֻכָּמִים:
25 הַנְּמָלִים עַם לֹא־עָז
וַיָּכִינוּ בַקַּיִץ לַחְמָם:
26 שְׁפַנִּים עַם לֹא־עָצוּם
וַיָּשִׂימוּ בַסֶּלַע בֵּיתָם:
27 מֶלֶךְ אֵין לָאַרְבֶּה
וַיֵּצֵא חֹצֵץ כֻּלּוֹ:
28 שְׂמָמִית בְּיָדַיִם תְּתַפֵּשׂ
וְהִיא בְּהֵיכְלֵי מֶלֶךְ: פ

29 שְׁלֹשָׁה הֵמָּה מֵיטִיבֵי צָעַד
וְאַרְבָּעָה מֵיטִבֵי לָכֶת:
30 לַיִשׁ גִּבּוֹר בַּבְּהֵמָה
וְלֹא־יָשׁוּב מִפְּנֵי־כֹל:
31 זַרְזִיר מָתְנַיִם אוֹ־תָיִשׁ
וּמֶלֶךְ אַלְקוּם עִמּוֹ:

32 אִם־נָבַלְתָּ בְהִתְנַשֵּׂא
וְאִם־זַמּוֹתָ יָד לְפֶה:
33 כִּי מִיץ חָלָב יוֹצִיא חֶמְאָה
וּמִיץ־אַף יוֹצִיא דָם
וּמִיץ אַפַּיִם יוֹצִיא רִיב: פ

לא דִּבְרֵי לְמוּאֵל מֶלֶךְ מַשָּׂא
אֲשֶׁר־יִסְּרַתּוּ אִמּוֹ:

2 מַה־בְּרִי
וּמַה־בַּר־בִּטְנִי
וּמֶה בַּר־נְדָרָי:

---

b   Or "spider."

1653

3Do not give your strength to women,

Your vigor,[a] [b-to those who destroy kings.-b]

4Wine is not for kings, O Lemuel;

Not for kings to drink,

Nor any strong drink for princes,

5Lest they drink and forget what has been ordained,

And infringe on the rights of the poor.

6Give strong drink to the hapless

And wine to the embittered.

7Let them drink and forget their poverty,

And put their troubles out of mind.

8Speak up for the dumb,

For the rights of all the unfortunate.

9Speak up, judge righteously,

Champion the poor and the needy.

3 אַל־תִּתֵּן לַנָּשִׁים חֵילֶךָ

וּדְרָכֶיךָ לַמְחוֹת מְלָכִין*:

4 אַל לַמְלָכִים ׀ לְמוֹאֵל

אַל לַמְלָכִים שְׁתוֹ־יָיִן

וּלְרוֹזְנִים אוֹ אֵי שֵׁכָר:

5 פֶּן־יִשְׁתֶּה וְיִשְׁכַּח מְחֻקָּק

וִישַׁנֶּה דִּין כָּל־בְּנֵי־עֹנִי:

6 תְּנוּ־שֵׁכָר לְאוֹבֵד

וְיַיִן לְמָרֵי נָפֶשׁ:

7 יִשְׁתֶּה וְיִשְׁכַּח רִישׁוֹ

וַעֲמָלוֹ לֹא יִזְכָּר־עוֹד:

8 פְּתַח־פִּיךָ לְאִלֵּם

אֶל־דִּין כָּל־בְּנֵי חֲלוֹף:

9 פְּתַח־פִּיךָ שְׁפָט־צֶדֶק

וְדִין עָנִי וְאֶבְיוֹן: פ

א 10What a rare find is a capable wife!

Her worth is far beyond that of rubies.

ב 11Her husband puts his confidence in her,

And lacks no good thing.

ג 12She is good to him, never bad,

All the days of her life.

ד 13She looks for wool and flax,

And sets her hand to them with a will.

ה 14She is like a merchant fleet,

Bringing her food from afar.

ו 15She rises while it is still night,

And supplies provisions for her household,

The daily fare of her maids.

ז 16She sets her mind on an estate and acquires it;

She plants a vineyard by her own labors.

ח 17She girds herself with strength,

[c-And performs her tasks with vigor.-c]

ט 18She sees[d] that her business thrives;

Her lamp never goes out at night.

י 19She sets her hand to the distaff;

Her fingers work the spindle.

10 אֵשֶׁת־חַיִל מִי יִמְצָא

וְרָחֹק מִפְּנִינִים מִכְרָהּ:

11 בָּטַח בָּהּ לֵב בַּעְלָהּ

וְשָׁלָל לֹא יֶחְסָר:

12 גְּמָלַתְהוּ טוֹב וְלֹא־רָע

כֹּל יְמֵי חַיֶּיהָ:

13 דָּרְשָׁה צֶמֶר וּפִשְׁתִּים

וַתַּעַשׂ בְּחֵפֶץ כַּפֶּיהָ:

14 הָיְתָה כָּאֳנִיּוֹת סוֹחֵר

מִמֶּרְחָק תָּבִיא לַחְמָהּ:

15 וַתָּקָם ׀ בְּעוֹד לַיְלָה

וַתִּתֵּן טֶרֶף לְבֵיתָהּ

וְחֹק לְנַעֲרֹתֶיהָ:

16 זָמְמָה שָׂדֶה וַתִּקָּחֵהוּ

מִפְּרִי כַפֶּיהָ נטע נָטְעָה כָּרֶם:

17 חָגְרָה בְעוֹז מָתְנֶיהָ

וַתְּאַמֵּץ זְרוֹעֹתֶיהָ:

18 טָעֲמָה כִּי־טוֹב סַחְרָהּ

לֹא־יִכְבֶּה בליל בַלַּיְלָה נֵרָהּ:

19 יָדֶיהָ שִׁלְּחָה בַכִּישׁוֹר

וְכַפֶּיהָ תָּמְכוּ פָלֶךְ:

---

a   Lit. "ways."

b-b   Meaning of Heb. uncertain.

c-c   Lit. "And exerts her arms."

d   Lit. "tastes."

ב 20She gives generously to the poor;
Her hands are stretched out to the needy.

ל 21She is not worried for her household because
   of snow,
For her whole household is dressed in crimson.

מ 22She makes covers for herself;
Her clothing is linen and purple.

נ 23Her husband is prominent in the gates,
As he sits among the elders of the land.

ס 24She makes cloth and sells it,
And offers a girdle to the merchant.

ע 25She is clothed with strength and splendor;
She looks to the future cheerfully.

פ 26Her mouth is full of wisdom,
Her tongue with kindly teaching.

צ 27She oversees the activities of her household
And never eats the bread of idleness.

ק 28Her children declare her happy;
Her husband praises her,

ר 29"Many women have done well,
But you surpass them all."

ש 30Grace is deceptive,
Beauty is illusory;
It is for her fear of the LORD
That a woman is to be praised.

ת 31Extol her for the fruit of her hand,
And let her works praise her in the gates.

20 כַּפָּהּ פָּרְשָׂה לֶעָנִי	
וְיָדֶיהָ שִׁלְּחָה לָאֶבְיוֹן:	
21 לֹא־תִירָא לְבֵיתָהּ מִשָּׁלֶג	
כִּי כָל־בֵּיתָהּ לָבֻשׁ שָׁנִים:	
22 מַרְבַדִּים עָשְׂתָה־לָּהּ	
שֵׁשׁ וְאַרְגָּמָן לְבוּשָׁהּ:	
23 נוֹדָע בַּשְּׁעָרִים בַּעְלָהּ	
בְּשִׁבְתּוֹ עִם־זִקְנֵי־אָרֶץ:	
24 סָדִין עָשְׂתָה וַתִּמְכֹּר	
וַחֲגוֹר נָתְנָה לַכְּנַעֲנִי:	
25 עֹז־וְהָדָר לְבוּשָׁהּ	
וַתִּשְׂחַק לְיוֹם אַחֲרוֹן:	
26 פִּיהָ פָּתְחָה בְחָכְמָה	
וְתוֹרַת־חֶסֶד עַל־לְשׁוֹנָהּ:	
27 צוֹפִיָּה הֲלִיכוֹת בֵּיתָהּ	
וְלֶחֶם עַצְלוּת לֹא תֹאכֵל:	
28 קָמוּ בָנֶיהָ וַיְאַשְּׁרוּהָ	
בַּעְלָהּ וַיְהַלְלָהּ:	
29 רַבּוֹת בָּנוֹת עָשׂוּ חָיִל	
וְאַתְּ עָלִית עַל־כֻּלָּנָה:	
30 שֶׁקֶר הַחֵן וְהֶבֶל הַיֹּפִי	
אִשָּׁה יִרְאַת־יְהֹוָה הִיא תִתְהַלָּל:	
31 תְּנוּ־לָהּ מִפְּרִי יָדֶיהָ	
וִיהַלְלוּהָ בַשְּׁעָרִים מַעֲשֶׂיהָ:*	

תם ונשלם תהילה לאל בורא עולם

JOB

1 There was a man in the land of Uz named Job. That man was blameless and upright; he feared God and shunned evil. ²Seven sons and three daughters were born to him; ³his possessions were seven thousand sheep, three thousand camels, five hundred yoke of oxen and five hundred she-asses, and a very large household. That man was wealthier than anyone in the East.

⁴It was the custom of his sons to hold feasts, each on his set day in his own home. They would invite their three sisters to eat and drink with them. ⁵When a round of feast days was over, Job would send word to them to sanctify themselves, and, rising early in the morning, he would make burnt offerings, one for each of them; for Job thought, "Perhaps my children have sinned and blasphemed God in their thoughts." This is what Job always used to do.

⁶One day the divine beings presented themselves before the Lᴏʀᴅ, ᵃ-and the Adversary-ᵃ came along with them. ⁷The Lᴏʀᴅ said to the Adversary, "Where have you been?" The Adversary answered the Lᴏʀᴅ, "I have been roaming all over the earth." ⁸The Lᴏʀᴅ said to the Adversary, "Have you noticed My servant Job? There is no one like him on earth, a blameless and upright man who fears God and shuns evil!" ⁹The Adversary answered the Lᴏʀᴅ, "Does Job not have good reason to fear God? ¹⁰Why, it is You who have fenced him round, him and his household and all that he has. You have blessed his efforts so that his possessions spread out in the land. ¹¹But lay Your hand upon all that he

אִ֗ישׁ הָיָ֥ה בְאֶֽרֶץ־ע֖וּץ אִיּ֣וֹב שְׁמ֑וֹ אִ֣ישׁ הַה֔וּא תָּ֧ם וְיָשָׁ֛ר וִירֵ֥א אֱלֹהִ֖ים וְסָ֥ר מֵרָֽע: ²וַיִּוָּ֥לְדוּ ל֖וֹ שִׁבְעָ֣ה בָנִ֑ים וְשָׁל֖וֹשׁ בָּנֽוֹת: ³וַיְהִ֣י מִ֠קְנֵ֠הוּ שִֽׁבְעַ֨ת אַלְפֵי־צֹ֜אן וּשְׁלֹ֧שֶׁת אַלְפֵ֣י גְמַלִּ֗ים וַחֲמֵ֨שׁ מֵא֤וֹת צֶֽמֶד־בָּקָר֙ וַחֲמֵ֣שׁ מֵא֣וֹת אֲתוֹנ֔וֹת וַעֲבֻדָּ֖ה רַבָּ֣ה מְאֹ֑ד וַיְהִי֙ הָאִ֣ישׁ הַה֔וּא גָּד֖וֹל מִכָּל־בְּנֵי־קֶֽדֶם:

⁴וְהָלְכ֤וּ בָנָיו֙ וְעָשׂ֣וּ מִשְׁתֶּ֔ה בֵּ֖ית אִ֣ישׁ יוֹמ֑וֹ וְשָֽׁלְח֗וּ וְקָרְאוּ֙ לִשְׁלֹ֣שֶׁת אַחְיֹתֵיהֶ֔ם לֶאֱכֹ֥ל וְלִשְׁתּ֖וֹת עִמָּהֶֽם: ⁵וַיְהִ֡י כִּ֣י הִקִּיפוּ֩ יְמֵ֨י הַמִּשְׁתֶּ֜ה וַיִּשְׁלַ֧ח אִיּ֣וֹב וַֽיְקַדְּשֵׁ֗ם וְהִשְׁכִּ֣ים בַּבֹּ֘קֶר֮ וְהֶעֱלָ֣ה עֹלוֹת֮ מִסְפַּ֣ר כֻּלָּם֒ כִּ֚י אָמַ֣ר אִיּ֔וֹב אוּלַי֙ חָטְא֣וּ בָנַ֔י וּבֵרֲכ֥וּ אֱלֹהִ֖ים בִּלְבָבָ֑ם כָּ֛כָה יַעֲשֶׂ֥ה אִיּ֖וֹב כָּל־הַיָּמִֽים: פ

⁶וַיְהִ֣י הַיּ֔וֹם וַיָּבֹ֙אוּ֙ בְּנֵ֣י הָאֱלֹהִ֔ים לְהִתְיַצֵּ֖ב עַל־יְהוָ֑ה וַיָּב֥וֹא גַֽם־הַשָּׂטָ֖ן בְּתוֹכָֽם: ⁷וַיֹּ֧אמֶר יְהוָ֛ה אֶל־הַשָּׂטָ֖ן מֵאַ֣יִן תָּבֹ֑א וַיַּ֨עַן הַשָּׂטָ֤ן אֶת־יְהוָה֙ וַיֹּאמַ֔ר מִשּׁ֣וּט בָּאָ֔רֶץ וּמֵֽהִתְהַלֵּ֖ךְ בָּֽהּ: ⁸וַיֹּ֤אמֶר יְהוָה֙ אֶל־הַשָּׂטָ֔ן הֲשַׂ֥מְתָּ לִבְּךָ֖ עַל־עַבְדִּ֣י אִיּ֑וֹב כִּ֣י אֵ֤ין כָּמֹ֙הוּ֙ בָּאָ֔רֶץ אִ֣ישׁ תָּ֧ם וְיָשָׁ֛ר יְרֵ֥א אֱלֹהִ֖ים וְסָ֥ר מֵרָֽע: ⁹וַיַּ֧עַן הַשָּׂטָ֛ן אֶת־יְהוָ֖ה וַיֹּאמַ֑ר הַֽחִנָּ֔ם יָרֵ֥א אִיּ֖וֹב אֱלֹהִֽים: ¹⁰הֲלֹֽא־אַ֠תְּ שַׂ֣כְתָּ בַעֲד֧וֹ וּבְעַד־בֵּית֛וֹ וּבְעַ֥ד כָּל־אֲשֶׁר־ל֖וֹ מִסָּבִ֑יב מַעֲשֵׂ֤ה יָדָיו֙ בֵּרַ֔כְתָּ וּמִקְנֵ֖הוּ פָּרַ֥ץ בָּאָֽרֶץ: ¹¹וְאוּלָם֙ שְֽׁלַח־נָ֣א יָֽדְךָ֔ וְגַ֖ע בְּכָל־אֲשֶׁר־ל֑וֹ אִם־לֹ֥א עַל־פָּנֶ֖יךָ

---

a-a Heb. *ha-satan.*

has and he will surely blaspheme You to Your face." [12]The Lord replied to the Adversary, "See, all that he has is in your power; only do not lay a hand on him." The Adversary departed from the presence of the Lord.

[13]One day, as his sons and daughters were eating and drinking wine in the house of their eldest brother, [14]a messenger came to Job and said, "The oxen were plowing and the she-asses were grazing alongside them [15]when Sabeans attacked them and carried them off, and put the boys to the sword; I alone have escaped to tell you." [16]This one was still speaking when another came and said, "God's fire fell from heaven, took hold of the sheep and the boys, and burned them up; I alone have escaped to tell you." [17]This one was still speaking when another came and said, "A Chaldean formation of three columns made a raid on the camels and carried them off and put the boys to the sword; I alone have escaped to tell you." [18]This one was still speaking when another came and said, "Your sons and daughters were eating and drinking wine in the house of their eldest brother [19]when suddenly a mighty wind came from the wilderness. It struck the four corners of the house so that it collapsed upon the young people and they died; I alone have escaped to tell you."

[20]Then Job arose, tore his robe, cut off his hair, and threw himself on the ground and worshiped. [21]He said, "Naked came I out of my mother's womb, and naked shall I return there; the Lord has given, and the Lord has taken away; blessed be the name of the Lord."

[22]For all that, Job did not sin nor did he cast reproach on God.

2 One day the divine beings presented themselves before the Lord. The Adversary came

יְבָרֲכֶֽךָּ׃ 12 וַיֹּ֨אמֶר יְהֹוָ֜ה אֶל־הַשָּׂטָ֗ן הִנֵּ֤ה כׇל־אֲשֶׁר־לוֹ֙ בְּיָדֶ֔ךָ רַ֣ק אֵלָ֔יו אַל־תִּשְׁלַ֖ח יָדֶ֑ךָ וַיֵּצֵא֙ הַשָּׂטָ֔ן מֵעִ֖ם פְּנֵ֥י יְהֹוָֽה׃ 13 וַיְהִ֖י הַיּ֑וֹם וּבָנָ֨יו וּבְנֹתָ֤יו אֹֽכְלִים֙ וְשֹׁתִ֣ים יַ֔יִן בְּבֵ֖ית אֲחִיהֶ֥ם הַבְּכֽוֹר׃ 14 וּמַלְאָ֛ךְ בָּ֥א אֶל־אִיּ֖וֹב וַיֹּאמַ֑ר הַבָּקָר֙ הָי֣וּ חֹֽרְשׁ֔וֹת וְהָאֲתֹנ֖וֹת רֹע֥וֹת עַל־יְדֵיהֶֽם׃ 15 וַתִּפֹּ֤ל שְׁבָא֙ וַתִּקָּחֵ֔ם וְאֶת־הַנְּעָרִ֖ים הִכּ֣וּ לְפִי־חָ֑רֶב וָאִמָּ֨לְטָ֧ה רַק־אֲנִ֛י לְבַדִּ֖י לְהַגִּ֥יד לָֽךְ׃ 16 ע֣וֹד ׀ זֶ֣ה מְדַבֵּ֗ר וְזֶה֮ בָּ֣א וַיֹּאמַר֒ אֵ֣שׁ אֱלֹהִ֗ים נָֽפְלָה֙ מִן־הַשָּׁמַ֔יִם וַתִּבְעַ֥ר בַּצֹּ֛אן וּבַנְּעָרִ֖ים וַתֹּאכְלֵ֑ם וָאִמָּ֨לְטָ֧ה רַק־אֲנִ֛י לְבַדִּ֖י לְהַגִּ֥יד לָֽךְ׃ 17 ע֣וֹד ׀ זֶ֣ה מְדַבֵּ֗ר וְזֶה֮ בָּ֣א וַיֹּאמַר֒ כַּשְׂדִּ֞ים שָׂ֣מוּ ׀ שְׁלֹשָׁ֣ה רָאשִׁ֗ים וַֽיִּפְשְׁט֤וּ עַל־הַגְּמַלִּים֙ וַיִּקָּח֔וּם וְאֶת־הַנְּעָרִ֖ים הִכּ֣וּ לְפִי־חָ֑רֶב וָאִמָּ֨לְטָ֧ה רַק־אֲנִ֛י לְבַדִּ֖י לְהַגִּ֥יד לָֽךְ׃ 18 עַ֚ד זֶ֣ה מְדַבֵּ֔ר וְזֶ֖ה בָּ֣א וַיֹּאמַ֑ר בָּנֶ֨יךָ וּבְנוֹתֶ֤יךָ אֹֽכְלִים֙ וְשֹׁתִ֣ים יַ֔יִן בְּבֵ֖ית אֲחִיהֶ֥ם הַבְּכֽוֹר׃ 19 וְהִנֵּה֩ ר֨וּחַ גְּדוֹלָ֜ה בָּ֣אָה ׀ מֵעֵ֣בֶר הַמִּדְבָּ֗ר וַיִּגַּע֙ בְּאַרְבַּע֙ פִּנּ֣וֹת הַבַּ֔יִת וַיִּפֹּ֥ל עַל־הַנְּעָרִ֖ים וַיָּמ֑וּתוּ וָאִמָּ֨לְטָ֧ה רַק־אֲנִ֛י לְבַדִּ֖י לְהַגִּ֥יד לָֽךְ׃ 20 וַיָּ֤קׇם אִיּוֹב֙ וַיִּקְרַ֣ע אֶת־מְעִל֔וֹ וַיָּ֖גׇז אֶת־רֹאשׁ֑וֹ וַיִּפֹּ֥ל אַ֖רְצָה וַיִּשְׁתָּֽחוּ׃ 21 וַיֹּאמֶר֩ עָרֹ֨ם יָצָ֜אתִי מִבֶּ֣טֶן אִמִּ֗י וְעָרֹם֙ אָשׁ֣וּב שָׁ֔מָּה יְהֹוָ֣ה נָתַ֔ן וַיהֹוָ֖ה לָקָ֑ח יְהִ֛י שֵׁ֥ם יְהֹוָ֖ה מְבֹרָֽךְ׃ 22 בְּכׇל־זֹ֖את לֹא־חָטָ֣א אִיּ֑וֹב וְלֹא־נָתַ֥ן תִּפְלָ֖ה לֵֽאלֹהִֽים׃ פ

ב 1 וַיְהִ֣י הַיּ֔וֹם וַיָּבֹ֙אוּ֙ בְּנֵ֣י הָֽאֱלֹהִ֔ים לְהִתְיַצֵּ֖ב עַל־יְהֹוָ֑ה וַיָּב֥וֹא גַֽם־הַשָּׂטָ֛ן

along with them to present himself before the LORD. ²The LORD said to the Adversary, "Where have you been?" The Adversary answered the LORD, "I have been roaming all over the earth." ³The LORD said to the Adversary, "Have you noticed My servant Job? There is no one like him on earth, a blameless and upright man who fears God and shuns evil. He still keeps his integrity; so you have incited Me against him to destroy him for no good reason." ⁴The Adversary answered the LORD, ᵃ-"Skin for skin-ᵃ—all that a man has he will give up for his life. ⁵But lay a hand on his bones and his flesh, and he will surely blaspheme You to Your face." ⁶So the LORD said to the Adversary, "See, he is in your power; only spare his life." ⁷The Adversary departed from the presence of the LORD and inflicted a severe inflammation on Job from the sole of his foot to the crown of his head. ⁸He took a potsherd to scratch himself as he sat in ashes. ⁹His wife said to him, "You still keep your integrity! Blaspheme God and die!" ¹⁰But he said to her, "You talk as any shameless woman might talk! Should we accept only good from God and not accept evil?" For all that, Job said nothing sinful.

¹¹When Job's three friends heard about all these calamities that had befallen him, each came from his home—Eliphaz the Temanite, Bildad the Shuhite, and Zophar the Naamathite. They met together to go and console and comfort him. ¹²When they saw him from a distance, they could not recognize him, and they broke into loud weeping; each one tore his robe and threw dust into the air onto his head. ¹³They sat with him on the ground seven days and seven nights. None spoke a word to him for they saw how very great was his suffering.

---

a-a   Apparently a proverb whose meaning is uncertain.

בְּתֹכָ֖ם לְהִתְיַצֵּ֥ב עַל־יְהֹוָֽה׃ 2 וַיֹּ֨אמֶר יְהֹוָ֤ה אֶל־הַשָּׂטָן֙ אֵ֣י מִזֶּ֣ה תָּבֹ֔א וַיַּ֨עַן הַשָּׂטָ֤ן אֶת־יְהֹוָה֙ וַיֹּאמַ֔ר מִשֻּׁ֣ט בָּאָ֔רֶץ וּמֵהִתְהַלֵּ֖ךְ בָּֽהּ׃ 3 וַיֹּ֨אמֶר יְהֹוָ֜ה אֶל־הַשָּׂטָ֗ן הֲשַׂ֤מְתָּ לִבְּךָ֙ אֶל־עַבְדִּ֣י אִיּ֔וֹב כִּ֣י אֵ֤ין כָּמֹ֙הוּ֙ בָּאָ֔רֶץ אִ֣ישׁ תָּ֧ם וְיָשָׁ֛ר יְרֵ֥א אֱלֹהִ֖ים וְסָ֣ר מֵרָ֑ע וְעֹדֶ֙נּוּ֙ מַחֲזִ֣יק בְּתֻמָּת֔וֹ וַתְּסִיתֵ֥נִי ב֖וֹ לְבַלְּע֥וֹ חִנָּֽם׃ 4 וַיַּ֧עַן הַשָּׂטָ֛ן אֶת־יְהֹוָ֖ה וַיֹּאמַ֑ר ע֣וֹר בְּעַד־ע֗וֹר וְכֹל֙ אֲשֶׁ֣ר לָאִ֔ישׁ יִתֵּ֖ן בְּעַ֥ד נַפְשֽׁוֹ׃ 5 אוּלָם֙ שְֽׁלַֽח־נָ֣א יָֽדְךָ֔ וְגַ֥ע אֶל־עַצְמ֖וֹ וְאֶל־בְּשָׂר֑וֹ אִם־לֹ֥א אֶל־פָּנֶ֖יךָ יְבָרְכֶֽךָּ׃ 6 וַיֹּ֧אמֶר יְהֹוָ֛ה אֶל־הַשָּׂטָ֖ן הִנּ֣וֹ בְיָדֶ֑ךָ אַ֖ךְ אֶת־נַפְשׁ֥וֹ שְׁמֹֽר׃ 7 וַיֵּצֵא֙ הַשָּׂטָ֔ן מֵאֵ֖ת פְּנֵ֣י יְהֹוָ֑ה וַיַּ֤ךְ אֶת־אִיּוֹב֙ בִּשְׁחִ֣ין רָ֔ע מִכַּ֥ף רַגְל֖וֹ עַ֥ד וְעַ֥ד קׇדְקֳדֽוֹ׃ 8 וַיִּֽקַּֽח־ל֣וֹ חֶ֔רֶשׂ לְהִתְגָּרֵ֖ד בּ֑וֹ וְה֖וּא יֹשֵׁ֥ב בְּתוֹךְ־הָאֵֽפֶר׃ 9 וַתֹּ֤אמֶר לוֹ֙ אִשְׁתּ֔וֹ עֹדְךָ֖ מַחֲזִ֣יק בְּתֻמָּתֶ֑ךָ בָּרֵ֥ךְ אֱלֹהִ֖ים וָמֻֽת׃ 10 וַיֹּ֣אמֶר אֵלֶ֗יהָ כְּדַבֵּ֞ר אַחַ֤ת הַנְּבָלוֹת֙ תְּדַבֵּ֔רִי גַּ֣ם אֶת־הַטּ֗וֹב נְקַבֵּל֙ מֵאֵ֣ת הָֽאֱלֹהִ֔ים וְאֶת־הָרָ֖ע לֹ֣א נְקַבֵּ֑ל בְּכׇל־זֹ֛את לֹא־חָטָ֥א אִיּ֖וֹב בִּשְׂפָתָֽיו׃ פ 11 וַֽיִּשְׁמְע֞וּ שְׁלֹ֣שֶׁת ׀ רֵעֵ֣י אִיּ֗וֹב אֵ֣ת כׇּל־הָרָעָ֣ה הַזֹּאת֮ הַבָּ֣אָה עָלָיו֒ וַיָּבֹ֙אוּ֙ אִ֣ישׁ מִמְּקֹמ֔וֹ אֱלִיפַ֤ז הַתֵּימָנִי֙ וּבִלְדַּ֣ד הַשּׁוּחִ֔י וְצוֹפַ֖ר הַנַּֽעֲמָתִ֑י וַיִּוָּעֲד֣וּ יַחְדָּ֔ו לָב֥וֹא לָנֽוּד־ל֖וֹ וּֽלְנַחֲמֽוֹ׃ 12 וַיִּשְׂא֨וּ אֶת־עֵינֵיהֶ֤ם מֵֽרָחוֹק֙ וְלֹ֣א הִכִּירֻ֔הוּ וַיִּשְׂא֥וּ קוֹלָ֖ם וַיִּבְכּ֑וּ וַֽיִּקְרְעוּ֙ אִ֣ישׁ מְעִל֔וֹ וַיִּזְרְק֥וּ עָפָ֛ר עַל־רָאשֵׁיהֶ֖ם הַשָּׁמָֽיְמָה׃ 13 וַיֵּשְׁב֤וּ אִתּוֹ֙ לָאָ֔רֶץ שִׁבְעַ֥ת יָמִ֖ים וְשִׁבְעַ֣ת לֵיל֑וֹת וְאֵין־דֹּבֵ֤ר אֵלָיו֙ דָּבָ֔ר כִּ֣י רָא֔וּ כִּֽי־גָדַ֥ל הַכְּאֵ֖ב מְאֹֽד׃

3 [a]Afterward, Job began to speak and cursed the day of his birth. [2]Job spoke up and said:

[3]Perish the day on which I was born,

And the night it was announced,

"A male has been conceived!"

[4]May that day be darkness;

May God above have no concern for it;

May light not shine on it;

[5]May darkness and deep gloom reclaim it;

May a pall lie over it;

May [b]what blackens[b] the day terrify it.

[6]May obscurity carry off that night;

May it not be counted among the days of the

year;

May it not appear in any of its months;

[7]May that night be desolate;

May no sound of joy be heard in it;

[8]May those who cast spells upon the day[c]

damn it,

Those prepared to disable Leviathan;

[9]May its twilight stars remain dark;

May it hope for light and have none;

May it not see the glimmerings of the dawn—

[10]Because it did not block my mother's

womb,

And hide trouble from my eyes.

[11]Why did I not die at birth,

Expire as I came forth from the womb?

[12]Why were there knees to receive me,

Or breasts for me to suck?

[13]For now would I be lying in repose, asleep

and at rest,

ג אַחֲרֵי־כֵ֗ן פָּתַ֣ח אִיּ֣וֹב אֶת־פִּ֑יהוּ וַיְקַלֵּ֥ל

אֶת־יוֹמֽוֹ׃ פ [2] וַיַּ֥עַן אִיּ֗וֹב וַיֹּאמַֽר׃

[3]* יֹ֣אבַד י֖וֹם אִוָּ֣לֶד בּ֑וֹ

וְהַלַּ֥יְלָה אָ֝מַ֗ר

הֹ֣רָה גָֽבֶר׃

[4] הַיּ֥וֹם הַה֗וּא יְֽהִי־חֹ֥שֶׁךְ

אַֽל־יִדְרְשֵׁ֣הוּ אֱל֣וֹהַּ מִמָּ֑עַל

וְאַל־תּוֹפַ֖ע עָלָ֣יו נְהָרָֽה׃

[5] יִגְאָלֻ֡הוּ חֹ֣שֶׁךְ וְ֭צַלְמָוֶת

תִּשְׁכָּן־עָלָ֣יו עֲנָנָ֑ה

יְ֝בַעֲתֻ֗הוּ כִּֽמְרִ֥ירֵי יֽוֹם׃

[6] הַלַּ֥יְלָה הַהוּא֮ יִקָּחֵ֢ה֫וּ אֹ֥פֶל

אַל־יִ֭חַדְּ בִּימֵ֣י שָׁנָ֑ה

בְּמִסְפַּ֥ר יְ֝רָחִ֗ים אַל־יָבֹֽא׃

[7] הִנֵּ֤ה הַלַּ֣יְלָה הַ֭הוּא יְהִ֣י גַלְמ֑וּד

אַל־תָּבֹ֖א רְנָנָ֣ה בֽוֹ׃

[8] יִקְּבֻ֥הוּ אֹרְרֵי־י֑וֹם

הָ֝עֲתִידִ֗ים עֹרֵ֥ר לִוְיָתָֽן׃

[9] יֶחְשְׁכוּ֮ כּוֹכְבֵ֢י נִ֫שְׁפּ֥וֹ

יְקַו־לְא֥וֹר וָאַ֑יִן

וְאַל־יִ֝רְאֶ֗ה בְּעַפְעַפֵּי־שָֽׁחַר׃

[10] כִּ֤י לֹ֣א סָ֭גַר דַּלְתֵ֣י בִטְנִ֑י

וַיַּסְתֵּ֥ר עָ֝מָ֗ל מֵעֵינָֽי׃

[11] לָ֤מָּה לֹּ֣א מֵרֶ֣חֶם אָמ֑וּת

מִבֶּ֖טֶן יָצָ֣אתִי וְאֶגְוָֽע׃

[12] מַ֭דּוּעַ קִדְּמ֣וּנִי בִרְכָּ֑יִם

וּמַה־שָּׁ֝דַ֗יִם כִּ֣י אִינָֽק׃

[13] כִּֽי־עַ֭תָּה שָׁכַ֣בְתִּי וְאֶשְׁק֑וֹט יָ֝שַׁ֗נְתִּי אָ֥ז ׀

יָנ֥וּחַֽ לִֽי׃

a   There are many difficulties in the poetry of Job, making the
    interpretation of words, verses, and even chapters uncertain. The
    rubric "Meaning of Heb. uncertain" in this book indicates only
    some of the extreme instances.

b-b Meaning of Heb. uncertain.

c   Or "sea," taking Heb. yom as equivalent of yam; compare the
    combination of sea with Leviathan in Ps. 74.13, 14 and with
    Dragon in Job 7.12; cf. also Isa. 27.1.

14With the world's kings and counselors who
   rebuild ruins for themselves,
15Or with nobles who possess gold and who
   fill their houses with silver.
16Or why was I not like a buried stillbirth,
Like babies who never saw the light?
17There the wicked cease from troubling;
There rest those whose strength is spent.
18Prisoners are wholly at ease;
They do not hear the taskmaster's voice.
19Small and great alike are there,
And the slave is free of his master.

20Why does He give light to the sufferer
And life to the bitter in spirit;
21To those who wait for death but it does not
   come,
Who search for it more than for treasure,
22Who rejoice to exultation,
And are glad to reach the grave;
23To the man who has lost his way,
Whom God has hedged about?

24My groaning serves as my bread;
My roaring pours forth as water.
25For what I feared has overtaken me;
What I dreaded has come upon me.
26I had no repose, no quiet, no rest,
And trouble came.

4

Then Eliphaz the Temanite said in reply:

2If one ventures a word with you, will it be
   too much?
But who can hold back his words?
3See, you have encouraged many;
You have strengthened failing hands.

עִם־מְלָכִים וְיֹעֲצֵי אֶרֶץ הַבֹּנִים 14
חֳרָבוֹת לָמוֹ:
אוֹ עִם־שָׂרִים זָהָב לָהֶם הַמְמַלְאִים 15
בָּתֵּיהֶם כָּסֶף:
אוֹ כְנֵפֶל טָמוּן לֹא אֶהְיֶה 16
כְּעֹלְלִים לֹא־רָאוּ אוֹר:
שָׁם רְשָׁעִים חָדְלוּ רֹגֶז 17
וְשָׁם יָנוּחוּ יְגִיעֵי כֹחַ:
יַחַד אֲסִירִים שַׁאֲנָנוּ 18
לֹא שָׁמְעוּ קוֹל נֹגֵשׂ:
קָטֹן וְגָדוֹל שָׁם הוּא 19
וְעֶבֶד חָפְשִׁי מֵאֲדֹנָיו:
לָמָּה יִתֵּן לְעָמֵל אוֹר 20
וְחַיִּים לְמָרֵי נָפֶשׁ:
הַמְחַכִּים לַמָּוֶת וְאֵינֶנּוּ 21
וַיַּחְפְּרֻהוּ מִמַּטְמוֹנִים:
הַשְּׂמֵחִים אֱלֵי־גִיל 22
יָשִׂישׂוּ כִּי יִמְצְאוּ־קָבֶר:
לְגֶבֶר אֲשֶׁר־דַּרְכּוֹ נִסְתָּרָה 23
וַיָּסֶךְ אֱלוֹהַּ בַּעֲדוֹ:
כִּי־לִפְנֵי לַחְמִי אַנְחָתִי תָבֹא 24
וַיִּתְּכוּ כַמַּיִם שַׁאֲגֹתָי:
כִּי פַחַד פָּחַדְתִּי וַיֶּאֱתָיֵנִי 25
וַאֲשֶׁר יָגֹרְתִּי יָבֹא לִי:
לֹא שָׁלַוְתִּי ׀ וְלֹא שָׁקַטְתִּי וְלֹא־נָחְתִּי 26
וַיָּבֹא רֹגֶז: פ

וַיַּעַן אֱלִיפַז הַתֵּימָנִי וַיֹּאמַר: ד

הֲנִסָּה דָבָר אֵלֶיךָ תִּלְאֶה 2
וַעְצֹר בְּמִלִּין מִי יוּכָל:
הִנֵּה יִסַּרְתָּ רַבִּים 3
וְיָדַיִם רָפוֹת תְּחַזֵּק:

4 Your words have kept him who stumbled
   from falling;
   You have braced knees that gave way.
5 But now that it overtakes you, it is too much;
   It reaches you, and you are unnerved.
6 Is not your piety your confidence,
   Your integrity your hope?
7 Think now, what innocent man ever perished?
   Where have the upright been destroyed?
8 As I have seen, those who plow evil
   And sow mischief reap them.
9 They perish by a blast from God,
   Are gone at the breath of His nostrils.
10 The lion may roar, the cub may howl,
   But the teeth of the king of beasts *a*-are
   broken.-*a*
11 The lion perishes for lack of prey,
   And its whelps are scattered.

12 A word came to me in stealth;
   My ear caught a whisper of it.
13 In thought-filled visions of the night,
   When deep sleep falls on men,
14 Fear and trembling came upon me,
   Causing all my bones to quake with fright.
15 A wind passed by me,
   Making the hair of my flesh bristle.
16 It halted; its appearance was strange to me;
   A form loomed before my eyes;
   I heard a murmur, a voice,
17 "Can mortals be acquitted by God?
   Can man be cleared by his Maker?
18 If He cannot trust His own servants,
   And casts reproach*a* on His angels,
19 How much less those who dwell in houses
   of clay,
   Whose origin is dust,
   Who are crushed like the moth,

4 כּוֹשֵׁל יְקִימוּן מִלֶּיךָ
וּבִרְכַּיִם כֹּרְעוֹת תְּאַמֵּץ:
5 כִּי עַתָּה ׀ תָּבוֹא אֵלֶיךָ וַתֵּלֶא
תִּגַּע עָדֶיךָ וַתִּבָּהֵל:
6 הֲלֹא יִרְאָתְךָ כִּסְלָתֶךָ
תִּקְוָתְךָ וְתֹם דְּרָכֶיךָ:
7 זְכָר־נָא מִי הוּא נָקִי אָבָד
וְאֵיפֹה יְשָׁרִים נִכְחָדוּ:
8 כַּאֲשֶׁר רָאִיתִי חֹרְשֵׁי אָוֶן
וְזֹרְעֵי עָמָל יִקְצְרֻהוּ:
9 מִנִּשְׁמַת אֱלוֹהַּ יֹאבֵדוּ
וּמֵרוּחַ אַפּוֹ יִכְלוּ:
10 שַׁאֲגַת אַרְיֵה וְקוֹל שָׁחַל
וְשִׁנֵּי כְפִירִים נִתָּעוּ:
11 לַיִשׁ אֹבֵד מִבְּלִי־טָרֶף
וּבְנֵי לָבִיא יִתְפָּרָדוּ:
12 וְאֵלַי דָּבָר יְגֻנָּב
וַתִּקַּח אָזְנִי שֵׁמֶץ מֶנְהוּ:
13 בִּשְׂעִפִּים מֵחֶזְיֹנוֹת לָיְלָה
בִּנְפֹל תַּרְדֵּמָה עַל־אֲנָשִׁים:
14 פַּחַד קְרָאַנִי וּרְעָדָה
וְרֹב עַצְמוֹתַי הִפְחִיד:
15 וְרוּחַ עַל־פָּנַי יַחֲלֹף
תְּסַמֵּר שַׂעֲרַת בְּשָׂרִי:
16 יַעֲמֹד ׀ וְלֹא־אַכִּיר מַרְאֵהוּ
תְּמוּנָה לְנֶגֶד עֵינָי
דְּמָמָה וָקוֹל אֶשְׁמָע:
17 הַאֱנוֹשׁ מֵאֱלוֹהַּ יִצְדָּק
אִם מֵעֹשֵׂהוּ יִטְהַר־גָּבֶר:
18 הֵן בַּעֲבָדָיו לֹא יַאֲמִין
וּבְמַלְאָכָיו יָשִׂים תָּהֳלָה:
19 אַף ׀ שֹׁכְנֵי בָתֵּי־חֹמֶר
אֲשֶׁר־בֶּעָפָר יְסוֹדָם
יְדַכְּאוּם לִפְנֵי־עָשׁ:

---

a-a Meaning of Heb. uncertain.

1662

20Shattered between daybreak and evening,
Perishing forever, unnoticed.
21Their cord is pulled up
And they die, and not with wisdom."

5 Call now! Will anyone answer you?
  To whom among the holy beings will you
    turn?
2Vexation kills the fool;
Passion slays the simpleton.
3I myself saw a fool who had struck roots;
Impulsively, I cursed his home:
4May his children be far from success;
May they be oppressed in the gate with none
    to deliver them;
5May the hungry devour his harvest,
a-Carrying it off in baskets;
May the thirsty swallow their wealth.-a
6Evil does not grow out of the soil,
Nor does mischief spring from the ground;
7For man is born to [do] mischief,
Just as sparks fly upward.

8But I would resort to God;
I would lay my case before God,
9Who performs great deeds which cannot be
    fathomed,
Wondrous things without number;
10Who gives rain to the earth,
And sends water over the fields;
11Who raises the lowly up high,
So that the dejected are secure in victory;
12Who thwarts the designs of the crafty,
So that their hands cannot gain success;
13Who traps the clever in their own wiles;
The plans of the crafty go awry.
14By day they encounter darkness,
At noon they grope as in the night.

---

a-a   Meaning of Heb. uncertain.

20 מִבֹּקֶר לָעֶרֶב יֻכַּתּוּ
מִבְּלִי מֵשִׂים לָנֶצַח יֹאבֵדוּ:
21 הֲלֹא־נִסַּע יִתְרָם בָּם
יָמוּתוּ וְלֹא בְחָכְמָה:

ה קְרָא־נָא הֲיֵשׁ עוֹנֶךָּ
וְאֶל־מִי מִקְּדֹשִׁים תִּפְנֶה:
2 כִּי־לֶאֱוִיל יַהֲרָג־כָּעַשׂ
וּפֹתֶה תָּמִית קִנְאָה:
3 אֲנִי־רָאִיתִי אֱוִיל מַשְׁרִישׁ
וָאֶקּוֹב נָוֵהוּ פִתְאֹם:
4 יִרְחֲקוּ בָנָיו מִיֶּשַׁע
וְיִדַּכְּאוּ בַשַּׁעַר וְאֵין מַצִּיל:
5 אֲשֶׁר קְצִירוֹ ׀ רָעֵב יֹאכֵל
וְאֶל־מִצִּנִּים יִקָּחֵהוּ
וְשָׁאַף צַמִּים חֵילָם:
6 כִּי ׀ לֹא־יֵצֵא מֵעָפָר אָוֶן
וּמֵאֲדָמָה לֹא־יִצְמַח עָמָל:
7 כִּי־אָדָם לְעָמָל יוּלָּד
וּבְנֵי־רֶשֶׁף יַגְבִּיהוּ עוּף:

8 אוּלָם אֲנִי אֶדְרֹשׁ אֶל־אֵל
וְאֶל־אֱלֹהִים אָשִׂים דִּבְרָתִי:
9 עֹשֶׂה גְדֹלוֹת וְאֵין חֵקֶר
נִפְלָאוֹת עַד־אֵין מִסְפָּר:
10 הַנֹּתֵן מָטָר עַל־פְּנֵי־אָרֶץ
וְשֹׁלֵחַ מַיִם עַל־פְּנֵי חוּצוֹת:
11 לָשׂוּם שְׁפָלִים לְמָרוֹם
וְקֹדְרִים שָׂגְבוּ יֶשַׁע:
12 מֵפֵר מַחְשְׁבוֹת עֲרוּמִים
וְלֹא־תַעֲשֶׂינָה יְדֵיהֶם תּוּשִׁיָּה:
13 לֹכֵד חֲכָמִים בְּעָרְמָם
וַעֲצַת נִפְתָּלִים נִמְהָרָה:
14 יוֹמָם יְפַגְּשׁוּ־חֹשֶׁךְ
וְכַלַּיְלָה יְמַשְׁשׁוּ בַצָּהֳרָיִם:

15But He saves the needy from the sword of
their mouth,
From the clutches of the strong.

16So there is hope for the wretched;
The mouth of wrongdoing is stopped.

17See how happy is the man whom God re-
proves;
Do not reject the discipline of the Almighty.

18He injures, but He binds up;
He wounds, but His hands heal.

19He will deliver you from six troubles;
In seven no harm will reach you:

20In famine He will redeem you from death,
In war, from the sword.

21You will be sheltered from the scourging
tongue;
You will have no fear when violence comes.

22You will laugh at violence and starvation,
And have no fear of wild beasts.

23For you will have a pact with the rocks in
the field,
And the beasts of the field will be your allies.

24You will know that all is well in your tent;
When you visit your wife^b you will never fail.

25You will see that your offspring are many,
Your descendants like the grass of the earth.

26You will come to the grave ^a-in ripe old
age,-^a
As shocks of grain are taken away in their season.

27See, we have inquired into this and it is so;
Hear it and accept it.

6 Then Job said in reply:

2If my anguish were weighed,
My full calamity laid on the scales,

15 וַיֹּשַׁע מֵחֶרֶב מִפִּיהֶם
וּמִיַּד חָזָק אֶבְיוֹן:
16 וַתְּהִי לַדַּל תִּקְוָה
וְעֹלָתָה קָפְצָה פִּיהָ:

17 הִנֵּה אַשְׁרֵי אֱנוֹשׁ יוֹכִחֶנּוּ אֱלוֹהַּ
וּמוּסַר שַׁדַּי אַל־תִּמְאָס:
18 כִּי הוּא יַכְאִיב וְיֶחְבָּשׁ
יִמְחַץ וְיָדָו תִּרְפֶּינָה:
19 בְּשֵׁשׁ צָרוֹת יַצִּילֶךָ
וּבְשֶׁבַע לֹא־יִגַּע בְּךָ רָע:
20 בְּרָעָב פָּדְךָ מִמָּוֶת
וּבְמִלְחָמָה מִידֵי חָרֶב:
21 בְּשׁוֹט לָשׁוֹן תֵּחָבֵא
וְלֹא־תִירָא מִשֹּׁד כִּי יָבוֹא:
22 לְשֹׁד וּלְכָפָן תִּשְׂחָק
וּמֵחַיַּת הָאָרֶץ אַל־תִּירָא:
23 כִּי עִם־אַבְנֵי הַשָּׂדֶה בְרִיתֶךָ
וְחַיַּת הַשָּׂדֶה הָשְׁלְמָה־לָךְ:
24 וְיָדַעְתָּ כִּי־שָׁלוֹם אָהֳלֶךָ
וּפָקַדְתָּ נָוְךָ וְלֹא תֶחֱטָא:
25 וְיָדַעְתָּ כִּי־רַב זַרְעֶךָ
וְצֶאֱצָאֶיךָ כְּעֵשֶׂב הָאָרֶץ:
26 תָּבוֹא בְכֶלַח אֱלֵי־קָבֶר
כַּעֲלוֹת גָּדִישׁ בְּעִתּוֹ:
27 הִנֵּה־זֹאת חֲקַרְנוּהָ כֶּן־הִיא
שְׁמָעֶנָּה וְאַתָּה דַע־לָךְ: פ

ו וַיַּעַן אִיּוֹב וַיֹּאמַר:

2 לוּ שָׁקוֹל יִשָּׁקֵל כַּעְשִׂי
וְהַוָּתִי בְּמֹאזְנַיִם יִשְׂאוּ־יָחַד:

---

b Lit. "home."

³It would be heavier than the sand of the sea;
That is why I spoke recklessly.*a*

⁴For the arrows of the Almighty are in me;
My spirit absorbs their poison;
God's terrors are arrayed against me.

⁵Does a wild ass bray when he has grass?
Does a bull bellow over his fodder?

⁶Can what is tasteless be eaten without salt?
Does *a*-mallow juice-*a* have any flavor?

⁷I refuse to touch them;
They are like food when I am sick.

⁸Would that my request were granted,
That God gave me what I wished for;

⁹Would that God consented to crush me,
Loosed His hand and cut me off.

¹⁰Then this would be my consolation,
a-As I writhed in unsparing-*a* pains:
That I did not *b*-suppress my words against
the Holy One.-*b*

¹¹What strength have I, that I should endure?
How long have I to live, that I should be patient?

¹²Is my strength the strength of rock?
Is my flesh bronze?

¹³Truly, I cannot help myself;
I have been deprived of resourcefulness.

¹⁴*a*-A friend owes loyalty to one who fails,
Though he forsakes the fear of the Almighty;-*a*

¹⁵My comrades are fickle, like a wadi,
Like a bed on which streams once ran.

¹⁶*a*-They are dark with ice;
Snow obscures them;-*a*

¹⁷But when they thaw, they vanish;
In the heat, they disappear where they are.

¹⁸Their course twists and turns;
They run into the desert and perish.

³ כִּי־עַתָּה מֵחוֹל יַמִּים יִכְבָּד
עַל־כֵּן דְּבָרַי לָעוּ:
⁴ כִּי חִצֵּי שַׁדַּי עִמָּדִי
אֲשֶׁר חֲמָתָם שֹׁתָה רוּחִי
בִּעוּתֵי אֱלוֹהַּ יַעַרְכוּנִי:
⁵ הֲיִנְהַק־פֶּרֶא עֲלֵי־דֶשֶׁא
אִם יִגְעֶה־שּׁוֹר עַל־בְּלִילוֹ:
⁶ הֲיֵאָכֵל תָּפֵל מִבְּלִי־מֶלַח
אִם־יֶשׁ־טַעַם בְּרִיר חַלָּמוּת:
⁷ מֵאֲנָה לִנְגּוֹעַ נַפְשִׁי
הֵמָּה כִּדְוֵי לַחְמִי:

⁸ מִי־יִתֵּן תָּבוֹא שֶׁאֱלָתִי
וְתִקְוָתִי יִתֵּן אֱלוֹהַּ:
⁹ וְיֹאֵל אֱלוֹהַּ וִידַכְּאֵנִי
יַתֵּר יָדוֹ וִיבַצְּעֵנִי:
¹⁰ וּתְהִי עוֹד ׀ נֶחָמָתִי
וַאֲסַלְּדָה בְחִילָה לֹא יַחְמוֹל
כִּי־לֹא כִחַדְתִּי אִמְרֵי קָדוֹשׁ:
¹¹ מַה־כֹּחִי כִי־אֲיַחֵל
וּמַה־קִּצִּי כִּי־אַאֲרִיךְ נַפְשִׁי:
¹² אִם־כֹּחַ אֲבָנִים כֹּחִי
אִם־בְּשָׂרִי נָחוּשׁ:
¹³ הַאִם אֵין עֶזְרָתִי בִי
וְתֻשִׁיָּה נִדְּחָה מִמֶּנִּי:

¹⁴ לַמָּס מֵרֵעֵהוּ חָסֶד
וְיִרְאַת שַׁדַּי יַעֲזוֹב:
¹⁵ אַחַי בָּגְדוּ כְמוֹ־נָחַל
כַּאֲפִיק נְחָלִים יַעֲבֹרוּ:
¹⁶ הַקֹּדְרִים מִנִּי־קָרַח
עָלֵימוֹ יִתְעַלֶּם־שָׁלֶג:
¹⁷ בְּעֵת יְזֹרְבוּ נִצְמָתוּ
בְּחֻמּוֹ נִדְעֲכוּ מִמְּקוֹמָם:
¹⁸ יִלָּפְתוּ אָרְחוֹת דַּרְכָּם
יַעֲלוּ בַתֹּהוּ וְיֹאבֵדוּ:

---

a Meaning of Heb. uncertain.
b-b Meaning of Heb. uncertain; others "deny the words of the Holy
 One."

19Caravans from Tema look to them;

Processions from Sheba count on them.

20They are disappointed in their hopes;

When they reach the place, they stand aghast.

21So you are as nothing:*c*

At the sight of misfortune, you take fright.

22Did I say to you, "I need your gift;

Pay a bribe for me out of your wealth;

23Deliver me from the clutches of my enemy;

Redeem me from violent men"?

24Teach me; I shall be silent;

Tell me where I am wrong.

25*a*-How trenchant honest words are;-*a*

But what sort of reproof comes from you?

26Do you devise words of reproof,

But count a hopeless man's words as wind?

27You would even cast lots over an orphan,

Or barter away your friend.

28Now be so good as to face me;

I will not lie to your face.

29Relent! Let there not be injustice;

Relent! I am still in the right.

30Is injustice on my tongue?

Can my palate not discern evil?

7 Truly man has a term of service on earth;

His days are like those of a hireling—

2Like a slave who longs for [evening's] shad-

ows,

Like a hireling who waits for his wage.

3So have I been allotted months of futility;

Nights of misery have been apportioned to

me.

4When I lie down, I think,

"When shall I rise?"

Night *a*-drags on,-*a*

---

19 הִבִּיטוּ אָרְחוֹת תֵּמָא

הֲלִיכֹת שְׁבָא קִוּוּ־לָמוֹ:

20 בֹּשׁוּ כִּי־בָטָח

בָּאוּ עָדֶיהָ וַיֶּחְפָּרוּ:

21 כִּי־עַתָּה הֱיִיתֶם לֹא

תִּרְאוּ חֲתַת וַתִּירָאוּ:

22 הֲכִי־אָמַרְתִּי הָבוּ לִי

וּמִכֹּחֲכֶם שִׁחֲדוּ בַעֲדִי:

23 וּמַלְּטוּנִי מִיַּד־צָר

וּמִיַּד עָרִיצִים תִּפְדּוּנִי:

24 הוֹרוּנִי וַאֲנִי אַחֲרִישׁ

וּמַה־שָּׁגִיתִי הָבִינוּ לִי:

25 מַה־נִּמְרְצוּ אִמְרֵי־יֹשֶׁר

וּמַה־יּוֹכִיחַ הוֹכֵחַ מִכֶּם:

26 הַלְהוֹכַח מִלִּים תַּחְשֹׁבוּ

וּלְרוּחַ אִמְרֵי נֹאָשׁ:

27 אַף־עַל־יָתוֹם תַּפִּילוּ

וְתִכְרוּ עַל־רֵיעֲכֶם:

28 וְעַתָּה הוֹאִילוּ פְנוּ־בִי

וְעַל־פְּנֵיכֶם אִם־אֲכַזֵּב:

29 שֻׁבוּ־נָא אַל־תְּהִי עַוְלָה

וּשֻׁבִי עוֹד צִדְקִי־בָהּ:

30 הֲיֵשׁ־בִּלְשׁוֹנִי עַוְלָה

אִם־חִכִּי לֹא־יָבִין הַוּוֹת:

ז

1 הֲלֹא־צָבָא לֶאֱנוֹשׁ עַל עֲלֵי־אָרֶץ

וְכִימֵי שָׂכִיר יָמָיו:

2 כְּעֶבֶד יִשְׁאַף־צֵל

וּכְשָׂכִיר יְקַוֶּה פָעֳלוֹ:

3 כֵּן הָנְחַלְתִּי לִי יַרְחֵי־שָׁוְא

וְלֵילוֹת עָמָל מִנּוּ־לִי:

4 אִם־שָׁכַבְתִּי וְאָמַרְתִּי

מָתַי אָקוּם

וּמִדַּד־עָרֶב

---

c Following kethib, with Targum; meaning of Heb. uncertain.

a-a Meaning of Heb. uncertain.

And I am sated with tossings till morning twilight.

⁵My flesh is covered with maggots and clods
of earth;

My skin is broken and festering.

⁶My days fly faster than a weaver's shuttle,

And come to their end ᵇ-without hope.-ᵇ

⁷Consider that my life is but wind;

I shall never see happiness again.

⁸The eye that gazes on me will not see me;

Your eye will seek me, but I shall be gone.

⁹As a cloud fades away,

So whoever goes down to Sheol does not
come up;

¹⁰He returns no more to his home;

His place does not know him.

¹¹On my part, I will not speak with restraint;

I will give voice to the anguish of my spirit;

I will complain in the bitterness of my soul.

¹²Am I the sea or the Dragon,ᶜ

That You have set a watch over me?

¹³When I think, "My bed will comfort me,

My couch will share my sorrow,"

¹⁴You frighten me with dreams,

And terrify me with visions,

¹⁵Till I prefer strangulation,

Death, to my wasted frame.

¹⁶I am sick of it.

I shall not live forever;

Let me be, for my days are a breath.

¹⁷What is man, that You make much of him,

That You fix Your attention upon him?

¹⁸You inspect him every morning,

Examine him every minute.

¹⁹Will You not look away from me for a while,

Let me be, till I swallow my spittle?

²⁰If I have sinned, what have I done to You,

וְשָׂבַ֥עְתִּי נְדֻדִ֗ים עֲדֵי־נָֽשֶׁף׃

⁵ לָ֘בַ֤שׁ בְּשָׂרִ֣י רִ֭מָּה וגיש וְג֣וּשׁ עָפָ֑ר
עוֹרִ֥י רָ֝גַ֗ע וַיִּמָּאֵֽס׃

⁶ יָמַ֣י קַ֭לּוּ מִנִּי־אָ֑רֶג
וַ֝יִּכְל֗וּ בְּאֶ֣פֶס תִּקְוָֽה׃

⁷ זְכֹ֗ר כִּי־ר֥וּחַ חַיָּ֑י
לֹא־תָשׁ֥וּב עֵ֝ינִ֗י לִרְא֥וֹת טֽוֹב׃

⁸ לֹֽא־תְ֭שׁוּרֵנִי עֵ֣ין רֹאִ֑י
עֵינֶ֖יךָ בִּ֣י וְאֵינֶֽנִּי׃

⁹ כָּלָ֣ה עָ֭נָן וַיֵּלַ֑ךְ
כֵּ֥ן יוֹרֵ֥ד שְׁ֝א֗וֹל לֹ֣א יַעֲלֶֽה׃

¹⁰ לֹא־יָשׁ֣וּב ע֣וֹד לְבֵית֑וֹ
וְלֹא־יַכִּירֶ֖נּוּ ע֣וֹד מְקֹמֽוֹ׃

¹¹ גַּם־אֲנִי֮ לֹ֤א אֶחֱשָׂ֫ךְ פִּ֥י
אֲֽדַבְּרָ֗ה בְּצַ֣ר רוּחִ֑י
אָ֝שִׂ֗יחָה בְּמַ֣ר נַפְשִֽׁי׃

¹² הֲיָם־אָ֭נִי אִם־תַּנִּ֑ין
כִּֽי־תָשִׂ֖ים עָלַ֣י מִשְׁמָֽר׃

¹³ כִּֽי־אָ֭מַרְתִּי תְּנַחֲמֵ֣נִי עַרְשִׂ֑י
יִשָּׂ֥א בְ֝שִׂיחִ֗י מִשְׁכָּבִֽי׃

¹⁴ וְחִתַּתַּ֥נִי בַחֲלֹמ֑וֹת
וּֽמֵחֶזְיֹנ֥וֹת תְּבַעֲתַֽנִּי׃

¹⁵ וַתִּבְחַ֣ר מַחֲנָ֣ק נַפְשִׁ֑י
מָ֝֗וֶת מֵֽעַצְמוֹתָֽי׃

¹⁶ מָ֭אַסְתִּי
לֹא־לְעֹלָ֣ם אֶֽחְיֶ֑ה
חֲדַ֥ל מִ֝מֶּ֗נִּי כִּי־הֶ֥בֶל יָמָֽי׃

¹⁷ מָֽה־אֱ֭נוֹשׁ כִּ֣י תְגַדְּלֶ֑נּוּ
וְכִֽי־תָשִׁ֖ית אֵלָ֣יו לִבֶּֽךָ׃

¹⁸ וַתִּפְקְדֶ֥נּוּ לִבְקָרִ֑ים
לִ֝רְגָעִ֗ים תִּבְחָנֶֽנּוּ׃

¹⁹ כַּ֭מָּה לֹא־תִשְׁעֶ֣ה מִמֶּ֑נִּי
לֹֽא־תַ֝רְפֵּ֗נִי עַד־בִּלְעִ֥י רֻקִּֽי׃

²⁰ חָטָ֡אתִי מָ֤ה אֶפְעַ֙ל ׀ לָ֜ךְ

ᵇ-ᵇ   Or "when the thread runs out."
ᶜ   See note at 3.8.

Watcher of men?

Why make of me Your target,

And a burden to myself?

21Why do You not pardon my transgression

And forgive my iniquity?

For soon I shall lie down in the dust;

When You seek me, I shall be gone.

8 Bildad the Shuhite said in reply:

2How long will you speak such things?

Your utterances are a mighty wind!

3Will God pervert the right?

Will the Almighty pervert justice?

4If your sons sinned against Him,

He dispatched them for their transgression.

5But if you seek God

And supplicate the Almighty,

6If you are blameless and upright,

He will protect you,

And grant well-being to your righteous home.

7Though your beginning be small,

In the end you will grow very great.

8Ask the generation past,

Study what their fathers have searched out—

9For we are of yesterday and know nothing;

Our days on earth are a shadow—

10Surely they will teach you and tell you,

Speaking out of their understanding.

11Can papyrus thrive without marsh?

Can rushes grow without water?

12While still tender, not yet plucked,

They would wither before any other grass.

13Such is the fate of all who forget God;

The hope of the impious man comes to naught—

נֹצֵ֥ר הָאָדָ֑ם

לָ֤מָה שַׂמְתַּ֣נִי לְמִפְגָּ֣ע לָ֑ךְ

וָאֶהְיֶ֖ה עָלַ֣י לְמַשָּֽׂא׃

21 וּמֶ֤ה ׀ לֹא־תִשָּׂ֣א פִשְׁעִי֮

וְתַעֲבִ֪יר אֶת־עֲו‍ֹ֫נִ֥י

כִּֽי־עַתָּ֥ה לֶעָפָ֣ר אֶשְׁכָּ֑ב

וְשִׁ֖חֲרְתַּ֣נִי וְאֵינֶֽנִּי׃ פ

ח וַ֭יַּעַן בִּלְדַּ֥ד הַשּׁוּחִ֗י וַיֹּאמַֽר׃

2 עַד־אָ֥ן תְּמַלֶּל־אֵ֑לֶּה

וְר֥וּחַ כַּ֝בִּ֗יר אִמְרֵי־פִֽיךָ׃

3 הַ֭אֵל יְעַוֵּ֣ת מִשְׁפָּ֑ט

וְאִם־שַׁ֝דַּ֗י יְעַוֵּֽת־צֶֽדֶק׃

4 אִם־בָּנֶ֥יךָ חָֽטְאוּ־ל֑וֹ

וַֽ֝יְשַׁלְּחֵ֗ם בְּיַד־פִּשְׁעָֽם׃

5 אִם־אַ֭תָּה תְּשַׁחֵ֣ר אֶל־אֵ֑ל

וְאֶל־שַׁ֝דַּ֗י תִּתְחַנָּֽן׃

6 אִם־זַ֥ךְ וְיָשָׁ֗ר אָ֫תָּ֥ה

כִּי־עַ֭תָּה יָעִ֣יר עָלֶ֑יךָ

וְ֝שִׁלַּ֗ם נְוַ֣ת צִדְקֶֽךָ׃

7 וְהָיָ֣ה רֵאשִׁיתְךָ֣ מִצְעָ֑ר

וְ֝אַחֲרִֽיתְךָ֗ יִשְׂגֶּ֥ה מְאֹֽד׃

8 כִּֽי־שְׁאַל־נָ֣א לְדֹ֣ר רִישׁ֑וֹן*

וְ֝כוֹנֵ֗ן לְחֵ֣קֶר אֲבוֹתָֽם׃

9 כִּֽי־תְמ֣וֹל אֲ֭נַחְנוּ וְלֹ֣א נֵדָ֑ע

כִּ֤י צֵ֖ל יָמֵ֣ינוּ עֲלֵי־אָֽרֶץ׃

10 הֲלֹא־הֵ֣ם י֭וֹרוּךָ יֹ֣אמְרוּ לָ֑ךְ

וּ֝מִלִּבָּ֗ם יוֹצִ֥אוּ מִלִּֽים׃

11 הֲיִֽגְאֶה־גֹּ֭מֶא בְּלֹ֣א בִצָּ֑ה

יִשְׂגֶּה־אָ֥חוּ בְלִי־מָֽיִם׃

12 עֹדֶ֣נּוּ בְ֭אִבּוֹ לֹ֣א יִקָּטֵ֑ף

וְלִפְנֵ֖י כָל־חָצִ֣יר יִיבָֽשׁ׃

13 כֵּ֗ן אָ֭רְחוֹת כָּל־שֹׁ֣כְחֵי אֵ֑ל

וְתִקְוַ֖ת חָנֵ֣ף תֹּאבֵֽד׃

י' במקום א' .v. 8

1668

14Whose confidence is a *a*-thread of gossa-
mer,-*a*

Whose trust is a spider's web.

15He leans on his house—it will not stand;

He seizes hold of it, but it will not hold.

16He stays fresh even in the sun;

His shoots spring up in his garden;

17*a*-His roots are twined around a heap,

They take hold of a house of stones.-*a*

18When he is uprooted from his place,

It denies him, [saying,]

"I never saw you."

19Such is his happy lot;

And from the earth others will grow.

20Surely God does not despise the blameless;

He gives no support to evildoers.

21He will yet fill your mouth with laughter,

And your lips with shouts of joy.

22Your enemies will be clothed in disgrace;

The tent of the wicked will vanish.

9

Job said in reply:

2Indeed I know that it is so:

Man cannot win a suit against God.

3If he insisted on a trial with Him,

He would not answer one charge in a thousand.

4Wise of heart and mighty in power—

Who ever challenged Him and came out
whole?—

5Him who moves mountains without their
knowing it,

Who overturns them in His anger;

6Who shakes the earth from its place,

Till its pillars quake;

7Who commands the sun not to shine;

Who seals up the stars;

אֲשֶׁר־יָקוֹט כִּסְלוֹ ‎14

וּבֵית עַכָּבִישׁ מִבְטַחוֹ:

יִשָּׁעֵן עַל־בֵּיתוֹ וְלֹא יַעֲמֹד ‎15

יַחֲזִיק בּוֹ וְלֹא יָקוּם:

רָטֹב הוּא לִפְנֵי־שָׁמֶשׁ ‎16

וְעַל גַּנָּתוֹ יֹנַקְתּוֹ תֵצֵא:

עַל־גַּל שָׁרָשָׁיו יְסֻבָּכוּ ‎17

בֵּית אֲבָנִים יֶחֱזֶה:

אִם־יְבַלְּעֶנּוּ מִמְּקֹמוֹ ‎18

וְכִחֶשׁ בּוֹ

לֹא רְאִיתִיךָ:

הֶן־הוּא מְשׂוֹשׂ דַּרְכּוֹ ‎19

וּמֵעָפָר אַחֵר יִצְמָחוּ:

הֶן־אֵל לֹא יִמְאַס־תָּם ‎20

וְלֹא־יַחֲזִיק בְּיַד־מְרֵעִים:

עַד־יְמַלֶּה* שְׂחוֹק פִּיךָ ‎21

וּשְׂפָתֶיךָ תְרוּעָה:

שֹׂנְאֶיךָ יִלְבְּשׁוּ־בֹשֶׁת ‎22

וְאֹהֶל רְשָׁעִים אֵינֶנּוּ: פ

וַיַּעַן אִיּוֹב וַיֹּאמַר: ט

אָמְנָם יָדַעְתִּי כִי־כֵן ‎2

וּמַה־יִּצְדַּק אֱנוֹשׁ עִם־אֵל:

אִם־יַחְפֹּץ לָרִיב עִמּוֹ ‎3

לֹא־יַעֲנֶנּוּ אַחַת מִנִּי־אָלֶף:

חֲכַם לֵבָב וְאַמִּיץ כֹּחַ ‎4

מִי־הִקְשָׁה אֵלָיו וַיִּשְׁלָם:

הַמַּעְתִּיק הָרִים וְלֹא יָדָעוּ ‎5

אֲשֶׁר הֲפָכָם בְּאַפּוֹ:

הַמַּרְגִּיז אֶרֶץ מִמְּקוֹמָהּ ‎6

וְעַמּוּדֶיהָ יִתְפַלָּצוּן:

הָאֹמֵר לַחֶרֶס וְלֹא יִזְרָח ‎7

וּבְעַד כּוֹכָבִים יַחְתֹּם:

a-a *Meaning of Heb. uncertain.*

8Who by Himself spread out the heavens,
And trod on the back of the sea;
9Who made the Bear[a] and Orion,
Pleiades, and the chambers of the south wind;
10Who performs great deeds which cannot be
   fathomed,
And wondrous things without number.
11He passes me by—I do not see Him;
He goes by me, but I do not perceive Him.
12He snatches away—who can stop Him?
Who can say to Him, "What are You doing?"
13God does not restrain His anger;
Under Him Rahab's[b] helpers sink down.
14How then can I answer Him,
Or choose my arguments against Him?
15Though I were in the right, I could not speak
   out,
But I would plead for mercy with my judge.
16If I summoned Him and He responded,
I do not believe He would lend me His ear.
17For He crushes me [c]for a hair;[c]
He wounds me much for no cause.
18He does not let me catch my breath,
But sates me with bitterness.
19If a trial of strength—He is the strong one;
If a trial in court—who will summon Him
   for me?
20Though I were innocent,
My mouth would condemn me;
Though I were blameless, He would prove me
   crooked.
21I am blameless—I am distraught;
I am sick of life.
22It is all one; therefore I say,
"He destroys the blameless and the guilty."
23When suddenly a scourge brings death,
He mocks as the innocent fail.
24The earth is handed over to the wicked one;

8 נֹטֶ֣ה שָׁמַ֣יִם לְבַדּ֑וֹ
וְ֝דוֹרֵ֗ךְ עַל־בָּ֥מֳתֵי יָֽם׃
9 עֹֽשֶׂה־עָ֭שׁ כְּסִ֥יל
וְכִימָ֗ה וְחַדְרֵ֥י תֵמָֽן׃
10 עֹשֶׂ֣ה גְ֭דֹלוֹת עַד־אֵ֣ין חֵ֑קֶר
וְ֝נִפְלָא֗וֹת עַד־אֵ֥ין מִסְפָּֽר׃
11 הֵ֤ן יַעֲבֹ֣ר עָ֭לַי וְלֹ֣א אֶרְאֶ֑ה
וְ֝יַחֲלֹ֗ף וְֽלֹא־אָבִ֥ין לֽוֹ׃
12 הֵ֣ן יַ֭חְתֹּף מִ֣י יְשִׁיבֶ֑נּוּ
מִֽי־יֹאמַ֥ר אֵ֝לָ֗יו מַֽה־תַּעֲשֶֽׂה׃
13 אֱ֭לוֹהַּ לֹא־יָשִׁ֣יב אַפּ֑וֹ
תַּחְתָּ֥ו שָׁ֝חֲח֗וּ עֹ֣זְרֵי רָֽהַב׃
14 אַ֭ף כִּֽי־אָנֹכִ֣י אֶֽעֱנֶ֑נּוּ
אֶבְחֲרָ֖ה דְבָרַ֣י עִמּֽוֹ׃
15 אֲשֶׁ֣ר אִם־צָ֭דַקְתִּי לֹ֣א אֶעֱנֶ֑ה
לִ֝מְשֹׁפְטִ֗י אֶתְחַנָּֽן׃
16 אִם־קָרָ֥אתִי וַֽיַּעֲנֵ֑נִי
לֹֽא־אַ֝אֲמִ֗ין כִּֽי־יַאֲזִ֥ין קוֹלִֽי׃
17 אֲשֶׁר־בִּשְׂעָרָ֥ה יְשׁוּפֵ֑נִי
וְהִרְבָּ֖ה פְצָעַ֣י חִנָּֽם׃
18 לֹֽא־יִ֭תְּנֵנִי הָשֵׁ֣ב רוּחִ֑י
כִּ֥י יַ֝שְׂבִּעַ֗נִי מַמְּרֹרִֽים׃
19 אִם־לְכֹ֣חַ אַמִּ֣יץ הִנֵּ֑ה
וְאִם־לְ֝מִשְׁפָּ֗ט מִ֣י יוֹעִידֵֽנִי׃
20 אִם־אֶ֭צְדָּק
פִּ֣י יַרְשִׁיעֵ֑נִי
תָּֽם־אָ֝֗נִי וַֽיַּעְקְשֵֽׁנִי׃
21 תָּֽם־אָ֭נִי לֹֽא־אֵדַ֣ע נַפְשִׁ֑י
אֶמְאַ֥ס חַיָּֽי׃
22 אַחַ֗ת הִ֥יא עַל־כֵּ֥ן אָמַ֑רְתִּי
תָּ֥ם וְ֝רָשָׁ֗ע ה֣וּא מְכַלֶּֽה׃
23 אִם־שׁ֭וֹט יָמִ֣ית פִּתְאֹ֑ם
לְמַסַּ֖ת נְקִיִּ֣ם יִלְעָֽג׃
24 אֶ֤רֶץ ׀ נִתְּנָ֬ה בְֽיַד־רָשָׁ֗ע

a   Meaning of Heb. uncertain.
b   A primeval monster.
c-c   With Targum and Peshitta; or "with a storm."

He covers the eyes of its judges.   פְּנֵי־שֹׁפְטֶיהָ יְכַסֶּה
If it is not He, then who?   אִם־לֹא אֵפוֹא מִי־הוּא:

25My days fly swifter than a runner;   25 וְיָמַי קַלּוּ מִנִּי־רָץ
They flee without seeing happiness;   בָּרְחוּ לֹא־רָאוּ טוֹבָה:
26They pass like reed-boats,   26 חָלְפוּ עִם־אֳנִיּוֹת אֵבֶה
Like an eagle swooping onto its prey.   כְּנֶשֶׁר יָטוּשׂ עֲלֵי־אֹכֶל:
27If I say, "I will forget my complaint;   27 אִם־אָמְרִי אֶשְׁכְּחָה שִׂיחִי
Abandon my sorrow[d] and be diverted,"   אֶעֶזְבָה פָנַי וְאַבְלִיגָה:
28I remain in dread of all my suffering;   28 יָגֹרְתִּי כָל־עַצְּבֹתָי
I know that You will not acquit me.   יָדַעְתִּי כִּי־לֹא תְנַקֵּנִי:
29It will be I who am in the wrong;   29 אָנֹכִי אֶרְשָׁע
Why then should I waste effort?   לָמָּה־זֶּה הֶבֶל אִיגָע:
30If I washed with soap,   30 אִם־הִתְרָחַצְתִּי במו־בְמֵי־שָׁלֶג
Cleansed my hands with lye,   וַהֲזִכּוֹתִי בְּבֹר כַּפָּי:
31You would dip me in muck   31 אָז בַּשַּׁחַת תִּטְבְּלֵנִי
Till my clothes would abhor me.   וְתִעֲבוּנִי שַׂלְמוֹתָי:
32He is not a man, like me, that I can answer   32 כִּי־לֹא־אִישׁ כָּמֹנִי אֶעֱנֶנּוּ
Him,
That we can go to law together.   נָבוֹא יַחְדָּו בַּמִּשְׁפָּט:
33No arbiter is between us   33 לֹא יֵשׁ־בֵּינֵינוּ מוֹכִיחַ
To lay his hand on us both.   יָשֵׁת יָדוֹ עַל־שְׁנֵינוּ:
34If He would only take His rod away from   34 יָסֵר מֵעָלַי שִׁבְטוֹ
me
And not let His terror frighten me,   וְאֵמָתוֹ אַל־תְּבַעֲתַנִּי:
35Then I would speak out without fear of   35 אֲדַבְּרָה וְלֹא אִירָאֶנּוּ
Him;
For I know myself not to be so.   כִּי לֹא־כֵן אָנֹכִי עִמָּדִי:

10

I am disgusted with life;   נָקְטָה נַפְשִׁי
I will give rein to my complaint,   בְּחַיָּי אֶעֶזְבָה עָלַי שִׂיחִי
Speak in the bitterness of my soul.   אֲדַבְּרָה בְּמַר נַפְשִׁי:
2I say to God, "Do not condemn me;   2 אֹמַר אֶל־אֱלוֹהַּ אַל־תַּרְשִׁיעֵנִי
Let me know what You charge me with.   הוֹדִיעֵנִי עַל מַה־תְּרִיבֵנִי:
3Does it benefit You to defraud,   3 הֲטוֹב לְךָ | כִּי־תַעֲשֹׁק
To despise the toil of Your hands,   כִּי־תִמְאַס יְגִיעַ כַּפֶּיךָ
While smiling on the counsel of the wicked?   וְעַל־עֲצַת רְשָׁעִים הוֹפָעְתָּ:
4Do You have the eyes of flesh?   4 הַעֵינֵי בָשָׂר לָךְ

d Lit. "face."

Is Your vision that of mere men?

5Are Your days the days of a mortal,

Are Your years the years of a man,

6That You seek my iniquity

And search out my sin?

7You know that I am not guilty,

And that there is none to deliver from Your
hand.

8"Your hands shaped and fashioned me,

Then destroyed every part of me.

9Consider that You fashioned me like clay;

Will You then turn me back into dust?

10You poured me out like milk,

Congealed me like cheese;

11You clothed me with skin and flesh

And wove me of bones and sinews;

12You bestowed on me life and care;

Your providence watched over my spirit.

13Yet these things You hid in Your heart;

I know that You had this in mind:

14To watch me when I sinned

And not clear me of my iniquity;

15Should I be guilty—the worse for me!

And even when innocent, I cannot lift my
head;

So sated am I with shame,

And drenched in my misery.

16a-It is something to be proud of-a to hunt
me like a lion,

To b-show Yourself wondrous through-b me
time and again!

17You keep sending fresh witnesses against
me,

Letting Your vexation with me grow.

a-I serve my term and am my own replacement.-a

אִם־כִּרְאוֹת אֱנוֹשׁ תִּרְאֶה:

5 הֲכִימֵי אֱנוֹשׁ יָמֶיךָ

אִם־שְׁנוֹתֶיךָ כִּימֵי גָבֶר:

6 כִּי־תְבַקֵּשׁ לַעֲוֺנִי

וּלְחַטָּאתִי תִדְרוֹשׁ:

7 עַל־דַּעְתְּךָ כִּי־לֹא אֶרְשָׁע

וְאֵין מִיָּדְךָ מַצִּיל:

8 יָדֶיךָ עִצְּבוּנִי וַיַּעֲשׂוּנִי

יַחַד סָבִיב וַתְּבַלְּעֵנִי:

9 זְכָר־נָא כִּי־כַחֹמֶר עֲשִׂיתָנִי

וְאֶל־עָפָר תְּשִׁיבֵנִי:

10 הֲלֹא כֶחָלָב תַּתִּיכֵנִי

וְכַגְּבִנָּה תַּקְפִּיאֵנִי:

11 עוֹר וּבָשָׂר תַּלְבִּישֵׁנִי

וּבַעֲצָמוֹת וְגִידִים תְּסֹכְכֵנִי:

12 חַיִּים וָחֶסֶד עָשִׂיתָ עִמָּדִי

וּפְקֻדָּתְךָ שָׁמְרָה רוּחִי:

13 וְאֵלֶּה צָפַנְתָּ בִלְבָבֶךָ

יָדַעְתִּי כִּי־זֹאת עִמָּךְ:

14 אִם־חָטָאתִי וּשְׁמַרְתָּנִי

וּמֵעֲוֺנִי לֹא תְנַקֵּנִי:

15 אִם־רָשַׁעְתִּי אַלְלַי לִי

וְצָדַקְתִּי לֹא־אֶשָּׂא רֹאשִׁי

שְׂבַע קָלוֹן

וּרְאֵה עָנְיִי:

16 וְיִגְאֶה כַּשַּׁחַל תְּצוּדֵנִי

וְתָשֹׁב תִּתְפַּלָּא־בִי:

17 תְּחַדֵּשׁ עֵדֶיךָ ׀ נֶגְדִּי

וְתֶרֶב כַּעַשְׂךָ עִמָּדִי

חֲלִיפוֹת וְצָבָא עִמִּי:

a-a   *Meaning of Heb. uncertain.*
b-b   Or *"make sport of"; cf. Pal. Aram.* 'afli.

¹⁸"Why did You let me come out of the womb?

Better had I expired before any eye saw me,

¹⁹Had I been as though I never was,

Had I been carried from the womb to the grave.

²⁰My days are few, so desist!

Leave me alone, let me be diverted a while

²¹Before I depart—never to return—

For the land of deepest gloom;

²²A land whose light is darkness,

All gloom and disarray,

Whose light is like darkness."

11 Then Zophar the Naamathite said in reply:

²Is a multitude of words unanswerable?

Must a loquacious person be right?

³Your prattle may silence men;

You may mock without being rebuked,

⁴And say, "My doctrine is pure,

And I have been innocent in Your sight."

⁵But would that God might speak,

And talk to you Himself.

⁶He would tell you the secrets of wisdom,

[a]-For there are many sides to sagacity;

And know that God has overlooked for you some of your iniquity.-[a]

⁷Would you discover the mystery of God?

Would you discover the limit of the Almighty?

⁸Higher than heaven—what can you do?

Deeper than Sheol—what can you know?

⁹Its measure is longer than the earth

And broader than the sea.

¹⁰[a]-Should He pass by, or confine,

Or call an assembly, who can stop Him?-[a]

---

[a]-[a] Meaning of Heb. uncertain.

18 וְלָמָּה מֵרֶחֶם הֹצֵאתָנִי

אֶגְוַע וְעַיִן לֹא־תִרְאֵנִי׃

19 כַּאֲשֶׁר לֹא־הָיִיתִי אֶהְיֶה

מִבֶּטֶן לַקֶּבֶר אוּבָל׃

20 הֲלֹא־מְעַט יָמַי יֶחְדָּל וַחֲדָל

יָשִׁית וְשִׁית מִמֶּנִּי וְאַבְלִיגָה מְעָט׃

21 בְּטֶרֶם אֵלֵךְ וְלֹא אָשׁוּב

אֶל־אֶרֶץ חֹשֶׁךְ וְצַלְמָוֶת׃

22 אֶרֶץ עֵיפָתָה ׀ כְּמוֹ אֹפֶל

צַלְמָוֶת וְלֹא סְדָרִים

וַתֹּפַע כְּמוֹ־אֹפֶל׃ פ

יא 1 וַיַּעַן צֹפַר הַנַּעֲמָתִי וַיֹּאמַר׃

2 הֲרֹב דְּבָרִים לֹא יֵעָנֶה

וְאִם־אִישׁ שְׂפָתַיִם יִצְדָּק׃

3 בַּדֶּיךָ מְתִים יַחֲרִישׁוּ

וַתִּלְעַג וְאֵין מַכְלִם׃

4 וַתֹּאמֶר זַךְ לִקְחִי

וּבַר הָיִיתִי בְעֵינֶיךָ׃

5 וְאוּלָם מִי־יִתֵּן אֱלוֹהַּ דַּבֵּר

וְיִפְתַּח שְׂפָתָיו עִמָּךְ׃

6 וְיַגֶּד־לְךָ ׀ תַּעֲלֻמוֹת חָכְמָה

כִּי־כִפְלַיִם לְתוּשִׁיָּה

וְדַע כִּי־יַשֶּׁה לְךָ אֱלוֹהַ מֵעֲוֹנֶךָ׃

7 הַחֵקֶר אֱלוֹהַ תִּמְצָא

אִם עַד־תַּכְלִית שַׁדַּי תִּמְצָא׃

8 גׇּבְהֵי שָׁמַיִם מַה־תִּפְעָל

עֲמֻקָּה מִשְּׁאוֹל מַה־תֵּדָע׃

9 אֲרֻכָּה מֵאֶרֶץ מִדָּהּ

וּרְחָבָה מִנִּי־יָם׃

10 אִם־יַחֲלֹף וְיַסְגִּיר

וְיַקְהִיל וּמִי יְשִׁיבֶנּוּ׃

11For He knows deceitful men;
When He sees iniquity, does He not discern
　it?
12a-A hollow man will get understanding,
When a wild ass is born a man.-a

13But if you direct your mind,
And spread forth your hands toward Him—
14If there is iniquity with you, remove it,
And do not let injustice reside in your tent—
15Then, free of blemish, you will hold your
　head high,
And, b-when in straits,-b be unafraid.
16You will then put your misery out of mind,
Consider it as water that has flowed past.
17a-Life will be brighter than noon;-a
You will shine, you will be like the morning.
18You will be secure, for there is hope,
a-And, entrenched,-a you will rest secure;
19You will lie down undisturbed;
The great will court your favor.
20But the eyes of the wicked pine away;
Escape is cut off from them;
They have only their last breath to look for-
　ward to.

12 Then Job said in reply:

2Indeed, you are the [voice of] the people,
And wisdom will die with you.
3But I, like you, have a mind,
And am not less than you.
Who does not know such things?
4I have become a laughingstock to my
　friend—
"One who calls to God and is answered,
Blamelessly innocent"—a laughingstock.
5a-In the thought of the complacent there is
　contempt for calamity;

כִּי־הוּא יָדַע מְתֵי־שָׁוְא 11
וַיַּרְא־אָוֶן וְלֹא יִתְבּוֹנָן:
וְאִישׁ נָבוּב יִלָּבֵב 12
וְעַיִר פֶּרֶא אָדָם יִוָּלֵד:

אִם־אַתָּה הֲכִינוֹתָ לִבֶּךָ 13
וּפָרַשְׂתָּ אֵלָיו כַּפֶּךָ:
אִם־אָוֶן בְּיָדְךָ הַרְחִיקֵהוּ 14
וְאַל־תַּשְׁכֵּן בְּאֹהָלֶיךָ עַוְלָה:
כִּי־אָז ׀ תִּשָּׂא פָנֶיךָ מִמּוּם 15
וְהָיִיתָ מֻצָק וְלֹא תִירָא:
כִּי־אַתָּה עָמָל תִּשְׁכָּח 16
כְּמַיִם עָבְרוּ תִזְכֹּר:
וּמִצָּהֳרַיִם יָקוּם חָלֶד 17
תָּעֻפָה כַּבֹּקֶר תִּהְיֶה:
וּבָטַחְתָּ כִּי־יֵשׁ תִּקְוָה 18
וְחָפַרְתָּ לָבֶטַח תִּשְׁכָּב:
וְרָבַצְתָּ וְאֵין מַחֲרִיד 19
וְחִלּוּ פָנֶיךָ רַבִּים:
וְעֵינֵי רְשָׁעִים תִּכְלֶינָה 20
וּמָנוֹס אָבַד מִנְהֶם
וְתִקְוָתָם מַפַּח־נָפֶשׁ: פ

וַיַּעַן אִיּוֹב וַיֹּאמַר: יב

אָמְנָם כִּי אַתֶּם־עָם 2
וְעִמָּכֶם תָּמוּת חָכְמָה:
גַּם־לִי לֵבָב ׀ כְּמוֹכֶם 3
לֹא־נֹפֵל אָנֹכִי מִכֶּם
וְאֶת־מִי־אֵין כְּמוֹ־אֵלֶּה:
שְׂחֹק לְרֵעֵהוּ ׀ אֶהְיֶה 4
קֹרֵא לֶאֱלוֹהַּ וַיַּעֲנֵהוּ
שְׂחוֹק צַדִּיק תָּמִים:
לַפִּיד בּוּז לְעַשְׁתּוּת שַׁאֲנָן 5

b-b　Heb. muṣaq; other Heb. editions muṣṣaq, "you will be firm."

1674

It is ready for those whose foot slips.-a

6Robbers live untroubled in their tents,

And those who provoke God are secure,

a-Those whom God's hands have produced.-a

7But ask the beasts, and they will teach you;

The birds of the sky, they will tell you,

8Or speak to the earth, it will teach you;

The fish of the sea, they will inform you.

9Who among all these does not know

That the hand of the LORD has done this?

10In His hand is every living soul

And the breath of all mankind.

11Truly, the ear tests arguments

As the palate tastes foods.

12Is wisdom in the aged

And understanding in the long-lived?

13With Him are wisdom and courage;

His are counsel and understanding.

14Whatever He tears down cannot be rebuilt;

Whomever He imprisons cannot be set free.

15When He holds back the waters, they dry
up;

When He lets them loose, they tear up the
land.

16With Him are strength and resourcefulness;

Erring and causing to err are from Him.

17He makes counselors go about naked[b]

And causes judges to go mad.

18He undoes the belts of kings,

And fastens loincloths on them.

19He makes priests go about naked,[b]

And leads temple-servants[c] astray.

20He deprives trusty men of speech,

And takes away the reason of elders.

21He pours disgrace upon great men,

And loosens the belt of the mighty.

22He draws mysteries out of the darkness,

And brings obscurities to light.

נָכוֹן לְמוֹעֲדֵי רָגֶל:

6 יִשְׁלָיוּ אֹהָלִים ׀ לְשֹׁדְדִים

וּבַטֻּחוֹת לְמַרְגִּיזֵי אֵל

לַאֲשֶׁר הֵבִיא אֱלוֹהַּ בְּיָדוֹ:

7 וְאוּלָם שְׁאַל־נָא בְהֵמוֹת וְתֹרֶךָּ

וְעוֹף הַשָּׁמַיִם וְיַגֶּד־לָךְ:

8 אוֹ שִׂיחַ לָאָרֶץ וְתֹרֶךָּ

וִיסַפְּרוּ לְךָ דְּגֵי הַיָּם:

9 מִי לֹא־יָדַע בְּכָל־אֵלֶּה

כִּי יַד־יְהֹוָה עָשְׂתָה זֹּאת:

10 אֲשֶׁר בְּיָדוֹ נֶפֶשׁ כָּל־חָי

וְרוּחַ כָּל־בְּשַׂר־אִישׁ:

11 הֲלֹא־אֹזֶן מִלִּין תִּבְחָן

וְחֵךְ אֹכֶל יִטְעַם־לוֹ:

12 בִּישִׁישִׁים חָכְמָה

וְאֹרֶךְ יָמִים תְּבוּנָה:

13 עִמּוֹ חָכְמָה וּגְבוּרָה

לוֹ עֵצָה וּתְבוּנָה:

14 הֵן יַהֲרוֹס וְלֹא יִבָּנֶה

יִסְגֹּר עַל־אִישׁ וְלֹא יִפָּתֵחַ:

15 הֵן יַעְצֹר בַּמַּיִם וְיִבָשׁוּ

וִישַׁלְּחֵם וְיַהַפְכוּ אָרֶץ:

16 עִמּוֹ עֹז וְתוּשִׁיָּה

לוֹ שֹׁגֵג וּמַשְׁגֶּה:

17 מוֹלִיךְ יוֹעֲצִים שׁוֹלָל

וְשֹׁפְטִים יְהוֹלֵל:

18 מוּסַר מְלָכִים פִּתֵּחַ

וַיֶּאְסֹר אֵזוֹר בְּמָתְנֵיהֶם:

19 מוֹלִיךְ כֹּהֲנִים שׁוֹלָל

וְאֵתָנִים יְסַלֵּף:

20 מֵסִיר שָׂפָה לְנֶאֱמָנִים

וְטַעַם זְקֵנִים יִקָּח:

21 שׁוֹפֵךְ בּוּז עַל־נְדִיבִים

וּמְזִיחַ אֲפִיקִים רִפָּה:

22 מְגַלֶּה עֲמֻקוֹת מִנִּי־חֹשֶׁךְ

וַיֹּצֵא לָאוֹר צַלְמָוֶת:

---

a-a Meaning of Heb. uncertain.

b A sign of madness.

c Cf. Ugaritic ytnm, a class of temple servants; others "the mighty."

23He exalts nations, then destroys them;
He expands nations, then leads them away.
24He deranges the leaders of the people,
And makes them wander in a trackless waste.
25They grope without light in the darkness;
He makes them wander as if drunk.

23 מַשְׂגִּיא לַגּוֹיִם וַיְאַבְּדֵם
שֹׁטֵחַ לַגּוֹיִם וַיַּנְחֵם:
24 מֵסִיר לֵב רָאשֵׁי עַם־הָאָרֶץ
וַיַּתְעֵם בְּתֹהוּ לֹא־דָרֶךְ:
25 יְמַשְׁשׁוּ־חֹשֶׁךְ וְלֹא־אוֹר
וַיַּתְעֵם כַּשִּׁכּוֹר:

13 My eye has seen all this;
My ear has heard and understood it.
2What you know, I know also;
I am not less than you.
3Indeed, I would speak to the Almighty;
I insist on arguing with God.
4But you invent lies;
All of you are quacks.
5If you would only keep quiet
It would be considered wisdom on your part.
6Hear now my arguments,
Listen to my pleading.
7Will you speak unjustly on God's behalf?
Will you speak deceitfully for Him?
8Will you be partial toward Him?
Will you plead God's cause?
9Will it go well when He examines you?
Will you fool Him as one fools men?
10He will surely reprove you
If in a-your heart-a you are partial toward
　Him.
11His threat will terrify you,
And His fear will seize you.
12Your briefs are emptyb platitudes;
Your responses are unsubstantial.c

13Keep quiet; I will have my say,
Come what may upon me.
14How long! I will take my flesh in my teeth;
I will take my life in my hands.

יג הֶן־כָּל רָאֲתָה עֵינִי
שָׁמְעָה אָזְנִי וַתָּבֶן לָהּ:
2 כְּדַעְתְּכֶם יָדַעְתִּי גַם־אָנִי
לֹא־נֹפֵל אָנֹכִי מִכֶּם:
3 אוּלָם אֲנִי אֶל־שַׁדַּי אֲדַבֵּר
וְהוֹכֵחַ אֶל־אֵל אֶחְפָּץ:
4 וְאוּלָם אַתֶּם טֹפְלֵי־שָׁקֶר
רֹפְאֵי אֱלִל כֻּלְּכֶם:
5 מִי־יִתֵּן הַחֲרֵשׁ תַּחֲרִישׁוּן
וּתְהִי לָכֶם לְחָכְמָה:
6 שִׁמְעוּ־נָא תוֹכַחְתִּי
וְרִבוֹת שְׂפָתַי הַקְשִׁיבוּ:
7 הַלְאֵל תְּדַבְּרוּ עַוְלָה
וְלוֹ תְּדַבְּרוּ רְמִיָּה:
8 הֲפָנָיו תִּשָּׂאוּן
אִם־לָאֵל תְּרִיבוּן:
9 הֲטוֹב כִּי־יַחְקֹר אֶתְכֶם
אִם־כְּהָתֵל בֶּאֱנוֹשׁ תְּהָתֵלּוּ בוֹ:
10 הוֹכֵחַ יוֹכִיחַ אֶתְכֶם
אִם־בַּסֵּתֶר פָּנִים תִּשָּׂאוּן:
11 הֲלֹא שְׂאֵתוֹ תְּבַעֵת אֶתְכֶם
וּפַחְדּוֹ יִפֹּל עֲלֵיכֶם:
12 זִכְרֹנֵיכֶם מִשְׁלֵי־אֵפֶר
לְגַבֵּי־חֹמֶר גַּבֵּיכֶם:

13 הַחֲרִישׁוּ מִמֶּנִּי וַאֲדַבְּרָה־אָנִי
וְיַעֲבֹר עָלַי מָה:
14 עַל־מָה | אֶשָּׂא בְשָׂרִי בְשִׁנָּי
וְנַפְשִׁי אָשִׂים בְּכַפִּי:

a-a　Lit. "secret."
b　Lit. "ashen."
c　Lit. "clayey."

15d-He may well slay me; I may have no hope;-d
Yet I will argue my case before Him.
16In this too is my salvation:
That no impious man can come into His presence.

17Listen closely to my words;
Give ear to my discourse.
18See now, I have prepared a case;
I know that I will win it.
19For who is it that would challenge me?
I should then keep silent and expire.
20But two things do not do to me,
So that I need not hide from You:
21Remove Your hand from me,
And let not Your terror frighten me.
22Then summon me and I will respond,
Or I will speak and You reply to me.
23How many are my iniquities and sins?
Advise me of my transgression and sin.
24Why do You hide Your face,
And treat me like an enemy?
25Will You harass a driven leaf,
Will You pursue dried-up straw,
26That You decree for me bitter things
And make me e-answer for-e the iniquities of
my youth,
27That You put my feet in the stocks
And watch all my ways,
f-Hemming in my footsteps?-f
28Man wastes away like a rotten thing,
Like a garment eaten by moths.

14
Man born of woman is short-lived and
sated with trouble.
2He blossoms like a flower and withers;
He vanishes like a shadow and does not endure.

15 הֵ֤ן יִקְטְלֵ֗נִי לֹ֥א לֹ֥ו אֲיַחֵ֑ל
אַךְ־דְּרָכַ֗י אֶל־פָּנָ֥יו אוֹכִֽיחַ׃
16 גַּם־ה֥וּא־לִ֥י לִֽישׁוּעָ֑ה
כִּי־לֹ֥א לְ֝פָנָ֗יו חָנֵ֥ף יָבֽוֹא׃

17 שִׁמְע֣וּ שָׁ֭מוֹעַ מִלָּתִ֑י
וְ֝אַֽחֲוָתִ֗י בְּאָזְנֵיכֶֽם׃
18 הִנֵּה־נָ֭א עָרַ֣כְתִּי מִשְׁפָּ֑ט
יָ֝דַ֗עְתִּי כִּֽי־אֲנִ֥י אֶצְדָּֽק׃
19 מִי־ה֭וּא יָרִ֣יב עִמָּדִ֑י
כִּֽי־עַתָּ֖ה אַחֲרִ֣ישׁ וְאֶגְוָֽע׃
20 אַךְ־שְׁ֭תַּיִם אַל־תַּ֣עַשׂ עִמָּדִ֑י
אָ֥ז מִ֝פָּנֶ֗יךָ לֹ֣א אֶסָּתֵֽר׃
21 כַּ֭פְּךָ מֵעָלַ֣י הַרְחַ֑ק
וְ֝אֵ֥מָתְךָ֗ אַֽל־תְּבַעֲתַֽנִּי׃
22 וּ֭קְרָא וְאָנֹכִ֣י אֶֽעֱנֶ֑ה
אֽוֹ־אֲ֝דַבֵּ֗ר וַהֲשִׁיבֵֽנִי׃
23 כַּמָּ֣ה לִ֭י עֲוֺנ֣וֹת וְחַטָּא֑וֹת
פִּֽשְׁעִ֥י וְ֝חַטָּאתִ֗י הֹדִיעֵֽנִי׃
24 לָמָּה־פָנֶ֥יךָ תַסְתִּ֑יר
וְתַחְשְׁבֵ֖נִי לְאוֹיֵ֣ב לָֽךְ׃
25 הֶעָלֶ֣ה נִדָּ֣ף תַּעֲר֑וֹץ
וְאֶת־קַ֖שׁ יָבֵ֣שׁ תִּרְדֹּֽף׃
26 כִּֽי־תִכְתֹּ֣ב עָלַ֣י מְרֹר֑וֹת
וְ֝תוֹרִישֵׁ֗נִי עֲוֺנ֥וֹת נְעוּרָֽי׃
27 וְתָשֵׂ֬ם בַּסַּ֨ד ׀ רַגְלַ֗י
וְתִשְׁמ֥וֹר כָּל־אָרְחוֹתָ֑י
עַל־שָׁרְשֵׁ֥י רַ֝גְלַ֗י תִּתְחַקֶּֽה׃
28 וְ֭הוּא כְּרָקָ֣ב יִבְלֶ֑ה
כְּ֝בֶ֗גֶד אֲכָ֥לוֹ עָֽשׁ׃

יד אָדָ֣ם יְל֣וּד אִשָּׁ֑ה קְצַ֥ר יָ֝מִ֗ים וּֽשְׂבַֽע־
רֹֽגֶז׃
2 כְּצִ֣יץ יָ֭צָא וַיִּמָּ֑ל
וַיִּבְרַ֥ח כַּ֝צֵּ֗ל וְלֹ֣א יַעֲמֽוֹד׃

---

d-d So with kethib; others with qere "Though He slay me, yet will
        I trust in Him."
e-e Lit. "inherit."
f-f Meaning of Heb. uncertain.

3Do You fix Your gaze on such a one?
Will You go to law with me?
4a-Who can produce a clean thing out of an
    unclean one? No one!-a
5His days are determined;
You know the number of his months;
You have set him limits that he cannot pass.
6Turn away from him, that he may be at ease
Until, like a hireling, he finishes out his day.

7There is hope for a tree;
If it is cut down it will renew itself;
Its shoots will not cease.
8If its roots are old in the earth,
And its stump dies in the ground,
9At the scent of water it will bud
And produce branches like a sapling.
10But mortals languish and die;
Man expires; where is he?
11The waters of the sea fail,
And the river dries up and is parched.
12So man lies down never to rise;
He will awake only when the heavens are no
    more,
Only then be aroused from his sleep.
13O that You would hide me in Sheol,
Conceal me until Your anger passes,
Set me a fixed time to attend to me.
14If a man dies, can he live again?
All the time of my service I wait
Until my replacement comes.
15You would call and I would answer You;
You would set Your heart on Your handi-
    work.
16Then You would not count my steps,
Or keep watch over my sin.
17My transgression would be sealed up in a
    pouch;
You would coat over my iniquity.

3 אַף־עַל־זֶה פָּקַחְתָּ עֵינֶךָ
וְאֹתִי תָבִיא בְמִשְׁפָּט עִמָּךְ:
4 מִי־יִתֵּן טָהוֹר מִטָּמֵא לֹא אֶחָד:
5 אִם חֲרוּצִים ׀ יָמָיו
מִסְפַּר־חֳדָשָׁיו אִתָּךְ
חֻקָּו עָשִׂיתָ וְלֹא יַעֲבוֹר:
6 שְׁעֵה מֵעָלָיו וְיֶחְדָּל
עַד־יִרְצֶה כְּשָׂכִיר יוֹמוֹ:

7 כִּי יֵשׁ לָעֵץ
תִּקְוָה אִם־יִכָּרֵת וְעוֹד יַחֲלִיף
וְיֹנַקְתּוֹ לֹא תֶחְדָּל:
8 אִם־יַזְקִין בָּאָרֶץ שָׁרְשׁוֹ
וּבֶעָפָר יָמוּת גִּזְעוֹ:
9 מֵרֵיחַ מַיִם יַפְרִחַ
וְעָשָׂה קָצִיר כְּמוֹ־נָטַע:
10 וְגֶבֶר יָמוּת וַיֶּחֱלָשׁ
וַיִּגְוַע אָדָם וְאַיּוֹ:
11 אָזְלוּ־מַיִם מִנִּי־יָם
וְנָהָר יֶחֱרַב וְיָבֵשׁ:
12 וְאִישׁ שָׁכַב וְלֹא־יָקוּם
עַד־בִּלְתִּי שָׁמַיִם לֹא יָקִיצוּ
וְלֹא־יֵעֹרוּ מִשְּׁנָתָם:
13 מִי יִתֵּן ׀ בִּשְׁאוֹל תַּצְפִּנֵנִי
תַּסְתִּירֵנִי עַד־שׁוּב אַפֶּךָ
תָּשִׁית לִי חֹק וְתִזְכְּרֵנִי:
14 אִם־יָמוּת גֶּבֶר הֲיִחְיֶה
כָּל־יְמֵי צְבָאִי אֲיַחֵל
עַד־בּוֹא חֲלִיפָתִי:
15 תִּקְרָא וְאָנֹכִי אֶעֱנֶךָּ
לְמַעֲשֵׂה יָדֶיךָ תִכְסֹף:
16 כִּי־עַתָּה צְעָדַי תִּסְפּוֹר
לֹא־תִשְׁמוֹר עַל־חַטָּאתִי:
17 חָתֻם בִּצְרוֹר פִּשְׁעִי
וַתִּטְפֹּל עַל־עֲוֹנִי:

a-a   *Meaning of Heb. uncertain.*

18Mountains collapse and crumble;
Rocks are dislodged from their place.
19Water wears away stone;
Torrents wash away earth;
So you destroy man's hope,
20You overpower him forever and he perishes;
You alter his visage and dispatch him.
21His sons attain honor and he does not know
it;
They are humbled and he is not aware of it.
22He feels only the pain of his flesh,
And his spirit mourns in him.

15 Eliphaz the Temanite said in reply:

2Does a wise man answer with windy opinions,
And fill his belly with the east wind?
3Should he argue with useless talk,
With words that are of no worth?
4You subvert piety
And restrain prayer to God.
5Your sinfulness dictates your speech,
So you choose crafty language.
6Your own mouth condemns you—not I;
Your lips testify against you.

7Were you the first man born?
Were you created before the hills?
8Have you listened in on the council of God?
Have you sole possession of wisdom?
9What do you know that we do not know,
Or understand that we do not?
10Among us are gray-haired old men,
Older by far than your father.
11Are God's consolations not enough for you,
And His gentle words to you?

18 וְאוּלָם הַר־נוֹפֵל יִבּוֹל
וְצוּר יֶעְתַּק מִמְּקֹמוֹ:
19 אֲבָנִים ׀ שָׁחֲקוּ מַיִם
תִּשְׁטֹף־סְפִיחֶיהָ עֲפַר־אָרֶץ
וְתִקְוַת אֱנוֹשׁ הֶאֱבַדְתָּ:
20 תִּתְקְפֵהוּ לָנֶצַח וַיַּהֲלֹךְ
מְשַׁנֶּה פָנָיו וַתְּשַׁלְּחֵהוּ:
21 יִכְבְּדוּ בָנָיו וְלֹא יֵדָע
וְיִצְעֲרוּ וְלֹא־יָבִין לָמוֹ:
22 אַךְ־בְּשָׂרוֹ עָלָיו יִכְאָב
וְנַפְשׁוֹ עָלָיו תֶּאֱבָל: פ

טו וַיַּעַן אֱלִיפַז הַתֵּימָנִי וַיֹּאמַר:

2 הֶחָכָם יַעֲנֶה דַעַת־רוּחַ
וִימַלֵּא קָדִים בִּטְנוֹ:
3 הוֹכֵחַ בְּדָבָר לֹא יִסְכּוֹן
וּמִלִּים לֹא־יוֹעִיל בָּם:
4 אַף־אַתָּה תָּפֵר יִרְאָה
וְתִגְרַע שִׂיחָה לִפְנֵי־אֵל:
5 כִּי יְאַלֵּף עֲוֹנְךָ פִיךָ
וְתִבְחַר לְשׁוֹן עֲרוּמִים:
6 יַרְשִׁיעֲךָ פִיךָ וְלֹא־אָנִי
וּשְׂפָתֶיךָ יַעֲנוּ־בָךְ:

7 הֲרִאישׁוֹן* אָדָם תִּוָּלֵד
וְלִפְנֵי גְבָעוֹת חוֹלָלְתָּ:
8 הַבְסוֹד אֱלוֹהַ תִּשְׁמָע
וְתִגְרַע אֵלֶיךָ חָכְמָה:
9 מַה־יָּדַעְתָּ וְלֹא נֵדָע
תָּבִין וְלֹא־עִמָּנוּ הוּא:
10 גַּם־שָׂב גַּם־יָשִׁישׁ בָּנוּ
כַּבִּיר מֵאָבִיךָ יָמִים:
11 הַמְעַט מִמְּךָ תַּנְחֻמוֹת אֵל
וְדָבָר לָאַט עִמָּךְ:

v. 7. יתיר י׳

12How your heart has carried you away,

How your eyes *a*-have failed-*a* you,

13That you could vent your anger on God,

And let such words out of your mouth!

14What is man that he can be cleared of guilt,

One born of woman, that he be in the right?

15He puts no trust in His holy ones;

The heavens are not guiltless in His sight;

16What then of one loathsome and foul,

Man, who drinks wrongdoing like water!

17I will hold forth; listen to me;

What I have seen, I will declare—

18That which wise men have transmitted

from their fathers,

And have not withheld,

19To whom alone the land was given,

No stranger passing among them:

20The wicked man writhes in torment all his

days;

Few years are reserved for the ruthless.

21Frightening sounds fill his ears;

When he is at ease a robber falls upon him.

22He is never sure he will come back from the

dark;

A sword stares him in the face.

23He wanders about for bread—where is it?

He knows that the day of darkness has been

readied for him.

24Troubles terrify him, anxiety overpowers

him,

Like a king *a*-expecting a siege.-*a*

25For he has raised his arm against God

And played the hero against the Almighty.

26He runs at Him defiantly*b*

a-With his thickly bossed shield.

27His face is covered with fat

And his loins with blubber.-*a*

28He dwells in cities doomed to ruin,

צ מַה־יִּקָּחֲךָ֣ לִבֶּ֑ךָ 12

וּֽמַה־יִּרְזְמ֥וּן עֵינֶֽיךָ׃

כִּֽי־תָשִׁ֣יב אֶל־אֵ֣ל רוּחֶ֑ךָ 13

וְהֹצֵ֖אתָ מִפִּ֣יךָ מִלִּֽין׃

מָֽה־אֱנ֥וֹשׁ כִּֽי־יִזְכֶּ֑ה 14

וְכִֽי־יִ֝צְדַּ֗ק יְל֣וּד אִשָּֽׁה׃

הֵ֣ן בקדשו בִּ֭קְדֹשָׁיו לֹ֣א יַאֲמִ֑ין 15

וְ֝שָׁמַ֗יִם לֹא־זַכּ֥וּ בְעֵינָֽיו׃

אַ֭ף כִּֽי־נִתְעָ֥ב וְֽנֶאֱלָ֑ח 16

אִישׁ־שֹׁתֶ֖ה כַמַּ֣יִם עַוְלָֽה׃

אֲחַוְךָ֥ שְֽׁמַֽע־לִ֑י 17

וְזֶֽה־חָ֝זִ֗יתִי וַאֲסַפֵּֽרָה׃

אֲשֶׁר־חֲכָמִ֥ים יַגִּ֑ידוּ 18

וְלֹ֥א כִֽ֝חֲד֗וּ מֵאֲבוֹתָֽם׃

לָהֶ֣ם לְ֭בַדָּם נִתְּנָ֣ה הָאָ֑רֶץ 19

וְלֹא־עָ֖בַר זָ֣ר בְּתוֹכָֽם׃

כָּל־יְמֵ֣י רָ֭שָׁע ה֣וּא מִתְחוֹלֵ֑ל 20

וּמִסְפַּ֥ר שָׁ֝נִ֗ים נִצְפְּנ֥וּ לֶעָרִֽיץ׃

ק֤וֹל־פְּחָדִ֥ים בְּאָזְנָ֑יו 21

בַּ֝שָּׁל֗וֹם שׁוֹדֵ֥ד יְבוֹאֶֽנּוּ׃

לֹא־יַאֲמִ֣ין שׁ֭וּב מִנִּי־חֹ֑שֶׁךְ 22

וצפו וְצָפ֖וּי ה֣וּא אֱלֵי־חָֽרֶב׃

נֹ֘דֵ֤ד ה֣וּא לַלֶּ֣חֶם אַיֵּ֑ה 23

יָדַ֓ע ׀ כִּֽי־נָכ֖וֹן בְּיָד֣וֹ יֽוֹם־חֹֽשֶׁךְ׃

יְֽ֭בַעֲתֻהוּ צַ֣ר וּמְצוּקָ֑ה 24

תִּ֝תְקְפֵ֗הוּ כְּמֶ֤לֶךְ ׀ עָתִ֬יד לַכִּידֽוֹר׃

כִּֽי־נָטָ֣ה אֶל־אֵ֣ל יָד֑וֹ 25

וְאֶל־שַׁ֝דַּ֗י יִתְגַּבָּֽר׃

יָר֣וּץ אֵלָ֣יו בְּצַוָּ֑אר 26

בַּ֝עֲבִ֗י גַּבֵּ֥י מָֽגִנָּֽיו׃

כִּֽי־כִסָּ֣ה פָנָ֣יו בְּחֶלְבּ֑וֹ 27

וַיַּ֖עַשׂ פִּימָ֣ה עֲלֵי־כָֽסֶל׃

וַיִּשְׁכּ֤וֹן ׀ עָרִ֬ים נִכְחָד֗וֹת 28

_____

a-a   Meaning of Heb. uncertain.

b   Lit. "with neck."

In houses that shall not be lived in,
That are destined to become heaps of rubble.
²⁹He will not be rich;
His wealth will not endure;
a-His produce shall not bend to the earth.-*a*
³⁰He will never get away from the darkness;
Flames will sear his shoots;
a-He will pass away by the breath of His mouth.
³¹He will not be trusted;
He will be misled by falsehood,
And falsehood will be his recompense.-*a*
³²He will wither before his time,
His boughs never having flourished.
³³He will drop his unripe grapes like a vine;
He will shed his blossoms like an olive tree.
³⁴For the company of the impious is desolate;
Fire consumes the tents of the briber;
³⁵For they have conceived mischief, given birth to evil,
And their womb has produced deceit.

בָּתִּים לֹא־יֵשְׁבוּ לָמוֹ
אֲשֶׁר הִתְעַתְּדוּ לְגַלִּים:
29 לֹא־יֶעְשַׁר
וְלֹא־יָקוּם חֵילוֹ
וְלֹא־יִטֶּה לָאָרֶץ מִנְלָם:
30 לֹא־יָסוּר ׀ מִנִּי־חֹשֶׁךְ
יֹנַקְתּוֹ תְּיַבֵּשׁ שַׁלְהָבֶת
וְיָסוּר בְּרוּחַ פִּיו:
31 אַל־יַאֲמֵן
בַּשׁוֹ בַּשָּׁיו נִתְעָה
כִּי־שָׁוְא תִּהְיֶה תְמוּרָתוֹ:
32 בְּלֹא־יוֹמוֹ תִּמָּלֵא
וְכִפָּתוֹ לֹא רַעֲנָנָה:
33 יַחְמֹס כַּגֶּפֶן בִּסְרוֹ
וְיַשְׁלֵךְ כַּזַּיִת נִצָּתוֹ:
34 כִּי־עֲדַת חָנֵף גַּלְמוּד
וְאֵשׁ אָכְלָה אָהֳלֵי־שֹׁחַד:
35 הָרֹה עָמָל וְיָלֹד אָוֶן
וּבִטְנָם תָּכִין מִרְמָה: ס

16 Job said in reply:

²I have often heard such things;
You are all mischievous comforters.
³Have windy words no limit?
What afflicts you that you speak on?
⁴I would also talk like you
If you were in my place;
I would barrage you with words,
I would wag my head over you.
⁵I would encourage you with words,*a*
My moving lips would bring relief.
⁶If I speak, my pain will not be relieved,
And if I do not—what have I lost?
⁷Now He has truly worn me out;
You have destroyed my whole community.

טז וַיַּעַן אִיּוֹב וַיֹּאמַר:

2 שָׁמַעְתִּי כְאֵלֶּה רַבּוֹת
מְנַחֲמֵי עָמָל כֻּלְּכֶם:
3 הֲקֵץ לְדִבְרֵי־רוּחַ
אוֹ מַה־יַּמְרִיצְךָ כִּי תַעֲנֶה:
4 גַּם ׀ אָנֹכִי כָּכֶם אֲדַבֵּרָה
לוּ־יֵשׁ נַפְשְׁכֶם תַּחַת נַפְשִׁי
אַחְבִּירָה עֲלֵיכֶם בְּמִלִּים
וְאָנִיעָה עֲלֵיכֶם בְּמוֹ רֹאשִׁי:
5 אֲאַמִּצְכֶם בְּמוֹ־פִי
וְנִיד שְׂפָתַי יַחְשֹׂךְ:
6 אִם־אֲדַבְּרָה לֹא־יֵחָשֵׂךְ כְּאֵבִי
וְאַחְדְּלָה מַה־מִנִּי יַהֲלֹךְ:
7 אַךְ־עַתָּה הֶלְאָנִי
הֲשִׁמּוֹתָ כָּל־עֲדָתִי:

a Lit. "my mouth."

8You have shriveled me;

My gauntness serves as a witness,

And testifies against me.

9In His anger He tears and persecutes me;

He gnashes His teeth at me;

My foe stabs me with his eyes.

10They open wide their mouths at me;

Reviling me, they strike my cheeks;

They inflame themselves against me.

11God hands me over to an evil man,

Thrusts me into the clutches of the wicked.

12I had been untroubled, and He broke me in pieces;

He took me by the scruff and shattered me;

He set me up as His target;

13His bowmen surrounded me;

He pierced my kidneys; He showed no mercy;

He spilled my bile onto the ground.

14He breached me, breach after breach;

He rushed at me like a warrior.

15I sewed sackcloth over my skin;

I *b*-buried my glory-*b* in the dust.

16My face is red with weeping;

Darkness covers my eyes

17*c*-For no injustice on my part

And for the purity of my prayer!-*c*

18Earth, do not cover my blood;

Let there be no resting place for my outcry!

19Surely now my witness is in heaven;

He who can testify for me is on high.

20O my advocates, my fellows,

Before God my eyes shed tears;

21Let Him arbitrate between a man and God

As between a man and his fellow.

22For a few more years will pass,

17

And I shall go the way of no return.

1My spirit is crushed, my days run out;

The graveyard waits for me.

8 וְתִּקְמְטֵנִי לְעֵד הָיָה
וַיָּקָם בִּי כַחֲשִׁי
בְּפָנַי יַעֲנֶה:
9 אַפּוֹ טָרַף ׀ וַיִּשְׂטְמֵנִי
חָרַק עָלַי בְּשִׁנָּיו
צָרִי ׀ יִלְטוֹשׁ עֵינָיו לִי:
10 פָּעֲרוּ עָלַי ׀ בְּפִיהֶם
בְּחֶרְפָּה הִכּוּ לְחָיָי
יַחַד עָלַי יִתְמַלָּאוּן:
11 יַסְגִּירֵנִי אֵל אֶל עֲוִיל
וְעַל יְדֵי רְשָׁעִים יִרְטֵנִי:
12 שָׁלֵו הָיִיתִי ׀ וַיְפַרְפְּרֵנִי
וְאָחַז בְּעָרְפִּי וַיְפַצְפְּצֵנִי
וַיְקִימֵנִי לוֹ לְמַטָּרָה:
13 יָסֹבּוּ עָלַי ׀ רַבָּיו
יְפַלַּח כִּלְיוֹתַי וְלֹא יַחְמוֹל
יִשְׁפֹּךְ לָאָרֶץ מְרֵרָתִי:
14 יִפְרְצֵנִי פֶרֶץ עַל פְּנֵי פָרֶץ
יָרֻץ עָלַי כְּגִבּוֹר:
15 שַׂק תָּפַרְתִּי עֲלֵי גִלְדִּי
וְעֹלַלְתִּי בֶעָפָר קַרְנִי:
16 פָּנַי חמרמרה חֳמַרְמְרוּ מִנִּי בֶכִי
וְעַל עַפְעַפַּי צַלְמָוֶת:
17 עַל לֹא חָמָס בְּכַפָּי
וּתְפִלָּתִי זַכָּה:
18 אֶרֶץ אַל תְּכַסִּי דָמִי
וְאַל יְהִי מָקוֹם לְזַעֲקָתִי:
19 גַּם עַתָּה הִנֵּה בַשָּׁמַיִם עֵדִי
וְשָׂהֲדִי בַּמְּרוֹמִים:
20 מְלִיצַי רֵעָי
אֶל אֱלוֹהַּ דָּלְפָה עֵינִי:
21 וְיוֹכַח לְגֶבֶר עִם אֱלוֹהַּ
וּבֶן אָדָם לְרֵעֵהוּ:
22 כִּי שְׁנוֹת מִסְפָּר יֶאֱתָיוּ
יז וְאֹרַח לֹא אָשׁוּב אֶהֱלֹךְ:
1 רוּחִי חֻבָּלָה יָמַי נִזְעָכוּ
קְבָרִים לִי:

b-b Lit. "made my horn enter into."

c-c Or "Though I did no injustice, / And my prayer was pure."

²Surely mocking men keep me company,
And with their provocations I close my eyes.
³Come now, stand surety for me!
Who will give his hand on my behalf?
⁴You have hidden understanding from their minds;
Therefore You must not exalt [them].
⁵He informs on his friends for a share [of their property],
And his children's eyes pine away.

⁶He made me a byword among people;
I have become like Tophet^a of old.
⁷My eyes fail from vexation;
All shapes seem to me like shadows.
⁸The upright are amazed at this;
The pure are aroused against the impious.
⁹The righteous man holds to his way;
He whose hands are clean grows stronger.
¹⁰But all of you, come back now;
I shall not find a wise man among you.
¹¹My days are done, my tendons severed,
The strings of my heart.
¹²They say that night is day,
That light is here—in the face of darkness.
¹³If I must look forward to Sheol as my home,
And make my bed in the dark place,
¹⁴Say to the Pit, "You are my father,"
To the maggots, "Mother," "Sister"—
¹⁵Where, then, is my hope?
Who can see hope for me?
¹⁶Will it descend to Sheol?
Shall we go down together to the dust?

18
Then Bildad the Shuhite said in reply:

²How long? Put an end to talk!
Consider, and then we shall speak.
³Why are we thought of as brutes,

אַם־לֹא הֲתֻלִים עִמָּדִי 2
וּבְהַמְּרוֹתָם תָּלַן עֵינִי:
שִׂימָה־נָּא עָרְבֵנִי עִמָּךְ 3
מִי־הוּא לְיָדִי יִתָּקֵעַ:
כִּי־לִבָּם צָפַנְתָּ מִּשָּׂכֶל 4
עַל־כֵּן לֹא תְרֹמֵם:
לְחֵלֶק יַגִּיד רֵעִים 5
וְעֵינֵי בָנָיו תִּכְלֶנָה:
וְהִצִּגַנִי לִמְשֹׁל עַמִּים 6
וְתֹפֶת לְפָנִים אֶהְיֶה:
וַתֵּכַהּ מִכַּעַשׂ עֵינִי 7
וִיצֻרַי כַּצֵּל כֻּלָּם:
יָשֹׁמּוּ יְשָׁרִים עַל־זֹאת 8
וְנָקִי עַל־חָנֵף יִתְעֹרָר:
וְיֹאחֵז צַדִּיק דַּרְכּוֹ 9
וּטְהָר־יָדַיִם יֹסִיף אֹמֶץ:
וְאוּלָם כֻּלָּם תָּשֻׁבוּ וּבֹאוּ נָא 10
וְלֹא־אֶמְצָא בָכֶם חָכָם:
יָמַי עָבְרוּ זִמֹּתַי נִתְּקוּ 11
מוֹרָשֵׁי לְבָבִי:
לַיְלָה לְיוֹם יָשִׂימוּ 12
אוֹר קָרוֹב מִפְּנֵי־חֹשֶׁךְ:
אִם־אֲקַוֶּה שְׁאוֹל בֵּיתִי 13
בַּחֹשֶׁךְ רִפַּדְתִּי יְצוּעָי:
לַשַּׁחַת קָרָאתִי אָבִי אָתָּה 14
אִמִּי וַאֲחֹתִי לָרִמָּה:
וְאַיֵּה אֵפוֹ תִקְוָתִי 15
וְתִקְוָתִי מִי יְשׁוּרֶנָּה:
בַּדֵּי שְׁאֹל תֵּרַדְנָה 16
אִם־יַחַד עַל־עָפָר נָחַת: ס

יח
וַיַּעַן בִּלְדַּד הַשֻּׁחִי וַיֹּאמַר:

עַד־אָנָה ׀ תְּשִׂימוּן קִנְצֵי לְמִלִּין 2
תָּבִינוּ וְאַחַר נְדַבֵּר:
מַדּוּעַ נֶחְשַׁבְנוּ כַבְּהֵמָה 3

---

^a *That consumed children; cf. Jer. 7.31.*

1683

Regarded by you as stupid?

⁴You who tear yourself to pieces in anger—

Will ᵃ-earth's order be disrupted-ᵃ for your
   sake?

Will rocks be dislodged from their place?

⁵Indeed, the light of the wicked fails;

The flame of his fire does not shine.

⁶The light in his tent darkens;

His lamp fails him.

⁷His iniquitous strides are hobbled;

His schemes overthrow him.

⁸He is led by his feet into the net;

He walks onto the toils.

⁹The trap seizes his heel;

The noose tightens on him.

¹⁰The rope for him lies hidden on the ground;

His snare, on the path.

¹¹Terrors assault him on all sides

And send his feet flying.

¹²His progeny hunger;

Disaster awaits his wife.ᵇ

¹³The tendons under his skin are consumed;

Death's first-born consumes his tendons.

¹⁴He is torn from the safety of his tent;

Terror marches him to the king.ᶜ

¹⁵It lodges in his desolate tent;

Sulfur is strewn upon his home.

¹⁶His roots below dry up,

And above, his branches wither.

¹⁷All mention of him vanishes from the earth;

He has no name abroad.

¹⁸He is thrust from light to darkness,

Driven from the world.

¹⁹He has no seed or breed among his people,

No survivor where he once lived.

²⁰Generations to come will be appalled at his
   fate,

As the previous ones are seized with horror.

נִטְמִ֖ינוּ בְּעֵינֵיכֶֽם׃

4 טֹרֵ֥ף נַפְשׁ֗וֹ בְּאַ֫פּ֥וֹ

הַלְמַעַנְךָ֮ תֵּעָ֪זַ֫ב אָ֥רֶץ

וְיֶעְתַּק־צ֝֗וּר מִמְּקֹמֽוֹ׃

5 גַּ֤ם א֣וֹר רְשָׁעִ֣ים יִדְעָ֑ךְ

וְלֹֽא־יִ֝גַּ֗הּ שְׁבִ֣יב אִשּֽׁוֹ׃

6 א֭וֹר חָשַׁ֣ךְ בְּאׇהֳל֑וֹ

וְ֝נֵר֗וֹ עָלָ֥יו יִדְעָֽךְ׃

7 יֵֽ֭צְרוּ צַעֲדֵ֣י אוֹנ֑וֹ

וְֽתַשְׁלִיכֵ֥הוּ עֲצָתֽוֹ׃

8 כִּֽי־שֻׁלַּ֣ח בְּרֶ֣שֶׁת בְּרַגְלָ֑יו

וְעַל־שְׂ֝בָכָ֗ה יִתְהַלָּֽךְ׃

9 יֹאחֵ֣ז בְּעָקֵ֣ב פָּ֑ח

יַחֲזֵ֖ק עָלָ֣יו צַמִּֽים׃

10 טָמ֣וּן בָּאָ֣רֶץ חַבְל֑וֹ

וּ֝מַלְכֻּדְתּ֗וֹ עֲלֵ֣י נָתִֽיב׃

11 סָ֭בִיב בִּֽעֲתֻ֣הוּ בַלָּה֑וֹת

וֶהֱפִיצֻ֥הוּ לְרַגְלָֽיו׃

12 יְהִי־רָעֵ֥ב אֹנ֑וֹ

וְ֝אֵ֗יד נָכ֥וֹן לְצַלְעֽוֹ׃

13 יֹ֭אכַל בַּדֵּ֣י עוֹר֑וֹ

יֹאכַ֥ל בַּ֝דָּ֗יו בְּכ֣וֹר מָֽוֶת׃

14 יִנָּתֵ֣ק מֵ֭אׇהֳל֣וֹ מִבְטַח֑וֹ

וְ֝תַצְעִדֵ֗הוּ לְמֶ֣לֶךְ בַּלָּהֽוֹת׃

15 תִּשְׁכּ֣וֹן בְּ֭אׇהֳלוֹ מִבְּלִי־ל֑וֹ

יְזֹרֶ֖ה עַל־נָוֵ֣הוּ גׇפְרִֽית׃

16 מִ֭תַּחַת שׇׁרָשָׁ֣יו יִבָ֑שׁוּ

וּ֝מִמַּ֗עַל יִמַּ֥ל קְצִירֽוֹ׃

17 זִֽכְרוֹ־אָ֭בַד מִנִּי־אָ֑רֶץ

וְלֹא־שֵׁ֥ם ל֝֗וֹ עַל־פְּנֵי־חֽוּץ׃

18 יֶהְדְּפֻ֣הוּ מֵא֣וֹר אֶל־חֹ֑שֶׁךְ

וּֽמִתֵּבֵ֥ל יְנִדֻּֽהוּ׃

19 לֹ֘א נִ֤ין ל֣וֹ וְלֹֽא־נֶ֣כֶד בְּעַמּ֑וֹ

וְאֵ֥ין שָׂ֝רִ֗יד בִּמְגוּרָֽיו׃

20 עַל־י֭וֹמוֹ נָשַׁ֣מּוּ אַחֲרֹנִ֑ים

וְ֝קַדְמֹנִ֗ים אָ֣חֲזוּ שָֽׂעַר׃

21"These were the haunts of the wicked;
Here was the place of him who knew not
   God."

21 אַךְ־אֵלֶּה מִשְׁכְּנוֹת עַוָּל
וְזֶה מְקוֹם לֹא־יָדַע־אֵל: ס

19 Job said in reply:

יט וַיַּעַן אִיּוֹב וַיֹּאמַר:

2How long will you grieve my spirit,
And crush me with words?
3a-Time and again-a you humiliate me,
And are not ashamed to abuse me.
4If indeed I have erred,
My error remains with me.
5Though you are overbearing toward me,
Reproaching me with my disgrace,
6Yet know that God has wronged me;
He has thrown up siege works around me.
7I cry, "Violence!" but am not answered;
I shout, but can get no justice.
8He has barred my way; I cannot pass;
He has laid darkness upon my path.
9He has stripped me of my glory,
Removed the crown from my head.
10He tears down every part of me; I perish;
He uproots my hope like a tree.
11He kindles His anger against me;
He regards me as one of His foes.
12His troops advance together;
They build their road toward me
And encamp around my tent.
13He alienated my kin from me;
My acquaintances disown me.
14My relatives are gone;
My friends have forgotten me.
15My dependents and maidservants regard
   me as a stranger;
I am an outsider to them.
16I summon my servant but he does not respond;

2 עַד־אָנָה תּוֹגְיוּן נַפְשִׁי
וּתְדַכְּאוּנַנִי* בְמִלִּים:
3 זֶה עֶשֶׂר פְּעָמִים תַּכְלִימוּנִי
לֹא־תֵבֹשׁוּ תַּהְכְּרוּ־לִי:
4 וְאַף־אָמְנָם שָׁגִיתִי
אִתִּי תָּלִין מְשׁוּגָתִי:
5 אִם־אָמְנָם עָלַי תַּגְדִּילוּ
וְתוֹכִיחוּ עָלַי חֶרְפָּתִי:
6 דְּעוּ־אֵפוֹ כִּי־אֱלוֹהַּ עִוְּתָנִי
וּמְצוּדוֹ עָלַי הִקִּיף:
7 הֵן אֶצְעַק חָמָס וְלֹא אֵעָנֶה
אֲשַׁוַּע וְאֵין מִשְׁפָּט:
8 אָרְחִי גָדַר וְלֹא אֶעֱבוֹר
וְעַל נְתִיבוֹתַי חֹשֶׁךְ יָשִׂים:
9 כְּבוֹדִי מֵעָלַי הִפְשִׁיט
וַיָּסַר עֲטֶרֶת רֹאשִׁי:
10 יִתְּצֵנִי סָבִיב וָאֵלַךְ
וַיַּסַּע כָּעֵץ תִּקְוָתִי:
11 וַיַּחַר עָלַי אַפּוֹ
וַיַּחְשְׁבֵנִי לוֹ כְצָרָיו:
12 יַחַד ׀ יָבֹאוּ גְדוּדָיו
וַיָּסֹלּוּ עָלַי דַּרְכָּם
וַיַּחֲנוּ סָבִיב לְאָהֳלִי:
13 אַחַי מֵעָלַי הִרְחִיק
וְיֹדְעַי אַךְ־זָרוּ מִמֶּנִּי:
14 חָדְלוּ קְרוֹבָי
וּמְיֻדָּעַי שְׁכֵחוּנִי:
15 גָּרֵי בֵיתִי וְאַמְהֹתַי לְזָר תַּחְשְׁבֻנִי
נָכְרִי הָיִיתִי בְעֵינֵיהֶם:
16 לְעַבְדִּי קָרָאתִי וְלֹא יַעֲנֶה

a-a Lit. "Ten times."   א׳ נחה v. 2.

I must myself entreat him.

17My odor is repulsive to my wife;

I am loathsome to my children.

18Even youngsters disdain me;

When I rise, they speak against me.

19All my bosom friends detest me;

Those I love have turned against me.

20My bones stick to my skin and flesh;

I escape with the skin of my teeth.

21Pity me, pity me! You are my friends;

For the hand of God has struck me!

22Why do you pursue me like God,

b-Maligning me insatiably?-b

23O that my words were written down;

Would they were inscribed in a record,

24Incised on a rock forever

With iron stylus and lead!

25But I know that my Vindicator lives;

In the end He will testify on earth—

26This, after my skin will have been peeled off.

But I would behold God while still in my flesh,

27I myself, not another, would behold Him;

Would see with my own eyes:

My heartc pines within me.

28You say, "How do we persecute him?

The root of the matter is in him."d

29Be in fear of the sword,

For [your] fury is iniquity worthy of the sword;

Know there is a judgment!

20 Zophar the Naamathite said in reply:

2In truth, my thoughts urge me to answer

(It is because of my feelings

3When I hear reproof that insults me);

בְּמוֹ־פִ֗י אֶתְחַנֶּן־לֽוֹ׃

17 ר֖וּחִֽי זָ֣רָה לְאִשְׁתִּ֑י וְ֝חַנֹּתִ֗י לִבְנֵ֣י בִטְנִֽי׃

18 גַּם־עֲ֭וִילִים מָ֣אֲסוּ בִ֑י אָ֝ק֗וּמָה וַיְדַבְּרוּ־בִֽי׃

19 תִּֽ֭עֲבוּנִי כָּל־מְתֵ֣י סוֹדִ֑י וְזֶֽה־אָ֝הַ֗בְתִּי נֶהְפְּכוּ־בִֽי׃

20 בְּעוֹרִ֣י וּ֭בִבְשָׂרִי דָּבְקָ֣ה עַצְמִ֑י וָ֝אֶתְמַלְּטָ֗ה בְּע֣וֹר שִׁנָּֽי׃

21 חָנֻּ֬נִי חָנֻּ֣נִי אַתֶּ֣ם רֵעָ֑י כִּ֥י יַד־אֱ֝ל֗וֹהַּ נָ֣גְעָה בִּֽי׃

22 לָ֭מָּה תִּרְדְּפֻ֣נִי כְמוֹ־אֵ֑ל וּ֝מִבְּשָׂרִ֗י לֹ֣א תִשְׂבָּֽעוּ׃

23 מִֽי־יִתֵּ֣ן אֵ֭פוֹ וְיִכָּתְב֣וּן מִלָּ֑י מִֽי־יִתֵּ֖ן בַּסֵּ֣פֶר וְיֻחָֽקוּ׃

24 בְּעֵט־בַּרְזֶ֥ל וְעֹפָ֑רֶת לָ֝עַ֗ד בַּצּ֥וּר יֵחָצְבֽוּן׃

25 וַאֲנִ֣י יָ֭דַעְתִּי גֹּ֣אֲלִי חָ֑י וְ֝אַחֲר֗וֹן עַל־עָפָ֥ר יָקֽוּם׃

26 וְאַחַ֣ר ע֭וֹרִֽי נִקְּפוּ־זֹ֑את וּ֝מִבְּשָׂרִ֗י אֶחֱזֶ֥ה אֱלֽוֹהַּ׃

27 אֲשֶׁ֤ר אֲנִ֨י ׀ אֶֽחֱזֶה־לִּ֗י וְעֵינַ֣י רָא֣וּ וְלֹא־זָ֑ר כָּל֖וּ כִלְיֹתַ֣י בְּחֵקִֽי׃

28 כִּ֣י תֹ֭אמְרוּ מַה־נִּרְדָּף־ל֑וֹ וְשֹׁ֥רֶשׁ דָּ֝בָ֗ר נִמְצָא־בִֽי*׃

29 גּ֤וּרוּ לָכֶ֨ם ׀ מִפְּנֵי־חֶ֗רֶב כִּֽי־חֵ֭מָה עֲוֺנ֣וֹת חָ֑רֶב לְמַ֖עַן תֵּדְע֣וּן שַׁדִּֽין שַׁדּֽוּן׃ ס

כ 20 וַ֭יַּעַן צֹפַ֥ר הַנַּֽעֲמָתִ֗י וַיֹּאמַֽר׃

2 לָ֭כֵן שְׂעִפַּ֣י יְשִׁיב֑וּנִי וּ֝בַעֲב֗וּר ח֣וּשִׁי בִֽי׃

3 מוּסַ֣ר כְּלִמָּתִ֣י אֶשְׁמָ֑ע

b-b Lit. "You are not satisfied with my flesh."

c   Lit. "kidneys."

d   With many mss. and versions; printed editions, "me."

A spirit out of my understanding makes me
reply:

⁴Do you not know this, that from time immemorial,

Since man was set on earth,

⁵The joy of the wicked has been brief,

The happiness of the impious, fleeting?

⁶Though he grows as high as the sky,

His head reaching the clouds,

⁷He perishes forever, like his dung;

Those who saw him will say, "Where is he?"

⁸He flies away like a dream and cannot be
found;

He is banished like a night vision.

⁹Eyes that glimpsed him do so no more;

They cannot see him in his place any longer.

¹⁰His sons ingratiate themselves with the
poor;

His own hands must give back his wealth.

¹¹His bones, still full of vigor,

Lie down in the dust with him.

¹²Though evil is sweet to his taste,

And he conceals it under his tongue;

¹³Though he saves it, does not let it go,

Holds it inside his mouth,

¹⁴His food in his bowels turns

Into asps' venom within him.

¹⁵The riches he swallows he vomits;

God empties it out of his stomach.

¹⁶He sucks the poison of asps;

The tongue of the viper kills him.

¹⁷Let him not enjoy the streams,

The rivers of honey, the brooks of cream.

¹⁸He will give back the goods unswallowed;

The value of the riches, undigested.

¹⁹Because he crushed and tortured the poor,

He will not build up the house he took by
force.

²⁰He will not see his children tranquil;

He will not preserve one of his dear ones.ᵃ

וְרוּחַ מִבִּינָתִי יַעֲנֵנִי׃
4 הֲזֹאת יָדַעְתָּ מִנִּי־עַד
מִנִּי שִׂים אָדָם עֲלֵי־אָרֶץ׃
5 כִּי רִנְנַת רְשָׁעִים מִקָּרוֹב
וְשִׂמְחַת חָנֵף עֲדֵי־רָגַע׃
6 אִם־יַעֲלֶה לַשָּׁמַיִם שִׂיאוֹ
וְרֹאשׁוֹ לָעָב יַגִּיעַ׃
7 כְּגֶלֲלוֹ לָנֶצַח יֹאבֵד
רֹאָיו יֹאמְרוּ אַיּוֹ׃
8 כַּחֲלוֹם יָעוּף וְלֹא יִמְצָאוּהוּ
וְיֻדַּד כְּחֶזְיוֹן לָיְלָה׃
9 עַיִן שְׁזָפַתּוּ וְלֹא תוֹסִיף
וְלֹא־עוֹד תְּשׁוּרֶנּוּ מְקוֹמוֹ׃
10 בָּנָיו יְרַצּוּ דַלִּים
וְיָדָיו תָּשֵׁבְנָה אוֹנוֹ׃
11 עַצְמוֹתָיו מָלְאוּ עֲלוּמוֹ עֲלוּמָיו
וְעִמּוֹ עַל־עָפָר תִּשְׁכָּב׃
12 אִם־תַּמְתִּיק בְּפִיו רָעָה
יַכְחִידֶנָּה תַּחַת לְשׁוֹנוֹ׃
13 יַחְמֹל עָלֶיהָ וְלֹא יַעַזְבֶנָּה
וְיִמְנָעֶנָּה בְּתוֹךְ חִכּוֹ׃
14 לַחְמוֹ בְּמֵעָיו נֶהְפָּךְ
מְרוֹרַת פְּתָנִים בְּקִרְבּוֹ׃
15 חַיִל בָּלַע וַיְקִאֶנּוּ
מִבִּטְנוֹ יוֹרִשֶׁנּוּ אֵל׃
16 רֹאשׁ־פְּתָנִים יִינָק
תַּהַרְגֵהוּ לְשׁוֹן אֶפְעֶה׃
17 אַל־יֵרֶא בִפְלַגּוֹת
נַהֲרֵי נַחֲלֵי דְּבַשׁ וְחֶמְאָה׃
18 מֵשִׁיב יָגָע וְלֹא יִבְלָע
כְּחֵיל תְּמוּרָתוֹ וְלֹא יַעֲלֹס׃
19 כִּי־רִצַּץ עָזַב דַּלִּים
בַּיִת גָּזַל וְלֹא יִבְנֵהוּ׃
20 כִּי ׀ לֹא־יָדַע שָׁלֵו בְּבִטְנוֹ
בַּחֲמוּדוֹ לֹא יְמַלֵּט׃

ᵃ For this meaning of beṭen and ḥamud, cf. Hos. 9.16.

1687

21With no survivor to enjoy it,
His fortune will not prosper.
22When he has all he wants, trouble will come;
Misfortunes of all kinds will batter him.
23Let that fill his belly;
Let Him loose His burning anger at him,
And rain down His weapons upon him.
24Fleeing from iron arrows,
He is shot through from a bow of bronze.
25Brandished and run through his body,
The blade, through his gall,
Strikes terror into him.
26Utter darkness waits for his treasured ones;
A fire fanned by no man will consume him;
Who survives in his tent will be crushed.
27Heaven will expose his iniquity;
Earth will rise up against him.
28His household will be cast forth by a flood,
Spilled out on the day of His wrath.
29This is the wicked man's portion from God,
The lot God has ordained for him.

21 Job said in reply:

2Listen well to what I say,
And let that be your consolation.
3Bear with me while I speak,
And after I have spoken, you may mock.
4Is my complaint directed toward a man?
Why should I not lose my patience?
5Look at me and be appalled,
And clap your hand to your mouth.
6When I think of it I am terrified;
My body is seized with shuddering.

7Why do the wicked live on,
Prosper and grow wealthy?

כתובים איוב כ

21 אֵין־שָׂרִ֥יד לְאָכְל֑וֹ
עַל־כֵּ֝֗ן לֹא־יָחִ֥יל טוּבֽוֹ׃
22 בִּמְלֹאות* שִׂפְק֣וֹ יֵ֣צֶר ל֑וֹ
כׇּל־יַ֥ד עָ֝מֵ֗ל תְּבוֹאֶֽנּוּ׃
23 יְהִ֤י ׀ לְמַלֵּ�֪א בִטְנ֡וֹ
יְֽשַׁלַּֽח־בּ֭וֹ חֲר֣וֹן אַפּ֑וֹ
וְיַמְטֵ֥ר עָ֝לֵ֗ימוֹ בִּלְחוּמֽוֹ׃
24 יִ֭בְרַח מִנֵּ֣שֶׁק בַּרְזֶ֑ל
תַּ֝חְלְפֵ֗הוּ קֶ֣שֶׁת נְחוּשָֽׁה׃
25 שָׁלַף֮ וַיֵּצֵ֢א מִגֵּ֫וָ֥ה
וּ֭בָרָק מִֽמְּרֹרָת֥וֹ יַהֲלֹ֗ךְ
עָלָ֥יו אֵמִֽים׃
26 כׇּל־חֹשֶׁךְ֮ טָמ֢וּן לִצְפּ֫וּנָ֥יו
תְּ֭אׇכְלֵהוּ אֵ֣שׁ לֹֽא־נֻפָּ֑ח
יֵ֥רַע שָׂ֝רִ֗יד בְּאׇהֳלֽוֹ׃
27 יְגַלּ֣וּ שָׁמַ֣יִם עֲוֺנ֑וֹ
וְ֝אֶ֗רֶץ מִתְקוֹמָ֥מָה לֽוֹ׃
28 יִ֭גֶל יְב֣וּל בֵּית֑וֹ
נִ֝גָּר֗וֹת בְּי֣וֹם אַפּֽוֹ׃
29 זֶ֤ה ׀ חֵֽלֶק־אָדָ֣ם רָ֭שָׁע מֵאֱלֹהִ֑ים
וְנַחֲלַ֖ת אִמְר֣וֹ מֵאֵֽל׃ פ

כא וַיַּ֥עַן אִיּ֗וֹב וַיֹּאמַֽר׃
2 שִׁמְע֣וּ שָׁ֭מוֹעַ מִלָּתִ֑י
וּתְהִי־זֹ֝֗את תַּנְח֥וּמֹֽתֵיכֶֽם׃
3 שָׂ֭אוּנִי וְאָנֹכִ֣י אֲדַבֵּ֑ר
וְאַחַ֖ר דַּבְּרִ֣י תַלְעִֽיג׃
4 הֶ֭אָנֹכִי לְאָדָ֣ם שִׂיחִ֑י
וְאִם־מַ֝דּ֗וּעַ לֹא־תִקְצַ֥ר רוּחִֽי׃
5 פְּנוּ־אֵלַ֥י וְהָשַׁ֑מּוּ
וְשִׂ֖ימוּ יָ֣ד עַל־פֶּֽה׃
6 וְאִם־זָכַ֥רְתִּי וְנִבְהָ֑לְתִּי
וְאָחַ֥ז בְּ֝שָׂרִ֗י פַּלָּצֽוּת׃

7 מַדּ֣וּעַ רְשָׁעִ֣ים יִחְי֑וּ
עָ֝תְק֗וּ גַּם־גָּ֥בְרוּ חָֽיִל׃

⁸Their children are with them always,
And they see their children's children.
⁹Their homes are secure, without fear;
They do not feel the rod of God.
¹⁰Their bull breeds and does not fail;
Their cow calves and never miscarries;
¹¹They let their infants run loose like sheep,
And their children skip about.
¹²They sing to the music of timbrel and lute,
And revel to the tune of the pipe;
¹³They spend their days in happiness,
And go down to Sheol in peace.
¹⁴They say to God, "Leave us alone,
We do not want to learn Your ways;
¹⁵What is Shaddai that we should serve Him?
What will we gain by praying to Him?"
¹⁶Their happiness is not their own doing.
(The thoughts of the wicked are beyond me!)
¹⁷How seldom does the lamp of the wicked
  fail,
Does the calamity they deserve befall them,
Does He apportion [their] lot in anger!
¹⁸Let them become like straw in the wind,
Like chaff carried off by a storm.
¹⁹[You say,] "God is reserving his punish-
  ment for his sons";
Let it be paid back to him that he may feel
  it,
²⁰Let his eyes see his ruin,
And let him drink the wrath of Shaddai!
²¹For what does he care about the fate of his
  family,
When his number of months runs out?
²²Can God be instructed in knowledge,
He who judges from such heights?
²³One man dies in robust health,
All tranquil and untroubled;
²⁴His pails are full of milk;
The marrow of his bones is juicy.
²⁵Another dies embittered,

זַרְעָם נָכוֹן לִפְנֵיהֶם עִמָּם 8
וְצֶאֱצָאֵיהֶם לְעֵינֵיהֶם:
בָּתֵּיהֶם שָׁלוֹם מִפָּחַד 9
וְלֹא שֵׁבֶט אֱלוֹהַּ עֲלֵיהֶם:
שׁוֹרוֹ עִבַּר וְלֹא יַגְעִל 10
תְּפַלֵּט פָּרָתוֹ וְלֹא תְשַׁכֵּל:
יְשַׁלְּחוּ כַצֹּאן עֲוִילֵיהֶם 11
וְיַלְדֵיהֶם יְרַקֵּדוּן:
יִשְׂאוּ כְּתֹף וְכִנּוֹר 12
וְיִשְׂמְחוּ לְקוֹל עוּגָב:
יבלו יְכַלּוּ בַטּוֹב יְמֵיהֶם 13
וּבְרֶגַע שְׁאוֹל יֵחָתּוּ:
וַיֹּאמְרוּ לָאֵל סוּר מִמֶּנּוּ 14
וְדַעַת דְּרָכֶיךָ לֹא חָפָצְנוּ:
מַה־שַּׁדַּי כִּי־נַעַבְדֶנּוּ 15
וּמַה־נּוֹעִיל כִּי נִפְגַּע־בּוֹ:
הֵן לֹא בְיָדָם טוּבָם 16
עֲצַת רְשָׁעִים רָחֲקָה מֶנִּי:
כַּמָּה ׀ נֵר־רְשָׁעִים יִדְעָךְ 17
וְיָבֹא עָלֵימוֹ אֵידָם
חֲבָלִים יְחַלֵּק בְּאַפּוֹ:
יִהְיוּ כְּתֶבֶן לִפְנֵי־רוּחַ 18
וּכְמֹץ גְּנָבַתּוּ סוּפָה:
אֱלוֹהַּ יִצְפֹּן־לְבָנָיו אוֹנוֹ 19
יְשַׁלֵּם אֵלָיו וְיֵדָע:
יִרְאוּ עֵינָו כִּידוֹ 20
וּמֵחֲמַת שַׁדַּי יִשְׁתֶּה:
כִּי מַה־חֶפְצוֹ בְּבֵיתוֹ אַחֲרָיו 21
וּמִסְפַּר חֳדָשָׁיו חֻצָּצוּ:
הַלְאֵל יְלַמֶּד־דָּעַת 22
וְהוּא רָמִים יִשְׁפּוֹט:
זֶה יָמוּת בְּעֶצֶם תֻּמּוֹ 23
כֻּלּוֹ שַׁלְאֲנַן וְשָׁלֵיו:
עֲטִינָיו מָלְאוּ חָלָב 24
וּמֹחַ עַצְמוֹתָיו יְשֻׁקֶּה:
וְזֶה יָמוּת בְּנֶפֶשׁ מָרָה 25

Never having tasted happiness.

26They both lie in the dust

And are covered with worms.

27Oh, I know your thoughts,

And the tactics you will devise against me.

28You will say, "Where is the house of the great man—

And where the tent in which the wicked dwelled?"

29You must have consulted the wayfarers;

You cannot deny their evidence.

30For the evil man is spared on the day of calamity,

On the day when wrath is led forth.

31Who will upbraid him to his face?

Who will requite him for what he has done?

32He is brought to the grave,

While a watch is kept at his tomb.

33The clods of the wadi are sweet to him,

Everyone follows behind him,

Innumerable are those who precede him.

34Why then do you offer me empty consolation?

Of your replies only the perfidy remains.

22 Eliphaz the Temanite said in reply:

2Can a man be of use to God,

A wise man benefit Him?

3Does Shaddai gain if you are righteous?

Does He profit if your conduct is blameless?

4Is it because of your piety that He arraigns you,

And enters into judgment with you?

5You know that your wickedness is great,

And that your iniquities have no limit.

6You exact pledges from your fellows without reason,

וְלֹא־אָכַל בַּטּוֹבָה:

26 יַחַד עַל־עָפָר יִשְׁכָּבוּ

וְרִמָּה תְּכַסֶּה עֲלֵיהֶם:

27 הֵן יָדַעְתִּי מַחְשְׁבוֹתֵיכֶם

וּמְזִמּוֹת עָלַי תַּחְמֹסוּ:

28 כִּי תֹאמְרוּ אַיֵּה בֵית־נָדִיב

וְאַיֵּה אֹהֶל ׀ מִשְׁכְּנוֹת רְשָׁעִים:

29 הֲלֹא שְׁאֶלְתֶּם עוֹבְרֵי דָרֶךְ

וְאֹתֹתָם לֹא תְנַכֵּרוּ:

30 כִּי לְיוֹם אֵיד יֵחָשֶׂךְ רָע

לְיוֹם עֲבָרוֹת יוּבָלוּ:

31 מִי־יַגִּיד עַל־פָּנָיו דַּרְכּוֹ

וְהוּא־עָשָׂה מִי יְשַׁלֶּם־לוֹ:

32 וְהוּא לִקְבָרוֹת יוּבָל

וְעַל־גָּדִישׁ יִשְׁקוֹד:

33 מָתְקוּ־לוֹ רִגְבֵי נָחַל

וְאַחֲרָיו כָּל־אָדָם יִמְשׁוֹךְ

וּלְפָנָיו אֵין מִסְפָּר:

34 וְאֵיךְ תְּנַחֲמוּנִי הָבֶל

וּתְשׁוּבֹתֵיכֶם נִשְׁאַר־מָעַל: ס

כב וַיַּעַן אֱלִיפַז הַתֵּמָנִי וַיֹּאמַר:

2 הַלְאֵל יִסְכָּן־גָּבֶר

כִּי־יִסְכֹּן עָלֵימוֹ מַשְׂכִּיל:

3 הַחֵפֶץ לְשַׁדַּי כִּי תִצְדָּק

וְאִם־בֶּצַע כִּי־תַתֵּם דְּרָכֶיךָ:

4 הֲמִיִּרְאָתְךָ יֹכִיחֶךָ

יָבוֹא עִמְּךָ בַּמִּשְׁפָּט:

5 הֲלֹא רָעָתְךָ רַבָּה

וְאֵין־קֵץ לַעֲוֺנֹתֶיךָ:

6 כִּי־תַחְבֹּל אַחֶיךָ חִנָּם

And leave them naked, stripped of their clothes;

⁷You do not give the thirsty water to drink;
You deny bread to the hungry.

⁸The land belongs to the strong;
The privileged occupy it.

⁹You have sent away widows empty-handed;
The strength of the fatherless is broken.

¹⁰Therefore snares are all around you,
And sudden terrors frighten you,

¹¹Or darkness, so you cannot see;
A flood of waters covers you.

¹²God is in the heavenly heights;
See the highest stars, how lofty!

¹³You say, "What can God know?
Can He govern through the dense cloud?

¹⁴The clouds screen Him so He cannot see
As He moves about the circuit of heaven."

¹⁵Have you observed the immemorial path
That evil men have trodden;

¹⁶How they were shriveled up before their time
And their foundation poured out like a river?

¹⁷They said to God, "Leave us alone;
What can Shaddai do about it?"

¹⁸But it was He who filled their houses with good things.
(The thoughts of the wicked are beyond me!)

¹⁹The righteous, seeing it,ᵃ rejoiced;
The innocent laughed with scorn.

²⁰Surely their substance was destroyed,
And their remnant consumed by fire.

²¹Be close to Him and wholehearted;
Good things will come to you thereby.

²²Accept instruction from His mouth;
Lay up His words in your heart.

²³If you return to Shaddai you will be restored,

וּבִגְדֵי עֲרוּמִּים תַּפְשִׁיט:
7 לֹא־מַיִם עָיֵף תַּשְׁקֶה
וּמֵרָעֵב תִּמְנַע־לָחֶם:
8 וְאִישׁ זְרוֹעַ לוֹ הָאָרֶץ
וּנְשׂוּא פָנִים יֵשֶׁב בָּהּ:
9 אַלְמָנוֹת שִׁלַּחְתָּ רֵיקָם
וּזְרֹעוֹת יְתֹמִים יְדֻכָּא:
10 עַל־כֵּן סְבִיבוֹתֶיךָ פַחִים
וִיבַהֶלְךָ פַּחַד פִּתְאֹם:
11 אוֹ־חֹשֶׁךְ לֹא־תִרְאֶה
וְשִׁפְעַת־מַיִם תְּכַסֶּךָּ:

12 הֲלֹא־אֱלוֹהַּ גֹּבַהּ שָׁמָיִם
וּרְאֵה רֹאשׁ כּוֹכָבִים כִּי־רָמּוּ:
13 וְאָמַרְתָּ מַה־יָּדַע אֵל
הַבְעַד עֲרָפֶל יִשְׁפּוֹט:
14 עָבִים סֵתֶר־לוֹ וְלֹא יִרְאֶה
וְחוּג שָׁמַיִם יִתְהַלָּךְ:
15 הַאֹרַח עוֹלָם תִּשְׁמֹר
אֲשֶׁר דָּרְכוּ מְתֵי־אָוֶן:
16* אֲשֶׁר־קֻמְּטוּ וְלֹא־עֵת
נָהָר יוּצַק יְסוֹדָם:
17 הָאֹמְרִים לָאֵל סוּר מִמֶּנּוּ
וּמַה־יִּפְעַל שַׁדַּי לָמוֹ:
18 וְהוּא מִלֵּא בָתֵּיהֶם טוֹב
וַעֲצַת רְשָׁעִים רָחֲקָה מֶנִּי:
19 יִרְאוּ צַדִּיקִים וְיִשְׂמָחוּ
וְנָקִי יִלְעַג־לָמוֹ:
20 אִם־לֹא נִכְחַד קִימָנוּ
וְיִתְרָם אָכְלָה אֵשׁ:

21 הַסְכֶּן־נָא עִמּוֹ וּשְׁלָם
בָּהֶם תְּבוֹאַתְךָ טוֹבָה:
22 קַח־נָא מִפִּיו תּוֹרָה
וְשִׂים אֲמָרָיו בִּלְבָבֶךָ:
23 אִם־תָּשׁוּב עַד־שַׁדַּי תִּבָּנֶה

v. 16. חֲצִי הַסֵּפֶר בִּפְסוּקִים

ᵃ Referring to v. 16.

If you banish iniquity from your tent;

24If you regard treasure as dirt,
Ophir-gold as stones of the wadi,

25And Shaddai be your treasure
And precious silver for you,

26When you seek the favor of Shaddai,
And lift up your face to God,

27You will pray to Him, and He will listen to you,
And you will pay your vows.

28You will decree and it will be fulfilled,
And light will shine upon your affairs.

29When others sink low, you will say it is pride;
For He saves the humble.

30He will deliver the guilty;
He will be delivered through the cleanness of your hands.

23 Job said in reply:

2Today again my complaint is bitter;
a-My strength is spent-a on account of my groaning.

3Would that I knew how to reach Him,
How to get to His dwelling-place.

4I would set out my case before Him
And fill my mouth with arguments.

5I would learn what answers He had for me
And know how He would reply to me.

6Would He contend with me overbearingly?
Surely He would not accuse me!

7There the upright would be cleared by Him,
And I would escape forever from my judge.

8But if I go East—He is not there;
West—I still do not perceive Him;

9North—since He is concealed, I do not behold Him;

תַּרְחִ֥יק עַוְלָ֗ה מֵאָהֳלֶֽךָ׃

24 וְשִׁית־עַל־עָפָ֥ר בָּ֑צֶר
וּבְצ֖וּר נְחָלִ֣ים אוֹפִֽיר׃

25 וְהָיָ֣ה שַׁדַּ֣י בְּצָרֶ֑יךָ
וְכֶ֖סֶף תּוֹעָפ֣וֹת לָֽךְ׃

26 כִּי־אָ֭ז עַל־שַׁדַּ֣י תִּתְעַנָּ֑ג
וְתִשָּׂ֖א אֶל־אֱל֣וֹהַּ פָּנֶֽיךָ׃

27 תַּעְתִּ֣יר אֵ֭לָיו וְיִשְׁמָעֶ֑ךָּ
וּנְדָרֶ֥יךָ תְשַׁלֵּֽם׃

28 וְֽתִגְזַר־א֭וֹמֶר וְיָ֣קָם לָ֑ךְ
וְעַל־דְּ֝רָכֶ֗יךָ נָ֣גַֽהּ אֽוֹר׃

29 כִּֽי־הִ֭שְׁפִּילוּ וַתֹּ֣אמֶר גֵּוָ֑ה
וְשַׁ֖ח עֵינַ֣יִם יוֹשִֽׁעַ׃

30 יְֽמַלֵּ֥ט אִֽי־נָקִ֑י
וְ֝נִמְלַ֗ט בְּבֹ֣ר כַּפֶּֽיךָ׃ פ

כג וַיַּ֥עַן אִיּ֗וֹב וַיֹּאמַֽר׃

2 גַּם־הַ֭יּוֹם מְרִ֣י שִׂחִ֑י
יָ֝דִ֗י כָּבְדָ֥ה עַל־אַנְחָתִֽי׃

3 מִֽי־יִתֵּ֣ן יָ֭דַעְתִּי וְאֶמְצָאֵ֑הוּ
אָ֝ב֗וֹא עַד־תְּכוּנָתֽוֹ׃

4 אֶעֶרְכָ֣ה לְפָנָ֣יו מִשְׁפָּ֑ט
וּ֝פִ֗י אֲמַלֵּ֥א תוֹכָחֽוֹת׃

5 אֵ֭דְעָה מִלִּ֣ים יַעֲנֵ֑נִי
וְאָבִ֥ינָה מַה־יֹּ֥אמַר לִֽי׃

6 הַבְּרָב־כֹּ֭חַ יָרִ֣יב עִמָּדִ֑י
לֹ֥א אַךְ־ה֝֗וּא יָשִׂ֥ם בִּֽי׃

7 שָׁ֗ם יָ֭שָׁר נוֹכָ֣ח עִמּ֑וֹ
וַאֲפַלְּטָ֥ה לָ֝נֶ֗צַח מִשֹּׁפְטִֽי׃

8 הֵ֤ן קֶ֣דֶם אֶהֱלֹ֣ךְ וְאֵינֶ֑נּוּ
וְ֝אָח֗וֹר וְֽלֹא־אָבִ֥ין לֽוֹ׃

9 שְׂמֹ֣אול בַּעֲשֹׂת֣וֹ וְלֹא־אָ֑חַז

a-a Lit. "My hand is heavy."

1692

South—He is hidden, and I cannot see Him.

10But He knows the way I take;
Would He assay me, I should emerge pure
as gold.

11I have followed in His tracks,
Kept His way without swerving,

12I have not deviated from what His lips commanded;
I have treasured His words more than my
daily bread.

13He is one; who can dissuade Him?
Whatever He desires, He does.

14For He will bring my term to an end,
But He has many more such at His disposal.

15Therefore I am terrified at His presence;
When I consider, I dread Him.

16God has made me fainthearted;
Shaddai has terrified me.

17Yet I am not cut off by the darkness;
He has concealed the thick gloom from me.

24

Why are times for judgment not reserved by Shaddai?
Even those close to Him cannot foresee His
actions.[a]

2People remove boundary-stones;
They carry off flocks and pasture them;

3They lead away the donkeys of the fatherless,
And seize the widow's bull as a pledge;

4They chase the needy off the roads;
All the poor of the land are forced into hiding.

5Like the wild asses of the wilderness,
They go about their tasks, seeking food;
The wilderness provides each with food for
his lads;

6They harvest fodder in the field,
And glean the late grapes in the vineyards of
the wicked.

יַעְטֹף יָמִין וְלֹא אֶרְאֶה:

10 כִּי־יָדַע דֶּרֶךְ עִמָּדִי
בְּחָנַנִי כַּזָּהָב אֵצֵא:

11 בַּאֲשֻׁרוֹ אָחֲזָה רַגְלִי
דַּרְכּוֹ שָׁמַרְתִּי וְלֹא־אָט:

12 מִצְוַת שְׂפָתָיו וְלֹא אָמִישׁ
מֵחֻקִּי צָפַנְתִּי אִמְרֵי־פִיו:

13 וְהוּא בְאֶחָד וּמִי יְשִׁיבֶנּוּ
וְנַפְשׁוֹ אִוְּתָה וַיָּעַשׂ:

14 כִּי יַשְׁלִים חֻקִּי
וְכָהֵנָּה רַבּוֹת עִמּוֹ:

15 עַל־כֵּן מִפָּנָיו אֶבָּהֵל
אֶתְבּוֹנֵן וְאֶפְחַד מִמֶּנּוּ:

16 וְאֵל הֵרַךְ לִבִּי
וְשַׁדַּי הִבְהִילָנִי:

17 כִּי־לֹא נִצְמַתִּי מִפְּנֵי־חֹשֶׁךְ
וּמִפָּנַי כִּסָּה־אֹפֶל:

כד מַדּוּעַ מִשַּׁדַּי לֹא־נִצְפְּנוּ עִתִּים
וְידעו וְיֹדְעָיו לֹא־חָזוּ יָמָיו:

2 גְּבֻלוֹת יַשִּׂיגוּ
עֵדֶר גָּזְלוּ וַיִּרְעוּ:

3 חֲמוֹר יְתוֹמִים יִנְהָגוּ
יַחְבְּלוּ שׁוֹר אַלְמָנָה:

4 יַטּוּ אֶבְיוֹנִים מִדָּרֶךְ
יַחַד חֻבְּאוּ עֲנִיֵּי־אָרֶץ:

5 הֵן פְּרָאִים בַּמִּדְבָּר
יָצְאוּ בְּפָעֳלָם מְשַׁחֲרֵי לַטָּרֶף
עֲרָבָה לוֹ לֶחֶם לַנְּעָרִים:

6 בַּשָּׂדֶה בְּלִילוֹ יקצירו יִקְצֹרוּ
וְכֶרֶם רָשָׁע יְלַקֵּשׁוּ:

---

a   Lit. "days."

7They pass the night naked for lack of clothing,

They have no covering against the cold;

8They are drenched by the mountain rains,

And huddle against the rock for lack of shelter.

9*b*They snatch the fatherless infant from the
breast,

And seize the child of the poor as a pledge.

10They go about naked for lack of clothing,

And, hungry, carry sheaves;

11Between rows [of olive trees] they make oil,

And, thirsty, they tread the winepresses.

12Men groan in the city;

The souls of the dying cry out;

Yet God does not regard it as a reproach.

13They are rebels against the light;

They are strangers to its ways,

And do not stay in its path.

14The murderer arises *c-*in the evening*-c*

To kill the poor and needy,

And at night he acts the thief.

15The eyes of the adulterer watch for twilight,

Thinking, "No one will glimpse me then."

He masks his face.

16In the dark they break into houses;

By day they shut themselves in;

They do not know the light.

17For all of them morning is darkness;

It is then that they discern the terror of darkness.

18*d*May they be flotsam on the face of the
water;

May their portion in the land be cursed;

May none turn aside by way of their vineyards.

---

7 עָר֣וֹם יָלִ֣ינוּ מִבְּלִ֣י לְב֑וּשׁ
וְאֵ֥ין כְּס֗וּת בַּקָּרָֽה׃

8 מִזֶּ֣רֶם הָרִ֣ים יִרְטָ֑בוּ
וּֽמִבְּלִ֥י מַ֝חְסֶ֗ה חִבְּקוּ־צֽוּר׃

9 יִ֭גְזְלוּ מִשֹּׁ֣ד יָת֑וֹם
וְֽעַל־עָנִ֥י יַחְבֹּֽלוּ׃

10 עָר֣וֹם הִ֭לְּכוּ בְּלִ֣י לְב֑וּשׁ
וּ֝רְעֵבִ֗ים נָ֣שְׂאוּ עֹֽמֶר׃

11 בֵּין־שׁוּרֹתָ֥ם יַצְהִ֑ירוּ
יְקָבִ֥ים דָּ֝רְכ֗וּ וַיִּצְמָֽאוּ׃

12 מֵ֘עִ֤יר מְתִ֨ים ׀ יִנְאָ֗קוּ
וְנֶֽפֶשׁ־חֲלָלִ֥ים תְּשַׁוֵּ֑עַ
וֶ֝אֱל֗וֹהַ לֹא־יָשִׂ֥ים תִּפְלָֽה׃

13 הֵ֤מָּה ׀ הָיוּ֮ בְּֽמֹרְדֵ֫י־א֥וֹר
לֹֽא־הִכִּ֥ירוּ דְרָכָ֑יו
וְלֹ֥א יָ֝שְׁב֗וּ בִּנְתִֽיבֹתָֽיו׃

14 לָא֡וֹר יָ֘ק֤וּם רוֹצֵ֗חַ
יִֽקְטָל־עָנִ֥י וְאֶבְי֑וֹן
וּ֝בַלַּ֗יְלָה יְהִ֥י כַגַּנָּֽב׃

15 וְעֵ֤ין נֹאֵ֨ף ׀ שָׁ֤מְרָֽה נֶ֨שֶׁף
לֵאמֹ֗ר לֹא־תְשׁוּרֵ֥נִי עָ֑יִן
וְסֵ֖תֶר פָּנִ֣ים יָשִֽׂים׃

16 חָתַ֥ר בַּחֹ֗שֶׁךְ בָּ֫תִּ֥ים
יוֹמָ֥ם חִתְּמוּ־לָ֑מוֹ
לֹא־יָ֥דְעוּ אֽוֹר׃

17 כִּ֤י יַחְדָּ֨ו ׀ בֹּ֣קֶר לָ֣מוֹ צַלְמָ֑וֶת
כִּֽי־יַ֝כִּ֗יר בַּלְה֥וֹת צַלְמָֽוֶת׃

18 קַֽל־ה֤וּא ׀ עַל־פְּנֵי־מַ֗יִם
תְּקֻלַּ֣ל חֶלְקָתָ֣ם בָּאָ֑רֶץ
לֹֽא־יִ֝פְנֶ֗ה דֶּ֣רֶךְ כְּרָמִֽים׃

---

b   *This verse belongs to the description of the wicked in vv. 2–4a.*
c-c *Cf. Mishnaic Heb. ʿor, Aramaic ʾorta, "evening"; others "with
     the light."*
d   *From here to the end of the chapter the translation is largely
     conjectural.*

1694

¹⁹May drought and heat snatch away their
   snow waters,
And Sheol, those who have sinned.
²⁰May the womb forget him;
May he be sweet to the worms;
May he be no longer remembered;
May wrongdoers be broken like a tree.
²¹May he consort with a barren woman who
   bears no child,
Leave his widow deprived of good.
²²Though he has the strength to seize bulls,
May he live with no assurance of survival.
²³Yet [God] gives him the security on which
   he relies,
And keeps watch over his affairs.
²⁴Exalted for a while, let them be gone;
Be brought low, and shrivel like mallows,
And wither like the heads of grain.

²⁵Surely no one can confute me,
Or prove that I am wrong.

25 Bildad the Shuhite said in reply:

²Dominion and dread are His;
He imposes peace in His heights.
³Can His troops be numbered?
On whom does His light not shine?
⁴How can man be in the right before God?
How can one born of woman be cleared of
   guilt?
⁵Even the moon is not bright,
And the stars are not pure in His sight.
⁶How much less man, a worm,
The son-of-man, a maggot.

19 צִיָּה גַם־חֹם יִגְזְלוּ מֵימֵי־שֶׁלֶג
שְׁאוֹל חָטָאוּ׃
20 יִשְׁכָּחֵהוּ רֶחֶם ׀
מְתָקוֹ רִמָּה
עוֹד לֹא־יִזָּכֵר
וַתִּשָּׁבֵר כָּעֵץ עַוְלָה׃
21 רֹעֶה עֲקָרָה לֹא תֵלֵד
וְאַלְמָנָה לֹא יְיֵטִיב׃
22 וּמָשַׁךְ אַבִּירִים בְּכֹחוֹ
יָקוּם וְלֹא־יַאֲמִין בַּחַיִּין׃
23 יִתֶּן־לוֹ לָבֶטַח וְיִשָּׁעֵן
וְעֵינֵיהוּ עַל־דַּרְכֵיהֶם׃
24 רוֹמּוּ מְּעַט ׀ וְאֵינֶנּוּ
וְהֻמְּכוּ כַּכֹּל יִקָּפְצוּן
וּכְרֹאשׁ שִׁבֹּלֶת יִמָּלוּ׃
25 וְאִם־לֹא אֵפוֹ מִי יַכְזִיבֵנִי
וְיָשֵׂם לְאַל מִלָּתִי׃ ס

כה וַיַּעַן בִּלְדַּד הַשֻּׁחִי וַיֹּאמַר׃
2 הַמְשֵׁל וָפַחַד עִמּוֹ
עֹשֶׂה שָׁלוֹם בִּמְרוֹמָיו׃
3 הֲיֵשׁ מִסְפָּר לִגְדוּדָיו
וְעַל־מִי לֹא־יָקוּם אוֹרֵהוּ׃
4 וּמַה־יִּצְדַּק אֱנוֹשׁ עִם־אֵל
וּמַה־יִּזְכֶּה יְלוּד אִשָּׁה׃
5 הֵן עַד־יָרֵחַ וְלֹא יַאֲהִיל
וְכוֹכָבִים לֹא־זַכּוּ בְעֵינָיו׃
6 אַף כִּי־אֱנוֹשׁ רִמָּה
וּבֶן־אָדָם תּוֹלֵעָה׃ פ

26 Then Job said in reply:

כו וַיַּעַן אִיּוֹב וַיֹּאמַר׃

2You would help without having the strength;

You would deliver with arms that have no power.

3Without having the wisdom, you offer advice

And freely give your counsel.

4To whom have you addressed words?

Whose breath issued from you?

2 מֶה־עָזַרְתָּ לְלֹא־כֹחַ
הוֹשַׁעְתָּ זְרוֹעַ לֹא־עֹז׃
3 מַה־יָּעַצְתָּ לְלֹא חָכְמָה
וְתוּשִׁיָּה לָרֹב הוֹדָעְתָּ׃
4 אֶת־מִי הִגַּדְתָּ מִלִּין
וְנִשְׁמַת־מִי יָצְאָה מִמֶּךָּ׃

5The shades tremble

Beneath the waters and their denizens.

6Sheol is naked before Him;

Abaddon has no cover.

7He it is who stretched out Zaphon[a] over chaos,

Who suspended earth over emptiness.

8He wrapped up the waters in His clouds;

Yet no cloud burst under their weight.

9b-He shuts off the view of His throne,

Spreading His cloud over it.-b

10He drew a boundary on the surface of the waters,

At the extreme where light and darkness meet.

11The pillars of heaven tremble,

Astounded at His blast.

12By His power He stilled the sea;

By His skill He struck down Rahab.

13By His wind the heavens were calmed;

His hand pierced the c-Elusive Serpent.-c

14These are but glimpses of His rule,

The mere whisper that we perceive of Him;

Who can absorb the thunder of His mighty deeds?

5 הָרְפָאִים יְחוֹלָלוּ
מִתַּחַת מַיִם וְשֹׁכְנֵיהֶם׃
6 עָרוֹם שְׁאוֹל נֶגְדּוֹ
וְאֵין כְּסוּת לָאֲבַדּוֹן׃
7 נֹטֶה צָפוֹן עַל־תֹּהוּ
תֹּלֶה אֶרֶץ עַל־בְּלִי־מָה׃
8 צֹרֵר־מַיִם בְּעָבָיו
וְלֹא־נִבְקַע עָנָן תַּחְתָּם׃
9 מְאַחֵז פְּנֵי־כִסֵּה*
פַּרְשֵׁז עָלָיו עֲנָנוֹ׃
10 חֹק־חָג עַל־פְּנֵי־מָיִם
עַד־תַּכְלִית אוֹר עִם־חֹשֶׁךְ׃
11 עַמּוּדֵי שָׁמַיִם יְרוֹפָפוּ
וְיִתְמְהוּ מִגַּעֲרָתוֹ׃
12 בְּכֹחוֹ רָגַע הַיָּם
וּבִתְבוּנָתוֹ מָחַץ רָהַב׃
13 בְּרוּחוֹ שָׁמַיִם שִׁפְרָה
חֹלֲלָה יָדוֹ נָחָשׁ בָּרִחַ׃
14 הֶן־אֵלֶּה ׀ קְצוֹת דְּרָכָיו
וּמַה־שֵּׁמֶץ דָּבָר נִשְׁמַע־בּוֹ
וְרַעַם גְּבוּרֹתָיו מִי יִתְבּוֹנָן׃ ס

---

a   Used for heaven; cf. Isa. 14.13; Ps. 48.3.
b-b   Meaning of Heb. uncertain.
c-c   Cf. Isa. 27.1.

ה' במקום א'   v. 9.

1696

27 Job again took up his theme and said:

²By God who has deprived me of justice!
By Shaddai who has embittered my life!
³As long as there is life in me,
And God's breath is in my nostrils,
⁴My lips will speak no wrong,
Nor my tongue utter deceit.
⁵Far be it from me to say you are right;
Until I die I will maintain my integrity.
⁶I persist in my righteousness and will not
yield;
ᵃ⁻I shall be free of reproach⁻ᵃ as long as I live.

⁷May my enemy be as the wicked;
My assailant, as the wrongdoer.
⁸For what hope has the impious man when
he is cut down,
When God takes away his life?
⁹Will God hear his cry
When trouble comes upon him,
¹⁰When he seeks the favor of Shaddai,
Calls upon God at all times?
¹¹I will teach you what is in God's power,
And what is with Shaddai I will not conceal.
¹²All of you have seen it,
So why talk nonsense?
¹³This is the evil man's portion from God,
The lot that the ruthless receive from Shaddai:
¹⁴Should he have many sons—they are
marked for the sword;
His descendants will never have their fill of
bread;
¹⁵Those who survive him will be buried in a
plague,
And their widows will not weep;
¹⁶Should he pile up silver like dust,
Lay up clothing like dirt—

כז וַיֹּ֣סֶף אִ֭יּוֹב שְׂאֵ֥ת מְשָׁל֗וֹ וַיֹּאמַֽר׃

² חַי־אֵ֭ל הֵסִ֣יר מִשְׁפָּטִ֑י
וְ֝שַׁדַּ֗י הֵמַ֥ר נַפְשִֽׁי׃
³ כִּֽי־כָל־ע֣וֹד נִשְׁמָתִ֣י בִ֑י
וְר֖וּחַ אֱל֣וֹהַּ בְּאַפִּֽי׃
⁴ אִם־תְּדַבֵּ֥רְנָה שְׂפָתַ֣י עַוְלָ֑ה
וּ֝לְשׁוֹנִ֗י אִם־יֶהְגֶּ֥ה רְמִיָּֽה׃
⁵ חָלִ֣ילָה לִּי֮ אִם־אַצְדִּ֪יק אֶ֫תְכֶ֥ם עַד־
אֶגְוָ֑ע
לֹא־אָסִ֖יר תֻּמָּתִ֣י מִמֶּֽנִּי׃
⁶ בְּצִדְקָתִ֣י הֶ֭חֱזַקְתִּי וְלֹ֣א אַרְפֶּ֑הָ
לֹֽא־יֶחֱרַ֥ף לְ֝בָבִ֗י מִיָּמָֽי׃
⁷ יְהִ֣י כְ֭רָשָׁע אֹֽיְבִ֑י
וּמִתְקוֹמְמִ֥י כְעַוָּֽל׃
⁸ כִּ֤י מַה־תִּקְוַ֣ת חָ֭נֵף כִּ֣י יִבְצָ֑ע
כִּ֤י יֵ֖שֶׁל אֱל֣וֹהַּ נַפְשֽׁוֹ׃
⁹ הַֽ֭צַעֲקָתוֹ יִשְׁמַ֥ע ׀ אֵ֑ל
כִּֽי־תָב֖וֹא עָלָ֣יו צָרָֽה׃
¹⁰ אִם־עַל־שַׁדַּ֥י יִתְעַנָּ֑ג
יִקְרָ֖א אֱל֣וֹהַּ בְּכָל־עֵֽת׃
¹¹ אוֹרֶ֣ה אֶתְכֶ֣ם בְּיַד־אֵ֑ל
אֲשֶׁ֥ר עִם־שַׁ֝דַּ֗י לֹ֣א אֲכַחֵֽד׃
¹² הֵן־אַתֶּ֣ם כֻּלְּכֶ֣ם חֲזִיתֶ֑ם
וְלָמָּה־זֶּ֝֗ה הֶ֣בֶל תֶּהְבָּֽלוּ׃
¹³ זֶ֤ה ׀ חֵֽלֶק־אָדָ֖ם רָשָׁ֥ע ׀ עִם־אֵ֑ל
וְֽנַחֲלַ֥ת עָ֝רִיצִ֗ים מִשַּׁדַּ֥י יִקָּֽחוּ׃
¹⁴ אִם־יִרְבּ֣וּ בָנָ֣יו לְמוֹ־חָ֑רֶב
וְ֝צֶאֱצָאָ֗יו לֹ֣א יִשְׂבְּעוּ־לָֽחֶם׃
¹⁵ שְׂ֭רִידָיו בַּמָּ֣וֶת יִקָּבֵ֑רוּ
וְ֝אַלְמְנֹתָ֗יו לֹ֣א תִבְכֶּֽינָה׃
¹⁶ אִם־יִצְבֹּ֣ר כֶּעָפָ֣ר כָּ֑סֶף
וְ֝כַחֹ֗מֶר יָכִ֥ין מַלְבּֽוּשׁ׃

---

a-a   *Meaning of Heb. uncertain.*

17He may lay it up, but the righteous will wear
  it,
And the innocent will share the silver.
18The house he built is like a bird's nest,
Like the booth a watchman makes.
19He lies down, a rich man, with [his wealth]
  intact;
When he opens his eyes it is gone.
20Terror overtakes him like a flood;
A storm wind makes off with him by night.
21The east wind carries him far away, and he
  is gone;
It sweeps him from his place.
22Then it hurls itself at him without mercy;
He tries to escape from its force.
23It claps its hands at him,
And whistles at him from its place.

28 There is a mine for silver,
And a place where gold is refined.
2Iron is taken out of the earth,
And copper smelted from rock.
3He sets bounds for darkness;
To every limit man probes,
To rocks in deepest darkness.
4a-They open up a shaft far from where men
  live,
[In places] forgotten by wayfarers,
Destitute of men, far removed.-a
5Earth, out of which food grows,
Is changed below as if into fire.
6Its rocks are a source of sapphires;
It contains gold dust too.
7No bird of prey knows the path to it;
The falcon's eye has not gazed upon it.
8The proud beasts have not reached it;
The lion has not crossed it.
9Man sets his hand against the flinty rock

17 יָכִין וְצַדִּיק יִלְבָּשׁ
וְכֶסֶף נָקִי יַחֲלֹק:
18 בָּנָה כָעָשׁ בֵּיתוֹ
וּכְסֻכָּה עָשָׂה נֹצֵר:
19 עָשִׁיר יִשְׁכַּב וְלֹא יֵאָסֵף
עֵינָיו פָּקַח וְאֵינֶנּוּ:
20 תַּשִּׂיגֵהוּ כַמַּיִם בַּלָּהוֹת
לַיְלָה גְּנָבַתּוּ סוּפָה:
21 יִשָּׂאֵהוּ קָדִים וְיֵלַךְ
וִישָׂעֲרֵהוּ מִמְּקֹמוֹ:
22 וְיַשְׁלֵךְ עָלָיו וְלֹא יַחְמֹל
מִיָּדוֹ בָּרוֹחַ יִבְרָח:
23 יִשְׂפֹּק עָלֵימוֹ כַפֵּימוֹ
וְיִשְׁרֹק עָלָיו מִמְּקֹמוֹ:

כח כִּי יֵשׁ לַכֶּסֶף מוֹצָא
וּמָקוֹם לַזָּהָב יָזֹקּוּ:
2 בַּרְזֶל מֵעָפָר יֻקָּח
וְאֶבֶן יָצוּק נְחוּשָׁה:
3 קֵץ שָׂם לַחֹשֶׁךְ
וּלְכָל־תַּכְלִית הוּא חוֹקֵר
אֶבֶן אֹפֶל וְצַלְמָוֶת:
4 פָּרַץ נַחַל מֵעִם־גָּר
הַנִּשְׁכָּחִים מִנִּי־רָגֶל
דַּלּוּ מֵאֱנוֹשׁ נָעוּ:
5 אֶרֶץ מִמֶּנָּה יֵצֵא־לָחֶם
וְתַחְתֶּיהָ נֶהְפַּךְ כְּמוֹ־אֵשׁ:
6 מְקוֹם־סַפִּיר אֲבָנֶיהָ
וְעַפְרֹת זָהָב לוֹ:
7 נָתִיב לֹא־יְדָעוֹ עָיִט
וְלֹא שְׁזָפַתּוּ עֵין אַיָּה:
8 לֹא־הִדְרִיכֻהוּ בְנֵי־שָׁחַץ
לֹא־עָדָה עָלָיו שָׁחַל:
9 בַּחַלָּמִישׁ שָׁלַח יָדוֹ

a-a Meaning of Heb. uncertain.

And overturns mountains by the roots.

10He carves out channels through rock;
His eyes behold every precious thing.

11He dams up the sources of the streams
So that hidden things may be brought to light.

12But where can wisdom be found;
Where is the source of understanding?

13No man can set a value on it;
It cannot be found in the land of the living.

14The deep says, "It is not in me";
The sea says, "I do not have it."

15It cannot be bartered for gold;
Silver cannot be paid out as its price.

16The finest gold of Ophir cannot be weighed
     against it,
Nor precious onyx, nor sapphire.

17Gold or glass cannot match its value,
Nor vessels of fine gold be exchanged for it.

18Coral and crystal cannot be mentioned with
     it;
A pouch of wisdom is better than rubies.

19Topaz from Nubia cannot match its value;
Pure gold cannot be weighed against it.

20But whence does wisdom come?
Where is the source of understanding?

21It is hidden from the eyes of all living,
Concealed from the fowl of heaven.

22Abaddon and Death say,
"We have only a report of it."

23God understands the way to it;
He knows its source;

24For He sees to the ends of the earth,
Observes all that is beneath the heavens.

25When He fixed the weight of the winds,
Set the measure of the waters;

26When He made a rule for the rain
And a course for the thunderstorms,

הָפַךְ מִשֹּׁרֶשׁ הָרִים׃

10 בַּצּוּרוֹת יְאֹרִים בִּקֵּעַ
וְכָל־יְקָר רָאֲתָה עֵינוֹ׃

11 מִבְּכִי נְהָרוֹת חִבֵּשׁ
וְתַעֲלֻמָהּ יֹצִא אוֹר׃ פ

12 וְהַחָכְמָה מֵאַיִן תִּמָּצֵא
וְאֵי זֶה מְקוֹם בִּינָה׃

13 לֹא־יָדַע אֱנוֹשׁ עֶרְכָּהּ
וְלֹא תִמָּצֵא בְּאֶרֶץ הַחַיִּים׃

14 תְּהוֹם אָמַר לֹא בִי־הִיא
וְיָם אָמַר אֵין עִמָּדִי׃

15 לֹא־יֻתַּן סְגוֹר תַּחְתֶּיהָ
וְלֹא יִשָּׁקֵל כֶּסֶף מְחִירָהּ׃

16 לֹא־תְסֻלֶּה בְּכֶתֶם אוֹפִיר
בְּשֹׁהַם יָקָר וְסַפִּיר׃

17 לֹא־יַעַרְכֶנָּה זָהָב וּזְכוֹכִית
וּתְמוּרָתָהּ כְּלִי־פָז׃

18 רָאמוֹת וְגָבִישׁ לֹא יִזָּכֵר
וּמֶשֶׁךְ חָכְמָה מִפְּנִינִים׃

19 לֹא־יַעַרְכֶנָּה פִּטְדַת־כּוּשׁ
בְּכֶתֶם טָהוֹר לֹא תְסֻלֶּה׃ פ

20 וְהַחָכְמָה מֵאַיִן תָּבוֹא
וְאֵי זֶה מְקוֹם בִּינָה׃

21 וְנֶעֶלְמָה מֵעֵינֵי כָל־חָי
וּמֵעוֹף הַשָּׁמַיִם נִסְתָּרָה׃

22 אֲבַדּוֹן וָמָוֶת אָמְרוּ
בְּאָזְנֵינוּ שָׁמַעְנוּ שִׁמְעָהּ׃

23 אֱלֹהִים הֵבִין דַּרְכָּהּ
וְהוּא יָדַע אֶת־מְקוֹמָהּ׃

24 כִּי־הוּא לִקְצוֹת־הָאָרֶץ יַבִּיט
תַּחַת כָּל־הַשָּׁמַיִם יִרְאֶה׃

25 לַעֲשׂוֹת לָרוּחַ מִשְׁקָל
וּמַיִם תִּכֵּן בְּמִדָּה׃

26 בַּעֲשֹׂתוֹ לַמָּטָר חֹק
וְדֶרֶךְ לַחֲזִיז קֹלוֹת׃

27Then He saw it and gauged it;
He measured it and probed it.
28He said to man,
"See! Fear of the Lord is wisdom;
To shun evil is understanding."

27 אָז רָאָה וַיְסַפְּרָהּ
הֱכִינָהּ וְגַם־חֲקָרָהּ:
28 וַיֹּאמֶר ׀ לָאָדָם
הֵן יִרְאַת אֲדֹנָי הִיא חָכְמָה
וְסוּר מֵרָע בִּינָה: ס

29

Job again took up his theme and said:

כט וַיֹּסֶף אִיּוֹב שְׂאֵת מְשָׁלוֹ וַיֹּאמַר:

2O that I were as in months gone by,
In the days when God watched over me,
3When His lamp shone over my head,
When I walked in the dark by its light,
4When I was in my prime,
When God's company graced my tent,
5When Shaddai was still with me,
When my lads surrounded me,
6When my feet were bathed in cream,
And rocks poured out streams of oil for me.
7When I passed through the city gates
To take my seat in the square,
8Young men saw me and hid,
Elders rose and stood;
9Nobles held back their words;
They clapped their hands to their mouths.
10The voices of princes were hushed;
Their tongues stuck to their palates.
11The ear that heard me acclaimed me;
The eye that saw, commended me.
12For I saved the poor man who cried out,
The orphan who had none to help him.
13I received the blessing of the lost;
I gladdened the heart of the widow.
14I clothed myself in righteousness and it
    robed me;
Justice was my cloak and turban.
15I was eyes to the blind
And feet to the lame.
16I was a father to the needy,

2 מִי־יִתְּנֵנִי כְיַרְחֵי־קֶדֶם
כִּימֵי אֱלוֹהַּ יִשְׁמְרֵנִי:
3 בְּהִלּוֹ נֵרוֹ עֲלֵי רֹאשִׁי
לְאוֹרוֹ אֵלֶךְ חֹשֶׁךְ:
4 כַּאֲשֶׁר הָיִיתִי בִּימֵי חָרְפִּי
בְּסוֹד אֱלוֹהַּ עֲלֵי אָהֳלִי:
5 בְּעוֹד שַׁדַּי עִמָּדִי
סְבִיבוֹתַי נְעָרָי:
6 בִּרְחֹץ הֲלִיכַי בְּחֵמָה
וְצוּר יָצוּק עִמָּדִי פַּלְגֵי־שָׁמֶן:
7 בְּצֵאתִי שַׁעַר עֲלֵי־קָרֶת
בָּרְחוֹב אָכִין מוֹשָׁבִי:
8 רָאוּנִי נְעָרִים וְנֶחְבָּאוּ
וִישִׁישִׁים קָמוּ עָמָדוּ:
9 שָׂרִים עָצְרוּ בְמִלִּים
וְכַף יָשִׂימוּ לְפִיהֶם:
10 קוֹל־נְגִידִים נֶחְבָּאוּ
וּלְשׁוֹנָם לְחִכָּם דָּבֵקָה:
11 כִּי אֹזֶן שָׁמְעָה וַתְּאַשְּׁרֵנִי
וְעַיִן רָאֲתָה וַתְּעִידֵנִי:
12 כִּי־אֲמַלֵּט עָנִי מְשַׁוֵּעַ
וְיָתוֹם וְלֹא־עֹזֵר לוֹ:
13 בִּרְכַּת אֹבֵד עָלַי תָּבֹא
וְלֵב אַלְמָנָה אַרְנִן:
14 צֶדֶק לָבַשְׁתִּי וַיִּלְבָּשֵׁנִי
כִּמְעִיל וְצָנִיף מִשְׁפָּטִי:
15 עֵינַיִם הָיִיתִי לַעִוֵּר
וְרַגְלַיִם לַפִּסֵּחַ אָנִי:
16 אָב אָנֹכִי לָאֶבְיוֹנִים

And I looked into the case of the stranger.
17I broke the jaws of the wrongdoer,
And I wrested prey from his teeth.
18I thought I would end my days with my
family,ᵃ
And ᵇ-be as long-lived as the phoenix,-ᵇ
19My roots reaching water,
And dew lying on my branches;
20My vigor refreshed,
My bow ever new in my hand.
21Men would listen to me expectantly,
And wait for my counsel.
22After I spoke they had nothing to say;
My words were as drops [of dew] upon them.
23They waited for me as for rain,
For the late rain, their mouths open wide.
24When I smiled at them, they would not believe it;
They never expectedᶜ a sign of my favor.
25I decided their course and presided over
them;
I lived like a king among his troops,
Like one who consoles mourners.

30 But now those younger than I deride
me,
[Men] whose fathers I would have disdained
to put among my sheep dogs.
2Of what use to me is the strength of their
hands?
All their vigorᵃ is gone.
3Wasted from want and starvation,
They flee to a parched land,
To the gloom of desolate wasteland.
4They pluck saltwort and wormwood;
The roots of broom are their food.
5Driven out ᵃ-from society,-ᵃ

וְרָב לֹא־יָדַעְתִּי אֶחְקְרֵהוּ:
17 וָאֲשַׁבְּרָה מְתַלְּעוֹת עַוָּל
וּמִשִּׁנָּיו אַשְׁלִיךְ טָרֶף:
18 וָאֹמַר עִם־קִנִּי אֶגְוָע
וְכַחוֹל אַרְבֶּה יָמִים:
19 שָׁרְשִׁי פָתוּחַ אֱלֵי־מָיִם
וְטַל יָלִין בִּקְצִירִי:
20 כְּבוֹדִי חָדָשׁ עִמָּדִי
וְקַשְׁתִּי בְּיָדִי תַחֲלִיף:
21 לִי־שָׁמְעוּ וְיִחֵלּוּ
וְיִדְּמוּ לְמוֹ עֲצָתִי:
22 אַחֲרֵי דְבָרִי לֹא יִשְׁנוּ
וְעָלֵימוֹ תִּטֹּף מִלָּתִי:
23 וְיִחֲלוּ כַמָּטָר לִי
וּפִיהֶם פָּעֲרוּ לְמַלְקוֹשׁ:
24 אֶשְׂחַק אֲלֵהֶם לֹא יַאֲמִינוּ
וְאוֹר פָּנַי לֹא יַפִּילוּן:
25 אֶבְחַר דַּרְכָּם וְאֵשֵׁב רֹאשׁ
וְאֶשְׁכּוֹן כְּמֶלֶךְ בַּגְּדוּד
כַּאֲשֶׁר אֲבֵלִים יְנַחֵם:

ל
וְעַתָּה שָׂחֲקוּ עָלַי צְעִירִים מִמֶּנִּי
לְיָמִים אֲשֶׁר־מָאַסְתִּי אֲבוֹתָם לָשִׁית
עִם־כַּלְבֵי צֹאנִי:
2 גַּם־כֹּחַ יְדֵיהֶם לָמָּה לִּי
עָלֵימוֹ אָבַד כָּלַח:
3 בְּחֶסֶר וּבְכָפָן גַּלְמוּד
הַעֹרְקִים צִיָּה
אֶמֶשׁ שׁוֹאָה וּמְשֹׁאָה:
4 הַקֹּטְפִים מַלּוּחַ עֲלֵי־שִׂיחַ
וְשֹׁרֶשׁ רְתָמִים לַחְמָם:
5 מִן־גֵּו יְגֹרָשׁוּ

ᵃ Lit. "nest."
ᵇ⁻ᵇ Others "multiply days like sand."
ᶜ Taking yappilun as from pll; cf. Gen. 48.11.

ᵃ Meaning of Heb. uncertain.

They are cried at like a thief.

6They live in the gullies of wadis,
In holes in the ground, and in rocks,

7Braying among the bushes,
Huddling among the nettles,

8Scoundrels, nobodies,
Stricken from the earth.

9Now I am the butt of their gibes;
I have become a byword to them.

10They abhor me; they keep their distance
  from me;
They do not withhold spittle from my face.

11Because God^b has disarmed^c and humbled
  me,
They have thrown off restraint in my presence.

12Mere striplings assail me at my right hand:
They put me to flight;
They build their roads for my ruin.

13They tear up my path;
They promote my fall,
Although it does them no good.

14They come as through a wide breach;
They roll in ^a-like raging billows.^{-a}

15Terror tumbles upon me;
It sweeps away my honor like the wind;
My dignity^d vanishes like a cloud.

16So now my life runs out;
Days of misery have taken hold of me.

17By night my bones feel gnawed;
My sinews never rest.

18^a-With great effort I change clothing;
The neck of my tunic fits my waist.^{-a}

19He regarded me as clay,
I have become like dust and ashes.

20I cry out to You, but You do not answer me;
I wait, but You do [not] consider me.

יָרִיעוּ עָלֵימוֹ כַּגַּנָּב:
6 בַּעֲרוּץ נְחָלִים לִשְׁכֹּן
חֹרֵי עָפָר וְכֵפִים:
7 בֵּין־שִׂיחִים יִנְהָקוּ
תַּחַת חָרוּל יְסֻפָּחוּ:
8 בְּנֵי־נָבָל גַּם־בְּנֵי בְלִי־שֵׁם
נִכְּאוּ מִן־הָאָרֶץ:

9 וְעַתָּה נְגִינָתָם הָיִיתִי
וָאֱהִי לָהֶם לְמִלָּה:
10 תִּעֲבוּנִי רָחֲקוּ מֶנִּי
וּמִפָּנַי לֹא־חָשְׂכוּ רֹק:
11 כִּי־יִתְרוֹ יִתְרִי פִתַּח וַיְעַנֵּנִי
וְרֶסֶן מִפָּנַי שִׁלֵּחוּ:
12 עַל־יָמִין פִּרְחַח יָקוּמוּ
רַגְלַי שִׁלֵּחוּ
וַיָּסֹלּוּ עָלַי אָרְחוֹת אֵידָם:
13 נָתְסוּ נְתִיבָתִי
לְהַוָּתִי יֹעִילוּ
לֹא עֹזֵר לָמוֹ:
14 כְּפֶרֶץ רָחָב יֶאֱתָיוּ
תַּחַת שֹׁאָה הִתְגַּלְגָּלוּ:
15 הָהְפַּךְ עָלַי
בַּלָּהוֹת תִּרְדֹּף כָּרוּחַ נְדִבָתִי
וּכְעָב עָבְרָה יְשֻׁעָתִי:
16 וְעַתָּה עָלַי תִּשְׁתַּפֵּךְ נַפְשִׁי
יֹאחֲזוּנִי יְמֵי־עֹנִי:
17 לַיְלָה עֲצָמַי נִקַּר מֵעָלָי
וְעֹרְקַי לֹא יִשְׁכָּבוּן:
18 בְּרָב־כֹּחַ יִתְחַפֵּשׂ לְבוּשִׁי
כְּפִי כֻתָּנְתִּי יַאַזְרֵנִי:
19 הֹרָנִי לַחֹמֶר
וָאֶתְמַשֵּׁל כֶּעָפָר וָאֵפֶר:

20 אֲשַׁוַּע אֵלֶיךָ וְלֹא תַעֲנֵנִי
עָמַדְתִּי וַתִּתְבֹּנֶן בִּי:

b   Lit. "He."
c   Lit. "loosened my [bow] string."
d   Heb. yeshuʻathi taken as related to shoaʻ, "noble."

²¹You have become cruel to me;
With Your powerful hand You harass me.
²²You lift me up and mount me on the wind;
You make my courage melt.
²³I know You will bring me to death,
The house assigned for all the living.
^{24a}-Surely He would not strike at a ruin
If, in calamity, one cried out to Him.-^a
²⁵Did I not weep for the unfortunate?
Did I not grieve for the needy?
²⁶I looked forward to good fortune, but evil
came;
I hoped for light, but darkness came.
²⁷My bowels are in turmoil without respite;
Days of misery confront me.
²⁸I walk about in sunless gloom;
I rise in the assembly and cry out.
²⁹I have become a brother to jackals,
A companion to ostriches.
³⁰My skin, blackened, is peeling off me;
My bones are charred by the heat.
³¹So my lyre is given over to mourning,
My pipe, to accompany weepers.

31

I have covenanted with my eyes
Not to gaze on a maiden.
²What fate is decreed by God above?
What lot, by Shaddai in the heights?
³Calamity is surely for the iniquitous;
Misfortune, for the worker of mischief.
⁴Surely He observes my ways,
Takes account of my every step.

⁵Have I walked with worthless men,
Or my feet hurried to deceit?
⁶Let Him weigh me on the scale of righteous-
ness;
Let God ascertain my integrity.
⁷If my feet have strayed from their course,

כא תֵּהָפֵךְ לְאַכְזָר לִי
בְּעֹצֶם יָדְךָ תִשְׂטְמֵנִי:
כב תִּשָּׂאֵנִי אֶל־רוּחַ תַּרְכִּיבֵנִי
וּתְמֹגְגֵנִי תשוה תֻּשִׁיָּה:
כג כִּי־יָדַעְתִּי מָוֶת תְּשִׁיבֵנִי
וּבֵית מוֹעֵד לְכָל־חָי:
כד אַךְ לֹא־בְעִי יִשְׁלַח־יָד
אִם־בְּפִידוֹ לָהֶן שׁוּעַ:
כה אִם־לֹא בָכִיתִי לִקְשֵׁה־יוֹם
עָגְמָה נַפְשִׁי לָאֶבְיוֹן:
כו כִּי טוֹב קִוִּיתִי וַיָּבֹא רָע
וַאֲיַחֲלָה לְאוֹר וַיָּבֹא אֹפֶל:
כז מֵעַי רֻתְּחוּ וְלֹא־דָמּוּ
קִדְּמֻנִי יְמֵי־עֹנִי:
כח קֹדֵר הִלַּכְתִּי בְּלֹא חַמָּה
קַמְתִּי בַקָּהָל אֲשַׁוֵּעַ:
כט אָח הָיִיתִי לְתַנִּים
וְרֵעַ לִבְנוֹת יַעֲנָה:
ל עוֹרִי שָׁחַר מֵעָלָי
וְעַצְמִי־חָרָה מִנִּי־חֹרֶב:
לא וַיְהִי לְאֵבֶל כִּנֹּרִי
וְעֻגָבִי לְקוֹל בֹּכִים:

לא בְּרִית כָּרַתִּי לְעֵינָי
וּמָה אֶתְבּוֹנֵן עַל־בְּתוּלָה:
ב וּמֶה חֵלֶק אֱלוֹהַּ מִמָּעַל
וְנַחֲלַת שַׁדַּי מִמְּרֹמִים:
ג הֲלֹא־אֵיד לְעַוָּל
וְנֵכֶר לְפֹעֲלֵי אָוֶן:
ד הֲלֹא־הוּא יִרְאֶה דְרָכָי
וְכָל־צְעָדַי יִסְפּוֹר:

ה אִם־הָלַכְתִּי עִם־שָׁוְא
וַתַּחַשׁ עַל־מִרְמָה רַגְלִי:
ו יִשְׁקְלֵנִי בְמֹאזְנֵי־צֶדֶק
וְיֵדַע אֱלוֹהַּ תֻּמָּתִי:
ז אִם תִּטֶּה אַשֻּׁרִי מִנִּי הַדֶּרֶךְ

My heart followed after my eyes,
And a stain sullied my hands,
8May I sow, but another reap,
May the growth of my field be uprooted!
9If my heart was ravished by the wife of my
   neighbor,
And I lay in wait at his door,
10May my wife grind for another,
May others kneel over her!
11For that would have been debauchery,
A criminal offense,
12A fire burning down to Abaddon,
Consuming the roots of all my increase.
13Did I ever brush aside the case of my ser-
   vants, man or maid,
When they made a complaint against me?
14What then should I do when God arises;
When He calls me to account, what should
   I answer Him?
15Did not He who made me in my mother's
   belly make him?
Did not One form us both in the womb?
16Did I deny the poor their needs,
Or let a*a* widow pine away,
17By eating my food alone,
The fatherless not eating of it also?
18Why, from my youth he grew up with me
   as though I were his father;
Since I left my mother's womb I was her*b*
   guide.
19I never saw an unclad wretch,
A needy man without clothing,
20Whose loins did not bless me
As he warmed himself with the shearings of
   my sheep.
21If I raised my hand against the fatherless,
Looking to my supporters in the gate,
22May my arm drop off my shoulder;
My forearm break off *c-*at the elbow.*-c*

וְאַחַר עֵינַי הָלַךְ לִבִּי
וּבְכַפַּי דָּבַק מאוּם*׃ פ
8 אֶזְרְעָה וְאַחֵר יֹאכֵל
וְצֶאֱצָאַי יְשֹׁרָשׁוּ׃
9 אִם־נִפְתָּה לִבִּי עַל־אִשָּׁה
וְעַל־פֶּתַח רֵעִי אָרָבְתִּי׃
10 תִּטְחַן לְאַחֵר אִשְׁתִּי
וְעָלֶיהָ יִכְרְעוּן אֲחֵרִין׃
11 כִּי־הוּא הִיא זִמָּה
וְהִיא וְהוּא עָוֹן פְּלִילִים׃
12 כִּי אֵשׁ הִיא עַד־אֲבַדּוֹן תֹּאכֵל
וּבְכָל־תְּבוּאָתִי תְשָׁרֵשׁ׃
13 אִם־אֶמְאַס מִשְׁפַּט עַבְדִּי וַאֲמָתִי
בְּרִבָם עִמָּדִי׃
14 וּמָה אֶעֱשֶׂה כִּי־יָקוּם אֵל
וְכִי־יִפְקֹד מָה אֲשִׁיבֶנּוּ׃
15 הֲלֹא־בַבֶּטֶן עֹשֵׂנִי עָשָׂהוּ
וַיְכֻנֶנּוּ בָּרֶחֶם אֶחָד׃
16 אִם־אֶמְנַע מֵחֵפֶץ דַּלִּים
וְעֵינֵי אַלְמָנָה אֲכַלֶּה׃
17 וְאֹכַל פִּתִּי לְבַדִּי
וְלֹא־אָכַל יָתוֹם מִמֶּנָּה׃
18 כִּי מִנְּעוּרַי גְּדֵלַנִי כְאָב
וּמִבֶּטֶן אִמִּי אַנְחֶנָּה׃
19 אִם־אֶרְאֶה אוֹבֵד מִבְּלִי לְבוּשׁ
וְאֵין כְּסוּת לָאֶבְיוֹן׃
20 אִם־לֹא בֵרֲכוּנִי חֲלָצוֹ חֲלָצָיו
וּמִגֵּז כְּבָשַׂי יִתְחַמָּם׃
21 אִם־הֲנִיפוֹתִי עַל־יָתוֹם יָדִי
כִּי־אֶרְאֶה בַשַּׁעַר עֶזְרָתִי׃
22 כְּתֵפִי מִשִּׁכְמָה תִפּוֹל
וְאֶזְרֹעִי מִקָּנָה תִשָּׁבֵר׃

---

a   Lit. "the eyes of a."
b   Viz., the widow's.
c-c Lit. "from its shaft," i.e., the humerus.

נחה א׳   v. 7.

²³For I am in dread of God-sent calamity; I cannot bear His threat. ²⁴Did I put my reliance on gold, Or regard fine gold as my bulwark? ²⁵Did I rejoice in my great wealth, In having attained plenty? ²⁶If ever I saw the light shining, The moon on its course in full glory, ²⁷And I secretly succumbed, And my hand touched my mouth in a kiss, ²⁸That, too, would have been a criminal offense, For I would have denied God above. ²⁹Did I rejoice over my enemy's misfortune? Did I thrill because evil befell him? ³⁰I never let my mouth^d sin By wishing his death in a curse. ³¹(Indeed, the men of my clan said, "We would consume his flesh insatiably!") ³²No sojourner spent the night in the open; I opened my doors to the road. ³³Did I hide my transgressions like Adam, Bury my wrongdoing in my bosom, ³⁴That I should [now] fear the great multitude, And am shattered by the contempt of families, So that I keep silent and do not step outdoors?

³⁵O that I had someone to give me a hearing; O that Shaddai would reply to my writ, Or my accuser draw up a true bill! ³⁶I would carry it on my shoulder; Tie it around me for a wreath. ³⁷I would give him an account of my steps, Offer it as to a commander.

³⁸If my land cries out against me, Its furrows weep together;

23 כִּי פַחַד אֵלַי אֵיד אֵל
וּמִשְּׂאֵתוֹ לֹא אוּכָל:
24 אִם־שַׂמְתִּי זָהָב כִּסְלִי
וְלַכֶּתֶם אָמַרְתִּי מִבְטַחִי:
25 אִם־אֶשְׂמַח כִּי־רַב חֵילִי
וְכִי־כַבִּיר מָצְאָה יָדִי:
26 אִם־אֶרְאֶה אוֹר כִּי יָהֵל
וְיָרֵחַ יָקָר הֹלֵךְ:
27 וַיִּפְתְּ בַּסֵּתֶר לִבִּי
וַתִּשַּׁק יָדִי לְפִי:
28 גַּם־הוּא עָוֺן פְּלִילִי
כִּי־כִחַשְׁתִּי לָאֵל מִמָּעַל:
29 אִם־אֶשְׂמַח בְּפִיד מְשַׂנְאִי
וְהִתְעֹרַרְתִּי כִּי־מְצָאוֹ רָע:
30 וְלֹא־נָתַתִּי לַחֲטֹא חִכִּי
לִשְׁאֹל בְּאָלָה נַפְשׁוֹ*:
31 אִם־לֹא אָמְרוּ מְתֵי אָהֳלִי
מִי־יִתֵּן מִבְּשָׂרוֹ לֹא נִשְׂבָּע:
32 בַּחוּץ לֹא־יָלִין גֵּר
דְּלָתַי לָאֹרַח אֶפְתָּח:
33 אִם־כִּסִּיתִי כְאָדָם פְּשָׁעָי
לִטְמוֹן בְּחֻבִּי עֲוֺנִי:
34 כִּי אֶעֱרוֹץ ׀ הָמוֹן רַבָּה
וּבוּז־מִשְׁפָּחוֹת יְחִתֵּנִי
וָאֶדֹּם לֹא־אֵצֵא פָתַח:

35 מִי יִתֶּן־לִי ׀ שֹׁמֵעַ לִי
הֶן־תָּוִי שַׁדַּי יַעֲנֵנִי
וְסֵפֶר כָּתַב אִישׁ רִיבִי:
36 אִם־לֹא עַל־שִׁכְמִי אֶשָּׂאֶנּוּ
אֶעֶנְדֶנּוּ עֲטָרוֹת לִי:
37 מִסְפַּר צְעָדַי אַגִּידֶנּוּ
כְּמוֹ־נָגִיד אֲקָרְבֶנּוּ:

38 אִם־עָלַי אַדְמָתִי תִזְעָק
וְיַחַד תְּלָמֶיהָ יִבְכָּיוּן:

39 If I have eaten its produce without payment,
And made its [rightful] owners despair,
40 May nettles grow there instead of wheat;
Instead of barley, stinkweed!

The words of Job are at an end.

39 אִם־כֹּחָהּ אָכַ֫לְתִּי בְלִי־כָ֑סֶף
וְנֶ֖פֶשׁ בְּעָלֶ֣יהָ הִפָּֽחְתִּי׃
40 תַּ֤חַת חִטָּ֨ה ׀ יֵ֥צֵא ח֗וֹחַ
וְתַֽחַת־שְׂעֹרָ֥ה בָאְשָׁ֑ה
תַּ֖מּוּ דִּבְרֵ֥י אִיּֽוֹב׃ פ

32 These three men ceased replying to Job, for he considered himself right. 2 Then Elihu son of Barachel the Buzite, of the family of Ram, was angry—angry at Job because he thought himself right against God. 3 He was angry as well at his three friends, because they found no reply, but merely condemned Job. 4 Elihu waited out Job's speech, for they were all older than he. 5 But when Elihu saw that the three men had nothing to reply, he was angry.

6 Then Elihu son of Barachel the Buzite said in reply:

I have but few years, while you are old;
Therefore I was too awestruck and fearful
To hold forth among you.
7 I thought, "Let age speak;
Let advanced years declare wise things."
8 But truly it is the spirit in men,
The breath of Shaddai, that gives them under-
standing.
9 It is not the aged who are wise,
The elders, who understand how to judge.
10 Therefore I say, "Listen to me;
I too would hold forth."
11 Here I have waited out your speeches,
I have given ear to your insights,
While you probed the issues;
12 But as I attended to you,
I saw that none of you could argue with Job,
Or offer replies to his statements.

לב וַיִּשְׁבְּת֗וּ שְׁלֹ֤שֶׁת הָאֲנָשִׁ֣ים הָאֵ֔לֶּה
מֵעֲנ֖וֹת אֶת־אִיּ֑וֹב כִּ֤י ה֖וּא צַדִּ֣יק בְּעֵינָֽיו׃
2 וַיִּ֤חַר אַ֨ף ׀ אֱלִיה֣וּא בֶן־בַּֽרַכְאֵ֣ל הַבּוּזִי֮
מִמִּשְׁפַּ֪חַת רָ֥ם בְּאִיּ֗וֹב חָרָ֣ה אַפּ֑וֹ עַל־צַדְּק֥וֹ
נַפְשׁ֗וֹ מֵֽאֱלֹהִֽים׃ 3 וּבִשְׁלֹ֤שֶׁת רֵעָיו֙ חָרָ֣ה
אַפּ֔וֹ עַ֤ל אֲשֶׁ֣ר לֹא־מָצְא֣וּ מַעֲנֶ֑ה וַֽיַּרְשִׁ֖יעוּ
אֶת־אִיּֽוֹב׃ 4 וֶֽאֱלִיה֗וּ חִכָּ֣ה אֶת־אִיּ֔וֹב
בִּדְבָרִ֑ים כִּ֤י זְקֵנִֽים־הֵ֨מָּה מִמֶּ֖נּוּ לְיָמִֽים׃
5 וַיַּ֤רְא אֱלִיה֗וּא כִּ֣י אֵ֤ין מַעֲנֶ֔ה בְּפִ֖י שְׁלֹ֣שֶׁת
הָאֲנָשִׁ֑ים וַיִּ֖חַר אַפּֽוֹ׃ פ

6 וַיַּ֤עַן ׀ אֱלִיה֣וּא בֶן־בַּֽרַכְאֵ֣ל הַבּוּזִי֮ וַיֹּאמַ֥ר

צָעִ֤יר אֲנִ֣י לְיָמִ֔ים וְאַתֶּ֣ם יְשִׁישִׁ֑ים
עַל־כֵּ֭ן זָחַ֥לְתִּי וָֽאִירָ֓א ׀
מֵֽחַוֺּ֖ת דֵּעִ֣י אֶתְכֶֽם׃
7 אָ֭מַרְתִּי יָמִ֣ים יְדַבֵּ֑רוּ
וְרֹ֥ב שָׁ֝נִ֗ים יֹדִ֥יעוּ חָכְמָֽה׃
8 אָ֭כֵן רֽוּחַ־הִ֣יא בֶאֱנ֑וֹשׁ
וְנִשְׁמַ֖ת שַׁדַּ֣י תְּבִינֵֽם׃
9 לֹֽא־רַבִּ֥ים יֶחְכָּ֑מוּ
וּ֝זְקֵנִ֗ים יָבִ֥ינוּ מִשְׁפָּֽט׃
10 לָכֵ֣ן אָ֭מַרְתִּי שִׁמְעָה־לִּ֑י
אֲחַוֶּ֖ה דֵּעִ֣י אַף־אָֽנִי׃
11 הֵ֤ן הוֹחַ֨לְתִּי לְֽדִבְרֵיכֶ֗ם
אָ֭זִין עַד־תְּב֣וּנֹֽתֵיכֶ֑ם
עַֽד־תַּחְקְר֥וּן מִלִּֽין׃
12 וְעָֽדֵיכֶ֗ם אֶתְבּ֫וֹנָ֥ן
וְהִנֵּ֤ה אֵ֣ין לְאִיּ֣וֹב מוֹכִ֑יחַ

¹³I fear you will say, "We have found the wise course;
God will defeat him, not man."

¹⁴He did not set out his case against me,
Nor shall I use your reasons to reply to him.

¹⁵They have been broken and can no longer reply;
Words fail them.

¹⁶I have waited till they stopped speaking,
Till they ended and no longer replied.

¹⁷Now I also would have my say;
I too would like to hold forth,

¹⁸For I am full of words;
The wind in my belly presses me.

¹⁹My belly is like wine not yet opened,
Like jugs of new wine ready to burst.

²⁰Let me speak, then, and get relief;
Let me open my lips and reply.

²¹I would not show regard for any man,
Or temper my speech for anyone's sake;

²²For I do not know how to temper my speech—
My Maker would soon carry me off!

33 But now, Job, listen to my words,
Give ear to all that I say.

²Now I open my lips;
My tongue forms words in my mouth.

³My words bespeak the uprightness of my heart;
My lips utter insight honestly.

⁴The spirit of God formed me;
The breath of Shaddai sustains me.

⁵If you can, answer me;
Argue against me, take your stand.

⁶You and I are the same before God;
I too was nipped from clay.

⁷You are not overwhelmed by fear of me;
My pressure does not weigh heavily on you.

עוֹנֶה אֲמָרָיו מִכֶּם׃

¹³ פֶּן־תֹּאמְרוּ מָצָאנוּ חָכְמָה
אֵל יִדְּפֶנּוּ לֹא־אִישׁ׃

¹⁴ וְלֹא־עָרַךְ אֵלַי מִלִּין
וּבְאִמְרֵיכֶם לֹא אֲשִׁיבֶנּוּ׃

¹⁵ חַתּוּ לֹא־עָנוּ עוֹד
הֶעְתִּיקוּ מֵהֶם מִלִּים׃

¹⁶ וְהוֹחַלְתִּי כִּי־לֹא יְדַבֵּרוּ
כִּי עָמְדוּ לֹא־עָנוּ עוֹד׃

¹⁷ אַעֲנֶה אַף־אֲנִי חֶלְקִי
אֲחַוֶּה דֵעִי אַף־אָנִי׃

¹⁸ כִּי מָלֵתִי* מִלִּים
הֱצִיקַתְנִי רוּחַ בִּטְנִי׃

¹⁹ הִנֵּה־בִטְנִי כְּיַיִן לֹא־יִפָּתֵחַ
כְּאֹבוֹת חֲדָשִׁים יִבָּקֵעַ׃

²⁰ אֲדַבְּרָה וְיִרְוַח־לִי
אֶפְתַּח שְׂפָתַי וְאֶעֱנֶה׃

²¹ אַל־נָא אֶשָּׂא פְנֵי־אִישׁ
וְאֶל־אָדָם לֹא אֲכַנֶּה׃

²² כִּי לֹא יָדַעְתִּי אֲכַנֶּה
כִּמְעַט יִשָּׂאֵנִי עֹשֵׂנִי׃

לג וְאוּלָם שְׁמַע־נָא אִיּוֹב מִלָּי
וְכָל־דְּבָרַי הַאֲזִינָה׃

² הִנֵּה־נָא פָּתַחְתִּי פִי
דִּבְּרָה לְשׁוֹנִי בְחִכִּי׃

³ יֹשֶׁר־לִבִּי אֲמָרָי
וְדַעַת שְׂפָתַי בָּרוּר מִלֵּלוּ׃

⁴ רוּחַ־אֵל עָשָׂתְנִי
וְנִשְׁמַת שַׁדַּי תְּחַיֵּנִי׃

⁵ אִם־תּוּכַל הֲשִׁיבֵנִי
עֶרְכָה לְפָנַי הִתְיַצָּבָה׃

⁶ הֵן־אֲנִי כְפִיךָ לָאֵל
מֵחֹמֶר קֹרַצְתִּי גַם־אָנִי׃

⁷ הִנֵּה אֵמָתִי לֹא תְבַעֲתֶךָּ
וְאַכְפִּי עָלֶיךָ לֹא־יִכְבָּד׃

8Indeed, you have stated in my hearing,
I heard the words spoken,
9"I am guiltless, free from transgression;
I am innocent, without iniquity.
10But He finds reasons to oppose me,
Considers me His enemy.
11He puts my feet in stocks,
Watches all my ways."

12In this you are not right;
I will answer you: God is greater than any
   man.
13Why do you complain against Him
That He does not reply to any of man's
   charges?
14For God speaks *a*-time and again-*a*—
Though man does not perceive it—
15In a dream, a night vision,
When deep sleep falls on men,
While they slumber on their beds.
16Then He opens men's understanding,
And by disciplining them leaves His signature
17To turn man away from an action,
To suppress pride in man.
18He spares him from the Pit,
His person, from perishing by the sword.
19He is reproved by pains on his bed,
And the trembling in his bones is constant.
20He detests food;
Fine food [is repulsive] to him.
21His flesh wastes away till it cannot be seen,
And his bones are rubbed away till they are
   invisible.
22He comes close to the Pit,
His life [verges] on death.
23If he has a representative,
One advocate against a thousand
To declare the man's uprightness,
24Then He has mercy on him and decrees,

8 אַ֤ךְ אָמַ֣רְתָּ בְאָזְנָ֑י
וְק֖וֹל מִלִּ֣ין אֶשְׁמָֽע׃
9 זַ֤ךְ אֲנִי֙ בְּלִ֣י פָ֔שַׁע חַ֖ף אָנֹכִ֑י
וְלֹ֖א עָוֺ֣ן לִֽי׃
10 הֵ֣ן תְּנוּא֣וֹת עָלַ֣י יִמְצָ֑א
יַחְשְׁבֵ֖נִי לְאוֹיֵ֣ב לֽוֹ׃
11 יָשֵׂ֣ם בַּסַּ֣ד רַגְלָ֑י
יִ֜שְׁמֹ֗ר כׇּל־אׇרְחֹתָֽי׃

12 הֶן־זֹ֣את לֹא־צָדַ֣קְתָּ אֶעֱנֶ֑ךָּ
כִּֽי־יִרְבֶּ֥ה אֱ֜ל֗וֹהַּ מֵאֱנֽוֹשׁ׃
13 מַ֭דּוּעַ אֵלָ֣יו רִיב֑וֹתָ
כִּ֥י כׇל־דְּ֜בָרָ֗יו לֹא־יַֽעֲנֶֽה׃
14 כִּֽי־בְאַחַ֥ת יְדַבֶּר־אֵ֑ל
וּ֜בִשְׁתַּ֗יִם לֹ֣א יְשׁוּרֶֽנָּה׃
15 בַּחֲל֤וֹם ׀ חֶזְי֬וֹן לַ֗יְלָה
בִּנְפֹ֣ל תַּ֭רְדֵּמָה עַל־אֲנָשִׁ֑ים
בִּ֜תְנוּמ֗וֹת עֲלֵ֣י מִשְׁכָּֽב׃
16 אָ֣ז יִ֭גְלֶה אֹ֣זֶן אֲנָשִׁ֑ים
וּבְמֹ֖סָרָ֣ם יַחְתֹּֽם׃
17 לְ֭הָסִיר אָדָ֣ם מַעֲשֶׂ֑ה
וְגֵוָ֖ה מִגֶּ֣בֶר יְכַסֶּֽה׃
18 יַחְשֹׂ֣ךְ נַ֭פְשׁוֹ מִנִּי־שָׁ֑חַת
וְ֜חַיָּת֗וֹ מֵעֲבֹ֥ר בַּשָּֽׁלַח׃
19 וְהוּכַ֣ח בְּ֭מַכְאוֹב עַל־מִשְׁכָּב֑וֹ
וריב וְ֖רֹ֣ב עֲצָמָ֣יו אֵתָֽן׃
20 וְזִֽהֲמַ֣תּוּ חַיָּת֣וֹ לָ֑חֶם
וְ֜נַפְשׁ֗וֹ מַאֲכַ֥ל תַּאֲוָֽה׃
21 יִ֣כֶל בְּשָׂר֣וֹ מֵרֹ֑אִי
ושפי וְשֻׁפּ֥וּ עַ֜צְמוֹתָ֗יו לֹ֣א רֻאּֽוּ׃*
22 וַתִּקְרַ֣ב לַשַּׁ֣חַת נַפְשׁ֑וֹ
וְ֜חַיָּת֗וֹ לַֽמְמִתִֽים׃
23 אִם־יֵ֤שׁ עָלָ֨יו ׀ מַלְאָ֗ךְ
מֵלִ֗יץ אֶחָ֥ד מִנִּי־אָ֑לֶף
לְהַגִּ֖יד לְאָדָ֣ם יׇשְׁרֽוֹ׃
24 וַיְחֻנֶּ֗נּוּ וַ֭יֹּאמֶר

v. 21. א׳ דגושה

a-a Lit. "once...twice."

"Redeem him from descending to the Pit,
For I have obtained his ransom;
[25]Let his flesh be healthier[b] than in his youth;
Let him return to his younger days."
[26]He prays to God and is accepted by Him;
He enters His presence with shouts of joy,
For He requites a man for his righteousness.
[27]He[c] declares[b] to men,
"I have sinned; I have perverted what was
     right;
But I was not paid back for it."
[28]He redeemed [d]-him from passing into the
     Pit;
He-[d] will enjoy the light.
[29]Truly, God does all these things
Two or three times to a man,
[30]To bring him back from the Pit,
That he may bask in the light of life.

[31]Pay heed, Job, and hear me;
Be still, and I will speak;
[32]If you have what to say, answer me;
Speak, for I am eager to vindicate you.
[33]But if not, you listen to me;
Be still, and I will teach you wisdom.

34 Elihu said in reply:

[2]Listen, O wise men, to my words;
You who have knowledge, give ear to me.
[3]For the ear tests arguments
As the palate tastes food.
[4]Let us decide for ourselves what is just;
Let us know among ourselves what is good.
[5]For Job has said, "I am right;
God has deprived me of justice.
[6]I declare the judgment against me false;

פְּדָעֵהוּ מֵרֶדֶת שָׁחַת
מָצָאתִי כֹפֶר׃
25 רֻטֲפַשׁ בְּשָׂרוֹ מִנֹּעַר
יָשׁוּב לִימֵי עֲלוּמָיו׃
26 יֶעְתַּר אֶל־אֱלוֹהַּ ׀ וַיִּרְצֵהוּ
וַיַּרְא פָּנָיו בִּתְרוּעָה
וַיָּשֶׁב לֶאֱנוֹשׁ צִדְקָתוֹ׃
27 יָשֹׁר ׀ עַל־אֲנָשִׁים וַיֹּאמֶר
חָטָאתִי וְיָשָׁר הֶעֱוֵיתִי
וְלֹא־שָׁוָה לִי׃
28 פָּדָה נפשי נַפְשׁוֹ מֵעֲבֹר בַּשָּׁחַת
וחיתי וְחַיָּתוֹ בָּאוֹר תִּרְאֶה׃
29 הֶן־כָּל־אֵלֶּה יִפְעַל־אֵל
פַּעֲמַיִם שָׁלוֹשׁ עִם־גָּבֶר׃
30 לְהָשִׁיב נַפְשׁוֹ מִנִּי־שָׁחַת
לֵאוֹר בְּאוֹר הַחַיִּים׃

31 הַקְשֵׁב אִיּוֹב שְׁמַע־לִי
הַחֲרֵשׁ וְאָנֹכִי אֲדַבֵּר׃
32 אִם־יֵשׁ־מִלִּין הֲשִׁיבֵנִי
דַּבֵּר כִּי־חָפַצְתִּי צַדְּקֶךָּ׃
33 אִם־אַיִן אַתָּה שְׁמַע־לִי
הַחֲרֵשׁ וַאֲאַלֶּפְךָ חָכְמָה׃ ס

לד וַיַּעַן אֱלִיהוּא וַיֹּאמַר׃

2 שִׁמְעוּ חֲכָמִים מִלָּי
וְיֹדְעִים הַאֲזִינוּ לִי׃
3 כִּי־אֹזֶן מִלִּין תִּבְחָן
וְחֵךְ יִטְעַם לֶאֱכֹל׃
4 מִשְׁפָּט נִבְחֲרָה־לָּנוּ
נֵדְעָה בֵינֵינוּ מַה־טּוֹב׃
5 כִּי־אָמַר אִיּוֹב צָדַקְתִּי
וְאֵל הֵסִיר מִשְׁפָּטִי׃
6 עַל־מִשְׁפָּטִי אֲכַזֵּב

---

b   *Meaning of Heb. uncertain.*
c   *I.e., the contrite man.*
d-d   *Or with kethib, "me...I."*

My arrow-wound is deadly, though I am free
  from transgression."

7What man is like Job,
Who drinks mockery like water;

8Who makes common cause with evildoers,
And goes with wicked men?

9For he says, "Man gains nothing
When he is in God's favor."

10Therefore, men of understanding, listen to
  me;
Wickedness be far from God,
Wrongdoing, from Shaddai!

11For He pays a man according to his actions,
And provides for him according to his conduct;

12For God surely does not act wickedly;
Shaddai does not pervert justice.

13Who placed the earth in His charge?
Who ordered the entire world?

14If He but intends it,
He can call back His spirit and breath;

15All flesh would at once expire,
And mankind return to dust.

16If you would understand, listen to this;
Give ear to what I say.

17Would one who hates justice govern?
Would you condemn the Just Mighty One?

18Would you call a king a scoundrel,
Great men, wicked?

19He is not partial to princes;
The noble are not preferred to the wretched;
For all of them are the work of His hands.

20Some die suddenly in the middle of the
  night;
People are in turmoil and pass on;
Even great men are removed—not by human
  hands.

21For His eyes are upon a man's ways;

אֱנ֣וּשׁ חִצִּ֣י בְלִי־פָֽשַׁע׃

7 מִי־גֶ֥בֶר כְּאִיּ֑וֹב
יִֽשְׁתֶּה־לַּ֖עַג כַּמָּֽיִם׃

8 וְאָרַ֣ח לְ֭חֶבְרָה עִם־פֹּ֣עֲלֵי אָ֑וֶן
וְ֝לָלֶ֗כֶת עִם־אַנְשֵׁי־רֶֽשַׁע׃

9 כִּֽי־אָ֭מַר לֹ֣א יִסְכָּן־גָּ֑בֶר
בִּ֝רְצֹת֗וֹ עִם־אֱלֹהִֽים׃

10 לָכֵ֤ן ׀ אַ֥נְשֵׁי לֵבָ֗ב שִׁמְע֫וּ לִ֥י
חָלִ֖לָה לָאֵ֥ל מֵרֶ֗שַׁע
וְשַׁדַּ֥י מֵעָֽוֶל׃

11 כִּ֤י פֹ֣עַל אָ֭דָם יְשַׁלֶּם־ל֑וֹ
וּֽכְאֹ֥רַח אִ֝֗ישׁ יַמְצִאֶֽנּוּ׃

12 אַף־אׇמְנָ֗ם אֵ֥ל לֹֽא־יַרְשִׁ֑יעַ
וְ֝שַׁדַּ֗י לֹֽא־יְעַוֵּ֥ת מִשְׁפָּֽט׃

13 מִֽי־פָקַ֣ד עָלָ֣יו אָ֑רְצָה
וּמִ֥י שָׂ֝֗ם תֵּבֵ֥ל כֻּלָּֽהּ׃

14 אִם־יָשִׂ֣ים אֵלָ֣יו לִבּ֑וֹ
רוּח֥וֹ וְ֝נִשְׁמָת֗וֹ אֵלָ֥יו יֶאֱסֹֽף׃

15 יִגְוַ֣ע כׇּל־בָּשָׂ֣ר יָ֑חַד
וְ֝אָדָ֗ם עַל־עָפָ֥ר יָשֽׁוּב׃

16 וְאִם־בִּ֥ינָה שִׁמְעָה־זֹּ֑את
הַ֝אֲזִ֗ינָה לְק֣וֹל מִלָּֽי׃

17 הַאַ֬ף שׂוֹנֵ֣א מִשְׁפָּ֣ט יַחֲב֑וֹשׁ
וְאִם־צַדִּ֖יק כַּבִּ֣יר תַּרְשִֽׁיעַ׃

18 הַאֲמֹ֣ר לְמֶ֣לֶךְ בְּלִיָּ֑עַל
רָ֝שָׁ֗ע אֶל־נְדִיבִֽים׃

19 אֲשֶׁ֤ר לֹֽא־נָשָׂ֨א ׀ פְּנֵ֥י שָׂרִ֗ים
וְלֹ֤א נִכַּר־שׁ֥וֹעַ לִפְנֵי־דָ֑ל
כִּֽי־מַעֲשֵׂ֖ה יָדָ֣יו כֻּלָּֽם׃

20 רֶ֤גַע ׀ יָמֻתוּ֮ וַחֲצ֢וֹת לָ֫יְלָה
יְגֹעֲשׁ֣וּ עָ֣ם וְיַעֲבֹ֑רוּ
וְיָסִ֥ירוּ אַ֝בִּ֗יר לֹ֣א בְיָֽד׃

21 כִּֽי־עֵ֭ינָיו עַל־דַּרְכֵי־אִ֑ישׁ

He observes his every step.
22Neither darkness nor gloom offers
A hiding-place for evildoers.
23He has no set time for man
To appear before God in judgment.
24He shatters mighty men without number
And sets others in their place.
25Truly, He knows their deeds;
Night is over, and they are crushed.
26He strikes them down with the wicked
Where people can see,
27Because they have been disloyal to Him
And have not understood any of His ways;
28Thus He lets the cry of the poor come before
  Him;
He listens to the cry of the needy.
29When He is silent, who will condemn?
If He hides His face, who will see Him,
Be it nation or man?
30The impious man rule no more,
Nor do those who ensnare the people.
31Has he said to God,
"I will bear [my punishment] and offend no
  more.
32What I cannot see You teach me.
If I have done iniquity, I shall not do so
  again"?
33Should He requite as you see fit?
But you have despised [Him]!
You must decide, not I;
Speak what you know.
34Men of understanding say to me,
Wise men who hear me,
35"Job does not speak with knowledge;
His words lack understanding."
36Would that Job were tried to the limit
For answers which befit sinful men.
37He adds to his sin;
He increases his transgression among us;
He multiplies his statements against God.

וְכָל־צְעָדָיו יִרְאֶה:
22 אֵין־חֹשֶׁךְ וְאֵין צַלְמָוֶת
לְהִסָּתֶר שָׁם פֹּעֲלֵי אָוֶן:
23 כִּי לֹא עַל־אִישׁ יָשִׂים עוֹד
לַהֲלֹךְ אֶל־אֵל בַּמִּשְׁפָּט:
24 יָרֹעַ כַּבִּירִים לֹא־חֵקֶר
וַיַּעֲמֵד אֲחֵרִים תַּחְתָּם:
25 לָכֵן יַכִּיר מַעְבָּדֵיהֶם
וְהָפַךְ לַיְלָה וְיִדַּכָּאוּ:
26 תַּחַת־רְשָׁעִים סְפָקָם
בִּמְקוֹם רֹאִים:
27 אֲשֶׁר עַל־כֵּן סָרוּ מֵאַחֲרָיו
וְכָל־דְּרָכָיו לֹא הִשְׂכִּילוּ:
28 לְהָבִיא עָלָיו צַעֲקַת־דָּל
וְצַעֲקַת עֲנִיִּים יִשְׁמָע:
29 וְהוּא יַשְׁקִט ׀ וּמִי יַרְשִׁעַ
וְיַסְתֵּר פָּנִים וּמִי יְשׁוּרֶנּוּ
וְעַל־גּוֹי וְעַל־אָדָם יָחַד:
30 מִמְּלֹךְ אָדָם חָנֵף
מִמֹּקְשֵׁי עָם:
31 כִּי־אֶל־אֵל הֶאָמַר
נָשָׂאתִי לֹא אֶחְבֹּל:
32 בִּלְעֲדֵי אֶחֱזֶה אַתָּה הֹרֵנִי
אִם־עָוֶל פָּעַלְתִּי לֹא אֹסִיף:
33 הֲמֵעִמְּךָ יְשַׁלְמֶנָּה
כִּי־מָאַסְתָּ
כִּי־אַתָּה תִבְחַר וְלֹא־אָנִי
וּמַה־יָדַעְתָּ דַבֵּר:
34 אַנְשֵׁי לֵבָב יֹאמְרוּ לִי
וְגֶבֶר חָכָם שֹׁמֵעַ לִי:
35 אִיּוֹב לֹא־בְדַעַת יְדַבֵּר
וּדְבָרָיו לֹא בְהַשְׂכֵּיל:
36 אָבִי יִבָּחֵן אִיּוֹב עַד־נֶצַח
עַל־תְּשֻׁבֹת בְּאַנְשֵׁי־אָוֶן:
37 כִּי יֹסִיף עַל־חַטָּאתוֹ
פֶשַׁע בֵּינֵינוּ יִסְפּוֹק
וְיֶרֶב אֲמָרָיו לָאֵל: ס

לה וַיַּעַן אֱלִיהוּ וַיֹּאמַר:

35 Elihu said in reply:

2Do you think it just
To say, "I am right against God"?
3If you ask how it benefits you,
"What have I gained from not sinning?"
4I shall give you a reply,
You, along with your friends.
5Behold the heavens and see;
Look at the skies high above you.
6If you sin, what do you do to Him?
If your transgressions are many,
How do you affect Him?
7If you are righteous,
What do you give Him;
What does He receive from your hand?
8Your wickedness affects men like yourself;
Your righteousness, mortals.

9Because of contention the oppressed cry out;
They shout because of the power of the great.
10But none says, "Where is my God, my
    Maker,
Who gives strength in the night;
11Who gives us more knowledge than the
    beasts of the earth,
Makes us wiser than the birds of the sky?"
12Then they cry out, but He does not respond
Because of the arrogance of evil men.
13Surely it is false that God does not listen,
That Shaddai does not take note of it.
14Though you say, "You do not take note of
    it,"
The case is before Him;
So wait for Him.
15a-But since now it does not seem so,
He vents his anger;
He does not realize that it may be long drawn
    out.-a

2 הֲזֹאת חָשַׁבְתָּ לְמִשְׁפָּט
אָמַרְתָּ צִדְקִי מֵאֵל:
3 כִּי־תֹאמַר מַה־יִּסְכָּן־לָךְ
מָה־אֹעִיל מֵחַטָּאתִי:
4 אֲנִי אֲשִׁיבְךָ מִלִּין
וְאֶת־רֵעֶיךָ עִמָּךְ:
5 הַבֵּט שָׁמַיִם וּרְאֵה
וְשׁוּר שְׁחָקִים גָּבְהוּ מִמֶּךָּ:
6 אִם־חָטָאתָ מַה־תִּפְעָל־בּוֹ
וְרַבּוּ פְשָׁעֶיךָ מַה־תַּעֲשֶׂה־לּוֹ:
7 אִם־צָדַקְתָּ מַה־תִּתֶּן־לוֹ
אוֹ מַה־מִּיָּדְךָ יִקָּח:
8 לְאִישׁ־כָּמוֹךָ רִשְׁעֶךָ
וּלְבֶן־אָדָם צִדְקָתֶךָ:

9 מֵרֹב עֲשׁוּקִים יַזְעִיקוּ
יְשַׁוְּעוּ מִזְּרוֹעַ רַבִּים:
10 וְלֹא־אָמַר אַיֵּה אֱלוֹהַּ עֹשָׂי
נֹתֵן זְמִרוֹת בַּלָּיְלָה:
11 מַלְּפֵנוּ מִבַּהֲמוֹת אָרֶץ
וּמֵעוֹף הַשָּׁמַיִם יְחַכְּמֵנוּ:
12 שָׁם יִצְעֲקוּ וְלֹא יַעֲנֶה
מִפְּנֵי גְּאוֹן רָעִים:
13 אַךְ־שָׁוְא לֹא־יִשְׁמַע ׀ אֵל
וְשַׁדַּי לֹא יְשׁוּרֶנָּה:
14 אַף כִּי־תֹאמַר לֹא תְשׁוּרֶנּוּ
דִּין לְפָנָיו וּתְחוֹלֵל לוֹ:
15 וְעַתָּה כִּי־אַיִן פָּקַד אַפּוֹ
וְלֹא־יָדַע בַּפַּשׁ מְאֹד:

a-a Meaning of Heb. uncertain.

16Hence Job mouths empty words,
And piles up words without knowledge.

16 וְאָיֹּוב הֶבֶל יִפְצֶה־פִּיהוּ
בִּבְלִי־דַעַת מִלִּין יַכְבִּר: פ

36 Then Elihu spoke once more.

לו 1 וַיֹּסֶף אֱלִיהוּא וַיֹּאמַר:

2Wait a little and let me hold forth;
There is still more to say for God.
3I will make my opinions widely known;
I will justify my Maker.
4In truth, my words are not false;
A man of sound opinions is before you.

2 כַּתַּר־לִי זְעֵיר וַאֲחַוֶּךָּ
כִּי עוֹד לֶאֱלוֹהַּ מִלִּים:
3 אֶשָּׂא דֵעִי לְמֵרָחוֹק
וּלְפֹעֲלִי אֶתֵּן־צֶדֶק:
4 כִּי־אָמְנָם לֹא־שֶׁקֶר מִלָּי
תְּמִים דֵּעוֹת עִמָּךְ:

5See, God is mighty; He is not contemptuous;
He is mighty in strength and mind.
6He does not let the wicked live;
He grants justice to the lowly.
7He does not withdraw His eyes from the
    righteous;
With kings on thrones
He seats them forever, and they are exalted.
8If they are bound in shackles
And caught in trammels of affliction,
9He declares to them what they have done,
And that their transgressions are excessive;
10He opens their understanding by discipline,
And orders them back from mischief.
11If they will serve obediently,
They shall spend their days in happiness,
Their years in delight.
12But if they are not obedient,
They shall perish by the sword,
Die for lack of understanding.
13But the impious in heart become enraged;
They do not cry for help when He afflicts
    them.
14They die in their youth;
[Expire] among the depraved.
15He rescues the lowly from their affliction,

5 הֶן־אֵל כַּבִּיר וְלֹא יִמְאָס
כַּבִּיר כֹּחַ לֵב:
6 לֹא־יְחַיֶּה רָשָׁע
וּמִשְׁפַּט עֲנִיִּים יִתֵּן:
7 לֹא־יִגְרַע מִצַּדִּיק עֵינָיו
וְאֶת־מְלָכִים לַכִּסֵּא
וַיֹּשִׁיבֵם לָנֶצַח וַיִּגְבָּהוּ:
8 וְאִם־אֲסוּרִים בַּזִּקִּים
יִלָּכְדוּן בְּחַבְלֵי־עֹנִי:
9 וַיַּגֵּד לָהֶם פָּעֳלָם
וּפִשְׁעֵיהֶם כִּי יִתְגַּבָּרוּ:
10 וַיִּגֶל אָזְנָם לַמּוּסָר
וַיֹּאמֶר כִּי־יְשֻׁבוּן מֵאָוֶן:
11 אִם־יִשְׁמְעוּ וְיַעֲבֹדוּ
יְכַלּוּ יְמֵיהֶם בַּטּוֹב
וּשְׁנֵיהֶם בַּנְּעִימִים:
12 וְאִם־לֹא יִשְׁמְעוּ
בְּשֶׁלַח יַעֲבֹרוּ
וְיִגְוְעוּ בִּבְלִי־דָעַת:
13 וְחַנְפֵי־לֵב יָשִׂימוּ אָף
לֹא יְשַׁוְּעוּ כִּי אֲסָרָם:
14 תָּמֹת בַּנֹּעַר נַפְשָׁם
וְחַיָּתָם בַּקְּדֵשִׁים:
15 יְחַלֵּץ עָנִי בְעָנְיוֹ

And opens their understanding through distress.

16Indeed, He draws you away from the brink
of distress

To a broad place where there is no constraint;
Your table is laid out with rich food.

17You are obsessed with the case of the wicked
man,

But the justice of the case will be upheld.

18Let anger at his affluence not mislead you;
Let much bribery not turn you aside.

19a-Will your limitless wealth avail you,-a
All your powerful efforts?

20Do not long for the night
When peoples vanish where they are.

21Beware! Do not turn to mischief;
Because of that you have been tried by
affliction.

22See, God is beyond reach in His power;
Who governs like Him?

23Who ever reproached Him for His conduct?
Who ever said, "You have done wrong"?

24Remember, then, to magnify His work,
Of which men have sung,

25Which all men have beheld,
Men have seen, from a distance.

26See, God is greater than we can know;
The number of His years cannot be counted.

27He forms the droplets of water,
Which cluster into rain, from His mist.

28The skies rain;
They pour down on all mankind.

29Can one, indeed, contemplate the expanse
of clouds,

The thunderings from His pavilion?

30See, He spreads His lightning over it;
It fills the bed of the sea.

31By these things He controls peoples;
He gives food in abundance.

וַיִּ֖גֶל בַּלַּ֣חַץ אָזְנָֽם׃

16 וְאַ֤ף הֲסִֽיתְךָ֨ ׀ מִפִּי־צָ֗ר
רַ֭חַב לֹא־מוּצָ֣ק תַּחְתֶּ֑יהָ
וְנַ֥חַת שֻׁ֝לְחָנְךָ֗ מָ֣לֵא דָֽשֶׁן׃

17 וְדִין־רָשָׁ֥ע מָלֵ֑אתָ
דִּ֖ין וּמִשְׁפָּ֣ט יִתְמֹֽכוּ׃

18 כִּֽי־חֵ֭מָה פֶּן־יְסִֽיתְךָ֣ בְסָ֑פֶק
וְרָב־כֹּ֝֗פֶר אַל־יַטֶּֽךָּ׃

19 הֲיַעֲרֹ֣ךְ שׁ֭וּעֲךָ לֹ֣א בְצָ֑ר
וְ֝כֹ֗ל מַאֲמַצֵּי־כֹֽחַ׃

20 אַל־תִּשְׁאַ֥ף הַלָּ֑יְלָה
לַעֲל֖וֹת עַמִּ֣ים תַּחְתָּֽם׃

21 הִ֭שָּׁמֶר אַל־תֵּ֣פֶן אֶל־אָ֑וֶן
כִּֽי־עַל־זֶ֝֗ה בָּחַ֥רְתָּ מֵעֹֽנִי׃

22 הֶן־אֵ֭ל יַשְׂגִּ֣יב בְּכֹח֑וֹ
מִ֖י כָמֹ֣הוּ מוֹרֶֽה׃

23 מִֽי־פָקַ֣ד עָלָ֣יו דַּרְכּ֑וֹ
וּמִֽי־אָ֝מַ֗ר פָּעַ֥לְתָּ עַוְלָֽה׃

24 זְ֭כֹר כִּֽי־תַשְׂגִּ֣יא פׇעֳל֑וֹ
אֲשֶׁ֖ר שֹׁרְר֣וּ אֲנָשִֽׁים׃

25 כׇּל־אָדָ֥ם חָֽזוּ־ב֑וֹ
אֱ֝נ֗וֹשׁ יַבִּ֥יט מֵרָחֽוֹק׃

26 הֶן־אֵ֣ל שַׂ֭גִּיא וְלֹ֣א נֵדָ֑ע
מִסְפַּ֖ר שָׁנָ֣יו וְלֹא־חֵֽקֶר׃

27 כִּ֤י יְגָרַ֥ע נִטְפֵי־מָ֑יִם
יָזֹ֖קּוּ מָטָ֣ר לְאֵדֽוֹ׃

28 אֲשֶׁ֣ר־יִזְּל֣וּ שְׁחָקִ֑ים
יִ֝רְעֲפ֗וּ עֲלֵ֤י ׀ אָדָ֥ם רָֽב׃

29 אַ֣ף אִם־יָ֭בִין מִפְרְשֵׂי־עָ֑ב
תְּ֝שֻׁא֗וֹת סֻכָּתֽוֹ׃

30 הֵן־פָּרַ֣שׂ עָלָ֣יו אוֹר֑וֹ
וְשׇׁרְשֵׁ֖י הַיָּ֣ם כִּסָּֽה׃

31 כִּי־בָ֭ם יָדִ֣ין עַמִּ֑ים
יִתֶּן־אֹ֥כֶל לְמַכְבִּֽיר׃

---

a-a Meaning of Heb. uncertain.

32Lightning fills His hands;
He orders it to hit the mark.
33Its noise tells of Him.
a-The kindling of anger against iniquity.-a

37 Because of this, too, my heart quakes,
And leaps from its place.
2Just listen to the noise of His rumbling,
To the sound that comes out of His mouth.
3He lets it loose beneath the entire heavens—
His lightning, to the ends of the earth.
4After it, He lets out a roar;
He thunders in His majestic voice.
No one can find a trace of it by the time His
voice is heard.
5God thunders marvelously with His voice;
He works wonders that we cannot understand.
6He commands the snow, "Fall to the
ground!"
And the downpour of rain, His mighty downpour of rain,
7Is as a sign on every man's hand,
That all men may know His doings.
8Then the beast enters its lair,
And remains in its den.
9The storm wind comes from its chamber,
And the cold from the constellations.
10By the breath of God ice is formed,
And the expanse of water becomes solid.
11He also loads the clouds with moisture
And scatters His lightning-clouds.
12a-He keeps turning events by His stratagems,-a
That they might accomplish all that He commands them
Throughout the inhabited earth,
13Causing each of them to happen to His land,
Whether as a scourge or as a blessing.

עַל־כַּפַּיִם כִּסָּה־אוֹר 32
וַיְצַו עָלֶיהָ בְמַפְגִּיעַ:
יַגִּיד עָלָיו רֵעוֹ 33
מִקְנֶה אַף עַל־עוֹלֶה:

לז אַף־לְזֹאת יֶחֱרַד לִבִּי
וְיִתַּר מִמְּקוֹמוֹ:
שִׁמְעוּ שָׁמוֹעַ בְּרֹגֶז קֹלוֹ 2
וְהֶגֶה מִפִּיו יֵצֵא:
תַּחַת־כָּל־הַשָּׁמַיִם יִשְׁרֵהוּ 3
וְאוֹרוֹ עַל־כַּנְפוֹת הָאָרֶץ:
אַחֲרָיו ׀ יִשְׁאַג־קוֹל 4
יַרְעֵם בְּקוֹל גְּאוֹנוֹ
וְלֹא יְעַקְּבֵם כִּי־יִשָּׁמַע קוֹלוֹ:
יַרְעֵם אֵל בְּקוֹלוֹ נִפְלָאוֹת 5
עֹשֶׂה גְדֹלוֹת וְלֹא נֵדָע:
כִּי לַשֶּׁלֶג ׀ יֹאמַר הֱוֵא אָרֶץ וְגֶשֶׁם 6
מָטָר
וְגֶשֶׁם מִטְרוֹת עֻזּוֹ:
בְּיַד־כָּל־אָדָם יַחְתּוֹם 7
לָדַעַת כָּל־אַנְשֵׁי מַעֲשֵׂהוּ:
וַתָּבֹא חַיָּה בְמוֹ־אָרֶב 8
וּבִמְעוֹנֹתֶיהָ תִשְׁכֹּן:
מִן־הַחֶדֶר תָּבוֹא סוּפָה 9
וּמִמְּזָרִים קָרָה:
מִנִּשְׁמַת־אֵל יִתֶּן־קָרַח 10
וְרֹחַב מַיִם בְּמוּצָק:
אַף־בְּרִי יַטְרִיחַ עָב 11
יָפִיץ עֲנַן אוֹרוֹ:
וְהוּא מְסִבּוֹת ׀ מִתְהַפֵּךְ בְּתַחְבּוּלֹתוֹ 12
בְּתַחְבּוּלֹתָיו
לְפָעֳלָם כֹּל אֲשֶׁר יְצַוֵּם ׀
עַל־פְּנֵי תֵבֵל אָרְצָה:
אִם־לְשֵׁבֶט אִם־לְאַרְצוֹ 13
אִם־לְחֶסֶד יַמְצִאֵהוּ:

a-a Meaning of Heb. uncertain.

¹⁴Give ear to this, Job;
Stop to consider the marvels of God.
¹⁵Do you know what charge God lays upon
them
When His lightning-clouds shine?
¹⁶Do you know the marvels worked upon the
expanse of clouds
By Him whose understanding is perfect,
¹⁷^a-Why your clothes become hot-^a
When the land is becalmed by the south wind?
¹⁸Can you help him stretch out the heavens,
Firm as a mirror of cast metal?
¹⁹Inform us, then, what we may say to Him;
We cannot argue because [we are in] dark-
ness.
²⁰Is anything conveyed to Him when I speak?
Can a man say anything when he is confused?
²¹Now, then, one cannot see the sun,
Though it be bright in the heavens,
Until the wind comes and clears them [of
clouds].
²²By the north wind the golden rays emerge;
The splendor about God is awesome.
²³Shaddai—we cannot attain to Him;
He is great in power and justice
And abundant in righteousness; He does not
torment.
²⁴Therefore, men are in awe of Him
Whom none of the wise can perceive.

38 Then the LORD replied to Job out of the
tempest and said:

²Who is this who darkens counsel,
Speaking without knowledge?
³Gird your loins like a man;
I will ask and you will inform Me.

14 הַאֲזִינָה זֹּאת אִיּוֹב
עֲמֹד וְהִתְבּוֹנֵן ׀ נִפְלְאוֹת אֵל:
15 הֲתֵדַע בְּשׂוּם־אֱלוֹהַּ עֲלֵיהֶם
וְהוֹפִיעַ אוֹר עֲנָנוֹ:
16 הֲתֵדַע עַל־מִפְלְשֵׂי־עָב
מִפְלְאוֹת תְּמִים דֵּעִים:
17 אֲשֶׁר־בְּגָדֶיךָ חַמִּים
בְּהַשְׁקִט אֶרֶץ מִדָּרוֹם:
18 תַּרְקִיעַ עִמּוֹ לִשְׁחָקִים
חֲזָקִים כִּרְאִי מוּצָק:
19 הוֹדִיעֵנוּ מַה־נֹּאמַר לוֹ
לֹא־נַעֲרֹךְ מִפְּנֵי־חֹשֶׁךְ:
20 הַיְסֻפַּר־לוֹ כִּי אֲדַבֵּר
אִם־אָמַר אִישׁ כִּי יְבֻלָּע:
21 וְעַתָּה ׀ לֹא רָאוּ אוֹר
בָּהִיר הוּא בַּשְּׁחָקִים
וְרוּחַ עָבְרָה וַתְּטַהֲרֵם:
22 מִצָּפוֹן זָהָב יֶאֱתֶה
עַל־אֱלוֹהַּ נוֹרָא הוֹד:
23 שַׁדַּי לֹא־מְצָאנֻהוּ
שַׂגִּיא־כֹחַ וּמִשְׁפָּט
וְרֹב־צְדָקָה לֹא יְעַנֶּה:
24 לָכֵן יְרֵאוּהוּ אֲנָשִׁים
לֹא־יִרְאֶה כָּל־חַכְמֵי־לֵב: פ

לח וַיַּעַן־יְהוָה אֶת־אִיּוֹב מנהסערה
מִן ׀ הַסְּעָרָה וַיֹּאמַר:
2 מִי זֶה ׀ מַחְשִׁיךְ עֵצָה
בְמִלִּין בְּלִי־דָעַת:
3 אֱזָר־נָא כְגֶבֶר חֲלָצֶיךָ
וְאֶשְׁאָלְךָ וְהוֹדִיעֵנִי:

⁴Where were you when I laid the earth's foun-
   dations?
Speak if you have understanding.
⁵Do you know who fixed its dimensions
Or who measured it with a line?
⁶Onto what were its bases sunk?
Who set its cornerstone
⁷When the morning stars sang together
And all the divine beings shouted for joy?

⁸Who closed the sea behind doors
When it gushed forth out of the womb,
⁹When I clothed it in clouds,
Swaddled it in dense clouds,
¹⁰When I made breakers My limit for it,
And set up its bar and doors,
¹¹And said, "You may come so far and no far-
   ther;
Here your surging waves will stop"?

¹²Have you ever commanded the day to
   break,
Assigned the dawn its place,
¹³So that it seizes the corners of the earth
And shakes the wicked out of it?
¹⁴It changes like clay under the seal
Till [its hues] are fixed like those of a garment.
¹⁵Their light is withheld from the wicked,
And the upraised arm is broken.

¹⁶Have you penetrated to the sources of the
   sea,
Or walked in the recesses of the deep?
¹⁷Have the gates of death been disclosed to
   you?
Have you seen the gates of deep darkness?
¹⁸Have you surveyed the expanses of the
   earth?
If you know of these—tell Me.

אֵיפֹ֣ה הָ֭יִיתָ בְּיָסְדִי־אָ֑רֶץ 4
הַ֝גֵּ֗ד אִם־יָדַ֥עְתָּ בִינָֽה׃
מִי־שָׂ֣ם מְ֭מַדֶּיהָ כִּ֣י תֵדָ֑ע 5
א֖וֹ מִֽי־נָטָ֣ה עָלֶ֣יהָ קָּֽו׃
עַל־מָ֭ה אֲדָנֶ֣יהָ הָטְבָּ֑עוּ 6
א֥וֹ מִֽי־יָ֝רָ֗ה אֶ֣בֶן פִּנָּתָֽהּ׃
בְּרָן־יַ֭חַד כּ֣וֹכְבֵי בֹ֑קֶר 7
וַ֝יָּרִ֗יעוּ כָּל־בְּנֵ֥י אֱלֹהִֽים׃
וַיָּ֣סֶךְ בִּדְלָתַ֣יִם יָ֑ם 8
בְּ֝גִיח֗וֹ מֵרֶ֥חֶם יֵצֵֽא׃
בְּשׂוּמִ֣י עָנָ֣ן לְבֻשׁ֑וֹ 9
וַ֝עֲרָפֶ֗ל חֲתֻלָּתֽוֹ׃
וָאֶשְׁבֹּ֣ר עָלָ֣יו חֻקִּ֑י 10
וָ֝אָשִׂ֗ים בְּרִ֥יחַ וּדְלָתָֽיִם׃
וָאֹמַ֗ר עַד־פֹּ֣ה תָ֭בוֹא וְלֹ֣א תֹסִ֑יף 11
וּפֹא*־יָ֝שִׁ֗ית בִּגְא֥וֹן גַּלֶּֽיךָ׃
הַֽ֭מִיָּמֶיךָ צִוִּ֣יתָ בֹּ֑קֶר 12
*יִדַּ֖עְתָּה שַׁ֣חַר*הַשָּׁ֣חַר מְקֹמֽוֹ׃
לֶ֭אֱחֹז בְּכַנְפ֣וֹת הָאָ֑רֶץ 13
וְיִנָּעֲר֖וּ רְשָׁעִ֣ים* מִמֶּֽנָּה׃
תִּ֭תְהַפֵּךְ כְּחֹ֣מֶר חוֹתָ֑ם 14
וְ֝יִֽתְיַצְּב֗וּ כְּמ֣וֹ לְבֽוּשׁ׃
וְיִמָּנַ֣ע מֵרְשָׁעִ֣ים* אוֹרָ֑ם 15
וּזְר֥וֹעַ רָ֝מָ֗ה תִּשָּׁבֵֽר׃
הֲ֭בָאתָ עַד־נִבְכֵי־יָ֑ם 16
וּבְחֵ֥קֶר תְּ֝ה֗וֹם הִתְהַלָּֽכְתָּ׃
הֲנִגְל֣וּ לְ֭ךָ שַׁעֲרֵי־מָ֑וֶת 17
וְשַׁעֲרֵ֖י צַלְמָ֣וֶת תִּרְאֶֽה׃
הִ֭תְבֹּנַנְתָּ עַד־רַחֲבֵי־אָ֑רֶץ 18
הַ֝גֵּ֗ד אִם־יָדַ֥עְתָּ כֻלָּֽהּ׃

¹⁹Which path leads to where light dwells,
And where is the place of darkness,
²⁰That you may take it to its domain
And know the way to its home?
²¹Surely you know, for you were born then,
And the number of your years is many!

²²Have you penetrated the vaults of snow,
Seen the vaults of hail,
²³Which I have put aside for a time of adversity,
For a day of war and battle?
²⁴By what path is the west wind^a dispersed,
The east wind scattered over the earth?
²⁵Who cut a channel for the torrents
And a path for the thunderstorms,
²⁶To rain down on uninhabited land,
On the wilderness where no man is,
²⁷To saturate the desolate wasteland,
And make the crop of grass sprout forth?
²⁸Does the rain have a father?
Who begot the dewdrops?
²⁹From whose belly came forth the ice?
Who gave birth to the frost of heaven?
³⁰Water congeals like stone,
And the surface of the deep compacts.

³¹Can you tie cords to Pleiades
Or undo the reins of Orion?
³²Can you lead out Mazzaroth^b in its season,
Conduct the Bear with her sons?
³³Do you know the laws of heaven
Or impose its authority on earth?

³⁴Can you send up an order to the clouds
For an abundance of water to cover you?
³⁵Can you dispatch the lightning on a mission
And have it answer you, "I am ready"?
³⁶Who put wisdom in the hidden parts?

---

^a *As Aramaic 'urya.*
^b *Evidently a constellation.*

19 אֵי־זֶה הַדֶּרֶךְ יִשְׁכָּן־אוֹר
וְחֹשֶׁךְ אֵי־זֶה מְקֹמוֹ:
20 כִּי תִקָּחֶנּוּ אֶל־גְּבוּלוֹ
וְכִי־תָבִין נְתִיבוֹת בֵּיתוֹ:
21 יָדַעְתָּ כִּי־אָז תִּוָּלֵד
וּמִסְפַּר יָמֶיךָ רַבִּים:

22 הֲבָאתָ אֶל־אֹצְרוֹת שָׁלֶג
וְאֹצְרוֹת בָּרָד תִּרְאֶה:
23 אֲשֶׁר־חָשַׂכְתִּי לְעֶת־צָר
לְיוֹם קְרָב וּמִלְחָמָה:
24 אֵי־זֶה הַדֶּרֶךְ יֵחָלֶק אוֹר
יָפֵץ קָדִים עֲלֵי־אָרֶץ:
25 מִי־פִלַּג לַשֶּׁטֶף תְּעָלָה
וְדֶרֶךְ לַחֲזִיז קֹלוֹת:
26 לְהַמְטִיר עַל־אֶרֶץ לֹא־אִישׁ
מִדְבָּר לֹא־אָדָם בּוֹ:
27 לְהַשְׂבִּיעַ שֹׁאָה וּמְשֹׁאָה
וּלְהַצְמִיחַ מֹצָא דֶשֶׁא:
28 הֲיֵשׁ־לַמָּטָר אָב
אוֹ מִי־הוֹלִיד אֶגְלֵי־טָל:
29 מִבֶּטֶן מִי יָצָא הַקָּרַח
וּכְפֹר שָׁמַיִם מִי יְלָדוֹ:
30 כָּאֶבֶן מַיִם יִתְחַבָּאוּ
וּפְנֵי תְהוֹם יִתְלַכָּדוּ:

31 הַתְקַשֵּׁר מַעֲדַנּוֹת כִּימָה
אוֹ־מֹשְׁכוֹת כְּסִיל תְּפַתֵּחַ:
32 הֲתֹצִיא מַזָּרוֹת בְּעִתּוֹ
וְעַיִשׁ עַל־בָּנֶיהָ תַנְחֵם:
33 הֲיָדַעְתָּ חֻקּוֹת שָׁמָיִם
אִם־תָּשִׂים מִשְׁטָרוֹ בָאָרֶץ:

34 הֲתָרִים לָעָב קוֹלֶךָ
וְשִׁפְעַת־מַיִם תְּכַסֶּךָּ:
35 הַתְשַׁלַּח בְּרָקִים וְיֵלֵכוּ
וְיֹאמְרוּ לְךָ הִנֵּנוּ:
36 מִי־שָׁת בַּטֻּחוֹת חָכְמָה

Who gave understanding to the mind?[c]

³⁷Who is wise enough to give an account of
the heavens?
Who can tilt the bottles of the sky,
³⁸Whereupon the earth melts into a mass,
And its clods stick together.

³⁹Can you hunt prey for the lion,
And satisfy the appetite of the king of beasts?
⁴⁰They crouch in their dens,
Lie in ambush in their lairs.
⁴¹Who provides food for the raven
When his young cry out to God
And wander about without food?

39

Do you know the season when the
mountain goats give birth?
Can you mark the time when the hinds calve?
²Can you count the months they must complete?
Do you know the season they give birth,
³When they couch to bring forth their offspring,
To deliver their young?
⁴Their young are healthy; they grow up in the
open;
They leave and return no more.

⁵Who sets the wild ass free?
Who loosens the bonds of the onager,
⁶Whose home I have made the wilderness,
The salt land his dwelling-place?
⁷He scoffs at the tumult of the city,
Does not hear the shouts of the driver.
⁸He roams the hills for his pasture;
He searches for any green thing.

⁹Would the wild ox agree to serve you?
Would he spend the night at your crib?

אוֹ מִי־נָתַן לַשֶּׂכְוִי בִינָה:

³⁷ מִי־יְסַפֵּר שְׁחָקִים בְּחָכְמָה
וְנִבְלֵי שָׁמַיִם מִי יַשְׁכִּיב:
³⁸ בְּצֶקֶת עָפָר לַמּוּצָק
וּרְגָבִים יְדֻבָּקוּ:

³⁹ הֲתָצוּד לְלָבִיא טָרֶף
וְחַיַּת כְּפִירִים תְּמַלֵּא:
⁴⁰ כִּי־יָשֹׁחוּ בַמְּעוֹנוֹת
יֵשְׁבוּ בַסֻּכָּה לְמוֹ־אָרֶב:
⁴¹ מִי יָכִין לָעֹרֵב צֵידוֹ
כִּי־יְלָדָיו אֶל־אֵל יְשַׁוֵּעוּ
יִתְעוּ לִבְלִי־אֹכֶל:

לט הֲיָדַעְתָּ עֵת לֶדֶת יַעֲלֵי־סָלַע
חֹלֵל אַיָּלוֹת תִּשְׁמֹר:
² תִּסְפֹּר יְרָחִים תְּמַלֶּאנָה
וְיָדַעְתָּ עֵת לִדְתָּנָה:
³ תִּכְרַעְנָה יַלְדֵיהֶן תְּפַלַּחְנָה
חֶבְלֵיהֶם תְּשַׁלַּחְנָה:
⁴ יַחְלְמוּ בְנֵיהֶם יִרְבּוּ בַבָּר
יָצְאוּ וְלֹא־שָׁבוּ לָמוֹ:

⁵ מִי־שִׁלַּח פֶּרֶא חָפְשִׁי
וּמֹסְרוֹת עָרוֹד מִי פִתֵּחַ:
⁶ אֲשֶׁר־שַׂמְתִּי עֲרָבָה בֵיתוֹ
וּמִשְׁכְּנוֹתָיו מְלֵחָה:
⁷ יִשְׂחַק לַהֲמוֹן קִרְיָה
תְּשֻׁאוֹת נוֹגֵשׂ לֹא יִשְׁמָע:
⁸ יְתוּר הָרִים מִרְעֵהוּ
וְאַחַר כָּל־יָרוֹק יִדְרוֹשׁ:

⁹ הֲיֹאבֶה רֵּים* עָבְדֶךָ
אִם־יָלִין עַל־אֲבוּסֶךָ:

v. 9. ר' דְּגוּשָׁה, חָסֵר א'

---

c   Or "rooster"; meaning of Heb. uncertain.

¹⁰Can you hold the wild ox by ropes to the furrow?
Would he plow up the valleys behind you?
¹¹Would you rely on his great strength
And leave your toil to him?
¹²Would you trust him to bring in the seed
And gather it in from your threshing floor?

¹³The wing of the ostrich beats joyously;
Are her pinions and plumage like the stork's?
¹⁴She leaves her eggs on the ground,
Letting them warm in the dirt,
¹⁵Forgetting they may be crushed underfoot,
Or trampled by a wild beast.
¹⁶Her young are cruelly abandoned as if they were not hers;
Her labor is in vain for lack of concern.
¹⁷For God deprived her of wisdom,
Gave her no share of understanding,
¹⁸Else she would soar on high,
Scoffing at the horse and its rider.

¹⁹Do you give the horse his strength?
Do you clothe his neck with a mane?
²⁰Do you make him quiver like locusts,
His majestic snorting [spreading] terror?
²¹He[a] paws with force, he runs with vigor,
Charging into battle.
²²He scoffs at fear; he cannot be frightened;
He does not recoil from the sword.
²³A quiverful of arrows whizzes by him,
And the flashing spear and the javelin.
²⁴Trembling with excitement, he swallows[b] the land;
He does not turn aside at the blast of the trumpet.
²⁵As the trumpet sounds, he says, "Aha!"
From afar he smells the battle,
The roaring and shouting of the officers.

הֲתִקְשָׁר־רֵים* בְּתֶלֶם עֲבֹתֹו 10
אִם־יְשַׂדֵּד עֲמָקִים אַחֲרֶיךָ:
הֲתִבְטַח־בֹּו כִּי־רַב כֹּחֹו 11
וְתַעֲזֹב אֵלָיו יְגִיעֶךָ:
הֲתַאֲמִין בֹּו כִּי־יָשִׁוב זַרְעֶךָ 12
וְגָרְנְךָ יֶאֱסֹף:

כְּנַף־רְנָנִים נֶעֱלָסָה 13
אִם־אֶבְרָה חֲסִידָה וְנֹצָה:
כִּי־תַעֲזֹב לָאָרֶץ בֵּצֶיהָ 14
וְעַל־עָפָר תְּחַמֵּם:
וַתִּשְׁכַּח כִּי־רֶגֶל תְּזוּרֶהָ 15
וְחַיַּת הַשָּׂדֶה תְּדוּשֶׁהָ:
הִקְשִׁיחַ בָּנֶיהָ לְּלֹא־לָהּ 16
לְרִיק יְגִיעָהּ בְּלִי־פָחַד:
כִּי־הִשָּׁהּ אֱלֹוהַּ חָכְמָה 17
וְלֹא־חָלַק לָהּ בַּבִּינָה:
כָּעֵת בַּמָּרֹום תַּמְרִיא 18
תִּשְׂחַק לַסּוּס וּלְרֹכְבֹו:

הֲתִתֵּן לַסּוּס גְּבוּרָה 19
הֲתַלְבִּישׁ צַוָּארֹו רַעְמָה:
הֲתַרְעִישֶׁנּוּ כָּאַרְבֶּה 20
הֹוד נַחְרֹו אֵימָה:
יַחְפְּרוּ בָעֵמֶק וְיָשִׂישׂ בְּכֹחַ 21
יֵצֵא לִקְרַאת־נָשֶׁק:
יִשְׂחַק לְפַחַד וְלֹא יֵחָת 22
וְלֹא־יָשׁוּב מִפְּנֵי־חָרֶב:
עָלָיו תִּרְנֶה אַשְׁפָּה 23
לַהַב חֲנִית וְכִידֹון:
בְּרַעַשׁ וְרֹגֶז יְגַמֶּא־אָרֶץ 24
וְלֹא־יַאֲמִין כִּי־קֹול שֹׁופָר:
בְּדֵי שֹׁפָר ׀ יֹאמַר הֶאָח 25
וּמֵרָחֹוק יָרִיחַ מִלְחָמָה
רַעַם שָׂרִים וּתְרוּעָה:

---

a *Lit. "They ..."*
b *Or "digs up."*

26Is it by your wisdom that the hawk grows
   pinions,
Spreads his wings to the south?

27Does the eagle soar at your command,
Building his nest high,

28Dwelling in the rock,
Lodging upon the fastness of a jutting rock?

29From there he spies out his food;
From afar his eyes see it.

30His young gulp blood;
Where the slain are, there is he.

40 The LORD said in reply to Job.

2a-Shall one who should be disciplined complain against Shaddai?-a
He who arraigns God must respond.

3Job said in reply to the LORD:

4See, I am of small worth; what can I answer
   You?
I clap my hand to my mouth.

5I have spoken once, and will not reply;
Twice, and will do so no more.

6Then the LORD replied to Job out of the tempest and said:

7Gird your loins like a man;
I will ask, and you will inform Me.

8Would you impugn My justice?
Would you condemn Me that you may be
   right?

9Have you an arm like God's?
Can you thunder with a voice like His?

10Deck yourself now with grandeur and eminence;
Clothe yourself in glory and majesty.

26הֲמִבִּינָתְךָ֫ יַאֲבֶר־נֵ֑ץ
יִפְרֹ֥שׂ כְּנָפָ֣יו לְתֵימָֽן׃

27אִם־עַל־פִּ֭יךָ יַגְבִּ֣יהַּ נָ֑שֶׁר
וְ֝כִ֗י יָרִ֥ים קִנּֽוֹ׃

28סֶ֣לַע יִ֭שְׁכֹּן וְיִתְלֹנָ֑ן
עַֽל־שֶׁן־סֶ֝֗לַע וּמְצוּדָֽה׃

29מִשָּׁ֥ם חָֽפַר־אֹ֑כֶל
לְ֝מֵרָח֗וֹק עֵינָ֥יו יַבִּֽיטוּ׃

30וְאֶפְרֹחָ֥ו יְעַלְעוּ־דָ֑ם
וּבַאֲשֶׁ֥ר חֲ֝לָלִ֗ים שָׁ֣ם הֽוּא׃ פ

מ וַיַּ֖עַן יְהֹוָ֥ה אֶת־אִיּ֗וֹב וַיֹּאמַֽר׃

2הֲ֭רֹב עִם־שַׁדַּ֣י יִסּ֑וֹר
מוֹכִ֖יחַ אֱל֣וֹהַּ יַעֲנֶֽנָּה׃ פ

3וַיַּ֖עַן אִיּ֥וֹב אֶת־יְהֹוָ֗ה וַיֹּאמַֽר׃

4הֵ֣ן קַ֭לֹּתִי מָ֣ה אֲשִׁיבֶ֑ךָּ
יָ֝דִ֗י שַׂ֣מְתִּי לְמוֹ־פִֽי׃

5אַחַ֣ת דִּ֭בַּרְתִּי וְלֹ֣א אֶֽעֱנֶ֑ה
וּ֝שְׁתַּ֗יִם וְלֹ֣א אוֹסִֽיף׃ פ

6וַיַּֽעַן־יְהֹוָ֣ה אֶת־אִ֭יּוֹב מנסערה מִן ׀
סְעָרָ֣ה וַיֹּאמַֽר׃

7אֱזׇר־נָ֣א כְגֶ֣בֶר חֲלָצֶ֑יךָ
אֶ֝שְׁאָלְךָ֗ וְהוֹדִיעֵֽנִי׃

8הַ֭אַף תָּפֵ֣ר מִשְׁפָּטִ֑י
תַּ֝רְשִׁיעֵ֗נִי לְמַ֣עַן תִּצְדָּֽק׃

9וְאִם־זְר֖וֹעַ כָּאֵ֥ל ׀ לָ֑ךְ
וּ֝בְק֗וֹל כָּמֹ֥הוּ תַרְעֵֽם׃

10עֲדֵ֥ה נָ֣א גָא֣וֹן וָגֹ֑בַהּ
וְה֖וֹד וְהָדָ֣ר תִּלְבָּֽשׁ׃

---

¹¹Scatter wide your raging anger;
See every proud man and bring him low.
¹²See every proud man and humble him,
And bring them down where they stand.
¹³Bury them all in the earth;
Hide their faces in obscurity.
¹⁴Then even I would praise you
For the triumph your right hand won you.

¹⁵Take now behemoth, whom I made as I did
    you;
He eats grass, like the cattle.
¹⁶His strength is in his loins,
His might in the muscles of his belly.
^{17a}-He makes his tail stand up-^a like a cedar;
The sinews of his thighs are knit together.
¹⁸His bones are like tubes of bronze,
His limbs like iron rods.
¹⁹He is the first of God's works;
Only his Maker can draw the sword against
    him.
²⁰The mountains yield him produce,
Where all the beasts of the field play.
²¹He lies down beneath the lotuses,
In the cover of the swamp reeds.
²²The lotuses embower him with shade;
The willows of the brook surround him.
²³He can restrain the river from its rushing;
He is confident the stream^b will gush at his
    command.
²⁴Can he be taken by his eyes?
Can his nose be pierced by hooks?
²⁵Can you draw out Leviathan by a fishhook?
Can you press down his tongue by a rope?
²⁶Can you put a ring through his nose,
Or pierce his jaw with a barb?
²⁷Will he plead with you at length?
Will he speak soft words to you?

11 הָפֵץ עֶבְרוֹת אַפֶּךָ
וּרְאֵה כָל־גֵּאֶה וְהַשְׁפִּילֵהוּ׃
12 רְאֵה כָל־גֵּאֶה הַכְנִיעֵהוּ
וַהֲדֹךְ רְשָׁעִים תַּחְתָּם׃
13 טָמְנֵם בֶּעָפָר יָחַד
פְּנֵיהֶם חֲבֹשׁ בַּטָּמוּן׃
14 וְגַם־אֲנִי אוֹדֶךָּ
כִּי־תוֹשִׁעַ לְךָ יְמִינֶךָ׃

15 הִנֵּה־נָא בְהֵמוֹת אֲשֶׁר־עָשִׂיתִי עִמָּךְ
חָצִיר כַּבָּקָר יֹאכֵל׃
16 הִנֵּה־נָא כֹחוֹ בְמָתְנָיו
וְאֹנוֹ בִּשְׁרִירֵי בִּטְנוֹ׃
17 יַחְפֹּץ זְנָבוֹ כְמוֹ־אָרֶז
גִּידֵי פַחֲדוֹ פַחֲדָיו יְשֹׂרָגוּ׃
18 עֲצָמָיו אֲפִיקֵי נְחוּשָׁה
גְּרָמָיו כִּמְטִיל בַּרְזֶל׃
19 הוּא רֵאשִׁית דַּרְכֵי־אֵל
הָעֹשׂוֹ יַגֵּשׁ חַרְבּוֹ׃
20 כִּי־בוּל הָרִים יִשְׂאוּ־לוֹ
וְכָל־חַיַּת הַשָּׂדֶה יְשַׂחֲקוּ־שָׁם׃
21 תַּחַת־צֶאֱלִים יִשְׁכָּב
בְּסֵתֶר קָנֶה וּבִצָּה׃
22 יְסֻכֻּהוּ צֶאֱלִים צִלֲלוֹ
יְסֹבּוּהוּ עַרְבֵי־נָחַל׃
23 הֵן יַעֲשֹׁק נָהָר לֹא יַחְפּוֹז
יִבְטַח ׀ כִּי־יָגִיחַ יַרְדֵּן אֶל־פִּיהוּ׃
24 בְּעֵינָיו יִקָּחֶנּוּ
בְּמוֹקְשִׁים יִנְקָב־אָף׃
25 תִּמְשֹׁךְ לִוְיָתָן בְּחַכָּה
וּבְחֶבֶל תַּשְׁקִיעַ לְשֹׁנוֹ׃
26 הֲתָשִׂים אַגְמוֹן בְּאַפּוֹ
וּבְחוֹחַ תִּקּוֹב לֶחֱיוֹ׃
27 הֲיַרְבֶּה אֵלֶיךָ תַּחֲנוּנִים
אִם־יְדַבֵּר אֵלֶיךָ רַכּוֹת׃

b Lit. "Jordan."

28Will he make an agreement with you
To be taken as your lifelong slave?
29Will you play with him like a bird,
And tie him down for your girls?
30a-Shall traders traffic in him?-a
Will he be divided up among merchants?
31Can you fill his skin with darts
Or his head with fish-spears?
32Lay a hand on him,
And you will never think of battle again.

41 See, any hope [of capturing] him must
be disappointed;
One is prostrated by the very sight of him.
2There is no one so fierce as to rouse him;
Who then can stand up to Me?
3Whoever confronts Me I will requite,
For everything under the heavens is Mine.
4a-I will not be silent concerning him
Or the praise of his martial exploits.-a
5Who can uncover his outer garment?
Who can penetrate the folds of his jowls?
6Who can pry open the doors of his face?
His bared teeth strike terror.
7His protective scales are his pride,
Locked with a binding seal.
8One scale touches the other;
Not even a breath can enter between them.
9Each clings to each;
They are interlocked so they cannot be
parted.
10His sneezings flash lightning,
And his eyes are like the glimmerings of dawn.
11Firebrands stream from his mouth;
Fiery sparks escape.
12Out of his nostrils comes smoke
As from a steaming, boiling cauldron.

28 הֲיִכְרֹת בְּרִית עִמָּךְ
תִּקָּחֶנּוּ לְעֶבֶד עוֹלָם:
29 הַתְשַׂחֶק־בּוֹ כַּצִּפּוֹר
וְתִקְשְׁרֶנּוּ לְנַעֲרוֹתֶיךָ:
30 יִכְרוּ עָלָיו חַבָּרִים
יֶחֱצוּהוּ בֵּין כְּנַעֲנִים:
31 הַתְמַלֵּא בְשֻׂכּוֹת עוֹרוֹ
וּבְצִלְצַל דָּגִים רֹאשׁוֹ:
32 שִׂים־עָלָיו כַּפֶּךָ
זְכֹר מִלְחָמָה אַל־תּוֹסַף:

מא הֶן־תֹּחַלְתּוֹ נִכְזָבָה
הֲגַם אֶל־מַרְאָיו יֻטָל:
2 לֹא־אַכְזָר כִּי יְעוּרֶנּוּ
וּמִי הוּא לְפָנַי יִתְיַצָּב:
3 מִי הִקְדִּימַנִי וַאֲשַׁלֵּם
תַּחַת כָּל־הַשָּׁמַיִם לִי־הוּא:
4 לֹא־לוֹ־אַחֲרִישׁ בַּדָּיו
וּדְבַר־גְּבוּרוֹת וְחִין עֶרְכּוֹ:
5 מִי־גִלָּה פְּנֵי לְבוּשׁוֹ
בְּכֶפֶל רִסְנוֹ מִי יָבוֹא:
6 דַּלְתֵי פָנָיו מִי פִתֵּחַ
סְבִיבוֹת שִׁנָּיו אֵימָה:
7 גַּאֲוָה אֲפִיקֵי מָגִנִּים
סָגוּר חוֹתָם צָר:
8 אֶחָד בְּאֶחָד יִגַּשׁוּ
וְרוּחַ לֹא־יָבוֹא בֵינֵיהֶם:
9 אִישׁ־בְּאָחִיהוּ יְדֻבָּקוּ
יִתְלַכְּדוּ וְלֹא יִתְפָּרָדוּ:
10 עֲטִישֹׁתָיו תָּהֶל אוֹר
וְעֵינָיו כְּעַפְעַפֵּי־שָׁחַר:
11 מִפִּיו לַפִּידִים יַהֲלֹכוּ
כִּידוֹדֵי אֵשׁ יִתְמַלָּטוּ:
12 מִנְּחִירָיו יֵצֵא עָשָׁן
כְּדוּד נָפוּחַ וְאַגְמֹן:

a-a Meaning of Heb. uncertain.

13His breath ignites coals;
Flames blaze from his mouth.

14Strength resides in his neck;
Power leaps before him.

15The layers of his flesh stick together;
He is as though cast hard; he does not totter.

16His heart is cast hard as a stone,
Hard as the nether millstone.

17Divine beings are in dread as he rears up;
As he crashes down, they cringe.

18No sword that overtakes him can prevail,
Nor spear, nor missile, nor lance.

19He regards iron as straw,
Bronze, as rotted wood.

20No arrow can put him to flight;
Slingstones turn into stubble for him.

21Clubsᵃ are regarded as stubble;
He scoffs at the quivering javelin.

22His underpart is jagged shards;
It spreads a threshing-sledge on the mud.

23He makes the depths seethe like a cauldron;
He makes the sea [boil] like an ointment-pot.

24His wake is a luminous path;
He makes the deep seem white-haired.

25There is no one on land who can dominate
  him,
Made as he is without fear.

26He sees all that is haughty;
He is king over all proud beasts.

13 נַפְשׁוֹ גֶּחָלִים תְּלַהֵט
וְלַהַב מִפִּיו יֵצֵא:

14 בְּצַוָּארוֹ יָלִין עֹז
וּלְפָנָיו תָּדוּץ דְּאָבָה:

15 מַפְּלֵי בְשָׂרוֹ דָבֵקוּ
יָצוּק עָלָיו בַּל־יִמּוֹט:

16 לִבּוֹ יָצוּק כְּמוֹ־אָבֶן
וְיָצוּק כְּפֶלַח תַּחְתִּית:

17 מִשֵּׂתוֹ* יָגוּרוּ אֵלִים
מִשְּׁבָרִים יִתְחַטָּאוּ:

18 מַשִּׂיגֵהוּ חֶרֶב בְּלִי תָקוּם
חֲנִית מַסָּע וְשִׁרְיָה:

19 יַחְשֹׁב לְתֶבֶן בַּרְזֶל
לְעֵץ רִקָּבוֹן נְחוּשָׁה:

20 לֹא־יַבְרִיחֶנּוּ בֶן־קָשֶׁת
לְקַשׁ נֶהְפְּכוּ־לוֹ אַבְנֵי־קָלַע:

21 כְּקַשׁ נֶחְשְׁבוּ תוֹתָח
וְיִשְׂחַק לְרַעַשׁ כִּידוֹן:

22 תַּחְתָּיו חַדּוּדֵי חָרֶשׂ
יִרְפַּד חָרוּץ עֲלֵי־טִיט:

23 יַרְתִּיחַ כַּסִּיר מְצוּלָה
יָם יָשִׂים כַּמֶּרְקָחָה:

24 אַחֲרָיו יָאִיר נָתִיב
יַחְשֹׁב תְּהוֹם לְשֵׂיבָה:

25 אֵין־עַל־עָפָר מָשְׁלוֹ
הֶעָשׂוּ לִבְלִי־חָת:

26 אֶת־כָּל־גָּבֹהַּ יִרְאֶה
הוּא מֶלֶךְ עַל־כָּל־בְּנֵי־שָׁחַץ: ס

42 Job said in reply to the Lord:

2I know that You can do everything,
That nothing you propose is impossible for
  You.

3Who is this who obscures counsel without
  knowledge?

מב וַיַּעַן אִיּוֹב אֶת־יְהֹוָה וַיֹּאמַר:

2 יָדַעְתָּ כִּי־כֹל תּוּכָל
וְלֹא־יִבָּצֵר מִמְּךָ מְזִמָּה:

3 מִי זֶה | מַעְלִים עֵצָה בְּלִי דָעַת

v. 17. חסר א'

Indeed, I spoke without understanding
Of things beyond me, which I did not know.
4Hear now, and I will speak;
I will ask, and You will inform me.
5I had heard You with my ears,
But now I see You with my eyes;
6Therefore, I recant and relent,
Being but dust and ashes.

7After the LORD had spoken these words to Job, the LORD said to Eliphaz the Temanite, "I am incensed at you and your two friends, for you have not spoken the truth about Me as did My servant Job. 8Now take seven bulls and seven rams and go to My servant Job and sacrifice a burnt offering for yourselves. And let Job, My servant, pray for you; for to him I will show favor and not treat you vilely, since you have not spoken the truth about Me as did My servant Job." 9Eliphaz the Temanite and Bildad the Shuhite and Zophar the Naamathite went and did as the LORD had told them, and the LORD showed favor to Job. 10The LORD restored Job's fortunes when he prayed on behalf of his friends, and the LORD gave Job twice what he had before.

11All his brothers and sisters and all his former friends came to him and had a meal with him in his house. They consoled and comforted him for all the misfortune that the LORD had brought upon him. Each gave him one *kesitah*[a] and each one gold ring. 12Thus the LORD blessed the latter years of Job's life more than the former. He had fourteen thousand sheep, six thousand camels, one thousand yoke of oxen, and one thousand she-asses. 13He also had seven sons and three daughters. 14The first he named Jemimah, the second Keziah, and the third Keren-happuch.

לָכֵ֣ן הִ֭גַּדְתִּי וְלֹ֣א אָבִ֑ין
נִפְלָא֥וֹת מִ֝מֶּ֗נִּי וְלֹ֣א אֵדָֽע׃
4 שְֽׁמַֽע־נָ֭א וְאָנֹכִ֣י אֲדַבֵּ֑ר
אֶ֝שְׁאָלְךָ֗ וְהוֹדִיעֵֽנִי׃
5 לְשֵֽׁמַע־אֹ֥זֶן שְׁמַעְתִּ֑יךָ
וְ֝עַתָּ֗ה עֵינִ֥י רָאָֽתְךָ׃
6 עַל־כֵּ֭ן אֶמְאַ֣ס וְנִחַ֑מְתִּי
עַל־עָפָ֥ר וָאֵֽפֶר׃ פ

7 וַיְהִ֗י אַחַ֨ר דִּבֶּ֧ר יְהֹוָ֛ה אֶת־הַדְּבָרִ֥ים הָאֵ֖לֶּה אֶל־אִיּ֑וֹב וַיֹּ֨אמֶר יְהֹוָ֜ה אֶל־אֱלִיפַ֣ז הַתֵּֽימָנִ֗י חָרָ֨ה אַפִּ֤י בְךָ֙ וּבִשְׁנֵ֣י רֵעֶ֔יךָ כִּ֠י לֹ֣א דִבַּרְתֶּ֥ם אֵלַ֛י נְכוֹנָ֖ה כְּעַבְדִּ֥י אִיּֽוֹב׃ 8 וְעַתָּ֡ה קְחֽוּ־לָכֶ֣ם שִׁבְעָֽה־פָרִים֩ וְשִׁבְעָ֨ה אֵילִ֜ים וּלְכ֣וּ ׀ אֶל־עַבְדִּ֣י אִיּ֗וֹב וְהַעֲלִיתֶ֤ם עוֹלָה֙ בַּֽעַדְכֶ֔ם וְאִיּ֣וֹב עַבְדִּ֔י יִתְפַּלֵּ֖ל עֲלֵיכֶ֑ם כִּ֣י אִם־פָּנָ֞יו אֶשָּׂ֗א לְבִלְתִּ֞י עֲשׂ֤וֹת עִמָּכֶם֙ נְבָלָ֔ה כִּ֠י לֹ֣א דִבַּרְתֶּ֥ם אֵלַ֛י נְכוֹנָ֖ה כְּעַבְדִּ֥י אִיּֽוֹב׃ 9 וַיֵּלְכ֞וּ אֱלִיפַ֣ז הַתֵּֽימָנִ֗י וּבִלְדַּד֙ הַשּׁ֣וּחִ֔י צֹפַר֙ הַנַּֽעֲמָתִ֔י וַיַּֽעֲשׂ֔וּ כַּֽאֲשֶׁ֛ר דִּבֶּ֥ר אֲלֵיהֶ֖ם יְהֹוָ֑ה וַיִּשָּׂ֥א יְהֹוָ֖ה אֶת־פְּנֵ֥י אִיּֽוֹב׃ 10 וַֽיהֹוָ֗ה שָׁ֚ב אֶת־*שבית* אִיּ֔וֹב בְּהִֽתְפַּלְל֖וֹ בְּעַ֣ד רֵעֵ֑הוּ וַיֹּ֧סֶף יְהֹוָ֛ה אֶת־כָּל־אֲשֶׁ֥ר לְאִיּ֖וֹב לְמִשְׁנֶֽה׃ 11 וַיָּבֹ֣אוּ אֵ֠לָיו כָּל־אֶחָ֨יו וְכָל־אַחְיוֹתָ֜יו וְכָל־יֹֽדְעָ֣יו לְפָנִ֗ים וַיֹּֽאכְל֨וּ עִמּ֣וֹ לֶחֶם֮ בְּבֵיתוֹ֒ וַיָּנֻ֤דוּ ל֙וֹ֙ וַיְנַֽחֲמ֣וּ אֹת֔וֹ עַ֚ל כָּל־הָ֣רָעָ֔ה אֲשֶׁר־הֵבִ֥יא יְהֹוָ֖ה עָלָ֑יו וַיִּתְּנוּ־ל֗וֹ אִ֚ישׁ קְשִׂיטָ֣ה אֶחָ֔ת וְאִ֕ישׁ נֶ֥זֶם זָהָ֖ב אֶחָֽד׃ ס 12 וַֽיהֹוָ֗ה בֵּרַ֛ךְ אֶת־אַֽחֲרִ֥ית אִיּ֖וֹב מֵרֵֽאשִׁת֑וֹ וַֽיְהִי־ל֡וֹ אַרְבָּעָה֩ עָשָׂ֨ר אֶ֜לֶף צֹ֗אן וְשֵׁ֤שֶׁת אֲלָפִים֙ גְּמַלִּ֔ים וְאֶֽלֶף־צֶ֥מֶד בָּקָ֖ר וְאֶ֥לֶף אֲתוֹנֽוֹת׃ 13 וַֽיְהִי־ל֛וֹ שִׁבְעָ֥נָה בָנִ֖ים וְשָׁל֥וֹשׁ בָּנֽוֹת׃ 14 וַיִּקְרָ֞א שֵׁם־הָֽאַחַת֙ יְמִימָ֔ה וְשֵׁ֥ם הַשֵּׁנִ֖ית קְצִיעָ֑ה וְשֵׁ֥ם הַשְּׁלִישִׁ֖ית קֶ֥רֶן הַפּֽוּךְ׃ 15 וְלֹ֣א נִמְצָ֞א

---

a   *A unit of unknown value.*

15Nowhere in the land were women as beautiful as Job's daughters to be found. Their father gave them estates together with their brothers. 16Afterward, Job lived one hundred and forty years to see four generations of sons and grandsons. 17So Job died old and contented.

נָשִׁ֣ים יָפ֔וֹת כִּבְנ֥וֹת אִיּ֖וֹב בְּכָל־הָאָ֑רֶץ וַיִּתֵּ֨ן לָהֶ֧ם אֲבִיהֶ֛ם נַחֲלָ֖ה בְּת֥וֹךְ אֲחֵיהֶֽם׃ ס

16 וַיְחִ֤י אִיּוֹב֙ אַֽחֲרֵי־זֹ֔את מֵאָ֥ה וְאַרְבָּעִ֖ים שָׁנָ֑ה וַיִּרְאֶ֣ה אֶת־בָּנָ֗יו וְאֶת־בְּנֵ֣י בָנָ֔יו אַרְבָּעָ֖ה דֹּרֽוֹת׃ 17 וַיָּ֣מָת אִיּ֔וֹב זָקֵ֖ן וּשְׂבַ֥ע יָמִֽים׃ *

תם ונשלם תהילה לאל בורא עולם

שִׁיר הַשִּׁירִים
THE SONG OF SONGS

1 The Song of Songs, by[a] Solomon.

[2b]-Oh, give me of the kisses of your mouth,-[b]
For your love is more delightful than wine.
[3]Your ointments yield a sweet fragrance,
Your name is like finest[c] oil—
Therefore do maidens love you.
[4]Draw me after you, let us run!
[d]-The king has brought me to his chambers.-[d]
Let us delight and rejoice in your love,
Savoring it more than wine—
[e]-Like new wine-[e] they love you!

[5]I am dark, but comely,
O daughters of Jerusalem—
Like the tents of Kedar,
Like the pavilions of Solomon.
[6]Don't stare at me because I am swarthy,
Because the sun has gazed upon me.
My mother's sons quarreled with me,
They made me guard the vineyards;
My own vineyard I did not guard.

[7]Tell me, you whom I love so well;
Where do you pasture your sheep?
Where do you rest them at noon?
Let me not be [c]-as one who strays-[c]
Beside the flocks of your fellows.
[8]If you do not know, O fairest of women,
Go follow the tracks of the sheep,

א שִׁ֥יר הַשִּׁירִ֖ים אֲשֶׁ֥ר לִשְׁלֹמֹֽה׃

2 יִשָּׁקֵ֙נִי֙ מִנְּשִׁיק֣וֹת פִּ֔יהוּ
כִּֽי־טוֹבִ֥ים דֹּדֶ֖יךָ מִיָּֽיִן׃
3 לְרֵ֙יחַ֙ שְׁמָנֶ֣יךָ טוֹבִ֔ים
שֶׁ֖מֶן תּוּרַ֣ק שְׁמֶ֑ךָ
עַל־כֵּ֖ן עֲלָמ֥וֹת אֲהֵבֽוּךָ׃
4 מָשְׁכֵ֖נִי אַחֲרֶ֣יךָ נָּר֑וּצָה
הֱבִיאַ֨נִי הַמֶּ֜לֶךְ חֲדָרָ֗יו
נָגִ֤ילָה וְנִשְׂמְחָה֙ בָּ֔ךְ
נַזְכִּ֤ירָה דֹדֶ֙יךָ֙
מִיַּ֔יִן מֵישָׁרִ֖ים אֲהֵבֽוּךָ׃ ס

5 שְׁחוֹרָ֤ה אֲנִי֙ וְֽנָאוָ֔ה
בְּנ֖וֹת יְרוּשָׁלָ֑͏ִם
כְּאׇהֳלֵ֣י קֵדָ֔ר
כִּירִיע֖וֹת שְׁלֹמֹֽה׃
6 אַל־תִּרְא֙וּנִי֙ שֶׁאֲנִ֣י שְׁחַרְחֹ֔רֶת
שֶׁשְּׁזָפַ֖תְנִי הַשָּׁ֑מֶשׁ
בְּנֵ֧י אִמִּ֣י נִֽחֲרוּ־בִ֗י
שָׂמֻ֙נִי֙ נֹטֵרָ֣ה אֶת־הַכְּרָמִ֔ים
כַּרְמִ֥י שֶׁלִּ֖י לֹ֥א נָטָֽרְתִּי׃

7 הַגִּ֣ידָה לִּ֗י שֶׁ֤אָהֲבָה֙ נַפְשִׁ֔י
אֵיכָ֣ה תִרְעֶ֔ה
אֵיכָ֖ה תַּרְבִּ֣יץ בַּֽצׇּהֳרָ֑יִם
שַׁלָּמָ֤ה אֶֽהְיֶה֙ כְּעֹ֣טְיָ֔ה
עַ֖ל עֶדְרֵ֥י חֲבֵרֶֽיךָ׃
8 אִם־לֹ֤א תֵֽדְעִי֙ לָ֔ךְ הַיָּפָ֖ה בַּנָּשִׁ֑ים
צְֽאִי־לָ֞ךְ בְּעִקְבֵ֣י הַצֹּ֗אן

---

a   Or "concerning."
b-b   Heb. "Let him give me of the kisses of his mouth!"
c   Meaning of Heb. uncertain.
d-d   Emendation yields "Bring me, O king, to your chambers."
e-e   Understanding *mesharim* as related to *tirosh*; cf. Aramaic *merath*.

And graze your kids/
By the tents of the shepherds.

וּרְעִי אֶת־גְּדִיֹּתַ֔יִךְ
עַ֖ל מִשְׁכְּנ֥וֹת הָרֹעִֽים׃ ס

⁹I have likened you, my darling,
To a mare in Pharaoh's chariots:
¹⁰Your cheeks are comely with plaited
  wreaths,
Your neck with strings of jewels.
¹¹We will add wreaths of gold
To your spangles of silver.

⁹ לְסֻסָתִי֙ בְּרִכְבֵ֣י פַרְעֹ֔ה
דִּמִּיתִ֖יךְ רַעְיָתִֽי׃
¹⁰ נָאו֤וּ לְחָיַ֙יִךְ֙ בַּתֹּרִ֔ים
צַוָּארֵ֖ךְ בַּחֲרוּזִֽים׃
¹¹ תּוֹרֵ֤י זָהָב֙ נַעֲשֶׂה־לָּ֔ךְ
עִ֖ם נְקֻדּ֥וֹת הַכָּֽסֶף׃

¹²While the king was on his couch,
My nard gave forth its fragrance.
¹³My beloved to me is a bag of myrrh
Lodged between my breasts.
¹⁴My beloved to me is a spray of henna
  blooms
From the vineyards of En-gedi.

¹² עַד־שֶׁ֤הַמֶּ֙לֶךְ֙ בִּמְסִבּ֔וֹ
נִרְדִּ֖י נָתַ֥ן רֵיחֽוֹ׃
¹³ צְר֨וֹר הַמֹּ֤ר ׀ דּוֹדִי֙ לִ֔י
בֵּ֥ין שָׁדַ֖י יָלִֽין׃
¹⁴ אֶשְׁכֹּ֨ל הַכֹּ֤פֶר ׀ דּוֹדִי֙ לִ֔י
בְּכַרְמֵ֖י עֵ֥ין גֶּֽדִי׃ ס

¹⁵Ah, you are fair, my darling,
Ah, you are fair,
With your dove-like eyes!
¹⁶And you, my beloved, are handsome,
Beautiful indeed!
Our couch is in a bower;
¹⁷Cedars are the beams of our house,
Cypresses the rafters.

¹⁵ הִנָּ֤ךְ יָפָה֙ רַעְיָתִ֔י
הִנָּ֥ךְ יָפָ֖ה
עֵינַ֥יִךְ יוֹנִֽים׃
¹⁶ הִנְּךָ֨ יָפֶ֤ה דוֹדִי֙
אַ֣ף נָעִ֔ים
אַף־עַרְשֵׂ֖נוּ רַעֲנָנָֽה׃
¹⁷ קֹר֤וֹת בָּתֵּ֙ינוּ֙ אֲרָזִ֔ים
רַהִיטֵ֖נוּ בְּרוֹתִֽים׃

2 I am a roseᵃ of Sharon,
A lily of the valleys.

ב אֲנִי֙ חֲבַצֶּ֣לֶת הַשָּׁר֔וֹן
שֽׁוֹשַׁנַּ֖ת הָעֲמָקִֽים׃

²Like a lily among thorns,
So is my darling among the maidens.

² כְּשֽׁוֹשַׁנָּה֙ בֵּ֣ין הַחוֹחִ֔ים
כֵּ֥ן רַעְיָתִ֖י בֵּ֥ין הַבָּנֽוֹת׃

³Like an apple tree among trees of the forest,
So is my beloved among the youths.
I delight to sit in his shade,
And his fruit is sweet to my mouth.

³ כְּתַפּ֙וּחַ֙ בַּעֲצֵ֣י הַיַּ֔עַר
כֵּ֥ן דּוֹדִ֖י בֵּ֣ין הַבָּנִ֑ים
בְּצִלּוֹ֙ חִמַּ֣דְתִּי וְיָשַׁ֔בְתִּי
וּפִרְי֖וֹ מָת֥וֹק לְחִכִּֽי׃

/   As a pretext for coming.

ᵃ   Lit. "crocus."

⁴He brought me to the banquet room
ᵇ-And his banner of love was over me.-ᵇ
⁵"Sustain me with raisin cakes,
Refresh me with apples,
For I am faint with love."
⁶His left hand was under my head,
His right arm embraced me.
⁷I adjure you, O maidens of Jerusalem,
By gazelles or by hinds of the field:
Do not wake or rouse
Love until it please!

⁸Hark! My beloved!
There he comes,
Leaping over mountains,
Bounding over hills.
⁹My beloved is like a gazelle
Or like a young stag.
There he stands behind our wall,
Gazing through the window,
Peering through the lattice.
¹⁰My beloved spoke thus to me,
"Arise, my darling;
My fair one, come away!
¹¹For now the winter is past,
The rains are over and gone.
¹²The blossoms have appeared in the land,
The time of pruningᶜ has come;
The song of the turtledove
Is heard in our land.
¹³The green figs form on the fig tree,
The vines in blossom give off fragrance.
Arise, my darling;
My fair one, come away!

¹⁴"O my dove, in the cranny of the rocks,
Hidden by the cliff,
Let me see your face,

4 הֱבִיאַ֙נִי֙ אֶל־בֵּ֣ית הַיַּ֔יִן
וְדִגְל֥וֹ עָלַ֖י אַהֲבָֽה:
5 סַמְּכ֙וּנִי֙ בָּֽאֲשִׁישׁ֔וֹת
רַפְּד֖וּנִי בַּתַּפּוּחִ֑ים
כִּי־חוֹלַ֥ת אַהֲבָ֖ה אָֽנִי:
6 שְׂמֹאלוֹ֙ תַּ֣חַת לְרֹאשִׁ֔י
וִימִינ֖וֹ תְּחַבְּקֵֽנִי:
7 הִשְׁבַּ֙עְתִּי אֶתְכֶ֜ם בְּנ֤וֹת יְרוּשָׁלִַ֙ם֙
בִּצְבָא֔וֹת א֖וֹ בְּאַיְל֣וֹת הַשָּׂדֶ֑ה
אִם־תָּעִ֧ירוּ ׀ וְֽאִם־תְּעֽוֹרְר֛וּ
אֶת־הָאַהֲבָ֖ה עַ֥ד שֶׁתֶּחְפָּֽץ: ס

8 ק֣וֹל דּוֹדִ֔י
הִנֵּה־זֶ֖ה בָּ֑א
מְדַלֵּג֙ עַל־הֶ֣הָרִ֔ים
מְקַפֵּ֖ץ עַל־הַגְּבָעֽוֹת:
9 דּוֹמֶ֤ה דוֹדִי֙ לִצְבִ֔י
א֖וֹ לְעֹ֣פֶר הָֽאַיָּלִ֑ים
הִנֵּה־זֶ֤ה עוֹמֵד֙ אַחַ֣ר כָּתְלֵ֔נוּ
מַשְׁגִּ֙יחַ֙ מִן־הַֽחַלֹּנ֔וֹת
מֵצִ֖יץ מִן־הַֽחֲרַכִּֽים:
10 עָנָ֥ה דוֹדִ֖י וְאָ֣מַר לִ֑י
ק֥וּמִי לָ֛ךְ רַעְיָתִ֥י
יָפָתִ֖י וּלְכִי־לָֽךְ:
11 כִּֽי־הִנֵּ֥ה הַסְּתָ֖יו עָבָ֑ר
הַגֶּ֕שֶׁם חָלַ֖ף הָלַ֥ךְ לֽוֹ:
12 הַנִּצָּנִים֙ נִרְא֣וּ בָאָ֔רֶץ
עֵ֥ת הַזָּמִ֖יר הִגִּ֑יעַ
וְק֥וֹל הַתּ֖וֹר
נִשְׁמַ֥ע בְּאַרְצֵֽנוּ:
13 הַתְּאֵנָה֙ חָֽנְטָ֣ה פַגֶּ֔יהָ
וְהַגְּפָנִ֥ים ׀ סְמָדַ֖ר נָ֣תְנוּ רֵ֑יחַ
ק֥וּמִי לְכִ֛י לָ֖ךְ רַעְיָתִ֥י
יָפָתִ֖י וּלְכִי־לָֽךְ: ס

14 יוֹנָתִ֞י בְּחַגְוֵ֣י הַסֶּ֗לַע
בְּסֵ֙תֶר֙ הַמַּדְרֵגָ֔ה
הַרְאִ֙ינִי֙ אֶת־מַרְאַ֔יִךְ

ᵇ⁻ᵇ *Meaning of Heb. uncertain.*
ᶜ *Or "singing."*

Let me hear your voice;

For your voice is sweet

And your face is comely."

15Catch us the foxes,

The little foxes

That ruin the vineyards—

For our vineyard is in blossom.

16My beloved is mine

And I am his

Who browses among the lilies.

17When the day d-blows gently-d

And the shadows flee,e

Set out, my beloved,

Swift as a gazelle

Or a young stag,

For the hills of spices!f

הַשְׁמִיעִינִי אֶת־קוֹלֵךְ

כִּי־קוֹלֵךְ עָרֵב

וּמַרְאֵיךְ נָאוֶה: ס

15 אֶחֱזוּ־לָנוּ שׁוּעָלִים

שׁוּעָלִים קְטַנִּים

מְחַבְּלִים כְּרָמִים

וּכְרָמֵינוּ סְמָדַר:

16 דּוֹדִי לִי

וַאֲנִי לוֹ

הָרֹעֶה בַּשּׁוֹשַׁנִּים:

17 עַד שֶׁיָּפוּחַ הַיּוֹם

וְנָסוּ הַצְּלָלִים

סֹבׄ דְּמֵה־לְךָ

דוֹדִי לִצְבִי

אוֹ לְעֹפֶר הָאַיָּלִים

עַל־הָרֵי בָתֶר: ס

3

Upon my couch at nighta

I sought the one I love—

I sought, but found him not.

2"I must rise and roam the town,

Through the streets and through the squares;

I must seek the one I love."

I sought but found him not.

3b-I met the watchmen-b

Who patrol the town.

"Have you seen the one I love?"

4Scarcely had I passed them

When I found the one I love.

I held him fast, I would not let him go

Till I brought him to my mother's house,

To the chamber of her who conceived me

5I adjure you, O maidens of Jerusalem,

By gazelles or by hinds of the field:

ג עַל־מִשְׁכָּבִי בַּלֵּילוֹת

בִּקַּשְׁתִּי אֵת שֶׁאָהֲבָה נַפְשִׁי

בִּקַּשְׁתִּיו וְלֹא מְצָאתִיו:

2 אָקוּמָה נָּא וַאֲסוֹבְבָה בָעִיר

בַּשְּׁוָקִים וּבָרְחֹבוֹת

אֲבַקְשָׁה אֵת שֶׁאָהֲבָה נַפְשִׁי

בִּקַּשְׁתִּיו וְלֹא מְצָאתִיו:

3 מְצָאוּנִי הַשֹּׁמְרִים

הַסֹּבְבִים בָּעִיר

אֵת שֶׁאָהֲבָה נַפְשִׁי רְאִיתֶם:

4 כִּמְעַט שֶׁעָבַרְתִּי מֵהֶם

עַד שֶׁמָּצָאתִי אֵת שֶׁאָהֲבָה נַפְשִׁי

אֲחַזְתִּיו וְלֹא אַרְפֶּנּוּ

עַד־שֶׁהֲבֵיאתִיו אֶל־בֵּית אִמִּי

וְאֶל־חֶדֶר הוֹרָתִי:

5 הִשְׁבַּעְתִּי אֶתְכֶם בְּנוֹת יְרוּשָׁלַ͏ִם

בִּצְבָאוֹת אוֹ בְּאַיְלוֹת הַשָּׂדֶה

---

d-d   Emendation yields "declines"; cf. Jer. 6.4.

e   Septuagint reads "lengthen"; cf. Jer. 6.4.

f   Heb. bather of uncertain meaning; 8.14 reads besamim, "spices."

a   I.e., in a dream.

b-b   Lit. "The watchmen met me."

Do not wake or rouse
Love until it please!
6Who is she that comes up from the desert
Like columns of smoke,
In clouds of myrrh and frankincense,
Of all the powders of the merchant?
7There is Solomon's couch,
Encircled by sixty warriors
Of the warriors of Israel,
8All of them trained[c] in warfare,
Skilled in battle,
Each with sword on thigh
Because of terror by night.

9King Solomon made him a palanquin
Of wood from Lebanon.
10He made its posts of silver,
Its back[d] of gold,
Its seat of purple wool.
Within, it was decked with [e]love
By the maidens of Jerusalem.[-e]
11O maidens of Zion, go forth
And gaze upon King Solomon
Wearing the crown that his mother
Gave him on his wedding day,
On his day of bliss.

אִם־תָּעִירוּ ׀ וְאִם־תְּעֽוֹרְרוּ
אֶת־הָאַהֲבָה עַד שֶׁתֶּחְפָּֽץ׃ ס
6 מִי זֹאת עֹלָה מִן־הַמִּדְבָּר
כְּתִֽימֲרוֹת עָשָׁן
מְקֻטֶּרֶת מוֹר וּלְבוֹנָה
מִכֹּל אַבְקַת רוֹכֵֽל׃
7 הִנֵּה מִטָּתוֹ שֶׁלִּשְׁלֹמֹה
שִׁשִּׁים גִּבֹּרִים סָבִיב לָהּ
מִגִּבֹּרֵי יִשְׂרָאֵֽל׃
8 כֻּלָּם אֲחֻזֵי חֶרֶב
מְלֻמְּדֵי מִלְחָמָה
אִישׁ חַרְבּוֹ עַל־יְרֵכוֹ
מִפַּחַד בַּלֵּילֽוֹת׃ ס

9 אַפִּרְיוֹן עָשָׂה לוֹ הַמֶּלֶךְ שְׁלֹמֹה
מֵעֲצֵי הַלְּבָנֽוֹן׃
10 עַמּוּדָיו עָשָׂה כֶסֶף
רְפִידָתוֹ זָהָב
מֶרְכָּבוֹ אַרְגָּמָן
תּוֹכוֹ רָצוּף אַהֲבָה
מִבְּנוֹת יְרוּשָׁלָֽ͏ִם׃
11 צְאֶינָה ׀ וּֽרְאֶינָה בְּנוֹת צִיּוֹן
בַּמֶּלֶךְ שְׁלֹמֹה
בָּעֲטָרָה שֶׁעִטְּרָה־לּוֹ אִמּוֹ
בְּיוֹם חֲתֻנָּתוֹ
וּבְיוֹם שִׂמְחַת לִבּֽוֹ׃ ס

4 Ah, you are fair, my darling,
Ah, you are fair.
Your eyes are like doves
Behind your veil.
Your hair is like a flock of goats
Streaming down Mount Gilead.
2Your teeth are like a flock of ewes[a]
Climbing up from the washing pool;

ד הִנָּךְ יָפָה רַעְיָתִי
הִנָּךְ יָפָה
עֵינַיִךְ יוֹנִים
מִבַּעַד לְצַמָּתֵךְ
שַׂעְרֵךְ כְּעֵדֶר הָֽעִזִּים
שֶׁגָּלְשׁוּ מֵהַר גִּלְעָֽד׃
2 שִׁנַּיִךְ כְּעֵדֶר הַקְּצוּבוֹת
שֶׁעָלוּ מִן־הָרַחְצָה

---

c Cf. Akkadian aḫāzu, "to learn."
d Meaning of Heb. uncertain.
e-e Emendation yields "ebony, / O maidens of Jerusalem!"
a Cf. 6.6; exact nuance of qeṣuboth uncertain, perhaps "shorn ones."

All of them bear twins,
And not one loses her young.
3Your lips are like a crimson thread,
Your mouth is lovely.
Your brow behind your veil
[Gleams] like a pomegranate split open.
4Your neck is like the Tower of David,
Built b-to hold weapons,-b
Hung with a thousand shields—
All the quivers of warriors.
5Your breasts are like two fawns,
Twins of a gazelle,
Browsing among the lilies.
6cWhen the day blows gently
And the shadows flee,
I will betake me to the mount of myrrh,
To the hill of frankincense.
7Every part of you is fair, my darling,
There is no blemish in you
8From Lebanon come with me;
From Lebanon, my bride, with me!
Trip down from Amana's peak,
From the peak of Senird and Hermon,
From the dens of lions,
From the hillse of leopards.

9You have captured my heart,
My own,f my bride,
You have captured my heart
With one [glance] of your eyes,
With one coil of your necklace.
10How sweet is your love,
My own, my bride!
How much more delightful your love than
    wine,
Your ointments more fragrant
Than any spice!

שֶׁכֻּלָּם֙ מַתְאִימ֔וֹת
וְשַׁכֻּלָ֖ה אֵ֥ין בָּהֶֽם׃
3 כְּח֤וּט הַשָּׁנִי֙ שִׂפְתוֹתַ֔יִךְ
וּמִדְבָּרֵ֖יךְ נָאוֶ֑ה
כְּפֶ֤לַח הָֽרִמּוֹן֙
רַקָּתֵ֔ךְ מִבַּ֖עַד לְצַמָּתֵֽךְ׃
4 כְּמִגְדַּ֤ל דָּוִיד֙ צַוָּארֵ֔ךְ
בָּנ֖וּי לְתַלְפִּיּ֑וֹת
אֶ֤לֶף הַמָּגֵן֙ תָּל֣וּי עָלָ֔יו
כֹּ֖ל שִׁלְטֵ֥י הַגִּבֹּרִֽים׃
5 שְׁנֵ֥י שָׁדַ֖יִךְ כִּשְׁנֵ֣י עֳפָרִ֑ים
תְּאוֹמֵ֖י צְבִיָּ֑ה
הָרוֹעִ֖ים בַּשּׁוֹשַׁנִּֽים׃
6 עַ֤ד שֶׁיָּפ֙וּחַ֙ הַיּ֔וֹם
וְנָ֖סוּ הַצְּלָלִ֑ים
אֵ֤לֶךְ לִי֙ אֶל־הַ֣ר הַמּ֔וֹר
וְאֶל־גִּבְעַ֖ת הַלְּבוֹנָֽה׃
7 כֻּלָּ֤ךְ יָפָה֙ רַעְיָתִ֔י
וּמ֖וּם אֵ֥ין בָּֽךְ׃ ס
8 אִתִּ֤י מִלְּבָנוֹן֙ כַּלָּ֔ה
אִתִּ֖י מִלְּבָנ֣וֹן תָּב֑וֹאִי
תָּשׁ֣וּרִי ׀ מֵרֹ֣אשׁ אֲמָנָ֗ה
מֵרֹ֤אשׁ שְׂנִיר֙ וְחֶרְמ֔וֹן
מִמְּעֹנ֣וֹת אֲרָי֔וֹת
מֵהַרְרֵ֖י נְמֵרִֽים׃

9 לִבַּבְתִּ֖נִי
אֲחֹתִ֣י כַלָּ֑ה
לִבַּבְתִּ֙ינִי֙
בְּאַחַ֣ת מֵעֵינַ֔יִךְ
בְּאַחַ֥ד עֲנָ֖ק מִצַּוְּרֹנָֽיִךְ׃
10 מַה־יָּפ֤וּ דֹדַ֙יִךְ֙
אֲחֹתִ֣י כַלָּ֑ה
מַה־טֹּ֤בוּ דֹדַ֙יִךְ֙ מִיַּ֔יִן
וְרֵ֥יחַ שְׁמָנַ֖יִךְ
מִכָּל־בְּשָׂמִֽים׃

---

b-b *Apparently a poetic figure for jewelry; meaning of Heb.*
      uncertain.
c   *See notes at 2.17.*
d   *Cf. Deut. 3.9.*
e   *Emendation yields "lairs"; cf. Nah. 2.13.*
f   *Lit. "sister"; and so frequently below.*

11Sweetness drops
From your lips, O bride;
Honey and milk
Are under your tongue;
And the scent of your robes
Is like the scent of Lebanon.

12A garden locked
Is my own, my bride,
A fountain locked,
A sealed-up spring.

13Your limbs are an orchard of pomegranates
And of all luscious fruits,
Of henna and of nard—

14Nard and saffron,
Fragrant reed and cinnamon,
With all aromatic woods,
Myrrh and aloes—
All the choice perfumes.

15g-[You are] a garden spring,
A well of fresh water,-g
A rill of Lebanon.

16Awake, O north wind,
Come, O south wind!
Blow upon my garden,
That its perfume may spread.
Let my beloved come to his garden
And enjoy its luscious fruits!

5 I have come to my garden,
My own, my bride;
I have plucked my myrrh and spice,
Eaten my honey and honeycomb,
Drunk my wine and my milk.

Eat, lovers, and drink:
Drink deep of love!

11 נֹפֶת תִּטֹּפְנָה
שִׂפְתוֹתַיִךְ כַּלָּה
דְּבַשׁ וְחָלָב
תַּחַת לְשׁוֹנֵךְ
וְרֵיחַ שַׂלְמֹתַיִךְ
כְּרֵיחַ לְבָנוֹן: ס

12 גַּן ׀ נָעוּל
אֲחֹתִי כַלָּה
גַּל נָעוּל
מַעְיָן חָתוּם:

13 שְׁלָחַיִךְ פַּרְדֵּס רִמּוֹנִים
עִם פְּרִי מְגָדִים
כְּפָרִים עִם־נְרָדִים:

14 *נֵרְדְּ ׀ וְכַרְכֹּם
קָנֶה וְקִנָּמוֹן
עִם כָּל־עֲצֵי לְבוֹנָה
מֹר וַאֲהָלוֹת
עִם כָּל־רָאשֵׁי בְשָׂמִים:

15 מַעְיַן גַּנִּים
בְּאֵר מַיִם חַיִּים
וְנֹזְלִים מִן־לְבָנוֹן:

16 עוּרִי צָפוֹן
וּבוֹאִי תֵימָן
הָפִיחִי גַנִּי
יִזְּלוּ בְשָׂמָיו
יָבֹא דוֹדִי לְגַנּוֹ
וְיֹאכַל פְּרִי מְגָדָיו:

ה בָּאתִי לְגַנִּי
אֲחֹתִי כַלָּה
אָרִיתִי מוֹרִי עִם־בְּשָׂמִי
אָכַלְתִּי יַעְרִי עִם־דִּבְשִׁי
שָׁתִיתִי יֵינִי עִם־חֲלָבִי
אִכְלוּ רֵעִים שְׁתוּ
וְשִׁכְרוּ דּוֹדִים: ס

---

g-g *Emendation yields "The spring in my garden / Is a well of fresh water."*

v. 14. חצי הספר בפסוקים

²ᵃI was asleep,
But my heart was wakeful.
Hark, my beloved knocks!
"Let me in, my own,
My darling, my faultless dove!
For my head is drenched with dew,
My locks with the damp of night."
³I had taken off my robe—
Was I to don it again?
I had bathed my feet—
Was I to soil them again?
⁴My beloved ᵇ-took his hand off the latch,-ᵇ
And my heart was stirred ᶜ-for him.-ᶜ
⁵I rose to let in my beloved;
My hands dripped myrrh—
My fingers, flowing myrrh—
Upon the handles of the bolt.
⁶I opened the door for my beloved,
But my beloved had turned and gone.
I was faint ᵈ-because of what he said.-ᵈ
I sought, but found him not;
I called, but he did not answer.
⁷I met the watchmenᵉ
Who patrol the town;
They struck me, they bruised me.
The guards of the walls
Stripped me of my mantle.
⁸I adjure you, O maidens of Jerusalem!
If you meet my beloved, tell him this:
That I am faint with love.

⁹How is your beloved better than another,ᶠ
O fairest of women?
How is your beloved better than anotherᶠ
That you adjure us so?

2 אֲנִי יְשֵׁנָה
וְלִבִּי עֵר
קוֹל ׀ דּוֹדִי דוֹפֵק
פִּתְחִי־לִי אֲחֹתִי
רַעְיָתִי יוֹנָתִי תַמָּתִי
שֶׁרֹאשִׁי* נִמְלָא־טָל
קְוֻצּוֹתַי רְסִיסֵי לָיְלָה:
3 פָּשַׁטְתִּי אֶת־כֻּתָּנְתִּי
אֵיכָכָה אֶלְבָּשֶׁנָּה
רָחַצְתִּי אֶת־רַגְלַי
אֵיכָכָה אֲטַנְּפֵם:
4 דּוֹדִי שָׁלַח יָדוֹ מִן־הַחֹר
וּמֵעַי הָמוּ עָלָיו:
5 קַמְתִּי אֲנִי לִפְתֹּחַ לְדוֹדִי
וְיָדַי נָטְפוּ־מוֹר
וְאֶצְבְּעֹתַי מוֹר עֹבֵר
עַל כַּפּוֹת הַמַּנְעוּל:
6 פָּתַחְתִּי אֲנִי לְדוֹדִי
וְדוֹדִי חָמַק עָבָר
נַפְשִׁי יָצְאָה בְדַבְּרוֹ
בִּקַּשְׁתִּיהוּ וְלֹא מְצָאתִיהוּ
קְרָאתִיו וְלֹא עָנָנִי:
7 מְצָאֻנִי הַשֹּׁמְרִים
הַסֹּבְבִים בָּעִיר
הִכּוּנִי פְצָעוּנִי
נָשְׂאוּ אֶת־רְדִידִי מֵעָלַי
שֹׁמְרֵי הַחֹמוֹת:
8 הִשְׁבַּעְתִּי אֶתְכֶם בְּנוֹת יְרוּשָׁלָ͏ִם
אִם־תִּמְצְאוּ אֶת־דּוֹדִי מַה־תַּגִּידוּ לוֹ
שֶׁחוֹלַת אַהֲבָה אָנִי:

9 מַה־דּוֹדֵךְ מִדּוֹד
הַיָּפָה בַּנָּשִׁים
מַה־דּוֹדֵךְ מִדּוֹד
שֶׁכָּכָה הִשְׁבַּעְתָּנוּ:

---

a   *In vv. 2–8 the maiden relates a dream.*
b-b   *Meaning of Heb. uncertain.*
c-c   *Many manuscripts and editions read "within me" ('alai).*
d-d   *Change of vocalization yields "because of him."*
e   *See note at 3.3.*
f   *Or "What sort of beloved is your beloved?"*

ר' דגושה   v. 2.

10My beloved is clear-skinned and ruddy,
Preeminent among ten thousand.
11His head is finest gold,
His locks are curled
And black as a raven.
12His eyes are like doves
By watercourses,
Bathed in milk,
b-Set by a brimming pool.-b
13His cheeks are like beds of spices,
g-Banks of-g perfume
His lips are like lilies;
They drip flowing myrrh.
14His hands are rods of gold,
Studded with beryl;
His belly a tablet of ivory,
Adorned with sapphires.
15His legs are like marble pillars
Set in sockets of fine gold.
He is majestic as Lebanon,
Stately as the cedars.
16His mouth is delicious
And all of him is delightful.
Such is my beloved,
Such is my darling,
O maidens of Jerusalem!

6 "Whither has your beloved gone,
O fairest of women?
Whither has your beloved turned?
Let us seek him with you."
2My beloved has gone down to his garden,
To the beds of spices,
To browse in the gardens
And to pick lilies.
3I am my beloved's

10 דּוֹדִי צַח וְאָדֹום
דָּגוּל מֵרְבָבָה:
11 רֹאשֹׁו כֶּתֶם פָּז
קְוֻצֹּותָיו תַּלְתַּלִּים
שְׁחֹרֹות כָּעֹורֵב:
12 עֵינָיו כְּיֹונִים
עַל־אֲפִיקֵי מָיִם
רֹחֲצֹות בֶּחָלָב
יֹשְׁבֹות עַל־מִלֵּאת:
13 לְחָיָו כַּעֲרוּגַת הַבֹּשֶׂם
מִגְדְּלֹות מֶרְקָחִים
שִׂפְתֹותָיו שֹׁושַׁנִּים
נֹטְפֹות מֹור עֹבֵר:
14 יָדָיו גְּלִילֵי זָהָב
מְמֻלָּאִים בַּתַּרְשִׁישׁ
מֵעָיו עֶשֶׁת שֵׁן
מְעֻלֶּפֶת סַפִּירִים:
15 שֹׁוקָיו עַמּוּדֵי שֵׁשׁ
מְיֻסָּדִים עַל־אַדְנֵי־פָז
מַרְאֵהוּ כַּלְּבָנֹון
בָּחוּר כָּאֲרָזִים:
16 חִכֹּו מַמְתַקִּים
וְכֻלֹּו מַחֲמַדִּים
זֶה דֹודִי
וְזֶה רֵעִי
בְּנֹות יְרוּשָׁלָם:

ו אָנָה הָלַךְ דֹּודֵךְ
הַיָּפָה בַּנָּשִׁים
אָנָה פָּנָה דֹודֵךְ
וּנְבַקְשֶׁנּוּ עִמָּךְ:
2 דֹּודִי יָרַד לְגַנֹּו
לַעֲרוּגֹות הַבֹּשֶׂם
לִרְעֹות בַּגַּנִּים
וְלִלְקֹט שֹׁושַׁנִּים:
3 אֲנִי לְדֹודִי

g-g *Septuagint vocalizes as participle, "producing."*

And my beloved is mine;
He browses among the lilies.

וְדוֹדִי לִי
הָרֹעֶה בַּשּׁוֹשַׁנִּים: ס

4You are beautiful, my darling, as Tirzah,
Comely as Jerusalem,
a-Awesome as bannered hosts.-a

4 יָפָה אַתְּ רַעְיָתִי כְּתִרְצָה
נָאוָה כִּירוּשָׁלָ͏ִם
אֲיֻמָּה כַּנִּדְגָּלוֹת:

5Turn your eyes away from me,
For they overwhelm me!
Your hair is like a flock of goats
Streaming down from Gilead.

5 הָסֵבִּי עֵינַיִךְ מִנֶּגְדִּי
שֶׁהֵם* הִרְהִיבֻנִי
שַׂעְרֵךְ כְּעֵדֶר הָעִזִּים
שֶׁגָּלְשׁוּ מִן־הַגִּלְעָד:

6Your teeth are like a flock of ewes
Climbing up from the washing pool;
All of them bear twins,
And not one loses her young.

6 שִׁנַּיִךְ כְּעֵדֶר הָרְחֵלִים
שֶׁעָלוּ מִן־הָרַחְצָה
שֶׁכֻּלָּם מַתְאִימוֹת
וְשַׁכֻּלָה אֵין בָּהֶם:

7Your brow behind your veil
[Gleams] like a pomegranate split open.

7 כְּפֶלַח הָרִמּוֹן
רַקָּתֵךְ מִבַּעַד לְצַמָּתֵךְ:

8There are sixty queens,
And eighty concubines,
And damsels without number.

8 שִׁשִּׁים הֵמָּה מְלָכוֹת
וּשְׁמֹנִים פִּילַגְשִׁים
וַעֲלָמוֹת אֵין מִסְפָּר:

9Only one is my dove,
My perfect one,
The only one of her mother,
The delight of her who bore her.
Maidens see and acclaim her;
Queens and concubines, and praise her.

9 אַחַת הִיא יוֹנָתִי
תַמָּתִי
אַחַת הִיא לְאִמָּהּ
בָּרָה הִיא לְיוֹלַדְתָּהּ
רָאוּהָ בָנוֹת וַיְאַשְּׁרוּהָ
מְלָכוֹת וּפִילַגְשִׁים וַיְהַלְלוּהָ: ס

10Who is she that shines through like the
    dawn,
Beautiful as the moon,
Radiant as the sun
a-Awesome as bannered hosts?-a

10 מִי־זֹאת הַנִּשְׁקָפָה כְּמוֹ־שָׁחַר
יָפָה כַלְּבָנָה
בָּרָה כַּחַמָּה
אֲיֻמָּה כַּנִּדְגָּלוֹת: ס

11I went down to the nut grove
To see the budding of the vale;
To see if the vines had blossomed,
If the pomegranates were in bloom.

11 אֶל־גִּנַּת אֱגוֹז יָרַדְתִּי
לִרְאוֹת בְּאִבֵּי הַנָּחַל
לִרְאוֹת הֲפָרְחָה הַגֶּפֶן
הֵנֵצוּ הָרִמֹּנִים:

12a-Before I knew it,
My desire set me
Mid the chariots of Ammi-nadib.-a

12 לֹא יָדַעְתִּי
נַפְשִׁי שָׂמַתְנִי
מַרְכְּבוֹת עַמִּי־נָדִיב:

---

a-a *Meaning of Heb. uncertain.*

7

Turn back, turn back,
O maid of Shulem!
Turn back, turn back,
That we may gaze upon you.
"Why will you gaze at the Shulammite
In[a] the Mahanaim dance?"
²How lovely are your feet in sandals,
O daughter of nobles!
Your rounded thighs are like jewels,
The work of a master's hand.
³Your navel is like a round goblet—
Let mixed wine not be lacking!—
Your belly like a heap of wheat
Hedged about with lilies.
⁴Your breasts are like two fawns,
Twins of a gazelle.
⁵Your neck is like a tower of ivory,
Your eyes like pools in Heshbon
By the gate of Bath-rabbim,
Your nose like the Lebanon tower
That faces toward Damascus.
⁶The head upon you is like [b]-crimson wool,-[b]
The locks of your head are like purple—
[c]-A king is held captive in the tresses.-[c]
⁷How fair you are, how beautiful!
O Love, with all its rapture!
⁸Your stately form is like the palm,
Your breasts are like clusters.
⁹I say: Let me climb the palm,
Let me take hold of its branches;
Let your breasts be like clusters of grapes,
Your breath like the fragrance of apples,
¹⁰And your mouth like choicest wine.
"Let it flow to my beloved as new wine[d]
[c]-Gliding over the lips of sleepers."-[c]

ז

שׁוּבִי שׁוּבִי
הַשּׁוּלַמִּית
שׁוּבִי שׁוּבִי
וְנֶחֱזֶה־בָּךְ
מַה־תֶּחֱזוּ בַּשּׁוּלַמִּית
כִּמְחֹלַת* הַמַּחֲנָיִם:
2 מַה־יָּפוּ פְעָמַיִךְ בַּנְּעָלִים
בַּת־נָדִיב
חַמּוּקֵי יְרֵכַיִךְ כְּמוֹ חֲלָאִים
מַעֲשֵׂה יְדֵי אָמָּן:
3 שָׁרְרֵךְ אַגַּן הַסַּהַר
אַל־יֶחְסַר הַמָּזֶג
בִּטְנֵךְ עֲרֵמַת חִטִּים
סוּגָה בַּשּׁוֹשַׁנִּים:
4 שְׁנֵי שָׁדַיִךְ כִּשְׁנֵי עֳפָרִים
תָּאֳמֵי צְבִיָּה:
5 צַוָּארֵךְ כְּמִגְדַּל הַשֵּׁן
עֵינַיִךְ בְּרֵכוֹת בְּחֶשְׁבּוֹן
עַל־שַׁעַר בַּת־רַבִּים
אַפֵּךְ כְּמִגְדַּל הַלְּבָנוֹן
צוֹפֶה פְּנֵי דַמָּשֶׂק:
6 רֹאשֵׁךְ עָלַיִךְ כַּכַּרְמֶל
וְדַלַּת רֹאשֵׁךְ כָּאַרְגָּמָן
מֶלֶךְ אָסוּר בָּרְהָטִים:
7 מַה־יָּפִית וּמַה־נָּעַמְתְּ
אַהֲבָה בַּתַּעֲנוּגִים:
8 זֹאת קוֹמָתֵךְ דָּמְתָה לְתָמָר
וְשָׁדַיִךְ לְאַשְׁכֹּלוֹת:
9 אָמַרְתִּי אֶעֱלֶה בְתָמָר
אֹחֲזָה בְּסַנְסִנָּיו
וְיִהְיוּ־נָא שָׁדַיִךְ כְּאֶשְׁכְּלוֹת הַגֶּפֶן
וְרֵיחַ אַפֵּךְ כַּתַּפּוּחִים:
10 וְחִכֵּךְ כְּיֵין הַטּוֹב
הוֹלֵךְ לְדוֹדִי לְמֵישָׁרִים
דּוֹבֵב שִׂפְתֵי יְשֵׁנִים:

---

a With many manuscripts and editions; others read "like."
   Meaning of entire line uncertain.
b-b So Ibn Janah and Ibn Ezra, taking karmel as a by-form of
     karmil: cf. 2 Chron. 2.6, 13; 3.14.
c-c Meaning of Heb. uncertain.
d See note at 1.4 end.

v. 1. בנוסח אחר "בְּמַחֲלַת"

¹¹I am my beloved's,
And his desire is for me.
¹²Come, my beloved,
Let us go into the open;
Let us lodge ^e-among the henna shrubs.-^e
¹³Let us go early to the vineyards;
Let us see if the vine has flowered,
If its blossoms have opened,
If the pomegranates are in bloom.
There I will give my love to you.
¹⁴The mandrakes yield their fragrance,
At our doors are all choice fruits;
Both freshly picked and long-stored
Have I kept, my beloved, for you.

11 אֲנִי לְדוֹדִי
וְעָלַי תְּשׁוּקָתוֹ: ס
12 לְכָה דוֹדִי
נֵצֵא הַשָּׂדֶה
נָלִינָה בַּכְּפָרִים:
13 נַשְׁכִּימָה לַכְּרָמִים
נִרְאֶה אִם־פָּרְחָה הַגֶּפֶן
פִּתַּח הַסְּמָדַר
הֵנֵצוּ הָרִמּוֹנִים
שָׁם אֶתֵּן אֶת־דֹּדַי לָךְ:
14 הַדּוּדָאִים נָתְנוּ־רֵיחַ
וְעַל־פְּתָחֵינוּ כָּל־מְגָדִים
חֲדָשִׁים גַּם־יְשָׁנִים
דּוֹדִי צָפַנְתִּי לָךְ:

8 If only it could be as with a brother,
As if you had nursed at my mother's breast:
Then I could kiss you
When I met you in the street,
And no one would despise me.
²I would lead you, I would bring you
To the house of my mother,
Of her who taught^a me—
I would let you drink of the spiced wine,
Of my pomegranate juice.

ח מִי יִתֶּנְךָ כְּאָח לִי
יוֹנֵק שְׁדֵי אִמִּי
אֶמְצָאֲךָ בַחוּץ
אֶשָּׁקְךָ
גַּם לֹא־יָבֻזוּ לִי:
2 אֶנְהָגְךָ אֲבִיאֲךָ
אֶל־בֵּית אִמִּי
תְּלַמְּדֵנִי
אַשְׁקְךָ מִיַּיִן הָרֶקַח
מֵעֲסִיס רִמֹּנִי:

³His left hand was under my head,
His right hand caressed me.
⁴I adjure you, O maidens of Jerusalem:
Do not wake or rouse
Love until it please!

3 שְׂמֹאלוֹ תַּחַת רֹאשִׁי
וִימִינוֹ תְּחַבְּקֵנִי:
4 הִשְׁבַּעְתִּי אֶתְכֶם בְּנוֹת יְרוּשָׁלָ͏ִם
מַה־תָּעִירוּ ׀ וּמַה־תְּעֹרְרוּ
אֶת־הָאַהֲבָה עַד שֶׁתֶּחְפָּץ: ס

⁵Who is she that comes up from the desert,
Leaning upon her beloved?

5 מִי זֹאת עֹלָה מִן־הַמִּדְבָּר
מִתְרַפֶּקֶת עַל־דּוֹדָהּ

e-e   *Or "in the villages."*

a   *Emendation yields "bore"; cf. 6.9; 8.5.*

Under the apple tree I roused you;
It was there your mother conceived you,
There she who bore you conceived you.

6Let me be a seal upon your heart,
Like the seal upon your hand.b
For love is fierce as death,
Passion is mighty as Sheol;
Its darts are darts of fire,
A blazing flame.
7Vast floods cannot quench love,
Nor rivers drown it.
If a man offered all his wealth for love,
He would be laughed to scorn.

8"We have a little sister,
Whose breasts are not yet formed.
What shall we do for our sister
When she is spoken for?
9If she be a wall,
We will build upon it a silver battlement;
If she be a door,
We will panel it in cedar."
10I am a wall,
My breasts are like towers.
So I became in his eyes
As one who finds favor.

11Solomon had a vineyard
In Baal-hamon.
He had to post guards in the vineyard:
A man would give for its fruit
A thousand pieces of silver.
12I have my very own vineyard:

b Lit. "arm."

תַּ֤חַת הַתַּפּ֙וּחַ֙ עֽוֹרַרְתִּ֔יךָ
שָׁ֚מָּה חִבְּלַ֣תְךָ אִמֶּ֔ךָ
שָׁ֖מָּה חִבְּלָ֥ה יְלָדַֽתְךָ׃

6 שִׂימֵ֨נִי כַֽחוֹתָ֜ם עַל־לִבֶּ֗ךָ
כַּֽחוֹתָם֙ עַל־זְרוֹעֶ֔ךָ
כִּֽי־עַזָּ֤ה כַמָּ֙וֶת֙ אַהֲבָ֔ה
קָשָׁ֥ה כִשְׁא֖וֹל קִנְאָ֑ה
רְשָׁפֶ֕יהָ רִשְׁפֵּ֖י אֵ֑שׁ
שַׁלְהֶֽבֶתְיָֽה׃*
7 מַ֣יִם רַבִּ֗ים לֹ֤א יֽוּכְלוּ֙ לְכַבּ֣וֹת אֶת־
הָֽאַהֲבָ֔ה
וּנְהָר֖וֹת לֹ֣א יִשְׁטְפ֑וּהָ
אִם־יִתֵּ֨ן אִ֜ישׁ אֶת־כָּל־ה֤וֹן בֵּיתוֹ֙ בָּֽאַהֲבָ֔ה
בּ֖וֹז יָב֥וּזוּ לֽוֹ׃ ס

8 אָח֥וֹת לָ֙נוּ֙ קְטַנָּ֔ה
וְשָׁדַ֖יִם אֵ֣ין לָ֑הּ
מַֽה־נַּעֲשֶׂה֙ לַֽאֲחֹתֵ֔נוּ
בַּיּ֖וֹם שֶׁיְּדֻבַּר־בָּֽהּ׃
9 אִם־חוֹמָ֣ה הִ֔יא
נִבְנֶ֥ה עָלֶ֖יהָ טִ֣ירַת כָּ֑סֶף
וְאִם־דֶּ֣לֶת הִ֔יא
נָצ֥וּר עָלֶ֖יהָ ל֥וּחַ אָֽרֶז׃
10 אֲנִ֣י חוֹמָ֔ה
וְשָׁדַ֖י כַּמִּגְדָּל֑וֹת
אָ֛ז הָיִ֥יתִי בְעֵינָ֖יו
כְּמֽוֹצְאֵ֥ת שָׁלֽוֹם׃ פ

11 כֶּ֣רֶם הָיָ֤ה לִשְׁלֹמֹה֙
בְּבַ֣עַל הָמ֔וֹן
נָתַ֥ן אֶת־הַכֶּ֖רֶם לַנֹּֽטְרִ֑ים
אִ֛ישׁ יָבִ֥א בְּפִרְי֖וֹ
אֶ֥לֶף כָּֽסֶף׃
12 כַּרְמִ֥י שֶׁלִּ֖י לְפָנָ֑י

You may have the thousand, O Solomon,
And the guards of the fruit two hundred!

13O you who linger in the garden,[c]
A lover[c] is listening;
Let me hear your voice.
14"Hurry, my beloved,
Swift as a gazelle or a young stag,
To the hills of spices!"

הָאֶ֥לֶף לְךָ֙ שְׁלֹמֹ֔ה
וּמָאתַ֖יִם לְנֹטְרִ֥ים אֶת־פִּרְיֽוֹ׃

13 הַיּוֹשֶׁ֣בֶת בַּגַּנִּ֗ים
חֲבֵרִ֛ים מַקְשִׁיבִ֥ים
לְקוֹלֵ֖ךְ הַשְׁמִיעִֽנִי׃
14 בְּרַ֣ח ׀ דּוֹדִ֗י
וּֽדְמֵה־לְךָ֤ לִצְבִי֙ א֚וֹ לְעֹ֣פֶר הָֽאַיָּלִ֔ים
עַ֖ל הָרֵ֥י בְשָׂמִֽים׃*

תם ונשלם תהילה לאל בורא עולם

---

c Heb. plural. Meaning of verse uncertain.   v. 14. סכום הפסוקים של ספר 117 וחציו 4.14

1740

RUTH

1 In the days when the chieftains[a] ruled, there was a famine in the land; and a man of Bethlehem in Judah, with his wife and two sons, went to reside in the country of Moab. [2]The man's name was Elimelech, his wife's name was Naomi, and his two sons were named Mahlon and Chilion—Ephrathites of Bethlehem in Judah. They came to the country of Moab and remained there.

[3]Elimelech, Naomi's husband, died; and she was left with her two sons. [4]They married Moabite women, one named Orpah and the other Ruth, and they lived there about ten years. [5]Then those two—Mahlon and Chilion—also died; so the woman was left without her two sons and without her husband.

[6]She started out with her daughters-in-law to return from the country of Moab; for in the country of Moab she had heard that the Lord had taken note of His people and given them food. [7]Accompanied by her two daughters-in-law, she left the place where she had been living; and they set out on the road back to the land of Judah.

[8]But Naomi said to her two daughters-in-law, "Turn back, each of you to her mother's house. May the Lord deal kindly with you, as you have dealt with the dead and with me! [9]May the Lord grant that each of you find security in the house of a husband!" And she kissed them farewell. They broke into weeping [10]and said to her, "No, we will return with you to your people."

[11]But Naomi replied, "Turn back, my daugh-

---

a I.e., the leaders who arose in the period before the monarchy; others "judges."

א וַיְהִי בִּימֵי שְׁפֹט הַשֹּׁפְטִים וַיְהִי רָעָב בָּאָרֶץ וַיֵּלֶךְ אִישׁ מִבֵּית לֶחֶם יְהוּדָה לָגוּר בִּשְׂדֵי מוֹאָב הוּא וְאִשְׁתּוֹ וּשְׁנֵי בָנָיו: 2 וְשֵׁם הָאִישׁ אֱלִימֶלֶךְ וְשֵׁם אִשְׁתּוֹ נׇעֳמִי וְשֵׁם שְׁנֵי־בָנָיו ׀ מַחְלוֹן וְכִלְיוֹן אֶפְרָתִים מִבֵּית לֶחֶם יְהוּדָה וַיָּבֹאוּ שְׂדֵי־מוֹאָב וַיִּהְיוּ־שָׁם: 3 וַיָּמׇת אֱלִימֶלֶךְ אִישׁ נׇעֳמִי וַתִּשָּׁאֵר הִיא וּשְׁנֵי בָנֶיהָ: 4 וַיִּשְׂאוּ לָהֶם נָשִׁים מֹאֲבִיּוֹת שֵׁם הָאַחַת עׇרְפָּה וְשֵׁם הַשֵּׁנִית רוּת וַיֵּשְׁבוּ שָׁם כְּעֶשֶׂר שָׁנִים: 5 וַיָּמֻתוּ גַם־שְׁנֵיהֶם מַחְלוֹן וְכִלְיוֹן וַתִּשָּׁאֵר הָאִשָּׁה מִשְּׁנֵי יְלָדֶיהָ וּמֵאִישָׁהּ: 6 וַתָּקׇם הִיא וְכַלֹּתֶיהָ וַתָּשׇׁב מִשְּׂדֵי מוֹאָב כִּי שָׁמְעָה בִּשְׂדֵה מוֹאָב כִּי־פָקַד יְהֹוָה אֶת־עַמּוֹ לָתֵת לָהֶם לָחֶם: 7 וַתֵּצֵא מִן־הַמָּקוֹם אֲשֶׁר הָיְתָה־שָּׁמָּה וּשְׁתֵּי כַלֹּתֶיהָ עִמָּהּ וַתֵּלַכְנָה בַדֶּרֶךְ לָשׁוּב אֶל־אֶרֶץ יְהוּדָה: 8 וַתֹּאמֶר נׇעֳמִי לִשְׁתֵּי כַלֹּתֶיהָ לֵכְנָה שֹּׁבְנָה אִשָּׁה לְבֵית אִמָּהּ יעשה יַעַשׂ יְהֹוָה עִמָּכֶם חֶסֶד כַּאֲשֶׁר עֲשִׂיתֶם עִם־הַמֵּתִים וְעִמָּדִי: 9 יִתֵּן יְהֹוָה לָכֶם וּמְצֶאןָ מְנוּחָה אִשָּׁה בֵּית אִישָׁהּ וַתִּשַּׁק לָהֶן וַתִּשֶּׂאנָה קוֹלָן וַתִּבְכֶּינָה: 10 וַתֹּאמַרְנָה־לָּהּ כִּי־אִתָּךְ נָשׁוּב לְעַמֵּךְ: 11 וַתֹּאמֶר נׇעֳמִי שֹׁבְנָה בְנֹתַי לָמָּה תֵלַכְנָה

ters! Why should you go with me? Have I any more sons in my body who might be husbands for you? [12]Turn back, my daughters, for I am too old to be married. Even if I thought there was hope for me, even if I were married tonight and I also bore sons, [13]should you wait for them to grow up? Should you on their account debar yourselves from marriage? Oh no, my daughters! My lot is far more bitter than yours, for the hand of the LORD has struck out against me."

[14]They broke into weeping again, and Orpah kissed her mother-in-law farewell. But Ruth clung to her. [15]So she said, "See, your sister-in-law has returned to her people and her gods. Go follow your sister-in-law." [16]But Ruth replied, "Do not urge me to leave you, to turn back and not follow you. For wherever you go, I will go; wherever you lodge, I will lodge; your people shall be my people, and your God my God. [17]Where you die, I will die, and there I will be buried. b-Thus and more may the LORD do to me-b if anything but death parts me from you." [18]When [Naomi] saw how determined she was to go with her, she ceased to argue with her; [19]and the two went on until they reached Bethlehem.

When they arrived in Bethlehem, the whole city buzzed with excitement over them. The women said, "Can this be Naomi?" [20]"Do not call me Naomi,"c she replied. "Call me Mara,d for Shaddaie has made my lot very bitter. [21]I went away full, and the LORD has brought me back empty. How can you call me Naomi, when the LORD has f-dealt harshly with-f me, when Shaddai has brought misfortune upon me!"

[22]Thus Naomi returned from the country of Moab; she returned with her daughter-in-law Ruth the Moabite. They arrived in Bethlehem at the beginning of the barley harvest.

עַמִּי הֲעֽוֹד־לִ֤י בָנִים֙ בְּמֵעַ֔י וְהָי֥וּ לָכֶ֖ם לַאֲנָשִֽׁים׃ 12 שֹׁ֤בְנָה בְנֹתַי֙ לֵ֔כְןָ כִּ֥י זָקַ֖נְתִּי מִהְי֣וֹת לְאִ֑ישׁ כִּ֤י אָמַ֙רְתִּי֙ יֶשׁ־לִ֣י תִקְוָ֔ה גַּ֣ם הָיִ֤יתִי הַלַּ֙יְלָה֙ לְאִ֔ישׁ וְגַ֖ם יָלַ֥דְתִּי בָנִֽים׃ 13 הֲלָהֵ֣ן ׀ תְּשַׂבֵּ֗רְנָה עַ֚ד אֲשֶׁ֣ר יִגְדָּ֔לוּ הֲלָהֵן֙ תֵּֽעָגֵ֔נָה לְבִלְתִּ֖י הֱי֣וֹת לְאִ֑ישׁ אַ֣ל בְּנֹתַ֗י כִּֽי־מַר־לִ֤י מְאֹד֙ מִכֶּ֔ם כִּֽי־יָצְאָ֥ה בִ֖י יַד־ יְהוָֽה׃ 14 וַתִּשֶּׂ֣נָה* קוֹלָ֔ן וַתִּבְכֶּ֖ינָה ע֑וֹד וַתִּשַּׁ֤ק עָרְפָּה֙ לַחֲמוֹתָ֔הּ וְר֖וּת דָּ֥בְקָה בָּֽהּ׃ 15 וַתֹּ֗אמֶר הִנֵּה֙ שָׁ֣בָה יְבִמְתֵּ֔ךְ אֶל־עַמָּ֖הּ וְאֶל־אֱלֹהֶ֑יהָ שׁ֖וּבִי אַחֲרֵ֥י יְבִמְתֵּֽךְ׃ 16 וַתֹּ֤אמֶר רוּת֙ אַל־תִּפְגְּעִי־בִ֔י לְעָזְבֵ֖ךְ לָשׁ֣וּב מֵאַחֲרָ֑יִךְ כִּ֠י אֶל־אֲשֶׁ֨ר תֵּלְכִ֜י אֵלֵ֗ךְ וּבַאֲשֶׁ֤ר תָּלִ֙ינִי֙ אָלִ֔ין עַמֵּ֣ךְ עַמִּ֔י וֵאלֹהַ֖יִךְ אֱלֹהָֽי׃ 17 בַּאֲשֶׁ֤ר תָּמ֙וּתִי֙ אָמ֔וּת וְשָׁ֖ם אֶקָּבֵ֑ר כֹּה֩ יַעֲשֶׂ֨ה יְהוָ֥ה לִי֙ וְכֹ֣ה יֹסִ֔יף כִּ֣י הַמָּ֔וֶת יַפְרִ֖יד בֵּינִ֥י וּבֵינֵֽךְ׃ 18 וַתֵּ֕רֶא כִּֽי־מִתְאַמֶּ֥צֶת הִ֖יא לָלֶ֣כֶת אִתָּ֑הּ וַתֶּחְדַּ֖ל לְדַבֵּ֥ר אֵלֶֽיהָ׃ 19 וַתֵּלַ֣כְנָה שְׁתֵּיהֶ֔ם עַד־ בֹּאָ֖נָה בֵּ֣ית לָ֑חֶם וַיְהִ֗י כְּבֹאָ֙נָה֙ בֵּ֣ית לֶ֔חֶם וַתֵּהֹ֤ם כָּל־הָעִיר֙ עֲלֵיהֶ֔ן וַתֹּאמַ֖רְנָה הֲזֹ֥את נָעֳמִֽי׃ 20 וַתֹּ֣אמֶר אֲלֵיהֶ֗ן אַל־תִּקְרֶ֤אנָה לִי֙ נָעֳמִ֔י קְרֶ֥אןָ לִ֖י מָרָ֑א* כִּי־הֵמַ֥ר שַׁדַּ֛י לִ֖י מְאֹֽד׃ 21 אֲנִי֙ מְלֵאָ֣ה הָלַ֔כְתִּי וְרֵיקָ֖ם הֱשִׁיבַ֣נִי יְהוָ֑ה לָ֣מָּה תִקְרֶ֤אנָה לִי֙ נָעֳמִ֔י וַֽיהוָה֙ עָ֣נָה בִ֔י וְשַׁדַּ֖י הֵ֥רַֽע לִֽי׃ 22 וַתָּ֣שָׁב נָעֳמִ֗י וְר֨וּת הַמּוֹאֲבִיָּ֤ה כַלָּתָהּ֙ עִמָּ֔הּ הַשָּׁ֖בָה מִשְּׂדֵ֣י מוֹאָ֑ב וְהֵ֗מָּה בָּ֚אוּ בֵּ֣ית לֶ֔חֶם בִּתְחִלַּ֖ת קְצִ֥יר שְׂעֹרִֽים׃

---

b-b A formula of imprecation.
c I.e., "Pleasantness."
d I.e., "Bitterness."
e Usually rendered "the Almighty."
f-f Others "testified against."

2

Now Naomi had a kinsman on her husband's side, a man of substance, of the family of Elimelech, whose name was Boaz.

[2]Ruth the Moabite said to Naomi, "I would like to go to the fields and glean among the ears of grain, behind someone who may show me kindness." "Yes, daughter, go," she replied; [3]and off she went. She came and gleaned in a field, behind the reapers; and, as luck would have it, it was the piece of land belonging to Boaz, who was of Elimelech's family.

[4]Presently Boaz arrived from Bethlehem. He greeted the reapers, "The LORD be with you!" And they responded, "The LORD bless you!" [5]Boaz said to the servant who was in charge of the reapers, "Whose girl is that?" [6]The servant in charge of the reapers replied, "She is a Moabite girl who came back with Naomi from the country of Moab. [7]She said, 'Please let me glean and gather among the sheaves behind the reapers.' She has been on her feet ever since she came this morning. [a]-She has rested but little in the hut."-[a]

[8]Boaz said to Ruth, [b]-"Listen to me, daughter.-[b] Don't go to glean in another field. Don't go elsewhere, but stay here close to my girls. [9]Keep your eyes on the field they are reaping, and follow them. I have ordered the men not to molest you. And when you are thirsty, go to the jars and drink some of [the water] that the men have drawn."

[10]She prostrated herself with her face to the ground, and said to him, "Why are you so kind as to single me out, when I am a foreigner?"

[11]Boaz said in reply, "I have been told of all that you did for your mother-in-law after the death of your husband, how you left your father and mother and the land of your birth and came to a people you had not known before. [12]May

ב וּלְנָעֳמִ֞י מידע מוֹדַ֣ע לְאִישָׁ֗הּ אִ֚ישׁ גִּבּ֣וֹר חַ֔יִל מִמִּשְׁפַּ֖חַת אֱלִימֶ֑לֶךְ וּשְׁמ֖וֹ בֹּֽעַז׃ [2]וַתֹּאמֶר֩ ר֨וּת הַמּוֹאֲבִיָּ֜ה אֶֽל־נָעֳמִ֗י אֵֽלְכָה־נָּ֤א הַשָּׂדֶה֙ וַאֲלַקֳטָ֣ה בַשִּׁבֳּלִ֔ים אַחַ֕ר אֲשֶׁ֥ר אֶמְצָא־חֵ֖ן בְּעֵינָ֑יו וַתֹּ֥אמֶר לָ֖הּ לְכִ֥י בִתִּֽי׃ [3]וַתֵּ֤לֶךְ וַתָּבוֹא֙ וַתְּלַקֵּ֣ט בַּשָּׂדֶ֔ה אַחֲרֵ֖י הַקֹּצְרִ֑ים וַיִּ֣קֶר מִקְרֶ֔הָ חֶלְקַ֤ת הַשָּׂדֶה֙ לְבֹ֔עַז אֲשֶׁ֖ר מִמִּשְׁפַּ֥חַת אֱלִימֶֽלֶךְ׃ [4]וְהִנֵּה־בֹ֗עַז בָּ֚א מִבֵּ֣ית לֶ֔חֶם וַיֹּ֥אמֶר לַקּוֹצְרִ֖ים יְהֹוָ֣ה עִמָּכֶ֑ם וַיֹּ֥אמְרוּ ל֖וֹ יְבָרֶכְךָ֥ יְהֹוָֽה׃ [5]וַיֹּ֤אמֶר בֹּ֙עַז֙ לְנַעֲר֔וֹ הַנִּצָּ֖ב עַל־הַקּֽוֹצְרִ֑ים לְמִ֖י הַנַּעֲרָ֥ה הַזֹּֽאת׃ [6]וַיַּ֗עַן הַנַּ֛עַר הַנִּצָּ֥ב עַל־הַקּוֹצְרִ֖ים וַיֹּאמַ֑ר נַעֲרָ֤ה מֽוֹאֲבִיָּה֙ הִ֔יא הַשָּׁ֥בָה עִֽם־נׇעֳמִ֖י מִשְּׂדֵ֥ה מוֹאָֽב׃ [7]וַתֹּ֗אמֶר אֲלַקֳטָה־נָּא֙ וְאָסַפְתִּ֣י בָעֳמָרִ֔ים אַחֲרֵ֖י הַקּוֹצְרִ֑ים וַתָּב֣וֹא וַֽתַּעֲמ֗וֹד מֵאָ֤ז הַבֹּ֙קֶר֙ וְעַד־עַ֔תָּה זֶ֛ה שִׁבְתָּ֥הּ הַבַּ֖יִת מְעָֽט׃ [8]וַיֹּאמֶר֩ בֹּ֨עַז אֶל־ר֜וּת הֲל֧וֹא שָׁמַ֣עַתְּ בִּתִּ֗י אַל־תֵּלְכִי֙ לִלְקֹט֙ בְּשָׂדֶ֣ה אַחֵ֔ר וְגַ֛ם לֹ֥א תַעֲבוּרִ֖י מִזֶּ֑ה וְכֹ֥ה תִדְבָּקִ֖ין עִם־נַעֲרֹתָֽי׃ [9]עֵינַ֜יִךְ בַּשָּׂדֶ֤ה אֲשֶׁר־יִקְצֹרוּן֙ וְהָלַ֣כְתְּ אַחֲרֵיהֶ֔ן הֲל֥וֹא צִוִּ֛יתִי אֶת־הַנְּעָרִ֖ים לְבִלְתִּ֣י נׇגְעֵ֑ךְ וְצָמִ֗ת וְהָלַכְתְּ֙ אֶל־הַכֵּלִ֔ים וְשָׁתִ֕ית מֵאֲשֶׁ֥ר יִשְׁאֲב֖וּן הַנְּעָרִֽים׃ [10]וַתִּפֹּל֙ עַל־פָּנֶ֔יהָ וַתִּשְׁתַּ֖חוּ אָ֑רְצָה וַתֹּ֣אמֶר אֵלָ֗יו מַדּוּעַ֩ מָצָ֨אתִי חֵ֤ן בְּעֵינֶ֙יךָ֙ לְהַכִּירֵ֔נִי וְאָנֹכִ֖י נׇכְרִיָּֽה׃ [11]וַיַּ֤עַן בֹּ֙עַז֙ וַיֹּ֣אמֶר לָ֔הּ הֻגֵּ֨ד הֻגַּ֜ד לִ֗י כֹּ֤ל אֲשֶׁר־עָשִׂית֙ אֶת־חֲמוֹתֵ֔ךְ אַחֲרֵ֖י מ֣וֹת אִישֵׁ֑ךְ וַתַּֽעַזְבִ֞י אָבִ֣יךְ וְאִמֵּ֗ךְ וְאֶ֙רֶץ֙ מֽוֹלַדְתֵּ֔ךְ וַתֵּ֣לְכִ֔י אֶל־עַ֕ם אֲשֶׁ֥ר לֹא־יָדַ֖עַתְּ תְּמ֥וֹל שִׁלְשֽׁוֹם׃ [12]יְשַׁלֵּ֥ם יְהֹוָ֖ה פׇּעֳלֵ֑ךְ וּתְהִ֨י

---

a-a   *Meaning of Heb. uncertain.*
b-b   *Lit. "Have you not heard, daughter?"*

the LORD reward your deeds. May you have a full recompense from the LORD, the God of Israel, under whose wings you have sought refuge!"

¹³She answered, "You are most kind, my lord, to comfort me and to speak gently to your maidservant—though I am not so much as one of your maidservants."

¹⁴At mealtime, Boaz said to her, "Come over here and partake of the meal, and dip your morsel in the vinegar." So she sat down beside the reapers. He handed her roasted grain, and she ate her fill and had some left over.

¹⁵When she got up again to glean, Boaz gave orders to his workers, "You are not only to let her glean among the sheaves, without interference, ¹⁶but you must also pull some [stalks] out of the heaps and leave them for her to glean, and not scold her."

¹⁷She gleaned in the field until evening. Then she beat out what she had gleaned—it was about an 'ephah of barley—¹⁸and carried it back with her to the town. When her mother-in-law saw what she had gleaned, and when she also took out and gave her what she had left over after eating her fill, ¹⁹her mother-in-law asked her, "Where did you glean today? Where did you work? Blessed be he who took such generous notice of you!" So she told her mother-in-law whom she had worked with, saying, "The name of the man with whom I worked today is Boaz."

²⁰Naomi said to her daughter-in-law, "Blessed be he of the LORD, who has not failed in His kindness to the living or to the dead! For," Naomi explained to her daughter-in-law, "the man is related to us; he is one of our redeeming kinsmen."ᶜ ²¹Ruth the Moabite said, "He even told me, 'Stay close by my workers until all my harvest is finished.'" ²²And Naomi answered her daughter-in-law Ruth, "It is best, daughter, that

מַשְׂכֻּרְתֵּ֣ךְ שְׁלֵמָ֗ה מֵעִ֤ם יְהוָה֙ אֱלֹהֵ֣י
יִשְׂרָאֵ֔ל אֲשֶׁר־בָּ֖את לַחֲס֥וֹת תַּֽחַת־כְּנָפָֽיו׃
13 וַ֠תֹּאמֶר אֶמְצָא־חֵ֨ן בְּעֵינֶ֤יךָ אֲדֹנִי֙ כִּ֣י
נִֽחַמְתָּ֔נִי וְכִ֥י דִבַּ֖רְתָּ עַל־לֵ֣ב שִׁפְחָתֶ֑ךָ וְאָ֣נֹכִ֔י
לֹ֣א אֶֽהְיֶ֔ה כְּאַחַ֖ת שִׁפְחֹתֶֽיךָ׃
14 וַיֹּאמֶר֩ לָ֨ה* בֹ֜עַז לְעֵ֣ת הָאֹ֗כֶל גֹּ֤שִֽׁי הֲלֹם֙
וְאָכַ֣לְתְּ מִן־הַלֶּ֔חֶם וְטָבַ֥לְתְּ פִּתֵּ֖ךְ בַּחֹ֑מֶץ
וַתֵּ֙שֶׁב֙ מִצַּ֣ד הַקּֽוֹצְרִ֔ים וַיִּצְבָּט־לָ֣הּ קָלִ֔י
וַתֹּ֥אכַל וַתִּשְׂבַּ֖ע וַתֹּתַֽר׃
15 וַתָּ֖קָם לְלַקֵּ֑ט וַיְצַו֩ בֹּ֨עַז אֶת־נְעָרָ֜יו לֵאמֹ֗ר
גַּ֣ם בֵּ֧ין הָעֳמָרִ֛ים תְּלַקֵּ֖ט וְלֹ֥א תַכְלִימֽוּהָ׃
16 וְגַ֛ם שֹׁל־תָּשֹׁ֥לּוּ לָ֖הּ מִן־הַצְּבָתִ֑ים
וַעֲזַבְתֶּ֥ם וְלִקְּטָ֖ה וְלֹ֥א תִגְעֲרוּ־בָֽהּ׃
17 וַתְּלַקֵּ֥ט בַּשָּׂדֶ֖ה עַד־הָעָ֑רֶב וַתַּחְבֹּט֙ אֵ֣ת
אֲשֶׁר־לִקֵּ֔טָה וַיְהִ֖י כְּאֵיפָ֥ה שְׂעֹרִֽים׃
18 וַתִּשָּׂ֖א וַתָּב֣וֹא הָעִ֑יר וַתֵּ֥רֶא חֲמוֹתָ֖הּ אֵ֣ת
אֲשֶׁר־לִקֵּ֑טָה וַתּוֹצֵא֙ וַתִּתֶּן־לָ֔הּ אֵ֥ת אֲשֶׁר־
הוֹתִ֖רָה מִשָּׂבְעָֽהּ׃ 19 וַתֹּאמֶר֩ לָ֨הּ חֲמוֹתָ֜הּ
אֵיפֹ֨ה לִקַּ֤טְתְּ הַיּוֹם֙ וְאָ֣נָה עָשִׂ֔ית יְהִ֥י
מַכִּירֵ֖ךְ בָּר֑וּךְ וַתַּגֵּ֣ד לַחֲמוֹתָ֗הּ אֵ֤ת אֲשֶׁר־
עָֽשְׂתָה֙ עִמּ֔וֹ וַתֹּ֗אמֶר שֵׁ֤ם הָאִישׁ֙ אֲשֶׁ֨ר
עָשִׂ֧יתִי עִמּ֛וֹ הַיּ֖וֹם בֹּֽעַז׃
20 וַתֹּ֨אמֶר נָעֳמִ֜י לְכַלָּתָ֗הּ בָּר֥וּךְ הוּא֙ לַֽיהוָ֔ה
אֲשֶׁר֙ לֹא־עָזַ֣ב חַסְדּ֔וֹ אֶת־הַֽחַיִּ֖ים וְאֶת־
הַמֵּתִ֑ים וַתֹּ֧אמֶר לָ֣הּ נָעֳמִ֗י קָר֥וֹב לָ֙נוּ֙
הָאִ֔ישׁ מִֽגֹּאֲלֵ֖נוּ הֽוּא׃ 21* וַתֹּ֖אמֶר ר֣וּת
הַמּוֹאֲבִיָּ֑ה גַּ֣ם ׀ כִּי־אָמַ֣ר אֵלַ֗י עִם־הַנְּעָרִ֤ים
אֲשֶׁר־לִי֙ תִּדְבָּקִ֔ין עַ֣ד אִם־כִּלּ֔וּ אֵ֖ת כָּל־
הַקָּצִ֥יר אֲשֶׁר־לִֽי׃ 22 וַתֹּ֧אמֶר נָעֳמִ֛י אֶל־ר֥וּת

c Cf. Lev. 25.25 and note and Deut. 25.5–6. The fact that Boaz was a kinsman of Ruth's dead husband opened up the possibility of providing an heir for the latter.

v. 14. ה' רפה
v. 21. חצי הספר בפסוקים

1744

you go out with his girls, and not be annoyed in some other field." ²³So she stayed close to the maidservants of Boaz, and gleaned until the barley harvest and the wheat harvest were finished. Then she stayed at home with her mother-in-law.

3 Naomi, her mother-in-law, said to her, "Daughter, I must seek a home for you, where you may be happy. ²Now there is our kinsman Boaz, whose girls you were close to. He will be winnowing barley on the threshing floor tonight. ³So bathe, anoint yourself, dress up, and go down to the threshing floor. But do not disclose yourself to the man until he has finished eating and drinking. ⁴When he lies down, note the place where he lies down, and go over and uncover his feet and lie down. He will tell you what you are to do." ⁵She replied, "I will do everything you tell me."

⁶She went down to the threshing floor and did just as her mother-in-law had instructed her. ⁷Boaz ate and drank, and in a cheerful mood went to lie down beside the grainpile. Then she went over stealthily and uncovered his feet and lay down. ⁸In the middle of the night, the man gave a start and pulled back—there was a woman lying at his feet!

⁹"Who are you?" he asked. And she replied, "I am your handmaid Ruth. ᵃ-Spread your robe over your handmaid,-ᵃ for you are a redeeming kinsman."

¹⁰He exclaimed, "Be blessed of the LORD, daughter! Your latest deed of loyalty is greater than the first, in that you have not turned to younger men, whether poor or rich.ᵇ ¹¹And now, daughter, have no fear. I will do in your behalf whatever you ask, for all the ᶜ-elders of

כַּלָּתֵהּ טוֹב בִּתִּי כִּי תֵצְאִי עִם־נַעֲרוֹתָיו וְלֹא יִפְגְּעוּ־בָךְ בְּשָׂדֶה אַחֵר: 23 וַתִּדְבַּ֫ק בְּנַעֲרוֹת בֹּעַז לְלַקֵּט עַד־כְּלוֹת קְצִיר־הַשְּׂעֹרִים וּקְצִיר הַחִטִּים וַתֵּשֶׁב אֶת־חֲמוֹתָהּ:

ג וַתֹּאמֶר לָהּ נָעֳמִי חֲמוֹתָהּ בִּתִּי הֲלֹא אֲבַקֶּשׁ־לָךְ מָנוֹחַ אֲשֶׁר יִיטַב־לָךְ: 2 וְעַתָּה הֲלֹא בֹעַז מֹדַעְתָּנוּ אֲשֶׁר הָיִית אֶת־נַעֲרוֹתָיו הִנֵּה־הוּא זֹרֶה אֶת־גֹּרֶן הַשְּׂעֹרִים הַלָּיְלָה: 3 וְרָחַצְתְּ ׀ וָסַכְתְּ וְשַׂמְתְּ שִׂמְלֹתַיִךְ עָלַיִךְ וְיָרַדְתִּי הַגֹּרֶן אַל־תִּוָּדְעִי לָאִישׁ עַד כַּלֹּתוֹ לֶאֱכֹל וְלִשְׁתּוֹת: 4 וִיהִי בְשָׁכְבוֹ וְיָדַעַתְּ אֶת־הַמָּקוֹם אֲשֶׁר יִשְׁכַּב־שָׁם וּבָאת וְגִלִּית מַרְגְּלֹתָיו וְשָׁכָבְתְּ וְהוּא יַגִּיד לָךְ אֵת אֲשֶׁר תַּעֲשִׂין: 5 וַתֹּאמֶר אֵלֶיהָ כֹּל אֲשֶׁר־תֹּאמְרִי [אֵלַי*] אֶעֱשֶׂה:

6 וַתֵּרֶד הַגֹּרֶן וַתַּעַשׂ כְּכֹל אֲשֶׁר־צִוַּתָּה חֲמוֹתָהּ: 7 וַיֹּאכַל בֹּעַז וַיֵּשְׁתְּ וַיִּיטַב לִבּוֹ וַיָּבֹא לִשְׁכַּב בִּקְצֵה הָעֲרֵמָה וַתָּבֹא בַלָּט וַתְּגַל מַרְגְּלֹתָיו וַתִּשְׁכָּב: 8 וַיְהִי בַּחֲצִי הַלַּיְלָה וַיֶּחֱרַד הָאִישׁ וַיִּלָּפֵת וְהִנֵּה אִשָּׁה שֹׁכֶבֶת מַרְגְּלֹתָיו: 9 וַיֹּאמֶר מִי־אָתּ וַתֹּאמֶר אָנֹכִי רוּת אֲמָתֶךָ וּפָרַשְׂתָּ כְנָפֶךָ עַל־אֲמָתְךָ כִּי גֹאֵל אָתָּה: 10 וַיֹּאמֶר בְּרוּכָה אַתְּ לַיהוָה בִּתִּי הֵיטַבְתְּ חַסְדֵּךְ הָאַחֲרוֹן מִן־הָרִאשׁוֹן לְבִלְתִּי־לֶכֶת אַחֲרֵי הַבַּחוּרִים אִם־דַּל וְאִם־עָשִׁיר: 11 וְעַתָּה בִּתִּי אַל־תִּירְאִי כֹּל אֲשֶׁר־תֹּאמְרִי אֶעֱשֶׂה־לָךְ כִּי יוֹדֵעַ כָּל־שַׁעַר עַמִּי כִּי אֵשֶׁת חַיִל אָתְּ: 12 וְעַתָּה כִּי אָמְנָם כִּי

v. 5. קְרִיא וְלֹא כְתִיב

---

a-a   *A formal act of espousal; cf. Ezek. 16.8.*
b   *I.e., she sought out a kinsman of her dead husband; see note at 2.20 above. Her first act of loyalty had been to return with Naomi.*
c-c   *Lit. "gate of my people."*

my town-c know what a fine woman you are. 12But while it is true I am a redeeming kinsman, there is another redeemer closer than I. 13Stay for the night. Then in the morning, if he will act as a redeemer, good! let him redeem. But if he does not want to act as redeemer for you, I will do so myself, as the Lord lives! Lie down until morning."

14So she lay at his feet until dawn. She rose before one person could distinguish another, for he thought, "Let it not be known that the woman came to the threshing floor." 15And he said, "Hold out the shawl you are wearing." She held it while he measured out six measures of barley, and he put it on her back.

When she-d got back to the town, 16she came to her mother-in-law, who asked, "How is it with you, daughter?" She told her all that the man had done for her; 17and she added, "He gave me these six measures of barley, saying to me, 'Do not go back to your mother-in-law empty-handed.'" 18And Naomi said, "Stay here, daughter, till you learn how the matter turns out. For the man will not rest, but will settle the matter today."

4 Meanwhile, Boaz had gone to the gate and sat down there. And now the redeemer whom Boaz had mentioned passed by. He called, "Come over and sit down here, So-and-so!" And he came over and sat down. 2Then [Boaz] took ten elders of the town and said, "Be seated here"; and they sat down.

3He said to the redeemer, "Naomi, now returned from the country of Moab, must sell the piece of land which belonged to our kinsman Elimelech. 4I thought I should disclose the matter to you and say: Acquire it in the presence of those seated here and in the presence of the

אִם־גָּאַל֙ אָנֹכִ֔י וְגַ֛ם יֵ֥שׁ גֹּאֵ֖ל קָר֥וֹב מִמֶּֽנִּי׃ 13 לִ֣ינִי ׀ הַלַּ֗יְלָה וְהָיָ֤ה בַבֹּ֙קֶר֙ אִם־יִגְאָלֵ֥ךְ טוֹב֙ יִגְאָ֔ל וְאִם־לֹ֨א יַחְפֹּ֜ץ לְגָֽאֳלֵ֗ךְ וּגְאַלְתִּ֤יךְ אָנֹ֙כִי֙ חַי־יְהוָ֔ה שִׁכְבִ֖י עַד־הַבֹּֽקֶר׃ 14 וַתִּשְׁכַּ֤ב מַרְגְּלוֹתָו֙ עַד־הַבֹּ֔קֶר וַתָּ֕קָם בטרום בְּטֶ֛רֶם יַכִּ֥יר אִ֖ישׁ אֶת־רֵעֵ֑הוּ וַיֹּ֙אמֶר֙ אַל־יִוָּדַ֔ע כִּי־בָ֥אָה הָאִשָּׁ֖ה הַגֹּֽרֶן׃ 15 וַיֹּ֗אמֶר הָ֠בִי הַמִּטְפַּ֤חַת אֲשֶׁר־עָלַ֙יִךְ֙ וְאֶֽחֳזִי־בָ֔הּ וַתֹּ֖אחֶז בָּ֑הּ וַיָּ֤מָד שֵׁשׁ־שְׂעֹרִים֙ וַיָּ֣שֶׁת עָלֶ֔יהָ וַיָּבֹ֖א הָעִֽיר׃ 16 וַתָּבוֹא֙ אֶל־חֲמוֹתָ֔הּ וַתֹּ֖אמֶר מִי־אַ֣תְּ בִּתִּ֑י וַתַּ֨גֶּד־לָ֔הּ אֵ֛ת כָּל־אֲשֶׁ֥ר עָֽשָׂה־לָ֖הּ הָאִֽישׁ׃ 17 וַתֹּ֕אמֶר שֵׁשׁ־הַשְּׂעֹרִ֥ים הָאֵ֖לֶּה נָ֣תַן לִ֑י כִּ֤י אָמַר֙ [אֵלַי֙*] אַל־תָּב֥וֹאִי רֵיקָ֖ם אֶל־חֲמוֹתֵֽךְ׃ 18 וַתֹּ֙אמֶר֙ שְׁבִ֣י בִתִּ֔י עַ֚ד אֲשֶׁ֣ר תֵּֽדְעִ֔ין אֵ֖יךְ יִפֹּ֣ל דָּבָ֑ר כִּ֣י לֹ֤א יִשְׁקֹט֙ הָאִ֔ישׁ כִּֽי־אִם־כִּלָּ֥ה הַדָּבָ֖ר הַיּֽוֹם׃

ד וּבֹ֨עַז עָלָ֣ה הַשַּׁעַר֮ וַיֵּ֣שֶׁב שָׁם֒ וְהִנֵּ֨ה הַגֹּאֵ֤ל עֹבֵר֙ אֲשֶׁ֣ר דִּבֶּר־בֹּ֔עַז וַיֹּ֛אמֶר ס֥וּרָה שְׁבָה־פֹּ֖ה פְּלֹנִ֣י אַלְמֹנִ֑י וַיָּ֖סַר וַיֵּשֵֽׁב׃ 2 וַיִּקַּ֞ח עֲשָׂרָ֤ה אֲנָשִׁים֙ מִזִּקְנֵ֣י הָעִ֔יר וַיֹּ֖אמֶר שְׁבוּ־פֹ֑ה וַיֵּשֵֽׁבוּ׃ 3 וַיֹּ֙אמֶר֙ לַגֹּאֵ֔ל חֶלְקַת֙ הַשָּׂדֶ֔ה אֲשֶׁ֥ר לְאָחִ֖ינוּ לֶאֱלִימֶ֑לֶךְ מָכְרָ֣ה נָעֳמִ֔י הַשָּׁ֖בָה מִשְּׂדֵ֥ה מוֹאָֽב׃ 4 וַאֲנִ֨י אָמַ֜רְתִּי אֶגְלֶ֧ה אָזְנְךָ֣ לֵאמֹ֗ר קְ֠נֵה נֶ֥גֶד הַיֹּֽשְׁבִים֙ וְנֶ֣גֶד זִקְנֵ֣י עַמִּ֔י

v. 12. כתיב ולא קריא
v. 15. בנוסח אחר "ותבא"
v. 17. קריא ולא כתיב

d So in many Heb. mss; most mss. read "he."

elders of my people. If you are willing to redeem it, redeem! But if you[a] will not redeem, tell me, that I may know. For there is no one to redeem but you, and I come after you." "I am willing to redeem it," he replied. [5]Boaz continued, "When you acquire the property from Naomi [b]-and from Ruth the Moabite, you must also acquire the wife of the deceased,-[b] so as to perpetuate the name of the deceased upon his estate." [6]The redeemer replied, "Then I cannot redeem it for myself, lest I impair my own estate.[c] You take over my right of redemption, for I am unable to exercise it."

[7]Now this was formerly done in Israel in cases of redemption or exchange: to validate any transaction, one man would take off his sandal and hand it to the other. Such was the practice[d] in Israel. [8]So when the redeemer said to Boaz, "Acquire for yourself," he drew off his sandal. [9]And Boaz said to the elders and to the rest of the people, "You are witnesses today that I am acquiring from Naomi all that belonged to Elimelech and all that belonged to Chilion and Mahlon. [10]I am also acquiring Ruth the Moabite, the wife of Mahlon, as my wife, so as to perpetuate the name of the deceased upon his estate, that the name of the deceased may not disappear from among his kinsmen and from the gate of his home town. You are witnesses today."

[11]All the people at the gate and the elders answered, "We are. May the LORD make the woman who is coming into your house like Rachel and Leah, both of whom built up the House of Israel! Prosper in Ephrathah[e] and perpetuate your name in Bethlehem! [12]And may

אִם־תִּגְאַל֙ גְּאָ֔ל וְאִם־לֹ֨א יִגְאַל֙* הַגִּ֣ידָה לִּ֔י וְאֵ֣דְעָ֔ה כִּ֣י אֵ֤ין זֽוּלָתְךָ֙ לִגְא֔וֹל וְאָנֹכִ֖י אַחֲרֶ֑יךָ וַיֹּ֖אמֶר אָנֹכִ֥י אֶגְאָֽל׃ [5]וַיֹּ֣אמֶר בֹּ֗עַז בְּיוֹם־קְנוֹתְךָ֧ הַשָּׂדֶ֛ה מִיַּ֣ד נָעֳמִ֑י וּ֠מֵאֵ֞ת ר֣וּת הַמּוֹאֲבִיָּ֤ה אֵֽשֶׁת־הַמֵּת֙ קָנִ֔יתָה לְהָקִ֥ים שֵׁם־הַמֵּ֖ת עַל־נַחֲלָתֽוֹ׃ [6]וַיֹּ֣אמֶר הַגֹּאֵ֗ל לֹ֤א אוּכַל֙ לִגְאׇל־לִ֔י פֶּן־אַשְׁחִ֖ית אֶת־נַחֲלָתִ֑י גְּאַל־לְךָ֤ אַתָּה֙ אֶת־גְּאֻלָּתִ֔י כִּ֥י לֹא־אוּכַ֖ל לִגְאֹֽל׃ [7]וְזֹאת֩ לְפָנִ֨ים בְּיִשְׂרָאֵ֜ל עַל־הַגְּאוּלָּ֤ה וְעַל־הַתְּמוּרָה֙ לְקַיֵּ֣ם כׇּל־דָּבָ֔ר שָׁלַ֥ף אִ֛ישׁ נַעֲל֖וֹ וְנָתַ֣ן לְרֵעֵ֑הוּ וְזֹ֥את הַתְּעוּדָ֖ה בְּיִשְׂרָאֵֽל׃ [8]וַיֹּ֧אמֶר הַגֹּאֵ֛ל לְבֹ֖עַז קְנֵה־לָ֑ךְ וַיִּשְׁלֹ֖ף נַעֲלֽוֹ׃ [9]וַיֹּ֩אמֶר֩ בֹּ֨עַז לַזְּקֵנִ֜ים וְכׇל־הָעָ֗ם עֵדִ֤ים אַתֶּם֙ הַיּ֔וֹם כִּ֤י קָנִ֙יתִי֙ אֶת־כׇּל־אֲשֶׁ֣ר לֶֽאֱלִימֶ֔לֶךְ וְאֵ֛ת כׇּל־אֲשֶׁ֥ר לְכִלְי֖וֹן וּמַחְל֑וֹן מִיַּ֖ד נׇעֳמִֽי׃ [10]וְגַ֣ם אֶת־ר֣וּת הַמֹּאֲבִיָּה֩ אֵ֨שֶׁת מַחְל֜וֹן קָנִ֧יתִי לִ֣י לְאִשָּׁ֗ה לְהָקִ֤ים שֵׁם־הַמֵּת֙ עַל־נַ֣חֲלָת֔וֹ וְלֹא־יִכָּרֵ֧ת שֵׁם־הַמֵּ֛ת מֵעִ֥ם אֶחָ֖יו וּמִשַּׁ֣עַר מְקוֹמ֑וֹ עֵדִ֥ים אַתֶּ֖ם הַיּֽוֹם׃ [11]וַיֹּ֨אמְר֜וּ כׇּל־הָעָ֧ם אֲשֶׁר־בַּשַּׁ֛עַר וְהַזְּקֵנִ֖ים עֵדִ֑ים יִתֵּן֩ יְהֹוָ֨ה אֶֽת־הָאִשָּׁ֜ה הַבָּאָ֣ה אֶל־בֵּיתֶ֗ךָ כְּרָחֵ֤ל ׀ וּכְלֵאָה֙ אֲשֶׁר֩ בָּנ֨וּ שְׁתֵּיהֶ֜ם אֶת־בֵּ֣ית יִשְׂרָאֵ֗ל וַעֲשֵׂה־חַ֙יִל֙ בְּאֶפְרָ֔תָה וּקְרָא־שֵׁ֖ם בְּבֵ֥ית לָֽחֶם׃ [12]וִיהִ֤י בֵֽיתְךָ֙

---

a So many Heb. mss., Septuagint, and Targum; most mss. read "he."

b-b Emendation yields "you must also acquire Ruth the Moabite, the wife of the deceased"; cf. v. 10.

c I.e., by expending capital for property which will go to the son legally regarded as Mahlon's; see Deut. 25.5–6.

d Understanding Heb. te'udah in the sense of the Arabic 'ādah and Syriac 'yādā. Cf. Ibn Ezra.

e Ephrathah is another name applied to Bethlehem; cf. 1.2; Gen. 35.16, 19; 48.7; Mic. 5.1.

your house be like the house of Perez whom Tamar bore to Judah—through the offspring which the LORD will give you by this young woman."

13So Boaz married Ruth; she became his wife, and he cohabited with her. The LORD let her conceive, and she bore a son. 14And the women said to Naomi, "Blessed be the LORD, who has not withheld a redeemer from you today! May his name be perpetuated in Israel! 15He will renew your life and sustain your old age; for he is born of your daughter-in-law, who loves you and is better to you than seven sons."

16Naomi took the child and held it to her bosom. She became its foster mother, 17and the women neighbors gave him a name, saying, "A son is born to Naomi!" They named him Obed; he was the father of Jesse, father of David.

18This is the line of Perez: Perez begot Hezron, 19Hezron begot Ram, Ram begot Amminadab, 20Amminadab begot Nahshon, Nahshon begot Salmon,f 21Salmon begot Boaz, Boaz begot Obed, 22Obed begot Jesse, and Jesse begot David.

כְּבֵית פֶּרֶץ אֲשֶׁר־יָלְדָה תָמָר לִיהוּדָה מִן־הַזֶּרַע אֲשֶׁר יִתֵּן יְהֹוָה לְךָ מִן־הַנַּעֲרָה הַזֹּאת: 13 וַיִּקַּח בֹּעַז אֶת־רוּת וַתְּהִי־לוֹ לְאִשָּׁה וַיָּבֹא אֵלֶיהָ וַיִּתֵּן יְהֹוָה לָהּ הֵרָיוֹן וַתֵּלֶד בֵּן: 14 וַתֹּאמַרְנָה הַנָּשִׁים אֶל־נָעֳמִי בָּרוּךְ יְהֹוָה אֲשֶׁר לֹא הִשְׁבִּית לָךְ גֹּאֵל הַיּוֹם וְיִקָּרֵא שְׁמוֹ בְּיִשְׂרָאֵל: 15 וְהָיָה לָךְ לְמֵשִׁיב נֶפֶשׁ וּלְכַלְכֵּל אֶת־שֵׂיבָתֵךְ כִּי כַלָּתֵךְ אֲשֶׁר־אֲהֵבַתֶךְ יְלָדַתּוּ אֲשֶׁר־הִיא טוֹבָה לָךְ מִשִּׁבְעָה בָּנִים: 16 וַתִּקַּח נָעֳמִי אֶת־הַיֶּלֶד וַתְּשִׁתֵהוּ בְחֵיקָהּ וַתְּהִי־לוֹ לְאֹמֶנֶת: 17 וַתִּקְרֶאנָה לוֹ הַשְּׁכֵנוֹת שֵׁם לֵאמֹר יֻלַּד־בֵּן לְנָעֳמִי וַתִּקְרֶאנָה שְׁמוֹ עוֹבֵד הוּא אֲבִי־יִשַׁי אֲבִי דָוִד: פ 18 וְאֵלֶּה תּוֹלְדוֹת פָּרֶץ פֶּרֶץ הוֹלִיד אֶת־חֶצְרוֹן: 19 וְחֶצְרוֹן הוֹלִיד אֶת־רָם וְרָם הוֹלִיד אֶת־עַמִּינָדָב: 20 וְעַמִּינָדָב הוֹלִיד אֶת־נַחְשׁוֹן וְנַחְשׁוֹן הוֹלִיד אֶת־שַׂלְמָה: 21 וְשַׂלְמוֹן הוֹלִיד אֶת־בֹּעַז וּבֹעַז הוֹלִיד אֶת־עוֹבֵד: 22 וְעֹבֵד הוֹלִיד אֶת־יִשַׁי וְיִשַׁי הוֹלִיד אֶת־דָּוִד: *

תם ונשלם תהילה לאל בורא עולם

---

f Heb. "Salmah."

LAMENTATIONS

1 א ᵃAlas!

Lonely sits the city
Once great with people!
She that was great among nations
Is become like a widow;
The princess among states
Is become a thrall.

ב ²Bitterly she weeps in the night,
Her cheek wet with tears.
There is none to comfort her
Of all her friends.
All her allies have betrayed her;
They have become her foes.

ג ³Judah has gone into exile
Because of misery and harsh oppression;
When she settled among the nations,
She found no rest;
All her pursuers overtook her
ᵇ-In the narrow places.-ᵇ

ד ⁴Zion's roads are in mourning,
Empty of festival pilgrims;
All her gates are deserted.
Her priests sigh,
Her maidens are unhappy—
She is utterly disconsolate!

ה ⁵Her enemies are now the masters,
Her foes are at ease,
Because the LORD has afflicted her
For her many transgressions;
Her infants have gone into captivity
Before the enemy.

א אֵיכָ֣ה ׀
יָשְׁבָ֣ה בָדָ֗ד הָעִיר֙
רַבָּ֣תִי עָ֔ם
הָיְתָ֖ה כְּאַלְמָנָ֑ה
רַבָּ֣תִי בַגּוֹיִ֗ם
שָׂרָ֙תִי֙ בַּמְּדִינ֔וֹת
הָיְתָ֖ה לָמַֽס׃ ס

² בָּכ֨וֹ תִבְכֶּ֜ה בַּלַּ֗יְלָה
וְדִמְעָתָהּ֙ עַ֣ל לֶֽחֱיָ֔הּ
אֵֽין־לָ֥הּ מְנַחֵ֖ם
מִכָּל־אֹֽהֲבֶ֑יהָ
כָּל־רֵעֶ֙יהָ֙ בָּ֣גְדוּ בָ֔הּ
הָ֥יוּ לָ֖הּ לְאֹיְבִֽים׃ ס

³ גָּֽלְתָ֨ה יְהוּדָ֤ה
מֵעֹ֙נִי֙ וּמֵרֹ֣ב עֲבֹדָ֔ה
הִ֚יא יָשְׁבָ֣ה בַגּוֹיִ֔ם
לֹ֥א מָצְאָ֖ה מָנ֑וֹחַ
כָּל־רֹֽדְפֶ֥יהָ הִשִּׂיג֖וּהָ
בֵּ֥ין הַמְּצָרִֽים׃ ס

⁴ דַּרְכֵ֨י צִיּ֜וֹן אֲבֵל֗וֹת
מִבְּלִי֙ בָּאֵ֣י מוֹעֵ֔ד
כָּל־שְׁעָרֶ֙יהָ֙ שֽׁוֹמֵמִ֔ין
כֹּהֲנֶ֣יהָ נֶאֱנָחִ֑ים
בְּתוּלֹתֶ֥יהָ נּוּג֖וֹת
וְהִ֥יא מַר־לָֽהּ׃ ס

⁵ הָי֨וּ צָרֶ֤יהָ לְרֹאשׁ֙
אֹיְבֶ֣יהָ שָׁל֔וּ
כִּֽי־יְהֹוָ֥ה הוֹגָ֖הּ
עַ֣ל רֹב־פְּשָׁעֶ֑יהָ
עוֹלָלֶ֛יהָ הָלְכ֥וּ שְׁבִ֖י
לִפְנֵי־צָֽר׃ ס

ᵃ Chaps. 1–4 are alphabetical acrostics, i.e., the verses begin with
the successive letters of the Heb. alphabet. Chap. 3 is a triple
acrostic. In chaps. 2–4 the letter *pe* precedes the 'ayin.
ᵇ-ᵇ Meaning of Heb. uncertain.

ו 6Gone from Fair Zion are all
That were her glory;
Her leaders were like stags
That found no pasture;
They could only walk feebly
Before the pursuer.

ז 7All the precious things she had
In the days of old
Jerusalem recalled
In her days of woe and sorrow,
When her people fell by enemy hands
With none to help her;
When enemies looked on and gloated
Over her downfall.

ח 8Jerusalem has greatly sinned,
Therefore she is become a mockery.
All who admired her despise her,
For they have seen her disgraced;
And she can only sigh
And shrink back.

ט 9Her uncleanness clings to her skirts.
She gave no thought to her future;
She has sunk appallingly,
With none to comfort her.—
See, O LORD, my misery;
How the enemy jeers!

י 10The foe has laid hands
On everything dear to her.
She has seen her Sanctuary
Invaded by nations
Which You have denied admission
Into Your community.

כ 11All her inhabitants sigh
As they search for bread;
They have bartered their treasures for food,
To keep themselves alive.—

6וַיֵּצֵא מן בת מִבַּת־צִיּוֹן
כָּל־הֲדָרָהּ
הָיוּ שָׂרֶיהָ כְּאַיָּלִים
לֹא־מָצְאוּ מִרְעֶה
וַיֵּלְכוּ בְלֹא־כֹחַ
לִפְנֵי רוֹדֵף: ס

7זָכְרָה יְרוּשָׁלִַם
יְמֵי עָנְיָהּ וּמְרוּדֶיהָ
כֹּל מַחֲמֻדֶיהָ אֲשֶׁר הָיוּ
מִימֵי קֶדֶם
בִּנְפֹל עַמָּהּ בְּיַד־צָר
וְאֵין עוֹזֵר לָהּ
רָאוּהָ צָרִים שָׂחֲקוּ
עַל מִשְׁבַּתֶּהָ: ס

8חֵטְא חָטְאָה יְרוּשָׁלִַם
עַל־כֵּן לְנִידָה הָיָתָה
כָּל־מְכַבְּדֶיהָ הִזִּילוּהָ
כִּי־רָאוּ עֶרְוָתָהּ
גַּם־הִיא נֶאֶנְחָה
וַתָּשָׁב אָחוֹר: ס

9טֻמְאָתָהּ בְּשׁוּלֶיהָ
לֹא זָכְרָה אַחֲרִיתָהּ
וַתֵּרֶד פְּלָאִים
אֵין מְנַחֵם לָהּ
רְאֵה יְהוָה אֶת־עָנְיִי
כִּי הִגְדִּיל אוֹיֵב: ס

10יָדוֹ פָּרַשׂ צָר
עַל כָּל־מַחֲמַדֶּיהָ
כִּי־רָאֲתָה
גוֹיִם בָּאוּ מִקְדָּשָׁהּ
אֲשֶׁר צִוִּיתָה לֹא־יָבֹאוּ
בַקָּהָל לָךְ: ס

11כָּל־עַמָּהּ נֶאֱנָחִים
מְבַקְשִׁים לֶחֶם
נָתְנוּ מחמודיהם מַחֲמַדֵּיהֶם בְּאֹכֶל
לְהָשִׁיב נָפֶשׁ

See, O Lord, and behold,
c-How abject-*c* I have become!

רְאֵה יְהוָה וְהַבִּיטָה
כִּי הָיִיתִי זוֹלֵלָה: ס

ל 12*b*-May it never befall you,-*b*
All who pass along the road—
Look about and see:
Is there any agony like mine,
Which was dealt out to me
When the Lord afflicted me
On His day of wrath?

12 לוֹא אֲלֵיכֶם
כָּל־עֹבְרֵי דֶרֶךְ
הַבִּיטוּ וּרְאוּ
אִם־יֵשׁ מַכְאוֹב כְּמַכְאֹבִי
אֲשֶׁר עוֹלַל לִי
אֲשֶׁר הוֹגָה יְהוָה
בְּיוֹם חֲרוֹן אַפּוֹ: ס

מ 13From above He sent a fire
Down into my bones.
He spread a net for my feet,
He hurled me backward;
He has left me forlorn,
In constant misery.

13 מִמָּרוֹם שָׁלַח־אֵשׁ
בְּעַצְמֹתַי וַיִּרְדֶּנָּה
פָּרַשׂ רֶשֶׁת לְרַגְלַי
הֱשִׁיבַנִי אָחוֹר
נְתָנַנִי שֹׁמֵמָה
כָּל־הַיּוֹם דָּוָה: ס

נ 14*d*The yoke of my offenses is bound fast,
Lashed tight by His hand;
Imposed upon my neck,
It saps my strength;
The Lord has delivered me into the hands
Of those I cannot withstand.

14 נִשְׂקַד עֹל פְּשָׁעַי
בְּיָדוֹ יִשְׂתָּרְגוּ
עָלוּ עַל־צַוָּארִי
הִכְשִׁיל כֹּחִי
נְתָנַנִי אֲדֹנָי בִּידֵי
לֹא־אוּכַל קוּם: ס

ס 15The Lord in my midst has rejected
All my heroes;
He has proclaimed a set time against me
To crush my young men.
As in a press the Lord has trodden
Fair Maiden Judah.

15 סִלָּה כָל־אַבִּירַי
אֲדֹנָי בְּקִרְבִּי
קָרָא עָלַי מוֹעֵד
לִשְׁבֹּר בַּחוּרָי
גַּת דָּרַךְ אֲדֹנָי
לִבְתוּלַת בַּת־יְהוּדָה: ס

ע 16For these things do I weep,
My eyes flow with tears:
Far from me is any comforter
Who might revive my spirit;
My children are forlorn,
For the foe has prevailed.

16 עַל־אֵלֶּה אֲנִי בוֹכִיָּה
עֵינִי עֵינִי יֹרְדָה מַּיִם
כִּי־רָחַק מִמֶּנִּי מְנַחֵם
מֵשִׁיב נַפְשִׁי
הָיוּ בָנַי שׁוֹמֵמִים
כִּי גָבַר אוֹיֵב: ס

פ 17Zion spreads out her hands,
She has no one to comfort her;
The Lord has summoned against Jacob

17 פֵּרְשָׂה צִיּוֹן בְּיָדֶיהָ
אֵין מְנַחֵם לָהּ
צִוָּה יְהוָה לְיַעֲקֹב

---

c-c   Or (ironically) "What a glutton"; cf. Prov. 23.20–21.
d   Meaning of parts of vv. 14 and 15 uncertain.

His enemies all about him;
Jerusalem has become among them
A thing unclean.

סְבִיבָיו צָרָיו
הָיְתָה יְרוּשָׁלַ͏ִם
לְנִדָּה בֵּינֵיהֶם: ס

צ 18The LORD is in the right,
For I have disobeyed Him.
Hear, all you peoples,
And behold my agony:
My maidens and my youths
Have gone into captivity!

18 צַדִּיק הוּא יְהֹוָה
כִּי פִיהוּ מָרִיתִי
שִׁמְעוּ־נָא כָל־עמים הָעַמִּים
וּרְאוּ מַכְאֹבִי
בְּתוּלֹתַי וּבַחוּרַי
הָלְכוּ בַשֶּׁבִי: ס

ק 19I cried out to my friends,
But they played me false.
My priests and my elders
Have perished in the city
As they searched for food
To keep themselves alive.

19 קָרָאתִי לַמְאַהֲבַי
הֵמָּה רִמּוּנִי
כֹּהֲנַי וּזְקֵנַי
בָּעִיר גָּוָעוּ
כִּי־בִקְשׁוּ אֹכֶל לָמוֹ
וְיָשִׁיבוּ אֶת־נַפְשָׁם: ס

ר 20See, O LORD, the distress I am in!
My heart is in anguish,
e-I know how wrong I was-e
To disobey.
Outside the sword deals death;
Indoors, the plague.

20 רְאֵה יְהֹוָה כִּי־צַר־לִי
מֵעַי חֳמַרְמָרוּ
נֶהְפַּךְ לִבִּי בְּקִרְבִּי
כִּי מָרוֹ מָרִיתִי
מִחוּץ שִׁכְּלָה־חֶרֶב
בַּבַּיִת כַּמָּוֶת: ס

ש 21When they heard how I was sighing,
There was none to comfort me;
All my foes heard of my plight and exulted.
For it is Your doing:
fYou have brought on the day that You
   threatened.
Oh, let them become like me!-f

21 שָׁמְעוּ כִּי נֶאֱנָחָה אָנִי
אֵין מְנַחֵם לִי
כָּל־אֹיְבַי שָׁמְעוּ רָעָתִי שָׂשׂוּ
כִּי אַתָּה עָשִׂיתָ
הֵבֵאתָ יוֹם־קָרָאתָ
וְיִהְיוּ כָמוֹנִי: ס

ת 22Let all their wrongdoing come before You,
And deal with them
As You have dealt with me
For all my transgressions.
For my sighs are many,
And my heart is sick.

22 תָּבֹא כָל־רָעָתָם לְפָנֶיךָ
וְעוֹלֵל לָמוֹ
כַּאֲשֶׁר עוֹלַלְתָּ לִי
עַל כָּל־פְּשָׁעָי
כִּי־רַבּוֹת אַנְחֹתַי
וְלִבִּי דַוָּי: פ

e-e Lit. "My heart has turned over within me"; cf. Exod. 14.5;
   Hos. 11.8.
f-f Emendation yields "Oh, bring on them what befell me, / And
   let them become like me!"

ב **אֵיכָה֙**

2 א Alas!

The Lord in His wrath
Has shamed[a] Fair Zion,
Has cast down from heaven to earth
The majesty of Israel.
He did not remember His Footstool[b]
On His day of wrath.

ב ²The Lord has laid waste without pity
All the habitations of Jacob;
He has razed in His anger
Fair Judah's strongholds.
He has brought low in dishonor
The kingdom and its leaders.

ג ³In blazing anger He has cut down
All the might of Israel;
He has withdrawn His right hand
In the presence of the foe;
He has ravaged Jacob like flaming fire,
Consuming on all sides.

ד ⁴He bent His bow like an enemy,
Poised His right hand like a foe;
He slew all who delighted the eye.
He poured out His wrath like fire
In the Tent of Fair Zion.

ה ⁵The Lord has acted like a foe,
He has laid waste Israel,
Laid waste all her citadels,
Destroyed her strongholds.
He has increased within Fair Judah
Mourning and moaning.

ו ⁶He has stripped His Booth[b] like a garden,
He has destroyed His Tabernacle;[c]
The Lᴏʀᴅ has ended in Zion
Festival and sabbath;
In His raging anger He has spurned
King and priest.

יָעִ֨יב בְּאַפּ֤וֹ ׀ אֲדֹנָי֙
אֶת־בַּת־צִיּ֔וֹן
הִשְׁלִ֤יךְ מִשָּׁמַ֙יִם֙ אֶ֔רֶץ
תִּפְאֶ֖רֶת יִשְׂרָאֵ֑ל
וְלֹא־זָכַ֥ר הֲדֹם־רַגְלָ֖יו
בְּי֥וֹם אַפּֽוֹ׃ ס

² בִּלַּ֨ע אֲדֹנָ֜י לֹ֤א וְלֹ֣א חָמַ֗ל
אֵ֚ת כָּל־נְא֣וֹת יַעֲקֹ֔ב
הָרַ֧ס בְּעֶבְרָת֛וֹ
מִבְצְרֵ֥י בַת־יְהוּדָ֖ה
הִגִּ֣יעַ לָאָ֣רֶץ חִלֵּ֑ל
מַמְלָכָ֖ה וְשָׂרֶֽיהָ׃ ס

³ גָּדַ֣ע בָּֽחֳרִי־אַ֗ף
כֹּ֚ל קֶ֣רֶן יִשְׂרָאֵ֔ל
הֵשִׁ֥יב אָח֛וֹר יְמִינ֖וֹ
מִפְּנֵ֣י אוֹיֵ֑ב
וַיִּבְעַ֤ר בְּיַעֲקֹב֙ כְּאֵ֣שׁ לֶֽהָבָ֔ה
אָכְלָ֖ה סָבִֽיב׃ ס

⁴ דָּרַ֨ךְ קַשְׁתּ֜וֹ כְּאוֹיֵ֗ב
נִצָּ֤ב יְמִינוֹ֙ כְּצָ֔ר
וַֽיַּהֲרֹ֔ג כֹּ֖ל מַחֲמַדֵּי־עָ֑יִן
בְּאֹ֙הֶל֙ בַּת־צִיּ֔וֹן
שָׁפַ֥ךְ כָּאֵ֖שׁ חֲמָתֽוֹ׃ ס

⁵ הָיָ֨ה אֲדֹנָ֤י ׀ כְּאוֹיֵב֙
בִּלַּ֣ע יִשְׂרָאֵ֔ל
בִּלַּע֙ כָּל־אַרְמְנוֹתֶ֔יהָ
שִׁחֵ֖ת מִבְצָרָ֑יו
וַיֶּ֙רֶב֙ בְּבַת־יְהוּדָ֔ה
תַּאֲנִיָּ֖ה וַאֲנִיָּֽה׃ ס

⁶ וַיַּחְמֹ֤ס כַּגַּן֙ שֻׂכּ֔וֹ
שִׁחֵ֖ת מוֹעֲד֑וֹ
שִׁכַּ֣ח יְהֹוָ֣ה ׀ בְּצִיּ֗וֹן
מוֹעֵ֣ד וְשַׁבָּ֔ת
וַיִּנְאַ֥ץ בְּזַֽעַם־אַפּ֖וֹ
מֶ֥לֶךְ וְכֹהֵֽן׃ ס

---

a   *Meaning of Heb. uncertain.*
b   *I.e., the Temple.*
c   *Lit. "(Tent of) Meeting."*

א 7The Lord has rejected His altar,
Disdained His Sanctuary.
He has handed over to the foe
The walls of its citadels;
They raised a shout in the House of the LORD
As on a festival day.

ח 8The LORD resolved to destroy
The wall of Fair Zion;
d-He measured with a line,-d refrained not
From bringing destruction.
He has made wall and rampart to mourn,
Together they languish.

ט 9Her gates have sunk into the ground,
He has smashed her bars to bits;
Her king and her leaders are e-in exile,-e
Instruction f is no more;
Her prophets, too, receive
No vision from the LORD.

י 10Silent sit on the ground
The elders of Fair Zion;
They have strewn dust on their heads
And girded themselves with sackcloth;
The maidens of Jerusalem have bowed
Their heads to the ground.

כ 11My eyes are spent with tears,
My heart is in tumult,
g-My being melts away-g
Over the ruin of h-my poor people,-h
As babes and sucklings languish
In the squares of the city.

ל 12They keep asking their mothers,
"Where is bread and wine?"
As they languish like battle-wounded
In the squares of the town,
As their life runs out
In their mothers' bosoms.

7 זָנַ֨ח אֲדֹנָ֤י ׀ מִזְבְּחוֹ֙
נִאֵ֣ר מִקְדָּשׁ֔וֹ
הִסְגִּיר֙ בְּיַד־אוֹיֵ֔ב
חוֹמֹ֖ת אַרְמְנוֹתֶ֑יהָ
ק֛וֹל נָתְנ֥וּ בְּבֵית־יְהוָ֖ה
כְּי֥וֹם מוֹעֵֽד׃ ס

8 חָשַׁ֨ב יְהוָ֤ה ׀ לְהַשְׁחִית֙
חוֹמַ֣ת בַּת־צִיּ֔וֹן
נָ֣טָה קָ֔ו לֹא־הֵשִׁ֥יב יָד֖וֹ
מִבַּלֵּ֑עַ
וַיַּֽאֲבֶל־חֵ֥ל וְחוֹמָ֖ה
יַחְדָּ֥ו אֻמְלָֽלוּ׃ ס

9 טָבְע֤וּ בָאָ֨רֶץ֙ שְׁעָרֶ֔יהָ
אִבַּ֥ד וְשִׁבַּ֖ר בְּרִיחֶ֑יהָ
מַלְכָּ֤הּ וְשָׂרֶ֨יהָ֙ בַגּוֹיִ֔ם
אֵ֣ין תּוֹרָ֔ה
גַּם־נְבִיאֶ֕יהָ לֹא־מָצְא֥וּ
חָז֖וֹן מֵיהוָֽה׃ ס

10 יֵשְׁב֤וּ לָאָ֨רֶץ֙ יִדְּמ֔וּ
זִקְנֵ֖י בַת־צִיּ֑וֹן
הֶֽעֱל֤וּ עָפָר֙ עַל־רֹאשָׁ֔ם
חָגְר֖וּ שַׂקִּ֑ים
הוֹרִ֤ידוּ לָאָ֨רֶץ֙ רֹאשָׁ֔ן
בְּתוּלֹ֖ת יְרוּשָׁלִָֽם׃ ס

11 כָּל֤וּ בַדְּמָעוֹת֙ עֵינַ֔י
חֳמַרְמְר֖וּ מֵעַ֑י
נִשְׁפַּ֤ךְ לָאָ֨רֶץ֙ כְּבֵדִ֔י
עַל־שֶׁ֖בֶר בַּת־עַמִּ֑י
בֵּֽעָטֵ֤ף עוֹלֵל֙ וְיוֹנֵ֔ק
בִּרְחֹב֖וֹת קִרְיָֽה׃ ס

12 לְאִמֹּתָם֙ יֹֽאמְר֔וּ
אַיֵּ֖ה דָּגָ֣ן וָיָ֑יִן
בְּהִֽתְעַטְּפָ֤ם כֶּֽחָלָל֙
בִּרְחֹב֣וֹת עִ֔יר
בְּהִשְׁתַּפֵּ֣ךְ נַפְשָׁ֔ם
אֶל־חֵ֖יק אִמֹּתָֽם׃ ס

d-d I.e., He made His plans.
e-e Lit. "among the nations."
f Heb. torah, here priestly instruction; cf. Jer. 18.18; Hag. 2.11;
  Mal. 2.6.
g-g Lit. "My liver spills on the ground."
h-h Lit. "the daughter of my people"; so elsewhere in poetry.

מ 13What can I *i*-take as witness-*i* or liken
To you, O Fair Jerusalem?
What can I match with you to console you,
O Fair Maiden Zion?
For your ruin is vast as the sea:
Who can heal you?

נ 14Your seers prophesied to you
Delusion and folly.
They did not expose your iniquity
So as to restore your fortunes,
But prophesied to you oracles
Of delusion and deception.

ס 15All who pass your way
Clap their hands at you;
They hiss and wag their head
At Fair Jerusalem:*j*
"Is this the city that was called
Perfect in Beauty,
Joy of All the Earth?"

פ 16All your enemies
Jeer at you;
They hiss and gnash their teeth,
And cry: "We've ruined her!
Ah, this is the day we hoped for;
k-We have lived to see it!"-*k*

ע 17The Lord has done what He purposed,
Has carried out the decree
That He ordained long ago;
He has torn down without pity.
He has let the foe rejoice over you,
Has exalted the might of your enemies.

צ 18*l*-Their heart cried out-*l* to the Lord.
O wall of Fair Zion,
Shed tears like a torrent
Day and night!
Give yourself no respite,
Your eyes no rest.

13 מֶה־אֲעִידֵ֣ךְ מָ֣ה אֲדַמֶּה־
לָּ֗ךְ הַבַּת֙ יְר֣וּשָׁלִַ֔ם
מָ֤ה אַשְׁוֶה־לָּךְ֙ וַאֲנַֽחֲמֵ֔ךְ
בְּתוּלַ֖ת בַּת־צִיּ֑וֹן
כִּֽי־גָד֥וֹל כַּיָּ֛ם שִׁבְרֵ֖ךְ
מִ֥י יִרְפָּא־לָֽךְ׃ ס
14 נְבִיאַ֗יִךְ חָ֤זוּ לָךְ֙
שָׁ֣וְא וְתָפֵ֔ל
וְלֹֽא־גִלּ֥וּ עַל־עֲוֺנֵ֖ךְ
לְהָשִׁ֣יב שביתך שְׁבוּתֵ֑ךְ
וַיֶּ֣חֱזוּ לָ֔ךְ מַשְׂא֥וֹת
שָׁ֖וְא וּמַדּוּחִֽים׃ ס
15 סָֽפְק֨וּ עָלַ֤יִךְ כַּפַּ֙יִם֙
כָּל־עֹ֣בְרֵי דֶ֔רֶךְ
שָֽׁרְקוּ֙ וַיָּנִ֣עוּ רֹאשָׁ֔ם
עַל־בַּ֖ת יְרוּשָׁלִָ֑ם
הֲזֹ֣את הָעִ֗יר שֶׁיֹּֽאמְרוּ֙
כְּלִ֣ילַת יֹ֔פִי
מָשׂ֖וֹשׂ לְכָל־הָאָֽרֶץ׃ ס
16 פָּצ֨וּ עָלַ֤יִךְ פִּיהֶם֙
כָּל־א֣וֹיְבַ֔יִךְ
שָֽׁרְקוּ֙ וַיַּֽחַרְקוּ־שֵׁ֔ן
אָמְר֖וּ בִּלָּ֑עְנוּ
אַ֣ךְ זֶ֥ה הַיּ֛וֹם שֶׁקִּוִּינֻ֖הוּ
מָצָ֥אנוּ רָאִֽינוּ׃ ס
17 עָשָׂ֨ה יְהֹוָ֜ה אֲשֶׁ֣ר זָמָ֗ם
בִּצַּ֤ע אֶמְרָתוֹ֙
אֲשֶׁ֣ר צִוָּ֣ה מִֽימֵי־קֶ֔דֶם
הָרַ֖ס וְלֹ֣א חָמָ֑ל
וַיְשַׂמַּ֤ח עָלַ֙יִךְ֙ אוֹיֵ֔ב
הֵרִ֖ים קֶ֥רֶן צָרָֽיִךְ׃ ס
18 צָעַ֥ק לִבָּ֖ם אֶל־אֲדֹנָ֑י
חוֹמַ֣ת בַּת־צִ֠יּוֹן
הוֹרִ֨ידִי כַנַּ֤חַל דִּמְעָה֙
יוֹמָ֣ם וָלַ֔יְלָה
אַל־תִּתְּנִ֤י פוּגַת֙ לָ֔ךְ
אַל־תִּדֹּ֖ם בַּת־עֵינֵֽךְ׃ ס

---

i-i Emendation yields "compare."

j These gestures were intended to ward off the calamity from the
viewer; cf., e.g., Jer. 18.16 and note; Job 27.23.

k-k Lit. "We have attained, we have seen."

l-l Emendation yields "Cry aloud."

ק ¹⁹Arise, cry out in the night
At the beginning of the watches,
Pour out your heart like water
In the presence of the Lord!
Lift up your hands to Him
For the life of your infants,
Who faint for hunger
At every street corner.

ר ²⁰See, O LORD, and behold,
To whom You have done this!
Alas, women eat their own fruit,
Their new-born^m babes!
Alas, priest and prophet are slain
In the Sanctuary of the Lord!

ש ²¹Prostrate in the streets lie
Both young and old.
My maidens and youths
Are fallen by the sword;
You slew them on Your day of wrath,
You slaughtered without pity.

ת ²²You summoned, as on a festival,
My neighbors from roundabout.
On the day of the wrath of the LORD,
None survived or escaped;
Those whom I bore^m and reared
My foe has consumed.

3 א I am the man ^{a-}who has known affliction
Under-^a the rod of His wrath;
²Me He drove on and on
In unrelieved darkness;
³On none but me He brings down His hand
Again and again, without cease.

ב ⁴He has worn away my flesh and skin;
He has shattered my bones.

---

m   *The root has this meaning in Arabic; others "dandled."*
a-a   *Emendation yields "whom the Lord has shepherded with."*

19 קוּמִי ׀ רֹנִּי בליל בַלַּ֫יְלָה
לְרֹאשׁ אַשְׁמֻרוֹת
שִׁפְכִי כַמַּ֫יִם לִבֵּךְ
נֹכַח פְּנֵי אֲדֹנָי
שְׂאִי אֵלָיו כַּפַּ֫יִךְ
עַל־נֶ֫פֶשׁ עוֹלָלַ֫יִךְ
הָעֲטוּפִים בְּרָעָב
בְּרֹאשׁ כָּל־חוּצוֹת׃ ס

20 רְאֵה יְהֹוָה וְהַבִּ֫יטָה
לְמִי עוֹלַלְתָּ כֹּה
אִם־תֹּאכַ֫לְנָה נָשִׁים פִּרְיָם
עֹלֲלֵי טִפֻּחִים
אִם־יֵהָרֵג בְּמִקְדַּשׁ אֲדֹנָי
כֹּהֵן וְנָבִיא׃ ס

21 שָׁכְבוּ לָאָ֫רֶץ חוּצוֹת
נַ֫עַר וְזָקֵן
בְּתוּלֹתַי וּבַחוּרַי
נָפְלוּ בֶחָ֫רֶב
הָרַ֫גְתָּ בְּיוֹם אַפֶּ֫ךָ
טָבַ֫חְתָּ לֹא חָמָ֫לְתָּ׃ ס

22 תִּקְרָא כְיוֹם מוֹעֵד
מְגוּרַי מִסָּבִיב
וְלֹא הָיָה בְּיוֹם אַף־יְהֹוָה
פָּלִיט וְשָׂרִיד
אֲשֶׁר־טִפַּ֫חְתִּי וְרִבִּ֫יתִי
אֹיְבִי כִלָּם׃ פ

ג אֲנִי הַגֶּ֫בֶר רָאָה עֳנִי
בְּשֵׁ֫בֶט עֶבְרָתוֹ׃
2 אוֹתִי נָהַג וַיֹּלַךְ
חֹ֫שֶׁךְ וְלֹא־אוֹר׃
3 אַךְ בִּי יָשֻׁב יַהֲפֹךְ יָדוֹ
כָּל־הַיּוֹם׃ ס
4 בִּלָּה בְשָׂרִי וְעוֹרִי
שִׁבַּר עַצְמוֹתָי׃

⁵All around me He has built
Misery^b and hardship;
⁶He has made me dwell in darkness,
Like those long dead.

ז ⁷He has walled me in and I cannot break out;
He has weighed me down with chains.
⁸And when I cry and plead,
He shuts out my prayer;
⁹He has walled in my ways with hewn blocks,
He has made my paths a maze.

ד ¹⁰He is a lurking bear to me,
A lion in hiding;
^{11c-}He has forced me off my way^{-c} and man-
gled me,
He has left me numb.
¹²He has bent His bow and made me
The target of His arrows:

ה ¹³He has shot into my vitals
The shafts of His quiver.
¹⁴I have become a laughingstock to all people,
The butt of their gibes all day long.
¹⁵He has filled me with bitterness,
Sated me with wormwood.

ו ¹⁶He has broken my teeth on gravel,
Has ground me into the dust.
¹⁷My life was bereft of peace,
I forgot what happiness was.
¹⁸I thought my strength and hope
Had perished before the Lord.

ז ¹⁹To recall my distress and my misery
Was wormwood and poison;
²⁰Whenever I thought of them,
I was bowed low.

²¹But this do I call to mind,
Therefore I have hope:

ח ²²The kindness of the Lord has not ended,

בָּנָ֥ה עָלַ֛י וַיַּקַּ֖ף 5
רֹ֥אשׁ וּתְלָאָֽה׃
בְּמַחֲשַׁכִּ֥ים הֽוֹשִׁיבַ֖נִי 6
כְּמֵתֵ֥י עוֹלָֽם׃ ס
גָּדַ֧ר בַּעֲדִ֛י וְלֹ֥א אֵצֵ֖א 7
הִכְבִּ֥יד נְחָשְׁתִּֽי׃
גַּ֣ם כִּ֤י אֶזְעַק֙ וַאֲשַׁוֵּ֔עַ 8
שָׂתַ֖ם תְּפִלָּתִֽי׃
גָּדַ֤ר דְּרָכַי֙ בְּגָזִ֔ית 9
נְתִֽיבֹתַ֖י עִוָּֽה׃ ס
דֹּ֣ב אֹרֵ֥ב הוּא֙ לִ֔י 10
אֲרִ֖יה בְּמִסְתָּרִֽים׃
דְּרָכַ֞י סוֹרֵ֤ר וַֽיְפַשְּׁחֵ֔נִי 11
שָׂמַ֖נִי שֹׁמֵֽם׃
דָּרַ֤ךְ קַשְׁתּוֹ֙ וַיַּצִּיבֵ֔נִי 12
כַּמַּטָּרָ֖א* לַחֵֽץ׃ ס
הֵבִיא֙ בְּכִלְיוֹתָ֔י 13
בְּנֵ֖י אַשְׁפָּתֽוֹ׃
הָיִ֤יתִי שְּׂחֹק֙ לְכָל־עַמִּ֔י* 14
נְגִֽינָתָ֖ם כָּל־הַיּֽוֹם׃
הִשְׂבִּיעַ֥נִי בַמְּרוֹרִ֖ים 15
הִרְוַ֥נִי לַעֲנָֽה׃ ס
וַיַּגְרֵ֤ס בֶּֽחָצָץ֙ שִׁנָּ֔י 16
הִכְפִּישַׁ֖נִי בָּאֵֽפֶר׃
וַתִּזְנַ֧ח מִשָּׁל֛וֹם נַפְשִׁ֖י 17
נָשִׁ֥יתִי טוֹבָֽה׃
וָאֹמַר֙ אָבַ֣ד נִצְחִ֔י 18
וְתֽוֹחַלְתִּ֖י מֵיְהוָֽה׃ ס
זְכָר־עָנְיִ֥י וּמְרוּדִ֖י 19
לַעֲנָ֥ה וָרֹֽאשׁ׃
זָכ֣וֹר תִּזְכּ֔וֹר 20
וְתָשׁ֥וֹחַ עָלַ֖י נַפְשִֽׁי׃
זֹ֛את אָשִׁ֥יב אֶל־לִבִּ֖י 21
עַל־כֵּ֥ן אוֹחִֽיל׃ ס
חַֽסְדֵ֤י יְהוָה֙ כִּ֣י לֹא־תָ֔מְנוּ 22

---

^b   Taking *rosh* as equivalent to *resh*.
^{c-c} Meaning of Heb. uncertain.

v. 12. א׳ במקום ה׳
v. 14. סבירין ומטעין "עמים"

1757

His mercies are not spent.

²³They are renewed every morning—
Ample is Your grace!

²⁴"The Lord is my portion," I say with full
   heart;
Therefore will I hope in Him.

ט ²⁵The Lord is good to those who trust in Him,
To the one who seeks Him;

²⁶It is good to wait patiently
Till rescue comes from the Lord.

²⁷It is good for a man, when young,
To bear a yoke;

י ²⁸Let him sit alone and be patient,
When He has laid it upon him.

²⁹Let him put his mouth to the dust—
There may yet be hope.

³⁰Let him offer his cheek to the smiter;
Let him be surfeited with mockery.

כ ³¹For the Lord does not
Reject forever,

³²But first afflicts, then pardons
In His abundant kindness.

³³For He does not willfully bring grief
Or affliction to man,

ל ³⁴Crushing under His feet
All the prisoners of the earth.

³⁵To deny a man his rights
In the presence of the Most High,

³⁶To wrong a man in his cause—
This the Lord does not choose.

מ ³⁷Whose decree was ever fulfilled,
Unless the Lord willed it?

³⁸Is it not at the word of the Most High,
That weal and woe befall?

³⁹Of what shall a living man complain?
Each one of his own sins!

נ ⁴⁰Let us search and examine our ways,
And turn back to the Lord;

כִּי לֹא־כָל֖וּ רַחֲמָֽיו׃

23 חֲדָשִׁים֙ לַבְּקָרִ֔ים
רַבָּ֖ה אֱמוּנָתֶֽךָ׃

24 חֶלְקִ֤י יְהוָה֙ אָמְרָ֣ה נַפְשִׁ֔י
עַל־כֵּ֖ן אוֹחִ֥יל לֽוֹ׃ ס

25 ט֤וֹב יְהוָה֙ לְקֹוָ֔ו
לְנֶ֖פֶשׁ תִּדְרְשֶֽׁנּוּ׃

26 ט֤וֹב וְיָחִיל֙ וְדוּמָ֔ם
לִתְשׁוּעַ֖ת יְהוָֽה׃

27 ט֣וֹב לַגֶּ֔בֶר
כִּֽי־יִשָּׂ֥א עֹ֖ל בִּנְעוּרָֽיו׃ ס

28 יֵשֵׁ֤ב בָּדָד֙ וְיִדֹּ֔ם
כִּ֥י נָטַ֖ל עָלָֽיו׃

29 יִתֵּ֤ן בֶּֽעָפָר֙ פִּ֔יהוּ
אוּלַ֖י יֵ֥שׁ תִּקְוָֽה׃

30 יִתֵּ֧ן לְמַכֵּ֛הוּ לֶ֖חִי
יִשְׂבַּ֥ע בְּחֶרְפָּֽה׃ ס

31 כִּ֣י לֹ֥א יִזְנַ֖ח
לְעוֹלָ֖ם אֲדֹנָֽי׃

32 כִּ֣י אִם־הוֹגָ֔ה וְרִחַ֖ם
כְּרֹ֥ב חֲסָדָֽיו׃

33 כִּ֣י לֹ֤א עִנָּה֙ מִלִּבּ֔וֹ
וַיַּגֶּ֖ה בְּנֵי־אִֽישׁ׃ ס

34 *לְדַכֵּא֙ תַּ֣חַת רַגְלָ֔יו
כֹּ֖ל אֲסִ֥ירֵי אָֽרֶץ׃

35 לְהַטּוֹת֙ מִשְׁפַּט־גֶּ֔בֶר
נֶ֖גֶד פְּנֵ֥י עֶלְיֽוֹן׃

36 לְעַוֵּ֤ת אָדָם֙ בְּרִיב֔וֹ
אֲדֹנָ֖י לֹ֥א רָאָֽה׃ ס

37 מִ֣י זֶ֤ה אָמַר֙ וַתֶּ֔הִי
אֲדֹנָ֖י לֹ֥א צִוָּֽה׃

38 מִפִּ֥י עֶלְיֽוֹן לֹ֣א
תֵצֵ֔א הָרָע֖וֹת וְהַטּֽוֹב׃

39 מַה־יִּתְאוֹנֵן֙ אָדָ֣ם חָ֔י
גֶּ֖בֶר עַל־חֲטָאָֽיו׃ ס

40 נַחְפְּשָׂ֤ה דְרָכֵ֙ינוּ֙ וְֽנַחְקֹ֔רָה
וְנָשׁ֖וּבָה עַד־יְהוָֽה׃

⁴¹Let us lift up our hearts with^d our hands
To God in heaven:
⁴²We have transgressed and rebelled,
And You have not forgiven.

ס ⁴³You have clothed Yourself in anger and
    pursued us,
You have slain without pity.
⁴⁴You have screened Yourself off with a cloud,
That no prayer may pass through.
⁴⁵You have made us filth and refuse
In the midst of the peoples.

פ ⁴⁶All our enemies loudly
Rail against us.
⁴⁷Panic and pitfall are our lot,
Death and destruction.
⁴⁸My eyes shed streams of water
Over the ruin of my poor^e people.

ע ⁴⁹My eyes shall flow without cease,
Without respite,
⁵⁰^{f-}Until the Lord looks down
And beholds from heaven.
⁵¹My eyes have brought me grief-^f
Over all the maidens of my city.

צ ⁵²My foes have snared me like a bird,
Without any cause.
⁵³They have ended my life in a pit
And cast stones at me.
⁵⁴Waters flowed over my head;
I said: I am lost!

ק ⁵⁵I have called on Your name, O Lord,
From the depths of the Pit.
⁵⁶Hear my plea;
Do not shut Your ear
To my groan, to my cry!
⁵⁷You have ever drawn nigh when I called
    You;

41 נָשָׂא לְבָבֵנוּ אֶל־כַּפָּיִם
אֶל־אֵל בַּשָּׁמָיִם:
42 נַחְנוּ פָשַׁעְנוּ וּמָרִינוּ
אַתָּה לֹא סָלָחְתָּ: ס
43 סַכֹּתָה בָאַף וַתִּרְדְּפֵנוּ
הָרַגְתָּ לֹא חָמָלְתָּ:
44 סַכּוֹתָה בֶעָנָן לָךְ
מֵעֲבוֹר תְּפִלָּה:
45 סְחִי וּמָאוֹס תְּשִׂימֵנוּ
בְּקֶרֶב הָעַמִּים: ס
46 פָּצוּ עָלֵינוּ
פִּיהֶם כָּל־אֹיְבֵינוּ:
47 פַּחַד וָפַחַת הָיָה לָנוּ
הַשֵּׁאת וְהַשָּׁבֶר:
48 פַּלְגֵי־מַיִם תֵּרַד עֵינִי
עַל־שֶׁבֶר בַּת־עַמִּי: ס
49 עֵינִי נִגְּרָה וְלֹא תִדְמֶה
מֵאֵין הֲפֻגוֹת:
50 עַד־יַשְׁקִיף
וְיֵרֶא יְהוָה מִשָּׁמָיִם:
51 עֵינִי עוֹלְלָה לְנַפְשִׁי
מִכֹּל בְּנוֹת עִירִי: ס
52 צוֹד צָדוּנִי כַּצִּפּוֹר אֹיְבַי
חִנָּם:
53 צָמְתוּ בַבּוֹר חַיָּי
וַיַּדּוּ־אֶבֶן בִּי:
54 צָפוּ־מַיִם עַל־רֹאשִׁי
אָמַרְתִּי נִגְזָרְתִּי: ס
55 קָרָאתִי שִׁמְךָ יְהוָה
מִבּוֹר תַּחְתִּיּוֹת:
56 קוֹלִי שָׁמָעְתָּ
אַל־תַּעְלֵם אָזְנְךָ
לְרַוְחָתִי לְשַׁוְעָתִי:
57 קָרַבְתָּ בְּיוֹם אֶקְרָאֶךָּ

---

d   Lit. "to"; emendation yields "rather than"; cf. Joel 2.13.
e   Lit. "the daughter of my"; so frequently in poetry.
f-f   Emendation yields: ⁵⁰"Until the Lord looks down from heaven /
    And beholds ⁵¹my affliction. / The Lord has brought me grief."

1759

You have said, "Do not fear!"　　　אָמַרְתָּ אַל־תִּירָא: ס

ר 58You championed my cause, O Lord,　　58רַבְתָּ אֲדֹנָי רִיבֵי נַפְשִׁי

You have redeemed my life.　　גָּאַלְתָּ חַיָּי:

59You have seen, O Lord, the wrong done me;　　59רָאִיתָה יְהוָה עַוָּתָתִי

Oh, vindicate my right!　　שָׁפְטָה מִשְׁפָּטִי:

60You have seen all their malice,　　60רָאִיתָה כָּל־נִקְמָתָם

All their designs against me;　　כָּל־מַחְשְׁבֹתָם לִי: ס

שׁ 61You have heard, O Lord, their taunts,　　61שָׁמַעְתָּ חֶרְפָּתָם יְהוָה

All their designs against me,　　כָּל־מַחְשְׁבֹתָם עָלָי:

62The mouthings and pratings of my adver-　　62שִׂפְתֵי קָמַי וְהֶגְיוֹנָם

saries　　

Against me all day long.　　עָלַי כָּל־הַיּוֹם:

63See how, at their ease or at work,　　63שִׁבְתָּם וְקִימָתָם הַבִּיטָה

I am the butt of their gibes.　　אֲנִי מַנְגִּינָתָם: ס

ת 64Give them, O Lord, their deserts　　64תָּשִׁיב לָהֶם גְּמוּל יְהוָה

According to their deeds.　　כְּמַעֲשֵׂה יְדֵיהֶם:

65Give them anguish[c] of heart;　　65תִּתֵּן לָהֶם מְגִנַּת־לֵב

Your curse be upon them!　　תַּאֲלָתְךָ לָהֶם:

66Oh, pursue them in wrath and destroy them　　66תִּרְדֹּף בְּאַף וְתַשְׁמִידֵם

From under the heavens of the Lord!　　מִתַּחַת שְׁמֵי יְהוָה: פ

4 א Alas!　　ד אֵיכָה

The gold is dulled,[a]　　יוּעַם זָהָב

Debased the finest gold!　　יִשְׁנֶא* הַכֶּתֶם הַטּוֹב

The sacred[b] gems are spilled　　תִּשְׁתַּפֵּכְנָה אַבְנֵי־קֹדֶשׁ

At every street corner.　　בְּרֹאשׁ כָּל־חוּצוֹת: ס

ב 2The precious children of Zion;　　2בְּנֵי צִיּוֹן הַיְקָרִים

Once valued as gold—　　הַמְסֻלָּאִים בַּפָּז

Alas, they are accounted as earthen pots,　　אֵיכָה נֶחְשְׁבוּ לְנִבְלֵי־חֶרֶשׂ

Work of a potter's hands!　　מַעֲשֵׂה יְדֵי יוֹצֵר: ס

ג 3Even jackals offer the breast　　3גַּם־תַּנִּין תַּנִּים חָלְצוּ שַׁד

And suckle their young;　　הֵינִיקוּ גּוּרֵיהֶן

But my poor people has turned cruel,　　בַּת־עַמִּי לְאַכְזָר

Like ostriches of the desert.　　כִּי עֵנִים כַּיְעֵנִים בַּמִּדְבָּר: ס

ד 4The tongue of the suckling cleaves　　4דָּבַק לְשׁוֹן יוֹנֵק

To its palate for thirst.　　אֶל־חִכּוֹ בַּצָּמָא

Little children beg for bread;　　עוֹלָלִים שָׁאֲלוּ לֶחֶם

None gives them a morsel.　　פֹּרֵשׂ אֵין לָהֶם: ס

---

a Meaning of Heb. uncertain.
b Emendation yields "precious."

v. 1. א׳ במקום ה׳ *

ה ⁵Those who feasted on dainties
Lie famished in the streets;
Those who were reared in purple
Have embraced refuse heaps.

ו ⁶The guilt^c of my poor^d people
Exceeded the iniquity^c of Sodom,
Which was overthrown in a moment,
Without a hand striking it.

ז ⁷Her elect were purer than snow,
Whiter than milk;
Their limbs were ruddier than coral,
Their bodies^a were like sapphire.

ח ⁸Now their faces are blacker than soot,
They are not recognized in the streets;
Their skin has shriveled on their bones,
It has become dry as wood.

ט ⁹Better off were the slain of the sword
Than those slain by famine,
^{a-}Who pined away, [as though] wounded,
For lack of-^a the fruits of the field.

י ¹⁰With their own hands, tenderhearted
   women
Have cooked their children;
Such became their fare,
In the disaster of my poor^d people.

כ ¹¹The Lord vented all His fury,
Poured out His blazing wrath;
He kindled a fire in Zion
Which consumed its foundations.

ל ¹²The kings of the earth did not believe,
Nor any of the inhabitants of the world,
That foe or adversary could enter
The gates of Jerusalem.

מ ¹³It was for the sins of her prophets,
The iniquities of her priests,
Who had shed in her midst
The blood of the just.

5 הָאֹכְלִים לְמַעֲדַנִּים
נָשַׁמּוּ בַּחוּצֹות
הָאֱמֻנִים עֲלֵי תֹולָע
חִבְּקוּ אַשְׁפַּתֹּות: ס

6 וַיִּגְדַּל עֲוֹן בַּת־עַמִּי
מֵחַטַּאת סְדֹם
הַהֲפוּכָה כְמֹו־רָגַע
וְלֹא־חָלוּ בָהּ יָדָיִם: ס

7 זַכּוּ נְזִירֶיהָ מִשֶּׁלֶג
צַחוּ מֵחָלָב
אָדְמוּ עֶצֶם מִפְּנִינִים
סַפִּיר גִּזְרָתָם: ס

8 חָשַׁךְ מִשְּׁחֹור תָּאֳרָם
לֹא נִכְּרוּ בַּחוּצֹות
צָפַד עֹורָם עַל־עַצְמָם
יָבֵשׁ הָיָה כָעֵץ: ס

9 טֹובִים הָיוּ חַלְלֵי־חֶרֶב
מֵחַלְלֵי רָעָב
שֶׁהֵם* יָזוּבוּ מְדֻקָּרִים
מִתְּנוּבֹת שָׂדָי: ס

10 יְדֵי נָשִׁים רַחֲמָנִיֹּות
בִּשְּׁלוּ יַלְדֵיהֶן
הָיוּ לְבָרֹות לָמֹו
בְּשֶׁבֶר בַּת־עַמִּי: ס

11 כִּלָּה יְהֹוָה אֶת־חֲמָתֹו
שָׁפַךְ חֲרֹון אַפֹּו
וַיַּצֶּת־אֵשׁ בְּצִיֹּון
וַתֹּאכַל יְסֹודֹתֶיהָ: ס

12 לֹא הֶאֱמִינוּ מַלְכֵי־אֶרֶץ
וכל כֹּל יֹשְׁבֵי תֵבֵל
כִּי יָבֹא צַר וְאֹויֵב
בְּשַׁעֲרֵי יְרוּשָׁלָם: ס

13 מֵחַטֹּאת נְבִיאֶיהָ
עֲוֹנֹת כֹּהֲנֶיהָ
הַשֹּׁפְכִים בְּקִרְבָּהּ
דַּם צַדִּיקִים: ס

---

c   I.e., punishment.
d   See note at 3.48.

v. 9. שני טעמים

‫נ‬ 14They wandered blindly through the streets,
Defiled with blood,
So that no one was able
To touch their garments.

‫ס‬ 15"Away! Unclean!" people shouted at them,
"Away! Away! Touch not!"
So they wandered and wandered again;
For the nations had resolved:
"They shall stay here no longer."

‫פ‬ 16*e*The LORD's countenance has turned away
from them,
He will look on them no more.
They showed no regard for priests,
No favor to elders.

‫ע‬ 17Even now our eyes pine away
In vain for deliverance.
As we waited, still we wait
For a nation that cannot help.

‫צ‬ 18Our steps were checked,
We could not walk *f*-in our squares.-*f*
Our doom is near, our days are done—
Alas, our doom has come!

‫ק‬ 19Our pursuers were swifter
Than the eagles in the sky;
They chased us in the mountains,
Lay in wait for us in the wilderness.

‫ר‬ 20The breath of our life, the LORD's anointed,
Was captured in their traps—
He in whose shade we had thought
To live among the nations.

‫ש‬ 21Rejoice and exult, Fair Edom,
Who dwell in the land of Uz!
To you, too, the cup shall pass,
You shall get drunk and expose your naked-
ness.

‫ת‬ 22Your iniquity, Fair Zion, is expiated;
He will exile you no longer.
Your iniquity, Fair Edom, He will note;
He will uncover your sins.

14 נָע֣וּ עִוְרִים֙ בַּֽחוּצ֔וֹת
נְגֹֽאֲל֖וּ בַּדָּ֑ם
בְּלֹ֣א יֽוּכְל֔וּ
יִגְּע֖וּ בִּלְבֻשֵׁיהֶֽם׃ ס

15 ס֤וּרוּ טָמֵא֙ קָ֣רְאוּ לָ֔מוֹ
ס֥וּרוּ ס֖וּרוּ אַל־תִּגָּ֑עוּ
כִּ֤י נָצוּ֙ גַּם־נָ֔עוּ
אָֽמְרוּ֙ בַּגּוֹיִ֔ם
לֹ֥א יוֹסִ֖פוּ לָגֽוּר׃ ס

16 פְּנֵ֤י יְהוָה֙ חִלְּקָ֔ם
לֹ֥א יוֹסִ֖יף לְהַבִּיטָ֑ם
פְּנֵ֤י כֹֽהֲנִים֙ לֹ֣א נָשָׂ֔אוּ
זְקֵנִ֖ים וּזְקֵנִ֥ים לֹ֥א חָנָֽנוּ׃ ס

17 עוֹדֵ֙ינָה֙ עוֹדֵ֙ינוּ֙ תִּכְלֶ֣ינָה עֵינֵ֔ינוּ
אֶל־עֶזְרָתֵ֖נוּ הָ֑בֶל
בְּצִפִּיָּתֵ֣נוּ צִפִּ֔ינוּ
אֶל־גּ֖וֹי לֹ֥א יוֹשִֽׁעַ׃ ס

18 צָד֣וּ צְעָדֵ֔ינוּ
מִלֶּ֖כֶת בִּרְחֹֽבֹתֵ֑ינוּ
קָרַ֣ב קִצֵּ֔ינוּ מָלְא֖וּ יָמֵ֑ינוּ
כִּי־בָ֥א קִצֵּֽינוּ׃ ס

19 קַלִּ֤ים הָיוּ֙ רֹֽדְפֵ֔ינוּ
מִנִּשְׁרֵ֖י שָׁמָ֑יִם
עַל־הֶֽהָרִ֣ים דְּלָקֻ֔נוּ
בַּמִּדְבָּ֖ר אָ֥רְבוּ לָֽנוּ׃ ס

20 ר֤וּחַ אַפֵּ֙ינוּ֙ מְשִׁ֣יחַ יְהוָ֔ה
נִלְכַּ֖ד בִּשְׁחִיתוֹתָ֑ם
אֲשֶׁ֣ר אָמַ֔רְנוּ בְּצִלּ֖וֹ
נִֽחְיֶ֥ה בַגּוֹיִֽם׃ ס

21 שִׂ֤ישִׂי וְשִׂמְחִי֙ בַּת־אֱד֔וֹם
ישבתי יוֹשֶׁ֖בֶת בְּאֶ֣רֶץ ע֑וּץ
גַּם־עָלַ֙יִךְ֙ תַּֽעֲבָר־כּ֔וֹס
תִּשְׁכְּרִ֖י וְתִתְעָרִֽי׃ ס

22 תַּם־עֲוֹנֵ֥ךְ בַּת־צִיּ֖וֹן
לֹ֥א יוֹסִ֖יף לְהַגְלוֹתֵ֑ךְ
פָּקַ֤ד עֲוֹנֵךְ֙ בַּת־אֱד֔וֹם
גִּלָּ֖ה עַל־חַטֹּאתָֽיִךְ׃ פ

---

e   Meaning of line uncertain.
f-f   Or "With long strides."

5

Remember, O LORD, what has befallen us;
Behold, and see our disgrace!
[2]Our heritage has passed to aliens,
Our homes to strangers.
[3]We have become orphans, fatherless;
Our mothers are like widows.
[4]We must pay to drink our own water,
Obtain our own kindling at a price.
[5]We are hotly[a] pursued;
Exhausted, we are given no rest.
[6]We hold out a hand to Egypt;
To Assyria, for our fill of bread.
[7]Our fathers sinned and are no more;
And we must bear their guilt.
[8]Slaves are ruling over us,
With none to rescue us from them.
[9]We get our bread at the peril of our lives,
Because of the [b]-sword of the wilderness.-[b]
[10]Our skin glows like an oven,
With the fever of famine.
[11]They[c] have ravished women in Zion,
Maidens in the towns of Judah.
[12]Princes have been hanged by them;[c]
No respect has been shown to elders.
[13]Young men must carry millstones,
And youths stagger under loads of wood.
[14]The old men are gone from the gate,
The young men from their music.
[15]Gone is the joy of our hearts;
Our dancing is turned into mourning.
[16]The crown has fallen from our head;
Woe to us that we have sinned!

[17]Because of this our hearts are sick,
Because of these our eyes are dimmed:
[18]Because of Mount Zion, which lies desolate;
Jackals prowl over it.

ה זְכֹ֤ר יְהוָה֙ מֶֽה־הָ֣יָה לָ֔נוּ
הַבִּ֖יטָה וּרְאֵ֥ה אֶת־חֶרְפָּתֵֽנוּ׃
[2] נַחֲלָתֵ֙נוּ֙ נֶֽהֶפְכָ֣ה לְזָרִ֔ים
בָּתֵּ֖ינוּ לְנָכְרִֽים׃
[3] יְתוֹמִ֤ים הָיִ֙ינוּ֙ אין וְאֵ֣ין אָ֔ב
אִמֹּתֵ֖ינוּ כְּאַלְמָנֽוֹת׃
[4] מֵימֵ֙ינוּ֙ בְּכֶ֣סֶף שָׁתִ֔ינוּ
עֵצֵ֖ינוּ בִּמְחִ֥יר יָבֹֽאוּ׃
[5] עַ֤ל צַוָּארֵ֙נוּ֙ נִרְדָּ֔פְנוּ
יָגַ֖עְנוּ לא וְלֹ֥א הֽוּנַֽח־לָֽנוּ׃
[6] מִצְרַ֙יִם֙ נָתַ֣נּוּ יָ֔ד
אַשּׁ֖וּר לִשְׂבֹּ֥עַ לָֽחֶם׃
[7] אֲבֹתֵ֤ינוּ חָֽטְאוּ֙ אינם וְאֵינָ֔ם
אנחנו וַאֲנַ֖חְנוּ עֲוֺנֹתֵיהֶ֥ם סָבָֽלְנוּ׃
[8] עֲבָדִים֙ מָ֣שְׁלוּ בָ֔נוּ
פֹּרֵ֖ק אֵ֥ין מִיָּדָֽם׃
[9] בְּנַפְשֵׁ֙נוּ֙ נָבִ֣יא לַחְמֵ֔נוּ
מִפְּנֵ֖י חֶ֥רֶב הַמִּדְבָּֽר׃
[10] עוֹרֵ֙נוּ֙ כְּתַנּ֣וּר נִכְמָ֔רוּ
מִפְּנֵ֖י זַלְעֲפ֥וֹת רָעָֽב׃
[11] נָשִׁים֙ בְּצִיּ֣וֹן עִנּ֔וּ
בְּתֻלֹ֖ת בְּעָרֵ֥י יְהוּדָֽה׃
[12] שָׂרִים֙ בְּיָדָ֣ם נִתְל֔וּ
פְּנֵ֥י זְקֵנִ֖ים לֹ֥א נֶהְדָּֽרוּ׃
[13] בַּחוּרִים֙ טְח֣וֹן נָשָׂ֔אוּ
וּנְעָרִ֖ים בָּעֵ֥ץ כָּשָֽׁלוּ׃
[14] זְקֵנִים֙ מִשַּׁ֣עַר שָׁבָ֔תוּ
בַּחוּרִ֖ים מִנְּגִינָתָֽם׃
[15] שָׁבַת֙ מְשׂ֣וֹשׂ לִבֵּ֔נוּ
נֶהְפַּ֥ךְ לְאֵ֖בֶל מְחֹלֵֽנוּ׃
[16] נָֽפְלָה֙ עֲטֶ֣רֶת רֹאשֵׁ֔נוּ
אֽוֹי־נָ֥א לָ֖נוּ כִּ֥י חָטָֽאנוּ׃

[17] עַל־זֶ֗ה הָיָ֤ה דָוֶה֙ לִבֵּ֔נוּ
עַל־אֵ֖לֶּה חָשְׁכ֥וּ עֵינֵֽינוּ׃
[18] עַ֤ל הַר־צִיּוֹן֙ שֶׁשָּׁמֵ֔ם
שֽׁוּעָלִ֖ים הִלְּכוּ־בֽוֹ׃ פ

---

a   Lit. "on our neck"; meaning of Heb. uncertain.
b-b   Or "heat (cf. Deut. 28.22) of the wilderness"; meaning of Heb.
     uncertain.
c   I.e., the slaves of v. 8.

19But You, O LORD, are enthroned forever,
Your throne endures through the ages.
20Why have You forgotten us utterly,
Forsaken us for all time?
21Take us back, O LORD, to Yourself,
And let us come back;
Renew our days as of old!
22For truly, You have rejected us,
Bitterly raged against us.

Take us back, O LORD, to Yourself,
And let us come back;
Renew our days as of old!

19 אַתָּה יְהוָה לְעוֹלָם תֵּשֵׁב
כִּסְאֲךָ לְדֹר וָדוֹר:
20 לָמָּה לָנֶצַח תִּשְׁכָּחֵנוּ
תַּעַזְבֵנוּ לְאֹרֶךְ יָמִים:
21 הֲשִׁיבֵנוּ יְהוָה ׀ אֵלֶיךָ
וְנָשׁוּבָה
חַדֵּשׁ יָמֵינוּ כְּקֶדֶם:
22 כִּי אִם־מָאֹס מְאַסְתָּנוּ
קָצַפְתָּ עָלֵינוּ עַד־מְאֹד:*

[הֲשִׁיבֵנוּ יְהוָה ׀ אֵלֶיךָ
וְנָשׁוּבָה
חַדֵּשׁ יָמֵינוּ כְּקֶדֶם:*]

תם ונשלם תהילה לאל בורא עולם

---

v. 22.   סכום הפסוקים של ספר 154 וחציו 3.34

end.   במסורת הקריאה נשנה הפסוק לפני האחרון

ECCLESIASTES

1 The words of Koheleth[a] son of David, king in Jerusalem.

: דִּבְרֵי קֹהֶלֶת בֶּן־דָּוִד מֶלֶךְ בִּירוּשָׁלָם א

2Utter futility!—said Koheleth—
Utter futility! All is futile!
3What real value is there for a man
In all the gains[b] he makes beneath the sun?

הֲבֵל הֲבָלִים אָמַר קֹהֶלֶת 2
: הֲבֵל הֲבָלִים הַכֹּל הָבֶל
מַה־יִּתְרוֹן לָאָדָם 3
: בְּכָל־עֲמָלוֹ שֶׁיַּעֲמֹל תַּחַת הַשָּׁמֶשׁ

4One generation goes, another comes,
But the earth remains the same forever.
5The sun rises, and the sun sets—
And glides[c] back to where it rises.
6Southward blowing,
Turning northward,
Ever turning blows the wind;
On its rounds the wind returns.
7All streams flow into the sea,
Yet the sea is never full;
To the place [from] which they flow
The streams flow back again.[d]
8All such things are wearisome:
No man can ever state them;
The eye never has enough of seeing,
Nor the ear enough of hearing.
9Only that shall happen
Which has happened,
Only that occur
Which has occurred;
There is nothing new
Beneath the sun!

דּוֹר הֹלֵךְ וְדוֹר בָּא 4
: וְהָאָרֶץ לְעוֹלָם עֹמָדֶת
וְזָרַח הַשֶּׁמֶשׁ וּבָא הַשָּׁמֶשׁ 5
: וְאֶל־מְקוֹמוֹ שׁוֹאֵף זוֹרֵחַ הוּא שָׁם
הוֹלֵךְ אֶל־דָּרוֹם 6
וְסוֹבֵב אֶל־צָפוֹן
סוֹבֵב | סֹבֵב הוֹלֵךְ הָרוּחַ
: וְעַל־סְבִיבֹתָיו שָׁב הָרוּחַ
כָּל־הַנְּחָלִים הֹלְכִים אֶל־הַיָּם 7
וְהַיָּם אֵינֶנּוּ מָלֵא
אֶל־מְקוֹם שֶׁהַנְּחָלִים הֹלְכִים
: שָׁם הֵם שָׁבִים לָלָכֶת
כָּל־הַדְּבָרִים יְגֵעִים 8
לֹא־יוּכַל אִישׁ לְדַבֵּר
לֹא־תִשְׂבַּע עַיִן לִרְאוֹת
: וְלֹא־תִמָּלֵא אֹזֶן מִשְּׁמֹעַ
מַה־שֶּׁהָיָה 9
הוּא שֶׁיִּהְיֶה
וּמַה־שֶּׁנַּעֲשָׂה
הוּא שֶׁיֵּעָשֶׂה
וְאֵין כָּל־חָדָשׁ
: תַּחַת הַשָּׁמֶשׁ

---

a Probably "the Assembler," i.e., of hearers or of sayings; cf. 12.9–11.
b So Rashbam. Heb. 'amal usually has this sense in Ecclesiastes; cf. Ps. 105.44.
c So Targum; cf. Bereshith Rabbah on Gen. 1.17.
d According to popular belief, through tunnels; so Targum and Rashi.

10Sometimes there is a phenomenon of which they say, "Look, this one is new!"—it occurred long since, in ages that went by before us. 11The earlier ones are not remembered; so too those that will occur later e-will no more be remembered than-e those that will occur at the very end.

12I, Koheleth, was king in Jerusalem over Israel. 13I set my mind to study and to probe with wisdom all that happens under the sun.—An unhappy business, that, which God gave men to be concerned with! 14I observed all the happenings beneath the sun, and I found that all is futile and pursuitf of wind:

15A twisted thing that cannot be made straight,

A lack that cannot be made good.

16I said to myself: "Here I have grown richer and wiser than any that ruled before me over Jerusalem, and my mind has zealously absorbed wisdom and learning." 17And so I set my mind to appraise wisdom and to appraise madness and folly. And I learned—that this too was pursuit of wind:

18For as wisdom grows, vexation grows;

To increase learning is to increase heartache.

2 I said to myself, "Come, I will treat you to merriment. Taste mirth!" That too, I found, was futile.

2Of revelry I said, "It's mad!"

Of merriment, "What good is that?"

3I ventured to tempt my flesh with wine, and to grasp folly, while letting my mind direct with wisdom, to the end that I might learn which of the two was better for men to practice in their few days of life under heaven. 4I multiplied my possessions. I built myself houses and I planted

10 יֵ֣שׁ דָּבָ֛ר שֶׁיֹּאמַ֥ר רְאֵה־זֶ֖ה חָדָ֣שׁ ה֑וּא כְּבָר֙ הָיָ֣ה לְעֹֽלָמִ֔ים אֲשֶׁ֥ר הָיָ֖ה מִלְּפָנֵֽנוּ׃
11 אֵ֥ין זִכְר֖וֹן לָרִֽאשֹׁנִ֑ים וְגַ֨ם לָאַחֲרֹנִ֜ים שֶׁיִּהְי֗וּ לֹֽא־יִהְיֶ֤ה לָהֶם֙ זִכָּר֔וֹן עִ֥ם שֶׁיִּהְי֖וּ לָאַחֲרֹנָֽה׃ פ

12 אֲנִ֣י קֹהֶ֗לֶת הָיִ֥יתִי מֶ֛לֶךְ עַל־יִשְׂרָאֵ֖ל בִּירֽוּשָׁלִָֽם׃ 13 וְנָתַ֣תִּי אֶת־לִבִּ֗י לִדְר֤וֹשׁ וְלָתוּר֙ בַּֽחָכְמָ֔ה עַ֛ל כָּל־אֲשֶׁ֥ר נַעֲשָׂ֖ה תַּ֣חַת הַשָּׁמָ֑יִם ה֣וּא ׀ עִנְיַ֣ן רָ֗ע נָתַ֧ן אֱלֹהִ֛ים לִבְנֵ֥י הָאָדָ֖ם לַעֲנ֥וֹת בּֽוֹ׃ 14 רָאִ֙יתִי֙ אֶת־כָּל־הַֽמַּעֲשִׂ֔ים שֶֽׁנַּעֲשׂ֖וּ תַּ֣חַת הַשָּׁ֑מֶשׁ וְהִנֵּ֥ה הַכֹּ֛ל הֶ֖בֶל וּרְע֥וּת רֽוּחַ׃
15 מְעֻוָּ֖ת לֹא־יוּכַ֣ל לִתְקֹ֑ן
וְחֶסְר֖וֹן לֹא־יוּכַ֥ל לְהִמָּנֽוֹת׃
16 דִּבַּ֨רְתִּי אֲנִ֤י עִם־לִבִּי֙ לֵאמֹ֔ר אֲנִ֗י הִנֵּ֨ה הִגְדַּ֤לְתִּי וְהוֹסַ֙פְתִּי֙ חָכְמָ֔ה עַ֥ל כָּל־אֲשֶׁר־הָיָ֥ה לְפָנַ֖י עַל־יְרֽוּשָׁלִָ֑ם וְלִבִּ֛י רָאָ֥ה הַרְבֵּ֖ה חָכְמָ֥ה וָדָֽעַת׃ 17 וָאֶתְּנָ֤ה לִבִּי֙ לָדַ֣עַת חָכְמָ֔ה וְדַ֥עַת הֽוֹלֵל֖וֹת וְשִׂכְל֑וּת יָדַ֕עְתִּי שֶׁגַּם־זֶ֥ה ה֖וּא רַעְי֥וֹן רֽוּחַ׃
18 כִּ֛י בְּרֹ֥ב חָכְמָ֖ה רָב־כָּ֑עַס
וְיוֹסִ֥יף דַּ֖עַת יוֹסִ֥יף מַכְאֽוֹב׃

ב אָמַ֤רְתִּֽי אֲנִי֙ בְּלִבִּ֔י לְכָה־נָּ֛א אֲנַסְּכָ֥ה בְשִׂמְחָ֖ה וּרְאֵ֣ה בְט֑וֹב וְהִנֵּ֥ה גַם־ה֖וּא הָֽבֶל׃
2 לִשְׂח֖וֹק אָמַ֣רְתִּי מְהוֹלָ֑ל
וּלְשִׂמְחָ֖ה מַה־זֹּ֥ה עֹשָֽׂה׃

3 תַּ֣רְתִּי בְלִבִּ֗י לִמְשׁ֤וֹךְ בַּיַּ֙יִן֙ אֶת־בְּשָׂרִ֔י וְלִבִּ֖י נֹהֵ֣ג בַּֽחָכְמָ֑ה וְלֶאֱחֹ֣ז בְּסִכְל֔וּת עַ֣ד אֲשֶׁר־אֶרְאֶ֗ה אֵי־זֶ֨ה ט֜וֹב לִבְנֵ֤י הָאָדָם֙ אֲשֶׁ֤ר יַעֲשׂוּ֙ תַּ֣חַת הַשָּׁמַ֔יִם מִסְפַּ֖ר יְמֵ֥י חַיֵּיהֶֽם׃ 4 הִגְדַּ֖לְתִּי מַעֲשָׂ֑י בָּנִ֤יתִי לִי֙ בָּתִּ֔ים נָטַ֥עְתִּי

e-e Lit. "will not be remembered like…" For 'im meaning "like," cf. 2.16; 7.11; Job 9.26.
f Lit. "tending," from root ra'ah, "to shepherd."

vineyards. [5]I laid out gardens and groves, in which I planted every kind of fruit tree. [6]I constructed pools of water, enough to irrigate a forest shooting up with trees. [7]I bought male and female slaves, and I acquired stewards. I also acquired more cattle, both herds and flocks, than all who were before me in Jerusalem. [8]I further amassed silver and gold and treasures of kings and provinces; and I got myself male and female singers, as well as the luxuries of commoners—coffers[a] and coffers of them. [9]Thus, I gained more wealth than anyone before me in Jerusalem. In addition, my wisdom remained with me: [10]I withheld from my eyes nothing they asked for, and denied myself no enjoyment; rather, I got enjoyment out of[b] all my wealth. And that was all I got out of my wealth.

[11]Then my thoughts turned to all the fortune my hands had built up, to the wealth I had acquired and won—and oh, it was all futile and pursuit of wind; there was no real value under the sun! [12c]For what will the man be like who will succeed [d]-the one who is ruling-[d] over what was built up long ago?

My thoughts also turned to appraising wisdom and madness and folly. [13]I found that

Wisdom is superior to folly

As light is superior to darkness;

[14]A wise man has his eyes in his head,

Whereas a fool walks in darkness.

But I also realized that the same fate awaits them both. [15]So I reflected: "The fate of the fool is also destined for me; to what advantage, then, have I been wise?" And I came to the conclusion that that too was futile, [16]because the wise man, just like[e] the fool, is not remembered forever;

---

a   The Heb. shiddah occurs only here in the Bible; in the Mishnah it designates a kind of chest.

b   Septuagint and a few Heb. manuscripts have "(in exchange) for"; cf. 2.24; 3.13, 22; 5.17.

c   The order of the two sentences in this verse is reversed in the translation for clarity.

d-d   Change of vocalization yields "me, and who is to rule"; cf. vv. 18–19.

e   See note on 1.11.

לִי כְּרָמִים: 5 עָשִׂיתִי לִי גַּנּוֹת וּפַרְדֵּסִים וְנָטַעְתִּי בָהֶם עֵץ כָּל־פֶּרִי: 6 עָשִׂיתִי לִי בְּרֵכוֹת מָיִם לְהַשְׁקוֹת מֵהֶם יַעַר צוֹמֵחַ עֵצִים: 7 קָנִיתִי עֲבָדִים וּשְׁפָחוֹת וּבְנֵי־ בַיִת הָיָה לִי גַּם מִקְנֶה בָקָר וָצֹאן הַרְבֵּה הָיָה לִי מִכֹּל שֶׁהָיוּ לְפָנַי בִּירוּשָׁלָם: 8 כָּנַסְתִּי לִי גַּם־כֶּסֶף וְזָהָב וּסְגֻלַּת מְלָכִים וְהַמְּדִינוֹת עָשִׂיתִי לִי שָׁרִים וְשָׁרוֹת וְתַעֲנוּגֹת בְּנֵי הָאָדָם שִׁדָּה וְשִׁדּוֹת: 9 וְגָדַלְתִּי וְהוֹסַפְתִּי מִכֹּל שֶׁהָיָה לְפָנַי בִּירוּשָׁלָם אַף חָכְמָתִי עָמְדָה לִּי: 10 וְכֹל אֲשֶׁר שָׁאֲלוּ עֵינַי לֹא אָצַלְתִּי מֵהֶם לֹא־ מָנַעְתִּי אֶת־לִבִּי מִכָּל־שִׂמְחָה כִּי־לִבִּי שָׂמֵחַ מִכָּל־עֲמָלִי וְזֶה־הָיָה חֶלְקִי מִכָּל־ עֲמָלִי: 11 וּפָנִיתִי אֲנִי בְּכָל־מַעֲשַׂי שֶׁעָשׂוּ יָדַי וּבֶעָמָל שֶׁעָמַלְתִּי לַעֲשׂוֹת וְהִנֵּה הַכֹּל הֶבֶל וּרְעוּת רוּחַ וְאֵין יִתְרוֹן תַּחַת הַשָּׁמֶשׁ: 12 וּפָנִיתִי אֲנִי לִרְאוֹת חָכְמָה וְהוֹלֵלוֹת וְסִכְלוּת כִּי ׀ מֶה הָאָדָם שֶׁיָּבוֹא אַחֲרֵי הַמֶּלֶךְ אֵת אֲשֶׁר־כְּבָר עָשׂוּהוּ: 13 וְרָאִיתִי אָנִי שֶׁיֵּשׁ יִתְרוֹן לַחָכְמָה מִן־הַסִּכְלוּת כִּיתְרוֹן הָאוֹר מִן־הַחֹשֶׁךְ: 14 הֶחָכָם עֵינָיו בְּרֹאשׁוֹ וְהַכְּסִיל בַּחֹשֶׁךְ הוֹלֵךְ וְיָדַעְתִּי גַם־אָנִי שֶׁמִּקְרֶה אֶחָד יִקְרֶה אֶת־כֻּלָּם: 15 וְאָמַרְתִּי אֲנִי בְּלִבִּי כְּמִקְרֵה הַכְּסִיל גַּם־אֲנִי יִקְרֵנִי וְלָמָּה חָכַמְתִּי אֲנִי אָז יוֹתֵר וְדִבַּרְתִּי בְלִבִּי שֶׁגַּם־זֶה הָבֶל: 16 כִּי אֵין זִכְרוֹן לֶחָכָם עִם־הַכְּסִיל לְעוֹלָם

for, as the succeeding days roll by, both are forgotten. Alas, the wise man dies, just like[e] the
fool!

17And so I loathed life. For I was distressed
by all that goes on under the sun, because everything is futile and pursuit of wind.

18So, too, I loathed all the wealth that I was
gaining under the sun. For I shall leave it to the
man who will succeed me—19and who knows
whether he will be wise or foolish?—and he will
control all the wealth that I gained by toil and
wisdom under the sun. That too is futile. 20And
so I came to view with despair all the gains I
had made under the sun. 21For sometimes a person whose fortune was made with wisdom,
knowledge, and skill must hand it on to be the
portion of somebody who did not toil for it.
That too is futile, and a grave evil. 22For what
does a man get for all the toiling and worrying
he does under the sun? 23All his days his
thoughts are grief and heartache, and even at
night his mind has no respite. That too is futile!

24There is nothing worthwhile for a man but
to eat and drink and afford himself enjoyment
with his means. And even that, I noted, comes
from God. 25For who eats and who enjoys but
myself?[f] 26To the man, namely, who pleases
Him He has given g-the wisdom and shrewdness
to enjoy himself;-g and to him who displeases,
He has given the urge to gather and amass—
only for handing on to one who is pleasing to
God. That too is futile and pursuit of wind.

3

A season is set for everything, a time for
every experience under heaven:[a]

2A time for b-being born-b and a time for
dying,

בְּשֶׁכְּבָר הַיָּמִים הַבָּאִים הַכֹּל נִשְׁכָּח וְאֵיךְ
יָמוּת הֶחָכָם עִם־הַכְּסִיל:
17 וְשָׂנֵאתִי אֶת־הַחַיִּים כִּי רַע עָלַי
הַמַּעֲשֶׂה שֶׁנַּעֲשָׂה תַּחַת הַשָּׁמֶשׁ כִּי־הַכֹּל
הֶבֶל וּרְעוּת רוּחַ:
18 וְשָׂנֵאתִי אֲנִי אֶת־כָּל־עֲמָלִי שֶׁאֲנִי עָמֵל
תַּחַת הַשָּׁמֶשׁ שֶׁאַנִּיחֶנּוּ לָאָדָם שֶׁיִּהְיֶה
אַחֲרָי: 19 וּמִי יוֹדֵעַ הֶחָכָם יִהְיֶה אוֹ סָכָל
וְיִשְׁלַט בְּכָל־עֲמָלִי שֶׁעָמַלְתִּי וְשֶׁחָכַמְתִּי
תַּחַת הַשָּׁמֶשׁ גַּם־זֶה הָבֶל: 20 וְסַבּוֹתִי אֲנִי
לְיַאֵשׁ אֶת־לִבִּי עַל כָּל־הֶעָמָל שֶׁעָמַלְתִּי
תַּחַת הַשָּׁמֶשׁ: 21 כִּי־יֵשׁ אָדָם שֶׁעֲמָלוֹ
בְּחָכְמָה וּבְדַעַת וּבְכִשְׁרוֹן וּלְאָדָם שֶׁלֹּא
עָמַל־בּוֹ יִתְּנֶנּוּ חֶלְקוֹ גַּם־זֶה הֶבֶל וְרָעָה
רַבָּה: 22 כִּי מֶה־הֹוֶה לָאָדָם בְּכָל־עֲמָלוֹ
וּבְרַעְיוֹן לִבּוֹ שֶׁהוּא עָמֵל תַּחַת הַשָּׁמֶשׁ:
23 כִּי כָל־יָמָיו מַכְאֹבִים וָכַעַס עִנְיָנוֹ
גַּם־בַּלַּיְלָה לֹא־שָׁכַב לִבּוֹ גַּם־זֶה הֶבֶל
הוּא:
24 אֵין־טוֹב בָּאָדָם שֶׁיֹּאכַל וְשָׁתָה וְהֶרְאָה
אֶת־נַפְשׁוֹ טוֹב בַּעֲמָלוֹ גַּם־זֹה רָאִיתִי אָנִי
כִּי מִיַּד הָאֱלֹהִים הִיא: 25 כִּי מִי יֹאכַל
וּמִי יָחוּשׁ חוּץ מִמֶּנִּי: 26 כִּי לְאָדָם שֶׁטּוֹב
לְפָנָיו נָתַן חָכְמָה וְדַעַת וְשִׂמְחָה וְלַחוֹטֶא
נָתַן עִנְיָן לֶאֱסוֹף וְלִכְנוֹס לָתֵת לְטוֹב לִפְנֵי
הָאֱלֹהִים גַּם־זֶה הֶבֶל וּרְעוּת רוּחַ:

ג לַכֹּל זְמָן וְעֵת לְכָל־חֵפֶץ תַּחַת
הַשָּׁמָיִם:* ס
2 עֵת לָלֶדֶת וְעֵת לָמוּת

f   Some mss. and ancient versions read mimmennu, "by His doing."
g-g   Lit. "wisdom and knowledge and enjoyment."

a   I.e., all human experiences are preordained by God; see v. 11.
b-b   Lit. "giving birth."

v. 1.   בכתב היד שלנו הרשימה בצורת שירה

1768

A time for planting and a time for uprooting
the planted;

3A time for c-slaying and a time for healing,-c
A time for tearing down and a time for building up;

4A time for weeping and a time for laughing,
A time for wailing and a time for dancing;

5A time for throwing stones and a time for
gathering stones,
A time for embracing and a time for shunning
embraces;

6A time for seeking and a time for losing,
A time for keeping and a time for discarding;

7A time for ripping and a time for sewing,
A time for silence and a time for speaking;

8A time for loving and a time for hating;
A time for war and a time for peace.

9What value, then, can the man of affairs get
from what he earns? 10I have observed the business that God gave man to be concerned with:
11He brings everything to pass precisely at its
time; He also puts eternity in their mind,d but
without man ever guessing, from first to last,
all the things that God brings to pass. 12Thus I
realized that the only worthwhile thing there is
for them is to enjoy themselves and do what is
goode in their lifetime; 13also, that whenever a
man does eat and drink and get enjoyment out
of all his wealth, it is a gift of God.

14I realized, too, that whatever God has
brought to pass will recur evermore:

Nothing can be added to it
And nothing taken from it—
and God has brought to pass that men revere
Him.

15f What is occurring occurred long since,
And what is to occur occurred long since:
and God seeks the pursued. 16And, indeed, I
have observed under the sun:

עֵת לָטַעַת וְעֵת לַעֲקוֹר נָטֽוּעַ׃

3 עֵת לַהֲרוֹג וְעֵת לִרְפּוֹא
עֵת לִפְרוֹץ וְעֵת לִבְנֽוֹת׃

4 עֵת לִבְכּוֹת וְעֵת לִשְׂחוֹק
עֵת סְפוֹד וְעֵת רְקֽוֹד׃

5 עֵת לְהַשְׁלִיךְ אֲבָנִים וְעֵת כְּנוֹס אֲבָנִים
עֵת לַחֲבוֹק וְעֵת לִרְחֹק מֵחַבֵּֽק׃

6 עֵת לְבַקֵּשׁ וְעֵת לְאַבֵּד
עֵת לִשְׁמוֹר וְעֵת לְהַשְׁלִֽיךְ׃

7 עֵת לִקְרוֹעַ וְעֵת לִתְפּוֹר
עֵת לַחֲשׁוֹת וְעֵת לְדַבֵּֽר׃

8 עֵת לֶאֱהֹב וְעֵת לִשְׂנֹא
עֵת מִלְחָמָה וְעֵת שָׁלֽוֹם׃ ס

9 מַה־יִּתְרוֹן הָעוֹשֶׂה בַּאֲשֶׁר הוּא עָמֵֽל׃

10 רָאִיתִי אֶת־הָעִנְיָן אֲשֶׁר נָתַן אֱלֹהִים
לִבְנֵי הָאָדָם לַעֲנוֹת בּֽוֹ׃ 11 אֶת־הַכֹּל עָשָׂה
יָפֶה בְעִתּוֹ גַּם אֶת־הָעֹלָם נָתַן בְּלִבָּם
מִבְּלִי אֲשֶׁר לֹא־יִמְצָא הָאָדָם אֶת־
הַמַּעֲשֶׂה אֲשֶׁר־עָשָׂה הָאֱלֹהִים מֵרֹאשׁ
וְעַד־סֽוֹף׃ 12 יָדַעְתִּי כִּי אֵין טוֹב בָּם כִּי
אִם־לִשְׂמוֹחַ וְלַעֲשׂוֹת טוֹב בְּחַיָּֽיו׃ 13 וְגַם
כָּל־הָאָדָם שֶׁיֹּאכַל וְשָׁתָה וְרָאָה טוֹב
בְּכָל־עֲמָלוֹ מַתַּת אֱלֹהִים הִֽיא׃
14 יָדַעְתִּי כִּי כָּל־אֲשֶׁר יַעֲשֶׂה הָאֱלֹהִים
הוּא יִהְיֶה לְעוֹלָם
עָלָיו אֵין לְהוֹסִיף
וּמִמֶּנּוּ אֵין לִגְרֹעַ
וְהָאֱלֹהִים עָשָׂה שֶׁיִּרְאוּ מִלְּפָנָֽיו׃
15 מַה־שֶּׁהָיָה כְּבָר הוּא
וַאֲשֶׁר לִהְיוֹת כְּבָר הָיָה
וְהָאֱלֹהִים יְבַקֵּשׁ אֶת־נִרְדָּֽף׃ 16 וְעוֹד
רָאִיתִי תַּחַת הַשָּֽׁמֶשׁ

---

c-c   *Emendation yields "wrecking...repairing"; cf. 1 Kings 18.30.*
d   *I.e., He preoccupies man with the attempt to discover the times
of future events; cf. 8.17.*
e   *I.e., what the author has already concluded (2.24) is good.*
f   *Meaning of parts of verse uncertain.*

Alongside justice there is wickedness,

Alongside righteousness there is wickedness. [17]I mused: "God will doom both righteous and wicked, for g-there is-g a time for every experience and for every happening." [18f]So I decided, as regards men, to dissociate them [from] the divine beings and to face the fact that they are beasts.[h] [19]For in respect of the fate of man and the fate of beast, they have one and the same fate: as the one dies so dies the other, and both have the same lifebreath; man has no superiority over beast, since both amount to nothing. [20]Both go to the same place; both came from dust and both return to dust. [21]Who knows if a man's lifebreath does rise upward and if a beast's breath does sink down into the earth?

[22]I saw that there is nothing better for man than to enjoy his possessions, since that is his portion. For who can enable him to see what will happen afterward?

4 I further observed[a] all the oppression that goes on under the sun: the tears of the oppressed, with none to comfort them; and the power of their oppressors—with none to comfort them. [2]Then I accounted those who died long since more fortunate than those who are still living; [3]and happier than either are those who have not yet come into being and have never witnessed the miseries that go on under the sun.

[4]I have also noted that all labor and skillful enterprise come from men's envy of each other—another futility and pursuit of wind! [5][True,]

The fool folds his hands together[b]

מְקוֹם הַמִּשְׁפָּט שָׁמָּה הָרֶשַׁע
וּמְקוֹם הַצֶּדֶק שָׁמָּה הָרָשַׁע:
17 אָמַרְתִּי אֲנִי בְּלִבִּי אֶת־הַצַּדִּיק וְאֶת־
הָרָשָׁע יִשְׁפֹּט הָאֱלֹהִים כִּי־עֵת לְכָל־
חֵפֶץ וְעַל כָּל־הַמַּעֲשֶׂה שָׁם: 18 אָמַרְתִּי
אֲנִי בְּלִבִּי עַל־דִּבְרַת בְּנֵי הָאָדָם לְבָרָם
הָאֱלֹהִים וְלִרְאוֹת שְׁהֶם־בְּהֵמָה הֵמָּה
לָהֶם: 19 כִּי מִקְרֶה בְנֵי־הָאָדָם וּמִקְרֶה
הַבְּהֵמָה וּמִקְרֶה אֶחָד לָהֶם כְּמוֹת זֶה כֵּן
מוֹת זֶה וְרוּחַ אֶחָד לַכֹּל וּמוֹתַר הָאָדָם
מִן־הַבְּהֵמָה אָיִן כִּי הַכֹּל הָבֶל: 20 הַכֹּל
הוֹלֵךְ אֶל־מָקוֹם אֶחָד הַכֹּל הָיָה מִן־הֶעָפָר
וְהַכֹּל שָׁב אֶל־הֶעָפָר: 21 מִי יוֹדֵעַ רוּחַ בְּנֵי
הָאָדָם הָעֹלָה הִיא לְמָעְלָה וְרוּחַ הַבְּהֵמָה
הַיֹּרֶדֶת הִיא לְמַטָּה לָאָרֶץ:
22 וְרָאִיתִי כִּי אֵין טוֹב מֵאֲשֶׁר יִשְׂמַח
הָאָדָם בְּמַעֲשָׂיו כִּי־הוּא חֶלְקוֹ כִּי מִי
יְבִיאֶנּוּ לִרְאוֹת בְּמֶה שֶׁיִּהְיֶה אַחֲרָיו:

ד
וְשַׁבְתִּי אֲנִי וָאֶרְאֶה אֶת־כָּל־
הָעֲשֻׁקִים אֲשֶׁר נַעֲשִׂים תַּחַת הַשָּׁמֶשׁ
וְהִנֵּה ׀ דִּמְעַת הָעֲשֻׁקִים וְאֵין לָהֶם מְנַחֵם
וּמִיַּד עֹשְׁקֵיהֶם כֹּחַ וְאֵין לָהֶם מְנַחֵם:
2 וְשַׁבֵּחַ אֲנִי אֶת־הַמֵּתִים שֶׁכְּבָר מֵתוּ
מִן־הַחַיִּים אֲשֶׁר הֵמָּה חַיִּים עֲדֶנָה: 3 וְטוֹב
מִשְּׁנֵיהֶם אֵת אֲשֶׁר־עֲדֶן לֹא הָיָה אֲשֶׁר
לֹא־רָאָה אֶת־הַמַּעֲשֶׂה הָרָע אֲשֶׁר נַעֲשָׂה
תַּחַת הַשָּׁמֶשׁ:

4 וְרָאִיתִי אֲנִי אֶת־כָּל־עָמָל וְאֵת כָּל־
כִּשְׁרוֹן הַמַּעֲשֶׂה כִּי הִיא קִנְאַת־אִישׁ
מֵרֵעֵהוּ גַּם־זֶה הֶבֶל וּרְעוּת רוּחַ:
5 הַכְּסִיל חֹבֵק אֶת־יָדָיו

---

g-g   *Shift of a diacritical point yields "He has set."*
h   *Contrast Ps. 8.5–6.*

a   *Cf. 3.16.*
b   *I.e., does not work; cf. Prov. 6.10; 24.33.*

And has to eat his own flesh.

6[But no less truly,]

Better is a handful of gratification

Than two fistfuls of labor which is pursuit of wind.

7And I have noted this further futility under the sun: 8the case of the man who is alone, with no companion, who has neither son nor brother; yet he amasses wealth without limit, and his eye is never sated with riches. For whom, now, c-is he amassing it while denying himself-c enjoyment? That too is a futility and an unhappy business.

9dTwo are better off than one, in that they have greater e-benefit from-e their earnings. 10For should they fall, one can raise the other; but woe betide him who is alone and falls with no companion to raise him! 11Further, when two lie together they are warm; but how can he who is alone get warm? 12Also, if one attacks, two can stand up to him. A threefold cord is not readily broken!

13Better a poor but wise youth than an old but foolish king who no longer has the sense to heed warnings. 14For the former can emerge from a dungeon to become king; while the latter, even if born to kingship, can become a pauper.f 15[However,] I reflected about g-all the living who walk under the sun with-g that youthful successor who steps into his place. 16Unnumbered are the multitudes of all those who preceded them;h and later generations will not acclaim him either.i For thatj too is futile and pursuit of wind.

וְאָכַל אֶת־בְּשָׂרוֹ:

6 טוֹב מְלֹא כַף נָחַת מִמְּלֹא חָפְנַיִם עָמָל וּרְעוּת רוּחַ: 7 וְשַׁבְתִּי אֲנִי וָאֶרְאֶה הֶבֶל תַּחַת הַשָּׁמֶשׁ: 8 יֵשׁ אֶחָד וְאֵין שֵׁנִי גַּם בֵּן וָאָח אֵין־לוֹ וְאֵין קֵץ לְכָל־עֲמָלוֹ גַּם־עֵינָיו עֵינוֹ לֹא־תִשְׂבַּע עֹשֶׁר וּלְמִי | אֲנִי עָמֵל וּמְחַסֵּר אֶת־נַפְשִׁי מִטּוֹבָה גַּם־זֶה הֶבֶל וְעִנְיַן רָע הוּא: 9 טוֹבִים הַשְּׁנַיִם מִן־הָאֶחָד אֲשֶׁר יֵשׁ־לָהֶם שָׂכָר טוֹב בַּעֲמָלָם: 10 כִּי אִם־יִפֹּלוּ הָאֶחָד יָקִים אֶת־חֲבֵרוֹ וְאִילוֹ* הָאֶחָד שֶׁיִּפּוֹל וְאֵין שֵׁנִי לַהֲקִימוֹ: 11 גַּם אִם־יִשְׁכְּבוּ שְׁנַיִם וְחַם לָהֶם וּלְאֶחָד אֵיךְ יֵחָם: 12 וְאִם־יִתְקְפוֹ הָאֶחָד הַשְּׁנַיִם יַעַמְדוּ נֶגְדּוֹ וְהַחוּט הַמְשֻׁלָּשׁ לֹא בִמְהֵרָה יִנָּתֵק: 13 טוֹב יֶלֶד מִסְכֵּן וְחָכָם מִמֶּלֶךְ זָקֵן וּכְסִיל אֲשֶׁר לֹא־יָדַע לְהִזָּהֵר עוֹד: 14 כִּי־מִבֵּית הָסוּרִים יָצָא לִמְלֹךְ כִּי גַּם בְּמַלְכוּתוֹ נוֹלַד רָשׁ: 15 רָאִיתִי אֶת־כָּל־הַחַיִּים הַמְהַלְּכִים תַּחַת הַשָּׁמֶשׁ עִם הַיֶּלֶד הַשֵּׁנִי אֲשֶׁר יַעֲמֹד תַּחְתָּיו: 16 אֵין־קֵץ לְכָל־הָעָם לְכֹל אֲשֶׁר־הָיָה לִפְנֵיהֶם גַּם הָאַחֲרוֹנִים לֹא יִשְׂמְחוּ־בוֹ כִּי־גַם־זֶה הֶבֶל וְרַעְיוֹן רוּחַ:

---

c-c   Lit. "am I amassing...myself."
d   4.9–5.8 consists of a series of observations, each of which is introduced by some slight association with what precedes. The theme of 4.4–8 is not resumed until 5.9.
e-e   Emendation yields "hope for"; cf. 2.20.
f   Taking rash as a verb; cf. Ps. 34.11.
g-g   I.e., "the contemporaries of."
h   And so never heard of the gifted youth.
i   For despite his wisdom, he too will be forgotten; cf. 2.16.
j   I.e., the advantage of wisdom over folly.

שני טעמים   v. 10.

17k-Be not overeager to go-k to the House of God: more acceptable is obedience than the offering of fools, for they know nothing [but] to do wrong.

5 Keep your mouth from being rash, and let not your throata be quick to bring forth speech before God. For God is in heaven and you are on earth; that is why your words should be few. 2Just as dreams come with much brooding, so does foolish utterance come with much speech. 3When you make a vow to God, do not delay to fulfill it. For He has no pleasure in fools; what you vow, fulfill. 4It is better not to vow at all than to vow and not fulfill. 5Don't let your mouth bring you into disfavor, and don't plead before the messengerb that it was an error, c-but fear God;c else God may be angered by your talk and destroy your possessions. 6dFor much dreaming leads to futility and to superfluous talk.

7If you see in a province oppression of the poor and suppression of right and justice, don't wonder at the fact; for one high official is protected by a higher one, and both of them by still higher ones. 8Thus the greatest advantage in all the land is his: he controls a field that is cultivated.e

9A lover of money never has his fill of money, nor a lover of wealth his fill of income. That too is futile. 10As his substance increases, so do those who consume it; what, then, does the success of its owner amount to but feasting his eyes? 11A worker'sf sleep is sweet, whether he has much

17 שְׁמֹר רגליך רַגְלְךָ כַּאֲשֶׁר תֵּלֵךְ אֶל־בֵּית הָאֱלֹהִים וְקָרוֹב לִשְׁמֹעַ מִתֵּת הַכְּסִילִים זָבַח כִּי־אֵינָם יוֹדְעִים לַעֲשׂוֹת רָע:

ה אַל־תְּבַהֵל עַל־פִּיךָ וְלִבְּךָ אַל־יְמַהֵר לְהוֹצִיא דָבָר לִפְנֵי הָאֱלֹהִים כִּי הָאֱלֹהִים בַּשָּׁמַיִם וְאַתָּה עַל־הָאָרֶץ עַל־כֵּן יִהְיוּ דְבָרֶיךָ מְעַטִּים: 2 כִּי בָּא הַחֲלוֹם בְּרֹב עִנְיָן וְקוֹל כְּסִיל בְּרֹב דְּבָרִים: 3 כַּאֲשֶׁר תִּדֹּר נֶדֶר לֵאלֹהִים אַל־תְּאַחֵר לְשַׁלְּמוֹ כִּי אֵין חֵפֶץ בַּכְּסִילִים אֵת אֲשֶׁר־תִּדֹּר שַׁלֵּם: 4 טוֹב אֲשֶׁר לֹא־תִדֹּר מִשֶּׁתִּדּוֹר וְלֹא תְשַׁלֵּם: 5 אַל־תִּתֵּן אֶת־פִּיךָ לַחֲטִיא אֶת־בְּשָׂרֶךָ וְאַל־תֹּאמַר לִפְנֵי הַמַּלְאָךְ כִּי שְׁגָגָה הִיא לָמָּה יִקְצֹף הָאֱלֹהִים עַל־קוֹלֶךָ וְחִבֵּל אֶת־מַעֲשֵׂה יָדֶיךָ: 6 כִּי בְרֹב חֲלֹמוֹת וַהֲבָלִים וּדְבָרִים הַרְבֵּה כִּי אֶת־הָאֱלֹהִים יְרָא:

7 אִם־עֹשֶׁק רָשׁ וְגֵזֶל מִשְׁפָּט וָצֶדֶק תִּרְאֶה בַמְּדִינָה אַל־תִּתְמַהּ עַל־הַחֵפֶץ כִּי גָבֹהַּ מֵעַל גָּבֹהַּ שֹׁמֵר וּגְבֹהִים עֲלֵיהֶם: 8 וְיִתְרוֹן אֶרֶץ בַּכֹּל הִיא הוּא מֶלֶךְ לְשָׂדֶה נֶעֱבָד:

9 אֹהֵב כֶּסֶף לֹא־יִשְׂבַּע כֶּסֶף וּמִי־אֹהֵב בֶּהָמוֹן לֹא תְבוּאָה גַּם־זֶה הָבֶל: 10 בִּרְבוֹת הַטּוֹבָה רַבּוּ אוֹכְלֶיהָ וּמַה־כִּשְׁרוֹן לִבְעָלֶיהָ כִּי אִם־רְאִית רְאוּת עֵינָיו: 11 מְתוּקָה שְׁנַת הָעֹבֵד אִם־מְעַט וְאִם־

---

k-k   Lit. "Guard your foot when it [or, you] would go."

a   Heb. leb, lit. "heart," sometimes designates the organ of speech; cf. Isa. 33.18; 59.13; Ps. 19.15; 49.4; Job. 8.10.
b   Some ancient versions read "God."
c-c   Moved up from v. 6 for clarity.
d   Meaning of verse uncertain. Emendation yields "Much brooding results in dreams; and much talk in futilities"; cf. v. 2.
e   I.e., the high official profits from the labor of others; but meaning of verse uncertain.
f   Some ancient versions have "slave's."

or little to eat; but the rich man's abundance doesn't let him sleep.

¹²Here is a grave evil I have observed under the sun: riches hoarded by their owner to his misfortune, ¹³in that those riches are lost in some unlucky venture; and if he begets a son, he has nothing in hand.

¹⁴g-Another grave evil is this: He must depart just as he came.-g As he came out of his mother's womb, so must he depart at last, naked as he came. He can take nothing of his wealth to carry with him. ¹⁵So what is the good of his toiling for the wind? ¹⁶Besides, all his days h-he eats in darkness,-h with much vexation and grief and anger.

¹⁷Only this, I have found, is a real good: that one should eat and drink and get pleasure with all the gains he makes under the sun, during the numbered days of life that God has given him; for that is his portion. ¹⁸Also, whenever a man is given riches and property by God, and is also permitted by Him to enjoy them and to take his portion and get pleasure for his gains—that is a gift of God. ¹⁹For [such a man] will not brood much over the days of his life,i because God keeps him busy enjoying himself.

6 There is an evil I have observed under the sun, and a grave one it is for man: ²that God sometimes grants a man riches, property, and wealth, so that he does not want for anything his appetite may crave, but God does not permit him to enjoy it; instead, a stranger will enjoy it. That is futility and a grievous ill. ³Even if a man should beget a hundred children and live many years—no matter how many the days of his years may come to, if his gullet is not sated through his wealth, I say: The stillbirth, though

הַרְבֵּה יֹאכֵל וְהַשָּׂבָע לֶעָשִׁיר אֵינֶנּוּ מַנִּיחַ לוֹ לִישׁוֹן:

¹² יֵשׁ רָעָה חוֹלָה רָאִיתִי תַּחַת הַשָּׁמֶשׁ עֹשֶׁר שָׁמוּר לִבְעָלָיו לְרָעָתוֹ: ¹³ וְאָבַד הָעֹשֶׁר הַהוּא בְּעִנְיָן רָע וְהוֹלִיד בֵּן וְאֵין בְּיָדוֹ מְאוּמָה:

¹⁴ כַּאֲשֶׁר יָצָא מִבֶּטֶן אִמּוֹ עָרוֹם יָשׁוּב לָלֶכֶת כְּשֶׁבָּא וּמְאוּמָה לֹא־יִשָּׂא בַעֲמָלוֹ שֶׁיֹּלֵךְ בְּיָדוֹ: ¹⁵ וְגַם־זֹה רָעָה חוֹלָה כָּל־עֻמַּת שֶׁבָּא כֵּן יֵלֵךְ וּמַה־יִּתְרוֹן לוֹ שֶׁיַּעֲמֹל לָרוּחַ: ¹⁶ גַּם כָּל־יָמָיו בַּחֹשֶׁךְ יֹאכֵל וְכָעַס הַרְבֵּה וְחָלְיוֹ וָקָצֶף:

¹⁷ הִנֵּה אֲשֶׁר־רָאִיתִי אָנִי טוֹב אֲשֶׁר־יָפֶה לֶאֱכוֹל־וְלִשְׁתּוֹת וְלִרְאוֹת טוֹבָה בְּכָל־עֲמָלוֹ ׀ שֶׁיַּעֲמֹל תַּחַת־הַשֶּׁמֶשׁ מִסְפַּר יְמֵי־חַיָּו* אֲשֶׁר־נָתַן־לוֹ הָאֱלֹהִים כִּי־הוּא חֶלְקוֹ: ¹⁸ גַּם כָּל־הָאָדָם אֲשֶׁר נָתַן־לוֹ הָאֱלֹהִים עֹשֶׁר וּנְכָסִים וְהִשְׁלִיטוֹ לֶאֱכֹל מִמֶּנּוּ וְלָשֵׂאת אֶת־חֶלְקוֹ וְלִשְׂמֹחַ בַּעֲמָלוֹ זֹה מַתַּת אֱלֹהִים הִיא: ¹⁹ כִּי לֹא הַרְבֵּה יִזְכֹּר אֶת־יְמֵי חַיָּיו כִּי הָאֱלֹהִים מַעֲנֶה בְּשִׂמְחַת לִבּוֹ:

ו יֵשׁ רָעָה אֲשֶׁר רָאִיתִי תַּחַת הַשָּׁמֶשׁ וְרַבָּה הִיא עַל־הָאָדָם: ² אִישׁ אֲשֶׁר יִתֶּן־לוֹ הָאֱלֹהִים עֹשֶׁר וּנְכָסִים וְכָבוֹד וְאֵינֶנּוּ חָסֵר לְנַפְשׁוֹ ׀ מִכֹּל אֲשֶׁר־יִתְאַוֶּה וְלֹא־יַשְׁלִיטֶנּוּ הָאֱלֹהִים לֶאֱכֹל מִמֶּנּוּ כִּי אִישׁ נָכְרִי יֹאכְלֶנּוּ זֶה הֶבֶל וָחֳלִי רָע הוּא: ³ אִם־יוֹלִיד אִישׁ מֵאָה וְשָׁנִים רַבּוֹת יִחְיֶה וְרַב ׀ שֶׁיִּהְיוּ יְמֵי־שָׁנָיו וְנַפְשׁוֹ לֹא־תִשְׂבַּע מִן־הַטּוֹבָה וְגַם־קְבוּרָה לֹא־הָיְתָה לּוֹ

v. 17. חסר י'

---

g-g   *Moved up from v. 15 for clarity.*
h-h   *Septuagint reads "are [spent] in darkness and mourning."*
i   *The thought of which is depressing; see v. 16.*

it was not even accorded a burial,[a] is more fortunate than he. [4]Though it comes into futility and departs into darkness, and its very name is covered with darkness, [5]though it has never seen or experienced the sun, it is better off than he—[6]yes, even if the other lived a thousand years twice over but never had his fill of enjoyment! For are not both of them bound for the same place? [7b]All of man's earning is for the sake of his mouth, [c]yet his gullet is not sated. [8]What advantage then has the wise man over the fool, what advantage has the pauper who knows how to get on in life?[-c] [9d]Is the feasting of the eyes more important than the pursuit of desire? That, too, is futility and pursuit of wind.

[10]Whatever happens, it was designated long ago and it was known that it would happen; as for man, he cannot contend with what is stronger than he. [11]Often, much talk means much futility. How does it benefit a man? [12]Who can possibly know what is best for a man to do in life—the few days of his fleeting life? For[e] who can tell him what the future holds for him under the sun?

7

[a]A good name is better than fragrant oil, and the day of death than the day of birth.[b]

[2]It is better to go to a house of mourning than to a house of feasting; for that is the end of every man, and a living one should take it to heart.

[3]Vexation is better than revelry;[c] for though the face be sad, the heart may be glad. [4]Wise

אָמַרְתִּי טוֹב מִמֶּנּוּ הַנָּפֶל : [4] כִּי־בַהֶבֶל בָּא וּבַחֹשֶׁךְ יֵלֵךְ וּבַחֹשֶׁךְ שְׁמוֹ יְכֻסֶּה : [5] גַּם־שֶׁמֶשׁ לֹא־רָאָה וְלֹא יָדָע נַחַת לָזֶה מִזֶּה : [6] וְאִלּוּ חָיָה אֶלֶף שָׁנִים פַּעֲמַיִם וְטוֹבָה לֹא רָאָה הֲלֹא אֶל־מָקוֹם אֶחָד הַכֹּל הוֹלֵךְ : [7] כָּל־עֲמַל הָאָדָם לְפִיהוּ וְגַם־הַנֶּפֶשׁ לֹא תִמָּלֵא : [8] כִּי מַה־יּוֹתֵר לֶחָכָם מִן־הַכְּסִיל מַה־לֶּעָנִי יוֹדֵעַ לַהֲלֹךְ נֶגֶד הַחַיִּים : [9] טוֹב מַרְאֵה עֵינַיִם מֵהֲלָךְ־נֶפֶשׁ גַּם־זֶה הֶבֶל וּרְעוּת רוּחַ :

[10]* מַה־שֶּׁהָיָה כְּבָר נִקְרָא שְׁמוֹ וְנוֹדָע אֲשֶׁר־הוּא אָדָם וְלֹא־יוּכַל לָדִין עִם שֶׁהַתְּקִיף מִמֶּנּוּ : [11] כִּי יֵשׁ־דְּבָרִים הַרְבֵּה מַרְבִּים הָבֶל מַה־יֹּתֵר לָאָדָם : [12] כִּי מִי־יוֹדֵעַ מַה־טּוֹב לָאָדָם בַּחַיִּים מִסְפַּר יְמֵי־חַיֵּי הֶבְלוֹ וְיַעֲשֵׂם כַּצֵּל אֲשֶׁר מִי־יַגִּיד לָאָדָם מַה־יִּהְיֶה אַחֲרָיו תַּחַת הַשָּׁמֶשׁ :

ז טוֹב שֵׁם מִשֶּׁמֶן טוֹב וְיוֹם הַמָּוֶת מִיּוֹם הִוָּלְדוֹ : [2] טוֹב לָלֶכֶת אֶל־בֵּית־אֵבֶל מִלֶּכֶת אֶל־בֵּית מִשְׁתֶּה בַּאֲשֶׁר הוּא סוֹף כָּל־הָאָדָם וְהַחַי יִתֵּן אֶל־לִבּוֹ : [3] טוֹב כַּעַס מִשְּׂחֹק כִּי־בְרֹעַ פָּנִים יִיטַב

---

a   *Stillbirths were cast into pits or hidden in the ground in no recognizable graves; cf. v. 4 end.*
b   *Cf. Prov. 16.26.*
c-c   *Meaning of Heb. uncertain; emendation yields "And if the gullet is not sated, [8]what advantage has the wise man over the fool, he who knows how to get on in life over the pauper?"*
d   *Meaning of first half of verse uncertain.*
e   *Lit. "according to the shadow that"; cf. Qumran Aramaic betel and Syriac meṭṭol; and see 8.13.*

a   *The author now offers a number of practical maxims, which, however, he concludes (vv. 23–24) are of limited value.*
b   *Until a man dies, there is always danger that he may forfeit his good name.*
c   *For empty revelry precludes real happiness; cf. 2.2.*

men are drawn to a house of mourning, and fools to a house of merrymaking.

⁵It is better to listen to a wise man's reproof than to listen to the praise of fools. ⁶For the levity*d* of the fool is like the crackling of nettles under a kettle. *e*But that too is illusory; ⁷for cheating*f* may rob the wise man of reason and destroy the prudence of the cautious.*g*

⁸The end of a matter is better than the beginning of it.

Better a patient spirit than a haughty spirit.

⁹Don't let your spirit be quickly vexed, for vexation abides in the breasts of fools.

¹⁰Don't say, "How has it happened that former times were better than these?" For it is not wise of you to ask that question.

¹¹Wisdom is as good as a patrimony, and even better, for those who behold the sun. ¹²For to be in the shelter of wisdom is to be also in the shelter of money,*h* and the advantage of intelligence is that wisdom preserves the life of him who possesses it.

¹³*i*Consider God's doing! Who can straighten what He has twisted? ¹⁴So in a time of good fortune enjoy the good fortune; and in a time of misfortune, reflect: The one no less than the other was God's doing; consequently, man may find no fault with Him.*j*

¹⁵In my own brief span of life, I have seen both these things: sometimes a good man perishes in spite of his goodness, and sometimes a wicked one endures in spite of his wickedness. ¹⁶So don't overdo goodness and don't act the wise man to excess, or you may be dumfounded. ¹⁷Don't overdo wickedness and don't be a fool, or you may die before your time. ¹⁸It is best that

לֵב: ⁴ לֵב חֲכָמִים בְּבֵית אֵבֶל וְלֵב כְּסִילִים בְּבֵית שִׂמְחָה:

⁵ טוֹב לִשְׁמֹעַ גַּעֲרַת חָכָם מֵאִישׁ שֹׁמֵעַ שִׁיר כְּסִילִים: ⁶ כִּי כְקוֹל הַסִּירִים תַּחַת הַסִּיר כֵּן שְׂחֹק הַכְּסִיל וְגַם־זֶה הָבֶל: ⁷ כִּי הָעֹשֶׁק יְהוֹלֵל חָכָם וִיאַבֵּד אֶת־לֵב מַתָּנָה:

⁸ טוֹב אַחֲרִית דָּבָר מֵרֵאשִׁיתוֹ טוֹב אֶרֶךְ־רוּחַ מִגְּבַהּ־רוּחַ:

⁹ אַל־תְּבַהֵל בְּרוּחֲךָ לִכְעוֹס כִּי כַעַס בְּחֵיק כְּסִילִים יָנוּחַ:

¹⁰ אַל־תֹּאמַר מֶה הָיָה שֶׁהַיָּמִים הָרִאשֹׁנִים הָיוּ טוֹבִים מֵאֵלֶּה כִּי לֹא מֵחָכְמָה שָׁאַלְתָּ עַל־זֶה:

¹¹ טוֹבָה חָכְמָה עִם־נַחֲלָה וְיֹתֵר לְרֹאֵי הַשָּׁמֶשׁ: ¹² כִּי בְּצֵל הַחָכְמָה בְּצֵל הַכָּסֶף וְיִתְרוֹן דַּעַת הַחָכְמָה תְּחַיֶּה בְעָלֶיהָ:

¹³ רְאֵה אֶת־מַעֲשֵׂה הָאֱלֹהִים כִּי מִי יוּכַל לְתַקֵּן אֵת אֲשֶׁר עִוְּתוֹ: ¹⁴ בְּיוֹם טוֹבָה הֱיֵה בְטוֹב וּבְיוֹם רָעָה רְאֵה גַּם אֶת־זֶה לְעֻמַּת־זֶה עָשָׂה הָאֱלֹהִים עַל־דִּבְרַת שֶׁלֹּא יִמְצָא הָאָדָם אַחֲרָיו מְאוּמָה:

¹⁵ אֶת־הַכֹּל רָאִיתִי בִּימֵי הֶבְלִי יֵשׁ צַדִּיק אֹבֵד בְּצִדְקוֹ וְיֵשׁ רָשָׁע מַאֲרִיךְ בְּרָעָתוֹ:

¹⁶ אַל־תְּהִי צַדִּיק הַרְבֵּה וְאַל־תִּתְחַכַּם יוֹתֵר לָמָּה תִּשּׁוֹמֵם: ¹⁷ אַל־תִּרְשַׁע הַרְבֵּה וְאַל־תְּהִי סָכָל לָמָּה תָמוּת בְּלֹא עִתֶּךָ:

¹⁸ טוֹב אֲשֶׁר תֶּאֱחֹז בָּזֶה וְגַם־מִזֶּה אַל

---

d   Emendation yields "praise" (shbḥ.)

e   This section, to end of verse 7, is apparently a continuation of the thought in vv. 11–12 and 19.

f   Emendation yields "riches."

g   Lit. "caution"; cf. postbiblical mathun, "cautious."

h   Emendation yields "For the possessor of wisdom becomes a possessor of money."

i   Vv. 13–14 continue the thought of v. 10.

j   So Rashi; cf. the same thought in Job 1.22; 2.10.

you grasp the one without letting go of the other, for one who fears God will do his duty[k] by both.

[19]Wisdom is more of a stronghold to a wise man than [l]-ten magnates-[l] that a city may contain.

[20][m]For there is not one good man on earth who does what is best[n] and doesn't err.

[21]Finally, don't pay attention to everything that is said, so that you may not hear your slave reviling you; [22]for well you remember[o] the many times that you yourself have reviled others.

[23]All this I tested with wisdom. I thought I could fathom it,[n] but it eludes me. [24][The secret of] what happens is elusive and deep, deep down; who can discover it? [25]I put my mind to studying, exploring, and seeking wisdom and the reason of things, and to studying wickedness, stupidity, madness, and folly. [26]Now, I find woman more bitter than death; she is all traps, her hands are fetters and her heart is snares. He who is pleasing to God escapes her, and he who is displeasing is caught by her. [27]See, this is what I found, said Koheleth, item by item in my search for the reason of things. [28]As for what I sought further but did not find, I found only one human being in a thousand, and the one I found among so many was never a woman. [29]But, see, this I did find: God made men plain, but they have engaged in too much reasoning.

8 [a]-Who is like the wise man,-[a] and who knows the meaning of the adage:

"A man's wisdom lights up his face,

So that his deep discontent[b] is dissembled"?

[2]I do! "Obey the king's orders—and [c]-don't

תַּנַּח אֶת־יָדֶךָ כִּי־יְרֵא אֱלֹהִים יֵצֵא אֶת־
כֻּלָּם:
19 הַחָכְמָה תָּעֹז לֶחָכָם מֵעֲשָׂרָה שַׁלִּיטִים
אֲשֶׁר הָיוּ בָּעִיר:
20 כִּי אָדָם אֵין צַדִּיק בָּאָרֶץ אֲשֶׁר יַעֲשֶׂה־
טּוֹב וְלֹא יֶחֱטָא:
21 גַּם לְכָל־הַדְּבָרִים אֲשֶׁר יְדַבֵּרוּ אַל־
תִּתֵּן לִבֶּךָ אֲשֶׁר לֹא־תִשְׁמַע אֶת־עַבְדְּךָ
מְקַלְלֶךָ: 22 כִּי גַּם־פְּעָמִים רַבּוֹת יָדַע לִבֶּךָ
אֲשֶׁר גַּם־אַתָּ קִלַּלְתָּ אֲחֵרִים:
23 כָּל־זֹה נִסִּיתִי בַחָכְמָה אָמַרְתִּי אֶחְכָּמָה
וְהִיא רְחוֹקָה מִמֶּנִּי: 24 רָחוֹק מַה־שֶּׁהָיָה
וְעָמֹק | עָמֹק מִי יִמְצָאֶנּוּ: 25 סַבּוֹתִי אֲנִי
וְלִבִּי לָדַעַת וְלָתוּר וּבַקֵּשׁ חָכְמָה וְחֶשְׁבּוֹן
וְלָדַעַת רֶשַׁע כֶּסֶל וְהַסִּכְלוּת הוֹלֵלוֹת:
26 וּמוֹצֵא אֲנִי מַר מִמָּוֶת אֶת־הָאִשָּׁה
אֲשֶׁר־הִיא מְצוֹדִים וַחֲרָמִים לִבָּהּ
אֲסוּרִים יָדֶיהָ טוֹב לִפְנֵי הָאֱלֹהִים יִמָּלֵט
מִמֶּנָּה וְחוֹטֵא יִלָּכֶד בָּהּ: 27 רְאֵה זֶה
מָצָאתִי אָמְרָה קֹהֶלֶת אַחַת לְאַחַת
לִמְצֹא חֶשְׁבּוֹן: 28 אֲשֶׁר עוֹד־בִּקְשָׁה נַפְשִׁי
וְלֹא מָצָאתִי אָדָם אֶחָד מֵאֶלֶף מָצָאתִי
וְאִשָּׁה בְכָל־אֵלֶּה לֹא מָצָאתִי: 29 לְבַד
רְאֵה־זֶה מָצָאתִי אֲשֶׁר עָשָׂה הָאֱלֹהִים
אֶת־הָאָדָם יָשָׁר וְהֵמָּה בִקְשׁוּ חִשְּׁבֹנוֹת
רַבִּים:

ח מִי כְּהֶחָכָם וּמִי יוֹדֵעַ פֵּשֶׁר דָּבָר
חָכְמַת אָדָם תָּאִיר פָּנָיו
וְעֹז פָּנָיו יְשֻׁנֶּא*:
2 אֲנִי פִּי־מֶלֶךְ שְׁמוֹר וְעַל דִּבְרַת שְׁבוּעַת

v. 1. א׳ במקום ה׳

---

k Cf. postbiblical yaṣa yede.
l-l Emendation yields "the riches of the magnates"; cf. Prov. 18.11.
m Apparently continuing the thought of v. 16.
n Refers back to 6.12.
o Lit. "your heart knows"; the same idiom occurs again in 8.5.

a-a Some ancient versions read "Who here is wise."
b Lit. "face"; cf. 1 Sam. 1.18; Job 9.27.
c-c Moved up from v. 3 for English word order.

rush-*c* into uttering an oath by God."*d* *3e*-Leave his presence; do not tarry-*e* in a dangerous situation, for he can do anything he pleases; [4]inasmuch as a king's command is authoritative, and none can say to him, "What are you doing?" [5]One who obeys orders will not suffer from the dangerous situation.

A wise man, however, will bear in mind*f* that there is a time of doom.*g* [6]For there is a time for every experience, including the doom; for a man's calamity*h* overwhelms him. [7]Indeed, he does not know what is to happen; even when it is on the point of happening, who can tell him? [8]No man has authority over the lifebreath—to hold back the lifebreath;*i* there is no authority over the day of death. There is no mustering out from that war; wickedness*j* is powerless to save its owner.

[9]All these things I observed; I noted all that went on under the sun, while men still had authority over men to treat them unjustly. [10]And then I saw scoundrels *k*-coming from the Holy Site and being brought to burial,-*k* while such as had acted righteously were forgotten in the city.

And here is another frustration: [11]the fact that the sentence imposed for evil deeds is not executed swiftly, which is why men are emboldened to do evil—[12]the fact that a sinner may do evil a hundred times and his [punishment] still be delayed. For although I am aware that "It will be well with those who revere God since they revere Him, [13]and it will not be well with the

---

d   The answer to the inquiry about the implications of the proverb in v. 1 is given in the form of another proverb, of which only the first half is relevant and is enlarged upon.

e-e   Or "Give ground before him; do not resist."

f   The same idiom as in 7.22.

g   Lit. "time and doom"; cf. the synonymous "time of misfortune," lit. "time and misfortune," 9.11.

h   Still another term for death; cf. "the time of calamity" for "the hour of death," 9.12.

i   From leaving the body when the time comes; see 12.7; cf. Ps. 104.29; 146.4.

j   Emendation yields "riches."

k-k   Meaning uncertain; emendation yields "approaching [to minister]. They would come and profane the Holy Site."

אֱלֹהִֽים׃ 3 אַל־תִּבָּהֵ֤ל מִפָּנָיו֙ תֵּלֵ֔ךְ אַֽל־תַּעֲמֹ֖ד בְּדָבָ֣ר רָ֑ע כִּ֛י כָּל־אֲשֶׁ֥ר יַחְפֹּ֖ץ יַעֲשֶֽׂה׃ 4 בַּאֲשֶׁ֥ר דְּבַר־מֶ֖לֶךְ שִׁלְט֑וֹן וּמִ֥י יֹֽאמַר־ל֖וֹ מַֽה־תַּעֲשֶֽׂה׃ 5 שׁוֹמֵ֣ר מִצְוָ֔ה לֹ֥א יֵדַ֖ע דָּבָ֣ר רָ֑ע וְעֵ֣ת וּמִשְׁפָּ֔ט יֵדַ֖ע לֵ֥ב חָכָֽם׃ 6 כִּ֣י לְכָל־חֵ֔פֶץ יֵ֖שׁ עֵ֣ת וּמִשְׁפָּ֑ט כִּֽי־רָעַ֥ת הָאָדָ֖ם רַבָּ֥ה עָלָֽיו׃ 7 כִּֽי־אֵינֶ֥נּוּ יֹדֵ֖עַ מַה־שֶּׁיִּֽהְיֶ֑ה כִּ֚י כַּאֲשֶׁ֣ר יִֽהְיֶ֔ה מִ֖י יַגִּ֥יד לֽוֹ׃ 8 אֵ֣ין אָדָ֞ם שַׁלִּ֤יט בָּר֙וּחַ֙ לִכְל֣וֹא אֶת־הָר֔וּחַ וְאֵ֤ין שִׁלְטוֹן֙ בְּי֣וֹם הַמָּ֔וֶת וְאֵ֥ין מִשְׁלַ֖חַת בַּמִּלְחָמָ֑ה וְלֹֽא־יְמַלֵּ֥ט רֶ֖שַׁע אֶת־בְּעָלָֽיו׃ 9 אֶת־כָּל־זֶ֤ה רָאִ֨יתִי֙ וְנָת֣וֹן אֶת־לִבִּ֔י לְכָל־מַעֲשֶׂ֔ה אֲשֶׁ֥ר נַעֲשָׂ֖ה תַּ֣חַת הַשָּׁ֑מֶשׁ עֵ֗ת אֲשֶׁ֨ר שָׁלַ֧ט הָאָדָ֛ם בְּאָדָ֖ם לְרַ֥ע לֽוֹ׃ 10 וּבְכֵ֡ן רָאִיתִי֩ רְשָׁעִ֨ים קְבֻרִ֜ים וָבָ֗אוּ וּמִמְּק֤וֹם קָדוֹשׁ֙ יְהַלֵּ֔כוּ וְיִֽשְׁתַּכְּח֥וּ בָעִ֖יר אֲשֶׁ֣ר כֵּן־עָשׂ֑וּ גַּם־זֶ֖ה הָֽבֶל׃ 11 אֲשֶׁר֙ אֵין־נַעֲשָׂ֣ה פִתְגָ֔ם מַעֲשֵׂ֥ה הָרָעָ֖ה מְהֵרָ֑ה עַל־כֵּ֡ן מָלֵ֞א לֵ֧ב בְּנֵֽי־הָאָדָ֛ם בָּהֶ֖ם לַעֲשׂ֥וֹת רָֽע׃ 12 אֲשֶׁ֣ר חֹטֶ֗א עֹשֶׂ֥ה רָ֛ע מְאַ֖ת וּמַאֲרִ֣יךְ ל֑וֹ כִּ֚י גַּם־יוֹדֵ֣עַ אָ֔נִי אֲשֶׁ֤ר יִֽהְיֶה־טּוֹב֙ לְיִרְאֵ֣י הָֽאֱלֹהִ֔ים אֲשֶׁ֥ר יִֽירְא֖וּ מִלְּפָנָֽיו׃ 13 וְטוֹב֙ לֹֽא־יִהְיֶ֣ה לָֽרָשָׁ֔ע וְלֹֽא־יַאֲרִ֥יךְ יָמִ֖ים כַּצֵּ֑ל אֲשֶׁ֛ר אֵינֶ֥נּוּ יָרֵ֖א מִלִּפְנֵ֥י אֱלֹהִֽים׃ 14 יֵשׁ־

scoundrel, and he will not live long, because[l] he does not revere God"—[14]here is a frustration that occurs in the world: sometimes an upright man is requited according to the conduct of the scoundrel; and sometimes the scoundrel is requited according to the conduct of the upright. I say all that is frustration.

[15]I therefore praised enjoyment. For the only good a man can have under the sun is to eat and drink and enjoy himself. That much can accompany him, in exchange for his wealth, through the days of life that God has granted him under the sun.

[16]For I have set my mind to learn wisdom and to observe the business that goes on in the world—even to the extent of going without sleep day and night—[17]and I have observed all that God brings to pass. Indeed, man cannot guess the events that occur under the sun. For man tries strenuously, but fails to guess them; and even if a sage should think to discover them he would not be able to guess them.

9

For all this I noted, and I ascertained[a] all this: that the actions of even the righteous and the wise are determined by God. [b]-Even love! Even hate! Man knows none of these in advance—[2]none!-[b] For the same fate is in store for all: for the righteous, and for the wicked; for the good and pure,[c] and for the impure; for him who sacrifices, and for him who does not;[d] for him who is pleasing,[e] and for him who is displeasing; and for him who swears, and for him who shuns oaths.[f] [3]That is the sad thing about

הֶ֫בֶל אֲשֶׁ֣ר נַעֲשָׂה֮ עַל־הָאָרֶץ֒ אֲשֶׁ֣ר ׀ יֵ֣שׁ
צַדִּיקִ֗ים אֲשֶׁ֨ר מַגִּ֤יעַ אֲלֵהֶם֙ כְּמַעֲשֵׂ֣ה
הָרְשָׁעִ֔ים וְיֵ֣שׁ רְשָׁעִ֔ים שֶׁמַּגִּ֥יעַ אֲלֵהֶ֖ם
כְּמַעֲשֵׂ֣ה הַצַּדִּיקִ֑ים אָמַ֕רְתִּי שֶׁגַּם־זֶ֖ה
הָֽבֶל׃
[15] וְשִׁבַּ֤חְתִּֽי אֲנִי֙ אֶת־הַשִּׂמְחָ֔ה אֲשֶׁ֨ר אֵֽין־
ט֤וֹב לָֽאָדָם֙ תַּ֣חַת הַשֶּׁ֔מֶשׁ כִּ֛י אִם־לֶֽאֱכ֥וֹל
וְלִשְׁתּ֖וֹת וְלִשְׂמ֑וֹחַ וְה֞וּא יִלְוֶ֣נּוּ בַעֲמָל֗וֹ
יְמֵ֥י חַיָּ֛יו אֲשֶׁר־נָֽתַן־ל֥וֹ הָאֱלֹהִ֖ים תַּ֥חַת
הַשָּֽׁמֶשׁ׃

[16] כַּאֲשֶׁ֨ר נָתַ֤תִּי אֶת־לִבִּי֙ לָדַ֣עַת חָכְמָ֔ה
וְלִרְאוֹת֙ אֶת־הָ֣עִנְיָ֔ן אֲשֶׁ֥ר נַעֲשָׂ֖ה עַל־
הָאָ֑רֶץ כִּ֣י גַ֤ם בַּיּוֹם֙ וּבַלַּ֔יְלָה שֵׁנָ֕ה בְּעֵינָ֖יו
אֵינֶ֥נּוּ רֹאֶֽה׃ [17] וְרָאִ֘יתִי֮ אֶת־כָּל־מַעֲשֵׂ֣ה
הָאֱלֹהִים֒ כִּ֡י לֹא֩ יוּכַ֨ל הָאָדָ֜ם לִמְצ֗וֹא
אֶת־הַֽמַּעֲשֶׂה֙ אֲשֶׁ֣ר נַעֲשָׂ֣ה תַֽחַת־הַשֶּׁ֔מֶשׁ
בְּ֠שֶׁל אֲשֶׁ֨ר יַעֲמֹ֤ל הָֽאָדָם֙ לְבַקֵּ֔שׁ וְלֹ֣א יִמְצָ֑א
וְגַ֨ם אִם־יֹאמַ֤ר הֶֽחָכָם֙ לָדַ֔עַת לֹ֥א יוּכַ֖ל
לִמְצֹֽא׃

ט [9] כִּ֣י אֶת־כָּל־זֶ֗ה נָתַ֤תִּי אֶל־לִבִּי֙ וְלָב֣וּר
אֶת־כָּל־זֶ֔ה אֲשֶׁ֨ר הַצַּדִּיקִ֧ים וְהַחֲכָמִ֛ים
וַעֲבָדֵיהֶ֖ם בְּיַ֣ד הָאֱלֹהִ֑ים גַּֽם־אַהֲבָ֣ה גַם־
שִׂנְאָ֗ה אֵ֤ין יוֹדֵ֙עַ֙ הָֽאָדָ֔ם הַכֹּ֖ל לִפְנֵיהֶֽם׃
[2] הַכֹּ֞ל כַּאֲשֶׁ֣ר לַכֹּ֗ל מִקְרֶ֨ה אֶחָ֜ד לַצַּדִּ֤יק
וְלָֽרָשָׁע֙ לַטּוֹב֙ וְלַטָּה֣וֹר וְלַטָּמֵ֔א וְלַ֨זֹּבֵ֔חַ
וְלַאֲשֶׁ֖ר אֵינֶ֣נּוּ זֹבֵ֑חַ כַּטּוֹב֙ כַּֽחֹטֶ֔א הַנִּשְׁבָּ֕ע
כַּאֲשֶׁ֖ר שְׁבוּעָ֥ה יָרֵֽא׃ [3] זֶ֣ה ׀ רָ֗ע בְּכֹ֤ל

---

l   *See note on 6.12.*

a   *Meaning of verb uncertain; construction as in Hos. 12.3; Ezra 3.12.*

b-b   *Emendation yields "Even love, even hate, no man can know in advance. All ²are insignificant."*

c   *I.e., those who observe the laws of ritual purity.*

d   *Cf. 4.17.*

e   *I.e., to God; cf. 2.26; 7.26.*

f   *Cf. 8.2.*

all that goes on under the sun: that the same fate is in store for all. (Not only that, but men's hearts are full of sadness, and their minds of madness, while they live; and then—to the dead!) [4]For he who is *g*-reckoned among-*g* the living has something to look forward to—even a live dog is better than a dead lion—[5]since the living know they will die. But the dead know nothing; they have no more recompense,*h* for even the memory of them has died. [6]Their loves, their hates, their jealousies have long since perished; and they have no more share till the end of time in all that goes on under the sun.

[7]Go, eat your bread in gladness, and drink your wine in joy; for your action was long ago approved by God.*i* [8]Let your clothes always be freshly washed, and your head never lack ointment. [9]Enjoy happiness with a woman you love all the fleeting days of life that have been granted to you under the sun—all your fleeting days. For that alone is what you can get out of life and out of the means you acquire under the sun. [10]Whatever it is in your power to do, do with all your might. For there is no action, no reasoning, no learning, no wisdom in Sheol, where you are going.

[11]I have further observed under the sun that
The race is not won by the swift,
Nor the battle by the valiant;
Nor is bread won by the wise,
Nor wealth by the intelligent,
Nor favor by the learned.
For the time of mischance*j* comes to all.*k* [12]And a man cannot even know his time. As fishes are enmeshed in a fatal net, and as birds are trapped in a snare, so men are caught at the time of

אֲשֶׁר־נַעֲשָׂה תַּחַת הַשָּׁמֶשׁ כִּי־מִקְרֶה אֶחָד לַכֹּל וְגַם לֵב בְּנֵי־הָאָדָם מָלֵא־רָע וְהוֹלֵלוֹת בִּלְבָבָם בְּחַיֵּיהֶם וְאַחֲרָיו אֶל־הַמֵּתִים: [4]כִּי־מִי אֲשֶׁר יבחר יְחֻבַּר אֶל כָּל־הַחַיִּים יֵשׁ בִּטָּחוֹן כִּי־לְכֶלֶב חַי הוּא טוֹב מִן־הָאַרְיֵה הַמֵּת: [5]כִּי הַחַיִּים יוֹדְעִים שֶׁיָּמֻתוּ וְהַמֵּתִים אֵינָם יוֹדְעִים מְאוּמָה וְאֵין־עוֹד לָהֶם שָׂכָר כִּי נִשְׁכַּח זִכְרָם: [6]גַּם אַהֲבָתָם גַּם־שִׂנְאָתָם גַּם־קִנְאָתָם כְּבָר אָבָדָה וְחֵלֶק אֵין־לָהֶם עוֹד לְעוֹלָם בְּכֹל אֲשֶׁר־נַעֲשָׂה תַּחַת הַשָּׁמֶשׁ:

[7]לֵךְ אֱכֹל בְּשִׂמְחָה לַחְמֶךָ וּשְׁתֵה בְלֶב־טוֹב יֵינֶךָ כִּי כְבָר רָצָה הָאֱלֹהִים אֶת־מַעֲשֶׂיךָ: [8]בְּכָל־עֵת יִהְיוּ בְגָדֶיךָ לְבָנִים וְשֶׁמֶן עַל־רֹאשְׁךָ אַל־יֶחְסָר: [9]רְאֵה חַיִּים עִם־אִשָּׁה אֲשֶׁר־אָהַבְתָּ כָּל־יְמֵי חַיֵּי הֶבְלֶךָ אֲשֶׁר נָתַן־לְךָ תַּחַת הַשֶּׁמֶשׁ כֹּל יְמֵי הֶבְלֶךָ כִּי הוּא חֶלְקְךָ בַּחַיִּים וּבַעֲמָלְךָ אֲשֶׁר־אַתָּה עָמֵל תַּחַת הַשָּׁמֶשׁ: [10]כֹּל אֲשֶׁר תִּמְצָא יָדְךָ לַעֲשׂוֹת בְּכֹחֲךָ עֲשֵׂה כִּי אֵין מַעֲשֶׂה וְחֶשְׁבּוֹן וְדַעַת וְחָכְמָה בִּשְׁאוֹל אֲשֶׁר אַתָּה הֹלֵךְ שָׁמָּה: ס

[11]שַׁבְתִּי וְרָאֹה תַחַת־הַשֶּׁמֶשׁ כִּי
לֹא לַקַּלִּים הַמֵּרוֹץ
וְלֹא לַגִּבּוֹרִים הַמִּלְחָמָה
וְגַם לֹא לַחֲכָמִים לֶחֶם
וְגַם לֹא לַנְּבֹנִים עֹשֶׁר
וְגַם לֹא לַיֹּדְעִים חֵן
כִּי־עֵת וָפֶגַע יִקְרֶה אֶת־כֻּלָּם: [12]כִּי גַּם לֹא־יֵדַע הָאָדָם אֶת־עִתּוֹ כַּדָּגִים שֶׁנֶּאֱחָזִים בִּמְצוֹדָה רָעָה וְכַצִּפֳּרִים

---

g-g Lit. "joined to all."
h Emendation yields "hope."
i Cf. 2.24–25; 3.13; 5.18.
j Euphemism for death.
k I.e., the insignificant duration of life renders all successes illusory; cf. 4.15–16.

calamity,*j* when it comes upon them without warning.

¹³This thing too I observed under the sun about wisdom, and it affected me profoundly. ¹⁴There was a little city, with few men in it; and to it came a great king, who invested it and built mighty siege works against it. ¹⁵Present in the city was a poor wise man *l*-who might have saved-*l* it with his wisdom, but nobody thought of that poor man. ¹⁶So I observed: Wisdom is better than valor; but

A poor man's wisdom is scorned,
And his words are not heeded.

¹⁷*m*Words spoken softly by wise men are heeded *n*-sooner than those shouted by a lord in folly.-*n*

¹⁸Wisdom is more valuable than *o*-weapons of war,-*o* but a single error destroys much of value.

10

Dead flies turn the perfumer's ointment fetid and putrid;*a* so a little folly outweighs massive wisdom.

²A wise man's mind tends toward the right hand, a fool's toward the left.*b* ³A fool's mind is also wanting when he travels, and he lets everybody know he is a fool.

⁴If the wrath of a lord flares up against you, don't give up your post;*c* for *d*-when wrath abates, grave offenses are pardoned.-*d*

⁵Here is an evil I have seen under the sun as great as an error committed by a ruler: ⁶Folly was placed on lofty heights, while rich men sat

הָאֲחֻזוֹת בַּפֶּ֔ח כָּהֵ֕ם יוּקָשִׁים֙ בְּנֵ֣י הָֽאָדָ֔ם
לְעֵ֣ת רָעָ֔ה כְּשֶׁתִּפּ֥וֹל עֲלֵיהֶ֖ם פִּתְאֹֽם׃

¹³ גַּם־זֹ֛ה רָאִ֥יתִי חָכְמָ֖ה תַּ֣חַת הַשָּׁ֑מֶשׁ
וּגְדוֹלָ֥ה הִ֖יא אֵלָֽי׃ ¹⁴ עִ֣יר קְטַנָּ֔ה וַאֲנָשִׁ֥ים
בָּ֖הּ מְעָ֑ט וּבָֽא־אֵלֶ֜יהָ מֶ֤לֶךְ גָּדוֹל֙ וְסָבַ֣ב
אֹתָ֔הּ וּבָנָ֥ה עָלֶ֖יהָ מְצוֹדִ֥ים גְּדֹלִֽים׃

¹⁵ וּמָ֣צָא בָ֗הּ אִ֤ישׁ מִסְכֵּן֙ חָכָ֔ם וּמִלַּט־ה֥וּא
אֶת־הָעִ֖יר בְּחָכְמָת֑וֹ וְאָדָם֙ לֹ֣א זָכַ֔ר אֶת־
הָאִ֥ישׁ הַמִּסְכֵּ֖ן הַהֽוּא׃ ¹⁶ וְאָמַ֣רְתִּי אָ֔נִי
טוֹבָ֥ה חָכְמָ֖ה מִגְּבוּרָ֑ה
וְחָכְמַ֤ת הַמִּסְכֵּן֙ בְּזוּיָ֔ה
וּדְבָרָ֖יו אֵינָ֥ם נִשְׁמָעִֽים׃

¹⁷ דִּבְרֵ֣י חֲכָמִ֔ים בְּנַ֖חַת נִשְׁמָעִ֑ים מִזַּעֲקַ֥ת
מוֹשֵׁ֖ל בַּכְּסִילִֽים׃

¹⁸ טוֹבָ֥ה חָכְמָ֖ה מִכְּלֵ֣י קְרָ֑ב וְחוֹטֶ֣א אֶחָ֔ד
יְאַבֵּ֖ד טוֹבָ֥ה הַרְבֵּֽה׃

י זְבוּבֵ֣י מָ֗וֶת יַבְאִ֛ישׁ יַבִּ֥יעַ שֶׁ֣מֶן רוֹקֵ֑חַ
יָקָ֛ר מֵחָכְמָ֥ה מִכָּב֖וֹד סִכְל֥וּת מְעָֽט׃

² לֵ֤ב חָכָם֙ לִֽימִינ֔וֹ וְלֵ֥ב כְּסִ֖יל לִשְׂמֹאלֽוֹ׃

³ וְגַם־בַּדֶּ֛רֶךְ כשהסכל כְּשֶׁסָּכָ֥ל הֹלֵ֖ךְ לִבּ֣וֹ
חָסֵ֑ר וְאָמַ֥ר לַכֹּ֖ל סָכָ֥ל הֽוּא׃

⁴ אִם־ר֤וּחַ הַמּוֹשֵׁל֙ תַּעֲלֶ֣ה עָלֶ֔יךָ מְקוֹמְךָ֖
אַל־תַּנַּ֑ח כִּ֣י מַרְפֵּ֔א יַנִּ֖יחַ חֲטָאִ֥ים גְּדוֹלִֽים׃

⁵ יֵ֣שׁ רָעָ֔ה רָאִ֖יתִי תַּ֣חַת הַשָּׁ֑מֶשׁ כִּשְׁגָגָ֕ה
שֶׁיֹּצָ֖א מִלִּפְנֵ֥י הַשַּׁלִּֽיט׃ ⁶ נִתַּן֙ הַסֶּ֣כֶל

---

l-l   Others "who saved."

m   Verses 9.17–10.19 constitute a group of loosely connected aphorisms.

n   Lit. "than the scream of a lord in [the manner of] the fools."

o-o   Emendation yields "everything precious."

a   Meaning of Heb. uncertain.

b   I.e., a wise man's mind brings him good luck; a fool's brings him bad luck.

c   Emendation yields "hope."

d-d   Lit. "abatement (2 Chron. 36.16) remits grave offenses." For hinniaḥ, "to remit," cf. Abodah Zarah 13a; cf. hanaḥah, "remission of taxes," Esth. 2.18.

in low estate. [7]I have seen slaves on horseback, and nobles walking on the ground like slaves.

[8]He who digs a pit will fall into it; he who breaches a stone fence will be bitten by a snake. [9]He who quarries stones will [e]-be hurt by them; he who splits wood will be harmed by-[e] it. [10][f]If the ax has become dull and he has not whetted the edge, he must exert more strength. Thus the advantage of a skill [depends on the exercise of] prudence. [11]If the snake bites because no spell was uttered, no advantage is gained by the trained charmer.

[12]A wise man's talk brings him favor, but a fool's lips are his undoing. [13]His talk begins as silliness and ends as disastrous madness. [14]Yet the fool talks and talks!

[g]A man cannot know what will happen; who can tell him what the future holds?

[15][h]A fool's exertions tire him out, for he doesn't know how to get to a town.

[16]Alas for you, O land whose king is a lackey and whose ministers dine in the morning! [17]Happy are you, O land whose king is a master and whose ministers dine at the proper time— with restraint, not with guzzling!

[18]Through slothfulness the ceiling sags,
Through lazy hands the house caves in.

[19]They[i] make a banquet for revelry; wine makes life merry, and money answers every need.

[20]Don't revile a king even among your intimates.[j]

Don't revile a rich man even in your bed-chamber;

For a bird of the air may carry the utterance,
And a winged creature may report the word.

בִּמְרוֹמִים רַבִּים וַעֲשִׁירִים בַּשֵּׁפֶל יֵשֵׁבוּ׃
7 רָאִיתִי עֲבָדִים עַל־סוּסִים וְשָׂרִים הֹלְכִים כַּעֲבָדִים עַל־הָאָרֶץ׃
8 חֹפֵר גּוּמָּץ בּוֹ יִפּוֹל וּפֹרֵץ גָּדֵר יִשְּׁכֶנּוּ נָחָשׁ׃ 9 מַסִּיעַ אֲבָנִים יֵעָצֵב בָּהֶם בּוֹקֵעַ עֵצִים יִסָּכֶן בָּם׃ 10 אִם־קֵהָה הַבַּרְזֶל וְהוּא לֹא־פָנִים קִלְקַל וַחֲיָלִים יְגַבֵּר וְיִתְרוֹן הַכְשֵׁיר חָכְמָה׃ 11 אִם־יִשֹּׁךְ הַנָּחָשׁ בְּלוֹא־לָחַשׁ וְאֵין יִתְרוֹן לְבַעַל הַלָּשׁוֹן׃
12 דִּבְרֵי פִי־חָכָם חֵן וְשִׂפְתוֹת כְּסִיל תְּבַלְּעֶנּוּ׃ 13 תְּחִלַּת דִּבְרֵי־פִיהוּ סִכְלוּת וְאַחֲרִית פִּיהוּ הוֹלֵלוּת רָעָה׃ 14 וְהַסָּכָל יַרְבֶּה דְבָרִים לֹא־יֵדַע הָאָדָם מַה־שֶׁיִּהְיֶה וַאֲשֶׁר יִהְיֶה מֵאַחֲרָיו מִי יַגִּיד לוֹ׃
15 עֲמַל הַכְּסִילִים תְּיַגְּעֶנּוּ אֲשֶׁר לֹא־יָדַע לָלֶכֶת אֶל־עִיר׃
16 אִי־לָךְ אֶרֶץ שֶׁמַּלְכֵּךְ נָעַר וְשָׂרַיִךְ בַּבֹּקֶר יֹאכֵלוּ׃ 17 אַשְׁרֵיךְ אֶרֶץ שֶׁמַּלְכֵּךְ בֶּן־חוֹרִים וְשָׂרַיִךְ בָּעֵת יֹאכֵלוּ בִּגְבוּרָה וְלֹא בַשְּׁתִי׃ 18 בַּעֲצַלְתַּיִם יִמַּךְ הַמְּקָרֶה וּבְשִׁפְלוּת יָדַיִם יִדְלֹף הַבָּיִת׃
19 לִשְׂחוֹק עֹשִׂים לֶחֶם וְיַיִן יְשַׂמַּח חַיִּים וְהַכֶּסֶף יַעֲנֶה אֶת־הַכֹּל׃
20 גַּם בְּמַדָּעֲךָ מֶלֶךְ אַל־תְּקַלֵּל וּבְחַדְרֵי מִשְׁכָּבְךָ אַל־תְּקַלֵּל עָשִׁיר כִּי עוֹף הַשָּׁמַיִם יוֹלִיךְ אֶת־הַקּוֹל וּבַעַל הכנפים כְּנָפַיִם יַגֵּיד דָּבָר׃

---

e-e   *Emendation yields "profit...shall make use of."*
f   *Meaning of verse uncertain.*
g   *The thought of this sentence is resumed at v. 20.*
h   *This verse continues the thought of v. 3.*
i   *I.e., the ministers of v. 16.*
j   *Others "thoughts"; meaning of Heb. uncertain.*

11

Send your bread forth upon the waters; for after many days you will find it. ²Distribute portions to seven or even to eight, for you cannot know what misfortune may occur on earth.

³If the clouds are filled, they will pour down rain on the earth; and *ª-if a tree falls to the south or to the north, the tree will stay where it falls.-ª* ⁴If one watches the wind, he will never sow; and if one observes the clouds, he will never reap. ⁵Just as you do not know how the lifebreath passes into*ᵇ* the limbs within the womb of the pregnant woman, so you cannot foresee the actions of God, who causes all things to happen. ⁶Sow your seed in the morning, and don't hold back your hand in the evening, since you don't know which is going to succeed, the one or the other, or if both are equally good.

⁷How sweet is the light, what a delight for the eyes to behold the sun! ⁸Even if a man lives many years, let him enjoy himself in all of them, remembering how many the days of darkness are going to be. The only future is nothingness!

⁹O youth, enjoy yourself while you are young! Let your heart lead you to enjoyment in the days of your youth. Follow the desires of your heart and the glances of your eyes—but know well that God will call you to account for all such things—¹⁰and banish care from your mind, and pluck sorrow out of your flesh! For youth and black hair are fleeting.

12

So appreciate your vigor*ª* in the days of your youth, before those days of sorrow come and those years arrive of which you will say, "I

יא שְׁלַ֥ח לַחְמְךָ֖ עַל־פְּנֵ֣י הַמָּ֑יִם כִּֽי־
בְרֹ֥ב הַיָּמִ֖ים תִּמְצָאֶֽנּוּ׃ ² תֶּן־חֵ֥לֶק לְשִׁבְעָ֖ה
וְגַ֣ם לִשְׁמוֹנָ֑ה כִּ֚י לֹ֣א תֵדַ֔ע מַה־יִּהְיֶ֥ה רָעָ֖ה
עַל־הָאָֽרֶץ׃ ³ אִם־יִמָּלְא֨וּ הֶעָבִ֜ים גֶּ֗שֶׁם עַל־הָאָ֙רֶץ֙
יָרִ֔יקוּ וְאִם־יִפּ֥וֹל עֵ֛ץ בַּדָּר֖וֹם וְאִ֣ם בַּצָּפ֑וֹן
מְק֛וֹם שֶׁיִּפּ֥וֹל הָעֵ֖ץ שָׁ֥ם יְהֽוּא׃ ⁴ שֹׁמֵ֥ר ר֙וּחַ֙
לֹ֣א יִזְרָ֔ע וְרֹאֶ֥ה בֶעָבִ֖ים לֹ֥א יִקְצֽוֹר׃
⁵ כַּאֲשֶׁ֨ר אֵֽינְךָ֤ יוֹדֵ֙עַ֙ מַה־דֶּ֣רֶךְ הָר֔וּחַ
כַּעֲצָמִים֙* בְּבֶ֣טֶן הַמְּלֵאָ֔ה כָּ֗כָה לֹ֤א תֵדַע֙
אֶֽת־מַעֲשֵׂ֣ה הָֽאֱלֹהִ֔ים אֲשֶׁ֥ר יַעֲשֶׂ֖ה אֶת־
הַכֹּֽל׃ ⁶ בַּבֹּ֙קֶר֙ זְרַ֣ע אֶת־זַרְעֶ֔ךָ וְלָעֶ֖רֶב אַל־
תַּנַּ֣ח יָדֶ֑ךָ כִּ֠י אֵֽינְךָ֤ יוֹדֵע֙ אֵ֣י זֶ֣ה יִכְשָׁ֗ר הֲזֶ֤ה
אֽוֹ־זֶה֙ וְאִם־שְׁנֵיהֶ֥ם כְּאֶחָ֖ד טוֹבִֽים׃

⁷ וּמָת֖וֹק הָא֑וֹר וְט֥וֹב לַֽעֵינַ֖יִם לִרְא֥וֹת אֶת־
הַשָּֽׁמֶשׁ׃ ⁸ כִּ֣י אִם־שָׁנִ֥ים הַרְבֵּ֛ה יִֽחְיֶ֥ה
הָאָדָ֖ם בְּכֻלָּ֣ם יִשְׂמָ֑ח וְיִזְכֹּר֙ אֶת־יְמֵ֣י
הַחֹ֔שֶׁךְ כִּֽי־הַרְבֵּ֥ה יִהְי֖וּ כָּל־שֶׁבָּ֥א הָֽבֶל׃

⁹ שְׂמַ֧ח בָּח֣וּר בְּיַלְדוּתֶ֗יךָ וִֽיטִֽיבְךָ֤ לִבְּךָ֙
בִּימֵ֣י בְחוּרוֹתֶ֔ךָ וְהַלֵּךְ֙ בְּדַרְכֵ֣י לִבְּךָ֔
וּבְמַרְאֵ֖י* עֵינֶ֑יךָ וְדָ֕ע כִּ֧י עַל־כָּל־אֵ֛לֶּה
יְבִֽיאֲךָ֥ הָאֱלֹהִ֖ים בַּמִּשְׁפָּֽט׃ ¹⁰ וְהָסֵ֥ר כַּ֙עַס֙
מִלִּבֶּ֔ךָ וְהַעֲבֵ֥ר רָעָ֖ה מִבְּשָׂרֶ֑ךָ כִּֽי־הַיַּלְד֥וּת
וְהַֽשַּׁחֲר֖וּת הָֽבֶל׃

יב וּזְכֹר֙ אֶת־בּ֣וֹרְאֶ֔יךָ בִּימֵ֖י בְּחוּרֹתֶ֑יךָ
עַ֣ד אֲשֶׁ֤ר לֹא־יָבֹ֙אוּ֙ יְמֵ֣י הָֽרָעָ֔ה וְהִגִּ֣יעוּ
שָׁנִ֔ים אֲשֶׁ֣ר תֹּאמַ֔ר אֵֽין־לִ֥י בָהֶ֖ם חֵֽפֶץ׃

---

a-a Emendation yields, "if a thunderbolt (lit. arrow, cf., e.g., 2 Sam. 22.15) falls…where the thunderbolt falls, only there will it strike."

b So many mss. and Targum; most mss. read "like."

a Cf. postbiblical bori; others "Remember thy Creator."

v. 5. בנוסח אחר "בעצמים"
v. 9. י' במקום ה'

have no pleasure in them"; [2]before sun and light and moon and stars grow dark, and the clouds come back again after the rain:

[3]When the guards of the house[b] become shaky,
And the men of valor[c] are bent,
And the maids that grind,[d] grown few, are idle,
And the ladies that peer through the windows[e] grow dim,
[4]And the doors to the street[f] are shut—
With the noise of the hand mill growing fainter,
And the song of the bird [g]-growing feebler,[g]
And all the strains of music dying down;[h]
[5]When one is afraid of heights
And there is terror on the road.—
For the almond tree may blossom,
[i]-The grasshopper be burdened,[i]
And the caper bush may bud again;[j]
But man sets out for his eternal abode,
With mourners all around in the street.—
[6]Before the silver cord snaps
And the golden bowl crashes,
The jar is shattered at the spring,
And the jug[k] is smashed at the cistern.[l]
[7]And the dust returns to the ground
As it was,
And the lifebreath returns to God
Who bestowed it.
[8]Utter futility—said Koheleth—
All is futile!

עַד֩ אֲשֶׁ֨ר לֹֽא־תֶחְשַׁ֤ךְ הַשֶּׁ֙מֶשׁ֙ וְהָא֔וֹר [2]
וְהַיָּרֵ֖חַ וְהַכּוֹכָבִ֑ים וְשָׁ֥בוּ הֶעָבִ֖ים אַחַ֥ר
הַגָּֽשֶׁם׃

בַּיּ֗וֹם שֶׁיָּזֻ֙עוּ֙ שֹׁמְרֵ֣י הַבַּ֔יִת [3]
וְהִֽתְעַוְּת֖וּ אַנְשֵׁ֣י הֶחָ֑יִל
וּבָטְל֤וּ הַטֹּֽחֲנוֹת֙ כִּ֣י מִעֵ֔טוּ
וְחָשְׁכ֥וּ הָרֹא֖וֹת בָּאֲרֻבּֽוֹת׃
וְסֻגְּר֤וּ דְלָתַ֙יִם֙ בַּשּׁ֔וּק [4]
בִּשְׁפַ֖ל ק֣וֹל הַֽטַּחֲנָ֑ה
וְיָקוּם֙ לְק֣וֹל הַצִּפּ֔וֹר
וְיִשַּׁ֖חוּ כָּל־בְּנ֥וֹת הַשִּֽׁיר׃
גַּ֣ם מִגָּבֹ֤הַּ יִרָ֙אוּ֙ [5]
וְחַתְחַתִּ֣ים בַּדֶּ֔רֶךְ
וְיָנֵ֤אץ הַשָּׁקֵד֙
וְיִסְתַּבֵּ֣ל הֶֽחָגָ֔ב
וְתָפֵ֖ר הָֽאֲבִיּוֹנָ֑ה
כִּֽי־הֹלֵ֤ךְ הָאָדָם֙ אֶל־בֵּ֣ית עוֹלָמ֔וֹ
וְסָבְב֥וּ בַשּׁ֖וּק הַסֹּפְדִֽים׃
עַ֣ד אֲשֶׁ֤ר לֹֽא־יֵרָתֵק֙ חֶ֣בֶל הַכֶּ֔סֶף [6]
וְתָרֻ֖ץ גֻּלַּ֣ת הַזָּהָ֑ב
וְתִשָּׁ֤בֶר כַּד֙ עַל־הַמַּבּ֔וּעַ
וְנָרֹ֥ץ הַגַּלְגַּ֖ל אֶל־הַבּֽוֹר׃
וְיָשֹׁ֧ב הֶעָפָ֛ר עַל־הָאָ֖רֶץ [7]
כְּשֶׁהָיָ֑ה
וְהָר֣וּחַ תָּשׁ֔וּב אֶל־הָאֱלֹהִ֖ים
אֲשֶׁ֥ר נְתָנָֽהּ׃
הֲבֵ֤ל הֲבָלִים֙ אָמַ֣ר הַקּוֹהֶ֔לֶת [8]
הַכֹּ֖ל הָֽבֶל׃

---

b   I.e., the arms.
c   I.e., the legs.
d   I.e., the teeth.
e   I.e., the eyes.
f   I.e., the ears.
g-g   Exact meaning of Heb. uncertain.
h   Cf. 2 Sam. 19.36.
i-i   Emendation yields "The squill (postbiblical Heb. ḥaṣab) resume its burden," i.e., its blossom-stalk and its leaves.
j   These plants, after seeming dead for part of the year, revive, unlike man; cf. Job 14.7–10.
k   So in Punic; others "wheel."
l   Poetic figure for the end of life.

⁹A further word: Because Koheleth was a sage, he continued to instruct the people. He listened to and tested the soundness*m* of many maxims. ¹⁰Koheleth sought to discover useful sayings and recorded*n* genuinely truthful sayings. ¹¹The sayings of the wise are like goads, like nails fixed *o*-in prodding sticks.-*o* *p*-They were given by one Shepherd.-*p*

¹²A further word: *q*-Against them,-*q* my son, be warned!

The making of many books is without limit
And much study*r* is a wearying of the flesh.
¹³The sum of the matter, when all is said and done: Revere God and observe His commandments! For this applies to all mankind: ¹⁴that God will call every creature to account for *s*-everything unknown,-*s* be it good or bad.

The sum of the matter, when all is said and
done: Revere God and observe His commandments! For this applies to all mankind.

9 וְיֹתֵ֕ר שֶׁהָיָ֥ה קֹהֶ֖לֶת חָכָ֑ם ע֗וֹד לִמַּד־
דַּ֙עַת֙ אֶת־הָעָ֔ם וְאִזֵּ֣ן וְחִקֵּ֔ר תִּקֵּ֖ן מְשָׁלִ֥ים
הַרְבֵּֽה׃ 10 בִּקֵּ֣שׁ קֹהֶ֔לֶת לִמְצֹ֖א דִּבְרֵי־חֵ֑פֶץ
וְכָת֥וּב יֹ֖שֶׁר דִּבְרֵ֥י אֱמֶֽת׃ 11 דִּבְרֵ֤י חֲכָמִים֙
כַּדָּ֣רְבֹנ֔וֹת וּֽכְמַשְׂמְר֥וֹת נְטוּעִ֖ים בַּעֲלֵ֣י
אֲסֻפּ֑וֹת נִתְּנ֖וּ מֵרֹעֶ֥ה אֶחָֽד׃

12 וְיֹתֵ֥ר מֵהֵ֖מָּה בְּנִ֣י הִזָּהֵ֑ר
עֲשׂ֙וֹת סְפָרִ֤ים הַרְבֵּה֙ אֵ֣ין קֵ֔ץ
וְלַ֥הַג הַרְבֵּ֖ה יְגִעַ֥ת בָּשָֽׂר׃
13 ס֚וֹף דָּבָ֣ר הַכֹּ֣ל נִשְׁמָ֔ע אֶת־הָאֱלֹהִ֥ים יְרָ֖א
וְאֶת־מִצְוֺתָ֣יו שְׁמ֑וֹר כִּי־זֶ֖ה כָּל־הָאָדָֽם׃
14 כִּ֤י אֶת־כָּל־מַ֙עֲשֶׂ֔ה הָאֱלֹהִ֖ים יָבִ֣א
בְמִשְׁפָּ֑ט עַ֖ל כָּל־נֶעְלָ֑ם אִם־ט֖וֹב וְאִם־
רָֽע׃*

[ס֚וֹף דָּבָ֣ר הַכֹּ֣ל נִשְׁמָ֔ע אֶת־הָאֱלֹהִ֥ים יְרָ֖א
וְאֶת־מִצְוֺתָ֣יו שְׁמ֑וֹר כִּי־זֶ֖ה כָּל־הָאָדָֽם׃*]

תם ונשלם תהילה לאל בורא עולם

---

m A noun, like dibber (Jer. 5.13), which occurs in such postbiblical
  phrases as shanim kethiq(qe)nan, "normal years" (lit. "years
  according to their propriety").
n Wekhathub is equivalent to wekhathob, an infinitive employed
  as in Esth. 9.16 and elsewhere.
o-o Meaning of Heb. uncertain. Others "are those that are
  composed in collections."
p-p Meaning of Heb. uncertain. Emendation yields "They are accounted as a sharp ox goad" (post-biblical mardea').
q-q Emendation yields "Slow, there!" Cf. Arabic mah and mah
  mah; so also mah (meh) in Prov. 31.2.
r Meaning of Heb. uncertain.
s-s Emendation yields "all their conduct."

ESTHER

1 It happened in the days of Ahasuerus—that Ahasuerus who reigned over a hundred and twenty-seven provinces from India to Ethiopia. 2In those days, when King Ahasuerus occupied the royal throne in the fortress[a] Shushan, 3in the third year of his reign, he gave a banquet for all the officials and courtiers—the administration of Persia and Media, the nobles and the governors of the provinces in his service. 4For no fewer than a hundred and eighty days he displayed the vast riches of his kingdom and the splendid glory of his majesty. 5At the end of this period, the king gave a banquet for seven days in the court of the king's palace garden for all the people who lived in the fortress Shushan, high and low alike. 6b[There were hangings of] white cotton and blue wool, caught up by cords of fine linen and purple wool to silver rods and alabaster columns; and there were couches of gold and silver on a pavement of marble, alabaster, mother-of-pearl, and mosaics. 7Royal wine was served in abundance, as befits a king, in golden beakers, beakers of varied design. 8And the rule for the drinking was, "No restrictions!" For the king had given orders to every palace steward to comply with each man's wishes. 9In addition, Queen Vashti gave a banquet for women, in the royal palace of King Ahasuerus.

10On the seventh day, when the king was merry with wine, he ordered Mehuman, Bizzetha, Harbona, Bigtha, Abagtha, Zethar, and Carcas, the seven eunuchs in attendance on

א וַיְהִי בִּימֵי אֲחַשְׁוֵרוֹשׁ הוּא אֲחַשְׁוֵרוֹשׁ הַמֹּלֵךְ מֵהֹדּוּ וְעַד־כּוּשׁ שֶׁבַע וְעֶשְׂרִים וּמֵאָה מְדִינָה: 2 בַּיָּמִים הָהֵם כְּשֶׁבֶת | הַמֶּלֶךְ אֲחַשְׁוֵרוֹשׁ עַל כִּסֵּא מַלְכוּתוֹ אֲשֶׁר בְּשׁוּשַׁן הַבִּירָה: 3 בִּשְׁנַת שָׁלוֹשׁ לְמָלְכוֹ עָשָׂה מִשְׁתֶּה לְכָל־שָׂרָיו וַעֲבָדָיו חֵיל | פָּרַס וּמָדַי הַפַּרְתְּמִים וְשָׂרֵי הַמְּדִינוֹת לְפָנָיו: 4 בְּהַרְאֹתוֹ אֶת־עֹשֶׁר כְּבוֹד מַלְכוּתוֹ וְאֶת־יְקָר תִּפְאֶרֶת גְּדוּלָּתוֹ יָמִים רַבִּים שְׁמוֹנִים וּמְאַת יוֹם: 5 וּבִמְלוֹאת | הַיָּמִים הָאֵלֶּה עָשָׂה הַמֶּלֶךְ לְכָל־הָעָם הַנִּמְצְאִים בְּשׁוּשַׁן הַבִּירָה לְמִגָּדוֹל וְעַד־קָטָן מִשְׁתֶּה שִׁבְעַת יָמִים בַּחֲצַר גִּנַּת בִּיתַן הַמֶּלֶךְ: 6 חוּר | כַּרְפַּס וּתְכֵלֶת אָחוּז בְּחַבְלֵי־בוּץ וְאַרְגָּמָן עַל־גְּלִילֵי כֶסֶף וְעַמּוּדֵי שֵׁשׁ מִטּוֹת | זָהָב וָכֶסֶף עַל רִצְפַת בַּהַט־וָשֵׁשׁ וְדַר וְסֹחָרֶת: 7 וְהַשְׁקוֹת בִּכְלֵי זָהָב וְכֵלִים מִכֵּלִים שׁוֹנִים וְיֵין מַלְכוּת רָב כְּיַד הַמֶּלֶךְ: 8 וְהַשְּׁתִיָּה כַדָּת אֵין אֹנֵס כִּי־כֵן | יִסַּד הַמֶּלֶךְ עַל כָּל־רַב בֵּיתוֹ לַעֲשׂוֹת כִּרְצוֹן אִישׁ־וָאִישׁ: 9 גַּם וַשְׁתִּי הַמַּלְכָּה עָשְׂתָה מִשְׁתֵּה נָשִׁים בֵּית הַמַּלְכוּת אֲשֶׁר לַמֶּלֶךְ אֲחַשְׁוֵרוֹשׁ: ס 10 בַּיּוֹם הַשְּׁבִיעִי כְּטוֹב לֵב־הַמֶּלֶךְ בַּיָּיִן אָמַר לִמְהוּמָן בִּזְּתָא חַרְבוֹנָא בִּגְתָא וַאֲבַגְתָא זֵתַר וְכַרְכַּס שִׁבְעַת הַסָּרִיסִים

---

a I.e., the fortified city.
b Meaning of part of this verse uncertain.

King Ahasuerus, [11]to bring Queen Vashti before the king wearing a royal diadem, to display her beauty to the peoples and the officials; for she was a beautiful woman. [12]But Queen Vashti refused to come at the king's command conveyed by the eunuchs. The king was greatly incensed, and his fury burned within him.

[13]Then the king consulted the sages learned in procedure.[c] (For it was the royal practice [to turn] to all who were versed in law and precedent. [14]His closest advisers were Carshena, Shethar, Admatha, Tarshish, Meres, Marsena, and Memucan, the seven ministers of Persia and Media who had access to the royal presence and occupied the first place in the kingdom.) [15]"What," [he asked,] "shall be done, according to law, to Queen Vashti for failing to obey the command of King Ahasuerus conveyed by the eunuchs?"

[16]Thereupon Memucan declared in the presence of the king and the ministers: "Queen Vashti has committed an offense not only against Your Majesty but also against all the officials and against all the peoples in all the provinces of King Ahasuerus. [17]For the queen's behavior will make all wives despise their husbands, as they reflect that King Ahasuerus himself ordered Queen Vashti to be brought before him, but she would not come. [18]This very day the ladies of Persia and Media, who have heard of the queen's behavior, will cite it to all Your Majesty's officials, and there will be no end of scorn and provocation!

[19]"If it please Your Majesty, let a royal edict be issued by you, and let it be written into the laws of Persia and Media, so that it cannot be abrogated, that Vashti shall never enter the presence of King Ahasuerus. And let Your Majesty bestow her royal state upon another who is more worthy than she. [20]Then will the judg-

---

c   Lit. "the times."

הַמְשָׁרְתִ֔ים אֶת־פְּנֵ֖י הַמֶּ֥לֶךְ אֲחַשְׁוֵרֽוֹשׁ׃

[11] לְ֠הָבִיא אֶת־וַשְׁתִּ֧י הַמַּלְכָּ֛ה לִפְנֵ֥י הַמֶּ֖לֶךְ בְּכֶ֣תֶר מַלְכ֑וּת לְהַרְא֨וֹת הָֽעַמִּ֤ים וְהַשָּׂרִים֙ אֶת־יָפְיָ֔הּ כִּֽי־טוֹבַ֥ת מַרְאֶ֖ה הִֽיא׃

[12] וַתְּמָאֵ֞ן הַמַּלְכָּ֣ה וַשְׁתִּ֗י לָבוֹא֙ בִּדְבַ֣ר הַמֶּ֔לֶךְ אֲשֶׁ֖ר בְּיַ֣ד הַסָּרִיסִ֑ים וַיִּקְצֹ֤ף הַמֶּ֨לֶךְ֙ מְאֹ֔ד וַחֲמָת֖וֹ בָּעֲרָ֥ה בֽוֹ׃

[13] וַיֹּ֣אמֶר הַמֶּ֔לֶךְ לַחֲכָמִ֖ים יֹדְעֵ֣י הָֽעִתִּ֑ים כִּי־כֵן֙ דְּבַ֣ר הַמֶּ֔לֶךְ לִפְנֵ֕י כָּל־יֹדְעֵ֖י דָּ֥ת וָדִֽין׃

[14] וְהַקָּרֹ֣ב אֵלָ֗יו כַּרְשְׁנָ֤א שֵׁתָר֙ אַדְמָ֣תָא תַרְשִׁ֔ישׁ מֶ֥רֶס מַרְסְנָ֖א מְמוּכָ֑ן שִׁבְעַ֞ת שָׂרֵ֣י ׀ פָּרַ֣ס וּמָדַ֗י רֹאֵי֙ פְּנֵ֣י הַמֶּ֔לֶךְ הַיֹּשְׁבִ֥ים רִאשֹׁנָ֖ה בַּמַּלְכֽוּת׃

[15] כְּדָת֙ מַֽה־לַּעֲשׂ֔וֹת בַּמַּלְכָּ֖ה וַשְׁתִּ֑י עַ֣ל ׀ אֲשֶׁ֣ר לֹֽא־עָשְׂתָ֗ה אֶֽת־מַאֲמַר֙ הַמֶּ֣לֶךְ אֲחַשְׁוֵר֔וֹשׁ בְּיַ֖ד הַסָּרִיסִֽים׃ ס

[16] וַיֹּ֣אמֶר מומכן מְמוּכָ֗ן לִפְנֵ֤י הַמֶּ֨לֶךְ֙ וְהַשָּׂרִ֔ים לֹ֤א עַל־הַמֶּ֨לֶךְ֙ לְבַדּ֔וֹ עָוְתָ֖ה וַשְׁתִּ֣י הַמַּלְכָּ֑ה כִּ֤י עַל־כָּל־הַשָּׂרִים֙ וְעַל־כָּל־הָ֣עַמִּ֔ים אֲשֶׁ֕ר בְּכָל־מְדִינ֖וֹת הַמֶּ֥לֶךְ אֲחַשְׁוֵרֽוֹשׁ׃

[17] כִּֽי־יֵצֵ֤א דְבַר־הַמַּלְכָּה֙ עַל־כָּל־הַנָּשִׁ֔ים לְהַבְז֥וֹת בַּעְלֵיהֶ֖ן בְּעֵינֵיהֶ֑ן בְּאָמְרָ֗ם הַמֶּ֣לֶךְ אֲחַשְׁוֵר֡וֹשׁ אָמַ֞ר לְהָבִ֨יא אֶת־וַשְׁתִּ֧י הַמַּלְכָּ֛ה לְפָנָ֖יו וְלֹא־בָֽאָה׃

[18] וְֽהַיּ֨וֹם הַזֶּ֜ה תֹּאמַ֣רְנָה ׀ שָׂר֣וֹת פָּֽרַס־וּמָדַ֗י אֲשֶׁ֤ר שָֽׁמְעוּ֙ אֶת־דְּבַ֣ר הַמַּלְכָּ֔ה לְכֹ֖ל שָׂרֵ֣י הַמֶּ֑לֶךְ וּכְדַ֖י בִּזָּי֥וֹן וָקָֽצֶף׃

[19] אִם־עַל־הַמֶּ֣לֶךְ ט֗וֹב יֵצֵ֤א דְבַר־מַלְכוּת֙ מִלְּפָנָ֔יו וְיִכָּתֵ֛ב בְּדָתֵ֥י פָֽרַס־וּמָדַ֖י וְלֹ֣א יַעֲב֑וֹר אֲשֶׁ֨ר לֹֽא־תָב֜וֹא וַשְׁתִּ֗י לִפְנֵי֙ הַמֶּ֣לֶךְ אֲחַשְׁוֵר֔וֹשׁ וּמַלְכוּתָהּ֙ יִתֵּ֣ן הַמֶּ֔לֶךְ לִרְעוּתָ֖הּ

ment executed by Your Majesty resound throughout your realm, vast though it is; and all wives will treat their husbands with respect, high and low alike."

21The proposal was approved by the king and the ministers, and the king did as Memucan proposed. 22Dispatches were sent to all the provinces of the king, to every province in its own script and to every nation in its own language, that every man should wield authority in his home and speak the language of his own people.

2 Some time afterward, when the anger of King Ahasuerus subsided, he thought of Vashti and what she had done and what had been decreed against her. 2The king's servants who attended him said, "Let beautiful young virgins be sought out for Your Majesty. 3Let Your Majesty appoint officers in every province of your realm to assemble all the beautiful young virgins at the fortress Shushan, in the harem under the supervision of Hege, the king's eunuch, guardian of the women. Let them be provided with their cosmetics. 4And let the maiden who pleases Your Majesty be queen instead of Vashti." The proposal pleased the king, and he acted upon it.

5In the fortress Shushan lived a Jew by the name of Mordecai, son of Jair son of Shimei son of Kish, a Benjaminite. 6[Kish] had been exiled from Jerusalem in the group that was carried into exile along with King Jeconiah of Judah, which had been driven into exile by King Nebuchadnezzar of Babylon.—7He was foster father to Hadassah—that is, Esther—his uncle's daughter, for she had neither father nor mother. The maiden was shapely and beautiful; and when her father and mother died, Mordecai adopted her as his own daughter.

הַטּוֹבָה מִמֶּנָּה: 20 וְנִשְׁמַע פִּתְגָם הַמֶּלֶךְ אֲשֶׁר־יַעֲשֶׂה בְּכָל־מַלְכוּתוֹ כִּי רַבָּה הִיא וְכָל־הַנָּשִׁים יִתְּנוּ יְקָר לְבַעְלֵיהֶן לְמִגָּדוֹל וְעַד־קָטָן:

21 וַיִּיטַב הַדָּבָר בְּעֵינֵי הַמֶּלֶךְ וְהַשָּׂרִים וַיַּעַשׂ הַמֶּלֶךְ כִּדְבַר מְמוּכָן: 22 וַיִּשְׁלַח סְפָרִים אֶל־כָּל־מְדִינוֹת הַמֶּלֶךְ אֶל־מְדִינָה וּמְדִינָה כִּכְתָבָהּ וְאֶל־עַם וָעָם כִּלְשׁוֹנוֹ לִהְיוֹת כָּל־אִישׁ שֹׂרֵר בְּבֵיתוֹ וּמְדַבֵּר כִּלְשׁוֹן עַמּוֹ: פ

ב אַחַר הַדְּבָרִים הָאֵלֶּה כְּשֹׁךְ חֲמַת הַמֶּלֶךְ אֲחַשְׁוֵרוֹשׁ זָכַר אֶת־וַשְׁתִּי וְאֵת אֲשֶׁר־עָשָׂתָה וְאֵת אֲשֶׁר־נִגְזַר עָלֶיהָ: 2 וַיֹּאמְרוּ נַעֲרֵי־הַמֶּלֶךְ מְשָׁרְתָיו יְבַקְשׁוּ לַמֶּלֶךְ נְעָרוֹת בְּתוּלוֹת טוֹבוֹת מַרְאֶה: 3 וְיַפְקֵד הַמֶּלֶךְ פְּקִידִים בְּכָל־מְדִינוֹת מַלְכוּתוֹ וְיִקְבְּצוּ אֶת־כָּל־נַעֲרָה־בְתוּלָה טוֹבַת מַרְאֶה אֶל־שׁוּשַׁן הַבִּירָה אֶל־בֵּית הַנָּשִׁים אֶל־יַד הֵגֶא סְרִיס הַמֶּלֶךְ שֹׁמֵר הַנָּשִׁים וְנָתוֹן תַּמְרוּקֵיהֶן: 4 וְהַנַּעֲרָה אֲשֶׁר תִּיטַב בְּעֵינֵי הַמֶּלֶךְ תִּמְלֹךְ תַּחַת וַשְׁתִּי וַיִּיטַב הַדָּבָר בְּעֵינֵי הַמֶּלֶךְ וַיַּעַשׂ כֵּן: ס

5 אִישׁ יְהוּדִי הָיָה בְּשׁוּשַׁן הַבִּירָה וּשְׁמוֹ מָרְדֳּכַי בֶּן יָאִיר בֶּן־שִׁמְעִי בֶּן־קִישׁ אִישׁ יְמִינִי: 6 אֲשֶׁר הָגְלָה מִירוּשָׁלַיִם עִם־הַגֹּלָה אֲשֶׁר הָגְלְתָה עִם יְכָנְיָה מֶלֶךְ־יְהוּדָה אֲשֶׁר הֶגְלָה נְבוּכַדְנֶאצַּר מֶלֶךְ בָּבֶל: 7 וַיְהִי אֹמֵן אֶת־הֲדַסָּה הִיא אֶסְתֵּר בַּת־דֹּדוֹ כִּי אֵין לָהּ אָב וָאֵם וְהַנַּעֲרָה יְפַת־תֹּאַר וְטוֹבַת מַרְאֶה וּבְמוֹת אָבִיהָ וְאִמָּהּ לְקָחָהּ מָרְדֳּכַי לוֹ לְבַת:

8When the king's order and edict was proclaimed, and when many girls were assembled in the fortress Shushan under the supervision of Hegai,ᵃ Esther too was taken into the king's palace under the supervision of Hegai, guardian of the women. 9The girl pleased him and won his favor, and he hastened to furnish her with her cosmetics and her rations, as well as with the seven maids who were her due from the king's palace; and he treated her and her maids with special kindness in the harem. 10Esther did not reveal her people or her kindred, for Mordecai had told her not to reveal it. 11Every single day Mordecai would walk about in front of the court of the harem, to learn how Esther was faring and what was happening to her.

12When each girl's turn came to go to King Ahasuerus at the end of the twelve months' treatment prescribed for women (for that was the period spent on beautifying them: six months with oil of myrrh and six months with perfumes and women's cosmetics, 13and it was after that that the girl would go to the king), whatever she asked for would be given her to take with her from the harem to the king's palace. 14She would go in the evening and leave in the morning for a second harem in charge of Shaashgaz, the king's eunuch, guardian of the concubines. She would not go again to the king unless the king wanted her, when she would be summoned by name. 15When the turn came for Esther daughter of Abihail—the uncle of Mordecai, who had adopted her as his own daughter—to go to the king, she did not ask for anything but what Hegai, the king's eunuch, guardian of the women, advised. Yet Esther won the admiration of all who saw her.

16Esther was taken to King Ahasuerus, in his royal palace, in the tenth month, which is the month of Tebeth, in the seventh year of his

ᵃ *Identical with Hege in v. 3.*

8 וַיְהִ֞י בְּהִשָּׁמַ֤ע דְּבַר־הַמֶּ֙לֶךְ֙ וְדָת֔וֹ וּֽבְהִקָּבֵ֞ץ נְעָר֥וֹת רַבּ֛וֹת אֶל־שׁוּשַׁ֥ן הַבִּירָ֖ה אֶל־יַ֣ד הֵגָ֑י וַתִּלָּקַ֤ח אֶסְתֵּר֙ אֶל־בֵּ֣ית הַמֶּ֔לֶךְ אֶל־יַ֥ד הֵגַ֖י שֹׁמֵ֥ר הַנָּשִֽׁים: 9 וַתִּיטַ֨ב הַנַּעֲרָ֣ה בְעֵינָיו֮ וַתִּשָּׂ֣א חֶ֣סֶד לְפָנָיו֒ וַ֠יְבַהֵ֤ל אֶת־תַּמְרוּקֶ֙יהָ֙ וְאֶת־מָ֣נוֹתֶ֔הָ לָתֵ֣ת לָ֔הּ וְאֵת֙ שֶׁ֣בַע הַנְּעָר֔וֹת הָרְאֻי֥וֹת לָֽתֶת־לָ֖הּ מִבֵּ֣ית הַמֶּ֑לֶךְ וַיְשַׁנֶּ֧הָ וְאֶת־נַעֲרוֹתֶ֛יהָ לְט֖וֹב בֵּ֥ית הַנָּשִֽׁים: 10 לֹא־הִגִּ֣ידָה אֶסְתֵּ֔ר אֶת־עַמָּ֖הּ וְאֶת־מֽוֹלַדְתָּ֑הּ כִּ֧י מָרְדֳּכַ֛י צִוָּ֥ה עָלֶ֖יהָ אֲשֶׁ֥ר לֹֽא־תַגִּֽיד: 11 וּבְכָל־י֣וֹם וָי֔וֹם מָרְדֳּכַי֙ מִתְהַלֵּ֔ךְ לִפְנֵ֖י חֲצַ֣ר בֵּית־הַנָּשִׁ֑ים לָדַ֙עַת֙ אֶת־שְׁל֣וֹם אֶסְתֵּ֔ר וּמַה־יֵּעָשֶׂ֖ה בָּֽהּ: 12 וּבְהַגִּ֡יעַ תֹּר֩ נַעֲרָ֨ה וְנַעֲרָ֜ה לָב֣וֹא ׀ אֶל־הַמֶּ֣לֶךְ אֲחַשְׁוֵר֗וֹשׁ מִקֵּץ֩ הֱי֨וֹת לָ֜הּ כְּדָ֤ת הַנָּשִׁים֙ שְׁנֵ֣ים עָשָׂ֣ר חֹ֔דֶשׁ כִּ֛י כֵּ֥ן יִמְלְא֖וּ יְמֵ֣י מְרוּקֵיהֶ֑ן שִׁשָּׁ֤ה חֳדָשִׁים֙ בְּשֶׁ֣מֶן הַמֹּ֔ר וְשִׁשָּׁ֤ה חֳדָשִׁים֙ בַּבְּשָׂמִ֔ים וּבְתַמְרוּקֵ֖י הַנָּשִֽׁים: 13 וּבָזֶ֕ה הַֽנַּעֲרָ֖ה בָּאָ֣ה אֶל־הַמֶּ֑לֶךְ אֵת֩ כָּל־אֲשֶׁ֨ר תֹּאמַ֜ר יִנָּ֤תֵֽן לָהּ֙ לָב֣וֹא עִמָּ֔הּ מִבֵּ֥ית הַנָּשִׁ֖ים עַד־בֵּ֥ית הַמֶּֽלֶךְ: 14 בָּעֶ֣רֶב ׀ הִ֣יא בָאָ֗ה וּ֠בַבֹּקֶר הִ֣יא שָׁבָ֞ה אֶל־בֵּ֤ית הַנָּשִׁים֙ שֵׁנִ֔י אֶל־יַ֧ד שַֽׁעֲשְׁגַ֛ז סְרִ֥יס הַמֶּ֖לֶךְ שֹׁמֵ֣ר הַפִּֽילַגְשִׁ֑ים לֹא־תָב֤וֹא עוֹד֙ אֶל־הַמֶּ֔לֶךְ כִּ֣י אִם־חָפֵ֥ץ בָּ֛הּ הַמֶּ֖לֶךְ וְנִקְרְאָ֥ה בְשֵֽׁם: 15 וּבְהַגִּ֣יעַ תֹּר־אֶסְתֵּ֣ר בַּת־אֲבִיחַ֣יִל דֹּ֣ד מָרְדֳּכַ֡י אֲשֶׁר֩ לָֽקַֽח־ל֨וֹ לְבַ֜ת לָב֣וֹא אֶל־הַמֶּ֗לֶךְ לֹ֤א בִקְשָׁה֙ דָּבָ֔ר כִּ֠י אִ֣ם אֶת־אֲשֶׁ֥ר יֹאמַ֛ר הֵגַ֥י סְרִיס־הַמֶּ֖לֶךְ שֹׁמֵ֣ר הַנָּשִׁ֑ים וַתְּהִ֤י אֶסְתֵּר֙ נֹשֵׂ֣את חֵ֔ן בְּעֵינֵ֖י כָּל־רֹאֶֽיהָ: 16 וַתִּלָּקַ֨ח אֶסְתֵּ֜ר אֶל־הַמֶּ֤לֶךְ אֲחַשְׁוֵרוֹשׁ֙ אֶל־בֵּ֣ית מַלְכוּת֔וֹ בַּחֹ֥דֶשׁ הָעֲשִׂירִ֖י הוּא־חֹ֣דֶשׁ טֵבֵ֑ת בִּשְׁנַת־שֶׁ֖בַע לְמַלְכוּתֽוֹ:

reign. [17]The king loved Esther more than all the other women, and she won his grace and favor more than all the virgins. So he set a royal diadem on her head and made her queen instead of Vashti. [18]The king gave a great banquet for all his officials and courtiers, "the banquet of Esther." He proclaimed a remission of taxes[b] for the provinces and distributed gifts as befits a king.

[19][c]When the virgins were assembled a second time, Mordecai sat in the palace gate. [20]But Esther still did not reveal her kindred or her people, as Mordecai had instructed her; for Esther obeyed Mordecai's bidding, as she had done when she was under his tutelage.

[21]At that time, when Mordecai was sitting in the palace gate, Bigthan and Teresh, two of the king's eunuchs who guarded the threshold, became angry, and plotted to do away with King Ahasuerus. [22]Mordecai learned of it and told it to Queen Esther, and Esther reported it to the king in Mordecai's name. [23]The matter was investigated and found to be so, and the two were impaled on stakes. This was recorded in the book of annals at the instance of the king.

3 Some time afterward, King Ahasuerus promoted Haman son of Hammedatha the Agagite; he advanced him and seated him higher than any of his fellow officials. [2]All the king's courtiers in the palace gate knelt and bowed low to Haman, for such was the king's order concerning him; but Mordecai would not kneel or bow low. [3]Then the king's courtiers who were in the palace gate said to Mordecai, "Why do you disobey the king's order?" [4]When they spoke to him day after day and he would not listen to them, they told Haman, in order to see whether Mordecai's resolve would prevail; for he had ex-

---

17 וַיֶּאֱהַ֨ב הַמֶּ֤לֶךְ אֶת־אֶסְתֵּר֙ מִכָּל־הַנָּשִׁ֔ים וַתִּשָּׂא־חֵ֥ן וָחֶ֛סֶד לְפָנָ֖יו מִכָּל־הַבְּתוּלֹ֑ת וַיָּ֤שֶׂם כֶּֽתֶר־מַלְכוּת֙ בְּרֹאשָׁ֔הּ וַיַּמְלִיכֶ֖הָ תַּ֥חַת וַשְׁתִּֽי׃ 18 וַיַּ֨עַשׂ הַמֶּ֜לֶךְ מִשְׁתֶּ֣ה גָד֗וֹל לְכָל־שָׂרָיו֙ וַעֲבָדָ֔יו אֵ֖ת מִשְׁתֵּ֣ה אֶסְתֵּ֑ר וַהֲנָחָ֤ה לַמְּדִינוֹת֙ עָשָׂ֔ה וַיִּתֵּ֥ן מַשְׂאֵ֖ת כְּיַ֥ד הַמֶּֽלֶךְ׃ 19 וּבְהִקָּבֵ֥ץ בְּתוּל֖וֹת שֵׁנִ֑ית וּמָרְדֳּכַ֖י יֹשֵׁ֥ב בְּשַֽׁעַר־הַמֶּֽלֶךְ׃ 20 אֵ֣ין אֶסְתֵּ֗ר מַגֶּ֤דֶת מֽוֹלַדְתָּהּ֙ וְאֶת־עַמָּ֔הּ כַּאֲשֶׁ֛ר צִוָּ֥ה עָלֶ֖יהָ מָרְדֳּכָ֑י וְאֶת־מַאֲמַ֤ר מָרְדֳּכַי֙ אֶסְתֵּ֣ר עֹשָׂ֔ה כַּאֲשֶׁ֛ר הָיְתָ֥ה בְאָמְנָ֖ה אִתּֽוֹ׃ ס 21 בַּיָּמִ֣ים הָהֵ֔ם וּמָרְדֳּכַ֖י יֹשֵׁ֣ב בְּשַֽׁעַר־הַמֶּ֑לֶךְ קָצַ֨ף בִּגְתָ֜ן וָתֶ֗רֶשׁ שְׁנֵֽי־סָרִיסֵ֤י הַמֶּ֙לֶךְ֙ מִשֹּׁמְרֵ֣י הַסַּ֔ף וַיְבַקְשׁוּ֙ לִשְׁלֹ֣חַ יָ֔ד בַּמֶּ֖לֶךְ אֲחַשְׁוֵֽרֹשׁ׃ 22 וַיִּוָּדַ֤ע הַדָּבָר֙ לְמָרְדֳּכַ֔י וַיַּגֵּ֖ד לְאֶסְתֵּ֣ר הַמַּלְכָּ֑ה וַתֹּ֧אמֶר אֶסְתֵּ֛ר לַמֶּ֖לֶךְ בְּשֵׁ֥ם מָרְדֳּכָֽי׃ 23 וַיְבֻקַּ֤שׁ הַדָּבָר֙ וַיִּמָּצֵ֔א וַיִּתָּל֥וּ שְׁנֵיהֶ֖ם עַל־עֵ֑ץ וַיִּכָּתֵ֗ב בְּסֵ֛פֶר דִּבְרֵ֥י הַיָּמִ֖ים לִפְנֵ֥י הַמֶּֽלֶךְ׃ פ

ג אַחַ֣ר ׀ הַדְּבָרִ֣ים הָאֵ֗לֶּה גִּדַּל֩ הַמֶּ֨לֶךְ אֲחַשְׁוֵר֜וֹשׁ אֶת־הָמָ֧ן בֶּֽן־הַמְּדָ֛תָא הָאֲגָגִ֖י וַֽיְנַשְּׂאֵ֑הוּ וַיָּ֙שֶׂם֙ אֶת־כִּסְא֔וֹ מֵעַ֕ל כָּל־הַשָּׂרִ֖ים אֲשֶׁ֥ר אִתּֽוֹ׃ 2 וְכָל־עַבְדֵ֨י הַמֶּ֜לֶךְ אֲשֶׁר־בְּשַׁ֣עַר הַמֶּ֗לֶךְ כֹּרְעִ֤ים וּמִֽשְׁתַּחֲוִים֙ לְהָמָ֔ן כִּי־כֵ֖ן צִוָּה־ל֣וֹ הַמֶּ֑לֶךְ וּמָ֨רְדֳּכַ֔י לֹ֥א יִכְרַ֖ע וְלֹ֥א יִֽשְׁתַּחֲוֶֽה׃ 3 וַיֹּ֨אמְר֜וּ עַבְדֵ֥י הַמֶּ֛לֶךְ אֲשֶׁר־בְּשַׁ֥עַר הַמֶּ֖לֶךְ לְמָרְדֳּכָ֑י מַדּ֙וּעַ֙ אַתָּ֣ה עוֹבֵ֔ר אֵ֖ת מִצְוַ֥ת הַמֶּֽלֶךְ׃ 4 וַיְהִ֗י באמרם [כְּאָמְרָ֤ם] אֵלָיו֙ י֣וֹם וָי֔וֹם וְלֹ֥א שָׁמַ֖ע אֲלֵיהֶ֑ם וַיַּגִּ֣ידוּ לְהָמָ֗ן לִרְאוֹת֙ הֲיַֽעַמְדוּ֙

---

b   Or "an amnesty."
c   Meaning of verse uncertain.

plained to them that he was a Jew.^a ⁵When Haman saw that Mordecai would not kneel or bow
low to him, Haman was filled with rage. ⁶But
he disdained to lay hands on Mordecai alone;
having been told who Mordecai's people were,
Haman plotted to do away with all the Jews,
Mordecai's people, throughout the kingdom of
Ahasuerus.

⁷In the first month, that is, the month of
Nisan, in the twelfth year of King Ahasuerus,
pur—which means "the lot"—was cast before
Haman concerning every day and every month,
[until it fell on] the twelfth month, that is, the
month of Adar. ⁸Haman then said to King Ahasuerus, "There is a certain people, scattered and
dispersed among the other peoples in all the
provinces of your realm, whose laws are different from those of any other people and who
do not obey the king's laws; and it is not in
Your Majesty's interest to tolerate them. ⁹If it
please Your Majesty, let an edict be drawn for
their destruction, and I will pay ten thousand
talents of silver to the stewards for deposit in
the royal treasury." ¹⁰Thereupon the king removed his signet ring from his hand and gave
it to Haman son of Hammedatha the Agagite,
the foe of the Jews. ¹¹And the king said, "The
money and the people are yours to do with as
you see fit."

¹²On the thirteenth day of the first month,
the king's scribes were summoned and a decree
was issued, as Haman directed, to the king's satraps, to the governors of every province, and
to the officials of every people, to every province
in its own script and to every people in its own
language. The orders were issued in the name
of King Ahasuerus and sealed with the king's
signet. ¹³Accordingly, written instructions were
dispatched by couriers to all the king's provinces to destroy, massacre, and exterminate all

---

*a   I.e., that as a Jew he could not bow to a descendant of Agag,
the Amalekite king; see 1 Sam. 15, and cf. Exod. 17.14–16; Deut.
25.17–19.*

דִּבְרֵי מָרְדֳּכַי כִּי־הִגִּיד לָהֶם אֲשֶׁר־הוּא
יְהוּדִי: 5 וַיַּרְא הָמָן כִּי־אֵין מָרְדֳּכַי כֹּרֵעַ
וּמִשְׁתַּחֲוֶה לוֹ וַיִּמָּלֵא הָמָן חֵמָה: 6 וַיִּבֶז
בְּעֵינָיו לִשְׁלֹחַ יָד בְּמָרְדֳּכַי לְבַדּוֹ כִּי־הִגִּידוּ
לוֹ אֶת־עַם מָרְדֳּכָי וַיְבַקֵּשׁ הָמָן לְהַשְׁמִיד
אֶת־כָּל־הַיְּהוּדִים אֲשֶׁר בְּכָל־מַלְכוּת
אֲחַשְׁוֵרוֹשׁ עַם מָרְדֳּכָי:

7 בַּחֹדֶשׁ הָרִאשׁוֹן הוּא־חֹדֶשׁ נִיסָן בִּשְׁנַת
שְׁתֵּים עֶשְׂרֵה לַמֶּלֶךְ אֲחַשְׁוֵרוֹשׁ הִפִּיל
פּוּר הוּא הַגּוֹרָל לִפְנֵי הָמָן מִיּוֹם ׀ לְיוֹם
וּמֵחֹדֶשׁ לְחֹדֶשׁ שְׁנֵים־עָשָׂר הוּא־חֹדֶשׁ
אֲדָר: ס 8 וַיֹּאמֶר הָמָן לַמֶּלֶךְ אֲחַשְׁוֵרוֹשׁ
יֶשְׁנוֹ עַם־אֶחָד מְפֻזָּר וּמְפֹרָד בֵּין הָעַמִּים
בְּכֹל מְדִינוֹת מַלְכוּתֶךָ וְדָתֵיהֶם שֹׁנוֹת
מִכָּל־עָם וְאֶת־דָּתֵי הַמֶּלֶךְ אֵינָם עֹשִׂים
וְלַמֶּלֶךְ אֵין־שֹׁוֶה לְהַנִּיחָם: 9 אִם־עַל־
הַמֶּלֶךְ טוֹב יִכָּתֵב לְאַבְּדָם וַעֲשֶׂרֶת אֲלָפִים
כִּכַּר־כֶּסֶף אֶשְׁקוֹל עַל־יְדֵי עֹשֵׂי הַמְּלָאכָה
לְהָבִיא אֶל־גִּנְזֵי הַמֶּלֶךְ: 10 וַיָּסַר הַמֶּלֶךְ
אֶת־טַבַּעְתּוֹ מֵעַל יָדוֹ וַיִּתְּנָהּ לְהָמָן בֶּן־
הַמְּדָתָא הָאֲגָגִי צֹרֵר הַיְּהוּדִים: 11 וַיֹּאמֶר
הַמֶּלֶךְ לְהָמָן הַכֶּסֶף נָתוּן לָךְ וְהָעָם
לַעֲשׂוֹת בּוֹ כַּטּוֹב בְּעֵינֶיךָ:

12 וַיִּקָּרְאוּ סֹפְרֵי הַמֶּלֶךְ בַּחֹדֶשׁ הָרִאשׁוֹן
בִּשְׁלוֹשָׁה עָשָׂר יוֹם בּוֹ וַיִּכָּתֵב כְּכָל־אֲשֶׁר־
צִוָּה הָמָן אֶל אֲחַשְׁדַּרְפְּנֵי־הַמֶּלֶךְ וְאֶל־
הַפַּחוֹת אֲשֶׁר ׀ עַל־מְדִינָה וּמְדִינָה וְאֶל־
שָׂרֵי עַם וָעָם מְדִינָה וּמְדִינָה כִּכְתָבָהּ
וְעַם וָעָם כִּלְשׁוֹנוֹ בְּשֵׁם הַמֶּלֶךְ אֲחַשְׁוֵרֹשׁ
נִכְתָּב וְנֶחְתָּם בְּטַבַּעַת הַמֶּלֶךְ: 13 וְנִשְׁלוֹחַ
סְפָרִים בְּיַד הָרָצִים אֶל־כָּל־מְדִינוֹת
הַמֶּלֶךְ לְהַשְׁמִיד לַהֲרֹג וּלְאַבֵּד אֶת־כָּל־

the Jews, young and old, children and women, on a single day, on the thirteenth day of the twelfth month—that is, the month of Adar—and to plunder their possessions. 14The text of the document was to the effect that a law should be proclaimed in every single province; it was to be publicly displayed to all the peoples, so that they might be ready for that day.

15The couriers went out posthaste on the royal mission, and the decree was proclaimed in the fortress Shushan. The king and Haman sat down to feast, but the city of Shushan was dumfounded.

4 When Mordecai learned all that had happened, Mordecai tore his clothes and put on sackcloth and ashes. He went through the city, crying out loudly and bitterly, 2until he came in front of the palace gate; for one could not enter the palace gate wearing sackcloth.—3Also, in every province that the king's command and decree reached, there was great mourning among the Jews, with fasting, weeping, and wailing, and everybody lay in sackcloth and ashes.—4When Esther's maidens and eunuchs came and informed her, the queen was greatly agitated. She sent clothing for Mordecai to wear, so that he might take off his sackcloth; but he refused. 5Thereupon Esther summoned Hathach, one of the eunuchs whom the king had appointed to serve her, and sent him to Mordecai to learn the why and wherefore of it all. 6Hathach went out to Mordecai in the city square in front of the palace gate; 7and Mordecai told him all that had happened to him, and all about the money that Haman had offered to pay into the royal treasury for the destruction of the Jews. 8He also gave him the written text of the law that had been proclaimed in Shushan for their destruction. [He bade him] show it to Es-

הַיְּהוּדִים מִנַּעַר וְעַד־זָקֵן טַף וְנָשִׁים בְּיוֹם
אֶחָד בִּשְׁלוֹשָׁה עָשָׂר לְחֹדֶשׁ שְׁנֵים־עָשָׂר
הוּא־חֹדֶשׁ אֲדָר וּשְׁלָלָם לָבוֹז: 14 פַּתְשֶׁגֶן
הַכְּתָב לְהִנָּתֵן דָּת בְּכָל־מְדִינָה וּמְדִינָה
גָּלוּי לְכָל־הָעַמִּים לִהְיוֹת עֲתִדִים לַיּוֹם
הַזֶּה:
15 הָרָצִים יָצְאוּ דְחוּפִים בִּדְבַר הַמֶּלֶךְ
וְהַדָּת נִתְּנָה בְּשׁוּשַׁן הַבִּירָה וְהַמֶּלֶךְ וְהָמָן
יָשְׁבוּ לִשְׁתּוֹת וְהָעִיר שׁוּשָׁן נָבוֹכָה: פ

ד וּמָרְדֳּכַי יָדַע אֶת־כָּל־אֲשֶׁר נַעֲשָׂה
וַיִּקְרַע מָרְדֳּכַי אֶת־בְּגָדָיו וַיִּלְבַּשׁ שַׂק וָאֵפֶר
וַיֵּצֵא בְּתוֹךְ הָעִיר וַיִּזְעַק זְעָקָה גְדֹלָה
וּמָרָה: 2 וַיָּבוֹא עַד לִפְנֵי שַׁעַר־הַמֶּלֶךְ כִּי
אֵין לָבוֹא אֶל־שַׁעַר הַמֶּלֶךְ בִּלְבוּשׁ שָׂק:
3 וּבְכָל־מְדִינָה וּמְדִינָה מְקוֹם אֲשֶׁר דְּבַר־
הַמֶּלֶךְ וְדָתוֹ מַגִּיעַ אֵבֶל גָּדוֹל לַיְּהוּדִים
וְצוֹם וּבְכִי וּמִסְפֵּד שַׂק וָאֵפֶר יֻצַּע לָרַבִּים:
4 וַתְּבוֹאֶינָה נַעֲרוֹת אֶסְתֵּר
וְסָרִיסֶיהָ וַיַּגִּידוּ לָהּ וַתִּתְחַלְחַל הַמַּלְכָּה
מְאֹד וַתִּשְׁלַח בְּגָדִים לְהַלְבִּישׁ אֶת־מָרְדֳּכַי
וּלְהָסִיר שַׂקּוֹ מֵעָלָיו וְלֹא קִבֵּל: 5 וַתִּקְרָא
אֶסְתֵּר לַהֲתָךְ מִסָּרִיסֵי הַמֶּלֶךְ אֲשֶׁר
הֶעֱמִיד לְפָנֶיהָ וַתְּצַוֵּהוּ עַל־מָרְדֳּכָי לָדַעַת
מַה־זֶּה וְעַל־מַה־זֶּה: 6 וַיֵּצֵא הֲתָךְ אֶל־
מָרְדֳּכָי אֶל־רְחוֹב הָעִיר אֲשֶׁר לִפְנֵי שַׁעַר־
הַמֶּלֶךְ: 7 וַיַּגֶּד־לוֹ מָרְדֳּכַי אֵת כָּל־אֲשֶׁר
קָרָהוּ וְאֵת פָּרָשַׁת הַכֶּסֶף אֲשֶׁר אָמַר
הָמָן לִשְׁקוֹל עַל־גִּנְזֵי הַמֶּלֶךְ בַּיְּהוּדִיים
בַּיְּהוּדִים לְאַבְּדָם: 8 וְאֶת־פַּתְשֶׁגֶן כְּתָב־
הַדָּת אֲשֶׁר־נִתַּן בְּשׁוּשָׁן לְהַשְׁמִידָם נָתַן
לוֹ לְהַרְאוֹת אֶת־אֶסְתֵּר וּלְהַגִּיד לָהּ

ther and inform her, and charge her to go to the king and to appeal to him and to plead with him for her people. [9]When Hathach came and delivered Mordecai's message to Esther, [10]Esther told Hathach to take back to Mordecai the following reply: [11]"All the king's courtiers and the people of the king's provinces know that if any person, man or woman, enters the king's presence in the inner court without having been summoned, there is but one law for him—that he be put to death. Only if the king extends the golden scepter to him may he live. Now I have not been summoned to visit the king for the last thirty days."

[12]When Mordecai was told what Esther had said, [13]Mordecai had this message delivered to Esther: "Do not imagine that you, of all the Jews, will escape with your life by being in the king's palace. [14]On the contrary, if you keep silent in this crisis, relief and deliverance will come to the Jews from another quarter, while you and your father's house will perish. And who knows, perhaps you have attained to royal position for just such a crisis." [15]Then Esther sent back this answer to Mordecai: [16]"Go, assemble all the Jews who live in Shushan, and fast in my behalf; do not eat or drink for three days, night or day. I and my maidens will observe the same fast. Then I shall go to the king, though it is contrary to the law; and if I am to perish, I shall perish!" [17]So Mordecai went about [the city] and did just as Esther had commanded him.

5 On the third day, Esther put on royal apparel and stood in the inner court of the king's palace, facing the king's palace, while the king was sitting on his royal throne in the throne room facing the entrance of the palace. [2]As soon as the king saw Queen Esther standing in the court, she won his favor. The king extended to

וּלְצַוּוֹת עָלֶיהָ לָבוֹא אֶל־הַמֶּלֶךְ לְהִתְחַנֶּן־לוֹ וּלְבַקֵּשׁ מִלְּפָנָיו עַל־עַמָּהּ: [9] וַיָּבוֹא הֲתָךְ וַיַּגֵּד לְאֶסְתֵּר אֵת דִּבְרֵי מָרְדֳּכָי: [10] וַתֹּאמֶר אֶסְתֵּר לַהֲתָךְ וַתְּצַוֵּהוּ אֶל־מָרְדֳּכָי: [11] כָּל־עַבְדֵי הַמֶּלֶךְ וְעַם־מְדִינוֹת הַמֶּלֶךְ יֹדְעִים אֲשֶׁר כָּל־אִישׁ וְאִשָּׁה אֲשֶׁר יָבוֹא־אֶל־הַמֶּלֶךְ אֶל־הֶחָצֵר הַפְּנִימִית אֲשֶׁר לֹא־יִקָּרֵא אַחַת דָּתוֹ לְהָמִית לְבַד מֵאֲשֶׁר יוֹשִׁיט־לוֹ הַמֶּלֶךְ אֶת־שַׁרְבִיט הַזָּהָב וְחָיָה וַאֲנִי לֹא נִקְרֵאתִי לָבוֹא אֶל־הַמֶּלֶךְ זֶה שְׁלוֹשִׁים יוֹם: [12] וַיַּגִּידוּ לְמָרְדֳּכָי אֵת דִּבְרֵי אֶסְתֵּר: פ [13] וַיֹּאמֶר מָרְדֳּכַי לְהָשִׁיב אֶל־אֶסְתֵּר אַל־תְּדַמִּי בְנַפְשֵׁךְ לְהִמָּלֵט בֵּית־הַמֶּלֶךְ מִכָּל־הַיְּהוּדִים: [14] כִּי אִם־הַחֲרֵשׁ תַּחֲרִישִׁי בָּעֵת הַזֹּאת רֶוַח וְהַצָּלָה יַעֲמוֹד לַיְּהוּדִים מִמָּקוֹם אַחֵר וְאַתְּ וּבֵית־אָבִיךְ תֹּאבֵדוּ וּמִי יוֹדֵעַ אִם־לְעֵת כָּזֹאת הִגַּעַתְּ לַמַּלְכוּת: [15] וַתֹּאמֶר אֶסְתֵּר לְהָשִׁיב אֶל־מָרְדֳּכָי: [16] לֵךְ כְּנוֹס אֶת־כָּל־הַיְּהוּדִים הַנִּמְצְאִים בְּשׁוּשָׁן וְצוּמוּ עָלַי וְאַל־תֹּאכְלוּ וְאַל־תִּשְׁתּוּ שְׁלֹשֶׁת יָמִים לַיְלָה וָיוֹם גַּם־אֲנִי וְנַעֲרֹתַי אָצוּם כֵּן וּבְכֵן אָבוֹא אֶל־הַמֶּלֶךְ אֲשֶׁר לֹא־כַדָּת וְכַאֲשֶׁר אָבַדְתִּי אָבָדְתִּי: [17] וַיַּעֲבֹר מָרְדֳּכָי וַיַּעַשׂ כְּכֹל אֲשֶׁר־צִוְּתָה עָלָיו אֶסְתֵּר: ס

ה [1] וַיְהִי ׀ בַּיּוֹם הַשְּׁלִישִׁי וַתִּלְבַּשׁ אֶסְתֵּר מַלְכוּת וַתַּעֲמֹד בַּחֲצַר בֵּית־הַמֶּלֶךְ הַפְּנִימִית נֹכַח בֵּית הַמֶּלֶךְ וְהַמֶּלֶךְ יוֹשֵׁב עַל־כִּסֵּא מַלְכוּתוֹ בְּבֵית הַמַּלְכוּת נֹכַח פֶּתַח הַבָּיִת: [2] וַיְהִי כִרְאוֹת הַמֶּלֶךְ אֶת־אֶסְתֵּר הַמַּלְכָּה עֹמֶדֶת בֶּחָצֵר נָשְׂאָה חֵן

Esther the golden scepter which he had in his hand, and Esther approached and touched the tip of the scepter. [3]"What troubles you, Queen Esther?" the king asked her. "And what is your request? Even to half the kingdom, it shall be granted you." [4]"If it please Your Majesty," Esther replied, "let Your Majesty and Haman come today to the feast that I have prepared for him." [5]The king commanded, "Tell Haman to hurry and do Esther's bidding." So the king and Haman came to the feast that Esther had prepared.

[6]At the wine feast, the king asked Esther, "What is your wish? It shall be granted you. And what is your request? Even to half the kingdom, it shall be fulfilled." [7]"My wish," replied Esther, "my request—[8]if Your Majesty will do me the favor, if it please Your Majesty to grant my wish and accede to my request—let Your Majesty and Haman come to the feast which I will prepare for them; and tomorrow I will do Your Majesty's bidding."

[9]That day Haman went out happy and light-hearted. But when Haman saw Mordecai in the palace gate, and Mordecai did not rise or even stir on his account, Haman was filled with rage at him. [10]Nevertheless, Haman controlled himself and went home. He sent for his friends and his wife Zeresh, [11]and Haman told them about his great wealth and his many sons, and all about how the king had promoted him and advanced him above the officials and the king's courtiers. [12]"What is more," said Haman, "Queen Esther gave a feast, and besides the king she did not have anyone but me. And tomorrow too I am invited by her along with the king. [13]Yet all this means nothing to me every time I see that Jew Mordecai sitting in the palace gate." [14]Then his wife Zeresh and all his friends said to him, "Let a stake be put up, fifty cubits high, and in the morning ask the king to have Mordecai impaled

בְּעֵינָיו וַיּ֣וֹשֶׁט הַמֶּ֗לֶךְ לְאֶסְתֵּ֔ר אֵ֖ת שַׁרְבִ֣יט הַזָּהָ֑ב אֲשֶׁ֣ר בְּיָד֔וֹ וַתִּקְרַ֣ב אֶסְתֵּ֔ר וַתִּגַּ֖ע בְּרֹ֥אשׁ הַשַּׁרְבִֽיט׃ ס 3 וַיֹּ֤אמֶר לָהּ֙ הַמֶּ֔לֶךְ מַה־לָּ֖ךְ אֶסְתֵּ֣ר הַמַּלְכָּ֑ה וּמַה־בַּקָּשָׁתֵ֛ךְ עַד־חֲצִ֥י הַמַּלְכ֖וּת וְיִנָּ֥תֵֽן לָֽךְ׃ 4 וַתֹּ֣אמֶר אֶסְתֵּ֔ר אִם־עַל־הַמֶּ֖לֶךְ ט֑וֹב יָב֨וֹא הַמֶּ֤לֶךְ וְהָמָן֙ הַיּ֔וֹם אֶל־הַמִּשְׁתֶּ֖ה אֲשֶׁר־עָשִׂ֥יתִי לֽוֹ׃ 5 וַיֹּ֣אמֶר הַמֶּ֔לֶךְ מַהֲרוּ֙ אֶת־הָמָ֔ן לַעֲשׂ֖וֹת אֶת־דְּבַ֣ר אֶסְתֵּ֑ר וַיָּבֹ֤א הַמֶּ֙לֶךְ֙ וְהָמָ֔ן אֶל־הַמִּשְׁתֶּ֖ה אֲשֶׁר־עָשְׂתָ֥ה אֶסְתֵּֽר׃

6 וַיֹּ֨אמֶר הַמֶּ֤לֶךְ לְאֶסְתֵּר֙ בְּמִשְׁתֵּ֣ה הַיַּ֔יִן מַה־שְּׁאֵלָתֵ֖ךְ וְיִנָּ֣תֵֽן לָ֑ךְ וּמַה־בַּקָּשָׁתֵ֛ךְ עַד־חֲצִ֥י הַמַּלְכ֖וּת וְתֵעָֽשׂ׃ *7 וַתַּ֥עַן אֶסְתֵּ֖ר וַתֹּאמַ֑ר שְׁאֵלָתִ֖י וּבַקָּשָׁתִֽי׃ 8 אִם־מָצָ֨אתִי חֵ֜ן בְּעֵינֵ֣י הַמֶּ֗לֶךְ וְאִם־עַל־הַמֶּ֙לֶךְ֙ ט֔וֹב לָתֵת֙ אֶת־שְׁאֵ֣לָתִ֔י וְלַעֲשׂ֖וֹת אֶת־בַּקָּשָׁתִ֑י יָב֧וֹא הַמֶּ֣לֶךְ וְהָמָ֗ן אֶל־הַמִּשְׁתֶּה֙ אֲשֶׁ֣ר אֶֽעֱשֶׂ֣ה לָהֶ֔ם וּמָחָ֥ר אֶֽעֱשֶׂ֖ה כִּדְבַ֥ר הַמֶּֽלֶךְ׃

9 וַיֵּצֵ֨א הָמָ֜ן בַּיּ֤וֹם הַהוּא֙ שָׂמֵ֣חַ וְט֣וֹב לֵ֔ב וְכִרְא֩וֹת֩ הָמָ֨ן אֶֽת־מָרְדֳּכַ֜י בְּשַׁ֣עַר הַמֶּ֗לֶךְ וְלֹא־קָם֙ וְלֹא־זָ֣ע מִמֶּ֔נּוּ וַיִּמָּלֵ֥א הָמָ֛ן עַֽל־מָרְדֳּכַ֖י חֵמָֽה׃ 10 וַיִּתְאַפַּ֣ק הָמָ֔ן וַיָּב֖וֹא אֶל־בֵּית֑וֹ וַיִּשְׁלַ֛ח וַיָּבֵ֥א אֶת־אֹהֲבָ֖יו וְאֶת־זֶ֥רֶשׁ אִשְׁתּֽוֹ׃ 11 וַיְסַפֵּ֨ר לָהֶ֤ם הָמָן֙ אֶת־כְּב֣וֹד עָשְׁר֔וֹ וְרֹ֖ב בָּנָ֑יו וְאֵת֩ כָּל־אֲשֶׁ֨ר גִּדְּל֤וֹ הַמֶּ֙לֶךְ֙ וְאֵ֣ת אֲשֶׁ֣ר נִשְּׂא֔וֹ עַל־הַשָּׂרִ֖ים וְעַבְדֵ֥י הַמֶּֽלֶךְ׃ 12 וַיֹּ֘אמֶר֮ הָמָן֒ אַ֣ף לֹא־הֵבִ֩יאָה֩ אֶסְתֵּ֨ר הַמַּלְכָּ֧ה עִם־הַמֶּ֛לֶךְ אֶל־הַמִּשְׁתֶּ֥ה אֲשֶׁר־עָשָׂ֖תָה כִּ֣י אִם־אוֹתִ֑י וְגַם־לְמָחָ֛ר אֲנִ֥י קָֽרוּא־לָ֖הּ עִם־הַמֶּֽלֶךְ׃ 13 וְכָל־זֶ֕ה אֵינֶ֥נּוּ שֹׁוֶ֖ה לִ֑י בְּכָל־עֵ֗ת אֲשֶׁ֨ר אֲנִ֤י רֹאֶה֙ אֶת־מָרְדֳּכַ֣י הַיְּהוּדִ֔י יוֹשֵׁ֖ב בְּשַׁ֥עַר הַמֶּֽלֶךְ׃ 14 וַתֹּ֣אמֶר לוֹ֩ זֶ֨רֶשׁ אִשְׁתּ֜וֹ וְכָל־אֹֽהֲבָ֗יו יַֽעֲשׂוּ־עֵץ֮ גָּבֹ֣הַּ חֲמִשִּׁ֣ים אַמָּה֒ וּבַבֹּ֣קֶר ׀ אֱמֹ֣ר לַמֶּ֗לֶךְ וְיִתְל֤וּ אֶֽת־מָרְדֳּכַי֙ עָלָ֔יו וּבֹֽא־

on it. Then you can go gaily with the king to the feast." The proposal pleased Haman, and he had the stake put up.

6 That night, sleep deserted the king, and he ordered the book of records, the annals, to be brought; and it was read to the king. [2]There it was found written that Mordecai had denounced Bigthana and Teresh, two of the king's eunuchs who guarded the threshold, who had plotted to do away with King Ahasuerus. [3]"What honor or advancement has been conferred on Mordecai for this?" the king inquired. "Nothing at all has been done for him," replied the king's servants who were in attendance on him. [4]"Who is in the court?" the king asked. For Haman had just entered the outer court of the royal palace, to speak to the king about having Mordecai impaled on the stake he had prepared for him. [5]"It is Haman standing in the court," the king's servants answered him. "Let him enter," said the king. [6]Haman entered, and the king asked him, "What should be done for a man whom the king desires to honor?" Haman said to himself, "Whom would the king desire to honor more than me?" [7]So Haman said to the king, "For the man whom the king desires to honor, [8]let royal garb which the king has worn be brought, and a horse on which the king has ridden and on whose head a royal diadem has been set; [9]and let the attire and the horse be put in the charge of one of the king's noble courtiers. And let the man whom the king desires to honor be attired and paraded on the horse through the city square, while they proclaim before him: This is what is done for the man whom the king desires to honor!" [10]"Quick, then!" said the king to Haman. "Get the garb and the horse, as you have said, and do this to Mordecai the Jew, who sits in the

עִם־הַמֶּלֶךְ אֶל־הַמִּשְׁתֶּה שָׂמֵחַ וָיֵיטַב הַדָּבָר לִפְנֵי הָמָן וַיַּעַשׂ הָעֵץ׃ פ

ו בַּלַּיְלָה הַהוּא נָדְדָה שְׁנַת הַמֶּלֶךְ וַיֹּאמֶר לְהָבִיא אֶת־סֵפֶר הַזִּכְרֹנוֹת דִּבְרֵי הַיָּמִים וַיִּהְיוּ נִקְרָאִים לִפְנֵי הַמֶּלֶךְ׃ [2]וַיִּמָּצֵא כָתוּב אֲשֶׁר הִגִּיד מָרְדֳּכַי עַל־בִּגְתָנָא וָתֶרֶשׁ שְׁנֵי סָרִיסֵי הַמֶּלֶךְ מִשֹּׁמְרֵי הַסַּף אֲשֶׁר בִּקְשׁוּ לִשְׁלֹחַ יָד בַּמֶּלֶךְ אֲחַשְׁוֵרוֹשׁ׃ [3]וַיֹּאמֶר הַמֶּלֶךְ מַה־נַּעֲשָׂה יְקָר וּגְדוּלָּה לְמָרְדֳּכַי עַל־זֶה וַיֹּאמְרוּ נַעֲרֵי הַמֶּלֶךְ מְשָׁרְתָיו לֹא־נַעֲשָׂה עִמּוֹ דָּבָר׃ [4]וַיֹּאמֶר הַמֶּלֶךְ מִי בֶחָצֵר וְהָמָן בָּא לַחֲצַר בֵּית־הַמֶּלֶךְ הַחִיצוֹנָה לֵאמֹר לַמֶּלֶךְ לִתְלוֹת אֶת־מָרְדֳּכַי עַל־הָעֵץ אֲשֶׁר־הֵכִין לוֹ׃ [5]וַיֹּאמְרוּ נַעֲרֵי הַמֶּלֶךְ אֵלָיו הִנֵּה הָמָן עֹמֵד בֶּחָצֵר וַיֹּאמֶר הַמֶּלֶךְ יָבוֹא׃ [6]וַיָּבוֹא הָמָן וַיֹּאמֶר לוֹ הַמֶּלֶךְ מַה־לַעֲשׂוֹת בָּאִישׁ אֲשֶׁר הַמֶּלֶךְ חָפֵץ בִּיקָרוֹ וַיֹּאמֶר הָמָן בְּלִבּוֹ לְמִי יַחְפֹּץ הַמֶּלֶךְ לַעֲשׂוֹת יְקָר יוֹתֵר מִמֶּנִּי׃ [7]וַיֹּאמֶר הָמָן אֶל־הַמֶּלֶךְ אִישׁ אֲשֶׁר הַמֶּלֶךְ חָפֵץ בִּיקָרוֹ׃ [8]יָבִיאוּ לְבוּשׁ מַלְכוּת אֲשֶׁר לָבַשׁ־בּוֹ הַמֶּלֶךְ וְסוּס אֲשֶׁר רָכַב עָלָיו הַמֶּלֶךְ וַאֲשֶׁר נִתַּן כֶּתֶר מַלְכוּת בְּרֹאשׁוֹ׃ [9]וְנָתוֹן הַלְּבוּשׁ וְהַסּוּס עַל־יַד־אִישׁ מִשָּׂרֵי הַמֶּלֶךְ הַפַּרְתְּמִים וְהִלְבִּישׁוּ אֶת־הָאִישׁ אֲשֶׁר הַמֶּלֶךְ חָפֵץ בִּיקָרוֹ וְהִרְכִּיבֻהוּ עַל־הַסּוּס בִּרְחוֹב הָעִיר וְקָרְאוּ לְפָנָיו כָּכָה יֵעָשֶׂה לָאִישׁ אֲשֶׁר הַמֶּלֶךְ חָפֵץ בִּיקָרוֹ׃ [10]וַיֹּאמֶר הַמֶּלֶךְ לְהָמָן מַהֵר קַח אֶת־הַלְּבוּשׁ וְאֶת־הַסּוּס כַּאֲשֶׁר דִּבַּרְתָּ וַעֲשֵׂה־כֵן לְמָרְדֳּכַי הַיְּהוּדִי הַיּוֹשֵׁב בְּשַׁעַר הַמֶּלֶךְ

king's gate. Omit nothing of all you have proposed." [11]So Haman took the garb and the horse and arrayed Mordecai and paraded him through the city square; and he proclaimed before him: This is what is done for the man whom the king desires to honor!

[12]Then Mordecai returned to the king's gate, while Haman hurried home, his head covered in mourning. [13]There Haman told his wife Zeresh and all his friends everything that had befallen him. His advisers and his wife Zeresh said to him, "If Mordecai, before whom you have begun to fall, is of Jewish stock, you will not overcome him; you will fall before him to your ruin."

[14]While they were still speaking with him, the king's eunuchs arrived and hurriedly brought Haman to the banquet which Esther had prepared.

7

So the king and Haman came to feast with Queen Esther. [2]On the second day, the king again asked Esther at the wine feast, "What is your wish, Queen Esther? It shall be granted you. And what is your request? Even to half the kingdom, it shall be fulfilled." [3]Queen Esther replied: "If Your Majesty will do me the favor, and if it pleases Your Majesty, let my life be granted me as my wish, and my people as my request. [4]For we have been sold, my people and I, to be destroyed, massacred, and exterminated. Had we only been sold as bondmen and bondwomen, I would have kept silent; for *a-the adversary-a* is not worthy of the king's trouble."

[5]Thereupon King Ahasuerus demanded of Queen Esther, "Who is he and where is he who dared to do this?" [6]"The adversary and enemy," replied Esther, "is this evil Haman!" And Ha-

אַל־תַּפֵּל דָּבָר מִכֹּל אֲשֶׁר דִּבַּֽרְתָּ׃ 11 וַיִּקַּח הָמָן אֶת־הַלְּבוּשׁ וְאֶת־הַסּוּס וַיַּלְבֵּשׁ אֶת־ מָרְדֳּכָי וַיַּרְכִּיבֵהוּ בִּרְחוֹב הָעִיר וַיִּקְרָא לְפָנָיו כָּֽכָה יֵעָשֶׂה לָאִישׁ אֲשֶׁר הַמֶּלֶךְ חָפֵץ בִּיקָרֽוֹ׃
12 וַיָּ֥שָׁב מָרְדֳּכַי אֶל־שַׁעַר הַמֶּלֶךְ וְהָמָן נִדְחַף אֶל־בֵּיתוֹ אָבֵל וַחֲפוּי רֹֽאשׁ׃
13 וַיְסַפֵּר הָמָן לְזֶרֶשׁ אִשְׁתּוֹ וּלְכָל־אֹֽהֲבָיו אֵת כָּל־אֲשֶׁר קָרָהוּ וַיֹּאמְרוּ לוֹ חֲכָמָיו וְזֶרֶשׁ אִשְׁתּוֹ אִם מִזֶּרַע הַיְּהוּדִים מָרְדֳּכַי אֲשֶׁר הַחִלּוֹתָ לִנְפֹּל לְפָנָיו לֹא־תוּכַל לוֹ כִּֽי־נָפוֹל תִּפּוֹל לְפָנָֽיו׃
14 עוֹדָם מְדַבְּרִים עִמּוֹ וְסָרִיסֵי הַמֶּלֶךְ הִגִּיעוּ וַיַּבְהִלוּ לְהָבִיא אֶת־הָמָן אֶל־ הַמִּשְׁתֶּה אֲשֶׁר־עָשְׂתָה אֶסְתֵּֽר׃

ז 1 וַיָּבֹא הַמֶּלֶךְ וְהָמָן לִשְׁתּוֹת עִם־אֶסְתֵּר הַמַּלְכָּֽה׃ 2 וַיֹּאמֶר הַמֶּלֶךְ לְאֶסְתֵּר גַּם בַּיּוֹם הַשֵּׁנִי בְּמִשְׁתֵּה הַיַּיִן מַה־שְּׁאֵלָתֵךְ אֶסְתֵּר הַמַּלְכָּה וְתִנָּתֵן לָךְ וּמַה־בַּקָּשָׁתֵךְ עַד־חֲצִי הַמַּלְכוּת וְתֵעָֽשׂ׃ 3 וַתַּעַן אֶסְתֵּר הַמַּלְכָּה וַתֹּאמַר אִם־מָצָאתִי חֵן בְּעֵינֶיךָ הַמֶּלֶךְ וְאִם־עַל־הַמֶּלֶךְ טוֹב תִּנָּתֶן־לִי נַפְשִׁי בִּשְׁאֵלָתִי וְעַמִּי בְּבַקָּשָׁתִֽי׃ 4 כִּי נִמְכַּרְנוּ אֲנִי וְעַמִּי לְהַשְׁמִיד לַהֲרוֹג וּלְאַבֵּד וְאִלּוּ לַעֲבָדִים וְלִשְׁפָחוֹת נִמְכַּרְנוּ הֶחֱרַשְׁתִּי כִּי אֵין הַצָּר שֹׁוֶה בְּנֵזֶק הַמֶּֽלֶךְ׃ ס 5 וַיֹּאמֶר הַמֶּלֶךְ אֲחַשְׁוֵרוֹשׁ וַיֹּאמֶר לְאֶסְתֵּר הַמַּלְכָּה מִי הוּא זֶה וְאֵי־זֶה הוּא אֲשֶׁר מְלָאוֹ לִבּוֹ לַעֲשׂוֹת כֵּֽן׃ 6 וַתֹּאמֶר־אֶסְתֵּר אִישׁ צַר וְאוֹיֵב הָמָן הָרָע הַזֶּה וְהָמָן נִבְעַת מִלִּפְנֵי הַמֶּלֶךְ וְהַמַּלְכָּֽה׃ 7 וְהַמֶּלֶךְ קָם

---

a-a Emendation yields "a trifle" (ḥiṣṣar), lit. "little finger."

man cringed in terror before the king and the queen. ⁷The king, in his fury, left the wine feast for the palace garden, while Haman remained to plead with Queen Esther for his life; for he saw that the king had resolved to destroy him. ⁸When the king returned from the palace garden to the banquet room, Haman was lying prostrate on the couch on which Esther reclined. "Does he mean," cried the king, "to ravish the queen in my own palace?" No sooner did these words leave the king's lips than Haman's face ᵇ-was covered.-ᵇ ⁹Then Harbonah, one of the eunuchs in attendance on the king, said, "What is more, a stake is standing at Haman's house, fifty cubits high, which Haman made for Mordecai—the man whose words saved the king." "Impale him on it!" the king ordered. ¹⁰So they impaled Haman on the stake which he had put up for Mordecai, and the king's fury abated.

8 That very day King Ahasuerus gave the property of Haman, the enemy of the Jews, to Queen Esther. Mordecai presented himself to the king, for Esther had revealed how he was related to her. ²The king slipped off his ring, which he had taken back from Haman, and gave it to Mordecai; and Esther put Mordecai in charge of Haman's property.

³Esther spoke to the king again, falling at his feet and weeping, and beseeching him to avert the evil plotted by Haman the Agagite against the Jews. ⁴The king extended the golden scepter to Esther, and Esther arose and stood before the king. ⁵"If it please Your Majesty," she said, "and if I have won your favor and the proposal seems right to Your Majesty, and if I am pleasing to you—let dispatches be written countermand-

---

בַּחֲמָתוֹ מִמִּשְׁתֵּה הַיַּיִן אֶל־גִּנַּת הַבִּיתָן וְהָמָן עָמַד לְבַקֵּשׁ עַל־נַפְשׁוֹ מֵאֶסְתֵּר הַמַּלְכָּה כִּי רָאָה כִּי־כָלְתָה אֵלָיו הָרָעָה מֵאֵת הַמֶּלֶךְ: ⁸ וְהַמֶּלֶךְ שָׁב מִגִּנַּת הַבִּיתָן אֶל־בֵּית ׀ מִשְׁתֵּה הַיַּיִן וְהָמָן נֹפֵל עַל־הַמִּטָּה אֲשֶׁר אֶסְתֵּר עָלֶיהָ וַיֹּאמֶר הַמֶּלֶךְ הֲגַם לִכְבּוֹשׁ אֶת־הַמַּלְכָּה עִמִּי בַּבָּיִת הַדָּבָר יָצָא מִפִּי הַמֶּלֶךְ וּפְנֵי הָמָן חָפוּ: ס ⁹ וַיֹּאמֶר חַרְבוֹנָה אֶחָד מִן־הַסָּרִיסִים לִפְנֵי הַמֶּלֶךְ גַּם הִנֵּה־הָעֵץ אֲשֶׁר־עָשָׂה הָמָן לְמָרְדֳּכַי אֲשֶׁר דִּבֶּר־טוֹב עַל־הַמֶּלֶךְ עֹמֵד בְּבֵית הָמָן גָּבֹהַּ חֲמִשִּׁים אַמָּה וַיֹּאמֶר הַמֶּלֶךְ תְּלֻהוּ עָלָיו: ¹⁰ וַיִּתְלוּ אֶת־הָמָן עַל־הָעֵץ אֲשֶׁר־הֵכִין לְמָרְדֳּכָי וַחֲמַת הַמֶּלֶךְ שָׁכָכָה: פ

ח בַּיּוֹם הַהוּא נָתַן הַמֶּלֶךְ אֲחַשְׁוֵרוֹשׁ לְאֶסְתֵּר הַמַּלְכָּה אֶת־בֵּית הָמָן צֹרֵר הַיְּהוּדִיִּים וּמָרְדֳּכַי בָּא לִפְנֵי הַמֶּלֶךְ כִּי־הִגִּידָה אֶסְתֵּר מַה הוּא־לָהּ: ² וַיָּסַר הַמֶּלֶךְ אֶת־טַבַּעְתּוֹ אֲשֶׁר הֶעֱבִיר מֵהָמָן וַיִּתְּנָהּ לְמָרְדֳּכָי וַתָּשֶׂם אֶסְתֵּר אֶת־מָרְדֳּכַי עַל־בֵּית הָמָן: פ ³ וַתּוֹסֶף אֶסְתֵּר וַתְּדַבֵּר לִפְנֵי הַמֶּלֶךְ וַתִּפֹּל לִפְנֵי רַגְלָיו וַתֵּבְךְּ וַתִּתְחַנֶּן־לוֹ לְהַעֲבִיר אֶת־רָעַת הָמָן הָאֲגָגִי וְאֵת מַחֲשַׁבְתּוֹ אֲשֶׁר חָשַׁב עַל־הַיְּהוּדִים: ⁴ וַיּוֹשֶׁט הַמֶּלֶךְ לְאֶסְתֵּר אֵת שַׁרְבִט הַזָּהָב וַתָּקָם אֶסְתֵּר וַתַּעֲמֹד לִפְנֵי הַמֶּלֶךְ: ⁵ וַתֹּאמֶר אִם־עַל־הַמֶּלֶךְ טוֹב וְאִם־מָצָאתִי חֵן לְפָנָיו וְכָשֵׁר הַדָּבָר לִפְנֵי הַמֶּלֶךְ וְטוֹבָה אֲנִי בְּעֵינָיו

---

b-b   *Meaning of Heb. uncertain. Emendation yields "blanched";*
    cf. Ps. 34.6.

ing those which were written by Haman son of Hammedatha the Agagite, embodying his plot to annihilate the Jews throughout the king's provinces. [6] For how can I bear to see the disaster which will befall my people! And how can I bear to see the destruction of my kindred!"

[7] Then King Ahasuerus said to Queen Esther and Mordecai the Jew, "I have given Haman's property to Esther, and he has been impaled on the stake for scheming against the Jews. [8] And you may further write with regard to the Jews as you see fit. [Write it] in the king's name and seal it with the king's signet, for an edict that has been written in the king's name and sealed with the king's signet may not be revoked."

[9] So the king's scribes were summoned at that time, on the twenty-third day of the third month, that is, the month of Sivan; and letters were written, at Mordecai's dictation, to the Jews and to the satraps, the governors and the officials of the one hundred and twenty-seven provinces from India to Ethiopia: to every province in its own script and to every people in its own language, and to the Jews in their own script and language. [10] He had them written in the name of King Ahasuerus and sealed with the king's signet. Letters were dispatched by mounted couriers, riding steeds a-used in the king's service, bred of the royal stud,-a [11] to this effect: The king has permitted the Jews of every city to assemble and fight for their lives; if any people or province attacks them, they may destroy, massacre, and exterminate its armed force together with women and children, and plunder their possessions—[12] on a single day in all the provinces of King Ahasuerus, namely, on the thirteenth day of the twelfth month, that is, the month of Adar. [13] The text of the document was to be issued as a law in every single province: it was to be publicly displayed to all the peoples, so that the Jews should be ready for that day

יִכָּתֵב לְהָשִׁיב אֶת־הַסְּפָרִים מַחֲשֶׁבֶת הָמָן בֶּן־הַמְּדָ֫תָא הָאֲגָגִי אֲשֶׁר כָּתַב לְאַבֵּד אֶת־הַיְּהוּדִים אֲשֶׁר בְּכָל־מְדִינוֹת הַמֶּֽלֶךְ׃ [6] כִּי אֵיכָכָ֫ה אוּכַל וְֽרָאִיתִי בָּרָעָה אֲשֶׁר־יִמְצָא אֶת־עַמִּי וְאֵיכָכָ֫ה אוּכַל וְֽרָאִיתִי בְּאָבְדַן מוֹלַדְתִּֽי׃ ס [7] וַיֹּ֫אמֶר הַמֶּ֫לֶךְ אֲחַשְׁוֵרֹשׁ לְאֶסְתֵּר הַמַּלְכָּ֫ה וּֽלְמָרְדֳּכַי הַיְּהוּדִי הִנֵּה בֵית־הָמָן נָתַ֫תִּי לְאֶסְתֵּר וְאֹתוֹ תָּלוּ עַל־הָעֵץ עַל אֲשֶׁר־שָׁלַח יָדוֹ בַּיְּהוּדִֽים׃ [8] וְאַתֶּם כִּתְבוּ עַל־הַיְּהוּדִים כַּטּוֹב בְּעֵֽינֵיכֶם בְּשֵׁם הַמֶּ֫לֶךְ וְחִתְמוּ בְּטַבַּעַת הַמֶּ֫לֶךְ כִּֽי־כְתָב אֲשֶׁר־נִכְתָּב בְּשֵׁם־הַמֶּ֫לֶךְ וְנַחְתּוֹם בְּטַבַּעַת הַמֶּ֫לֶךְ אֵין לְהָשִֽׁיב׃ [9] וַיִּקָּרְאוּ סֹפְרֵי־הַמֶּ֫לֶךְ בָּֽעֵת־הַהִיא בַּחֹ֫דֶשׁ הַשְּׁלִישִׁי הוּא־חֹ֫דֶשׁ סִיוָ֫ן בִּשְׁלוֹשָׁה וְעֶשְׂרִים בּוֹ וַיִּכָּתֵב כְּֽכָל־אֲשֶׁר־צִוָּה מָרְדֳּכַי אֶל־הַיְּהוּדִים וְאֶל הָאֲחַשְׁדַּרְפְּנִים־ וְֽהַפַּחוֹת וְשָׂרֵי הַמְּדִינוֹת אֲשֶׁר ׀ מֵהֹ֫דּוּ וְעַד־כּוּשׁ שֶׁבַע וְעֶשְׂרִים וּמֵאָה מְדִינָה מְדִינָה וּמְדִינָה כִּכְתָבָהּ וְעַם וָעָם כִּלְשֹׁנוֹ וְאֶל־הַיְּהוּדִים כִּכְתָבָם וְכִלְשׁוֹנָֽם׃ [10] וַיִּכְתֹּב בְּשֵׁם֙ הַמֶּ֫לֶךְ אֲחַשְׁוֵרֹשׁ וַיַּחְתֹּם בְּטַבַּעַת הַמֶּ֫לֶךְ וַיִּשְׁלַח סְפָרִים בְּיַד הָרָצִים בַּסּוּסִים רֹכְבֵי הָרֶ֫כֶשׁ הָֽאֲחַשְׁתְּרָנִים בְּנֵי הָֽרַמָּכִֽים׃ [11] אֲשֶׁר נָתַן הַמֶּ֫לֶךְ לַיְּהוּדִים ׀ אֲשֶׁר בְּכָל־עִיר־וָעִיר לְהִקָּהֵל֙ וְלַעֲמֹד עַל־נַפְשָׁם לְהַשְׁמִיד וְלַהֲרֹג וּלְאַבֵּד אֶת־כָּל־חֵיל עַם וּמְדִינָה הַצָּרִים אֹתָם טַף וְנָשִׁים וּשְׁלָלָם לָבֽוֹז׃ [12] בְּיוֹם אֶחָד בְּכָל־מְדִינוֹת הַמֶּ֫לֶךְ אֲחַשְׁוֵרוֹשׁ בִּשְׁלוֹשָׁה עָשָׂר לְחֹ֫דֶשׁ שְׁנֵים־עָשָׂר הוּא־חֹ֫דֶשׁ אֲדָֽר׃ [13] פַּתְשֶׁגֶן הַכְּתָב לְהִנָּתֵן דָּת֙ בְּכָל־מְדִינָה וּמְדִינָה גָּלוּי לְכָל־הָֽעַמִּים וְלִהְיוֹת היהודיים הַיְּהוּדִים עֲתוּדִים עֲתִידִים לַיּוֹם הַזֶּה לְהִנָּקֵם

a-a *Meaning of Heb. uncertain.*

to avenge themselves on their enemies. [14]The couriers, mounted on royal steeds, went out in urgent haste at the king's command; and the decree was proclaimed in the fortress Shushan.

[15]Mordecai left the king's presence in royal robes of blue and white, with a magnificent crown of gold and a mantle of fine linen and purple wool. And the city of Shushan rang with joyous cries. [16]The Jews enjoyed light and gladness, happiness and honor. [17]And in every province and in every city, when the king's command and decree arrived, there was gladness and joy among the Jews, a feast and a holiday. And many of the people of the land professed to be Jews, for the fear of the Jews had fallen upon them.

9 And so, on the thirteenth day of the twelfth month—that is, the month of Adar—when the king's command and decree were to be executed, the very day on which the enemies of the Jews had expected to get them in their power, the opposite happened, and the Jews got their enemies in their power. [2]Throughout the provinces of King Ahasuerus, the Jews mustered in their cities to attack those who sought their hurt; and no one could withstand them, for the fear of them had fallen upon all the peoples. [3]Indeed, all the officials of the provinces—the satraps, the governors, and the king's stewards—showed deference to the Jews, because the fear of Mordecai had fallen upon them. [4]For Mordecai was now powerful in the royal palace, and his fame was spreading through all the provinces; the man Mordecai was growing ever more powerful. [5]So the Jews struck at their enemies with the sword, slaying and destroying; they wreaked their will upon their enemies.

[6]In the fortress Shushan the Jews killed a total of five hundred men. [7]They also killed[a]

מֵאֹיְבֵיהֶֽם: 14 הָרָצִ֞ים רֹכְבֵ֤י הָרֶ֙כֶשׁ֙ הָֽאֲחַשְׁתְּרָנִ֔ים יָֽצְא֛וּ מְבֹהָלִ֥ים וּדְחוּפִ֖ים בִּדְבַ֣ר הַמֶּ֑לֶךְ וְהַדָּ֥ת נִתְּנָ֖ה בְּשׁוּשַׁ֥ן הַבִּירָֽה: פ

15 וּמָרְדֳּכַ֞י יָצָ֣א ׀ מִלִּפְנֵ֣י הַמֶּ֗לֶךְ בִּלְב֤וּשׁ מַלְכוּת֙ תְּכֵ֣לֶת וָח֔וּר וַעֲטֶ֤רֶת זָהָב֙ גְּדוֹלָ֔ה וְתַכְרִ֥יךְ בּ֖וּץ וְאַרְגָּמָ֑ן וְהָעִ֣יר שׁוּשָׁ֔ן צָהֲלָ֖ה וְשָׂמֵֽחָה: 16 לַיְּהוּדִ֕ים הָֽיְתָ֥ה אוֹרָ֖ה וְשִׂמְחָ֑ה וְשָׂשֹׂ֖ן וִיקָֽר: 17 וּבְכָל־מְדִינָ֣ה וּמְדִינָ֗ה וּבְכָל־עִ֣יר וָעִ֔יר מְקוֹם֙ אֲשֶׁ֣ר דְּבַר־ הַמֶּ֤לֶךְ וְדָתוֹ֙ מַגִּ֔יעַ שִׂמְחָ֤ה וְשָׂשׂוֹן֙ לַיְּהוּדִ֔ים מִשְׁתֶּ֖ה וְי֣וֹם ט֑וֹב וְרַבִּ֞ים מֵֽעַמֵּ֤י הָאָ֙רֶץ֙ מִֽתְיַהֲדִ֔ים כִּֽי־נָפַ֥ל פַּֽחַד־הַיְּהוּדִ֖ים עֲלֵיהֶֽם:

ט וּבִשְׁנֵים֩ עָשָׂ֨ר חֹ֜דֶשׁ הוּא־חֹ֣דֶשׁ אֲדָ֗ר בִּשְׁלוֹשָׁ֨ה עָשָׂ֥ר יוֹם֙ בּ֔וֹ אֲשֶׁ֨ר הִגִּ֧יעַ דְּבַר־ הַמֶּ֛לֶךְ וְדָת֖וֹ לְהֵֽעָשׂ֑וֹת בַּיּ֗וֹם אֲשֶׁ֨ר שִׂבְּר֜וּ אֹיְבֵ֤י הַיְּהוּדִים֙ לִשְׁל֣וֹט בָּהֶ֔ם וְנַהֲפ֣וֹךְ ה֔וּא אֲשֶׁ֨ר יִשְׁלְט֧וּ הַיְּהוּדִ֛ים הֵ֖מָּה בְּשֹׂנְאֵיהֶֽם: 2 נִקְהֲל֣וּ הַיְּהוּדִ֗ים בְּעָֽרֵיהֶם֙ בְּכָל־מְדִינוֹת֙ הַמֶּ֣לֶךְ אֲחַשְׁוֵר֔וֹשׁ לִשְׁלֹ֣חַ יָ֔ד בִּמְבַקְשֵׁ֖י רָֽעָתָ֑ם וְאִישׁ֙ לֹא־עָמַ֣ד לִפְנֵיהֶ֔ם כִּֽי־ נָפַ֥ל פַּחְדָּ֖ם עַל־כָּל־הָעַמִּֽים: 3 וְכָל־שָׂרֵ֣י הַמְּדִינ֡וֹת וְהָ֠אֲחַשְׁדַּרְפְּנִ֤ים וְהַפַּחוֹת֙ וְעֹשֵׂ֣י הַמְּלָאכָ֗ה אֲשֶׁ֤ר לַמֶּ֙לֶךְ֙ מְנַשְּׂאִ֣ים אֶת־ הַיְּהוּדִ֔ים כִּֽי־נָפַ֥ל פַּֽחַד־מָרְדֳּכַ֖י עֲלֵיהֶֽם: 4 כִּֽי־גָד֤וֹל מָרְדֳּכַי֙ בְּבֵ֣ית הַמֶּ֔לֶךְ וְשָׁמְע֖וֹ הוֹלֵ֣ךְ בְּכָל־הַמְּדִינ֑וֹת כִּֽי־הָאִ֥ישׁ מָרְדֳּכַ֖י הוֹלֵ֥ךְ וְגָדֽוֹל: פ 5 וַיַּכּ֤וּ הַיְּהוּדִים֙ בְּכָל־ אֹ֣יְבֵיהֶ֔ם מַכַּת־חֶ֥רֶב וְהֶ֖רֶג וְאַבְדָּ֑ן וַיַּעֲשׂ֥וּ בְשֹׂנְאֵיהֶ֖ם כִּרְצוֹנָֽם: 6 וּבְשׁוּשַׁ֣ן הַבִּירָ֗ה הָרְג֤וּ הַיְּהוּדִים֙ וְאַבֵּ֔ד חֲמֵ֥שׁ מֵא֖וֹת אִֽישׁ: 7 וְאֵ֣ת ׀

---

a   *Moved up from v. 10 for greater clarity.*

Parshandatha,

Dalphon,

Aspatha,

8Poratha,

Adalia,

Aridatha,

9Parmashta,

Arisai,

Aridai,

and Vaizatha,

10the ten sons of Haman son of Hammedatha, the foe of the Jews. But they did not lay hands on the spoil. 11When the number of those slain in the fortress Shushan was reported on that same day to the king, 12the king said to Queen Esther, "In the fortress Shushan alone the Jews have killed a total of five hundred men, as well as the ten sons of Haman. What then must they have done in the provinces of the realm! What is your wish now? It shall be granted you. And what else is your request? It shall be fulfilled." 13"If it please Your Majesty," Esther replied, "let the Jews in Shushan be permitted to act tomorrow also as they did today; and let Haman's ten sons be impaled on the stake." 14The king ordered that this should be done, and the decree was proclaimed in Shushan. Haman's ten sons were impaled: 15and the Jews in Shushan mustered again on the fourteenth day of Adar and slew three hundred men in Shushan. But they did not lay hands on the spoil.

16The rest of the Jews, those in the king's provinces, likewise mustered and fought for their lives. They disposed of their enemies, killing seventy-five thousand of their foes; but they did not lay hands on the spoil. 17That was on the thirteenth day of the month of Adar; and they rested on the fourteenth day and made it a day of feasting and merrymaking. (18But the Jews in Shushan mustered on both the thirteenth and fourteenth days, and so rested on the fifteenth,

אֵת ׀ פַּרְשַׁנְדָּתָא

אֵת ׀ דַּלְפוֹן

8 וְאֵת ׀ אַסְפָּתָא:

וְאֵת ׀ פּוֹרָתָא

וְאֵת ׀ אֲדַלְיָא

9 וְאֵת ׀ אֲרִידָתָא:

וְאֵת ׀ פַּרְמַשְׁתָּא

וְאֵת ׀ אֲרִיסַי

וְאֵת ׀ אֲרִדַי

10 וַיְזָתָא:

בְּנֵי הָמָן בֶּן־הַמְּדָתָא צֹרֵר הַיְּהוּדִים הָרָגוּ וּבַבִּזָּה לֹא שָׁלְחוּ אֶת־יָדָם: 11 בַּיּוֹם הַהוּא בָּא מִסְפַּר הַהֲרוּגִים בְּשׁוּשַׁן הַבִּירָה לִפְנֵי הַמֶּלֶךְ: ס 12 וַיֹּאמֶר הַמֶּלֶךְ לְאֶסְתֵּר הַמַּלְכָּה בְּשׁוּשַׁן הַבִּירָה הָרְגוּ הַיְּהוּדִים וְאַבֵּד חֲמֵשׁ מֵאוֹת אִישׁ וְאֵת עֲשֶׂרֶת בְּנֵי־הָמָן בִּשְׁאָר מְדִינוֹת הַמֶּלֶךְ מֶה עָשׂוּ וּמַה־שְּׁאֵלָתֵךְ וְיִנָּתֵן לָךְ וּמַה־בַּקָּשָׁתֵךְ עוֹד וְתֵעָשׂ: 13 וַתֹּאמֶר אֶסְתֵּר אִם־עַל־הַמֶּלֶךְ טוֹב יִנָּתֵן גַּם־מָחָר לַיְּהוּדִים אֲשֶׁר בְּשׁוּשָׁן לַעֲשׂוֹת כְּדָת הַיּוֹם וְאֵת עֲשֶׂרֶת בְּנֵי־הָמָן יִתְלוּ עַל־הָעֵץ: 14 וַיֹּאמֶר הַמֶּלֶךְ לְהֵעָשׂוֹת כֵּן וַתִּנָּתֵן דָּת בְּשׁוּשָׁן וְאֵת עֲשֶׂרֶת בְּנֵי־הָמָן תָּלוּ: 15 וַיִּקָּהֲלוּ הַיְּהוּדִיים אֲשֶׁר־בְּשׁוּשָׁן גַּם בְּיוֹם אַרְבָּעָה עָשָׂר לְחֹדֶשׁ אֲדָר וַיַּהַרְגוּ בְשׁוּשָׁן שְׁלֹשׁ מֵאוֹת אִישׁ וּבַבִּזָּה לֹא שָׁלְחוּ אֶת־יָדָם: 16 וּשְׁאָר הַיְּהוּדִים אֲשֶׁר בִּמְדִינוֹת הַמֶּלֶךְ נִקְהֲלוּ ׀ וְעָמֹד עַל־נַפְשָׁם וְנוֹחַ מֵאֹיְבֵיהֶם וְהָרֹג בְּשֹׂנְאֵיהֶם חֲמִשָּׁה וְשִׁבְעִים אָלֶף וּבַבִּזָּה לֹא שָׁלְחוּ אֶת־יָדָם: 17 בְּיוֹם־שְׁלֹשָׁה עָשָׂר לְחֹדֶשׁ אֲדָר וְנוֹחַ בְּאַרְבָּעָה עָשָׂר בּוֹ וְעָשֹׂה אֹתוֹ יוֹם מִשְׁתֶּה וְשִׂמְחָה: 18 וְהַיְּהוּדִיים אֲשֶׁר־בְּשׁוּשָׁן נִקְהֲלוּ בִּשְׁלֹשָׁה עָשָׂר בּוֹ וּבְאַרְבָּעָה עָשָׂר

and made it a day of feasting and merrymaking.) ¹⁹That is why village Jews, who live in unwalled towns, observe the fourteenth day of the month of Adar and make it a day of merrymaking and feasting, and as a holiday and an occasion for sending gifts to one another.

²⁰Mordecai recorded these events. And he sent dispatches to all the Jews throughout the provinces of King Ahasuerus, near and far, ²¹charging them to observe the fourteenth and fifteenth days of Adar, every year—²²the same days on which the Jews enjoyed relief from their foes and the same month which had been transformed for them from one of grief and mourning to one of festive joy. They were to observe them as days of feasting and merrymaking, and as an occasion for sending gifts to one another and presents to the poor. ²³The Jews accordingly assumed as an obligation that which they had begun to practice and which Mordecai prescribed for them.

²⁴For Haman son of Hammedatha the Agagite, the foe of all the Jews, had plotted to destroy the Jews, and had cast *pur*—that is, the lot—with intent to crush and exterminate them. ²⁵But when [Esther] came before the king, he commanded: ^b-"With the promulgation of this decree,-^b let the evil plot, which he devised against the Jews, recoil on his own head!" So they impaled him and his sons on the stake. ²⁶For that reason these days were named Purim, after *pur*.

In view, then, of all the instructions in the said letter and of what they had experienced in that matter and what had befallen them, ²⁷the Jews undertook and irrevocably obligated themselves and their descendants, and all who might join them, to observe these two days in the manner prescribed and at the proper time each year. ²⁸Consequently, these days are recalled and observed in every generation: by every family,

בּוֹ וְנ֕וֹחַ בַּחֲמִשָּׁ֥ה עָשָׂ֖ר בּ֑וֹ וְעָשֹׂ֣ה אֹת֔וֹ י֖וֹם מִשְׁתֶּ֥ה וְשִׂמְחָֽה׃ 19 עַל־כֵּ֞ן הַיְּהוּדִ֣ים הַפְּרוֹזִ֗ים הַיֹּשְׁבִים֮ בְּעָרֵ֣י הַפְּרָזוֹת֒ עֹשִׂ֗ים אֵ֠ת י֣וֹם אַרְבָּעָ֤ה עָשָׂר֙ לְחֹ֣דֶשׁ אֲדָ֔ר שִׂמְחָ֥ה וּמִשְׁתֶּ֖ה וְי֣וֹם ט֑וֹב וּמִשְׁל֥וֹחַ מָנ֖וֹת אִ֥ישׁ לְרֵעֵֽהוּ׃ פ

20 וַיִּכְתֹּ֣ב מָרְדֳּכַ֔י אֶת־הַדְּבָרִ֖ים הָאֵ֑לֶּה וַיִּשְׁלַ֣ח סְפָרִ֗ים אֶל־כָּל־הַיְּהוּדִ֗ים אֲשֶׁר֙ בְּכָל־מְדִינוֹת֙ הַמֶּ֣לֶךְ אֲחַשְׁוֵר֔וֹשׁ הַקְּרוֹבִ֖ים וְהָרְחוֹקִֽים׃ 21 לְקַיֵּ֖ם עֲלֵיהֶ֑ם לִהְי֣וֹת עֹשִׂ֗ים אֵ֠ת י֣וֹם אַרְבָּעָ֤ה עָשָׂר֙ לְחֹ֣דֶשׁ אֲדָ֔ר וְאֵ֛ת יוֹם־חֲמִשָּׁ֥ה עָשָׂ֖ר בּ֑וֹ בְּכָל־שָׁנָ֥ה וְשָׁנָֽה׃ 22 כַּיָּמִ֗ים אֲשֶׁר־נָ֨חוּ בָהֶ֤ם הַיְּהוּדִים֙ מֵאֹ֣יְבֵיהֶ֔ם וְהַחֹ֗דֶשׁ אֲשֶׁר֩ נֶהְפַּ֨ךְ לָהֶ֤ם מִיָּגוֹן֙ לְשִׂמְחָ֔ה וּמֵאֵ֖בֶל לְי֣וֹם ט֑וֹב לַעֲשׂ֣וֹת אוֹתָ֗ם יְמֵי֙ מִשְׁתֶּ֣ה וְשִׂמְחָ֔ה וּמִשְׁל֤וֹחַ מָנוֹת֙ אִ֣ישׁ לְרֵעֵ֔הוּ וּמַתָּנ֖וֹת לָֽאֶבְיוֹנִֽים׃ 23 וְקִבֵּל֙ הַיְּהוּדִ֔ים אֵ֥ת אֲשֶׁר־הֵחֵ֖לּוּ לַעֲשׂ֑וֹת וְאֵ֛ת אֲשֶׁר־כָּתַ֥ב מָרְדֳּכַ֖י אֲלֵיהֶֽם׃

24 כִּי֩ הָמָ֨ן בֶּֽן־הַמְּדָ֜תָא הָֽאֲגָגִ֗י צֹרֵר֙ כָּל־הַיְּהוּדִ֔ים חָשַׁ֥ב עַל־הַיְּהוּדִ֖ים לְאַבְּדָ֑ם וְהִפִּ֥יל פּוּר֙ ה֣וּא הַגּוֹרָ֔ל לְהֻמָּ֖ם וּֽלְאַבְּדָֽם׃ 25 וּבְבֹאָהּ֮ לִפְנֵ֣י הַמֶּלֶךְ֒ אָמַ֣ר עִם־הַסֵּ֔פֶר יָשׁ֞וּב מַחֲשַׁבְתּ֧וֹ הָרָעָ֛ה אֲשֶׁר־חָשַׁ֥ב עַל־הַיְּהוּדִ֖ים עַל־רֹאשׁ֑וֹ וְתָל֥וּ אֹת֛וֹ וְאֶת־בָּנָ֖יו עַל־הָעֵֽץ׃ 26 עַל־כֵּ֡ן קָֽרְאוּ֩ לַיָּמִ֨ים הָאֵ֤לֶּה פוּרִים֙ עַל־שֵׁ֣ם הַפּ֔וּר עַל־כֵּ֕ן עַל־כָּל־דִּבְרֵ֖י הָאִגֶּ֣רֶת הַזֹּ֑את וּמָֽה־רָא֣וּ עַל־כָּ֔כָה וּמָ֥ה הִגִּ֖יעַ אֲלֵיהֶֽם׃ 27 קִיְּמ֣וּ וקבל וְקִבְּל֣וּ הַיְּהוּדִים֩ ׀ עֲלֵיהֶ֨ם ׀ וְעַל־זַרְעָ֜ם וְעַ֨ל כָּל־הַנִּלְוִ֤ים עֲלֵיהֶם֙ וְלֹ֣א יַעֲב֔וֹר לִהְי֣וֹת עֹשִׂ֗ים אֵ֣ת שְׁנֵ֤י הַיָּמִים֙ הָאֵ֔לֶּה כִּכְתָבָ֖ם וְכִזְמַנָּ֑ם בְּכָל־שָׁנָ֖ה וְשָׁנָֽה׃ 28 וְהַיָּמִ֣ים הָ֠אֵלֶּה נִזְכָּרִ֨ים וְנַעֲשִׂ֜ים בְּכָל־דּ֣וֹר וָד֗וֹר מִשְׁפָּחָה֙ וּמִשְׁפָּחָ֔ה מְדִינָ֥ה

every province, and every city. And these days of Purim shall never cease among the Jews, and the memory of them shall never perish among their descendants.

²⁹ᶜThen Queen Esther daughter of Abihail wrote a second letter of Purim for the purpose of confirming with full authority the aforementioned one of Mordecai the Jew. ³⁰Dispatches were sent to all the Jews in the hundred and twenty-seven provinces of the realm of Ahasuerus with an ordinance of "equity and honesty:"ᵈ ³¹These days of Purim shall be observed at their proper time, as Mordecai the Jew—and now Queen Esther—has obligated them to do, and just as they have assumed for themselves and their descendants the obligation of the fasts with their lamentations.ᵉ

³²And Esther's ordinance validating these observances of Purim was recorded in a scroll.

10

King Ahasuerus imposed tribute on the mainland and the islands. ²All his mighty and powerful acts, and a full account of the greatness to which the king advanced Mordecai, are recorded in the Annals of the Kings of Media and Persia. ³For Mordecai the Jew ranked next to King Ahasuerus and was highly regarded by the Jews and popular with the multitude of his brethren; he sought the good of his people and interceded for the welfare of all his kindred.

וּמְדִינָה וְעִיר וָעִיר וִימֵי הַפּוּרִים הָאֵלֶּה לֹא יַעַבְרוּ מִתּוֹךְ הַיְּהוּדִים וְזִכְרָם לֹא־יָסוּף מִזַּרְעָם: ס
²⁹ וַתִּכְתֹּב אֶסְתֵּר הַמַּלְכָּה בַת־אֲבִיחַיִל וּמָרְדֳּכַי הַיְּהוּדִי אֶת־כָּל־תֹּקֶף לְקַיֵּם אֵת אִגֶּרֶת הַפֻּרִים הַזֹּאת הַשֵּׁנִית: ³⁰ וַיִּשְׁלַח סְפָרִים אֶל־כָּל־הַיְּהוּדִים אֶל־שֶׁבַע וְעֶשְׂרִים וּמֵאָה מְדִינָה מַלְכוּת אֲחַשְׁוֵרוֹשׁ דִּבְרֵי שָׁלוֹם וֶאֱמֶת: ³¹ לְקַיֵּם אֶת־יְמֵי הַפֻּרִים הָאֵלֶּה בִּזְמַנֵּיהֶם כַּאֲשֶׁר קִיַּם עֲלֵיהֶם מָרְדֳּכַי הַיְּהוּדִי וְאֶסְתֵּר הַמַּלְכָּה וְכַאֲשֶׁר קִיְּמוּ עַל־נַפְשָׁם וְעַל־זַרְעָם דִּבְרֵי הַצֹּמוֹת וְזַעֲקָתָם: ³² וּמַאֲמַר אֶסְתֵּר קִיַּם דִּבְרֵי הַפֻּרִים הָאֵלֶּה וְנִכְתָּב בַּסֵּפֶר: פ

י וַיָּשֶׂם הַמֶּלֶךְ אחשרש אֲחַשְׁוֵרוֹשׁ ׀ מַס עַל־הָאָרֶץ וְאִיֵּי הַיָּם: ² וְכָל־מַעֲשֵׂה תָקְפּוֹ וּגְבוּרָתוֹ וּפָרָשַׁת גְּדֻלַּת מָרְדֳּכַי אֲשֶׁר גִּדְּלוֹ הַמֶּלֶךְ הֲלוֹא־הֵם כְּתוּבִים עַל־סֵפֶר דִּבְרֵי הַיָּמִים לְמַלְכֵי מָדַי וּפָרָס: ³ כִּי ׀ מָרְדֳּכַי הַיְּהוּדִי מִשְׁנֶה לַמֶּלֶךְ אֲחַשְׁוֵרוֹשׁ וְגָדוֹל לַיְּהוּדִים וְרָצוּי לְרֹב אֶחָיו דֹּרֵשׁ טוֹב לְעַמּוֹ וְדֹבֵר שָׁלוֹם לְכָל־זַרְעוֹ: *

תם ונשלם תהילה לאל בורא עולם

ᶜ Force of vv. 29–31 uncertain in part. Verse 29 reads literally, "Then Queen Esther, daughter of Abihail, and Mordecai the Jew, wrote with full authority to confirm this second letter of Purim."

ᵈ I.e., of new holidays, the instituting of which is linked to love of equity and honesty in Zech. 8.19.

ᵉ The Jews had long been observing fast days in commemoration of national calamities; see Zech. 7.5; 8.19.

v. 3. סכום הפסוקים של ספר 167 (אף על פי שכתוב 168 בכתב היד שלנו) וחציו 5.7

DANIEL

1 In the third year of the reign of King Jehoiakim of Judah, King Nebuchadnezzar of Babylon came to Jerusalem and laid siege to it. [2]The Lord delivered King Jehoiakim of Judah into his power, together with some of the vessels of the House of God, and he brought them to the land of Shinar to the house of his god; he deposited the vessels in the treasury of his god. [3]Then the king ordered Ashpenaz, his chief officer, to bring some Israelites of royal descent and of the nobility—[4]youths without blemish, handsome, proficient in all wisdom, knowledgeable and intelligent, and capable of serving in the royal palace—and teach them the writings and the language of the Chaldeans. [5]The king allotted daily rations to them from the king's food and from the wine he drank. They were to be educated for three years, [a-]at the end of which they[-a] were to enter the king's service.

[6]Among them were the Judahites Daniel, Hananiah, Mishael and Azariah. [7]The chief officer gave them new names; he named Daniel Belteshazzar, Hananiah Shadrach, Mishael Meshach, and Azariah Abed-nego. [8]Daniel resolved not to defile himself with the king's food or the wine he drank, so he sought permission of the chief officer not to defile himself, [9]and God disposed the chief officer to be kind and compassionate toward Daniel. [10]The chief officer said to Daniel, "I fear that my lord the king, who allotted food and drink to you, will notice that you look out of sorts, unlike the other youths of your age—and you will put my

א בִּשְׁנַת שָׁלוֹשׁ לְמַלְכוּת יְהוֹיָקִים מֶלֶךְ־יְהוּדָה בָּא נְבוּכַדְנֶאצַּר מֶלֶךְ־בָּבֶל יְרוּשָׁלַם וַיָּצַר עָלֶיהָ: 2 וַיִּתֵּן אֲדֹנָי בְּיָדוֹ אֶת־יְהוֹיָקִים מֶלֶךְ־יְהוּדָה וּמִקְצָת כְּלֵי בֵית־הָאֱלֹהִים וַיְבִיאֵם אֶרֶץ־שִׁנְעָר בֵּית אֱלֹהָיו וְאֶת־הַכֵּלִים הֵבִיא בֵּית אוֹצַר אֱלֹהָיו: 3 וַיֹּאמֶר הַמֶּלֶךְ לְאַשְׁפְּנַז רַב סָרִיסָיו לְהָבִיא מִבְּנֵי יִשְׂרָאֵל וּמִזֶּרַע הַמְּלוּכָה וּמִן־הַפַּרְתְּמִים: 4 יְלָדִים אֲשֶׁר אֵין־בָּהֶם כָּל־מאום מוּם וְטוֹבֵי מַרְאֶה וּמַשְׂכִּילִים בְּכָל־חָכְמָה וְיֹדְעֵי דַעַת וּמְבִינֵי מַדָּע וַאֲשֶׁר כֹּחַ בָּהֶם לַעֲמֹד בְּהֵיכַל הַמֶּלֶךְ וּלְלַמְּדָם סֵפֶר וּלְשׁוֹן כַּשְׂדִּים: 5 וַיְמַן לָהֶם הַמֶּלֶךְ דְּבַר־יוֹם בְּיוֹמוֹ מִפַּת־בַּג הַמֶּלֶךְ וּמִיֵּין מִשְׁתָּיו וּלְגַדְּלָם שָׁנִים שָׁלוֹשׁ וּמִקְצָתָם יַעַמְדוּ לִפְנֵי הַמֶּלֶךְ: 6 וַיְהִי בָהֶם מִבְּנֵי יְהוּדָה דָּנִיֵּאל חֲנַנְיָה מִישָׁאֵל וַעֲזַרְיָה: 7 וַיָּשֶׂם לָהֶם שַׂר הַסָּרִיסִים שֵׁמוֹת וַיָּשֶׂם לְדָנִיֵּאל בֵּלְטְשַׁאצַּר וְלַחֲנַנְיָה שַׁדְרַךְ וּלְמִישָׁאֵל מֵישַׁךְ וְלַעֲזַרְיָה עֲבֵד נְגוֹ: 8 וַיָּשֶׂם דָּנִיֵּאל עַל־לִבּוֹ אֲשֶׁר לֹא־יִתְגָּאַל בְּפַתְבַּג הַמֶּלֶךְ וּבְיֵין מִשְׁתָּיו וַיְבַקֵּשׁ מִשַּׂר הַסָּרִיסִים אֲשֶׁר לֹא יִתְגָּאָל: 9 וַיִּתֵּן הָאֱלֹהִים אֶת־דָּנִיֵּאל לְחֶסֶד וּלְרַחֲמִים לִפְנֵי שַׂר הַסָּרִיסִים: 10 וַיֹּאמֶר שַׂר הַסָּרִיסִים לְדָנִיֵּאל יָרֵא אֲנִי אֶת־אֲדֹנִי הַמֶּלֶךְ אֲשֶׁר מִנָּה אֶת־מַאֲכַלְכֶם וְאֶת־מִשְׁתֵּיכֶם אֲשֶׁר לָמָּה יִרְאֶה אֶת־פְּנֵיכֶם זֹעֲפִים מִן־הַיְלָדִים אֲשֶׁר כְּגִילְכֶם

a-a Or "and some of them."

life[b] in jeopardy with the king." [11]Daniel replied to the guard whom the chief officer had put in charge of Daniel, Hananiah, Mishael and Azariah, [12]"Please test your servants for ten days, giving us legumes to eat and water to drink. [13]Then compare our appearance with that of the youths who eat of the king's food, and do with your servants as you see fit." [14]He agreed to this plan of theirs, and tested them for ten days. [15]When the ten days were over, they looked better and healthier than all the youths who were eating of the king's food. [16]So the guard kept on removing their food, and the wine they were supposed to drink, and gave them legumes. [17]God made all four of these young men intelligent and proficient in all writings and wisdom, and Daniel had understanding of visions and dreams of all kinds. [18]When the time the king had set for their presentation had come, the chief officer presented them to Nebuchadnezzar. [19]The king spoke with them, and of them all none was equal to Daniel, Hananiah, Mishael and Azariah; so these entered the king's service. [20]Whenever the king put a question to them requiring wisdom and understanding, he found them to be ten times better than all the magicians and exorcists throughout his realm. [21]Daniel was there until the first year of King Cyrus.

2 In the second year of the reign of Nebuchadnezzar, Nebuchadnezzar had a dream; his spirit was agitated, [a]-yet he was overcome by-[a] sleep. [2]The king ordered the magicians, exorcists, sorcerers, and Chaldeans to be summoned in order to tell the king what he had dreamed. They came and stood before the king, [3]and the king said to them, "I have had a dream and I am full

11 וְחִיַּבְתֶּ֥ם אֶת־רֹאשִׁ֖י לַמֶּ֑לֶךְ: וַיֹּ֣אמֶר דָּנִיֵּ֗אל אֶל־הַמֶּלְצַ֔ר אֲשֶׁ֤ר מִנָּה֙ שַׂ֣ר הַסָּֽרִיסִ֔ים עַל־דָּנִיֵּ֣אל חֲנַנְיָ֔ה מִֽישָׁאֵ֖ל וַעֲזַרְיָֽה: 12 נַס־נָ֥א אֶת־עֲבָדֶ֖יךָ יָמִ֣ים עֲשָׂרָ֑ה וְיִתְּנוּ־לָ֜נוּ מִן־הַזֵּרֹעִ֛ים וְנֹאכְלָ֖ה וּמַ֥יִם וְנִשְׁתֶּֽה: 13 וְיֵרָא֤וּ לְפָנֶ֨יךָ֙ מַרְאֵ֔ינוּ וּמַרְאֵה֙ הַיְלָדִ֔ים הָאֹ֣כְלִ֔ים אֵ֖ת פַּתְבַּ֣ג הַמֶּ֑לֶךְ וְכַאֲשֶׁ֣ר תִּרְאֵ֔ה עֲשֵׂ֖ה עִם־עֲבָדֶֽיךָ: 14 וַיִּשְׁמַ֥ע לָהֶ֖ם לַדָּבָ֣ר הַזֶּ֑ה וַיְנַסֵּ֖ם יָמִ֥ים עֲשָׂרָֽה: 15 וּמִקְצָת֙ יָמִ֣ים עֲשָׂרָ֔ה נִרְאָ֧ה מַרְאֵיהֶ֛ם ט֖וֹב וּבְרִיאֵ֣י בָּשָׂ֑ר מִן־כָּל־הַ֨יְלָדִ֔ים הָאֹ֣כְלִ֔ים אֵ֖ת פַּתְבַּ֥ג הַמֶּֽלֶךְ: 16 וַיְהִ֣י הַמֶּלְצַ֗ר נֹשֵׂא֙ אֶת־פַּתְבָּגָ֔ם וְיֵ֖ין מִשְׁתֵּיהֶ֑ם וְנֹתֵ֥ן לָהֶ֖ם זֵרְעֹנִֽים: 17 וְהַיְלָדִ֤ים הָאֵ֨לֶּה֙ אַרְבַּעְתָּ֔ם נָתַ֨ן לָהֶ֧ם הָאֱלֹהִ֛ים מַדָּ֥ע וְהַשְׂכֵּ֖ל בְּכָל־סֵ֣פֶר וְחָכְמָ֑ה וְדָנִיֵּ֣אל הֵבִ֔ין בְּכָל־חָז֖וֹן וַחֲלֹמֽוֹת: 18 וּלְמִקְצָת֙ הַיָּמִ֔ים אֲשֶׁר־אָמַ֥ר הַמֶּ֖לֶךְ לַהֲבִיאָ֑ם וַיְבִיאֵם֙ שַׂ֣ר הַסָּֽרִיסִ֔ים לִפְנֵ֖י נְבֻכַדְנֶצַּֽר: 19 וַיְדַבֵּ֣ר אִתָּם֮ הַמֶּלֶךְ֒ וְלֹ֤א נִמְצָא֙ מִכֻּלָּ֔ם כְּדָנִיֵּ֣אל חֲנַנְיָ֔ה מִֽישָׁאֵ֖ל וַעֲזַרְיָ֑ה וַיַּֽעַמְד֖וּ לִפְנֵ֥י הַמֶּֽלֶךְ: 20 וְכֹ֗ל דְּבַ֨ר חָכְמַ֤ת בִּינָה֙ אֲשֶׁר־בִּקֵּ֤שׁ מֵהֶם֙ הַמֶּ֔לֶךְ וַֽיִּמְצָאֵ֔ם עֶ֖שֶׂר יָד֑וֹת עַ֣ל כָּל־הַֽחַרְטֻמִּים֙ הָֽאַשָּׁפִ֔ים אֲשֶׁ֖ר בְּכָל־מַלְכוּתֽוֹ: 21 וַֽיְהִי֙ דָּנִיֵּ֔אל עַד־שְׁנַ֥ת אַחַ֖ת לְכ֥וֹרֶשׁ הַמֶּֽלֶךְ: פ

ב וּבִשְׁנַ֣ת שְׁתַּ֗יִם לְמַלְכוּת֙ נְבֻֽכַדְנֶצַּ֔ר חָלַ֥ם נְבֻֽכַדְנֶצַּ֖ר חֲלֹמ֑וֹת וַתִּתְפָּ֣עֶם רוּח֔וֹ וּשְׁנָת֖וֹ נִהְיְתָ֥ה עָלָֽיו: 2 וַיֹּ֣אמֶר הַמֶּ֗לֶךְ לִקְרֹ֤א לַֽחַרְטֻמִּים֙ וְלָ֣אַשָּׁפִ֔ים וְלַֽמְכַשְּׁפִ֖ים וְלַכַּשְׂדִּ֑ים לְהַגִּ֥יד לַמֶּ֖לֶךְ חֲלֹמֹתָ֑יו וַיָּבֹ֕אוּ וַיַּֽעַמְד֖וּ לִפְנֵ֥י הַמֶּֽלֶךְ: 3 וַיֹּ֧אמֶר לָהֶ֛ם הַמֶּ֖לֶךְ חֲל֣וֹם חָלָ֑מְתִּי וַתִּפָּ֥עֶם רוּחִ֖י לָדַ֥עַת אֶת־

---

b   *Lit. "head."*

a-a   *Meaning of Heb. uncertain; others "and he could not."*

of anxiety to know what I have dreamed." [4]The Chaldeans spoke to the king in Aramaic, "O king, live forever! Relate the dream to your servants, and we will tell its meaning." [5]The king said in reply to the Chaldeans, "I hereby decree: If you will not make the dream and its meaning known to me, you shall be torn limb from limb and your houses confiscated.[b] [6]But if you tell the dream and its meaning, you shall receive from me gifts, presents, and great honor; therefore, tell me the dream and its meaning." [7]Once again they answered, "Let the king relate the dream to his servants, and we will tell its meaning." [8]The king said in reply, "It is clear to me that you are playing for time, since you see that I have decreed [9]that if you do not make the dream known to me, there is but one verdict for you. You have conspired to tell me something false and fraudulent until circumstances change; so relate the dream to me, and I will then know that you can tell its meaning." [10]The Chaldeans said in reply to the king, "There is no one on earth who can [c-]satisfy the king's demand,[-c] for great king or ruler—none has ever asked such a thing of any magician, exorcist, or Chaldean. [11]The thing asked by the king is difficult; there is no one who can tell it to the king except the gods whose abode is not among mortals."[d] [12]Whereupon the king flew into a violent rage, and gave an order to do away with all the wise men of Babylon.

[13]The decree condemning the wise men to death was issued. Daniel and his companions were about to be put to death [14]when Daniel remonstrated with Arioch, the captain of the royal guard who had set out to put the wise men of Babylon to death. [15]He spoke up and said to Arioch, the royal officer, "Why is the decree of the king so urgent?" Thereupon Arioch informed Daniel of the matter. [16]So Daniel went

b   *Meaning uncertain; or "turned into ruins."*
c-c *Lit. "tell the king's matter."*
d   *Lit. "flesh."*

הַחֲלוֹם: 4 וַיְדַבְּרוּ הַכַּשְׂדִּים לַמֶּלֶךְ אֲרָמִית מַלְכָּא לְעָלְמִין חֱיִי אֱמַר חֶלְמָא לְעַבְדָיךְ וּפִשְׁרָא נְחַוֵּא: 5 עָנֵה מַלְכָּא וְאָמַר לְכַשְׂדָּיֵא מִלְּתָא מִנִּי אַזְדָּא הֵן לָא תְהוֹדְעוּנַּנִי חֶלְמָא וּפִשְׁרֵהּ הַדָּמִין תִּתְעַבְדוּן וּבָתֵּיכוֹן נְוָלִי יִתְּשָׂמוּן: 6 וְהֵן חֶלְמָא וּפִשְׁרֵהּ תְּהַחֲוֺן מַתְּנָן וּנְבִזְבָּה וִיקָר שַׂגִּיא תְּקַבְּלוּן מִן־קֳדָמָי לָהֵן חֶלְמָא וּפִשְׁרֵהּ הַחֲוֺנִי: 7 עֲנוֹ תִנְיָנוּת וְאָמְרִין מַלְכָּא חֶלְמָא יֵאמַר לְעַבְדוֹהִי וּפִשְׁרָה נְהַחֲוֵה: 8 עָנֵה מַלְכָּא וְאָמַר מִן־יַצִּיב יָדַע אֲנָה דִּי עִדָּנָא אַנְתּוּן זָבְנִין כָּל־קֳבֵל דִּי חֲזֵיתוֹן דִּי אַזְדָּא מִנִּי מִלְּתָא: 9 דִּי הֵן־חֶלְמָא לָא תְהוֹדְעֻנַּנִי חֲדָה־הִיא דָתְכוֹן וּמִלָּה כִדְבָה וּשְׁחִיתָה הִזְמִנְתּוּן לְמֵאמַר קֳדָמַי עַד דִּי עִדָּנָא יִשְׁתַּנֵּא לָהֵן חֶלְמָא אֱמַרוּ לִי וְאִנְדַּע דִּי פִשְׁרֵהּ תְּהַחֲוֻנַּנִי: 10 עֲנוֹ כַשְׂדָּיֵא קֳדָם־מַלְכָּא וְאָמְרִין לָא־אִיתַי אֱנָשׁ עַל־יַבֶּשְׁתָּא דִּי מִלַּת מַלְכָּא יוּכַל לְהַחֲוָיָה כָּל־קֳבֵל דִּי כָּל־מֶלֶךְ רַב וְשַׁלִּיט מִלָּה כִדְנָה לָא שְׁאֵל לְכָל־חַרְטֹם וְאָשַׁף וְכַשְׂדָּי: 11 וּמִלְּתָא דִי־מַלְכָּה שָׁאֵל יַקִּירָה וְאָחֳרָן לָא אִיתַי דִּי יְחַוִּנַּהּ קֳדָם מַלְכָּא לָהֵן אֱלָהִין דִּי מְדָרְהוֹן עִם־בִּשְׂרָא לָא אִיתוֹהִי: 12 כָּל־קֳבֵל דְּנָה מַלְכָּא בְּנַס וּקְצַף שַׂגִּיא וַאֲמַר לְהוֹבָדָה לְכֹל חַכִּימֵי בָבֶל: 13 וְדָתָא נֶפְקַת וְחַכִּימַיָּא מִתְקַטְּלִין וּבְעוֹ דָּנִיֵּאל וְחַבְרוֹהִי לְהִתְקְטָלָה: פ 14 בֵּאדַיִן דָּנִיֵּאל הֲתִיב עֵטָא וּטְעֵם לְאַרְיוֹךְ רַב־טַבָּחַיָּא דִּי מַלְכָּא דִּי נְפַק לְקַטָּלָה לְחַכִּימֵי בָּבֶל: 15 עָנֵה וְאָמַר לְאַרְיוֹךְ שַׁלִּיטָא דִי־מַלְכָּא עַל־מָה דָתָא מְהַחְצְפָה מִן־קֳדָם מַלְכָּא אֱדַיִן מִלְּתָא הוֹדַע אַרְיוֹךְ

to ask the king for time, that he might tell the meaning to the king. [17]Then Daniel went to his house and informed his companions, Hananiah, Mishael, and Azariah, of the matter,[18]that they might implore the God of Heaven for help regarding this mystery, so that Daniel and his colleagues would not be put to death together with the other wise men of Babylon.

[19]The mystery was revealed to Daniel in a night vision; then Daniel blessed the God of Heaven. [20]Daniel spoke up and said:

"Let the name of God be blessed forever and
    ever,
For wisdom and power are His.
[21]He changes times and seasons,
Removes kings and installs kings;
He gives the wise their wisdom
And knowledge to those who know.
[22]He reveals deep and hidden things,
Knows what is in the darkness,
And light dwells with Him.
[23]I acknowledge and praise You,
O God of my fathers,
You who have given me wisdom and power,
For now You have let me know what we asked
    of You;
You have let us know what concerns the
    king."

[24]Thereupon Daniel went to Arioch, whom the king had appointed to do away with the wise men of Babylon; he came and said to him as follows, "Do not do away with the wise men of Babylon; bring me to the king and I will tell the king the meaning!" [25]So Arioch rushed Daniel into the king's presence and said to him, "I have found among the exiles of Judah a man who can make the meaning known to the king!" [26]The king said in reply to Daniel (who was called Belteshazzar), "Can you really make known to me the dream that I saw and its meaning?" [27]Daniel answered the king and said, "The mystery about

לְדָנִיֵּאל: 16 וְדָנִיֵּאל עַל וּבְעָה מִן־מַלְכָּא
דִּי זְמָן יִנְתֶּן־לֵהּ וּפִשְׁרָא לְהַחֲוָיָה
לְמַלְכָּא: פ 17 אֱדַיִן דָּנִיֵּאל לְבַיְתֵהּ אֲזַל
וְלַחֲנַנְיָה מִישָׁאֵל וַעֲזַרְיָה חַבְרוֹהִי מִלְּתָא
הוֹדַע: 18 וְרַחֲמִין לְמִבְעֵא מִן־קֳדָם אֱלָהּ
שְׁמַיָּא עַל־רָזָה דְּנָה דִּי לָא יְהֹבְדוּן דָּנִיֵּאל
וְחַבְרוֹהִי עִם־שְׁאָר חַכִּימֵי בָבֶל:
19 אֱדַיִן לְדָנִיֵּאל בְּחֶזְוָא דִי־לֵילְיָא רָזָה גֲלִי
אֱדַיִן דָּנִיֵּאל בָּרִךְ לֶאֱלָהּ שְׁמַיָּא: 20 עָנֵה
דָנִיֵּאל וְאָמַר
לֶהֱוֵא שְׁמֵהּ דִּי־אֱלָהָא מְבָרַךְ מִן־עָלְמָא
    וְעַד־עָלְמָא
דִּי חָכְמְתָא וּגְבוּרְתָא דִּי לֵהּ־הִיא:
21 וְהוּא מְהַשְׁנֵא עִדָּנַיָּא וְזִמְנַיָּא
מְהַעְדֵּה מַלְכִין וּמְהָקֵים מַלְכִין
יָהֵב חָכְמְתָא לְחַכִּימִין
וּמַנְדְּעָא לְיָדְעֵי בִינָה:
22 הוּא גָּלֵא עַמִּיקָתָא וּמְסַתְּרָתָא
יָדַע מָה בַחֲשׁוֹכָא
וּנְהִירָא וּנְהוֹרָא עִמֵּהּ שְׁרֵא:
23 לָךְ ׀ אֱלָהּ אֲבָהָתִי
מְהוֹדֵא וּמְשַׁבַּח אֲנָה
דִּי חָכְמְתָא וּגְבוּרְתָא יְהַבְתְּ לִי
וּכְעַן הוֹדַעְתַּנִי דִּי־בְעֵינָא מִנָּךְ
דִּי־מִלַּת מַלְכָּא הוֹדַעְתֶּנָא:
24 כָּל־קֳבֵל דְּנָה דָּנִיֵּאל עַל עַל־אַרְיוֹךְ דִּי
מַנִּי מַלְכָּא לְהוֹבָדָה לְחַכִּימֵי בָבֶל אֲזַל ׀
וְכֵן אֲמַר־לֵהּ לְחַכִּימֵי בָבֶל אַל־תְּהוֹבֵד
הַעֵלַנִי קֳדָם מַלְכָּא וּפִשְׁרָא לְמַלְכָּא
אֲחַוֵּא: ס 25 אֱדַיִן אַרְיוֹךְ בְּהִתְבְּהָלָה
הַנְעֵל לְדָנִיֵּאל קֳדָם מַלְכָּא וְכֵן אֲמַר־לֵהּ
דִּי־הַשְׁכַּחַת גְּבַר מִן־בְּנֵי גָלוּתָא דִּי יְהוּד
דִּי פִשְׁרָא לְמַלְכָּא יְהוֹדַע: 26 עָנֵה מַלְכָּא
וְאָמַר לְדָנִיֵּאל דִּי שְׁמֵהּ בֵּלְטְשַׁאצַּר
הַאִיתָךְ כָּהֵל לְהוֹדַעֻתַנִי חֶלְמָא
דִי־חֲזֵית וּפִשְׁרֵהּ: 27 עָנֵה דָנִיֵּאל קֳדָם

which the king has inquired—wise men, exorcists, magicians, and diviners cannot tell to the king. [28]But there is a God in heaven who reveals mysteries, and He has made known to King Nebuchadnezzar what is to be at the end of days. This is your dream and the vision that entered your mind in bed: [29]O king, the thoughts that came to your mind in your bed are about future events; He who reveals mysteries has let you know what is to happen. [30]Not because my wisdom is greater than that of other creatures has this mystery been revealed to me, but in order that the meaning should be made known to the king, and that you may know the thoughts of your mind.

[31]"O king, as you looked on, there appeared a great statue. This statue, which was huge and its brightness surpassing, stood before you, and its appearance was awesome. [32]The head of that statue was of fine gold; its breast and arms were of silver; its belly and thighs, of bronze; [33]its legs were of iron, and its feet part iron and part clay. [34]As you looked on, a stone was hewn out, not by hands, and struck the statue on its feet of iron and clay and crushed them. [35]All at once, the iron, clay, bronze, silver, and gold were crushed, and became like chaff of the threshing floors of summer; a wind carried them off until no trace of them was left. But the stone that struck the statue became a great mountain and filled the whole earth.

[36]"Such was the dream, and we will now tell the king its meaning. [37]You, O king—king of kings, to whom the God of Heaven has given kingdom, power, might, and glory; [38]into whose hands He has given men, wild beasts, and the fowl of heaven, wherever they may dwell; and to whom He has given dominion over them all—you are the head of gold. [39]But another kingdom will arise after you, inferior to yours; then yet a third kingdom, of bronze, which will

מַלְכָּא וְאָמַר רָזָה דִּי־מַלְכָּא שָׁאֵל לָא
חַכִּימִין אָשְׁפִין חַרְטֻמִּין גָּזְרִין יָכְלִין
לְהַחֲוָיָה לְמַלְכָּא: 28 בְּרַם אִיתַי אֱלָהּ
בִּשְׁמַיָּא גָּלֵא רָזִין וְהוֹדַע לְמַלְכָּא
נְבוּכַדְנֶצַּר מָה דִּי לֶהֱוֵא בְּאַחֲרִית יוֹמַיָּא
חֶלְמָךְ וְחֶזְוֵי רֵאשָׁךְ עַל־מִשְׁכְּבָךְ דְּנָה
הוּא: פ 29 אנתה אַנְתְּ מַלְכָּא רַעְיוֹנָךְ
עַל־מִשְׁכְּבָךְ סְלִקוּ מָה דִּי לֶהֱוֵא אַחֲרֵי
דְנָה וְגָלֵא רָזַיָּא הוֹדְעָךְ מָה־דִי לֶהֱוֵא:
30 וַאֲנָה לָא בְחָכְמָה דִּי־אִיתַי בִּי מִן־כָּל־
חַיַּיָּא רָזָא דְנָה גֱּלִי לִי לָהֵן עַל־דִּבְרַת דִּי
פִשְׁרָא לְמַלְכָּא יְהוֹדְעוּן וְרַעְיוֹנֵי לִבְבָךְ
תִּנְדַּע:

31 אנתה אַנְתְּ מַלְכָּא חָזֵה הֲוַיְתָ וַאֲלוּ צְלֵם
חַד שַׂגִּיא צַלְמָא דִּכֵּן רַב וְזִיוֵהּ יַתִּיר קָאֵם
לְקָבְלָךְ וְרֵוֵהּ דְּחִיל: 32 הוּא צַלְמָא רֵאשֵׁהּ
דִּי־דְהַב טָב חֲדוֹהִי וּדְרָעוֹהִי דִּי כְסַף
מְעוֹהִי וְיַרְכָתֵהּ דִּי נְחָשׁ: 33 שָׁקוֹהִי דִּי
פַרְזֶל רַגְלוֹהִי מנהון מִנְּהֵין דִּי פַרְזֶל וּמִנְּהוֹן
וּמִנְּהֵין דִּי חֲסַף: 34 חָזֵה הֲוַיְתָ עַד דִּי
הִתְגְּזֶרֶת אֶבֶן דִּי־לָא בִידַיִן וּמְחָת לְצַלְמָא
עַל־רַגְלוֹהִי דִּי פַרְזְלָא וְחַסְפָּא וְהַדֵּקֶת
הִמּוֹן: 35 בֵּאדַיִן דָּקוּ כַחֲדָה פַּרְזְלָא חַסְפָּא
נְחָשָׁא כַּסְפָּא וְדַהֲבָא וַהֲווֹ כְּעוּר מִן־אִדְּרֵי־
קַיִט וּנְשָׂא הִמּוֹן רוּחָא וְכָל־אֲתַר לָא־
הִשְׁתֲּכַח לְהוֹן וְאַבְנָא ׀ דִּי־מְחָת לְצַלְמָא
הֲוָת לְטוּר רַב וּמְלָת כָּל־אַרְעָא:
36 דְּנָה חֶלְמָא וּפִשְׁרֵהּ נֵאמַר קֳדָם־מַלְכָּא:
37 אנתה אַנְתְּ מַלְכָּא מֶלֶךְ מַלְכַיָּא דִּי אֱלָהּ
שְׁמַיָּא מַלְכוּתָא חִסְנָא וְתָקְפָּא וִיקָרָא
יְהַב־לָךְ: 38 וּבְכָל־דִּי דארין דָאְרִין בְּנֵי־
אֲנָשָׁא חֵיוַת בָּרָא וְעוֹף־שְׁמַיָּא יְהַב בִּידָךְ
וְהַשְׁלְטָךְ בְּכָלְּהוֹן אנתה אַנְתְּ־הוּא רֵאשָׁה
דִּי דַהֲבָא: 39 וּבָתְרָךְ תְּקוּם מַלְכוּ אָחֳרִי
אֲרַע* מִנָּךְ וּמַלְכוּ תליתיא תְלִיתָאָה
אָחֳרִי דִּי נְחָשָׁא דִּי תִשְׁלַט בְּכָל־אַרְעָא:

rule over the whole earth. ⁴⁰But the fourth kingdom will be as strong as iron; just as iron crushes and shatters everything—and like iron that smashes—so will it crush and smash all these. ⁴¹You saw the feet and the toes, part potter's clay and part iron; that means it will be a divided kingdom; it will have only some of the stability of iron, inasmuch as you saw iron mixed with common clay. ⁴²And the toes were part iron and part clay; that [means] the kingdom will be in part strong and in part brittle. ⁴³You saw iron mixed with common clay; that means: *e-*they shall intermingle with the offspring of men,*-e* but shall not hold together, just as iron does not mix with clay. ⁴⁴And in the time of those kings, the God of Heaven will establish a kingdom that shall never be destroyed, a kingdom that shall not be transferred to another people. It will crush and wipe out all these kingdoms, but shall itself last forever—⁴⁵just as you saw how a stone was hewn from the mountain, not by hands, and crushed the iron, bronze, clay, silver, and gold. The great God has made known to the king what will happen in the future. The dream is sure and its interpretation reliable."

⁴⁶Then King Nebuchadnezzar prostrated himself and paid homage to Daniel and ordered that a meal offering and pleasing offerings be made to him. ⁴⁷The king said in reply to Daniel, "Truly your God must be the God of gods and Lord of kings and the revealer of mysteries to have enabled you to reveal this mystery." ⁴⁸The king then elevated Daniel and gave him very many gifts, and made him governor of the whole province of Babylon and chief prefect of all the wise men of Babylon. ⁴⁹At Daniel's request, the king appointed Shadrach, Meshach, and Abed-nego to administer the province of Babylon; while Daniel himself was at the king's court.

---

e-e Meaning uncertain.

⁴⁰ וּמַלְכוּ רְבִיעָיָה תֶּהֱוֵא תַקִּיפָה
כְּפַרְזְלָא כָּל־קֳבֵל דִּי פַרְזְלָא מְהַדֵּק וְחָשֵׁל
כֹּלָּא וּכְפַרְזְלָא דִּי־מְרָעַע כָּל־אִלֵּין תַּדִּק
וְתֵרֹעַ: ⁴¹ וְדִי־חֲזַיְתָה רַגְלַיָּא וְאֶצְבְּעָתָא
מִנְּהוֹן מִנְּהֵין חֲסַף דִּי־פֶחָר וּמִנְּהוֹן וּמִנְּהֵין
פַּרְזֶל מַלְכוּ פְלִיגָה תֶּהֱוֵה וּמִן־נִצְבְּתָא דִי
פַרְזְלָא לֶהֱוֵא־בַהּ כָּל־קֳבֵל דִּי חֲזַיְתָה
פַּרְזְלָא מְעָרַב בַּחֲסַף טִינָא: ⁴² וְאֶצְבְּעָת
רַגְלַיָּא מִנְּהוֹן מִנְּהֵין פַּרְזֶל וּמִנְּהוֹן וּמִנְּהֵין
חֲסַף מִן־קְצָת מַלְכוּתָא תֶּהֱוֵה תַקִּיפָה
וּמִנַּהּ תֶּהֱוֵה תְבִירָה: ⁴³ דִּי וְדִי חֲזַיְת
פַּרְזְלָא מְעָרַב בַּחֲסַף טִינָא מִתְעָרְבִין לֶהֱוֹן
בִּזְרַע אֲנָשָׁא וְלָא־לֶהֱוֹן דָּבְקִין דְּנָה עִם־
דְּנָה הֵא־כְדִי פַרְזְלָא לָא מִתְעָרַב עִם־
חַסְפָּא: ⁴⁴ וּבְיוֹמֵיהוֹן דִּי מַלְכַיָּא אִנּוּן יְקִים
אֱלָהּ שְׁמַיָּא מַלְכוּ דִּי לְעָלְמִין לָא תִתְחַבַּל
וּמַלְכוּתָה לְעַם אָחֳרָן לָא תִשְׁתְּבִק תַּדִּק
וְתָסֵיף כָּל־אִלֵּין מַלְכְוָתָא וְהִיא תְּקוּם
לְעָלְמַיָּא: ⁴⁵ כָּל־קֳבֵל דִּי־חֲזַיְת דִּי מִטּוּרָא
אִתְגְּזֶרֶת אֶבֶן דִּי־לָא בִידַיִן וְהַדֵּקֶת פַּרְזְלָא
נְחָשָׁא חַסְפָּא כַּסְפָּא וְדַהֲבָא אֱלָהּ רַב
הוֹדַע לְמַלְכָּא מָה דִּי לֶהֱוֵא אַחֲרֵי דְנָה
וְיַצִּיב חֶלְמָא וּמְהֵימַן פִּשְׁרֵהּ: פ
⁴⁶ בֵּאדַיִן מַלְכָּא נְבוּכַדְנֶצַּר נְפַל עַל־
אַנְפּוֹהִי וּלְדָנִיֵּאל סְגִד וּמִנְחָה וְנִיחֹחִין
אֲמַר לְנַסָּכָה לֵהּ: ⁴⁷ עָנֵה מַלְכָּא לְדָנִיֵּאל
וְאָמַר מִן־קְשֹׁט דִּי אֱלָהֲכוֹן הוּא אֱלָהּ
אֱלָהִין וּמָרֵא מַלְכִין וְגָלֵה רָזִין דִּי יְכֵלְתָּ
לְמִגְלֵא רָזָה דְנָה: ⁴⁸ אֱדַיִן מַלְכָּא לְדָנִיֵּאל
רַבִּי וּמַתְּנָן רַבְרְבָן שַׂגִּיאָן יְהַב־לֵהּ
וְהַשְׁלְטֵהּ עַל כָּל־מְדִינַת בָּבֶל וְרַב־סִגְנִין
עַל כָּל־חַכִּימֵי בָבֶל: ⁴⁹ וְדָנִיֵּאל בְּעָא מִן־
מַלְכָּא וּמַנִּי עַל עֲבִידְתָּא דִּי מְדִינַת בָּבֶל
לְשַׁדְרַךְ מֵישַׁךְ וַעֲבֵד נְגוֹ וְדָנִיֵּאל בִּתְרַע
מַלְכָּא: פ

3 King Nebuchadnezzar made a statue of gold sixty cubits high and six cubits broad. He set it up in the plain of Dura in the province of Babylon. [2]King Nebuchadnezzar then sent word to gather the satraps, prefects, governors, counselors, treasurers, judges, officers, and all the provincial officials to attend the dedication of the statue that King Nebuchadnezzar had set up. [3]So the satraps, prefects, governors, counselors, treasurers, judges, officers, and all the provincial officials assembled for the dedication of the statue that King Nebuchadnezzar had set up, and stood before the statue that Nebuchadnezzar had set up. [4]The herald proclaimed in a loud voice, "You are commanded, O peoples and nations of every language, [5]when you hear the sound of the horn, pipe, zither, lyre, psaltery, bagpipe, and all other types of instruments, to fall down and worship the statue of gold that King Nebuchadnezzar has set up. [6]Whoever will not fall down and worship shall at once be thrown into a burning fiery furnace." [7]And so, as soon as all the peoples heard the sound of the horn, pipe, zither, lyre, psaltery, and all other types of instruments, all peoples and nations of every language fell down and worshiped the statue of gold that King Nebuchadnezzar had set up.

[8]Seizing the occasion, certain Chaldeans came forward to slander the Jews. [9]They spoke up and said to King Nebuchadnezzar, "O king, live forever! [10]You, O king, gave an order that everyone who hears the horn, pipe, zither, lyre, psaltery, bagpipe, and all types of instruments must fall down and worship the golden statue, [11]and whoever does not fall down and worship shall be thrown into a burning fiery furnace.

ג נְבוּכַדְנֶצַּר מַלְכָּא עֲבַד צְלֵם דִּי־דְהַב
רוּמֵהּ אַמִּין שִׁתִּין פְּתָיֵהּ אַמִּין שֵׁת
אֲקִימֵהּ בְּבִקְעַת דּוּרָא בִּמְדִינַת בָּבֶל:
2 וּנְבוּכַדְנֶצַּר מַלְכָּא שְׁלַח לְמִכְנַשׁ |
לַאֲחַשְׁדַּרְפְּנַיָּא סִגְנַיָּא וּפַחֲוָתָא אֲדַרְגָּזְרַיָּא
גְדָבְרַיָּא דְּתָבְרַיָּא תִּפְתָּיֵא וְכֹל שִׁלְטֹנֵי
מְדִינָתָא לְמֵתֵא לַחֲנֻכַּת צַלְמָא דִּי הֲקֵים
נְבוּכַדְנֶצַּר מַלְכָּא: 3 בֵּאדַיִן מִתְכַּנְּשִׁין
אֲחַשְׁדַּרְפְּנַיָּא סִגְנַיָּא וּפַחֲוָתָא אֲדַרְגָּזְרַיָּא
גְדָבְרַיָּא דְּתָבְרַיָּא תִּפְתָּיֵא וְכֹל שִׁלְטֹנֵי
מְדִינָתָא לַחֲנֻכַּת צַלְמָא דִּי הֲקֵים
נְבוּכַדְנֶצַּר מַלְכָּא וקאמין וְקָיְמִין לָקֳבֵל
צַלְמָא דִּי הֲקֵים נְבוּכַדְנֶצַּר: 4 וְכָרוֹזָא קָרֵא
בְחָיִל לְכוֹן אָמְרִין עַמְמַיָּא אֻמַּיָּא
וְלִשָּׁנַיָּא: 5 בְּעִדָּנָא דִּי־תִשְׁמְעוּן קָל קַרְנָא
מַשְׁרוֹקִיתָא קיתרוס קַתְרוֹס סַבְּכָא
פְסַנְתֵּרִין סוּמְפֹּנְיָה וְכֹל זְנֵי זְמָרָא תִּפְּלוּן
וְתִסְגְּדוּן לְצֶלֶם דַּהֲבָא דִּי הֲקֵים
נְבוּכַדְנֶצַּר מַלְכָּא: 6 וּמַן־דִּי־לָא יִפֵּל וְיִסְגֻּד
בַּהּ־שַׁעֲתָא יִתְרְמֵא לְגוֹא־אַתּוּן נוּרָא
יָקִדְתָּא: 7 כָּל־קֳבֵל דְּנָה בֵּהּ־זִמְנָא כְּדִי
שָׁמְעִין כָּל־עַמְמַיָּא קָל קַרְנָא מַשְׁרוֹקִיתָא
קיתרס קַתְרוֹס שַׂבְּכָא פְּסַנְטֵרִין וְכֹל זְנֵי
זְמָרָא נָפְלִין כָּל־עַמְמַיָּא אֻמַיָּא וְלִשָׁנַיָּא
סָגְדִין לְצֶלֶם דַּהֲבָא דִּי הֲקֵים נְבוּכַדְנֶצַּר
מַלְכָּא:

8 כָּל־קֳבֵל דְּנָה בֵּהּ־זִמְנָא קְרִבוּ גֻּבְרִין
כַּשְׂדָּאִין וַאֲכַלוּ קַרְצֵיהוֹן דִּי יְהוּדָיֵא:
9 עֲנוֹ וְאָמְרִין לִנְבוּכַדְנֶצַּר מַלְכָּא מַלְכָּא
לְעָלְמִין חֱיִי: 10 אנתה אַנְתְּ מַלְכָּא שָׂמְתָּ
טְּעֵם דִּי כָל־אֱנָשׁ דִּי־יִשְׁמַע קָל קַרְנָא
מַשְׁרֹקִיתָא קיתרס קַתְרוֹס שַׂבְּכָא
פְסַנְתֵּרִין וסיפניה וְסוּפֹּנְיָה וְכֹל זְנֵי זְמָרָא
יִפֵּל וְיִסְגֻּד לְצֶלֶם דַּהֲבָא: 11 וּמַן־דִּי־לָא
יִפֵּל וְיִסְגֻּד יִתְרְמֵא לְגוֹא־אַתּוּן נוּרָא

12There are certain Jews whom you appointed to administer the province of Babylon, Shadrach, Meshach, and Abed-nego; those men pay no heed to you, O king; they do not serve your god or worship the statue of gold that you have set up."

13Then Nebuchadnezzar, in raging fury, ordered Shadrach, Meshach, and Abed-nego to be brought; so those men were brought before the king. 14Nebuchadnezzar spoke to them and said, "Is it true, Shadrach, Meshach, and Abed-nego, that you do not serve my god or worship the statue of gold that I have set up? 15Now if you are ready to fall down and worship the statue that I have made when you hear the sound of the horn, pipe, zither, lyre, psaltery, and bagpipe, and all other types of instruments, [well and good]; but if you will not worship, you shall at once be thrown into a burning fiery furnace, and what god is there that can save you from my power?" 16Shadrach, Meshach, and Abed-nego said in reply to the king, "O Nebuchadnezzar, we have no need to answer you in this matter, 17for if so it must be, our God whom we serve is able to save us from the burning fiery furnace, and He will save us from your power, O king. 18But even if He does not, be it known to you, O king, that we will not serve your god or worship the statue of gold that you have set up."

19Nebuchadnezzar was so filled with rage at Shadrach, Meshach, and Abed-nego that his visage was distorted, and he gave an order to heat up the furnace to seven times its usual heat. 20He commanded some of the strongest men of his army to bind Shadrach, Meshach, and Abed-nego, and to throw them into the burning fiery furnace. 21So these men, in their shirts, trousers, hats, and other garments, were bound and thrown into the burning fiery furnace. 22Be-

יְקַדְתָּא: 12 אִיתַי גֻּבְרִין יְהוּדָאיִן דִּי־מַנִּיתָ
יָתְהוֹן עַל־עֲבִידַת מְדִינַת בָּבֶל שַׁדְרַךְ
מֵישַׁךְ וַעֲבֵד נְגוֹ גֻּבְרַיָּא אִלֵּךְ לָא־שָׂמוּ
עֲלָיךְ מַלְכָּא טְעֵם לֵאלָהָיךְ לָא פָלְחִין וּלְצֶלֶם דַּהֲבָא דִּי הֲקֵימְתָּ לָא
סָגְדִין: ס

13 בֵּאדַיִן נְבוּכַדְנֶצַּר בִּרְגַז וַחֲמָה אֲמַר
לְהַיְתָיָה לְשַׁדְרַךְ מֵישַׁךְ וַעֲבֵד נְגוֹ בֵּאדַיִן
גֻּבְרַיָּא אִלֵּךְ הֵיתָיוּ קֳדָם מַלְכָּא: 14 עָנֵה
נְבֻכַדְנֶצַּר וְאָמַר לְהוֹן הַצְדָּא שַׁדְרַךְ מֵישַׁךְ
וַעֲבֵד נְגוֹ לֵאלָהַי לָא אִיתֵיכוֹן פָּלְחִין
וּלְצֶלֶם דַּהֲבָא דִּי הֲקֵימֵת לָא סָגְדִין:
15 כְּעַן הֵן אִיתֵיכוֹן עֲתִידִין דִּי בְעִדָּנָא
דִּי־תִשְׁמְעוּן קָל קַרְנָא מַשְׁרוֹקִיתָא קיתרס
קַתְרוֹס שַׂבְּכָא פְּסַנְתֵּרִין וְסוּמְפֹּנְיָה וְכֹל |
זְנֵי זְמָרָא תִּפְּלוּן וְתִסְגְּדוּן לְצַלְמָא דִּי־
עַבְדֵת וְהֵן לָא תִסְגְּדוּן בַּהּ־שַׁעֲתָה
תִתְרְמוֹן לְגוֹא־אַתּוּן נוּרָא יָקִדְתָּא וּמַן־
הוּא אֱלָהּ דִּי יְשֵׁיזְבִנְכוֹן מִן־יְדָי: 16 עֲנוֹ
שַׁדְרַךְ מֵישַׁךְ וַעֲבֵד נְגוֹ וְאָמְרִין לְמַלְכָּא
נְבוּכַדְנֶצַּר לָא־חַשְׁחִין אֲנַחְנָה עַל־דְּנָה
פִּתְגָם לַהֲתָבוּתָךְ: 17 הֵן אִיתַי אֱלָהַנָא
דִּי־אֲנַחְנָא פָלְחִין יָכִל לְשֵׁיזָבוּתַנָא מִן־
אַתּוּן נוּרָא יָקִדְתָּא וּמִן־יְדָךְ מַלְכָּא
יְשֵׁיזִב: 18 וְהֵן לָא יְדִיעַ לֶהֱוֵא־לָךְ מַלְכָּא
דִּי לֵאלָהָיךְ* לָא־אִיתַנָא פָלְחִין
וּלְצֶלֶם דַּהֲבָא דִּי הֲקֵימְתָּ לָא נִסְגֻּד: ס

19 בֵּאדַיִן נְבוּכַדְנֶצַּר הִתְמְלִי חֱמָא וּצְלֵם
אַנְפּוֹהִי אשתנו אֶשְׁתַּנִּי עַל־שַׁדְרַךְ מֵישַׁךְ
וַעֲבֵד נְגוֹ עָנֵה וְאָמַר לְמֵזֵא לְאַתּוּנָא
חַד־שִׁבְעָה עַל דִּי חֲזֵה לְמֵזְיֵהּ: 20 וּלְגֻבְרִין
גִּבָּרֵי־חַיִל דִּי בְחַילֵהּ אֲמַר לְכַפָּתָה
לְשַׁדְרַךְ מֵישַׁךְ וַעֲבֵד נְגוֹ לְמִרְמֵא לְאַתּוּן
נוּרָא יָקִדְתָּא: 21 בֵּאדַיִן גֻּבְרַיָּא אִלֵּךְ
כְּפִתוּ בְּסַרְבָּלֵיהוֹן פטישיהון פַּטְּשֵׁיהוֹן
וְכַרְבְּלָתְהוֹן וּלְבֻשֵׁיהוֹן וּרְמִיו לְגוֹא־אַתּוּן

cause the king's order was urgent, and the furnace was heated to excess, a tongue of flame killed the men who carried up Shadrach, Meshach, and Abed-nego. ²³But those three men, Shadrach, Meshach, and Abed-nego, dropped, bound, into the burning fiery furnace.

²⁴Then King Nebuchadnezzar was astonished and, rising in haste, addressed his companions, saying, "Did we not throw three men, bound, into the fire?" They spoke in reply, "Surely, O king." ²⁵He answered, "But I see four men walking about unbound and unharmed in the fire and the fourth looks like a divine being." ²⁶Nebuchadnezzar then approached the hatch of the burning fiery furnace and called, "Shadrach, Meshach, Abed-nego, servants of the Most High God, come out!" So Shadrach, Meshach, and Abed-nego came out of the fire. ²⁷The satraps, the prefects, the governors, and the royal companions gathered around to look at those men, on whose bodies the fire had had no effect, the hair of whose heads had not been singed, whose shirts looked no different, to whom not even the odor of fire clung. ²⁸Nebuchadnezzar spoke up and said, "Blessed be the God of Shadrach, Meshach, and Abed-nego, who sent His angel to save His servants who, trusting in Him, flouted the king's decree at the risk of their lives rather than serve or worship any god but their own God. ²⁹I hereby give an order that [anyone of] any people or nation of whatever language who blasphemes the God of Shadrach, Meshach, and Abed-nego shall be torn limb from limb, and his house confiscated, for there is no other God who is able to save in this way."

³⁰Thereupon the king promoted Shadrach, Meshach, and Abed-nego in the province of Babylon.

נוּרָא יָקֵדְתָּא: 22 כָּל־קֳבֵל דְּנָה מִן־דִּי מִלַּת מַלְכָּא מַחְצְפָה וְאַתּוּנָא אֵזֵה יַתִּירָא גֻּבְרַיָּא אִלֵּךְ דִּי הַסִּקוּ לְשַׁדְרַךְ מֵישַׁךְ וַעֲבֵד נְגוֹ קַטִּל הִמּוֹן שְׁבִיבָא דִּי נוּרָא: 23 וְגֻבְרַיָּא אִלֵּךְ תְּלָתֵּהוֹן שַׁדְרַךְ מֵישַׁךְ וַעֲבֵד נְגוֹ נְפַלוּ לְגוֹא־אַתּוּן־נוּרָא יָקֵדְתָּא מְכַפְּתִין: פ

24 אֱדַיִן נְבוּכַדְנֶצַּר מַלְכָּא תְּוַהּ וְקָם בְּהִתְבְּהָלָה עָנֵה וְאָמַר לְהַדָּבְרוֹהִי הֲלָא גֻבְרִין תְּלָתָא רְמֵינָא לְגוֹא־נוּרָא מְכַפְּתִין עָנַיִן וְאָמְרִין לְמַלְכָּא יַצִּיבָא מַלְכָּא: 25 עָנֵה וְאָמַר הָא־אֲנָה חָזֵה גֻּבְרִין אַרְבְּעָה שְׁרַיִן מַהְלְכִין בְּגוֹא־נוּרָא וַחֲבָל לָא־אִיתַי בְּהוֹן וְרֵוֵהּ דִּי רְבִיעָיָא דָּמֵה לְבַר־אֱלָהִין: ס 26 בֵּאדַיִן קְרֵב נְבוּכַדְנֶצַּר לִתְרַע אַתּוּן נוּרָא יָקֵדְתָּא עָנֵה וְאָמַר שַׁדְרַךְ מֵישַׁךְ וַעֲבֵד־נְגוֹ עַבְדוֹהִי דִּי־אֱלָהָא עליא עִלָּאָה פֻּקוּ וֶאֱתוֹ בֵּאדַיִן נָפְקִין שַׁדְרַךְ מֵישַׁךְ וַעֲבֵד נְגוֹ מִן־גּוֹא נוּרָא: 27 וּמִתְכַּנְּשִׁין אֲחַשְׁדַּרְפְּנַיָּא סִגְנַיָּא וּפַחֲוָתָא וְהַדָּבְרֵי מַלְכָּא חָזַיִן לְגֻבְרַיָּא אִלֵּךְ דִּי לָא־שְׁלֵט נוּרָא בְּגֶשְׁמְהוֹן וּשְׂעַר רֵאשְׁהוֹן לָא הִתְחָרַךְ וְסָרְבָּלֵיהוֹן לָא שְׁנוֹ וְרֵיחַ נוּר לָא עֲדָת בְּהוֹן: 28 עָנֵה נְבוּכַדְנֶצַּר וְאָמַר בְּרִיךְ אֱלָהֲהוֹן דִּי־שַׁדְרַךְ מֵישַׁךְ וַעֲבֵד נְגוֹ דִּי־שְׁלַח מַלְאֲכֵהּ וְשֵׁיזִב לְעַבְדוֹהִי דִּי הִתְרְחִצוּ עֲלוֹהִי וּמִלַּת מַלְכָּא שַׁנִּיו וִיהַבוּ גשמיהון גֶשְׁמְהוֹן דִּי לָא־יִפְלְחוּן וְלָא־יִסְגְּדוּן לְכָל־אֱלָהּ לָהֵן לֵאלָהֲהוֹן: 29 וּמִנִּי שִׂים טְעֵם דִּי כָל־עַם אֻמָּה וְלִשָּׁן דִּי־יֵאמַר שלה שָׁלוּ עַל אֱלָהֲהוֹן דִּי־שַׁדְרַךְ מֵישַׁךְ וַעֲבֵד נְגוֹא* הַדָּמִין יִתְעֲבֵד וּבַיְתֵהּ נְוָלִי יִשְׁתַּוֵּה כָּל־קֳבֵל דִּי לָא אִיתַי אֱלָהּ אָחֳרָן דִּי־יִכֻל לְהַצָּלָה כִּדְנָה:

30 בֵּאדַיִן מַלְכָּא הַצְלַח לְשַׁדְרַךְ מֵישַׁךְ וַעֲבֵד נְגוֹ בִּמְדִינַת בָּבֶל: פ

³¹"King Nebuchadnezzar to all people and nations of every language that inhabit the whole earth: May your well-being abound! ³²The signs and wonders that the Most High God has worked for me I am pleased to relate. ³³How great are His signs; how mighty His wonders! His kingdom is an everlasting kingdom, and His dominion endures throughout the generations."

4 I, Nebuchadnezzar, was living serenely in my house, flourishing in my palace. ²I had a dream that frightened me, and my thoughts in bed and the vision of my mind alarmed me. ³I gave an order to bring all the wise men of Babylon before me to let me know the meaning of the dream. ⁴The magicians, exorcists, Chaldeans, and diviners came, and I related the dream to them, but they could not make its meaning known to me. ⁵Finally, Daniel, called Belteshazzar after the name of my god, in whom the spirit of the holy gods was, came to me, and I related the dream to him, [saying], ⁶"Belteshazzar, chief magician, in whom I know the spirit of the holy gods to be, and whom no mystery baffles, tell me the meaning of my dream vision that I have seen. ⁷In the visions of my mind in bed

    I saw a tree of great height in the midst of the earth;
⁸The tree grew and became mighty;
Its top reached heaven,
And it was visible to the ends of the earth.
⁹Its foliage was beautiful
And its fruit abundant;
There was food for all in it.
Beneath it the beasts of the field found shade,
And the birds of the sky dwelt on its branches;
All creatures fed on it.

³¹ נְבוּכַדְנֶצַּר מַלְכָּא לְכָל־עַמְמַיָּא אֻמַיָּא וְלִשָּׁנַיָּא דִּי־דארין בְּכָל־אַרְעָא שְׁלָמְכוֹן יִשְׂגֵּא: ³² אָתַיָּא וְתִמְהַיָּא דִּי עֲבַד עִמִּי אֱלָהָא עליא עִלָּאָה שְׁפַר קָדָמַי לְהַחֲוָיָה: ³³ אָתוֹהִי כְּמָה רַבְרְבִין וְתִמְהוֹהִי כְּמָה תַקִּיפִין מַלְכוּתֵהּ מַלְכוּת עָלַם וְשָׁלְטָנֵהּ עִם־דָּר וְדָר:

ד אֲנָה נְבוּכַדְנֶצַּר שְׁלֵה הֲוֵית בְּבֵיתִי וְרַעְנַן בְּהֵיכְלִי: ² חֵלֶם חֲזֵית וִידַחֲלִנַּנִי וְהַרְהֹרִין עַל־מִשְׁכְּבִי וְחֶזְוֵי רֵאשִׁי יְבַהֲלֻנַּנִי: ³ וּמִנִּי שִׂים טְעֵם לְהַנְעָלָה קָדָמַי לְכֹל חַכִּימֵי בָבֶל דִּי־פְשַׁר חֶלְמָא יְהוֹדְעֻנַּנִי: ⁴ בֵּאדַיִן עללין עָלִּין חַרְטֻמַיָּא אָשְׁפַיָּא כשדיא כַּשְׂדָּאֵי וְגָזְרַיָּא וְחֶלְמָא אָמַר אֲנָה קֳדָמֵיהוֹן וּפִשְׁרֵהּ לָא־מְהוֹדְעִין לִי: ⁵ וְעַד אָחֳרֵין* עַל קָדָמַי דָּנִיֵּאל דִּי־שְׁמֵהּ בֵּלְטְשַׁאצַּר כְּשֻׁם אֱלָהִי וְדִי רוּחַ־אֱלָהִין קַדִּישִׁין בֵּהּ וְחֶלְמָא קָדָמוֹהִי אַמְרֵת: ⁶ בֵּלְטְשַׁאצַּר רַב חַרְטֻמַיָּא דִּי | אֲנָה יִדְעֵת דִּי רוּחַ אֱלָהִין קַדִּישִׁין בָּךְ וְכָל־רָז לָא־אָנֵס לָךְ חֶזְוֵי חֶלְמִי דִי־חֲזֵית וּפִשְׁרֵהּ אֱמַר: ⁷ וְחֶזְוֵי רֵאשִׁי עַל־מִשְׁכְּבִי חָזֵה הֲוֵית וַאֲלוּ אִילָן בְּגוֹא אַרְעָא וְרוּמֵהּ שַׂגִּיא:
⁸ רְבָה אִילָנָא וּתְקִף וְרוּמֵהּ יִמְטֵא לִשְׁמַיָּא וַחֲזוֹתֵהּ לְסוֹף כָּל־אַרְעָא:
⁹ עָפְיֵהּ שַׁפִּיר וְאִנְבֵּהּ שַׂגִּיא וּמָזוֹן לְכֹלָּא־בֵהּ תְּחֹתוֹהִי תַּטְלֵל | חֵיוַת בָּרָא וּבְעַנְפוֹהִי ידורן יְדֻרָן צִפֲּרֵי שְׁמַיָּא וּמִנֵּהּ יִתְּזִין כָּל־בִּשְׂרָא:

¹⁰In the vision of my mind in bed, I looked and saw a holy Watcher coming down from heaven. ¹¹He called loudly and said:

'Hew down the tree, lop off its branches,
Strip off its foliage, scatter its fruit.
Let the beasts of the field flee from beneath it
And the birds from its branches,
¹²But leave the stump with its roots in the ground.
In fetters of iron and bronze
In the grass of the field,
Let him be drenched with the dew of heaven,
And share earth's verdure with the beasts.
¹³Let his mind be altered from that of a man,
And let him be given the mind of a beast,
And let seven seasons pass over him.
¹⁴This sentence is decreed by the Watchers;
This verdict is commanded by the Holy Ones
So that all creatures may know
That the Most High is sovereign over the realm of man,
And He gives it to whom He wishes
And He may set over it even the lowest of men.'

¹⁵"I, King Nebuchadnezzar, had this dream; now you, Belteshazzar, tell me its meaning, since all the wise men of my kingdom are not able to make its meaning known to me, but you are able, for the spirit of the holy gods is in you."

¹⁶Then Daniel, called Belteshazzar, was perplexed for a while, and alarmed by his thoughts. The king addressed him, "Let the dream and its meaning not alarm you." Belteshazzar replied, "My lord, would that the dream were for your enemy and its meaning for your foe! ¹⁷The tree that you saw grow and become mighty, whose top reached heaven, which was visible throughout the earth, ¹⁸whose foliage was beautiful, whose fruit was so abundant that there was food for all in it, beneath which the beasts of the field

¹⁰חָזֵ֥ה הֲוֵ֛ית בְּחֶזְוֵ֥י רֵאשִׁ֖י עַֽל־מִשְׁכְּבִ֑י
וַאֲל֣וּ עִ֤יר וְקַדִּישׁ֙ מִן־שְׁמַיָּ֣א נָחִֽת׃ ¹¹קָרֵ֣א
בְחַ֗יִל וְכֵ֣ן אָמַ֔ר
גֹּ֤דּוּ אִֽילָנָא֙ וְקַצִּ֣צוּ עַנְפ֔וֹהִי
אַתַּ֥רוּ עׇפְיֵ֖הּ וּבַדַּ֣רוּ אִנְבֵּ֑הּ
תְּנֻ֤ד חֵֽיוְתָא֙ מִן־תַּחְתּ֔וֹהִי
וְצִפְּרַיָּ֖א מִן־עַנְפֽוֹהִי׃
¹²בְּרַ֨ם עִקַּ֤ר שׇׁרְשׁ֙וֹהִי֙ בְּאַרְעָ֣א שְׁבֻ֔קוּ
וּבֶאֱסוּר֙ דִּֽי־פַרְזֶ֣ל וּנְחָ֔שׁ
בְּדִתְאָ֖א דִּ֣י בָרָ֑א
וּבְטַ֤ל שְׁמַיָּא֙ יִצְטַבַּ֔ע
וְעִם־חֵיוְתָ֥א חֲלָקֵ֖הּ בַּעֲשַׂ֥ב אַרְעָֽא׃
¹³לִבְבֵהּ֙ מִן־[אֲנָשָׁא֙] אֲנוֹשָׁ֣א יְשַׁנּ֔וֹן
וּלְבַ֥ב חֵיוָ֖ה יִתְיְהִ֣ב לֵ֑הּ
וְשִׁבְעָ֥ה עִדָּנִ֖ין יַחְלְפ֥וּן עֲלֽוֹהִי׃
¹⁴בִּגְזֵרַ֤ת עִירִין֙ פִּתְגָמָ֔א
וּמֵאמַ֥ר קַדִּישִׁ֖ין שְׁאֵֽלְתָ֑א
עַד־דִּבְרַ֡ת דִּ֣י יִנְדְּע֣וּן חַ֠יַּיָּ֠א
דִּֽי־שַׁלִּ֨יט [עִלָּאָה] עִלָּיָ֜א בְּמַלְכ֣וּת אֲנָשָׁ֗א
[אֲנָשָׁ֗א]
וּלְמַן־דִּ֤י יִצְבֵּא֙ יִתְּנִנַּ֔הּ
וּשְׁפַ֥ל אֲנָשִׁ֖ים יְקִ֥ים עֲלַֽהּ׃
¹⁵דְּנָ֤ה חֶלְמָא֙ חֲזֵ֔ית אֲנָ֖ה מַלְכָּ֣א
נְבוּכַדְנֶצַּ֑ר וְאַ֣נְתְּ [וְאַנְתְּ] בֵּלְטְשַׁאצַּ֞ר
פִּשְׁרֵ֣א ׀ אֱמַ֗ר כׇּל־קֳבֵ֤ל דִּי֙ ׀ כׇּל־חַכִּימֵ֣י
מַלְכוּתִ֗י לָֽא־יָכְלִ֛ין פִּשְׁרָ֖א לְהוֹדָעֻתַ֑נִי
וְאַ֣נְתְּ [וְאַנְתְּ] כָּהֵ֔ל דִּ֛י רֽוּחַ־אֱלָהִ֥ין קַדִּישִׁ֖ין
בָּֽךְ׃
¹⁶אֱדַ֨יִן דָּֽנִיֵּ֜אל דִּֽי־שְׁמֵ֣הּ בֵּלְטְשַׁאצַּ֗ר
אֶשְׁתּוֹמַם֙ כְּשָׁעָ֣ה חֲדָ֔ה וְרַעְיֹנֹ֖הִי יְבַהֲלֻנֵּ֑הּ
עָנֵ֨ה מַלְכָּ֜א וְאָמַ֗ר בֵּלְטְשַׁאצַּר֙ חֶלְמָ֤א
וּפִשְׁרֵא֙ [וּפִשְׁרֵהּ] אַֽל־יְבַהֲלָ֔ךְ עָנֵ֤ה בֵלְטְשַׁאצַּר֙
וְאָמַ֔ר מָרִ֕י חֶלְמָ֥א [לְשָֽׂנְאָ֖ךְ] לשנאיך
וּפִשְׁרֵ֥הּ לְעָרָֽךְ׃ ¹⁷אִֽילָנָא֙ דִּ֣י חֲזַ֔יְתָ
דִּ֥י רְבָ֖ה וּתְקִ֑ף וְרוּמֵהּ֙ יִמְטֵ֣א לִשְׁמַיָּ֔א
וַחֲזוֹתֵ֖הּ לְכׇל־אַרְעָֽא׃ ¹⁸וְעׇפְיֵ֣הּ שַׁפִּ֣יר

dwelt, and in whose branches the birds of the sky lodged—[19]it is you, O king, you who have grown and become mighty, whose greatness has grown to reach heaven, and whose dominion is to the end of the earth. [20]The holy Watcher whom the king saw descend from heaven and say,

Hew down the tree and destroy it,
But leave the stump with its roots in the ground.
In fetters of iron and bronze
In the grass of the field,
Let him be drenched with the dew of heaven,
And share the lot of the beasts of the field
Until seven seasons pass over him—

[21]this is its meaning, O king; it is the decree of the Most High which has overtaken my lord the king. [22]You will be driven away from men and have your habitation with the beasts of the field. You will be fed grass like cattle, and be drenched with the dew of heaven; seven seasons will pass over you until you come to know that the Most High is sovereign over the realm of man, and He gives it to whom He wishes. [23]And the meaning of the command to leave the stump of the tree with its roots is that the kingdom will remain yours from the time you come to know that Heaven is sovereign. [24]Therefore, O king, may my advice be acceptable to you: Redeem your sins by beneficence and your iniquities by generosity to the poor; then your serenity may be extended."

[25]All this befell King Nebuchadnezzar. [26]Twelve months later, as he was walking on the roof of the royal palace at Babylon, [27]the king exclaimed, "There is great Babylon, which I have built by my vast power to be a royal residence for the glory of my majesty!" [28]The words were still on the king's lips, when a voice fell from heaven, "It has been decreed for you, O King Nebuchadnezzar: The kingdom has

וְאׇנְבֵּהּ שַׂגִּיא וּמָזוֹן לְכֹלָּא־בֵהּ תְּחֹתֹוהִי
תְּדוּר חֵיוַת בָּרָא וּבְעַנְפֹוהִי יִשְׁכְּנָן צִפֲּרֵי
שְׁמַיָּא: 19 אַנְתְּ־הוּא מַלְכָּא דִּי
רְבַית* וּתְקֵפְתְּ וּרְבוּתָךְ רְבָת וּמְטָת
לִשְׁמַיָּא וְשָׁלְטָנָךְ לְסוֹף אַרְעָא: 20 וְדִי חֲזָה
מַלְכָּא עִיר וְקַדִּישׁ נָחֵת ׀ מִן־שְׁמַיָּא וְאָמַר
גֹּדּוּ אִילָנָא וְחַבְּלוּהִי
בְּרַם עִקַּר שָׁרְשֹׁוהִי בְּאַרְעָא
שְׁבֻקוּ וּבֶאֱסוּר דִּי־פַרְזֶל וּנְחָשׁ
בְּדִתְאָא דִּי בָרָא
וּבְטַל שְׁמַיָּא יִצְטַבַּע
וְעִם־חֵיוַת בָּרָא חֲלָקֵהּ
עַד דִּי־שִׁבְעָה עִדָּנִין יַחְלְפוּן עֲלֹוהִי:
21 דְּנָה פִשְׁרָא מַלְכָּא וּגְזֵרַת עִלָּיא עֲלָאָה
הִיא דִּי מְטָת עַל־מָרִאי מָרֵי מַלְכָּא: 22 וְלָךְ
טָרְדִין מִן־אֲנָשָׁא וְעִם־חֵיוַת בָּרָא לֶהֱוֵה
מְדֹרָךְ וְעִשְׂבָּא כְתוֹרִין ׀ לָךְ יְטַעֲמוּן וּמִטַּל
שְׁמַיָּא לָךְ מְצַבְּעִין וְשִׁבְעָה עִדָּנִין יַחְלְפוּן
עֲלַיךְ עַד דִּי־תִנְדַּע דִּי־שַׁלִּיט עִלָּיא
עֲלָאָה בְּמַלְכוּת אֲנָשָׁא וּלְמַן־דִּי יִצְבֵּא
יִתְּנִנַּהּ: 23 וְדִי אֲמַרוּ לְמִשְׁבַּק עִקַּר
שָׁרְשֹׁוהִי דִּי אִילָנָא מַלְכוּתָךְ לָךְ קַיָּמָה
מִן־דִּי תִנְדַּע דִּי שַׁלִּטִן שְׁמַיָּא: 24 לָהֵן
מַלְכָּא מִלְכִּי יִשְׁפַּר עֲלַיךְ וַחֲטָיַךְ
וַחֲטָאָךְ בְּצִדְקָה פְרֻק וַעֲוָיָתָךְ בְּמִחַן עֲנָיִן
הֵן תֶּהֱוֵא אַרְכָה לִשְׁלֵוְתָךְ:
25 כֹּלָּא מְטָא עַל־נְבוּכַדְנֶצַּר מַלְכָּא: פ
26 לִקְצָת יַרְחִין תְּרֵי־עֲשַׂר עַל־הֵיכַל
מַלְכוּתָא דִּי בָבֶל מְהַלֵּךְ הֲוָה: 27 עָנֵה
מַלְכָּא וְאָמַר הֲלָא דָא־הִיא בָּבֶל רַבְּתָא
דִּי־אֲנָה בֱנַיְתַהּ לְבֵית מַלְכוּ בִּתְקָף חִסְנִי
וְלִיקָר הַדְרִי: 28 עוֹד מִלְּתָא בְּפֻם מַלְכָּא
קָל מִן־שְׁמַיָּא נְפַל לָךְ אָמְרִין נְבוּכַדְנֶצַּר
מַלְכָּא מַלְכוּתָה עֲדָת מִנָּךְ: 29 וּמִן־אֲנָשָׁא
לָךְ טָרְדִין וְעִם־חֵיוַת בָּרָא מְדֹרָךְ עִשְׂבָּא

passed out of your hands. ²⁹You are being driven away from men, and your habitation is to be with the beasts of the field. You are to be fed grass like cattle, and seven seasons will pass over you until you come to know that the Most High is sovereign over the realm of man and He gives it to whom He wishes." ³⁰There and then the sentence was carried out upon Nebuchadnezzar. He was driven away from men, he ate grass like cattle, and his body was drenched with the dew of heaven until his hair grew like eagle's [feathers] and his nails like [the talons of] birds.

³¹"When the time had passed, I, Nebuchadnezzar, lifted my eyes to heaven, and my reason was restored to me. I blessed the Most High, and praised and glorified the Ever-Living One,

Whose dominion is an everlasting dominion

And whose kingdom endures throughout the generations.

³²All the inhabitants of the earth are of no account.

He does as He wishes with the host of heaven,

And with the inhabitants of the earth.

There is none to stay His hand

Or say to Him, 'What have You done?'

³³There and then my reason was restored to me, and my majesty and splendor were restored to me for the glory of my kingdom. My companions and nobles sought me out, and I was reestablished over my kingdom, and added greatness was given me. ³⁴So now I, Nebuchadnezzar, praise, exalt, and glorify the King of Heaven, all of whose works are just and whose ways are right, and who is able to humble those who behave arrogantly."

5 King Belshazzar gave a great banquet for his thousand nobles, and in the presence of the thousand he drank wine. ²Under the influence

כְּתוֹרִין לָךְ יְטַעֲמוּן וְשִׁבְעָה עִדָּנִין יַחְלְפוּן עֲלָיךְ עַד דִּי־תִנְדַּע דִּי־שַׁלִּיט עִלָּאָה עִלָּאָה בְּמַלְכוּת אֲנָשָׁא וּלְמַן־דִּי יִצְבֵּא יִתְּנִנַּהּ: 30 בַּהּ־שַׁעֲתָא מִלְּתָא סָפַת עַל־נְבוּכַדְנֶצַּר וּמִן־אֲנָשָׁא טְרִיד וְעִשְׂבָּא כְתוֹרִין יֵאכֻל וּמִטַּל שְׁמַיָּא גִּשְׁמֵהּ יִצְטַבַּע עַד דִּי שַׂעְרֵהּ כְּנִשְׁרִין רְבָה וְטִפְרוֹהִי כְצִפְּרִין:

31 וְלִקְצָת יוֹמַיָּה אֲנָה נְבוּכַדְנֶצַּר עַיְנַי לִשְׁמַיָּא נִטְלֵת וּמַנְדְּעִי עֲלַי יְתוּב וּלְעִלָּיָא וּלְעִלָּאָה בָּרְכֵת וּלְחַי עָלְמָא שַׁבְּחֵת וְהַדְּרֵת

דִּי שָׁלְטָנֵהּ שָׁלְטָן עָלַם וּמַלְכוּתֵהּ עִם־דָּר וְדָר:

32 וְכָל־דָּאְרֵי אַרְעָא כְּלָה חֲשִׁיבִין וּכְמִצְבְּיֵהּ עָבֵד בְּחֵיל שְׁמַיָּא

וְדָאְרֵי אַרְעָא

וְלָא אִיתַי דִּי־יְמַחֵא בִידֵהּ

וְיֵאמַר לֵהּ מָה עֲבַדְתְּ:

33 בֵּהּ־זִמְנָא מַנְדְּעִי | יְתוּב עֲלַי וְלִיקַר מַלְכוּתִי הַדְרִי וְזִוִי יְתוּב עֲלַי וְלִי הַדָּבְרַי וְרַבְרְבָנַי יְבַעוֹן וְעַל־מַלְכוּתִי הָתְקְנַת וּרְבוּ יַתִּירָה הוּסְפַת לִי: 34 כְּעַן אֲנָה נְבוּכַדְנֶצַּר מְשַׁבַּח וּמְרוֹמֵם וּמְהַדַּר לְמֶלֶךְ שְׁמַיָּא דִּי כָל־מַעֲבָדוֹהִי קְשֹׁט וְאֹרְחָתֵהּ דִּין וְדִי מַהְלְכִין בְּגֵוָה יָכִל לְהַשְׁפָּלָה: פ

ה בֵּלְשַׁאצַּר מַלְכָּא עֲבַד לְחֶם רַב לְרַבְרְבָנוֹהִי אֲלַף וְלָקֳבֵל אַלְפָּא חַמְרָא שָׁתֵה: 2 בֵּלְשַׁאצַּר אֲמַר | בִּטְעֵם חַמְרָא

of the wine, Belshazzar ordered the gold and silver vessels that his father Nebuchadnezzar had taken out of the temple at Jerusalem to be brought so that the king and his nobles, his consorts, and his concubines could drink from them. [3]The golden vessels that had been taken out of the sanctuary of the House of God in Jerusalem were then brought, and the king, his nobles, his consorts, and his concubines drank from them. [4]They drank wine and praised the gods of gold and silver, bronze, iron, wood, and stone. [5]Just then, the fingers of a human hand appeared and wrote on the plaster of the wall of the king's palace opposite the lampstand, so that the king could see the hand as it wrote. [6]The king's face darkened, and his thoughts alarmed him; the joints of his loins were loosened and his knees knocked together. [7]The king called loudly for the exorcists, Chaldeans, and diviners to be brought. The king addressed the wise men of Babylon, "Whoever can read this writing and tell me its meaning shall be clothed in purple and wear a golden chain on his neck, and shall rule as *a*-one of three-*a* in the kingdom."

[8]Then all the king's wise men came, but they could not read the writing or make known its meaning to the king. [9]King Belshazzar grew exceedingly alarmed and his face darkened, and his nobles were dismayed. [10]Because of the state of the king and his nobles, the queen came to the banquet hall. The queen spoke up and said, "O king, live forever! Let your thoughts not alarm you or your face darken. [11]There is a man in your kingdom who has the spirit of the holy gods in him; in your father's time, illumination, understanding, and wisdom like that of the gods were to be found in him, and your father, King Nebuchadnezzar, appointed him chief of the magicians, exorcists, Chaldeans, and diviners. [12]Seeing that there is to be found in Daniel

---

לְהַיְתָיָה֩ לְמָאנֵ֨י דַהֲבָ֜א וְכַסְפָּ֗א דִּ֤י הַנְפֵּק֙ נְבוּכַדְנֶצַּ֣ר אֲב֔וּהִי מִן־הֵיכְלָ֖א דִּ֣י בִירוּשְׁלֶ֑ם וְיִשְׁתּ֣וֹן בְּה֗וֹן מַלְכָּא֙ וְרַבְרְבָנ֔וֹהִי שֵׁגְלָתֵ֖הּ וּלְחֵנָתֵֽהּ: 3 בֵּאדַ֗יִן הַיְתִיו֙ מָאנֵ֣י דַהֲבָ֔א דִּ֣י הַנְפִּ֗קוּ מִן־הֵֽיכְלָ֛א דִּֽי־בֵ֥ית אֱלָהָ֖א דִּ֣י בִירֽוּשְׁלֶ֑ם וְאִשְׁתִּ֣יו בְּה֗וֹן מַלְכָּא֙ וְרַבְרְבָנ֔וֹהִי שֵׁגְלָתֵ֖הּ וּלְחֵנָתֵֽהּ: 4 אִשְׁתִּ֖יו חַמְרָ֑א וְ֠שַׁבַּחוּ לֵֽאלָהֵ֞י דַּהֲבָ֧א וְכַסְפָּ֛א נְחָשָׁ֥א פַרְזְלָ֖א אָעָ֥א וְאַבְנָֽא: 5 בַּהּ־שַׁעֲתָ֗ה נְפַ֙קוּ֙ אֶצְבְּעָן֙ דִּ֣י יַד־אֱנָ֔שׁ וְכָֽתְבָ֗ן לָקֳבֵל֙ נֶבְרַשְׁתָּ֔א עַל־גִּירָ֕א דִּֽי־כְתַ֥ל הֵיכְלָ֖א דִּ֣י מַלְכָּ֑א וּמַלְכָּ֣א חָזֵ֔ה פַּ֥ס יְדָ֖ה דִּ֥י כָתְבָֽה: 6 אֱדַ֤יִן מַלְכָּא֙ זִיו֣וֹהִי שְׁנ֔וֹהִי וְרַעְיֹנֹ֖הִי יְבַהֲלוּנֵּ֑הּ וְקִטְרֵ֤י חַרְצֵהּ֙ מִשְׁתָּרַ֔יִן וְאַרְכֻבָּתֵ֖הּ דָּ֥א לְדָ֖א נָֽקְשָֽׁן: 7 קָרֵ֤א מַלְכָּא֙ בְּחַ֔יִל לְהֶֽעָלָ֖ה לְאָֽשְׁפַיָּ֑א כַּשְׂדָּאֵ֖י וְגָֽזְרַיָּ֑א עָנֵ֨ה מַלְכָּ֜א וְאָמַ֣ר ׀ לְחַכִּימֵ֣י בָבֶ֗ל דִּ֣י כָל־אֱ֠נָשׁ דִּֽי־יִקְרֵ֞ה כְּתָבָ֤ה דְנָה֙ וּפִשְׁרֵ֣הּ יְחַוִּנַּ֗נִי אַרְגְּוָנָ֤א יִלְבַּשׁ֙ והמונכא והַֽמְנִיכָ֤א דִֽי־דַהֲבָא֙ עַֽל־צַוְּארֵ֔הּ וְתַלְתִּ֥י בְמַלְכוּתָ֖א יִשְׁלַֽט: ס 8 אֱדַ֙יִן֙ עללין עָֽלִּ֔ין כֹּ֖ל חַכִּימֵ֣י מַלְכָּ֑א וְלָֽא־כָהֲלִ֤ין כְּתָבָא֙ לְמִקְרֵ֔א ופשרא וּפִשְׁרֵ֖הּ לְהוֹדָעָ֥ה לְמַלְכָּֽא: 9 אֱ֠דַיִן מַלְכָּ֤א בֵלְשַׁאצַּר֙ שַׂגִּ֣יא מִתְבָּהַ֔ל וְזִיו֖וֹהִי שָׁנַ֣יִן עֲל֑וֹהִי וְרַבְרְבָנ֖וֹהִי מִֽשְׁתַּבְּשִֽׁין: 10 מַלְכְּתָ֕א לָקֳבֵ֨ל מִלֵּ֤י מַלְכָּא֙ וְרַבְרְבָנ֔וֹהִי לְבֵ֥ית מִשְׁתְּיָ֖א עללת עַלַּ֑ת עֲנָ֨ת מַלְכְּתָ֜א וַאֲמֶ֗רֶת מַלְכָּא֙ לְעָלְמִ֣ין חֱיִ֔י אַֽל־יְבַהֲל֙וּךְ֙ רַעְיוֹנָ֔ךְ וזיויך* וְזִיוָ֖יךְ אַל־יִשְׁתַּנּֽוֹ: 11 אִיתַ֨י גְּבַ֜ר בְּמַלְכוּתָ֗ךְ דִּ֠י ר֣וּחַ אֱלָהִ֣ין קַדִּישִׁין֮ בֵּהּ֒ וּבְיוֹמֵ֣י אֲב֗וּךְ נַהִיר֧וּ וְשָׂכְלְתָנ֛וּ וְחָכְמָ֥ה כְּחָכְמַת־אֱלָהִ֖ין הִשְׁתְּכַ֣חַת בֵּ֑הּ וּמַלְכָּ֤א נְבֻֽכַדְנֶצַּר֙ אֲב֔וּךְ רַ֧ב חַרְטֻמִּ֣ין אָֽשְׁפִ֗ין כַּשְׂדָּאִין֙ גָּזְרִ֔ין הֲקִימֵ֖הּ אֲב֥וּךְ מַלְכָּֽא: 12 כָּל־קֳבֵ֡ל דִּ֣י ר֣וּחַ ׀ יַתִּירָ֡ה וּמַנְדַּ֡ע

(whom the king called Belteshazzar) extraordinary spirit, knowledge, and understanding to interpret dreams, to explain riddles and solve problems, let Daniel now be called to tell the meaning [of the writing]."

13Daniel was then brought before the king. The king addressed Daniel, "You are Daniel, one of the exiles of Judah whom my father, the king, brought from Judah. 14I have heard about you that you have the spirit of the gods in you, and that illumination, knowledge, and extraordinary wisdom are to be found in you. 15Now the wise men and exorcists have been brought before me to read this writing and to make known its meaning to me. But they could not tell what it meant. 16I have heard about you, that you can give interpretations and solve problems. Now if you can read the writing and make known its meaning to me, you shall be clothed in purple and wear a golden chain on your neck and rule as one of three in the kingdom."

17Then Daniel said in reply to the king, "You may keep your gifts for yourself, and give your presents to others. But I will read the writing for the king, and make its meaning known to him. 18O king, the Most High God bestowed kingship, grandeur, glory, and majesty upon your father Nebuchadnezzar. 19And because of the grandeur that He bestowed upon him, all the peoples and nations of every language trembled in fear of him. He put to death whom he wished, and whom he wished he let live; he raised high whom he wished and whom he wished he brought low. 20But when he grew haughty and willfully presumptuous, he was deposed from his royal throne and his glory was removed from him. 21He was driven away from men, and his mind made like that of a beast, and his habitation was with wild asses. He was fed grass like cattle, and his body was drenched with the dew of heaven until he came to know

וְשָׂכְלְתָנוּ מְפַשַּׁר חֶלְמִין וַאַחֲוָיַת אֲחִידָן
וּמְשָׁרֵא קִטְרִין הִשְׁתְּכַחַת בֵּהּ בְּדָנִיֵּאל
דִּי־מַלְכָּא שָׂם־שְׁמֵהּ בֵּלְטְשַׁאצַּר כְּעַן
דָּנִיֵּאל יִתְקְרֵי וּפִשְׁרָה יְהַחֲוֵה: פ
13 בֵּאדַיִן דָּנִיֵּאל הֻעַל קֳדָם מַלְכָּא עָנֵה
מַלְכָּא וְאָמַר לְדָנִיֵּאל אנתה (אַנְתְּ)־הוּא
דָנִיֵּאל דִּי־מִן־בְּנֵי גָלוּתָא דִּי יְהוּד דִּי הַיְתִי
מַלְכָּא אַבִי מִן־יְהוּד: 14 וְשִׁמְעֵת עליך (עֲלָךְ)
דִּי רוּחַ אֱלָהִין בָּךְ וְנַהִירוּ וְשָׂכְלְתָנוּ
וְחָכְמָה יַתִּירָה הִשְׁתְּכַחַת בָּךְ: 15 וּכְעַן
הֻעַלּוּ קֳדָמַי חַכִּימַיָּא אָשְׁפַיָּא דִּי־כְתָבָה
דְנָה יִקְרוֹן וּפִשְׁרֵהּ לְהוֹדָעֻתַנִי וְלָא־כָהֲלִין
פְּשַׁר־מִלְּתָא לְהַחֲוָיָה: 16 וַאֲנָה שִׁמְעֵת
עליך (עֲלָךְ) דִּי־תוכל (תִיכּוּל) פִּשְׁרִין לְמִפְשַׁר
וְקִטְרִין לְמִשְׁרֵא כְּעַן הֵן תוכל (תִּיכּוּל) תָּבוּל
כְּתָבָא לְמִקְרֵא וּפִשְׁרֵהּ לְהוֹדָעֻתַנִי
אַרְגְּוָנָא תִלְבַּשׁ והמונכא (וְהַמְנִיכָא) דִי־
דַהֲבָא עַל־צַוְּארָךְ וְתַלְתָּא בְמַלְכוּתָא
תִּשְׁלַט: פ
17 בֵּאדַיִן עָנֵה דָנִיֵּאל וְאָמַר קֳדָם מַלְכָּא
מַתְּנָתָךְ לָךְ לֶהֶוְיָן וּנְבָזְבְּיָתָךְ לְאָחֳרָן הַב
בְּרַם כְּתָבָא אֶקְרֵא לְמַלְכָּא וּפִשְׁרָא
אֲהוֹדְעִנֵּהּ: 18 אנתה (אַנְתְּ) מַלְכָּא אֱלָהָא
עליא (עִלָּאָה) מַלְכוּתָא וּרְבוּתָא וִיקָרָא
וְהַדְרָה יְהַב לִנְבֻכַדְנֶצַּר אֲבוּךְ: 19 וּמִן־
רְבוּתָא דִּי יְהַב־לֵהּ כֹּל עַמְמַיָּא אֻמַּיָּא
וְלִשָׁנַיָּא הֲווֹ זאעין (זָיְעִין) וְדָחֲלִין מִן־
קֳדָמוֹהִי דִּי־הֲוָה צָבֵא הֲוָא קָטֵל וְדִי־הֲוָה
צָבֵא הֲוָה מַחֵא וְדִי־הֲוָה צָבֵא הֲוָה מָרִים
וְדִי־הֲוָה צָבֵא הֲוָה מַשְׁפִּיל: 20 וּכְדִי רִם
לִבְבֵהּ וְרוּחֵהּ תִּקְפַת לַהֲזָדָה הָנְחַת מִן־
כָּרְסֵא מַלְכוּתֵהּ וִיקָרָה* הֶעְדִּיו מִנֵּהּ:
21 וּמִן־בְּנֵי אֲנָשָׁא טְרִיד וְלִבְבֵהּ | עִם־
חֵיוְתָא שוי (שַׁוִּיו) וְעִם־עֲרָדַיָּא מְדוֹרֵהּ
עִשְׂבָּא כְתוֹרִין יְטַעֲמוּנֵהּ וּמִטַּל שְׁמַיָּא
גִּשְׁמֵהּ יִצְטַבַּע עַד דִּי־יְדַע דִּי־שַׁלִּיט

that the Most High God is sovereign over the realm of man, and sets over it whom He wishes. ²²But you, Belshazzar his son, did not humble yourself although you knew all this. ²³You exalted yourself against the Lord of Heaven, and had the vessels of His temple brought to you. You and your nobles, your consorts, and your concubines drank wine from them and praised the gods of silver and gold, bronze and iron, wood and stone, which do not see, hear, or understand; but the God who controls your lifebreath and every move you make—Him you did not glorify! ²⁴He therefore made the hand appear, and caused the writing to be inscribed. ²⁵This is the writing that is inscribed: MENE MENE TEKEL UPHARSIN. ²⁶And this is its meaning: MENE—God has numbered[b] [the days of] your kingdom and brought it to an end; ²⁷TEKEL—[c]-you have been weighed-[c] in the balance and found wanting; ²⁸PERES—your kingdom [d]-has been divided-[d] and given to the Medes and the Persians." ²⁹Then, at Belshazzar's command, they clothed Daniel in purple, placed a golden chain on his neck, and proclaimed that he should rule as one of three in the kingdom.

6 ³⁰That very night, Belshazzar, the Chaldean king, was killed, ¹and Darius the Mede received the kingdom, being about sixty-two years old. ²It pleased Darius to appoint over the kingdom one hundred and twenty satraps to be in charge of the whole kingdom; ³over them were three ministers, one of them Daniel, to whom these satraps reported, in order that the king not be troubled. ⁴This man Daniel surpassed the other ministers and satraps by virtue of his extraordinary spirit, and the king considered setting him over the whole kingdom. ⁵The ministers and satraps looked for some fault in Daniel's conduct in matters of state, but

אֱלָהָא עלִיָא בְּמַלְכוּת אֲנָשָׁא וּלְמַן־
דִּי יִצְבֵּה יְהָקֵים עליה עֲלַהּ: 22 ואנתה
וְאַנְתְּ בְּרֵהּ בֵּלְשַׁאצַּר לָא הַשְׁפֵּלְתְּ לִבְבָךְ
כָּל־קָבֵל דִּי כָל־דְּנָה יְדַעְתָּ: 23 וְעַל
מָרֵא־שְׁמַיָּא | הִתְרוֹמַמְתָּ וּלְמָאנַיָּא דִי־
בַיְתֵהּ הַיְתִיו קדמיך קָדָמָךְ ואנתה וְאַנְתְּ
ורברבניך וְרַבְרְבָנָךְ שֵׁגְלָתָךְ וּלְחֵנָתָךְ
חַמְרָא שָׁתַיִן בְּהוֹן וְלֵאלָהֵי כַסְפָּא־וְדַהֲבָא
נְחָשָׁא פַרְזְלָא אָעָא וְאַבְנָא דִּי לָא־חָזַיִן
וְלָא־שָׁמְעִין וְלָא יָדְעִין שַׁבַּחְתָּ וְלֵאלָהָא
דִּי־נִשְׁמְתָךְ בִּידֵהּ וְכָל־אֹרְחָתָךְ לֵהּ לָא
הַדַּרְתָּ: 24 בֵּאדַיִן מִן־קֳדָמוֹהִי שְׁלִיחַ פַּסָּא
דִי־יְדָא וּכְתָבָא דְּנָה רְשִׁים: 25 וּדְנָה
כְתָבָא דִּי רְשִׁים מְנֵא מְנֵא תְּקֵל וּפַרְסִין:
26 דְּנָה פְּשַׁר־מִלְּתָא מְנֵא מְנָה־אֱלָהָא
מַלְכוּתָךְ וְהַשְׁלְמַהּ: 27 תְּקֵל תְּקִילְתָּה
בְמֹאזַנְיָא וְהִשְׁתְּכַחַתְּ חַסִּיר: 28 פְּרֵס
פְּרִיסַת מַלְכוּתָךְ וִיהִיבַת לְמָדַי וּפָרָס:
29 בֵּאדַיִן | אֲמַר בֵּלְשַׁאצַּר וְהַלְבִּישׁו
לְדָנִיֵּאל אַרְגְּוָנָא והמונכא וְהַמְנִיכָא דִי־
דַהֲבָא עַל־צַוְּארֵהּ וְהַכְרִזוּ עֲלוֹהִי דִּי־
לֶהֱוֵא שַׁלִּיט תַּלְתָּא בְּמַלְכוּתָא:
30 בֵּהּ בְּלֵילְיָא קְטִיל בֵּלְאשַׁצַּר מַלְכָּא
כשדיא כַשְׂדָּאָה: פ 1 וְדָרְיָוֶשׁ מדיא
מָדָאָה קַבֵּל מַלְכוּתָא כְּבַר שְׁנִין שִׁתִּין
וְתַרְתֵּין: 2 שְׁפַר קֳדָם דָּרְיָוֶשׁ וַהֲקֵים עַל־
מַלְכוּתָא לַאֲחַשְׁדַּרְפְּנַיָּא מְאָה וְעֶשְׂרִין
דִּי לֶהֱוֹן בְּכָל־מַלְכוּתָא: 3 וְעֵלָּא מִנְּהוֹן
סָרְכִין תְּלָתָא דִּי דָנִיֵּאל חַד־מִנְּהוֹן דִּי־
לֶהֱוֹן אֲחַשְׁדַּרְפְּנַיָּא אִלֵּין יָהֲבִין לְהוֹן
טַעְמָא וּמַלְכָּא לָא־לֶהֱוֵא נָזִק: 4 אֱדַיִן
דָּנִיֵּאל דְּנָה הֲוָא מִתְנַצַּח עַל־סָרְכַיָּא
וַאֲחַשְׁדַּרְפְּנַיָּא כָּל־קֳבֵל דִּי רוּחַ יַתִּירָא
בֵּהּ וּמַלְכָּא עֲשִׁית לַהֲקָמוּתֵהּ עַל־כָּל־
מַלְכוּתָא: 5 אֱדַיִן סָרְכַיָּא וַאֲחַשְׁדַּרְפְּנַיָּא

---

b   *Aramaic mena.*
c-c   *Aramaic tekilta.*
d-d   *Aramaic perisat.*

they could find neither fault nor corruption, inasmuch as he was trustworthy, and no negligence or corruption was to be found in him. [6]Those men then said, "We are not going to find any fault with this Daniel, unless we find something against him in connection with the laws of his God." [7]Then these ministers and satraps came thronging in to the king and said to him, "O King Darius, live forever! [8]All the ministers of the kingdom, the prefects, satraps, companions, and governors are in agreement that a royal ban should be issued under sanction of an oath that whoever shall address a petition to any god or man, besides you, O king, during the next thirty days shall be thrown into a lions' den. [9]So issue the ban, O king, and put it in writing so that it be unalterable as a law of the Medes and Persians that may not be abrogated." [10]Thereupon King Darius put the ban in writing.

[11]When Daniel learned that it had been put in writing, he went to his house, in whose upper chamber he had had windows made facing Jerusalem, and three times a day he knelt down, prayed, and made confession to his God, as he had always done. [12]Then those men came thronging in and found Daniel petitioning his God in supplication. [13]They then approached the king and reminded him of the royal ban: "Did you not put in writing a ban that whoever addresses a petition to any god or man besides you, O king, during the next thirty days, shall be thrown into a lions' den?" The king said in reply, "The order stands firm, as a law of the Medes and Persians that may not be abrogated." [14]Thereupon they said to the king, "Daniel, one of the exiles of Judah, pays no heed to you, O king, or to the ban that you put in writing; three times a day he offers his petitions [to his God]." [15]Upon hearing that, the king was very disturbed, and he set his heart upon saving Daniel,

הֲוֹו בָעַיִן עִלָּה לְהַשְׁכָּחָה לְדָנִיֵּאל מִצַּד מַלְכוּתָא וְכָל־עִלָּה וּשְׁחִיתָה לָא־יָכְלִין לְהַשְׁכָּחָה כָּל־קֳבֵל דִּי־מְהֵימַן הוּא וְכָל־שָׁלוּ וּשְׁחִיתָה לָא הִשְׁתְּכַחַת עֲלוֹהִי: [6]אֱדַיִן גֻּבְרַיָּא אִלֵּךְ אָמְרִין דִּי לָא נְהַשְׁכַּח לְדָנִיֵּאל דְּנָה כָּל־עִלָּא לָהֵן הַשְׁכַּחְנָה עֲלוֹהִי בְּדָת אֱלָהֵהּ: ס [7]אֱדַיִן סָרְכַיָּא וַאֲחַשְׁדַּרְפְּנַיָּא אִלֵּן הַרְגִּשׁוּ עַל־מַלְכָּא וְכֵן אָמְרִין לֵהּ דָּרְיָוֶשׁ מַלְכָּא לְעָלְמִין חֱיִי: [8]אִתְיָעַטוּ כֹּל | סָרְכֵי מַלְכוּתָא סִגְנַיָּא וַאֲחַשְׁדַּרְפְּנַיָּא הַדָּבְרַיָּא וּפַחֲוָתָא לְקַיָּמָה קְיָם מַלְכָּא וּלְתַקָּפָה אֱסָר דִּי כָל־דִּי־יִבְעֵה בָעוּ מִן־כָּל־אֱלָהּ וֶאֱנָשׁ עַד־יוֹמִין תְּלָתִין לָהֵן מִנָּךְ מַלְכָּא יִתְרְמֵא לְגֹב אַרְיָוָתָא: [9]כְּעַן מַלְכָּא תְּקִים אֱסָרָא וְתִרְשֻׁם כְּתָבָא דִּי לָא לְהַשְׁנָיָה כְּדָת־מָדַי וּפָרַס דִּי־לָא תֶעְדֵּא: [10]כָּל־קֳבֵל דְּנָה מַלְכָּא דָּרְיָוֶשׁ רְשַׁם כְּתָבָא וֶאֱסָרָא:

[11]וְדָנִיֵּאל כְּדִי יְדַע דִּי־רְשִׁים כְּתָבָא עַל לְבַיְתֵהּ וְכַוִּין פְּתִיחָן לֵהּ בְּעִלִּיתֵהּ נֶגֶד יְרוּשְׁלֶם וְזִמְנִין תְּלָתָה בְיוֹמָא הוּא | בָּרֵךְ עַל־בִּרְכוֹהִי וּמְצַלֵּא וּמוֹדֵא קֳדָם אֱלָהֵהּ כָּל־קֳבֵל דִּי־הֲוָא עָבֵד מִן־קַדְמַת דְּנָה: ס [12]אֱדַיִן גֻּבְרַיָּא אִלֵּךְ הַרְגִּשׁוּ וְהַשְׁכַּחוּ לְדָנִיֵּאל בָּעֵא וּמִתְחַנַּן קֳדָם אֱלָהֵהּ: [13]בֵּאדַיִן קְרִיבוּ וְאָמְרִין קֳדָם־מַלְכָּא עַל־אֱסָר מַלְכָּא הֲלָא אֱסָר רְשַׁמְתָּ דִּי כָל־אֱנָשׁ דִּי־יִבְעֵה מִן־כָּל־אֱלָהּ וֶאֱנָשׁ עַד־יוֹמִין תְּלָתִין לָהֵן מִנָּךְ מַלְכָּא יִתְרְמֵא לְגוֹב אַרְיָוָתָא עָנֵה מַלְכָּא וְאָמַר יַצִּיבָא מִלְּתָא כְּדָת־מָדַי וּפָרַס דִּי־לָא תֶעְדֵּא: [14]בֵּאדַיִן עֲנוֹ וְאָמְרִין קֳדָם מַלְכָּא דִּי דָנִיֵּאל דִּי מִן־בְּנֵי גָלוּתָא דִּי יְהוּד לָא־שָׂם עֲלָךְ מַלְכָּא טְעֵם וְעַל־אֱסָרָא דִּי רְשַׁמְתָּ וְזִמְנִין תְּלָתָה בְּיוֹמָא בָּעֵא בָּעוּתֵהּ: [15]אֱדַיִן מַלְכָּא כְּדִי מִלְּתָא שְׁמַע

1819

and until the sun set made every effort to rescue him. [16]Then those men came thronging in to the king and said to the king, "Know, O king, that it is a law of the Medes and Persians that any ban that the king issues under sanction of oath is unalterable." [17]By the king's order, Daniel was then brought and thrown into the lions' den. The king spoke to Daniel and said, "Your God, whom you serve so regularly, will deliver you." [18]A rock was brought and placed over the mouth of the den; the king sealed it with his signet and with the signet of his nobles, so that nothing might be altered concerning Daniel.

[19]The king then went to his palace and spent the night fasting; no diversions were brought to him, and his sleep fled from him. [20]Then, at the first light of dawn, the king arose and rushed to the lions' den. [21]As he approached the den, he cried to Daniel in a mournful voice; the king said to Daniel, "Daniel, servant of the living God, was the God whom you served so regularly able to deliver you from the lions?" [22]Daniel then talked with the king, "O king, live forever! [23]My God sent His angel, who shut the mouths of the lions so that they did not injure me, inasmuch as I was found innocent by Him, nor have I, O king, done you any injury." [24]The king was very glad, and ordered Daniel to be brought up out of the den. Daniel was brought up out of the den, and no injury was found on him, for he had trusted in his God. [25]Then, by order of the king, those men who had slandered Daniel were brought and, together with their children and wives, were thrown into the lions' den. They had hardly reached the bottom of the den when the lions overpowered them and crushed all their bones.

[26]Then King Darius wrote to all peoples and

שַׂגִּיא בְּאֵשׁ עֲלֹוהִי וְעַל דָּנִיֵּאל שָׂם בָּל לְשֵׁיזָבוּתֵהּ וְעַד מֶעָלֵי שִׁמְשָׁא הֲוָא מִשְׁתַּדַּר לְהַצָּלוּתֵהּ: 16 בֵּאדַיִן גֻּבְרַיָּא אִלֵּךְ הַרְגִּשׁוּ עַל־מַלְכָּא וְאָמְרִין לְמַלְכָּא דַּע מַלְכָּא דִּי־דָת לְמָדַי וּפָרַס דִּי־כָל־אֱסָר וּקְיָם דִּי־מַלְכָּא יְהָקֵים לָא לְהַשְׁנָיָה: 17 בֵּאדַיִן מַלְכָּא אֲמַר וְהַיְתִיו לְדָנִיֵּאל וּרְמֹו לְגֻבָּא דִּי אַרְיָוָתָא עָנֵה מַלְכָּא וְאָמַר לְדָנִיֵּאל אֱלָהָךְ דִּי אַנתְּ פָּלַח־לֵהּ בִּתְדִירָא הוּא יְשֵׁיזְבִנָּךְ: 18 וְהֵיתָיִת אֶבֶן חֲדָה וְשֻׂמַת עַל־פֻּם גֻּבָּא וְחַתְמַהּ מַלְכָּא בְּעִזְקְתֵהּ וּבְעִזְקָת רַבְרְבָנֹוהִי דִּי לָא־ תִשְׁנֵא צְבוּ בְּדָנִיֵּאל: 19 אֱדַיִן אֲזַל מַלְכָּא לְהֵיכְלֵהּ וּבָת טְוָת וְדַחֲוָן לָא־הַנְעֵל קָדָמֹוהִי וְשִׁנְתֵּהּ נַדַּת עֲלֹוהִי: 20 בֵּאדַיִן מַלְכָּא בִּשְׁפַּרְפָּרָא יְקוּם בְּנָגְהָא וּבְהִתְבְּהָלָה לְגֻבָּא דִי־אַרְיָוָתָא אֲזַל: 21 וּכְמִקְרְבֵהּ לְגֻבָּא לְדָנִיֵּאל בְּקָל עֲצִיב זְעִק עָנֵה מַלְכָּא וְאָמַר לְדָנִיֵּאל דָּנִיֵּאל עֲבֵד אֱלָהָא חַיָּא אֱלָהָךְ דִּי אַנתְּ אַנתְּ פָּלַח־לֵהּ בִּתְדִירָא הַיְכֵל לְשֵׁיזָבוּתָךְ מִן־אַרְיָוָתָא: 22 אֱדַיִן דָּנִיֵּאל עִם־מַלְכָּא מַלִּל מַלְכָּא לְעָלְמִין חֱיִי: 23 אֱלָהִי שְׁלַח מַלְאֲכֵהּ וּסֲגַר פֻּם אַרְיָוָתָא וְלָא חַבְּלוּנִי כָּל־קֳבֵל דִּי קָדָמֹוהִי זָכוּ הִשְׁתְּכַחַת לִי וְאַף קָדָמָיִךְ קֳדָמָךְ מַלְכָּא חֲבוּלָה לָא עַבְדֵת: 24 בֵּאדַיִן מַלְכָּא שַׂגִּיא טְאֵב עֲלֹוהִי וּלְדָנִיֵּאל אֲמַר לְהַנְסָקָה מִן־גֻּבָּא וְהֻסַּק דָּנִיֵּאל מִן־גֻּבָּא וְכָל־חֲבָל לָא־ הִשְׁתְּכַח בֵּהּ דִּי הֵימִן בֵּאלָהֵהּ: 25 וַאֲמַר מַלְכָּא וְהַיְתִיו גֻּבְרַיָּא אִלֵּךְ דִּי־אֲכַלוּ קַרְצֹוהִי דִּי דָנִיֵּאל וּלְגֹב אַרְיָוָתָא רְמֹו אִנּוּן בְּנֵיהֹון וּנְשֵׁיהֹון וְלָא־מְטֹו לְאַרְעִית גֻּבָּא עַד דִּי־שְׁלִטוּ בְהֹון אַרְיָוָתָא וְכָל־ גַּרְמֵיהֹון הַדִּקוּ: 26 בֵּאדַיִן דָּרְיָוֶשׁ מַלְכָּא כְּתַב לְכָל־עַמְמַיָּא

nations of every language that inhabit the earth, "May your well-being abound! 27I have hereby given an order that throughout my royal domain men must tremble in fear before the God of Daniel, for He is the living God who endures forever; His kingdom is indestructible, and His dominion is to the end of time; 28He delivers and saves, and performs signs and wonders in heaven and on earth, for He delivered Daniel from the power of the lions." 29Thus Daniel prospered during the reign of Darius and during the reign of Cyrus the Persian.

7 In the first year of King Belshazzar of Babylon, Daniel saw a dream and a vision of his mind in bed; afterward he wrote down the dream. Beginning the account, 2Daniel related the following:

"In my vision at night, I saw the four winds of heaven stirring up the great sea. 3Four mighty beasts different from each other emerged from the sea. 4The first was like a lion but had eagles' wings. As I looked on, its wings were plucked off, and it was lifted off the ground and set on its feet like a man and given the mind of a man. 5Then I saw a second, different beast, which was like a bear but raised on one side, and with three fangs in its mouth among its teeth; it was told, 'Arise, eat much meat!' 6After that, as I looked on, there was another one, like a leopard, and it had on its back four wings like those of a bird; the beast had four heads, and dominion was given to it. 7After that, as I looked on in the night vision, there was a fourth beast—fearsome, dreadful, and very powerful, with great iron teeth—that devoured and crushed, and stamped the remains with its feet. It was different from all the other beasts which had gone before it; and it had ten horns. 8While I was gazing upon these horns, a new little horn

אֻמַּיָּא וְלִשָׁנַיָּא דִּי־דָארִין דָּיְרִין בְּכָל־אַרְעָא שְׁלָמְכוֹן יִשְׂגֵּא: 27 מִן־קֳדָמַי שִׂים טְעֵם דִּי ׀ בְּכָל־שָׁלְטָן מַלְכוּתִי לֶהֱוֺן זָאעִין זָיְעִין וְדָחֲלִין מִן־קֳדָם אֱלָהֵהּ דִּי־דָנִיֵּאל דִּי־הוּא ׀ אֱלָהָא חַיָּא וְקַיָּם לְעָלְמִין וּמַלְכוּתֵהּ דִּי־לָא תִתְחַבַּל וְשָׁלְטָנֵהּ עַד־סוֹפָא: 28 מְשֵׁיזִב וּמַצִּל וְעָבֵד אָתִין וְתִמְהִין בִּשְׁמַיָּא וּבְאַרְעָא דִּי שֵׁיזִיב לְדָנִיֵּאל מִן־יַד אַרְיָוָתָא: 29 וְדָנִיֵּאל דְּנָה הַצְלַח בְּמַלְכוּת דָּרְיָוֶשׁ וּבְמַלְכוּת כּוֹרֶשׁ פָּרְסָאָה: פ

ז בִּשְׁנַת חֲדָה לְבֵלְאשַׁצַּר מֶלֶךְ בָּבֶל דָּנִיֵּאל חֵלֶם חֲזָה וְחֶזְוֵי רֵאשֵׁהּ עַל־מִשְׁכְּבֵהּ בֵּאדַיִן חֶלְמָא כְתַב רֵאשׁ מִלִּין אֲמַר: 2 עָנֵה דָנִיֵּאל וְאָמַר חָזֵה הֲוֵית בְּחֶזְוִי עִם־לֵילְיָא וַאֲרוּ אַרְבַּע רוּחֵי שְׁמַיָּא מְגִיחָן לְיַמָּא רַבָּא: 3 וְאַרְבַּע חֵיוָן רַבְרְבָן סָלְקָן מִן־יַמָּא שָׁנְיָן דָּא מִן־דָּא: 4 קַדְמָיְתָא כְאַרְיֵה וְגַפִּין דִּי־נְשַׁר לַהּ חָזֵה הֲוֵית עַד דִּי־מְּרִיטוּ גַפַּיהּ וּנְטִילַת מִן־אַרְעָא וְעַל־רַגְלַיִן כֶּאֱנָשׁ הֳקִימַת וּלְבַב אֱנָשׁ יְהִיב לַהּ: 5 וַאֲרוּ חֵיוָה אָחֳרִי תִנְיָנָה דָּמְיָה לְדֹב וְלִשְׂטַר־חַד הֳקִמַת וּתְלָת עִלְעִין בְּפֻמַּהּ בֵּין שִׁנַּהּ וְכֵן אָמְרִין לַהּ קוּמִי אֲכֻלִי בְּשַׂר שַׂגִּיא: 6 בָּאתַר דְּנָה חָזֵה הֲוֵית וַאֲרוּ אָחֳרִי כִּנְמַר וְלַהּ גַּפִּין אַרְבַּע דִּי־עוֹף עַל־גַּבַּהּ וְאַרְבְּעָה רֵאשִׁין לְחֵיוְתָא וְשָׁלְטָן יְהִיב לַהּ: 7 בָּאתַר דְּנָה חָזֵה הֲוֵית בְּחֶזְוֵי לֵילְיָא וַאֲרוּ חֵיוָה רְבִיעָיָה רְבִיעָיָה דְּחִילָה וְאֵימְתָנִי וְתַקִּיפָא יַתִּירָא וְשִׁנַּיִן דִּי־פַרְזֶל לַהּ רַבְרְבָן אָכְלָה וּמַדֱּקָה וּשְׁאָרָא בְּרַגְלַהּ רָפְסָה וְהִיא מְשַׁנְּיָה מִן־כָּל־חֵיוָתָא דִּי קָדָמַיהּ* וְקַרְנַיִן עֲשַׂר לַהּ: 8 מִשְׂתַּכַּל הֲוֵית בְּקַרְנַיָּא וַאֲלוּ קֶרֶן אָחֳרִי

sprouted up among them; three of the older horns were uprooted to make room for it. There were eyes in this horn like those of a man, and a mouth that spoke arrogantly. [9]As I looked on,

Thrones were set in place,
And the Ancient of Days took His seat.
His garment was like white snow,
And the hair of His head was like lamb's[a] wool.
His throne was tongues of flame;
Its wheels were blazing fire.

[10]A river of fire streamed forth before Him;
Thousands upon thousands served Him;
Myriads upon myriads attended Him;
The court sat and the books were opened.

[11]I looked on. Then, because of the arrogant words that the horn spoke, the beast was killed as I looked on; its body was destroyed and it was consigned to the flames. [12]The dominion of the other beasts was taken away, but an extension of life was given to them for a time and season. [13]As I looked on, in the night vision,

One like a human being
Came with the clouds of heaven;
He reached the Ancient of Days
And was presented to Him.

[14]Dominion, glory, and kingship were given to him;
All peoples and nations of every language must serve him.
His dominion is an everlasting dominion that shall not pass away,
And his kingship, one that shall not be destroyed.

[15]As for me, Daniel, my spirit was disturbed within me and the vision of my mind alarmed me. [16]I approached one of the attendants and asked him the true meaning of all this. He gave me this interpretation of the matter: [17]'These great beasts, four in number [mean] four kingdoms[b] will arise out of the earth; [18]then holy

זְעֵירָה֙ סִלְקָ֣ת בֵּֽינֵיהֵ֔ן וּתְלָ֣ת מִן־
קַרְנַיָּ֣א קַדְמָיָתָ֗א אתעקרו אתְעֲקַ֖רָה מִן־
קדמֵיה וַאֲל֥וּ עַיְנִ֛ין כְּעַיְנֵ֥י אֲנָשָׁ֖א
בְּקַרְנָא־דָ֑א וּפֻ֖ם מְמַלִּ֥ל רַבְרְבָֽן׃ [9] חָזֵ֣ה
הֲוֵ֗ית עַ֣ד דִּ֤י
כָרְסָוָן֙ רְמִ֔יו
וְעַתִּ֥יק יֹומִ֖ין יְתִ֑ב
לְבוּשֵׁ֣הּ ׀ כִּתְלַ֣ג חִוָּ֗ר
וּשְׂעַ֤ר רֵאשֵׁהּ֙ כַּעֲמַ֣ר נְקֵ֔א
כָּרְסְיֵהּ֙ שְׁבִיבִ֣ין דִּי־נ֔וּר
גַּלְגִּלֹּ֖והִי נ֥וּר דָּלִֽק׃
[10] נְהַ֣ר דִּֽי־נ֗וּר נָגֵ֤ד וְנָפֵק֙ מִן־קֳדָמֹ֔והִי
אֶ֤לֶף אלפים אַלְפִ֣ין יְשַׁמְּשׁוּנֵּ֔הּ
וְרִבֹּ֥ו רבון רִבְבָ֖ן קָֽדָמֹ֣והִי יְקוּמ֑וּן
דִּינָ֣א יְתִ֔ב וְסִפְרִ֖ין פְּתִֽיחוּ׃
[11] חָזֵ֣ה הֲוֵ֗ית בֵּאדַ֙יִן֙ מִן־קָ֤ל מִלַּיָּא֙
רַבְרְבָתָ֔א דִּ֥י קַרְנָ֖א מְמַלֱּלָ֑ה חָזֵ֣ה הֲוֵ֗ית
עַ֣ד דִּ֤י קְטִילַת֙ חֵֽיוְתָ֔א וְהוּבַ֖ד גִּשְׁמַ֑הּ
וִיהִיבַ֖ת לִיקֵדַ֥ת אֶשָּֽׁא׃ [12] וּשְׁאָר֙ חֵֽיוָתָ֔א
הֶעְדִּ֖יו שָׁלְטָנְהֹ֑ון וְאַרְכָ֧ה בְחַיִּ֛ין יְהִ֥יבַת
לְהֹ֖ון עַד־זְמַ֥ן וְעִדָּֽן׃ [13] חָזֵ֤ה הֲוֵית֙ בְּחֶזְוֵ֣י
לֵֽילְיָ֔א
וַאֲר֙וּ עִם־עֲנָנֵ֣י שְׁמַיָּ֔א
כְּבַ֥ר אֱנָ֖שׁ אָתֵ֣ה הֲוָ֑ה
וְעַד־עַתִּ֤יק יֹֽומַיָּא֙ מְטָ֔ה
וּקְדָמֹ֖והִי הַקְרְבֽוּהִי׃
[14] וְלֵ֨הּ יְהִ֤יב שָׁלְטָן֙ וִיקָ֣ר וּמַלְכ֔וּ
וְכֹ֣ל עַֽמְמַיָּ֗א אֻמַיָּ֛א וְלִשָּׁנַיָּ֖א לֵ֣הּ יִפְלְח֑וּן
שָׁלְטָנֵ֞הּ שָׁלְטָ֤ן עָלַם֙ דִּֽי־לָ֣א יֶעְדֵּ֔ה
וּמַלְכוּתֵ֖הּ דִּי־לָ֥א תִתְחַבַּֽל׃ פ
[15] אֶתְכְּרִיַּ֥ת רוּחִ֛י אֲנָ֥ה דָנִיֵּ֖אל בְּגֹ֣וא נִדְנֶ֑ה
וְחֶזְוֵ֥י רֵאשִׁ֖י יְבַהֲלֻנַּֽנִי׃ [16] קִרְבֵ֗ת עַל־חַד֙
מִן־קָ֣אֲמַיָּ֔א וְיַצִּיבָ֥א אֶבְעֵֽא־מִנֵּ֖הּ עַל־כָּל־
דְּנָ֑ה וַאֲמַר־לִ֕י וּפְשַׁ֥ר מִלַּיָּ֖א יְהֹודְעִנַּֽנִי׃
[17] אִלֵּין֙ חֵיוָתָ֣א רַבְרְבָתָ֔א דִּ֥י אִנִּ֖ין אַרְבַּ֑ע
אַרְבְּעָ֥ה מַלְכִ֖ין יְקוּמ֥וּן מִן־אַרְעָֽא׃

ones of the Most High will receive the kingdom, and will possess the kingdom forever—forever and ever.' ¹⁹Then I wanted to ascertain the true meaning of the fourth beast, which was different from them all, very fearsome, with teeth of iron, claws of bronze, that devoured and crushed, and stamped the remains; ²⁰and of the ten horns on its head; and of the new one that sprouted, to make room for which three fell—the horn that had eyes, and a mouth that spoke arrogantly, and which was more conspicuous than its fellows. ²¹(I looked on as that horn made war with the holy ones and overcame them, ²²until the Ancient of Days came and judgment was rendered in favor of the holy ones of the Most High, for the time had come, and the holy ones took possession of the kingdom.) ²³This is what he said: 'The fourth beast [means]—there will be a fourth kingdom upon the earth which will be different from all the kingdoms; it will devour the whole earth, tread it down, and crush it. ²⁴And the ten horns [mean]—from that kingdom, ten kings will arise, and after them another will arise. He will be different from the former ones, and will bring low three kings. ²⁵He will speak words against the Most High, and will harass the holy ones of the Most High. He will think of changing times and laws, and they will be delivered into his power for a ᶜtime, times, and half a time.⁻ᶜ ²⁶Then the court will sit and his dominion will be taken away, to be destroyed and abolished for all time. ²⁷The kingship and dominion and grandeur belonging to all the kingdoms under Heaven will be given to the people of the holy ones of the Most High. Their kingdom shall be an everlasting kingdom, and all dominions shall serve and obey them.'" ²⁸Here the account ends.

I, Daniel, was very alarmed by my thoughts, and my face darkened; and I could not put the matter out of my mind.

---

¹⁸ וִיקַבְּלוּן֙ מַלְכוּתָ֔א קַדִּישֵׁ֖י עֶלְיוֹנִ֑ין וְיַחְסְנ֤וּן מַלְכוּתָא֙ עַד־עָ֣לְמָ֔א וְעַ֖ד עָלַ֥ם עָלְמַיָּֽא׃ ¹⁹ אֱדַ֗יִן צְבִית֙ לְיַצָּבָ֔א עַל־חֵֽיוְתָא֙ רְבִיעָ֣יְתָ֔א דִּֽי־הֲוָ֥ת שָֽׁנְיָ֖ה מִן־כלהון כָּלְּהֵ֑ין דְּחִילָ֤ה יַתִּ֙ירָה֙ שניה דִּֽי־פַרְזֶ֥ל וְטִפְרַ֖יהּ* דִּֽי־נְחָ֑שׁ אָֽכְלָ֤ה מַדֱּקָה֙ וּשְׁאָרָ֔א בְּרַגְלַ֥יהּ* רָֽפְסָֽה׃ ²⁰ וְעַל־קַרְנַיָּ֣א עֲשַׂ֗ר דִּ֣י בְרֵאשַׁ֔הּ וְאָֽחֳרִי֙ דִּ֣י סִלְקַ֔ת וּנְפַ֥לָה מִן־קדמיה קֳדָמַ֖הּ תְּלָ֑ת וְקַרְנָ֨א דִכֵּ֜ן וְעַיְנִ֣ין לַ֗הּ וּפֻם֙ מְמַלִּ֣ל רַבְרְבָ֔ן וְחֶזְוַ֖הּ רַ֥ב מִן־חַבְרָתַֽהּ׃ ²¹ חָזֵ֣ה הֲוֵ֔ית וְקַרְנָ֣א דִכֵּ֔ן עָֽבְדָ֥ה קְרָ֖ב עִם־קַדִּישִׁ֑ין וְיָכְלָ֖ה לְהֽוֹן׃ ²² עַ֣ד דִּֽי־אֲתָ֗ה עַתִּיק֙ יֽוֹמַיָּ֔א וְדִינָ֣א יְהִ֔ב לְקַדִּישֵׁ֖י עֶלְיוֹנִ֑ין וְזִמְנָ֣א מְטָ֔ה וּמַלְכוּתָ֖א הֶחֱסִ֥נוּ קַדִּישִֽׁין׃ ²³ כֵּן֮ אֲמַר֒ חֵֽיוְתָא֙ רְבִיעָ֣יְתָ֔א מַלְכ֤וּ רביעיא רְבִיעָאָה֙ תֶּהֱוֵ֣א בְאַרְעָ֔א דִּ֥י תִשְׁנֵ֖א מִן־כָּל־מַלְכְוָתָ֑א וְתֵאכֻל֙ כָּל־אַרְעָ֔א וּתְדוּשִׁנַּ֖הּ וְתַדְּקִנַּֽהּ׃ ²⁴ וְקַרְנַיָּ֣א עֲשַׂ֗ר מִנַּהּ֙ מַלְכוּתָ֔ה עַשְׂרָ֥ה מַלְכִ֖ין יְקֻמ֑וּן וְאָֽחֳרָ֞ן יְק֣וּם אַֽחֲרֵיה֗וֹן וְה֤וּא יִשְׁנֵא֙ מִן־קַדְמָיֵ֔א וּתְלָתָ֥ה מַלְכִ֖ין יְהַשְׁפִּֽל׃ ²⁵ וּמִלִּ֗ין לְצַ֤ד עליא עִלָּאָה֙ יְמַלִּ֔ל וּלְקַדִּישֵׁ֥י עֶלְיוֹנִ֖ין יְבַלֵּ֑א וְיִסְבַּ֗ר לְהַשְׁנָיָה֙ זִמְנִ֣ין וְדָ֔ת וְיִתְיַהֲב֣וּן בִּידֵ֔הּ עַד־עִדָּ֥ן וְעִדָּנִ֖ין וּפְלַ֥ג עִדָּֽן׃ ²⁶ וְדִינָ֖א יִתִּ֑ב וְשָׁלְטָנֵ֣הּ יְהַעְדּ֔וֹן לְהַשְׁמָדָ֥ה וּלְהוֹבָדָ֖ה עַד־סוֹפָֽא׃ ²⁷ וּמַלְכוּתָ֨ה וְשָׁלְטָנָ֜א וּרְבוּתָ֗א דִּ֚י מַלְכְוָת֙ תְּח֣וֹת כָּל־שְׁמַיָּ֔א יְהִיבַ֕ת לְעַ֖ם קַדִּישֵׁ֣י עֶלְיוֹנִ֑ין מַלְכוּתֵהּ֙ מַלְכ֣וּת עָלַ֔ם וְכֹל֙ שָׁלְטָ֣נַיָּ֔א לֵ֥הּ יִפְלְח֖וּן וְיִֽשְׁתַּמְּעֽוּן׃ ²⁸ עַד־כָּ֖ה סוֹפָ֣א דִֽי־מִלְּתָ֑א אֲנָ֨ה דָֽנִיֵּ֜אל שַׂגִּ֣יא ׀ רַעְיוֹנַ֣י יְבַהֲלֻנַּ֗נִי וְזִיוַי֙ יִשְׁתַּנּ֣וֹן עֲלַ֔י וּמִלְּתָ֖א בְּלִבִּ֥י נִטְרֵֽת׃ פ

---

8 In the third year of the reign of King Belshazzar, a vision appeared to me, to me, Daniel, after the one that had appeared to me earlier. ²I saw in the vision—at the time I saw it I was in the fortress of Shushan, in the province of Elam—I saw in the vision that I was beside the Ulai River. ³I looked and saw a ram standing between me and the river; he had two horns; the horns were high, with one higher than the other, and the higher sprouting last. ⁴I saw the ram butting westward, northward, and southward. No beast could withstand him, and there was none to deliver from his power. He did as he pleased and grew great. ⁵As I looked on, a he-goat came from the west, passing over the entire earth without touching the ground. The goat had a conspicuous horn on its forehead. ⁶He came up to the two-horned ram that I had seen standing between me and the river and charged at him with furious force. ⁷I saw him reach the ram and rage at him; he struck the ram and broke its two horns, and the ram was powerless to withstand him. He threw him to the ground and trampled him, and there was none to deliver the ram from his power. ⁸Then the he-goat grew very great, but at the peak of his power his big horn was broken. In its place, four conspicuous horns sprouted toward the four winds of heaven. ⁹From one of them emerged a small horn, which extended itself greatly toward the south, toward the east, and toward the beautiful land. ¹⁰It grew as high as the host of heaven and it hurled some stars of the [heavenly] host to the ground and trampled them. ¹¹It vaunted itself against the very chief of the host; on its account the regular offering was suspended, and His holy place was abandoned. ¹²ᵃ⁻An army was arrayed iniquitously against the regular offering;⁻ᵃ it hurled truth to the ground and prospered in what it did.

ח בִּשְׁנַ֣ת שָׁל֔וֹשׁ לְמַלְכ֖וּת בֵּלְאשַׁצַּ֣ר
הַמֶּ֑לֶךְ חָז֞וֹן נִרְאָ֤ה אֵלַי֙ אֲנִ֣י דָֽנִיֵּ֔אל אַחֲרֵ֛י
הַנִּרְאָ֥ה אֵלַ֖י בַּתְּחִלָּֽה: ²וָֽאֶרְאֶה֮ בֶּֽחָזוֹן֒
וַיְהִי֙ בִּרְאֹתִ֔י וַאֲנִי֙ בְּשׁוּשַׁ֣ן הַבִּירָ֔ה אֲשֶׁ֖ר
בְּעֵילָ֣ם הַמְּדִינָ֑ה וָֽאֶרְאֶה֙ בֶּֽחָז֔וֹן וַאֲנִ֣י
הָיִ֔יתִי עַל־אוּבַ֖ל אוּלָֽי: ³וָאֶשָּׂ֣א עֵינַ֗י
וָֽאֶרְאֶה֮ וְהִנֵּ֣ה ׀ אַ֣יִל אֶחָ֗ד עֹמֵ֛ד לִפְנֵ֥י
הָאֻבָ֖ל וְל֣וֹ קְרָנָ֑יִם וְהַקְּרָנַ֣יִם גְּבֹה֗וֹת
וְהָֽאַחַת֙ גְּבֹהָ֣ה מִן־הַשֵּׁנִ֔ית וְהַ֨גְּבֹהָ֔ה עֹלָ֖ה
בָּאַחֲרֹנָֽה: ⁴רָאִ֣יתִי אֶת־הָאַ֡יִל מְנַגֵּ֩חַ יָ֨מָּה
וְצָפ֜וֹנָה וָנֶ֗גְבָּה וְכָל־חַיּוֹת֙ לֹא־יַֽעַמְד֣וּ
לְפָנָ֔יו וְאֵ֥ין מַצִּ֖יל מִיָּד֑וֹ וְעָשָׂ֥ה כִרְצֹנ֖וֹ
וְהִגְדִּֽיל: ⁵וַאֲנִ֣י ׀ הָיִ֣יתִי מֵבִ֗ין וְהִנֵּ֤ה צְפִיר־
הָֽעִזִּים֙ בָּ֤א מִן־הַֽמַּעֲרָב֙ עַל־פְּנֵ֣י כָל־הָאָ֔רֶץ
וְאֵ֥ין נוֹגֵ֖עַ בָּאָ֑רֶץ וְהַ֨צָּפִ֔יר קֶ֥רֶן חָז֖וּת בֵּ֥ין
עֵינָֽיו: ⁶וַיָּבֹ֗א עַד־הָאַ֙יִל֙ בַּ֣עַל הַקְּרָנַ֔יִם
אֲשֶׁ֣ר רָאִ֔יתִי עֹמֵ֖ד לִפְנֵ֣י הָאֻבָ֑ל וַיָּ֤רָץ אֵלָיו֙
בַּחֲמַ֥ת כֹּחֽוֹ: ⁷וּרְאִיתִ֞יו מַגִּ֣יעַ ׀ אֵ֣צֶל הָאַ֗יִל
וַיִּתְמַרְמַ֤ר אֵלָיו֙ וַיַּ֣ךְ אֶת־הָאַ֔יִל וַיְשַׁבֵּר֙
אֶת־שְׁתֵּ֣י קְרָנָ֔יו וְלֹא־הָ֥יָה כֹ֛חַ בָּאַ֖יִל
לַעֲמֹ֣ד לְפָנָ֑יו וַיַּשְׁלִיכֵ֤הוּ אַ֙רְצָה֙ וַֽיִּרְמְסֵ֔הוּ
וְלֹא־הָיָ֥ה מַצִּ֛יל לָאַ֖יִל מִיָּדֽוֹ: ⁸וּצְפִ֥יר
הָעִזִּ֖ים הִגְדִּ֣יל עַד־מְאֹ֑ד וּכְעָצְמ֗וֹ נִשְׁבְּרָה֙
הַקֶּ֣רֶן הַגְּדוֹלָ֔ה וַֽתַּעֲלֶ֜נָה חָז֤וּת אַרְבַּע֙
תַּחְתֶּ֔יהָ לְאַרְבַּ֖ע רוּח֥וֹת הַשָּׁמָֽיִם: ⁹וּמִן־
הָאַחַ֣ת מֵהֶ֗ם יָצָ֤א קֶֽרֶן־אַחַת֙ מִצְּעִירָ֔ה
וַתִּגְדַּל־יֶ֛תֶר אֶל־הַנֶּ֥גֶב וְאֶל־הַמִּזְרָ֖ח וְאֶל־
הַצֶּֽבִי: ¹⁰וַתִּגְדַּ֖ל עַד־צְבָ֣א הַשָּׁמָ֑יִם
וַתַּפֵּ֥ל אַ֙רְצָה֙ מִן־הַצָּבָ֣א וּמִן־הַכּֽוֹכָבִ֖ים
וַֽתִּרְמְסֵֽם: ¹¹וְעַ֥ד שַׂר־הַצָּבָ֖א הִגְדִּ֑יל וּמִמֶּ֙נּוּ֙
הֵרִ֣ים הַתָּמִ֔יד וְהֻשְׁלַ֖ךְ מְכ֥וֹן
מִקְדָּשֽׁוֹ: ¹²וְצָבָ֛א תִּנָּתֵ֥ן עַל־הַתָּמִ֖יד
בְּפָ֑שַׁע וְתַשְׁלֵ֤ךְ אֱמֶת֙ אַ֔רְצָה וְעָשְׂתָ֖ה
וְהִצְלִֽיחָה:

ᵃ⁻ᵃ Meaning of Heb. uncertain.

13Then I heard a holy being speaking, and another holy being said to whoever it was who was speaking, "How long will [what was seen in] the vision last—*-a*-the regular offering be forsaken because of transgression; the sanctuary be surrendered and the [heavenly] host be trampled?"*-a* 14He answered me,*b* "For twenty-three hundred evenings and mornings; then the sanctuary shall be cleansed." 15While I, Daniel, was seeing the vision, and trying to understand it, there appeared before me one who looked like a man. 16I heard a human voice from the middle of Ulai calling out, "Gabriel, make that man understand the vision." 17He came near to where I was standing, and as he came I was terrified, and fell prostrate. He said to me, "Understand, O man, that the vision refers to the time of the end." 18When he spoke with me, I was overcome by a deep sleep as I lay prostrate on the ground. Then he touched me and made me stand up, 19and said, "I am going to inform you of what will happen when wrath is at an end, for [it refers] to the time appointed for the end.

20"The two-horned ram that you saw [signifies] the kings of Media and Persia; 21and the buck, the he-goat--the king of Greece; and the large horn on his forehead, that is the first king. 22One was broken and four came in its stead—that [means]: four kingdoms will arise out of a nation, but without its power. 23When their kingdoms are at an end, when the measure of transgression*c* has been filled, then a king will arise, impudent and versed in intrigue. 24He will have great strength, but not through his own strength. He will be extraordinarily destructive; he will prosper in what he does, and destroy the mighty and the people of holy ones. 25By his cunning, he will use deceit successfully. He will make great plans, will destroy many, taking them unawares, and will rise up against the chief

13 וָאֶשְׁמְעָה אֶחָד־קָדוֹשׁ מְדַבֵּר וַיֹּאמֶר אֶחָד קָדוֹשׁ לַפַּלְמוֹנִי הַמְדַבֵּר עַד־מָתַי הֶחָזוֹן הַתָּמִיד וְהַפֶּשַׁע שֹׁמֵם תֵּת וְקֹדֶשׁ וְצָבָא מִרְמָס: 14 וַיֹּאמֶר אֵלַי עַד עֶרֶב בֹּקֶר אַלְפַּיִם וּשְׁלֹשׁ מֵאוֹת וְנִצְדַּק קֹדֶשׁ: 15 וַיְהִי בִּרְאֹתִי אֲנִי דָנִיֵּאל אֶת־הֶחָזוֹן וָאֲבַקְשָׁה בִינָה וְהִנֵּה עֹמֵד לְנֶגְדִּי כְּמַרְאֵה־גָבֶר: 16 וָאֶשְׁמַע קוֹל־אָדָם בֵּין אוּלָי וַיִּקְרָא וַיֹּאמַר גַּבְרִיאֵל הָבֵן לְהַלָּז אֶת־הַמַּרְאֶה: 17 וַיָּבֹא אֵצֶל עָמְדִי וּבְבֹאוֹ נִבְעַתִּי וָאֶפְּלָה עַל־פָּנָי וַיֹּאמֶר אֵלַי הָבֵן בֶּן־אָדָם כִּי לְעֶת־קֵץ הֶחָזוֹן: 18 וּבְדַבְּרוֹ עִמִּי נִרְדַּמְתִּי עַל־פָּנַי אָרְצָה וַיִּגַּע־בִּי וַיַּעֲמִידֵנִי עַל־עָמְדִי: 19 וַיֹּאמֶר הִנְנִי מוֹדִיעֲךָ אֵת אֲשֶׁר־יִהְיֶה בְּאַחֲרִית הַזָּעַם כִּי לְמוֹעֵד קֵץ: 20 הָאַיִל אֲשֶׁר־רָאִיתָ בַּעַל הַקְּרָנָיִם מַלְכֵי מָדַי וּפָרָס: 21 וְהַצָּפִיר הַשָּׂעִיר מֶלֶךְ יָוָן וְהַקֶּרֶן הַגְּדוֹלָה אֲשֶׁר בֵּין־עֵינָיו הוּא הַמֶּלֶךְ הָרִאשׁוֹן: 22 וְהַנִּשְׁבֶּרֶת וַתַּעֲמֹדְנָה אַרְבַּע תַּחְתֶּיהָ אַרְבַּע מַלְכֻיּוֹת מִגּוֹי יַעֲמֹדְנָה וְלֹא בְכֹחוֹ: 23 וּבְאַחֲרִית מַלְכוּתָם כְּהָתֵם הַפֹּשְׁעִים יַעֲמֹד מֶלֶךְ עַז־פָּנִים וּמֵבִין חִידוֹת: 24 וְעָצַם כֹּחוֹ וְלֹא בְכֹחוֹ וְנִפְלָאוֹת יַשְׁחִית וְהִצְלִיחַ וְעָשָׂה וְהִשְׁחִית עֲצוּמִים וְעַם־קְדֹשִׁים: 25 וְעַל־שִׂכְלוֹ וְהִצְלִיחַ מִרְמָה בְּיָדוֹ וּבִלְבָבוֹ יַגְדִּיל

---

b Several ancient versions "him."
c Lit. "transgressors."

of chiefs, but will be broken, not by [human] hands. [26]What was said in the vision about evenings and mornings is true. Now you keep the vision a secret, for it pertains to far-off days." [27]So I, Daniel, was stricken,[a] and languished many days. Then I arose and attended to the king's business, but I was dismayed by the vision and no one could explain it.

9 In the first year of Darius son of Ahasuerus, of Median descent, who was made king over the kingdom of the Chaldeans—[2]in the first year of his reign, I, Daniel, consulted the books concerning the number of years that, according to the word of the Lord that had come to Jeremiah the prophet, were to be the term of Jerusalem's desolation—seventy years. [3]I turned my face to the Lord God, devoting myself to prayer and supplication, in fasting, in sackcloth and ashes. [4]I prayed to the Lord my God, making confession thus: "O Lord, great and awesome God, who stays faithful to His covenant with those who love Him and keep His commandments! [5]We have sinned; we have gone astray; we have acted wickedly; we have been rebellious and have deviated from Your commandments and Your rules, [6]and have not obeyed Your servants the prophets who spoke in Your name to our kings, our officers, our fathers, and all the people of the land. [7]With You, O Lord, is the right, and the shame is on us to this very day, on the men of Judah and the inhabitants of Jerusalem, all Israel, near and far, in all the lands where You have banished them, for the trespass they committed against You. [8]The shame, O Lord, is on us, on our kings, our officers, and our fathers, because we have sinned against You. [9]To the Lord our God belong mercy and forgiveness, for we rebelled against Him, [10]and did not obey the Lord our God by following His teachings that

וּבְשַׁלְוָ֣ה יַשְׁחִ֣ית רַבִּ֑ים וְעַל־שַׂר־שָׂרִים֙ יַעֲמֹ֔ד וּבְאֶ֥פֶס יָ֖ד יִשָּׁבֵֽר׃ 26 וּמַרְאֵ֨ה הָעֶ֧רֶב וְהַבֹּ֛קֶר אֲשֶׁ֥ר נֶאֱמַ֖ר אֱמֶ֣ת ה֑וּא וְאַתָּה֙ סְתֹ֣ם הֶֽחָז֔וֹן כִּ֖י לְיָמִ֥ים רַבִּֽים׃ 27 וַאֲנִ֣י דָנִיֵּ֗אל נִהְיֵ֤יתִי֙ וְנֶֽחֱלֵ֣יתִי֙ יָמִ֔ים וָאָק֕וּם וָאֶֽעֱשֶׂ֖ה אֶת־מְלֶ֣אכֶת הַמֶּ֑לֶךְ וָאֶשְׁתּוֹמֵ֥ם עַל־הַמַּרְאֶ֖ה וְאֵ֥ין מֵבִֽין׃ פ

ט בִּשְׁנַ֣ת אַחַ֗ת לְדָרְיָ֛וֶשׁ בֶּן־אֲחַשְׁוֵר֖וֹשׁ מִזֶּ֣רַע מָדָ֑י אֲשֶׁ֣ר הָמְלַ֔ךְ עַ֖ל מַלְכ֥וּת כַּשְׂדִּֽים׃ 2 בִּשְׁנַ֤ת אַחַת֙ לְמָלְכ֔וֹ אֲנִי֙ דָּֽנִיֵּ֔אל בִּינֹ֥תִי בַּסְּפָרִ֑ים מִסְפַּ֣ר הַשָּׁנִ֗ים אֲשֶׁ֨ר הָיָ֤ה דְבַר־יְהוָה֙ אֶל־יִרְמְיָ֣ה הַנָּבִ֔יא לְמַלֹּ֛אות לְחָרְב֥וֹת יְרוּשָׁלִַ֖ם שִׁבְעִ֥ים שָׁנָֽה׃ 3 וָאֶתְּנָ֣ה אֶת־פָּנַ֗י אֶל־אֲדֹנָי֙ הָֽאֱלֹהִ֔ים לְבַקֵּ֥שׁ תְּפִלָּ֖ה וְתַחֲנוּנִ֑ים בְּצ֖וֹם וְשַׂ֥ק וָאֵֽפֶר׃ 4 וָאֶתְפַּֽלְלָ֛ה לַיהוָ֥ה אֱלֹהַ֖י וָאֶתְוַדֶּ֑ה וָאֹמְרָ֗ה אָֽנָּ֤א אֲדֹנָי֙ הָאֵ֤ל הַגָּדוֹל֙ וְהַנּוֹרָ֔א שֹׁמֵ֤ר הַבְּרִית֙ וְהַחֶ֔סֶד לְאֹהֲבָ֖יו וּלְשֹׁמְרֵ֥י מִצְוֺתָֽיו׃ 5 חָטָ֥אנוּ וְעָוִ֖ינוּ והִרְשַׁ֣עְנוּ וּמָרָ֑דְנוּ וְס֥וֹר מִמִּצְוֺתֶ֖ךָ וּמִמִּשְׁפָּטֶֽיךָ׃ 6 וְלֹ֤א שָׁמַ֙עְנוּ֙ אֶל־עֲבָדֶ֣יךָ הַנְּבִיאִ֔ים אֲשֶׁ֤ר דִּבְּרוּ֙ בְּשִׁמְךָ֔ אֶל־מְלָכֵ֧ינוּ שָׂרֵ֛ינוּ וַאֲבֹתֵ֖ינוּ וְאֶ֥ל כָּל־עַ֥ם הָאָֽרֶץ׃ 7 לְךָ֤ אֲדֹנָי֙ הַצְּדָקָ֔ה וְלָ֛נוּ בֹּ֥שֶׁת הַפָּנִ֖ים כַּיּ֣וֹם הַזֶּ֑ה לְאִ֤ישׁ יְהוּדָה֙ וּלְיוֹשְׁבֵ֣י יְרוּשָׁלִַ֔ם וּֽלְכָל־יִשְׂרָאֵ֞ל הַקְּרֹבִ֣ים וְהָרְחֹקִ֗ים בְּכָל־הָֽאֲרָצוֹת֙ אֲשֶׁ֣ר הִדַּחְתָּ֣ם שָׁ֔ם בְּמַעֲלָ֖ם אֲשֶׁ֥ר מָֽעֲלוּ־בָֽךְ׃ 8 יְהוָ֗ה לָ֚נוּ בֹּ֣שֶׁת הַפָּנִ֔ים לִמְלָכֵ֥ינוּ לְשָׂרֵ֖ינוּ וְלַאֲבֹתֵ֑ינוּ אֲשֶׁ֥ר חָטָ֖אנוּ לָֽךְ׃ 9 לַֽאדֹנָ֣י אֱלֹהֵ֔ינוּ הָרַחֲמִ֖ים וְהַסְּלִח֑וֹת כִּ֥י מָרַ֖דְנוּ בּֽוֹ׃ 10 וְלֹ֣א שָׁמַ֔עְנוּ בְּק֖וֹל יְהוָ֣ה אֱלֹהֵ֑ינוּ לָלֶ֤כֶת בְּתֹֽרֹתָיו֙ אֲשֶׁ֣ר נָתַ֣ן לְפָנֵ֔ינוּ

He set before us through His servants the prophets. [11]All Israel has violated Your teaching and gone astray, disobeying You; so the curse and the oath written in the Teaching of Moses, the servant of God, have been poured down upon us, for we have sinned against Him. [12]He carried out the threat that He made against us, and against our rulers who ruled us, to bring upon us great misfortune; under the whole heaven there has never been done the like of what was done to Jerusalem. [13]All that calamity, just as is written in the Teaching of Moses, came upon us, yet we did not supplicate the LORD our God, did not repent of our iniquity or become wise through Your truth. [14]Hence the LORD was intent upon bringing calamity upon us, for the LORD our God is in the right in all that He has done, but we have not obeyed Him.

[15]"Now, O Lord our God—You who brought Your people out of the land of Egypt with a mighty hand, winning fame for Yourself to this very day—we have sinned, we have acted wickedly. [16]O Lord, as befits Your abundant benevolence, let Your wrathful fury turn back from Your city Jerusalem, Your holy mountain; for because of our sins and the iniquities of our fathers, Jerusalem and Your people have become a mockery among all who are around us.

[17]"O our God, hear now the prayer of Your servant and his plea, and show Your favor to Your desolate sanctuary, for the Lord's sake. [18]Incline Your ear, O my God, and hear; open Your eyes and see our desolation and the city to which Your name is attached. Not because of any merit of ours do we lay our plea before You but because of Your abundant mercies. [19]O Lord, hear! O Lord, forgive! O Lord, listen, and act without delay for Your own sake, O my God; for Your name is attached to Your city and Your people!"

בְּיַ֖ד עֲבָדָ֣יו הַנְּבִיאִֽים׃ 11 וְכָל־יִשְׂרָאֵ֗ל עָבְרוּ֙ אֶת־תּ֣וֹרָתֶ֔ךָ וְס֕וֹר לְבִלְתִּ֖י שְׁמ֣וֹעַ בְּקֹלֶ֑ךָ וַתִּתַּ֨ךְ עָלֵ֜ינוּ הָאָלָ֣ה וְהַשְּׁבֻעָ֗ה אֲשֶׁ֤ר כְּתוּבָה֙ בְּתוֹרַת֙ מֹשֶׁ֣ה עֶֽבֶד־הָֽאֱלֹהִ֔ים כִּ֥י חָטָ֖אנוּ לֽוֹ׃ 12 וַיָּ֜קֶם אֶת־דְּבָרָ֣יו ׀ אֲשֶׁר־דִּבֶּ֣ר עָלֵ֗ינוּ וְעַ֤ל שֹֽׁפְטֵ֙ינוּ֙ אֲשֶׁ֣ר שְׁפָט֔וּנוּ לְהָבִ֥יא עָלֵ֖ינוּ רָעָ֣ה גְדֹלָ֑ה אֲשֶׁ֣ר לֹֽא־נֶעֶשְׂתָ֗ה תַּ֚חַת כָּל־הַשָּׁמַ֔יִם כַּאֲשֶׁ֥ר נֶעֶשְׂתָ֖ה בִּירוּשָׁלָֽ͏ִם׃ 13 כַּאֲשֶׁ֤ר כָּתוּב֙ בְּתוֹרַ֣ת מֹשֶׁ֔ה אֵ֛ת כָּל־הָרָעָ֥ה הַזֹּ֖את בָּ֣אָה עָלֵ֑ינוּ וְלֹֽא־חִלִּ֜ינוּ אֶת־פְּנֵ֣י ׀ יְהוָ֣ה אֱלֹהֵ֗ינוּ לָשׁוּב֙ מֵֽעֲוֺנֵ֔נוּ וּלְהַשְׂכִּ֖יל בַּאֲמִתֶּֽךָ׃ 14 וַיִּשְׁקֹ֤ד יְהוָה֙ עַל־הָ֣רָעָ֔ה וַיְבִיאֶ֖הָ עָלֵ֑ינוּ כִּֽי־צַדִּ֞יק יְהוָ֣ה אֱלֹהֵ֗ינוּ עַל־כָּל־מַעֲשָׂיו֙ אֲשֶׁ֣ר עָשָׂ֔ה וְלֹ֥א שָׁמַ֖עְנוּ בְּקֹלֽוֹ׃ 15 וְעַתָּ֣ה ׀ אֲדֹנָ֣י אֱלֹהֵ֗ינוּ אֲשֶׁר֩ הוֹצֵ֨אתָ אֶֽת־עַמְּךָ֜ מֵאֶ֤רֶץ מִצְרַ֙יִם֙ בְּיָ֣ד חֲזָקָ֔ה וַתַּֽעַשׂ־לְךָ֥ שֵׁ֖ם כַּיּ֣וֹם הַזֶּ֑ה חָטָ֖אנוּ רָשָֽׁעְנוּ׃ 16 אֲדֹנָ֗י כְּכָל־צִדְקֹתֶ֙ךָ֙ יָֽשָׁב־נָ֣א אַפְּךָ֣ וַחֲמָֽתְךָ֔ מֵעִֽירְךָ֥ יְרוּשָׁלַ֖͏ִם הַר־קָדְשֶׁ֑ךָ כִּ֤י בַחֲטָאֵ֙ינוּ֙ וּבַעֲוֺנ֣וֹת אֲבֹתֵ֔ינוּ יְרוּשָׁלַ֥͏ִם וְעַמְּךָ֛ לְחֶרְפָּ֖ה לְכָל־סְבִיבֹתֵֽינוּ׃ 17 וְעַתָּ֣ה ׀ שְׁמַ֣ע אֱלֹהֵ֗ינוּ אֶל־תְּפִלַּ֤ת עַבְדְּךָ֙ וְאֶל־תַּ֣חֲנוּנָ֔יו וְהָאֵ֣ר פָּנֶ֔יךָ עַל־מִקְדָּשְׁךָ֖ הַשָּׁמֵ֑ם לְמַ֖עַן אֲדֹנָֽי׃ 18 הַטֵּ֨ה אֱלֹהַ֥י ׀ אָזְנְךָ֮ וּֽשֲׁמָע֒ פְּקַ֣ח עֵינֶ֗יךָ וּרְאֵה֙ שֹֽׁמְמֹתֵ֔ינוּ וְהָעִ֕יר אֲשֶׁר־נִקְרָ֥א שִׁמְךָ֖ עָלֶ֑יהָ כִּ֣י ׀ לֹ֣א עַל־צִדְקֹתֵ֗ינוּ אֲנַ֙חְנוּ֙ מַפִּילִ֤ים תַּחֲנוּנֵ֙ינוּ֙ לְפָנֶ֔יךָ כִּ֖י עַל־רַחֲמֶ֥יךָ הָרַבִּֽים׃ 19 אֲדֹנָ֤י ׀ שְׁמָ֙עָה֙ אֲדֹנָ֣י ׀ סְלָ֔חָה אֲדֹנָ֛י הַֽקְשִׁ֥יבָה וַעֲשֵׂ֖ה אַל־תְּאַחַ֑ר לְמַֽעֲנְךָ֣ אֱלֹהַ֔י כִּֽי־שִׁמְךָ֣ נִקְרָ֔א עַל־עִֽירְךָ֖ וְעַל־עַמֶּֽךָ׃

20While I was speaking, praying, and confessing my sin and the sin of my people Israel, and laying my supplication before the Lord my God on behalf of the holy mountain of my God—21while I was uttering my prayer, the man Gabriel, whom I had previously seen in the vision, was sent forth in flight and reached me about the time of the evening offering. 22He made me understand by speaking to me and saying, "Daniel, I have just come forth to give you understanding. 23A word went forth as you began your plea, and I have come to tell it, for you are precious; so mark the word and understand the vision.

24"Seventy weeks*a* have been decreed for your people and your holy city until the measure of transgression is filled and that of sin complete, until iniquity is expiated, and eternal righteousness ushered in; and prophetic vision ratified,*b* and the Holy of Holies anointed. 25You must know and understand: From the issuance of the word to restore and rebuild Jerusalem until the [time of the] anointed leader is seven weeks; and for sixty-two weeks it will be rebuilt, square and moat, but in a time of distress. 26And after those sixty-two weeks, the anointed one will disappear and vanish.*c* The army of a leader who is to come will destroy the city and the sanctuary, but its end will come through a flood. Desolation is decreed until the end of war. 27During one week he will make a firm covenant with many. For half a week he will put a stop to the sacrifice and the meal offering. At the *c*-corner [of the altar]-*c* will be an appalling abomination until the decreed destruction will be poured down upon the appalling thing."

10

In the third year of King Cyrus of Persia, an oracle was revealed to Daniel, who was called

וְעוֹד אֲנִי מְדַבֵּר וּמִתְפַּלֵּל וּמִתְוַדֶּה 20 חַטָּאתִי וְחַטַּאת עַמִּי יִשְׂרָאֵל וּמַפִּיל תְּחִנָּתִי לִפְנֵי יְהוָה אֱלֹהַי עַל הַר־קֹדֶשׁ אֱלֹהָי׃ 21 וְעוֹד אֲנִי מְדַבֵּר בַּתְּפִלָּה וְהָאִישׁ גַּבְרִיאֵל אֲשֶׁר רָאִיתִי בֶחָזוֹן בַּתְּחִלָּה מֻעָף בִּיעָף נֹגֵעַ אֵלַי כְּעֵת מִנְחַת־עָרֶב׃ 22 וַיָּבֶן וַיְדַבֵּר עִמִּי וַיֹּאמַר דָּנִיֵּאל עַתָּה יָצָאתִי לְהַשְׂכִּילְךָ בִינָה׃ 23 בִּתְחִלַּת תַּחֲנוּנֶיךָ יָצָא דָבָר וַאֲנִי בָּאתִי לְהַגִּיד כִּי חֲמוּדוֹת אָתָּה וּבִין בַּדָּבָר וְהָבֵן בַּמַּרְאֶה׃ 24 שָׁבֻעִים שִׁבְעִים נֶחְתַּךְ עַל־עַמְּךָ וְעַל־ עִיר קָדְשֶׁךָ לְכַלֵּא הַפֶּשַׁע וּלְחָתֵם [וּלְהָתֵם] חטאות [חַטָּאת] וּלְכַפֵּר עָוֹן וּלְהָבִיא צֶדֶק עֹלָמִים וְלַחְתֹּם חָזוֹן וְנָבִיא וְלִמְשֹׁחַ קֹדֶשׁ קָדָשִׁים׃ 25 וְתֵדַע וְתַשְׂכֵּל מִן־מֹצָא דָבָר לְהָשִׁיב וְלִבְנוֹת יְרוּשָׁלַ͏ִם עַד־מָשִׁיחַ נָגִיד שָׁבֻעִים שִׁבְעָה וְשָׁבֻעִים שִׁשִּׁים וּשְׁנַיִם תָּשׁוּב וְנִבְנְתָה רְחוֹב וְחָרוּץ וּבְצוֹק הָעִתִּים׃ 26 וְאַחֲרֵי הַשָּׁבֻעִים שִׁשִּׁים וּשְׁנַיִם יִכָּרֵת מָשִׁיחַ וְאֵין לוֹ וְהָעִיר וְהַקֹּדֶשׁ יַשְׁחִית עַם נָגִיד הַבָּא וְקִצּוֹ בַשֶּׁטֶף וְעַד קֵץ מִלְחָמָה נֶחֱרֶצֶת שֹׁמֵמוֹת׃ 27 וְהִגְבִּיר בְּרִית לָרַבִּים שָׁבוּעַ אֶחָד וַחֲצִי הַשָּׁבוּעַ יַשְׁבִּית זֶבַח וּמִנְחָה וְעַל כְּנַף שִׁקּוּצִים מְשֹׁמֵם וְעַד־כָּלָה וְנֶחֱרָצָה תִּתַּךְ עַל־שֹׁמֵם׃ פ

רְ בִּשְׁנַת שָׁלוֹשׁ לְכוֹרֶשׁ מֶלֶךְ פָּרַס דָּבָר נִגְלָה לְדָנִיֵּאל אֲשֶׁר־נִקְרָא שְׁמוֹ בֵּלְטְשַׁאצַּר

---

a   Viz., of years.
b   Lit. "sealed."
c   Meaning of Heb. uncertain.

Belteshazzar. That oracle was true, *a*-but it was a great task to understand the prophecy; understanding came to him through the vision.-*a*

²At that time, I, Daniel, kept three full weeks of mourning. ³I ate no tasty food, nor did any meat or wine enter my mouth. I did not anoint myself until the three weeks were over. ⁴It was on the twenty-fourth day of the first month, when I was on the bank of the great river—the Tigris—⁵that I looked and saw a man dressed in linen, his loins girt in *b*-fine gold.-*b* ⁶His body was like beryl, his face had the appearance of lightning, his eyes were like flaming torches, his arms and legs had the color of burnished bronze, and the sound of his speech was like the noise of a multitude.

⁷I, Daniel, alone saw the vision; the men who were with me did not see the vision, yet they were seized with a great terror and fled into hiding. ⁸So I was left alone to see this great vision. I was drained of strength, my vigor was destroyed, and I could not summon up strength. ⁹I heard him speaking; and when I heard him speaking, overcome by a deep sleep, I lay prostrate on the ground. ¹⁰Then a hand touched me, and shook me onto my hands and knees. ¹¹He said to me, "O Daniel, precious man, mark what I say to you and stand up, for I have been sent to you." After he said this to me, I stood up, trembling. ¹²He then said to me, "Have no fear, Daniel, for from the first day that you set your mind to get understanding, practicing abstinence before your God, your prayer was heard, and I have come because of your prayer. ¹³However, the prince of the Persian kingdom opposed me for twenty-one days; now Michael, a prince of the first rank, has come to my aid, after I was detained there with the kings of Persia. ¹⁴So I have come to make you understand what is to

וֶאֱמֶת הַדָּבָר וְצָבָא גָדוֹל וּבִין אֶת־הַדָּבָר וּבִינָה לוֹ בַּמַּרְאֶה: ² בַּיָּמִים הָהֵם אֲנִי דָנִיֵּאל הָיִיתִי מִתְאַבֵּל שְׁלֹשָׁה שָׁבֻעִים יָמִים: ³ לֶחֶם חֲמֻדוֹת לֹא אָכַלְתִּי וּבָשָׂר וָיַיִן לֹא־בָא אֶל־פִּי וְסוֹךְ לֹא־סָכְתִּי עַד־מְלֹאת שְׁלֹשֶׁת שָׁבֻעִים יָמִים: פ ⁴ וּבְיוֹם עֶשְׂרִים וְאַרְבָּעָה לַחֹדֶשׁ הָרִאשׁוֹן וַאֲנִי הָיִיתִי עַל יַד הַנָּהָר הַגָּדוֹל הוּא חִדָּקֶל: ⁵ וָאֶשָּׂא אֶת־עֵינַי וָאֵרֶא וְהִנֵּה אִישׁ־אֶחָד לָבוּשׁ בַּדִּים וּמָתְנָיו חֲגֻרִים בְּכֶתֶם אוּפָז: ⁶ וּגְוִיָּתוֹ כְתַרְשִׁישׁ וּפָנָיו כְּמַרְאֵה בָרָק וְעֵינָיו כְּלַפִּידֵי אֵשׁ וּזְרֹעֹתָיו וּמַרְגְּלֹתָיו כְּעֵין נְחֹשֶׁת קָלָל וְקוֹל דְּבָרָיו כְּקוֹל הָמוֹן: ⁷ וְרָאִיתִי אֲנִי דָנִיֵּאל לְבַדִּי אֶת־הַמַּרְאָה וְהָאֲנָשִׁים אֲשֶׁר הָיוּ עִמִּי לֹא רָאוּ אֶת־הַמַּרְאָה אֲבָל חֲרָדָה גְדֹלָה נָפְלָה עֲלֵיהֶם וַיִּבְרְחוּ בְּהֵחָבֵא: ⁸ וַאֲנִי נִשְׁאַרְתִּי לְבַדִּי וָאֶרְאֶה אֶת־הַמַּרְאָה הַגְּדֹלָה הַזֹּאת וְלֹא נִשְׁאַר־בִּי כֹּחַ וְהוֹדִי נֶהְפַּךְ עָלַי לְמַשְׁחִית וְלֹא עָצַרְתִּי כֹּחַ: ⁹ וָאֶשְׁמַע אֶת־קוֹל דְּבָרָיו וּכְשָׁמְעִי אֶת־קוֹל דְּבָרָיו וַאֲנִי הָיִיתִי נִרְדָּם עַל־פָּנַי וּפָנַי אָרְצָה: ¹⁰ וְהִנֵּה־יָד נָגְעָה בִּי וַתְּנִיעֵנִי עַל־בִּרְכַּי וְכַפּוֹת יָדָי: ¹¹ וַיֹּאמֶר אֵלַי דָּנִיֵּאל אִישׁ־חֲמֻדוֹת הָבֵן בַּדְּבָרִים אֲשֶׁר אָנֹכִי דֹבֵר אֵלֶיךָ וַעֲמֹד עַל־עָמְדֶךָ כִּי עַתָּה שֻׁלַּחְתִּי אֵלֶיךָ וּבְדַבְּרוֹ עִמִּי אֶת־הַדָּבָר הַזֶּה עָמַדְתִּי מַרְעִיד: ¹² וַיֹּאמֶר אֵלַי אַל־תִּירָא דָנִיֵּאל כִּי מִן־הַיּוֹם הָרִאשׁוֹן אֲשֶׁר נָתַתָּ אֶת־לִבְּךָ לְהָבִין וּלְהִתְעַנּוֹת לִפְנֵי אֱלֹהֶיךָ נִשְׁמְעוּ דְבָרֶיךָ וַאֲנִי־בָאתִי בִּדְבָרֶיךָ: ¹³ וְשַׂר מַלְכוּת פָּרַס עֹמֵד לְנֶגְדִּי עֶשְׂרִים וְאֶחָד יוֹם וְהִנֵּה מִיכָאֵל אַחַד הַשָּׂרִים הָרִאשֹׁנִים בָּא לְעָזְרֵנִי וַאֲנִי נוֹתַרְתִּי שָׁם אֵצֶל מַלְכֵי פָרָס: ¹⁴ וּבָאתִי לַהֲבִינְךָ אֵת אֲשֶׁר־יִקְרָה

befall your people in the days to come, for there is yet a vision for those days."

¹⁵While he was saying these things to me, I looked down and kept silent. ¹⁶Then one who looked like a man touched my lips, and I opened my mouth and spoke, saying to him who stood before me, "My lord, because of the vision, I have been seized with pangs and cannot summon strength. ¹⁷How can this servant of my lord speak with my lord, seeing that my strength has failed and no spirit is left in me?" ¹⁸He who looked like a man touched me again, and strengthened me. ¹⁹He said, "Have no fear, precious man, all will be well with you; be strong, be strong!" As he spoke with me, I was strengthened, and said, "Speak on, my lord, for you have strengthened me!" ²⁰Then he said, "Do you know why I have come to you? Now I must go back to fight the prince of Persia. When I go off, the prince of Greece will come in. ²¹ᶜNo one is helping me against them except your prince, Michael. However, I will tell you what is recorded in the book of truth.-ᶜ

11 "In the first year of Darius the Mede, I took my stand to strengthen and fortify him. ²And now I will tell you the truth: Persia will have three more kings, and the fourth will be wealthier than them all; by the power he obtains through his wealth, he will stir everyone up against the kingdom of Greece. ³Then a warrior king will appear who will have an extensive dominion and do as he pleases. ⁴But after his appearance, his kingdom will be broken up and scattered to the four winds of heaven, but not for any of his posterity, nor with dominion like that which he had; for his kingdom will be uprooted and belong to others beside these.

⁵"The king of the south will grow powerful; however, one of his officers will overpower him and rule, having an extensive dominion. ⁶After

לְעַמְּךָ בְּאַחֲרִית הַיָּמִים כִּי־עוֹד חָזוֹן לַיָּמִים: ¹⁵ וּבְדַבְּרוֹ עִמִּי כַּדְּבָרִים הָאֵלֶּה נָתַתִּי פָנַי אַרְצָה וְנֶאֱלָמְתִּי: ¹⁶ וְהִנֵּה כִּדְמוּת בְּנֵי אָדָם נֹגֵעַ עַל־שְׂפָתָי וָאֶפְתַּח־פִּי וָאֲדַבְּרָה וָאֹמְרָה אֶל־הָעֹמֵד לְנֶגְדִּי אֲדֹנִי בַּמַּרְאָה נֶהֶפְכוּ צִירַי עָלַי וְלֹא עָצַרְתִּי כֹּחַ: ¹⁷ וְהֵיךְ יוּכַל עֶבֶד אֲדֹנִי זֶה לְדַבֵּר עִם־אֲדֹנִי זֶה וַאֲנִי מֵעַתָּה לֹא־יַעֲמָד־בִּי כֹחַ וּנְשָׁמָה לֹא נִשְׁאֲרָה־בִי: ¹⁸ וַיֹּסֶף וַיִּגַּע־בִּי כְּמַרְאֵה אָדָם וַיְחַזְּקֵנִי: ¹⁹ וַיֹּאמֶר אַל־תִּירָא אִישׁ־חֲמֻדוֹת שָׁלוֹם לָךְ חֲזַק וַחֲזָק וּכְדַבְּרוֹ עִמִּי הִתְחַזַּקְתִּי וָאֹמְרָה יְדַבֵּר אֲדֹנִי כִּי חִזַּקְתָּנִי: ²⁰ וַיֹּאמֶר הֲיָדַעְתָּ לָמָּה־בָּאתִי אֵלֶיךָ וְעַתָּה אָשׁוּב לְהִלָּחֵם עִם־שַׂר פָּרָס וַאֲנִי יוֹצֵא וְהִנֵּה שַׂר־יָוָן בָּא: ²¹ אֲבָל אַגִּיד לְךָ אֶת־הָרָשׁוּם בִּכְתָב אֱמֶת וְאֵין אֶחָד מִתְחַזֵּק עִמִּי עַל־אֵלֶּה כִּי אִם־מִיכָאֵל שַׂרְכֶם: פ

יא וַאֲנִי בִּשְׁנַת אַחַת לְדָרְיָוֶשׁ הַמָּדִי עָמְדִי לְמַחֲזִיק וּלְמָעוֹז לוֹ: ² וְעַתָּה אֱמֶת אַגִּיד לָךְ הִנֵּה־עוֹד שְׁלֹשָׁה מְלָכִים עֹמְדִים לְפָרַס וְהָרְבִיעִי יַעֲשִׁיר עֹשֶׁר־גָּדוֹל מִכֹּל וּכְחֶזְקָתוֹ בְעָשְׁרוֹ יָעִיר הַכֹּל אֵת מַלְכוּת יָוָן: ³ וְעָמַד מֶלֶךְ גִּבּוֹר וּמָשַׁל מִמְשָׁל רַב וְעָשָׂה כִּרְצוֹנוֹ: ⁴ וּכְעָמְדוֹ תִּשָּׁבֵר מַלְכוּתוֹ וְתֵחָץ לְאַרְבַּע רוּחוֹת הַשָּׁמָיִם וְלֹא לְאַחֲרִיתוֹ וְלֹא כְמָשְׁלוֹ אֲשֶׁר מָשָׁל כִּי תִנָּתֵשׁ מַלְכוּתוֹ וְלַאֲחֵרִים מִלְּבַד־אֵלֶּה: ⁵ וְיֶחֱזַק מֶלֶךְ־הַנֶּגֶב וּמִן־שָׂרָיו וְיֶחֱזַק עָלָיו וּמָשָׁל מִמְשָׁל רַב מֶמְשַׁלְתּוֹ: ⁶ וּלְקֵץ שָׁנִים

ᶜ⁻ᶜ   *Order of clauses inverted for clarity.*

some years, an alliance will be made, and the daughter of the king of the south will come to the king of the north to effect the agreement, but she will not maintain her strength, nor will his strength endure. She will be surrendered together with those who escorted her and the one who begot her and helped her during those times. ⁷A shoot from her stock will appear in his place, will come against the army and enter the fortress of the king of the north; he will fight and overpower them. ⁸He will also take their gods with their molten images and their precious vessels of silver and gold back to Egypt as booty. For some years he will leave the king of the north alone, ⁹who will [later] invade the realm of the king of the south, but will go back to his land.

¹⁰"His sons will wage war, collecting a multitude of great armies; he will advance and sweep through as a flood, and will again wage war as far as his stronghold. ¹¹Then the king of the south, in a rage, will go out to do battle with him, with the king of the north. He will muster a great multitude, but the multitude will be delivered into his [foe's] power. ¹²But when the multitude is carried off, he will grow arrogant; he will cause myriads to perish, but will not prevail. ¹³Then the king of the north will again muster a multitude even greater than the first. After a time, a matter of years, he will advance with a great army and much baggage. ¹⁴In those times, many will resist the king of the south, and the lawless sons of your people will assert themselves to confirm the vision, but they will fail. ¹⁵The king of the north will advance and throw up siege ramps and capture a fortress city, and the forces of the south will not hold out; even the elite of his army will be powerless to resist. ¹⁶His opponent will do as he pleases, for none will hold out against him; he will install himself in the beautiful land with destruction within his

יִתְחַבָּ֔רוּ וּבַ֣ת מֶֽלֶךְ־הַנֶּ֗גֶב תָּבוֹא֙ אֶל־מֶ֣לֶךְ הַצָּפ֔וֹן לַעֲשׂ֖וֹת מֵישָׁרִ֑ים וְלֹא־תַעְצֹ֞ר כּ֣וֹחַ הַזְּר֗וֹעַ וְלֹ֤א יַעֲמֹד֙ וּזְרֹע֔וֹ וְתִנָּתֵ֥ן הִ֛יא וּמְבִיאֶ֥יהָ וְהַיֹּֽלְדָ֖הּ וּמַחֲזִקָ֥הּ בָּעִתִּֽים׃ ⁷וְעָמַ֛ד מִנֵּ֥צֶר שָׁרָשֶׁ֖יהָ כַּנּ֑וֹ וְיָבֹ֣א אֶל־הַחַ֗יִל וְיָבֹא֙ בְּמָעוֹז֙ מֶ֣לֶךְ הַצָּפ֔וֹן וְעָשָׂ֥ה בָהֶ֖ם וְהֶחֱזִֽיק׃ ⁸וְגַ֣ם אֱלֹֽהֵיהֶ֡ם עִם־נְסִכֵיהֶם֩ עִם־כְּלֵ֨י חֶמְדָּתָ֜ם כֶּ֧סֶף וְזָהָ֛ב בַּשְּׁבִ֖י יָבִ֣א מִצְרָ֑יִם וְהוּא֙ שָׁנִ֣ים יַעֲמֹ֔ד מִמֶּ֖לֶךְ הַצָּפֽוֹן׃ ⁹וּבָ֗א בְּמַלְכוּת֙ מֶ֣לֶךְ הַנֶּ֔גֶב וְשָׁ֖ב אֶל־אַדְמָתֽוֹ׃

¹⁰וּבנו וּבָנָ֣יו יִתְגָּר֗וּ וְאָֽסְפוּ֙ הֲמוֹן֙ חֲיָלִ֣ים רַבִּ֔ים וּבָ֥א ב֖וֹא וְשָׁטַ֣ף וְעָבָ֑ר וְיָשֹׁ֥ב וְיִתְגָּר֖וּ עַד־מעזה מָעֻזּֽוֹ׃ ¹¹וְיִתְמַרְמַר֙ מֶ֣לֶךְ הַנֶּ֔גֶב וְיָצָ֕א וְנִלְחַ֥ם עִמּ֖וֹ עִם־מֶ֣לֶךְ הַצָּפ֑וֹן וְהֶעֱמִיד֙ הָמ֣וֹן רָ֔ב וְנִתַּ֥ן הֶהָמ֖וֹן בְּיָדֽוֹ׃ ¹²וְנִשָּׂ֥א הֶהָמ֖וֹן ירום וְרָ֣ם לְבָב֑וֹ וְהִפִּ֛יל רִבֹּא֖וֹת וְלֹ֥א יָעֽוֹז׃ ¹³וְשָׁב֙ מֶ֣לֶךְ הַצָּפ֔וֹן וְהֶעֱמִ֣יד הָמ֔וֹן רַ֖ב מִן־הָרִאשׁ֑וֹן וּלְקֵ֨ץ הָעִתִּ֤ים שָׁנִים֙ יָ֣בוֹא ב֔וֹא בְּחַ֥יִל גָּד֖וֹל וּבִרְכ֥וּשׁ רָֽב׃ ¹⁴וּבָעִתִּ֣ים הָהֵ֔ם רַבִּ֥ים יַֽעַמְד֖וּ עַל־מֶ֣לֶךְ הַנֶּ֑גֶב וּבְנֵ֣י ׀ פָּרִיצֵ֣י עַמְּךָ֗ יִֽנַּשְּׂא֛וּ לְהַעֲמִ֥יד חָז֖וֹן וְנִכְשָֽׁלוּ׃ ¹⁵וְיָבֹא֙ מֶ֣לֶךְ הַצָּפ֔וֹן וְיִשְׁפֹּךְ֙ סֹֽלְלָ֔ה וְלָכַ֖ד עִ֣יר מִבְצָר֑וֹת וּזְרֹע֤וֹת הַנֶּ֙גֶב֙ לֹ֣א יַעֲמֹ֔דוּ וְעַם֙ מִבְחָרָ֔יו וְאֵ֥ין כֹּ֖חַ לַעֲמֹֽד׃ ¹⁶וְיַ֨עַשׂ הַבָּ֤א אֵלָיו֙ כִּרְצוֹנ֔וֹ וְאֵ֥ין עוֹמֵ֖ד לְפָנָ֑יו וְיַעֲמֹ֤ד

reach. 17He will set his mind upon invading the strongholds throughout his [foe's] kingdom, but in order to destroy it he will effect an agreement with him and give him a daughter in marriage; he will not succeed at it and it will not come about. 18He will turn to the coastlands and capture many; but a consul will put an end to his insults, nay pay him back for his insults. 19He will head back to the strongholds of his own land, but will stumble, and fall, and vanish. 20His place will be taken by one who will dispatch an officer to exact tribute for royal glory, but he will be broken in a few days, not by wrath or by war. 21His place will be taken by a contemptible man, on whom royal majesty was not conferred; he will come in unawares and seize the kingdom through trickery. 22The forces of the flood will be overwhelmed by him and will be broken, and so too the covenant leader. 23And, from the time an alliance is made with him, he will practice deceit; and he will rise to power with a small band. 24He will invade the richest of provinces unawares, and will do what his father and forefathers never did, lavishing on them*a* spoil, booty, and wealth; he will have designs upon strongholds, but only for a time.

25"He will muster his strength and courage against the king of the south with a great army. The king of the south will wage war with a very great and powerful army but will not stand fast, for they will devise plans against him. 26Those who eat of his food will ruin him. His army will be overwhelmed, and many will fall slain. 27The minds of both kings will be bent on evil; while sitting at the table together, they will lie to each other, but to no avail, for there is yet an appointed term. 28He will return to his land with great wealth, his mind set against the holy covenant. Having done his pleasure, he will return to his land. 29At the appointed time, he will again invade the south, but the second time will not

בְּאֶרֶץ־הַצְּבִי וְכָלָה בְיָדוֹ: 17 וְיָשֵׂם ׀ פָּנָיו לָבוֹא בְּתֹקֶף כָּל־מַלְכוּתוֹ וִישָׁרִים עִמּוֹ וְעָשָׂה וּבַת הַנָּשִׁים יִתֶּן־לוֹ לְהַשְׁחִיתָהּ וְלֹא תַעֲמֹד וְלֹא־לוֹ תִהְיֶה: 18 וְיָשֵׁב ׀ פָּנָיו לְאִיִּים וְלָכַד רַבִּים וְהִשְׁבִּית קָצִין חֶרְפָּתוֹ לוֹ בִּלְתִּי חֶרְפָּתוֹ יָשִׁיב לוֹ: 19 וְיָשֵׁב פָּנָיו לְמָעוּזֵּי אַרְצוֹ וְנִכְשַׁל וְנָפַל וְלֹא יִמָּצֵא: 20 וְעָמַד עַל־כַּנּוֹ מַעֲבִיר נוֹגֵשׂ הֶדֶר מַלְכוּת וּבְיָמִים אֲחָדִים יִשָּׁבֵר וְלֹא בְאַפַּיִם וְלֹא בְמִלְחָמָה: 21 וְעָמַד עַל־כַּנּוֹ נִבְזֶה וְלֹא־נָתְנוּ עָלָיו הוֹד מַלְכוּת וּבָא בְשַׁלְוָה וְהֶחֱזִיק מַלְכוּת בַּחֲלַקְלַקּוֹת: 22 וּזְרֹעוֹת הַשֶּׁטֶף יִשָּׁטְפוּ מִלְּפָנָיו וְיִשָּׁבֵרוּ וְגַם נְגִיד בְּרִית: 23 וּמִן־הִתְחַבְּרוּת אֵלָיו יַעֲשֶׂה מִרְמָה וְעָלָה וְעָצַם בִּמְעַט־גּוֹי: 24 בְּשַׁלְוָה וּבְמִשְׁמַנֵּי מְדִינָה יָבוֹא וְעָשָׂה אֲשֶׁר לֹא־עָשׂוּ אֲבֹתָיו וַאֲבוֹת אֲבֹתָיו בִּזָּה וְשָׁלָל וּרְכוּשׁ לָהֶם יִבְזוֹר וְעַל מִבְצָרִים יְחַשֵּׁב מַחְשְׁבֹתָיו וְעַד־עֵת: 25 וְיָעֵר כֹּחוֹ וּלְבָבוֹ עַל־מֶלֶךְ הַנֶּגֶב בְּחַיִל גָּדוֹל וּמֶלֶךְ הַנֶּגֶב יִתְגָּרֶה לַמִּלְחָמָה בְּחַיִל־גָּדוֹל וְעָצוּם עַד־מְאֹד וְלֹא יַעֲמֹד כִּי־יַחְשְׁבוּ עָלָיו מַחֲשָׁבוֹת: 26 וְאֹכְלֵי פַת־בָּגוֹ יִשְׁבְּרוּהוּ וְחֵילוֹ יִשְׁטוֹף וְנָפְלוּ חֲלָלִים רַבִּים: 27 וּשְׁנֵיהֶם הַמְּלָכִים לְבָבָם לְמֵרָע וְעַל־שֻׁלְחָן אֶחָד כָּזָב יְדַבֵּרוּ וְלֹא תִצְלָח כִּי־עוֹד קֵץ לַמּוֹעֵד: 28 וְיָשֹׁב אַרְצוֹ בִּרְכוּשׁ גָּדוֹל וּלְבָבוֹ עַל־בְּרִית קֹדֶשׁ וְעָשָׂה וְשָׁב לְאַרְצוֹ: 29 לַמּוֹעֵד יָשׁוּב וּבָא בַנֶּגֶב וְלֹא־

---

a   I.e., his followers.

be like the first. ³⁰Ships from Kittim will come against him. He will be checked, and will turn back, raging against the holy covenant. Having done his pleasure, he will then attend to those who forsake the holy covenant. ³¹Forces will be levied by him; they will desecrate the temple, the fortress; they will abolish the regular offering and set up the appalling abomination. ³²He will flatter with smooth words those who act wickedly toward the covenant, but the people devoted to their God will stand firm. ³³The knowledgeable among the people will make the many understand; and for a while they shall fall by sword and flame, suffer captivity and spoliation. ³⁴In defeat, they will receive a little help, and many will join them insincerely. ³⁵Some of the knowledgeable will fall, that they may be refined and purged and whitened until the time of the end, for an interval still remains until the appointed time.

³⁶"The king will do as he pleases; he will exalt and magnify himself above every god, and he will speak awful things against the God of gods. He will prosper until wrath is spent, and what has been decreed is accomplished. ³⁷He will not have regard for the god of his ancestors or for the one dear to women; he will not have regard for any god, but will magnify himself above all. ³⁸He will honor the god of fortresses on his stand; he will honor with gold and silver, with precious stones and costly things, a god that his ancestors never knew. ³⁹He will deal with fortified strongholds with the help of an alien god. He will heap honor on those who acknowledge him, and will make them master over many; he will distribute land for a price. ⁴⁰At the time of the end, the king of the south will lock horns with him, but the king of the north will attack him with chariots and riders and many ships. He will invade lands, sweeping through them like a flood; ⁴¹he will invade the

תִּהְיֶ֣ה כָרִאשֹׁנָ֖ה וְכָאַחֲרֹנָֽה׃ 30 וּבָ֣אוּ ב֗וֹ צִיִּ֣ים כִּתִּים֮ וְנִכְאָ֣ה וְשָׁב֒ וְזָעַ֣ם עַל־בְּרִית־ ק֔וֹדֶשׁ וְעָשָׂ֖ה וְשָׁ֑ב וְיָבֵ֕ן עַל־עֹזְבֵ֖י בְּרִ֥ית קֹֽדֶשׁ׃ 31 וּזְרֹעִ֖ים מִמֶּ֣נּוּ יַעֲמֹ֑דוּ וְחִלְּל֞וּ הַמִּקְדָּ֤שׁ הַמָּעוֹז֙ וְהֵסִ֣ירוּ הַתָּמִ֔יד וְנָתְנ֖וּ הַשִּׁקּ֥וּץ מְשׁוֹמֵֽם׃ 32 וּמַרְשִׁיעֵ֣י בְרִ֔ית יַחֲנִ֖יף בַּחֲלַקּ֑וֹת וְעַ֛ם יֹדְעֵ֥י אֱלֹהָ֖יו יַחֲזִ֥קוּ וְעָשֽׂוּ׃ 33 וּמַשְׂכִּ֣ילֵי עָ֔ם יָבִ֖ינוּ לָֽרַבִּ֑ים וְנִכְשְׁל֞וּ בְּחֶ֧רֶב וּבְלֶהָבָ֛ה בִּשְׁבִ֥י וּבְבִזָּ֖ה יָמִֽים׃ 34 וּבְהִכָּ֣שְׁלָ֔ם יֵעָזְר֖וּ עֵ֣זֶר מְעָ֑ט וְנִלְו֧וּ עֲלֵיהֶ֛ם רַבִּ֖ים בַּחֲלַקְלַקּֽוֹת׃ 35 וּמִן־ הַמַּשְׂכִּילִ֣ים יִכָּ֣שְׁל֗וּ לִצְר֥וֹף בָּהֶ֛ם וּלְבָרֵ֥ר וְלַלְבֵּ֖ן עַד־עֵ֣ת קֵ֑ץ כִּי־ע֖וֹד לַמּוֹעֵֽד׃

36 וְעָשָׂ֨ה כִרְצוֹנ֜וֹ הַמֶּ֗לֶךְ וְיִתְרוֹמֵ֤ם וְיִתְגַּדֵּל֙ עַל־כָּל־אֵ֔ל וְעַל֙ אֵ֣ל אֵלִ֔ים יְדַבֵּ֖ר נִפְלָא֑וֹת וְהִצְלִ֙יחַ֙ עַד־כָּ֣לָה זַ֔עַם כִּ֥י נֶחֱרָצָ֖ה נֶעֱשָֽׂתָה׃ 37 וְעַל־אֱלֹהֵ֤י אֲבֹתָיו֙ לֹ֣א יָבִ֔ין וְעַל־חֶמְדַּ֥ת נָשִׁ֛ים וְעַֽל־כָּל־אֱל֖וֹהַּ לֹ֣א יָבִ֑ין כִּ֥י עַל־כֹּ֖ל יִתְגַּדָּֽל׃ 38 וְלֶאֱלֹ֙הַּ֙ מָֽעֻזִּ֔ים עַל־ כַּנּ֖וֹ יְכַבֵּ֑ד וְלֶאֱל֜וֹהַּ אֲשֶׁ֧ר לֹא־יְדָעֻ֣הוּ אֲבֹתָ֗יו יְכַבֵּ֛ד בְּזָהָ֥ב וּבְכֶ֖סֶף וּבְאֶ֣בֶן יְקָרָ֖ה וּבַחֲמֻדֽוֹת׃ 39 וְעָשָׂ֞ה לְמִבְצְרֵ֤י מָֽעֻזִּים֙ עִם־ אֱל֣וֹהַּ נֵכָ֔ר אֲשֶׁ֥ר הִכִּ֖יר יַרְבֶּ֣ה כָב֑וֹד וְהִמְשִׁילָם֙ בָּֽרַבִּ֔ים וַאֲדָמָ֖ה יְחַלֵּ֥ק בִּמְחִֽיר׃ 40 וּבְעֵ֣ת קֵ֗ץ יִתְנַגַּ֤ח עִמּוֹ֙ מֶ֣לֶךְ הַנֶּ֔גֶב וְיִשְׂתָּעֵ֨ר עָלָ֜יו מֶ֣לֶךְ הַצָּפ֗וֹן בְּרֶ֙כֶב֙ וּבְפָ֣רָשִׁ֔ים וּבׇאֳנִיּ֖וֹת רַבּ֑וֹת וּבָ֥א בַאֲרָצ֛וֹת וְשָׁטַ֖ף וְעָבָֽר׃ 41 וּבָא֙ בְּאֶ֣רֶץ הַצְּבִ֔י וְרַבּ֖וֹת

beautiful land, too, and many will fall, but these will escape his clutches: Edom, Moab, and the chief part of the Ammonites. [42]He will lay his hands on lands; not even the land of Egypt will escape. [43]He will gain control over treasures of gold and silver and over all the precious things of Egypt, and the Libyans and Cushites will follow at his heel. [44]But reports from east and north will alarm him, and he will march forth in a great fury to destroy and annihilate many. [45]He will pitch his royal pavilion between the sea and the beautiful holy mountain, and he will meet his doom with no one to help him.

12 "At that time, the great prince, Michael, who stands beside the sons of your people, will appear. It will be a time of trouble, the like of which has never been since the nation came into being. At that time, your people will be rescued, all who are found inscribed in the book. [2]Many of those that sleep in the dust of the earth will awake, some to eternal life, others to reproaches, to everlasting abhorrence. [3]And the knowledgeable will be radiant like the bright expanse of sky, and those who lead the many to righteousness will be like the stars forever and ever.

[4]"But you, Daniel, keep the words secret, and seal the book until the time of the end. Many will range far and wide and knowledge will increase."

[5]Then I, Daniel, looked and saw two others standing, one on one bank of the river, the other on the other bank of the river. [6]One said to the man clothed in linen, who was above the water of the river, "How long until the end of these awful things?" [7]Then I heard the man dressed in linen, who was above the water of the river, swear by the Ever-Living One as he lifted his right hand and his left hand to heaven: "For a [a]-time, times, and half a time;-[a] and when the

יִכָּשֵׁ֑לוּ וְאֵ֙לֶּה֙ יִמָּלְט֣וּ מִיָּד֔וֹ אֱד֥וֹם וּמוֹאָ֖ב וְרֵאשִׁ֖ית בְּנֵ֥י עַמּֽוֹן׃ 42 וְיִשְׁלַ֥ח יָד֖וֹ בָּאֲרָצ֑וֹת וְאֶ֣רֶץ מִצְרַ֔יִם לֹ֥א תִהְיֶ֖ה לִפְלֵיטָֽה׃ 43 וּמָשַׁ֗ל בְּמִכְמַנֵּי֙ הַזָּהָ֣ב וְהַכֶּ֔סֶף וּבְכֹ֖ל חֲמֻד֣וֹת מִצְרָ֑יִם וְלֻבִ֥ים וְכֻשִׁ֖ים בְּמִצְעָדָֽיו׃ 44 וּשְׁמֻע֣וֹת יְבַהֲלֻ֔הוּ מִמִּזְרָ֖ח וּמִצָּפ֑וֹן וְיָצָא֙ בְּחֵמָ֣א* גְדֹלָ֔ה לְהַשְׁמִ֥יד וּֽלְהַחֲרִ֖ים רַבִּֽים׃ 45 וְיִטַּע֙ אָהֳלֵ֣י אַפַּדְנ֔וֹ בֵּ֥ין יַמִּ֖ים לְהַר־צְבִי־קֹ֑דֶשׁ וּבָא֙ עַד־קִצּ֔וֹ וְאֵ֥ין עוֹזֵ֖ר לֽוֹ׃

יב וּבָעֵ֣ת הַהִ֗יא יַעֲמֹ֙ד מִֽיכָאֵ֜ל הַשַּׂ֣ר הַגָּד֗וֹל הָעֹמֵד֮ עַל־בְּנֵ֣י עַמֶּךָ֒ וְהָיְתָה֙ עֵ֣ת צָרָ֔ה אֲשֶׁ֤ר לֹֽא־נִהְיְתָה֙ מִֽהְי֣וֹת גּ֔וֹי עַ֖ד הָעֵ֣ת הַהִ֑יא וּבָעֵ֤ת הַהִיא֙ יִמָּלֵ֣ט עַמְּךָ֔ כָּל־הַנִּמְצָ֖א כָּת֥וּב בַּסֵּֽפֶר׃ 2 וְרַבִּ֕ים מִיְּשֵׁנֵ֥י אַדְמַת־עָפָ֖ר יָקִ֑יצוּ אֵ֚לֶּה לְחַיֵּ֣י עוֹלָ֔ם וְאֵ֥לֶּה לַחֲרָפ֖וֹת לְדִרְא֥וֹן עוֹלָֽם׃ ס 3 וְהַ֨מַּשְׂכִּלִ֔ים יַזְהִ֖רוּ כְּזֹ֣הַר הָרָקִ֑יעַ וּמַצְדִּיקֵי֙ הָֽרַבִּ֔ים כַּכּוֹכָבִ֖ים לְעוֹלָ֥ם וָעֶֽד׃ פ 4 וְאַתָּ֣ה דָֽנִיֵּ֗אל סְתֹ֧ם הַדְּבָרִ֛ים וַחֲתֹ֥ם הַסֵּ֖פֶר עַד־עֵ֣ת קֵ֑ץ יְשֹׁטְט֥וּ רַבִּ֖ים וְתִרְבֶּ֥ה הַדָּֽעַת׃ 5 וְרָאִ֙יתִי֙ אֲנִ֣י דָֽנִיֵּ֔אל וְהִנֵּ֛ה שְׁנַ֥יִם אֲחֵרִ֖ים עֹמְדִ֑ים אֶחָ֥ד הֵ֙נָּה֙ לִשְׂפַ֣ת הַיְאֹ֔ר וְאֶחָ֥ד הֵ֖נָּה לִשְׂפַ֥ת הַיְאֹֽר׃ 6 וַיֹּ֗אמֶר לָאִישׁ֙ לְב֣וּשׁ הַבַּדִּ֔ים אֲשֶׁ֥ר מִמַּ֖עַל לְמֵימֵ֣י הַיְאֹ֑ר עַד־מָתַ֖י קֵ֥ץ הַפְּלָאֽוֹת׃ 7 וָאֶשְׁמַ֞ע אֶת־הָאִ֣ישׁ ׀ לְב֣וּשׁ הַבַּדִּ֗ים אֲשֶׁ֣ר מִמַּ֘עַל֮ לְמֵימֵ֣י הַיְאֹר֒ וַיָּ֨רֶם יְמִינ֤וֹ וּשְׂמֹאלוֹ֙ אֶל־הַשָּׁמַ֔יִם וַיִּשָּׁבַ֖ע בְּחֵ֣י הָעוֹלָ֑ם כִּי֩ לְמוֹעֵ֙ד מֽוֹעֲדִ֜ים וָחֵ֗צִי

---

breaking of the power of the holy people comes to an end, then shall all these things be fulfilled."

8I heard and did not understand, so I said, "My lord, what will be the outcome of these things?" 9He said, "Go, Daniel, for these words are secret and sealed to the time of the end. 10Many will be purified and purged and refined; the wicked will act wickedly and none of the wicked will understand; but the knowledgeable will understand. (11From the time the regular offering is abolished, and an appalling abomination is set up—it will be a thousand two hundred and ninety days. 12Happy the one who waits and reaches one thousand three hundred and thirty-five days.) 13But you, go on to the end; you shall rest, and arise to your destiny at the end of the days."

וּבְכַלּ֞וֹת נַפֵּ֤ץ יַד־עַם־קֹ֙דֶשׁ֙ תִּכְלֶ֣ינָה כָל־
אֵֽלֶּה׃
8 וַאֲנִ֥י שָׁמַ֖עְתִּי וְלֹ֣א אָבִ֑ין וָאֹ֣מְרָ֔ה אֲדֹנִ֕י
מָ֥ה אַחֲרִ֖ית אֵֽלֶּה׃ פ 9 וַיֹּ֖אמֶר לֵ֣ךְ דָּנִיֵּ֑אל
כִּֽי־סְתֻמִ֧ים וַחֲתֻמִ֛ים הַדְּבָרִ֖ים עַד־עֵ֥ת
קֵֽץ׃ 10 יִתְבָּֽרֲר֤וּ וְיִֽתְלַבְּנוּ֙ וְיִצָּ֣רְפוּ֔ רַבִּ֔ים
וְהִרְשִׁ֖יעוּ רְשָׁעִ֑ים וְלֹ֤א יָבִ֙ינוּ֙ כָּל־רְשָׁעִ֔ים
וְהַמַּשְׂכִּלִ֖ים יָבִֽינוּ׃ 11 וּמֵעֵת֙ הוּסַ֣ר הַתָּמִ֔יד
וְלָתֵ֖ת שִׁקּ֣וּץ שֹׁמֵ֑ם יָמִ֕ים אֶ֖לֶף מָאתַ֥יִם
וְתִשְׁעִֽים׃ 12 אַשְׁרֵ֥י הַֽמְחַכֶּ֖ה וְיַגִּ֑יעַ לְיָמִ֕ים
אֶ֕לֶף שְׁלֹ֥שׁ מֵא֖וֹת שְׁלֹשִׁ֥ים וַחֲמִשָּֽׁה׃
13 וְאַתָּ֖ה לֵ֣ךְ לַקֵּ֑ץ וְתָנ֛וּחַ וְתַעֲמֹ֥ד לְגֹרָלְךָ֖
לְקֵ֥ץ הַיָּמִֽין׃*

תם ונשלם תהילה לאל בורא עולם

EZRA

1 In the first year of King Cyrus of Persia, when the word of the Lord spoken by Jeremiah was fulfilled,[a] the Lord roused the spirit of King Cyrus of Persia to issue a proclamation throughout his realm by word of mouth and in writing as follows:

2"Thus said King Cyrus of Persia: The Lord God of Heaven has given me all the kingdoms of the earth and has charged me with building Him a house in Jerusalem, which is in Judah. 3Anyone of you of all His people—may his God be with him, and let him go up to Jerusalem that is in Judah and build the House of the Lord God of Israel, the God that is in Jerusalem; 4and all who stay behind, wherever he may be living, let the people of his place assist him with silver, gold, goods, and livestock, besides the freewill offering to the House of God that is in Jerusalem."

5So the chiefs of the clans of Judah and Benjamin, and the priests and Levites, all whose spirit had been roused by God, got ready to go up to build the House of the Lord that is in Jerusalem. 6All their neighbors supported them with silver vessels, with gold, with goods, with livestock, and with precious objects, besides what had been given as a freewill offering. 7King Cyrus of Persia released the vessels of the Lord's house which Nebuchadnezzar had taken away from Jerusalem and had put in the house of his god. 8These King Cyrus of Persia released through the office of Mithredath the treasurer, who gave an inventory of them to Sheshbazzar the prince of Judah. 9This is the inventory: 30

א וּבִשְׁנַ֣ת אַחַ֗ת לְכ֙וֹרֶשׁ֙ מֶ֣לֶךְ פָּרַ֔ס לִכְל֥וֹת דְּבַר־יְהֹוָ֖ה מִפִּ֣י יִרְמְיָ֑ה הֵעִ֣יר יְהֹוָ֗ה אֶת־ר֙וּחַ֙ כֹּ֣רֶשׁ מֶֽלֶךְ־פָּרַ֔ס וַיַּֽעֲבֶר־קוֹל֙ בְּכׇל־מַלְכוּת֔וֹ וְגַם־בְּמִכְתָּ֖ב לֵאמֹֽר׃ 2 כֹּ֣ה אָמַ֗ר כֹּ֚רֶשׁ מֶ֣לֶךְ פָּרַ֔ס כֹּ֚ל מַמְלְכ֣וֹת הָאָ֔רֶץ נָ֣תַן לִ֔י יְהֹוָ֖ה אֱלֹהֵ֣י הַשָּׁמָ֑יִם וְהֽוּא־פָקַ֤ד עָלַי֙ לִבְנֽוֹת־ל֣וֹ בַ֔יִת בִּירֽוּשָׁלַ֖͏ִם אֲשֶׁ֥ר בִּֽיהוּדָֽה׃ 3 מִֽי־בָכֶ֣ם מִכׇּל־עַמּ֗וֹ יְהִ֤י אֱלֹהָיו֙ עִמּ֔וֹ וְיַ֕עַל לִירֽוּשָׁלַ֖͏ִם אֲשֶׁ֣ר בִּֽיהוּדָ֑ה וְיִ֗בֶן אֶת־בֵּ֤ית יְהֹוָה֙ אֱלֹהֵ֣י יִשְׂרָאֵ֔ל ה֥וּא הָאֱלֹהִ֖ים אֲשֶׁ֥ר בִּירֽוּשָׁלָֽ͏ִם׃ 4 וְכׇל־הַנִּשְׁאָ֗ר מִֽכׇּל־הַמְּקֹמוֹת֮ אֲשֶׁ֣ר ה֣וּא גָֽר־שָׁם֒ יְנַשְּׂא֙וּהוּ֙ אַנְשֵׁ֣י מְקֹמ֔וֹ בְּכֶ֥סֶף וּבְזָהָ֖ב וּבִרְכ֣וּשׁ וּבִבְהֵמָ֑ה עִם־הַ֨נְּדָבָ֔ה לְבֵ֥ית הָאֱלֹהִ֖ים אֲשֶׁ֥ר בִּירֽוּשָׁלָֽ͏ִם׃ 5 וַיָּק֜וּמוּ רָאשֵׁ֣י הָאָב֗וֹת לִֽיהוּדָה֙ וּבִנְיָמִ֔ן וְהַכֹּֽהֲנִ֖ים וְהַלְוִיִּ֑ם לְכֹ֨ל הֵעִ֤יר הָאֱלֹהִים֙ אֶת־רוּח֔וֹ לַעֲל֣וֹת לִבְנ֔וֹת אֶת־בֵּ֥ית יְהֹוָ֖ה אֲשֶׁ֥ר בִּירֽוּשָׁלָֽ͏ִם׃ 6 וְכׇל־סְבִיבֹֽתֵיהֶם֙ חִזְּק֣וּ בִֽידֵיהֶ֔ם בִּכְלֵי־כֶ֧סֶף בַּזָּהָ֛ב בָּרְכ֥וּשׁ וּבַבְּהֵמָ֖ה וּבַמִּגְדָּנ֑וֹת לְבַ֖ד עַל־כׇּל־הִתְנַדֵּֽב׃ ס 7 וְהַמֶּ֣לֶךְ כּ֔וֹרֶשׁ הוֹצִ֖יא אֶת־כְּלֵ֣י בֵית־יְהֹוָ֑ה אֲשֶׁ֨ר הוֹצִ֤יא נְבֽוּכַדְנֶצַּר֙ מִיר֣וּשָׁלַ֔͏ִם וַיִּתְּנֵ֖ם בְּבֵ֥ית אֱלֹהָֽיו׃ 8 וַיּֽוֹצִיאֵ֗ם כּ֚וֹרֶשׁ מֶ֣לֶךְ פָּרַ֔ס עַל־יַ֖ד מִתְרְדָ֣ת הַגִּזְבָּ֑ר וַֽיִּסְפְּרֵם֙ לְשֵׁשְׁבַּצַּ֔ר הַנָּשִׂ֖יא לִֽיהוּדָֽה׃ 9 וְאֵ֖לֶּה מִסְפָּרָ֑ם אֲגַרְטְלֵ֨י זָהָ֜ב שְׁלֹשִׁ֗ים אֲגַרְטְלֵי־כֶ֙סֶף֙ אָ֔לֶף מַֽחֲלָפִ֖ים תִּשְׁעָ֥ה וְעֶשְׂרִֽים׃ ס 10 כְּפוֹרֵ֤י זָהָב֙ שְׁלֹשִׁ֔ים כְּפ֤וֹרֵי כֶ֙סֶף֙ מִשְׁנִ֔ים

a Cf. Jer. 29.10.

gold basins, 1,000 silver basins, 29 knives, [10]30 gold bowls, 410 silver *b-double bowls,-b* 1,000 other vessels; [11]in all, 5,400 gold and silver vessels. Sheshbazzar brought all these back when the exiles came back from Babylon to Jerusalem.

2 *a*These are the people of the province who came up from among the captive exiles whom King Nebuchadnezzar of Babylon had carried into exile to Babylon, who returned to Jerusalem and Judah, each to his own city, [2]who came with Zerubbabel, Jeshua, Nehemiah, Seraiah, Reelaiah, Mordecai, Bilshan, Mispar, Bigvai, Rehum, Baanah:

The list of the men of the people of Israel: [3]the sons of Parosh—2,172; [4]the sons of Shephatiah—372; [5]the sons of Arah—775; [6]the sons of Pahath-moab: the sons of Jeshua and Joab—2,812; [7]the sons of Elam—1,254; [8]the sons of Zattu—945; [9]the sons of Zaccai—760; [10]the sons of Bani—642; [11]the sons of Bebai—623; [12]the sons of Azgad—1,222; [13]the sons of Adonikam—666; [14]the sons of Bigvai—2,056; [15]the sons of Adin—454; [16]the sons of Ater: Hezekiah—98; [17]the sons of Bezai—323; [18]the sons of Jorah—112; [19]the sons of Hashum—223; [20]the sons of Gibbar—95; [21]the sons of Bethlehem—

אַרְבַּע מֵאוֹת וַעֲשָׂרָה כָּל כְּפוֹרֵי כֶסֶף מִשְׁנִים אַרְבַּע מֵאוֹת וַעֲשָׂרָה כֵּלִים אֲחֵרִים אָלֶף: ס 11 כָּל־כֵּלִים לַזָּהָב וְלַכֶּסֶף חֲמֵשֶׁת אֲלָפִים וְאַרְבַּע מֵאוֹת הַכֹּל הֶעֱלָה שֵׁשְׁבַּצַּר עִם הֵעָלוֹת הַגּוֹלָה מִבָּבֶל לִירוּשָׁלִָם: פ

ב וְאֵלֶּה ׀ בְּנֵי הַמְּדִינָה הָעֹלִים מִשְּׁבִי הַגּוֹלָה אֲשֶׁר הֶגְלָה נבוכדנצור נְבוּכַדְנֶצַּר מֶלֶךְ־בָּבֶל לְבָבֶל וַיָּשׁוּבוּ לִירוּשָׁלַםִ וִיהוּדָה אִישׁ לְעִירוֹ: 2 אֲשֶׁר־בָּאוּ עִם־ זְרֻבָּבֶל יֵשׁוּעַ נְחֶמְיָה שְׂרָיָה רְעֵלָיָה מָרְדֳּכַי בִּלְשָׁן מִסְפָּר בִּגְוַי רְחוּם בַּעֲנָה מִסְפַּר אַנְשֵׁי עַם יִשְׂרָאֵל: ס 3 בְּנֵי פַרְעֹשׁ אַלְפַּיִם מֵאָה שִׁבְעִים וּשְׁנָיִם: ס 4 בְּנֵי שְׁפַטְיָה שְׁלֹשׁ מֵאוֹת שִׁבְעִים וּשְׁנָיִם: ס 5 בְּנֵי אָרַח שְׁבַע מֵאוֹת חֲמִשָּׁה וְשִׁבְעִים: ס 6 בְּנֵי־פַחַת מוֹאָב לִבְנֵי יֵשׁוּעַ יוֹאָב אַלְפַּיִם שְׁמֹנֶה מֵאוֹת וּשְׁנֵים עָשָׂר: ס 7 בְּנֵי עֵילָם אֶלֶף מָאתַיִם חֲמִשִּׁים וְאַרְבָּעָה: ס 8 בְּנֵי זַתּוּא תְּשַׁע מֵאוֹת וְאַרְבָּעִים וַחֲמִשָּׁה: ס 9 בְּנֵי זַכָּי שְׁבַע מֵאוֹת וְשִׁשִּׁים: ס 10 בְּנֵי בָנִי שֵׁשׁ מֵאוֹת אַרְבָּעִים וּשְׁנָיִם: ס 11 בְּנֵי בֵבָי שֵׁשׁ מֵאוֹת עֶשְׂרִים וּשְׁלֹשָׁה: ס 12 בְּנֵי עַזְגָּד אֶלֶף מָאתַיִם עֶשְׂרִים וּשְׁנָיִם: ס 13 בְּנֵי אֲדֹנִיקָם שֵׁשׁ מֵאוֹת שִׁשִּׁים וְשִׁשָּׁה: ס 14 בְּנֵי בִגְוָי אַלְפַּיִם חֲמִשִּׁים וְשִׁשָּׁה: ס 15 בְּנֵי עָדִין אַרְבַּע מֵאוֹת חֲמִשִּׁים וְאַרְבָּעָה: ס 16 בְּנֵי־אָטֵר לִיחִזְקִיָּה תִּשְׁעִים וּשְׁמֹנָה: ס 17 בְּנֵי בֵצָי שְׁלֹשׁ מֵאוֹת עֶשְׂרִים וּשְׁלֹשָׁה: ס 18 בְּנֵי יוֹרָה מֵאָה וּשְׁנֵים עָשָׂר: ס 19 בְּנֵי חָשֻׁם מָאתַיִם עֶשְׂרִים וּשְׁלֹשָׁה: ס 20 בְּנֵי גִבָּר תִּשְׁעִים וַחֲמִשָּׁה: ס 21 בְּנֵי בֵית־לֶחֶם מֵאָה

---

b-b   Meaning of Heb. uncertain.

a   This chapter appears as Neh. 7.6–73 with variations in the names and numbers.

123; 22the sons of Netophah—56; 23the sons of Anathoth—128; 24the sons of Azmaveth—42; 25the sons of Kiriath-arim: Chephirah and Beeroth—743; 26the sons of Ramah and Geba—621; 27the men of Michmas—122; 28the men of Beth-el and Ai—223; 29the men of Nebo—52; 30the sons of Magbish—156; 31the sons of the other Elam—1,254; 32the sons of Harim—320; 33the sons of Lod, Hadid, and Ono—725; 34the sons of Jericho—345; 35the sons of Senaah—3,630.

36The priests: the sons of Jedaiah: the house of Jeshua—973; 37the sons of Immer—1,052; 38the sons of Pashhur—1,247; 39the sons of Harim—1,017.

40The Levites: the sons of Jeshua and Kadmiel: the sons of Hodaviah—74.

41The singers: the sons of Asaph—128.

42The gatekeepers: the sons of Shallum, the sons of Ater, the sons of Talmon, the sons of Akkub, the sons of Hatita, the sons of Shobai, all told—139.

43The temple servants: the sons of Ziha, the sons of Hasupha, the sons of Tabbaoth, 44the sons of Keros, the sons of Siaha, the sons of Padon, 45the sons of Lebanah, the sons of Hagabah, the sons of Akkub, 46the sons of Hagab, the sons of Salmai, the sons of Hanan, 47the sons of Giddel, the sons of Gahar, the sons of Reaiah, 48the sons of Rezin, the sons of Nekoda, the sons of Gazzam, 49the sons of Uzza, the sons of Paseah, the sons of Besai, 50the sons of Asnah, the sons of Meunim, the sons of Nephusim, 51the sons of Bakbuk, the sons of

עֶשְׂרִים וּשְׁלֹשָׁה: ס 22 אַנְשֵׁי נְטֹפָה
חֲמִשִּׁים וְשִׁשָּׁה: 23 אַנְשֵׁי עֲנָתוֹת מֵאָה
עֶשְׂרִים וּשְׁמֹנָה: ס 24 בְּנֵי עַזְמָוֶת
אַרְבָּעִים וּשְׁנָיִם: ס 25 בְּנֵי קִרְיַת עָרִים
כְּפִירָה וּבְאֵרוֹת שְׁבַע מֵאוֹת וְאַרְבָּעִים
וּשְׁלֹשָׁה: ס 26 בְּנֵי הָרָמָה וָגֶבַע שֵׁשׁ
מֵאוֹת עֶשְׂרִים וְאֶחָד: ס 27 אַנְשֵׁי
מִכְמָס מֵאָה עֶשְׂרִים וּשְׁנָיִם: ס 28 אַנְשֵׁי
בֵית־אֵל וְהָעָי מָאתַיִם עֶשְׂרִים
וּשְׁלֹשָׁה: ס 29 בְּנֵי נְבוֹ חֲמִשִּׁים
וּשְׁנָיִם: ס 30 בְּנֵי מַגְבִּישׁ מֵאָה חֲמִשִּׁים
וְשִׁשָּׁה: ס 31 בְּנֵי עֵילָם אַחֵר אֶלֶף
מָאתַיִם חֲמִשִּׁים וְאַרְבָּעָה: ס 32 בְּנֵי
חָרִם שְׁלֹשׁ מֵאוֹת וְעֶשְׂרִים: ס 33 בְּנֵי־
לֹד חָדִיד וְאוֹנוֹ שְׁבַע מֵאוֹת עֶשְׂרִים
וַחֲמִשָּׁה: ס 34 בְּנֵי יְרֵחוֹ שְׁלֹשׁ מֵאוֹת
אַרְבָּעִים וַחֲמִשָּׁה: 35 בְּנֵי סְנָאָה
שְׁלֹשֶׁת אֲלָפִים וְשֵׁשׁ מֵאוֹת וּשְׁלֹשִׁים: ס
36 הַכֹּהֲנִים בְּנֵי יְדַעְיָה לְבֵית יֵשׁוּעַ תֵּשַׁע
מֵאוֹת שִׁבְעִים וּשְׁלֹשָׁה: ס 37 בְּנֵי אִמֵּר
אֶלֶף חֲמִשִּׁים וּשְׁנָיִם: ס 38 בְּנֵי פַשְׁחוּר
אֶלֶף מָאתַיִם אַרְבָּעִים וְשִׁבְעָה: ס
39 בְּנֵי חָרִם אֶלֶף וְשִׁבְעָה עָשָׂר: ס
40 הַלְוִיִּם בְּנֵי־יֵשׁוּעַ וְקַדְמִיאֵל לִבְנֵי
הוֹדַוְיָה שִׁבְעִים וְאַרְבָּעָה: ס
41 הַמְשֹׁרְרִים בְּנֵי אָסָף מֵאָה עֶשְׂרִים
וּשְׁמֹנָה: פ 42 בְּנֵי הַשֹּׁעֲרִים בְּנֵי־שַׁלּוּם
בְּנֵי־אָטֵר בְּנֵי־טַלְמוֹן בְּנֵי־עַקּוּב בְּנֵי
חֲטִיטָא בְּנֵי שֹׁבָי הַכֹּל מֵאָה שְׁלֹשִׁים
וְתִשְׁעָה: פ 43 הַנְּתִינִים* בְּנֵי־צִיחָא
בְּנֵי־חֲשׂוּפָא בְּנֵי טַבָּעוֹת: 44 בְּנֵי־קֵרֹס בְּנֵי־
סִיעֲהָא בְּנֵי פָדוֹן: 45 בְּנֵי־לְבָנָה בְּנֵי־חֲגָבָה
בְּנֵי עַקּוּב: 46 בְּנֵי־חָגָב בְּנֵי־שַׁמְלַי שַׁלְמָי
בְּנֵי חָנָן: 47 בְּנֵי־גִדֵּל בְּנֵי־גַחַר בְּנֵי רְאָיָה:
48 בְּנֵי־רְצִין בְּנֵי־נְקוֹדָא בְּנֵי גַזָּם: 49 בְּנֵי־
עֻזָּא בְּנֵי־פָסֵחַ בְּנֵי בֵסָי: 50 בְּנֵי־אַסְנָה

Hakupha, the sons of Harhur, 52the sons of Bazluth, the sons of Mehida, the sons of Harsha, 53the sons of Barkos, the sons of Sisera, the sons of Temah, 54the sons of Neziah, the sons of Hatipha.

55The sons of Solomon's servants: the sons of Sotai, the sons of Hassophereth, the sons of Peruda, 56the sons of Jaalah, the sons of Darkon, the sons of Giddel, 57the sons of Shephatiah, the sons of Hattil, the sons of Pochereth-hazzebaim, the sons of Ami.

58The total of temple servants and the sons of Solomon's servants—392.

59The following were those who came up from Tel-melah, Tel-harsha, Cherub, Addan, and Immer—they were unable to tell whether their father's house and descent were Israelite: 60the sons of Delaiah, the sons of Tobiah, the sons of Nekoda—652.

61Of the sons of the priests, the sons of Habaiah, the sons of Hakkoz, the sons of Barzillai who had married a daughter of Barzillai and had taken his[b] name—62these searched for their genealogical records, but they could not be found, so they were disqualified for the priesthood. 63The Tirshatha[c] ordered them not to eat of the most holy things until a priest with Urim and Thummim should appear.

64The sum of the entire community was 42,360, 65not counting their male and female servants, those being 7,337; they also had 200 male and female singers. 66Their horses—736; their mules—245; 67their camels—435; their asses—6,720.

68Some of the chiefs of the clans, on arriving at the House of the Lord in Jerusalem, gave a freewill offering to erect the House of God on its site. 69In accord with their means, they donated to the treasury of the work: gold—6,100 drachmas, silver—5,000 minas, and priestly robes—100.

בְּנֵי־מְעִינִים מְעוֹנִים בְּנֵי נְפִיסִים נְפוּסִים׃
51 בְּנֵי־בַקְבּוּק בְּנֵי־חֲקוּפָא בְּנֵי חַרְחוּר׃
52 בְּנֵי־בַצְלוּת בְּנֵי־מְחִידָא בְּנֵי חַרְשָׁא׃
53 בְּנֵי־בַרְקוֹס בְּנֵי־סִיסְרָא בְּנֵי־תָמַח׃
54 בְּנֵי נְצִיחַ בְּנֵי חֲטִיפָא׃ 55 בְּנֵי עַבְדֵי שְׁלֹמֹה בְּנֵי־סֹטַי בְּנֵי־הַסֹּפֶרֶת בְּנֵי פְרוּדָא׃
56 בְּנֵי־יַעְלָה בְנֵי־דַרְקוֹן בְּנֵי גִדֵּל׃ 57 בְּנֵי שְׁפַטְיָה בְנֵי־חַטִּיל בְּנֵי פֹּכֶרֶת הַצְּבָיִים בְּנֵי אָמִי׃ 58 כָּל־הַנְּתִינִים וּבְנֵי עַבְדֵי שְׁלֹמֹה שְׁלֹשׁ מֵאוֹת תִּשְׁעִים וּשְׁנָיִם׃ ס
59 וְאֵלֶּה הָעֹלִים מִתֵּל מֶלַח תֵּל חַרְשָׁא כְּרוּב אַדָּן אִמֵּר וְלֹא יָכְלוּ לְהַגִּיד בֵּית־אֲבוֹתָם וְזַרְעָם אִם מִיִּשְׂרָאֵל הֵם׃ 60 בְּנֵי־דְלָיָה בְנֵי־טוֹבִיָּה בְּנֵי נְקוֹדָא שֵׁשׁ מֵאוֹת חֲמִשִּׁים וּשְׁנָיִם׃ ס 61 וּמִבְּנֵי הַכֹּהֲנִים בְּנֵי חֳבַיָּה בְּנֵי הַקּוֹץ בְּנֵי בַרְזִלַּי אֲשֶׁר לָקַח מִבְּנוֹת בַּרְזִלַּי הַגִּלְעָדִי אִשָּׁה* וַיִּקָּרֵא עַל־שְׁמָם׃ 62 אֵלֶּה בִּקְשׁוּ כְתָבָם הַמִּתְיַחְשִׂים וְלֹא נִמְצָאוּ וַיְגֹאֲלוּ מִן־הַכְּהֻנָּה׃ 63 וַיֹּאמֶר הַתִּרְשָׁתָא לָהֶם אֲשֶׁר לֹא־יֹאכְלוּ מִקֹּדֶשׁ הַקֳּדָשִׁים עַד עֲמֹד כֹּהֵן לְאוּרִים וּלְתֻמִּים׃ 64 כָּל־הַקָּהָל כְּאֶחָד אַרְבַּע רִבּוֹא אַלְפַּיִם שְׁלֹשׁ־מֵאוֹת שִׁשִּׁים׃ 65 מִלְּבַד עַבְדֵיהֶם וְאַמְהֹתֵיהֶם אֵלֶּה שִׁבְעַת אֲלָפִים שְׁלֹשׁ מֵאוֹת שְׁלֹשִׁים וְשִׁבְעָה וְלָהֶם מְשֹׁרְרִים וּמְשֹׁרְרוֹת מָאתָיִם׃ 66 סוּסֵיהֶם שְׁבַע מֵאוֹת שְׁלֹשִׁים וְשִׁשָּׁה פִּרְדֵיהֶם מָאתַיִם אַרְבָּעִים וַחֲמִשָּׁה׃ 67 גְּמַלֵּיהֶם אַרְבַּע מֵאוֹת שְׁלֹשִׁים וַחֲמִשָּׁה חֲמֹרִים שֵׁשֶׁת אֲלָפִים שְׁבַע מֵאוֹת וְעֶשְׂרִים׃ פ
68 וּמֵרָאשֵׁי הָאָבוֹת בְּבוֹאָם לְבֵית יְהוָה אֲשֶׁר בִּירוּשָׁלִָם הִתְנַדְּבוּ לְבֵית הָאֱלֹהִים לְהַעֲמִידוֹ עַל־מְכוֹנוֹ׃ 69 כְּכֹחָם נָתְנוּ לְאוֹצַר הַמְּלָאכָה זָהָב דַּרְכְּמוֹנִים שֵׁשׁ־רִבֹּאות וָאֶלֶף ס וְכֶסֶף מָנִים חֲמֵשֶׁת אֲלָפִים וְכָתְנֹת כֹּהֲנִים מֵאָה׃ ס

v. 61. סבירין ומטעין "לאשה"

70The priests, the Levites and some of the people, and the singers, gatekeepers, and the temple servants took up residence in their towns and all Israel in their towns.

3 When the seventh month arrived—the Israelites being settled in their towns—the entire people assembled as one man in Jerusalem. 2Then Jeshua son of Jozadak and his brother priests, and Zerubbabel son of Shealtiel and his brothers set to and built the altar of the God of Israel to offer burnt offerings upon it as is written in the Teaching of Moses, the man of God. 3They set up the altar on its site because they were in fear of the peoples of the land, and they offered burnt offerings on it to the Lord, burnt offerings each morning and evening. 4Then they celebrated the festival of Tabernacles as is written, with its daily burnt offerings in the proper quantities, on each day as is prescribed for it, 5followed by the regular burnt offering and the offerings for the new moons and for all the sacred fixed times of the Lord, and whatever freewill offerings were made to the Lord. 6From the first day of the seventh month they began to make burnt offerings to the Lord, though the foundation of the Temple of the Lord had not been laid. 7They paid the hewers and craftsmen with money, and the Sidonians and Tyrians with food, drink, and oil to bring cedarwood from Lebanon by sea to Joppa, in accord with the authorization granted them by King Cyrus of Persia.

8In the second year after their arrival at the House of God, at Jerusalem, in the second month, Zerubbabel son of Shealtiel and Jeshua son of Jozadak, and the rest of their brother priests and Levites, and all who had come from the captivity to Jerusalem, as their first step ap-

70 וַיֵּשְׁב֣וּ הַכֹּהֲנִ֣ים וְֽהַלְוִיִּ֡ם וּמִן־הָעָ֡ם וְהַמְשֹׁרְרִ֨ים וְהַשּׁוֹעֲרִ֜ים וְהַנְּתִינִ֗ים בְּעָרֵיהֶ֛ם וְכׇל־יִשְׂרָאֵ֖ל בְּעָרֵיהֶֽם׃ ס

ג וַיִּגַּע֙ הַחֹ֣דֶשׁ הַשְּׁבִיעִ֔י וּבְנֵ֥י יִשְׂרָאֵ֖ל בֶּעָרִ֑ים ס וַיֵּאָסְפ֥וּ הָעָ֛ם כְּאִ֥ישׁ אֶחָ֖ד אֶל־יְרוּשָׁלָֽ͏ִם׃ ס 2וַיָּ֩קׇם֩ יֵשׁ֨וּעַ בֶּן־יֽוֹצָדָ֜ק וְאֶחָ֣יו הַכֹּהֲנִ֗ים וּזְרֻבָּבֶ֤ל בֶּן־שְׁאַלְתִּיאֵל֙ וְאֶחָ֔יו וַיִּבְנ֕וּ אֶת־מִזְבַּ֖ח אֱלֹהֵ֣י יִשְׂרָאֵ֑ל לְהַעֲל֤וֹת עָלָיו֙ עֹל֔וֹת כַּכָּת֕וּב בְּתוֹרַ֖ת מֹשֶׁ֥ה אִישׁ־הָאֱלֹהִֽים׃ 3וַיָּכִ֤ינוּ הַמִּזְבֵּ֙חַ֙ עַל־מְכ֣וֹנֹתָ֔יו כִּ֚י בְּאֵימָ֣ה עֲלֵיהֶ֔ם מֵעַמֵּ֖י הָאֲרָצ֑וֹת ויעל וַיַּעֲל֨וּ עָלָ֤יו עֹלוֹת֙ לַֽיהֹוָ֔ה עֹל֖וֹת לַבֹּ֥קֶר וְלָעָֽרֶב׃ 4וַֽיַּעֲשׂ֛וּ אֶת־חַ֥ג הַסֻּכּ֖וֹת כַּכָּת֑וּב וְעֹלַ֨ת י֤וֹם בְּיוֹם֙ בְּמִסְפָּ֔ר כְּמִשְׁפַּ֖ט דְּבַר־י֥וֹם בְּיוֹמֽוֹ׃ 5וְאַחֲרֵיכֵ֞ן עֹלַ֤ת תָּמִיד֙ וְלֶ֣חֳדָשִׁ֔ים וּלְכׇל־מוֹעֲדֵ֥י יְהֹוָ֖ה הַמְקֻדָּשִׁ֑ים וּלְכֹ֛ל מִתְנַדֵּ֥ב נְדָבָ֖ה לַֽיהֹוָֽה׃ 6מִיּ֤וֹם אֶחָד֙ לַחֹ֣דֶשׁ הַשְּׁבִיעִ֔י הֵחֵ֕לּוּ לְהַעֲל֥וֹת עֹל֖וֹת לַֽיהֹוָ֑ה וְהֵיכַ֥ל יְהֹוָ֖ה לֹ֥א יֻסָּֽד׃ 7וַיִּתְּנוּ־כֶ֔סֶף לַחֹצְבִ֖ים וְלֶחָרָשִׁ֑ים וּמַאֲכָ֨ל וּמִשְׁתֶּ֜ה וָשֶׁ֗מֶן לַצִּֽדֹנִים֙ וְלַצֹּרִ֔ים לְהָבִיא֩ עֲצֵ֨י אֲרָזִ֤ים מִן־הַלְּבָנוֹן֙ אֶל־יָ֣ם יָפ֔וֹא* כְּרִשְׁי֛וֹן כּ֥וֹרֶשׁ מֶֽלֶךְ־פָּרַ֖ס עֲלֵיהֶֽם׃ פ

8וּבַשָּׁנָ֣ה הַשֵּׁנִ֗ית לְבוֹאָ֞ם אֶל־בֵּ֤ית הָֽאֱלֹהִים֙ לִיר֣וּשָׁלַ֔͏ִם בַּחֹ֖דֶשׁ הַשֵּׁנִ֑י הֵחֵ֡לּוּ זְרֻבָּבֶ֣ל בֶּן־שְׁ֠אַלְתִּיאֵ֠ל וְיֵשׁ֨וּעַ בֶּן־יֽוֹצָדָ֜ק וּשְׁאָ֥ר אֲחֵיהֶ֣ם ׀ הַכֹּהֲנִ֣ים וְהַלְוִיִּ֗ם וְכׇל־הַבָּאִים֙ מֵהַשְּׁבִ֣י יְר֣וּשָׁלַ֔͏ִם וַיַּעֲמִ֗ידוּ אֶת־

pointed Levites from the age of twenty and upward to supervise the work of the House of the LORD. [9]Jeshua, his sons and brothers, Kadmiel and his sons, -ᵃthe sons of Judah,-ᵃ together were appointed in charge of those who did the work in the House of God; also the sons of Henadad, their sons and brother Levites.

[10]When the builders had laid the foundation of the Temple of the LORD, priests in their vestments with trumpets, and Levites sons of Asaph with cymbals were stationed to give praise to the LORD, as King David of Israel had ordained. [11]They sang songs extolling and praising the LORD, ᵇ"For He is good, His steadfast love for Israel is eternal."-ᵇ All the people raised a great shout extolling the LORD because the foundation of the House of the LORD had been laid. [12]Many of the priests and Levites and the chiefs of the clans, the old men who had seen the first house, wept loudly at the sight of the founding of this house. Many others shouted joyously at the top of their voices. [13]The people could not distinguish the shouts of joy from the people's weeping, for the people raised a great shout, the sound of which could be heard from afar.

4 When the adversaries of Judah and Benjamin heard that the returned exiles were building a temple to the LORD God of Israel, [2]they approached Zerubbabel and the chiefs of the clans and said to them, "Let us build with you, since we too worship your God, having offered sacrifices to Him since the time of King Esarhaddon of Assyria, who brought us here." [3]Zerubbabel, Jeshua, and the rest of the chiefs of the clans of Israel answered them, "It is not for you and us to build a House to our God, but we alone will build it to the LORD God of Israel, in accord with the charge that the king, King Cyrus of Persia, laid upon us." [4]Thereupon

הַלְוִיִּם מִבֶּ֨ן עֶשְׂרִ֤ים שָׁנָה֙ וָמַ֔עְלָה לְנַצֵּ֖חַ עַל־מְלֶ֥אכֶת בֵּית־יְהֹוָֽה׃ פ 9 וַיַּֽעֲמֹ֣ד יֵשׁ֡וּעַ בָּנָ֣יו וְ֠אֶחָיו קַדְמִיאֵ֨ל וּבָנָ֜יו בְּנֵֽי־ יְהוּדָה֙ כְּאֶחָ֔ד לְנַצֵּ֥חַ עַל־עֹשֵׂ֖ה הַמְּלָאכָ֑ה בְּבֵ֖ית הָאֱלֹהִ֑ים ס בְּנֵ֣י חֵֽנָדָ֔ד בְּנֵיהֶ֥ם וַאֲחֵיהֶ֖ם הַלְוִיִּֽם׃

10 וְיִסְּד֥וּ הַבֹּנִ֖ים אֶת־הֵיכַ֣ל יְהֹוָ֑ה וַיַּעֲמִ֨ידוּ הַכֹּהֲנִ֜ים מְלֻבָּשִׁ֤ים בַּחֲצֹֽצְרוֹת֙ וְהַלְוִיִּ֣ם בְּנֵֽי־אָסָ֗ף בַּֽמְצִלְתַּ֔יִם לְהַלֵּל֙ אֶת־יְהֹוָ֔ה עַל־יְדֵ֖י דָּוִ֥יד מֶֽלֶךְ־יִשְׂרָאֵֽל׃ 11 וַ֠יַּעֲנ֠וּ בְּהַלֵּ֨ל וּבְהוֹדֹ֤ת לַֽיהֹוָה֙ כִּ֣י ט֔וֹב כִּֽי־לְעוֹלָ֥ם חַסְדּ֖וֹ עַל־יִשְׂרָאֵ֑ל וְכׇל־הָעָ֡ם הֵרִ֩יעוּ֩ תְרוּעָ֨ה גְדוֹלָ֤ה בְהַלֵּל֙ לַֽיהֹוָ֔ה עַ֖ל הוּסַ֥ד בֵּית־ יְהֹוָֽה׃ ס 12 וְרַבִּ֣ים מֵהַכֹּהֲנִ֣ים וְהַלְוִיִּ֡ם וְרָאשֵׁ֣י הָאָבוֹת֩ הַזְּקֵנִ֨ים אֲשֶׁ֤ר רָאוּ֙ אֶת־ הַבַּ֣יִת הָרִאשׁ֔וֹן בְּיׇסְד֕וֹ זֶ֤ה הַבַּ֙יִת֙ בְּעֵ֣ינֵיהֶ֔ם בֹּכִ֖ים בְּק֣וֹל גָּד֑וֹל וְרַבִּ֛ים בִּתְרוּעָ֥ה בְשִׂמְחָ֖ה לְהָרִ֥ים ק֥וֹל׃ 13 וְאֵ֣ין הָעָ֗ם מַכִּירִים֙ ק֚וֹל תְּרוּעַ֣ת הַשִּׂמְחָ֔ה לְק֖וֹל בְּכִ֣י הָעָ֑ם כִּ֣י הָעָ֗ם מְרִיעִים֙ תְּרוּעָ֣ה גְדוֹלָ֔ה וְהַקּ֥וֹל נִשְׁמַ֖ע עַד־לְמֵרָחֽוֹק׃ פ

ד וַֽיִּשְׁמְע֔וּ צָרֵ֥י יְהוּדָ֖ה וּבִנְיָמִ֑ן כִּֽי־בְנֵ֤י הַגּוֹלָה֙ בּוֹנִ֣ים הֵיכָ֔ל לַֽיהֹוָ֖ה אֱלֹהֵ֥י יִשְׂרָאֵֽל׃ 2 וַיִּגְּשׁ֨וּ אֶל־זְרֻבָּבֶ֜ל וְאֶל־רָאשֵׁ֣י הָֽאָב֗וֹת וַיֹּאמְר֤וּ לָהֶם֙ נִבְנֶ֣ה עִמָּכֶ֔ם כִּ֣י כָכֶ֔ם נִדְר֖וֹשׁ לֵאלֹֽהֵיכֶ֑ם ולא וְלֹ֣א ׀ אֲנַ֣חְנוּ זֹבְחִ֗ים מִימֵי֙ אֵסַ֤ר חַדֹּן֙ מֶ֣לֶךְ אַשּׁ֔וּר הַמַּֽעֲלֶ֥ה אֹתָ֖נוּ פֹּֽה׃ 3 וַיֹּ֩אמֶר֩ לָהֶ֨ם זְרֻבָּבֶ֜ל וְיֵשׁ֗וּעַ וּשְׁאָ֨ר רָאשֵׁ֤י הָֽאָבוֹת֙ לְיִשְׂרָאֵ֔ל לֹֽא־לָכֶ֣ם וָלָ֔נוּ לִבְנ֥וֹת בַּ֖יִת לֵאלֹהֵ֑ינוּ כִּי֩ אֲנַ֨חְנוּ יַ֜חַד נִבְנֶ֗ה לַֽיהֹוָה֙ אֱלֹהֵ֣י יִשְׂרָאֵ֔ל כַּאֲשֶׁ֣ר צִוָּ֔נוּ הַמֶּ֖לֶךְ כּ֥וֹרֶשׁ מֶֽלֶךְ־פָּרָֽס׃ 4 וַיְהִי֙ עַם־הָאָ֔רֶץ מְרַפִּ֖ים יְדֵ֥י

ᵃ-ᵃ I.e., Hodaviah of 2.40.
ᵇ-ᵇ Cf. Pss. 106.1; 136.

the people of the land undermined the resolve of the people of Judah, and made them afraid to build. [5]They bribed ministers in order to thwart their plans all the years of King Cyrus of Persia and until the reign of King Darius of Persia.

[6]And in the reign of Ahasuerus, at the start of his reign, they drew up an accusation against the inhabitants of Judah and Jerusalem.

[7]And in the time of Artaxerxes, Bishlam, Mithredath, Tabeel, and the rest of their colleagues wrote to King Artaxerxes of Persia, a letter written in Aramaic and translated.[a]

Aramaic:[b] [8]Rehum the commissioner and Shimshai the scribe wrote a letter concerning Jerusalem to King Artaxerxes as follows: ([9c]Then Rehum the commissioner and Shimshai the scribe, and the rest of their colleagues, the judges, officials, officers, and overseers, the men of Erech, and of Babylon, and of Susa—that is the Elamites—[10]and other peoples whom the great and glorious Osnappar deported and settled in the city of Samaria and the rest of the province Beyond the River [wrote]—and now [11]this is the text of the letter which they sent to him:)—"To King Artaxerxes [from] your servants, men of the province Beyond the River. And now [12]be it known to the king that the Jews who came up from you to us have reached Jerusalem and are rebuilding that rebellious and wicked city; they are completing the walls and repairing the foundation. [13]Now be it known to the king that if this city is rebuilt and the walls completed, they will not pay tribute, poll-tax, or land-tax, and in the end it will harm the kingdom. [14]Now since we eat the salt of the palace, and it is not right that we should see the king dishonored, we have written to advise the king [of this] [15]so that you may

עַם־יְהוּדָה וּמְבַלֲהִים וּמְבַהֲלִים אוֹתָם לִבְנוֹת: 5 וְסֹכְרִים עֲלֵיהֶם יוֹעֲצִים לְהָפֵר עֲצָתָם כָּל־יְמֵי כּוֹרֶשׁ מֶלֶךְ פָּרַס וְעַד־מַלְכוּת דָּרְיָוֶשׁ מֶלֶךְ־פָּרָס: 6 וּבְמַלְכוּת אֲחַשְׁוֵרוֹשׁ בִּתְחִלַּת מַלְכוּתוֹ כָּתְבוּ שִׂטְנָה עַל־יֹשְׁבֵי יְהוּדָה וִירוּשָׁלָ͏ִם: ס

7 וּבִימֵי אַרְתַּחְשַׁשְׂתָּא כָּתַב בִּשְׁלָם מִתְרְדָת טָבְאֵל וּשְׁאָר כנותו כְּנָוֺתָיו עַל־אַרְתַּחְשַׁשְׂתְּא מֶלֶךְ פָּרָס וּכְתָב הַנִּשְׁתְּוָן כָּתוּב אֲרָמִית וּמְתֻרְגָּם

אֲרָמִית: פ 8 רְחוּם בְּעֵל־טְעֵם וְשִׁמְשַׁי סָפְרָא כְּתַבוּ אִגְּרָה חֲדָה עַל־יְרוּשְׁלֶם לְאַרְתַּחְשַׁשְׂתְּא מַלְכָּא כְּנֵמָא: 9 אֱדַיִן רְחוּם בְּעֵל־טְעֵם וְשִׁמְשַׁי סָפְרָא וּשְׁאָר כְּנָוָתְהוֹן דִּינָיֵא וַאֲפַרְסַתְכָיֵא טַרְפְּלָיֵא אֲפָרְסָיֵא ארכוי אַרְכְּוָיֵא בָבְלָיֵא שׁוּשַׁנְכָיֵא דהוא דֶּהָיֵא עֵלְמָיֵא: 10 וּשְׁאָר אֻמַּיָּא דִּי הַגְלִי אָסְנַפַּר רַבָּא וְיַקִּירָא וְהוֹתֵב הִמּוֹ בְּקִרְיָה דִּי שָׁמְרָיִן וּשְׁאָר עֲבַר־נַהֲרָה וּכְעֶנֶת: 11 דְּנָה פַּרְשֶׁגֶן אִגַּרְתָּא דִּי שְׁלַחוּ עֲלוֹהִי עַל־אַרְתַּחְשַׁשְׂתְּא מַלְכָּא עבדיך עַבְדָךְ אֱנָשׁ עֲבַר־נַהֲרָה וּכְעֶנֶת: פ

12 יְדִיעַ לֶהֱוֵא לְמַלְכָּא דִּי יְהוּדָיֵא דִּי סְלִקוּ מִן־לְוָתָךְ עֲלֶינָא אֲתוֹ לִירוּשְׁלֶם קִרְיְתָא מָרָדְתָּא ובאישתא וּבִאישְׁתָּא בָּנַיִן וְשׁוּרֵי ושׁוריא וְשׁוּרַיָּא אשכללו אַשְׁכְלִלוּ וְאֻשַּׁיָּא יַחִיטוּ: 13 כְּעַן יְדִיעַ לֶהֱוֵא לְמַלְכָּא דִּי הֵן קִרְיְתָא דָךְ תִּתְבְּנֵא וְשׁוּרַיָּה יִשְׁתַּכְלְלוּן מִנְדָּה־בְלוֹ וַהֲלָךְ לָא יִנְתְּנוּן וְאַפְּתֹם מַלְכִים תְּהַנְזִק: 14 כְּעַן כָּל־קֳבֵל דִּי־מְלַח הֵיכְלָא מְלַחְנָא וְעַרְוַת מַלְכָּא לָא אֲרִיךְ לַנָא לְמֶחֱזֵא עַל־דְּנָה שְׁלַחְנָא וְהוֹדַעְנָא לְמַלְכָּא: 15 דִּי יְבַקַּר בִּסְפַר־דָּכְרָנַיָּא דִּי אֲבָהָתָךְ וּתְהַשְׁכַּח בִּסְפַר דָּכְרָנַיָּא וְתִנְדַּע

a Cf. below v. 18 and note d.
b A note indicating that what follows is in the Aramaic language.
c Vv. 9–11 amplify v. 8.

search the records of your fathers and find in the records and know that this city is a rebellious city, harmful to kings and states. Sedition has been rife in it from early times; on that account this city was destroyed. [16]We advise the king that if this city is rebuilt and its walls are completed, you will no longer have any portion in the province Beyond the River."

[17]The king sent back the following message: "To Rehum the commissioner and Shimshai the scribe, and the rest of their colleagues, who dwell in Samaria and in the rest of the province of Beyond the River, greetings. [18]Now the letter that you wrote me has been read to me in translation.*d* [19]At my order a search has been made, and it has been found that this city has from earliest times risen against kings, and that rebellion and sedition have been rife in it. [20]Powerful kings have ruled over Jerusalem and exercised authority over the whole province of Beyond the River, and tribute, poll-tax, and land-tax were paid to them. [21]Now issue an order to stop these men; this city is not to be rebuilt until I so order. [22]Take care not to be lax in this matter or there will be much damage and harm to the kingdom."

[23]When the text of the letter of King Artaxerxes was read before Rehum and Shimshai the scribe and their colleagues, they hurried to Jerusalem, to the Jews, and stopped them by main force. [24]At that time, work on the House of God in Jerusalem stopped and remained in abeyance until the second year of the reign of King Darius of Persia.

5 Then the prophets, Haggai the prophet and Zechariah son of Iddo, prophesied to the Jews in Judah and Jerusalem, *a*-inspired by the God of Israel.-*a* [2]Thereupon Zerubbabel son of

---

d   I.e., from Aramaic to Persian.

a-a   Lit. "with the name of the God of Israel upon them."

דִּי קִרְיְתָא דָךְ קִרְיָא מָרָדָא וּמְהַנְזְקַת
מַלְכִין וּמְדִנָן וְאֶשְׁתַּדּוּר עָבְדִין בְּגַוַּהּ מִן־
יוֹמָת עָלְמָא עַל־דְּנָה קִרְיְתָא דָךְ
הָחָרְבַת: 16 מְהוֹדְעִין אֲנַחְנָה לְמַלְכָּא דִּי
הֵן קִרְיְתָא דָךְ תִּתְבְּנֵא וְשׁוּרַיָּה יִשְׁתַּכְלְלוּן
לָקֳבֵל דְּנָה חֲלָק בַּעֲבַר נַהֲרָא לָא אִיתַי
לָךְ: פ 17 פִּתְגָמָא שְׁלַח מַלְכָּא עַל־רְחוּם בְּעֵל־
טְעֵם וְשִׁמְשַׁי סָפְרָא וּשְׁאָר כְּנָוָתְהוֹן דִּי
יָתְבִין בְּשָׁמְרָיִן וּשְׁאָר עֲבַר־נַהֲרָה שְׁלָם
וּכְעֶת: ס 18 נִשְׁתְּוָנָא דִּי שְׁלַחְתּוּן
עֲלֶינָא מְפָרַשׁ קֱרִי קָדָמָי: 19 וּמִנִּי שִׂים
טְעֵם וּבַקַּרוּ וְהַשְׁכַּחוּ דִּי קִרְיְתָא דָךְ
מִן־יוֹמָת עָלְמָא עַל־מַלְכִין מִתְנַשְּׂאָה
וּמְרַד וְאֶשְׁתַּדּוּר מִתְעֲבֶד־בַּהּ: 20 וּמַלְכִין
תַּקִּיפִין הֲווֹ עַל־יְרוּשְׁלֶם וְשַׁלִּיטִין בְּכֹל
עֲבַר נַהֲרָה וּמִדָּה בְלוֹ וַהֲלָךְ מִתְיְהֵב
לְהוֹן: 21 כְּעַן שִׂימוּ טְּעֵם לְבַטָּלָא גֻּבְרַיָּא
אִלֵּךְ וְקִרְיְתָא דָךְ לָא תִתְבְּנֵא עַד־מִנִּי
טַעְמָא יִתְּשָׂם: 22 וּזְהִירִין הֱווֹ שָׁלוּ
לְמֶעְבַּד עַל־דְּנָה לְמָה יִשְׂגֵּא חֲבָלָא
לְהַנְזָקַת מַלְכִין: ס 23 אֱדַיִן מִן־דִּי פַּרְשֶׁגֶן נִשְׁתְּוָנָא דִּי
אַרְתַּחְשַׁשְׂתְּא אַרְתַּחְשַׁשְׂתְּ מַלְכָּא קֱרִי
קֳדָם־רְחוּם וְשִׁמְשַׁי סָפְרָא וּכְנָוָתְהוֹן אֲזַלוּ
בִבְהִילוּ לִירוּשְׁלֶם עַל־יְהוּדָיֵא וּבַטִּלוּ
הִמּוֹ בְּאֶדְרָע וְחָיִל: ס 24 בֵּאדַיִן בְּטֵלַת
עֲבִידַת בֵּית־אֱלָהָא דִּי בִּירוּשְׁלֶם וַהֲוָת
בָּטְלָא עַד שְׁנַת תַּרְתֵּין לְמַלְכוּת דָּרְיָוֶשׁ
מֶלֶךְ־פָּרָס: פ

ה וְהִתְנַבִּי חַגַּי נביאה נְבִיָּא וּזְכַרְיָה
בַר־עִדּוֹא נביאיא נְבִיַּיָּא עַל־יְהוּדָיֵא דִּי
בִיהוּד וּבִירוּשְׁלֶם בְּשֻׁם אֱלָהּ יִשְׂרָאֵל
עֲלֵיהוֹן: ס 2 בֵּאדַיִן קָמוּ זְרֻבָּבֶל בַּר־

Shealtiel and Jeshua son of Jozadak began rebuilding the House of God in Jerusalem, with the full support of the prophets of God. ³At once Tattenai, governor of the province of Beyond the River, Shethar-bozenai, and their colleagues descended upon them and said this to them, "Who issued orders to you to rebuild this house and complete its furnishing?" ⁴Then we*b* said to them, "What are the names of the men who are engaged in the building?" ⁵But God watched over the elders of the Jews and they were not stopped while a report went to Darius and a letter was sent back in reply to it.

⁶This is the text of the letter that Tattenai, governor of the province of Beyond the River, and Shethar-bozenai and his colleagues, the officials of Beyond the River, sent to King Darius. ⁷They sent a message to him and this is what was written in it: "To King Darius, greetings, and so forth. ⁸Be it known to the king, that we went to the province of Judah, to the house of the great God. It is being rebuilt of hewn stone, and wood is being laid in the walls. The work is being done with dispatch and is going well. ⁹Thereupon we directed this question to these elders, 'Who issued orders to you to rebuild this house and to complete its furnishings?' ¹⁰We also asked their names so that we could write down the names of their leaders for your information. ¹¹This is what they answered us: 'We are the servants of the God of heaven and earth; we are rebuilding the house that was originally built many years ago; a great king of Israel built it and completed it. ¹²But because our fathers angered the God of Heaven, He handed them over to Nebuchadnezzar the Chaldean, king of Babylon, who demolished this house and exiled the people to Babylon. ¹³But in the first year of King Cyrus of Babylon, King Cyrus issued an order

---

b   The officials of v. 3; cf. v. 10. Greek and Syriac read "they."

שְׁאַלְתִּיאֵל וְיֵשׁוּעַ בַּר־יוֹצָדָק וְשָׁרִיו לְמִבְנֵא בֵּית אֱלָהָא דִּי בִירוּשְׁלֶם וְעִמְּהוֹן נְבִיַּיָּא דִי־אֱלָהָא מְסַעֲדִין לְהוֹן: פ ³ בֵּהּ־זִמְנָא אֲתָא עֲלֵיהוֹן תַּתְּנַי פַּחַת עֲבַר־נַהֲרָה וּשְׁתַר בּוֹזְנַי וּכְנָוָתְהוֹן וְכֵן אָמְרִין לְהֹם מַן־שָׂם לְכֹם טְעֵם בַּיְתָא דְנָה לִבְּנֵא וְאֻשַּׁרְנָא דְנָה לְשַׁכְלָלָה: ס ⁴ אֱדַיִן כְּנֵמָא אֲמַרְנָא לְהֹם מַן־אִנּוּן שְׁמָהָת גֻּבְרַיָּא דִּי־דְנָה בִּנְיָנָא בָּנַיִן: ⁵ וְעֵין אֱלָהֲהֹם הֲוָת עַל־שָׂבֵי יְהוּדָיֵא וְלָא־בַטִּלוּ הִמּוֹ עַד־טַעְמָא לְדָרְיָוֶשׁ יְהָךְ וֶאֱדַיִן יְתִיבוּן נִשְׁתְּוָנָא עַל־דְּנָה: פ

⁶ פַּרְשֶׁגֶן אִגַּרְתָּא דִּי־שְׁלַח תַּתְּנַי | פַּחַת עֲבַר־נַהֲרָה וּשְׁתַר בּוֹזְנַי וּכְנָוָתֵהּ אֲפַרְסְכָיֵא דִּי בַּעֲבַר נַהֲרָה עַל־דָּרְיָוֶשׁ מַלְכָּא: ⁷ פִּתְגָמָא שְׁלַחוּ עֲלוֹהִי וְכִדְנָה כְּתִיב בְּגַוֵּהּ לְדָרְיָוֶשׁ מַלְכָּא שְׁלָמָא כֹלָּא: ⁸ ס יְדִיעַ | לֶהֱוֵא לְמַלְכָּא דִּי־אֲזַלְנָא לִיהוּד מְדִינְתָּא לְבֵית אֱלָהָא רַבָּא וְהוּא מִתְבְּנֵא אֶבֶן גְּלָל וְאָע מִתְּשָׂם בְּכֻתְלַיָּא וַעֲבִידְתָּא דָךְ אָסְפַּרְנָא מִתְעַבְדָא וּמַצְלַח בְּיֶדְהֹם: ס ⁹ אֱדַיִן שְׁאֵלְנָא לְשָׂבַיָּא אִלֵּךְ כְּנֵמָא אֲמַרְנָא לְהֹם מַן־שָׂם לְכֹם טְעֵם בַּיְתָא דְנָה לְמִבְנְיָה וְאֻשַּׁרְנָא דְנָה לְשַׁכְלָלָה: ¹⁰ וְאַף שְׁמָהָתְהֹם שְׁאֵלְנָא לְּהֹם לְהוֹדָעוּתָךְ דִּי נִכְתֻּב שֻׁם־גֻּבְרַיָּא דִּי בְרָאשֵׁיהֹם: ס

¹¹ וּכְנֵמָא פִתְגָמָא הֲתִיבוּנָא לְמֵמַר אֲנַחְנָא הִמּוֹ עַבְדוֹהִי דִּי־אֱלָהּ שְׁמַיָּא וְאַרְעָא וּבָנַיִן בַּיְתָא דִּי־הֲוָא בְנֵה מִקַּדְמַת דְּנָה שְׁנִין שַׂגִּיאָן וּמֶלֶךְ לְיִשְׂרָאֵל רַב בְּנָהִי וְשַׁכְלְלֵהּ: ¹² לָהֵן מִן־דִּי הַרְגִּזוּ אֲבָהֳתַנָא לֶאֱלָהּ שְׁמַיָּא יְהַב הִמּוֹ בְּיַד נְבוּכַדְנֶצַּר מֶלֶךְ־בָּבֶל כסדיא כַּסְדָּאָה וּבַיְתָה דְנָה סַתְרֵהּ וְעַמָּה הַגְלִי לְבָבֶל: ס ¹³ בְּרַם

to rebuild this House of God. ¹⁴Also the silver and gold vessels of the House of God that Nebuchadnezzar had taken away from the temple in Jerusalem and brought to the temple in Babylon—King Cyrus released them from the temple in Babylon to be given to the one called Sheshbazzar whom he had appointed governor. ¹⁵He said to him, "Take these vessels, go, deposit them in the temple in Jerusalem, and let the House of God be rebuilt on its original site." ¹⁶That same Sheshbazzar then came and laid the foundations for the House of God in Jerusalem; and ever since then it has been under construction, but is not yet finished.' ¹⁷And now, if it please the king, let the royal archives there in Babylon be searched to see whether indeed an order had been issued by King Cyrus to rebuild this House of God in Jerusalem. May the king convey to us his pleasure in this matter."

6 Thereupon, at the order of King Darius, they searched the archives where the treasures were stored in Babylon. ²But it was in the citadel of Ecbatana, in the province of Media, that a scroll was found in which the following was written: "Memorandum: ³In the first year of King Cyrus, King Cyrus issued an order concerning the House of God in Jerusalem: 'Let the house be rebuilt, a place for offering sacrifices, with a base built up high. Let it be sixty cubits high and sixty cubits wide, ⁴with a course of unused timber for each three courses of hewn stone. The expenses shall be paid by the palace. ⁵And the gold and silver vessels of the House of God which Nebuchadnezzar had taken away from the temple in Jerusalem and transported to Babylon shall be returned, and let each go back to the temple in Jerusalem where it belongs; you shall deposit it in the House of God.'

בִּשְׁנַת חֲדָה לְכוֹרֶשׁ מַלְכָּא דִּי בָבֶל כּוֹרֶשׁ מַלְכָּא שָׂם טְעֵם בֵּית־אֱלָהָא דְנָה לִבְּנֵא: ¹⁴ וְאַף מָאנַיָּא דִי־בֵית־אֱלָהָא דִּי דַהֲבָה וְכַסְפָּא דִּי נְבוּכַדְנֶצַּר הַנְפֵּק מִן־הֵיכְלָא דִּי בִירוּשְׁלֶם וְהֵיבֵל הִמּוֹ לְהֵיכְלָא דִּי בָבֶל הַנְפֵּק הִמּוֹ כּוֹרֶשׁ מַלְכָּא מִן־הֵיכְלָא דִּי בָבֶל וִיהִיבוּ לְשֵׁשְׁבַּצַּר שְׁמֵהּ דִּי פֶחָה שָׂמֵהּ: ¹⁵ וַאֲמַר־לֵהּ ׀ אלה אֵל מָאנַיָּא שֵׂא אֵזֶל־אֲחֵת הִמּוֹ בְּהֵיכְלָא דִּי בִירוּשְׁלֶם וּבֵית אֱלָהָא יִתְבְּנֵא עַל־אַתְרֵהּ: ס ¹⁶ אֱדַיִן שֵׁשְׁבַּצַּר דֵּךְ אֲתָא יְהַב אֻשַּׁיָּא דִּי־בֵית אֱלָהָא דִּי בִירוּשְׁלֶם וּמִן־אֱדַיִן וְעַד־כְּעַן מִתְבְּנֵא וְלָא שְׁלִם: ¹⁷ וּכְעַן הֵן עַל־מַלְכָּא טָב יִתְבַּקַּר בְּבֵית גִּנְזַיָּא דִּי־מַלְכָּא תַמָּה דִּי בְּבָבֶל הֵן אִיתַי דִּי־מִן־כּוֹרֶשׁ מַלְכָּא שִׂים טְעֵם לְמִבְנֵא בֵּית־אֱלָהָא דֵךְ בִּירוּשְׁלֶם וּרְעוּת מַלְכָּא עַל־דְּנָה יִשְׁלַח עֲלֶינָא: ס

ו בֵּאדַיִן דָּרְיָוֶשׁ מַלְכָּא שָׂם טְעֵם וּבַקַּרוּ ׀ בְּבֵית סִפְרַיָּא דִּי גִנְזַיָּא מְהַחֲתִין תַּמָּה בְּבָבֶל: ² וְהִשְׁתְּכַח בְּאַחְמְתָא בְּבִירְתָא דִּי בְּמָדַי מְדִינְתָּה מְגִלָּה חֲדָה וְכֵן־כְּתִיב בְּגַוַּהּ דִּכְרוֹנָה: פ ³ בִּשְׁנַת חֲדָה לְכוֹרֶשׁ מַלְכָּא כּוֹרֶשׁ מַלְכָּא שָׂם טְעֵם בֵּית־אֱלָהָא בִירוּשְׁלֶם בַּיְתָא יִתְבְּנֵא אֲתַר דִּי־דָבְחִין דִּבְחִין וְאֻשּׁוֹהִי מְסוֹבְלִין רוּמֵהּ אַמִּין שִׁתִּין פְּתָיֵהּ אַמִּין שִׁתִּין: ⁴ נִדְבָּכִין דִּי־אֶבֶן גְּלָל תְּלָתָא וְנִדְבָּךְ דִּי־אָע חֲדַת וְנִפְקְתָא מִן־בֵּית מַלְכָּא תִּתְיְהִב: ⁵ וְאַף מָאנֵי בֵית־אֱלָהָא דִּי דַהֲבָה וְכַסְפָּא דִּי נְבוּכַדְנֶצַּר הַנְפֵּק מִן־הֵיכְלָא דִי־בִירוּשְׁלֶם וְהֵיבֵל לְבָבֶל יַהֲתִיבוּן וִיהָךְ לְהֵיכְלָא דִי־בִירוּשְׁלֶם לְאַתְרֵהּ וְתַחֵת בְּבֵית אֱלָהָא: ס

6"Now[a] you, Tattenai, governor of the province of Beyond the River, Shethar-bozenai and colleagues, the officials of the province of Beyond the River, stay away from that place. 7Allow the work of this House of God to go on; let the governor of the Jews and the elders of the Jews rebuild this House of God on its site. 8And I hereby issue an order concerning what you must do to help these elders of the Jews rebuild this House of God: the expenses are to be paid to these men with dispatch out of the resources of the king, derived from the taxes of the province of Beyond the River, so that the work not be stopped. 9They are to be given daily, without fail, whatever they need of young bulls, rams, or lambs as burnt offerings for the God of Heaven, and wheat, salt, wine, and oil, at the order of the priests in Jerusalem, 10so that they may offer pleasing sacrifices to the God of Heaven and pray for the life of the king and his sons. 11I also issue an order that whoever alters this decree shall have a beam removed from his house, and he shall be impaled on it and his house confiscated.[b] 12And may the God who established His name there cause the downfall of any king or nation that undertakes to alter or damage that House of God in Jerusalem. I, Darius, have issued the decree; let it be carried out with dispatch."

13Then Tattenai, governor of the province of Beyond the River, Shethar-bozenai, and their colleagues carried out with dispatch what King Darius had written. 14So the elders of the Jews progressed in the building, urged on by the prophesying of Haggai the prophet and Zechariah son of Iddo, and they brought the building to completion under the aegis of the God of Israel and by the order of Cyrus and Darius and King Artaxerxes of Persia. 15The house was finished on the third of the month of Adar in

6 כְּעַ֡ן תַּתְּנַי֩ פַּחַ֨ת עֲבַֽר־נַהֲרָ֜ה שְׁתַ֤ר בּוֹזְנַי֙ וּכְנָוָ֣תְה֔וֹן אֲפַרְסְכָיֵ֔א דִּ֖י בַּעֲבַ֣ר נַהֲרָ֑ה רַחִיקִ֥ין הֲו֖וֹ מִן־תַּמָּֽה: 7 שְׁבֻ֕קוּ לַעֲבִידַ֖ת בֵּית־אֱלָהָ֣א דֵ֑ךְ פַּחַ֤ת יְהוּדָיֵא֙ וּלְשָׂבֵ֣י יְהוּדָיֵ֔א בֵּית־אֱלָהָ֥א דֵ֖ךְ יִבְנ֥וֹן עַל־אַתְרֵֽהּ: 8 וּמִנִּי֮ שִׂ֣ים טְעֵם֒ לְמָ֣א דִֽי־תַעַבְד֗וּן עִם־שָׂבֵ֤י יְהוּדָיֵא֙ אִלֵּ֔ךְ לְמִבְנֵ֖א בֵּית־אֱלָהָ֣א דֵ֑ךְ וּמִנִּכְסֵ֣י מַלְכָּ֗א דִּ֚י מִדַּת֙ עֲבַ֣ר נַהֲרָ֔ה אָסְפַּ֗רְנָא נִפְקְתָ֛א תֶּהֱוֵ֧א מִֽתְיַהֲבָ֛א לְגֻבְרַיָּ֥א אִלֵּ֖ךְ דִּי־לָ֥א לְבַטָּלָֽא: 9 וּמָ֣ה חַשְׁחָ֡ן וּבְנֵ֣י תוֹרִ֣ין וְדִכְרִ֣ין וְאִמְּרִ֣ין | לַעֲלָוָ֣ן | לֶאֱלָ֣הּ שְׁמַיָּ֡א חִנְטִ֣ין מְלַ֣ח | חֲמַ֣ר וּמְשַׁ֣ח כְּמֵאמַ֣ר כָּהֲנַיָּ֤א דִֽי־בִירֽוּשְׁלֶם֙ לֶהֱוֵ֨א מִתְיְהֵ֥ב לְהֹ֛ם י֥וֹם | בְּי֖וֹם דִּי־לָ֥א שָׁלֽוּ: 10 דִּֽי־לֶהֱוֺ֧ן מְהַקְרְבִ֛ין נִיחוֹחִ֖ין לֶאֱלָ֣הּ שְׁמַיָּ֑א וּמְצַלַּ֕יִן לְחַיֵּ֥י מַלְכָּ֖א וּבְנֽוֹהִי: 11 וּמִנִּי֮ שִׂ֣ים טְעֵם֒ דִּ֣י כָל־אֱנָ֗שׁ דִּ֤י יְהַשְׁנֵא֙ פִּתְגָמָ֣א דְנָ֔ה יִתְנְסַ֥ח אָע֙ מִן־בַּיְתֵ֔הּ וּזְקִ֖יף יִתְמְחֵ֣א עֲלֹ֑הִי וּבַיְתֵ֛הּ נְוָל֥וּ יִתְעֲבֵ֖ד עַל־דְּנָֽה: 12 וֵֽאלָהָ֞א דִּ֣י שַׁכִּ֧ן שְׁמֵ֣הּ תַּמָּ֗ה יְמַגַּ֞ר כָּל־מֶ֤לֶךְ וְעַם֙ דִּ֣י | יִשְׁלַ֣ח יְדֵ֗הּ לְהַשְׁנָיָ֛ה לְחַבָּלָ֛ה בֵּית־אֱלָהָ֥א דֵ֖ךְ דִּ֣י בִירֽוּשְׁלֶ֑ם אֲנָ֤ה דָרְיָ֨וֶשׁ֙ שָׂ֣מֶת טְעֵ֔ם אָסְפַּ֖רְנָא יִתְעֲבִֽד: פ

13 אֱדַ֡יִן תַּתְּנַ֞י פַּחַ֧ת עֲבַֽר־נַהֲרָ֛ה שְׁתַ֥ר בּוֹזְנַ֖י וּכְנָוָתְה֑וֹן לָקֳבֵ֗ל דִּֽי־שְׁלַ֞ח דָּרְיָ֧וֶשׁ מַלְכָּ֛א כְּנֵ֖מָא אָסְפַּ֥רְנָא עֲבַֽדוּ: 14 וְשָׂבֵ֤י יְהוּדָיֵא֙ בָּנַ֣יִן וּמַצְלְחִ֔ין בִּנְבוּאַת֙ חַגַּ֣י נְבִיָּ֔א וּזְכַרְיָ֖ה בַּר־עִדּ֑וֹא וּבְנ֣וֹ וְשַׁכְלִ֗לוּ מִן־טַ֨עַם֙ אֱלָ֣הּ יִשְׂרָאֵ֔ל וּמִטְּעֵם֙ כּ֣וֹרֶשׁ וְדָרְיָ֔וֶשׁ וְאַרְתַּחְשַׁ֖שְׂתְּא מֶ֥לֶךְ פָּרָֽס:

---

a *This introduces the text of the reply of Darius that doubtless contained the preceding narrative (vv. 1–5) as a preliminary.*

b *Meaning uncertain; or "turned into ruins."*

1847

the sixth year of the reign of King Darius. [16]The Israelites, the priests, and the Levites, and all the other exiles celebrated the dedication of the House of God with joy. [17]And they sacrificed for the dedication of this House of God one hundred bulls, two hundred rams, four hundred lambs, and twelve goats as a purification offering for all of Israel, according to the number of the tribes of Israel. [18]They appointed the priests in their courses and the Levites in their divisions for the service of God in Jerusalem, according to the prescription in the Book of Moses.

[19c]The returned exiles celebrated the Passover on the fourteenth day of the first month, [20]for the priests and Levites had purified themselves to a man; they were all pure. They slaughtered the passover offering for all the returned exiles, and for their brother priests and for themselves. [21]The children of Israel who had returned from the exile, together with all who joined them in separating themselves from the uncleanliness of the nations of the lands to worship the LORD God of Israel, ate of it. [22]They joyfully celebrated the Feast of Unleavened Bread for seven days, for the LORD had given them cause for joy by inclining the heart of the Assyrian king toward them so as to give them support in the work of the House of God, the God of Israel.

7 After these events, during the reign of King Artaxerxes of Persia, Ezra son of Seraiah son of Azariah son of Hilkiah [2]son of Shallum son of Zadok son of Ahitub [3]son of Amariah son of Azariah son of Meraioth [4]son of Zerahiah son of Uzzi son of Bukki [5]son of Abishua son of Phinehas son of Eleazar son of Aaron the chief priest—[6]that Ezra came up from Babylon, a

---

c   *Hebrew resumes here.*

---

15 וְשֵׁיצִיא* בַּיְתָה דְנָה עַד יוֹם תְּלָתָה לִירַח אֲדָר דִּי־הִיא שְׁנַת־שֵׁת לְמַלְכוּת דָּרְיָוֶשׁ מַלְכָּא: פ 16 וַעֲבַדוּ בְנֵי־יִשְׂרָאֵל כָּהֲנַיָּא וְלֵוָיֵא וּשְׁאָר בְּנֵי־גָלוּתָא חֲנֻכַּת בֵּית־אֱלָהָא דְנָה בְּחֶדְוָה: 17 וְהַקְרִבוּ לַחֲנֻכַּת בֵּית־אֱלָהָא דְנָה תּוֹרִין מְאָה דִּכְרִין מָאתַיִן אִמְּרִין אַרְבַּע מְאָה וּצְפִירֵי עִזִּין לְחַטָּאָה עַל־כָּל־יִשְׂרָאֵל תְּרֵי־עֲשַׂר לְמִנְיָן שִׁבְטֵי יִשְׂרָאֵל: 18 וַהֲקִימוּ כָהֲנַיָּא בִּפְלֻגָּתְהוֹן וְלֵוָיֵא בְּמַחְלְקָתְהוֹן עַל־עֲבִידַת אֱלָהָא דִּי בִירוּשְׁלֶם כִּכְתָב סְפַר מֹשֶׁה: פ

19 וַיַּעֲשׂוּ בְנֵי־הַגּוֹלָה אֶת־הַפָּסַח בְּאַרְבָּעָה עָשָׂר לַחֹדֶשׁ הָרִאשׁוֹן: 20 כִּי הִטַּהֲרוּ הַכֹּהֲנִים וְהַלְוִיִּם כְּאֶחָד כֻּלָּם טְהוֹרִים וַיִּשְׁחֲטוּ הַפֶּסַח לְכָל־בְּנֵי הַגּוֹלָה וְלַאֲחֵיהֶם הַכֹּהֲנִים וְלָהֶם: 21 וַיֹּאכְלוּ בְנֵי־יִשְׂרָאֵל הַשָּׁבִים מֵהַגּוֹלָה וְכֹל הַנִּבְדָּל מִטֻּמְאַת גּוֹיֵ־הָאָרֶץ אֲלֵהֶם לִדְרֹשׁ לַיהֹוָה אֱלֹהֵי יִשְׂרָאֵל: 22 וַיַּעֲשׂוּ חַג־מַצּוֹת שִׁבְעַת יָמִים בְּשִׂמְחָה כִּי ׀ שִׂמְּחָם יְהֹוָה וְהֵסֵב לֵב מֶלֶךְ־אַשּׁוּר עֲלֵיהֶם לְחַזֵּק יְדֵיהֶם בִּמְלֶאכֶת בֵּית־הָאֱלֹהִים אֱלֹהֵי יִשְׂרָאֵל: פ

ז וְאַחַר הַדְּבָרִים הָאֵלֶּה בְּמַלְכוּת אַרְתַּחְשַׁסְתְּא מֶלֶךְ־פָּרָס עֶזְרָא בֶּן־שְׂרָיָה בֶּן־עֲזַרְיָה בֶּן־חִלְקִיָּה: 2 בֶּן־שַׁלּוּם בֶּן־צָדוֹק בֶּן־אֲחִיטוּב: 3 בֶּן־אֲמַרְיָה בֶן־עֲזַרְיָה בֶּן־מְרָיוֹת: 4 בֶּן־זְרַחְיָה בֶן־עֻזִּי בֶּן־בֻּקִּי: 5 בֶּן־אֲבִישׁוּעַ בֶּן־פִּינְחָס בֶּן־אֶלְעָזָר בֶּן־אַהֲרֹן הַכֹּהֵן הָרֹאשׁ: 6 הוּא עֶזְרָא עָלָה

scribe expert in the Teaching of Moses which the Lord God of Israel had given, whose request the king had granted in its entirety, thanks to the benevolence of the Lord toward him.

(7Some of the Israelites, the priests and Levites, the singers, the gatekeepers, and the temple servants set out for Jerusalem in the seventh year of King Artaxerxes, 8arriving in Jerusalem in the fifth month in the seventh year of the king.) 9On the first day of the first month the journey up from Babylon was started, and on the first day of the fifth month he arrived in Jerusalem, thanks to the benevolent care of his God for him. 10For Ezra had dedicated himself to study the Teaching of the Lord so as to observe it, and to teach laws and rules to Israel.

11The following is the text of the letter which King Artaxerxes gave Ezra the priest-scribe, a scholar in matters concerning the commandments of the Lord and His laws to Israel:

12a"Artaxerxes king of kings, to Ezra the priest, scholar in the law of the God of heaven, b-and so forth.-b And now, 13I hereby issue an order that anyone in my kingdom who is of the people of Israel and its priests and Levites who feels impelled to go to Jerusalem may go with you. 14For you are commissioned by the king and his seven advisers to regulate Judah and Jerusalem according to the law of your God, which is in your care, 15and to bring the freewill offering of silver and gold, which the king and his advisers made to the God of Israel, whose dwelling is in Jerusalem, 16and whatever silver and gold that you find throughout the province of Babylon, together with the freewill offerings that the people and the priests will give for the House of their God, which is in Jerusalem. 17You shall, therefore, with dispatch acquire with this money bulls, rams, and lambs, with their meal offerings and libations, and offer them on the altar of the House of your God in

מִבָּבֶל וְהוּא־סֹפֵר מָהִיר בְּתוֹרַת מֹשֶׁה אֲשֶׁר־נָתַן יְהוָה אֱלֹהֵי יִשְׂרָאֵל וַיִּתֶּן־לוֹ הַמֶּלֶךְ כְּיַד־יְהוָה אֱלֹהָיו עָלָיו כֹּל בַּקָּשָׁתוֹ: פ

7 וַיַּעֲלוּ מִבְּנֵי־יִשְׂרָאֵל וּמִן־הַכֹּהֲנִים וְהַלְוִיִּם וְהַמְשֹׁרְרִים וְהַשֹּׁעֲרִים וְהַנְּתִינִים אֶל־יְרוּשָׁלִָם בִּשְׁנַת־שֶׁבַע לְאַרְתַּחְשַׁסְתְּא הַמֶּלֶךְ: 8 וַיָּבֹא יְרוּשָׁלִַם בַּחֹדֶשׁ הַחֲמִישִׁי הִיא שְׁנַת הַשְּׁבִיעִית לַמֶּלֶךְ: 9 כִּי בְּאֶחָד לַחֹדֶשׁ הָרִאשׁוֹן הוּא יְסֻד הַמַּעֲלָה מִבָּבֶל וּבְאֶחָד לַחֹדֶשׁ הַחֲמִישִׁי בָּא אֶל־יְרוּשָׁלִַם כְּיַד־אֱלֹהָיו הַטּוֹבָה עָלָיו: 10 כִּי עֶזְרָא הֵכִין לְבָבוֹ לִדְרוֹשׁ אֶת־תּוֹרַת יְהוָה וְלַעֲשֹׂת וּלְלַמֵּד בְּיִשְׂרָאֵל חֹק וּמִשְׁפָּט: ס

11 וְזֶה | פַּרְשֶׁגֶן הַנִּשְׁתְּוָן אֲשֶׁר נָתַן הַמֶּלֶךְ אַרְתַּחְשַׁסְתְּא לְעֶזְרָא הַכֹּהֵן הַסֹּפֵר סֹפֵר דִּבְרֵי מִצְוֹת־יְהוָה וְחֻקָּיו עַל־יִשְׂרָאֵל: פ

12 אַרְתַּחְשַׁסְתְּא מֶלֶךְ מַלְכַיָּא לְעֶזְרָא כָהֲנָא סָפַר דָּתָא דִּי־אֱלָהּ שְׁמַיָּא גְּמִיר וּכְעֶנֶת: 13 מִנִּי שִׂים טְעֵם דִּי כָל־מִתְנַדַּב בְּמַלְכוּתִי מִן־עַמָּה יִשְׂרָאֵל וְכָהֲנוֹהִי וְלֵוָיֵא לִמְהָךְ לִירוּשְׁלֶם עִמָּךְ יְהָךְ: 14 כָּל־קֳבֵל דִּי מִן־קֳדָם מַלְכָּא וְשִׁבְעַת יָעֲטֹהִי שְׁלִיחַ לְבַקָּרָא עַל־יְהוּד וְלִירוּשְׁלֶם בְּדָת אֱלָהָךְ דִּי בִידָךְ: 15 וּלְהֵיבָלָה כְּסַף וּדְהַב דִּי־מַלְכָּא וְיָעֲטוֹהִי הִתְנַדַּבוּ לֶאֱלָהּ יִשְׂרָאֵל דִּי בִירוּשְׁלֶם מִשְׁכְּנֵהּ: 16 וְכֹל כְּסַף וּדְהַב דִּי תְהַשְׁכַּח בְּכֹל מְדִינַת בָּבֶל עִם הִתְנַדָּבוּת עַמָּא וְכָהֲנַיָּא מִתְנַדְּבִין לְבֵית אֱלָהֲהֹם דִּי בִירוּשְׁלֶם: 17 כָּל־קֳבֵל דְּנָה אָסְפַּרְנָא תִקְנֵא בְּכַסְפָּא דְנָה תּוֹרִין | דִּכְרִין אִמְּרִין וּמִנְחָתְהוֹן וְנִסְכֵּיהוֹן וּתְקָרֵב

---

a   Aramaic resumes here through v. 26.
b-b   Meaning uncertain.

Jerusalem. ¹⁸And whatever you wish to do with the leftover silver and gold, you and your kinsmen may do, in accord with the will of your God. ¹⁹The vessels for the service of the House of your God that are given to you, deliver to God in Jerusalem, ²⁰and any other needs of the House of your God that it falls to you to supply, do so from the royal treasury. ²¹I, King Artaxerxes, for my part, hereby issue an order to all the treasurers in the province of Beyond the River that whatever request Ezra the priest, scholar in the law of the God of Heaven, makes of you is to be fulfilled with dispatch ²²up to the sum of one hundred talents of silver, one hundred *kor* of wheat, one hundred *bath* of wine, one hundred *bath* of oil, and salt without limit. ²³Whatever is by order of the God of Heaven must be carried out diligently for the House of the God of Heaven, else wrath will come upon the king and his sons. ²⁴We further advise you that it is not permissible to impose tribute, poll tax, or land tax on any priest, Levite, singer, gatekeeper, temple servant, or other servant of this House of God. ²⁵And you, Ezra, by the divine wisdom you possess, appoint magistrates and judges to judge all the people in the province of Beyond the River who know the laws of your God, and to teach those who do not know them. ²⁶Let anyone who does not obey the law of your God and the law of the king be punished with dispatch, whether by death, corporal punishment, confiscation of possessions, or imprisonment."

^{27c}Blessed is the L ORD God of our fathers, who put it into the mind of the king to glorify the House of the L ORD in Jerusalem, ²⁸and who inclined the king and his counselors and the king's military officers to be favorably disposed toward me. For my part, thanks to the care of the L ORD for me, I summoned up courage and assembled leading men in Israel to go with me.

---

c   Hebrew resumes here.

הִמּוֹ עַל־מַדְבְּחָה דִּי בֵּית אֱלָהֲכֹם דִּי
בִירוּשְׁלֶם: 18 וּמָה דִּי עליך וְעַל־אחיך
אֱנָךְ יֵיטַב בִּשְׁאָר כַּסְפָּא וְדַהֲבָה לְמֶעְבַּד
כִּרְעוּת אֱלָהֲכֹם תַּעַבְדוּן: 19 וּמָאנַיָּא
דִּי־מִתְיַהֲבִין לָךְ לְפָלְחָן בֵּית אֱלָהָךְ
הַשְׁלֵם קֳדָם אֱלָהּ יְרוּשְׁלֶם: 20 וּשְׁאָר
חַשְׁחוּת בֵּית אֱלָהָךְ דִּי יִפֶּל־לָךְ לְמִנְתַּן
תִּנְתֵּן מִן־בֵּית גִּנְזֵי מַלְכָּא: 21 וּמִנִּי אֲנָה
אַרְתַּחְשַׁסְתְּא מַלְכָּא שִׂים טְעֵם לְכֹל
גִּזַּבְרַיָּא דִּי בַּעֲבַר נַהֲרָה דִּי כָל־דִּי
יִשְׁאֲלֶנְכוֹן עֶזְרָא כָהֲנָה סָפַר דָּתָא דִּי־אֱלָהּ
שְׁמַיָּא אָסְפַּרְנָא יִתְעֲבִד: 22 עַד־כְּסַף
כַּכְּרִין מְאָה וְעַד־חִנְטִין כֹּרִין מְאָה וְעַד־
חֲמַר בַּתִּין מְאָה וְעַד־בַּתִּין מְשַׁח מְאָה
וּמְלַח דִּי־לָא כְתָב: 23 כָּל־דִּי מִן־טַעַם
אֱלָהּ שְׁמַיָּא יִתְעֲבֵד אַדְרַזְדָּא לְבֵית אֱלָהּ
שְׁמַיָּא דִּי־לְמָה לֶהֱוֵא קְצַף עַל־מַלְכוּת
מַלְכָּא וּבְנוֹהִי: 24 וּלְכֹם מְהוֹדְעִין דִּי כָל־
כָּהֲנַיָּא וְלֵוָיֵא זַמָּרַיָּא תָרָעַיָּא נְתִינַיָּא
וּפָלְחֵי בֵּית אֱלָהָא דְנָה מִנְדָּה בְלוֹ וַהֲלָךְ
לָא שַׁלִּיט לְמִרְמֵא עֲלֵיהֹם: 25 וְאַנְתְּ עֶזְרָא
כְּחָכְמַת אֱלָהָךְ דִּי־בִידָךְ מֶנִּי שָׁפְטִין וְדַיָּנִין
דִּי־לֶהֱוֹן דאנין דָּאֲנִין לְכָל־עַמָּה דִּי בַּעֲבַר
נַהֲרָה לְכָל־יָדְעֵי דָּתֵי אֱלָהָךְ וְדִי לָא יָדַע
תְּהוֹדְעוּן: 26 וְכָל־דִּי־לָא לֶהֱוֵא עָבֵד דָּתָא
דִּי־אֱלָהָךְ וְדָתָא דִּי מַלְכָּא אָסְפַּרְנָא דִּינָה
לֶהֱוֵא מִתְעֲבֵד מִנֵּהּ הֵן לְמוֹת הֵן לשרשו
לִשְׁרֹשִׁי הֵן־לַעֲנָשׁ נִכְסִין וְלֶאֱסוּרִין: פ
27 בָּרוּךְ יְהוָה אֱלֹהֵי אֲבוֹתֵינוּ אֲשֶׁר נָתַן
כָּזֹאת בְּלֵב הַמֶּלֶךְ לְפָאֵר אֶת־בֵּית יְהוָה
אֲשֶׁר בִּירוּשָׁלָ͏ִם: 28 וְעָלַי הִטָּה־חֶסֶד לִפְנֵי
הַמֶּלֶךְ וְיוֹעֲצָיו וּלְכָל־שָׂרֵי הַמֶּלֶךְ הַגִּבֹּרִים
וַאֲנִי הִתְחַזַּקְתִּי כְּיַד־יְהוָה אֱלֹהַי עָלַי
וָאֶקְבְּצָה מִיִּשְׂרָאֵל רָאשִׁים לַעֲלוֹת
עִמִּי: פ

8 These are the chiefs of the clans and the register of the genealogy of those who came up with me from Babylon in the reign of King Artaxerxes: [2]Of the sons of Phinehas, Gershom; of the sons of Ithamar, Daniel; of the sons of David, Hattush. [3]Of the sons of Shecaniah: of the sons of Parosh, Zechariah; through him the genealogy of 150 males was registered. [4]Elieho-enai son of Zerahiah, of the sons of Pahath-moab, and with him 200 males. [5]Of the sons of Shecaniah son of Jahaziel; and with him 300 males. [6]And of the sons of Adin, Ebed son of Jonathan; and with him 50 males. [7]And of the sons of Elam, Jeshaiah son of Athaliah; and with him 70 males. [8]And of the sons of Shephatiah, Zebadiah son of Michael; and with him 80 males. [9]Of the sons of Joab, Obadiah son of Jehiel; and with him 218 males. [10]And of the sons of Shelomith, the son of Josiphiah; and with him 160 males. [11]And of the sons of Bebai, Zechariah son of Bebai; and with him 28 males. [12]And of the sons of Azgad, Johanan son of Hakkatan; and with him 110 males. [13]And of the sons of Adonikam, who were the last; and these are their names: Eliphelet, Jeiel, and Shemaiah; and with them 60 males. [14]And of the sons of Bigvai, Uthai and Zaccur; and with them 70 males.

[15]These I assembled by the river that enters Ahava, and we encamped there for three days. I reviewed the people and the priests, but I did not find any Levites there. [16]I sent for Eliezer, Ariel, Shemaiah, Elnathan, Jarib, Elnathan, Na-than, Zechariah, and Meshullam, the leading men, and also for Joiarib and Elnathan, the in-structors, [17]and I gave them an order for Iddo, the leader at the place [called] Casiphia. I gave them a message to convey to Iddo [and] his brother, temple-servants at the place [called] Casiphia, that they should bring us attendants for the House of our God. [18]Thanks to the be-

ח וְאֵ֣לֶּה רָאשֵׁ֧י אֲבֹתֵיהֶ֛ם וְהִתְיַחְשָׂ֑ם הָעֹלִ֣ים עִמִּ֗י בְּמַלְכ֛וּת אַרְתַּחְשַׁ֥סְתְּא הַמֶּ֖לֶךְ מִבָּבֶֽל: ס 2 מִבְּנֵ֤י פִֽינְחָס֙ גֵּ֣רְשֹׁ֔ם ס מִבְּנֵ֥י אִיתָמָ֖ר דָּנִיֵּ֑אל ס מִבְּנֵ֥י דָוִ֖ד חַטּֽוּשׁ: ס 3 מִבְּנֵ֥י שְׁכַנְיָ֖ה ס מִבְּנֵ֣י פַרְעֹ֗שׁ זְכַרְיָ֔ה וְעִמּ֖וֹ הִתְיַחֵ֣שׂ לִזְכָרִ֑ים מֵאָ֥ה וַחֲמִשִּֽׁים: ס 4 מִבְּנֵי֙ פַּחַ֣ת מוֹאָ֔ב אֶלְיְהוֹעֵינַ֖י בֶּן־זְרַֽחְיָ֑ה וְעִמּ֖וֹ מָאתַ֥יִם הַזְּכָרִֽים: ס 5 מִבְּנֵ֥י שְׁכַנְיָ֖ה בֶּן־יַחֲזִיאֵ֑ל וְעִמּ֕וֹ שְׁלֹ֥שׁ מֵא֖וֹת הַזְּכָרִֽים: ס 6 וּמִבְּנֵ֣י עָדִ֗ין עֶ֚בֶד בֶּן־י֣וֹנָתָ֔ן וְעִמּ֖וֹ חֲמִשִּׁ֥ים הַזְּכָרִֽים: ס 7 וּמִבְּנֵ֤י עֵילָם֙ יְשַֽׁעְיָ֣ה בֶּן־עֲתַלְיָ֔ה וְעִמּ֖וֹ שִׁבְעִ֥ים הַזְּכָרִֽים: ס 8 וּמִבְּנֵ֣י שְׁפַטְיָ֗ה זְבַדְיָ֛ה בֶּן־מִֽיכָאֵ֖ל וְעִמּ֖וֹ שְׁמֹנִ֥ים הַזְּכָרִֽים: ס 9 מִבְּנֵ֣י יוֹאָ֔ב עֹבַדְיָ֖ה בֶּן־יְחִיאֵ֑ל וְעִמּ֕וֹ מָאתַ֥יִם וּשְׁמֹנָ֥ה עָשָׂ֖ר הַזְּכָרִֽים: ס 10 וּמִבְּנֵ֥י שְׁלוֹמִ֖ית בֶּן־יוֹסִפְיָ֑ה וְעִמּ֕וֹ מֵאָ֥ה וְשִׁשִּׁ֖ים הַזְּכָרִֽים: ס 11 וּמִבְּנֵ֣י בֵבַ֗י זְכַרְיָ֣ה בֶּן־בֵּבָ֑י וְעִמּ֕וֹ עֶשְׂרִ֥ים וּשְׁמֹנָ֖ה הַזְּכָרִֽים: ס 12 וּמִבְּנֵ֣י עַזְגָּ֔ד יֽוֹחָנָ֖ן בֶּן־הַקָּטָ֑ן וְעִמּ֕וֹ מֵאָ֥ה וַעֲשָׂרָ֖ה הַזְּכָרִֽים: ס 13 וּמִבְּנֵ֣י אֲדֹנִיקָם֮ אַחֲרֹנִים֒ וְאֵ֣לֶּה שְׁמוֹתָ֔ם אֱלִיפֶ֖לֶט יְעִיאֵ֣ל וּֽשְׁמַעְיָ֑ה וְעִמָּהֶ֖ם שִׁשִּׁ֥ים הַזְּכָרִֽים: ס 14 וּמִבְּנֵ֥י בִגְוַ֖י עוּתַ֣י וזָבּ֑וּד וְעִמּ֖וֹ* שִׁבְעִ֥ים הַזְּכָרִֽים: פ

15 וָאֶקְבְּצֵ֗ם אֶל־הַנָּהָר֙ הַבָּ֣א אֶֽל־אַהֲוָ֔א וַנַּחֲנֶ֥ה שָׁ֖ם יָמִ֣ים שְׁלֹשָׁ֑ה וָאָבִ֤ינָה בָעָם֙ וּבַכֹּ֣הֲנִ֔ים וּמִבְּנֵ֥י לֵוִ֖י לֹא־מָצָ֥אתִי שָֽׁם: 16 וָאֶשְׁלְחָ֡ה לֶאֱלִיעֶ֡זֶר לַאֲרִיאֵ֡ל לִ֠שְׁמַעְיָ֡ה וּלְאֶלְנָתָ֣ן וּלְיָרִיב֩ וּלְאֶלְנָתָ֨ן וּלְנָתָ֜ן וְלִזְכַרְיָ֧ה וְלִמְשֻׁלָּ֛ם רָאשִׁ֖ים וּלְיוֹיָרִ֥יב וּלְאֶלְנָתָ֖ן מְבִינִֽים: 17 וָאוֹצִאָ֤ה אוֹתָם֙ עַל־אִדּ֣וֹ הָרֹ֔אשׁ בְּכָסִפְיָ֖א הַמָּק֑וֹם וָאָשִׂימָה֩ בְּפִיהֶ֨ם דְּבָרִ֜ים לְדַבֵּ֣ר אֶל־אִדּ֗וֹ

nevolent care of our God for us, they brought us a capable man of the family of Mahli son of Levi son of Israel, and Sherebiah and his sons and brothers, 18 in all, ¹⁹and Hashabiah, and with him Jeshaiah of the family of Merari, his brothers and their sons, 20 in all; ²⁰and of the temple servants whom David and the officers had appointed for the service of the Levites— 220 temple servants, all of them listed by name.

²¹I proclaimed a fast there by the Ahava River to afflict ourselves before our God to beseech Him for a smooth journey for us and for our children and for all our possessions; ²²for I was ashamed to ask the king for soldiers and horsemen to protect us against any enemy on the way, since we had told the king, "The benevolent care of our God is for all who seek Him, while His fierce anger is against all who forsake Him." ²³So we fasted and besought our God for this, and He responded to our plea. ²⁴Then I selected twelve of the chiefs of the priests, namely Sherebiah and Hashabiah with ten of their brothers, ²⁵and I weighed out to them the silver, the gold, and the vessels, the contribution to the House of our God which the king, his counselors and officers, and all Israel who were present had made. ²⁶I entrusted to their safekeeping the weight of six hundred and fifty talents of silver, one hundred silver vessels of one talent each, one hundred talents of gold; ²⁷also, twenty gold bowls worth one thousand *darics* and two vessels of good, shining bronze, as precious as gold. ²⁸I said to them, "You are consecrated to the LORD, and the vessels are consecrated, and the silver and gold are a freewill offering to the LORD God of your fathers. ²⁹Guard them diligently until such time as you weigh them out in the presence of the officers of the priests and the Levites and the officers of the clans of Israel in Jerusalem in the chambers of the House of the LORD."

אֲחֵיהֶ֖ם הַנְּתוּנִ֥ים בְּכַסְפְיָ֖א הַמָּק֑וֹם לְהָבִיא־לָ֣נוּ מְשָׁרְתִ֔ים לְבֵ֖ית אֱלֹהֵֽינוּ׃ 18 וַיָּבִ֣יאוּ* לָ֡נוּ כְּיַד־אֱלֹהֵ֩ינוּ֩ הַטּוֹבָ֨ה עָלֵ֜ינוּ אִ֣ישׁ שֶׂ֗כֶל מִבְּנֵ֛י מַחְלִ֥י בֶן־לֵוִ֖י בֶּן־יִשְׂרָאֵ֑ל וְשֵׁרֵֽבְיָ֥ה וּבָנָ֛יו וְאֶחָ֖יו שְׁמֹנָ֥ה עָשָֽׂר׃ 19 וְאֶת־חֲשַׁבְיָ֔ה וְאִתּ֥וֹ יְשַֽׁעְיָ֖ה מִבְּנֵ֣י מְרָרִ֑י אֶחָ֥יו וּבְנֵיהֶ֖ם עֶשְׂרִֽים׃ ס 20 וּמִן־ הַנְּתִינִ֗ים שֶׁנָּתַ֨ן דָּוִ֤יד וְהַשָּׂרִים֙ לַעֲבֹדַ֣ת הַלְוִיִּ֔ם נְתִינִ֖ים מָאתַ֣יִם וְעֶשְׂרִ֑ים כֻּלָּ֖ם נִקְּב֥וּ בְשֵׁמֽוֹת׃ 21 וָאֶקְרָ֨א שָׁ֥ם צוֹם֙ עַל־הַנָּהָ֣ר אַהֲוָ֔א לְהִתְעַנּ֖וֹת לִפְנֵ֣י אֱלֹהֵ֑ינוּ לְבַקֵּ֤שׁ מִמֶּ֨נּוּ֙ דֶּ֣רֶךְ יְשָׁרָ֔ה לָ֥נוּ וּלְטַפֵּ֖נוּ וּלְכָל־רְכוּשֵֽׁנוּ׃ 22 כִּ֣י בֹ֗שְׁתִּי לִשְׁא֤וֹל מִן־הַמֶּ֨לֶךְ֙ חַ֣יִל וּפָרָשִׁ֔ים לְעָזְרֵ֥נוּ מֵאוֹיֵ֖ב בַּדָּ֑רֶךְ כִּֽי־אָמַ֤רְנוּ לַמֶּ֨לֶךְ֙ לֵאמֹ֔ר יַד־אֱלֹהֵ֤ינוּ עַל־כָּל־מְבַקְשָׁיו֙ לְטוֹבָ֔ה וְעֻזּ֣וֹ וְאַפּ֔וֹ עַ֖ל כָּל־עֹזְבָֽיו׃ 23 וַנָּצ֛וּמָה וַנְּבַקְשָׁ֥ה מֵאֱלֹהֵ֖ינוּ עַל־זֹ֑את וַיֵּעָתֵ֖ר לָֽנוּ׃ 24 וָאַבְדִּ֛ילָה מִשָּׂרֵ֥י הַכֹּהֲנִ֖ים שְׁנֵ֣ים עָשָׂ֑ר לְשֵׁרֵֽבְיָ֣ה חֲשַׁבְיָ֔ה וְעִמָּהֶ֥ם מֵאֲחֵיהֶ֖ם עֲשָׂרָֽה׃ 25 ואשקולה וָֽאֶשְׁקֳלָ֣ה לָהֶ֗ם אֶת־הַכֶּ֨סֶף וְאֶת־הַזָּהָ֜ב וְאֶת־הַכֵּלִ֗ים תְּרוּמַ֤ת בֵּית־אֱלֹהֵ֨ינוּ֙ הַהֵרִ֣ימוּ הַמֶּ֔לֶךְ וְיֹעֲצָ֖יו וְשָׂרָ֑יו וְכָל־יִשְׂרָאֵ֖ל הַנִּמְצָאִֽים׃ 26 וָאֶשְׁקֳלָ֨ה עַל־יָדָ֜ם כֶּ֗סֶף כִּכָּרִים֙ שֵֽׁשׁ־ מֵא֣וֹת וַחֲמִשִּׁ֔ים וּכְלֵי־כֶ֖סֶף מֵאָ֣ה לְכִכָּרִ֑ים זָהָ֖ב מֵאָ֥ה כִכָּֽר׃ 27 וּכְפֹרֵ֤י זָהָב֙ עֶשְׂרִ֔ים לַאֲדַרְכֹנִ֖ים אָ֑לֶף וּכְלֵ֨י נְחֹ֜שֶׁת מֻצְהָ֤ב טוֹבָה֙ שְׁנַ֔יִם חֲמוּדֹ֖ת כַּזָּהָֽב׃ 28 וָאֹמְרָ֣ה אֲלֵהֶ֗ם אַתֶּ֥ם קֹ֨דֶשׁ֙ לַֽיהוָ֔ה וְהַכֵּלִ֖ים קֹ֑דֶשׁ וְהַכֶּ֨סֶף וְהַזָּהָ֔ב נְדָבָ֕ה לַיהוָ֖ה אֱלֹהֵ֥י אֲבֹתֵיכֶֽם׃ 29 שִׁקְד֣וּ וְשִׁמְר֗וּ עַֽד־תִּשְׁקְלוּ֙ לִפְנֵ֞י שָׂרֵ֧י הַכֹּהֲנִ֣ים וְהַלְוִיִּ֗ם וְשָֽׂרֵי־הָאָב֛וֹת לְיִשְׂרָאֵ֖ל בִּירוּשָׁלָ֑͏ִם הַלִּשְׁכ֖וֹת בֵּ֥ית יְהוָֽה׃

א׳ דגושה v. 18.

30So the priests and the Levites received the cargo of silver and gold and vessels by weight, to bring them to Jerusalem to the House of our God. 31We set out for Jerusalem from the Ahava River on the twelfth of the first month. We enjoyed the care of our God, who saved us from enemy ambush on the journey.

32We arrived in Jerusalem and stayed there three days. 33On the fourth day the silver, gold, and vessels were weighed out in the House of our God into the keeping of Meremoth son of Uriah the priest, with whom was Eleazar son of Phinehas. Jozabad son of Jeshua, and Noadiah son of Binnui, the Levites, were with them. 34Everything accorded as to number and weight, the entire cargo being recorded at that time.

35The returning exiles who arrived from captivity made burnt offerings to the God of Israel: twelve bulls for all Israel, ninety-six rams, seventy-seven lambs and twelve he-goats as a purification offering, all this a burnt offering to the LORD. 36They handed the royal orders to the king's satraps and the governors of the province of Beyond the River who gave support to the people and the House of God.

9 When this was over, the officers approached me, saying, "The people of Israel and the priests and Levites have not separated themselves from the peoples of the land whose abhorrent practices are like those of the Canaanites, the Hittites, the Perizzites, the Jebusites, the Ammonites, the Moabites, the Egyptians, and the Amorites. 2They have taken their daughters as wives for themselves and for their sons, so that the holy seed has become intermingled with the peoples of the land; and it is the officers and prefects who have taken the lead in this trespass."

30 וְקִבְּל֣וּ הַכֹּהֲנִ֣ים וְהַלְוִיִּ֗ם מִשְׁקַ֤ל הַכֶּ֙סֶף֙ וְהַזָּהָ֣ב וְהַכֵּלִ֔ים לְהָבִ֥יא לִירוּשָׁלִַ֖ם לְבֵ֥ית אֱלֹהֵֽינוּ׃ פ 31 וַנִּסְעָ֞ה מִנְּהַ֣ר אַֽהֲוָ֗א בִּשְׁנֵ֤ים עָשָׂר֙ לַחֹ֣דֶשׁ הָֽרִאשׁ֔וֹן לָלֶ֖כֶת יְרוּשָׁלָ֑͏ִם וְיַד־אֱלֹהֵ֙ינוּ֙ הָֽיְתָ֣ה עָלֵ֔ינוּ וַיַּ֙צִּילֵ֔נוּ מִכַּ֥ף אוֹיֵ֛ב וְאוֹרֵ֖ב עַל־הַדָּֽרֶךְ׃ 32 וַנָּב֖וֹא יְרֽוּשָׁלָ֑͏ִם וַנֵּ֥שֶׁב שָׁ֖ם יָמִ֥ים שְׁלֹשָֽׁה׃ 33 וּבַיּ֣וֹם הָֽרְבִיעִ֗י נִשְׁקַ֤ל הַכֶּ֙סֶף֙ וְהַזָּהָ֣ב וְהַכֵּלִ֔ים בְּבֵ֖ית אֱלֹהֵ֑ינוּ עַ֣ל יַד־מְרֵמ֧וֹת בֶּן־אֽוּרִיָּ֣ה הַכֹּהֵ֗ן וְעִמּ֣וֹ אֶלְעָזָ֣ר בֶּן־פִּֽינְחָ֑ס וְעִמָּהֶ֞ם יוֹזָבָ֧ד בֶּן־יֵשׁ֛וּעַ וְנֽוֹעַדְיָ֥ה בֶן־בִּנּ֖וּי הַלְוִיִּֽם׃ 34 בְּמִסְפָּ֥ר בְּמִשְׁקָ֖ל לַכֹּ֑ל וַיִּכָּתֵ֥ב כָּֽל־הַמִּשְׁקָ֖ל בָּעֵ֥ת הַהִֽיא׃ פ 35 הַ֠בָּאִ֠ים מֵֽהַשְּׁבִ֞י בְנֵ֣י הַגּוֹלָ֗ה הִקְרִ֚יבוּ עֹלוֹת֮ לֵֽאלֹהֵ֣י יִשְׂרָאֵל֒ פָּרִ֨ים שְׁנֵֽים־עָשָׂ֜ר עַל־כָּל־יִשְׂרָאֵ֗ל אֵילִ֣ים ׀ תִּשְׁעִ֣ים וְשִׁשָּׁ֗ה כְּבָשִׂים֙ שִׁבְעִ֣ים וְשִׁבְעָ֔ה צְפִירֵ֥י חַטָּ֖את שְׁנֵ֣ים עָשָׂ֑ר הַכֹּ֖ל עוֹלָ֥ה לַֽיהֹוָֽה׃ פ 36 וַֽיִּתְּנ֣וּ ׀ אֶת־דָּתֵ֣י הַמֶּ֗לֶךְ לַֽאֲחַשְׁדַּרְפְּנֵי֙ הַמֶּ֔לֶךְ וּפַֽחֲו֖וֹת עֵ֣בֶר הַנָּהָ֑ר וְנִשְּׂא֥וּ אֶת־הָעָ֖ם וְאֶת־בֵּֽית־הָֽאֱלֹהִֽים׃ ס

ט 1 וּכְכַלּ֣וֹת אֵ֗לֶּה נִגְּשׁ֚וּ אֵלַי֙ הַשָּׂרִ֣ים לֵאמֹ֔ר לֹֽא־נִבְדְּל֞וּ הָעָ֤ם יִשְׂרָאֵל֙ וְהַכֹּֽהֲנִ֣ים וְהַלְוִיִּ֔ם מֵֽעַמֵּ֖י הָֽאֲרָצ֑וֹת כְּ֠תֽוֹעֲבֹ֠תֵיהֶ֟ם לַכְּנַעֲנִ֣י הַֽחִתִּ֗י הַפְּרִזִּי֙ הַיְבוּסִ֣י הָֽעַמֹּנִ֔י הַמֹּֽאָבִי֙ הַמִּצְרִ֔י וְהָֽאֱמֹרִֽי׃ 2 כִּֽי־נָֽשְׂא֣וּ מִבְּנֹֽתֵיהֶ֗ם לָהֶם֙ וְלִבְנֵיהֶ֔ם וְהִתְעָֽרְבוּ֙ זֶ֣רַע הַקֹּ֔דֶשׁ בְּעַמֵּ֖י הָֽאֲרָצ֑וֹת וְיַ֧ד הַשָּׂרִ֣ים וְהַסְּגָנִ֗ים הָ֥יְתָ֛ה בַּמַּ֥עַל הַזֶּ֖ה רִֽאשׁוֹנָֽה׃ ס

3When I heard this, I rent my garment and robe, I tore hair out of my head and beard, and I sat desolate. 4Around me gathered all who were concerned over the words of the God of Israel because of the returning exiles' trespass, while I sat desolate until the evening offering. 5At the time of the evening offering I ended my self-affliction; still in my torn garment and robe, I got down on my knees and spread out my hands to the LORD my God, 6and said, "O my God, I am too ashamed and mortified to lift my face to You, O my God, for our iniquities a-are overwhelming-a and our guilt has grown high as heaven. 7From the time of our fathers to this very day we have been deep in guilt. Because of our iniquities, we, our kings, and our priests have been handed over to foreign kings, to the sword, to captivity, to pillage, and to humiliation, as is now the case.

8"But now, for a short while, there has been a reprieve from the LORD our God, who has granted us a surviving remnant and given us a stake in His holy place; our God has restored the luster to our eyes and furnished us with a little sustenance in our bondage. 9For bondsmen we are, though even in our bondage God has not forsaken us, but has disposed the king of Persia favorably toward us, to furnish us with sustenance and to raise again the House of our God, repairing its ruins and giving us a holdb in Judah and Jerusalem.

10"Now, what can we say in the face of this, O our God, for we have forsaken Your commandments, 11which You gave us through Your servants the prophets when You said, 'The land that you are about to possess is a land unclean through the uncleanness of the peoples of the land, through their abhorrent practices with which they, in their impurity, have filled it from

---

a-a Lit. "are numerous above the head."
b Lit. "fence."

3 וּכְשָׁמְעִי אֶת־הַדָּבָר הַזֶּה קָרַעְתִּי אֶת־
בִּגְדִי וּמְעִילִי וָאֶמְרְטָה מִשְּׂעַר רֹאשִׁי וּזְקָנִי
וָאֵשְׁבָה מְשׁוֹמֵם: 4 וְאֵלַי יֵאָסְפוּ כֹּל חָרֵד
בְּדִבְרֵי אֱלֹהֵי־יִשְׂרָאֵל עַל מַעַל הַגּוֹלָה
וַאֲנִי יֹשֵׁב מְשׁוֹמֵם עַד לְמִנְחַת הָעָרֶב:
5 וּבְמִנְחַת הָעֶרֶב קַמְתִּי מִתַּעֲנִיתִי וּבְקָרְעִי
בִגְדִי וּמְעִילִי וָאֶכְרְעָה עַל־בִּרְכַּי וָאֶפְרְשָׂה
כַפַּי אֶל־יְהוָה אֱלֹהָי: 6 וָאֹמְרָה אֱלֹהַי
בֹּשְׁתִּי וְנִכְלַמְתִּי לְהָרִים אֱלֹהַי פָּנַי אֵלֶיךָ
כִּי עֲוֺנֹתֵינוּ רָבוּ לְמַעְלָה רֹּאשׁ* וְאַשְׁמָתֵנוּ
גָדְלָה עַד לַשָּׁמָיִם: 7 מִימֵי אֲבֹתֵינוּ אֲנַחְנוּ
בְּאַשְׁמָה גְדֹלָה עַד הַיּוֹם הַזֶּה וּבַעֲוֺנֹתֵינוּ
נִתַּנּוּ אֲנַחְנוּ מְלָכֵינוּ כֹהֲנֵינוּ בְּיַד | מַלְכֵי
הָאֲרָצוֹת בַּחֶרֶב בַּשְּׁבִי וּבַבִּזָּה וּבְבֹשֶׁת
פָּנִים כְּהַיּוֹם הַזֶּה:
8 וְעַתָּה כִּמְעַט־רֶגַע הָיְתָה תְחִנָּה מֵאֵת |
יְהוָה אֱלֹהֵינוּ לְהַשְׁאִיר לָנוּ פְּלֵיטָה
וְלָתֶת־לָנוּ יָתֵד בִּמְקוֹם קָדְשׁוֹ לְהָאִיר
עֵינֵינוּ אֱלֹהֵינוּ וּלְתִתֵּנוּ מִחְיָה מְעַט
בְּעַבְדֻתֵנוּ: 9 כִּי־עֲבָדִים אֲנַחְנוּ וּבְעַבְדֻתֵנוּ
לֹא עֲזָבָנוּ אֱלֹהֵינוּ וַיַּט־עָלֵינוּ חֶסֶד לִפְנֵי
מַלְכֵי פָרַס לָתֶת־לָנוּ מִחְיָה לְרוֹמֵם
אֶת־בֵּית אֱלֹהֵינוּ וּלְהַעֲמִיד אֶת־חָרְבֹתָיו
וְלָתֶת־לָנוּ גָדֵר בִּיהוּדָה וּבִירוּשָׁלָ͏ִם: ס
10 וְעַתָּה מַה־נֹּאמַר אֱלֹהֵינוּ אַחֲרֵי־זֹאת
כִּי עָזַבְנוּ מִצְוֺתֶיךָ: 11 אֲשֶׁר צִוִּיתָ בְּיַד
עֲבָדֶיךָ הַנְּבִיאִים לֵאמֹר הָאָרֶץ אֲשֶׁר
אַתֶּם בָּאִים לְרִשְׁתָּהּ אֶרֶץ נִדָּה הִיא
בְּנִדַּת עַמֵּי הָאֲרָצוֹת בְּתוֹעֲבֹתֵיהֶם אֲשֶׁר
מִלְאוּהָ מִפֶּה אֶל־פֶּה בְּטֻמְאָתָם: 12 וְעַתָּה

one end to the other. 12Now then, do not give your daughters in marriage to their sons or let their daughters marry your sons; do nothing for their well-being or advantage, then you will be strong and enjoy the bounty of the land and bequeath it to your children forever.' 13After all that has happened to us because of our evil deeds and our deep guilt—though You, our God, have been forbearing, [punishing us] less than our iniquity [deserves] in that You have granted us such a remnant as this—14shall we once again violate Your commandments by intermarrying with these peoples who follow such abhorrent practices? Will You not rage against us till we are destroyed without remnant or survivor? 15O LORD, God of Israel, You are benevolent,c for we have survived as a remnant, as is now the case. We stand before You in all our guilt, for we cannot face You on this account."

10 While Ezra was praying and making confession, weeping and prostrating himself before the House of God, a very great crowd of Israelites gathered about him, men, women, and children; the people were weeping bitterly. 2Then Shecaniah son of Jehiel of the family of Elam spoke up and said to Ezra, "We have trespassed against our God by bringing into our homes foreign women from the peoples of the land; a-but there is still hope for Israel despite this.-a 3Now then, let us make a covenant with our God to expel all these women and those who have been born to them, in accordance with the bidding of the Lord and of all who are concerned over the commandment of our God, and let the Teaching be obeyed. 4Take action, for the responsibility is yours and we are with you. Act with resolve!"

---

c   Or "in the right."
a-a   Or "Is there…?"

בְּנֹתֵיכֶ֞ם אַל־תִּתְּנ֣וּ לִבְנֵיהֶ֗ם וּבְנֹֽתֵיהֶם֙ אַל־תִּשְׂא֣וּ לִבְנֵיכֶ֔ם וְלֹֽא־תִדְרְשׁ֧וּ שְׁלֹמָ֛ם וְטוֹבָתָ֖ם עַד־עוֹלָ֑ם לְמַ֣עַן תֶּחֶזְק֗וּ וַאֲכַלְתֶּם֙ אֶת־ט֣וּב הָאָ֔רֶץ וְהוֹרַשְׁתֶּ֥ם לִבְנֵיכֶ֖ם עַד־עוֹלָֽם׃ 13 וְאַֽחֲרֵי֙ כָּל־הַבָּ֣א עָלֵ֔ינוּ בְּמַעֲשֵׂ֖ינוּ הָרָעִ֑ים וּבְאַשְׁמָתֵ֖נוּ הַגְּדֹלָ֑ה כִּ֣י ׀ אַתָּ֣ה אֱלֹהֵ֗ינוּ חָשַׂ֙כְתָּ֙ לְמַ֣טָּה מֵֽעֲוֺנֵ֔נוּ וְנָתַ֧תָּה לָּ֛נוּ פְּלֵיטָ֖ה כָּזֹֽאת׃ 14 הֲנָשׁוּב֩ לְהָפֵ֨ר מִצְוֺתֶ֜יךָ וּֽלְהִתְחַתֵּ֗ן בְּעַמֵּ֤י הַתֹּֽעֵבוֹת֙ הָאֵ֔לֶּה הֲל֤וֹא תֶֽאֱנַף־בָּ֙נוּ֙ עַד־כַּלֵּ֔ה לְאֵ֥ין שְׁאֵרִ֖ית וּפְלֵיטָֽה׃ פ 15 יְהוָ֞ה אֱלֹהֵ֤י יִשְׂרָאֵל֙ צַדִּ֣יק אַ֔תָּה כִּֽי־נִשְׁאַ֥רְנוּ פְלֵיטָ֖ה כְּהַיּ֣וֹם הַזֶּ֑ה הִנְנ֤וּ לְפָנֶ֙יךָ֙ בְּאַשְׁמָתֵ֔ינוּ כִּ֣י אֵ֥ין לַעֲמ֛וֹד לְפָנֶ֖יךָ עַל־זֹֽאת׃ פ

י וּכְהִתְפַּלֵּ֤ל עֶזְרָא֙ וּכְהִ֨תְוַדֹּת֔וֹ בֹּכֶה֙ וּמִתְנַפֵּ֔ל לִפְנֵ֖י בֵּ֣ית הָאֱלֹהִ֑ים נִקְבְּצוּ֩ אֵלָ֨יו מִיִּשְׂרָאֵ֜ל קָהָ֣ל רַב־מְאֹ֗ד אֲנָשִׁ֤ים וְנָשִׁים֙ וִֽילָדִ֔ים כִּֽי־בָכ֥וּ הָעָ֖ם הַרְבֵּֽה־בֶֽכֶה׃ ס 2 וַיַּעַן֩ שְׁכַנְיָ֨ה בֶן־יְחִיאֵ֜ל מִבְּנֵ֣י עֵילָ֗ם וַיֹּ֙אמֶר֙ לְעֶזְרָ֔א אֲנַ֙חְנוּ֙ מָעַ֣לְנוּ בֵֽאלֹהֵ֔ינוּ וַנֹּ֛שֶׁב נָשִׁ֥ים נָכְרִיּ֖וֹת מֵעַמֵּ֣י הָאָ֑רֶץ וְעַתָּ֛ה יֵשׁ־מִקְוֶ֥ה לְיִשְׂרָאֵ֖ל עַל־זֹֽאת׃ 3 וְעַתָּ֣ה נִֽכְרָת־בְּרִ֣ית לֵֽאלֹהֵ֡ינוּ לְהוֹצִ֣יא כָל־נָשִׁ֣ים וְהַנּוֹלָ֣ד מֵהֶ֗ם בַּעֲצַ֣ת אֲדֹנָי֮ וְהַחֲרֵדִים֒ בְּמִצְוַ֖ת אֱלֹהֵ֑ינוּ וְכַתּוֹרָ֖ה יֵעָשֶֽׂה׃ 4 ק֛וּם כִּֽי־עָלֶ֥יךָ הַדָּבָ֖ר וַאֲנַ֣חְנוּ עִמָּ֑ךְ חֲזַ֖ק וַעֲשֵֽׂה׃ פ

⁵So Ezra at once put the officers of the priests and the Levites and all Israel under oath to act accordingly, and they took the oath. ⁶Then Ezra rose from his place in front of the House of God and went into the chamber of Jehohanan son of Eliashib; there, he ate no bread and drank no water, for he was in mourning over the trespass of those who had returned from exile. ⁷Then a proclamation was issued in Judah and Jerusalem that all who had returned from the exile should assemble in Jerusalem, ⁸and that anyone who did not come in three days would, by decision of the officers and elders, have his property confiscated and himself excluded from the congregation of the returning exiles.

⁹All the men of Judah and Benjamin assembled in Jerusalem in three days; it was the ninth month, the twentieth of the month. All the people sat in the square of the House of God, trembling on account of the event and because of the rains. ¹⁰Then Ezra the priest got up and said to them, "You have trespassed by bringing home foreign women, thus aggravating the guilt of Israel. ¹¹So now, make confession to the LORD, God of your fathers, and do His will, and separate yourselves from the peoples of the land and from the foreign women."

¹²The entire congregation responded in a loud voice, "We must surely do just as you say. ¹³However, many people are involved, and it is the rainy season; it is not possible to remain out in the open, nor is this the work of a day or two, because we have transgressed extensively in this matter. ¹⁴Let our officers remain on behalf of the entire congregation, and all our townspeople who have brought home foreign women shall appear before them at scheduled times, together with the elders and judges of each town, in order to avert the burning anger of our God from us on this account." ¹⁵Only Jonathan son of Asahel and Jahzeiah son of Tikvah remained

---

5 וַיָּ֣קָם עֶזְרָ֗א וַיַּשְׁבַּ֣ע אֶת־שָׂרֵי֩ הַכֹּהֲנִ֨ים
הַלְוִיִּ֜ם וְכָל־יִשְׂרָאֵ֗ל לַעֲשׂ֛וֹת כַּדָּבָ֥ר הַזֶּ֖ה
וַיִּשָּׁבֵֽעוּ׃ 6 וַיָּ֣קָם עֶזְרָ֗א מִלִּפְנֵי֙ בֵּ֣ית
הָֽאֱלֹהִ֔ים וַיֵּ֕לֶךְ אֶל־לִשְׁכַּ֖ת יְהוֹחָנָ֣ן בֶּן־
אֶלְיָשִׁ֑יב וַיֵּ֣לֶךְ שָׁ֗ם לֶ֤חֶם לֹֽא־אָכַל֙
וּמַ֣יִם לֹֽא־שָׁתָ֔ה כִּ֥י מִתְאַבֵּ֖ל עַל־מַ֥עַל
הַגּוֹלָֽה׃ ס 7 וַיַּעֲבִ֨ירוּ ק֜וֹל בִּֽיהוּדָ֣ה
וִֽירוּשָׁלִַ֗ם לְכֹל֙ בְּנֵ֣י הַגּוֹלָ֔ה לְהִקָּבֵ֖ץ
יְרוּשָׁלָֽ͏ִם׃ 8 וְכֹ֣ל אֲשֶׁ֣ר לֹֽא־יָב֣וֹא לִשְׁלֹ֣שֶׁת
הַיָּמִ֗ים כַּעֲצַ֤ת הַשָּׂרִים֙ וְהַזְּקֵנִ֔ים
יׇחֳרַ֖ם כָּל־רְכוּשׁ֑וֹ וְה֥וּא יִבָּדֵ֖ל מִקְּהַ֥ל
הַגּוֹלָֽה׃ ס

9 וַיִּקָּבְצ֣וּ כָל־אַנְשֵֽׁי־יְהוּדָ֣ה וּבִנְיָמִ֣ן ׀
יְרוּשָׁלִַ֨ם֙ לִשְׁלֹ֣שֶׁת הַיָּמִ֔ים ה֛וּא חֹ֥דֶשׁ
הַתְּשִׁיעִ֖י בְּעֶשְׂרִ֣ים בַּחֹ֑דֶשׁ וַיֵּשְׁב֣וּ כָל־הָעָ֗ם
בִּרְחוֹב֙ בֵּ֣ית הָֽאֱלֹהִ֔ים מַרְעִידִ֖ים עַל־
הַדָּבָ֖ר וּמֵהַגְּשָׁמִֽים׃ פ 10 וַיָּ֛קׇם עֶזְרָ֥א
הַכֹּהֵ֖ן וַיֹּ֣אמֶר אֲלֵהֶ֑ם אַתֶּ֣ם מְעַלְתֶּ֗ם
וַתֹּשִׁ֨יבוּ֙ נָשִׁ֣ים נׇכְרִיּ֔וֹת לְהוֹסִ֖יף עַל־
אַשְׁמַ֥ת יִשְׂרָאֵֽל׃ 11 וְעַתָּ֗ה תְּנ֤וּ תוֹדָה֙
לַיהֹוָ֛ה אֱלֹהֵֽי־אֲבֹתֵיכֶ֖ם וַעֲשׂ֣וּ רְצוֹנ֑וֹ
וְהִבָּֽדְלוּ֙ מֵעַמֵּ֣י הָאָ֔רֶץ וּמִן־הַנָּשִׁ֖ים
הַנׇּכְרִיּֽוֹת׃

12 וַיַּֽעֲנ֧וּ כׇֽל־הַקָּהָ֛ל וַיֹּאמְר֖וּ ק֣וֹל גָּד֑וֹל כֵּ֛ן
כדברך כִּדְבָרְךָ֥ עָלֵ֖ינוּ לַעֲשֽׂוֹת׃ 13 אֲבָ֞ל
הָעָ֥ם רָב֙ וְהָעֵ֣ת גְּשָׁמִ֔ים וְאֵ֥ין כֹּ֖חַ לַעֲמ֣וֹד
בַּח֑וּץ וְהַמְּלָאכָ֗ה לֹֽא־לְי֤וֹם אֶחָד֙ וְלֹ֣א
לִשְׁנַ֔יִם כִּֽי־הִרְבִּ֥ינוּ לִפְשֹׁ֖עַ בַּדָּבָ֥ר הַזֶּֽה׃
14 יַֽעֲמְדוּ־נָ֣א שָׂרֵ֣ינוּ לְֽכׇל־הַקָּהָ֗ל וְכֹ֣ל ׀
אֲשֶׁ֣ר בְּעָרֵ֗ינוּ הַהֹשִׁ֞יב נָשִׁ֤ים נׇכְרִיּוֹת֙ יָבֹ֣א
לְעִתִּ֣ים מְזֻמָּנִ֔ים וְעִמָּהֶ֛ם זִקְנֵי־עִ֥יר וָעִ֖יר
וְשֹׁפְטֶ֑יהָ עַ֠ד לְהָשִׁ֞יב חֲר֤וֹן אַף־אֱלֹהֵ֙ינוּ֙
מִמֶּ֔נּוּ עַ֖ד לַדָּבָ֥ר הַזֶּֽה׃ פ 15 אַ֣ךְ יוֹנָתָ֧ן
בֶּן־עֲשָׂהאֵ֛ל וְיַחְזְיָ֥ה בֶן־תִּקְוָ֖ה עָמְד֣וּ עַל־

for this purpose, assisted by Meshullam and Shabbethai, the Levites. [16]The returning exiles did so. Ezra the priest and the men who were the chiefs of the ancestral clans—all listed by name—sequestered themselves on the first day of the tenth month to study the matter. [17]By the first day of the first month they were done with all the men who had brought home foreign women. [18]Among the priestly families who were found to have brought foreign women were Jeshua son of Jozadak and his brothers Maaseiah, Eliezer, Jarib, and Gedaliah. [19]They gave their word[b] to expel their wives and, acknowledging their guilt, offered a ram from the flock to expiate it. [20]Of the sons of Immer: Hanani and Zebadiah; [21]of the sons of Harim: Maaseiah, Elijah, Shemaiah, Jehiel, and Uzziah; [22]of the sons of Pashhur: Elioenai, Maaseiah, Ishmael, Nethanel, Jozabad, and Elasah; [23]of the Levites: Jozabad, Shimei, Kelaiah who is Kelita, Pethahiah, Judah, and Eliezer. [24]Of the singers: Eliashib. Of the gatekeepers: Shallum, Telem, and Uri. [25]Of the Israelites: of the sons of Parosh: Ramiah, Izziah, Malchijah, Mijamin, Eleazar, Malchijah, and Benaiah; [26]of the sons of Elam: Mattaniah, Zechariah, Jehiel, Abdi, Jeremoth, and Elijah; [27]of the sons of Zattu: Elioenai, Eliashib, Mattaniah, Jeremoth, Zabad, and Aziza; [28]of the sons of Bebai: Jehohanan, Hananiah, Zabbai, and Athlai; [29]of the sons of Bani: Meshullam, Malluch, Adaiah, Jashub, Sheal, and Ramoth; [30]of the sons of Pahath-moab: Adna, Chelal, Benaiah, Maaseiah, Mattaniah, Bezalel, Binnui, and Manasseh; [31]of the sons of Harim: Eliezer, Isshijah, Malchijah, Shemaiah, and Shimeon; [32]also Benjamin, Malluch, and Shemariah; [33]of the sons of Hashum: Mattenai, Mattattah, Zabad, Eliphelet, Jeremai, Manasseh, and Shimei; [34]of the sons of Bani: Maadai, Amram, and Uel;

---

b Lit. "hand."

זֹאת וּמְשֻׁלָּם וְשַׁבְּתַי הַלֵּוִי עֹזְרָם:
16 וַיַּעֲשׂוּ־כֵן בְּנֵי הַגּוֹלָה וַיִּבָּדְלוּ עֶזְרָא הַכֹּהֵן אֲנָשִׁים רָאשֵׁי הָאָבוֹת לְבֵית אֲבֹתָם וְכֻלָּם בְּשֵׁמוֹת וַיֵּשְׁבוּ בְּיוֹם אֶחָד לַחֹדֶשׁ הָעֲשִׂירִי לְדַרְיוֹשׁ הַדָּבָר: 17 וַיְכַלּוּ בַכֹּל אֲנָשִׁים הַהֹשִׁיבוּ נָשִׁים נָכְרִיּוֹת עַד יוֹם אֶחָד לַחֹדֶשׁ הָרִאשׁוֹן: פ 18 וַיִּמָּצֵא מִבְּנֵי הַכֹּהֲנִים אֲשֶׁר הֹשִׁיבוּ נָשִׁים נָכְרִיּוֹת מִבְּנֵי יֵשׁוּעַ בֶּן־יוֹצָדָק וְאֶחָיו מַעֲשֵׂיָה וֶאֱלִיעֶזֶר וְיָרִיב וּגְדַלְיָה: 19 וַיִּתְּנוּ יָדָם לְהוֹצִיא נְשֵׁיהֶם וַאֲשֵׁמִים אֵיל־צֹאן עַל־אַשְׁמָתָם: ס 20 וּמִבְּנֵי אִמֵּר חֲנָנִי וּזְבַדְיָה: ס 21 וּמִבְּנֵי חָרִם מַעֲשֵׂיָה וְאֵלִיָּה וּשְׁמַעְיָה וִיחִיאֵל וְעֻזִּיָּה: 22 וּמִבְּנֵי פַשְׁחוּר אֶלְיוֹעֵינַי מַעֲשֵׂיָה יִשְׁמָעֵאל נְתַנְאֵל יוֹזָבָד וְאֶלְעָשָׂה: ס 23 וּמִן־הַלְוִיִּם יוֹזָבָד וְשִׁמְעִי וְקֵלָיָה הוּא קְלִיטָא פְּתַחְיָה יְהוּדָה וֶאֱלִיעֶזֶר: ס 24 וּמִן־הַמְשֹׁרְרִים אֶלְיָשִׁיב וּמִן־הַשֹּׁעֲרִים שַׁלֻּם וָטֶלֶם וְאוּרִי: ס 25 וּמִיִּשְׂרָאֵל מִבְּנֵי פַרְעֹשׁ רַמְיָה וְיִזִּיָּה וּמַלְכִּיָּה וּמִיָּמִן וְאֶלְעָזָר וּמַלְכִּיָּה וּבְנָיָה: ס 26 וּמִבְּנֵי עֵילָם מַתַּנְיָה זְכַרְיָה וִיחִיאֵל וְעַבְדִּי וִירֵמוֹת וְאֵלִיָּה: ס 27 וּמִבְּנֵי זַתּוּא אֶלְיוֹעֵנַי אֶלְיָשִׁיב מַתַּנְיָה וִירֵמוֹת וְזָבָד וַעֲזִיזָא: ס 28 וּמִבְּנֵי בֵּבָי יְהוֹחָנָן חֲנַנְיָה זַבַּי עַתְלָי: ס 29 וּמִבְּנֵי בָנִי מְשֻׁלָּם מַלּוּךְ וַעֲדָיָה יָשׁוּב וּשְׁאָל יְרֵמוֹת וְרָמוֹת: ס 30 וּמִבְּנֵי פַחַת מוֹאָב עַדְנָא וּכְלָל בְּנָיָה מַעֲשֵׂיָה מַתַּנְיָה בְצַלְאֵל וּבִנּוּי וּמְנַשֶּׁה: ס 31 וּבְנֵי חָרִם אֱלִיעֶזֶר יִשִּׁיָּה מַלְכִּיָּה שְׁמַעְיָה שִׁמְעוֹן: 32 בְּנְיָמִן מַלּוּךְ שְׁמַרְיָה: ס 33 מִבְּנֵי חָשֻׁם מַתְּנַי מַתַּתָּה זָבָד אֱלִיפֶלֶט יְרֵמַי מְנַשֶּׁה שִׁמְעִי: ס 34 מִבְּנֵי בָנִי מַעֲדַי עַמְרָם וְאוּאֵל: ס 35 בְּנָיָה

35also Benaiah, Bedeiah, Cheluhu, 36Vaniah, Meremoth, Eliashib, 37Mattaniah, Mattenai, Jaasai, 38Bani, Binnui, Shimei, 39Shelemiah, Nathan, Adaiah, 40Machnadebai, Shashai, Sharai, 41Azarel, Shelemiah, Shemariah, 42Shallum, Amariah, and Joseph; 43of the sons of Nebo: Jeiel, Mattithiah, Zabad, Zebina, Jaddai, Joel, and Benaiah.

44All these had married foreign women, among whom were some women c-who had borne children.-c

בֵּדְיָה כְלוּהִי כְלוּהוּ׃ 36 וַנְיָה מְרֵמוֹת
אֶלְיָשִׁיב׃ 37 מַתַּנְיָה מַתְּנַי וְיַעֲשָׂו וְיַעֲשָׂי׃
38 וּבָנִי וּבִנּוּי שִׁמְעִי׃ 39 וְשֶׁלֶמְיָה וְנָתָן
וַעֲדָיָה׃ 40 מַכְנַדְבַי שָׁשַׁי שָׁרָי׃ 41 עֲזַרְאֵל
וְשֶׁלֶמְיָהוּ שְׁמַרְיָה׃ 42 שַׁלּוּם אֲמַרְיָה
יוֹסֵף׃ ס 43 מִבְּנֵי נְבוֹ יְעִיאֵל מַתִּתְיָה
זָבָד זְבִינָא יַדַּי יַדּוֹ וְיוֹאֵל בְּנָיָה׃
44 כָּל־אֵלֶּה נשאו נָשְׂאוּ נָשִׁים נָכְרִיּוֹת וְיֵשׁ
מֵהֶם נָשִׁים וַיָּשִׂימוּ בָּנִים׃ פ

---

c-c *Meaning of Heb. uncertain.*

NEHEMIAH

1 The narrative of Nehemiah son of Hacaliah:
In the month of Kislev of the twentieth year,[a]
when I was in the fortress of Shushan, ²Hanani,
one of my brothers, together with some men
of Judah, arrived, and I asked them about the
Jews, the remnant who had survived the
captivity, and about Jerusalem. ³They replied,
"The survivors who have survived the captivity
there in the province are in dire trouble and
disgrace; Jerusalem's wall is full of breaches, and
its gates have been destroyed by fire."

⁴When I heard that, I sat and wept, and was
in mourning for days, fasting and praying to
the God of Heaven. ⁵I said, "O LORD, God of
Heaven, great and awesome God, who stays
faithful to His covenant with those who love
Him and keep His commandments! ⁶Let Your
ear be attentive and Your eyes open to receive
the prayer of Your servant that I am praying to
You now, day and night, on behalf of the Israelites, Your servants, confessing the sins that we
Israelites have committed against You, sins that
I and my father's house have committed. ⁷We
have offended You by not keeping the commandments, the laws, and the rules that You
gave to Your servant Moses. ⁸Be mindful of the
promise You gave to Your servant Moses: 'If you
are unfaithful, I will scatter you among the peoples; ⁹but if you turn back to Me, faithfully keep
My commandments, even if your dispersed are
at the ends of the earth,[b] I will gather them from
there and bring them to the place where I have
chosen to establish My name.' ¹⁰For they are

---

a   I.e., of King Artaxerxes; cf. 2.1.
b   Lit. "sky."

א דִּבְרֵי נְחֶמְיָה בֶּן־חֲכַלְיָה
וַיְהִי בְחֹדֶשׁ־כִּסְלֵו שְׁנַת עֶשְׂרִים
וַאֲנִי הָיִיתִי בְּשׁוּשַׁן הַבִּירָה: 2 וַיָּבֹא חֲנָנִי
אֶחָד מֵאַחַי הוּא וַאֲנָשִׁים מִיהוּדָה
וָאֶשְׁאָלֵם עַל־הַיְּהוּדִים הַפְּלֵיטָה אֲשֶׁר־
נִשְׁאֲרוּ מִן־הַשֶּׁבִי וְעַל־יְרוּשָׁלָם: 3 וַיֹּאמְרוּ
לִי הַנִּשְׁאָרִים אֲשֶׁר־נִשְׁאֲרוּ מִן־הַשְּׁבִי שָׁם
בַּמְּדִינָה בְּרָעָה גְדֹלָה וּבְחֶרְפָּה וְחוֹמַת
יְרוּשָׁלַם מְפֹרָצֶת וּשְׁעָרֶיהָ נִצְּתוּ בָאֵשׁ:
4 וַיְהִי כְּשָׁמְעִי ׀ אֶת־הַדְּבָרִים הָאֵלֶּה
יָשַׁבְתִּי וָאֶבְכֶּה וָאֶתְאַבְּלָה יָמִים וָאֱהִי
צָם וּמִתְפַּלֵּל לִפְנֵי אֱלֹהֵי הַשָּׁמָיִם: 5 וָאֹמַר
אָנָּא יְהוָה אֱלֹהֵי הַשָּׁמַיִם הָאֵל הַגָּדוֹל
וְהַנּוֹרָא שֹׁמֵר הַבְּרִית וָחֶסֶד לְאֹהֲבָיו
וּלְשֹׁמְרֵי מִצְוֹתָיו: 6 תְּהִי נָא אָזְנְךָ־קַשֶּׁבֶת
וְעֵינֶיךָ פְתֻחוֹת לִשְׁמֹעַ אֶל־תְּפִלַּת עַבְדְּךָ
אֲשֶׁר אָנֹכִי מִתְפַּלֵּל לְפָנֶיךָ הַיּוֹם יוֹמָם
וָלַיְלָה עַל־בְּנֵי יִשְׂרָאֵל עֲבָדֶיךָ וּמִתְוַדֶּה
עַל־חַטֹּאות בְּנֵי־יִשְׂרָאֵל אֲשֶׁר חָטָאנוּ לָךְ
וַאֲנִי וּבֵית־אָבִי חָטָאנוּ: 7 חֲבֹל חָבַלְנוּ לָךְ
וְלֹא־שָׁמַרְנוּ אֶת־הַמִּצְוֹת וְאֶת־הַחֻקִּים
וְאֶת־הַמִּשְׁפָּטִים אֲשֶׁר צִוִּיתָ אֶת־מֹשֶׁה
עַבְדֶּךָ: 8 זְכָר־נָא אֶת־הַדָּבָר אֲשֶׁר צִוִּיתָ
אֶת־מֹשֶׁה עַבְדְּךָ לֵאמֹר אַתֶּם תִּמְעָלוּ אֲנִי
אָפִיץ אֶתְכֶם בָּעַמִּים: 9 וְשַׁבְתֶּם אֵלַי
וּשְׁמַרְתֶּם מִצְוֹתַי וַעֲשִׂיתֶם אֹתָם אִם־
יִהְיֶה נִדַּחֲכֶם בִּקְצֵה הַשָּׁמַיִם מִשָּׁם
אֲקַבְּצֵם והבואתים וַהֲבִיאוֹתִים אֶל־
הַמָּקוֹם אֲשֶׁר בָּחַרְתִּי לְשַׁכֵּן אֶת־שְׁמִי

Your servants and Your people whom You redeemed by Your great power and Your mighty hand. [11] O Lord! Let Your ear be attentive to the prayer of Your servant, and to the prayer of Your servants who desire to hold Your name in awe. Grant Your servant success today, and dispose that man to be compassionate toward him!"

I was the king's cupbearer at the time.

2 In the month of Nisan, in the twentieth year of King Artaxerxes, wine was set before him; I took the wine and gave it to the king—I had never been out of sorts in his presence. [2] The king said to me, "How is it that you look bad, though you are not ill? It must be bad thoughts." I was very frightened, [3] but I answered the king, "May the king live forever! How should I not look bad when the city of the graveyard of my ancestors lies in ruins, and its gates have been consumed by fire?" [4] The king said to me, "What is your request?" With a prayer to the God of Heaven, [5] I answered the king, "If it please the king, and if your servant has found favor with you, send me to Judah, to the city of my ancestors' graves, to rebuild it." [6] With the consort seated at his side, the king said to me, "How long will you be gone and when will you return?" So it was agreeable to the king to send me, and I gave him a date. [7] Then I said to the king, "If it please the king, let me have letters to the governors of the province of Beyond the River, directing them to grant me passage until I reach Judah; [8] likewise, a letter to Asaph, the keeper of the King's Park, directing him to give me timber for roofing the gatehouses of the temple fortress and the city walls and for the house I shall occupy." The king gave me these, thanks to my God's benevolent care for me. [9] When I came to the governors of the province of Beyond the

שָׁם: 10 וְהֵם עֲבָדֶיךָ וְעַמֶּךָ אֲשֶׁר פָּדִיתָ בְּכֹחֲךָ הַגָּדוֹל וּבְיָדְךָ הַחֲזָקָה: 11 אָנָּא אֲדֹנָי תְּהִי נָא אָזְנְךָ־קַשֶּׁבֶת אֶל־תְּפִלַּת עַבְדְּךָ וְאֶל־תְּפִלַּת עֲבָדֶיךָ הַחֲפֵצִים לְיִרְאָה אֶת־שְׁמֶךָ וְהַצְלִיחָה־נָּא לְעַבְדְּךָ הַיּוֹם וּתְנֵהוּ לְרַחֲמִים לִפְנֵי הָאִישׁ הַזֶּה וַאֲנִי הָיִיתִי מַשְׁקֶה לַמֶּלֶךְ: פ

ב וַיְהִי ׀ בְּחֹדֶשׁ נִיסָן שְׁנַת עֶשְׂרִים לְאַרְתַּחְשַׁסְתְּא הַמֶּלֶךְ יַיִן לְפָנָיו וָאֶשָּׂא אֶת־הַיַּיִן וָאֶתְּנָה לַמֶּלֶךְ וְלֹא־הָיִיתִי רַע לְפָנָיו: 2 וַיֹּאמֶר לִי הַמֶּלֶךְ מַדּוּעַ ׀ פָּנֶיךָ רָעִים וְאַתָּה אֵינְךָ חוֹלֶה אֵין זֶה כִּי־אִם רֹעַ לֵב וָאִירָא הַרְבֵּה מְאֹד: 3 וָאֹמַר לַמֶּלֶךְ הַמֶּלֶךְ לְעוֹלָם יִחְיֶה מַדּוּעַ לֹא־יֵרְעוּ פָנַי אֲשֶׁר הָעִיר בֵּית־קִבְרוֹת אֲבֹתַי חֲרֵבָה וּשְׁעָרֶיהָ אֻכְּלוּ בָאֵשׁ: 4 וַיֹּאמֶר לִי הַמֶּלֶךְ עַל־מַה־זֶּה אַתָּה מְבַקֵּשׁ וָאֶתְפַּלֵּל אֶל־אֱלֹהֵי הַשָּׁמָיִם: 5 וָאֹמַר לַמֶּלֶךְ אִם־עַל־הַמֶּלֶךְ טוֹב וְאִם־יִיטַב עַבְדְּךָ לְפָנֶיךָ אֲשֶׁר תִּשְׁלָחֵנִי אֶל־יְהוּדָה אֶל־עִיר קִבְרוֹת אֲבֹתַי וְאֶבְנֶנָּה: 6 וַיֹּאמֶר לִי הַמֶּלֶךְ וְהַשֵּׁגַל ׀ יוֹשֶׁבֶת אֶצְלוֹ עַד־מָתַי יִהְיֶה מַהֲלָכֲךָ וּמָתַי תָּשׁוּב וַיִּיטַב לִפְנֵי־הַמֶּלֶךְ וַיִּשְׁלָחֵנִי וָאֶתְּנָה לוֹ זְמָן: 7 וָאוֹמַר לַמֶּלֶךְ אִם־עַל־הַמֶּלֶךְ טוֹב אִגְּרוֹת יִתְּנוּ־לִי עַל־פַּחֲווֹת עֵבֶר הַנָּהָר אֲשֶׁר יַעֲבִירוּנִי עַד אֲשֶׁר־אָבוֹא אֶל־יְהוּדָה: 8 וְאִגֶּרֶת אֶל־אָסָף שֹׁמֵר הַפַּרְדֵּס אֲשֶׁר לַמֶּלֶךְ אֲשֶׁר יִתֶּן־לִי עֵצִים לְקָרוֹת אֶת־שַׁעֲרֵי הַבִּירָה אֲשֶׁר־לַבַּיִת וּלְחוֹמַת הָעִיר וְלַבַּיִת אֲשֶׁר־אָבוֹא אֵלָיו וַיִּתֶּן־לִי הַמֶּלֶךְ כְּיַד־אֱלֹהַי הַטּוֹבָה עָלָי: 9 וָאָבוֹא אֶל־פַּחֲווֹת עֵבֶר הַנָּהָר וָאֶתְּנָה לָהֶם אֵת אִגְּרוֹת

River I gave them the king's letters. The king also sent army officers and cavalry with me.

10When Sanballat the Horonite and Tobiah the Ammonite servant heard, it displeased them greatly that someone had come, intent on improving the condition of the Israelites.

11I arrived in Jerusalem. After I was there three days 12I got up at night, I and a few men with me, and telling no one what my God had put into my mind to do for Jerusalem, and taking no other beast than the one on which I was riding, 13I went out by the Valley Gate, at night, toward the Jackals' Spring and the Dung Gate; and I surveyed the walls of Jerusalem that were breached, and its gates, consumed by fire. 14I proceeded to the Fountain Gate and to the King's Pool, where there was no room for the beast under me to continue. 15So I went up the wadi by night, surveying the wall, and, entering again by the Valley Gate, I returned. 16The prefects knew nothing of where I had gone or what I had done, since I had not yet divulged it to the Jews—the priests, the nobles, the prefects, or the rest of the officials.

17Then I said to them, "You see the bad state we are in—Jerusalem lying in ruins and its gates destroyed by fire. Come, let us rebuild the wall of Jerusalem and suffer no more disgrace." 18I told them of my God's benevolent care for me, also of the things that the king had said to me, and they said, "Let us start building!" They were encouraged by [His] benevolence.

19When Sanballat the Horonite and Tobiah the Ammonite servant and Geshem the Arab heard, they mocked us and held us in contempt and said, "What is this that you are doing? Are you rebelling against the king?" 20I said to them in reply, "The God of Heaven will grant us success, and we, His servants, will start building. But you have no share or claim or stake[a] in Jerusalem!"

---

a Lit. "record."

הַמֶּלֶךְ וַיִּשְׁלַח עִמִּי הַמֶּלֶךְ שָׂרֵי חַיִל
וּפָרָשִׁים: פ 10 וַיִּשְׁמַע סַנְבַלַּט הַחֹרֹנִי וְטוֹבִיָּה הָעֶבֶד
הָעַמּוֹנִי וַיֵּרַע לָהֶם רָעָה גְדֹלָה אֲשֶׁר־בָּא
אָדָם לְבַקֵּשׁ טוֹבָה לִבְנֵי יִשְׂרָאֵל: 11 וָאָבוֹא אֶל־יְרוּשָׁלָ͏ִם וָאֱהִי־שָׁם יָמִים
שְׁלֹשָׁה: 12 וָאָקוּם ׀ לַיְלָה אֲנִי וַאֲנָשִׁים ׀
מְעַט עִמִּי וְלֹא־הִגַּדְתִּי לְאָדָם מָה אֱלֹהַי
נֹתֵן אֶל־לִבִּי לַעֲשׂוֹת לִירוּשָׁלָ͏ִם וּבְהֵמָה
אֵין עִמִּי כִּי אִם־הַבְּהֵמָה אֲשֶׁר אֲנִי רֹכֵב
בָּהּ: 13 וָאֵצְאָה בְשַׁעַר־הַגַּיְא לַיְלָה וְאֶל־
פְּנֵי עֵין הַתַּנִּין וְאֶל־שַׁעַר הָאַשְׁפֹּת וָאֱהִי
שֹׂבֵר בְּחוֹמֹת יְרוּשָׁלַ͏ִם אֲשֶׁר־הַמְפֹרוּצִים
הֵם ׀ פְּרוּצִים וּשְׁעָרֶיהָ אֻכְּלוּ בָאֵשׁ: 14 וָאֶעֱבֹר אֶל־שַׁעַר הָעַיִן וְאֶל־בְּרֵכַת
הַמֶּלֶךְ וְאֵין־מָקוֹם לַבְּהֵמָה לַעֲבֹר תַּחְתָּי: 15 וָאֱהִי עֹלֶה בַנַּחַל לַיְלָה וָאֱהִי שֹׂבֵר
בַּחוֹמָה וָאָשׁוּב וָאָבוֹא בְּשַׁעַר הַגַּיְא
וָאָשׁוּב: 16 וְהַסְּגָנִים לֹא יָדְעוּ אָנָה הָלַכְתִּי
וּמָה אֲנִי עֹשֶׂה וְלַיְּהוּדִים וְלַכֹּהֲנִים
וְלַחֹרִים וְלַסְּגָנִים וּלְיֶתֶר עֹשֵׂה הַמְּלָאכָה
עַד־כֵּן לֹא הִגַּדְתִּי: 17 וָאוֹמַר אֲלֵהֶם אַתֶּם רֹאִים הָרָעָה אֲשֶׁר
אֲנַחְנוּ בָהּ אֲשֶׁר יְרוּשָׁלַ͏ִם חֲרֵבָה וּשְׁעָרֶיהָ
נִצְּתוּ בָאֵשׁ לְכוּ וְנִבְנֶה אֶת־חוֹמַת
יְרוּשָׁלַ͏ִם וְלֹא־נִהְיֶה עוֹד חֶרְפָּה: 18 וָאַגִּיד
לָהֶם אֶת־יַד אֱלֹהַי אֲשֶׁר־הִיא טוֹבָה עָלַי
וְאַף־דִּבְרֵי הַמֶּלֶךְ אֲשֶׁר אָמַר־לִי וַיֹּאמְרוּ
נָקוּם וּבָנִינוּ וַיְחַזְּקוּ יְדֵיהֶם לַטּוֹבָה: פ 19 וַיִּשְׁמַע סַנְבַלַּט הַחֹרֹנִי וְטֹבִיָּה ׀ הָעֶבֶד
הָעַמּוֹנִי וְגֶשֶׁם הָעַרְבִי וַיַּלְעִגוּ לָנוּ וַיִּבְזוּ
עָלֵינוּ וַיֹּאמְרוּ מָה־הַדָּבָר הַזֶּה אֲשֶׁר אַתֶּם
עֹשִׂים הַעַל הַמֶּלֶךְ אַתֶּם מֹרְדִים: 20 וָאָשִׁיב אוֹתָם דָּבָר וָאוֹמַר לָהֶם אֱלֹהֵי
הַשָּׁמַיִם הוּא יַצְלִיחַ לָנוּ וַאֲנַחְנוּ עֲבָדָיו
נָקוּם וּבָנִינוּ וְלָכֶם אֵין־חֵלֶק וּצְדָקָה
וְזִכָּרוֹן בִּירוּשָׁלָ͏ִם:

3

Then Eliashib the high priest and his fellow priests set to and rebuilt the Sheep Gate; they consecrated it and set up its doors, consecrating it as far as the Hundred's Tower, as far as the Tower of Hananel. [2]Next to him, the men of Jericho built. Next to them,[a] Zaccur son of Imri. [3]The sons of Hassenaah rebuilt the Fish Gate; they roofed it and set up its doors, locks, and bars. [4]Next to them, Meremoth son of Uriah son of Hakkoz repaired; and next to him,[b] Meshullam son of Berechiah son of Meshezabel. Next to him,[b] Zadok son of Baana repaired. [5]Next to him,[b] the Tekoites repaired, though their nobles would not [c]take upon their shoulders[c] the work of their lord. [6]Joiada son of Paseah and Meshullam son of Besodeiah repaired the Jeshanah Gate; they roofed it and set up its doors, locks, and bars. [7]Next to them, Melatiah the Gibeonite and Jadon the Meronothite repaired, [with] the men of Gibeon and Mizpah, [d]under the jurisdiction[d] of the governor of the province of Beyond the River. [8]Next to them,[a] Uzziel son of Harhaiah, [of the] smiths, repaired. Next to him, Hananiah, of[e] the perfumers. They restored Jerusalem as far as the Broad Wall. [9]Next to them, Rephaiah son of Hur, chief of half the district of Jerusalem, repaired. [10]Next to him,[b] Jedaiah son of Harumaph repaired in front of his house. Next to him, Hattush son of Hashabneiah repaired. [11]Malchijah son of Harim and Hasshub son of Pahath-moab repaired a second stretch, including the Tower of Ovens. [12]Next to them,[a] Shallum son of Hallohesh,[f] chief of half the district of Jerusalem, repaired—he and his daughters. [13]Hanun and the inhabitants of Zanoah repaired the Valley Gate; they rebuilt it and set

ג וַיָּ֡קָם אֶלְיָשִׁיב֩ הַכֹּהֵ֨ן הַגָּד֜וֹל וְאֶחָ֣יו הַכֹּהֲנִ֗ים וַיִּבְנוּ֙ אֶת־שַׁ֣עַר הַצֹּ֔אן הֵ֣מָּה קִדְּשׁ֔וּהוּ וַֽיַּעֲמִ֖ידוּ דַּלְתֹתָ֑יו וְעַד־מִגְדַּ֤ל הַמֵּאָה֙ קִדְּשׁ֔וּהוּ עַ֖ד מִגְדַּ֥ל חֲנַנְאֵֽל׃ ס ²וְעַל־יָד֥וֹ בָנ֖וּ אַנְשֵׁ֣י יְרֵח֑וֹ ס וְעַל־יָד֥וֹ בָנָ֖ה זַכּ֥וּר בֶּן־אִמְרִֽי׃ ס ³וְאֵת֙ שַׁ֣עַר הַדָּגִ֔ים בָּנ֖וּ בְּנֵ֣י הַסְּנָאָ֑ה הֵ֣מָּה קֵר֔וּהוּ וַֽיַּעֲמִ֨ידוּ֙ דַּלְתֹתָ֔יו מַנְעוּלָ֖יו וּבְרִיחָֽיו׃ ס ⁴וְעַל־יָדָ֣ם הֶחֱזִ֗יק מְרֵמ֤וֹת בֶּן־אוּרִיָּה֙ בֶּן־הַקּ֔וֹץ ס וְעַל־יָדָ֣ם הֶחֱזִ֔יק מְשֻׁלָּ֥ם בֶּן־בֶּרֶכְיָ֖ה בֶּן־מְשֵׁיזַבְאֵ֑ל ס וְעַל־יָדָ֣ם הֶחֱזִ֔יק צָד֖וֹק בֶּן־בַּעֲנָֽא׃ ס ⁵וְעַל־יָדָ֣ם הֶחֱזִ֔יקוּ הַתְּקוֹעִ֑ים וְאַדִּֽירֵיהֶם֙ לֹא־הֵבִ֣יאוּ צַוָּרָ֔ם* בַּעֲבֹדַ֖ת אֲדֹנֵיהֶֽם׃ ס ⁶וְאֵת֩ שַׁ֨עַר הַיְשָׁנָ֜ה הֶחֱזִ֗יקוּ יֽוֹיָדָע֙ בֶּן־פָּסֵ֔חַ וּמְשֻׁלָּ֖ם בֶּן־בְּסֽוֹדְיָ֑ה הֵ֣מָּה קֵר֔וּהוּ וַֽיַּעֲמִ֨ידוּ֙ דַּלְתֹתָ֔יו וּמַנְעֻלָ֖יו וּבְרִיחָֽיו׃ ס ⁷וְעַל־יָדָ֨ם הֶחֱזִ֜יק מְלַטְיָ֣ה הַגִּבְעֹנִ֗י וְיָדוֹן֙ הַמֵּרֹ֣נֹתִ֔י אַנְשֵׁ֥י גִבְע֖וֹן וְהַמִּצְפָּ֑ה לְכִסֵּ֕א פַּחַ֖ת עֵ֥בֶר הַנָּהָֽר׃ ס ⁸עַל־יָד֣וֹ הֶחֱזִ֗יק עֻזִּיאֵ֤ל בֶּן־חַרְהֲיָה֙ צֽוֹרְפִ֔ים ס וְעַל־יָד֣וֹ הֶחֱזִ֔יק חֲנַנְיָ֖ה בֶּן־הָרַקָּחִ֑ים וַיַּֽעַזְבוּ֙ יְר֣וּשָׁלַ֔͏ִם עַ֖ד הַחוֹמָ֥ה הָרְחָבָֽה׃ ס ⁹וְעַל־יָדָ֤ם הֶחֱזִיק֙ רְפָיָ֣ה בֶן־ח֔וּר שַׂ֖ר חֲצִ֥י פֶּ֥לֶךְ יְרוּשָׁלָֽ͏ִם׃ ס ¹⁰וְעַל־יָדָ֧ם הֶחֱזִ֛יק יְדָיָ֥ה בֶן־חֲרוּמַ֖ף וְנֶ֣גֶד בֵּית֑וֹ ס וְעַל־יָד֣וֹ הֶחֱזִ֔יק חַטּ֖וּשׁ בֶּן־חֲשַׁבְנְיָֽה׃ ¹¹מִדָּ֤ה שֵׁנִית֙ הֶחֱזִ֔יק מַלְכִּיָּ֣ה בֶן־חָרִ֔ם וְחַשּׁ֖וּב בֶּן־פַּחַ֣ת מוֹאָ֑ב וְאֵ֖ת מִגְדַּ֥ל הַתַּנּוּרִֽים׃ ס ¹²וְעַל־יָד֣וֹ הֶחֱזִ֗יק שַׁלּוּם֙ בֶּן־הַלּוֹחֵ֔שׁ שַׂ֕ר חֲצִ֖י פֶּ֣לֶךְ יְרוּשָׁלָ֑͏ִם ה֖וּא וּבְנוֹתָֽיו׃ ס ¹³אֵ֣ת שַׁ֣עַר הַגַּ֗יְא הֶחֱזִ֤יק חָנוּן֙ וְיֹשְׁבֵ֣י זָנ֔וֹחַ הֵ֣מָּה בָנ֔וּהוּ

---

a   Lit. "him."
b   Lit. "them."
c-c   Lit. "bring their neck into."
d-d   Lit. "of the throne"; meaning of Heb. uncertain.
e   Lit. "son of," i.e., member of the guild of.
f   I.e., the charmer.

v. 5. חסר א'

up its doors, locks, and bars. And [they also repaired] a thousand cubits of wall to the Dung Gate. [14]Malchijah son of Rechab, chief of the district of Beth-haccerem, repaired the Dung Gate; he rebuilt it and set up its doors, locks, and bars. [15]Shallun son of Col-hozeh, chief of the district of Mizpah, repaired the Fountain Gate; he rebuilt it and covered it, and set up its doors, locks, and bars, as well as the wall of the irrigation*pool of the King's Garden as far as the steps going down from the City of David. [16]After him, Nehemiah son of Azbuk, chief of half the district of Beth-zur, repaired, from in front of the graves of David as far as the artificial pool, and as far as the House of the Warriors. [17]After him, the Levites repaired: Rehum son of Bani. Next to him, Hashabiah, chief of half the district of Keilah, repaired for his district. [18]After him, their brothers repaired: Bavvai son of Henadad, chief of half the district of Keilah. [19]Next to him, Ezer son of Jeshua, the chief of Mizpah, repaired a second stretch, from in front of the ascent to the armory [at] the angle [of the wall]. [20]After him, Baruch son of Zaccai zealously repaired a second stretch, from the angle to the entrance to the house of Eliashib, the high priest. [21]After him, Meremoth son of Uriah son of Hakkoz repaired a second stretch, from the entrance to Eliashib's house to the end of Eliashib's house. [22]After him, the priests, inhabitants of the plain, repaired. [23]After them,[g] Benjamin and Hasshub repaired in front of their houses. After them,[g] Azariah son of Maaseiah son of Ananiah repaired beside his house. [24]After him, Binnui son of Henadad repaired a second stretch, from the house of Azariah to the angle, to the corner. [25]Palal son of Uzai—from in front of the angle and the tower that juts out of the house of the king, the upper [tower] of the prison compound. After him,

---

g   *Following Kimhi; cf. Mishnaic Heb.* bet hashelaḥin, *irrigated field.*

וַיַּעֲמִידוּ֙ דַּלְתֹתָ֔יו מַנְעֻלָ֖יו וּבְרִיחָ֑יו וְאֶ֤לֶף אַמָּה֙ בַּֽחוֹמָ֔ה עַ֖ד שַׁ֥עַר הָשְׁפֽוֹת*׃ 14 וְאֵ֣ת ׀ שַׁ֣עַר הָֽאַשְׁפּ֗וֹת הֶֽחֱזִיק֙ מַלְכִּיָּ֣ה בֶן־רֵכָ֔ב שַׂ֖ר פֶּ֣לֶךְ בֵּית־הַכָּ֑רֶם ה֣וּא יִבְנֶ֔נּוּ וְיַעֲמִיד֙ דַּלְתֹתָ֔יו מַנְעֻלָ֖יו וּבְרִיחָֽיו׃ ס 15 וְאֵ֣ת שַׁ֣עַר הָעַ֡יִן הֶחֱזִיק֩ שַׁלּ֨וּן בֶּן־כָּל־חֹ֜זֶה שַׂ֣ר פֶּ֣לֶךְ הַמִּצְפָּ֗ה ה֤וּא יִבְנֶ֨נּוּ֙ וִיטַֽלְלֶ֔נּוּ וְיַעֲמִידוּ֙ [וְ]יַעֲמִיד֙ דַּלְתֹתָ֔יו מַנְעֻלָ֖יו וּבְרִיחָ֑יו וְאֵ֣ת חוֹמַ֣ת בְּרֵכַ֣ת הַשֶּׁ֗לַח לְגַן־הַמֶּ֔לֶךְ וְעַד־הַֽמַּעֲל֔וֹת הַיּֽוֹרְד֖וֹת מֵעִ֥יר דָּוִֽיד׃ ס 16 אַחֲרָ֣יו הֶחֱזִ֗יק נְחֶמְיָ֣ה בֶן־עַזְבּוּק֮ שַׂ֣ר חֲצִ֣י פֶּ֣לֶךְ בֵּֽית־צ֒וּר֒ עַד־נֶ֨גֶד֙ קִבְרֵ֣י דָוִ֔יד וְעַד־הַבְּרֵכָה֙ הָעֲשׂוּיָ֔ה וְעַ֖ד בֵּ֥ית הַגִּבֹּרִֽים׃ ס 17 אַחֲרָ֛יו הֶחֱזִ֥יקוּ הַלְוִיִּ֖ם רְח֣וּם בֶּן־בָּנִ֑י עַל־יָד֣וֹ הֶחֱזִ֗יק חֲשַׁבְיָ֛ה שַׂר־חֲצִי־פֶ֥לֶךְ קְעִילָ֖ה לְפִלְכּֽוֹ׃ 18 ס אַחֲרָיו֙ הֶחֱזִ֣יקוּ אֲחֵיהֶ֔ם בַּוַּ֖י בֶּן־חֵנָדָ֑ד שַׂ֕ר חֲצִ֖י פֶּ֥לֶךְ קְעִילָֽה׃ ס 19 וַיְחַזֵּ֨ק עַל־יָד֜וֹ עֵ֗זֶר בֶּן־יֵשׁ֛וּעַ שַׂ֥ר הַמִּצְפָּ֖ה מִדָּ֣ה שֵׁנִ֑ית מִנֶּ֕גֶד עֲלֹ֥ת הַנֶּ֖שֶׁק הַמִּקְצֹֽעַ׃ ס 20 אַחֲרָ֣יו הֶֽחֱרָ֡ה הֶחֱזִ֞יק בָּר֧וּךְ בֶּן־זבי [זַכַּ֛י] מִדָּ֥ה שֵׁנִ֖ית מִן־הַמִּקְצ֑וֹעַ עַד־פֶּ֙תַח֙ בֵּ֣ית אֶלְיָשִׁ֣יב הַכֹּהֵ֔ן הַגָּדֽוֹל׃ ס 21 אַחֲרָ֣יו הֶחֱזִ֗יק מְרֵמ֧וֹת בֶּן־אֽוּרִיָּ֛ה בֶּן־הַקּ֖וֹץ מִדָּ֣ה שֵׁנִ֑ית מִפֶּ֙תַח֙ בֵּ֣ית אֶלְיָשִׁ֔יב וְעַד־תַּכְלִ֖ית בֵּ֥ית אֶלְיָשִֽׁיב׃ ס 22 וְאַחֲרָ֛יו הֶחֱזִ֥יקוּ הַכֹּהֲנִ֖ים אַנְשֵׁ֥י הַכִּכָּֽר׃ 23 אַחֲרָ֞יו הֶחֱזִ֧יק בִּנְיָמִ֛ן וְחַשּׁ֖וּב נֶ֣גֶד בֵּיתָ֑ם ס אַחֲרָ֣יו הֶחֱזִ֗יק עֲזַרְיָ֧ה בֶן־מַעֲשֵׂיָ֛ה בֶּן־עֲנָֽנְיָ֖ה אֵ֥צֶל בֵּיתֽוֹ׃ ס 24 אַחֲרָ֣יו הֶחֱזִ֗יק בִּנּ֛וּי בֶּן־חֵנָדָ֖ד מִדָּ֣ה שֵׁנִ֑ית מִבֵּ֣ית עֲזַרְיָ֔ה עַד־הַמִּקְצ֖וֹעַ וְעַד־הַפִּנָּֽה׃ 25 פָּלָ֣ל בֶּן־אוּזַי֮ מִנֶּ֣גֶד הַמִּקְצוֹעַ֒ וְהַמִּגְדָּ֗ל הַיּוֹצֵא֙ מִבֵּ֤ית הַמֶּ֙לֶךְ֙ הָֽעֶלְי֔וֹן אֲשֶׁ֖ר לַחֲצַ֣ר הַמַּטָּרָ֑ה אַחֲרָ֖יו פְּדָיָ֥ה בֶן־פַּרְעֹֽשׁ׃ ס

Pedaiah son of Parosh. (²⁶The temple servants were living on the Ophel, as far as a point in front of the Water Gate in the east, and the jutting tower.) ²⁷After him, the Tekoites repaired a second stretch, from in front of the great jutting tower to the wall of the Ophel. ²⁸Above the Horse Gate, the priests repaired, each in front of his house. ²⁹After them,ᵃ Zadok son of Immer repaired in front of his house. After him, Shemaiah son of Shechaniah, keeper of the East Gate, repaired. ³⁰After him, Hananiah son of Shelemiah and Hanun, the sixth son of Zalaph, repaired a second stretch. After them,ᵃ Meshullam son of Berechiah repaired in front of his chamber. ³¹After him, Malchijah of the smiths repaired as far as the house of the temple servants and the merchants, [from] in front of the Muster Gate to the corner loft. ³²And between the corner loft to the Sheep Gate the smiths and the merchants repaired.

³³When Sanballat heard that we were rebuilding the wall, it angered him, and he was extremely vexed. He mocked the Jews, ³⁴saying in the presence of his brothers and the Samarian force, "What are the miserable Jews doing? Will they restore, offer sacrifice, and finish one day? Can they revive those stones out of the dust heaps, burned as they are?" ³⁵Tobiah the Ammonite, alongside him, said, "That stone wall they are building—if a fox climbed it he would breach it!"

³⁶Hear, our God, how we have become a mockery, and return their taunts upon their heads! Let them be taken as spoil to a land of captivity! ³⁷Do not cover up their iniquity or let their sin be blotted out before You, for they hurled provocations at the builders.

³⁸We rebuilt the wall till it was continuous all around to half its height; for the people's heart was in the work.

26 וְהַ֨נְּתִינִ֔ים הָי֥וּ יֹשְׁבִ֖ים בָּעֹ֑פֶל עַ֗ד נֶ֨גֶד שַׁ֤עַר הַמַּ֨יִם֙ לַמִּזְרָ֔ח וְהַמִּגְדָּ֖ל הַיּוֹצֵֽא׃ ס 27 אַחֲרָ֛יו הֶחֱזִ֥יקוּ הַתְּקֹעִ֖ים מִדָּ֣ה שֵׁנִ֑ית מִנֶּ֜גֶד הַמִּגְדָּ֤ל הַגָּדוֹל֙ הַיּוֹצֵ֔א וְעַ֖ד חוֹמַ֥ת הָעֹֽפֶל׃ 28 מֵעַ֣ל ׀ שַׁ֣עַר הַסּוּסִ֗ים הֶחֱזִ֨יקוּ֙ הַכֹּ֣הֲנִ֔ים אִ֖ישׁ לְנֶ֥גֶד בֵּיתֽוֹ׃ ס 29 אַחֲרָ֧יו הֶחֱזִ֛יק צָד֥וֹק בֶּן־אִמֵּ֖ר נֶ֣גֶד בֵּיתֹ֑ו ס וְאַחֲרָ֤יו הֶחֱזִיק֙ שְׁמַֽעְיָ֣ה בֶן־שְׁכַנְיָ֔ה שֹׁמֵ֖ר שַׁ֥עַר הַמִּזְרָֽח׃ ס 30 אחרי אַחֲרָ֣יו הֶחֱזִ֗יק חֲנַנְיָ֤ה בֶן־שֶׁלֶמְיָה֙ וְחָנ֧וּן בֶּן־צָלָ֛ף הַשִּׁשִּׁ֖י מִדָּ֣ה שֵׁנִ֑י ס אַחֲרָ֣יו הֶחֱזִ֗יק מְשֻׁלָּם֙ בֶּן־בֶּ֣רֶכְיָ֔ה נֶ֖גֶד נִשְׁכָּתֽוֹ׃ ס 31 אחרי אַחֲרָ֣יו הֶחֱזִ֗יק מַלְכִּיָּה֙ בֶּן־הַצֹּ֣רְפִ֔י עַד־בֵּ֥ית הַנְּתִינִ֖ים וְהָרֹכְלִ֑ים נֶ֚גֶד שַׁ֣עַר הַמִּפְקָ֔ד וְעַ֖ד עֲלִיַּ֥ת הַפִּנָּֽה׃ 32 *וּבֵ֨ין עֲלִיַּ֤ת הַפִּנָּה֙ לְשַׁ֣עַר הַצֹּ֔אן הֶחֱזִ֥יקוּ הַצֹּרְפִ֖ים וְהָרֹכְלִֽים׃ פ

33 וַיְהִ֞י כַּאֲשֶׁ֧ר שָׁמַ֣ע סַנְבַלַּ֗ט כִּֽי־אֲנַ֨חְנוּ֙ בוֹנִ֣ים אֶת־הַֽחוֹמָ֔ה וַיִּ֣חַר ל֔וֹ וַיִּכְעַ֖ס הַרְבֵּ֑ה וַיַּלְעֵ֖ג עַל־הַיְּהוּדִֽים׃ 34 וַיֹּ֣אמֶר ׀ לִפְנֵ֣י אֶחָ֗יו וְחֵיל֙ שֹׁ֣מְר֔וֹן וַיֹּ֕אמֶר מָ֛ה הַיְּהוּדִ֥ים הָאֲמֵלָלִ֖ים עֹשִׂ֑ים הֲיַעַזְב֤וּ לָהֶם֙ הֲיִזְבָּ֔חוּ הַיְכַלּ֣וּ בַיּ֔וֹם הַיְחַיּ֧וּ אֶת־הָאֲבָנִ֛ים מֵעֲרֵמ֥וֹת הֶעָפָ֖ר וְהֵ֥מָּה שְׂרוּפֽוֹת׃ 35 וְטוֹבִיָּ֥ה הָעַמֹּנִ֖י אֶצְל֑וֹ וַיֹּ֗אמֶר גַּ֚ם אֲשֶׁר־הֵ֣ם בּוֹנִ֔ים אִם־יַעֲלֶ֣ה שׁוּעָ֔ל וּפָרַ֖ץ חוֹמַ֥ת אַבְנֵיהֶֽם׃ פ

36 שְׁמַ֤ע אֱלֹהֵ֨ינוּ֙ כִּֽי־הָיִ֣ינוּ בוּזָ֔ה וְהָשֵׁ֥ב חֶרְפָּתָ֖ם אֶל־רֹאשָׁ֑ם וּתְנֵ֥ם לְבִזָּ֖ה בְּאֶ֥רֶץ שִׁבְיָֽה׃ 37 וְאַל־תְּכַס֙ עַל־עֲוֹנָ֔ם וְחַטָּאתָ֥ם מִלְּפָנֶ֖יךָ אַל־תִּמָּחֶ֑ה כִּ֥י הִכְעִ֖יסוּ לְנֶ֥גֶד הַבּוֹנִֽים׃

38 וַנִּבְנֶה֙ אֶת־הַ֣חוֹמָ֔ה וַתִּקָּשֵׁ֥ר כָּל־הַחוֹמָ֖ה עַד־חֶצְיָ֑הּ וַיְהִ֧י לֵ֦ב לָעָ֖ם לַעֲשֽׂוֹת׃ פ

v. 32.　חצי הספר בפסוקים

1864

כתובים נחמיה ד

4 When Sanballat and Tobiah, and the Arabs, the Ammonites, and the Ashdodites heard that healing had come to the walls of Jerusalem, that the breached parts had begun to be filled, it angered them very much, ²and they all conspired together to come and fight against Jerusalem and to throw it into confusion. ³Because of them we prayed to our God, and set up a watch over them[a] day and night.

⁴Judah was saying,

"The strength of the basket-carrier has failed,
And there is so much rubble;
We are not able ourselves
To rebuild the wall."

⁵And our foes were saying, "Before they know or see it, we shall be in among them and kill them, and put a stop to the work." ⁶When the Jews living near them[b] would arrive, they would tell us [c]time and again-[c] [d]"... from all the places where...you shall come back to us..."-[d] ⁷I stationed, on the lower levels of the place, behind the walls, on the bare rock—I stationed the people by families with their swords, their lances, and their bows. ⁸Then I decided to exhort the nobles, the prefects, and the rest of the people, "Do not be afraid of them! Think of the great and awesome Lord, and fight for your brothers, your sons and daughters, your wives and homes!"

⁹When our enemies learned that it had become known to us, since God had thus frustrated their plan, we could all return to the wall, each to his work. ¹⁰From that day on, half my servants did work and half held lances and shields, bows and armor. And the officers stood behind the whole house of Judah ¹¹who were

---

ד וַיְהִי כַאֲשֶׁר שָׁמַע סַנְבַלַּט וְטוֹבִיָּה וְהָעַרְבִים וְהָעַמֹּנִים וְהָאַשְׁדּוֹדִים כִּי־עָלְתָה אֲרוּכָה לְחֹמוֹת יְרוּשָׁלַ͏ִם כִּי־הֵחֵלּוּ הַפְּרֻצִים לְהִסָּתֵם וַיִּחַר לָהֶם מְאֹד: ² וַיִּקְשְׁרוּ כֻלָּם יַחְדָּו לָבוֹא לְהִלָּחֵם בִּירוּשָׁלָ͏ִם וְלַעֲשׂוֹת לוֹ תּוֹעָה: ³ וַנִּתְפַּלֵּל אֶל־אֱלֹהֵינוּ וַנַּעֲמִיד מִשְׁמָר עֲלֵיהֶם יוֹמָם וָלַיְלָה מִפְּנֵיהֶם: ⁴ וַיֹּאמֶר יְהוּדָה כָּשַׁל כֹּחַ הַסַּבָּל וְהֶעָפָר הַרְבֵּה וַאֲנַחְנוּ לֹא נוּכַל לִבְנוֹת בַּחוֹמָה: ⁵ וַיֹּאמְרוּ צָרֵינוּ לֹא יֵדְעוּ וְלֹא יִרְאוּ עַד אֲשֶׁר־נָבוֹא אֶל־תּוֹכָם וַהֲרַגְנוּם וְהִשְׁבַּתְנוּ אֶת־הַמְּלָאכָה: ⁶ וַיְהִי כַּאֲשֶׁר־בָּאוּ הַיְּהוּדִים הַיֹּשְׁבִים אֶצְלָם וַיֹּאמְרוּ לָנוּ עֶשֶׂר פְּעָמִים מִכָּל־הַמְּקֹמוֹת אֲשֶׁר־תָּשׁוּבוּ עָלֵינוּ: ⁷ וָאַעֲמִיד מִתַּחְתִּיּוֹת לַמָּקוֹם מֵאַחֲרֵי לַחוֹמָה בצחחיים בַּצְּחִחִיִּם וָאַעֲמִיד אֶת־הָעָם לְמִשְׁפָּחוֹת עִם־חַרְבֹתֵיהֶם רָמְחֵיהֶם וְקַשְּׁתֹתֵיהֶם: ⁸ וָאֵרֶא וָאָקוּם וָאֹמַר אֶל־הַחֹרִים וְאֶל־הַסְּגָנִים וְאֶל־יֶתֶר הָעָם אַל־תִּירְאוּ מִפְּנֵיהֶם אֶת־אֲדֹנָי הַגָּדוֹל וְהַנּוֹרָא זְכֹרוּ וְהִלָּחֲמוּ עַל־אֲחֵיכֶם בְּנֵיכֶם וּבְנֹתֵיכֶם נְשֵׁיכֶם וּבָתֵּיכֶם: פ

⁹ וַיְהִי כַּאֲשֶׁר־שָׁמְעוּ אוֹיְבֵינוּ כִּי־נוֹדַע לָנוּ וַיָּפֶר הָאֱלֹהִים אֶת־עֲצָתָם ונשוב וַנָּשָׁב כֻּלָּנוּ אֶל־הַחוֹמָה אִישׁ אֶל־מְלַאכְתּוֹ: ¹⁰ וַיְהִי ׀ מִן־הַיּוֹם הַהוּא חֲצִי נְעָרַי עֹשִׂים בַּמְּלָאכָה וְחֶצְיָם מַחֲזִיקִים וְהָרְמָחִים הַמָּגִנִּים וְהַקְּשָׁתוֹת וְהַשִּׁרְיֹנִים וְהַשָּׂרִים אַחֲרֵי כָּל־בֵּית יְהוּדָה: ¹¹ הַבּוֹנִים בַּחוֹמָה

---

a   I.e., the workers on the walls.
b   I.e., the foes.
c-c Lit. "ten times."
d-d Heb. seems to be abbreviated; a possible restoration of the sentence, with the missing elements enclosed in brackets, is: [of their evil plan; and we would say to them,] "From all the places where [you get such information] you shall come back to us [and convey it]."

rebuilding the wall. The basket-carriers were burdened, doing work with one hand while the other held a weapon. [12]As for the builders, each had his sword girded at his side as he was building. The trumpeter stood beside me. [13]I said to the nobles, the prefects, and the rest of the people, "There is much work and it is spread out; we are scattered over the wall, far from one another. [14]When you hear a trumpet call, gather yourselves to me at that place; our God will fight for us!" [15]And so we worked on, while half were holding lances, from the break of day until the stars appeared.

[16]I further said to the people at that time, "Let every man with his servant lodge in Jerusalem, that we may use the night to stand guard and the day to work." [17]Nor did I, my brothers, my servants, or the guards following me ever take off our clothes, e-[or] each his weapon, even at the water.-e

5

There was a great outcry by the common folk and their wives against their brother Jews. [2]Some said, "Our sons and daughters are numerous; we must get grain to eat in order that we may live!" [3]Others said, "We must pawn our fields, our vineyards, and our homes to get grain to stave off hunger." [4]Yet others said, "We have borrowed money against our fields and vineyards to pay the king's tax. [5]Now a-we are as good as-a our brothers, and our children as good as theirs; yet here we are subjecting our sons and daughters to slavery—some of our daughters are already subjected—and we are powerless, while our fields and vineyards belong to others."

[6]It angered me very much to hear their outcry and these complaints. [7]After pondering the matter carefully, I censured the nobles and the prefects, saying, "Are you pressing claims on

וְהַנֹּשְׂאִים בַּסֶּבֶל עֹמְשִׂים בְּאַחַת יָדוֹ
עֹשֶׂה בַמְּלָאכָה וְאַחַת מַחֲזֶקֶת הַשָּׁלַח:
12 וְהַבּוֹנִים אִישׁ חַרְבּוֹ אֲסוּרִים עַל־מָתְנָיו
וּבוֹנִים וְהַתּוֹקֵעַ בַּשּׁוֹפָר אֶצְלִי: 13 וָאֹמַר
אֶל־הַחֹרִים וְאֶל־הַסְּגָנִים וְאֶל־יֶתֶר הָעָם
הַמְּלָאכָה הַרְבֵּה וּרְחָבָה וַאֲנַחְנוּ נִפְרָדִים
עַל־הַחוֹמָה רְחוֹקִים אִישׁ מֵאָחִיו:
14 בִּמְקוֹם אֲשֶׁר תִּשְׁמְעוּ אֶת־קוֹל הַשּׁוֹפָר
שָׁמָּה תִּקָּבְצוּ אֵלֵינוּ אֱלֹהֵינוּ יִלָּחֶם
לָנוּ: 15 וַאֲנַחְנוּ עֹשִׂים בַּמְּלָאכָה וְחֶצְיָם
מַחֲזִיקִים בָּרְמָחִים מֵעֲלוֹת הַשַּׁחַר עַד
צֵאת הַכּוֹכָבִים:
16 גַּם בָּעֵת הַהִיא אָמַרְתִּי לָעָם אִישׁ וְנַעֲרוֹ
יָלִינוּ בְּתוֹךְ יְרוּשָׁלִָם וְהָיוּ־לָנוּ הַלַּיְלָה
מִשְׁמָר וְהַיּוֹם מְלָאכָה: 17 וְאֵין אֲנִי וְאַחַי
וּנְעָרַי וְאַנְשֵׁי הַמִּשְׁמָר אֲשֶׁר אַחֲרַי אֵין־
אֲנַחְנוּ פֹשְׁטִים בְּגָדֵינוּ אִישׁ שִׁלְחוֹ
הַמָּיִם: ס

ה וַתְּהִי צַעֲקַת הָעָם וּנְשֵׁיהֶם גְּדוֹלָה
אֶל־אֲחֵיהֶם הַיְּהוּדִים: 2 וְיֵשׁ אֲשֶׁר אֹמְרִים
בָּנֵינוּ וּבְנֹתֵינוּ אֲנַחְנוּ רַבִּים וְנִקְחָה דָגָן
וְנֹאכְלָה וְנִחְיֶה: 3 וְיֵשׁ אֲשֶׁר אֹמְרִים
שְׂדֹתֵינוּ וּכְרָמֵינוּ וּבָתֵּינוּ אֲנַחְנוּ עֹרְבִים
וְנִקְחָה דָגָן בָּרָעָב: 4 וְיֵשׁ אֲשֶׁר אֹמְרִים
לָוִינוּ כֶסֶף לְמִדַּת הַמֶּלֶךְ שְׂדֹתֵינוּ
וּכְרָמֵינוּ: 5 וְעַתָּה כִּבְשַׂר אַחֵינוּ בְּשָׂרֵנוּ
כִּבְנֵיהֶם בָּנֵינוּ וְהִנֵּה אֲנַחְנוּ כֹבְשִׁים אֶת־
בָּנֵינוּ וְאֶת־בְּנֹתֵינוּ לַעֲבָדִים וְיֵשׁ מִבְּנֹתֵינוּ
נִכְבָּשׁוֹת וְאֵין לְאֵל יָדֵנוּ וּשְׂדֹתֵינוּ וּכְרָמֵינוּ
לַאֲחֵרִים:
6 וַיִּחַר לִי מְאֹד כַּאֲשֶׁר שָׁמַעְתִּי אֶת־
זַעֲקָתָם וְאֵת הַדְּבָרִים הָאֵלֶּה: 7 וַיִּמָּלֵךְ
לִבִּי עָלַי וָאָרִיבָה אֶת־הַחֹרִים וְאֶת־
הַסְּגָנִים וָאֹמְרָה לָהֶם מַשָּׁא אִישׁ־בְּאָחִיו

---

e-e   Meaning of Heb. uncertain.

a-a   Lit. "our flesh is as good as the flesh of."

loans made to your brothers?" Then I raised a large crowd against them [8]and said to them, "We have done our best to buy back our Jewish brothers who were sold to the nations; will you now sell your brothers so that they must be sold [back] to us?" They kept silent, for they found nothing to answer. [9]So I continued, "What you are doing is not right. You ought to act in a God-fearing way so as not to give our enemies, the nations, room to reproach us. [10]I, my brothers, and my servants also have claims of money and grain against them; let us now abandon those claims! [11]Give back at once their fields, their vineyards, their olive trees, and their homes, and [abandon] the claims for the hundred pieces of silver, the grain, the wine, and the oil that you have been pressing against them!" [12]They replied, "We shall give them back, and not demand anything of them; we shall do just as you say." Summoning the priests, I put them under oath to keep this promise. [13]I also shook out the bosom of my garment and said, "So may God shake free of his household and property any man who fails to keep this promise; may he be thus shaken out and stripped." All the assembled answered, "Amen," and praised the LORD.

The people kept this promise.

[14]Furthermore, from the day I was commissioned to be governor in the land of Judah—from the twentieth year of King Artaxerxes until his thirty-second year, twelve years in all—neither I nor my brothers ever ate of the governor's food allowance. [15]The former governors who preceded me laid heavy burdens on the people, and took from them for bread and wine more than[b] forty shekels of silver. Their servants also tyrannized over the people. But I, out of the fear of God, did not do so. [16]I also supported the work on this wall; we did not buy any land, and all my servants were gathered there at the

---

b Lit. "after"; meaning of Heb. uncertain.

אַתֶּם נֹשִׁאים* וָאֶתֵּן עֲלֵיהֶם קְהִלָּה גְדוֹלָה: [8]וָאֹמְרָה לָהֶם אֲנַחְנוּ קָנִינוּ אֶת־אַחֵינוּ הַיְּהוּדִים הַנִּמְכָּרִים לַגּוֹיִם כְּדֵי בָנוּ וְגַם־אַתֶּם תִּמְכְּרוּ אֶת־אֲחֵיכֶם וְנִמְכְּרוּ־לָנוּ וַיַּחֲרִישׁוּ וְלֹא מָצְאוּ דָּבָר: ס [9]וַיֹּאמֶר וָאֹמַר לֹא־טוֹב הַדָּבָר אֲשֶׁר־אַתֶּם עֹשִׂים הֲלוֹא בְּיִרְאַת אֱלֹהֵינוּ תֵּלֵכוּ מֵחֶרְפַּת הַגּוֹיִם אוֹיְבֵינוּ: [10]וְגַם־אֲנִי אַחַי וּנְעָרַי נֹשִׁים בָּהֶם כֶּסֶף וְדָגָן נַעַזְבָה־נָּא אֶת־הַמַּשָּׁא הַזֶּה: [11]הָשִׁיבוּ נָא לָהֶם כְּהַיּוֹם שְׂדֹתֵיהֶם כַּרְמֵיהֶם זֵיתֵיהֶם וּבָתֵּיהֶם וּמְאַת הַכֶּסֶף וְהַדָּגָן הַתִּירוֹשׁ וְהַיִּצְהָר אֲשֶׁר אַתֶּם נֹשִׁים בָּהֶם: [12]וַיֹּאמְרוּ נָשִׁיב וּמֵהֶם לֹא נְבַקֵּשׁ כֵּן נַעֲשֶׂה כַּאֲשֶׁר אַתָּה אוֹמֵר וָאֶקְרָא אֶת־הַכֹּהֲנִים וָאַשְׁבִּיעֵם לַעֲשׂוֹת כַּדָּבָר הַזֶּה: [13]גַּם־חָצְנִי נָעַרְתִּי וָאֹמְרָה כָּכָה יְנַעֵר הָאֱלֹהִים אֶת־כָּל־הָאִישׁ אֲשֶׁר לֹא־יָקִים אֶת־הַדָּבָר הַזֶּה מִבֵּיתוֹ וּמִיגִיעוֹ וְכָכָה יִהְיֶה נָעוּר וָרֵק וַיֹּאמְרוּ כָל־הַקָּהָל אָמֵן וַיְהַלְלוּ אֶת־יְהוָה וַיַּעַשׂ הָעָם כַּדָּבָר הַזֶּה: [14]גַּם מִיּוֹם ׀ אֲשֶׁר־צִוָּה אֹתִי לִהְיוֹת פֶּחָם בְּאֶרֶץ יְהוּדָה מִשְּׁנַת עֶשְׂרִים וְעַד שְׁנַת שְׁלֹשִׁים וּשְׁתַּיִם לְאַרְתַּחְשַׁסְתְּא הַמֶּלֶךְ שָׁנִים שְׁתֵּים עֶשְׂרֵה אֲנִי וְאַחַי לֶחֶם הַפֶּחָה לֹא אָכַלְתִּי: [15]וְהַפַּחוֹת הָרִאשֹׁנִים אֲשֶׁר־לְפָנַי הִכְבִּידוּ עַל־הָעָם וַיִּקְחוּ מֵהֶם בְּלֶחֶם וָיַיִן אַחַר כֶּסֶף־שְׁקָלִים אַרְבָּעִים גַּם נַעֲרֵיהֶם שָׁלְטוּ עַל־הָעָם וַאֲנִי לֹא־עָשִׂיתִי כֵן מִפְּנֵי יִרְאַת אֱלֹהִים: [16]וְגַם בִּמְלֶאכֶת הַחוֹמָה הַזֹּאת הֶחֱזַקְתִּי וְשָׂדֶה

work. ¹⁷Although there were at my table, between Jews and prefects, one hundred and fifty
men in all, beside those who came to us from
surrounding nations; ¹⁸and although what was
prepared for each day came to one ox, six
select sheep, and fowl, all prepared for me,
and at ten-day intervals all sorts of wine in
abundance—yet I did not resort to the governor's food allowance, for the [king's] service lay
heavily on the people.

¹⁹O my God, remember to my credit all that
I have done for this people!

6 When word reached Sanballat, Tobiah,
Geshem the Arab, and the rest of our enemies
that I had rebuilt the wall and not a breach remained in it—though at that time I had not yet
set up doors in the gateways—²Sanballat and
Geshem sent a message to me, saying, "Come,
let us get together in Kephirim in the Ono valley"; they planned to do me harm. ³I sent them
messengers, saying, "I am engaged in a great
work and cannot come down, for the work will
stop if I leave it in order to come down to you."
⁴They sent me the same message four times, and
I gave them the same answer. ⁵Sanballat sent
me the same message a fifth time by his servant,
who had an open letter with him. ⁶Its text was:
"Word has reached the nations, and Geshem*a*
too says that you and the Jews are planning to
rebel—for which reason you are building the
wall—and that you are to be their king. *b-*Such
is the word.*-b* ⁷You have also set up prophets
in Jerusalem to proclaim about you, 'There is
a king in Judah!' Word of these things will surely
reach the king; so come, let us confer together."

⁸I sent back a message to him, saying, "None
of these things you mention has occurred; they

---

a   Heb. Gashmu.
b-b   Meaning of Heb. uncertain.

לֹא קָנִינוּ וְכָל־נְעָרַי קְבוּצִים שָׁם עַל־
הַמְּלָאכָֽה: 17 וְהַיְּהוּדִים וְהַסְּגָנִים מֵאָה
וַחֲמִשִּׁים אִישׁ וְהַבָּאִים אֵלֵינוּ מִן־הַגּוֹיִם
אֲשֶׁר־סְבִיבֹתֵינוּ עַל־שֻׁלְחָנִֽי: 18 וַאֲשֶׁר
הָיָה נַעֲשֶׂה לְיוֹם אֶחָד שׁוֹר אֶחָד צֹאן
שֵׁשׁ־בְּרֻרוֹת וְצִפֳּרִים נַעֲשׂוּ־לִי וּבֵין עֲשֶׂרֶת
יָמִים בְּכָל־יַיִן לְהַרְבֵּה וְעִם־זֶה לֶחֶם
הַפֶּחָה לֹא בִקַּשְׁתִּי כִּֽי־כָבְדָה הָעֲבֹדָה
עַל־הָעָם הַזֶּֽה: 19 זָכְרָה־לִּי אֱלֹהַי לְטוֹבָה כֹּל אֲשֶׁר־
עָשִׂיתִי עַל־הָעָם הַזֶּֽה: פ

ו וַיְהִי כַאֲשֶׁר נִשְׁמַע לְסַנְבַלַּט וְטוֹבִיָּה
וּלְגֶשֶׁם הָעַרְבִי וּלְיֶתֶר אֹֽיְבֵינוּ כִּי בָנִיתִי
אֶת־הַֽחוֹמָה וְלֹא־נוֹתַר בָּהּ פָּרֶץ גַּם
עַד־הָעֵת הַהִיא דְּלָתוֹת לֹא־הֶעֱמַדְתִּי
בַשְּׁעָרִֽים: 2 וַיִּשְׁלַח סַנְבַלַּט וְגֶשֶׁם אֵלַי
לֵאמֹר לְכָה וְנִֽוָּעֲדָה יַחְדָּו בַּכְּפִירִים
בְּבִקְעַת אוֹנוֹ וְהֵמָּה חֹֽשְׁבִים לַעֲשׂוֹת לִי
רָעָֽה: 3 וָאֶשְׁלְחָה עֲלֵיהֶם מַלְאָכִים לֵאמֹר
מְלָאכָה גְדוֹלָה אֲנִי עֹשֶׂה וְלֹא אוּכַל
לָרֶדֶת לָמָּה תִשְׁבַּת הַמְּלָאכָה כַּאֲשֶׁר
אַרְפֶּהָ וְיָרַדְתִּי אֲלֵיכֶֽם: 4 וַיִּשְׁלְחוּ אֵלַי
כַּדָּבָר הַזֶּה אַרְבַּע פְּעָמִים וָאָשִׁיב אוֹתָם
כַּדָּבָר הַזֶּֽה: ס 5 וַיִּשְׁלַח אֵלַי סַנְבַלַּט
כַּדָּבָר הַזֶּה פַּעַם חֲמִישִׁית אֶת־נַעֲרוֹ
וְאִגֶּרֶת פְּתוּחָה בְּיָדֽוֹ: 6 כָּתוּב בָּהּ בַּגּוֹיִם
נִשְׁמָע וְגַשְׁמוּ אֹמֵר אַתָּה וְהַיְּהוּדִים
חֹשְׁבִים לִמְרוֹד עַל־כֵּן אַתָּה בוֹנֶה הַחוֹמָה
וְאַתָּה הֹוֶה לָהֶם לְמֶלֶךְ כַּדְּבָרִים הָאֵֽלֶּה:
7 וְגַם־נְבִיאִים הֶעֱמַדְתָּ לִקְרֹא עָלֶיךָ
בִירוּשָׁלִַם לֵאמֹר מֶלֶךְ בִּֽיהוּדָה וְעַתָּה
יִשָּׁמַע לַמֶּלֶךְ כַּדְּבָרִים הָאֵלֶּה וְעַתָּה לְכָה
וְנִֽוָּעֲצָה יַחְדָּֽו: ס
8 וָאֶשְׁלְחָה אֵלָיו לֵאמֹר לֹא נִהְיָה כַּדְּבָרִים
הָאֵלֶּה אֲשֶׁר אַתָּה אוֹמֵר כִּי מִלִּבְּךָ אַתָּה

are figments of your imagination"—⁹for they all wished to intimidate us, thinking, "They will desist from the work, and it will not get done." Now strengthen my hands!

¹⁰Then I visited Shemaiah son of Delaiah son of Mehetabel when he was housebound, and he said,

"Let us meet in the House of God, inside the sanctuary,

And let us shut the doors of the sanctuary, for they are coming to kill you,

By night they are coming to kill you."

¹¹I replied, "Will a man like me take flight? Besides, who such as I can go into the sanctuary and live? I will not go in." ¹²Then I realized that it was not God who sent him, but that he uttered that prophecy about me—Tobiah and Sanballat having hired him—¹³because he was a hireling, that I might be intimidated and act thus and commit a sin, and so provide them a scandal with which to reproach me.

¹⁴"O my God, remember against Tobiah and Sanballat these deeds of theirs,ᶜ and against Noadiah the prophetess, and against the other prophets that they wished to intimidate me!"

¹⁵The wall was finished on the twenty-fifth of Elul, after fifty-two days. ¹⁶When all our enemies heard it, all the nations round about us were intimidated, and fell very low in their own estimation; they realized that this work had been accomplished by the help of our God.

¹⁷Also in those days, the nobles of Judah kept up a brisk correspondence with Tobiah, and Tobiah with them. ¹⁸Many in Judah were his confederates, for he was a son-in-law of Shecaniah son of Arah, and his son Jehohanan had married the daughter of Meshullam son of Berechiah. ¹⁹They would also speak well of him to me, and would divulge my affairs to him. Tobiah sent letters to intimidate me.

ᶜ Lit. "his."

בּוֹדְאָם*‎ : 9‏ כִּי כֻלָּם מְיָרְאִים אוֹתָ֫נוּ לֵאמֹר יִרְפּוּ יְדֵיהֶם מִן־הַמְּלָאכָה וְלֹא תֵעָשֶׂה וְעַתָּה חַזֵּק אֶת־יָדָי:

10‏ וַאֲנִי־בָאתִי בֵּית שְׁמַעְיָה בֶן־דְּלָיָה בֶּן־מְהֵיטַבְאֵל וְהוּא עָצוּר וַיֹּאמֶר נִוָּעֵד אֶל־בֵּית הָאֱלֹהִים אֶל־תּוֹךְ הַהֵיכָל וְנִסְגְּרָה דַּלְתוֹת הַהֵיכָל כִּי בָּאִים לְהָרְגֶךָ וְלַיְלָה בָּאִים לְהָרְגֶךָ:

11‏ וָאֹמְרָה הַאִישׁ כָּמוֹנִי יִבְרָח וּמִי כָמוֹנִי אֲשֶׁר־יָבוֹא אֶל־הַהֵיכָל וָחָי לֹא אָבוֹא:

12‏ וָאַכִּירָה וְהִנֵּה לֹא־אֱלֹהִים שְׁלָחוֹ כִּי הַנְּבוּאָה דִּבֶּר עָלַי וְטוֹבִיָּה וְסַנְבַלַּט שְׂכָרוֹ:

13‏ לְמַעַן שָׂכוּר הוּא לְמַעַן־אִירָא וְאֶעֱשֶׂה־כֵּן וְחָטָאתִי וְהָיָה לָהֶם לְשֵׁם רָע לְמַעַן יְחָרְפוּנִי: פ

14‏ זָכְרָה אֱלֹהַי לְטוֹבִיָּה וּלְסַנְבַלַּט כְּמַעֲשָׂיו אֵלֶּה וְגַם לְנוֹעַדְיָה הַנְּבִיאָה וּלְיֶתֶר הַנְּבִיאִים אֲשֶׁר הָיוּ מְיָרְאִים אוֹתִי:

15‏ וַתִּשְׁלַם הַחוֹמָה בְּעֶשְׂרִים וַחֲמִשָּׁה לֶאֱלוּל לַחֲמִשִּׁים וּשְׁנַיִם יוֹם: פ 16‏ וַיְהִי כַּאֲשֶׁר שָׁמְעוּ כָּל־אוֹיְבֵינוּ וַיִּרְאוּ כָּל־הַגּוֹיִם אֲשֶׁר סְבִיבֹתֵינוּ וַיִּפְּלוּ מְאֹד בְּעֵינֵיהֶם וַיֵּדְעוּ כִּי מֵאֵת אֱלֹהֵינוּ נֶעֶשְׂתָה הַמְּלָאכָה הַזֹּאת:

17‏ גַּם | בַּיָּמִים הָהֵם מַרְבִּים חֹרֵי יְהוּדָה אִגְּרֹתֵיהֶם הוֹלְכוֹת עַל־טוֹבִיָּה וַאֲשֶׁר לְטוֹבִיָּה בָּאוֹת אֲלֵיהֶם: 18‏ כִּי־רַבִּים בִּיהוּדָה בַּעֲלֵי שְׁבוּעָה לוֹ כִּי־חָתָן הוּא לִשְׁכַנְיָה בֶן־אָרַח וִיהוֹחָנָן בְּנוֹ לָקַח אֶת־בַּת־מְשֻׁלָּם בֶּן בֶּרֶכְיָה: 19‏ גַּם טוֹבֹתָיו הָיוּ אֹמְרִים לְפָנַי וּדְבָרַי הָיוּ מוֹצִיאִים לוֹ אִגְּרוֹת שָׁלַח טוֹבִיָּה לְיָרְאֵנִי:

v. 8. ‏נ"חא א'

7 When the wall was rebuilt and I had set up the doors, tasks were assigned to the gatekeepers, the singers, and the Levites. ²I put Hanani my brother and Hananiah, the captain of the fortress, in charge of Jerusalem, for he was a more trustworthy and God-fearing man than most. ³I said to them, "The gates of Jerusalem are not to be opened until the heat of the day,ᵃ and ᵇ-before you leave your posts-ᵇ let the doors be closed and barred. And assign the inhabitants of Jerusalem to watches, each man to his watch, and each in front of his own house."

⁴The city was broad and large, the people in it were few, and houses were not yet built. ⁵My God put it into my mind to assemble the nobles, the prefects, and the people, in order to register them by families. I found the genealogical register of those who were the first to come up, and there I found written:

⁶ᶜThese are the people of the province who came up from among the captive exiles that Nebuchadnezzar, king of Babylon, had deported, and who returned to Jerusalem and to Judah, each to his own city, ⁷who came with Zerubbabel, Jeshua, Nehemiah, Azariah, Raamiah, Nahamani, Mordecai, Bilshan, Mispereth, Bigvai, Nehum, Baanah.

The number of the men of the people of Israel: ⁸the sons of Parosh—2,172; ⁹the sons of Shephatiah—372; ¹⁰the sons of Arah—652; ¹¹the sons of Pahath-moab: the sons of Jeshua and Joab—2,818; ¹²the sons of Elam—1,254; ¹³the sons of Zattu—845; ¹⁴the sons of Zaccai—760; ¹⁵the sons of Binnui—648; ¹⁶the sons of Bebai—628;

ז וַיְהִי כַּאֲשֶׁר נִבְנְתָה הַחוֹמָה וָאַעֲמִיד הַדְּלָתֽוֹת וַיִּפָּקְדֽוּ הַשּׁוֹעֲרִים וְהַמְשֹׁרְרִים וְהַלְוִיִּם: ² וָאֲצַוֶּה אֶת־חֲנָנִי אָחִי וְאֶת־חֲנַנְיָה שַׂר הַבִּירָה עַל־יְרוּשָׁלָ͏ִם כִּי־הוּא כְּאִישׁ אֱמֶת וְיָרֵא אֶת־הָאֱלֹהִים מֵרַבִּים: ³ וַיֹּאמֶר לָהֶם לֹא יִפָּתְחוּ שַׁעֲרֵי יְרוּשָׁלַ͏ִם עַד־חֹם הַשֶּׁמֶשׁ וְעַד הֵם עֹמְדִים יָגִיפוּ הַדְּלָתוֹת וֶאֱחֹזוּ וְהַעֲמֵיד מִשְׁמְרוֹת יֹשְׁבֵי יְרוּשָׁלָ͏ִם אִישׁ בְּמִשְׁמָרוֹ וְאִישׁ נֶגֶד בֵּיתֽוֹ: ⁴ וְהָעִיר רַחֲבַת יָדַיִם וּגְדוֹלָה וְהָעָם מְעַט בְּתוֹכָהּ וְאֵין בָּתִּים בְּנוּיִם: ⁵ וַיִּתֵּן אֱלֹהַי אֶל־לִבִּי וָאֶקְבְּצָה אֶת־הַחֹרִים וְאֶת־הַסְּגָנִים וְאֶת־הָעָם לְהִתְיַחֵשׂ וָאֶמְצָא סֵפֶר הַיַּחַשׂ הָעוֹלִים בָּרִאשׁוֹנָה וָאֶמְצָא כָּתוּב בּֽוֹ: פ

⁶ אֵלֶּה ׀ בְּנֵי הַמְּדִינָה הָעֹלִים מִשְּׁבִי הַגּוֹלָה אֲשֶׁר הֶגְלָה נְבוּכַדְנֶצַּר מֶלֶךְ בָּבֶל וַיָּשׁוּבוּ לִירוּשָׁלַ͏ִם וְלִיהוּדָה אִישׁ לְעִירֽוֹ: ⁷ הַבָּאִים עִם־זְרֻבָּבֶל יֵשׁוּעַ נְחֶמְיָה עֲזַרְיָה רַֽעַמְיָה נַחֲמָנִי מָרְדֳּכַי בִּלְשָׁן מִסְפֶּרֶת בִּגְוַי נְחוּם בַּעֲנָה מִסְפַּר אַנְשֵׁי עַם יִשְׂרָאֵל: ס ⁸ בְּנֵי פַרְעֹשׁ אַלְפַּיִם מֵאָה וְשִׁבְעִים וּשְׁנָֽיִם: ס ⁹ בְּנֵי שְׁפַטְיָה שְׁלֹשׁ מֵאוֹת שִׁבְעִים וּשְׁנָֽיִם: ס ¹⁰ בְּנֵי אָרַח שֵׁשׁ מֵאוֹת חֲמִשִּׁים וּשְׁנָֽיִם: ס ¹¹ בְּנֵי־פַחַת מוֹאָב לִבְנֵי יֵשׁוּעַ וְיוֹאָב אַלְפַּיִם וּשְׁמֹנֶה מֵאוֹת שְׁמֹנָה עָשָׂר: ס ¹² בְּנֵי עֵילָם אֶלֶף מָאתַיִם חֲמִשִּׁים וְאַרְבָּעָֽה: ס ¹³ בְּנֵי זַתּוּא שְׁמֹנֶה מֵאוֹת אַרְבָּעִים וַחֲמִשָּֽׁה: ס ¹⁴ בְּנֵי זַכָּי שְׁבַע מֵאוֹת וְשִׁשִּֽׁים: ס ¹⁵ בְּנֵי בִנּוּי שֵׁשׁ מֵאוֹת אַרְבָּעִים וּשְׁמֹנָֽה: ¹⁶ בְּנֵי בֵבָי שֵׁשׁ מֵאוֹת עֶשְׂרִים וּשְׁמֹנָֽה: ס ¹⁷ בְּנֵי עַזְגָּד אַלְפַּיִם שְׁלֹשׁ מֵאוֹת

ᵃ Lit. "sun."
ᵇ⁻ᵇ Lit. "while they are still standing."
ᶜ Vv. 6–43 appear as Ezra 2 with variations in the names and numbers.

the sons of Azgad—2,322; ¹⁸the sons of Adoni-kam—667; ¹⁹the sons of Bigvai—2,067; ²⁰the sons of Adin—655; ²¹the sons of Ater: Hezekiah—98; ²²the sons of Hashum—328; ²³the sons of Bezai—324; ²⁴the sons of Hariph—112; ²⁵the sons of Gibeon—95; ²⁶the men of Bethlehem and Netophah—188; ²⁷the men of Anathoth—128; ²⁸the men of Beth-azmaveth—42; ²⁹the men of Kiriath-jearim, Chephirah, and Beeroth—743; ³⁰the men of Ramah and Geba—621; ³¹the men of Michmas—122; ³²the men of Bethel and Ai—123; ³³the men of the other Nebo—52; ³⁴the sons of the other Elam—1,254; ³⁵the sons of Harim—320; ³⁶the sons of Jericho—345; ³⁷the sons of Lod, Hadid, and Ono—721; ³⁸the sons of Senaah—3,930.

³⁹The priests: the sons of Jedaiah: the house of Jeshua—973; ⁴⁰the sons of Immer—1,052; ⁴¹the sons of Pashhur—1,247; ⁴²the sons of Harim—1,017.

⁴³The Levites: the sons of Jeshua: Kadmiel, the sons of Hodeiah—74.

⁴⁴The singers: the sons of Asaph—148.

⁴⁵The gatekeepers: the sons of Shallum, the sons of Ater, the sons of Talmon, the sons of Akkub, the sons of Hatita, the sons of Shobai—138.

עֶשְׂרִים וּשְׁנָיִם: ס 18 בְּנֵי אֲדֹנִיקָם שֵׁשׁ מֵאוֹת שִׁשִּׁים וְשִׁבְעָה: ס 19 בְּנֵי בִגְוָי אַלְפַּיִם שִׁשִּׁים וְשִׁבְעָה: ס 20 בְּנֵי עָדִין שֵׁשׁ מֵאוֹת חֲמִשִּׁים וַחֲמִשָּׁה: ס 21 בְּנֵי־ אָטֵר לְחִזְקִיָּה תִּשְׁעִים וּשְׁמֹנָה: ס 22 בְּנֵי חָשֻׁם שְׁלֹשׁ מֵאוֹת עֶשְׂרִים וּשְׁמֹנָה: ס 23 בְּנֵי בֵצָי שְׁלֹשׁ מֵאוֹת עֶשְׂרִים וְאַרְבָּעָה: ס 24 בְּנֵי חָרִיף מֵאָה שְׁנֵים עָשָׂר: ס 25 בְּנֵי גִבְעוֹן תִּשְׁעִים וַחֲמִשָּׁה: 26 אַנְשֵׁי בֵית־לֶחֶם וּנְטֹפָה מֵאָה שְׁמֹנִים וּשְׁמֹנָה: ס 27 אַנְשֵׁי עֲנָתוֹת מֵאָה עֶשְׂרִים וּשְׁמֹנָה: ס 28 אַנְשֵׁי בֵית־עַזְמָוֶת אַרְבָּעִים וּשְׁנָיִם: ס 29 אַנְשֵׁי קִרְיַת יְעָרִים כְּפִירָה וּבְאֵרוֹת שְׁבַע מֵאוֹת אַרְבָּעִים וּשְׁלֹשָׁה: ס 30 אַנְשֵׁי הָרָמָה וָגֶבַע שֵׁשׁ מֵאוֹת עֶשְׂרִים וְאֶחָד: ס 31 אַנְשֵׁי מִכְמָס מֵאָה וְעֶשְׂרִים וּשְׁנָיִם: ס 32 אַנְשֵׁי בֵית־אֵל וְהָעָי מֵאָה עֶשְׂרִים וּשְׁלֹשָׁה: ס 33 אַנְשֵׁי נְבוֹ אַחֵר חֲמִשִּׁים וּשְׁנָיִם: ס 34 בְּנֵי עֵילָם אַחֵר אֶלֶף מָאתַיִם חֲמִשִּׁים וְאַרְבָּעָה: ס 35 בְּנֵי חָרִם שְׁלֹשׁ מֵאוֹת וְעֶשְׂרִים: ס 36 בְּנֵי יְרֵחוֹ שְׁלֹשׁ מֵאוֹת אַרְבָּעִים וַחֲמִשָּׁה: ס 37 בְּנֵי־לֹד חָדִיד וְאוֹנוֹ שְׁבַע מֵאוֹת עֶשְׂרִים וְאֶחָד: ס 38 בְּנֵי סְנָאָה שְׁלֹשֶׁת אֲלָפִים תְּשַׁע מֵאוֹת וּשְׁלֹשִׁים: פ 39 הַכֹּהֲנִים בְּנֵי יְדַעְיָה לְבֵית יֵשׁוּעַ תְּשַׁע מֵאוֹת שִׁבְעִים וּשְׁלֹשָׁה: ס 40 בְּנֵי אִמֵּר אֶלֶף חֲמִשִּׁים וּשְׁנָיִם: ס 41 בְּנֵי פַשְׁחוּר אֶלֶף מָאתַיִם אַרְבָּעִים וְשִׁבְעָה: ס 42 בְּנֵי חָרִם אֶלֶף שִׁבְעָה עָשָׂר: פ 43 הַלְוִיִּם בְּנֵי־יֵשׁוּעַ לְקַדְמִיאֵל לִבְנֵי לְהוֹדְוָה שִׁבְעִים וְאַרְבָּעָה: ס 44 הַמְשֹׁרְרִים בְּנֵי אָסָף מֵאָה אַרְבָּעִים וּשְׁמֹנָה: ס

46The temple servants: the sons of Ziha, the sons of Hasupha, the sons of Tabbaoth, 47the sons of Keros, the sons of Siah, the sons of Padon, 48the sons of Lebanah, the sons of Hagabah, the sons of Shalmai, 49the sons of Hanan, the sons of Giddel, the sons of Gahar, 50the sons of Reaiah, the sons of Rezin, the sons of Nekoda, 51the sons of Gazzam, the sons of Uzza, the sons of Paseah, 52the sons of Besai, the sons of Meunim, the sons of Nephishesim, 53the sons of Bakbuk, the sons of Hakupha, the sons of Harhur, 54the sons of Bazlith, the sons of Mehida, the sons of Harsha, 55the sons of Barkos, the sons of Sisera, the sons of Temah, 56the sons of Neziah, the sons of Hatipha.

57The sons of Solomon's servants: the sons of Sotai, the sons of Sophereth, the sons of Perida, 58the sons of Jala, the sons of Darkon, the sons of Giddel, 59the sons of Shephatiah, the sons of Hattil, the sons of Pochereth-hazzebaim, the sons of Amon.

60The total of temple servants and the sons of Solomon's servants—392.

61The following were those who came up from Tel-melah, Tel-harsha, Cherub, Addon, and Immer—they were unable to tell whether their father's house and descent were Israelite: 62the sons of Delaiah, the sons of Tobiah, the sons of Nekoda—642.

63Of the priests: the sons of Habaiah, the sons of Hakkoz, the sons of Barzillai who had married a daughter of Barzillai the Gileadite and had taken his^d name—64these searched for their genealogical records, but they could not be found, so they were disqualified for the priesthood. 65The Tirshatha^e ordered them not to eat of the most holy things until a priest with Urim and Thummim should appear.

66The sum of the entire community was 42,360, 67not counting their male and female

---

45 הַשֹּׁעֲרִים בְּנֵי־שַׁלֻּם בְּנֵי־אָטֵר בְּנֵי־טַלְמֹן בְּנֵי־עַקּוּב בְּנֵי חֲטִיטָא בְּנֵי שֹׁבָי מֵאָה שְׁלֹשִׁים וּשְׁמֹנָה: ס

46 הַנְּתִינִים* בְּנֵי־צִחָא בְנֵי־חֲשֻׂפָא בְּנֵי טַבָּעוֹת: 47 בְּנֵי־קֵרֹס בְּנֵי־סִיעָא בְּנֵי פָדוֹן: 48 בְּנֵי־לְבָנָה בְנֵי־חֲגָבָה בְּנֵי שַׁלְמָי: 49 בְּנֵי־חָנָן בְּנֵי־גִדֵּל בְּנֵי־גָחַר: 50 בְּנֵי־רְאָיָה בְנֵי־רְצִין בְּנֵי נְקוֹדָא: 51 בְּנֵי־גַזָּם בְּנֵי־עֻזָּא בְּנֵי פָסֵחַ: 52 בְּנֵי־בֵסַי בְּנֵי־מְעוּנִים בְּנֵי נפושסים נְפִישְׁסִים: 53 בְּנֵי־בַקְבּוּק בְּנֵי־חֲקוּפָא בְּנֵי חַרְחוּר: 54 בְּנֵי־בַצְלִית בְּנֵי־מְחִידָא בְּנֵי חַרְשָׁא: 55 בְּנֵי־בַרְקוֹס בְּנֵי־סִיסְרָא בְּנֵי־תָמַח: 56 בְּנֵי נְצִיחַ בְּנֵי חֲטִיפָא:

57 בְּנֵי עַבְדֵי שְׁלֹמֹה בְּנֵי־סוֹטַי בְּנֵי־סוֹפֶרֶת בְּנֵי פְרִידָא: 58 בְּנֵי־יַעְלָא בְנֵי־דַרְקוֹן בְּנֵי גִדֵּל: 59 בְּנֵי שְׁפַטְיָה בְנֵי־חַטִּיל בְּנֵי פֹכֶרֶת הַצְּבָיִים בְּנֵי אָמוֹן:

60 כָּל־הַנְּתִינִים וּבְנֵי עַבְדֵי שְׁלֹמֹה שְׁלֹשׁ מֵאוֹת תִּשְׁעִים וּשְׁנָיִם: פ

61 וְאֵלֶּה הָעוֹלִים מִתֵּל מֶלַח תֵּל חַרְשָׁא כְּרוּב אַדּוֹן וְאִמֵּר וְלֹא יָכְלוּ לְהַגִּיד בֵּית־אֲבוֹתָם וְזַרְעָם אִם מִיִּשְׂרָאֵל הֵם: 62 בְּנֵי־דְלָיָה בְנֵי־טוֹבִיָּה בְּנֵי נְקוֹדָא שֵׁשׁ מֵאוֹת וְאַרְבָּעִים וּשְׁנָיִם: ס

63 וּמִן־הַכֹּהֲנִים בְּנֵי חֲבַיָּה בְּנֵי הַקּוֹץ בְּנֵי בַרְזִלַּי אֲשֶׁר לָקַח מִבְּנוֹת בַּרְזִלַּי הַגִּלְעָדִי אִשָּׁה* וַיִּקָּרֵא עַל־שְׁמָם: 64 אֵלֶּה בִּקְשׁוּ כְתָבָם הַמִּתְיַחְשִׂים וְלֹא נִמְצָא וַיִּגֹּאֲלוּ מִן־הַכְּהֻנָּה: 65 וַיֹּאמֶר הַתִּרְשָׁתָא לָהֶם אֲשֶׁר לֹא־יֹאכְלוּ מִקֹּדֶשׁ הַקֳּדָשִׁים עַד עֲמֹד הַכֹּהֵן לְאוּרִים וְתֻמִּים:

66 כָּל־הַקָּהָל כְּאֶחָד אַרְבַּע רִבּוֹא אַלְפַּיִם שְׁלֹשׁ־מֵאוֹת וְשִׁשִּׁים: 67 מִלְּבַד עַבְדֵיהֶם וְאַמְהֹתֵיהֶם אֵלֶּה שִׁבְעַת אֲלָפִים שְׁלֹשׁ

---

^d Lit. "their."
^e A Persian title.

v. 46. בכתב היד שלנו, חלק הרשימה בצורת שירה
v. 63. סבירין ומטעין "לְאִשָּׁה"

1872

servants, these being 7,337; they also had 245 male and female singers. [68f]-[Their horses—736, their mules—245,]-[f] camels—435, asses—6,720.

[69]Some of the heads of the clans made donations for the work. The Tirshatha donated to the treasury: gold—1,000 drachmas, basins—50, priestly robes—530.

[70]Some of the heads of the clans donated to the work treasury: gold—20,000 drachmas, and silver—2,200 minas.

[71]The rest of the people donated: gold—20,000 drachmas, silver—2,000, and priestly robes—67.

[72]The priests, the Levites, the gatekeepers, the singers, some of the people, the temple servants, and all Israel took up residence in their towns.

8 When the seventh month arrived—the Israelites being [settled] in their towns—[1]the entire people assembled as one man in the square before the Water Gate, and they asked Ezra the scribe to bring the scroll of the Teaching of Moses with which the Lord had charged Israel. [2]On the first day of the seventh month, Ezra the priest brought the Teaching before the congregation, men and women and all who could listen with understanding. [3]He read from it, facing the square before the Water Gate, from the first light until midday, to the men and the women and those who could understand; the ears of all the people were given to the scroll of the Teaching.

[4]Ezra the scribe stood upon a wooden tower made for the purpose, and beside him stood Mattithiah, Shema, Anaiah, Uriah, Hilkiah, and Maaseiah at his right, and at his left Pedaiah, Mishael, Malchijah, Hashum, Hashbaddanah, Zechariah, Meshullam. [5]Ezra opened the scroll

---

מֵאוֹת שְׁלֹשִׁים וְשִׁבְעָה וְלָהֶם מְשֹׁרְרִים וּמְשֹׁרְרוֹת מָאתַיִם וְאַרְבָּעִים וַחֲמִשָּׁה: ס 68 * גְּמַלִּים אַרְבַּע מֵאוֹת שְׁלֹשִׁים וַחֲמִשָּׁה ס חֲמֹרִים שֵׁשֶׁת אֲלָפִים שְׁבַע מֵאוֹת וְעֶשְׂרִים: 69 וּמִקְצָת רָאשֵׁי הָאָבוֹת נָתְנוּ לַמְּלָאכָה הַתִּרְשָׁתָא נָתַן לָאוֹצָר זָהָב דַּרְכְּמֹנִים אֶלֶף מִזְרָקוֹת חֲמִשִּׁים כָּתְנוֹת כֹּהֲנִים שְׁלֹשִׁים וַחֲמֵשׁ מֵאוֹת: 70 וּמֵרָאשֵׁי הָאָבוֹת נָתְנוּ לְאוֹצַר הַמְּלָאכָה זָהָב דַּרְכְּמוֹנִים שְׁתֵּי רִבּוֹת וְכֶסֶף מָנִים אַלְפַּיִם וּמָאתָיִם: 71 וַאֲשֶׁר נָתְנוּ שְׁאֵרִית הָעָם זָהָב דַּרְכְּמוֹנִים שְׁתֵּי רִבּוֹא וְכֶסֶף מָנִים אַלְפַּיִם וְכָתְנֹת כֹּהֲנִים שִׁשִּׁים וְשִׁבְעָה: פ 72 וַיֵּשְׁבוּ הַכֹּהֲנִים וְהַלְוִיִּם וְהַשּׁוֹעֲרִים וְהַמְשֹׁרְרִים וּמִן־הָעָם וְהַנְּתִינִים וְכָל־יִשְׂרָאֵל בְּעָרֵיהֶם

ח וַיִּגַּע הַחֹדֶשׁ הַשְּׁבִיעִי וּבְנֵי יִשְׂרָאֵל בְּעָרֵיהֶם: 1 וַיֵּאָסְפוּ כָל־הָעָם כְּאִישׁ אֶחָד אֶל־הָרְחוֹב אֲשֶׁר לִפְנֵי שַׁעַר־הַמָּיִם וַיֹּאמְרוּ לְעֶזְרָא הַסֹּפֵר לְהָבִיא אֶת־סֵפֶר תּוֹרַת מֹשֶׁה אֲשֶׁר־צִוָּה יְהוָה אֶת־יִשְׂרָאֵל: 2 וַיָּבִיא עֶזְרָא הַכֹּהֵן אֶת־הַתּוֹרָה לִפְנֵי הַקָּהָל מֵאִישׁ וְעַד־אִשָּׁה וְכֹל מֵבִין לִשְׁמֹעַ בְּיוֹם אֶחָד לַחֹדֶשׁ הַשְּׁבִיעִי: 3 וַיִּקְרָא־בוֹ לִפְנֵי הָרְחוֹב אֲשֶׁר | לִפְנֵי שַׁעַר־הַמַּיִם מִן־הָאוֹר עַד־מַחֲצִית הַיּוֹם נֶגֶד הָאֲנָשִׁים וְהַנָּשִׁים וְהַמְּבִינִים וְאָזְנֵי כָל־הָעָם אֶל־סֵפֶר הַתּוֹרָה: 4 וַיַּעֲמֹד עֶזְרָא הַסֹּפֵר עַל־מִגְדַּל־עֵץ אֲשֶׁר עָשׂוּ לַדָּבָר וַיַּעֲמֹד אֶצְלוֹ מַתִּתְיָה וְשֶׁמַע וַעֲנָיָה וְאוּרִיָּה וְחִלְקִיָּה וּמַעֲשֵׂיָה עַל־יְמִינוֹ וּמִשְּׂמֹאלוֹ פְּדָיָה וּמִישָׁאֵל וּמַלְכִּיָּה וְחָשֻׁם וְחַשְׁבַּדָּנָה זְכַרְיָה מְשֻׁלָּם: פ

v. 68. בנוסח אחר נחחבר פסוק "סוסיהם שבע מאות שלשים וששה פרדיהם מאתים ארבעים וחמשה"

[f-f] These words are missing in some mss. and editions; but cf. Ezra 2.66.

in the sight of all the people, for he was above all the people; as he opened it, all the people stood up. [6]Ezra blessed the Lord, the great God, and all the people answered, "Amen, Amen," with hands upraised. Then they bowed their heads and prostrated themselves before the Lord with their faces to the ground. [7]Jeshua, Bani, Sherebiah, Jamin, Akkub, Shabbethai, Hodiah, Maaseiah, Kelita, Azariah, Jozabad, Hanan, Pelaiah, and the Levites explained the Teaching to the people, while the people stood in their places. [8]They read from the scroll of the Teaching of God, translating it and giving the sense; so they understood the reading.

[9]Nehemiah the Tirshatha, Ezra the priest and scribe, and the Levites who were explaining to the people said to all the people, "This day is holy to the Lord your God: you must not mourn or weep," for all the people were weeping as they listened to the words of the Teaching. [10]He further said to them, "Go, eat choice foods and drink sweet drinks and send portions to whoever has nothing prepared, for the day is holy to our Lord. Do not be sad, for your rejoicing in the Lord is the source of your strength." [11]The Levites were quieting the people, saying, "Hush, for the day is holy; do not be sad." [12]Then all the people went to eat and drink and send portions and make great merriment, for they understood the things they were told.

[13]On the second day, the heads of the clans of all the people and the priests and Levites gathered to Ezra the scribe to study the words of the Teaching. [14]They found written in the Teaching that the Lord had commanded Moses that the Israelites must dwell in booths during the festival of the seventh month, [15]and that they must announce and proclaim throughout all their towns and Jerusalem as follows, "Go out to the mountains and bring leafy branches of olive

5 וַיִּפְתַּ֨ח עֶזְרָ֤א הַסֵּ֨פֶר֙ לְעֵינֵ֣י כָל־הָעָ֔ם כִּֽי־מֵעַ֥ל כָּל־הָעָ֖ם הָיָ֑ה וּכְפִתְח֖וֹ עָֽמְד֥וּ כָל־הָעָֽם׃ 6 וַיְבָ֣רֶךְ עֶזְרָ֔א אֶת־יְהוָ֥ה הָאֱלֹהִ֖ים הַגָּד֑וֹל וַיַּֽעֲנ֨וּ כָל־הָעָ֜ם אָמֵ֤ן ׀ אָמֵן֙ בְּמֹ֣עַל יְדֵיהֶ֔ם וַיִּקְּד֧וּ וַיִּֽשְׁתַּחֲוֻ֛ לַיהוָ֖ה אַפַּ֥יִם אָֽרְצָה׃ 7 וְיֵשׁ֡וּעַ וּבָנִ֡י וְשֵׁרֵ֣בְיָ֣ה ׀ יָמִ֡ין עַקּ֡וּב שַׁבְּתַ֣י ׀ הֽוֹדִיָּ֡ה מַֽעֲשֵׂיָ֡ה קְלִיטָ֣א עֲזַרְיָ֣ה יֽוֹזָבָ֡ד חָנָ֣ן פְּלָאיָ֗ה וְהַלְוִיִּ֖ם מְבִינִ֣ים אֶת־הָעָ֣ם לַתּוֹרָ֑ה וְהָעָ֖ם עַל־עָמְדָֽם׃ 8 וַיִּקְרְא֥וּ בַסֵּ֛פֶר בְּתוֹרַ֥ת הָאֱלֹהִ֖ים מְפֹרָ֑שׁ וְשׂ֣וֹם שֶׂ֔כֶל וַיָּבִ֖ינוּ בַּמִּקְרָֽא׃ ס
9 וַיֹּ֣אמֶר נְחֶמְיָ֣ה ה֣וּא הַתִּרְשָׁ֡תָא וְעֶזְרָ֣א הַכֹּהֵ֣ן ׀ הַסֹּפֵ֡ר וְהַלְוִיִּם֩ הַמְּבִינִ֨ים אֶת־הָעָ֜ם לְכָל־הָעָ֗ם הַיּ֤וֹם קָדֹֽשׁ־הוּא֙ לַיהוָ֣ה אֱלֹֽהֵיכֶ֔ם אַל־תִּֽתְאַבְּל֖וּ וְאַל־תִּבְכּ֑וּ כִּ֤י בוֹכִים֙ כָּל־הָעָ֔ם כְּשָׁמְעָ֖ם אֶת־דִּבְרֵ֥י הַתּוֹרָֽה׃ 10 וַיֹּ֣אמֶר לָהֶ֗ם לְכוּ֩ אִכְל֨וּ מַשְׁמַנִּ֜ים וּשְׁת֣וּ מַֽמְתַקִּ֗ים וְשִׁלְח֤וּ מָנוֹת֙ לְאֵ֣ין נָכ֣וֹן ל֔וֹ כִּֽי־קָד֥וֹשׁ הַיּ֖וֹם לַֽאֲדֹנֵ֑ינוּ וְאַל־תֵּ֣עָצֵ֔בוּ כִּֽי־חֶדְוַ֥ת יְהוָ֖ה הִ֥יא מָֽעֻזְּכֶֽם׃ 11 וְהַלְוִיִּ֞ם מַחְשִׁ֤ים לְכָל־הָעָם֙ לֵאמֹ֣ר הַ֔סּוּ כִּ֥י הַיּ֖וֹם קָדֹ֑שׁ וְאַל־תֵּֽעָצֵֽבוּ׃ 12 וַיֵּֽלְכ֨וּ כָל־הָעָ֜ם לֶֽאֱכֹ֤ל וְלִשְׁתּוֹת֙ וּלְשַׁלַּ֣ח מָנ֔וֹת וְלַֽעֲשׂ֖וֹת שִׂמְחָ֣ה גְדוֹלָ֑ה כִּ֤י הֵבִ֨ינוּ֙ בַּדְּבָרִ֔ים אֲשֶׁ֥ר הוֹדִ֖יעוּ לָהֶֽם׃ ס
13 וּבַיּ֣וֹם הַשֵּׁנִ֡י נֶֽאֶסְפוּ֩ רָאשֵׁ֨י הָֽאָב֜וֹת לְכָל־הָעָ֗ם הַכֹּֽהֲנִים֙ וְהַלְוִיִּ֔ם אֶל־עֶזְרָ֖א הַסֹּפֵ֑ר וּלְהַשְׂכִּ֖יל אֶל־דִּבְרֵ֥י הַתּוֹרָֽה׃ 14 וַיִּמְצְא֖וּ כָּת֣וּב בַּתּוֹרָ֑ה אֲשֶׁ֨ר צִוָּ֤ה יְהוָה֙ בְּיַד־מֹשֶׁ֔ה אֲשֶׁר֩ יֵֽשְׁב֨וּ בְנֵֽי־יִשְׂרָאֵ֧ל בַּסֻּכּ֛וֹת בֶּחָ֖ג בַּחֹ֥דֶשׁ הַשְּׁבִיעִֽי׃ 15 וַֽאֲשֶׁ֣ר יַשְׁמִ֗יעוּ וְיַֽעֲבִ֨ירוּ ק֜וֹל בְּכָל־עָֽרֵיהֶ֗ם וּבִירֽוּשָׁלִַ֙ם֙ לֵאמֹ֔ר צְא֣וּ הָהָ֔ר וְהָבִ֙יאוּ֙ עֲלֵי־זַ֔יִת וַֽעֲלֵי־

trees, pine[a] trees, myrtles, palms and [other] leafy[a] trees to make booths, as it is written." [16]So the people went out and brought them, and made themselves booths on their roofs, in their courtyards, in the courtyards of the House of God, in the square of the Water Gate and in the square of the Ephraim Gate. [17]The whole community that returned from the captivity made booths and dwelt in the booths—the Israelites had not done so from the days of Joshua[b] son of Nun to that day—and there was very great rejoicing. [18]He read from the scroll of the Teaching of God each day, from the first to the last day. They celebrated the festival seven days, and there was a solemn gathering on the eighth, as prescribed.

9 On the twenty-fourth day of this month, the Israelites assembled, fasting, in sackcloth, and with earth upon them. [2]Those of the stock of Israel separated themselves from all foreigners, and stood and confessed their sins and the iniquities of their fathers. [3]Standing in their places, they read from the scroll of the Teaching of the Lord their God for one-fourth of the day, and for another fourth they confessed and prostrated themselves before the Lord their God. [4]On the raised platform of the Levites stood Jeshua and Bani, Kadmiel, Shebaniah, Bunni, Sherebiah, Bani, and Chenani, and cried in a loud voice to the Lord their God. [5]The Levites Jeshua, Kadmiel, Bani, Hashabniah, Sherebiah, Hodiah, and Pethahiah said, "Rise, bless the Lord your God who is from eternity to eternity: 'May Your glorious name be blessed, exalted though it is above every blessing and praise!'

[6]"You alone are the Lord. You made the heavens, the highest[a] heavens, and all their host, the earth and everything upon it, the seas and

עֵץ שֶׁמֶן וַעֲלֵי הֲדַס וַעֲלֵי תְמָרִים וַעֲלֵי עֵץ עָבֹת לַעֲשֹׂת סֻכֹּת כַּכָּתוּב: פ [16] וַיֵּצְאוּ הָעָם וַיָּבִיאוּ וַיַּעֲשׂוּ לָהֶם סֻכּוֹת אִישׁ עַל־גַּגּוֹ וּבְחַצְרֹתֵיהֶם וּבְחַצְרוֹת בֵּית הָאֱלֹהִים וּבִרְחוֹב שַׁעַר הַמַּיִם וּבִרְחוֹב שַׁעַר אֶפְרָיִם: [17] וַיַּעֲשׂוּ כָל־הַקָּהָל הַשָּׁבִים מִן־הַשְּׁבִי | סֻכּוֹת וַיֵּשְׁבוּ בַסֻּכּוֹת כִּי לֹא־עָשׂוּ מִימֵי יֵשׁוּעַ בִּן־נוּן כֵּן בְּנֵי יִשְׂרָאֵל עַד הַיּוֹם הַהוּא וַתְּהִי שִׂמְחָה גְדוֹלָה מְאֹד: [18] וַיִּקְרָא בְּסֵפֶר תּוֹרַת הָאֱלֹהִים יוֹם | בְּיוֹם מִן־הַיּוֹם הָרִאשׁוֹן עַד הַיּוֹם הָאַחֲרוֹן וַיַּעֲשׂוּ־חָג שִׁבְעַת יָמִים וּבַיּוֹם הַשְּׁמִינִי עֲצֶרֶת כַּמִּשְׁפָּט: פ

ט וּבְיוֹם עֶשְׂרִים וְאַרְבָּעָה לַחֹדֶשׁ הַזֶּה נֶאֶסְפוּ בְנֵי־יִשְׂרָאֵל בְּצוֹם וּבְשַׂקִּים וַאֲדָמָה עֲלֵיהֶם: [2] וַיִּבָּדְלוּ זֶרַע יִשְׂרָאֵל מִכֹּל בְּנֵי נֵכָר וַיַּעַמְדוּ וַיִּתְוַדּוּ עַל־חַטֹּאתֵיהֶם וַעֲוֹנוֹת אֲבֹתֵיהֶם: [3] וַיָּקוּמוּ עַל־עָמְדָם וַיִּקְרְאוּ בְּסֵפֶר תּוֹרַת יְהוָה אֱלֹהֵיהֶם רְבִעִית הַיּוֹם וּרְבִעִית מִתְוַדִּים וּמִשְׁתַּחֲוִים לַיהוָה אֱלֹהֵיהֶם: פ [4] וַיָּקָם עַל־מַעֲלֵה הַלְוִיִּם יֵשׁוּעַ וּבָנִי קַדְמִיאֵל שְׁבַנְיָה בֻּנִּי שֵׁרֵבְיָה בָּנִי כְנָנִי וַיִּזְעֲקוּ בְּקוֹל גָּדוֹל אֶל־יְהוָה אֱלֹהֵיהֶם: [5] וַיֹּאמְרוּ הַלְוִיִּם יֵשׁוּעַ וְקַדְמִיאֵל בָּנִי חֲשַׁבְנְיָה שֵׁרֵבְיָה הוֹדִיָּה שְׁבַנְיָה פְתַחְיָה קוּמוּ בָּרֲכוּ אֶת־יְהוָה אֱלֹהֵיכֶם מִן־הָעוֹלָם עַד־הָעוֹלָם וִיבָרְכוּ שֵׁם כְּבוֹדֶךָ וּמְרוֹמַם עַל־כָּל־בְּרָכָה וּתְהִלָּה: [6] אַתָּה־הוּא יְהוָה לְבַדֶּךָ אַתָּ עָשִׂיתָ אֶת־הַשָּׁמַיִם שְׁמֵי הַשָּׁמַיִם וְכָל־צְבָאָם הָאָרֶץ וְכָל־אֲשֶׁר עָלֶיהָ הַיַּמִּים וְכָל־אֲשֶׁר

---

a   *Meaning of Heb. uncertain.*
b   *Heb. Jeshua.*
a   *Lit. "the heavens of the."*

everything in them. You keep them all alive, and the host of heaven prostrate themselves before You. [7] You are the LORD God, who chose Abram, who brought him out of Ur of the Chaldeans and changed his name to Abraham. [8] Finding his heart true to You, You made a covenant with him to give the land of the Canaanite, the Hittite, the Amorite, the Perizzite, the Jebusite, and the Girgashite—to give it to his descendants. And You kept Your word, for You are righteous. [9] You took note of our fathers' affliction in Egypt, and heard their cry at the Sea of Reeds. [10] You performed signs and wonders against Pharaoh, all his servants, and all the people of his land, for You knew that they acted presumptuously toward them. You made a name for Yourself that endures to this day. [11] You split the sea before them; they passed through the sea on dry land, but You threw their pursuers into the depths, like a stone into the raging waters.

[12] "You led them by day with a pillar of cloud, and by night with a pillar of fire, to give them light in the way they were to go. [13] You came down on Mount Sinai and spoke to them from heaven; You gave them right rules and true teachings, good laws and commandments. [14] You made known to them Your holy sabbath, and You ordained for them laws, commandments and Teaching, through Moses Your servant. [15] You gave them bread from heaven when they were hungry, and produced water from a rock when they were thirsty. You told them to go and possess the land that You swore to give them. [16] But they—our fathers—acted presumptuously; they stiffened their necks and did not obey Your commandments. [17] Refusing to obey, unmindful of Your wonders that You did for them, they stiffened their necks, and in their defiance resolved to return to their slavery. But You, being a forgiving God, gracious and compassionate, long-suffering and abounding in

בָּהֶם וְאַתָּה מְחַיֶּה אֶת־כֻּלָּם וּצְבָא הַשָּׁמַיִם לְךָ מִשְׁתַּחֲוִים: 7 אַתָּה־הוּא יְהֹוָה הָאֱלֹהִים אֲשֶׁר בָּחַרְתָּ בְּאַבְרָם וְהוֹצֵאתוֹ מֵאוּר כַּשְׂדִּים וְשַׂמְתָּ שְּׁמוֹ אַבְרָהָם: 8 וּמָצָאתָ אֶת־לְבָבוֹ נֶאֱמָן לְפָנֶיךָ וְכָרוֹת עִמּוֹ הַבְּרִית לָתֵת אֶת־אֶרֶץ הַכְּנַעֲנִי הַחִתִּי הָאֱמֹרִי וְהַפְּרִזִּי וְהַיְבוּסִי וְהַגִּרְגָּשִׁי לָתֵת לְזַרְעוֹ וַתָּקֶם אֶת־דְּבָרֶיךָ כִּי צַדִּיק אָתָּה: 9 וַתֵּרֶא אֶת־עֳנִי אֲבֹתֵינוּ בְּמִצְרָיִם וְאֶת־זַעֲקָתָם שָׁמַעְתָּ עַל־יַם־ סוּף: 10 וַתִּתֵּן אֹתֹת וּמֹפְתִים בְּפַרְעֹה וּבְכָל־עֲבָדָיו וּבְכָל־עַם אַרְצוֹ כִּי יָדַעְתָּ כִּי הֵזִידוּ עֲלֵיהֶם וַתַּעַשׂ־לְךָ שֵׁם כְּהַיּוֹם הַזֶּה: 11 וְהַיָּם בָּקַעְתָּ לִפְנֵיהֶם וַיַּעַבְרוּ בְתוֹךְ־ הַיָּם בַּיַּבָּשָׁה וְאֶת־רֹדְפֵיהֶם הִשְׁלַכְתָּ בִמְצוֹלֹת כְּמוֹ־אֶבֶן בְּמַיִם עַזִּים: 12 וּבְעַמּוּד עָנָן הִנְחִיתָם יוֹמָם וּבְעַמּוּד אֵשׁ לַיְלָה לְהָאִיר לָהֶם אֶת־הַדֶּרֶךְ אֲשֶׁר יֵלְכוּ־בָהּ: 13 וְעַל הַר־סִינַי יָרַדְתָּ וְדַבֵּר עִמָּהֶם מִשָּׁמָיִם וַתִּתֵּן לָהֶם מִשְׁפָּטִים יְשָׁרִים וְתוֹרוֹת אֱמֶת חֻקִּים וּמִצְוֹת טוֹבִים: 14 וְאֶת־שַׁבַּת קָדְשְׁךָ הוֹדַעְתָּ לָהֶם וּמִצְווֹת וְחֻקִּים וְתוֹרָה צִוִּיתָ לָהֶם בְּיַד מֹשֶׁה עַבְדֶּךָ: 15 וְלֶחֶם מִשָּׁמַיִם נָתַתָּה לָהֶם לִרְעָבָם וּמַיִם מִסֶּלַע הוֹצֵאתָ לָהֶם לִצְמָאָם וַתֹּאמֶר לָהֶם לָבוֹא לָרֶשֶׁת אֶת־ הָאָרֶץ אֲשֶׁר נָשָׂאתָ אֶת־יָדְךָ לָתֵת לָהֶם: 16 וְהֵם וַאֲבֹתֵינוּ הֵזִידוּ וַיַּקְשׁוּ אֶת־עָרְפָּם וְלֹא שָׁמְעוּ אֶל־מִצְוֹתֶיךָ: 17 וַיְמָאֲנוּ לִשְׁמֹעַ וְלֹא־זָכְרוּ נִפְלְאֹתֶיךָ אֲשֶׁר עָשִׂיתָ עִמָּהֶם וַיַּקְשׁוּ אֶת־עָרְפָּם וַיִּתְּנוּ־רֹאשׁ לָשׁוּב לְעַבְדֻתָם בְּמִרְיָם וְאַתָּה אֱלוֹהַּ סְלִיחוֹת חַנּוּן וְרַחוּם אֶרֶךְ־אַפַּיִם וְרַב־וְחֶסֶד חֶסֶד

faithfulness, did not abandon them. ¹⁸Even though they made themselves a molten calf and said, 'This is your God who brought you out of Egypt,' thus committing great impieties, ¹⁹You, in Your abundant compassion, did not abandon them in the wilderness. The pillar of cloud did not depart from them to lead them on the way by day, nor the pillar of fire by night to give them light in the way they were to go. ²⁰You endowed them with Your good spirit to instruct them. You did not withhold Your manna from their mouth; You gave them water when they were thirsty. ²¹Forty years You sustained them in the wilderness so that they lacked nothing; their clothes did not wear out, and their feet did not swell.

²²"You gave them kingdoms and peoples, and *b*-allotted them territory.-*b* They took possession of the land of Sihon, the land of the king of Heshbon, and the land of Og, king of Bashan. ²³You made their children as numerous as the stars of heaven, and brought them to the land which You told their fathers to go and possess. ²⁴The sons came and took possession of the land: You subdued the Canaanite inhabitants of the land before them; You delivered them into their power, both their kings and the peoples of the land, to do with them as they pleased. ²⁵They captured fortified cities and rich lands; they took possession of houses filled with every good thing, of hewn cisterns, vineyards, olive trees, and fruit trees in abundance. They ate, they were filled, they grew fat; they luxuriated in Your great bounty. ²⁶Then, defying You, they rebelled; they cast Your Teaching behind their back. They killed Your prophets who admonished them to turn them back to You; they committed great impieties.

²⁷"You delivered them into the power of their adversaries who oppressed them. In their time of trouble they cried to You; You in heaven

וְלֹא עֲזַבְתָּם: 18 אַף כִּי־עָשׂוּ לָהֶם עֵגֶל מַסֵּכָה וַיֹּאמְרוּ זֶה אֱלֹהֶיךָ אֲשֶׁר הֶעֶלְךָ מִמִּצְרָיִם וַיַּעֲשׂוּ נֶאָצוֹת גְּדֹלוֹת: 19 וְאַתָּה בְּרַחֲמֶיךָ הָרַבִּים לֹא עֲזַבְתָּם בַּמִּדְבָּר אֶת־עַמּוּד הֶעָנָן לֹא־סָר מֵעֲלֵיהֶם בְּיוֹמָם לְהַנְחֹתָם בְּהַדֶּרֶךְ וְאֶת־עַמּוּד הָאֵשׁ בְּלַיְלָה לְהָאִיר לָהֶם וְאֶת־הַדֶּרֶךְ אֲשֶׁר יֵלְכוּ־בָהּ: 20 וְרוּחֲךָ הַטּוֹבָה נָתַתָּ לְהַשְׂכִּילָם וּמַנְךָ לֹא־מָנַעְתָּ מִפִּיהֶם וּמַיִם נָתַתָּה לָהֶם לִצְמָאָם: 21 וְאַרְבָּעִים שָׁנָה כִּלְכַּלְתָּם בַּמִּדְבָּר לֹא חָסֵרוּ שַׂלְמֹתֵיהֶם לֹא בָלוּ וְרַגְלֵיהֶם לֹא בָצֵקוּ:

22 וַתִּתֵּן לָהֶם מַמְלָכוֹת וַעֲמָמִים וַתַּחְלְקֵם לְפֵאָה וַיִּירְשׁוּ אֶת־אֶרֶץ סִיחוֹן וְאֶת־אֶרֶץ מֶלֶךְ חֶשְׁבּוֹן וְאֶת־אֶרֶץ עוֹג מֶלֶךְ־הַבָּשָׁן: 23 וּבְנֵיהֶם הִרְבִּיתָ כְּכֹכְבֵי הַשָּׁמָיִם וַתְּבִיאֵם אֶל־הָאָרֶץ אֲשֶׁר־אָמַרְתָּ לַאֲבֹתֵיהֶם לָבוֹא לָרָשֶׁת: 24 וַיָּבֹאוּ הַבָּנִים וַיִּירְשׁוּ אֶת־הָאָרֶץ וַתַּכְנַע לִפְנֵיהֶם אֶת־ יֹשְׁבֵי הָאָרֶץ הַכְּנַעֲנִים וַתִּתְּנֵם בְּיָדָם וְאֶת־מַלְכֵיהֶם וְאֶת־עַמְמֵי הָאָרֶץ לַעֲשׂוֹת בָּהֶם כִּרְצוֹנָם: 25 וַיִּלְכְּדוּ עָרִים בְּצֻרוֹת וַאֲדָמָה שְׁמֵנָה וַיִּירְשׁוּ בָּתִּים מְלֵאִים כָּל־ טוּב בֹּרוֹת חֲצוּבִים כְּרָמִים וְזֵיתִים וְעֵץ מַאֲכָל לָרֹב וַיֹּאכְלוּ וַיִּשְׂבְּעוּ וַיַּשְׁמִינוּ וַיִּתְעַדְּנוּ בְּטוּבְךָ הַגָּדוֹל: 26 וַיַּמְרוּ וַיִּמְרְדוּ בָּךְ וַיַּשְׁלִכוּ אֶת־תּוֹרָתְךָ אַחֲרֵי גַוָּם וְאֶת־ נְבִיאֶיךָ הָרָגוּ אֲשֶׁר־הֵעִידוּ בָם לַהֲשִׁיבָם אֵלֶיךָ וַיַּעֲשׂוּ נֶאָצוֹת גְּדוֹלֹת:

27 וַתִּתְּנֵם בְּיַד צָרֵיהֶם וַיָּצֵרוּ לָהֶם וּבְעֵת צָרָתָם יִצְעֲקוּ אֵלֶיךָ וְאַתָּה מִשָּׁמַיִם

---

b-b Meaning of Heb. uncertain.

heard them, and in Your abundant compassion gave them saviors who saved them from the power of their adversaries. [28]But when they had relief, they again did what was evil in Your sight, so You abandoned them to the power of their enemies, who subjugated them. Again they cried to You, and You in heaven heard and rescued them in Your compassion, time after time. [29]You admonished them in order to turn them back to Your Teaching, but they acted presumptuously and disobeyed Your commandments, and sinned against Your rules, by following which a man shall live. They turned a defiant shoulder, stiffened their neck, and would not obey. [30]You bore with them for many years, admonished them by Your spirit through Your prophets, but they would not give ear, so You delivered them into the power of the peoples of the lands. [31]Still, in Your great compassion You did not make an end of them or abandon them, for You are a gracious and compassionate God.

[32]"And now, our God, great, mighty, and awesome God, who stays faithful to His covenant, do not treat lightly all the suffering that has overtaken us—our kings, our officers, our priests, our prophets, our fathers, and all Your people—from the time of the Assyrian kings to this day. [33]Surely You are in the right with respect to all that has come upon us, for You have acted faithfully, and we have been wicked. [34]Our kings, officers, priests, and fathers did not follow Your Teaching, and did not listen to Your commandments or to the warnings that You gave them. [35]When they had their own kings and enjoyed the good that You lavished upon them, and the broad and rich land that You put at their disposal, they would not serve You, and did not turn from their wicked deeds. [36]Today we are slaves, and the land that You gave our fathers to enjoy its fruit and bounty—here we

תִּשְׁמָע וּבְרַחֲמֶיךָ הָרַבִּים תִּתֵּן לָהֶם מוֹשִׁיעִים וְיוֹשִׁיעוּם מִיַּד צָרֵיהֶם: [28] וּכְנוֹחַ לָהֶם יָשׁוּבוּ לַעֲשׂוֹת רַע לְפָנֶיךָ וַתַּעַזְבֵם בְּיַד אֹיְבֵיהֶם וַיִּרְדּוּ בָהֶם וַיָּשׁוּבוּ וַיִּזְעָקוּךָ וְאַתָּה מִשָּׁמַיִם תִּשְׁמַע וְתַצִּילֵם כְּרַחֲמֶיךָ רַבּוֹת עִתִּים: [29] וַתָּעַד בָּהֶם לַהֲשִׁיבָם אֶל־תּוֹרָתֶךָ וְהֵמָּה הֵזִידוּ וְלֹא־שָׁמְעוּ לְמִצְוֹתֶיךָ וּבְמִשְׁפָּטֶיךָ חָטְאוּ־בָם אֲשֶׁר־יַעֲשֶׂה אָדָם וְחָיָה בָהֶם וַיִּתְּנוּ כָתֵף סוֹרֶרֶת וְעָרְפָּם הִקְשׁוּ וְלֹא שָׁמֵעוּ: [30] וַתִּמְשֹׁךְ עֲלֵיהֶם שָׁנִים רַבּוֹת וַתָּעַד בָּם בְּרוּחֲךָ בְּיַד־נְבִיאֶיךָ וְלֹא הֶאֱזִינוּ וַתִּתְּנֵם בְּיַד עַמֵּי הָאֲרָצֹת: [31] וּבְרַחֲמֶיךָ הָרַבִּים לֹא־עֲשִׂיתָם כָּלָה וְלֹא עֲזַבְתָּם כִּי אֵל־חַנּוּן וְרַחוּם אָתָּה: [32] וְעַתָּה אֱלֹהֵינוּ הָאֵל הַגָּדוֹל הַגִּבּוֹר וְהַנּוֹרָא שׁוֹמֵר הַבְּרִית וְהַחֶסֶד אַל־יִמְעַט לְפָנֶיךָ אֵת כָּל־הַתְּלָאָה אֲשֶׁר־מְצָאַתְנוּ לִמְלָכֵינוּ לְשָׂרֵינוּ וּלְכֹהֲנֵינוּ וְלִנְבִיאֵנוּ וְלַאֲבֹתֵינוּ וּלְכָל־עַמֶּךָ מִימֵי מַלְכֵי אַשּׁוּר עַד הַיּוֹם הַזֶּה: [33] וְאַתָּה צַדִּיק עַל כָּל־הַבָּא עָלֵינוּ כִּי־אֱמֶת עָשִׂיתָ וַאֲנַחְנוּ הִרְשָׁעְנוּ: [34] וְאֶת־מְלָכֵינוּ שָׂרֵינוּ כֹּהֲנֵינוּ וַאֲבֹתֵינוּ לֹא עָשׂוּ תּוֹרָתֶךָ וְלֹא הִקְשִׁיבוּ אֶל־מִצְוֹתֶיךָ וּלְעֵדְוֹתֶיךָ אֲשֶׁר הַעִידֹתָ בָּהֶם: [35] וְהֵם בְּמַלְכוּתָם וּבְטוּבְךָ הָרָב אֲשֶׁר־נָתַתָּ לָהֶם וּבְאֶרֶץ הָרְחָבָה וְהַשְּׁמֵנָה אֲשֶׁר־נָתַתָּ לִפְנֵיהֶם לֹא עֲבָדוּךָ וְלֹא־שָׁבוּ מִמַּעַלְלֵיהֶם הָרָעִים: [36] הִנֵּה אֲנַחְנוּ הַיּוֹם עֲבָדִים וְהָאָרֶץ אֲשֶׁר־נָתַתָּה לַאֲבֹתֵינוּ לֶאֱכֹל אֶת־פִּרְיָהּ וְאֶת־טוּבָהּ הִנֵּה אֲנַחְנוּ עֲבָדִים עָלֶיהָ: [37] וּתְבוּאָתָהּ מַרְבָּה לַמְּלָכִים אֲשֶׁר־נָתַתָּה עָלֵינוּ

are slaves on it! [37]On account of our sins it yields its abundant crops to kings whom You have set over us. They rule over our bodies and our beasts as they please, and we are in great distress.

10 "In view of all this, we make this pledge and put it in writing; and on the sealed copy [are subscribed] our officials, our Levites, and our priests.

[2]"On the sealed copy[a] [are subscribed]: Nehemiah the Tirshatha son of Hacaliah and Zedekiah, [3]Seraiah, Azariah, Jeremiah, [4]Pashhur, Amariah, Malchijah, [5]Hattush, Shebaniah, Malluch, [6]Harim, Meremoth, Obadiah, [7]Daniel, Ginnethon, Baruch, [8]Meshullam, Abijah, Mijamin, [9]Maaziah, Bilgai, Shemaiah; these are the priests.

[10]"And the Levites: Jeshua son of Azaniah, Binnui of the sons of Henadad, and Kadmiel. [11]And their brothers: Shebaniah, Hodiah, Kelita, Pelaiah, Hanan, [12]Mica, Rehob, Hashabiah, [13]Zaccur, Sherebiah, Shebaniah, [14]Hodiah, Bani, and Beninu.

[15]"The heads of the people: Parosh, Pahath-moab, Elam, Zattu, Bani, [16]Bunni, Azgad, Bebai, [17]Adonijah, Bigvai, Adin, [18]Ater, Hezekiah, Azzur, [19]Hodiah, Hashum, Bezai, [20]Hariph, Anathoth, Nebai, [21]Magpiash, Meshullam, Hezir, [22]Meshezabel, Zadok, Jaddua, [23]Pelatiah, Hanan, Anaiah, [24]Hoshea, Hananiah, Hasshub, [25]Hallohesh, Pilha, Shobek, [26]Rehum, Hashabnah, Maaseiah,[27]and Ahiah, Hanan, Anan, [28]Malluch, Harim, Baanah.

[29]"And the rest of the people, the priests, the Levites, the gatekeepers, the singers, the temple servants, and all who separated themselves from the peoples of the lands to [follow] the Teaching of God, their wives, sons and daughters, all who know enough to understand, [30]join with their

---

a Heb. plural.

בְּחַטֹּאותֵינוּ וְעַל גְּוִיֹּתֵינוּ מֹשְׁלִים
וּבִבְהֶמְתֵּנוּ כִּרְצוֹנָם וּבְצָרָה גְדוֹלָה
אֲנָחְנוּ: פ

ל וּבְכָל־זֹאת אֲנַחְנוּ כֹּרְתִים אֲמָנָה
וְכֹתְבִים וְעַל הֶחָתוּם שָׂרֵינוּ לְוִיֵּנוּ
כֹּהֲנֵינוּ:

[2] וְעַל הַחֲתוּמִים נְחֶמְיָה הַתִּרְשָׁתָא בֶּן־
חֲכַלְיָה וְצִדְקִיָּה: [3] שְׂרָיָה עֲזַרְיָה יִרְמְיָה:
[4] פַּשְׁחוּר אֲמַרְיָה מַלְכִּיָּה: [5] חַטּוּשׁ
שְׁבַנְיָה מַלּוּךְ: [6] חָרִם מְרֵמוֹת עֹבַדְיָה:
[7] דָּנִיֵּאל גִּנְּתוֹן בָּרוּךְ: [8] מְשֻׁלָּם אֲבִיָּה
מִיָּמִן: [9] מַעַזְיָה בִלְגַּי שְׁמַעְיָה אֵלֶּה
הַכֹּהֲנִים: ס

[10] וְהַלְוִיִּם וְיֵשׁוּעַ בֶּן־אֲזַנְיָה בִּנּוּי מִבְּנֵי
חֵנָדָד קַדְמִיאֵל: [11] וַאֲחֵיהֶם שְׁבַנְיָה
הוֹדִיָּה קְלִיטָא פְּלָאיָה חָנָן: [12] מִיכָא
רְחוֹב חֲשַׁבְיָה: [13] זַכּוּר שֵׁרֵבְיָה שְׁבַנְיָה:
[14] הוֹדִיָּה בָנִי בְּנִינוּ: ס

[15] רָאשֵׁי הָעָם פַּרְעֹשׁ פַּחַת מוֹאָב עֵילָם
זַתּוּא בָּנִי: [16] בֻּנִּי עַזְגָּד בֵּבָי: [17] אֲדֹנִיָּה בִגְוַי
עָדִין: [18] אָטֵר חִזְקִיָּה עַזּוּר: [19] הוֹדִיָּה
חָשֻׁם בֵּצָי: [20] חָרִיף עֲנָתוֹת נוֹבָי נֵיבָי:
[21] מַגְפִּיעָשׁ מְשֻׁלָּם חֵזִיר: [22] מְשֵׁיזַבְאֵל
צָדוֹק יַדּוּעַ: [23] פְּלַטְיָה חָנָן עֲנָיָה: [24] הוֹשֵׁעַ
חֲנַנְיָה חַשּׁוּב: [25] הַלּוֹחֵשׁ פִּלְחָא שׁוֹבֵק:
[26] רְחוּם חֲשַׁבְנָה מַעֲשֵׂיָה: [27] וַאֲחִיָּה חָנָן
עָנָן: [28] מַלּוּךְ חָרִם בַּעֲנָה:
[29] וּשְׁאָר הָעָם הַכֹּהֲנִים הַלְוִיִּם הַשּׁוֹעֲרִים
הַמְשֹׁרְרִים הַנְּתִינִים וְכָל־הַנִּבְדָּל מֵעַמֵּי
הָאֲרָצוֹת אֶל־תּוֹרַת הָאֱלֹהִים נְשֵׁיהֶם
בְּנֵיהֶם וּבְנֹתֵיהֶם כֹּל יוֹדֵעַ מֵבִין:
[30] מַחֲזִיקִים עַל־אֲחֵיהֶם אַדִּירֵיהֶם וּבָאִים

noble brothers, and take an oath with sanctions to follow the Teaching of God, given through Moses the servant of God, and to observe carefully all the commandments of the LORD our Lord, His rules and laws.

31"Namely: We will not give our daughters in marriage to the peoples of the land, or take their daughters for our sons.

32"The peoples of the land who bring their wares and all sorts of foodstuff for sale on the sabbath day—we will not buy from them on the sabbath or a holy day.

"We will forgo [the produce of] the seventh year, and every outstanding debt.

33"We have laid upon ourselves obligations: To charge ourselves one-third of a shekel yearly for the service of the House of our God—34for the rows of bread, for the regular meal offering and for the regular burnt offering, [for those of the] sabbaths, new moons, festivals, for consecrations, for sin offerings to atone for Israel, and for all the work in the House of our God.

35"We have cast lots [among] the priests, the Levites, and the people, to bring the wood offering to the House of our God by clans annually at set times in order to provide fuel for the altar of the LORD our God, as is written in the Teaching.

36"And [we undertake] to bring to the House of the LORD annually the first fruits of our soil, and of every fruit of every tree; 37also, the firstborn of our sons and our beasts, as is written in the Teaching; and to bring the firstlings of our cattle and flocks to the House of our God for the priests who minister in the House of our God.

38"We will bring to the storerooms of the House of our God the first part of our dough, and our gifts [of grain], and of the fruit of every tree, wine and oil for the priests, and the tithes

בְּאָלָה וּבִשְׁבוּעָה לָלֶכֶת בְּתוֹרַת הָאֱלֹהִים
אֲשֶׁר נִתְּנָה בְּיַד מֹשֶׁה עֶבֶד־הָאֱלֹהִים
וְלִשְׁמוֹר וְלַעֲשׂוֹת אֶת־כָּל־מִצְוֹת יְהוָה
אֲדֹנֵינוּ וּמִשְׁפָּטָיו וְחֻקָּיו:
31 וַאֲשֶׁר לֹא־נִתֵּן בְּנֹתֵינוּ לְעַמֵּי הָאָרֶץ
וְאֶת־בְּנֹתֵיהֶם לֹא נִקַּח לְבָנֵינוּ:
32 וְעַמֵּי הָאָרֶץ הַמְבִיאִים אֶת־הַמַּקָּחוֹת
וְכָל־שֶׁבֶר בְּיוֹם הַשַּׁבָּת לִמְכּוֹר לֹא־נִקַּח
מֵהֶם בַּשַּׁבָּת וּבְיוֹם קֹדֶשׁ
וְנִטֹּשׁ אֶת־הַשָּׁנָה הַשְּׁבִיעִית וּמַשָּׁא כָל־
יָד:
33 וְהֶעֱמַדְנוּ עָלֵינוּ מִצְוֹת לָתֵת עָלֵינוּ
שְׁלִשִׁית הַשֶּׁקֶל בַּשָּׁנָה לַעֲבֹדַת בֵּית
אֱלֹהֵינוּ: 34 לְלֶחֶם הַמַּעֲרֶכֶת וּמִנְחַת
הַתָּמִיד וּלְעוֹלַת הַתָּמִיד הַשַּׁבָּתוֹת
הֶחֳדָשִׁים לַמּוֹעֲדִים וְלַקֳּדָשִׁים וְלַחַטָּאוֹת
לְכַפֵּר עַל־יִשְׂרָאֵל וְכֹל מְלֶאכֶת בֵּית־
אֱלֹהֵינוּ: ס
35 וְהַגּוֹרָלוֹת הִפַּלְנוּ עַל־קֻרְבָּן* הָעֵצִים
הַכֹּהֲנִים הַלְוִיִּם וְהָעָם לְהָבִיא לְבֵית
אֱלֹהֵינוּ לְבֵית־אֲבֹתֵינוּ לְעִתִּים מְזֻמָּנִים
שָׁנָה בְשָׁנָה לְבַעֵר עַל־מִזְבַּח יְהוָה אֱלֹהֵינוּ
כַּכָּתוּב בַּתּוֹרָה:
36 וּלְהָבִיא אֶת־בִּכּוּרֵי אַדְמָתֵנוּ וּבִכּוּרֵי
כָל־פְּרִי כָל־עֵץ שָׁנָה בְשָׁנָה לְבֵית
יְהוָה: 37 וְאֶת־בְּכֹרוֹת בָּנֵינוּ וּבְהֶמְתֵּינוּ
כַּכָּתוּב בַּתּוֹרָה וְאֶת־בְּכוֹרֵי בְקָרֵינוּ
וְצֹאנֵינוּ לְהָבִיא לְבֵית אֱלֹהֵינוּ לַכֹּהֲנִים
הַמְשָׁרְתִים בְּבֵית אֱלֹהֵינוּ:
38 וְאֶת־רֵאשִׁית עֲרִיסֹתֵינוּ וּתְרוּמֹתֵינוּ
וּפְרִי כָל־עֵץ תִּירוֹשׁ וְיִצְהָר נָבִיא
לַכֹּהֲנִים אֶל־לִשְׁכוֹת בֵּית־אֱלֹהֵינוּ וּמַעְשַׂר
אַדְמָתֵנוּ לַלְוִיִּם וְהֵם הַלְוִיִּם הַמְעַשְּׂרִים

v. 35. מנוקד בקיבוץ

1880

of our land for the Levites—the Levites who collect the tithe in all our towns *b-subject to royal
service.-b* 39An Aaronite priest must be with the
Levites when they collect the tithe, and the Levites must bring up a tithe of the tithe to the
House of our God, to the storerooms of the
treasury. 40For it is to the storerooms that the
Israelites and the Levites must bring the gifts of
grain, wine, and oil. The equipment of the sanctuary and of the ministering priests and the
gatekeepers and the singers is also there.

    "We will not neglect the House of our God."

11

The officers of the people settled in Jerusalem; the rest of the people cast lots for one
out of ten to come and settle in the holy city
of Jerusalem, and the other nine-tenths to stay
in the towns. 2The people gave their blessing to
all the men who willingly settled in Jerusalem.

3These are the heads of the province who lived
in Jerusalem—in the countryside*a* of Judah, the
people lived in their towns, each on his own
property, Israelites, priests, Levites, temple servants, and the sons of Solomon's servants,
4while in Jerusalem some of the Judahites and
some of the Benjaminites lived:

    Of the Judahites: Athaiah son of Uzziah son
of Zechariah son of Amariah son of Shephatiah
son of Mahalalel, of the clan of Periz, 5and
Maaseiah son of Baruch son of Col-hozeh son
of Hazaiah son of Adaiah son of Joiarib son of
Zechariah son of the Shilohite. 6All the clan of
Periz who were living in Jerusalem—468 valorous men.

7These are the Benjaminites: Sallu son of
Meshullam son of Joed son of Pedaiah son of
Kolaiah son of Maaseiah son of Ithiel son of
Jesaiah. 8After him, Gabbai and Sallai—928.

9Joel son of Zichri was the official in charge

39 וְהָיָ֧ה הַכֹּהֵ֣ן בֶּֽן־ בְּכֹל֙ עָרֵ֣י עֲבֹדָתֵ֔נוּ:
אַהֲרֹ֛ן עִם־הַלְוִיִּ֖ם בַּעְשֵׂ֣ר הַלְוִיִּ֑ם וְהַלְוִיִּ֞ם
יַעֲל֨וּ אֶת־מַעֲשַׂ֤ר הַֽמַּעֲשֵׂר֙ לְבֵ֣ית אֱלֹהֵ֔ינוּ
אֶל־הַלְּשָׁכ֖וֹת לְבֵ֥ית הָאוֹצָֽר: 40 כִּ֣י אֶל־
הַ֠לְּשָׁכוֹת יָבִ֨יאוּ בְנֵֽי־יִשְׂרָאֵ֜ל וּבְנֵ֣י הַלֵּוִ֗י
אֶת־תְּרוּמַ֤ת הַדָּגָן֙ הַתִּיר֣וֹשׁ וְהַיִּצְהָ֔ר וְשָׁ֨ם
כְּלֵ֤י הַמִּקְדָּשׁ֙ וְהַכֹּ֣הֲנִ֔ים הַֽמְשָׁרְתִ֔ים
וְהַשּׁוֹעֲרִ֖ים וְהַמְשֹׁרְרִ֑ים
וְלֹ֥א נַעֲזֹ֖ב אֶת־בֵּ֥ית אֱלֹהֵֽינוּ:

יא וַיֵּשְׁב֥וּ שָׂרֵֽי־הָעָ֖ם בִּירוּשָׁלִָ֑ם
וּשְׁאָ֣ר הָ֠עָם הִפִּ֨ילוּ גוֹרָל֜וֹת לְהָבִ֣יא ׀
אֶחָ֣ד מִן־הָעֲשָׂרָ֗ה לָשֶׁ֙בֶת֙ בִּירֽוּשָׁלִַ֙ם֙ עִ֣יר
הַקֹּ֔דֶשׁ וְתֵ֥שַׁע הַיָּד֖וֹת בֶּעָרִֽים: 2 וַֽיְבָרֲכ֣וּ
הָעָ֑ם לְכֹל֙ הָֽאֲנָשִׁ֔ים הַמִּֽתְנַדְּבִ֖ים לָשֶׁ֣בֶת
בִּירוּשָׁלִָֽם: פ

3 וְאֵ֣לֶּה ׀ רָאשֵׁ֣י הַמְּדִינָ֗ה אֲשֶׁ֤ר יָֽשְׁבוּ֙
בִּיר֣וּשָׁלִָ֔ם וּבְעָרֵ֣י יְהוּדָ֗ה יָֽשְׁב֞וּ אִ֤ישׁ
בַּאֲחֻזָּתוֹ֙ בְּעָ֣רֵיהֶ֔ם יִשְׂרָאֵ֖ל הַכֹּהֲנִ֣ים
וְהַלְוִיִּם֙ וְהַנְּתִינִ֔ים וּבְנֵ֖י עַבְדֵ֥י שְׁלֹמֹֽה:
4 וּבִירֽוּשָׁלִַ֙ם֙ יָֽשְׁב֔וּ מִבְּנֵ֥י יְהוּדָ֖ה וּמִבְּנֵ֣י
בִנְיָמִ֑ן

מִבְּנֵ֣י יְ֠הוּדָה עֲתָיָ֨ה בֶן־עֻזִּיָּ֜ה בֶּן־זְכַרְיָ֧ה
בֶן־אֲמַרְיָ֛ה בֶּן־שְׁפַטְיָ֥ה בֶּן־מַֽהֲלַלְאֵ֖ל
מִבְּנֵי־פָֽרֶץ: 5 וּמַעֲשֵׂיָ֨ה בֶן־בָּר֪וּךְ בֶּן־
כָּל־חֹ֠זֶה בֶּן־חֲזָיָ֨ה בֶן־עֲדָיָ֧ה בֶן־יוֹיָרִ֛יב
בֶּן־זְכַרְיָ֖ה בֶּן־הַשִּׁלֹנִֽי: 6 כָּל־בְּנֵי־פֶ֕רֶץ
הַיֹּשְׁבִ֖ים בִּירוּשָׁלִָ֑ם אַרְבַּ֣ע מֵא֧וֹת שִׁשִּׁ֛ים
וּשְׁמֹנָ֖ה אַנְשֵׁי־חָֽיִל: ס

7 וְאֵ֖לֶּה בְּנֵ֣י בִנְיָמִ֑ן סַלֻּ֡א בֶּן־מְשֻׁלָּ֡ם בֶּן־
יוֹעֵ֡ד בֶּן־פְּדָיָה֩ בֶּן־ק֨וֹלָיָ֧ה בֶן־מַעֲשֵׂיָ֛ה בֶּן־
אִֽיתִיאֵ֖ל בֶּן־יְשַֽׁעְיָֽה: 8 וְאַחֲרָ֖יו גַּבַּ֣י סַלָּ֑י
תְּשַׁ֥ע מֵא֛וֹת עֶשְׂרִ֥ים וּשְׁמֹנָֽה:

of them, and Judah son of Hassenuah was the second-in-command of the city.

10Of the priests: Jedaiah son of Joiarib, Jachin, 11Seraiah son of Hilkiah son of Meshullam son of Zadok son of Meraioth son of Ahitub, chief officer of the House of God, 12and their brothers, who did the work of the House—822; and Adaiah son of Jeroham son of Pelaliah son of Amzi son of Zechariah son of Pashhur son of Malchijah, 13and his brothers, heads of clans—242; and Amashsai son of Azarel son of Ahzai son of Meshillemoth son of Immer, 14and their brothers, valorous warriors—128. Zabdiel son of Haggedolim was the official in charge of them.

15Of the Levites: Shemaiah son of Hasshub son of Azrikam son of Hashabiah son of Bunni, 16and Shabbethai and Jozabad of the heads of the Levites were in charge of the external work of the House of God. 17Mattaniah son of Micha son of Zabdi son of Asaph was the head; at prayer, he would lead off with praise; and Bakbukiah, one of his brothers, was his second-in-command; and Abda son of Shammua son of Galal son of Jeduthun. 18All the Levites in the holy city—284.

19And the gatekeepers: Akkub, Talmon, and their brothers, who stood watch at the gates—172.

20And the rest of the Israelites, the priests, and the Levites in all the towns of Judah [lived] each on his estate.

21The temple servants lived on the Ophel; Ziha and Gishpa were in charge of the temple servants.

22The overseer of the Levites in Jerusalem was Uzzi son of Bani son of Hashabiah son of Mattaniah son of Micha, of the Asaphite singers, over the work of the House of God. 23There was a royal order concerning them, a stipulation concerning the daily duties of the singers.

9 וְיוֹאֵל בֶּן־זִכְרִי פָּקִיד עֲלֵיהֶם וִיהוּדָה בֶן־הַסְּנוּאָה עַל־הָעִיר מִשְׁנֶה: פ

10 מִן־הַכֹּהֲנִים יְדַעְיָה בֶן־יוֹיָרִיב יָכִין:

11 שְׂרָיָה בֶן־חִלְקִיָּה בֶּן־מְשֻׁלָּם בֶּן־צָדוֹק בֶּן־מְרָיוֹת בֶּן־אֲחִיטוּב נְגִד בֵּית הָאֱלֹהִים:

12 וַאֲחֵיהֶם עֹשֵׂי הַמְּלָאכָה לַבַּיִת שְׁמֹנֶה מֵאוֹת עֶשְׂרִים וּשְׁנָיִם וַעֲדָיָה בֶּן־יְרֹחָם בֶּן־פְּלַלְיָה בֶּן־אַמְצִי בֶן־זְכַרְיָה בֶּן־פַּשְׁחוּר בֶּן־מַלְכִּיָּה:

13 וְאֶחָיו רָאשִׁים לְאָבוֹת מָאתַיִם אַרְבָּעִים וּשְׁנָיִם וַעֲמַשְׁסַי בֶּן־עֲזַרְאֵל בֶּן־אַחְזַי בֶּן־מְשִׁלֵּמוֹת בֶּן־אִמֵּר:

14 וַאֲחֵיהֶם גִּבּוֹרֵי חַיִל מֵאָה עֶשְׂרִים וּשְׁמֹנָה וּפָקִיד עֲלֵיהֶם זַבְדִּיאֵל בֶּן־הַגְּדוֹלִים: ס

15 וּמִן־הַלְוִיִּם שְׁמַעְיָה בֶן־חַשּׁוּב בֶּן־עַזְרִיקָם בֶּן־חֲשַׁבְיָה בֶּן־בּוּנִּי:

16 וְשַׁבְּתַי וְיוֹזָבָד עַל־הַמְּלָאכָה הַחִיצֹנָה לְבֵית הָאֱלֹהִים מֵרָאשֵׁי הַלְוִיִּם:

17 וּמַתַּנְיָה בֶן־מִיכָה בֶּן־זַבְדִּי בֶן־אָסָף רֹאשׁ הַתְּחִלָּה יְהוֹדֶה לַתְּפִלָּה וּבַקְבֻּקְיָה מִשְׁנֶה מֵאֶחָיו וְעַבְדָּא בֶּן־שַׁמּוּעַ בֶּן־גָּלָל בֶּן־יְדִיתוּן יְדוּתוּן:

18 כָּל־הַלְוִיִּם בְּעִיר הַקֹּדֶשׁ מָאתַיִם שְׁמֹנִים וְאַרְבָּעָה: פ

19 וְהַשּׁוֹעֲרִים עַקּוּב טַלְמוֹן וַאֲחֵיהֶם הַשֹּׁמְרִים בַּשְּׁעָרִים מֵאָה שִׁבְעִים וּשְׁנָיִם:

20 וּשְׁאָר יִשְׂרָאֵל הַכֹּהֲנִים הַלְוִיִּם בְּכָל־עָרֵי יְהוּדָה אִישׁ בְּנַחֲלָתוֹ:

21 וְהַנְּתִינִים יֹשְׁבִים בָּעֹפֶל וְצִיחָא וְגִשְׁפָּא עַל־הַנְּתִינִים: פ

22 וּפְקִיד הַלְוִיִּם בִּירוּשָׁלַ͏ִם עֻזִּי בֶן־בָּנִי בֶּן־חֲשַׁבְיָה בֶּן־מַתַּנְיָה בֶּן־מִיכָא מִבְּנֵי אָסָף הַמְשֹׁרְרִים לְנֶגֶד מְלֶאכֶת בֵּית־הָאֱלֹהִים:

23 כִּי־מִצְוַת הַמֶּלֶךְ עֲלֵיהֶם וַאֲמָנָה עַל־הַמְשֹׁרְרִים דְּבַר־יוֹם בְּיוֹמוֹ:

24Petahiah son of Meshezabel, of the sons of Zerah son of Judah, advised the king concerning all the affairs of the people.

25As concerns the villages with their fields: Some of the Judahites lived in Kiriath-arba and its outlying hamlets, in Dibon and its outlying hamlets, and in Jekabzeel and its villages; 26in Jeshua, in Moladah, and in Beth-pelet; 27in Hazar-shual, in Beer-sheba and its outlying hamlets; 28and in Ziklag and in Meconah and its outlying hamlets; 29in En-rimmon, in Zorah and in Jarmuth; 30Zanoah, Adullam, and their villages; Lachish and its fields; Azekah and its outlying hamlets. They settled from Beer-sheba to the Valley of Hinnom.

31The Benjaminites: from Geba, Michmash, Aija, and Bethel and its outlying hamlets; 32Anathoth, Nob, Ananiah, 33Hazor, Ramah, Gittaim, 34Hadid, Zeboim, Neballat, 35Lod, Ono, Ge-harashim. 36Some of the Judahite divisions of Levites were [shifted] to Benjamin.

12 These are the priests and the Levites who came up with Zerubbabel son of Shealtiel and Jeshua:

Seraiah, Jeremiah, Ezra, 2Amariah, Malluch, Hattush, 3Shecaniah, Rehum, Meramoth, 4Iddo, Ginnethoi, Abijah, 5Mijamin, Maadiah, Bilgah, 6Shemaiah, Joiarib, Jedaiah, 7Sallu, Amok, Hilkiah, Jedaiah. These were the heads of the priests and their brothers in the time of Jeshua.

8The Levites: Jeshua, Binnui, Kadmiel, Sherebiah, Judah, and Mattaniah, in charge of thanksgiving songs,a he and his brothers; 9and Bakbukiah and Unni [and] their brothers served opposite them by shifts.

10Jeshua begot Joiakim; Joiakim begot Eliashib; Eliashib begot Joiada; 11Joiada begot Jonathan; Jonathan begot Jaddua.

---

24 וּפְתַֽחְיָ֨ה בֶּן־מְשֵֽׁיזַבְאֵ֜ל מִבְּנֵי־זֶ֤רַח בֶּן־
יְהוּדָה֙ לְיַ֣ד הַמֶּ֔לֶךְ לְכָל־דָּבָ֖ר לָעָֽם׃
וְאֶל־הַחֲצֵרִ֖ים בִּשְׂדֹתָ֑ם מִבְּנֵ֣י יְהוּדָ֗ה 25
יָֽשְׁבוּ֙ בְּקִרְיַ֣ת הָֽאַרְבַּ֔ע וּבְנֹתֶ֖יהָ וּבְדִיבֹן֙
וּבְנֹתֶ֔יהָ וּבִיקַבְצְאֵ֖ל וַחֲצֵרֶֽיהָ׃ 26 וּבְיֵשׁ֨וּעַ
וּבְמֽוֹלָדָ֖ה וּבְבֵ֥ית פָּֽלֶט׃ 27 וּבַחֲצַ֣ר שׁוּעָ֗ל
וּבִבְאֵ֥ר שֶׁ֖בַע וּבְנֹתֶֽיהָ׃ 28 וּבְצִֽקְלַ֖ג וּבִמְכֹנָ֥ה
וּבִבְנֹתֶֽיהָ׃ 29 וּבְעֵ֥ין רִמּ֖וֹן וּבְצָרְעָ֥ה
וּבְיַרְמֽוּת׃ 30 זָנֹ֨חַ עֲדֻלָּ֜ם וְחַצְרֵיהֶ֗ם לָכִ֣ישׁ
וּשְׂדֹתֶ֔יהָ עֲזֵקָ֖ה וּבְנֹתֶ֑יהָ וַיַּחֲנ֥וּ מִבְּאֵר־
שֶׁ֖בַע עַד־גֵּֽיא־הִנֹּֽם׃
וּבְנֵ֣י בִנְיָמִ֗ן מִגֶּ֤בַע מִכְמָשׂ֙ וְעַיָּ֔ה וּבֵית־ 31
אֵ֖ל וּבְנֹתֶֽיהָ׃ 32 עֲנָת֥וֹת נֹ֖ב עֲנַנְיָֽה׃
33 חָצ֥וֹר ׀ רָמָ֖ה גִּתָּֽיִם׃ 34 חָדִ֥יד צְבֹעִ֖ים
נְבַלָּֽט׃ 35 לֹ֥ד וְאוֹנ֖וֹ גֵּ֣י הַחֲרָשִֽׁים׃ 36 וּמִן־
הַלְוִיִּ֛ם מַחְלְק֥וֹת יְהוּדָ֖ה לְבִנְיָמִֽין׃ פ

יב וְאֵ֙לֶּה֙ הַכֹּ֣הֲנִ֔ים וְהַלְוִיִּ֔ם אֲשֶׁ֥ר עָל֖וּ
עִם־זְרֻבָּבֶ֥ל בֶּן־שְׁאַלְתִּיאֵ֖ל וְיֵשׁ֑וּעַ
שְׂרָיָ֥ה יִרְמְיָ֖ה עֶזְרָֽא׃ 2 אֲמַרְיָ֥ה מַלּ֖וּךְ
חַטּֽוּשׁ׃ 3 שְׁכַנְיָ֥ה רְחֻ֖ם מְרֵמֹֽת׃ 4 עִדּ֥וֹא
גִנְּת֖וֹי אֲבִיָּֽה׃ 5 מִיָּמִ֥ין מַֽעַדְיָ֖ה בִּלְגָּֽה׃
6 שְׁמַֽעְיָ֥ה וְיוֹיָרִ֖יב יְדַֽעְיָֽה׃ 7 סַלּ֣וּ עָמ֔וֹק
חִלְקִיָּ֖ה יְדַֽעְיָ֑ה אֵ֛לֶּה רָאשֵׁ֥י הַכֹּהֲנִ֖ים
וַאֲחֵיהֶ֖ם בִּימֵ֥י יֵשֽׁוּעַ׃ פ
וְהַלְוִיִּ֗ם יֵשׁ֤וּעַ בִּנּוּי֙ קַדְמִיאֵ֣ל שֵׁרֵֽבְיָ֔ה 8
יְהוּדָ֖ה מַתַּנְיָ֑ה עַל־הֻיְּד֔וֹת ה֖וּא וְאֶחָֽיו׃
9 וּבַקְבֻּקְיָ֨ה וְעֻנּ֜וֹ אֲחֵיהֶ֛ם לְנֶגְדָּ֖ם
לְמִשְׁמָרֽוֹת׃
10 וְיֵשׁ֖וּעַ הוֹלִ֣יד אֶת־יֽוֹיָקִ֑ים וְיֽוֹיָקִ֗ים
הוֹלִ֤יד אֶת־אֶלְיָשִׁיב֙ וְאֶלְיָשִׁיב֙* אֶת־
יֽוֹיָדָ֔ע׃ 11 וְיֽוֹיָדָע֙ הוֹלִ֣יד אֶת־יֽוֹנָתָ֔ן וְיֽוֹנָתָ֖ן
הוֹלִ֥יד אֶת־יַדּֽוּעַ׃

---

a   Meaning of Heb. uncertain.   בנוסח אחר נתחבר תיבה "הוליד"   v. 10.

12In the time of Joiakim, the heads of the priestly clans were: Meriaiah—of the Seraiah clan; Hananiah—of the Jeremiah clan; 13Meshullam—of the Ezra clan; Jehohanan—of the Amariah clan; 14Jonathan—of the Melicu clan; Joseph—of the Shebaniah clan; 15Adna—of the Harim clan; Helkai—of the Meraioth clan; 16Zechariah—of the Iddo clan; Meshullam—of the Ginnethon clan; 17Zichri—of the Abijah clan ... of the Miniamin clan; Piltai—of the Moadiah clan; 18Shammua—of the Bilgah clan; Jehonathan—of the Shemaiah clan; 19Mattenai—of the Joiarib clan; Uzzi—of the Jedaiah clan; 20Kallai—of the Sallai clan; Eber—of the Amok clan; 21Hashabiah—of the Hilkiah clan; Nethanel—of the Jedaiah clan.

22The Levites and the priests were listed by heads of clans in the days of Eliashib, Joiada, Johanan, and Jaddua, down to the reign of Darius the Persian. 23But the Levite heads of clans are listed in the book of the chronicles to the time of Johanan son of Eliashib.

24The heads of the Levites: Hashabiah, Sherebiah, Jeshua son of Kadmiel, and their brothers served opposite them, singing praise and thanksgiving hymns by the ordinance of David the man of God—served opposite them in shifts; 25Mattaniah, Bakbukiah, Obadiah, Meshullam, Talmon, and Akkub, guarding as gatekeepers by shifts at the vestibules of the gates.

26These were in the time of Joiakim son of Jeshua son of Jozadak, and in the time of Nehemiah the governor, and of Ezra the priest, the scribe.

27At the dedication of the wall of Jerusalem, the Levites, wherever they lived, were sought out and brought to Jerusalem to celebrate a joyful dedication with thanksgiving and with song, accompanied by cymbals, harps, and lyres. 28The companies of singers assembled from the [Jor-

12 וּבִימֵי יוֹיָקִים הָיוּ כֹהֲנִים רָאשֵׁי הָאָבוֹת לִשְׂרָיָה מְרָיָה לְיִרְמְיָה חֲנַנְיָה: 13 לְעֶזְרָא מְשֻׁלָּם לַאֲמַרְיָה יְהוֹחָנָן: 14 למלוכי לִמְלִיכוּ יוֹנָתָן לִשְׁבַנְיָה יוֹסֵף: 15 לְחָרִם עַדְנָא לִמְרָיוֹת חֶלְקָי: 16 לַעִדּוֹא לְעִדּוֹא זְכַרְיָה לְגִנְּתוֹן מְשֻׁלָּם: 17 לַאֲבִיָּה זִכְרִי לְמִנְיָמִין לְמוֹעַדְיָה פִּלְטָי: 18 לְבִלְגָּה שַׁמּוּעַ לִשְׁמַעְיָה יְהוֹנָתָן: 19 וּלְיוֹיָרִיב מַתְּנַי לִידַעְיָה עֻזִּי: 20 לְסַלַּי קַלָּי לְעָמוֹק עֵבֶר: 21 לְחִלְקִיָּה חֲשַׁבְיָה לִידַעְיָה נְתַנְאֵל:

22 הַלְוִיִּם בִּימֵי אֶלְיָשִׁיב יוֹיָדָע וְיוֹחָנָן וְיַדּוּעַ כְּתוּבִים רָאשֵׁי אָבוֹת וְהַכֹּהֲנִים עַל־מַלְכוּת דָּרְיָוֶשׁ הַפָּרְסִי: פ 23 בְּנֵי לֵוִי רָאשֵׁי הָאָבוֹת כְּתוּבִים עַל־סֵפֶר דִּבְרֵי הַיָּמִים וְעַד־יְמֵי יוֹחָנָן בֶּן־אֶלְיָשִׁיב: 24 וְרָאשֵׁי הַלְוִיִּם חֲשַׁבְיָה שֵׁרֵבְיָה וְיֵשׁוּעַ בֶּן־קַדְמִיאֵל וַאֲחֵיהֶם לְנֶגְדָּם לְהַלֵּל לְהוֹדוֹת בְּמִצְוַת דָּוִיד אִישׁ־הָאֱלֹהִים מִשְׁמָר לְעֻמַּת מִשְׁמָר: 25 מַתַּנְיָה וּבַקְבֻּקְיָה עֹבַדְיָה מְשֻׁלָּם טַלְמוֹן עַקּוּב שֹׁמְרִים שׁוֹעֲרִים מִשְׁמָר בַּאֲסֻפֵּי הַשְּׁעָרִים: 26 אֵלֶּה בִּימֵי יוֹיָקִים בֶּן־יֵשׁוּעַ בֶּן־יוֹצָדָק וּבִימֵי נְחֶמְיָה הַפֶּחָה וְעֶזְרָא הַכֹּהֵן הַסּוֹפֵר: פ 27 וּבַחֲנֻכַּת חוֹמַת יְרוּשָׁלַ͏ִם בִּקְשׁוּ אֶת־הַלְוִיִּם מִכָּל־מְקוֹמֹתָם לַהֲבִיאָם לִירוּשָׁלָ͏ִם לַעֲשֹׂת חֲנֻכָּה וְשִׂמְחָה וּבְתוֹדוֹת וּבְשִׁיר מְצִלְתַּיִם נְבָלִים וּבְכִנֹּרוֹת: 28 וַיֵּאָסְפוּ בְּנֵי הַמְשֹׁרְרִים וּמִן־הַכִּכָּר סְבִיבוֹת יְרוּשָׁלַ͏ִם וּמִן־חַצְרֵי

dan] plain, the environs of Jerusalem, and from the Netophathite villages; [29]from Beth-hagilgal, from the countryside of Geba and Azmaveth, for the singers built themselves villages in the environs of Jerusalem.

[30]The priests and Levites purified themselves; then they purified the people, and the gates, and the wall.

[31]I had the officers of Judah go up onto the wall, and I appointed two large thanksgiving [choirs] and processions. [One marched] south on the wall, to the Dung Gate; [32]behind them were Hoshaiah and half the officers of Judah, [33]and Azariah, Ezra, Meshullam, [34]Judah, Benjamin, Shemaiah, and Jeremiah, [35]and some of the young priests, with trumpets; Zechariah son of Jonathan son of Shemaiah son of Mattaniah son of Micaiah son of Zaccur son of Asaph, [36]and his brothers Shemaiah, and Azarel, Milalai, Gilalai, Maai, Nethanel, Judah, and Hanani, with the musical instruments of David, the man of God; and Ezra the scribe went ahead of them. [37]From there to the Fountain Gate, where they ascended the steps of the City of David directly before them, by the ascent on the wall, above the house of David, [and onward] to the Water Gate on the east.

[38]The other thanksgiving [choir] marched on the wall in the opposite direction, with me and half the people behind it, above the Tower of Ovens to the Broad Wall; [39]and above the Gate of Ephraim, the Jeshanah Gate, the Fish Gate, the Tower of Hananel, the Tower of the Hundred, to the Sheep Gate; and they halted at the Gate of the Prison Compound. [40]Both thanksgiving choirs halted at the House of God, and I and half the prefects with me, [41]and the priests Eliakim, Maaseiah, Miniamin, Micaiah, Elioenai, Zechariah, Hananiah, with trumpets, [42]and Maaseiah and Shemaiah, Eleazar, Uzzi, Jehohanan, Malchijah, Elam, and Ezer. Then

נְטֹפָתִי: 29 וּמִבֵּית הַגִּלְגָּל וּמִשְּׂדוֹת גֶּבַע וְעַזְמָוֶת כִּי חֲצֵרִים בָּנוּ לָהֶם הַמְשֹׁרֲרִים סְבִיבוֹת יְרוּשָׁלָ͏ִם: 30 וַיִּטַּהֲרוּ הַכֹּהֲנִים וְהַלְוִיִּם וַיְטַהֲרוּ אֶת־הָעָם וְאֶת־הַשְּׁעָרִים וְאֶת־הַחוֹמָה: 31 וָאַעֲלֶה אֶת־שָׂרֵי יְהוּדָה מֵעַל לַחוֹמָה וָאַעֲמִידָה שְׁתֵּי תוֹדֹת גְּדוֹלֹת וְתַהֲלֻכֹת לַיָּמִין מֵעַל לַחוֹמָה לְשַׁעַר הָאַשְׁפֹּת: 32 וַיֵּלֶךְ אַחֲרֵיהֶם הוֹשַׁעְיָה וַחֲצִי שָׂרֵי יְהוּדָה: 33 וַעֲזַרְיָה עֶזְרָא וּמְשֻׁלָּם: 34 יְהוּדָה וּבִנְיָמִן וּשְׁמַעְיָה וְיִרְמְיָה: ס 35 וּמִבְּנֵי הַכֹּהֲנִים בַּחֲצֹצְרוֹת זְכַרְיָה בֶן־יוֹנָתָן בֶּן־שְׁמַעְיָה בֶּן־מַתַּנְיָה בֶּן־מִיכָיָה בֶּן־זַכּוּר בֶּן־אָסָף: 36 וְאֶחָיו שְׁמַעְיָה וַעֲזַרְאֵל מִלֲלַי גִּלֲלַי מָעַי נְתַנְאֵל וִיהוּדָה חֲנָנִי בִּכְלֵי־שִׁיר דָּוִיד אִישׁ הָאֱלֹהִים וְעֶזְרָא הַסּוֹפֵר לִפְנֵיהֶם: 37 וְעַל שַׁעַר הָעַיִן וְנֶגְדָּם עָלוּ עַל־מַעֲלוֹת עִיר דָּוִיד בַּמַּעֲלֶה לַחוֹמָה מֵעַל לְבֵית דָּוִיד וְעַד שַׁעַר הַמַּיִם מִזְרָח: 38 וְהַתּוֹדָה הַשֵּׁנִית הַהוֹלֶכֶת לְמוֹאל* וַאֲנִי אַחֲרֶיהָ וַחֲצִי הָעָם מֵעַל לְהַחוֹמָ֑ה מֵעַל לְמִגְדַּל הַתַּנּוּרִים וְעַד הַחוֹמָה הָרְחָבָה: 39 וּמֵעַל לְשַׁעַר־אֶפְרַיִם וְעַל־שַׁעַר הַיְשָׁנָה וְעַל־שַׁעַר הַדָּגִים וּמִגְדַּל חֲנַנְאֵל וּמִגְדַּל הַמֵּאָה וְעַד שַׁעַר הַצֹּאן וְעָמְדוּ בְּשַׁעַר הַמַּטָּרָה: 40 וַתַּעֲמֹדְנָה שְׁתֵּי הַתּוֹדֹת בְּבֵית הָאֱלֹהִים וַאֲנִי וַחֲצִי הַסְּגָנִים עִמִּי: 41 וְהַכֹּהֲנִים אֶלְיָקִים מַעֲשֵׂיָה מִנְיָמִין מִיכָיָה אֶלְיוֹעֵינַי זְכַרְיָה חֲנַנְיָה בַּחֲצֹצְרוֹת: 42 וּמַעֲשֵׂיָה וּשְׁמַעְיָה וְאֶלְעָזָר וְעֻזִּי וִיהוֹחָנָן וּמַלְכִּיָּה וְעֵילָם וָעָזֶר

the singers sounded forth, with Jezrahiah in charge.

⁴³On that day, they offered great sacrifices and rejoiced, for God made them rejoice greatly; the women and children also rejoiced, and the rejoicing in Jerusalem could be heard from afar.

⁴⁴At that time men were appointed over the chambers that served as treasuries for the gifts, the first fruits, and the tithes, into which the portions prescribed by the Teaching for the priests and Levites were gathered from the fields of the towns; for the people of Judah were grateful to the priests and Levites who were in attendance, ⁴⁵who kept the charge of their God and the charge of purity, as well as to the singers and gatekeepers [serving] in accord with the ordinance of David and Solomon his son—⁴⁶for the chiefs of the singers and songs of praise and thanksgiving to God already existed in the time of David and Asaph. ⁴⁷And in the time of Zerubbabel, and in the time of Nehemiah, all Israel contributed the daily portions of the singers and the gatekeepers, and made sacred contributions for the Levites, and the Levites made sacred contributions for the Aaronites.

13 At that time they read to the people from the Book of Moses, and it was found written that no Ammonite or Moabite might ever enter the congregation of God, ²since they did not meet Israel with bread and water, and hired Balaam against them to curse them; but our God turned the curse into a blessing. ³When they heard the Teaching, they separated all the alien admixture from Israel.

⁴Earlier, the priest Eliashib, a relative of Tobiah, who had been appointed over the rooms in the House of our God, ⁵had assigned to him*a* a large room where they used to store the meal offering, the frankincense, the equip-

---

וָעֵזֶר וַיַּשְׁמִיעוּ הַמְשֹׁרְרִים וְיִזְרַחְיָה הַפָּקִיד:

⁴³ וַיִּזְבְּחוּ בַיּוֹם־הַהוּא זְבָחִים גְּדוֹלִים וַיִּשְׂמָחוּ כִּי הָאֱלֹהִים שִׂמְּחָם שִׂמְחָה גְדוֹלָה וְגַם הַנָּשִׁים וְהַיְלָדִים שָׂמֵחוּ וַתִּשָּׁמַע שִׂמְחַת יְרוּשָׁלַם מֵרָחוֹק:

⁴⁴ וַיִּפָּקְדוּ בַיּוֹם הַהוּא אֲנָשִׁים עַל־הַנְּשָׁכוֹת לָאוֹצָרוֹת* לַתְּרוּמוֹת לָרֵאשִׁית וְלַמַּעַשְׂרוֹת לִכְנוֹס בָּהֶם לִשְׂדֵי הֶעָרִים מְנָאוֹת הַתּוֹרָה לַכֹּהֲנִים וְלַלְוִיִּם כִּי שִׂמְחַת יְהוּדָה עַל־הַכֹּהֲנִים וְעַל־הַלְוִיִּם הָעֹמְדִים: ⁴⁵ וַיִּשְׁמְרוּ מִשְׁמֶרֶת אֱלֹהֵיהֶם וּמִשְׁמֶרֶת הַטָּהֳרָה וְהַמְשֹׁרְרִים וְהַשֹּׁעֲרִים כְּמִצְוַת דָּוִיד שְׁלֹמֹה בְנוֹ: ⁴⁶ כִּי־בִימֵי דָוִיד וְאָסָף מִקֶּדֶם רֹאשׁ רָאשֵׁי הַמְשֹׁרְרִים וְשִׁיר־תְּהִלָּה וְהֹדוֹת לֵאלֹהִים: ⁴⁷ וְכָל־יִשְׂרָאֵל בִּימֵי זְרֻבָּבֶל וּבִימֵי נְחֶמְיָה נֹתְנִים מְנָיוֹת הַמְשֹׁרְרִים וְהַשֹּׁעֲרִים דְּבַר־יוֹם בְּיוֹמוֹ וּמַקְדִּשִׁים לַלְוִיִּם וְהַלְוִיִּם מַקְדִּשִׁים לִבְנֵי אַהֲרֹן: פ

יג בַּיּוֹם הַהוּא נִקְרָא בְּסֵפֶר מֹשֶׁה בְּאָזְנֵי הָעָם וְנִמְצָא כָּתוּב בּוֹ אֲשֶׁר לֹא־יָבוֹא עַמֹּנִי וּמֹאָבִי בִּקְהַל הָאֱלֹהִים עַד־עוֹלָם: ² כִּי לֹא קִדְּמוּ אֶת־בְּנֵי יִשְׂרָאֵל בַּלֶּחֶם וּבַמָּיִם וַיִּשְׂכֹּר עָלָיו אֶת־בִּלְעָם לְקַלְלוֹ וַיַּהֲפֹךְ אֱלֹהֵינוּ הַקְּלָלָה לִבְרָכָה: ³ וַיְהִי כְּשָׁמְעָם אֶת־הַתּוֹרָה וַיַּבְדִּילוּ כָל־עֵרֶב מִיִּשְׂרָאֵל:

⁴ וְלִפְנֵי מִזֶּה אֶלְיָשִׁיב הַכֹּהֵן נָתוּן בְּלִשְׁכַּת בֵּית־אֱלֹהֵינוּ קָרוֹב לְטוֹבִיָּה: ⁵ וַיַּעַשׂ לוֹ לִשְׁכָּה גְדוֹלָה וְשָׁם הָיוּ לְפָנִים נֹתְנִים אֶת־הַמִּנְחָה הַלְּבוֹנָה וְהַכֵּלִים וּמַעְשַׂר

---

a I.e., Tobiah.

ment, the tithes of grain, wine, and oil, the dues of the Levites, singers and gatekeepers, and the gifts for the priests. ⁶During all this time, I was not in Jerusalem, for in the thirty-second year of King Artaxerxes of Babylon, I went to the king, and only after a while did I ask leave of the king [to return]. ⁷When I arrived in Jerusalem, I learned of the outrage perpetrated by Eliashib on behalf of Tobiah in assigning him a room in the courts of the House of God. ⁸I was greatly displeased, and had all the household gear of Tobiah thrown out of the room; ⁹I gave orders to purify the rooms, and had the equipment of the House of God and the meal offering and the frankincense put back.

¹⁰I then discovered that the portions of the Levites had not been contributed, and that the Levites and the singers who performed the [temple] service had made off, each to his fields. ¹¹I censured the prefects, saying, "How is it that the House of God has been neglected?" Then I recalled [the Levites] and installed them again in their posts; ¹²and all Judah brought the tithes of grain, wine, and oil into the treasuries. ¹³I put the treasuries in the charge of the priest Shelemiah, the scribe Zadok, and Pedaiah of the Levites; and assisting them was Hanan son of Zaccur son of Mattaniah—for they were regarded as trustworthy persons, and it was their duty to distribute the portions to their brothers.

¹⁴O my God, remember me favorably for this, and do not blot out the devotion I showed toward the House of my God and its attendants.

¹⁵At that time I saw men in Judah treading winepresses on the sabbath, and others bringing heaps of grain and loading them onto asses, also wine, grapes, figs, and all sorts of goods, and bringing them into Jerusalem on the sabbath. I admonished them there and then for selling provisions. ¹⁶Tyrians who lived there brought fish and all sorts of wares and sold them on the

הַדָּגָן֩ הַתִּיר֨וֹשׁ וְהַיִּצְהָ֜ר מִצְוַ֣ת הַלְוִיִּ֗ם וְהַמְשֹׁרְרִ֖ים וְהַשֹּׁעֲרִ֑ים וּתְרוּמַ֖ת הַכֹּהֲנִֽים: ⁶וּבְכָל־זֶ֕ה לֹ֥א הָיִ֖יתִי בִּירוּשָׁלִָ֑ם כִּ֡י בִּשְׁנַת֩ שְׁלֹשִׁ֨ים וּשְׁתַּ֜יִם לְאַרְתַּחְשַׁ֤סְתְּא מֶֽלֶךְ־בָּבֶל֙ בָּ֣אתִי אֶל־הַמֶּ֔לֶךְ וּלְקֵ֥ץ יָמִ֖ים נִשְׁאַ֥לְתִּי מִן־הַמֶּֽלֶךְ: ⁷וָאָב֖וֹא לִירוּשָׁלִָ֑ם וָאָבִ֣ינָה בָרָעָ֗ה אֲשֶׁ֨ר עָשָׂ֤ה אֶלְיָשִׁיב֙ לְט֣וֹבִיָּ֔ה לַעֲשׂ֥וֹת לוֹ֙ נִשְׁכָּ֔ה בְּחַצְרֵ֖י בֵּ֥ית הָאֱלֹהִֽים: ⁸וַיֵּ֥רַע לִ֖י מְאֹ֑ד וָאַשְׁלִ֜יכָה אֶֽת־כָּל־כְּלֵ֧י בֵית־טֽוֹבִיָּ֛ה הַח֖וּץ מִן־הַלִּשְׁכָּֽה: ⁹וָאֹ֣מְרָ֔ה וַֽיְטַהֲר֖וּ הַלְּשָׁכ֑וֹת וָאָשִׁ֣יבָה שָּׁ֗ם כְּלֵי֙ בֵּ֣ית הָאֱלֹהִ֔ים אֶת־הַמִּנְחָ֖ה וְהַלְּבוֹנָֽה: פ

¹⁰וָאֵ֣דְעָ֔ה כִּֽי־מְנָי֥וֹת הַלְוִיִּ֖ם לֹ֣א נִתָּ֑נָה וַיִּבְרְח֧וּ אִישׁ־לְשָׂדֵ֛הוּ הַלְוִיִּ֥ם וְהַמְשֹׁרְרִ֖ים עֹשֵׂ֥י הַמְּלָאכָֽה: ¹¹וָאָרִ֙יבָה֙ אֶת־הַסְּגָנִ֔ים וָאֹ֣מְרָ֔ה מַדּ֖וּעַ נֶעֱזַ֣ב בֵּית־הָאֱלֹהִ֑ים וָֽאֶ֨קְבְּצֵ֔ם וָאַֽעֲמִדֵ֖ם עַל־עָמְדָֽם: ¹²וְכָל־יְהוּדָ֗ה הֵבִ֜יאוּ מַעְשַׂ֧ר הַדָּגָ֛ן וְהַתִּיר֥וֹשׁ וְהַיִּצְהָ֖ר לָאוֹצָרֽוֹת: ¹³וָאוֹצְרָ֣ה עַל־א֣וֹצָר֡וֹת שֶׁלֶמְיָ֣ה הַכֹּהֵן֩ וְצָד֨וֹק הַסּוֹפֵ֜ר וּפְדָיָ֣ה מִן־הַלְוִיִּ֗ם וְעַל־יָדָ֞ם חָנָ֧ן בֶּן־זַכּ֛וּר בֶּן־מַתַּנְיָ֖ה כִּ֣י נֶאֱמָנִ֣ים נֶחְשָׁ֑בוּ וַעֲלֵיהֶ֖ם לַחֲלֹ֥ק לַאֲחֵיהֶֽם: פ

¹⁴זָכְרָה־לִּ֥י אֱלֹהַ֖י עַל־זֹ֑את וְאַל־תֶּ֣מַח חֲסָדַ֗י אֲשֶׁ֥ר עָשִׂ֛יתִי בְּבֵ֥ית אֱלֹהַ֖י וּבְמִשְׁמָרָֽיו:

¹⁵בַּיָּמִ֣ים הָהֵ֡מָּה רָאִ֣יתִי בִֽיהוּדָ֣ה | דֹּרְכִֽים־גִּתּ֣וֹת | בַּשַּׁבָּ֡ת וּמְבִיאִ֣ים הָעֲרֵמ֣וֹת וְֽעֹמְסִ֪ים עַל־הַחֲמֹרִ֟ים וְאַף־יַ֜יִן עֲנָבִ֤ים וּתְאֵנִים֙ וְכָל־מַשָּׂ֔א וּמְבִיאִ֥ים יְרוּשָׁלִַ֖ם בְּי֣וֹם הַשַּׁבָּ֑ת וָאָעִ֕יד בְּי֖וֹם מִכְרָ֥ם צָֽיִד: ¹⁶וְהַצֹּרִים֙ יָ֣שְׁבוּ בָ֔הּ מְבִיאִ֥ים דָּ֖אג* וְכָל־מֶ֑כֶר וּמֹכְרִ֧ים בַּשַּׁבָּ֛ת לִבְנֵ֥י יְהוּדָ֖ה

v. 16. יתיר א'

sabbath to the Judahites in Jerusalem. ¹⁷I censured the nobles of Judah, saying to them, "What evil thing is this that you are doing, profaning the sabbath day! ¹⁸This is just what your ancestors did, and for it God brought all this misfortune on this city; and now you give cause for further wrath against Israel by profaning the sabbath!"

¹⁹When shadows filled the gateways of Jerusalem at the approach of the sabbath, I gave orders that the doors be closed, and ordered them not to be opened until after the sabbath. I stationed some of my servants at the gates, so that no goods should enter on the sabbath. ²⁰Once or twice the merchants and the vendors of all sorts of wares spent the night outside Jerusalem, ²¹but I warned them, saying, "What do you mean by spending the night alongside the wall? If you do so again, I will lay hands upon you!" From then on they did not come on the sabbath. ²²I gave orders to the Levites to purify themselves and come and guard the gates, to preserve the sanctity of the sabbath.

This too, O my God, remember to my credit, and spare me in accord with your abundant faithfulness.

²³Also at that time, I saw that Jews had married Ashdodite, Ammonite, and Moabite women; ²⁴a good number of their children spoke the language of Ashdod and the language of those various peoples, and did not know how to speak Judean. ²⁵I censured them, cursed them, flogged them, tore out their hair, and adjured them by God, saying, "You shall not give your daughters in marriage to their sons, or take any of their daughters for your sons or yourselves. ²⁶It was just in such things that King Solomon of Israel sinned! Among the many nations there was not a king like him, and so well loved was he by his God that God made him king of all Israel, yet foreign wives caused even

וּבִירוּשָׁלָֽ͏ִם: 17 וָאָרִ֕יבָה אֵ֖ת חֹרֵ֣י יְהוּדָ֑ה וָאֹמְרָ֣ה לָהֶ֗ם מָֽה־הַדָּבָ֨ר הָרָ֤ע הַזֶּה֙ אֲשֶׁ֣ר אַתֶּ֣ם עֹשִׂ֔ים וּֽמְחַלְּלִ֖ים אֶת־י֥וֹם הַשַּׁבָּֽת: 18 הֲל֨וֹא כֹ֤ה עָשׂוּ֙ אֲבֹ֣תֵיכֶ֔ם וַיָּבֵ֨א אֱלֹהֵ֜ינוּ עָלֵ֗ינוּ אֵ֚ת כָּל־הָרָעָ֣ה הַזֹּ֔את וְעַ֖ל הָעִ֣יר הַזֹּ֑את וְאַתֶּ֞ם מוֹסִיפִ֤ים חָרוֹן֙ עַל־יִשְׂרָאֵ֔ל לְחַלֵּ֖ל אֶת־הַשַּׁבָּֽת: פ

19 וַיְהִ֡י כַּאֲשֶׁ֣ר צָֽלֲלוּ֩ שַׁעֲרֵ֨י יְרוּשָׁלַ֜͏ִם לִפְנֵ֣י הַשַּׁבָּ֗ת וָאֹֽמְרָה֙ וַיִּסָּ֣גְר֣וּ הַדְּלָת֔וֹת וָאֹ֣מְרָ֔ה אֲשֶׁר֙ לֹ֣א יִפְתָּח֔וּם עַ֖ד אַחַ֣ר הַשַּׁבָּ֑ת וּמִנְּעָרַ֗י הֶֽעֱמַ֨דְתִּי֙ עַל־הַשְּׁעָרִ֔ים לֹא־יָב֥וֹא מַשָּׂ֖א בְּי֥וֹם הַשַּׁבָּֽת: 20 וַיָּלִ֨ינוּ הָרֹכְלִ֜ים וּמֹכְרֵ֧י כָל־מִמְכָּ֛ר מִח֥וּץ לִירוּשָׁלָ֖͏ִם פַּ֥עַם וּשְׁתָּֽיִם: 21 וָאָעִ֣ידָה בָהֶ֗ם וָאֹמְרָ֤ה אֲלֵיהֶם֙ מַדּ֜וּעַ אַתֶּ֤ם לֵנִים֙ נֶ֣גֶד הַחוֹמָ֔ה אִם־תִּשְׁנ֕וּ יָ֖ד אֶשְׁלַ֣ח בָּכֶ֑ם מִן־הָעֵ֣ת הַהִ֔יא לֹא־בָ֖אוּ בַּשַּׁבָּֽת: ס 22 וָאֹמְרָ֣ה לַלְוִיִּ֗ם אֲשֶׁ֨ר יִֽהְי֤וּ מִֽטַּהֲרִים֙ וּבָאִים֙ שֹׁמְרִ֣ים הַשְּׁעָרִ֔ים לְקַדֵּ֖שׁ אֶת־י֣וֹם הַשַּׁבָּ֑ת

גַּם־זֹאת֙ זָכְרָה־לִּ֣י אֱלֹהַ֔י וְח֥וּסָה עָלַ֖י כְּרֹ֥ב חַסְדֶּֽךָ: פ

23 גַּ֣ם ׀ בַּיָּמִ֣ים הָהֵ֗ם רָאִ֤יתִי אֶת־הַיְּהוּדִים֙ הֹשִׁ֗יבוּ נָשִׁים֙ אשדודיות [אַשְׁדֳּדִיּ֔וֹת] עמוניות [עַמֳּנִיּ֖וֹת] מוֹאֲבִיּֽוֹת: 24 וּבְנֵיהֶ֗ם חֲצִי֙ מְדַבֵּ֣ר אַשְׁדּוֹדִ֔ית וְאֵינָ֥ם מַכִּירִ֖ים לְדַבֵּ֣ר יְהוּדִ֑ית וְכִלְשׁ֥וֹן עַ֥ם וָעָֽם: 25 וָאָרִ֤יב עִמָּם֙ וָאֲקַֽלְלֵ֔ם וָאַכֶּ֥ה מֵהֶ֛ם אֲנָשִׁ֖ים וָאֶמְרְטֵ֑ם וָאַשְׁבִּיעֵ֣ם בֵּֽאלֹהִ֗ים אִם־תִּתְּנ֤וּ בְנֹֽתֵיכֶם֙ לִבְנֵיהֶ֔ם וְאִם־תִּשְׂאוּ֙ מִבְּנֹ֣תֵיהֶ֔ם לִבְנֵיכֶ֖ם וְלָכֶֽם: 26 הֲל֣וֹא עַל־אֵ֣לֶּה חָטָֽא־שְׁלֹמֹ֣ה מֶ֣לֶךְ יִשְׂרָאֵ֗ל וּבַגּוֹיִ֤ם הָרַבִּים֙ לֹֽא־הָיָ֣ה מֶ֔לֶךְ כָּמֹ֗הוּ וְאָה֤וּב לֵֽאלֹהָיו֙ הָיָ֔ה וַיִּתְּנֵ֣הוּ אֱלֹהִ֔ים מֶ֖לֶךְ עַל־כָּל־יִשְׂרָאֵ֑ל גַּם־אוֹת֣וֹ

him to sin. 27How, then, can we acquiesce in your doing this great wrong, breaking faith with our God by marrying foreign women?" 28One of the sons of Joiada son of the high priest Eliashib was a son-in-law of Sanballat the Horonite; I drove him away from me.

29Remember to their discredit, O my God, how they polluted the priesthood, the covenant of the priests and Levites. 30I purged them of every foreign element, and arranged for the priests and the Levites to work each at his task by shifts, 31and for the wood offering [to be brought] at fixed times and for the first fruits.

O my God, remember it to my credit!

27 וְלָכֶם הַחֱטִיאוּ הַנָּשִׁים הַנָּכְרִיּֽוֹת: הֲנִשְׁמַע לַעֲשֹׂת אֵת כָּל־הָרָעָה הַגְּדוֹלָה הַזֹּאת לִמְעֹל בֵּאלֹהֵינוּ לְהֹשִׁיב נָשִׁים נָכְרִיּֽוֹת: 28 וּמִבְּנֵי יוֹיָדָע בֶּן־אֶלְיָשִׁיב הַכֹּהֵן הַגָּדוֹל חָתָן לְסַנְבַלַּט הַחֹרֹנִי וָאַבְרִיחֵהוּ מֵעָלָֽי:

29 זָכְרָה לָהֶם אֱלֹהָי עַל גָּאֳלֵי הַכְּהֻנָּה וּבְרִית הַכְּהֻנָּה וְהַלְוִיִּֽם: 30 וְטִֽהַרְתִּים מִכָּל־נֵכָר וָאַעֲמִידָה מִשְׁמָרוֹת לַכֹּהֲנִים וְלַלְוִיִּם אִישׁ בִּמְלַאכְתּֽוֹ: 31 וּלְקֻרְבַּן* הָעֵצִים בְּעִתִּים מְזֻמָּנוֹת וְלַבִּכּוּרִים זָכְרָה־לִּי אֱלֹהַי לְטוֹבָֽה:*

תם ונשלם תהילה לאל בורא עולם

1 CHRONICLES

1 Adam, Seth, Enosh; ²Kenan, Mahalalel, Jared; ³Enoch, Methuselah, Lamech; ⁴Noah, Shem, Ham, and Japheth.

⁵*a*The sons of Japheth: Gomer, Magog, Madai, Javan, Tubal, Meshech, and Tiras. ⁶The sons of Gomer: Ashkenaz, Diphath, and Togarmah. ⁷The sons of Javan: Elishah, Tarshish, Kittim, and Rodanim.

⁸The sons of Ham: Cush, Mizraim, Put, and Canaan. ⁹The sons of Cush: Seba, Havilah, Sabta, Raama, and Sabteca. The sons of Raama: Sheba and Dedan. ¹⁰Cush begot Nimrod; he was the first mighty one on earth.

¹¹Mizraim begot the Ludim, the Anamim, the Lehabim, the Naphtuhim, ¹²the Pathrusim, the Casluhim (whence the Philistines came forth), and the Caphtorim.

¹³Canaan begot Sidon his first-born, and Heth, ¹⁴and the Jebusites, the Amorites, the Girgashites, ¹⁵the Hivites, the Arkites, the Sinites, ¹⁶the Arvadites, the Zemarites, and the Hamathites.

¹⁷The sons of Shem: Elam, Asshur, Arpachshad, Lud, Aram, Uz, Hul, Gether, and Meshech. ¹⁸Arpachshad begot Shelah; and Shelah begot Eber. ¹⁹Two sons were born to Eber: the name of the one was Peleg (for in his days the earth was divided), and the name of his brother Joktan. ²⁰Joktan begot Almodad,

אָדָם שֵׁת אֱנֽוֹשׁ׃ 2 קֵינָן מַהֲלַלְאֵל
יָֽרֶד׃ 3 חֲנוֹךְ מְתוּשֶׁלַח לָֽמֶךְ׃ 4 נֹחַ שֵׁם חָם
וָיָֽפֶת׃ ס
5 בְּנֵי יֶפֶת גֹּמֶר וּמָגוֹג וּמָדַי וְיָוָן וְתֻבָל
וּמֶשֶׁךְ וְתִירָֽס׃ ס 6 וּבְנֵי גֹּמֶר אַשְׁכֲּנַז
וְדִיפַת וְתוֹגַרְמָֽה׃ 7 וּבְנֵי יָוָן אֱלִישָׁה
וְתַרְשִׁישָׁה כִּתִּים וְרוֹדָנִֽים׃ ס
8 בְּנֵי חָם כּוּשׁ וּמִצְרַיִם פּוּט וּכְנָֽעַן׃ 9 וּבְנֵי
כוּשׁ סְבָא וַחֲוִילָה וְסַבְתָּא וְרַעְמָא
וְסַבְתְּכָא וּבְנֵי רַעְמָא שְׁבָא וּדְדָֽן׃ ס
10 וְכוּשׁ יָלַד אֶת־נִמְרוֹד הוּא הֵחֵל לִהְיוֹת
גִּבּוֹר בָּאָֽרֶץ׃ ס
11 וּמִצְרַיִם יָלַד אֶת־לוּדִים וְאֶת־
עֲנָמִים וְאֶת־לְהָבִים וְאֶת־נַפְתֻּחִֽים׃
12 וְאֶת־פַּתְרֻסִים וְאֶת־כַּסְלֻחִים אֲשֶׁר
יָצְאוּ מִשָּׁם פְּלִשְׁתִּים וְאֶת־כַּפְתֹּרִֽים׃ ס
13 וּכְנַעַן יָלַד אֶת־צִידוֹן בְּכֹרוֹ וְאֶת־חֵֽת׃
14 וְאֶת־הַיְבוּסִי וְאֶת־הָאֱמֹרִי וְאֶת
הַגִּרְגָּשִֽׁי׃ 15 וְאֶת־הַחִוִּי וְאֶת־הָעַרְקִי וְאֶת־
הַסִּינִֽי׃ 16 וְאֶת־הָאַרְוָדִי וְאֶת־הַצְּמָרִי
וְאֶת־הַחֲמָתִֽי׃ ס
17 בְּנֵי שֵׁם עֵילָם וְאַשּׁוּר וְאַרְפַּכְשַׁד וְלוּד
וַאֲרָם וְעוּץ וְחוּל וְגֶתֶר וָמֶֽשֶׁךְ׃ ס
18 וְאַרְפַּכְשַׁד יָלַד אֶת־שָׁלַח וְשֶׁלַח יָלַד
אֶת־עֵֽבֶר׃ 19 וּלְעֵבֶר יֻלַּד שְׁנֵי בָנִים שֵׁם
הָאֶחָד פֶּלֶג כִּי בְיָמָיו נִפְלְגָה הָאָרֶץ וְשֵׁם
אָחִיו יָקְטָֽן׃ 20 וְיָקְטָן יָלַד אֶת־אַלְמוֹדָד
וְאֶת־שָׁלֶף וְאֶת־חֲצַרְמָוֶת וְאֶת־יָֽרַח׃
21 וְאֶת־הֲדוֹרָם וְאֶת־אוּזָל וְאֶת־דִּקְלָֽה׃

---

a   With vv. 5–23, cf. Gen. 10.1–30.

Sheleph, Hazarmaveth, Jerah, [21]Hadoram, Uzal, Diklah, [22]Ebal, Abimael, Sheba, [23]Ophir, Havilah, and Jobab; all these were the sons of Joktan.

[24]Shem, Arpachshad, Shelah; [25]Eber, Peleg, Reu; [26]Serug, Nahor, Terah; [27]Abram, that is, Abraham.

[28b]The sons of Abraham: Isaac and Ishmael. [29]This is their line: The first-born of Ishmael, Nebaioth; and Kedar, Abdeel, Mibsam, [30]Mishma, Dumah, Massa, Hadad, Tema, [31]Jetur, Naphish, and Kedmah. These are the sons of Ishmael. [32]The sons of Keturah, Abraham's concubine: she bore Zimran, Jokshan, Medan, Midian, Ishbak, and Shuah. The sons of Jokshan: Sheba and Dedan. [33]The sons of Midian: Ephah, Epher, Enoch, Abida, and Eldaah. All these were the descendants of Keturah.

[34]Abraham begot Isaac. The sons of Isaac: Esau and Israel. [35]The sons of Esau: Eliphaz, Reuel, Jeush, Jalam, and Korah. [36]The sons of Eliphaz: Teman, Omar, Zephi, Gatam, Kenaz, Timna, and Amalek. [37]The sons of Reuel: Nahath, Zerah, Shammah, and Mizzah.

[38]The sons of Seir: Lotan, Shobal, Zibeon, Anah, Dishon, Ezer, and Dishan. [39]The sons of Lotan: Hori and Homam; and Lotan's sister was Timna. [40]The sons of Shobal: Alian, Manahath, Ebal, Shephi, and Onam. The sons of Zibeon: Aiah and Anah. [41]The sons of Anah: Dishon. The sons of Dishon: Hamran, Eshban, Ithran, and Cheran. [42]The sons of Ezer: Bilhan, Zaavan, and Jaakan. The sons of Dishan: Uz and Aran.

[43c]These are the kings who reigned in the land of Edom before any king reigned over the Israelites: Bela son of Beor, and the name of his city was Dinhabah. [44]When Bela died, Jobab son of Zerah from Bozrah succeeded him as king. [45]When Jobab died, Husham of the land of the

---

b   With vv. 28–33, cf. Gen. 25.1–16.
c   With vv. 43–50, cf. Gen. 36.31–43.

כתובים דברי הימים א א

22 וְאֶת־עֵיבָל וְאֶת־אֲבִימָאֵל וְאֶת־שְׁבָא׃
23 וְאֶת־אוֹפִיר וְאֶת־חֲוִילָה וְאֶת־יוֹבָב
כָּל־אֵלֶּה בְּנֵי יׇקְטָן׃ ס 25 עֵבֶר פֶּלֶג רְעוּ׃
24 שֵׁם ׀ אַרְפַּכְשַׁד שָׁלַח׃
26 שְׂרוּג נָחוֹר תָּרַח׃ 27 אַבְרָם הוּא
אַבְרָהָם׃ ס

28 בְּנֵי אַבְרָהָם יִצְחָק וְיִשְׁמָעֵאל׃ ס
29 אֵלֶּה תֹּלְדֹתָם בְּכוֹר יִשְׁמָעֵאל נְבָיוֹת
וְקֵדָר וְאַדְבְּאֵל וּמִבְשָׂם׃ 30 מִשְׁמָע וְדוּמָה
מַשָּׂא חֲדַד וְתֵימָא׃ 31 יְטוּר נָפִישׁ וָקֵדְמָה
אֵלֶּה הֵם בְּנֵי יִשְׁמָעֵאל׃ ס 32 וּבְנֵי
קְטוּרָה פִּילֶגֶשׁ אַבְרָהָם יָלְדָה אֶת־זִמְרָן
וְיׇקְשָׁן וּמְדָן וּמִדְיָן וְיִשְׁבָּק וְשׁוּחַ וּבְנֵי יׇקְשָׁן
שְׁבָא וּדְדָן׃ ס 33 וּבְנֵי מִדְיָן עֵיפָה וָעֵפֶר
וַחֲנוֹךְ וַאֲבִידָע וְאֶלְדָּעָה כָּל־אֵלֶּה בְּנֵי
קְטוּרָה׃ ס

34 וַיּוֹלֶד אַבְרָהָם אֶת־יִצְחָק ס בְּנֵי
יִצְחָק עֵשָׂו וְיִשְׂרָאֵל׃ ס 35 בְּנֵי עֵשָׂו
אֱלִיפַז רְעוּאֵל וִיעוּשׁ וְיַעְלָם וְקֹרַח׃ ס
36 בְּנֵי אֱלִיפַז תֵּימָן וְאוֹמָר צְפִי וְגַעְתָּם
קְנַז וְתִמְנָע וַעֲמָלֵק׃ ס 37 בְּנֵי רְעוּאֵל
נַחַת זֶרַח שַׁמָּה וּמִזָּה׃ ס

38 וּבְנֵי שֵׂעִיר לוֹטָן וְשׁוֹבָל וְצִבְעוֹן וַעֲנָה
וְדִישֹׁן וְאֵצֶר וְדִישָׁן׃ 39 וּבְנֵי לוֹטָן חֹרִי
וְהוֹמָם וַאֲחוֹת לוֹטָן תִּמְנָע׃ ס 40 בְּנֵי
שׁוֹבָל עַלְיָן וּמָנַחַת וְעֵיבָל שְׁפִי
וְאוֹנָם ס וּבְנֵי צִבְעוֹן אַיָּה וַעֲנָה׃ 41 בְּנֵי
עֲנָה דִּישׁוֹן ס וּבְנֵי דִישׁוֹן חַמְרָן וְאֶשְׁבָּן
וְיִתְרָן וּכְרָן׃ ס 42 בְּנֵי־אֵצֶר בִּלְהָן וְזַעֲוָן
יַעֲקָן בְּנֵי דִישׁוֹן עוּץ וַאֲרָן׃ פ

43 וְאֵלֶּה הַמְּלָכִים אֲשֶׁר מָלְכוּ בְּאֶרֶץ
אֱדוֹם לִפְנֵי מְלׇךְ־מֶלֶךְ לִבְנֵי יִשְׂרָאֵל בֶּלַע
בֶּן־בְּעוֹר וְשֵׁם עִירוֹ דִּנְהָבָה׃ 44 וַיָּמׇת בֶּלַע
וַיִּמְלֹךְ תַּחְתָּיו יוֹבָב בֶּן־זֶרַח מִבׇּצְרָה׃
45 וַיָּמׇת יוֹבָב וַיִּמְלֹךְ תַּחְתָּיו חוּשָׁם מֵאֶרֶץ

Temanites succeeded him as king. ⁴⁶When Husham died, Hadad son of Bedad, who defeated the Midianites in the country of Moab, succeeded him as king, and the name of his city was Avith. ⁴⁷When Hadad died, Samlah of Masrekah succeeded him as king. ⁴⁸When Samlah died, Saul of Rehoboth-on-the-River succeeded him as king. ⁴⁹When Saul died, Baal-hanan son of Achbor succeeded him as king. ⁵⁰When Baal-hanan died, Hadad succeeded him as king; and the name of his city was Pai, and his wife's name Mehetabel daughter of Matred daughter of Me-zahab. ⁵¹And Hadad died.

The clans of Edom were the clans of Timna, Alvah, Jetheth, ⁵²Oholibamah, Elah, Pinon, ⁵³Kenaz, Teman, Mibzar, ⁵⁴Magdiel, and Iram; these are the clans of Edom.

2 These are the sons of Israel: Reuben, Simeon, Levi, Judah, Issachar, Zebulun, ²Dan, Joseph, Benjamin, Naphtali, Gad, and Asher. ³The sons of Judah: Er, Onan, and Shelah; these three, Bath-shua the Canaanite woman bore to him. But Er, Judah's first-born, was displeasing to the Lord, and He took his life. ⁴His daughter-in-law Tamar also bore him Perez and Zerah. Judah's sons were five in all.

⁵The sons of Perez: Hezron and Hamul. ⁶The sons of Zerah: Zimri, Ethan, Heman, Calcol, and Dara, five in all. ⁷The sons of Carmi: Achar, the troubler of Israel, who committed a trespass against the proscribed thing; ⁸and Ethan's son was Azariah.

⁹The sons of Hezron that were born to him: Jerahmeel, Ram, and Chelubai. ¹⁰Ram begot Amminadab, and Amminadab begot Nahshon, prince of the sons of Judah. ¹¹Nahshon was the father of Salma, Salma of Boaz, ¹²Boaz of Obed, Obed of Jesse. ¹³Jesse begot Eliab his first-born,

הַתֵּימָנִי: 46 וַיָּמָת חוּשָׁם וַיִּמְלֹךְ תַּחְתָּיו הֲדַד בֶּן־בְּדַד הַמַּכֶּה אֶת־מִדְיָן בִּשְׂדֵה מוֹאָב וְשֵׁם עִירוֹ עיות עֲוִית: 47 וַיָּמָת הֲדָד וַיִּמְלֹךְ תַּחְתָּיו שַׂמְלָה מִמַּשְׂרֵקָה: 48 וַיָּמָת שַׂמְלָה וַיִּמְלֹךְ תַּחְתָּיו שָׁאוּל מֵרְחֹבוֹת הַנָּהָר: 49 וַיָּמָת שָׁאוּל וַיִּמְלֹךְ תַּחְתָּיו בַּעַל חָנָן בֶּן־עַכְבּוֹר: 50 וַיָּמָת בַּעַל חָנָן וַיִּמְלֹךְ תַּחְתָּיו הֲדַד וְשֵׁם עִירוֹ פָּעִי וְשֵׁם אִשְׁתּוֹ מְהֵיטַבְאֵל בַּת־מַטְרֵד בַּת מֵי זָהָב: 51 וַיָּמָת הֲדָד ס

וַיִּהְיוּ אַלּוּפֵי אֱדוֹם אַלּוּף תִּמְנָע אַלּוּף עַלְיָה אַלּוּף יְתֵת: 52 אַלּוּף אָהֳלִיבָמָה אַלּוּף אֵלָה אַלּוּף פִּינֹן: 53 אַלּוּף קְנַז אַלּוּף תֵּימָן אַלּוּף מִבְצָר: 54 אַלּוּף מַגְדִּיאֵל אַלּוּף עִירָם אֵלֶּה אַלּוּפֵי אֱדוֹם: פ

ב אֵלֶּה בְּנֵי יִשְׂרָאֵל רְאוּבֵן שִׁמְעוֹן לֵוִי וִיהוּדָה יִשָּׂשכָר וּזְבֻלוּן: 2 דָּן יוֹסֵף וּבִנְיָמִן נַפְתָּלִי גָּד וְאָשֵׁר: ס 3 בְּנֵי יְהוּדָה עֵר וְאוֹנָן וְשֵׁלָה שְׁלוֹשָׁה נוֹלַד לוֹ מִבַּת־שׁוּעַ הַכְּנַעֲנִית וַיְהִי עֵר ׀ בְּכוֹר יְהוּדָה רַע בְּעֵינֵי יְהוָה וַיְמִיתֵהוּ: ס 4 וְתָמָר כַּלָּתוֹ יָלְדָה לּוֹ אֶת־פֶּרֶץ וְאֶת־זָרַח כָּל־בְּנֵי יְהוּדָה חֲמִשָּׁה: ס

5 בְּנֵי־פֶרֶץ חֶצְרוֹן וְחָמוּל: ס 6 וּבְנֵי זֶרַח זִמְרִי וְאֵיתָן וְהֵימָן וְכַלְכֹּל וָדָרַע כֻּלָּם חֲמִשָּׁה: ס 7 וּבְנֵי כַּרְמִי עָכָר עוֹכֵר יִשְׂרָאֵל אֲשֶׁר מָעַל בַּחֵרֶם: ס 8 וּבְנֵי אֵיתָן עֲזַרְיָה:

9 וּבְנֵי חֶצְרוֹן אֲשֶׁר נוֹלַד־לוֹ אֶת־יְרַחְמְאֵל וְאֶת־רָם וְאֶת־כְּלוּבָי: 10 וְרָם הוֹלִיד אֶת־עַמִּינָדָב וְעַמִּינָדָב הוֹלִיד אֶת־נַחְשׁוֹן נְשִׂיא בְּנֵי יְהוּדָה: 11 וְנַחְשׁוֹן הוֹלִיד אֶת־שַׂלְמָא וְשַׂלְמָא הוֹלִיד אֶת־בֹּעַז: 12 וּבֹעַז הוֹלִיד אֶת־עוֹבֵד וְעוֹבֵד הוֹלִיד אֶת־יִשָׁי:

Abinadab the second, Shimea the third, ¹⁴Nethanel the fourth, Raddai the fifth, ¹⁵Ozem the sixth, David the seventh; ¹⁶their sisters were Zeruiah and Abigail. The sons of Zeruiah: Abishai, Joab, and Asahel, three. ¹⁷Abigail bore Amasa, and the father of Amasa was Jether the Ishmaelite.

¹⁸Caleb son of Hezron had children by his wife Azubah, and by Jerioth; these were her sons: Jesher, Shobab, and Ardon. ¹⁹When Azubah died, Caleb married Ephrath, who bore him Hur. ²⁰Hur begot Uri, and Uri begot Bezalel.

²¹Afterward Hezron had relations with the daughter of Machir father of Gilead—he had married her when he was sixty years old—and she bore him Segub; ²²and Segub begot Jair; he had twenty-three cities in the land of Gilead. ²³But Geshur and Aram took from them Havvoth-jair, Kenath and its dependencies, sixty towns. All these were the sons of Machir, the father of Gilead. ²⁴After the death of Hezron, in Caleb-ephrathah, Abijah, wife of Hezron, bore Ashhur, the father of Tekoa.

²⁵The sons of Jerahmeel the first-born of Hezron: Ram his first-born, Bunah, Oren, Ozem, and Ahijah. ²⁶Jerahmeel had another wife, whose name was Atarah; she was the mother of Onam. ²⁷The sons of Ram the first-born of Jerahmeel: Maaz, Jamin, and Eker. ²⁸The sons of Onam: Shammai and Jada. The sons of Shammai: Nadab and Abishur. ²⁹The name of Abishur's wife was Abihail, and she bore him Ahban and Molid. ³⁰The sons of Nadab: Seled and Appaim; Seled died childless. ³¹The sons of Appaim: Ishi. The sons of Ishi: Sheshan. The sons of Sheshan: Ahlai. ³²The sons of Jada, Shammai's brother: Jether and Jona-

13 וְאִישַׁי* הוֹלִיד אֶת־בְּכֹרוֹ אֶת־אֱלִיאָב
וַאֲבִינָדָב֙ הַשֵּׁנִ֔י וְשִׁמְעָ֖א הַשְּׁלִשִֽׁי׃
14 נְתַנְאֵ֣ל הָֽרְבִיעִ֔י רַדַּ֖י הַֽחֲמִישִֽׁי׃ 15 אֹ֤צֶם
הַשִּׁשִּׁי֙ דָּוִ֣יד הַשְּׁבִעִֽי׃ 16 וְאַחְיֹתֵיהֶ֖ם
צְרוּיָ֣ה וַֽאֲבִיגָ֑יִל וּבְנֵ֣י צְרוּיָ֗ה
אַבְשַׁ֤י וְיוֹאָב֙ וַֽעֲשָׂהאֵ֔ל שְׁלֹשָֽׁה׃
17 וַֽאֲבִיגַ֙יִל֙ יָֽלְדָ֣ה אֶת־עֲמָשָׂ֔א וַֽאֲבִ֖י
עֲמָשָׂ֑א יֶ֖תֶר הַיִּשְׁמְעֵאלִֽי׃
18 וְכָלֵ֣ב בֶּן־חֶצְר֗וֹן הוֹלִ֛יד אֶת־עֲזוּבָ֥ה
אִשָּׁ֖ה וְאֶת־יְרִיע֑וֹת וְאֵ֣לֶּה בָנֶ֔יהָ יֵ֥שֶׁר
וְשׁוֹבָ֖ב וְאַרְדּֽוֹן׃ 19 וַתָּ֣מָת עֲזוּבָ֔ה וַיִּֽקַּֽח־ל֤וֹ
כָלֵב֙ אֶת־אֶפְרָ֔ת וַתֵּ֥לֶד ל֖וֹ אֶת־חֽוּר׃
20 וְח֕וּר הוֹלִ֖יד אֶת־אוּרִ֑י וְאוּרִ֖י הוֹלִ֥יד
אֶת־בְּצַלְאֵֽל׃ ס
21 וְאַחַ֗ר בָּ֤א חֶצְרוֹן֙ אֶל־בַּת־מָכִיר֙ אֲבִ֣י
גִלְעָ֔ד וְה֣וּא לְקָחָ֔הּ וְה֖וּא בֶּן־שִׁשִּׁ֣ים שָׁנָ֑ה
וַתֵּ֥לֶד ל֖וֹ אֶת־שְׂגֽוּב׃ 22 וּשְׂג֖וּב הוֹלִ֣יד
אֶת־יָאִ֑יר וַֽיְהִי־ל֗וֹ עֶשְׂרִ֤ים וְשָׁלוֹשׁ֙ עָרִ֔ים
בְּאֶ֖רֶץ הַגִּלְעָֽד׃ 23 וַיִּקַּ֣ח גְּשֽׁוּר־וַֽאֲרָם֩ אֶת־
חַוֺּ֙ת יָאִ֜יר מֵֽאִתָּ֗ם אֶת־קְנָ֛ת וְאֶת־בְּנֹתֶ֖יהָ
שִׁשִּׁ֣ים עִ֑יר כָּל־אֵ֕לֶּה בְּנֵ֖י מָכִ֥יר אֲבִי־
גִלְעָֽד׃ 24 וְאַחַ֣ר מוֹת־חֶצְרוֹן֮ בְּכָלֵ֣ב
אֶפְרָ֒תָה֒ וְאֵ֣שֶׁת חֶצְרוֹן֙ אֲבִיָּ֔ה וַתֵּ֣לֶד ל֔וֹ
אֶת־אַשְׁח֖וּר אֲבִ֥י תְקֽוֹעַ׃
25 וַיִּֽהְי֤וּ בְנֵי־יְרַחְמְאֵל֙ בְּכ֣וֹר חֶצְר֔וֹן
הַבְּכ֖וֹר ׀ רָ֣ם וּבוּנָ֑ה וָאֹ֖רֶן וָאֹ֥צֶם אֲחִיָּֽה׃
26 וַתְּהִ֨י אִשָּׁ֥ה אַחֶ֛רֶת לִֽירַחְמְאֵ֖ל וּשְׁמָ֣הּ
עֲטָרָ֑ה הִ֖יא אֵ֥ם אוֹנָֽם׃ 27 ס וַיִּֽהְי֥וּ בְנֵֽי־
רָ֖ם בְּכ֣וֹר יְרַחְמְאֵ֑ל מַ֥עַץ וְיָמִ֖ין וָעֵֽקֶר׃
28 וַיִּֽהְי֥וּ בְנֵֽי־אוֹנָ֖ם שַׁמַּ֣י וְיָדָ֑ע וּבְנֵ֣י שַׁמַּ֔י
נָדָ֖ב וַֽאֲבִישֽׁוּר׃ 29 וְשֵׁ֛ם אֵ֥שֶׁת אֲבִישׁ֖וּר
אֲבִיהָ֑יִל וַתֵּ֣לֶד ל֔וֹ אֶת־אַחְבָּ֖ן וְאֶת־מוֹלִֽיד׃
30 וּבְנֵ֣י נָדָ֔ב סֶ֖לֶד וְאַפָּ֑יִם וַיָּ֥מָת סֶ֖לֶד לֹ֥א
בָנִֽים׃ ס 31 וּבְנֵ֤י אַפַּ֙יִם֙ יִשְׁעִ֔י וּבְנֵ֥י יִשְׁעִ֖י
שֵׁשָׁ֑ן וּבְנֵ֥י שֵׁשָׁ֖ן אַחְלָֽי׃ 32 וּבְנֵ֤י יָדָע֙ אֲחִ֣י
שַׁמַּ֔י יֶ֖תֶר וְיֽוֹנָתָ֑ן וַיָּ֧מָת יֶ֖תֶר לֹ֥א

than; Jether died childless. 33The sons of Jonathan: Peleth and Zaza. These were the descendants of Jerahmeel. 34Sheshan had no sons, only daughters; Sheshan had an Egyptian slave, whose name was Jarha. 35So Sheshan gave his daughter in marriage to Jarha his slave; and she bore him Attai. 36Attai begot Nathan, and Nathan begot Zabad. 37Zabad begot Ephlal, and Ephlal begot Obed. 38Obed begot Jehu, and Jehu begot Azariah. 39Azariah begot Helez, and Helez begot Eleasah. 40Eleasah begot Sisamai, and Sisamai begot Shallum. 41Shallum begot Jekamiah, and Jekamiah begot Elishama.

42The sons of Caleb brother of Jerahmeel: Meshah his first-born, who was the father of Ziph. The sons of Mareshah father of Hebron. 43The sons of Hebron: Korah, Tappuah, Rekem, and Shema. 44Shema begot Raham the father of Jorkeam, and Rekem begot Shammai. 45The son of Shammai: Maon, and Maon begot Bethzur. 46Ephah, Caleb's concubine, bore Haran, Moza, and Gazez; Haran begot Gazez. 47The sons of Jahdai: Regem, Jotham, Geshan, Pelet, Ephah, and Shaaph. 48Maacah, Caleb's concubine, bore Sheber and Tirhanah. 49She also bore Shaaph father of Madmannah, Sheva father of Machbenah and father of Gibea; the daughter of Caleb was Achsah. 50These were the descendants of Caleb.

The sons of Hur the first-born of Ephrathah: Shobal father of Kiriath-jearim, 51Salma father of Bethlehem, Hareph father of Beth-gader. 52Shobal father of Kiriath-jearim had sons: Haroeh, half of the Menuhoth. 53And the families of Kiriath-jearim: the Ithrites, the Puthites, the Shumathites, and the Mishraites; from these came the Zorathites and the Eshtaolites. 54The sons of Salma: Bethlehem, the Netophathites, Atroth-beth-joab, and half of the Manahathites, the Zorites. 55The families of the scribes that dwelt at Jabez: the Tirathites, the Shimeathites,

---

33 וּבְנֵי יוֹנָתָן פֶּלֶת וְזָזָא ס בָּנִים:
אֵלֶּה הָיוּ בְּנֵי יְרַחְמְאֵל: 34 וְלֹא־הָיָה
לְשֵׁשָׁן בָּנִים כִּי אִם־בָּנוֹת וּלְשֵׁשָׁן עֶבֶד
מִצְרִי וּשְׁמוֹ יַרְחָע: 35 וַיִּתֵּן שֵׁשָׁן אֶת־
בִּתּוֹ לְיַרְחָע עַבְדּוֹ לְאִשָּׁה וַתֵּלֶד לוֹ
אֶת־עַתָּי: 36 וְעַתַּי הוֹלִיד אֶת־נָתָן וְנָתָן
הוֹלִיד אֶת־זָבָד: 37 וְזָבָד הוֹלִיד אֶת־
אֶפְלָל וְאֶפְלָל הוֹלִיד אֶת־עוֹבֵד: 38 וְעוֹבֵד
הוֹלִיד אֶת־יֵהוּא וְיֵהוּא הוֹלִיד אֶת־
עֲזַרְיָה: 39 וַעֲזַרְיָה הוֹלִיד אֶת־חָלֶץ וְחֶלֶץ
הוֹלִיד אֶת־אֶלְעָשָׂה: 40 וְאֶלְעָשָׂה הוֹלִיד
אֶת־סִסְמָי וְסִסְמַי הוֹלִיד אֶת־שַׁלּוּם:
41 וְשַׁלּוּם הוֹלִיד אֶת־יְקַמְיָה וִיקַמְיָה
הוֹלִיד אֶת־אֱלִישָׁמָע:
42 וּבְנֵי כָלֵב אֲחִי יְרַחְמְאֵל מֵישָׁע בְּכֹרוֹ
הוּא אֲבִי־זִיף וּבְנֵי מָרֵשָׁה אֲבִי חֶבְרוֹן:
43 וּבְנֵי חֶבְרוֹן קֹרַח וְתַפֻּחַ וְרֶקֶם וָשָׁמַע:
44 וְשֶׁמַע הוֹלִיד אֶת־רַחַם אֲבִי יָרְקְעָם
וְרֶקֶם הוֹלִיד אֶת־שַׁמָּי: 45 וּבֶן־שַׁמַּי מָעוֹן
וּמָעוֹן אֲבִי בֵית־צוּר: 46 וְעֵיפָה פִּילֶגֶשׁ
כָּלֵב יָלְדָה אֶת־חָרָן וְאֶת־מוֹצָא וְאֶת־גָּזֵז
וְחָרָן הוֹלִיד אֶת־גָּזֵז: ס 47 וּבְנֵי יָהְדָּי
רֶגֶם וְיוֹתָם וְגֵישָׁן וָפֶלֶט וְעֵיפָה וָשָׁעַף:
48 פִּלֶגֶשׁ כָּלֵב מַעֲכָה יָלַד שֶׁבֶר וְאֶת־
תִּרְחֲנָה: 49 וַתֵּלֶד שַׁעַף אֲבִי מַדְמַנָּה אֶת־
שְׁוָא אֲבִי מַכְבֵּנָה וַאֲבִי גִבְעָא וּבַת־כָּלֵב
עַכְסָה: 50 אֵלֶּה הָיוּ בְּנֵי כָלֵב ס
בֶּן־חוּר בְּכוֹר אֶפְרָתָה שׁוֹבָל אֲבִי קִרְיַת
יְעָרִים: 51 שַׂלְמָא אֲבִי בֵית־לָחֶם חָרֵף
אֲבִי בֵית־גָּדֵר: 52 וַיִּהְיוּ בָנִים לְשׁוֹבָל אֲבִי
קִרְיַת יְעָרִים הָרֹאֶה חֲצִי הַמְּנֻחוֹת:
53 וּמִשְׁפְּחוֹת קִרְיַת יְעָרִים הַיִּתְרִי וְהַפּוּתִי
וְהַשֻּׁמָתִי וְהַמִּשְׁרָעִי מֵאֵלֶּה יָצְאוּ
הַצָּרְעָתִי וְהָאֶשְׁתָּאֻלִי: ס 54 בְּנֵי שַׂלְמָא
בֵּית לֶחֶם וּנְטוֹפָתִי עַטְרוֹת בֵּית יוֹאָב
וַחֲצִי הַמָּנַחְתִּי הַצָּרְעִי: 55 וּמִשְׁפְּחוֹת
סֹפְרִים ישבו יֹשְׁבֵי יַעְבֵּץ תִּרְעָתִים

the Sucathites; these are the Kenites who came from Hammath, father of the house of Rechab.

3 These are the sons of David who were born to him in Hebron: the first-born Amnon, by Ahinoam the Jezreelite; the second Daniel, by Abigail the Carmelite; ²the third Absalom, son of Maacah daughter of King Talmai of Geshur; the fourth Adonijah, son of Haggith; ³the fifth Shephatiah, by Abital; the sixth Ithream, by his wife Eglah; ⁴six were born to him in Hebron. He reigned there seven years and six months, and in Jerusalem he reigned thirty-three years. ⁵These were born to him in Jerusalem: Shimea, Shobab, Nathan, and Solomon, four by Bathshua daughter of Ammiel; ⁶then Ibhar, Elishama, Eliphelet, ⁷Nogah, Nepheg, Japhia, ⁸Elishama, Eliada, and Eliphelet—nine. ⁹All were David's sons, besides the sons of the concubines; and Tamar was their sister.

¹⁰The son of Solomon: Rehoboam; his son Abijah, his son Asa, his son Jehoshaphat, ¹¹his son Joram, his son Ahaziah, his son Joash, ¹²his son Amaziah, his son Azariah, his son Jotham, ¹³his son Ahaz, his son Hezekiah, his son Manasseh, ¹⁴his son Amon, and his son Josiah. ¹⁵The sons of Josiah: Johanan the first-born, the second Jehoiakim, the third Zedekiah, the fourth Shallum. ¹⁶The descendants of Jehoiakim: his son Jeconiah, his son Zedekiah; ¹⁷and the sons of Jeconiah, the captive: Shealtiel his son, ¹⁸Malchiram, Pedaiah, Shenazzar, Jekamiah, Hoshama, and Nedabiah; ¹⁹the sons of Pedaiah: Zerubbabel and Shimei; the sons of Zerubbabel: Meshullam and Hananiah, and Shelomith was their sister; ²⁰Hashubah, Ohel, Berechiah, Hasadiah, and Jushabhesed—five. ²¹And the sons of Hananiah: Pelatiah and Jeshaiah; the sons of [Jeshaiah]:

שְׁמָעָתִים שׁוּכָתִים הֵמָּה הַקִּינִים הַבָּאִים מֵחַמַּת אֲבִי בֵית־רֵכָב: ס

ג וְאֵלֶּה הָיוּ בְּנֵי דָוִיד אֲשֶׁר נוֹלַד־לוֹ בְּחֶבְרוֹן הַבְּכוֹר ׀ אַמְנֹן לַאֲחִינֹעַם הַיִּזְרְעֵאלִית שֵׁנִי דָּנִיֵּאל לַאֲבִיגַיִל הַכַּרְמְלִית: 2 הַשְּׁלִשִׁי לְאַבְשָׁלוֹם בֶּן־מַעֲכָה בַּת־תַּלְמַי מֶלֶךְ גְּשׁוּר הָרְבִיעִי אֲדֹנִיָּה בֶן־חַגִּית: 3 הַחֲמִישִׁי שְׁפַטְיָה לַאֲבִיטָל הַשִּׁשִּׁי יִתְרְעָם לְעֶגְלָה אִשְׁתּוֹ: 4 שִׁשָּׁה נוֹלַד־לוֹ בְחֶבְרוֹן וַיִּמְלָךְ־שָׁם שֶׁבַע שָׁנִים וְשִׁשָּׁה חֳדָשִׁים וּשְׁלֹשִׁים וְשָׁלוֹשׁ שָׁנָה מָלַךְ בִּירוּשָׁלָ͏ִם: ס 5 וְאֵלֶּה נוּלְּדוּ־לוֹ בִּירוּשָׁלָיִם שִׁמְעָא וְשׁוֹבָב וְנָתָן וּשְׁלֹמֹה אַרְבָּעָה לְבַת־שׁוּעַ בַּת־עַמִּיאֵל: 6 וְיִבְחָר וֶאֱלִישָׁמָע וֶאֱלִיפָלֶט: 7 וְנֹגַהּ וְנֶפֶג וְיָפִיעַ: 8 וֶאֱלִישָׁמָע וְאֶלְיָדָע וֶאֱלִיפֶלֶט תִּשְׁעָה: 9 כֹּל בְּנֵי דָוִיד מִלְּבַד בְּנֵי־פִילַגְשִׁים וְתָמָר אֲחוֹתָם: פ

10 וּבֶן־שְׁלֹמֹה רְחַבְעָם אֲבִיָּה בְנוֹ אָסָא בְנוֹ יְהוֹשָׁפָט בְּנוֹ: 11 יוֹרָם בְּנוֹ אֲחַזְיָהוּ בְנוֹ יוֹאָשׁ בְּנוֹ: 12 אֲמַצְיָהוּ בְנוֹ עֲזַרְיָה בְנוֹ יוֹתָם בְּנוֹ: 13 אָחָז בְּנוֹ חִזְקִיָּהוּ בְנוֹ מְנַשֶּׁה בְּנוֹ: 14 אָמוֹן בְּנוֹ יֹאשִׁיָּהוּ בְנוֹ: 15 וּבְנֵי יֹאשִׁיָּהוּ הַבְּכוֹר יוֹחָנָן הַשֵּׁנִי יְהוֹיָקִים הַשְּׁלִשִׁי צִדְקִיָּהוּ הָרְבִיעִי שַׁלּוּם: 16 וּבְנֵי יְהוֹיָקִים יְכָנְיָה בְנוֹ צִדְקִיָּה בְנוֹ: 17 וּבְנֵי יְכָנְיָה אַסִּר שְׁאַלְתִּיאֵל בְּנוֹ: 18 וּמַלְכִּירָם וּפְדָיָה וְשֶׁנְאַצַּר יְקַמְיָה הוֹשָׁמָע וּנְדַבְיָה: 19 וּבְנֵי פְדָיָה זְרֻבָּבֶל וְשִׁמְעִי וּבֶן*־זְרֻבָּבֶל מְשֻׁלָּם וַחֲנַנְיָה וּשְׁלֹמִית אֲחוֹתָם: 20 וַחֲשֻׁבָה וָאֹהֶל וּבֶרֶכְיָה וַחֲסַדְיָה יוּשַׁב חֶסֶד חָמֵשׁ: 21 וּבֶן*־חֲנַנְיָה פְּלַטְיָה וִישַׁעְיָה בְּנֵי רְפָיָה בְּנֵי אַרְנָן בְּנֵי עֹבַדְיָה בְּנֵי שְׁכַנְיָה: 22 וּבְנֵי שְׁכַנְיָה שְׁמַעְיָה

Rephaiah; the sons of [Rephaiah]: Arnan; the sons of [Arnan]: Obadiah; the sons of [Obadiah]: Shecaniah. 22And the sons of Shecaniah: Shemaiah; and the sons of Shemaiah: Hattush, and Igal, and Bariah, and Neariah, and Shaphat—six. 23And the sons of Neariah: Elioenai, and Hizkiah, and Azrikam—three. 24And the sons of Elioenai: Hodaviah, and Eliashib, and Pelaiah, and Akkub, and Johanan, and Delaiah, and Anani—seven.

4 The sons of Judah: Perez, Hezron, Carmi, Hur, and Shobal. 2Reaiah son of Shobal begot Jahath, and Jahath begot Ahumai and Lahad. These were the families of the Zorathites. 3These were [the sons of] the father of Etam: Jezreel, Ishma, and Idbash; and the name of their sister was Hazlelponi, 4and Penuel was the father of Gedor, and Ezer the father of Hushah. These were the sons of Hur, the first-born of Ephrathah, the father of Bethlehem. 5Ashhur the father of Tekoa had two wives, Helah and Naarah; 6Naarah bore him Ahuzam, Hepher, Temeni, and Ahashtari. These were the sons of Naarah. 7The sons of Helah: Zereth, Zohar, and Ethnan. 8Koz was the father of Anub, Zobebah, and the families of Aharhel son of Harum. 9Jabez was more esteemed than his brothers; and his mother named him Jabez, "Because," she said, "I bore him in pain."[a] 10Jabez invoked the God of Israel, saying, "Oh, bless me, enlarge my territory, stand by me, and make me not suffer pain from misfortune!" And God granted what he asked. 11Chelub the brother of Shuhah begot Mehir, who was the father of Eshton. 12Eshton begot Bethrapha, Paseah, and Tehinnah father of Ir-nahash. These were the men of Recah. 13The sons of Kenaz: Othniel and Seraiah; and the sons of Othniel: 14Hathath and Meonothai. He begot Ophrah. Seraiah begot Joab father of

---

a   Heb. 'oṣeb, connected with "Jabez."

ד   וּבְנֵי שְׁמַעְיָה חַטּוּשׁ וְיִגְאָל וּבָרִיחַ וּנְעַרְיָה וְשָׁפָט שִׁשָּׁה: 23 וּבֶן־*נְעַרְיָה אֶלְיוֹעֵינַי וְחִזְקִיָּה וְעַזְרִיקָם שְׁלֹשָׁה: 24 וּבְנֵי אֶלְיוֹעֵינַי הוֹדַיְוָהוּ וְאֶלְיָשִׁיב וּפְלָיָה וְעַקּוּב וְיוֹחָנָן וּדְלָיָה וַעֲנָנִי שִׁבְעָה: ס

ד   בְּנֵי יְהוּדָה פֶּרֶץ חֶצְרוֹן וְכַרְמִי וְחוּר וְשׁוֹבָל: 2 וּרְאָיָה בֶן־שׁוֹבָל הוֹלִיד אֶת־יַחַת וְיַחַת הֹלִיד אֶת־אֲחוּמַי וְאֶת־לָהַד אֵלֶּה מִשְׁפְּחוֹת הַצָּרְעָתִי: ס 3 וְאֵלֶּה אֲבִי עֵיטָם יִזְרְעֶאל וְיִשְׁמָא וְיִדְבָּשׁ וְשֵׁם אֲחוֹתָם הַצְלֶלְפּוֹנִי: 4 וּפְנוּאֵל אֲבִי גְדֹר וְעֵזֶר אֲבִי חוּשָׁה אֵלֶּה בְנֵי־חוּר בְּכוֹר אֶפְרָתָה אֲבִי בֵּית לָחֶם: 5 וּלְאַשְׁחוּר אֲבִי תְקוֹעַ הָיוּ שְׁתֵּי נָשִׁים חֶלְאָה וְנַעֲרָה: 6 וַתֵּלֶד לוֹ נַעֲרָה אֶת־אֲחֻזָּם וְאֶת־חֵפֶר וְאֶת־תֵּימְנִי וְאֶת־הָאֲחַשְׁתָּרִי אֵלֶּה בְּנֵי נַעֲרָה: 7 וּבְנֵי חֶלְאָה צֶרֶת יִצְחַר וְאֶתְנָן: 8 וְקוֹץ הוֹלִיד אֶת־עָנוּב וְאֶת־הַצֹּבֵבָה וּמִשְׁפְּחוֹת אֲחַרְחֵל בֶּן־הָרוּם: 9 וַיְהִי יַעְבֵּץ נִכְבָּד מֵאֶחָיו וְאִמּוֹ קָרְאָה שְׁמוֹ יַעְבֵּץ לֵאמֹר כִּי יָלַדְתִּי בְּעֹצֶב: 10 וַיִּקְרָא יַעְבֵּץ לֵאלֹהֵי יִשְׂרָאֵל לֵאמֹר אִם־בָּרֵךְ תְּבָרֲכֵנִי וְהִרְבִּיתָ אֶת־גְּבוּלִי וְהָיְתָה יָדְךָ עִמִּי וְעָשִׂיתָ מֵּרָעָה לְבִלְתִּי עָצְבִּי וַיָּבֵא אֱלֹהִים אֵת אֲשֶׁר־שָׁאָל: 11 וּכְלוּב אֲחִי־שׁוּחָה הוֹלִיד אֶת־מְחִיר הוּא אֲבִי אֶשְׁתּוֹן: 12 וְאֶשְׁתּוֹן הוֹלִיד אֶת־בֵּית רָפָא וְאֶת־פָּסֵחַ וְאֶת־תְּחִנָּה אֲבִי עִיר נָחָשׁ אֵלֶּה אַנְשֵׁי רֵכָה: ס 13 וּבְנֵי קְנַז עָתְנִיאֵל וּשְׂרָיָה וּבְנֵי עָתְנִיאֵל חֲתַת: 14 וּמְעוֹנֹתַי הוֹלִיד אֶת־עָפְרָה וּשְׂרָיָה

סבירין ומטעין "ובני"   v. 23.

Ge-harashim,[b] so-called because they were craftsmen. [15]The sons of Caleb son of Jephunneh: Iru, Elah, and Naam; and the sons of Elah: Kenaz. [16]The sons of Jehallelel: Ziph, Ziphah, Tiria, and Asarel. [17]The sons of Ezrah: Jether, Mered, Epher, and Jalon. She[c] conceived and bore Miriam, Shammai, and Ishbah father of Eshtemoa. [18]And his Judahite wife bore Jered father of Gedor, Heber father of Soco, and Jekuthiel father of Zanoah. These were the sons of Bithiah daughter of Pharaoh, whom Mered married. [19]The sons of the wife of Hodiah sister of Naham were the fathers of Keilah the Garmite and Eshtemoa the Maacathite. [20]The sons of Shimon: Amnon, Rinnah, Ben-hanan, and Tilon. The sons of Ishi: Zoheth and Ben-zoheth. [21]The sons of Shelah son of Judah: Er father of Lecah, Laadah father of Mareshah, and the families of the linen factory at Beth-ashbea; [22]and Jokim, and the men of Cozeba and Joash, and Saraph, who married into Moab and Jashubi Lehem (the records are ancient). [23]These were the potters who dwelt at Netaim and Gederah; they dwelt there in the king's service.

[24]The sons of Simeon: Nemuel, Jamin, Jarib, Zerah, Shaul; [25]his son Shallum, his son Mibsam, his son Mishma. [26]The sons of Mishma: his son Hammuel, his son Zaccur, his son Shimei. [27]Shimei had sixteen sons and six daughters; but his brothers had not many children; in all, their families were not as prolific as the Judahites. [28]They dwelt in Beersheba, Moladah, Hazar-shual, [29]Bilhah, Ezem, Tolad, [30]Bethuel, Hormah, Ziklag, [31]Beth-marcaboth, Hazarsusim, Beth-biri, and Shaaraim. These were their towns until David became king, [32]together with their villages, Etam, Ain, Rimmon, Tochen, and Ashan—five towns, [33]along with all their villages that were around these towns as far as Baal; such were their settlements.

הוֹלִיד אֶת־יוֹאָב אֲבִי גֵּיא חֲרָשִׁים כִּי
חֲרָשִׁים הָיוּ: פ 15 וּבְנֵי כָּלֵב בֶּן־יְפֻנֶּה
עִירוּ אֵלָה וָנָעַם וּבְנֵי אֵלָה וּקְנַז: 16 וּבְנֵי
יְהַלֶּלְאֵל זִיף וְזִיפָה תִּירְיָא וַאֲשַׂרְאֵל:
17 וּבֶן־עֶזְרָה יֶתֶר וּמֶרֶד וְעֵפֶר וְיָלוֹן וַתַּהַר
אֶת־מִרְיָם וְאֶת־שַׁמַּי וְאֶת־יִשְׁבָּח אֲבִי
אֶשְׁתְּמֹעַ: 18 וְאִשְׁתּוֹ הַיְהֻדִיָּה יָלְדָה אֶת־
יֶרֶד אֲבִי גְדוֹר וְאֶת־חֶבֶר אֲבִי שׂוֹכוֹ
וְאֶת־יְקוּתִיאֵל אֲבִי זָנוֹחַ וְאֵלֶּה בְּנֵי בִּתְיָה
בַת־פַּרְעֹה אֲשֶׁר לָקַח מָרֶד: ס 19 וּבְנֵי
אֵשֶׁת הוֹדִיָּה אֲחוֹת נַחַם אֲבִי קְעִילָה
הַגַּרְמִי וְאֶשְׁתְּמֹעַ הַמַּעֲכָתִי: 20 וּבְנֵי שִׁימוֹן
אַמְנוֹן וְרִנָּה בֶּן־חָנָן וָתוֹלוֹן וְתִילוֹן וּבְנֵי
יִשְׁעִי זוֹחֵת וּבֶן־זוֹחֵת: 21 בְּנֵי שֵׁלָה בֶן־
יְהוּדָה עֵר אֲבִי לֵכָה וְלַעְדָּה אֲבִי מָרֵשָׁה
וּמִשְׁפְּחוֹת בֵּית־עֲבֹדַת הַבֻּץ לְבֵית
אַשְׁבֵּעַ: 22 וְיוֹקִים וְאַנְשֵׁי כֹזֵבָא וְיוֹאָשׁ
וְשָׂרָף אֲשֶׁר־בָּעֲלוּ לְמוֹאָב וְיָשֻׁבִי לָחֶם
וְהַדְּבָרִים עַתִּיקִים: 23 הֵמָּה הַיּוֹצְרִים
וְיֹשְׁבֵי נְטָעִים וּגְדֵרָה עִם־הַמֶּלֶךְ
בִּמְלַאכְתּוֹ יָשְׁבוּ שָׁם: ס

24 בְּנֵי שִׁמְעוֹן נְמוּאֵל וְיָמִין יָרִיב זֶרַח
שָׁאוּל: 25 שַׁלֻּם בְּנוֹ מִבְשָׂם בְּנוֹ מִשְׁמָע
בְּנוֹ: 26 וּבְנֵי מִשְׁמָע חַמּוּאֵל בְּנוֹ זַכּוּר בְּנוֹ
שִׁמְעִי בְנוֹ: 27 וּלְשִׁמְעִי בָּנִים שִׁשָּׁה עָשָׂר
וּבָנוֹת שֵׁשׁ וּלְאֶחָיו אֵין בָּנִים רַבִּים וְכֹל
מִשְׁפַּחְתָּם לֹא הִרְבּוּ עַד־בְּנֵי יְהוּדָה: ס
28 וַיֵּשְׁבוּ בִּבְאֵר־שֶׁבַע וּמוֹלָדָה וַחֲצַר
שׁוּעָל: 29 וּבְבִלְהָה וּבְעֶצֶם וּבְתוֹלָד:
30 וּבִבְתוּאֵל וּבְחָרְמָה וּבְצִיקְלָג: 31 וּבְבֵית
מַרְכָּבוֹת וּבַחֲצַר סוּסִים וּבְבֵית בִּרְאִי
וּבְשַׁעֲרַיִם אֵלֶּה עָרֵיהֶם עַד־מְלֹךְ דָּוִיד:
32 וְחַצְרֵיהֶם עֵיטָם וָעַיִן רִמּוֹן וְתֹכֶן וְעָשָׁן
עָרִים חָמֵשׁ: 33 וְכָל־חַצְרֵיהֶם אֲשֶׁר
סְבִיבוֹת הֶעָרִים הָאֵלֶּה עַד־בָּעַל זֹאת
מוֹשְׁבֹתָם

---

b   Lit. "the valley of the craftsmen."
c   Apparently Bithiah; cf. v. 18.

Registered in their genealogy were: ³⁴Mesho-bab, Jamlech, Joshah son of Amaziah,³⁵Joel, Jehu son of Joshibiah son of Seraiah son of Asiel. ³⁶Elioenai, Jaakobah, Jeshohaiah, Asaiah, Adiel, Jesimiel, Benaiah, ³⁷Ziza son of Shiphi son of Allon son of Jedaiah son of Shimri son of Shemaiah—³⁸these mentioned by name were chiefs in their families, and their clans increased greatly. ³⁹They went to the approaches to Gedor, to the eastern side of the valley, in search of pasture for their flocks. ⁴⁰They found rich, good pasture, and the land was ample, quiet, and peaceful. The former inhabitants were of Ham; ⁴¹those recorded by name came in the days of King Hezekiah of Judah, and attacked their encampments and the Meunim who were found there, and wiped them out forever, and settled in their place, because there was pasture there for their flocks. ⁴²And some of them, five hundred of the Simeonites, went to Mount Seir, with Pelatiah, Neariah, Rephaiah, and Uzziel, sons of Ishi, at their head, ⁴³and they destroyed the last surviving Amalekites, and they live there to this day.

5 The sons of Reuben the first-born of Israel. (He was the first-born; but when he defiled his father's bed, his birthright was given to the sons of Joseph son of Israel, so he is not reckoned as first-born in the genealogy; ²though Judah became more powerful than his brothers and a leader came from him, yet the birthright belonged to Joseph.) ³The sons of Reuben, the first-born of Israel: Enoch, Pallu, Hezron, and Carmi. ⁴The sons of Joel: his son Shemaiah, his son Gog, his son Shimei, ⁵his son Micah, his son Reaiah, his son Baal, ⁶his son Beerah—whom King Tillegath-pilneser of Assyria exiled—was chieftain of the Reubenites. ⁷And his kinsmen,

34 וּמְשׁוֹבָ֣ב וַיַּמְלֵ֑ךְ וְיוֹשָׁ֖ה בֶּן־אֲמַצְיָֽה: 35 וְיוֹאֵ֣ל וְיֵה֗וּא בֶּן־יֽוֹשִׁבְיָ֛ה בֶּן־שְׂרָיָ֖ה בֶּן־עֲשִׂיאֵֽל: 36 וְאֶלְיֽוֹעֵינַ֡י וְיַֽעֲקֹ֡בָה וִֽישֽׁוֹחָיָ֡ה וַֽעֲשָׂיָ֡ה וַֽעֲדִיאֵ֡ל וִישִׂימִאֵ֡ל וּבְנָיָֽה: 37 וְזִיזָ֨א בֶן־שִׁפְעִ֧י בֶן־אַלּ֛וֹן בֶּן־יְדָיָ֥ה בֶן־שִׁמְרִ֖י בֶּן־שְׁמַעְיָֽה: 38 אֵ֣לֶּה הַבָּאִ֣ים בְּשֵׁמ֗וֹת נְשִׂיאִים֙ בְּמִשְׁפְּחוֹתָ֔ם וּבֵ֖ית אֲבֽוֹתֵיהֶ֑ם פָּרְצ֖וּ לָרֽוֹב: 39 וַיֵּֽלְכוּ֙ לִמְב֣וֹא גְדֹ֔ר עַ֖ד לְמִזְרַ֣ח הַגָּ֑יְא לְבַקֵּ֥שׁ מִרְעֶ֖ה לְצֹאנָֽם: 40 וַֽיִּמְצְא֤וּ מִרְעֶה֙ שָׁמֵ֣ן וָט֔וֹב וְהָאָ֙רֶץ֙ רַֽחֲבַ֣ת יָדַ֔יִם וְשֹׁקֶ֖טֶת וּשְׁלֵוָ֑ה כִּ֣י מִן־חָ֔ם הַיֹּֽשְׁבִ֥ים שָׁ֖ם לְפָנִֽים: 41 וַיָּבֹ֡אוּ אֵ֩לֶּה֩ הַכְּתוּבִ֨ים בְּשֵׁמ֜וֹת בִּימֵ֣י ׀ יְחִזְקִיָּ֣הוּ מֶֽלֶךְ־יְהוּדָ֗ה וַיַּכּ֣וּ אֶת־אָֽהֳלֵיהֶ֡ם וְאֶת־הַמְּעוּנִ֣ים אֲשֶׁ֣ר נִמְצְאוּ־שָׁ֩מָּה֩ וַיַּֽחֲרִימֻ֨ם עַד־הַיּ֤וֹם הַזֶּ֔ה וַיֵּֽשְׁב֖וּ תַּחְתֵּיהֶ֑ם כִּֽי־מִרְעֶ֥ה לְצֹאנָ֖ם שָֽׁם: 42 וּמֵהֶ֣ם ׀ מִן־בְּנֵ֣י שִׁמְע֗וֹן הָֽלְכוּ֙ לְהַ֣ר שֵׂעִ֔יר אֲנָשִׁ֖ים חֲמֵ֣שׁ מֵא֑וֹת וּפְלַטְיָ֡ה וּֽנְעַרְיָ֧ה וּרְפָיָ֣ה וְעֻזִּיאֵ֗ל בְּנֵ֥י יִשְׁעִ֖י בְּרֹאשָֽׁם: 43 וַיַּכּ֕וּ אֶת־שְׁאֵרִ֥ית הַפְּלֵטָ֖ה לַֽעֲמָלֵ֑ק וַיֵּ֣שְׁבוּ שָׁ֔ם עַ֖ד הַיּ֥וֹם הַזֶּֽה:

ה 1 וּבְנֵ֨י רְאוּבֵ֥ן בְּכֽוֹר־יִשְׂרָאֵל�»ֹ כִּ֣י ה֣וּא הַבְּכוֹר֒ וּֽבְחַלְּלוֹ֙ יְצוּעֵ֣י אָבִ֔יו נִתְּנָה֙ בְּכֹ֣רָת֔וֹ לִבְנֵ֥י יוֹסֵ֖ף בֶּן־יִשְׂרָאֵ֑ל וְלֹ֥א לְהִתְיַחֵ֖שׂ לַבְּכֹרָֽה: 2 כִּ֤י יְהוּדָה֙ גָּבַ֣ר בְּאֶחָ֔יו וּלְנָגִ֖יד מִמֶּ֑נּוּ וְהַבְּכֹרָ֖ה לְיוֹסֵֽף: ס 3 בְּנֵ֣י רְאוּבֵ֔ן בְּכ֖וֹר יִשְׂרָאֵ֑ל חֲנ֥וֹךְ וּפַלּ֖וּא חֶצְר֥וֹן וְכַרְמִֽי: 4 בְּנֵ֖י יוֹאֵ֑ל שְׁמַעְיָ֥ה בְנ֛וֹ גּ֥וֹג בְּנ֖וֹ שִׁמְעִ֥י בְנֽוֹ: 5 מִיכָ֥ה בְנ֛וֹ רְאָיָ֥ה בְנ֖וֹ בַּ֥עַל בְּנֽוֹ: 6 בְּאֵרָ֣ה בְנ֗וֹ אֲשֶׁ֤ר הֶגְלָה֙ תִּלְּגַ֣ת פִּלְנְאֶ֔סֶר מֶ֖לֶךְ אַשֻּׁ֑ר ה֥וּא נָשִׂ֖יא לָראֽוּבֵנִֽי: 7 וְאֶחָיו֙

by their families, according to their lines in the genealogy: the head, Jeiel, and Zechariah, 8and Bela son of Azaz son of Shema son of Joel; he dwelt in Aroer as far as Nebo and Baal-meon. 9He also dwelt to the east as far as the fringe of the wilderness this side of the Euphrates, because their cattle had increased in the land of Gilead. 10And in the days of Saul they made war on the Hagrites, who fell by their hand; and they occupied their tents throughout all the region east of Gilead.

11The sons of Gad dwelt facing them in the land of Bashan as far as Salcah: 12Joel the chief, Shapham the second, Janai, and Shaphat in Bashan. 13And by clans: Michael, Meshullam, Sheba, Jorai, Jacan, Zia, and Eber—seven. 14These were the sons of Abihail son of Huri son of Jaroah son of Gilead son of Michael son of Jeshishai son of Jahdo son of Buz; 15Ahi son of Abdiel son of Guni was chief of their clan, 16and they dwelt in Gilead, in Bashan, and in its dependencies, and in all the pasturelands of Sharon, to their limits. 17All of them were registered by genealogies in the days of King Jotham of Judah, and in the days of King Jeroboam of Israel.

18The Reubenites, the Gadites, and the half-tribe of Manasseh had warriors who carried shield and sword, drew the bow, and were experienced at war—44,760, ready for service. 19They made war on the Hagrites—Jetur, Naphish, and Nodab. 20They prevailed against them; the Hagrites and all who were with them were delivered into their hands, for they cried to God in the battle, and He responded to their entreaty because they trusted in Him. 21They carried off their livestock: 50,000 of their camels, 250,000 sheep, 2,000 asses, and 100,000 people. 22For many fell slain, because it was God's battle. And they dwelt in their place until the exile.

לְמִשְׁפְּחֹתָיו בְּהִתְיַחֵשׂ לְתֹלְדוֹתָם הָרֹאשׁ
יְעִיאֵל וּזְכַרְיָהוּ: 8 וּבֶלַע בֶּן־עָזָז בֶּן־שֶׁמַע
בֶּן־יוֹאֵל הוּא יוֹשֵׁב בַּעֲרֹעֵר וְעַד־נְבוֹ
וּבַעַל מְעוֹן: 9 וְלַמִּזְרָח יָשַׁב עַד־לְבוֹא
מִדְבָּרָה לְמִן־הַנָּהָר פְּרָת כִּי מִקְנֵיהֶם רָבוּ
בְּאֶרֶץ גִּלְעָד: 10 וּבִימֵי שָׁאוּל עָשׂוּ
מִלְחָמָה עִם־הַהַגְרִאִים וַיִּפְּלוּ בְּיָדָם
וַיֵּשְׁבוּ בְּאָהֳלֵיהֶם עַל־כָּל־פְּנֵי מִזְרָח
לַגִּלְעָד: פ

11 וּבְנֵי־גָד לְנֶגְדָּם יָשְׁבוּ בְּאֶרֶץ הַבָּשָׁן
עַד־סַלְכָה: 12 יוֹאֵל הָרֹאשׁ וְשָׁפָם הַמִּשְׁנֶה
וְיַעְנַי וְשָׁפָט בַּבָּשָׁן: 13 וַאֲחֵיהֶם לְבֵית
אֲבוֹתֵיהֶם מִיכָאֵל וּמְשֻׁלָּם וְשֶׁבַע וְיוֹרַי
וְיַעְכָּן וְזִיעַ וָעֵבֶר שִׁבְעָה: ס 14 אֵלֶּה |
בְּנֵי אֲבִיחַיִל בֶּן־חוּרִי בֶּן־יָרוֹחַ בֶּן־גִּלְעָד
בֶּן־מִיכָאֵל בֶּן־יְשִׁישַׁי בֶּן־יַחְדּוֹ בֶּן־בּוּז:
15 אֲחִי בֶּן־עַבְדִּיאֵל בֶּן־גּוּנִי רֹאשׁ לְבֵית
אֲבוֹתָם: 16 וַיֵּשְׁבוּ בַּגִּלְעָד בַּבָּשָׁן וּבִבְנֹתֶיהָ
וּבְכָל־מִגְרְשֵׁי שָׁרוֹן עַל־תּוֹצְאוֹתָם:
17 כֻּלָּם הִתְיַחְשׂוּ בִּימֵי יוֹתָם מֶלֶךְ־יְהוּדָה
וּבִימֵי יָרָבְעָם מֶלֶךְ־יִשְׂרָאֵל: פ

18 בְּנֵי־רְאוּבֵן וְגָדִי וַחֲצִי שֵׁבֶט־מְנַשֶּׁה מִן־
בְּנֵי־חַיִל אֲנָשִׁים נֹשְׂאֵי מָגֵן וְחֶרֶב וְדֹרְכֵי
קֶשֶׁת וּלְמוּדֵי מִלְחָמָה אַרְבָּעִים וְאַרְבָּעָה
אֶלֶף וּשְׁבַע־מֵאוֹת וְשִׁשִּׁים יֹצְאֵי צָבָא:
19 וַיַּעֲשׂוּ מִלְחָמָה עִם־הַהַגְרִיאִים וִיטוּר
וְנָפִישׁ וְנוֹדָב: 20 וַיֵּעָזְרוּ עֲלֵיהֶם וַיִּנָּתְנוּ
בְּיָדָם הַהַגְרִיאִים וְכֹל שֶׁעִמָּהֶם כִּי
לֵאלֹהִים זָעֲקוּ בַּמִּלְחָמָה וְנַעְתּוֹר לָהֶם
כִּי־בָטְחוּ בוֹ: 21 וַיִּשְׁבּוּ מִקְנֵיהֶם גְּמַלֵּיהֶם
חֲמִשִּׁים אֶלֶף וְצֹאן מָאתַיִם וַחֲמִשִּׁים אֶלֶף
וַחֲמוֹרִים אַלְפָּיִם וְנֶפֶשׁ אָדָם מֵאָה אָלֶף:
22 כִּי חֲלָלִים רַבִּים נָפָלוּ כִּי מֵהָאֱלֹהִים
הַמִּלְחָמָה וַיֵּשְׁבוּ תַחְתֵּיהֶם עַד־הַגֹּלָה: פ

²³The members of the half-tribe of Manasseh dwelt in the land; they were very numerous from Bashan to Baal-hermon, Senir, and Mount Hermon. ²⁴These were the chiefs of their clans: Epher, Ishi, Eliel, Azriel, Jeremiah, Hodaviah, and Jahdiel, men of substance, famous men, chiefs of their clans. ²⁵But they trespassed against the God of their fathers by going astray after the gods of the peoples of the land, whom God had destroyed before them. ²⁶So the God of Israel roused the spirit of King Pul of Assyria—the spirit of King Tillegath-pilneser of Assyria—and he carried them away, namely, the Reubenites, the Gadites, and the half-tribe of Manasseh, and brought them to Halah, Habor, Hara, and the river Gozan, to this day.

²⁷ᵃThe sons of Levi: Gershom, Kohath, and Merari. ²⁸The sons of Kohath: Amram, Izhar, Hebron, and Uzziel. ²⁹The children of Amram: Aaron, Moses, and Miriam. The sons of Aaron: Nadab, Abihu, Eleazar, and Ithamar. ³⁰Eleazar begot Phinehas, Phinehas begot Abishua, ³¹Abishua begot Bukki, Bukki begot Uzzi, ³²Uzzi begot Zerahiah, Zerahiah begot Meraioth, ³³Meraioth begot Amariah, Amariah begot Ahitub, ³⁴Ahitub begot Zadok, Zadok begot Ahimaaz, ³⁵Ahimaaz begot Azariah, Azariah begot Johanan, ³⁶and Johanan begot Azariah (it was he who served as priest in the House that Solomon built in Jerusalem). ³⁷Azariah begot Amariah, Amariah begot Ahitub, ³⁸Ahitub begot Zadok, Zadok begot Shallum, ³⁹Shallum begot Hilkiah, Hilkiah begot Azariah, ⁴⁰Azariah begot Seraiah, Seraiah begot Jehozadak; ⁴¹and Jehozadak went into exile when the LORD exiled Judah and Jerusalem by the hand of Nebuchadnezzar.

²³ וּבְנֵי חֲצִי שֵׁבֶט מְנַשֶּׁה יָשְׁבוּ בָּאָרֶץ מִבָּשָׁן עַד־בַּעַל חֶרְמוֹן וּשְׂנִיר וְהַר־חֶרְמוֹן הֵמָּה רָבוּ: ²⁴ וְאֵלֶּה רָאשֵׁי בֵית־אֲבוֹתָם וְעֵפֶר וְיִשְׁעִי וֶאֱלִיאֵל וְעַזְרִיאֵל וְיִרְמְיָה וְהוֹדַוְיָה וְיַחְדִּיאֵל אֲנָשִׁים גִּבּוֹרֵי חַיִל אַנְשֵׁי שֵׁמוֹת רָאשִׁים לְבֵית אֲבוֹתָם: ²⁵ וַיִּמְעֲלוּ בֵּאלֹהֵי אֲבוֹתֵיהֶם וַיִּזְנוּ אַחֲרֵי אֱלֹהֵי עַמֵּי־הָאָרֶץ אֲשֶׁר־הִשְׁמִיד אֱלֹהִים מִפְּנֵיהֶם: ²⁶ וַיָּעַר אֱלֹהֵי יִשְׂרָאֵל אֶת־רוּחַ ׀ פּוּל מֶלֶךְ־אַשּׁוּר וְאֶת־רוּחַ תִּלְּגַת פִּלְנֶסֶר מֶלֶךְ אַשּׁוּר וַיַּגְלֵם לָראוּבֵנִי* וְלַגָּדִי וְלַחֲצִי שֵׁבֶט מְנַשֶּׁה וַיְבִיאֵם לַחְלַח וְחָבוֹר וְהָרָא וּנְהַר גּוֹזָן עַד הַיּוֹם הַזֶּה: פ

²⁷ בְּנֵי לֵוִי גֵּרְשׁוֹן קְהָת וּמְרָרִי: ²⁸ וּבְנֵי קְהָת עַמְרָם יִצְהָר וְחֶבְרוֹן וְעֻזִּיאֵל: ס ²⁹ וּבְנֵי עַמְרָם אַהֲרֹן וּמֹשֶׁה וּמִרְיָם ס וּבְנֵי אַהֲרֹן נָדָב וַאֲבִיהוּא אֶלְעָזָר וְאִיתָמָר: ס ³⁰ אֶלְעָזָר הוֹלִיד אֶת־פִּינְחָס פִּינְחָס הוֹלִיד אֶת־אֲבִישׁוּעַ: ³¹ וַאֲבִישׁוּעַ הוֹלִיד אֶת־בֻּקִּי וּבֻקִּי הוֹלִיד אֶת־עֻזִּי: ³² וְעֻזִּי הוֹלִיד אֶת־זְרַחְיָה וּזְרַחְיָה הוֹלִיד אֶת־מְרָיוֹת: ³³ מְרָיוֹת הוֹלִיד אֶת־אֲמַרְיָה וַאֲמַרְיָה הוֹלִיד אֶת־אֲחִיטוּב: ³⁴ וַאֲחִיטוּב הוֹלִיד אֶת־צָדוֹק וְצָדוֹק הוֹלִיד אֶת־אֲחִימַעַץ: ³⁵ וַאֲחִימַעַץ הוֹלִיד אֶת־עֲזַרְיָה וַעֲזַרְיָה הוֹלִיד אֶת־יוֹחָנָן: ³⁶ וְיוֹחָנָן הוֹלִיד אֶת־עֲזַרְיָה הוּא אֲשֶׁר כִּהֵן בַּבַּיִת אֲשֶׁר־בָּנָה שְׁלֹמֹה בִּירוּשָׁלָ͏ִם: ³⁷ וַיּוֹלֶד עֲזַרְיָה אֶת־אֲמַרְיָה וַאֲמַרְיָה הוֹלִיד אֶת־אֲחִיטוּב: ³⁸ וַאֲחִיטוּב הוֹלִיד אֶת־צָדוֹק וְצָדוֹק הוֹלִיד אֶת־שַׁלּוּם: ³⁹ וְשַׁלּוּם הוֹלִיד אֶת־חִלְקִיָּה וְחִלְקִיָּה הוֹלִיד אֶת־עֲזַרְיָה: ⁴⁰ וַעֲזַרְיָה הוֹלִיד אֶת־שְׂרָיָה וּשְׂרָיָה הוֹלִיד אֶת־יְהוֹצָדָק: ⁴¹ וִיהוֹצָדָק הָלַךְ בְּהַגְלוֹת יְהוָה אֶת־יְהוּדָה וִירוּשָׁלָ͏ִם בְּיַד נְבֻכַדְנֶאצַּר: ס

ᵃ   *In some editions, chap. 6 begins here.*

6 The sons of Levi: Gershom, Kohath, and Merari. ²And these are the names of the sons of Gershom: Libni and Shimei. ³The sons of Kohath: Amram, Izhar, Hebron, and Uzziel. ⁴The sons of Merari: Mahli and Mushi. These were the families of the Levites according to their clans. ⁵Of Gershom: his son Libni, his son Jahath, his son Zimmah, ⁶his son Joah, his son Iddo, his son Zerah, his son Jeatherai. ⁷The sons of Kohath: his son Amminadab, his son Korah, his son Assir, ⁸his son Elkanah, his son Ebiasaph, his son Assir, ⁹his son Tahath, his son Uriel, his son Uzziah, and his son Shaul. ¹⁰The sons of El-kanah: Amasai and Ahimoth, ¹¹his son Elkanah, his son Zophai, his son Nahath, ¹²his son Eliab, his son Jeroham, his son Elkanah. ¹³The sons of Samuel: his first-born ᵃ-Vashni, and-ᵃ Abijah. ¹⁴The sons of Merari: Mahli, his son Libni, his son Shimei, his son Uzzah, ¹⁵his son Shimea, his son Haggiah, and his son Asaiah.

¹⁶These were appointed by David to be in charge of song in the House of the Lord, from the time the Ark came to rest. ¹⁷They served at the Tabernacle of the Tent of Meeting with song until Solomon built the House of the Lord in Jerusalem; and they carried out their duties as prescribed for them. ¹⁸Those were the ap-pointed men; and their sons were: the Kohath-ites: Heman the singer, son of Joel son of Sam-uel ¹⁹son of Elkanah son of Jeroham son of Eliel of Toah ²⁰son of Zuph son of Elkanah son of Mahath son of Amasai ²¹son of Elka-nah son of Joel son of Azariah son of Zeph-aniah ²²son of Tahath son of Assir son of Ebiasaph son of Korah ²³son of Izhar son of Kohath son of Levi son of Israel; ²⁴and his kins-man Asaph, who stood on his right, namely, Asaph son of Berechiah son of Shimea ²⁵son of Michael son of Baaseiah son of Malchijah ²⁶son of Ethni son of Zerah son of Adaiah ²⁷son of

² בְּנֵי לֵוִי גֵּרְשֹׁם קְהָת וּמְרָרִי: וְאֵלֶּה שְׁמוֹת בְּנֵי־גֵרְשׁוֹם לִבְנִי וְשִׁמְעִי: ³ וּבְנֵי קְהָת עַמְרָם וְיִצְהָר וְחֶבְרוֹן וְעֻזִּיאֵל: ⁴ בְּנֵי מְרָרִי מַחְלִי וּמֻשִׁי וְאֵלֶּה מִשְׁפְּחוֹת הַלֵּוִי לַאֲבֹתֵיהֶם: ⁵ לְגֵרְשׁוֹם לִבְנִי בְנוֹ יַחַת בְּנוֹ זִמָּה בְנוֹ: ⁶ יוֹאָח בְּנוֹ עִדּוֹ בְנוֹ זֶרַח בְּנוֹ יְאָתְרַי בְּנוֹ: ⁷ בְּנֵי קְהָת עַמִּינָדָב בְּנוֹ קֹרַח בְּנוֹ אַסִּיר בְּנוֹ: ⁸ אֶלְקָנָה בְנוֹ וְאֶבְיָסָף בְּנוֹ וְאַסִּיר בְּנוֹ: ⁹ תַּחַת בְּנוֹ אוּרִיאֵל בְּנוֹ עֻזִּיָּה בְנוֹ וְשָׁאוּל בְּנוֹ: ¹⁰ וּבְנֵי אֶלְקָנָה עֲמָשַׂי וַאֲחִימוֹת: ¹¹ אֶלְקָנָה בנו בְּנֵי אֶלְקָנָה צוֹפַי בְנוֹ וְנַחַת בְּנוֹ: ¹² אֱלִיאָב בְּנוֹ יְרֹחָם בְּנוֹ אֶלְקָנָה בְנוֹ: ¹³ וּבְנֵי שְׁמוּאֵל הַבְּכֹר וַשְׁנִי וַאֲבִיָּה: ס ¹⁴ בְּנֵי מְרָרִי מַחְלִי לִבְנִי בְנוֹ שִׁמְעִי בְנוֹ עֻזָּה בְנוֹ: ¹⁵ שִׁמְעָא בְנוֹ חַגִּיָּה בְנוֹ עֲשָׂיָה בְנוֹ: פ

¹⁶ וְאֵלֶּה אֲשֶׁר הֶעֱמִיד דָּוִיד עַל־יְדֵי־שִׁיר בֵּית יְהוָה מִמְּנוֹחַ הָאָרוֹן: ¹⁷ וַיִּהְיוּ מְשָׁרְתִים לִפְנֵי מִשְׁכַּן אֹהֶל־מוֹעֵד בַּשִּׁיר עַד־בְּנוֹת שְׁלֹמֹה אֶת־בֵּית יְהוָה בִּירוּשָׁלָ͏ִם וַיַּעַמְדוּ כְמִשְׁפָּטָם עַל־עֲבוֹדָתָם: ¹⁸ וְאֵלֶּה הָעֹמְדִים וּבְנֵיהֶם מִבְּנֵי הַקְּהָתִי הֵימָן הַמְשׁוֹרֵר בֶּן־יוֹאֵל בֶּן־שְׁמוּאֵל: ¹⁹ בֶּן־אֶלְקָנָה בֶּן־יְרֹחָם בֶּן־אֱלִיאֵל בֶּן־תּוֹחַ: ²⁰ בֶּן־צִיף צוּף בֶּן־אֶלְקָנָה בֶּן־מַחַת בֶּן־עֲמָשָׂי: ²¹ בֶּן־אֶלְקָנָה בֶּן־יוֹאֵל בֶּן־עֲזַרְיָה בֶּן־צְפַנְיָה: ²² בֶּן־תַּחַת בֶּן־אַסִּיר בֶּן־אֶבְיָסָף בֶּן־קֹרַח: ²³ בֶּן־יִצְהָר בֶּן־קְהָת בֶּן־לֵוִי בֶּן־יִשְׂרָאֵל: ²⁴ וְאָחִיו אָסָף הָעֹמֵד עַל־יְמִינוֹ אָסָף בֶּן־בֶּרֶכְיָהוּ בֶּן־שִׁמְעָא: ²⁵ בֶּן־מִיכָאֵל בֶּן־בַּעֲשֵׂיָה בֶּן־מַלְכִּיָּה: ²⁶ בֶּן־אֶתְנִי בֶן־זֶרַח בֶּן־עֲדָיָה: ²⁷ בֶּן־אֵיתָן

---

a-a Some ancient vv. read "Joel, and the second"; cf. 1 Sam. 8.2.

1902

Ethan son of Zimmah son of Shimei ²⁸son of Jahath son of Gershom son of Levi. ²⁹On the left were their kinsmen: the sons of Merari: Ethan son of Kishi son of Abdi son of Malluch ³⁰son of Hashabiah son of Amaziah son of Hilkiah ³¹son of Amzi son of Bani son of Shemer ³²son of Mahli son of Mushi son of Merari son of Levi; ³³and their kinsmen the Levites were appointed for all the service of the Tabernacle of the House of God.

³⁴But Aaron and his sons made offerings upon the altar of burnt offering and upon the altar of incense, performing all the tasks of the most holy place, to make atonement for Israel, according to all that Moses the servant of God had commanded. ³⁵These are the sons of Aaron: his son Eleazar, his son Phinehas, his son Abishua, ³⁶his son Bukki, his son Uzzi, his son Zerahiah, ³⁷his son Meraioth, his son Amariah, his son Ahitub, ³⁸his son Zadok, his son Ahimaaz. ³⁹ᵇThese are their dwelling-places according to their settlements within their borders: to the sons of Aaron of the families of Kohathites, for theirs was the [first] lot; ⁴⁰they gave them Hebron in the land of Judah and its surrounding pasturelands, ⁴¹but the fields of the city and its villages they gave to Caleb son of Jephunneh. ⁴²To the sons of Aaron they gave the citiesᶜ of refuge: Hebron and Libnah with its pasturelands, Jattir and Eshtemoa with its pasturelands, ⁴³Hilen with its pasturelands, Debir with its pasturelands, ⁴⁴Ashan with its pasturelands, and Beth-shemesh with its pasturelands. ⁴⁵From the tribe of Benjamin, Geba with its pasturelands, Alemeth with its pasturelands, and Anathoth with its pasturelands. All their cities throughout their families were thirteen.

⁴⁶To the remaining Kohathites were given by lot out of the family of the tribe, out of the

בֶּן־זִמָּה בֶן־שִׁמְעִי׃ 28 בֶּן־יַחַת בֶּן־גֵּרְשֹׁם בֶּן־לֵוִי׃ ס 29 וּבְנֵי מְרָרִי אֲחֵיהֶם עַל־הַשְּׂמְאוֹל אֵיתָן בֶּן־קִישִׁי בֶן־עַבְדִּי בֶּן־מַלּוּךְ׃ 30 בֶּן־חֲשַׁבְיָה בֶן־אֲמַצְיָה בֶּן־חִלְקִיָּה׃ 31 בֶּן־אַמְצִי בֶן־בָּנִי בֶּן־שָׁמֶר׃ 32 בֶּן־מַחְלִי בֶּן־מוּשִׁי בֶּן־מְרָרִי בֶּן־לֵוִי׃ ס 33 וַאֲחֵיהֶם הַלְוִיִּם נְתוּנִים לְכָל־עֲבוֹדַת מִשְׁכַּן בֵּית הָאֱלֹהִים׃ 34 וְאַהֲרֹן וּבָנָיו מַקְטִירִים עַל־מִזְבַּח הָעוֹלָה וְעַל־מִזְבַּח הַקְּטֹרֶת לְכֹל מְלֶאכֶת קֹדֶשׁ הַקֳּדָשִׁים וּלְכַפֵּר עַל־יִשְׂרָאֵל כְּכֹל אֲשֶׁר צִוָּה מֹשֶׁה עֶבֶד הָאֱלֹהִים׃ פ 35 וְאֵלֶּה בְּנֵי אַהֲרֹן אֶלְעָזָר בְּנוֹ פִּינְחָס בְּנוֹ אֲבִישׁוּעַ בְּנוֹ׃ 36 בֻּקִּי בְנוֹ עֻזִּי בְנוֹ זְרַחְיָה בְנוֹ׃ 37 מְרָיוֹת בְּנוֹ אֲמַרְיָה בְנוֹ אֲחִיטוּב בְּנוֹ׃ 38 צָדוֹק בְּנוֹ אֲחִימַעַץ בְּנוֹ׃ ס 39 וְאֵלֶּה מוֹשְׁבוֹתָם לְטִירוֹתָם בִּגְבוּלָם לִבְנֵי אַהֲרֹן לְמִשְׁפַּחַת הַקְּהָתִי כִּי לָהֶם הָיָה הַגּוֹרָל׃ 40 וַיִּתְּנוּ לָהֶם אֶת־חֶבְרוֹן בְּאֶרֶץ יְהוּדָה וְאֶת־מִגְרָשֶׁיהָ סְבִיבֹתֶיהָ׃ 41 וְאֶת־שְׂדֵה הָעִיר וְאֶת־חֲצֵרֶיהָ נָתְנוּ לְכָלֵב בֶּן־יְפֻנֶּה׃ ס 42 וְלִבְנֵי אַהֲרֹן נָתְנוּ אֶת־עָרֵי הַמִּקְלָט אֶת־חֶבְרוֹן וְאֶת־לִבְנָה וְאֶת־מִגְרָשֶׁיהָ וְאֶת־יַתִּר וְאֶת־אֶשְׁתְּמֹעַ וְאֶת־מִגְרָשֶׁיהָ׃ 43 וְאֶת־חִילֵז* וְאֶת־מִגְרָשֶׁיהָ אֶת־דְּבִיר וְאֶת־מִגְרָשֶׁיהָ׃ 44 וְאֶת־עָשָׁן וְאֶת־מִגְרָשֶׁיהָ וְאֶת־בֵּית שֶׁמֶשׁ וְאֶת־מִגְרָשֶׁיהָ׃ ס 45 וּמִמַּטֵּה בִנְיָמִן אֶת־גֶּבַע וְאֶת־מִגְרָשֶׁיהָ וְאֶת־עָלֶמֶת וְאֶת־מִגְרָשֶׁיהָ וְאֶת־עֲנָתוֹת וְאֶת־מִגְרָשֶׁיהָ כָּל־עָרֵיהֶם שְׁלֹשׁ־עֶשְׂרֵה עִיר בְּמִשְׁפְּחוֹתֵיהֶם׃ ס 46 וְלִבְנֵי קְהָת הַנּוֹתָרִים מִמִּשְׁפַּחַת הַמַּטֶּה מִמַּחֲצִית מַטֵּה חֲצִי מְנַשֶּׁה בַּגּוֹרָל עָרִים

v. 43. בנוסח אחר "חילן״

b With vv. 24–51, cf. Josh. 21.3–42.
c Josh. 21.13, "city."

half-tribe, the half of Manasseh, ten cities. 47To the Gershomites according to their families were allotted thirteen cities out of the tribes of Issachar, Asher, Naphtali, and Manasseh in Bashan. 48To the Merarites according to their families were allotted twelve cities out of the tribes of Reuben, Gad, and Zebulun. 49So the people of Israel gave the Levites the cities with their pasturelands. 50They gave them by lot out of the tribe of the Judahites these cities that are mentioned by name, and out of the tribe of the Simeonites, and out of the tribe of the Benjaminites.

51And some of the families of the sons of Kohath had cities of their territory out of the tribe of Ephraim. 52They gave them the cities of refuge: Shechem with its pasturelands in the hill country of Ephraim, Gezer with its pasturelands, 53Jokmeam with its pasturelands, Beth-horon with its pasturelands, 54Aijalon with its pasturelands, Gath-rimmon with its pasturelands; 55and out of the half-tribe of Manasseh: Aner with its pasturelands, and Bileam with its pasturelands, for the rest of the families of the Kohathites.

56To the Gershomites; out of the half-tribe of Manasseh: Golan in Bashan with its pasturelands and Ashtaroth with its pasturelands; 57and out of the tribe of Issachar: Kedesh with its pasturelands, Dobrath with its pasturelands, 58Ramoth with its pasturelands, and Anem with its pasturelands; 59out of the tribe of Asher: Mashal with its pasturelands, Abdon with its pasturelands, 60Hukok with its pasturelands, and Rehob with its pasturelands; 61and out of the tribe of Naphtali: Kedesh in Galilee with its pasturelands; Hammon with its pasturelands, and Kiriathaim with its pasturelands. 62To the rest of the Merarites, out of the tribe of Zebulun: Rimmono with its

עֶשֶׂר: ס 47 וְלִבְנֵי גֵרְשׁוֹם לְמִשְׁפְּחוֹתָם מִמַּטֵּה יִשָּׂשכָר וּמִמַּטֵּה אָשֵׁר וּמִמַּטֵּה נַפְתָּלִי וּמִמַּטֵּה מְנַשֶּׁה בַּבָּשָׁן עָרִים שְׁלֹשׁ עֶשְׂרֵה: ס 48 לִבְנֵי מְרָרִי לְמִשְׁפְּחוֹתָם מִמַּטֵּה רְאוּבֵן וּמִמַּטֵּה־גָד וּמִמַּטֵּה זְבוּלֻן בַּגּוֹרָל עָרִים שְׁתֵּים עֶשְׂרֵה: 49 וַיִּתְּנוּ בְנֵי־יִשְׂרָאֵל לַלְוִיִּם אֶת־הֶעָרִים וְאֶת־מִגְרְשֵׁיהֶם: 50 וַיִּתְּנוּ בַגּוֹרָל מִמַּטֵּה בְנֵי־יְהוּדָה וּמִמַּטֵּה בְנֵי־שִׁמְעוֹן וּמִמַּטֵּה בְּנֵי בִנְיָמִן אֵת הֶעָרִים הָאֵלֶּה אֲשֶׁר־יִקְרְאוּ אֶתְהֶם בְּשֵׁמוֹת: ס

51 וּמִמִּשְׁפְּחוֹת בְּנֵי קְהָת וַיְהִי עָרֵי גְבוּלָם מִמַּטֵּה אֶפְרָיִם: 52 וַיִּתְּנוּ לָהֶם אֶת־עָרֵי הַמִּקְלָט אֶת־שְׁכֶם וְאֶת־מִגְרָשֶׁיהָ בְּהַר אֶפְרָיִם וְאֶת־גֶּזֶר וְאֶת־מִגְרָשֶׁיהָ: 53 וְאֶת־יָקְמְעָם וְאֶת־מִגְרָשֶׁיהָ וְאֶת־בֵּית חוֹרוֹן וְאֶת־מִגְרָשֶׁיהָ: 54 וְאֶת־אַיָּלוֹן וְאֶת־מִגְרָשֶׁיהָ וְאֶת־גַּת־רִמּוֹן וְאֶת־מִגְרָשֶׁיהָ: פ 55 וּמִמַּחֲצִית מַטֵּה מְנַשֶּׁה אֶת־עָנֵר וְאֶת־מִגְרָשֶׁיהָ וְאֶת־בִּלְעָם וְאֶת־מִגְרָשֶׁיהָ לְמִשְׁפַּחַת לִבְנֵי־קְהָת הַנּוֹתָרִים: פ 56 לִבְנֵי גֵרְשׁוֹם מִמִּשְׁפַּחַת חֲצִי מַטֵּה מְנַשֶּׁה אֶת־גּוֹלָן בַּבָּשָׁן וְאֶת־מִגְרָשֶׁיהָ וְאֶת־עַשְׁתָּרוֹת וְאֶת־מִגְרָשֶׁיהָ: ס 57 וּמִמַּטֵּה יִשָּׂשכָר אֶת־קֶדֶשׁ וְאֶת־מִגְרָשֶׁיהָ אֶת־דָּבְרַת וְאֶת־מִגְרָשֶׁיהָ: 58 וְאֶת־רָאמוֹת וְאֶת־מִגְרָשֶׁיהָ וְאֶת־עָנֵם וְאֶת־מִגְרָשֶׁיהָ: ס 59 וּמִמַּטֵּה אָשֵׁר אֶת־מָשָׁל וְאֶת־מִגְרָשֶׁיהָ וְאֶת־עַבְדּוֹן וְאֶת־מִגְרָשֶׁיהָ: 60 וְאֶת־חוּקֹק וְאֶת־מִגְרָשֶׁיהָ וְאֶת־רְחֹב וְאֶת־מִגְרָשֶׁיהָ: 61 וּמִמַּטֵּה נַפְתָּלִי אֶת־קֶדֶשׁ בַּגָּלִיל וְאֶת־מִגְרָשֶׁיהָ וְאֶת־חַמּוֹן וְאֶת־מִגְרָשֶׁיהָ וְאֶת־קִרְיָתַיִם וְאֶת־מִגְרָשֶׁיהָ: ס 62 לִבְנֵי מְרָרִי הַנּוֹתָרִים מִמַּטֵּה זְבוּלֻן אֶת־רִמּוֹנוֹ וְאֶת־

pasturelands, Tabor with its pasturelands; [63]and beyond the Jordan at Jericho, on the east side of the Jordan, out of the tribe of Reuben: Bezer in the wilderness with its pasturelands, Jahaz with its pasturelands, [64]Kedemoth with its pasturelands, and Mephaath with its pasture lands; [65]and out of the tribe of Gad: Ramoth in Gilead with its pasturelands, Mahanaim with its pasturelands, [66]Heshbon with its pasturelands, and Jazer with its pasturelands.

מִגְרָשֶׁיהָ אֶת־תָּבוֹר וְאֶת־מִגְרָשֶׁיהָ: [63] וּמֵעֵבֶר לְיַרְדֵּן יְרֵחוֹ לְמִזְרַח הַיַּרְדֵּן מִמַּטֵּה רְאוּבֵן אֶת־בֶּצֶר בַּמִּדְבָּר וְאֶת־מִגְרָשֶׁיהָ וְאֶת־יַהְצָה וְאֶת־מִגְרָשֶׁיהָ: [64] וְאֶת־קְדֵמוֹת וְאֶת־מִגְרָשֶׁיהָ וְאֶת־מֵיפַעַת וְאֶת־מִגְרָשֶׁיהָ: [65] וּמִמַּטֵּה־גָד אֶת־רָאמוֹת בַּגִּלְעָד וְאֶת־מִגְרָשֶׁיהָ וְאֶת־מַחֲנַיִם וְאֶת־מִגְרָשֶׁיהָ: [66] וְאֶת־חֶשְׁבּוֹן וְאֶת־מִגְרָשֶׁיהָ וְאֶת־יַעְזֵיר וְאֶת־מִגְרָשֶׁיהָ: ס

7 The sons of Issachar: Tola, Puah, Jashub, and Shimron—four. [2]The sons of Tola: Uzzi, Rephaiah, Jeriel, Jahmai, Ibsam, Shemuel, chiefs of their clans, men of substance according to their lines; their number in the days of David was 22,600. [3]The sons of Uzzi: Izrahiah. And the sons of Izrahiah: Michael, Obadiah, Joel, and Isshiah—five. All of them were chiefs. [4]And together with them, by their lines, according to their clans, were units of the fighting force, 36,000, for they had many wives and sons. [5]Their kinsmen belonging to all the families of Issachar were in all 87,000 men of substance; they were all registered by genealogy.

[6][The sons of] Benjamin: Bela, Becher, and Jediael—three. [7]The sons of Bela: Ezbon, Uzzi, Uzziel, Jerimoth, and Iri—five, chiefs of clans, men of substance, registered by genealogy— 22,034. [8]The sons of Becher: Zemirah, Joash, Eliezer, Elioenai, Omri, Jeremoth, Abijah, Anathoth, and Alemeth. All these were the sons of Becher; [9]and they were registered by genealogy according to their lines, as chiefs of their clans, men of substance—20,200. [10]The sons of Jediael: Bilhan. And the sons of Bilhan: Jeush, Benjamin, Ehud, Chenaanah, Zethan, Tarshish,

ז וְלִבְנֵי יִשָּׂשכָר תּוֹלָע וּפוּאָה* יָשִׁיב יָשׁוּב וְשִׁמְרוֹן אַרְבָּעָה: ס [2] וּבְנֵי תוֹלָע עֻזִּי וּרְפָיָה וִירִיאֵל וְיַחְמַי וְיִבְשָׂם וּשְׁמוּאֵל רָאשִׁים לְבֵית־אֲבוֹתָם לְתוֹלָע גִּבּוֹרֵי חַיִל לְתֹלְדוֹתָם מִסְפָּרָם בִּימֵי דָוִיד עֶשְׂרִים־ וּשְׁנַיִם אֶלֶף וְשֵׁשׁ מֵאוֹת: ס [3] וּבְנֵי עֻזִּי יִזְרַחְיָה וּבְנֵי יִזְרַחְיָה מִיכָאֵל וְעֹבַדְיָה וְיוֹאֵל יִשִּׁיָּה חֲמִשָּׁה רָאשִׁים כֻּלָּם: [4] וַעֲלֵיהֶם לְתֹלְדוֹתָם לְבֵית אֲבוֹתָם גְּדוּדֵי צְבָא מִלְחָמָה שְׁלֹשִׁים וְשִׁשָּׁה אֶלֶף כִּי־ הִרְבּוּ נָשִׁים וּבָנִים: [5] וַאֲחֵיהֶם לְכֹל מִשְׁפְּחוֹת יִשָּׂשכָר גִּבּוֹרֵי חֲיָלִים שְׁמוֹנִים וְשִׁבְעָה אֶלֶף הִתְיַחְשָׂם לַכֹּל: פ [6] בִּנְיָמִן בֶּלַע וָבֶכֶר וִידִיעֲאֵל שְׁלֹשָׁה: [7] וּבְנֵי בֶלַע אֶצְבּוֹן וְעֻזִּי וְעֻזִּיאֵל וִירִימוֹת וְעִירִי חֲמִשָּׁה רָאשֵׁי בֵּית אָבוֹת גִּבּוֹרֵי חֲיָלִים וְהִתְיַחְשָׂם עֶשְׂרִים וּשְׁנַיִם אֶלֶף וּשְׁלֹשִׁים וְאַרְבָּעָה: ס [8] וּבְנֵי בֶכֶר זְמִירָה וְיוֹעָשׁ וֶאֱלִיעֶזֶר וְאֶלְיוֹעֵינַי וְעָמְרִי וִירֵמוֹת וַאֲבִיָּה וַעֲנָתוֹת וָעָלֶמֶת כָּל־אֵלֶּה בְּנֵי־בָכֶר: [9] וְהִתְיַחְשָׂם לְתֹלְדוֹתָם רָאשֵׁי בֵּית אֲבוֹתָם גִּבּוֹרֵי חָיִל עֶשְׂרִים אֶלֶף וּמָאתָיִם: ס [10] וּבְנֵי יְדִיעֲאֵל בִּלְהָן וּבְנֵי בִלְהָן יעיש יְעוּשׁ וּבִנְיָמִן וְאֵהוּד וּכְנַעֲנָה

מלא א' v. 1.

and Ahishahar. 11All these were the sons of Jediael, chiefs of the clans, men of substance—17,200, who made up the fighting force. 12And Shuppim and Huppim were the sons of Ir; Hushim the sons of Aher.

13The sons of Naphtali: Jahziel, Guni, Jezer, and Shallum, the descendants of Bilhah.

14The sons of Manasseh: Asriel, whom his Aramean concubine bore; she bore Machir the father of Gilead. 15And Machir took wives for Huppim and for Shuppim. The name of his sister was Maacah. And the name of the second was Zelophehad; and Zelophehad had daughters. 16And Maacah the wife of Machir bore a son, and she named him Peresh; and the name of his brother was Sheresh; and his sons were Ulam and Rekem. 17The sons of Ulam: Bedan. These were the sons of Gilead son of Machir son of Manasseh. 18And his sister Hammolecheth bore Ishhod, Abiezer, and Mahlah. 19The sons of Shemida were Ahian, Shechem, Likhi, and Aniam.

20The sons of Ephraim: Shuthelah, his son Bered, his son Tahath, his son Eleadah, his son Tahath, 21his son Zabad, his son Shuthelah, also Ezer and Elead. The men of Gath, born in the land, killed them because they had gone down to take their cattle. 22And Ephraim their father mourned many days, and his brothers came to comfort him. 23He cohabited with his wife, who conceived and bore a son; and she named him Beriah, because it occurred when there was misfortune*a* in his house. 24His daughter was Sheerah, who built both Lower and Upper Beth-horon, and Uzzen-sheerah. 25His son Rephah, his son Resheph, his son Telah, his son Tahan, 26his son Ladan, his son Ammihud, his son Elishama, 27his son Non, his son Joshua. 28Their possessions and settlements were Bethel and its dependencies, and on the east Naaran, and on the west Gezer and its dependencies, Shechem

11 כָּל־אֵ֫לֶּה
בְּנֵ֣י יְדִֽיעֲאֵ֗ל לְרָאשֵׁ֤י הָֽאָבוֹת֙ גִּבּוֹרֵ֣י חֲיָלִ֔ים
שִׁבְעָֽה־עָשָׂ֥ר אֶ֖לֶף וּמָאתַ֑יִם יֹצְאֵ֥י צָבָ֖א
לַמִּלְחָמָֽה׃ 12 וְשֻׁפִּ֤ם וְחֻפִּם֙ בְּנֵ֣י עִ֔יר חֻשִׁ֖ם
בְּנֵ֥י אַחֵֽר׃

13 בְּנֵ֣י נַפְתָּלִ֗י יַחֲצִיאֵ֧ל וְגוּנִ֛י וְיֵ֖צֶר וְשַׁלּ֑וּם
בְּנֵ֥י בִלְהָֽה׃ פ

14 בְּנֵ֣י מְנַשֶּׁ֗ה אַשְׂרִיאֵל֙ אֲשֶׁ֣ר יָלָ֔דָה פִּֽילַגְשׁ֖וֹ
הָֽאֲרַמִּיָּ֑ה יָֽלְדָ֔ה אֶת־מָכִ֖יר אֲבִ֥י גִלְעָֽד׃
15 וּמָכִ֞יר לָקַ֤ח אִשָּׁה֙ לְחֻפִּ֣ים וּלְשֻׁפִּ֔ים וְשֵׁ֤ם
אֲחֹתוֹ֙ מַֽעֲכָ֔ה וְשֵׁ֥ם הַשֵּׁנִ֖י צְלׇפְחָ֑ד וַתִּהְיֶ֥נָה
לִצְלׇפְחָ֖ד בָּנֽוֹת׃ 16 וַתֵּ֨לֶד מַֽעֲכָ֣ה אֵֽשֶׁת־
מָכִיר֮ בֵּן֒ וַתִּקְרָ֤א שְׁמוֹ֙ פֶּ֔רֶשׁ וְשֵׁ֥ם
אָחִ֖יו שָׁ֑רֶשׁ וּבָנָ֖יו אוּלָ֥ם וָרָֽקֶם׃ 17 וּבְנֵ֥י
אוּלָ֖ם בְּדָ֑ן אֵ֚לֶּה בְּנֵ֣י גִלְעָ֔ד בֶּן־מָכִ֖יר
בֶּן־מְנַשֶּֽׁה׃ 18 וַֽאֲחֹתוֹ֙ הַמֹּלֶ֔כֶת יָֽלְדָ֖ה אֶת־
אִישְׁה֑וֹד וְאֶת־אֲבִיעֶ֖זֶר וְאֶת־מַחְלָֽה׃
19 וַיִּֽהְי֖וּ בְּנֵ֣י שְׁמִידָ֑ע אַחְיָ֣ן וָשֶׁ֔כֶם וְלִקְחִ֖י
וְאַנְיעָֽם׃ פ

20 וּבְנֵ֣י אֶפְרַ֔יִם שׁוּתֶ֖לַח וּבֶ֤רֶד בְּנוֹ֙ וְתַ֣חַת
בְּנ֔וֹ וְאֶלְעָדָ֥ה בְנ֖וֹ וְתַ֥חַת בְּנֽוֹ׃ 21 וְזָבָ֤ד בְּנוֹ֙
וְשׁוּתֶ֣לַח בְּנ֔וֹ וְעֵ֥זֶר וְאֶלְעָ֖ד וַֽהֲרָג֗וּם אַנְשֵׁי־
גַת֙ הַנּֽוֹלָדִ֣ים בָּאָ֔רֶץ כִּ֥י יָֽרְד֖וּ לָקַ֥חַת
אֶת־מִקְנֵיהֶֽם׃ 22 וַיִּתְאַבֵּ֛ל אֶפְרַ֥יִם אֲבִיהֶ֖ם
יָמִ֣ים רַבִּ֑ים וַיָּבֹ֥אוּ אֶחָ֖יו לְנַֽחֲמֽוֹ׃ 23 וַיָּבֹא֙
אֶל־אִשְׁתּ֔וֹ וַתַּ֖הַר וַתֵּ֣לֶד בֵּ֑ן וַיִּקְרָ֤א אֶת־
שְׁמוֹ֙ בְּרִיעָ֔ה כִּ֥י בְרָעָ֖ה הָֽיְתָ֥ה בְּבֵיתֽוֹ׃
24 וּבִתּ֣וֹ שֶֽׁאֱרָ֔ה וַתִּ֧בֶן אֶת־בֵּית־חוֹר֛וֹן
הַתַּחְתּ֖וֹן וְאֶת־הָֽעֶלְי֑וֹן וְאֵ֖ת אֻזֵּ֥ן שֶֽׁאֱרָֽה׃
25 וְרֶ֥פַח בְּנ֛וֹ וְרֶ֥שֶׁף וְתֶ֥לַח בְּנ֖וֹ וְתַ֥חַן בְּנֽוֹ׃
26 לַעְדָּ֥ן בְּנ֛וֹ עַמִּיה֥וּד בְּנ֖וֹ אֱלִֽישָׁמָ֥ע בְּנֽוֹ׃
27 נ֥וֹן בְּנ֖וֹ יְהוֹשֻׁ֥עַ בְּנֽוֹ׃ 28 וַֽאֲחֻזָּתָם֙
וּמֹֽשְׁבוֹתָ֔ם בֵּֽית־אֵ֖ל וּבְנֹתֶ֑יהָ וְלַמִּזְרָ֣ח נַֽעֲרָ֔ן
וְלַֽמַּעֲרָ֗ב גֶּ֤זֶר וּבְנֹתֶ֙יהָ֙ וּשְׁכֶ֣ם וּבְנֹתֶ֔יהָ עַד־

---

a Heb. bera'ah.

and its dependencies, and Aiah and its dependencies; ²⁹also along the borders of the Manassites, Beth-shean and its dependencies, Taanach and its dependencies, Megiddo and its dependencies, Dor and its dependencies. In these dwelt the sons of Joseph son of Israel.

³⁰The sons of Asher: Imnah, Ishvah, Ishvi, Beriah, and their sister Serah. ³¹The sons of Beriah: Heber and Malchiel, who was the father of Birzaith. ³²Heber begot Japhlet, Shomer, Hotham, and their sister, Shua. ³³The sons of Japhlet: Pasach, Bimhal, and Ashvath. These were the sons of Japhlet. ³⁴The sons of Shemer: Ahi, Rohgah, Hubbah, and Aram. ³⁵The sons of Helem his brother: Zophah, Imna, Shelesh, and Amal. ³⁶The sons of Zophah: Suah, Harnepher, Shual, Beri, Imrah, ³⁷Bezer, Hod, Shamma, Shilshah, Ithran, and Beera. ³⁸The sons of Jether: Jephunneh, Pispa, and Ara. ³⁹The sons of Ulla: Arah, Hanniel, and Rizia. ⁴⁰All of these men of Asher, chiefs of the clans, select men, men of substance, heads of the chieftains. And they were registered by genealogy according to fighting force; the number of the men was 26,000 men.

8 Benjamin begot Bela his first-born, Ashbel the second, Aharah the third, ²Nohah the fourth, and Rapha the fifth. ³And Bela had sons: Addar, Gera, Abihud, ⁴Abishua, Naaman, Ahoah, ⁵Gera, Shephuphan, and Huram. ⁶These were the sons of Ehud—they were chiefs of clans of the inhabitants of Geba, and they were exiled to Manahath: ⁷Naaman, Ahijah, and Gera—he exiled them and begot Uzza and Ahihud. ⁸And Shaharaim had sons in the country of Moab after he had sent away Hushim and Baara his wives. ⁹He had sons by Hodesh his wife: Jobab, Zibia, Mesha, Malcam, ¹⁰Jeuz,

עֲזָּה וּבְנֹתֶיהָ: ²⁹ וְעַל־יְדֵי בְנֵי־מְנַשֶּׁה בֵּית־שְׁאָן וּבְנֹתֶיהָ תַּעְנַךְ וּבְנֹתֶיהָ מְגִדּוֹ וּבְנוֹתֶיהָ דּוֹר וּבְנוֹתֶיהָ בְּאֵלֶּה יָשְׁבוּ בְּנֵי יוֹסֵף בֶּן־יִשְׂרָאֵל: פ
³⁰ בְּנֵי אָשֵׁר יִמְנָה וְיִשְׁוָה וְיִשְׁוִי וּבְרִיעָה וְשֶׂרַח אֲחוֹתָם: ³¹ וּבְנֵי בְרִיעָה חֶבֶר וּמַלְכִּיאֵל הוּא אֲבִי בִרְזָוִת: ³² וְחֶבֶר הוֹלִיד אֶת־יַפְלֵט וְאֶת־שׁוֹמֵר וְאֶת־חוֹתָם וְאֵת שׁוּעָא אֲחוֹתָם: ³³ וּבְנֵי יַפְלֵט פָּסַךְ וּבִמְהָל וְעַשְׁוָת אֵלֶּה בְּנֵי יַפְלֵט: ³⁴ וּבְנֵי שֶׁמֶר אֲחִי וְרוֹהְגָּה יְחֻבָּה וַֽאֲרָם: ³⁵ וּבֶן*־הֵלֶם אָחִיו צוֹפַח וְיִמְנָע וְשֵׁלֶשׁ וְעָמָל: ³⁶ בְּנֵי צוֹפַח סוּחַ וְחַרְנֶפֶר וְשׁוּעָל וּבֵרִי וְיִמְרָה: ³⁷ בֶּצֶר וָהוֹד וְשַׁמָּא וְשִׁלְשָׁה וְיִתְרָן וּבְאֵרָא: ³⁸ וּבְנֵי יֶתֶר יְפֻנֶּה וּפִסְפָּה וַאֲרָא: ³⁹ וּבְנֵי עֻלָּא אָרַח וְחַנִּיאֵל וְרִֽצְיָא: ⁴⁰ כָּל־אֵלֶּה בְנֵי־אָשֵׁר רָאשֵׁי בֵית־הָאָבוֹת בְּרוּרִים גִּבּוֹרֵי חֲיָלִים רָאשֵׁי הַנְּשִׂיאִים וְהִתְיַחְשָׂם בַּצָּבָא בַּמִּלְחָמָה מִסְפָּרָם אֲנָשִׁים עֶשְׂרִים וְשִׁשָּׁה אָלֶף: ס

ח וּבִנְיָמִן הוֹלִיד אֶת־בֶּלַע בְּכֹרוֹ אַשְׁבֵּל הַשֵּׁנִי וְאַחְרַח הַשְּׁלִישִׁי: ² נוֹחָה הָרְבִיעִי וְרָפָא הַחֲמִישִׁי: ס ³ וַיִּהְיוּ בָנִים לְבָלַע אַדָּר וְגֵרָא וַאֲבִיהוּד: ⁴ וַאֲבִישׁוּעַ וְנַעֲמָן וַאֲחוֹחַ: ⁵ וְגֵרָא וּשְׁפוּפָן וְחוּרָם: ⁶ וְאֵלֶּה בְּנֵי אֵחוּד אֵלֶּה הֵם רָאשֵׁי אָבוֹת לְיוֹשְׁבֵי גֶבַע וַיַּגְלוּם אֶל־מָנָחַת: ⁷ וְנַעֲמָן וַאֲחִיָּה וְגֵרָא הוּא הֶגְלָם וְהוֹלִיד אֶת־עֻזָּא וְאֶת־אֲחִיחֻד: ⁸ וְשַׁחֲרַיִם הוֹלִיד בִּשְׂדֵה מוֹאָב מִן־שִׁלְחוֹ אֹתָם חוּשִׁים וְאֶת־בַּעֲרָא נָשָׁיו: ⁹ וַיּוֹלֶד מִן־חֹדֶשׁ אִשְׁתּוֹ אֶת־יוֹבָב וְאֶת־צִבְיָא וְאֶת־מֵישָׁא וְאֶת־מַלְכָּם: ¹⁰ וְאֶת־

Sachiah, and Mirmah. These were his sons, chiefs of clans. ¹¹He also begot by Hushim: Abitub and Elpaal. ¹²The sons of Elpaal: Eber, Misham, and Shemed, who built Ono and Lod with its dependencies, ¹³and Beriah and Shema—they were chiefs of clans of the inhabitants of Aijalon, who put to flight the inhabitants of Gath; ¹⁴and Ahio, Shashak, and Jeremoth. ¹⁵Zebadiah, Arad, Eder, ¹⁶Michael, Ishpah, and Joha were sons of Beriah. ¹⁷Zebadiah, Meshullam, Hizki, Heber, ¹⁸Ishmerai, Izliah, and Jobab were the sons of Elpaal. ¹⁹Jakim, Zichri, Zabdi, ²⁰Elienai, Zillethai, Eliel, ²¹Adaiah, Beraiah, and Shimrath were the sons of Shimei. ²²Ishpan, Eber, Eliel, ²³Abdon, Zichri, Hanan, ²⁴Hananiah, Elam, Anthothiah, ²⁵Iphdeiah, and Penuel were the sons of Shashak. ²⁶Shamsherai, Shehariah, Athaliah, ²⁷Jaareshiah, Elijah, and Zichri were the sons of Jeroham. ²⁸These were the chiefs of the clans, according to their lines. These chiefs dwelt in Jerusalem.

²⁹The father of Gibeon dwelt in Gibeon, and the name of his wife was Maacah. ³⁰His first-born son: Abdon; then Zur, Kish, Baal, Nadab, ³¹Gedor, Ahio, Zecher. ³²Mikloth begot Shimeah. And they dwelt in Jerusalem opposite their kinsmen, with their kinsmen. ³³Ner begot Kish, Kish begot Saul, Saul begot Jonathan, Malchi-shua, Abinadab, and Eshbaal; ³⁴and the son of Jonathan was Merib-baal; and Merib-baal begot Micah. ³⁵The sons of Micah: Pithon, Melech, Taarea, and Ahaz. ³⁶Ahaz begot Jehoaddah; and Jehoaddah begot Alemeth, Azmaveth, and Zimri; Zimri begot Moza. ³⁷Moza begot Binea; his son Raphah; his son Eleasah, his son Azel. ³⁸Azel had six sons, and

יְעוּץ וְאֶת־שָׂכְיָה וְאֶת־מִרְמָה אֵלֶּה בָנָיו
רָאשֵׁי אָבוֹת: 11 וּמַחְשִׁים הוֹלִיד אֶת־
אֲבִיטוּב וְאֶת־אֶלְפָּעַל: 12 וּבְנֵי אֶלְפַּעַל
עֵבֶר וּמִשְׁעָם וָשֶׁמֶד הוּא בָּנָה אֶת־
אוֹנוֹ וְאֶת־לֹד וּבְנֹתֶיהָ: 13 וּבְרִעָה וָשֶׁמַע
הֵמָּה רָאשֵׁי הָאָבוֹת לְיוֹשְׁבֵי אַיָּלוֹן
הֵמָּה הִבְרִיחוּ אֶת־יוֹשְׁבֵי גַת: 14 וְאַחְיוֹ
שָׁשָׁק וִירֵמוֹת: 15 וּזְבַדְיָה וַעֲרָד וָעָדֶר:
16 וּמִיכָאֵל וְיִשְׁפָּה וְיוֹחָא בְּנֵי בְרִיעָה:
17 וּזְבַדְיָה וּמְשֻׁלָּם וְחִזְקִי וָחָבֶר: 18 וְיִשְׁמְרַי
וְיִזְלִיאָה וְיוֹבָב בְּנֵי אֶלְפָּעַל: 19 וְיָקִים
וְזִכְרִי וְזַבְדִּי: 20 וָאֱלִיעֵנַי וְצִלְּתַי וֶאֱלִיאֵל:
21 וַעֲדָיָה וּבְרָאיָה וְשִׁמְרָת בְּנֵי שִׁמְעִי:
22 וְיִשְׁפָּן וָעֵבֶר וֶאֱלִיאֵל: 23 וְעַבְדּוֹן וְזִכְרִי
וְחָנָן: 24 וַחֲנַנְיָה וְעֵילָם וְעַנְתֹתִיָּה:
25 וְיִפְדְּיָה וּפְנוּאֵל בְּנֵי שָׁשָׁק:
26 וְשַׁמְשְׁרַי וּשְׁחַרְיָה וַעֲתַלְיָה: 27 וְיַעֲרֶשְׁיָה
וְאֵלִיָּה וְזִכְרִי בְּנֵי יְרֹחָם: 28 אֵלֶּה רָאשֵׁי
אָבוֹת לְתֹלְדוֹתָם רָאשִׁים אֵלֶּה יָשְׁבוּ
בִירוּשָׁלִָם: ס
29 וּבְגִבְעוֹן יָשְׁבוּ אֲבִי גִבְעוֹן וְשֵׁם אִשְׁתּוֹ
מַעֲכָה: 30 וּבְנוֹ הַבְּכוֹר עַבְדּוֹן וְצוּר וְקִישׁ
וּבַעַל וְנָדָב: 31 וּגְדוֹר וְאַחְיוֹ וָזָכֶר:
32 וּמִקְלוֹת הוֹלִיד אֶת־שִׁמְאָה וְאַף־הֵמָּה
נֶגֶד אֲחֵיהֶם יָשְׁבוּ בִירוּשָׁלִַם עִם־
אֲחֵיהֶם: ס 33 וְנֵר הוֹלִיד אֶת־קִישׁ
וְקִישׁ הוֹלִיד אֶת־שָׁאוּל וְשָׁאוּל הוֹלִיד
אֶת־יְהוֹנָתָן וְאֶת־מַלְכִּי־שׁוּעַ וְאֶת־
אֲבִינָדָב וְאֶת־אֶשְׁבָּעַל: 34 וּבֶן־יְהוֹנָתָן
מְרִיב בָּעַל וּמְרִיב בַּעַל הוֹלִיד אֶת־
מִיכָה: ס 35 וּבְנֵי מִיכָה פִּיתוֹן וָמֶלֶךְ
וְתַאְרֵעַ וְאָחָז: 36 וְאָחָז הוֹלִיד אֶת־
יְהוֹעַדָּה וִיהוֹעַדָּה הוֹלִיד אֶת־עָלֶמֶת
וְאֶת־עַזְמָוֶת וְאֶת־זִמְרִי וְזִמְרִי הוֹלִיד אֶת־
מוֹצָא: 37 וּמוֹצָא הוֹלִיד אֶת־בִּנְעָא רָפָה
בְנוֹ אֶלְעָשָׂה בְנוֹ אָצֵל בְּנוֹ: 38 וּלְאָצֵל

these are their names: Azrikam, Bocheru, Ishmael, Sheariah, Obadiah, and Hanan. All these were the sons of Azel. 39The sons of Eshek his brother: Ulam his first-born, Jeush the second, and Eliphelet the third. 40The descendants of Ulam—men of substance, who drew the bow, had many children and grandchildren—one hundred and fifty; all these were Benjaminites.

9 All Israel was registered by genealogies; and these are in the book of the kings of Israel. And Judah was taken into exile in Babylon because of their trespass. 2aThe first to settle in their towns, on their property, were Israelites, priests, Levites, and temple servants, 3while some of the Judahites and some of the Benjaminites and some of the Ephraimites and Manassehites settled in Jerusalem; 4Uthai son of Ammihud son of Omri son of Imri son of Bani, from the sons of Perez son of Judah; 5and of the Shilonites: Asaiah the first-born and his sons. 6Of the sons of Zerah: Jeuel and their kinsmen—690. 7Of the Benjaminites: Sallu son of Meshullam son of Hodaviah son of Hassenuah, 8Ibneiah son of Jeroham, Elah son of Uzzi son of Michri, and Meshullam son of Shephatiah son of Reuel son of Ibneiah; 9and their kinsmen, according to their lines—956. All these were chiefs of their ancestral clans.

10Of the priests: Jedaiah, Jehoiarib, Jachin, 11and Azariah son of Hilkiah son of Meshullam son of Zadok son of Meraioth son of Ahitub, chief officer of the House of God; 12and Adaiah son of Jeroham son of Pashhur son of Malchijah, and Maasai son of Adiel son of Jahzerah son of Meshullam son of Meshillemith son of Immer, 13together with their kinsmen, chiefs of their clans—1,760, men of substance for the work of the service of the House of God.

---

a With vv. 2–17, cf. Neh. 11.3–19.

שִׁשָּׁה בָנִים֙ וְאֵ֣לֶּה שְׁמוֹתָ֔ם עַזְרִיקָ֣ם ׀ בֹּ֣כְרוּ
וְיִשְׁמָעֵ֧אל וּשְׁעַרְיָ֛ה וְעֹבַדְיָ֖ה וְחָנָ֑ן כָּל־אֵ֖לֶּה
בְּנֵ֥י אָצַֽל׃ 39 וּבְנֵ֖י עֵ֣שֶׁק אָחִ֑יו אוּלָ֣ם בְּכֹר֗וֹ
יְע֤וּשׁ הַשֵּׁנִי֙ וֶֽאֱלִיפֶ֖לֶט הַשְּׁלִשִֽׁי׃ 40 וַיִּהְי֣וּ
בְנֵי־א֠וּלָם אֲנָשִׁ֨ים גִּבּ֥וֹרֵי־חַ֙יִל֙ דֹּ֣רְכֵי קֶ֔שֶׁת
וּמַרְבִּ֣ים בָּנִ֔ים וּבְנֵ֥י בָנִ֖ים מֵאָ֣ה וַחֲמִשִּׁ֑ים
כָּל־אֵ֖לֶּה מִבְּנֵ֥י בִנְיָמִֽן׃ פ

ט וְכָל־יִשְׂרָאֵל֙ הִתְיַחְשׂ֔וּ וְהִנָּ֥ם כְּתוּבִ֖ים
עַל־סֵ֣פֶר מַלְכֵ֣י יִשְׂרָאֵ֑ל וִיהוּדָ֛ה הָגְל֥וּ לְבָבֶ֖ל
בְּמַעֲלָֽם׃ ס 2 וְהַיּֽוֹשְׁבִים֙ הָרִ֣אשֹׁנִ֔ים
אֲשֶׁ֥ר בַּאֲחֻזָּתָ֖ם בְּעָרֵיהֶ֑ם יִשְׂרָאֵל֙ הַכֹּ֣הֲנִ֔ים
הַלְוִיִּ֖ם וְהַנְּתִינִֽים׃ 3 וּבִירֽוּשָׁלַ֙͏ִם֙ יָֽשְׁב֔וּ מִן־
בְּנֵ֣י יְהוּדָ֔ה וּמִן־בְּנֵ֥י בִנְיָמִ֖ן וּמִן־בְּנֵ֥י אֶפְרַ֖יִם
וּמְנַשֶּֽׁה׃ 4 עוּתַ֨י בֶּן־עַמִּיה֜וּד בֶּן־עָמְרִ֣י בֶּן־
אִמְרִ֤י בֶן־בנימן בָּנִ֔י מִן־בְּנֵי־פֶ֖רֶץ בֶּן־
יְהוּדָֽה׃ 5 וּמִן־הַשִּֽׁילוֹנִ֑י עֲשָׂיָ֥ה הַבְּכ֖וֹר
וּבָנָֽיו׃ 6 וּמִן־בְּנֵי־זֶ֖רַח יְעוּאֵ֣ל וַאֲחֵיהֶ֑ם
שֵׁשׁ־מֵא֖וֹת וְתִשְׁעִֽים׃ 7 וּמִן־בְּנֵ֖י בִּנְיָמִ֑ן
סַלּוּא֙ בֶּן־מְשֻׁלָּ֔ם בֶּן־הֽוֹדַוְיָ֖ה בֶּן־הַסְּנֻאָֽה׃
8 וְיִבְנְיָ֣ה בֶּן־יְרֹחָ֔ם וְאֵלָ֥ה בֶן־עֻזִּ֖י בֶּן־מִכְרִ֑י
וּמְשֻׁלָּם֙ בֶּן־שְׁפַטְיָ֔ה בֶּן־רְעוּאֵ֖ל בֶּן־יִבְנִיָּֽה׃
9 וַאֲחֵיהֶ֣ם לְתֹלְדוֹתָ֔ם תְּשַׁ֥ע מֵא֖וֹת
וַחֲמִשִּׁ֣ים וְשִׁשָּׁ֑ה כָּל־אֵ֣לֶּה אֲנָשִׁים֙ רָאשֵׁ֣י
אָב֔וֹת לְבֵ֖ית אֲבֹתֵיהֶֽם׃ ס
10 וּמִן־הַכֹּהֲנִ֑ים יְדַֽעְיָ֥ה וִיהוֹיָרִ֖יב וְיָכִֽין׃
11 וַעֲזַרְיָ֨ה בֶן־חִלְקִיָּ֜ה בֶּן־מְשֻׁלָּ֣ם בֶּן־
צָד֗וֹק בֶּן־מְרָיוֹת֙ בֶּן־אֲחִיט֔וּב נְגִ֖יד בֵּ֣ית
הָאֱלֹהִֽים׃ ס 12 וַעֲדָיָה֙ בֶּן־יְרֹחָ֔ם בֶּן־
פַּשְׁח֖וּר בֶּן־מַלְכִּיָּ֑ה וּמַעְשַׂ֨י בֶּן־עֲדִיאֵ֧ל בֶּן־
יַחְזֵ֛רָה בֶּן־מְשֻׁלָּ֥ם בֶּן־מְשִׁלֵּמִ֖ית בֶּן־אִמֵּֽר׃
13 וַאֲחֵיהֶ֗ם רָאשִׁים֙ לְבֵ֣ית אֲבוֹתָ֔ם אֶ֕לֶף
וּשְׁבַ֥ע מֵא֖וֹת וְשִׁשִּׁ֑ים גִּבּ֥וֹרֵי חֵ֖יל מְלֶ֣אכֶת
עֲבוֹדַ֥ת בֵּית־הָאֱלֹהִֽים׃

14Of the Levites: Shemaiah son of Hasshub son of Azrikam son of Hashabiah, of the sons of Merari; 15and Bakbakkar, Heresh, Galal, and Mattaniah son of Mica son of Zichri son of Asaph; 16and Obadiah son of Shemaiah son of Galal son of Jeduthun, and Berechiah son of Asa son of Elkanah, who dwelt in the villages of the Netophathites.

17The gatekeepers were: Shallum, Akkub, Talmon, Ahiman; and their kinsman Shallum was the chief 18hitherto in the King's Gate on the east. They were the keepers belonging to the Levite camp. 19Shallum son of Kore son of Ebiasaph son of Korah, and his kinsmen of his clan, the Korahites, were in charge of the work of the service, guards of the threshold of the Tent; their fathers had been guards of the entrance to the camp of the LORD. 20And Phinehas son of Eleazar was the chief officer over them in time past; the LORD was with him. 21Zechariah the son of Meshelemiah was gatekeeper at the entrance of the Tent of Meeting. 22All these, who were selected as gatekeepers at the thresholds, were 212. They were selected by genealogies in their villages. David and Samuel the seer established them in their office of trust. 23They and their descendants were in charge of the gates of the House of the LORD, that is, the House of the Tent, as guards. 24The gatekeepers were on the four sides, east, west, north, and south; 25and their kinsmen in their villages were obliged to join them every seven days, according to a fixed schedule. 26The four chief gatekeepers, who were Levites, were entrusted to be over the chambers and the treasuries of the House of God. 27They spent the night near the House of God; for they had to do guard duty, and they were in charge of opening it every morning.

28Some of them had charge of the service vessels, for they were counted when they were

14 וּמִן־הַלְוִיִּם שְׁמַעְיָה בֶן־חַשּׁוּב בֶּן־עַזְרִיקָם בֶּן־חֲשַׁבְיָה מִן־בְּנֵי מְרָרִי: 15 וּבַקְבַּקַּר חֶרֶשׁ וְגָלָל וּמַתַּנְיָה בֶּן־מִיכָא בֶּן־זִכְרִי בֶּן־אָסָף: 16 וְעֹבַדְיָה בֶּן־שְׁמַעְיָה בֶּן־גָּלָל בֶּן־יְדוּתוּן וּבֶרֶכְיָה בֶן־אָסָא בֶּן־אֶלְקָנָה הַיּוֹשֵׁב בְּחַצְרֵי נְטוֹפָתִי: 17 וְהַשֹּׁעֲרִים שַׁלּוּם וְעַקּוּב וְטַלְמֹן וַאֲחִימָן וַאֲחִיהֶם שַׁלּוּם הָרֹאשׁ: 18 וְעַד־הֵנָּה בְּשַׁעַר הַמֶּלֶךְ מִזְרָחָה הֵמָּה הַשֹּׁעֲרִים לְמַחֲנוֹת בְּנֵי לֵוִי: 19 וְשַׁלּוּם בֶּן־קוֹרֵא בֶּן־אֶבְיָסָף בֶּן־קֹרַח וְאֶחָיו לְבֵית־אָבִיו הַקָּרְחִים עַל מְלֶאכֶת הָעֲבוֹדָה שֹׁמְרֵי הַסִּפִּים לָאֹהֶל וַאֲבֹתֵיהֶם עַל־מַחֲנֵה יְהוָה שֹׁמְרֵי הַמָּבוֹא: 20 וּפִינְחָס בֶּן־אֶלְעָזָר נָגִיד הָיָה עֲלֵיהֶם לְפָנִים יְהוָה | עִמּוֹ: 21 זְכַרְיָה בֶּן מְשֶׁלֶמְיָה שֹׁעֵר פֶּתַח לְאֹהֶל מוֹעֵד: 22 כֻּלָּם הַבְּרוּרִים לְשֹׁעֲרִים בַּסִּפִּים מָאתַיִם וּשְׁנֵים עָשָׂר הֵמָּה בְחַצְרֵיהֶם הִתְיַחְשָׂם הֵמָּה יִסַּד דָּוִיד וּשְׁמוּאֵל הָרֹאֶה בֶּאֱמוּנָתָם: 23 וְהֵם וּבְנֵיהֶם עַל־הַשְּׁעָרִים לְבֵית־יְהוָה לְבֵית־הָאֹהֶל לְמִשְׁמָרוֹת: 24 לְאַרְבַּע רוּחוֹת יִהְיוּ הַשֹּׁעֲרִים מִזְרָח יָמָּה צָפוֹנָה וָנֶגְבָּה: 25 וַאֲחֵיהֶם בְּחַצְרֵיהֶם לָבוֹא לְשִׁבְעַת הַיָּמִים מֵעֵת אֶל־עֵת עִם־אֵלֶּה: 26 כִּי בֶאֱמוּנָה הֵמָּה אַרְבַּעַת גִּבֹּרֵי הַשֹּׁעֲרִים הֵם הַלְוִיִּם וְהָיוּ עַל־הַלְּשָׁכוֹת וְעַל הָאֹצָרוֹת בֵּית הָאֱלֹהִים: 27 וּסְבִיבוֹת בֵּית־הָאֱלֹהִים יָלִינוּ כִּי־עֲלֵיהֶם מִשְׁמֶרֶת וְהֵם עַל־הַמַּפְתֵּחַ וְלַבֹּקֶר לַבֹּקֶר: 28 וּמֵהֶם עַל־כְּלֵי הָעֲבוֹדָה כִּי־בְמִסְפָּר יְבִיאוּם וּבְמִסְפָּר יוֹצִיאוּם: 29 וּמֵהֶם מְמֻנִּים עַל־הַכֵּלִים וְעַל כָּל־כְּלֵי הַקֹּדֶשׁ

brought back and taken out. 29Some of them were in charge of the vessels and all the holy vessels, and of the flour, wine, oil, incense, and spices. 30Some of the priests blended the compound of spices. 31Mattithiah, one of the Levites, the first-born of Shallum the Korahite, was entrusted with making the flat cakes. 32Also some of their Kohathite kinsmen had charge of the rows of bread, to prepare them for each sabbath.

33Now these are the singers, the chiefs of Levitical clans who remained in the chambers free of other service, for they were on duty day and night. 34These were chiefs of Levitical clans, according to their lines; these chiefs lived in Jerusalem.

35The father of Gibeon, Jeiel, lived in Gibeon, and the name of his wife was Maacah. 36His first-born son, Abdon; then Zur, Kish, Baal, Ner, Nadab, 37Gedor, Ahio, Zechariah, and Mikloth; 38Mikloth begot Shimeam; and they lived in Jerusalem opposite their kinsmen, with their kinsmen. 39Ner begot Kish, Kish begot Saul, Saul begot Jonathan, Malchi-shua, Abinadab, and Eshbaal; 40and the son of Jonathan was Merib-baal; and Merib-baal begot Micah. 41The sons of Micah: Pithon, Melech, Taharea; 42Ahaz begot Jarah, and Jarah begot Alemeth, Azmaveth, and Zimri; Zimri begot Moza. 43Moza begot Binea; his son was Rephaiah, his son Eleasah, his son Azel. 44Azel had six sons and these were their names: Azrikam, Bocheru, Ishmael, Sheariah, Obadiah, and Hanan. These were the sons of Azel.

10 aThe Philistines attacked Israel, and the men of Israel fled before the Philistines and [many] fell on Mount Gilboa. 2The Philistines pursued Saul and his sons, and the Philistines

וְעַל־הַסֹּ֫לֶת וְהַיַּ֫יִן וְהַשֶּׁ֫מֶן וְהַלְּבוֹנָ֖ה וְהַבְּשָׂמִֽים׃ 30 וּמִן־בְּנֵי֙ הַכֹּ֣הֲנִ֔ים רֹקְחֵ֥י הַמִּרְקַ֖חַת לַבְּשָׂמִֽים׃ 31 וּמַתִּתְיָה֙ מִן־הַלְוִיִּ֔ם ה֥וּא הַבְּכ֖וֹר לְשַׁלֻּ֣ם הַקָּרְחִ֑י בֶּאֱמוּנָ֖ה עַ֥ל מַעֲשֵׂ֥ה הַחֲבִתִּֽים׃ 32 וּמִן־בְּנֵ֧י הַקְּהָתִ֣י מִן־אֲחֵיהֶ֗ם עַל־לֶ֣חֶם הַֽמַּעֲרָ֑כֶת לְהָכִ֖ין שַׁבַּ֥ת שַׁבָּֽת׃ ס

33 וְאֵ֙לֶּה֙ הַמְשֹׁ֣רְרִ֔ים רָאשֵׁ֥י אָב֖וֹת לַלְוִיִּ֑ם בַּלְּשָׁכֹ֣ת פְּטוּרִ֔ים כִּֽי־יוֹמָ֥ם וָלַ֖יְלָה עֲלֵיהֶ֥ם בַּמְּלָאכָֽה׃ 34 אֵ֜לֶּה רָאשֵׁ֧י הָאָב֛וֹת לַלְוִיִּ֖ם לְתֹלְדוֹתָ֣ם רָאשִׁ֑ים אֵ֖לֶּה יָשְׁב֥וּ בִירֽוּשָׁלָֽ͏ִם׃ פ

35 וּבְגִבְע֛וֹן יָשְׁב֥וּ אֲבִֽי־גִבְע֖וֹן יְעִיאֵ֑ל וְשֵׁ֥ם אִשְׁתּ֖וֹ מַעֲכָֽה׃ 36 וּבְנ֥וֹ הַבְּכ֖וֹר עַבְדּ֑וֹן וְצ֣וּר וְקִ֔ישׁ וּבַ֥עַל וְנֵ֖ר וְנָדָֽב׃ 37 וּגְד֣וֹר וְאַחְי֗וֹ וּזְכַרְיָ֖ה וּמִקְלֽוֹת׃ 38 וּמִקְל֖וֹת הוֹלִ֣יד אֶת־שִׁמְאָ֑ם וְאַף־הֵ֗ם נֶ֧גֶד אֲחֵיהֶ֛ם יָשְׁב֥וּ בִירוּשָׁלַ֖͏ִם עִם־אֲחֵיהֶֽם׃ ס 39 וְנֵר֙ הוֹלִ֣יד אֶת־קִ֔ישׁ וְקִ֖ישׁ הוֹלִ֣יד אֶת־שָׁא֑וּל וְשָׁא֗וּל הוֹלִ֤יד אֶת־יְהֽוֹנָתָן֙ וְאֶת־מַלְכִּי־שׁ֔וּעַ וְאֶת־אֲבִינָדָ֖ב וְאֶת־אֶשְׁבָּֽעַל׃ 40 וּבֶן־יְה֖וֹנָתָ֑ן מְרִ֣יב בָּ֑עַל וּמְרִי־בַ֖עַל הוֹלִ֥יד אֶת־מִיכָֽה׃ 41 וּבְנֵ֖י מִיכָ֑ה פִּית֥וֹן וָמֶ֖לֶךְ וְתַחְרֵֽעַ׃ 42 וְאָחָז֙ הוֹלִ֣יד אֶת־יַעְרָ֔ה וְיַעְרָ֕ה הוֹלִ֖יד אֶת־עָלֶ֣מֶת וְאֶת־עַזְמָ֑וֶת וְאֶת־זִמְרִ֕י וְזִמְרִ֖י הוֹלִ֥יד אֶת־מוֹצָֽא׃ 43 וּמוֹצָ֖א הוֹלִ֣יד אֶת־בִּנְעָ֑א וּרְפָיָ֥ה בְנ֛וֹ אֶלְעָשָׂ֥ה בְנ֖וֹ אָצֵ֥ל בְּנֽוֹ׃ 44 וּלְאָצֵל֮ שִׁשָּׁ֣ה בָנִים֒ וְאֵ֣לֶּה שְׁמוֹתָ֗ם עַזְרִיקָ֣ם ׀ בֹּ֠כְרוּ וְיִשְׁמָעֵ֧אל וּשְׁעַרְיָ֛ה וְעֹבַדְיָ֥ה וְחָנָ֖ן אֵ֥לֶּה בְּנֵ֥י אָצַֽל׃ פ

י וּפְלִשְׁתִּ֖ים נִלְחֲמ֣וּ בְיִשְׂרָאֵ֑ל וַיָּ֣נָס אִֽישׁ־יִשְׂרָאֵ֗ל מִפְּנֵ֣י פְלִשְׁתִּ֔ים וַיִּפְּל֥וּ חֲלָלִ֖ים בְּהַ֥ר גִּלְבֹּֽעַ׃ 2 וַיַּדְבְּק֣וּ פְלִשְׁתִּ֔ים אַחֲרֵ֥י

---

a   With vv. 1–12, cf. 1 Sam. 31.1–13.

struck down Jonathan, Abinadab, and Malchi-shua, sons of Saul. ³The battle raged around Saul, and the archers hit him, and he *b-was wounded-b* by the archers. ⁴Saul said to his arms-bearer, "Draw your sword and run me through, so that these uncircumcised may not come and make sport of me." But his arms-bearer, out of great awe, refused; whereupon Saul grasped the sword and fell upon it. ⁵When the arms-bearer saw that Saul was dead, he too fell on his sword and died. ⁶Thus Saul and his three sons and his entire house died together. ⁷And when all the men of Israel who were in the valley saw that they*c* had fled and that Saul and his sons were dead, they abandoned their towns and fled; the Philistines then came and occupied them.

⁸The next day the Philistines came to strip the slain, and they found Saul and his sons lying on Mount Gilboa. ⁹They stripped him, and carried off his head and his armor, and sent them throughout the land of the Philistines to spread the news to their idols and among the people. ¹⁰They placed his armor in the temple of their god, and they impaled his head in the temple of Dagan. ¹¹When all Jabesh-gilead heard everything that the Philistines had done to Saul, ¹²all their stalwart men set out, removed the bodies of Saul and his sons, and brought them to Jabesh. They buried the bones under the oak tree in Jabesh, and they fasted for seven days. ¹³Saul died for the trespass that he had committed against the Lord in not having fulfilled the command of the Lord; moreover, he had consulted a ghost to seek advice, ¹⁴and did not seek advice of the Lord; so He had him slain and the kingdom transferred to David son of Jesse.

---

b-b *Meaning of Heb. uncertain.*
c   *I.e., Israel.*

שָׁא֔וּל וְאַחֲרֵ֖י בָנָ֑יו וַיַּכּ֣וּ פְלִשְׁתִּ֗ים אֶת־
יֽוֹנָתָ֤ן וְאֶת־אֲבִֽינָדָב֙ וְאֶת־מַלְכִּי־שׁ֔וּעַ בְּנֵ֖י
שָׁאֽוּל׃ ³ וַתִּכְבַּ֤ד הַמִּלְחָמָה֙ עַל־שָׁא֔וּל
וַיִּמְצָאֻ֥הוּ הַמּוֹרִ֖ים בַּקָּ֑שֶׁת וַיָּ֖חֶל מִן־
הַיּוֹרִֽים׃ ⁴ וַיֹּ֣אמֶר שָׁאוּל֩ אֶל־נֹשֵׂ֨א כֵלָ֜יו
שְׁלֹ֥ף חַרְבְּךָ֣ ׀ וְדָקְרֵ֣נִי בָ֗הּ פֶּן־יָבֹ֜אוּ
הָעֲרֵלִ֤ים הָאֵ֙לֶּה֙ וְהִתְעַלְּלוּ־בִ֔י וְלֹ֤א אָבָה֙
נֹשֵׂ֣א כֵלָ֔יו כִּ֥י יָרֵ֖א מְאֹ֑ד ס וַיִּקַּ֤ח שָׁאוּל֙
אֶת־הַחֶ֔רֶב וַיִּפֹּ֖ל עָלֶֽיהָ׃ ⁵ וַיַּ֥רְא נֹשֵֽׂא־כֵלָ֖יו
כִּ֣י מֵ֣ת שָׁא֑וּל וַיִּפֹּ֥ל גַּם־ה֛וּא עַל־הַחֶ֖רֶב
וַיָּמֹֽת׃ ⁶ ס וַיָּ֤מָת שָׁאוּל֙ וּשְׁלֹ֣שֶׁת בָּנָ֔יו
וְכָל־בֵּית֖וֹ יַחְדָּ֥ו מֵֽתוּ׃ ⁷ וַֽיִּרְאוּ֩ כָּל־אִ֨ישׁ
יִשְׂרָאֵ֜ל אֲשֶׁר־בָּעֵ֗מֶק כִּ֤י נָ֙סוּ֙ וְכִי־מֵ֣תוּ
שָׁא֣וּל וּבָנָ֔יו וַיַּעַזְב֥וּ עָרֵיהֶ֖ם וַיָּנֻ֑סוּ וַיָּבֹ֣אוּ
פְלִשְׁתִּ֔ים וַיֵּשְׁב֖וּ בָּהֶֽם׃ ס
⁸ וַֽיְהִי֙ מִֽמָּחֳרָ֔ת וַיָּבֹ֣אוּ פְלִשְׁתִּ֔ים לְפַשֵּׁ֖ט
אֶת־הַֽחֲלָלִ֑ים וַֽיִּמְצְא֤וּ אֶת־שָׁאוּל֙ וְאֶת־
בָּנָ֔יו נֹפְלִ֖ים בְּהַ֥ר גִּלְבֹּֽעַ׃ ⁹ וַיַּ֨פְשִׁיטֻ֔הוּ
וַיִּשְׂא֥וּ אֶת־רֹאשׁ֖וֹ וְאֶת־כֵּלָ֑יו וַיְשַׁלְּח֧וּ
בְאֶֽרֶץ־פְלִשְׁתִּ֛ים סָבִ֖יב לְבַשֵּׂ֥ר אֶת־
עֲצַבֵּיהֶ֖ם וְאֶת־הָעָֽם׃ ¹⁰ וַיָּשִׂ֙ימוּ֙ אֶת־כֵּלָ֔יו
בֵּ֖ית אֱלֹהֵיהֶ֑ם וְאֶת־גֻּלְגָּלְתּ֣וֹ תָֽקְע֔וּ בֵּ֥ית
דָּגֽוֹן׃ ס ¹¹ וַֽיִּשְׁמְע֔וּ כֹּ֖ל יָבֵ֣ישׁ גִּלְעָ֑ד
אֵ֛ת כָּל־אֲשֶׁר־עָשׂ֥וּ פְלִשְׁתִּ֖ים לְשָׁאֽוּל׃
¹² וַיָּק֜וּמוּ כָּל־אִ֣ישׁ חַ֗יִל וַיִּשְׂאוּ֙ אֶת־גּוּפַ֣ת
שָׁא֗וּל וְאֵת֙ גּוּפֹ֣ת בָּנָ֔יו וַיְבִיא֖וּם יָבֵ֑ישָׁה
וַיִּקְבְּר֧וּ אֶת־עַצְמוֹתֵיהֶ֛ם תַּ֥חַת הָאֵלָ֖ה
בְּיָבֵ֑שׁ וַיָּצ֖וּמוּ שִׁבְעַ֥ת יָמִֽים׃ ¹³ וַיָּ֣מָת
שָׁא֗וּל בְּמַֽעֲלוֹ֙ אֲשֶׁ֣ר מָעַ֣ל בַּֽיהוָ֔ה עַל־דְּבַ֤ר
יְהוָה֙ אֲשֶׁ֣ר לֹֽא־שָׁמָ֔ר וְגַם־לִשְׁא֥וֹל בָּא֖וֹב
לִדְרֽוֹשׁ׃ ¹⁴ וְלֹֽא־דָרַ֥שׁ בַּֽיהוָ֖ה וַיְמִיתֵ֑הוּ
וַיַּסֵּב֙ אֶת־הַמְּלוּכָ֔ה לְדָוִ֖יד בֶּן־יִשָֽׁי׃ פ

11 [a]All Israel gathered to David at Hebron and said, "We are your own flesh and blood. [2]Long before now, even when Saul was king, you were the leader of Israel; and the LORD your God said to you: You shall shepherd My people Israel; you shall be ruler of My people Israel." [3]All the elders of Israel came to the king at Hebron, and David made a pact with them in Hebron before the LORD. And they anointed David king over Israel, according to the word of the LORD through Samuel.

[4]David and all Israel set out for Jerusalem, that is Jebus, where the Jebusite inhabitants of the land lived. [5]David was told by the inhabitants of Jebus, "You will never get in here!" But David captured the stronghold of Zion; it is now the City of David. [6]David said, "Whoever attacks the Jebusites first will be the chief officer"; Joab son of Zeruiah attacked first, and became the chief.

[7]David occupied the stronghold; therefore it was renamed the City of David. [8]David also fortified the surrounding area, from the Millo roundabout, and Joab rebuilt the rest of the city. [9]David kept growing stronger, for the LORD of Hosts was with him.

[10]And these were David's chief warriors who strongly supported him in his kingdom, together with all Israel, to make him king, according to the word of the LORD concerning Israel.

[11]This is the list of David's warriors: Jashobeam son of Hachmoni, the chief officer; he wielded his spear against three hundred and slew them all on one occasion. [12]Next to him was Eleazar son of Dodo, the Ahohite; he was one of the three warriors. [13]He was with David at Pas Dammim when the Philistines gathered there for battle. There was a plot of ground full

יא וַיִּקָּבְצ֧וּ כָל־יִשְׂרָאֵ֛ל אֶל־דָּוִ֖יד חֶבְר֣וֹנָה לֵאמֹ֑ר הִנֵּ֨ה עַצְמְךָ֧ וּֽבְשָׂרְךָ֛ אֲנָֽחְנוּ: 2 גַּם־תְּמ֣וֹל גַּם־שִׁלְשׁ֗וֹם גַּ֚ם בִּהְי֣וֹת שָׁא֣וּל מֶ֔לֶךְ אַתָּ֛ה הַמּוֹצִ֥יא וְהַמֵּבִ֖יא אֶת־יִשְׂרָאֵ֑ל וַיֹּ֩אמֶר֩ יְהֹוָ֨ה אֱלֹהֶ֜יךָ לְךָ֗ אַתָּ֨ה תִרְעֶ֤ה אֶת־עַמִּי֙ אֶת־יִשְׂרָאֵ֔ל וְאַתָּה֙ תִּהְיֶ֣ה נָגִ֔יד עַ֖ל עַמִּ֥י יִשְׂרָאֵֽל: 3 וַ֠יָּבֹ֠אוּ כָּל־זִקְנֵ֨י יִשְׂרָאֵ֤ל אֶל־הַמֶּ֙לֶךְ֙ חֶבְר֔וֹנָה וַיִּכְרֹת֩ לָהֶ֨ם דָּוִ֥יד בְּרִ֛ית בְּחֶבְר֖וֹן לִפְנֵ֣י יְהֹוָ֑ה וַיִּמְשְׁח֨וּ אֶת־דָּוִ֤יד לְמֶ֙לֶךְ֙ עַל־יִשְׂרָאֵ֔ל כִּדְבַ֥ר יְהֹוָ֖ה בְּיַד־שְׁמוּאֵֽל: ס 4 וַיֵּ֨לֶךְ דָּוִ֧יד וְכָל־יִשְׂרָאֵ֛ל יְרוּשָׁלִַ֖ם הִ֣יא יְב֑וּס וְשָׁ֙ם֙ הַיְבוּסִ֔י יֹשְׁבֵ֖י הָאָֽרֶץ: 5 וַיֹּ֩אמְרוּ֩ יֹשְׁבֵ֨י יְב֜וּס לְדָוִ֗יד לֹ֤א תָבוֹא֙ הֵ֔נָּה וַיִּלְכֹּ֤ד דָּוִיד֙ אֶת־מְצֻדַ֣ת צִיּ֔וֹן הִ֖יא עִ֥יר דָּוִֽיד: 6 וַיֹּ֣אמֶר דָּוִ֗יד כָּל־מַכֵּ֤ה יְבוּסִי֙ בָּרִ֣אשׁוֹנָ֔ה יִֽהְיֶ֥ה לְרֹ֖אשׁ וּלְשָׂ֑ר וַיַּ֧עַל בָּרִאשׁוֹנָ֛ה יוֹאָ֥ב בֶּן־צְרוּיָ֖ה וַיְהִ֥י לְרֹֽאשׁ: 7 וַיֵּ֥שֶׁב דָּוִ֖יד בַּמְּצָ֑ד עַל־כֵּ֥ן קָרְאוּ־ל֖וֹ עִ֥יר דָּוִֽיד: 8 וַיִּ֤בֶן הָעִיר֙ מִסָּבִ֔יב מִן־הַמִּלּ֖וֹא וְעַד־הַסָּבִ֑יב וְיוֹאָ֣ב יְחַיֶּ֔ה אֶת־שְׁאָ֖ר הָעִֽיר: 9 וַיֵּ֤לֶךְ דָּוִיד֙ הָל֣וֹךְ וְגָד֔וֹל וַיהֹוָ֥ה צְבָא֖וֹת עִמּֽוֹ: פ 10 וְאֵ֜לֶּה רָאשֵׁ֤י הַגִּבּוֹרִים֙ אֲשֶׁ֣ר לְדָוִ֔יד הַמִּֽתְחַזְּקִ֥ים עִמּ֛וֹ בְמַלְכוּת֖וֹ עִם־כָּל־יִשְׂרָאֵ֑ל לְהַמְלִיכ֖וֹ כִּדְבַ֥ר יְהֹוָ֖ה עַל־יִשְׂרָאֵֽל: ס 11 וְאֵ֛לֶּה מִסְפַּ֥ר הַגִּבֹּרִ֖ים אֲשֶׁ֣ר לְדָוִ֑יד יָשָׁבְעָ֣ם בֶּן־חַכְמוֹנִ֗י רֹ֚אשׁ הַשָּׁ֣לִישִׁ֔ים הֽוּא־עוֹרֵ֣ר אֶת־חֲנִית֗וֹ עַל־שְׁלֹשׁ־מֵא֥וֹת חָלָ֖ל בְּפַ֥עַם אֶחָֽת: 12 וְאַחֲרָ֛יו אֶלְעָזָ֥ר בֶּן־דּוֹד֖וֹ הָאֲחוֹחִ֑י ה֕וּא בִּשְׁלוֹשָׁ֖ה הַגִּבֹּרִֽים: 13 הֽוּא־הָיָ֨ה עִם־דָּוִ֜יד בַּפַּ֣ס דַּמִּ֗ים וְהַפְּלִשְׁתִּים֙ נֶאֶסְפוּ־שָׁ֣ם לַמִּלְחָמָ֔ה

---

a With vv. 1–9, cf. 2 Sam. 5.1–10, and with vv. 11–41, cf. 2 Sam. 23.8–39.

1913

of barley there; the troops had fled from the Philistines, [14]but they took their stand in the middle of the plot and defended it, and they routed the Philistines. Thus the LORD wrought a great victory.

[15]Three of the thirty chiefs went down to the rock to David, at the cave of Adullam, while a force of Philistines was encamped in the Valley of Rephaim. [16]David was then in the stronghold, and a Philistine garrison was then at Bethlehem. [17]David felt a craving and said, "If only I could get a drink of water from the cistern which is by the gate of Bethlehem!" [18]So the three got through the Philistine camp, and drew water from the cistern which is by the gate of Bethlehem, and they carried it back to David. But David would not drink it, and he poured it out as a libation to the LORD. [19]For he said, "God forbid that I should do this! Can I drink the blood of these men who risked their lives?"—for they had brought it at the risk of their lives, and he would not drink it. Such were the exploits of the three warriors.

[20]Abshai, the brother of Joab, was head of another three. He once wielded his spear against three hundred and slew them. He won a name among the three; [21]among the three he was more highly regarded than the other two, and so he became their commander. However, he did not attain to the other three.

[22]Benaiah son of Jehoiada from Kabzeel was a brave soldier who performed great deeds. He killed the two [sons] of Ariel of Moab. Once, on a snowy day, he went down into a pit and killed a lion. [23]He also killed an Egyptian, a giant of a man five cubits tall. The Egyptian had a spear in his hand, like a weaver's beam, yet [Benaiah] went down against him with a club, wrenched the spear out of the Egyptian's hand, and killed him with his own spear. [24]Such were the exploits of Benaiah son of Jehoiada; and he

וַתְּהִי חֶלְקַת הַשָּׂדֶה מְלֵאָה שְׂעוֹרִים וְהָעָם נָסוּ מִפְּנֵי פְלִשְׁתִּים: 14 וַיִּתְיַצְּבוּ בְתוֹךְ־הַחֶלְקָה וַיַּצִּילוּהָ וַיַּכּוּ אֶת־פְּלִשְׁתִּים וַיּוֹשַׁע יְהוָה תְּשׁוּעָה גְדוֹלָה: 15 וַיֵּרְדוּ שְׁלוֹשָׁה מִן־הַשְּׁלוֹשִׁים רֹאשׁ עַל־הַצֻּר אֶל־דָּוִיד אֶל־מְעָרַת עֲדֻלָּם וּמַחֲנֵה פְלִשְׁתִּים חֹנָה בְּעֵמֶק רְפָאִים: 16 וְדָוִיד אָז בַּמְּצוּדָה וּנְצִיב פְּלִשְׁתִּים אָז בְּבֵית לָחֶם: 17 וַיִּתְאָו דָּוִיד וַיֹּאמַר מִי יַשְׁקֵנִי מַיִם מִבּוֹר בֵּית־לֶחֶם אֲשֶׁר בַּשָּׁעַר: 18 וַיִּבְקְעוּ הַשְּׁלֹשָׁה בְּמַחֲנֵה פְלִשְׁתִּים וַיִּשְׁאֲבוּ־מַיִם מִבּוֹר בֵּית־לֶחֶם אֲשֶׁר בַּשַּׁעַר וַיִּשְׂאוּ וַיָּבִאוּ אֶל־דָּוִיד וְלֹא־אָבָה דָוִיד לִשְׁתּוֹתָם וַיְנַסֵּךְ אֹתָם לַיהוָה: 19 וַיֹּאמֶר חָלִילָה לִּי מֵאֱלֹהַי מֵעֲשׂוֹת זֹאת הֲדַם הָאֲנָשִׁים הָאֵלֶּה אֶשְׁתֶּה בְּנַפְשׁוֹתָם כִּי בְנַפְשׁוֹתָם הֱבִיאוּם וְלֹא אָבָה לִשְׁתּוֹתָם אֵלֶּה עָשׂוּ שְׁלֹשֶׁת הַגִּבּוֹרִים: 20 וְאַבְשַׁי אֲחִי־יוֹאָב הוּא הָיָה רֹאשׁ הַשְּׁלוֹשָׁה וְהוּא עוֹרֵר אֶת־חֲנִיתוֹ עַל־שְׁלֹשׁ מֵאוֹת חָלָל וְלֹא־שֵׁם בַּשְּׁלוֹשָׁה: 21 מִן־הַשְּׁלוֹשָׁה בַשְּׁנַיִם נִכְבָּד וַיְהִי לָהֶם לְשָׂר וְעַד־הַשְּׁלוֹשָׁה לֹא־בָא: ס 22 בְּנָיָה בֶן־יְהוֹיָדָע בֶּן־אִישׁ־חַיִל רַב־פְּעָלִים מִן־קַבְצְאֵל הוּא הִכָּה אֵת שְׁנֵי אֲרִיאֵל מוֹאָב וְהוּא יָרַד וְהִכָּה אֶת־הָאֲרִי בְּתוֹךְ הַבּוֹר בְּיוֹם הַשָּׁלֶג: 23 וְהוּא־הִכָּה אֶת־הָאִישׁ הַמִּצְרִי אִישׁ מִדָּה | חָמֵשׁ בָּאַמָּה וּבְיַד הַמִּצְרִי חֲנִית כִּמְנוֹר אֹרְגִים וַיֵּרֶד אֵלָיו בַּשָּׁבֶט וַיִּגְזֹל אֶת־הַחֲנִית מִיַּד הַמִּצְרִי וַיַּהַרְגֵהוּ בַּחֲנִיתוֹ: 24 אֵלֶּה עָשָׂה בְּנָיָהוּ בֶּן־יְהוֹיָדָע וְלוֹ־שֵׁם בִּשְׁלוֹשָׁה הַגִּבֹּרִים: 25 מִן־הַשְּׁלוֹשִׁים הִנּוֹ נִכְבָּד הוּא

won a name among the three warriors. 25He was highly regarded among the thirty, but he did not attain to the three. David put him in charge of his bodyguard.[b]

26The valiant warriors: Asahel brother of Joab, Elhanan son of Dodo from Bethlehem, 27Shammoth the Harorite, Helez the Pelonite, 28Ira son of Ikkesh from Tekoa, Abiezer of Anathoth, 29Sibbecai the Hushathite, Ilai the Ahohite, 30Mahrai the Netophathite, Heled son of Baanah the Netophathite, 31Ittai son of Ribai from Gibeah of the Benjaminites, Benaiah of Pirathon, 32Hurai of Nahale-gaash, Abiel the Arbathite, 33Azmaveth the Bahrumite, Eliahba of Shaalbon, 34the sons of Hashem the Gizonite, Jonathan son of Shageh the Hararite, 35Ahiam son of Sacar the Hararite, Eliphal son of Ur, 36Hepher the Mecherathite, Ahijah the Pelonite, 37Hezro the Carmelite, Naarai son of Ezbai, 38Joel brother of Nathan, Mibhar son of Hagri, 39Zelek the Ammonite, Naharai the Berothite—the arms-bearer of Joab son of Zeruiah—40Ira the Ithrite, Gareb the Ithrite, 41Uriah the Hittite, Zabad son of Ahlai. 42Adina son of Shiza the Reubenite, a chief of the Reubenites, and thirty with him; 43Hanan son of Maacah, and Joshaphat the Mithnite; 44Uzziah the Ashterathite, Shama and Jeiel sons of Hotham the Aroerite; 45Jedaiael son of Shimri, and Joha his brother, the Tizite; 46Eliel the Mahavite, and Jeribai and Joshaviah sons of Elnaam, and Ithmah the Moabite; 47Eliel, Obed, and Jaassiel the Mezobaite.

12

The following joined David at Ziklag while he was still in hiding from Saul son of Kish; these were the warriors who gave support in battle; 2they were armed with the bow and could

---

b   *Meaning of Heb. uncertain.*

וְאֶל־הַשְּׁלוֹשָׁה לֹא־בָא וַיְשִׂימֵהוּ דָוִיד עַל־
מִשְׁמַעְתּוֹ: ס
26 וְגִבּוֹרֵי הַחֲיָלִים עֲשָׂה־אֵל אֲחִי יוֹאָב אֶלְחָנָן בֶּן־דּוֹדוֹ מִבֵּית לָחֶם: ס
27 שַׁמּוֹת הַהֲרוֹרִי חֶלֶץ הַפְּלוֹנִי: ס
28 עִירָא בֶן־עִקֵּשׁ הַתְּקוֹעִי אֲבִיעֶזֶר הָעֲנְּתוֹתִי: ס 29 סִבְּכַי הַחֻשָׁתִי עִילַי הָאֲחוֹחִי: ס 30 מַהְרַי הַנְּטֹפָתִי חֵלֶד בֶּן־בַּעֲנָה הַנְּטוֹפָתִי: ס 31 אִיתַי בֶּן־רִיבַי מִגִּבְעַת בְּנֵי בִנְיָמִן ס בְּנָיָה הַפִּרְעָתֹנִי: 32 חוּרַי מִנַּחֲלֵי גָעַשׁ ס אֲבִיאֵל הָעַרְבָתִי: ס 33 עַזְמָוֶת הַבַּחֲרוּמִי אֶלְיַחְבָּא הַשַּׁעַלְבֹנִי: ס 34 בְּנֵי הָשֵׁם הַגִּזוֹנִי יוֹנָתָן בֶּן־שָׁגֵה הַהֲרָרִי: ס 35 אֲחִיאָם בֶּן־שָׂכָר הַהֲרָרִי אֱלִיפַל בֶּן־אוּר: ס 36 חֵפֶר הַמְּכֵרָתִי אֲחִיָּה הַפְּלֹנִי: ס 37 חֶצְרוֹ הַכַּרְמְלִי נַעֲרַי בֶּן־אֶזְבָּי: ס 38 יוֹאֵל אֲחִי נָתָן מִבְחָר בֶּן־הַגְרִי: ס 39 צֶלֶק הָעַמּוֹנִי נַחְרַי הַבֵּרֹתִי נֹשֵׂא כְּלֵי יוֹאָב בֶּן־צְרוּיָה: ס 40 עִירָא הַיִּתְרִי גָּרֵב הַיִּתְרִי: ס 41 אוּרִיָּה הַחִתִּי זָבָד בֶּן־אַחְלָי: ס 42 עֲדִינָא בֶן־שִׁיזָא הָרְאוּבֵנִי רֹאשׁ לָרְאוּבֵנִי וְעָלָיו שְׁלוֹשִׁים: ס 43 חָנָן בֶּן־מַעֲכָה וְיוֹשָׁפָט הַמִּתְנִי: 44 עֻזִּיָּא הָעַשְׁתְּרָתִי שָׁמָע וִיעוּאֵל וִיעִיאֵל בְּנֵי חוֹתָם הָעֲרֹעֵרִי: ס 45 יְדִיעֲאֵל בֶּן־שִׁמְרִי וְיֹחָא אָחִיו הַתִּיצִי: ס 46 אֱלִיאֵל הַמַּחֲוִים וִירִיבַי וְיוֹשַׁוְיָה בְּנֵי אֶלְנָעַם וְיִתְמָה הַמּוֹאָבִי: 47 אֱלִיאֵל וְעוֹבֵד וְיַעֲשִׂיאֵל הַמְּצֹבָיָה: פ

יב וְאֵלֶּה הַבָּאִים אֶל־דָּוִיד לְצִיקְלַג עוֹד עָצוּר מִפְּנֵי שָׁאוּל בֶּן־קִישׁ וְהֵמָּה בַּגִּבּוֹרִים עֹזְרֵי הַמִּלְחָמָה: 2 נֹשְׁקֵי קֶשֶׁת

use both right hand and left hand to sling stones or shoot arrows with the bow; they were kinsmen of Saul from Benjamin. ³At the head were Ahiezer and Joash, sons of Shemaah of Gibeah; and Jeziel and Pelet, sons of Azmaveth; and Beracah and Jehu of Anathoth; ⁴Ishmaiah of Gibeon, a warrior among the thirty, leading the thirty; ⁵Jeremiah, Jahaziel, Johanan, and Jozabad of Gederah; ⁶Eluzai, Jerimoth, Bealiah, Shemariah, and Shephatiah the Hariphite; ⁷Elkanah, Isshiah, Azarel, Joezer, and Jashobeam the Korahites; ⁸Joelah and Zebadiah, sons of Jeroham of Gedor.ᵃ ⁹Of the Gadites, there withdrew to follow David to the wilderness stronghold valiant men, fighters fit for battle, armed with shield and spear; they had the appearance of lions, and were as swift as gazelles upon the mountains: ¹⁰Ezer the chief, Obadiah the second, Eliab the third, ¹¹Mashmannah the fourth, Jeremiah the fifth, ¹²Attai the sixth, Eliel the seventh, ¹³Johanan the eighth, Elzabad the ninth, ¹⁴Jeremiah the tenth, Machbannai the eleventh. ¹⁵Those were the Gadites, heads of the army. The least was equal to a hundred, the greatest to a thousand. ¹⁶These were the ones who crossed the Jordan in the first month, when it was at its crest, and they put to flight all the lowlanders to the east and west. ¹⁷Some of the Benjaminites and Judahites came to the stronghold to David, ¹⁸and David went out to meet them, saying to them, "If you come on a peaceful errand, to support me, then I will make common cause with you, but if to betray me to my foes, for no injustice on my part, then let the God of our fathers take notice and give judgment." ¹⁹Then the spirit seized Amasai, chief of the captains:

"We are yours, David,
On your side, son of Jesse;
At peace, at peace with you,
And at peace with him who supports you,

מִימִינִ֤ים וּמַשְׂמִאלִים֙ בָּֽאֲבָנִ֔ים וּבַחִצִּ֖ים בַּקָּ֑שֶׁת מֵאֲחֵ֥י שָׁא֖וּל מִבִּנְיָמִֽן׃ 3 הָרֹ֗אשׁ אֲחִיעֶ֣זֶר וְיוֹאָ֘שׁ֮ בְּנֵ֣י הַשְּׁמָעָ֣ה הַגִּבְעָתִי֒ ויזיאל [וִיזִיאֵ֣ל] וָפֶ֔לֶט בְּנֵ֖י עַזְמָ֑וֶת וּבְרָכָ֕ה וְיֵה֖וּא הָעֲנְּתֹתִֽי׃ 4 וְיִֽשְׁמַעְיָ֤ה הַגִּבְעוֹנִי֙ גִּבּ֣וֹר בַּשְּׁלֹשִׁ֔ים וְעַל־הַשְּׁלֹשִֽׁים׃ 5 וְיִרְמְיָ֤ה וְיַחֲזִיאֵל֙ וְי֣וֹחָנָ֔ן וְיוֹזָבָ֖ד הַגְּדֵרָתִֽי׃ 6 אֶלְעוּזַ֤י וִֽירִימוֹת֙ וּבְעַלְיָ֣ה וּשְׁמַרְיָ֔הוּ וּשְׁפַטְיָ֖הוּ הַחֲרוּפִֽי׃ 7 אֶלְקָנָ֣ה וְיִשִּׁיָּ֗הוּ וַעֲזַרְאֵ֧ל וְיֽוֹעֶ֛זֶר וְיָשָׁבְעָ֖ם הַקָּרְחִֽים׃ 8 וְיוֹעֵאלָ֥ה וּזְבַדְיָ֖ה בְּנֵ֣י יְרֹחָ֑ם מִן־הַגְּדֽוֹר׃ 9 וּמִן־הַגָּדִ֡י נִבְדְּל֣וּ אֶל־דָּוִיד֩ לַמְצַ֨ד מִדְבָּ֜רָה גִּבֹּרֵ֣י הַחַ֗יִל אַנְשֵׁ֤י צָבָא֙ לַמִּלְחָמָ֔ה עֹרְכֵ֥י צִנָּ֖ה וָרֹ֑מַח וּפְנֵ֤י אַרְיֵה֙ פְּנֵיהֶ֔ם וְכִצְבָאיִ֥ם עַל־הֶהָרִ֖ים לְמַהֵֽר׃ ס 10 עֵ֖זֶר הָרֹ֑אשׁ עֹבַדְיָה֙ הַשֵּׁנִ֔י אֱלִיאָ֖ב הַשְּׁלִשִֽׁי׃ 11 מִשְׁמַנָּה֙ הָרְבִיעִ֔י יִרְמְיָ֖ה הַחֲמִשִֽׁי׃ 12 עַתַּי֙ הַשִּׁשִּׁ֔י אֱלִיאֵ֖ל הַשְּׁבִעִֽי׃ 13 יֽוֹחָנָן֙ הַשְּׁמִינִ֔י אֶלְזָבָ֖ד הַתְּשִׁיעִֽי׃ 14 יִרְמְיָ֙הוּ֙ הָעֲשִׂירִ֔י ס מַכְבַּנַּ֖י עַשְׁתֵּ֥י עָשָֽׂר׃ 15 אֵ֥לֶּה מִבְּנֵי־גָ֖ד רָאשֵׁ֣י הַצָּבָ֑א אֶחָ֤ד לְמֵאָה֙ הַקָּטָ֔ן וְהַגָּד֖וֹל לְאָֽלֶף׃ 16 אֵ֣לֶּה הֵ֗ם אֲשֶׁ֨ר עָבְר֤וּ אֶת־הַיַּרְדֵּן֙ בַּחֹ֣דֶשׁ הָרִאשׁ֔וֹן וְה֥וּא מְמַלֵּ֖א עַל־כָּל־גדיתיו [גְּדוֹתָ֑יו] וַיַּבְרִ�liרֿ֙ אֶת־כָּל־הָ֣עֲמָקִ֔ים לַמִּזְרָ֖ח וְלַֽמַּעֲרָֽב׃ ס 17 וַיָּבֹ֙אוּ֙ מִן־בְּנֵ֣י בִנְיָמִ֔ן וִיהוּדָ֖ה עַד־לַמְצָ֥ד לְדָוִֽיד׃ 18 וַיֵּצֵ֣א דָוִ֗יד לִפְנֵיהֶם֮ וַיַּ֣עַן וַיֹּ֣אמֶר לָהֶם֒ אִם־לְשָׁל֞וֹם בָּאתֶ֤ם אֵלַי֙ לְעָזְרֵ֔נִי יִֽהְיֶה־לִּ֧י עֲלֵיכֶ֛ם לֵבָ֖ב לְיָ֑חַד וְאִם־לְרַמּוֹתַ֣נִי לְצָרַ֗י בְּלֹ֤א חָמָס֙ בְּכַפַּ֔י יֵ֛רֶא אֱלֹהֵ֥י אֲבוֹתֵ֖ינוּ וְיוֹכַֽח׃ ס 19 וְר֣וּחַ לָבְשָׁ֗ה אֶת־עֲמָשַׂי֙ רֹ֣אשׁ השלושים [הַשָּׁלִישִׁ֔ים]

לְךָ֤ דָוִיד֙
וְעִמְּךָ֣ בֶן־יִשַׁ֔י
שָׁל֧וֹם ׀ שָׁל֣וֹם לְךָ֗
וְשָׁל֖וֹם לְעֹזְרֶ֑ךָ

---

a   Or, "the troop," reading Heb. gedud with several mss.

For your God supports you."
So David accepted them, and placed them at the head of his band.

²⁰Some Manassites went over to David's side when he came with the Philistines to make war against Saul, but they were of no help to them, because the lords of the Philistines in council dismissed him, saying, "He will go over to the side of his lord, Saul, and it will cost us our heads"; ²¹when he went to Ziklag, these Manassites went over to his side—Adnah, Jozabad, Jediael, Michael, Jozabad, Elihu, and Zillethai, chiefs of the clans of Manasseh.

²²It was they who gave support to David against the band,^b for all were valiant men; and they were officers of the force.

²³Day in day out, people came to David to give him support, until there was an army as vast as the army of God.

²⁴These are the numbers of the [men of the] armed bands who joined David at Hebron to transfer Saul's kingdom to him, in accordance with the word of the Lord:

²⁵Judahites, equipped with shield and spear—6,800 armed men; ²⁶Simeonites, valiant men, fighting troops—7,100; ²⁷of the Levites—4,600; ²⁸Jehoiada, chief officer of the Aaronides; with him, 3,700; ²⁹Zadok, a young valiant man, with his clan—22 officers; ³⁰of the Benjaminites, kinsmen of Saul, 3,000 in their great numbers, hitherto protecting the interests of the house of Saul; ³¹of the Ephraimites, 20,800 valiant men, famous in their clans; ³²of the half-tribe of Manasseh, 18,000, who were designated by name to come and make David king; ³³of the Issacharites, men who knew how to interpret the signs of the times, to determine how Israel should act; their chiefs were 200, and all their kinsmen followed them; ³⁴of Zebulun, those

---

b *I.e., the band of Amalekite raiders; cf. 1 Sam. 30.8, 15.*

כִּי עֲזָרְךָ אֱלֹהֶיךָ

וַיְקַבְּלֵם דָּוִיד וַיִּתְּנֵם בְּרָאשֵׁי הַגְּדוּד׃ פ

20 וּמִמְּנַשֶּׁה נָפְלוּ עַל־דָּוִיד בְּבֹאוֹ עִם־
פְלִשְׁתִּים עַל־שָׁאוּל לַמִּלְחָמָה וְלֹא עֲזָרֻם
כִּי בְעֵצָה שִׁלְּחֻהוּ סַרְנֵי פְלִשְׁתִּים
לֵאמֹר בְּרָאשֵׁינוּ יִפּוֹל אֶל־אֲדֹנָיו שָׁאוּל׃
21 בְּלֶכְתּוֹ אֶל־צִיקְלַג נָפְלוּ עָלָיו ׀ מִמְּנַשֶּׁה
עַדְנַח וְיוֹזָבָד וִידִיעֲאֵל וּמִיכָאֵל וְיוֹזָבָד
וֶאֱלִיהוּא וְצִלְּתַי רָאשֵׁי הָאֲלָפִים אֲשֶׁר
לִמְנַשֶּׁה׃
22 וְהֵמָּה עָזְרוּ עִם־דָּוִיד עַל־הַגְּדוּד כִּי־
גִבּוֹרֵי חַיִל כֻּלָּם וַיִּהְיוּ שָׂרִים בַּצָּבָא׃
23 כִּי לְעֶת־יוֹם בְּיוֹם יָבֹאוּ עַל־דָּוִיד לְעָזְרוֹ
עַד־לְמַחֲנֶה גָדוֹל כְּמַחֲנֵה אֱלֹהִים׃ פ
24 וְאֵלֶּה מִסְפְּרֵי רָאשֵׁי הֶחָלוּץ לַצָּבָא בָּאוּ
עַל־דָּוִיד חֶבְרוֹנָה לְהָסֵב מַלְכוּת שָׁאוּל
אֵלָיו כְּפִי יְהוָה׃ ס
25 בְּנֵי יְהוּדָה נֹשְׂאֵי צִנָּה וָרֹמַח שֵׁשֶׁת
אֲלָפִים וּשְׁמוֹנָה מֵאוֹת חֲלוּצֵי צָבָא׃ ס
26 מִן־בְּנֵי שִׁמְעוֹן גִּבּוֹרֵי חַיִל לַצָּבָא שִׁבְעַת
אֲלָפִים וּמֵאָה׃ ס 27 מִן־בְּנֵי הַלֵּוִי
אַרְבַּעַת אֲלָפִים וְשֵׁשׁ מֵאוֹת׃ ס
28 וִיהוֹיָדָע הַנָּגִיד לְאַהֲרֹן וְעִמּוֹ שְׁלֹשֶׁת
אֲלָפִים וּשְׁבַע מֵאוֹת׃ ס 29 וְצָדוֹק נַעַר
גִּבּוֹר חָיִל וּבֵית־אָבִיו שָׂרִים עֶשְׂרִים
וּשְׁנָיִם׃ ס 30 וּמִן־בְּנֵי בִנְיָמִן אֲחֵי שָׁאוּל
שְׁלֹשֶׁת אֲלָפִים וְעַד־הֵנָּה מַרְבִּיתָם
שֹׁמְרִים מִשְׁמֶרֶת בֵּית שָׁאוּל׃ ס
31 וּמִן־בְּנֵי אֶפְרַיִם עֶשְׂרִים אֶלֶף וּשְׁמוֹנֶה
מֵאוֹת גִּבּוֹרֵי חָיִל אַנְשֵׁי שֵׁמוֹת לְבֵית
אֲבוֹתָם׃ ס 32 וּמֵחֲצִי מַטֵּה מְנַשֶּׁה
שְׁמוֹנָה עָשָׂר אָלֶף אֲשֶׁר נִקְּבוּ בְּשֵׁמוֹת
לָבוֹא לְהַמְלִיךְ אֶת־דָּוִיד׃ ס 33 וּמִבְּנֵי
יִשָׂשכָר יוֹדְעֵי בִינָה לַעִתִּים לָדַעַת מַה־
יַּעֲשֶׂה יִשְׂרָאֵל רָאשֵׁיהֶם מָאתַיִם וְכָל־
אֲחֵיהֶם עַל־פִּיהֶם׃ ס 34 מִזְּבֻלוּן יוֹצְאֵי

ready for service, able to man a battle line with all kinds of weapons, 50,000, giving support wholeheartedly; [35]of Naphtali, 1,000 chieftains with their shields and lances—37,000; [36]of the Danites, able to man the battle line—28,600; [37]of Asher, those ready for service to man the battle line—40,000; [38]from beyond the Jordan, of the Reubenites, the Gadites, and the half-tribe of Manasseh, together with all kinds of military weapons—120,000.

[39]All these, fighting men, manning the battle line with whole heart, came to Hebron to make David king over all Israel. Likewise, all the rest of Israel was of one mind to make David king.

[40]They were there with David three days, eating and drinking, for their kinsmen had provided for them.

[41]And also, their relatives as far away as Issachar, Zebulun, and Naphtali brought food by ass, camel, mule, and ox—provisions of flour, cakes of figs, raisin cakes, wine, oil, cattle, and sheep in abundance, for there was joy in Israel.

13 Then David consulted with the officers of the thousands and the hundreds, with every chief officer. [2]David said to the entire assembly of Israel, "If you approve, and if the LORD our God concurs,[a] let us send far and wide to our remaining kinsmen throughout the territories of Israel, including the priests and Levites in the towns where they have pasturelands, that they should gather together to us [3]in order to transfer the Ark of our God to us, for throughout the days of Saul we paid no regard to it." [4]The entire assembly agreed to do so, for the proposal pleased all the people. [5]David then assembled all Israel from Shihor of Egypt to Lebo-hamath,

---

צָבָא עֹרְכֵי מִלְחָמָה בְּכָל־כְּלֵי מִלְחָמָה
חֲמִשִּׁים אָלֶף וְלַעֲדֹר בְּלֹא־לֵב וָלֵב: ס
35 וּמִנַּפְתָּלִי שָׂרִים אָלֶף וְעִמָּהֶם בְּצִנָּה
וַחֲנִית שְׁלֹשִׁים וְשִׁבְעָה אָלֶף: ס 36 וּמִן־
הַדָּנִי עֹרְכֵי מִלְחָמָה עֶשְׂרִים־וּשְׁמוֹנָה
אֶלֶף וְשֵׁשׁ מֵאוֹת: ס 37 וּמֵאָשֵׁר יוֹצְאֵי
צָבָא לַעֲרֹךְ מִלְחָמָה אַרְבָּעִים אָלֶף: ס
38 וּמֵעֵבֶר לַיַּרְדֵּן מִן־הָראוּבֵנִי וְהַגָּדִי
וַחֲצִי | שֵׁבֶט מְנַשֶּׁה בְּכֹל כְּלֵי צְבָא
מִלְחָמָה מֵאָה וְעֶשְׂרִים אָלֶף:
39 כָּל־אֵלֶּה אַנְשֵׁי מִלְחָמָה עֹדְרֵי מַעֲרָכָה
בְּלֵבָב שָׁלֵם בָּאוּ חֶבְרוֹנָה לְהַמְלִיךְ אֶת־
דָּוִיד עַל־כָּל־יִשְׂרָאֵל וְגַם כָּל־שֵׁרִית*
יִשְׂרָאֵל לֵב אֶחָד לְהַמְלִיךְ אֶת־דָּוִיד:
40 וַיִּהְיוּ־שָׁם עִם־דָּוִיד יָמִים שְׁלוֹשָׁה
אֹכְלִים וְשׁוֹתִים כִּי־הֵכִינוּ לָהֶם אֲחֵיהֶם:
41 וְגַם הַקְּרוֹבִים־אֲלֵיהֶם עַד־יִשָּׂשׂכָר
וּזְבֻלוּן וְנַפְתָּלִי מְבִיאִים לֶחֶם בַּחֲמוֹרִים
וּבַגְּמַלִּים וּבַפְּרָדִים | וּבַבָּקָר מַאֲכָל קֶמַח
דְּבֵלִים וְצִמּוּקִים וְיַיִן־וְשֶׁמֶן וּבָקָר וְצֹאן
לָרֹב כִּי שִׂמְחָה בְּיִשְׂרָאֵל: פ

יג וַיִּוָּעַץ דָּוִיד עִם־שָׂרֵי הָאֲלָפִים
וְהַמֵּאוֹת לְכָל־נָגִיד: 2 וַיֹּאמֶר דָּוִיד לְכֹל |
קְהַל יִשְׂרָאֵל אִם־עֲלֵיכֶם טוֹב וּמִן־יְהֹוָה
אֱלֹהֵינוּ נִפְרְצָה נִשְׁלְחָה עַל־אַחֵינוּ
הַנִּשְׁאָרִים בְּכֹל אַרְצוֹת יִשְׂרָאֵל וְעִמָּהֶם
הַכֹּהֲנִים וְהַלְוִיִּם בְּעָרֵי מִגְרְשֵׁיהֶם וְיִקָּבְצוּ
אֵלֵינוּ: 3 וְנָסֵבָּה אֶת־אֲרוֹן אֱלֹהֵינוּ אֵלֵינוּ
כִּי־לֹא דְרַשְׁנֻהוּ בִּימֵי שָׁאוּל: 4 וַיֹּאמְרוּ
כָל־הַקָּהָל לַעֲשׂוֹת כֵּן כִּי־יָשַׁר הַדָּבָר
בְּעֵינֵי כָל־הָעָם: 5 וַיַּקְהֵל דָּוִיד אֶת־כָּל־
יִשְׂרָאֵל מִן־שִׁיחוֹר מִצְרַיִם וְעַד־לְבוֹא
חֲמָת לְהָבִיא אֶת־אֲרוֹן הָאֱלֹהִים מִקִּרְיַת

---

a   *Meaning of Heb. uncertain.*

in order to bring the Ark of God from Kiriath-jearim. ⁶ᵇDavid and all Israel went up to Baalah, Kiriath-jearim of Judah, to bring up from there the Ark of God, the Lord, Enthroned on the Cherubim, to which the Name was attached. ⁷They transported the Ark of God on a new cart from the house of Abinadab; Uzza and Ahio guided the cart, ⁸and David and all Israel danced before God with all their might—with songs, lyres, harps, timbrels, cymbals, and trumpets. ⁹But when they came to the threshing floor of Chidon, Uzza put out his hand to hold the Ark of God because the oxen had stumbled.ᵃ ¹⁰The Lord was incensed at Uzza, and struck him down, because he laid a hand on the Ark; and so he died there before God. ¹¹David was distressed because the Lord ᶜhad burst out-ᶜ against Uzza; and that place was named Perez-uzzah, as it is still called.

¹²David was afraid of God that day; he said, "How can I bring the Ark of God here?" ¹³So David did not remove the Ark to his place in the City of David; instead, he diverted it to the house of Obed-edom the Gittite. ¹⁴The Ark of God remained in the house of Obed-edom, in its own abode, three months, and the Lord blessed the house of Obed-edom and all he had.

14 ᵃKing Hiram of Tyre sent envoys to David with cedar logs, stonemasons, and carpenters to build a palace for him. ²Thus David knew that the Lord had established him as king over Israel, and that his kingship was highly exalted for the sake of His people Israel.

³David took more wives in Jerusalem, and David begot more sons and daughters. ⁴These are the names of the children born to him in Jerusalem:ᵇ Shammua, Shobab, Nathan, and

יְעָרִֽים׃ 6 וַיַּ֧עַל דָּוִ֛יד וְכׇל־יִשְׂרָאֵ֖ל בַּעֲלָ֑תָה אֶל־קִרְיַ֥ת יְעָרִ֖ים אֲשֶׁ֣ר לִֽיהוּדָ֑ה לְהַעֲל֣וֹת מִשָּׁ֗ם אֵ֚ת אֲר֣וֹן הָאֱלֹהִ֔ים ׀ יְהֹוָה֙ יוֹשֵׁ֣ב הַכְּרוּבִ֔ים אֲשֶׁר־נִקְרָ֖א שֵֽׁם׃ 7 וַיַּרְכִּ֜יבוּ אֶת־אֲר֤וֹן הָֽאֱלֹהִים֙ עַל־עֲגָלָ֣ה חֲדָשָׁ֔ה מִבֵּ֖ית אֲבִינָדָ֑ב וְעֻזָּ֣א וְאַחְי֔וֹ נֹהֲגִ֖ים בָּעֲגָלָֽה׃ 8 וְדָוִ֣יד וְכׇל־יִשְׂרָאֵ֗ל מְשַׂחֲקִ֛ים לִפְנֵ֥י הָאֱלֹהִ֖ים בְּכׇל־עֹ֑ז וּבְשִׁירִ֣ים וּבְכִנֹּר֤וֹת וּבִנְבָלִים֙ וּבְתֻפִּ֔ים וּבִמְצִלְתַּ֖יִם וּבַחֲצֹצְרֽוֹת׃ 9 וַיָּבֹ֖אוּ עַד־גֹּ֣רֶן כִּידֹ֑ן וַיִּשְׁלַ֨ח עֻזָּ֜א אֶת־יָד֗וֹ לֶֽאֱחֹז֙ אֶת־הָ֣אָר֔וֹן כִּ֥י שָׁמְט֖וּ הַבָּקָֽר׃ 10 וַיִּֽחַר־אַ֤ף יְהֹוָה֙ בְּעֻזָּ֔א וַיַּכֵּ֕הוּ עַ֛ל אֲשֶׁר־שָׁלַ֥ח יָד֖וֹ עַל־הָאָר֑וֹן וַיָּ֥מׇת שָׁ֖ם לִפְנֵ֥י אֱלֹהִֽים׃ 11 וַיִּ֣חַר לְדָוִ֔יד כִּֽי־פָרַ֧ץ יְהֹוָ֛ה פֶּ֖רֶץ בְּעֻזָּ֑א וַיִּקְרָ֞א לַמָּק֤וֹם הַהוּא֙ פֶּ֣רֶץ עֻזָּ֔א עַ֖ד הַיּ֥וֹם הַזֶּֽה׃

12 וַיִּירָ֤א דָוִיד֙ אֶת־הָ֣אֱלֹהִ֔ים בַּיּ֥וֹם הַה֖וּא לֵאמֹ֑ר הֵ֚יךְ אָבִ֣יא אֵלַ֔י אֵ֖ת אֲר֥וֹן הָאֱלֹהִֽים׃ 13 וְלֹֽא־הֵסִ֨יר דָּוִ֧יד אֶת־הָאָר֛וֹן אֵלָ֖יו אֶל־עִ֣יר דָּוִ֑יד וַיַּטֵּ֕הוּ אֶל־בֵּ֖ית עֹבֵֽד־אֱדֹ֥ם הַגִּתִּֽי׃ 14 וַיֵּ֩שֶׁב֩ אֲר֨וֹן הָאֱלֹהִ֜ים עִם־בֵּ֨ית עֹבֵ֥ד אֱדֹ֛ם בְּבֵית֖וֹ שְׁלֹשָׁ֣ה חֳדָשִׁ֑ים וַיְבָ֣רֶךְ יְהֹוָ֗ה אֶת־בֵּ֛ית עֹבֵֽד־אֱדֹ֖ם וְאֶת־כׇּל־אֲשֶׁר־ל֑וֹ פ

יד וַיִּשְׁלַ֞ח חִירָ֤ם מֶֽלֶךְ־צֹר֙ מַלְאָכִים֙ אֶל־דָּוִ֔יד וַעֲצֵ֖י אֲרָזִ֑ים וְחָרָשֵׁ֣י קִ֔יר וְחָרָשֵׁ֖י עֵצִ֑ים לִבְנ֥וֹת ל֖וֹ בָּֽיִת׃ 2 וַיֵּ֣דַע דָּוִ֔יד כִּֽי־הֱכִינ֧וֹ יְהֹוָ֛ה לְמֶ֖לֶךְ עַל־יִשְׂרָאֵ֑ל כִּֽי־נִשֵּׂ֤את לְמַ֙עְלָה֙ מַלְכוּת֔וֹ בַּעֲב֖וּר עַמּ֥וֹ יִשְׂרָאֵֽל׃ פ

3 וַיִּקַּ֨ח דָּוִ֥יד ע֛וֹד נָשִׁ֖ים בִּירוּשָׁלָ֑͏ִם וַיּ֧וֹלֶד דָּוִ֛יד ע֖וֹד בָּנִ֥ים וּבָנֽוֹת׃ 4 וְאֵ֙לֶּה֙ שְׁמ֣וֹת הַיְלוּדִ֔ים אֲשֶׁ֥ר הָיוּ־ל֖וֹ בִּירוּשָׁלָ֑͏ִם שַׁמּ֖וּעַ

ᵇ With vv. 6–14, cf. 2 Sam. 6.2–11.
ᶜ⁻ᶜ Heb. paraṣ…pereṣ.

ᵃ With vv. 1–16, cf. 2 Sam. 5.11–25.
ᵇ With the list in vv. 4–7, cf. also 1 Chron. 3.5–8.

Solomon; [5]Ibhar, Elishua, and Elpelet; [6]Nogah, Nepheg, and Japhia; [7]Elishama, Beeliada, and Eliphelet.

[8]When the Philistines heard that David had been anointed king over all Israel, all the Philistines went up in search of David; but David heard of it, and he went out to them. [9]The Philistines came and raided the Valley of Rephaim. [10]David inquired of God, "Shall I go up against the Philistines? Will You deliver them into my hands?" And the LORD answered him, "Go up, and I will deliver them into your hands." [11]Thereupon David ascended Baal-perazim, and David defeated them there. David said, "God c-burst out-c against my enemies by my hands as waters burst out." That is why that place was named Baal-perazim. [12]They abandoned their gods there, and David ordered these to be burned.

[13]Once again the Philistines raided the valley. [14]David inquired of God once more, and God answered, "Do not go up after them, but circle around them and confront them at the baca[d] trees. [15]And when you hear the sound of marching in the tops of the baca trees, then go out to battle, for God will be going in front of you to attack the Philistine forces." [16]David did as God had commanded him; and they routed the Philistines from Gibeon all the way to Gezer. [17]David became famous throughout the lands, and the LORD put the fear of him in all the nations.

15

He had houses made for himself in the City of David, and he prepared a place for the Ark of God, and pitched a tent for it. [2]Then David gave orders that none but the Levites were to carry the Ark of God, for the LORD had chosen them to carry the Ark of the LORD and to minister to Him forever. [3]David assembled all Israel

---

5 וְשׁוֹבָ֣ב נָתָ֖ן וּשְׁלֹמֹֽה׃ 5 וְיִבְחָ֥ר וֶאֱלִישׁ֖וּעַ
וְאֶלְפָּֽלֶט׃ 6 וְנֹ֥גַהּ וְנֶ֖פֶג וְיָפִ֑יעַ׃ 7 וֶאֱלִישָׁמָ֥ע
וּבְעֶלְיָדָ֖ע וֶאֱלִיפָֽלֶט׃ 8 וַיִּשְׁמְע֣וּ פְלִשְׁתִּ֗ים כִּֽי־נִמְשַׁ֨ח דָּוִ֤יד לְמֶ֙לֶךְ֙
עַל־כָּל־יִשְׂרָאֵ֔ל וַיַּעֲל֥וּ כָל־פְּלִשְׁתִּ֖ים
לְבַקֵּ֣שׁ אֶת־דָּוִ֑יד וַיִּשְׁמַ֣ע דָּוִ֔יד וַיֵּצֵ֖א
לִפְנֵיהֶֽם׃ 9 וּפְלִשְׁתִּ֖ים בָּ֑אוּ וַֽיִּפְשְׁט֖וּ בְּעֵ֥מֶק
רְפָאִֽים׃ 10 וַיִּשְׁאַ֨ל דָּוִ֤יד בֵּֽאלֹהִים֙ לֵאמֹ֔ר
הַאֶֽעֱלֶה֙ עַל־פְּלִשְׁתִּ֔ים וּנְתַתָּ֖ם
בְּיָדִ֑י וַיֹּ֨אמֶר ל֤וֹ יְהוָה֙ עֲלֵ֔ה וּנְתַתִּ֖ים בְּיָדֶֽךָ׃
11 וַיַּעֲל֣וּ בְּבַֽעַל־פְּרָצִים֮ וַיַּכֵּ֣ם שָׁם֒ דָּוִ֗יד
וַיֹּ֣אמֶר דָּוִ֔יד פָּרַ֨ץ הָאֱלֹהִ֤ים אֶת־אוֹיְבַי֙
בְּיָדִ֔י כְּפֶ֖רֶץ מָ֑יִם עַל־כֵּ֗ן קָרְא֛וּ שֵֽׁם־הַמָּק֥וֹם
הַה֖וּא בַּ֥עַל פְּרָצִֽים׃ 12 וַיַּֽעַזְבוּ־שָׁ֖ם אֶת־
אֱלֹֽהֵיהֶ֑ם וַיֹּ֣אמֶר דָּוִ֔יד וַיִּשָּׂרְפ֖וּ בָּאֵֽשׁ׃ פ
13 וַיֹּסִ֤יפוּ עוֹד֙ פְּלִשְׁתִּ֔ים וַֽיִּפְשְׁט֖וּ בָּעֵֽמֶק׃
14 וַיִּשְׁאַ֨ל ע֤וֹד דָּוִיד֙ בֵּֽאלֹהִ֔ים וַיֹּ֨אמֶר ל֜וֹ
הָאֱלֹהִ֗ים לֹ֤א תַֽעֲלֶה֙ אַחֲרֵיהֶ֔ם הָסֵב֙
מֵֽעֲלֵיהֶ֔ם וּבָאתָ֥ לָהֶ֖ם מִמּ֥וּל הַבְּכָאִֽים׃
15 וִ֠יהִי כְּֽשָׁמְעֲךָ֞ אֶת־ק֤וֹל הַצְּעָדָה֙ בְּרָאשֵׁ֣י
הַבְּכָאִ֔ים אָ֖ז תֵּצֵ֣א בַמִּלְחָמָ֑ה כִּֽי־יָצָ֧א
הָאֱלֹהִים֙ לְפָנֶ֔יךָ לְהַכּ֖וֹת אֶת־מַחֲנֵ֥ה
פְלִשְׁתִּֽים׃ 16 וַיַּ֣עַשׂ דָּוִ֔יד כַּֽאֲשֶׁ֥ר צִוָּ֖הוּ
הָאֱלֹהִ֑ים וַיַּכּוּ֙ אֶת־מַחֲנֵ֣ה פְלִשְׁתִּ֔ים
מִגִּבְע֖וֹן וְעַד־גָּֽזְרָה׃ 17 וַיֵּצֵ֥א שֵֽׁם־דָּוִ֖יד
בְּכָל־הָֽאֲרָצ֑וֹת וַֽיהוָ֗ה נָתַ֥ן אֶת־פַּחְדּ֖וֹ עַל־
כָּל־הַגּוֹיִֽם׃

טו

וַיַּֽעַשׂ־ל֥וֹ בָתִּ֖ים בְּעִ֣יר דָּוִ֑יד וַיָּ֧כֶן
מָק֣וֹם לַֽאֲר֣וֹן הָֽאֱלֹהִ֗ים וַיֶּט־ל֖וֹ אֹֽהֶל׃ 2 אָ֚ז
אָמַ֣ר דָּוִ֔יד לֹ֣א לָשֵׂ֥את אֶת־אֲר֖וֹן הָֽאֱלֹהִ֑ים
כִּ֣י אִם־הַלְוִיִּ֔ם כִּי־בָ֣ם ׀ בָּחַ֤ר יְהוָה֙ לָשֵׂאת֙
אֶת־אֲר֣וֹן יְהוָ֔ה וּֽלְשָׁרְת֖וֹ עַד־עוֹלָֽם׃ ס
3 וַיַּקְהֵ֧ל דָּוִ֛יד אֶת־כָּל־יִשְׂרָאֵ֖ל אֶל־

---

c-c Heb. paras.
d Meaning of Heb. uncertain.

in Jerusalem to bring up the Ark of the LORD to its place, which he had prepared for it. ⁴Then David gathered together the Aaronides and the Levites: ⁵the sons of Kohath: Uriel the officer and his kinsmen—120; ⁶the sons of Merari: Asaiah the officer and his kinsmen—220; ⁷the sons of Gershom: Joel the officer and his kinsmen—130; ⁸the sons of Elizaphan: Shemaiah the officer and his kinsmen—200; ⁹the sons of Hebron: Eliel the officer and his kinsmen—80; ¹⁰the sons of Uzziel: Amminadab the officer and his kinsmen—112.

¹¹David sent for Zadok and Abiathar the priests, and for the Levites: Uriel, Asaiah, Joel, Shemaiah, Eliel, and Amminadab. ¹²He said to them, "You are the heads of the clans of the Levites; sanctify yourselves, you and your kinsmen, and bring up the Ark of the LORD God of Israel to [the place] I have prepared for it. ¹³ᵃ-Because you were not there the first time,-ᵃ the LORD our God burst out against us, for we did not show due regard for Him."

¹⁴The priests and Levites sanctified themselves in order to bring up the Ark of the LORD God of Israel. ¹⁵The Levites carried the Ark of God by means of poles on their shoulders, as Moses had commanded in accordance with the word of the LORD. ¹⁶David ordered the officers of the Levites to install their kinsmen, the singers, with musical instruments, harps, lyres, and cymbals, joyfully making their voices heard. ¹⁷So the Levites installed Heman son of Joel and, of his kinsmen, Asaph son of Berechiah; and, of the sons of Merari their kinsmen, Ethan son of Kushaiah. ¹⁸Together with them were their kinsmen of second rank, Zechariah, Ben, Jaaziel, Shemiramoth, Jehiel, Unni, Eliab, Benaiah, Maaseiah, Mattithiah, Eliphalehu, Mikneiah, Obed-edom and Jeiel the gatekeepers. ¹⁹Also the singers Heman, Asaph, and Ethan to sound the bronze cymbals, ²⁰and Zechariah,

a-a *Meaning of Heb. uncertain.*

יְרוּשָׁלִַם לְהַעֲלוֹת אֶת־אֲרוֹן יְהֹוָה אֶל־מְקוֹמוֹ אֲשֶׁר־הֵכִין לוֹ: 4 וַיֶּאֱסֹף דָּוִיד אֶת־בְּנֵי אַהֲרֹן וְאֶת־הַלְוִיִּם: 5 לִבְנֵי קְהָת אוּרִיאֵל הַשָּׂר וְאֶחָיו מֵאָה וְעֶשְׂרִים: ס 6 לִבְנֵי מְרָרִי עֲשָׂיָה הַשָּׂר וְאֶחָיו מָאתַיִם וְעֶשְׂרִים: ס 7 לִבְנֵי גֵרְשׁוֹם יוֹאֵל הַשָּׂר וְאֶחָיו מֵאָה וּשְׁלֹשִׁים: ס 8 לִבְנֵי אֱלִיצָפָן שְׁמַעְיָה הַשָּׂר וְאֶחָיו מָאתָיִם: ס 9 לִבְנֵי חֶבְרוֹן אֱלִיאֵל הַשָּׂר וְאֶחָיו שְׁמוֹנִים: ס 10 לִבְנֵי עֻזִּיאֵל עַמִּינָדָב הַשָּׂר וְאֶחָיו מֵאָה וּשְׁנֵים עָשָׂר: ס
11 וַיִּקְרָא דָוִיד לְצָדוֹק וּלְאֶבְיָתָר הַכֹּהֲנִים וְלַלְוִיִּם לְאוּרִיאֵל עֲשָׂיָה וְיוֹאֵל שְׁמַעְיָה וֶאֱלִיאֵל וְעַמִּינָדָב: 12 וַיֹּאמֶר לָהֶם אַתֶּם רָאשֵׁי הָאָבוֹת לַלְוִיִּם הִתְקַדְּשׁוּ אַתֶּם וַאֲחֵיכֶם וְהַעֲלִיתֶם אֵת אֲרוֹן יְהֹוָה אֱלֹהֵי יִשְׂרָאֵל אֶל־הֲכִינוֹתִי לוֹ: 13 כִּי לְמַבָּרִאשׁוֹנָה לֹא אַתֶּם פָּרַץ יְהֹוָה אֱלֹהֵינוּ בָּנוּ כִּי־לֹא דְרַשְׁנֻהוּ כַּמִּשְׁפָּט: 14 וַיִּתְקַדְּשׁוּ הַכֹּהֲנִים וְהַלְוִיִּם לְהַעֲלוֹת אֶת־אֲרוֹן יְהֹוָה אֱלֹהֵי יִשְׂרָאֵל: 15 וַיִּשְׂאוּ בְנֵי־הַלְוִיִּם אֵת אֲרוֹן הָאֱלֹהִים כַּאֲשֶׁר צִוָּה מֹשֶׁה כִּדְבַר יְהֹוָה בִּכְתֵפָם בַּמֹּטוֹת עֲלֵיהֶם: פ 16 וַיֹּאמֶר דָּוִיד לְשָׂרֵי הַלְוִיִּם לְהַעֲמִיד אֶת־אֲחֵיהֶם הַמְשֹׁרְרִים בִּכְלֵי־שִׁיר נְבָלִים וְכִנֹּרוֹת וּמְצִלְתָּיִם מַשְׁמִיעִים לְהָרִים־בְּקוֹל לְשִׂמְחָה: פ 17 וַיַּעֲמִידוּ הַלְוִיִּם אֵת הֵימָן בֶּן־יוֹאֵל וּמִן־אֶחָיו אָסָף בֶּן־בֶּרֶכְיָהוּ ס וּמִן־בְּנֵי מְרָרִי אֲחֵיהֶם אֵיתָן בֶּן־קוּשָׁיָהוּ: 18 וְעִמָּהֶם אֲחֵיהֶם הַמִּשְׁנִים זְכַרְיָהוּ בֵּן וְיַעֲזִיאֵל וּשְׁמִירָמוֹת וִיחִיאֵל | וְעֻנִּי אֱלִיאָב וּבְנָיָהוּ וּמַעֲשֵׂיָהוּ וּמַתִּתְיָהוּ וֶאֱלִיפְלֵהוּ וּמִקְנֵיָהוּ וְעֹבֵד אֱדֹם וִיעִיאֵל הַשֹּׁעֲרִים: 19 וְהַמְשֹׁרְרִים הֵימָן אָסָף וְאֵיתָן בִּמְצִלְתַּיִם נְחֹשֶׁת לְהַשְׁמִיעַ:

Aziel, Shemiramoth, Jehiel, Unni, Eliab, Maaseiah, and Benaiah with harps a-on *alamoth;-a* 21also Mattithiah, Eliphalehu, Mikneiah, Obed-edom, Jeiel, and Azaziah, with lyres to lead a-on the *sheminith;-a* 22also Chenaniah, officer of the Levites in song;a he was in charge of the songa because he was a master. 23Berechiah and Elkanah were gatekeepers for the Ark. 24Shebaniah, Joshaphat, Nethanel, Amasai, Zechariah, Benaiah, and Eliezer the priests sounded the trumpets before the Ark of God, and Obed-edom and Jehiah were gatekeepers for the Ark. 25bThen David and the elders of Israel and the officers of the thousands who were going to bring up the Ark of the Covenant of the Lord from the house of Obed-edom were joyful. 26Since God helped the Levites who were carrying the Ark of the Covenant of the Lord, they sacrificed seven bulls and seven rams. 27Now David and all the Levites who were carrying the Ark, and the singers and Chenaniah, officer of song of the singers, a-were wrapped-a in robes of fine linen, and David wore a linen ephod. 28All Israel brought up the Ark of the Covenant of the Lord with shouts and with blasts of the horn, with trumpets and cymbals, playing on harps and lyres. 29As the Ark of the Covenant of the Lord arrived at the City of David, Michal daughter of Saul looked out of the window and saw King David leaping and dancing, and she despised him for it.

16

aThey brought in the Ark of God and set it up inside the tent that David had pitched for it, and they sacrificed burnt offerings and offerings of well-being before God. 2When David finished sacrificing the burnt offerings and the offerings of well-being, he blessed the people in the name of the Lord. 3And he distributed

---

20 וּזְכַרְיָ֗ה וַעֲזִיאֵ֤ל וּשְׁמִֽירָמוֹת֙ וִיחִיאֵ֣ל וְעֻנִּ֔י וֶאֱלִיאָ֤ב וּמַעֲשֵׂיָ֙הוּ֙ וּבְנָיָ֔הוּ בִּנְבָלִ֖ים עַל־עֲלָמֽוֹת׃ 21 וּמַתִּתְיָ֣הוּ וֶאֱלִ֣יפְלֵ֗הוּ וּמִקְנֵיָ֛הוּ וְעֹבֵ֥ד אֱדֹ֖ם וִֽיעִיאֵ֣ל וַעֲזַזְיָ֑הוּ בְּכִנֹּר֥וֹת עַל־הַשְּׁמִינִ֖ית לְנַצֵּֽחַ׃ 22 וּכְנַנְיָ֥הוּ שַֽׂר־הַלְוִיִּ֖ם בְּמַשָּׂ֑א יָסֹ֣ר בַּמַּשָּׂ֔א כִּ֥י מֵבִ֖ין הֽוּא׃ 23 וּבֶֽרֶכְיָ֙ה וְאֶלְקָנָ֔ה שֹׁעֲרִ֖ים לָאָרֽוֹן׃ 24 וּשְׁבַנְיָ֡הוּ וְיֽוֹשָׁפָ֡ט וּנְתַנְאֵ֡ל וַעֲמָשַׂ֡י וּזְכַרְיָ֡הוּ וּבְנָיָ֡הוּ וֶאֱלִיעֶ֣זֶר הַכֹּהֲנִ֡ים מַחְצְרִים֩ בַּחֲצֹ֨צְר֜וֹת לִפְנֵ֨י אֲר֤וֹן הָֽאֱלֹהִים֙ וְעֹבֵ֣ד אֱדֹ֔ם וִיחִיָּ֥ה שֹׁעֲרִ֖ים לָאָרֽוֹן׃ 25 וַיְהִ֣י דָוִ֣יד וְזִקְנֵ֣י יִשְׂרָאֵ֡ל וְשָׂרֵ֣י הָֽאֲלָפִ֡ים הַהֹלְכִים֩ לְֽהַעֲל֨וֹת אֶת־אֲר֧וֹן בְּרִית־יְהוָ֛ה מִן־בֵּ֥ית עֹבֵֽד־אֱדֹ֖ם בְּשִׂמְחָֽה׃ ס 26 וַֽיְהִי֙ בֶּעְזֹ֣ר הָֽאֱלֹהִ֔ים אֶת־הַ֣לְוִיִּ֔ם נֹשְׂאֵ֖י אֲר֣וֹן בְּרִית־יְהוָ֑ה וַיִּזְבְּח֥וּ שִׁבְעָֽה־פָרִ֖ים וְשִׁבְעָ֥ה אֵילִֽים׃ 27 וְדָוִ֞יד מְכֻרְבָּ֣ל ׀ בִּמְעִ֣יל בּ֗וּץ וְכָל־הַלְוִיִּם֙ הַנֹּשְׂאִ֣ים אֶת־הָֽאָר֔וֹן וְהַמְשֹׁ֣רְרִ֔ים וּכְנַנְיָ֛ה הַשַּׂ֥ר הַמַּשָּׂ֖א הַמְשֹׁרְרִ֑ים וְעַל־דָּוִ֖יד אֵפ֥וֹד בָּֽד׃ 28 וְכָל־יִשְׂרָאֵ֗ל מַעֲלִים֙ אֶת־אֲר֣וֹן בְּרִית־יְהוָ֔ה בִּתְרוּעָ֥ה וּבְק֣וֹל שׁוֹפָ֗ר וּבַחֲצֹֽצְרוֹת֙ וּבִמְצִלְתָּ֔יִם מַשְׁמִעִ֖ים בִּנְבָלִ֥ים וְכִנֹּרֽוֹת׃ 29 וַיְהִ֗י אֲרוֹן֙ בְּרִ֣ית יְהוָ֔ה בָּ֖א עַד־עִ֣יר דָּוִ֑יד וּמִיכַ֨ל בַּת־שָׁא֜וּל נִשְׁקְפָ֣ה ׀ בְּעַ֣ד הַחַלּ֗וֹן וַתֵּ֨רֶא אֶת־הַמֶּ֤לֶךְ דָּוִיד֙ מְרַקֵּ֣ד וּמְשַׂחֵ֔ק וַתִּ֥בֶז ל֖וֹ בְּלִבָּֽהּ׃ פ

טז

וַיָּבִ֙יאוּ֙ אֶת־אֲר֣וֹן הָֽאֱלֹהִ֔ים וַיַּצִּ֣יגוּ אֹת֔וֹ בְּת֣וֹךְ הָאֹ֔הֶל אֲשֶׁ֥ר נָֽטָה־ל֖וֹ דָּוִ֑יד וַיַּקְרִ֛יבוּ עֹל֥וֹת וּשְׁלָמִ֖ים לִפְנֵ֥י הָֽאֱלֹהִֽים׃ 2 וַיְכַ֣ל דָּוִ֔יד מֵֽהַעֲל֥וֹת הָעֹלָ֖ה וְהַשְּׁלָמִ֑ים וַיְבָ֥רֶךְ אֶת־הָעָ֖ם בְּשֵׁ֥ם יְהוָֽה׃ 3 וַיְחַלֵּק֩

---

b   Vv. 25–29 are found also in 2 Sam. 6.12–16.

a   With vv. 1–3, cf. 2 Sam. 6.17–19.

to every person in Israel—man and woman alike—to each a loaf of bread, *b-*a cake made in a pan, and a raisin cake.*-b* 4He appointed Levites to minister before the Ark of the Lord, to invoke, to praise, and to extol the Lord God of Israel: 5Asaph the chief, Zechariah second in rank, Jeiel, Shemiramoth, Jehiel, Mattithiah, Eliab, Benaiah, Obed-edom, and Jeiel, with harps and lyres, and Asaph sounding the cymbals, 6and Benaiah and Jahaziel the priests, with trumpets, regularly before the Ark of the Covenant of God. 7Then, on that day, David first commissioned Asaph and his kinsmen to give praise to the Lord:

8c"Praise the Lord;
call on His name;
proclaim His deeds among the peoples.
9Sing praises unto Him;
speak of all His wondrous acts.
10Exult in His holy name;
let all who seek the Lord rejoice.
11Turn to the Lord, to His might;*d*
seek His presence constantly.
12Remember the wonders He has done;
His portents and the judgments He has pronounced,
13O offspring of Israel, His servant,
O descendants of Jacob, His chosen ones.
14He is the Lord our God;
His judgments are throughout the earth.
15Be ever mindful of His covenant,
the promise He gave for a thousand generations,
16that He made with Abraham,
swore to Isaac,
17and confirmed in a decree for Jacob,
for Israel, as an eternal covenant,
18saying, 'To you I will give the land of Canaan as your allotted heritage.'
19You were then few in number,

לְכָל־אִישׁ יִשְׂרָאֵל מֵאִישׁ וְעַד־אִשָּׁה לְאִישׁ כִּכַּר־לֶחֶם וְאֶשְׁפָּר וַאֲשִׁישָׁה: 4 וַיִּתֵּן לִפְנֵי אֲרוֹן יְהוָה מִן־הַלְוִיִּם מְשָׁרְתִים וּלְהַזְכִּיר וּלְהוֹדוֹת וּלְהַלֵּל לַיהוָה אֱלֹהֵי יִשְׂרָאֵל: פ 5 אָסָף הָרֹאשׁ וּמִשְׁנֵהוּ זְכַרְיָה יְעִיאֵל וּשְׁמִירָמוֹת וִיחִיאֵל וּמַתִּתְיָה וֶאֱלִיאָב וּבְנָיָהוּ וְעֹבֵד אֱדֹם וִיעִיאֵל בִּכְלֵי נְבָלִים וּבְכִנֹּרוֹת וְאָסָף בַּמְצִלְתַּיִם מַשְׁמִיעַ: 6 וּבְנָיָהוּ וְיַחֲזִיאֵל הַכֹּהֲנִים בַּחֲצֹצְרוֹת תָּמִיד לִפְנֵי אֲרוֹן בְּרִית־הָאֱלֹהִים: 7 בַּיּוֹם הַהוּא אָז נָתַן דָּוִיד בָּרֹאשׁ לְהֹדוֹת לַיהוָה בְּיַד־אָסָף וְאֶחָיו: פ

8 * הוֹדוּ לַיהוָה
קִרְאוּ בִשְׁמוֹ
הוֹדִיעוּ בָעַמִּים עֲלִילֹתָיו:
9 שִׁירוּ לוֹ זַמְּרוּ־לוֹ
שִׂיחוּ בְּכָל־נִפְלְאֹתָיו:
10 הִתְהַלְלוּ בְּשֵׁם קָדְשׁוֹ
יִשְׂמַח לֵב מְבַקְשֵׁי יְהוָה:
11 דִּרְשׁוּ יְהוָה וְעֻזּוֹ
בַּקְּשׁוּ פָנָיו תָּמִיד:
12 זִכְרוּ נִפְלְאֹתָיו אֲשֶׁר עָשָׂה
מֹפְתָיו וּמִשְׁפְּטֵי־פִיהוּ:
13 זֶרַע יִשְׂרָאֵל עַבְדּוֹ
בְּנֵי יַעֲקֹב בְּחִירָיו:
14 הוּא יְהוָה אֱלֹהֵינוּ
בְּכָל־הָאָרֶץ מִשְׁפָּטָיו:
15 זִכְרוּ לְעוֹלָם בְּרִיתוֹ
דָּבָר צִוָּה לְאֶלֶף דּוֹר:
16 אֲשֶׁר כָּרַת אֶת־אַבְרָהָם
וּשְׁבוּעָתוֹ לְיִצְחָק:
17 וַיַּעֲמִידֶהָ לְיַעֲקֹב לְחֹק
לְיִשְׂרָאֵל בְּרִית עוֹלָם:
18 לֵאמֹר לְךָ אֶתֵּן אֶרֶץ־כְּנָעַן
חֶבֶל נַחֲלַתְכֶם:

b-b Meaning of Heb. uncertain.
c With vv. 8–22, cf. Ps. 105.1–15.
d I.e., the Ark; cf. Pss. 78.61; 132.8.

vv. 8–36. בכתב היד שלנו, כתוב בצורת שירה

a handful, merely sojourning there,
²⁰wandering from nation to nation,
from one kingdom to another.
²¹He allowed no one to oppress them;
He reproved kings on their account,
²²'Do not touch My anointed ones;
do not harm My prophets.'

²³e"Sing to the Lord, all the earth.
proclaim His victory day after day.
²⁴Tell of His glory among the nations,
His wondrous deeds among all peoples.
²⁵For the Lord is great and much acclaimed,
He is held in awe by all divine beings.
²⁶All the gods of the peoples are mere idols,
but the Lord made the heavens.
²⁷Glory and majesty are before Him;
strength and joy are in His place.

²⁸"Ascribe to the Lord, O families of the peo-
ples,
ascribe to the Lord glory and strength.
²⁹Ascribe to the Lord the glory of His name,
bring tribute and enter before Him,
bow down to the Lord majestic in holiness.
³⁰Tremble in His presence, all the earth!
The world stands firm; it cannot be shaken.
³¹Let the heavens rejoice and the earth exult;
let them declare among the nations, "The
Lord is King!"
³²Let the sea and all within it thunder,
the fields and everything in them exult;
³³then shall all the trees of the forest shout
for joy
at the presence of the Lord,
for He is coming to rule the earth.
³⁴Praise the Lord for He is good;
His steadfast love is eternal.
³⁵f-Declare:

---

e   With vv. 23–33, cf. Ps. 96.1–13.
f-f   Cf. Ps. 106.47–48.

19 בִּהְיֽוֹתְכֶם֙ מְתֵ֣י מִסְפָּ֔ר
כִּמְעַ֖ט וְגָרִ֥ים בָּֽהּ׃
20 וַיִּֽתְהַלְּכוּ֙ מִגּ֣וֹי אֶל־גּ֔וֹי
וּמִמַּמְלָכָ֖ה אֶל־עַ֥ם אַחֵֽר׃
21 לֹא־הִנִּ֣יחַ לְאִ֣ישׁ לְעָשְׁקָ֑ם
וַיּ֖וֹכַח עֲלֵיהֶ֣ם מְלָכִֽים׃
22 אַֽל־תִּגְּעוּ֙ בִּמְשִׁיחָ֔י
וּבִנְבִיאַ֖י אַל־תָּרֵֽעוּ׃ פ

23 שִׁ֤ירוּ לַֽיהֹוָה֙ כָּל־הָאָ֔רֶץ
בַּשְּׂר֥וּ מִיּֽוֹם־אֶל־י֖וֹם יְשֽׁוּעָתֽוֹ׃
24 סַפְּר֤וּ בַגּוֹיִם֙ אֶת־כְּבוֹד֔וֹ
בְּכָל־הָ֣עַמִּ֔ים נִפְלְאֹתָֽיו׃
25 כִּ֥י גָד֣וֹל יְהֹוָ� ה וּמְהֻלָּ֣ל מְאֹ֑ד
וְנוֹרָ֥א ה֖וּא עַל־כָּל־אֱלֹהִֽים׃
26 כִּ֠י כָּל־אֱלֹהֵ֤י הָעַמִּים֙ אֱלִילִ֔ים
וַֽיהֹוָ֖ה שָׁמַ֥יִם עָשָֽׂה׃
27 ה֤וֹד וְהָדָר֙ לְפָנָ֔יו
עֹ֥ז וְחֶדְוָ֖ה בִּמְקֹמֽוֹ׃

28 הָב֤וּ לַֽיהֹוָה֙ מִשְׁפְּח֣וֹת עַמִּ֔ים
הָב֥וּ לַֽיהֹוָ֖ה כָּב֥וֹד וָעֹֽז׃
29 הָב֥וּ לַֽיהֹוָ֖ה כְּב֣וֹד שְׁמ֑וֹ
שְׂא֤וּ מִנְחָה֙ וּבֹ֣אוּ לְפָנָ֔יו
הִשְׁתַּֽחֲו֥וּ לַֽיהֹוָ֖ה בְּהַדְרַת־קֹֽדֶשׁ׃
30 חִ֤ילוּ מִלְּפָנָיו֙ כָּל־הָאָ֔רֶץ
אַף־תִּכּ֥וֹן תֵּבֵ֖ל בַּל־תִּמּֽוֹט׃
31 יִשְׂמְח֤וּ הַשָּׁמַ֙יִם֙ וְתָגֵ֣ל הָאָ֔רֶץ
וְיֹאמְר֥וּ בַגּוֹיִ֖ם יְהֹוָ֥ה מָלָֽךְ׃
32 יִרְעַ֥ם הַיָּ֖ם וּמְלוֹא֑וֹ
יַעֲלֹ֥ץ הַשָּׂדֶ֖ה וְכָל־אֲשֶׁר־בּֽוֹ׃
33 אָ֥ז יְרַנְּנ֖וּ עֲצֵ֣י הַיָּ֑עַר
מִלִּפְנֵ֣י יְהֹוָ֔ה
כִּי־בָ֖א לִשְׁפּ֥וֹט אֶת־הָאָֽרֶץ׃
34 הוֹד֥וּ לַֽיהֹוָ֖ה כִּ֣י ט֑וֹב
כִּ֥י לְעוֹלָ֖ם חַסְדּֽוֹ׃
35 וְאִמְרֽוּ

Deliver us, O God, our deliverer,
and gather us and save us from the nations,
to acclaim Your holy name,
to glory in Your praise.
36Blessed is the LORD, God of Israel, from eternity to eternity." And all the people said, "Amen" and "Praise the LORD."-f

37He left Asaph and his kinsmen there before the Ark of the Covenant of the LORD to minister before the Ark regularly as each day required, 38as well as Obed-edom with their kinsmen—68; also Obed-edom son of Jedithun and Hosah as gatekeepers; 39also Zadok the priest and his fellow priests before the Tabernacle of the LORD at the shrine which was in Gibeon; 40to sacrifice burnt offerings to the LORD on the altar of the burnt offering regularly, morning and evening, in accordance with what was prescribed in the Teaching of the LORD with which He charged Israel. 41With them were Heman and Jeduthun and the other selected men designated by name to give praise to the LORD, "For His steadfast love is eternal." 42Heman and Jeduthun had with them trumpets and cymbals to sound, and instruments for the songs of God; and the sons of Jeduthun were to be at the gate. 43Then all the people went every one to his home, and David returned to greet his household.

17 aWhen David settled in his palace, David said to the prophet Nathan, "Here I am dwelling in a house of cedar, while the Ark of the Covenant of the LORD is under tent-cloths." 2Nathan said to David, "Do whatever you have in mind, for God is with you."

3But that same night the word of God came to Nathan: 4"Go and say to My servant David: Thus said the LORD: You are not the one to build a house for Me to dwell in. 5From the day that I brought out Israel to this day, I have not dwelt

הוֹשִׁיעֵ֙נוּ֙ אֱלֹהֵ֣י יִשְׁעֵ֔נוּ
וְקַבְּצֵ֙נוּ֙ וְהַצִּילֵ֔נוּ מִן־הַגּוֹיִ֔ם
לְהֹדוֹת֙ לְשֵׁ֣ם קָדְשֶׁ֔ךָ
לְהִשְׁתַּבֵּ֖חַ בִּתְהִלָּתֶֽךָ׃
36 בָּר֤וּךְ יְהֹוָה֙ אֱלֹהֵ֣י יִשְׂרָאֵ֔ל מִן־הָ֣עוֹלָ֔ם וְעַ֖ד הָעֹלָ֑ם וַיֹּאמְר֤וּ כׇל־הָעָם֙ אָמֵ֔ן וְהַלֵּ֖ל לַיהֹוָֽה׃ פ
37 וַיַּֽעֲזׇב־שָׁ֗ם לִפְנֵ֛י אֲר֥וֹן בְּרִית־יְהֹוָ֖ה לְאָסָ֣ף וּלְאֶחָ֑יו לְשָׁרֵ֞ת לִפְנֵ֧י הָאָר֛וֹן תָּמִ֖יד לִדְבַר־י֥וֹם בְּיוֹמֽוֹ׃ 38 וְעֹבֵ֤ד אֱדֹם֙ וַאֲחֵיהֶ֔ם שִׁשִּׁ֖ים וּשְׁמוֹנָ֑ה וְעֹבֵ֨ד אֱדֹ֧ם בֶּן־יְדִיתֻ֛ן וְחֹסָ֖ה לְשֹׁעֲרִֽים׃ 39 וְאֵ֣ת ׀ צָד֣וֹק הַכֹּהֵ֗ן וְאֶחָיו֙ הַכֹּ֣הֲנִ֔ים לִפְנֵ֖י מִשְׁכַּ֣ן יְהֹוָ֑ה בַּבָּמָ֖ה אֲשֶׁ֥ר בְּגִבְעֽוֹן׃ 40 לְֽהַעֲל֩וֹת֩ עֹל֨וֹת לַיהֹוָ֜ה עַל־מִזְבַּ֧ח הָעֹלָ֛ה תָּמִ֖יד לַבֹּ֣קֶר וְלָעָ֑רֶב וּלְכׇל־הַכָּתוּב֙ בְּתוֹרַ֣ת יְהֹוָ֔ה אֲשֶׁ֥ר צִוָּ֖ה עַל־יִשְׂרָאֵֽל׃ 41 וְעִמָּהֶם֙ הֵימָ֣ן וִידוּת֔וּן וּשְׁאָר֙ הַבְּרוּרִ֔ים אֲשֶׁ֥ר נִקְּב֖וּ בְּשֵׁמ֑וֹת לְהֹדוֹת֙ לַֽיהֹוָ֔ה כִּ֥י לְעוֹלָ֖ם חַסְדּֽוֹ׃ 42 וְעִמָּהֶ֣ם הֵימָ֣ן וִֽידוּת֗וּן חֲצֹֽצְרוֹת֙ וּמְצִלְתַּ֔יִם לְמַשְׁמִעִ֕ים וּכְלֵ֖י שִׁ֣יר הָאֱלֹהִ֑ים וּבְנֵ֥י יְדוּת֖וּן לַשָּֽׁעַר׃ 43 וַיֵּלְכ֥וּ כׇל־הָעָ֖ם אִ֣ישׁ לְבֵית֑וֹ וַיִּסֹּ֥ב דָּוִ֖יד לְבָרֵ֥ךְ אֶת־בֵּיתֽוֹ׃ פ

יז וַיְהִ֕י כַּאֲשֶׁ֛ר יָשַׁ֥ב דָּוִ֖יד בְּבֵית֑וֹ וַיֹּ֨אמֶר דָּוִ֜יד אֶל־נָתָ֣ן הַנָּבִ֗יא הִנֵּ֨ה אָנֹכִ֤י יוֹשֵׁב֙ בְּבֵ֣ית הָאֲרָזִ֔ים וַאֲר֥וֹן בְּרִית־יְהֹוָ֖ה תַּ֣חַת יְרִיעֽוֹת׃ 2 וַיֹּ֤אמֶר נָתָן֙ אֶל־דָּוִ֔יד כֹּ֛ל אֲשֶׁ֥ר בִּֽלְבָבְךָ֖ עֲשֵׂ֑ה כִּ֥י הָאֱלֹהִ֖ים עִמָּֽךְ׃ ס 3 וַֽיְהִ֖י בַּלַּ֣יְלָה הַה֑וּא וַֽיְהִי֙ דְּבַר־אֱלֹהִ֔ים אֶל־נָתָ֖ן לֵאמֹֽר׃ 4 לֵ֤ךְ וְאָֽמַרְתָּ֙ אֶל־דָּוִ֣יד עַבְדִּ֔י כֹּ֖ה אָמַ֣ר יְהֹוָ֑ה לֹ֥א אַתָּ֛ה תִּבְנֶה־לִּ֥י הַבַּ֖יִת לָשָֽׁבֶת׃ 5 כִּ֣י לֹ֤א יָשַׁ֙בְתִּי֙ בְּבַ֔יִת מִן־הַיּ֗וֹם אֲשֶׁ֤ר הֶעֱלֵ֙יתִי֙ אֶת־יִשְׂרָאֵ֔ל עַ֖ד

in a house, but have [gone] from tent to tent and from one Tabernacle [to another]. 6As I moved about wherever Israel went, did I ever reproach any of the judges of Israel whom I appointed to care for My people Israel: Why have you not built Me a house of cedar?

7"Further, say thus to My servant David: Thus said the LORD of Hosts: I took you from the pasture, from following the flock, to be ruler of My people Israel, 8and I have been with you wherever you went, and have cut down all your enemies before you. Moreover, I will give you renown like that of the greatest men on earth. 9I will establish a home for My people Israel and will plant them firm, so that they shall dwell secure and shall tremble no more. Evil men shall not wear them down anymore as in the past, 10ever since I appointed judges over My people Israel. I will subdue all your enemies.

And I declare to you: The LORD will build a house[b] for you. 11When your days are done and you follow your fathers, I will raise up your offspring after you, one of your own sons, and I will establish his kingship. 12He shall build a house for Me, and I will establish his throne forever. 13I will be a father to him, and he shall be a son to Me, but I will never withdraw My favor from him as I withdrew it from your predecessor. 14I will install him in My house and in My kingship forever, and his throne shall be established forever."

15Nathan spoke to David in accordance with all these words and all this prophecy. 16Then King David came and sat before the LORD, and he said, "What am I, O LORD God, and what is my family, that You have brought me thus far? 17Yet even this, O God, has seemed too little to You; for You have spoken of Your servant's house for the future. c-You regard me as a man of distinction,-c O LORD God. 18What more can

הַיּ֣וֹם הַזֶּ֑ה וָאֶֽהְיֶ֛ה מֵאֹ֥הֶל אֶל־אֹ֖הֶל וּמִמִּשְׁכָּֽן׃ 6בְּכֹ֥ל אֲשֶׁר־הִתְהַלַּ֙כְתִּי֙ בְּכָל־יִשְׂרָאֵ֔ל הֲדָבָ֣ר דִּבַּ֗רְתִּי אֶת־אַחַד֙ שֹֽׁפְטֵ֣י יִשְׂרָאֵ֔ל אֲשֶׁ֥ר צִוִּ֖יתִי לִרְע֣וֹת אֶת־עַמִּ֑י לֵאמֹ֕ר לָ֛מָּה לֹֽא־בְנִיתֶ֥ם לִ֖י בֵּ֥ית אֲרָזִֽים׃ 7וְ֠עַתָּה כֹּֽה־תֹאמַ֞ר לְעַבְדִּ֣י לְדָוִ֗יד ס כֹּ֤ה אָמַר֙ יְהֹוָ֣ה צְבָא֔וֹת אֲנִ֤י לְקַחְתִּ֙יךָ֙ מִן־הַנָּוֶ֔ה מִֽן־אַחֲרֵ֖י הַצֹּ֑אן לִֽהְי֣וֹת נָגִ֔יד עַ֖ל עַמִּ֥י יִשְׂרָאֵֽל׃ 8וָאֶֽהְיֶ֣ה עִמְּךָ֗ בְּכֹל֙ אֲשֶׁ֣ר הָלַ֔כְתָּ וָאַכְרִ֥ית אֶת־כָּל־אוֹיְבֶ֖יךָ מִפָּנֶ֑יךָ וְעָשִׂ֤יתִי לְךָ֙ שֵׁ֔ם כְּשֵׁ֥ם הַגְּדוֹלִ֖ים אֲשֶׁ֥ר בָּאָֽרֶץ׃ 9וְשַׂמְתִּ֣י מָ֠קוֹם לְעַמִּ֨י יִשְׂרָאֵ֜ל וּנְטַעְתִּ֗יהוּ וְשָׁכַ֤ן תַּחְתָּיו֙ וְלֹ֣א יִרְגַּ֣ז ע֔וֹד וְלֹֽא־יוֹסִ֜יפוּ בְנֵי־עַוְלָ֛ה לְבַלֹּת֖וֹ כַּאֲשֶׁ֥ר בָּרִאשׁוֹנָֽה׃ 10וּלְמִיָּמִ֗ים אֲשֶׁ֨ר צִוִּ֤יתִי שֹֽׁפְטִים֙ עַל־עַמִּ֣י יִשְׂרָאֵ֔ל וְהִכְנַעְתִּ֖י אֶת־כָּל־אוֹיְבֶ֑יךָ וָאַגִּ֣ד לָ֔ךְ וּבַ֖יִת יִבְנֶה־לְּךָ֥ יְהֹוָֽה׃ 11וְהָיָ֗ה כִּֽי־מָלְא֤וּ יָמֶ֙יךָ֙ לָלֶ֣כֶת עִם־אֲבֹתֶ֔יךָ וַהֲקִֽימוֹתִ֤י אֶֽת־זַרְעֲךָ֙ אַחֲרֶ֔יךָ אֲשֶׁ֥ר יִהְיֶ֖ה מִבָּנֶ֑יךָ וַהֲכִינוֹתִ֖י אֶת־מַלְכוּתֽוֹ׃ 12ה֣וּא יִבְנֶה־לִּ֖י בָּ֑יִת וְכֹנַנְתִּ֥י אֶת־כִּסְא֖וֹ עַד־עוֹלָֽם׃ 13אֲנִי֙ אֶֽהְיֶה־לּ֣וֹ לְאָ֔ב וְה֖וּא יִֽהְיֶה־לִּ֣י לְבֵ֑ן וְחַסְדִּי֙ לֹֽא־אָסִ֣יר מֵֽעִמּ֔וֹ כַּאֲשֶׁ֣ר הֲסִיר֔וֹתִי מֵאֲשֶׁ֥ר הָיָ֖ה לְפָנֶֽיךָ׃ 14וְהַֽעֲמַדְתִּ֧יהוּ בְּבֵיתִ֛י וּבְמַלְכוּתִ֖י עַד־הָעוֹלָ֑ם וְכִסְא֕וֹ יִהְיֶ֥ה נָכ֖וֹן עַד־עוֹלָֽם׃ 15כְּכֹל֙ הַדְּבָרִ֣ים הָאֵ֔לֶּה וּכְכֹ֖ל הֶחָז֣וֹן הַזֶּ֑ה כֵּ֛ן דִּבֶּ֥ר נָתָ֖ן אֶל־דָּוִֽיד׃ פ 16וַיָּבֹא֙ הַמֶּ֣לֶךְ דָּוִ֔יד וַיֵּ֖שֶׁב לִפְנֵ֣י יְהֹוָ֑ה וַיֹּ֗אמֶר מִֽי־אֲנִ֞י יְהֹוָ֣ה אֱלֹהִ֗ים וּמִ֤י בֵיתִי֙ כִּ֣י הֲבִיאֹתַ֔נִי עַד־הֲלֹֽם׃ 17וַתִּקְטַ֨ן זֹ֤את בְּעֵינֶ֙יךָ֙ אֱלֹהִ֔ים וַתְּדַבֵּ֥ר עַל־בֵּֽית־עַבְדְּךָ֖ לְמֵרָח֑וֹק וּרְאִיתַ֗נִי כְּת֧וֹר הָאָדָ֛ם הַֽמַּעֲלָ֖ה יְהֹוָ֥ה אֱלֹהִֽים׃ 18מַה־יּוֹסִ֙יף ע֤וֹד דָּוִיד֙ אֵלֶ֣יךָ לְכָב֖וֹד אֶת־

b   *I.e., a dynasty; play on "house" (i.e., Temple) in v. 4.*
c-c *Meaning of Heb. uncertain.*

David add regarding the honoring of Your servant? You know Your servant. [19]O Lord, c-for Your servant's sake, and of Your own accord,-c You have wrought this great thing, and made known all these great things. [20]O Lord, there is none like You, and there is no other God but You, as we have always heard. [21]And who is like Your people Israel, a unique nation on earth, whom God went and redeemed as His people, winning renown for Yourself for great and marvelous deeds, driving out nations before Your people whom You redeemed from Egypt. [22]You have established Your people Israel as Your very own people forever; and You, O Lord, have become their God.

[23]"And now, O Lord, let Your promise concerning Your servant and his house be fulfilled forever; and do as You have promised. [24]Let it be fulfilled that Your name be glorified forever, in that men will say, 'The Lord of Hosts, God of Israel, is Israel's God'; and may the house of Your servant David be established before You. [25]Because You, my God, have revealed to Your servant that You will build a house for him, Your servant has ventured to pray to You. [26]And now, O Lord, You are God and You have made this gracious promise to Your servant. [27]Now, it has pleased You to bless Your servant's house, that it abide before You forever; for You, O Lord, have blessed and are blessed forever."

18 [a]Sometime afterward, David attacked the Philistines and subdued them; and David took Gath and its dependencies from the Philistines. [2]He also defeated the Moabites; the Moabites became tributary vassals of David.

[3]David defeated Hadadezer, king of Zobah-hamath, who was on his way to set up his monument at the Euphrates River. [4]David captured 1,000 chariots and 7,000 horsemen and 20,000

---

19 יְהוָ֗ה עַבְדְּךָ֙ וְאַתָּ֖ה אֶת־עַבְדְּךָ֥ יָדָֽעְתָּ׃ בַּעֲב֤וּר עַבְדְּךָ֙ וּֽכְלִבְּךָ֔ עָשִׂ֕יתָ אֵ֖ת כָּל־הַגְּדוּלָּ֣ה הַזֹּ֑את לְהֹדִ֕יעַ אֶת־כָּל־הַגְּדֻלּֽוֹת׃ 20 יְהוָה֙ אֵ֣ין כָּמ֔וֹךָ וְאֵ֥ין אֱלֹהִ֖ים זוּלָתֶ֑ךָ בְּכֹ֥ל אֲשֶׁר־שָׁמַ֖עְנוּ בְּאָזְנֵֽינוּ׃ 21 וּמִי֙ כְּעַמְּךָ֣ יִשְׂרָאֵ֔ל גּ֥וֹי אֶחָ֖ד בָּאָ֑רֶץ אֲשֶׁר֩ הָלַ֨ךְ הָאֱלֹהִ֜ים לִפְדּ֧וֹת ל֣וֹ עָ֗ם לָשׂ֤וּם לְךָ֙ שֵׁ֣ם גְּדֻלּ֣וֹת וְנֹרָא֔וֹת לְגָרֵ֗שׁ מִפְּנֵ֧י עַמְּךָ֛ אֲשֶׁר־פָּדִ֥יתָ מִמִּצְרַ֖יִם גּוֹיִֽם׃ 22 וַ֠תִּתֵּן אֶת־עַמְּךָ֨ יִשְׂרָאֵ֧ל ׀ לְךָ֛ לְעָ֖ם עַד־עוֹלָ֑ם וְאַתָּ֣ה יְהוָ֔ה הָיִ֥יתָ לָהֶ֖ם לֵאלֹהִֽים׃

23 וְעַתָּ֣ה יְהוָ֔ה הַדָּבָ֗ר אֲשֶׁ֤ר דִּבַּ֙רְתָּ֙ עַל־עַבְדְּךָ֔ וְעַל־בֵּית֖וֹ יֵאָמֵ֣ן עַד־עוֹלָ֑ם וַעֲשֵׂ֖ה כַּאֲשֶׁ֥ר דִּבַּֽרְתָּ׃ 24 וְ֠יֵאָמֵן וְיִגְדַּ֨ל שִׁמְךָ֤ עַד־עוֹלָם֙ לֵאמֹ֔ר יְהוָ֤ה צְבָאוֹת֙ אֱלֹהֵ֣י יִשְׂרָאֵ֔ל אֱלֹהִ֖ים לְיִשְׂרָאֵ֑ל וּבֵ֥ית־דָּוִ֛יד עַבְדְּךָ֖ נָכ֥וֹן לְפָנֶֽיךָ׃ 25 כִּ֣י ׀ אַתָּ֣ה אֱלֹהַ֗י גָּלִ֙יתָ֙ אֶת־אֹ֣זֶן עַבְדְּךָ֔ לִבְנ֥וֹת ל֖וֹ בָּ֑יִת עַל־כֵּן֙ מָצָ֣א עַבְדְּךָ֔ לְהִתְפַּלֵּ֖ל לְפָנֶֽיךָ׃ 26 וְעַתָּ֣ה יְהוָ֔ה אַתָּה־ה֖וּא הָאֱלֹהִ֑ים וַתְּדַבֵּר֙ עַֽל־עַבְדְּךָ֔ הַטּוֹבָ֖ה הַזֹּֽאת׃ 27 וְעַתָּ֗ה הוֹאַ֙לְתָּ֙ לְבָרֵךְ֙ אֶת־בֵּ֣ית עַבְדְּךָ֔ לִהְי֥וֹת לְעוֹלָ֖ם לְפָנֶ֑יךָ כִּֽי־אַתָּ֤ה יְהוָה֙ בֵּרַ֔כְתָּ וּמְבֹרָ֖ךְ לְעוֹלָֽם׃ פ

יח וַיְהִ֣י אַחֲרֵי־כֵ֗ן וַיַּ֤ךְ דָּוִיד֙ אֶת־פְּלִשְׁתִּ֖ים וַיַּכְנִיעֵ֑ם וַיִּקַּ֞ח אֶת־גַּ֧ת וּבְנֹתֶ֛יהָ מִיַּ֖ד פְּלִשְׁתִּֽים׃ 2 וַיַּ֖ךְ אֶת־מוֹאָ֑ב וַיִּהְי֤וּ מוֹאָב֙ עֲבָדִ֣ים לְדָוִ֔יד נֹשְׂאֵ֖י מִנְחָֽה׃ 3 וַיַּ֥ךְ דָּוִ֛יד אֶת־הֲדַדְעֶ֥זֶר מֶֽלֶךְ־צוֹבָ֖ה חֲמָ֑תָה בְּלֶכְתּ֕וֹ לְהַצִּ֥יב יָד֖וֹ בִּֽנְהַר־פְּרָֽת׃ 4 וַיִּלְכֹּ֣ד דָּוִ֣יד מִמֶּ֡נּוּ אֶ֣לֶף רֶ֠כֶב וְשִׁבְעַ֨ת אֲלָפִ֤ים פָּֽרָשִׁים֙ וְעֶשְׂרִ֣ים אֶ֣לֶף אִ֣ישׁ רַגְלִ֔י

---

a   *With this chapter, cf. 2 Sam. 8.*

foot soldiers of his force; and David hamstrung all the chariot horses except for 100, which he retained. [5]And when the Arameans of Damascus came to the aid of King Hadadezer of Zobah-hamath, David struck down 22,000 of the Arameans. [6]David stationed [garrisons] in Aram of Damascus, and the Arameans became tributary vassals of David. The LORD gave David victory wherever he went. [7]David took the gold shields[b] carried by Hadadezer's retinue and brought them to Jerusalem; [8]and from Tibbath and Cun, towns of Hadadezer, David took a vast amount of copper, from which Solomon made the bronze tank, the columns, and the bronze vessels.

[9]When King Tou of Hamath heard that David had defeated the entire army of King Hadadezer of Zobah, [10]he sent his son Hadoram to King David to greet him and to congratulate him on his military victory over Hadadezer— for Hadadezer had been at war with Tou; [he brought with him] all manner of gold, silver, and copper objects. [11]King David dedicated these to the LORD, along with the other silver and gold that he had taken from all the nations: from Edom, Moab, and Ammon; from the Philistines and the Amalekites.

[12]Abshai son of Zeruiah struck down Edom in the Valley of Salt, 18,000 in all. [13]He stationed garrisons in Edom, and all the Edomites became vassals of David. The LORD gave David victory wherever he went.

[14]David reigned over all Israel, and David executed true justice among all his people. [15]Joab son of Zeruiah was commander of the army; Jehoshaphat son of Ahilud was recorder; [16]Zadok son of Ahitub and Abimelech son of Abiathar were priests; Shavsha was scribe; [17]Benaiah son of Jehoiada was commander of the Cherethites and the Pelethites; and David's sons were first ministers of the king.

וַיְעַקֵּר דָּוִיד אֶת־כָּל־הָרֶכֶב וַיּוֹתֵר מִמֶּנּוּ מֵאָה רָכֶב: 5 וַיָּבֹא אֲרַם דַּרְמֶשֶׂק לַעְזוֹר לַהֲדַדְעֶזֶר מֶלֶךְ צוֹבָה וַיַּךְ דָּוִיד בַּאֲרָם עֶשְׂרִים־וּשְׁנַיִם אֶלֶף אִישׁ: 6 וַיָּשֶׂם דָּוִיד בַּאֲרַם דַּרְמֶשֶׂק וַיְהִי אֲרָם לְדָוִיד עֲבָדִים נֹשְׂאֵי מִנְחָה וַיּוֹשַׁע יְהֹוָה לְדָוִיד בְּכֹל אֲשֶׁר הָלָךְ: 7 וַיִּקַּח דָּוִיד אֵת שִׁלְטֵי הַזָּהָב אֲשֶׁר הָיוּ עַל עַבְדֵי הֲדַדְעֶזֶר וַיְבִיאֵם יְרוּשָׁלָ͏ִם: 8 וּמִטִּבְחַת וּמִכּוּן עָרֵי הֲדַדְעֶזֶר לָקַח דָּוִיד נְחֹשֶׁת רַבָּה מְאֹד בָּהּ | עָשָׂה שְׁלֹמֹה אֶת־יָם הַנְּחֹשֶׁת וְאֶת־הָעַמּוּדִים וְאֵת כְּלֵי הַנְּחֹשֶׁת: פ 9 וַיִּשְׁמַע תֹּעוּ מֶלֶךְ חֲמָת כִּי הִכָּה דָוִיד אֶת־כָּל־חֵיל הֲדַדְעֶזֶר מֶלֶךְ־צוֹבָה: 10 וַיִּשְׁלַח אֶת־הֲדוֹרָם־בְּנוֹ אֶל־הַמֶּלֶךְ־ דָּוִיד לִשְׁאָול־לוֹ לְשָׁלוֹם וּלְבָרֲכוֹ עַל אֲשֶׁר נִלְחַם בַּהֲדַדְעֶזֶר וַיַּכֵּהוּ כִּי־אִישׁ מִלְחֲמוֹת תֹּעוּ הָיָה הֲדַדְעֶזֶר וְכֹל כְּלֵי זָהָב וָכֶסֶף וּנְחֹשֶׁת: 11 גַּם־אֹתָם הִקְדִּישׁ הַמֶּלֶךְ דָּוִיד לַיהֹוָה עִם־הַכֶּסֶף וְהַזָּהָב אֲשֶׁר נָשָׂא מִכָּל־הַגּוֹיִם מֵאֱדוֹם וּמִמּוֹאָב וּמִבְּנֵי עַמּוֹן וּמִפְּלִשְׁתִּים וּמֵעֲמָלֵק: 12 וְאַבְשַׁי בֶּן־צְרוּיָה הִכָּה אֶת־אֱדוֹם בְּגֵיא הַמֶּלַח שְׁמוֹנָה עָשָׂר אָלֶף: 13 וַיָּשֶׂם בֶּאֱדוֹם נְצִיבִים וַיִּהְיוּ כָל־אֱדוֹם עֲבָדִים לְדָוִיד וַיּוֹשַׁע יְהֹוָה אֶת־דָּוִיד בְּכֹל אֲשֶׁר הָלָךְ: 14 וַיִּמְלֹךְ דָּוִיד עַל־כָּל־יִשְׂרָאֵל וַיְהִי עֹשֶׂה מִשְׁפָּט וּצְדָקָה לְכָל־עַמּוֹ: 15 וְיוֹאָב בֶּן־ צְרוּיָה עַל־הַצָּבָא וִיהוֹשָׁפָט בֶּן־אֲחִילוּד מַזְכִּיר: 16 וְצָדוֹק בֶּן־אֲחִיטוּב וַאֲבִימֶלֶךְ בֶּן־אֶבְיָתָר כֹּהֲנִים וְשַׁוְשָׁא סוֹפֵר: 17 וּבְנָיָהוּ בֶּן־יְהוֹיָדָע עַל־הַכְּרֵתִי וְהַפְּלֵתִי וּבְנֵי־דָוִיד הָרִאשֹׁנִים לְיַד הַמֶּלֶךְ: פ

---

b   Or "quivers."

19

^aSometime afterward, Nahash the king of the Ammonites died, and his son succeeded him as king. ²David said, "I will keep faith with Hanun son of Nahash, since his father kept faith with me." David sent messengers with condolences to him over his father. But when David's courtiers came to the land of Ammon to Hanun, with condolences, ³the Ammonite officials said to Hanun, "Do you think David is really honoring your father just because he sent you men with condolences? Why, it is to explore, to subvert, and to spy out the land that his courtiers have come to you." ⁴So Hanun seized David's courtiers, shaved them, and cut away half of their garments up to the buttocks, and sent them off. ⁵When David was told about the men, he dispatched others to meet them, for the men were greatly embarrassed. And the king gave orders, "Stay in Jericho until your beards grow back; then you can return."

⁶The Ammonites realized that they had incurred the wrath of David; so Hanun and the Ammonites sent 1,000 silver talents to hire chariots and horsemen from Aram-naharaim, Aram-maacah, and Zobah. ⁷They hired 32,000 chariots, the king of Maacah, and his army, who came and encamped before Medeba. The Ammonites were mobilized from their cities and came to do battle.

⁸On learning this, David sent out Joab and the whole army, [including] the professional fighters. ⁹The Ammonites marched out and took up their battle position at the entrance of the city, while the kings who came [took their stand] separately in the open. ¹⁰Joab saw that there was a battle line against him both front and rear. So he made a selection from all the picked men of Israel and arrayed them against the Arameans, ¹¹and the rest of the troops he put under the command of his brother Abishai

---

יט וַיְהִי אַחֲרֵי־כֵן וַיָּמָת נָחָשׁ מֶלֶךְ בְּנֵי־עַמּוֹן וַיִּמְלֹךְ בְּנוֹ תַּחְתָּיו: ²וַיֹּאמֶר דָּוִיד אֶעֱשֶׂה־חֶסֶד ׀ עִם־חָנוּן בֶּן־נָחָשׁ כִּי־עָשָׂה אָבִיו עִמִּי חֶסֶד וַיִּשְׁלַח דָּוִיד מַלְאָכִים לְנַחֲמוֹ עַל־אָבִיו וַיָּבֹאוּ עַבְדֵי דָוִיד אֶל־אֶרֶץ בְּנֵי־עַמּוֹן אֶל־חָנוּן לְנַחֲמוֹ: ³וַיֹּאמְרוּ שָׂרֵי בְנֵי־עַמּוֹן לְחָנוּן הַמְכַבֵּד דָּוִיד אֶת־אָבִיךָ בְּעֵינֶיךָ כִּי־שָׁלַח לְךָ מְנַחֲמִים הֲלֹא בַּעֲבוּר לַחְקֹר וְלַהֲפֹךְ וּלְרַגֵּל הָאָרֶץ בָּאוּ עֲבָדָיו אֵלֶיךָ: פ ⁴וַיִּקַּח חָנוּן אֶת־עַבְדֵי דָוִיד וַיְגַלְּחֵם וַיִּכְרֹת אֶת־מַדְוֵיהֶם בַּחֵצִי עַד־הַמִּפְשָׂעָה וַיְשַׁלְּחֵם: ⁵וַיֵּלְכוּ וַיַּגִּידוּ לְדָוִיד עַל־הָאֲנָשִׁים וַיִּשְׁלַח לִקְרָאתָם כִּי־הָיוּ הָאֲנָשִׁים נִכְלָמִים מְאֹד וַיֹּאמֶר הַמֶּלֶךְ שְׁבוּ בִירֵחוֹ עַד אֲשֶׁר־יְצַמַּח זְקַנְכֶם וְשַׁבְתֶּם:

⁶וַיִּרְאוּ בְּנֵי עַמּוֹן כִּי הִתְבָּאֲשׁוּ עִם־דָּוִיד וַיִּשְׁלַח חָנוּן וּבְנֵי עַמּוֹן אֶלֶף כִּכַּר־כֶּסֶף לִשְׂכֹּר לָהֶם מִן־אֲרַם נַהֲרַיִם וּמִן־אֲרַם מַעֲכָה וּמִצּוֹבָה רֶכֶב וּפָרָשִׁים: ⁷וַיִּשְׂכְּרוּ לָהֶם שְׁנַיִם וּשְׁלֹשִׁים אֶלֶף רֶכֶב וְאֶת־מֶלֶךְ מַעֲכָה וְאֶת־עַמּוֹ וַיָּבֹאוּ וַיַּחֲנוּ לִפְנֵי מֵידְבָא וּבְנֵי עַמּוֹן נֶאֶסְפוּ מֵעָרֵיהֶם וַיָּבֹאוּ לַמִּלְחָמָה: פ

⁸וַיִּשְׁמַע דָּוִיד וַיִּשְׁלַח אֶת־יוֹאָב וְאֵת כָּל־צָבָא הַגִּבּוֹרִים: ⁹וַיֵּצְאוּ בְּנֵי עַמּוֹן וַיַּעַרְכוּ מִלְחָמָה פֶּתַח הָעִיר וְהַמְּלָכִים אֲשֶׁר־בָּאוּ לְבַדָּם בַּשָּׂדֶה: ¹⁰וַיַּרְא יוֹאָב כִּי־הָיְתָה פְנֵי־הַמִּלְחָמָה אֵלָיו פָּנִים וְאָחוֹר וַיִּבְחַר מִכָּל־בָּחוּר בְּיִשְׂרָאֵל וַיַּעֲרֹךְ לִקְרַאת אֲרָם: ¹¹וְאֵת יֶתֶר הָעָם נָתַן בְּיַד אַבְשַׁי אָחִיו וַיַּעַרְכוּ לִקְרַאת בְּנֵי עַמּוֹן:

---

^a With this chapter, cf. 2 Sam. 10.

and arrayed them against the Ammonites. 12Joab said, "If the Arameans prove too strong for me, you come to my aid; and if the Ammonites prove too strong for you, I will come to your aid. 13Let us be strong and resolute for the sake of our people and the towns of our God; and the LORD will do what He deems right."

14Joab and the troops with him marched into battle against the Arameans, who fled before him. 15And when the Ammonites saw that the Arameans had fled, they too fled before his brother Abishai, and withdrew into the city. So Joab went to Jerusalem.

16When the Arameans saw that they had been routed by Israel, they sent messengers to bring out the Arameans from across the Euphrates; Shophach, Hadadezer's army commander, led them. 17David was informed of it; he assembled all Israel, crossed the Jordan, and came and took up positions against them. David drew up his forces against Aram; and they fought with him. 18But the Arameans were put to flight by Israel. David killed 7,000 Aramean charioteers and 40,000 footmen; he also killed Shophach, the army commander. 19And when all the vassals of Hadadezer saw that they had been routed by Israel, they submitted to David and became his vassals. And the Arameans would not help the Ammonites anymore.

20

aAt the turn of the year, the season when kings go out [to battle], Joab led out the army force and devastated the land of Ammon, and then besieged Rabbah, while David remained in Jerusalem; Joab reduced Rabbah and left it in ruins. 2David took the crown from the head of their king; he found that it weighed a talent of gold, and in it were precious stones. It was placed on David's head. He also carried off a vast amount of booty from the city. 3He led out

a With vv. 1–3, cf. 2 Sam. 11.1; 12.30–31.

12 וַיֹּאמֶר אִם־תֶּחֱזַק מִמֶּ֫נִּי אֲרָם וְהָיִ֥יתָ לִּ֖י לִתְשׁוּעָ֑ה ס וְאִם־בְּנֵ֣י עַמּוֹן֩ יֶחֶזְק֨וּ מִמְּךָ֜ וְהוֹשַׁעְתִּֽיךָ׃ 13 חֲזַ֞ק וְנִֽתְחַזְּקָ֗ה בְּֽעַד־עַמֵּ֙נוּ֙ וּבְעַ֖ד עָרֵ֣י אֱלֹהֵ֑ינוּ וַֽיהוָ֔ה הַטּ֥וֹב בְּעֵינָ֖יו יַעֲשֶֽׂה׃

14 וַיִּגַּ֣שׁ יוֹאָ֗ב וְהָעָם֙ אֲשֶׁר־עִמּ֔וֹ לִפְנֵ֥י אֲרָ֖ם לַמִּלְחָמָ֑ה וַיָּנ֖וּסוּ מִפָּנָֽיו׃ 15 וּבְנֵ֣י עַמּ֗וֹן רָאוּ֙ כִּי־נָ֣ס אֲרָ֔ם וַיָּנ֙וּסוּ֙ גַּם־הֵ֔ם מִפְּנֵ֙י אַבְשַׁ֣י אָחִ֔יו וַיָּבֹ֖אוּ הָעִ֑ירָה וַיָּבֹ֥א יוֹאָ֖ב יְרוּשָׁלִָֽם׃ פ

16 וַיַּ֣רְא אֲרָ֗ם כִּ֤י נִגְּפוּ֙ לִפְנֵ֣י יִשְׂרָאֵ֔ל וַיִּשְׁלְחוּ֙ מַלְאָכִ֔ים וַיּוֹצִ֣יאוּ אֶת־אֲרָ֔ם אֲשֶׁ֖ר מֵעֵ֣בֶר הַנָּהָ֑ר וְשׁוֹפַ֛ךְ שַׂר־צְבָ֥א הֲדַדְעֶ֖זֶר לִפְנֵיהֶֽם׃ 17 וַיֻּגַּ֣ד לְדָוִ֗יד וַיֶּאֱסֹ֤ף אֶת־כָּל־יִשְׂרָאֵל֙ וַיַּעֲבֹ֣ר הַיַּרְדֵּ֔ן וַיָּבֹ֣א אֲלֵהֶ֔ם וַֽיַּעֲרֹ֖ךְ אֲלֵהֶ֑ם וַיַּעֲרֹ֙ךְ דָּוִ֜יד לִקְרַ֤את אֲרָם֙ מִלְחָמָ֔ה וַיִּֽלָּחֲמ֖וּ עִמּֽוֹ׃ 18 וַיָּ֣נָס אֲרָם֮ מִלִּפְנֵ֣י יִשְׂרָאֵל֒ וַיַּהֲרֹ֨ג דָּוִ֜יד מֵאֲרָ֗ם שִׁבְעַ֤ת אֲלָפִים֙ רֶ֔כֶב וְאַרְבָּעִ֥ים אֶ֖לֶף אִ֣ישׁ רַגְלִ֑י וְאֵ֛ת שׁוֹפַ֥ךְ שַׂר־הַצָּבָ֖א הֵמִֽית׃ 19 וַיִּרְא֞וּ עַבְדֵ֣י הֲדַדְעֶ֗זֶר כִּ֤י נִגְּפוּ֙ לִפְנֵ֣י יִשְׂרָאֵ֔ל וַיַּשְׁלִ֥ימוּ עִם־דָּוִ֖יד וַיַּֽעַבְדֻ֑הוּ וְלֹֽא־אָבָ֣ה אֲרָ֗ם לְהוֹשִׁ֛יעַ אֶת־בְּנֵֽי־עַמּ֖וֹן עֽוֹד׃ פ

כ וַיְהִ֡י לְעֵת֩ תְּשׁוּבַ֨ת הַשָּׁנָ֜ה לְעֵ֣ת ׀ צֵ֣את הַמְּלָכִ֗ים וַיִּנְהַ֣ג יוֹאָ֡ב אֶת־חֵ֣יל הַצָּבָ֡א וַיַּשְׁחֵת֩ ׀ אֶת־אֶ֨רֶץ בְּנֵֽי־עַמּ֜וֹן וַיָּבֹ֗א וַיָּ֙צַר֙ אֶת־רַבָּ֔ה וְדָוִ֖יד יֹשֵׁ֣ב בִּירוּשָׁלִָ֑ם וַיַּ֥ךְ יוֹאָ֛ב אֶת־רַבָּ֖ה וַיֶּֽהֶרְסֶֽהָ׃ 2 וַיִּקַּ֣ח דָּוִ֣יד אֶת־עֲטֶֽרֶת־מַלְכָּם֩ מֵעַ֨ל רֹאשׁ֜וֹ וַֽיִּמְצָאָ֣הּ ׀ מִשְׁקַ֣ל כִּכַּר־זָהָ֗ב וּבָהּ֙ אֶ֣בֶן יְקָרָ֔ה וַתְּהִ֖י עַל־רֹ֣אשׁ דָּוִ֑יד וּשְׁלַ֥ל הָעִ֛יר הוֹצִ֖יא הַרְבֵּ֥ה

the people who lived there and [b]he hacked them[b] with saws and iron threshing boards and axes;[c] David did thus to all the towns of Ammon. Then David and all the troops returned to Jerusalem. [4]After this, fighting broke out with the Philistines at Gezer; that was when Sibbecai the Hushathite killed Sippai, a descendant of the Rephaim, and they were humbled.

[5]Again there was fighting with the Philistines, and Elhanan son of Jair killed Lahmi, the brother of Goliath the Gittite; his spear had a shaft like a weaver's beam. [6]Once again there was fighting at Gath. There was a giant of a man who had twenty-four fingers [and toes], six [on each hand] and six [on each foot]; he too was descended from the Raphah. [7]When he taunted Israel, Jonathan son of David's brother Shimea killed him. [8]These were descended from the Raphah in Gath, and they fell by the hands of David and his men.

21

[a]Satan arose against Israel and incited David to number Israel. [2]David said to Joab and to the commanders of the army, "Go and count Israel from Beer-sheba to Dan and bring me information as to their number." [3]Joab answered, "May the LORD increase His people a hundredfold; my lord king, are they not all subjects of my lord? Why should my lord require this? Why should it be a cause of guilt for Israel?"

[4]However, the king's command to Joab remained firm, so Joab set out and traversed all Israel; he then came to Jerusalem. [5]Joab reported to David the number of the people that had been recorded. All Israel comprised 1,100,000 ready to draw the sword, while in Judah there were 470,000 men ready to draw the sword. [6]He did not record among them Levi and

מְאֹד: ‏3 וְאֶת־הָעָם אֲשֶׁר־בָּהּ הוֹצִיא וַיָּשַׂר בַּמְּגֵרָה וּבַחֲרִיצֵי הַבַּרְזֶל וּבַמְּגֵרוֹת וְכֵן יַעֲשֶׂה דָוִיד לְכֹל עָרֵי בְנֵי־עַמּוֹן וַיָּשָׁב דָּוִיד וְכָל־הָעָם יְרוּשָׁלָ͏ִם: פ ‏4 וַיְהִי אַחֲרֵיכֵן וַתַּעֲמֹד מִלְחָמָה בְּגֶזֶר עִם־פְּלִשְׁתִּים אָז הִכָּה סִבְּכַי הַחֻשָׁתִי אֶת־סִפַּי מִילִדֵי הָרְפָאִים וַיִּכָּנֵעוּ:

‏5 וַתְּהִי־עוֹד מִלְחָמָה אֶת־פְּלִשְׁתִּים וַיַּךְ אֶלְחָנָן בֶּן־יָעוּר אֶת־לַחְמִי אֲחִי גָּלְיָת הַגִּתִּי וְעֵץ חֲנִיתוֹ כִּמְנוֹר אֹרְגִים: ‏6 וַתְּהִי־ עוֹד מִלְחָמָה בְּגַת וַיְהִי ׀ אִישׁ מִדָּה וְאֶצְבְּעֹתָיו שֵׁשׁ־וָשֵׁשׁ עֶשְׂרִים וְאַרְבַּע וְגַם־הוּא נוֹלַד לְהָרָפָא: ‏7 וַיְחָרֵף אֶת־ יִשְׂרָאֵל וַיַּכֵּהוּ יְהוֹנָתָן בֶּן־שִׁמְעָא אֲחִי דָוִיד: ‏8 אֵל נוּלְּדוּ לְהָרָפָא בְּגַת וַיִּפְּלוּ בְיַד־דָּוִיד וּבְיַד־עֲבָדָיו: פ

כא

וַיַּעֲמֹד שָׂטָן עַל־יִשְׂרָאֵל וַיָּסֶת אֶת־דָּוִיד לִמְנוֹת אֶת־יִשְׂרָאֵל: ‏2 וַיֹּאמֶר דָּוִיד אֶל־יוֹאָב וְאֶל־שָׂרֵי הָעָם לְכוּ סִפְרוּ אֶת־יִשְׂרָאֵל מִבְּאֵר שֶׁבַע וְעַד־דָּן וְהָבִיאוּ אֵלַי וְאֵדְעָה אֶת־מִסְפָּרָם: ‏3 וַיֹּאמֶר יוֹאָב יוֹסֵף יְהֹוָה עַל־עַמּוֹ ׀ כָּהֵם מֵאָה פְעָמִים הֲלֹא אֲדֹנִי הַמֶּלֶךְ כֻּלָּם לַאדֹנִי לַעֲבָדִים לָמָּה יְבַקֵּשׁ זֹאת אֲדֹנִי לָמָּה יִהְיֶה לְאַשְׁמָה לְיִשְׂרָאֵל: ‏4 וּדְבַר־הַמֶּלֶךְ חָזַק עַל־יוֹאָב וַיֵּצֵא יוֹאָב וַיִּתְהַלֵּךְ בְּכָל־יִשְׂרָאֵל וַיָּבֹא יְרוּשָׁלָ͏ִם: ‏5 וַיִּתֵּן יוֹאָב אֶת־מִסְפַּר מִפְקַד־הָעָם אֶל־ דָּוִיד וַיְהִי כָל־יִשְׂרָאֵל אֶלֶף אֲלָפִים וּמֵאָה אֶלֶף אִישׁ שֹׁלֵף חֶרֶב וִיהוּדָה אַרְבַּע מֵאוֹת וְשִׁבְעִים אֶלֶף אִישׁ שֹׁלֵף חָרֶב: ‏6 וְלֵוִי

---

b-b   *Meaning of Heb. uncertain. 2 Sam. 12.31 has "set them to work."*

c   *Heb. megeroth; cf. 2 Sam. 12.31 magzeroth, "axes."*

a   *With vv. 1–26, cf. 2 Sam. 24.*

Benjamin, because the king's command had become repugnant to Joab. ⁷God was displeased about this matter and He struck Israel.

⁸David said to God, "I have sinned grievously in having done this thing; please remit the guilt of Your servant, for I have acted foolishly." ⁹The Lord ordered Gad, David's seer: ¹⁰"Go and tell David: Thus said the Lord: I offer you three things; choose one of them and I will bring it upon you." ¹¹Gad came to David and told him, "Thus said the Lord: Select for yourself ¹²a three-year famine; or that you be swept away three months before your adversaries with the sword of your enemies overtaking you; or three days of the sword of the Lord, pestilence in the land, the angel of the Lord wreaking destruction throughout the territory of Israel. Now consider what reply I shall take back to Him who sent me." ¹³David said to Gad, "I am in great distress. Let me fall into the hands of the Lord, for His compassion is very great; and let me not fall into the hands of men."

¹⁴The Lord sent a pestilence upon Israel, and 70,000 men fell in Israel. ¹⁵God sent an angel to Jerusalem to destroy it, but as he was about to wreak destruction, the Lord saw and renounced further punishment and said to the destroying angel, "Enough! Stay your hand!" The angel of the Lord was then standing by the threshing floor of Ornan the Jebusite. ¹⁶David looked up and saw the angel of the Lord standing between heaven and earth, with a drawn sword in his hand directed against Jerusalem. David and the elders, covered in sackcloth, threw themselves on their faces. ¹⁷David said to God, "Was it not I alone who ordered the numbering of the people? I alone am guilty, and have caused severe harm; but these sheep, what have they done? O Lord my God, let Your hand fall upon me and my father's house, and let not

וּבִנְיָמִ֗ן לֹ֤א פָקַד֙ בְּתוֹכָ֔ם כִּֽי־נִתְעַ֥ב דְּבַר־
הַמֶּ֖לֶךְ אֶת־יוֹאָֽב׃ ⁷וַיֵּ֛רַע בְּעֵינֵ֥י הָאֱלֹהִ֖ים
עַל־הַדָּבָ֣ר הַזֶּ֑ה וַיַּ֖ךְ אֶת־יִשְׂרָאֵֽל׃ פ
⁸וַיֹּ֨אמֶר דָּוִ֜יד אֶל־הָאֱלֹהִ֗ים חָטָ֤אתִי מְאֹד֙
אֲשֶׁ֤ר עָשִׂ֙יתִי֙ אֶת־הַדָּבָ֣ר הַזֶּ֔ה וְעַתָּ֗ה
הַֽעֲבֶר־נָא֙ אֶת־עֲו֣וֹן עַבְדְּךָ֔ כִּ֥י נִסְכַּ֖לְתִּי
מְאֹֽד׃ פ ⁹וַיְדַבֵּ֥ר יְהֹוָ֖ה אֶל־גָּ֣ד חֹזֵ֥ה דָוִ֖יד
לֵאמֹֽר׃ ¹⁰לֵ֣ךְ וְדִבַּרְתָּ֤ אֶל־דָּוִיד֙ לֵאמֹ֔ר כֹּ֚ה
אָמַ֣ר יְהֹוָ֔ה שָׁל֕וֹשׁ אֲנִ֖י נֹטֶ֣ה עָלֶ֑יךָ בְּחַר־לְךָ֛
אַחַ֥ת מֵהֵ֖נָּה וְאֶעֱשֶׂה־לָּֽךְ׃ ¹¹וַיָּבֹ֥א גָ֖ד
אֶל־דָּוִ֑יד וַיֹּ֤אמֶר לוֹ֙ כֹּֽה־אָמַ֣ר יְהֹוָ֔ה קַבֶּל־
לָֽךְ׃ ¹²אִם־שָׁל֧וֹשׁ שָׁנִ֣ים רָעָ֗ב וְאִם־שְׁלֹשָׁ֨ה
חֳדָשִׁ֜ים נִסְפֶּ֥ה מִפְּנֵי־צָרֶ֘יךָ֮ וְחֶ֣רֶב אוֹיְבֶ֣ךָ ׀
לְמַשֶּׂגֶת֒ וְאִם־שְׁלֹ֣שֶׁת יָמִ֗ים חֶ֤רֶב יְהֹוָה֙
וְדֶ֣בֶר בָּאָ֔רֶץ וּמַלְאַ֣ךְ יְהֹוָ֔ה מַשְׁחִ֖ית בְּכָל־
גְּב֣וּל יִשְׂרָאֵ֑ל וְעַתָּ֣ה רְאֵ֔ה מָֽה־אָשִׁ֥יב
אֶת־שֹׁלְחִ֖י דָּבָֽר׃ פ ¹³וַיֹּ֧אמֶר דָּוִ֛יד אֶל־
גָּ֖ד צַר־לִ֣י מְאֹ֑ד אֶפְּלָה־נָּ֣א בְיַד־יְהֹוָ֗ה
כִּֽי־רַבִּ֤ים רַחֲמָיו֙ מְאֹ֔ד וּבְיַד־אָדָ֖ם אַל־
אֶפֹּֽל׃

¹⁴וַיִּתֵּ֤ן יְהֹוָה֙ דֶּ֣בֶר בְּיִשְׂרָאֵ֑ל וַיִּפֹּל֙ מִיִּשְׂרָאֵ֔ל
שִׁבְעִ֥ים אֶ֖לֶף אִֽישׁ׃ ¹⁵וַיִּשְׁלַ֣ח הָאֱלֹהִ֣ים ׀
מַלְאָ֣ךְ ׀ לִירֽוּשָׁלַ֘͏ִם֮ לְהַשְׁחִיתָהּ֒ וּכְהַשְׁחִ֗ית
רָאָ֤ה יְהֹוָה֙ וַיִּנָּ֣חֶם עַל־הָרָעָ֔ה וַיֹּ֨אמֶר
לַמַּלְאָ֤ךְ הַמַּשְׁחִית֙ רַ֣ב עַתָּ֔ה הֶ֖רֶף יָדֶ֑ךָ
וּמַלְאַ֤ךְ יְהֹוָה֙ עֹמֵ֔ד עִם־גֹּ֖רֶן אָרְנָ֥ן
הַיְבוּסִֽי׃ ס ¹⁶וַיִּשָּׂ֨א דָוִ֜יד אֶת־עֵינָ֗יו
וַיַּ֞רְא אֶת־מַלְאַ֤ךְ יְהֹוָה֙ עֹמֵ֗ד בֵּ֤ין הָאָ֙רֶץ֙
וּבֵ֣ין הַשָּׁמַ֔יִם וְחַרְבּ֤וֹ שְׁלוּפָה֙ בְּיָד֔וֹ נְטוּיָ֖ה
עַל־יְרֽוּשָׁלָ֑͏ִם וַיִּפֹּ֨ל דָּוִ֤יד וְהַזְּקֵנִים֙ מְכֻסִּ֣ים
בַּשַּׂקִּ֔ים עַל־פְּנֵיהֶֽם׃ ¹⁷וַיֹּ֣אמֶר דָּוִ֣יד אֶל־
הָאֱלֹהִ֡ים הֲלֹא֩ אֲנִ֨י אָמַ֜רְתִּי לִמְנ֣וֹת בָּעָ֗ם
וַאֲנִי־ה֤וּא אֲשֶׁר־חָטָ֙אתִי֙ וְהָרֵ֣עַ הֲרֵע֔וֹתִי
וְאֵ֥לֶּה הַצֹּ֖אן מֶ֣ה עָשׂ֑וּ יְהֹוָ֣ה אֱלֹהַ֗י תְּהִ֨י
נָ֤א יָֽדְךָ֙ בִּ֔י וּבְבֵ֣ית אָבִ֔י וּֽבְעַמְּךָ֖ לֹ֣א
לְמַגֵּפָֽה׃ ס ¹⁸וּמַלְאַ֣ךְ יְהֹוָ֗ה אָמַר֙ אֶל־

Your people be plagued!" [18]The angel of the Lord told Gad to inform David that David should go and set up an altar to the Lord on the threshing floor of Ornan the Jebusite. [19]David went up, following Gad's instructions, which he had delivered in the name of the Lord. [20]Ornan too saw the angel; his four sons who were with him hid themselves while Ornan kept on threshing wheat. [21]David came to Ornan; when Ornan looked up, he saw David and came off the threshing floor and bowed low to David, with his face to the ground. [22]David said to Ornan, "Sell me the site of the threshing floor, that I may build on it an altar to the Lord. Sell it to me at the full price, that the plague against the people will be checked." [23]Ornan said to David, "Take it and let my lord the king do whatever he sees fit. See, I donate oxen for burnt offerings, and the threshing boards for wood, as well as wheat for a meal offering—I donate all of it." [24]But King David replied to Ornan, "No, I will buy them at the full price. I cannot make a present to the Lord of what belongs to you, or sacrifice a burnt offering that has cost me nothing." [25]So David paid Ornan for the site 600 shekels' worth of gold. [26]And David built there an altar to the Lord and sacrificed burnt offerings and offerings of well-being. He invoked the Lord, who answered him with fire from heaven on the altar of burnt offerings. [27]The Lord ordered the angel to return his sword to its sheath. [28]At that time, when David saw that the Lord answered him at the threshing floor of Ornan the Jebusite, then he sacrificed there—[29]for the Tabernacle of the Lord, which Moses had made in the wilderness, and the altar of burnt offerings, were at that time in the shrine at Gibeon, [30]and David was unable to go to it to worship God because he was terrified by the sword of the angel of the Lord.

גָּד לֵאמֹר לְדָוִיד כִּי ׀ יַעֲלֶה דָוִיד לְהָקִים מִזְבֵּחַ לַיהוָה בְּגֹרֶן אָרְנָן הַיְבֻסִי: 19 וַיַּעַל דָּוִיד בִּדְבַר־גָּד אֲשֶׁר דִּבֶּר בְּשֵׁם יְהוָה: 20 וַיָּשָׁב אָרְנָן וַיַּרְא אֶת־הַמַּלְאָךְ וְאַרְבַּעַת בָּנָיו עִמּוֹ מִתְחַבְּאִים וְאָרְנָן דָּשׁ חִטִּים: 21 וַיָּבֹא דָוִיד עַד־אָרְנָן וַיַּבֵּט אָרְנָן וַיַּרְא אֶת־דָּוִיד וַיֵּצֵא מִן־הַגֹּרֶן וַיִּשְׁתַּחוּ לְדָוִיד אַפַּיִם אָרְצָה: 22 וַיֹּאמֶר דָּוִיד אֶל־אָרְנָן תְּנָה־לִּי מְקוֹם הַגֹּרֶן וְאֶבְנֶה־בּוֹ מִזְבֵּחַ לַיהוָה בְּכֶסֶף מָלֵא תְּנֵהוּ לִי וְתֵעָצַר הַמַּגֵּפָה מֵעַל הָעָם: 23 וַיֹּאמֶר אָרְנָן אֶל־דָּוִיד קַח־לָךְ וְיַעַשׂ אֲדֹנִי הַמֶּלֶךְ הַטּוֹב בְּעֵינָיו רְאֵה נָתַתִּי הַבָּקָר לָעֹלוֹת וְהַמּוֹרִגִּים לָעֵצִים וְהַחִטִּים לַמִּנְחָה הַכֹּל נָתָתִּי: 24 וַיֹּאמֶר הַמֶּלֶךְ דָּוִיד לְאָרְנָן לֹא כִּי־קָנֹה אֶקְנֶה בְּכֶסֶף מָלֵא כִּי לֹא־אֶשָּׂא אֲשֶׁר־לְךָ לַיהוָה וְהַעֲלוֹת עוֹלָה חִנָּם: 25 וַיִּתֵּן דָּוִיד לְאָרְנָן בַּמָּקוֹם שִׁקְלֵי זָהָב מִשְׁקָל שֵׁשׁ מֵאוֹת: 26 וַיִּבֶן שָׁם דָּוִיד מִזְבֵּחַ לַיהוָה וַיַּעַל עֹלוֹת וּשְׁלָמִים וַיִּקְרָא אֶל־יְהוָה וַיַּעֲנֵהוּ בָאֵשׁ מִן־הַשָּׁמַיִם עַל מִזְבַּח הָעֹלָה: 27 וַיֹּאמֶר יְהוָה לַמַּלְאָךְ ס וַיָּשֶׁב חַרְבּוֹ אֶל־נְדָנָהּ: 28 בָּעֵת הַהִיא בִּרְאוֹת דָּוִיד כִּי־עָנָהוּ יְהוָה בְּגֹרֶן אָרְנָן הַיְבוּסִי וַיִּזְבַּח שָׁם: 29 וּמִשְׁכַּן יְהוָה אֲשֶׁר־עָשָׂה מֹשֶׁה בַמִּדְבָּר וּמִזְבַּח הָעוֹלָה בָּעֵת הַהִיא בַּבָּמָה בְּגִבְעוֹן: 30 וְלֹא־יָכֹל דָּוִיד לָלֶכֶת לְפָנָיו לִדְרֹשׁ אֱלֹהִים כִּי נִבְעַת מִפְּנֵי חֶרֶב מַלְאַךְ יְהוָה: ס 1 וַיֹּאמֶר

22 ¹David said, "Here will be the House of the LORD and here the altar of burnt offerings for Israel."

²David gave orders to assemble the aliens living in the land of Israel, and assigned them to be hewers, to quarry and dress stones for building the House of God. ³Much iron for nails for the doors of the gates and for clasps did David lay aside, and so much copper it could not be weighed, ⁴and cedar logs without number—for the Sidonians and the Tyrians brought many cedar logs to David.

⁵For David thought, "My son Solomon is an untried youth, and the House to be built for the LORD is to be made exceedingly great to win fame and glory throughout all the lands; let me then lay aside material for him." So David laid aside much material before he died. ⁶Then he summoned his son Solomon and charged him with building the House for the LORD God of Israel.

⁷David said to Solomon, "My son, I wanted to build a House for the name of the LORD my God. ⁸But the word of the LORD came to me, saying, 'You have shed much blood and fought great battles; you shall not build a House for My name for you have shed much blood on the earth in My sight. ⁹But you will have a son who will be a man at rest, for I will give him rest from all his enemies on all sides; Solomon[a] will be his name and I shall confer peace[b] and quiet on Israel in his time. ¹⁰He will build a House for My name; he shall be a son to Me and I to him a father, and I will establish his throne of kingship over Israel forever.' ¹¹Now, my son, may the LORD be with you, and may you succeed in building the House of the LORD your God as He promised you would. ¹²Only let God give you sense and understanding and put you in charge of Israel and the observance of the

---

a   Heb. Shelomoh.
b   Heb. shalom.

כב דָּוִיד זֶה הוּא בֵּית יְהוָה הָאֱלֹהִים וְזֶה־מִּזְבֵּחַ לְעֹלָה לְיִשְׂרָאֵל׃ ס

²וַיֹּאמֶר דָּוִיד לִכְנוֹס אֶת־הַגֵּרִים אֲשֶׁר בְּאֶרֶץ יִשְׂרָאֵל וַיַּעֲמֵד חֹצְבִים לַחְצוֹב אַבְנֵי גָזִית לִבְנוֹת בֵּית הָאֱלֹהִים׃ ³וּבַרְזֶל ׀ לָרֹב לַמִּסְמְרִים לְדַלְתוֹת הַשְּׁעָרִים וְלַמְחַבְּרוֹת הֵכִין דָּוִיד וּנְחֹשֶׁת לָרֹב אֵין מִשְׁקָל׃ ⁴וַעֲצֵי אֲרָזִים לְאֵין מִסְפָּר כִּי הֵבִיאוּ הַצִּידֹנִים וְהַצֹּרִים עֲצֵי אֲרָזִים לָרֹב לְדָוִיד׃ פ

⁵וַיֹּאמֶר דָּוִיד שְׁלֹמֹה בְנִי נַעַר וָרָךְ וְהַבַּיִת לִבְנוֹת לַיהוָה לְהַגְדִּיל ׀ לְמַעְלָה לְשֵׁם וּלְתִפְאֶרֶת לְכָל־הָאֲרָצוֹת אָכִינָה נָּא לוֹ וַיָּכֶן דָּוִיד לָרֹב לִפְנֵי מוֹתוֹ׃ ⁶וַיִּקְרָא לִשְׁלֹמֹה בְנוֹ וַיְצַוֵּהוּ לִבְנוֹת בַּיִת לַיהוָה אֱלֹהֵי יִשְׂרָאֵל׃ ס

⁷וַיֹּאמֶר דָּוִיד לִשְׁלֹמֹה בנו בְּנִי אֲנִי הָיָה עִם־לְבָבִי לִבְנוֹת בַּיִת לְשֵׁם יְהוָה אֱלֹהָי׃ ⁸וַיְהִי עָלַי דְּבַר־יְהוָה לֵאמֹר דָּם לָרֹב שָׁפַכְתָּ וּמִלְחָמוֹת גְּדֹלוֹת עָשִׂיתָ לֹא־תִבְנֶה בַיִת לִשְׁמִי כִּי דָּמִים רַבִּים שָׁפַכְתָּ אַרְצָה לְפָנָי׃ ⁹הִנֵּה־בֵן נוֹלָד לָךְ הוּא יִהְיֶה אִישׁ מְנוּחָה וַהֲנִחוֹתִי לוֹ מִכָּל־אוֹיְבָיו מִסָּבִיב כִּי שְׁלֹמֹה יִהְיֶה שְׁמוֹ וְשָׁלוֹם וָשֶׁקֶט אֶתֵּן עַל־יִשְׂרָאֵל בְּיָמָיו׃ ¹⁰הוּא־יִבְנֶה בַיִת לִשְׁמִי וְהוּא יִהְיֶה־לִּי לְבֵן וַאֲנִי־לוֹ לְאָב וַהֲכִינוֹתִי כִּסֵּא מַלְכוּתוֹ עַל־יִשְׂרָאֵל עַד־עוֹלָם׃ ¹¹עַתָּה בְנִי יְהִי יְהוָה עִמָּךְ וְהִצְלַחְתָּ וּבָנִיתָ בֵּית יְהוָה אֱלֹהֶיךָ כַּאֲשֶׁר דִּבֶּר עָלֶיךָ׃ ¹²אַךְ יִתֶּן־לְךָ יְהוָה שֵׂכֶל וּבִינָה וִיצַוְּךָ עַל־יִשְׂרָאֵל

Teaching of the Lord your God. [13]Then you shall succeed, if you observantly carry out the laws and the rules that the Lord charged Moses to lay upon Israel. Be strong and of good courage; do not be afraid or dismayed. [14]See, _c_-by denying myself,-_c_ I have laid aside for the House of the Lord one hundred thousand talents of gold and one million talents of silver, and so much copper and iron it cannot be weighed; I have also laid aside wood and stone, and you shall add to them. [15]An abundance of workmen is at your disposal—hewers, workers in stone and wood, and every kind of craftsman in every kind of material—[16]gold, silver, copper, and iron without limit. Go and do it, and may the Lord be with you."

[17]David charged all the officers of Israel to support his son Solomon, [18]"See, the Lord your God is with you, and He will give you rest on every side, for He delivered the inhabitants of the land into my hand so that the land lies conquered before the Lord and before His people. [19]Now, set your minds and hearts on worshiping the Lord your God, and go build the Sanctuary of the Lord your God so that you may bring the Ark of the Covenant of the Lord and the holy vessels of God to the house that is built for the name of the Lord."

23

When David reached a ripe old age, he made his son Solomon king over Israel. [2]Then David assembled all the officers of Israel and the priests and the Levites. [3]The Levites, from the age of thirty and upward, were counted; the head-count of their males was 38,000: [4]of these there were 24,000 in charge of the work of the House of the Lord, 6,000 officers and magistrates, [5]4,000 gatekeepers, and 4,000 for praising the Lord "with instruments I devised for

13 וְלִשְׁמֹר אֶת־תּוֹרַת יְהוָה אֱלֹהֶיךָ: אָז תַּצְלִיחַ אִם־תִּשְׁמוֹר לַעֲשׂוֹת אֶת־הַחֻקִּים וְאֶת־הַמִּשְׁפָּטִים אֲשֶׁר צִוָּה יְהוָה אֶת־מֹשֶׁה עַל־יִשְׂרָאֵל חֲזַק וֶאֱמָץ אַל־תִּירָא וְאַל־תֵּחָת: 14 וְהִנֵּה בְעָנְיִי הֲכִינוֹתִי לְבֵית־יְהוָה זָהָב כִּכָּרִים מֵאָה־אֶלֶף וְכֶסֶף אֶלֶף אֲלָפִים כִּכָּרִים וְלַנְּחֹשֶׁת וְלַבַּרְזֶל אֵין מִשְׁקָל כִּי לָרֹב הָיָה וְעֵצִים וַאֲבָנִים הֲכִינוֹתִי וַעֲלֵיהֶם תּוֹסִיף: 15 וְעִמְּךָ לָרֹב עֹשֵׂי מְלָאכָה חֹצְבִים וְחָרָשֵׁי אֶבֶן וָעֵץ וְכָל־חָכָם בְּכָל־מְלָאכָה: 16 לַזָּהָב לַכֶּסֶף וְלַנְּחֹשֶׁת וְלַבַּרְזֶל אֵין מִסְפָּר קוּם וַעֲשֵׂה וִיהִי יְהוָה עִמָּךְ: 17 וַיְצַו דָּוִיד לְכָל־שָׂרֵי יִשְׂרָאֵל לַעְזֹר לִשְׁלֹמֹה בְנוֹ: 18 הֲלֹא יְהוָה אֱלֹהֵיכֶם עִמָּכֶם וְהֵנִיחַ לָכֶם מִסָּבִיב כִּי ׀ נָתַן בְּיָדִי אֵת יֹשְׁבֵי הָאָרֶץ וְנִכְבְּשָׁה הָאָרֶץ לִפְנֵי יְהוָה וְלִפְנֵי עַמּוֹ: 19 עַתָּה תְּנוּ לְבַבְכֶם וְנַפְשְׁכֶם לִדְרוֹשׁ לַיהוָה אֱלֹהֵיכֶם וְקוּמוּ וּבְנוּ אֶת־מִקְדַּשׁ יְהוָה הָאֱלֹהִים לְהָבִיא אֶת־אֲרוֹן בְּרִית־יְהוָה וּכְלֵי קֹדֶשׁ הָאֱלֹהִים לַבַּיִת הַנִּבְנֶה לְשֵׁם־יְהוָה: פ

כג וְדָוִיד זָקֵן וְשָׂבַע יָמִים וַיַּמְלֵךְ אֶת־שְׁלֹמֹה בְנוֹ עַל־יִשְׂרָאֵל: 2 וַיֶּאֱסֹף אֶת־כָּל־שָׂרֵי יִשְׂרָאֵל וְהַכֹּהֲנִים וְהַלְוִיִּם: 3 וַיִּסָּפְרוּ הַלְוִיִּם מִבֶּן שְׁלֹשִׁים שָׁנָה וָמַעְלָה וַיְהִי מִסְפָּרָם לְגֻלְגְּלֹתָם לִגְבָרִים שְׁלֹשִׁים וּשְׁמוֹנָה אָלֶף: 4 מֵאֵלֶּה לְנַצֵּחַ עַל־מְלֶאכֶת בֵּית־יְהוָה עֶשְׂרִים וְאַרְבָּעָה אָלֶף וְשֹׁטְרִים וְשֹׁפְטִים שֵׁשֶׁת אֲלָפִים: 5 וְאַרְבַּעַת אֲלָפִים שֹׁעֲרִים

_c-c_ With Targum; or "in my poverty."

singing praises." [6]David formed them into divisions:

The sons of Levi: Gershon, Kohath, and Merari. [7]The Gershonites: Ladan and Shimei. [8]The sons of Ladan: Jehiel the chief, Zetham, and Joel—3. [9]The sons of Shimei: Shelomith, Haziel, and Haran—3. These were the chiefs of the clans of the Ladanites. [10]And the sons of Shimei: Jahath, Zina, Jeush, and Beriah; these were the sons of Shimei—4. [11]Jahath was the chief and Zizah the second, but Jeush and Beriah did not have many children, so they were enrolled together as a single clan. [12]The sons of Kohath: Amram, Izhar, Hebron, and Uzziel—4. [13]The sons of Amram: Aaron and Moses. Aaron was set apart, he and his sons, forever, to be consecrated as most holy, to make burnt offerings to the Lord and serve Him and pronounce blessings in His name forever. [14]As for Moses, the man of God, his sons were named after the tribe of Levi. [15]The sons of Moses: Gershom and Eliezer. [16]The sons of Gershom: Shebuel the chief. [17]And the sons of Eliezer were: Rehabiah the chief. Eliezer had no other sons, but the sons of Rehabiah were very numerous. [18]The sons of Izhar: Shelomith the chief. [19]The sons of Hebron: Jeriah the chief, Amariah the second, Jahaziel the third, and Jekameam the fourth. [20]The sons of Uzziel: Micah the chief and Isshiah the second. [21]The sons of Merari: Mahli and Mushi. The sons of Mahli: Eleazar and Kish. [22]Eleazar died having no sons but only daughters; the sons of Kish, their kinsmen, married them. [23]The sons of Mushi: Mahli, Eder, and Jeremoth—3.

[24]These are the sons of Levi by clans, with their clan chiefs as they were enrolled, with a list of their names by heads, who did the work of the service of the House of the Lord from the age of twenty and upward. [25]For David said, "The Lord God of Israel has given rest to His

וְאַרְבַּ֣עַת אֲלָפִים֩ מְהַֽלְלִ֨ים לַיהֹוָ֤ה בַּכֵּלִים֙ אֲשֶׁ֣ר עָשִׂ֣יתִי לְהַלֵּ֔ל: 6 וַיֶּחָלְקֵ֥ם דָּוִ֖יד מַחְלְק֑וֹת ס
לִבְנֵ֣י לֵוִ֔י לְגֵרְשׁ֖וֹן קְהָ֥ת וּמְרָרִֽי: ס 7 לַגֵּ֣רְשֻׁנִּ֔י לַעְדָּ֖ן וְשִׁמְעִֽי: ס 8 בְּנֵ֣י לַעְדָּ֗ן הָרֹ֛אשׁ יְחִיאֵ֥ל וְזֵתָ֖ם וְיוֹאֵ֥ל שְׁלֹשָֽׁה: ס 9 בְּנֵ֣י שִׁמְעִ֗י שְׁלֹמ֤וֹת וַחֲזִיאֵל֙ וְהָרָ֔ן שְׁלֹשָׁ֑ה אֵ֛לֶּה רָאשֵׁ֥י הָאָב֖וֹת לְלַעְדָּֽן: ס 10 וּבְנֵ֣י שִׁמְעִ֔י יַ֣חַת זִינָ֔א וִיע֖וּשׁ וּבְרִיעָ֑ה אֵ֛לֶּה בְנֵי־שִׁמְעִ֖י אַרְבָּעָֽה: 11 וַֽיְהִי־יַ֣חַת הָרֹ֗אשׁ וְזִיזָ֣ה הַשֵּׁנִ֔י וִיע֥וּשׁ וּבְרִיעָ֖ה לֹא־הִרְבּ֣וּ בָנִ֑ים וַיִּֽהְיוּ֙ לְבֵ֣ית אָ֔ב לִפְקֻדָּ֖ה אֶחָֽת: ס 12 בְּנֵ֣י קְהָ֗ת עַמְרָ֥ם יִצְהָ֛ר חֶבְר֥וֹן וְעֻזִּיאֵ֖ל אַרְבָּעָֽה: ס 13 בְּנֵ֣י עַמְרָ֔ם אַהֲרֹ֖ן וּמֹשֶׁ֑ה וַיִּבָּדֵ֣ל אַֽהֲרֹ֡ן לְהַקְדִּישׁוֹ֩ קֹ֨דֶשׁ קָֽדָשִׁ֜ים הֽוּא־וּבָנָ֣יו עַד־עוֹלָ֗ם לְהַקְטִיר֩ לִפְנֵ֨י יְהֹוָ֤ה לְשָֽׁרְתוֹ֙ וּלְבָרֵ֣ךְ בִּשְׁמ֖וֹ עַד־עוֹלָֽם: 14 וּמֹשֶׁ֖ה אִ֣ישׁ הָאֱלֹהִ֑ים בָּנָ֕יו יִקָּרְא֖וּ עַל־שֵׁ֥בֶט הַלֵּוִֽי: 15 בְּנֵ֣י מֹשֶׁ֔ה גֵּרְשֹׁ֖ם וֶאֱלִיעֶֽזֶר: 16 בְּנֵ֥י גֵרְשׁ֖וֹם שְׁבוּאֵ֥ל הָרֹֽאשׁ: 17 וַיִּֽהְי֣וּ בְנֵֽי־אֱלִיעֶ֗זֶר רְחַבְיָ֣ה הָרֹ֑אשׁ וְלֹא־הָיָ֤ה לֶאֱלִיעֶ֙זֶר֙ בָּנִ֣ים אֲחֵרִ֔ים וּבְנֵ֥י רְחַבְיָ֖ה רָב֥וּ לְמָֽעְלָה: 18 בְּנֵ֣י יִצְהָ֑ר שְׁלֹמִ֖ית הָרֹֽאשׁ: ס 19 בְּנֵ֣י חֶבְר֗וֹן יְרִיָּ֤הֽוּ הָרֹאשׁ֙ אֲמַרְיָ֣ה הַשֵּׁנִ֔י יַחֲזִיאֵל֙ הַשְּׁלִ֣ישִׁ֔י וִֽיקַמְעָ֖ם הָרְבִיעִֽי: 20 בְּנֵ֣י עֻזִּיאֵ֔ל מִיכָ֥ה הָרֹ֖אשׁ וְיִשִּׁיָּ֥ה הַשֵּׁנִֽי: ס 21 בְּנֵ֣י מְרָרִ֔י מַחְלִ֖י וּמוּשִׁ֑י בְּנֵ֣י מַחְלִ֔י אֶלְעָזָ֖ר וְקִֽישׁ: 22 וַיָּ֣מׇת אֶלְעָזָ֗ר וְלֹא־הָ֥יוּ ל֛וֹ בָּנִ֖ים כִּ֣י אִם־בָּנ֑וֹת וַיִּשָּׂא֥וּם בְּנֵי־קִ֖ישׁ אֲחֵיהֶֽם: 23 בְּנֵ֣י מוּשִׁ֗י מַחְלִ֥י וְעֵ֛דֶר וִירֵמ֖וֹת שְׁלֹשָֽׁה: 24 אֵ֣לֶּה בְנֵֽי־לֵוִי֩ לְבֵ֨ית אֲבֹתֵיהֶ֜ם רָאשֵׁ֣י הָאָב֗וֹת לִפְקוּדֵיהֶם֙ בְּמִסְפַּ֣ר שֵׁמ֔וֹת לְגֻלְגְּלֹתָ֔ם עֹשֵׂה֙ הַמְּלָאכָ֔ה לַעֲבֹדַ֖ת בֵּ֣ית יְהֹוָ֑ה מִבֶּ֛ן עֶשְׂרִ֥ים שָׁנָ֖ה וָמָֽעְלָה: 25 כִּ֚י אָמַ֣ר דָּוִ֔יד הֵנִ֛יחַ יְהֹוָ֥ה אֱלֹהֵֽי־יִשְׂרָאֵ֖ל

people and made His dwelling in Jerusalem forever. ²⁶Therefore the Levites need not carry the Tabernacle and all its various service vessels." ²⁷Among the last acts of David was the counting of the Levites from the age of twenty and upward. ²⁸For their appointment was alongside the Aaronites for the service of the House of the LORD, to look after the courts and the chambers, and the purity of all the holy things, and the performance of the service of the House of God, ²⁹and the rows of bread, and the fine flour for the meal offering, and the unleavened wafers, and the cakes made on the griddle and soaked, and every measure of capacity and length; ³⁰and to be present every morning to praise and extol the LORD, and at evening too, ³¹and whenever offerings were made to the LORD, according to the quantities prescribed for them, on sabbaths, new moons and holidays, regularly, before the LORD; ³²and so to keep watch over the Tent of Meeting, over the holy things, and over the Aaronites their kinsmen, for the service of the House of the LORD.

24

The divisions of the Aaronites were: The sons of Aaron: Nadab and Abihu, Eleazar and Ithamar. ²Nadab and Abihu died in the lifetime of their father, and they had no children, so Eleazar and Ithamar served as priests.

³David, Zadok of the sons of Eleazar, and Ahimelech of the sons of Ithamar divided them into offices by their tasks. ⁴The sons of Eleazar turned out to be more numerous by male heads than the sons of Ithamar, so they divided the sons of Eleazar into sixteen chiefs of clans and the sons of Ithamar into eight clans. ⁵They divided them by lot, both on an equal footing, since they were all sanctuary officers and officers

לְעַמּוֹ וַיִּשְׁכֹּן בִּירוּשָׁלַ‍ִם עַד־לְעוֹלָם: 26 וְגַם לַלְוִיִּם אֵין־לָשֵׂאת אֶת־הַמִּשְׁכָּן וְאֶת־ כָּל־כֵּלָיו לַעֲבֹדָתוֹ: 27 כִּי בְדִבְרֵי דָוִיד הָאַחֲרֹנִים הֵמָּה מִסְפַּר בְּנֵי־לֵוִי מִבֶּן עֶשְׂרִים שָׁנָה וּלְמָעְלָה: 28 כִּי מַעֲמָדָם לְיַד־בְּנֵי אַהֲרֹן לַעֲבֹדַת בֵּית יְהֹוָה עַל־ הַחֲצֵרוֹת וְעַל־הַלְּשָׁכוֹת וְעַל־טָהֳרַת לְכָל־קֹדֶשׁ וּמַעֲשֵׂה עֲבֹדַת בֵּית הָאֱלֹהִים: 29 וּלְלֶחֶם הַמַּעֲרֶכֶת וּלְסֹלֶת לְמִנְחָה וְלִרְקִיקֵי הַמַּצּוֹת וְלַמַּחֲבַת וְלַמֻּרְבָּכֶת וּלְכָל־מְשׂוּרָה וּמִדָּה: 30 וְלַעֲמֹד בַּבֹּקֶר בַּבֹּקֶר לְהֹדוֹת וּלְהַלֵּל לַיהֹוָה וְכֵן לָעָרֶב: 31 וּלְכֹל הַעֲלוֹת עֹלוֹת לַיהֹוָה לַשַּׁבָּתוֹת לֶחֳדָשִׁים וְלַמֹּעֲדִים בְּמִסְפָּר כְּמִשְׁפָּט עֲלֵיהֶם תָּמִיד לִפְנֵי יְהֹוָה: 32 וְשָׁמְרוּ אֶת־ מִשְׁמֶרֶת אֹהֶל־מוֹעֵד וְאֵת מִשְׁמֶרֶת הַקֹּדֶשׁ וּמִשְׁמֶרֶת בְּנֵי אַהֲרֹן אֲחֵיהֶם לַעֲבֹדַת בֵּית יְהֹוָה: פ

כד וְלִבְנֵי אַהֲרֹן מַחְלְקוֹתָם בְּנֵי אַהֲרֹן נָדָב וַאֲבִיהוּא אֶלְעָזָר וְאִיתָמָר: 2 וַיָּמָת נָדָב וַאֲבִיהוּא לִפְנֵי אֲבִיהֶם וּבָנִים לֹא־הָיוּ לָהֶם וַיְכַהֲנוּ אֶלְעָזָר וְאִיתָמָר: 3 וַיֶּחָלְקֵם דָּוִיד וְצָדוֹק מִן־בְּנֵי אֶלְעָזָר וַאֲחִימֶלֶךְ מִן־בְּנֵי אִיתָמָר לִפְקֻדָּתָם בַּעֲבֹדָתָם: 4 וַיִּמָּצְאוּ בְנֵי־אֶלְעָזָר רַבִּים לְרָאשֵׁי הַגְּבָרִים מִן־בְּנֵי אִיתָמָר וַיַּחְלְקוּם לִבְנֵי אֶלְעָזָר רָאשִׁים לְבֵית־אָבוֹת שִׁשָּׁה עָשָׂר וְלִבְנֵי אִיתָמָר לְבֵית אֲבוֹתָם שְׁמוֹנָה: 5 וַיַּחְלְקוּם בְּגוֹרָלוֹת אֵלֶּה עִם־ אֵלֶּה כִּי־הָיוּ שָׂרֵי־קֹדֶשׁ וְשָׂרֵי הָאֱלֹהִים

of God—the sons of Eleazar and the sons of Ithamar. [6]Shemaiah son of Nathanel, the scribe, who was of the Levites, registered them under the eye of the king, the officers, and Zadok the priest, and Ahimelech son of Abiathar, and the chiefs of clans of the priests and Levites—*a*one clan more taken for Eleazar for each one taken of Ithamar.*-a*

[7]The first lot fell on Jehoiarib; the second on Jedaiah; [8]the third on Harim; the fourth on Seorim; [9]the fifth on Malchijah; the sixth on Mijamin; [10]the seventh on Hakkoz; the eighth on Abijah; [11]the ninth on Jeshua; the tenth on Shecaniah; [12]the eleventh on Eliashib; the twelfth on Jakim; [13]the thirteenth on Huppah; the fourteenth on Jeshebeab; [14]the fifteenth on Bilgah; the sixteenth on Immer; [15]the seventeenth on Hezir; the eighteenth on Happizzez; [16]the nineteenth on Pethahiah; the twentieth on Jehezkel; [17]the twenty-first on Jachin; the twenty-second on Gamul; [18]the twenty-third on Delaiah; the twenty-fourth on Maaziah.

[19]According to this allocation of offices by tasks, they were to enter the House of the Lord as was laid down for them by Aaron their father, as the Lord God of Israel had commanded him.

[20]The remaining Levites: the sons of Amram: Shubael; the sons of Shubael: Jehdeiah; [21]Rehabiah. The sons of Rehabiah: Isshiah, the chief. [22]Izharites: Shelomoth. The sons of Shelomoth: Jahath [23]and Benai, Jeriah; the second, Amariah; the third, Jahaziel; the fourth, Jekameam. [24]The sons of Uzziel: Micah. The sons of Micah: Shamir. [25]The brother of Micah: Isshiah. The sons of Isshiah: Zechariah. [26]The sons of Merari: Mahli and Mushi. The sons of Jaazaiah, his son—[27]the sons of Merari by Jaazaiah his son: Shoham, Zakkur, and Ibri. [28]Mahli: Eleazar; he had no sons. [29]Kish: the sons of Kish: Jerahmeel. [30]The sons of Mushi:

מִבְּנֵי אֶלְעָזָר וּבִבְנֵי אִיתָמָר: ס
6 וַיִּכְתְּבֵם שְׁמַעְיָה בֶן־נְתַנְאֵל הַסּוֹפֵר מִן־
הַלֵּוִי לִפְנֵי הַמֶּלֶךְ וְהַשָּׂרִים וְצָדוֹק הַכֹּהֵן
וַאֲחִימֶלֶךְ בֶּן־אֶבְיָתָר וְרָאשֵׁי הָאָבוֹת
לַכֹּהֲנִים וְלַלְוִיִּם בֵּית־אָב אֶחָד אָחֻז
לְאֶלְעָזָר וְאָחֻז | אָחֻז לְאִיתָמָר: פ
7 *וַיֵּצֵא הַגּוֹרָל הָרִאשׁוֹן לִיהוֹיָרִיב
לִידַעְיָה הַשֵּׁנִי: 8 לְחָרִם הַשְּׁלִישִׁי
לִשְׂעֹרִים הָרְבִיעִי: 9 לְמַלְכִּיָּה הַחֲמִישִׁי
לְמִיָּמִן הַשִּׁשִּׁי: 10 לְהַקּוֹץ הַשְּׁבִעִי לַאֲבִיָּה
הַשְּׁמִינִי: 11 לְיֵשׁוּעַ הַתְּשִׁעִי לִשְׁכַנְיָהוּ
הָעֲשִׂרִי: 12 לְאֶלְיָשִׁיב עַשְׁתֵּי עָשָׂר לְיָקִים
שְׁנֵים עָשָׂר: 13 לְחֻפָּה שְׁלֹשָׁה עָשָׂר
לְיֶשֶׁבְאָב אַרְבָּעָה עָשָׂר: 14 לְבִלְגָּה חֲמִשָּׁה
עָשָׂר לְאִמֵּר שִׁשָּׁה עָשָׂר: 15 לְחֵזִיר שִׁבְעָה
עָשָׂר לְהַפִּצֵּץ שְׁמוֹנָה עָשָׂר: 16 לִפְתַחְיָה
תִּשְׁעָה עָשָׂר לִיחֶזְקֵאל הָעֶשְׂרִים: 17 לְיָכִין
אֶחָד וְעֶשְׂרִים לְגָמוּל שְׁנַיִם וְעֶשְׂרִים:
18 לִדְלָיָהוּ שְׁלֹשָׁה וְעֶשְׂרִים לְמַעַזְיָהוּ
אַרְבָּעָה וְעֶשְׂרִים: פ
19 אֵלֶּה פְקֻדָּתָם לַעֲבֹדָתָם לָבוֹא לְבֵית־
יְהוָה כְּמִשְׁפָּטָם בְּיַד אַהֲרֹן אֲבִיהֶם כַּאֲשֶׁר
צִוָּהוּ יְהוָה אֱלֹהֵי יִשְׂרָאֵל: פ
20 וְלִבְנֵי לֵוִי הַנּוֹתָרִים לִבְנֵי עַמְרָם שׁוּבָאֵל
לִבְנֵי שׁוּבָאֵל יֶחְדְּיָהוּ: 21 לִרְחַבְיָהוּ לִבְנֵי
רְחַבְיָהוּ הָרֹאשׁ יִשִּׁיָּה: 22 לַיִּצְהָרִי שְׁלֹמוֹת
לִבְנֵי שְׁלֹמוֹת יָחַת: 23 וּבְנֵי יְרִיָּהוּ אֲמַרְיָהוּ
הַשֵּׁנִי יַחֲזִיאֵל הַשְּׁלִישִׁי יְקַמְעָם הָרְבִיעִי:
24 בְּנֵי עֻזִּיאֵל מִיכָה לִבְנֵי מִיכָה שָׁמוֹר
שָׁמִיר: 25 אֲחִי מִיכָה יִשִּׁיָּה לִבְנֵי יִשִּׁיָּה
זְכַרְיָהוּ: 26 בְּנֵי מְרָרִי מַחְלִי וּמוּשִׁי
בְּנֵי יַעֲזִיָּהוּ בְנוֹ: 27 בְּנֵי מְרָרִי לְיַעֲזִיָּהוּ
בְנוֹ וְשֹׁהַם וְזַכּוּר וְעִבְרִי: 28 לְמַחְלִי
אֶלְעָזָר וְלֹא־הָיָה לוֹ בָּנִים: 29 לְקִישׁ בְּנֵי־
קִישׁ יְרַחְמְאֵל: 30 וּבְנֵי מוּשִׁי מַחְלִי

vv. 7–18.　　בכתב היד שלנו, הרשימה בצורת שירה

---

a-a Meaning of Heb. uncertain.

Mahli, Eder, and Jerimoth. These were the sons of the Levites by their clans.

³¹These too cast lots corresponding to their kinsmen, the sons of Aaron, under the eye of King David and Zadok and Ahimelech and the chiefs of the clans of the priests and Levites, on the principle of "chief and youngest brother alike."

25

David and the officers of the army set apart for service the sons of Asaph, of Heman, and of Jeduthun, who prophesied to the accompaniment of lyres, harps, and cymbals. The list of men who performed this work, according to their service, was:

²Sons of Asaph: Zaccur, Joseph, Nethaniah, and Asarelah—sons of Asaph under the charge of Asaph, who prophesied by order of the king. ³Jeduthun—the sons of Jeduthun: Gedaliah, Zeri, Jeshaiah, Hashabiah, Mattithiah—6, under the charge of their father Jeduthun, who, accompanied on the harp, prophesied, praising and extolling the LORD. ⁴Heman—the sons of Heman: Bukkiah, Mattaniah, Uzziel, Shebuel, Jerimoth, Hananiah, Hanani, Eliathah, Giddalti, Romamti-ezer, Joshbekashah, Mallothi, Hothir, and Mahazioth; ⁵all these were sons of Heman, the seer of the king, [who uttered] prophecies of God for His greater glory. God gave Heman fourteen sons and three daughters; ⁶all these were under the charge of their father for the singing in the House of the LORD, to the accompaniment of cymbals, harps, and lyres, for the service of the House of God by order of the king. Asaph, Jeduthun, and Heman—⁷their total number with their kinsmen, trained singers of the LORD—all the masters, 288.

⁸They cast lots for shifts on the principle of "small and great alike, like master like apprentice."

וְעֶ֫דֶר וִירִימ֑וֹת אֵ֣לֶּה בְּנֵ֤י הַלְוִיִּם֙ לְבֵ֣ית אֲבֹתֵיהֶֽם׃

31 וַיַּפִּ֜ילוּ גַם־הֵ֗ם גּוֹרָלוֹת֙ לְעֻמַּת֙ ׀ אֲחֵיהֶ֣ם בְּנֵֽי־אַהֲרֹ֔ן לִפְנֵ֤י דָוִיד֙ הַמֶּ֔לֶךְ וְצָד֖וֹק וַאֲחִימֶ֑לֶךְ וְרָאשֵׁי֙ הָֽאָב֔וֹת לַכֹּהֲנִ֖ים וְלַלְוִיִּ֑ם אָב֤וֹת הָרֹאשׁ֙ לְעֻמַּ֣ת אָחִ֣יו הַקָּטָֽן׃ ס

כה וַיַּבְדֵּ֣ל דָּוִ֡יד וְשָׂרֵ֣י הַצָּבָ֡א לַעֲבֹדָ֞ה לִבְנֵ֧י אָסָ֛ף וְהֵימָ֥ן וִֽידוּת֖וּן הַֽנִּבְּאִ֑ים בְּכִנֹּר֥וֹת בִּנְבָלִ֖ים וּבִֽמְצִלְתָּ֑יִם וַֽיְהִי֙ מִסְפָּרָ֔ם אַנְשֵׁ֥י מְלָאכָ֖ה לַעֲבֹדָתָֽם׃ 2 לִבְנֵ֣י אָסָ֗ף זַכּ֧וּר וְיוֹסֵ֛ף וּנְתַנְיָ֥ה וַֽאֲשַׂרְאֵ֑לָה בְּנֵ֣י אָסָ֔ף עַ֚ל יַד־אָסָ֔ף הַנִּבָּ֖א עַל־יְדֵ֥י הַמֶּֽלֶךְ׃ 3 לִֽידוּת֗וּן בְּנֵ֣י יְדוּת֘וּן֘ גְּדַלְיָ֣הוּ וּצְרִ֣י וִֽישַׁעְיָ֔הוּ חֲשַׁבְיָ֖הוּ וּמַתִּתְיָ֑הוּ שִׁשָּׁ֗ה עַ֚ל יְדֵ֣י אֲבִיהֶ֣ם יְדוּת֔וּן בַּכִּנּ֕וֹר הַנִּבָּ֕א עַל־הֹד֥וֹת וְהַלֵּ֖ל לַֽיהוָֽה׃ ס 4 לְהֵימָ֗ן בְּנֵ֣י הֵימָ֔ן בֻּקִּיָּ֨הוּ מַתַּנְיָ֜הוּ עֻזִּיאֵ֤ל שְׁבוּאֵל֙ וִירִימ֔וֹת חֲנַנְיָ֣ה חֲנָ֔נִי אֱלִיאָ֖תָה גִּדַּ֑לְתִּי וְרֹמַ֣מְתִּי עֶ֔זֶר יָשְׁבְּקָ֖שָׁה מַלּ֥וֹתִי הוֹתִ֖יר מַחֲזִיאֽוֹת׃ 5 כָּל־אֵ֨לֶּה בָנִ֜ים לְהֵימָ֣ן חֹזֵ֣ה הַמֶּ֗לֶךְ בְּדִבְרֵ֤י הָֽאֱלֹהִים֙ לְהָרִ֣ים קָ֑רֶן וַיִּתֵּ֤ן הָֽאֱלֹהִים֙ לְהֵימָ֔ן בָּנִ֥ים אַרְבָּעָ֥ה עָשָׂ֖ר וּבָנ֥וֹת שָׁלֽוֹשׁ׃ 6 כָּל־אֵ֣לֶּה עַל־יְדֵי֩ אֲבִיהֶ֨ם בַּשִּׁ֜יר בֵּ֣ית יְהוָ֗ה בִּמְצִלְתַּ֙יִם֙ נְבָלִ֣ים וְכִנֹּר֔וֹת לַעֲבֹדַ֖ת בֵּ֣ית הָאֱלֹהִ֑ים עַ֚ל יְדֵ֣י הַמֶּ֔לֶךְ ס אָסָ֖ף וִידוּת֥וּן וְהֵימָֽן׃ 7 וַֽיְהִ֤י מִסְפָּרָם֙ עִם־אֲחֵיהֶ֔ם מְלֻמְּדֵי־שִׁ֖יר לַֽיהוָ֑ה כָּל־הַמֵּבִ֕ין מָאתַ֖יִם שְׁמוֹנִ֥ים וּשְׁמוֹנָֽה׃ 8 וַיַּפִּ֜ילוּ גּוֹרָל֗וֹת מִשְׁמֶ֙רֶת֙ לְעֻמַּת֙ כַּקָּטֹ֣ן כַּגָּד֔וֹל מֵבִ֖ין עִם־תַּלְמִֽיד׃ פ

⁹The first lot fell to Asaph—to Joseph; the second, to Gedaliah, he and his brothers and his sons—12; ¹⁰the third, to Zaccur: his sons and his brothers—12; ¹¹the fourth, to Izri: his sons and his brothers—12; ¹²the fifth, to Nethaniah: his sons and his brothers—12; ¹³the sixth, to Bukkiah: his sons and his brothers—12; ¹⁴the seventh, to Jesarelah: his sons and his brothers—12; ¹⁵the eighth, to Jeshaiah: his sons and his brothers—12; ¹⁶the ninth, to Mattaniah: his sons and his brothers—12; ¹⁷the tenth, to Shimei: his sons and his brothers—12; ¹⁸the eleventh to Azarel: his sons and his brothers—12; ¹⁹the twelfth, to Hashabiah: his sons and his brothers—12; ²⁰the thirteenth, to Shubael: his sons and his brothers—12; ²¹the fourteenth, to Mattithiah: his sons and his brothers—12; ²²the fifteenth, to Jeremoth: his sons and his brothers—12; ²³the sixteenth, to Hananiah: his sons and his brothers—12; ²⁴the seventeenth, to Joshbekashah: his sons and his brothers—12; ²⁵the eighteenth, to Hanani: his sons and his brothers—12; ²⁶the nineteenth, to Mallothi: his sons and his brothers—12; ²⁷the twentieth, to Eliathah: his sons and his brothers—12; ²⁸the twenty-first, to Hothir: his sons and his brothers—12; ²⁹the twenty-second, to Giddalti: his sons and his brothers—12; ³⁰the twenty-third, to Mahazioth: his sons and his brothers—12; ³¹the twenty-fourth, to Romamti-ezer: his sons and his brothers—12.

26

The divisions of the gatekeepers: Korahites: Meshelemiah son of Kore, of the sons of Asaph. ²Sons of Meshelemiah: Zechariah the

⁹וַיֵּצֵא הַגּוֹרָל הָרִאשׁוֹן לְאָסָף לְיוֹסֵף גְּדַלְיָהוּ הַשֵּׁנִי הוּא־וְאֶחָיו וּבָנָיו שְׁנֵים עָשָׂר: ¹⁰הַשְּׁלִשִׁי זַכּוּר בָּנָיו וְאֶחָיו שְׁנֵים עָשָׂר: ¹¹הָרְבִיעִי לַיִּצְרִי בָּנָיו וְאֶחָיו שְׁנֵים עָשָׂר: ¹²הַחֲמִישִׁי נְתַנְיָהוּ בָּנָיו וְאֶחָיו שְׁנֵים עָשָׂר: ¹³הַשִּׁשִּׁי בֻקִּיָּהוּ בָּנָיו וְאֶחָיו שְׁנֵים עָשָׂר: ¹⁴הַשְּׁבִעִי יְשַׂרְאֵלָה בָּנָיו וְאֶחָיו שְׁנֵים עָשָׂר: ¹⁵הַשְּׁמִינִי יְשַׁעְיָהוּ בָּנָיו וְאֶחָיו שְׁנֵים עָשָׂר: ¹⁶הַתְּשִׁיעִי מַתַּנְיָהוּ בָּנָיו וְאֶחָיו שְׁנֵים עָשָׂר: ¹⁷הָעֲשִׂירִי שִׁמְעִי בָּנָיו וְאֶחָיו שְׁנֵים עָשָׂר: ¹⁸עַשְׁתֵּי־עָשָׂר עֲזַרְאֵל בָּנָיו וְאֶחָיו שְׁנֵים עָשָׂר: ¹⁹הַשְּׁנֵים עָשָׂר לַחֲשַׁבְיָה בָּנָיו וְאֶחָיו שְׁנֵים עָשָׂר: ²⁰לִשְׁלֹשָׁה עָשָׂר שׁוּבָאֵל בָּנָיו וְאֶחָיו שְׁנֵים עָשָׂר: ²¹לְאַרְבָּעָה עָשָׂר מַתִּתְיָהוּ בָּנָיו וְאֶחָיו שְׁנֵים עָשָׂר: ²²לַחֲמִשָּׁה עָשָׂר לִירֵמוֹת בָּנָיו וְאֶחָיו שְׁנֵים עָשָׂר: ²³לְשִׁשָּׁה עָשָׂר לַחֲנַנְיָהוּ בָּנָיו וְאֶחָיו שְׁנֵים עָשָׂר: ²⁴לְשִׁבְעָה עָשָׂר לְיָשְׁבְּקָשָׁה בָּנָיו וְאֶחָיו שְׁנֵים עָשָׂר: ²⁵לִשְׁמוֹנָה עָשָׂר לַחֲנָנִי בָּנָיו וְאֶחָיו שְׁנֵים עָשָׂר: ²⁶לְתִשְׁעָה עָשָׂר לְמַלּוֹתִי בָּנָיו וְאֶחָיו שְׁנֵים עָשָׂר: ²⁷לְעֶשְׂרִים לֶאֱלִיָּתָה בָּנָיו וְאֶחָיו שְׁנֵים עָשָׂר: ²⁸לְאֶחָד וְעֶשְׂרִים לְהוֹתִיר בָּנָיו וְאֶחָיו שְׁנֵים עָשָׂר: ²⁹לִשְׁנַיִם וְעֶשְׂרִים לְגִדַּלְתִּי בָּנָיו וְאֶחָיו שְׁנֵים עָשָׂר: ³⁰לִשְׁלֹשָׁה וְעֶשְׂרִים לְמַחֲזִיאוֹת בָּנָיו וְאֶחָיו שְׁנֵים עָשָׂר: ³¹לְאַרְבָּעָה וְעֶשְׂרִים לְרוֹמַמְתִּי עָזֶר בָּנָיו וְאֶחָיו שְׁנֵים עָשָׂר: פ

כו לְמַחְלְקוֹת לְשֹׁעֲרִים לַקָּרְחִים מְשֶׁלֶמְיָהוּ בֶן־קֹרֵא מִן־בְּנֵי אָסָף: ²וְלִמְשֶׁלֶמְיָהוּ בָּנִים זְכַרְיָהוּ הַבְּכוֹר

firstborn, Jediael the second, Zebadiah the third, Jathniel the fourth, ³Elam the fifth, Jehohanan the sixth, Eliehoenai the seventh. ⁴Sons of Obed-edom: Shemaiah the first-born, Jehozabad the second, Joah the third, Sacar the fourth, Nethanel the fifth, ⁵Ammiel the sixth, Issachar the seventh, Peullethai the eighth—for God had blessed him. ⁶To his son Shemaiah were born sons who exercised authority in their clans because they were men of substance. ⁷The sons of Shemaiah: Othni, Rephael, Obed, Elzabad—his brothers, men of ability, were Elihu and Semachiah. ⁸All these, sons of Obed-edom; they and their sons and brothers, strong and able men for the service—62 of Obed-edom. ⁹Meshelemiah had sons and brothers, able men—18. ¹⁰Hosah of the Merarites had sons: Shimri the chief (he was not the first-born, but his father designated him chief), ¹¹Hilkiah the second, Tebaliah the third, Zechariah the fourth. All the sons and brothers of Hosah—13.

¹²These are the divisions of the gatekeepers, by their chief men, [who worked in] shifts corresponding to their kinsmen, ministering in the House of the Lord. ¹³They cast lots, small and great alike, by clans, for each gate.

¹⁴The lot for the east [gate] fell to Shelemiah. Then they cast lots [for] Zechariah his son, a prudent counselor, and his lot came out to be the north [gate]. ¹⁵For Obed-edom, the south [gate], and for his sons, the vestibule. ¹⁶For Shuppim and for Hosah, the west [gate], with the Shallecheth gate on the ascending highway. Watch corresponded to watch: ¹⁷At the east—six Levites; at the north—four daily; at the south—four daily; at the vestibule—two by two; ¹⁸at the colonnade on the west—four at the causeway and two at the colonnade. ¹⁹These were the divisions of the gatekeepers of the sons of Korah and the sons of Merari.

יְדִיעֲאֵ֣ל הַשֵּׁנִ֗י זְבַדְיָ֙הוּ֙ הַשְּׁלִשִׁ֔י יַתְנִיאֵ֖ל הָרְבִיעִֽי׃ ³עֵילָ֤ם הַחֲמִישִׁי֙ יְהֽוֹחָנָ֣ן הַשִּׁשִּׁ֔י אֶלְיְהֽוֹעֵינַ֖י הַשְּׁבִיעִֽי׃ ⁴וּלְעֹבֵ֥ד אֱדֹ֖ם בָּנִ֑ים שְׁמַֽעְיָ֣ה הַבְּכ֗וֹר יְהוֹזָבָ֤ד הַשֵּׁנִי֙ יוֹאָ֣ח הַשְּׁלִשִׁ֗י וְשָׂכָר֙ הָרְבִיעִ֔י וּנְתַנְאֵ֖ל הַחֲמִישִֽׁי׃ ⁵עַמִּיאֵ֤ל הַשִּׁשִּׁי֙ יִשָׂשכָ֣ר הַשְּׁבִיעִ֔י פְּעֻלְּתַ֖י הַשְּׁמִינִ֑י כִּ֥י בֵרְכ֖וֹ אֱלֹהִֽים׃ פ ⁶וְלִשְׁמַֽעְיָ֤ה בְנוֹ֙ נוֹלַ֣ד בָּנִ֔ים הַמִּמְשָׁלִ֖ים לְבֵ֣ית אֲבִיהֶ֑ם כִּֽי־גִבּ֥וֹרֵי חַ֖יִל הֵֽמָּה׃ ⁷בְּנֵ֣י שְׁמַֽעְיָ֗ה עָתְנִ֤י וּרְפָאֵל֙ וְעוֹבֵ֣ד אֶלְזָבָ֔ד אֶחָ֖יו בְּנֵי־חָ֑יִל אֱלִיה֖וּ וּסְמַכְיָֽהוּ׃ ⁸כָּל־אֵ֜לֶּה מִבְּנֵ֣י ׀ עֹבֵ֣ד אֱדֹ֗ם הֵ֤מָּה וּבְנֵיהֶם֙ וַֽאֲחֵיהֶ֔ם אִֽישׁ־חַ֥יִל בַּכֹּ֖חַ לַֽעֲבֹדָ֑ה שִׁשִּׁ֥ים וּשְׁנַ֖יִם לְעֹבֵ֥ד אֱדֹֽם׃ ⁹וְלִמְשֶֽׁלֶמְיָ֗הוּ בָּנִ֧ים וְאַחִ֛ים בְּנֵי־חָ֖יִל שְׁמוֹנָ֥ה עָשָֽׂר׃ ס ¹⁰וּלְחֹסָ֥ה מִן־בְּנֵֽי־מְרָרִ֖י בָּנִ֑ים שִׁמְרִ֤י הָרֹאשׁ֙ כִּ֣י לֹֽא־הָיָ֣ה בְכ֔וֹר וַיְשִׂימֵ֥הוּ אָבִ֖יהוּ לְרֹֽאשׁ׃ ¹¹חִלְקִיָּ֣הוּ הַשֵּׁנִ֗י טְבַלְיָ֙הוּ֙ הַשְּׁלִשִׁ֔י זְכַרְיָ֖הוּ הָֽרְבִעִ֑י כָּל־בָּנִ֧ים וְאַחִ֛ים לְחֹסָ֖ה שְׁלֹשָׁ֥ה עָשָֽׂר׃

¹²לְ֠אֵ֠לֶּה מַחְלְק֨וֹת הַשֹּֽׁעֲרִ֜ים לְרָאשֵׁ֣י הַגְּבָרִ֗ים מִשְׁמָרוֹת֙ לְעֻמַּ֣ת אֲחֵיהֶ֔ם לְשָׁרֵ֖ת בְּבֵ֥ית יְהוָֽה׃ ¹³וַיַּפִּ֥ילוּ גֽוֹרָל֖וֹת כַּקָּטֹ֣ן כַּגָּד֑וֹל לְבֵ֥ית אֲבוֹתָ֖ם לְשַׁ֥עַר וָשָֽׁעַר׃ פ ¹⁴וַיִּפֹּ֧ל הַגּוֹרָ֛ל מִזְרָ֖חָה לְשֶֽׁלֶמְיָ֑הוּ וּזְכַרְיָ֙הוּ֙ בְנ֣וֹ יוֹעֵ֣ץ ׀ בְּשֶׂ֔כֶל הִפִּ֙ילוּ֙ גּֽוֹרָל֔וֹת וַיֵּצֵ֥א גוֹרָל֖וֹ צָפֽוֹנָה׃ ס ¹⁵לְעֹבֵ֥ד אֱדֹ֖ם נֶ֑גְבָּה וּלְבָנָ֖יו בֵּ֥ית הָֽאֲסֻפִּֽים׃ ¹⁶לְשֻׁפִּ֤ים וּלְחֹסָה֙ לַֽמַּֽעֲרָ֔ב עִ֚ם שַׁ֣עַר שַׁלֶּ֔כֶת בַּֽמְסִלָּ֖ה הָֽעוֹלָ֑ה מִשְׁמָ֖ר לְעֻמַּ֥ת מִשְׁמָֽר׃ ¹⁷לַמִּזְרָח֙ הַֽלְוִיִּ֣ם שִׁשָּׁ֔ה לַצָּפ֥וֹנָה לַיּ֖וֹם אַרְבָּעָ֑ה לַנֶּ֙גְבָּה֙ לַיּ֣וֹם אַרְבָּעָ֔ה וְלָֽאֲסֻפִּ֖ים שְׁנַ֥יִם שְׁנָֽיִם׃ ¹⁸לַפַּרְבָּ֗ר לַֽמַּֽעֲרָב֙ אַרְבָּעָ֣ה לַֽמְסִלָּ֔ה שְׁנַ֖יִם לַפַּרְבָּֽר׃ ¹⁹אֵ֣לֶּה מַחְלְק֖וֹת הַשֹּֽׁעֲרִ֑ים לִבְנֵ֥י הַקָּֽרְחִ֖י וְלִבְנֵ֥י מְרָרִֽי׃

20And the Levites: Ahijah over the treasuries of the House of God and the treasuries of the dedicated things. 21The sons of Ladan: the sons of the Gershonites belonging to Ladan; the chiefs of the clans of Ladan, the Gershonite—Jehieli. 22The sons of Jehieli: Zetham and Joel; his brother was over the treasuries of the House of the Lord.

23Of the Amramites, the Izharites, the Hebronites, the Uzzielites: 24Shebuel son of Gershom son of Moses was the chief officer over the treasuries. 25And his brothers: Eliezer, his son Rehabiah, his son Jeshaiah, his son Joram, his son Zichri, his son Shelomith—26that Shelomith and his brothers were over all the treasuries of dedicated things that were dedicated by King David and the chiefs of the clans, and the officers of thousands and hundreds and the other army officers; 27they dedicated some of the booty of the wars to maintain the House of the Lord. 28All that Samuel the seer had dedicated, and Saul son of Kish, and Abner son of Ner, and Joab son of Zeruiah—or [what] any other man had dedicated, was under the charge of Shelomith and his brothers.

29The Izharites: Chenaniah and his sons were over Israel as clerks and magistrates for affairs outside [the sanctuary]. 30The Hebronites: Hashabiah and his brothers, capable men, 1,700, supervising Israel on the west side of the Jordan in all matters of the Lord and the service of the king. 31The Hebronites: Jeriah, the chief of the Hebronites—they were investigated in the fortieth year of David's reign by clans of all their lines, and men of substance were found among them in Jazer-gilead. 32His brothers, able men, 2,700, chiefs of clans—David put them in charge of the Reubenites, the Gadites, and the half-tribe of Manasseh in all matters of God and matters of the king.

20 וְהַלְוִיִּ֖ם אֲחִיָּ֑ה עַל־אוֹצְרוֹת֙ בֵּ֣ית הָאֱלֹהִ֔ים וּלְאֹצְר֖וֹת הַקֳּדָשִֽׁים׃ 21 בְּנֵ֣י לַעְדָּ֗ן בְּנֵ֤י הַגֵּרְשֻׁנִּי֙ לְלַעְדָּ֔ן רָאשֵׁ֥י הָאָב֖וֹת לְלַעְדָּ֣ן הַגֵּרְשֻׁנִּ֑י יְחִיאֵלִֽי׃ 22 בְּנֵ֖י יְחִיאֵלִ֑י זֵתָם֙ וְיוֹאֵ֣ל אָחִ֔יו עַל־אֹצְר֖וֹת בֵּ֥ית יְהֹוָֽה׃

23 לַֽעַמְרָמִי֙ לַיִּצְהָרִ֔י לַֽחֶבְרוֹנִ֖י לָֽעָזִּיאֵלִֽי׃ 24 וּשְׁבֻאֵ֛ל בֶּן־גֵּרְשׁ֥וֹם בֶּן־מֹשֶׁ֖ה נָגִ֥יד עַל־הָאֹצָרֽוֹת׃ 25 וְאֶחָ֖יו לֶֽאֱלִיעֶ֑זֶר רְחַבְיָ֣הוּ בְנ֗וֹ וִישַֽׁעְיָ֤הוּ בְנוֹ֙ וְיֹרָ֣ם בְּנ֔וֹ וְזִכְרִ֥י בְנ֖וֹ וׁשְׁלֹמִ֥ות וּשְׁלֹמִ֖ית בְּנֽוֹ׃ 26 ה֧וּא שְׁלֹמ֣וֹת* וְאֶחָ֗יו עַ֣ל כָּל־אֹצְר֣וֹת הַקֳּדָשִׁ֗ים אֲשֶׁ֨ר הִקְדִּ֜ישׁ דָּוִ֣יד הַמֶּ֗לֶךְ וְרָאשֵׁ֧י הָאָב֛וֹת לְשָׂרֵֽי־הָאֲלָפִ֥ים וְהַמֵּא֖וֹת וְשָׂרֵ֥י הַצָּבָֽא׃ 27 מִן־הַמִּלְחָמ֤וֹת וּמִן־הַשָּׁלָל֙ הִקְדִּ֔ישׁוּ לְחַזֵּ֖ק לְבֵ֥ית יְהֹוָֽה׃ 28 וְכֹ֨ל הַהִקְדִּ֜ישׁ שְׁמוּאֵ֤ל הָרֹאֶה֙ וְשָׁא֣וּל בֶּן־קִ֔ישׁ וְאַבְנֵ֣ר בֶּן־נֵ֔ר וְיוֹאָ֖ב בֶּן־צְרוּיָ֑ה כֹּ֚ל הַמַּקְדִּ֔ישׁ עַ֥ל יַד־שְׁלֹמִ֖ית וְאֶחָֽיו׃ פ 29 לַיִּצְהָרִ֗י כְּנַנְיָ֙הוּ֙ וּבָנָ֣יו לַמְּלָאכָ֤ה הַחִֽיצוֹנָה֙ עַל־יִשְׂרָאֵ֔ל לְשֹׁטְרִ֖ים וּלְשֹׁפְטִֽים׃ 30 לַֽחֶבְרוֹנִ֡י חֲשַׁבְיָ֣הוּ וְ֠אֶחָ֠יו בְּנֵי־חַ֜יִל אֶ֣לֶף וּשְׁבַע־מֵא֗וֹת עַ֚ל פְּקֻדַּ֣ת יִשְׂרָאֵ֔ל מֵעֵ֥בֶר לַיַּרְדֵּ֖ן מַעְרָ֑בָה לְכֹל֙ מְלֶ֣אכֶת יְהֹוָ֔ה וְלַעֲבֹדַ֖ת הַמֶּֽלֶךְ׃ 31 לַחֶבְרוֹנִי֙ יְרִיָּ֣ה הָרֹ֔אשׁ לַֽחֶבְרוֹנִ֥י לְתֹלְדֹתָ֖יו לְאָב֑וֹת בִּשְׁנַ֣ת הָֽאַרְבָּעִ֗ים לְמַלְכ֤וּת דָּוִיד֙ נִדְרָ֔שׁוּ וַיִּמָּצֵ֥א בָהֶ֛ם גִּבּ֥וֹרֵי חַ֖יִל בְּיַעְזֵ֥יר גִּלְעָֽד׃ 32 וְאֶחָ֣יו בְּנֵי־חַ֗יִל אַלְפַּ֥יִם וּשְׁבַ֖ע מֵא֣וֹת רָאשֵׁ֣י הָֽאָב֑וֹת וַיַּפְקִידֵ֞ם דָּוִ֣יד הַמֶּ֗לֶךְ עַל־הָראוּבֵנִ֤י וְהַגָּדִי֙ וַחֲצִי֙ שֵׁ֣בֶט הַֽמְנַשִּׁ֔י לְכָל־דְּבַ֥ר הָֽאֱלֹהִ֖ים וּדְבַ֥ר הַמֶּֽלֶךְ׃ פ

v. 26. בנוסח אחר "שְׁלוֹמִית"

27

The number of Israelites—chiefs of clans, officers of thousands and hundreds and their clerks, who served the king in all matters of the divisions, who worked in monthly shifts during all the months of the year—each division, 24,000. ²Over the first division for the first month—Jashobeam son of Zabdiel; his division had 24,000. ³Of the sons of Perez, he, the chief of all the officers of the army, [served] for the first month. ⁴Over the division of the second month—Dodai the Ahohite; Mikloth was chief officer of his division; his division had 24,000. ⁵The third army officer for the third month— Benaiah son of Jehoiada, the chief priest; his division had 24,000. ⁶That was Benaiah, one of the warriors of the thirty and over the thirty; and [over] his division was Ammizabad his son. ⁷The fourth, for the fourth month, Asahel brother of Joab, and his son Zebadiah after him; his division had 24,000. ⁸The fifth, for the fifth month, the officer Shamhut the Izrahite; his division had 24,000. ⁹The sixth, for the sixth month, Ira son of Ikkesh the Tekoite; his division had 24,000. ¹⁰The seventh, for the seventh month, Helez the Pelonite, of the Ephraimites; his division had 24,000. ¹¹The eighth, for the eighth month, Sibbecai the Hushathite, of Zerah; his division had 24,000. ¹²The ninth, for the ninth month, Abiezer the Anathothite, of Benjamin; his division had 24,000. ¹³The tenth, for the tenth month, Mahrai the Netophathite,

כז וּבְנֵ֣י יִשְׂרָאֵ֣ל ׀ לְֽמִסְפָּרָ֗ם רָאשֵׁ֣י הָאָב֡וֹת וְשָׂרֵ֣י הָֽאֲלָפִ֣ים ׀ וְהַמֵּא֗וֹת וְשֹׁ֣טְרֵיהֶם֮ הַמְשָׁרְתִ֣ים אֶת־הַמֶּלֶךְ֒ לְכֹ֣ל ׀ דְּבַ֣ר הַֽמַּחְלְק֗וֹת הַבָּאָ֤ה וְהַיֹּצֵאת֙ חֹ֣דֶשׁ בְּחֹ֔דֶשׁ לְכֹ֖ל חָדְשֵׁ֣י הַשָּׁנָ֑ה הַֽמַּחֲלֹ֣קֶת הָֽאַחַ֔ת עֶשְׂרִ֥ים וְאַרְבָּעָ֖ה אָֽלֶף׃ ס ²עַ֞ל הַמַּחֲלֹ֤קֶת הָרִֽאשׁוֹנָה֙ לַחֹ֣דֶשׁ הָֽרִאשׁ֔וֹן יָֽשָׁבְעָ֖ם בֶּן־זַבְדִּיאֵ֑ל וְעַל֙ מַחֲלֻקְתּ֔וֹ עֶשְׂרִ֥ים וְאַרְבָּעָ֖ה אָֽלֶף׃ ³מִן־בְּנֵי־פֶ֗רֶץ הָרֹ֛אשׁ לְכָל־שָׂרֵ֥י הַצְּבָא֖וֹת לַחֹ֥דֶשׁ הָרִאשֽׁוֹן׃ ⁴וְעַ֣ל מַחֲלֹ֣קֶת ׀ הַחֹ֣דֶשׁ הַשֵּׁנִי֮ דּוֹדַ֣י הָאֲחוֹחִי֒ וּמַ֣חֲלֻקְתּ֔וֹ וּמִקְל֖וֹת הַנָּגִ֑יד וְעַל֙ מַחֲלֻקְתּ֔וֹ עֶשְׂרִ֥ים וְאַרְבָּעָ֖ה אָֽלֶף׃ ס ⁵שַׂ֣ר הַצָּבָ֤א הַשְּׁלִישִׁי֙ לַחֹ֣דֶשׁ הַשְּׁלִישִׁ֔י בְּנָיָ֧הוּ בֶן־יְהוֹיָדָ֛ע הַכֹּהֵ֖ן רֹ֑אשׁ וְעַל֙ מַחֲלֻקְתּ֔וֹ עֶשְׂרִ֥ים וְאַרְבָּעָ֖ה אָֽלֶף׃ ⁶ה֧וּא בְנָיָ֛הוּ גִּבּ֥וֹר הַשְּׁלֹשִׁ֖ים וְעַל־הַשְּׁלֹשִׁ֑ים וּמַ֣חֲלֻקְתּ֔וֹ עַמִּיזָבָ֖ד בְּנֽוֹ׃ ס ⁷הָֽרְבִיעִ֞י לַחֹ֣דֶשׁ הָֽרְבִיעִ֗י עֲשָׂהאֵל֙ אֲחִ֣י יוֹאָ֔ב וּזְבַדְיָ֥ה בְנ֖וֹ אַחֲרָ֑יו וְעַל֙ מַחֲלֻקְתּ֔וֹ עֶשְׂרִ֥ים וְאַרְבָּעָ֖ה אָֽלֶף׃ ס ⁸הַֽחֲמִישִׁי֙ לַחֹ֣דֶשׁ הַֽחֲמִישִׁ֔י הַשַּׂ֖ר שַׁמְה֣וּת הַיִּזְרָ֑ח וְעַל֙ מַחֲלֻקְתּ֔וֹ עֶשְׂרִ֥ים וְאַרְבָּעָ֖ה אָֽלֶף׃ ס ⁹הַשִּׁשִּׁי֙ לַחֹ֣דֶשׁ הַשִּׁשִּׁ֔י עִירָ֥א בֶן־עִקֵּ֖שׁ הַתְּקוֹעִ֑י וְעַל֙ מַחֲלֻקְתּ֔וֹ עֶשְׂרִ֥ים וְאַרְבָּעָ֖ה אָֽלֶף׃ ס ¹⁰הַשְּׁבִיעִ֞י לַחֹ֣דֶשׁ הַשְּׁבִיעִ֗י חֶ֚לֶץ הַפְּל֣וֹנִ֔י מִן־בְּנֵ֖י אֶפְרָ֑יִם וְעַל֙ מַחֲלֻקְתּ֔וֹ עֶשְׂרִ֥ים וְאַרְבָּעָ֖ה אָֽלֶף׃ ס ¹¹הַשְּׁמִינִי֙ לַחֹ֣דֶשׁ הַשְּׁמִינִ֔י סִבְּכַ֥י הַחֻשָׁתִ֖י לַזַּרְחִ֑י וְעַל֙ מַחֲלֻקְתּ֔וֹ עֶשְׂרִ֥ים וְאַרְבָּעָ֖ה אָֽלֶף׃ ס ¹²הַתְּשִׁיעִי֙ לַחֹ֣דֶשׁ הַתְּשִׁיעִ֔י אֲבִיעֶ֥זֶר הָעֲנְּתֹתִ֖י לבנימיני לַבֶּן־ ׀ יְמִינִ֑י וְעַל֙ מַחֲלֻקְתּ֔וֹ עֶשְׂרִ֥ים וְאַרְבָּעָ֖ה אָֽלֶף׃ ס ¹³הָעֲשִׂירִי֙ לַחֹ֣דֶשׁ הָֽעֲשִׂירִ֔י מַהְרַ֖י הַנְּטוֹפָתִ֑י לַזַּרְחִ֑י וְעַל֙ מַחֲלֻקְתּ֔וֹ

of Zerah; his division had 24,000. ¹⁴The eleventh, for the eleventh month, Benaiah the Pirathonite, of the Ephraimites; his division had 24,000. ¹⁵The twelfth, for the twelfth month, Heldai the Netophathite, of Othniel; his division had 24,000.

¹⁶Over the tribes of Israel: Reuben: the chief officer, Eliezer son of Zichri. Simeon: Shephatiah son of Maaca. ¹⁷Levi: Hashabiah son of Kemuel. Aaron: Zadok. ¹⁸Judah: Elihu, of the brothers of David. Issachar: Omri son of Michael. ¹⁹Zebulun: Ishmaiah son of Obadiah. Naphtali: Jerimoth son of Azriel. ²⁰Ephraimites: Hoshea son of Azaziah. The half-tribe of Manasseh: Joel son of Pedaiah. ²¹Half Manasseh in Gilead: Iddo son of Zechariah. Benjamin: Jaasiel son of Abner. ²²Dan: Azarel son of Jeroham. These were the officers of the tribes of Israel.

²³David did not take a census of those under twenty years of age, for the LORD had promised to make Israel as numerous as the stars of heaven. ²⁴Joab son of Zeruiah did begin to count them, but he did not finish; wrath struck Israel on account of this, and the census was not entered into the account of the chronicles of King David.

²⁵Over the royal treasuries: Azmaveth son of Adiel. Over the treasuries in the country—in the towns, the hamlets, and the citadels: Jonathan son of Uzziah. ²⁶Over the field laborers in agricultural work: Ezri son of Chelub. ²⁷Over the vineyards: Shimei the Ramathite. And over the produce in the vineyards for wine cellars: Zabdi the Shiphmite. ²⁸Over the olive trees and the sycamores in the Shephelah: Baal-hanan the Gederite. Over the oil-stores: Joash. ²⁹Over the

עֶשְׂרִים וְאַרְבָּעָה אֶלֶף: ס ‏14‏ עַשְׁתֵּי־עָשָׂר לְעַשְׁתֵּי־עָשָׂר הַחֹדֶשׁ בְּנָיָה הַפִּרְעָתוֹנִי מִן־בְּנֵי אֶפְרָיִם וְעַל מַחֲלֻקְתּוֹ עֶשְׂרִים וְאַרְבָּעָה אֶלֶף: ס ‏15‏ הַשְּׁנֵים עָשָׂר לִשְׁנֵים עָשָׂר הַחֹדֶשׁ חֶלְדַּי הַנְּטוֹפָתִי לְעָתְנִיאֵל וְעַל מַחֲלֻקְתּוֹ עֶשְׂרִים וְאַרְבָּעָה אָלֶף: פ

‏16‏ וְעַל שִׁבְטֵי יִשְׂרָאֵל לָרֻאוּבֵנִי נָגִיד אֱלִיעֶזֶר בֶּן־זִכְרִי ס לַשִּׁמְעוֹנִי שְׁפַטְיָהוּ בֶן־מַעֲכָה: ס ‏17‏ לְלֵוִי חֲשַׁבְיָה בֶן־קְמוּאֵל לְאַהֲרֹן צָדוֹק: ס ‏18‏ לִיהוּדָה אֱלִיהוּ מֵאֲחֵי דָוִיד לְיִשָּׂשכָר עָמְרִי בֶּן־מִיכָאֵל: ס ‏19‏ לִזְבוּלֻן יִשְׁמַעְיָהוּ בֶּן־עֹבַדְיָהוּ לְנַפְתָּלִי יְרִימוֹת בֶּן־עַזְרִיאֵל: ס ‏20‏ לִבְנֵי אֶפְרַיִם הוֹשֵׁעַ בֶּן־עֲזַזְיָהוּ לַחֲצִי שֵׁבֶט מְנַשֶּׁה יוֹאֵל בֶּן־פְּדָיָהוּ: ס ‏21‏ לַחֲצִי הַמְנַשֶּׁה גִּלְעָדָה יִדּוֹ בֶּן־זְכַרְיָהוּ ס לְבִנְיָמִן יַעֲשִׂיאֵל בֶּן־אַבְנֵר: ס ‏22‏ לְדָן עֲזַרְאֵל בֶּן־יְרֹחָם אֵלֶּה שָׂרֵי שִׁבְטֵי יִשְׂרָאֵל:

‏23‏ וְלֹא־נָשָׂא דָוִיד מִסְפָּרָם לְמִבֶּן עֶשְׂרִים שָׁנָה וּלְמָטָּה כִּי אָמַר יְהֹוָה לְהַרְבּוֹת אֶת־יִשְׂרָאֵל כְּכוֹכְבֵי הַשָּׁמָיִם: ‏24‏ יוֹאָב בֶּן־צְרוּיָה הֵחֵל לִמְנוֹת וְלֹא כִלָּה וַיְהִי בָזֹאת קֶצֶף עַל־יִשְׂרָאֵל וְלֹא עָלָה הַמִּסְפָּר בְּמִסְפַּר דִּבְרֵי־הַיָּמִים לַמֶּלֶךְ דָּוִיד: ס ‏25‏ *וְעַל אֹצְרוֹת הַמֶּלֶךְ עַזְמָוֶת בֶּן־עֲדִיאֵל ס וְעַל הָאֹצָרוֹת בַּשָּׂדֶה בֶּעָרִים וּבַכְּפָרִים וּבַמִּגְדָּלוֹת יְהוֹנָתָן בֶּן־עֻזִּיָּהוּ ס ‏26‏ וְעַל עֹשֵׂי מְלֶאכֶת הַשָּׂדֶה לַעֲבֹדַת הָאֲדָמָה עֶזְרִי בֶּן־כְּלוּב: ‏27‏ וְעַל־הַכְּרָמִים שִׁמְעִי הָרָמָתִי וְעַל שֶׁבַּכְּרָמִים לְאֹצְרוֹת הַיַּיִן זַבְדִּי הַשִּׁפְמִי: ‏28‏ וְעַל־הַזֵּיתִים וְהַשִּׁקְמִים אֲשֶׁר בַּשְּׁפֵלָה בַּעַל חָנָן הַגְּדֵרִי ס וְעַל־אֹצְרוֹת הַשֶּׁמֶן יוֹעָשׁ:

cattle pasturing in Sharon: Shirtai the Sharonite. And over the cattle in the valleys: Shaphat son of Adlai. ³⁰Over the camels: Obil the Ishmaelite. And over the she-asses: Jehdeiah the Meronothite. ³¹Over the flocks: Jaziz the Hagrite. All these were stewards of the property of King David. ³²Jonathan, David's uncle, was a counselor, a master, and a scribe: Jehiel son of Hachmoni was with the king's sons. ³³Ahitophel was a counselor to the king. Hushai the Archite was the king's friend. ³⁴After Ahitophel were Jehoiada son of Benaiah and Abiathar. The commander of the king's army was Joab.

28

David assembled all the officers of Israel—the tribal officers, the divisional officers who served the king, the captains of thousands and the captains of hundreds, and the stewards of all the property and cattle of the king and his sons, with the eunuchs and the warriors, all the men of substance—to Jerusalem. ²King David rose to his feet and said, "Hear me, my brothers, my people! I wanted to build a resting-place for the Ark of the Covenant of the LORD, for the footstool of our God, and I laid aside material for building. ³But God said to me, 'You will not build a house for My name, for you are a man of battles and have shed blood.' ⁴The LORD God of Israel chose me of all my father's house to be king over Israel forever. For He chose Judah to be ruler, and of the family of Judah, my father's house; and of my father's sons, He preferred to make me king over all Israel; ⁵and of all my sons—for many are the sons the LORD gave me—He chose my son Solomon to sit on the throne of the kingdom of the LORD over Israel. ⁶He said to me, 'It will be your son Solomon who will build My House and My courts, for I

כט וְעַל־הַבָּקָר הָרֹעִים בַּשָּׁרוֹן שִׁטְרַי הַשָּׁרוֹנִי וְעַל־הַבָּקָר בָּעֲמָקִים שָׁפָט בֶּן־עַדְלָי׃ ס ל וְעַל־הַגְּמַלִּים אוֹבִיל הַיִּשְׁמְעֵלִי וְעַל־הָאֲתֹנוֹת יֶחְדְּיָהוּ הַמֵּרֹנֹתִי׃ ס לא וְעַל־הַצֹּאן יָזִיז הַהַגְרִי כָּל־אֵלֶּה שָׂרֵי הָרְכוּשׁ אֲשֶׁר לַמֶּלֶךְ דָּוִיד׃ לב וִיהוֹנָתָן דּוֹד־דָּוִיד יוֹעֵץ אִישׁ־מֵבִין וְסוֹפֵר הוּא וִיחִיאֵל בֶּן־חַכְמוֹנִי עִם־בְּנֵי הַמֶּלֶךְ׃ לג וַאֲחִיתֹפֶל יוֹעֵץ לַמֶּלֶךְ ס וְחוּשַׁי הָאַרְכִּי רֵעַ הַמֶּלֶךְ׃ לד וְאַחֲרֵי אֲחִיתֹפֶל יְהוֹיָדָע בֶּן־בְּנָיָהוּ וְאֶבְיָתָר וְשַׂר־צָבָא לַמֶּלֶךְ יוֹאָב׃ פ

כח וַיַּקְהֵל דָּוִיד אֶת־כָּל־שָׂרֵי יִשְׂרָאֵל שָׂרֵי הַשְּׁבָטִים וְשָׂרֵי הַמַּחְלְקוֹת הַמְשָׁרְתִים אֶת־הַמֶּלֶךְ וְשָׂרֵי הָאֲלָפִים וְשָׂרֵי הַמֵּאוֹת וְשָׂרֵי כָל־רְכוּשׁ־וּמִקְנֶה ׀ לַמֶּלֶךְ וּלְבָנָיו עִם־הַסָּרִיסִים וְהַגִּבּוֹרִים וּלְכָל־גִּבּוֹר חָיִל אֶל־יְרוּשָׁלָ͏ִם׃ ב וַיָּקָם דָּוִיד הַמֶּלֶךְ עַל־רַגְלָיו וַיֹּאמֶר שְׁמָעוּנִי אַחַי וְעַמִּי אֲנִי עִם־לְבָבִי לִבְנוֹת בֵּית מְנוּחָה לַאֲרוֹן בְּרִית־יְהוָה וְלַהֲדֹם רַגְלֵי אֱלֹהֵינוּ וַהֲכִינוֹתִי לִבְנוֹת׃ ג וְהָאֱלֹהִים אָמַר לִי לֹא־תִבְנֶה בַיִת לִשְׁמִי כִּי אִישׁ מִלְחָמוֹת אַתָּה וְדָמִים שָׁפָכְתָּ׃ ד וַיִּבְחַר יְהוָה אֱלֹהֵי יִשְׂרָאֵל בִּי מִכֹּל בֵּית־אָבִי לִהְיוֹת לְמֶלֶךְ עַל־יִשְׂרָאֵל לְעוֹלָם כִּי בִיהוּדָה בָּחַר לְנָגִיד וּבְבֵית יְהוּדָה בֵּית אָבִי וּבִבְנֵי אָבִי בִּי רָצָה לְהַמְלִיךְ עַל־כָּל־יִשְׂרָאֵל׃ ה וּמִכָּל־בָּנַי כִּי רַבִּים בָּנִים נָתַן לִי יְהוָה וַיִּבְחַר בִּשְׁלֹמֹה בְנִי לָשֶׁבֶת עַל־כִּסֵּא מַלְכוּת יְהוָה עַל־יִשְׂרָאֵל׃ ו וַיֹּאמֶר לִי שְׁלֹמֹה בִנְךָ הוּא־יִבְנֶה בֵיתִי וַחֲצֵרוֹתָי כִּי־בָחַרְתִּי בוֹ לִי לְבֵן וַאֲנִי אֶהְיֶה־

have chosen him to be a son to Me, and I will be a father to him. [7]I will establish his kingdom forever, if he keeps firmly to the observance of My commandments and rules as he does now.' [8]And now, in the sight of all Israel, the congregation of the LORD, and in the hearing of our God, [I say:] Observe and apply yourselves to all the commandments of the LORD your God in order that you may possess this good land and bequeath it to your children after you forever.

[9]"And you, my son Solomon, know the God of your father, and serve Him with single mind and fervent heart, for the LORD searches all minds and discerns the design of every thought; if you seek Him He will be available to you, but if you forsake Him He will abandon you forever. [10]See then, the LORD chose you to build a house as the sanctuary; be strong and do it."

[11]David gave his son Solomon the plan of the porch and its houses, its storerooms and its upper chambers and inner chambers; and of the place of the Ark-cover; [12]and the plan of all that he had by the spirit: of the courts of the House of the LORD and all its surrounding chambers, and of the treasuries of the House of God and of the treasuries of the holy things; [13]the divisions of priests and Levites for all the work of the service of the House of the LORD and all the vessels of the service of the House of the LORD; [14]and gold, the weight of gold for vessels of every sort of use; silver for all the vessels of silver by weight, for all the vessels of every kind of service; [15]the weight of the gold lampstands and their gold lamps, and the weight of the silver lampstands, each lampstand and its silver lamps, according to the use of every lampstand; [16]and the weight of gold for the tables of the rows of bread, for each table, and of silver for the silver tables; [17]and of the pure gold for the forks and the basins and the jars; and the weight of

לוֹ לְאָב: [7]וַהֲכִינוֹתִי אֶת־מַלְכוּתוֹ עַד־
לְעוֹלָם אִם־יֶחֱזַק לַעֲשׂוֹת מִצְוֹתַי
וּמִשְׁפָּטַי כַּיּוֹם הַזֶּה: [8]וְעַתָּה לְעֵינֵי כָל־
יִשְׂרָאֵל קְהַל־יְהוָה וּבְאָזְנֵי אֱלֹהֵינוּ שִׁמְרוּ
וְדִרְשׁוּ כָּל־מִצְוֹת יְהוָה אֱלֹהֵיכֶם לְמַעַן
תִּירְשׁוּ אֶת־הָאָרֶץ הַטּוֹבָה וְהִנְחַלְתֶּם
לִבְנֵיכֶם אַחֲרֵיכֶם עַד־עוֹלָם: פ
[9]וְאַתָּה שְׁלֹמֹה־בְנִי דַּע אֶת־אֱלֹהֵי אָבִיךָ
וְעָבְדֵהוּ בְּלֵב שָׁלֵם וּבְנֶפֶשׁ חֲפֵצָה כִּי
כָל־לְבָבוֹת דּוֹרֵשׁ יְהוָה וְכָל־יֵצֶר
מַחֲשָׁבוֹת מֵבִין אִם־תִּדְרְשֶׁנּוּ יִמָּצֵא לָךְ
וְאִם־תַּעַזְבֶנּוּ יַזְנִיחֲךָ לָעַד: [10]רְאֵה ׀ עַתָּה
כִּי־יְהוָה בָּחַר בְּךָ לִבְנוֹת־בַּיִת לַמִּקְדָּשׁ
חֲזַק וַעֲשֵׂה: פ
[11]וַיִּתֵּן דָּוִיד לִשְׁלֹמֹה בְנוֹ אֶת־תַּבְנִית
הָאוּלָם וְאֶת־בָּתָּיו וְגַנְזַכָּיו וַעֲלִיֹּתָיו
וַחֲדָרָיו הַפְּנִימִים וּבֵית הַכַּפֹּרֶת:
[12]וְתַבְנִית כֹּל אֲשֶׁר הָיָה בָרוּחַ עִמּוֹ
לְחַצְרוֹת בֵּית־יְהוָה וּלְכָל־הַלְּשָׁכוֹת
סָבִיב לְאֹצְרוֹת בֵּית הָאֱלֹהִים וּלְאֹצְרוֹת
הַקֳּדָשִׁים: [13]וּלְמַחְלְקוֹת הַכֹּהֲנִים וְהַלְוִיִּם
וּלְכָל־מְלֶאכֶת עֲבוֹדַת בֵּית־יְהוָה וּלְכָל־
כְּלֵי עֲבוֹדַת בֵּית־יְהוָה: [14]לַזָּהָב בַּמִּשְׁקָל
לַזָּהָב לְכָל־כְּלֵי עֲבוֹדָה וַעֲבוֹדָה לְכֹל כְּלֵי
הַכֶּסֶף בְּמִשְׁקָל לְכָל־כְּלֵי עֲבוֹדָה וַעֲבוֹדָה:
[15]וּמִשְׁקָל לִמְנֹרוֹת הַזָּהָב וְנֵרֹתֵיהֶם זָהָב
בְּמִשְׁקַל־מְנוֹרָה וּמְנוֹרָה וְנֵרֹתֶיהָ וְלִמְנֹרוֹת
הַכֶּסֶף בְּמִשְׁקָל לִמְנוֹרָה וְנֵרֹתֶיהָ כַּעֲבוֹדַת
מְנוֹרָה וּמְנוֹרָה: [16]וְאֶת־הַזָּהָב מִשְׁקָל
לְשֻׁלְחֲנוֹת הַמַּעֲרֶכֶת לְשֻׁלְחַן וְשֻׁלְחָן
וְכֶסֶף לְשֻׁלְחֲנוֹת הַכָּסֶף: [17]וְהַמִּזְלָגוֹת

the gold bowls, every bowl; and the weight of the silver bowls, each and every bowl; [18]the weight of refined gold for the incense altar and the gold for the figure of the chariot—the cherubs—those with outspread wings screening the Ark of the Covenant of the LORD. [19]"All this that the LORD made me understand by His hand on me, I give you in writing—the plan of all the works."

[20]David said to his son Solomon, "Be strong and of good courage and do it; do not be afraid or dismayed, for the LORD God my God is with you; He will not fail you or forsake you till all the work on the House of the LORD is done. [21]Here are the divisions of the priests and Levites for all kinds of service of the House of God, and with you in all the work are willing men, skilled in all sorts of tasks; also the officers and all the people are at your command."

29 King David said to the entire assemblage, "God has chosen my son Solomon alone, an untried lad, although the work to be done is vast—for the temple[a] is not for a man but for the LORD God. [2]I have spared no effort to lay up for the House of my God gold for golden objects, silver for silver, copper for copper, iron for iron, wood for wooden, onyx-stone and inlay-stone, stone of antimony and variegated colors—every kind of precious stone and much marble. [3]Besides, out of my solicitude for the House of my God, I gave over my private hoard of gold and silver to the House of my God—in addition to all that I laid aside for the holy House: [4]3,000 gold talents of Ophir gold, and 7,000 talents of refined silver for covering the walls of the houses [5](gold for golden objects, silver for silver for all the work)—into the hands of craftsmen. Now who is going to make a free-

---

a Lit. "fortress."

וְהַמִּזְרָקוֹת וְהַקְּשָׂוֹת זָהָב טָהוֹר וְלִכְפוֹרֵי הַזָּהָב בְּמִשְׁקָל לִכְפוֹר וּכְפוֹר וְלִכְפוֹרֵי הַכֶּסֶף בְּמִשְׁקָל לִכְפוֹר וּכְפוֹר: 18 וּלְמִזְבַּח הַקְּטֹרֶת זָהָב מְזֻקָּק בַּמִּשְׁקָל וּלְתַבְנִית הַמֶּרְכָּבָה הַכְּרֻבִים זָהָב לְפֹרְשִׂים וְסֹכְכִים עַל־אֲרוֹן בְּרִית־יְהוָה: 19 הַכֹּל בִּכְתָב מִיַּד יְהוָה עָלַי הִשְׂכִּיל כֹּל מַלְאֲכוֹת הַתַּבְנִית: פ

20 וַיֹּאמֶר דָּוִיד לִשְׁלֹמֹה בְנוֹ חֲזַק וֶאֱמַץ וַעֲשֵׂה אַל־תִּירָא וְאַל־תֵּחָת כִּי יְהוָה אֱלֹהִים אֱלֹהַי עִמָּךְ לֹא יַרְפְּךָ וְלֹא יַעַזְבֶךָּ עַד־לִכְלוֹת כָּל־מְלֶאכֶת עֲבוֹדַת בֵּית־יְהוָה: 21 וְהִנֵּה מַחְלְקוֹת הַכֹּהֲנִים וְהַלְוִיִּם לְכָל־עֲבוֹדַת בֵּית הָאֱלֹהִים וְעִמְּךָ בְכָל־מְלָאכָה לְכָל־נָדִיב בַּחָכְמָה לְכָל־עֲבוֹדָה וְהַשָּׂרִים וְכָל־הָעָם לְכָל־דְּבָרֶיךָ: פ

כט וַיֹּאמֶר דָּוִיד הַמֶּלֶךְ לְכָל־הַקָּהָל שְׁלֹמֹה בְנִי אֶחָד בָּחַר־בּוֹ אֱלֹהִים נַעַר וָרָךְ וְהַמְּלָאכָה גְדוֹלָה כִּי לֹא לְאָדָם הַבִּירָה כִּי לַיהוָה אֱלֹהִים: 2 וּכְכָל־כֹּחִי הֲכִינוֹתִי לְבֵית־אֱלֹהַי הַזָּהָב לַזָּהָב וְהַכֶּסֶף לַכֶּסֶף וְהַנְּחֹשֶׁת לַנְּחֹשֶׁת הַבַּרְזֶל לַבַּרְזֶל וְהָעֵצִים לָעֵצִים אַבְנֵי־שֹׁהַם וּמִלּוּאִים אַבְנֵי־פוּךְ וְרִקְמָה וְכֹל אֶבֶן יְקָרָה וְאַבְנֵי־שַׁיִשׁ לָרֹב: 3 וְעוֹד בִּרְצוֹתִי בְּבֵית אֱלֹהַי יֶשׁ־לִי סְגֻלָּה זָהָב וָכָסֶף נָתַתִּי לְבֵית־אֱלֹהַי לְמַעְלָה מִכָּל־הֲכִינוֹתִי לְבֵית הַקֹּדֶשׁ: 4 שְׁלֹשֶׁת אֲלָפִים כִּכְּרֵי זָהָב מִזְּהַב אוֹפִיר וְשִׁבְעַת אֲלָפִים כִּכַּר־כֶּסֶף מְזֻקָּק לָטוּחַ קִירוֹת הַבָּתִּים: 5 לַזָּהָב לַזָּהָב וְלַכֶּסֶף לַכֶּסֶף

will offering and devote himself today to the LORD?"

⁶The officers of the clans and the officers of the tribes of Israel and the captains of thousands and hundreds and the supervisors of the king's work made freewill offerings, ⁷giving for the work of the House of God: 5,000 talents of gold, 10,000 darics, 10,000 talents of silver, 18,000 talents of copper, 100,000 talents of iron. ⁸Whoever had stones in his possession gave them to the treasury of the House of the LORD in the charge of Jehiel the Gershonite. ⁹The people rejoiced over the freewill offerings they made, for with a whole heart they made freewill offerings to the LORD; King David also rejoiced very much.

¹⁰David blessed the LORD in front of all the assemblage; David said, "Blessed are You, LORD, God of Israel our father, from eternity to eternity. ¹¹Yours, LORD, are greatness, might, splendor, triumph, and majesty—yes, all that is in heaven and on earth; to You, LORD, belong kingship and preeminence above all. ¹²Riches and honor are Yours to dispense; You have dominion over all; with You are strength and might, and it is in Your power to make anyone great and strong. ¹³Now, God, we praise You and extol Your glorious name. ¹⁴Who am I and who are my people, that we should have the means to make such a freewill offering; but all is from You, and it is Your gift that we have given to You. ¹⁵For we are sojourners with You, mere transients like our fathers; our days on earth are like a shadow, with nothing in prospect. ¹⁶O LORD our God, all this great mass that we have laid aside to build You a House for Your holy name is from You, and it is all Yours. ¹⁷I know, God, that You search the heart and desire uprightness; I, with upright heart, freely offered all these things; now Your people, who are pre-

וּלְכָל־מְלָאכָה בְּיַד חָרָשִׁים וּמִי מִתְנַדֵּב לְמַלֹּאות יָדוֹ הַיּוֹם לַיהוָה: ⁶ וַיִּתְנַדְּבוּ שָׂרֵי הָאָבוֹת וְשָׂרֵי | שִׁבְטֵי יִשְׂרָאֵל וְשָׂרֵי הָאֲלָפִים וְהַמֵּאוֹת וּלְשָׂרֵי מְלֶאכֶת הַמֶּלֶךְ: ⁷ וַיִּתְּנוּ לַעֲבוֹדַת בֵּית־הָאֱלֹהִים זָהָב כִּכָּרִים חֲמֵשֶׁת־אֲלָפִים וַאֲדַרְכֹנִים רִבּוֹ וְכֶסֶף כִּכָּרִים עֲשֶׂרֶת אֲלָפִים וּנְחֹשֶׁת רִבּוֹ וּשְׁמוֹנַת אֲלָפִים כִּכָּרִים וּבַרְזֶל מֵאָה־אֶלֶף כִּכָּרִים: ⁸ וְהַנִּמְצָא אִתּוֹ אֲבָנִים נָתְנוּ לְאוֹצַר בֵּית־יְהוָה עַל יַד־יְחִיאֵל הַגֵּרְשֻׁנִּי: ⁹ וַיִּשְׂמְחוּ הָעָם עַל־הִתְנַדְּבָם כִּי בְּלֵב שָׁלֵם הִתְנַדְּבוּ לַיהוָה וְגַם דָּוִיד הַמֶּלֶךְ שָׂמַח שִׂמְחָה גְדוֹלָה: פ ¹⁰ וַיְבָרֶךְ דָּוִיד אֶת־יְהוָה לְעֵינֵי כָּל־הַקָּהָל וַיֹּאמֶר דָּוִיד בָּרוּךְ אַתָּה יְהוָה אֱלֹהֵי יִשְׂרָאֵל אָבִינוּ מֵעוֹלָם וְעַד־עוֹלָם: ¹¹ לְךָ יְהוָה הַגְּדֻלָּה וְהַגְּבוּרָה וְהַתִּפְאֶרֶת וְהַנֵּצַח וְהַהוֹד כִּי־כֹל בַּשָּׁמַיִם וּבָאָרֶץ לְךָ יְהוָה הַמַּמְלָכָה וְהַמִּתְנַשֵּׂא לְכֹל | לְרֹאשׁ: ¹² וְהָעֹשֶׁר וְהַכָּבוֹד מִלְּפָנֶיךָ וְאַתָּה מוֹשֵׁל בַּכֹּל וּבְיָדְךָ כֹּחַ וּגְבוּרָה וּבְיָדְךָ לְגַדֵּל וּלְחַזֵּק לַכֹּל: ¹³ וְעַתָּה אֱלֹהֵינוּ מוֹדִים אֲנַחְנוּ לָךְ וּמְהַלְלִים לְשֵׁם תִּפְאַרְתֶּךָ: ¹⁴ וְכִי מִי אֲנִי וּמִי עַמִּי כִּי־נַעְצֹר כֹּחַ לְהִתְנַדֵּב כָּזֹאת כִּי־מִמְּךָ הַכֹּל וּמִיָּדְךָ נָתַנּוּ לָךְ: ¹⁵ כִּי־גֵרִים אֲנַחְנוּ לְפָנֶיךָ וְתוֹשָׁבִים כְּכָל־אֲבֹתֵינוּ כַּצֵּל | יָמֵינוּ עַל־הָאָרֶץ וְאֵין מִקְוֶה: ¹⁶ יְהוָה אֱלֹהֵינוּ כֹּל הֶהָמוֹן הַזֶּה אֲשֶׁר הֲכִינֹנוּ לִבְנוֹת־לְךָ בַיִת לְשֵׁם קָדְשֶׁךָ מִיָּדְךָ הִיא וּלְךָ הַכֹּל: ¹⁷ וְיָדַעְתִּי אֱלֹהַי כִּי אַתָּה בֹּחֵן לֵבָב וּמֵישָׁרִים תִּרְצֶה אֲנִי בְּיֹשֶׁר לְבָבִי הִתְנַדַּבְתִּי כָל־אֵלֶּה וְעַתָּה עַמְּךָ הַנִּמְצְאוּ־פֹה רָאִיתִי בְשִׂמְחָה לְהִתְנַדֶּב־לָךְ: ¹⁸ יְהוָה אֱלֹהֵי אַבְרָהָם

sent here—I saw them joyously making freewill offerings. [18]O LORD God of Abraham, Isaac, and Israel, our fathers, remember this to the eternal credit of the thoughts of Your people's hearts, and make their hearts constant toward You. [19]As to my son Solomon, give him a whole heart to observe Your commandments, Your admonitions, and Your laws, and to fulfill them all, and to build this temple[a] for which I have made provision."

[20]David said to the whole assemblage, "Now bless the LORD your God." All the assemblage blessed the LORD God of their fathers, and bowed their heads low to the LORD and the king. [21]They offered sacrifices to the LORD and made burnt offerings to the LORD on the morrow of that day: 1,000 bulls, 1,000 rams, 1,000 lambs, with their libations; [they made] sacrifices in great number for all Israel, [22]and they ate and drank in the presence of the LORD on that day with great joy. They again proclaimed Solomon son of David king, and they anointed him as ruler before the LORD, and Zadok as high priest. [23]Solomon successfully took over the throne of the LORD as king instead of his father David, and all went well with him. All Israel accepted him; [24]all the officials and the warriors, and the sons of King David as well, gave their hand in support of King Solomon. [25]The LORD made Solomon exceedingly great in the eyes of all Israel, and endowed him with a regal majesty that no king of Israel before him ever had.

[26]Thus David son of Jesse reigned over all Israel; [27]the length of his reign over Israel was forty years: he reigned seven years in Hebron and thirty-three years in Jerusalem. [28]He died at a ripe old age, having enjoyed long life, riches and honor, and his son Solomon reigned in his stead. [29]The acts of King David, early and late, are recorded in the history of Samuel the seer,

יִצְחָ֤ק וְיִשְׂרָאֵל֙ אֲבֹתֵ֔ינוּ שָׁמְרָה־זֹּ֣את
לְעוֹלָ֔ם לְיֵ֥צֶר מַחְשְׁב֖וֹת לְבַ֣ב עַמֶּ֑ךָ וְהָכֵ֥ן
לְבָבָ֖ם אֵלֶֽיךָ׃ [19] וְלִשְׁלֹמֹ֣ה בְנִ֗י תֵּ֚ן לֵבָ֣ב
שָׁלֵ֔ם לִשְׁמוֹר֙ מִצְוֺתֶ֣יךָ עֵדְוֺתֶ֖יךָ וְחֻקֶּ֑יךָ
וְלַעֲשׂ֣וֹת הַכֹּ֔ל וְלִבְנ֖וֹת הַבִּירָ֖ה אֲשֶׁר־
הֲכִינֽוֹתִי׃ פ

[20] וַיֹּ֤אמֶר דָּוִיד֙ לְכָל־הַקָּהָ֔ל בָּרְכוּ־נָ֕א אֶת־
יְהוָ֖ה אֱלֹהֵיכֶ֑ם וַיְבָרְכ֣וּ כָֽל־הַקָּהָ֗ל לַיהוָה֙
אֱלֹהֵ֣י אֲבֹֽתֵיהֶ֔ם וַיִּקְּד֧וּ וַיִּֽשְׁתַּחֲו֛וּ לַיהוָ֖ה
וְלַמֶּֽלֶךְ׃ [21] וַיִּזְבְּח֣וּ לַיהוָ֡ה ׀ וַיַּעֲל֣וּ
עֹלוֹת֩ לַיהוָ֨ה לְמׇֽחֳרַ֜ת הַיּ֣וֹם הַה֗וּא פָּרִ֨ים
אֶ֜לֶף אֵילִ֥ים אֶ֛לֶף כְּבָשִׂ֥ים אֶ֖לֶף וְנִסְכֵּיהֶ֑ם
וּזְבָחִ֥ים לָרֹ֖ב לְכָל־יִשְׂרָאֵֽל׃ [22] וַיֹּאכְל֨וּ
וַיִּשְׁתּ֜וּ לִפְנֵ֧י יְהוָ֛ה בַּיּ֥וֹם הַה֖וּא בְּשִׂמְחָ֣ה
גְדוֹלָ֑ה וַיַּמְלִ֤יכוּ שֵׁנִית֙ לִשְׁלֹמֹ֣ה בֶן־דָּוִ֔יד
וַיִּמְשְׁח֧וּ לַיהוָ֛ה לְנָגִ֖יד וּלְצָד֥וֹק לְכֹהֵֽן׃ [23] וַיֵּ֣שֶׁב שְׁ֠לֹמֹ֠ה עַל־כִּסֵּ֨א יְהוָ֧ה ׀ לְמֶ֛לֶךְ
תַּֽחַת־דָּוִ֥יד אָבִ֖יו וַיַּצְלַ֑ח וַיִּשְׁמְע֥וּ אֵלָ֖יו
כָּל־יִשְׂרָאֵֽל׃ [24] וְכׇל־הַשָּׂרִים֙ וְהַגִּבֹּרִ֔ים וְגַ֕ם
כָּל־בְּנֵ֖י הַמֶּ֣לֶךְ דָּוִ֑יד נָתְנ֣וּ יָ֔ד תַּ֖חַת
שְׁלֹמֹ֥ה הַמֶּֽלֶךְ׃ [25] וַיְגַדֵּ֨ל יְהוָ֤ה אֶת־שְׁלֹמֹה֙
לְמַ֔עְלָה לְעֵינֵ֖י כָּל־יִשְׂרָאֵ֑ל וַיִּתֵּ֤ן עָלָיו֙ ה֣וֹד
מַלְכ֔וּת אֲשֶׁ֧ר לֹֽא־הָיָ֛ה עַל־כָּל־מֶ֖לֶךְ לְפָנָ֑יו
עַל־יִשְׂרָאֵֽל׃ פ

[26] וְדָוִיד֙ בֶּן־יִשָׁ֑י מָלַ֖ךְ עַל־כָּל־יִשְׂרָאֵֽל׃
[27] וְהַיָּמִ֗ים אֲשֶׁ֤ר מָלַךְ֙ עַל־יִשְׂרָאֵ֔ל
אַרְבָּעִ֖ים שָׁנָ֑ה בְּחֶבְר֤וֹן מָלַךְ֙ שֶׁ֣בַע שָׁנִ֔ים
וּבִירוּשָׁלַ֖͏ִם מָלַ֖ךְ שְׁלֹשִׁ֥ים וְשָׁלֽוֹשׁ׃ [28] וַיָּ֗מׇת
בְּשֵׂיבָ֣ה טוֹבָ֔ה שְׂבַ֥ע יָמִ֖ים עֹ֣שֶׁר וְכָב֑וֹד
וַיִּמְלֹ֛ךְ שְׁלֹמֹ֥ה בְנ֖וֹ תַּחְתָּֽיו׃ [29] וְדִבְרֵי֙ דָּוִ֣יד
הַמֶּ֔לֶךְ הָרִאשֹׁנִ֖ים וְהָאַחֲרֹנִ֑ים הִנָּ֣ם
כְּתוּבִ֗ים עַל־דִּבְרֵי֙ שְׁמוּאֵ֣ל הָרֹאֶ֔ה וְעַל־

the history of Nathan the prophet, and the history of Gad the seer, ³⁰together with all the mighty deeds of his kingship and the events that befell him and Israel and all the kingdoms of the earth.

דִּבְרֵי נָתָן הַנָּבִיא וְעַל־דִּבְרֵי גָּד הַחֹזֶה:
³⁰ עִם כָּל־מַלְכוּתוֹ וּגְבוּרָתוֹ וְהָעִתִּים אֲשֶׁר
עָבְרוּ עָלָיו וְעַל־יִשְׂרָאֵל וְעַל כָּל־מַמְלְכוֹת
הָאֲרָצוֹת: פ

2 CHRONICLES

1 *a*Solomon son of David took firm hold of his kingdom, for the LORD his God was with him and made him exceedingly great. 2Solomon summoned all Israel—the officers of thousands and of hundreds, and the judges, and all the chiefs of all Israel, the heads of the clans. 3Then Solomon, and all the assemblage with him, went to the shrine at Gibeon, for the Tent of Meeting, which Moses the servant of the LORD had made in the wilderness, was there. (4But the Ark of God David had brought up from Kiriath-jearim to the place which David had prepared for it; for he had pitched a tent for it in Jerusalem.) 5The bronze altar, which Bezalel son of Uri son of Hur had made, was also there before the Tabernacle of the LORD, and Solomon and the assemblage resorted to it. 6There Solomon ascended the bronze altar before the LORD, which was at the Tent of Meeting, and on it sacrificed a thousand burnt offerings.

7That night, God appeared to Solomon and said to him, "Ask, what shall I grant you?" 8Solomon said to God, "You dealt most graciously with my father David, and now You have made me king in his stead. 9Now, O LORD God, let Your promise to my father David be fulfilled; for You have made me king over a people as numerous as the dust of the earth. 10Grant me then the wisdom and the knowledge *b*-to lead this people,-*b* for who can govern Your great people?" 11God said to Solomon, "Because you want this, and have not asked for wealth, prop-

א וַיִּתְחַזֵּק שְׁלֹמֹה בֶן־דָּוִיד עַל־מַלְכוּתוֹ וַיהוָה אֱלֹהָיו עִמּוֹ וַיְגַדְּלֵהוּ לְמָעְלָה: 2 וַיֹּאמֶר שְׁלֹמֹה לְכָל־יִשְׂרָאֵל לְשָׂרֵי הָאֲלָפִים וְהַמֵּאוֹת וְלַשֹּׁפְטִים וּלְכֹל נָשִׂיא לְכָל־יִשְׂרָאֵל רָאשֵׁי הָאָבוֹת: 3 וַיֵּלְכוּ שְׁלֹמֹה וְכָל־הַקָּהָל עִמּוֹ לַבָּמָה אֲשֶׁר בְּגִבְעוֹן כִּי־שָׁם הָיָה אֹהֶל מוֹעֵד הָאֱלֹהִים אֲשֶׁר עָשָׂה מֹשֶׁה עֶבֶד־יְהוָה בַּמִּדְבָּר: 4 אֲבָל אֲרוֹן הָאֱלֹהִים הֶעֱלָה דָוִיד מִקִּרְיַת יְעָרִים בַּהֵכִין לוֹ דָּוִיד כִּי נָטָה־לוֹ אֹהֶל בִּירוּשָׁלָ͏ִם: 5 וּמִזְבַּח הַנְּחֹשֶׁת אֲשֶׁר עָשָׂה בְּצַלְאֵל בֶּן־אוּרִי בֶן־חוּר שָׂם לִפְנֵי מִשְׁכַּן יְהוָה וַיִּדְרְשֵׁהוּ שְׁלֹמֹה וְהַקָּהָל: 6 וַיַּעַל שְׁלֹמֹה שָׁם עַל־מִזְבַּח הַנְּחֹשֶׁת לִפְנֵי יְהוָה אֲשֶׁר לְאֹהֶל מוֹעֵד וַיַּעַל עָלָיו עֹלוֹת אָלֶף: 7 בַּלַּיְלָה הַהוּא נִרְאָה אֱלֹהִים לִשְׁלֹמֹה וַיֹּאמֶר לוֹ שְׁאַל מָה אֶתֶּן־לָךְ: 8 וַיֹּאמֶר שְׁלֹמֹה לֵאלֹהִים אַתָּה עָשִׂיתָ עִם־דָּוִיד אָבִי חֶסֶד גָּדוֹל וְהִמְלַכְתַּנִי תַּחְתָּיו: 9 עַתָּה יְהוָה אֱלֹהִים יֵאָמֵן דְּבָרְךָ עִם דָּוִיד אָבִי כִּי אַתָּה הִמְלַכְתַּנִי עַל־עַם רַב כַּעֲפַר הָאָרֶץ: 10 עַתָּה חָכְמָה וּמַדָּע תֶּן־לִי וְאֵצְאָה לִפְנֵי הָעָם־הַזֶּה וְאָבוֹאָה כִּי־מִי יִשְׁפֹּט אֶת־עַמְּךָ הַזֶּה הַגָּדוֹל: ס 11 וַיֹּאמֶר־אֱלֹהִים לִשְׁלֹמֹה יַעַן אֲשֶׁר הָיְתָה זֹאת עִם־לְבָבֶךָ וְלֹא־שָׁאַלְתָּ עֹשֶׁר

---

a With vv. 3–13, cf. 1 Kings 3.4–15; with vv. 14–17, cf. 1 Kings 10.26–29.
b-b Lit. "that I may go out before this people and come in."

erty, and glory, nor have you asked for the life of your enemy, or long life for yourself, but you have asked for the wisdom and the knowledge to be able to govern My people over whom I have made you king, [12]wisdom and knowledge are granted to you, and I grant you also wealth, property, and glory, the like of which no king before you has had, nor shall any after you have." [13]From the shrine at Gibeon, from the Tent of Meeting, Solomon went to Jerusalem and reigned over Israel.

[14]Solomon assembled chariots and horsemen; he had 1,400 chariots and 12,000 horses that he stationed in the chariot towns and with the king in Jerusalem. [15]The king made silver and gold as plentiful in Jerusalem as stones, and cedars as plentiful as the sycamores in the Shephelah. [16]Solomon's horses were imported from Egypt and from Que; the king's traders would buy them from Que at the market price. [17]A chariot imported from Egypt cost 600 shekels of silver, and a horse 150. These in turn were exported by them[c] to all the kings of the Hittites and the kings of the Arameans.

[18]Then Solomon resolved to build a House for the name of the Lord and a royal palace for himself.

2 [a]Solomon mustered 70,000 basket carriers and 80,000 quarriers in the hills, with 3,600 men supervising them. [2]Solomon sent this message to King Huram of Tyre, "In view of what you did for my father David in sending him cedars to build a palace for his residence—[3]see, I intend to build a House for the name of the Lord my God; I will dedicate it to Him for making incense offering of sweet spices in His honor, for the regular rows of bread, and for the morning and evening burnt offerings on sabbaths, new moons, and festivals, as is Israel's

---

c   *That is, Solomon's dealers.*

a   *Cf. 1 Kings 5.*

נְכָסִ֤ים וְכָבוֹד֙ וְאֵת֙ נֶ֣פֶשׁ שֹׂנְאֶ֔יךָ וְגַם־יָמִ֥ים רַבִּ֖ים לֹ֣א שָׁאָ֑לְתָּ וַתִּֽשְׁאַל־לְךָ֤ חׇכְמָה֙ וּמַדָּ֔ע אֲשֶׁ֥ר תִּשְׁפּוֹט֙ אֶת־עַמִּ֔י אֲשֶׁ֥ר הִמְלַכְתִּ֖יךָ עָלָֽיו: [12] הַֽחׇכְמָ֥ה וְהַמַּדָּ֖ע נָת֣וּן לָ֑ךְ וְעֹ֨שֶׁר וּנְכָסִ֤ים וְכָבוֹד֙ אֶתֶּן־לְךָ֗ אֲשֶׁ֣ר ׀ לֹא־הָ֤יָה כֵן֙ לַמְּלָכִ֔ים אֲשֶׁ֣ר לְפָנֶ֔יךָ וְאַחֲרֶ֖יךָ לֹ֥א יִֽהְיֶה־כֵּֽן: [13] וַיָּבֹ֣א שְׁלֹמֹ֡ה לַבָּמָ֣ה אֲשֶׁר־בְּגִבְעוֹן֩ יְרוּשָׁלַ֨͏ִם מִלִּפְנֵ֛י אֹ֥הֶל מוֹעֵ֖ד וַיִּמְלֹ֥ךְ עַל־יִשְׂרָאֵֽל: פ

[14] וַיֶּאֱסֹ֣ף שְׁלֹמֹה֮ רֶ֣כֶב וּפָרָשִׁים֒ וַֽיְהִי־ל֗וֹ אֶ֤לֶף וְאַרְבַּע־מֵאוֹת֙ רֶ֔כֶב וּשְׁנֵֽים־עָשָׂ֥ר אֶ֖לֶף פָּרָשִׁ֑ים וַיַּנִּיחֵם֙ בְּעָרֵ֣י הָרֶ֔כֶב וְעִם־הַמֶּ֖לֶךְ בִּירֽוּשָׁלָֽͅם: [15] וַיִּתֵּ֨ן הַמֶּ֜לֶךְ אֶת־הַכֶּ֣סֶף וְאֶת־הַזָּהָ֗ב בִּירֽוּשָׁלַ֨͏ִם֙ כָּֽאֲבָנִ֔ים וְאֵ֣ת הָאֲרָזִ֗ים נָתַ֛ן כַּשִּׁקְמִ֥ים אֲשֶׁר־בַּשְּׁפֵלָ֖ה לָרֹֽב: [16] וּמוֹצָ֧א הַסּוּסִ֛ים אֲשֶׁ֥ר לִשְׁלֹמֹ֖ה מִמִּצְרָ֑יִם וּמִקְוֵ֕א סֹחֲרֵ֣י הַמֶּ֔לֶךְ מִקְוֵ֥א יִקְח֖וּ בִּמְחִֽיר: [17] וַֽ֠יַּעֲל֠וּ וַיּוֹצִ֨יאוּ מִמִּצְרַ֜יִם מֶרְכָּבָ֗ה בְּשֵׁ֤שׁ מֵאוֹת֙ כֶּ֔סֶף וְס֖וּס בַּחֲמִשִּׁ֣ים וּמֵאָ֑ה וְ֠כֵ֠ן לְכׇל־מַלְכֵ֧י הַֽחִתִּ֛ים וּמַלְכֵ֥י אֲרָ֖ם בְּיָדָ֥ם יוֹצִֽיאוּ:

[18] וַיֹּ֣אמֶר שְׁלֹמֹ֗ה לִבְנ֥וֹת בַּ֙יִת֙ לְשֵׁ֣ם יְהֹוָ֔ה וּבַ֖יִת לְמַלְכוּתֽוֹ:

ב וַיִּסְפֹּ֨ר שְׁלֹמֹ֜ה שִׁבְעִ֥ים אֶ֣לֶף אִישׁ֮ סַבָּ֒ל֒ וּשְׁמוֹנִ֥ים אֶ֛לֶף אִ֖ישׁ חֹצֵ֣ב בָּהָ֑ר וּמְנַצְּחִ֣ים עֲלֵיהֶ֔ם שְׁלֹ֥שֶׁת אֲלָפִ֖ים וְשֵׁ֥שׁ מֵאֽוֹת: פ [2] וַיִּשְׁלַ֣ח שְׁלֹמֹ֔ה אֶל־חוּרָ֥ם מֶֽלֶךְ־צֹ֖ר לֵאמֹ֑ר כַּאֲשֶׁ֤ר עָשִׂ֙יתָ֙ עִם־דָּוִ֣יד אָבִ֔י וַתִּֽשְׁלַֽח־ל֣וֹ אֲרָזִ֔ים לִבְנֽוֹת־ל֥וֹ בַ֖יִת לָשֶׁ֥בֶת בּֽוֹ: [3] הִנֵּה֩ אֲנִ֨י בֽוֹנֶה־בַּ֜יִת לְשֵׁ֣ם ׀ יְהֹוָ֣ה אֱלֹהָ֗י לְהַקְדִּ֣ישׁ ל֡וֹ לְהַקְטִ֣יר לְפָנָ֣יו קְטֹֽרֶת־סַמִּים֩ וּמַעֲרֶ֨כֶת תָּמִ֜יד וְעֹל֣וֹת לַבֹּ֣קֶר וְלָעֶ֗רֶב לַשַּׁבָּתוֹת֙ וְלֶ֣חֳדָשִׁ֔ים וּֽלְמוֹעֲדֵ֖י יְהֹוָ֣ה אֱלֹהֵ֑ינוּ לְעוֹלָ֖ם זֹ֥את עַל־

eternal duty. ⁴The House that I intend to build will be great, inasmuch as our God is greater than all gods. ⁵Who indeed is capable of building a House for Him! Even the heavens to their uttermost reaches cannot contain Him, and who am I that I should build Him a House—except as a place for making burnt offerings to Him? ⁶Now send me a craftsman to work in gold, silver, bronze, and iron, and in purple, crimson, and blue yarn, and who knows how to engrave, alongside the craftsmen I have here in Judah and in Jerusalem, whom my father David provided. ⁷Send me cedars, cypress, and algum wood from the Lebanon, for I know that your servants are skilled at cutting the trees of Lebanon. My servants will work with yours ⁸to provide me with a great stock of timber; for the House that I intend to build will be singularly great. ⁹I have allocated for your servants, the wood-cutters who fell the trees, 20,000 *kor* of crushed wheat and 20,000 *kor* of barley, 20,000 *bath* of wine and 20,000 *bath* of oil.”

¹⁰Huram, king of Tyre, sent Solomon this written message in reply, “Because the Lord loved His people, He made you king over them.”

¹¹Huram continued, “Blessed is the Lord, God of Israel, who made the heavens and the earth, who gave King David a wise son, endowed with intelligence and understanding, to build a House for the Lord and a royal palace for himself. ¹²Now I am sending you a skillful and intelligent man, my master[b] Huram, ¹³the son of a Danite woman, his father a Tyrian. He is skilled at working in gold, silver, bronze, iron, precious stones, and wood; in purple, blue, and crimson yarn and in fine linen; and at engraving and designing whatever will be required of him, alongside your craftsmen and the craftsmen of my lord, your father David. ¹⁴As to the wheat,

---

b   *Lit. “my father.”*

1953

barley, oil, and wine which my lord mentioned, let him send them to his servants. [15]We undertake to cut down as many trees of Lebanon as you need, and deliver them to you as rafts by sea to Jaffa; you will transport them to Jerusalem."

[16]Solomon took a census of all the aliens who were in the land of Israel, besides the census taken by his father David, and they were found to be 153,600. [17]He made 70,000 of them basket carriers, and 80,000 of them quarriers, with 3,600 supervisors to see that the people worked.

3

[a]Then Solomon began to build the House of the LORD in Jerusalem on Mount Moriah, where [the LORD] had appeared to his father David, at the place which David had designated, at the threshing floor of Ornan the Jebusite. [2]He began to build on the second day of the second month of the fourth year of his reign. [3]These were the dimensions Solomon established for building the House of God: its length in cubits, by the former measure, was 60, and its breadth was 20. [4]The length of the porch in front [was equal] to the breadth of the House—20 cubits, and its height was 120. Inside he overlaid it with pure gold. [5]The House itself he paneled with cypress wood. He overlaid it with fine gold and embossed on it palms and chains. [6]He studded the House with precious stones for decoration; the gold was from Parvaim. [7]He overlaid the House with gold—the beams, the thresholds, its walls and doors; he carved cherubim on the walls. [8]He made the Holy of Holies: its length was [equal to] the breadth of the house—20 cubits, and its breadth was 20 cubits. He overlaid it with 600 talents of fine gold. [9]The weight of the nails was 50 shekels of gold; the upper cham-

וְהַשְּׂעֹרִים הַשֶּׁמֶן וְהַיַּיִן אֲשֶׁר אָמַר אֲדֹנִי יִשְׁלַח לַעֲבָדָיו: 15 וַאֲנַחְנוּ נִכְרֹת עֵצִים מִן־הַלְּבָנוֹן כְּכָל־צָרְכֶּךָ וּנְבִיאֵם לְךָ רַפְסֹדוֹת עַל־יָם יָפוֹ וְאַתָּה תַּעֲלֶה אֹתָם יְרוּשָׁלָ͏ִם: פ

16 וַיִּסְפֹּר שְׁלֹמֹה כָּל־הָאֲנָשִׁים הַגֵּירִים אֲשֶׁר בְּאֶרֶץ יִשְׂרָאֵל אַחֲרֵי הַסְּפָר אֲשֶׁר סְפָרָם דָּוִיד אָבִיו וַיִּמָּצְאוּ מֵאָה וַחֲמִשִּׁים אֶלֶף וּשְׁלֹשֶׁת אֲלָפִים וְשֵׁשׁ מֵאוֹת: 17 וַיַּעַשׂ מֵהֶם שִׁבְעִים אֶלֶף סַבָּל וּשְׁמֹנִים אֶלֶף חֹצֵב בָּהָר וּשְׁלֹשֶׁת אֲלָפִים וְשֵׁשׁ מֵאוֹת מְנַצְּחִים לְהַעֲבִיד אֶת־הָעָם:

ג וַיָּחֶל שְׁלֹמֹה לִבְנוֹת אֶת־בֵּית־יְהוָה בִּירוּשָׁלַ͏ִם בְּהַר הַמּוֹרִיָּה אֲשֶׁר נִרְאָה לְדָוִיד אָבִיהוּ אֲשֶׁר הֵכִין בִּמְקוֹם דָּוִיד בְּגֹרֶן אָרְנָן הַיְבוּסִי: 2 וַיָּחֶל לִבְנוֹת בַּחֹדֶשׁ הַשֵּׁנִי בַּשֵּׁנִי בִּשְׁנַת אַרְבַּע לְמַלְכוּתוֹ: 3 וְאֵלֶּה הוּסַד שְׁלֹמֹה לִבְנוֹת אֶת־בֵּית הָאֱלֹהִים הָאֹרֶךְ אַמּוֹת בַּמִּדָּה הָרִאשׁוֹנָה אַמּוֹת שִׁשִּׁים וְרֹחַב אַמּוֹת עֶשְׂרִים: 4 וְהָאוּלָם אֲשֶׁר עַל־פְּנֵי הָאֹרֶךְ עַל־פְּנֵי רֹחַב־הַבַּיִת אַמּוֹת עֶשְׂרִים וְהַגֹּבַהּ מֵאָה וְעֶשְׂרִים וַיְצַפֵּהוּ מִפְּנִימָה זָהָב טָהוֹר: 5 וְאֵת ׀ הַבַּיִת הַגָּדוֹל חִפָּה עֵץ בְּרוֹשִׁים וַיְחַפֵּהוּ זָהָב טוֹב וַיַּעַל עָלָיו תִּמֹרִים וְשַׁרְשְׁרוֹת: 6 וַיְצַף אֶת־הַבַּיִת אֶבֶן יְקָרָה לְתִפְאָרֶת וְהַזָּהָב זְהַב פַּרְוָיִם: 7 וַיְחַף אֶת־הַבַּיִת הַקֹּרוֹת הַסִּפִּים וְקִירוֹתָיו וְדַלְתוֹתָיו זָהָב וּפִתַּח כְּרוּבִים עַל־הַקִּירוֹת: 8 ס וַיַּעַשׂ אֶת־בֵּית־קֹדֶשׁ הַקֳּדָשִׁים אָרְכּוֹ עַל־פְּנֵי רֹחַב־הַבַּיִת אַמּוֹת עֶשְׂרִים וְרָחְבּוֹ אַמּוֹת עֶשְׂרִים וַיְחַפֵּהוּ זָהָב טוֹב לְכִכָּרִים שֵׁשׁ מֵאוֹת: 9 וּמִשְׁקָל לְמִסְמְרוֹת לִשְׁקָלִים חֲמִשִּׁים

---

a   With vv. 2–17, cf. 1 Kings 6; 7.1–22.

bers he overlaid with gold. ¹⁰He made two sculptured cherubim in the Holy of Holies, and they were overlaid with gold. ¹¹The outspread wings of the cherubim were 20 cubits across: one wing 5 cubits long touching one wall of the House, and the other wing 5 cubits long touching the wing of the other cherub; ¹²one wing of the other [cherub] 5 cubits long extending to the other wall of the House, and its other wing 5 cubits long touching the wing of the first cherub. ¹³The wingspread of these cherubim was thus 20 cubits across, and they were standing up facing the House. ¹⁴He made the curtain of blue, purple, and crimson yarn and fine linen, and he worked cherubim into it. ¹⁵At the front of the House he made two columns 35 cubits high; the capitals[b] on top of them were 5 cubits high. ¹⁶He made chainwork in the inner Sanctuary and set it on the top of the columns; he made a hundred pomegranates and set them into the chainwork. ¹⁷He erected the columns in front of the Great Hall, one to its right and one to its left; the one to the right was called Jachin, and the one to the left, Boaz.

4 *ᵃ*He made an altar of bronze 20 cubits long, 20 cubits wide, and 10 cubits high.

²He made the sea[b] of cast metal 10 cubits across from brim to brim, perfectly round; it was 5 cubits high, and its circumference was 30 cubits. ³Beneath were figures of oxen set all around it, of 10 cubits, encircling the sea; the oxen were in two rows, cast in one piece with it. ⁴It stood upon twelve oxen: three faced north, three faced west, three faced south, and three faced east, with the sea resting upon them; their haunches were all turned inward. ⁵It was a

---

b   *Meaning of Heb. uncertain.*

a   *Cf. 1 Kings 7.23–50.*
b   *I.e., a large basin.*

---

10 וַיַּ֣עַשׂ בְּבֵית־ זָהָ֖ב וְהָעֲלִיּ֥וֹת חִפָּ֥ה זָהָ֑ב: קֹ֤דֶשׁ הַקֳּדָשִׁים֙ כְּרוּבִ֣ים שְׁנַ֔יִם מַעֲשֵׂ֖ה צַעֲצֻעִ֑ים וַיְצַפּ֥וּ אֹתָ֖ם זָהָֽב: 11 וְכַנְפֵ֣י הַכְּרוּבִ֗ים אָרְכָּ֘ם֮ אַמּ֣וֹת עֶשְׂרִ֒ים֒ כְּנַ֣ף הָאֶחָ֞ד לְאַמּ֣וֹת חָמֵשׁ֮ מַגַּ֣עַת לְקִ֣יר הַבַּ֒יִת֒ וְהַכָּנָ֣ף הָאַחֶ֗רֶת אַמּ֣וֹת חָמֵ֔שׁ מַגִּ֕יעַ לִכְנַ֖ף הַכְּר֥וּב הָאַחֵֽר: 12 וּכְנַ֨ף הַכְּר֤וּב הָאֶחָד֙ אַמּ֣וֹת חָמֵ֔שׁ מַגִּ֖יעַ לְקִ֣יר הַבָּ֑יִת וְהַכָּנָ֣ף הָאַחֶ֗רֶת אַמּ֣וֹת חָמֵ֔שׁ דְּבֵקָ֕ה לִכְנַ֖ף הַכְּר֥וּב הָאַחֵֽר: 13 כַּנְפֵי֙ הַכְּרוּבִ֣ים הָאֵ֔לֶּה פֹּרְשִׂ֥ים אַמּ֖וֹת עֶשְׂרִ֑ים וְהֵ֛ם עֹמְדִ֥ים עַל־רַגְלֵיהֶ֖ם וּפְנֵיהֶ֥ם לַבָּֽיִת: ס 14 וַיַּ֖עַשׂ אֶת־הַפָּרֹ֑כֶת תְּכֵ֤לֶת וְאַרְגָּמָן֙ וְכַרְמִ֣יל וּב֔וּץ וַיַּ֥עַל עָלָ֖יו כְּרוּבִֽים: ס 15 וַיַּ֜עַשׂ לִפְנֵ֤י הַבַּ֙יִת֙ עַמּוּדִ֣ים שְׁנַ֔יִם אַמּ֕וֹת שְׁלֹשִׁ֥ים וְחָמֵ֖שׁ אֹ֑רֶךְ וְהַצֶּ֥פֶת אֲשֶׁר־עַל־רֹאשׁ֖וֹ אַמּ֥וֹת חָמֵֽשׁ: ס 16 וַיַּ֤עַשׂ שַׁרְשְׁרוֹת֙ בַּדְּבִ֔יר וַיִּתֵּ֖ן עַל־רֹ֣אשׁ הָעַמֻּדִ֑ים וַיַּ֤עַשׂ רִמּוֹנִים֙ מֵאָ֔ה וַיִּתֵּ֖ן בַּֽשַּׁרְשְׁרֽוֹת: 17 וַיָּ֤קֶם אֶת־הָֽעַמּוּדִים֙ עַל־פְּנֵ֣י הַהֵיכָ֔ל אֶחָ֥ד מִיָּמִ֖ין וְאֶחָ֣ד מֵֽהַשְּׂמֹ֑אול* וַיִּקְרָ֤א שֵֽׁם־הַיְמָנִי֙ יָכִ֔ין וְשֵׁ֥ם הַשְּׂמָאלִ֖י בֹּֽעַז: ס

ד וַיַּ֛עַשׂ מִזְבַּ֥ח נְחֹ֖שֶׁת עֶשְׂרִ֣ים אַמָּה֩ אָרְכּ֜וֹ וְעֶשְׂרִ֤ים אַמָּה֙ רָחְבּ֔וֹ וְעֶ֥שֶׂר אַמּ֖וֹת קוֹמָתֽוֹ: ס 2 וַיַּ֥עַשׂ אֶת־הַיָּ֖ם מוּצָ֑ק עֶ֣שֶׂר בָּ֠אַמָּה מִשְּׂפָת֨וֹ אֶל־שְׂפָת֜וֹ עָג֣וֹל ׀ סָבִ֗יב וְחָמֵ֤שׁ בָּֽאַמָּה֙ קֽוֹמָת֔וֹ וְקָו֙ שְׁלֹשִׁ֣ים בָּֽאַמָּ֔ה יָסֹ֥ב אֹת֖וֹ סָבִֽיב: 3 וּדְמ֣וּת בְּקָרִים֩ תַּ֨חַת ל֜וֹ סָבִ֤יב ׀ סָבִיב֙ סוֹבְבִ֣ים אֹת֔וֹ עֶ֚שֶׂר בָּֽאַמָּ֔ה מַקִּיפִ֥ים אֶת־הַיָּ֖ם סָבִ֑יב שְׁנַ֤יִם טוּרִים֙ הַבָּקָ֔ר יְצוּקִ֖ים בְּמֻֽצַקְתּֽוֹ: 4 עֹמֵ֞ד עַל־ שְׁנֵ֧ים עָשָׂ֣ר בָּקָ֗ר שְׁלֹשָׁ֣ה פֹנִ֣ים ׀ צָפ֡וֹנָה וּשְׁלוֹשָׁה֩ פֹנִ֨ים ׀ יָ֜מָּה וּשְׁלֹשָׁ֣ה ׀ פֹּנִ֣ים נֶ֗גְבָּה וּשְׁלֹשָׁה֙ פֹּנִ֣ים מִזְרָ֔חָה וְהַיָּ֥ם עֲלֵיהֶ֖ם

handbreadth thick, and its brim was made like that of a cup, like the petals of a lily. It held 3,000 *bath.*

6He made ten bronze lavers for washing; he set five on the right and five on the left; they would rinse off in them the parts of the burnt offering; but the sea served the priests for washing. 7He made ten lampstands of gold as prescribed, and placed them in the Great Hall, five on the right and five on the left. 8He made ten tables and placed them in the Great Hall, five on the right and five on the left. He made one hundred gold basins. 9He built the court of the priests and the great court, and doors for the great court; he overlaid the doors with bronze. 10He set the sea on the right side, at the southeast corner.

11Huram made the pails, the shovels, and the basins. With that Huram completed the work he had undertaken for King Solomon in the House of God: 12the two columns, the globes, and the two capitals on top of the columns; and the two pieces of network to cover the two globes of the capitals on top of the columns; 13the four hundred pomegranates for the two pieces of network, two rows of pomegranates for each network, to cover the two globes of the capitals on top of the columns; 14he made the stands and the lavers upon the stands; 15one sea with the twelve oxen beneath it; 16the pails, the shovels, and the bowls.c And all the vessels made for King Solomon for the House of the Lord by Huram his master were of burnished bronze. 17The king had them cast in molds dug out of the earth, in the plain of the Jordan between Succoth and Zeredah. 18Solomon made a very

---

c Or "forks."

מִלְמַ֫עְלָה וְכָל־אַחֲרֵיהֶ֖ם בָּֽיְתָה׃ 5 וְעָבְי֣וֹ
טֶ֔פַח וּשְׂפָתוֹ֙ כְּמַעֲשֵׂ֣ה שְׂפַת־כּ֔וֹס פֶּ֖רַח
שֽׁוֹשַׁנָּ֑ה מַחֲזִ֣יק בַּתִּ֔ים שְׁלֹ֥שֶׁת אֲלָפִ֖ים
יָכִ֑יל׃ ס

6 וַיַּ֣עַשׂ כִּיּוֹרִים֮ עֲשָׂרָה֒ וַ֠יִּתֵּן חֲמִשָּׁ֨ה מִיָּמִ֜ין
וַחֲמִשָּׁ֤ה מִשְּׂמֹאול֙* לְרָחְצָ֣ה בָהֶ֔ם אֶת־
מַעֲשֵׂ֤ה הָעוֹלָה֙ יָדִ֣יחוּ בָ֔ם וְהַיָּ֕ם לְרָחְצָ֖ה
לַכֹּהֲנִ֥ים בּֽוֹ׃ ס 7 וַיַּ֜עַשׂ אֶת־מְנֹר֥וֹת
הַזָּהָ֛ב עֶ֖שֶׂר כְּמִשְׁפָּטָ֑ם וַיִּתֵּן֙ בַּֽהֵיכָ֔ל חָמֵ֤שׁ
מִיָּמִין֙ וְחָמֵ֣שׁ מִשְּׂמֹאול֒* ס 8 וַיַּ֣עַשׂ
שֻׁלְחָנוֹת֮ עֲשָׂרָה֒ וַיַּנַּ֣ח בַּֽהֵיכָ֔ל חֲמִשָּׁ֤ה
מִיָּמִין֙ וַחֲמִשָּׁ֣ה מִשְּׂמֹאול֒* וַיַּ֛עַשׂ מִזְרְקֵ֥י
זָהָ֖ב מֵאָֽה׃ 9 וַיַּ֙עַשׂ֙ חֲצַ֣ר הַכֹּהֲנִ֔ים וְהָעֲזָרָ֖ה
הַגְּדוֹלָ֑ה וּדְלָת֥וֹת לָעֲזָרָ֖ה וְדַלְתוֹתֵיהֶ֛ם
צִפָּ֥ה נְחֹֽשֶׁת׃ 10 וְאֶת־הַיָּ֗ם נָתַ֤ן מִכֶּ֙תֶף֙
הַיְמָנִ֣ית קֵ֔דְמָה מִמּ֖וּל נֶֽגְבָּה׃

11 וַיַּ֣עַשׂ חוּרָ֔ם אֶת־הַ֨סִּיר֔וֹת וְאֶת־הַיָּעִ֖ים
וְאֶת־הַמִּזְרָק֑וֹת ס וַיְכַ֣ל חירם חוּרָ֗ם
לַעֲשׂוֹת֙ אֶת־הַמְּלָאכָ֔ה אֲשֶׁ֥ר עָשָׂ֖ה לַמֶּ֣לֶךְ
שְׁלֹמֹ֑ה בְּבֵ֖ית הָאֱלֹהִֽים׃ 12 עַמּוּדִ֣ים שְׁנַ֔יִם
וְהַגֻּלּ֧וֹת וְהַכֹּֽתָר֛וֹת עַל־רֹ֥אשׁ הָעַמּוּדִ֖ים
שְׁתָּ֑יִם וְהַשְּׂבָכ֣וֹת שְׁתַּ֔יִם לְכַסּ֗וֹת אֶת־שְׁתֵּי֙
גֻּלּ֣וֹת הַכֹּֽתָר֔וֹת אֲשֶׁ֖ר עַל־רֹ֥אשׁ הָעַמּוּדִֽים׃
13 וְאֶת־הָרִמּוֹנִ֛ים אַרְבַּ֥ע מֵא֖וֹת לִשְׁתֵּ֣י
הַשְּׂבָכ֑וֹת שְׁנַ֨יִם טוּרִ֤ים רִמּוֹנִים֙ לַשְּׂבָכָ֣ה
הָֽאֶחָ֔ת לְכַסּ֗וֹת אֶת־שְׁתֵּי֙ גֻּלּ֣וֹת הַכֹּֽתָר֔וֹת
אֲשֶׁ֖ר עַל־פְּנֵ֥י הָעַמּוּדִֽים׃ 14 וְאֶת־הַמְּכֹנ֖וֹת
עָשָׂ֑ה וְאֶת־הַכִּיֹּר֛וֹת עָשָׂ֖ה עַל־הַמְּכֹנֽוֹת׃
15 אֶת־הַיָּ֣ם אֶחָ֑ד וְאֶת־הַבָּקָ֥ר שְׁנֵים־עָשָׂ֖ר
תַּחְתָּֽיו׃ 16 וְאֶת־הַסִּיר֥וֹת וְאֶת־הַיָּעִ֖ים
וְאֶת־הַמִּזְלָגוֹת֙ וְאֶת־כָּל־כְּלֵיהֶ֔ם עָשָׂ֞ה
חוּרָ֥ם אָבִ֛יו לַמֶּ֥לֶךְ שְׁלֹמֹ֖ה לְבֵ֣ית יְהוָ֑ה
נְחֹ֥שֶׁת מָרֽוּק׃ 17 בְּכִכַּ֤ר הַיַּרְדֵּן֙ יְצָקָ֣ם
הַמֶּ֔לֶךְ בַּעֲבִ֖י הָאֲדָמָ֑ה בֵּ֥ין סֻכּ֖וֹת וּבֵ֥ין
צְרֵדָֽתָה׃ 18 וַיַּ֧עַשׂ שְׁלֹמֹ֛ה כָּל־הַכֵּלִ֖ים

מלא ו׳   v. 6.
מלא ו׳   v. 7.
מלא ו׳   v. 8.

1956

large number of vessels; the weight of the bronze used could not be reckoned. [19]And Solomon made all the furnishings that were in the House of God: the altar of gold; the tables for the bread of display; [20]the lampstands and their lamps, to burn as prescribed in front of the inner Sanctuary, of solid gold; [21]and the petals, lamps, and tongs, of purest gold; [22]the snuffers, basins, ladles, and fire pans, of solid gold; and the entrance to the House: the doors of the innermost part of the House, the Holy of Holies, and the doors of the Great Hall of the House, of gold.

5 [a]When all the work that King Solomon undertook for the House of the LORD was completed, Solomon brought the things that his father David had consecrated—the silver, the gold, and the utensils—and deposited them in the treasury of the House of God.

[2]Then Solomon convoked the elders of Israel—all the heads of the tribes and the ancestral chiefs of the Israelites—in Jerusalem, to bring up the Ark of the Covenant of the LORD from the City of David, that is, Zion.

[3]All the men of Israel assembled before the king at the Feast,[b] in the seventh month. [4]When all the elders of Israel had come, the Levites carried the Ark. [5]They brought up the Ark and the Tent of Meeting and all the holy vessels that were in the Tent—the Levite priests brought them up. [6]Meanwhile, King Solomon and the whole community of Israel, who had gathered to him before the Ark, were sacrificing sheep and oxen in such abundance that they could not be numbered or counted.

[7]The priests brought the Ark of the LORD's Covenant to its place in the inner Sanctuary of the House, in the Holy of Holies, beneath the

---

אֵ֣לֶּה לָרֹ֣ב מְאֹ֑ד כִּ֥י לֹ֥א נֶחְקַ֖ר מִשְׁקַ֥ל הַנְּחֹֽשֶׁת: פ 19 וַיַּ֣עַשׂ שְׁלֹמֹ֔ה אֵ֖ת כָּל־הַכֵּלִ֔ים אֲשֶׁ֖ר בֵּ֣ית הָאֱלֹהִ֑ים וְאֵת֙ מִזְבַּ֣ח הַזָּהָ֔ב וְאֶת־הַשֻּׁלְחָנ֔וֹת וַעֲלֵיהֶ֖ם לֶ֥חֶם הַפָּנִֽים: 20 וְאֶת־הַמְּנֹר֣וֹת וְנֵרֹתֵיהֶ֗ם לְבַעֲרָ֛ם כַּמִּשְׁפָּ֖ט לִפְנֵ֣י הַדְּבִ֑יר זָהָ֥ב סָגֽוּר: 21 וְהַפֶּ֤רַח וְהַנֵּרֹת֙ וְהַמֶּלְקָחַ֔יִם זָהָ֖ב ה֣וּא מִכְל֥וֹת זָהָֽב: 22 וְהַֽמְזַמְּרֹ֣ות וְהַמִּזְרָקֹ֗ות וְהַכַּפּ֛וֹת וְהַמַּחְתּ֖וֹת זָהָ֣ב סָג֑וּר וּפֶ֣תַח הַבַּ֡יִת דַּלְתוֹתָיו֩ הַפְּנִימִיּ֨וֹת לְקֹ֤דֶשׁ הַקֳּדָשִׁים֙ וְדַלְתֵ֥י הַבַּ֛יִת לַהֵיכָ֖ל זָהָֽב:

ה וַתִּשְׁלַ֕ם כָּל־הַמְּלָאכָ֔ה אֲשֶׁר־עָשָׂ֥ה שְׁלֹמֹ֖ה לְבֵ֣ית יְהוָ֑ה ס וַיָּבֵ֨א שְׁלֹמֹ֜ה אֶת־קָדְשֵׁ֣י ׀ דָּוִ֣יד אָבִ֗יו וְאֶת־הַכֶּ֤סֶף וְאֶת־הַזָּהָב֙ וְאֶת־כָּל־הַכֵּלִ֔ים נָתַ֕ן בְּאֹצְר֖וֹת בֵּ֥ית הָאֱלֹהִֽים: פ 2 אָ֣ז יַקְהֵ֣יל שְׁלֹמֹ֣ה אֶת־זִקְנֵ֣י יִשְׂרָאֵ֡ל וְאֶת־כָּל־רָאשֵׁ֣י הַמַּטּ֡וֹת נְשִׂיאֵ֣י הָאָב֣וֹת לִבְנֵ֣י יִשְׂרָאֵ֖ל אֶל־יְרוּשָׁלִָ֑ם לְֽהַעֲל֞וֹת אֶת־אֲר֧וֹן בְּרִית־יְהוָ֛ה מֵעִ֥יר דָּוִ֖יד הִ֥יא צִיּֽוֹן: 3 וַיִּקָּהֲל֧וּ אֶל־הַמֶּ֛לֶךְ כָּל־אִ֥ישׁ יִשְׂרָאֵ֖ל בֶּחָ֑ג ה֥וּא הַחֹ֖דֶשׁ הַשְּׁבִעִֽי: 4 וַיָּבֹ֕אוּ כֹּ֖ל זִקְנֵ֣י יִשְׂרָאֵ֑ל וַיִּשְׂא֥וּ הַלְוִיִּ֖ם אֶת־הָאָרֽוֹן: 5 וַיַּעֲל֤וּ אֶת־הָֽאָרוֹן֙ וְאֶת־אֹ֣הֶל מוֹעֵ֔ד וְאֶת־כָּל־כְּלֵ֥י הַקֹּ֖דֶשׁ אֲשֶׁ֣ר בָּאֹ֑הֶל הֶעֱל֣וּ אֹתָ֔ם הַכֹּהֲנִ֖ים הַלְוִיִּֽם: 6 וְהַמֶּ֣לֶךְ שְׁלֹמֹ֗ה וְכָל־עֲדַ֤ת יִשְׂרָאֵל֙ הַנּוֹעָדִ֣ים עָלָ֔יו לִפְנֵ֖י הָאָר֑וֹן מְזַבְּחִים֙ צֹ֣אן וּבָקָ֔ר אֲשֶׁ֧ר לֹֽא־יִסָּפְר֛וּ וְלֹ֥א יִמָּנ֖וּ מֵרֹֽב: 7 וַיָּבִ֣יאוּ הַכֹּהֲנִ֗ים אֶת־אֲר֤וֹן בְּרִית־יְהוָה֙ אֶל־מְקוֹמ֔וֹ אֶל־דְּבִ֥יר הַבַּ֖יִת אֶל־קֹ֣דֶשׁ הַקֳּדָשִׁ֑ים אֶל־תַּ֖חַת כַּנְפֵ֥י הַכְּרוּבִֽים:

---

wings of the cherubim; 8for the cherubim had their wings spread out over the place of the Ark so that the cherubim covered the Ark and its poles from above. 9The poles projected beyond the Ark and the ends of the poles were visible from the front of the inner Sanctuary, but they could not be seen from the outside; and there they remain to this day. 10There was nothing inside the Ark but the two tablets that Moses placed [there] at Horeb, when the LORD made [a Covenant] with the Israelites after their departure from Egypt. 11When the priests came out of the Sanctuary—all the priests present had sanctified themselves, without keeping to the set divisions—12all the Levite singers, Asaph, Heman, Jeduthun, their sons and their brothers, dressed in fine linen, holding cymbals, harps, and lyres, were standing to the east of the altar, and with them were 120 priests who blew trumpets. 13The trumpeters and the singers joined in unison to praise and extol the LORD; and as the sound of the trumpets, cymbals, and other musical instruments, and the praise of the LORD, "For He is good, for His steadfast love is eternal," grew louder, the House, the House of the LORD, was filled with a cloud. 14The priests could not stay and perform the service because of the cloud, for the glory of the LORD filled the House of God.

6 aThen Solomon declared:
"The LORD has chosen
To abide in a thick cloud;
2I have built for You
A stately House,
And a place where You
May dwell forever."
3Then, as the whole congregation of Israel stood, the king turned and blessed the whole congregation of Israel. 4He said, "Blessed is the

8 וַיִּהְי֣וּ הַכְּרוּבִ֗ים פֹּרְשִׂ֤ים כְּנָפַ֙יִם֙ עַל־מְק֣וֹם הָאָר֔וֹן וַיְכַסּ֧וּ הַכְּרוּבִ֛ים עַל־הָאָר֖וֹן וְעַל־בַּדָּ֑יו מִלְמָֽעְלָה׃ 9 וַֽיַּאֲרִ֙יכוּ֙ הַבַּדִּ֔ים וַיֵּרָאוּ֩ רָאשֵׁ֨י הַבַּדִּ֤ים מִן־הָֽאָרוֹן֙ עַל־פְּנֵ֣י הַדְּבִ֔יר וְלֹ֥א יֵרָא֖וּ הַח֑וּצָה וַֽיְהִי־שָׁ֔ם עַ֖ד הַיּ֥וֹם הַזֶּֽה׃ 10 אֵ֚ין בָּֽאָר֔וֹן רַ֚ק שְׁנֵ֣י הַלֻּח֔וֹת אֲשֶׁר־נָתַ֥ן מֹשֶׁ֖ה בְּחֹרֵ֑ב אֲשֶׁ֨ר כָּרַ֤ת יְהֹוָה֙ עִם־בְּנֵ֣י יִשְׂרָאֵ֔ל בְּצֵאתָ֖ם מִמִּצְרָֽיִם׃ פ 11 וַיְהִ֞י בְּצֵ֤את הַכֹּֽהֲנִים֙ מִן־הַקֹּ֔דֶשׁ כִּ֠י כׇּל־הַכֹּהֲנִ֤ים הַנִּמְצְאִים֙ הִתְקַדָּ֔שׁוּ אֵ֖ין לִשְׁמ֥וֹר לְמַחְלְקֽוֹת׃ 12 וְהַלְוִיִּ֣ם הַמְשֹׁרֲרִ֣ים לְכֻלָּ֡ם לְאָסָ֡ף לְהֵימָ֣ן לִֽ֠ידֻתוּן וְלִבְנֵיהֶ֨ם וְלַאֲחֵיהֶ֜ם מְלֻבָּשִׁ֣ים בּ֗וּץ בִּמְצִלְתַּ֙יִם֙ וּבִנְבָלִ֣ים וְכִנֹּר֔וֹת עֹמְדִ֖ים מִזְרָ֣ח לַמִּזְבֵּ֑חַ וְעִמָּהֶ֤ם כֹּֽהֲנִים֙ לְמֵאָ֣ה וְעֶשְׂרִ֔ים מַחְצְרִ֖ים בַּחֲצֹצְרֽוֹת׃ 13 וַיְהִ֣י כְ֠אֶחָד לַֽמְחַצְּרִ֨ים וְלַמְשֹׁרְרִ֜ים לְהַשְׁמִ֣יעַ קוֹל־אֶחָ֗ד לְהַלֵּ֣ל וּלְהֹד֘וֹת לַיהֹוָה֒ וּכְהָרִ֣ים ק֠וֹל בַּחֲצֹצְר֨וֹת וּבִמְצִלְתַּ֜יִם וּבִכְלֵ֣י הַשִּׁ֗יר וּבְהַלֵּ֤ל לַיהֹוָה֙ כִּ֣י ט֔וֹב כִּ֥י לְעוֹלָ֖ם חַסְדּ֑וֹ וְהַבַּ֛יִת מָלֵ֥א עָנָ֖ן בֵּ֥ית יְהֹוָֽה׃ 14 וְלֹא־יָֽכְל֧וּ הַכֹּהֲנִ֛ים לַעֲמ֥וֹד לְשָׁרֵ֖ת מִפְּנֵ֣י הֶעָנָ֑ן כִּֽי־מָלֵ֥א כְבוֹד־יְהֹוָ֖ה אֶת־בֵּ֥ית הָאֱלֹהִֽים׃ פ

ו אָ֖ז אָמַ֣ר שְׁלֹמֹ֑ה
יְהֹוָ֣ה אָמַ֔ר
לִשְׁכּ֖וֹן בָּעֲרָפֶֽל׃
2 וַאֲנִ֛י בָּנִ֥יתִי
בֵית־זְבֻ֖ל לָ֑ךְ
וּמָכ֖וֹן
לְשִׁבְתְּךָ֥ עוֹלָמִֽים׃
3 וַיַּסֵּ֤ב הַמֶּ֙לֶךְ֙ אֶת־פָּנָ֔יו וַיְבָ֕רֶךְ אֵ֖ת כׇּל־קְהַ֣ל יִשְׂרָאֵ֑ל וְכׇל־קְהַ֥ל יִשְׂרָאֵ֖ל עוֹמֵֽד׃

---

a Cf. 1 Kings 8.12–53.

Lord God of Israel, b-who made a promise to my father David and fulfilled it.-b For He said, 5'From the time I brought My people out of the land of Egypt, I never chose a city from among all the tribes of Israel to build a House where My name might abide; nor did I choose anyone to be the leader of my people Israel. 6But then I chose Jerusalem for My name to abide there, and I chose David to rule My people Israel.'

7"Now my father David had wanted to build a House for the name of the Lord God of Israel. 8But the Lord said to my father David, 'As for your wanting to build a House for My name, you do well to want that. 9However, you shall not build the House; your son, the issue of your loins, he shall build the House for My name.' 10Now the Lord has fulfilled the promise that He made. I have succeededc my father David and have ascended the throne of Israel, as the Lord promised. I have built the House for the name of the Lord God of Israel, 11and there I have set the Ark containing the Covenant that the Lord made with the Israelites."

12Then, standing before the altar of the Lord in front of the whole congregation of Israel, he spread forth his hands. 13Solomon had made a bronze platformd and placed it in the midst of the Great Court; it was 5 cubits long and 5 cubits wide and 3 cubits high. He stood on it; then, kneeling in front of the whole congregation of Israel, he spread forth his hands to heaven 14and said, "O Lord God of Israel, there is no god like You in the heavens and on the earth, You who steadfastly maintain the Covenant with Your servants who walk before You with all their heart; 15You who have kept the promises You made to Your servant, my father David; You made a promise and have fulfilled it—as is now the case. 16And now, O Lord God of Israel, keep

4 וַיֹּאמֶר בָּרוּךְ יְהוָה אֱלֹהֵי יִשְׂרָאֵל אֲשֶׁר דִּבֶּר בְּפִיו אֵת דָּוִיד אָבִי וּבְיָדָיו מִלֵּא לֵאמֹר: 5 מִן־הַיּוֹם אֲשֶׁר הוֹצֵאתִי אֶת־עַמִּי מֵאֶרֶץ מִצְרַיִם לֹא־בָחַרְתִּי בְעִיר מִכֹּל שִׁבְטֵי יִשְׂרָאֵל לִבְנוֹת בַּיִת לִהְיוֹת שְׁמִי שָׁם וְלֹא־בָחַרְתִּי בְאִישׁ לִהְיוֹת נָגִיד עַל־עַמִּי יִשְׂרָאֵל: 6 וָאֶבְחַר בִּירוּשָׁלַ͏ִם לִהְיוֹת שְׁמִי שָׁם וָאֶבְחַר בְּדָוִיד לִהְיוֹת עַל־עַמִּי יִשְׂרָאֵל: 7 וַיְהִי עִם־לְבַב דָּוִיד אָבִי לִבְנוֹת בַּיִת לְשֵׁם יְהוָה אֱלֹהֵי יִשְׂרָאֵל: 8 וַיֹּאמֶר יְהוָה אֶל־דָּוִיד אָבִי יַעַן אֲשֶׁר הָיָה עִם־לְבָבְךָ לִבְנוֹת בַּיִת לִשְׁמִי הֱטִיבוֹתָ כִּי הָיָה עִם־לְבָבֶךָ: 9 רַק אַתָּה לֹא תִבְנֶה הַבָּיִת כִּי בִנְךָ הַיּוֹצֵא מֵחֲלָצֶיךָ הוּא־יִבְנֶה הַבַּיִת לִשְׁמִי: 10 וַיָּקֶם יְהוָה אֶת־דְּבָרוֹ אֲשֶׁר דִּבֵּר וָאָקוּם תַּחַת דָּוִיד אָבִי וָאֵשֵׁב ׀ עַל־כִּסֵּא יִשְׂרָאֵל כַּאֲשֶׁר דִּבֶּר יְהוָה וָאֶבְנֶה הַבַּיִת לְשֵׁם יְהוָה אֱלֹהֵי יִשְׂרָאֵל: 11 וָאָשִׂים שָׁם אֶת־הָאָרוֹן אֲשֶׁר־שָׁם בְּרִית יְהוָה אֲשֶׁר כָּרַת עִם־בְּנֵי יִשְׂרָאֵל: 12 וַיַּעֲמֹד לִפְנֵי מִזְבַּח יְהוָה נֶגֶד כָּל־קְהַל יִשְׂרָאֵל וַיִּפְרֹשׂ כַּפָּיו: 13 כִּי־עָשָׂה שְׁלֹמֹה כִּיּוֹר נְחֹשֶׁת וַיִּתְּנֵהוּ בְּתוֹךְ הָעֲזָרָה חָמֵשׁ אַמּוֹת אָרְכּוֹ וְחָמֵשׁ אַמּוֹת רָחְבּוֹ וְאַמּוֹת שָׁלוֹשׁ קוֹמָתוֹ וַיַּעֲמֹד עָלָיו וַיִּבְרַךְ עַל־בִּרְכָּיו נֶגֶד כָּל־קְהַל יִשְׂרָאֵל וַיִּפְרֹשׂ כַּפָּיו הַשָּׁמָיְמָה: 14 וַיֹּאמַר יְהוָה אֱלֹהֵי יִשְׂרָאֵל אֵין־כָּמוֹךָ אֱלֹהִים בַּשָּׁמַיִם וּבָאָרֶץ שֹׁמֵר הַבְּרִית וְהַחֶסֶד לַעֲבָדֶיךָ הַהֹלְכִים לְפָנֶיךָ בְּכָל־לִבָּם: 15 אֲשֶׁר שָׁמַרְתָּ לְעַבְדְּךָ דָּוִיד אָבִי אֵת אֲשֶׁר־דִּבַּרְתָּ לוֹ וַתְּדַבֵּר בְּפִיךָ וּבְיָדְךָ מִלֵּאתָ כַּיּוֹם הַזֶּה: 16 וְעַתָּה יְהוָה ׀

b-b   Lit. "who spoke with His own mouth a promise to my father David and has fulfilled with His own hands."
c   Lit. "risen in place of."
d   Meaning of Heb. uncertain.

1959

that promise that You made to Your servant, my father David, 'You shall never lack a descendant in My sight sitting on the throne of Israel if only your children will look to their way and walk in the [path] of My teachings as you have walked before Me.' 17Now, therefore, O God of Israel, let the promise that You made to Your servant, my father David, be confirmed.

18"Does God really dwell with man on earth? Even the heavens to their uttermost reaches cannot contain You; how much less this House that I have built! 19Yet turn, O LORD my God, to the prayer and supplication of Your servant, and hear the cry and the prayer that Your servant offers to You. 20May Your eyes be open day and night toward this House, toward the place where You have resolved to make Your name abide; may You heed the prayers that Your servant offers toward this place. 21And when You hear the supplications that Your servant and Your people Israel offer toward this place, give heed in Your heavenly abode—give heed and pardon.

22"If a man commits an offense against his fellow, and an oath is exacted from him, causing him to utter an imprecation against himself, and he comes with his imprecation before Your altar in this House, 23may You hear in heaven and take action to judge Your servants, requiting him who is in the wrong by bringing down the punishment of his conduct on his head, vindicating him who is in the right by rewarding him according to his righteousness.

24"Should Your people Israel be defeated by an enemy because they have sinned against You, and then once again acknowledge Your name and offer prayer and supplication to You in this House, 25may You hear in heaven and pardon the sin of Your people Israel, and restore them to the land that You gave to them and to their fathers.

אֱלֹהֵ֣י יִשְׂרָאֵ֔ל שְׁמֹר֙ לְעַבְדְּךָ֤ דָוִיד֙ אָבִ֔י אֵ֚ת אֲשֶׁ֣ר דִּבַּ֣רְתָּ לּ֔וֹ לֵאמֹ֕ר לֹא־יִכָּרֵ֨ת לְךָ֥ אִ֛ישׁ מִלְּפָנַ֔י יוֹשֵׁ֖ב עַל־כִּסֵּ֣א יִשְׂרָאֵ֑ל רַ֣ק אִם־ יִשְׁמְר֣וּ בָנֶ֗יךָ אֶת־דַּרְכָּם֙ לָלֶ֣כֶת בְּתֽוֹרָתִ֔י כַּאֲשֶׁ֥ר הָלַ֖כְתָּ לְפָנָֽי: 17 וְעַתָּ֛ה יְהוָ֥ה אֱלֹהֵ֖י יִשְׂרָאֵ֑ל יֵֽאָמֵן֙ דְּבָ֣רְךָ֔ אֲשֶׁ֥ר דִּבַּ֖רְתָּ לְעַבְדְּךָ֥ לְדָוִֽיד:

18 כִּ֚י הַֽאֻמְנָ֔ם יֵשֵׁ֧ב אֱלֹהִ֛ים אֶת־הָֽאָדָ֖ם עַל־הָאָ֑רֶץ הִ֠נֵּה שָׁמַ֜יִם וּשְׁמֵ֤י הַשָּׁמַ֙יִם֙ לֹ֣א יְכַלְכְּל֔וּךָ אַ֕ף כִּֽי־הַבַּ֥יִת הַזֶּ֖ה אֲשֶׁ֥ר בָּנִֽיתִי: 19 וּפָנִ֜יתָ אֶל־תְּפִלַּ֧ת עַבְדְּךָ֛ וְאֶל־תְּחִנָּת֖וֹ יְהוָ֣ה אֱלֹהָ֑י לִשְׁמֹ֤עַ אֶל־הָֽרִנָּה֙ וְאֶל־ הַתְּפִלָּ֔ה אֲשֶׁ֥ר עַבְדְּךָ֖ מִתְפַּלֵּ֥ל לְפָנֶֽיךָ: 20 לִהְי֨וֹת עֵינֶ֜יךָ פְתֻח֤וֹת אֶל־הַבַּ֣יִת הַזֶּ֗ה יוֹמָ֣ם וָלַ֔יְלָה אֶל־הַ֨מָּק֔וֹם אֲשֶׁ֣ר אָמַ֔רְתָּ לָשׂ֥וּם שִׁמְךָ֖ שָׁ֑ם לִשְׁמ֙וֹעַ֙ אֶל־הַתְּפִלָּ֔ה אֲשֶׁ֣ר יִתְפַּלֵּ֣ל עַבְדְּךָ֔ אֶל־הַמָּק֖וֹם הַזֶּֽה: 21 וְשָׁ֣מַעְתָּ֔ אֶל־תַּחֲנוּנֵ֛י עַבְדְּךָ֥ וְעַמְּךָ֖ יִשְׂרָאֵ֑ל אֲשֶׁ֥ר יִֽתְפַּֽלְל֖וּ אֶל־הַמָּק֣וֹם הַזֶּ֑ה וְ֠אַתָּה תִּשְׁמַ֞ע מִמְּק֤וֹם שִׁבְתְּךָ֙ מִן־הַשָּׁמַ֔יִם וְשָׁמַעְתָּ֖ וְסָלָֽחְתָּ:

22 אִם־יֶֽחֱטָ֥א אִישׁ֙ לְרֵעֵ֔הוּ וְנָֽשָׁא*־ב֖וֹ אָלָ֣ה לְהַֽאֲלֹת֑וֹ וּבָ֣א אָלָ֗ה לִפְנֵ֛י מִֽזְבַּחֲךָ֖ בַּבַּ֥יִת הַזֶּֽה: 23 וְאַתָּ֣ה ׀ תִּשְׁמַ֣ע מִן־הַשָּׁמַ֗יִם וְעָשִׂ֙יתָ֙ וְשָׁפַטְתָּ֣ אֶת־עֲבָדֶ֔יךָ לְהָשִׁ֣יב לְרָשָׁ֔ע לָתֵ֥ת דַּרְכּ֖וֹ בְּרֹאשׁ֑וֹ וּלְהַצְדִּ֣יק צַדִּ֔יק לָ֥תֶת ל֖וֹ כְּצִדְקָתֽוֹ: ס

24 וְֽאִם־יִנָּגֵ֞ף עַמְּךָ֧ יִשְׂרָאֵ֛ל לִפְנֵ֥י אוֹיֵ֖ב כִּ֣י יֶחֶטְאוּ־לָ֑ךְ וְשָׁ֙בוּ֙ וְהוֹד֣וּ אֶת־שְׁמֶ֔ךָ וְהִתְפַּֽלְל֧וּ וְהִֽתְחַנְּנ֛וּ לְפָנֶ֖יךָ בַּבַּ֥יִת הַזֶּֽה: 25 וְאַתָּה֙ תִּשְׁמַ֣ע מִן־הַשָּׁמַ֔יִם וְסָ֣לַחְתָּ֔ לְחַטַּ֖את עַמְּךָ֣ יִשְׂרָאֵ֑ל וַהֲשֵֽׁיבוֹתָ֞ם אֶל־הָ֣אֲדָמָ֔ה אֲשֶׁר־נָתַ֥תָּה לָהֶ֖ם וְלַֽאֲבֹתֵיהֶֽם: פ

v. 22. בנוסח אחר "וְנָשָׁא", כלומר בסימן השמאלית

26"Should the heavens be shut up and there be no rain because they have sinned against You, and then they pray toward this place and acknowledge Your name and repent of their sins, because You humbled them, 27may You hear in heaven and pardon the sin of Your servants, Your people Israel, when You have shown them the proper way in which they are to walk, and send down rain upon the land that You gave to Your people as their heritage. 28So, too, if there is a famine in the land, if there is pestilence, blight, mildew, locusts, or caterpillars, or if an enemy oppresses them in any of the settlements of their land.

"In any plague and in any disease, 29any prayer or supplication offered by any person among all Your people Israel—each of whom knows his affliction and his pain—when he spreads forth his hands toward this House, 30may You hear in Your heavenly abode, and pardon. Deal with each man according to his ways as You know his heart to be—for You alone know the hearts of all men—31so that they may revere You all the days that they live on the land that You gave to our fathers.

32"Or if a foreigner who is not of Your people Israel comes from a distant land for the sake of Your great name, Your mighty hand, and Your outstretched arm, if he comes to pray toward this House, 33may You hear in Your heavenly abode and grant whatever the foreigner appeals to You for. Thus all the peoples of the earth will know Your name and revere You, as does Your people Israel; and they will recognize that Your name is attached to this House that I have built.

34"When Your people take the field against their enemies in a campaign on which You send them, and they pray to You in the direction of the city which You have chosen and the House which I have built to Your name, 35may You

כו בְּהֵעָצֵר הַשָּׁמַיִם וְלֹא־יִהְיֶה מָטָר כִּי יֶחֶטְאוּ־לָךְ וְהִתְפַּלְלוּ אֶל־הַמָּקוֹם הַזֶּה וְהוֹדוּ אֶת־שְׁמֶךָ מֵחַטָּאתָם יְשׁוּבוּן כִּי תַעֲנֵם: כז וְאַתָּה ׀ תִּשְׁמַע הַשָּׁמַיִם וְסָלַחְתָּ לְחַטַּאת עֲבָדֶיךָ וְעַמְּךָ יִשְׂרָאֵל כִּי תוֹרֵם אֶל־הַדֶּרֶךְ הַטּוֹבָה אֲשֶׁר יֵלְכוּ־בָהּ וְנָתַתָּה מָטָר עַל־אַרְצְךָ אֲשֶׁר־נָתַתָּה לְעַמְּךָ לְנַחֲלָה: ס כח רָעָב כִּי־יִהְיֶה בָאָרֶץ דֶּבֶר כִּי־יִהְיֶה שִׁדָּפוֹן וְיֵרָקוֹן אַרְבֶּה וְחָסִיל כִּי יִהְיֶה כִּי יָצַר־לוֹ אוֹיְבָיו בְּאֶרֶץ שְׁעָרָיו כָּל־נֶגַע וְכָל־מַחֲלָה: כט כָּל־תְּפִלָּה כָל־תְּחִנָּה אֲשֶׁר יִהְיֶה לְכָל־הָאָדָם וּלְכֹל עַמְּךָ יִשְׂרָאֵל אֲשֶׁר יֵדְעוּ אִישׁ נִגְעוֹ וּמַכְאֹבוֹ וּפָרַשׂ כַּפָּיו אֶל־הַבַּיִת הַזֶּה: ל וְאַתָּה תִּשְׁמַע מִן־הַשָּׁמַיִם מְכוֹן שִׁבְתֶּךָ וְסָלַחְתָּ וְנָתַתָּה לָאִישׁ כְּכָל־דְּרָכָיו אֲשֶׁר תֵּדַע אֶת־לְבָבוֹ כִּי אַתָּה לְבַדְּךָ יָדַעְתָּ אֶת־לְבַב בְּנֵי הָאָדָם: לא לְמַעַן יִירָאוּךָ לָלֶכֶת בִּדְרָכֶיךָ כָּל־הַיָּמִים אֲשֶׁר־הֵם חַיִּים עַל־פְּנֵי הָאֲדָמָה אֲשֶׁר נָתַתָּה לַאֲבֹתֵינוּ: ס לב וְגַם אֶל־הַנָּכְרִי אֲשֶׁר לֹא מֵעַמְּךָ יִשְׂרָאֵל הוּא וּבָא ׀ מֵאֶרֶץ רְחוֹקָה לְמַעַן שִׁמְךָ הַגָּדוֹל וְיָדְךָ הַחֲזָקָה וּזְרוֹעֲךָ הַנְּטוּיָה וּבָאוּ וְהִתְפַּלְלוּ אֶל־הַבַּיִת הַזֶּה: לג וְאַתָּה תִּשְׁמַע מִן־הַשָּׁמַיִם מִמְּכוֹן שִׁבְתֶּךָ וְעָשִׂיתָ כְּכֹל אֲשֶׁר־יִקְרָא אֵלֶיךָ הַנָּכְרִי לְמַעַן יֵדְעוּ כָל־עַמֵּי הָאָרֶץ אֶת־שְׁמֶךָ וּלְיִרְאָה אֹתְךָ כְּעַמְּךָ יִשְׂרָאֵל וְלָדַעַת כִּי־שִׁמְךָ נִקְרָא עַל־הַבַּיִת הַזֶּה אֲשֶׁר בָּנִיתִי: לד כִּי־יֵצֵא עַמְּךָ לַמִּלְחָמָה עַל־אוֹיְבָיו בַּדֶּרֶךְ אֲשֶׁר תִּשְׁלָחֵם וְהִתְפַּלְלוּ אֵלֶיךָ דֶּרֶךְ הָעִיר הַזֹּאת אֲשֶׁר בָּחַרְתָּ בָּהּ וְהַבַּיִת אֲשֶׁר־בָּנִיתִי לִשְׁמֶךָ: לה וְשָׁמַעְתָּ

hear in heaven their prayer and supplication and uphold their cause.

36"When they sin against You—for there is no person who does not sin—and You are angry with them and deliver them to the enemy, and their captors carry them off to an enemy land, near or far; 37and they take it to heart in the land to which they have been carried off, and repent and make supplication to You in the land of their captivity, saying, 'We have sinned, we have acted perversely, we have acted wickedly,' 38and they turn back to You with all their heart and soul, in the land of their captivity where they were carried off, and pray in the direction of their land which You gave to their fathers and the city which You have chosen, and toward the House which I have built for Your name—39may You hear their prayer and supplication in Your heavenly abode, uphold their cause, and pardon Your people who have sinned against You. 40Now My God, may Your eyes be open and Your ears attentive to prayer from this place, and now,

41Advance, O Lord God, to your resting-place,

You and Your mighty Ark.

Your priests, O Lord God, are clothed in triumph;

Your loyal ones will rejoice in [Your] goodness.

42O Lord God,

do not reject Your anointed one;

remember the loyalty of Your servant David."

7 ªWhen Solomon finished praying, fire descended from heaven and consumed the burnt offering and the sacrifices, and the glory of the Lord filled the House. 2The priests could not enter the House of the Lord, for the glory of the Lord filled the House of the Lord. 3All the

מִן־הַשָּׁמַיִם אֶת־תְּפִלָּתָם וְאֶת־תְּחִנָּתָם וְעָשִׂיתָ מִשְׁפָּטָם:

36 כִּי יֶחֶטְאוּ־לָךְ כִּי אֵין אָדָם אֲשֶׁר לֹא־יֶחֱטָא וְאָנַפְתָּ בָם וּנְתַתָּם לִפְנֵי אוֹיֵב וְשָׁבוּם שֹׁבֵיהֶם אֶל־אֶרֶץ רְחוֹקָה אוֹ קְרוֹבָה: 37 וְהֵשִׁיבוּ אֶל־לְבָבָם בָּאָרֶץ אֲשֶׁר נִשְׁבּוּ־שָׁם וְשָׁבוּ ׀ וְהִתְחַנְּנוּ אֵלֶיךָ בְּאֶרֶץ שִׁבְיָם לֵאמֹר חָטָאנוּ הֶעֱוִינוּ וְרָשָׁעְנוּ: 38 וְשָׁבוּ אֵלֶיךָ בְּכָל־לִבָּם וּבְכָל־נַפְשָׁם בְּאֶרֶץ שִׁבְיָם אֲשֶׁר־שָׁבוּ אֹתָם וְהִתְפַּלְלוּ דֶּרֶךְ אַרְצָם אֲשֶׁר נָתַתָּה לַאֲבוֹתָם וְהָעִיר אֲשֶׁר בָּחַרְתָּ וְלַבַּיִת אֲשֶׁר־בָּנִיתִי לִשְׁמֶךָ: 39 וְשָׁמַעְתָּ מִן־הַשָּׁמַיִם מִמְּכוֹן שִׁבְתְּךָ אֶת־תְּפִלָּתָם וְאֶת־תְּחִנֹּתֵיהֶם וְעָשִׂיתָ מִשְׁפָּטָם וְסָלַחְתָּ לְעַמְּךָ אֲשֶׁר חָטְאוּ־לָךְ: 40 עַתָּה אֱלֹהַי יִהְיוּ־נָא עֵינֶיךָ פְּתֻחוֹת וְאָזְנֶיךָ קַשֻּׁבוֹת לִתְפִלַּת הַמָּקוֹם הַזֶּה: ס 41 וְעַתָּה

קוּמָה יְהוָה אֱלֹהִים לְנוּחֶךָ אַתָּה וַאֲרוֹן עֻזֶּךָ

כֹּהֲנֶיךָ יְהוָה אֱלֹהִים יִלְבְּשׁוּ תְשׁוּעָה וַחֲסִידֶיךָ יִשְׂמְחוּ בַטּוֹב:

42 יְהוָה אֱלֹהִים אַל־תָּשֵׁב פְּנֵי מְשִׁיחֶיךָ* זָכְרָה לְחַסְדֵי דָּוִיד עַבְדֶּךָ: פ

ז וּכְכַלּוֹת שְׁלֹמֹה לְהִתְפַּלֵּל וְהָאֵשׁ יָרְדָה מֵהַשָּׁמַיִם וַתֹּאכַל הָעֹלָה וְהַזְּבָחִים וּכְבוֹד יְהוָה מָלֵא אֶת־הַבָּיִת: 2 וְלֹא יָכְלוּ הַכֹּהֲנִים לָבוֹא אֶל־בֵּית יְהוָה כִּי־מָלֵא כְבוֹד־יְהוָה אֶת־בֵּית יְהוָה: 3 וְכֹל ׀ בְּנֵי

Israelites witnessed the descent of the fire and the glory of the LORD on the House; they knelt with their faces to the ground and prostrated themselves, praising the LORD, "For He is good, for His steadfast love is eternal."

⁴Then the king and all the people offered sacrifices before the LORD. ⁵King Solomon offered as sacrifices 22,000 oxen and 120,000 sheep; thus the king and all the people dedicated the House of God. ⁶The priests stood at their watches; the Levites with the instruments for the LORD's music that King David had made to praise the LORD, "For His steadfast love is eternal," by means of the psalms of David that they knew. The priests opposite them blew trumpets while all Israel were standing.

⁷Solomon consecrated the center of the court in front of the House of the LORD, because he presented there the burnt offerings and the fat parts of the offerings of well-being, since the bronze altar that Solomon had made was not able to hold the burnt offerings, the meal offerings, and the fat parts. ⁸At that time Solomon kept the Feast for seven days—all Israel with him—a great assemblage from Lebo-hamath to the Wadi of Egypt.

⁹On the eighth day they held a solemn gathering; they observed the dedication of the altar seven days, and the Feast seven days. ¹⁰On the twenty-third day of the seventh month he dismissed the people to their homes, rejoicing and in good spirits over the goodness that the LORD had shown to David and Solomon and His people Israel.

¹¹Thus Solomon finished building the House of the LORD and the royal palace; Solomon succeeded in everything he had set his heart on accomplishing with regard to the House of the LORD and his palace. ¹²The LORD appeared to Solomon at night and said to him, "I have heard your prayer and have chosen this site as My

יִשְׂרָאֵל רֹאִים בְּרֶ֫דֶת הָאֵשׁ וּכְב֣וֹד יְהוָ֔ה עַל־הַבָּ֑יִת וַיִּכְרְעוּ֩ אַפַּ֨יִם אַ֤רְצָה עַל־הָרִֽצְפָה֙ וַיִּֽשְׁתַּֽחֲו֔וּ וְהוֹד֥וֹת לַֽיהוָ֖ה כִּ֣י ט֑וֹב כִּ֥י לְעוֹלָ֖ם חַסְדּֽוֹ׃

⁴ וְהַמֶּ֥לֶךְ וְכָל־הָעָ֛ם זֹבְחִ֥ים זֶ֖בַח לִפְנֵ֥י יְהוָֽה׃ ס ⁵ וַיִּזְבַּ֞ח הַמֶּ֣לֶךְ שְׁלֹמֹה֮ אֶת־זֶ֣בַח הַבָּקָר֒ עֶשְׂרִ֣ים וּשְׁנַ֨יִם֙ אֶ֔לֶף וְצֹ֕אן מֵאָ֥ה וְעֶשְׂרִ֖ים אָ֑לֶף וַֽיַּחְנְכוּ֙ אֶת־בֵּ֣ית הָֽאֱלֹהִ֔ים הַמֶּ֖לֶךְ וְכָל־הָעָֽם׃ ⁶ וְהַכֹּֽהֲנִ֞ים עַל־מִשְׁמְרוֹתָ֣ם עֹמְדִ֗ים וְהַלְוִיִּ֞ם בִּכְלֵי־שִׁ֣יר יְהוָ֗ה אֲשֶׁ֨ר עָשָׂ֜ה דָּוִ֤יד הַמֶּ֙לֶךְ֙ לְהֹד֣וֹת לַֽיהוָ֗ה כִּֽי־לְעוֹלָם֙ חַסְדּ֔וֹ בְּהַלֵּ֥ל דָּוִ֖יד בְּיָדָ֑ם וְהַכֹּהֲנִים֙ מַחְצְרִ֣ים נֶגְדָּ֔ם וְכָל־יִשְׂרָאֵ֖ל עֹמְדִֽים׃ ס

⁷ וַיְקַדֵּ֣שׁ שְׁלֹמֹ֗ה אֶת־תּ֤וֹךְ הֶֽחָצֵר֙ אֲשֶׁר֙ לִפְנֵ֣י בֵית־יְהוָ֔ה כִּֽי־עָ֥שָׂה שָׁ֖ם הָֽעֹל֑וֹת וְאֵ֖ת חֶלְבֵ֣י הַשְּׁלָמִ֑ים כִּֽי־מִזְבַּ֤ח הַנְּחֹ֙שֶׁת֙ אֲשֶׁ֣ר עָשָׂ֣ה שְׁלֹמֹ֔ה לֹ֣א יָכ֗וֹל לְהָכִ֛יל אֶת־הָעֹלָ֥ה וְאֶת־הַמִּנְחָ֖ה וְאֶת־הַחֲלָבִֽים׃ ⁸ וַיַּ֣עַשׂ שְׁלֹמֹ֣ה אֶת־הֶ֠חָג בָּעֵ֨ת הַהִ֜יא שִׁבְעַ֤ת יָמִים֙ וְכָל־יִשְׂרָאֵ֣ל עִמּ֔וֹ קָהָ֖ל גָּד֣וֹל מְאֹ֑ד מִלְּב֥וֹא חֲמָ֖ת עַד־נַ֥חַל מִצְרָֽיִם׃ ⁹ וַֽיַּעֲשׂ֞וּ בַּיּ֧וֹם הַשְּׁמִינִ֛י עֲצָ֖רֶת כִּ֣י ׀ חֲנֻכַּ֣ת הַמִּזְבֵּ֗חַ עָשׂוּ֙ שִׁבְעַ֣ת יָמִ֔ים וְהֶחָ֖ג שִׁבְעַ֥ת יָמִֽים׃ ¹⁰ וּבְי֨וֹם עֶשְׂרִ֤ים וּשְׁלֹשָׁה֙ לַחֹ֣דֶשׁ הַשְּׁבִיעִ֔י שִׁלַּ֥ח אֶת־הָעָ֖ם לְאׇהֳלֵיהֶ֑ם שְׂמֵחִים֙ וְט֣וֹבֵי לֵ֔ב עַל־הַטּוֹבָ֗ה אֲשֶׁ֨ר עָשָׂ֤ה יְהוָה֙ לְדָוִ֣יד וְלִשְׁלֹמֹ֔ה וּלְיִשְׂרָאֵ֖ל עַמּֽוֹ׃ ¹¹ וַיְכַ֧ל שְׁלֹמֹ֛ה אֶת־בֵּ֥ית יְהוָ֖ה וְאֶת־בֵּ֣ית הַמֶּ֑לֶךְ וְאֵ֨ת כָּל־הַבָּ֜א עַל־לֵ֣ב שְׁלֹמֹ֗ה לַעֲשׂ֛וֹת בְּבֵית־יְהוָ֥ה וּבְבֵית֖וֹ הִצְלִֽיחַ׃ פ ¹² וַיֵּרָ֧א יְהוָ֛ה אֶל־שְׁלֹמֹ֖ה בַּלָּ֑יְלָה וַיֹּ֣אמֶר ל֗וֹ שָׁמַ֙עְתִּי֙ אֶת־תְּפִלָּתֶ֔ךָ וּבָחַ֥רְתִּי בַּמָּק֛וֹם

House of sacrifice. [13]If I shut up the heavens and there is no rain; if I command the locusts to ravage the land; or if I let loose pestilence against My people, [14]when My people, who bear My name, humble themselves, pray, and seek My favor and turn from their evil ways, I will hear in My heavenly abode and forgive their sins and heal their land. [15]Now My eyes will be open and My ears attentive to the prayers from this place. [16]And now I have chosen and consecrated this House that My name be there forever. My eyes and My heart shall always be there. [17]As for you, if you walk before Me as your father David walked before Me, doing all that I have commanded you, keeping My laws and rules, [18]then I will establish your royal throne over Israel forever, in accordance with the Covenant I made with your father David, saying, 'You shall never lack a descendant ruling over Israel.' [19]But if you turn away from Me and forsake My laws and commandments that I set before you, and go and serve other gods and worship them, [20]then I will uproot them[b] from My land that I gave them, and this House that I consecrated to My name I shall cast out of my sight, and make it a proverb and a byword among all peoples. [21]And as for this House, once so exalted, everyone passing by it shall be appalled and say, 'Why did the Lord do thus to this land and to this House?' [22]And the reply will be, 'It is because they forsook the Lord God of their fathers who freed them from the land of Egypt, and adopted other gods and worshiped them and served them; therefore He brought all this calamity upon them.'"

8 [a]At the end of twenty years, during which Solomon constructed the House of the Lord and his palace—[2]Solomon also rebuilt the cities

הַזֶּה לִי לְבֵית זָבַח: 13 הֵן אֶעֱצֹר הַשָּׁמַיִם
וְלֹא־יִהְיֶה מָטָר וְהֵן־אֲצַוֶּה עַל־חָגָב
לֶאֱכוֹל הָאָרֶץ וְאִם־אֲשַׁלַּח דֶּבֶר בְּעַמִּי:
14 וְיִכָּנְעוּ עַמִּי אֲשֶׁר נִקְרָא־שְׁמִי עֲלֵיהֶם
וְיִתְפַּלְלוּ וִיבַקְשׁוּ פָנַי וְיָשֻׁבוּ מִדַּרְכֵיהֶם
הָרָעִים וַאֲנִי אֶשְׁמַע מִן־הַשָּׁמַיִם וְאֶסְלַח
לְחַטָּאתָם וְאֶרְפָּא אֶת־אַרְצָם: 15 עַתָּה
עֵינַי יִהְיוּ פְתֻחוֹת וְאָזְנַי קַשֻּׁבוֹת לִתְפִלַּת
הַמָּקוֹם הַזֶּה: 16 וְעַתָּה בָּחַרְתִּי וְהִקְדַּשְׁתִּי
אֶת־הַבַּיִת הַזֶּה לִהְיוֹת־שְׁמִי שָׁם עַד־
עוֹלָם וְהָיוּ עֵינַי וְלִבִּי שָׁם כָּל־הַיָּמִים:
17 וְאַתָּה אִם־תֵּלֵךְ לְפָנַי כַּאֲשֶׁר הָלַךְ דָּוִיד
אָבִיךָ וְלַעֲשׂוֹת כְּכֹל אֲשֶׁר צִוִּיתִיךָ וְחֻקַּי
וּמִשְׁפָּטַי תִּשְׁמוֹר: 18 וַהֲקִימוֹתִי אֵת כִּסֵּא
מַלְכוּתֶךָ כַּאֲשֶׁר כָּרַתִּי לְדָוִיד אָבִיךָ לֵאמֹר
לֹא־יִכָּרֵת לְךָ אִישׁ מוֹשֵׁל בְּיִשְׂרָאֵל:
19 וְאִם־תְּשׁוּבוּן אַתֶּם וַעֲזַבְתֶּם חֻקּוֹתַי
וּמִצְוֺתַי אֲשֶׁר נָתַתִּי לִפְנֵיכֶם וַהֲלַכְתֶּם
וַעֲבַדְתֶּם אֱלֹהִים אֲחֵרִים וְהִשְׁתַּחֲוִיתֶם
לָהֶם: 20 וּנְתַשְׁתִּים מֵעַל אַדְמָתִי אֲשֶׁר
נָתַתִּי לָהֶם וְאֶת־הַבַּיִת הַזֶּה אֲשֶׁר
הִקְדַּשְׁתִּי לִשְׁמִי אַשְׁלִיךְ מֵעַל פָּנָי וְאֶתְּנֶנּוּ
לְמָשָׁל וְלִשְׁנִינָה בְּכָל־הָעַמִּים: 21 וְהַבַּיִת
הַזֶּה אֲשֶׁר הָיָה עֶלְיוֹן לְכָל־עֹבֵר עָלָיו
יִשֹּׁם וְאָמַר בַּמֶּה עָשָׂה יְהוָה כָּכָה לָאָרֶץ
הַזֹּאת וְלַבַּיִת הַזֶּה: 22 וְאָמְרוּ עַל אֲשֶׁר
עָזְבוּ אֶת־יְהוָה ׀ אֱלֹהֵי אֲבֹתֵיהֶם אֲשֶׁר
הוֹצִיאָם מֵאֶרֶץ מִצְרַיִם וַיַּחֲזִיקוּ בֵּאלֹהִים
אֲחֵרִים וַיִּשְׁתַּחֲווּ לָהֶם וַיַּעַבְדוּם עַל־כֵּן
הֵבִיא עֲלֵיהֶם אֵת כָּל־הָרָעָה הַזֹּאת: פ

ח וַיְהִי מִקֵּץ ׀ עֶשְׂרִים שָׁנָה אֲשֶׁר בָּנָה
שְׁלֹמֹה אֶת־בֵּית יְהוָה וְאֶת־בֵּיתוֹ:
2 וְהֶעָרִים אֲשֶׁר נָתַן חוּרָם לִשְׁלֹמֹה בָּנָה

---

b   I.e., Israel; cf. 1 Kings 9.7.

a   Cf. 1 Kings 9.10–28.

that Huram had given to him,*b* and settled Israelites in them—³Solomon marched against Hamath-zobah and overpowered it. ⁴He built Tadmor in the desert and all the garrison towns that he built in Hamath. ⁵He built Upper Beth-horon and Lower Beth-horon as fortified cities with walls, gates, and bars, ⁶as well as Baalath and all of Solomon's garrison towns, chariot towns, and cavalry towns—everything that Solomon desired to build in Jerusalem and in the Lebanon, and throughout the territory that he ruled. ⁷All the people that were left of the Hittites, Amorites, Perizzites, Hivites, and Jebusites, none of whom were of Israelite stock—⁸those of their descendants who were left after them in the land, whom the Israelites had not annihilated—these Solomon subjected to forced labor, as is still the case. ⁹But the Israelites, none of whom Solomon enslaved for his works, served as soldiers and as his chief officers, and as commanders of his chariotry and cavalry. ¹⁰These were King Solomon's prefects—250 foremen over the people. ¹¹Solomon brought up Pharaoh's daughter from the City of David to the palace that he had built for her, for he said, "No wife of mine shall dwell in a palace of King David of Israel, for [the area] is sacred since the Ark of the LORD has entered it."

¹²At that time, Solomon offered burnt offerings on the altar that he had built in front of the porch. ¹³What was due for each day he sacrificed according to the commandment of Moses for the sabbaths, the new moons, and the thrice-yearly festivals—the Feast of Unleavened Bread, the Feast of Weeks, and the Feast of Booths. ¹⁴Following the prescription of his father David, he set up the divisions of the priests for their duties, and the Levites for their watches, to praise and to serve alongside the priests, according to each day's requirement,

---

b Lit. "Solomon."

שְׁלֹמֹה אֹתָם וַיּוֹשֶׁב שָׁם אֶת־בְּנֵי יִשְׂרָאֵל׃
3 וַיֵּלֶךְ שְׁלֹמֹה חֲמָת צוֹבָה וַיֶּחֱזַק עָלֶיהָ׃
4 וַיִּבֶן אֶת־תַּדְמֹר בַּמִּדְבָּר וְאֵת כָּל־עָרֵי הַמִּסְכְּנוֹת אֲשֶׁר בָּנָה בַּחֲמָת׃ 5 וַיִּבֶן אֶת־בֵּית חוֹרוֹן הָעֶלְיוֹן וְאֶת־בֵּית חוֹרוֹן הַתַּחְתּוֹן עָרֵי מָצוֹר חוֹמוֹת דְּלָתַיִם וּבְרִיחַ׃ 6 וְאֶת־בַּעֲלָת וְאֵת כָּל־עָרֵי הַמִּסְכְּנוֹת אֲשֶׁר הָיוּ לִשְׁלֹמֹה וְאֵת כָּל־עָרֵי הָרֶכֶב וְאֵת עָרֵי הַפָּרָשִׁים וְאֵת ׀ כָּל־חֵשֶׁק שְׁלֹמֹה אֲשֶׁר חָשַׁק לִבְנוֹת בִּירוּשָׁלַ͏ִם וּבַלְּבָנוֹן וּבְכֹל אֶרֶץ מֶמְשַׁלְתּוֹ׃ 7 כָּל־הָעָם הַנּוֹתָר מִן־הַחִתִּי וְהָאֱמֹרִי וְהַפְּרִזִּי וְהַחִוִּי וְהַיְבוּסִי אֲשֶׁר לֹא מִיִּשְׂרָאֵל הֵמָּה׃ 8 מִן־בְּנֵיהֶם אֲשֶׁר נוֹתְרוּ אַחֲרֵיהֶם בָּאָרֶץ אֲשֶׁר לֹא־כִלּוּם בְּנֵי יִשְׂרָאֵל וַיַּעֲלֵם שְׁלֹמֹה לְמַס עַד הַיּוֹם הַזֶּה׃ 9 וּמִן־בְּנֵי יִשְׂרָאֵל אֲשֶׁר לֹא־נָתַן שְׁלֹמֹה לַעֲבָדִים לִמְלַאכְתּוֹ כִּי־הֵמָּה אַנְשֵׁי מִלְחָמָה וְשָׂרֵי שָׁלִישָׁיו וְשָׂרֵי רִכְבּוֹ וּפָרָשָׁיו׃ פ
10 וְאֵלֶּה שָׂרֵי הַנִּצָּבִים אֲשֶׁר־לַמֶּלֶךְ שְׁלֹמֹה חֲמִשִּׁים וּמָאתָיִם הָרֹדִים בָּעָם׃ 11 וְאֶת־בַּת־פַּרְעֹה הֶעֱלָה שְׁלֹמֹה מֵעִיר דָּוִיד לַבַּיִת אֲשֶׁר בָּנָה־לָהּ כִּי אָמַר לֹא־תֵשֵׁב אִשָּׁה לִי בְּבֵית דָּוִיד מֶלֶךְ־יִשְׂרָאֵל כִּי־קֹדֶשׁ הֵמָּה אֲשֶׁר־בָּאָה אֲלֵיהֶם אֲרוֹן יְהֹוָה׃ פ
12 אָז הֶעֱלָה שְׁלֹמֹה עֹלוֹת לַיהֹוָה עַל מִזְבַּח יְהֹוָה אֲשֶׁר בָּנָה לִפְנֵי הָאוּלָם׃ 13 וּבִדְבַר־יוֹם בְּיוֹם לְהַעֲלוֹת כְּמִצְוַת מֹשֶׁה לַשַּׁבָּתוֹת וְלֶחֳדָשִׁים וְלַמּוֹעֲדוֹת שָׁלוֹשׁ פְּעָמִים בַּשָּׁנָה בְּחַג הַמַּצּוֹת וּבְחַג הַשָּׁבֻעוֹת וּבְחַג הַסֻּכּוֹת׃ 14 וַיַּעֲמֵד כְּמִשְׁפַּט דָּוִיד־אָבִיו אֶת־מַחְלְקוֹת הַכֹּהֲנִים עַל־עֲבֹדָתָם וְהַלְוִיִּם עַל־מִשְׁמְרוֹתָם לְהַלֵּל וּלְשָׁרֵת נֶגֶד הַכֹּהֲנִים לִדְבַר־יוֹם בְּיוֹמוֹ וְהַשּׁוֹעֲרִים בְּמַחְלְקוֹתָם

and the gatekeepers in their watches, gate by gate, for such was the commandment of David, the man of God. [15]They did not depart from the commandment of the king relating to the priests and the Levites in all these matters and also relating to the treasuries. [16]And all of Solomon's work was well executed from the day the House of the LORD was founded until the House of the LORD was completed to perfection.

[17]At that time Solomon went to Ezion-geber and to Eloth on the seacoast of the land of Edom. [18]Huram sent him, under the charge of servants, a fleet with a crew of expert seamen; they went with Solomon's men to Ophir, and obtained gold there in the amount of 450 talents, which they brought to King Solomon.

9

[a]The queen of Sheba heard of Solomon's fame, and came to Jerusalem to test Solomon with hard questions, accompanied by a very large retinue, including camels bearing spices, a great quantity of gold, and precious stones. When she came to Solomon, she spoke to him of all that she had on her mind. [2]Solomon had answers for all her questions; there was nothing that Solomon did not know, nothing to which he could not give her an answer.

[3]When the queen of Sheba saw how wise Solomon was and the palace he had built, [4]the fare of his table, the seating of his courtiers, the service and attire of his attendants, his butlers and their attire, and the procession with which he went up to the House of the LORD, it took her breath away. [5]She said to the king, "What I heard in my own land about you and your wisdom was true. [6]I did not believe what they said until I came and saw with my own eyes that not even the half of your great wisdom had been described to me; you surpass the report that I heard. [7]How fortunate are your men and how

לְשֹׁעֵר וָשֹׁעֵר כִּי כֵן מִצְוַת דָּוִיד אִישׁ־
הָאֱלֹהִֽים׃ 15 וְלֹא סָרוּ מִצְוַת הַמֶּלֶךְ עַל־
הַכֹּהֲנִים וְהַלְוִיִּם לְכָל־דָּבָר וְלָאֹצָרֽוֹת׃
16 וַתִּכֹּן כָּל־מְלֶאכֶת שְׁלֹמֹה עַד־הַיּוֹם
מוּסַד בֵּית־יְהוָה וְעַד־כְּלֹתוֹ שָׁלֵם בֵּית
יְהוָֽה׃ ס
17 אָז הָלַךְ שְׁלֹמֹה לְעֶצְיֽוֹן־גֶּבֶר וְאֶל־
אֵילוֹת עַל־שְׂפַת הַיָּם בְּאֶרֶץ אֱדֽוֹם׃
18 וַיִּֽשְׁלַֽח־לוֹ חוּרָם בְּיַד־עֲבָדָיו אֳנִיּוֹת
אֳנִיּוֹת וַעֲבָדִים יוֹדְעֵי יָם וַיָּבֹאוּ עִם־עַבְדֵי
שְׁלֹמֹה אוֹפִירָה וַיִּקְחוּ מִשָּׁם אַרְבַּע־מֵאוֹת
וַחֲמִשִּׁים כִּכַּר זָהָב וַיָּבִיאוּ אֶל־הַמֶּלֶךְ
שְׁלֹמֹֽה׃ פ

ט וּמַֽלְכַּת־שְׁבָא שָׁמְעָה אֶת־שֵׁמַע
שְׁלֹמֹה וַתָּבוֹא לְנַסּוֹת אֶת־שְׁלֹמֹה
בְחִידוֹת בִּירֽוּשָׁלַ͏ִם בְּחַיִל כָּבֵד מְאֹד
וּגְמַלִּים נֹשְׂאִים בְּשָׂמִים וְזָהָב לָרֹב וְאֶבֶן
יְקָרָה וַתָּבוֹא אֶל־שְׁלֹמֹה וַתְּדַבֵּר עִמּוֹ אֵת
כָּל־אֲשֶׁר הָיָה עִם־לְבָבָֽהּ׃ 2 וַיַּגֶּד־לָהּ
שְׁלֹמֹה אֶת־כָּל־דְּבָרֶיהָ וְלֹא־נֶעְלַם דָּבָר
מִשְּׁלֹמֹה אֲשֶׁר לֹא הִגִּיד לָֽהּ׃
3 וַתֵּרֶא מַֽלְכַּת־שְׁבָא אֵת חָכְמַת שְׁלֹמֹה
וְהַבַּיִת אֲשֶׁר בָּנָֽה׃ 4 וּמַאֲכַל שֻׁלְחָנוֹ
וּמוֹשַׁב עֲבָדָיו וּמַעֲמַד מְשָׁרְתָיו
וּמַלְבּֽוּשֵׁיהֶם וּמַשְׁקָיו וּמַלְבּֽוּשֵׁיהֶם
וַעֲלִיָּתוֹ אֲשֶׁר יַעֲלֶה בֵּית יְהוָה וְלֹא־הָיָה
עוֹד בָּהּ רֽוּחַ׃ 5 וַתֹּאמֶר אֶל־הַמֶּלֶךְ אֱמֶת
הַדָּבָר אֲשֶׁר שָׁמַעְתִּי בְּאַרְצִי עַל־דְּבָרֶיךָ
וְעַל־חָכְמָתֶֽךָ׃ 6 וְלֹא־הֶאֱמַנְתִּי לְדִבְרֵיהֶם
עַד אֲשֶׁר־בָּאתִי וַתִּרְאֶינָה עֵינַי וְהִנֵּה לֹא
הֻגַּד־לִי חֲצִי מַרְבִּית חָכְמָתֶךָ יָסַפְתָּ עַל־
הַשְּׁמוּעָה אֲשֶׁר שָׁמָֽעְתִּי׃ 7 אַשְׁרֵי אֲנָשֶׁיךָ
וְאַשְׁרֵי עֲבָדֶיךָ אֵלֶּה הָעֹמְדִים לְפָנֶיךָ

a Cf. 1 Kings 10; 11.41–43.

fortunate are these courtiers of yours who are always in attendance on you and can hear your wisdom! 8Blessed is the LORD your God, who favored you and set you on His throne as a king before the LORD. It is because of your God's love for Israel and in order to establish them forever that He made you king over them to execute righteous justice."

9She presented the king with 120 talents of gold, and a vast quantity of spices and precious stones. There were no such spices as those which the queen of Sheba gave to King Solomon—10also, the servants of Huram and Solomon who brought gold from Ophir brought algum-wood and precious stones. 11The king made of the algum-wood ramps for the House of the LORD and for the royal palace, and lyres and harps for the musicians, whose like had never before been seen in the land of Judah—12King Solomon, in turn, gave the queen of Sheba everything she expressed a desire for, exceeding a return for what she had brought to the king. Then she and her courtiers left and returned to her own land.

13The gold that Solomon received every year weighed 666 gold talents, 14besides what traders and merchants brought, and the gold and silver that all the kings of Arabia and governors of the regions brought to Solomon. 15King Solomon made 200 shields of beaten gold—600 shekels of beaten gold for each shield, 16and 300 bucklers of beaten gold—300 [shekels] of gold for each buckler. The king placed them in the Lebanon Forest House. 17The king also made a large throne of ivory, overlaid with pure gold. 18Six steps led up to the throne; and the throne had a golden footstool attached to it, and arms on either side of the seat. Two lions stood beside the arms, 19and twelve lions stood on the six steps, six on either side. None such was ever

8 וִיהִי יְהוָה תָּמִיד וְשֹׁמְעִים אֶת־חָכְמָתֶךָ: אֱלֹהֶיךָ בָּרוּךְ אֲשֶׁר ׀ חָפֵץ בְּךָ לְתִתְּךָ עַל־כִּסְאוֹ לְמֶלֶךְ לַיהוָה אֱלֹהֶיךָ בְּאַהֲבַת אֱלֹהֶיךָ אֶת־יִשְׂרָאֵל לְהַעֲמִידוֹ לְעוֹלָם וַיִּתֶּנְךָ עֲלֵיהֶם לְמֶלֶךְ לַעֲשׂוֹת מִשְׁפָּט וּצְדָקָה:

9 וַתִּתֵּן לַמֶּלֶךְ מֵאָה וְעֶשְׂרִים ׀ כִּכַּר זָהָב וּבְשָׂמִים לָרֹב מְאֹד וְאֶבֶן יְקָרָה וְלֹא הָיָה כַּבֹּשֶׂם הַהוּא אֲשֶׁר־נָתְנָה מַלְכַּת־שְׁבָא לַמֶּלֶךְ שְׁלֹמֹה: 10 וְגַם־עַבְדֵי חִירָם חוּרָם וְעַבְדֵי שְׁלֹמֹה אֲשֶׁר־הֵבִיאוּ זָהָב מֵאוֹפִיר הֵבִיאוּ עֲצֵי אַלְגּוּמִּים וְאֶבֶן יְקָרָה: 11 וַיַּעַשׂ הַמֶּלֶךְ אֶת־עֲצֵי הָאַלְגּוּמִּים מְסִלּוֹת לְבֵית־יְהוָה וּלְבֵית הַמֶּלֶךְ וְכִנֹּרוֹת וּנְבָלִים לַשָּׁרִים וְלֹא־נִרְאוּ כָהֵם לְפָנִים בְּאֶרֶץ יְהוּדָה: 12 וְהַמֶּלֶךְ שְׁלֹמֹה נָתַן לְמַלְכַּת־שְׁבָא אֶת־כָּל־חֶפְצָהּ אֲשֶׁר שָׁאָלָה מִלְּבַד אֲשֶׁר־הֵבִיאָה אֶל־הַמֶּלֶךְ וַתַּהֲפֹךְ וַתֵּלֶךְ לְאַרְצָהּ הִיא וַעֲבָדֶיהָ: פ

13 וַיְהִי מִשְׁקַל הַזָּהָב אֲשֶׁר־בָּא לִשְׁלֹמֹה בְּשָׁנָה אֶחָת שֵׁשׁ מֵאוֹת וְשִׁשִּׁים וָשֵׁשׁ כִּכְּרֵי זָהָב: 14 לְבַד מֵאַנְשֵׁי הַתָּרִים וְהַסֹּחֲרִים מְבִיאִים וְכָל־מַלְכֵי עֲרַב וּפַחוֹת הָאָרֶץ מְבִיאִים זָהָב וָכֶסֶף לִשְׁלֹמֹה: 15 וַיַּעַשׂ הַמֶּלֶךְ שְׁלֹמֹה מָאתַיִם צִנָּה זָהָב שָׁחוּט שֵׁשׁ מֵאוֹת זָהָב שָׁחוּט יַעֲלֶה עַל־הַצִּנָּה הָאֶחָת: 16 וּשְׁלֹשׁ־מֵאוֹת מָגִנִּים זָהָב שָׁחוּט שְׁלֹשׁ מֵאוֹת זָהָב יַעֲלֶה עַל־הַמָּגֵן הָאֶחָת וַיִּתְּנֵם הַמֶּלֶךְ בְּבֵית יַעַר הַלְּבָנוֹן: פ 17 וַיַּעַשׂ הַמֶּלֶךְ כִּסֵּא־שֵׁן גָּדוֹל וַיְצַפֵּהוּ זָהָב טָהוֹר: 18 וְשֵׁשׁ מַעֲלוֹת לַכִּסֵּא וְכֶבֶשׁ בַּזָּהָב לַכִּסֵּא מָאֳחָזִים וְיָדוֹת מִזֶּה וּמִזֶּה עַל־מְקוֹם הַשָּׁבֶת וּשְׁנַיִם אֲרָיוֹת עֹמְדִים אֵצֶל הַיָּדוֹת: 19 וּשְׁנֵים עָשָׂר אֲרָיוֹת עֹמְדִים שָׁם עַל־שֵׁשׁ הַמַּעֲלוֹת מִזֶּה וּמִזֶּה לֹא־נַעֲשָׂה כֵן לְכָל־

made for any other kingdom. ²⁰All of King Solomon's drinking vessels were of gold, and all the utensils of the Lebanon Forest House were of pure gold; silver counted for nothing in Solomon's days. ²¹The king's fleet traveled to Tarshish with Huram's servants. Once every three years, the Tarshish fleet came in, bearing gold and silver, ivory, apes, and peacocks.

²²King Solomon surpassed all the kings of the earth in wealth and wisdom. ²³All the kings of the earth came to pay homage to Solomon and to listen to the wisdom with which God had endowed him. ²⁴Each brought his tribute—silver and gold objects, robes, weapons, and spices, horses and mules—in the amount due each year. ²⁵Solomon had 4,000 stalls for horses and chariots, and 12,000 horsemen, which he stationed in the chariot towns and with the king in Jerusalem. ²⁶He ruled over all the kings from the Euphrates to the land of the Philistines and to the border of Egypt. ²⁷The king made silver as plentiful in Jerusalem as stones, and cedars as plentiful as sycamores in the Shephelah. ²⁸Horses were brought for Solomon from Egypt and all the lands. ²⁹The other events of Solomon's reign, early and late, are recorded in the chronicle of the prophet Nathan and in the prophecies of Ahijah the Shilonite and in the visions of Jedo the seer concerning Jeroboam son of Nebat. ³⁰Solomon reigned forty years over all Israel in Jerusalem. ³¹Solomon slept with his fathers and was buried in the city of his father David; his son Rehoboam succeeded him as king.

10 ^aRehoboam went to Shechem, for all Israel had come to Shechem to acclaim him king. ²Jeroboam son of Nebat learned of it while he

---

מַמְלָכָה: 20 וְכֹל כְּלֵי מַשְׁקֵה הַמֶּלֶךְ שְׁלֹמֹה זָהָב וְכֹל כְּלֵי בֵית־יַעַר הַלְּבָנוֹן זָהָב סָגוּר אֵין כֶּסֶף נֶחְשָׁב בִּימֵי שְׁלֹמֹה לִמְאוּמָה: 21 כִּי־אֳנִיּוֹת לַמֶּלֶךְ הֹלְכוֹת תַּרְשִׁישׁ עִם עַבְדֵי חוּרָם אַחַת לְשָׁלוֹשׁ שָׁנִים תָּבוֹאנָה | אֳנִיּוֹת תַּרְשִׁישׁ נֹשְׂאוֹת זָהָב וָכֶסֶף שֶׁנְהַבִּים וְקוֹפִים וְתֻכִּיִּים: פ

22 וַיִּגְדַּל הַמֶּלֶךְ שְׁלֹמֹה מִכֹּל מַלְכֵי הָאָרֶץ לְעֹשֶׁר וְחָכְמָה: 23 וְכֹל מַלְכֵי הָאָרֶץ מְבַקְשִׁים אֶת־פְּנֵי שְׁלֹמֹה לִשְׁמֹעַ אֶת־חָכְמָתוֹ אֲשֶׁר־נָתַן הָאֱלֹהִים בְּלִבּוֹ: 24 וְהֵם מְבִיאִים אִישׁ מִנְחָתוֹ כְּלֵי כֶסֶף וּכְלֵי זָהָב וּשְׂלָמוֹת נֵשֶׁק וּבְשָׂמִים סוּסִים וּפְרָדִים דְּבַר־שָׁנָה בְּשָׁנָה: פ 25 וַיְהִי לִשְׁלֹמֹה אַרְבַּעַת אֲלָפִים אֻרְיוֹת סוּסִים וּמַרְכָּבוֹת וּשְׁנֵים־עָשָׂר אֶלֶף פָּרָשִׁים וַיַּנִּיחֵם בְּעָרֵי הָרֶכֶב וְעִם־הַמֶּלֶךְ בִּירוּשָׁלָ͏ִם: 26 וַיְהִי מוֹשֵׁל בְּכָל־הַמְּלָכִים מִן־הַנָּהָר וְעַד־אֶרֶץ פְּלִשְׁתִּים וְעַד גְּבוּל מִצְרָיִם: 27 וַיִּתֵּן הַמֶּלֶךְ אֶת־הַכֶּסֶף בִּירוּשָׁלַ͏ִם כָּאֲבָנִים וְאֵת הָאֲרָזִים נָתַן כַּשִּׁקְמִים אֲשֶׁר־בַּשְּׁפֵלָה לָרֹב: 28 וּמוֹצִיאִים סוּסִים מִמִּצְרַיִם לִשְׁלֹמֹה וּמִכָּל־הָאֲרָצוֹת: 29 וּשְׁאָר דִּבְרֵי שְׁלֹמֹה הָרִאשֹׁנִים וְהָאַחֲרוֹנִים הֲלֹא־הֵם כְּתוּבִים עַל־דִּבְרֵי נָתָן הַנָּבִיא וְעַל־נְבוּאַת אֲחִיָּה הַשִּׁילוֹנִי וּבַחֲזוֹת יֶעְדִּי יֶעְדּוֹ הַחֹזֶה עַל־יָרָבְעָם בֶּן־נְבָט: 30 וַיִּמְלֹךְ שְׁלֹמֹה בִירוּשָׁלַ͏ִם עַל־כָּל־יִשְׂרָאֵל אַרְבָּעִים שָׁנָה: 31 וַיִּשְׁכַּב שְׁלֹמֹה עִם־אֲבֹתָיו וַיִּקְבְּרֻהוּ בְּעִיר דָּוִיד אָבִיו וַיִּמְלֹךְ רְחַבְעָם בְּנוֹ תַּחְתָּיו: פ

י וַיֵּלֶךְ רְחַבְעָם שְׁכֶמָה כִּי שְׁכֶם בָּאוּ כָל־יִשְׂרָאֵל לְהַמְלִיךְ אֹתוֹ: 2 וַיְהִי כִּשְׁמֹעַ יָרָבְעָם בֶּן־נְבָט וְהוּא בְמִצְרַיִם אֲשֶׁר

---

was in Egypt where he had fled from King Solomon, and Jeroboam returned from Egypt. ³They sent for him; and Jeroboam and all Israel came and spoke to Rehoboam as follows: ⁴"Your father made our yoke heavy. Now lighten the harsh labor and the heavy yoke that your father laid on us, and we will serve you." ⁵He answered them, "Come back to me in three days." So the people went away.

⁶King Rehoboam took counsel with the elders who had served during the lifetime of his father Solomon. He said, "What answer do you counsel to give these people?" ⁷They answered him, "If you will be good to these people and appease them and speak to them with kind words, they will be your servants always." ⁸But he ignored the counsel that the elders gave him, and took counsel with the young men who had grown up with him and were serving him. ⁹"What," he asked, "do you counsel that we reply to these people who said to me, 'Lighten the yoke that your father laid on us'?" ¹⁰And the young men who had grown up with him answered, "Speak thus to the people who said to you, 'Your father made our yoke heavy, now you make it lighter for us.' Say to them, 'My little finger is thicker than my father's loins. ¹¹My father imposed a heavy yoke on you, and I will add to your yoke; my father flogged you with whips, but I [will do so] with scorpions.'"

¹²Jeroboam and all the people came to Rehoboam on the third day, since the king had told them, "Come back on the third day." ¹³The king answered them harshly; thus King Rehoboam ignored the elders' counsel. ¹⁴He spoke to them in accordance with the counsel of the young men, and said, ᵇ-"I will make-ᵇ your yoke heavy, and I will add to it; my father flogged you with whips, but I [will do so] with scorpions." ¹⁵The king did not listen to the people, for God had

b-b Some mss. and printed editions read "my father made"; cf. 1 Kings 12.14.

brought it about in order that the LORD might fulfill the promise that He had made through Ahijah the Shilonite to Jeroboam son of Nebat. [16]When all Israel [saw] that the king had not listened to them, the people answered the king:

"We have no portion in David,
No share in Jesse's son!
To your tents, O Israel!
Now look to your own house, O David."

So all Israel returned to their homes.[c] [17]But Rehoboam continued to reign over the Israelites who lived in the towns of Judah. [18]King Rehoboam sent out Hadoram, who was in charge of the forced labor, but the Israelites pelted him to death with stones. Thereupon, King Rehoboam hurriedly mounted his chariot and fled to Jerusalem. [19]Israel has been in revolt against the house of David to this day.

11 [a]When Rehoboam arrived in Jerusalem, he mustered the house of Judah and Benjamin, 180,000 picked fighting men, to make war with Israel in order to restore the kingdom to Rehoboam. [2]But the word of the LORD came to Shemaiah, the man of God: [3]"Say to Rehoboam son of Solomon king of Judah, and to all Israel in Judah and Benjamin: [4]Thus said the LORD: You shall not set out to make war on your kinsmen. Let every man return to his home, for this thing has been brought about by Me." They heeded the words of the LORD and refrained from marching against Jeroboam. [5]Rehoboam dwelt in Jerusalem and built fortified towns in Judah. [6]He built up Bethlehem, and Etam, and Tekoa, [7]and Beth-zur, and Soco, and Adullam, [8]and Gath, and Mareshah, and Ziph, [9]and Adoraim, and Lachish, and Azekah, [10]and

c   Lit. "tents."
a   With 11.1–4, cf. 1 Kings 12.21–24.

נְסִבָּה֙ מֵעִ֣ם הָֽאֱלֹהִ֔ים לְמַ֨עַן֙ הָקִ֣ים יְהֹוָ֔ה אֶת־דְּבָר֗וֹ אֲשֶׁ֤ר דִּבֶּר֙ בְּיַד֙ אֲחִיָּ֣הוּ הַשִּׁילוֹנִ֔י אֶל־יָרׇבְעָ֖ם בֶּן־נְבָֽט׃ 16 וְכׇל־יִשְׂרָאֵ֗ל כִּ֠י לֹֽא־שָׁמַ֨ע הַמֶּ֜לֶךְ לָהֶ֗ם וַיָּשִׁ֣יבוּ הָעָ֣ם אֶת־הַמֶּ֣לֶךְ ׀ לֵאמֹ֗ר

מַה־לָּ֨נוּ חֵ֜לֶק בְּדָוִ֗יד
וְלֹֽא־נַחֲלָה֙ בְּבֶן־יִשַׁ֔י
אִ֥ישׁ לְאֹהָלֶ֖יךָ יִשְׂרָאֵ֑ל
עַתָּ֕ה רְאֵ֥ה בֵֽיתְךָ֖ דָּוִ֑יד

וַיֵּ֥לֶךְ כׇּל־יִשְׂרָאֵ֖ל לְאֹהָלָֽיו׃ 17 וּבְנֵ֣י יִשְׂרָאֵ֔ל הַיֹּֽשְׁבִ֖ים בְּעָרֵ֣י יְהוּדָ֑ה וַיִּמְלֹ֥ךְ עֲלֵיהֶ֖ם רְחַבְעָֽם׃ 18 וַיִּשְׁלַ֞ח הַמֶּ֣לֶךְ רְחַבְעָ֗ם אֶת־הֲדֹרָם֙ אֲשֶׁ֣ר עַל־הַמַּ֔ס וַיִּרְגְּמוּ־ב֧וֹ בְנֵֽי־יִשְׂרָאֵ֛ל אֶ֖בֶן וַיָּמֹ֑ת וְהַמֶּ֣לֶךְ רְחַבְעָ֗ם הִתְאַמֵּץ֙ לַֽעֲל֣וֹת בַּמֶּרְכָּבָ֔ה לָנ֖וּס יְרֽוּשָׁלָֽ͏ִם׃ 19 וַיִּפְשְׁע֤וּ יִשְׂרָאֵל֙ בְּבֵ֣ית דָּוִ֔יד עַ֖ד הַיּ֥וֹם הַזֶּֽה׃

לא וַיָּבֹ֤א רְחַבְעָם֙ יְר֣וּשָׁלַ֔͏ִם וַיַּקְהֵל֙ אֶת־בֵּ֤ית יְהוּדָה֙ וּבִנְיָמִ֔ן מֵאָ֧ה וּשְׁמוֹנִ֛ים אֶ֖לֶף בָּח֣וּר עֹשֵׂ֣ה מִלְחָמָ֑ה לְהִלָּחֵם֙ עִם־יִשְׂרָאֵ֔ל לְהָשִׁ֥יב אֶת־הַמַּמְלָכָ֖ה לִרְחַבְעָֽם׃ 2 וַֽיְהִי֙ דְּבַר־יְהֹוָ֔ה אֶל־שְׁמַֽעְיָ֥הוּ אִישׁ־הָאֱלֹהִ֖ים לֵאמֹֽר׃ 3 אֱמֹ֗ר אֶל־רְחַבְעָ֤ם בֶּן־שְׁלֹמֹה֙ מֶ֣לֶךְ יְהוּדָ֔ה וְאֶל֙ כׇּל־יִשְׂרָאֵ֔ל בִּיהוּדָ֖ה וּבִנְיָמִ֥ן לֵאמֹֽר׃ 4 כֹּ֣ה אָמַ֣ר יְהֹוָ֗ה לֹא־תַֽעֲלוּ֙ וְלֹֽא־תִלָּ֣חֲמ֔וּ עִם־אֲחֵיכֶ֔ם שׁ֚וּבוּ אִ֣ישׁ לְבֵית֔וֹ כִּ֧י מֵֽאִתִּ֛י נִהְיָ֖ה הַדָּבָ֣ר הַזֶּ֑ה וַיִּשְׁמְעוּ֙ אֶת־דִּבְרֵ֣י יְהֹוָ֔ה וַיָּשֻׁ֖בוּ מִלֶּ֥כֶת אֶל־יָרׇבְעָֽם׃ 5 וַיֵּ֥שֶׁב רְחַבְעָ֖ם בִּירֽוּשָׁלָ֑͏ִם וַיִּ֧בֶן עָרִ֛ים לְמָצ֖וֹר בִּיהוּדָֽה׃ 6 וַיִּ֥בֶן אֶת־בֵּֽית־לֶ֖חֶם וְאֶת־עֵיטָ֑ם וְאֶת־תְּקֽוֹעַ׃ 7 וְאֶת־בֵּֽית־צ֥וּר וְאֶת־שׂוֹכ֖וֹ וְאֶת־עֲדֻלָּֽם׃ 8 וְאֶת־גַּ֥ת וְאֶת־מָרֵשָׁ֖ה וְאֶת־זִֽיף׃ 9 וְאֶת־אֲדוֹרַ֥יִם וְאֶת־לָכִ֖ישׁ וְאֶת־עֲזֵקָֽה׃ 10 וְאֶת־צׇרְעָ֥ה וְאֶת־אַיָּל֖וֹן

Zorah, and Aijalon, and Hebron, which are in Judah and in Benjamin, as fortified towns. ¹¹He strengthened the fortified towns and put commanders in them, along with stores of food, oil, and wine, ¹²and shields and spears in every town. He strengthened them exceedingly; thus Judah and Benjamin were his.

¹³The priests and the Levites, from all their territories throughout Israel, presented themselves to him. ¹⁴The Levites had left their pasturelands and their holdings and had set out for Judah and Jerusalem, for Jeroboam and his sons had prevented them from serving the Lord, ¹⁵having appointed his own priests for the shrines, goat-demons, and calves which he had made. ¹⁶From all the tribes of Israel, those intent on seeking the Lord God of Israel followed them to Jerusalem, to sacrifice to the Lord God of their fathers. ¹⁷They strengthened the kingdom of Judah, and supported Rehoboam son of Solomon for three years, for they followed the ways of David and Solomon for three years.

¹⁸Rehoboam married Mahalath daughter of Jerimoth son of David, and Abihail daughter of Eliab son of Jesse. ¹⁹She bore him sons: Jeush, Shemariah, and Zaham. ²⁰He then took Maacah daughter of Absalom; she bore him Abijah, Attai, Ziza, and Shelomith. ²¹Rehoboam loved Maacah daughter of Absalom more than his other wives and concubines—for he took eighteen wives and sixty concubines; he begot twenty-eight sons and sixty daughters. ²²Rehoboam designated Abijah son of Maacah as chief and leader among his brothers, for he intended him to be his successor. ²³He prudently distributed all his sons throughout the regions of Judah and Benjamin and throughout the fortified towns; he provided them with abundant food, and he sought many wives for them.

וְאֶת־חֶבְרוֹן אֲשֶׁר בִּיהוּדָה וּבְבִנְיָמִן עָרֵי מְצֻרוֹת: ¹¹ וַיְחַזֵּק אֶת־הַמְּצֻרוֹת וַיִּתֵּן בָּהֶם נְגִידִים וְאֹצְרוֹת מַאֲכָל וְשֶׁמֶן וָיָיִן: ¹² וּבְכָל־עִיר וָעִיר צִנּוֹת וּרְמָחִים וַיְחַזְּקֵם לְהַרְבֵּה מְאֹד וַיְהִי־לוֹ יְהוּדָה וּבִנְיָמִן: ס

¹³ וְהַכֹּהֲנִים וְהַלְוִיִּם אֲשֶׁר בְּכָל־יִשְׂרָאֵל הִתְיַצְּבוּ עָלָיו מִכָּל־גְּבוּלָם: ¹⁴ כִּי־עָזְבוּ הַלְוִיִּם אֶת־מִגְרְשֵׁיהֶם וַאֲחֻזָּתָם וַיֵּלְכוּ לִיהוּדָה וְלִירוּשָׁלִָם כִּי־הִזְנִיחָם יָרָבְעָם וּבָנָיו מִכַּהֵן לַיהוָה: ¹⁵ וַיַּעֲמֶד־לוֹ כֹּהֲנִים לַבָּמוֹת וְלַשְּׂעִירִים וְלָעֲגָלִים אֲשֶׁר עָשָׂה: ¹⁶ וְאַחֲרֵיהֶם מִכֹּל שִׁבְטֵי יִשְׂרָאֵל הַנֹּתְנִים אֶת־לְבָבָם לְבַקֵּשׁ אֶת־יְהוָה אֱלֹהֵי יִשְׂרָאֵל בָּאוּ יְרוּשָׁלִַם לִזְבּוֹחַ לַיהוָה אֱלֹהֵי אֲבוֹתֵיהֶם: ¹⁷ וַיְחַזְּקוּ אֶת־מַלְכוּת יְהוּדָה וַיְאַמְּצוּ אֶת־רְחַבְעָם בֶּן־שְׁלֹמֹה לְשָׁנִים שָׁלוֹשׁ כִּי הָלְכוּ בְּדֶרֶךְ דָּוִיד וּשְׁלֹמֹה לְשָׁנִים שָׁלוֹשׁ: ¹⁸ וַיִּקַּח־לוֹ רְחַבְעָם אִשָּׁה אֶת־מָחֲלַת בֶּן־יְרִימוֹת בֶּן־דָּוִיד אֲבִיהַיִל בַּת־אֱלִיאָב בֶּן־יִשָׁי: ¹⁹ וַתֵּלֶד לוֹ בָּנִים אֶת־יְעוּשׁ וְאֶת־שְׁמַרְיָה וְאֶת־זָהַם: ²⁰ וְאַחֲרֶיהָ לָקַח אֶת־מַעֲכָה בַּת־אַבְשָׁלוֹם וַתֵּלֶד לוֹ אֶת־אֲבִיָּה וְאֶת־עַתַּי וְאֶת־זִיזָא וְאֶת־שְׁלֹמִית: ²¹ וַיֶּאֱהַב רְחַבְעָם אֶת־מַעֲכָה בַת־אַבְשָׁלוֹם מִכָּל־נָשָׁיו וּפִילַגְשָׁיו כִּי נָשִׁים שְׁמוֹנֶה־עֶשְׂרֵה נָשָׂא וּפִילַגְשִׁים שִׁשִּׁים וַיּוֹלֶד עֶשְׂרִים וּשְׁמוֹנָה בָּנִים וְשִׁשִּׁים בָּנוֹת: ²² וַיַּעֲמֵד לָרֹאשׁ רְחַבְעָם אֶת־אֲבִיָּה בֶן־מַעֲכָה לְנָגִיד בְּאֶחָיו כִּי לְהַמְלִיכוֹ: ²³ וַיָּבֶן וַיִּפְרֹץ מִכָּל־בָּנָיו לְכָל־אַרְצוֹת יְהוּדָה וּבִנְיָמִן לְכֹל עָרֵי הַמְּצֻרוֹת וַיִּתֵּן לָהֶם הַמָּזוֹן לָרֹב וַיִּשְׁאַל הֲמוֹן נָשִׁים:

12

When the kingship of Rehoboam was firmly established, and he grew strong, he abandoned the Teaching of the LORD, he and all Israel with him.

²In the fifth year of King Rehoboam, King Shishak of Egypt marched against Jerusalem—for they had trespassed against the LORD—³with 1,200 chariots, 60,000 horsemen and innumerable troops who came with him from Egypt: Lybians, Sukkites, and Kushites. ⁴He took the fortified towns of Judah and advanced on Jerusalem. ⁵The prophet Shemaiah came to Rehoboam and the officers of Judah, who had assembled in Jerusalem because of Shishak, and said to them, "Thus said the LORD: You have abandoned Me, so I am abandoning you to Shishak." ⁶Then the officers of Israel and the king humbled themselves and declared, "The LORD is in the right." ⁷When the LORD saw that they had submitted, the word of the LORD came to Shemaiah, saying, "Since they have humbled themselves, I will not destroy them but will grant them some measure of deliverance, and My wrath will not be poured out on Jerusalem through Shishak. ⁸They will be subject to him, and they will know the difference between serving Me and serving the kingdoms of the earth." King Shishak of Egypt marched against Jerusalem. ⁹ᵃHe took away the treasures of the House of the LORD and the treasures of the royal palace; he took away everything; he took away the golden shields that Solomon had made. ¹⁰King Rehoboam had bronze shields made in their place, and entrusted them to the officers of the guardᵇ who guarded the entrance to the royal palace. ¹¹Whenever the king entered the House of the LORD, the guards would carry them and then bring them back to the armory of the guards. ¹²After he had humbled himself,

יב וַיְהִי כְּהָכִין מַלְכוּת רְחַבְעָם
וּכְחֶזְקָתוֹ עָזַב אֶת־תּוֹרַת יְהֹוָה וְכָל־
יִשְׂרָאֵל עִמּוֹ: פ

2 וַיְהִי בַּשָּׁנָה הַחֲמִישִׁית לַמֶּלֶךְ רְחַבְעָם
עָלָה שִׁישַׁק מֶלֶךְ־מִצְרַיִם עַל־יְרוּשָׁלָ͏ִם כִּי
מָעֲלוּ בַּיהֹוָה: 3 בְּאֶלֶף וּמָאתַיִם רֶכֶב
וּבְשִׁשִּׁים אֶלֶף פָּרָשִׁים וְאֵין מִסְפָּר לָעָם
אֲשֶׁר־בָּאוּ עִמּוֹ מִמִּצְרַיִם לוּבִים סֻכִּיִּים
וְכוּשִׁים: 4 וַיִּלְכֹּד אֶת־עָרֵי הַמְּצֻרוֹת
אֲשֶׁר לִיהוּדָה וַיָּבֹא עַד־יְרוּשָׁלָ͏ִם: ס
5 וּשְׁמַעְיָה הַנָּבִיא בָּא אֶל־רְחַבְעָם וְשָׂרֵי
יְהוּדָה אֲשֶׁר־נֶאֶסְפוּ אֶל־יְרוּשָׁלַ͏ִם מִפְּנֵי
שִׁישָׁק וַיֹּאמֶר לָהֶם כֹּה־אָמַר יְהֹוָה אַתֶּם
עֲזַבְתֶּם אֹתִי וְאַף־אֲנִי עָזַבְתִּי אֶתְכֶם
בְּיַד־שִׁישָׁק: 6 וַיִּכָּנְעוּ שָׂרֵי־יִשְׂרָאֵל וְהַמֶּלֶךְ
וַיֹּאמְרוּ צַדִּיק | יְהֹוָה: 7 וּבִרְאוֹת יְהֹוָה כִּי
נִכְנָעוּ הָיָה דְבַר־יְהֹוָה אֶל־שְׁמַעְיָה |
לֵאמֹר נִכְנְעוּ לֹא אַשְׁחִיתֵם וְנָתַתִּי
לָהֶם כִּמְעַט לִפְלֵיטָה וְלֹא־תִתַּךְ חֲמָתִי
בִּירוּשָׁלַ͏ִם בְּיַד־שִׁישָׁק: 8 כִּי יִהְיוּ־לוֹ
לַעֲבָדִים וְיֵדְעוּ עֲבוֹדָתִי וַעֲבוֹדַת מַמְלְכוֹת
הָאֲרָצוֹת: ס 9 וַיַּעַל שִׁישַׁק מֶלֶךְ־
מִצְרַיִם עַל־יְרוּשָׁלַ͏ִם וַיִּקַּח אֶת־אֹצְרוֹת
בֵּית־יְהֹוָה וְאֶת־אֹצְרוֹת בֵּית הַמֶּלֶךְ אֶת־
הַכֹּל לָקָח וַיִּקַּח אֶת־מָגִנֵּי הַזָּהָב אֲשֶׁר
עָשָׂה שְׁלֹמֹה: 10 וַיַּעַשׂ הַמֶּלֶךְ רְחַבְעָם
תַּחְתֵּיהֶם מָגִנֵּי נְחֹשֶׁת וְהִפְקִיד עַל־יַד
שָׂרֵי הָרָצִים הַשֹּׁמְרִים פֶּתַח בֵּית הַמֶּלֶךְ:
11 וַיְהִי מִדֵּי־בוֹא הַמֶּלֶךְ בֵּית יְהֹוָה
בָּאוּ הָרָצִים וּנְשָׂאוּם וֶהֱשִׁיבוּם אֶל־תָּא
הָרָצִים: 12 וּבְהִכָּנְעוֹ שָׁב מִמֶּנּוּ אַף־יְהֹוָה

ᵃ With vv. 9–16, cf. 1 Kings 14.26–31.
ᵇ Lit. "runners."

the anger of the LORD was averted and He did not destroy him entirely; in Judah, too, good things were found.

[13]King Rehoboam grew strong in Jerusalem and exercised kingship. Rehoboam was forty-one years old when he became king, and he reigned seventeen years in Jerusalem—the city the LORD had chosen out of all the tribes of Israel to establish His name there. His mother's name was Naamah the Ammonitess. [14]He did what was wrong, for he had not set his heart to seek the LORD. [15]The deeds of Rehoboam, early and late, are recorded in the chronicles of the prophet Shemaiah and Iddo the seer, in the manner of genealogy. There was continuous war between Rehoboam and Jeroboam. [16]Rehoboam slept with his fathers and was buried in the City of David. His son Abijah succeeded him as king.

13 In the eighteenth year of King Jeroboam, Abijah became king over Judah. [2]He reigned three years in Jerusalem; his mother's name was Micaiah daughter of Uriel of Gibeah. There was war between Abijah and Jeroboam. [3]Abijah joined battle with a force of warriors, 400,000 picked men. Jeroboam arrayed for battle against him 800,000 picked men, warriors. [4]Abijah stood on top of Mount Zemaraim in the hill country of Ephraim and said, "Listen to me, Jeroboam and all Israel. [5]Surely you know that the LORD God of Israel gave David kingship over Israel forever—to him and his sons—by a covenant of salt. [6]Jeroboam son of Nebat had been in the service of Solomon son of David, but he rose up and rebelled against his master. [7]Riffraff and scoundrels gathered around him and pressed hard upon Rehoboam son of Solomon.

וְלֹא לְהַשְׁחִית לְכַלֵּה וְגַם בִּיהוּדָה הָיָה דְּבָרִים טוֹבִים: ס
[13] וַיִּתְחַזֵּק הַמֶּלֶךְ רְחַבְעָם בִּירוּשָׁלִַם וַיִּמְלֹךְ כִּי בֶן־אַרְבָּעִים וְאַחַת שָׁנָה רְחַבְעָם בְּמָלְכוֹ וּשֲׁבַע עֶשְׂרֵה שָׁנָה ׀ מָלַךְ בִּירוּשָׁלִַם הָעִיר אֲשֶׁר־בָּחַר יְהֹוָה לָשׂוּם אֶת־שְׁמוֹ שָׁם מִכֹּל שִׁבְטֵי יִשְׂרָאֵל וְשֵׁם אִמּוֹ נַעֲמָה הָעַמֹּנִית: [14] וַיַּעַשׂ הָרָע כִּי לֹא הֵכִין לִבּוֹ לִדְרוֹשׁ אֶת־יְהֹוָה: ס
[15] וְדִבְרֵי רְחַבְעָם הָרִאשֹׁנִים וְהָאַחֲרוֹנִים הֲלֹא־הֵם כְּתוּבִים בְּדִבְרֵי שְׁמַעְיָה הַנָּבִיא וְעִדּוֹ הַחֹזֶה לְהִתְיַחֵשׂ וּמִלְחֲמוֹת רְחַבְעָם וְיָרָבְעָם כָּל־הַיָּמִים: [16] וַיִּשְׁכַּב רְחַבְעָם עִם־אֲבֹתָיו וַיִּקָּבֵר בְּעִיר דָּוִיד וַיִּמְלֹךְ אֲבִיָּה בְנוֹ תַּחְתָּיו: פ

יג בִּשְׁנַת שְׁמוֹנֶה עֶשְׂרֵה לַמֶּלֶךְ יָרָבְעָם וַיִּמְלֹךְ אֲבִיָּה עַל־יְהוּדָה: [2] שָׁלוֹשׁ שָׁנִים מָלַךְ בִּירוּשָׁלִַם וְשֵׁם אִמּוֹ מִיכָיָהוּ בַת־אוּרִיאֵל מִן־גִּבְעָה וּמִלְחָמָה הָיְתָה בֵּין אֲבִיָּה וּבֵין יָרָבְעָם: [3] וַיֶּאְסֹר אֲבִיָּה אֶת־הַמִּלְחָמָה בְּחַיִל גִּבּוֹרֵי מִלְחָמָה אַרְבַּע־מֵאוֹת אֶלֶף אִישׁ בָּחוּר ס וְיָרָבְעָם עָרַךְ עִמּוֹ מִלְחָמָה בִּשְׁמוֹנֶה מֵאוֹת אֶלֶף אִישׁ בָּחוּר גִּבּוֹר* חָיִל: [4] ס וַיָּקָם אֲבִיָּה מֵעַל לְהַר צְמָרַיִם אֲשֶׁר בְּהַר אֶפְרָיִם וַיֹּאמֶר שְׁמָעוּנִי יָרָבְעָם וְכָל־יִשְׂרָאֵל: [5] הֲלֹא לָכֶם לָדַעַת כִּי יְהֹוָה ׀ אֱלֹהֵי יִשְׂרָאֵל נָתַן מַמְלָכָה לְדָוִיד עַל־יִשְׂרָאֵל לְעוֹלָם לוֹ וּלְבָנָיו בְּרִית מֶלַח: [6] ס וַיָּקָם יָרָבְעָם בֶּן־נְבָט עֶבֶד שְׁלֹמֹה בֶן־דָּוִיד וַיִּמְרֹד עַל־אֲדֹנָיו: [7] וַיִּקָּבְצוּ עָלָיו אֲנָשִׁים רֵקִים בְּנֵי בְלִיַּעַל וַיִּתְאַמְּצוּ עַל־רְחַבְעָם בֶּן־שְׁלֹמֹה

v. 3.   סבירין ומטעין "גבורי"

Rehoboam was inexperienced and fainthearted and could not stand up to them. 8Now you are bent on opposing the kingdom of the Lord, which is in the charge of the sons of David, because you are a great multitude and possess the golden calves that Jeroboam made for you as gods. 9Did you not banish the priests of the Lord, the sons of Aaron and the Levites, and, like the peoples of the land, appoint your own priests? Anyone who offered himself for ordination with a young bull of the herd and seven rams became a priest of no-gods! 10As for us, the Lord is our God, and we have not forsaken Him. The priests who minister to the Lord are the sons of Aaron, and the Levites are at their tasks. 11They offer burnt offerings in smoke each morning and each evening, and the aromatic incense, the rows of bread on the pure table; they kindle the golden lampstand with its lamps burning each evening, for we keep the charge of the Lord our God, while you have forsaken it. 12See, God is with us as our chief, and His priests have the trumpets for sounding blasts against you. O children of Israel, do not fight the Lord God of your fathers, because you will not succeed." 13Jeroboam, however, had directed the ambush to go around and come from the rear, thus a-the main body was-a in front of Judah, while the ambush was behind them. 14When Judah turned around and saw that the fighting was before and behind them, they cried out to the Lord, and the priests blew the trumpets. 15The men of Judah raised a shout; and when the men of Judah raised a shout, God routed Jeroboam and all Israel before Abijah and Judah. 16The Israelites fled before Judah, and God delivered them into their hands. 17Abijah and his army inflicted a severe defeat on them; 500,000 men of Israel fell slain. 18The Israelites were crushed at that time, while the people of Judah triumphed because they relied

a-a Lit. "they were."

וּרְחַבְעָם הָיָה נַעַר וְרַךְ־לֵבָב וְלֹא הִתְחַזַּק לִפְנֵיהֶם: 8 וְעַתָּה ׀ אַתֶּם אֹמְרִים לְהִתְחַזֵּק לִפְנֵי מַמְלֶכֶת יְהוָה בְּיַד בְּנֵי דָוִיד וְאַתֶּם הָמוֹן רָב וְעִמָּכֶם עֶגְלֵי זָהָב אֲשֶׁר עָשָׂה לָכֶם יָרָבְעָם לֵאלֹהִים: 9 הֲלֹא הִדַּחְתֶּם אֶת־כֹּהֲנֵי יְהוָה אֶת־בְּנֵי אַהֲרֹן וְהַלְוִיִּם וַתַּעֲשׂוּ לָכֶם כֹּהֲנִים כְּעַמֵּי הָאֲרָצוֹת כָּל־הַבָּא לְמַלֵּא יָדוֹ בְּפַר בֶּן־בָּקָר וְאֵילִם שִׁבְעָה וְהָיָה כֹהֵן לְלֹא אֱלֹהִים: ס 10 וַאֲנַחְנוּ יְהוָה אֱלֹהֵינוּ וְלֹא עֲזַבְנֻהוּ וְכֹהֲנִים מְשָׁרְתִים לַיהוָה בְּנֵי אַהֲרֹן וְהַלְוִיִּם בַּמְּלָאכֶת: 11 וּמַקְטִרִים לַיהוָה עֹלוֹת בַּבֹּקֶר־בַּבֹּקֶר וּבָעֶרֶב־בָּעֶרֶב וּקְטֹרֶת־סַמִּים וּמַעֲרֶכֶת לֶחֶם עַל־הַשֻּׁלְחָן הַטָּהוֹר וּמְנוֹרַת הַזָּהָב וְנֵרֹתֶיהָ לְבָעֵר בָּעֶרֶב בָּעֶרֶב כִּי־שֹׁמְרִים אֲנַחְנוּ אֶת־מִשְׁמֶרֶת יְהוָה אֱלֹהֵינוּ וְאַתֶּם עֲזַבְתֶּם אֹתוֹ: 12 וְהִנֵּה עִמָּנוּ בָרֹאשׁ הָאֱלֹהִים ׀ וְכֹהֲנָיו וַחֲצֹצְרוֹת הַתְּרוּעָה לְהָרִיעַ עֲלֵיכֶם בְּנֵי יִשְׂרָאֵל אַל־תִּלָּחֲמוּ עִם־יְהוָה אֱלֹהֵי־אֲבֹתֵיכֶם כִּי־לֹא תַצְלִיחוּ: 13 וְיָרָבְעָם הֵסֵב אֶת־הַמַּאְרָב לָבוֹא מֵאַחֲרֵיהֶם וַיִּהְיוּ לִפְנֵי יְהוּדָה וְהַמַּאְרָב מֵאַחֲרֵיהֶם: 14 וַיִּפְנוּ יְהוּדָה וְהִנֵּה לָהֶם הַמִּלְחָמָה פָּנִים וְאָחוֹר וַיִּצְעֲקוּ לַיהוָה וְהַכֹּהֲנִים מחצרים מַחְצְרִים בַּחֲצֹצְרוֹת: 15 וַיָּרִיעוּ אִישׁ יְהוּדָה וַיְהִי בְּהָרִיעַ אִישׁ יְהוּדָה וְהָאֱלֹהִים נָגַף אֶת־יָרָבְעָם וְכָל־יִשְׂרָאֵל לִפְנֵי אֲבִיָּה וִיהוּדָה: 16 וַיָּנוּסוּ בְנֵי־יִשְׂרָאֵל מִפְּנֵי יְהוּדָה וַיִּתְּנֵם אֱלֹהִים בְּיָדָם: 17 וַיַּכּוּ בָהֶם אֲבִיָּה וְעַמּוֹ מַכָּה רַבָּה וַיִּפְּלוּ חֲלָלִים מִיִּשְׂרָאֵל חֲמֵשׁ־מֵאוֹת אֶלֶף אִישׁ בָּחוּר: 18 וַיִּכָּנְעוּ בְנֵי־יִשְׂרָאֵל בָּעֵת הַהִיא וַיֶּאֶמְצוּ בְּנֵי יְהוּדָה כִּי נִשְׁעֲנוּ

on the Lord God of their fathers. ¹⁹Abijah pursued Jeroboam and captured some of his cities—Bethel with its dependencies, Jeshanah with its dependencies, and Ephrain with its dependencies. ²⁰Jeroboam could not muster strength again during the days of Abijah. The Lord struck him down and he died. ²¹But Abijah grew powerful; he married fourteen wives and begat twenty-two sons and sixteen daughters.

²²The other events of Abijah's reign, his conduct and his acts, are recorded in the story of the prophet Iddo. ²³Abijah slept with his fathers and was buried in the City of David; his son Asa succeeded him as king. The land was untroubled for ten years.

14 Asa did what was good and pleasing to the Lord his God. ²He abolished the alien altars and shrines; he smashed the pillars and cut down the sacred posts. ³He ordered Judah to turn to the Lord God of their fathers and to observe the Teaching and the Commandment. ⁴He abolished the shrines and the incense stands throughout the cities of Judah, and the kingdom was untroubled under him. ⁵He built fortified towns in Judah, since the land was untroubled and he was not engaged in warfare during those years, for the Lord had granted him respite. ⁶He said to Judah, "Let us build up these cities and surround them with walls and towers, gates and bars, while the land is at our disposal because we turned to the Lord our God—we turned [to Him] and He gave us respite on all sides." They were successful in their building.

⁷Asa had an army of 300,000 men from Judah bearing shields and spears, and 280,000 from Benjamin bearing bucklers and drawing the bow; all these were valiant men. ⁸Zerah the Cushite marched out against them with an army

עַל־יְהוָה אֱלֹהֵי אֲבוֹתֵיהֶם: ¹⁹ וַיִּרְדֹּף אֲבִיָּה אַחֲרֵי יָרָבְעָם וַיִּלְכֹּד מִמֶּנּוּ עָרִים אֶת־בֵּית־אֵל וְאֶת־בְּנוֹתֶיהָ וְאֶת־יְשָׁנָה וְאֶת־בְּנוֹתֶיהָ וְאֶת־עֶפְרוֹן וּבְנֹתֶיהָ: ²⁰ וְלֹא־עָצַר כֹּחַ־יָרָבְעָם עוֹד בִּימֵי אֲבִיָּהוּ וַיִּגְּפֵהוּ יְהוָה וַיָּמֹת: פ ²¹ וַיִּתְחַזֵּק אֲבִיָּהוּ וַיִּשָּׂא־לוֹ נָשִׁים אַרְבַּע עֶשְׂרֵה וַיּוֹלֶד עֶשְׂרִים וּשְׁנַיִם בָּנִים וְשֵׁשׁ עֶשְׂרֵה בָּנוֹת: ס

²² וְיֶתֶר דִּבְרֵי אֲבִיָּה וּדְרָכָיו וּדְבָרָיו כְּתוּבִים בְּמִדְרַשׁ הַנָּבִיא עִדּוֹ: ²³ וַיִּשְׁכַּב אֲבִיָּה עִם־אֲבֹתָיו וַיִּקְבְּרוּ אֹתוֹ בְּעִיר דָּוִיד וַיִּמְלֹךְ אָסָא בְנוֹ תַּחְתָּיו בְּיָמָיו שָׁקְטָה הָאָרֶץ עֶשֶׂר שָׁנִים: פ

יד וַיַּעַשׂ אָסָא הַטּוֹב וְהַיָּשָׁר בְּעֵינֵי יְהוָה אֱלֹהָיו: ² וַיָּסַר אֶת־מִזְבְּחוֹת הַנֵּכָר וְהַבָּמוֹת וַיְשַׁבֵּר אֶת־הַמַּצֵּבוֹת וַיְגַדַּע אֶת־הָאֲשֵׁרִים: ³ וַיֹּאמֶר לִיהוּדָה לִדְרוֹשׁ אֶת־יְהוָה אֱלֹהֵי אֲבוֹתֵיהֶם וְלַעֲשׂוֹת הַתּוֹרָה וְהַמִּצְוָה: ⁴ וַיָּסַר מִכָּל־עָרֵי יְהוּדָה אֶת־הַבָּמוֹת וְאֶת־הַחַמָּנִים וַתִּשְׁקֹט הַמַּמְלָכָה לְפָנָיו: ⁵ וַיִּבֶן עָרֵי מְצוּרָה בִּיהוּדָה כִּי־שָׁקְטָה הָאָרֶץ וְאֵין־עִמּוֹ מִלְחָמָה בַּשָּׁנִים הָאֵלֶּה כִּי־הֵנִיחַ יְהוָה לוֹ: ⁶ וַיֹּאמֶר לִיהוּדָה נִבְנֶה | אֶת־הֶעָרִים הָאֵלֶּה וְנָסֵב חוֹמָה וּמִגְדָּלִים דְּלָתַיִם וּבְרִיחִים עוֹדֶנּוּ הָאָרֶץ לְפָנֵינוּ כִּי דָרַשְׁנוּ אֶת־יְהוָה אֱלֹהֵינוּ דָּרַשְׁנוּ וַיָּנַח לָנוּ מִסָּבִיב וַיִּבְנוּ וַיַּצְלִיחוּ: פ

⁷ וַיְהִי לְאָסָא חַיִל נֹשֵׂא צִנָּה וָרֹמַח מִיהוּדָה שְׁלֹשׁ מֵאוֹת אֶלֶף ס וּמִבִּנְיָמִן נֹשְׂאֵי מָגֵן וְדֹרְכֵי קֶשֶׁת מָאתַיִם וּשְׁמוֹנִים אֶלֶף כָּל־אֵלֶּה גִּבּוֹרֵי חָיִל: ⁸ וַיֵּצֵא אֲלֵיהֶם זֶרַח הַכּוּשִׁי בְּחַיִל אֶלֶף אֲלָפִים וּמַרְכָּבוֹת

of a thousand thousand and 300 chariots. When he reached Mareshah ⁹Asa confronted him, and the battle lines were drawn in the valley of Zephat by Mareshah. ¹⁰Asa called to the LORD his God, and said, "O LORD, it is all the same to You to help the numerous and the powerless. Help us, O LORD our God, for we rely on You, and in Your name we have come against this great multitude. You are the LORD our God. Let no mortal hinder You." ¹¹So the LORD routed the Cushites before Asa and Judah, and the Cushites fled. ¹²Asa and the army with him pursued them as far as Gerar. Many of the Cushites fell wounded beyond recovery, for they broke before the LORD and His camp. Very much spoil was taken. ¹³All the cities in the vicinity of Gerar were ravaged, for a terror of the LORD seized them. All the cities were plundered, and they yielded much booty. ¹⁴They also ravaged the encampment of herdsmen, capturing much sheep and camels. Then they returned to Jerusalem.

15

The spirit of God came upon Azariah son of Oded. ²He came to Asa and said to him, "Listen to me, Asa and all Judah and Benjamin; the LORD is with you as long as you are with Him. If you turn to Him, He will respond to you, but if you forsake Him, He will forsake you. ³Israel has gone many days without the true God, without a priest to give instruction and without Teaching. ⁴But in distress it returned to the LORD God of Israel, and sought Him, and He responded to them. ⁵At those times, ᵃ-no wayfarer-ᵃ was safe, for there was much tumult among all the inhabitants of the lands. ⁶Nation was crushed by nation and city by city, for God threw them into panic with every kind of trouble. ⁷As for you, be strong, do not be disheartened, for there is reward for your labor."

ᵃ⁻ᵃ   Lit. "one who goes out and one who comes in."

שְׁלֹשׁ מֵאֹ֔ות וַיָּבֹ֖א עַד־מָרֵשָֽׁה׃ ⁹וַיֵּצֵ֣א אָסָא֮ לְפָנָיו֒ וַיַּעַרְכ֣וּ מִלְחָמָ֔ה בְּגֵ֥יא צְפַ֖תָה לְמָרֵשָֽׁה׃ ¹⁰וַיִּקְרָ֣א אָסָ֗א אֶל־יְהוָ֣ה אֱלֹהָיו֮ וַיֹּאמַר֒ יְהוָ֗ה אֵֽין־עִמְּךָ֤ לַעְזֹור֙ בֵּ֥ין רַ֣ב לְאֵ֣ין כֹּ֔חַ עָזְרֵ֜נוּ יְהוָ֤ה אֱלֹהֵ֙ינוּ֙ כִּֽי־עָלֶ֣יךָ נִשְׁעַ֔נּוּ וּבְשִׁמְךָ֣ בָ֗אנוּ עַל־הֶהָמֹ֣ון הַזֶּ֑ה יְהוָ֤ה אֱלֹהֵ֙ינוּ֙ אַתָּ֔ה אַל־יַעְצֹ֥ר עִמְּךָ֖ אֱנֹֽושׁ׃ ס ¹¹וַיִּגֹּ֤ף יְהוָה֙ אֶת־הַכּוּשִׁ֔ים לִפְנֵ֥י אָסָ֖א וְלִפְנֵ֣י יְהוּדָ֑ה וַיָּנֻ֖סוּ הַכּוּשִֽׁים׃ ¹²וַיִּרְדְּפֵ֣ם אָסָ֗א וְהָעָם֙ אֲשֶׁר־עִמֹּ֔ו עַד־לִגְרָ֔ר וַיִּפֹּ֤ל מִכּוּשִׁים֙ לְאֵ֣ין לָהֶ֣ם מִֽחְיָ֔ה כִּֽי־נִשְׁבְּר֥וּ לִפְנֵֽי־יְהוָ֖ה וְלִפְנֵ֣י מַחֲנֵ֑הוּ וַיִּשְׂא֥וּ שָׁלָ֖ל הַרְבֵּ֥ה מְאֹֽד׃ ¹³וַיַּכּ֗וּ אֵ֤ת כָּל־הֶֽעָרִים֙ סְבִיבֹ֣ות גְּרָ֔ר כִּֽי־הָיָ֥ה פַֽחַד־יְהוָ֖ה עֲלֵיהֶ֑ם וַיָּבֹ֙זּוּ֙ אֶת־כָּל־הֶ֣עָרִ֔ים כִּֽי־בִזָּ֥ה רַבָּ֖ה הָיְתָ֥ה בָהֶֽם׃ ¹⁴וְגַם־אָהֳלֵ֥י מִקְנֶ֖ה הִכּ֑וּ וַיִּשְׁבּ֨וּ צֹ֤אן לָרֹב֙ וּגְמַלִּ֔ים וַיָּשֻׁ֖בוּ יְרוּשָׁלָֽ͏ִם׃ ס

טו וַֽעֲזַרְיָ֙הוּ֙ בֶּן־עֹודֵ֔ד הָיְתָ֥ה עָלָ֖יו ר֣וּחַ אֱלֹהִֽים׃ ²וַיֵּצֵא֮ לִפְנֵ֣י אָסָא֒ וַיֹּ֣אמֶר לֹ֔ו שְׁמָע֕וּנִי אָסָ֖א וְכָל־יְהוּדָ֣ה וּבִנְיָמִ֑ן יְהוָ֤ה עִמָּכֶם֙ בִּֽהְיֹֽותְכֶ֣ם עִמֹּ֔ו וְאִם־תִּדְרְשֻׁ֙הוּ֙ יִמָּצֵ֣א לָכֶ֔ם וְאִם־תַּעַזְבֻ֖הוּ יַעֲזֹ֥ב אֶתְכֶֽם׃ ס ³וְיָמִ֥ים רַבִּ֖ים לְיִשְׂרָאֵ֑ל לְלֹ֣א ׀ אֱלֹהֵ֣י אֱמֶ֗ת וּלְלֹ֛א כֹּהֵ֥ן מֹורֶ֖ה וּלְלֹ֥א תֹורָֽה׃ ⁴וַיָּ֙שָׁב֙ בַּצַּר־לֹ֔ו עַל־יְהוָ֖ה אֱלֹהֵ֣י יִשְׂרָאֵ֑ל וַיְבַקְשֻׁ֖הוּ וַיִּמָּצֵ֥א לָהֶֽם׃ ⁵וּבָעִתִּ֣ים הָהֵ֔ם אֵ֥ין שָׁלֹ֖ום לַיֹּוצֵ֣א וְלַבָּ֑א כִּ֚י מְהוּמֹ֣ת רַבֹּ֔ות עַ֥ל כָּל־יֹושְׁבֵ֖י הָאֲרָצֹֽות׃ ⁶וְכֻתְּת֤וּ גֹוי־בְּגֹוי֙ וְעִ֣יר בְּעִ֔יר כִּֽי־אֱלֹהִ֥ים הֲמָמָ֖ם בְּכָל־צָרָֽה׃ ⁷וְאַתֶּ֣ם חִזְק֔וּ וְאַל־יִרְפּ֖וּ יְדֵיכֶ֑ם כִּ֛י יֵ֥שׁ שָׂכָ֖ר לִפְעֻלַּתְכֶֽם׃ ס

8When Asa heard these words, the prophecy of Oded the prophet, he took courage and removed the abominations from the entire land of Judah and Benjamin and from the cities that he had captured in the hill country of Ephraim. He restored the altar of the LORD in front of the porch of the LORD. 9He assembled all the people of Judah and Benjamin and those people of Ephraim, Manasseh, and Simeon who sojourned among them, for many in Israel had thrown in their lot with him when they saw that the LORD his God was with him. 10They were assembled in Jerusalem in the third month of the fifteenth year of the reign of Asa. 11They brought sacrifices to the LORD on that day; they brought 700 oxen and 7,000 sheep of the spoil. 12They entered into a covenant to worship the LORD God of their fathers with all their heart and with all their soul. 13Whoever would not worship the LORD God of Israel would be put to death, whether small or great, whether man or woman. 14So they took an oath to the LORD in a loud voice and with shouts, with trumpeting and blasts of the horn. 15All Judah rejoiced over the oath, for they swore with all their heart and sought Him with all their will. He responded to them and gave them respite on every side.

16bHec also deposed Maacah mother of King Asa from the rank of queen mother, because she had made an abominable thing for [the goddess] Asherah. Asa cut down her abominable thing, reduced it to dust, and burned it in the Wadi Kidron. 17The shrines, indeed, were not abolished in Israel; however, Asa was wholehearted [with the LORD] all his life. 18He brought into the House of God the things that he and his father had consecrated—silver, gold, and utensils. 19There was no war until the thirty-fifth year of the reign of Asa.

---

b   *With vv. 16–19, cf. 1 Kings 15.13–16.*
c   *I.e., Asa.*

8 וְכִשְׁמֹ֩עַ אָסָ֨א הַדְּבָרִ֤ים הָאֵ֙לֶּה֙ וְהַנְּבוּאָה֙ עֹדֵ֣ד הַנָּבִ֔יא הִתְחַזַּ֗ק וַיַּעֲבֵ֤ר הַשִּׁקּוּצִים֙ מִכָּל־אֶ֤רֶץ יְהוּדָה֙ וּבִנְיָמִ֔ן וּמִן־הֶ֣עָרִ֔ים אֲשֶׁ֥ר לָכַ֖ד מֵהַ֣ר אֶפְרָ֑יִם וַיְחַדֵּשׁ֙ אֶת־מִזְבַּ֣ח יְהוָ֔ה אֲשֶׁ֖ר לִפְנֵ֥י אוּלָ֥ם יְהוָֽה׃ 9 וַיִּקְבֹּ֗ץ אֶת־כָּל־יְהוּדָה֙ וּבִנְיָמִ֔ן וְהַגָּרִים֙ עִמָּהֶ֔ם מֵאֶפְרַ֥יִם וּמְנַשֶּׁ֖ה וּמִשִּׁמְע֑וֹן כִּֽי־נָפְל֨וּ עָלָ֤יו מִיִּשְׂרָאֵל֙ לָרֹ֔ב בִּרְאֹתָ֕ם כִּֽי־יְהוָ֥ה אֱלֹהָ֖יו עִמּֽוֹ׃ פ 10 וַיִּקָּבְצ֥וּ יְרוּשָׁלַ֖͏ִם בַּחֹ֣דֶשׁ הַשְּׁלִישִׁ֑י לִשְׁנַ֥ת חֲמֵשׁ־עֶשְׂרֵ֖ה לְמַלְכ֥וּת אָסָֽא׃ 11 וַיִּזְבְּח֤וּ לַֽיהוָה֙ בַּיּ֣וֹם הַה֔וּא מִן־הַשָּׁלָ֖ל הֵבִ֑יאוּ בָּקָר֙ שְׁבַ֣ע מֵא֔וֹת וְצֹ֖אן שִׁבְעַ֥ת אֲלָפִֽים׃ 12 וַיָּבֹ֣אוּ בַבְּרִ֔ית לִדְרֹ֕ושׁ אֶת־יְהוָ֖ה אֱלֹהֵ֣י אֲבוֹתֵיהֶ֑ם בְּכָל־לְבָבָ֖ם וּבְכָל־נַפְשָֽׁם׃ 13 וְכֹ֨ל אֲשֶׁ֧ר לֹֽא־יִדְרֹ֛שׁ לַיהוָ֥ה אֱלֹהֵֽי־יִשְׂרָאֵ֖ל יוּמָ֑ת לְמִן־קָטֹן֙ וְעַד־גָּד֔וֹל לְמֵאִ֖ישׁ וְעַד־אִשָּֽׁה׃ 14 וַיִּשָּֽׁבְעוּ֙ לַֽיהוָ֔ה בְּק֣וֹל גָּד֔וֹל וּבִתְרוּעָ֖ה וּבַחֲצֹצְר֥וֹת וּבְשׁוֹפָרֽוֹת׃ 15 וַיִּשְׂמְח֤וּ כָל־יְהוּדָה֙ עַל־הַשְּׁבוּעָ֔ה כִּ֤י בְכָל־לְבָבָם֙ נִשְׁבָּ֔עוּ וּבְכָל־רְצוֹנָ֣ם בִּקְשֻׁ֔הוּ וַיִּמָּצֵ֖א לָהֶ֑ם וַיָּ֧נַח יְהוָ֛ה לָהֶ֖ם מִסָּבִֽיב׃

16 וְגַם־מַעֲכָ֣ה אֵ֣ם ׀ אָסָ֣א הַמֶּ֗לֶךְ הֱסִירָהּ֙ מִגְּבִירָ֔ה אֲשֶׁר־עָשְׂתָ֥ה לַאֲשֵׁרָ֖ה מִפְלָ֑צֶת וַיִּכְרֹ֤ת אָסָא֙ אֶת־מִפְלַצְתָּ֔הּ וַיָּ֕דֶק וַיִּשְׂרֹ֖ף בְּנַ֥חַל קִדְרֽוֹן׃ 17 וְהַ֨בָּמ֔וֹת לֹא־סָ֖רוּ מִיִּשְׂרָאֵ֑ל רַ֧ק לְבַב־אָסָ֛א הָיָ֥ה שָׁלֵ֖ם כָּל־יָמָֽיו׃ 18 וַיָּבֵ֞א אֶת־קָדְשֵׁ֣י אָבִ֗יו וְקָֽדָשָׁ֛יו בֵּ֥ית הָאֱלֹהִ֖ים כֶּ֣סֶף וְזָהָ֑ב וְכֵלִֽים׃ 19 וּמִלְחָמָ֖ה לֹ֣א הָיָ֑תָה עַ֛ד שְׁנַת־שְׁלֹשִׁ֥ים וְחָמֵ֖שׁ לְמַלְכ֥וּת אָסָֽא׃ ס

16 [a]In the thirty-sixth year of the reign of Asa, King Baasha of Israel marched against Judah and built up Ramah to block [b]all movement-[b] of King Asa of Judah. [2]Asa took all the silver and gold from the treasuries of the House of the LORD and the royal palace, and sent them to King Ben-hadad of Aram, who resided in Damascus, with this message: [3]"There is a pact between me and you, as there was between my father and your father. I herewith send you silver and gold; go and break your pact with King Baasha of Israel so that he may withdraw from me." [4]Ben-hadad acceded to King Asa's request; he sent his army commanders against the towns of Israel and ravaged Ijon, Dan, Abel-maim, and all the garrison towns of Naphtali. [5]When Baasha heard about it, he stopped building up Ramah and put an end to the work on it. [6]Then King Asa mustered all Judah, and they carried away the stones and timber with which Baasha had built up Ramah; with these King Asa built up Geba and Mizpah.

[7]At that time, Hanani the seer came to King Asa of Judah and said to him, "Because you relied on the king of Aram and did not rely on the LORD your God, therefore the army of the king of Aram has slipped out of your hands. [8]The Cushites and Lybians were a mighty army with chariots and horsemen in very great numbers, yet because you relied on the LORD He delivered them into your hands. [9]For the eyes of the LORD range over the entire earth, to give support to those who are wholeheartedly with Him. You have acted foolishly in this matter, and henceforth you will be beset by wars." [10]Asa was vexed at the seer and put him into the stocks,[c] for he was furious with him because of that. Asa inflicted cruelties on some of the people at that time.

טז בִּשְׁנַ֨ת שְׁלֹשִׁ֤ים וָשֵׁשׁ֙ לְמַלְכ֣וּת אָסָ֔א עָלָ֞ה בַּעְשָׁ֤א מֶֽלֶךְ־יִשְׂרָאֵל֙ עַל־יְהוּדָ֔ה וַיִּ֖בֶן אֶת־הָרָמָ֑ה לְבִלְתִּ֗י תֵּ֤ת יוֹצֵא֙ וָבָ֔א לְאָסָ֖א מֶ֥לֶךְ יְהוּדָֽה׃ [2] וַיֹּצֵ֣א אָסָ֗א כֶּ֣סֶף וְזָהָ֗ב מֵאֹצְרוֹת֙ בֵּ֤ית יְהוָה֙ וּבֵ֣ית הַמֶּ֔לֶךְ וַיִּשְׁלַ֗ח אֶל־בֶּן־הֲדַד֙ מֶ֣לֶךְ אֲרָ֔ם הַיּוֹשֵׁ֥ב בְּדַרְמֶ֖שֶׂק לֵאמֹֽר׃ [3] בְּרִית֙ בֵּינִ֣י וּבֵינֶ֔ךָ וּבֵ֥ין אָבִ֖י וּבֵ֣ין אָבִ֑יךָ הִנֵּ֨ה שָׁלַ֤חְתִּי לְךָ֙ כֶּ֣סֶף וְזָהָ֔ב לֵ֞ךְ הָפֵ֣ר בְּרִֽיתְךָ֗ אֶת־בַּעְשָׁא֙ מֶ֣לֶךְ יִשְׂרָאֵ֔ל וְיַעֲלֶ֖ה מֵעָלָֽי׃ [4] וַיִּשְׁמַ֨ע בֶּן־הֲדַ֜ד אֶל־הַמֶּ֣לֶךְ אָסָ֗א וַ֠יִּשְׁלַח אֶת־שָׂרֵ֨י הַחֲיָלִ֤ים אֲשֶׁר־לוֹ֙ אֶל־עָרֵ֣י יִשְׂרָאֵ֔ל וַיַּכּוּ֙ אֶת־עִיּ֣וֹן וְאֶת־דָּ֔ן וְאֵ֖ת אָבֵ֣ל מָ֑יִם וְאֵ֥ת כָּֽל־מִסְכְּנ֖וֹת עָרֵ֥י נַפְתָּלִֽי׃ [5] וַֽיְהִי֙ כִּשְׁמֹ֣עַ בַּעְשָׁ֔א וַיֶּחְדַּ֕ל מִבְּנ֖וֹת אֶת־הָרָמָ֑ה וַיַּשְׁבֵּ֖ת אֶת־מְלַאכְתּֽוֹ׃ ס [6] וְאָסָ֣א הַמֶּ֗לֶךְ לָקַח֙ אֶת־כָּל־יְהוּדָ֔ה וַיִּשְׂא֞וּ אֶת־אַבְנֵ֤י הָֽרָמָה֙ וְאֶת־עֵצֶ֔יהָ אֲשֶׁ֥ר בָּנָ֖ה בַּעְשָׁ֑א וַיִּ֣בֶן בָּהֶ֔ם אֶת־גֶּ֖בַע וְאֶת־הַמִּצְפָּֽה׃ ס [7] וּבָעֵ֣ת הַהִ֗יא בָּ֚א חֲנָ֣נִי הָרֹאֶ֔ה אֶל־אָסָ֖א מֶ֣לֶךְ יְהוּדָ֑ה וַיֹּ֣אמֶר אֵלָ֗יו בְּהִשָּׁ֨עֶנְךָ֜ עַל־מֶ֤לֶךְ אֲרָם֙ וְלֹ֣א נִשְׁעַ֔נְתָּ עַל־יְהוָ֣ה אֱלֹהֶ֔יךָ עַל־כֵּ֗ן נִמְלַ֛ט חֵ֥יל מֶֽלֶךְ־אֲרָ֖ם מִיָּדֶֽךָ׃ [8] הֲלֹ֧א הַכּוּשִׁ֣ים וְהַלּוּבִ֗ים הָי֣וּ לְחַ֣יִל ׀ לָרֹ֤ב לְרֶ֨כֶב֙ וּלְפָ֣רָשִׁ֔ים לְהַרְבֵּ֖ה מְאֹ֑ד וּבְהִשָּֽׁעֶנְךָ֤ עַל־יְהוָה֙ נְתָנָ֣ם בְּיָדֶ֔ךָ׃ [9] כִּ֣י יְהוָ֗ה עֵינָ֞יו מְשֹׁטְט֤וֹת בְּכָל־הָאָ֨רֶץ֙ לְ֠הִתְחַזֵּק עִם־לְבָבָ֥ם שָׁלֵ֛ם אֵלָ֖יו נִסְכַּ֣לְתָּ עַל־זֹ֑את כִּ֣י מֵעַ֔תָּה יֵ֥שׁ עִמְּךָ֖ מִלְחָמֽוֹת׃ [10] וַיִּכְעַ֨ס אָסָ֜א אֶל־הָֽרֹאֶ֗ה וַֽיִּתְּנֵ֨הוּ֙ בֵּ֣ית הַמַּהְפֶּ֔כֶת כִּֽי־בְזַ֥עַף עִמּ֖וֹ עַל־זֹ֑את וַיְרַצֵּ֥ץ אָסָ֛א מִן־הָעָ֖ם בָּעֵ֥ת הַהִֽיא׃

---

a   *Cf. 1 Kings 15.17–24.*
b-b   *Lit. "one who goes out and one who comes in."*
c   *Meaning of Heb. uncertain.*

11The acts of Asa, early and late, are recorded in the annals of the kings of Judah and Israel. 12In the thirty-ninth year of his reign, Asa suffered from an acute foot ailment; but ill as he was, he still did not turn to the LORD but to physicians. 13Asa slept with his fathers. He died in the forty-first year of his reign 14and was buried in the grave that he had made for himself in the City of David. He was laid in his resting-place, which was filled with spices of all kinds, expertly blended; a very great fire was made in his honor.

17

His son Jehoshaphat succeeded him as king, and took firm hold of Israel. 2He stationed troops in all the fortified towns of Judah, and stationed garrisons throughout the land of Judah and the cities of Ephraim which his father Asa had captured. 3The LORD was with Jehoshaphat because he followed the earlier ways of his father David, and did not worship the Baalim, 4but worshiped the God of his father and followed His commandments—unlike the behavior of Israel. 5So the LORD established the kingdom in his hands, and all Judah gave presents to Jehoshaphat. He had wealth and glory in abundance. 6His mind was elevated in the ways of the LORD. Moreover, he abolished the shrines and the sacred posts from Judah.

7In the third year of his reign he sent his officers Ben-hail, Obadiah, Zechariah, Nethanel, and Micaiah throughout the cities of Judah to offer instruction. 8With them were the Levites, Shemaiah, Nethaniah, Zebadiah, Asahel, Shemiramoth, Jehonathan, Adonijah, Tobijah and Tob-adonijah the Levites; with them were Elishama and Jehoram the priests. 9They offered instruction throughout Judah, having

11 וְהִנֵּה֙ דִּבְרֵ֣י אָסָ֔א הָרִאשׁוֹנִ֖ים וְהָאַחֲרוֹנִ֑ים הִנָּ֣ם כְּתוּבִ֗ים עַל־סֵ֥פֶר הַמְּלָכִ֖ים לִֽיהוּדָ֥ה וְיִשְׂרָאֵֽל׃ 12 וַיֶּחֱלֶ֣א אָסָ֡א בִּשְׁנַת֩ שְׁלוֹשִׁ֨ים וָתֵ֤שַׁע לְמַלְכוּתוֹ֙ בְּרַגְלָ֔יו עַד־לְמַ֖עְלָה חָלְי֑וֹ וְגַם־בְּחׇלְי֛וֹ לֹא־דָרַ֥שׁ אֶת־יְהֹוָ֖ה כִּ֥י בָּרֹפְאִֽים׃ 13 וַיִּשְׁכַּ֤ב אָסָא֙ עִם־אֲבֹתָ֔יו וַיָּ֕מׇת בִּשְׁנַ֛ת אַרְבָּעִ֥ים וְאַחַ֖ת לְמׇלְכֽוֹ׃ 14 וַיִּקְבְּרֻ֣הוּ בְקִבְרֹתָ֗יו אֲשֶׁ֤ר כָּרָה־לוֹ֙ בְּעִ֣יר דָּוִ֔יד וַיַּשְׁכִּיבֻ֗הוּ בַּמִּשְׁכָּב֙ אֲשֶׁ֤ר מִלֵּא֙ בְּשָׂמִ֣ים וּזְנִ֔ים מְרֻקָּחִ֖ים בְּמִרְקַ֣חַת מַעֲשֶׂ֑ה וַיִּשְׂרְפוּ־ל֥וֹ שְׂרֵפָ֖ה גְדוֹלָ֥ה עַד־לִמְאֹֽד׃ פ

יז

וַיִּמְלֹ֛ךְ יְהוֹשָׁפָ֥ט בְּנ֖וֹ תַּחְתָּ֑יו וַיִּתְחַזֵּ֖ק עַל־יִשְׂרָאֵֽל׃ 2 וַיִּ֨תֶּן־חַ֔יִל בְּכׇל־עָרֵ֥י יְהוּדָ֖ה הַבְּצֻר֑וֹת וַיִּתֵּ֤ן נְצִיבִים֙ בְּאֶ֣רֶץ יְהוּדָ֔ה וּבְעָרֵ֣י אֶפְרַ֔יִם אֲשֶׁ֥ר לָכַ֖ד אָסָ֥א אָבִֽיו׃ 3 וַיְהִ֥י יְהֹוָ֖ה עִם־יְהוֹשָׁפָ֑ט כִּ֣י הָלַ֗ךְ בְּדַרְכֵ֞י דָּוִ֤יד אָבִיו֙ הָרִ֣אשֹׁנִ֔ים וְלֹ֥א דָרַ֖שׁ לַבְּעָלִֽים׃ 4 כִּ֠י לֵאלֹהֵ֤י אָבִיו֙ דָּרָ֔שׁ וּבְמִצְוֺתָ֖יו הָלָ֑ךְ וְלֹ֖א כְּמַעֲשֵׂ֥ה יִשְׂרָאֵֽל׃ 5 וַיָּ֨כֶן יְהֹוָ֤ה אֶת־הַמַּמְלָכָה֙ בְּיָד֔וֹ וַיִּתְּנ֧וּ כׇל־יְהוּדָ֛ה מִנְחָ֖ה לִיהוֹשָׁפָ֑ט וַיְהִי־ל֥וֹ עֹֽשֶׁר־וְכָב֖וֹד לָרֹֽב׃ 6 וַיִּגְבַּ֥הּ לִבּ֖וֹ בְּדַרְכֵ֣י יְהֹוָ֑ה וְע֗וֹד הֵסִ֛יר אֶת־הַבָּמ֥וֹת וְאֶת־הָאֲשֵׁרִ֖ים מִיהוּדָֽה׃ פ

7 וּבִשְׁנַ֨ת שָׁל֜וֹשׁ לְמׇלְכ֗וֹ שָׁלַ֤ח לְשָׂרָיו֙ לְבֶן־חַ֙יִל֙ וּלְעֹבַדְיָ֣ה וְלִזְכַרְיָ֔ה וְלִנְתַנְאֵ֖ל וּלְמִ֣יכָיָ֑הוּ לְלַמֵּ֖ד בְּעָרֵ֥י יְהוּדָֽה׃ 8 וְעִמָּהֶ֣ם הַלְוִיִּ֗ם שְֽׁמַֽעְיָ֡הוּ וּנְתַנְיָ֡הוּ וּזְבַדְיָ֡הוּ וַעֲשָׂהאֵ֣ל ושמרימות וּֽשְׁמִֽירָמ֡וֹת וִיה֣וֹנָתָ֣ן וַאֲדֹ֨נִיָּ֤הֽוּ וְטֽוֹבִיָּ֙הוּ֙ וְט֣וֹב אֲדֽוֹנִיָּ֔ה הַלְוִיִּ֑ם וְעִמָּהֶ֛ם אֱלִישָׁמָ֥ע וִֽיהוֹרָ֖ם הַכֹּהֲנִֽים׃ 9 וַֽיְלַמְּדוּ֙ בִּֽיהוּדָ֔ה וְעִ֨מָּהֶ֔ם סֵ֖פֶר תּוֹרַ֣ת יְהֹוָ֑ה וַיָּסֹ֙בּוּ֙ בְּכׇל־עָרֵ֣י יְהוּדָ֔ה וַיְלַמְּד֖וּ

with them the Book of the Teaching of the LORD. They made the rounds of all the cities of Judah and instructed the people. [10]A terror of the LORD seized all the kingdoms of the lands around Judah, and they did not go to war with Jehoshaphat. [11]From Philistia a load of silver was brought to Jehoshaphat as tribute. The Arabs, too, brought him flocks: 7,700 rams and 7,700 he-goats. [12]Jehoshaphat grew greater and greater, and he built up fortresses and garrison towns in Judah. [13]He carried out extensive works in the towns of Judah, and had soldiers, valiant men, in Jerusalem. [14]They were enrolled according to their clans. Judah: chiefs of thousands, Adnah the chief, who had 300,000 valiant men; [15]next to him was Jehohanan the captain, who had 280,000; [16]next to him was Amasiah son of Zichri, who made a freewill offering to the LORD. He had 200,000 valiant men. [17]Benjamin: Eliada, a valiant man, who had 200,000 men armed with bow and buckler; [18]next to him was Jehozabad, who had 180,000 armed men. [19]These served the king, besides those whom the king assigned to the fortified towns throughout Judah.

18

[a]So Jehoshaphat had wealth and honor in abundance, and he allied himself by marriage to Ahab. [2]After some years had passed, he came to visit Ahab at Samaria. Ahab slaughtered sheep and oxen in abundance for him and for the people with him, and persuaded him to march against Ramoth-gilead. [3]King Ahab of Israel said to King Jehoshaphat of Judah, "Will you accompany me to Ramoth-gilead?" He answered him, "I will do what you do; my troops shall be your troops and shall accompany you in battle." [4]Jehoshaphat then said to the king

a   *Cf. 1 Kings 22.*

בָּעָם: 10 וַיְהִי ׀ פַּחַד יְהוָה עַל כָּל־מַמְלְכוֹת הָאֲרָצוֹת אֲשֶׁר סְבִיבוֹת יְהוּדָה וְלֹא נִלְחֲמוּ עִם־יְהוֹשָׁפָט: 11 וּמִן־פְּלִשְׁתִּים מְבִיאִים לִיהוֹשָׁפָט מִנְחָה וְכֶסֶף מַשָּׂא גַּם הָעַרְבִיאִים מְבִיאִים לוֹ צֹאן אֵילִים שִׁבְעַת אֲלָפִים וּשְׁבַע מֵאוֹת וּתְיָשִׁים שִׁבְעַת אֲלָפִים וּשְׁבַע מֵאוֹת: פ 12 וַיְהִי יְהוֹשָׁפָט הֹלֵךְ וְגָדֵל עַד־לְמָעְלָה וַיִּבֶן בִּיהוּדָה בִּירָנִיּוֹת וְעָרֵי מִסְכְּנוֹת: 13 וּמְלָאכָה רַבָּה הָיָה לוֹ בְּעָרֵי יְהוּדָה וְאַנְשֵׁי מִלְחָמָה גִּבּוֹרֵי חַיִל בִּירוּשָׁלָ͏ִם: 14 וְאֵלֶּה פְּקֻדָּתָם לְבֵית אֲבוֹתֵיהֶם לִיהוּדָה שָׂרֵי אֲלָפִים עַדְנָה הַשָּׂר וְעִמּוֹ גִּבּוֹרֵי חַיִל שְׁלֹשׁ מֵאוֹת אָלֶף: ס 15 וְעַל־יָדוֹ יְהוֹחָנָן הַשָּׂר וְעִמּוֹ מָאתַיִם וּשְׁמוֹנִים אָלֶף: ס 16 וְעַל־יָדוֹ עֲמַסְיָה בֶן־זִכְרִי הַמִּתְנַדֵּב לַיהוָה וְעִמּוֹ מָאתַיִם אֶלֶף גִּבּוֹר* חָיִל: ס 17 וּמִן־בִּנְיָמִן גִּבּוֹר חַיִל אֶלְיָדָע וְעִמּוֹ נֹשְׁקֵי־קֶשֶׁת וּמָגֵן מָאתַיִם אָלֶף: ס 18 וְעַל־יָדוֹ יְהוֹזָבָד וְעִמּוֹ מֵאָה־וּשְׁמוֹנִים אֶלֶף חֲלוּצֵי צָבָא: ס 19 אֵלֶּה הַמְשָׁרְתִים אֶת־הַמֶּלֶךְ מִלְּבַד אֲשֶׁר־נָתַן הַמֶּלֶךְ בְּעָרֵי הַמִּבְצָר בְּכָל־יְהוּדָה: פ

יח

וַיְהִי לִיהוֹשָׁפָט עֹשֶׁר וְכָבוֹד לָרֹב וַיִּתְחַתֵּן לְאַחְאָב: 2 וַיֵּרֶד לְקֵץ שָׁנִים אֶל־אַחְאָב לְשֹׁמְרוֹן וַיִּזְבַּח־לוֹ אַחְאָב צֹאן וּבָקָר לָרֹב וְלָעָם אֲשֶׁר עִמּוֹ וַיְסִיתֵהוּ לַעֲלוֹת אֶל־רָמוֹת גִּלְעָד: 3 וַיֹּאמֶר אַחְאָב מֶלֶךְ־יִשְׂרָאֵל אֶל־יְהוֹשָׁפָט מֶלֶךְ יְהוּדָה הֲתֵלֵךְ עִמִּי רָמֹת גִּלְעָד וַיֹּאמֶר לוֹ כָּמוֹנִי כָמוֹךָ וּכְעַמְּךָ עַמִּי וְעִמְּךָ בַּמִּלְחָמָה:

v. 16.   סבירין ומטעין "גבורי"

of Israel, "But first inquire for the word of the LORD."

⁵So the king of Israel gathered the prophets, four hundred men, and asked them, "Shall I march upon Ramoth-gilead for battle, or shall I not?" "March," they said, "and God will deliver it into the king's hands." ⁶Then Jehoshaphat asked, "Is there not another prophet of the LORD here through whom we can inquire?" ⁷And the king of Israel answered Jehoshaphat, "There is one more man through whom we can inquire of the LORD; but I hate him, because he never prophesies anything good for me but always misfortune. He is Micaiah son of Imlah." Jehoshaphat replied, "Let the king not say such a thing." ⁸So the king of Israel summoned an officer and said, "Bring Micaiah son of Imlah at once."

⁹The king of Israel and King Jehoshaphat of Judah, wearing their robes, were seated on their thrones situated in the threshing floor at the entrance of the gate of Samaria; and all the prophets were prophesying before them. ¹⁰Zedekiah son of Chenaanah had provided himself with iron horns; and he said, "Thus said the LORD: With these you shall gore the Arameans till you make an end of them." ¹¹All the other prophets were prophesying similarly, "March against Ramoth-gilead and be victorious! The LORD will deliver it into Your Majesty's hands."

¹²The messenger who had gone to summon Micaiah said to him, "Look, the words of the prophets are unanimously favorable to the king. Let your word be like that of the rest of them; speak a favorable word." ¹³"By the life of the LORD," Micaiah answered, "I will speak only what my God tells me." ¹⁴When he came before the king, the king said to him, "Micah,ᵇ shall we march against Ramoth-gilead for battle or shall we not?" He answered him, "March and be victorious! They will be delivered into your

---

ᵇ   *A shortened form of Micaiah.*

4 וַיֹּ֙אמֶר֙ יְהוֹשָׁפָ֔ט אֶל־מֶ֖לֶךְ יִשְׂרָאֵ֑ל דְּרָשׁ־נָ֥א כַיּ֖וֹם אֶת־דְּבַ֥ר יְהֹוָֽה׃ 5 וַיִּקְבֹּ֣ץ מֶֽלֶךְ־יִ֠שְׂרָאֵל אֶֽת־הַנְּבִאִ֞ים אַרְבַּ֧ע מֵא֣וֹת אִ֗ישׁ וַיֹּ֤אמֶר אֲלֵהֶם֙ הֲנֵלֵ֞ךְ אֶל־רָמֹ֥ת גִּלְעָ֛ד לַמִּלְחָמָ֖ה אִם־אֶחְדָּ֑ל וַיֹּאמְר֣וּ עֲלֵ֔ה וְיִתֵּ֥ן הָאֱלֹהִ֖ים בְּיַ֥ד הַמֶּֽלֶךְ׃ 6 וַיֹּ֙אמֶר֙ יְה֣וֹשָׁפָ֔ט הַאֵ֨ין פֹּ֥ה נָבִ֛יא לַיהֹוָ֖ה ע֑וֹד וְנִדְרְשָׁ֖ה מֵאֹתֽוֹ׃ 7 וַיֹּ֣אמֶר מֶֽלֶךְ־יִשְׂרָאֵ֣ל ׀ אֶֽל־יְהוֹשָׁפָ֡ט ע֣וֹד אִישׁ־אֶחָ֡ד לִדְרֹושׁ֩ אֶת־יְהֹוָ֨ה מֵאֹת֜וֹ וַאֲנִ֣י שְׂנֵאתִ֗יהוּ כִּֽי־אֵינֶ֜נּוּ מִתְנַבֵּ֤א עָלַי֙ לְטוֹבָ֔ה כִּ֥י כָל־יָמָ֖יו לְרָעָ֑ה ה֣וּא מִיכָ֣יְהוּ בֶן־יִמְלָ֔א וַיֹּ֙אמֶר֙ יְה֣וֹשָׁפָ֔ט אַל־יֹאמַ֥ר הַמֶּ֖לֶךְ כֵּֽן׃ 8 וַיִּקְרָא֙ מֶ֣לֶךְ יִשְׂרָאֵ֔ל אֶל־סָרִ֖יס אֶחָ֑ד וַיֹּ֕אמֶר מַהֵ֖ר מִיכָ֥הוּ מִיכָ֥יְהוּ בֶן־יִמְלָֽא׃ 9 וּמֶ֣לֶךְ יִשְׂרָאֵ֡ל וִֽיהוֹשָׁפָ֣ט מֶֽלֶךְ־יְהוּדָ֡ה יֽוֹשְׁבִים֩ אִ֨ישׁ עַל־כִּסְא֜וֹ מְלֻבָּשִׁ֣ים בְּגָדִ֗ים וְיֹֽשְׁבִים֙ בְּגֹ֔רֶן פֶּ֖תַח שַׁ֣עַר שֹֽׁמְר֑וֹן וְכָ֨ל־הַנְּבִיאִ֔ים מִֽתְנַבְּאִ֖ים לִפְנֵיהֶֽם׃ 10 וַיַּ֥עַשׂ ל֛וֹ צִדְקִיָּ֥הוּ בֶן־כְּנַעֲנָ֖ה קַרְנֵ֣י בַרְזֶ֑ל וַיֹּ֙אמֶר֙ כֹּֽה־אָמַ֣ר יְהֹוָ֔ה בְּאֵ֛לֶּה תְּנַגַּ֥ח אֶת־אֲרָ֖ם עַד־כַּלּוֹתָֽם׃ 11 וְכָ֨ל־הַנְּבִאִ֔ים נִבְּאִ֖ים כֵּ֣ן לֵאמֹ֑ר עֲלֵ֞ה רָמֹ֤ת גִּלְעָד֙ וְהַצְלַ֔ח וְנָתַ֥ן יְהֹוָ֖ה בְּיַ֥ד הַמֶּֽלֶךְ׃ 12 וְהַמַּלְאָ֞ךְ אֲשֶׁר־הָלַ֣ךְ ׀ לִקְרֹ֣א לְמִיכָ֗יְהוּ דִּבֶּ֤ר אֵלָיו֙ לֵאמֹ֔ר הִנֵּ֞ה דִּבְרֵ֧י הַנְּבִאִ֛ים פֶּֽה־אֶחָ֥ד ט֖וֹב אֶל־הַמֶּ֑לֶךְ וִֽיהִי־נָ֣א דְבָרְךָ֗ כְּאַחַ֥ד מֵהֶ֖ם וְדִבַּ֥רְתָּ טּֽוֹב׃ 13 וַיֹּ֖אמֶר מִיכָ֑יְהוּ חַי־יְהֹוָ֔ה כִּ֠י אֶת־אֲשֶׁר־יֹאמַ֥ר אֱלֹהַ֛י אֹת֥וֹ אֲדַבֵּֽר׃ 14 וַיָּבֹא֮ אֶל־הַמֶּלֶךְ֒ וַיֹּ֨אמֶר הַמֶּ֜לֶךְ אֵלָ֗יו מִיכָה֙ הֲנֵלֵ֞ךְ אֶל־רָמֹ֥ת גִּלְעָ֛ד לַמִּלְחָמָ֖ה אִם־אֶחְדָּ֑ל וַיֹּ֙אמֶר֙ עֲל֣וּ וְהַצְלִ֔יחוּ וְיִנָּתְנ֖וּ בְּיֶדְכֶֽם׃ 15 וַיֹּ֤אמֶר אֵלָיו֙

hands." 15The king said to him, "How many times must I adjure you to tell me nothing but the truth in the name of the Lord?" 16Then he said, "I saw all Israel scattered over the hills like sheep without a shepherd; and the Lord said, 'These have no master; let everyone return to his home in safety.'" 17The king of Israel said to Jehoshaphat, "Did I not tell you that he would not prophesy good fortune for me, but only misfortune?"

18Then [Micaiah] said, "Indeed, hear now the word of the Lord! I saw the Lord seated upon His throne, with all the host of heaven standing in attendance to the right and to the left of Him. 19The Lord asked, 'Who will entice King Ahab of Israel so that he will march and fall at Ramoth-gilead?' Then one said this and another said that, 20until a certain spirit came forward and stood before the Lord and said, 'I will entice him.' 'How?' said the Lord to him. 21And he replied, 'I will go forth and become a lying spirit in the mouth of all his prophets.' Then He said, 'You will entice with success. Go forth and do it.' 22Thus the Lord has put a lying spirit in the mouth of all these prophets of yours; for the Lord has decreed misfortune for you."

23Thereupon Zedekiah son of Chenaanah came up and struck Micaiah on the cheek, and exclaimed, "However did the spirit of the Lord pass from me to speak with you!" 24Micaiah replied, "You will see on the day when you try to hide in the innermost room." 25Then the king of Israel said, "Take Micaiah and turn him over to Amon, the governor of the city, and to Prince Joash, 26and say, 'The king's orders are: Put this fellow in prison, and let his fare be scant bread and scant water until I come home safe.'" 27To which Micaiah retorted, "If you ever come home safe, the Lord has not spoken through me." He said further, c-"Listen, all you peoples!"-c

c-c Cf. Mic. 1.2.

הַמֶּלֶךְ עַד־כַּמֶּה פְעָמִים אֲנִי מַשְׁבִּיעֶךָ אֲשֶׁר לֹא־תְדַבֵּר אֵלַי רַק־אֱמֶת בְּשֵׁם יְהוָה: 16 וַיֹּאמֶר רָאִיתִי אֶת־כָּל־יִשְׂרָאֵל נְפוֹצִים עַל־הֶהָרִים כַּצֹּאן אֲשֶׁר אֵין־לָהֶן רֹעֶה וַיֹּאמֶר יְהוָה לֹא־אֲדֹנִים לָאֵלֶּה יָשׁוּבוּ אִישׁ־לְבֵיתוֹ בְּשָׁלוֹם: 17 וַיֹּאמֶר מֶלֶךְ־יִשְׂרָאֵל אֶל־יְהוֹשָׁפָט הֲלֹא אָמַרְתִּי אֵלֶיךָ לֹא־יִתְנַבֵּא עָלַי טוֹב כִּי אִם־לְרָע: ס

18 וַיֹּאמֶר לָכֵן שִׁמְעוּ דְבַר־יְהוָה רָאִיתִי אֶת־יְהוָה יוֹשֵׁב עַל־כִּסְאוֹ וְכָל־צְבָא הַשָּׁמַיִם עֹמְדִים עַל־יְמִינוֹ וּשְׂמֹאלוֹ: 19 וַיֹּאמֶר יְהוָה מִי יְפַתֶּה אֶת־אַחְאָב מֶלֶךְ־יִשְׂרָאֵל וְיַעַל וְיִפֹּל בְּרָמוֹת גִּלְעָד וַיֹּאמֶר זֶה אֹמֵר כָּכָה וְזֶה אֹמֵר כָּכָה: 20 וַיֵּצֵא הָרוּחַ וַיַּעֲמֹד לִפְנֵי יְהוָה וַיֹּאמֶר אֲנִי אֲפַתֶּנּוּ וַיֹּאמֶר יְהוָה אֵלָיו בַּמֶּה: 21 וַיֹּאמֶר אֵצֵא וְהָיִיתִי לְרוּחַ שֶׁקֶר בְּפִי כָּל־נְבִיאָיו וַיֹּאמֶר תְּפַתֶּה וְגַם־תּוּכָל צֵא וַעֲשֵׂה־כֵן: 22 וְעַתָּה הִנֵּה נָתַן יְהוָה רוּחַ שֶׁקֶר בְּפִי נְבִיאֶיךָ אֵלֶּה וַיהוָה דִּבֶּר עָלֶיךָ רָעָה: ס

23 וַיִּגַּשׁ צִדְקִיָּהוּ בֶן־כְּנַעֲנָה וַיַּךְ אֶת־מִיכָיְהוּ עַל־הַלֶּחִי וַיֹּאמֶר אֵי זֶה הַדֶּרֶךְ עָבַר רוּחַ־יְהוָה מֵאִתִּי לְדַבֵּר אֹתָךְ: 24 וַיֹּאמֶר מִיכָיְהוּ הִנְּךָ רֹאֶה בַּיּוֹם הַהוּא אֲשֶׁר תָּבוֹא חֶדֶר בְּחֶדֶר לְהֵחָבֵא: 25 וַיֹּאמֶר מֶלֶךְ יִשְׂרָאֵל קְחוּ אֶת־מִיכָיְהוּ וַהֲשִׁיבֻהוּ אֶל־אָמוֹן שַׂר־הָעִיר וְאֶל־יוֹאָשׁ בֶּן־הַמֶּלֶךְ: 26 וַאֲמַרְתֶּם כֹּה אָמַר הַמֶּלֶךְ שִׂימוּ זֶה בֵּית הַכֶּלֶא וְהַאֲכִלֻהוּ לֶחֶם לַחַץ וּמַיִם לַחַץ עַד שׁוּבִי בְשָׁלוֹם: 27 וַיֹּאמֶר מִיכָיְהוּ אִם־שׁוֹב תָּשׁוּב בְּשָׁלוֹם לֹא־דִבֶּר יְהוָה בִּי וַיֹּאמֶר שִׁמְעוּ עַמִּים כֻּלָּם: פ

28The king of Israel and King Jehoshaphat of Judah marched against Ramoth-gilead. 29The king of Israel said to Jehoshaphat, d-"I will disguise myself and go-d into the battle, but you, wear your robes." So the king of Israel disguised himself, and they went into the battle. 30The king of Aram had given these instructions to his chariot officers: "Do not attack anyone, small or great, except the king of Israel." 31When the chariot officers saw Jehoshaphat, whom they took for the king of Israel, they wheeled around to attack him, and Jehoshaphat cried out and the Lord helped him, and God diverted them from him. 32And when the chariot officers realized that he was not the king of Israel, they gave up the pursuit. 33Then a man drew his bow at random and hit the king of Israel between the e-plates of the-e armor and he said to his charioteer, "Turn around and get me behind the lines; I am wounded." 34The battle e-raged all day long,-e and the king remained propped up in the chariot facing Aram until dusk; he died as the sun was setting.

19 King Jehoshaphat of Judah returned safely to his palace, to Jerusalem. 2Jehu son of Hanani the seer went out to meet King Jehoshaphat and said to him, "Should one give aid to the wicked and befriend those who hate the Lord? For this, wrath is upon you from the Lord. 3However, there is some good in you, for you have purged the land of the sacred posts and have dedicated yourself to worship God."

4Jehoshaphat remained in Jerusalem a while and then went out among the people from Beer-sheba to the hill country of Ephraim; he brought them back to the Lord God of their fathers. 5He appointed judges in the land in all the fortified towns of Judah, in each and every

28 וַיַּעַל מֶלֶךְ־יִשְׂרָאֵל וִיהוֹשָׁפָט מֶלֶךְ־יְהוּדָה אֶל־רָמֹת גִּלְעָד: 29 וַיֹּאמֶר מֶלֶךְ יִשְׂרָאֵל אֶל־יְהוֹשָׁפָט הִתְחַפֵּשׂ וָבוֹא בַמִּלְחָמָה וְאַתָּה לְבַשׁ בְּגָדֶיךָ וַיִּתְחַפֵּשׂ מֶלֶךְ יִשְׂרָאֵל וַיָּבֹאוּ בַּמִּלְחָמָה: 30 וּמֶלֶךְ אֲרָם צִוָּה אֶת־שָׂרֵי הָרֶכֶב אֲשֶׁר־לוֹ לֵאמֹר לֹא תִּלָּחֲמוּ אֶת־הַקָּטֹן אֶת־הַגָּדוֹל כִּי אִם־אֶת־מֶלֶךְ יִשְׂרָאֵל לְבַדּוֹ: 31 וַיְהִי כִּרְאוֹת שָׂרֵי הָרֶכֶב אֶת־יְהוֹשָׁפָט וְהֵמָּה אָמְרוּ מֶלֶךְ יִשְׂרָאֵל הוּא וַיָּסֹבּוּ עָלָיו לְהִלָּחֵם וַיִּזְעַק יְהוֹשָׁפָט וַיהוָה עֲזָרוֹ וַיְסִיתֵם אֱלֹהִים מִמֶּנּוּ: 32 וַיְהִי כִּרְאוֹת שָׂרֵי הָרֶכֶב כִּי לֹא־הָיָה מֶלֶךְ יִשְׂרָאֵל וַיָּשֻׁבוּ מֵאַחֲרָיו: 33 וְאִישׁ מָשַׁךְ בַּקֶּשֶׁת לְתֻמּוֹ וַיַּךְ אֶת־מֶלֶךְ יִשְׂרָאֵל בֵּין הַדְּבָקִים וּבֵין הַשִּׁרְיָן וַיֹּאמֶר לָרַכָּב הֲפֹךְ יָדֶיךָ וְהוֹצֵאתַנִי מִן־הַמַּחֲנֶה כִּי הָחֳלֵיתִי: 34 וַתַּעַל הַמִּלְחָמָה בַּיּוֹם הַהוּא וּמֶלֶךְ יִשְׂרָאֵל הָיָה מַעֲמִיד בַּמֶּרְכָּבָה נֹכַח אֲרָם עַד־הָעֶרֶב וַיָּמָת לְעֵת בּוֹא הַשָּׁמֶשׁ:

יט וַיָּשָׁב יְהוֹשָׁפָט מֶלֶךְ־יְהוּדָה אֶל־בֵּיתוֹ בְּשָׁלוֹם לִירוּשָׁלָ͏ִם: 2 וַיֵּצֵא אֶל־פָּנָיו יֵהוּא בֶן־חֲנָנִי הַחֹזֶה וַיֹּאמֶר אֶל־הַמֶּלֶךְ יְהוֹשָׁפָט הֲלָרָשָׁע לַעְזֹר וּלְשֹׂנְאֵי יְהוָה תֶּאֱהָב וּבָזֹאת עָלֶיךָ קֶּצֶף מִלִּפְנֵי יְהוָה: 3 אֲבָל דְּבָרִים טוֹבִים נִמְצְאוּ עִמָּךְ כִּי־בִעַרְתָּ הָאֲשֵׁרוֹת מִן־הָאָרֶץ וַהֲכִינוֹתָ לְבָבְךָ לִדְרֹשׁ הָאֱלֹהִים: 4 וַיֵּשֶׁב יְהוֹשָׁפָט בִּירוּשָׁלָ͏ִם ס וַיָּשָׁב וַיֵּצֵא בָעָם מִבְּאֵר שֶׁבַע עַד־הַר אֶפְרַיִם וַיְשִׁיבֵם אֶל־יְהוָה אֱלֹהֵי אֲבוֹתֵיהֶם: 5 וַיַּעֲמֵד שֹׁפְטִים בָּאָרֶץ בְּכָל־עָרֵי יְהוּדָה הַבְּצֻרוֹת לְעִיר וָעִיר: 6 וַיֹּאמֶר אֶל־

d-d Infinitives used for finite verb; cf. note at 1 Kings 22.30.
e-e Meaning of Heb. uncertain.

town. ⁶He charged the judges: "Consider what you are doing, for you judge not on behalf of man, but on behalf of the LORD, and He is with you when you pass judgment. ⁷Now let the dread of the LORD be upon you; act with care, for there is no injustice or favoritism or bribe-taking with the LORD our God." ⁸Jehosha-phat also appointed in Jerusalem some Levites and priests and heads of the clans of Israelites for rendering judgment in matters of the LORD, and for disputes. Then they returned to Jeru-salem. ⁹He charged them, "This is how you shall act: in fear of the LORD, with fidelity, and with whole heart. ¹⁰When a dispute comes before you from your brothers living in their towns, whether about homicide, or about ritual, or laws or rules, you must instruct them so that they do not incur guilt before the LORD and wrath be upon you and your brothers. Act so and you will not incur guilt. ¹¹See, Amariah the chief priest is over you in all cases concerning the LORD, and Zebadiah son of Ishmael is the commander of the house of Judah in all cases concerning the king; the Levitical officials are at your disposal; act with resolve and the LORD be with the good."

20 After that, Moabites, Ammonites, to-gether with some Ammonim,ᵃ came against Jehoshaphat to wage war. ²The report was brought to Jehoshaphat: "A great multitude is coming against you from beyond the sea, from Aram, and is now in Hazazon-tamar"—that is, Ein-gedi. ³Jehoshaphat was afraid; he decided to resort to the LORD and proclaimed a fast for all Judah. ⁴Judah assembled to beseech the LORD. They also came from all the towns of Ju-dah to seek the LORD.

⁵Jehoshaphat stood in the congregation of Judah and Jerusalem in the House of the LORD

הַשֹּׁפְטִים רְאוּ מָה־אַתֶּם עֹשִׂים כִּי לֹא
לְאָדָם תִּשְׁפְּטוּ כִּי לַיהוָה וְעִמָּכֶם בִּדְבַר
מִשְׁפָּט: ⁷וְעַתָּה יְהִי פַחַד־יְהוָה עֲלֵיכֶם
שִׁמְרוּ וַעֲשׂוּ כִּי־אֵין עִם־יְהוָה אֱלֹהֵינוּ
עַוְלָה וּמַשֹּׂא פָנִים וּמִקַּח־שֹׁחַד: ⁸וְגַם
בִּירוּשָׁלִַם הֶעֱמִיד יְהוֹשָׁפָט מִן־הַלְוִיִּם
וְהַכֹּהֲנִים וּמֵרָאשֵׁי הָאָבוֹת לְיִשְׂרָאֵל
לְמִשְׁפַּט יְהוָה וְלָרִיב וַיָּשֻׁבוּ יְרוּשָׁלִָם:
⁹וַיְצַו עֲלֵיהֶם לֵאמֹר כֹּה תַעֲשׂוּן בְּיִרְאַת
יְהוָה בֶּאֱמוּנָה וּבְלֵבָב שָׁלֵם: ¹⁰וְכָל־רִיב
אֲשֶׁר־יָבוֹא עֲלֵיכֶם מֵאֲחֵיכֶם ׀ הַיֹּשְׁבִים
בְּעָרֵיהֶם בֵּין־דָּם ׀ לְדָם בֵּין־תּוֹרָה לְמִצְוָה
לְחֻקִּים וּלְמִשְׁפָּטִים וְהִזְהַרְתֶּם אֹתָם וְלֹא
יֶאְשְׁמוּ לַיהוָה וְהָיָה־קֶצֶף עֲלֵיכֶם וְעַל־
אֲחֵיכֶם כֹּה תַעֲשׂוּן וְלֹא תֶאְשָׁמוּ: ¹¹וְהִנֵּה
אֲמַרְיָהוּ כֹהֵן הָרֹאשׁ עֲלֵיכֶם לְכֹל דְּבַר־
יְהוָה וּזְבַדְיָהוּ בֶן־יִשְׁמָעֵאל הַנָּגִיד לְבֵית־
יְהוּדָה לְכֹל דְּבַר־הַמֶּלֶךְ וְשֹׁטְרִים הַלְוִיִּם
לִפְנֵיכֶם חִזְקוּ וַעֲשׂוּ וִיהִי יְהוָה עִם־
הַטּוֹב: פ

כ וַיְהִי אַחֲרֵיכֵן בָּאוּ בְנֵי־מוֹאָב וּבְנֵי
עַמּוֹן וְעִמָּהֶם ׀ מֵהָעַמּוֹנִים עַל־יְהוֹשָׁפָט
לַמִּלְחָמָה: ²וַיָּבֹאוּ וַיַּגִּידוּ לִיהוֹשָׁפָט
לֵאמֹר בָּא עָלֶיךָ הָמוֹן רָב מֵעֵבֶר לַיָּם
מֵאֲרָם וְהִנָּם בְּחַצְצוֹן תָּמָר הִיא עֵין גֶּדִי:
³וַיִּרָא* וַיִּתֵּן יְהוֹשָׁפָט אֶת־פָּנָיו לִדְרוֹשׁ
לַיהוָה וַיִּקְרָא־צוֹם עַל־כָּל־יְהוּדָה:
⁴וַיִּקָּבְצוּ יְהוּדָה לְבַקֵּשׁ מֵיְהוָה גַּם מִכָּל־
עָרֵי יְהוּדָה בָּאוּ לְבַקֵּשׁ אֶת־יְהוָה:
⁵וַיַּעֲמֹד יְהוֹשָׁפָט בִּקְהַל יְהוּדָה וִירוּשָׁלִַם
בְּבֵית יְהוָה לִפְנֵי הֶחָצֵר הַחֲדָשָׁה:

v. 3. חסר י' בשורש

ᵃ Probably for m'nym "Meunites" (1 Chron. 4.41); cf. Kimhi.

at the front of the new court. 6He said, "Lord God of our fathers, truly You are the God in heaven and You rule over the kingdoms of the nations; power and strength are Yours; none can oppose You. 7O our God, you dispossessed the inhabitants of this land before Your people Israel, and You gave it to the descendants of Your friend Abraham forever. 8They settled in it and in it built for You a House for Your name. They said, 9'Should misfortune befall us—the punishing sword, pestilence, or famine, we shall stand before this House and before You—for Your name is in this House—and we shall cry out to You in our distress, and You will listen and deliver us.' 10Now the people of Ammon, Moab, and the hill country of Seir, into whose [land] You did not let Israel come when they came from Egypt, but they turned aside from them and did not wipe them out, 11these now repay us by coming to expel us from Your possession which You gave us as ours. 12O our God, surely You will punish them, for we are powerless before this great multitude that has come against us, and do not know what to do, but our eyes are on You." 13All Judah stood before the Lord with their little ones, their womenfolk, and their children.

14Then in the midst of the congregation the spirit of the Lord came upon Jahaziel son of Zechariah son of Benaiah son of Jeiel son of Mattaniah the Levite, of the sons of Asaph, 15and he said, "Give heed, all Judah and the inhabitants of Jerusalem and King Jehoshaphat; thus said the Lord to you, 'Do not fear or be dismayed by this great multitude, for the battle is God's, not yours. 16March down against them tomorrow as they come up by the Ascent of Ziz; you will find them at the end of the wadi in the direction of the wilderness of Jeruel. 17It is not for you to fight this battle; stand by, wait, and witness your deliverance by the Lord, O Judah

6 וַיֹּאמַ֗ר יְהוָ֞ה אֱלֹהֵ֤י אֲבֹתֵ֙ינוּ֙ הֲלֹ֣א אַתָּה־ ה֣וּא אֱלֹהִים֮ בַּשָּׁמַ֒יִם֒ וְאַתָּ֣ה מוֹשֵׁ֗ל בְּכֹל֙ מַמְלְכ֣וֹת הַגּוֹיִ֔ם וּבְיָדְךָ֖ כֹּ֣חַ וּגְבוּרָ֑ה וְאֵ֥ין עִמְּךָ֖ לְהִתְיַצֵּֽב: 7 הֲלֹ֣א ׀ אַתָּ֣ה אֱלֹהֵ֗ינוּ הוֹרַ֙שְׁתָּ֙ אֶת־יֹשְׁבֵי֙ הָאָ֣רֶץ הַזֹּ֔את מִלִּפְנֵ֖י עַמְּךָ֣ יִשְׂרָאֵ֑ל וַֽתִּתְּנָ֗הּ לְזֶ֛רַע אַבְרָהָ֥ם אֹֽהַבְךָ֖ לְעוֹלָֽם: 8 וַיֵּשְׁבוּ־בָ֑הּ וַיִּבְנ֣וּ לְךָ֣ ׀ בָּהּ֮ מִקְדָּשׁ֮ לְשִׁמְךָ֣ לֵאמֹֽר: 9 אִם־תָּב֙וֹא עָלֵ֜ינוּ רָעָ֗ה חֶ֣רֶב֙ שְׁפוֹט֙ וְדֶ֣בֶר וְרָעָ֔ב נַֽעַמְדָ֞ה לִפְנֵ֫י הַבַּ֣יִת הַזֶּה֮ וּלְפָנֶיךָ֒ כִּ֣י שִׁמְךָ֣ בַּבַּ֣יִת הַזֶּ֑ה וְנִזְעַ֥ק אֵלֶ֛יךָ מִצָּרָתֵ֖נוּ וְתִשְׁמַ֥ע וְתוֹשִֽׁיעַ: 10 וְעַתָּ֡ה הִנֵּה֩ בְנֵֽי־עַמּ֨וֹן וּמוֹאָ֜ב וְהַר־שֵׂעִ֗יר אֲשֶׁ֣ר לֹֽא־נָתַ֧תָּה לְיִשְׂרָאֵ֛ל לָב֥וֹא בָהֶ֖ם בְּבֹאָ֣ם מֵאֶ֣רֶץ מִצְרָ֑יִם כִּ֛י סָ֥רוּ מֵעֲלֵיהֶ֖ם וְלֹ֥א הִשְׁמִידֽוּם: 11 וְהִ֨נֵּה־הֵ֔ם גֹּֽמְלִ֖ים עָלֵ֑ינוּ לָבוֹא֙ לְגָ֣רְשֵׁ֔נוּ מִיְּרֻשָּׁ֣תְךָ֔ אֲשֶׁ֥ר הֽוֹרַשְׁתָּֽנוּ: 12 אֱלֹהֵ֙ינוּ֙ הֲלֹ֣א תִשְׁפָּט־בָּ֔ם כִּ֣י אֵ֥ין בָּ֙נוּ֙ כֹּ֔חַ לִ֠פְנֵי הֶהָמ֥וֹן הָרָ֛ב הַזֶּ֖ה הַבָּ֣א עָלֵ֑ינוּ וַאֲנַ֗חְנוּ לֹ֤א נֵדַע֙ מַֽה־נַּעֲשֶׂ֔ה כִּ֥י עָלֶ֖יךָ עֵינֵֽינוּ: 13 וְכָ֙ל־יְהוּדָ֔ה עֹמְדִ֖ים לִפְנֵ֣י יְהוָ֑ה גַּם־טַפָּ֖ם נְשֵׁיהֶ֥ם וּבְנֵיהֶֽם: פ

14 וְיַחֲזִיאֵ֡ל בֶּן־זְכַרְיָ֡הוּ בֶּן־בְּנָיָה֩ בֶּן־יְעִיאֵ֨ל בֶּן־מַתַּנְיָ֜ה הַלֵּוִ֗י מִן־בְּנֵ֣י אָסָ֔ף הָיְתָ֤ה עָלָיו֙ ר֣וּחַ יְהוָ֔ה בְּת֖וֹךְ הַקָּהָֽל: 15 וַיֹּ֡אמֶר הַקְשִׁ֣יבוּ כָל־יְהוּדָה֩ וְיֹשְׁבֵ֨י יְרוּשָׁלַ֜͏ִם וְהַמֶּ֣לֶךְ יְהוֹשָׁפָ֗ט כֹּֽה־אָמַ֤ר יְהוָה֙ לָכֶ֔ם אַ֠תֶּם אַל־תִּֽירְא֣וּ וְאַל־תֵּחַ֗תּוּ מִפְּנֵי֙ הֶהָמ֤וֹן הָרָב֙ הַזֶּ֔ה כִּ֣י לֹ֥א לָכֶ֛ם הַמִּלְחָמָ֖ה כִּ֥י לֵאלֹהִֽים: 16 מָחָר֙ רְד֣וּ עֲלֵיהֶ֔ם הִנָּ֥ם עֹלִ֖ים בְּמַעֲלֵ֣ה הַצִּ֑יץ וּמְצָאתֶ֤ם אֹתָם֙ בְּס֣וֹף הַנַּ֔חַל פְּנֵ֖י מִדְבַּ֥ר יְרוּאֵֽל: 17 לֹ֥א לָכֶ֖ם לְהִלָּ֣חֵם בָּזֹ֑את הִתְיַצְּב֣וּ עִמְד֡וּ וּרְא֣וּ אֶת־ יְשׁוּעַ֣ת יְהוָה֩ עִמָּכֶ֨ם יְהוּדָ֜ה וִירֽוּשָׁלַ֗͏ִם

and Jerusalem; do not fear or be dismayed; go forth to meet them tomorrow and the Lord will be with you.'" [18]Jehoshaphat bowed low with his face to the ground, and all Judah and the inhabitants of Jerusalem threw themselves down before the Lord to worship the Lord. [19]Levites of the sons of Kohath and of the sons of Korah got up to extol the Lord God of Israel at the top of their voices.

[20]Early the next morning they arose and went forth to the wilderness of Tekoa. As they went forth, Jehoshaphat stood and said, "Listen to me, O Judah and inhabitants of Jerusalem: Trust firmly in the Lord your God and you will stand firm; trust firmly in His prophets and you will succeed." [21]After taking counsel with the people, he stationed singers to the Lord extolling the One majestic in holiness as they went forth ahead of the vanguard, saying, "Praise the Lord, for His steadfast love is eternal." [22]As they began their joyous shouts and hymns, the Lord set ambushes for the men of Amon, Moab, and the hill country of Seir, who were marching against Judah, and they were routed. [23]The Ammonites and Moabites turned against the men of the hill country of Seir to exterminate and annihilate them. When they had made an end of the men of Seir, each helped to destroy his fellow.

[24]When Judah reached the lookout in the wilderness and looked for the multitude, they saw them lying on the ground as corpses; not one had survived. [25]Jehoshaphat and his army came to take the booty, and found an abundance of goods, corpses, and precious objects, which they pillaged, more than they could carry off. For three days they were taking booty, there was so much of it. [26]On the fourth day they assembled in the Valley of Blessing—for there they blessed the Lord; that is why that place is called the Valley of Blessing to this day. [27]All the men

אַל־תִּֽירְאוּ֙ וְאַל־תֵּחַ֔תּוּ מָחָר֙ צְא֣וּ לִפְנֵיהֶ֔ם וַיהֹוָ֖ה עִמָּכֶֽם׃ 18 וַיִּקֹּ֧ד יְהוֹשָׁפָ֛ט אַפַּ֖יִם אָ֑רְצָה וְכׇל־יְהוּדָ֞ה וְיֹשְׁבֵ֣י יְרוּשָׁלַ֗͏ִם נָֽפְלוּ֙ לִפְנֵ֣י יְהֹוָ֔ה לְהִֽשְׁתַּחֲוֺ֖ת לַיהֹוָֽה׃ 19 וַיָּקֻ֧מוּ הַלְוִיִּ֛ם מִן־בְּנֵ֥י הַקְּהָתִ֖ים וּמִן־בְּנֵ֣י הַקׇּרְחִ֑ים לְהַלֵּ֗ל לַיהֹוָה֙ אֱלֹהֵ֣י יִשְׂרָאֵ֔ל בְּק֥וֹל גָּד֖וֹל לְמָֽעְלָה׃

20 וַיַּשְׁכִּ֣ימוּ בַבֹּ֔קֶר וַיֵּצְא֖וּ לְמִדְבַּ֣ר תְּק֑וֹעַ וּבְצֵאתָ֞ם עָמַ֣ד יְהוֹשָׁפָ֗ט וַיֹּ֙אמֶר֙ שְׁמָע֣וּנִי יְהוּדָה֙ וְיֹשְׁבֵ֣י יְרוּשָׁלַ֔͏ִם הַאֲמִ֜ינוּ בַּיהֹוָ֧ה אֱלֹֽהֵיכֶ֛ם וְתֵאָמֵ֖נוּ הַאֲמִ֥ינוּ בִנְבִיאָ֖יו וְהַצְלִֽיחוּ׃ 21 וַיִּוָּעַץ֙ אֶל־הָעָ֔ם וַיַּעֲמֵ֤ד מְשֹׁרְרִים֙ לַֽיהֹוָ֔ה וּֽמְהַֽלְלִ֖ים לְהַדְרַת־קֹ֑דֶשׁ בְּצֵאת֙ לִפְנֵ֣י הֶֽחָל֔וּץ וְאֹֽמְרִים֙ הוֹד֣וּ לַֽיהֹוָ֔ה כִּ֥י לְעוֹלָ֖ם חַסְדּֽוֹ׃ 22 וּבְעֵת֩ הֵחֵ֨לּוּ בְרִנָּ֜ה וּתְהִלָּ֗ה נָתַ֣ן יְהֹוָ֣ה ׀ מְֽאָרְבִ֡ים עַל־בְּנֵי֩ עַמּ֨וֹן מוֹאָ֜ב וְהַר־שֵׂעִ֛יר הַבָּאִ֥ים לִֽיהוּדָ֖ה וַיִּנָּגֵֽפוּ׃ 23 וַ֠יַּֽעַמְד֠וּ בְּנֵ֨י עַמּ֧וֹן וּמוֹאָ֛ב עַל־יֹשְׁבֵ֥י הַר־שֵׂעִ֖יר לְהַחֲרִ֣ים וּלְהַשְׁמִ֑יד וּכְכַלּוֹתָם֙ בְּיוֹשְׁבֵ֣י שֵׂעִ֔יר עָזְר֥וּ אִ֖ישׁ־בְּרֵעֵ֥הוּ לְמַשְׁחִֽית׃

24 וִֽיהוּדָ֞ה בָּ֣א עַל־הַמִּצְפֶּה֮ לַמִּדְבָּר֒ וַיִּפְנוּ֙ אֶל־הֶ֣הָמ֔וֹן וְהִנָּ֧ם פְּגָרִ֛ים נֹפְלִ֖ים אַ֑רְצָה וְאֵ֖ין פְּלֵיטָֽה׃ 25 וַיָּבֹ֨א יְהוֹשָׁפָ֣ט וְעַמּוֹ֮ לָבֹ֣ז אֶת־שְׁלָלָם֒ וַיִּמְצְא֨וּ בָהֶ֜ם לָרֹ֣ב וּרְכ֗וּשׁ וּפְגָרִים֙ וּכְלֵ֣י חֲמֻד֔וֹת וַיְנַצְּל֥וּ לָהֶ֖ם לְאֵ֣ין מַשָּׂ֑א וַיִּֽהְי֞וּ יָמִ֧ים שְׁלוֹשָׁ֛ה בֹּזְזִ֥ים אֶת־הַשָּׁלָ֖ל כִּ֥י רַב־הֽוּא׃ 26 וּבַיּ֣וֹם הָרְבִעִ֗י נִקְהֲלוּ֙ לְעֵ֣מֶק בְּרָכָ֔ה כִּי־שָׁ֖ם בֵּרְכ֣וּ אֶת־יְהֹוָ֑ה עַל־כֵּ֗ן קָרְא֞וּ אֶת־שֵׁ֤ם הַמָּקוֹם֙ הַה֔וּא עֵ֥מֶק בְּרָכָ֖ה עַד־הַיּֽוֹם׃ 27 וַ֠יָּשֻׁ֠בוּ כׇּל־אִ֨ישׁ

of Judah and Jerusalem with Jehoshaphat at their head returned joyfully to Jerusalem, for the Lord had given them cause for rejoicing over their enemies. 28They came to Jerusalem to the House of the Lord, to the accompaniment of harps, lyres, and trumpets. 29The terror of God seized all the kingdoms of the lands when they heard that the Lord had fought the enemies of Israel. 30The kingdom of Jehoshaphat was untroubled, and his God granted him respite on all sides.

31bJehoshaphat reigned over Judah. He was thirty-five years old when he became king, and he reigned in Jerusalem for twenty-five years. His mother's name was Azubah daughter of Shilhi. 32He followed the course of his father Asa and did not deviate from it, doing what was pleasing to the Lord. 33However, the shrines did not cease; the people still did not direct their heart toward the God of their fathers. 34As for the other events of Jehoshaphat's reign, early and late, they are recorded in the annals of Jehu son of Hanani, which were included in the book of the kings of Israel.

35Afterward, King Jehoshaphat of Judah entered into a partnership with King Ahaziah of Israel, thereby acting wickedly. 36He joined with him in constructing ships to go to Tarshish; the ships were constructed in Ezion-geber. 37Eliezer son of Dodavahu of Mareshah prophesied against Jehoshaphat, "As you have made a partnership with Ahaziah, the Lord will break up your work." The ships were wrecked and were unable to go to Tarshish.

21 aJehoshaphat slept with his fathers and was buried with his fathers in the City of David; his son Jehoram succeeded him as king. 2He had brothers, sons of Jehoshaphat: Azariah, Jehiel,

יְהוּדָה וִירוּשָׁלַ֙͏ִם֙ וִיהוֹשָׁפָ֣ט בְּרֹאשָׁ֔ם לָשׁ֥וּב אֶל־יְרוּשָׁלַ֖͏ִם בְּשִׂמְחָ֑ה כִּֽי־שִׂמְּחָ֥ם יְהוָ֖ה מֵאֽוֹיְבֵיהֶֽם׃ 28 וַיָּבֹ֙אוּ֙ יְר֣וּשָׁלַ֔͏ִם בִּנְבָלִ֥ים וּבְכִנֹּר֖וֹת וּבַחֲצֹצְר֑וֹת אֶל־בֵּ֖ית יְהוָֽה׃ 29 וַיְהִי֙ פַּ֣חַד אֱלֹהִ֔ים עַ֖ל כָּל־מַמְלְכ֣וֹת הָאֲרָצ֑וֹת בְּשָׁמְעָ֕ם כִּ֚י נִלְחַ֣ם יְהוָ֔ה עִ֖ם אֽוֹיְבֵ֥י יִשְׂרָאֵֽל׃ 30 וַתִּשְׁקֹ֖ט מַלְכ֣וּת יְהוֹשָׁפָ֑ט וַיָּ֧נַֽח ל֦וֹ אֱלֹהָ֖יו מִסָּבִֽיב׃ פ

31 וַיִּמְלֹ֥ךְ יְהוֹשָׁפָ֖ט עַל־יְהוּדָ֑ה בֶּן־שְׁלֹשִׁ֨ים וְחָמֵ֜שׁ שָׁנָ֣ה בְמָלְכ֗וֹ וְעֶשְׂרִ֨ים וְחָמֵ֤שׁ שָׁנָה֙ מָלַךְ֙ בִּיר֣וּשָׁלַ֔͏ִם וְשֵׁ֣ם אִמּ֔וֹ עֲזוּבָ֖ה בַּת־שִׁלְחִֽי׃ 32 וַיֵּ֗לֶךְ בְּדֶ֛רֶךְ אָבִ֥יו אָסָ֖א וְלֹא־סָ֣ר מִמֶּ֑נָּה לַעֲשׂ֥וֹת הַיָּשָׁ֖ר בְּעֵינֵ֥י יְהוָֽה׃ 33 אַ֥ךְ הַבָּמ֖וֹת לֹא־סָ֑רוּ וְע֤וֹד הָעָם֙ לֹא־הֵכִ֣ינוּ לְבָבָ֔ם לֵאלֹהֵ֖י אֲבֹתֵיהֶֽם׃ 34 וְיֶ֙תֶר֙ דִּבְרֵ֣י יְהוֹשָׁפָ֔ט הָרִאשֹׁנִ֖ים וְהָאַחֲרֹנִ֑ים הִנָּ֣ם כְּתוּבִ֗ים בְּדִבְרֵי֙ יֵה֣וּא בֶן־חֲנָ֔נִי אֲשֶׁ֣ר הֹֽעֲלָ֔ה עַל־סֵ֖פֶר מַלְכֵ֥י יִשְׂרָאֵֽל׃

35 וְאַחֲרֵי־כֵ֗ן אֶתְחַבַּר֙ יְהוֹשָׁפָ֣ט מֶֽלֶךְ־יְהוּדָ֔ה עִ֖ם אֲחַזְיָ֣ה מֶֽלֶךְ־יִשְׂרָאֵ֑ל ה֥וּא הִרְשִׁ֖יעַ לַעֲשֽׂוֹת׃ 36 וַֽיְחַבְּרֵ֣הוּ עִמּ֔וֹ לַעֲשׂ֥וֹת אֳנִיּ֖וֹת לָלֶ֣כֶת תַּרְשִׁ֑ישׁ וַיַּעֲשׂ֥וּ אֳנִיּ֖וֹת בְּעֶצְי֥וֹן גָּֽבֶר׃ 37 וַיִּתְנַבֵּ֞א אֱלִיעֶ֤זֶר בֶּן־דֹּֽדָוָ֙הוּ֙ מִמָּ֣רֵשָׁ֔ה עַל־יְהוֹשָׁפָ֖ט לֵאמֹ֑ר כְּהִֽתְחַבֶּרְךָ֣ עִם־אֲחַזְיָ֗הוּ פָּרַ֤ץ יְהוָה֙ אֶֽת־מַעֲשֶׂ֔יךָ וַיִּשָּׁבְר֣וּ אֳנִיּ֔וֹת וְלֹ֥א עָצְר֖וּ לָלֶ֥כֶת אֶל־תַּרְשִֽׁישׁ׃

כא וַיִּשְׁכַּ֤ב יְהֽוֹשָׁפָט֙ עִם־אֲבֹתָ֔יו וַיִּקָּבֵ֥ר עִם־אֲבֹתָ֖יו בְּעִ֣יר דָּוִ֑יד וַיִּמְלֹ֛ךְ יְהוֹרָ֥ם בְּנ֖וֹ תַּחְתָּֽיו׃ 2 וְלֽוֹ־אַחִ֣ים בְּנֵ֣י

b   With vv. 31–37, cf. 1 Kings 22.41–49.

a   Cf. 2 Kings 8.17–24.

Zechariah, Azariahu, Michael, and Shephatiah; all these were sons of King Jehoshaphat of Israel. ³Their father gave them many gifts of silver, gold, and [other] presents, as well as fortified towns in Judah, but he gave the kingdom to Jehoram because he was the first-born.

⁴Jehoram proceeded to take firm hold of his father's kingdom and put to the sword all his brothers, as well as some of the officers of Israel. ⁵Jehoram was thirty-two years old when he became king, and he reigned in Jerusalem eight years. ⁶He followed the practices of the kings of Israel doing what the House of Ahab had done, for he married a daughter of Ahab; he did what was displeasing to the LORD. ⁷However, the LORD refrained from destroying the House of David for the sake of the covenant he had made with David, and in accordance with his promise to maintain a lamp for him and his descendants for all time. ⁸During his reign, the Edomites rebelled against Judah's rule and set up a king of their own. ⁹Jehoram advanced [against them] with his officers and all his chariotry. He arose by night and attacked the Edomites, who surrounded him and the chariot commanders. ¹⁰Edom has been in rebellion against Judah, to this day; Libnah also rebelled against him at that time, because he had forsaken the LORD God of his fathers. ¹¹Moreover, he built shrines in the hill country of Judah; he led astray the inhabitants of Jerusalem and made Judah wayward.

¹²A letter from Elijah the prophet came to him which read, "Thus says the LORD God of your father David: Since you have not followed the practices of your father Jehoshaphat and the practices of King Asa of Judah, ¹³but have followed the practices of the kings of Israel, leading astray Judah and the inhabitants of Jerusalem as the House of Ahab led them astray, and have also killed your brothers of your father's house,

יְהוֹשָׁפָט עֲזַרְיָה וִיחִיאֵל וּזְכַרְיָהוּ וַעֲזַרְיָהוּ וּמִיכָאֵל וּשְׁפַטְיָהוּ כָּל־אֵלֶּה בְּנֵי יְהוֹשָׁפָט מֶלֶךְ־יִשְׂרָאֵל: ³וַיִּתֵּן לָהֶם | אֲבִיהֶם מַתָּנוֹת רַבּוֹת לְכֶסֶף וּלְזָהָב וּלְמִגְדָּנוֹת עִם־עָרֵי מְצֻרוֹת בִּיהוּדָה וְאֶת־הַמַּמְלָכָה נָתַן לִיהוֹרָם כִּי־הוּא הַבְּכוֹר: פ

⁴וַיָּקָם יְהוֹרָם עַל־מַמְלֶכֶת אָבִיו וַיִּתְחַזַּק וַיַּהֲרֹג אֶת־כָּל־אֶחָיו בֶּחָרֶב וְגַם מִשָּׂרֵי יִשְׂרָאֵל: ⁵בֶּן־שְׁלֹשִׁים וּשְׁתַּיִם שָׁנָה יְהוֹרָם בְּמָלְכוֹ וּשְׁמוֹנֶה שָׁנִים מָלַךְ בִּירוּשָׁלָ͏ִם: ⁶וַיֵּלֶךְ בְּדֶרֶךְ | מַלְכֵי יִשְׂרָאֵל כַּאֲשֶׁר עָשׂוּ בֵּית אַחְאָב כִּי בַּת־אַחְאָב הָיְתָה לּוֹ אִשָּׁה* וַיַּעַשׂ הָרַע בְּעֵינֵי יְהוָה: ⁷וְלֹא־אָבָה יְהוָה לְהַשְׁחִית אֶת־בֵּית דָּוִיד לְמַעַן הַבְּרִית אֲשֶׁר כָּרַת לְדָוִיד וְכַאֲשֶׁר אָמַר לָתֵת לוֹ נִיר וּלְבָנָיו כָּל־הַיָּמִים: ⁸בְּיָמָיו פָּשַׁע אֱדוֹם מִתַּחַת יַד־יְהוּדָה וַיַּמְלִיכוּ עֲלֵיהֶם מֶלֶךְ: ⁹וַיַּעֲבֹר יְהוֹרָם עִם־שָׂרָיו וְכָל־הָרֶכֶב עִמּוֹ וַיְהִי קָם לַיְלָה וַיַּךְ אֶת־אֱדוֹם הַסּוֹבֵב אֵלָיו וְאֵת שָׂרֵי הָרָכֶב: ¹⁰וַיִּפְשַׁע אֱדוֹם מִתַּחַת יַד־יְהוּדָה עַד הַיּוֹם הַזֶּה אָז תִּפְשַׁע לִבְנָה בָּעֵת הַהִיא מִתַּחַת יָדוֹ כִּי עָזַב אֶת־יְהוָה אֱלֹהֵי אֲבֹתָיו: ¹¹גַּם־הוּא עָשָׂה־בָמוֹת בְּהָרֵי יְהוּדָה וַיֶּזֶן אֶת־יֹשְׁבֵי יְרוּשָׁלַ͏ִם וַיַּדַּח אֶת־יְהוּדָה: פ

¹²וַיָּבֹא אֵלָיו מִכְתָּב מֵאֵלִיָּהוּ הַנָּבִיא לֵאמֹר כֹּה | אָמַר יְהוָה אֱלֹהֵי דָּוִיד אָבִיךָ תַּחַת אֲשֶׁר לֹא־הָלַכְתָּ בְּדַרְכֵי יְהוֹשָׁפָט אָבִיךָ וּבְדַרְכֵי אָסָא מֶלֶךְ־יְהוּדָה: ¹³וַתֵּלֶךְ בְּדֶרֶךְ מַלְכֵי יִשְׂרָאֵל וַתַּזְנֶה אֶת־יְהוּדָה וְאֶת־יֹשְׁבֵי יְרוּשָׁלַ͏ִם כְּהַזְנוֹת בֵּית אַחְאָב וְגַם אֶת־אַחֶיךָ בֵית־אָבִיךָ הַטּוֹבִים מִמְּךָ הָרָגְתָּ: ¹⁴הִנֵּה יְהוָה נֹגֵף מַגֵּפָה

who were better than you, [14]therefore, the LORD will inflict a great blow upon your people, your sons, and your wives and all your possessions. [15]As for you, you will be severely stricken with a disorder of the bowels year after year until your bowels drop out."

[16]The LORD stirred up the spirit of the Philistines and the Arabs who were neighbors of the Cushites against Jehoram. [17]They marched against Judah, breached its defenses, and carried off all the property that was found in the king's palace, as well as his sons and his wives. The only son who remained was Jehoahaz, his youngest. [18]After this, the LORD afflicted him with an incurable disease of the bowels. [19]Some years later, when a period of two years had elapsed, his bowels dropped out because of his disease, and he died a gruesome death. His people did not make a fire for him like the fire for his fathers. [20]He was thirty-two years old when he became king, and he reigned in Jerusalem eight years. He departed unpraised,[b] and was buried in the City of David, but not in the tombs of the kings.

22 [a]The inhabitants of Jerusalem made

Ahaziah, his youngest son, king in his stead, because all the older ones had been killed by the troops that penetrated the camp with the Arabs. Ahaziah son of Jehoram reigned as king of Judah. [2]Ahaziah was forty-two years old when he became king, and he reigned in Jerusalem one year; his mother's name was Athaliah daughter of Omri. [3]He too followed the practices of the house of Ahab, for his mother counseled him to do evil. [4]He did what was displeasing to the LORD, like the house of Ahab, for they became his counselors after his father's death, to his ruination. [5]Moreover, he followed their coun-

גְדוֹלָה בְּעַמֶּךָ וּבְבָנֶיךָ וּבְנָשֶׁיךָ וּבְכָל־
רְכוּשֶׁךָ: [15] וְאַתָּה בָּחֳלָיִים רַבִּים בְּמַחֲלֵה
מֵעֶיךָ עַד־יֵצְאוּ מֵעֶיךָ מִן־הַחֹלִי יָמִים
עַל־יָמִים:

[16] וַיָּעַר יְהוָה עַל־יְהוֹרָם אֵת רוּחַ
הַפְּלִשְׁתִּים וְהָעַרְבִים אֲשֶׁר עַל־יַד
כּוּשִׁים: [17] וַיַּעֲלוּ בִיהוּדָה וַיִּבְקָעוּהָ וַיִּשְׁבּוּ
אֵת כָּל־הָרְכוּשׁ הַנִּמְצָא לְבֵית־הַמֶּלֶךְ
וְגַם־בָּנָיו וְנָשָׁיו וְלֹא נִשְׁאַר־לוֹ בֵּן כִּי
אִם־יְהוֹאָחָז קְטֹן בָּנָיו: [18] וְאַחֲרֵי כָּל־זֹאת
נְגָפוֹ יְהוָה | בְּמֵעָיו לָחֳלִי לְאֵין מַרְפֵּא:
[19] וַיְהִי לְיָמִים | מִיָּמִים וּכְעֵת צֵאת
הַקֵּץ לְיָמִים שְׁנַיִם יָצְאוּ מֵעָיו עִם־חָלְיוֹ
וַיָּמָת בְּתַחֲלֻאִים רָעִים וְלֹא־עָשׂוּ לוֹ עַמּוֹ
שְׂרֵפָה כִּשְׂרֵפַת אֲבֹתָיו: [20] בֶּן־שְׁלֹשִׁים
וּשְׁתַּיִם הָיָה בְמָלְכוֹ וּשְׁמוֹנֶה שָׁנִים מָלַךְ
בִּירוּשָׁלָ͏ִם וַיֵּלֶךְ בְּלֹא חֶמְדָּה וַיִּקְבְּרֻהוּ
בְּעִיר דָּוִיד וְלֹא בְּקִבְרוֹת הַמְּלָכִים:

כב

[1] וַיַּמְלִיכוּ יוֹשְׁבֵי יְרוּשָׁלַ͏ִם אֶת־
אֲחַזְיָהוּ בְנוֹ הַקָּטֹן תַּחְתָּיו כִּי כָל־
הָרִאשֹׁנִים הָרַג הַגְּדוּד הַבָּא בָעַרְבִים
לַמַּחֲנֶה וַיִּמְלֹךְ אֲחַזְיָהוּ בֶן־יְהוֹרָם מֶלֶךְ
יְהוּדָה: פ [2] בֶּן־אַרְבָּעִים וּשְׁתַּיִם
שָׁנָה אֲחַזְיָהוּ בְמָלְכוֹ וְשָׁנָה אַחַת מָלַךְ
בִּירוּשָׁלָ͏ִם וְשֵׁם אִמּוֹ עֲתַלְיָהוּ בַּת־עָמְרִי:
[3] גַּם־הוּא הָלַךְ בְּדַרְכֵי בֵּית אַחְאָב כִּי
אִמּוֹ הָיְתָה יוֹעַצְתּוֹ לְהַרְשִׁיעַ: [4] וַיַּעַשׂ
הָרַע בְּעֵינֵי יְהוָה כְּבֵית אַחְאָב כִּי־הֵמָּה
הָיוּ־לוֹ יוֹעֲצִים אַחֲרֵי מוֹת אָבִיו לְמַשְׁחִית
לוֹ: [5] גַּם בַּעֲצָתָם הָלַךְ וַיֵּלֶךְ אֶת־יְהוֹרָם

---

b   *Following Septuagint; cf. Arabic* ḥamada, *"praise."*

a   *With vv. 1–6, cf. 2 Kings 8.25–29; with vv. 8–9, cf. 2 Kings 9.27–28; with vv. 10–12, cf. 2 Kings 11.1–3.*

sel and marched with Jehoram son of King Ahab of Israel to battle against King Hazael of Aram at Ramoth-gilead, where the Arameans wounded Joram. [6]He returned to Jezreel to recover from the wounds inflicted on him at Ramah when he fought against King Hazael of Aram. King Azariah son of Jehoram of Judah went down to Jezreel to visit Jehoram son of Ahab while he was ill. [7]God caused the downfall of Ahaziah because he visited Joram. During his visit he went out with Jehoram to Jehu son of Nimshi, whom the LORD had anointed to cut off the house of Ahab. [8]In the course of bringing the house of Ahab to judgment, Jehu came upon the officers of Judah and the nephews of Ahaziah, ministers of Ahaziah, and killed them. [9]He sent in search of Ahaziah, who was caught hiding in Samaria, was brought to Jehu, and put to death. He was given a burial, because it was said, "He is the son of Jehoshaphat who worshiped the LORD wholeheartedly." So the house of Ahaziah could not muster the strength to rule.

[10]When Athaliah, Ahaziah's mother, learned that her son was dead, she promptly did away with all who were of the royal stock of the house of Judah. [11]But Jehoshabeath, daughter of the king, spirited away Ahaziah's son Joash from among the princes who were being slain, and put him and his nurse in a bedroom. Jehoshabeath, daughter of King Jehoram, wife of the priest Jehoiada—she was the sister of Ahaziah—kept him hidden from Athaliah so that he was not put to death. [12]He stayed with them for six years, hidden in the House of God, while Athaliah reigned over the land.

23 [a]In the seventh year, Jehoiada took courage and brought the chiefs of the hundreds, Azariah son of Jeroham, Ishmael son of

---

בֶּן־אַחְאָב מֶלֶךְ יִשְׂרָאֵל לַמִּלְחָמָה עַל־חֲזָאֵל מֶלֶךְ־אֲרָם בְּרָמוֹת גִּלְעָד וַיַּכּוּ הָרַמִּים אֶת־יוֹרָם׃ [6]וַיָּשָׁב לְהִתְרַפֵּא בְיִזְרְעֶאל כִּי הַמַּכִּים אֲשֶׁר הִכֻּהוּ בָרָמָה בְּהִלָּחֲמוֹ אֶת־חֲזָהאֵל מֶלֶךְ אֲרָם וַעֲזַרְיָהוּ בֶן־יְהוֹרָם מֶלֶךְ יְהוּדָה יָרַד לִרְאוֹת אֶת־יְהוֹרָם בֶּן־אַחְאָב בְּיִזְרְעֶאל כִּי־חֹלֶה הוּא׃ [7]וּמֵאֱלֹהִים הָיְתָה תְּבוּסַת אֲחַזְיָהוּ לָבוֹא אֶל־יוֹרָם וּבְבֹאוֹ יָצָא עִם־יְהוֹרָם אֶל־יֵהוּא בֶּן־נִמְשִׁי אֲשֶׁר מְשָׁחוֹ יְהוָה לְהַכְרִית אֶת־בֵּית אַחְאָב׃ [8]וַיְהִי כְּהִשָּׁפֵט יֵהוּא עִם־בֵּית אַחְאָב וַיִּמְצָא אֶת־שָׂרֵי יְהוּדָה וּבְנֵי אֲחֵי אֲחַזְיָהוּ מְשָׁרְתִים לַאֲחַזְיָהוּ וַיַּהַרְגֵם׃ [9]וַיְבַקֵּשׁ אֶת־אֲחַזְיָהוּ וַיִּלְכְּדֻהוּ וְהוּא מִתְחַבֵּא בְשֹׁמְרוֹן וַיְבִאֻהוּ אֶל־יֵהוּא וַיְמִתֻהוּ וַיִּקְבְּרֻהוּ כִּי אָמְרוּ בֶּן־יְהוֹשָׁפָט הוּא אֲשֶׁר־דָּרַשׁ אֶת־יְהוָה בְּכָל־לְבָבוֹ וְאֵין לְבֵית אֲחַזְיָהוּ לַעְצֹר כֹּחַ לְמַמְלָכָה׃ [10]וַעֲתַלְיָהוּ אֵם אֲחַזְיָהוּ רָאֲתָה כִּי מֵת בְּנָהּ וַתָּקָם וַתְּדַבֵּר אֶת־כָּל־זֶרַע הַמַּמְלָכָה לְבֵית יְהוּדָה׃ [11]וַתִּקַּח יְהוֹשַׁבְעַת בַּת־הַמֶּלֶךְ אֶת־יוֹאָשׁ בֶּן־אֲחַזְיָהוּ וַתִּגְנֹב אֹתוֹ מִתּוֹךְ בְּנֵי־הַמֶּלֶךְ הַמּוּמָתִים וַתִּתֵּן אֹתוֹ וְאֶת־מֵינִקְתּוֹ בַּחֲדַר הַמִּטּוֹת וַתַּסְתִּירֵהוּ יְהוֹשַׁבְעַת בַּת־הַמֶּלֶךְ יְהוֹרָם אֵשֶׁת יְהוֹיָדָע הַכֹּהֵן כִּי הִיא הָיְתָה אֲחוֹת אֲחַזְיָהוּ מִפְּנֵי עֲתַלְיָהוּ וְלֹא הֱמִיתָתְהוּ׃ [12]וַיְהִי אִתָּם בְּבֵית הָאֱלֹהִים מִתְחַבֵּא שֵׁשׁ שָׁנִים וַעֲתַלְיָה מֹלֶכֶת עַל־הָאָרֶץ׃ פ

כג וּבַשָּׁנָה הַשְּׁבִעִית הִתְחַזַּק יְהוֹיָדָע וַיִּקַּח אֶת־שָׂרֵי הַמֵּאוֹת לַעֲזַרְיָהוּ בֶן־יְרֹחָם

---

[a] Cf. 2 Kings 11.4–20.

Jehohanan, Azariah son of Obed, Maaseiah son of Adaiah, and Elishaphat son of Zichri, into a compact with him. ²They went through Judah and assembled the Levites from all the towns of Judah, and the chiefs of the clans of Israel. They came to Jerusalem ³and the entire assembly made a covenant with the king in the House of God. He*b* said to them, "The son of the king shall be king according to the promise the Lord made concerning the sons of David. ⁴This is what you must do: One third of you, priests and Levites, who are on duty for the week, shall be gatekeepers at the thresholds; ⁵another third shall be stationed in the royal palace, and the other third at the Foundation Gate. All the people shall be in the courts of the House of the Lord. ⁶Let no one enter the House of the Lord except the priests and the ministering Levites. They may enter because they are sanctified, but all the people shall obey the proscription of the Lord. ⁷The Levites shall surround the king on every side, every man with his weapons at the ready; and whoever enters the House shall be killed. Stay close to the king in his comings and goings." ⁸The Levites and all Judah did just as Jehoiada the priest ordered: each took his men—those who were on duty that week and those who were off duty that week, for Jehoiada the priest had not dismissed the divisions. ⁹Jehoiada the priest gave the chiefs of the hundreds King David's spears and shields and quivers that were kept in the House of God. ¹⁰He stationed the entire force, each man with his weapons at the ready, from the south end of the House to the north end of the House, at the altar and the House, to guard the king on every side. ¹¹Then they brought out the king's son, and placed upon him the crown and the insignia. They proclaimed him king, and Jehoiada and his sons anointed him and shouted, "Long live the king!"

¹²When Athaliah heard the shouting of the

b I.e., Jehoiada.

people and the guards and the acclamation of the king, she came out to the people, to the House of the Lord. [13]She looked about and saw the king standing by his pillar at the entrance, the chiefs with their trumpets beside the king, and all the people of the land rejoicing and blowing trumpets, and the singers with musical instruments leading the hymns. Athaliah rent her garments and cried out, "Treason, treason!" [14]Then the priest Jehoiada ordered out the army officers, the chiefs of hundreds, and said to them, "Take her out between the ranks, and if anyone follows her, put him to the sword." For the priest thought, "Let her not be put to death in the House of the Lord." [15]They cleared a passage for her and she came to the entrance of the Horse Gate to the royal palace; there she was put to death.

[16]Then Jehoiada solemnized a covenant between himself and the people and the king that they should be the people of the Lord. [17]All the people then went to the temple of Baal; they tore it down and smashed its altars and images to bits, and they slew Mattan, the priest of Baal, in front of the altars. [18]Jehoiada put the officers of the House of the Lord in the charge of Levite priests whom David had assigned over the House of the Lord to offer up burnt offerings, as is prescribed in the Teaching of Moses, accompanied by joyful song as ordained by David. [19]He stationed the gatekeepers at the gates of the House of the Lord to prevent the entry of anyone unclean for any reason. [20]He took the chiefs of hundreds, the nobles, and the rulers of the people and all the people of the land, and they escorted the king down from the House of the Lord into the royal palace by the upper gate, and seated the king on the royal throne. [21]All the people of the land rejoiced, and the city was quiet. As for Athaliah, she had been put to the sword.

וְהַמְהַלְלִים אֶת־הַמֶּלֶךְ וַתָּבוֹא אֶל־הָעָם בֵּית יְהֹוָה: 13 וַתֵּרֶא וְהִנֵּה הַמֶּלֶךְ עוֹמֵד עַל־עַמּוּדוֹ בַּמָּבוֹא וְהַשָּׂרִים וְהַחֲצֹצְרוֹת עַל־הַמֶּלֶךְ וְכָל־עַם הָאָרֶץ שָׂמֵחַ וְתוֹקֵעַ בַּחֲצֹצְרוֹת וְהַמְשׁוֹרְרִים בִּכְלֵי הַשִּׁיר וּמוֹדִיעִים לְהַלֵּל וַתִּקְרַע עֲתַלְיָהוּ אֶת־בְּגָדֶיהָ וַתֹּאמֶר קֶשֶׁר קָשֶׁר: ס 14 וַיּוֹצֵא יְהוֹיָדָע הַכֹּהֵן אֶת־שָׂרֵי הַמֵּאוֹת ׀ פְּקוּדֵי הַחַיִל וַיֹּאמֶר אֲלֵהֶם הוֹצִיאוּהָ אֶל־מִבֵּית הַשְּׂדֵרוֹת וְהַבָּא אַחֲרֶיהָ יוּמַת בֶּחָרֶב כִּי אָמַר הַכֹּהֵן לֹא תְמִיתוּהָ בֵּית יְהֹוָה: 15 וַיָּשִׂימוּ לָהּ יָדַיִם וַתָּבוֹא אֶל־מְבוֹא שַׁעַר־הַסּוּסִים בֵּית הַמֶּלֶךְ וַיְמִיתוּהָ שָׁם: פ

16 וַיִּכְרֹת יְהוֹיָדָע בְּרִית בֵּינוֹ וּבֵין כָּל־הָעָם וּבֵין הַמֶּלֶךְ לִהְיוֹת לְעָם לַיהֹוָה: 17 וַיָּבֹאוּ כָל־הָעָם בֵּית־הַבַּעַל וַיִּתְּצֻהוּ וְאֶת־מִזְבְּחֹתָיו וְאֶת־צְלָמָיו שִׁבֵּרוּ וְאֵת מַתָּן כֹּהֵן הַבַּעַל הָרְגוּ לִפְנֵי הַמִּזְבְּחוֹת: 18 וַיָּשֶׂם יְהוֹיָדָע פְּקֻדֹּת בֵּית יְהֹוָה בְּיַד הַכֹּהֲנִים הַלְוִיִּם אֲשֶׁר חָלַק דָּוִיד עַל־בֵּית יְהֹוָה לְהַעֲלוֹת עֹלוֹת יְהֹוָה כַּכָּתוּב בְּתוֹרַת מֹשֶׁה בְּשִׂמְחָה וּבְשִׁיר עַל יְדֵי דָוִיד: 19 וַיַּעֲמֵד הַשּׁוֹעֲרִים עַל־שַׁעֲרֵי בֵּית יְהֹוָה וְלֹא־יָבֹא טָמֵא לְכָל־דָּבָר: 20 וַיִּקַּח אֶת־שָׂרֵי הַמֵּאוֹת וְאֶת־הָאַדִּירִים וְאֶת־הַמּוֹשְׁלִים בָּעָם וְאֵת ׀ כָּל־עַם הָאָרֶץ וַיּוֹרֶד אֶת־הַמֶּלֶךְ מִבֵּית יְהֹוָה וַיָּבֹאוּ בְּתוֹךְ־שַׁעַר הָעֶלְיוֹן בֵּית הַמֶּלֶךְ וַיּוֹשִׁיבוּ אֶת־הַמֶּלֶךְ עַל כִּסֵּא הַמַּמְלָכָה: 21 וַיִּשְׂמְחוּ כָל־עַם־הָאָרֶץ וְהָעִיר שָׁקָטָה וְאֶת־עֲתַלְיָהוּ הֵמִיתוּ בֶחָרֶב: ס

24

^{a}Jehoash was seven years old when he became king, and he reigned in Jerusalem forty years. His mother's name was Zibiah of Beer-sheba. ^{2}All the days of the priest Jehoiada, Jehoash did what was pleasing to the LORD. ^{3}Jehoiada took two wives for him, by whom he had sons and daughters.

^{4}Afterward, Joash decided to renovate the House of the LORD. ^{5}He assembled the priests and the Levites and charged them as follows: "Go out to the towns of Judah and collect money from all Israel for the annual repair of the House of your God. Do it quickly." But the Levites did not act quickly. ^{6}The king summoned Jehoiada the chief and said to him, "Why have you not seen to it that the Levites brought the tax imposed by Moses, the servant of the LORD, and the congregation of Israel from Judah and Jerusalem to the Tent of the Pact?" ^{7}For the children of the wicked Athaliah had violated the House of God and had even used the sacred things of the House of the LORD for the Baals. ^{8}The king ordered that a chest be made and placed on the outside of the gate of the House of the LORD. ^{9}A proclamation was issued in Judah and Jerusalem to bring the tax imposed on Israel in the wilderness by Moses, the servant of God. ^{10}All the officers and all the people gladly brought it and threw it into the chest till it was full. ^{11}Whenever the chest was brought to the royal officers by the Levites, and they saw that it contained much money, the royal scribe and the agent of the chief priest came and emptied out the chest and carried it back to its place. They did this day by day, and much money was collected. ^{12}The king and Jehoiada delivered the money to those who oversaw the tasks connected with the work of the House of the LORD. They hired masons and carpenters to renovate the House of the LORD, as well as craftsmen in

<hr>

a   Cf. 2 Kings 12.1–22.

1993

כד בֶּן־שֶׁבַע שָׁנִים יֹאָשׁ בְּמָלְכוֹ וְאַרְבָּעִים שָׁנָה מָלַךְ בִּירוּשָׁלִָם וְשֵׁם אִמּוֹ צִבְיָה מִבְּאֵר שָׁבַע: 2 וַיַּעַשׂ יוֹאָשׁ הַיָּשָׁר בְּעֵינֵי יְהוָה כָּל־יְמֵי יְהוֹיָדָע הַכֹּהֵן: 3 וַיִּשָּׂא־לוֹ יְהוֹיָדָע נָשִׁים שְׁתָּיִם וַיּוֹלֶד בָּנִים וּבָנוֹת:

4 וַיְהִי אַחֲרֵיכֵן הָיָה עִם־לֵב יוֹאָשׁ לְחַדֵּשׁ אֶת־בֵּית יְהוָה: 5 וַיִּקְבֹּץ אֶת־הַכֹּהֲנִים וְהַלְוִיִּם וַיֹּאמֶר לָהֶם צְאוּ לְעָרֵי יְהוּדָה וְקִבְצוּ מִכָּל־יִשְׂרָאֵל כֶּסֶף לְחַזֵּק ׀ אֶת־בֵּית אֱלֹהֵיכֶם מִדֵּי שָׁנָה בְּשָׁנָה וְאַתֶּם תְּמַהֲרוּ לַדָּבָר וְלֹא מִהֲרוּ הַלְוִיִּם: 6 וַיִּקְרָא הַמֶּלֶךְ לִיהוֹיָדָע הָרֹאשׁ וַיֹּאמֶר לוֹ מַדּוּעַ לֹא־דָרַשְׁתָּ עַל־הַלְוִיִּם לְהָבִיא מִיהוּדָה וּמִירוּשָׁלִַם אֶת־מַשְׂאַת מֹשֶׁה עֶבֶד־יְהוָה וְהַקָּהָל לְיִשְׂרָאֵל לְאֹהֶל הָעֵדוּת: 7 כִּי עֲתַלְיָהוּ הַמִּרְשַׁעַת בָּנֶיהָ פָרְצוּ אֶת־בֵּית הָאֱלֹהִים וְגַם כָּל־קָדְשֵׁי בֵית־יְהוָה עָשׂוּ לַבְּעָלִים: 8 וַיֹּאמֶר הַמֶּלֶךְ וַיַּעֲשׂוּ אֲרוֹן אֶחָד וַיִּתְּנֻהוּ בְּשַׁעַר בֵּית־יְהוָה חוּצָה: 9 וַיִּתְּנוּ־קוֹל בִּיהוּדָה וּבִירוּשָׁלַם לְהָבִיא לַיהוָה מַשְׂאַת מֹשֶׁה עֶבֶד־הָאֱלֹהִים עַל־יִשְׂרָאֵל בַּמִּדְבָּר: 10 וַיִּשְׂמְחוּ כָל־הַשָּׂרִים וְכָל־הָעָם וַיָּבִיאוּ וַיַּשְׁלִיכוּ לָאָרוֹן עַד־לְכַלֵּה: 11 וַיְהִי בְּעֵת יָבִיא אֶת־הָאָרוֹן אֶל־פְּקֻדַּת הַמֶּלֶךְ בְּיַד הַלְוִיִּם וְכִרְאוֹתָם כִּי־רַב הַכֶּסֶף וּבָא סוֹפֵר הַמֶּלֶךְ וּפְקִיד כֹּהֵן הָרֹאשׁ וִיעָרוּ אֶת־הָאָרוֹן וְיִשָּׂאֻהוּ וִישִׁיבֻהוּ אֶל־מְקֹמוֹ כֹּה עָשׂוּ לְיוֹם ׀ בְּיוֹם וַיַּאַסְפוּ־כֶסֶף לָרֹב: 12 וַיִּתְּנֵהוּ הַמֶּלֶךְ וִיהוֹיָדָע אֶל־עוֹשֵׂה מְלֶאכֶת עֲבוֹדַת בֵּית־יְהוָה וַיִּהְיוּ שֹׂכְרִים חֹצְבִים וְחָרָשִׁים לְחַדֵּשׁ בֵּית יְהוָה וְגַם לְחָרָשֵׁי בַרְזֶל

iron and bronze to repair the House of the LORD. ¹³The overseers did their work; under them the work went well and they restored the House of God to its original form and repaired it. ¹⁴When they had finished, they brought the money that was left over to the king and Jehoiada; it was made into utensils for the House of the LORD, service vessels: buckets and ladles, golden and silver vessels. Burnt offerings were offered up regularly in the House of the LORD all the days of Jehoiada. ¹⁵Jehoiada reached a ripe old age and died; he was one hundred and thirty years old at his death. ¹⁶They buried him in the City of David together with the kings, because he had done good in Israel, and on behalf of God and His House.

¹⁷But after the death of Jehoiada, the officers of Judah came, bowing low to the king; and the king listened to them. ¹⁸They forsook the House of the LORD God of their fathers to serve the sacred posts and idols; and there was wrath upon Judah and Jerusalem because of this guilt of theirs. ¹⁹The LORD sent prophets among them to bring them back to Him; they admonished them but they would not pay heed. ²⁰Then the spirit of God enveloped Zechariah son of Jehoiada the priest; he stood above the people and said to them, "Thus God said: Why do you transgress the commandments of the LORD when you cannot succeed? Since you have forsaken the LORD, He has forsaken you." ²¹They conspired against him and pelted him with stones in the court of the House of the LORD, by order of the king. ²²King Joash disregarded the loyalty that his father Jehoiada had shown to him, and killed his son. As he was dying, he said, "May the LORD see and requite it."

²³At the turn of the year, the army of Aram marched against him; they invaded Judah and Jerusalem, and wiped out all the officers of the people from among the people, and sent all the

וּנְחֹ֖שֶׁת לְחַזֵּ֥ק אֶת־בֵּ֣ית יְהֹוָ֑ה: 13 וַֽיַּעֲשׂוּ֩ עֹשֵׂ֨י הַמְּלָאכָ֜ה וַתַּ֧עַל אֲרוּכָ֣ה לַמְּלָאכָ֛ה בְּיָדָ֖ם וַיַּֽעֲמִ֜ידוּ אֶת־בֵּ֧ית הָֽאֱלֹהִ֛ים עַל־מַתְכֻּנְתּ֖וֹ וַֽיְאַמְּצֻֽהוּ: 14 וּֽכְכַלּוֹתָ֡ם הֵבִ֣יאוּ לִפְנֵ֣י הַמֶּ֩לֶךְ֩ וִֽיהֽוֹיָדָ֨ע אֶת־שְׁאָ֜ר הַכֶּ֗סֶף וַיַּֽעֲשֵׂ֨הוּ כֵלִ֜ים לְבֵית־יְהֹוָ֗ה כְּלֵ֤י שָׁרֵת֙ וְהַעֲל֣וֹת וְכַפּ֔וֹת וּכְלֵ֥י זָהָ֖ב וָכָ֑סֶף וַיִּֽהְי֨וּ מַֽעֲלִ֤ים עֹלוֹת֙ בְּבֵית־יְהֹוָ֔ה תָּמִ֖יד כֹּ֥ל יְמֵ֥י יְהֽוֹיָדָֽע: פ 15 וַיִּזְקַ֧ן יְהֽוֹיָדָ֛ע וַיִּשְׂבַּ֥ע יָמִ֖ים וַיָּמֹ֑ת בֶּן־מֵאָ֧ה וּשְׁלֹשִׁ֛ים שָׁנָ֖ה בְּמוֹתֽוֹ: 16 וַיִּקְבְּרֻ֥הוּ בְעִיר־דָּוִ֖יד עִם־הַמְּלָכִ֑ים כִּֽי־עָשָׂ֤ה טוֹבָה֙ בְּיִשְׂרָאֵ֔ל וְעִ֥ם הָֽאֱלֹהִ֖ים וּבֵיתֽוֹ: ס

17 וְאַֽחֲרֵ֥י מוֹת֙ יְה֣וֹיָדָ֔ע בָּ֚אוּ שָׂרֵ֣י יְהוּדָ֔ה וַיִּֽשְׁתַּֽחֲו֖וּ לַמֶּ֑לֶךְ אָ֛ז שָׁמַ֥ע הַמֶּ֖לֶךְ אֲלֵיהֶֽם: 18 וַיַּֽעַזְב֗וּ אֶת־בֵּ֤ית יְהֹוָה֙ אֱלֹהֵ֣י אֲבֽוֹתֵיהֶ֔ם וַיַּֽעַבְד֥וּ אֶת־הָֽאֲשֵׁרִ֖ים וְאֶת־הָֽעֲצַבִּ֑ים וַֽיְהִי־קֶ֗צֶף עַל־יְהוּדָה֙ וִיר֣וּשָׁלַ֔͏ִם בְּאַשְׁמָתָ֖ם זֹֽאת: 19 וַיִּשְׁלַ֤ח בָּהֶם֙ נְבִאִ֔ים לַֽהֲשִׁיבָ֖ם אֶל־יְהֹוָ֑ה וַיָּעִ֥ידוּ בָ֖ם וְלֹ֥א הֶֽאֱזִֽינוּ: ס 20 וְר֣וּחַ אֱלֹהִ֗ים לָֽבְשָׁה֙ אֶת־זְכַרְיָה֙ בֶּן־יְהֽוֹיָדָ֣ע הַכֹּהֵ֔ן וַיַּֽעֲמֹ֖ד מֵעַ֣ל לָעָ֑ם וַיֹּ֨אמֶר לָהֶ֜ם כֹּ֣ה ׀ אָמַ֣ר הָֽאֱלֹהִ֗ים לָ֤מָה אַתֶּם֙ עֹֽבְרִים֙ אֶת־מִצְוֺ֣ת יְהֹוָ֔ה וְלֹ֣א תַצְלִ֔יחוּ כִּֽי־עֲזַבְתֶּ֥ם אֶת־יְהֹוָ֖ה וַיַּֽעֲזֹ֥ב אֶתְכֶֽם: 21 וַיִּקְשְׁר֣וּ עָלָ֗יו וַיִּרְגְּמֻ֥הוּ אֶ֨בֶן֙ בְּמִצְוַ֣ת הַמֶּ֔לֶךְ בַּֽחֲצַ֖ר בֵּ֣ית יְהֹוָֽה: 22 וְלֹֽא־זָכַ֞ר יוֹאָ֣שׁ הַמֶּ֗לֶךְ הַחֶ֨סֶד֙ אֲשֶׁ֨ר עָשָׂ֜ה יְהֽוֹיָדָ֤ע אָבִיו֙ עִמּ֔וֹ וַיַּֽהֲרֹ֖ג אֶת־בְּנ֑וֹ וּכְמוֹת֣וֹ אָמַ֔ר יֵ֥רֶא יְהֹוָ֖ה וְיִדְרֹֽשׁ: פ

23 וַיְהִ֣י ׀ לִתְקוּפַ֣ת הַשָּׁנָ֗ה עָלָ֣ה עָלָיו֮ חֵ֣יל אֲרָם֒ וַיָּבֹ֨אוּ אֶל־יְהוּדָ֜ה וִיר֣וּשָׁלַ֗͏ִם וַיַּשְׁחִ֜יתוּ אֶת־כָּל־שָׂרֵ֤י הָעָם֙ מֵעָ֔ם וְכָל־שְׁלָלָ֖ם

booty they took to the king of Damascus. [24]The invading army of Aram had come with but a few men, but the LORD delivered a very large army into their hands, because they had forsaken the LORD God of their fathers. They inflicted punishments on Joash. [25]When they withdrew, having left him with many wounds, his courtiers plotted against him because of the murder[b] of the sons of Jehoiada the priest, and they killed him in bed. He died and was buried in the City of David; he was not buried in the tombs of the kings. [26]These were the men who conspired against him: Zabad son of Shimeath the Ammonitess, and Jehozabad son of Shimrith the Moabitess. [27]As to his sons, and the many pronouncements against him, and his rebuilding of the House of God, they are recorded in the story in the book of the kings. His son Amaziah succeeded him as king.

25

[a]Amaziah was twenty-five years old when he became king, and he reigned twenty-nine years in Jerusalem; his mother's name was Jehoaddan of Jerusalem. [2]He did what was pleasing to the LORD, but not with a whole heart. [3]Once he had the kingdom firmly under control, he executed the courtiers who had assassinated his father the king. [4]But he did not put their children to death for [he acted] in accordance with what is written in the Teaching, in the Book of Moses, where the LORD commanded, [b]"Parents shall not die for children, nor shall children die for parents, but every person shall die only for his own crime."[-b]

[5]Amaziah assembled the men of Judah, and he put all the men of Judah and Benjamin under officers of thousands and officers of hundreds, by clans. He mustered them from the age of twenty upward, and found them to be 300,000

שָׁלְח֖וּ לְמֶ֥לֶךְ דַּרְמָֽשֶׂק׃ 24 כִּ֣י בְמִצְעָ֣ר אֲנָשִׁים֮ בָּ֣אוּ ׀ חֵ֣יל אֲרָם֒ וַֽיהוָ֗ה נָתַ֨ן בְּיָדָ֜ם חַ֤יִל לָרֹ֣ב מְאֹ֔ד כִּ֣י עָֽזְב֔וּ אֶת־יְהוָ֖ה אֱלֹהֵ֣י אֲבוֹתֵיהֶ֑ם וְאֶת־יוֹאָ֖שׁ עָשׂ֥וּ שְׁפָטִֽים׃ 25 וּבְלֶכְתָּ֣ם מִמֶּ֗נּוּ כִּֽי־עָזְב֣וּ אֹתוֹ֮ בְּמַחֲלֻיִ֣ם רַבִּים֒ הִתְקַשְּׁר֨וּ עָלָ֜יו עֲבָדָ֗יו בִּדְמֵ֗י בְּנֵי֙ יְהוֹיָדָ֣ע הַכֹּהֵ֔ן וַיַּֽהַרְגֻ֥הוּ עַל־ מִטָּת֖וֹ וַיָּמֹ֑ת וַֽיִּקְבְּרֻ֙הוּ֙ בְּעִ֣יר דָּוִ֔יד וְלֹ֥א קְבָרֻ֖הוּ בְּקִבְר֥וֹת הַמְּלָכִֽים׃ ס 26 וְאֵ֖לֶּה הַמִּתְקַשְּׁרִ֣ים עָלָ֔יו זָבָ֕ד בֶּן־שִׁמְעָת֙ הָֽעַמּוֹנִ֔ית וִיהוֹזָבָ֕ד בֶּן־שִׁמְרִ֖ית הַמּוֹאָבִֽית׃ 27 וּבָנָ֞יו ורב יֶ֣רֶב הַמַּשָּׂ֤א עָלָיו֙ וִיס֖וֹד בֵּ֣ית הָֽאֱלֹהִ֑ים הִנָּ֣ם כְּתוּבִ֗ים עַל־מִדְרַשׁ֙ סֵ֣פֶר הַמְּלָכִ֔ים וַיִּמְלֹ֛ךְ אֲמַצְיָ֥הוּ בְנ֖וֹ תַּחְתָּֽיו׃ פ

כה בֶּן־עֶשְׂרִ֨ים וְחָמֵ֤שׁ שָׁנָה֙ מָלַ֣ךְ אֲמַצְיָ֔הוּ וְעֶשְׂרִ֣ים וָתֵ֙שַׁע֙ שָׁנָ֔ה מָלַ֖ךְ בִּֽירוּשָׁלָ֑͏ִם וְשֵׁ֣ם אִמּ֔וֹ יְהוֹעַדָּ֖ן מִירֽוּשָׁלָֽיִם׃ 2 וַיַּ֥עַשׂ הַיָּשָׁ֖ר בְּעֵינֵ֣י יְהוָ֑ה רַ֕ק לֹ֖א בְּלֵבָ֥ב שָׁלֵֽם׃ 3 וַיְהִ֕י כַּאֲשֶׁ֛ר חָזְקָ֥ה הַמַּמְלָכָ֖ה עָלָ֑יו וַֽיַּהֲרֹג֙ אֶת־עֲבָדָ֔יו הַמַּכִּ֖ים אֶת־הַמֶּ֥לֶךְ אָבִֽיו׃ 4 וְאֶת־בְּנֵיהֶ֖ם לֹ֣א הֵמִ֑ית כִּ֣י כַכָּת֣וּב בַּתּוֹרָ֡ה בְּסֵ֣פֶר מֹשֶׁה֩ אֲשֶׁר־צִוָּ֨ה יְהוָ֜ה לֵאמֹ֗ר לֹא־יָמ֨וּתוּ אָב֤וֹת עַל־בָּנִים֙ וּבָנִ֣ים לֹא־יָמ֣וּתוּ עַל־אָב֔וֹת כִּ֛י אִ֥ישׁ בְּחֶטְא֖וֹ יָמֽוּתוּ׃ פ 5 וַיִּקְבֹּ֣ץ אֲמַצְיָ֣הוּ אֶת־יְהוּדָ֗ה וַיַּֽעֲמִידֵ֞ם לְבֵ֣ית־אָב֗וֹת לְשָׂרֵ֤י הָֽאֲלָפִים֙ וּלְשָׂרֵ֣י הַמֵּא֔וֹת לְכָל־יְהוּדָ֖ה וּבִנְיָמִ֑ן וַֽיִּפְקְדֵ֗ם לְמִבֶּ֨ן עֶשְׂרִ֤ים שָׁנָה֙ וָמַ֔עְלָה וַיִּמְצָאֵ֗ם שְׁלֹֽשׁ־מֵא֤וֹת אֶ֙לֶף֙ בָּח֔וּר יוֹצֵ֣א צָבָ֔א אֹחֵ֖ז

---

picked men fit for service, able to bear spear and shield. [6]He hired 100,000 warriors from Israel for 100 talents of silver. [7]Then a man of God came to him and said, "O king! Do not let the army of Israel go with you, for the LORD is not with Israel—all these Ephraimites. [8]But go by yourself and do it; take courage for battle, [else] God will make you fall before the enemy. For in God there is power to help one or make one fall!" [9]Amaziah said to the man of God, "And what am I to do about the 100 talents I gave for the Israelite force?" The man of God replied, "The LORD has the means to give you much more than that." [10]So Amaziah detached the force that came to him from Ephraim, [ordering them] to go back to their place. They were greatly enraged against Judah and returned to their place in a rage.

[11]Amaziah took courage and, leading his army, he marched to the Valley of Salt. He slew 10,000 men of Seir; [12]another 10,000 the men of Judah captured alive and brought to the top of Sela. They threw them down from the top of Sela and every one of them was burst open. [13]The men of the force that Amaziah had sent back so they would not go with him into battle made forays against the towns of Judah from Samaria to Beth-horon. They slew 3,000 of them, and took much booty.

[14]After Amaziah returned from defeating the Edomites, he had the gods of the men of Seir brought, and installed them as his gods; he prostrated himself before them, and to them he made sacrifice. [15]The LORD was enraged at Amaziah, and sent a prophet to him who said to him, "Why are you worshiping the gods of a people who could not save their people from you?" [16]As he spoke to him, [Amaziah] said to him, "Have we appointed you a counselor to the king? Stop, else you will be killed!" The prophet stopped, saying, "I see God has coun-

רֶמַח וְצִנָּה׃ 6 וַיִּשְׂכֹּר מִיִּשְׂרָאֵל מֵאָה אֶלֶף גִּבּוֹר* חָיִל בְּמֵאָה כִכַּר־כָּסֶף׃ 7 וְאִישׁ הָאֱלֹהִים בָּא אֵלָיו לֵאמֹר הַמֶּלֶךְ אַל־יָבֹא עִמְּךָ צְבָא יִשְׂרָאֵל כִּי אֵין יְהוָה עִם־יִשְׂרָאֵל כֹּל בְּנֵי אֶפְרָיִם׃ 8 כִּי אִם־בֹּא אַתָּה עֲשֵׂה חֲזַק לַמִּלְחָמָה יַכְשִׁילְךָ הָאֱלֹהִים לִפְנֵי אוֹיֵב כִּי יֶשׁ־כֹּחַ בֵּאלֹהִים לַעְזוֹר וּלְהַכְשִׁיל׃ 9 וַיֹּאמֶר אֲמַצְיָהוּ לְאִישׁ הָאֱלֹהִים וּמַה־לַּעֲשׂוֹת לִמְאַת הַכִּכָּר אֲשֶׁר נָתַתִּי לִגְדוּד יִשְׂרָאֵל וַיֹּאמֶר אִישׁ הָאֱלֹהִים יֵשׁ לַיהוָה לָתֶת לְךָ הַרְבֵּה מִזֶּה׃ 10 וַיַּבְדִּילֵם אֲמַצְיָהוּ לְהַגְּדוּד אֲשֶׁר־בָּא אֵלָיו מֵאֶפְרַיִם לָלֶכֶת לִמְקוֹמָם וַיִּחַר אַפָּם מְאֹד בִּיהוּדָה וַיָּשׁוּבוּ לִמְקוֹמָם בׇּחֳרִי־אָף׃ פ

11 וַאֲמַצְיָהוּ הִתְחַזַּק וַיִּנְהַג אֶת־עַמּוֹ וַיֵּלֶךְ גֵּיא הַמֶּלַח וַיַּךְ אֶת־בְּנֵי־שֵׂעִיר עֲשֶׂרֶת אֲלָפִים׃ 12 וַעֲשֶׂרֶת אֲלָפִים חַיִּים שָׁבוּ בְּנֵי יְהוּדָה וַיְבִיאוּם לְרֹאשׁ הַסָּלַע וַיַּשְׁלִיכוּם מֵרֹאשׁ־הַסֶּלַע וְכֻלָּם נִבְקָעוּ׃ ס 13 וּבְנֵי הַגְּדוּד אֲשֶׁר הֵשִׁיב אֲמַצְיָהוּ מִלֶּכֶת עִמּוֹ לַמִּלְחָמָה וַיִּפְשְׁטוּ בְּעָרֵי יְהוּדָה מִשֹּׁמְרוֹן וְעַד־בֵּית חוֹרוֹן וַיַּכּוּ מֵהֶם שְׁלֹשֶׁת אֲלָפִים וַיָּבֹזּוּ בִּזָּה רַבָּה׃ ס

14 וַיְהִי אַחֲרֵי בוֹא אֲמַצְיָהוּ מֵהַכּוֹת אֶת־אֲדוֹמִים וַיָּבֵא אֶת־אֱלֹהֵי בְּנֵי שֵׂעִיר וַיַּעֲמִידֵם לוֹ לֵאלֹהִים וְלִפְנֵיהֶם יִשְׁתַּחֲוֶה וְלָהֶם יְקַטֵּר׃ 15 וַיִּחַר־אַף יְהוָה בַּאֲמַצְיָהוּ וַיִּשְׁלַח אֵלָיו נָבִיא וַיֹּאמֶר לוֹ לָמָּה דָרַשְׁתָּ אֶת־אֱלֹהֵי הָעָם אֲשֶׁר לֹא־הִצִּילוּ אֶת־עַמָּם מִיָּדֶךָ׃ 16 וַיְהִי ׀ בְּדַבְּרוֹ אֵלָיו וַיֹּאמֶר לוֹ הַלְיוֹעֵץ לַמֶּלֶךְ נְתַנּוּךָ חֲדַל־לְךָ לָמָּה יַכּוּךָ וַיֶּחְדַּל הַנָּבִיא וַיֹּאמֶר יָדַעְתִּי כִּי־יָעַץ

v. 6. ‏ סבירין ומטעין "גבורי"

seled that you be destroyed, since you act this way and disregard my counsel."

¹⁷Then King Amaziah of Judah took counsel and sent this message to Joash son of Jehoahaz son of Jehu, king of Israel, "Come, let us confront each other!" ¹⁸King Joash of Israel sent back this message to King Amaziah of Judah, "The thistle in Lebanon sent this message to the cedar in Lebanon, 'Give your daughter to my son in marriage.' But a wild beast in Lebanon passed by and trampled the thistle. ¹⁹You boast that you have defeated the Edomites and you are ambitious to get more glory. Now stay at home, lest, provoking disaster you fall, dragging Judah down with you." ²⁰But Amaziah paid no heed—it was God's doing, in order to deliver them up because they worshiped the gods of Edom. ²¹King Joash of Israel marched up, and he and King Amaziah of Judah confronted each other at Beth-shemesh in Judah. ²²The men of Judah were routed by Israel, and they all fled to their homes. ²³King Joash of Israel captured Amaziah son of Joash son of Jehoahaz, king of Judah, in Beth-shemesh. He brought him to Jerusalem and made a breach of 400 cubits in the wall of Jerusalem, from the Ephraim Gate to the Corner Gate. ²⁴Then, with all the gold and silver and all the utensils that were to be found in the House of God in the custody of Obed-edom, and with the treasuries of the royal palace, and with the hostages, he returned to Samaria.

²⁵King Amaziah son of Joash of Judah lived fifteen years after the death of King Joash son of Jehoahaz of Israel. ²⁶The other events of Amaziah's reign, early and late, are recorded in the book of the kings of Judah and Israel. ²⁷From the time that Amaziah turned from following the Lord, a conspiracy was formed against him in Jerusalem, and he fled to Lachish; but they sent men after him to Lachish and they put him to death there. ²⁸They brought his body back

אֱלֹהִים֙ לְהַשְׁחִיתֶ֔ךָ כִּי־עָשִׂ֣יתָ זֹּ֔את וְלֹ֥א שָׁמַ֖עְתָּ לַעֲצָתִֽי׃ פ

¹⁷ וַיִּוָּעַ֞ץ אֲמַצְיָ֣הוּ מֶ֣לֶךְ יְהוּדָ֗ה וַ֠יִּשְׁלַח אֶל־יוֹאָ֨שׁ בֶּן־יְהוֹאָחָ֤ז בֶּן־יֵהוּא֙ מֶ֣לֶךְ יִשְׂרָאֵ֣ל לֵאמֹ֑ר לְכָ֖ה נִתְרָאֶ֥ה פָנִֽים׃ ¹⁸ וַיִּשְׁלַ֞ח יוֹאָ֣שׁ מֶֽלֶךְ־יִשְׂרָאֵ֗ל אֶל־אֲמַצְיָ֣הוּ מֶֽלֶךְ־יְהוּדָה֮ לֵאמֹר֒ הַח֜וֹחַ אֲשֶׁ֣ר בַּלְּבָנ֗וֹן שָׁ֠לַח אֶל־הָאֶ֜רֶז אֲשֶׁ֤ר בַּלְּבָנוֹן֙ לֵאמֹ֔ר תְּנָֽה־אֶת־בִּתְּךָ֥ לִבְנִ֖י לְאִשָּׁ֑ה וַֽתַּעֲבֹ֞ר חַיַּ֤ת הַשָּׂדֶה֙ אֲשֶׁ֣ר בַּלְּבָנ֔וֹן וַתִּרְמֹ֖ס אֶת־הַחֽוֹחַ׃ ¹⁹ אָמַ֗רְתָּ הִנֵּ֤ה הִכִּ֙יתָ֙ אֶת־אֱד֔וֹם וּנְשָׂאֲךָ֥ לִבְּךָ֖ לְהַכְבִּ֑יד עַתָּה֙ שְׁבָ֣ה בְּבֵיתֶ֔ךָ לָ֤מָּה תִתְגָּרֶה֙ בְּרָעָ֔ה וְנָ֣פַלְתָּ֔ אַתָּ֖ה וִיהוּדָ֥ה עִמָּֽךְ׃ ²⁰ וְלֹא־שָׁמַ֣ע אֲמַצְיָ֔הוּ כִּ֤י מֵהָֽאֱלֹהִים֙ הִ֔יא לְמַ֖עַן תִּתָּ֣ם בְּיָ֑ד כִּ֣י דָֽרְשׁ֔וּ אֵ֖ת אֱלֹהֵ֥י אֱדֽוֹם׃ ²¹ וַיַּ֨עַל יוֹאָ֤שׁ מֶֽלֶךְ־יִשְׂרָאֵל֙ וַיִּתְרָא֣וּ פָנִ֔ים ה֖וּא וַאֲמַצְיָ֣הוּ מֶֽלֶךְ־יְהוּדָ֑ה בְּבֵ֥ית שֶׁ֖מֶשׁ אֲשֶׁ֥ר לִֽיהוּדָֽה׃ ²² וַיִּנָּ֥גֶף יְהוּדָ֖ה לִפְנֵ֣י יִשְׂרָאֵ֑ל וַיָּנֻ֖סוּ אִ֥ישׁ לְאֹהָלָֽיו׃ ²³ וְאֵת֩ אֲמַצְיָ֨הוּ מֶֽלֶךְ־יְהוּדָ֜ה בֶּן־יוֹאָ֣שׁ בֶּן־יְהוֹאָחָ֗ז תָּפַ֛שׂ יוֹאָ֥שׁ מֶֽלֶךְ־יִשְׂרָאֵ֖ל בְּבֵ֣ית שָׁ֑מֶשׁ וַיְבִיאֵ֙הוּ֙ יְר֣וּשָׁלִַ֔ם וַיִּפְרֹ֞ץ בְּחוֹמַ֣ת יְרוּשָׁלִַ֗ם מִשַּׁ֤עַר אֶפְרַ֙יִם֙ עַד־שַׁ֣עַר הַפּוֹנֶ֔ה אַרְבַּ֥ע מֵא֖וֹת אַמָּֽה׃ ²⁴ וְכָֽל־הַזָּהָ֣ב וְהַכֶּ֡סֶף וְאֵ֣ת כָּל־הַ֠כֵּלִים הַנִּמְצְאִ֨ים בְּבֵית־הָאֱלֹהִ֜ים עִם־עֹבֵ֣ד אֱד֗וֹם וְאֶת־אֹצְר֤וֹת בֵּ֣ית הַמֶּ֔לֶךְ וְאֵ֖ת בְּנֵ֣י הַתַּֽעֲרֻב֑וֹת וַיָּ֖שָׁב שֹׁמְרֽוֹן׃ פ

²⁵ וַיְחִ֨י אֲמַצְיָ֧הוּ בֶן־יוֹאָ֛שׁ מֶ֥לֶךְ יְהוּדָ֖ה אַחֲרֵ֣י מ֥וֹת יוֹאָ֛שׁ בֶּן־יְהוֹאָחָ֖ז מֶ֣לֶךְ יִשְׂרָאֵ֑ל חֲמֵ֥שׁ עֶשְׂרֵ֖ה שָׁנָֽה׃ ²⁶ וְיֶ֙תֶר֙ דִּבְרֵ֣י אֲמַצְיָ֔הוּ הָרִֽאשֹׁנִ֖ים וְהָאַחֲרוֹנִ֑ים הֲלֹא֙ הִנָּ֣ם כְּתוּבִ֔ים עַל־סֵ֥פֶר מַלְכֵֽי־יְהוּדָ֖ה וְיִשְׂרָאֵֽל׃ ²⁷ וּמֵעֵ֗ת אֲשֶׁר־סָ֤ר אֲמַצְיָ֙הוּ֙ מֵאַחֲרֵ֣י יְהֹוָ֔ה וַיִּקְשְׁר֨וּ עָלָ֥יו קֶ֛שֶׁר בִּירוּשָׁלִַ֖ם וַיָּ֣נָס לָכִ֑ישָׁה וַיִּשְׁלְח֤וּ אַֽחֲרָיו֙ לָכִ֔ישָׁה וַיְמִיתֻ֖הוּ שָֽׁם׃

on horses and buried him with his fathers in the city of Judah.

26 Then all the people of Judah took Uzziah, who was sixteen years old, and proclaimed him king to succeed his father Amaziah. [2]It was he who rebuilt Eloth and restored it to Judah after King [Amaziah] slept with his fathers.

[3]Uzziah was sixteen years old when he became king, and he reigned fifty-two years in Jerusalem; his mother's name was Jecoliah of Jerusalem. [4]He did what was pleasing to the LORD just as his father Amaziah had done. [5]He applied himself to the worship of God during the time of Zechariah, instructor in the visions[a] of God; during the time he worshiped the LORD, God made him prosper. [6]He went forth to fight the Philistines, and breached the wall of Gath and the wall of Jabneh and the wall of Ashdod; he built towns in [the region of] Ashdod and among the Philistines. [7]God helped him against the Philistines, against the Arabs who lived in Gur-baal, and the Meunites. [8]The Ammonites paid tribute to Uzziah, and his fame spread to the approaches of Egypt, for he grew exceedingly strong. [9]Uzziah built towers in Jerusalem on the Corner Gate and the Valley Gate and on the Angle, and fortified them. [10]He built towers in the wilderness and hewed out many cisterns, for he had much cattle, and farmers in the foothills and on the plain, and vine dressers in the mountains and on the fertile lands, for he loved the soil.

[11]Uzziah had an army of warriors, a battle-ready force who were mustered by Jeiel the scribe and Maasseiah the adjutant under Hananiah, one of the king's officers. [12]The clan chiefs, valiants, totaled 2,600; [13]under them was the trained army of 307,500, who made war with

---

28 וַיִּשָּׂאֻ֙הוּ עַל־הַסּוּסִ֔ים וַיִּקְבְּר֥וּ אֹת֖וֹ עִם־אֲבֹתָ֖יו בְּעִ֥יר יְהוּדָֽה:

כו וַיִּקְח֞וּ כָּל־עַ֤ם יְהוּדָה֙ אֶת־עֻזִּיָּ֔הוּ וְה֕וּא בֶּן־שֵׁ֥שׁ עֶשְׂרֵ֖ה שָׁנָ֑ה וַיַּמְלִ֤יכוּ אֹתוֹ֙ תַּ֣חַת אָבִ֔יו אֲמַצְיָֽהוּ: [2] ה֚וּא בָּנָ֣ה אֶת־אֵיל֔וֹת וַיְשִׁבֶ֖הָ לִֽיהוּדָ֑ה אַחֲרֵ֥י שְׁכַֽב־הַמֶּ֖לֶךְ עִם־אֲבֹתָֽיו: פ

[3] בֶּן־שֵׁ֨שׁ עֶשְׂרֵ֤ה שָׁנָה֙ עֻזִּיָּ֔הוּ בְּמָלְכ֔וֹ וַחֲמִשִּׁ֤ים וּשְׁתַּ֙יִם֙ שָׁנָ֔ה מָלַ֖ךְ בִּירֽוּשָׁלִָ֑ם וְשֵׁ֣ם אִמּ֔וֹ יְכׇלְיָ֖ה מִן־יְרֽוּשָׁלָֽיִם: [4] וַיַּ֥עַשׂ הַיָּשָׁ֖ר בְּעֵינֵ֣י יְהֹוָ֑ה כְּכֹ֥ל אֲשֶׁר־עָשָׂ֖ה אֲמַצְיָ֥הוּ אָבִֽיו: [5] וַיְהִי֙ לִדְרֹ֣שׁ אֱלֹהִ֔ים בִּימֵ֣י זְכַרְיָ֔הוּ הַמֵּבִ֖ין בִּרְאֹ֣ת הָאֱלֹהִ֑ים וּבִימֵ֤י דׇרְשׁוֹ֙ אֶת־יְהֹוָ֔ה הִצְלִיח֖וֹ הָאֱלֹהִֽים: ס [6] וַיֵּצֵא֙ וַיִּלָּ֣חֶם בַּפְּלִשְׁתִּ֔ים וַיִּפְרֹ֞ץ אֶת־חוֹמַ֣ת גַּ֗ת וְאֵת֙ חוֹמַ֣ת יַבְנֵ֔ה וְאֵ֖ת חוֹמַ֣ת אַשְׁדּ֑וֹד וַיִּבְנֶ֣ה עָרִ֔ים בְּאַשְׁדּ֖וֹד וּבַפְּלִשְׁתִּֽים: [7] וַיַּעְזְרֵ֨הוּ הָֽאֱלֹהִ֜ים עַל־פְּלִשְׁתִּ֗ים וְעַל־הָעַרְבִים֙ הַיֹּשְׁבִ֣ים בְּגוּר־בָּ֔עַל וְהַמְּעוּנִֽים: [8] וַיִּתְּנ֤וּ הָֽעַמּוֹנִים֙ מִנְחָ֣ה לְעֻזִּיָּ֔הוּ וַיֵּ֥לֶךְ שְׁמ֖וֹ עַד־לְב֣וֹא מִצְרַ֔יִם כִּ֥י הֶחֱזִ֖יק עַד־לְמָֽעְלָה: [9] וַיִּ֨בֶן עֻזִּיָּ֤הוּ מִגְדָּלִים֙ בִּיר֣וּשָׁלִַ֔ם עַל־שַׁ֧עַר הַפִּנָּ֛ה וְעַל־שַׁ֥עַר הַגַּ֖יְא וְעַל־הַמִּקְצ֑וֹעַ וַֽיְחַזְּקֵֽם: [10] וַיִּ֨בֶן מִגְדָּלִ֣ים בַּמִּדְבָּר֮ וַיַּחְצֹ֣ב בֹּר֣וֹת רַבִּים֒ כִּ֤י מִקְנֶה־רַּב֙* הָ֣יָה ל֔וֹ וּבַשְּׁפֵלָ֖ה וּבַמִּישׁ֑וֹר אִכָּרִ֣ים וְכֹֽרְמִ֗ים בֶּהָרִ֤ים וּבַכַּרְמֶל֙ כִּי־אֹהֵ֥ב אֲדָמָ֖ה הָיָֽה: ס [11] וַיְהִ֣י לְעֻזִּיָּ֡הוּ חַ֩יִל֩ עֹ֨שֵׂה מִלְחָמָ֜ה יוֹצְאֵ֧י צָבָ֣א לִגְד֗וּד בְּמִסְפַּר֙ פְּקֻדָּתָ֔ם בְּיַד֙ יְעִיאֵ֣ל הַסּוֹפֵ֔ר וּמַעֲשֵׂיָ֖הוּ הַשּׁוֹטֵ֑ר עַ֕ל יַד־חֲנַנְיָ֖הוּ מִשָּׂרֵ֥י הַמֶּֽלֶךְ: [12] כֹּ֠ל מִסְפַּ֞ר רָאשֵׁ֤י הָאָבוֹת֙ לְגִבּ֣וֹרֵי חָ֔יִל אַלְפַּ֖יִם וְשֵׁ֥שׁ מֵאֽוֹת: [13] וְעַל־יָדָ֞ם חֵ֣יל צָבָ֗א שְׁלֹ֤שׁ מֵאוֹת֙

might and power to aid the king against the enemy. ¹⁴Uzziah provided them—the whole army—with shields and spears, and helmets and mail, and bows and slingstones. ¹⁵He made clever devices in Jerusalem, set on the towers and the corners, for shooting arrows and large stones. His fame spread far, for he was helped wonderfully, and he became strong.

¹⁶When he was strong, he grew so arrogant he acted corruptly: he trespassed against his God by entering the Temple of the LORD to offer incense on the incense altar. ¹⁷The priest Azariah, with eighty other brave priests of the LORD, followed him in ¹⁸and, confronting King Uzziah, said to him, "It is not for you, Uzziah, to offer incense to the LORD, but for the Aaronite priests, who have been consecrated, to offer incense. Get out of the Sanctuary, for you have trespassed; there will be no glory in it for you from the LORD God." ¹⁹Uzziah, holding the censer and ready to burn incense, got angry; but as he got angry with the priests, leprosy broke out on his forehead in front of the priests in the House of the LORD beside the incense altar. ²⁰When the chief priest Azariah and all the other priests looked at him, his forehead was leprous, so they rushed him out of there; he too made haste to get out, for the LORD had struck him with a plague. ²¹King Uzziah was a leper until the day of his death. He lived in ^b-isolated quarters-^b as a leper, for he was cut off from the House of the LORD—while Jotham his son was in charge of the king's house and governed the people of the land.

²²The other events of Uzziah's reign, early and late, were recorded by the prophet Isaiah son of Amoz. ²³Uzziah slept with his fathers in the burial field of the kings, because, they said, he was a leper; his son Jotham succeeded him as king.

---

b-b   *Meaning of Heb. uncertain.*

אֶלֶף וְשִׁבְעַת אֲלָפִים וַחֲמֵשׁ מֵאוֹת עוֹשֵׂי מִלְחָמָה בְּכֹחַ חָיִל לַעְזֹר לַמֶּלֶךְ עַל־הָאוֹיֵב: 14 וַיָּכֶן לָהֶם עֻזִּיָּהוּ לְכָל־הַצָּבָא מָגִנִּים וּרְמָחִים וְכוֹבָעִים וְשִׁרְיֹנוֹת וּקְשָׁתוֹת וּלְאַבְנֵי קְלָעִים: 15 וַיַּעַשׂ ׀ בִּירוּשָׁלִַם חִשְּׁבֹנוֹת מַחֲשֶׁבֶת חוֹשֵׁב לִהְיוֹת עַל־הַמִּגְדָּלִים וְעַל־הַפִּנּוֹת לִירוֹא בַּחִצִּים וּבָאֲבָנִים גְּדֹלוֹת וַיֵּצֵא שְׁמוֹ עַד־לְמֵרָחוֹק כִּי־הִפְלִיא לְהֵעָזֵר עַד כִּי־חָזָק:

16 וּכְחֶזְקָתוֹ גָּבַהּ לִבּוֹ עַד־לְהַשְׁחִית וַיִּמְעַל בַּיהוָה אֱלֹהָיו וַיָּבֹא אֶל־הֵיכַל יְהוָה לְהַקְטִיר עַל־מִזְבַּח הַקְּטֹרֶת: 17 וַיָּבֹא אַחֲרָיו עֲזַרְיָהוּ הַכֹּהֵן וְעִמּוֹ כֹּהֲנִים לַיהוָה שְׁמוֹנִים בְּנֵי־חָיִל: 18 וַיַּעַמְדוּ עַל־עֻזִּיָּהוּ הַמֶּלֶךְ וַיֹּאמְרוּ לוֹ לֹא־לְךָ עֻזִּיָּהוּ לְהַקְטִיר לַיהוָה כִּי לַכֹּהֲנִים בְּנֵי־אַהֲרֹן הַמְקֻדָּשִׁים לְהַקְטִיר צֵא מִן־הַמִּקְדָּשׁ כִּי מָעַלְתָּ וְלֹא־לְךָ לְכָבוֹד מֵיְהוָה אֱלֹהִים: 19 וַיִּזְעַף עֻזִּיָּהוּ וּבְיָדוֹ מִקְטֶרֶת לְהַקְטִיר וּבְזַעְפּוֹ עִם־הַכֹּהֲנִים וְהַצָּרַעַת זָרְחָה בְמִצְחוֹ לִפְנֵי הַכֹּהֲנִים בְּבֵית יְהוָה מֵעַל לְמִזְבַּח הַקְּטֹרֶת: 20 וַיִּפֶן אֵלָיו עֲזַרְיָהוּ כֹהֵן הָרֹאשׁ וְכָל־הַכֹּהֲנִים וְהִנֵּה־הוּא מְצֹרָע בְּמִצְחוֹ וַיַּבְהִלוּהוּ מִשָּׁם וְגַם־הוּא נִדְחַף לָצֵאת כִּי נִגְּעוֹ יְהוָה: 21 וַיְהִי עֻזִּיָּהוּ הַמֶּלֶךְ מְצֹרָע ׀ עַד־יוֹם מוֹתוֹ וַיֵּשֶׁב בֵּית הַחָפְשׁית הַחָפְשִׁית מְצֹרָע כִּי נִגְזַר מִבֵּית יְהוָה וְיוֹתָם בְּנוֹ עַל־בֵּית הַמֶּלֶךְ שׁוֹפֵט אֶת־עַם הָאָרֶץ:

22 וְיֶתֶר דִּבְרֵי עֻזִּיָּהוּ הָרִאשֹׁנִים וְהָאַחֲרֹנִים כָּתַב יְשַׁעְיָהוּ בֶן־אָמוֹץ הַנָּבִיא: 23 וַיִּשְׁכַּב עֻזִּיָּהוּ עִם־אֲבֹתָיו וַיִּקְבְּרוּ אֹתוֹ עִם־אֲבֹתָיו בִּשְׂדֵה הַקְּבוּרָה אֲשֶׁר לַמְּלָכִים כִּי אָמְרוּ מְצוֹרָע הוּא וַיִּמְלֹךְ יוֹתָם בְּנוֹ תַּחְתָּיו: פ

27

Jotham was twenty-five years old when he became king, and he reigned sixteen years in Jerusalem; his mother's name was Jerushah daughter of Zadok. ²He did what was pleasing to the LORD just as his father Uzziah had done, but he did not enter the Temple of the LORD; however, the people still acted corruptly. ³It was he who built the Upper Gate of the House of the LORD; he also built extensively on the wall of Ophel. ⁴He built towns in the hill country of Judah, and in the woods he built fortresses and towers. ⁵Moreover, he fought with the king of the Ammonites and overcame them; the Ammonites gave him that year 100 talents of silver and 10,000 *kor* of wheat and another 10,000 of barley; that is what the Ammonites paid him, and [likewise] in the second and third years. ⁶Jotham was strong because he maintained a faithful course before the LORD his God.

⁷The other events of Jotham's reign, and all his battles and his conduct, are recorded in the book of the kings of Israel and Judah. ⁸He was twenty-five years old when he became king, and he reigned sixteen years in Jerusalem. ⁹Jotham slept with his fathers, and was buried in the City of David; his son Ahaz succeeded him as king.

28

Ahaz was twenty years old when he became king, and he reigned sixteen years in Jerusalem. He did not do what was pleasing to the LORD as his father David had done, ²but followed the ways of the kings of Israel; he even made molten images for the Baals. ³He made offerings in the Valley of Ben-hinnom and burned his sons in fire, in the abhorrent fashion of the nations which the LORD had dispossessed before the Israelites. ⁴He sacrificed and made offerings at the shrines, on the hills, and under every leafy tree. ⁵The LORD his God delivered

כז בֶּן־עֶשְׂרִ֨ים וְחָמֵ֤שׁ שָׁנָה֙ יוֹתָ֔ם בְּמָלְכ֔וֹ וְשֵׁשׁ־עֶשְׂרֵ֣ה שָׁנָ֔ה מָלַ֖ךְ בִּירֽוּשָׁלָ֑͏ִם וְשֵׁ֣ם אִמּ֔וֹ יְרוּשָׁ֖ה בַּת־צָדֽוֹק׃ ²וַיַּ֨עַשׂ הַיָּשָׁ֜ר בְּעֵינֵ֣י יְהוָ֗ה כְּכֹ֤ל אֲשֶׁר־עָשָׂה֙ עֻזִּיָּ֣הוּ אָבִ֔יו רַ֕ק לֹא־בָ֖א אֶל־הֵיכַ֣ל יְהוָ֑ה וְע֖וֹד הָעָ֥ם מַשְׁחִיתִֽים׃ ³ה֗וּא בָּנָ֛ה אֶת־שַׁ֥עַר בֵּית־יְהוָ֖ה הָעֶלְי֑וֹן וּבְחוֹמַ֥ת הָעֹ֖פֶל בָּנָ֥ה לָרֹֽב׃ ⁴וְעָרִ֥ים בָּנָ֖ה בְּהַר־יְהוּדָ֑ה וּבֶחֳרָשִׁ֣ים בָּנָ֔ה בִּֽירָנִיּ֖וֹת וּמִגְדָּלֽים׃ ⁵וְ֠ה֠וּא נִלְחַ֞ם עִם־מֶ֣לֶךְ בְּנֵֽי־עַמּוֹן֮ וַיֶּחֱזַ֣ק עֲלֵיהֶם֒ וַיִּתְּנוּ־ל֨וֹ בְנֵֽי־עַמּ֜וֹן בַּשָּׁנָ֣ה הַהִ֗יא מֵאָה֙ כִּכַּר־כֶּ֔סֶף וַעֲשֶׂ֨רֶת אֲלָפִ֤ים כֹּרִים֙ חִטִּ֔ים וּשְׂעוֹרִ֖ים עֲשֶׂ֣רֶת אֲלָפִ֑ים זֹ֗את הֵשִׁ֤יבוּ לוֹ֙ בְּנֵ֣י עַמּ֔וֹן ס וּבַשָּׁנָ֥ה הַשֵּׁנִ֖ית וְהַשְּׁלִשִֽׁית׃ ⁶וַיִּתְחַזֵּ֖ק יוֹתָ֑ם כִּ֚י הֵכִ֣ין דְּרָכָ֔יו לִפְנֵ֖י יְהוָ֥ה אֱלֹהָֽיו׃

⁷וְיֶ֨תֶר֙ דִּבְרֵ֣י יוֹתָ֔ם וְכָל־מִלְחֲמֹתָ֖יו וּדְרָכָ֑יו הִנָּ֣ם כְּתוּבִ֔ים עַל־סֵ֥פֶר מַלְכֵֽי־יִשְׂרָאֵ֖ל וִיהוּדָֽה׃ ⁸בֶּן־עֶשְׂרִ֨ים וְחָמֵ֤שׁ שָׁנָה֙ הָיָ֣ה בְמָלְכ֔וֹ וְשֵׁשׁ־עֶשְׂרֵ֣ה שָׁנָ֔ה מָלַ֖ךְ בִּירֽוּשָׁלָֽ͏ִם׃ ⁹וַיִּשְׁכַּ֤ב יוֹתָם֙ עִם־אֲבֹתָ֔יו וַיִּקְבְּר֥וּ אֹת֖וֹ בְּעִ֣יר דָּוִ֑יד וַיִּמְלֹ֛ךְ אָחָ֥ז בְּנ֖וֹ תַּחְתָּֽיו׃ פ

כח בֶּן־עֶשְׂרִ֤ים שָׁנָה֙ אָחָ֣ז בְּמָלְכ֔וֹ וְשֵׁשׁ־עֶשְׂרֵ֣ה שָׁנָ֔ה מָלַ֖ךְ בִּירוּשָׁלָ֑͏ִם וְלֹא־עָשָׂ֧ה הַיָּשָׁ֛ר בְּעֵינֵ֥י יְהוָ֖ה כְּדָוִ֥יד אָבִֽיו׃ ²וַיֵּ֕לֶךְ בְּדַרְכֵ֖י מַלְכֵ֣י יִשְׂרָאֵ֑ל וְגַ֧ם מַסֵּכ֛וֹת עָשָׂ֖ה לַבְּעָלִֽים׃ ³וְה֤וּא הִקְטִיר֙ בְּגֵ֣יא בֶן־הִנֹּ֔ם וַיַּבְעֵ֥ר אֶת־בָּנָ֖יו בָּאֵ֑שׁ כְּתֹֽעֲבוֹת֙ הַגּוֹיִ֔ם אֲשֶׁר֙ הֹרִ֣ישׁ יְהוָ֔ה מִפְּנֵ֖י בְּנֵ֥י יִשְׂרָאֵֽל׃ ⁴וַיְזַבֵּ֧חַ וַיְקַטֵּ֛ר בַּבָּמ֖וֹת וְעַל־הַגְּבָע֑וֹת וְתַ֖חַת כָּל־עֵ֥ץ רַעֲנָֽן׃ ⁵וַיִּתְּנֵ֡הוּ יְהוָ֣ה אֱלֹהָיו֮ בְּיַ֣ד מֶ֣לֶךְ אֲרָם֒ וַיַּ֨כּוּ־ב֔וֹ וַיִּשְׁבּ֣וּ

him over to the king of Aram, who defeated him and took many of his men captive, and brought them to Damascus. He was also delivered over to the king of Israel, who inflicted a great defeat on him. [6]Pekah son of Remaliah killed 120,000 in Judah—all brave men—in one day, because they had forsaken the Lord God of their fathers. [7]Zichri, the champion of Ephraim, killed Maaseiah the king's son, and Azrikam chief of the palace, and Elkanah, the second to the king. [8]The Israelites captured 200,000 of their kinsmen, women, boys, and girls; they also took a large amount of booty from them and brought the booty to Samaria.

[9]A prophet of the Lord by the name of Oded was there, who went out to meet the army on its return to Samaria. He said to them, "Because of the fury of the Lord God of your fathers against Judah, He delivered them over to you, and you killed them in a rage that reached heaven. [10]Do you now intend to subjugate the men and women of Judah and Jerusalem to be your slaves? As it is, you have nothing but offenses against the Lord your God. [11]Now then, listen to me, and send back the captives you have taken from your kinsmen, for the wrath of the Lord is upon you!" [12]Some of the chief men of the Ephraimites—Azariah son of Jehohanan, Berechiah son of Meshillemoth, Jehizkiah son of Shallum, and Amasa son of Hadlai—confronted those returning from the campaign [13]and said to them, "Do not bring these captives here, for it would mean our offending the Lord, adding to our sins and our offenses; for our offense is grave enough, and there is already wrath upon Israel." [14]So the soldiers released the captives and the booty in the presence of the officers and all the congregation. [15]Then the men named above proceeded to take the captives in hand, and with the booty they clothed all the naked among them—they

מִמֶּ֙נּוּ֙ שִׁבְיָ֣ה גְדוֹלָ֔ה וַיָּבִ֖יאוּ דַּרְמָ֑שֶׂק וְ֠גַם בְּיַד־מֶ֧לֶךְ יִשְׂרָאֵ֛ל נִתָּ֖ן וַיַּךְ־בּ֥וֹ מַכָּ֖ה גְדוֹלָֽה׃ ס [6]וַיַּהֲרֹ֞ג פֶּ֣קַח בֶּן־רְמַלְיָ֗הוּ בִּיהוּדָ֜ה מֵאָ֧ה וְעֶשְׂרִ֛ים אֶ֖לֶף בְּי֣וֹם אֶחָ֑ד הַכֹּ֖ל בְּנֵי־חָ֑יִל בְּעׇזְבָ֕ם אֶת־יְהוָ֖ה אֱלֹהֵ֥י אֲבוֹתָֽם׃ [7]וַיַּהֲרֹ֞ג זִכְרִ֣י ׀ גִּבּ֣וֹר אֶפְרַ֗יִם אֶת־מַעֲשֵׂיָ֙הוּ֙ בֶּן־הַמֶּ֔לֶךְ וְאֶת־עַזְרִיקָ֖ם נְגִ֣יד הַבָּ֑יִת וְאֶת־אֶלְקָנָ֖ה מִשְׁנֵ֥ה הַמֶּֽלֶךְ׃ ס [8]וַיִּשְׁבּוּ֩ בְנֵֽי־יִשְׂרָאֵ֙ל מֵֽאֲחֵיהֶ֜ם מָאתַ֣יִם אֶ֗לֶף נָשִׁ֤ים בָּנִים֙ וּבָנ֔וֹת וְגַם־שָׁלָ֥ל רָ֖ב בָּזְז֣וּ מֵהֶ֑ם וַיָּבִ֥יאוּ אֶת־הַשָּׁלָ֖ל לְשֹׁמְרֽוֹן׃ ס [9]וְ֠שָׁם הָיָ֙ה נָבִ֤יא לַֽיהוָה֙ עֹדֵ֣ד שְׁמ֔וֹ וַיֵּצֵ֗א לִפְנֵ֤י הַצָּבָא֙ הַבָּ֣א לְשֹׁמְר֔וֹן וַיֹּ֣אמֶר לָהֶ֗ם הִ֠נֵּה בַּחֲמַ֙ת יְהוָ֧ה אֱלֹהֵֽי־אֲבוֹתֵיכֶ֛ם עַל־יְהוּדָ֖ה נְתָנָ֣ם בְּיֶדְכֶ֑ם וַתַּֽהַרְגוּ־בָ֣ם בְּזַ֔עַף עַ֥ד לַשָּׁמַ֖יִם הִגִּֽיעַ׃ [10]וְ֠עַתָּה בְּנֵֽי־יְהוּדָ֣ה וִֽירוּשָׁלַ֗͏ִם אַתֶּ֤ם אֹֽמְרִים֙ לִכְבֹּ֣שׁ לַעֲבָדִ֥ים וְלִשְׁפָח֖וֹת לָכֶ֑ם הֲלֹ֣א רַק־אַתֶּ֗ם עִמָּכֶ֛ם אֲשָׁמ֖וֹת לַיהוָ֥ה אֱלֹהֵיכֶֽם׃ [11]וְעַתָּ֣ה שְׁמָע֔וּנִי וְהָשִׁ֙יבוּ֙ הַשִּׁבְיָ֔ה אֲשֶׁ֥ר שְׁבִיתֶ֖ם מֵאֲחֵיכֶ֑ם כִּ֛י חֲר֥וֹן אַף־יְהוָ֖ה עֲלֵיכֶֽם׃ ס [12]וַיָּקֻ֙מוּ אֲנָשִׁ֜ים מֵרָאשֵׁ֣י בְנֵֽי־אֶפְרַ֗יִם עֲזַרְיָ֤הוּ בֶן־יְהֽוֹחָנָן֙ בֶּֽרֶכְיָ֣הוּ בֶן־מְשִׁלֵּמ֔וֹת וִֽיחִזְקִיָּ֙הוּ֙ בֶּן־שַׁלֻּ֔ם וַעֲמָשָׂ֖א בֶּן־חַדְלָ֑י עַל־הַבָּאִ֖ים מִן־הַצָּבָֽא׃ [13]וַיֹּאמְר֣וּ לָהֶ֗ם לֹא־תָבִ֤יאוּ אֶת־הַשִּׁבְיָה֙ הֵ֔נָּה כִּי֩ לְאַשְׁמַ֙ת יְהוָ֤ה עָלֵ֙ינוּ֙ אַתֶּ֣ם אֹמְרִ֔ים לְהֹסִ֥יף עַל־חַטֹּאתֵ֖ינוּ וְעַל־אַשְׁמָתֵ֑ינוּ כִּֽי־רַבָּ֤ה אַשְׁמָה֙ לָ֔נוּ וַחֲר֥וֹן אָ֖ף עַל־יִשְׂרָאֵֽל׃ ס [14]וַיַּעֲזֹ֣ב הֶֽחָל֗וּץ אֶת־הַשִּׁבְיָה֙ וְאֶת־הַבִּזָּ֔ה לִפְנֵ֥י הַשָּׂרִ֖ים וְכׇל־הַקָּהָֽל׃ [15]וַיָּקֻ֣מוּ הָאֲנָשִׁים֮ אֲשֶׁר־נִקְּב֣וּ בְשֵׁמוֹת֒ וַיַּחֲזִ֙יקוּ֙ בַשִּׁבְיָ֔ה וְכׇֽל־מַעֲרֻמֵּיהֶ֜ם הִלְבִּ֣ישׁוּ מִן־הַשָּׁלָ֗ל וַיַּלְבִּשׁ֙וּם

clothed them and shod them and gave them to eat and drink and anointed them and provided donkeys for all who were failing and brought them to Jericho, the city of palms, back to their kinsmen. Then they returned to Samaria.

[16]At that time, King Ahaz sent to the king of Assyria for help. [17]Again the Edomites came and inflicted a defeat on Judah and took captives. [18]And the Philistines made forays against the cities of the Shephelah and the Negeb of Judah; they seized Beth-shemesh and Aijalon and Gederoth, and Soco with its villages, and Timnah with its villages, and Gimzo with its villages; and they settled there. [19]Thus the LORD brought Judah low on account of King Ahaz of Israel,[a] for he threw off restraint in Judah and trespassed against the LORD. [20]Tillegath-pilneser, king of Assyria, marched against him and gave him trouble, instead of supporting him. [21]For Ahaz plundered the House of the LORD and the house of the king and the officers, and made a gift to the king of Assyria—to no avail.

[22]In his time of trouble, this King Ahaz trespassed even more against the LORD, [23]sacrificing to the gods of Damascus which had defeated him, for he thought, "The gods of the kings of Aram help them; I shall sacrifice to them and they will help me"; but they were his ruin and that of all Israel. [24]Ahaz collected the utensils of the House of God, and cut the utensils of the House of God to pieces. He shut the doors of the House of the LORD and made himself altars in every corner of Jerusalem. [25]In every town in Judah he set up shrines to make offerings to other gods, vexing the LORD God of his fathers.

[26]The other events of his reign and all his conduct, early and late, are recorded in the book of the kings of Judah and Israel. [27]Ahaz slept with his fathers and was buried in the city, in Jerusalem; his body was not brought to the

וַיַּנְעִלוּם וַיַּאֲכִלוּם וַיַּשְׁקוּם וַיְסֻכוּם וַיְנַהֲלוּם בַּחֲמֹרִים לְכָל־כּוֹשֵׁל וַיְבִיאוּם יְרֵחוֹ עִיר־הַתְּמָרִים אֵצֶל אֲחֵיהֶם וַיָּשׁוּבוּ שֹׁמְרוֹן׃ פ

16 בָּעֵת הַהִיא שָׁלַח הַמֶּלֶךְ אָחָז עַל־מַלְכֵי אַשּׁוּר לַעְזֹר לוֹ׃ 17 וְעוֹד אֲדוֹמִים בָּאוּ וַיַּכּוּ בִיהוּדָה וַיִּשְׁבּוּ־שֶׁבִי׃ 18 וּפְלִשְׁתִּים פָּשְׁטוּ בְּעָרֵי הַשְּׁפֵלָה וְהַנֶּגֶב לִיהוּדָה וַיִּלְכְּדוּ אֶת־בֵּית־שֶׁמֶשׁ וְאֶת־אַיָּלוֹן וְאֶת־הַגְּדֵרוֹת וְאֶת־שׂוֹכוֹ וּבְנוֹתֶיהָ וְאֶת־תִּמְנָה וּבְנוֹתֶיהָ וְאֶת־גִּמְזוֹ וְאֶת־בְּנֹתֶיהָ וַיֵּשְׁבוּ שָׁם׃ 19 כִּי־הִכְנִיעַ יְהוָה אֶת־יְהוּדָה בַּעֲבוּר אָחָז מֶלֶךְ־יִשְׂרָאֵל* כִּי הִפְרִיעַ בִּיהוּדָה וּמָעוֹל מַעַל בַּיהוָה׃ 20 וַיָּבֹא עָלָיו תִּלְּגַת פִּלְנְאֶסֶר מֶלֶךְ אַשּׁוּר וַיָּצַר לוֹ וְלֹא חֲזָקוֹ׃ 21 כִּי־חָלַק אָחָז אֶת־בֵּית יְהוָה וְאֶת־בֵּית הַמֶּלֶךְ וְהַשָּׂרִים וַיִּתֵּן לְמֶלֶךְ אַשּׁוּר וְלֹא לְעֶזְרָה לוֹ׃ 22 וּבְעֵת הָצֵר לוֹ וַיּוֹסֶף לִמְעוֹל בַּיהוָה הוּא הַמֶּלֶךְ אָחָז׃ 23 וַיִּזְבַּח לֵאלֹהֵי דַרְמֶשֶׂק הַמַּכִּים בּוֹ וַיֹּאמֶר כִּי אֱלֹהֵי מַלְכֵי־אֲרָם הֵם מַעְזְרִים אוֹתָם לָהֶם אֲזַבֵּחַ וְיַעְזְרוּנִי וְהֵם הָיוּ־לוֹ לְהַכְשִׁילוֹ וּלְכָל־יִשְׂרָאֵל׃ 24 וַיֶּאֱסֹף אָחָז אֶת־כְּלֵי בֵית־הָאֱלֹהִים וַיְקַצֵּץ אֶת־כְּלֵי בֵית־הָאֱלֹהִים וַיִּסְגֹּר אֶת־דַּלְתוֹת בֵּית־יְהוָה וַיַּעַשׂ לוֹ מִזְבְּחוֹת בְּכָל־פִּנָּה בִּירוּשָׁלִָם׃ 25 וּבְכָל־עִיר וָעִיר לִיהוּדָה עָשָׂה בָמוֹת לְקַטֵּר לֵאלֹהִים אֲחֵרִים וַיַּכְעֵס אֶת־יְהוָה אֱלֹהֵי אֲבֹתָיו׃ 26 וְיֶתֶר דְּבָרָיו וְכָל־דְּרָכָיו הָרִאשֹׁנִים וְהָאַחֲרוֹנִים הִנָּם כְּתוּבִים עַל־סֵפֶר מַלְכֵי־יְהוּדָה וְיִשְׂרָאֵל׃ 27 וַיִּשְׁכַּב אָחָז עִם־אֲבֹתָיו וַיִּקְבְּרֻהוּ בָעִיר בִּירוּשָׁלִַם כִּי

v. 19. סבירין ומטען "יְהוּדָה"

---

[a] Some mss. and ancient versions read "Judah."

tombs of the kings of Israel. His son Hezekiah succeeded him as king.

29

Hezekiah became king at the age of twenty-five, and he reigned twenty-nine years in Jerusalem; his mother's name was Abijah daughter of Zechariah. [2]He did what was pleasing to the LORD, just as his father David had done.

[3]He, in the first month of the first year of his reign, opened the doors of the House of the LORD and repaired them. [4]He summoned the priests and the Levites and assembled them in the east square. [5]He said to them, "Listen to me, Levites! Sanctify yourselves and sanctify the House of the LORD God of your fathers, and take the abhorrent things out of the holy place. [6]For our fathers trespassed and did what displeased the LORD our God; they forsook Him and turned their faces away from the dwelling-place of the LORD, turning their backs on it. [7]They also shut the doors of the porch and put out the lights; they did not offer incense and did not make burnt offerings in the holy place to the God of Israel. [8]The wrath of the LORD was upon Judah and Jerusalem; He made them an object of horror, amazement, and hissing[a] as you see with your own eyes. [9]Our fathers died by the sword, and our sons and daughters and wives are in captivity on account of this. [10]Now I wish to make a covenant with the LORD God of Israel, so that His rage may be withdrawn from us. [11]Now, my sons, do not be slack, for the LORD chose you to attend upon Him, to serve Him, to be His ministers and to make offerings to Him."

[12]So the Levites set to—Mahath son of Amasai and Joel son of Azariah of the sons of Kohath; and of the sons of Merari, Kish son of Abdi and Azariah son of Jehallelel; and of the

לֹא הֱבִיאֻהוּ לְקִבְרֵי מַלְכֵי יִשְׂרָאֵל וַיִּמְלֹךְ יְחִזְקִיָּהוּ בְנוֹ תַּחְתָּיו: פ

כט

יְחִזְקִיָּהוּ מָלַךְ בֶּן־עֶשְׂרִים וְחָמֵשׁ שָׁנָה וְעֶשְׂרִים וָתֵשַׁע שָׁנָה מָלַךְ בִּירוּשָׁלָ͏ִם וְשֵׁם אִמּוֹ אֲבִיָּה בַּת־זְכַרְיָהוּ: 2 וַיַּעַשׂ הַיָּשָׁר בְּעֵינֵי יְהוָה כְּכֹל אֲשֶׁר־עָשָׂה דָּוִיד אָבִיו: 3 הוּא בַשָּׁנָה הָרִאשׁוֹנָה לְמָלְכוֹ בַּחֹדֶשׁ הָרִאשׁוֹן פָּתַח אֶת־דַּלְתוֹת בֵּית־יְהוָה וַיְחַזְּקֵם: 4 וַיָּבֵא אֶת־הַכֹּהֲנִים וְאֶת־הַלְוִיִּם וַיַּאַסְפֵם לִרְחוֹב הַמִּזְרָח: 5 וַיֹּאמֶר לָהֶם שְׁמָעוּנִי הַלְוִיִּם עַתָּה הִתְקַדְּשׁוּ וְקַדְּשׁוּ אֶת־בֵּית יְהוָה אֱלֹהֵי אֲבֹתֵיכֶם וְהוֹצִיאוּ אֶת־הַנִּדָּה מִן־הַקֹּדֶשׁ: 6 כִּי־מָעֲלוּ אֲבֹתֵינוּ וְעָשׂוּ הָרַע בְּעֵינֵי יְהוָה־אֱלֹהֵינוּ וַיַּעַזְבֻהוּ וַיַּסֵּבּוּ פְנֵיהֶם מִמִּשְׁכַּן יְהוָה וַיִּתְּנוּ־עֹרֶף: 7 גַּם סָגְרוּ דַלְתוֹת הָאוּלָם וַיְכַבּוּ אֶת־הַנֵּרוֹת וּקְטֹרֶת לֹא הִקְטִירוּ וְעֹלָה לֹא־הֶעֱלוּ בַקֹּדֶשׁ לֵאלֹהֵי יִשְׂרָאֵל: 8 וַיְהִי קֶצֶף יְהוָה עַל־יְהוּדָה וִירוּשָׁלָ͏ִם וַיִּתְּנֵם לְזַעֲוָה לְשַׁמָּה וְלִשְׁרֵקָה כַּאֲשֶׁר אַתֶּם רֹאִים בְּעֵינֵיכֶם: 9 וְהִנֵּה נָפְלוּ אֲבוֹתֵינוּ בֶּחָרֶב וּבָנֵינוּ וּבְנוֹתֵינוּ וְנָשֵׁינוּ בַּשְּׁבִי עַל־זֹאת: 10 עַתָּה עִם־לְבָבִי לִכְרוֹת בְּרִית לַיהוָה אֱלֹהֵי יִשְׂרָאֵל וְיָשֹׁב מִמֶּנּוּ חֲרוֹן אַפּוֹ: 11 בָּנַי עַתָּה אַל־תִּשָּׁלוּ כִּי־בָכֶם בָּחַר יְהוָה לַעֲמֹד לְפָנָיו לְשָׁרְתוֹ וְלִהְיוֹת לוֹ מְשָׁרְתִים וּמַקְטִרִים: ס 12 וַיָּקֻמוּ הַלְוִיִּם מַחַת בֶּן־עֲמָשַׂי וְיוֹאֵל בֶּן־עֲזַרְיָהוּ מִן־בְּנֵי הַקְּהָתִי וּמִן־בְּנֵי מְרָרִי קִישׁ בֶּן־עַבְדִּי וַעֲזַרְיָהוּ בֶּן־יְהַלֶּלְאֵל וּמִן־

Gershonites, Joah son of Zimmah and Eden son of Joah; [13]and of the sons of Elizaphan, Shimri and Jeiel; and of the sons of Asaph, Zechariah and Mattaniah;[14]and of the sons of Heman, Jehiel and Shimei; and of the sons of Jeduthun, Shemaiah and Uzziel—[15]and, gathering their brothers, they sanctified themselves and came, by a command of the king concerning the LORD's ordinances, to purify the House of the LORD. [16]The priests went into the House of the LORD to purify it, and brought all the unclean things they found in the Temple of the LORD out into the court of the House of the LORD; [there] the Levites received them, to take them outside to Wadi Kidron. [17]They began the sanctification on the first day of the first month; on the eighth day of the month they reached the porch of the LORD. They sanctified the House of the LORD for eight days, and on the sixteenth day of the first month they finished. [18]Then they went into the palace of King Hezekiah and said, "We have purified the whole House of the LORD and the altar of burnt offering and all its utensils, and the table of the bread of display and all its utensils; [19]and all the utensils that King Ahaz had befouled during his reign, when he trespassed, we have made ready and sanctified. They are standing in front of the altar of the LORD."

[20]King Hezekiah rose early, gathered the officers of the city, and went up to the House of the LORD. [21]They brought seven bulls and seven rams and seven lambs and seven he-goats as a sin offering for the kingdom and for the Sanctuary and for Judah. He ordered the Aaronite priests to offer them on the altar of the LORD. [22]The cattle were slaughtered, and the priests received the blood and dashed it against the altar; the rams were slaughtered and the blood was dashed against the altar; the lambs were slaughtered and the blood was dashed

הַגֵּרְשֻׁנִּי יוֹאָח בֶּן־זִמָּה וְעֵדֶן בֶּן־יוֹאָח:
13 וּמִן־בְּנֵי אֱלִיצָפָן שִׁמְרִי ויעואל וִיעִיאֵל
וּמִן־בְּנֵי אָסָף זְכַרְיָהוּ וּמַתַּנְיָהוּ: ס
14 וּמִן־בְּנֵי הֵימָן יְחוּאֵל וְשִׁמְעִי ס
וּמִן־בְּנֵי יְדוּתוּן שְׁמַעְיָה וְעֻזִּיאֵל:
15 וַיַּאַסְפוּ אֶת־אֲחֵיהֶם וַיִּתְקַדְּשׁוּ וַיָּבֹאוּ
כְמִצְוַת־הַמֶּלֶךְ בְּדִבְרֵי יְהוָה לְטַהֵר בֵּית
יְהוָה: 16 וַיָּבֹאוּ הַכֹּהֲנִים לִפְנִימָה בֵית־
יְהוָה לְטַהֵר וַיּוֹצִיאוּ אֵת כָּל־הַטֻּמְאָה
אֲשֶׁר מָצְאוּ בְּהֵיכַל יְהוָה לַחֲצַר בֵּית
יְהוָה וַיְקַבְּלוּ הַלְוִיִּם לְהוֹצִיא לְנַחַל־
קִדְרוֹן חוּצָה: 17 וַיָּחֵלּוּ בְּאֶחָד לַחֹדֶשׁ
הָרִאשׁוֹן לְקַדֵּשׁ וּבְיוֹם שְׁמוֹנָה לַחֹדֶשׁ בָּאוּ
לְאוּלָם יְהוָה וַיְקַדְּשׁוּ אֶת־בֵּית־יְהוָה
לְיָמִים שְׁמוֹנָה וּבְיוֹם שִׁשָּׁה עָשָׂר לַחֹדֶשׁ
הָרִאשׁוֹן כִּלּוּ: ס 18 וַיָּבוֹאוּ פְנִימָה אֶל־
חִזְקִיָּהוּ הַמֶּלֶךְ וַיֹּאמְרוּ טִהַרְנוּ אֶת־כָּל־
בֵּית יְהוָה אֶת־מִזְבַּח הָעוֹלָה וְאֶת־כָּל־
כֵּלָיו וְאֶת־שֻׁלְחַן הַמַּעֲרֶכֶת וְאֶת־כָּל־
כֵּלָיו: 19 וְאֵת כָּל־הַכֵּלִים אֲשֶׁר הִזְנִיחַ
הַמֶּלֶךְ אָחָז בְּמַלְכוּתוֹ בְּמַעֲלוֹ הֵכַנּוּ
וְהִקְדַּשְׁנוּ וְהִנָּם לִפְנֵי מִזְבַּח יְהוָה: ס
20 וַיַּשְׁכֵּם יְחִזְקִיָּהוּ הַמֶּלֶךְ וַיֶּאֱסֹף אֵת
שָׂרֵי הָעִיר וַיַּעַל בֵּית יְהוָה: 21 וַיָּבִיאוּ
פָרִים־שִׁבְעָה וְאֵילִים שִׁבְעָה וּכְבָשִׂים
שִׁבְעָה וּצְפִירֵי עִזִּים שִׁבְעָה לְחַטָּאת
עַל־הַמַּמְלָכָה וְעַל־הַמִּקְדָּשׁ וְעַל־יְהוּדָה
וַיֹּאמֶר לִבְנֵי אַהֲרֹן הַכֹּהֲנִים לְהַעֲלוֹת
עַל־מִזְבַּח יְהוָה: 22 וַיִּשְׁחֲטוּ הַבָּקָר וַיְקַבְּלוּ
הַכֹּהֲנִים אֶת־הַדָּם וַיִּזְרְקוּ הַמִּזְבֵּחָה
וַיִּשְׁחֲטוּ הָאֵלִים וַיִּזְרְקוּ הַדָּם הַמִּזְבֵּחָה
וַיִּשְׁחֲטוּ הַכְּבָשִׂים וַיִּזְרְקוּ הַדָּם הַמִּזְבֵּחָה:

against the altar. 23The he-goats for the sin offering were presented to the king and the congregation, who laid their hands upon them. 24The priests slaughtered them and performed the purgation rite with the blood against the altar, to expiate for all Israel, for the king had designated the burnt offering and the sin offering to be for all Israel. 25He stationed the Levites in the House of the LORD with cymbals and harps and lyres, as David and Gad the king's seer and Nathan the prophet had ordained, for the ordinance was by the LORD through His prophets.

26When the Levites were in place with the instruments of David, and the priests with their trumpets, 27Hezekiah gave the order to offer the burnt offering on the altar. When the burnt offering began, the song of the LORD and the trumpets began also, together with the instruments of King David of Israel. 28All the congregation prostrated themselves, the song was sung and the trumpets were blown—all this until the end of the burnt offering. 29When the offering was finished, the king and all who were there with him knelt and prostrated themselves. 30King Hezekiah and the officers ordered the Levites to praise the LORD in the words of David and Asaph the seer; so they praised rapturously, and they bowed and prostrated themselves.

31Then Hezekiah said, "Now you have consecrated yourselves to the LORD; come, bring sacrifices of well-being and thanksgiving to the House of the LORD." The congregation brought sacrifices of well-being and thanksgiving, and all who felt so moved brought burnt offerings. 32The number of burnt offerings that the congregation brought was 70 cattle, 100 rams, 200 lambs—all these for burnt offerings to the LORD. 33The sacred offerings were 600 large cattle and 3,000 small cattle. 34The priests were too few to be able to flay all the burnt offerings, so

23 וַיַּגִּ֙ישׁוּ֙ אֶת־שְׂעִירֵ֣י הַֽחַטָּ֔את לִפְנֵ֥י הַמֶּ֖לֶךְ וְהַקָּהָ֑ל וַיִּסְמְכ֥וּ יְדֵיהֶ֖ם עֲלֵיהֶֽם׃ 24 וַיִּשְׁחָטוּם֙ הַכֹּ֣הֲנִ֔ים וַֽיְחַטְּא֤וּ אֶת־דָּמָם֙ הַמִּזְבֵּ֔חָה לְכַפֵּ֖ר עַל־כָּל־יִשְׂרָאֵ֑ל כִּ֤י לְכָל־יִשְׂרָאֵל֙ אָמַ֣ר הַמֶּ֔לֶךְ הָעוֹלָ֖ה וְהַחַטָּֽאת׃ 25 וַיַּֽעֲמֵ֨ד אֶת־הַלְוִיִּ֜ם בֵּ֣ית יְהֹוָ֗ה בִּמְצִלְתַּ֙יִם֙ בִּנְבָלִ֣ים וּבְכִנֹּר֔וֹת בְּמִצְוַ֥ת דָּוִ֛יד וְגָ֥ד חֹזֵֽה־הַמֶּ֖לֶךְ וְנָתָ֣ן הַנָּבִ֑יא כִּ֧י בְיַד־יְהֹוָ֛ה הַמִּצְוָ֖ה בְּיַד־נְבִיאָֽיו׃ ס 26 וַיַּֽעַמְד֤וּ הַלְוִיִּם֙ בִּכְלֵ֣י דָוִ֔יד וְהַכֹּֽהֲנִ֖ים בַּחֲצֹֽצְרֽוֹת׃ ס 27 וַיֹּ֙אמֶר֙ חִזְקִיָּ֔הוּ לְהַעֲל֥וֹת הָֽעֹלָ֖ה לְהַמִּזְבֵּ֑חַ וּבְעֵ֞ת הֵחֵ֣ל הָֽעוֹלָ֗ה הֵחֵ֤ל שִׁיר־יְהֹוָה֙ וְהַֽחֲצֹ֣צְר֔וֹת וְעַ֨ל־יְדֵ֔י כְּלֵ֖י דָּוִ֥יד מֶֽלֶךְ־יִשְׂרָאֵֽל׃ 28 וְכָל־הַקָּהָל֙ מִֽשְׁתַּֽחֲוִ֔ים וְהַשִּׁ֣יר מְשׁוֹרֵ֔ר וְהַחֲצֹ֣צְר֖וֹת מַחְצְרִ֑ים הַכֹּ֕ל עַ֖ד לִכְל֥וֹת הָעֹלָֽה׃ 29 וּכְכַלּ֖וֹת לְהַֽעֲל֑וֹת כָּֽרְע֥וּ הַמֶּ֛לֶךְ וְכָל־הַנִּמְצְאִ֥ים אִתּ֖וֹ וַיִּֽשְׁתַּחֲוֽוּ׃ 30 וַ֠יֹּ֠אמֶר יְחִזְקִיָּ֨הוּ הַמֶּ֤לֶךְ וְהַשָּׂרִים֙ לַלְוִיִּ֔ם לְהַלֵּ֣ל לַֽיהֹוָ֔ה בְּדִבְרֵ֥י דָוִ֖יד וְאָסָ֣ף הַחֹזֶ֑ה וַֽיְהַלְלוּ֙ עַד־לְשִׂמְחָ֔ה וַיִּקְּד֖וּ וַיִּֽשְׁתַּחֲוֽוּ׃ פ 31 וַיַּ֙עַן֙ יְחִזְקִיָּ֔הוּ וַיֹּ֕אמֶר עַתָּ֛ה מִלֵּאתֶ֥ם יֶדְכֶ֖ם לַֽיהֹוָ֑ה גֹּ֙שׁוּ֙ וְהָבִ֣יאוּ זְבָחִ֣ים וְתוֹד֔וֹת לְבֵ֖ית יְהֹוָ֑ה וַיָּבִ֤יאוּ הַקָּהָל֙ זְבָחִ֣ים וְתוֹד֔וֹת וְכָל־נְדִ֥יב לֵ֖ב עֹלֽוֹת׃ 32 וַיְהִ֞י מִסְפַּ֣ר הָֽעֹלָ֗ה אֲשֶׁ֙ר הֵבִ֣יאוּ הַקָּהָל֮ בָּקָ֣ר שִׁבְעִים֒ אֵילִ֣ים מֵאָ֔ה כְּבָשִׂ֖ים מָאתָ֑יִם לְעֹלָ֥ה לַֽיהֹוָ֖ה כָּל־אֵֽלֶּה׃ 33 וְהַ֨קֳּדָשִׁ֔ים בָּקָ֖ר שֵׁ֣שׁ מֵא֑וֹת וְצֹ֖אן שְׁלֹ֥שֶׁת אֲלָפִֽים׃ 34 רַ֤ק הַכֹּֽהֲנִים֙ הָי֣וּ לִמְעָ֔ט וְלֹ֣א יָֽכְל֔וּ לְהַפְשִׁ֖יט אֶת־כָּל־

their kinsmen, the Levites, reinforced them till the end of the work, and till the [rest of the] priests sanctified themselves. (The Levites were more conscientious about sanctifying themselves than the priests.) 35For beside the large number of burnt offerings, there were the fat parts of the sacrifices of well-being and the libations for the burnt offerings; so the service of the House of the LORD was properly accomplished. 36Hezekiah and all the people rejoiced over what God had enabled the people to accomplish, because it had happened so suddenly.

הָעֹלֹ֑ות וַֽיְחַזְּק֞וּם אֲחֵיהֶ֤ם הַלְוִיִּם֙ עַד־כְּלֹ֣ות הַמְּלָאכָ֔ה וְעַ֥ד יִתְקַדְּשׁ֖וּ הַכֹּהֲנִ֑ים כִּ֤י הַלְוִיִּם֙ יִשְׁרֵ֣י לֵבָ֔ב לְהִתְקַדֵּ֖שׁ מֵֽהַכֹּהֲנִֽים׃ 35 וְגַם־עֹלָ֨ה לָרֹ֜ב בְּחֶלְבֵ֣י הַשְּׁלָמִ֗ים וּבַנְּסָכִים֙ לָֽעֹלָ֔ה וַתִּכֹּ֖ון עֲבֹודַ֣ת בֵּית־יְהֹוָֽה׃ 36 וַיִּשְׂמַ֤ח יְחִזְקִיָּ֙הוּ֙ וְכָל־הָעָ֔ם עַ֛ל הַהֵכִ֥ין הָאֱלֹהִ֖ים לָעָ֑ם כִּ֥י בְּפִתְאֹ֖ם הָיָ֥ה הַדָּבָֽר׃ פ

30 Hezekiah sent word to all Israel and Judah; he also wrote letters to Ephraim and Manasseh to come to the House of the LORD in Jerusalem to keep the Passover for the LORD God of Israel. 2The king and his officers and the congregation in Jerusalem had agreed to keep the Passover in the second month, 3for at the time, they were unable to keep it,[a] for not enough priests had sanctified themselves, nor had the people assembled in Jerusalem. 4The king and the whole congregation thought it proper 5to issue a decree and proclaim throughout all Israel from Beer-sheba to Dan that they come and keep the Passover for the LORD God of Israel in Jerusalem—not often did they act in accord with what was written. 6The couriers went out with the letters from the king and his officers through all Israel and Judah, by order of the king, proclaiming, "O you Israelites! Return to the LORD God of your fathers, Abraham, Isaac, and Israel, and He will return to the remnant of you who escaped from the hand of the kings of Assyria. 7Do not be like your fathers and brothers who trespassed against the LORD God of their fathers and He turned them into a horror, as you see. 8Now do not be stiffnecked like your fathers; submit yourselves to the LORD and

ל וַיִּשְׁלַ֣ח יְחִזְקִיָּ֗הוּ עַל־כָּל־יִשְׂרָאֵל֙ וִֽיהוּדָ֔ה וְגַֽם־אִגְּרֹות֙ כָּתַב֙ עַל־אֶפְרַ֣יִם וּמְנַשֶּׁ֔ה לָבֹ֥וא לְבֵית־יְהֹוָ֖ה בִּירוּשָׁלִָ֑ם לַעֲשֹׂ֣ות פֶּ֔סַח לַיהֹוָ֖ה אֱלֹהֵ֥י יִשְׂרָאֵֽל׃ 2 וַיִּוָּעַ֨ץ הַמֶּ֧לֶךְ וְשָׂרָ֛יו וְכָל־הַקָּהָ֖ל בִּירוּשָׁלִָ֑ם לַעֲשֹׂ֥ות הַפֶּ֖סַח בַּחֹ֥דֶשׁ הַשֵּׁנִֽי׃ 3 כִּ֣י לֹ֤א יָכְלוּ֙ לַעֲשֹׂתֹ֣ו בָּעֵ֣ת הַהִ֔יא כִּ֧י הַכֹּהֲנִ֛ים לֹֽא־הִתְקַדְּשׁ֥וּ לְמַדַּ֖י וְהָעָ֑ם לֹא־נֶאֶסְפ֖וּ לִירוּשָׁלִָֽם׃ 4 וַיִּישַׁ֥ר הַדָּבָ֖ר בְּעֵינֵ֣י הַמֶּ֑לֶךְ וּבְעֵינֵ֖י כָּל־הַקָּהָֽל׃ 5 וַיַּֽעֲמִ֣ידוּ דָבָ֗ר לְהַעֲבִ֨יר קֹ֜ול בְּכָל־יִשְׂרָאֵ֗ל מִבְּאֵֽר־שֶׁ֙בַע֙ וְעַד־דָּ֔ן לָבֹ֞וא לַעֲשֹׂ֥ות פֶּ֛סַח לַיהֹוָ֥ה אֱלֹהֵֽי־יִשְׂרָאֵ֖ל בִּירוּשָׁלִָ֑ם כִּ֣י לֹ֥א לָרֹ֛ב עָשׂ֖וּ כַּכָּתֽוּב׃ 6 וַיֵּלְכ֣וּ הָרָצִ֡ים בָּֽאִגְּרֹ֣ות מִיַּ֣ד הַמֶּלֶךְ֩ וְשָׂרָ֨יו בְּכָל־יִשְׂרָאֵ֜ל וִֽיהוּדָ֗ה וּכְמִצְוַ֤ת הַמֶּ֙לֶךְ֙ לֵאמֹ֔ר בְּנֵ֣י יִשְׂרָאֵ֗ל שׁ֚וּבוּ אֶל־יְהֹוָ֗ה אֱלֹהֵ֤י אַבְרָהָם֙ יִצְחָ֣ק וְיִשְׂרָאֵ֔ל וְיָשֹׁב֙ אֶל־הַפְּלֵיטָ֔ה הַנִּשְׁאֶ֥רֶת לָכֶ֖ם מִכַּ֑ף מַלְכֵ֥י אַשּֽׁוּר׃ 7 וְאַל־תִּֽהְי֗וּ כַּאֲבֹֽותֵיכֶם֙ וְכַ֣אֲחֵיכֶ֔ם אֲשֶׁ֣ר מָעֲל֔וּ בַּיהֹוָ֖ה אֱלֹהֵ֣י אֲבֹותֵיהֶ֑ם וַיִּתְּנֵ֣ם לְשַׁמָּ֔ה כַּאֲשֶׁ֖ר אַתֶּ֥ם רֹאִֽים׃ 8 עַתָּ֕ה אַל־תַּקְשׁ֥וּ עָרְפְּכֶ֖ם כַּאֲבֹֽותֵיכֶ֑ם תְּנוּ־יָד֙ לַֽיהֹוָ֔ה וּבֹ֙אוּ֙ לְמִקְדָּשֹׁ֔ו

---

a I.e., on its proper date; cf. Num. 9.1–14.

come to His sanctuary, which He consecrated forever, and serve the LORD your God so that His anger may turn back from you. 9If you return to the LORD, your brothers and children will be regarded with compassion by their captors, and will return to this land; for the LORD your God is gracious and merciful; He will not turn His face from you if you return to Him."

10As the couriers passed from town to town in the land of Ephraim and Manasseh till they reached Zebulun, they were laughed at and mocked. 11Some of the people of Asher and Manasseh and Zebulun, however, were contrite, and came to Jerusalem. 12The hand of God was on Judah, too, making them of a single mind to carry out the command of the king and officers concerning the ordinance of the LORD. 13A great crowd assembled at Jerusalem to keep the Feast of Unleavened Bread in the second month, a very great congregation. 14They set to and removed the altars that were in Jerusalem, and they removed all the incense stands and threw them into Wadi Kidron. 15They slaughtered the paschal sacrifice on the fourteenth of the second month. The priests and Levites were ashamed, and they sanctified themselves and brought burnt offerings to the House of the LORD. 16They took their stations, as was their rule according to the Teaching of Moses, man of God. The priests dashed the blood [which they received] from the Levites. 17Since many in the congregation had not sanctified themselves, the Levites were in charge of slaughtering the paschal sacrifice for everyone who was not clean, so as to consecrate them to the LORD. 18For most of the people—many from Ephraim and Manasseh, Issachar and Zebulun—had not purified themselves, yet they ate the paschal sacrifice in violation of what was written. Hezekiah prayed for them, saying, "The good LORD will provide atonement for 19everyone who set

אֲשֶׁ֣ר הִקְדִּ֣ישׁ לְעוֹלָ֔ם וְעִבְד֖וּ אֶת־יְהוָ֣ה אֱלֹֽהֵיכֶ֑ם וְיָשֹׁ֥ב מִכֶּ֖ם חֲר֥וֹן אַפּֽוֹ׃ 9 כִּ֣י בְשׁוּבְכֶ֞ם עַל־יְהוָ֗ה אֲחֵיכֶ֤ם וּבְנֵיכֶם֙ לְרַחֲמִ֔ים לִפְנֵ֖י שֽׁוֹבֵיהֶ֑ם וְלָשׁ֖וּב לָאָ֣רֶץ הַזֹּ֑את כִּֽי־חַנּ֤וּן וְרַחוּם֙ יְהוָ֣ה אֱלֹֽהֵיכֶ֔ם וְלֹא־יָסִ֥יר פָּנִ֖ים מִכֶּ֑ם אִם־תָּשׁ֖וּבוּ אֵלָֽיו׃ פ

10 וַיִּהְי֨וּ הָרָצִ֜ים עֹבְרִ֨ים מֵעִ֧יר ׀ לָעִ֛יר בְּאֶֽרֶץ־אֶפְרַ֥יִם וּמְנַשֶּׁ֖ה וְעַד־זְבֻל֑וּן וַיִּֽהְי֤וּ מַשְׂחִיקִים֙ עֲלֵיהֶ֔ם וּמַלְעִגִ֖ים בָּֽם׃ 11 אַ֣ךְ אֲנָשִׁ֞ים מֵאָשֵׁ֧ר וּמְנַשֶּׁ֛ה וּמִזְּבֻל֖וּן נִכְנְע֑וּ וַיָּבֹ֖אוּ לִירוּשָׁלָֽ͏ִם׃ 12 גַּ֣ם בִּיהוּדָ֗ה הָֽיְתָה֙ יַ֣ד הָאֱלֹהִ֔ים לָתֵ֥ת לָהֶ֖ם לֵ֣ב אֶחָ֑ד לַעֲשׂ֞וֹת מִצְוַ֥ת הַמֶּ֛לֶךְ וְהַשָּׂרִ֖ים בִּדְבַ֥ר יְהוָֽה׃ 13 וַיֵּאָסְפ֣וּ יְרוּשָׁלַ֗͏ִם עַם־רָ֔ב לַעֲשׂ֣וֹת אֶת־ חַ֧ג הַמַּצּ֛וֹת בַּחֹ֥דֶשׁ הַשֵּׁנִ֖י קָהָ֣ל לָרֹ֥ב מְאֹֽד׃ 14 וַיָּקֻ֗מוּ וַיָּסִ֙ירוּ֙ אֶת־הַֽמִּזְבְּח֔וֹת אֲשֶׁ֖ר בִּירוּשָׁלָ֑͏ִם וְאֵ֤ת כָּל־הַֽמְקַטְּרוֹת֙ הֵסִ֔ירוּ וַיַּשְׁלִ֖יכוּ לְנַ֥חַל קִדְרֽוֹן׃ 15 וַיִּשְׁחֲט֣וּ הַפֶּ֔סַח בְּאַרְבָּעָ֥ה עָשָׂ֖ר לַחֹ֣דֶשׁ הַשֵּׁנִ֑י וְהַכֹּהֲנִ֣ים וְהַלְוִיִּ֗ם נִכְלְמוּ֙ וַיִּֽתְקַדְּשׁ֔וּ וַיָּבִ֥יאוּ עֹל֖וֹת בֵּ֥ית יְהוָֽה׃ 16 וַיַּֽעַמְד֤וּ עַל־עָמְדָם֙ כְּמִשְׁפָּטָ֔ם כְּתוֹרַ֖ת מֹשֶׁ֣ה אִישׁ־הָאֱלֹהִ֑ים הַכֹּֽהֲנִים֙ זֹרְקִ֣ים אֶת־הַדָּ֔ם מִיַּ֖ד הַלְוִיִּֽם׃ 17 כִּי־רַבַּ֥ת בַּקָּהָ֖ל אֲשֶׁ֣ר לֹא־הִתְקַדָּ֑שׁוּ וְהַלְוִיִּ֞ם עַל־שְׁחִיטַ֣ת הַפְּסָחִ֗ים לְכֹל֙ לֹ֣א טָה֔וֹר לְהַקְדִּ֖ישׁ לַיהוָֽה׃ 18 כִּ֤י מַרְבִּ֣ית הָעָ֗ם רַבַּ֞ת מֵֽאֶפְרַ֤יִם וּמְנַשֶּׁה֙ יִשָּׂשכָ֣ר וּזְבֻל֔וּן לֹ֣א הִטֶּהָ֔רוּ כִּֽי־אָכְל֥וּ אֶת־הַפֶּ֖סַח בְּלֹ֣א כַכָּת֑וּב כִּי֩ הִתְפַּלֵּ֨ל יְחִזְקִיָּ֤הוּ עֲלֵיהֶם֙ לֵאמֹ֔ר יְהוָ֥ה הַטּ֖וֹב יְכַפֵּ֥ר בְּעַֽד׃ 19 כָּל־ לְבָב֣וֹ הֵכִ֔ין לִדְר֛וֹשׁ הָאֱלֹהִ֖ים ׀ יְהוָ֗ה

his mind on worshiping God, the LORD God of his fathers, even if he is not purified for the sanctuary." [20]The LORD heard Hezekiah and healed the people.

[21]The Israelites who were in Jerusalem kept the Feast of Unleavened Bread seven days, with great rejoicing, the Levites and the priests praising the LORD daily with powerful instruments for the LORD. [22]Hezekiah persuaded all the Levites who performed skillfully for the LORD to spend the seven days of the festival making offerings of well-being, and confessing to the LORD God of their fathers. [23]All the congregation resolved to keep seven more days, so they kept seven more days of rejoicing. [24]King Hezekiah of Judah contributed to the congregation 1,000 bulls and 7,000 sheep. And the officers contributed to the congregation 1,000 bulls and 10,000 sheep. And the priests sanctified themselves in large numbers. [25]All the congregation of Judah and the priests and the Levites and all the congregation that came from Israel, and the resident aliens who came from the land of Israel and who lived in Judah, rejoiced. [26]There was great rejoicing in Jerusalem, for since the time of King Solomon son of David of Israel nothing like it had happened in Jerusalem. [27]The Levite priests rose and blessed the people, and their voice was heard, and their prayer went up to His holy abode, to heaven.

31 When all this was finished, all Israel who were present went out into the towns of Judah and smashed the pillars, cut down the sacred posts, demolished the shrines and altars throughout Judah and Benjamin, and throughout Ephraim and Manasseh, to the very last one. Then all the Israelites returned to their towns, each to his possession.

אֱלֹהֵי אֲבוֹתָיו וְלֹא כְּטָהֳרַת הַקֹּדֶשׁ: ס
20 וַיִּשְׁמַע יְהוָה אֶל־יְחִזְקִיָּהוּ וַיִּרְפָּא אֶת־
הָעָם: ס
21 וַיַּעֲשׂוּ בְנֵי־יִשְׂרָאֵל הַנִּמְצְאִים בִּירוּשָׁלַ͏ִם
אֶת־חַג הַמַּצּוֹת שִׁבְעַת יָמִים בְּשִׂמְחָה
גְדוֹלָה וּמְהַלְלִים לַיהוָה יוֹם ׀ בְּיוֹם
הַלְוִיִּם וְהַכֹּהֲנִים בִּכְלֵי־עֹז לַיהוָה: ס
22 וַיְדַבֵּר יְחִזְקִיָּהוּ עַל־לֵב כָּל־הַלְוִיִּם
הַמַּשְׂכִּילִים שֵׂכֶל־טוֹב לַיהוָה וַיֹּאכְלוּ
אֶת־הַמּוֹעֵד שִׁבְעַת הַיָּמִים מְזַבְּחִים
זִבְחֵי שְׁלָמִים וּמִתְוַדִּים לַיהוָה אֱלֹהֵי
אֲבוֹתֵיהֶם: ס 23 וַיִּוָּעֲצוּ כָּל־הַקָּהָל
לַעֲשׂוֹת שִׁבְעַת יָמִים אֲחֵרִים וַיַּעֲשׂוּ
שִׁבְעַת־יָמִים שִׂמְחָה: 24 כִּי חִזְקִיָּהוּ מֶלֶךְ־
יְהוּדָה הֵרִים לַקָּהָל אֶלֶף פָּרִים וְשִׁבְעַת
אֲלָפִים צֹאן וְהַשָּׂרִים הֵרִימוּ לַקָּהָל
פָּרִים אֶלֶף וְצֹאן עֲשֶׂרֶת אֲלָפִים וַיִּתְקַדְּשׁוּ
כֹהֲנִים לָרֹב: 25 וַיִּשְׂמְחוּ ׀ כָּל־קְהַל יְהוּדָה
וְהַכֹּהֲנִים וְהַלְוִיִּם וְכָל־הַקָּהָל הַבָּאִים
מִיִּשְׂרָאֵל וְהַגֵּרִים הַבָּאִים מֵאֶרֶץ יִשְׂרָאֵל
וְהַיּוֹשְׁבִים בִּיהוּדָה: 26 וַתְּהִי שִׂמְחָה־
גְדוֹלָה בִּירוּשָׁלָ͏ִם כִּי מִימֵי שְׁלֹמֹה בֶן־דָּוִיד
מֶלֶךְ יִשְׂרָאֵל לֹא כָזֹאת בִּירוּשָׁלָ͏ִם: ס
27 וַיָּקֻמוּ הַכֹּהֲנִים הַלְוִיִּם וַיְבָרְכוּ אֶת־
הָעָם וַיִּשָּׁמַע בְּקוֹלָם וַתָּבוֹא תְפִלָּתָם
לִמְעוֹן קָדְשׁוֹ לַשָּׁמָיִם: פ

לא וּכְכַלּוֹת כָּל־זֹאת יָצְאוּ כָל־
יִשְׂרָאֵל הַנִּמְצְאִים לְעָרֵי יְהוּדָה וַיְשַׁבְּרוּ
הַמַּצֵּבוֹת וַיְגַדְּעוּ הָאֲשֵׁרִים וַיְנַתְּצוּ אֶת־
הַבָּמוֹת וְאֶת־הַמִּזְבְּחֹת מִכָּל־יְהוּדָה
וּבִנְיָמִן וּבְאֶפְרַיִם וּמְנַשֶּׁה עַד־לְכַלֵּה
וַיָּשׁוּבוּ כָּל־בְּנֵי יִשְׂרָאֵל אִישׁ לַאֲחֻזָּתוֹ
לְעָרֵיהֶם: ס

2Hezekiah reconstituted the divisions of the priests and Levites, each man of the priests and Levites according to his office, for the burnt offerings, the offerings of well-being, to minister, and to sing hymns and praises in the gates of the courts of the LORD; 3also the king's portion, from his property, for the burnt offerings—the morning and evening burnt offering, and the burnt offerings for sabbaths, and new moons, and festivals, as prescribed in the Teaching of the LORD.

4He ordered the people, the inhabitants of Jerusalem, to deliver the portions of the priests and the Levites, so that they might devote themselves to the Teaching of the LORD. 5When the word spread, the Israelites brought large quantities of grain, wine, oil, honey, and all kinds of agricultural produce, and tithes of all, in large amounts. 6The men of Israel and Judah living in the towns of Judah—they too brought tithes of cattle and sheep and tithes of sacred things consecrated to the LORD their God, piling them in heaps. 7In the third month the heaps began to accumulate, and were finished in the seventh month. 8When Hezekiah and the officers came and saw the heaps, they blessed the LORD and his people Israel. 9Hezekiah asked the priests and Levites about the heaps. 10The chief priest Azariah, of the house of Zadok, replied to him, saying, "Ever since the gifts began to be brought to the House of the LORD, people have been eating to satiety and leaving over in great amounts, for the LORD has blessed His people; this huge amount is left over!" 11Hezekiah then gave orders to prepare store-chambers in the House of the LORD; and they were prepared. 12They brought in the gifts and the tithes and the sacred things faithfully. Their supervisor was Conaniah the Levite, and Shimei his brother was second in rank. 13Jehiel and Azaziah and Nahath

2 וַיַּעֲמֵ֣ד יְחִזְקִיָּ֗הוּ אֶת־מַחְלְק֣וֹת הַכֹּהֲנִ֣ים
וְהַלְוִיִּם֮ עַל־מַחְלְקוֹתָם֒ אִ֣ישׁ ׀ כְּפִ֣י עֲבֹדָת֗וֹ
לַכֹּהֲנִ֣ים וְלַלְוִיִּ֔ם לְעֹלָ֖ה וְלִשְׁלָמִ֑ים לְשָׁרֵ֨ת
וּלְהֹד֤וֹת וּלְהַלֵּל֙ בְּשַׁעֲרֵ֖י מַחֲנ֥וֹת יְהֹוָֽה׃ ס
3 וּמְנָת֩ הַמֶּ֨לֶךְ מִן־רְכוּשׁ֜וֹ לָעֹל֗וֹת לְעֹל֣וֹת
הַבֹּ֣קֶר וְהָעֶ֔רֶב וְהָ֣עֹל֔וֹת לַשַּׁבָּת֖וֹת
וְלֶחֳדָשִׁ֣ים וְלַמֹּעֲדִ֑ים כַּכָּת֖וּב בְּתוֹרַ֥ת
יְהֹוָֽה׃
4 וַיֹּ֣אמֶר לָעָ֗ם לְיוֹשְׁבֵ֣י יְרוּשָׁלַ֔͏ִם לָתֵ֕ת מְנָ֖ת
הַכֹּהֲנִ֣ים וְהַלְוִיִּ֑ם לְמַ֥עַן יֶחֶזְק֖וּ בְּתוֹרַ֥ת
יְהֹוָֽה׃ 5 וְכִפְרֹ֣ץ הַדָּבָ֗ר הִרְבּ֤וּ בְנֵֽי־יִשְׂרָאֵל֙
רֵאשִׁ֣ית דָּגָ֜ן תִּיר֣וֹשׁ וְיִצְהָ֣ר וּדְבַ֗שׁ וְכֹל֙
תְּבוּאַ֣ת שָׂדֶ֔ה וּמַעֲשַׂ֥ר הַכֹּ֖ל לָרֹ֥ב הֵבִֽיאוּ׃
6 וּבְנֵ֧י יִשְׂרָאֵ֣ל וִֽיהוּדָ֗ה הַיּֽוֹשְׁבִים֮ בְּעָרֵ֣י
יְהוּדָה֒ גַּם־הֵ֗ם מַעְשַׂ֤ר בָּקָר֙ וָצֹ֔אן וּמַעְשַׂ֣ר
קָֽדָשִׁ֗ים הַמְקֻדָּשִׁ֛ים לַיהֹוָ֥ה אֱלֹהֵיהֶ֖ם
הֵבִ֑יאוּ וַֽיִּתְּנ֖וּ עֲרֵמ֥וֹת עֲרֵמֽוֹת׃ ס
7 בַּחֹ֙דֶשׁ֙ הַשְּׁלִשִׁ֔י הֵחֵ֥לּוּ הָעֲרֵמ֖וֹת לְיִסּ֑וֹד
וּבַחֹ֥דֶשׁ הַשְּׁבִיעִ֖י כִּלּֽוּ׃ ס 8 וַיָּבֹ֙אוּ֙
יְחִזְקִיָּ֣הוּ וְהַשָּׂרִ֔ים וַֽיִּרְא֖וּ אֶת־הָעֲרֵמ֑וֹת
וַֽיְבָרְכוּ֙ אֶת־יְהֹוָ֔ה וְאֵ֖ת עַמּ֥וֹ יִשְׂרָאֵֽל׃ פ
9 וַיִּדְרֹ֣שׁ יְחִזְקִיָּ֗הוּ עַל־הַכֹּהֲנִ֛ים וְהַלְוִיִּ֖ם
עַל־הָעֲרֵמֽוֹת׃ 10 וַיֹּ֣אמֶר אֵלָ֡יו עֲזַרְיָ֣הוּ
הַכֹּהֵ֨ן הָרֹ֜אשׁ לְבֵ֣ית צָד֗וֹק וַיֹּ֙אמֶר֙ מֵהָחֵ֤ל
הַתְּרוּמָה֙ לָבִ֣יא* בֵית־יְהֹוָ֔ה אָכ֥וֹל וְשָׂב֖וֹעַ
וְהוֹתֵ֣ר עַד־לָר֑וֹב כִּ֤י יְהֹוָה֙ בֵּרַ֣ךְ אֶת־עַמּ֔וֹ
וְהַנּוֹתָ֥ר אֶת־הֶהָמ֖וֹן הַזֶּֽה׃ ס 11 וַיֹּ֣אמֶר
יְחִזְקִיָּ֗הוּ לְהָכִ֧ין לְשָׁכ֛וֹת בְּבֵ֥ית יְהֹוָ֖ה
וַיָּכִֽינוּ׃ 12 וַיָּבִ֨יאוּ אֶת־הַתְּרוּמָ֧ה וְהַמַּעֲשֵׂ֛ר
וְהַקֳּדָשִׁ֖ים בֶּאֱמוּנָ֑ה וַעֲלֵיהֶ֤ם נָגִיד֙ כֹּונַנְיָ֣הוּ
כׇּנַנְיָ֣הוּ הַלֵּוִ֔י וְשִׁמְעִ֥י אָחִ֖יהוּ מִשְׁנֶֽה׃
13 וִיחִיאֵ֡ל וַ֠עֲזַזְיָ֠הוּ וְנַ֨חַת וַעֲשָׂהאֵ֜ל

and Asahel and Jerimoth and Jozabad and Eliel and Ismachiah and Mahath and Benaiah were commissioners under Conaniah and Shimei his brother by appointment of King Hezekiah; Azariah was supervisor of the House of God. ¹⁴Kore son of Imnah the Levite, the keeper of the East Gate, was in charge of the freewill offerings to God, of the allocation of gifts to the Lᴏʀᴅ, and the most sacred things. ¹⁵Under him were Eden, Miniamin, Jeshua, Shemaiah, Amariah, and Shecaniah, in offices of trust in the priestly towns, making allocation to their brothers by divisions, to great and small alike; ¹⁶besides allocating their daily rations to those males registered by families from three years old and up, all who entered the House of the Lᴏʀᴅ according to their service and their shift by division; ¹⁷and in charge of the registry of priests by clans, and of the Levites, from twenty years old and up, by shifts, in their divisions; ¹⁸and the registry of the dependents of their whole company—wives, sons, and daughters—for, relying upon them, they sanctified themselves in holiness. ¹⁹And for the Aaronite priests, in each and every one of their towns with adjoining fields, the above-named men were to allocate portions to every male of the priests and to every registered Levite. ²⁰Hezekiah did this throughout Judah. He acted in a way that was good, upright, and faithful before the Lᴏʀᴅ his God. ²¹Every work he undertook in the service of the House of God or in the Teaching and the Commandment, to worship his God, he did with all his heart; and he prospered.

32

ᵃAfter these faithful deeds, King Sennacherib of Assyria invaded Judah and encamped against its fortified towns with the aim of taking them over. ²When Hezekiah saw that

---

a Cf. 2 Kings 18–20; Isa. 36–39.

וִירֵמוֹת וְיוֹזָבָד וֶאֱלִיאֵל וְיִסְמַכְיָהוּ וּמַחַת
וּבְנָיָהוּ פְּקִידִים מִיַּד כּונניהו כֵּנַנְיָהוּ
וְשִׁמְעִי אָחִיו בְּמִפְקַד יְחִזְקִיָּהוּ הַמֶּלֶךְ
וַעֲזַרְיָהוּ נְגִיד בֵּית־הָאֱלֹהִים׃ 14 וְקוֹרֵא
בֶן־יִמְנָה הַלֵּוִי הַשּׁוֹעֵר לַמִּזְרָחָה עַל
נִדְבוֹת הָאֱלֹהִים לָתֵת תְּרוּמַת יְהוָה
וְקָדְשֵׁי הַקֳּדָשִׁים׃ 15 וְעַל־יָדוֹ עֵדֶן וּמִנְיָמִן
וְיֵשׁוּעַ וּשְׁמַעְיָהוּ אֲמַרְיָהוּ וּשְׁכַנְיָהוּ
בְּעָרֵי הַכֹּהֲנִים בֶּאֱמוּנָה לָתֵת לַאֲחֵיהֶם
בְּמַחְלְקוֹת כַּגָּדוֹל כַּקָּטָן׃ 16 מִלְּבַד
הִתְיַחְשָׂם לִזְכָרִים מִבֶּן שָׁלוֹשׁ שָׁנִים
וּלְמַעְלָה לְכָל־הַבָּא לְבֵית־יְהוָה לִדְבַר־
יוֹם בְּיוֹמוֹ לַעֲבוֹדָתָם בְּמִשְׁמְרוֹתָם
כְּמַחְלְקוֹתֵיהֶם׃ 17 וְאֵת הִתְיַחֵשׂ הַכֹּהֲנִים
לְבֵית אֲבוֹתֵיהֶם וְהַלְוִיִּם מִבֶּן עֶשְׂרִים שָׁנָה
וּלְמַעְלָה בְּמִשְׁמְרוֹתֵיהֶם בְּמַחְלְקוֹתֵיהֶם׃
18 וּלְהִתְיַחֵשׂ בְּכָל־טַפָּם נְשֵׁיהֶם וּבְנֵיהֶם
וּבְנוֹתֵיהֶם לְכָל־קָהָל כִּי בֶאֱמוּנָתָם
יִתְקַדְּשׁוּ־קֹדֶשׁ׃ 19 וְלִבְנֵי אַהֲרֹן הַכֹּהֲנִים
בִּשְׂדֵי מִגְרַשׁ עָרֵיהֶם בְּכָל־עִיר וָעִיר
אֲנָשִׁים אֲשֶׁר נִקְּבוּ בְּשֵׁמוֹת לָתֵת מָנוֹת
לְכָל־זָכָר בַּכֹּהֲנִים וּלְכָל־הִתְיַחֵשׂ בַּלְוִיִּם׃
20 וַיַּעַשׂ כָּזֹאת יְחִזְקִיָּהוּ בְּכָל־יְהוּדָה וַיַּעַשׂ
הַטּוֹב וְהַיָּשָׁר וְהָאֱמֶת לִפְנֵי יְהוָה אֱלֹהָיו׃
21 וּבְכָל־מַעֲשֶׂה אֲשֶׁר־הֵחֵל ׀ בַּעֲבוֹדַת
בֵּית־הָאֱלֹהִים וּבַתּוֹרָה וּבַמִּצְוָה לִדְרֹשׁ
לֵאלֹהָיו בְּכָל־לְבָבוֹ עָשָׂה וְהִצְלִיחַ׃ פ

לב אַחֲרֵי הַדְּבָרִים וְהָאֱמֶת הָאֵלֶּה
בָּא סַנְחֵרִיב מֶלֶךְ־אַשּׁוּר וַיָּבֹא בִיהוּדָה
וַיִּחַן עַל־הֶעָרִים הַבְּצֻרוֹת וַיֹּאמֶר לְבִקְעָם
אֵלָיו׃ 2 וַיַּרְא יְחִזְקִיָּהוּ כִּי־בָא סַנְחֵרִיב

Sennacherib had come, intent on making war against Jerusalem, ³he consulted with his officers and warriors about stopping the flow of the springs outside the city, and they supported him. ⁴A large force was assembled to stop up all the springs and the wadi that flowed through the land, for otherwise, they thought, the king of Assyria would come and find water in abundance. ⁵He acted with vigor, rebuilding the whole breached wall, raising towers on it, and building another wall outside it. He fortified the Millo of the City of David, and made a great quantity of arms and shields. ⁶He appointed battle officers over the people; then, gathering them to him in the square of the city gate, he rallied them, saying, ⁷"Be strong and of good courage; do not be frightened or dismayed by the king of Assyria or by the horde that is with him, for we have more with us than he has with him. ⁸With him is an arm of flesh, but with us is the Lord our God, to help us and to fight our battles." The people were encouraged by the speech of King Hezekiah of Judah.

⁹Afterward, King Sennacherib of Assyria sent his officers to Jerusalem—he and all his staff being at Lachish—with this message to King Hezekiah of Judah and to all the people of Judah who were in Jerusalem: ¹⁰"Thus said King Sennacherib of Assyria: On what do you trust to enable you to endure a siege in Jerusalem? ¹¹Hezekiah is seducing you to a death of hunger and thirst, saying, 'The Lord our God will save us from the king of Assyria.' ¹²But is not Hezekiah the one who removed His shrines and His altars and commanded the people of Judah and Jerusalem saying, 'Before this one altar you shall prostrate yourselves, and upon it make your burnt offerings'? ¹³Surely you know what I and my fathers have done to the peoples of the lands? Were the gods of the nations of the lands able to save their lands from me? ¹⁴Which of all the

³ וַיִּוָּעַ֗ץ עִם־שָׂרָ֤יו וְגִבֹּרָיו֙ לִסְתּוֹם֙ אֶת־מֵימֵ֣י הָעֲיָנ֔וֹת אֲשֶׁ֖ר מִח֣וּץ לָעִ֑יר וַֽיַּעְזְרֽוּהוּ׃ ⁴ וַיִּקָּבְצ֣וּ עַם־רָ֗ב וַֽיִּסְתְּמוּ֙ אֶת־כׇּל־הַמַּעְיָנ֔וֹת וְאֶת־הַנַּ֛חַל הַשּׁוֹטֵ֥ף בְּתוֹךְ־הָאָ֖רֶץ לֵאמֹ֑ר לָ֤מָּה יָב֙וֹאוּ֙ מַלְכֵ֣י אַשּׁ֔וּר וּמָצְא֖וּ מַ֥יִם רַבִּֽים׃ ⁵ וַיִּתְחַזַּ֡ק וַיִּ֩בֶן֩ אֶת־כׇּל־הַחוֹמָ֨ה הַפְּרוּצָ֜ה וַיַּ֣עַל עַל־הַמִּגְדָּל֗וֹת וְלַח֙וּצָה֙ הַחוֹמָ֣ה אַחֶ֔רֶת וַיְחַזֵּ֖ק אֶת־הַמִּלּ֣וֹא עִ֣יר דָּוִ֑יד וַיַּ֥עַשׂ שֶׁ֛לַח לָרֹ֖ב וּמָגִנִּֽים׃ ⁶ וַיִּתֵּ֛ן שָׂרֵ֥י מִלְחָמ֖וֹת עַל־הָעָ֑ם וַיִּקְבְּצֵ֣ם אֵלָ֗יו אֶל־רְחוֹב֙ שַׁ֣עַר הָעִ֔יר וַיְדַבֵּ֥ר עַל־לְבָבָ֖ם לֵאמֹֽר׃ ⁷ חִזְק֣וּ וְאִמְצ֔וּ אַל־תִּֽירְא֣וּ וְאַל־תֵּחַ֗תּוּ מִפְּנֵי֙ מֶ֣לֶךְ אַשּׁ֔וּר וּמִלִּפְנֵ֖י כׇּל־הֶהָמ֣וֹן אֲשֶׁר־עִמּ֑וֹ כִּֽי־עִמָּ֥נוּ רַ֖ב מֵעִמּֽוֹ׃ ⁸ עִמּוֹ֙ זְר֣וֹעַ בָּשָׂ֔ר וְעִמָּ֜נוּ יְהֹוָ֤ה אֱלֹהֵ֙ינוּ֙ לְעׇזְרֵ֔נוּ וּלְהִלָּחֵ֖ם מִלְחֲמֹתֵ֑נוּ וַיִּסָּמְכ֣וּ הָעָ֔ם עַל־דִּבְרֵ֖י יְחִזְקִיָּ֥הוּ מֶֽלֶךְ־יְהוּדָֽה׃ פ

⁹ אַ֣חַר זֶ֗ה שָׁ֠לַ֠ח סַנְחֵרִ֨יב מֶלֶךְ־אַשּׁ֤וּר עֲבָדָיו֙ יְרֽוּשָׁלַ֔יְמָה וְהוּא֙ עַל־לָכִ֔ישׁ וְכׇל־מֶמְשַׁלְתּ֖וֹ עִמּ֑וֹ עַל־יְחִזְקִיָּ֙הוּ֙ מֶ֣לֶךְ יְהוּדָ֔ה וְעַֽל־כׇּל־יְהוּדָ֛ה אֲשֶׁ֥ר בִּירוּשָׁלַ֖͏ִם לֵאמֹֽר׃ ¹⁰ כֹּ֣ה אָמַ֔ר סַנְחֵרִ֖יב מֶ֣לֶךְ אַשּׁ֑וּר עַל־מָ֗ה אַתֶּ֤ם בֹּֽטְחִים֙ וְיֹֽשְׁבִ֔ים בְּמָצ֖וֹר בִּירוּשָׁלָֽ͏ִם׃ ¹¹ הֲלֹ֤א יְחִזְקִיָּ֙הוּ֙ מַסִּ֣ית אֶתְכֶ֔ם לָתֵ֣ת אֶתְכֶ֗ם לָמ֛וּת בְּרָעָ֥ב וּבְצָמָ֖א לֵאמֹ֑ר יְהֹוָ֣ה אֱלֹהֵ֔ינוּ יַצִּילֵ֕נוּ מִכַּ֖ף מֶ֥לֶךְ אַשּֽׁוּר׃ ¹² הֲלֹא־ה֗וּא יְחִזְקִיָּ֙הוּ֙ הֵסִ֣יר אֶת־בָּמֹתָ֖יו וְאֶת־מִזְבְּחֹתָ֑יו וַיֹּ֤אמֶר לִֽיהוּדָה֙ וְלִיר֣וּשָׁלַ֔͏ִם לֵאמֹ֗ר לִפְנֵ֨י מִזְבֵּ֧חַ אֶחָ֛ד תִּֽשְׁתַּחֲו֖וּ וְעָלָ֥יו תַּקְטִֽירוּ׃ ¹³ הֲלֹ֣א תֵדְע֗וּ מֶ֤ה עָשִׂ֙יתִי֙ אֲנִ֣י וַאֲבוֹתַ֔י לְכֹ֖ל עַמֵּ֣י הָאֲרָצ֑וֹת הֲיָכ֣וֹל יָֽכְל֗וּ אֱלֹהֵי֙ גּוֹיֵ֣ הָאֲרָצ֔וֹת לְהַצִּ֥יל אֶת־אַרְצָ֖ם מִיָּדִֽי׃ ¹⁴ מִ֠י בְּכׇל־אֱלֹהֵ֞י הַגּוֹיִ֤ם הָאֵ֙לֶּה֙

gods of any of those nations whom my fathers destroyed was able to save his people from me, that your God should be able to save you from me? 15Now then, do not let Hezekiah delude you; do not let him seduce you in this way; do not believe him. For no god of any nation or kingdom has been able to save his people from me or from my fathers—much less your God, to save you from me!" 16His officers said still more things against the Lord God and against His servant Hezekiah. 17He also wrote letters reviling the Lord God of Israel, saying of Him, "Just as the gods of the other nations of the earth did not save their people from me, so the God of Hezekiah will not save his people from me." 18They called loudly in the language of Judah to the people of Jerusalem who were on the wall, to frighten them into panic, so as to capture the city. 19They spoke of the God of Jerusalem as though He were like the gods of the other peoples of the earth, made by human hands. 20Then King Hezekiah and the prophet Isaiah son of Amoz prayed about this, and cried out to heaven.

21The Lord sent an angel who annihilated every mighty warrior, commander, and officer in the army of the king of Assyria, and he returned in disgrace to his land. He entered the house of his god, and there some of his own offspring struck him down by the sword. 22Thus the Lord delivered Hezekiah and the inhabitants of Jerusalem from King Sennacherib of Assyria, and from everyone; He provided for them on all sides. 23Many brought tribute to the Lord to Jerusalem, and gifts to King Hezekiah of Judah; thereafter he was exalted in the eyes of all the nations.

24At that time, Hezekiah fell deathly sick. He prayed to the Lord, who responded to him and gave him a sign. 25Hezekiah made no return for what had been bestowed upon him, for he grew

אֲשֶׁר הֶחֱרִימוּ אֲבוֹתַי אֲשֶׁר יָכוֹל לְהַצִּיל
אֶת־עַמּוֹ מִיָּדִי כִּי יוּכַל אֱלֹהֵיכֶם לְהַצִּיל
אֶתְכֶם מִיָּדִי: 15 וְעַתָּה אַל־יַשִּׁיא אֶתְכֶם
חִזְקִיָּהוּ וְאַל־יַסִּית אֶתְכֶם כָּזֹאת וְאַל־
תַּאֲמִינוּ לוֹ כִּי־לֹא יוּכַל כָּל־אֱלוֹהַּ כָּל־גּוֹי
וּמַמְלָכָה לְהַצִּיל עַמּוֹ מִיָּדִי וּמִיַּד אֲבוֹתָי
אַף כִּי אֱלֹהֵיכֶם לֹא־יַצִּילוּ אֶתְכֶם מִיָּדִי:
16 וְעוֹד דִּבְּרוּ עֲבָדָיו עַל־יְהוָה הָאֱלֹהִים
וְעַל יְחִזְקִיָּהוּ עַבְדּוֹ: 17 וּסְפָרִים כָּתַב
לְחָרֵף לַיהוָה אֱלֹהֵי יִשְׂרָאֵל וְלֵאמֹר עָלָיו
לֵאמֹר כֵּאלֹהֵי גּוֹיֵ הָאֲרָצוֹת אֲשֶׁר לֹא־
הִצִּילוּ עַמָּם מִיָּדִי כֵּן לֹא־יַצִּיל אֱלֹהֵי
יְחִזְקִיָּהוּ עַמּוֹ מִיָּדִי: 18 וַיִּקְרְאוּ בְקוֹל־גָּדוֹל
יְהוּדִית עַל־עַם יְרוּשָׁלִַם אֲשֶׁר עַל־
הַחוֹמָה לְיָרְאָם וּלְבַהֲלָם לְמַעַן יִלְכְּדוּ
אֶת־הָעִיר: 19 וַיְדַבְּרוּ אֶל־אֱלֹהֵי יְרוּשָׁלִָם
כְּעַל אֱלֹהֵי עַמֵּי הָאָרֶץ מַעֲשֵׂה יְדֵי
הָאָדָם: ס 20 וַיִּתְפַּלֵּל יְחִזְקִיָּהוּ הַמֶּלֶךְ
וִישַׁעְיָהוּ בֶן־אָמוֹץ הַנָּבִיא עַל־זֹאת
וַיִּזְעֲקוּ הַשָּׁמָיִם: פ
21 וַיִּשְׁלַח יְהוָה מַלְאָךְ וַיַּכְחֵד כָּל־גִּבּוֹר
חַיִל וְנָגִיד וְשָׂר בְּמַחֲנֵה מֶלֶךְ אַשּׁוּר וַיָּשָׁב
בְּבֹשֶׁת פָּנִים לְאַרְצוֹ וַיָּבֹא בֵּית אֱלֹהָיו
וּמִיצִיאֵי וּמִיצִיאֵי מֵעָיו שָׁם הִפִּילֻהוּ
בֶחָרֶב: 22 וַיּוֹשַׁע יְהוָה אֶת־יְחִזְקִיָּהוּ וְאֵת
יֹשְׁבֵי יְרוּשָׁלִַם מִיַּד סַנְחֵרִיב מֶלֶךְ־אַשּׁוּר
וּמִיַּד־כֹּל וַיְנַהֲלֵם מִסָּבִיב: 23 וְרַבִּים
מְבִיאִים מִנְחָה לַיהוָה לִירוּשָׁלִָם
וּמִגְדָּנוֹת לִיחִזְקִיָּהוּ מֶלֶךְ יְהוּדָה וַיִּנַּשֵּׂא
לְעֵינֵי כָל־הַגּוֹיִם מֵאַחֲרֵי־כֵן: ס
24 בַּיָּמִים הָהֵם חָלָה יְחִזְקִיָּהוּ עַד־לָמוּת
וַיִּתְפַּלֵּל אֶל־יְהוָה וַיֹּאמֶר לוֹ וּמוֹפֵת נָתַן
לוֹ: 25 וְלֹא־כִגְמֻל עָלָיו הֵשִׁיב יְחִזְקִיָּהוּ כִּי
גָבַהּ לִבּוֹ וַיְהִי עָלָיו קֶצֶף וְעַל־יְהוּדָה

arrogant; so wrath was decreed for him and for Judah and Jerusalem. [26]Then Hezekiah humbled himself where he had been arrogant, he and the inhabitants of Jerusalem, and no wrath of the Lord came on them during the reign of Hezekiah. [27]Hezekiah enjoyed riches and glory in abundance; he filled treasuries with silver and gold, precious stones, spices, shields, and all lovely objects; [28]and store-cities with the produce of grain, wine, and oil, and stalls for all kinds of beasts, and flocks for sheepfolds. [29]And he acquired towns, and flocks of small and large cattle in great number, for God endowed him with very many possessions. [30]It was Hezekiah who stopped up the spring of water of Upper Gihon, leading it downward west of the City of David; Hezekiah prospered in all that he did. [31]So too in the matter of the ambassadors of the princes of Babylon, who were sent to him to inquire about the sign that was in the land, when God forsook him in order to test him, to learn all that was in his mind.

[32]The other events of Hezekiah's reign, and his faithful acts, are recorded in the visions of the prophet Isaiah son of Amoz and in the book of the kings of Judah and Israel. [33]Hezekiah slept with his fathers, and was buried on the upper part of the tombs of the sons of David. When he died, all the people of Judah and the inhabitants of Jerusalem accorded him much honor. Manasseh, his son, succeeded him.

33

[a]Manasseh was twelve years old when he became king, and he reigned fifty-five years in Jerusalem. [2]He did what was displeasing to the Lord, following the abhorrent practices of the nations that the Lord had dispossessed before the Israelites. [3]He rebuilt the shrines that his father Hezekiah had demolished; he erected altars for the Baals and made sacred posts. He bowed

a   *Cf. 2 Kings 21.*

כו : וַיִּכָּנַע יְחִזְקִיָּהוּ בְּגֹבַהּ לִבּוֹ הוּא וְיֹשְׁבֵי יְרוּשָׁלִָם וְלֹא־בָא עֲלֵיהֶם קֶצֶף יְהֹוָה בִּימֵי יְחִזְקִיָּהוּ : כז וַיְהִי לִיחִזְקִיָּהוּ עֹשֶׁר וְכָבוֹד הַרְבֵּה מְאֹד וְאֹצָרוֹת עָשָׂה־לוֹ לְכֶסֶף וּלְזָהָב וּלְאֶבֶן יְקָרָה וְלִבְשָׂמִים וּלְמָגִנִּים וּלְכֹל כְּלֵי חֶמְדָּה : כח וּמִסְכְּנוֹת לִתְבוּאַת דָּגָן וְתִירוֹשׁ וְיִצְהָר וְאֻרָוֹת לְכָל־בְּהֵמָה וּבְהֵמָה וַעֲדָרִים לָאֲוֵרוֹת : כט וְעָרִים עָשָׂה לוֹ וּמִקְנֵה־צֹאן וּבָקָר לָרֹב כִּי נָתַן־לוֹ אֱלֹהִים רְכוּשׁ רַב מְאֹד : ל וְהוּא יְחִזְקִיָּהוּ סָתַם אֶת־מוֹצָא מֵימֵי גִיחוֹן הָעֶלְיוֹן וַיַּישְּׁרֵם לְמַטָּה־מַּעְרָבָה לְעִיר דָּוִיד וַיַּצְלַח יְחִזְקִיָּהוּ בְּכָל־מַעֲשֵׂהוּ : לא וְכֵן בִּמְלִיצֵי | שָׂרֵי בָּבֶל הַמְשַׁלְּחִים עָלָיו לִדְרֹשׁ הַמּוֹפֵת אֲשֶׁר הָיָה בָאָרֶץ עֲזָבוֹ הָאֱלֹהִים לְנַסּוֹתוֹ לָדַעַת כָּל־בִּלְבָבוֹ : לב וְיֶתֶר דִּבְרֵי יְחִזְקִיָּהוּ וַחֲסָדָיו הִנָּם כְּתוּבִים בַּחֲזוֹן יְשַׁעְיָהוּ בֶן־אָמוֹץ הַנָּבִיא עַל־סֵפֶר מַלְכֵי־יְהוּדָה וְיִשְׂרָאֵל : לג וַיִּשְׁכַּב יְחִזְקִיָּהוּ עִם־אֲבֹתָיו וַיִּקְבְּרֻהוּ בְּמַעֲלֵה קִבְרֵי בְנֵי־דָוִיד וְכָבוֹד עָשׂוּ־לוֹ בְמוֹתוֹ כָּל־יְהוּדָה וְיֹשְׁבֵי יְרוּשָׁלִַם וַיִּמְלֹךְ מְנַשֶּׁה בְנוֹ תַּחְתָּיו : פ

לג

בֶּן־שְׁתֵּים עֶשְׂרֵה שָׁנָה מְנַשֶּׁה בְמָלְכוֹ וַחֲמִשִּׁים וְחָמֵשׁ שָׁנָה מָלַךְ בִּירוּשָׁלִָם : ב וַיַּעַשׂ הָרַע בְּעֵינֵי יְהֹוָה כְּתוֹעֲבוֹת הַגּוֹיִם אֲשֶׁר הוֹרִישׁ יְהֹוָה מִפְּנֵי בְּנֵי יִשְׂרָאֵל : ג וַיָּשָׁב וַיִּבֶן אֶת־הַבָּמוֹת אֲשֶׁר נִתַּץ יְחִזְקִיָּהוּ אָבִיו וַיָּקֶם מִזְבְּחוֹת לַבְּעָלִים וַיַּעַשׂ אֲשֵׁרוֹת וַיִּשְׁתַּחוּ לְכָל־

down to all the host of heaven and worshiped them, ⁴and he built altars [to them] in the House of the LORD, of which the LORD had said, "My name will be in Jerusalem forever." ⁵He built altars for all the host of heaven in the two courts of the House of the LORD. ⁶He consigned his sons to the fire in the Valley of Ben-hinnom, and he practiced soothsaying, divination, and sorcery, and consulted ghosts and familiar spirits; he did much that was displeasing to the LORD in order to vex Him. ⁷He placed a sculptured image that he made in the House of God, of which God had said to David and to his son Solomon, "In this House and in Jerusalem, which I chose out of all the tribes of Israel, I will establish My name forever. ⁸And I will never again remove the feet of Israel from the land that I assigned to their fathers, if only they observe faithfully all that I have commanded them—all the teaching and the laws and the rules given by Moses." ⁹Manasseh led Judah and the inhabitants of Jerusalem astray into evil greater than that done by the nations that the LORD had destroyed before the Israelites.

¹⁰The LORD spoke to Manasseh and his people, but they would not pay heed, ¹¹so the LORD brought against them the officers of the army of the king of Assyria, who took Manasseh captive in manacles, bound him in fetters, and led him off to Babylon. ¹²In his distress, he entreated the LORD his God and humbled himself greatly before the God of his fathers. ¹³He prayed to Him, and He granted his prayer, heard his plea, and returned him to Jerusalem to his kingdom. Then Manasseh knew that the LORD alone was God. ¹⁴Afterward he built the outer wall of the City of David west of Gihon in the wadi on the way to the Fish Gate, and it encircled Ophel; he raised it very high. He also placed army officers in all the fortified towns of Judah. ¹⁵He removed the foreign gods and

צְבָא הַשָּׁמַ֫יִם וַיַּעֲבֹ֖ד אֹתָֽם׃ 4 וּבָנָ֣ה מִזְבְּח֔וֹת בְּבֵ֖ית יְהֹוָ֑ה אֲשֶׁר֙ אָמַ֣ר יְהֹוָ֔ה בִּירוּשָׁלַ֥͏ִם יִֽהְיֶה־שְּׁמִ֖י לְעוֹלָֽם׃ 5 וַיִּ֥בֶן מִזְבְּח֖וֹת לְכׇל־צְבָ֣א הַשָּׁמָ֑יִם בִּשְׁתֵּ֖י חַצְר֥וֹת בֵּית־יְהֹוָֽה׃ 6 וְה֣וּא הֶעֱבִ֣יר אֶת־בָּנָ֣יו בָּאֵשׁ֮ בְּגֵ֣י בֶן־הִנֹּם֒ וְעוֹנֵ֤ן וְנִחֵשׁ֙ וְכִשֵּׁ֔ף וְעָ֗שָׂה א֥וֹב וְיִדְּעוֹנִ֖י הִרְבָּ֑ה לַעֲשׂ֥וֹת הָרַ֛ע בְּעֵינֵ֥י יְהֹוָ֖ה לְהַכְעִיסֽוֹ׃ 7 וַיָּ֕שֶׂם אֶת־פֶּ֥סֶל הַסֶּ֖מֶל אֲשֶׁ֣ר עָשָׂ֑ה בְּבֵ֣ית הָאֱלֹהִ֗ים אֲשֶׁ֨ר אָמַ֤ר אֱלֹהִים֙ אֶל־דָּוִ֔יד וְאֶל־שְׁלֹמֹ֣ה בְנ֔וֹ בַּבַּ֤יִת הַזֶּה֙ וּבִ֣ירוּשָׁלַ֔͏ִם אֲשֶׁ֣ר בָּחַ֗רְתִּי מִכֹּל֙ שִׁבְטֵ֣י יִשְׂרָאֵ֔ל אָשִׂ֥ים אֶת־שְׁמִ֖י לְעֵילֽוֹם׃ 8 וְלֹ֣א אוֹסִ֗יף לְהָסִיר֙ אֶת־רֶ֣גֶל יִשְׂרָאֵ֔ל מֵעַל֙ הָֽאֲדָמָ֔ה אֲשֶׁ֥ר הֶעֱמַ֖דְתִּי לַאֲבֹֽתֵיכֶ֑ם רַ֣ק ׀ אִם־יִשְׁמְר֣וּ לַעֲשׂ֗וֹת אֵ֚ת כׇּל־אֲשֶׁ֣ר צִוִּיתִ֔ים לְכׇל־הַתּוֹרָ֖ה וְהַחֻקִּ֣ים וְהַמִּשְׁפָּטִ֑ים בְּיַד־מֹשֶֽׁה׃ 9 וַיֶּ֣תַע מְנַשֶּׁ֗ה אֶת־יְהוּדָ֛ה וְיֹשְׁבֵ֥י יְרוּשָׁלַ֖͏ִם לַעֲשׂ֣וֹת רָ֑ע מִן־הַ֨גּוֹיִ֔ם אֲשֶׁר֙ הִשְׁמִ֣יד יְהֹוָ֔ה מִפְּנֵ֖י בְּנֵ֥י יִשְׂרָאֵֽל׃ פ

10 וַיְדַבֵּ֧ר יְהֹוָ֛ה אֶל־מְנַשֶּׁ֥ה וְאֶל־עַמּ֖וֹ וְלֹ֥א הִקְשִֽׁיבוּ׃ 11 וַיָּבֵ֨א יְהֹוָ֜ה עֲלֵיהֶ֗ם אֶת־שָׂרֵ֤י הַצָּבָא֙ אֲשֶׁר֙ לְמֶ֣לֶךְ אַשּׁ֔וּר וַיִּלְכְּד֥וּ אֶת־מְנַשֶּׁ֖ה בַּחֹחִ֑ים וַיַּֽאַסְרֻ֙הוּ֙ בַּֽנְחֻשְׁתַּ֔יִם וַיּוֹלִיכֻ֖הוּ בָּבֶֽלָה׃ 12 וּכְהָצֵ֣ר ל֔וֹ חִלָּ֕ה אֶת־פְּנֵ֖י יְהֹוָ֣ה אֱלֹהָ֑יו וַיִּכָּנַ֣ע מְאֹ֔ד מִלִּפְנֵ֖י אֱלֹהֵ֥י אֲבֹתָֽיו׃ 13 וַיִּתְפַּלֵּ֣ל אֵלָ֗יו וַיֵּעָ֤תֶר לוֹ֙ וַיִּשְׁמַ֣ע תְּחִנָּת֔וֹ וַיְשִׁיבֵ֥הוּ יְרוּשָׁלַ֖͏ִם לְמַלְכוּת֑וֹ וַיֵּ֣דַע מְנַשֶּׁ֔ה כִּ֥י יְהֹוָ֖ה ה֥וּא הָאֱלֹהִֽים׃ 14 וְאַחֲרֵי־כֵ֡ן בָּנָ֣ה חוֹמָ֣ה חִיצוֹנָ֣ה ׀ לְעִיר־דָּוִ֡יד מַעְרָ֩בָה֩ לְגִיח֨וֹן בַּנַּ֜חַל וְלָב֨וֹא בְשַׁ֤עַר הַדָּגִים֙ וְסָבַ֣ב לָעֹ֔פֶל וַיַּגְבִּיהֶ֖הָ מְאֹ֑ד וַיָּ֧שֶׂם שָֽׂרֵי־חַ֛יִל בְּכׇל־הֶעָרִ֥ים הַבְּצֻר֖וֹת בִּיהוּדָֽה׃ 15 וַיָּ֡סַר אֶת־אֱלֹהֵ֣י הַנֵּכָר֩ וְאֶת־הַסֶּ֨מֶל

the image from the House of the Lord, as well as all the altars that he had built on the Mount of the House of the Lord and in Jerusalem, and dumped them outside the city. [16]He rebuilt the altar of the Lord and offered on it sacrifices of well-being and thanksgiving, and commanded the people of Judah to worship the Lord God of Israel. [17]To be sure, the people continued sacrificing at the shrines, but only to the Lord their God.

[18]The other events of Manasseh's reign, and his prayer to his God, and the words of the seers who spoke to him in the name of the Lord God of Israel are found in the chronicles of the kings of Israel. [19]His prayer and how it was granted to him, the whole account of his sin and trespass, and the places in which he built shrines and installed sacred posts and images before he humbled himself are recorded in the words of Hozai.[b] [20]Manasseh slept with his fathers and was buried on his palace grounds; his son Amon succeeded him as king.

[21]Amon was twenty-two years old when he became king, and he reigned two years in Jerusalem. [22]He did what was displeasing to the Lord, as his father Manasseh had done. Amon sacrificed to all the idols that his father Manasseh had made and worshiped them. [23]He did not humble himself before the Lord, as his father Manasseh had humbled himself; instead, Amon incurred much guilt. [24]His courtiers conspired against him and killed him in his palace. [25]But the people of the land struck down all who had conspired against King Amon; and the people of the land made his son Josiah king in his stead.

34

[a]Josiah was eight years old when he became king, and he reigned thirty-one years in

---

b Or "seers."

a Cf. 2 Kings 22; 23.1–20.

מִבֵּית יְהֹוָה וְכָל־הַמִּזְבְּחוֹת אֲשֶׁר בָּנָה בְּהַר בֵּית־יְהֹוָה וּבִירוּשָׁלָ͏ִם וַיַּשְׁלֵךְ חוּצָה לָעִיר: [16]וַיִּ֨כֶן֙ וַיִּ֨בֶן֙ אֶת־מִזְבַּ֣ח יְהֹוָ֔ה וַיִּזְבַּ֣ח עָלָ֗יו זִבְחֵ֤י שְׁלָמִים֙ וְתוֹדָ֔ה וַיֹּ֙אמֶר֙ לִֽיהוּדָ֔ה לַעֲבֹ֕וד אֶת־יְהֹוָ֖ה אֱלֹהֵ֣י יִשְׂרָאֵֽל: [17]אֲבָ֗ל ע֥וֹד הָעָ֛ם זֹבְחִ֖ים בַּבָּמ֑וֹת רַ֖ק לַֽיהֹוָ֥ה אֱלֹהֵיהֶֽם:

[18]וְיֶ֨תֶר דִּבְרֵ֤י מְנַשֶּׁה֙ וּתְפִלָּת֣וֹ אֶל־אֱלֹהָ֔יו וְדִבְרֵי֙ הַֽחֹזִ֔ים הַֽמְדַבְּרִ֣ים אֵלָ֔יו בְּשֵׁ֥ם יְהֹוָ֖ה אֱלֹהֵ֣י יִשְׂרָאֵ֑ל הִנָּ֕ם עַל־דִּבְרֵ֖י מַלְכֵ֥י יִשְׂרָאֵֽל: [19]וּתְפִלָּת֣וֹ וְהֵעָֽתֶר־ל֣וֹ וְכָל־חַטָּאת֣וֹ וּמַ֠עְל֠וֹ וְהַמְּקֹמ֞וֹת אֲשֶׁר֩ בָּנָ֨ה בָהֶ֜ם בָּמ֗וֹת וְהֶעֱמִיד֙ הָאֲשֵׁרִ֣ים וְהַפְּסִלִ֔ים לִפְנֵ֖י הִכָּֽנְע֑וֹ הִנָּ֣ם כְּתוּבִ֔ים עַ֖ל דִּבְרֵ֥י חוֹזָֽי: [20]וַיִּשְׁכַּ֤ב מְנַשֶּׁה֙ עִם־אֲבֹתָ֔יו וַֽיִּקְבְּרֻ֖הוּ בֵית֑וֹ וַיִּמְלֹ֛ךְ אָמ֥וֹן בְּנ֖וֹ תַּחְתָּֽיו: פ

[21]בֶּן־עֶשְׂרִ֨ים וּשְׁתַּ֤יִם שָׁנָה֙ אָמ֣וֹן בְּמָלְכ֔וֹ וּשְׁתַּ֣יִם שָׁנִ֔ים מָלַ֖ךְ בִּירֽוּשָׁלָ͏ִם: [22]וַיַּ֨עַשׂ הָרַ֜ע בְּעֵינֵ֤י יְהֹוָה֙ כַּאֲשֶׁ֣ר עָשָׂ֣ה מְנַשֶּׁ֣ה אָבִ֑יו וּֽלְכָל־הַפְּסִילִ֞ים אֲשֶׁ֣ר עָשָׂה֙ מְנַשֶּׁ֣ה אָבִ֗יו זִבַּ֧ח אָמ֛וֹן וַיַּֽעַבְדֵֽם: [23]וְלֹ֤א נִכְנַע֙ מִלִּפְנֵ֣י יְהֹוָ֔ה כְּהִכָּנַ֖ע מְנַשֶּׁ֣ה אָבִ֑יו כִּ֛י ה֥וּא אָמ֖וֹן הִרְבָּ֥ה אַשְׁמָֽה: [24]וַיִּקְשְׁר֤וּ עָלָיו֙ עֲבָדָ֔יו וַיְמִית֖וּהוּ בְּבֵיתֽוֹ: [25]וַיַּכּוּ֩ עַם־הָאָ֨רֶץ אֵ֣ת כָּל־הַקֹּֽשְׁרִ֖ים עַל־הַמֶּ֣לֶךְ אָמ֑וֹן וַיַּמְלִ֧יכוּ עַם־הָאָ֛רֶץ אֶת־יֹֽאשִׁיָּ֥הוּ בְנ֖וֹ תַּחְתָּֽיו: פ

לד בֶּן־שְׁמוֹנֶ֤ה שָׁנִים֙ יֹֽאשִׁיָּ֣הוּ בְמָלְכ֔וֹ וּשְׁלֹשִׁ֤ים וְאַחַת֙ שָׁנָ֔ה מָלַ֖ךְ בִּירוּשָׁלָ͏ִֽם:

Jerusalem. [2]He did what was pleasing to the LORD, following the ways of his father David without deviating to the right or to the left. [3]In the eighth year of his reign, while he was still young, he began to seek the God of his father David, and in the twelfth year he began to purge Judah and Jerusalem of the shrines, the sacred posts, the idols, and the molten images. [4]At his bidding, they demolished the altars of the Baals, and he had the incense stands above them cut down; he smashed the sacred posts, the idols, and the images, ground them into dust, and strewed it onto the graves of those who had sacrificed to them. [5]He burned the bones of priests on their altars and purged Judah and Jerusalem. [6]In the towns of Manasseh and Ephraim and Simeon, as far as Naphtali, [lying] in ruins on every side, [7]he demolished the altars and the sacred posts and smashed the idols and ground them into dust; and he hewed down all the incense stands throughout the land of Israel. Then he returned to Jerusalem.

[8]In the eighteenth year of his reign, after purging the land and the House, he commissioned Shaphan son of Azaliah, Maaseiah the governor of the city, and Joah son of Joahaz the recorder to repair the House of the LORD his God. [9]They came to the high priest Hilkiah and delivered to him the silver brought to the House of God, which the Levites, the guards of the threshold, had collected from Manasseh and Ephraim and from all the remnant of Israel and from all Judah and Benjamin and [b]-the inhabitants of Jerusalem.-[b] [10]They delivered it into the custody of the overseers who were in charge at the House of the LORD, and the overseers who worked in the House of the LORD spent it on examining and repairing the House. [11]They paid it out to the artisans and the masons to buy quarried stone and wood for the couplings and for making roof-beams for the buildings that

2 וַיַּ֙עַשׂ֙ הַיָּשָׁ֣ר בְּעֵינֵ֣י יְהוָ֔ה וַיֵּ֕לֶךְ בְּדַרְכֵ֖י דָּוִ֣יד אָבִ֑יו וְלֹא־סָ֖ר יָמִ֥ין וּשְׂמֹֽאול׃* 3 וּבִשְׁמוֹנֶ֨ה שָׁנִ֜ים לְמָלְכ֗וֹ וְהוּא֙ עוֹדֶ֣נּוּ נַ֔עַר הֵחֵ֕ל לִדְר֕וֹשׁ לֵאלֹהֵ֖י דָּוִ֣יד אָבִ֑יו וּבִשְׁתֵּ֣ים עֶשְׂרֵ֣ה שָׁנָ֗ה הֵחֵל֙ לְטַהֵ֣ר אֶת־יְהוּדָ֣ה וִירֽוּשָׁלַ֔͏ִם מִן־הַבָּמוֹת֙ וְהָ֣אֲשֵׁרִ֔ים וְהַפְּסִלִ֖ים וְהַמַּסֵּכֽוֹת׃ 4 וַיְנַתְּצ֣וּ לְפָנָ֗יו אֵ֚ת מִזְבְּח֣וֹת הַבְּעָלִ֔ים וְהַֽחַמָּנִ֥ים אֲשֶׁר־לְמַ֖עְלָה מֵעֲלֵיהֶ֖ם גִּדֵּ֑עַ וְֽהָאֲשֵׁרִ֞ים וְהַפְּסִלִ֣ים וְהַמַּסֵּכ֗וֹת שִׁבַּ֤ר וְהֵדַק֙ וַיִּזְרֹ֔ק עַל־פְּנֵי֙ הַקְּבָרִ֔ים הַזֹּבְחִ֖ים לָהֶֽם׃ 5 וְעַצְמוֹת֙ כֹּ֣הֲנִ֔ים שָׂרַ֖ף עַל־מִזְבְּחוֹתָ֑ם מִזְבְּחוֹתָ֑ם וַיְטַהֵ֥ר אֶת־יְהוּדָ֖ה וְאֶת־יְרוּשָׁלָֽ͏ִם׃ 6 וּבְעָרֵ֨י מְנַשֶּׁ֧ה וְאֶפְרַ֛יִם וְשִׁמְע֖וֹן וְעַד־נַפְתָּלִ֑י בהר בְּחַרְבֹתֵיהֶ֖ם סָבִֽיב׃ 7 וַיְנַתֵּ֣ץ אֶת־הַֽמִּזְבְּח֗וֹת וְאֶת־הָאֲשֵׁרִ֤ים וְהַפְּסִלִים֙ כִּתַּ֣ת לְהֵדַ֔ק וְכָל־הַֽחַמָּנִ֥ים גִּדַּ֖ע בְּכָל־אֶ֣רֶץ יִשְׂרָאֵ֑ל וַיָּ֖שָׁב לִירוּשָׁלָֽ͏ִם׃ ס 8 וּבִשְׁנַ֨ת שְׁמוֹנֶ֤ה עֶשְׂרֵה֙ לְמָלְכ֔וֹ לְטַהֵ֥ר הָאָ֖רֶץ וְהַבָּ֑יִת שָׁלַ֡ח אֶת־שָׁפָ֣ן בֶּן־אֲצַלְיָ֡הוּ וְאֶת־מַעֲשֵׂיָ֣הוּ שַׂר־הָעִ֗יר וְ֠אֵת יוֹאָ֨ח בֶּן־יֽוֹאָחָ֤ז הַמַּזְכִּיר֙ לְחַזֵּ֕ק אֶת־בֵּ֖ית יְהוָ֥ה אֱלֹהָֽיו׃ 9 וַיָּבֹ֜אוּ אֶל־חִלְקִיָּ֣הוּ ׀ הַכֹּהֵ֣ן הַגָּד֗וֹל וַֽיִּתְּנוּ֙ אֶת־הַכֶּ֨סֶף֙ הַמּוּבָ֣א בֵית־אֱלֹהִ֔ים אֲשֶׁ֣ר אָסְפֽוּ־הַלְוִיִּם֩ שֹׁמְרֵ֨י הַסַּ֜ף מִיַּ֣ד מְנַשֶּׁ֣ה וְאֶפְרַ֗יִם וּמִכֹּל֙ שְׁאֵרִ֣ית יִשְׂרָאֵ֔ל וּמִכָּל־יְהוּדָ֥ה וּבִנְיָמִ֖ן וישבי וַיָּשֻׁ֖בוּ יְרֽוּשָׁלָֽ͏ִם׃ 10 וַֽיִּתְּנ֗וּ עַל־יַד֙ עֹשֵׂ֣ה הַמְּלָאכָ֔ה הַמֻּפְקָדִ֖ים בְּבֵ֣ית יְהוָ֑ה וַיִּתְּנ֣וּ אֹת֗וֹ עוֹשֵׂ֤י הַמְּלָאכָה֙ אֲשֶׁ֣ר עֹשִׂ֣ים בְּבֵ֣ית יְהוָ֔ה לִבְדּ֖וֹק וּלְחַזֵּ֥ק הַבָּֽיִת׃ 11 וַֽיִּתְּנ֣וּ לֶֽחָרָשִׁים֮ וְלַבֹּנִים֒ לִקְנוֹת֙ אַבְנֵ֣י מַחְצֵ֔ב וְעֵצִ֖ים לַֽמְחַבְּר֑וֹת וּלְקָרוֹת֙ אֶת־הַבָּ֣תִּ֔ים אֲשֶׁ֥ר הִשְׁחִ֖יתוּ מַלְכֵ֥י יְהוּדָֽה׃ 12 וְהָאֲנָשִׁים֩ עֹשִׂ֨ים

---

b-b *With kethib and ancient versions; qere, "they returned to Jerusalem."*

the kings of Judah had allowed to fall into ruin. 12The men did the work honestly; over them were appointed the Levites Jahath and Obadiah, of the sons of Merari, and Zechariah and Meshullam, of the sons of Kohath, to supervise; while other Levites, all the master musicians, 13were over the porters, supervising all who worked at each and every task; some of the Levites were scribes and officials and gatekeepers.

14As they took out the silver that had been brought to the House of the LORD, the priest Hilkiah found a scroll of the LORD's Teaching given by Moses. 15Hilkiah spoke up and said to the scribe Shaphan, "I have found a scroll of the Teaching in the House of the LORD"; and Hilkiah gave the scroll to Shaphan. 16Shaphan brought the scroll to the king and also reported to the king, "All that was entrusted to your servants is being done; 17they have melted down the silver that was found in the House of the LORD and delivered it to those who were in charge, to the overseers." 18The scribe Shaphan also told the king, "The priest Hilkiah has given me a scroll"; and Shaphan read from it to the king. 19When the king heard the words of the Teaching, he tore his clothes. 20The king gave orders to Hilkiah, and Ahikam son of Shaphan, and Abdon son of Micah, and the scribe Shaphan, and Asaiah the king's minister, saying, 21"Go, inquire of the LORD on my behalf and on behalf of those who remain in Israel and Judah concerning the words of the scroll that has been found, for great indeed must be the wrath of the LORD that has been poured down upon us because our fathers did not obey the word of the LORD and do all that is written in this scroll."

22Hilkiah and those whom the king [had ordered] went to the prophetess Huldah, wife of Shallum son of Tokhath son of Hasrah, keeper of the wardrobe, who was living in Jerusalem

בֶּאֱמוּנָה בַּמְּלָאכָה וַעֲלֵיהֶם ׀ מֻפְקָדִים יַחַת וְעֹבַדְיָהוּ הַלְוִיִּם מִן־בְּנֵי מְרָרִי וּזְכַרְיָה וּמְשֻׁלָּם מִן־בְּנֵי הַקְּהָתִים לְנַצֵּחַ וְהַלְוִיִּם כָּל־מֵבִין בִּכְלֵי־שִׁיר: 13 וְעַל הַסַּבָּלִים וּמְנַצְּחִים לְכֹל עֹשֵׂה מְלָאכָה לַעֲבוֹדָה וַעֲבוֹדָה וּמֵהַלְוִיִּם סוֹפְרִים וְשֹׁטְרִים וְשׁוֹעֲרִים: 14 וּבְהוֹצִיאָם אֶת־הַכֶּסֶף הַמּוּבָא בֵּית יְהוָה מָצָא חִלְקִיָּהוּ הַכֹּהֵן אֶת־סֵפֶר תּוֹרַת־יְהוָה בְּיַד־מֹשֶׁה: 15 וַיַּעַן חִלְקִיָּהוּ וַיֹּאמֶר אֶל־שָׁפָן הַסּוֹפֵר סֵפֶר הַתּוֹרָה מָצָאתִי בְּבֵית יְהוָה וַיִּתֵּן חִלְקִיָּהוּ אֶת־הַסֵּפֶר אֶל־שָׁפָן: 16 וַיָּבֵא שָׁפָן אֶת־הַסֵּפֶר אֶל־הַמֶּלֶךְ וַיָּשֶׁב עוֹד אֶת־הַמֶּלֶךְ דָּבָר לֵאמֹר כֹּל אֲשֶׁר־נִתַּן בְּיַד־עֲבָדֶיךָ הֵם עֹשִׂים: 17 וַיַּתִּיכוּ אֶת־הַכֶּסֶף הַנִּמְצָא בְּבֵית־יְהוָה וַיִּתְּנוּהוּ עַל־יַד הַמֻּפְקָדִים וְעַל־יַד עֹשֵׂי הַמְּלָאכָה: 18 וַיַּגֵּד שָׁפָן הַסּוֹפֵר לַמֶּלֶךְ לֵאמֹר סֵפֶר נָתַן לִי חִלְקִיָּהוּ הַכֹּהֵן וַיִּקְרָא־בוֹ שָׁפָן לִפְנֵי הַמֶּלֶךְ: 19 וַיְהִי כִּשְׁמֹעַ הַמֶּלֶךְ אֵת דִּבְרֵי הַתּוֹרָה וַיִּקְרַע אֶת־בְּגָדָיו: 20 וַיְצַו הַמֶּלֶךְ אֶת־חִלְקִיָּהוּ וְאֶת־אֲחִיקָם בֶּן־שָׁפָן וְאֶת־עַבְדּוֹן בֶּן־מִיכָה וְאֵת ׀ שָׁפָן הַסּוֹפֵר וְאֵת עֲשָׂיָה עֶבֶד־הַמֶּלֶךְ לֵאמֹר: 21 לְכוּ דִרְשׁוּ אֶת־יְהוָה בַּעֲדִי וּבְעַד הַנִּשְׁאָר בְּיִשְׂרָאֵל וּבִיהוּדָה עַל־דִּבְרֵי הַסֵּפֶר אֲשֶׁר נִמְצָא כִּי־גְדוֹלָה חֲמַת־יְהוָה אֲשֶׁר נִתְּכָה בָנוּ עַל אֲשֶׁר לֹא־שָׁמְרוּ אֲבוֹתֵינוּ אֶת־דְּבַר יְהוָה לַעֲשׂוֹת כְּכָל־הַכָּתוּב עַל־הַסֵּפֶר הַזֶּה: פ 22 וַיֵּלֶךְ חִלְקִיָּהוּ וַאֲשֶׁר הַמֶּלֶךְ אֶל־חֻלְדָּה הַנְּבִיאָה אֵשֶׁת ׀ שַׁלֻּם בֶּן־תּוֹקְהַת בֶּן־חַסְרָה שׁוֹמֵר הַבְּגָדִים וְהִיא יוֹשֶׁבֶת בִּירוּשָׁלַםִ בַּמִּשְׁנֶה וַיְדַבְּרוּ אֵלֶיהָ

in the Mishneh,[c] and spoke to her accordingly. [23]She responded to them: "Thus said the Lord God of Israel: Say to the man who sent you to Me, [24]'Thus said the Lord: I am going to bring disaster upon this place and its inhabitants—all the curses that are written in the scroll that was read to the king of Judah—[25]because they forsook Me and made offerings to other gods in order to vex Me with all the works of their hands; My wrath shall be poured out against this place and not be quenched.' [26]But say this to the king of Judah who sent you to inquire of the Lord: 'Thus said the Lord God of Israel: As for the words which you have heard, [27]since your heart was softened and you humbled yourself before God when you heard His words concerning this place and its inhabitants, and you humbled yourself before Me and tore your clothes and wept before Me, I for My part have listened, declares the Lord. [28]Assuredly, I will gather you to your fathers, and you will be laid in your grave in peace; your eyes shall see nothing of the disaster that I will bring upon this place and its inhabitants.'" They reported this back to the king.

[29]Then the king sent word and assembled all the elders of Judah and Jerusalem. [30]The king went up to the House of the Lord with all the men of Judah and the inhabitants of Jerusalem and the priests and the Levites—all the people, young and old—and he read to them the entire text of the covenant scroll that was found in the House of the Lord. [31]The king stood in his place and solemnized the covenant before the Lord: to follow the Lord and observe His commandments, His injunctions, and His laws with all his heart and soul, to fulfill all the terms of the covenant written in this scroll. [32]He obligated all the men of Jerusalem and Benjamin who were present; and the inhabitants of Jerusalem acted in accord with the Covenant of God, God of their fathers. [33]Josiah removed all the abom-

---

c   *A quarter in Jerusalem; cf. Zeph. 1.10.*

inations from the whole territory of the Israelites and obliged all who were in Israel to worship the LORD their God. Throughout his reign they did not deviate from following the LORD God of their fathers.

35 [a]Josiah kept the Passover for the LORD in Jerusalem; the passover sacrifice was slaughtered on the fourteenth day of the first month. [2]He reinstated the priests in their shifts and rallied them to the service of the House of the LORD. [3]He said to the Levites, consecrated to the LORD, who taught all Israel, "Put the Holy Ark in the House that Solomon son of David, king of Israel, built; as you no longer carry it on your shoulders, see now to the service of the LORD your God and His people Israel, [4]and dispose yourselves by clans according to your divisions, as prescribed in the writing of King David of Israel and in the document of his son Solomon, [5]and attend in the Sanctuary, by clan divisions, on your kinsmen, the people—by clan divisions of the Levites. [6]Having sanctified yourselves, slaughter the passover sacrifice and prepare it for your kinsmen, according to the word of God given by Moses." [7]Josiah donated to the people small cattle—lambs and goats, all for passover sacrifices for all present—to the sum of 30,000, and large cattle, 3,000—these from the property of the king. [8]His officers gave a freewill offering to the people, to the priests, and to the Levites. Hilkiah and Zechariah and Jehiel, the chiefs of the House of God, donated to the priests for passover sacrifices 2,600 [small cattle] and 300 large cattle. [9]Conaniah, Shemaiah, and Nethanel, his brothers, and Hashabiah and Jeiel and Jozabad, officers of the Levites, donated 5,000 [small cattle] and 500 large cattle to the Levites for passover sacrifices.

---

a Cf. 2 Kings 23.21–30.

יִשְׂרָאֵל וַיַּעֲבֵ֨ד אֵ֜ת כָּל־הַנִּמְצָ֣א בְּיִשְׂרָאֵ֗ל לַעֲבֹ֖וד אֶת־יְהֹוָ֣ה אֱלֹהֵיהֶ֑ם כָּל־יָמָ֕יו לֹ֣א סָ֔רוּ מֵאַחֲרֵ֕י יְהֹוָ֖ה אֱלֹהֵ֥י אֲבוֹתֵיהֶֽם׃ פ

לה וַיַּ֨עַשׂ יֹאשִׁיָּ֧הוּ בִירוּשָׁלַ֛͏ִם פֶּ֖סַח לַֽיהֹוָ֑ה וַיִּשְׁחֲט֣וּ הַפֶּ֔סַח בְּאַרְבָּעָ֥ה עָשָׂ֖ר לַחֹ֥דֶשׁ הָרִאשֽׁוֹן׃ [2]וַיַּעֲמֵ֥ד הַכֹּהֲנִ֖ים עַל־מִשְׁמְרוֹתָ֑ם וַֽיְחַזְּקֵ֔ם לַעֲבוֹדַ֖ת בֵּ֥ית יְהֹוָֽה׃ [3]וַיֹּ֣אמֶר לַ֠לְוִיִּ֠ם הַמְּבִינִ֨ים לְכָל־יִשְׂרָאֵ֜ל הַקְּדוֹשִׁ֣ים לַֽיהֹוָ֗ה תְּנ֣וּ אֶת־אֲרֽוֹן־הַקֹּ֨דֶשׁ֙ בַּ֠בַּ֠יִת אֲשֶׁ֨ר בָּנָ֜ה שְׁלֹמֹ֤ה בֶן־דָּוִיד֙ מֶ֣לֶךְ יִשְׂרָאֵ֔ל אֵין־לָכֶ֥ם מַשָּׂ֖א בַּכָּתֵ֑ף עַתָּ֗ה עִבְדוּ֙ אֶת־יְהֹוָ֣ה אֱלֹֽהֵיכֶ֔ם וְאֵ֖ת עַמּ֥וֹ יִשְׂרָאֵֽל׃ [4]והכונו וְהָכִ֨ינוּ לְבֵית־אֲבוֹתֵיכֶ֜ם כְּמַחְלְקוֹתֵיכֶ֗ם בִּכְתָ֗ב דָּוִיד֙ מֶ֣לֶךְ יִשְׂרָאֵ֔ל וּבְמִכְתַּ֖ב שְׁלֹמֹ֥ה בְנֽוֹ׃ [5]וְעִמְד֣וּ בַקֹּ֗דֶשׁ לִפְלֻגּוֹת֙ בֵּ֣ית הָֽאָב֔וֹת לַאֲחֵיכֶ֖ם בְּנֵ֣י הָעָ֑ם וַחֲלֻקַּ֥ת בֵּֽית־אָ֖ב לַלְוִיִּֽם׃ [6]וְשַׁחֲט֖וּ הַפָּ֑סַח וְהִתְקַדְּשׁוּ֙ וְהָכִ֣ינוּ לַאֲחֵיכֶ֔ם לַעֲשׂ֖וֹת כִּדְבַר־יְהֹוָ֖ה בְּיַד־מֹשֶֽׁה׃ פ [7]וַיָּ֣רֶם יֹֽאשִׁיָּ֣הוּ לִבְנֵ֣י הָעָ֡ם צֹאן֩ כְּבָשִׂ֨ים וּבְנֵֽי־עִזִּ֜ים הַכֹּ֣ל לַפְּסָחִ֗ים לְכָל־הַנִּמְצָא֙ לְמִסְפַּ֤ר שְׁלֹשִׁ֣ים אֶ֔לֶף וּבָקָ֖ר שְׁלֹ֣שֶׁת אֲלָפִ֑ים אֵ֖לֶּה מֵרְכ֥וּשׁ הַמֶּֽלֶךְ׃ ס [8]וְשָׂרָ֞יו לִנְדָבָ֣ה לָעָ֡ם לַכֹּהֲנִ֣ים וְלַלְוִיִּם֮ הֵרִימוּ֒ חִלְקִיָּ֤ה וּזְכַרְיָ֨הוּ֙ וִֽיחִיאֵ֔ל נְגִידֵ֖י בֵּ֣ית הָאֱלֹהִ֑ים לַכֹּהֲנִ֞ים נָתְנ֣וּ לַפְּסָחִ֗ים אַלְפַּ֙יִם֙ וְשֵׁ֣שׁ מֵא֔וֹת וּבָקָ֖ר שְׁלֹ֥שׁ מֵאֽוֹת׃ [9]וכונניהו [וְכָ֠נַנְיָ֠הוּ] וּשְׁמַֽעְיָ֨הוּ וּנְתַנְאֵ֜ל אֶחָ֗יו וַחֲשַׁבְיָ֧הוּ וִיעִיאֵ֛ל וְיוֹזָבָ֖ד שָׂרֵ֣י הַלְוִיִּ֑ם הֵרִ֤ימוּ לַלְוִיִּם֙ לַפְּסָחִ֔ים חֲמֵ֣שֶׁת אֲלָפִ֔ים וּבָקָ֖ר חֲמֵ֥שׁ מֵאֽוֹת׃

10The service was arranged well: the priests stood at their posts and the Levites in their divisions, by the king's command. 11They slaughtered the passover sacrifice and the priests [received its blood] from them and dashed it, while the Levites flayed the animals. 12They removed the parts to be burnt, distributing them to divisions of the people by clans, and making the sacrifices to the Lord, as prescribed in the scroll of Moses; they did the same for the cattle. 13They roasted the passover sacrifice in fire, as prescribed, while the sacred offerings they cooked in pots, cauldrons, and pans, and conveyed them with dispatch to all the people. 14Afterward they provided for themselves and the priests, for the Aaronite priests were busy offering the burnt offerings and the fatty parts until nightfall, so the Levites provided both for themselves and for the Aaronite priests. 15The Asaphite singers were at their stations, by command of David and Asaph and Heman and Jeduthun, the seer of the king; and the gatekeepers were at each and every gate. They did not have to leave their tasks, because their Levite brothers provided for them. 16The entire service of the Lord was arranged well that day, to keep the Passover and to make the burnt offerings on the altar of the Lord, according to the command of King Josiah. 17All the Israelites present kept the Passover at that time, and the Feast of Unleavened Bread for seven days. 18Since the time of the prophet Samuel, no Passover like that one had ever been kept in Israel; none of the kings of Israel had kept a Passover like the one kept by Josiah and the priests and the Levites and all Judah and Israel there present and the inhabitants of Jerusalem. 19That Passover was kept in the eighteenth year of the reign of Josiah.

20After all this furbishing of the Temple by Josiah, King Necho of Egypt came up to fight at Carchemish on the Euphrates, and Josiah

10 וַתִּכּוֹן הָעֲבוֹדָה וַיַּעַמְדוּ הַכֹּהֲנִים עַל־עָמְדָם וְהַלְוִיִּם עַל־מַחְלְקוֹתָם כְּמִצְוַת הַמֶּלֶךְ: 11 וַיִּשְׁחֲטוּ הַפָּסַח וַיִּזְרְקוּ הַכֹּהֲנִים מִיָּדָם וְהַלְוִיִּם מַפְשִׁיטִים: 12 וַיָּסִירוּ הָעֹלָה לְתִתָּם לְמִפְלַגּוֹת לְבֵית־אָבוֹת לִבְנֵי הָעָם לְהַקְרִיב לַיהוָה כַּכָּתוּב בְּסֵפֶר מֹשֶׁה וְכֵן לַבָּקָר: 13 וַיְבַשְּׁלוּ הַפֶּסַח בָּאֵשׁ כַּמִּשְׁפָּט וְהַקֳּדָשִׁים בִּשְּׁלוּ בַּסִּירוֹת וּבַדְּוָדִים וּבַצֵּלָחוֹת וַיָּרִיצוּ לְכָל־בְּנֵי הָעָם: 14 וְאַחַר הֵכִינוּ לָהֶם וְלַכֹּהֲנִים כִּי הַכֹּהֲנִים בְּנֵי אַהֲרֹן בְּהַעֲלוֹת הָעוֹלָה וְהַחֲלָבִים עַד־לָיְלָה וְהַלְוִיִּם הֵכִינוּ לָהֶם וְלַכֹּהֲנִים בְּנֵי אַהֲרֹן: 15 וְהַמְשֹׁרְרִים בְּנֵי־אָסָף עַל־מַעֲמָדָם כְּמִצְוַת דָּוִיד וְאָסָף וְהֵימָן וִידֻתוּן חוֹזֵה הַמֶּלֶךְ וְהַשֹּׁעֲרִים לְשַׁעַר וָשָׁעַר אֵין לָהֶם לָסוּר מֵעַל עֲבֹדָתָם כִּי־אֲחֵיהֶם הַלְוִיִּם הֵכִינוּ לָהֶם: 16 וַתִּכּוֹן כָּל־עֲבוֹדַת יְהוָה בַּיּוֹם הַהוּא לַעֲשׂוֹת הַפֶּסַח וְהַעֲלוֹת עֹלוֹת עַל מִזְבַּח יְהוָה כְּמִצְוַת הַמֶּלֶךְ יֹאשִׁיָּהוּ: 17 וַיַּעֲשׂוּ בְנֵי־יִשְׂרָאֵל הַנִּמְצָאִים אֶת־הַפֶּסַח בָּעֵת הַהִיא וְאֶת־חַג הַמַּצּוֹת שִׁבְעַת יָמִים: 18 וְלֹא־נַעֲשָׂה פֶסַח כָּמֹהוּ בְּיִשְׂרָאֵל מִימֵי שְׁמוּאֵל הַנָּבִיא וְכָל־מַלְכֵי יִשְׂרָאֵל ׀ לֹא־עָשׂוּ כַּפֶּסַח אֲשֶׁר־עָשָׂה יֹאשִׁיָּהוּ וְהַכֹּהֲנִים וְהַלְוִיִּם וְכָל־יְהוּדָה וְיִשְׂרָאֵל הַנִּמְצָא וְיוֹשְׁבֵי יְרוּשָׁלָ͏ִם: ס 19 בִּשְׁמוֹנֶה עֶשְׂרֵה שָׁנָה לְמַלְכוּת יֹאשִׁיָּהוּ נַעֲשָׂה הַפֶּסַח הַזֶּה: 20 אַחֲרֵי כָל־זֹאת אֲשֶׁר הֵכִין יֹאשִׁיָּהוּ אֶת־הַבַּיִת עָלָה נְכוֹ מֶלֶךְ־מִצְרַיִם לְהִלָּחֵם בְּכַרְכְּמִישׁ עַל־פְּרָת וַיֵּצֵא לִקְרָאתוֹ

went out against him. ²¹[Necho] sent messengers to him, saying, "What have I to do with you, king of Judah? I do not march against you this day but against the kingdom that wars with me, and it is God's will that I hurry. Refrain, then, from interfering with God who is with me, that He not destroy you." ²²But Josiah would not let him alone; instead, *b*-he donned [his armor]-*b* to fight him, heedless of Necho's words from the mouth of God; and he came to fight in the plain of Megiddo. ²³Archers shot King Josiah, and the king said to his servants, "Get me away from here, for I am badly wounded." ²⁴His servants carried him out of his chariot and put him in the wagon of his second-in-command, and conveyed him to Jerusalem. There he died, and was buried in the grave of his fathers, and all Judah and Jerusalem went into mourning over Josiah. ²⁵Jeremiah composed laments for Josiah which all the singers, male and female, recited in their laments for Josiah, as is done to this day; they became customary in Israel and were incorporated into the laments. ²⁶The other events of Josiah's reign and his faithful deeds, in accord with the Teaching of the LORD, ²⁷and his acts, early and late, are recorded in the book of the kings of Israel and Judah.

36

^aThe people of the land took Jehoahaz son of Josiah and made him king instead of his father in Jerusalem. ²Jehoahaz was twenty-three years old when he became king and he reigned three months in Jerusalem. ³The king of Egypt deposed him in Jerusalem and laid a fine on the land of 100 silver talents and one gold talent. ⁴The king of Egypt made his brother Eliakim king over Judah and Jerusalem, and changed his name to Jehoiakim; Necho took his brother Joahaz and brought him to Egypt.

יֹאשִׁיָּהוּ: 21 וַיִּשְׁלַ֣ח אֵלָיו֮ מַלְאָכִ֣ים ׀ לֵאמֹר֒ מַה־לִּ֣י וָלָ֗ךְ מֶ֚לֶךְ יְהוּדָ֔ה לֹא־עָלֶ֛יךָ אַתָּ֥ה הַיּ֖וֹם כִּ֚י אֶל־בֵּ֣ית מִלְחַמְתִּ֔י וֵאלֹהִ֖ים אָמַ֣ר לְבַהֲלֵ֑נִי חֲדַל־לְךָ֛ מֵאֱלֹהִ֥ים אֲשֶׁר־עִמִּ֖י וְאַל־יַשְׁחִיתֶֽךָ: 22 וְלֹא־הֵסֵ֨ב יֹאשִׁיָּ֜הוּ פָּנָ֣יו מִמֶּ֗נּוּ כִּ֤י לְהִלָּ֣חֶם־בּוֹ֙ הִתְחַפֵּ֔שׂ וְלֹ֣א שָׁמַ֗ע אֶל־דִּבְרֵ֥י נְכ֖וֹ מִפִּ֣י אֱלֹהִ֑ים וַיָּבֹ֕א לְהִלָּחֵ֖ם בְּבִקְעַ֥ת מְגִדּֽוֹ: 23 וַיֹּרוּ֙ הַיֹּרִ֔ים לַמֶּ֖לֶךְ יֹאשִׁיָּ֑הוּ וַיֹּ֨אמֶר הַמֶּ֜לֶךְ לַעֲבָדָ֗יו הַעֲבִיר֙וּנִי֙ כִּ֥י הׇחֳלֵ֖יתִי מְאֹֽד: 24 וַיַּֽעֲבִירֻ֨הוּ עֲבָדָ֜יו מִן־הַמֶּרְכָּבָ֗ה וַיַּרְכִּיבֻ֙הוּ֙ עַ֣ל רֶ֤כֶב הַמִּשְׁנֶה֙ אֲשֶׁר־ל֔וֹ וַיּוֹלִיכֻ֖הוּ יְרֽוּשָׁלַ֑͏ִם וַיָּ֗מׇת וַיִּקָּבֵר֙ בְּקִבְר֣וֹת אֲבֹתָ֔יו וְכׇל־יְהוּדָ֣ה וִיר֣וּשָׁלַ֔͏ִם מִֽתְאַבְּלִ֖ים עַל־יֹאשִׁיָּֽהוּ: פ 25 וַיְקוֹנֵ֣ן יִרְמְיָ֘הוּ֮ עַל־יֹאשִׁיָּהוּ֒ וַיֹּאמְר֣וּ כׇל־הַשָּׁרִ֣ים ׀ וְֽהַשָּׁר֣וֹת בְּקִינֽוֹתֵיהֶם֮ עַל־יֹאשִׁיָּהוּ֒ עַד־הַיּ֔וֹם וַיִּתְּנ֥וּם לְחֹ֖ק עַל־יִשְׂרָאֵ֑ל וְהִנָּ֥ם כְּתוּבִ֖ים עַל־הַקִּינֽוֹת: 26 וְיֶ֛תֶר דִּבְרֵ֥י יֹאשִׁיָּ֖הוּ וַחֲסָדָ֑יו כַּכָּת֖וּב בְּתוֹרַ֥ת יְהֹוָֽה: 27 וּדְבָרָ֖יו הָרִֽאשֹׁנִ֣ים וְהָאַחֲרֹנִ֑ים הִנָּ֣ם כְּתוּבִ֗ים עַל־סֵ֛פֶר מַלְכֵֽי־יִשְׂרָאֵ֖ל וִיהוּדָֽה:

לו
וַיִּקְח֣וּ עַם־הָאָ֗רֶץ אֶת־יְהֽוֹאָחָ֣ז בֶּן־יֹֽאשִׁיָּ֔הוּ וַיַּמְלִיכֻ֥הוּ תַֽחַת־אָבִ֖יו בִּירֽוּשָׁלָֽ͏ִם: 2 בֶּן־שָׁל֧וֹשׁ וְעֶשְׂרִ֛ים שָׁנָ֖ה יוֹאָחָ֣ז בְּמׇלְכ֑וֹ וּשְׁלֹשָׁ֣ה חֳדָשִׁ֔ים מָלַ֖ךְ בִּירֽוּשָׁלָֽ͏ִם: 3 וַיְסִירֵ֥הוּ מֶֽלֶךְ־מִצְרַ֖יִם בִּירֽוּשָׁלָ֑͏ִם וַיַּֽעֲנֹשׁ֙ אֶת־הָאָ֔רֶץ מֵאָ֥ה כִכַּר־כֶּ֖סֶף וְכִכַּ֥ר זָהָֽב: 4 וַיַּמְלֵ֨ךְ מֶֽלֶךְ־מִצְרַ֤יִם אֶת־אֶלְיָקִים֙ אָחִ֔יו עַל־יְהוּדָ֖ה וִירֽוּשָׁלַ֑͏ִם וַיַּסֵּ֥ב אֶת־שְׁמ֖וֹ יְהֽוֹיָקִ֑ים וְאֶת־יוֹאָחָ֣ז אָחִ֔יו לָקַ֥ח נְכ֖וֹ וַיְבִיאֵ֥הוּ מִצְרָֽיְמָה: פ

---

b-b With Targum.

   a With vv. 1–13, cf. 2 Kings 23.28–37; 24.1–20.

⁵Jehoiakim was twenty-five years old when he became king, and he reigned eleven years in Jerusalem; he did what was displeasing to the LORD his God. ⁶King Nebuchadnezzar of Babylon marched against him; he bound him in fetters to convey him to Babylon. ⁷Nebuchadnezzar also brought some vessels of the House of the LORD to Babylon, and set them in his palace in Babylon. ⁸The other events of Jehoiakim's reign, and the abominable things he did, and what was found against him, are recorded in the book of the kings of Israel and Judah. His son Jehoiachin succeeded him as king.

⁹Jehoiachin was eight years old when he became king, and he reigned three months and ten days in Jerusalem; he did what was displeasing to the LORD. ¹⁰At the turn of the year, King Nebuchadnezzar sent to have him brought to Babylon with the precious vessels of the House of the LORD, and he made his kinsman Zedekiah king over Judah and Jerusalem.

¹¹Zedekiah was twenty-one years old when he became king, and he reigned eleven years in Jerusalem. ¹²He did what was displeasing to the LORD his God; he did not humble himself before the prophet Jeremiah, who spoke for the LORD. ¹³He also rebelled against Nebuchadnezzar, who made him take an oath[b] by God; he stiffened his neck and hardened his heart so as not to turn to the LORD God of Israel. ¹⁴All the officers of the priests and the people committed many trespasses, following all the abominable practices of the nations. They polluted the House of the LORD, which He had consecrated in Jerusalem. ¹⁵The LORD God of their fathers had sent word to them through His messengers daily without fail, for He had pity on His people and His dwelling-place. ¹⁶But they mocked the messengers of God and disdained His words and taunted His prophets until the wrath of the LORD against His people grew be-

5 בֶּן־עֶשְׂרִים וְחָמֵשׁ שָׁנָה יְהוֹיָקִים בְּמָלְכוֹ
וְאַחַת עֶשְׂרֵה שָׁנָה מָלַךְ בִּירוּשָׁלָ֑͏ִם
וַיַּעַשׂ הָרַע בְּעֵינֵי יְהוָה אֱלֹהָיו: 6 עָלָיו
עָלָה נְבוּכַדְנֶאצַּר מֶלֶךְ בָּבֶל וַיַּאַסְרֵהוּ
בַּנְחֻשְׁתַּיִם לְהֹלִיכוֹ בָּבֶלָה: 7 וּמִכְּלֵי בֵּית
יְהוָה הֵבִיא נְבוּכַדְנֶאצַּר לְבָבֶל וַיִּתְּנֵם
בְּהֵיכָלוֹ בְּבָבֶל: 8 וְיֶתֶר דִּבְרֵי יְהוֹיָקִים
וְתֹעֲבֹתָיו אֲשֶׁר־עָשָׂה וְהַנִּמְצָא עָלָיו הִנָּם
כְּתוּבִים עַל־סֵפֶר מַלְכֵי יִשְׂרָאֵל וִיהוּדָה
וַיִּמְלֹךְ יְהוֹיָכִין בְּנוֹ תַּחְתָּיו: פ

9 בֶּן־שְׁמוֹנֶה שָׁנִים יְהוֹיָכִין בְּמָלְכוֹ
וּשְׁלֹשָׁה חֳדָשִׁים וַעֲשֶׂרֶת יָמִים מָלַךְ
בִּירוּשָׁלָ֑͏ִם וַיַּעַשׂ הָרַע בְּעֵינֵי יְהוָה:
10 וְלִתְשׁוּבַת הַשָּׁנָה שָׁלַח הַמֶּלֶךְ
נְבוּכַדְנֶאצַּר וַיְבִאֵהוּ בָבֶלָה עִם־כְּלֵי
חֶמְדַּת בֵּית־יְהוָה וַיַּמְלֵךְ אֶת־צִדְקִיָּהוּ
אָחִיו עַל־יְהוּדָה וִירוּשָׁלָ͏ִם: פ

11 בֶּן־עֶשְׂרִים וְאַחַת שָׁנָה צִדְקִיָּהוּ בְמָלְכוֹ
וְאַחַת עֶשְׂרֵה שָׁנָה מָלַךְ בִּירוּשָׁלָ͏ִם:
12 וַיַּעַשׂ הָרַע בְּעֵינֵי יְהוָה אֱלֹהָיו לֹא נִכְנַע
מִלִּפְנֵי יִרְמְיָהוּ הַנָּבִיא מִפִּי יְהוָה: 13 וְגַם
בַּמֶּלֶךְ נְבוּכַדְנֶאצַּר מָרָד אֲשֶׁר הִשְׁבִּיעוֹ
בֵּאלֹהִים וַיֶּקֶשׁ אֶת־עָרְפּוֹ וַיְאַמֵּץ אֶת־
לְבָבוֹ מִשּׁוּב אֶל־יְהוָה אֱלֹהֵי יִשְׂרָאֵל:
14 גַּם כָּל־שָׂרֵי הַכֹּהֲנִים וְהָעָם הִרְבּוּ
למעול־מַעַל כְּכֹל תֹּעֲבוֹת הַגּוֹיִם
וַיְטַמְּאוּ אֶת־בֵּית יְהוָה אֲשֶׁר הִקְדִּישׁ
בִּירוּשָׁלָ͏ִם: 15 וַיִּשְׁלַח יְהוָה אֱלֹהֵי
אֲבוֹתֵיהֶם עֲלֵיהֶם בְּיַד מַלְאָכָיו הַשְׁכֵּם
וְשָׁלוֹחַ כִּי־חָמַל עַל־עַמּוֹ וְעַל־מְעוֹנוֹ:
16 וַיִּהְיוּ מַלְעִבִים בְּמַלְאֲכֵי הָאֱלֹהִים
וּבוֹזִים דְּבָרָיו וּמִתַּעְתְּעִים בִּנְבִאָיו עַד
עֲלוֹת חֲמַת־יְהוָה בְּעַמּוֹ עַד־לְאֵין מַרְפֵּא

---

b   *Viz., a vassal oath.*

yond remedy. [17]He therefore brought the king of the Chaldeans upon them, who killed their youths by the sword in their sanctuary; He did not spare youth, maiden, elder, or graybeard, but delivered all into his hands. [18]All the vessels of the House of God, large and small, and the treasures of the House of the LORD and the treasures of the king and his officers were all brought to Babylon. [19]They burned the House of God and tore down the wall of Jerusalem, burned down all its mansions, and consigned all its precious objects to destruction. [20]Those who survived the sword he exiled to Babylon, and they became his and his sons' servants till the rise of the Persian kingdom, [21]in fulfillment of the word of the LORD spoken by Jeremiah, until the land paid back its sabbaths; as long as it lay desolate it kept sabbath, till seventy years were completed.

[22]And in the first year of King Cyrus of Persia, when the word of the LORD spoken by Jeremiah was fulfilled, the LORD roused the spirit of King Cyrus of Persia to issue a proclamation throughout his realm by word of mouth and in writing, as follows: [23]"Thus said King Cyrus of Persia: The LORD God of Heaven has given me all the kingdoms of the earth, and has charged me with building Him a House in Jerusalem, which is in Judah. Any one of you of all His people, the LORD his God be with him and let him go up."

17 וַיַּעַל עֲלֵיהֶם אֶת־מֶלֶךְ כשדיים כַּשְׂדִּים וַיַּהֲרֹג בַּחוּרֵיהֶם בַּחֶרֶב בְּבֵית מִקְדָּשָׁם וְלֹא חָמַל עַל־בָּחוּר וּבְתוּלָה זָקֵן וְיָשֵׁשׁ הַכֹּל נָתַן בְּיָדוֹ: 18 וְכֹל כְּלֵי בֵּית הָאֱלֹהִים הַגְּדֹלִים וְהַקְּטַנִּים וְאֹצְרוֹת בֵּית יְהֹוָה וְאֹצְרוֹת הַמֶּלֶךְ וְשָׂרָיו הַכֹּל הֵבִיא בָבֶל: 19 וַיִּשְׂרְפוּ אֶת־בֵּית הָאֱלֹהִים וַיְנַתְּצוּ אֵת חוֹמַת יְרוּשָׁלָ͏ִם וְכָל־אַרְמְנוֹתֶיהָ שָׂרְפוּ בָאֵשׁ וְכָל־כְּלֵי מַחֲמַדֶּיהָ לְהַשְׁחִית: ס 20 וַיֶּגֶל הַשְּׁאֵרִית מִן־הַחֶרֶב אֶל־בָּבֶל וַיִּהְיוּ־לוֹ וּלְבָנָיו לַעֲבָדִים עַד־מְלֹךְ מַלְכוּת פָּרָס: 21 לְמַלֹּאות דְּבַר־יְהֹוָה בְּפִי יִרְמְיָהוּ עַד־רָצְתָה הָאָרֶץ אֶת־שַׁבְּתוֹתֶיהָ כָּל־יְמֵי הׇשַּׁמָּה שָׁבָתָה לְמַלֹּאות שִׁבְעִים שָׁנָה: פ

22 וּבִשְׁנַת אַחַת לְכוֹרֶשׁ מֶלֶךְ פָּרַס לִכְלוֹת דְּבַר־יְהֹוָה בְּפִי יִרְמְיָהוּ הֵעִיר יְהֹוָה אֶת־רוּחַ כּוֹרֶשׁ מֶלֶךְ־פָּרַס וַיַּעֲבֶר־קוֹל בְּכָל־מַלְכוּתוֹ וְגַם־בְּמִכְתָּב לֵאמֹר: ס 23 כֹּה אָמַר כּוֹרֶשׁ ׀ מֶלֶךְ פָּרַס כָּל־מַמְלְכוֹת הָאָרֶץ נָתַן לִי יְהֹוָה אֱלֹהֵי הַשָּׁמַיִם וְהוּא־פָקַד עָלַי לִבְנוֹת־לוֹ בַיִת בִּירוּשָׁלַ͏ִם אֲשֶׁר בִּיהוּדָה מִי־בָכֶם מִכָּל־עַמּוֹ יְהֹוָה אֱלֹהָיו עִמּוֹ וְיָעַל: * * ::

תם ונשלם תהילה לאל בורא עולם

v. 23. סכום הפסוקים של ספר 1,765 וחציו 27.25 בחלק הראשון

v. 23. סכום הפסוקים של המקרא 23,194 (אף על פי שכתוב 23,203 בכתב היד שלנו) וחציו ירמיה 6.5

GUIDE TO ENGLISH FOOTNOTES

Glossary for the Footnotes

Akkadian
An ancient Semitic language spoken in Mesopotamia; its chief dialects were Babylonian and Assyrian.

Aquila
A second-century convert to Judaism who made a literal translation of the Bible into Greek.

Berakhot
One of the treatises of the Mishnah and the Talmud.

Ibn Ezra
Rabbi Abraham ibn Ezra, a Bible commentator and grammarian who lived in Spain in the twelfth century.

Kethib
The way a word, usually unvocalized, is written in the Bible; see *qere*.

Kimhi
Rabbi David Kimḥi (Radak), a Bible commentator and grammarian who lived in southern France in the late twelfth and early thirteenth centuries.

Masorah
The text of the Bible as transmitted, with vowel signs and accents.

Mishnah
The code of Jewish law prepared by Rabbi Judah ha-Nasi about 200 C.E. The word is usually followed by the name of the relevant treatise.

Peshitta
A translation of the Bible into Syriac, parts of which are said to have been made in the first century C.E.

Qere
The way the Masorah requires a word to be read, especially when it diverges from the *kethib*.

Qumran
The site of the caves where Bible manuscripts were found in 1949–50. The manuscripts are identified by such symbols as 4QSam^a (for manuscript *a* of Samuel, found in the fourth cave of Qumran); 1QIs^a (for manuscript *a* of Isaiah found in the first cave of Qumran).

Rashbam	Rabbi Shmuel ben Meir, a grandson of Rashi, who commented on the Torah.
Rashi	Rabbi Shlomo Yitzḥaki, the best-known Jewish commentator on the Bible. He lived in France at the end of the eleventh century.
Saadia	A *gaon*, i.e., a head of a Babylonian talmudic academy, in the early part of the tenth century. His works include the famous translation of the Bible into Arabic.
Septuagint	The oldest Jewish translation of the Bible, into Greek. The Torah translation dates from the third century B.C.E.; other books of the Bible were translated somewhat later.
Syriac	See *Peshitta*.
Targum	A Jewish translation of the Bible into Aramaic, a language once widely spoken in western Asia, of which Syriac was a later development.
Ugaritic	A language of inscriptions found at Ras Shamra, on the Syrian coast, in the second millennium B.C.E. Both the language and its literature have shed much light on the Hebrew Bible.
Vulgate	The Latin translation of the Bible made by the Church father Jerome about the year 400 C.E. It became the official Bible of the Roman Catholic Church.

Abbreviations and Terms

Cf.	A reference to another version, or to a cognate language, that justified the translation adopted.
Heb.	The Hebrew word or phrase in transliteration, especially when necessary to point out a pun, homonym, or the like. *Heb.* is also used to indicate the literal wording for which a superior rendering was employed; see Genesis 46.23, note *d*, or 49.9, note *a*. An example of a somewhat different type may be seen at Exodus 21.22, note *e*.
I.e.	An explanation, to avoid adding words to the text, in order to clarify the translation; see Exodus 22.29, note *j*.

Lit.	For the literal translation of a word or phrase that was given an idiomatic or somewhat free translation in the text; see Genesis 30.27, note *j*, and 30.38, *k*; or 43.21, note *b*, and 43.43, note *c*; or Deuteronomy 18.1, note *a* (where the Hebrew and English cannot agree in number).
Meaning of Heb. uncertain	Where the translation represents the best that the committee could achieve with an elusive or difficult text. In some cases the text may be unintelligible because of corruption.
Moved up	Where clarity required the shifting of a word or phrase within a verse or from one verse to another; see Genesis 10.14, note *d*.
Or	Indicates an alternative reading that the committee found almost as acceptable as the one adopted for the text.
Others	Indicates a well-known traditional translation, especially if it was used in the older (1917) JPS version, that the committee does not find acceptable even as an alternate reading.
See	Frequently used in place of *cf.*, but usually intended to begin a note attached to another passage in the Bible.

GUIDE TO HEBREW FOOTNOTES

The footnotes were designed for readers having a general knowledge of Hebrew.* Three basic rules apply:

- No abbreviations (*ra'shei teivot*) are used.
- Numbers are indicated only with Arabic numerals, not with Hebrew letters.
- A note refers to a certain letter by using a single hatch mark, not by spelling out the name of the letter.

For example, the fifth letter of the Hebrew alphabet is written as 'ה, which stands only for that letter—and not for God's name or the number five, as in other books.

The following glossary of terms is in alphabetical order—without prefixed conjunctions, prepositions, or the definite article.

Glossary for the Footnotes

אהרן בן אשר	Aaron ben Asher (renowned tenth-century masorete)—vocalization here was at issue in his day
"את"	direct-object marker
בתראה	latter; last
דגושה	pointed with a *dagesh*—which is unexpected in this particular case, or, for 'א and 'ר, is rare altogether
דרך המדרש	according to midrash (rather than arithmetic)
הלכה	rabbinic law governing scrolls for ritual use
המשך	continuation
הפוכה	inverted

---

* For background on issues treated in the footnotes, see the preface. Per tradition, the footnotes are composed in a shorthand (not literary) style. Deciphering them requires awareness of the context; a footnote either marks a special juncture in the text, or else the marked item is extraordinary in some way.

For example, the footnote 'חסר ה means "The letter ה is missing." Yet its full import becomes clear after taking into account that this must be both unusual and intended, yielding something like: "According to how the text has come down to us, the letter ה—which is normal in the spelling of this word—is missing in this instance. So when you *write* the text, leave out that letter here; but when you *read* the text, supply that missing letter in your mind."

זעירא	small
חלוקה	division
חסר	unusual spelling—the stated letter is missing
חצי	halfway point[1]—measured in verses, words, or letters
טעם, טעמים	accent; trope; punctuation (singular and plural)
טעם התחתון	the "lower" trope (used for study rather than worship)
יתיר	unusual spelling—the stated letter ('א, 'ה, 'ו, or 'י) is superfluous (not part of root or grammatical form)
כתב היד שלנו	our base manuscript; the Leningrad Codex
כתיב ולא קריא	written but not read aloud; part of the written tradition but omitted in the reading tradition
כתר ארם צובה	Aleppo Codex—a careful, early medieval manuscript
לשון יחיד	singular verb form
לשון ענן	"clouds" (rather than "leaders")—a rare meaning of a common word
לשון רבים	plural verb form
לשון שנאה	means "enmity, enemy"—a rare homonym
מדינחאי	"easterners"—scribal tradition in Babylonia (present-day Iraq), more than 1300 years ago (compare מערבאי)[2]
מהדורת לעטעריס	edition of R. Meir Halevi Letteris (c. 1860), reproduced in the Hertz Pentateuch, Aryeh Kaplan *Living Torah*, KTAV *Tiqqun*, and elsewhere
מהדורת שטוטגארט	Stuttgart edition; *Biblia Hebraica Stuttgartensia* (BHS)
מלא	unusual spelling—the stated vowel-letter ('ו or 'י) is superfluous given the way this word is vocalized
מנוקד, מנוקדת	pointed or vocalized
מסורה	masoretic notes
מסורת הקריאה	reading tradition
מערבאי	"westerners"—scribal tradition in the Levant, more than 1300 years ago (compare מדינחאי)
מקף	hyphen
מקרא	Scripture; Bible; Tanakh
נדפס	printed (in this edition)

1   By masoretic convention, whenever the total verse count is an even number, the first verse of the second half is called the "halfway point."
2   Verse count methods and vocalization methods differed among various early scribal schools. Extant Tiberian masoretic manuscripts did not use any one source consistently.

נוסח אחר	a version that differs from our codex; a variant in other masoretic manuscripts or in a proto-masoretic Qumran ("Dead Sea") scroll[3]
נוסחים המקובלים	accepted or "received" versions—editions of *Miqra'ot Gedolot,* Letteris (see מהדורת לעטעריס), Koren, Artscroll, and Breuer (Yemenite); *textus receptus*
נחה	silent
נסמן	marked
נספר	counted
נקוד	extraordinary dot (*niqud*)
נקרא	called
נשנה	repeated
נתחבר	included
סבירין ומטעין	caution: those who think (using logic or rules of grammar) that the text should read here as follows will mislead others (i.e., are mistaken)
סגול	the vowel *segol* (short "e")
סוף פסוק	end of the verse; period
סימן ימנית	a dot on the right side (*shin* rather than *sin*)
סימן שמאלית	a dot on the left side (*sin* rather than *shin*)
סימנית מנוזרת	separating sign; bracket
סכום הפסוקים	count of verses; total number of verses
פיסקא באמצע פסוק	a break or gap appears in the middle of the verse
צורה	layout; format
צורת שירה	poetry format
קיבוץ	the vowel *kibbuts* (long "u")
קריא ולא כתיב	read aloud but not written down; part of the reading tradition but omitted in the written tradition
רבתי	large
רפה	without the expected dot (*dagesh* or *mappiq*)
רשימה	list
שורש	root; spelling that shows a word's basic meaning
שירה	poem; poetry; psalm
שנאה	literally, "hatred"—see לשון שנאה
שנוי	a change (of)
שני טעמים	Two accents on a single word
תחתון	literally, "lower"—see טעם התחתון
תיבה, תיבות	word(s)
תלויה	suspended; raised above the line
תנועה, תנועות	vowel(s)

---

3   See the corresponding English footnote for details.

TABLE OF SCRIPTURAL READINGS

TORAH			NEVI'IM

Local practice may differ from the selections listed.

a   Parentheses indicate Sephardi ritual.

	TORAH		NEVI'IM

LEVITICUS

ויקרא	Va-yikra'	1.1–5.26	Isaiah 43.21–44.23
צו	Tsav	6.1–8.36	Jeremiah 7.21–8.3; 9.22, 23
שמיני	Shemini	9.1–11.47	2 Samuel 6.1–7.17 (6.1–19)
תזריע	Tazria'	12.1–13.59	2 Kings 4.42–5.19
מצרע	Metsora'	14.1–15.33	2 Kings 7.3–20
אחרי מות	'Aharei Mot	16.1–18.30	Ezekiel 22.1–19 (22.1–16)
קדשים	Kedoshim	19.1–20.27	Amos 9.7–15 (Ezekiel 20.2–20)
אמר	'Emor	21.1–24.23	Ezekiel 44.15–31
בהר	Be-har	25.1–26.2	Jeremiah 32.6–27
בחקתי	Be-ḥukkotai	26.3–27.34	Jeremiah 16.19–17.14

NUMBERS

במדבר	Be-midbar	1.1–4.20	Hosea 2.1–22
נשא	Naso'	4.21–7.89	Judges 13.2–25
בהעלתך	Be-ha'alotekha	8.1–12.16	Zechariah 2.14–4.7
שלח לך	Shelaḥ-Lekha	13.1–15.41	Joshua 2.1–24
קרח	Koraḥ	16.1–18.32	1 Samuel 11.14–12.22
חקת	Ḥukkat	19.1–22.1	Judges 11.1–33
בלק	Balak	22.2–25.9	Micah 5.6–6.8
פינחס	Pinḥas	25.10–30.1	1 Kings 18.46–19.21
מטות	Mattot	30.2–32.42	Jeremiah 1.1–2.3
מסעי	Mase'ei	33.1–36.13	Jeremiah 2.4–28; 3.4 (2.4–28; 4.1, 2)

DEUTERONOMY

דברים	Devarim	1.1–3.22	Isaiah 1.1–27
ואתחנן	Va-'ethannan	3.23–7.11	Isaiah 40.1–26
עקב	'Ekev	7.12–11.25	Isaiah 49.14–51.3
ראה	Re'eh	11.26–16.17	Isaiah 54.11–55.5
שפטים	Shofetim	16.18–21.9	Isaiah 51.12–52.12
כי תצא	Ki Tetse'	21.10–25.19	Isaiah 54.1–10
כי תבוא	Ki Tavo'	26.1–29.8	Isaiah 60.1–22
נצבים	Nitsavim	29.9–30.20	Isaiah 61.10–63.9
וילך	Va-yelekh	31.1–30	—
האזינו	Ha'azinu	32.1–52	2 Samuel 22.1–51
וזאת הברכה	Ve-zo't		
	Ha-berakhah	33.1–34.12	Joshua 1.1–18 (1.1–9)

TORAH   NEVI'IM

READINGS FOR SPECIAL SABBATHS

	TORAH	NEVI'IM
Sabbath coinciding with Rosh Ḥodesh	Weekly portion and Numbers 28.9–15	Isaiah 66.1–24
Sabbath immediately preceding Rosh Ḥodesh	Weekly portion	1 Samuel 20.18–42
Shekalim	Weekly portion and Exodus 30.11–16	2 Kings 12.1–17 (11.17–12.17)
Zakhor	Weekly portion and Deuteronomy 25.17–19	1 Samuel 15.2–34 (15.1–34)
Parah	Weekly portion and Numbers 19.1–22	Ezekiel 36.16–38 (36.16–36)
Ha-Ḥodesh	Weekly portion and Exodus 12.1–20	Ezekiel 45.16–46.18 (45.18–46.15)
Ha-Gadol	Weekly portion	Malachi 3.4–24
First Sabbath Hanukkah	Weekly portion plus the verses relating the prince (*nasi*) of the day corresponding to the day of Hanukkah	Zechariah 2.14–4.7
Second Sabbath Hanukkah	Weekly portion and Hanukkah portions as above	1 Kings 7.40–50

TORAH NEVI'IM

READINGS FOR THE DAYS OF AWE

Rosh Ha-Shanah

	TORAH	NEVI'IM
First Day	Genesis 21.1–34; Numbers 29.1–6	1 Samuel 1.1–2.10
Second Day	Genesis 22.1–24; Numbers 29.1–6	Jeremiah 31.2–20
Sabbath Shuvah	Weekly portion	Hosea 14.2–10; Micah 7.18–20; Joel 2.15–27 (Hosea 14.2–10; Micah 7.18–20)

Yom Kippur

	TORAH	NEVI'IM
Morning	Leviticus 16.1–34; Numbers 29.7–11	Isaiah 57.14–58.14
Afternoon	Leviticus 18.1–30	Jonah 1.1–4.11; Micah 7.18–20

READINGS FOR THE FESTIVALS

Sukkot (Tabernacles)

	TORAH	NEVI'IM
First Day	Leviticus 22.26–23.44 Numbers 29.12–16	Zechariah 14.1–21
Second Day	Leviticus 22.26–23.44 Numbers 29.12–16	1 Kings 8.2–21
Sabbath during the Middle Days	Exodus 33.12–34.26; Daily portion from Numbers 29	Ezekiel 38.18–39.16
Eighth Day	Deuteronomy 14.22–16.17; Numbers 29.35–30.1	1 Kings 8.54–66

TORAH   NEVI'IM

READINGS FOR THE FESTIVALS (*continued*)

	TORAH	NEVI'IM
Simḥat Torah	Deuteronomy 33.1–34.12; Genesis 1.1–2.3; Numbers 29.35–30.1	Joshua 1.1–18 (1.1–9)
Pesaḥ (Passover)		
First Day	Exodus 12.21–51; Numbers 28.16–25	Joshua 5.2–6.1; 6.27
Second Day	Leviticus 22.26–23.44; Numbers 28.16–25	2 Kings 23.1–9; 21–25
Sabbath during the Middle Days	Exodus 33.12–34.26; Numbers 28.19–25	Ezekiel 37.1–14
Seventh Day	Exodus 13.17–15.26; Numbers 28.19–25	2 Samuel 22.1–51
Eighth Day	Deuteronomy 15.19–16.17; Numbers 28.19–25	Isaiah 10.32–12.6
Shavuot (Pentecost)		
First Day	Exodus 19.1–20.23; Numbers 28.26–31	Ezekiel 1.1–28; 3.12
Second Day	Deuteronomy 15.19–16.17;[a] Numbers 28.26–31	Habakkuk 3.1–19 (2.20–3.19)

---

a   On the Sabbath, 14.22–16.17.

TORAH   NEVI'IM

READINGS ON WEEKDAY OCCASIONS

Purim   Exodus 17.8–16   —

Ninth of Av
Morning   Deuteronomy 4.25–40   Jeremiah 8.13–9.23

Afternoon   Exodus 32.11–14;   Isaiah 55.6–56.8
                         34.1–10

Public Fast Days
Morning   Exodus 32.11–14;   —
                         34.1–10

Afternoon   Exodus 32.11–14;   Isaiah 55.6–56.8
                         34.1–10

READINGS OF THE FIVE MEGILLOTH

The Song of Songs   Sabbath during Pesaḥ (Passover)
Ruth   Shavuot (Pentecost)
Lamentations   Ninth of Av
Ecclesiastes   Sabbath during Sukkot (Tabernacles)
Esther   Purim